# 2006 ESPN®
## SPORTS ALMANAC

### With Exclusive Year in Review Commentary from ESPN Anchors and Analysts

YEAR IN REVIEW

BASEBALL

COLLEGE FOOTBALL

PRO FOOTBALL

COLLEGE BASKETBALL

PRO BASKETBALL

HOCKEY

COLLEGE SPORTS

HALLS OF FAME & AWARDS

WHO'S WHO

**Stuart Scott**

**Chris Berman**

**Dan Patrick**

**Dick Vitale**

**Karl Ravech**

**Lee Corso**

**Chris Fowler**

**Trey Wingo**

ALSO CONTRIBUTING

sportsnation

Jerry Bembry
Mike Greenberg

Jim Caple
Andy Katz

# The Champions of 2005

## Auto Racing
For all the statistics, see the Auto Racing section.

**NASCAR Circuit**

| | |
|---|---|
| Daytona 500 | Jeff Gordon |
| Coca-Cola 600 | Jimmie Johnson |
| Allstate 400 at the Brickyard | Tony Stewart |
| UAW-Ford 500 | Dale Jarrett |
| Nextel Cup Points Leader | Tony Stewart, 6100 pts (through Oct. 31) |

**Champ Car World Series Circuit**

| | |
|---|---|
| Points Championship | Sebastien Bourdais, 310 pts (through Oct. 31) |

**Indy Racing League Circuit**

| | |
|---|---|
| Indianapolis 500 | Dan Wheldon |
| IndyCar Championship | Dan Wheldon, 628 pts |

**Formula One Circuit**

| | |
|---|---|
| U.S. Grand Prix | Michael Schumacher |
| World Driving Champion | Fernando Alonso, 133 pts |

## Baseball
For all the statistics, see the Baseball section.

| | |
|---|---|
| **World Series** | Chicago-AL def. Houston, 4 games to 0 |
| MVP | Jermaine Dye, Chicago, OF |
| **ALCS** | Chicago def. Los Angeles, 4 games to 1 |
| **NLCS** | Houston def. St. Louis, 4 games to 2 |
| **All-Star Game** | American League 7, National League 5 |
| MVP | Miguel Tejada, AL (Baltimore), SS |
| **Coll. World Series** | Texas def. Florida, 2 games to 0 |
| MVP | David Maroul, Texas, 3B |

## College Basketball
For all the statistics, see the College Basketball section.

**Men's NCAA Tournament**

| | |
|---|---|
| Championship | North Carolina 75, Illinois 70 |
| MVP | Sean May, North Carolina, C |

**Women's NCAA Tournament**

| | |
|---|---|
| Championship | Baylor 84, Michigan St. 62 |
| MVP | Sophia Young, Baylor, F |

## Pro Basketball
For all the statistics, see the Pro Basketball section.

| | |
|---|---|
| **NBA Finals** | San Antonio def. Detroit, 4 games to 3 |
| MVP | Tim Duncan, San Antonio, F/C |
| **Eastern Final** | Detroit def. Miami, 4 games to 3 |
| **Western Final** | San Antonio def. Phoenix, 4 games to 1 |
| **All-Star Game** | East 125, West 115 |
| MVP | Allen Iverson, East (Philadelphia), G |

## Bowling
For all the statistics, see the Bowling section.

**Men's Major Championships**

| | |
|---|---|
| Miller High Life Masters | Danny Wiseman |
| U.S. Open | Chris Barnes |
| PBA World Championship | Patrick Allen |
| Tournament of Champions | Steve Jaros |

**Women's Major Championships**

| | |
|---|---|
| WIBC Queens | Tennelle Milligan |

## College Football (2004)
For all the statistics, see the College Football section.

**National Champions**

| | |
|---|---|
| AP | USC (13-0) |
| ESPN/*USA Today* Coaches' | USC (13-0) |

**Major Bowls**

| | |
|---|---|
| Orange | USC 55, Oklahoma 19 |
| Sugar | Auburn 16, Virginia Tech 13 |
| Rose | Texas 38, Michigan 37 |
| Fiesta | Utah 35, Pittsburgh 7 |
| **Heisman Trophy** | Matt Leinart, USC, QB |

## Pro Football (2004)
For all the statistics, see the Pro Football section.

| | |
|---|---|
| **Super Bowl XXXIX** | New England 24, Philadelphia 21 |
| MVP | Deion Branch, New England, WR |
| **AFC Championship** | New England 41, Pittsburgh 27 |
| **NFC Championship** | Philadelphia 27, Atlanta 10 |
| **Pro Bowl** | AFC 38, NFC 27 |
| MVP | Peyton Manning, Indianapolis, QB |
| **CFL Grey Cup Final** | Toronto 27, British Columbia 19 |
| MVP | Damon Allen, Toronto, QB |

## Golf
For all the statistics, see the Golf section.

**Men's Major Championships**

| | |
|---|---|
| Masters | Tiger Woods |
| U.S. Open | Michael Campbell |
| British Open | Tiger Woods |
| PGA Championship | Phil Mickelson |

**Champions (Seniors) Major Championships**

| | |
|---|---|
| The Tradition | Loren Roberts |
| Senior PGA Championship | Mike Reid |
| U.S. Senior Open | Allen Doyle |
| Senior Players Championship | Peter Jacobsen |
| Senior British Open | Tom Watson |

**Women's Major Championships**

| | |
|---|---|
| Kraft Nabisco Championship | Annika Sorenstam |
| LPGA Championship | Annika Sorenstam |
| U.S. Women's Open | Birdie Kim |
| Women's British Open | Jeong Jang |

**National Team Competition**

| | |
|---|---|
| Presidents Cup | United States 18½, International 15½ |
| Solheim Cup | United States 15½, Europe 12½ |

## Hockey

| | |
|---|---|
| **Stanley Cup** | not held |
| MVP | not awarded |
| **Eastern Final** | not held |
| **Western Final** | not held |
| **All-Star Game** | not held |
| MVP | not awarded |

## Horse Racing
For all the statistics, see the Horse Racing section.

**Triple Crown Champions**

| | |
|---|---|
| Kentucky Derby | Giacomo (Mike Smith) |
| Preakness Stakes | Afleet Alex (Jeremy Rose) |
| Belmont Stakes | Afleet Alex (Jeremy Rose) |

**Harness Racing**

| | |
|---|---|
| Hambletonian | Vivid Photo (Roger Hammer) |
| Little Brown Jug | P-Forty-Seven (Dave Palone) |

## Soccer
For all the statistics, see the Soccer section.

| | |
|---|---|
| **MLS Cup 2004** | D.C. United 3, Kansas City 2 |
| MVP | Alecko Eskandarian, D.C. United, F |

## Tennis
For all the statistics, see the Tennis section.

**Men's Grand Slam Championships**

| | |
|---|---|
| Australian Open | Marat Safin |
| French Open | Rafael Nadal |
| Wimbledon | Roger Federer |
| U.S. Open | Roger Federer |

**Women's Grand Slam Championships**

| | |
|---|---|
| Australian Open | Serena Williams |
| French Open | Justine Henin-Hardenne |
| Wimbledon | Venus Williams |
| U.S. Open | Kim Clijsters |

## Miscellaneous Champions
For more, see the Miscellaneous & Int'l Sports sections.

| | |
|---|---|
| **Little League World Series** | West Oahu, Hawaii |
| **Tour de France** | Lance Armstrong (USA) |
| **Iditarod** | Robert Sorlie |
| **World Series of Poker** | Joseph Hachem |

# 2006
# ESPN
# Sports
# Almanac

## Gerry Brown
## Michael Morrison
### Editors

ESPN
BOOKS

**Editors**
Gerry Brown
Michael Morrison

Comments and suggestions from readers are invited. Because of the many letters received, however, it is not possible to respond personally to every correspondent. Nevertheless, all letters are welcome and each will be carefully considered. The **ESPN Sports Almanac** does not rule on bets or wagers. Address all correspondence to: Sports Almanac, Inc., P.O. Box 542281, Lake Worth, FL 33454-2281.
Email: info@espnalmanac.com.

ISBN 1-933060-04-2

FIRST EDITION

10 9 8 7 6 5 4 3 2 1

# CONTENTS 5

Despite what you may have seen on the Chinese calendar, 2005 was the year of the hurricane. Two pro franchises became homeless and scores of college teams along the gulf coast were displaced by Hurricane Katrina. We here at the sports almanac didn't escape the stormy weather either, losing power for nearly a week in our Florida headquarters during our annual deadline scramble in the days following Wilma. A poll on ESPN.com's SportsNation ranked Katrina's impact as the top sports story of the year. Who are we to argue with the Nation? We're too busy taking down the storm shutters anyway.

We certainly don't argue to often with the following people because their advice and guidance continues to blow us away.

At ESPN Books, our mightiest thanks go to Chris Raymond for believing in the unique value of this book in the sports landscape and for continuing to work to grow it. Also sincere thanks to Hyperion's Gretchen Young for pushing hard on our behalf. To co-opt the White Sox post-season anthem, "Don't Stop Believin'."

Thanks as always to John Hassan for his steadying hand and after-hours assistance.

Our respect for and appreciation of Almanac father Mike Meserole grows with each passing year. Rick Sommers of Command Web never ceases to make us look good. We're glad that you finally got your New Jersey Devils back.

We'd be remiss if we failed to acknowledge the assistance of SportsNation's Daniel Dodd, Barbara Zidovsky from Nielsen Media Research and Elvis Brathwaite from AP/Wide World Photos. Also we can't forget Barbara Blake at ESPN Creative Services and Jerry Baltz at the International Bowling Museum & Hall of Fame.

Thanks once again to Rick Campbell and Gary Johnson at the NCAA, U.S. Trotting's Paul Ramlow, the PBA Tour's Rosie Leutzinger and "Outbound" Bill Magrath from the *Sports Business Daily.*

Also, our continued appreciation goes out to the usually anonymous pro and college sports media relations folks from coast to coast that made our jobs easier.

We must also make sure to mention how much we needed the constant input from junior assistant editor Molly Brown and all the hot meals and support from our better halves Lisa and Lori.

But by far the best news this year in the Almanac family was the arrival of import Avery Kai Morrison. Hurricane Avery was the best thing to hit the Morrison household in quite some time and even during the darkest moments of the year she lit up the room.

Gerry Brown
Michael Morrison

October 30, 2005

## Major League Cities & Teams

As of Oct. 31, 2005, there were 134 major league teams playing or scheduled to play baseball, men's basketball, NFL football, hockey and soccer in 53 cities in the United States and Canada. Listed below are the cities and the teams that play there.

**Anaheim**
AL      Los Angeles Angels of Anaheim
NHL     Mighty Ducks of Anaheim

**Atlanta**
NL      Braves
NBA     Hawks
NFL     Falcons
NHL     Thrashers

**Baltimore**
AL      Orioles      NFL      Ravens

**Baton Rouge**
NBA     New Orleans Hornets
NFL     New Orleans Saints

**Boston**
AL      Red Sox
NBA     Celtics
NFL     N.E. Patriots (Foxboro)
NHL     Bruins
MLS     N.E. Revolution (Foxboro)

**Buffalo**
NFL     Bills (Orchard Park)
NHL     Sabres

**Calgary**
NHL     Flames

**Charlotte**
NBA     Bobcats
NFL     Carolina Panthers

**Chicago**
AL      White Sox
NL      Cubs
NBA     Bulls
NFL     Bears
NHL     Blackhawks
MLS     Fire

**Cincinnati**
NL      Reds      NFL      Bengals

**Cleveland**
AL      Indians      NBA      Cavaliers
NFL     Browns

**Columbus**
NHL     Blue Jackets
MLS     Crew

**Dallas**
AL      Texas Rangers (Arlington)
NBA     Mavericks
NFL     Cowboys (Irving)
NHL     Stars
MLS     FC Dallas

**Denver**
NL      Colorado Rockies
NBA     Nuggets
NFL     Broncos
NHL     Colorado Avalanche
MLS     Colorado Rapids

**Detroit**
AL      Tigers
NBA     Pistons (Auburn Hills)
NFL     Lions
NHL     Red Wings

**East Rutherford**
NBA     New Jersey Nets
NFL     New York Giants
NFL     New York Jets
NHL     New Jersey Devils
MLS     MetroStars

**Edmonton**
NHL     Oilers

**Green Bay**
NFL     Packers

**Houston**
NL      Astros
NBA     Rockets
NFL     Texans

**Indianapolis**
NBA     Indiana Pacers
NFL     Colts

**Jacksonville**
NFL     Jaguars

**Kansas City**
AL      Royals
NFL     Chiefs
MLS     Wizards

**Los Angeles**
NL      Dodgers
NBA     Clippers
NBA     Lakers
NHL     Kings
MLS     Galaxy (Carson)
MLS     Club Chivas USA (Carson)

**Memphis**
NBA     Grizzlies

**Miami**
NL      Florida Marlins
NBA     Heat
NFL     Dolphins
NHL     Florida Panthers (Sunrise)

**Milwaukee**
NL      Brewers
NBA     Bucks

**Minneapolis**
AL      Minnesota Twins
NBA     Minnesota Timberwolves
NFL     Minnesota Vikings

**Montreal**
NHL     Canadiens

**Nashville**
NFL     Tennessee Titans
NHL     Predators

**New York**
AL      Yankees
NL      Mets (Flushing)
NBA     Knicks
NHL     Rangers
NHL     Islanders (Uniondale)

**Oakland**
AL      Athletics
NBA     Golden St. Warriors
NFL     Raiders

**Oklahoma City**
NBA     New Orleans Hornets

**Orlando**
NBA     Magic

**Ottawa**
NHL     Senators (Kanata)

**Philadelphia**
NL      Phillies
NBA     76ers
NFL     Eagles
NHL     Flyers

**Phoenix**
NL      Arizona Diamondbacks
NBA     Suns
NFL     Arizona Cardinals (Tempe)
NHL     Coyotes

**Pittsburgh**
NL      Pirates
NFL     Steelers
NHL     Penguins

**Portland**
NBA     Trail Blazers

**Raleigh**
NHL     Carolina Hurricanes

**Sacramento**
NBA     Kings

**St. Louis**
NL      Cardinals
NFL     Rams
NHL     Blues

**St. Paul**
NHL     Minnesota Wild

**Salt Lake City**
NBA     Utah Jazz
MLS     Real Salt Lake

**San Antonio**
NBA     Spurs
NFL     New Orleans Saints

**San Diego**
NL      Padres
NFL     Chargers

**San Francisco**
NL      Giants
NFL     49ers

**San Jose**
NHL     Sharks
MLS     Earthquakes

**Seattle**
AL      Mariners
NBA     SuperSonics
NFL     Seahawks

**Tampa**
AL      T.B. Devil Rays (St. Petersburg)
NFL     T.B. Buccaneers
NHL     T.B. Lightning

**Toronto**
AL      Blue Jays
NBA     Raptors
NHL     Maple Leafs

**Vancouver**
NHL     Canucks

**Washington**
NL      Nationals
NBA     Wizards
NFL     Redskins (Raljon, Md.)
NHL     Capitals
MLS     D.C. United

# Year in Review

Katrina made life miserable on the Gulf
Coast and may force the Saints and
Hornets from New Orleans permanently.

AP/Wide World Photos

# 2004-05: A Look Back

by **Jim Caple**

You'll have to forgive us for going to press before the 2005 calendar year ended but we have early deadlines here at the ESPN Almanac. So tell us, how did that Astros-Braves playoff game come out anyway?

Ha! Just kidding. We know Houston's Chris Burke hit a walk-off home run in the bottom of the 18th inning to end the longest postseason game in baseball history. Even more remarkable than the game's length, however, was that the fan who caught Burke's home run was the same fan who caught Lance Berkman's game-tying grand slam in the eighth inning.

What are the chances of that? Said Sean Dean: "I had several people say I should buy a lottery ticket or go to Vegas."

**Jim Caple** is a senior writer at ESPN.com. His first book, "The Devil Wears Pinstripes," is on sale at bookstores nationwide. It can also be ordered through his Web site, Jimcaple.com.

*It was a year worth shouting about for plenty of reasons. For all the details see below.*

Well, we all sort of felt that way this past year when the sports world hit us almost more than we could handle.

The 12-month ride since last year's Almanac was the wildest and most rewarding that didn't include a Giacomo-Closing Argument exacta ticket.

We shared our beer with Ron Artest in Detroit and discussed . . . ummm..."vitamins" with our favorite Congressmen in D.C. We caught touchdown passes from Peyton Manning and took dance lessons with Matt Leinart. We rode around the Brickyard with Danica Patrick and cycled through the Pyrenees with Lance Armstrong. We pitched 94-mile gas from 60-feet-six inches with 43-year-old Roger Clemens and pitched in physics-defying shots from 25 feet with Tiger Woods. And in perhaps the most amazing, pinch-yourself moment of all, we watched World Series games in Chicago.

Yes, really. A World Series in

AP/Wide World Photos

*The New England Patriots and* **Bill Belichick** *made another big splash in 2005 winning their third Super Bowl in four seasons.*

Chicago. We may spend the rest of the winter on the couch with Dr. Phil before we get over that one. But we're getting a little ahead of ourselves. Let's go back to where we left off last year.

Remember when Boston had a reputation for its suffering fans (a reputation that somehow thrived despite all those Celtics titles)?

Hopefully we won't have to endure any tales of Boston suffering ever again other than those involving that *Queer Eye for the Straight Guy* Red Sox makeover. Not only are Boston fans still celebrating their 2004 world championship—boom! there goes another David Ortiz ninth inning home run—Tom Brady and their Patriots won the Super Bowl for the third time in four years.

The ESPN Almanac would like to first, congratulate them on their success, and second, thank them for not making a Jimmy Fallon movie about their angst.

Do the Patriots belong in the dynasty category of earlier Steelers and Cowboys teams? "I'll leave the comparisons and historical perspectives to everybody else," coach Bill

nator was moonlighting as Notre Dame's head coach.

Charlie Weis went to Notre Dame after the school that is supposed to be above such things tarnished its

AP/Wide World Photos

Belichick said after his team's 24-21 victory over the Eagles. Well, OK.

Then we'll say it. They do. Remember, the Patriots were so good they defeated Philadelphia even though their offensive coordi-

reputation by firing Tyrone Willingham despite a winning record, the first time the Irish have let a coach go before his contract ran out. Notre Dame fans hailed Weis, with one popular t-shirt putting it this way: "New Coach, New Pope, New Era. Same Old Jesus."

Well, we'll see how they feel in two years.

The verdict is in, however, on

won the Heisman Trophy, led USC to an Orange Bowl rout over Oklahoma for its second consecutive national title and passed up the NFL draft so he could enjoy another year

AP/Wide World Photos

Southern Cal's Pete Carroll, who, last we checked, had a 30-game winning streak and a table at any LA restaurant he wanted (Westwood locations excluded).

Trojans quarterback Matt Leinart

of higher education: a three-credit course in ballroom dancing (or as it would be called at Ohio State - advanced calculus). Leinart's biggest play, however, was when the scholar/athlete/dancer twisted his way into the end zone to beat green-shirted Notre Dame in an edge-of-your-seat game so thrilling it should have been broadcast on ESPN Classic.

Spike TV would have been a fitting channel for the Thanksgiving weekend Pacers-Pistons game. Evidently upset with the method with which he had been served his beer, Ron Artest went into the stands in Detroit, triggering a players-fan clash that resulted in nine suspensions and the NBA's biggest black eye since the release of "Space Jam." (And just think how harsh the punishment would have been had David Stern's new dress code been in effect.)

Four Detroit players were suspended but the Pistons recovered to win the Eastern Conference before losing the finals to Tim Duncan and the San Antonio Spurs.

Meanwhile, Steve Nash became the first Canadian to win the NBA's MVP award, which nearly made up for Celine Dion's recording of "My Heart Will Go On."

In quieter basketball news, Roy Williams finally won the big one

AP/Wide World Photos

*Indiana's **Ron Artest** and some teammates missed some serious minutes due to suspension following the Pacers-Pistons brawl at the Palace of Auburn Hills in November 2004.*

AP/Wide World Photos

*Disgraced slugger **Rafael Palmeiro** had a lot of questions to answer upon his return to baseball following a suspension for a positive steroid test.*

when he coached North Carolina to the Final Four championship despite the enormous disadvantage of not having his own American Express commercial.

Baylor won the women's Final Four in the tournament where coaches do not get national Chevrolet commercials.

With so much chaos elsewhere, it was nice to see the golf world return to normal with Tiger Woods showing he isn't over-the-hill quite yet despite turning 30 at the end of the year (Tiger 30? The next thing you know Britney Spears will be a mother). He snapped a 34-month drought by winning two more majors—the Masters and the British Open—and finishing two strokes back at the U.S. Open and PGA Championship.

He also had the most amazing golf shot that did not involve Bill Murray and a gopher when his 25-foot chip from the second rough on Augusta's 16th hole caught the green, curled down toward the hole, rolled slowly to the cup and stopped briefly on the lip to ask directions before dropping in for a birdie.

"You expect the unexpected," Chris DiMarco said after Tiger beat him in a one-hole playoff, "and unfortunately it's not unexpected when he's doing it."

Roger Federer continued his tennis

AP/Wide World Photos

*Indy Racing League rookie **Danica Patrick** got plenty of attention in 2005. She almost deserved it running an impressive fourth at the Indianapolis 500.*

dominance as well, winning Wimbledon and the U.S. Open and drawing further raves that he might be the greatest player ever. He also was completely overshadowed by people Googling Maria Sharapova images.

The woman of the year, however, was Danica Patrick, who single-handedly revived interest in the Indianapolis 500 and created a need for more women's restrooms in the pits. In the best showing ever by a woman driver, she led the race until the final laps before finishing in fourth place and on TV more than celebrity poker. To really appreciate how big a moment this was though, consider that *Sports Illustrated* put Patrick on the cover even though she was wearing her clothes.

Patrick might have won Indy with a little more fuel in the tank but we all could appreciate that feeling in a year that saw gasoline reach $3 a gallon.

With such high prices, no wonder the NHL shrewdly saved on those breathtaking Zamboni fuel costs by canceling the 2004-05 season. Hockey finally returned in the fall with new salaries (24 percent smaller), new rules and a new hope Sidney Crosby.

The 18-year-old Pittsburgh Penguins rookie may be the most anticipated hockey player in years, but we still have a special place for that Montreal Canadiens rookie -Youppi!, the former Expos mascot who somehow never cleared customs when Les Expos moved to Washington and became the first baseball team in 33 years to relocate.

The re-named Washington Nationals weren't baseball's only presence in D.C. this year, though. In addition to those high gas prices, the United States remained at war in Iraq, its budget deficit was staggering, the President said social security needed overhauling, General Motors and the airline industry faced bankruptcy, the dollar fell, health insurance was a disaster and scientists increasingly warned about global warming.

So what did Congress focus on in the spring? Steroids, naturally. In perhaps the greatest threat to television viewers not involving Yankee-ography, C-Span brought Donald Fehr, Bud Selig *and* Congress onto a single screen when baseball was called to Washington to testify on its steroid policy.

(Of course, Congress needed to hold the hearings in 2005 so it could clear the deck for next year's election year topic: the infield fly rule.)

Rafael Palmeiro vigorously denied ever using steroids during those hearings only to be suspended later for testing positive shortly after reaching the 3,000 hit mark. But if Palmeiro was less than truthful with Congress, so what? He was simply returning the favor.

Not that you should read anything into this transition but...Barry Bonds sat out the first five months of the season with that stubborn knee that needed draining every five minutes. The planets and stars finally aligned properly Sept. 12 and he returned to the lineup long enough to hit five home runs before shutting himself down the final weekend with 708 career home runs, six shy of Babe Ruth's total and an increasingly daunting 47 behind Hank Aaron's record.

George Steinbrenner has had better years as well. His Yankees failed to reach the World Series despite

> *"Danica Patrick might have won Indy with a little more fuel in the tank but we all could appreciate that feeling in a year that saw gasoline reach $3 a gallon."*

their $206 million payroll and his horse, Bellamy Road, finished seventh at the Kentucky Derby despite being the 5-2 favorite. Apparently, Alex Rodriguez was the jockey.

When all was said and done, baseball fans were left watching something most of us had never seen: Nomar Garciaparra going an entire at-bat without adjusting his cup.

No, actually it was something even more amazing. The White Sox played Chicago's first World Series since Oprah weighed less than 50 pounds, and won it for the first time since 1917 (and Red Sox fans thought *they* went a long time without winning). The only headline more surprising than "Chicago Wins World Series!!!" would have been "Ozzie To Reporters: 'No Comment'."

AP/Wide World Photos

Given all of the above, there's obviously a lot of competition for the year's biggest sports star. But for our money, it's the future Mr. Sheryl Crow.

In what he repeatedly maintained as his career finale (yeah, we'll see about that, too), Lance Armstrong won the Tour de France for the seventh consecutive year.

Armstrong has been so dominating that it's as if the rest of the pack is riding Schwinn Stingrays with banana seats and baseball cards clothespinned to the spokes.

Lance had become such an American hero that he should have ridden off into the sunset. Instead he simply went the traditional route by circling the Arc de Triomphe.

He also took the opportunity to

scold the European cycling reporters who had so often been suspicious of him. "I'm sorry you don't believe in miracles. But this is a hell of a race," he said. "You should believe in these athletes, and you should believe in these people. I'll be a fan of the Tour de France for as long as I live."

And there are no secrets—this is a hard sporting event and hard work wins it."

That sounded good at the time but not so much a month later when a report claimed that urine samples from 1999 showed Armstrong took EPO during his first Tour title. He vehemently denied the charges but then again, so did Palmeiro.

Well, that's the modern fan's dilemma in an era when even some golfers are so muscled (well, not you, Phil) they look as if they should be fighting Jean-Claude Van Damme. Do you suspect everyone of being on steroids other than Michelle Wie?

Or do you try not to think about it and instead appreciate the performances for what they are?

After all, when 50-to-1 shot Giacomo or Danica Patrick raced down the back stretch, Tiger chipped in on 16, Lance pedalled through the Alps, Federer served at Wimbledon, the White Sox starters took the mound, Big Papi stepped to the plate or simply when Notre Dame came rushing out of the tunnel in their green jerseys, it was nice to remember that the most notable human growth enhancer in sports is its ability to produce goose bumps up and down our bodies.

AP/Wide World Photos

# Overheard in Bristol...

## Original takes from ESPN's best and brightest on the year's biggest stories

"This generation of basketball fans thinks of NBA brawls and conjures up images of Jeff Van Gundy swinging on Alonzo Mourning's leg, or a few shoves and some wild fists. But talk to old school NBA players. They'll tell you, the brawls back in the day rivaled some of the hockey fights we see. They were brutal, scary face-offs where you often wondered if some of these players were more skilled at fighting than ballin'.

I swear Maurice Lucas could've survived as a club heavyweight and the Kermit Washington punch that caved in the face of Rudy Tomjanovich is *still* one of the most lethal blows we've ever seen on a court *or* in a ring. But for the most part, our generation has been spared that type of brutality until that memorable night in November.

Watching it was scary. Some snapshots: big muscular players running into the stands punching fans, big muscular fans punching players, players and fans alike punching each other, even one fan ripping a chair from its mooring and flinging it into the crowd.

This wasn't as simplistic as a bunch of thuggish NBA stars creating havoc. Jermaine O'Neal is one of the most respected, classy men in the NBA. A man who dotes on his daughter and respects the game. He's also a man who saw a teammate attacked ON THE COURT and lost his cool enough to connect with the most solid blow of the entire brawl.

Which means what? It means the entire event was so scary, especially for those involved, it created what so many harrowing experiences create--chaos.

The line that divides fans and athletes is so small, it's almost transparent and AS A PARENT, it'll make you THINK the next time you get an offer to sit courtside at a game."

**–Stuart Scott**

*II* No matter what else happens, 2005 will go down as the year of the steroid. From the ongoing BALCO investigation, to the congressional hearings in March, to the shocking positive test of Rafael Palmeiro. It simply dominated the sporting landscape. And quite frankly, it will for years to come.

Can we realistically look at ANY record set before 2005 and say for certain it's a clean record? Can we realistically accuse everyone of being dirty? Or is that being guilty of widespread discrimination?

All we have at our disposal is the body of evidence. And in the case of people like Mark McGwire and Barry Bonds, that body seems to tell us an awful lot. We can only judge by what we see. And right now, our eyes are telling us more than any test, positive or negative, ever could."

**–Trey Wingo**

*II* It might be remembered as the year two sporting franchises were literally washed away from their hometown. The damage of Hurricane Katrina and subsequent flooding may have forced both the New Orleans Saints and the New Orleans Hornets to relocate to cities not ravaged by nature. And it's not just the physical damage caused to their facilites. There are real economic decisions that need to be made. The Saints are the only NFL team that are subsidized by the state. Considering the massive amout of relief and reconstruction needed, can Louisiana seriously afford to spend millions to keep an NFL team? Can businesses deciding whether or not to move back to New Orleans afford to spend the money on luxury boxes to keep both the Saints and the Hornets in the game. As is always the case the bottom line is the bottom line and that, more than anything else, may be the death knell of sports in New Orleans."

**–Trey Wingo**

*II* The Cubs own the Windy City but the White Sox had a short-term lease in 2005. On their dominating run to their first World Series title since 1917, culminating in a sweep of the Houston Astros, the White Sox had all the answers. The only thing the Southsiders and their fans, despite their ill-fated best efforts, could not accomplish in 2005 was to make *Journey* cool. The theme song of their playoff run was unfortunately 1981's "Don't Stop Believing" and due to that reason alone I fell off the bandwagon early on."

**–Dan Patrick**

**"** Jack Nicklaus bidding farewell to the game he elevated into an art form on the course where it was invented was a moment too perfect to capture in words. Every once in a while in sports, the past and the present meld into one. On that Friday in Scotland, Jack arrived at the place where yesterday meets tomorrow. It was a moment no one who was watching will ever forget."

**–Mike Greenberg**

**"** Sports are all about indelible images. Pictures cast individuals in our memories forever. Is there a person of appropriate age that will ever forget Rafael Palmeiro pointing his finger on Capitol Hill claiming, "I have never done steroids, period."? Five months later he was suspended for steroid use and his Hall of Fame status was plummeted into uncertainty."

**–Karl Ravech**

## SportsNation asked you to rank the top stories of the year. And here is how you voted...

1   Hurricane Katrina dislocates Saints and Hornets.

2   Lance Armstrong wins seventh Tour de France.

3   Ron Artest suspended in wake of brawl.

4   Rafael Palmeiro testifies, then tests positive for steroids.

5   New England Patriots win Super Bowl XXXIX.

6   USC Trojans win second straight national title.

7   Peyton Manning breaks NFL single season record for TD passes.

8   NHL lockout causes cancellation of season.

9   San Antonio Spurs win NBA title.

10   Roy Williams finally gets his national championship.

11   Tiger Woods wins two more majors.

12   Andre Agassi makes magical run at U.S. Open.

**Note:** White Sox fans don't flip out! Due to time constraints, this poll was taken prior to Chicago's historic World Series win.

# *Extra Points*

Now really...is jumping through a flaming hoop while
wearing a furry, oversized wolf suit ever a good idea?

AP/Wide World Photos

# Extra Points

*A look back at some of the more offbeat sports moments, quotes and personalities from the past year.*

## "Bird" Man of Alcatraz

In October the lawyers for Eric James Torpy reached a plea agreement that would send the Oklahoma man to prison for 30 years for robbery and shooting with an intent to kill.

There was just one problem — Torpy wasn't happy with the prison term. He wanted more! Evidently a huge Larry Bird fan, he asked the judge for 33 years instead of 30, to match Bird's Celtics uniform number.

"He said if he was going down, he was going to go down in Larry Bird's jersey," said Judge Ray Elliott. "We accommodated his request and he was just as happy as he could be."

---

### Best Yogi Berra Impression

"The more you can take high-percentage shots, the greater chance you have to make a higher percentage of them.

— Mavericks coach Avery Johnson

---

## Got Milk?

Florida Marlins batboy Nick Cirillo was suspended for six games in late August for accepting a bet from Dodgers (and former Marlins) pitcher Brad Penny that he couldn't drink a gallon of milk in under an hour without throwing up.

What actually happened appears to be the source of even more controversy. Penny told the media that Cirillo drank the milk and didn't throw up, but didn't do so in the appropriate time frame.

Cirillo claimed on "The Late Show With David Letterman" that he drank the milk in 59 minutes but then vomited outside the clubhouse. He got an unpaid vacation either way.

"It's kind of ridiculous that you get a 10-game suspension for steroids and a six-game suspension for milk," said Penny.

So in the end, not only did he not win the $500, but he's out six day's pay as well. On the bright side, he now has exceptionally strong teeth and bones.

AP/Wide World Photos

## Select a Caption:

1. *Wookie of the Year!*
2. *That last pitch had a little hair on it.*
3. *Johnny Damon throws out the first pitch at Fenway Park.*

## Rusty Wallace Shows Tony Danza Who's The Boss

Tony Danza received quite a scare during a taping of a segment for "The Tony Danza Show" in which he raced go-karts with NASCAR driver Rusty Wallace.

As the two entered the final lap of the "DayTony 500," Wallace gave Danza a little "bump and run" causing the show's host to lose control of his cart and flip over. Wallace rushed over and yelled, "I thought I killed ya!"

Danza was a little shaken up but escaped without serious injury. Neither driver was wearing a helmet.

## Wheaton vs. Wheaton

In the 2004 NCAA Division III Women's Soccer Final Four, Wheaton, Mass. faced off with Wheaton, Ill. for the first time in history.

Wheaton scored two goals to open the second half but Wheaton quickly cut the lead to one at the 63-minute mark. Wheaton would get no closer however, as the stingy Wheaton defense stiffened, keeping the Wheaton offense at bay. Wheaton added a late goal to make the final score 3-1.

Wheaton improved to 24-1 and advanced to the finals while Wheaton dropped to 23-1-2 with the loss.

AP/Wide World Photos

*Yes, that's **John Daly**. And yes, he's trying to hit a golf ball over the mother of all water hazards — Niagara Falls. On August 3 Daly smacked 20 balls from a platform, trying to span the 342-yard distance across the Falls from Canada into the United States. The closest he came was on his second try when the ball caromed off the bottom of a wall just short of the target. The other 19 disappeared into the mist.*

### Legal Eagle

When Philadelphia linebacker Jeremiah Trotter was fined $5,000 for his role in the pregame fight with the Atlanta Falcons on Sept. 12, he threatened to take his appeal all the way to the Supreme Court...or higher!

"Any of you know Matlock? Give me his number. I heard he's never lost," Trotter said.

### Nickname of the Year

"The Germanator"

— given by Rockets guard Jon Barry to teammate Ryan Bowen, who had the tough task of guarding Dallas forward and German-born Dirk Nowitzki during the first round of the playoffs. The Mavs won the series but Nowitzki was held five points below his season average.

### 100m dash record for 95-year-olds is shattered!

On June 21, Kozo Haraguchi, 95, set a new world record in the 100meters for men aged 95-99. As the only runner in the race, he clocked a 22.04 to beat the old mark of 24.01. Haraguchi also holds the mark for men aged 90-94 (18.08 seconds). No word on whether the tennis balls on his walker caught fire.

## Whiz Kid

Vikings running back Onterrio Smith was stopped at the Minneapolis-St. Paul Airport on April 21, after something in his luggage set off an airport security alarm. Turns out the "something" was several vials of dried urine and a device for beating drug tests called "The Original Whizzinator."

What exactly is an "Original Whizzinator" you may ask? According to the product's website, it is "an easy to conceal urinating device with a realistic prosthetic penis. And our quality production and materials assures you that the Whizzinator will let it flow, again and again, anytime, anywhere you need it!"

Smith claimed he was taking the device to his cousin (it's always the cousin's fault, isn't it?). While no charges were filed, he wasn't so lucky with the league office, who suspended him for the entire season (he already had two strikes in the NFL's substance abuse program).

Hey at least he splurged on an Original. You should see what they're trying to pass off as a Whizzinator these days.

## ...and in somewhat related news...

The second half of the Pistons-Magic game on January 18 was delayed after a seeing-eye dog wandered onto the court and relieved itself during halftime. Rasheed Wallace came out for warmups, saw what was waiting for him in the middle of the lane and could only stop and stare in disbelief.

## Giving the Finger...Twice

Portuguese soccer player **Paolo Diogo** lost a finger while climbing a fence in celebration of a goal. Reportedly his wedding ring got caught on the top of the fence and tore the top of his finger off. Adding insult to injury, the ref penalized him for excessive celebration.

Australian Rules football player **Brett Backwell** told the Australian Broadcasting Corp. that he plans to have one of his fingers amputated to improve his game. He says he's been in pain since breaking the finger three years ago. "To chop a finger off, that's a bit drastic, but I love my footy."

### Hold That Thought, Doc...Manny's Up

A study published in the Annals of Emergency Medicine shows that traffic in Boston-area emergency rooms "slowed significantly" during the Red Sox 2004 championship run. "The patient with pneumonia, the patient with an asthma attack will say, 'Maybe I can ride this out at home,'" said Doctor Alasdair Conn, ER chief at Mass. General Hospital. "It's as if when they look at the TV and see what's happening, they say, 'My infected lung, it's not so bad.'"

## Injuries of the Year

1. The Mets placed first baseman **Doug Mientkiewicz** on the 15-day DL after he suffered a slight tear in his right hamstring while warming up in the on-deck circle.

2. Rockies rookie **Clint Barmes** missed three months of the season with a broken collarbone after falling while carrying a package of deer meat up the stairs.

3. Devil Rays first baseman **Eduardo Perez** missed the final game of the season after injuring his knee while posing for the team picture.

4. Pitcher **Mike Remlinger** broke the little finger on his left hand when it was caught between two chairs in the Cubs clubhouse.

5. Minnesota Twins veteran **Terry Mulholland** rolled over in his hotel bed and got a feather from his pillow caught in his right eye. Two days later he was back in action. "I got some eye-drops and I'm ready to go," he said.

6. **Manny Fernandez** was supposed to start in net for the Minnesota Wild on Oct. 5, but had to pass after suffering neck and back spasms toweling off after a shower.

7. The Cubs told righthander **Carlos Zambrano** to cut back on his e-mailing because it's possible that the four hours a day he spends on the computer is contributing to his elbow problems. "I have to spend one hour a day and take it easy." he said.

---

### Juan Gone Faster Than Big Hurt Hurt

After spending the first two months on the disabled list, White Sox slugger Frank Thomas finally returned to the lineup on May 30...and left the game with a hip flexor injury in the seventh, after going 0-for-2 with a walk.

A day later, Indians outfielder Juan Gonzalez was activated from the DL...and lasted all of one at-bat, pulling up lame with a hamstring injury while running out a ground ball in the first inning. He was done for the year.

---

### Dolphin Rescued at Sea

Former Miami Dolphins running back **Larry Csonka** was among six people rescued by a helicopter after their boat was stranded overnight near Anchorage, Alaska. "It was a cold, dark, lonely night on the Bering Sea," said the hall of famer.

Csonka runs an outdoor sports TV show and was returning from filming a hunting trip when the boat ran into some nasty weather and called the Coast Guard.

### Derek Jeter Center?

Manhattan attorney and Harvard grad Kerry Konrad figured out the perfect way to get back at some of his former classmates, still beaming and talking trash after the Sox' come-from-behind victory over the Yankees in the ALCS.

When the operators of Boston's FleetCenter offered to sell one-day naming rights for the arena on eBay, Konrad posted a bid of $2,325...and won. When he told officials he wanted to name it the Derek Jeter Center, officials were at a loss...and then his bid was rejected.

"All names have to be rated 'G,'" said FleetCenter president Richard Krezwick. "We determined that 'Derek Jeter Center' is an obscene and vulgar use of the English language in Boston."

Eventually Konrad decided to deliver his bid and call the arena the "Jimmy Fund Center" after the Boston-based charity.

### Shaq Dishes Out an Assist

Miami Heat center Shaquille O'Neal, who is currently in the process of becoming a reserve police officer on Miami Beach, helped make his first arrest.

While driving on South Beach at around 3 a.m. on September 11, he heard a passenger in a car make anti-gay slurs to a couple, and then throw a bottle at them. The man then sped off but a quick-thinking Shaq flagged down an officer, who caught up to the car and arrested an 18-year-old on charges of aggravated assault and assault with a deadly weapon.

Shaquille O'Neal        Derek Jeter

### Open Mouth, Insert Foot

" I feel like they're a 1½-man team. I want to respect them just because I have to play them, but then I watch them on tape and everything, and I realize they're an average team, besides Reggie Bush."

—Oklahoma defensive end **Larry Birdine**, Dec. 22, 2004, two weeks before the average team, USC, pasted the Sooners, 55-19, in the Orange Bowl to win their second straight national championship.

### ...and the other foot...

"The U.S. is a small team. They play like my sister, my aunt and my grandmother."

—Mexican soccer coach **Ricardo Lavolpe**, *after* the United States' 2-0 whitewash of the Mexicans to clinch a berth in the 2006 World Cup. Lavolpe's sister, aunt and grandmother may very well be outstanding players, but we'll assume this is meant to be an insult.

## Who is That Masked Man?

Ultimate Pros and
www.therealrandymoss.com

Looking for a Halloween costume for next year? Why not go as your favorite Oakland Raiders wide receiver? For just $49.95 you can have your very own **Randy Moss mask**, created from an actual face cast and complete with a "deluxe afro wig." They're available at: www.therealrandymoss.com.

By the way, if your favorite Oakland Raiders receiver happens to be Jerry Porter or Doug Gabriel...you're on your own.

## NBA Dresses For Success

In October 2005, the NBA instituted a new, stricter dress code with the hopes of improving the league's image. Players are required to dress in "business casual" when engaged in team or league business – so no more jeans, 'do rags or throwbacks jerseys. Not surprisingly, many players didn't receive the change too well:

" You can put a murderer in a suit and he's still a murderer."

—Philadelphia 76ers all-star **Allen Iverson**

" I don't see it happening unless every NBA player is given a stipend to buy clothes."

—Denver Nuggets center **Marcus Camby**. Camby, incidentally, is due to make more than $7 million in the 2005-06 season.

" We don't know where the cutoff is – maybe if you earn less than $8 million, you'll get a scholarship from the commissioner."

—NBA Commissioner **David Stern**, presumably in response to Camby's comments.

"Oh I've got all kinds of suits I'm gonna break out – yellow and orange, suede, velvet. And a Cat in the Hat suit."

—Indiana Pacers **Ron Artest**

**Marcus Camby**      **Ron Artest**

AP/Wide World Photos

*Patriots owner **Bob Kraft**, left, shows off his 4.94-carat, diamond-encrusted Super Bowl ring to Russian president **Vladimir Putin** at a meeting in June. And that's the last Kraft would see of the ring as Putin quietly put it into his pocket and said good-bye. Whether it was miscommunication or simply a gift is still unknown. Kraft insists it was a gift, claiming, "I have ancestors from Russia, so it added significance for me to know that something so cherished reside at the Kremlin along with other special gifts given to Russian presidents." Fortunately for Kraft, he has two more just like it.*

### Van de Velde to Women's Tour?

On October 27 French golfer Jean Van de Velde, upset that women may be able to qualify for the men's British Open in 2006, said he will get an application and attempt to qualify for the 2006 Women's British Open at Royal Lytham.

"I am making a point. I'm not trying to make a sexist stance." He then added, "I'll even wear a kilt and shave my legs."

### Playing Through

What happens when one of the PGA Tour's fastest players gets paired up with one of its slowest? We found out on June 12 when Rory Sabbatini, fed up with partner Ben Crane's deliberate style, finished up out of turn on the 17th hole and walked to the 18th while Crane was still on the 17th fairway. PGA player Paul Azinger called Sabbatini's actions, "as inconsiderate as anything I've ever seen."

## Mascots Finally Get Their Due

What Ty Cobb, Babe Ruth, Honus Wagner, Christy Mathewson and Walter Johnson are to the National Baseball Hall of Fame — the San Diego Chicken, Phillie Fanatic and Phoenix Suns Gorilla are to the brand new Mascot Hall of Fame.

Those three beloved figures make up the inaugural class and were selected from a group of 14 finalists that included Ronald McDonald, the Denver Nuggets' Rocky and America's favorite rodent, Mickey Mouse. The inaugural induction ceremony was August 16 in Philadelphia and was attended by over 40 mascots.

"The Gorilla has meant so much to the city of Phoenix and he has taken on a life of his own," said Suns owner Robert Sarver.

Not everyone was as enthused however.

"The chicken is alright," said former Marlins manager and Padres front office employee. "Do your act and get the hell off the field."

To be considered for enshrinement, a mascot must be in existence for at least 10 years; have a major impact on its sport, industry and community; and have a performance that is consistently memorable and groundbreaking.

## When Mascots Attack

Sadly, not all mascot-related news was positive during the past year. In late 2004 in Dallas, Saints kicker Mitch Berger was practicing his kickoffs before his game with the Cowboys, when out of nowhere flew Rowdy, the Cowboys mascot, who tried to block the kick.

Berger landed awkwardly and a nasty skirmish ensued.

"I yelled a few expletives at him, and he's screaming back at me..." Berger said. "I tried to rip his head off and throw it, but I couldn't get it off. The referee saw it all, but what's he going to do? Throw a flag?

Rowdy was unavailable for comment.

## "A Political Animal"

Al the Ice Gorilla, mascot for the American Hockey League's Syracuse Crunch, is fed up with the state of affairs in his beloved city and he's doing something about it — he's running for mayor as a write-in candidate.

Though some clearly see a mascot running for mayor as nothing but a joke, there's no denying Al's constructive, well-thought out plans for the future development of Syracuse – in his opinion, more so than incumbent Matt Driscoll.

"The gorilla is skating on thin ice," said Driscoll.

## Free Agent Youppi! Signed by Canadiens

With the Montreal Expos now located in Washington, D.C., their longtime mascot Youppi! has been hired by the Montreal Canadiens. He is believed to be the first mascot in pro sports history to move from one league to another.

# Calendar

Skateboarder **Danny Way** jumps the Great Wall of China in Beijing on July 9. Why? Because it's there.

AP/Wide World Photos

# November 2004

| Sun | Mon | Tue | Wed | Thu | Fri | Sat |
|-----|-----|-----|-----|-----|-----|-----|
|     | 1   | 2   | 3   | 4   | 5   | 6   |
| 7   | 8   | 9   | 10  | 11  | 12  | 13  |
| 14  | 15  | 16  | 17  | 18  | 19  | 20  |
| 21  | 22  | 23  | 24  | 25  | 26  | 27  |
| 28  | 29  | 30  |     |     |     |     |

### Brawl at the Palace

**Who is most to blame for the brawl in Detroit?**

| | |
|---|---|
| 46.3% — | Detroit fans |
| 39.0% — | Ron Artest |
| 9.3% — | Ben Wallace |
| 4.8% — | Detroit Security |
| 0.6% — | Referees |

**Do you fault Ron Artest for going into the stands after being hit by a full cup of beer?**

| | |
|---|---|
| 58.8% — | Yes, he has to have a cooler head and let security handle it. |
| 41.2% — | No, any person has a right to defend himself in that situation. |

**Which was the worst incident between fans and players?**

| | |
|---|---|
| 68.7% — | Ron Artest and Pacers battle Detroit fans in the stands. |
| 24.8% — | Royals coach Tom Gamboa attacked on field in Chicago. |
| 6.4% — | Texas pitcher Frank Francisco throws chair into stands. |

**What should happen to Ron Artest?**

| | |
|---|---|
| 52.9% — | Suspended more than 10 games |
| 19.6% — | Suspended 1-5 games |
| 16.8% — | Suspended 6-10 games |
| 15.4% — | Monetary fine, no suspension |

**Total Votes:** 206,997

**3 The 2004-05 NBA season tips off** with Shaq's Heat blowing out the New Jersey Nets, 100-77, and LeBron scoring 28 in the Cavs' 109-104 loss to the Indiana Pacers.

**4 And then there were 30.** The expansion Charlotte Bobcats open their inaugural NBA season with a 103-96 loss to the Washington Wizards.

**U.S. Olympic swimming star Michael Phelps** is busted for DUI after running a top sign in Maryland.

**5 The Arizona Diamondbacks fire** new manager Wally Backman just four days after he was hired after the team learned of an arrest stemming from a domestic dispute and a DUI charge in 2000. Bob Melvin is hired as the new manager.

**6 David Ortiz blasts** a 514-foot home run in Tokyo in a game between major league all-stars and Japanese stars. "I thought for a second that it might land in the Dominican [Republic]," he said.

**7 Paula Radcliffe wins the NY Marathon** (2:23:10), finishing just four seconds in front of Kenyan Susan Chepchemei in the tightest women's race in NY Marathon history. Hendrik Ramaala wins the men's event in 2:09:28, ahead of USA's Meb Keflezighi (2:09:53).

**Sebastien Bourdais edges** teammate Bruno Junqueira at the Gran Premio Telmex-Tecate in Mexico City to wrap up the 2004 Champ Car title.

**8 Defensemen Ray Bourque,** Paul Coffey and Larry Murphy are inducted into the Hockey Hall of Fame along with Coyotes exec. Cliff Fletcher.

**9 Dave Wannstedt resigns** as head coach of the 1-8 Miami Dolphins.

**14 With three goals in a seven-minute span,** the D.C. United defeats the Kansas City Wizards, 3-2, in MLS Cup 2004.

**15 Giants slugger Barry Bonds** is awarded his record seventh National League MVP award and fourth in a row. The 40-year old batted .362 and hit his 700th home run in 2004. Dodgers 3B Adrian Beltre finishes in second.

**ABC's Monday Night Football opens** with a suggestive skit in which Desperate Housewives star Nicollette Sheridan drops her towel and attempts to seduce wide receiver Terrell Owens in the Eagles' locker room. ABC Sports, and Owens, later apologize after a slew of viewer complaints.

AP/Wide World Photos

*Indiana Pacers forward **Ron Artest** has his jersey partially torn after venturing into the crowd at the Palace to fight with a fan he thought threw a cup of beer on him. He had plenty of time to sew his ripped shirt as he was suspended for the remainder of the season.*

**16 Vladimir Guerrero** of the Anaheim Angels wins the American League MVP award over runner-up Gary Sheffield.

**19 Friday Night Fights at the Palace.** Indiana Pacers forward Ron Artest storms into the crowd after he is struck by a cup of beer, setting off a brutal melee between fans and the Pacers in one of the ugliest incidents in NBA, and sports, history.

Artest is later suspended for the entire season while Stephen Jackson and Jermaine O'Neal are 'handed 30 games and 25 games, respectively (O'Neal's is later cut to 15). In all, nine players are suspended, including Pistons' forward Ben Wallace, who shoved Artest after a hard foul, setting the chain of events in motion.

"The events were shocking, repulsive and inexcusable," said commissioner David Stern. "A humiliation for everyone associated with the NBA.

**21 Kurt Busch finishes fifth** at Homestead—despite losing his front-right wheel earlier in the race—and earns enough points to win NASCAR's first Nextel Cup championship. Jimmie Johnson ends the season in second place, while fellow Chevy driver Jeff Gordon takes third.

**24 Phil Mickelson shoots** a 59 at the PGA Grand Slam of Golf and misses a nine-foot putt for a 58 by mere inches. The tournament is an unofficial exhibition match, however, leaving Al Geiberger, Chip Beck and David Duval as the only men to card a sub-60 score in an official PGA event.

**25 Quarterback Peyton Manning throws** six touchdown passes to lead the Indianapolis Colts to a 41-9 drubbing of the Lions in early Thanksgiving Day NFL action. The Dallas Cowboys take care of the Chicago Bears, 21-7, in the later game.

**28 The Cincinnati Bengals** defeat the Cleveland Browns, 58-48, in the second-highest scoring game in NFL history (behind the Redskins 72-41 win over the Giants in 1966).

**30 Tyrone Willingham is fired** as the head coach of Notre Dame football after three seasons, in which his teams went a combined 21-15. After an exhaustive search, New England Patriots offensive coordinator Charlie Weis is hired 13 days later and entrusted with bringing the program back into the national championship picture.

## December 2004

| Sun | Mon | Tue | Wed | Thu | Fri | Sat |
|-----|-----|-----|-----|-----|-----|-----|
|     |     |     | 1   | 2   | 3   | 4   |
| 5   | 6   | 7   | 8   | 9   | 10  | 11  |
| 12  | 13  | 14  | 15  | 16  | 17  | 18  |
| 19  | 20  | 21  | 22  | 23  | 24  | 25  |
| 26  | 27  | 28  | 29  | 30  | 31  |     |

### Giambi in a Jam

**How many home runs will Jason Giambi hit in the 2005 season?**

| 44.1% | — | 21-30 |
| 28.7% | — | 11-20 |
| 15.5% | — | 31 or more |
| 11.6% | — | 10 or less |

**Total Votes:** 33,210

**How should records set by any player who admits to having used steroids be treated?**

| 38.4% | — | Noted with asterisk |
| 33.3% | — | Expunged from the books |
| 28.3% | — | Left as is |

**Who do you recognize as baseball's single-season home run leader?**

| 42.5% | — | Roger Maris |
| 35.2% | — | Barry Bonds |
| 14.6% | — | Mark McGwire |
| 6.2%  | — | Babe Ruth |
| 1.6%  | — | Sammy Sosa |

**Nine players hit at least 40 home runs last season. How many would you guess used steroids?**

| 47.7% | — | Two or three |
| 40.9% | — | More than half |
| 6.4%  | — | All of them |
| 5.0%  | — | None |

**Total Votes:** 19,348

**1  Move over Dean.** Harry Statham, head basketball coach of the NAIA's McKendree College, records win number 880 with an 83-72 win over Maryvale. The win gives him one more than former North Carolina head coach Dean Smith (879).

**2  Busted!** *The San Francisco Chronicle* publishes the testimony of Yankees slugger Jason Giambi from December 2003 in which he testified that he used steroids for at least three seasons and injected himself with human growth hormones in 2003.

The following night on ABC's "20/20," BALCO founder Victor Conte says he supplied track star Marion Jones with performance-enhancing drugs prior to the 2000 Olympics in Sydney.

"After I instructed her how to do it and dialed it up, she did the injection with me sitting right there next to her," he says. Jones denies all charges and later sues Conte.

**6  Nine tournament victories** and a record $10.9 million in season earnings is enough for Fiji-native Vijay Singh to end Tiger Woods' five-year reign as PGA Tour Player of the Year.

"This was kind of a landslide," said Singh. "I really didn't have to wait for a vote."

**9  Ohio State imposes** a one-year postseason ban on its men's basketball team, stemming from former coach Jim O'Brien's payment of $6,000 to a former recruit.

**11  USC quarterback Matt Leinart** wins the Heisman Trophy, beating out Oklahoma teammates Adrian Peterson (a true freshman) and 2003 winner Jason White.

**15  Pitcher Pedro Martinez,** claiming he didn't get the respect he deserved from the Red Sox, says goodbye to the team he just won the World Series with and signs a four-year, $53 million deal to become the ace of the New York Mets.

**17  The Toronto Raptors** grant forward Vince Carter his wish for a change of scenery, dealing the five-time all-star to the New Jersey Nets for Alonzo Mourning, Aaron Williams, Erik Williams and two first-round draft picks.

**19  Ouch! The Philadelphia Eagles** improve their record to 13-1 with a 12-7 win over the Dallas Cowboys, but lose star wide receiver Terrell Owens in the process, after a horse collar tackle by safety Roy Williams leaves him with a broken leg and torn ligaments in his ankle.

AP/Wide World Photos

BALCO founder **Victor Conte** holds up an autographed Marion Jones photo in his office outside of San Francisco. On December 3 Conte gave an interview with ABC's "20/20" and described, in detail, how he helped Jones inject steroids. Jones angrily denied all charges.

**21 The long-awaited relocation** of the Montreal Expos to Washington, D.C. clears another important hurdle when the District of Columbia votes, 7-6, to approve legislation that will allow the team to move to the nation's capital and become the Nationals, beginning with the upcoming 2005 season.

**The Associated Press** officially tells the BCS to stop using its Top-25 college football poll to determine which teams should play in BCS bowl games.

**26 Indianapolis Colts quarterback Peyton Manning** tosses a 21-yard strike to wide receiver Brandon Stokley for his 49th touchdown pass of the season, breaking former Dolphins star Dan Marino's single-season mark of 48. Perhaps more importantly to Manning, the score is instrumental in leading the Colts to a 34-31, come-from-behind overtime victory against the San Diego Chargers.

**Reggie White,** the affable defensive end dubbed the "Minister of Defense," dies at his home in North Carolina at the age of 43. He played 15 seasons for the Philadelphia Eagles, Green Bay Packers and Carolina Panthers

**27 Cyclist Lance Armstrong** is named Associated Press Male Athlete of the Year for the third year in a row. Armstrong won his unprecedented sixth Tour de France in 2004.

**28 For the second straight year,** golfer Annika Sorenstam is voted AP Female Athlete of the Year after a season in which she won eight tournaments including the McDonald's LPGA Championship. Connecticut hoopster Diana Taurasi places second.

**30 An uninspired Cal team,** still smarting after being snubbed by the BCS, falls, 45-31, to Texas Tech in the Holiday Bowl in San Diego. Also, Boston College beats North Carolina, 37-24, in the Continental Tire Bowl, and Navy (10-2) caps its best season in 99 years with a 34-19 win over New Mexico in the Emerald Bowl in San Francisco.

**31 In major college football bowl** game action, Miami crushes Florida, 27-10, in the Peach Bowl to win state bragging rights, Louisville wins a thriller, 44-40, over Boise State in the Liberty Bowl and Minnesota ekes out a 20-16 win over Alabama in the Music City Bowl in Nashville.

# January 2005

| Sun | Mon | Tue | Wed | Thu | Fri | Sat |
|-----|-----|-----|-----|-----|-----|-----|
|     |     |     |     |     |     | 1   |
| 2   | 3   | 4   | 5   | 6   | 7   | 8   |
| 9   | 10  | 11  | 12  | 13  | 14  | 15  |
| 16  | 17  | 18  | 19  | 20  | 21  | 22  |
| 23/30 | 24/31 | 25 | 26 | 27 | 28 | 29 |

## Sammy wears out his welcome

**Sammy Sosa was dealt to the Orioles for Jerry Hairston Jr. and two minor leaguers. Who got the better end of the deal?**

52.1% — Orioles...Sosa just needs a change of scenery

47.9% — Cubs...Sosa was becoming a liability

**How has your opinion changed from his record-chasing 1998 season to his late-season problems with the Cubs?**

41.2% — I used to love Sosa but last year's actions lessened my opinion of him

30.4% — I was never high on Sosa and last year's actions reaffirmed my feelings

18.1% — I used to love Sosa and still do

10.2% — I was never high on Sosa but he was not treated fairly by the Cubs

**The Orioles were 78-84 in 2004. Will they finish above .500 this year?**

55.2% — Yes

44.8% — No

**Total Votes:** 74,672

**1** **Texas kicker Dusty Mangum** boots a 37-yard field goal as time expires to give the Longhorns a 38-37 win over Michigan in the Rose Bowl. In other New Year's Day action, Georgia edges Wisconsin, 24-21, in the Outback Bowl, Tennessee pounds Texas A&M, 38-7, in the Cotton Bowl and Urban Meyer's Utah team stays undefeated with a 35-7 win over Pitt in the Fiesta Bowl.

**3** **Auburn keeps its national title hopes** alive with a 16-13 victory over Virginia Tech in the Sugar Bowl.

**Dan Gilbert, founder** of online mortgage company Quicken Loans, buys the Cleveland Cavaliers and Gund Arena for $375 million.

**First Los Angeles, then California,** then Anaheim and now...Angels owner Arte Moreno announces that his team will be called the Los Angeles Angels of Anaheim. They are promptly sued by the City of Anaheim.

"Name another team that has two destinations in it!" said city spokesman John Nicoletti.

**4** **Top-ranked USC pummels** No. 2 Oklahoma, 55-19, in the Orange Bowl as Pete Carroll and Co. win their second consecutive National Championship. Trojan quarterback Matt Leinart throws an Orange Bowl-record five touchdown passes and earns the game's MVP award.

**Wade Boggs and Ryne Sandberg** are elected to the Baseball Hall of Fame, Boggs on his first try and Sandberg on his third. Boggs is an overwhelming selection with 91.9 percent of the vote, while Sandberg receives 76.2 percent (75 is needed for election).

**8** **NY Jets kicker Doug Brien** nails a 28-yard field goal in overtime, minutes after Chargers kicker Nate Kaeding misses a 40-yarder, to lead the Jets to a 20-17 win and into the next round of the playoffs. Elsewhere, the Rams defeat the Seahawks when a last-second Matt Hasselbeck pass goes through the hands of Bobby Engram in the end zone.

**9** **The Vikings and Colts earn** first-round playoff victories, but Vikings wide receiver Randy Moss steals the headlines with his "fake moon" of the Lambeau Field crowd after one of his two touchdowns.

**10** **"Don't get in my face, and don't talk back to me, alright?"** Randy Johnson's welcome to New York is an unpleasant one after a confrontation with a cameraman on the way to his physical.

**Colts quarterback Peyton Manning** wins his second straight AP MVP award.

AP/Wide World Photos

*Vikings receiver **Randy Moss** bends over and pretends to "moon" the Lambeau Field crowd after his 34-yard touchdown against the Packers on January 9.*

**11 Coveted free agent Carlos Beltran** inks a seven-year, $119 million deal to patrol centerfield for the NY Mets.

**13 Major League Baseball** and its players' union announce a new steroid policy that includes a 10-day suspension for a first positive test, 30 days for the second, 60 days for a third and a one-year ban for a fourth.

**15 The Pittsburgh Steelers advance** to the AFC Championship Game with a 20-17 overtime win over the Jets, after Jets kicker Doug Brien misses two field goals in the last 2:02 of regulation. The Falcons also advance, with a 47-17 trouncing of the Rams.

**Michelle Kwan joins** Maribel Vinson as the only two women to win nine U.S. Figure Skating Championships. Johnny Weir successfully defends his title in the men's division.

**16 The New England Patriots dominate** the high-octane Colts, 20-3, while the Terrell Owens-less Eagles beat the Vikings, 27-14.

**22 Sixty seven-year-old Lenny Wilkens,** the winningest (and losingest) coach in NBA history, steps down as coach of the 17-22 New York Knicks.

**23 The Patriots power** to a 41-27 win in Pittsburgh while the Eagles finally win the NFC Championship Game after three straight losses, 27-10, over the Falcons to set up a Super Bowl showdown.

**24 Ghostzapper wins** the Eclipse Award for Horse of the Year—besting runner-up Smarty Jones—and adds another one for Top Older Male.

**28 Serena Williams rallies** to a come-from-behind 2-6, 6-3, 6-0 victory over Lindsay Davenport at the finals of the Australian Open for her seventh Grand Slam singles title.

**Slammin' Sammy Sosa takes** his familiar, albeit less frequent, home run hop to Baltimore. The rightfielder, currently in seventh place on the all-time home run list with 574, is dealt from the Chicago Cubs to the Orioles for Jerry Hairston Jr. and two prospects.

**30 Russian Marat Safin defeats** hometown favorite Lleyton Hewitt, in four sets, 1-6, 6-3, 6-4, 6-4, to win the men's Australian Open. It is Safin's second major title (he also won the 2000 U.S. Open over then-hometown favorite Pete Sampras).

# February 2005

| Sun | Mon | Tue | Wed | Thu | Fri | Sat |
|-----|-----|-----|-----|-----|-----|-----|
|     |     | 1   | 2   | 3   | 4   | 5   |
| 6   | 7   | 8   | 9   | 10  | 11  | 12  |
| 13  | 14  | 15  | 16  | 17  | 18  | 19  |
| 20  | 21  | 22  | 23  | 24  | 25  | 26  |
| 27  | 28  |     |     |     |     |     |

## Pats a Dynasty?

**Are the New England Patriots a dynasty?**

| 85.5% | — | Yes |
|-------|---|-----|
| 14.5% | — | No  |

**Does the fact that the Patriots have not won a Super Bowl in convincing fashion diminish their legacy at all?**

| 80.5% | — | No  |
|-------|---|-----|
| 19.5% | — | Yes |

**How will Super Bowl XXXIX be remembered?**

| 75.4% | — | Patriots fulfill dynasty talk with third win in four years. |
|-------|---|----|
| 24.6% | — | Donovan McNabb and Eagles watch clock tick away |

**Total Votes:** 77,381

## Chaney Sends in his Goon

**Should [Temple coach] John Chaney be fired?**

| 55.5% | — | Yes |
|-------|---|-----|
| 44.5% | — | No  |

**Which is the ugliest incident between a college player and coach?**

| 45.8% | — | Woody Hayes punching a Clemson football player |
|-------|---|----|
| 37.5% | — | Bob Knight putting his hands around Neil Reed's throat |
| 16.8% | — | Chaney ordering Nehemiah Ingram to give "hard fouls" |

**2  Rudy Tomjanovich walks** away from a $30 million contract, quitting as head coach of the Los Angeles Lakers (24-19) due to the "immense pressure he put on himself."

**3  In an emotional, tear-filled press conference,** Emmitt Smith, the leading rusher of all-time with 18,355 yards, announces his retirement after a 15-year NFL career.

**5  Quarterbacks Dan Marino, Steve Young** and Benny Friedman and running back and NFL pioneer Fritz Pollard are elected into the Pro Football Hall of Fame.

**6  If this isn't a dynasty, then what is?** The New England Patriots win their second consecutive Super Bowl and third in the last four years with a 24-21 victory over the Philadelphia Eagles in Super Bowl XXXIX. Wide receiver Deion Branch hauls in 11 of Tom Brady's passes for 133 yards to earn game MVP honors.

Terrell Owens returns from injury and delivers a gutsy performance in a losing effort, catching nine balls for 122 yards. The Pats' defense picks off Donovan McNabb three times (two by Rodney Harrison) and sack him four more times. With the win, Tom Brady improves to 9-0 in playoff games over his stellar career.

**8  Boston College is handed** its first loss of the season, 68-65, to Notre Dame, dropping them to 20-1 and leaving Illinois (24-0) as the only undefeated men's Division I college basketball team in the country.

**The WNBA announces** its new expansion team will be located in Chicago and will begin play in 2006 (it is later announced that the team will be known as the Sky).

**Excerpts are released** from Jose Canseco's book, *Juiced: Wild Times, Rampant 'Roids, Smash Hits, and How Baseball Got Big* and cause an uproar before the book officially hits the shelves on Valentine's Day. Canseco claims he introduced Juan Gonzalez, Pudge Rodriguez and Rafael Palmeiro to steroids...and actually injected former A's teammate Mark McGwire on more than one occasion.

**10  In a strange (but true) press conference,** Jason Giambi apologizes to fans, the media and his Yankee teammates, but never utters the word *steroid* or explains to anyone the reasons for his apology. Nonetheless, Yankees owner George Steinbrenner praises Giambi, saying it took a "hell of a man" to apologize to the New York fans.

**12  Allen Iverson scores** 60 points in the 76ers' 112-99 win over the Orlando Magic.

AP/Wide World Photos

NFL all-time leading rusher **Emmitt Smith** cries as he announces his retirement from football on February 3 after a 15-year career. He is consoled by his wife, Pat.

**13 Dale Jarrett, 48, records** a qualifying speed of 188.312 mph to grab the pole at next week's NASCAR season-opening Daytona 500. it is the third Daytona 500 pole of his career. Jimmie Johnson's lap at 188.170 is good enough for second, putting him in the front row alongside Jarrett.

**Regular season MVP** Peyton Manning can now add Pro Bowl MVP to his resume after tossing three touchdown passes in the AFC's 38-27 victory in Honolulu.

**14 Chris Bourque, son of former great Ray,** scores the game-winning goal 14:10 into overtime to lead Boston University to a 3-2 win over Northeastern in the annual Beanpot championship game in Boston. It is the Terriers' 26th win in the tournament's 53-year history.

**Savannah State finishes** its season at 0-28, making it the second Division I men's basketball team in the last 50 years (Prairie View, 0-28, 1991-92) to go winless for an entire season. The team officially has a 55-game losing streak.

**15 Carlee, a German short-haired pointer,** wows the crowd with her amazing "free stack" and wins Best in Show at the annual Westminster Dog Show.

**16 "This is a sad, regrettable day** that all of us wish could have been avoided," says NHL commissioner Gary Bettman, just after he officially cancels the entire 2004-05 season. It is the first time the Stanley Cup won't be awarded since 1919.

**Patriots linebacker Tedy Bruschi** is admitted to Mass. General Hospital for what is later learned to be a mild stroke.

**19 The NHL calls in the big guns**—legends Wayne Gretzky and Mario Lemieux—with the hopes of reaching an agreement and "uncanceling" the season.

**21 Game MVP Allen Iverson** scores 15 points and dishes out 10 assists to lead the East to a 125-115 win in the NBA All-Star Game.

**Jeff Gordon wins his third** Daytona 500, edging Kurt Busch and Dale Earnhardt Jr. in "overtime" after a late caution flag adds two extra laps. It is the 70th win of Gordon's career.

**25 Temple suspends head coach John Chaney** for the rest of the regular season for sending in "goon" Nehemiah Ingram to "send a message" during their game with St. Joe's. Unfortunately one of Ingram's hard fouls breaks senior forward John Bryant's arm.

# March 2005

| Sun | Mon | Tue | Wed | Thu | Fri | Sat |
|-----|-----|-----|-----|-----|-----|-----|
|     |     | 1   | 2   | 3   | 4   | 5   |
| 6   | 7   | 8   | 9   | 10  | 11  | 12  |
| 13  | 14  | 15  | 16  | 17  | 18  | 19  |
| 20  | 21  | 22  | 23  | 24  | 25  | 26  |
| 27  | 28  | 29  | 30  | 31  |     |     |

## Congress Hammers MLB

**Whose testimony was the most compelling?**

| | |
|---|---|
| 28.4% — | Mark McGwire |
| 12.7% — | Senator Jim Bunning |
| 12.6% — | Curt Schilling |
| 12.2% — | Donald Hooten Sr. |
| 11.2% — | Jose Canseco |
| 10.6% — | Dr. Denise & Raymond Garibaldi |
| 8.9% — | Rafael Palmeiro |
| 1.9% — | Dr. Elliot Pellman, MLB medical adviser |
| 1.4% — | Sammy Sosa |

**What do you feel was the primary purpose of the hearing?**

| | |
|---|---|
| 59.8% — | To force MLB to enact tougher testing policies |
| 27.5% — | To gain airtime and headlines for committee members |
| 12.7% — | To raise awareness of the potential dangers of steroids |

**What is your opinion of Sammy Sosa's statement under oath that he had not used steroids?**

| | |
|---|---|
| 69.3% — | I don't believe him |
| 30.7% — | I believe him |

**What is your opinion of Rafael Palmeiro's statement under oath that he had not used steroids?**

| | |
|---|---|
| 70.3% — | I believe him |
| 29.7% — | I don't believe him |

**Total Votes:** 73,115

**2** **Highly controversial, yet immensely talented** wide receiver Randy Moss is traded from the Minnesota Vikings to the Oakland Raiders for linebacker Napoleon Harris, a first-round pick in the upcoming draft and another late-round pick.

**6** **Ohio State's Matt Sylvester** nails a three-pointer with 5.1 seconds left to give the Buckeyes a 65-64 win over top-ranked Illinois and hand the Illini their first loss of the season. The loss drops Illinois to 29-1 and ensures that the 1976 Indiana squad will remain the last undefeated national champion for at least another season.

**Tiger Woods sinks a 30-foot birdie putt** on the 17th hole and records a thrilling, come-from-behind, one-stroke victory over playing partner Phil Mickelson in the Ford Championship at Doral. With the win, Tiger reclaims his familiar spot as the No. 1 ranked player in the world.

**7** **Rick Neuheisel's lawsuit** stemming from his 2003 dismissal as Washington football coach comes to an end with the former coach hitting the jackpot. Neuheisel, the school and the NCAA agreed to a settlement that pays him a total of $4.5 million.

**12** **New Hampshire's Bode Miller**, often criticized for his unorthodox style, becomes the first American since Phil Mahre and Tamara McKinney in 1983 to win alpine skiing's World Cup overall title.

**13** **The NCAA Division I men's** basketball brackets are set with Illinois, North Carolina, Washington and Duke grabbing the top seeds. Miami-OH is probably the most surprising omission while Rick Pitino's Louisville (29-4), who was expected to get either a one or two seed is shocked to find themselves with the No. 4 seed in the Albuquerque bracket.

**New York's** *Daily News* reports that a 1990s FBI investigation uncovered a California man, Curtis Wenzlaff, giving "Bash Brothers" Jose Canseco and Mark McGwire illegal anabolic steroids. McGwire is already reeling after Canseco's book, released last month, leveled scathing accusations at the former A's and Cardinals slugger.

**15** **The NCAA Tournament** is underway! Well...sort of. Oakland (13-18) defeats Alabama A&M in the play-in game and earns a No. 16 seed in the Syracuse bracket. As a reward, they get to play top-seeded North Carolina (27-4) in Charlotte.

AP/Wide World Photos

*Mark McGwire* is sworn in before giving his uncomfortable and uninspiring testimony on Capitol Hill regarding steroid use in Major League Baseball. He is flanked from left to right by Sammy Sosa, Sosa's interpreter Patricia Rosell, Rafael Palmeiro and Curt Schilling.

**16 Norwegian Robert Sorlie** wins his second Iditarod Trail Sled Dog Race in three tries, completing the 1,100-mile race from Anchorage to Nome in nine days, 18 hours, 39 minutes and 31 seconds.

**17 Congress takes aim** at Major League Baseball, prodding players on their use and blasting commissioner Bud Selig and players' union executive director Donald Fehr on the league's current drug policy, which is at worst pitiful, and at best, confusing.

"They owe it to us to prove that they are fixing this terrible problem," said hall of famer Jim Bunning, R-Ky. "If not, we will have to do it for them."

Players Mark McGwire, Sammy Sosa, Rafael Palmeiro and Curt Schilling are in attendance, along with former player Jose Canseco, whose book sparked the scandal. Palmeiro points and emphatically states that he never used steroids, Sosa loses his ability to speak English and McGwire comes away smelling the worst of all, as he fails to state under oath that he never took illegal steroids. "I didn't come here to talk about the past," said McGwire. When pressed further, he added, "Steroids is bad. Don't do 'em."

**18 Major upsets abound** at the NCAA Tourney as No. 13 seed Vermont nips fourth-seeded Syracuse, 60-57, in overtime, and No. 14 seed Bucknell, with five scholarship players and eight walk-ons, shocks No. 3 Kansas, 64-63.

**20 LeBron James scores 56** in a 105-98 loss to the Toronto Raptors. He becomes the youngest player in NBA history (20 years, 80 days) with a 50-point game.

**Russian Irina Slutskaya wins** her second World Figure Skating Championship as American Sasha Cohen places second. A disappointed Michelle Kwan finishes in fourth.

**22 Barry Bonds conducts a depressing** press conference and announces he may not play at all during the upcoming baseball season. Bonds chastises the media, claiming they "finally brought me and my family down."

**26 Illinois, trailing 75-60** with four minutes left, roars back to beat Arizona in overtime, 90-89. Louisville rallies from 20 down to beat West Virginia in overtime, 93-85.

**27 Michigan State completes** a thrilling weekend of NCAA hoops, staging a two-overtime victory over Kentucky to reach the Final Four.

# April 2005

| Sun | Mon | Tue | Wed | Thu | Fri | Sat |
|-----|-----|-----|-----|-----|-----|-----|
|     |     |     |     |     | 1   | 2   |
| 3   | 4   | 5   | 6   | 7   | 8   | 9   |
| 10  | 11  | 12  | 13  | 14  | 15  | 16  |
| 17  | 18  | 19  | 20  | 21  | 22  | 23  |
| 24  | 25  | 26  | 27  | 28  | 29  | 30  |

## Sheffield vs. Fenway Fan

**Who was more at fault for the incident on April 14?**

| 80.7% — | The Boston fan |
| 19.3% — | Gary Sheffield |

**What do you think was the fan's intention?**

| 40.8% — | He was trying to distract Sheffield but didn't mean to touch him |
| 32.9% — | He was trying to swipe at Sheffield |
| 26.4% — | He was reaching for the ball |

**What do you think of Gary Sheffield's reaction?**

| 39.1% — | He did what should be expected of a player |
| 35.9% — | He should be commended for showing remarkable restraint |
| 25.0% — | He overreacted |

**If placed in the same situation as Sheffield, do you think you would have gone after the fan?**

| 56.5% — | No |
| 43.5% — | Yes |

**Total Votes: 91,577**

**2** **After a slow start puts them** down by five at halftime, North Carolina turns on the jets and cruises to a 87-71 win over Michigan State to advance to the NCAA Championship Game. Sean May pours in 22 points, all but four coming in the second half.

The Heels will play Illinois, who puts an end to Louisville's season with a 72-57. Luther Head and Roger Powell Jr. each score 20 to lead the Illini.

**3** **The 2005 Major League baseball season** gets underway...with the Yankees and Red Sox meeting for the first time since the Sox' stirring come-from-behind 4-3 series win in the ALCS just over five months ago. The host Yankees, behind new ace Randy Johnson, get the better of Boston this time with a 9-2 win over former Yankee David Wells.

**Tampa Bay speedster** Alex Sanchez becomes the first victim of baseball's new steroid policy. He is given a 10-day suspension, but blames the positive test on a dietary supplement he purchased over the counter. He adds, "I'm surprised because look at what kind of player I am. I'm a leadoff hitter. I never hit home runs."

**4** **North Carolina beats Illinois,** 75-70, to win its fourth men's national basketball championship and first since 1993. Team leader Sean May has a very happy 21st birthday, scoring a game-high 26 points on 10-of-11 shooting and grabbing 10 rebounds. Head coach Roy Williams can finally cut down the nets as champion, after losing in the Final Four four times with Kansas, twice in the final game. Illinois (37-2) was looking for its first hoops title ever. They were led by Luther Head's 21 points.

**5** **Baylor wins its first women's** basketball title with an 84-62 trouncing of Michigan State in Indianapolis. Coach Kim Mulkey-Robertson becomes the first person to win the championship as a head coach, assistant coach and player. Sophia Young scores 26 and is named most outstanding player of the Final Four.

**9** **The second round of the Masters** is complete and Jack Nicklaus, playing in his 45th and final Masters, fails to make the cut.

**10** **Tiger Woods beats Chris DiMarco** with a 15-foot birdie putt on the first sudden-death playoff hole at the Masters for his fourth green jacket. His tournament will be remembered for his seven straight birdies leading to a third-round 65, and his amazing chip on 16 in which the ball rolled down the slope of the green, stopped on the lip of the cup and finally dropped in.

AP/Wide World Photos

*President George W. Bush* throws out the first pitch at the Washington Nationals-Arizona Diamondbacks game, the first regular-season baseball game in the nation's capital in 34 years.

**13 TiVo, a digital video recorder** company, announces that Tiger Woods' chip shot on the 16th hole of the Masters received a 116 ranking for replays, out of a possible 200. By comparison, Janet Jackson's "wardrobe malfunction" during halftime of the 2004 Super Bowl received a score of 180, while the Madonna-Britney Spears kiss at the 2003 MTV Video Music Awards received a 140.

**14 Baseball returns to the nation's capital** for the first time since 1971 as the Washington Nationals win their home opener, 5-3, over the Arizona Diamondbacks at RFK Stadium in front of 45,596 fans. President George Bush, donning a nationals jacket, throws out the ceremonial first pitch, a changeup high and away.

**A fan at friendly Fenway** takes a swipe at Yankee oufielder Gary Sheffield as he is fielding Jason Varitek's triple in the right field corner. Sheffield pushes the fan before throwing the ball to the cutoff man, then turns with a cocked fist before regaining his composure. "I don't know if he hit me or not," said Sheffield. "It felt like it. I thought my lip was busted." The fan later claimed he was simply going for the ball — apparently by swinging at it.

**18 The NFL inks new television** contracts with CBS, FOX, NBC and ESPN to begin in 2006. NBC, which returns to the NFL after an eight-year hiatus, gets Sunday Night Football, while ESPN takes over the Monday Night Football schedule from Disney partner ABC. CBS continues to broadcast AFC games on Sunday, while FOX continues with Sunday NFC games.

**20 Cubs shortstop Nomar Garciaparra** take one step out of the batters box and pulls up lame with a severely torn groin, causing him to miss the majority of the 2005 season.

**23 The San Francisco 49ers** select Utah quarterback Alex Smith with the first overall selection in the NFL Draft. Running back Ronnie Brown is taken second by the Miami Dolphins and his backfield partner at Auburn, Cadillac Williams, is taken three picks later by the Tampa Bay Buccaneers. Denver chooses former Ohio State running back Maurice Clarett with the last pick in the third round.

**26 Alex Rodriguez swats** three home runs in his first three at-bats and drives in 10 — becoming the 11th player with at least 10 RBI in a game — in the Yankees' 12-4 win over Angels.

# May 2005

| Sun | Mon | Tue | Wed | Thu | Fri | Sat |
|-----|-----|-----|-----|-----|-----|-----|
| 1 | 2 | 3 | 4 | 5 | 6 | 7 |
| 8 | 9 | 10 | 11 | 12 | 13 | 14 |
| 15 | 16 | 17 | 18 | 19 | 20 | 21 |
| 22 | 23 | 24 | 25 | 26 | 27 | 28 |
| 29 | 30 | 31 | | | | |

## Interest in Indy?

**Are you more interested in this year's Indy 500 because of Danica Patrick?**

| | | |
|---|---|---|
| 94.8% | — | No |
| 5.2% | — | Yes |

**What is the world's most prestigious auto race?**

| | | |
|---|---|---|
| 75.7% | — | Monaco Grand Prix |
| 11.9% | — | Daytona 500 |
| 6.6% | — | 24 Hours at Le Mans |
| 5.7% | — | Indianapolis 500 |

**What is your favorite racing circuit?**

| | | |
|---|---|---|
| 72.9% | — | Champ Car |
| 11.0% | — | NASCAR Nextel Cup |
| 5.0% | — | Formula One |
| 4.9% | — | Other |
| 4.3% | — | IRL |
| 1.9% | — | Not a racing fan |

**Who is the greatest driver in Indianapolis 500 history?**

| | | |
|---|---|---|
| 81.2% | — | Mario Andretti |
| 6.2% | — | Rick Mears |
| 4.4% | — | A.J. Foyt |
| 4.3% | — | Al Unser Jr. |
| 4.0% | — | Al Unser |

**Total Votes:** 47,960

**1  Kellen Winslow, tight end** for the Cleveland Browns, suffers injuries in a motorcycle accident that will keep him out for the entire 2005-06 season. Adding insult to injury, he may owe the team his $4.4 million signing bonus because his contract prohibits him from engaging in dangerous activities, which is what many would consider his actions to be.

**2  Furious NBA commissioner David Stern** fines Houston Rockets head coach Jeff Van Gundy a record $100,000 for accusing officials of targeting center Yao Ming during the Rockets' playoff series with the Dallas Mavericks. Van Gundy said he was told by an off-duty referee that officials "were looking at Yao harder because of Mark [Cuban's] complaints."

**7  Giacomo, a 50-1 longshot,** rallies down the stretch under jockey Mike Smith, to win the $2.3 million Kentucky Derby at Churchill Downs. His stunning victory is by a half-length over 71-1 longshot Closing Argument. Afleet Alex takes third, while pre-race favorite Bellamy Road—owned by George Steinbrenner—finishes in seventh.

**In what is widely considered the fight of the year, lightweight** Diego Corrales picks himself up off the canvas twice and comes back to knock out Luis Castillo at 2:06 of the 10th round.

**8  Phoenix Suns guard Steve Nash** wins his first NBA most valuable player award in the fourth-closest margin in the last 25 years. Nash earned 65 first-place votes and 1,066 total points while Miami Heat center Shaquille O'Neal garnered 58 first-place votes and 1,032 points.

**10  Jason Giambi, mired** in a 4-for-38 slump and batting just .195 on the season, is asked by the Yankees to consider taking a minor league assignment. Adding to what is already a lousy week for him, six days later in Oakland, he is doused with beer by a fan upon returning to the dugout after a flyout.

**13  Tiger Woods misses** a 15-foot par putt on the 18th hole of the second round at the Byron Nelson Championship and misses a cut for the first time in seven years and 142 tournaments.

AP/Wide World Photos

*England's **Dan Wheldon** is only too happy to find out how tough it is to get milk stains out of a racing suit as he pours the traditional bottle over his head after winning the Indy 500 on May 29. America's sweetheart Danica Patrick finishes fourth.*

**21 Favorite Afleet Alex nearly falls** after colliding with Scrappy T at the top of the stretch, then somehow gets his legs back underneath him — and his jockey Jeremy Rose back in the saddle — and surges ahead to win the 130th Preakness Stakes. Scrappy T finishes in second and Kentucky Derby winner Giacomo places third.

**The Texas Rangers blast** eight home runs, four in the second inning alone, in an 18-3 rout of the Houston Astros in Arlington. David Dellucci (2), Mark Texeira, Rod Barajas, Hank Blalock, Laynce Nix, Richard Hidalgo and Kevin Mench all go yard for the Rangers. "We didn't pitch very good," said Astros manager Phil Garner in what may be the understatement of the year. Five weeks later, the Rangers would hit eight homers in a game once again in an 18-5 victory over the Angels. By the way, the record for homers in an inning is five.

**22 Paula Creamer, 18,** becomes the youngest winner of an LPGA event in 53 years with her victory at the Sybase Classic. Her win at the age of 18 years, nine months and 17 days is second only to Marlene Hagge's win at the 1952 Sarasota Open at 18 years, 14 days. Creamer receives her high school diploma four days later.

**29 Dan Wheldon** passes rookie Danica Patrick with six laps remaining to become the first Englishman in 39 years to win the Indianapolis 500. Patrick finishes fourth, the highest finish by a woman in Indy 500 history. She leads 19 laps, becoming the first woman to lead a lap at Indy. With a nearly empty gas tank, she is forced to take conservation measures and has to sit back as Wheldon, Vitor Meira and Bryan Herta pass her.

**Jimmie Johnson overcomes** a Nextel Cup series record 22 cautions and a myriad of accidents and outlasts the rest of the field to win his third consecutive Coca-Cola 600 at Lowe's Motor Speedway. He overtakes Bobby Labonte on the final lap and wins by 0.027 seconds.

**30 Johns Hopkins wins** its eighth NCAA Division I lacrosse title and first since 1987 with a 9-8 squeaker over Duke.

**31 International soccer superstar David Beckham** plays his first game in the U.S., as England takes on Colombia at Giants Stadium.

# June 2005

| Sun | Mon | Tue | Wed | Thu | Fri | Sat |
|-----|-----|-----|-----|-----|-----|-----|
|     |     |     | 1   | 2   | 3   | 4   |
| 5   | 6   | 7   | 8   | 9   | 10  | 11  |
| 12  | 13  | 14  | 15  | 16  | 17  | 18  |
| 19  | 20  | 21  | 22  | 23  | 24  | 25  |
| 26  | 27  | 28  | 29  | 30  |     |     |

## Mike Tyson Fading Into Bolivia?

**What would you like to see Mike Tyson do after his fighting days are over?**

| 41.0% | — | Pro wrestling |
|-------|---|---------------|
| 30.5% | — | TV commentator |
| 17.8% | — | Boxing Promoter |
| 10.7% | — | Actor |

**Where will Tyson rank on a list with the following heavyweight champs: Muhammad Ali, Rocky Marciano, Joe Louis, Jack Dempsey?**

| 44.2% | — | Just outside that top five |
|-------|---|----------------------------|
| 26.3% | — | Among the top three |
| 23.1% | — | Not even in the same league |
| 6.4%  | — | At the top of the list |

**Total Votes:** 21,646

### Top Coaches

**With Phil Jackson returning to the Lakers and Larry Brown joining the Knicks, SportsNation ranks the top current pro coaches:**

| 1. Bill Belichick | 7. Bobby Cox |
|-------------------|--------------|
| 2. Phil Jackson | 8. Tony La Russa |
| 3. Larry Brown | 9. Andy Reid |
| 4. Joe Torre | 10. Bill Cowher |
| 5. Bill Parcells | 11. Rick Carlisle |
| 6. Gregg Popovich | 12. Ron Gardenhire |

**1** **The San Antonio Spurs** are back in the NBA Finals as they overcome a 42-point effort from Phoenix' Amare Stoudemire to beat the Suns, 101-95, and complete their 4-1 series win.

**2** **Basketball hall of famer George Mikan dies** in Scottsdale, Ariz. at the age of 80. The 6-10 Mikan was such a dominant force inside, the NBA had to make rule changes solely because of him. The 24-second clock was implemented and the lane was widened from six feet to 12 feet to keep him further away from the basket.

**3** **Spanish teenager Rafael Nadal** celebrates his 19th birthday by beating top-ranked Roger Federer in four sets to advance to the finals of the French Open. The unusually sloppy Federer commits 62 unforced errors in the loss. Two days later, Nadal would beat unseeded Argentine Mariano Puerta, 6-7 (6-8), 6-3, 6-1, 7-5 for the first Grand Slam title of his brief career.

**4** **Belgium's Justine Henin-Hardenne** proves her comeback from illness and injury in 2004 is complete as she crushes fan-favorite Mary Pierce, 6-1, 6-1, in the Finals of the French Open for her fourth Grand Slam singles title. The entire match takes just 62 minutes.

**6** **The Detroit Pistons return** to the NBA Finals for the second straight year after beating the Miami Heat, 88-82, in Game 7 of the Eastern Conference Finals. Rip Hamilton scores 22 points for Detroit, Shaquille O'Neal leads the Heat with 27 and Dwayne Wayne, playing with a strained rib muscle, adds 20.

**7** **The Arizona Diamondbacks** make 17-year-old Virginia high school infielder Justin Upton the top pick in baseball's First-Year Player Draft. Upton's brother B.J. was the second overall pick by Tampa Bay in the 2002 draft.

**8** **Former Boston Bruins great Cam Neely** is elected to the Hockey Hall of Fame along with two-time Soviet gold-medalist Valeri Kharlamov.

**Samantha Findlay's** three-run homer in the 10th inning gives Michigan a 4-1 win over UCLA, making the Wolverines the first school east of the Mississippi River to win the NCAA Division I Softball World Series.

**11** **Heavyweight Mike Tyson loses** to little-known Kevin McBride, three days after saying he would "gut him like a fish." Tyson tires after winning the opening rounds and fails to come out for the seventh. It is the third loss in the last four fights for Tyson, who is contemplating retirement.

ROGERS RAGE
ARLINGTON
AMERIQUEST FIELD

NEWS at 6:00

AP/Wide World Photos

*In this image made from television, Texas Rangers pitcher **Kenny Rogers** pushes photographer Larry Rodriguez's camera to the ground during warm-ups on June 28. He is originally given a 20-game suspension but it is later reduced to 13 games.*

**There's no question** who the top 3-year-old horse in the world is after Preakness winner Afleet Alex roars to a seven-length victory at the Belmont Stakes. Andromeda's Hero, trained by Nick Zito, places second and Nolan's Cat finishes third. Kentucky Derby winner Giacomo tires down the stretch to finish a disappointing seventh.

**14 Asafa Powell of Jamaica** sets a new world record in the 100 meters, running a 9.77 at Olympic Stadium in Athens. He betters the previous mark (9.78) set by American Tim Montgomery in 2002 and claims the title of "World's Fastest Man."

**Phil Jackson is rehired** as coach of the Los Angeles Lakers, inking a three-year deal worth an estimated $7-10 million per year. Star Kobe Bryant, who Jackson once referred to as "uncoachable," is in favor of the hiring. "In Phil Jackson, they [management] chose a proven winner. That is something I support."

**Sparks fly** between managers Mike Scioscia and Frank Robinson after Angels reliever Brendan Donnelly is caught with pine tar on his glove. Donnelly is immediately ejected (and later given a 10-day suspension).

**19 New Zealander Michael Campbell** holds off a charging Tiger and powers to a two-stroke win at the U.S. Open at Pinehurst. It is the first major title of his career.

**"Big Shot Bob" strikes again!** Robert Horry hits yet another clutch 3-pointer, this one coming with 5.9 seconds left in overtime to give the Spurs a 96-95 victory over the Pistons and a 3-2 NBA Finals lead.

**Just six racers compete** in Formula One's U.S. Grand Prix in Indianapolis after Michelin informs its teams that there could be safety issues with its tires.

**21 NBA owners and players agree** to a six-year collective bargaining agreement, thus avoiding a potential lockout. The deal raises the league's minimum age to 19.

**23 The San Antonio Spurs win** Game 7, 81-74, over the Pistons for their third NBA title in the last seven years. Tim Duncan wins his third Finals MVP award.

**28 Utah center Andrew Bogut** is chosen by the Milwaukee Bucks with the first overall pick at the NBA draft. North Carolina's Marvin Williams goes second to the Atlanta Hawks.

# July 2005

| Sun | Mon | Tue | Wed | Thu | Fri | Sat |
|-----|-----|-----|-----|-----|-----|-----|
|     |     |     |     |     | 1   | 2   |
| 3   | 4   | 5   | 6   | 7   | 8   | 9   |
| 10  | 11  | 12  | 13  | 14  | 15  | 16  |
| 17  | 18  | 19  | 20  | 21  | 22  | 23  |
| 24/31 | 25 | 26 | 27 | 28 | 29 | 30 |

ESPN SN sportsnation

## NHL Unlocked

**What's your status as an NHL fan?**

| 77.3% | — | Still a fan |
|-------|---|-------------|
| 12.7% | — | Never was a fan |
| 10.0% | — | No longer a fan |

**Who do you think "won" the labor war?**

| 65.9% | — | Owners |
|-------|---|--------|
| 32.5% | — | Neither side benefited |
| 1.6%  | — | Players |

**What is the most important thing for the NHL to do to win back fans?**

| 46.8% | — | Lower ticket prices |
|-------|---|---------------------|
| 26.5% | — | Alter rules to open up offense |
| 21.4% | — | Secure a place on American TV |
| 5.3%  | — | Nothing – fans will come back anyway |

**How good will super prospect Sidney Crosby be?**

| 57.7% | — | Perennial all-star/award candidate |
|-------|---|------------------------------------|
| 25.7% | — | Occasional all-star |
| 9.5%  | — | The next Gretzky or Lemieux |
| 7.1%  | — | Total disappointment |

**Total Votes:** 74,015

**1 Venus Williams jumps for joy** after her dramatic, come-from-behind 4-6, 7-6(4), 9-7 victory over Lindsay Davenport in the women's Wimbledon final. It is Williams' third Wimbledon singles title but first win at a Grand Slam event since her win at the U.S. Open in 2001. She becomes the lowest seed (14) to win the women's title and the first woman since 1935 to face match point in the final and come back to win. At two hours, 45 minutes, it is the longest women's final in the history of Wimbledon.

**3 Roger Federer makes it look so easy,** cruising past Andy Roddick, 6-2, 7-5(2), 6-4, in the men's Wimbledon final. He becomes the fourth man in the last 70 years to win three consecutive Wimbledon titles, joining Pete Sampras, Bjorn Borg and Fred Perry.

**4 It's Kobayashi again!** For the fifth year in a row the superstar of competitive eating easily wins the annual Nathan's Famous hot dog eating contest at Coney Island, this time swallowing 49 of the tasty red hots in 12 minutes.

**6 The city of London is jubilant** after it is awarded the 2012 Summer Olympic by four votes over runner-up Paris. Madrid finishes third in the voting, followed by New York City and Moscow. "I'm terribly disappointed that it wasn't us," said New York mayor Michael Bloomberg, "but we have no regrets." London last hosted the Summer Games in 1948.

**8 Michelle Wie comes close** but fails in her bid to become the first woman in 60 years to make a cut in a PGA Tour event. The 15-year-old shoots an even-par 71 in the second round of the John Deere Classic but misses the cut by two strokes. She is above the cut line after 14 holes, but late misses eventually do her in.

**9 Skateboarder Danny Way** speeds 50 mph down a huge ramp and flies over the Great Wall of China, becoming the first person to jump over China's famous landmark without the use of a motorized aid.

**11 Phillies OF Bobby Abreu blasts** a record 24 home runs in the first round and goes on to defeat Ivan Rodriguez in the finals of the Home Run Derby. Abreu hits a total of 41 homers in the competition's three rounds, including a 517-foot shot to the back row of the bleachers.

**12 The American League wins** its eighth consecutive MLB All-Star Game, 7-5, over the National League at Comerica Park in Detroit. Orioles shortstop Miguel Tejada hits a second-inning home run and is named MVP.

AP/Wide World Photos

*Well it's about time! NHL commissioner **Gary Bettman**, left, shakes hands with NHLPA Executive Director **Bob Goodenow,** signaling the official end of the NHL lockout in late July.*

**13 The NHL lockout comes to an end** as the owners and players finally come to an agreement on a six-year labor deal that includes a salary cap at $39 million. The league now begins its arduous task of wooing back fans.

**15 Jack Nicklaus wraps up** his final major with a birdie on the 18th hole in the second round of the British Open at St. Andrews. "I knew the hole would move wherever I hit it," he joked. His three-over-par 147 misses the cut by two strokes. Oh by the way, Tiger Woods (66-67) holds a four-shot lead.

**Rafael Palmeiro hits an RBI double** off Seattle's Joel Pineiro for the 3,000th hit of his career. he becomes the fourth player (joining Willie Mays, Hank Aaron and Eddie Murray) to record 3,000 hits and 500 home runs.

**In related news,** BALCO founder Victor Conte pleads guilty to conspiracy to distribute steroids and money laundering.

**17 Tiger Woods roars** to an impressive wire-to-wire victory at the British Open for his second Claret Jug, second major title of the year and second career Grand Slam. His 14-under 274 is five strokes ahead of runner-up Colin Montgomerie.

**22 In a ceremony to officially "re-launch" the NHL,** commissioner Gary Bettman announces a host of rule changes — including the introduction of a shootout to break a tie, and offers an apology to fans.

**24 American Lance Armstrong**, in his familiar yellow jersey, cruises down the Champs-Elysees one last time as he wins his unprecedented seventh consecutive Tour de France. He averages 25.88 mph over the entire Tour and beats runner-up Ivan Basso of Italy by four minutes, 40 seconds.

**25 All is forgiven as Ricky Williams returns** to the Miami Dolphins on the first day of NFL training camp.

**26 Chicago hurler Greg Maddux** fans Omar Vizquel in the third inning of the Cubs' 3-2 loss to the Giants to become the 13th member of Major League Baseball's 3,000-strikeout club.

**27 Well-traveled Larry Brown signs** a deal to become the 22nd head coach of the New York Knicks. Terms of the contract are not disclosed.

**30 Savior Sidney Crosby** is selected by the Penguins with the top pick in the NHL Draft.

# August 2005

| Sun | Mon | Tue | Wed | Thu | Fri | Sat |
|-----|-----|-----|-----|-----|-----|-----|
|     |  1  |  2  |  3  |  4  |  5  |  6  |
|  7  |  8  |  9  | 10  | 11  | 12  | 13  |
| 14  | 15  | 16  | 17  | 18  | 19  | 20  |
| 21  | 22  | 23  | 24  | 25  | 26  | 27  |
| 28  | 29  | 30  | 31  |     |     |     |

## Terrell Owens Too Much Trouble?

**Is Terrell Owens' production on the field worth the headaches he causes off the field?**

| | |
|---|---|
| 70.0% — | No |
| 30.0% — | Yes |

**Where will Owens be by the end of the 2005 regular season?**

| | |
|---|---|
| 52.0% — | Playing for the Eagles |
| 30.5% — | Suspended by the Eagles |
| 14.9% — | Playing for another team |
| 2.6% — | Out of the NFL |

**What's your take on Owens?**

| | |
|---|---|
| 51.2% — | He's a bad guy who will always cause problems |
| 43.0% — | He's probably a decent guy; he just has some issues |
| 5.9% — | He's totally misunderstood; the media needs to get off his back |

**Who should be the NFL's highest-paid receiver?**

| | |
|---|---|
| 43.2% — | Marvin Harrison |
| 34.2% — | Randy Moss |
| 12.4% — | Terrell Owens |
| 7.0% — | Hines Ward |
| 3.3% — | Torry Holt |

**Total Votes:** 43,483

**1** **Rafael Palmeiro's image** takes a severe beating after the newest member of the 3,000-hit club tests positive for steroids. In March, under oath in front of a Congressional panel, he strongly denied ever taking steroids: "I have never used steroids. Period."

His latest quote echoes that sentiment, with one all-important alteration: "I have never *intentionally* used steroids. Never. Ever. Period." He is handed a 10-game suspension.

**4** **Hall of fame basketball coach Sue Gunter** dies at the age of 66 in Baton Rouge. She coached women for 40 years, 22 at LSU, and guided her teams to 708 wins and 13 NCAA tournaments.

**5** **Golfer Jason Gore,** who became a crowd favorite with his performance at the U.S. Open, cards a 12-under-par 59 at the Nationwide Tour's Cox Classic.

**7** **Indiana-native Tony Stewart** finally wins at his favorite track, the Indianapolis Motor Speedway, as he holds off runner-up Kasey Kahne and third-place finisher Brian Vickers to capture the Allstate 400 at the Brickyard. Dale Earnhardt Jr. finishes dead last (43rd) and has his hopes for the Chase for the Nextel Cup all but wiped away.

**American sprinter Justin Gatlin**, gold-medalist at the 2004 Olympics, runs a 9.88 to win the 100-meter dash at the World Track & Field Championships in Helsinki. His 0.17-second winning margin is the largest in the history of the world championships.

**Dan Marino fires one last pass** to Mark Clayton as the former Dolphins quarterback is enshrined in the Pro Football Hall of Fame in Canton, Ohio, along with Steve Young, Fritz Pollard and Benny Friedman.

**8** **Wayne Gretzky accepts a new challenge,** signing a multiyear deal to become head coach of the Phoenix Coyotes, of which he is also part-owner.

**10** **"Terrell Owens has been sent home** from training camp due to undisclosed team issues," Eagles head coach Andy Reid explains. Owens has squabbled with team management over contract issues, and with quarterback Donovan McNabb, and has appeared quiet and distant with his teammates at training camp.

Being tossed from camp hardly affects him, however, as he is later photographed working out at home in his yard in front of a throng of neighbors and media.

AP/Wide World Photos

*The Louisiana Superdome* is littered with debris, and beams of light filter in from holes in the roof after Hurricane Katrina pounds New Orleans and the Gulf Coast in late August. The facility is deemed unusable for the foreseeable future.

**15 Phil Mickelson captures major No. 2,** after sinking a three-foot birdie putt on the final hole at Baltusrol Golf Club to defeat Steve Elkington and Thomas Bjorn by one stroke. Rain and lightning delays the tournament's finish, forcing Lefty to finish the event's final five holes on Monday morning. He cards a four-round total of 276, four shots below par. Tiger Woods, who was one shot away from missing the cut, finishes tied for third, two shots behind Mickelson.

**17 The NCAA purchases** the preseason and postseason National Invitation Tournaments for $56.5 million from the Metropolitan Intercollegiate Basketball Association. The NCAA will now control the two postseason hoops tournaments, involving 105 Division I teams (65 in the NCAA tourney, 40 in the NIT).

**18 In an interview with** HBO's *Real Sports with Bryant Gumbel,* Randy Moss admits to using marijuana "every once in a while." While his candor is refreshing, he can expect a call from the NFL offices any day now.

**20 The Associated Press preseason** college football poll is released and, to virtually no one's surprise, USC has the top spot with 60 out of a possible 65 first-place votes.

**The Kansas City Royals win a game!** Their 2-1 win over the Oakland A's ends a 19-game losing streak, two off the American League mark for futility (21) set by Baltimore at the start of the 1988 season.

**22 Maria Sharapova** unseats Lindsay Davenport as the top-ranked player on the WTA Tour. The 18-year-old is the fifth-youngest player, and the first Russian woman, to hold the top ranking.

**23 Florida State, the first school** to challenge the NCAA's new policy prohibiting Native American imagery in postseason events, wins its appeal, primarily because of the university's relationship with the Seminole Tribe of Florida.

**Lance Armstrong is on the defensive** yet again after the French newspaper *L'Equipe* reports that urine samples taken from Armstrong in 1999 tested positive for EPO, a performance-enhancing drug. Armstrong angrily denies the charges, calling it a "witch hunt."

**28 Hurricane Katrina decimates** much of New Orleans and rips off part of the Superdome roof, which is being used to shelter evacuees. The Saints eventually opt to play most of their home games in San Antonio, while the Hornets head for Oklahoma City and Baton Rouge.

# September 2005

| Sun | Mon | Tue | Wed | Thu | Fri | Sat |
|-----|-----|-----|-----|-----|-----|-----|
|     |     |     |     | 1   | 2   | 3   |
| 4   | 5   | 6   | 7   | 8   | 9   | 10  |
| 11  | 12  | 13  | 14  | 15  | 16  | 17  |
| 18  | 19  | 20  | 21  | 22  | 23  | 24  |
| 25  | 26  | 27  | 28  | 29  | 30  |     |

### Tennis' All-time Best

**Where do U.S. Open finalists Andre Agassi and Roger Federer rank all-time?**

**SportsNation gives its take on the top 15 (men only):**

1. Pete Sampras
2. Andre Agassi
3. Bjorn Borg
4. Roger Federer
5. John McEnroe
6. Rod Laver
7. Jimmy Connors
8. Roy Emerson
9. Ivan Lendl
10. Arthur Ashe
11. Boris Becker
12. Bill Tilden
13. Stefan Edberg
14. Mats Wilander
15. Jim Courier

### Bonds Returns

**Will Barry Bonds (703 HRs) break Hank Aaron's record (755) next season?**

| 66.5% | — | No  |
|-------|---|-----|
| 33.5% | — | Yes |

**Total Votes:** 14,537

**3** **In Week 1 of the NCAA** college football schedule, USC picks up right where it left off with a 63-17 win over Hawaii, and Orange Bowl loser Oklahoma also picks up where it left off, losing a stunner to TCU, 17-10. Notre Dame cruises to a 42-21 upset win over Pittsburgh in Charlie Weis' and Dave Wannstedt's first games.

**The United States men's soccer team** defeats Mexico, 2-0, to clinch a berth in the 2006 World Cup in Germany. Steve Ralston and DaMarcus Beasley score within a five-minute span of the second half. It will be the fifth straight U.S. appearance in the World Cup.

**4** **Kyle Busch, 20,** becomes the youngest driver ever to win a Nextel Cup race, holding off Greg Biffle to win the Sony HD 400 at California Speedway.

**5** **Jerry Rice, the greatest receiver** of all-time, retires from the NFL after 20 years, 1,549 receptions and a record 208 touchdowns — 197 via the pass.

**7** **Andre Agassi records a stirring** come-from-behind victory over fellow American James Blake, 3-6, 3-6, 6-3, 6-3, 7-6(6) to advance to the semifinals of the U.S. Open.

**8** **The New England Patriots** begin their quest for a third straight Super Bowl title with a 30-20 win over the Oakland Raiders in Foxborough. Tom Brady throws for 306 yards to lead the Pats while newcomer Randy Moss makes an immediate impact, hauling in a 73-yard touchdown pass from Kerry Collins.

**9** **Connecticut men's coach Jim Calhoun** and Syracuse coach Jim Boeheim are inducted into the Basketball Hall of Fame in Springfield, Mass. along with late LSU coach Sue Gunter, coach and broadcaster Hubie Brown and Brazilian women's star Hortencia Marcari.

**10** **In her 23rd Grand Slam** singles event, Kim Clijsters finally breaks through with her first major title, defeating Mary Pierce in straight sets, 6-3, 6-1, in the finals of the U.S. Open.

**Crowd favorite Andre Agassi,** 35, continues his improbable run for his ninth Grand Slam singles title, defeating Robby Ginepri in five sets in U.S. Open semifinal action. Agassi will face the world's top player Roger Federer, who advances with a win over Lleyton Hewitt.

**NASCAR's "regular season" ends** with Kurt Busch winning the Chevy Rock & Roll 400 in Richmond. The top 10 drivers are now set for the "Chase for the Nextel Cup" with Roush Racing accounting for half of the playoff field.

AP/Wide World Photos

*In this scene reminiscent of their Ryder Cup win in 1999, **the United States team** rushes onto the green to celebrate their Cup-winning putt. This time, it's Chris DiMarco's turn to be the hero as he sinks a 15-footer to clinch The Presidents Cup win on Sept. 25.*

**Notre Dame's second game** in the Charlie Weis era is much like the first — a rousing success, as the Irish snap Michigan's 16-game home winning streak with a 17-10 victory in Ann Arbor. Elsewhere, No. 2 Texas travels to No. 4 Ohio State and comes away with a 25-22 win on a late touchdown pass from Vince Young.

**11 Roger Federer puts a stop** to Andre Agassi's fairytale bid for a third U.S Open title with a 6-3, 2-6, 7-6(1), 6-1 victory in the finals. The win gives Federer back-to-back U.S. Open wins, not to mention a 34-match winning streak.

**With a ravaged city and** practically the entire country rooting for them, the New Orleans Saints record an emotional 23-20 win over Carolina on a 47-yard John Carney field goal with seven seconds remaining.

**The USA takes back the Solheim Cup** with a 15½-12½ victory over the Europeans in Carmel, Indiana. Youngsters Paula Creamer, Christina Kim and Natalie Gulbis all win their singles matches to pace the Americans.

**Chris Schenkel,** the Emmy Award-winning sportscaster and longtime voice of the PBA, dies after a long battle with emphysema at the age of 82.

**12 Barry Bonds makes his return** to the field in a 4-3 Giants' win over the Padres. He goes 1-for-4 with a double.

**Sure first-ballot hockey hall of famer** Mark Messier hangs up his skates after 25 years and six Stanley Cups. He leaves as the NHL's No. 2 scorer, behind only former teammate Wayne Gretzky.

**14 ESPN and Major League Baseball** agree to a new eight-year deal worth an average of $296 million a year to begin in 2006. Aside from the TV rights, ESPN also receives rights to show live MLB action via cell-phones.

**19 The New Orleans Saints play** a "home game" against the Giants at Giants Stadium and lose 27-10. An accompanying telethon raises $5 million for victims of Hurricane Katrina.

**20 Finals MVP Yolanda Griffith** scores 14 points and grabs 10 boards to lead the Sacramento Monarchs to a 62-59 win over Connecticut and their first WNBA Championship.

**25 Chris DiMarco rolls in a 15-footer** on the 18th hole to defeat Australian Stuart Appleby and give the Americans an 18½-15½ victory over the International Team in The Presidents Cup.

# October 2005

| Sun | Mon | Tue | Wed | Thu | Fri | Sat |
|-----|-----|-----|-----|-----|-----|-----|
|     |     |     |     |     |     | 1   |
| 2   | 3   | 4   | 5   | 6   | 7   | 8   |
| 9   | 10  | 11  | 12  | 13  | 14  | 15  |
| 16  | 17  | 18  | 19  | 20  | 21  | 22  |
| 23/30 | 24/31 | 25 | 26 | 27 | 28 | 29 |

## NBA Dress Code

**Are you in favor of the dress code implemented by the NBA for its players?**

58.9% — Yes
41.1% — No

**Do you think the dress code is an attempt to minimize the "hip-hop" image associated with NBA players?**

82.9% — Yes
17.1% — No

**Who should determine what players wear when engaged in team or league business?**

41.5% — The team
39.3% — The league
19.2% — The player

**Total Votes:** 134,943

## The Best World Series

**SportsNation ranks the best World Series of the past 20 years. Listed are the top 10:**

1. D'Backs-Yankees '01
2. Twins-Braves '91
3. Dodgers-A's '88
4. Mets-Red Sox '86
5. Red Sox-Cardinals '04
6. Marlins-Indians '97
7. Blue Jays-Phillies '93
8. Angels-Giants '02
9. Royals-Cardinals '85
10. Marlins-Yankees '03

**2** **Antonio Tarver scores** a unanimous 12-round decision over Roy Jones Jr. to hang onto his IBO light heavyweight title. it is Tarver's second win over Jones in the last 16 months. Tarver improves to 24-3 while Jones drops to 49-3.

**The Astros and Red Sox clinch** playoff berths, while the Indians and Phillies are edged out on the final day of the baseball regular season. The Red Sox pound the Yankees, 10-1, but they clinch earlier in the day when the Indians fall 3-1 to the White Sox, their third consecutive loss to end the season. Houston hurler Roy Oswalt pitches the Astros to a 6-4 victory against the Cubs to make them the NL wildcard representative for the second year in a row.

**4** **Jon Daniels, 28,** becomes the youngest general manager in MLB history, taking over for the Rangers' John Hart, who steps down. Daniels is 10 months younger than Theo Epstein was when he became GM of the Red Sox in 2002. "He's a walking baseball encyclopedia," says Rangers owner Tom Hicks.

**5** **NHL hockey is back on the ice** for the first time in 16 months. Among the highlights — the Tampa Bay Lightning finally get to raise their championship banner, 18-year-old Sidney Crosby assists on the Penguins' only goal of the night and Ottawa's Dany Heatley beats Toronto goalie Ed Belfour for the deciding goal in the league's first shootout after Senators' goalie Dominik Hasek stops Jason Allison and Eric Lindros.

**Never before has skipping school been so profitable.** Michelle Wie, 15, plays hooky to announce her intentions for becoming a professional on the LPGA Tour. With endorsement deals already in place with Nike and Sony, she becomes an instant millionaire.

**7** **The Chicago White Sox make short work** of the defending champion Red Sox, winning 5-3 to complete their 3-0 ALDS sweep.

**Only in boxing.** Jose Luis Castillo weighs in well over the 135-pound lightweight limit for his upcoming rematch with Diego Corrales, so the promoters stepped in with a solution — he must pay a fine up front and weigh in at no more than 147 pounds the following day or pay Corrales $75,000 more for every pound over. Yes, it's confusing, but that's boxing.

**8** **In the longest postseason game** in major league history, Chris Burke delivers a walk-off home run in the bottom of the 18th inning to give the Astros a 7-6 win against the Braves to advance to the NLCS. They will face the St. Louis Cardinals, who swept the Padres.

AP/Wide World Photos

*White Sox catcher **A.J. Pierzynski** swings at strike three from Angels hurler Kelvim Escobar in the bottom of the ninth in Game 2 of the ALCS. Seconds later, Pierzynski would be on first base when umpire Doug Eddings ruled catcher Josh Paul didn't catch the ball cleanly.*

**Jose Luis Castillo knocks out** Diego Corrales in the fourth round, but due to the weight fiasco of a day earlier, Corrales retains the WBO and WBC titles. Even without the controversy, the fight is a pale comparison to their first fight, won by Corrales earlier in the year.

**10 Rookie Ervin Santana takes over** for injured starter Bartolo Colon and pitches the Angels to a 5-3 win over the Yankees and into the ALCS against the White Sox.

**12 The Minnesota Vikings' rocky season** gets even rockier when allegations arise that several Vikings players participated in various forms of lewd behavior at a private party aboard two chartered boats on Lake Minnetonka. "Sex?" asked running back Mewelde Moore. "That's crazy. Come on. I'm engaged!"

**A.J. Pierzynski is ruled safe** at first on a controversial ninth-inning play in Game 2 of the ALCS. Despite what appears to be a clear fist pump to signal an "out," umpire Doug Eddings rules that catcher Josh Paul drops a swinging third strike. With the inning extended, the Sox go on to win the game, 2-1, and even the series at one game apiece.

**15 Matt Leinart twists** his way into the end zone to give No. 1 USC a thrilling 34-31 win over Notre Dame in South Bend. On the previous play, Leinart is popped on his way into the end zone and fumbles the ball out of bounds, giving the Trojans time for one more play.

**16 Michelle Wie is disqualified** from the Samsung World Championship, her first professional tournament, when it is ruled that she took an improper drop during the third round.

**17 The Chicago White Sox are already in,** and the Astros are one strike away from the World Series when Albert Pujols stuns the Houston crowd with a three-run homer off of closer Brad Lidge. Two days later, however, the Astros would leave no doubt with a 5-1 victory to reach their first World Series in team history.

**25 Geoff Blum homers** in the top of the 14th inning to give the White Sox a 7-5 win and a commanding 3-0 series lead. It is the longest game in World Series history.

**26 The White Sox are the champs!** Chicago wins its first World Series since 1917, winning Game 4, 1-0, to complete their 4-0 series sweep. OF Jermaine Dye is named series MVP.

## W2W4: What To Watch For in 2006

A brief look at some of the upcoming events in 2006.

AP/Wide World Photos

***Michelle Kwan*** *seeks her first Olympic gold medal at the Turin Winter Olympics, Feb. 10-26.*

AP/Wide World Photos

*The **U.S men's soccer team** has a legitimate shot at its first World Cup title, June 9-July 9.*

AP/Wide World Photos

*Teenager **Michelle Wie** looks for her first win on the LPGA Tour.*

AP/Wide World Photos

***Barry Bonds*** *needs seven home runs to pass the Babe and 48 to pass Hank Aaron.*

# Baseball

Orioles first baseman **Rafael Palmeiro** testifies in front of Congress that he never used steroids. Months later, he tests positive.

AP/Wide World Photos

# South Side Satisfied

*The White Sox, under manager Ozzie Guillen, win Chicago's first World Series title since 1917.*

**Karl Ravech**
*is an analyst for ESPN's baseball coverage.*

Upon further review, the 2005 Major League Baseball season remains as much a mystery as the truth behind the 1919 Black Sox. The 2005 Chicago White Sox successfully buried the franchise's past scandals, and the south side of Chicago celebrated the team's first World Series title since 1917.

In doing so a segment of that town's population was freed from a perpetual inferiority complex, if not within the confines of the city limits, then certainly on a national and international landscape that ranks the Cubs as the Second City's first baseball team, and the White Sox as nothing more than a footnote to one of baseball's darkest chapters. How this team emerged from  a season that seemingly was constantly being threatened is a tribute to its grittiness.

As the season began the usual suspects lined up as favorites to win it all. The Yankees with a payroll over $200 million had acquired Randy Johnson, arguably the greatest left-handed pitcher of his generation. Along with Johnson, the pinstripes pinned their hopes on newly acquired pitchers Carl Pavano and Jaret Wright. In the end neither of those two were a factor at all. Instead the Yankees were carried by no-name, no-career arms like Aaron Small and Chien-Ming Wang — and yet they still won their eighth straight division title. But their road was a bumpy one. Rumors of manager Joe Torre's firing erupted from the Yankees' Tampa offices as often as Tom Cruise claimed to be "so happy and so in love." Yet Torre survived and will return for what will be his 11th season in pinstripes —no small feat with the Boss constantly watching.

AP/Wide World Photos

*__The Chicago White Sox celebrate__ their first World Series title since 1917 after sweeping the Houston Astros, 4 games to 0.*

The Red Sox won the wild card in the American League but never regained the footing that led them to the title in 2004. A big reason was that the foot that was bleeding last October never healed, and an unhealthy Curt Schilling made a return to glory close to impossible.

The newly named Los Angeles Angels of Anaheim played exactly like the Anaheim Angels from previous years and won the West, mostly because they were the same team, save for the marketing dollars gained by the name change.

The National League's power base was once again located in St. Louis. The Cardinals rolled to another 100-win season and celebrated every home game as if it was their last. The countdown began on opening day as Busch Stadium was set to be demolished in favor of another Busch Stadium being built an Albert Pujols home run away.

San Diego, almost by default, won the West. Their record was barely above .500 (82-80). In fact when you consider that they were swept in three games by the Cardinals in the playoffs,

AP/Wide World Photos

*Rookie **Chris Burke's** walk-off home run in the bottom of the 18th gave the Astros a win over the Braves in the longest game in postseason history — and a ticket to the NLCS.*

the Padres lost more games than they won in 2005.

The Atlanta Braves, like the Yankees, keep winning the East. We're now at 14 straight division titles and counting, but they keep losing in the postseason. The Astros, behind incredibly strong starting pitching featuring the ageless Roger Clemens, made it all the way to the World Series but unlike years past, the Wild Card was not the ticket to glory.

Baseballs biggest threat this season appeared to come in the shape of a syringe. Steroids became the buzz-word, and increased testing had many fans rubber-necking the sports pages on a daily basis to see "who got nailed."

That list turned out to be far less glamorous than the All-Star team that appeared before Congress in March. Mark McGwire, Sammy Sosa, Curt Schilling and Rafael Palmeiro all took turns either denying ever using steroids or flat-out refusing to recognize the road they may have traveled. While McGwire repeatedly said, "I'm not here to talk about the past," the most indelible image of the proceedings was of Rafael Palmeiro pointing his

*continued on page 64* ▸

# The Ten Biggest Stories of the Year in Baseball

**10**   **The Cleveland Indians** improve from a sub-.500 team in 2004 to a team with 93 wins in 2005 under manager Eric Wedge. Though they collapse in the final weekend and miss the playoffs, their foundation of young stars like Grady Sizemore, Travis Hafner and Victor Martinez should give Tribe fans reason to cheer in 2006.

**9**   **The Cubs' Derrek Lee** threatens to become the first Triple Crown winner since Yaz in 1967. In the end he finishes five back of Andruw Jones in homers and well back in RBIs, but gives the north side of Chicago something to cheer about in an otherwise disappointing season.

**8**   With steroid speculation now a daily issue, **Jason Giambi bats** .195 through the first month of the season and is almost sent to the minors. The near demotion lights a fire under him and he finishes the season with a .440 on base percentage, 32 home runs and the AL Comeback Player of the Year Award.

**7**   **The St. Louis Cardinals** record the majors' only 100-win season behind the pitching of Chris Carpenter and the lethal bat of Albert Pujols, but again come up short in the postseason.

**6**   Just when you think he couldn't possibly do it again, designated hitter **David Ortiz comes through** one more time with a game-winning hit to will the Boston Red Sox into the postseason for the third straight season.

**5**   **The Houston Astros roll** past the Braves on Chris Burke's 18th-inning home run, then take down defending NL champs St. Louis to reach the World Series for the first time in the franchise's 43-year existence. Roger Clemens delivers a 1.87 ERA at the age of 43.

**4**   In Game 2 of the ALCS, White Sox catcher **A.J. Pierzynski alertly runs** to first on a swinging third strike that Angels catcher Josh Paul appears to catch. When umpire Doug Eddings rules that the ball was trapped, Pierzynski is ruled safe and the White Sox win on the next at-bat.

**3**   President Bush throws out the first pitch at RFK Stadium as **baseball returns to the nation's capital** for the first time in 34 years. The Nationals improve by 14 games from 2004, their final season in Montreal.

**2**   Likely spurred on by Jose Canseco's best-selling tell-all book, **the steroid issue** jumps to the front and center in 2005. Mark McGwire's pristine image takes a beating when he gives vague answers to Congress and never denies taking steroids. Rafael Palmeiro takes an even bigger hit when he tests positive in August, after having emphatically denied ever using steroids less than five months earlier.

**1**   Behind outstanding pitching, timely hitting and the managing of Ozzie Guillen, the **White Sox roll** through the postseason with just one loss and win their first World Series since 1917.

finger straight at the Congressional panel and proclaiming, "I have never used steroids, period." Less than five months later, Palmeiro was suspended for having failed baseball's steroid test. Does anyone even remember that Palmeiro also got his 3000th career hit this past season?

Barry Bonds was injured for almost the entire season and will have to wait till 2006 to make his run at the Babe. Though he played in only a handful of games, his every move was magnified more than any decision Ozzie Guillen made from the White Sox dugout.

So in this season that lacked any true identity, at least one thing stayed true. Baseball's golden rule applies in 2005 the same way it did back in 1917. Pitching and defense win championships. And that's exactly why on the south side of Chicago, the White Sox identity crisis is over.

## Power Outage

Oakland A's catcher Jason Kendall, who once hit as many as 14 home runs in a season as a member of the Pittsburgh Pirates, has hit just 12 over the past four seasons — and *none* in 2005. He was one of seven players in the 2005 regular season to have at least 200 at-bats without going deep.

| Player | AB | R | H | HR | RBI | Avg. |
|---|---|---|---|---|---|---|
| Jason Kendall, Oak . . . .601 | 70 | 163 | 0 | 53 | .271 |
| Scott Podsednik, ChW . .507 | 80 | 147 | 0 | 25 | .290 |
| Tony Womack, NYY . . . .329 | 46 | 82 | 0 | 15 | .249 |
| Jamey Carroll, Wash . . .303 | 44 | 76 | 0 | 22 | .251 |
| Willie Bloomquist, Sea . .249 | 27 | 64 | 0 | 22 | .257 |
| Pablo Ozuna, ChW . . . .203 | 27 | 56 | 0 | 11 | .276 |
| Joey Gathright, TB . . . . .203 | 29 | 56 | 0 | 13 | .276 |

**Note:** Amazingly, Podsednik hit two home runs in 49 at-bats during the 2005 postseason.

In 2005, Minnesota Twins starting pitcher Carlos Silva allowed just nine walks in 188.1 innings, before shutting down his season due to a knee injury with a record of 9-8.

**Did you know**, the only starter since 1920 to record more wins than walks over the course of a season was Bret Saberhagen, who went 14-4 with 13 walks in 1994 as a member of the New York Mets

# 2005
# *Season in Review*

SPORTS ALMANAC

## Final Major League Standings

Division champions (*) and Wild Card (†) winners are noted. Number of seasons listed after each manager refers to current tenure with club.

## American League

### East Division

| | W | L | Pct | GB | Home | Road |
|---|---|---|---|---|---|---|
| *New York | 95 | 67 | .586 | — | 53-28 | 42-39 |
| †Boston | 95 | 67 | .586 | — | 54-27 | 41-40 |
| Toronto | 80 | 82 | .494 | 15 | 43-38 | 37-44 |
| Baltimore | 74 | 88 | .457 | 21 | 36-45 | 38-43 |
| Tampa Bay | 67 | 95 | .414 | 28 | 40-41 | 27-54 |

**2005 Managers: NY**–Joe Torre (10th season); **Bos**–Terry Francona (2nd); **Tor**–John Gibbons (2nd); **Bal**–Lee Mazzilli (2nd, 51-56) was fired on Aug. 4 and replaced by bench coach Sam Perlozzo (23-32); **TB**–Lou Piniella (3rd).
**2004 Standings:** 1. New York (101-61); 2. Boston (98-64); 3. Baltimore (78-84); 4. Tampa Bay (70-91); 5. Toronto (67-94).
**Note:** The Yankees won the division due to a better head-to-head record (10-9) against the Red Sox.

### Central Division

| | W | L | Pct | GB | Home | Road |
|---|---|---|---|---|---|---|
| *Chicago | 99 | 63 | .611 | — | 47-34 | 52-29 |
| Cleveland | 93 | 69 | .574 | 6 | 43-38 | 50-31 |
| Minnesota | 83 | 79 | .512 | 16 | 45-36 | 38-43 |
| Detroit | 71 | 91 | .438 | 28 | 39-42 | 32-49 |
| Kansas City | 56 | 106 | .346 | 43 | 34-47 | 22-59 |

**2005 Managers: Chi**–Ozzie Guillen (2nd season); **Cle**–Eric Wedge (3rd); **Min**–Ron Gardenhire (4th); **Det**–Alan Trammell (3rd); **KC**–Tony Pena (4th, 8-25) resigned on May 10 and was replaced by bench coach Bob Schaefer (5-12), then Buddy Bell (43-69) on May 31.
**2004 Standings:** 1. Minnesota (92-70); 2. Chicago (83-79); 3. Cleveland (80-82); 4. Detroit (72-90); 5. Kansas City (58-104).

### West Division

| | W | L | Pct | GB | Home | Road |
|---|---|---|---|---|---|---|
| *Los Angeles | 95 | 67 | .586 | — | 49-32 | 46-35 |
| Oakland | 88 | 74 | .543 | 7 | 45-36 | 43-38 |
| Texas | 79 | 83 | .488 | 16 | 44-37 | 35-46 |
| Seattle | 69 | 93 | .426 | 26 | 39-42 | 30-51 |

**2005 Managers: LAA**–Mike Scioscia (6th season); **Oak**–Ken Macha (3rd); **Tex**–Buck Showalter (3rd); **Sea**–Mike Hargrove (1st).
**2004 Standings:** 1. Anaheim (92-70); 2. Oakland (91-71); 3. Texas (89-73); 4. Seattle (63-99).

## National League

### East Division

| | W | L | Pct | GB | Home | Road |
|---|---|---|---|---|---|---|
| *Atlanta | 90 | 72 | .556 | — | 53-28 | 37-44 |
| Philadelphia | 88 | 74 | .543 | 2 | 46-35 | 42-39 |
| Florida | 83 | 79 | .512 | 7 | 45-36 | 38-43 |
| New York | 83 | 79 | .512 | 7 | 48-33 | 35-46 |
| Washington | 81 | 81 | .500 | 9 | 41-40 | 40-41 |

**2005 Managers: Atl**–Bobby Cox (16th season); **Phi**–Charlie Manuel (1st); **Fla**–Jack McKeon (3rd); **NY**–Willie Randolph (1st); **Wash**–Frank Robinson (4th).
**2004 Standings:** 1. Atlanta (96-66); 2. Philadelphia (86-76); 3. Florida (83-79); 4. New York (71-91); 5. Montreal (67-95).

### Central Division

| | W | L | Pct | GB | Home | Road |
|---|---|---|---|---|---|---|
| *St. Louis | 100 | 62 | .617 | — | 50-31 | 50-31 |
| †Houston | 89 | 73 | .549 | 11 | 53-28 | 36-45 |
| Milwaukee | 81 | 81 | .500 | 19 | 46-35 | 35-46 |
| Chicago | 79 | 83 | .488 | 21 | 38-43 | 41-40 |
| Cincinnati | 73 | 89 | .451 | 27 | 42-39 | 31-50 |
| Pittsburgh | 67 | 95 | .414 | 33 | 34-47 | 33-48 |

**2005 Managers: St.L**–Tony La Russa (10th season); **Hou**–Phil Garner (2nd); **Mil**–Ned Yost (3rd); **Chi**–Dusty Baker (3rd); **Cin**–Dave Miley (3rd, 27-43) was fired on June 21 and replaced by bench coach Jerry Narron (46-46); **Pit**–Lloyd McClendon (5th, 55-81) was fired on Sept. 6 and replaced by bench coach Pete Mackanin (12-14).
**2004 Standings:** 1. St. Louis (105-57); 2. Houston (92-70); 3. Chicago (89-73); 4. Cincinnati (76-86); 5. Pittsburgh (72-89); 6. Milwaukee (67-94).

### West Division

| | W | L | Pct | GB | Home | Road |
|---|---|---|---|---|---|---|
| *San Diego | 82 | 80 | .506 | — | 46-35 | 36-45 |
| Arizona | 77 | 85 | .475 | 5 | 36-45 | 41-40 |
| San Francisco | 75 | 87 | .463 | 7 | 37-44 | 38-43 |
| Los Angeles | 71 | 91 | .438 | 11 | 40-41 | 31-50 |
| Colorado | 67 | 95 | .414 | 15 | 40-41 | 27-54 |

**2005 Managers: SD**–Bruce Bochy (11th season); **Ari**–Bob Melvin (1st); **SF**–Felipe Alou (3rd); **LA**–Jim Tracy (5th); **Col**– Clint Hurdle (4th).
**2004 Standings:** 1. Los Angeles (93-69); 2. San Francisco (91-71); 3. San Diego (87-75); 4. Colorado (68-94); 5. Arizona (51-111).

## Interleague Play Standings

### American League

| | W-L | Pct | | W-L | Pct |
|---|---|---|---|---|---|
| Cleveland | 15-3 | .833 | Kansas City | 9-9 | .500 |
| Boston | 12-6 | .667 | Texas | 9-9 | .500 |
| Chicago | 12-6 | .667 | Toronto | 8-10 | .444 |
| Los Angeles | 12-6 | .667 | Baltimore | 8-10 | .444 |
| New York | 11-7 | .611 | Minnesota | 8-10 | .444 |
| Oakland | 10-8 | .556 | Tampa Bay | 3-15 | .167 |
| Seattle | 10-8 | .556 | **Totals** | **136-116** | **.540** |
| Detroit | 9-9 | .500 | | | |

### National League

| | W-L | Pct | | W-L | Pct |
|---|---|---|---|---|---|
| Washington | 12-6 | .667 | Pittsburgh | 5-7 | .417 |
| Florida | 10-5 | .667 | Chicago | 6-9 | .400 |
| St. Louis | 10-5 | .667 | Colorado | 6-9 | .400 |
| Milwaukee | 8-7 | .533 | San Diego | 7-11 | .389 |
| Atlanta | 7-8 | .467 | San Francisco | 6-12 | .333 |
| Philadelphia | 7-8 | .467 | New York | 5-10 | .333 |
| Houston | 7-8 | .467 | Los Angeles | 5-13 | .278 |
| Cincinnati | 7-8 | .467 | **Totals** | **116-136** | **.460** |
| Arizona | 8-10 | .444 | | | |

Texas Rangers
**Michael Young**
Batting Avg., Hits

New York Yankees
**Alex Rodriguez**
Home Runs, Runs, SLG

Boston Red Sox
**David Ortiz**
RBI

Cleveland Indians
**Kevin Millwood**
ERA

## American League Leaders
(*) indicates rookie.

### Batting

| | Bat | Gm | AB | R | H | Avg | TB | 2B | 3B | HR | RBI | BB | SO | SB | Slg Pct | OBP |
|---|---|---|---|---|---|---|---|---|---|---|---|---|---|---|---|---|
| Michael Young, Tex | R | 159 | 668 | 114 | 221 | **.331** | 343 | 40 | 5 | 24 | 91 | 58 | 91 | 5 | .513 | .385 |
| Alex Rodriguez, NY | R | 162 | 605 | 124 | 194 | **.321** | 369 | 29 | 1 | 48 | 130 | 91 | 139 | 21 | .610 | .421 |
| Vladimir Guerrero, LAA | R | 141 | 520 | 95 | 165 | **.317** | 294 | 29 | 2 | 32 | 108 | 61 | 48 | 13 | .565 | .394 |
| Johnny Damon, Bos | L | 148 | 624 | 117 | 197 | **.316** | 274 | 35 | 6 | 10 | 75 | 53 | 69 | 18 | .439 | .366 |
| Brian Roberts, Bal | S | 143 | 561 | 92 | 176 | **.314** | 289 | 45 | 7 | 18 | 73 | 67 | 83 | 27 | .515 | .387 |
| Derek Jeter, NY | R | 159 | 654 | 122 | 202 | **.309** | 294 | 25 | 5 | 19 | 70 | 77 | 117 | 14 | .450 | .389 |
| Victor Martinez, Cle | S | 147 | 547 | 73 | 167 | **.305** | 260 | 33 | 0 | 20 | 80 | 63 | 78 | 0 | .475 | .378 |
| Hideki Matsui, NY | L | 162 | 629 | 108 | 192 | **.305** | 312 | 45 | 3 | 23 | 116 | 63 | 78 | 2 | .496 | .367 |
| Travis Hafner, Cle | L | 137 | 486 | 94 | 148 | **.305** | 289 | 42 | 0 | 33 | 108 | 79 | 123 | 0 | .595 | .408 |
| Miguel Tejada, Bal | R | 162 | 654 | 89 | 199 | **.304** | 337 | 50 | 5 | 26 | 98 | 40 | 83 | 5 | .515 | .349 |
| Ichiro Suzuki, Sea | L | 162 | 679 | 111 | 206 | **.303** | 296 | 21 | 12 | 15 | 68 | 48 | 66 | 33 | .436 | .350 |
| Mark Texeira, Tex | S | 162 | 644 | 112 | 194 | **.301** | 370 | 41 | 3 | 43 | 144 | 72 | 124 | 4 | .575 | .379 |
| Carl Crawford, TB | L | 156 | 644 | 101 | 194 | **.301** | 302 | 33 | 15 | 15 | 81 | 27 | 84 | 46 | .469 | .331 |
| Mike Sweeney, KC | R | 122 | 470 | 63 | 141 | **.300** | 243 | 39 | 0 | 21 | 83 | 33 | 61 | 3 | .517 | .347 |
| Coco Crisp, Cle | S | 145 | 594 | 86 | 178 | **.300** | 276 | 42 | 4 | 16 | 69 | 44 | 81 | 15 | .465 | .345 |

**Note:** Batters must have 3.1 plate appearances per their team's games played to qualify.

### Home Runs

| | |
|---|---|
| Rodriguez, NY | 48 |
| Ortiz, Bos | 47 |
| Ramirez, Bos | 45 |
| Texeira, Tex | 43 |
| Konerko, Chi | 40 |
| Sexson, Sea | 39 |
| Soriano, Tex | 36 |
| Sheffield, NY | 34 |
| Hafner, Cle | 33 |
| Giambi, NY | 32 |
| Guerrero, LAA | 32 |

### Triples

| | |
|---|---|
| Crawford, TB | 15 |
| Suzuki, Sea | 12 |
| Sizemore, Cle | 11 |
| Figgins, LAA | 10 |
| Inge, Det | 9 |
| Roberts, Bal | 7 |

### On Base Pct.

| | |
|---|---|
| Giambi, NY | .440 |
| Rodriguez, NY | .421 |
| Hafner, Cle | .408 |
| Ortiz, Bos | .397 |
| Guerrero, LAA | .394 |
| Jeter, NY | .389 |
| Ramirez, Bos | .388 |
| Roberts, Bal | .387 |

### Runs Batted In

| | |
|---|---|
| Ortiz, Bos | 148 |
| Texeira, Tex | 144 |
| Ramirez, Bos | 144 |
| Rodriguez, NY | 130 |
| Sheffield, NY | 123 |
| Sexson, Sea | 121 |
| Cantu, TB | 117 |
| Matsui, NY | 116 |
| Hafner, Cle | 108 |
| Guerrero, LAA | 108 |

### Doubles

| | |
|---|---|
| Tejada, Bal | 50 |
| Matsui, NY | 45 |
| Roberts, Bal | 45 |
| Soriano, Tex | 43 |
| Crisp, Cle | 42 |
| Hafner, Cle | 42 |
| Texeira, Tex | 41 |

### Slugging Pct.

| | |
|---|---|
| Rodriguez, NY | .610 |
| Ortiz, Bos | .604 |
| Hafner, Cle | .595 |
| Ramirez, Bos | .594 |
| Texeira, Tex | .575 |
| Guerrero, LAA | .565 |
| Sexson, Sea | .541 |
| Giambi, NY | .535 |

### Hits

| | |
|---|---|
| Young, Tex | 221 |
| Suzuki, Sea | 206 |
| Jeter, NY | 202 |
| Tejada, Bal | 199 |
| Damon, Bos | 197 |
| Texeira, Tex | 194 |
| Crawford, TB | 194 |
| Rodriguez, NY | 194 |
| Matsui, NY | 192 |

### Runs

| | |
|---|---|
| Rodriguez, NY | 124 |
| Jeter, NY | 122 |
| Ortiz, Bos | 119 |
| Damon, Bos | 117 |
| Young, Tex | 114 |
| Figgins, LAA | 113 |
| Texeira, Tex | 112 |
| Ramirez, Bos | 112 |
| Suzuki, Sea | 111 |
| Sizemore, Cle | 111 |

### Walks

| | |
|---|---|
| Giambi, NY | 108 |
| Ortiz, Bos | 102 |
| Rodriguez, NY | 91 |
| Sexson, Sea | 89 |
| Konerko, Chi | 81 |
| Ramirez, Bos | 80 |

### Stolen Bases

| | SB | CS |
|---|---|---|
| Figgins, LAA | 62 | 17 |
| Podsednik, Chi | 59 | 23 |
| Crawford, TB | 46 | 8 |
| Lugo, TB | 39 | 11 |
| Suzuki, Sea | 33 | 8 |
| Soriano, Tex | 30 | 2 |
| Roberts, Bal | 27 | 10 |
| Womack, NY | 27 | 5 |

### Total Bases

| | |
|---|---|
| Texeira, Tex | 370 |
| Rodriguez, NY | 369 |
| Ortiz, Bos | 363 |
| Young, Tex | 343 |
| Tejada, Bal | 337 |
| Ramirez, Bos | 329 |
| Soriano, Tex | 326 |
| Matsui, NY | 312 |

### Strikeouts

| | |
|---|---|
| Sexson, Sea | 167 |
| Inge, Det | 140 |
| Rodriguez, NY | 139 |
| Sizemore, Cle | 132 |
| Blalock, Tex | 132 |
| Chavez, Oak | 129 |
| Peralta, Cle | 128 |

## Pitching

| | Arm | W | L | ERA | Gm | GS | CG | ShO | Sv | IP | H | R | ER | HR | HB | BB | SO | WP |
|---|---|---|---|---|---|---|---|---|---|---|---|---|---|---|---|---|---|---|
| Kevin Millwood, Cle | R | 9 | 11 | **2.86** | 30 | 30 | 1 | 0 | 0 | 192.0 | 182 | 72 | 61 | 20 | 4 | 52 | 146 | 2 |
| Johan Santana, Min | L | 16 | 7 | **2.87** | 33 | 33 | 3 | 2 | 0 | 231.2 | 180 | 77 | 74 | 22 | 1 | 45 | 238 | 8 |
| Mark Buehrle, Chi | L | 16 | 8 | **3.12** | 33 | 33 | 3 | 1 | 0 | 236.2 | 240 | 99 | 82 | 20 | 4 | 40 | 149 | 2 |
| Jarrod Washburn, LAA | L | 8 | 8 | **3.20** | 29 | 29 | 1 | 1 | 0 | 177.1 | 184 | 66 | 63 | 19 | 8 | 51 | 94 | 2 |
| Carlos Silva, Min | R | 9 | 8 | **3.44** | 27 | 27 | 2 | 0 | 0 | 188.1 | 212 | 83 | 72 | 25 | 3 | 9 | 71 | 0 |
| John Lackey, LAA | R | 14 | 5 | **3.44** | 33 | 33 | 1 | 0 | 0 | 209.0 | 208 | 85 | 80 | 13 | 11 | 71 | 199 | 18 |
| Kenny Rogers, Tex | L | 14 | 8 | **3.46** | 30 | 30 | 1 | 0 | 0 | 195.1 | 205 | 86 | 75 | 15 | 8 | 53 | 87 | 0 |
| Bartolo Colon, LAA | R | 21 | 8 | **3.48** | 33 | 33 | 2 | 0 | 0 | 222.2 | 215 | 93 | 86 | 26 | 3 | 43 | 157 | 2 |
| Jon Garland, Chi | R | 18 | 10 | **3.50** | 33 | 33 | 3 | 3 | 0 | 221.0 | 212 | 93 | 86 | 26 | 7 | 47 | 115 | 2 |
| Joe Blanton*, Oak | R | 12 | 12 | **3.53** | 33 | 33 | 2 | 0 | 0 | 201.1 | 178 | 86 | 79 | 23 | 5 | 67 | 116 | 4 |
| Jose Contreras, Chi | R | 15 | 7 | **3.61** | 32 | 32 | 1 | 0 | 0 | 204.2 | 177 | 91 | 82 | 23 | 9 | 75 | 154 | 20 |
| Josh Towers, Tor | R | 13 | 12 | **3.71** | 33 | 33 | 2 | 1 | 0 | 208.2 | 237 | 101 | 86 | 24 | 6 | 29 | 112 | 1 |
| Gustavo Chacin*, Tor | L | 13 | 9 | **3.72** | 34 | 34 | 0 | 0 | 0 | 203.0 | 213 | 93 | 84 | 20 | 8 | 70 | 121 | 3 |
| Danny Haren, Oak | R | 14 | 12 | **3.73** | 34 | 34 | 3 | 0 | 0 | 217.0 | 212 | 101 | 90 | 26 | 6 | 53 | 163 | 6 |
| Paul Byrd, LAA | R | 12 | 11 | **3.74** | 31 | 31 | 2 | 1 | 0 | 204.1 | 216 | 95 | 85 | 22 | 7 | 28 | 102 | 1 |

**Note:** Pitchers must have one inning pitched per their team's games played to qualify.

### Wins

Colon, LAA . . . . . . . . 21-8
Garland, Chi . . . . . . 18-10
Lee, Cle . . . . . . . . . . 18-5
Johnson, NY . . . . . . 17-8
Wakefield, Bos . . 16-12
Santana, Min . . . . . 16-7
Buehrle, Chi . . . . . 16-8
Five tied with 15 each.

### Losses

Greinke, KC . . . . . . . 5-17
Lima, KC . . . . . . . . . 5-16
Robertson, Det . . . . . 7-16
Franklin, Sea . . . . . . 8-15
Westbrook, Cle . . . 15-15
Maroth, Det . . . . . . 14-14
Hernandez, KC . . . . 8-14
Five tied with 13 each.

### Walks

Kazmir*, TB . . . . . . . . 100
Zito, Oak . . . . . . . . . 89
Cabrera, Bal . . . . . . . 87
Contreras, Chi . . . . . 75
Meche, Sea . . . . . . . . 72
Lackey, LAA . . . . . . . 71
Chacin*, Tor . . . . . . . 70
Hernandez, KC . . . . . 70

### Strikeouts

Santana, Min . . . . . . . 238
Johnson, NY . . . . . . . 211
Lackey, LAA . . . . . . . 199
Kazmir*, TB . . . . . . . 174
Zito, Oak . . . . . . . . . 171
Haren, Oak . . . . . . . 163
Sabathia, Cle . . . . . . 161
Cabrera, Bal . . . . . . . 157
Colon, LAA . . . . . . . . 157
Contreras, Chi . . . . . 154

### Appearances

Timlin, Bos . . . . . . . . 81
Schoeneweis, Tor . . . . 80
Howry, Cle . . . . . . . . 79
Gordon, NY . . . . . . . . 79
Shields, Ana . . . . . . . 78
Crain*, Min . . . . . . . 75
Rincon, Min . . . . . . . 75
Williams, Bal . . . . . . 72

### Innings

Buehrle, Chi . . . . . 236.2
Santana, Min . . . . 231.2
Zito, Oak . . . . . . . 228.1
Garcia, Chi . . . . . . 228.0
Johnson, NY . . . . . 225.2
Wakefield, Bos . . . 225.1
Colon, LAA . . . . . . 222.2
Garland, Chi . . . . . 221.0
Haren, Oak . . . . . . 217.0
Westbrook, Cle . . . 210.2

### HRs Allowed

Wakefield, Bos . . . . . 35
Chen, Bal . . . . . . . . . 33
Radke, Min . . . . . . . . 33
Elarton, Cle . . . . . . . 32
Johnson, NY . . . . . . . 32
Lima, KC . . . . . . . . . 31
Maroth, Det . . . . . . . 30

### Opp. Batting Average

Santana, Min . . . . . .210
Zito, Oak . . . . . . . . .221
Contreras, Chi . . . . .232
Blanton*, Oak . . . . .236
Johnson, NY . . . . . .243
Wakefield, Bos . . . . .245
Chen, Bal . . . . . . . . .248
Kazmir*, TB . . . . . .248
Millwood, Cle . . . . .248
Sabathia, Cle . . . . .248

### Complete Games

Halladay, Tor . . . . . . . 5
Bonderman, Det . . . . . 4
Johnson, NY . . . . . . . 4
Haren, Oak . . . . . . . . 3
Buehrle, Chi . . . . . . . 3
Garland, Chi . . . . . . . 3
Santana, Min . . . . . . . 3
Wakefield, Bos . . . . . 3
Radke, Min . . . . . . . . 3

### Saves

| | SV | BS |
|---|---|---|
| Rodriguez, LAA . . | .45 | 5 |
| Wickman, Cle . . | .45 | 5 |
| Nathan, Min . . . | .43 | 5 |
| Rivera, NY . . . | .43 | 4 |
| Baez, TB . . . | .41 | 8 |
| Cordero, Tex . . | .37 | 8 |
| Ryan, Bal . . . | .36 | 5 |
| Guardado, Sea . . | .36 | 5 |
| Hermanson, Chi . . | .34 | 5 |
| Batista, Tor . . . | .31 | 8 |
| Street*, Oak . . | .23 | 4 |
| MacDougal, KC . . | .21 | 4 |

### Wild Pitches

Contreras, Chi . . . . . 20
Garcia, Chi . . . . . . . 20
Lackey, LAA . . . . . . . 18
Johnson, Det . . . . . . 17
Clement, Bos . . . . . . 13
Shields, LAA . . . . . . 12

### WHIP

(Walks + Hits/IP)
Santana, Min . . . 0.97
Johnson, NY . . . . 1.13
Colon, LAA . . . . . 1.16
Garland, Chi . . . . 1.17
Silva, Min . . . . . . 1.17
Radke, Min . . . . . 1.18
Buehrle, Chi . . . . 1.18
Byrd, LAA . . . . . . 1.19
Zito, Oak . . . . . . . 1.20
Blanton*, Oak . . . 1.22

### Shutouts

Garland, Chi . . . . . . . 3
Santana, Min . . . . . . . 2
Halladay, Tor . . . . . . . 2
Mussina, NY . . . . . . . 2
14 tied with 1 each.

### Hit Batters

Arroyo, Bos . . . . . . . 20
Martinez, Bos . . . . . . 16
Wakefield, Bos . . . . . 16
Zambrano, TB . . . . . . 16
Park, Tex . . . . . . . . . 13
Villone, Sea . . . . . . . 12
Hudson, Oak . . . . . . . 12
Mulder, Oak . . . . . . . 12

## Fielding

### Put Outs

Texeira, Tex . . . . . . 1378
Konerko, Chi . . . . . 1321
Erstad, LAA . . . . . . 1218
Morneau, Min . . . . 1191
Sexson, Sea . . . . . . 1147
Broussard, Cle . . . . 1082
Kendall, Cle . . . . . . 986
Martinez, Cle . . . . . 904
Johnson, Oak . . . . . 896
Two tied with 874 each.

### Assists

Tejada, Bal . . . . . . . 479
Jeter, NY . . . . . . . . 454
Soriano, Tex . . . . . . 448
Berroa, KC . . . . . . . 441
Young, Tex . . . . . . . 427
Lugo, TB . . . . . . . . 424
Uribe, Chi . . . . . . . 422
Peralta, Cle . . . . . . 413
Belliard, Cle . . . . . 413
Roberts, Bal . . . . . . 413

### OF Assists

Ramirez, Bos . . . . . . 17
Wells, Tor . . . . . . . . 12
Long, KC . . . . . . . . . 12
Suzuki, Sea . . . . . . . 10
Monroe, Det . . . . . . . 10
Jones, Min . . . . . . . . 10
Hunter, Min . . . . . . . 9
Ford, Min . . . . . . . . 9
Dye, Chi . . . . . . . . . 9
Brown, KC . . . . . . . . 9

### Errors

Renteria, Bos . . . . . . 30
Adams*, Tor . . . . . . 26
Berroa, KC . . . . . . . 25
Lugo, TB . . . . . . . . . 24
Inge, Det . . . . . . . . . 23
Tejada, Bal . . . . . . . 22
Soriano, Tex . . . . . . 21
Teahen, KC . . . . . . . 20
Peralta, Cle . . . . . . . 19
Three tied with 18 each.

Chicago Cubs
**Derrek Lee**
BA, Hits, 2B, TB, SLG

Atlanta Braves
**Andruw Jones**
Home Runs, RBI

Houston Astros
**Roger Clemens**
ERA, Opp. BA

Florida Marlins
**Dontrelle Willis**
Wins, CG, ShO

## National League Leaders

(*) indicates rookie.

### Batting

| | Bat | Gm | AB | R | H | Avg | TB | 2B | 3B | HR | RBI | BB | SO | SB | Slg Pct | OBP |
|---|---|---|---|---|---|---|---|---|---|---|---|---|---|---|---|---|
| Derrek Lee, Chi | R | 158 | 594 | 120 | 199 | **.335** | 393 | 50 | 3 | 46 | 107 | 85 | 109 | 15 | .662 | .418 |
| Albert Pujols, St.L | R | 161 | 591 | 129 | 195 | **.330** | 360 | 38 | 2 | 41 | 117 | 97 | 65 | 16 | .609 | .430 |
| Miguel Cabrera, Fla | R | 158 | 613 | 106 | 198 | **.323** | 344 | 43 | 2 | 33 | 116 | 64 | 125 | 1 | .561 | .385 |
| Todd Helton, Col | L | 144 | 509 | 92 | 163 | **.320** | 272 | 45 | 2 | 20 | 79 | 106 | 80 | 3 | .534 | .445 |
| Sean Casey, Cin | L | 137 | 529 | 75 | 165 | **.312** | 224 | 32 | 0 | 9 | 58 | 48 | 48 | 2 | .423 | .371 |
| Chad Tracy, Ari | L | 145 | 503 | 73 | 155 | **.308** | 278 | 34 | 4 | 27 | 72 | 35 | 78 | 3 | .553 | .359 |
| Matt Holliday, Col | R | 125 | 479 | 68 | 147 | **.307** | 242 | 24 | 7 | 19 | 87 | 36 | 79 | 14 | .505 | .361 |
| David Wright, NY | R | 160 | 575 | 99 | 176 | **.306** | 301 | 42 | 1 | 27 | 102 | 72 | 113 | 17 | .523 | .388 |
| Brady Clark, Mil | R | 145 | 599 | 94 | 183 | **.306** | 255 | 31 | 1 | 13 | 53 | 47 | 55 | 10 | .426 | .372 |
| Jason Bay, Pit | R | 162 | 599 | 110 | 183 | **.306** | 335 | 44 | 6 | 32 | 101 | 95 | 142 | 21 | .559 | .402 |
| Aramis Ramirez, Chi | R | 123 | 463 | 72 | 140 | **.302** | 263 | 30 | 0 | 31 | 92 | 35 | 60 | 0 | .568 | .358 |
| Ken Griffey Jr. | L | 128 | 491 | 85 | 148 | **.301** | 283 | 30 | 0 | 35 | 92 | 54 | 93 | 0 | .576 | .369 |
| Carlos Delgado, Fla | L | 144 | 521 | 81 | 157 | **.301** | 303 | 41 | 3 | 33 | 115 | 72 | 121 | 0 | .582 | .399 |
| Brian Giles, SD | L | 158 | 545 | 92 | 164 | **.301** | 263 | 38 | 8 | 15 | 83 | 119 | 64 | 13 | .483 | .423 |
| Luis Castillo, Fla | S | 122 | 439 | 72 | 132 | **.301** | 164 | 12 | 4 | 4 | 30 | 65 | 32 | 10 | .374 | .391 |

**Note:** Batters must have 3.1 plate appearances per their team's games played to qualify.

### Home Runs

| | |
|---|---|
| A. Jones, Atl | 51 |
| Lee, Chi | 46 |
| Pujols, St.L | 41 |
| Dunn, Cin | 40 |
| Glaus, Ari | 37 |
| Ensberg, Hou | 36 |
| Griffey Jr., Cin | 35 |
| Floyd, NY | 34 |
| Cabrera, Fla | 33 |
| Delgado, Fla | 33 |

### Runs Batted In

| | |
|---|---|
| A. Jones, Atl | 128 |
| Pujols, St.L | 117 |
| Burrell, Phi | 117 |
| Cabrera, Fla | 116 |
| Delgado, Fla | 115 |
| Lee, Mil | 114 |
| Lee, Chi | 107 |
| Utley, Phi | 105 |
| Kent, LA | 105 |

### Hits

| | |
|---|---|
| Lee, Chi | 199 |
| Cabrera, Fla | 198 |
| Rollins, Phi | 196 |
| Pujols, St.L | 195 |
| Reyes, NY | 190 |
| Eckstein, St.L | 185 |
| Bay, Pit | 183 |
| Clark, Mil | 183 |
| Pierre, Fla | 181 |

### Stolen Bases

| | SB | CS |
|---|---|---|
| Reyes, NY | 60 | 15 |
| Pierre, Fla | 57 | 17 |
| Furcal, Atl | 46 | 10 |
| Rollins, Phi | 41 | 6 |
| Freel, Cin | 36 | 10 |
| Taveras*, Hou | 34 | 11 |
| Abreu, Phi | 31 | 9 |
| Counsell, Ari | 26 | 7 |

### Triples

| | |
|---|---|
| Reyes, NY | 17 |
| Pierre, Fla | 13 |
| Furcal, Atl | 11 |
| Rollins, Phi | 11 |
| Roberts, SD | 10 |
| Giles, SD | 8 |

### Doubles

| | |
|---|---|
| Lee, Chi | 50 |
| Giles, Atl | 45 |
| Helton, Col | 45 |
| Bay, Pit | 44 |
| Cabrera, Fla | 43 |
| Randa, SD | 43 |
| Three tied with 42 each. | |

### Runs

| | |
|---|---|
| Pujols, St.L | 129 |
| Lee, Chi | 120 |
| Rollins, Phi | 115 |
| Bay, Pit | 110 |
| Dunn, Cin | 107 |
| Cabrera, Fla | 106 |
| Giles, Atl | 104 |
| Abreu, Phi | 104 |

### Total Bases

| | |
|---|---|
| Lee, Chi | 393 |
| Pujols, St.L | 360 |
| Cabrera, Fla | 344 |
| A. Jones, Atl | 337 |
| Bay, Pit | 335 |
| Delgado, Fla | 303 |
| Wright, NY | 301 |
| Lee, Mil | 301 |

### On Base Pct.

| | |
|---|---|
| Helton, Col | .445 |
| Pujols, St.L | .430 |
| Giles, SD | .423 |
| Lee, Chi | .418 |
| Berkman, Hou | .411 |
| Johnson, Wash. | .408 |
| Abreu, Phi | .405 |
| Bay, Pit | .402 |

### Slugging Pct.

| | |
|---|---|
| Lee, Chi | .662 |
| Pujols, St.L | .609 |
| Delgado, Fla | .582 |
| Griffey Jr., Cin | .576 |
| A. Jones, Atl | .575 |
| Ramirez, Chi | .568 |
| Cabrera, Fla | .561 |
| Bay, Pit | .559 |

### Walks

| | |
|---|---|
| Giles, SD | 119 |
| Abreu, Phi | 117 |
| Dunn, Cin | 114 |
| Helton, Col | 106 |
| Burrell, Phi | 99 |
| Pujols, St.L | 97 |
| Bay, Pit | 95 |

### Strikeouts

| | |
|---|---|
| Dunn, Cin | 168 |
| Burrell, Phi | 160 |
| Wilson, Col-Wash | 148 |
| Wilkerson, Wash | 147 |
| Glaus, Ari | 145 |
| Bay, Pit | 142 |
| Edmonds, St.L | 139 |

## Pitching

| | Arm | W | L | ERA | Gm | GS | CG | ShO | Sv | IP | H | R | ER | HR | HB | BB | SO | WP |
|---|---|---|---|---|---|---|---|---|---|---|---|---|---|---|---|---|---|---|
| Roger Clemens, Hou | R | 13 | 8 | **1.87** | 32 | 32 | 1 | 0 | 0 | 211.1 | 151 | 51 | 44 | 11 | 3 | 62 | 185 | 3 |
| Andy Pettitte, Hou | L | 17 | 9 | **2.39** | 33 | 33 | 0 | 0 | 0 | 222.1 | 188 | 66 | 59 | 17 | 3 | 41 | 171 | 2 |
| Dontrelle Willis, Fla | L | 22 | 10 | **2.63** | 34 | 34 | 7 | 5 | 0 | 236.1 | 213 | 79 | 69 | 11 | 8 | 55 | 170 | 2 |
| Pedro Martinez, NY | R | 15 | 8 | **2.82** | 31 | 31 | 4 | 1 | 0 | 217.0 | 159 | 69 | 68 | 19 | 4 | 47 | 208 | 4 |
| Chris Carpenter, St.L | R | 21 | 5 | **2.83** | 33 | 33 | 7 | 4 | 0 | 241.2 | 204 | 82 | 76 | 18 | 3 | 51 | 213 | 5 |
| Jake Peavy, SD | R | 13 | 7 | **2.88** | 30 | 30 | 3 | 3 | 0 | 203.0 | 162 | 70 | 65 | 18 | 7 | 50 | 216 | 3 |
| Roy Oswalt, Hou | R | 20 | 12 | **2.94** | 35 | 35 | 4 | 1 | 0 | 241.2 | 243 | 85 | 79 | 18 | 8 | 48 | 184 | 5 |
| John Smoltz, Atl | R | 14 | 7 | **3.06** | 33 | 33 | 3 | 1 | 0 | 229.2 | 210 | 83 | 78 | 18 | 1 | 53 | 169 | 2 |
| John Patterson, Wash | R | 9 | 7 | **3.13** | 31 | 31 | 2 | 1 | 0 | 198.1 | 172 | 71 | 69 | 19 | 5 | 65 | 185 | 9 |
| Carlos Zambrano, Chi | R | 14 | 6 | **3.26** | 33 | 33 | 2 | 0 | 0 | 223.1 | 170 | 88 | 81 | 21 | 8 | 86 | 202 | 7 |
| Josh Beckett, Fla | R | 15 | 8 | **3.38** | 29 | 29 | 2 | 1 | 0 | 178.2 | 153 | 75 | 67 | 14 | 7 | 58 | 166 | 5 |
| A.J. Burnett, Fla | R | 12 | 12 | **3.44** | 32 | 32 | 4 | 2 | 0 | 209.0 | 184 | 97 | 80 | 12 | 7 | 79 | 198 | 12 |
| Tim Hudson, Atl | R | 14 | 9 | **3.52** | 29 | 29 | 2 | 0 | 0 | 192.0 | 194 | 79 | 75 | 20 | 9 | 65 | 115 | 4 |
| Tom Glavine, NY | L | 13 | 13 | **3.53** | 33 | 33 | 2 | 1 | 0 | 211.1 | 227 | 88 | 83 | 12 | 3 | 61 | 105 | 1 |
| Brandon Webb, Ari | R | 14 | 12 | **3.54** | 33 | 33 | 1 | 0 | 0 | 229.0 | 229 | 98 | 90 | 21 | 2 | 59 | 172 | 14 |

**Note:** Pitchers must have one inning pitched per their team's games played to qualify.

## Wins

| | |
|---|---|
| Willis, Fla | 22-10 |
| Carpenter, St.L | 21-5 |
| Oswalt, Hou | 20-12 |
| Capuano, Mil | 18-12 |
| Lieber, Phi | 17-13 |
| Pettitte, Hou | 17-9 |
| Suppan, St.L | 16-10 |
| Mulder, St.L | 16-8 |
| Three tied with 15 each. | |

## Losses

| | |
|---|---|
| Wells, Pit | 8-18 |
| Wright, Col | 8-16 |
| Redman, Pit | 5-15 |
| Lawrence, SD | 7-15 |
| Milton, Cin | 8-15 |
| Tomko, SF | 8-15 |
| Vazquez, Ari | 11-15 |
| Lowe, LA | 12-15 |
| Maddux, Chi | 13-15 |

## Walks

| | |
|---|---|
| Wells, Pit | 99 |
| Davis, Mil | 93 |
| Capuano, Mil | 91 |
| Zambrano, Chi | 86 |
| Schmidt, SF | 85 |
| Hernandez, Wash | 84 |
| Wright, Col | 81 |
| Burnett, Fla | 79 |

## Strikeouts

| | |
|---|---|
| Peavy, SD | 216 |
| Carpenter, St.L | 213 |
| Myers, Phi | 208 |
| Davis, Mil | 208 |
| Martinez, NY | 208 |
| Zambrano, Chi | 202 |
| Burnett, Fla | 198 |
| Vazquez, Ari | 192 |
| Prior, Chi | 188 |
| Clemens, Hou | 185 |
| Patterson, Wash | 185 |

## Appearances

| | |
|---|---|
| Eyre, SF | 86 |
| Majewski*, Wash | 79 |
| Sanchez, LA | 79 |
| Madson, Phi | 78 |
| Fuentes, Col | 78 |
| Mercker, Cin | 78 |
| Torres, Pit | 78 |
| Qualls*, Hou | 77 |
| King, St.L | 77 |

## Innings

| | |
|---|---|
| Hernandez, Wash | 246.1 |
| Oswalt, Hou | 241.2 |
| Carpenter, St.L | 241.2 |
| Willis, Fla | 236.1 |
| Smoltz, Atl | 229.2 |
| Webb, Ari | 229.0 |
| Maddux, Chi | 225.0 |
| Weaver, LA | 224.0 |
| Zambrano, Chi | 223.1 |

## HR Allowed

| | |
|---|---|
| Milton, Cin | 40 |
| Weaver, LA | 35 |
| Vazquez, Ari | 35 |
| Ortiz, Cin | 34 |
| Lieber, Phi | 33 |
| Capuano, Mil | 31 |
| Myers, Phi | 31 |
| Ramirez, Atl | 31 |

## Opp. Batting Average

| | |
|---|---|
| Clemens, Hou | .198 |
| Martinez, NY | .204 |
| Zambrano, Chi | .212 |
| Peavy, SD | .217 |
| Prior, Chi | .227 |
| Pettitte, Hou | .230 |
| Carpenter, St.L | .231 |
| Patterson, Wash | .233 |
| Beckett, Fla | .234 |

## Complete Games

| | |
|---|---|
| Willis, Fla | 7 |
| Carpenter, St.L | 7 |
| Oswalt, Hou | 4 |
| Burnett, Fla | 4 |
| Martinez, NY | 4 |
| Nine tied with 3 each. | |

## Saves

| | SV | BS |
|---|---|---|
| Cordero, Wash | 47 | 7 |
| Hoffman, SD | 43 | 3 |
| Lidge, Hou | 42 | 4 |
| Jones, Fla | 40 | 5 |
| Turnbow, Mil | 39 | 4 |
| Isringhausen, St.L | 39 | 4 |
| Wagner, Phi | 38 | 3 |
| Dempster, Chi | 33 | 2 |
| Fuentes, Col | 31 | 3 |
| Looper, NY | 28 | 8 |
| Mesa, Pit | 27 | 7 |

## Wild Pitches

| | |
|---|---|
| Webb, Ari | 14 |
| Burnett, Fla | 12 |
| Kim, Col | 11 |
| Marquis, St.L | 10 |
| Mulder, St.L | 9 |
| Turnbow, Mil | 9 |
| Patterson, Wash | 9 |

## Hit Batters

| | |
|---|---|
| Weaver, LA | 18 |
| Zambrano, NY | 15 |
| Wright, Col | 15 |
| Kim, Col | 14 |
| Hernandez, Wash | 13 |

## WHIP
(Walks + Hits/IP)

| | |
|---|---|
| Martinez, NY | 0.95 |
| Clemens, Hou | 1.01 |
| Pettitte, Hou | 1.03 |
| Peavy, SD | 1.04 |
| Carpenter, St.L | 1.06 |
| Willis, Fla | 1.13 |
| Smoltz, Atl | 1.15 |
| Zambrano, Chi | 1.15 |

## Shutouts

| | |
|---|---|
| Willis, Fla | 5 |
| Carpenter, St.L | 4 |
| Peavy, SD | 3 |
| Four tied with 2 each. | |

## Fielding

## Put Outs

| | |
|---|---|
| Pujols, St.L | 1597 |
| Lee, Chi | 1323 |
| Helton, Col | 1236 |
| Casey, Cin | 1153 |
| Delgado, Fla | 1147 |
| Overbay, Mil | 1133 |
| LaRoche, Atl | 1070 |
| Johnson, Wash | 1017 |
| Ausmus, Hou | 884 |
| Barrett, Chi | 870 |

## Assists

| | |
|---|---|
| J. Wilson, Pit | 523 |
| Eckstein, St.L | 517 |
| Furcal, Atl | 504 |
| Giles, Atl | 469 |
| Counsell, Ari | 459 |
| Grudzielanek, St.L | 442 |
| Reyes, NY | 428 |
| Vizquel, SF | 426 |
| Kent, LA | 424 |
| Everett, Hou | 421 |

## OF Assists

| | |
|---|---|
| Floyd, NY | 15 |
| Francoeur*, Atl | 13 |
| Cabrera, Fla | 12 |
| A. Jones, Atl | 11 |
| Taveras*, Hou | 10 |
| Jenkins, Mil | 10 |
| Hawpe, Col | 10 |
| Guillen, Wash | 10 |
| Burrell, Phi | 10 |
| Three tied with 8 each. | |

## Errors

| | |
|---|---|
| Wright, NY | 24 |
| Glaus, Ari | 24 |
| Bell, Phi | 21 |
| Weeks*, Mil | 21 |
| Atkins*, Col | 18 |
| Reyes, NY | 18 |
| Lopez, Cin | 17 |
| Barmes*, Col | 17 |
| Four tied with 16 each. | |

# Team Batting Statistics

## American League

| Team | Avg | AB | R | H | HR | RBI | SB |
|---|---|---|---|---|---|---|---|
| Boston | .281 | 5626 | 910 | 1579 | 199 | 863 | 45 |
| New York | .276 | 5624 | 886 | 1552 | 229 | 847 | 84 |
| Tampa Bay | .274 | 5552 | 750 | 1519 | 157 | 717 | 151 |
| Detroit | .272 | 5602 | 723 | 1521 | 168 | 678 | 66 |
| Cleveland | .271 | 5609 | 790 | 1522 | 207 | 760 | 62 |
| Los Angeles | .270 | 5624 | 761 | 1520 | 147 | 726 | 161 |
| Baltimore | .269 | 5551 | 729 | 1492 | 189 | 700 | 83 |
| Texas | .267 | 5716 | 865 | 1528 | 260 | 834 | 67 |
| Toronto | .265 | 5581 | 775 | 1480 | 136 | 735 | 72 |
| Kansas City | .263 | 5503 | 701 | 1445 | 126 | 653 | 53 |
| Oakland | .262 | 5627 | 772 | 1476 | 155 | 739 | 31 |
| Chicago | .262 | 5529 | 741 | 1450 | 200 | 713 | 137 |
| Minnesota | .259 | 5564 | 688 | 1441 | 134 | 644 | 102 |
| Seattle | .256 | 5507 | 699 | 1408 | 130 | 657 | 102 |

## National League

| Team | Avg | AB | R | H | HR | RBI | SB |
|---|---|---|---|---|---|---|---|
| Florida | .272 | 5502 | 717 | 1499 | 128 | 678 | 96 |
| St. Louis | .270 | 5538 | 805 | 1494 | 170 | 757 | 83 |
| Chicago | .270 | 5584 | 703 | 1506 | 194 | 674 | 65 |
| Philadelphia | .270 | 5542 | 807 | 1494 | 167 | 760 | 116 |
| Colorado | .267 | 5542 | 740 | 1477 | 150 | 704 | 65 |
| Atlanta | .265 | 5486 | 769 | 1453 | 184 | 733 | 92 |
| San Francisco | .261 | 5462 | 649 | 1427 | 128 | 617 | 71 |
| Cincinnati | .261 | 5565 | 820 | 1453 | 222 | 784 | 72 |
| Milwaukee | .259 | 5448 | 726 | 1413 | 175 | 689 | 79 |
| Pittsburgh | .259 | 5573 | 680 | 1445 | 139 | 656 | 73 |
| New York | .258 | 5505 | 722 | 1421 | 175 | 683 | 153 |
| San Diego | .257 | 5502 | 684 | 1416 | 130 | 655 | 99 |
| Houston | .256 | 5462 | 693 | 1400 | 161 | 654 | 115 |
| Arizona | .256 | 5550 | 696 | 1419 | 191 | 670 | 67 |
| Los Angeles | .253 | 5433 | 685 | 1374 | 149 | 653 | 58 |
| Washington | .252 | 5426 | 639 | 1367 | 117 | 615 | 45 |

# Team Pitching Statistics

## American League

| Team | ERA | W | Sv | CG | ShO | HR | BB | SO |
|---|---|---|---|---|---|---|---|---|
| Cleveland | 3.61 | 93 | 51 | 6 | 10 | 157 | 413 | 1050 |
| Chicago | 3.61 | 99 | 54 | 9 | 10 | 167 | 459 | 1040 |
| Los Angeles | 3.68 | 95 | 54 | 7 | 11 | 158 | 443 | 1126 |
| Oakland | 3.69 | 88 | 38 | 9 | 12 | 154 | 504 | 1075 |
| Minnesota | 3.71 | 83 | 44 | 9 | 8 | 169 | 348 | 965 |
| Toronto | 4.06 | 80 | 35 | 9 | 8 | 185 | 444 | 958 |
| Seattle | 4.49 | 69 | 39 | 6 | 7 | 179 | 496 | 892 |
| Detroit | 4.51 | 71 | 37 | 7 | 2 | 193 | 461 | 907 |
| New York | 4.52 | 95 | 46 | 8 | 14 | 164 | 463 | 985 |
| Baltimore | 4.56 | 74 | 38 | 2 | 9 | 180 | 580 | 1052 |
| Boston | 4.74 | 95 | 38 | 6 | 8 | 164 | 440 | 959 |
| Texas | 4.96 | 79 | 46 | 2 | 6 | 159 | 522 | 932 |
| Tampa Bay | 5.39 | 67 | 43 | 1 | 4 | 194 | 615 | 949 |
| Kansas City | 5.49 | 56 | 25 | 4 | 4 | 178 | 580 | 924 |

## National League

| Team | ERA | W | Sv | CG | ShO | HR | BB | SO |
|---|---|---|---|---|---|---|---|---|
| St. Louis | 3.49 | 100 | 48 | 15 | 14 | 153 | 443 | 974 |
| Houston | 3.51 | 89 | 45 | 6 | 11 | 155 | 440 | 1164 |
| New York | 3.76 | 83 | 38 | 8 | 11 | 135 | 491 | 1012 |
| Washington | 3.87 | 81 | 51 | 4 | 9 | 140 | 539 | 997 |
| Milwaukee | 3.97 | 81 | 46 | 7 | 6 | 169 | 569 | 1173 |
| Atlanta | 3.98 | 90 | 38 | 8 | 12 | 145 | 520 | 929 |
| San Diego | 4.13 | 82 | 45 | 4 | 8 | 146 | 503 | 1133 |
| Florida | 4.16 | 83 | 42 | 14 | 15 | 116 | 563 | 1125 |
| Chicago | 4.19 | 79 | 39 | 8 | 10 | 186 | 576 | 1256 |
| Philadelphia | 4.21 | 88 | 40 | 4 | 6 | 189 | 487 | 1159 |
| San Francisco | 4.33 | 75 | 46 | 4 | 8 | 151 | 592 | 972 |
| Los Angeles | 4.38 | 71 | 40 | 6 | 9 | 182 | 471 | 1004 |
| Pittsburgh | 4.42 | 67 | 35 | 4 | 14 | 162 | 612 | 958 |
| Arizona | 4.84 | 77 | 45 | 6 | 10 | 193 | 537 | 1038 |
| Colorado | 5.13 | 67 | 37 | 4 | 4 | 175 | 604 | 981 |
| Cincinnati | 5.15 | 73 | 31 | 2 | 1 | 219 | 492 | 955 |

# Team Fielding Statistics

## American League

| Team | Pct | TC | E | PO | A | DP | TP |
|---|---|---|---|---|---|---|---|
| Oakland | .986 | 6088 | 88 | 4351 | 1649 | 166 | 0 |
| Seattle | .986 | 5944 | 86 | 4283 | 1575 | 144 | 0 |
| Los Angeles | .986 | 6001 | 87 | 4393 | 1521 | 139 | 0 |
| Chicago | .985 | 6191 | 94 | 4427 | 1670 | 166 | 0 |
| Toronto | .985 | 6193 | 95 | 4341 | 1757 | 154 | 0 |
| New York | .984 | 6075 | 95 | 4292 | 1688 | 151 | 0 |
| Minnesota | .984 | 6259 | 102 | 4393 | 1764 | 171 | 0 |
| Cleveland | .983 | 6110 | 106 | 4358 | 1646 | 156 | 0 |
| Baltimore | .982 | 6069 | 107 | 4283 | 1679 | 154 | 0 |
| Texas | .982 | 6106 | 108 | 4320 | 1678 | 149 | 0 |
| Detroit | .982 | 6208 | 110 | 4307 | 1791 | 171 | 0 |
| Boston | .982 | 6019 | 109 | 4287 | 1623 | 135 | 0 |
| Kansas City | .979 | 6011 | 125 | 4240 | 1646 | 163 | 0 |
| Tampa Bay | .979 | 5835 | 124 | 4265 | 1446 | 139 | 0 |

## National League

| Team | Pct | TC | E | PO | A | DP | TP |
|---|---|---|---|---|---|---|---|
| Atlanta | .986 | 6219 | 86 | 4331 | 1802 | 170 | 0 |
| Houston | .985 | 6118 | 89 | 4329 | 1700 | 146 | 0 |
| San Francisco | .985 | 6053 | 90 | 4333 | 1630 | 146 | 0 |
| Philadelphia | .985 | 6003 | 90 | 4305 | 1608 | 132 | 0 |
| Arizona | .985 | 6257 | 94 | 4369 | 1794 | 159 | 0 |
| Washington | .985 | 6014 | 92 | 4374 | 1548 | 156 | 0 |
| St. Louis | .984 | 6388 | 100 | 4337 | 1951 | 196 | 1 |
| Chicago | .983 | 6079 | 101 | 4320 | 1658 | 136 | 0 |
| Florida | .983 | 6089 | 103 | 4327 | 1659 | 177 | 0 |
| Los Angeles | .983 | 6115 | 106 | 4282 | 1727 | 141 | 0 |
| Cincinnati | .983 | 5990 | 104 | 4299 | 1587 | 133 | 0 |
| New York | .983 | 6070 | 106 | 4307 | 1657 | 146 | 0 |
| San Diego | .982 | 6004 | 109 | 4366 | 1529 | 136 | 0 |
| Pittsburgh | .981 | 6228 | 117 | 4308 | 1803 | 193 | 0 |
| Colorado | .981 | 6080 | 118 | 4256 | 1706 | 158 | 0 |
| Milwaukee | .980 | 5915 | 119 | 4314 | 1482 | 139 | 0 |

**Pct**—Fielding Percentage; **TC**—Total Chances; **E**—Errors; **PO**—Put Outs; **A**—Assists; **DP**—Double Plays; **TP**—Triple Plays.

## 2005 All-Star Game

76th Baseball All-Star Game. **Date:** July 12 at Comerica Park, Detroit, Michigan; **Managers:** Tony La Russa, St. Louis (NL) and Terry Francona, Boston (AL); **Ted Williams MVP Award:** Miguel Tejada (AL) 1-for-3 with a HR and 2 RBI.

**Note:** The league that wins the All-Star Game also secures home-field advantage for the World Series.

### National League

| | AB | R | H | BI | BB | SO | Avg |
|---|---|---|---|---|---|---|---|
| Bobby Abreu, Phi, rf | 2 | 0 | 1 | 0 | 1 | 0 | .500 |
| Jimmy Rollins, Phi, ss | 1 | 0 | 1 | 0 | 0 | 0 | 1.000 |
| Luis Gonzalez, Ari, ph | 1 | 1 | 1 | 1 | 0 | 0 | 1.000 |
| Carlos Beltran, NY, lf | 3 | 0 | 1 | 0 | 0 | 1 | .333 |
| Paul LoDuca, Fla, c | 2 | 0 | 0 | 0 | 0 | 0 | .000 |
| Albert Pujols, St.L, dh | 2 | 0 | 1 | 0 | 0 | 0 | .500 |
| Carlos Lee, Mil, ph-dh | 3 | 0 | 0 | 1 | 0 | 1 | .000 |
| Derrek Lee, Chi, 1b | 3 | 0 | 1 | 0 | 0 | 1 | .333 |
| Morgan Ensberg, Hou, 1b | 2 | 0 | 0 | 0 | 0 | 1 | .000 |
| Jim Edmonds, St.L, cf-rf | 1 | 0 | 0 | 0 | 1 | 0 | .000 |
| Moises Alou, SF, ph-rf | 1 | 1 | 1 | 0 | 1 | 0 | 1.000 |
| Aramis Ramirez, Chi, 3b | 2 | 0 | 1 | 0 | 0 | 0 | .500 |
| Felipe Lopez, Cin, 3b | 1 | 0 | 1 | 0 | 0 | 0 | 1.000 |
| Mike Piazza, NY, c | 2 | 0 | 0 | 0 | 0 | 1 | .000 |
| Miguel Cabrera, Fla, lf | 2 | 0 | 1 | 0 | 0 | 0 | .000 |
| Jeff Kent, LA, 2b | 1 | 0 | 0 | 0 | 0 | 0 | .000 |
| Luis Castillo, Fla, 2b | 3 | 1 | 1 | 0 | 0 | 0 | .333 |
| David Eckstein, St.L, ss | 2 | 0 | 0 | 0 | 0 | 0 | .000 |
| Andruw Jones, Atl, cf | 1 | 2 | 1 | 2 | 1 | 0 | 1.000 |
| TOTALS | 35 | 5 | 11 | 5 | 5 | 6 | .314 |

### American League

| | AB | R | H | BI | BB | SO | Avg |
|---|---|---|---|---|---|---|---|
| Johnny Damon, Bos, cf | 2 | 1 | 1 | 0 | 0 | 0 | .500 |
| Ichiro Suzuki, Sea, cf-rf | 2 | 0 | 1 | 2 | 0 | 0 | .500 |
| Alex Rodriguez, NY, 3b | 2 | 1 | 1 | 0 | 1 | 0 | .500 |
| Melvin Mora, Bal, 3b | 1 | 0 | 0 | 0 | 0 | 1 | .000 |
| Shea Hillenbrand, Tor, 3b | 0 | 0 | 0 | 0 | 0 | 0 | — |
| David Ortiz, Bos, dh | 3 | 0 | 2 | 1 | 0 | 0 | .667 |
| Mike Sweeney, KC, ph-dh | 1 | 0 | 0 | 0 | 0 | 1 | .000 |
| Manny Ramirez, Bos, lf | 2 | 0 | 0 | 0 | 0 | 1 | .000 |
| Garret Anderson, LAA, lf | 2 | 0 | 0 | 0 | 0 | 1 | .000 |
| Miguel Tejada, Bal, ss | 3 | 1 | 1 | 2 | 0 | 0 | .333 |
| Michael Young, Tex, ss | 1 | 0 | 1 | 0 | 0 | 0 | 1.000 |
| Vladimir Guerrero, LAA, rf | 3 | 0 | 1 | 0 | 0 | 0 | .333 |
| Alfonso Soriano, pr-2b | 1 | 1 | 0 | 0 | 0 | 0 | .000 |
| Mark Teixera, Tex, 1b | 3 | 1 | 1 | 2 | 0 | 0 | .333 |
| Paul Konerko, Chi, 1b | 1 | 0 | 0 | 0 | 0 | 1 | .000 |
| Jason Varitek, Bos, c | 1 | 1 | 1 | 0 | 1 | 0 | 1.000 |
| Ivan Rodriguez, Det, c | 1 | 0 | 0 | 0 | 1 | 0 | .000 |
| Brian Roberts, Bal, 2b | 2 | 1 | 1 | 0 | 0 | 0 | .500 |
| Gary Sheffield, NY, ph-rf | 1 | 0 | 0 | 0 | 0 | 0 | .000 |
| Scott Podsednik, Chi, cf | 0 | 0 | 0 | 0 | 0 | 0 | — |
| TOTALS | 32 | 7 | 11 | 7 | 3 | 6 | .344 |

| | 1 | 2 | 3 | 4 | 5 | 6 | 7 | 8 | 9 | | R | H | E |
|---|---|---|---|---|---|---|---|---|---|---|---|---|---|
| **National League** | 0 | 0 | 0 | 0 | 0 | 0 | 2 | 1 | 2 | – | 5 | 11 | 0 |
| **American League** | 0 | 1 | 2 | 2 | 0 | 2 | 0 | 0 | x | – | 7 | 11 | 1 |

**E**—Colon (AL). **LOB**—National 8, American 4. **2B**—Gonzalez, D. Lee, Alou (NL); Young, Roberts (AL). **HR**—A. Jones (NL, off Rogers, 1 on); Tejada (AL, off Smoltz, 0 on), Texeira (AL, off Willis, 1 on). **SB**—none. **SF**—none. **GIDP**—Beltran, Lo Duca, A. Ramirez (NL); M. Ramirez, Sheffield (AL).

| NL Pitching | IP | H | R | ER | BB | SO |
|---|---|---|---|---|---|---|
| Chris Carpenter, St.L | 1.0 | 2 | 0 | 0 | 0 | 0 |
| John Smoltz, Atl (L, 0-1) | 1.0 | 2 | 1 | 1 | 0 | 0 |
| Roy Oswalt, Hou | 1.0 | 2 | 2 | 2 | 1 | 1 |
| Livan Hernandez, Wash | 1.0 | 2 | 2 | 2 | 1 | 0 |
| Roger Clemens, Hou | 1.0 | 0 | 0 | 0 | 0 | 1 |
| Dontrelle Willis, Fla | 1.0 | 2 | 2 | 2 | 1 | 0 |
| Brad Lidge, Hou | 1.0 | 0 | 0 | 0 | 0 | 3 |
| Jake Peavy, SD | 0.2 | 1 | 0 | 0 | 0 | 1 |
| Chad Cordero, Wash | 0.1 | 0 | 0 | 0 | 0 | 1 |
| TOTALS | 8.0 | 11 | 7 | 7 | 3 | 6 |

| AL Pitching | IP | H | R | ER | BB | SO |
|---|---|---|---|---|---|---|
| Mark Buehrle, Chi (W, 1-0) | 2.0 | 3 | 0 | 0 | 0 | 3 |
| Bartolo Colon, LAA | 1.0 | 1 | 0 | 0 | 0 | 0 |
| Johan Santana, Min | 1.0 | 1 | 0 | 0 | 1 | 0 |
| Matt Clement, Bos | 1.0 | 0 | 0 | 0 | 1 | 1 |
| Jon Garland, Chi | 1.0 | 0 | 0 | 0 | 0 | 1 |
| Kenny Rogers, Tex | 1.0 | 3 | 2 | 2 | 0 | 1 |
| Joe Nathan, Min | 1.0 | 2 | 1 | 1 | 0 | 0 |
| Bob Wickman, Cle | 0.0 | 0 | 1 | 1 | 1 | 0 |
| B.J. Ryan, Bal | 0.2 | 1 | 1 | 1 | 0 | 0 |
| Mariano Rivera, NY (S, 1) | 0.1 | 0 | 0 | 0 | 0 | 1 |
| TOTALS | 9.0 | 11 | 5 | 5 | 5 | 6 |

Wickman pitched to 1 batter in the 9th. **WP**—Garland (AL). **Umpires**—Joe West (plate); Tim Welke (1b); Eric Cooper (2b); Mike DiMuro (3b); C.B. Bucknor (lf); Andy Fletcher (rf). **Attendance**—41,617 (40,120 cap.). **Time**—2:41. **TV Rating**—8.1/14 share (FOX).

## Home Run Derby

Results of the 2005 All-Star Home Run Derby held at Comerica Park in Detroit, Michigan on July 11: For the first time in the Derby's 20-year history, the eight participating players represented their native countries, as opposed to the previous format that included four American League sluggers and four from the National League.

### First Round

| | Country | No. |
|---|---|---|
| Bobby Abreu, Phi. | Venezuela | 24 |
| David Ortiz, Bos | Dominican Republic | 17 |
| Carlos Lee, Mil | Panama | 11 |
| Ivan Rodriguez, Det. | Puerto Rico | 7 |
| Hee-Sop Choi, LA | Korea | 5 |
| Andruw Jones, Atl | Netherlands | 5 |
| Mark Teixera, Tex | United States | 2 |
| Jason Bay, Pit | Canada | 0 |
| (Top four advance to second round) | | |

### Second Round

| | Country | No. |
|---|---|---|
| Ivan Rodriguez, Det. | Puerto Rico | 8 |
| Bobby Abreu, Phi. | Venezuela | 6 |
| Carlos Lee, Mil | Panama | 4 |
| David Ortiz, Bos | Dominican Republic | 3 |
| (Top two advance to Finals) | | |

### Finals

| | Country | No. |
|---|---|---|
| Bobby Abreu, Phi. | Venezuela | 11 |
| Ivan Rodriguez, Det. | Puerto Rico | 5 |

# AL Team by Team Statistics

At least 135 at bats or 40 innings pitched during the regular season, unless otherwise indicated. Players who competed for more than one AL team are listed with their final club. Players traded from the NL are listed with AL team only if they have 135 AB or 40 IP. Note that (*) indicates rookie and PTBN indicates player to be named.

## Baltimore Orioles

| Batting (140 AB) | Avg | AB | R | H | HR | RBI | SB |
|---|---|---|---|---|---|---|---|
| Brian Roberts | .314 | 561 | 92 | 176 | 18 | 73 | 27 |
| Miguel Tejada | .304 | 654 | 89 | 199 | 26 | 98 | 5 |
| Melvin Mora | .283 | 593 | 86 | 168 | 27 | 88 | 7 |
| Luis Matos | .280 | 389 | 53 | 109 | 4 | 32 | 17 |
| Chris Gomez | .279 | 219 | 27 | 61 | 1 | 18 | 2 |
| Javy Lopez | .278 | 395 | 47 | 110 | 15 | 49 | 0 |
| Jay Gibbons | .277 | 488 | 72 | 135 | 26 | 79 | 0 |
| Rafael Palmeiro | .266 | 369 | 47 | 98 | 18 | 60 | 2 |
| B.J. Surhoff | .257 | 303 | 30 | 78 | 5 | 34 | 0 |
| Sal Fasano | .250 | 160 | 25 | 40 | 11 | 20 | 0 |
| Larry Bigbie | .248 | 206 | 22 | 51 | 5 | 21 | 3 |
| Eric Byrnes | .231 | 359 | 47 | 83 | 10 | 35 | 5 |
| Sammy Sosa | .221 | 380 | 39 | 84 | 14 | 45 | 1 |
| David Newham | .202 | 218 | 31 | 44 | 5 | 21 | 9 |

**Acquired:** OF Byrnes from Col. for OF Bigbie (July 29). **Claimed:** P Baldwin off waivers from Tex. (Aug, 23).

| Pitching (40 IP) | ERA | W-L | Gm | IP | BB | SO |
|---|---|---|---|---|---|---|
| B.J. Ryan | 2.43 | 1-1 | 69 | 70.1 | 26 | 100 |
| Chris Ray* | 2.66 | 1-3 | 41 | 40.2 | 18 | 43 |
| Todd Williams | 3.30 | 5-5 | 72 | 76.1 | 26 | 38 |
| James Baldwin | 3.81 | 0-2 | 28 | 56.2 | 16 | 29 |
| Bruce Chen | 3.83 | 13-10 | 34 | 197.1 | 63 | 133 |
| Erik Bedard | 4.00 | 6-8 | 24 | 141.2 | 57 | 125 |
| Steve Kline | 4.28 | 2-4 | 67 | 61.0 | 30 | 36 |
| Daniel Cabrera | 4.52 | 10-13 | 29 | 161.1 | 87 | 157 |
| Rodrigo Lopez | 4.90 | 15-12 | 35 | 209.1 | 63 | 118 |
| Jorge Julio | 5.90 | 3-5 | 67 | 71.2 | 24 | 58 |
| Sidney Ponson | 6.21 | 7-11 | 23 | 130.1 | 48 | 68 |
| John Maine* | 6.30 | 2-3 | 10 | 40.0 | 24 | 24 |

**Saves:** Ryan (36), Williams, Baldwin and Tim Byrdak (1). **Complete games:** Chen and Ponson (1). **Shutouts:** none.

## Boston Red Sox

| Batting (135 AB) | Avg | AB | R | H | HR | RBI | SB |
|---|---|---|---|---|---|---|---|
| Johnny Damon | .316 | 624 | 117 | 197 | 10 | 75 | 18 |
| Tony Graffanino | .309 | 379 | 68 | 117 | 7 | 38 | 7 |
| David Ortiz | .300 | 601 | 119 | 180 | 47 | 148 | 1 |
| Bill Mueller | .295 | 519 | 69 | 153 | 10 | 62 | 0 |
| Manny Ramirez | .292 | 554 | 112 | 162 | 45 | 144 | 1 |
| John Olerud | .289 | 173 | 18 | 50 | 7 | 37 | 0 |
| Jason Varitek | .281 | 470 | 70 | 132 | 22 | 70 | 2 |
| Edgar Renteria | .276 | 623 | 100 | 172 | 8 | 70 | 9 |
| Trot Nixon | .275 | 408 | 64 | 112 | 13 | 67 | 2 |
| Kevin Millar | .272 | 449 | 57 | 122 | 9 | 50 | 0 |
| Alex Cora | .232 | 250 | 25 | 58 | 3 | 24 | 7 |
| Doug Mirabelli | .228 | 136 | 16 | 31 | 6 | 18 | 2 |

**Acquired:** IF Cora from Cle. for IF Ramon Vazquez (July 7); IF Graffanino from KC for 2 minor leaguers (July 19). **Designated:** P Halama for assignment (July 26).

| Pitching (40 IP) | ERA | W-L | Gm | IP | BB | SO |
|---|---|---|---|---|---|---|
| Mike Timlin | 2.24 | 7-3 | 81 | 80.1 | 20 | 59 |
| Tim Wakefield | 4.15 | 16-12 | 33 | 225.1 | 68 | 151 |
| David Wells | 4.45 | 15-7 | 30 | 184.0 | 21 | 107 |
| Bronson Arroyo | 4.51 | 14-10 | 35 | 205.1 | 54 | 100 |
| Matt Clement | 4.57 | 13-6 | 32 | 191.0 | 68 | 146 |
| Wade Miller | 4.95 | 4-4 | 16 | 91.0 | 47 | 64 |
| Curt Schilling | 5.69 | 8-8 | 32 | 93.1 | 22 | 87 |
| Keith Foulke | 5.91 | 5-5 | 43 | 45.2 | 18 | 34 |
| Jeremi Gonzalez | 6.11 | 2-1 | 28 | 56.0 | 16 | 28 |
| John Halama | 6.18 | 1-1 | 30 | 43.2 | 9 | 26 |

**Saves:** Foulke (15), Timlin (13), Schilling (9). **Complete games:** Wakefield (3), Wells (2), Clement (1). **Shutouts:** none.

## Chicago White Sox

| Batting (140 AB) | Avg | AB | R | H | HR | RBI | SB |
|---|---|---|---|---|---|---|---|
| Scott Podsednik | .290 | 507 | 80 | 147 | 0 | 25 | 59 |
| Paul Konerko | .283 | 575 | 98 | 163 | 40 | 100 | 0 |
| Tadahito Iguchi* | .278 | 511 | 74 | 142 | 15 | 71 | 15 |
| Pablo Ozuna | .276 | 203 | 27 | 56 | 0 | 11 | 14 |
| Jermaine Dye | .274 | 529 | 74 | 145 | 31 | 86 | 11 |
| Aaron Rowand | .270 | 578 | 77 | 156 | 13 | 69 | 16 |
| A.J. Pierzynski | .257 | 460 | 61 | 118 | 18 | 56 | 0 |
| Joe Crede | .252 | 432 | 54 | 109 | 22 | 62 | 1 |
| Juan Uribe | .252 | 481 | 58 | 121 | 16 | 71 | 4 |
| Carl Everett | .251 | 490 | 58 | 123 | 23 | 87 | 4 |
| Timo Perez | .218 | 179 | 13 | 39 | 2 | 15 | 2 |

| Pitching (35 IP) | ERA | W-L | Gm | IP | BB | SO |
|---|---|---|---|---|---|---|
| Neal Cotts | 1.94 | 4-0 | 69 | 60.1 | 29 | 58 |
| Cliff Politte | 2.00 | 7-1 | 68 | 67.1 | 21 | 57 |
| Dustin Hermanson | 2.04 | 2-4 | 57 | 57.1 | 17 | 33 |
| Bobby Jenks* | 2.75 | 1-1 | 32 | 39.1 | 15 | 50 |
| Mark Buehrle | 3.12 | 16-8 | 33 | 236.2 | 40 | 149 |
| Jon Garland | 3.50 | 18-10 | 32 | 221.0 | 47 | 115 |
| Jose Contreras | 3.61 | 15-7 | 32 | 204.2 | 75 | 154 |
| Luis Vizcaino | 3.73 | 6-5 | 65 | 70.0 | 29 | 43 |
| Damaso Marte | 3.77 | 3-4 | 66 | 45.1 | 33 | 54 |
| Freddy Garcia | 3.87 | 14-8 | 33 | 228.0 | 60 | 146 |
| Brandon McCarthy* | 4.03 | 3-2 | 12 | 67.0 | 17 | 48 |
| Orlando Hernandez | 5.12 | 9-9 | 24 | 128.1 | 50 | 91 |

**Saves:** Hermanson (34), Shingo Takatsu (8), Jenks (6), Marte (4), Hernandez and Politte (1). **Complete games:** Buehrle and Garland (3), Garcia (2), Contreras (1). **Shutouts:** Garland (3), Buehrle (1).

## Cleveland Indians

| Batting (135 AB) | Avg | AB | R | H | HR | RBI | SB |
|---|---|---|---|---|---|---|---|
| Victor Martinez | .305 | 547 | 73 | 167 | 20 | 80 | 0 |
| Travis Hafner | .305 | 486 | 94 | 148 | 33 | 108 | 0 |
| Coco Crisp | .300 | 594 | 86 | 178 | 16 | 69 | 15 |
| Jhonny Peralta | .292 | 504 | 82 | 147 | 24 | 78 | 0 |
| Grady Sizemore | .289 | 640 | 111 | 187 | 22 | 81 | 22 |
| Ronnie Belliard | .284 | 536 | 71 | 152 | 17 | 78 | 2 |
| Jody Gerut | .275 | 138 | 12 | 38 | 1 | 12 | 1 |
| Ben Broussard | .255 | 466 | 59 | 119 | 19 | 68 | 2 |
| Aaron Boone | .243 | 511 | 61 | 124 | 16 | 60 | 9 |
| Casey Blake | .241 | 523 | 72 | 126 | 23 | 58 | 4 |
| Jose Hernandez | .231 | 234 | 28 | 54 | 6 | 31 | 1 |

**Traded:** OF Gerut to ChC for OF Jason Dubois (July 18).

| Pitching (40 IP) | ERA | W-L | Gm | IP | BB | SO |
|---|---|---|---|---|---|---|
| Arthur Rhodes | 2.08 | 3-1 | 47 | 43.1 | 12 | 43 |
| Bob Howry | 2.47 | 7-4 | 79 | 73.0 | 16 | 48 |
| Bob Wickman | 2.47 | 0-4 | 64 | 62.0 | 21 | 41 |
| Rafael Betancourt | 2.79 | 4-3 | 54 | 67.2 | 17 | 73 |
| Kevin Millwood | 2.86 | 9-11 | 30 | 192.0 | 52 | 146 |
| David Riske | 3.10 | 3-4 | 58 | 72.2 | 15 | 48 |
| Cliff Lee | 3.79 | 18-5 | 32 | 202.0 | 52 | 143 |
| C.C. Sabathia | 4.03 | 15-10 | 31 | 196.2 | 62 | 161 |
| Jake Westbrook | 4.49 | 15-15 | 34 | 210.2 | 56 | 119 |
| Scott Elarton | 4.61 | 11-9 | 31 | 181.2 | 48 | 103 |
| Jason Davis | 4.69 | 4-2 | 11 | 40.1 | 20 | 32 |

**Saves:** Wickman (45), Howry (3), Betancourt, Riske and Matt Miller (1). **Complete games:** Westbrook (2), Millwood, Lee, Sabathia and Elarton (1). **Shutouts:** none.

## Detroit Tigers

| Batting (135 AB) | Avg | AB | R | H | HR | RBI | SB |
|---|---|---|---|---|---|---|---|
| Placido Polanco | .338 | 343 | 58 | 116 | 6 | 36 | 4 |
| Carlos Guillen | .320 | 334 | 48 | 107 | 5 | 23 | 2 |
| Rondell White | .313 | 374 | 49 | 117 | 12 | 53 | 1 |
| Magglio Ordonez | .302 | 305 | 38 | 92 | 8 | 46 | 0 |
| Chris Shelton | .299 | 388 | 61 | 116 | 18 | 59 | 0 |
| John McDonald | .277 | 166 | 18 | 46 | 0 | 16 | 6 |
| Craig Monroe | .277 | 567 | 69 | 157 | 20 | 89 | 8 |
| Ivan Rodriguez | .276 | 504 | 71 | 139 | 14 | 50 | 7 |
| Curtis Granderson* | .272 | 162 | 18 | 44 | 8 | 20 | 1 |
| Dmitri Young | .271 | 469 | 61 | 127 | 21 | 72 | 1 |
| Brandon Inge | .261 | 616 | 75 | 161 | 16 | 72 | 7 |
| Nook Logan | .258 | 322 | 47 | 83 | 1 | 17 | 23 |
| Carlos Pena | .235 | 260 | 37 | 61 | 18 | 44 | 0 |
| Omar Infante | .222 | 406 | 36 | 90 | 9 | 43 | 8 |
| Vance Wilson | .197 | 152 | 18 | 30 | 3 | 19 | 0 |

**Acquired:** IF Polanco from Phi. for P Ugueth Urbina and IF Ramon Martinez (June 8); IF McDonald from Tor. for a PTBN (July 22). **Traded:** P Farnsworth to Atl. for P Roman Colon and a minor leaguer (July 31).

| Pitching (40 IP) | ERA | W-L | Gm | IP | BB | SO |
|---|---|---|---|---|---|---|
| Kyle Farnsworth | 2.31 | 1-1 | 46 | 42.2 | 20 | 55 |
| Fernando Rodney | 2.86 | 2-3 | 39 | 44.0 | 17 | 42 |
| Chris Spurling | 3.44 | 3-4 | 56 | 70.2 | 22 | 26 |
| Franklyn German | 3.66 | 4-0 | 58 | 59.0 | 34 | 38 |
| Jamie Walker | 3.70 | 4-3 | 66 | 48.2 | 13 | 30 |
| Nate Robertson | 4.48 | 7-16 | 32 | 196.2 | 65 | 122 |
| Jason Johnson | 4.54 | 8-13 | 33 | 210.0 | 49 | 93 |
| Jeremy Bonderman | 4.57 | 14-13 | 29 | 189.0 | 57 | 145 |
| Mike Maroth | 4.74 | 14-14 | 34 | 209.0 | 51 | 115 |
| Sean Douglass | 5.56 | 5-5 | 18 | 87.1 | 33 | 55 |
| Wilfredo Ledezma | 7.07 | 2-4 | 10 | 49.2 | 24 | 30 |

**Saves:** Rodney and Ugueth Urbina (9), Troy Percival (8), Farnsworth (6), Craig Dingman (4), German (1). **Complete games:** Bonderman (4), Robertson (2), Johnson (1). **Shutouts:** none.

## Kansas City Royals

| Batting (135 AB) | Avg | AB | R | H | HR | RBI | SB |
|---|---|---|---|---|---|---|---|
| Mike Sweeney | .300 | 470 | 63 | 141 | 21 | 83 | 3 |
| David DeJesus | .293 | 461 | 69 | 135 | 9 | 56 | 5 |
| Emil Brown | .286 | 545 | 75 | 156 | 17 | 86 | 10 |
| Terrence Long | .279 | 455 | 62 | 127 | 6 | 53 | 3 |
| Matt Stairs | .275 | 396 | 55 | 109 | 13 | 66 | 1 |
| Angel Berroa | .270 | 608 | 68 | 164 | 11 | 55 | 7 |
| Mark Teahen* | .246 | 447 | 60 | 110 | 7 | 55 | 7 |
| John Buck | .242 | 401 | 40 | 97 | 12 | 47 | 2 |
| Chip Ambres* | .241 | 145 | 25 | 35 | 4 | 9 | 3 |
| Joe McEwing | .239 | 180 | 16 | 43 | 1 | 6 | 4 |
| Ruben Gotay | .227 | 282 | 32 | 64 | 5 | 29 | 2 |

| Pitching (40 IP) | ERA | W-L | Gm | IP | BB | SO |
|---|---|---|---|---|---|---|
| Andrew Sisco* | 3.11 | 2-5 | 67 | 75.1 | 42 | 76 |
| Mike MacDougal | 3.33 | 5-6 | 68 | 70.1 | 24 | 72 |
| Ambiorix Burgos* | 3.98 | 3-5 | 59 | 63.1 | 31 | 65 |
| Mike Wood | 4.46 | 5-8 | 47 | 115.0 | 52 | 60 |
| D.J. Carrasco | 4.79 | 6-8 | 21 | 114.2 | 51 | 49 |
| Jeremy Affeldt | 5.26 | 0-2 | 49 | 49.2 | 29 | 39 |
| Runelvys Hernandez | 5.52 | 8-14 | 29 | 159.2 | 70 | 88 |
| Jimmy Gobble | 5.70 | 1-1 | 28 | 53.2 | 30 | 38 |
| Zack Greinke | 5.80 | 5-17 | 33 | 183.0 | 53 | 114 |
| J.P. Howell* | 6.19 | 3-5 | 15 | 72.2 | 39 | 54 |
| Shawn Camp | 6.43 | 1-4 | 29 | 49.0 | 13 | 28 |
| Jose Lima | 6.99 | 5-16 | 32 | 168.2 | 61 | 80 |
| Leo Nunez* | 7.55 | 3-2 | 41 | 53.2 | 18 | 32 |

**Saves:** MacDougal (21), Burgos and Wood (2). **Complete games:** Greinke (2), Carrasco and Lima (1). **Shutouts:** none.

## Los Angeles Angels of Anaheim

| Batting (135 AB) | Avg | AB | R | H | HR | RBI | SB |
|---|---|---|---|---|---|---|---|
| Vladimir Guerrero | .317 | 520 | 95 | 165 | 32 | 108 | 13 |
| Adam Kennedy | .300 | 416 | 49 | 125 | 2 | 37 | 19 |
| Bengie Molina | .295 | 410 | 45 | 121 | 15 | 69 | 0 |
| Chone Figgins | .290 | 642 | 113 | 186 | 8 | 57 | 62 |
| Garret Anderson | .283 | 575 | 68 | 163 | 17 | 96 | 1 |
| Darin Erstad | .273 | 609 | 86 | 166 | 7 | 66 | 10 |
| Juan Rivera | .271 | 350 | 46 | 95 | 15 | 59 | 1 |
| Orlando Cabrera | .257 | 540 | 70 | 139 | 8 | 57 | 21 |
| Maicer Izturis* | .246 | 191 | 18 | 47 | 1 | 15 | 9 |
| Dallas McPherson* | .244 | 205 | 29 | 50 | 8 | 26 | 3 |
| Jeff DaVanon | .231 | 225 | 42 | 52 | 2 | 15 | 11 |
| Jose Molina | .228 | 184 | 14 | 42 | 6 | 25 | 2 |
| Steve Finley | .222 | 406 | 41 | 90 | 12 | 54 | 8 |

| Pitching (40 IP) | ERA | W-L | Gm | IP | BB | SO |
|---|---|---|---|---|---|---|
| Francisco Rodriguez | 2.67 | 2-5 | 66 | 67.1 | 32 | 91 |
| Scot Shields | 2.75 | 10-11 | 78 | 91.2 | 37 | 98 |
| Kelvim Escobar | 3.02 | 3-2 | 16 | 59.2 | 21 | 63 |
| Jarrod Wasburn | 3.20 | 8-8 | 29 | 177.1 | 51 | 94 |
| John Lackey | 3.44 | 14-5 | 33 | 209.0 | 71 | 199 |
| Bartolo Colon | 3.48 | 21-8 | 33 | 222.2 | 43 | 157 |
| Brendan Donnelly | 3.72 | 9-3 | 65 | 65.1 | 19 | 53 |
| Paul Byrd | 3.74 | 12-11 | 31 | 204.1 | 28 | 102 |
| Esteban Yan | 4.59 | 1-1 | 49 | 66.2 | 30 | 45 |
| Ervin Santana* | 4.65 | 12-8 | 23 | 133.2 | 47 | 99 |
| Kevin Gregg | 5.04 | 1-3 | 33 | 64.1 | 29 | 52 |

**Saves:** Rodriguez (45), Shields (7), Escobar and Chris Bootcheck (1). **Complete games:** Colon and Byrd (2), Washburn, Lackey and Santana (1). **Shutouts:** Washburn, Byrd and Santana (1).

## Minnesota Twins

| Batting (135 AB) | Avg | AB | R | H | HR | RBI | SB |
|---|---|---|---|---|---|---|---|
| Mike Redmond | .311 | 148 | 17 | 46 | 1 | 26 | 0 |
| Joe Mauer | .294 | 489 | 61 | 144 | 9 | 55 | 13 |
| Shannon Stewart | .274 | 551 | 69 | 151 | 10 | 56 | 7 |
| Torii Hunter | .269 | 372 | 63 | 100 | 14 | 56 | 23 |
| Luis Rodriguez* | .269 | 175 | 21 | 47 | 2 | 20 | 2 |
| Lew Ford | .264 | 522 | 70 | 138 | 7 | 53 | 13 |
| Michael Cuddyer | .263 | 422 | 55 | 111 | 12 | 42 | 3 |
| Matthew LeCroy | .260 | 304 | 33 | 79 | 17 | 50 | 0 |
| Juan Castro | .257 | 272 | 27 | 70 | 5 | 33 | 0 |
| Luis Rivas | .257 | 136 | 21 | 35 | 1 | 12 | 4 |
| Jacque Jones | .249 | 523 | 74 | 130 | 23 | 73 | 13 |
| Jason Bartlett | .241 | 224 | 33 | 54 | 3 | 16 | 4 |
| Justin Morneau | .239 | 490 | 62 | 117 | 22 | 79 | 0 |
| Nick Punto | .239 | 394 | 45 | 94 | 4 | 26 | 13 |
| Bret Boone | .221 | 326 | 33 | 72 | 7 | 37 | 4 |
| Terry Tiffee* | .207 | 150 | 9 | 31 | 1 | 15 | 1 |

**Acquired:** IF Boone from Sea. for cash and a PTBN (July 12). **Released:** Boone (Aug. 2).

| Pitching (35 IP) | ERA | W-L | Gm | IP | BB | SO |
|---|---|---|---|---|---|---|
| Juan Rincon | 2.45 | 6-6 | 75 | 77.0 | 30 | 84 |
| Joe Nathan | 2.70 | 7-4 | 69 | 70.0 | 22 | 94 |
| Jesse Crain* | 2.71 | 12-5 | 75 | 79.2 | 29 | 25 |
| Johan Santana | 2.87 | 16-7 | 33 | 231.2 | 45 | 238 |
| Scott Baker* | 3.35 | 3-3 | 10 | 53.2 | 14 | 32 |
| Matt Guerrier* | 3.39 | 0-3 | 43 | 71.2 | 24 | 46 |
| Carlos Silva | 3.44 | 9-8 | 27 | 188.1 | 9 | 71 |
| J.C. Romero | 3.47 | 4-3 | 68 | 57.0 | 39 | 48 |
| Brad Radke | 4.04 | 9-12 | 31 | 200.2 | 23 | 117 |
| Kyle Lohse | 4.18 | 9-13 | 31 | 178.2 | 44 | 86 |
| Terry Mulholland | 4.27 | 0-2 | 49 | 59.0 | 17 | 18 |
| Joe Mays | 5.65 | 6-10 | 31 | 156.0 | 41 | 59 |

**Saves:** Nathan (43), Crain (1). **Complete games:** Santana and Radke (3), Silva (2), Mays (1). **Shutouts:** Santana (2), Radke and Mays (1).

## New York Yankees

| Batting (135 AB) | Avg | AB | R | H | HR | RBI | SB |
|---|---|---|---|---|---|---|---|
| Alex Rodriguez | .321 | 605 | 124 | 194 | 48 | 130 | 21 |
| Derek Jeter | .309 | 654 | 122 | 202 | 19 | 70 | 14 |
| Hideki Matsui | .305 | 629 | 108 | 192 | 23 | 116 | 2 |
| Robinson Cano* | .297 | 522 | 78 | 155 | 14 | 62 | 1 |
| Gary Sheffield | .291 | 584 | 104 | 170 | 34 | 123 | 10 |
| Jason Giambi | .271 | 417 | 74 | 113 | 32 | 87 | 0 |
| Jorge Posada | .262 | 474 | 67 | 124 | 19 | 71 | 1 |
| Bernie Williams | .249 | 485 | 53 | 121 | 12 | 64 | 1 |
| Tony Womack | .249 | 329 | 46 | 82 | 0 | 15 | 27 |
| Tino Martinez | .241 | 303 | 43 | 73 | 17 | 49 | 2 |
| Ruben Sierra | .229 | 170 | 14 | 39 | 4 | 29 | 0 |
| Mark Bellhorn | .210 | 300 | 43 | 63 | 8 | 30 | 3 |

**Acquired:** P Leiter from Fla. for cash (July 16); P Chacon from Col. for 2 minor league pitchers (July 28). **Signed:** free agent P Embree (July 31); free agent IF Bellhorn (Aug. 31).

| Pitching (40 IP) | ERA | W-L | Gm | IP | BB | SO |
|---|---|---|---|---|---|---|
| Mariano Rivera | 1.38 | 7-4 | 71 | 78.1 | 18 | 80 |
| Tom Gordon | 2.57 | 5-4 | 79 | 80.2 | 29 | 69 |
| Shawn Chacon | 2.85 | 7-3 | 14 | 79.0 | 30 | 40 |
| Aaron Small | 3.20 | 10-0 | 15 | 76.0 | 24 | 37 |
| Randy Johnson | 3.79 | 17-8 | 34 | 225.2 | 47 | 211 |
| Chien-Ming Wang* | 4.02 | 8-5 | 18 | 116.1 | 32 | 47 |
| Mike Mussina | 4.41 | 13-8 | 30 | 179.2 | 47 | 142 |
| Tanyon Sturtze | 4.73 | 5-3 | 64 | 78.0 | 27 | 45 |
| Carl Pavano | 4.77 | 4-6 | 17 | 100.0 | 18 | 56 |
| Al Leiter | 5.49 | 4-5 | 16 | 62.1 | 38 | 45 |
| Scott Proctor | 6.04 | 1-0 | 29 | 44.2 | 17 | 36 |
| Jaret Wright | 6.08 | 5-5 | 13 | 63.2 | 32 | 34 |
| Kevin Brown | 6.50 | 4-7 | 13 | 73.1 | 19 | 50 |
| Alan Embree | 7.62 | 2-5 | 15 | 52.0 | 14 | 38 |

**Saves:** Rivera (43), Gordon (2), Sturtze (1), Embree (1). **Complete games:** Johnson (4), Mussina (3), Small and Pavano (1). **Shutouts:** Mussina (2), Small and Pavano (1).

## Oakland Athletics

| Batting (135 AB) | Avg | AB | R | H | HR | RBI | SB |
|---|---|---|---|---|---|---|---|
| Mark Ellis | .316 | 434 | 76 | 137 | 13 | 52 | 1 |
| Mark Kotsay | .280 | 582 | 75 | 163 | 15 | 82 | 5 |
| Bobby Crosby | .276 | 333 | 66 | 92 | 9 | 38 | 0 |
| Dan Johnson* | .275 | 375 | 54 | 103 | 15 | 58 | 0 |
| Jason Kendall | .271 | 601 | 70 | 163 | 0 | 53 | 8 |
| Eric Chavez | .269 | 625 | 92 | 168 | 27 | 101 | 6 |
| Jay Payton | .267 | 408 | 62 | 109 | 18 | 63 | 0 |
| Bobby Kielty | .263 | 377 | 55 | 99 | 10 | 57 | 3 |
| Scott Hatteberg | .256 | 464 | 52 | 119 | 7 | 59 | 0 |
| Marco Scutaro | .247 | 381 | 48 | 94 | 9 | 37 | 5 |
| Erubiel Durazo | .237 | 152 | 15 | 36 | 4 | 16 | 1 |
| Nick Swisher* | .236 | 462 | 66 | 109 | 21 | 74 | 0 |
| Keith Ginter | .161 | 137 | 12 | 22 | 3 | 25 | 0 |

**Acquired:** OF Payton from Bos. for P Chad Bradford (July 8); P Kennedy and P Jay Witasick from Col. for OF Eric Byrnes and IF Omar Quintanilla (July 13).

| Pitching (40 IP) | ERA | W-L | Gm | IP | BB | SO |
|---|---|---|---|---|---|---|
| Huston Street* | 1.72 | 5-1 | 67 | 78.1 | 26 | 72 |
| Justin Duchscherer | 2.21 | 7-4 | 65 | 85.2 | 19 | 85 |
| Rich Harden | 2.53 | 10-5 | 22 | 128.0 | 43 | 121 |
| Kiko Calero | 3.23 | 4-1 | 58 | 55.2 | 18 | 52 |
| Joe Blanton* | 3.53 | 12-12 | 33 | 201.1 | 67 | 116 |
| Danny Haren | 3.73 | 14-12 | 34 | 217.0 | 53 | 163 |
| Barry Zito | 3.86 | 14-13 | 35 | 228.1 | 89 | 171 |
| Kirk Saarloos | 4.17 | 10-9 | 29 | 159.2 | 54 | 53 |
| Joe Kennedy | 4.45 | 4-5 | 19 | 60.2 | 20 | 45 |
| Keiichi Yabu* | 4.50 | 4-0 | 40 | 58.0 | 26 | 44 |

**Saves:** Street (23), Octavio Dotel (7), Duchscherer (5), Calero, Yabu and Jay Witasick (1). **Complete games:** Haren (3), Harden, Blanton and Saarloos (2). **Shutouts:** Harden and Saarloos (1).

## Seattle Mariners

| Batting (135 AB) | Avg | AB | R | H | HR | RBI | SB |
|---|---|---|---|---|---|---|---|
| Ichiro Suzuki | .303 | 679 | 111 | 206 | 15 | 68 | 33 |
| Raul Ibanez | .280 | 614 | 92 | 172 | 20 | 89 | 9 |
| Mike Morse* | .278 | 230 | 27 | 64 | 3 | 23 | 3 |
| Randy Winn | .275 | 386 | 46 | 106 | 6 | 37 | 12 |
| Richie Sexson | .263 | 558 | 99 | 147 | 39 | 121 | 1 |
| Willie Bloomquist | .257 | 249 | 27 | 64 | 0 | 22 | 14 |
| Yuniesky Betancourt* | .256 | 211 | 24 | 54 | 1 | 15 | 1 |
| Adrian Beltre | .255 | 603 | 69 | 154 | 19 | 87 | 3 |
| Jeremy Reed* | .254 | 488 | 61 | 124 | 3 | 45 | 12 |
| Jose Lopez | .247 | 190 | 18 | 47 | 2 | 25 | 4 |
| Greg Dobbs* | .246 | 142 | 8 | 35 | 1 | 20 | 1 |
| Miguel Olivo | .151 | 152 | 14 | 23 | 5 | 18 | 1 |

**Traded:** OF Winn to SF for P Jesse Foppert and C Yorvit Torrealba (July 30); P Villone to Fla. for 2 minor leaguers (July 31); C Olivo to SD for C Miguel Ojeda and a minor leaguer (July 31).

| Pitching (35 IP) | ERA | W-L | Gm | IP | BB | SO |
|---|---|---|---|---|---|---|
| Ron Villone | 2.45 | 2-3 | 52 | 40.1 | 23 | 41 |
| Felix Hernandez* | 2.67 | 4-4 | 12 | 84.1 | 23 | 77 |
| Eddie Guardado | 2.72 | 2-3 | 58 | 56.1 | 15 | 48 |
| Julio Mateo | 3.06 | 3-6 | 55 | 88.1 | 17 | 52 |
| J.J. Putz | 3.60 | 6-5 | 64 | 60.0 | 23 | 45 |
| Jeff Nelson | 3.93 | 1-3 | 49 | 36.2 | 22 | 34 |
| Shigetoshi Hasegawa | 4.19 | 1-3 | 46 | 66.2 | 16 | 30 |
| Jeff Harris* | 4.19 | 2-5 | 11 | 53.2 | 20 | 25 |
| Jamie Moyer | 4.28 | 13-7 | 32 | 200.0 | 52 | 102 |
| Gil Meche | 5.09 | 10-8 | 29 | 143.1 | 72 | 83 |
| Ryan Franklin | 5.10 | 8-15 | 32 | 190.2 | 62 | 93 |
| Matt Thornton | 5.21 | 0-4 | 55 | 57.0 | 42 | 57 |
| Joel Pineiro | 5.62 | 7-11 | 30 | 189.0 | 56 | 107 |
| Aaron Sele | 5.66 | 6-12 | 21 | 116.0 | 41 | 53 |

**Saves:** Guardado (36), Villone, Putz and Nelson (1). **Complete games:** Franklin and Pineiro (2), Moyer and Sele (1). **Shutouts:** Franklin and Sele (1).

## Tampa Bay Devil Rays

| Batting (135 AB) | Avg | AB | R | H | HR | RBI | SB |
|---|---|---|---|---|---|---|---|
| Carl Crawford | .301 | 644 | 101 | 194 | 15 | 81 | 46 |
| Julio Lugo | .295 | 616 | 89 | 182 | 6 | 57 | 39 |
| Toby Hall | .287 | 432 | 28 | 124 | 5 | 48 | 0 |
| Jorge Cantu | .286 | 598 | 73 | 171 | 28 | 117 | 1 |
| Jonny Gomes* | .282 | 348 | 61 | 98 | 21 | 54 | 9 |
| Joey Gathright* | .276 | 203 | 29 | 56 | 0 | 13 | 20 |
| Travis Lee | .272 | 404 | 54 | 110 | 12 | 49 | 7 |
| Alex Gonzalez | .269 | 349 | 47 | 94 | 9 | 38 | 2 |
| Josh Phelps | .266 | 158 | 21 | 42 | 5 | 26 | 0 |
| Aubrey Huff | .261 | 575 | 70 | 150 | 22 | 92 | 8 |
| Eduardo Perez | .255 | 161 | 23 | 41 | 11 | 28 | 0 |
| Damon Hollins* | .249 | 342 | 44 | 85 | 13 | 46 | 8 |
| Nick Green | .239 | 318 | 53 | 76 | 5 | 29 | 3 |

**Traded:**

| Pitching (40 IP) | ERA | W-L | Gm | IP | BB | SO |
|---|---|---|---|---|---|---|
| Danys Baez | 2.86 | 5-4 | 67 | 72.1 | 30 | 51 |
| Chad Orvella* | 3.60 | 3-3 | 37 | 50.0 | 23 | 43 |
| Scott Kazmir | 3.77 | 10-9 | 32 | 186.0 | 100 | 174 |
| Trever Miller | 4.06 | 2-2 | 61 | 44.1 | 29 | 35 |
| Jesus Colome | 4.57 | 2-3 | 36 | 45.1 | 18 | 28 |
| Lance Carter | 4.89 | 1-2 | 39 | 57.0 | 15 | 22 |
| Casey Fossum | 4.92 | 8-12 | 16 | 162.2 | 60 | 128 |
| Doug Waechter | 5.62 | 5-12 | 29 | 157.0 | 38 | 87 |
| Mark Hendrickson | 5.90 | 11-8 | 31 | 178.1 | 49 | 89 |
| Seth McClung | 6.59 | 7-11 | 34 | 109.1 | 62 | 92 |
| Travis Harper | 6.75 | 4-6 | 52 | 73.1 | 24 | 40 |
| Hideo Nomo | 7.24 | 5-8 | 19 | 100.2 | 51 | 59 |
| Dewon Brazelton | 7.61 | 1-8 | 20 | 71.0 | 60 | 43 |

**Saves:** Baez (41), Orvella and Carter (1). **Complete games:** Hendrickson (1). **Shutouts:** none.

## Texas Rangers

**Batting** (100 AB)

| | Avg | AB | R | H | HR | RBI | SB |
|---|---|---|---|---|---|---|---|
| Michael Young | .331 | 668 | 114 | 221 | 24 | 91 | 5 |
| Mark Texeira | .301 | 644 | 112 | 194 | 43 | 144 | 4 |
| Sandy Alomar Jr. | .273 | 128 | 11 | 35 | 0 | 14 | 0 |
| Alfonso Soriano | .268 | 637 | 102 | 171 | 36 | 104 | 30 |
| Kevin Mench | .264 | 557 | 71 | 147 | 25 | 73 | 4 |
| Hank Blalock | .263 | 647 | 80 | 170 | 25 | 92 | 1 |
| Gary Matthews Jr. | .255 | 475 | 72 | 121 | 17 | 55 | 9 |
| Rod Barajas | .254 | 410 | 53 | 104 | 21 | 60 | 0 |
| David Dellucci | .251 | 435 | 97 | 109 | 29 | 65 | 5 |
| Mark DeRosa | .243 | 148 | 26 | 36 | 8 | 20 | 1 |
| Laynce Nix | .240 | 229 | 28 | 55 | 6 | 32 | 2 |
| Adrian Gonzalez* | .227 | 150 | 17 | 34 | 6 | 17 | 0 |
| Richard Hidalgo | .221 | 308 | 43 | 68 | 16 | 43 | 1 |

**Traded:** P Park to SD for IF Phil Nevin (July 30). **Released:** P Drese (June 8); P Astacio (June 22).

**Pitching** (35 IP)

| | ERA | W-L | Gm | IP | BB | SO |
|---|---|---|---|---|---|---|
| Francisco Cordero | 3.39 | 3-1 | 69 | 69.0 | 30 | 79 |
| Kameron Loe* | 3.42 | 9-6 | 48 | 92.0 | 31 | 45 |
| Kenny Rogers | 3.46 | 14-8 | 30 | 195.1 | 53 | 87 |
| Joaquin Benoit | 3.72 | 4-4 | 32 | 87.0 | 38 | 78 |
| Juan Dominguez* | 4.22 | 4-6 | 22 | 70.1 | 25 | 45 |
| Chris Young* | 4.26 | 12-7 | 31 | 164.2 | 45 | 137 |
| John Wasdin | 4.28 | 3-2 | 31 | 75.2 | 20 | 44 |
| Brian Shouse | 5.23 | 3-2 | 64 | 53.1 | 18 | 35 |
| Doug Brocail | 5.52 | 5-3 | 61 | 73.1 | 34 | 61 |
| Ricardo Rodriguez | 5.53 | 2-3 | 12 | 57.0 | 17 | 24 |
| Chan Ho Park | 5.66 | 8-5 | 20 | 109.2 | 54 | 80 |
| Pedro Astacio | 6.04 | 2-8 | 12 | 67.0 | 11 | 45 |
| Ryan Drese | 6.46 | 4-6 | 12 | 69.2 | 24 | 20 |
| Ron Mahay | 6.81 | 0-2 | 30 | 35.2 | 16 | 30 |
| C.J. Wilson* | 6.94 | 1-7 | 24 | 48.0 | 18 | 30 |

**Saves:** Cordero (37), Wasdin (4), Loe, Brocail, Mahay and Wilson (1). **Complete games:** Drese and Rogers (1). **Shutouts:** Rogers (1).

## Toronto Blue Jays

**Batting** (100 AB)

| | Avg | AB | R | H | HR | RBI | SB |
|---|---|---|---|---|---|---|---|
| Frank Catalanotto | .301 | 419 | 56 | 126 | 8 | 59 | 0 |
| Shea Hillenbrand | .291 | 594 | 91 | 173 | 18 | 82 | 5 |
| Aaron Hill* | .274 | 361 | 49 | 99 | 3 | 40 | 2 |
| Orlando Hudson | .271 | 461 | 62 | 125 | 10 | 63 | 7 |
| Vernon Wells | .269 | 620 | 78 | 167 | 28 | 97 | 8 |
| Reed Johnson | .269 | 398 | 55 | 107 | 8 | 58 | 5 |
| Eric Hinske | .262 | 477 | 79 | 125 | 15 | 68 | 8 |
| Alex Rios | .262 | 481 | 71 | 126 | 10 | 59 | 14 |
| Russ Adams* | .256 | 481 | 68 | 123 | 8 | 63 | 11 |
| Gregg Zaun | .251 | 434 | 61 | 109 | 11 | 61 | 2 |
| Corey Koskie | .249 | 354 | 49 | 88 | 11 | 36 | 4 |
| Frank Menechino | .216 | 148 | 22 | 32 | 4 | 13 | 0 |

**Pitching** (25 IP)

| | ERA | W-L | Gm | IP | BB | SO |
|---|---|---|---|---|---|---|
| Roy Halladay | 2.41 | 12-4 | 19 | 141.2 | 18 | 108 |
| Justin Speier | 2.57 | 3-2 | 65 | 66.2 | 15 | 56 |
| Jason Frasor | 3.25 | 3-5 | 67 | 74.2 | 28 | 62 |
| Scott Schoeneweis | 3.32 | 3-4 | 80 | 57.0 | 25 | 43 |
| Pete Walker | 3.54 | 6-6 | 41 | 84.0 | 33 | 43 |
| Josh Towers | 3.71 | 13-12 | 33 | 208.2 | 29 | 112 |
| Gustavo Chacin* | 3.72 | 13-9 | 34 | 203.0 | 70 | 121 |
| Vinnie Chulk | 3.88 | 0-1 | 62 | 72.0 | 26 | 39 |
| Miguel Batista | 4.10 | 5-8 | 71 | 74.2 | 27 | 54 |
| Scott Downs | 4.31 | 4-3 | 26 | 94.0 | 34 | 75 |
| Dave Bush | 4.49 | 5-11 | 25 | 136.1 | 29 | 75 |
| Ted Lilly | 5.56 | 10-11 | 25 | 126.1 | 58 | 96 |
| Dustin McGowan* | 6.35 | 1-3 | 13 | 45.1 | 17 | 34 |
| Brandon League* | 6.56 | 1-0 | 20 | 35.2 | 20 | 17 |

**Saves:** Batista (31), Walker (2), Frasor and Schoeneweis (1). **Complete games:** Halladay (5), Towers and Bush (2). **Shutouts:** Halladay (2), Towers (1).

## Home Attendance

Overall 2005 MLB regular season attendance (based on tickets sold) was 74,915,268, the highest total in history. The average per game crowd of 30,970 was the third-highest in history. Numbers in parentheses indicate ranking in 2002. HD indicates home dates. **Note:** Washington moved from Montreal before the 2005 season.

### American League

| | | Attendance | HD | Average |
|---|---|---|---|---|
| 1 | New York (1) | 4,090,696 | 81 | 50,502 |
| 2 | Los Angeles (2) | 3,404,686 | 81 | 42,033 |
| 3 | Boston (4) | 2,847,888 | 81 | 35,159 |
| 4 | Seattle (3) | 2,725,459 | 81 | 33,648 |
| 5 | Baltimore (5) | 2,624,740 | 81 | 32,404 |
| 6 | Texas (6) | 2,525,221 | 80 | 31,565 |
| 7 | Chicago (8) | 2,342,833 | 81 | 28,924 |
| 8 | Oakland (7) | 2,109,118 | 81 | 26,038 |
| 9 | Detroit (9) | 2,024,431 | 80 | 25,306 |
| 10 | Minnesota (10) | 2,034,243 | 81 | 25,114 |
| 11 | Toronto (11) | 2,014,995 | 81 | 24,876 |
| 12 | Cleveland (12) | 2,013,763 | 81 | 24,861 |
| 13 | Kansas City (13) | 1,371,181 | 79 | 17,357 |
| 14 | Tampa Bay (14) | 1,141,669 | 81 | 14,094 |
| | TOTALS | 33,270,923 | 1130 | 29,443 |

### National League

| | | Attendance | HD | Average |
|---|---|---|---|---|
| 1 | Los Angeles (1) | 3,603,646 | 81 | 44,489 |
| 2 | St. Louis (6) | 3,538,988 | 81 | 43,691 |
| 3 | San Francisco (3) | 3,181,023 | 81 | 39,272 |
| 4 | Chicago (4) | 3,099,992 | 80 | 38,750 |
| 5 | San Diego (7) | 2,869,787 | 81 | 35,429 |
| 6 | New York (11) | 2,829,929 | 80 | 35,374 |
| 7 | Houston (5) | 2,804,760 | 81 | 34,627 |
| 8 | Washington (16) | 2,731,993 | 81 | 33,728 |
| 9 | Philadelphia (2) | 2,665,304 | 80 | 33,316 |
| 10 | Atlanta (10) | 2,521,167 | 80 | 31,515 |
| 11 | Milwaukee (13) | 2,211,023 | 81 | 27,296 |
| 12 | Arizona (8) | 2,059,424 | 81 | 25,425 |
| 13 | Cincinnati (12) | 1,943,067 | 81 | 23,988 |
| 14 | Colorado (9) | 1,914,389 | 80 | 23,930 |
| 15 | Pittsburgh (15) | 1,817,245 | 79 | 23,003 |
| 16 | Florida (14) | 1,852,608 | 81 | 22,872 |
| | TOTALS | 41,644,345 | 1289 | 32,307 |

# NL Team by Team Statistics

At least 135 at bats or 40 innings pitched during the regular season unless otherwise indicated. Players who competed for more than one NL team are listed with their final club. Players traded from the AL are listed with NL team only if they have 135 AB or 40 IP. Note that (*) indicates rookie and PTBN indicates player to be named.

## Arizona Diamondbacks

| Batting (135 AB) | Avg | AB | R | H | HR | RBI | SB |
|---|---|---|---|---|---|---|---|
| Chad Tracy | .308 | 503 | 73 | 155 | 27 | 72 | 3 |
| Tony Clark | .306 | 349 | 47 | 106 | 30 | 87 | 0 |
| Shawn Green | .286 | 581 | 87 | 166 | 22 | 73 | 8 |
| Alex Cintron | .273 | 330 | 36 | 90 | 8 | 48 | 1 |
| Luis Gonzalez | .271 | 579 | 90 | 157 | 24 | 79 | 4 |
| Royce Clayton | .270 | 522 | 59 | 141 | 2 | 44 | 13 |
| Troy Glaus | .258 | 538 | 78 | 139 | 37 | 97 | 4 |
| Craig Counsell | .256 | 578 | 85 | 148 | 9 | 42 | 26 |
| Quinton McCracken | .237 | 215 | 23 | 51 | 1 | 13 | 4 |
| Luis Terrero | .230 | 161 | 23 | 37 | 4 | 20 | 3 |
| Chris Snyder* | .202 | 326 | 24 | 66 | 6 | 28 | 0 |

**Acquired:** P Worrell from Phi. for IF Matt Kata (July 21). **Claimed:** P Vargas off waivers from Wash. (June 3).

| Pitching (40 IP) | ERA | W-L | Gm | IP | BB | SO |
|---|---|---|---|---|---|---|
| Jose Valverde | 2.44 | 3-4 | 61 | 66.1 | 20 | 75 |
| Brandon Webb | 3.54 | 14-12 | 33 | 229.0 | 59 | 172 |
| Tim Worrell | 4.07 | 1-2 | 51 | 48.2 | 12 | 39 |
| Javier Vazquez | 4.42 | 11-15 | 33 | 215.2 | 46 | 192 |
| Brad Halsey* | 4.61 | 8-12 | 28 | 160.0 | 39 | 82 |
| Shawn Estes | 4.80 | 7-8 | 21 | 123.2 | 45 | 63 |
| Mike Kolove | 5.07 | 2-1 | 44 | 49.2 | 20 | 28 |
| Lance Cormier* | 5.11 | 7-3 | 67 | 79.1 | 43 | 63 |
| Claudio Vargas | 5.24 | 9-9 | 25 | 132.1 | 47 | 95 |
| Russ Ortiz | 6.89 | 5-11 | 22 | 115.0 | 65 | 46 |
| Brian Bruney | 7.43 | 1-3 | 47 | 46.0 | 35 | 51 |

**Saves:** Valverde (15), Lyon (14), Bruney (12), Javier Lopez (2), Worrell, Groom and Greg Aquino (1). **Complete games:** Vazquez (3), Estes (2), Webb (1). **Shutouts:** Vazquez (1).

## Atlanta Braves

| Batting (155 AB) | Avg | AB | R | H | HR | RBI | SB |
|---|---|---|---|---|---|---|---|
| Wilson Betemit* | .305 | 246 | 36 | 75 | 4 | 20 | 1 |
| Jeff Francouer* | .300 | 257 | 41 | 77 | 14 | 45 | 3 |
| Chipper Jones | .296 | 358 | 66 | 106 | 21 | 72 | 5 |
| Marcus Giles | .291 | 577 | 104 | 168 | 15 | 63 | 16 |
| Rafael Furcal | .284 | 616 | 100 | 175 | 12 | 58 | 46 |
| Brian McCann* | .278 | 180 | 20 | 50 | 5 | 23 | 1 |
| Julio Franco | .275 | 233 | 30 | 64 | 9 | 42 | 4 |
| Ryan Langerhans* | .267 | 326 | 48 | 87 | 8 | 42 | 0 |
| Andruw Jones | .263 | 586 | 95 | 154 | 51 | 128 | 5 |
| Johnny Estrada | .261 | 357 | 31 | 93 | 4 | 39 | 0 |
| Adam LaRoche | .259 | 451 | 53 | 117 | 20 | 78 | 0 |
| Brian Jordan | .247 | 231 | 25 | 57 | 3 | 24 | 2 |
| Todd Hollandsworth | .244 | 303 | 26 | 74 | 6 | 36 | 4 |
| Kelly Johnson | .241 | 290 | 46 | 70 | 9 | 40 | 2 |

**Acquired:** OF Hollandsworth from ChC for 2 minor leaguers (Aug. 30). **Traded:** P Colon and a minor leaguer to Det. for P Kyle Farnsworth (July 31). **Signed:** P Brower (June 16).

| Pitching (40 IP) | ERA | W-L | Gm | IP | BB | SO |
|---|---|---|---|---|---|---|
| Jorge Sosa | 2.55 | 13-3 | 44 | 134.0 | 64 | 85 |
| John Smoltz | 3.06 | 14-7 | 33 | 229.2 | 53 | 169 |
| Mike Hampton | 3.50 | 5-3 | 12 | 69.1 | 18 | 27 |
| Tim Hudson | 3.52 | 14-9 | 29 | 192.0 | 65 | 115 |
| Chris Reitsma | 3.93 | 3-6 | 76 | 73.1 | 14 | 42 |
| John Thomson | 4.47 | 4-6 | 17 | 98.2 | 28 | 61 |
| Horacio Ramirez | 4.63 | 11-9 | 33 | 202.1 | 67 | 80 |
| Kyle Davies* | 4.93 | 7-6 | 21 | 87.2 | 49 | 62 |
| Roman Colon* | 5.28 | 1-5 | 23 | 44.1 | 14 | 30 |
| Jim Brower | 5.37 | 3-3 | 69 | 60.1 | 32 | 53 |
| Dan Kolb | 5.93 | 3-8 | 65 | 57.2 | 29 | 39 |
| Adam Bernero | 6.51 | 4-3 | 36 | 47.0 | 12 | 37 |

**Saves:** Reitsma (15), Kolb (11), Farnsworth (10), Brower, Macay McBride and John Foster (1). **Complete games:** Smoltz (3), Hudson (2), Hampton, Thomson and Ramirez (1). **Shutouts:** Smoltz, Hampton and Ramirez (1).

## Chicago Cubs

| Batting (140 AB) | Avg | AB | R | H | HR | RBI | SB |
|---|---|---|---|---|---|---|---|
| Derrek Lee | .335 | 594 | 120 | 199 | 46 | 107 | 15 |
| Matt Murton* | .321 | 140 | 19 | 45 | 7 | 14 | 2 |
| Todd Walker | .305 | 397 | 50 | 121 | 12 | 40 | 1 |
| Aramis Ramirez | .302 | 463 | 72 | 140 | 31 | 92 | 0 |
| Nomar Garciaparra | .283 | 230 | 28 | 65 | 9 | 30 | 0 |
| Michael Barrett | .276 | 424 | 48 | 117 | 16 | 61 | 0 |
| Neifi Perez | .274 | 572 | 59 | 157 | 9 | 54 | 8 |
| Matt Lawton | .268 | 452 | 61 | 121 | 11 | 49 | 17 |
| Jerry Hairston Jr. | .261 | 380 | 51 | 99 | 4 | 30 | 8 |
| Jeromy Burnitz | .258 | 605 | 84 | 156 | 24 | 87 | 5 |
| Jose Macias | .254 | 177 | 15 | 45 | 1 | 13 | 4 |
| Henry Blanco | .242 | 161 | 16 | 39 | 6 | 25 | 0 |
| Jason Dubois | .239 | 142 | 15 | 34 | 7 | 22 | 0 |
| Corey Patterson | .215 | 451 | 47 | 97 | 13 | 34 | 15 |

**Acquired:** P Williams and P David Aardsma from SF for P LaTroy Hawkins (May 28); OF Jody Gerut from Cle. for OF Dubois (July 18); OF Lawton from Pit. for OF Gerut (July 31). **Traded:** P Lawton to NYY for P Justin Berg (Aug. 28).

| Pitching (40 IP) | ERA | W-L | Gm | IP | BB | SO |
|---|---|---|---|---|---|---|
| Will Ohman* | 2.91 | 2-2 | 69 | 43.1 | 24 | 45 |
| Ryan Dempster | 3.13 | 5-3 | 63 | 92.0 | 49 | 89 |
| Carlos Zambrano | 3.26 | 14-6 | 33 | 223.1 | 86 | 202 |
| Mark Prior | 3.67 | 11-7 | 27 | 166.2 | 59 | 188 |
| Michael Wuertz | 3.81 | 6-2 | 75 | 75.2 | 40 | 89 |
| Kerry Wood | 4.23 | 3-4 | 21 | 66.0 | 26 | 77 |
| Greg Maddux | 4.24 | 13-15 | 35 | 225.0 | 36 | 136 |
| Jerome Williams | 4.26 | 6-10 | 22 | 122.2 | 49 | 70 |
| Roberto Novoa* | 4.43 | 4-5 | 49 | 44.2 | 25 | 47 |
| Glendon Rusch | 4.52 | 9-8 | 46 | 145.1 | 53 | 111 |
| Sergio Mitre | 5.37 | 2-5 | 21 | 60.1 | 23 | 37 |

**Saves:** Dempster (33), Todd Wellemeyer and Chad Fox (1). **Complete games:** Maddux (3), Zambrano (2), Prior, Rusch and Mitre (1). **Shutouts:** Rusch and Mitre (1).

## Cincinnati Reds

| Batting (135 AB) | Avg | AB | R | H | HR | RBI | SB |
|---|---|---|---|---|---|---|---|
| Sean Casey | .312 | 529 | 75 | 165 | 9 | 58 | 2 |
| Ken Griffey Jr. | .301 | 491 | 85 | 148 | 35 | 92 | 0 |
| Felipe Lopez | .291 | 580 | 97 | 169 | 23 | 85 | 15 |
| Rich Aurilia | .282 | 426 | 61 | 120 | 14 | 68 | 2 |
| Javier Valentin | .281 | 221 | 36 | 62 | 14 | 50 | 0 |
| Ryan Freel | .271 | 369 | 69 | 100 | 4 | 21 | 36 |
| Jason LaRue | .260 | 361 | 38 | 94 | 14 | 60 | 0 |
| Willy Mo Pena | .254 | 311 | 42 | 79 | 19 | 51 | 2 |
| Adam Dunn | .247 | 543 | 107 | 134 | 40 | 101 | 4 |
| Austin Kearns | .240 | 387 | 62 | 93 | 18 | 67 | 0 |
| Edwin Encarnacion* | .232 | 211 | 25 | 49 | 9 | 31 | 3 |

| Pitching (40 IP) | ERA | W-L | Gm | IP | BB | SO |
|---|---|---|---|---|---|---|
| Kent Mercker | 3.65 | 3-1 | 78 | 61.2 | 19 | 45 |
| Aaron Harang | 3.83 | 11-13 | 32 | 211.2 | 51 | 163 |
| David Weathers | 3.94 | 7-4 | 73 | 77.2 | 29 | 61 |
| Brandon Claussen | 4.21 | 10-11 | 29 | 166.2 | 57 | 121 |
| Matt Belisle* | 4.41 | 4-8 | 60 | 85.2 | 26 | 59 |
| Todd Coffey* | 4.50 | 4-1 | 57 | 58.0 | 11 | 26 |
| Ramon Ortiz | 5.36 | 9-11 | 30 | 171.1 | 51 | 96 |
| Ryan Wagner | 6.11 | 3-2 | 42 | 45.2 | 17 | 39 |
| Randy Keisler | 6.27 | 2-1 | 24 | 56.0 | 28 | 43 |
| Luke Hudson | 6.38 | 6-9 | 19 | 84.2 | 50 | 53 |
| Eric Milton | 6.47 | 8-15 | 34 | 186.1 | 52 | 123 |
| Paul Wilson | 7.77 | 1-5 | 9 | 46.1 | 17 | 30 |

**Saves:** Weathers (15), Mercker (4), Belisle and Coffey (1). **Complete games:** Harang and Ortiz (1). **Shutouts:** none.

### Colorado Rockies

**Batting** (120 AB)

| | Avg | AB | R | H | HR | RBI | SB |
|---|---|---|---|---|---|---|---|
| Todd Helton | .320 | 509 | 92 | 163 | 20 | 79 | 3 |
| Matt Holliday | .307 | 479 | 68 | 147 | 19 | 87 | 14 |
| Cory Sullivan* | .294 | 378 | 64 | 111 | 4 | 30 | 12 |
| Luis Gonzalez | .292 | 404 | 51 | 118 | 9 | 44 | 3 |
| Clint Barmes* | .289 | 350 | 55 | 101 | 10 | 46 | 6 |
| Garrett Atkins | .287 | 519 | 62 | 149 | 13 | 89 | 0 |
| Aaron Miles | .281 | 324 | 37 | 91 | 2 | 28 | 4 |
| Brad Hawpe* | .262 | 305 | 38 | 80 | 9 | 47 | 2 |
| Todd Greene | .254 | 126 | 10 | 32 | 7 | 23 | 0 |
| Danny Ardoin | .229 | 210 | 28 | 48 | 6 | 22 | 1 |
| Desi Relaford | .224 | 210 | 24 | 47 | 1 | 16 | 3 |
| J.D. Closser | .219 | 237 | 31 | 52 | 7 | 27 | 1 |
| Omar Quintanilla* | .219 | 128 | 16 | 28 | 0 | 7 | 2 |
| Dustan Mohr | .214 | 266 | 34 | 57 | 17 | 38 | 1 |

**Acquired:** IF Quintanilla and OF Eric Byrnes from Oak. for P Kennedy and P Jay Witasick (July 13); P Day, OF J.J. Davis and a PTBN from Wash. for OF Preston Wilson (July 13). **Traded:** Chacon to NYY for 2 minor league pitchers (July 28). **Claimed:** P Sunny Kim off waivers from Wash. (Aug. 5). **Signed:** P DeJean (June 25).

**Pitching** (40 IP)

| | ERA | W-L | Gm | IP | BB | SO |
|---|---|---|---|---|---|---|
| Brian Fuentes | 2.91 | 2-5 | 78 | 74.1 | 34 | 91 |
| Aaron Cook | 3.67 | 7-2 | 13 | 83.1 | 16 | 24 |
| Shawn Chacon | 4.09 | 1-7 | 13 | 72.2 | 36 | 39 |
| David Cortes* | 4.10 | 2-0 | 50 | 52.2 | 10 | 36 |
| Mike DeJean | 4.48 | 5-4 | 66 | 62.1 | 30 | 52 |
| Byung-Hyun Kim | 4.86 | 5-12 | 40 | 148.0 | 71 | 115 |
| Sunny Kim | 4.90 | 6-3 | 24 | 82.2 | 21 | 55 |
| Jason Jennings | 5.02 | 6-9 | 20 | 122.0 | 62 | 75 |
| Marcos Carvajal* | 5.09 | 0-2 | 39 | 53.0 | 21 | 47 |
| Jamey Wright | 5.46 | 8-16 | 34 | 171.1 | 81 | 101 |
| Jeff Francis* | 5.68 | 14-12 | 33 | 183.2 | 70 | 128 |
| Jose Acevedo | 6.47 | 2-4 | 36 | 64.0 | 16 | 31 |
| Zach Day | 6.85 | 1-3 | 17 | 47.1 | 32 | 23 |
| Joe Kennedy | 7.04 | 4-8 | 16 | 92.0 | 44 | 52 |

**Saves:** Fuentes (31), Chin-hui Tsao (3), Cortes (2), Acevedo (1). **Complete games:** Cook (2), S. Kim and Jennings (1). **Shutouts:** S. Kim.

### Florida Marlins

**Batting** (135 AB)

| | Avg | AB | R | H | HR | RBI | SB |
|---|---|---|---|---|---|---|---|
| Miguel Cabrera | .323 | 613 | 106 | 198 | 33 | 116 | 1 |
| Jeff Conine | .304 | 335 | 42 | 102 | 3 | 33 | 2 |
| Carlos Delgado | .301 | 521 | 81 | 157 | 33 | 115 | 0 |
| Luis Castillo | .301 | 439 | 72 | 132 | 4 | 30 | 10 |
| Juan Encarnacion | .287 | 506 | 59 | 145 | 16 | 76 | 6 |
| Paul Lo Duca | .283 | 445 | 45 | 126 | 6 | 57 | 4 |
| Juan Pierre | .276 | 656 | 96 | 181 | 2 | 47 | 57 |
| Alex Gonzalez | .264 | 435 | 45 | 115 | 5 | 45 | 5 |
| Damion Easley | .240 | 267 | 37 | 64 | 9 | 30 | 4 |
| Mike Lowell | .236 | 500 | 56 | 118 | 8 | 58 | 4 |

**Traded:** P Leiter to NYY for cash (July 16).

**Pitching** (30 IP)

| | ERA | W-L | Gm | IP | BB | SO |
|---|---|---|---|---|---|---|
| Todd Jones | 2.10 | 1-5 | 68 | 73.0 | 14 | 62 |
| Dontrelle Willis | 2.63 | 22-10 | 34 | 236.1 | 55 | 170 |
| Jim Mecir | 3.12 | 1-4 | 52 | 43.1 | 17 | 34 |
| Josh Beckett | 3.38 | 15-8 | 29 | 178.2 | 58 | 166 |
| A.J. Burnett | 3.44 | 12-12 | 32 | 209.0 | 79 | 198 |
| Nate Bump | 4.03 | 0-3 | 31 | 38.0 | 12 | 18 |
| Jason Vargas* | 4.03 | 5-5 | 17 | 73.2 | 31 | 59 |
| Paul Quantrill | 4.14 | 1-2 | 28 | 37.0 | 7 | 25 |
| Brian Moehler | 4.55 | 6-12 | 37 | 158.1 | 42 | 95 |
| Guillermo Mota | 4.70 | 2-2 | 56 | 67.0 | 32 | 60 |
| Ismael Valdez | 5.33 | 2-2 | 14 | 50.2 | 22 | 27 |
| Randy Messenger* | 5.35 | 0-0 | 29 | 37.0 | 30 | 29 |
| Al Leiter | 6.64 | 3-7 | 17 | 80.0 | 60 | 52 |

**Saves:** Jones (40), Mota (2). **Complete games:** Willis (7), Burnett (4), Beckett (2), Vargas (1). **Shutouts:** Willis (5), Burnett (2), Beckett (1).

### Houston Astros

**Batting** (135 AB)

| | Avg | AB | R | H | HR | RBI | SB |
|---|---|---|---|---|---|---|---|
| Lance Berkman | .293 | 468 | 76 | 137 | 24 | 82 | 4 |
| Willy Taveras* | .291 | 592 | 82 | 172 | 3 | 29 | 34 |
| Orlando Palmeiro | .284 | 204 | 22 | 58 | 3 | 20 | 3 |
| Morgan Ensberg | .283 | 526 | 86 | 149 | 36 | 101 | 6 |
| Jason Lane | .267 | 517 | 65 | 138 | 26 | 78 | 6 |
| Craig Biggio | .264 | 590 | 94 | 156 | 26 | 69 | 11 |
| Brad Ausmus | .258 | 387 | 35 | 100 | 3 | 47 | 5 |
| Chris Burke* | .248 | 318 | 49 | 79 | 5 | 26 | 11 |
| Adam Everett | .248 | 549 | 58 | 136 | 11 | 54 | 21 |
| Jose Vizcaino | .246 | 187 | 15 | 46 | 1 | 23 | 2 |
| Mike Lamb | .236 | 322 | 41 | 76 | 12 | 53 | 1 |

**Pitchers** (40 IP)

| | ERA | W-L | Gm | IP | BB | SO |
|---|---|---|---|---|---|---|
| Roger Clemens | 1.87 | 13-8 | 32 | 211.1 | 62 | 185 |
| Dan Wheeler | 2.21 | 2-3 | 71 | 73.1 | 19 | 69 |
| Brad Lidge | 2.29 | 4-4 | 70 | 70.2 | 23 | 103 |
| Andy Pettitte | 2.39 | 17-9 | 33 | 222.1 | 41 | 171 |
| Roy Oswalt | 2.94 | 20-12 | 35 | 241.2 | 48 | 184 |
| Chad Qualls* | 3.28 | 6-4 | 77 | 79.2 | 23 | 60 |
| Russ Springer | 4.73 | 4-4 | 62 | 59.0 | 21 | 54 |
| Brandon Backe | 4.76 | 10-8 | 26 | 149.1 | 67 | 97 |
| Wandy Rodriguez* | 5.53 | 10-10 | 25 | 128.2 | 53 | 80 |
| Ezequiel Astacio* | 5.67 | 3-6 | 22 | 81.0 | 25 | 66 |

**Saves:** Lidge (29), Octavio Dotel (14), Miceli (2), Chad Qualls and Kirk Bullinger (1). **Complete games:** Oswalt (2). **Shutouts:** Oswalt (2).

### Los Angeles Dodgers

**Batting** (135 AB)

| | Avg | AB | R | H | HR | RBI | SB |
|---|---|---|---|---|---|---|---|
| Antonio Perez | .297 | 259 | 28 | 77 | 3 | 23 | 11 |
| Milton Bradley | .290 | 283 | 49 | 82 | 13 | 38 | 6 |
| Jeff Kent | .289 | 553 | 100 | 160 | 29 | 105 | 6 |
| J.D. Drew | .286 | 252 | 48 | 72 | 15 | 36 | 1 |
| Ricky Ledee | .278 | 237 | 31 | 66 | 7 | 39 | 0 |
| Dioner Navarro | .273 | 176 | 21 | 48 | 3 | 14 | 0 |
| Oscar Robles* | .272 | 364 | 44 | 99 | 5 | 34 | 0 |
| Olmedo Saenz | .263 | 319 | 39 | 84 | 15 | 63 | 0 |
| Cesar Izturis | .257 | 444 | 48 | 114 | 2 | 31 | 8 |
| Hee-Seop Choi | .253 | 320 | 40 | 81 | 15 | 42 | 1 |
| Jose Cruz Jr. | .251 | 358 | 46 | 90 | 18 | 50 | 0 |
| Mike Edwards* | .247 | 239 | 23 | 59 | 3 | 15 | 1 |
| Jason Phillips | .238 | 399 | 38 | 95 | 10 | 55 | 0 |
| Jayson Werth | .234 | 337 | 46 | 79 | 7 | 43 | 11 |
| Jason Repko* | .221 | 276 | 43 | 61 | 8 | 30 | 5 |
| Jose Valentin | .170 | 147 | 17 | 25 | 2 | 14 | 3 |

**Acquired:** OF Cruz Jr. from Bos. for a PTBN (Aug. 9).

**Pitching** (40 IP)

| | ERA | W-L | Gm | IP | BB | SO |
|---|---|---|---|---|---|---|
| Elmer Dessens | 3.56 | 1-2 | 28 | 65.2 | 19 | 37 |
| Derek Lowe | 3.61 | 12-15 | 35 | 222.0 | 55 | 146 |
| Duaner Sanchez | 3.73 | 4-7 | 79 | 82.0 | 36 | 71 |
| Brad Penny | 3.90 | 7-9 | 29 | 175.1 | 41 | 122 |
| Giovanni Carrara | 3.93 | 7-4 | 72 | 75.2 | 38 | 56 |
| Jeff Weaver | 4.22 | 14-11 | 34 | 224.0 | 43 | 157 |
| Odalis Perez | 4.56 | 7-8 | 19 | 108.2 | 28 | 74 |
| Steve Schmoll* | 5.01 | 2-2 | 48 | 46.2 | 22 | 29 |
| D.J. Houlton* | 5.16 | 6-9 | 35 | 129.0 | 52 | 90 |
| Yhency Brazoban | 5.33 | 4-10 | 74 | 72.2 | 32 | 61 |
| Scott Erickson | 6.02 | 1-4 | 19 | 55.1 | 25 | 15 |

**Saves:** Brazoban (21), Gagne and Sanchez (8), Schmoll (3). **Complete games:** Weaver (3), Lowe (2), Penny (1). **Shutouts:** Lowe and Weaver (2).

## Milwaukee Brewers

| Batting (135 AB) | Avg | AB | R | H | HR | RBI | SB |
|---|---|---|---|---|---|---|---|
| Brady Clark | .306 | 599 | 94 | 183 | 13 | 53 | 10 |
| Wes Helms | .298 | 168 | 18 | 50 | 4 | 24 | 0 |
| Geoff Jenkins | .292 | 538 | 87 | 157 | 25 | 86 | 0 |
| Bill Hall | .291 | 501 | 69 | 146 | 17 | 62 | 18 |
| Jeff Cirillo | .281 | 185 | 29 | 52 | 4 | 23 | 4 |
| Lyle Overbay | .276 | 537 | 80 | 148 | 19 | 72 | 1 |
| Damian Miller | .273 | 385 | 50 | 105 | 9 | 43 | 0 |
| Carlos Lee | .265 | 618 | 85 | 164 | 32 | 114 | 13 |
| Russell Branyan | .257 | 202 | 23 | 52 | 12 | 31 | 1 |
| J.J. Hardy* | .247 | 372 | 46 | 92 | 9 | 50 | 0 |
| Rickie Weeks* | .239 | 360 | 56 | 86 | 13 | 42 | 15 |
| Chad Moeller | .206 | 199 | 23 | 41 | 7 | 23 | 0 |
| Chris Magruder | .203 | 138 | 16 | 28 | 2 | 13 | 3 |

**Acquired:** P Ohka from Wash. for IF Junior Spivey (June 11).

| Pitching (40 IP) | ERA | W-L | Gm | IP | BB | SO |
|---|---|---|---|---|---|---|
| Derrick Turnbow | 1.74 | 7-1 | 69 | 67.1 | 24 | 64 |
| Rick Helling | 2.39 | 3-1 | 15 | 49.0 | 18 | 42 |
| Ben Sheets | 3.33 | 10-9 | 22 | 156.2 | 25 | 141 |
| Matt Wise | 3.36 | 4-4 | 49 | 64.1 | 25 | 62 |
| Doug Davis | 3.84 | 11-11 | 35 | 222.2 | 93 | 208 |
| Chris Capuano | 3.99 | 18-12 | 35 | 219.0 | 91 | 176 |
| Tomo Ohka | 4.04 | 11-9 | 32 | 180.1 | 55 | 98 |
| Jorge de la Rosa* | 4.46 | 2-2 | 38 | 42.1 | 38 | 42 |
| Julio Santana | 4.50 | 3-5 | 41 | 42.0 | 19 | 49 |
| Ricky Bottalico | 4.54 | 2-2 | 40 | 41.2 | 19 | 29 |
| Victor Santos | 4.57 | 4-13 | 29 | 141.2 | 60 | 89 |
| Wes Obermueller | 5.26 | 1-4 | 23 | 65.0 | 36 | 33 |
| Gary Glover | 5.57 | 5-4 | 15 | 64.2 | 20 | 58 |

**Saves:** Turnbow (39), Bottalico (2), Wise, Santana, Mike Adams, Tommy Phelps and Dana Eveland (1). **Complete games:** Sheets (3), D. Davis (2), Ohka and Santos (1). **Shutouts:** D. Davis and Ohka (1).

## New York Mets

| Batting (135 AB) | Avg | AB | R | H | HR | RBI | SB |
|---|---|---|---|---|---|---|---|
| David Wright | .306 | 575 | 99 | 176 | 27 | 102 | 17 |
| Chris Woodward | .283 | 173 | 16 | 49 | 3 | 18 | 0 |
| Jose Reyes | .273 | 696 | 99 | 190 | 7 | 58 | 60 |
| Mike Cameron | .273 | 308 | 47 | 84 | 12 | 39 | 13 |
| Cliff Floyd | .273 | 550 | 85 | 150 | 34 | 98 | 12 |
| Carlos Beltran | .266 | 582 | 83 | 155 | 16 | 78 | 17 |
| Marlon Anderson | .264 | 235 | 31 | 62 | 7 | 19 | 6 |
| Victor Diaz* | .257 | 280 | 41 | 72 | 12 | 38 | 6 |
| Kazuo Matsui | .255 | 267 | 31 | 68 | 3 | 24 | 6 |
| Mike Piazza | .251 | 398 | 41 | 100 | 19 | 62 | 0 |
| Miguel Cairo | .251 | 327 | 31 | 82 | 2 | 19 | 13 |
| Ramon Castro | .244 | 209 | 26 | 51 | 8 | 41 | 1 |
| Doug Mientkiewicz | .240 | 275 | 36 | 66 | 11 | 29 | 0 |

| Pitching (40 IP) | ERA | W-L | Gm | IP | BB | SO |
|---|---|---|---|---|---|---|
| Roberto Hernandez | 2.58 | 8-6 | 67 | 69.2 | 28 | 61 |
| Jae Seo | 2.59 | 8-2 | 14 | 90.1 | 16 | 59 |
| Pedro Martinez | 2.82 | 15-8 | 31 | 217.0 | 47 | 208 |
| Aaron Heilman | 3.17 | 5-3 | 53 | 108.0 | 37 | 106 |
| Tom Glavine | 3.53 | 13-13 | 33 | 211.1 | 61 | 105 |
| Braden Looper | 3.94 | 4-7 | 60 | 59.1 | 22 | 27 |
| Kris Benson | 4.13 | 10-8 | 28 | 174.1 | 49 | 95 |
| Victor Zambrano | 4.17 | 7-12 | 31 | 166.1 | 77 | 112 |
| Kazuhisa Ishii | 5.14 | 3-9 | 19 | 91.0 | 49 | 53 |
| Heath Bell* | 5.59 | 1-3 | 42 | 46.2 | 13 | 43 |

**Saves:** Looper (28), Danny Graves (10), Heilman (5), Hernandez (4), Juan Padilla (1). **Complete games:** Martinez (4), Glavine (2), Seo and Heilman (1). **Shutouts:** Martinez, Heilman and Glavine (1).

## Philadelphia Phillies

| Batting (135 AB) | Avg | AB | R | H | HR | RBI | SB |
|---|---|---|---|---|---|---|---|
| Kenny Lofton | .335 | 367 | 67 | 123 | 2 | 36 | 22 |
| Placido Polanco | .316 | 158 | 26 | 50 | 3 | 20 | 0 |
| Jason Michaels | .304 | 289 | 54 | 88 | 4 | 31 | 3 |
| Chase Utley | .291 | 543 | 93 | 158 | 28 | 105 | 16 |
| Jimmy Rollins | .290 | 677 | 115 | 196 | 12 | 54 | 41 |
| Ryan Howard* | .288 | 312 | 52 | 90 | 22 | 63 | 0 |
| Bobby Abreu | .286 | 588 | 104 | 168 | 24 | 102 | 31 |
| Pat Burrell | .281 | 562 | 78 | 158 | 32 | 117 | 0 |
| Mike Lieberthal | .263 | 392 | 48 | 103 | 12 | 47 | 0 |
| Todd Pratt | .251 | 175 | 17 | 44 | 7 | 23 | 0 |
| David Bell | .248 | 557 | 53 | 138 | 10 | 61 | 0 |
| Michael Tucker | .239 | 268 | 35 | 64 | 5 | 36 | 4 |
| Tomas Perez | .233 | 159 | 17 | 37 | 0 | 22 | 1 |
| Jim Thome | .207 | 193 | 26 | 40 | 7 | 30 | 0 |

**Acquired:** P Urbina and IF Ramon Martinez from Det. for IF Polanco (June 8); OF Tucker from SF for P Kelvin Pichardo and cash (Aug. 28).

| Pitchers (40 IP) | ERA | W-L | Gm | IP | BB | SO |
|---|---|---|---|---|---|---|
| Billy Wagner | 1.51 | 4-3 | 75 | 77.2 | 20 | 87 |
| Aaron Fultz | 2.24 | 4-0 | 62 | 72.1 | 23 | 54 |
| Robinson Tejeda* | 3.57 | 4-3 | 26 | 85.2 | 51 | 72 |
| Brett Myers | 3.72 | 13-8 | 34 | 215.1 | 68 | 208 |
| Geoff Geary | 3.72 | 2-1 | 40 | 58.0 | 21 | 42 |
| Ugueth Urbina | 4.13 | 4-3 | 56 | 52.1 | 25 | 66 |
| Ryan Madson | 4.14 | 6-5 | 78 | 87.0 | 25 | 79 |
| Jon Lieber | 4.20 | 17-13 | 35 | 218.1 | 41 | 149 |
| Randy Wolf | 4.39 | 6-4 | 13 | 80.0 | 26 | 61 |
| Cory Lidle | 4.53 | 13-11 | 31 | 184.2 | 40 | 121 |
| Vicente Padilla | 4.71 | 9-12 | 27 | 147.0 | 74 | 103 |
| Rheal Cormier | 5.89 | 4-2 | 57 | 47.1 | 16 | 34 |

**Saves:** Wagner (38), Urbina (1). **Complete games:** Myers (2), Lieber and Lidle (1). **Shutouts:** none.

## Pittsburgh Pirates

| Batting (135 AB) | Avg | AB | R | H | HR | RBI | SB |
|---|---|---|---|---|---|---|---|
| Jason Bay | .306 | 599 | 110 | 183 | 32 | 101 | 21 |
| Freddy Sanchez | .291 | 453 | 54 | 132 | 5 | 35 | 2 |
| Rob Mackowiak | .272 | 463 | 57 | 126 | 9 | 58 | 8 |
| Jose Castillo | .268 | 370 | 49 | 99 | 11 | 53 | 2 |
| Craig Wilson | .264 | 197 | 23 | 52 | 5 | 22 | 3 |
| Daryle Ward | .260 | 407 | 46 | 106 | 12 | 63 | 0 |
| Ty Wigginton | .258 | 155 | 20 | 40 | 7 | 25 | 0 |
| Jack Wilson | .257 | 587 | 60 | 151 | 8 | 52 | 7 |
| Ryan Doumit | .255 | 231 | 25 | 59 | 6 | 35 | 2 |
| Tike Redman | .251 | 319 | 33 | 80 | 2 | 26 | 4 |
| Humberto Cota | .242 | 297 | 29 | 72 | 7 | 43 | 0 |
| Brad Eldred* | .221 | 190 | 23 | 42 | 12 | 27 | 1 |

| Pitching (40 IP) | ERA | W-L | Gm | IP | BB | SO |
|---|---|---|---|---|---|---|
| Zach Duke* | 1.81 | 8-2 | 14 | 84.2 | 23 | 58 |
| Paul Maholm* | 2.18 | 3-1 | 6 | 41.1 | 17 | 26 |
| Mike Gonzalez | 2.70 | 1-3 | 51 | 50.0 | 31 | 58 |
| Salomon Torres | 2.76 | 5-5 | 78 | 94.2 | 36 | 55 |
| Rick White | 3.72 | 4-7 | 71 | 75.0 | 29 | 40 |
| Dave Williams | 4.41 | 10-11 | 25 | 138.2 | 58 | 88 |
| Ryan Vogelsong | 4.43 | 2-2 | 44 | 81.1 | 40 | 52 |
| Brian Meadows | 4.58 | 3-1 | 65 | 74.2 | 21 | 44 |
| Jose Mesa | 4.76 | 2-8 | 55 | 56.2 | 26 | 37 |
| John Grabow | 4.85 | 2-3 | 63 | 52.0 | 25 | 42 |
| Mark Redman | 4.90 | 5-15 | 30 | 178.1 | 56 | 101 |
| Josh Fogg | 5.05 | 6-11 | 34 | 169.1 | 53 | 85 |
| Kip Wells | 5.09 | 8-18 | 33 | 182.0 | 99 | 132 |
| Ian Snell* | 5.14 | 1-2 | 15 | 42.0 | 24 | 34 |
| Oliver Perez | 5.85 | 7-5 | 20 | 103.0 | 70 | 97 |

**Saves:** Mesa (27), Gonzalez and Torres (3), White (2). **Complete games:** Redman (2), Williams and Wells (1). **Shutouts:** Williams, Redman and Wells (1).

## St. Louis Cardinals

| Batting (135 AB) | Avg | AB | R | H | HR | RBI | SB |
|---|---|---|---|---|---|---|---|
| Albert Pujols | .330 | 591 | 129 | 195 | 41 | 117 | 16 |
| John Rodriguez | .295 | 149 | 15 | 44 | 5 | 24 | 2 |
| David Eckstein | .294 | 630 | 90 | 185 | 8 | 61 | 11 |
| Mark Grudzielanek | .294 | 528 | 64 | 155 | 8 | 59 | 8 |
| Larry Walker | .289 | 315 | 66 | 91 | 15 | 52 | 2 |
| So Taguchi | .288 | 396 | 45 | 114 | 8 | 53 | 11 |
| Abraham Nunez | .285 | 421 | 64 | 120 | 5 | 44 | 0 |
| Hector Luna | .285 | 137 | 26 | 39 | 1 | 18 | 10 |
| Reggie Sanders | .271 | 295 | 49 | 80 | 21 | 54 | 14 |
| Jim Edmonds | .263 | 467 | 88 | 123 | 29 | 89 | 5 |
| Yadier Molina | .252 | 385 | 36 | 97 | 8 | 49 | 2 |
| John Mabry | .240 | 246 | 26 | 59 | 8 | 32 | 0 |
| Scott Rolen | .235 | 196 | 28 | 46 | 5 | 28 | 1 |

| Pitching (35 IP) | ERA | W-L | Gm | IP | BB | SO |
|---|---|---|---|---|---|---|
| Jason Isringhausen | 2.14 | 1-2 | 63 | 59.0 | 27 | 51 |
| Al Reyes | 2.15 | 4-2 | 65 | 62.2 | 20 | 67 |
| Cal Eldred | 2.19 | 1-0 | 31 | 37.0 | 18 | 29 |
| Chris Carpenter | 2.83 | 21-5 | 33 | 241.2 | 51 | 213 |
| Brad Thompson* | 2.95 | 4-0 | 40 | 55.0 | 15 | 29 |
| Ray King | 3.38 | 4-4 | 77 | 40.0 | 16 | 23 |
| Julian Tavarez | 3.43 | 2-3 | 74 | 65.2 | 19 | 47 |
| Randy Flores | 3.46 | 3-1 | 50 | 41.2 | 13 | 43 |
| Jeff Suppan | 3.57 | 16-10 | 32 | 194.1 | 63 | 114 |
| Mark Mulder | 3.64 | 16-8 | 32 | 205.0 | 70 | 111 |
| Matt Morris | 4.11 | 14-10 | 31 | 192.2 | 37 | 117 |
| Jason Marquis | 4.13 | 13-14 | 33 | 207.0 | 69 | 100 |

**Saves:** Isringhausen (39), Tavarez (4), Reyes (3), Flores and Thompson (1). **Complete games:** Carpenter (7), Mulder and Marquis (3), Morris (2). **Shutouts:** Carpenter (4), Mulder (2), Marquis (1).

## San Diego Padres

| Batting (135 AB) | Avg | AB | R | H | HR | RBI | SB |
|---|---|---|---|---|---|---|---|
| Brian Giles | .301 | 545 | 92 | 164 | 15 | 83 | 13 |
| Mark Sweeney | .294 | 221 | 31 | 65 | 8 | 40 | 4 |
| Ramon Hernandez | .290 | 369 | 36 | 107 | 12 | 58 | 1 |
| Mark Loretta | .280 | 404 | 54 | 113 | 3 | 38 | 8 |
| Joe Randa | .276 | 555 | 71 | 153 | 17 | 68 | 0 |
| Dave Roberts | .275 | 411 | 65 | 113 | 8 | 38 | 23 |
| Eric Young | .275 | 142 | 22 | 39 | 2 | 12 | 7 |
| Robert Fick | .265 | 230 | 25 | 61 | 3 | 30 | 0 |
| Xavier Nady | .261 | 326 | 40 | 85 | 13 | 43 | 2 |
| Phil Nevin | .256 | 281 | 31 | 72 | 9 | 47 | 1 |
| Damian Jackson | .255 | 275 | 44 | 70 | 5 | 23 | 15 |
| Sean Burroughs | .250 | 284 | 20 | 71 | 1 | 17 | 4 |
| Khalil Greene | .250 | 436 | 51 | 109 | 15 | 70 | 5 |
| Ryan Klesko | .248 | 443 | 61 | 110 | 18 | 58 | 3 |
| Geoff Blum | .241 | 224 | 26 | 54 | 5 | 22 | 3 |

**Acquired:** IF Randa from Cin. for 2 minor league pitchers (July 23); P Park from Tex. for IF Nevin (July 30). **Traded:** P May and P Tim Redding to NYY for P Paul Quantrill (July 2); IF Blum to ChW for a minor leaguer (July 31). **Signed:** P Astacio (June 30).

| Pitching (45 IP) | ERA | W-L | Gm | IP | BB | SO |
|---|---|---|---|---|---|---|
| Clay Hensley* | 1.70 | 1-1 | 24 | 47.2 | 17 | 28 |
| Scott Linebrink | 1.83 | 8-1 | 73 | 73.2 | 23 | 70 |
| Rudy Seanez | 2.69 | 7-1 | 57 | 60.1 | 22 | 84 |
| Jake Peavy | 2.88 | 13-7 | 30 | 203.0 | 50 | 216 |
| Trevor Hoffman | 2.97 | 1-6 | 60 | 57.2 | 12 | 54 |
| Pedro Astacio | 3.17 | 4-2 | 12 | 59.2 | 26 | 33 |
| Akinori Otsuka | 3.59 | 2-8 | 66 | 62.2 | 34 | 60 |
| Chris Hammond | 3.84 | 5-1 | 55 | 58.2 | 14 | 34 |
| Adam Eaton | 4.27 | 11-5 | 24 | 128.2 | 44 | 100 |
| Brian Lawrence | 4.83 | 7-15 | 33 | 195.2 | 57 | 109 |
| Woody Williams | 4.85 | 9-12 | 28 | 159.2 | 51 | 106 |
| Tim Stauffer* | 5.33 | 3-6 | 15 | 81.0 | 29 | 49 |
| Darrell May | 5.61 | 1-3 | 22 | 59.1 | 20 | 42 |
| Chan Ho Park | 5.91 | 4-3 | 10 | 45.2 | 26 | 33 |

**Saves:** Hoffman (43), Linebrink and Otsuka (1). **Complete games:** Peavy (3), Lawrence (1). **Shutouts:** Peavy (3).

## San Francisco Giants

| Batting (135 AB) | Avg | AB | R | H | HR | RBI | SB |
|---|---|---|---|---|---|---|---|
| Randy Winn | .359 | 231 | 39 | 83 | 14 | 26 | 7 |
| Moises Alou | .321 | 427 | 67 | 137 | 19 | 63 | 5 |
| Ray Durham | .290 | 497 | 67 | 144 | 12 | 62 | 6 |
| Edgardo Alfonzo | .277 | 368 | 36 | 102 | 2 | 43 | 2 |
| J.T. Snow | .275 | 367 | 40 | 101 | 4 | 40 | 1 |
| Omar Vizquel | .271 | 568 | 66 | 154 | 3 | 45 | 24 |
| Jason Ellison* | .264 | 352 | 49 | 93 | 4 | 24 | 14 |
| Lance Niekro* | .252 | 278 | 32 | 70 | 12 | 46 | 0 |
| Pedro Feliz | .250 | 569 | 69 | 142 | 20 | 81 | 0 |
| Mike Matheny | .242 | 443 | 42 | 107 | 13 | 59 | 0 |
| Todd Linden* | .216 | 171 | 20 | 37 | 4 | 13 | 3 |
| Marquis Grissom | .212 | 137 | 8 | 29 | 2 | 15 | 1 |

**Acquired:** P Hawkins from ChC for P Jerome Williams and P David Aardsma (May 28); OF Winn from Sea. for P Jesse Foppert and C Yorvit Torrealba (July 30). **Traded:** P Christiansen to LAA for 2 minor league pitchers (Aug. 31).

| Pitching (40 IP) | ERA | W-L | Gm | IP | BB | SO |
|---|---|---|---|---|---|---|
| Matt Cain* | 2.33 | 2-1 | 7 | 46.1 | 19 | 30 |
| Scott Munter* | 2.56 | 2-0 | 45 | 38.2 | 12 | 11 |
| Scott Eyre | 2.63 | 2-2 | 86 | 68.1 | 26 | 65 |
| Noah Lowry | 3.78 | 13-13 | 33 | 204.2 | 76 | 172 |
| LaTroy Hawkins | 3.83 | 2-8 | 66 | 56.1 | 24 | 43 |
| Jeff Fassero | 4.05 | 4-7 | 48 | 91.0 | 31 | 60 |
| Tyler Walker | 4.23 | 6-4 | 67 | 61.2 | 27 | 54 |
| Jason Schmidt | 4.40 | 12-7 | 29 | 172.0 | 85 | 165 |
| Brett Tomko | 4.48 | 8-15 | 33 | 190.2 | 57 | 114 |
| Kevin Correia | 4.63 | 2-5 | 16 | 58.1 | 31 | 44 |
| Brad Hennessey* | 4.64 | 5-8 | 21 | 118.1 | 52 | 64 |
| Jason Christiansen | 5.36 | 6-1 | 56 | 42.0 | 15 | 17 |
| Kirk Rueter | 5.95 | 2-7 | 20 | 107.1 | 47 | 25 |

**Saves:** Walker (23), Benitez (19), Hawkins (6), Tomko (1).
**Complete games:** Tomko (3), Cain (1). **Shutouts:** none.

## Washington Nationals

| Batting (135 AB) | Avg | AB | R | H | HR | RBI | SB |
|---|---|---|---|---|---|---|---|
| Nick Johnson | .289 | 453 | 66 | 131 | 15 | 74 | 3 |
| Ryan Church* | .287 | 268 | 41 | 77 | 9 | 42 | 3 |
| Jose Guillen | .283 | 551 | 81 | 156 | 24 | 76 | 1 |
| Jose Vidro | .275 | 309 | 38 | 85 | 7 | 32 | 0 |
| Brian Schneider | .268 | 369 | 38 | 99 | 10 | 44 | 1 |
| Marlon Byrd | .266 | 229 | 20 | 61 | 2 | 26 | 5 |
| Deivi Cruz | .265 | 260 | 28 | 69 | 5 | 20 | 0 |
| Preston Wilson | .260 | 520 | 73 | 135 | 25 | 90 | 6 |
| Carlos Baerga | .253 | 158 | 18 | 40 | 2 | 19 | 0 |
| Vinny Castilla | .253 | 494 | 53 | 125 | 12 | 66 | 4 |
| Jamey Carroll | .251 | 303 | 44 | 76 | 0 | 22 | 3 |
| Brad Wilkerson | .248 | 565 | 76 | 140 | 11 | 57 | 8 |
| Junior Spivey | .232 | 259 | 37 | 60 | 7 | 24 | 9 |
| Gary Bennett | .221 | 199 | 11 | 44 | 1 | 21 | 0 |
| Cristian Guzman | .219 | 456 | 39 | 100 | 4 | 31 | 7 |

**Acquired:** OF Byrd from Phi. for OF Endy Chavez (May 15); IF Spivey from Mil. for P. Tomo Ohka (June 11); OF Wilson from Col. for P Zach Day, OF J.J. Davis and a PTBN (July 13); IF Cruz from SF for a minor leaguer (Aug. 31). **Claimed:** P Drese off waivers from Tex. (June 10).

| Pitching (35 IP) | ERA | W-L | Gm | IP | BB | SO |
|---|---|---|---|---|---|---|
| Chad Cordero | 1.82 | 2-4 | 74 | 74.1 | 17 | 61 |
| Hector Carrasco | 2.04 | 5-4 | 64 | 88.1 | 38 | 75 |
| Luis Ayala | 2.66 | 8-7 | 68 | 71.0 | 14 | 40 |
| Gary Majewski* | 2.93 | 4-4 | 79 | 86.0 | 37 | 50 |
| John Patterson | 3.13 | 9-7 | 31 | 198.1 | 65 | 185 |
| Joey Eischen | 3.22 | 2-1 | 57 | 36.1 | 19 | 30 |
| Esteban Loaiza | 3.77 | 12-10 | 34 | 217.0 | 55 | 173 |
| Livan Hernandez | 3.98 | 15-10 | 35 | 246.1 | 84 | 147 |
| Tony Armas | 4.97 | 7-7 | 19 | 101.1 | 54 | 59 |
| Ryan Drese | 4.98 | 3-6 | 11 | 59.2 | 22 | 26 |

**Saves:** Cordero (47), Carrasco (2), Ayala and Majewski (1). **Complete games:** Patterson and Hernandez (2). **Shutouts:** Patterson (1).

## Players Who Played in Both Leagues in 2005

While all individual major league statistics count for career records, players cannot transfer their stats from one league to the other if they are traded during the regular season. Here are the combined stats for batters with at least 150 at bats and pitchers with at least 50 innings pitched, who played in both leagues in 2005. Players listed alphabetically.

### Batters (150 AB)

| | Avg | AB | R | H | HR | RBI | SB |
|---|---|---|---|---|---|---|---|
| Larry Bigbie .... | .239 | 272 | 27 | 65 | 5 | 23 | 5 |
| BAL ........ | .248 | 206 | 22 | 51 | 5 | 21 | 3 |
| COL ........ | .212 | 66 | 5 | 14 | 0 | 2 | 2 |
| Geoff Blum ...... | .229 | 319 | 32 | 73 | 6 | 25 | 3 |
| SD .......... | .241 | 224 | 26 | 54 | 5 | 22 | 3 |
| ChW ........ | .200 | 95 | 6 | 19 | 1 | 3 | 0 |
| Eric Byrnes ...... | .226 | 412 | 49 | 93 | 10 | 40 | 7 |
| OAK ........ | .266 | 192 | 30 | 51 | 7 | 24 | 2 |
| COL ........ | .189 | 53 | 2 | 10 | 0 | 5 | 2 |
| BAL ........ | .192 | 167 | 17 | 32 | 3 | 11 | 3 |
| Jose Cruz Jr. .... | .251 | 370 | 46 | 93 | 18 | 50 | 0 |
| ARI ........ | .213 | 202 | 23 | 43 | 12 | 28 | 0 |
| BOS ........ | .250 | 12 | 0 | 3 | 0 | 0 | 0 |
| LAD ........ | .301 | 156 | 23 | 47 | 6 | 22 | 0 |
| Jason Dubois .... | .235 | 187 | 21 | 44 | 9 | 24 | 0 |
| ChC ........ | .239 | 142 | 15 | 34 | 7 | 22 | 0 |
| CLE ........ | .222 | 45 | 6 | 10 | 2 | 2 | 0 |
| Jody Gerut ...... | .253 | 170 | 15 | 43 | 1 | 14 | 1 |
| CLE ........ | .275 | 138 | 12 | 38 | 1 | 12 | 1 |
| ChC ........ | .071 | 14 | 1 | 1 | 0 | 0 | 0 |
| PIT ........ | .222 | 18 | 2 | 4 | 0 | 2 | 0 |
| Matt Lawton ..... | .254 | 500 | 67 | 127 | 13 | 53 | 18 |
| PIT ........ | .273 | 374 | 53 | 102 | 10 | 44 | 16 |
| ChC ........ | .244 | 78 | 8 | 19 | 1 | 5 | 1 |
| NYY ........ | .125 | 48 | 6 | 6 | 2 | 4 | 1 |
| Phil Nevin ...... | .237 | 380 | 46 | 90 | 12 | 55 | 3 |
| SD .......... | .256 | 281 | 31 | 72 | 9 | 47 | 1 |
| TEX ........ | .182 | 99 | 15 | 18 | 3 | 8 | 2 |
| Miguel Olivo ..... | .217 | 267 | 30 | 58 | 9 | 34 | 7 |
| SEA ........ | .151 | 152 | 14 | 23 | 5 | 18 | 1 |
| SD .......... | .304 | 115 | 16 | 35 | 4 | 16 | 6 |
| Placido Polanco .. | .331 | 501 | 84 | 166 | 9 | 56 | 4 |
| PHI ........ | .316 | 158 | 26 | 50 | 3 | 20 | 0 |
| DET ........ | .338 | 343 | 58 | 116 | 6 | 36 | 4 |
| Alex Sanchez ... | .324 | 176 | 32 | 57 | 2 | 16 | 8 |
| TB .......... | .346 | 133 | 28 | 46 | 2 | 13 | 6 |
| SF .......... | .256 | 43 | 4 | 11 | 0 | 3 | 2 |
| Yorvit Torrealba .. | .234 | 201 | 32 | 47 | 3 | 15 | 1 |
| SF .......... | .226 | 93 | 18 | 21 | 1 | 7 | 1 |
| SEA ........ | .241 | 108 | 14 | 26 | 2 | 8 | 0 |
| Randy Winn .... | .306 | 617 | 85 | 189 | 20 | 63 | 19 |
| SEA ........ | .275 | 386 | 46 | 106 | 6 | 37 | 12 |
| SF .......... | .359 | 231 | 39 | 83 | 14 | 26 | 7 |

### Pitchers (50 IP)

| | ERA | W-L | Gm | IP | BB | SO |
|---|---|---|---|---|---|---|
| Pedro Astacio ... | .4.69 | 6-10 | 24 | 127.2 | 37 | 78 |
| TEX ........ | .6.05 | 2-8 | 12 | 67.0 | 11 | 45 |
| SD ........ | .3.17 | 4-2 | 12 | 60.2 | 26 | 33 |
| Shawn Chacon .. | .3.44 | 8-10 | 24 | 151.2 | 66 | 79 |
| COL ........ | .4.09 | 1-7 | 13 | 73.2 | 36 | 39 |
| NYY ........ | .2.85 | 7-3 | 14 | 79.0 | 30 | 40 |
| Roman Colon .... | .5.58 | 2-6 | 35 | 69.1 | 21 | 47 |
| ATL ........ | .5.28 | 1-5 | 23 | 44.1 | 14 | 30 |
| DET ........ | .6.12 | 1-1 | 12 | 25.0 | 7 | 17 |
| Ryan Drese ..... | .5.78 | 7-12 | 23 | 129.1 | 46 | 46 |
| TEX ........ | .6.46 | 4-6 | 12 | 70.2 | 24 | 20 |
| WASH ........ | .4.98 | 3-6 | 11 | 60.2 | 22 | 26 |
| Kyle Farnsworth .. | .2.19 | 1-1 | 72 | 70.0 | 27 | 87 |
| DET ........ | .2.32 | 1-1 | 46 | 43.2 | 20 | 55 |
| ATL ........ | .1.98 | 0-0 | 26 | 27.1 | 7 | 32 |
| John Halama .... | .5.68 | 1-4 | 40 | 65.0 | 17 | 37 |
| BOS ........ | .6.18 | 1-1 | 30 | 44.2 | 9 | 26 |
| WASH ........ | .4.64 | 0-3 | 10 | 21.1 | 8 | 11 |
| Joe Kennedy .... | .6.01 | 8-13 | 35 | 152.2 | 64 | 97 |
| COL ........ | .7.04 | 4-8 | 16 | 92.0 | 44 | 52 |
| OAK ........ | .4.45 | 4-5 | 19 | 61.2 | 20 | 45 |
| Al Leiter ....... | .6.13 | 7-12 | 33 | 142.1 | 98 | 97 |
| FLA ........ | .6.64 | 3-7 | 17 | 80.0 | 60 | 52 |
| NYY ........ | .5.49 | 4-5 | 16 | 62.1 | 38 | 45 |
| Darrell May ..... | .6.78 | 1-4 | 24 | 66.1 | 23 | 35 |
| SD ........ | .5.61 | 1-3 | 22 | 59.1 | 20 | 32 |
| NYY ........ | .16.71 | 0-1 | 2 | 7.0 | 3 | 3 |
| Chan Ho Park ... | .5.74 | 12-8 | 30 | 155.1 | 80 | 113 |
| TEX ........ | .5.66 | 8-5 | 20 | 110.2 | 54 | 80 |
| SD ........ | .5.91 | 4-3 | 10 | 46.2 | 26 | 33 |
| Paul Quantrill ... | .5.35 | 2-2 | 50 | 40.0 | 14 | 36 |
| NYY ........ | .6.75 | 1-0 | 22 | 32.0 | 7 | 11 |
| SD ........ | .3.41 | 1-1 | 22 | 32.2 | 2 | 24 |
| FLA ........ | .8.44 | 0-1 | 6 | 5.1 | 5 | 1 |
| Ugueth Urbina .. | .3.62 | 5-6 | 81 | 79.2 | 39 | 97 |
| DET ........ | .2.63 | 1-3 | 25 | 27.1 | 14 | 31 |
| PHI ........ | .4.13 | 4-3 | 56 | 52.1 | 25 | 66 |
| Ron Villone ..... | .4.08 | 5-5 | 79 | 64.0 | 35 | 70 |
| SEA ........ | .2.46 | 2-3 | 52 | 40.1 | 23 | 41 |
| FLA ........ | .6.85 | 3-2 | 27 | 24.2 | 12 | 29 |
| Jay Witasick .... | .2.84 | 1-5 | 60 | 63.1 | 29 | 73 |
| COL ........ | .2.52 | 0-4 | 32 | 36.2 | 12 | 40 |
| OAK ........ | .3.25 | 1-1 | 28 | 28.2 | 17 | 33 |

**Placido Polanco**
Phillies to Tigers

**Randy Winn**
Mariners to Giants

**Shawn Chacon**
Rockies to Yankees

**Kyle Farnsworth**
Tigers to Braves

## BASEBALL PLAYOFFS

DIVISIONAL SERIES — LCS — WORLD SERIES '05 — LCS — DIVISIONAL SERIES

Chicago   3
†Boston   0
    Chicago   4

**AMERICAN LEAGUE**

Los Angeles   3
New York   2
    Los Angeles   1

Chicago   4
Houston   0

†Houston   3
Atlanta   1
    Houston   4

**NATIONAL LEAGUE**

St. Louis   3
San Diego   0
    St. Louis   2

†Wild Card Team      †Wild Card Team

## Divisional Series Summaries

### AMERICAN LEAGUE

### White Sox, 3-0

| Date | Winner | Home Field |
|------|--------|-----------|
| Oct. 4 . . . . . . . . . . . | White Sox, 14-2 | at Chicago |
| Oct. 5 . . . . . . . . . . . | White Sox, 5-4 | at Chicago |
| Oct. 7 . . . . . . . . . . . | White Sox, 5-3 | at Boston |

### Game 1

Tuesday, Oct. 4, at Chicago

| | 1 2 3 | 4 5 6 | 7 8 9 | R H E |
|---|---|---|---|---|
| Boston . . . . . . | 0 0 0 | 2 0 0 | 0 0 0 | - 2 9 0 |
| Chicago . . . . . | 5 0 1 | 2 0 4 | 0 2 x | -14 11 1 |

**Win:** Contreras, Chi. (1-0). **Loss:** Clement, Bos. (0-1).
**2B:** Boston—Renteria (1), Graffanino (1), Millar (1), Ortiz (1), Olerud (1); Chicago—Pierzynski (1). **HR:** Chicago—Pierzynski 2 (2, off Clement, 2 on; off Arroyo, 0 on), Konerko (1, off Clement, 0 on), Uribe (1, off Clement, 1 on), Podsednik (1, off Gonzalez, 2 on). **RBI:** Boston—Millar (1); Chicago—Konerko 2 (2), Rowand (1), Pierzynski 4 (4), Uribe 3 (3), Podsednik 3 (3), Harris (1). **SB:** Chicago—Podsednik (1). **CS:** Chicago—Podsednik (1). **E:** Chicago—Crede (1).
**Attendance:** 40,717 (40,615). **Time:** 2:56.

### Game 2

Wednesday, Oct. 5, at Chicago

| | 1 2 3 | 4 5 6 | 7 8 9 | R H E |
|---|---|---|---|---|
| Boston . . . . . . | 2 0 2 | 0 0 0 | 0 0 0 | - 4 9 1 |
| Chicago . . . . . | 0 0 0 | 0 5 0 | 0 x | - 5 9 0 |

**Win:** Buehrle, Chi. (1-0). **Loss:** Wells, Bos. (0-1). **Save:** Jenks, Chi. (1).
**2B:** Boston—Renteria (2), Graffanino (2), Ortiz (2); Chicago—Rowand (1). **HR:** Chicago—Iguchi (1, off Wells, 2 on). **RBI:** Boston—Ramirez 2 (2), Varitek (1), Nixon (1); Chicago—Rowand (2), Crede (1), Iguchi 3 (3). **E:** Boston—Graffanino (1).
**Attendance:** 40,799 (40,615). **Time:** 2:29.

### Game 3

Friday, Oct. 7, at Boston

| | 1 2 3 | 4 5 6 | 7 8 9 | R H E |
|---|---|---|---|---|
| Chicago . . . . . | 0 0 2 | 0 0 2 | 0 0 1 | - 5 8 0 |
| Boston . . . . . . | 0 0 0 | 2 0 1 | 0 0 0 | - 3 7 1 |

**Win:** Garcia, Chi. (1-0). **Loss:** Wakefield, Bos. (0-1). **Save:** Jenks, Chi. (2).
**2B:** Chicago—Uribe (1), Podsednik (1), Rowand (2), Pierzynski (2); Boston—Damon (1). **HR:** Chicago—Konerko (2, off Wakefield, 1 on); Boston—Ortiz (1, off Garcia, 0 on). **RBI:** Chicago—Podsednik (4), Iguchi (4), Konerko 2 (4), Uribe (4); Boston—Ortiz (1), Ramirez 2 (4). **SB:** Chicago—Rowand (1), Pierzynski (1). **CS:** Chicago—Podsednik (2). **E:** Boston—Timlin (1).
**Attendance:** 35,496 (35,095). **Time:** 3:28.

**DID YOU KNOW?**

The White Sox' 3-0 win over the Red Sox in the ALDS was their first postseason series sweep in the 105-year history of the franchise, and first postseason series win of any kind since their World Series win over the New York Giants...in 1917.

## Divisional Series Summaries (Cont.)

### Angels, 3-2

| Date | Winner | Home Field |
|---|---|---|
| Oct. 4 | Yankees, 4-2 | at Anaheim |
| Oct. 5 | Angels, 5-3 | at Anaheim |
| Oct. 7 | Angels, 11-7 | at New York |
| Oct. 9 | Yankees, 3-2 | at New York |
| Oct. 10 | Angels, 5-3 | at Anaheim |

#### Game 1

Tuesday, Oct. 4, at Anaheim

| | 1 2 3 | 4 5 6 | 7 8 9 | R H E |
|---|---|---|---|---|
| New York | 3 1 0 | 0 0 0 | 0 0 0 | 4 9 0 |
| Los Angeles | 0 0 0 | 0 0 0 | 1 0 1 | 2 7 0 |

**Win:** Mussina, NY (1-0). **Loss:** Colon, LA (0-1). **Save:** Rivera, NY (1).
**2B:** New York—Cano (1), Giambi (1), Williams (1); Los Angeles—Finley (1). **HR:** Los Angeles—B. Molina (1, off Sturtze, 0 on). **RBI:** New York—Cano 3 (3), Giambi (1); Los Angeles—B. Molina (1), Erstad (1). **SB:** New York—Jeter (1); Los Angeles—Guerrero (1). **CS:** Los Angeles—Guerrero (1).
**Attendance:** 45,142 (45,037). **Time:** 2:59.

#### Game 2

Wednesday, Oct. 5, at Anaheim

| | 1 2 3 | 4 5 6 | 7 8 9 | R H E |
|---|---|---|---|---|
| New York | 0 1 0 | 0 1 0 | 0 0 1 | 3 6 3 |
| Los Angeles | 0 0 0 | 0 1 1 | 2 1 x | 5 7 0 |

**Win:** Escobar, LA (1-0). **Loss:** Wang, NY (0-1). **Save:** Rodriguez, LA (1).
**2B:** New York—Matsui (1), Cano (2), Giambi (2), Williams (2). **HR:** New York—Posada (1, off Rodriguez, 0 on); Los Angeles—Rivera (1, off Wang, 0 on), B. Molina (2, off Leiter, 0 on). **RBI:** New York—Cano (4), Sheffield (1), Posada (1); Los Angeles—Rivera (1), Molina 2 (3), Cabrera 2 (2). **SB:** New York—Rodriguez (1). **CS:** New York—Rodriguez (1); Los Angeles—Kennedy (1). **E:** New York—Cano (1), Rodriguez (1), Wang (1).
**Attendance:** 45,150 (45,037). **Time:** 3:05.

#### Game 3

Friday, Oct. 7, at New York

| | 1 2 3 | 4 5 6 | 7 8 9 | R H E |
|---|---|---|---|---|
| Los Angeles | 3 0 2 | 0 0 2 | 2 2 0 | 11 19 1 |
| New York | 0 0 0 | 4 2 0 | 0 1 0 | 7 12 2 |

**Win:** Shields, LA (1-0). **Loss:** Small, NY (0-1).
**2B:** Los Angeles—Cabrera (1), Erstad (1), Rivera (1); New York—Rodriguez (1), Cano (3). **3B:** Los Angeles—Anderson (1), Figgins (1). **HR:** Los Angeles—Anderson (1, off Johnson, 2 on), B. Molina (3, off Johnson, 1 on); New York—Matsui (1, off Byrd, 0 on), Jeter (1, off Escobar, 0 on). **RBI:** Los Angeles—Anderson 5 (5), B. Molina 2 (5), Erstad (2), Figgins (1), Finley (1), J. Molina (1); New York—Matsui (1), Posada (2), Jeter 2 (2), Giambi (2), Cano (5), Williams (1). **CS:** Los Angeles—Kennedy (2). **E:** Los Angeles—Cabrera (1); New York—Sheffield (1), Cano (2).
**Attendance:** 56,277 (57,478). **Time:** 4:00.

#### Game 4

Sunday, Oct. 9, at New York

| | 1 2 3 | 4 5 6 | 7 8 9 | R H E |
|---|---|---|---|---|
| Los Angeles | 0 0 0 | 0 0 2 | 0 0 0 | 2 4 0 |
| New York | 0 0 0 | 0 0 1 | 2 0 x | 3 4 1 |

**Win:** Leiter, NY (1-0). **Loss:** Shields, LA (1-1). **Loss:** Rivera, NY (2).
**2B:** Los Angeles—Figgins (1), Cabrera (2); New York—Posada (1). **RBI:** Los Angeles—Figgins (2), Cabrera (3); New York—Sheffield (2), Sierra (1), Jeter (3). **CS:** Los Angeles—Figgins (1). **E:** New York—Matsui (1).
**Attendance:** 56,226 (57,478). **Time:** 3:13.

#### Game 5

Monday, Oct. 10, at Anaheim

| | 1 2 3 | 4 5 6 | 7 8 9 | R H E |
|---|---|---|---|---|
| New York | 0 2 0 | 0 0 0 | 1 0 0 | 3 11 0 |
| Los Angeles | 0 3 2 | 0 0 0 | 0 0 x | 5 9 0 |

**Win:** Santana, LA (1-0). **Loss:** Mussina, NY (1-1). **Save:** Rodriguez, LA (2).
**2B:** New York—Giambi (3); Los Angeles—Erstad (2). **3B:** Los Angeles—Kennedy (1). **HR:** New York—Jeter (2, off Santana, 0 on); Los Angeles—Anderson (2, off Mussina, 0 on). **RBI:** New York—Crosby (1), Jeter 2 (5); Los Angeles—Anderson 2 (7), Kennedy 2 (2), Erstad (3). **SB:** New York—Crosby (1). **CS:** New York—Cano (1).
**Attendance:** 45,133 (45,037). **Time:** 3:29.

## NATIONAL LEAGUE

### Cardinals, 3-0

| Date | Winner | Home Field |
|---|---|---|
| Oct. 4 | Cardinals, 8-5 | at St. Louis |
| Oct. 6 | Cardinals, 6-2 | at St. Louis |
| Oct. 8 | Cardinals, 7-4 | at San Diego |

#### Game 1

Tuesday, Oct. 4, at St. Louis

| | 1 2 3 | 4 5 6 | 7 8 9 | R H E |
|---|---|---|---|---|
| San Diego | 0 0 0 | 0 0 0 | 1 1 3 | 5 13 1 |
| St. Louis | 1 0 3 | 0 4 0 | 0 0 x | 8 10 1 |

**Win:** Carpenter, St.L (1-0). **Loss:** Peavy, SD (0-1).
**2B:** San Diego—Sweeney (1), Greene (1); St. Louis—Edmonds (1). **HR:** San Diego—Young (1, off Flores, 0 on); St. Louis—Edmonds (1, off Peavy, 0 on), Sanders (1, off Peavy, 3 on). **RBI:** San Diego—Greene (1), Young 2 (2), Loretta (1), Giles (1); St. Louis—Edmonds (1), Sanders 6 (6). **SB:** San Diego—Giles (1), Jackson (1). **E:** San Diego—Greene (1); St. Louis—Eckstein (1).
**Attendance:** 52,349 (50,345). **Time:** 2:57.

## Game 2

Thursday, Oct. 6, at St. Louis

| | 1 2 3 | 4 5 6 | 7 8 9 | R H E |
|---|---|---|---|---|
| San Diego | 0 0 0 | 0 0 0 | 1 1 0 - | 2 10 1 |
| St. Louis | 0 0 2 | 2 0 0 | 2 0 x - | 6 6 0 |

**Win:** Mulder, St.L (1-0). **Loss:** Astacio, SD (0-1).

**2B:** San Diego—Greene (2); St. Louis—Nunez (1), Sanders (1). **RBI:** San Diego—Nady 2 (2); St. Louis—Eckstein 2 (2), Pujols (1), Molina (1), Sanders 2 (8), Nunez (1). **E:** San Diego—Greene (2).

**Attendance:** 52,599 (50,345). **Time:** 2:54.

## Game 3

Saturday, Oct. 8, at San Diego

| | 1 2 3 | 4 5 6 | 7 8 9 | R H E |
|---|---|---|---|---|
| St. Louis | 1 4 0 | 0 2 0 | 0 0 0 - | 7 13 1 |
| San Diego | 0 0 0 | 0 2 0 | 1 1 0 - | 4 9 0 |

**Win:** Morris, St.L (1-0). **Loss:** Williams, SD (0-1). **Save:** Isringhausen, St.L (1).

**2B:** St. Louis—Pujols 2 (2), Edmonds (2), Sanders (2); San Diego—Randa (1). **HR:** St. Louis—Eckstein (1, off Williams, 1 on); San Diego—Roberts (1, off Thompson, 0 on), Hernandez (1, off Tavarez, 0 on). **RBI:** St. Louis—Pujols (2), Eckstein 2 (4), Sanders 2 (10); San Diego—Young (3), Loretta (2), Roberts (1), Hernandez (1). **SB:** St. Louis—Nunez (1). **E:** St. Louis—Eckstein (2).

**Attendance:** 45,093 (42,445). **Time:** 3:07.

## Astros, 3-1

| Date | Winner | Home Field |
|---|---|---|
| Oct. 5 | Astros, 10-5 | at Atlanta |
| Oct. 6 | Braves, 7-1 | at Atlanta |
| Oct. 8 | Astros, 7-3 | at Houston |
| Oct. 9 | Astros, 7-6 (18 inn.) | at Houston |

## Game 1

Wednesday, Oct. 5, at Atlanta

| | 1 2 3 | 4 5 6 | 7 8 9 | R H E |
|---|---|---|---|---|
| Houston | 1 0 2 | 1 0 0 | 1 5 0 - | 10 11 1 |
| Atlanta | 1 0 0 | 2 0 0 | 0 1 1 - | 5 9 0 |

**Win:** Pettitte, Hou. (1-0). **Loss:** Hudson, Atl. (0-1).

**2B:** Houston—Biggio (1), Ausmus (1), Pettitte (1); Atlanta—Giles (1), C. Jones (1). **3B:** Atlanta—Francoeur (1). **HR:** Atlanta—C. Jones (1, off Pettitte, 0 on), A. Jones (1, off Pettitte, 1 on). **RBI:** Houston—Ensberg 5 (5), Biggio (1), Bagwell (1), Palmeiro 2 (2); Atlanta—C. Jones 2 (2), A. Jones 2 (2), Estrada (1). **E:** Houston—Ensberg (1).

**Attendance:** 40,590 (50,091). **Time:** 3:11.

## Game 2

Thursday, Oct. 6, at Atlanta

| | 1 2 3 | 4 5 6 | 7 8 9 | R H E |
|---|---|---|---|---|
| Houston | 1 0 0 | 0 0 0 | 0 0 0 - | 1 8 1 |
| Atlanta | 0 3 2 | 0 0 0 | 2 0 x - | 7 11 0 |

**Win:** Smoltz, Atl. (1-0). **Loss:** Clemens, Hou. (0-1).

**2B:** Houston—Burke (1); Atlanta—LaRoche (1). **HR:** Atlanta—McCann (1, off Clemens, 0 on). **RBI:** Houston—Lane (1); Atlanta—McCann 3 (3), LaRoche 2 (2), A. Jones (3), Francoeur (1). **SB:** Atlanta—Furcal (1). **E:** Houston—Qualls (1).

**Attendance:** 46,181 (50,091). **Time:** 2:52.

## Game 3

Saturday, Oct. 8, at Houston

| | 1 2 3 | 4 5 6 | 7 8 9 | R H E |
|---|---|---|---|---|
| Atlanta | 0 2 0 | 0 0 0 | 0 1 0 - | 3 8 0 |
| Houston | 2 0 1 | 0 0 0 | 4 0 x - | 7 12 1 |

**Win:** Oswalt, Hou. (1-0). **Loss:** Sosa, Atl. (0-1).

**2B:** Atlanta—A. Jones 2 (2); Houston—Biggio 3 (4), Ensberg 2 (2), Taveras (1), Lane (1). **HR:** Houston—Lamb (1, off Sosa, 0 on). **RBI:** Atlanta—McCann (4), Sosa (1), A. Jones (4); Houston—Ensberg 2 (7), Lane 2 (3), Lamb (1), Berkman (1), Everett (1). **E:** Houston—Everett (1).

**Attendance:** 43,759 (40,950). **Time:** 2:50.

## Game 4

Sunday, Oct. 9, at Houston

| | 1 2 3 | 4 5 6 | 7 8 9 | 10 11 12 |
|---|---|---|---|---|
| Atlanta | 0 0 4 | 0 1 0 | 0 1 0 | 0 0 0 |
| Houston | 0 0 0 | 0 1 0 | 0 4 1 | 0 0 0 |

| | 13 14 15 | 16 17 18 | R H E |
|---|---|---|---|
| Atlanta | 0 0 0 | 0 0 0 - | 6 13 0 |
| Houston | 0 0 0 | 0 0 1 - | 7 10 1 |

**Win:** Clemens, Hou. (1-1). **Loss:** Devine, Atl. (0-1).

**2B:** Atlanta—A. Jones (3), C. Jones (2), Hudson (1), Francoeur (1), Langerhans (1), Jordan (1); Houston—Berkman (2). **HR:** Atlanta—LaRoche (1, off Backe, 3 on), McCann (2, off Rodriguez, 0 on); Houston—Berkman (1, off Farnsworth, 3 on), Ausmus (1, off Farnsworth, 0 on), Burke (1, off Devine, 0 on). **RBI:** Atlanta—LaRoche 4 (6), A. Jones (5), McCann (5); Houston—Palmeiro (3), Berkman 4 (5), Ausmus (1), Burke (1). **SB:** Atlanta—Furcal 2 (3), Langerhans (1); Houston—Bruntlett (1), Biggio (1). **E:** Houston—Vizcaino (1).

**Attendance:** 43,413 (40,950). **Time:** 5:50.

## Longest Postseason Games

### (By innings)

| Year | Series | Result | Inn. |
|---|---|---|---|
| 2005 | NLDS | Astros 7, Braves 6 | 18 |
| 1986 | NLCS | Mets 7, Astros 6 | 16 |
| 1999 | NLCS | Mets 4, Braves 3 | 15 |
| 1995 | ALDS | Yankees 7, Mariners 5 | 15 |
| 2004 | ALCS | Red Sox 5, Yankees 4 | 14 |
| 1916 | WS | Red Sox 2, Dodgers 1 | 14 |
| 2000 | NLDS | Mets 3, Giants 2 | 13 |
| 1995 | ALDS | Indians 5, Red Sox 4 | 13 |

## American League Championship Series

### White Sox, 4-1

| Date | Winner | Home Field |
|------|--------|-----------|
| Oct. 11. . . . . . . . . . | Angels, 3-2 | at Chicago |
| Oct. 12. . . . . . . . . . | White Sox, 2-1 | at Chicago |
| Oct. 14. . . . . . . . . . | White Sox, 5-2 | at Anaheim |
| Oct. 15. . . . . . . . . . | White Sox, 8-2 | at Anaheim |
| Oct. 16. . . . . . . . . . | White Sox, 6-3 | at Anaheim |

### Game 1
Tuesday, Oct. 11, at Chicago

```
              1 2 3  4 5 6  7 8 9    R H E
Los Angeles ..0 1 2  0 0 0  0 0 0 -  3 7 1
Chicago .....0 0 1  1 0 0  0 0 0 -  2 7 0
```

**Win:** Byrd, LA (1-0). **Loss:** Contreras, Chi. (1-1). **Save:** Rodriguez, LA (3).

**HR:** Los Angeles—Anderson (3, off Contreras, 0 on); Chicago—Crede (1, off Byrd, 0 on). **RBI:** Los Angeles—Anderson (8), Cabrera (4), Guerrero (1); Chicago—Crede (2), Pierzynski (5). **SB:** Los Angeles—Erstad (1), Figgins (1). **CS:** Chicago—Podsednik (3), Pierzynski (1). **E:** Los Angeles—Figgins (1).

**Attendance:** 40,659 (40,615). **Time:** 2:47.

### Game 2
Wednesday, Oct. 12, at Chicago

```
              1 2 3  4 5 6  7 8 9    R H E
Los Angeles ..0 0 0  0 1 0  0 0 0 -  1 5 3
Chicago .....1 0 0  0 0 0  0 0 1 -  2 7 1
```

**Win:** Buehrle, Chi. (2-0). **Loss:** Escobar, LA (1-1).

**2B:** Los Angeles—Cabrera (1); Chicago—Rowand (1), Crede 2 (2). **HR:** Los Angeles—Quinlan (1, off Buehrle, 0 on). **RBI:** Los Angeles—Quinlan (1); Chicago—Dye (2), Crede (2). **SB:** Chicago—Ozuna (1). **E:** Chicago—Uribe (1).

**Attendance:** 41,013 (40,615). **Time:** 2:34.

### Most Valuable Player
**Paul Konerko, Chicago, 1B**

| AVG | AB | R | H | HR | RBI | BB |
|-----|----|----|----|----|----|----|
| .286 | 21 | 2 | 6 | 2 | 7 | 1 |

### Game 3
Friday, Oct. 14, at Anaheim

```
              1 2 3  4 5 6  7 8 9    R H  E
Chicago .....3 0 1  0 1 0  0 0 0 -  5 11 0
Los Angeles ..0 0 0  0 0 2  0 0 0 -  2 4  0
```

**Win:** Garland, Chi. (1-0). **Loss:** Lackey, LA (0-1).

**2B:** Chicago—Dye (1), Iguchi (1); Los Angeles—Erstad (1). **HR:** Chicago—Konerko (1, off Lackey, 1 on); Los Angeles—Cabrera (1, off Garland, 1 on). **RBI:** Chicago—Dye (2), Konerko 3 (3), Everett (1); Los Angeles—Cabrera 2 (3).

**Attendance:** 44,725 (45,037). **Time:** 2:42.

### Game 4
Saturday, Oct. 15, at Anaheim

```
              1 2 3  4 5 6  7 8 9    R H E
Chicago .....3 0  1 1 0  0 2 0 -  8 8 1
Los Angeles ..0 1 0  1 0 0  0 0 0 -  2 6 1
```

**Win:** Garcia, Chi. (2-0). **Loss:** Santana, LA (1-1).

**2B:** Chicago—Rowand (2); Los Angeles—Kotchman (1). **HR:** Chicago—Konerko (2, off Santana, 2 on), Pierzynski (1, off Santana, 0 on). **RBI:** Chicago—Konerko 3 (6), Everett 2 (3), Pierzynski (2), Crede 2 (4); Los Angeles—B. Molina (6), Kotchman (1). **SB:** Chicago—Dye (1), Podsednik 2 (2). **CS:** Chicago—Crede (1). **E:** Los Angeles—Cabrera (1).

**Attendance:** 44,857 (45,037). **Time:** 2:46.

### Game 5
Sunday, Oct. 16, at Anaheim

```
              1 2 3  4 5 6  7 8 9    R H E
Chicago .....0 1 0  0 1 0  1 1 2 -  6 8 1
Los Angeles ..0 0 1  0 2 0  0 0 0 -  3 5 2
```

**Win:** Contreras, Chi. (2-1). **Loss:** Escobar, LA (1-2).

**2B:** Chicago—Rowand (3), Uribe (1), Dye (2), Konerko (1); Los Angeles—Rivera (1), Figgins (1). **HR:** Chicago—Crede (2, off Escobar, 0 on). **RBI:** Chicago—Crede 3 (7), Dye (3), Konerko (7), Rowand (1); Los Angeles—Kennedy (1), Figgins (1), Anderson (2). **SB:** Chicago—Podsednik (3). **CS:** Chicago—Iguchi (1). **E:** Chicago—Contreras (1); Los Angeles—Escobar (1), Kennedy (1).

**Attendance:** 44,712 (45,037). **Time:** 3:11.

## ALCS Composite Box Score

### Chicago White Sox

| Batting | LCS vs. Los Angeles | | | | | | | | Overall AL Playoffs | | | | | | | |
|---------|------|----|----|----|----|-----|----|----|------|----|----|----|----|-----|----|----|
| | Avg | AB | R | H | HR | RBI | BB | SO | Avg | AB | R | H | HR | RBI | BB | SO |
| Joe Crede . . . . . . . . . . . | .368 | 19 | 2 | 7 | 2 | 7 | 0 | 3 | .286 | 28 | 4 | 8 | 2 | 8 | 1 | 4 |
| Scott Podsednik . . . . . . . | .294 | 17 | 4 | 5 | 0 | 0 | 6 | 5 | .286 | 28 | 7 | 8 | 1 | 4 | 7 | 6 |
| Paul Konerko . . . . . . . . . | .286 | 21 | 2 | 6 | 2 | 7 | 1 | 4 | .273 | 33 | 5 | 9 | 4 | 11 | 1 | 5 |
| Jermaine Dye . . . . . . . . . | .263 | 19 | 3 | 5 | 0 | 3 | 3 | 3 | .241 | 29 | 4 | 7 | 0 | 3 | 4 | 5 |
| Carl Everett . . . . . . . . . | .250 | 20 | 2 | 5 | 0 | 3 | 1 | 4 | .258 | 31 | 4 | 8 | 0 | 3 | 1 | 4 |
| Juan Uribe . . . . . . . . . . | .250 | 16 | 1 | 4 | 0 | 0 | 2 | 3 | .308 | 26 | 5 | 8 | 1 | 4 | 2 | 5 |
| Tadahito Iguchi . . . . . . . | .176 | 17 | 4 | 3 | 0 | 0 | 1 | 6 | .207 | 29 | 5 | 6 | 1 | 4 | 1 | 9 |
| A.J. Pierzynski . . . . . . . | .167 | 18 | 1 | 3 | 1 | 2 | 1 | 6 | .259 | 27 | 6 | 7 | 3 | 6 | 2 | 6 |
| Aaron Rowand . . . . . . . . | .167 | 18 | 3 | 3 | 0 | 1 | 1 | 2 | .250 | 28 | 6 | 7 | 0 | 3 | 2 | 3 |
| Pablo Ozuna . . . . . . . . . | — | 0 | 1 | 0 | 0 | 0 | 0 | 0 | — | 0 | 1 | 0 | 0 | 0 | 0 | 0 |
| Geoff Blum . . . . . . . . . . | — | 0 | 0 | 0 | 0 | 0 | 0 | 0 | .000 | 1 | 0 | 0 | 0 | 0 | 0 | 0 |
| Timo Perez . . . . . . . . . . | — | 0 | 0 | 0 | 0 | 0 | 0 | 0 | .000 | 1 | 0 | 0 | 0 | 0 | 0 | 0 |
| Willie Harris . . . . . . . . | — | 0 | 0 | 0 | 0 | 0 | 0 | 0 | 1.000 | 1 | 0 | 1 | 0 | 1 | 0 | 0 |
| TOTALS. . . . . . . . . . . . | .248 | 165 | 23 | 41 | 5 | 23 | 16 | 36 | | 262 | 47 | 28 | 12 | 47 | 21 | 47 |

| Pitching | LCS vs. Los Angeles | | | | | | | | Overall AL Playoffs | | | | | | | |
|---|---|---|---|---|---|---|---|---|---|---|---|---|---|---|---|---|
| | ERA | W-L | Sv | Gm | IP | H | BB | SO | ERA | W-L | Sv | Gm | IP | H | BB | SO |
| Neal Cotts | 0.00 | 0-0 | 0 | 1 | 0.2 | 0 | 0 | 0 | 0.00 | 0-0 | 0 | 2 | 1.0 | 0 | 0 | 0 |
| Mark Buehrle | 1.00 | 1-0 | 0 | 1 | 9.0 | 5 | 0 | 4 | 2.81 | 2-0 | 0 | 2 | 16.0 | 13 | 1 | 6 |
| Freddy Garcia | 2.00 | 1-0 | 0 | 1 | 9.0 | 6 | 1 | 5 | 3.21 | 2-0 | 0 | 2 | 14.0 | 11 | 5 | 6 |
| Jon Garland | 2.00 | 1-0 | 0 | 1 | 9.0 | 4 | 1 | 7 | 2.00 | 1-0 | 0 | 1 | 9.0 | 4 | 1 | 7 |
| Jose Contreras | 3.12 | 1-1 | 0 | 2 | 17.1 | 12 | 2 | 6 | 2.88 | 2-1 | 0 | 3 | 25.0 | 20 | 2 | 12 |
| Cliff Politte | — | 0-0 | 0 | 0 | 0.0 | 0 | 0 | 0 | 0.00 | 0-0 | 0 | 1 | 1.0 | 1 | 0 | 0 |
| Orlando Hernandez | — | 0-0 | 0 | 0 | 0.0 | 0 | 0 | 0 | 0.00 | 0-0 | 0 | 1 | 3.0 | 1 | 0 | 4 |
| Bobby Jenks | — | 0-0 | 0 | 0 | 0.0 | 0 | 0 | 0 | 0.00 | 0-0 | 2 | 2 | 3.0 | 1 | 1 | 1 |
| Damaso Marte | — | 0-0 | 0 | 0 | 0.0 | 0 | 0 | 0 | — | 0-0 | 0 | 1 | 0.0 | 1 | 2 | 0 |
| TOTALS | 2.20 | 4-1 | 0 | 5 | 45.0 | 27 | 4 | 22 | 2.50 | 7-1 | 2 | 8 | 72.0 | 52 | 12 | 36 |

## Los Angeles Angels of Anaheim

| Batting | LCS vs. Chicago | | | | | | | | Overall AL Playoffs | | | | | | | |
|---|---|---|---|---|---|---|---|---|---|---|---|---|---|---|---|---|
| | Avg | AB | R | H | HR | RBI | BB | SO | Avg | AB | R | H | HR | RBI | BB | SO |
| Jose Molina | .333 | 3 | 0 | 1 | 0 | 0 | 0 | 0 | .500 | 4 | 1 | 2 | 0 | 1 | 0 | 0 |
| Robb Quinlan | .333 | 3 | 1 | 1 | 1 | 1 | 0 | 2 | .400 | 5 | 1 | 2 | 1 | 1 | 0 | 2 |
| Adam Kennedy | .286 | 14 | 3 | 4 | 0 | 1 | 0 | 1 | .258 | 31 | 3 | 8 | 0 | 3 | 0 | 4 |
| Casey Kotchman | .286 | 7 | 0 | 2 | 0 | 1 | 1 | 1 | .222 | 9 | 0 | 2 | 0 | 1 | 1 | 1 |
| Darin Erstad | .235 | 17 | 1 | 4 | 0 | 0 | 1 | 2 | .270 | 37 | 2 | 10 | 0 | 3 | 1 | 8 |
| Steve Finley | .222 | 9 | 1 | 2 | 0 | 0 | 0 | 2 | .150 | 20 | 3 | 3 | 0 | 1 | 1 | 6 |
| Orlando Cabrera | .200 | 20 | 1 | 4 | 1 | 3 | 0 | 2 | .220 | 41 | 4 | 9 | 1 | 6 | 0 | 3 |
| Garret Anderson | .176 | 17 | 2 | 3 | 1 | 2 | 1 | 5 | .222 | 36 | 4 | 8 | 3 | 9 | 1 | 5 |
| Bengie Molina | .118 | 17 | 0 | 2 | 0 | 1 | 0 | 2 | .286 | 35 | 5 | 10 | 3 | 6 | 0 | 2 |
| Chone Figgins | .118 | 17 | 1 | 2 | 0 | 1 | 1 | 3 | .132 | 38 | 3 | 5 | 0 | 3 | 2 | 11 |
| Juan Rivera | .111 | 9 | 1 | 1 | 0 | 0 | 0 | 1 | .269 | 26 | 4 | 7 | 1 | 1 | 1 | 3 |
| Vladimir Guerrero | .050 | 20 | 0 | 1 | 0 | 1 | 0 | 1 | .184 | 38 | 5 | 7 | 0 | 1 | 2 | 3 |
| Jeff DaVanon | .000 | 1 | 0 | 0 | 0 | 0 | 0 | 0 | .000 | 1 | 1 | 0 | 0 | 0 | 0 | 0 |
| Josh Paul | — | 0 | 0 | 0 | 0 | 0 | 0 | 0 | — | 0 | 0 | 0 | 0 | 0 | 0 | 0 |
| Maicer Izturis | — | 0 | 0 | 0 | 0 | 0 | 0 | 0 | — | 0 | 0 | 0 | 0 | 0 | 0 | 0 |
| TOTALS | .175 | 154 | 11 | 27 | 3 | 11 | 4 | 22 | .227 | 321 | 36 | 73 | 9 | 36 | 9 | 48 |

| Pitching | ERA | W-L | Sv | Gm | IP | H | BB | SO | ERA | W-L | Sv | Gm | IP | H | BB | SO |
|---|---|---|---|---|---|---|---|---|---|---|---|---|---|---|---|---|
| Jarrod Washburn | 0.00 | 0-0 | 0 | 1 | 4.2 | 4 | 1 | 1 | 0.00 | 0-0 | 0 | 1 | 4.2 | 4 | 1 | 1 |
| Scot Shields | 0.00 | 0-0 | 0 | 4 | 6.0 | 4 | 1 | 5 | 1.64 | 1-1 | 0 | 8 | 11.0 | 8 | 4 | 10 |
| Brendan Donnelly | 0.00 | 0-0 | 0 | 3 | 3.1 | 2 | 1 | 5 | 2.45 | 0-0 | 0 | 4 | 3.2 | 4 | 2 | 5 |
| Francisco Rodriguez | 0.00 | 0-0 | 1 | 2 | 2.1 | 2 | 3 | 3 | 1.59 | 0-0 | 3 | 5 | 5.2 | 7 | 3 | 5 |
| Kevin Gregg | 0.00 | 0-0 | 0 | 1 | 2.0 | 1 | 1 | 3 | 0.00 | 0-0 | 0 | 1 | 2.0 | 1 | 1 | 3 |
| Kelvim Escobar | 2.08 | 0-2 | 0 | 2 | 4.1 | 4 | 2 | 10 | 1.59 | 1-2 | 0 | 6 | 11.1 | 6 | 7 | 15 |
| Paul Byrd | 3.38 | 1-0 | 0 | 2 | 10.2 | 10 | 2 | 2 | 5.02 | 1-0 | 0 | 3 | 14.1 | 17 | 4 | 4 |
| Esteban Yan | 9.00 | 0-0 | 0 | 1 | 2.0 | 3 | 1 | 2 | 9.00 | 0-0 | 0 | 1 | 2.0 | 3 | 1 | 2 |
| John Lackey | 9.00 | 0-1 | 0 | 1 | 5.0 | 8 | 1 | 3 | 4.41 | 0-1 | 0 | 3 | 16.1 | 15 | 10 | 12 |
| Ervin Santana | 10.38 | 0-1 | 0 | 1 | 4.1 | 3 | 3 | 2 | 7.45 | 1-1 | 0 | 2 | 9.2 | 8 | 5 | 4 |
| Bartolo Colon | — | 0-0 | 0 | 0 | 0.0 | 0 | 0 | 0 | 4.50 | 0-1 | 0 | 2 | 8.0 | 10 | 2 | 7 |
| TOTALS | 3.43 | 1-4 | 1 | 5 | 44.2 | 41 | 16 | 36 | 3.65 | 4-6 | 3 | 10 | 88.2 | 83 | 40 | 68 |

## Score by Innings

| | 1 | 2 | 3 | 4 | 5 | 6 | 7 | 8 | 9 | | R | H | E |
|---|---|---|---|---|---|---|---|---|---|---|---|---|---|
| Los Angeles | 0 | 2 | 3 | 1 | 3 | 2 | 0 | 0 | 0 | – | 11 | 27 | 7 |
| Chicago | 7 | 1 | 3 | 2 | 3 | 0 | 1 | 3 | 3 | – | 23 | 41 | 3 |

E: Los Angeles—Figgins, Guerrero, Paul, Washburn, Cabrera, Kennedy, Escobar; Chicago—Uribe, Garcia, Contreras.
2B: Los Angeles—Kotchman, Erstad, Cabrera, Figgins, Rivera; Chicago—Crede 2, Dye 2, Rowand 2, Konerko, Uribe, Iguchi.
3B: Chicago—Podsednik. HR: Los Angeles—Quinlan, Anderson; Chicago—Crede 2, Konerko 2, Pierzynski. SB: Los Angeles—Kennedy.
S: Los Angeles—Figgins, Erstad; Chicago—Podsednik 3, Ozuna, Dye. CS: Chicago—Podsednik, Pierzynski, Crede, Iguchi.
S: Los Angeles—Figgins 2, Kennedy; Chicago—Iguchi 2, Pierzynski. SF: Los Angeles—Anderson; Chicago—Rowand, Crede.
PB: Chicago—Pierzynski 2. HBP: by Byrd (Rowand, Iguchi), by Washburn (Iguchi), by Santana (Iguchi), by Buehrle (B. Molina). WP: none. Balk: none. LOB: Los Angeles—17; Chicago—33.
Umpires: Jerry Crawford, Doug Eddings, Ted Barrett, Ron Kulpa, Ed Rapuano, Randy Marsh.

## National League Championship Series

### Astros, 4-2

| Date | Winner | Home Field |
|---|---|---|
| Oct. 12 . . . . . . . . . . | Cardinals, 5-3 | at St. Louis |
| Oct. 13 . . . . . . . . . | Astros, 4-1 | at St. Louis |
| Oct. 15 . . . . . . . . . | Astros, 4-3 | at Houston |
| Oct. 16 . . . . . . . . . | Astros, 2-1 | at Houston |
| Oct. 17 . . . . . . . . . | Cardinals, 5-4 | at Houston |
| Oct. 19 . . . . . . . . . | Astros, 5-1 | at St. Louis |

### Most Valuable Player
#### Roy Oswalt, Houston, P

| G | W-L | IP | H | BB | K | ERA |
|---|---|---|---|---|---|---|
| 2 | 2-0 | 14.0 | 8 | 4 | 12 | 1.29 |

### Game 1
Wednesday, Oct. 12, at St. Louis

|  | 1 2 3 | 4 5 6 | 7 8 9 | R | H | E |
|---|---|---|---|---|---|---|
| **Houston** . . . . | 0 0 0 | 0 0 0 | 2 0 1 | - 3 | 7 | 0 |
| **St. Louis** . . . . | 2 1 0 | 0 2 0 | 0 0 x | - 5 | 8 | 1 |

**Win:** Carpenter, St.L (2-0). **Loss:** Pettitte, Hou. (1-1). **Save:** Isringhausen, St.L (2).

**2B:** Houston—Berkman (1), Ensberg (1); **HR:** Houston—Burke (1, off Carpenter, 1 on); St. Louis—Sanders (1, off Pettitte, 1 on). **RBI:** Houston—Burke 2 (2), Ausmus (1); St. Louis—Sanders 2 (2), Carpenter (1), Eckstein (1), Pujols (1). **E:** St. Louis—Eckstein (1).
**Attendance:** 52,332 (50,345). **Time:** 2:29.

### Game 2
Thursday, Oct. 13, at St. Louis

|  | 1 2 3 | 4 5 6 | 7 8 9 | R | H | E |
|---|---|---|---|---|---|---|
| **Houston** . . . . . | 0 1 0 | 0 1 0 | 0 2 0 | - 4 | 11 | 1 |
| **St. Louis** . . . . | 0 0 0 | 0 0 1 | 0 0 0 | - 1 | 6 | 0 |

**Win:** Oswalt, Hou. (2-0). **Loss:** Mulder, St.L (1-1). **Save:** Lidge, Hou. (1).

**2B:** Houston—Ausmus (1), Berkman (2); St. Louis—Molina (2). **3B:** Houston—Burke (1), Everett (1). **HR:** St. Louis—Pujols (1, off Oswalt, 0 on). **RBI:** Houston—Biggio (1), Burke (3), Everett (1); St. Louis—Pujols (2). **SB:** Houston—Ausmus (1). **CS:** Houston—Taveras (1). **E:** Houston—Ensberg (1).
**Attendance:** 52,358 (50,345). **Time:** 3:03.

### Game 3
Saturday, Oct. 15, at Houston

|  | 1 2 3 | 4 5 6 | 7 8 9 | R | H | E |
|---|---|---|---|---|---|---|
| **St. Louis** . . . . | 0 0 0 | 0 1 1 | 0 0 1 | - 3 | 7 | 1 |
| **Houston** . . . . | 0 0 0 | 2 0 2 | 0 0 x | - 4 | 11 | 0 |

**Win:** Clemens, Hou. (2-1). **Loss:** Morris, St.L (1-1). **Save:** Lidge, Hou. (2).

**2B:** St. Louis—Mabry (1); Houston—Lamb (1), Everett (1). **HR:** Houston—Lamb (1, off Morris, 1 on). **RBI:** St. Louis—Eckstein (2), Walker (1), Mabry (1); Houston—Lamb 2 (2), Lane (1). **SB:** St. Louis—Edmonds (1). **E:** St. Louis—Luna (1).
**Attendance:** 42,823 (40,950). **Time:** 3:00.

### Game 4
Sunday, Oct. 16, at Houston

|  | 1 2 3 | 4 5 6 | 7 8 9 | R | H | E |
|---|---|---|---|---|---|---|
| **St. Louis** . . . . | 0 0 0 | 1 0 0 | 0 0 0 | - 1 | 5 | 1 |
| **Houston** . . . . | 0 0 0 | 1 0 0 | 1 0 x | - 2 | 6 | 0 |

**Win:** Qualls, Hou. (1-0). **Loss:** Marquis, St.L (0-1). **Save:** Lidge, Hou. (3).

**2B:** St. Louis—Edmonds (1). **HR:** Houston—Lane (1, off Suppan, 0 on). **RBI:** St. Louis—Pujols (3); Houston—Lane (2), Ensberg (1). **E:** St. Louis—Marquis (1).
**Attendance:** 43,010 (40,950). **Time:** 3:11.

### Game 5
Monday, Oct. 17, at Houston

|  | 1 2 3 | 4 5 6 | 7 8 9 | R | H | E |
|---|---|---|---|---|---|---|
| **St. Louis** . . . . | 0 0 2 | 0 0 0 | 0 0 3 | - 5 | 9 | 1 |
| **Houston** . . . . | 0 1 0 | 0 0 0 | 3 0 0 | - 4 | 9 | 2 |

**Win:** Isringhausen, St.L (1-0). **Loss:** Lidge, Hou. (0-1).

**2B:** St. Louis—Molina (3); Houston—Ausmus (2). **HR:** St. Louis—Pujols (2, off Lidge, 2 on); Houston—Berkman (1, off Carpenter, 2 on). **RBI:** St. Louis—Grudzielanek 2 (2), Pujols 3 (6); Houston—Biggio (2), Berkman 3 (3). **SB:** St. Louis—Eckstein (1), Sanders (1). **CS:** St. Louis—Eckstein (1). **E:** St. Louis—Luna (2); Houston—Everett (1), Lamb (1).
**Attendance:** 43,470 (40,950). **Time:** 3:19.

### Game 6
Wednesday, Oct. 19, at St. Louis

|  | 1 2 3 | 4 5 6 | 7 8 9 | R | H | E |
|---|---|---|---|---|---|---|
| **Houston** . . . . | 0 0 2 | 1 0 1 | 1 0 0 | - 5 | 11 | 0 |
| **St. Louis** . . . . | 0 0 0 | 0 1 0 | 0 0 0 | - 1 | 4 | 1 |

**Win:** Oswalt, Hou. (3-0). **Loss:** Mulder, St.L (1-2).

**2B:** St. Louis—Walker (1). **HR:** Houston—Lane (2, off Mulder, 0 on). **RBI:** Houston—Biggio (3), Lane (3), Everett (2), Ensberg (2) St. Louis—Rodriguez (1). **E:** St. Louis—Edmonds (1).
**Attendance:** 52,438 (50,345). **Time:** 2:53.

## NLCS Composite Box Score
### Houston Astros

| | LCS vs. St. Louis | | | | | | | Overall NL Playoffs | | | | | | |
| Batting | Avg | AB | R | H | HR | RBI | BB | SO | Avg | AB | R | H | HR | RBI | BB | SO |
|---|---|---|---|---|---|---|---|---|---|---|---|---|---|---|---|---|
| Roger Clemens . . . . . . . . | .500 | 2 | 0 | 1 | 0 | 0 | 0 | 1 | .200 | 5 | 0 | 1 | 0 | 0 | 0 | 3 |
| Willy Taveras . . . . . . . . . | .357 | 14 | 1 | 5 | 0 | 0 | 1 | 1 | .357 | 28 | 3 | 10 | 0 | 0 | 2 | 2 |
| Craig Biggio . . . . . . . . | .333 | 24 | 2 | 8 | 0 | 3 | 2 | 3 | .326 | 43 | 8 | 14 | 0 | 4 | 4 | 8 |
| Orlando Palmeiro . . . . . . | .333 | 3 | 0 | 1 | 0 | 0 | 1 | 0 | .200 | 10 | 0 | 2 | 0 | 3 | 3 | 0 |
| Roy Oswalt . . . . . . . . | .333 | 3 | 0 | 1 | 0 | 0 | 1 | 1 | .167 | 6 | 0 | 1 | 0 | 0 | 1 | 1 |
| Brad Ausmus . . . . . . . . | .318 | 22 | 3 | 7 | 0 | 1 | 1 | 6 | .275 | 40 | 6 | 11 | 1 | 2 | 3 | 10 |
| Adam Everett . . . . . . . . | .304 | 23 | 2 | 7 | 0 | 2 | 0 | 4 | .270 | 37 | 3 | 10 | 0 | 3 | 1 | 5 |
| Chris Burke . . . . . . . . | .300 | 20 | 5 | 6 | 1 | 3 | 1 | 3 | .348 | 23 | 6 | 8 | 2 | 4 | 2 | 3 |
| Lance Berkman . . . . . . . | .286 | 21 | 2 | 6 | 1 | 3 | 4 | 3 | .314 | 35 | 6 | 11 | 2 | 8 | 7 | 7 |
| Morgan Ensberg . . . . . . | .238 | 21 | 1 | 5 | 0 | 2 | 2 | 2 | .256 | 39 | 3 | 10 | 0 | 9 | 4 | 5 |
| Jason Lane . . . . . . . . . | .238 | 21 | 3 | 5 | 2 | 4 | 2 | 4 | .237 | 38 | 4 | 9 | 2 | 6 | 3 | 7 |

## LCS vs. St. Louis / Overall NL Playoffs

| Batting (Cont) | Avg | AB | R | H | HR | RBI | BB | SO | Avg | AB | R | H | HR | RBI | BB | SO |
|---|---|---|---|---|---|---|---|---|---|---|---|---|---|---|---|---|
| Mike Lamb . . . . . . . . . . | .188 | 16 | 3 | 3 | 1 | 2 | 0 | 3 | .273 | 22 | 4 | 6 | 2 | 3 | 2 | 3 |
| Jose Vizcaino . . . . . . . . | .000 | 2 | 0 | 0 | 0 | 0 | 0 | 0 | .000 | 7 | 0 | 0 | 0 | 0 | 0 | 1 |
| Jeff Bagwell . . . . . . . . . | .000 | 1 | 0 | 0 | 0 | 0 | 0 | 0 | .333 | 3 | 1 | 1 | 0 | 1 | 0 | 0 |
| Andy Pettite . . . . . . . . . | .000 | 2 | 0 | 0 | 0 | 0 | 0 | 0 | .250 | 4 | 1 | 1 | 0 | 0 | 0 | 1 |
| Brandon Backe . . . . . . . | .000 | 2 | 0 | 0 | 0 | 0 | 0 | 1 | .000 | 3 | 0 | 0 | 0 | 0 | 0 | 1 |
| Eric Bruntlett . . . . . . . . | .000 | 1 | 0 | 0 | 0 | 0 | 0 | 0 | .143 | 7 | 1 | 1 | 0 | 0 | 0 | 5 |
| Luke Scott . . . . . . . . . . . | — | 0 | 0 | 0 | 0 | 0 | 0 | 0 | .000 | 2 | 1 | 0 | 0 | 0 | 1 | 1 |
| Raul Chavez . . . . . . . . . . | — | 0 | 0 | 0 | 0 | 0 | 0 | 0 | .000 | 1 | 0 | 0 | 0 | 0 | 0 | 0 |
| TOTALS . . . . . . . . . . . . | .278 | 198 | 22 | 55 | 5 | 19 | 15 | 33 | .272 | 353 | 47 | 96 | 9 | 43 | 34 | 63 |

| Pitching | ERA | W-L | Sv | Gm | IP | H | BB | SO | ERA | W-L | Sv | Gm | IP | H | BB | SO |
|---|---|---|---|---|---|---|---|---|---|---|---|---|---|---|---|---|
| Russ Springer . . . . . . . . | 0.00 | 0-0 | 0 | 1 | 1.0 | 0 | 1 | 1 | 3.00 | 0-0 | 0 | 3 | 3.0 | 5 | 2 | 2 |
| Dan Wheeler . . . . . . . . . | 0.00 | 0-0 | 0 | 3 | 2.2 | 2 | 0 | 2 | 1.29 | 0-0 | 0 | 6 | 7.0 | 6 | 3 | 7 |
| Mike Gallo . . . . . . . . . . . | 0.00 | 0-0 | 0 | 2 | 0.2 | 0 | 0 | 0 | 0.00 | 0-0 | 0 | 5 | 2.1 | 1 | 1 | 0 |
| Chad Qualls . . . . . . . . . | 0.00 | 1-0 | 0 | 4 | 4.2 | 0 | 0 | 4 | 2.45 | 1-0 | 0 | 6 | 7.2 | 5 | 2 | 5 |
| Ezequiel Astacio . . . . . . | 0.00 | 0-0 | 0 | 1 | 1.0 | 0 | 0 | 2 | 0.00 | 0-0 | 0 | 1 | 1.0 | 0 | 0 | 2 |
| Roy Oswalt . . . . . . . . . | 1.29 | 2-0 | 0 | 2 | 14.0 | 8 | 4 | 12 | 2.11 | 3-0 | 0 | 3 | 21.1 | 14 | 6 | 19 |
| Brandon Backe . . . . . . . | 1.59 | 0-0 | 0 | 1 | 5.2 | 2 | 3 | 7 | 4.91 | 0-0 | 0 | 3 | 11.0 | 8 | 6 | 10 |
| Roger Clemens . . . . . . . | 3.00 | 1-0 | 0 | 1 | 6.0 | 6 | 2 | 1 | 4.50 | 2-1 | 0 | 3 | 14.0 | 13 | 5 | 7 |
| Andy Pettitte . . . . . . . | 5.11 | 0-1 | 0 | 2 | 12.1 | 15 | 4 | 6 | 4.66 | 1-1 | 0 | 3 | 19.1 | 19 | 6 | 12 |
| Brad Lidge . . . . . . . . . | 7.20 | 0-1 | 3 | 4 | 5.0 | 6 | 2 | 7 | 4.00 | 0-1 | 3 | 7 | 9.0 | 8 | 6 | 12 |
| Wandy Rodriguez . . . . . . . | — | 0-0 | 0 | 0 | 0.0 | 0 | 0 | 0 | 9.00 | 0-0 | 0 | 1 | 1.0 | 1 | 0 | 2 |
| TOTALS . . . . . . . . . . . | 2.72 | 4-2 | 3 | 6 | 53.0 | 39 | 16 | 42 | 3.43 | 7-3 | 3 | 10 | 97.0 | 80 | 37 | 78 |

## St. Louis Cardinals

### LCS vs. Houston / Overall NL Playoffs

| Batting | Avg | AB | R | H | HR | RBI | BB | SO | Avg | AB | R | H | HR | RBI | BB | SO |
|---|---|---|---|---|---|---|---|---|---|---|---|---|---|---|---|---|
| Abraham Nunez . . . . . . | .385 | 13 | 1 | 5 | 0 | 0 | 0 | 1 | .375 | 24 | 4 | 9 | 0 | 0 | 2 | 4 |
| Yadier Molina . . . . . . . . | .318 | 22 | 1 | 7 | 0 | 0 | 0 | 2 | .286 | 35 | 2 | 10 | 0 | 3 | 0 | 3 |
| Albert Pujols . . . . . . . . | .304 | 23 | 3 | 7 | 2 | 6 | 1 | 3 | .375 | 32 | 7 | 12 | 2 | 8 | 5 | 3 |
| Mark Grudzielanek . . . . | .227 | 22 | 2 | 5 | 0 | 2 | 0 | 3 | .200 | 35 | 4 | 7 | 0 | 2 | 0 | 4 |
| Jim Edmonds . . . . . . . . | .211 | 19 | 2 | 4 | 0 | 0 | 5 | 5 | .267 | 30 | 7 | 8 | 1 | 1 | 7 | 7 |
| David Eckstein . . . . . . . | .200 | 20 | 5 | 4 | 0 | 2 | 3 | 2 | .273 | 33 | 8 | 9 | 1 | 6 | 4 | 3 |
| Reggie Sanders . . . . . . . | .167 | 18 | 1 | 3 | 1 | 2 | 1 | 8 | .233 | 30 | 2 | 7 | 2 | 12 | 2 | 10 |
| Larry Walker . . . . . . . . . | .158 | 19 | 0 | 3 | 0 | 1 | 4 | 4 | .107 | 28 | 1 | 3 | 0 | 1 | 6 | 9 |
| John Mabry . . . . . . . . . | .125 | 8 | 0 | 1 | 0 | 1 | 0 | 3 | .200 | 10 | 0 | 2 | 0 | 1 | 0 | 3 |
| Jeff Suppan . . . . . . . . . | .000 | 2 | 0 | 0 | 0 | 0 | 0 | 1 | .000 | 2 | 0 | 0 | 0 | 0 | 0 | 1 |
| Chris Carpenter . . . . . . | .000 | 4 | 0 | 0 | 0 | 1 | 0 | 1 | .000 | 7 | 0 | 0 | 0 | 1 | 0 | 2 |
| Matt Morris . . . . . . . . . | .000 | 1 | 0 | 0 | 0 | 0 | 0 | 0 | .333 | 3 | 1 | 1 | 0 | 0 | 0 | 0 |
| Mark Mulder . . . . . . . . | .000 | 3 | 0 | 0 | 0 | 0 | 0 | 3 | .000 | 4 | 0 | 0 | 0 | 0 | 1 | 4 |
| Jason Marquis . . . . . . . | .000 | 1 | 0 | 0 | 0 | 0 | 0 | 0 | .000 | 1 | 0 | 0 | 0 | 0 | 0 | 0 |
| So Taguchi . . . . . . . . . . | .000 | 6 | 0 | 0 | 0 | 0 | 0 | 3 | .000 | 7 | 0 | 0 | 0 | 0 | 0 | 3 |
| Hector Luna . . . . . . . . . | .000 | 4 | 0 | 0 | 0 | 0 | 0 | 2 | .000 | 4 | 0 | 0 | 0 | 0 | 0 | 2 |
| John Rodriguez . . . . . . | .000 | 2 | 1 | 0 | 0 | 1 | 2 | 1 | .000 | 3 | 1 | 0 | 0 | 1 | 2 | 1 |
| John Gall . . . . . . . . . . . | — | 0 | 0 | 0 | 0 | 0 | 0 | 0 | .000 | 1 | 0 | 0 | 0 | 0 | 0 | 0 |
| TOTALS . . . . . . . . . . . | .209 | 187 | 16 | 39 | 3 | 16 | 16 | 42 | .235 | 289 | 37 | 68 | 6 | 36 | 29 | 59 |

| Pitching | ERA | W-L | Sv | Gm | IP | H | BB | SO | ERA | W-L | Sv | Gm | IP | H | BB | SO |
|---|---|---|---|---|---|---|---|---|---|---|---|---|---|---|---|---|
| Jason Isringhausen . . . . | 0.00 | 1-0 | 1 | 3 | 4.0 | 3 | 0 | 2 | 1.29 | 1-0 | 2 | 6 | 7.0 | 8 | 1 | 6 |
| Randy Flores . . . . . . . . . | 0.00 | 0-0 | 0 | 2 | 1.1 | 0 | 1 | 3 | 2.70 | 0-0 | 0 | 5 | 3.1 | 2 | 1 | 3 |
| Brad Thompson . . . . . . | 0.00 | 0-0 | 0 | 2 | 1.0 | 2 | 0 | 0 | 7.71 | 0-0 | 0 | 4 | 2.1 | 5 | 0 | 1 |
| Jeff Suppan . . . . . . . . . | 1.80 | 0-0 | 0 | 1 | 5.0 | 3 | 3 | 5 | 1.80 | 0-0 | 0 | 1 | 5.0 | 3 | 3 | 5 |
| Chris Carpenter . . . . . . | 3.00 | 1-0 | 0 | 2 | 15.0 | 14 | 3 | 9 | 2.14 | 2-0 | 0 | 3 | 21.0 | 17 | 7 | 12 |
| Mark Mulder . . . . . . . . | 3.09 | 0-2 | 0 | 2 | 11.2 | 14 | 3 | 8 | 2.45 | 1-2 | 0 | 3 | 18.1 | 22 | 4 | 10 |
| Jason Marquis . . . . . . . | 3.38 | 0-1 | 0 | 3 | 5.1 | 6 | 3 | 4 | 3.38 | 0-1 | 0 | 3 | 5.1 | 6 | 3 | 4 |
| Matt Morris . . . . . . . . . | 5.06 | 0-1 | 0 | 1 | 5.1 | 8 | 1 | 3 | 3.97 | 1-1 | 0 | 2 | 11.1 | 13 | 4 | 7 |
| Julian Tavarez . . . . . . . | 5.40 | 0-0 | 0 | 3 | 3.1 | 5 | 0 | 2 | 7.71 | 0-0 | 0 | 5 | 4.2 | 9 | 1 | 2 |
| Cal Eldred . . . . . . . . . . | — | 0-0 | 0 | 0 | 0.0 | 0 | 0 | 0 | 27.00 | 0-0 | 0 | 1 | 0.2 | 2 | 1 | 0 |
| TOTALS . . . . . . . . . . . | 2.94 | 2-4 | 1 | 6 | 52.0 | 55 | 15 | 33 | 3.19 | 5-4 | 2 | 9 | 79.0 | 87 | 25 | 50 |

## Score by Innings

| | 1 | 2 | 3 | 4 | 5 | 6 | 7 | 8 | 9 | | R | H | E |
|---|---|---|---|---|---|---|---|---|---|---|---|---|---|
| Houston . . . . . . . . . . . . . . . . . . . | .0 | 2 | 2 | | 4 | 1 | 3 | 7 | 2 | 1 | – | 22 | 55 | 3 |
| St. Louis . . . . . . . . . . . . . . . . . . . | .2 | 1 | 2 | | 1 | 4 | 2 | 0 | 0 | 4 | – | 16 | 39 | 3 |

**E:** Houston—Ensberg, Lamb, Everett; St. Louis—Luna, Eckstein, Marquis. **2B:** Houston—Ausmus 2, Berkman 2, Everett, Ensberg, Lamb; St. Louis—Molina 3, Edmonds, Walker, Mabry. **3B:** Houston—Everett, Burke. **HR:** Houston—Lane 2, Burke, Berkman, Lamb; St. Louis—Pujols 2, Sanders. **SB:** Houston—Ausmus; St. Louis—Edmonds, Eckstein, Sanders. **CS:** Houston—Taveras; St. Louis—Eckstein. **S:** Houston—Pettitte 2, Oswalt 2, Biggio, Burke, Taveras, Everett; St. Louis—Carpenter 2, Morris. **SF:** Houston—Ausmus, Ensberg; St. Louis—Eckstein, Walker, Pujols, Rodriguez. **PB:** St. Louis—Molina. **HBP:** by Carpenter (Lane), by Pettitte (Eckstein), by Oswalt (Grudzielanek, Eckstein). **WP:** none. **Balk:** none. **LOB:** Houston—46; St. Louis—38.

**Umpires:** Tim McClelland, Greg Gibson, Wally Bell, Phil Cuzzi, Larry Poncino, Gerry Davis.

## WORLD SERIES

### White Sox, 4-0

| Date | Winner | Home Field | Date | Winner | Home Field |
|---|---|---|---|---|---|
| Oct. 22 . . . . . . . | White Sox, 5-3 | at Chicago | Oct. 25 . . . . . . . | White Sox, 7-5 | at Houston |
| Oct. 23 . . . . . . . | White Sox, 7-6 | at Chicago | Oct. 26 . . . . . . . | White Sox, 1-0 | at Houston |

### Game 1

Saturday, Oct. 22, at Chicago

| Houston | AB | R | H | RBI | Chicago | AB | R | H | RBI |
|---|---|---|---|---|---|---|---|---|---|
| Biggio, 2b | 4 | 1 | 1 | 0 | Podsednik, lf | 5 | 0 | 2 | 1 |
| Taveras, cf | 3 | 0 | 2 | 0 | Iguchi, 2b | 5 | 0 | 0 | 0 |
| Berkman, lf | 4 | 0 | 2 | 0 | Dye, rf | 2 | 1 | 1 | 1 |
| Burke, pr-lf | 0 | 0 | 0 | 0 | Konerko, 1b | 4 | 0 | 2 | 0 |
| Ensberg, 3b | 4 | 0 | 0 | 0 | C. Everett, dh | 3 | 1 | 1 | 0 |
| Lamb, 1b | 4 | 1 | 1 | 1 | Rowand, cf | 3 | 0 | 1 | 0 |
| Bagwell, dh | 2 | 0 | 0 | 0 | Pierzynski, c | 4 | 2 | 1 | 1 |
| Lane, rf | 4 | 0 | 0 | 0 | Crede, 3b | 4 | 1 | 1 | 1 |
| Ausmus, c | 3 | 0 | 1 | 0 | Uribe, ss | 2 | 0 | 1 | 1 |
| A. Everett, ss | 4 | 1 | 0 | 0 | | | | | |
| **Totals** | **32** | **3** | **7** | **3** | **Totals** | **32** | **5** | **10** | **5** |

```
            R  H  E
Houston ...... 012  000  000  —  3  7  1
Chicago ...... 120  100  01x  —  5 10  0
```

**E:** Houston—A. Everett (1). **2B:** Houston—Berkman (1), Taveras 2 (2); Chicago—Uribe (1). **3B:** Chicago—Podsednik (1). **HR:** Houston—Lamb (1, off Contreras, 0 on); Chicago—Dye (1, off Clemens, 0 on), Crede (1, off Rodriguez, 0 on). **SB:** Houston—Burke (1); Chicago—Podsednik (1), Pierzynski (1). **BB:** Chicago—Dye 2, Uribe 2, Rowand. **S:** Houston—Taveras; Chicago—C. Everett.

| Houston | IP | H | R | ER | BB | SO | HR | ERA |
|---|---|---|---|---|---|---|---|---|
| Clemens | 2 | 4 | 3 | 3 | 0 | 1 | 1 | 13.50 |
| Rodriguez (L, 0-1) | 3⅓ | 4 | 1 | 1 | 5 | 1 | 1 | 2.70 |
| Qualls | 1⅔ | 0 | 0 | 0 | 0 | 2 | 0 | 0.00 |
| Springer | 1 | 2 | 1 | 1 | 0 | 0 | 0 | 9.00 |

| Chicago | IP | H | R | ER | BB | SO | HR | ERA |
|---|---|---|---|---|---|---|---|---|
| Contreras (W, 1-0) | 7 | 6 | 3 | 3 | 0 | 2 | 1 | 3.86 |
| Cotts | ⅔ | 1 | 0 | 0 | 0 | 2 | 0 | 0.00 |
| Jenks (S, 1) | 1⅓ | 0 | 0 | 0 | 0 | 3 | 0 | 0.00 |

**HBP:** by Contreras (Ausmus), by Contreras (Bagwell 2). **IBB:** by Rodriguez (Rowand).

**Attendance:** 41,206 (40,615). **Time:** 3:13.

### Game 2

Sunday, Oct. 23, at Chicago

| Houston | AB | R | H | RBI | Chicago | AB | R | H | RBI |
|---|---|---|---|---|---|---|---|---|---|
| Biggio, 2b | 4 | 0 | 0 | 0 | Podsednik, lf | 5 | 1 | 1 | 1 |
| Bruntlett, 2b | 0 | 0 | 0 | 0 | Iguchi, 2b | 3 | 1 | 1 | 0 |
| Lamb, ph-1b | 1 | 0 | 0 | 0 | Dye, rf | 3 | 1 | 1 | 0 |
| Taveras, cf | 4 | 2 | 2 | 0 | Konerko, 1b | 4 | 1 | 1 | 4 |
| Berkman, 1b-lf | 3 | 0 | 1 | 3 | C. Everett, dh | 4 | 0 | 2 | 0 |
| Ensberg, 3b | 4 | 1 | 1 | 0 | Rowand, cf | 4 | 1 | 2 | 0 |
| Bagwell, dh | 4 | 1 | 1 | 0 | Pierzynski, c | 4 | 1 | 1 | 0 |
| Lane, rf | 4 | 0 | 1 | 0 | Crede, 3b | 4 | 0 | 1 | 1 |
| Burke, lf-2b | 3 | 1 | 0 | 0 | Uribe, ss | 4 | 1 | 2 | 1 |
| Ausmus, c | 4 | 1 | 2 | 0 | | | | | |
| A. Everett, ss | 3 | 0 | 0 | 0 | | | | | |
| J. Vizcaino, ph-ss | 1 | 0 | 1 | 2 | | | | | |
| **Totals** | **35** | **6** | **9** | **6** | **Totals** | **35** | **7** | **12** | **7** |

```
            R  H  E
Houston ...... 011  020  002  —  6  9  0
Chicago ...... 020  000  401  —  7 12  0
```

**2B:** Houston—Ausmus (1), Berkman (2); Chicago—Uribe 2 (3), Rowand (1). **3B:** Houston—Taveras (1). **HR:** Houston—Ensberg (1, off Buehrle, 0 on); Chicago—Konerko (1, off Qualls, 3 on), Podsednik (1, off Lidge, 0 on). **SB:** Houston—Lane (1); Chicago—Uribe (1). **CS:** Chicago—C. Everett (1). **Picked off:** Chicago—Iguchi (1). **BB:** Houston—Burke; Chicago—Iguchi. **SF:** Houston—Berkman.

| Houston | IP | H | R | ER | BB | SO | HR | ERA |
|---|---|---|---|---|---|---|---|---|
| Pettitte | 6 | 8 | 2 | 2 | 0 | 4 | 0 | 3.00 |
| Wheeler | ⅔ | 1 | 3 | 3 | 1 | 1 | 0 | 40.50 |
| Qualls | ⅔ | 2 | 1 | 1 | 0 | 0 | 1 | 3.86 |
| Gallo | ⅔ | 0 | 0 | 0 | 0 | 0 | 0 | 0.00 |
| Lidge (L, 0-1) | ⅓ | 1 | 1 | 1 | 0 | 1 | 1 | 27.00 |

| Chicago | IP | H | R | ER | BB | SO | HR | ERA |
|---|---|---|---|---|---|---|---|---|
| Buehrle | 7 | 7 | 4 | 4 | 0 | 6 | 1 | 5.14 |
| Politte | 1 | 0 | 0 | 0 | 0 | 1 | 0 | 0.00 |
| Jenks | ⅔ | 2 | 2 | 2 | 1 | 1 | 0 | 9.00 |
| Cotts (W, 1-0) | ⅓ | 0 | 0 | 0 | 0 | 0 | 0 | 0.00 |

**HBP:** by Wheeler (Dye).

**Attendance:** 41,432 (40,615). **Time:** 3:11.

### World Series
### Most Valuable Player

**Jermaine Dye, Chicago, OF**

| AVG | AB | R | H | HR | RBI | BB |
|---|---|---|---|---|---|---|
| .438 | 16 | 3 | 7 | 1 | 3 | 2 |

### Game 3
Tuesday, Oct. 25, at Houston

| Chicago | AB | R | H | RBI | Houston | AB | R | H | RBI |
|---|---|---|---|---|---|---|---|---|---|
| Podsednik, lf | 8 | 1 | 2 | 0 | Biggio, 2b | 6 | 2 | 2 | 1 |
| Iguchi, 2b | 7 | 1 | 2 | 1 | Taveras, cf | 6 | 0 | 0 | 0 |
| Dye, rf | 7 | 1 | 2 | 1 | Berkman, lf-1b | 5 | 0 | 2 | 1 |
| Konerko, 1b | 4 | 0 | 1 | 0 | Ensberg, 3b | 6 | 1 | 1 | 1 |
| Pierzynski, c | 3 | 0 | 1 | 2 | Lamb, 1b | 3 | 0 | 0 | 0 |
| Perez, ph | 1 | 0 | 0 | 0 | Bruntlett, pr-lf | 0 | 0 | 0 | 0 |
| Blum, 2b | 1 | 1 | 1 | 1 | Palmeiro, ph-lf | 1 | 0 | 0 | 0 |
| Rowand, cf | 6 | 1 | 1 | 0 | Lane, rf | 6 | 1 | 2 | 2 |
| Crede, 3b | 5 | 1 | 2 | 1 | Ausmus, c | 6 | 0 | 0 | 0 |
| Uribe, ss | 6 | 1 | 1 | 0 | Everett, ss | 5 | 1 | 1 | 0 |
| Garland, p | 3 | 0 | 0 | 0 | Oswalt, p | 1 | 0 | 0 | 0 |
| C. Everett, ph | 1 | 0 | 1 | 0 | Bagwell, ph | 1 | 0 | 0 | 0 |
| Harris, pr | 0 | 0 | 0 | 0 | Burke, lf | 1 | 0 | 0 | 0 |
| Widger, c | 1 | 0 | 0 | 1 | | | | | |
| **Totals** | **53** | **7** | **14** | **7** | **Totals** | **47** | **5** | **8** | **5** |

```
                         R   H   E
Chicago . . . . . 000 050 000 000 02 — 7  14  2
Houston . . . . . 102 100 010 000 00 — 5   8  1
```

**E:** Chicago—Uribe 2 (2), Hernandez (1); Houston—Ensberg (1). **2B:** Chicago—Konerko (1), Pierzynski (1); Houston—Biggio (1), Lane (1). **HR:** Chicago—Crede (2, off Oswalt, 0 on), Blum (1, off Astacio, 0 on); Houston—Lane (1, off Garland, 0 on). **SB:** Chicago—Harris (1), Podsednik (2); Houston—Burke (2). **CS:** Houston—A. Everett (1). **BB:** Chicago—Konerko 2, Pierzynski 2, Widger 2, Rowand, Crede, Uribe; Houston—Berkman 2, Palmeiro 2, Biggio, Ensberg, Lamb, Lane, Ausmus, A. Everett, Burke, J. Vizcaino. **S:** Houston—Oswalt, A. Everett.

| Chicago | IP | H | R | ER | BB | SO | HR | ERA |
|---|---|---|---|---|---|---|---|---|
| Garland | 7 | 7 | 4 | 2 | 2 | 4 | 1 | 2.57 |
| Polite | ⅔ | 0 | 1 | 1 | 1 | 1 | 0 | 5.40 |
| Cotts | 0 | 0 | 0 | 0 | 0 | 1 | 0 | 0.00 |
| Hermanson | ⅓ | 1 | 0 | 0 | 0 | 1 | 0 | 0.00 |
| Hernandez | 1 | 0 | 0 | 0 | 4 | 2 | 0 | 0.00 |
| L. Vizcaino | 1 | 0 | 0 | 0 | 1 | 0 | 0 | 0.00 |
| Jenks | 2 | 0 | 0 | 0 | 1 | 3 | 0 | 4.50 |
| Marte (W, 1-0) | 1⅔ | 0 | 0 | 0 | 2 | 3 | 0 | 0.00 |
| Buehrle (S, 1) | ⅓ | 0 | 0 | 0 | 0 | 0 | 0 | 4.91 |
| **Houston** | **IP** | **H** | **R** | **ER** | **BB** | **SO** | **HR** | **ERA** |
| Oswalt | 6 | 8 | 5 | 5 | 5 | 3 | 1 | 7.50 |
| Springer | 1 | 0 | 0 | 0 | 0 | 1 | 0 | 4.50 |
| Wheeler | 1⅓ | 1 | 0 | 0 | 0 | 0 | 0 | 13.50 |
| Gallo | ⅓ | 0 | 0 | 0 | 0 | 0 | 0 | 0.00 |
| Lidge | 1⅓ | 0 | 0 | 0 | 0 | 3 | 0 | 5.40 |
| Qualls | 3 | 1 | 0 | 0 | 2 | 3 | 0 | 1.69 |
| Astacio (L, 0-1) | ⅔ | 4 | 2 | 2 | 0 | 1 | 1 | 27.00 |
| Rodriguez | ⅓ | 0 | 0 | 0 | 0 | 1 | 0 | 2.45 |

**HBP:** by Oswalt (Crede), by Wheeler (Konerko), by Jenks (Taveras). **IBB:** by Hernandez (Berkman), by Qualls (Konerko).
**Attendance:** 42,848 (40,950). **Time:** 5:41.

### Game 4
Wednesday, Oct. 26, at Houston

| Chicago | AB | R | H | RBI | Houston | AB | R | H | RBI |
|---|---|---|---|---|---|---|---|---|---|
| Podsednik, lf | 3 | 0 | 1 | 0 | Biggio, 2b | 4 | 0 | 1 | 0 |
| Iguchi, 2b | 3 | 0 | 0 | 0 | Taveras, cf | 2 | 0 | 1 | 0 |
| C. Everett, ph | 1 | 0 | 0 | 0 | Berkman, lf | 1 | 0 | 0 | 0 |
| Dye, rf | 4 | 0 | 3 | 1 | Ensberg, 3b | 4 | 0 | 0 | 0 |
| Konerko, 1b | 4 | 0 | 0 | 0 | Lamb, 1b | 2 | 0 | 1 | 0 |
| Pierzynski, c | 4 | 0 | 1 | 0 | Vizcaino, ph-1b | 1 | 0 | 0 | 0 |
| Rowand, cf | 4 | 0 | 1 | 0 | Lane, rf | 4 | 0 | 1 | 0 |
| Crede, 3b | 4 | 0 | 1 | 0 | Ausmus, c | 3 | 0 | 1 | 0 |
| Uribe, ss | 4 | 0 | 0 | 0 | Everett, ss | 3 | 0 | 0 | 0 |
| Garcia, p | 2 | 0 | 0 | 0 | Burke, ph | 1 | 0 | 0 | 0 |
| Harris, ph-2b | 1 | 1 | 1 | 0 | Backe, p | 2 | 0 | 0 | 0 |
| | | | | | Bagwell, ph | 1 | 0 | 0 | 0 |
| | | | | | Palmeiro, ph | 1 | 0 | 0 | 0 |
| **Totals** | **34** | **1** | **8** | **1** | **Totals** | **29** | **0** | **5** | **0** |

```
                      R  H  E
Chicago . . . . . . 000  000 010  —  1  8  0
Houston . . . . . . 000  000 000  —  0  5  0
```

**2B:** Chicago—Dye (1), Crede (1), Pierzynski (2); Houston—Lamb (1). **3B:** Chicago—Podsednik (2). **SB:** Houston—Taveras (1), Berkman (1). **BB:** Houston—Berkman 3, Lamb. **S:** Chicago—Podsednik; Houston—Ausmus, Taveras.

| Chicago | IP | H | R | ER | BB | SO | HR | ERA |
|---|---|---|---|---|---|---|---|---|
| Garcia (W, 1-0) | 7 | 4 | 0 | 0 | 3 | 7 | 0 | 0.00 |
| Polite | ⅔ | 0 | 0 | 0 | 1 | 0 | 0 | 3.86 |
| Cotts | ⅓ | 0 | 0 | 0 | 0 | 0 | 0 | 0.00 |
| Jenks (S, 2) | 1 | 1 | 0 | 0 | 0 | 0 | 0 | 3.60 |
| **Houston** | **IP** | **H** | **R** | **ER** | **BB** | **SO** | **HR** | **ERA** |
| Backe | 7 | 5 | 0 | 0 | 0 | 7 | 0 | 0.00 |
| Lidge (L, 0-2) | 2 | 3 | 1 | 1 | 0 | 3 | 0 | 4.91 |

**HBP:** by Polite (Taveras). **IBB:** by Garcia (Lamb), by Polite (Berkman). **WP:** Polite.

**Attendance:** 42,936 (40,950). **Time:** 3:20.

## World Series Composite Box Score
### Chicago White Sox

| Batting | | WS vs. Houston | | | | | | | Overall Playoffs | | | | | | | |
|---|---|---|---|---|---|---|---|---|---|---|---|---|---|---|---|---|
| | Avg | AB | R | H | HR | RBI | BB | SO | Avg | AB | R | H | HR | RBI | BB | SO |
| Geoff Blum | 1.000 | 1 | 1 | 1 | 1 | 1 | 0 | 0 | .500 | 2 | 1 | 1 | 1 | 1 | 0 | 0 |
| Willie Harris | 1.000 | 1 | 1 | 1 | 0 | 0 | 0 | 0 | 1.000 | 2 | 1 | 2 | 0 | 1 | 0 | 0 |
| Carl Everett | .444 | 9 | 1 | 4 | 0 | 0 | 0 | 2 | .300 | 40 | 5 | 12 | 0 | 3 | 1 | 6 |
| Jermaine Dye | .438 | 16 | 3 | 7 | 1 | 3 | 2 | 2 | .311 | 45 | 7 | 14 | 1 | 6 | 6 | 7 |
| Joe Crede | .294 | 17 | 2 | 5 | 2 | 3 | 1 | 2 | .289 | 45 | 6 | 13 | 4 | 11 | 2 | 6 |
| Aaron Rowand | .294 | 17 | 2 | 5 | 0 | 0 | 2 | 6 | .267 | 45 | 8 | 12 | 0 | 3 | 4 | 9 |
| Scott Podsednik | .286 | 21 | 2 | 6 | 1 | 2 | 0 | 4 | .286 | 49 | 9 | 14 | 2 | 6 | 7 | 10 |
| A.J. Pierzynski | .267 | 15 | 3 | 4 | 0 | 3 | 2 | 1 | .262 | 42 | 9 | 11 | 3 | 9 | 4 | 8 |
| Paul Konerko | .250 | 16 | 1 | 4 | 1 | 4 | 2 | 3 | .265 | 49 | 6 | 13 | 5 | 15 | 3 | 8 |
| Juan Uribe | .250 | 16 | 2 | 4 | 0 | 2 | 3 | 3 | .286 | 42 | 7 | 12 | 1 | 6 | 5 | 8 |
| Tadahito Iguchi | .167 | 18 | 2 | 3 | 0 | 1 | 1 | 3 | .191 | 47 | 7 | 9 | 1 | 5 | 2 | 12 |

## World Series Composite Box Score (Cont.)

### Chicago White Sox

| Batting (Cont.) | WS vs. Houston Avg | AB | R | H | HR | RBI | BB | SO | Overall Playoffs Avg | AB | R | H | HR | RBI | BB | SO |
|---|---|---|---|---|---|---|---|---|---|---|---|---|---|---|---|---|
| Chris Widger | .000 | 1 | 0 | 0 | 0 | 1 | 2 | 1 | .000 | 1 | 0 | 0 | 0 | 1 | 2 | 1 |
| Freddy Garcia | .000 | 2 | 0 | 0 | 0 | 0 | 0 | 0 | .000 | 2 | 0 | 0 | 0 | 0 | 0 | 0 |
| Jon Garland | .000 | 3 | 0 | 0 | 0 | 0 | 0 | 2 | .000 | 3 | 0 | 0 | 0 | 0 | 0 | 2 |
| Timo Perez | .000 | 1 | 0 | 0 | 0 | 0 | 0 | 0 | .000 | 5 | 0 | 0 | 0 | 0 | 0 | 0 |
| Pablo Ozuna | — | 0 | 0 | 0 | 0 | 0 | 0 | 0 | .000 | 1 | 0 | 0 | 0 | 0 | 0 | 0 |
| TOTALS | .286 | 154 | 20 | 44 | 6 | 20 | 15 | 30 | .272 | 416 | 67 | 113 | 18 | 67 | 36 | 77 |

| Pitching | ERA | W-L | Sv | Gm | IP | H | BB | SO | ERA | W-L | Sv | Gm | IP | H | BB | SO |
|---|---|---|---|---|---|---|---|---|---|---|---|---|---|---|---|---|
| Dustin Hermanson | 0.00 | 0-0 | 0 | 1 | 0.1 | 1 | 0 | 1 | 0.00 | 0-0 | 0 | 1 | 0.1 | 1 | 0 | 1 |
| Orlando Hernandez | 0.00 | 0-0 | 0 | 1 | 1.0 | 0 | 4 | 2 | 0.00 | 0-0 | 0 | 2 | 4.0 | 1 | 4 | 6 |
| Freddy Garcia | 0.00 | 1-0 | 0 | 1 | 7.0 | 4 | 3 | 7 | 2.14 | 3-0 | 0 | 3 | 21.0 | 15 | 8 | 13 |
| Damaso Marte | 0.00 | 1-0 | 0 | 1 | 1.2 | 0 | 2 | 3 | 0.00 | 1-0 | 0 | 2 | 1.2 | 1 | 4 | 3 |
| Luis Vizcaino | 0.00 | 0-0 | 0 | 1 | 1.0 | 0 | 1 | 0 | 0.00 | 0-0 | 0 | 1 | 1.0 | 0 | 1 | 0 |
| Neal Cotts | 0.00 | 1-0 | 0 | 4 | 1.1 | 1 | 1 | 2 | 0.00 | 1-0 | 0 | 6 | 2.1 | 1 | 1 | 2 |
| Jon Garland | 2.57 | 0-0 | 0 | 1 | 7.0 | 7 | 2 | 4 | 2.25 | 1-0 | 0 | 2 | 16.0 | 11 | 3 | 11 |
| Bobby Jenks | 3.60 | 0-0 | 2 | 4 | 5.0 | 3 | 2 | 7 | 2.25 | 0-0 | 4 | 6 | 8.0 | 4 | 3 | 8 |
| Cliff Politte | 3.86 | 0-0 | 0 | 3 | 2.1 | 0 | 2 | 2 | 2.70 | 0-0 | 0 | 4 | 3.1 | 1 | 2 | 2 |
| Jose Contreras | 3.86 | 1-0 | 0 | 1 | 7.0 | 6 | 0 | 2 | 3.09 | 3-1 | 0 | 4 | 32.0 | 26 | 2 | 14 |
| Mark Buehrle | 4.91 | 0-0 | 1 | 2 | 7.1 | 7 | 0 | 6 | 3.47 | 2-0 | 1 | 4 | 23.1 | 20 | 1 | 12 |
| TOTALS | 2.63 | 4-0 | 3 | 4 | 41.0 | 29 | 17 | 36 | 2.55 | 11-1 | 5 | 12 | 113.0 | 81 | 29 | 72 |

## Houston Astros

### Batting

| Batting | WS vs. Chicago Avg | AB | R | H | HR | RBI | BB | SO | Overall Playoffs Avg | AB | R | H | HR | RBI | BB | SO |
|---|---|---|---|---|---|---|---|---|---|---|---|---|---|---|---|---|
| Jose Vizcaino | .500 | 2 | 0 | 1 | 0 | 2 | 1 | 0 | .111 | 9 | 0 | 1 | 0 | 2 | 1 | 1 |
| Lance Berkman | .385 | 13 | 0 | 5 | 0 | 6 | 5 | 5 | .333 | 48 | 6 | 16 | 2 | 14 | 12 | 12 |
| Willy Taveras | .333 | 15 | 2 | 5 | 0 | 0 | 0 | 3 | .349 | 43 | 5 | 15 | 0 | 0 | 2 | 5 |
| Brad Ausmus | .250 | 16 | 1 | 4 | 0 | 0 | 1 | 3 | .268 | 56 | 7 | 15 | 1 | 2 | 4 | 13 |
| Craig Biggio | .222 | 18 | 3 | 4 | 0 | 1 | 1 | 4 | .295 | 61 | 11 | 18 | 0 | 5 | 5 | 12 |
| Jason Lane | .222 | 18 | 1 | 4 | 1 | 2 | 1 | 5 | .232 | 56 | 5 | 13 | 3 | 8 | 4 | 12 |
| Mike Lamb | .200 | 10 | 1 | 2 | 1 | 1 | 2 | 3 | .250 | 32 | 5 | 8 | 3 | 4 | 4 | 6 |
| Jeff Bagwell | .125 | 8 | 1 | 1 | 0 | 0 | 0 | 1 | .182 | 11 | 2 | 2 | 0 | 1 | 0 | 1 |
| Morgan Ensberg | .111 | 18 | 2 | 2 | 1 | 2 | 1 | 7 | .211 | 57 | 5 | 12 | 1 | 11 | 5 | 12 |
| Adam Everett | .067 | 15 | 2 | 1 | 0 | 0 | 1 | 4 | .212 | 52 | 5 | 11 | 0 | 3 | 2 | 9 |
| Orlando Palmeiro | .000 | 2 | 0 | 0 | 0 | 0 | 2 | 0 | .167 | 12 | 0 | 2 | 0 | 3 | 5 | 0 |
| Roy Oswalt | .000 | 1 | 0 | 0 | 0 | 0 | 0 | 0 | .143 | 7 | 0 | 1 | 0 | 0 | 0 | 0 |
| Brandon Backe | .000 | 2 | 0 | 0 | 0 | 0 | 0 | 0 | .000 | 5 | 0 | 0 | 0 | 0 | 0 | 2 |
| Chris Burke | .000 | 5 | 1 | 0 | 0 | 0 | 2 | 0 | .286 | 28 | 7 | 8 | 2 | 4 | 4 | 3 |
| Eric Bruntlett | — | 0 | 0 | 0 | 0 | 0 | 0 | 0 | .143 | 7 | 1 | 1 | 0 | 0 | 0 | 3 |
| Roger Clemens | — | 0 | 0 | 0 | 0 | 0 | 0 | 0 | .200 | 5 | 0 | 1 | 0 | 0 | 0 | 1 |
| Andy Pettitte | — | 0 | 0 | 0 | 0 | 0 | 0 | 0 | .250 | 4 | 1 | 1 | 0 | 0 | 0 | 1 |
| Luke Scott | — | 0 | 0 | 0 | 0 | 0 | 0 | 0 | .000 | 2 | 1 | 0 | 0 | 0 | 1 | 0 |
| Raul Chavez | — | 0 | 0 | 0 | 0 | 0 | 0 | 0 | .000 | 1 | 0 | 0 | 0 | 0 | 1 | 0 |
| TOTALS | .203 | 143 | 14 | 29 | 3 | 14 | 17 | 36 | .252 | 496 | 61 | 125 | 12 | 57 | 51 | 99 |

### Pitching

| Pitching | ERA | W-L | Sv | Gm | IP | H | BB | SO | ERA | W-L | Sv | Gm | IP | H | BB | SO |
|---|---|---|---|---|---|---|---|---|---|---|---|---|---|---|---|---|
| Brandon Backe | 0.00 | 0-0 | 0 | 1 | 7.0 | 5 | 0 | 7 | 3.00 | 0-0 | 0 | 4 | 18.0 | 13 | 6 | 17 |
| Mike Gallo | 0.00 | 0-0 | 0 | 2 | 1.0 | 0 | 0 | 0 | 0.00 | 0-0 | 0 | 7 | 3.1 | 1 | 1 | 0 |
| Chad Qualls | 1.69 | 0-0 | 0 | 3 | 5.1 | 3 | 2 | 5 | 2.08 | 1-0 | 0 | 9 | 13.0 | 8 | 4 | 10 |
| Wandy Rodriguez | 2.45 | 0-1 | 0 | 2 | 3.2 | 4 | 5 | 2 | 3.86 | 0-1 | 0 | 3 | 4.2 | 5 | 5 | 4 |
| Andy Pettitte | 3.00 | 0-0 | 0 | 1 | 6.0 | 8 | 0 | 4 | 4.26 | 1-1 | 0 | 4 | 25.1 | 27 | 6 | 16 |
| Russ Springer | 4.50 | 0-0 | 0 | 2 | 2.0 | 2 | 0 | 1 | 3.38 | 0-0 | 0 | 5 | 5.1 | 7 | 2 | 3 |
| Brad Lidge | 4.91 | 0-2 | 0 | 3 | 3.2 | 4 | 0 | 6 | 4.26 | 0-3 | 3 | 10 | 12.2 | 12 | 6 | 18 |
| Roy Oswalt | 7.50 | 0-0 | 0 | 1 | 6.0 | 8 | 5 | 3 | 3.29 | 3-0 | 0 | 4 | 27.1 | 22 | 11 | 22 |
| Roger Clemens | 13.50 | 0-0 | 0 | 1 | 2.0 | 4 | 0 | 1 | 5.63 | 2-1 | 0 | 4 | 16.0 | 17 | 5 | 9 |
| Dan Wheeler | 13.50 | 0-0 | 0 | 2 | 2.0 | 2 | 1 | 1 | 4.00 | 0-0 | 0 | 8 | 9.0 | 8 | 4 | 8 |
| Ezequiel Astacio | 27.00 | 0-1 | 0 | 2 | 1.0 | 4 | 2 | 0 | 10.80 | 0-1 | 0 | 2 | 1.2 | 4 | 2 | 2 |
| TOTALS | 4.58 | 0-4 | 0 | 4 | 39.1 | 44 | 15 | 30 | 3.76 | 7-7 | 3 | 14 | 136.1 | 124 | 52 | 108 |

## Score by Innings

| | 1 | 2 | 3 | 4 | 5 | 6 | 7 | 8 | 9 | 10 | 11 | 12 | 13 | 14 | | R | H | E |
|---|---|---|---|---|---|---|---|---|---|---|---|---|---|---|---|---|---|---|
| Houston | 1 | 2 | 5 | 1 | 2 | 0 | 0 | 1 | 2 | 0 | 0 | 0 | 0 | 0 | – | 14 | 29 | 2 |
| Chicago | 1 | 4 | 0 | 1 | 5 | 0 | 4 | 2 | 1 | 0 | 0 | 0 | 0 | 2 | – | 20 | 44 | 3 |

**E:** Houston—A. Everett, Ensberg; Chicago—Uribe 2, Hernandez. **2B:** Houston—Berkman 2, Taveras 2, Ausmus, Biggio, Lane, Lamb; Chicago—Uribe 3, Pierzynski 2, Dye, Crede, Rowand, Konerko. **3B:** Houston—Taveras; Chicago—Podsednik 2. **HR:** Houston—Lane, Lamb, Ensberg; Chicago—Crede 2, Blum, Dye, Podsednik, Konerko. **SB:** Houston—Burke 2, Berkman, Taveras, Lane; Chicago—Podsednik 2, Harris, Pierzynski, Uribe. **S:** Houston—Taveras 2, A. Everett, Ausmus, Oswalt; Chicago—C. Everett, Podsednik. **SF:** Houston—Berkman. **HBP:** by Contreras (Bagwell 2, Ausmus), by Wheeler (Dye, Konerko), by Jenks (Taveras), by Oswalt (Crede), by Politte (Taveras). **LOB:** Houston—34; Chicago—36.
**Umpires:** Joe West, Jeff Nelson, Jerry Layne, Derryl Cousins, Gary Cederstrom, Angel Hernandez.

**COLLEGE**

## Final *Baseball America* Top 25

Final 2005 Division I Top 25, voted on by the editors of *Baseball America* and released after the NCAA CollegeWorld Series. Given are final records (excluding ties) and winning percentage (including all postseason games); records in College World Series and team eliminated by (DNP indicates team did not play in tourney); head coach (career years and four-year college record including 2005 postseason); preseason ranking and rank before start of CWS.

| | Record | Pct | CWS Recap | Head Coach | Preseason Rank | Rank before CWS |
|---|---|---|---|---|---|---|
| 1 Texas | 56-16 | .778 | 5-0 | Augie Garrido (37 yrs: 1542-717-8) | 4 | 5 |
| 2 Florida | 48-23 | .676 | 3-3 (Texas) | Pat McMahon (13 yrs: 527-259-1) | 15 | 7 |
| 3 Tulane | 56-12 | .824 | 1-2 (Baylor) | Rick Jones (17 yrs: 697-299-1) | 1 | 1 |
| 4 Baylor | 46-24 | 657 | 2-2 (Texas) | Steve Smith (11 yrs: 418-258-1) | 11 | 4 |
| 5 Nebraska | 57-15 | .792 | 1-2 (Arizona St.) | Mike Anderson (3 yrs: 140-56) | 50 | 3 |
| 6 Arizona St. | 42-25 | .627 | 3-2 (Florida) | Pat Murphy (21 yrs: 814-394-4) | 9 | 11 |
| 7 Oregon St. | 46-12 | .793 | 0-2 (Baylor) | Pat Casey (11 yrs: 336-234-4) | NR | 3 |
| 8 Tennessee | 46-21 | .687 | 0-2 (Arizona St.) | Rod Delmonico (16 yrs: 634-347) | 34 | 6 |
| 9 CS-Fullerton | 46-18 | .719 | DNP | George Horton (9 yrs: 402-172-1) | 3 | 9 |
| 10 Mississippi | 48-20 | .706 | DNP | Mike Bianco (8 yrs: 298-181-1) | 16 | 9 |
| 11 Georgia Tech | 45-19 | .703 | DNP | Danny Hall (18 yrs: 737-347) | 19 | 10 |
| 12 Arizona | 39-21 | .650 | DNP | Andy Lopez (23 yrs: 828-513-7) | 12 | 12 |
| 13 Rice | 45-19 | .703 | DNP | Wayne Graham (14 yrs: 627-257) | 18 | 13 |
| 14 Clemson | 43-23 | 652 | DNP | Jack Legett (26 yrs: 932-533) | 36 | 14 |
| 15 Miami-FL | 41-19 | .683 | DNP | Jim Morris (24 yrs: 1067-441-3) | 5 | 15 |
| 16 Florida State | 53-20 | .726 | DNP | Mike Martin (26 yrs: 1391-472-4) | 27 | 16 |
| 17 Southern California | 41-22 | 651 | DNP | Mike Gillespie (19 yrs: 738-438-2) | 30 | 17 |
| 18 Louisiana St. | 40-22 | .645 | DNP | Smoke Laval (11 yrs: 416-244) | 2 | 18 |
| 19 Long Beach St | 37-22 | .627 | DNP | Mike Weathers (6 yrs: 197-123) | 22 | 19 |
| 20 Alabama | 40-23 | .635 | DNP | Jim Wells (15 yrs: 670-314) | 43 | 20 |
| 21 Missouri | 40-23 | .635 | DNP | Tim Jamieson (11 yrs: 389-275-9) | NR | 21 |
| 22 Mississippi St. | 43-22 | .662 | DNP | Ron Polk (32 yrs: 1276-624-2) | 28 | 22 |
| 23 Coastal Carolina | 50-16 | .758 | DNP | Gary Gilmore (16 yrs: 637-317) | NR | 23 |
| 24 Pepperdine | 41-23 | .641 | DNP | Steve Rodriguez (2 yrs: 71-55) | 32 | 24 |
| 25 South Carolina | 41-23 | .641 | DNP | Ray Tanner (18 yrs: 808-348-3) | 7 | 25 |

## College World Series

**CWS participants:** Arizona St. (39-23), Baylor (44-22), Florida (45-20), Nebraska (56-13), Oregon St. (46-10), Tennessee (46-19), Texas (51-16), Tulane (55-10).

### Bracket One

June 17—Florida 6 . . . . . . . . . . . . . . . . . . . . . Tennessee 4
June 17—Nebraska 5 . . . . . . . . . . . . . . . . . . . . Arizona St. 3
June 19—Arizona St. 4 . . . . . . . . . . . . . Tennessee 2 (out)
June 19—Florida 7 . . . . . . . . . . . . . . . . . . . . . . Nebraska 4
June 21—Arizona St. 8 . . . . . . . . . . . . . . Nebraska 7 (out)
June 22—Arizona St. 6 . . . . . . . . . . . . . . . . . . . . Florida 1
June 23—Florida 6 . . . . . . . . . . . . . . . . . . . Arizona St. 3

### Bracket Two

June 18—Tulane 3 . . . . . . . . . . . . . . . . . . . . . Oregon St. 1
June 18—Texas 5 . . . . . . . . . . . . . . . . . . . . . . . . Baylor 1
June 20—Baylor 4 . . . . . . . . . . . . . . . . . Oregon St. 3 (out)
June 20—Texas 5 . . . . . . . . . . . . . . . . . . . . . . . . Tulane 0
June 21—Baylor 8 . . . . . . . . . . . . . . . . . . . . Tulane 7 (out)
June 22—Texas 4 . . . . . . . . . . . . . . . . . . . . Baylor 3 (out)

### Championship Series

June 26—Texas 4 . . . . . . . . . . . . . . . . . . . . . . . Florida 2
June 27—Texas 6 . . . . . . . . . . . . . . . . . . . Florida 2 (out)

### Most Outstanding Player

David Maroul, Texas, 3B

| AB | R | H | HR | RBI | AVG |
|---|---|---|---|---|---|
| 16 | 3 | 8 | 2 | 8 | .500 |

### All-Tournament Team

**C**–Taylor Teargarden, Texas; **1B**–Jeff Larish, Arizona St.; **2B**–Joey Hooft, Arizona St.; **3B**–David Maroul, Texas; **SS**–Seth Johnston, Texas; **OF**–Colin Curtis, Arizona St.; Travis Buck, Arizona St.; Andy Gerch, Nebraska; **DH**–Will Crouch, Texas; **P**–Kyle McCulloch, Texas; J. Brent Cox, Texas.

## Annual Awards

Chosen by *Baseball America*, *Collegiate Baseball*, National Collegiate Baseball Writers Association, American Baseball Coaches Association and USA Baseball.

### Player of the Year

Alex Gordon, Nebraska, IF . . . . . . . . . . . . .*BA*, ABCA, Golden Spikes (USA Baseball) Dick Howser (NCBWA)

Shane Robinson, Florida St. OF . . . . . . . . . . . . . .*CB*

### Coach of the Year

Augie Garrido, Texas . . . . . . . . . . . . . . . . .*CB*, ABCA
Rick Jones, Tulane . . . . . . . . . . . . . . . . . . . . . . . .*BA*

## *Baseball America* All-America Team

NCAA Division I All-Americans. Holdover from 2004 First Team in **bold**.

### First Team

| Pos | | Cl | Avg | HR | RBI |
|---|---|---|---|---|---|
| C | Jeff Clement, USC | Jr. | .348 | 15 | 54 |
| 1B | Matt LaPorta, Florida | Jr. | .328 | 26 | 79 |
| 2B | Jim Negrych, Pittsburgh | So. | .349 | 16 | 59 |
| 3B | **Alex Gordon**, Nebraska | Jr. | .372 | 19 | 66 |
| SS | Tyler Greene, Georgia Tech | Jr. | .372 | 12 | 72 |
| OF | Trevor Crowe, Arizona | Jr. | .403 | 9 | 54 |
| OF | Jacoby Ellsbury, Oregon St. | Jr. | .413 | 6 | 47 |
| OF | Shane Robinson, Florida St. | So. | .427 | 6 | 43 |
| DH | Ryan Braun, Miami-FL | Jr. | .388 | 18 | 76 |
| UT | Mike Costanzo, Coastal Car. | Jr. | .379 | 16 | 67 |

| Pos | | Cl | W-L | Sv | ERA |
|---|---|---|---|---|---|
| SP | Lance Broadway, TCU | Jr. | 15-1 | 0 | 1.62 |
| SP | Dallas Buck, Oregon St. | So. | 12-1 | 1 | 2.12 |
| SP | Luke Hochevar, Tennessee | Jr. | 15-3 | 0 | 2.26 |
| SP | Ian Kennedy, USC | So. | 12-3 | 0 | 2.54 |
| RP | Craig Hansen, St. John's | Jr. | 3-2 | 14 | 1.68 |

### Second Team

| Pos | | Cl | Avg | HR | RBI |
|---|---|---|---|---|---|
| C | Nick Hundley, Arizona | Jr. | .352 | 15 | 46 |
| 1B | Steve Pearce, South Carolina | Sr. | .358 | 21 | 63 |
| 2B | Chris Campbell, Charleston | So. | .379 | 15 | 87 |
| 3B | Ryan Zimmerman, Virginia | Jr. | .393 | 6 | 59 |
| SS | Seth Johnston, Texas | Sr. | .378 | 9 | 66 |
| OF | Daniel Carte, Winthrop | Jr. | .344 | 19 | 74 |
| OF | Eli Jorg, Tennessee | Jr. | .381 | 15 | 72 |
| OF | Brian Pettway, Mississippi | Jr. | .383 | 21 | 70 |
| DH | Kris Harvey, Clemson | Jr. | .341 | 25 | 70 |
| UT | Joe Savery, Rice | Fr. | .382 | 5 | 43 |

| Pos | | Cl | W-L | Sv | ERA |
|---|---|---|---|---|---|
| SP | Cesar Carrillo, Miami-FL | Jr. | 13-3 | 1 | 2.22 |
| SP | Mike Pelfrey, Wichita St. | Jr. | 12-3 | 0 | 1.93 |
| SP | Ricky Romero, CS-Fullerton | Jr. | 13-5 | 0 | 2.89 |
| SP | Max Scherzer, Missouri | So. | 9-4 | 0 | 1.86 |
| RP | J. Brent Cox, Texas | Jr. | 8-3 | 19 | 1.73 |

## NCAA Division I Leaders

### Batting

#### Average

| (At least 100 AB & 2.5/Gm) | Cl | Gm | AB | H | Avg |
|---|---|---|---|---|---|
| Corey Wimberley, Alcorn St. | So. | 38 | 132 | 61 | .462 |
| Jay Heafner, Davidson | Jr. | 50 | 203 | 91 | .448 |
| Brett Gardner, Col. of Charles. | Sr. | 63 | 273 | 122 | .447 |
| Carl Lipsey, Jackson St. | Sr. | 46 | 169 | 73 | .432 |
| Matt Kutler, Brown | Jr. | 42 | 171 | 73 | .427 |
| Shane Robinson, Florida St. | So. | 73 | 286 | 122 | .427 |
| Jaime Landin, Texas A&M-CC | Sr. | 53 | 211 | 90 | .427 |
| Aaron Bates, N.C. State | So. | 58 | 214 | 91 | .425 |
| Ryan Roberson, George Wash. | Sr. | 53 | 194 | 82 | .423 |
| Joe Ercolano, Lehigh | Fr. | 43 | 147 | 62 | .422 |

#### Home Runs (per game)

| | Cl | Gm | HR | Avg |
|---|---|---|---|---|
| Adam Tucker, Birmingham-So. | Jr. | 57 | 25 | 0.44 |
| Mark Aranda, New Mexico St. | Sr. | 54 | 22 | 0.41 |
| Jason Maxey, Towson | Sr. | 57 | 23 | 0.40 |
| Nolan Reimold, Bowling Green | Jr. | 50 | 20 | 0.40 |
| Jason Twomley, Massachusetts | Sr. | 41 | 16 | 0.39 |
| Kris Harvey, Clemson | Jr. | 65 | 25 | 0.38 |
| Adam Carr, Oklahoma St. | Jr. | 59 | 22 | 0.37 |
| Beau Mills, Fresno St. | Fr. | 59 | 22 | 0.37 |
| Matt Laporta, Florida | So. | 70 | 26 | 0.37 |
| Steve Pearce, South Carolina | Sr. | 58 | 21 | 0.36 |

#### Runs Batted In (per game)

| (At least 50 RBI) | Cl | Gm | RBI | Avg |
|---|---|---|---|---|
| Mark Aranda, New Mexico St. | Sr. | 54 | 85 | 1.57 |
| Adam Carr, Oklahoma St. | Jr. | 59 | 86 | 1.46 |
| Brandon Taylor, Brigham Young | Jr. | 58 | 83 | 1.43 |
| Luke Hopkins, New Mexico St. | Fr. | 56 | 79 | 1.41 |
| Caleb Moore, East Tennessee St. | Sr. | 52 | 73 | 1.40 |
| Chris Carlson, New Mexico | So. | 57 | 79 | 1.39 |
| Chris Campbell, Col. of Charles. | So. | 63 | 87 | 1.38 |
| Jordan Brown, Arizona | Jr. | 60 | 80 | 1.33 |
| Brad Willcutt, Southern Miss. | Sr. | 62 | 82 | 1.32 |
| Ryan Braun, Miami-FL | Jr. | 58 | 76 | 1.31 |

#### Stolen Bases (per game)

| (At least 25) | Cl | Gm | SB | CS | Avg |
|---|---|---|---|---|---|
| Adam Godwin, Troy | Sr. | 58 | 84 | 9 | 1.45 |
| Carl Lipsey, Jackson St. | Sr. | 46 | 55 | 9 | 1.20 |
| Corey Wimberley, Alcorn St. | So. | 38 | 42 | 5 | 1.11 |
| Zach Penprase, Miss. Valley St. | So. | 48 | 44 | 6 | 0.92 |
| Will Bashelor, Dartmouth | So. | 34 | 30 | 3 | 0.88 |
| Carlos Picornell, Beth.-Cookman | Jr. | 50 | 41 | 10 | 0.82 |
| Jonathan Sakurai, Chicago St. | So. | 55 | 38 | 11 | 0.69 |
| Matt Cooksey, George Mason | Sr. | 50 | 34 | 4 | 0.68 |
| Kraig Binick, NYIT | So. | 46 | 31 | 3 | 0.67 |
| Ryan Keena, IPFW | Jr. | 49 | 33 | 5 | 0.67 |

### Pitching

#### Earned Run Avg.

| (At least 50 inn.) | Cl | Gm | IP | ERA |
|---|---|---|---|---|
| Matt Torra, Massachusetts | Jr. | 14 | 94.2 | 1.14 |
| Nick Hill, Army | So. | 14 | 89.0 | 1.21 |
| Lance Broadway, TCU | Jr. | 19 | 117.0 | 1.62 |
| Craig Hansen, St. John's | Jr. | 31 | 64.1 | 1.68 |
| Mickey Storey, Florida Atlantic | Fr. | 23 | 95.1 | 1.70 |
| Gerard Breslin, La Salle | So. | 27 | 58.0 | 1.71 |
| J. Brent Cox, Texas | Jr. | 42 | 78.0 | 1.73 |
| John Madden, Auburn | Sr. | 44 | 86.1 | 1.77 |
| Josh Schmidt, Pacific | Sr. | 36 | 60.1 | 1.79 |
| Dennis Bigley, Oral Roberts | Sr. | 17 | 109.1 | 1.81 |

#### Wins

| | Cl | Gm | IP | W-L |
|---|---|---|---|---|
| Lance Broadway, TCU | Jr. | 19 | 117.0 | 15-1 |
| Luke Hochevar, Tennessee | Jr. | 19 | 139.2 | 15-3 |
| Kevin Slowey, Winthrop | Jr. | 19 | 136.1 | 14-2 |
| Brian Bogusevic, Tulane | Jr. | 19 | 130.1 | 13-3 |
| Cesar Carrillo, Miami-FL | Jr. | 19 | 125.2 | 13-3 |
| Ricky Romero, Cal St.-Fullerton | Jr. | 18 | 134.0 | |
| Thirteen tied with 12 wins each. | | | | |

### Strikeouts (per 9 inn.)

| (At least 50 inn.) | Cl | IP | SO | Avg |
|---|---|---|---|---|
| Dan Griffin, Niagara | So. | 78.1 | 120 | 13.8 |
| Josh Schmidt, Pacific | Sr. | 60.1 | 89 | 13.3 |
| David Robertson, Alabama | Fr. | 74.0 | 105 | 12.8 |
| Chris Blazek, Vermont | Jr. | 67.1 | 94 | 12.6 |
| Ian Kennedy, Southern California | So. | 117.0 | 158 | 12.2 |
| Anthony Varvaro, St. John's | Jr. | 85.1 | 115 | 12.1 |
| Matt Green, La.-Monroe | Jr. | 105.1 | 141 | 12.1 |
| David Price, Vanderbilt | Fr. | 69.1 | 92 | 11.9 |
| Craig Hansen, St. John's | Jr. | 64.1 | 85 | 11.9 |
| Lance Broadway, TCU | Jr. | 117.0 | 151 | 11.6 |

### Saves

| | Cl | Gm | IP | Sv |
|---|---|---|---|---|
| J. Brent Cox, Texas | Jr. | 42 | 78.0 | 19 |
| Steven Kleen, Pepperdine | Sr. | 29 | 51.1 | 17 |
| Brett Jensen, Nebraska | Jr. | 33 | 46.0 | 16 |
| Brett Harker, Col. of Charles. | Jr. | 28 | 51.0 | 15 |
| Erik Morrison, Ball St. | Sr. | 28 | 41.0 | 15 |
| Tyler Chambliss, Florida St. | So. | 39 | 52.1 | 15 |
| Eight tied with 14 each. | | | | |

## Other College World Series
Participants' final records in parentheses.

### NCAA Div. II
at Montgomery, Ala. (May 28-June 4)

**Participants:** CS-Chico (42-16-1); Central Missouri St. (57-9); Delta St., Miss. (52-10); Florida Southern (51-11); Grand Valley St., Mich. (36-17); North Florida (48-16); Southern Conn. St. (31-14); West Virginia St. (44-16).

**Championship:** Florida Southern def. North Florida, 12-9.

### NCAA Div. III
at Appleton, Wis. (May 27-31)

**Participants:** Chapman (37-11); Cortland St., N.Y. (43-9-1); Hampden-Sydney (27-15); Rowan, N.J. (42-10), Trinity, Conn. (35-9); Wartburg (37-11); Wis.-Whitewater (45-7); Wooster (39-9).

**Championship:** Wis-Whitewater def. Cortland St., 11-4.

## 2005 MLB First-Year Player Draft

First round selections at the 41st First-Year Player Draft held June 7-8, 2005 in New York. Clubs select in reverse order of their standing from the preceding season. In 2005 the Arizona Diamondbacks chose 17-year-old high school shortstop Justin Upton with the top overall pick. It was the sixth time in the last seven years that a high school player has gone in the top spot. Upton's brother, B.J., was the No. 2 overall selection (by the Tampa Bay Devil Rays) in 2002. Note that picks 31-48 are supplemental compensatory selections.

### First Round

| No | | Pos |
|---|---|---|
| 1 | Arizona . . . . . . . Justin Upton, Great Bridge HS San Diego, Calif. | SS |
| 2 | Kansas City . . . . . . . . Alex Gordon, Nebraska | 3B |
| 3 | Seattle . . . . . . . . . . . . . . Jeffrey Clement, USC | C |
| 4 | Washington . . . . . . . Ryan Zimmerman, Virginia | 3B |
| 5 | Milwaukee . . . . . . . . . . . Ryan Braun, Miami-FL | 3B |
| 6 | Toronto . . . . . . . . Ricardo Romero, CS-Fullerton | LHP |
| 7 | Colorado . . . . . . Troy Tulowizki, CS-Long Beach | SS |
| 8 | Tampa Bay . . . . . . . . . . Wade Townsend, Rice | RHP |
| 9 | NY Mets . . . . . . . . Michael Pelfrey, Wichita St. | RHP |
| 10 | Detroit . . . . . . . . . . . . . . . Cameron Maybin | CF |
| 11 | Pittsburgh . . . . Andrew McCutchen, Fort Meade (Fla.) HS | CF |
| 12 | Cincinnati . . . . . . . . Jay Bruce, Westbrook HS Beaumont, Texas | CF |
| 13 | Baltimore . . . . . .Brandon Snyder, Westfield HS Centreville, Va. | C |
| 14 | Cleveland . . . . . . . . . . .Trevor Crowe, Arizona | CF |
| 15 | Chicago-AL . . . . . . . . . . .Lance Broadway, TCU | RHP |
| 16 | Florida . . . . . . Christopher Volstad, Palm Beach Gardens (Fla.) HS | RHP |
| 17 | NY Yankees . . . . . . Carl Henry, Putnam City HS Oklahoma City, Okla. | SS |
| 18 | San Diego . . . . . . . . Cesar Carrillo, Miami-FL | RHP |
| 19 | Texas . . . . . . . . . . . . John Mayberry, Stanford | RF |
| 20 | Chicago-NL Mark Pawelek, Springville (Utah) HS | LHP |
| 21 | Oakland . . . . . .Clifton Pennington, Texas A&M | SS |
| 22 | Florida . . .Aaron Thompson, Second Baptist HS Houston, Texas | LHP |
| 23 | Boston . . . . . . . . . Jacoby Ellsbury, Oregon St. | CF |
| 24 | Houston . . . . . . . . . .Brian Bogusevic, Tulane | LHP |
| 25 | Minnesota . Matthew Albidrez-Garza, Fresno St. | RHP |

| No | | Pos |
|---|---|---|
| 26 | Boston . . . . . . . . . . . Craig Hansen, St. John's | RHP |
| 27 | Atlanta . . . . . . . . . .Joseph Devine, N.C. State | RHP |
| 28 | St. Louis . . . . . Colby Rasmus, Russell County HS Phenix City, Ala. | CF |
| 29 | Florida . . . . . . . Jacob Marceaux, McNeese St. | RHP |
| 30 | St. Louis . . . . . . . . James Greene, Georgia Tech | SS |
| 31 | Arizona . . . . . . . . Matthew Tora, Massachusetts | RHP |
| 32 | Colorado . . . . . . . . . . Chaz Roe, Lafayette HS Lexington, Ky. | RHP |
| 33 | Cleveland . John Drennen, Rancho Bernardo HS San Diego, Calif. | CF |
| 34 | Florida . . . Ryan Tucker, Temple City (Calif) HS | RHP |
| 35 | San Diego . . . . . Cesar Ramos, CS-Long Beach | LHP |
| 36 | Oakland . . . . . . . . . . Travis Buck, Arizona St. | RF |
| 37 | LA Angels . . . . Trevor Bell, Crescenta Valley HS Shadow Hills, Calif. | RHP |
| 38 | Houston . . . . . . . . . . . . . . Eli Iorg, Tennessee | OF |
| 39 | Minnesota . . . . Henry Sanchez, Mission Bay HS San Diego, Calif. | 1B |
| 40 | LA Dodgers . . . . . . .Luke Hochevar, Tennessee | RHP |
| 41 | Atlanta . . . . . . Beau Jones, Destrehan (La.) HS | LHP |
| 42 | Boston . . . . . .Clay Buchholz, Angelina College | RF |
| 43 | St. Louis . . . . . . . . .Mark McCormick, Baylor | RHP |
| 44 | Florida . . . . . . Sean West, Captain Shreve HS Shreveport, La. | LHP |
| 45 | Boston . . . . . . . . . . . . . Jed Lowrie, Stanford | 2B |
| 46 | St. Louis . . . .Tyler Herron, Wellington (Fla.) HS | RHP |
| 47 | Boston .Michael Bowden, Waubonsie Valley HS Aurora, Ill. | RHP |
| 48 | Baltimore . . . . . . .Garrett Olson, Cal Poly-SLO | LHP |

## Minor League Triple-A Final Standings

Division champions (*) and Wild Card (†) winners are noted.

### International League

| North Division | W | L | Pct | GB |
|---|---|---|---|---|
| *Buffalo (Indians) | 82 | 62 | .569 | — |
| Pawtucket (Red Sox) | 75 | 69 | .521 | 7 |
| Rochester (Twins) | 75 | 69 | .521 | 7 |
| Syracuse (Blue Jays) | 71 | 73 | .493 | 11 |
| Ottawa (Orioles) | 69 | 75 | .479 | 13 |
| Scranton-Wilkes Barre (Phillies) | 69 | 75 | .479 | 13 |

| South Division | W | L | Pct | GB |
|---|---|---|---|---|
| *Norfolk (Mets) | 79 | 65 | .549 | — |
| Durham (Devil Rays) | 65 | 79 | .451 | 14 |
| Charlotte (White Sox) | 57 | 87 | .396 | 22 |
| Richmond (Braves) | 56 | 88 | .389 | 23 |

| West Division | W | L | Pct | GB |
|---|---|---|---|---|
| *Toledo (Tigers) | 89 | 55 | .618 | — |
| †Indianapolis (Pirates) | 78 | 66 | .542 | 11 |
| Columbus (Yankees) | 77 | 67 | .535 | 12 |
| Louisville (Reds) | 66 | 78 | .458 | 23 |

#### Playoffs

**First Round** (Best-of-Five)

| | | |
|---|---|---|
| Toledo 3 | ........................... | Norfolk 2 |
| Indianapolis 3 | ........................... | Buffalo 2 |

**Championship** (Best-of-Five)

Toledo vs. Indianapolis

| Sept. 13 | Toledo, 10-8 | at Toledo |
|---|---|---|
| Sept. 14 | Toledo, 6-3 | at Toledo |
| Sept. 15 | Toledo, 8-3 | at Indianapolis |

**Toledo wins Governors' Cup, 3-0**

### Pacific Coast League

#### American Conference

| Northern Division | W | L | Pct | GB |
|---|---|---|---|---|
| *Nashville (Brewers) | 75 | 69 | .521 | — |
| Omaha (Royals) | 72 | 72 | .500 | 3 |
| Memphis (Cardinals) | 71 | 72 | .497 | 3½ |
| Iowa (Cubs) | 64 | 75 | .460 | 8½ |

| Southern Division | W | L | Pct | GB |
|---|---|---|---|---|
| *Oklahoma (Rangers) | 80 | 63 | .559 | — |
| Albuquerque (Marlins) | 78 | 66 | .542 | 2½ |
| Round Rock (Astros) | 74 | 70 | .514 | 6½ |
| New Orleans (Nationals) | 64 | 76 | .457 | 14½ |

#### Pacific Conference

| Northern Division | W | L | Pct | GB |
|---|---|---|---|---|
| *Tacoma (Mariners) | 80 | 64 | .556 | — |
| Salt Lake (Angels) | 79 | 65 | .549 | 1 |
| Portland (Padres) | 70 | 73 | .490 | 9½ |
| Colorado Springs (Rockies) | 65 | 78 | .455 | 14½ |

| Southern Division | W | L | Pct | GB |
|---|---|---|---|---|
| *Sacramento (A's) | 80 | 64 | .556 | — |
| Fresno (Giants) | 68 | 76 | .472 | 12 |
| Tucscon (Diamondbacks) | 68 | 76 | .472 | 12 |
| Las Vegas (Dodgers) | 57 | 86 | .399 | 22½ |

#### Playoffs

**Conference Finals** (Best-of-Five)

| | | |
|---|---|---|
| Nashville 3 | ........................... | Oklahoma 2 |
| Tacoma 3 | ........................... | Sacramento 2 |

**Championship** (Best-of-Five)

Nashville vs. Tacoma

| Sept. 13 | Nashville, 8-6 | at Nashville |
|---|---|---|
| Sept. 14 | Nashville, 11-5 | at Nashville |
| Sept. 16 | Nashville, 5-2 (13 Inn) | at Tacoma |

**Nashville wins PCL Championship, 3-0**

### 2005 International League All-Star Team

As selected by IL managers, coaches and media.

| Pos | Name/Team |
|---|---|
| C | Kelly Shoppach, Pawtucket |
| 1B | Mitch Jones, Columbus |
| 2B | Bernie Castro, Ottawa |
| SS | B.J. Upton, Durham |
| 3B | Edwin Encarnacion, Louisville |
| DH | Brian Daubach, Norfolk |
| OF | John-Ford Griffin, Syracuse |
| OF | Curtis Granderson, Toledo |
| OF | Shane Victorino, Scanton/WB |
| UT | Ryan Garko, Buffalo |
| SP | Zach Duke, Indianapolis |
| REL | Travis Bowyer, Rochester |

### 2005 Pacific Coast League All-Star Team

As selected by PCL managers and media representatives.

| Pos | Name/Team |
|---|---|
| C | Jeff Mathis, Salt Lake |
| 1B | Conor Jackson, Tucson |
| 2B | Andy Green, Tucson |
| SS | Danny Klassen, Round Rock |
| 3B | Mike Coolbaugh, Round Rock |
| DH | Rick Short, New Orleans |
| OF | Todd Linden, Fresno |
| OF | Brandon Watson, New Orleans |
| OF | Aaron Guiel, Omaha |
| RHP | Felix Hernandez, Tacoma |
| LHP | Matt White, New Orleans |
| REL | Jermaine Van Buren, Iowa |

# 1876-2005
# Through the Years

SPORTS ALMANAC

## The World Series

The World Series began in 1903 when Pittsburgh of the older National League (founded in 1876) invited Boston of the American League (founded in 1901) to play a best-of-9 game series to determine which of the two league champions was the best. Boston was the surprise winner, 5 games to 3. The 1904 NL champion New York Giants refused to play Boston the following year, so there was no Series. Giants' owner John T. Brush and his manager John McGraw both despised AL president Ban Johnson and considered the junior circuit to be a minor league. By the following year, however, Brush and Johnson had smoothed out their differences and the Giants agreed to play Philadelphia in a best-of-7 game series. Since then the World Series has been a best-of-7 format, except from 1919-21 when it returned to best-of-9.

In the chart below, the National League teams are listed in CAPITAL letters. Also, each World Series champion's wins and losses are noted in parentheses after the Series score in games.

**Multiple champions:** New York Yankees (26); Philadelphia-Oakland A's and St. Louis Cardinals (9); Boston Red Sox and Brooklyn-Los Angeles Dodgers (6); Cincinnati Reds, New York-San Francisco Giants and Pittsburgh Pirates (5); Detroit Tigers (4); Baltimore Orioles, Boston-Milwaukee-Atlanta Braves, Chicago White Sox and Washington Senators-Minnesota Twins (3); Chicago Cubs, Cleveland Indians, Florida Marlins, New York Mets and Toronto Blue Jays (2).

| Year | Winner | Manager | Series | Loser | Manager |
|------|--------|---------|--------|-------|---------|
| 1903 | Boston Red Sox | Jimmy Collins | 5-3 (LWLLWWWW) | PITTSBURGH | Fred Clarke |
| 1904 | Not held | | | | |
| 1905 | NY GIANTS | John McGraw | 4-1 (WLWWW) | Philadelphia A's | Connie Mack |
| 1906 | Chicago White Sox | Fielder Jones | 4-2 (WLWLWW) | CHICAGO CUBS | Frank Chance |
| 1907 | CHICAGO CUBS | Frank Chance | 4-0-1 (TWWWW) | Detroit | Hughie Jennings |
| 1908 | CHICAGO CUBS | Frank Chance | 4-1 (WWLWW) | Detroit | Hughie Jennings |
| 1909 | PITTSBURGH | Fred Clarke | 4-3 (WLWLWLW) | Detroit | Hughie Jennings |
| 1910 | Philadelphia A's | Connie Mack | 4-1 (WWWLW) | CHICAGO CUBS | Frank Chance |
| 1911 | Philadelphia A's | Connie Mack | 4-2 (LWWWLW) | NY GIANTS | John McGraw |
| 1912 | Boston Red Sox | Jake Stahl | 4-3-1 (WTLWWLLW) | NY GIANTS | John McGraw |
| 1913 | Philadelphia A's | Connie Mack | 4-1 (WLWWW) | NY GIANTS | John McGraw |
| 1914 | BOSTON BRAVES | George Stallings | 4-0 | Philadelphia A's | Connie Mack |
| 1915 | Boston Red Sox | Bill Carrigan | 4-1 (LWWWW) | PHILA. PHILLIES | Pat Moran |
| 1916 | Boston Red Sox | Bill Carrigan | 4-1 (WWLWW) | BROOKLYN | Wilbert Robinson |
| 1917 | Chicago White Sox | Pants Rowland | 4-2 (WWLLWW) | NY GIANTS | John McGraw |
| 1918 | Boston Red Sox | Ed Barrow | 4-2 (WWLWLW) | CHICAGO CUBS | Fred Mitchell |
| 1919 | CINCINNATI | Pat Moran | 5-3 (WWLWWLLW) | Chicago White Sox | Kid Gleason |
| 1920 | Cleveland | Tris Speaker | 5-2 (WLLWWWW) | BROOKLYN | Wilbert Robinson |
| 1921 | NY GIANTS | John McGraw | 5-3 (LLWWLWWW) | NY Yankees | Miller Huggins |
| 1922 | NY GIANTS | John McGraw | 4-0-1 (WTWWW) | NY Yankees | Miller Huggins |
| 1923 | NY Yankees | Miller Huggins | 4-2 (LWLWWW) | NY GIANTS | John McGraw |
| 1924 | Washington | Bucky Harris | 4-3 (LWLWLWW) | NY GIANTS | John McGraw |
| 1925 | PITTSBURGH | Bill McKechnie | 4-3 (LWLLWWW) | Washington | Bucky Harris |
| 1926 | ST.L. CARDINALS | Rogers Hornsby | 4-3 (LWWLLWW) | NY Yankees | Miller Huggins |
| 1927 | NY Yankees | Miller Huggins | 4-0 | PITTSBURGH | Donie Bush |
| 1928 | NY Yankees | Miller Huggins | 4-0 | ST.L. CARDINALS | Bill McKechnie |
| 1929 | Philadelphia A's | Connie Mack | 4-1 (WWLWW) | CHICAGO CUBS | Joe McCarthy |
| 1930 | Philadelphia A's | Connie Mack | 4-2 (WWLLWW) | ST.L. CARDINALS | Gabby Street |
| 1931 | ST.L. CARDINALS | Gabby Street | 4-3 (LWWLWLW) | Philadelphia A's | Connie Mack |
| 1932 | NY Yankees | Joe McCarthy | 4-0 | CHICAGO CUBS | Charlie Grimm |
| 1933 | NY GIANTS | Bill Terry | 4-1 (WWLWW) | Washington | Joe Cronin |
| 1934 | ST.L. CARDINALS | Frankie Frisch | 4-3 (WLWLLWW) | Detroit | Mickey Cochrane |
| 1935 | Detroit | Mickey Cochrane | 4-2 (LWWWLW) | CHICAGO CUBS | Charlie Grimm |
| 1936 | NY Yankees | Joe McCarthy | 4-2 (LWWWLW) | NY GIANTS | Bill Terry |
| 1937 | NY Yankees | Joe McCarthy | 4-1 (WWWLW) | NY GIANTS | Bill Terry |
| 1938 | NY Yankees | Joe McCarthy | 4-0 | CHICAGO CUBS | Gabby Hartnett |
| 1939 | NY Yankees | Joe McCarthy | 4-0 | CINCINNATI | Bill McKechnie |
| 1940 | CINCINNATI | Bill McKechnie | 4-3 (LWLWLW) | Detroit | Del Baker |
| 1941 | NY Yankees | Joe McCarthy | 4-1 (WLWWW) | BKLN. DODGERS | Leo Durocher |
| 1942 | ST.L. CARDINALS | Billy Southworth | 4-1 (LWWWW) | NY Yankees | Joe McCarthy |
| 1943 | NY Yankees | Joe McCarthy | 4-1 (WLWWW) | ST.L. CARDINALS | Billy Southworth |
| 1944 | ST.L. CARDINALS | Billy Southworth | 4-2 (LWWLWW) | St. Louis Browns | Luke Sewell |
| 1945 | Detroit | Steve O'Neill | 4-3 (LWLWLW) | CHICAGO CUBS | Charlie Grimm |
| 1946 | ST.L. CARDINALS | Eddie Dyer | 4-3 (LWLWLWW) | Boston Red Sox | Joe Cronin |

## The World Series (Cont.)

| Year | Winner | Manager | Series | Loser | Manager |
|------|--------|---------|--------|-------|---------|
| 1947 | NY Yankees | Bucky Harris | 4-3 (WWLLWLW) | BKLN. DODGERS | Burt Shotton |
| 1948 | Cleveland | Lou Boudreau | 4-2 (LWWWLW) | BOSTON BRAVES | Billy Southworth |
| 1949 | NY Yankees | Casey Stengel | 4-1 (WLWWW) | BKLN. DODGERS | Burt Shotton |
| 1950 | NY Yankees | Casey Stengel | 4-0 | PHILA. PHILLIES | Eddie Sawyer |
| 1951 | NY Yankees | Casey Stengel | 4-2 (LWLWWW) | NY GIANTS | Leo Durocher |
| 1952 | NY Yankees | Casey Stengel | 4-3 (LWLWLWW) | BKLN. DODGERS | Charlie Dressen |
| 1953 | NY Yankees | Casey Stengel | 4-2 (WWLLWW) | BKLN. DODGERS | Charlie Dressen |
| 1954 | NY GIANTS | Leo Durocher | 4-0 | Cleveland | Al Lopez |
| 1955 | BKLN. DODGERS | Walter Alston | 4-3 (LLWWWLW) | NY Yankees | Casey Stengel |
| 1956 | NY Yankees | Casey Stengel | 4-3 (LLWWWLW) | BKLN. DODGERS | Walter Alston |
| 1957 | MILW. BRAVES | Fred Haney | 4-3 (LWLWWLW) | NY Yankees | Casey Stengel |
| 1958 | NY Yankees | Casey Stengel | 4-3 (LLWLWWW) | MILW. BRAVES | Fred Haney |
| 1959 | LA DODGERS | Walter Alston | 4-2 (LWWWLW) | Chicago White Sox | Al Lopez |
| 1960 | PITTSBURGH | Danny Murtaugh | 4-3 (WLLWLWW) | NY Yankees | Casey Stengel |
| 1961 | NY Yankees | Ralph Houk | 4-1 (WLWWW) | CINCINNATI | Fred Hutchinson |
| 1962 | NY Yankees | Ralph Houk | 4-3 (WLWLWLW) | SF GIANTS | Alvin Dark |
| 1963 | LA DODGERS | Walter Alston | 4-0 | NY Yankees | Ralph Houk |
| 1964 | ST.L. CARDINALS | Johnny Keane | 4-3 (WLLLWWLW) | NY Yankees | Yogi Berra |
| 1965 | LA DODGERS | Walter Alston | 4-3 (LLWWWLW) | Minnesota | Sam Mele |
| 1966 | Baltimore | Hank Bauer | 4-0 | LA DODGERS | Walter Alston |
| 1967 | ST.L. CARDINALS | Red Schoendienst | 4-3 (WLWWLLW) | Boston Red Sox | Dick Williams |
| 1968 | Detroit | Mayo Smith | 4-3 (LWLLWWW) | ST.L. CARDINALS | Red Schoendienst |
| 1969 | NY METS | Gil Hodges | 4-1 (LWWWW) | Baltimore | Earl Weaver |
| 1970 | Baltimore | Earl Weaver | 4-1 (WWWLW) | CINCINNATI | Sparky Anderson |
| 1971 | PITTSBURGH | Danny Murtaugh | 4-3 (LLWWWLW) | Baltimore | Earl Weaver |
| 1972 | Oakland A's | Dick Williams | 4-3 (WWLWLLW) | CINCINNATI | Sparky Anderson |
| 1973 | Oakland A's | Dick Williams | 4-3 (WLWLLWW) | NY METS | Yogi Berra |
| 1974 | Oakland A's | Alvin Dark | 4-1 (WLWWW) | LA DODGERS | Walter Alston |
| 1975 | CINCINNATI | Sparky Anderson | 4-3 (LWWLWLW) | Boston Red Sox | Darrell Johnson |
| 1976 | CINCINNATI | Sparky Anderson | 4-0 | NY Yankees | Billy Martin |
| 1977 | NY Yankees | Billy Martin | 4-2 (WLWWLW) | LA DODGERS | Tommy Lasorda |
| 1978 | NY Yankees | Bob Lemon | 4-2 (LLWWWW) | LA DODGERS | Tommy Lasorda |
| 1979 | PITTSBURGH | Chuck Tanner | 4-3 (LWLLWWW) | Baltimore | Earl Weaver |
| 1980 | PHILA. PHILLIES | Dallas Green | 4-2 (WWLLWW) | Kansas City | Jim Frey |
| 1981 | LA DODGERS | Tommy Lasorda | 4-2 (LLWWWW) | NY Yankees | Bob Lemon |
| 1982 | ST.L. CARDINALS | Whitey Herzog | 4-3 (LWWLLWW) | Milwaukee Brewers | Harvey Kuenn |
| 1983 | Baltimore | Joe Altobelli | 4-1 (LWWWW) | PHILA. PHILLIES | Paul Owens |
| 1984 | Detroit | Sparky Anderson | 4-1 (WWLWW) | SAN DIEGO | Dick Williams |
| 1985 | Kansas City | Dick Howser | 4-3 (LLWWLWW) | ST.L. CARDINALS | Whitey Herzog |
| 1986 | NY METS | Davey Johnson | 4-3 (LLWWLWW) | Boston Red Sox | John McNamara |
| 1987 | Minnesota | Tom Kelly | 4-3 (WWLLLWW) | ST.L. CARDINALS | Whitey Herzog |
| 1988 | LA DODGERS | Tommy Lasorda | 4-1 (WWLWW) | Oakland A's | Tony La Russa |
| 1989 | Oakland A's | Tony La Russa | 4-0 | SF GIANTS | Roger Craig |
| 1990 | CINCINNATI | Lou Piniella | 4-0 | Oakland A's | Tony La Russa |
| 1991 | Minnesota | Tom Kelly | 4-3 (WWLLLWW) | ATLANTA BRAVES | Bobby Cox |
| 1992 | Toronto | Cito Gaston | 4-2 (LWWWLW) | ATLANTA BRAVES | Bobby Cox |
| 1993 | Toronto | Cito Gaston | 4-2 (WLWWLW) | PHILA. PHILLIES | Jim Fregosi |
| 1994 | Not held | | | | |
| 1995 | ATLANTA BRAVES | Bobby Cox | 4-2 (WWLWLW) | Cleveland | Mike Hargrove |
| 1996 | NY Yankees | Joe Torre | 4-2 (LLWWWW) | ATLANTA BRAVES | Bobby Cox |
| 1997 | FLORIDA | Jim Leyland | 4-3 (WLWLWLW) | Cleveland | Mike Hargrove |
| 1998 | NY Yankees | Joe Torre | 4-0 | SAN DIEGO | Bruce Bochy |
| 1999 | NY Yankees | Joe Torre | 4-0 | ATLANTA BRAVES | Bobby Cox |
| 2000 | NY Yankees | Joe Torre | 4-1 (WWLWW) | NY METS | Bobby Valentine |
| 2001 | ARIZONA | Bob Brenly | 4-3 (WWLLLWW) | NY Yankees | Joe Torre |
| 2002 | Anaheim | Mike Scioscia | 4-3 (LWWLWLW) | SF GIANTS | Dusty Baker |
| 2003 | FLORIDA | Jack McKeon | 4-2 (WLLWWW) | NY Yankees | Joe Torre |
| 2004 | Boston | Terry Francona | 4-0 | ST. LOUIS | Tony La Russa |
| 2005 | Chicago White Sox | Ozzie Guillen | 4-0 | HOUSTON | Phil Garner |

## Walk-off HR to Win a Postseason Series

| Year | Player | Team | Series, Game | Opponent | Final Score |
|------|--------|------|--------------|----------|-------------|
| 2005 | Chris Burke | Houston | NLDS Game 4 | Atlanta | 7-6 (18 inn.) |
| 2004 | David Ortiz | Boston | ALDS Game 3 | Anaheim | 8-6 (10 inn.) |
| 2003 | Aaron Boone | NY Yankees | ALCS Game 7 | Boston | 6-5 (11 inn.) |
| 1999 | Todd Pratt | NY Mets | NLDS Game 4 | Arizona | 4-3 (10 inn.) |
| 1993 | Joe Carter | Toronto | WS, Game 6 | Philadelphia | 8-6 |
| 1976 | Chris Chambliss | NY Yankees | ALCS, Game 5 | Kansas City | 7-6 |
| 1960 | Bill Mazeroski | Pittsburgh | WS, Game 7 | NY Yankees | 10-9 |

## Most Valuable Players

Currently selected by media panel and World Series official scorers. Presented by *Sport* magazine from 1955-88 and by Major League Baseball since 1989. Winner who did not play for World Series champions is in **bold** type.

**Multiple winners:** Bob Gibson, Reggie Jackson and Sandy Koufax (2).

| Year | Year | Year |
|------|------|------|
| 1955 Johnny Podres, Bklyn, P | 1974 Rollie Fingers, Oak., P | 1991 Jack Morris, Min., P |
| 1956 Don Larsen, NY, P | 1975 Pete Rose, Cin., 3B | 1992 Pat Borders, Tor., C |
| 1957 Lew Burdette, Mil., P | 1976 Johnny Bench, Cin., C | 1993 Paul Molitor, Tor., DH/1B/3B |
| 1958 Bob Turley, NY, P | 1977 Reggie Jackson, NY, OF | 1994 Series not held. |
| 1959 Larry Sherry, LA, P | 1978 Bucky Dent, NY, SS | 1995 Tom Glavine, Atl., P |
| | 1979 Willie Stargell, Pit., 1B | 1996 John Wetteland, NY, P |
| 1960 **Bobby Richardson**, NY, 2B | | 1997 Livan Hernandez, Fla., P |
| 1961 Whitey Ford, NY, P | 1980 Mike Schmidt, Phi., 3B | 1998 Scott Brosius, NY, 3B |
| 1962 Ralph Terry, NY, P | 1981 Pedro Guerrero, LA, OF; | 1999 Mariano Rivera, NY, P |
| 1963 Sandy Koufax, LA, P | Ron Cey, LA, 3B; | |
| 1964 Bob Gibson, St.L., P | & Steve Yeager, LA, C | 2000 Derek Jeter, NY, SS |
| 1965 Sandy Koufax, LA, P | 1982 Darrell Porter, St.L., C | 2001 Curt Schilling, Ari., P |
| 1966 Frank Robinson, Bal., OF | 1983 Rick Dempsey, Bal., C | & Randy Johnson, Ari., P |
| 1967 Bob Gibson, St.L., P | 1984 Alan Trammell, Det., SS | 2002 Troy Glaus, Ana., 3B |
| 1968 Mickey Lolich, Det., P | 1985 Bret Saberhagen, KC, P | 2003 Josh Beckett, Fla., P |
| 1969 Donn Clendenon, NY, 1B | 1986 Ray Knight, NY, 3B | 2004 Manny Ramirez, Bos., OF |
| | 1987 Frank Viola, Min., P | 2005 Jermaine Dye, Chi., OF |
| 1970 Brooks Robinson, Bal., 3B | 1988 Orel Hershiser, LA, P | |
| 1971 Roberto Clemente, Pit., OF | 1989 Dave Stewart, Oak., P | |
| 1972 Gene Tenace, Oak., C | | |
| 1973 Reggie Jackson, Oak., OF | 1990 Jose Rijo, Cin., P | |

# All-Time World Series Leaders

## CAREER

World Series leaders through 2005. Years listed indicate number of World Series appearances.

## Hitting

### Games

| | Yrs | Gm |
|---|---|---|
| Yogi Berra, NY Yankees | 14 | 75 |
| Mickey Mantle, NY Yankees | 12 | 65 |
| Elston Howard, NY Yankees—Boston | 10 | 54 |
| Hank Bauer, NY Yankees | 9 | 53 |
| Gil McDougald, NY Yankees | 8 | 53 |

### At Bats

| | Yrs | AB |
|---|---|---|
| Yogi Berra, NY Yankees | 14 | 259 |
| Mickey Mantle, NY Yankees | 12 | 230 |
| Joe DiMaggio, NY Yankees | 10 | 199 |
| Frankie Frisch, NY Giants-St.L. Cards | 8 | 197 |
| Gil McDougald, NY Yankees | 8 | 190 |

### Batting Avg. (minimum 50 AB)

| | AB | H | Avg |
|---|---|---|---|
| Pepper Martin, St.L. Cards | 55 | 23 | .418 |
| Paul Molitor, Mil. Brewers-Tor. Blue Jays | 55 | 23 | .418 |
| Lou Brock, St. Louis | 87 | 34 | .391 |
| Marquis Grissom, Atl-Cle | 77 | 30 | .390 |
| Thurman Munson, NY Yankees | 67 | 25 | .373 |
| George Brett, Kansas City | 51 | 19 | .373 |
| Hank Aaron, Milw. Braves | 55 | 20 | .364 |

### Hits

| | AB | H | Avg |
|---|---|---|---|
| Yogi Berra, NY Yankees | 259 | 71 | .274 |
| Mickey Mantle, NY Yankees | 230 | 59 | .257 |
| Frankie Frisch, NYG-St.L. Cards | 197 | 58 | .294 |
| Joe DiMaggio, NY Yankees | 199 | 54 | .271 |
| Hank Bauer, NY Yankees | 188 | 46 | .245 |
| Pee Wee Reese, Brooklyn | 169 | 46 | .272 |

### Runs

| | Gm | R |
|---|---|---|
| Mickey Mantle, NY Yankees | 65 | 42 |
| Yogi Berra, NY Yankees | 75 | 41 |
| Babe Ruth, Boston Red Sox-NY Yankees | 41 | 37 |
| Lou Gehrig, NY Yankees | 34 | 30 |
| Joe DiMaggio, NY Yankees | 51 | 27 |
| Derek Jeter, NY Yankees | 32 | 27 |

### Home Runs

| | AB | HR |
|---|---|---|
| Mickey Mantle, NY Yankees | 230 | 18 |
| Babe Ruth, Boston Red Sox-NY Yankees | 129 | 15 |
| Yogi Berra, NY Yankees | 259 | 12 |
| Duke Snider, Brooklyn-LA | 133 | 11 |
| Lou Gehrig, NY Yankees | 119 | 10 |
| Reggie Jackson, Oakland-NY Yankees | 98 | 10 |

### Runs Batted In

| | Gm | RBI |
|---|---|---|
| Mickey Mantle, NY Yankees | 65 | 40 |
| Yogi Berra, NY Yankees | 75 | 39 |
| Lou Gehrig, NY Yankees | 34 | 35 |
| Babe Ruth, Boston Red Sox-NY Yankees | 41 | 33 |
| Joe DiMaggio, NY Yankees | 51 | 30 |

### Stolen Bases

| | Gm | SB |
|---|---|---|
| Lou Brock, St. Louis | 21 | 14 |
| Eddie Collins, Phi. A's-Chisox | 34 | 14 |
| Frank Chance, Chi. Cubs | 20 | 10 |
| Davey Lopes, Los Angeles | 23 | 10 |
| Phil Rizzuto, NY Yankees | 52 | 10 |

## All-Time World Series Leaders (Cont.)

### Total Bases

| | Gm | TB |
|---|---|---|
| Mickey Mantle, NY Yankees | .65 | 123 |
| Yogi Berra, NY Yankees | .75 | 117 |
| Babe Ruth, Boston Red Sox-NY Yankees | .41 | 96 |
| Lou Gehrig, NY Yankees | .34 | 87 |
| Joe DiMaggio, NY Yankees | .51 | 84 |

### Slugging Pct. (minimum 50 AB)

| | AB | Pct |
|---|---|---|
| Reggie Jackson, Oakland-NY Yankees | .98 | .755 |
| Babe Ruth, Boston Red Sox-NY Yankees | .129 | .744 |
| Lou Gehrig, NY Yankees | .119 | .731 |
| Al Simmons, Phi. A's-Cincinnati | .73 | .658 |
| Lou Brock, St. Louis | .87 | .655 |

## Pitching

### Games

| | Yrs | Gm |
|---|---|---|
| Whitey Ford, NY Yankees | .11 | 22 |
| Mike Stanton, Atlanta-NY Yankees | .6 | 20 |
| Mariano Rivera, NY Yankees | .6 | 20 |
| Rollie Fingers, Oakland | .3 | 16 |
| Jeff Nelson, NY Yankees | .5 | 16 |
| Allie Reynolds, NY Yankees | .6 | 15 |
| Bob Turley, NY Yankees | .5 | 15 |

### Wins

| | Gm | W-L |
|---|---|---|
| Whitey Ford, NY Yankees | .22 | 10-8 |
| Bob Gibson, St. Louis | .9 | 7-2 |
| Allie Reynolds, NY Yankees | .15 | 7-2 |
| Red Ruffing, NY Yankees | .10 | 7-2 |
| Lefty Gomez, NY Yankees | .7 | 6-0 |
| Chief Bender, Philadelphia A's | .10 | 6-4 |
| Waite Hoyt, NY Yankees-Phi. A's | .12 | 6-4 |

### ERA (minimum 25 IP)

| | Gm | IP | ERA |
|---|---|---|---|
| Jack Billingham, Cincinnati | .7 | 25.1 | 0.36 |
| Harry Brecheen, St. Louis | .7 | 32.2 | 0.83 |
| Babe Ruth, Boston Red Sox | .3 | 31.0 | 0.87 |
| Sherry Smith, Brooklyn | .3 | 30.1 | 0.89 |
| Sandy Koufax, Los Angeles | .8 | 57.0 | 0.95 |

### Saves

| | Gm | IP | Sv |
|---|---|---|---|
| Mariano Rivera, NY Yankees | .20 | 31.0 | 9 |
| Rollie Fingers, Oakland | .16 | 33.1 | 6 |
| Allie Reynolds, NY Yankees | .15 | 77.1 | 4 |
| Johnny Murphy, NY Yankees | .8 | 16.1 | 4 |
| John Wetteland, NY Yankees | .5 | 4.1 | 4 |
| Robb Nen, Florida-SF | .7 | 7.2 | 4 |
| Nine pitchers tied with 3 each. | | | |

### Shutouts

| | GS | CG | ShO |
|---|---|---|---|
| Christy Mathewson, NY Giants | .11 | 10 | 4 |
| Three Finger Brown, Chi. Cubs | .7 | 5 | 3 |
| Whitey Ford, NY Yankees | .22 | 7 | 3 |
| Seven pitchers tied with 2 each. | | | |

### Innings Pitched

| | Gm | IP |
|---|---|---|
| Whitey Ford, NY Yankees | .22 | 146.0 |
| Christy Mathewson, NY Giants | .11 | 101.2 |
| Red Ruffing, NY Yankees | .10 | 85.2 |
| Chief Bender, Philadelphia A's | .10 | 85.0 |
| Waite Hoyt, NY Yankees-Phi. A's | .12 | 83.2 |

### Complete Games

| | GS | CG | W-L |
|---|---|---|---|
| Christy Mathewson, NY Giants | .11 | 10 | 5-5 |
| Chief Bender, Philadelphia A's | .10 | 9 | 6-4 |
| Bob Gibson, St. Louis | .9 | 8 | 7-2 |
| Whitey Ford, NY Yankees | .22 | 7 | 10-8 |
| Red Ruffing, NY Yankees | .10 | 7 | 7-2 |

### Strikeouts

| | Gm | IP | SO |
|---|---|---|---|
| Whitey Ford, NY Yankees | .22 | 146.0 | 94 |
| Bob Gibson, St. Louis | .9 | 81.0 | 92 |
| Allie Reynolds, NY Yankees | .15 | 77.1 | 62 |
| Sandy Koufax, Los Angeles | .8 | 57.0 | 61 |
| Red Ruffing, NY Yankees | .10 | 85.2 | 61 |

### Losses

| | Gm | W-L |
|---|---|---|
| Whitey Ford, NY Yankees | .22 | 10-8 |
| Christy Mathewson, NY Giants | .11 | 5-5 |
| Joe Bush, Phi. A's-Bosox-NY Yankees | .9 | 2-5 |
| Rube Marquard, NY Giants-Brooklyn | .11 | 2-5 |
| Eddie Plank, Philadelphia A's | .7 | 2-5 |
| Schoolboy Rowe, Detroit | .8 | 2-5 |

## World Series Appearances

In the 101 years that the World Series has been contested, American League teams have won 60 championships while National League teams have won 41. Note that the Brewers, now in the NL, were in the AL when they won their title. The following teams are ranked by number of appearances through the 2005 World Series; (*) indicates AL teams.

| | App | W | L | Pct. | Last Series | Last Title |
|---|---|---|---|---|---|---|
| NY Yankees* | .39 | 26 | 13 | .667 | 2003 | 2000 |
| Bklyn/LA Dodgers | .18 | 6 | 12 | .333 | 1988 | 1988 |
| NY/SF Giants | .17 | 5 | 12 | .294 | 2002 | 1954 |
| St.L. Cardinals | .16 | 9 | 7 | .563 | 2004 | 1982 |
| Phi/KC/Oak.A's* | .14 | 9 | 5 | .643 | 1990 | 1989 |
| Boston Red Sox* | .10 | 6 | 4 | .600 | 2004 | 2004 |
| Chicago Cubs | .10 | 2 | 8 | .200 | 1945 | 1908 |
| Cincinnati Reds | .9 | 5 | 4 | .556 | 1990 | 1990 |
| Detroit Tigers* | .9 | 4 | 5 | .444 | 1984 | 1984 |
| Bos/Mil/Atl.Braves | .9 | 3 | 6 | .333 | 1999 | 1995 |
| Pittsburgh Pirates | .7 | 5 | 2 | .714 | 1979 | 1979 |
| St.L/Bal.Orioles* | .7 | 3 | 4 | .429 | 1983 | 1983 |
| Wash/Min.Twins* | .6 | 3 | 3 | .500 | 1991 | 1991 |
| Chi. White Sox* | .5 | 3 | 2 | .600 | 2005 | 2005 |
| Cle. Indians* | .5 | 2 | 3 | .400 | 1997 | 1948 |
| Phi. Phillies | .5 | 1 | 4 | .200 | 1993 | 1980 |
| NY Mets | .4 | 2 | 2 | .500 | 2000 | 1986 |
| Fla. Marlins | .2 | 2 | 0 | 1.000 | 2003 | 2003 |
| Tor. Blue Jays* | .2 | 2 | 0 | 1.000 | 1993 | 1993 |
| KC Royals* | .2 | 1 | 1 | .500 | 1985 | 1985 |
| SD Padres | .2 | 0 | 2 | .000 | 1998 | — |
| LA Angels of Anaheim* | 1 | 1 | 0 | 1.000 | 2002 | 2002 |
| Ari. Diamondbacks | .1 | 1 | 0 | 1.000 | 2001 | 2001 |
| Sea/Mil.Brewers* | .1 | 0 | 1 | .000 | 1982 | — |
| Houston Astros | .1 | 0 | 1 | .000 | 2005 | — |

## League Championship Series

Division play came to the major leagues in 1969 when both the American and National Leagues expanded to 12 teams. With an East and West Division in each league, League Championship Series (LCS) became necessary to determine the NL and AL pennant winners. In 1994, teams were realigned into three divisions, the East, Central, and West with division winners and one wildcard team playing a best-of-5 League Divisional Series (see following pages for LDS results) to determine the LCS competitors.

In the tables below, the East Division champions are noted by the letter E, the Central division champions by C and the West Division champions by W. Wildcard winners are noted by WC. Also, each playoff winner's wins and losses are noted in parentheses after the series score. The LCS changed from best-of-5 to best-of-7 in 1985. Each league's LCS was cancelled in 1994 due to the players' strike.

## National League

**Multiple champions:** Atlanta, Cincinnati and LA Dodgers (5); NY Mets and St. Louis (4); Philadelphia (3); Florida, Pittsburgh, San Diego and San Francisco (2).

| Year | Winner | Manager | Series | Loser | Manager |
|------|--------|---------|--------|-------|---------|
| 1969 | E–New York | Gil Hodges | 3-0 | W–Atlanta | Lum Harris |
| 1970 | W–Cincinnati | Sparky Anderson | 3-0 | E–Pittsburgh | Danny Murtaugh |
| 1971 | E–Pittsburgh | Danny Murtaugh | 3-1 (LWWW) | W–San Francisco | Charlie Fox |
| 1972 | W–Cincinnati | Sparky Anderson | 3-2 (LWLWW) | E–Pittsburgh | Bill Virdon |
| 1973 | E–New York | Yogi Berra | 3-2 (LWLWW) | W–Cincinnati | Sparky Anderson |
| 1974 | W–Los Angeles | Walter Alston | 3-1 (WWLW) | E–Pittsburgh | Danny Murtaugh |
| 1975 | W–Cincinnati | Sparky Anderson | 3-0 | E–Pittsburgh | Danny Murtaugh |
| 1976 | W–Cincinnati | Sparky Anderson | 3-0 | E–Philadelphia | Danny Ozark |
| 1977 | W–Los Angeles | Tommy Lasorda | 3-1 (LWWW) | E–Philadelphia | Danny Ozark |
| 1978 | W–Los Angeles | Tommy Lasorda | 3-1 (WWLW) | E–Philadelphia | Danny Ozark |
| 1979 | E–Pittsburgh | Chuck Tanner | 3-0 | W–Cincinnati | John McNamara |
| 1980 | E–Philadelphia | Dallas Green | 3-2 (WLLWW) | W–Houston | Bill Virdon |
| 1981 | W–Los Angeles | Tommy Lasorda | 3-2 (WLLWW) | E–Montreal | Jim Fanning |
| 1982 | E–St. Louis | Whitey Herzog | 3-0 | W–Atlanta | Joe Torre |
| 1983 | E–Philadelphia | Paul Owens | 3-1 (WLWW) | W–Los Angeles | Tommy Lasorda |
| 1984 | W–San Diego | Dick Williams | 3-2 (LLWWW) | E–Chicago | Jim Frey |
| 1985 | E–St. Louis | Whitey Herzog | 4-2 (LLWWWW) | W–Los Angeles | Tommy Lasorda |
| 1986 | E–New York | Davey Johnson | 4-2 (LWWLWW) | W–Houston | Hal Lanier |
| 1987 | E–St. Louis | Whitey Herzog | 4-3 (WLWLLWW) | W–San Francisco | Roger Craig |
| 1988 | W–Los Angeles | Tommy Lasorda | 4-3 (LWLWWLW) | E–New York | Davey Johnson |
| 1989 | W–San Francisco | Roger Craig | 4-1 (WLWWW) | E–Chicago | Don Zimmer |
| 1990 | W–Cincinnati | Lou Piniella | 4-2 (LWWWLW) | E–Pittsburgh | Jim Leyland |
| 1991 | W–Atlanta | Bobby Cox | 4-3 (LWWLLWW) | E–Pittsburgh | Jim Leyland |
| 1992 | W–Atlanta | Bobby Cox | 4-3 (WWLWLLW) | E–Pittsburgh | Jim Leyland |
| 1993 | E–Philadelphia | Jim Fregosi | 4-2 (WLLWWW) | W–Atlanta | Bobby Cox |
| 1994 | Not held | | | | |
| 1995 | E–Atlanta | Bobby Cox | 4-0 | C–Cincinnati | Davey Johnson |
| 1996 | E–Atlanta | Bobby Cox | 4-3 (WLLLWWW) | C–St. Louis | Tony La Russa |
| 1997 | WC–Florida | Jim Leyland | 4-2 (WLWLWW) | E–Atlanta | Bobby Cox |
| 1998 | W–San Diego | Bruce Bochy | 4-2 (WWWLLW) | E–Atlanta | Bobby Cox |
| 1999 | E–Atlanta | Bobby Cox | 4-2 (WWWLLW) | WC–New York | Bobby Valentine |
| 2000 | WC–New York | Bobby Valentine | 4-1 (WWLWW) | C–St. Louis | Tony La Russa |
| 2001 | W–Arizona | Bob Brenly | 4-1 (WLWWW) | E–Atlanta | Bobby Cox |
| 2002 | WC–San Francisco | Dusty Baker | 4-1 (WWLWW) | C–St. Louis | Tony La Russa |
| 2003 | WC–Florida | Jack McKeon | 4-3 (WLLLWWW) | C–Chicago | Dusty Baker |
| 2004 | C–St. Louis | Tony La Russa | 4-3 (WWLLLWW) | WC–Houston | Phil Garner |
| 2005 | WC–Houston | Phil Garner | 4-2 (LWWWLW) | C–St. Louis | Tony La Russa |

## NLCS Most Valuable Players

Winners who did not play for NLCS champions are in **bold** type.

**Multiple winner:** Steve Garvey (2).

| Year | Year | Year |
|------|------|------|
| 1977 Dusty Baker, LA, OF | 1987 **Jeff Leonard,** SF, OF | 1996 Javy Lopez, Atl., C |
| 1978 Steve Garvey, LA, 1B | 1988 Orel Hershiser, LA, P | 1997 Livan Hernandez, Fla., P |
| 1979 Willie Stargell, Pit., 1B | 1989 Will Clark, SF, 1B | 1998 Sterling Hitchcock, SD, P |
| 1980 Manny Trillo, Phi., 2B | 1990 Rob Dibble, Cin., P | 1999 Eddie Perez, Atl., C |
| 1981 Burt Hooton, LA, P | & Randy Myers, Cin., P | 2000 Mike Hampton, NY, P |
| 1982 Darrell Porter, St.L., C | 1991 Steve Avery, Atl., P | 2001 Craig Counsell, Ari., 2B |
| 1983 Gary Matthews, Phi., OF | 1992 John Smoltz, Atl., P | 2002 Benito Santiago, SF, C |
| 1984 Steve Garvey, SD, 1B | 1993 Curt Schilling, Phi., P | 2003 Ivan Rodriguez, Fla., C |
| 1985 Ozzie Smith, St.L., SS | 1994 LCS not held. | 2004 Albert Pujols, St.L, 1B |
| 1986 **Mike Scott,** Hou., P | 1995 Mike Devereaux, Atl., OF | 2005 Roy Oswalt, Hou., P |

## League Championship Series (Cont.)

### American League

**Multiple champions:** NY Yankees (10); Oakland (6); Baltimore (5); Boston (3); Cleveland, Kansas City, Minnesota and Toronto (2).

| Year | Winner | Manager | Series | Loser | Manager |
|------|--------|---------|--------|-------|---------|
| 1969 | E–Baltimore | Earl Weaver | 3-0 | W–Minnesota | Billy Martin |
| 1970 | E–Baltimore | Earl Weaver | 3-0 | W–Minnesota | Bill Rigney |
| 1971 | E–Baltimore | Earl Weaver | 3-0 | W–Oakland | Dick Williams |
| 1972 | W–Oakland | Dick Williams | 3-2 (WWLLW) | E–Detroit | Billy Martin |
| 1973 | W–Oakland | Dick Williams | 3-2 (LWWLW) | E–Baltimore | Earl Weaver |
| 1974 | W–Oakland | Alvin Dark | 3-1 (LWWW) | E–Baltimore | Earl Weaver |
| 1975 | E–Boston | Darrell Johnson | 3-0 | W–Oakland | Alvin Dark |
| 1976 | E–New York | Billy Martin | 3-2 (WLWLW) | W–Kansas City | Whitey Herzog |
| 1977 | E–New York | Billy Martin | 3-2 (LWLWW) | W–Kansas City | Whitey Herzog |
| 1978 | E–New York | Bob Lemon | 3-1 (WLWW) | W–Kansas City | Whitey Herzog |
| 1979 | E–Baltimore | Earl Weaver | 3-1 (WWLW) | W–California | Jim Fregosi |
| 1980 | W–Kansas City | Jim Frey | 3-0 | E–New York | Dick Howser |
| 1981 | E–New York | Bob Lemon | 3-0 | W–Oakland | Billy Martin |
| 1982 | E–Milwaukee | Harvey Kuenn | 3-2 (LLWWW) | W–California | Gene Mauch |
| 1983 | E–Baltimore | Joe Altobelli | 3-1 (LWWW) | W–Chicago | Tony La Russa |
| 1984 | E–Detroit | Sparky Anderson | 3-0 | W–Kansas City | Dick Howser |
| 1985 | W–Kansas City | Dick Howser | 4-3 (LLWLWWW) | E–Toronto | Bobby Cox |
| 1986 | E–Boston | John McNamara | 4-3 (LWLLWWW) | W–California | Gene Mauch |
| 1987 | W–Minnesota | Tom Kelly | 4-1 (WWLWW) | E–Detroit | Sparky Anderson |
| 1988 | W–Oakland | Tony La Russa | 4-0 | E–Boston | Joe Morgan |
| 1989 | W–Oakland | Tony La Russa | 4-1 (WWLWW) | E–Toronto | Cito Gaston |
| 1990 | W–Oakland | Tony La Russa | 4-0 | E–Boston | Joe Morgan |
| 1991 | W–Minnesota | Tom Kelly | 4-1 (WLWWW) | E–Toronto | Cito Gaston |
| 1992 | E–Toronto | Cito Gaston | 4-2 (LWWWLW) | W–Oakland | Tony La Russa |
| 1993 | E–Toronto | Cito Gaston | 4-2 (WWLLWW) | W–Chicago | Gene Lamont |
| 1994 | Not held | | | | |
| 1995 | C–Cleveland | Mike Hargrove | 4-2 (LWLWWW) | W–Seattle | Lou Piniella |
| 1996 | E–New York | Joe Torre | 4-1 (WLWWW) | WC–Baltimore | Davey Johnson |
| 1997 | C–Cleveland | Mike Hargrove | 4-2 (LWWWLW) | E–Baltimore | Davey Johnson |
| 1998 | E–New York | Joe Torre | 4-2 (WLLWWW) | C–Cleveland | Mike Hargrove |
| 1999 | E–New York | Joe Torre | 4-1 (WWLWW) | WC–Boston | Jimy Williams |
| 2000 | E–New York | Joe Torre | 4-2 (LWWWLW) | WC–Seattle | Lou Piniella |
| 2001 | E–New York | Joe Torre | 4-1 (WWLWW) | W–Seattle | Lou Piniella |
| 2002 | WC–Anaheim | Mike Scioscia | 4-1 (LWWWW) | C–Minnesota | Ron Gardenhire |
| 2003 | E–New York | Joe Torre | 4-3 (LWWLWLW) | WC–Boston | Grady Little |
| 2004 | WC–Boston | Terry Francona | 4-3 (LLLWWWW) | E–New York | Joe Torre |
| 2005 | C–Chicago | Ozzie Guillen | 4-1 (LWWWW) | W–Los Angeles | Mike Scioscia |

### ALCS Most Valuable Players

Winner who did not play for ALCS champions is in **bold** type.

**Multiple winner:** Dave Stewart (2).

| Year | Year | Year |
|------|------|------|
| 1980 Frank White, KC, 2B | 1989 Rickey Henderson, Oak., OF | 1998 David Wells, NY, P |
| 1981 Graig Nettles, NY, 3B | 1990 Dave Stewart, Oak., P | 1999 Orlando Hernandez, NY, P |
| 1982 **Fred Lynn**, Cal., OF | 1991 Kirby Puckett, Min., OF | 2000 Dave Justice, NY, OF |
| 1983 Mike Boddicker, Bal., P | 1992 Roberto Alomar, Tor., 2B | 2001 Andy Pettitte, NY, P |
| 1984 Kirk Gibson, Det., OF | 1993 Dave Stewart, Tor., P | 2002 Adam Kennedy, Ana., 2B |
| 1985 George Brett, KC, 3B | 1994 LCS not held. | 2003 Mariano Rivera, NY, P |
| 1986 Marty Barrett, Bos., 2B | 1995 Orel Hershiser, Cle., P | 2004 David Ortiz, Bos., DH |
| 1987 Gary Gaetti, Min., 3B | 1996 Bernie Williams, NY, OF | 2005 Paul Konerko, Chi. 1B |
| 1988 Dennis Eckersley, Oak., P | 1997 Marquis Grissom, Cle., OF | |

*Chicago's Mark Buehrle, Jon Garland, Freddy Garcia and Jose Contreras all pitched complete games in the White Sox' ALCS victory over the Angles in 2005.*

***Did you know***, *the last team to pitch four complete games in a postseason series was the New York Yankees in the 1956 World Series against the Brooklyn Dodgers — Whitey Ford, Tom Sturdivant, Don Larsen (perfect game) and Bob Turley.*

## League Divisional Series

In 1994, leagues were realigned into three divisions, the East, Central, and West with division winners and one wildcard team playing a best-of-5 League Divisional Series to determine the LCS competitors. In the tables below, the East Division champions are noted by the letter E, the Central division champions by C and the West Division champions by W. Wildcard winners are noted by WC. Also, each playoff winner's wins and losses are noted in parentheses after the series score. Each league's LDS was cancelled in 1994 due to the players' strike.

## National League

**Multiple champions:** Atlanta (6); St. Louis (5); Florida, Houston and NY Mets (2).

| Year | Winner | Manager | Series | Loser | Manager |
|---|---|---|---|---|---|
| 1995 | E–Atlanta | Bobby Cox | 3-1 (WWLW) | WC–Colorado | Don Baylor |
| | C–Cincinnati | Davey Johnson | 3-0 | W–Los Angeles | Tommy Lasorda |
| 1996 | E–Atlanta | Bobby Cox | 3-0 | WC–Los Angeles | Bill Russell |
| | C–St. Louis | Tony La Russa | 3-0 | W–San Diego | Bruce Bochy |
| 1997 | E–Atlanta | Bobby Cox | 3-0 | C–Houston | Larry Dierker |
| | WC–Florida | Jim Leyland | 3-0 | W–San Francisco | Dusty Baker |
| 1998 | E–Atlanta | Bobby Cox | 3-0 | WC–Chicago | Jim Riggleman |
| | W–San Diego | Bruce Bochy | 3-1 (WLWW) | C–Houston | Larry Dierker |
| 1999 | E–Atlanta | Bobby Cox | 3-1 (LWWW) | C–Houston | Larry Dierker |
| | WC–New York | Bobby Valentine | 3-1 (WLWW) | W–Arizona | Buck Showalter |
| 2000 | C–St. Louis | Tony La Russa | 3-0 | E–Atlanta | Bobby Cox |
| | WC–New York | Bobby Valentine | 3-1 (LWWW) | W–San Francisco | Dusty Baker |
| 2001 | E–Atlanta | Bobby Cox | 3-0 | C–Houston | Larry Dierker |
| | W–Arizona | Bob Brenly | 3-2 (WLWLW) | WC–St. Louis | Tony La Russa |
| 2002 | WC–San Francisco | Dusty Baker | 3-2 (WLLWW) | E–Atlanta | Bobby Cox |
| | C–St. Louis | Tony La Russa | 3-0 | W–Arizona | Bob Brenly |
| 2003 | C–Chicago | Dusty Baker | 3-2 (WLWLW) | E–Atlanta | Bobby Cox |
| | WC–Florida | Jack McKeon | 3-1 (LWWW) | W–San Francisco | Felipe Alou |
| 2004 | C–St. Louis | Tony La Russa | 3-1 (LWWW) | W–Los Angeles | Jim Tracy |
| | WC–Houston | Phil Garner | 3-2 (WLWLW) | E–Atlanta | Bobby Cox |
| 2005 | C–St. Louis | Tony La Russa | 3-0 | W–San Diego | Bruce Bochy |
| | WC–Houston | Phil Garner | 3-1 (WLWW) | E–Atlanta | Bobby Cox |

## American League

**Multiple champions:** NY Yankees (7); Boston, Cleveland and Seattle (3); Anaheim-Los Angeles Angels, Baltimore (2).

| Year | Winner | Manager | Series | Loser | Manager |
|---|---|---|---|---|---|
| 1995 | C–Cleveland | Mike Hargrove | 3-0 | E–Boston | Kevin Kennedy |
| | W–Seattle | Lou Piniella | 3-2 (LLWWW) | WC–New York | Buck Showalter |
| 1996 | E–New York | Joe Torre | 3-1 (LWWW) | W–Texas | Johnny Oates |
| | WC–Baltimore | Davey Johnson | 3-1 (WWLW) | C–Cleveland | Mike Hargrove |
| 1997 | E–Baltimore | Davey Johnson | 3-1 (WWLW) | W–Seattle | Lou Piniella |
| | C–Cleveland | Mike Hargrove | 3-2 (LWLWW) | WC–New York | Joe Torre |
| 1998 | E–New York | Joe Torre | 3-0 | W–Texas | Johnny Oates |
| | C–Cleveland | Mike Hargrove | 3-1 (LWWW) | WC–Boston | Jimy Williams |
| 1999 | E–New York | Joe Torre | 3-0 | W–Texas | Johnny Oates |
| | WC–Boston | Jimy Williams | 3-2 (LLWWW) | C–Cleveland | Mike Hargrove |
| 2000 | E–New York | Joe Torre | 3-2 (LWWLW) | W–Oakland | Art Howe |
| | WC–Seattle | Lou Piniella | 3-0 | C–Chicago | Jerry Manuel |
| 2001 | E–New York | Joe Torre | 3-2 (LLWWW) | WC–Oakland | Art Howe |
| | W–Seattle | Lou Piniella | 3-2 (LWLWW) | C–Cleveland | Charlie Manuel |
| 2002 | WC–Anaheim | Mike Scioscia | 3-1 (LWWW) | E–New York | Joe Torre |
| | C–Minnesota | Ron Gardenhire | 3-2 (WLLWW) | W–Oakland | Art Howe |
| 2003 | E–New York | Joe Torre | 3-1 (LWWW) | C–Minnesota | Ron Gardenhire |
| | WC–Boston | Grady Little | 3-2 (LLWWW) | W–Oakland | Ken Macha |
| 2004 | E–New York | Joe Torre | 3-1 (LWWW) | C–Minnesota | Ron Gardenhire |
| | WC–Boston | Terry Francona | 3-0 | W–Anaheim | Mike Scioscia |
| 2005 | W–Los Angeles | Mike Scioscia | 3-2 (LWWLW) | E–New York | Joe Torre |
| | C–Chicago | Ozzie Guillen | 3-0 | WC–Boston | Terry Francona |

## Other Playoffs

Ten times since 1946, playoffs have been necessary to decide league or division championships or wild card berths when two teams were tied at the end of the regular season. Additionally, in the strike year of 1981 there were playoffs between the first and second half-season champions in both leagues.

### National League

| Year | NL | W | L | Manager | Year | NL East | W | L | Manager |
|------|-----|-----|-----|----------|------|---------|-----|-----|----------|
| 1946 | Brooklyn . . . . . . . . . .96 | 58 | | Leo Durocher | 1981 | (1st Half) Philadelphia 34 | 21 | | Dallas Green |
| | St. Louis . . . . . . . . .96 | 58 | | Eddie Dyer | | (2nd Half) Montreal . .30 | 23 | | Jim Fanning |
| | Playoff: (Best-of-3) St. Louis, 2-0 | | | | | Playoff: (Best-of-5) Montreal, 3-2 (WWLLW) | | | |

| Year | NL | W | L | Manager | Year | NL West | W | L | Manager |
|------|-----|-----|-----|----------|------|---------|-----|-----|----------|
| 1951 | Brooklyn . . . . . . . . . .96 | 58 | | Charlie Dressen | 1981 | (1st Half) Los Angeles .36 | 21 | | Tommy Lasorda |
| | New York . . . . . . . . .96 | 58 | | Leo Durocher | | (2nd Half) Houston . . .33 | 20 | | Bill Virdon |
| | Playoff: (Best-of-3) New York, 2-1 (WLW) | | | | | Playoff: (Best-of-5) Los Angeles, 3-2 (LLWWW) | | | |

| Year | NL | W | L | Manager | Year | NL Wild Card | W | L | Manager |
|------|-----|-----|-----|----------|------|---------|-----|-----|----------|
| 1959 | Milwaukee . . . . . . . .86 | 68 | | Fred Haney | 1998 | Chicago . . . . . . . . .89 | 73 | | Jim Riggleman |
| | Los Angeles . . . . . . .86 | 68 | | Walter Alston | | San Francisco . . . . . .89 | 73 | | Dusty Baker |
| | Playoff: (Best-of-3) Los Angeles, 2-0 | | | | | Playoff: (1 game) Chicago, 5-3 (at Chicago) | | | |

| Year | NL | W | L | Manager | Year | NL Wild Card | W | L | Manager |
|------|-----|-----|-----|----------|------|---------|-----|-----|----------|
| 1962 | Los Angeles . . . . . .101 | 61 | | Walter Alston | 1999 | Cincinnati . . . . . . . .96 | 66 | | Jack McKeon |
| | San Francisco . . . . .101 | 61 | | Alvin Dark | | New York . . . . . . . . .96 | 66 | | Bobby Valentine |
| | Playoff: (Best-of-3) San Francisco, 2-1 (WLW) | | | | | Playoff: (1 game) New York, 5-0 (at Cincinnati) | | | |

| Year | NL West | W | L | Manager |
|------|---------|-----|-----|----------|
| 1980 | Houston . . . . . . . . .92 | 70 | | Bill Virdon |
| | Los Angeles . . . . . . .92 | 70 | | Tommy Lasorda |
| | Playoff: (1 game) Houston, 7-1 (at LA) | | | |

### American League

| Year | AL | W | L | Manager | Year | AL West | W | L | Manager |
|------|-----|-----|-----|----------|------|---------|-----|-----|----------|
| 1948 | Boston . . . . . . . . . . .96 | 58 | | Joe McCarthy | 1981 | (1st Half) Oakland . .37 | 23 | | Billy Martin |
| | Cleveland . . . . . . . .96 | 58 | | Lou Boudreau | | (2nd Half) Kan. City . .30 | 23 | | Jim Frey |
| | Playoff: (1 game) Cleveland, 8-3 (at Boston) | | | | | Playoff: (Best-of-5), Oakland, 3-0 | | | |

| Year | AL East | W | L | Manager | Year | AL West | W | L | Manager |
|------|---------|-----|-----|----------|------|---------|-----|-----|----------|
| 1978 | Boston . . . . . . . . . .99 | 63 | | Don Zimmer | 1995 | Seattle . . . . . . . . .78 | 66 | | Lou Piniella |
| | New York . . . . . . . .99 | 63 | | Bob Lemon | | California . . . . . . . .78 | 66 | | M. Lachemann |
| | Playoff: (1 game) New York, 5-4 (at Boston) | | | | | Playoff: (1 game) Seattle, 9-1 (at Seattle) | | | |

| Year | AL East | W | L | Manager |
|------|---------|-----|-----|----------|
| 1981 | (1st Half) N.Y . . . . . .34 | 22 | | Bob Lemon |
| | (2nd Half) Milw . . . . .31 | 22 | | Buck Rodgers |
| | Playoff: (Best-of-5) New York, 3-2 (WWLLW) | | | |

## Regular Season League & Division Winners

Regular season National and American League pennant winners from 1900-68, as well as West and East divisional champions from 1969-93. In 1994, both leagues went to three divisions, West, Central and East, and each league also sent a wild card (WC) team to the playoffs. Note that (*) indicates 1994 divisional champion is unofficial (due to the players' strike). Note that **GA** column indicates games ahead of the second place club.

### National League

| Year | | W | L | Pct | GA | Year | | W | L | Pct | GA |
|------|-----|-----|-----|-----|-----|------|-----|-----|-----|-----|-----|
| 1900 | Brooklyn . . . . . . . . . . . . . .82 | 54 | .603 | 4½ | | 1919 | Cincinnati . . . . . . . . . . . . .96 | 44 | .686 | 9 |
| 1901 | Pittsburgh . . . . . . . . . . .90 | 49 | .647 | 7½ | | 1920 | Brooklyn . . . . . . . . . . . . .93 | 61 | .604 | 7 |
| 1902 | Pittsburgh . . . . . . . . . .103 | 36 | .741 | 27½ | | 1921 | New York . . . . . . . . . . .94 | 59 | .614 | 4 |
| 1903 | Pittsburgh . . . . . . . . . . .91 | 49 | .650 | 6½ | | 1922 | New York . . . . . . . . . . .93 | 61 | .604 | 7 |
| 1904 | New York . . . . . . . . . .106 | 47 | .693 | 13 | | 1923 | New York . . . . . . . . . . .95 | 58 | .621 | 4½ |
| 1905 | New York . . . . . . . . . .105 | 48 | .686 | 9 | | 1924 | New York . . . . . . . . . . .93 | 60 | .608 | 1½ |
| 1906 | Chicago . . . . . . . . . . .116 | 36 | .763 | 20 | | 1925 | Pittsburgh . . . . . . . . . .95 | 58 | .621 | 8½ |
| 1907 | Chicago . . . . . . . . . . .107 | 45 | .704 | 17 | | 1926 | St. Louis . . . . . . . . . . .89 | 65 | .578 | 2 |
| 1908 | Chicago . . . . . . . . . . . .99 | 55 | .643 | 1 | | 1927 | Pittsburgh . . . . . . . . . .94 | 60 | .610 | 1½ |
| 1909 | Pittsburgh . . . . . . . . . .110 | 42 | .724 | 6½ | | 1928 | St. Louis . . . . . . . . . . .95 | 59 | .617 | 2 |
| 1910 | Chicago . . . . . . . . . . .104 | 50 | .675 | 13 | | 1929 | Chicago . . . . . . . . . . .98 | 54 | .645 | 10½ |
| 1911 | New York . . . . . . . . . . .99 | 54 | .647 | 7½ | | 1930 | St. Louis . . . . . . . . . . .92 | 62 | .597 | 2 |
| 1912 | New York . . . . . . . . . .103 | 48 | .682 | 10 | | 1931 | St. Louis . . . . . . . . . .101 | 53 | .656 | 13 |
| 1913 | New York . . . . . . . . . .101 | 51 | .664 | 12½ | | 1932 | Chicago . . . . . . . . . . .90 | 64 | .584 | 4 |
| 1914 | Boston . . . . . . . . . . . . .94 | 59 | .614 | 10½ | | 1933 | New York . . . . . . . . . . .91 | 61 | .599 | 5 |
| 1915 | Philadelphia . . . . . . . . .90 | 62 | .592 | 7 | | 1934 | St. Louis . . . . . . . . . . .95 | 58 | .621 | 2 |
| 1916 | Brooklyn . . . . . . . . . . . .94 | 60 | .610 | 2½ | | 1935 | Chicago . . . . . . . . . .100 | 54 | .649 | 4 |
| 1917 | New York . . . . . . . . . . .98 | 56 | .636 | 10 | | 1936 | New York . . . . . . . . . . .92 | 62 | .597 | 5 |
| 1918 | Chicago . . . . . . . . . . . .84 | 45 | .651 | 10½ | | 1937 | New York . . . . . . . . . . .95 | 57 | .625 | 3 |

| Year | | W | L | Pct | GA |
|------|------|-----|----|------|------|
| 1938 | Chicago | 89 | 63 | .586 | 2 |
| 1939 | Cincinnati | 97 | 57 | .630 | 4½ |
| 1940 | Cincinnati | 100 | 53 | .654 | 12 |
| 1941 | Brooklyn | 100 | 54 | .649 | 2½ |
| 1942 | St. Louis | 106 | 48 | .688 | 2 |
| 1943 | St. Louis | 105 | 49 | .682 | 18 |
| 1944 | St. Louis | 105 | 49 | .682 | 14½ |
| 1945 | Chicago | 98 | 56 | .636 | 3 |
| 1946 | St. Louis† | 98 | 58 | .628 | 2 |
| 1947 | Brooklyn | 94 | 60 | .610 | 5 |
| 1948 | Boston | 91 | 62 | .595 | 6½ |
| 1949 | Brooklyn | 97 | 57 | .630 | 1 |
| 1950 | Philadelphia | 91 | 63 | .591 | 2 |
| 1951 | New York† | 98 | 59 | .624 | 1 |
| 1952 | Brooklyn | 96 | 57 | .627 | 4½ |
| 1953 | Brooklyn | 105 | 49 | .682 | 13 |
| 1954 | New York | 97 | 57 | .630 | 5 |
| 1955 | Brooklyn | 98 | 55 | .641 | 13½ |
| 1956 | Brooklyn | 93 | 61 | .604 | 1 |
| 1957 | Milwaukee | 95 | 59 | .617 | 8 |
| 1958 | Milwaukee | 92 | 62 | .597 | 8 |
| 1959 | Los Angeles† | 88 | 68 | .564 | 2 |
| 1960 | Pittsburgh | 95 | 59 | .617 | 7 |
| 1961 | Cincinnati | 93 | 61 | .604 | 4 |
| 1962 | San Francisco† | 103 | 62 | .624 | 1 |
| 1963 | Los Angeles | 99 | 63 | .611 | 6 |
| 1964 | St. Louis | 93 | 69 | .574 | 1 |
| 1965 | Los Angeles | 97 | 65 | .599 | 2 |
| 1966 | Los Angeles | 95 | 67 | .586 | 1½ |
| 1967 | St. Louis | 101 | 60 | .627 | 10½ |
| 1968 | St. Louis | 97 | 65 | .599 | 9 |
| 1969 | West—Atlanta | 93 | 69 | .574 | 3 |
| | East—N.Y. Mets | 100 | 62 | .617 | 8 |
| 1970 | West—Cincinnati | 102 | 60 | .630 | 14½ |
| | East—Pittsburgh | 89 | 73 | .549 | 5 |
| 1971 | West—San Francisco | 90 | 72 | .556 | 1 |
| | East—Pittsburgh | 97 | 65 | .599 | 7 |
| 1972 | West—Cincinnati | 95 | 59 | .617 | 10½ |
| | East—Pittsburgh | 96 | 59 | .619 | 11 |
| 1973 | West—Cincinnati | 99 | 63 | .611 | 3½ |
| | East—N.Y. Mets | 82 | 79 | .509 | 1½ |
| 1974 | West—Los Angeles | 102 | 60 | .630 | 4 |
| | East—Pittsburgh | 88 | 74 | .543 | 1½ |
| 1975 | West—Cincinnati | 108 | 54 | .667 | 20 |
| | East—Pittsburgh | 92 | 69 | .571 | 6½ |
| 1976 | West—Cincinnati | 102 | 60 | .630 | 10 |
| | East—Philadelphia | 101 | 61 | .623 | 9 |
| 1977 | West—Los Angeles | 98 | 64 | .605 | 10 |
| | East—Philadelphia | 101 | 61 | .623 | 5 |
| 1978 | West—Los Angeles | 95 | 67 | .586 | 2½ |
| | East—Philadelphia | 90 | 72 | .556 | 1½ |
| 1979 | West—Cincinnati | 90 | 71 | .559 | 1½ |
| | East—Pittsburgh | 98 | 64 | .605 | 2 |
| 1980 | West—Houston† | 93 | 70 | .571 | 1 |
| | East—Philadelphia | 91 | 71 | .562 | 1 |
| 1981 | West—Los Angeles$ | 63 | 47 | .573 | — |
| | East—Montreal$ | 60 | 48 | .556 | — |
| 1982 | West—Atlanta | 89 | 73 | .549 | 1 |
| | East—St. Louis | 92 | 70 | .568 | 3 |
| 1983 | West—Los Angeles | 91 | 71 | .562 | 3 |
| | East—Philadelphia | 90 | 72 | .556 | 6 |
| 1984 | West—San Diego | 92 | 70 | .568 | 12 |
| | East—Chicago | 96 | 65 | .596 | 6½ |
| 1985 | West—Los Angeles | 95 | 67 | .586 | 5½ |
| | East—St. Louis | 101 | 61 | .623 | 3 |
| 1986 | West—Houston | 96 | 66 | .593 | 10 |
| | East—N.Y. Mets | 108 | 54 | .667 | 21½ |
| 1987 | West—San Francisco | 90 | 72 | .556 | 6 |
| | East—St. Louis | 95 | 67 | .586 | 3 |
| 1988 | West—Los Angeles | 94 | 67 | .584 | 7 |
| | East—N.Y. Mets | 100 | 60 | .625 | 15 |
| 1989 | West—San Francisco | 92 | 70 | .568 | 3 |
| | East—Chicago | 93 | 69 | .574 | 6 |
| 1990 | West—Cincinnati | 91 | 71 | .562 | 5 |
| | East—Pittsburgh | 95 | 67 | .586 | 4 |
| 1991 | West—Atlanta | 94 | 68 | .580 | 1 |
| | East—Pittsburgh | 98 | 64 | .605 | 14 |
| 1992 | West—Atlanta | 98 | 64 | .605 | 8 |
| | East—Pittsburgh | 96 | 66 | .593 | 9 |
| 1993 | West—Atlanta | 104 | 58 | .642 | 1 |
| | East—Philadelphia | 97 | 65 | .599 | 3 |
| 1994 | West—Los Angeles* | 58 | 56 | .509 | 3½ |
| | Central—Cincinnati* | 66 | 48 | .579 | ½ |
| | East—Montreal* | 74 | 40 | .649 | 6 |
| 1995 | West—Los Angeles | 78 | 66 | .542 | 1 |
| | Central—Cincinnati | 85 | 59 | .590 | 9 |
| | East—Atlanta | 90 | 54 | .625 | 21 |
| | WC—Colorado | 77 | 67 | .535 | — |
| 1996 | West—San Diego | 91 | 71 | .562 | 1 |
| | Central—St. Louis | 88 | 74 | .543 | 6 |
| | East—Atlanta | 96 | 66 | .593 | 8 |
| | WC—Los Angeles | 90 | 72 | .556 | — |
| 1997 | West—San Francisco | 90 | 72 | .556 | 2 |
| | Central—Houston | 84 | 78 | .519 | 5 |
| | East—Atlanta | 101 | 61 | .623 | 9 |
| | WC—Florida | 92 | 70 | .568 | — |
| 1998 | West—San Diego | 98 | 64 | .605 | 9½ |
| | Central—Houston | 102 | 60 | .630 | 12½ |
| | East—Atlanta | 106 | 56 | .654 | 18 |
| | WC—Chicago† | 90 | 73 | .552 | — |
| 1999 | West—Arizona | 100 | 62 | .617 | 14 |
| | Central—Houston | 97 | 65 | .599 | 1½ |
| | East—Atlanta | 103 | 59 | .636 | 6½ |
| | WC—N.Y. Mets† | 97 | 66 | .595 | — |
| 2000 | West—San Francisco | 97 | 65 | .599 | 11 |
| | Central—St. Louis | 95 | 67 | .586 | 10 |
| | East—Atlanta | 95 | 67 | .586 | 1 |
| | WC—N.Y. Mets | 94 | 68 | .580 | — |
| 2001 | West—Arizona | 92 | 70 | .568 | 2 |
| | Central—Houston@ | 93 | 69 | .574 | — |
| | East—Atlanta | 88 | 74 | .543 | 2 |
| | WC—St. Louis | 93 | 69 | .574 | — |
| 2002 | West—Arizona | 98 | 64 | .605 | 2½ |
| | Central—St. Louis | 97 | 65 | .599 | 13 |
| | East—Atlanta | 101 | 59 | .631 | 19 |
| | WC—San Diego | 95 | 66 | .590 | — |
| 2003 | West—San Francisco | 100 | 61 | .621 | 15½ |
| | Central—Chicago | 88 | 74 | .543 | 1 |
| | East—Atlanta | 101 | 61 | .623 | 10 |
| | WC—Florida | 91 | 71 | .562 | — |
| 2004 | West—Los Angeles | 93 | 69 | .574 | 2 |
| | Central—St. Louis | 105 | 57 | .648 | 13 |
| | East—Atlanta | 96 | 66 | .593 | 10 |
| | WC—Houston | 92 | 70 | .568 | — |
| 2005 | West—San Diego | 82 | 80 | .506 | 5 |
| | Central—St. Louis | 100 | 62 | .617 | 11 |
| | East—Atlanta | 90 | 72 | .556 | 2 |
| | WC—Houston | 89 | 73 | .549 | — |

†**Regular season playoffs:** See "Other Playoffs" on page 102 for details.
$**Divisional playoffs:** See "Other Playoffs" on page 102 for details.
@In 2001, Houston (93-69) won the Central over St. Louis (93-69) due to a better head-to-head record.

## Regular Season League & Division Winners (Cont.)
### American League

| Year | | W | L | Pct | GA | Year | | W | L | Pct | GA |
|---|---|---|---|---|---|---|---|---|---|---|---|
| 1901 | Chicago | .83 | 53 | .610 | 4 | 1967 | Boston | .92 | 70 | .568 | 1 |
| 1902 | Philadelphia | .83 | 53 | .610 | 5 | 1968 | Detroit | .103 | 59 | .636 | 12 |
| 1903 | Boston | .91 | 47 | .659 | 14½ | 1969 | West—Minnesota | .97 | 65 | .599 | 9 |
| 1904 | Boston | .95 | 59 | .617 | 1½ | | East—Baltimore | .109 | 53 | .673 | 19 |
| 1905 | Philadelphia | .92 | 56 | .622 | 2 | 1970 | West—Minnesota | .98 | 64 | .605 | 9 |
| 1906 | Chicago | .93 | 58 | .616 | 3 | | East—Baltimore | .108 | 54 | .667 | 15 |
| 1907 | Detroit | .92 | 58 | .613 | 1½ | 1971 | West—Oakland | .101 | 60 | .627 | 16 |
| 1908 | Detroit | .90 | 63 | .588 | ½ | | East—Baltimore | .101 | 57 | .639 | 12 |
| 1909 | Detroit | .98 | 54 | .645 | 3½ | 1972 | West—Oakland | .93 | 62 | .600 | 5½ |
| 1910 | Philadelphia | .102 | 48 | .680 | 14½ | | East—Detroit | .86 | 70 | .551 | ½ |
| 1911 | Philadelphia | .101 | 50 | .669 | 13½ | 1973 | West—Oakland | .94 | 68 | .580 | 6 |
| 1912 | Boston | .105 | 47 | .691 | 14 | | East—Baltimore | .97 | 65 | .599 | 8 |
| 1913 | Philadelphia | .96 | 57 | .627 | 6½ | 1974 | West—Oakland | .90 | 72 | .556 | 5 |
| 1914 | Philadelphia | .99 | 53 | .651 | 8½ | | East—Baltimore | .91 | 71 | .562 | 2 |
| 1915 | Boston | .101 | 50 | .669 | 2½ | 1975 | West—Oakland | .98 | 64 | .605 | 7 |
| 1916 | Boston | .91 | 63 | .591 | 2 | | East—Boston | .95 | 65 | .594 | 4½ |
| 1917 | Chicago | .100 | 54 | .649 | 9 | 1976 | West—KansasCity | .90 | 72 | .556 | 2½ |
| 1918 | Boston | .75 | 51 | .595 | 2½ | | East—New York | .97 | 62 | .610 | 10½ |
| 1919 | Chicago | .88 | 52 | .629 | 3½ | 1977 | West—Kansas City | .102 | 60 | .630 | 8 |
| 1920 | Cleveland | .98 | 56 | .636 | 2 | | East—New York | .100 | 62 | .617 | 2½ |
| 1921 | New York | .98 | 55 | .641 | 4½ | 1978 | West—Kansas City | .92 | 70 | .568 | 5 |
| 1922 | New York | .94 | 60 | .610 | 1 | | East—New York† | .100 | 63 | .613 | 1 |
| 1923 | New York | .98 | 54 | .645 | 16 | 1979 | West—California | .88 | 74 | .543 | 3 |
| 1924 | Washington | .92 | 62 | .597 | 2 | | East—Baltimore | .102 | 57 | .642 | 8 |
| 1925 | Washington | .96 | 55 | .636 | 8½ | 1980 | West—Kansas City | .97 | 65 | .599 | 14 |
| 1926 | New York | .91 | 63 | .591 | 3 | | East—New York | .103 | 59 | .636 | 3 |
| 1927 | New York | .110 | 44 | .714 | 19 | 1981 | West—Oakland$ | .64 | 45 | .587 | — |
| 1928 | New York | .101 | 53 | .656 | 2½ | | East—New York$ | .59 | 48 | .551 | — |
| 1929 | Philadelphia | .104 | 46 | .693 | 18 | 1982 | West—California | .93 | 69 | .574 | 3 |
| 1930 | Philadelphia | .102 | 52 | .662 | 8 | | East—Milwaukee | .95 | 67 | .586 | 1 |
| 1931 | Philadelphia | .107 | 45 | .704 | 13½ | 1983 | West—Chicago | .99 | 63 | .611 | 20 |
| 1932 | New York | .107 | 47 | .695 | 13 | | East—Baltimore | .98 | 64 | .605 | 6 |
| 1933 | Washington | .99 | 53 | .651 | 7 | 1984 | West—Kansas City | .84 | 78 | .519 | 3 |
| 1934 | Detroit | .101 | 53 | .656 | 7 | | East—Detroit | .104 | 58 | .642 | 15 |
| 1935 | Detroit | .93 | 58 | .616 | 3 | 1985 | West—Kansas City | .91 | 71 | .562 | 1 |
| 1936 | New York | .102 | 51 | .667 | 19½ | | East—Toronto | .99 | 62 | .615 | 2 |
| 1937 | New York | .102 | 52 | .662 | 13 | 1986 | West—California | .92 | 70 | .568 | 5 |
| 1938 | New York | .99 | 53 | .651 | 9½ | | East—Boston | .95 | 66 | .590 | 5½ |
| 1939 | New York | .106 | 45 | .702 | 17 | 1987 | West—Minnesota | .85 | 77 | .525 | 2 |
| 1940 | Detroit | .90 | 64 | .584 | 1 | | East—Detroit | .98 | 64 | .605 | 2 |
| 1941 | New York | .101 | 53 | .656 | 17 | 1988 | West—Oakland | .104 | 58 | .642 | 13 |
| 1942 | New York | .103 | 51 | .669 | 9 | | East—Boston | .89 | 73 | .549 | 1 |
| 1943 | New York | .98 | 56 | .636 | 13½ | 1989 | West—Oakland | .99 | 63 | .611 | 7 |
| 1944 | St. Louis | .89 | 65 | .578 | 1 | | East—Toronto | .89 | 73 | .549 | 2 |
| 1945 | Detroit | .88 | 65 | .575 | 1½ | 1990 | West—Oakland | .103 | 59 | .636 | 9 |
| 1946 | Boston | .104 | 50 | .675 | 12 | | East—Boston | .88 | 74 | .543 | 2 |
| 1947 | New York | .97 | 57 | .630 | 12 | 1991 | West—Minnesota | .95 | 67 | .586 | 8 |
| 1948 | Cleveland† | .97 | 58 | .626 | 1 | | East—Toronto | .91 | 71 | .562 | 7 |
| 1949 | New York | .97 | 57 | .630 | 1 | 1992 | West—Oakland | .96 | 66 | .593 | 6 |
| 1950 | New York | .98 | 56 | .636 | 3 | | East—Toronto | .96 | 66 | .593 | 4 |
| 1951 | New York | .98 | 56 | .636 | 5 | 1993 | West—Chicago | .94 | 68 | .580 | 8 |
| 1952 | New York | .95 | 59 | .617 | 2 | | East—Toronto | .95 | 67 | .586 | 7 |
| 1953 | New York | .99 | 52 | .656 | 8½ | 1994 | West—Texas* | .52 | 62 | .456 | 1 |
| 1954 | Cleveland | .111 | 43 | .721 | 8 | | Central—Chicago* | .67 | 46 | .593 | 1 |
| 1955 | New York | .96 | 58 | .623 | 3 | | East—New York* | .70 | 43 | .619 | 6½ |
| 1956 | New York | .97 | 57 | .630 | 9 | 1995 | West—Seattle† | .79 | 66 | .545 | 1 |
| 1957 | New York | .98 | 56 | .636 | 8 | | Central—Cleveland | .100 | 44 | .694 | 30 |
| 1958 | New York | .92 | 62 | .597 | 10 | | East—Boston | .86 | 58 | .597 | 7 |
| 1959 | Chicago | .94 | 60 | .610 | 5 | | WC—New York | .79 | 65 | .549 | — |
| 1960 | New York | .97 | 57 | .630 | 8 | 1996 | West—Texas | .90 | 72 | .556 | 4½ |
| 1961 | New York | .109 | 53 | .673 | 8 | | Central—Cleveland | .99 | 62 | .615 | 14½ |
| 1962 | New York | .96 | 66 | .593 | 5 | | East—New York | .92 | 70 | .568 | 4 |
| 1963 | New York | .104 | 57 | .646 | 10½ | | WC—Baltimore | .88 | 74 | .543 | — |
| 1964 | New York | .99 | 63 | .611 | 1 | 1997 | West—Seattle | .90 | 72 | .556 | 6 |
| 1965 | Minnesota | .102 | 60 | .630 | 7 | | Central—Cleveland | .86 | 75 | .534 | 6 |
| 1966 | Baltimore | .97 | 63 | .606 | 9 | | East—Baltimore | .98 | 64 | .605 | 2 |
| | | | | | | | WC—New York | .96 | 66 | .593 | — |

| Year | | W | L | Pct | GA | Year | | W | L | Pct | GA |
|------|--|---|---|-----|-----|------|--|---|---|-----|-----|
| 1998 | West—Texas | 88 | 74 | .543 | 3 | 2002 | West—Oakland | 103 | 59 | .636 | 4 |
| | Central—Cleveland | 89 | 73 | .549 | 9 | | Central—Minnesota | 94 | 67 | .584 | 13½ |
| | East—New York | 114 | 48 | .704 | 22 | | East—New York | 103 | 58 | .640 | 10½ |
| | WC—Boston | 92 | 70 | .568 | — | | WC—Anaheim | 99 | 63 | .611 | — |
| 1999 | West—Texas | 95 | 67 | .586 | 8 | 2003 | West—Oakland | 96 | 66 | .593 | 3 |
| | Central—Cleveland | 97 | 65 | .599 | 21½ | | Central—Minnesota | 90 | 72 | .556 | 4 |
| | East—New York | 98 | 64 | .605 | 4 | | East—New York | 101 | 61 | .623 | 6 |
| | WC—Boston | 94 | 68 | .580 | - | | WC—Boston | 95 | 67 | .586 | — |
| 2000 | West—Oakland | 91 | 70 | .565 | ½ | 2004 | West—Anaheim | 92 | 70 | .568 | 1 |
| | Central—Chicago | 95 | 67 | .586 | 5 | | Central—Minnesota | 92 | 70 | .568 | 9 |
| | East—New York | 87 | 74 | .540 | 2½ | | East—New York | 101 | 61 | .623 | 3 |
| | WC—Seattle | 91 | 71 | .562 | — | | WC—Boston | 98 | 64 | .605 | — |
| 2001 | West—Seattle | 116 | 46 | .716 | 14 | 2005 | West—Los Angeles | 95 | 67 | .586 | 7 |
| | Central—Cleveland | 91 | 71 | .562 | 6 | | Central—Chicago | 99 | 63 | .611 | 6 |
| | East—New York | 95 | 65 | .594 | 13½ | | East—New York@ | 95 | 67 | .586 | — |
| | WC—Oakland | 102 | 60 | .630 | — | | WC—Boston | 95 | 67 | .586 | — |

†**Regular season playoffs:** See "Other Playoffs" on page 102 for details.
$**Divisional playoffs:** See "Other Playoffs" on page 102 for details.
@In 2005, New York (95-67) won the East over Boston (95-67) due to a better head-to-head record.

## The All-Star Game

Baseball's first All-Star Game was held on July 6, 1933, before 47,595 at Comiskey Park in Chicago. From that year on, the All-Star Game has matched the best players in the American League against the best in the National. From 1959-62, two All-Star Games were played. The only year an All-Star Game wasn't played was 1945, when World War II travel restrictions made it necessary to cancel the meeting. The NL leads the series, 40-34-2. In the chart below, the American League is listed in **bold** type.

Since 2002, the game's MVP award has been named the Ted Williams Award, after the Red Sox Hall of Famer. Beginning in 2003, the league that won the All-Star Game received home-field advantage in that season's World Series.

**MVP Multiple winners:** Gary Carter, Steve Garvey, Willie Mays and Cal Ripken Jr. (2).

| Year | | Host | AL Manager | NL Manager | MVP |
|------|--|------|------------|------------|-----|
| 1933 | **American,** 4-2 | Chicago (AL) | Connie Mack | John McGraw | No award |
| 1934 | **American,** 9-7 | New York (NL) | Joe Cronin | Bill Terry | No award |
| 1935 | **American,** 4-1 | Cleveland | Mickey Cochrane | Frankie Frisch | No award |
| 1936 | National, 4-3 | Boston (NL) | Joe McCarthy | Charlie Grimm | No award |
| 1937 | **American,** 8-3 | Washington | Joe McCarthy | Bill Terry | No award |
| 1938 | National, 4-1 | Cincinnati | Joe McCarthy | Bill Terry | No award |
| 1939 | **American,** 3-1 | New York (AL) | Joe McCarthy | Gabby Hartnett | No award |
| 1940 | National, 4-0 | St. Louis (NL) | Joe Cronin | Bill McKechnie | No award |
| 1941 | **American,** 7-5 | Detroit | Del Baker | Bill McKechnie | No award |
| 1942 | **American,** 3-1 | New York (NL) | Joe McCarthy | Leo Durocher | No award |
| 1943 | **American,** 5-3 | Philadelphia (AL) | Joe McCarthy | Billy Southworth | No award |
| 1944 | National, 7-1 | Pittsburgh | Joe McCarthy | Billy Southworth | No award |
| 1945 | Not held | | | | |
| 1946 | **American,** 12-0 | Boston (AL) | Steve O'Neill | Charlie Grimm | No award |
| 1947 | **American,** 2-1 | Chicago (NL) | Joe Cronin | Eddie Dyer | No award |
| 1948 | **American,** 5-2 | St. Louis (AL) | Bucky Harris | Leo Durocher | No award |
| 1949 | **American,** 11-7 | Brooklyn | Lou Boudreau | Billy Southworth | No award |
| 1950 | National, 4-3 (14) | Chicago (AL) | Casey Stengel | Burt Shotton | No award |
| 1951 | National, 8-3 | Detroit | Casey Stengel | Eddie Sawyer | No award |
| 1952 | National, 3-2 (5, rain) | Philadelphia (NL) | Casey Stengel | Leo Durocher | No award |
| 1953 | National, 5-1 | Cincinnati | Casey Stengel | Charlie Dressen | No award |
| 1954 | **American,** 11-9 | Cleveland | Casey Stengel | Walter Alston | No award |
| 1955 | National, 6-5 (12) | Milwaukee | Al Lopez | Leo Durocher | No award |
| 1956 | National, 7-3 | Washington | Casey Stengel | Walter Alston | No award |
| 1957 | **American,** 6-5 | St. Louis | Casey Stengel | Walter Alston | No award |
| 1958 | **American,** 4-3 | Baltimore | Casey Stengel | Fred Haney | No award |
| 1959-a | National, 5-4 | Pittsburgh | Casey Stengel | Fred Haney | No award |
| 1959-b | **American,** 5-3 | Los Angeles | Casey Stengel | Fred Haney | No award |
| 1960-a | National, 5-3 | Kansas City | Al Lopez | Walter Alston | No award |
| 1960-b | National, 6-0 | New York | Al Lopez | Walter Alston | No award |
| 1961-a | National, 5-4 (10) | San Francisco | Paul Richards | Danny Murtaugh | No award |
| 1961-b | TIE, 1-1 (9, rain) | Boston | Paul Richards | Danny Murtaugh | No award |
| 1962-a | National, 3-1 | Washington | Ralph Houk | Fred Hutchinson | Maury Wills, LA (NL), SS |
| 1962-b | **American,** 9-4 | Chicago (NL) | Ralph Houk | Fred Hutchinson | Leon Wagner, LA (AL), OF |
| 1963 | National, 5-3 | Cleveland | Ralph Houk | Alvin Dark | Willie Mays, SF, OF |
| 1964 | National, 7-4 | New York (NL) | Al Lopez | Walter Alston | Johnny Callison, Phi., OF |
| 1965 | National, 6-5 | Minnesota | Al Lopez | Gene Mauch | Juan Marichal, SF, P |
| 1966 | National, 2-1 (10) | St. Louis | Sam Mele | Walter Alston | Brooks Robinson, Bal., 3B |
| 1967 | National, 2-1 (15) | California | Hank Bauer | Walter Alston | Tony Perez, Cin., 3B |

## The All-Star Game (Cont.)

| Year | | Host | AL Manager | NL Manager | MVP |
|------|------|------|------------|------------|-----|
| 1968 | National, 1-0 | Houston | Dick Williams | Red Schoendienst | Willie Mays, SF, OF |
| 1969 | National, 9-3 | Washington | Mayo Smith | Red Schoendienst | Willie McCovey, SF, 1B |
| 1970 | National, 5-4 (12) | Cincinnati | Earl Weaver | Gil Hodges | Carl Yastrzemski, Bos., OF-1B |
| 1971 | **American,** 6-4 | Detroit | Earl Weaver | Sparky Anderson | Frank Robinson, Bal., OF |
| 1972 | National, 4-3 (10) | Atlanta | Earl Weaver | Danny Murtaugh | Joe Morgan, Con., 2B |
| 1973 | National, 7-1 | Kansas | Dick Williams | Sparky Anderson | Bobby Bonds, SF, OF |
| 1974 | National, 7-2 | Pittsburgh | Dick Williams | Yogi Berra | Steve Garvey, LA, 1B |
| 1975 | National, 6-3 | Milwaukee | Alvin Dark | Walter Alston | Bill Madlock, Chi. (NL), 3B & Jon Matlack, NY (NL), P |
| 1976 | National, 7-1 | Philadelphia | Darrell Johnson | Sparky Anderson | George Foster, Cin., OF |
| 1977 | National, 7-5 | New York (AL) | Billy Martin | Sparky Anderson | Don Sutton, LA, P |
| 1978 | National, 7-3 | San Diego | Billy Martin | Tommy Lasorda | Steve Garvey, LA, 1B |
| 1979 | National, 7-6 | Seattle | Bob Lemon | Tommy Lasorda | Dave Parker, Pit, OF |
| 1980 | National, 4-2 | Los Angeles | Earl Weaver | Chuck Tanner | Ken Griffey, Cin., OF |
| 1981 | National, 5-4 | Cleveland | Jim Frey | Dallas Green | Gary Carter, Mon., C |
| 1982 | National, 4-1 | Montreal | Billy Martin | Tommy Lasorda | Dave Concepcion, Cin., SS |
| 1983 | **American,** 13-3 | Chicago (AL) | Harvey Kuenn | Whitey Herzog | Fred Lynn, Cal., OF |
| 1984 | National, 3-1 | San Francisco | Joe Altobelli | Paul Owens | Gary Carter, Mon., C |
| 1985 | National, 6-1 | Minnesota | Sparky Anderson | Dick Williams | LaMarr Hoyt, SD, P |
| 1986 | **American,** 3-2 | Houston | Dick Howser | Whitey Herzog | Roger Clemens, Bos., P |
| 1987 | National, 2-0 (13) | Oakland | John McNamara | Davey Johnson | Tim Raines, Mon., OF |
| 1988 | **American,** 2-1 | Cincinnati | Tom Kelly | Whitey Herzog | Terry Steinbach, Oak., C |
| 1989 | **American,** 5-3 | California | Tony La Russa | Tommy Lasorda | Bo Jackson, KC, OF |
| 1990 | **American,** 2-0 | Chicago (NL) | Tony La Russa | Roger Craig | Julio Franco, Tex., 2B |
| 1991 | **American,** 4-2 | Toronto | Tony La Russa | Lou Piniella | Cal Ripken Jr., Bal., SS |
| 1992 | **American,** 13-6 | San Diego | Tom Kelly | Bobby Cox | Ken Griffey Jr., Sea., OF |
| 1993 | **American,** 9-3 | Baltimore | Cito Gaston | Bobby Cox | Kirby Puckett, Min., OF |
| 1994 | National, 8-7 (10) | Pittsburgh | Cito Gaston | Jim Fregosi | Fred McGriff, Atl., 1B |
| 1995 | National, 3-2 | Texas | Buck Showalter | Felipe Alou | Jeff Conine, Fla., PH |
| 1996 | National, 6-0 | Philadelphia | Mike Hargrove | Bobby Cox | Mike Piazza, LA, C |
| 1997 | **American,** 3-1 | Cleveland | Joe Torre | Bobby Cox | Sandy Alomar Jr., Cle., C |
| 1998 | **American,** 13-8 | Colorado | Mike Hargrove | Jim Leyland | Roberto Alomar, Bal., 2B |
| 1999 | **American,** 4-1 | Boston | Joe Torre | Bruce Bochy | Pedro Martinez, Bos., P |
| 2000 | **American,** 6-3 | Atlanta | Joe Torre | Bobby Cox | Derek Jeter, NY (AL), SS |
| 2001 | **American,** 4-1 | Seattle | Joe Torre | Bobby Valentine | Cal Ripken Jr., Bal., SS-3B |
| 2002 | TIE, 7-7 (11 inn.) * | Milwaukee | Joe Torre | Bob Brenly | No award |
| 2003 | **American,** 7-6 | Chicago (AL) | Mike Scioscia | Dusty Baker | Garret Anderson, Ana., OF |
| 2004 | **American,** 9-4 | Houston | Joe Torre | Jack McKeon | Alfonso Soriano, Tex., 2B |
| 2005 | **American,** 7-5 | Detroit | Terry Francona | Tony La Russa | Miguel Tejada, Bal., SS |

* Due to the depletion of both the AL and NL rosters, the 2002 game was called a tie after 11 innings.

AP/Wide World Photos

***Pete Rose***, *left, is hugged by teammate Dick Dietz after decking A.L. catcher Ray Fosse while scoring the winning run in the 1970 All-Star Game. Fosse suffered a fractured shoulder on the play.*

## Major League Franchise Origins

Here is what the current 30 teams in Major League Baseball have to show for the years they have put in as members of the National League (NL) and American League (AL). Pennants and World Series championships are since 1901.

## National League

| | 1st Year | Pennants & World Series | Franchise Stops |
|---|---|---|---|
| **Arizona Diamondbacks** | ..1998 | 1 NL (2001)<br>1 WS (2001) | • Phoenix (1998– ) |
| **Atlanta Braves** | .........1876 | 9 NL (1914,48,57-58,91-92,95,96,99)<br>3 WS (1914,57,95) | • Boston (1876–1952)<br>  Milwaukee (1953–65)<br>  Atlanta (1966– ) |
| **Chicago Cubs** | ...........1876 | 10 NL (1906-08,10,18,29,32,35,38,45)<br>2 WS (1907-08) | • Chicago (1876– ) |
| **Cincinnati Reds** | ........1876 | 9 NL (1919,39-40,61,70,72,75-76,90)<br>5 WS (1919,40,75-76,90) | • Cincinnati (1876–80)<br>  Cincinnati (1890– ) |
| **Colorado Rockies** | .......1993 | None | • Denver (1993– ) |
| **Florida Marlins** | .........1993 | 2 NL (1997, 2003)<br>2 WS (1997, 2003) | • Miami (1993– ) |
| **Houston Astros** | .......1962 | 1 NL (2005) | • Houston (1962– ) |
| **Los Angeles Dodgers** | .....1890 | 18 NL (1916,20,41,47,49,52-53,55-56,<br>59,63, 65-66,74,77-78, 81,88)<br>6 WS (1955,59,63,65,81,88) | • Brooklyn (1890-1957)<br>  Los Angeles (1958– ) |
| **Milwaukee Brewers** | .....1969 | 1 AL (1982) | • Seattle (1969)<br>  Milwaukee (1970– ) |
| **New York Mets** | ........1962 | 4 NL (1969,73,86,00)<br>2 WS (1969,86) | • New York (1962– ) |
| **Philadelphia Phillies** | .....1883 | 5 NL (1915,50,80,83,93)<br>1 WS (1980) | • Philadelphia (1883– ) |
| **Pittsburgh Pirates** | .......1887 | 7 NL (1903,09,25,27,60,71,79)<br>5 WS (1909,25,60,71,79) | • Pittsburgh (1887– ) |
| **St. Louis Cardinals** | .......1892 | 16 NL (1926,28,30-31,34,42-44,46,64,<br>67-68,82,85,87,2004)<br>9 WS (1926,31,34,42,44,46,64,67,82) | • St. Louis (1892– ) |
| **San Diego Padres** | .......1969 | 2 NL (1984,98) | • San Diego (1969– ) |
| **San Francisco Giants** | .....1883 | 17 NL (1905,11-13,17,21-24,33,36-37,51,<br>54,62,89,2002)<br>5 WS (1905,21-22,33,54) | • New York (1883–1957)<br>  San Francisco (1958– ) |
| **Washington Nationals** | ...1969 | None | • Montreal (1969–2004)<br>  Washington, DC (2005– ) |

## American League

| | 1st Year | Pennants & World Series | Franchise Stops |
|---|---|---|---|
| **Baltimore Orioles** | ........1901 | 7 AL (1944,66,69-71,79,83)<br>3 WS (1966,70,83) | • Milwaukee (1901)<br>  St. Louis (1902–53)<br>  Baltimore (1954– ) |
| **Boston Red Sox** | .........1901 | 10 AL (1903,12,15-16,18,46,67,75,86,2004)<br>6 WS (1903,12,15-16,18,2004) | • Boston (1901– ) |
| **Chicago White Sox** | ......1901 | 5 AL (1906,17,19,59,2005)<br>3 WS (1906,17,2005) | • Chicago (1901– ) |
| **Cleveland Indians** | .......1901 | 5 AL (1920,48,54,95,97)<br>2 WS (1920,48) | • Cleveland (1901– ) |
| **Detroit Tigers** | ...........1901 | 9 AL (1907-09,34-35,40,45,68,84)<br>4 WS (1935,45,68,84) | • Detroit (1901– ) |
| **Kansas City Royals** | ......1969 | 2 AL (1980,85)<br>1 WS (1985) | • Kansas City (1969– ) |
| **Los Angeles Angels<br>of Anaheim** | ......1961 | 1 AL (2002)<br>1 WS (2002) | • Los Angeles (1961–65)<br>  Anaheim, CA (1966– ) |
| **Minnesota Twins** | ........1901 | 6 AL (1924-25,33,65,87,91)<br>3 WS (1924,87,91) | • Washington, DC (1901–60)<br>  Bloomington, MN (1961–81)<br>  Minneapolis (1982– ) |
| **New York Yankees** | ....1901 | 39 AL (1921-23,26-28,32,36-39,41-43,47,<br>49-53,55-58,60-64,76-78,81,96,98-01,03)<br>26 WS (1923,27-28,32,36-39,41,43,47,<br>49-53,56,58,61-62,77-78,96,98-00) | • Baltimore (1901–02)<br>  New York (1903– ) |
| **Oakland Athletics** | .......1901 | 14 AL (1905,10-11,13-14,29-31,72-74,<br>88-90)<br>9 WS (1910-11,13,29-30,72-74,89) | • Philadelphia (1901-54)<br>  Kansas City (1955–67)<br>  Oakland (1968– ) |
| **Seattle Mariners** | ........1977 | None | • Seattle (1977– ) |
| **Tampa Bay Devil Rays** | ...1998 | None | • Tampa Bay (1998– ) |
| **Texas Rangers** | ...........1961 | None | • Washington, DC (1961–71)<br>  Arlington, TX (1972– ) |
| **Toronto Blue Jays** | .......1977 | 2 AL (1992-93)<br>2 WS (1992-93) | • Toronto (1977– ) |

## The Growth of Major League Baseball

The National League (founded in 1876) and the American League (founded in 1901) were both eight-team circuits at the turn of the century and remained that way until expansion finally came to Major League Baseball in the 1960s. The AL added two teams in 1961 and the NL did the same a year later. Both leagues went to 12 teams and split into two divisions in 1969. The AL then grew by two more teams to 14 in 1977, but the NL didn't follow suit until adding its 13th and 14th clubs in 1993. The NL added two teams (making it 16) in 1998 when the expansion Arizona Diamondbacks entered the league and the Milwaukee Brewers moved over from the AL. The Tampa Bay Devil Rays joined the AL in 1998, keeping the AL at 14 teams.

### Expansion Timetable (Since 1901)

**1961**—Los Angeles Angels and Washington Senators (now Texas Rangers) join AL; **1962**—Houston Colt .45s (now Astros) and New York Mets join NL; **1969**—Kansas City Royals and Seattle Pilots (now Milwaukee Brewers) join AL, while Montreal Expos (now Washington Nationals) and San Diego Padres join NL; **1977**—Seattle Mariners and Toronto Blue Jays join AL; **1993**—Colorado Rockies and Florida Marlins join NL; **1998**—Arizona Diamondbacks join NL and Tampa Bay Devil Rays join AL.

### City and Nickname Changes
#### National League

**1953**—Boston Braves move to Milwaukee; **1958**—Brooklyn Dodgers move to Los Angeles and New York Giants move to San Francisco; **1965**—Houston Colt .45s renamed Astros; **1966**—Milwaukee Braves move to Atlanta; **2004**—Montreal Expos move to Washington, D.C. and become Washington Nationals.

    **Other nicknames: Boston** (Beaneaters and Doves through 1908, and Bees from 1936-40); **Brooklyn** (Superbas through 1926, then Robins from 1927-31; then Dodgers from 1932-57); **Cincinnati** (Red Legs from 1944-45, then Redlegs from 1954-60, then Reds since 1961); **Philadelphia** (Blue Jays from 1943-44).

#### American League

**1902**—Milwaukee Brewers move to St. Louis and become Browns; **1903**—Baltimore Orioles move to New York and become Highlanders; **1913**—NY Highlanders renamed Yankees; **1954**—St. Louis Browns move to Baltimore and become Orioles; **1955**—Philadelphia Athletics move to Kansas City; **1961**—Washington Senators move to Bloomington, Minn., and become Minnesota Twins; **1965**—LA Angels renamed California Angels; **1966**—California Angels move to Anaheim; **1968**—KC Athletics move to Oakland and become A's; **1970**—Seattle Pilots move to Milwaukee and become Brewers; **1972**—Washington Senators move to Arlington, Texas, and become Rangers; **1982**—Minnesota Twins move to Minneapolis; **1987**—Oakland A's renamed Athletics; **1997**—California Angels renamed Anaheim Angels; **2005**—Anaheim Angels renamed Los Angeles Angels of Anaheim.

    **Other nicknames: Boston** (Pilgrims, Puritans, Plymouth Rocks and Somersets through 1906); **Cleveland** (Bronchos, Blues, Naps and Molly McGuires through 1914); **Washington** (Senators through 1904, then Nationals from 1905-44, then Senators again from 1945-60).

### National League Pennant Winners from 1876-99

Founded in 1876, the National League played 24 seasons before the turn of the century and its eventual rivalry with the younger American League.

    **Multiple winners:** Boston (8); Chicago (6); Baltimore (3); Brooklyn, New York and Providence (2).

| Year | | Year | | Year | | Year | |
|------|------------|------|------------|------|----------|------|-----------|
| 1876 | Chicago | 1882 | Chicago | 1888 | New York | 1894 | Baltimore |
| 1877 | Boston | 1883 | Boston | 1889 | New York | 1895 | Baltimore |
| 1878 | Boston | 1884 | Providence | 1890 | Brooklyn | 1896 | Baltimore |
| 1879 | Providence | 1885 | Chicago | 1891 | Boston | 1897 | Boston |
| 1880 | Chicago | 1886 | Chicago | 1892 | Boston | 1898 | Boston |
| 1881 | Chicago | 1887 | Detroit | 1893 | Boston | 1899 | Brooklyn |

### Champions of Leagues That No Longer Exist

A Special Baseball Records Committee appointed by the commissioner found in 1968 that four extinct leagues qualified for major league status—the American Association (1882-91), the Union Association (1884), the Players' League (1890) and the Federal League (1914-15). The first years of the American League (1900) and Federal League (1913) were not recognized.

#### American Association

| Year | Champion | Manager | Year | Champion | Manager | Year | Champion | Manager |
|------|----------|---------|------|----------|---------|------|----------|---------|
| 1882 | Cincinnati | Pop Snyder | 1886 | St. Louis | Charlie Comiskey | 1890 | Louisville | Jack Chapman |
| 1883 | Philadelphia | Lew Simmons | 1887 | St. Louis | Charlie Comiskey | 1891 | Boston | Arthur Irwin |
| 1884 | New York | Jim Mutrie | 1888 | St. Louis | Charlie Comiskey | | | |
| 1885 | St. Louis | Charlie Comiskey | 1889 | Brooklyn | Bill McGunnigle | | | |

#### Union Association

| Year | Champion | Manager |
|------|----------|---------|
| 1884 | St. Louis | Henry Lucas |

#### Players' League

| Year | Champion | Manager |
|------|----------|---------|
| 1890 | Boston | King Kelly |

#### Federal League

| Year | Champion | Manager |
|------|----------|---------|
| 1914 | Indianapolis | Bill Phillips |
| 1915 | Chicago | Joe Tinker |

## Annual Batting Leaders (since 1900)
### Batting Average
#### National League

**Multiple winners:** Tony Gwynn and Honus Wagner (8); Rogers Hornsby and Stan Musial (7); Roberto Clemente and Bill Madlock (4); Pete Rose, Larry Walker and Paul Waner (3); Hank Aaron, Richie Ashburn, Barry Bonds, Jake Daubert, Tommy Davis, Ernie Lombardi, Willie McGee, Lefty O'Doul, Dave Parker and Edd Roush (2).

| Year | | Avg | Year | | Avg | Year | | Avg |
|---|---|---|---|---|---|---|---|---|
| 1900 | Honus Wagner, Pit | .381 | 1936 | Paul Waner, Pit. | .373 | 1972 | Billy Williams, Chi | .333 |
| 1901 | Jesse Burkett, St.L | .382 | 1937 | Joe Medwick, St.L | .374 | 1973 | Pete Rose, Cin | .338 |
| 1902 | Ginger Beaumont, Pit | .357 | 1938 | Ernie Lombardi, Cin | .342 | 1974 | Ralph Garr, Atl | .353 |
| 1903 | Honus Wagner, Pit | .355 | 1939 | Johnny Mize, St.L | .349 | 1975 | Bill Madlock, Chi | .354 |
| 1904 | Honus Wagner, Pit | .349 | 1940 | Debs Garms, Pit | .355 | 1976 | Bill Madlock, Chi | .339 |
| 1905 | Cy Seymour, Cin | .377 | 1941 | Pete Reiser, Bklyn | .343 | 1977 | Dave Parker, Pit | .338 |
| 1906 | Honus Wagner, Pit | .339 | 1942 | Ernie Lombardi, Bos | .330 | 1978 | Dave Parker, Pit | .334 |
| 1907 | Honus Wagner, Pit | .350 | 1943 | Stan Musial, St.L | .357 | 1979 | Keith Hernandez, St.L | .344 |
| 1908 | Honus Wagner, Pit | .354 | 1944 | Dixie Walker, Bklyn | .357 | 1980 | Bill Buckner, Chi | .324 |
| 1909 | Honus Wagner, Pit | .339 | 1945 | Phil Cavarretta, Chi. | .355 | 1981 | Bill Madlock, Pit | .341 |
| 1910 | Sherry Magee, Phi | .331 | 1946 | Stan Musial, St.L | .365 | 1982 | Al Oliver, Mon | .331 |
| 1911 | Honus Wagner, Pit | .334 | 1947 | Harry Walker, St.L-Phi | .363 | 1983 | Bill Madlock, Pit | .323 |
| 1912 | Heinie Zimmerman, Chi. | .372 | 1948 | Stan Musial, St.L | .376 | 1984 | Tony Gwynn, SD. | .351 |
| 1913 | Jake Daubert, Bklyn | .350 | 1949 | Jackie Robinson, Bklyn | .342 | 1985 | Willie McGee, St.L | .353 |
| 1914 | Jake Daubert, Bklyn | .329 | 1950 | Stan Musial, St.L | .346 | 1986 | Tim Raines, Mon | .334 |
| 1915 | Larry Doyle, NY | .320 | 1951 | Stan Musial, St.L | .355 | 1987 | Tony Gwynn, SD. | .370 |
| 1916 | Hal Chase, Cin. | .339 | 1952 | Stan Musial, St.L | .336 | 1988 | Tony Gwynn, SD. | .313 |
| 1917 | Edd Roush, Cin. | .341 | 1953 | Carl Furillo, Bklyn | .344 | 1989 | Tony Gwynn, SD. | .336 |
| 1918 | Zack Wheat, Bklyn | .335 | 1954 | Willie Mays, NY | .345 | 1990 | Willie McGee, St.L | .335 |
| 1919 | Edd Roush, Cin. | .321 | 1955 | Richie Ashburn, Phi | .338 | 1991 | Terry Pendleton, Atl | .319 |
| 1920 | Rogers Hornsby, St.L | .370 | 1956 | Hank Aaron, Mil. | .328 | 1992 | Gary Sheffield, SD | .330 |
| 1921 | Rogers Hornsby, St.L | .397 | 1957 | Stan Musial, St.L | .351 | 1993 | Andres Galarraga, Col | .370 |
| 1922 | Rogers Hornsby, St.L | .401 | 1958 | Richie Ashburn, Phi | .350 | 1994 | Tony Gwynn, SD. | .394 |
| 1923 | Rogers Hornsby, St.L | .384 | 1959 | Hank Aaron, Mil. | .355 | 1995 | Tony Gwynn, SD. | .368 |
| 1924 | Rogers Hornsby, St.L | .424 | 1960 | Dick Groat, Pit | .325 | 1996 | Tony Gwynn, SD. | .353 |
| 1925 | Rogers Hornsby, St.L | .403 | 1961 | Roberto Clemente, Pit | .351 | 1997 | Tony Gwynn, SD. | .372 |
| 1926 | Bubbles Hargrave, Cin | .353 | 1962 | Tommy Davis, LA | .346 | 1998 | Larry Walker, Col. | .363 |
| 1927 | Paul Waner, Pit. | .380 | 1963 | Tommy Davis, LA | .326 | 1999 | Larry Walker, Col. | .379 |
| 1928 | Rogers Hornsby, Bos | .387 | 1964 | Roberto Clemente, Pit | .339 | 2000 | Todd Helton, Col. | .372 |
| 1929 | Lefty O'Doul, Phi. | .398 | 1965 | Roberto Clemente, Pit | .329 | 2001 | Larry Walker, Col. | .350 |
| 1930 | Bill Terry, NY | .401 | 1966 | Matty Alou, Pit | .342 | 2002 | Barry Bonds, SF | .370 |
| 1931 | Chick Hafey, St.L | .349 | 1967 | Roberto Clemente, Pit | .357 | 2003 | Albert Pujols, St.L | .359 |
| 1932 | Lefty O'Doul, Bklyn | .368 | 1968 | Pete Rose, Cin | .335 | 2004 | Barry Bonds, SF | .362 |
| 1933 | Chuck Klein, Phi | .368 | 1969 | Pete Rose, Cin | .348 | 2005 | Derrek Lee, Chi. | .335 |
| 1934 | Paul Waner, Pit. | .362 | 1970 | Rico Carty, Atl | .366 | | | |
| 1935 | Arky Vaughan, Pit. | .385 | 1971 | Joe Torre, St.L | .363 | | | |

#### American League

**Multiple winners:** Ty Cobb (12); Rod Carew (7); Ted Williams (6); Wade Boggs (5); Harry Heilmann (4); George Brett, Nap Lajoie, Tony Oliva and Carl Yastrzemski (3); Luke Appling, Joe DiMaggio, Ferris Fain, Jimmie Foxx, Nomar Garciaparra, Edgar Martinez, Pete Runnels, Al Simmons, George Sisler, Ichiro Suzuki and Mickey Vernon (2).

| Year | | Avg | Year | | Avg | Year | | Avg |
|---|---|---|---|---|---|---|---|---|
| 1901 | Nap Lajoie, Phi. | .422 | 1924 | Babe Ruth, NY | .378 | 1947 | Ted Williams, Bos | .343 |
| 1902 | Ed Delahanty, Wash. | .376 | 1925 | Harry Heilmann, Det | .393 | 1948 | Ted Williams, Bos | .369 |
| 1903 | Nap Lajoie, Cle | .355 | 1926 | Heinie Manush, Det | .378 | 1949 | George Kell, Det. | .343 |
| 1904 | Nap Lajoie, Cle | .381 | 1927 | Harry Heilmann, Det | .398 | 1950 | Billy Goodman, Bos | .354 |
| 1905 | Elmer Flick, Cle. | .306 | 1928 | Goose Goslin, Wash. | .379 | 1951 | Ferris Fain, Phi | .344 |
| 1906 | George Stone, St.L | .358 | 1929 | Lew Fonseca, Cle | .369 | 1952 | Ferris Fain, Phi | .327 |
| 1907 | Ty Cobb, Det | .350 | 1930 | Al Simmons, Phi | .381 | 1953 | Mickey Vernon, Wash. | .337 |
| 1908 | Ty Cobb, Det | .324 | 1931 | Al Simmons, Phi | .390 | 1954 | Bobby Avila, Clev. | .341 |
| 1909 | Ty Cobb, Det | .377 | 1932 | Dale Alexander, Det-Bos | .367 | 1955 | Al Kaline, Det. | .340 |
| 1910 | Ty Cobb, Det | .383 | 1933 | Jimmie Foxx, Phi | .356 | 1956 | Mickey Mantle, NY | .353 |
| 1911 | Ty Cobb, Det | .420 | 1934 | Lou Gehrig, NY. | .363 | 1957 | Ted Williams, Bos | .388 |
| 1912 | Ty Cobb, Det | .409 | 1935 | Buddy Myer, Wash. | .349 | 1958 | Ted Williams, Bos | .328 |
| 1913 | Ty Cobb, Det | .390 | 1936 | Luke Appling, Chi. | .388 | 1959 | Harvey Kuenn, Det | .353 |
| 1914 | Ty Cobb, Det | .368 | 1937 | Charlie Gehringer, Det | .371 | 1960 | Pete Runnels, Bos | .320 |
| 1915 | Ty Cobb, Det | .369 | 1938 | Jimmie Foxx, Bos. | .349 | 1961 | Norm Cash, Det. | .361* |
| 1916 | Tris Speaker, Cle. | .386 | 1939 | Joe DiMaggio, NY | .381 | 1962 | Pete Runnels, Bos | .326 |
| 1917 | Ty Cobb, Det | .383 | 1940 | Joe DiMaggio, NY | .352 | 1963 | Carl Yastrzemski, Bos. | .321 |
| 1918 | Ty Cobb, Det | .382 | 1941 | Ted Williams, Bos | .406 | 1964 | Tony Oliva, Min | .323 |
| 1919 | Ty Cobb, Det | .384 | 1942 | Ted Williams, Bos | .356 | 1965 | Tony Oliva, Min | .321 |
| 1920 | George Sisler, St.L | .407 | 1943 | Luke Appling, Chi. | .328 | 1966 | Frank Robinson, Bal | .316 |
| 1921 | Harry Heilmann, Det | .394 | 1944 | Lou Boudreau, Clev. | .327 | 1967 | Carl Yastrzemski, Bos. | .326 |
| 1922 | George Sisler, St.L | .420 | 1945 | Snuffy Stirnweiss, NY. | .309 | 1968 | Carl Yastrzemski, Bos. | .301 |
| 1923 | Harry Heilmann, Det | .403 | 1946 | Mickey Vernon, Wash | .353 | 1969 | Rod Carew, Min | .332 |

## Batting Average (Cont.)

| Year | | Avg | Year | | Avg | Year | | Avg |
|------|------|-----|------|------|-----|------|------|-----|
| 1970 | Alex Johnson, Cal. | .329 | 1982 | Willie Wilson, KC | .332 | 1994 | Paul O'Neill, NY | .359 |
| 1971 | Tony Oliva, Min | .337 | 1983 | Wade Boggs, Bos. | .361 | 1995 | Edgar Martinez, Sea | .356 |
| 1972 | Rod Carew, Min | .318 | 1984 | Don Mattingly, NY | .343 | 1996 | Alex Rodriguez, Sea | .358 |
| 1973 | Rod Carew, Min | .350 | 1985 | Wade Boggs, Bos. | .368 | 1997 | Frank Thomas, Chi | .347 |
| 1974 | Rod Carew, Min | .364 | 1986 | Wade Boggs, Bos. | .357 | 1998 | Bernie Williams, NY. | .339 |
| 1975 | Rod Carew, Min | .359 | 1987 | Wade Boggs, Bos. | .363 | 1999 | Nomar Garciaparra, Bos. | .357 |
| 1976 | George Brett, KC | .333 | 1988 | Wade Boggs, Bos. | .366 | 2000 | Nomar Garciaparra, Bos. | .372 |
| 1977 | Rod Carew, Min | .388 | 1989 | Kirby Puckett, Min. | .339 | 2001 | Ichiro Suzuki, Sea. | .350 |
| 1978 | Rod Carew, Min | .333 | 1990 | George Brett, KC | .329 | 2002 | Manny Ramirez, Bos | .349 |
| 1979 | Fred Lynn, Bos | .333 | 1991 | Julio Franco, Tex | .341 | 2003 | Bill Mueller, Bos. | .326 |
| 1980 | George Brett, KC | .390 | 1992 | Edgar Martinez, Sea. | .343 | 2004 | Ichiro Suzuki, Sea. | .372 |
| 1981 | Carney Lansford, Bos. | .336 | 1993 | John Olerud, Tor | .363 | 2005 | Michael Young, Tex. | .331 |

*Norm Cash later admitted to using a corked bat the entire season. He played 16 other seasons and never hit better than .286.

## Home Runs
### National League

**Multiple winners:** Mike Schmidt (8); Ralph Kiner (7); Gavvy Cravath and Mel Ott (6); Hank Aaron, Chuck Klein, Willie Mays, Johnny Mize, Cy Williams and Hack Wilson (4); Willie McCovey (3); Ernie Banks, Johnny Bench, Barry Bonds, George Foster, Rogers Hornsby, Tim Jordan, Dave Kingman, Eddie Mathews, Mark McGwire, Dale Murphy, Bill Nicholson, Dave Robertson, Wildfire Schulte, Sammy Sosa and Willie Stargell (2).

| Year | | HR | Year | | HR | Year | | HR |
|------|------|-----|------|------|-----|------|------|-----|
| 1900 | Herman Long, Bos | 12 | 1934 | Rip Collins, St.L | 35 | 1968 | Willie McCovey, SF | 36 |
| 1901 | Sam Crawford, Cin | 16 | | & Mel Ott, NY. | 35 | 1969 | Willie McCovey, SF | 45 |
| 1902 | Tommy Leach, Pit | 6 | 1935 | Wally Berger, Bos. | 34 | 1970 | Johnny Bench, Cin | 45 |
| 1903 | Jimmy Sheckard, Bklyn | 9 | 1936 | Mel Ott, NY. | 33 | 1971 | Willie Stargell, Pit | 48 |
| 1904 | Harry Lumley, Bklyn | 9 | 1937 | Joe Medwick, St.L. | 31 | 1972 | Johnny Bench, Cin | 40 |
| 1905 | Fred Odwell, Cin. | 9 | | & Mel Ott, NY. | 31 | 1973 | Willie Stargell, Pit | 44 |
| 1906 | Tim Jordan, Bklyn | 12 | 1938 | Mel Ott, NY. | 36 | 1974 | Mike Schmidt, Phi. | 36 |
| 1907 | Dave Brain, Bos | 10 | 1939 | Johnny Mize, St.L | 28 | 1975 | Mike Schmidt, Phi. | 38 |
| 1908 | Tim Jordan, Bklyn | 12 | 1940 | Johnny Mize, St.L. | 43 | 1976 | Mike Schmidt, Phi. | 38 |
| 1909 | Red Murray, NY | 7 | 1941 | Dolph Camilli, Bklyn. | 34 | 1977 | George Foster, Cin | 52 |
| 1910 | Fred Beck, Bos. | 10 | 1942 | Mel Ott, NY. | 30 | 1978 | George Foster, Cin | 40 |
| | & Wildfire Schulte, Chi | 10 | 1943 | Bill Nicholson, Chi | 29 | 1979 | Dave Kingman, Chi | 48 |
| 1911 | Wildfire Schulte, Chi. | 21 | 1944 | Bill Nicholson, Chi | 33 | 1980 | Mike Schmidt, Phi. | 48 |
| 1912 | Heinie Zimmerman, Chi. | 14 | 1945 | Tommy Holmes, Bos | 28 | 1981 | Mike Schmidt, Phi. | 31 |
| 1913 | Gavvy Cravath, Phi. | 19 | 1946 | Ralph Kiner, Pit. | 23 | 1982 | Dave Kingman, NY. | 37 |
| 1914 | Gavvy Cravath, Phi. | 19 | 1947 | Ralph Kiner, Pit. | 51 | 1983 | Mike Schmidt, Phi. | 40 |
| 1915 | Gavvy Cravath, Phi. | 24 | | & Johnny Mize, NY | 51 | 1984 | Dale Murphy, Atl. | 36 |
| 1916 | Cy Williams, Chi | 12 | 1948 | Ralph Kiner, Pit. | 40 | | & Mike Schmidt, Phi. | 36 |
| | & Dave Robertson, NY. | 12 | | & Johnny Mize, NY | 40 | 1985 | Dale Murphy, Atl. | 37 |
| 1917 | Gavvy Cravath, Phi. | 12 | 1949 | Ralph Kiner, Pit. | 54 | 1986 | Mike Schmidt, Phi. | 37 |
| | & Dave Robertson, NY. | 12 | 1950 | Ralph Kiner, Pit. | 47 | 1987 | Andre Dawson, Chi | 49 |
| 1918 | Gavvy Cravath, Phi. | 8 | 1951 | Ralph Kiner, Pit. | 42 | 1988 | Darryl Strawberry, NY. | 39 |
| 1919 | Gavvy Cravath, Phi. | 12 | 1952 | Ralph Kiner, Pit. | 37 | 1989 | Kevin Mitchell, SF | 47 |
| 1920 | Cy Williams, Phi. | 15 | | & Hank Sauer, Chi | 37 | 1990 | Ryne Sandberg, Chi | 40 |
| 1921 | George Kelly, NY | 23 | 1953 | Eddie Mathews, Mil | 47 | 1991 | Howard Johnson, NY. | 38 |
| 1922 | Rogers Hornsby, St.L. | 42 | 1954 | Ted Kluszewski, Cin | 49 | 1992 | Fred McGriff, SD | 35 |
| 1923 | Cy Williams, Phi. | 41 | 1955 | Willie Mays, NY. | 51 | 1993 | Barry Bonds, SF | 46 |
| 1924 | Jack Fournier, Bklyn | 27 | 1956 | Duke Snider, Bklyn | 43 | 1994 | Matt Williams, SF | 43 |
| 1925 | Rogers Hornsby, St.L. | 39 | 1957 | Hank Aaron, Mil. | 44 | 1995 | Dante Bichette, Col. | 40 |
| 1926 | Hack Wilson, Chi. | 21 | 1958 | Ernie Banks, Chi. | 47 | 1996 | Andres Galarraga, Col | 47 |
| 1927 | Cy Williams, Phi. | 30 | 1959 | Eddie Mathews, Mil | 46 | 1997 | Larry Walker, Col | 49 |
| | & Hack Wilson, Chi | 30 | 1960 | Ernie Banks, Chi. | 41 | 1998 | Mark McGwire, St.L | 70 |
| 1928 | Jim Bottomley, St.L. | 31 | 1961 | Orlando Cepeda, SF. | 46 | 1999 | Mark McGwire, St.L | 65 |
| | & Hack Wilson, Chi | 31 | 1962 | Willie Mays, SF | 49 | 2000 | Sammy Sosa, Chi | 50 |
| 1929 | Chuck Klein, Phi. | 43 | 1963 | Hank Aaron, Mil. | 44 | 2001 | Barry Bonds, SF | 73 |
| 1930 | Hack Wilson, Chi. | 56 | | & Willie McCovey, SF. | 44 | 2002 | Sammy Sosa, Chi | 49 |
| 1931 | Chuck Klein, Phi. | 31 | 1964 | Willie Mays, SF | 47 | 2003 | Jim Thome, Phi | 47 |
| 1932 | Chuck Klein, Phi. | 38 | 1965 | Willie Mays, SF | 52 | 2004 | Adrian Beltre, LA | 48 |
| | & Mel Ott, NY. | 38 | 1966 | Hank Aaron, Atl | 44 | 2005 | Andruw Jones, Atl. | 51 |
| 1933 | Chuck Klein, Phi. | 28 | 1967 | Hank Aaron, Atl | 39 | | | |

**Note:** In 1997 Mark McGwire hit 58 home runs but hit 34 of them in the AL with Oakland before his trade to St. Louis.

### American League

**Multiple winners:** Babe Ruth (12); Harmon Killebrew (6); Home Run Baker, Harry Davis, Jimmie Foxx, Hank Greenberg, Ken Griffey Jr., Reggie Jackson, Mickey Mantle, Alex Rodriguez and Ted Williams (4); Lou Gehrig and Jim Rice (3); Dick Allen, Tony Armas, Jose Canseco, Joe DiMaggio, Larry Doby, Cecil Fielder, Juan Gonzalez, Mark McGwire, Wally Pipp, Al Rosen and Gorman Thomas (2).

| Year | | HR | Year | | HR | Year | | HR |
|------|------|-----|------|------|-----|------|------|-----|
| 1901 | Nap Lajoie, Phi | 14 | 1904 | Harry Davis, Phi. | 10 | 1907 | Harry Davis, Phi. | 8 |
| 1902 | Socks Seybold, Phi | 16 | 1905 | Harry Davis, Phi. | 8 | 1908 | Sam Crawford, Det. | 7 |
| 1903 | Buck Freeman, Bos | 13 | 1906 | Harry Davis, Phi. | 12 | 1909 | Ty Cobb, Det | 9 |

| Year | | HR |
|---|---|---|
| 1910 | Jake Stahl, Bos | 10 |
| 1911 | Home Run Baker, Phi. | 11 |
| 1912 | Home Run Baker, Phi. | 10 |
| | & Tris Speaker, Bos. | 10 |
| 1913 | Home Run Baker, Phi. | 12 |
| 1914 | Home Run Baker, Phi. | 9 |
| 1915 | Braggo Roth, Chi-Cle | 7 |
| 1916 | Wally Pipp, NY. | 12 |
| 1917 | Wally Pipp, NY | 9 |
| 1918 | Babe Ruth, Bos | 11 |
| | & Tilly Walker, Phi | 11 |
| 1919 | Babe Ruth, Bos | 29 |
| 1920 | Babe Ruth, NY | 54 |
| 1921 | Babe Ruth, NY. | 59 |
| 1922 | Ken Williams, St.L. | 39 |
| 1923 | Babe Ruth, NY | 41 |
| 1924 | Babe Ruth, NY. | 46 |
| 1925 | Bob Meusel, NY | 33 |
| 1926 | Babe Ruth, NY. | 47 |
| 1927 | Babe Ruth, NY. | 60 |
| 1928 | Babe Ruth, NY. | 54 |
| 1929 | Babe Ruth, NY. | 46 |
| 1930 | Babe Ruth, NY. | 49 |
| 1931 | Lou Gehrig, NY. | 46 |
| | & Babe Ruth, NY | 46 |
| 1932 | Jimmie Foxx, Phi. | 58 |
| 1933 | Jimmie Foxx, Phi. | 48 |
| 1934 | Lou Gehrig, NY. | 49 |
| 1935 | Jimmie Foxx, Phi. | 36 |
| | & Hank Greenberg, Det. | 36 |
| 1936 | Lou Gehrig, NY. | 49 |
| 1937 | Joe DiMaggio, NY | 46 |
| 1938 | Hank Greenberg, Det. | 58 |
| 1939 | Jimmie Foxx, Bos. | 35 |
| 1940 | Hank Greenberg, Det. | 41 |
| 1941 | Ted Williams, Bos | 37 |
| 1942 | Ted Williams, Bos | 36 |
| 1943 | Rudy York, Det. | 34 |
| 1944 | Nick Etten, NY | 22 |
| 1945 | Vern Stephens, St.L | 24 |
| 1946 | Hank Greenberg, Det. | 44 |
| 1947 | Ted Williams, Bos. | 32 |
| 1948 | Joe DiMaggio, NY | 39 |
| 1949 | Ted Williams, Bos | 43 |
| 1950 | Al Rosen, Cle. | 37 |
| 1951 | Gus Zernial, Chi-Phi | 33 |
| 1952 | Larry Doby, Cle. | 32 |
| 1953 | Al Rosen, Cle. | 43 |
| 1954 | Larry Doby, Cle. | 32 |
| 1955 | Mickey Mantle, NY. | 37 |
| 1956 | Mickey Mantle, NY. | 52 |
| 1957 | Roy Sievers, Wash | 42 |
| 1958 | Mickey Mantle, NY. | 42 |
| 1959 | Rocky Colavito, Cle | 42 |
| | & Harmon Killebrew, Wash | 42 |
| 1960 | Mickey Mantle, NY. | 40 |
| 1961 | Roger Maris, NY. | 61 |
| 1962 | Harmon Killebrew, Min | 48 |
| 1963 | Harmon Killebrew, Min | 45 |
| 1964 | Harmon Killebrew, Min | 49 |
| 1965 | Tony Conigliaro, Bos. | 32 |
| 1966 | Frank Robinson, Bal | 49 |
| 1967 | Harmon Killebrew, Min | 44 |
| | & Carl Yastrzemski, Bos. | 44 |
| 1968 | Frank Howard, Wash. | 44 |
| 1969 | Harmon Killebrew, Min | 49 |
| 1970 | Frank Howard, Wash. | 44 |
| 1971 | Bill Melton, Chi | 33 |
| 1972 | Dick Allen, Chi | 37 |
| 1973 | Reggie Jackson, Oak | 32 |
| 1974 | Dick Allen, Chi. | 32 |
| 1975 | Reggie Jackson, Oak | 36 |
| | & George Scott, Mil | 36 |
| 1976 | Graig Nettles, NY | 32 |
| 1977 | Jim Rice, Bos | 39 |
| 1978 | Jim Rice, Bos | 46 |
| 1979 | Gorman Thomas, Mil | 45 |
| 1980 | Reggie Jackson, NY | 41 |
| | & Ben Oglivie, Mil | 41 |
| 1981 | Tony Armas, Oak | 22 |
| | Dwight Evans, Bos | 22 |
| | Bobby Grich, Cal | 22 |
| | & Eddie Murray, Bal. | 22 |
| 1982 | Reggie Jackson, Cal. | 39 |
| | & Gorman Thomas, Mil. | 39 |
| 1983 | Jim Rice, Bos | 39 |
| 1984 | Tony Armas, Bos | 43 |
| 1985 | Darrell Evans, Det. | 40 |
| 1986 | Jesse Barfield, Tor | 40 |
| 1987 | Mark McGwire, Oak | 49 |
| 1988 | Jose Canseco, Oak. | 42 |
| 1989 | Fred McGriff, Tor | 36 |
| 1990 | Cecil Fielder, Det | 51 |
| 1991 | Jose Canseco, Oak. | 44 |
| | & Cecil Fielder, Det. | 44 |
| 1992 | Juan Gonzalez, Tex. | 43 |
| 1993 | Juan Gonzalez, Tex. | 46 |
| 1994 | Ken Griffey Jr., Sea. | 40 |
| 1995 | Albert Belle, Cle. | 50 |
| 1996 | Mark McGwire, Oak | 52 |
| 1997 | Ken Griffey Jr., Sea. | 56 |
| 1998 | Ken Griffey Jr., Sea. | 56 |
| 1999 | Ken Griffey Jr., Sea. | 48 |
| 2000 | Troy Glaus, Ana | 47 |
| 2001 | Alex Rodriguez, Tex | 52 |
| 2002 | Alex Rodriguez, Tex | 57 |
| 2003 | Alex Rodriguez, Tex | 47 |
| 2004 | Manny Ramirez, Bos. | 43 |
| 2005 | Alex Rodriguez, NY | 48 |

## Runs Batted In
### National League

**Multiple winners:** Hank Aaron, Rogers Hornsby, Sherry Magee, Mike Schmidt and Honus Wagner (4); Johnny Bench, George Foster, Joe Medwick, Johnny Mize and Heinie Zimmerman (3); Ernie Banks, Jim Bottomley, Orlando Cepeda, Gavvy Cravath, Andres Galarraga, George Kelly, Chuck Klein, Willie McCovey, Dale Murphy, Stan Musial, Bill Nicholson, Sammy Sosa and Hack Wilson (2).

| Year | | RBI |
|---|---|---|
| 1900 | Elmer Flick, Phi | 110 |
| 1901 | Honus Wagner, Pit | 126 |
| 1902 | Honus Wagner, Pit | 91 |
| 1903 | Sam Mertes, NY. | 104 |
| 1904 | Bill Dahlen, NY | 80 |
| 1905 | Cy Seymour, Cin | 121 |
| 1906 | Jim Nealon, Pit. | 83 |
| | & Harry Steinfeldt, Chi. | 83 |
| 1907 | Sherry Magee, Phi | 85 |
| 1908 | Honus Wagner, Pit | 109 |
| 1909 | Honus Wagner, Pit | 100 |
| 1910 | Sherry Magee, Phi | 123 |
| 1911 | Wildfire Schulte, Chi. | 121 |
| 1912 | Heinie Zimmerman, Chi. | 103 |
| 1913 | Gavvy Cravath, Phi. | 128 |
| 1914 | Sherry Magee, Phi | 103 |
| 1915 | Gavvy Cravath, Phi. | 115 |
| 1916 | Heinie Zimmerman, Chi-NY | 83 |
| 1917 | Heinie Zimmerman, NY. | 102 |
| 1918 | Sherry Magee, Cin. | 76 |
| 1919 | Hy Myers, Bklyn | 73 |
| 1920 | Rogers Hornsby, St.L. | 94 |
| | & George Kelly, NY | 94 |
| 1921 | Rogers Hornsby, St.L. | 126 |
| 1922 | Rogers Hornsby, St.L. | 152 |
| 1923 | Irish Meusel, NY. | 125 |
| 1924 | George Kelly, NY. | 136 |
| 1925 | Rogers Hornsby, St.L | 143 |
| 1926 | Jim Bottomley, St.L | 120 |
| 1927 | Paul Waner, Pit. | 131 |
| 1928 | Jim Bottomley, St.L. | 136 |
| 1929 | Hack Wilson, Chi. | 159 |
| 1930 | Hack Wilson, Chi. | 191 |
| 1931 | Chuck Klein, Phi. | 121 |
| 1932 | Don Hurst, Phi. | 143 |
| 1933 | Chuck Klein, Phi. | 120 |
| 1934 | Mel Ott, NY. | 135 |
| 1935 | Wally Berger, Bos. | 130 |
| 1936 | Joe Medwick, St.L. | 138 |
| 1937 | Joe Medwick, St.L. | 154 |
| 1938 | Joe Medwick, St.L. | 122 |
| 1939 | Frank McCormick, Cin | 128 |
| 1940 | Johnny Mize, St.L | 137 |
| 1941 | Dolph Camilli, Bklyn | 120 |
| 1942 | Johnny Mize, NY | 110 |
| 1943 | Bill Nicholson, Chi | 128 |
| 1944 | Bill Nicholson, Chi | 122 |
| 1945 | Dixie Walker, Bklyn. | 124 |
| 1946 | Enos Slaughter, St.L. | 130 |
| 1947 | Johnny Mize, NY | 138 |
| 1948 | Stan Musial, St.L. | 131 |
| 1949 | Ralph Kiner, Pit. | 127 |
| 1950 | Del Ennis, Phi. | 126 |
| 1951 | Monte Irvin, NY | 121 |
| 1952 | Hank Sauer, Chi. | 121 |
| 1953 | Roy Campanella, Bklyn | 142 |
| 1954 | Ted Kluszewski, Cin | 141 |
| 1955 | Duke Snider, Bklyn | 136 |
| 1956 | Stan Musial, St.L. | 109 |
| 1957 | Hank Aaron, Mil | 132 |
| 1958 | Ernie Banks, Chi. | 129 |
| 1959 | Ernie Banks, Chi. | 143 |
| 1960 | Hank Aaron, Mil | 126 |
| 1961 | Orlando Cepeda, SF. | 142 |
| 1962 | Tommy Davis, LA | 153 |
| 1963 | Hank Aaron, Mil | 130 |
| 1964 | Ken Boyer, St.L. | 119 |
| 1965 | Deron Johnson, Cin. | 130 |
| 1966 | Hank Aaron, Atl | 127 |
| 1967 | Orlando Cepeda, St.L. | 111 |
| 1968 | Willie McCovey, SF | 105 |
| 1969 | Willie McCovey, SF | 126 |
| 1970 | Johnny Bench, Cin | 148 |
| 1971 | Joe Torre, St.L. | 137 |
| 1972 | Johnny Bench, Cin | 125 |
| 1973 | Willie Stargell, Pit. | 119 |
| 1974 | Johnny Bench, Cin | 129 |
| 1975 | Greg Luzinski, Phi. | 120 |
| 1976 | George Foster, Cin. | 121 |
| 1977 | George Foster, Cin. | 149 |
| 1978 | George Foster, Cin. | 120 |
| 1979 | Dave Winfield, SD | 118 |
| 1980 | Mike Schmidt, Phi. | 121 |
| 1981 | Mike Schmidt, Phi. | 91 |

## Runs Batted In (Cont.)

| Year | | RBI |
|---|---|---|
| 1982 | Dale Murphy, Atl | 109 |
| | & Al Oliver, Mon | 109 |
| 1983 | Dale Murphy, Atl | 121 |
| 1984 | Gary Carter, Mon | 106 |
| | & Mike Schmidt, Phi | 106 |
| 1985 | Dave Parker, Cin | 125 |
| 1986 | Mike Schmidt, Phi | 119 |
| 1987 | Andre Dawson, Chi | 137 |
| 1988 | Will Clark, SF | 109 |

| Year | | RBI |
|---|---|---|
| 1989 | Kevin Mitchell, SF | 125 |
| 1990 | Matt Williams, SF | 122 |
| 1991 | Howard Johnson, NY | 117 |
| 1992 | Darren Daulton, Phi | 109 |
| 1993 | Barry Bonds, SF | 123 |
| 1994 | Jeff Bagwell, Hou | 116 |
| 1995 | Dante Bichette, Col | 128 |
| 1996 | Andres Galarraga, Col | 150 |
| 1997 | Andres Galarraga, Col | 140 |

| Year | | RBI |
|---|---|---|
| 1998 | Sammy Sosa, Chi | 158 |
| 1999 | Mark McGwire, St.L | 147 |
| 2000 | Todd Helton, Col | 147 |
| 2001 | Sammy Sosa, Chi | 160 |
| 2002 | Lance Berkman, Hou | 128 |
| 2003 | Preston Wilson, Col | 141 |
| 2004 | Vinny Castilla, Col | 131 |
| 2005 | Andruw Jones, Atl | 128 |

### American League

**Multiple winners:** Babe Ruth (6); Lou Gehrig (5); Ty Cobb, Hank Greenberg and Ted Williams (4); Albert Belle, Sam Crawford, Cecil Fielder, Jimmie Foxx, Jackie Jensen, Harmon Killebrew, Vern Stephens and Bobby Veach (3); Home Run Baker, Cecil Cooper, Harry Davis, Joe DiMaggio, Buck Freeman, Nap Lajoie, Roger Maris, Jim Rice, Al Rosen, and Bobby Veach (2).

| Year | | RBI |
|---|---|---|
| 1901 | Nap Lajoie, Phi | 125 |
| 1902 | Buck Freeman, Bos | 121 |
| 1903 | Buck Freeman, Bos | 104 |
| 1904 | Nap Lajoie, Cle | 102 |
| 1905 | Harry Davis, Phi | 83 |
| 1906 | Harry Davis, Phi | 96 |
| 1907 | Ty Cobb, Det | 116 |
| 1908 | Ty Cobb, Det | 108 |
| 1909 | Ty Cobb, Det | 107 |
| 1910 | Sam Crawford, Det | 120 |
| 1911 | Ty Cobb, Det | 144 |
| 1912 | Home Run Baker, Phi | 133 |
| 1913 | Home Run Baker, Phi | 126 |
| 1914 | Sam Crawford, Det | 104 |
| 1915 | Sam Crawford, Det | 112 |
| | & Bobby Veach, Det | 112 |
| 1916 | Del Pratt, St.L | 103 |
| 1917 | Bobby Veach, Det | 103 |
| 1918 | Bobby Veach, Det | 78 |
| 1919 | Babe Ruth, Bos | 114 |
| 1920 | Babe Ruth, NY | 137 |
| 1921 | Babe Ruth, NY | 171 |
| 1922 | Ken Williams, St.L | 155 |
| 1923 | Babe Ruth, NY | 131 |
| 1924 | Goose Goslin, Wash | 129 |
| 1925 | Bob Meusel, NY | 138 |
| 1926 | Babe Ruth, NY | 145 |
| 1927 | Lou Gehrig, NY | 175 |
| 1928 | Lou Gehrig, NY | 142 |
| | & Babe Ruth, NY | 142 |
| 1929 | Al Simmons, Phi | 157 |
| 1930 | Lou Gehrig, NY | 174 |
| 1931 | Lou Gehrig, NY | 184 |
| 1932 | Jimmie Foxx, Phi | 169 |
| 1933 | Jimmie Foxx, Phi | 163 |
| 1934 | Lou Gehrig, NY | 165 |
| 1935 | Hank Greenberg, Det | 170 |
| 1936 | Hal Trosky, Cle | 162 |

| Year | | RBI |
|---|---|---|
| 1937 | Hank Greenberg, Det | 183 |
| 1938 | Jimmie Foxx, Bos | 175 |
| 1939 | Ted Williams, Bos | 145 |
| 1940 | Hank Greenberg, Det | 150 |
| 1941 | Joe DiMaggio, NY | 125 |
| 1942 | Ted Williams, Bos | 137 |
| 1943 | Rudy York, Det | 118 |
| 1944 | Vern Stephens, St.L | 109 |
| 1945 | Nick Etten, NY | 111 |
| 1946 | Hank Greenberg, Det | 127 |
| 1947 | Ted Williams, Bos | 114 |
| 1948 | Joe DiMaggio, NY | 155 |
| 1949 | Ted Williams, Bos | 159 |
| | & Vern Stephens, Bos | 159 |
| 1950 | Walt Dropo, Bos | 144 |
| | & Vern Stephens, Bos | 144 |
| 1951 | Gus Zernial, Chi-Phi | 129 |
| 1952 | Al Rosen, Cle | 105 |
| 1953 | Al Rosen, Cle | 145 |
| 1954 | Larry Doby, Cle | 126 |
| 1955 | Ray Boone, Det | 116 |
| | & Jackie Jensen, Bos | 116 |
| 1956 | Mickey Mantle, NY | 130 |
| 1957 | Roy Sievers, Wash | 114 |
| 1958 | Jackie Jensen, Bos | 122 |
| 1959 | Jackie Jensen, Bos | 112 |
| 1960 | Roger Maris, NY | 112 |
| 1961 | Roger Maris, NY | 142 |
| 1962 | Harmon Killebrew, Min | 126 |
| 1963 | Dick Stuart, Bos | 118 |
| 1964 | Brooks Robinson, Bal | 118 |
| 1965 | Rocky Colavito, Cle | 108 |
| 1966 | Frank Robinson, Bal | 122 |
| 1967 | Carl Yastrzemski, Bos | 121 |
| 1968 | Ken Harrelson, Bos | 109 |
| 1969 | Harmon Killebrew, Min | 140 |
| 1970 | Frank Howard, Wash | 126 |
| 1971 | Harmon Killebrew, Min | 119 |

| Year | | RBI |
|---|---|---|
| 1972 | Dick Allen, Chi | 113 |
| 1973 | Reggie Jackson, Oak | 117 |
| 1974 | Jeff Burroughs, Tex | 118 |
| 1975 | George Scott, Mil | 109 |
| 1976 | Lee May, Bal | 109 |
| 1977 | Larry Hisle, Min | 119 |
| 1978 | Jim Rice, Bos | 139 |
| 1979 | Don Baylor, Cal | 139 |
| 1980 | Cecil Cooper, Mil | 122 |
| 1981 | Eddie Murray, Bal | 78 |
| 1982 | Hal McRae, KC | 133 |
| 1983 | Cecil Cooper, Mil | 126 |
| | & Jim Rice, Bos | 126 |
| 1984 | Tony Armas, Bos | 123 |
| 1985 | Don Mattingly, NY | 145 |
| 1986 | Joe Carter, Cle | 121 |
| 1987 | George Bell, Tor | 134 |
| 1988 | Jose Canseco, Oak | 124 |
| 1989 | Ruben Sierra, Tex | 119 |
| 1990 | Cecil Fielder, Det | 132 |
| 1991 | Cecil Fielder, Det | 133 |
| 1992 | Cecil Fielder, Det | 124 |
| 1993 | Albert Belle, Cle | 129 |
| 1994 | Kirby Puckett, Min | 112 |
| 1995 | Albert Belle, Cle | 126 |
| | & Mo Vaughn, Bos | 126 |
| 1996 | Albert Belle, Cle | 148 |
| 1997 | Ken Griffey Jr., Sea | 147 |
| 1998 | Juan Gonzalez, Tex | 157 |
| 1999 | Manny Ramirez, Cle | 165 |
| 2000 | Edgar Martinez, Sea | 145 |
| 2001 | Bret Boone, Sea | 141 |
| 2002 | Alex Rodriguez, Tex | 142 |
| 2003 | Carlos Delgado, Tor | 145 |
| 2004 | Miguel Tejada, Bal | 150 |
| 2005 | David Ortiz, Bos | 148 |

---

## Batting Triple Crown Winners

Players who led either league in Batting Average, Home Runs and Runs Batted In over a single season.

### National League

| | Year | Avg | HR | RBI |
|---|---|---|---|---|
| Paul Hines, Providence | 1878 | .358 | 4 | 50 |
| Hugh Duffy, Boston | 1894 | .438 | 18 | 145 |
| Heinie Zimmerman, Chicago | 1912 | .372 | 14 | 103 |
| Rogers Hornsby, St. Louis | 1922 | .401 | 42 | 152 |
| Rogers Hornsby, St. Louis | 1925 | .403 | 39 | 143 |
| Chuck Klein, Philadelphia | 1933 | .368 | 28 | 120 |
| Joe Medwick, St. Louis | 1937 | .374 | 31*| 154 |

*Tied for league lead in HRs with Mel Ott, NY.

### American League

| | Year | Avg | HR | RBI |
|---|---|---|---|---|
| Nap Lajoie, Philadelphia | 1901 | .422 | 14 | 125 |
| Ty Cobb, Detroit | 1909 | .377 | 9 | 115 |
| Jimmie Foxx, Philadelphia | 1933 | .356 | 48 | 163 |
| Lou Gehrig, New York | 1934 | .363 | 49 | 165 |
| Ted Williams, Boston | 1942 | .356 | 36 | 137 |
| Ted Williams, Boston | 1947 | .343 | 32 | 114 |
| Mickey Mantle, New York | 1956 | .353 | 52 | 130 |
| Frank Robinson, Baltimore | 1966 | .316 | 49 | 122 |
| Carl Yastrzemski, Boston | 1967 | .326 | 44*| 121 |

*Tied for league lead in HRs with Harmon Killebrew, Min.

## Stolen Bases
### National League

**Multiple winners:** Max Carey (10); Lou Brock (8); Vince Coleman and Maury Wills (6); Honus Wagner (5); Bob Bescher, Kiki Cuyler, Willie Mays and Tim Raines (4); Bill Bruton, Frankie Frisch, Pepper Martin and Tony Womack (3); George Burns, Luis Castillo, Frank Chance, Augie Galan, Marquis Grissom, Stan Hack, Sam Jethroe, Davey Lopes, Omar Moreno, Pete Reiser and Jackie Robinson (2).

| Year | | SB | Year | | SB | Year | | SB |
|---|---|---|---|---|---|---|---|---|
| 1900 | Patsy Donovan, St.L | 45 | 1934 | Pepper Martin, St.L. | 23 | 1970 | Bobby Tolan, Cin | 57 |
| | & George Van Haltren, NY. | 45 | 1935 | Augie Galan, Chi | 22 | 1971 | Lou Brock, St.L | 64 |
| 1901 | Honus Wagner, Pit | 49 | 1936 | Pepper Martin, St.L. | 23 | 1972 | Lou Brock, St.L | 63 |
| 1902 | Honus Wagner, Pit | 42 | 1937 | Augie Galan, Chi | 23 | 1973 | Lou Brock, St.L | 70 |
| 1903 | Frank Chance, Chi | 67 | 1938 | Stan Hack, Chi | 16 | 1974 | Lou Brock, St.L. | 118 |
| | & Jimmy Sheckard, Bklyn. | 67 | 1939 | Stan Hack, Chi. | 17 | 1975 | Davey Lopes, LA. | 77 |
| 1904 | Honus Wagner, Pit | 53 | | & Lee Handley, Pit | 17 | 1976 | Davey Lopes, LA. | 63 |
| 1905 | Art Devlin, NY. | 59 | | | | 1977 | Frank Taveras, Pit | 70 |
| | & Billy Maloney, Chi | 59 | 1940 | Lonny Frey, Cin | 22 | 1978 | Omar Moreno, Pit. | 71 |
| 1906 | Frank Chance, Chi | 57 | 1941 | Danny Murtaugh, Phi | 18 | 1979 | Omar Moreno, Pit. | 77 |
| 1907 | Honus Wagner, Pit | 61 | 1942 | Pete Reiser, Bklyn | 20 | | | |
| 1908 | Honus Wagner, Pit | 53 | 1943 | Arky Vaughan, Bklyn. | 20 | 1980 | Ron LeFlore, Mon | 97 |
| 1909 | Bob Bescher, Cin | 54 | 1944 | Johnny Barrett, Pit | 28 | 1981 | Tim Raines, Mon. | 71 |
| | | | 1945 | Red Schoendienst, St.L. | 26 | 1982 | Tim Raines, Mon. | 78 |
| 1910 | Bob Bescher, Cin | 70 | 1946 | Pete Reiser, Bklyn | 34 | 1983 | Tim Raines, Mon. | 90 |
| 1911 | Bob Bescher, Cin | 81 | 1947 | Jackie Robinson, Bklyn. | 29 | 1984 | Tim Raines, Mon. | 75 |
| 1912 | Bob Bescher, Cin | 67 | 1948 | Richie Ashburn, Phi. | 32 | 1985 | Vince Coleman, St.L. | 110 |
| 1913 | Max Carey, Pit | 61 | 1949 | Jackie Robinson, Bklyn. | 37 | 1986 | Vince Coleman, St.L. | 107 |
| 1914 | George Burns, NY | 62 | | | | 1987 | Vince Coleman, St.L. | 109 |
| 1915 | Max Carey, Pit | 36 | 1950 | Sam Jethroe, Bos. | 35 | 1988 | Vince Coleman, St.L | 81 |
| 1916 | Max Carey, Pit | 63 | 1951 | Sam Jethroe, Bos. | 35 | 1989 | Vince Coleman, St.L | 65 |
| 1917 | Max Carey, Pit | 46 | 1952 | Pee Wee Reese, Bklyn | 30 | | | |
| 1918 | Max Carey, Pit | 58 | 1953 | Bill Bruton, Mil. | 26 | 1990 | Vince Coleman, St.L | 77 |
| 1919 | George Burns, NY | 40 | 1954 | Bill Bruton, Mil. | 34 | 1991 | Marquis Grissom, Mon | 76 |
| | | | 1955 | Bill Bruton, Mil. | 25 | 1992 | Marquis Grissom, Mon | 78 |
| 1920 | Max Carey, Pit | 52 | 1956 | Willie Mays, NY | 40 | 1993 | Chuck Carr, Fla. | 58 |
| 1921 | Frankie Frisch, NY | 49 | 1957 | Willie Mays, NY | 38 | 1994 | Craig Biggio, Hou | 39 |
| 1922 | Max Carey, Pit | 51 | 1958 | Willie Mays, SF | 31 | 1995 | Quilvio Veras, Fla. | 56 |
| 1923 | Max Carey, Pit | 51 | 1959 | Willie Mays, SF | 27 | 1996 | Eric Young, Col | 53 |
| 1924 | Max Carey, Pit | 49 | 1960 | Maury Wills, LA | 50 | 1997 | Tony Womack, Pit | 60 |
| 1925 | Max Carey, Pit | 46 | 1961 | Maury Wills, LA | 35 | 1998 | Tony Womack, Pit. | 58 |
| 1926 | Kiki Cuyler, Pit. | 35 | 1962 | Maury Wills, LA | 104 | 1999 | Tony Womack, Ari | 72 |
| 1927 | Frankie Frisch, St.L | 48 | 1963 | Maury Wills, LA | 40 | | | |
| 1928 | Kiki Cuyler, Chi. | 37 | 1964 | Maury Wills, LA | 53 | 2000 | Luis Castillo, Fla | 62 |
| 1929 | Kiki Cuyler, Chi. | 43 | 1965 | Maury Wills, LA | 94 | 2001 | Juan Pierre, Col. | 46 |
| 1930 | Kiki Cuyler, Chi. | 37 | 1966 | Lou Brock, St.L | 74 | | & Jimmy Rollins, Phi | 46 |
| 1931 | Frankie Frisch, St.L | 28 | 1967 | Lou Brock, St.L | 52 | 2002 | Luis Castillo, Fla. | 48 |
| 1932 | Chuck Klein, Phi | 20 | 1968 | Lou Brock, St.L | 62 | 2003 | Juan Pierre, Fla. | 65 |
| 1933 | Pepper Martin, St.L. | 26 | 1969 | Lou Brock, St.L | 53 | 2004 | Scott Podsednik, Mil | 70 |
| | | | | | | 2005 | Jose Reyes, NY. | 60 |

## 30 Homers & 30 Stolen Bases in One Season

### National League

| | Year | Gm | HR | SB |
|---|---|---|---|---|
| Willie Mays, NY Giants | 1956 | 152 | 36 | 40 |
| Willie Mays, NY Giants | 1957 | 152 | 35 | 38 |
| Hank Aaron, Milwaukee | 1963 | 161 | 44 | 31 |
| Bobby Bonds, San Francisco | 1969 | 158 | 32 | 45 |
| Bobby Bonds, San Francisco | 1973 | 160 | 39 | 43 |
| Dale Murphy, Atlanta | 1983 | 162 | 36 | 30 |
| Eric Davis, Cincinnati | 1987 | 129 | 37 | 50 |
| Howard Johnson, NY Mets. | 1987 | 157 | 36 | 32 |
| Darryl Strawberry, NY Mets | 1987 | 154 | 39 | 36 |
| Howard Johnson, NY Mets. | 1989 | 153 | 36 | 41 |
| Ron Gant, Atlanta | 1990 | 152 | 32 | 33 |
| Barry Bonds, Pittsburgh | 1990 | 151 | 33 | 52 |
| Ron Gant, Atlanta | 1991 | 154 | 32 | 34 |
| Howard Johnson, NY Mets. | 1991 | 156 | 38 | 30 |
| Barry Bonds, Pittsburgh | 1992 | 140 | 34 | 39 |
| Sammy Sosa, Chicago | 1993 | 159 | 33 | 36 |
| Barry Bonds, San Francisco | 1995 | 144 | 33 | 31 |
| Sammy Sosa, Chicago | 1995 | 144 | 36 | 34 |
| Barry Bonds, San Francisco | 1996 | 158 | 42 | 40 |
| Ellis Burks, Colorado | 1996 | 156 | 40 | 32 |
| Dante Bichette, Colorado | 1996 | 159 | 31 | 31 |
| Barry Larkin, Cincinnati. | 1996 | 152 | 33 | 36 |
| Larry Walker, Colorado | 1997 | 153 | 49 | 33 |
| Barry Bonds, San Francisco | 1997 | 159 | 40 | 37 |

| | Year | Gm | HR | SB |
|---|---|---|---|---|
| Raul Mondesi, Los Angeles. | 1997 | 159 | 30 | 32 |
| Jeff Bagwell, Houston | 1997 | 162 | 43 | 31 |
| Jeff Bagwell, Houston | 1999 | 162 | 42 | 30 |
| Raul Mondesi, Los Angeles. | 1999 | 159 | 33 | 36 |
| Preston Wilson, Florida | 2000 | 161 | 31 | 36 |
| Vladimir Guerrero, Montreal | 2001 | 159 | 34 | 37 |
| Bobby Abreu, Philadelphia. | 2001 | 162 | 31 | 36 |
| Vladimir Guerrero, Montreal | 2002 | 161 | 39 | 40 |
| Bobby Abreu, Philadelphia | 2004 | 159 | 30 | 40 |

### American League

| | Year | Gm | HR | SB |
|---|---|---|---|---|
| Kenny Williams, St. Louis | 1922 | 153 | 39 | 37 |
| Tommy Harper, Milwaukee. | 1970 | 154 | 31 | 38 |
| Bobby Bonds, New York. | 1975 | 145 | 32 | 30 |
| Bobby Bonds, California. | 1977 | 158 | 37 | 41 |
| Bobby Bonds, Chicago-Texas. | 1978 | 156 | 31 | 43 |
| Joe Carter, Cleveland | 1987 | 149 | 32 | 31 |
| Jose Canseco, Oakland | 1988 | 158 | 42 | 40 |
| Alex Rodriguez, Seattle. | 1998 | 161 | 42 | 46 |
| Shawn Green, Toronto. | 1998 | 158 | 35 | 35 |
| Jose Cruz Jr., Toronto. | 2001 | 146 | 34 | 32 |
| Alfonso Soriano, New York | 2002 | 156 | 39 | 41 |
| Alfonso Soriano, New York | 2003 | 156 | 38 | 35 |
| Alfonso Soriano, Texas. | 2005 | 156 | 36 | 30 |

**Note:** In 2004, Carlos Beltran switched leagues mid-season. Combining his AL and NL totals, he hit 38 HR and stole 42 bases.

## Stolen Bases (Cont.)
### American League

**Multiple winners:** Rickey Henderson (12); Luis Aparicio (9); Bert Campaneris, George Case and Ty Cobb (6); Kenny Lofton (5); Ben Chapman, Eddie Collins and George Sisler (4); Bob Dillinger, Minnie Minoso and Bill Werber (3); Carl Crawford, Elmer Flick, Tommy Harper, Brian Hunter, Clyde Milan, Johnny Mostil, Bill North and Snuffy Stirnweiss (2).

| Year | | SB | Year | | SB | Year | | SB |
|---|---|---|---|---|---|---|---|---|
| 1901 | Frank Isbell, Chi | 52 | 1936 | Lyn Lary, St.L | 37 | 1970 | Bert Campaneris, Oak. | 42 |
| 1902 | Topsy Hartsel, Phi | 47 | 1937 | Ben Chapman, Wash-Bos | 35 | 1971 | Amos Otis, KC. | 52 |
| 1903 | Harry Bay, Cle. | 45 | | & Bill Werber, Phi. | 35 | 1972 | Bert Campaneris, Oak. | 52 |
| 1904 | Elmer Flick, Cle | 42 | 1938 | Frank Crosetti, NY | 27 | 1973 | Tommy Harper, Bos | 54 |
| 1905 | Danny Hoffman, Phi | 46 | 1939 | George Case, Wash. | 51 | 1974 | Bill North, Oak. | 54 |
| 1906 | John Anderson, Wash | 39 | 1940 | George Case, Wash. | 35 | 1975 | Mickey Rivers, CA | 70 |
| | & Elmer Flick, Cle. | 39 | 1941 | George Case, Wash. | 33 | 1976 | Bill North, Oak. | 75 |
| 1907 | Ty Cobb, Det | 49 | 1942 | George Case, Wash. | 44 | 1977 | Freddie Patek, KC. | 53 |
| 1908 | Patsy Dougherty, Chi | 47 | 1943 | George Case, Wash. | 61 | 1978 | Ron LeFlore, Det | 68 |
| 1909 | Ty Cobb, Det | 76 | 1944 | Snuffy Stirnweiss, NY. | 55 | 1979 | Willie Wilson, KC. | 83 |
| 1910 | Eddie Collins, Phi | 81 | 1945 | Snuffy Stirnweiss, NY. | 33 | 1980 | Rickey Henderson, Oak. | 100 |
| 1911 | Ty Cobb, Det | 83 | 1946 | George Case, Cle | 28 | 1981 | Rickey Henderson, Oak. | 56 |
| 1912 | Clyde Milan, Wash. | 88 | 1947 | Bob Dillinger, St.L | 34 | 1982 | Rickey Henderson, Oak. | 130 |
| 1913 | Clyde Milan, Wash. | 75 | 1948 | Bob Dillinger, St.L | 28 | 1983 | Rickey Henderson, Oak. | 108 |
| 1914 | Fritz Maisel, NY | 74 | 1949 | Bob Dillinger, St.L | 20 | 1984 | Rickey Henderson, Oak. | 66 |
| 1915 | Ty Cobb, Det | 96 | 1950 | Dom DiMaggio, Bos. | 15 | 1985 | Rickey Henderson, NY. | 80 |
| 1916 | Ty Cobb, Det | 68 | 1951 | Minnie Minoso, Cle-Chi. | 31 | 1986 | Rickey Henderson, NY. | 87 |
| 1917 | Ty Cobb, Det | 55 | 1952 | Minnie Minoso, Chi | 22 | 1987 | Harold Reynolds, Sea | 60 |
| 1918 | George Sisler, St.L | 45 | 1953 | Minnie Minoso, Chi | 25 | 1988 | Rickey Henderson, NY. | 93 |
| 1919 | Eddie Collins, Chi. | 33 | 1954 | Jackie Jensen, Bos. | 22 | 1989 | R. Henderson, NY-Oak | 77 |
| 1920 | Sam Rice, Wash. | 63 | 1955 | Jim Rivera, Chi | 25 | 1990 | Rickey Henderson, Oak. | 65 |
| 1921 | George Sisler, St.L | 35 | 1956 | Luis Aparicio, Chi | 21 | 1991 | Rickey Henderson, Oak. | 58 |
| 1922 | George Sisler, St.L | 51 | 1957 | Luis Aparicio, Chi | 28 | 1992 | Kenny Lofton, Cle | 66 |
| 1923 | Eddie Collins, Chi. | 47 | 1958 | Luis Aparicio, Chi | 29 | 1993 | Kenny Lofton, Cle | 70 |
| 1924 | Eddie Collins, Chi. | 42 | 1959 | Luis Aparicio, Chi | 56 | 1994 | Kenny Lofton, Cle | 60 |
| 1925 | Johnny Mostil, Chi | 43 | 1960 | Luis Aparicio, Chi | 51 | 1995 | Kenny Lofton, Cle | 54 |
| 1926 | Johnny Mostil, Chi | 35 | 1961 | Luis Aparicio, Chi | 53 | 1996 | Kenny Lofton, Cle | 75 |
| 1927 | George Sisler, St.L | 27 | 1962 | Luis Aparicio, Chi | 31 | 1997 | Brian Hunter, Det | 74 |
| 1928 | Buddy Myer, Bos. | 30 | 1963 | Luis Aparicio, Bal | 40 | 1998 | Rickey Henderson, Oak. | 66 |
| 1929 | Charlie Gehringer, Det. | 28 | 1964 | Luis Aparicio, Bal | 57 | 1999 | Brian Hunter, Det-Sea. | 44 |
| 1930 | Marty McManus, Det | 23 | 1965 | Bert Campaneris, KC | 51 | 2000 | Johnny Damon, KC. | 46 |
| 1931 | Ben Chapman, NY. | 61 | 1966 | Bert Campaneris, KC | 52 | 2001 | Ichiro Suzuki, Sea. | 56 |
| 1932 | Ben Chapman, NY. | 38 | 1967 | Bert Campaneris, KC | 55 | 2002 | Alfonso Soriano, NY | 41 |
| 1933 | Ben Chapman, NY. | 27 | 1968 | Bert Campaneris, Oak. | 62 | 2003 | Carl Crawford, TB | 55 |
| 1934 | Bill Werber, Bos | 40 | 1969 | Tommy Harper, Sea | 73 | 2004 | Carl Crawford, TB | 59 |
| 1935 | Bill Werber, Bos | 29 | | | | 2005 | Chone Figgins, LAA | 62 |

# Consecutive Game Streaks
(Regular season games through 2005)

## Games Played

| Gm | | Dates of Streak |
|---|---|---|
| 2632 | Cal Ripken Jr., Bal | 5/30/82 to 9/19/98 |
| 2130 | Lou Gehrig, NY | 6/1/25 to 4/30/39 |
| 1307 | Everett Scott, Bos-NY | 6/20/16 to 5/5/25 |
| 1207 | Steve Garvey, LA-SD. | 9/3/75 to 7/29/83 |
| 1117 | Billy Williams, Cubs | 9/22/63 to 9/2/70 |
| 1103 | Joe Sewell, Cle | 9/13/22 to 4/30/30 |
| 918 | Miguel Tejada, Oak-Bal | 6/1/00 to present |
| 895 | Stan Musial, St.L | 4/15/52 to 8/23/57 |
| 829 | Eddie Yost, Wash | 4/30/49 to 5/11/55 |
| 822 | Gus Suhr, Pit | 9/11/31 to 6/4/37 |
| 798 | Nellie Fox, Chisox. | 8/8/55 to 9/3/60 |
| 745 | Pete Rose, Cin-Phi | 9/2/78 to 8/23/83 |
| 740 | Dale Murphy, Atl. | 9/26/81 to 7/8/86 |
| 730 | Richie Ashburn, Phi | 6/7/50 to 4/13/55 |
| 717 | Ernie Banks, Cubs. | 8/28/56 to 6/22/61 |
| 678 | Pete Rose, Cin | 9/28/73 to 5/7/78 |

### Others

| Gm | | Gm | |
|---|---|---|---|
| 673 | Earl Averill | 577 | George Pinckney |
| 652 | Frank McCormick | 574 | Steve Brodie |
| 648 | Sandy Alomar Sr. | 565 | Aaron Ward |
| 618 | Eddie Brown | 546 | Alex Rodriguez |
| 585 | Roy McMillan | 540 | Candy LaChance |

## Hitting

| | Gm | Year |
|---|---|---|
| Joe DiMaggio, New York (AL) | 56 | 1941 |
| Willie Keeler, Baltimore (NL) | 44 | 1897 |
| Pete Rose, Cincinnati (NL) | 44 | 1978 |
| Bill Dahlen, Chicago (NL) | 42 | 1894 |
| George Sisler, St. Louis (AL) | 41 | 1922 |
| Ty Cobb, Detroit (AL) | 40 | 1911 |
| Paul Molitor, Milwaukee (AL) | 39 | 1987 |
| Tommy Holmes, Boston (NL) | 37 | 1945 |
| Billy Hamilton, Philadelphia (NL) | 36 | 1894 |
| Jimmy Rollins, Philadelphia (NL) | 36* | 2005 |
| Fred Clarke, Louisville (NL) | 35 | 1895 |
| Ty Cobb, Detroit (AL) | 35 | 1917 |
| Luis Castillo, Florida (NL). | 35 | 2002 |
| Ty Cobb, Detroit (AL) | 34 | 1912 |
| George Sisler, St. Louis (AL) | 34 | 1925 |
| George McQuinn, St. Louis (AL). | 34 | 1938 |
| Dom DiMaggio, Boston (AL) | 34 | 1949 |
| Benito Santiago, San Diego (NL) | 34 | 1987 |
| George Davis, New York (NL) | 33 | 1893 |
| Hal Chase, New York (AL) | 33 | 1907 |
| Rogers Hornsby, St. Louis (NL) | 33 | 1922 |
| Heinie Manush, Washington (AL). | 33 | 1933 |

*current

## Annual Pitching Leaders (since 1900)
### Winning Percentage
At least 15 wins, except in strike years of 1981 and 1994 (when the minimum was 10).

#### National League

**Multiple winners:** Ed Reulbach and Tom Seaver (3); Larry Benton, Harry Brecheen, Jack Chesbro, Paul Derringer, Freddie Fitzsimmons, Don Gullett, Claude Hendrix, Carl Hubbell, Randy Johnson, Sandy Koufax, Bill Lee, Greg Maddux, Christy Mathewson, Don Newcombe, Preacher Roe and John Smoltz (2).

| Year | | W-L | Pct | Year | | W-L | Pct |
|---|---|---|---|---|---|---|---|
| 1900 | Jesse Tannehill, Pittsburgh | .20-6 | .769 | 1956 | Don Newcombe, Brooklyn | .27-7 | .794 |
| 1901 | Jack Chesbro, Pittsburgh | .21-10 | .677 | 1957 | Bob Buhl, Milwaukee | .18-7 | .720 |
| 1902 | Jack Chesbro, Pittsburgh | .28-6 | .824 | 1958 | Warren Spahn, Milwaukee | .22-11 | .667 |
| 1903 | Sam Leever, Pittsburgh | .25-7 | .781 | | & Lew Burdette, Milwaukee | .20-10 | .667 |
| 1904 | Joe McGinnity, New York | .35-8 | .814 | 1959 | Roy Face, Pittsburgh | .18-1 | .947 |
| 1905 | Christy Mathewson, New York | .31-8 | .795 | | | | |
| 1906 | Ed Reulbach, Chicago | .19-4 | .826 | 1960 | Ernie Broglio, St. Louis | .21-9 | .700 |
| 1907 | Ed Reulbach, Chicago | .17-4 | .810 | 1961 | Johnny Podres, Los Angeles | .18-5 | .783 |
| 1908 | Ed Reulbach, Chicago | .24-7 | .774 | 1962 | Bob Purkey, Cincinnati | .23-5 | .821 |
| 1909 | Howie Camnitz, Pittsburgh | .25-6 | .806 | 1963 | Ron Perranoski, Los Angeles | .16-3 | .842 |
| | & Christy Mathewson, New York | .25-6 | .806 | 1964 | Sandy Koufax, Los Angeles | .19-5 | .792 |
| | | | | 1965 | Sandy Koufax, Los Angeles | .26-8 | .765 |
| 1910 | King Cole, Chicago | .20-4 | .833 | 1966 | Juan Marichal, San Francisco | .25-6 | .806 |
| 1911 | Rube Marquard, New York | .24-7 | .774 | 1967 | Dick Hughes, St. Louis | .16-6 | .727 |
| 1912 | Claude Hendrix, Pittsburgh | .24-9 | .727 | 1968 | Steve Blass, Pittsburgh | .18-6 | .750 |
| 1913 | Bert Humphries, Chicago | .16-4 | .800 | 1969 | Tom Seaver, New York | .25-7 | .781 |
| 1914 | Bill James, Boston | .26-7 | .788 | | | | |
| 1915 | Grover Alexander, Phila. | .31-10 | .756 | 1970 | Bob Gibson, St. Louis | .23-7 | .767 |
| 1916 | Tom Hughes, Boston | .16-3 | .842 | 1971 | Don Gullett, Cincinnati | .16-6 | .727 |
| 1917 | Ferdie Schupp, New York | .21-7 | .750 | 1972 | Gary Nolan, Cincinnati | .15-5 | .750 |
| 1918 | Claude Hendrix, Chicago | .19-7 | .731 | 1973 | Tommy John, Los Angeles | .16-7 | .696 |
| 1919 | Dutch Ruether, Cincinnati | .19-6 | .760 | 1974 | Andy Messersmith, Los Angeles | .20-6 | .769 |
| | | | | 1975 | Don Gullett, Cincinnati | .15-4 | .789 |
| 1920 | Burleigh Grimes, Brooklyn | .23-11 | .676 | 1976 | Steve Carlton, Philadelphia | .20-7 | .741 |
| 1921 | Bill Doak, St. Louis | .15-6 | .714 | 1977 | John Candelaria, Pittsburgh | .20-5 | .800 |
| 1922 | Pete Donohue, Cincinnati | .18-9 | .667 | 1978 | Gaylord Perry, San Diego | .21-6 | .778 |
| 1923 | Dolf Luque, Cincinnati | .27-8 | .771 | 1979 | Tom Seaver, Cincinnati | .16-6 | .727 |
| 1924 | Emil Yde, Pittsburgh | .16-3 | .842 | | | | |
| 1925 | Bill Sherdel, St. Louis | .15-6 | .714 | 1980 | Jim Bibby, Pittsburgh | .19-6 | .760 |
| 1926 | Ray Kremer, Pittsburgh | .20-6 | .769 | 1981 | Tom Seaver, Cincinnati | .14-2 | .875 |
| 1927 | Larry Benton, Boston-NY. | .17-7 | .708 | 1982 | Phil Niekro, Atlanta | .17-4 | .810 |
| 1928 | Larry Benton, New York | .25-9 | .735 | 1983 | John Denny, Philadelphia | .19-6 | .760 |
| 1929 | Charlie Root, Chicago | .19-6 | .760 | 1984 | Rick Sutcliffe, Chicago | .16-1 | .941 |
| | | | | 1985 | Orel Hershiser, Los Angeles | .19-3 | .864 |
| 1930 | Freddie Fitzsimmons, NY | .19-7 | .731 | 1986 | Bob Ojeda, New York | .18-5 | .783 |
| 1931 | Paul Derringer, St. Louis | .18-8 | .692 | 1987 | Dwight Gooden, New York | .15-7 | .682 |
| 1932 | Lon Warneke, Chicago | .22-6 | .786 | 1988 | David Cone, New York | .20-3 | .870 |
| 1933 | Ben Cantwell, Boston | .20-10 | .667 | 1989 | Mike Bielecki, Chicago | .18-7 | .720 |
| 1934 | Dizzy Dean, St. Louis | .30-7 | .811 | | | | |
| 1935 | Bill Lee, Chicago | .20-6 | .769 | 1990 | Doug Drabek, Pittsburgh | .22-6 | .786 |
| 1936 | Carl Hubbell, New York | .26-6 | .813 | 1991 | John Smiley, Pittsburgh | .20-8 | .714 |
| 1937 | Carl Hubbell, New York | .22-8 | .733 | | & Jose Rijo, Cincinnati | .15-6 | .714 |
| 1938 | Bill Lee, Chicago | .22-9 | .710 | 1992 | Bob Tewksbury, St. Louis | .16-5 | .762 |
| 1939 | Paul Derringer, Cincinnati | .25-7 | .781 | 1993 | Mark Portugal, Houston | .18-4 | .818 |
| | | | | 1994 | Marvin Freeman, Colorado | .10-2 | .833 |
| 1940 | Freddie Fitzsimmons, Bklyn | .16-2 | .889 | 1995 | Greg Maddux, Atlanta | .19-2 | .905 |
| 1941 | Elmer Riddle, Cincinnati | .19-4 | .826 | 1996 | John Smoltz, Atlanta | .24-8 | .750 |
| 1942 | Larry French, Brooklyn | .15-4 | .789 | 1997 | Greg Maddux, Atlanta | .19-4 | .826 |
| 1943 | Mort Cooper, St. Louis | .21-8 | .724 | 1998 | John Smoltz, Atlanta | .17-3 | .850 |
| 1944 | Ted Wilks, St. Louis | .17-4 | .810 | 1999 | Mike Hampton, Houston | .22-4 | .846 |
| 1945 | Harry Brecheen, St. Louis | .14-4 | .778 | | | | |
| 1946 | Murray Dickson, St. Louis | .15-6 | .714 | 2000 | Randy Johnson, Arizona | .19-7 | .731 |
| 1947 | Larry Jansen, New York | .21-5 | .808 | 2001 | Curt Schilling, Arizona | .22-6 | .786 |
| 1948 | Harry Brecheen, St. Louis | .20-7 | .741 | 2002 | Randy Johnson, Arizona | .24-5 | .828 |
| 1949 | Preacher Roe, Brooklyn | .15-6 | .714 | 2003 | Jason Schmidt, San Francisco | .17-5 | .773 |
| | | | | 2004 | Roger Clemens, Houston | .18-4 | .818 |
| 1950 | Sal Maglie, New York | .18-4 | .818 | 2005 | Chris Carpenter, St. Louis | .21-5 | .808 |
| 1951 | Preacher Roe, Brooklyn | .22-3 | .880 | | | | |
| 1952 | Hoyt Wilhelm, New York | .15-3 | .833 | | | | |
| 1953 | Carl Erskine, Brooklyn | .20-6 | .769 | | | | |
| 1954 | Johnny Antonelli, New York | .21-7 | .750 | | | | |
| 1955 | Don Newcombe, Brooklyn | .20-5 | .800 | | | | |

**Note:** In 1984, Sutcliffe was also 4-5 with Cleveland for a combined AL-NL record of 20-6 (.769).

## Winning Percentage (Cont.)

### American League

**Multiple winners:** Lefty Grove (5); Chief Bender, Roger Clemens and Whitey Ford (3); Johnny Allen, Eddie Cicotte, Mike Cuellar, Lefty Gomez, Ron Guidry, Catfish Hunter, Randy Johnson, Walter Johnson, Pedro Martinez, Jim Palmer, Pete Vuckovich and Smokey Joe Wood (2).

| Year | | W-L | Pct | Year | | W-L | Pct |
|---|---|---|---|---|---|---|---|
| 1901 | Clark Griffith, Chicago | .24-7 | .774 | 1957 | Dick Donovan, Chicago | .16-6 | .727 |
| 1902 | Bill Bernhard, Phila-Cleve | .18-5 | .783 | | & Tom Sturdivant, New York | .16-6 | .727 |
| 1903 | Cy Young, Boston | .28-9 | .757 | 1958 | Bob Turley, New York | .21-7 | .750 |
| 1904 | Jack Chesbro, New York | .41-12 | .774 | 1959 | Bob Shaw, Chicago | .18-6 | .750 |
| 1905 | Andy Coakley, Philadelphia | .20-7 | .741 | | | | |
| 1906 | Eddie Plank, Philadelphia | .19-6 | .760 | 1960 | Jim Perry, Cleveland | .18-10 | .643 |
| 1907 | Wild Bill Donovan, Detroit | .25-4 | .862 | 1961 | Whitey Ford, New York | .25-4 | .862 |
| 1908 | Ed Walsh, Chicago | .40-15 | .727 | 1962 | Ray Herbert, Chicago | .20-9 | .690 |
| 1909 | George Mullin, Detroit | .29-8 | .784 | 1963 | Whitey Ford, New York | .24-7 | .774 |
| | | | | 1964 | Wally Bunker, Baltimore | .19-5 | .792 |
| 1910 | Chief Bender, Philadelphia | .23-5 | .821 | 1965 | Mudcat Grant, Minnesota | .21-7 | .750 |
| 1911 | Chief Bender, Philadelphia | .17-5 | .773 | 1966 | Sonny Siebert, Cleveland | .16-8 | .667 |
| 1912 | Smokey Joe Wood, Boston | .34-5 | .872 | 1967 | Joe Horlen, Chicago | .19-7 | .731 |
| 1913 | Walter Johnson, Washington | .36-7 | .837 | 1968 | Denny McLain, Detroit | .31-6 | .838 |
| 1914 | Chief Bender, Philadelphia | .17-3 | .850 | 1969 | Jim Palmer, Baltimore | .16-4 | .800 |
| 1915 | Smokey Joe Wood, Boston | .15-5 | .750 | | | | |
| 1916 | Eddie Cicotte, Chicago | .15-7 | .682 | 1970 | Mike Cuellar, Baltimore | .24-8 | .750 |
| 1917 | Reb Russell, Chicago | .15-5 | .750 | 1971 | Dave McNally, Baltimore | .21-5 | .808 |
| 1918 | Sad Sam Jones, Boston | .16-5 | .762 | 1972 | Catfish Hunter, Oakland | .21-7 | .750 |
| 1919 | Eddie Cicotte, Chicago | .29-7 | .806 | 1973 | Catfish Hunter, Oakland | .21-5 | .808 |
| | | | | 1974 | Mike Cuellar, Baltimore | .22-10 | .688 |
| 1920 | Jim Bagby, Cleveland | .31-12 | .721 | 1975 | Mike Torrez, Baltimore | .20-9 | .690 |
| 1921 | Carl Mays, New York | .27-9 | .750 | 1976 | Bill Campbell, Minnesota | .17-5 | .773 |
| 1922 | Joe Bush, New York | .26-7 | .788 | 1977 | Paul Splittorff, Kansas City | .16-6 | .727 |
| 1923 | Herb Pennock, New York | .19-6 | .760 | 1978 | Ron Guidry, New York | .25-3 | .893 |
| 1924 | Walter Johnson, Washington | .23-7 | .767 | 1979 | Mike Caldwell, Milwaukee | .16-6 | .727 |
| 1925 | Stan Coveleski, Washington | .20-5 | .800 | | | | |
| 1926 | George Uhle, Cleveland | .27-11 | .711 | 1980 | Steve Stone, Baltimore | .25-7 | .781 |
| 1927 | Waite Hoyt, New York | .22-7 | .759 | 1981 | Pete Vuckovich, Milwaukee | .14-4 | .778 |
| 1928 | General Crowder, St. Louis | .21-5 | .808 | 1982 | Pete Vuckovich, Milwaukee | .18-6 | .750 |
| 1929 | Lefty Grove, Philadelphia | .20-6 | .769 | | & Jim Palmer, Baltimore | .15-5 | .750 |
| | | | | 1983 | Rich Dotson, Chicago | .22-7 | .759 |
| 1930 | Lefty Grove, Philadelphia | .28-5 | .848 | 1984 | Doyle Alexander, Toronto | .17-6 | .739 |
| 1931 | Lefty Grove, Philadelphia | .31-4 | .886 | 1985 | Ron Guidry, New York | .22-6 | .786 |
| 1932 | Johnny Allen, New York | .17-4 | .810 | 1986 | Roger Clemens, Boston | .24-4 | .857 |
| 1933 | Lefty Grove, Philadelphia | .24-8 | .750 | 1987 | Roger Clemens, Boston | .20-9 | .690 |
| 1934 | Lefty Gomez, New York | .26-5 | .839 | 1988 | Frank Viola, Minnesota | .24-7 | .774 |
| 1935 | Eldon Auker, Detroit | .18-7 | .720 | 1989 | Bret Saberhagen, Kansas City | .23-6 | .793 |
| 1936 | Monte Pearson, New York | .19-7 | .731 | | | | |
| 1937 | Johnny Allen, Cleveland | .15-1 | .938 | 1990 | Bob Welch, Oakland | .27-6 | .818 |
| 1938 | Red Ruffing, New York | .21-7 | .750 | 1991 | Scott Erickson, Minnesota | .20-8 | .714 |
| 1939 | Lefty Grove, Boston | .15-4 | .789 | 1992 | Mike Mussina, Baltimore | .18-5 | .783 |
| | | | | 1993 | Jimmy Key, New York | .18-6 | .750 |
| 1940 | Schoolboy Rowe, Detroit | .16-3 | .842 | 1994 | Jason Bere, Chicago | .12-2 | .857 |
| 1941 | Lefty Gomez, New York | .15-5 | .750 | 1995 | Randy Johnson, Seattle | .18-2 | .900 |
| 1942 | Ernie Bonham, New York | .21-5 | .808 | 1996 | Charles Nagy, Cleveland | .17-5 | .773 |
| 1943 | Spud Chandler, New York | .20-4 | .833 | 1997 | Randy Johnson, Seattle | .20-4 | .833 |
| 1944 | Tex Hughson, Boston | .18-5 | .783 | 1998 | David Wells, New York | .18-4 | .818 |
| 1945 | Hal Newhouser, Detroit | .25-9 | .735 | 1999 | Pedro Martinez, Boston | .23-4 | .852 |
| 1946 | Boo Ferriss, Boston | .25-6 | .806 | | | | |
| 1947 | Allie Reynolds, New York | .19-8 | .704 | 2000 | Tim Hudson, Oakland | .20-6 | .769 |
| 1948 | Jack Kramer, Boston | .18-5 | .783 | 2001 | Roger Clemens, New York | .20-3 | .870 |
| 1949 | Ellis Kinder, Boston | .23-6 | .793 | 2002 | Pedro Martinez, Boston | .20-4 | .833 |
| | | | | 2003 | Roy Halladay, Toronto | .22-7 | .759 |
| 1950 | Vic Raschi, New York | .21-8 | .724 | 2004 | Curt Schilling, Boston | .21-6 | .778 |
| 1951 | Bob Feller, Cleveland | .22-8 | .733 | 2005 | Cliff Lee, Cleveland | .18-5 | .783 |
| 1952 | Bobby Shantz, Philadelphia | .24-7 | .774 | | | | |
| 1953 | Ed Lopat, New York | .16-4 | .800 | | | | |
| 1954 | Sandy Consuegra, Chicago | .16-3 | .842 | | | | |
| 1955 | Tommy Byrne, New York | .16-5 | .762 | | | | |
| 1956 | Whitey Ford, New York | .19-6 | .760 | | | | |

## Earned Run Average

Earned Run Averages were based on at least 10 complete games pitched (1900-49), at least 154 innings pitched (1950-60), and at least 162 innings pitched since 1961 in the AL and 1962 in the NL. In the strike years of 1981, '94 and '95, qualifiers had to pitch at least as many innings as the total number of games their team played that season.

### National League

**Multiple winners:** Grover Alexander, Sandy Koufax and Christy Mathewson (5); Greg Maddux (4); Carl Hubbell, Randy Johnson, Tom Seaver, Warren Spahn and Dazzy Vance (3); Kevin Brown, Bill Doak, Ray Kremer, Dolf Luque, Howie Pollet, Nolan Ryan, Bill Walker and Bucky Walters (2).

| Year | | ERA | Year | | ERA | Year | | ERA |
|---|---|---|---|---|---|---|---|---|
| 1900 | Rube Waddell, Pit | 2.37 | 1936 | Carl Hubbell, NY | 2.31 | 1972 | Steve Carlton, Phi | 1.97 |
| 1901 | Jesse Tannehill, Pit | 2.18 | 1937 | Jim Turner, Bos | 2.38 | 1973 | Tom Seaver, NY | 2.08 |
| 1902 | Jack Taylor, Chi | 1.33 | 1938 | Bill Lee, Chi | 2.66 | 1974 | Buzz Capra, Atl | 2.28 |
| 1903 | Sam Leever, Pit | 2.06 | 1939 | Bucky Walters, Cin | 2.29 | 1975 | Randy Jones, SD | 2.24 |
| 1904 | Joe McGinnity, NY | 1.61 | 1940 | Bucky Walters, Cin | 2.48 | 1976 | John Denny, St.L | 2.52 |
| 1905 | Christy Mathewson, NY | 1.27 | 1941 | Elmer Riddle, Cin | 2.24 | 1977 | John Candelaria, Pit | 2.34 |
| 1906 | Three Finger Brown, Chi | 1.04 | 1942 | Mort Cooper, St.L | 1.78 | 1978 | Craig Swan, NY | 2.43 |
| 1907 | Jack Pfiester, Chi | 1.15 | 1943 | Howie Pollet, St.L | 1.75 | 1979 | J.R. Richard, Hou | 2.71 |
| 1908 | Christy Mathewson, NY | 1.43 | 1944 | Ed Heusser, Cin | 2.38 | 1980 | Don Sutton, LA | 2.21 |
| 1909 | Christy Mathewson, NY | 1.14 | 1945 | Hank Borowy, Chi | 2.13 | 1981 | Nolan Ryan, Hou | 1.69 |
| 1910 | George McQuillan, Phi | 1.60 | 1946 | Howie Pollet, St.L | 2.10 | 1982 | Steve Rogers, Mon | 2.40 |
| 1911 | Christy Mathewson, NY | 1.99 | 1947 | Warren Spahn, Bos | 2.33 | 1983 | Atlee Hammaker, SF | 2.25 |
| 1912 | Jeff Tesreau, NY | 1.96 | 1948 | Harry Brecheen, St.L | 2.24 | 1984 | Alejandro Peña, LA | 2.48 |
| 1913 | Christy Mathewson, NY | 2.06 | 1949 | Dave Koslo, NY | 2.50 | 1985 | Dwight Gooden, NY | 1.53 |
| 1914 | Bill Doak, St.L | 1.72 | 1950 | Jim Hearn, St.L-NY | 2.49 | 1986 | Mike Scott, Hou | 2.22 |
| 1915 | Grover Alexander, Phi | 1.22 | 1951 | Chet Nichols, Bos | 2.88 | 1987 | Nolan Ryan, Hou | 2.76 |
| 1916 | Grover Alexander, Phi | 1.55 | 1952 | Hoyt Wilhelm, NY | 2.43 | 1988 | Joe Magrane, St.L | 2.18 |
| 1917 | Grover Alexander, Phi | 1.86 | 1953 | Warren Spahn, Mil | 2.10 | 1989 | Scott Garrelts, SF | 2.28 |
| 1918 | Hippo Vaughn, Chi | 1.74 | 1954 | Johnny Antonelli, NY | 2.30 | 1990 | Danny Darwin, Hou | 2.21 |
| 1919 | Grover Alexander, Chi | 1.72 | 1955 | Bob Friend, Pit | 2.83 | 1991 | Dennis Martinez, Mon | 2.39 |
| 1920 | Grover Alexander, Chi | 1.91 | 1956 | Lew Burdette, Mil | 2.70 | 1992 | Bill Swift, SF | 2.08 |
| 1921 | Bill Doak, St.L | 2.59 | 1957 | Johnny Podres, Bklyn | 2.66 | 1993 | Greg Maddux, Atl | 2.36 |
| 1922 | Rosy Ryan, NY | 3.01 | 1958 | Stu Miller, SF | 2.47 | 1994 | Greg Maddux, Atl | 1.56 |
| 1923 | Dolf Luque, Cin | 1.93 | 1959 | Sam Jones, SF | 2.83 | 1995 | Greg Maddux, Atl | 1.63 |
| 1924 | Dazzy Vance, Bklyn | 2.16 | 1960 | Mike McCormick, SF | 2.70 | 1996 | Kevin Brown, Fla. | 1.89 |
| 1925 | Dolf Luque, Cin | 2.63 | 1961 | Warren Spahn, Mil | 3.02 | 1997 | Pedro Martinez, Mon | 1.90 |
| 1926 | Ray Kremer, Pit | 2.61 | 1962 | Sandy Koufax, LA | 2.54 | 1998 | Greg Maddux, Atl | 2.22 |
| 1927 | Ray Kremer, Pit | 2.47 | 1963 | Sandy Koufax, LA | 1.88 | 1999 | Randy Johnson, Ari. | 2.48 |
| 1928 | Dazzy Vance, Bklyn | 2.09 | 1964 | Sandy Koufax, LA | 1.74 | 2000 | Kevin Brown, LA | 2.58 |
| 1929 | Bill Walker, NY | 3.09 | 1965 | Sandy Koufax, LA | 2.04 | 2001 | Randy Johnson, Ari. | 2.49 |
| 1930 | Dazzy Vance, Bklyn | 2.61 | 1966 | Sandy Koufax, LA | 1.73 | 2002 | Randy Johnson, Ari. | 2.32 |
| 1931 | Bill Walker, NY | 2.26 | 1967 | Phil Niekro, Atl | 1.87 | 2003 | Jason Schmidt, SF | 2.34 |
| 1932 | Lon Warneke, Chi | 2.37 | 1968 | Bob Gibson, St.L | 1.12 | 2004 | Jake Peavy, SD | 2.27 |
| 1933 | Carl Hubbell, NY | 1.66 | 1969 | Juan Marichal, SF | 2.10 | 2005 | Roger Clemens, Hou | 1.87 |
| 1934 | Carl Hubbell, NY | 2.30 | 1970 | Tom Seaver, NY | 2.81 | | | |
| 1935 | Cy Blanton, Pit | 2.58 | 1971 | Tom Seaver, NY | 1.76 | | | |

**Note:** In 1945, Borowy had a 3.13 ERA in 18 games with New York (AL) for a combined ERA of 2.65.

### American League

**Multiple winners:** Lefty Grove (9); Roger Clemens (6); Walter Johnson (5); Pedro Martinez (4); Spud Chandler, Stan Coveleski, Red Faber, Whitey Ford, Lefty Gomez, Ron Guidry, Addie Joss, Hal Newhouser, Jim Palmer, Gary Peters, Luis Tiant and Ed Walsh (2).

| Year | | ERA | Year | | ERA | Year | | ERA |
|---|---|---|---|---|---|---|---|---|
| 1901 | Cy Young, Bos | 1.62 | 1918 | Walter Johnson, Wash | 1.27 | 1934 | Lefty Gomez, NY | 2.33 |
| 1902 | Ed Siever, Det | 1.91 | 1919 | Walter Johnson, Wash | 1.49 | 1935 | Lefty Grove, Bos | 2.70 |
| 1903 | Earl Moore, Cle | 1.77 | 1920 | Bob Shawkey, NY | 2.45 | 1936 | Lefty Grove, Bos | 2.81 |
| 1904 | Addie Joss, Cle | 1.59 | 1921 | Red Faber, Chi | 2.48 | 1937 | Lefty Gomez, NY | 2.33 |
| 1905 | Rube Waddell, Phi | 1.48 | 1922 | Red Faber, Chi | 2.80 | 1938 | Lefty Grove, Bos | 3.08 |
| 1906 | Doc White, Chi | 1.52 | 1923 | Stan Coveleski, Cle | 2.76 | 1939 | Lefty Grove, Bos | 2.54 |
| 1907 | Ed Walsh, Chi | 1.60 | 1924 | Walter Johnson, Wash | 2.72 | 1940 | Ernie Bonham, NY | 1.90 |
| 1908 | Addie Joss, Cle | 1.16 | 1925 | Stan Coveleski, Wash | 2.84 | 1941 | Thornton Lee, Chi | 2.37 |
| 1909 | Harry Krause, Phi | 1.39 | 1926 | Lefty Grove, Phi | 2.51 | 1942 | Ted Lyons, Chi | 2.10 |
| 1910 | Ed Walsh, Chi | 1.27 | 1927 | Wilcy Moore, NY | 2.28 | 1943 | Spud Chandler, NY | 1.64 |
| 1911 | Vean Gregg, Cle | 1.81 | 1928 | Garland Braxton, Wash | 2.51 | 1944 | Dizzy Trout, Det. | 2.12 |
| 1912 | Walter Johnson, Wash | 1.39 | 1929 | Lefty Grove, Phi | 2.81 | 1945 | Hal Newhouser, Det | 1.81 |
| 1913 | Walter Johnson, Wash | 1.09 | 1930 | Lefty Grove, Phi. | 2.54 | 1946 | Hal Newhouser, Det | 1.94 |
| 1914 | Dutch Leonard, Bos | 1.01 | 1931 | Lefty Grove, Phi. | 2.06 | 1947 | Spud Chandler, NY | 2.46 |
| 1915 | Smokey Joe Wood, Bos | 1.49 | 1932 | Lefty Grove, Phi. | 2.84 | 1948 | Gene Bearden, Cle | 2.43 |
| 1916 | Babe Ruth, Bos | 1.75 | 1933 | Monte Pearson, Cle | 2.33 | 1949 | Mel Parnell, Bos | 2.77 |
| 1917 | Eddie Cicotte, Chi | 1.53 | | | | | | |

## Earned Run Average (Cont.)

| Year | | ERA |
|------|------|------|
| 1950 | Early Wynn, Cle | 3.20 |
| 1951 | Saul Rogovin, Det-Chi | 2.78 |
| 1952 | Allie Reynolds, NY | 2.06 |
| 1953 | Ed Lopat, NY | 2.42 |
| 1954 | Mike Garcia, Cle | 2.64 |
| 1955 | Billy Pierce, Chi | 1.97 |
| 1956 | Whitey Ford, NY | 2.47 |
| 1957 | Bobby Shantz, NY | 2.45 |
| 1958 | Whitey Ford, NY | 2.01 |
| 1959 | Hoyt Wilhelm, Bal. | 2.19 |
| 1960 | Frank Baumann, Chi | 2.67 |
| 1961 | Dick Donovan, Wash | 2.40 |
| 1962 | Hank Aguirre, Det. | 2.21 |
| 1963 | Gary Peters, Chi | 2.33 |
| 1964 | Dean Chance, LA | 1.65 |
| 1965 | Sam McDowell, Cle | 2.18 |
| 1966 | Gary Peters, Chi | 1.98 |
| 1967 | Joe Horlen, Chi | 2.06 |
| 1968 | Luis Tiant, Cle | 1.60 |
| 1969 | Dick Bosman, Wash | 2.19 |

| Year | | ERA |
|------|------|------|
| 1970 | Diego Segui, Oak. | 2.56 |
| 1971 | Vida Blue, Oak | 1.82 |
| 1972 | Luis Tiant, Bos | 1.91 |
| 1973 | Jim Palmer, Bal | 2.40 |
| 1974 | Catfish Hunter, Oak | 2.49 |
| 1975 | Jim Palmer, Bal | 2.09 |
| 1976 | Mark Fidrych, Det. | 2.34 |
| 1977 | Frank Tanana, Cal | 2.54 |
| 1978 | Ron Guidry, NY | 1.74 |
| 1979 | Ron Guidry, NY | 2.78 |
| 1980 | Rudy May, NY | 2.47 |
| 1981 | Steve McCatty, Oak | 2.32 |
| 1982 | Rick Sutcliffe, Cle | 2.96 |
| 1983 | Rick Honeycutt, Tex | 2.42 |
| 1984 | Mike Boddicker, Bal | 2.79 |
| 1985 | Dave Stieb, Tor | 2.48 |
| 1986 | Roger Clemens, Bos | 2.48 |
| 1987 | Jimmy Key, Tor | 2.76 |
| 1988 | Allan Anderson, Min | 2.45 |
| 1989 | Bret Saberhagen, KC | 2.16 |

| Year | | ERA |
|------|------|------|
| 1990 | Roger Clemens, Bos | 1.93 |
| 1991 | Roger Clemens, Bos | 2.62 |
| 1992 | Roger Clemens, Bos | 2.41 |
| 1993 | Kevin Appier, KC | 2.56 |
| 1994 | Steve Ontiveros, Oak | 2.65 |
| 1995 | Randy Johnson, Sea | 2.48 |
| 1996 | Juan Guzman, Tor. | 2.93 |
| 1997 | Roger Clemens, Tor | 2.05 |
| 1998 | Roger Clemens, Tor | 2.65 |
| 1999 | Pedro Martinez, Bos | 2.07 |
| 2000 | Pedro Martinez, Bos | 1.74 |
| 2001 | Freddy Garcia, Sea | 3.05 |
| 2002 | Pedro Martinez, Bos | 2.26 |
| 2003 | Pedro Martinez, Bos | 2.22 |
| 2004 | Johan Santana, Min | 2.61 |
| 2005 | Kevin Millwood, Cle | 2.86 |

## Strikeouts

### National League

**Multiple winners:** Dazzy Vance (7); Grover Alexander (6); Steve Carlton, Randy Johnson, Christy Mathewson and Tom Seaver (5); Dizzy Dean, Sandy Koufax and Warren Spahn (4); Don Drysdale, Sam Jones and Johnny Vander Meer (3); David Cone, Dwight Gooden, Bill Hallahan, J.R. Richard, Robin Roberts, Nolan Ryan, Curt Schilling, John Smoltz and Hippo Vaughn (2).

| Year | | SO |
|------|------|------|
| 1900 | Rube Waddell, Pit | 130 |
| 1901 | Noodles Hahn, Cin | 239 |
| 1902 | Vic Willis, Bos | 225 |
| 1903 | Christy Mathewson, NY | 267 |
| 1904 | Christy Mathewson, NY | 212 |
| 1905 | Christy Mathewson, NY | 206 |
| 1906 | Fred Beebe, Chi-St.L. | 171 |
| 1907 | Christy Mathewson, NY | 178 |
| 1908 | Christy Mathewson, NY | 259 |
| 1909 | Orval Overall, Chi | 205 |
| 1910 | Earl Moore, Phi | 185 |
| 1911 | Rube Marquard, NY | 237 |
| 1912 | Grover Alexander, Phi | 195 |
| 1913 | Tom Seaton, Phi | 168 |
| 1914 | Grover Alexander, Phi | 214 |
| 1915 | Grover Alexander, Phi | 241 |
| 1916 | Grover Alexander, Phi | 167 |
| 1917 | Grover Alexander, Phi | 201 |
| 1918 | Hippo Vaughn, Chi | 148 |
| 1919 | Hippo Vaughn, Chi | 141 |
| 1920 | Grover Alexander, Chi | 173 |
| 1921 | Burleigh Grimes, Bklyn | 136 |
| 1922 | Dazzy Vance, Bklyn | 134 |
| 1923 | Dazzy Vance, Bklyn | 197 |
| 1924 | Dazzy Vance, Bklyn | 262 |
| 1925 | Dazzy Vance, Bklyn | 221 |
| 1926 | Dazzy Vance, Bklyn | 140 |
| 1927 | Dazzy Vance, Bklyn | 184 |
| 1928 | Dazzy Vance, Bklyn | 200 |
| 1929 | Pat Malone, Chi | 166 |
| 1930 | Bill Hallahan, St.L | 177 |
| 1931 | Bill Hallahan, St.L | 159 |
| 1932 | Dizzy Dean, St.L | 191 |
| 1933 | Dizzy Dean, St.L | 199 |
| 1934 | Dizzy Dean, St.L | 195 |
| 1935 | Dizzy Dean, St.L | 190 |

| Year | | SO |
|------|------|------|
| 1936 | Van Lingle Mungo, Bklyn | 238 |
| 1937 | Carl Hubbell, NY | 159 |
| 1938 | Clay Bryant, Chi | 135 |
| 1939 | Claude Passeau, Phi-Chi | 137 |
| | & Bucky Walters, Cin | 137 |
| 1940 | Kirby Higbe, Phi | 137 |
| 1941 | John Vander Meer, Cin | 202 |
| 1942 | John Vander Meer, Cin | 186 |
| 1943 | John Vander Meer, Cin | 174 |
| 1944 | Bill Voiselle, NY | 161 |
| 1945 | Preacher Roe, Pit | 148 |
| 1946 | Johnny Schmitz, Chi. | 135 |
| 1947 | Ewell Blackwell, Cin. | 193 |
| 1948 | Harry Brecheen, St.L | 149 |
| 1949 | Warren Spahn, Bos | 151 |
| 1950 | Warren Spahn, Bos | 191 |
| 1951 | Don Newcombe, Bklyn | 164 |
| | & Warren Spahn, Bos | 164 |
| 1952 | Warren Spahn, Bos | 183 |
| 1953 | Robin Roberts, Phi | 198 |
| 1954 | Robin Roberts, Phi | 185 |
| 1955 | Sam Jones, Chi | 198 |
| 1956 | Sam Jones, Chi | 176 |
| 1957 | Jack Sanford, Phi | 188 |
| 1958 | Sam Jones, St.L | 225 |
| 1959 | Don Drysdale, LA | 242 |
| 1960 | Don Drysdale, LA | 246 |
| 1961 | Sandy Koufax, LA | 269 |
| 1962 | Don Drysdale, LA | 232 |
| 1963 | Sandy Koufax, LA | 306 |
| 1964 | Bob Veale, Pit | 250 |
| 1965 | Sandy Koufax, LA | 382 |
| 1966 | Sandy Koufax, LA | 317 |
| 1967 | Jim Bunning, Phi | 253 |
| 1968 | Bob Gibson, St.L | 268 |
| 1969 | Ferguson Jenkins, Chi | 273 |

| Year | | SO |
|------|------|------|
| 1970 | Tom Seaver, NY | 283 |
| 1971 | Tom Seaver, NY | 289 |
| 1972 | Steve Carlton, Phi | 310 |
| 1973 | Tom Seaver, NY | 251 |
| 1974 | Steve Carlton, Phi | 240 |
| 1975 | Tom Seaver, NY | 243 |
| 1976 | Tom Seaver, NY | 235 |
| 1977 | Phil Niekro, Atl | 262 |
| 1978 | J.R. Richard, Hou | 303 |
| 1979 | J.R. Richard, Hou | 313 |
| 1980 | Steve Carlton, Phi | 286 |
| 1981 | F. Valenzuela, LA | 180 |
| 1982 | Steve Carlton, Phi | 286 |
| 1983 | Steve Carlton, Phi | 275 |
| 1984 | Dwight Gooden, NY | 276 |
| 1985 | Dwight Gooden, NY | 268 |
| 1986 | Mike Scott, Hou | 306 |
| 1987 | Nolan Ryan, Hou | 270 |
| 1988 | Nolan Ryan, Hou | 228 |
| 1989 | Jose DeLeon, St.L | 201 |
| 1990 | David Cone, NY | 233 |
| 1991 | David Cone, NY | 241 |
| 1992 | John Smoltz, Atl. | 215 |
| 1993 | Jose Rijo, Cin | 227 |
| 1994 | Andy Benes, SD | 189 |
| 1995 | Hideo Nomo, LA | 236 |
| 1996 | John Smoltz, Atl | 276 |
| 1997 | Curt Schilling, Phi | 319 |
| 1998 | Curt Schilling, Phi | 300 |
| 1999 | Randy Johnson, Ari | 364 |
| 2000 | Randy Johnson, Ari | 347 |
| 2001 | Randy Johnson, Ari | 372 |
| 2002 | Randy Johnson, Ari | 334 |
| 2003 | Kerry Wood, Chi | 266 |
| 2004 | Randy Johnson, Ari | 290 |
| 2005 | Jake Peavy, SD | 216 |

**Note:** In 1998, Randy Johnson struck out 329 batters — 213 in the AL with Seattle, then 116 in the NL with Houston.

### American League

**Multiple winners:** Walter Johnson (12); Nolan Ryan (9); Bob Feller and Lefty Grove (7); Rube Waddell (6); Roger Clemens and Sam McDowell (5); Randy Johnson (4); Lefty Gomez, Mark Langston, Pedro Martinez and Camilo Pascual (3); Len Barker, Tommy Bridges, Jim Bunning, Hal Newhouser, Allie Reynolds, Johan Santana, Herb Score, Ed Walsh and Early Wynn (2).

| Year | | SO |
|---|---|---|
| 1901 | Cy Young, Bos | .158 |
| 1902 | Rube Waddell, Phi | .210 |
| 1903 | Rube Waddell, Phi | .302 |
| 1904 | Rube Waddell, Phi | .349 |
| 1905 | Rube Waddell, Phi | .287 |
| 1906 | Rube Waddell, Phi | .196 |
| 1907 | Rube Waddell, Phi | .232 |
| 1908 | Ed Walsh, Chi | .269 |
| 1909 | Frank Smith, Chi. | .177 |
| 1910 | Walter Johnson, Wash | .313 |
| 1911 | Ed Walsh, Chi | .255 |
| 1912 | Walter Johnson, Wash | .303 |
| 1913 | Walter Johnson, Wash | .243 |
| 1914 | Walter Johnson, Wash | .225 |
| 1915 | Walter Johnson, Wash | .203 |
| 1916 | Walter Johnson, Wash | .228 |
| 1917 | Walter Johnson, Wash | .188 |
| 1918 | Walter Johnson, Wash | .162 |
| 1919 | Walter Johnson, Wash | .147 |
| 1920 | Stan Coveleski, Cle | .133 |
| 1921 | Walter Johnson, Wash | .143 |
| 1922 | Urban Shocker, St.L | .149 |
| 1923 | Walter Johnson, Wash | .130 |
| 1924 | Walter Johnson, Wash | .158 |
| 1925 | Lefty Grove, Phi | .116 |
| 1926 | Lefty Grove, Phi | .194 |
| 1927 | Lefty Grove, Phi | .174 |
| 1928 | Lefty Grove, Phi | .183 |
| 1929 | Lefty Grove, Phi | .170 |
| 1930 | Lefty Grove, Phi | .209 |
| 1931 | Lefty Grove, Phi | .175 |
| 1932 | Red Ruffing, NY | .190 |
| 1933 | Lefty Gomez, NY | .163 |
| 1934 | Lefty Gomez, NY | .158 |
| 1935 | Tommy Bridges, Det | .163 |
| 1936 | Tommy Bridges, Det | .175 |

| Year | | SO |
|---|---|---|
| 1937 | Lefty Gomez, NY | .194 |
| 1938 | Bob Feller, Cle | .240 |
| 1939 | Bob Feller, Cle | .246 |
| 1940 | Bob Feller, Cle | .261 |
| 1941 | Bob Feller, Cle | .260 |
| 1942 | Tex Hughson, Bos | .113 |
| | & Bobo Newsom, Wash | .113 |
| 1943 | Allie Reynolds, Cle | .151 |
| 1944 | Hal Newhouser, Det | .187 |
| 1945 | Hal Newhouser, Det | .212 |
| 1946 | Bob Feller, Cle | .348 |
| 1947 | Bob Feller, Cle | .196 |
| 1948 | Bob Feller, Cle | .164 |
| 1949 | Virgil Trucks, Det | .153 |
| 1950 | Bob Lemon, Cle | .170 |
| 1951 | Vic Raschi, NY | .164 |
| 1952 | Allie Reynolds, NY | .160 |
| 1953 | Billy Pierce, Chi | .186 |
| 1954 | Bob Turley, Bal | .185 |
| 1955 | Herb Score, Cle | .245 |
| 1956 | Herb Score, Cle | .263 |
| 1957 | Early Wynn, Cle. | .184 |
| 1958 | Early Wynn, Chi. | .179 |
| 1959 | Jim Bunning, Det | .201 |
| 1960 | Jim Bunning, Det | .201 |
| 1961 | Camilo Pascual, Min | .221 |
| 1962 | Camilo Pascual, Min | .206 |
| 1963 | Camilo Pascual, Min | .202 |
| 1964 | Al Downing, NY | .217 |
| 1965 | Sam McDowell, Cle | .325 |
| 1966 | Sam McDowell, Cle | .225 |
| 1967 | Jim Lonborg, Bos | .246 |
| 1968 | Sam McDowell, Cle | .283 |
| 1969 | Sam McDowell, Cle | .279 |
| 1970 | Sam McDowell, Cle | .304 |

| Year | | SO |
|---|---|---|
| 1971 | Mickey Lolich, Det | .308 |
| 1972 | Nolan Ryan, Cal | .329 |
| 1973 | Nolan Ryan, Cal | .383 |
| 1974 | Nolan Ryan, Cal | .367 |
| 1975 | Frank Tanana, Cal | .269 |
| 1976 | Nolan Ryan, Cal | .327 |
| 1977 | Nolan Ryan, Cal | .341 |
| 1978 | Nolan Ryan, Cal | .260 |
| 1979 | Nolan Ryan, Cal | .223 |
| 1980 | Len Barker, Cle | .187 |
| 1981 | Len Barker, Cle | .127 |
| 1982 | Floyd Bannister, Sea | .209 |
| 1983 | Jack Morris, Det | .232 |
| 1984 | Mark Langston, Sea | .204 |
| 1985 | Bert Blyleven, Cle-Min | .206 |
| 1986 | Mark Langston, Sea | .245 |
| 1987 | Mark Langston, Sea | .262 |
| 1988 | Roger Clemens, Bos | .291 |
| 1989 | Nolan Ryan, Tex | .301 |
| 1990 | Nolan Ryan, Tex | .232 |
| 1991 | Roger Clemens, Bos | .241 |
| 1992 | Randy Johnson, Sea | .241 |
| 1993 | Randy Johnson, Sea | .308 |
| 1994 | Randy Johnson, Sea | .204 |
| 1995 | Randy Johnson, Sea | .294 |
| 1996 | Roger Clemens, Bos | .257 |
| 1997 | Roger Clemens, Tor | .292 |
| 1998 | Roger Clemens, Tor | .271 |
| 1999 | Pedro Martinez, Bos | .313 |
| 2000 | Pedro Martinez, Bos | .284 |
| 2001 | Hideo Nomo, Bos | .220 |
| 2002 | Pedro Martinez, Bos | .239 |
| 2003 | Esteban Loaiza, Chi | .207 |
| 2004 | Johan Santana, Min | .265 |
| 2005 | Johan Santana, Min | .238 |

## Pitching Triple Crown Winners

Pitchers who led either league in Earned Run Average, Wins and Strikeouts over a single season.

### National League

| | Year | ERA | W-L | SO |
|---|---|---|---|---|
| Tommy Bond, Bos | 1877 | 2.11 | 40-17 | 170 |
| Hoss Radbourn, Prov | 1884 | 1.38 | 60-12 | 441 |
| Tim Keefe, NY | 1888 | 1.74 | 35-12 | 333 |
| John Clarkson, Bos | 1889 | 2.73 | 49-19 | 284 |
| Amos Rusie, NY | 1894 | 2.78 | 36-13 | 195 |
| Christy Mathewson, NY | 1905 | 1.27 | 31-8 | 206 |
| Christy Mathewson, NY | 1908 | 1.43 | 37-11 | 259 |
| Grover Alexander, Phi | 1915 | 1.22 | 31-10 | 241 |
| Grover Alexander, Phi | 1916 | 1.55 | 33-12 | 167 |
| Grover Alexander, Phi | 1917 | 1.86 | 30-13 | 201 |
| Hippo Vaughn, Chi | 1918 | 1.74 | 22-10 | 148 |
| Grover Alexander, Chi | 1920 | 1.91 | 27-14 | 173 |
| Dazzy Vance, Bklyn | 1924 | 2.16 | 28-6 | 262 |
| Bucky Walters, Cin | 1939 | 2.29 | 27-11 | 137 |
| Sandy Koufax, LA | 1963 | 1.88 | 25-5 | 306 |
| Sandy Koufax, LA | 1965 | 2.04 | 26-8 | 382 |
| Sandy Koufax, LA | 1966 | 1.73 | 27-9 | 317 |
| Steve Carlton, Phi | 1972 | 1.97 | 27-10 | 310 |
| Dwight Gooden, NY | 1985 | 1.53 | 24-4 | 268 |
| Randy Johnson, Ari | 2002 | 2.32 | 24-5 | 334 |

**Ties:** In 1894, Rusie tied for league lead in wins with Jouett Meekin, NY (36-10); in 1939, Walters tied for league lead in strikeouts with Claude Passeau, Phi-Chi; in 1963, Koufax tied for the league lead in wins with Juan Marichal, SF.

### American League

| | Year | ERA | W-L | SO |
|---|---|---|---|---|
| Cy Young, Bos | 1901 | 1.62 | 33-10 | 158 |
| Rube Waddell, Phi. | 1905 | 1.48 | 26-11 | 287 |
| Walter Johnson, Wash | 1913 | 1.09 | 36-7 | 243 |
| Walter Johnson, Wash | 1918 | 1.27 | 23-13 | 162 |
| Walter Johnson, Wash | 1924 | 2.72 | 23-7 | 158 |
| Lefty Grove, Phi | 1930 | 2.54 | 28-5 | 209 |
| Lefty Grove, Phi | 1931 | 2.06 | 31-4 | 175 |
| Lefty Gomez, NY | 1934 | 2.33 | 26-5 | 158 |
| Lefty Gomez, NY | 1937 | 2.33 | 21-11 | 194 |
| Hal Newhouser, Det | 1945 | 1.81 | 25-9 | 212 |
| Roger Clemens, Tor | 1997 | 2.05 | 21-7 | 292 |
| Roger Clemens, Tor | 1998 | 2.65 | 20-6 | 271 |
| Pedro Martinez, Bos | 1999 | 2.07 | 23-4 | 313 |

**Ties:** In 1998, Clemens tied for league lead in wins with David Cone, NY (20-7) and Rick Helling, Tex (20-7).

## Saves

The "save" was created by Chicago baseball writer Jerome Holtzman in the 1960's and accepted as an official statistic by the Official Rules Committee of Major League Baseball in 1969. From 1969-72, a save was credited to a pitcher who finished a game his team won. From 1973-74, a save was credited to a pitcher who finished a game his team won with the tying or winning run on base or at bat. Since 1975 a pitcher has been credited with a save when he meets all three of the following conditions: (1) He is the finishing pitcher in a game won by his club; (2) He is not the winning pitcher; (3) He qualifies under one of the following conditions: (a) He enters the game with a lead of no more than three runs and pitches for at least one inning; (b) He enters the game with the potential tying run either on base, or at bat, or on deck; (c) He pitches effectively for at least three innings. No more than one save may be credited in each game.

### National League

**Multiple winners:** Bruce Sutter (5); John Franco and Lee Smith (3); Rawly Eastwick, Rollie Fingers, Mike Marshall, Randy Myers and Todd Worrell (2).

| Year | | Svs | Year | | Svs | Year | | Svs |
|---|---|---|---|---|---|---|---|---|
| 1969 | Fred Gladding, Hou | .29 | 1982 | Bruce Sutter, St.L | .36 | 1996 | Jeff Brantley, Cin | .44 |
| 1970 | Wayne Granger, Cin | .35 | 1983 | Lee Smith, Chi | .29 | | & Todd Worrell, LA | .44 |
| 1971 | Dave Giusti, Pit | .30 | 1984 | Bruce Sutter, St.L | .45 | 1997 | Jeff Shaw, Cin | .42 |
| 1972 | Clay Carroll, Cin | .37 | 1985 | Jeff Reardon, Mon | .41 | 1998 | Trevor Hoffman, SD | .53 |
| 1973 | Mike Marshall, Mon | .31 | 1986 | Todd Worrell, St.L | .36 | 1999 | Ugueth Urbina, Mon | .41 |
| 1974 | Mike Marshall, LA | .21 | 1987 | Steve Bedrosian, Phi. | .40 | 2000 | Antonio Alfonseca, Fla | .45 |
| 1975 | Rawly Eastwick, Cin | .22 | 1988 | John Franco, Cin | .39 | 2001 | Robb Nen, SF | .45 |
| | & Al Hrabosky, St.L | .22 | 1989 | Mark Davis, SD. | .44 | 2002 | John Smoltz, Atl | .55 |
| 1976 | Rawly Eastwick, Cin | .26 | 1990 | John Franco, NY | .33 | 2003 | Eric Gagne, LA | .55 |
| 1977 | Rollie Fingers, SD | .35 | 1991 | Lee Smith, St.L | .47 | 2004 | Armando Benitez, Fla | .47 |
| 1978 | Rollie Fingers, SD | .37 | 1992 | Lee Smith, St.L | .43 | | & Jason Isringhausen, St.L | .47 |
| 1979 | Bruce Sutter, Chi | .37 | 1993 | Randy Myers, Chi | .53 | 2005 | Chad Cordero, Wash | .47 |
| 1980 | Bruce Sutter, Chi | .28 | 1994 | John Franco, NY | .30 | | | |
| 1981 | Bruce Sutter, St.L | .25 | 1995 | Randy Myers, Chi | .38 | | | |

### American League

**Multiple winners:** Dan Quisenberry (5); Rich Gossage and Mariano Rivera (3); Dennis Eckersley, Sparky Lyle and Ron Perranoski (2).

| Year | | Svs | Year | | Svs | Year | | Svs |
|---|---|---|---|---|---|---|---|---|
| 1969 | Ron Perranoski, Min | .31 | 1982 | Dan Quisenberry, KC | .35 | 1995 | Jose Mesa, Cle | .46 |
| 1970 | Ron Perranoski, Min | .34 | 1983 | Dan Quisenberry, KC. | .45 | 1996 | John Wetteland, NY | .43 |
| 1971 | Ken Sanders, Mil. | .31 | 1984 | Dan Quisenberry, KC. | .44 | 1997 | Randy Myers, Bal | .45 |
| 1972 | Sparky Lyle, NY. | .35 | 1985 | Dan Quisenberry, KC. | .37 | 1998 | Tom Gordon, Bos | .46 |
| 1973 | John Hiller, Det | .38 | 1986 | Dave Righetti, NY | .46 | 1999 | Mariano Rivera, NY | .45 |
| 1974 | Terry Forster, Chi | .24 | 1987 | Tom Henke, Tor | .34 | 2000 | Todd Jones, Det. | .42 |
| 1975 | Rich Gossage, Chi | .26 | 1988 | Dennis Eckersley, Oak | .45 | | & Derek Lowe, Bos | .42 |
| 1976 | Sparky Lyle, NY. | .23 | 1989 | Jeff Russell, Tex | .38 | 2001 | Mariano Rivera, NY. | .50 |
| 1977 | Bill Campbell, Bos | .31 | 1990 | Bobby Thigpen, Chi | .57 | 2002 | Eddie Guardado, Min | .45 |
| 1978 | Rich Gossage, NY | .27 | 1991 | Bryan Harvey, Cal | .46 | 2003 | Keith Foulke, Oak | .43 |
| 1979 | Mike Marshall, Min | .32 | 1992 | Dennis Eckersley, Oak | .51 | 2004 | Mariano Rivera, NY. | .53 |
| 1980 | Rich Gossage, NY | .33 | 1993 | Jeff Montgomery, KC | .45 | 2005 | Francisco Rodriguez, LA | .45 |
| | & Dan Quisenberry, KC | .33 | | & Duane Ward, Tor | .45 | | & Bob Wickman, Cle | .45 |
| 1981 | Rollie Fingers, Mil | .28 | 1994 | Lee Smith, Bal | .33 | | | |

## Perfect Games

Eighteen pitchers have thrown perfect games (27 up, 27 down) in major league history. However, the game pitched by Ernie Shore is not considered to be official.

### National League

| | Game | Date | Score |
|---|---|---|---|
| Lee Richmond | Wor. vs Cle. | 6/12/1880 | 1-0 |
| Monte Ward | Prov. vs Buf. | 6/17/1880 | 5-0 |
| Jim Bunning. | Phi. at NY | 6/21/1964 | 6-0 |
| Sandy Koufax | LA vs Chi. | 9/9/1965 | 1-0 |
| Tom Browning | Cin. vs LA | 9/16/1988 | 1-0 |
| Dennis Martinez | Mon. at LA | 7/28/1991 | 2-0 |
| Randy Johnson | Ari. at Atl. | 5/18/2004 | 2-0 |

**Note:** Pittsburgh's Harvey Haddix pitched 12 perfect innings against the Milwaukee Braves on May 26, 1959 before losing, 1-0, in the 13th. Braves' lead-off batter Felix Mantilla reached on a throwing error by Pirates 3B Don Hoak, Eddie Mathews sacrificed Mantilla to 2nd, Hank Aaron was walked intentionally, and Joe Adcock hit a 3-run HR. Adcock, however, passed Aaron on the bases and was only credited with a 1-run double.

**Note:** Montreal's Pedro Martinez pitched nine perfect innings against the San Diego Padres on June 3, 1995 before surrendering a leadoff double to Bip Roberts in the 10th. He was then relieved by Mel Rojas, who finished the game, which Montreal won, 1-0.

### American League

| | Game | Date | Score |
|---|---|---|---|
| Cy Young | Bos. vs Phi. | 5/5/1904 | 3-0 |
| Addie Joss | Cle. vs Chi. | 10/2/1908 | 1-0 |
| Ernie Shore | Bos. vs Wash. | 6/23/1917 | 4-0* |
| Charlie Robertson | Chi. at Det. | 4/30/1922 | 2-0 |
| Catfish Hunter | Oak. vs Min. | 5/8/1968 | 4-0 |
| Len Barker | Cle. vs Tor. | 5/15/1981 | 3-0 |
| Mike Witt | Cal. at Tex. | 9/30/1984 | 1-0 |
| Kenny Rogers | Tex. vs Cal. | 7/28/1994 | 4-0 |
| David Wells | NY vs Min. | 5/17/1998 | 4-0 |
| David Cone | NY vs Mon. | 7/18/1999 | 6-0 |

*Babe Ruth started for Boston, walking Senators' lead-off batter Ray Morgan, then was thrown out of game by umpire Brick Owens for arguing the call. Shore came on in relief. Morgan was caught stealing and Shore retired the next 26 batters in a row. While technically not a perfect game—since he didn't start—Shore gets credit anyway.

### World Series

| Pitcher | Game | Date | Score |
|---|---|---|---|
| Don Larsen | NY vs Bklyn | 10/8/1956 | 2-0 |

## No-Hit Games

Nine innings or more, including perfect games, since 1876. Losing pitchers in **bold** type. **Multiple no-hitters:** Nolan Ryan (7); Sandy Koufax (4); Larry Corcoran, Bob Feller and Cy Young (3); Jim Bunning, Steve Busby, Carl Erskine, Bob Forsch, Pud Galvin, Ken Holtzman, Randy Johnson, Addie Joss, Hub (Dutch) Leonard, Jim Maloney, Christy Mathewson, Hideo Nomo, Allie Reynolds, Warren Spahn, Bill Stoneman, Virgil Trucks, Johnny Vander Meer and Don Wilson (2).

## National League

| Year | Date | Pitcher | Result |
|---|---|---|---|
| 1876 | 7/15 | George Bradley | St.L vs Har, 2-0 |
| 1880 | 6/12 | Lee Richmond | Wor vs Cle, 1-0 (perfect game) |
| | 6/17 | Monte Ward | Prov vs Buf, 5-0 (perfect game) |
| | 8/19 | Larry Corcoran | Chi vs Bos, 6-0 |
| | 8/20 | Pud Galvin | Buf at Wor, 1-0 |
| 1882 | 9/20 | Larry Corcoran | Chi vs Wor, 5-0 |
| 1883 | 7/25 | Old Hoss Radbourn | Prov at Cle, 8-0 |
| | 9/13 | Hugh Daily | Cle at Phi, 1-0 |
| 1884 | 6/27 | Larry Corcoran | Chi vs Prov, 6-0 |
| | 8/4 | Pud Galvin | Buf at Det, 18-0 |
| 1885 | 7/27 | John Clarkson | Chi vs Prov, 4-0 |
| | 8/29 | Charlie Ferguson | Phi vs Prov, 1-0 |
| 1891 | 6/22 | Tom Lovett | Bklyn vs NY, 4-0 |
| | 7/31 | Amos Rusie | NY vs Bklyn, 6-0 |
| 1892 | 8/6 | John Stivetts | Bos vs Bklyn, 11-0 |
| | 8/22 | Ben Sanders | Lou vs Bal, 6-2 |
| | 10/15 | Bumpus Jones | Cin vs Pit, 7-1 (1st major league game) |
| 1893 | 8/16 | Bill Hawke | Bal vs Wash, 5-0 |
| 1897 | 9/18 | Cy Young | Cle vs Cin, 6-0 |
| 1898 | 4/22 | Ted Breitenstein | Cin vs Pit, 11-0 |
| | 4/22 | Jim Hughes | Bal vs Bos, 8-0 |
| | 7/8 | Red Donahue | Phi vs Bos, 5-0 |
| | 8/21 | Walter Thornton | Chi vs Bklyn, 2-0 |
| 1899 | 5/25 | Deacon Phillippe | Lou vs NY, 7-0 |
| 1900 | 7/12 | Noodles Hahn | Cin vs Phi, 4-0 |
| 1901 | 7/15 | Christy Mathewson | NY at St.L, 5-0 |
| 1903 | 9/18 | Chick Fraser | Phi at Chi, 10-0 |
| 1905 | 6/13 | Christy Mathewson | NY at Chi, 1-0 |
| 1906 | 5/1 | John Lush | Phi at Bklyn, 6-0 |
| | 7/20 | Mal Eason | Bklyn at St.L, 2-0 |
| 1907 | 5/8 | Frank Pfeffer | Bos vs Cin, 6-0 |
| | 9/20 | Nick Maddox | Pit vs Bkn, 2-1 |
| 1908 | 7/4 | Hooks Wiltse | NY vs Phi, 1-0 (10) |
| | 9/5 | Nap Rucker | Bklyn vs Bos, 6-0 |
| 1912 | 9/6 | Jeff Tesreau | NY vs Phi, 3-0 |
| 1914 | 9/9 | George Davis | Bos vs Phi, 7-0 |
| 1915 | 4/15 | Rube Marquard | NY vs Bklyn, 2-0 |
| | 8/31 | Jimmy Lavender | Chi at N.Y, 2-0 |
| 1916 | 6/16 | Tom Hughes | Bos vs. Pit, 2-0 |
| 1917 | 5/2 | Fred Toney | Cin at Chi, 1-0 (10) |
| 1919 | 5/11 | Hod Eller | Cin at St.L, 6-0 |
| 1922 | 5/7 | Jesse Barnes | NY vs Phi, 6-0 |
| 1924 | 7/17 | Jesse Haines | St.L vs Bos, 5-0 |
| 1925 | 9/13 | Dazzy Vance | Bklyn vs Phi, 10-1 |
| 1929 | 5/8 | Carl Hubbell | NY vs Pit, 11-0 |
| 1934 | 9/21 | Paul Dean | St.L at Bklyn, 3-0 |
| 1938 | 6/11 | Johnny Vander Meer | Cin vs Bos, 3-0 |
| | 6/15 | Johnny Vander Meer | Cin at Bklyn, 6-0 (consecutive starts) |
| 1940 | 4/30 | Tex Carleton | Bklyn at Cin, 3-0 |
| 1941 | 8/30 | Lon Warneke | St.L at Cin, 2-0 |
| 1944 | 4/27 | Jim Tobin | Bos vs Bklyn, 2-0 |
| | 5/15 | Clyde Shoun | Cin vs Bos, 1-0 |
| 1946 | 4/23 | Ed Head | Bklyn vs Bos, 2-0 |
| 1947 | 6/18 | Ewell Blackwell | Cin vs Bos, 6-0 |
| 1948 | 9/9 | Rex Barney | Bklyn at NY, 2-0 |
| 1950 | 8/11 | Vern Bickford | Bos vs Bklyn, 7-0 |
| 1951 | 5/6 | Cliff Chambers | Pit at Bos, 3-0 |
| 1952 | 6/19 | Carl Erskine | Bklyn vs Chi, 5-0 |
| 1954 | 5/12 | Jim Wilson | Mil vs Phi, 2-0 |
| 1955 | 5/12 | Sam Jones | Chi vs Pit, 4-0 |
| 1956 | 5/12 | Carl Erskine | Bklyn vs NY, 3-0 |
| | 9/25 | Sal Maglie | Bklyn vs Phi, 5-0 |
| 1960 | 5/15 | Don Cardwell | Chi vs St.L, 4-0 |
| | 8/18 | Lew Burdette | Mil vs Phi, 1-0 |
| | 9/16 | Warren Spahn | Mil vs Phi, 4-0 |
| 1961 | 4/28 | Warren Spahn | Mil vs SF, 1-0 |
| 1962 | 6/30 | Sandy Koufax | LA vs NY, 5-0 |
| 1963 | 5/11 | Sandy Koufax | LA vs SF, 8-0 |
| | 5/17 | Don Nottebart | Hou vs Phi, 4-1 |
| | 6/15 | Juan Marichal | SF vs Hou, 1-0 |
| 1964 | 4/23 | **Ken Johnson** | Hou vs Cin, 0-1 |
| | 6/4 | Sandy Koufax | LA at Phi, 3-0 |
| | 6/21 | Jim Bunning | Phi at NY, 6-0 (perfect game) |
| 1965 | 8/19 | Jim Maloney | Cin at Chi, 1-0 (10) |
| | 9/9 | Sandy Koufax | LA vs Chi, 1-0 (perfect game) |
| 1967 | 6/18 | Don Wilson | Hou vs Atl, 2-0 |
| 1968 | 7/29 | George Culver | Cin at Phi, 6-1 |
| | 9/17 | Gaylord Perry | SF vs St.L, 1-0 |
| | 9/18 | Ray Washburn | St.L at SF, 2-0 (next day, same park) |
| 1969 | 4/17 | Bill Stoneman | Mon at Phi, 7-0 |
| | 4/30 | Jim Maloney | Cin vs Hou, 10-0 |
| | 5/1 | Don Wilson | Hou at Cin, 4-0 |
| | 8/19 | Ken Holtzman | Chi vs Atl, 3-0 |
| | 9/20 | Bob Moose | Pit at NY, 4-0 |
| 1970 | 6/12 | Dock Ellis | Pit at SD, 2-0 |
| | 7/20 | Bill Singer | LA vs Phi, 5-0 |
| 1971 | 6/3 | Ken Holtzman | Chi at Cin, 1-0 |
| | 6/23 | Rick Wise | Phi at Cin, 4-0 |
| | 8/14 | Bob Gibson | St.L at Pit, 11-0 |
| 1972 | 4/16 | Burt Hooton | Chi vs Phi, 4-0 |
| | 9/2 | Milt Pappas | Chi vs SD, 8-0 |
| | 10/2 | Bill Stoneman | Mon vs NY, 7-0 |
| 1973 | 8/5 | Phil Niekro | Atl vs SD, 9-0 |
| 1975 | 8/24 | Ed Halicki | SF vs NY, 6-0 |
| 1976 | 7/9 | Larry Dierker | Hou vs Mon, 6-0 |
| | 8/9 | John Candelaria | Pit vs LA, 2-0 |
| | 9/29 | John Montefusco | SF vs Atl, 9-0 |
| 1978 | 4/16 | Bob Forsch | St.L vs Phi, 5-0 |
| | 6/16 | Tom Seaver | Cin vs St.L, 4-0 |
| 1979 | 4/7 | Ken Forsch | Hou vs Atl, 6-0 |
| 1980 | 6/27 | Jerry Reuss | LA at SF, 8-0 |
| 1981 | 5/10 | Charlie Lea | Mon vs SF, 4-0 |
| | 9/26 | Nolan Ryan | Hou vs LA, 5-0 |
| 1983 | 9/25 | Bob Forsch | St.L vs Mon, 3-0 |
| 1986 | 9/25 | Mike Scott | Hou vs SF, 2-0 |
| 1988 | 9/16 | Tom Browning | Cin vs LA, 1-0 (perfect game) |
| 1990 | 6/29 | Fernando Valenzuela | LA vs St.L, 6-0 |
| | 8/15 | Terry Mulholland | Phi vs SF, 6-0 |
| 1991 | 5/23 | Tommy Greene | Phi at Mon, 2-0 |
| | 7/28 | Dennis Martinez | Mon at LA, 2-0 (perfect game) |
| | 9/11 | Mercker (6), Wohlers (2) & Peña (1) | Atl vs SD, 1-0 (combined no-hitter) |
| 1992 | 8/17 | Kevin Gross | LA vs SF, 2-0 |
| 1993 | 9/8 | Darryl Kile | Hou vs NY, 7-1 |
| 1994 | 4/8 | Kent Mercker | Atl at LA, 6-0 |
| 1995 | 7/14 | Ramon Martinez | LA vs Fla, 7-0 |
| 1996 | 5/11 | Al Leiter | Fla vs Col, 11-0 |
| | 9/17 | Hideo Nomo | LA at Col, 9-0 |
| 1997 | 6/10 | Kevin Brown | Fla at SF, 9-0 |
| | 7/12 | Francisco Cordova (9) Ricardo Rincon (1) | Pit vs. Hou, 3-0 (10 inn.) (combined no-hitter) |
| 1999 | 6/25 | Jose Jimenez | St.L at Ari, 1-0 |
| 2001 | 5/12 | A.J. Burnett | Fla vs SD, 3-0 |
| | 9/3 | Bud Smith | St.L at SD, 4-0 |
| 2003 | 4/27 | Kevin Millwood | Phi vs SF, 1-0 |
| | 6/11 | Oswalt (1), Munro (2.2) Saarloos (1.1), Lidge (2), Dotel (1) & Wagner (1) | Hou at NY-AL, 8-0 (combined no-hitter) |
| 2004 | 5/18 | Randy Johnson | Ari at Atl, 2-0 (perfect game) |

## No-Hit Games (Cont.)
### American League

| Year | Date | Pitcher | Result |
|---|---|---|---|
| 1902 | 9/20 | Jimmy Callahan | Chi vs Det, 3-0 |
| 1904 | 5/5 | Cy Young | Bos vs Phi, 3-0 |
| | | | (perfect game) |
| | 8/17 | Jesse Tannehill | Bos at Chi, 6-0 |
| 1905 | 7/22 | Weldon Henley | Phi at St. L, 6-0 |
| | 9/6 | Frank Smith | Chi at Det, 15-0 |
| | 9/27 | Bill Dinneen | Bos vs Chi, 2-0 |
| 1908 | 6/30 | Cy Young | Bos at NY, 8-0 |
| | 9/18 | Dusty Rhoades | Cle vs Bos, 2-1 |
| | 9/20 | Frank Smith | Chi vs Phi, 1-0 |
| | 10/2 | Addie Joss | Cle vs Chi, 1-0 |
| | | | (perfect game) |
| 1910 | 4/20 | Addie Joss | Cle at Chi, 1-0 |
| | 5/12 | Chief Bender | Phi vs Cle, 4-0 |
| 1911 | 7/29 | Smokey Joe Wood | Bos vs St. L, 5-0 |
| | 8/27 | Ed Walsh | Chi vs Bos, 5-0 |
| 1912 | 7/4 | George Mullin | Det vs St. L, 7-0 |
| | 8/30 | Earl Hamilton | St. L at Det, 5-1 |
| 1914 | 5/31 | Joe Benz | Chi vs Cle, 6-1 |
| 1916 | 6/16 | Rube Foster | Bos vs NY, 2-0 |
| | 8/26 | Joe Bush | Phi vs Cle, 5-0 |
| | 8/30 | Hub (Dutch) Leonard | Bos vs St. L, 4-0 |
| 1917 | 4/14 | Ed Cicotte | Chi at St. L, 11-0 |
| | 4/24 | George Mogridge | NY at Bos, 2-1 |
| | 5/5 | Ernie Koob | St. L vs Chi, 1-0 |
| | 5/6 | Bob Groom | St. L vs Chi, 3-0 |
| | | | (next day, same park) |
| | 6/23 | Babe Ruth (0) | Bos vs Wash, 4-0 |
| | | & Ernie Shore (9) | (combined no-hitter) |
| 1918 | 6/3 | Hub (Dutch) Leonard | Bos at Det, 5-0 |
| 1919 | 9/10 | Ray Caldwell | Cle at NY, 3-0 |
| 1920 | 7/1 | Walter Johnson | Wash at Bos, 1-0 |
| 1922 | 4/30 | Charlie Robertson | Chi at Det, 2-0 |
| | | | (perfect game) |
| 1923 | 9/4 | Sam Jones | NY at Phi, 2-0 |
| | 9/7 | Howard Ehmke | Bos at Phi, 4-0 |
| 1926 | 8/21 | Ted Lyons | Chi at Bos, 6-0 |
| 1931 | 4/29 | Wes Ferrell | Cle vs St. L, 9-0 |
| | 8/8 | Bob Burke | Wash vs Bos, 5-0 |
| 1935 | 8/31 | Vern Kennedy | Chi vs Cle, 5-0 |
| 1937 | 6/1 | Bill Dietrich | Chi vs St. L, 8-0 |
| 1938 | 8/27 | Monte Pearson | NY vs Cle, 13-0 |
| 1940 | 4/16 | Bob Feller | Cle at Chi, 1-0 |
| | | | (Opening Day) |
| 1945 | 9/9 | Dick Fowler | Phi vs St. L, 1-0 |
| 1946 | 4/30 | Bob Feller | Cle at NY, 1-0 |
| 1947 | 7/10 | Don Black | Cle vs Phi, 3-0 |
| | 9/3 | Bill McCahan | Phi vs Wash, 3-0 |
| 1948 | 6/30 | Bob Lemon | Cle at Det, 2-0 |
| 1951 | 7/1 | Bob Feller | Cle vs Det, 2-1 |
| | 7/12 | Allie Reynolds | NY at Cle, 1-0 |
| | 9/28 | Allie Reynolds | NY vs Bos, 8-0 |
| 1952 | 5/15 | Virgil Trucks | Det vs Wash, 1-0 |
| | 8/25 | Virgil Trucks | Det at NY, 1-0 |
| 1953 | 5/6 | Bobo Holloman | St. L vs Phi, 6-0 |
| | | | (first major league start) |
| 1956 | 7/14 | Mel Parnell | Bos vs Chi, 4-0 |
| | 10/8 | Don Larsen | NY vs Bklyn, 2-0 |
| | | | (perfect W. Series game) |
| 1957 | 8/20 | Bob Keegan | Chi vs Wash, 6-0 |
| 1958 | 7/20 | Jim Bunning | Det at Bos, 3-0 |
| | 9/20 | Hoyt Wilhelm | Bal vs NY, 1-0 |
| 1962 | 5/5 | Bo Belinsky | LA vs Bal, 2-0 |
| | 6/26 | Earl Wilson | Bos vs LA, 2-0 |
| | 8/1 | Bill Monbouquette | Bos at Chi, 1-0 |
| | 8/26 | Jack Kralick | Min vs KC, 1-0 |

| Year | Date | Pitcher | Result |
|---|---|---|---|
| 1965 | 9/16 | Dave Morehead | Bos vs Cle, 2-0 |
| 1966 | 6/10 | Sonny Siebert | Cle vs Wash, 2-0 |
| 1967 | 4/30 | **Steve Barber** (8⅔) | Bal vs Det, 1-2 |
| | | **& Stu Miller** (⅓) | (combined no-hitter) |
| | 8/25 | Dean Chance | Min at Cle, 2-1 |
| | 9/10 | Joel Horlen | Chi vs Det, 6-0 |
| 1968 | 4/27 | Tom Phoebus | Bal vs Bos, 6-0 |
| | 5/8 | Catfish Hunter | Oak vs Min, 4-0 |
| | | | (perfect game) |
| 1969 | 8/13 | Jim Palmer | Bal vs Oak, 8-0 |
| 1970 | 7/3 | Clyde Wright | Cal vs Oak, 4-0 |
| | 9/21 | Vida Blue | Oak vs Min, 6-0 |
| 1973 | 4/27 | Steve Busby | KC at Det, 3-0 |
| | 5/15 | Nolan Ryan | Cal at KC, 3-0 |
| | 7/15 | Nolan Ryan | Cal at Det, 6-0 |
| | 7/30 | Jim Bibby | Tex at Oak, 6-0 |
| 1974 | 6/19 | Steve Busby | KC at Mil, 2-0 |
| | 7/19 | Dick Bosman | Cle vs Oak, 4-0 |
| | 9/28 | Nolan Ryan | Cal vs Min, 4-0 |
| 1975 | 6/1 | Nolan Ryan | Cal vs Bal, 1-0 |
| | 9/28 | Vida Blue (5), | Oak vs Cal, 5-0 |
| | | Glenn Abbott (1), | (combined no-hitter) |
| | | Paul Lindblad (1), | |
| | | & Rollie Fingers (2) | |
| 1976 | 7/28 | John Odom (5) & | Chi at Oak, 2-1 |
| | | Francisco Barrios (4) | (combined no-hitter) |
| 1977 | 5/14 | Jim Colborn | KC vs Tex, 6-0 |
| | 5/30 | Dennis Eckersley | Cle vs Cal, 1-0 |
| | 9/22 | Bert Blyleven | Tex at Cal, 6-0 |
| 1981 | 5/15 | Len Barker | Cle vs Tor, 3-0 |
| | | | (perfect game) |
| 1983 | 7/4 | Dave Righetti | NY vs Bos, 4-0 |
| | 9/29 | Mike Warren | Oak vs Chi, 3-0 |
| 1984 | 4/7 | Jack Morris | Det at Chi, 4-0 |
| | 9/30 | Mike Witt | Cal at Tex, 1-0 |
| | | | (perfect game) |
| 1986 | 9/19 | Joe Cowley | Chi at Cal, 7-1 |
| 1987 | 4/15 | Juan Nieves | Mil at Bal, 7-0 |
| 1990 | 4/11 | Mark Langston (7) | Cal vs Sea, 1-0 |
| | | & Mike Witt (2) | (combined no-hitter) |
| | 6/2 | Randy Johnson | Sea vs Det, 2-0 |
| | 6/11 | Nolan Ryan | Tex at Oak, 5-0 |
| | 6/29 | Dave Stewart | Oak at Tor, 5-0 |
| | 9/2 | Dave Stieb | Tor at Cle, 3-0 |
| 1991 | 5/1 | Nolan Ryan | Tex vs Tor, 3-0 |
| | 7/13 | Bob Milacki (6), | Bal at Oak, 2-0 |
| | | Mike Flanagan (1), | (combined no-hitter) |
| | | Mark Williamson (1) | |
| | | & Gregg Olson (1) | |
| | 8/11 | Wilson Alvarez | Chi at Bal, 7-0 |
| | 8/26 | Bret Saberhagen | KC vs Chi, 7-0 |
| 1993 | 4/22 | Chris Bosio | Sea vs Bos, 7-0 |
| | 9/4 | Jim Abbott | NY vs Cle, 4-0 |
| 1994 | 4/27 | Scott Erickson | Min vs Mil, 6-0 |
| | 7/28 | Kenny Rogers | Tex vs Cal, 4-0 |
| | | | (perfect game) |
| 1996 | 5/14 | Dwight Gooden | NY vs Sea, 2-0 |
| 1998 | 5/17 | David Wells | NY vs Min, 4-0 |
| | | | (perfect game) |
| 1999 | 7/18 | David Cone | NY vs Mon, 6-0 |
| | | | (perfect game) |
| | 9/11 | Eric Milton | Min vs Ana, 7-0 |
| 2001 | 4/4 | Hideo Nomo | Bos at Bal, 3-0 |
| 2002 | 4/27 | Derek Lowe | Bos vs TB, 10-0 |

## All-Time Major League Leaders

Through the 2005 regular season.

### CAREER

Players active in 2005 in **bold** type.

### Batting

Note that (*) indicates left-handed hitter and (†) indicates switch-hitter.

#### Batting Average

(Minimum 3,000 AB)

| | | Yrs | AB | H | Avg |
|---|---|---|---|---|---|
| 1 | Ty Cobb* | 24 | 11,434 | 4189 | .366 |
| 2 | Rogers Hornsby | 23 | 8,173 | 2930 | .358 |
| 3 | Joe Jackson* | 13 | 4,981 | 1772 | .356 |
| 4 | Ed Delahanty* | 16 | 7,505 | 2596 | .346 |
| 5 | Tris Speaker* | 22 | 10,195 | 3514 | .345 |
| 6 | Ted Williams* | 19 | 7,706 | 2654 | .344 |
| 7 | Billy Hamilton* | 14 | 6,269 | 2159 | .344 |
| 8 | Dan Brouthers* | 19 | 6,711 | 2296 | .342 |
| 9 | Babe Ruth* | 22 | 8,399 | 2873 | .342 |
| 10 | Harry Heilmann* | 17 | 7,787 | 2660 | .342 |
| 11 | Pete Browning | 13 | 4,820 | 1646 | .341 |
| 12 | Willie Keeler* | 19 | 8,591 | 2932 | .341 |
| 13 | Bill Terry* | 14 | 6,428 | 2193 | .341 |
| 14 | George Sisler* | 15 | 8,267 | 2812 | .340 |
| 15 | Lou Gehrig* | 17 | 8,001 | 2721 | .340 |
| 16 | Jesse Burkett* | 16 | 8,421 | 2850 | .338 |
| 17 | Tony Gwynn* | 20 | 9,288 | 3141 | .338 |
| 18 | Nap Lajoie | 21 | 9,589 | 3242 | .338 |
| 19 | **Todd Helton*** | 9 | 4,560 | 1535 | .337 |
| 20 | Riggs Stephenson | 14 | 4,508 | 1515 | .336 |
| 21 | Al Simmons | 20 | 8,759 | 2927 | .334 |
| 22 | Paul Waner* | 20 | 9,459 | 3152 | .333 |
| 23 | Eddie Collins* | 25 | 9,949 | 3315 | .333 |
| 24 | **Ichiro Suzuki*** | 5 | 3,401 | 1130 | .332 |
| 25 | Stan Musial* | 22 | 10,972 | 3630 | .331 |

##### Players Active in 2005

| | | Yrs | AB | H | Avg |
|---|---|---|---|---|---|
| 1 | Todd Helton* | 9 | 4,560 | 1535 | .337 |
| 2 | Ichiro Suzuki* | 5 | 3,401 | 1130 | .332 |
| 3 | Vladimir Guerrero | 10 | 4,895 | 1586 | .324 |
| 4 | Nomar Garciaparra | 10 | 4,363 | 1395 | .320 |
| 5 | Derek Jeter | 11 | 6,167 | 1936 | .314 |
| 6 | Manny Ramirez | 13 | 6,126 | 1922 | .314 |
| 7 | Larry Walker* | 17 | 6,907 | 2160 | .313 |
| 8 | Mike Piazza | 14 | 6,203 | 1929 | .311 |
| 9 | Frank Thomas | 16 | 6,956 | 2136 | .307 |
| 10 | Alex Rodriguez | 12 | 6,195 | 1901 | .307 |
| 11 | Magglio Ordonez | 9 | 4,112 | 1259 | .306 |
| 12 | Sean Casey* | 9 | 4,017 | 1225 | .305 |
| 13 | Juan Pierre* | 6 | 3,411 | 1040 | .305 |

#### Hits

| | | Yrs | AB | H | Avg |
|---|---|---|---|---|---|
| 1 | Pete Rose† | 24 | 14,053 | **4256** | .303 |
| 2 | Ty Cobb* | 24 | 11,434 | **4189** | .366 |
| 3 | Hank Aaron | 23 | 12,364 | **3771** | .305 |
| 4 | Stan Musial* | 22 | 10,972 | **3630** | .331 |
| 5 | Tris Speaker* | 22 | 10,195 | **3514** | .345 |
| 6 | Carl Yastrzemski* | 23 | 11,988 | **3419** | .285 |
| 7 | Honus Wagner | 21 | 10,430 | **3415** | .327 |
| 8 | Paul Molitor | 21 | 10,835 | **3319** | .306 |
| 9 | Eddie Collins* | 25 | 9,949 | **3315** | .333 |
| 10 | Willie Mays | 22 | 10,881 | **3283** | .302 |
| 11 | Eddie Murray† | 21 | 11,336 | **3255** | .287 |
| 12 | Nap Lajoie | 21 | 9,589 | **3242** | .338 |
| 13 | Cal Ripken Jr. | 21 | 11,551 | **3184** | .276 |
| 14 | George Brett* | 21 | 10,349 | **3154** | .305 |
| 15 | Paul Waner* | 20 | 9,459 | **3152** | .333 |
| 16 | Robin Yount | 20 | 11,008 | **3142** | .285 |
| 17 | Tony Gwynn* | 20 | 9,288 | **3141** | .338 |
| 18 | Dave Winfield | 22 | 11,003 | **3110** | .283 |
| 19 | Rickey Henderson | 25 | 10,961 | **3055** | .279 |
| 20 | Rod Carew* | 19 | 9,315 | **3053** | .328 |
| 21 | Lou Brock* | 19 | 10,332 | **3023** | .293 |
| 22 | **Rafael Palmeiro*** | 20 | 10,472 | **3020** | .288 |
| 23 | Wade Boggs* | 18 | 9,180 | **3010** | .328 |
| 24 | Al Kaline | 22 | 10,116 | **3007** | .297 |
| 25 | Cap Anson | 22 | 9,108 | **3000** | .329 |
| | Roberto Clemente | 18 | 9,454 | **3000** | .317 |

##### Players Active in 2005

| | | Yrs | AB | H | Avg |
|---|---|---|---|---|---|
| 1 | Rafael Palmeiro* | 20 | 10,472 | **3020** | .288 |
| 2 | Craig Biggio | 18 | 9,811 | **2795** | .285 |
| 3 | Barry Bonds* | 20 | 9,140 | **2742** | .300 |
| 4 | Julio Franco | 21 | 8,422 | **2521** | .299 |
| 5 | Steve Finley* | 17 | 8,877 | **2426** | .273 |
| 6 | Gary Sheffield | 18 | 7,886 | **2345** | .297 |
| 7 | B.J. Surhoff* | 19 | 8,258 | **2326** | .282 |
| 8 | Jeff Bagwell | 15 | 7,797 | **2314** | .297 |
| 9 | Ken Griffey Jr.* | 17 | 7,870 | **2304** | .293 |
| | Sammy Sosa | 17 | 8,401 | **2304** | .275 |
| 11 | Omar Vizquel† | 17 | 8,387 | **2301** | .274 |
| 12 | Marquis Grissom | 17 | 8,275 | **2251** | .272 |

#### Games Played

| | | |
|---|---|---|
| 1 | Pete Rose | 3562 |
| 2 | Carl Yastrzemski | 3308 |
| 3 | Hank Aaron | 3298 |
| 4 | Rickey Henderson | 3081 |
| 5 | Ty Cobb | 3035 |
| 6 | Stan Musial | 3026 |
| | Eddie Murray | 3026 |
| 8 | Cal Ripken Jr. | 3001 |
| 9 | Willie Mays | 2992 |
| 10 | Dave Winfield | 2973 |
| 11 | Rusty Staub | 2951 |
| 12 | Brooks Robinson | 2896 |
| 13 | Robin Yount | 2856 |
| 14 | Al Kaline | 2834 |
| 15 | **Rafael Palmeiro** | 2831 |
| 16 | Harold Baines | 2830 |
| 17 | Eddie Collins | 2826 |
| 18 | Reggie Jackson | 2820 |
| 19 | Frank Robinson | 2808 |
| 20 | Honus Wagner | 2792 |

#### At Bats

| | | |
|---|---|---|
| 1 | Pete Rose | 14,053 |
| 2 | Hank Aaron | 12,364 |
| 3 | Carl Yastrzemski | 11,988 |
| 4 | Cal Ripken Jr. | 11,551 |
| 5 | Ty Cobb | 11,434 |
| 6 | Eddie Murray | 11,336 |
| 7 | Robin Yount | 11,008 |
| 8 | Dave Winfield | 11,003 |
| 9 | Stan Musial | 10,972 |
| 10 | Rickey Henderson | 10,961 |
| 11 | Willie Mays | 10,881 |
| 12 | Paul Molitor | 10,835 |
| 13 | Brooks Robinson | 10,654 |
| 14 | **Rafael Palmeiro** | 10,472 |
| 15 | Honus Wagner | 10,430 |
| 16 | George Brett | 10,349 |
| 17 | Lou Brock | 10,332 |
| 18 | Luis Aparicio | 10,230 |
| 19 | Tris Speaker | 10,195 |
| 20 | Al Kaline | 10,116 |

#### Total Bases

| | | |
|---|---|---|
| 1 | Hank Aaron | 6856 |
| 2 | Stan Musial | 6134 |
| 3 | Willie Mays | 6066 |
| 4 | Ty Cobb | 5854 |
| 5 | Babe Ruth | 5793 |
| 6 | Pete Rose | 5752 |
| 7 | **Barry Bonds** | 5584 |
| 8 | Carl Yastrzemski | 5539 |
| 9 | Eddie Murray | 5397 |
| 10 | **Rafael Palmeiro** | 5388 |
| 11 | Frank Robinson | 5373 |
| 12 | Dave Winfield | 5221 |
| 13 | Cal Ripken Jr. | 5168 |
| 14 | Tris Speaker | 5101 |
| 15 | Lou Gehrig | 5060 |
| 16 | George Brett | 5044 |
| 17 | Mel Ott | 5041 |
| 18 | Jimmie Foxx | 4956 |
| 19 | Ted Williams | 4884 |
| 20 | Honus Wagner | 4862 |

## Home Runs

| | | Yrs | AB | HR | AB/HR |
|---|---|---|---|---|---|
| 1 | Hank Aaron | .23 | 12,364 | **755** | 16.4 |
| 2 | Babe Ruth* | .22 | 8,399 | **714** | 11.8 |
| 3 | **Barry Bonds*** | .20 | 9,140 | **708** | 12.9 |
| 4 | Willie Mays | .22 | 10,881 | **660** | 16.5 |
| 5 | **Sammy Sosa** | .17 | 8,401 | **588** | 14.3 |
| 6 | Frank Robinson | .21 | 10,006 | **586** | 17.1 |
| 7 | Mark McGwire | .16 | 6,187 | **583** | 10.6 |
| 8 | Harmon Killebrew | .22 | 8,147 | **573** | 14.2 |
| 9 | **Rafael Palmeiro*** | .20 | 10,472 | **569** | 18.4 |
| 10 | Reggie Jackson* | .21 | 9,864 | **563** | 17.5 |
| 11 | Mike Schmidt | .18 | 8,352 | **548** | 15.2 |
| 12 | Mickey Mantle† | .18 | 8,102 | **536** | 15.1 |
| | **Ken Griffey Jr.*** | .17 | 7,870 | **536** | 14.7 |
| 14 | Jimmie Foxx | .20 | 8,134 | **534** | 15.2 |
| 15 | Ted Williams* | .19 | 7,706 | **521** | 14.8 |
| | Willie McCovey* | .22 | 8,197 | **521** | 15.7 |
| 17 | Eddie Mathews* | .17 | 8,537 | **512** | 16.7 |
| | Ernie Banks | .19 | 9,421 | **512** | 18.4 |
| 19 | Mel Ott* | .22 | 9,456 | **511** | 18.5 |
| 20 | Eddie Murray† | .21 | 11,336 | **504** | 22.5 |
| 21 | Lou Gehrig* | .17 | 8,001 | **493** | 16.2 |
| | Fred McGriff* | .19 | 8,757 | **493** | 17.8 |
| 23 | Willie Stargell* | .21 | 7,927 | **475** | 16.7 |
| | Stan Musial* | .22 | 10,972 | **475** | 23.1 |
| 25 | Dave Winfield | .22 | 11,003 | **465** | 23.7 |

## Runs Batted In

| | | Yrs | Gm | RBI | P/G |
|---|---|---|---|---|---|
| 1 | Hank Aaron | .23 | 3298 | **2297** | .70 |
| 2 | Babe Ruth* | .22 | 2503 | **2213** | .88 |
| 3 | Lou Gehrig* | .17 | 2164 | **1995** | .92 |
| 4 | Stan Musial* | .22 | 3026 | **1951** | .64 |
| 5 | Ty Cobb* | .24 | 3034 | **1938** | .64 |
| 6 | Jimmie Foxx | .20 | 2317 | **1922** | .83 |
| 7 | Eddie Murray† | .21 | 2980 | **1917** | .64 |
| 8 | Willie Mays | .22 | 2992 | **1903** | .64 |
| 9 | Mel Ott* | .22 | 2730 | **1860** | .68 |
| 10 | **Barry Bonds*** | .20 | 2730 | **1853** | .68 |
| 11 | Carl Yastrzemski* | .23 | 3308 | **1844** | .56 |
| 12 | Ted Williams* | .19 | 2292 | **1839** | .80 |
| 13 | **Rafael Palmeiro** | .20 | 2831 | **1835** | .65 |
| 14 | Dave Winfield | .22 | 2973 | **1833** | .62 |
| 15 | Al Simmons | .20 | 2215 | **1827** | .82 |
| 16 | Frank Robinson | .21 | 2808 | **1812** | .65 |
| 17 | Honus Wagner | .21 | 2792 | **1732** | .62 |
| 18 | Cap Anson | .22 | 2276 | **1715** | .75 |
| 19 | Reggie Jackson* | .21 | 2820 | **1702** | .60 |
| 20 | Cal Ripken Jr. | .21 | 3001 | **1695** | .56 |
| 21 | Tony Perez | .23 | 2777 | **1652** | .59 |
| 22 | Ernie Banks | .19 | 2528 | **1636** | .65 |
| 23 | Harold Baines* | .22 | 2830 | **1628** | .58 |
| 24 | Goose Goslin* | .18 | 2287 | **1609** | .70 |
| 25 | Nap Lajoie | .21 | 2480 | **1599** | .64 |

## Players Active in 2005

| | | Yrs | AB | HR | AB/HR |
|---|---|---|---|---|---|
| 1 | Barry Bonds* | .20 | 9,140 | **708** | 12.9 |
| 2 | Sammy Sosa | .17 | 8,401 | **588** | 14.3 |
| 3 | Rafael Palmeiro* | .20 | 10,472 | **569** | 18.4 |
| 4 | Ken Griffey Jr.* | .17 | 7,870 | **536** | 14.7 |
| 5 | Jeff Bagwell | .15 | 7,797 | **449** | 17.4 |
| | Gary Sheffield | .18 | 7,886 | **449** | 17.6 |
| 7 | Frank Thomas | .16 | 6,956 | **448** | 15.5 |
| 8 | Manny Ramirez | .13 | 6,126 | **435** | 14.1 |
| 9 | Juan Gonzalez | .17 | 6,556 | **434** | 15.1 |
| 10 | Jim Thome* | .15 | 5,919 | **430** | 13.8 |
| 11 | Alex Rodriguez | .12 | 6,195 | **429** | 14.4 |
| 12 | Mike Piazza* | .14 | 6,203 | **397** | 15.6 |
| 13 | Larry Walker* | .17 | 6,907 | **383** | 18.0 |
| 14 | Carlos Delgado* | .13 | 5,529 | **369** | 15.0 |
| 15 | Tino Martinez* | .16 | 7,111 | **339** | 21.0 |

## Players Active in 2005

| | | Yrs | Gm | RBI | P/G |
|---|---|---|---|---|---|
| 1 | Barry Bonds* | .20 | 2730 | **1853** | .68 |
| 2 | Rafael Palmeiro* | .20 | 2831 | **1835** | .65 |
| 3 | Sammy Sosa | .17 | 2240 | **1575** | .70 |
| 4 | Ken Griffey Jr.* | .17 | 2125 | **1536** | .72 |
| 5 | Jeff Bagwell | .15 | 2150 | **1529** | .71 |
| 6 | Gary Sheffield | .18 | 2190 | **1476** | .67 |
| 7 | Frank Thomas | .16 | 1959 | **1465** | .75 |
| 8 | Manny Ramirez | .13 | 1687 | **1414** | .84 |
| 9 | Juan Gonzalez | .17 | 1689 | **1404** | .83 |
| 10 | Ruben Sierra† | .19 | 2172 | **1318** | .61 |
| 11 | Jeff Kent | .15 | 1926 | **1312** | .68 |
| 12 | Larry Walker* | .17 | 1988 | **1311** | .66 |
| 13 | Tino Martinez* | .16 | 2023 | **1271** | .63 |
| 14 | Luis Gonzalez* | .16 | 2163 | **1251** | .58 |
| 15 | John Olerud* | .17 | 2234 | **1230** | .55 |

## Runs

| | | |
|---|---|---|
| 1 | Rickey Henderson | .2295 |
| 2 | Ty Cobb | .2246 |
| 3 | Babe Ruth | .2174 |
| | Hank Aaron | .2174 |
| 5 | Pete Rose | .2165 |
| 6 | **Barry Bonds** | .2078 |
| 7 | Willie Mays | .2062 |
| 8 | Stan Musial | .1949 |
| 9 | Lou Gehrig | .1888 |
| 10 | Tris Speaker | .1882 |
| 11 | Mel Ott | .1859 |
| 12 | Frank Robinson | .1829 |
| 13 | Eddie Collins | .1821 |
| 14 | Carl Yastrzemski | .1816 |
| 15 | Ted Williams | .1798 |
| 16 | Paul Molitor | .1782 |
| 17 | Charlie Gehringer | .1774 |
| 18 | Jimmie Foxx | .1751 |
| 19 | Honus Wagner | .1736 |
| 20 | Willie Keeler | .1727 |

## Extra Base Hits

| | | |
|---|---|---|
| 1 | Hank Aaron | .1477 |
| 2 | Stan Musial | .1377 |
| 3 | Babe Ruth | .1356 |
| 4 | **Barry Bonds** | .1349 |
| 5 | Willie Mays | .1323 |
| 6 | **Rafael Palmeiro** | .1192 |
| 7 | Lou Gehrig | .1190 |
| 8 | Frank Robinson | .1186 |
| 9 | Carl Yastrzemski | .1157 |
| 10 | Ty Cobb | .1136 |
| 11 | Tris Speaker | .1131 |
| 12 | George Brett | .1119 |
| 13 | Ted Williams | .1117 |
| | Jimmie Foxx | .1117 |
| 15 | Eddie Murray | .1099 |
| 16 | Dave Winfield | .1093 |
| 17 | Cal Ripken Jr. | .1078 |
| 18 | Reggie Jackson | .1075 |
| 19 | Mel Ott | .1071 |
| 20 | Pete Rose | .1041 |

## Slugging Percentage
(Minimum 3,000 AB)

| | | |
|---|---|---|
| 1 | Babe Ruth | .690 |
| 2 | Ted Williams | .634 |
| 3 | Lou Gehrig | .632 |
| 4 | **Barry Bonds** | .611 |
| 5 | Jimmie Foxx | .609 |
| 6 | **Todd Helton** | .607 |
| 7 | Hank Greenberg | .605 |
| 8 | **Manny Ramirez** | .599 |
| 9 | Mark McGwire | .588 |
| 10 | **Vladimir Guerrero** | .587 |
| 11 | Joe DiMaggio | .579 |
| 12 | **Alex Rodriguez** | .577 |
| 13 | Rogers Hornsby | .577 |
| 14 | **Frank Thomas** | .568 |
| 15 | **Larry Walker** | .565 |
| 16 | Albert Belle | .564 |
| 17 | **Jim Thome** | .562 |
| 18 | Johnny Mize | .562 |
| 19 | **Ken Griffey Jr.** | .561 |
| 20 | **Juan Gonzalez** | .561 |

## Stolen Bases

| | | |
|---|---|---|
| 1 | Rickey Henderson | 1406 |
| 2 | Lou Brock | 938 |
| 3 | Billy Hamilton | 912 |
| 4 | Ty Cobb | 892 |
| 5 | Tim Raines | 808 |
| 6 | Vince Coleman | 752 |
| 7 | Eddie Collins | 745 |
| 8 | Max Carey | 738 |
| 9 | Honus Wagner | 722 |
| 10 | Joe Morgan | 689 |
| 11 | Arlie Latham | 679 |
| 12 | Willie Wilson | 668 |
| 13 | Bert Campaneris | 649 |
| 14 | Tom Brown | 627 |
| 15 | Otis Nixon | 620 |
| 16 | George Davis | 616 |
| 17 | Dummy Hoy | 594 |
| 18 | Maury Wills | 586 |
| 19 | George Van Haltren | 583 |
| 20 | Ozzie Smith | 580 |

## Walks

| | | |
|---|---|---|
| 1 | **Barry Bonds** | 2311 |
| 2 | Rickey Henderson | 2190 |
| 3 | Babe Ruth | 2062 |
| 4 | Ted Williams | 2019 |
| 5 | Joe Morgan | 1865 |
| 6 | Carl Yastrzemski | 1845 |
| 7 | Mickey Mantle | 1733 |
| 8 | Mel Ott | 1708 |
| 9 | Eddie Yost | 1614 |
| 10 | Darrell Evans | 1605 |
| 11 | Stan Musial | 1599 |
| 12 | Pete Rose | 1566 |
| 13 | Harmon Killebrew | 1559 |
| 14 | Lou Gehrig | 1508 |
| 15 | Mike Schmidt | 1507 |
| 16 | Eddie Collins | 1499 |
| 17 | **Frank Thomas** | 1466 |
| 18 | Willie Mays | 1464 |
| 19 | Jimmie Foxx | 1452 |
| 20 | Eddie Mathews | 1444 |

## Strikeouts

| | | |
|---|---|---|
| 1 | Reggie Jackson | 2597 |
| 2 | **Sammy Sosa** | 2194 |
| 3 | Andres Galarraga | 2003 |
| 4 | Jose Canseco | 1942 |
| 5 | Willie Stargell | 1936 |
| 6 | Mike Schmidt | 1883 |
| 7 | Fred McGriff | 1882 |
| 8 | Tony Perez | 1867 |
| 9 | Dave Kingman | 1816 |
| 10 | **Jim Thome** | 1762 |
| 11 | Bobby Bonds | 1757 |
| 12 | Dale Murphy | 1748 |
| 13 | Lou Brock | 1730 |
| 14 | Mickey Mantle | 1710 |
| 15 | Harmon Killebrew | 1699 |
| 16 | Chili Davis | 1698 |
| 17 | Dwight Evans | 1697 |
| 18 | Rickey Henderson | 1694 |
| 19 | Dave Winfield | 1686 |
| 20 | Gary Gaetti | 1602 |

## Pitching

Note that (*) indicates left-handed pitcher. Active pitching leaders are listed for wins and strikeouts.

### Wins

| | | Yrs | GS | W | L | Pct |
|---|---|---|---|---|---|---|
| 1 | Cy Young | 22 | 815 | **511** | 316 | .618 |
| 2 | Walter Johnson | 21 | 666 | **417** | 279 | .599 |
| 3 | Christy Mathewson | 17 | 551 | **373** | 188 | .665 |
| | Grover Alexander | 20 | 598 | **373** | 208 | .642 |
| 5 | Pud Galvin | 15 | 688 | **365** | 310 | .541 |
| 6 | Warren Spahn* | 21 | 665 | **363** | 245 | .597 |
| 7 | Kid Nichols | 15 | 561 | **361** | 208 | .634 |
| 8 | Tim Keefe | 14 | 594 | **342** | 225 | .603 |
| 9 | **Roger Clemens** | 22 | 671 | **341** | 172 | .665 |
| 10 | Steve Carlton* | 24 | 709 | **329** | 244 | .574 |
| 11 | John Clarkson | 12 | 518 | **328** | 178 | .648 |
| 12 | Eddie Plank* | 17 | 529 | **326** | 194 | .627 |
| 13 | Don Sutton | 23 | 756 | **324** | 256 | .559 |
| | Nolan Ryan | 27 | 773 | **324** | 292 | .526 |
| 15 | **Greg Maddux** | 20 | 639 | **318** | 189 | .627 |
| | Phil Niekro | 24 | 716 | **318** | 274 | .537 |
| 17 | Gaylord Perry | 22 | 690 | **314** | 265 | .542 |
| 18 | Tom Seaver | 20 | 647 | **311** | 205 | .603 |
| 19 | Old Hoss Radbourn | 12 | 503 | **309** | 195 | .613 |
| 20 | Mickey Welch | 13 | 549 | **307** | 210 | .594 |
| 21 | Lefty Grove* | 17 | 456 | **300** | 141 | .680 |
| | Early Wynn | 23 | 612 | **300** | 244 | .551 |
| 23 | Bobby Mathews | 15 | 568 | **297** | 248 | .545 |
| 24 | Tommy John* | 26 | 700 | **288** | 231 | .555 |
| 25 | Bert Blyleven | 22 | 685 | **287** | 250 | .534 |
| 26 | Robin Roberts | 19 | 609 | **286** | 245 | .539 |
| 27 | Tony Mullane | 13 | 504 | **284** | 220 | .563 |
| | Ferguson Jenkins | 19 | 594 | **284** | 226 | .557 |
| 29 | Jim Kaat* | 25 | 625 | **283** | 237 | .544 |
| 30 | **Tom Glavine*** | 19 | 603 | **275** | 184 | .599 |

### Strikeouts

| | | Yrs | IP | SO | P/9 |
|---|---|---|---|---|---|
| 1 | Nolan Ryan | 27 | 5386.0 | **5714** | 9.55 |
| 2 | **Roger Clemens** | 22 | 4704.1 | **4502** | 8.61 |
| 3 | **Randy Johnson*** | 18 | 3593.2 | **4372** | 10.95 |
| 4 | Steve Carlton* | 24 | 5217.1 | **4136** | 7.13 |
| 5 | Bert Blyleven | 22 | 4970.0 | **3701** | 6.70 |
| 6 | Tom Seaver | 20 | 4782.2 | **3640** | 6.85 |
| 7 | Don Sutton | 23 | 5282.1 | **3574** | 6.09 |
| 8 | Gaylord Perry | 22 | 5350.1 | **3534** | 5.94 |
| 9 | Walter Johnson | 21 | 5914.1 | **3508** | 5.34 |
| 10 | Phil Niekro | 24 | 5404.1 | **3342** | 5.57 |
| 11 | Ferguson Jenkins | 19 | 4500.2 | **3192** | 6.38 |
| 12 | Bob Gibson | 17 | 3884.1 | **3117** | 7.22 |
| 13 | **Greg Maddux** | 20 | 4406.1 | **3052** | 6.23 |
| 14 | **Pedro Martinez** | 14 | 2513.0 | **2861** | 10.25 |
| 15 | Jim Bunning | 17 | 3760.1 | **2855** | 6.83 |
| 16 | **Curt Schilling** | 18 | 2906.0 | **2832** | 8.77 |
| | Mickey Lolich* | 16 | 3638.1 | **2832** | 7.01 |
| 18 | Cy Young | 22 | 7356.0 | **2803** | 3.43 |
| 19 | Frank Tanana* | 21 | 4186.2 | **2773** | 5.96 |
| 20 | David Cone | 17 | 2898.2 | **2668** | 8.28 |
| 21 | Chuck Finley* | 17 | 3197.1 | **2610** | 7.35 |
| 22 | Warren Spahn* | 21 | 5243.2 | **2583** | 4.43 |
| 23 | Bob Feller | 18 | 3827.0 | **2581** | 6.07 |
| 24 | **John Smoltz** | 18 | 2929.1 | **2567** | 7.89 |
| 25 | Tim Keefe | 14 | 5049.2 | **2564** | 4.57 |
| 26 | Jerry Koosman* | 19 | 3839.1 | **2556** | 5.99 |
| 27 | Christy Mathewson | 17 | 4781.0 | **2502** | 4.71 |
| 28 | Don Drysdale | 14 | 3432.0 | **2486** | 6.52 |
| 29 | Jack Morris | 18 | 3824.2 | **2478** | 5.83 |
| 30 | Mark Langston* | 16 | 2962.2 | **2464** | 7.49 |

### Pitchers Active in 2005

| | | Yrs | GS | W | L | Pct |
|---|---|---|---|---|---|---|
| 1 | Roger Clemens | 22 | 671 | **341** | 172 | .665 |
| 2 | Greg Maddux | 20 | 639 | **318** | 189 | .627 |
| 3 | Tom Glavine* | 19 | 603 | **275** | 184 | .599 |
| 4 | Randy Johnson* | 18 | 513 | **263** | 136 | .659 |
| 5 | David Wells* | 19 | 447 | **227** | 143 | .614 |
| 6 | Mike Mussina | 15 | 443 | **224** | 127 | .638 |
| 7 | Kevin Brown | 19 | 476 | **211** | 144 | .594 |
| 8 | Jamie Moyer* | 19 | 485 | **205** | 152 | .574 |
| 9 | Pedro Martinez | 14 | 352 | **197** | 84 | .701 |
| 10 | Curt Schilling | 18 | 381 | **192** | 131 | .594 |

### Pitchers Active in 2005

| | | Yrs | IP | SO | P/9 |
|---|---|---|---|---|---|
| 1 | Roger Clemens | 22 | 4704.1 | **4502** | 8.61 |
| 2 | Randy Johnson* | 18 | 3593.2 | **4372** | 10.95 |
| 3 | Greg Maddux | 20 | 4406.1 | **3052** | 6.23 |
| 4 | Pedro Martinez | 14 | 2513.0 | **2861** | 10.25 |
| 5 | Curt Schilling | 18 | 2906.0 | **2832** | 8.77 |
| 6 | John Smoltz | 18 | 2929.1 | **2567** | 7.89 |
| 7 | Mike Mussina | 15 | 3013.0 | **2400** | 7.17 |
| 8 | Kevin Brown | 19 | 3256.1 | **2397** | 6.62 |
| 9 | Tom Glavine* | 19 | 3951.2 | **2350** | 5.35 |
| 10 | David Wells* | 19 | 3206.1 | **2081** | 5.84 |

## Winning Pct.
(Minimum 100 wins)

| | | Yrs | W-L | Pct |
|---|---|---|---|---|
| 1 | Al Spalding | .7 | 252-65 | .795 |
| 2 | Spud Chandler | .11 | 109-43 | .717 |
| 3 | **Pedro Martinez** | .14 | 197-84 | .701 |
| 4 | Dave Foutz | .11 | 147-66 | .690 |
| 5 | Whitey Ford* | .16 | 236-106 | .690 |
| 6 | **Tim Hudson** | .7 | 106-48 | .688 |
| 7 | Bob Caruthers | .9 | 218-99 | .688 |
| 8 | Don Gullett* | .9 | 109-50 | .686 |
| 9 | Lefty Grove* | .17 | 300-141 | .680 |
| 10 | Smokey Joe Wood | .11 | 117-57 | .672 |
| 11 | Vic Raschi | .10 | 132-66 | .667 |
| 12 | Larry Corcoran | .8 | 177-89 | .665 |
| 13 | Christy Mathewson | .17 | 373-188 | .665 |
| 14 | **Roger Clemens** | .22 | 341-172 | .665 |
| 15 | Sam Leever | .13 | 194-100 | .660 |

## Losses

| | | Yrs | GS | W | L | Pct |
|---|---|---|---|---|---|---|
| 1 | Cy Young | .22 | 815 | 511 | **316** | .618 |
| 2 | Pud Galvin | .15 | 688 | 365 | **310** | .541 |
| 3 | Nolan Ryan | .27 | 773 | 324 | **292** | .526 |
| 4 | Walter Johnson | .21 | 666 | 417 | **279** | .599 |
| 5 | Phil Niekro | .24 | 716 | 318 | **274** | .537 |
| 6 | Gaylord Perry | .22 | 690 | 314 | **265** | .542 |
| 7 | Don Sutton | .23 | 756 | 324 | **256** | .559 |
| 8 | Jack Powell | .16 | 516 | 245 | **254** | .491 |
| 9 | Eppa Rixey* | .21 | 552 | 266 | **251** | .515 |
| 10 | Bert Blyleven | .22 | 685 | 287 | **250** | .534 |
| 11 | Bobby Mathews | .15 | 568 | 297 | **248** | .545 |
| 12 | Robin Roberts | .19 | 609 | 286 | **245** | .539 |
| | Warren Spahn* | .21 | 665 | 363 | **245** | .597 |
| 14 | Early Wynn | .23 | 612 | 300 | **244** | .551 |
| | Steve Carlton* | .24 | 709 | 329 | **244** | .574 |

## Appearances

| | | |
|---|---|---|
| 1 | Jesse Orosco | 1252 |
| 2 | **John Franco** | 1119 |
| 3 | Dennis Eckersley | 1071 |
| 4 | Hoyt Wilhelm | 1070 |
| 5 | Dan Plesac | 1064 |
| 6 | Kent Tekulve | 1050 |
| 7 | **Mike Stanton** | 1027 |
| 8 | Lee Smith | 1022 |
| 9 | Mike Jackson | 1005 |
| 10 | Rich Gossage | 1002 |
| 11 | Lindy McDaniel | 987 |
| 12 | Rollie Fingers | 944 |
| 13 | Gene Garber | 931 |
| 14 | Cy Young | 906 |
| 15 | Sparky Lyle | 899 |

## Innings Pitched

| | | |
|---|---|---|
| 1 | Cy Young | 7356.0 |
| 2 | Pud Galvin | 6003.1 |
| 3 | Walter Johnson | 5914.1 |
| 4 | Phil Niekro | 5404.1 |
| 5 | Nolan Ryan | 5386.0 |
| 6 | Gaylord Perry | 5350.1 |
| 7 | Don Sutton | 5282.1 |
| 8 | Warren Spahn | 5243.2 |
| 9 | Steve Carlton | 5217.1 |
| 10 | Grover Alexander | 5190.0 |
| 11 | Kid Nichols | 5056.1 |
| 12 | Tim Keefe | 5049.2 |
| 13 | Bert Blyleven | 4970.0 |
| 14 | Bobby Mathews | 4956.0 |
| 15 | Mickey Welch | 4802.0 |

## Earned Run Avg.
(Minimum 1500 IP)

| | | |
|---|---|---|
| 1 | Ed Walsh | 1.82 |
| 2 | Addie Joss | 1.89 |
| 3 | Al Spalding | 2.04 |
| 4 | Three Finger Brown | 2.06 |
| 5 | Monte Ward | 2.10 |
| 6 | Christy Mathewson | 2.13 |
| 7 | Rube Waddell | 2.16 |
| 8 | Walter Johnson | 2.17 |
| 9 | Orval Overall | 2.23 |
| 10 | Tommy Bond | 2.25 |
| 11 | Will White | 2.28 |
| 12 | Ed Reulbach | 2.28 |
| 13 | Jim Scott | 2.30 |
| 14 | Eddie Plank | 2.35 |
| 15 | Larry Corcoran | 2.36 |

## Shutouts

| | | |
|---|---|---|
| 1 | Walter Johnson | 110 |
| 2 | Grover Alexander | 90 |
| 3 | Christy Mathewson | 79 |
| 4 | Cy Young | 76 |
| 5 | Eddie Plank | 69 |
| 6 | Warren Spahn | 63 |
| 7 | Nolan Ryan | 61 |
| | Tom Seaver | 61 |
| 9 | Bert Blyleven | 60 |
| 10 | Don Sutton | 58 |
| 11 | Pud Galvin | 57 |
| | Ed Walsh | 57 |
| 13 | Bob Gibson | 56 |
| 14 | Three Finger Brown | 55 |
| | Steve Carlton | 55 |

## Walks Allowed

| | | |
|---|---|---|
| 1 | Nolan Ryan | 2795 |
| 2 | Steve Carlton | 1833 |
| 3 | Phil Niekro | 1809 |
| 4 | Early Wynn | 1775 |
| 5 | Bob Feller | 1764 |
| 6 | Bobo Newsom | 1732 |
| 7 | Amos Rusie | 1704 |
| 8 | Charlie Hough | 1665 |
| 9 | Gus Weyhing | 1566 |
| 10 | Red Ruffing | 1541 |
| 11 | **Roger Clemens** | 1520 |
| 12 | Bump Hadley | 1442 |
| 13 | Warren Spahn | 1434 |
| 14 | Earl Whitehill | 1431 |
| 15 | Tony Mullane | 1408 |

## HRs Allowed

| | | |
|---|---|---|
| 1 | Robin Roberts | 505 |
| 2 | Ferguson Jenkins | 484 |
| 3 | Phil Niekro | 482 |
| 4 | Don Sutton | 472 |
| 5 | Frank Tanana | 448 |
| 6 | Warren Spahn | 434 |
| 7 | Bert Blyleven | 430 |
| 8 | Steve Carlton | 414 |
| 9 | Gaylord Perry | 399 |
| 10 | Jim Kaat | 395 |
| 11 | Jack Morris | 389 |
| 12 | Charlie Hough | 383 |
| 13 | **Jamie Moyer** | 381 |
| 14 | Tom Seaver | 380 |
| 15 | Catfish Hunter | 374 |
| | **David Wells** | 374 |

## Saves

| | | |
|---|---|---|
| 1 | Lee Smith | 478 |
| 2 | **Trevor Hoffman** | 436 |
| 3 | **John Franco** | 424 |
| 4 | Dennis Eckersley | 390 |
| 5 | **Mariano Rivera** | 379 |
| 6 | Jeff Reardon | 367 |
| 7 | Randy Myers | 347 |
| 8 | Rollie Fingers | 341 |
| 9 | John Wetteland | 330 |
| 10 | **Roberto Hernandez** | 324 |
| | **Troy Percival** | 324 |
| 12 | **Jose Mesa** | 319 |
| 13 | Rick Aguilera | 318 |
| 14 | Robb Nen | 314 |
| 15 | Tom Henke | 311 |
| 16 | Rich Gossage | 310 |
| 17 | Jeff Montgomery | 304 |
| 18 | Doug Jones | 303 |
| 19 | Bruce Sutter | 300 |
| 20 | Rod Beck | 286 |
| 21 | **Billy Wagner** | 284 |
| 22 | **Armando Benitez** | 263 |
| 23 | Todd Worrell | 256 |
| 24 | Dave Righetti | 252 |
| 25 | Dan Quisenberry | 244 |
| 26 | Sparky Lyle | 238 |
| 27 | **Ugueth Urbina** | 237 |
| 28 | Hoyt Wilhelm | 227 |
| 29 | **Todd Jones** | 226 |
| 30 | Gene Garber | 218 |

## SINGLE SEASON

Through 2005 regular season.

### Batting

#### Home Runs

| | | Year | Gm | AB | HR |
|---|---|---|---|---|---|
| 1 | Barry Bonds, SF | 2001 | 153 | 476 | 73 |
| 2 | Mark McGwire, St.L | 1998 | 155 | 509 | 70 |
| 3 | Sammy Sosa, Chi-NL | 1998 | 159 | 643 | 66 |
| 4 | Mark McGwire, St.L | 1999 | 153 | 521 | 65 |
| 5 | Sammy Sosa, Chi-NL | 2001 | 160 | 577 | 64 |
| 6 | Sammy Sosa, Chi-NL | 1999 | 162 | 625 | 63 |
| 7 | Roger Maris, NY-AL | 1961 | 162 | 590 | 61 |
| 8 | Babe Ruth, NY-AL | 1927 | 151 | 540 | 60 |
| 9 | Babe Ruth, NY-AL | 1921 | 152 | 540 | 59 |
| 10 | Mark McGwire, Oak-St.L | 1997 | 156 | 540 | 58 |
| | Hank Greenberg, Det | 1938 | 155 | 556 | 58 |
| | Jimmie Foxx, Phi-AL | 1932 | 154 | 585 | 58 |
| 13 | Alex Rodriguez, Tex | 2002 | 162 | 624 | 57 |
| | Luis Gonzalez, Ari | 2001 | 162 | 609 | 57 |
| 15 | Hack Wilson, Chi-NL | 1930 | 155 | 585 | 56 |
| | Ken Griffey Jr., Sea | 1997 | 157 | 608 | 56 |
| | Ken Griffey Jr., Sea | 1998 | 161 | 633 | 56 |
| 18 | Babe Ruth, NY-AL | 1920 | 142 | 458 | 54 |
| | Mickey Mantle, NY-AL | 1961 | 153 | 514 | 54 |
| | Babe Ruth, NY-AL | 1928 | 154 | 536 | 54 |
| | Ralph Kiner, Pit | 1949 | 152 | 549 | 54 |

#### Hits

| | | Year | AB | H | Avg |
|---|---|---|---|---|---|
| 1 | Ichiro Suzuki, Sea. | 2004 | 704 | 262 | .372 |
| 2 | George Sisler, StL-AL | 1920 | 631 | 257 | .407 |
| 3 | Bill Terry, NY-NL | 1930 | 633 | 254 | .401 |
| | Lefty O'Doul, Phi-NL | 1929 | 638 | 254 | .398 |
| 5 | Al Simmons, Phi-AL | 1925 | 658 | 253 | .384 |
| 6 | Rogers Hornsby, StL-NL | 1922 | 623 | 250 | .401 |
| | Chuck Klein, Phi-NL | 1930 | 648 | 250 | .386 |
| 8 | Ty Cobb, Det | 1911 | 591 | 248 | .420 |
| 9 | George Sisler, StL-AL | 1922 | 586 | 246 | .420 |
| 10 | Ichiro Suzuki, Sea | 2001 | 692 | 242 | .350 |
| 11 | Babe Herman, Bklyn | 1930 | 614 | 241 | .393 |
| | Heinie Manush, StL-AL | 1928 | 638 | 241 | .378 |
| 13 | Wade Boggs, Bos | 1985 | 653 | 240 | .368 |
| | Darin Erstad, Ana | 2000 | 676 | 240 | .355 |
| 15 | Rod Carew, Min | 1977 | 616 | 239 | .388 |
| 16 | Don Mattingly, NY-AL | 1986 | 677 | 238 | .352 |
| 17 | Harry Heilmann, Det | 1921 | 602 | 237 | .394 |
| | Paul Waner, Pit | 1927 | 623 | 237 | .380 |
| | Joe Medwick, StL-NL | 1937 | 633 | 237 | .374 |
| 20 | Jack Tobin, StL-AL | 1921 | 671 | 236 | .352 |

### Batting Average

#### From 1900-49

| | | Year | AB | H | Avg |
|---|---|---|---|---|---|
| 1 | Rogers Hornsby, StL-NL | 1924 | 536 | 227 | .424 |
| 2 | Nap Lajoie, Phi-AL | 1901 | 543 | 229 | .422 |
| 3 | George Sisler, StL-AL | 1922 | 586 | 246 | .420 |
| 4 | Ty Cobb, Det | 1911 | 591 | 248 | .420 |
| 5 | Ty Cobb, Det | 1912 | 533 | 227 | .410 |
| 6 | Joe Jackson, Cle | 1911 | 571 | 233 | .408 |
| 7 | George Sisler, StL-AL | 1920 | 631 | 257 | .407 |
| 8 | Ted Williams, Bos-AL | 1941 | 456 | 185 | .406 |
| 9 | Rogers Hornsby, StL-NL | 1925 | 504 | 203 | .403 |
| 10 | Harry Heilmann, Det | 1923 | 524 | 211 | .403 |

#### Since 1950

| | | Year | AB | H | Avg |
|---|---|---|---|---|---|
| 1 | Tony Gwynn, SD | 1994 | 419 | 175 | .394 |
| 2 | George Brett, KC | 1980 | 449 | 175 | .390 |
| 3 | Ted Williams, Bos | 1957 | 420 | 163 | .388 |
| 4 | Rod Carew, Min | 1977 | 616 | 239 | .388 |
| 5 | Larry Walker, Col | 1999 | 438 | 166 | .379 |
| 6 | Todd Helton, Col | 2000 | 580 | 216 | .372 |
| 7 | Nomar Garciaparra, Bos | 2000 | 529 | 197 | .372 |
| 8 | Ichiro Suzuki, Sea | 2004 | 704 | 262 | .372 |
| 9 | Tony Gwynn, SD | 1997 | 592 | 220 | .372 |
| 10 | Andres Galarraga, Col | 1993 | 470 | 174 | .370 |

### Total Bases

#### From 1900-49

| | | Year | TB |
|---|---|---|---|
| 1 | Babe Ruth, New York-AL | 1921 | 457 |
| 2 | Rogers Hornsby, St. Louis-NL | 1922 | 450 |
| 3 | Lou Gehrig, New York-AL | 1927 | 447 |
| 4 | Chuck Klein, Philadelphia-NL | 1930 | 445 |
| 5 | Jimmie Foxx, Philadelphia-AL | 1932 | 438 |
| 6 | Stan Musial, St. Louis-NL | 1948 | 429 |
| 7 | Hack Wilson, Chicago-NL | 1930 | 423 |
| 8 | Chuck Klein, Philadelphia-NL | 1932 | 420 |
| 9 | Lou Gehrig, New York-AL | 1930 | 419 |
| 10 | Joe DiMaggio, New York-AL | 1937 | 418 |

#### Since 1950

| | | Year | TB |
|---|---|---|---|
| 1 | Sammy Sosa, Chicago-NL | 2001 | 425 |
| 2 | Luis Gonzalez, Arizona | 2001 | 419 |
| 3 | Sammy Sosa, Chicago-NL | 1998 | 416 |
| 4 | Barry Bonds, San Francisco | 2001 | 411 |
| 5 | Larry Walker, Colorado | 1997 | 409 |
| 6 | Jim Rice, Boston | 1978 | 406 |
| 7 | Todd Helton, Colorado | 2000 | 405 |
| 8 | Todd Helton, Colorado | 2001 | 402 |
| 9 | Hank Aaron, Milwaukee | 1959 | 400 |
| 10 | Albert Belle, Chicago-AL | 1998 | 399 |

### Runs Batted In

#### From 1900-49

| | | Year | Avg | HR | RBI |
|---|---|---|---|---|---|
| 1 | Hack Wilson, Chi-NL | 1930 | .356 | 56 | 191 |
| 2 | Lou Gehrig, NY-AL | 1931 | .341 | 46 | 184 |
| 3 | Hank Greenberg, Det | 1937 | .337 | 40 | 183 |
| 4 | Lou Gehrig, NY-AL | 1927 | .373 | 47 | 175 |
| | Jimmie Foxx, Bos-AL | 1938 | .349 | 50 | 175 |
| 6 | Lou Gehrig, NY-AL | 1930 | .379 | 41 | 174 |
| 7 | Babe Ruth, NY-AL | 1921 | .378 | 59 | 171 |
| 8 | Chuck Klein, Phi-NL | 1930 | .386 | 40 | 170 |
| | Hank Greenberg, Det | 1935 | .328 | 36 | 170 |
| 10 | Jimmie Foxx, Phi-AL | 1932 | .364 | 58 | 169 |

#### Since 1950

| | | Year | Avg | HR | RBI |
|---|---|---|---|---|---|
| 1 | Manny Ramirez, Cle | 1999 | .333 | 44 | 165 |
| 2 | Sammy Sosa, Chi-NL | 2001 | .328 | 64 | 160 |
| 3 | Sammy Sosa, Chi-NL | 1998 | .308 | 66 | 158 |
| 4 | Juan Gonzalez, Tex | 1998 | .318 | 45 | 157 |
| 5 | Tommy Davis, LA-NL | 1962 | .346 | 27 | 153* |
| 6 | Albert Belle, Chi-AL | 1998 | .328 | 49 | 152 |
| 7 | Andres Galarraga, Col | 1996 | .304 | 47 | 150 |
| | Miguel Tejada, Bal | 2004 | .311 | 34 | 150 |
| 9 | George Foster, Cin | 1977 | .320 | 52 | 149 |
| 10 | Johnny Bench, Cin | 1970 | .293 | 45 | 148 |
| | Albert Belle, Cle | 1996 | .311 | 48 | 148 |
| | Rafael Palmeiro, Tex | 1999 | .324 | 47 | 148 |
| | **David Ortiz**, Bos | 2005 | .300 | 47 | 148 |

## Runs

| | | Year | Runs |
|---|---|---|---|
| 1 | Babe Ruth, New York-AL | 1921 | 177 |
| 2 | Lou Gehrig, New York-AL | 1936 | 167 |
| 3 | Babe Ruth, New York-AL | 1928 | 163 |
| | Lou Gehrig, New York-AL | 1931 | 163 |
| 5 | Babe Ruth, New York-AL | 1920 | 158 |
| | Babe Ruth, New York-AL | 1927 | 158 |
| | Chuck Klein, Philadelphia-NL | 1930 | 158 |
| 8 | Rogers Hornsby, Chicago-NL | 1929 | 156 |
| 9 | Kiki Cuyler, Chicago-NL | 1930 | 155 |
| 10 | Lefty O'Doul, Philadelphia-NL | 1929 | 152 |
| | Woody English, Chicago-NL | 1930 | 152 |
| | Al Simmons, Philadelphia-AL | 1930 | 152 |
| | Chuck Klein, Philadelphia-NL | 1932 | 152 |
| | Jeff Bagwell, Houston | 2000 | 152 |
| 15 | Babe Ruth, New York-AL | 1923 | 151 |
| | Jimmie Foxx, Philadelphia-AL | 1932 | 151 |
| | Joe DiMaggio, New York-AL | 1937 | 151 |
| 18 | Babe Ruth, New York-AL | 1930 | 150 |
| | Ted Williams, Boston-AL | 1949 | 150 |
| 20 | Lou Gehrig, New York-AL | 1927 | 149 |
| | Babe Ruth, New York-AL | 1931 | 149 |

## Walks

| | | Year | BB |
|---|---|---|---|
| 1 | Barry Bonds, San Francisco | 2004 | 232 |
| 2 | Barry Bonds, San Francisco | 2002 | 198 |
| 3 | Barry Bonds, San Francisco | 2001 | 177 |
| 4 | Babe Ruth, New York-AL | 1923 | 170 |
| 5 | Ted Williams, Boston-AL | 1947 | 162 |
| | Ted Williams, Boston-AL | 1949 | 162 |
| | Mark McGwire, St. Louis | 1998 | 162 |
| 8 | Ted Williams, Boston-AL | 1946 | 156 |
| 9 | Barry Bonds, San Francisco | 1996 | 151 |
| | Eddie Yost, Washington | 1956 | 151 |

## Extra Base Hits

| | | Year | EBH |
|---|---|---|---|
| 1 | Babe Ruth, New York-AL | 1921 | 119 |
| 2 | Lou Gehrig, New York-AL | 1927 | 117 |
| 3 | Chuck Klein, Philadelphia-NL | 1930 | 107 |
| | Barry Bonds, San Francisco | 2001 | 107 |
| 5 | Todd Helton, Colorado | 2001 | 105 |
| 6 | Chuck Klein, Philadelphia-NL | 1932 | 103 |
| | Hank Greenberg, Detroit | 1937 | 103 |
| | Stan Musial, St. Louis-NL | 1948 | 103 |
| | Albert Belle, Cleveland | 1995 | 103 |
| | Todd Helton, Colorado | 2000 | 103 |
| | Sammy Sosa, Chicago-NL | 2001 | 103 |

## Slugging Percentage
### From 1900-49

| | | Year | Pct |
|---|---|---|---|
| 1 | Babe Ruth, New York-AL | 1920 | .847 |
| 2 | Babe Ruth, New York-AL | 1921 | .846 |
| 3 | Babe Ruth, New York-AL | 1927 | .772 |
| 4 | Lou Gehrig, New York-AL | 1927 | .765 |
| 5 | Babe Ruth, New York-AL | 1923 | .764 |
| 6 | Rogers Hornsby, St. Louis-NL | 1925 | .756 |
| 7 | Jimmie Foxx, Philadelphia-AL | 1932 | .749 |
| 8 | Babe Ruth, New York-AL | 1924 | .739 |
| 9 | Babe Ruth, New York-AL | 1926 | .737 |
| 10 | Ted Williams, Boston-AL | 1941 | .735 |

### Since 1950

| | | Year | Pct |
|---|---|---|---|
| 1 | Barry Bonds, San Francisco | 2001 | .863 |
| 2 | Barry Bonds, San Francisco | 2004 | .812 |
| 3 | Barry Bonds, San Francisco | 2002 | .799 |
| 4 | Mark McGwire, St. Louis | 1998 | .752 |
| 5 | Jeff Bagwell, Houston | 1994 | .750 |
| 6 | Barry Bonds, San Francisco | 2003 | .749 |
| 7 | Sammy Sosa, Chicago-NL | 2001 | .737 |
| 8 | Ted Williams, Boston | 1957 | .731 |
| 9 | Mark McGwire, Oakland | 1996 | .730 |
| 10 | Frank Thomas, Chicago-AL | 1994 | .729 |

## Doubles

| | | Year | 2B |
|---|---|---|---|
| 1 | Earl Webb, Boston-AL | 1931 | 67 |
| 2 | George Burns, Cleveland | 1926 | 64 |
| | Joe Medwick, St. Louis-NL | 1936 | 64 |
| 4 | Hank Greenberg, Detroit | 1934 | 63 |
| 5 | Paul Waner, Pittsburgh | 1932 | 62 |
| 6 | Charlie Gehringer, Detroit | 1936 | 60 |
| 7 | Tris Speaker, Cleveland | 1923 | 59 |
| | Chuck Klein, Philadelphia-NL | 1930 | 59 |
| | Todd Helton, Colorado | 2000 | 59 |
| 10 | Three tied with 57 each. | | |

## Triples
### From 1900-49

| | | Year | 3B |
|---|---|---|---|
| 1 | Chief Wilson, Pittsburgh | 1912 | 36 |
| 2 | Joe Jackson, Cleveland | 1912 | 26 |
| 3 | Sam Crawford, Detroit | 1914 | 26 |
| 4 | Kiki Cuyler, Pittsburgh | 1925 | 26 |
| 5 | Three tied with 25 each. | | |

### Since 1950

| | | Year | 3B |
|---|---|---|---|
| 1 | Willie Wilson, Kansas City | 1985 | 21 |
| | Lance Johnson, New York-NL | 1996 | 21 |
| 3 | Willie Mays, New York-NL | 1957 | 20 |
| | George Brett, Kansas City | 1979 | 20 |
| | Cristian Guzman, Minnesota | 2000 | 20 |

## Stolen Bases

| | | Year | SB |
|---|---|---|---|
| 1 | Rickey Henderson, Oakland | 1982 | 130 |
| 2 | Lou Brock, St. Louis | 1974 | 118 |
| 3 | Vince Coleman, St. Louis | 1985 | 110 |
| 4 | Vince Coleman, St. Louis | 1987 | 109 |
| 5 | Rickey Henderson, Oakland | 1983 | 108 |
| 6 | Vince Coleman, St. Louis | 1986 | 107 |
| 7 | Maury Wills, Los Angeles-NL | 1962 | 104 |
| 8 | Rickey Henderson, Oakland | 1980 | 100 |
| 9 | Ron LeFlore, Montreal | 1980 | 97 |
| 10 | Ty Cobb, Detroit | 1915 | 96 |
| | Omar Moreno, Pittsburgh | 1980 | 96 |
| 12 | Maury Wills, Los Angeles | 1965 | 94 |
| 13 | Rickey Henderson, New York-AL | 1988 | 93 |
| 14 | Tim Raines, Montreal | 1983 | 90 |
| 15 | Clyde Milan, Washington | 1912 | 88 |

## Strikeouts

| | | Year | SO |
|---|---|---|---|
| 1 | Adam Dunn, Cincinnati | 2004 | 195 |
| 2 | Bobby Bonds, San Francisco | 1970 | 189 |
| 3 | Jose Hernandez, Milwaukee | 2002 | 188 |
| 4 | Bobby Bonds, San Francisco | 1969 | 187 |
| | Preston Wilson, Florida | 2000 | 187 |
| 6 | Rob Deer, Milwaukee | 1987 | 186 |
| 7 | Pete Incaviglia, Texas | 1986 | 185 |
| | Jose Hernandez, Milwaukee | 2001 | 185 |
| | Jim Thome, Cleveland | 2001 | 185 |
| 10 | Cecil Fielder, Detroit | 1990 | 182 |
| | Jim Thome, Philadelphia | 2003 | 182 |

## Pinch Hits
Career pinch hits in parentheses.

| | | Year | PH | |
|---|---|---|---|---|
| 1 | John Vander Wal, Colorado | 1995 | 28 | (129) |
| 2 | Lenny Harris, Col-Ari | 1999 | 26 | (212) |
| 3 | Jose Morales, Montreal | 1976 | 25 | (123) |
| 4 | Dave Philley, Baltimore | 1961 | 24 | (93) |
| | Vic Davalillo, St. Louis | 1970 | 24 | (95) |
| | Rusty Staub, New York-NL | 1983 | 24 | (100) |
| | Gerald Perry, St. Louis | 1993 | 24 | (95) |

**Note:** Harris (212) is the career leader.

## Pitching
### Wins

#### From 1900-49

| | | Year | W | L | Pct |
|---|---|---|---|---|---|
| 1 | Jack Chesbro, NY-AL | 1904 | 41 | 12 | .774 |
| 2 | Ed Walsh, Chi-AL | 1908 | 40 | 15 | .727 |
| 3 | Christy Mathewson, NY-NL | 1908 | 37 | 11 | .771 |
| 4 | Walter Johnson, Wash | 1913 | 36 | 7 | .837 |
| 5 | Joe McGinnity, NY-NL | 1904 | 35 | 8 | .814 |
| 6 | Smokey Joe Wood, Bos-AL | 1912 | 34 | 5 | .872 |
| 7 | Cy Young, Bos-AL | 1901 | 33 | 10 | .767 |
| | Grover Alexander, Phi-NL | 1916 | 33 | 12 | .733 |
| | Christy Mathewson, NY-NL | 1904 | 33 | 12 | .733 |
| 10 | Cy Young, Bos-AL | 1902 | 32 | 11 | .744 |

#### Since 1950

| | | Year | W | L | Pct |
|---|---|---|---|---|---|
| 1 | Denny McLain, Det | 1968 | 31 | 6 | .838 |
| 2 | Robin Roberts, Phi-NL | 1952 | 28 | 7 | .800 |
| 3 | Bob Welch, Oak | 1990 | 27 | 6 | .818 |
| | Don Newcombe, Bklyn | 1956 | 27 | 7 | .794 |
| | Sandy Koufax, LA | 1966 | 27 | 9 | .750 |
| | Steve Carlton, Phi | 1972 | 27 | 10 | .730 |
| 7 | Sandy Koufax, LA | 1965 | 26 | 8 | .765 |
| | Juan Marichal, SF | 1968 | 26 | 9 | .743 |

**Note:** 11 pitchers tied with 25 wins, including Marichal twice.

### Earned Run Average

#### From 1900-49

| | | Year | ShO | ERA |
|---|---|---|---|---|
| 1 | Dutch Leonard, Bos-AL | 1914 | 7 | 1.01 |
| 2 | Three Finger Brown, Chi-NL | 1906 | 10 | 1.04 |
| 3 | Walter Johnson, Wash | 1913 | 11 | 1.09 |
| 4 | Christy Mathewson, NY-NL | 1909 | 8 | 1.14 |
| 5 | Jack Pfiester, Chi-NL | 1907 | 3 | 1.15 |
| 6 | Addie Joss, Cle | 1908 | 9 | 1.16 |
| 7 | Carl Lundgren, Chi-NL | 1907 | 7 | 1.17 |
| 8 | Grover Alexander, Phi-NL | 1915 | 12 | 1.22 |
| 9 | Cy Young, Bos-AL | 1908 | 3 | 1.26 |
| 10 | Three pitchers tied at 1.27 | | | |

#### Since 1950

| | | Year | ShO | ERA |
|---|---|---|---|---|
| 1 | Bob Gibson, St.L | 1968 | 13 | 1.12 |
| 2 | Dwight Gooden, NY-NL | 1985 | 8 | 1.53 |
| 3 | Greg Maddux, Atl | 1994 | 3 | 1.56 |
| 4 | Luis Tiant, Cle | 1968 | 9 | 1.60 |
| 5 | Greg Maddux, Atl | 1995 | 3 | 1.63 |
| 6 | Dean Chance, LA-AL | 1964 | 11 | 1.65 |
| 7 | Nolan Ryan, Cal | 1981 | 3 | 1.69 |
| 8 | Sandy Koufax, LA | 1966 | 5 | 1.73 |
| 9 | Sandy Koufax, LA | 1964 | 7 | 1.74 |
| 10 | Pedro Martinez, Bos | 2000 | 4 | 1.74 |

**Note:** Koufax's ERA in 1964 was 1.735. Martinez' ERA in 2000 was 1.742. The Yankees' Ron Guidry narrowly missed the top 10 list with an ERA of 1.743 in 1978.

### Winning Pct.

| | | Year | W-L | Pct |
|---|---|---|---|---|
| 1 | Roy Face, Pit | 1959 | 18-1 | .947 |
| 2 | Rick Sutcliffe, Chi-NL* | 1984 | 16-1 | .941 |
| 3 | Johnny Allen, Cle | 1937 | 15-1 | .938 |
| 4 | Greg Maddux, Atl | 1995 | 19-2 | .904 |
| 5 | Randy Johnson, Sea | 1995 | 18-2 | .900 |
| 6 | Ron Guidry, NY-AL | 1978 | 25-3 | .893 |
| 7 | Freddie Fitzsimmons, Bklyn | 1940 | 16-2 | .889 |
| 8 | Lefty Grove, Phi-AL | 1931 | 31-4 | .886 |
| 9 | Bob Stanley, Bos | 1978 | 15-2 | .882 |
| 10 | Preacher Roe, Bklyn | 1951 | 22-3 | .880 |

*Sutcliffe began 1984 with Cleveland and was 4-5 before being traded to the Cubs; his overall winning pct. was .769 (20-6).

### Strikeouts

| | | Year | SO | P/9 |
|---|---|---|---|---|
| 1 | Nolan Ryan, Cal | 1973 | 383 | 10.57 |
| 2 | Sandy Koufax, LA | 1965 | 382 | 10.24 |
| 3 | Randy Johnson, Ari | 2001 | 372 | 13.41 |
| 4 | Nolan Ryan, Cal | 1974 | 367 | 9.93 |
| 5 | Randy Johnson, Ari | 1999 | 364 | 12.06 |
| 6 | Rube Waddell, Phi-AL | 1904 | 349 | 8.20 |
| 7 | Bob Feller, Cle | 1946 | 348 | 8.43 |
| 8 | Randy Johnson, Ari | 2000 | 347 | 12.56 |
| 9 | Nolan Ryan, Cal | 1977 | 341 | 10.26 |
| 10 | Randy Johnson, Ari | 2002 | 334 | 11.56 |

### Appearances

| | | Year | App | Sv |
|---|---|---|---|---|
| 1 | Mike Marshall, LA | 1974 | 106 | 21 |
| 2 | Kent Tekulve, Pit | 1979 | 94 | 31 |
| 3 | Mike Marshall, LA | 1973 | 92 | 31 |
| 4 | Kent Tekulve, Pit | 1978 | 91 | 31 |
| 5 | Wayne Granger, Cin | 1969 | 90 | 27 |
| | Mike Marshall, Min | 1979 | 90 | 32 |
| | Kent Tekulve, Phi | 1987 | 90 | 3 |

### Saves

| | | Year | App | Sv |
|---|---|---|---|---|
| 1 | Bobby Thigpen, Chi-AL | 1990 | 77 | 57 |
| 2 | John Smoltz, Atl | 2002 | 75 | 55 |
| | Eric Gagne, LA | 2003 | 77 | 55 |
| 4 | Randy Myers, Chi-NL | 1993 | 73 | 53 |
| | Trevor Hoffman, SD | 1998 | 66 | 53 |
| | Mariano Rivera, NY-AL | 2004 | 74 | 53 |
| 7 | Eric Gagne, LA | 2002 | 77 | 52 |
| 8 | Dennis Eckersley, Oak | 1992 | 69 | 51 |
| | Rod Beck, Chi-NL | 1998 | 81 | 51 |
| 10 | Mariano Rivera, NY-AL | 2001 | 71 | 50 |

### Innings Pitched (since 1920)

| | | Year | IP | W-L |
|---|---|---|---|---|
| 1 | Wilbur Wood, Chi-AL | 1972 | 376.2 | 24-17 |
| 2 | Mickey Lolich, Det | 1971 | 376.0 | 25-14 |
| 3 | Bob Feller, Cle | 1946 | 371.1 | 26-15 |
| 4 | Grover Alexander, Chi-NL | 1920 | 363.1 | 27-14 |
| 5 | Wilbur Wood, Chi-AL | 1973 | 359.1 | 24-20 |

### Shutouts

| | | Year | ShO | ERA |
|---|---|---|---|---|
| 1 | Grover Alexander, Phi-NL | 1916 | 16 | 1.55 |
| 2 | Jack Coombs, Phi-AL | 1910 | 13 | 1.30 |
| | Bob Gibson, St.L | 1968 | 13 | 1.12 |
| 4 | Christy Mathewson, NY-NL | 1908 | 12 | 1.43 |
| | Grover Alexander, Phi-NL | 1915 | 12 | 1.22 |

### Walks Allowed (since 1920)

| | | Year | BB | SO |
|---|---|---|---|---|
| 1 | Bob Feller, Cle | 1938 | 208 | 240 |
| 2 | Nolan Ryan, Cal | 1977 | 204 | 341 |
| 3 | Nolan Ryan, Cal | 1974 | 202 | 367 |
| 4 | Bob Feller, Cle | 1941 | 194 | 260 |
| 5 | Bobo Newsom, St.L-AL | 1938 | 192 | 226 |

### Home Runs Allowed

| | | Year | HRs |
|---|---|---|---|
| 1 | Bert Blyleven, Minnesota | 1986 | 50 |
| 2 | Jose Lima, Houston | 2000 | 48 |
| 3 | Robin Roberts, Philadelphia | 1956 | 46 |
| | Bert Blyleven, Minnesota | 1987 | 46 |
| 5 | Jamie Moyer, Seattle | 2004 | 44 |

## SINGLE GAME
Through 2005 regular season.
### Batting

### Home Runs

| No | | Date | Inn |
|---|---|---|---|
| 4 | Bobby Lowe, Boston-NL | 5/30/1894 | 9 |
| | Ed Delahanty, Philadelphia-NL | 7/13/1896 | 9 |
| | Lou Gehrig, New York-AL | 6/3/1932 | 9 |
| | Chuck Klein, Philadelphia-NL | 7/10/1936 | 10 |
| | Pat Seerey, Chicago-AL | 7/18/1948 | 11 |
| | Gil Hodges, Brooklyn | 8/31/1950 | 9 |
| | Joe Adcock, Milwaukee | 7/31/1954 | 9 |
| | Rocky Colavito, Cleveland | 6/10/1959 | 9 |
| | Willie Mays, San Francisco | 4/30/1961 | 9 |
| | Mike Schmidt, Philadelphia | 4/17/1976 | 10 |
| | Bob Horner, Atlanta | 7/6/1986 | 9 |
| | Mark Whiten, St. Louis | 9/7/1993 | 9 |
| | Mike Cameron, Seattle | 5/2/2002 | 9 |
| | Shawn Green, Los Angeles | 5/23/2002 | 9 |
| | Carlos Delgado, Toronto | 9/25/2003 | 9 |

### Runs

| No | | Date | Inn |
|---|---|---|---|
| 7 | Guy Hecker, Louisville | 8/15/1886 | 9 |

### Hits

| No | | Date | Inn |
|---|---|---|---|
| 9 | Johnny Burnett, Cleveland (9-for-11) | 7/10/1932 | 18 |
| 7 | Wilbert Robinson, Baltimore (7-for-7) | 6/10/1892 | 9 |
| | Rennie Stennett, Pittsburgh (7-for-7) | 9/16/1975 | 9 |
| | Cesar Gutierrez, Detroit (7-for-7) | 6/21/1970 | 12 |
| | Rocky Colavito, Detroit (7-for-10) | 6/24/1962 | 22 |

### Runs Batted In

| No | | Date | Inn |
|---|---|---|---|
| 12 | Jim Bottomley, St. Louis-NL | 9/16/1924 | 9 |
| | Mark Whiten, St. Louis | 9/7/1993 | 9 |

### Pitching

### Strikeouts

| No | | Date | Inn |
|---|---|---|---|
| 21 | Tom Cheney, Washington | 9/12/1962 | 16 |
| 20 | Roger Clemens, Boston | 4/29/1986 | 9 |
| | Roger Clemens, Boston | 9/18/1996 | 9 |
| | Kerry Wood, Chicago-NL | 5/6/1998 | 9 |
| | Randy Johnson, Arizona | 5/8/2001 | 9* |

*Johnson struck out 20 in nine innings and was removed with the game tied, 1-1. Arizona beat Cincinnati, 4-3, in 11 innings.

### Innings Pitched

| No | | Date |
|---|---|---|
| 26 | Leon Cadore, Brooklyn (tie, 1-1) | 5/1/1920 |
| | Joe Oeschger, Boston-NL (tie, 1-1) | 5/1/1920 |

## Unassisted Triple Plays

One of the rarest feats in baseball, the unassisted triple play has been accomplished only 13 times in major league history. Ironically, in what can only be described as a statistic anomaly, the trick was turned twice in two days in May of 1927.

| Player, Position, Team | Date | Opponent |
|---|---|---|
| Paul Hines, OF, Providence | May 8, 1878 | Boston-NL |
| Neal Ball, SS, Cleveland | July 19, 1909 | Boston-AL |
| Bill Wambsganss, 2B, Cleveland* | Oct. 10, 1920 | Brooklyn |
| George Burns, 1B, Boston-AL | Sept. 14, 1923 | Cleveland |
| Ernie Padgett, SS, Boston-NL | Oct. 6, 1923 | Philadelphia |
| Glenn Wright, SS, Pittsburgh | May 7, 1925 | St.Louis-NL |
| Jimmy Cooney, SS, Chicago-NL | May 30, 1927 | Pittsburgh |
| Johnny Neun, 1B, Detroit | May 31, 1927 | Cleveland |
| Ron Hansen, SS, Washington | July 30, 1968 | Cleveland |
| Mickey Morandini, 2B, Philadelphia | Sept. 20, 1992 | Pittsburgh |
| John Valentin, SS, Boston | July 8, 1994 | Seattle |
| Randy Velarde, 2B, Oakland | May 29, 2000 | NY Yankees |
| Rafael Furcal, SS, Atlanta | Aug. 10, 2003 | St. Louis |

* World Series game

## Most Gold Gloves (by position)

Gold Gloves have been awarded since the 1957 season by Rawlings Sporting Goods to superior major league fielders at each position in both leagues. Voting has been conducted by a panel of sportswriters appointed by The Sporting News publisher J.G. Taylor Spink (1957), major league players (1958-1964) and managers and coaches (1965-present). Top 5 in each position are listed, through the 2004 season.

| Pitchers | No | Catchers | No | First Basemen | No | Second Basemen | No |
|---|---|---|---|---|---|---|---|
| 1 Jim Kaat | 16 | 1 Ivan Rodriguez | 11 | 1 Keith Hernandez | 11 | 1 Roberto Alomar | 10 |
| 2 Greg Maddux | 14 | 2 Johnny Bench | 10 | 2 Don Mattingly | 9 | 2 Ryne Sandberg | 9 |
| 3 Bob Gibson | 9 | 3 Bob Boone | 7 | 3 George Scott | 8 | 3 Bill Mazeroski | 8 |
| 4 Bobby Shantz | 8 | 4 Jim Sundberg | 6 | 4 Vic Power | 7 | Frank White | 8 |
| 5 Mark Langston | 7 | 5 Bill Freehan | 5 | Bill White | 7 | 5 Joe Morgan | 5 |
| | | | | | | Bobby Richardson | 5 |

| Third Basemen | No | Shortstops | No | Outfielders | No |
|---|---|---|---|---|---|
| 1 Brooks Robinson | 16 | 1 Ozzie Smith | 13 | 1 Roberto Clemente | 12 |
| 2 Mike Schmidt | 10 | 2 Luis Aparicio | 9 | Willie Mays | 12 |
| 3 Buddy Bell | 6 | Omar Vizquel | 9 | 3 Ken Griffey Jr. | 10 |
| Robin Ventura | 6 | 4 Mark Belanger | 8 | Al Kaline | 10 |
| Scott Rolen | 6 | 5 Dave Concepcion | 5 | 5 Five tied with 8 each | |

## All-Time Winningest Managers

Top 20 Major League career victories through the 2005 season. Career, regular season and postseason (playoffs and World Series) records are noted along with AL and NL pennants and World Series titles won. Managers active during 2005 season in **bold** type.

| | | Career | | | | Regular Season | | | Postseason | | | |
|---|---|---|---|---|---|---|---|---|---|---|---|---|
| | | Yrs | W | L | Pct | W | L | Pct | W | L | Pct | Titles |
| 1 | Connie Mack | 53 | **3755** | 3967 | .486 | 3731 | 3948 | .486 | 24 | 19 | .558 | 9 AL, 5 WS |
| 2 | John McGraw | 33 | **2866** | 2012 | .588 | 2840 | 1984 | .589 | 26 | 28 | .482 | 10 NL, 3 WS |
| 3 | **Tony La Russa** | 27 | **2262** | 1951 | .537 | 2214 | 1908 | .537 | 48 | 43 | .527 | 3 AL, 1 NL, 1 WS |
| 4 | Sparky Anderson | 26 | **2228** | 1855 | .547 | 2194 | 1834 | .545 | 34 | 21 | .618 | 4 NL, 1 AL, 3 WS |
| 5 | Bucky Harris | 29 | **2168** | 2228 | .493 | 2157 | 2218 | .493 | 11 | 10 | .524 | 3 AL, 2 WS |
| 6 | **Bobby Cox** | 24 | **2158** | 1669 | .564 | 2092 | 1603 | .566 | 66 | 66 | .500 | 5 NL, 1 WS |
| 7 | Joe McCarthy | 24 | **2155** | 1346 | .616 | 2125 | 1333 | .615 | 30 | 13 | .698 | 1 NL, 8 AL, 7 WS |
| 8 | Walter Alston | 23 | **2063** | 1634 | .558 | 2040 | 1613 | .558 | 23 | 21 | .523 | 7 NL, 4 WS |
| 9 | Leo Durocher | 24 | **2015** | 1717 | .540 | 2008 | 1709 | .540 | 7 | 8 | .467 | 3 NL, 1 WS |
| 10 | **Joe Torre** | 24 | **1950** | 1681 | .537 | 1876 | 1637 | .534 | 74 | 44 | .627 | 6 AL, 4 WS |
| 11 | Casey Stengel | 25 | **1942** | 1868 | .510 | 1905 | 1842 | .508 | 37 | 26 | .587 | 10 AL, 7 WS |
| 12 | Gene Mauch | 26 | **1907** | 2044 | .483 | 1902 | 2037 | .483 | 5 | 7 | .417 | —None— |
| 13 | Bill McKechnie | 25 | **1904** | 1737 | .523 | 1896 | 1723 | .524 | 8 | 14 | .364 | 4 NL, 2 WS |
| 14 | Tommy Lasorda | 21 | **1630** | 1469 | .526 | 1599 | 1439 | .526 | 31 | 30 | .508 | 4 NL, 2 WS |
| 15 | Ralph Houk | 20 | **1627** | 1539 | .514 | 1619 | 1531 | .514 | 8 | 8 | .500 | 3 AL, 2 WS |
| 16 | Fred Clarke | 19 | **1609** | 1189 | .575 | 1602 | 1181 | .576 | 7 | 8 | .467 | 4 NL, 1 WS |
| 17 | Dick Williams | 21 | **1592** | 1474 | .519 | 1571 | 1451 | .520 | 21 | 23 | .477 | 3 AL, 1 NL, 2 WS |
| 18 | **Lou Piniella** | 19 | **1542** | 1441 | .517 | 1519 | 1420 | .517 | 23 | 21 | .523 | 1 NL, 1 WS |
| 19 | Earl Weaver | 17 | **1506** | 1080 | .582 | 1480 | 1060 | .583 | 26 | 20 | .565 | 4 AL, 1 WS |
| 20 | Clark Griffith | 20 | **1491** | 1367 | .522 | 1491 | 1367 | .522 | 0 | 0 | .000 | 1 AL (1901) |

**Notes:** John McGraw's postseason record also includes two World Series tie games (1912, '22).

### Where They Managed

**Alston**—Brooklyn/Los Angeles NL (1954-76); **Anderson**—Cincinnati NL (1970-78), Detroit AL (1979-95); **Clarke**— Louisville NL (1897-99), Pittsburgh NL (1900-15); **Cox**—Atlanta (1978-81, 1990-), Toronto (1982-85); **Durocher**—Brooklyn NL (1939-46,48), New York NL (1948-55), Chicago NL (1966-72), Houston NL (1972-73); **Griffith**—Chicago AL (1901-02), New York AL (1903-08), Cincinnati NL (1909-11), Washington AL (1912-20); **Harris**—Washington AL (1924- 28,35-42,50-54), Detroit AL (1929-33,55-56), Boston AL (1934), Philadelphia NL (1943), New York AL (1947-48); **Houk**—New York AL (1961-63,66-73), Detroit AL (1974-78), Boston AL (1981-84); **La Russa**—Chicago AL (1979-86), Oakland (1986-95), St. Louis (1996-) **Lasorda**—Los Angeles NL (1976-96). **Mack**—Pittsburgh NL (1894-96), Philadelphia AL (1901-50); **Mauch**—Philadelphia NL (1960-68), Montreal NL (1969-75), Minnesota NL (1976-80), California AL (1981-82,85-87); **McCarthy**—Chicago NL (1926-30), New York AL (1931-46), Boston AL (1948-50); **McGraw**—Baltimore NL (1899), Baltimore AL (1901-02), New York NL (1902-32); **McKechnie**—Newark FL (1915), Pittsburgh NL (1922-26), St. Louis NL (1928-29), Boston NL (1930-37), Cincinnati NL (1938-46); **Piniella**—New York AL (1986-88), Cincinnati (1990-92), Seattle (1993-2002), Tampa Bay (2003-05); **Stengel**—Brooklyn NL (1934-36), Boston NL (1938-43), New York AL (1949-60), New York NL (1962-65); **Torre**—New York NL (1977-81), Atlanta (1982-84), St. Louis (1990-95), New York AL (1996-); **Weaver**—Baltimore AL (1968-82,85-86); **Williams**—Boston AL (1967-69), Oakland AL (1971-73), California AL (1974-76), Montreal NL (1977-81), San Diego NL (1982-85), Seattle AL (1986-88).

## Regular Season Winning Pct.

Minimum of 750 victories.

| | | Yrs | W | L | Pct | Pen |
|---|---|---|---|---|---|---|
| 1 | Joe McCarthy | 24 | 2125 | 1333 | **.615** | 9 |
| 2 | Charlie Comiskey | 12 | 838 | 541 | **.608** | 4 |
| 3 | Frank Selee | 16 | 1284 | 862 | **.598** | 5 |
| 4 | Billy Southworth | 13 | 1044 | 704 | **.597** | 4 |
| 5 | Frank Chance | 11 | 946 | 648 | **.593** | 4 |
| 6 | John McGraw | 33 | 2840 | 1984 | **.589** | 10 |
| 7 | Al Lopez | 17 | 1410 | 1004 | **.584** | 2 |
| 8 | Earl Weaver | 17 | 1480 | 1060 | **.583** | 4 |
| 9 | Cap Anson | 20 | 1296 | 947 | **.578** | 5 |
| 10 | Fred Clarke | 19 | 1602 | 1181 | **.576** | 4 |
| 11 | **Bobby Cox** | 24 | 2092 | 1603 | **.566** | 5 |
| 12 | Davey Johnson | 14 | 1148 | 888 | **.564** | 1 |
| 13 | Steve O'Neill | 14 | 1040 | 821 | **.559** | 1 |
| 14 | Walter Alston | 23 | 2040 | 1613 | **.558** | 7 |
| 15 | Bill Terry | 10 | 823 | 661 | **.555** | 3 |
| 16 | Miller Huggins | 17 | 1413 | 1134 | **.555** | 6 |
| 17 | Billy Martin | 16 | 1253 | 1013 | **.553** | 2 |
| 18 | Harry Wright | 18 | 1000 | 825 | **.548** | 2 |
| 19 | Charlie Grimm | 19 | 1287 | 1067 | **.547** | 3 |
| 20 | Sparky Anderson | 26 | 2194 | 1834 | **.545** | 5 |

## World Series Victories

| | | App | W | L | T | Pct | WS |
|---|---|---|---|---|---|---|---|
| 1 | Casey Stengel | 10 | 37 | 26 | 0 | .587 | 7 |
| 2 | Joe McCarthy | 9 | 30 | 13 | 0 | .698 | 7 |
| 3 | John McGraw | 9 | 26 | 28 | 2 | .482 | 3 |
| 4 | Connie Mack | 8 | 24 | 19 | 0 | .558 | 5 |
| 5 | **Joe Torre** | 6 | 21 | 11 | 0 | .656 | 4 |
| 6 | Walter Alston | 7 | 20 | 20 | 0 | .500 | 4 |
| 7 | Miller Huggins | 6 | 18 | 15 | 1 | .544 | 3 |
| 8 | Sparky Anderson | 5 | 16 | 12 | 0 | .571 | 3 |
| | Tommy Lasorda | 4 | 12 | 11 | 0 | .522 | 2 |
| | Dick Williams | 4 | 12 | 14 | 0 | .462 | 2 |
| 11 | Frank Chance | 4 | 11 | 9 | 1 | .548 | 2 |
| | Bucky Harris | 4 | 11 | 10 | 0 | .524 | 2 |
| | Billy Southworth | 4 | 11 | 11 | 0 | .500 | 2 |
| | Earl Weaver | 4 | 11 | 13 | 0 | .458 | 1 |
| | **Bobby Cox** | 5 | 11 | 18 | 0 | .379 | 1 |
| 16 | Whitey Herzog | 3 | 10 | 11 | 0 | .476 | 1 |
| 17 | Bill Carrigan | 2 | 8 | 2 | 0 | .800 | 2 |
| | Danny Murtaugh | 2 | 8 | 6 | 0 | .571 | 2 |
| | Cito Gaston | 2 | 8 | 6 | 0 | .571 | 2 |
| | Tom Kelly | 2 | 8 | 6 | 0 | .571 | 2 |
| | Ralph Houk | 3 | 8 | 8 | 0 | .500 | 2 |
| | Bill McKechnie | 4 | 8 | 14 | 0 | .364 | 2 |

## Active Managers' Records
Regular season games only; through 2005 (updated as of Oct. 28).

### National League

| | | Yrs | W | L | Pct |
|---|---|---|---|---|---|
| 1 | Tony La Russa, St.L | 27 | 2214 | 1908 | .537 |
| 2 | Bobby Cox, Atl. | 24 | 2092 | 1603 | .566 |
| 3 | Dusty Baker, Chi | 13 | 1096 | 945 | .537 |
| 4 | Frank Robinson, Wash. | 15 | 994 | 1085 | .478 |
| 5 | Felipe Alou, SF | 13 | 957 | 936 | .506 |
| 6 | Bruce Bochy, SD | 11 | 863 | 901 | .489 |
| 7 | Phil Garner, Hou. | 13 | 845 | 901 | .484 |
| 8 | Jim Tracy, Pit. | 5 | 427 | 383 | .527 |
| 9 | Charlie Manuel, Phi | 4 | 308 | 265 | .538 |
| 10 | Clint Hurdle, Col | 4 | 276 | 350 | .441 |
| 11 | Bob Melvin, Ari | 3 | 233 | 253 | .479 |
| 12 | Ned Yost, Mil | 3 | 216 | 269 | .445 |
| 13 | Jerry Narron, Cin | 3 | 180 | 208 | .464 |
| 14 | Willie Randolph, NY | 1 | 83 | 79 | .512 |
| 15 | Joe Girardi, Fla. | 0 | 0 | 0 | .000 |
| | Los Angeles | | | | |

### American League

| | | Yrs | W | L | Pct |
|---|---|---|---|---|---|
| 1 | Joe Torre, NY | 24 | 1876 | 1637 | .534 |
| 2 | Jim Leyland, Det. | 14 | 1069 | 1131 | .486 |
| 3 | Mike Hargrove, Sea | 14 | 1065 | 1056 | .502 |
| 4 | Buck Showalter, Tex. | 10 | 802 | 751 | .516 |
| 5 | Mike Scioscia, Ana. | 6 | 520 | 452 | .535 |
| 6 | Terry Francona, Bos. | 6 | 478 | 494 | .492 |
| 7 | Buddy Bell, KC | 7 | 388 | 531 | .422 |
| 8 | Ron Gardenhire, Min. | 4 | 359 | 288 | .555 |
| 9 | Ken Macha, Oak | 3 | 275 | 211 | .566 |
| 10 | Eric Wedge, Cle. | 3 | 241 | 246 | .495 |
| 11 | Ozzie Guillen, Chi | 2 | 182 | 142 | .562 |
| 12 | John Gibbons, Tor. | 2 | 100 | 112 | .472 |
| 13 | Sam Perlozzo, Bal | 1 | 23 | 32 | .418 |
| | Tampa Bay | | | | |

## Annual Awards

### MOST VALUABLE PLAYER

There have been three different Most Valuable Player awards in baseball since 1911—the Chalmers Award (1911-14), presented by the Detroit-based automobile company; the League Award (1922-29), presented by the National and American Leagues; and the Baseball Writers' Award (since 1931), presented by the Baseball Writers' Association of America. Statistics for winning players are provided below. Stats for winning pitchers before advent of Cy Young Award are in MVP Pitchers' Statistics table.

**Multiple winners: NL**—Barry Bonds (7); Roy Campanella, Stan Musial and Mike Schmidt (3); Ernie Banks, Johnny Bench, Rogers Hornsby, Carl Hubbell, Willie Mays, Joe Morgan and Dale Murphy (2). **AL**—Yogi Berra, Joe DiMaggio, Jimmie Foxx and Mickey Mantle (3); Mickey Cochrane, Lou Gehrig, Juan Gonzalez, Hank Greenberg, Walter Johnson, Roger Maris, Hal Newhouser, Cal Ripken Jr., Frank Thomas, Ted Williams and Robin Yount (2). **NL & AL**—Frank Robinson (2, one in each).

### Chalmers Award

#### National League

| Year | | Pos | HR | RBI | Avg |
|---|---|---|---|---|---|
| 1911 | Wildfire Schulte, Chi | OF | 21 | 121 | .300 |
| 1912 | Larry Doyle, NY | 2B | 10 | 90 | .330 |
| 1913 | Jake Daubert, Bklyn | 1B | 2 | 52 | .350 |
| 1914 | Johnny Evers, Bos | 2B | 1 | 40 | .279 |

#### American League

| Year | | Pos | HR | RBI | Avg |
|---|---|---|---|---|---|
| 1911 | Ty Cobb, Det | OF | 8 | 144 | .420 |
| 1912 | Tris Speaker, Bos | OF | 10 | 98 | .383 |
| 1913 | Walter Johnson, Wash | P | — | — | — |
| 1914 | Eddie Collins, Phi | 2B | 2 | 85 | .344 |

### League Award

#### National League

| Year | | Pos | HR | RBI | Avg |
|---|---|---|---|---|---|
| 1922 | No selection | | | | |
| 1923 | No selection | | | | |
| 1924 | Dazzy Vance, Bklyn | P | — | — | — |
| 1925 | Rogers Hornsby, St.L | 2B-Mgr | 39 | 143 | .403 |
| 1926 | Bob O'Farrell, St.L | C | 7 | 68 | .293 |
| 1927 | Paul Waner, Pit | OF | 9 | 131 | .380 |
| 1928 | Jim Bottomley, St.L | 1B | 31 | 136 | .325 |
| 1929 | Rogers Hornsby, Chi | 2B | 39 | 149 | .380 |

#### American League

| Year | | Pos | HR | RBI | Avg |
|---|---|---|---|---|---|
| 1922 | George Sisler, St.L | 1B | 8 | 105 | .420 |
| 1923 | Babe Ruth, NY | OF | 41 | 131 | .393 |
| 1924 | Walter Johnson, Wash | P | — | — | — |
| 1925 | Roger Peckinpaugh, Wash | SS | 4 | 64 | .294 |
| 1926 | George Burns, Cle | 1B | 4 | 114 | .358 |
| 1927 | Lou Gehrig, NY | 1B | 47 | 175 | .373 |
| 1928 | Mickey Cochrane, Phi | C | 10 | 57 | .293 |
| 1929 | No selection | | | | |

### Most Valuable Player
#### National League

| Year | | Pos | HR | RBI | Avg | Year | | Pos | HR | RBI | Avg |
|---|---|---|---|---|---|---|---|---|---|---|---|
| 1931 | Frankie Frisch, St.L | 2B | 4 | 82 | .311 | 1950 | Jim Konstanty, Phi | P | — | — | — |
| 1932 | Chuck Klein, Phi | OF | 38 | 137 | .348 | 1951 | Roy Campanella, Bklyn | C | 33 | 108 | .325 |
| 1933 | Carl Hubbell, NY | P | — | — | — | 1952 | Hank Sauer, Chi | OF | 37 | 121 | .270 |
| 1934 | Dizzy Dean, St.L | P | — | — | — | 1953 | Roy Campanella, Bklyn | C | 41 | 142 | .312 |
| 1935 | Gabby Hartnett, Chi | C | 13 | 91 | .344 | 1954 | Willie Mays, NY | OF | 41 | 110 | .345 |
| 1936 | Carl Hubbell, NY | P | — | — | — | 1955 | Roy Campanella, Bklyn | C | 32 | 107 | .318 |
| 1937 | Joe Medwick, St.L | OF | 31 | 154 | .374 | 1956 | Don Newcombe, Bklyn | P | — | — | — |
| 1938 | Ernie Lombardi, Cin | C | 19 | 95 | .342 | 1957 | Hank Aaron, Mil | OF | 44 | 132 | .322 |
| 1939 | Bucky Walters, Cin | P | — | — | — | 1958 | Ernie Banks, Chi | SS | 47 | 129 | .313 |
| 1940 | Frank McCormick, Cin | 1B | 19 | 127 | .309 | 1959 | Ernie Banks, Chi | SS | 45 | 143 | .304 |
| 1941 | Dolf Camilli, Bklyn | 1B | 34 | 120 | .285 | 1960 | Dick Groat, Pit | SS | 2 | 50 | .325 |
| 1942 | Mort Cooper, St.L | P | — | — | — | 1961 | Frank Robinson, Cin | OF | 37 | 124 | .323 |
| 1943 | Stan Musial, St.L | OF | 13 | 81 | .357 | 1962 | Maury Wills, LA | SS | 6 | 48 | .299 |
| 1944 | Marty Marion, St.L | SS | 6 | 63 | .267 | 1963 | Sandy Koufax, LA | P | — | — | — |
| 1945 | Phil Cavarretta, Chi | 1B | 6 | 97 | .355 | 1964 | Ken Boyer, St.L | 3B | 24 | 119 | .295 |
| 1946 | Stan Musial, St.L | 1B-Of | 16 | 103 | .365 | 1965 | Willie Mays, SF | OF | 52 | 112 | .317 |
| 1947 | Bob Elliott, Bos | 3B | 22 | 113 | .317 | 1966 | Roberto Clemente, Pit | OF | 29 | 119 | .317 |
| 1948 | Stan Musial, St.L | OF | 39 | 131 | .376 | 1967 | Orlando Cepeda, St.L | 1B | 25 | 111 | .325 |
| 1949 | Jackie Robinson, Bklyn | 2B | 16 | 124 | .342 | 1968 | Bob Gibson, St.L | P | — | — | — |

| Year | | Pos | HR | RBI | Avg | Year | | Pos | HR | RBI | Avg |
|---|---|---|---|---|---|---|---|---|---|---|---|
| 1969 | Willie McCovey, SF | 1B | 45 | 126 | .320 | 1987 | Andre Dawson, Chi | OF | 49 | 137 | .287 |
| 1970 | Johnny Bench, Cin | C | 45 | 148 | .293 | 1988 | Kirk Gibson, LA | OF | 25 | 76 | .290 |
| 1971 | Joe Torre, St.L | 3B | 24 | 137 | .363 | 1989 | Kevin Mitchell, SF | OF | 47 | 125 | .291 |
| 1972 | Johnny Bench, Cin | C | 40 | 125 | .270 | 1990 | Barry Bonds, Pit | OF | 33 | 114 | .301 |
| 1973 | Pete Rose, Cin | OF | 5 | 64 | .338 | 1991 | Terry Pendleton, Atl | 3B | 22 | 86 | .319 |
| 1974 | Steve Garvey, LA | 1B | 21 | 111 | .312 | 1992 | Barry Bonds, Pit | OF | 34 | 103 | .311 |
| 1975 | Joe Morgan, Cin | 2B | 17 | 94 | .327 | 1993 | Barry Bonds, SF | OF | 46 | 123 | .336 |
| 1976 | Joe Morgan, Cin | 2B | 27 | 111 | .320 | 1994 | Jeff Bagwell, Hou | 1B | 39 | 116 | .368 |
| 1977 | George Foster, Cin | OF | 52 | 149 | .320 | 1995 | Barry Larkin, Cin | SS | 15 | 66 | .319 |
| 1978 | Dave Parker, Pit | OF | 30 | 117 | .334 | 1996 | Ken Caminiti, SD | 3B | 40 | 130 | .326 |
| 1979 | Keith Hernandez, St.L | 1B | 11 | 105 | .344 | 1997 | Larry Walker, Col | OF | 49 | 130 | .366 |
| | Willie Stargell, Pit | 1B | 32 | 82 | .281 | 1998 | Sammy Sosa, Chi | OF | 66 | 158 | .308 |
| | | | | | | 1999 | Chipper Jones, Atl | 3B | 45 | 110 | .319 |
| 1980 | Mike Schmidt, Phi | 3B | 48 | 121 | .286 | 2000 | Jeff Kent, SF | 2B | 33 | 125 | .334 |
| 1981 | Mike Schmidt, Phi | 3B | 31 | 91 | .316 | 2001 | Barry Bonds, SF | OF | 73 | 137 | .328 |
| 1982 | Dale Murphy, Atl | OF | 36 | 109 | .281 | 2002 | Barry Bonds, SF | OF | 46 | 110 | .370 |
| 1983 | Dale Murphy, Atl | OF | 36 | 121 | .302 | 2003 | Barry Bonds, SF | OF | 45 | 90 | .341 |
| 1984 | Ryne Sandberg, Chi | 2B | 19 | 84 | .314 | 2004 | Barry Bonds, SF | OF | 45 | 101 | .362 |
| 1985 | Willie McGee, St.L | OF | 10 | 82 | .353 | | | | | | |
| 1986 | Mike Schmidt, Phi | 3B | 37 | 119 | .290 | | | | | | |

## American League

| Year | | Pos | HR | RBI | Avg | Year | | Pos | HR | RBI | Avg |
|---|---|---|---|---|---|---|---|---|---|---|---|
| 1931 | Lefty Grove, Phi | P | — | — | — | 1968 | Denny McLain, Det | P | — | — | — |
| 1932 | Jimmie Foxx, Phi | 1B | 58 | 169 | .364 | 1969 | Harmon Killebrew, Min | 3B-1B | 49 | 140 | .276 |
| 1933 | Jimmie Foxx, Phi | 1B | 48 | 163 | .356 | 1970 | Boog Powell, Bal | 1B | 35 | 114 | .297 |
| 1934 | Mickey Cochrane, Det | C-Mgr | 2 | 76 | .320 | 1971 | Vida Blue, Oak | P | — | — | — |
| 1935 | Hank Greenberg, Det | 1B | 36 | 170 | .328 | 1972 | Dick Allen, Chi | 1B | 37 | 113 | .308 |
| 1936 | Lou Gehrig, NY | 1B | 49 | 152 | .354 | 1973 | Reggie Jackson, Oak | OF | 32 | 117 | .293 |
| 1937 | Charlie Gehringer, Det | 2B | 14 | 96 | .371 | 1974 | Jeff Burroughs, Tex | OF | 25 | 118 | .301 |
| 1938 | Jimmie Foxx, Bos | 1B | 50 | 175 | .349 | 1975 | Fred Lynn, Bos | OF | 21 | 105 | .331 |
| 1939 | Joe DiMaggio, NY | OF | 30 | 126 | .381 | 1976 | Thurman Munson, NY | C | 17 | 105 | .302 |
| 1940 | Hank Greenberg, Det | OF | 41 | 150 | .340 | 1977 | Rod Carew, Min | 1B | 14 | 100 | .388 |
| 1941 | Joe DiMaggio, NY | OF | 30 | 125 | .357 | 1978 | Jim Rice, Bos | OF-DH | 46 | 139 | .315 |
| 1942 | Joe Gordon, NY | 2B | 18 | 103 | .322 | 1979 | Don Baylor, Cal | OF-DH | 36 | 139 | .296 |
| 1943 | Spud Chandler, NY | P | — | — | — | 1980 | George Brett, KC | 3B | 24 | 118 | .390 |
| 1944 | Hal Newhouser, Det | P | — | — | — | 1981 | Rollie Fingers, Mil | P | — | — | — |
| 1945 | Hal Newhouser, Det | P | — | — | — | 1982 | Robin Yount, Mil | SS | 29 | 114 | .331 |
| 1946 | Ted Williams, Bos | OF | 38 | 123 | .342 | 1983 | Cal Ripken Jr., Bal | SS | 27 | 102 | .318 |
| 1947 | Joe DiMaggio, NY | OF | 20 | 97 | .315 | 1984 | Willie Hernandez, Det | P | — | — | — |
| 1948 | Lou Boudreau, Cle | SS-Mgr | 18 | 106 | .355 | 1985 | Don Mattingly, NY | 1B | 35 | 145 | .324 |
| 1949 | Ted Williams, Bos | OF | 43 | 159 | .343 | 1986 | Roger Clemens, Bos | P | — | — | — |
| 1950 | Phil Rizzuto, NY | SS | 7 | 66 | .324 | 1987 | George Bell, Tor | OF | 47 | 134 | .308 |
| 1951 | Yogi Berra, NY | C | 27 | 88 | .294 | 1988 | Jose Canseco, Oak | OF | 42 | 124 | .307 |
| 1952 | Bobby Shantz, Phi | P | — | — | — | 1989 | Robin Yount, Mil | OF | 21 | 103 | .318 |
| 1953 | Al Rosen, Cle | 3B | 43 | 145 | .336 | 1990 | Rickey Henderson, Oak | OF | 28 | 61 | .325 |
| 1954 | Yogi Berra, NY | C | 22 | 125 | .307 | 1991 | Cal Ripken Jr., Bal | SS | 34 | 114 | .323 |
| 1955 | Yogi Berra, NY | C | 27 | 108 | .272 | 1992 | Dennis Eckersley, Oak | P | — | — | — |
| 1956 | Mickey Mantle, NY | OF | 52 | 130 | .353 | 1993 | Frank Thomas, Chi | 1B | 41 | 128 | .317 |
| 1957 | Mickey Mantle, NY | OF | 34 | 94 | .365 | 1994 | Frank Thomas, Chi | 1B | 38 | 101 | .353 |
| 1958 | Jackie Jensen, Bos | OF | 35 | 122 | .286 | 1995 | Mo Vaughn, Bos | 1B | 39 | 126 | .300 |
| 1959 | Nellie Fox, Chi | 2B | 2 | 70 | .306 | 1996 | Juan Gonzalez, Tex | OF-DH | 47 | 144 | .314 |
| 1960 | Roger Maris, NY | OF | 39 | 112 | .283 | 1997 | Ken Griffey Jr., Sea | OF | 56 | 147 | .304 |
| 1961 | Roger Maris, NY | OF | 61 | 142 | .269 | 1998 | Juan Gonzalez, Tex | OF | 45 | 157 | .318 |
| 1962 | Mickey Mantle, NY | OF | 30 | 89 | .321 | 1999 | Ivan Rodriguez, Tex | C | 35 | 113 | .332 |
| 1963 | Elston Howard, NY | C | 28 | 85 | .287 | 2000 | Jason Giambi, Oak | 1B | 43 | 137 | .333 |
| 1964 | Brooks Robinson, Bal | 3B | 28 | 118 | .317 | 2001 | Ichiro Suzuki, Sea | OF | 8 | 69 | .350 |
| 1965 | Zoilo Versalles, Min | SS | 19 | 77 | .273 | 2002 | Miguel Tejada, Oak | SS | 34 | 131 | .308 |
| 1966 | Frank Robinson, Bal | OF | 49 | 122 | .316 | 2003 | Alex Rodriguez, Tex | SS | 47 | 118 | .298 |
| 1967 | Carl Yastrzemski, Bos | OF | 44 | 121 | .326 | 2004 | Vladimir Guerrero, Ana | OF | 39 | 126 | .337 |

## MVP Pitchers' Statistics

Pitchers have been named Most Valuable Player on 23 occasions, 10 times in the NL and 13 in the AL. Four have been relief pitchers—Jim Konstanty, Rollie Fingers, Willie Hernandez and Dennis Eckersley. For statistics of MVP pitchers since 1956, see Cy Young Award tables on following page.

### National League

| Year | | Gm | W-L | SV | ERA |
|---|---|---|---|---|---|
| 1924 | Dazzy Vance, Bklyn | 35 | 28-6 | 0 | 2.16 |
| 1933 | Carl Hubbell, NY | 45 | 23-12 | 5 | 1.66 |
| 1934 | Dizzy Dean, St.L | 50 | 30-7 | 7 | 2.66 |
| 1936 | Carl Hubbell, NY | 42 | 26-6 | 3 | 2.31 |
| 1939 | Bucky Walters, Cin | 39 | 27-11 | 0 | 2.29 |
| 1942 | Mort Cooper, St.L | 37 | 22-7 | 0 | 1.78 |
| 1950 | Jim Konstanty, Phi | 74 | 16-7 | 22 | 2.66 |

### American League

| Year | | Gm | W-L | SV | ERA |
|---|---|---|---|---|---|
| 1913 | Walter Johnson, Wash | 47 | 36-7 | 2 | 1.09 |
| 1924 | Walter Johnson, Wash | 38 | 23-7 | 0 | 2.72 |
| 1931 | Lefty Grove, Phi | 41 | 31-4 | 5 | 2.06 |
| 1943 | Spud Chandler, NY | 30 | 20-4 | 0 | 1.64 |
| 1944 | Hal Newhouser, Det | 47 | 29-9 | 2 | 2.22 |
| 1945 | Hal Newhouser, Det | 40 | 25-9 | 2 | 1.81 |
| 1952 | Bobby Shantz, Phi | 33 | 24-7 | 0 | 2.48 |

## CY YOUNG AWARD

Voted on by the Baseball Writers Association of America. One award was presented from 1956-66, two since 1967. Pitchers who won the MVP and Cy Young awards in the same season are in **bold** type.

**Multiple winners: NL**—Steve Carlton, Greg Maddux and Randy Johnson (4); Sandy Koufax and Tom Seaver (3); Bob Gibson and Tom Glavine (2). **AL**—Roger Clemens (6); Jim Palmer (3); Pedro Martinez and Denny McLain (2). **NL & AL**—Roger Clemens (7, six in AL, one in NL); Randy Johnson (5, four in NL, one in AL); Pedro Martinez (3, two in AL, one in NL) and Gaylord Perry (2, one in each).

### NL and AL Combined

| Year | National League | Gm | W-L | SV | ERA | Year | American League | Gm | W-L | SV | ERA |
|------|-----------------|-----|------|-----|------|------|-----------------|-----|------|-----|------|
| 1956 | **Don Newcombe**, Bklyn | 38 | 27-7 | 0 | 3.06 | 1958 | Bob Turley, NY | 33 | 21-7 | 1 | 2.97 |
| 1957 | Warren Spahn, Mil | 39 | 21-11 | 3 | 2.69 | 1959 | Early Wynn, Chi | 37 | 22-10 | 0 | 3.17 |
| 1960 | Vernon Law, Pitt | 35 | 20-9 | 0 | 3.08 | 1961 | Whitey Ford, NY | 39 | 25-4 | 0 | 3.21 |
| 1962 | Don Drysdale, LA | 43 | 25-9 | 1 | 2.83 | 1964 | Dean Chance, LA | 46 | 20-9 | 4 | 1.65 |
| 1963 | **Sandy Koufax**, LA | 40 | 25-5 | 0 | 1.88 | | | | | | |
| 1965 | Sandy Koufax, LA | 43 | 26-8 | 2 | 2.04 | | | | | | |
| 1966 | Sandy Koufax, LA | 41 | 27-9 | 0 | 1.73 | | | | | | |

### Separate League Awards

| | National League | | | | | | American League | | | | |
|------|-----------------|-----|------|-----|------|------|-----------------|-----|------|-----|------|
| Year | | Gm | W-L | SV | ERA | Year | | Gm | W-L | SV | ERA |
| 1967 | Mike McCormick, SF | 40 | 22-10 | 0 | 2.85 | 1967 | Jim Lonborg, Bos | 39 | 22-9 | 0 | 3.16 |
| 1968 | **Bob Gibson**, St.L | 34 | 22-9 | 0 | 1.12 | 1968 | **Denny McLain**, Det | 41 | 31-6 | 0 | 1.96 |
| 1969 | Tom Seaver, NY | 36 | 25-7 | 0 | 2.21 | 1969 | Denny McLain, Det | 42 | 24-9 | 0 | 2.80 |
| 1970 | Bob Gibson, St.L | 34 | 23-7 | 0 | 3.12 | | Mike Cuellar, Bal | 39 | 23-11 | 0 | 2.38 |
| 1971 | Ferguson Jenkins, Chi | 39 | 24-13 | 0 | 2.77 | 1970 | Jim Perry, Min | 40 | 24-12 | 0 | 3.03 |
| 1972 | Steve Carlton, Phi | 41 | 27-10 | 0 | 1.97 | 1971 | Vida Blue, Oak | 39 | 24-8 | 0 | 1.82 |
| 1973 | Tom Seaver, NY | 36 | 19-10 | 0 | 2.08 | 1972 | Gaylord Perry, Cle | 41 | 24-16 | 1 | 1.92 |
| 1974 | Mike Marshall, LA | 106 | 15-12 | 21 | 2.42 | 1973 | Jim Palmer, Bal | 38 | 22-9 | 1 | 2.40 |
| 1975 | Tom Seaver, NY | 36 | 22-9 | 0 | 2.38 | 1974 | Catfish Hunter, Oak | 41 | 25-12 | 0 | 2.49 |
| 1976 | Randy Jones, SD | 40 | 22-14 | 0 | 2.74 | 1975 | Jim Palmer, Bal | 39 | 23-11 | 1 | 2.09 |
| 1977 | Steve Carlton, Phi | 36 | 23-10 | 0 | 2.64 | 1976 | Jim Palmer, Bal | 40 | 22-13 | 0 | 2.51 |
| 1978 | Gaylord Perry, SD | 37 | 21-6 | 0 | 2.72 | 1977 | Sparky Lyle, NY | 72 | 13-5 | 26 | 2.17 |
| 1979 | Bruce Sutter, Chi | 62 | 6-6 | 37 | 2.23 | 1978 | Ron Guidry, NY | 35 | 25-3 | 0 | 1.74 |
| 1980 | Steve Carlton, Phi | 38 | 24-9 | 0 | 2.34 | 1979 | Mike Flanagan, Bal | 39 | 23-9 | 0 | 3.08 |
| 1981 | Fernando Valenzuela, LA | 25 | 13-7 | 0 | 2.48 | 1980 | Steve Stone, Bal | 37 | 25-7 | 0 | 3.23 |
| 1982 | Steve Carlton, Phi | 38 | 23-11 | 0 | 3.10 | 1981 | **Rollie Fingers**, Mil | 47 | 6-3 | 28 | 1.04 |
| 1983 | John Denny, Phi | 36 | 19-6 | 0 | 2.37 | 1982 | Pete Vuckovich, Mil | 30 | 18-6 | 0 | 3.34 |
| 1984 | Rick Sutcliffe, Chi | 20* | 16-1 | 0 | 2.69 | 1983 | LaMarr Hoyt, Chi | 36 | 24-10 | 0 | 3.66 |
| 1985 | Dwight Gooden, NY | 35 | 24-4 | 0 | 1.53 | 1984 | **Willie Hernandez**, Det | 80 | 9-3 | 32 | 1.92 |
| 1986 | Mike Scott, Hou | 37 | 18-10 | 0 | 2.22 | 1985 | Bret Saberhagen, KC | 32 | 20-6 | 0 | 2.87 |
| 1987 | Steve Bedrosian, Phi | 65 | 5-3 | 40 | 2.83 | 1986 | **Roger Clemens**, Bos | 33 | 24-4 | 0 | 2.48 |
| 1988 | Orel Hershiser, LA | 35 | 23-8 | 1 | 2.26 | 1987 | Roger Clemens, Bos | 36 | 20-9 | 0 | 2.97 |
| 1989 | Mark Davis, SD | 70 | 4-3 | 44 | 1.85 | 1988 | Frank Viola, Min | 35 | 24-7 | 0 | 2.64 |
| 1990 | Doug Drabek, Pit | 33 | 22-6 | 0 | 2.76 | 1989 | Bret Saberhagen, KC | 36 | 23-6 | 0 | 2.16 |
| 1991 | Tom Glavine, Atl | 34 | 20-11 | 0 | 2.55 | 1990 | Bob Welch, Oak | 35 | 27-6 | 0 | 2.95 |
| 1992 | Greg Maddux, Chi | 35 | 20-11 | 0 | 2.18 | 1991 | Roger Clemens, Bos | 35 | 18-10 | 0 | 2.62 |
| 1993 | Greg Maddux, Atl | 36 | 20-10 | 0 | 2.36 | 1992 | **Dennis Eckersley**, Oak | 69 | 7-1 | 51 | 1.91 |
| 1994 | Greg Maddux, Atl | 25 | 16-6 | 0 | 1.56 | 1993 | Jack McDowell, Chi | 34 | 22-10 | 0 | 3.37 |
| 1995 | Greg Maddux, Atl | 28 | 19-2 | 0 | 1.63 | 1994 | David Cone, KC | 23 | 16-5 | 0 | 2.94 |
| 1996 | John Smoltz, Atl | 35 | 24-8 | 0 | 2.94 | 1995 | Randy Johnson, Sea | 30 | 18-2 | 0 | 2.48 |
| 1997 | Pedro Martinez, Mon | 31 | 17-8 | 0 | 1.90 | 1996 | Pat Hentgen, Tor | 35 | 20-10 | 0 | 3.22 |
| 1998 | Tom Glavine, Atl | 33 | 20-6 | 0 | 2.47 | 1997 | Roger Clemens, Tor | 34 | 21-7 | 0 | 2.05 |
| 1999 | Randy Johnson, Ari | 35 | 17-9 | 0 | 2.48 | 1998 | Roger Clemens, Tor | 33 | 20-6 | 0 | 2.65 |
| 2000 | Randy Johnson, Ari | 35 | 19-7 | 0 | 2.64 | 1999 | Pedro Martinez, Bos | 31 | 23-4 | 0 | 2.07 |
| 2001 | Randy Johnson, Ari | 35 | 21-6 | 0 | 2.49 | 2000 | Pedro Martinez, Bos | 29 | 18-6 | 0 | 1.74 |
| 2002 | Randy Johnson, Ari | 35 | 24-5 | 0 | 2.32 | 2001 | Roger Clemens, NY | 33 | 20-3 | 0 | 3.51 |
| 2003 | Eric Gagne, LA | 77 | 2-3 | 55 | 1.20 | 2002 | Barry Zito, Oak | 35 | 23-5 | 0 | 2.75 |
| 2004 | Roger Clemens, Hou | 33 | 18-4 | 0 | 2.98 | 2003 | Roy Halladay, Tor | 36 | 22-7 | 0 | 3.25 |
| | | | | | | 2004 | Johan Santana, Min | 34 | 20-6 | 0 | 2.61 |

*NL games only, Sutcliffe pitched 15 games with Cleveland before being traded to the Cubs.

## ROOKIE OF THE YEAR

Voted on by the Baseball Writers Assn. of America. One award was presented from 1947-48. Two awards (one for each league) have been presented since 1949. Winners who were also named MVP in the same season are in **bold** type.

### NL and AL Combined

| Year | | Pos | Year | | Pos |
|------|--|-----|------|--|-----|
| 1947 | Jackie Robinson, Brooklyn | 1B | 1948 | Alvin Dark, Boston-NL | SS |

### National League

| Year | | Pos | Year | | Pos | Year | | Pos |
|------|--|-----|------|--|-----|------|--|-----|
| 1949 | Don Newcombe, Bklyn | P | 1951 | Willie Mays, NY | OF | 1953 | Jim Gilliam, Bklyn | 2B |
| 1950 | Sam Jethroe, Bos | OF | 1952 | Joe Black, Bklyn | P | 1954 | Wally Moon, St.L | OF |

| Year | | Pos | Year | | Pos | Year | | Pos |
|---|---|---|---|---|---|---|---|---|
| 1955 | Bill Virdon, St.L. | OF | 1972 | Jon Matlack, NY | P | 1988 | Chris Sabo, Cin | 3B |
| 1956 | Frank Howard, Cin | OF | 1973 | Gary Matthews, SF | OF | 1989 | Jerome Walton, Chi | OF |
| 1957 | Jack Sanford, Phi | P | 1974 | Bake McBride, St.L. | OF | 1990 | David Justice, Atl | OF |
| 1958 | Orlando Cepeda, SF | 1B | 1975 | John Montefusco, SF | P | 1991 | Jeff Bagwell, Hou. | 1B |
| 1959 | Willie McCovey, SF | 1B | 1976 | Butch Metzger, SD | P | 1992 | Eric Karros, LA | 1B |
| 1960 | Frank Howard, LA | OF | | & Pat Zachry, Cin | P | 1993 | Mike Piazza, LA | C |
| 1961 | Billy Williams, Chi | OF | 1977 | Andre Dawson, Mon | OF | 1994 | Raul Mondesi, LA | OF |
| 1962 | Ken Hubbs, Chi | 2B | 1978 | Bob Horner, Atl | 3B | 1995 | Hideo Nomo, LA | P |
| 1963 | Pete Rose, Cin | 2B | 1979 | Rick Sutcliffe, LA | P | 1996 | Todd Hollandsworth, LA | OF |
| 1964 | Richie Allen, Phi | 3B | 1980 | Steve Howe, LA | P | 1997 | Scott Rolen, Phi | 3B |
| 1965 | Jim Lefebvre, LA | 2B | 1981 | Fernando Valenzuela, LA | P | 1998 | Kerry Wood, Chi | P |
| 1966 | Tommy Helms, Cin | 3B | 1982 | Steve Sax, LA | 2B | 1999 | Scott Williamson, Cin | P |
| 1967 | Tom Seaver, NY | P | 1983 | Darryl Strawberry, NY | OF | 2000 | Rafael Furcal, Atl | SS |
| 1968 | Johnny Bench, Cin | C | 1984 | Dwight Gooden, NY | P | 2001 | Albert Pujols, St.L. | OF-3B |
| 1969 | Ted Sizemore, LA | 2B | 1985 | Vince Coleman, St.L. | OF | 2002 | Jason Jennings, Col | P |
| 1970 | Carl Morton, Mon | P | 1986 | Todd Worrell, St.L. | P | 2003 | Dontrelle Willis, Fla | P |
| 1971 | Earl Williams, Atl | C | 1987 | Benito Santiago, SD | C | 2004 | Jason Bay, Pit | OF |

## American League

| Year | | Pos | Year | | Pos | Year | | Pos |
|---|---|---|---|---|---|---|---|---|
| 1949 | Roy Sievers, St.L | OF | 1968 | Stan Bahnsen, NY | P | 1986 | Jose Canseco, Oak | OF |
| 1950 | Walt Dropo, Bos | 1B | 1969 | Lou Piniella, KC | OF | 1987 | Mark McGwire, Oak | 1B |
| 1951 | Gil McDougald, NY | 3B | 1970 | Thurman Munson, NY | C | 1988 | Walt Weiss, Oak | SS |
| 1952 | Harry Byrd, Phi | P | 1971 | Chris Chambliss, Cle | 1B | 1989 | Gregg Olson, Bal | P |
| 1953 | Harvey Kuenn, Det | SS | 1972 | Carlton Fisk, Bos | C | 1990 | Sandy Alomar Jr., Cle | C |
| 1954 | Bob Grim, NY | P | 1973 | Al Bumbry, Bal | OF | 1991 | Chuck Knoblauch, Min | 2B |
| 1955 | Herb Score, Cle | P | 1974 | Mike Hargrove, Tex | 1B | 1992 | Pat Listach, Mil | SS |
| 1956 | Luis Aparicio, Chi | SS | 1975 | Fred Lynn, Bos | OF | 1993 | Tim Salmon, Cal | OF |
| 1957 | Tony Kubek, NY | INF-OF | 1976 | Mark Fidrych, Det | P | 1994 | Bob Hamelin, KC | DH |
| 1958 | Albie Pearson, Wash | OF | 1977 | Eddie Murray, Bal | DH-1B | 1995 | Marty Cordova, Min | OF |
| 1959 | Bob Allison, Wash | OF | 1978 | Lou Whitaker, Det | 2B | 1996 | Derek Jeter, NY | SS |
| 1960 | Ron Hansen, Bal | SS | 1979 | John Castino, Min | 3B | 1997 | Nomar Garciaparra, Bos | SS |
| 1961 | Don Schwall, Bos | P | | & Alfredo Griffin, Tor | SS | 1998 | Ben Grieve, Oak | OF |
| 1962 | Tom Tresh, NY | SS-OF | 1980 | Joe Charboneau, Cle | OF-DH | 1999 | Carlos Beltran, KC | OF |
| 1963 | Gary Peters, Chi | P | 1981 | Dave Righetti, NY | P | 2000 | Kazuhiro Sasaki, Sea | P |
| 1964 | Tony Oliva, Min | OF | 1982 | Cal Ripken Jr., Bal | SS-3B | 2001 | Ichiro Suzuki, Sea | OF |
| 1965 | Curt Blefary, Bal | OF | 1983 | Ron Kittle, Chi | OF | 2002 | Eric Hinske, Tor | 3B |
| 1966 | Tommie Agee, Chi | OF | 1984 | Alvin Davis, Sea | 1B | 2003 | Angel Berroa, KC | SS |
| 1967 | Rod Carew, Min | 2B | 1985 | Ozzie Guillen, Chi | SS | 2004 | Bobby Crosby, Oak | SS |

## MANAGER OF THE YEAR

Voted on by the Baseball Writers Association of America. Two awards (one for each league) presented since 1983. Note that (*) indicates manager's team won division championship and (†) indicates unofficial division won in 1994.

**Multiple winners:** Tony La Russa (4); Dusty Baker and Bobby Cox (3); Sparky Anderson, Tommy Lasorda, Jim Leyland, Jack McKeon, Lou Piniella, Buck Showalter and Joe Torre (2).

### National League

| Year | | Diff. from previous year | | |
|---|---|---|---|---|
| 1983 | Tommy Lasorda, LA. | 88-74 | to | 91-71* |
| 1984 | Jim Frey, Chi | 71-91 | to | 96-75* |
| 1985 | Whitey Herzog, St. L | 84-78 | to | 101-61* |
| 1986 | Hal Lanier, Hou. | 83-79 | to | 96-66* |
| 1987 | Buck Rodgers, Mon | 78-83 | to | 91-71 |
| 1988 | Tommy Lasorda, LA. | 73-89 | to | 94-67* |
| 1989 | Don Zimmer, Chi | 77-85 | to | 93-69* |
| 1990 | Jim Leyland, Pit | 74-88 | to | 95-67* |
| 1991 | Bobby Cox, Atl | 65-97 | to | 94-68* |
| 1992 | Jim Leyland, Pit | 98-64* | to | 96-66* |
| 1993 | Dusty Baker, SF | 72-90 | to | 103-59 |
| 1994 | Felipe Alou, Mon | 94-68 | to | 74-40† |
| 1995 | Don Baylor, Col | 53-64 | to | 77-67 |
| 1996 | Bruce Bochy, SD. | 70-74 | to | 91-71 |
| 1997 | Dusty Baker, SF | 68-94 | to | 90-72 |
| 1998 | Larry Dierker, Hou | 84-78 | to | 102-60* |
| 1999 | Jack McKeon, Cin | 77-85 | to | 96-67 |
| 2000 | Dusty Baker, SF | 86-76 | to | 97-65* |
| 2001 | Larry Bowa, Phi | 65-97 | to | 86-76 |
| 2002 | Tony La Russa, St.L. | 93-69 | to | 97-65* |
| 2003 | Jack McKeon, Fla. | 79-83 | to | 91-71 |
| 2004 | Bobby Cox | 101-61 | to | 96-66* |

### American League

| Year | | Diff. from previous year | | |
|---|---|---|---|---|
| 1983 | Tony La Russa, Chi | 87-75 | to | 99-63* |
| 1984 | Sparky Anderson, Det. | 92-70 | to | 104-58* |
| 1985 | Bobby Cox, Tor | 89-73 | to | 99-62* |
| 1986 | John McNamara, Bos. | 81-81 | to | 95-66* |
| 1987 | Sparky Anderson, Det. | 87-75 | to | 98-64* |
| 1988 | Tony La Russa, Oak | 81-81 | to | 104-58* |
| 1989 | Frank Robinson, Bal | 54-107 | to | 87-75 |
| 1990 | Jeff Torborg, Chi. | 69-92 | to | 94-68 |
| 1991 | Tom Kelly, Min | 74-88 | to | 95-67* |
| 1992 | Tony La Russa, Oak | 84-78 | to | 96-66* |
| 1993 | Gene Lamont, Chi. | 86-76 | to | 94-68* |
| 1994 | Buck Showalter, NY | 88-74 | to | 70-43† |
| 1995 | Lou Piniella, Sea. | 49-63 | to | 79-66* |
| 1996 | Joe Torre, NY | 79-65 | to | 92-70 |
| | & Johnny Oates, Tex. | 74-70 | to | 90-72 |
| 1997 | Davey Johnson, Bal | 88-74 | to | 98-64 |
| 1998 | Joe Torre, NY. | 96-66 | to | 114-48* |
| 1999 | Jimy Williams, Bos | 92-70 | to | 94-68 |
| 2000 | Jerry Manuel, Chi. | 75-86 | to | 95-67* |
| 2001 | Lou Piniella, Sea. | 91-71 | to | 116-46* |
| 2002 | Mike Scioscia, Ana | 75-87 | to | 99-63 |
| 2003 | Tony Pena, KC | 62-100 | to | 83-79 |
| 2004 | Buck Showalter, Tex. | 71-91 | to | 89-73 |

## COLLEGE BASEBALL

### College World Series

The NCAA Division I College World Series has been held in Kalamazoo, Mich. (1947-48), Wichita, Kan. (1949) and Omaha, Neb. (since 1950). Beginning in 2003, the championship series has been best-of-three series.

**Multiple winners:** USC (12); Texas (6); Arizona St. and LSU (5); CS-Fullerton and Miami-FL (4); Arizona and Minnesota (3); California; Michigan, Oklahoma and Stanford (2).

| Year | Winner | Coach | Score | Runner-up | Year | Winner | Coach | Score | Runner-up |
|------|--------|-------|-------|-----------|------|--------|-------|-------|-----------|
| 1947 | California | Clint Evans | 8-7 | Yale | 1980 | Arizona | Jerry Kindall | 5-3 | Hawaii |
| 1948 | USC | Sam Barry | 9-2 | Yale | 1981 | Arizona St. | Jim Brock | 7-4 | Okla. St. |
| 1949 | Texas | Bibb Falk | 10-3 | W. Forest | 1982 | Miami-FL | Ron Fraser | 9-3 | Wichita St. |
| 1950 | Texas | Bibb Falk | 3-0 | Wash. St. | 1983 | Texas | Cliff Gustafson | 4-3 | Alabama |
| 1951 | Oklahoma | Jack Baer | 3-2 | Tennessee | 1984 | CS-Fullerton | Augie Garrido | 3-1 | Texas |
| 1952 | Holy Cross | Jack Barry | 8-4 | Missouri | 1985 | Miami-FL | Ron Fraser | 10-6 | Texas |
| 1953 | Michigan | Ray Fisher | 7-5 | Texas | 1986 | Arizona | Jerry Kindall | 10-2 | Fla. St. |
| 1954 | Missouri | Hi Simmons | 4-1 | Rollins | 1987 | Stanford | M. Marquess | 9-5 | Okla. St. |
| 1955 | Wake Forest | Taylor Sanford | 7-6 | W. Mich. | 1988 | Stanford | M. Marquess | 9-4 | Ariz. St. |
| 1956 | Minnesota | Dick Siebert | 12-1 | Arizona | 1989 | Wichita St. | G. Stephenson | 5-3 | Texas |
| 1957 | California | Geo. Wolfman | 1-0 | Penn St. | 1990 | Georgia | Steve Webber | 2-1 | Okla. St. |
| 1958 | USC | Rod Dedeaux | 8-7 | Missouri | 1991 | LSU | Skip Bertman | 6-3 | Wichita St. |
| 1959 | Oklahoma St. | Toby Greene | 5-3 | Arizona | 1992 | Pepperdine | Andy Lopez | 3-2 | CS-Fullerton |
| 1960 | Minnesota | Dick Siebert | 2-1 | USC | 1993 | LSU | Skip Bertman | 8-0 | Wichita St. |
| 1961 | USC | Rod Dedeaux | 1-0 | Okla. St. | 1994 | Oklahoma | Larry Cochell | 13-5 | Ga. Tech |
| 1962 | Michigan | Don Lund | 5-4 | S. Clara | 1995 | CS-Fullerton | Augie Garrido | 11-5 | USC |
| 1963 | USC | Rod Dedeaux | 5-2 | Arizona | 1996 | LSU | Skip Bertman | 9-8 | Miami-FL |
| 1964 | Minnesota | Dick Siebert | 5-1 | Missouri | 1997 | LSU | Skip Bertman | 13-6 | Alabama |
| 1965 | Arizona St. | Bobby Winkles | 2-1 | Ohio St. | 1998 | USC | Mike Gillespie | 21-14 | Arizona St. |
| 1966 | Ohio St. | Marty Karow | 8-2 | Okla. St. | 1999 | Miami-FL | Jim Morris | 6-5 | Fla. St. |
| 1967 | Arizona St. | Bobby Winkles | 11-2 | Houston | 2000 | LSU | Skip Bertman | 6-5 | Stanford |
| 1968 | USC | Rod Dedeaux | 4-3 | So. Ill. | 2001 | Miami-FL | Jim Morris | 12-1 | Stanford |
| 1969 | Arizona St. | Bobby Winkles | 10-1 | Tulsa | 2002 | Texas | Augie Garrido | 12-6 | S.Carolina |
| 1970 | USC | Rod Dedeaux | 2-1 | Fla. St. | 2003 | Rice | Wayne Graham | 4-3<br>3-8<br>14-2 | Stanford |
| 1971 | USC | Rod Dedeaux | 7-2 | So. Ill. | | | | | |
| 1972 | USC | Rod Dedeaux | 1-0 | Ariz. St. | 2004 | CS-Fullerton | George Horton | 6-4<br>3-2 | Texas |
| 1973 | USC | Rod Dedeaux | 4-3 | Ariz. St. | | | | | |
| 1974 | USC | Rod Dedeaux | 7-3 | Miami-FL | 2005 | Texas | Augie Garrido | 4-2<br>6-2 | Florida |
| 1975 | Texas | Cliff Gustafson | 5-1 | S. Carolina | | | | | |
| 1976 | Arizona | Jerry Kindall | 7-1 | E. Michigan | | | | | |
| 1977 | Arizona St. | Jim Brock | 2-1 | S. Carolina | | | | | |
| 1978 | USC | Rod Dedeaux | 10-3 | Ariz. St. | | | | | |
| 1979 | CS-Fullerton | Augie Garrido | 2-1 | Arkansas | | | | | |

### Most Outstanding Player

The Most Outstanding Player has been selected every year of the College World Series since 1949. Winners who did not play for the CWS champion are listed in **bold** type. No player has won the award more than once.

| Year | | Year | | Year | |
|------|--|------|--|------|--|
| 1949 | **Charles Teague,** W. Forest, 2B | 1970 | **Gene Ammann,** Fla. St., P | 1991 | Gary Hymel, LSU, C |
| 1950 | **Ray VanCleef,** Rutgers, CF | 1971 | **Jerry Tabb,** Tulsa, 1B | 1992 | **Phil Nevin,** CS-Fullerton, 3B |
| 1951 | **Sidney Hatfield,** Tenn., P-1B | 1972 | Russ McQueen, USC, P | 1993 | Todd Walker, LSU, 2B |
| 1952 | James O'Neill, Holy Cross, P | 1973 | **Dave Winfield,** Minn., P-OF | 1994 | Chip Glass, Oklahoma, OF |
| 1953 | **J.L. Smith,** Texas, P | 1974 | George Milke, USC, P | 1995 | Mark Kotsay, CS-Fullerton, OF |
| 1954 | **Tom Yewcic,** Mich. St., C | 1975 | Mickey Reichenbach, Texas, 1B | 1996 | **Pat Burrell,** Miami-FL, 3B |
| 1955 | **Tom Borland,** Okla. St., P | 1976 | Steve Powers, Arizona, P-DH | 1997 | Brandon Larson, LSU, SS |
| 1956 | Jerry Thomas, Minn., P | 1977 | Bob Horner, Ariz. St., 3B | 1998 | Wes Rachels, USC, 2B |
| 1957 | **Cal Emery,** Penn St., P-1B | 1978 | Rod Boxberger, USC, P | 1999 | **Marshall McDougall,** Fla. St., 2B |
| 1958 | Bill Thom, USC, P | 1979 | Tony Hudson, CS-Fullerton, P | 2000 | Trey Hodges, LSU, P |
| 1959 | Jim Dobson, Okla. St., 3B | 1980 | Terry Francona, Arizona, LF | 2001 | Charlton Jimerson, Miami-FL, CF |
| 1960 | John Erickson, Minn., 2B | 1981 | Stan Holmes, Ariz. St., LF | 2002 | Huston Street, Texas, P |
| 1961 | **Littleton Fowler,** Okla. St., P | 1982 | Dan Smith, Miami-FL, P | 2003 | **John Hudgins,** Stanford, P |
| 1962 | **Bob Garibaldi,** Santa Clara, P | 1983 | Calvin Schiraldi, Texas, P | 2004 | Jason Windsor, CS-Fullerton, P |
| 1963 | Bud Hollowell, USC, C | 1984 | John Fishel, CS-Fullerton, LF | 2005 | David Maroul, Texas, 3B |
| 1964 | **Joe Ferris,** Maine, P | 1985 | Greg Ellena, Miami-FL, LF | | |
| 1965 | Sal Bando, Ariz. St., 3B | 1986 | Mike Senne, Arizona, DH | | |
| 1966 | Steve Arlin, Ohio St., P | 1987 | Paul Carey, Stanford, RF | | |
| 1967 | Ron Davini, Ariz. St., C | 1988 | Lee Plemel, Stanford, P | | |
| 1968 | Bill Seinsoth, USC, 1B | 1989 | Greg Brummett, Wich. St., P | | |
| 1969 | John Dolinsek, Ariz. St., LF | 1990 | Mike Rebhan, Georgia, P | | |

## Annual Awards
## Golden Spikes Award

First presented in 1978 by USA Baseball, honoring the nation's best amateur player; sponsored by the Major League Baseball Players Association. Alex Fernandez, the 1990 winner, has been the only junior college player chosen.

| Year | | Year | | Year | |
|------|------|------|------|------|------|
| 1978 | Bob Horner, Ariz. St, 2B | 1988 | Robin Ventura, Okla. St., 3B | 1998 | Pat Burrell, Miami-FL, 3B |
| 1979 | Tim Wallach, CS-Fullerton, 1B | 1989 | Ben McDonald, LSU, P | 1999 | Jason Jennings, Baylor, DH/P |
| 1980 | Terry Francona, Arizona, OF | 1990 | Alex Fernandez, Miami-Dade, P | 2000 | Kip Bouknight, South Carolina, P |
| 1981 | Mike Fuentes, Fla. St., OF | 1991 | Mike Kelly, Ariz. St., OF | 2001 | Mark Prior, USC, P |
| 1982 | Augie Schmidt, N. Orleans, SS | 1992 | Phil Nevin, CS-Fullerton, 3B | 2002 | Khalil Greene, Clemson, SS |
| 1983 | Dave Magadan, Alabama, 1B | 1993 | Darren Dreifort, Wichita St., P | 2003 | Rickie Weeks, Southern, 2B |
| 1984 | Oddibe McDowell, Ariz. St., OF | 1994 | Jason Varitek, Ga. Tech, C | 2004 | Jered Weaver, Long Beach St., P |
| 1985 | Will Clark, Miss. St., 1B | 1995 | Mark Kotsay, CS-Fullerton, OF | 2005 | Alex Gordon, Nebraska, IF |
| 1986 | Mike Loynd, Fla. St., P | 1996 | Travis Lee, San Diego St., 1B | | |
| 1987 | Jim Abbott, Michigan, P | 1997 | J.D. Drew, Florida St., OF | | |

## *Baseball America* Player of the Year

Presented to the College Player of the Year since 1981 by *Baseball America*.

| Year | | Year | | Year | |
|------|------|------|------|------|------|
| 1981 | Mike Sodders, Ariz. St., 3B | 1990 | Mike Kelly, Ariz. St., OF | 1999 | Jason Jennings, Baylor, DH/P |
| 1982 | Jeff Ledbetter, Fla. St., OF/P | 1991 | David McCarty, Stanford, 1B | 2000 | Mark Teixeira, Ga. Tech, 3B |
| 1983 | Dave Magadan, Alabama, 1B | 1992 | Phil Nevin, CS-Fullerton, 3B | 2001 | Mark Prior, USC, P |
| 1984 | Oddibe McDowell, Ariz. St., OF | 1993 | Brooks Kieschnick, Texas, DH/P | 2002 | Khalil Greene, Clemson, SS |
| 1985 | Pete Incaviglia, Okla. St., OF | 1994 | Jason Varitek, Ga. Tech, C | 2003 | Rickie Weeks, Southern, 2B |
| 1986 | Casey Close, Michigan, OF | 1995 | Todd Helton, Tenn., 1B/P | 2004 | Jered Weaver, Long Beach St., P |
| 1987 | Robin Ventura, Okla. St., 3B | 1996 | Kris Benson, Clemson, P | 2005 | Alex Gordon, Nebraska, IF |
| 1988 | John Olerud, Wash. St., 1B/P | 1997 | J.D. Drew, Florida St., OF | | |
| 1989 | Ben McDonald, LSU, P | 1998 | Jeff Austin, Stanford, P | | |

## Dick Howser Trophy

Sponsored by Xanthus and presented to the College Player of the Year since 1987, by the American Baseball Coaches Association (ABCA) from 1987-98 and the National Collegiate Baseball Writers Association (NCBWA) beginning in 1999. Founded and owned by the St. Petersburg (Fla.) Area Chamber of Commerce. Named after the late two-time All-America shortstop and college coach at Florida State. Howser was also a major league manager with Kansas City and the New York Yankees.
**Multiple winner:** Brooks Kieschnick (2).

| Year | | Year | | Year | |
|------|------|------|------|------|------|
| 1987 | Mike Fiore, Miami-FL, OF | 1994 | Jason Varitek, Ga. Tech, C | 2001 | Mark Prior, USC, P |
| 1988 | Robin Ventura, Okla. St., 3B | 1995 | Todd Helton, Tenn., 1B/P | 2002 | Khalil Greene, Clemson, SS |
| 1989 | Scott Bryant, Texas, DH | 1996 | Kris Benson, Clemson, P | 2003 | Rickie Weeks, Southern, 2B |
| 1990 | Paul Ellis, UCLA, C | 1997 | J.D. Drew, Florida St., OF | 2004 | Jered Weaver, Long Beach St., P |
| 1991 | Bobby Jones, Fresno St., P | 1998 | Eddie Furniss, LSU, 1B | 2005 | Alex Gordon, Nebraska, IF |
| 1992 | Brooks Kieschnick, Texas, DH/P | 1999 | Jason Jennings, Baylor, DH/P | | |
| 1993 | Brooks Kieschnick, Texas, DH/P | 2000 | Mark Teixeira, Ga. Tech, 3B | | |

## *Baseball America* Coach of the Year

Presented to the College Coach of the Year since 1981 by *Baseball America*.
**Multiple winners:** Skip Bertman, Augie Garrido, Dave Snow and Gene Stephenson (2).

| Year | | Year | | Year | |
|------|------|------|------|------|------|
| 1981 | Ron Fraser, Miami-FL | 1989 | Dave Snow, Long Beach St. | 1998 | Pat Murphy, Arizona St. |
| 1982 | Gene Stephenson, Wichita St. | 1990 | Steve Webber, Georgia | 1999 | Wayne Graham, Rice |
| 1983 | Barry Shollenberger, Alabama | 1991 | Jim Hendry, Creighton | 2000 | Ray Tanner, S. Carolina |
| 1984 | Augie Garrido, CS-Fullerton | 1992 | Andy Lopez, Pepperdine | 2001 | Dave Van Horn, Nebraska |
| 1985 | Ron Polk, Mississippi St. | 1993 | Gene Stephenson, Wichita St. | 2002 | Augie Garrido, Texas |
| 1986 | Skip Bertman, LSU | 1994 | Jim Morris, Miami-FL | 2003 | George Horton, CS-Fullerton |
| | & Dave Snow, Loyola-CA | 1995 | Rod Delmonico, Tennessee | 2004 | Dave Perno, Georgia |
| 1987 | Mark Marquess, Stanford | 1996 | Skip Bertman, LSU | 2005 | Rick Jones, Tulane |
| 1988 | Jim Brock, Arizona St. | 1997 | Jim Wells, Alabama | | |

## All-Time Winningest Division I Coaches

Coaches active in 2005 are in **bold** type. Records given are for four-year colleges only. For winning percentage, a minimum 10 years in Division I is required.

### Top 10 Winning Percentage

| | | Yrs | W | L | T | Pct |
|---|---|---|---|---|---|---|
| 1 | John Barry | .40 | 619 | 146 | 5 | .807 |
| 2 | Cliff Gustafson | .29 | 1427 | 373 | 2 | .792 |
| 3 | Harry Carlson | .17 | 143 | 41 | 0 | .777 |
| 4 | **Gene Stephenson** | .28 | 1506 | 489 | 3 | .755 |
| 5 | Bobby Winkles | .13 | 524 | 173 | 0 | .752 |
| 6 | **Mike Martin** | .26 | 1391 | 472 | 4 | .746 |
| 7 | Frank Sancet | .23 | 831 | 283 | 8 | .744 |
| 8 | Bob Wren | .23 | 464 | 160 | 4 | .742 |
| 9 | George Jacobs | .11 | 106 | 37 | 0 | .741 |
| 10 | Ron Fraser | .30 | 1267 | 440 | 9 | .741 |

### Top 25 Victories

| | | Yrs | W | L | T | Pct |
|---|---|---|---|---|---|---|
| 1 | **Augie Garrido** | .37 | **1542** | 717 | 8 | .682 |
| 2 | **Gene Stephenson** | .28 | **1506** | 489 | 3 | .755 |
| 3 | Cliff Gustafson | .29 | **1427** | 373 | 2 | .792 |
| 4 | **Larry Hays** | .35 | **1424** | 777 | 2 | .647 |
| | **Chuck Hartman** | .46 | **1424** | 783 | 8 | .645 |
| 6 | **Mike Martin** | .26 | **1391** | 472 | 4 | .746 |
| 7 | Rod Dedeaux | .44 | **1342** | 597 | 16 | .691 |
| 8 | **Larry Cochell** | .39 | **1330** | 814 | 3 | .620 |
| 9 | Bob Bennett | .34 | **1300** | 757 | 8 | .631 |
| 10 | **Ron Polk** | .32 | **1276** | 624 | 2 | .671 |

## Other NCAA Champions

### Division II

**Multiple winners:** Florida Southern (9); Cal Poly Pomona and Tampa (3); Central Missouri St., CS-Chico, CS-Northridge, Jacksonville St., Troy St., UC-Irvine and UC-Riverside (2).

| Year | | Year | | Year | | Year | |
|---|---|---|---|---|---|---|---|
| 1968 | Chapman, CA | 1978 | Florida Southern | 1988 | Florida Southern | 1998 | Tampa |
| 1969 | Illinois St. | 1979 | Valdosta St., GA | 1989 | Cal Poly SLO | 1999 | CS-Chico |
| 1970 | CS-Northridge | 1980 | Cal Poly Pomona | 1990 | Jacksonville St., AL | 2000 | Southeastern Okla. |
| 1971 | Florida Southern | 1981 | Florida Southern | 1991 | Jacksonville St., AL | 2001 | St. Mary's, TX |
| 1972 | Florida Southern | 1982 | UC-Riverside | 1992 | Tampa | 2002 | Columbus St., GA |
| 1973 | UC-Irvine | 1983 | Cal Poly Pomona | 1993 | Tampa | 2003 | Central Missouri St. |
| 1974 | UC-Irvine | 1984 | CS-Northridge | 1994 | Central Missouri St. | 2004 | Delta St., MS |
| 1975 | Florida Southern | 1985 | Florida Southern | 1995 | Florida Southern | 2005 | Florida Southern |
| 1976 | Cal Poly Pomona | 1986 | Troy St., AL | 1996 | Kennesaw St., GA | | |
| 1977 | UC-Riverside | 1987 | Troy St., AL | 1997 | CS-Chico | | |

### Division III

**Multiple winners:** Eastern Conn. St. (4); Marietta and Montclair St. (3); CS-Stanislaus, Glassboro St., Ithaca, NC-Wesleyan, Southern Maine and Wm. Paterson, NJ (2).

| Year | | Year | | Year | | Year | |
|---|---|---|---|---|---|---|---|
| 1976 | CS-Stanislaus | 1984 | Ramapo, NJ | 1992 | Wm. Paterson, NJ | 2000 | Montclair St., NJ |
| 1977 | CS-Stanislaus | 1985 | Wisconsin-Oshkosh | 1993 | Montclair St., NJ | 2001 | St. Thomas, MN |
| 1978 | Glassboro St., NJ | 1986 | Marietta, OH | 1994 | Wisconsin-Oshkosh | 2002 | Eastern Conn. St. |
| 1979 | Glassboro St., NJ | 1987 | Monclair St., NJ | 1995 | La Verne, CA | 2003 | Chapman, CA |
| 1980 | Ithaca, NY | 1988 | Ithaca, NY | 1996 | Wm. Paterson, NJ | 2004 | George Fox, OR |
| 1981 | Marietta, OH | 1989 | NC-Wesleyan | 1997 | Southern Maine | 2005 | Wis.-Whitewater |
| 1982 | Eastern Conn. St. | 1990 | Eastern Conn. St. | 1998 | Eastern Conn. St. | | |
| 1983 | Marietta, OH | 1991 | Southern Maine | 1999 | NC-Wesleyan | | |

## Major League Number One Draft Picks

The Major League First-Year Player Draft has been held every year since 1965. Clubs select in reverse order of their won-loss records from the previous regular season. Until 2005, the National League and American League teams alternated, with AL teams selecting first in odd-numbered years and NL teams going first in even-numbered years. Now, league affiliation does not come into play. Listed are the top selections from each draft.

| Year | | Pos | Team | Year | | Pos | Team |
|---|---|---|---|---|---|---|---|
| 1965 | Rick Monday | OF | Kansas City Athletics | 1986 | Jeff King | IF | Pittsburgh Pirates |
| 1966 | Steve Chilcott | C | New York Mets | 1987 | Ken Griffey Jr. | OF | Seattle Mariners |
| 1967 | Rom Blomberg | 1B | New York Yankees | 1988 | Andy Benes | P | San Diego Padres |
| 1968 | Tim Foli | IF | New York Mets | 1989 | Ben McDonald | P | Baltimore Orioles |
| 1969 | Jeff Burroughs | OF | Washington Senators | 1990 | Chipper Jones | SS | Atlanta Braves |
| 1970 | Mike Ivie | C | San Diego Padres | 1991 | Brien Taylor | P | New York Yankees |
| 1971 | Danny Goodwin | C | Chicago White Sox | 1992 | Phil Nevin | 3B | Houston Astros |
| 1972 | Dave Roberts | IF | San Diego Padres | 1993 | Alex Rodriguez | SS | Seattle Mariners |
| 1973 | David Clyde | P | Texas Rangers | 1994 | Paul Wilson | P | New York Mets |
| 1974 | Bill Almon | IF | San Diego Padres | 1995 | Darin Erstad | OF/P | California Angels |
| 1975 | Danny Goodwin | C | California Angels | 1996 | Kris Benson | P | Pittsburgh Pirates |
| 1976 | Floyd Bannister | P | Houston Astros | 1997 | Matt Anderson | P | Detroit Tigers |
| 1977 | Harold Baines | OF | Chicago White Sox | 1998 | Pat Burrell | 3B | Philadelphia Phillies |
| 1978 | Bob Horner | 3B | Atlanta Braves | 1999 | Josh Hamilton | OF | T.B. Devil Rays |
| 1979 | Al Chambers | OF | Seattle Mariners | 2000 | Adrian Gonzalez | 1B | Florida Marlins |
| 1980 | Darryl Strawberry | OF | New York Mets | 2001 | Joe Mauer | C | Minnesota Twins |
| 1981 | Mike Moore | P | Seattle Mariners | 2002 | Bryan Bullington | P | Pittsburgh Pirates |
| 1982 | Shawon Dunston | SS | Chicago Cubs | 2003 | Delmon Young | OF | T.B. Devil Rays |
| 1983 | Tim Belcher | P | Minnesota Twins | 2004 | Matt Bush | SS | San Diego Padres |
| 1984 | Shawn Abner | OF | New York Mets | 2005 | Justin Upton | SS | Ariz. Diamondbacks |
| 1985 | B.J. Surhoff | C | Milwaukee Brewers | | | | |

# College Football

USC head coach **Pete Carroll** and quarterback **Matt Leinart**, who passed on the NFL, will go for a third consecutive national title in 2005.

AP/Wide World Photos

# Trojan Horses

*Pete Carroll's Trojans, led by Matt Leinart and Reggie Bush, conquer Oklahoma to claim a second straight national championship.*

**Chris Fowler**
*is the host of ESPN's College GameDay*

The Sooners had surrendered. The same players who had huffed for a month that they'd hammer Matt Leinart and let the USC quarterback know that the Heisman still belonged to their guy, were now pleading for mercy in the BCS Championship game.

Between plays, Oklahoma's top pass rusher was asking Leinart if the Trojan braintrust couldn't just do OU's guys a favor.

"Please, can't y'all just run the ball?"

In other words, get this over with quicker. End the pain. Let previously perfect OU slink back to Norman humbled by a slaughter few saw coming.

Oh, by the way, this conversation took place in the middle of the third quarter. The white flag was being waved by a proud team that had crushed its three previous opponents, by a combined score of 107-6.

Eventually, mercy would be shown. The carnage could have been worse than the final score of 55-19 even indicated.

If the Trojans had really wanted to, they might have hit a hundred.

The tone had been set early, when Dominique Byrd made the crowd in Miami gasp with a one-handed circus grab for the Trojans' first touchdown. Uh, wasn't Byrd the guy who started the season at third-string tight end?

That pretty much characterizes Pete Carroll's payload of talent at Troy. For the top athletes in Southern California, he's made it fun and cool to stay home for school. The Trojans no longer recruit, they select. The practice field contains numerous no-names with enormous talent, waiting to make their mark.

And there is no end in sight.

Other programs peak, then fall-off and rebuild. For Auburn, 2004 was a pinnacle, a perfect season that featured three backfield stars bound for the NFL draft's first round.

Undefeated, but unfulfilled, might describe the Tigers, odd men out in the logjam atop the final BCS standings. One of my enduring memories of the 2004 season came after Auburn held

AP/Wide World Photos

*USC linebacker **Lofa Tatupu** and the rest of the Trojans flexed their muscles in the Orange Bowl and Oklahoma quarterback **Jason White** couldn't do much about it.*

off Tennessee in the SEC championship game. Outside the Georgia Dome, a middle-aged Auburn man with blood in his eye (and beer in his belly) was screaming; not in delight, at his team's 12-0 record and conference title and not in celebration of perhaps the best Tigers' season he'll ever see.

He was screaming in rage, at the stupidity of the pollsters and the computers that would rank his team third, at the injustice of the whole system. Even as a target of his anger, I almost couldn't blame the guy.

Even in Utah, the overwhelming joy of the post-game goalpost assault after beating BYU (my favorite memory of the regular season) quickly became tempered as the euphoria wore off.

The unbeaten Utes of the Mountain West Conference had broken through the BCS monopoly on the big bowl bids, but the system dictated that in their showcase opportunity for respect they would be matched against lackluster Pitt, the 8-3 co-champs of the depleted Big East.

It was an historic mess, the 2004 championship chase. The odds were defied, and the chaos scenario played out. For the first time in the seven-year history of the BCS, more than two teams were unbeaten from the major conferences. Auburn could (and did) go undefeated and not get anything more than a peek at the national title. The system will be tweaked *for the sixth time* in the off-season. In fact, the

AP/Wide World Photos

*Undefeated **Utah** crashed the BCS party, earning a Fiesta Bowl bid despite their Mountain West Conference pedigree. Head coach **Urban Meyer** parlayed the team's success into the top job at Florida, who as part of the SEC are founding members of the BCS.*

Associated Press decided that it doesn't like being involved so deeply in the process any more and announced that it wouldn't (and technically never had) allow the BCS to use its venerable media poll, which was one-third of the formula in 2004, in compiling the BCS standings going forward.

What can you do, until the system is overhauled? Not tweaked again, but overhauled.

Well, we can keep our sense of humor. You need one when trying to figure out college football this past year. How can anyone explain some of the other wackiness of 2004:

• Mississippi State scores just seven points and loses to the Div. 1-AA Maine Black Bears, possibly a low point for the mighty SEC, then snaps a five-game skid by hanging 38 points on perennial power Florida.

• Wisconsin allows 81 points in nine games, all wins, then surrenders 49 to lowly Michigan State and blows its Rose Bowl chance.

• Boston College's Fiesta Bowl bid and Big East Conference finale are spoiled in a 26-point home beating from a Syracuse team that had just lost to a 1-9 Temple team!

• Nebraska gives up 70 points to Texas Tech in the worst loss in Huskers history. The Red Raiders ring up seven touchdowns in the second half alone and Nebraska goes on to miss a bowl game for the first time since 1968.

# Lee Corso's Ten Biggest Stories of the Year in College Football

**10 Timmy Chang.** The University of Hawaii quarterback shatters Ty Detmer's NCAA career passing record which had stood for 13 years. After a 4,258-yard season in 2004, Chang finishes his career with 17,072 passing yards (over 2,000 more than Detmer) and legions of fans in his native Hawaii.

**9 A rookie wins the ACC.** Almost everyone felt Miami would be the newcomer that would win the Atlantic Coast Conference in 2004, however it is Virginia Tech who overcomes two close early-season losses to USC and N.C. State, then beats the Hurricanes in their own backyard on the final day of the regular season to clinch the ACC title. Then the Hokies give undefeated Auburn all they can handle in the Sugar Bowl before falling to the Tigers, 16-13.

**8 OU's Adrian Peterson.** Oklahoma running back Peterson bursts on the national scene, doing things that are very rarely done by a true freshman. Physically, Peterson looks and dominates like a senior and, despite a shoulder injury suffered late in the season, finishes the year with 1,925 yards and 15 touchdowns. He becomes the first freshman ever to finish second in the Heisman Trophy balloting.

**7 Utah.** Boise State and Louisville each have special seasons, but the "non-BCS conference" team that steals the headlines is Utah. Behind eventual top draft pick Alex Smith and a high-powered offensive attack that averaged 45.3 points per game and 500 yards a game, Urban Meyer's Utes earn a berth into the BCS and blow out Pittsburgh 35-7 to cap an undefeated 12-0 season. Meyer also moves on, taking the head coaching job at Florida.

**6 A new era in Nebraska.** One thing had been certain for the previous 42 years, Nebraska was assured a winning season. But that all changes in 2004. Year one of the Bill Callahan era brought a shift in offensive philosophy, a once-feared "blackshirt" defense is non-existent and the Huskers have their first losing season since 1968 and miss a bowl game for the first time in 35 years.

**5 Willingham fired by Notre Dame.** After a third straight blowout loss to USC, Tyrone Willingham is fired by Notre Dame. He had a 21-15 record in South Bend, but after an 8-0 start in 2002, the Irish lost 15 of 28 games. And by year's end, Michigan passes Notre Dame for the top spot on the All-Time NCAA Win Percentage list. Willingham is later hired at Washington.

**4    Matt Leinart.** Leinart becomes the second USC QB in three seasons to win the Heisman Trophy, throwing for 3,322 yards, 33 touchdowns, and just six interceptions. He immortalizes himself by capturing a second consecutive national title and then opts to return to school for his senior season and a chance at a third title.

**3    Auburn.** After a disappointing 2003 which saw university officials attempt to fire head coach Tommy Tuberville in very controversial fashion, the Tigers respond with the school's first outright SEC title since 1987 and a school-record 13-0 season, capped by a Sugar Bowl win over Virginia Tech. Behind the senior-laden backfield of Jason Campbell, Ronnie Brown and Cadillac Williams and a dominating defense, Auburn proves their national championship worthiness.

**2    USC repeats.** After a close call with Cal in October and a first half struggle in the fog at Oregon State, nothing stands in USC's path towards a second national title. The defending national champs, an underdog in the Orange Bowl to Oklahoma, pound the Sooners every way possible, winning, 55-19, leaving the game's outcome in little doubt midway through the second quarter. USC rolls up 525 total yards and leads 38-10 at halftime. Pete Carroll's Trojans have laid the foundation for a dynasty, as they take a 22-game winning streak into the 2005 season.

**1    BCS Controversy.** It's everywhere. Whether it's for the 1-2 spots among USC, Oklahoma and Auburn, or between Cal and Texas for the final at-large berth, 2004 is another controversial year for the BCS. It's the fourth time in five years there is a debate as to who should be in the BCS title game and a change in the voting of the final regular season polls enables Texas to jump Cal in the final BCS standings and gain the final at-large berth. As a result of all this, the AP elects to pull its poll from the BCS formula and ESPN removes its name from the Coaches' Poll.

---

Former Florida head coach Steve Spurrier was named head coach at South Carolina in 2004 and with his next bowl appearance will become the 19th man in history to take three different schools to a bowl game. **Did you know**, the man Spurrier replaced, Lou Holtz, is the only man in college football to take five different teams (William & Mary, N.C. State, Arkansas, Notre Dame and South Carolina) to a bowl?

# 2004-2005
# *Season in Review*

SPORTS ALMANAC

## Final AP Top 25 Poll

Voted on by panel of 65 sportswriters & broadcasters and released on Jan. 5, 2005, following the Fiesta Bowl: winning team receives the Bear Bryant Trophy, given since 1983; first place votes in parentheses, records, total points (based on 25 for 1st, 24 for 2nd, etc.) bowl game result, head coach and career record, preseason rank (released Aug. 14, 2004) and final regular season rank (released Dec. 5, 2004).

| | | Final Record | Points | Bowl Game | Head Coach | Aug. 15 Rank | Dec. 5 Rank |
|---|---|---|---|---|---|---|---|
| 1 | USC (62) | 13-0 | 1,622 | won Orange | Pete Carroll (4 yrs: 42-9) | 1 | 1 |
| 2 | Auburn (3) | 13-0 | 1,559 | won Sugar | Tommy Tuberville (10 yrs: 76-44) | 17 | 3 |
| 3 | Oklahoma | 12-1 | 1,454 | lost Orange | Bob Stoops (7 yrs: 78-14) | 2 | 2 |
| 4 | Utah | 12-0 | 1,438 | won Fiesta | Urban Meyer (4 yrs: 39-8) | 20 | 5 |
| 5 | Texas | 11-1 | 1,391 | won Rose | Mack Brown (21 yrs: 156-93-1) | 7 | 6 |
| 6 | Louisville | 11-1 | 1,261 | won Liberty | Bobby Petrino (2 yrs: 20-5) | NR | 7 |
| 7 | Georgia | 10-2 | 1,204 | won Outback | Mark Richt (4 yrs: 42-10) | 3 | 8 |
| 8 | Iowa | 10-2 | 1,111 | won Capital One | Kirk Ferentz (9 yrs: 54-52) | 19 | 11 |
| 9 | California | 10-2 | 1,060 | lost Holiday | Jeff Tedford (3 yrs: 25-13) | 13 | 4 |
| 10 | Virginia Tech | 10-3 | 996 | lost Sugar | Frank Beamer (24 yrs: 177-77-2) | NR | 9 |
| 11 | Miami-FL | 9-3 | 917 | won Peach | Larry Coker (4 yrs: 44-6) | 6 | 14 |
| 12 | Boise St. | 11-1 | 888 | lost Liberty | Dan Hawkins (9 yrs: 83-18-1) | NR | 10 |
| 13 | Tennessee | 10-3 | 868 | won Cotton | Philip Fullmer (13 yrs: 123-31) | 14 | 15 |
| 14 | Michigan | 9-3 | 842 | lost Rose | Lloyd Carr (10 yrs: 95-27) | 8 | 13 |
| 15 | Florida St. | 9-3 | 754 | won Gator | Bobby Bowden (39 yrs: 351-100-4) | 5 | 17 |
| 16 | LSU | 9-3 | 711 | lost Capital One | Nick Saban (11 yrs: 91-42-1) | 4 | 12 |
| 17 | Wisconsin | 9-3 | 482 | lost Outback | Barry Alvarez (15 yrs: 108-70-4) | 21 | 16 |
| 18 | Texas Tech | 8-4 | 476 | won Holiday | Mike Leach (5 yrs: 39-25) | NR | 23 |
| 19 | Arizona St. | 9-3 | 463 | won Sun | Dirk Koetter (5 yrs: 52-33) | NR | 21 |
| 20 | Ohio St. | 8-4 | 423 | won Alamo | Jim Tressel (19 yrs: 175-68-2) | 9 | 24 |
| 21 | Boston College | 9-3 | 314 | won Cont. Tire | Tom O'Brien (8 yrs: 57-39) | NR | 25 |
| 22 | Fresno St. | 9-3 | 203 | won MPC | Pat Hill (8 yrs: 64-38) | NR | NR |
| 23 | Virginia | 8-4 | 157 | lost MPC | Al Groh (10 yrs: 56-61) | NR | 18 |
| 24 | Navy | 10-2 | 126 | won Emerald | Paul Johnson (9 yrs: 82-27) | NR | NR |
| 25 | Pittsburgh | 8-4 | 99 | lost Fiesta | Walt Harris (11 yrs: 63-68) | NR | 19 |

**Other teams receiving votes:** 26. **Florida** (7-5, lost Peach, 85 pts); 27. **Bowling Green** (9-3, won GMAC, 74 pts); 28. **Texas A&M** (7-5, lost Cotton, 29 pts); 29. **Northern Illinois** (9-3, won Silicon Valley Classic, 27 pts); 30. **West Virginia** (8-4, lost Gator, 26 pts); 31. **Colorado** (8-5, won Houston, 13 pts); 32. **Connecticut** (8-4, won Motor City, 11 pts); 33. **Purdue** (7-5, lost Sun, 10 pts); 34. **Georgia Tech** (7-5, won Champs Sports) and **Minnesota** (7-5, won Music City, 6 pts); 36. **Southern Miss.** (7-5, won New Orleans) and **UTEP** (8-4, lost Houston, 1 pt).

## AP Preseason and Final Regular Season Polls
First place votes in parentheses.

### Top 25
(Aug. 14, 2004)

| | | Pts | | | | Pts |
|---|---|---|---|---|---|---|
| 1 | USC (48) | 1,603 | | 14 | Tennessee | 658 |
| 2 | Oklahoma (11) | 1,529 | | 15 | Clemson | 638 |
| 3 | Georgia (5) | 1,480 | | 16 | Virginia | 627 |
| 4 | LSU (1) | 1,446 | | 17 | Auburn | 540 |
| 5 | Florida St. | 1,291 | | 18 | Missouri | 525 |
| 6 | Miami-FL | 1,287 | | 19 | Iowa | 518 |
| 7 | Texas | 1,236 | | 20 | Utah | 446 |
| 8 | Michigan | 1,223 | | 21 | Wisconsin | 328 |
| 9 | Ohio St. | 1,005 | | 22 | Maryland | 310 |
| 10 | West Virginia | 937 | | 23 | Oregon | 200 |
| 11 | Florida | 836 | | 24 | Purdue | 153 |
| 12 | Kansas St. | 763 | | 25 | Minnesota | 142 |
| 13 | California | 744 | | | | |

### Top 25
(Dec. 5, 2004)

| | | Pts | | | | Pts |
|---|---|---|---|---|---|---|
| 1 | USC (44) | 1,599 | | 14 | Miami-FL | 776 |
| 2 | Oklahoma (14) | 1,556 | | 15 | Tennessee | 651 |
| 3 | Auburn (7) | 1,525 | | 16 | Wisconsin | 648 |
| 4 | California | 1,399 | | 17 | Florida St. | 647 |
| 5 | Utah | 1,345 | | 18 | Virginia | 482 |
| 6 | Texas | 1,337 | | 19 | Pittsburgh | 415 |
| 7 | Louisville | 1,183 | | 20 | Florida | 325 |
| 8 | Georgia | 1,117 | | 21 | Arizona St. | 222 |
| 9 | Virginia Tech | 1,111 | | 22 | Texas A&M | 213 |
| 10 | Boise St. | 960 | | 23 | Texas Tech | 168 |
| 11 | Iowa | 948 | | 24 | Ohio St. | 155 |
| 12 | LSU | 929 | | 25 | Boston College | 150 |
| 13 | Michigan | 917 | | | | |

## 2004-2005 Bowl Games

Listed by bowls matching highest-ranked teams as of final regular season AP poll (released Dec. 5, 2004). Attendance figures indicate tickets sold.

| Bowl | Winner | Regular Season | Loser | Regular Season | Score | Date | Attendance |
|------|--------|----------------|-------|----------------|-------|------|------------|
| Orange . . . . . . . . . . . .#1 | USC | 12-0 | #2 Oklahoma | 12-0 | 55-19 | Jan. 4 | 77,912 |
| Sugar . . . . . . . . . . . .#3 | Auburn | 12-0 | #9 Virginia Tech | 10-2 | 16-13 | Jan. 3 | 77,349 |
| Holiday . . . . . . . . . .#23 | Texas Tech | 7-4 | #4 California | 10-1 | 45-31 | Dec. 30 | 63,711 |
| Fiesta . . . . . . . . . . . .#5 | Utah | 11-0 | #19 Pittsburgh | 8-3 | 35-7 | Jan. 1 | 73,519 |
| Rose . . . . . . . . . . . .#6 | Texas | 10-1 | #13 Michigan | 9-2 | 38-37 | Jan. 1 | 93,468 |
| Liberty . . . . . . . . . . .#7 | Louisville | 10-1 | #10 Boise St. | 11-0 | 44-40 | Dec. 31 | 58,355 |
| Outback . . . . . . . . . .#8 | Georgia | 9-2 | #16 Wisconsin | 9-2 | 24-21 | Jan. 1 | 62,414 |
| Capital One . . . . . . .#11 | Iowa | 9-2 | #12 LSU | 9-2 | 30-25 | Jan. 1 | 70,229 |
| Peach . . . . . . . . . . .#14 | Miami-FL | 8-3 | #20 Florida | 7-4 | 27-10 | Dec. 31 | 69,322 |
| Cotton . . . . . . . . . . .#15 | Tennessee | 9-3 | #22 Texas A&M | 7-4 | 38-7 | Jan. 1 | 75,704 |
| Gator . . . . . . . . . . . .#17 | Florida St. | 8-3 | West Virginia | 8-3 | 30-18 | Jan. 1 | 70,112 |
| MPC Computers . . . . . . . . | Fresno St. | 8-3 | #18 Virginia | 8-3 | 37-34 (OT) | Dec. 27 | 28,516 |
| Sun . . . . . . . . . . . .#21 | Arizona St. | 8-3 | Purdue | 7-4 | 27-23 | Dec. 31 | 51,288 |
| Alamo . . . . . . . . . . .#24 | Ohio St. | 7-4 | Oklahoma St. | 7-4 | 33-7 | Dec. 29 | 65,265 |
| Continental Tire . . . . .#25 | Boston College | 8-3 | North Carolina | 6-5 | 37-24 | Dec. 30 | 70,412 |
| New Orleans | Southern Miss. | 6-5 | North Texas | 7-4 | 31-10 | Dec. 14 | 27,253 |
| Champs Sports . . . . . . . . | Georgia Tech | 6-5 | Syracuse | 6-5 | 51-14 | Dec. 21 | 28,237 |
| GMAC . . . . . . . . . . . . | Bowling Green | 8-3 | Memphis | 8-3 | 52-35 | Dec. 22 | 29,500 |
| Fort Worth . . . . . . . . . . | Cincinnati | 6-5 | Marshall | 6-5 | 32-14 | Dec. 23 | 27,902 |
| Las Vegas . . . . . . . . . . | Wyoming | 6-5 | UCLA | 6-5 | 24-21 | Dec. 23 | 29,062 |
| Hawaii . . . . . . . . . . . . | Hawaii | 7-5 | UAB | 7-4 | 59-40 | Dec. 24 | 39,754 |
| Motor City . . . . . . . . . . | Connecticut | 7-4 | Toledo | 9-3 | 39-10 | Dec. 27 | 52,552 |
| Independence . . . . . . . . | Iowa St. | 6-5 | Miami-OH | 8-4 | 17-13 | Dec. 28 | 43,000 |
| Insight . . . . . . . . . . . . | Oregon St. | 6-5 | Notre Dame | 6-5 | 38-21 | Dec. 28 | 45,917 |
| Houston . . . . . . . . . . . | Colorado | 7-5 | UTEP | 8-3 | 33-28 | Dec. 29 | 27,235 |
| Emerald . . . . . . . . . . . | Navy | 9-2 | New Mexico | 7-4 | 34-19 | Dec. 30 | 30,563 |
| Silicon Valley Classic . . . . | Northern Illinois | 8-3 | Troy | 7-4 | 34-21 | Dec. 30 | 21,456 |
| Music City . . . . . . . . . . | Minnesota | 6-5 | Alabama | 6-5 | 20-16 | Dec. 31 | 66,089 |

## 2004 Final BCS Rankings

The Bowl Championship Series rankings were used for the first time during the 1998 season to determine BCS bowl match-ups and revised slightly for the 1999, 2001, 2002 and 2004 seasons. The final rankings were released Dec. 5, 2004.

| | | Polls | | | | | Computer Rankings | | | | | | | | BCS |
| | AP | Pts | % | ESPN | Pts | % | A&H | RB | CM | KM | JS | PW | % | Avg | Avg |
|---|---|---|---|---|---|---|---|---|---|---|---|---|---|---|---|
| 1 USC . . . . . . . .1 | 1599 | .9840 | 1 | 1490 | .9770 | 24 | 24 | 25 | 25 | 25 | 24 | .970 | 2 | .9770 |
| 2 Oklahoma . . . .2 | 1556 | .9575 | 2 | 1459 | .9567 | 25 | 25 | 24 | 24 | 25 | 25 | .990 | 1 | .9681 |
| 3 USC . . . . . . . .3 | 1525 | .9385 | 3 | 1435 | .9410 | 23 | 23 | 23 | 23 | 23 | 23 | .920 | 3 | .9331 |
| 4 Texas . . . . . . .6 | 1337 | .8228 | 5 | 1281 | .8400 | 21 | 22 | 22 | 22 | 22 | 22 | .880 | 4 | .8476 |
| 5 California . . . .4 | 1399 | .8609 | 4 | 1286 | .8433 | 20 | 18 | 20 | 20 | 21 | 20 | .800 | 6 | .8347 |
| 6 Utah . . . . . . . .5 | 1345 | .8277 | 6 | 1215 | .7967 | 22 | 20 | 21 | 21 | 20 | 21 | .830 | 5 | .8181 |
| 7 Georgia . . . . .8 | 1117 | .6874 | 7 | 1117 | .7325 | 17 | 19 | 18 | 17 | 15 | 15 | .670 | 8 | .6966 |
| 8 Virginia Tech . .9 | 1111 | .6837 | 9 | 1037 | .6800 | 13 | 15 | 14 | 18 | 18 | 18 | .650 | 9 | .6712 |
| 9 Boise St. . . . .10 | 960 | .5908 | 10 | 943 | .6184 | 19 | 21 | 19 | 19 | 19 | 19 | .760 | 7 | .6564 |
| 10 Louisville . . . .7 | 1183 | .7280 | 8 | 1066 | .6990 | 9 | 12 | 13 | 11 | 17 | 16 | .520 | 13 | .6490 |
| 11 LSU . . . . . . .12 | 929 | .5717 | 11 | 932 | .6111 | 16 | 17 | 15 | 16 | 16 | 17 | .650 | 9 | .6109 |
| 12 Iowa . . . . . . .11 | 948 | .5834 | 13 | 812 | .5325 | 18 | 14 | 17 | 10 | 9 | 14 | .550 | 12 | .5553 |
| 13 Michigan . . . .13 | 917 | .5643 | 12 | 874 | .5731 | 14 | 16 | 12 | 3 | 2 | 9 | .380 | 17 | .5058 |
| 14 Miami-FL . . . .14 | 776 | .4775 | 14 | 738 | .4839 | 11 | 13 | 10 | 12 | 12 | 10 | .450 | 14 | .4705 |
| 15 Tennessee . . .15 | 651 | .4006 | 17 | 559 | .3666 | 12 | 11 | 11 | 14 | 11 | 11 | .450 | 14 | .4057 |
| 16 Florida St. . . .17 | 647 | .3982 | 15 | 643 | .4216 | 8 | 4 | 8 | 5 | 5 | 4 | .220 | 21 | .3466 |
| 17 Wisconsin . . .16 | 648 | .3988 | 16 | 599 | .3928 | 7 | 10 | 6 | 1 | 3 | 8 | .240 | 20 | .3439 |
| 18 Virginia . . . . .18 | 482 | .2966 | 18 | 455 | .2984 | 6 | 9 | 7 | 9 | 8 | 6 | .300 | 18 | .2983 |
| 19 Arizona St. . . .21 | 222 | .1366 | 24 | 173 | .1134 | 15 | 0 | 16 | 15 | 13 | 13 | .560 | 11 | .2700 |
| 20 Texas A&M . . .22 | 213 | .1311 | 25 | 147 | .0964 | 10 | 0 | 9 | 13 | 14 | 12 | .440 | 16 | .2225 |
| 21 Pittsburgh . . .19 | 415 | .2554 | 20 | 318 | .2085 | 0 | 6 | 0 | 0 | 0 | 0 | .000 | NR | .1546 |
| 22 Texas Tech . . .23 | 168 | .1034 | 21 | 234 | .1534 | 4 | 0 | 4 | 6 | 7 | 5 | .190 | 22 | .1489 |
| 23 Florida . . . . .20 | 325 | .2000 | 19 | 324 | .2125 | 0 | 5 | 0 | 0 | 0 | 0 | .000 | NR | .1375 |
| 24 Oklahoma St. . .32 | 16 | .0098 | 28 | 35 | .0230 | 5 | 0 | 5 | 8 | 10 | 7 | .250 | 19 | .0943 |
| 25 Ohio St. . . . . .24 | 155 | .0954 | 22 | 181 | .1187 | 3 | 8 | 1 | 0 | 0 | 0 | .040 | NR | .0847 |

**Note:** Team percentages are derived by dividing a team's actual voting points by a maximum 1625 possible points in the AP Poll and 1525 in the *USA Today*/ESPN Coaches Poll. Six computer rankings calculated in inverse points order (25 for #1, 24 for #2, etc.) are used to determine the overall computer component. The best and worst ranking for each team is dropped, and the remaining four are added and divided by 100 (the maximum possible points) to produce a Computer Rankings Percentage. Each computer ranking accounts for schedule strength and home/away performance in its formula. The BCS Average is calculated by averaging the percent totals of the AP, USA Today/ESPN Coaches, and Computer polls. *Computer Rankings*—A&H = Anderson & Hester, RB = Richard Billingsley, CM = Colley Matrix, KM = Kenneth Massey, JS = Jeff Sagarin, PW = Peter Wolfe, Avg. refers to the teams average position in the computer rankings.

## BCS Championship Game

Undefeated USC and Oklahoma were ranked first and second, respectively, in the final Bowl Championship Series standings (as well as the AP and ESPN/*USA Today* Coaches polls) and met in the Orange Bowl to decide Div. 1 college football's national championship. Opponents' records and AP rank listed below are day of game. Final statistics listed below include the bowl games.

### USC Trojans (12-0)

| Date | AP Rank | Opponent | Result |
|------|---------|----------|--------|
| Aug. 28 | #1 | Virginia Tech (0-0)* | W, 24-13 |
| Sept. 11 | #1 | Colorado St. (0-1) | W, 49-0 |
| Sept. 18 | #1 | at BYU (1-1) | W, 42-10 |
| Sept. 25 | #1 | at Stanford (2-0) | W, 31-28 |
| Oct. 9 | #1 | #7 California (3-0) | W, 23-17 |
| Oct. 16 | #1 | #15 Arizona St. (5-0) | W, 45-7 |
| Oct. 23 | #1 | Washington (1-5) | W, 38-0 |
| Oct. 30 | #1 | at Washington St. (3-4) | W, 42-12 |
| Nov. 6 | #1 | at Oregon St. (4-4) | W, 28-20 |
| Nov. 13 | #1 | Arizona (2-7) | W, 49-9 |
| Nov. 27 | #1 | Notre Dame (6-4) | W, 41-10 |
| Dec. 4 | #1 | at UCLA (6-4) | W, 29-24 |
| Jan. 4 | #1 | #2 Oklahoma (12-0)† | W, 55-19 |

*BCA Football Classic at Landover, Md.
†Orange Bowl

### Oklahoma Sooners (12-1)

| Date | AP Rank | Opponent | Result |
|------|---------|----------|--------|
| Sept. 4 | #2 | Bowling Green (0-0) | W, 40-24 |
| Sept. 11 | #2 | Houston (0-1) | W, 63-13 |
| Sept. 18 | #2 | Oregon (0-1) | W, 31-7 |
| Oct. 2 | #2 | Texas Tech (3-1) | W, 28-13 |
| Oct. 9 | #2 | #5 Texas* (4-0) | W, 12-0 |
| Oct. 16 | #2 | at Kansas St. (2-3) | W, 31-21 |
| Oct. 23 | #2 | Kansas (3-3) | W, 41-10 |
| Oct. 30 | #2 | at #20 Oklahoma St. (6-1) | W, 38-35 |
| Nov. 6 | #2 | at #22 Texas A&M (6-2) | W, 42-35 |
| Nov. 13 | #2 | Nebraska (5-4) | W, 30-3 |
| Nov. 20 | #2 | at Baylor (3-7) | W, 35-0 |
| Dec. 4 | #2 | # Colorado† (7-4) | W, 42-3 |
| Jan. 4 | #2 | #1 USC‡ (11-0) | L, 19-55 |

*at Dallas
†Big 12 Championship at Kansas City, Mo.
‡Orange Bowl

## Final Individual Statistics

| Passing (5 Att) | Att | Cmp | Pct. | Yds | TD | Rate |
|-----------------|-----|-----|------|-----|----|----|
| Matt Leinart | .412 | 269 | 65.3 | 3322 | 33 | 156.5 |
| Matt Cassel | .14 | 10 | 71.4 | 97 | 0 | 115.3 |

**Interceptions:** Leinart 6, Cassel 1.

| Top Receivers | No | Yds | Avg | Long | TD |
|---------------|-----|-----|-----|------|-----|
| Dwayne Jarrett | .55 | 849 | 15.4 | 57 | 13 |
| Reggie Bush | .43 | 509 | 11.8 | 69 | 7 |
| Steve Smith | .42 | 660 | 15.7 | 51 | 6 |
| Dominique Byrd | .37 | 384 | 10.4 | 33 | 3 |
| Alex Holmes | .24 | 244 | 10.2 | 48 | 0 |
| Chris McFoy | .21 | 272 | 13.0 | 31 | 0 |
| David Kirtman | .19 | 161 | 8.5 | 26 | 1 |

| Top Rushers | Car | Yds | Avg | Long | TD |
|-------------|-----|-----|-----|------|-----|
| LenDale White | .203 | 1103 | 5.4 | 54 | 15 |
| Reggie Bush | .143 | 908 | 6.3 | 81 | 6 |
| Desmond Reed | .31 | 173 | 5.6 | 28 | 1 |
| Hershel Dennis | .28 | 109 | 3.9 | 13 | 1 |
| David Kirtman | .8 | 45 | 5.6 | 14 | 0 |
| Lee Webb | .6 | 29 | 4.8 | 9 | 1 |

| Most Touchdowns | TD | Run | Rec | Ret | Pts |
|-----------------|-----|-----|-----|-----|-----|
| LenDale White | .17 | 15 | 2 | 0 | 102 |
| Reggie Bush | .15 | 6 | 7 | 2 | 90 |
| Dwayne Jarrett | .13 | 0 | 13 | 0 | 78 |
| Steve Smith | .6 | 0 | 6 | 0 | 36 |
| Matt Leinart | .3 | 3 | 0 | 0 | 18 |
| Dominique Byrd | .3 | 0 | 3 | 0 | 18 |

**2-Pt. Conversions:** none.

| Kicking | FG/Att | Lg | PAT/Att | Pts |
|---------|--------|----|---------|-----|
| Ryan Killeen | .16/25 | 44 | 64/64 | 112 |

| Punting | No | Yds | Long | Blkd | Avg |
|---------|-----|-----|------|------|-----|
| Tom Malone | .49 | 2144 | 62 | 1 | 43.8 |

| Most Interceptions | | Most Sacks | |
|--------------------|----|-----------|----|
| M. Grootegoed | .5 | Shaun Cody | .10.0 |
| Jason Leach | .3 | Lofa Tatupu | .6.0 |
| Lofa Tatupu | .3 | Mike Patterson | .6.0 |
| | | Lawrence Jackson | .6.0 |

## Final Individual Statistics

| Passing (5 Att) | Att | Cmp | Pct. | Yds | TD | Rate |
|-----------------|-----|-----|------|-----|----|----|
| Jason White | .390 | 255 | 65.4 | 3205 | 35 | 159.4 |
| Tommy Grady | .14 | 12 | 85.7 | 63 | 1 | 147.1 |

**Interceptions:** White 9.

| Top Receivers | No | Yds | Avg | Long | TD |
|---------------|-----|-----|-----|------|-----|
| Mark Clayton | .66 | 876 | 13.3 | 61 | 8 |
| Travis Wilson | .50 | 660 | 13.2 | 41 | 11 |
| Brandon Jones | .27 | 345 | 12.8 | 69 | 3 |
| Mark Bradley | .23 | 491 | 21.3 | 72 | 7 |
| Kejuan Jones | .22 | 196 | 8.9 | 25 | 0 |
| Will Peoples | .20 | 224 | 11.2 | 28 | 2 |
| James Moses | .17 | 151 | 8.9 | 40 | 2 |

| Top Rushers | Car | Yds | Avg | Long | TD |
|-------------|-----|-----|-----|------|-----|
| Adrian Peterson | .339 | 1925 | 5.7 | 80 | 15 |
| Kejuan Jones | .129 | 513 | 4.0 | 26 | 5 |
| D.J. Wolfe | .25 | 107 | 4.3 | 31 | 0 |
| Tashard Choice | .22 | 100 | 4.5 | 14 | 0 |
| Mark Bradley | .4 | 73 | 18.2 | 51 | 1 |
| Donta Hickson | .10 | 52 | 5.2 | 25 | 1 |

| Most Touchdowns | TD | Run | Rec | Ret | Pts |
|-----------------|-----|-----|-----|-----|-----|
| Adrian Peterson | .15 | 15 | 0 | 0 | 90 |
| Travis Wilson | .11 | 0 | 11 | 0 | 66 |
| Mark Clayton | .9 | 8 | 0 | 1 | 54 |
| Mark Bradley | .8 | 1 | 7 | 0 | 48 |
| Kejuan Jones | .5 | 5 | 0 | 0 | 30 |
| Brandon Jones | .3 | 0 | 3 | 0 | 18 |

**2-Pt. Conversions:** none.

| Kicking | FG/Att | Lg | PAT/Att | Pts |
|---------|--------|----|---------|-----|
| Tony DiCarlo | .8/16 | 35 | 45/48 | 69 |
| Garret Hartley | .1/1 | 29 | 12/12 | 15 |

| Punting | No | Yds | Long | Blkd | Avg |
|---------|-----|-----|------|------|-----|
| Blake Ferguson | .52 | 2183 | 58 | 1 | 42.0 |

| Most Interceptions | | Most Sacks | |
|--------------------|----|-----------|----|
| Brodney Pool | .2 | Dan Cody | .10.0 |
| Six tied | .1 | Jonathan Jackson | .8.0 |
| | | Larry Birdine | .7.0 |

*When quarterbacks Matt Leinart of USC and Jason White of Oklahoma faced off for a national title at the Orange Bowl in 2005 it was the first meeting of Heisman Trophy winners in college football history.*

## Orange Bowl

Tuesday, Jan. 4, 2005 at Pro Player Stadium, Miami, Fla.

### USC 55, Oklahoma 19

|  | 1 | 2 | 3 | 4 | F |
|---|---|---|---|---|---|
| #1 USC (Pac 10) . . . . . . . . . . . | 14 | 24 | 10 | 7 | 55 |
| #2 Oklahoma (Big 12) . . . . . . . | 7 | 3 | 0 | 9 | 19 |

**Favorite:** USC by 1
**Field:** Grass
**Time:** 3:52

**Attendance:** 77,912
**Weather:** humid but clear
**TV Rating:** 13.7/22 (ABC)

### Scoring Summary

**1st:** 07:44; **OU**—Travis Wilson 5-yd pass from Jason White (Garret Hartley kick), 12 plays, 92 yards, 5:56.

**1st:** 04:27; **USC**—Dominique Byrd 33-yd pass from Matt Leinart (Ryan Killeen kick), 6 plays, 75 yards, 3:17.

**1st:** 00:17; **USC**—LenDale White 6-yd run (Killeen kick), 1 play, 6 yards, 0:06.

**2nd:** 11:46; **USC**—Dwayne Jarrett 54-yd pass from Leinart (Killeen kick), 6 plays, 89 yards, 1:41.

**2nd:** 09:17; **USC**—Steve Smith 5-yd pass from Leinart (Killeen kick), 3 plays, 10 yards, 0:49.

**2nd:** 03:10; **OU**—Hartley 29-yd field goal, 13 plays, 68 yards, 6:07.

**2nd:** 01:56; **USC**— Smith 33-yd pass from Leinart (Killeen kick), 4 plays, 79 yards, 1:41.

**2nd:** 00:03; **USC**—Killeen 44-yd field goal, 7 plays, 8 yards, 0:50.

**3rd:** 10:42; **USC**—Smith 4-yd pass from Leinart (Killeen kick), 8 plays, 85 yards, 3:07.

**3rd:** 04:01; **USC**—Killeen 42-yd field goal, 9 plays, 45 yards, 2:34.

**4th:** 09:46; **USC**—White 8-yd run (Killeen kick), 5 plays, 56 yards, 3:00.

**4th:** 06:34; **OU**—Team safety.

**4th:** 03:59; **OU**—Wilson 9-yd pass from White (Hartley kick), 6 plays, 49 yards, 2:35.

### Team Statistics

|  | OU | USC |
|---|---|---|
| First downs . . . . . . . . . . . . . . . . . . . . . | 19 | 19 |
| Total Plays . . . . . . . . . . . . . . . . . . . . . . | 76 | 63 |
| Total Net Yards . . . . . . . . . . . . . . . . | 372 | 525 |
| Carries/yards (includ. sacks) . . . . . | 40/128 | 28/193 |
| Passing yards . . . . . . . . . . . . . . . . . | 244 | 332 |
| Completions/attempts . . . . . . . . . . | 24/36 | 18/35 |
| Had intercepted . . . . . . . . . . . . . . . . . | 3 | 0 |
| Fumbles/lost . . . . . . . . . . . . . . . . . . | 0/0 | 0/0 |

|  | OU | USC |
|---|---|---|
| Penalties/yards . . . . . . . . . . . . . . . . | 3/30 | 9/75 |
| Punts/average . . . . . . . . . . . . . . . . | 4/44.5 | 4/43.5 |
| 3rd down conversions . . . . . . . . . . | 8/17 | 6/14 |
| 4th down conversions . . . . . . . . . . . . | 0/1 | 2/2 |
| Red-Zone scores/chances . . . . . . . | 3/3 | 5/5 |
| Sacks by/yards . . . . . . . . . . . . . . . . | 1/9 | 2/20 |
| Time of possession . . . . . . . . . . . . | 35:06 | 24:54 |

### Individual Statistics

#### Oklahoma Sooners

| Passing | Att | Cmp | Int | Yds | TD | Sack |
|---|---|---|---|---|---|---|
| Jason White . . . . . . . | 36 | 24 | 3 | 244 | 2 | 2 |

| Receivers | No | Yds | Avg | Long | TD |
|---|---|---|---|---|---|
| Travis Wilson . . . . . . . . . . . | 7 | 59 | 8.4 | 20 | 2 |
| Mark Clayton . . . . . . . . . . | 4 | 21 | 5.3 | 9 | 0 |
| Mark Bradley . . . . . . . . . . | 2 | 66 | 33.0 | 34 | 0 |
| Kejuan Jones . . . . . . . . . | 2 | 30 | 15.0 | 25 | 0 |
| Brandon Jones . . . . . . . . | 2 | 13 | 6.5 | 7 | 0 |
| Adrian Peterson . . . . . . . | 2 | 6 | 3.0 | 5 | 0 |
| Jejuan Rankins . . . . . . . | 2 | 0 | 0.0 | 4 | 0 |
| Joe Jon Finley . . . . . . . . | 1 | 23 | 23.0 | 23 | 0 |
| Will Peoples . . . . . . . . . . | 1 | 18 | 18.0 | 18 | 0 |
| James Moses . . . . . . . . . | 1 | 8 | 8.0 | 8 | 0 |
| TOTALS . . . . . . . . . . . . | 24 | 244 | 10.2 | 34 | 2 |

| Rushers | Car | Yds | Avg | Long | TD |
|---|---|---|---|---|---|
| Adrian Peterson . . . . . . . | 339 | 1925 | 5.7 | 80 | 15 |
| Kejuan Jones . . . . . . . | 129 | 513 | 4.0 | 26 | 5 |
| D.J. Wolfe . . . . . . . . | 25 | 107 | 4.3 | 31 | 0 |
| Tashard Choice . . . . . . . | 22 | 100 | 4.5 | 14 | 0 |
| Mark Bradley . . . . . . . | 4 | 73 | 18.2 | 51 | 0 |
| Donta Hickson . . . . . . | 10 | 52 | 5.2 | 25 | 1 |
| TOTALS . . . . . . . . . . | 40 | 128 | 3.2 | 27 | 0 |

| Field Goals | 20-29 | 30-39 | 40-49 | 50-59 | Total |
|---|---|---|---|---|---|
| Garret Hartley . . . . | 1-1 | 0-0 | 0-0 | 0-0 | 1-1 |

| Punting | No | Yds | Long | Blkd | Avg |
|---|---|---|---|---|---|
| Blake Ferguson . . . . . . . | 4 | 178 | 51 | 0 | 44.5 |

| Punt Returns | No | Yds | Long | Avg | TD |
|---|---|---|---|---|---|
| Mark Bradley . . . . . . . | 1 | 3 | 3 | 3.0 | 0 |

| Kickoff Returns | No | Yds | Long | Avg | TD |
|---|---|---|---|---|---|
| Travis Wilson . . . . . . . | 3 | 51 | 26 | 17.0 | 0 |
| Mark Bradley . . . . . . . | 3 | 70 | 28 | 23.3 | 0 |
| Brandon Jones . . . . . | 1 | 18 | 18 | 18.0 | 0 |
| TOTALS . . . . . . . . . . | 7 | 139 | 28 | 19.9 | 0 |

#### USC Trojans

| Passing | Att | Cmp | Int | Yds | TD | Sack |
|---|---|---|---|---|---|---|
| Matt Leinart . . . . . . . | 35 | 18 | 0 | 332 | 5 | 1 |

| Receivers | No | Yds | Avg | Long | TD |
|---|---|---|---|---|---|
| Steve Smith . . . . . . . . . | 7 | 113 | 16.1 | 50 | 3 |
| Dwayne Jarrett . . . . . . . | 5 | 115 | 23.0 | 54 | 1 |
| Dominique Byrd . . . . . | 3 | 58 | 19.3 | 33 | 1 |
| Reggie Bush . . . . . . . . | 2 | 31 | 15.5 | 27 | 0 |
| David Kirtman . . . . . . . | 1 | 15 | 15.0 | 15 | 0 |
| TOTALS . . . . . . . . . . | 18 | 332 | 18.4 | 54 | 5 |

| Rushers | Car | Yds | Avg | Long | TD |
|---|---|---|---|---|---|
| LenDale White . . . . . . . | 15 | 118 | 7.9 | 39 | 2 |
| Reggie Bush . . . . . . . | 6 | 75 | 12.5 | 45 | 0 |
| Lee Webb . . . . . . . . . | 1 | 4 | 4.0 | 4 | 0 |
| David Kirtman . . . . . . | 1 | 4 | 4.0 | 4 | 0 |
| Desmond Reed . . . . . . | 2 | 2 | 1.0 | 1 | 0 |
| Dominique Byrd . . . . . | 1 | 1 | 1.0 | 1 | 0 |
| Matt Leinart . . . . . . . | 2 | -11 | -5.5 | 0 | 0 |
| TOTALS . . . . . . . . . . | 28 | 193 | 6.9 | 45 | 2 |

| Field Goals | 20-29 | 30-39 | 40-49 | 50-59 | Total |
|---|---|---|---|---|---|
| Ryan Killeen . . . . | 0-0 | 0-0 | 2-2 | 0-0 | 2-2 |

| Punting | No | Yds | Long | Blkd | Avg |
|---|---|---|---|---|---|
| Tom Malone . . . . . . . . | 4 | 174 | 56 | 0 | 43.5 |

| Punt Returns | No | Yds | Long | Avg | TD |
|---|---|---|---|---|---|
| Reggie Bush . . . . . . . | 1 | 7 | 7 | 7.0 | 0 |

| Kickoff Returns | No | Yds | Long | Avg | TD |
|---|---|---|---|---|---|
| Reggie Bush . . . . . . . | 2 | 36 | 19 | 18.0 | 0 |

## Other Final Division I-A Polls
### USA Today/ESPN Coaches Poll

Voted on by panel of 61 Division I-A head coaches; winning team receives the Sears Trophy (originally the McDonald's Trophy, 1991-93); first place votes in parentheses with total points (based on 25 for 1st, 24 for 2nd, etc.).

| Rank | Team | Pts |
|---|---|---|
| 1 | USC (61) | 1525 |
| 2 | Auburn | 1460 |
| 3 | Oklahoma | 1366 |
| 4 | Texas | 1324 |
| 5 | Utah | 1300 |
| 6 | Georgia | 1191 |
| 7 | Louisville | 1166 |
| 8 | Iowa | 1022 |
| 9 | California | 937 |
| 10 | Virginia Tech | 906 |
| 11 | Miami-FL | 903 |
| 12 | Michigan | 802 |
| 13 | Boise St. | 792 |
| 14 | Florida St. | 776 |
| 15 | Tennessee | 771 |
| 16 | LSU | 693 |
| 17 | Texas Tech | 478 |
| 18 | Wisconsin | 449 |
| 19 | Ohio St. | 430 |
| 20 | Arizona St. | 377 |
| 21 | Boston College | 245 |
| 22 | Fresno St. | 206 |
| 23 | Virginia | 157 |
| 24 | Navy | 129 |
| 25 | Florida | 101 |

**Other teams receiving votes:** 26. West Virginia (96 points), 27. Bowling Green (57), 28. Pittsburgh (45), 29. No. Illinois (40), 30. Texas A&M (16), 31. Colorado (15), 32. Minnesota (13), 33. Oregon St. (11), 34. Iowa St. (7), 35. Purdue (5), 36. Connecticut (4), 37. Georgia Tech (3), 38. Toledo, UTEP and Wyoming (2), 41. Hawaii (1).

## AP Weekly Rankings

The Associated Press Top 25 college football polls on a weekly basis are listed below. The table starts with the preseason and progresses through the season.

| | Pre | Sep 4 | Sep 11 | Sep 18 | Sep 26 | Oct 3 | Oct 9 | Oct 16 | Oct 23 | Oct 30 | Nov 6 | Nov 13 | Nov 20 | Nov 27 | Dec 4 | Jan 5 |
|---|---|---|---|---|---|---|---|---|---|---|---|---|---|---|---|---|
| USC | 1 | 1 | 1 | 1 | 1 | 1 | 1 | 1 | 1 | 1 | 1 | 1 | 1 | 1 | 1 | 1 |
| Oklahoma | 2 | 2 | 2 | 2 | 2 | 2 | 2 | 2 | 2 | 2 | 2 | 2 | 2 | 2 | 2 | 3 |
| Georgia | 3 | 3 | 3 | 3 | 3 | 3 | 12 | 10 | 10 | 8 | 8 | 11 | 8 | 8 | 8 | 7 |
| LSU | 4 | 6 | 5 | 13 | 13 | 24 | 20 | 18 | 19 | 17 | 17 | 14 | 14 | 13 | 12 | 16 |
| Florida St. | 5 | 4 | 8 | 8 | 9 | 8 | 7 | 5 | 5 | 13 | 11 | 10 | 19 | 16 | 17 | 15 |
| Miami-FL | 6 | 5 | 4 | 4 | 4 | 4 | 3 | 4 | 4 | 11 | 18 | 12 | 9 | 9 | 14 | 11 |
| Texas | 7 | 7 | 6 | 5 | 5 | 5 | 9 | 8 | 8 | 6 | 6 | 6 | 6 | 6 | 6 | 5 |
| Michigan | 8 | 8 | 17 | 18 | 19 | 14 | 14 | 13 | 12 | 10 | 9 | 7 | 13 | 14 | 13 | 14 |
| Ohio St. | 9 | 9 | 9 | 7 | 7 | 18 | 25 | - | - | - | - | - | - | 25 | 24 | 20 |
| West Virginia | 10 | 10 | 7 | 6 | 6 | 16 | 17 | 15 | 15 | 15 | 13 | 21 | 21 | - | - | - |
| Florida | 11 | 11 | 11 | 16 | 16 | 12 | 22 | 20 | - | - | - | - | 25 | 20 | 20 | - |
| Kansas St. | 12 | 13 | - | - | - | - | - | - | - | - | - | - | - | - | - | - |
| California | 13 | 12 | 10 | 10 | 10 | 7 | 8 | 7 | 7 | 4 | 5 | 4 | 4 | 4 | 4 | 9 |
| Tennessee | 14 | 14 | 13 | 11 | 10 | 17 | 13 | 11 | 11 | 9 | 15 | 15 | 15 | 15 | 15 | 13 |
| Clemson | 15 | 20 | - | - | - | - | - | - | - | - | - | - | - | - | - | - |
| Virginia | 16 | 15 | 12 | 12 | 12 | 10 | 6 | 14 | 13 | 12 | 10 | 18 | 16 | 18 | 18 | 23 |
| Auburn | 17 | 18 | 14 | 9 | 8 | 6 | 4 | 3 | 3 | 3 | 3 | 2 | 3 | 3 | 3 | 2 |
| Missouri | 18 | 19 | - | - | - | - | - | - | - | - | - | - | - | - | - | - |
| Iowa | 19 | 16 | 16 | - | - | - | 25 | 23 | - | 19 | 17 | 12 | 12 | 11 | 11 | 8 |
| Utah | 20 | 17 | 15 | 14 | 14 | 11 | 11 | 9 | 9 | 7 | 7 | 5 | 5 | 5 | 5 | 4 |
| Wisconsin | 21 | 21 | 20 | 20 | 20 | 15 | 10 | 6 | 6 | 5 | 4 | 9 | 20 | 17 | 16 | 17 |
| Maryland | 22 | 23 | 21 | 23 | 24 | 23 | - | - | - | - | - | - | - | - | - | - |
| Oregon | 23 | 24 | - | - | - | - | - | - | - | - | - | - | - | - | - | - |
| Purdue | 24 | 25 | 18 | 15 | 15 | 9 | 5 | 12 | 17 | - | - | - | - | - | - | - |
| Minnesota | 25 | 22 | 22 | 19 | 18 | 13 | 19 | - | 24 | - | - | - | - | - | - | - |
| Fresno St. | - | - | 19 | 17 | 17 | - | - | - | - | - | - | - | - | - | - | 22 |
| Boise St. | - | - | 23 | 21 | 23 | 21 | 21 | 19 | 18 | 16 | 14 | 13 | 10 | 11 | 10 | 12 |
| Louisville | - | - | 24 | 24 | 22 | 20 | 18 | 15 | 14 | 14 | 12 | 8 | 7 | 7 | 7 | 6 |
| Memphis | - | - | 25 | - | - | - | - | - | - | - | - | - | - | - | - | - |
| Arizona St. | - | - | - | 22 | 21 | 19 | 15 | 21 | 20 | 23 | 20 | 20 | 18 | 21 | 21 | 19 |
| Oklahoma St. | - | - | - | 25 | 25 | 22 | 16 | 22 | 20 | 19 | 25 | 23 | 23 | - | - | - |
| South Carolina | - | - | - | - | 25 | - | - | - | - | - | - | - | - | - | - | - |
| Texas A&M | - | - | - | - | - | - | 23 | 17 | 16 | 22 | 22 | 22 | 22 | 22 | 22 | - |
| Southern Miss. | - | - | - | - | - | 24 | - | 25 | 21 | - | - | - | - | - | - | - |
| Virginia Tech | - | - | - | - | - | - | - | 23 | 22 | 18 | 16 | 15 | 11 | 10 | 9 | 10 |
| Notre Dame | - | - | - | - | - | - | - | 24 | - | 24 | - | - | - | - | - | - |
| Boston College | - | - | - | - | - | - | - | - | - | 24 | 21 | 19 | 17 | 23 | 25 | 21 |
| UTEP | - | - | - | - | - | - | - | - | - | 25 | 23 | 24 | 24 | - | - | - |
| Bowling Green | - | - | - | - | - | - | - | - | - | - | 25 | - | - | - | - | - |
| Pittsburgh | - | - | - | - | - | - | - | - | - | - | - | - | - | 19 | 19 | 25 |
| Texas Tech | - | - | - | - | - | - | - | - | - | - | - | - | - | 24 | 23 | 18 |
| Navy | - | - | - | - | - | - | - | - | - | - | - | - | - | - | - | 24 |

*The USC Trojans became just the second team to go wire-to-wire as the nation's No. 1 team since the AP started a preseason poll in 1950. Can you name the other?*

Answer: 1999 Florida State Seminoles

# NCAA Division I-A Final Standings

Standings based on conference games only; overall records include postseason games.

## Atlantic Coast Conference

| | Conference | | | | Overall | | | |
|---|---|---|---|---|---|---|---|---|
| | W | L | PF | PA | W | L | PF | PA |
| *Virginia Tech | ....7 | 1 | 230 | 114 | 10 | 3 | 400 | 167 |
| *Florida St. | ......6 | 2 | 208 | 111 | 9 | 3 | 302 | 169 |
| *Miami-FL | .......5 | 3 | 226 | 143 | 9 | 3 | 380 | 204 |
| *Virginia | ........5 | 3 | 203 | 151 | 8 | 4 | 363 | 212 |
| *North Carolina | ..5 | 3 | 230 | 227 | 6 | 6 | 214 | 382 |
| *Georgia Tech | ...4 | 4 | 142 | 177 | 7 | 5 | 264 | 227 |
| Clemson | ......4 | 4 | 166 | 189 | 6 | 5 | 236 | 259 |
| Maryland | .....3 | 5 | 111 | 159 | 5 | 6 | 195 | 220 |
| N.C. State | .....3 | 5 | 156 | 182 | 5 | 6 | 264 | 218 |
| Wake Forest | ....1 | 7 | 140 | 219 | 4 | 7 | 230 | 253 |
| Duke | .........1 | 7 | 123 | 263 | 2 | 9 | 183 | 322 |

**Bowls (3-3):** Virginia Tech (lost Sugar); Florida St. (won Gator); Miami-FL (won Peach); Virginia (lost MPC Computers); North Carolina (lost Continental Tire); Georgia Tech (won Champs Sports).

## Big East Conference

| | Conference | | | | Overall | | | |
|---|---|---|---|---|---|---|---|---|
| | W | L | PF | PA | W | L | PF | PA |
| *Pittsburgh | ......4 | 2 | 152 | 136 | 8 | 4 | 325 | 288 |
| *Boston College | ..4 | 2 | 152 | 114 | 9 | 3 | 296 | 203 |
| *West Virginia | ...4 | 2 | 165 | 128 | 8 | 4 | 361 | 246 |
| *Syracuse | .....4 | 2 | 194 | 170 | 6 | 6 | 287 | 344 |
| *Connecticut | .....3 | 3 | 171 | 183 | 8 | 4 | 363 | 260 |
| Rutgers | .......1 | 5 | 139 | 185 | 4 | 7 | 269 | 343 |
| Temple | ........1 | 5 | 131 | 188 | 2 | 9 | 238 | 399 |

**Bowls (2-3):** Pittsburgh (lost Fiesta); Boston College (won Continental Tire); West Virginia (lost Gator); Syracuse (lost Champs Sports); Connecticut (won Motor City).

## Big Ten Conference

| | Conference | | | | Overall | | | |
|---|---|---|---|---|---|---|---|---|
| | W | L | PF | PA | W | L | PF | PA |
| *Iowa | .........7 | 1 | 199 | 125 | 10 | 2 | 292 | 211 |
| *Michigan | ......7 | 1 | 246 | 182 | 9 | 3 | 370 | 279 |
| *Wisconsin | .....6 | 2 | 167 | 145 | 9 | 3 | 249 | 185 |
| Northwestern | ....5 | 3 | 168 | 198 | 6 | 6 | 295 | 342 |
| *Ohio St. | .......4 | 4 | 184 | 171 | 8 | 4 | 290 | 219 |
| *Purdue | ........4 | 4 | 207 | 156 | 7 | 5 | 381 | 206 |
| Michigan St. | ....4 | 4 | 184 | 171 | 5 | 7 | 353 | 326 |
| *Minnesota | .....3 | 5 | 207 | 199 | 7 | 5 | 361 | 273 |
| Penn St. | ........2 | 6 | 103 | 124 | 4 | 7 | 195 | 168 |
| Indiana | .........1 | 7 | 159 | 258 | 3 | 8 | 262 | 343 |
| Illinois | .........1 | 7 | 141 | 248 | 3 | 8 | 240 | 323 |

**Bowls (3-3):** Iowa (won Capital One); Michigan (lost Rose); Wisconsin (lost Outback); Ohio St. (won Alamo); Purdue (lost Sun); Minnesota (won Music City).

---

### I-A Independents

| | W | L | PF | PA |
|---|---|---|---|---|
| *Navy | ..................10 | 2 | 334 | 238 |
| *Notre Dame | ...............6 | 6 | 289 | 289 |

**Bowls (1-1):** Navy (won Emerald); Notre Dame (lost Insight).

---

## Big 12 Conference

| | Conference | | | | Overall | | | |
|---|---|---|---|---|---|---|---|---|
| North | W | L | PF | PA | W | L | PF | PA |
| *Colorado | ....4 | 4 | 169 | 205 | 8 | 5 | 304 | 332 |
| *Iowa St. | .......4 | 4 | 148 | 188 | 7 | 5 | 246 | 259 |
| Nebraska | ......3 | 5 | 178 | 243 | 5 | 6 | 275 | 298 |
| Missouri | .......3 | 5 | 142 | 171 | 5 | 6 | 256 | 215 |
| Kansas | ........2 | 6 | 161 | 198 | 4 | 7 | 262 | 235 |
| Kansas St. | ......2 | 6 | 238 | 259 | 4 | 7 | 326 | 337 |

| | Conference | | | | Overall | | | |
|---|---|---|---|---|---|---|---|---|
| South | W | L | PF | PA | W | L | PF | PA |
| *Oklahoma | .......8 | 0 | 257 | 117 | 12 | 1 | 452 | 219 |
| *Texas | ........7 | 1 | 263 | 145 | 11 | 1 | 423 | 215 |
| *Texas A&M | .....5 | 3 | 255 | 207 | 7 | 5 | 341 | 292 |
| *Texas Tech | ......5 | 3 | 258 | 208 | 8 | 4 | 434 | 314 |
| *Oklahoma St. | ...4 | 4 | 252 | 220 | 7 | 5 | 387 | 301 |
| Baylor | .........1 | 7 | 149 | 319 | 3 | 8 | 224 | 396 |

**Big 12 championship game:** Oklahoma 42, Colorado 3 (Dec. 4, 2004).

**Bowls (4-3):** Oklahoma (lost Orange); Texas (won Rose); Texas A&M (lost Cotton); Texas Tech (won Holiday); Oklahoma St. (lost Alamo); Colorado (won Houston); Iowa St. (won Independence).

## Conference USA

| | Conference | | | | Overall | | | |
|---|---|---|---|---|---|---|---|---|
| | W | L | PF | PA | W | L | PF | PA |
| *Louisville | .......8 | 0 | 453 | 155 | 11 | 1 | 597 | 236 |
| *Memphis | .......5 | 3 | 276 | 254 | 8 | 4 | 430 | 375 |
| *UAB | ...........5 | 3 | 241 | 231 | 7 | 5 | 372 | 351 |
| *Southern Miss | ...5 | 3 | 238 | 218 | 7 | 5 | 309 | 308 |
| *Cincinnati | ......5 | 3 | 254 | 244 | 7 | 5 | 344 | 320 |
| Tulane | ........3 | 5 | 204 | 294 | 5 | 6 | 300 | 361 |
| TCU | ...........3 | 5 | 235 | 258 | 5 | 6 | 362 | 373 |
| South Florida | ...3 | 5 | 233 | 265 | 4 | 6 | 257 | 308 |
| Houston | .......3 | 5 | 197 | 243 | 3 | 8 | 230 | 354 |
| East Carolina | ...2 | 6 | 177 | 300 | 2 | 9 | 231 | 439 |
| Army | ..........2 | 6 | 222 | 275 | 2 | 9 | 260 | 388 |

**Bowls (3-2):** Louisville (won Liberty); UAB (lost Hawaii); Southern Miss (won New Orleans); Cincinnati (won Fort Worth); Memphis (lost GMAC).

## Mid-American Conference

| | Conference | | | | Overall | | | |
|---|---|---|---|---|---|---|---|---|
| East | W | L | PF | PA | W | L | PF | PA |
| *Miami-OH | ......7 | 1 | 282 | 158 | 8 | 5 | 407 | 298 |
| Akron | ..........6 | 2 | 237 | 217 | 6 | 5 | 271 | 347 |
| *Marshall | .......6 | 2 | 238 | 180 | 6 | 6 | 291 | 266 |
| Kent St. | ........4 | 4 | 269 | 186 | 5 | 6 | 335 | 264 |
| Ohio | ..........2 | 6 | 148 | 217 | 4 | 7 | 221 | 271 |
| Buffalo | ........2 | 6 | 167 | 247 | 2 | 9 | 197 | 351 |
| Central Florida | ..0 | 8 | 136 | 246 | 0 | 11 | 175 | 362 |

| | Conference | | | | Overall | | | |
|---|---|---|---|---|---|---|---|---|
| West | W | L | PF | PA | W | L | PF | PA |
| *Toledo | ........7 | 1 | 307 | 195 | 9 | 4 | 432 | 404 |
| *Northern Illinois | .7 | 1 | 303 | 180 | 9 | 3 | 421 | 304 |
| *Bowling Green | ..6 | 2 | 337 | 180 | 9 | 3 | 532 | 282 |
| Eastern Michigan | .4 | 4 | 249 | 333 | 4 | 7 | 328 | 458 |
| Central Michigan | .3 | 5 | 199 | 286 | 4 | 7 | 260 | 378 |
| Ball St. | ........2 | 6 | 207 | 279 | 2 | 9 | 225 | 405 |
| Western Michigan | 0 | 8 | 179 | 343 | 1 | 10 | 248 | 456 |

**MAC championship game:** Toledo 35, Miami-OH 27 (Dec. 2, 2004).

**Bowls (2-3):** Miami-OH (lost Independence); Northern Illinois (won Silicon Valley); Marshall (lost Fort Worth); Toledo (lost Motor City); Bowling Green (won GMAC).

## Mountain West Conference

| | Conference | | | | Overall | | |
|---|---|---|---|---|---|---|---|
| | W | L | PF | PA | W | L | PF | PA |
| *Utah | 7 | 0 | 351 | 178 | 12 | 0 | 544 | 234 |
| *New Mexico | 5 | 2 | 136 | 125 | 7 | 5 | 244 | 224 |
| BYU | 4 | 3 | 200 | 171 | 5 | 6 | 267 | 295 |
| *Wyoming | 3 | 4 | 173 | 196 | 7 | 5 | 315 | 297 |
| Air Force | 3 | 4 | 218 | 220 | 5 | 6 | 326 | 342 |
| Colorado State | 3 | 4 | 182 | 201 | 4 | 7 | 261 | 325 |
| San Diego St. | 2 | 5 | 138 | 194 | 4 | 7 | 234 | 282 |
| UNLV | 1 | 6 | 140 | 253 | 2 | 9 | 229 | 357 |

**Bowls (2-1):** Utah (won Fiesta); New Mexico (lost Emerald); Wyoming (won Las Vegas).

## Pacific-10 Conference

| | Conference | | | | Overall | | |
|---|---|---|---|---|---|---|---|
| | W | L | PF | PA | W | L | PF | PA |
| *USC | 8 | 0 | 285 | 117 | 13 | 0 | 496 | 169 |
| *California | 7 | 1 | 287 | 103 | 10 | 2 | 441 | 192 |
| *Arizona St. | 5 | 3 | 216 | 234 | 9 | 3 | 358 | 294 |
| *Oregon St. | 5 | 3 | 210 | 191 | 7 | 5 | 320 | 294 |
| *UCLA | 4 | 4 | 252 | 227 | 6 | 6 | 361 | 309 |
| Oregon | 4 | 4 | 203 | 211 | 5 | 6 | 282 | 282 |
| Washington St. | 3 | 5 | 193 | 262 | 5 | 6 | 273 | 307 |
| Stanford | 2 | 6 | 147 | 197 | 4 | 7 | 242 | 233 |
| Arizona | 2 | 6 | 130 | 240 | 3 | 8 | 164 | 275 |
| Washington | 0 | 8 | 114 | 255 | 1 | 10 | 154 | 334 |

**Bowls (3-2):** USC (won Orange); California (lost Holiday); Arizona St. (won Sun); Oregon St. (won Insight); UCLA (lost Las Vegas).

## Sun Belt Conference

| | Conference | | | | Overall | | |
|---|---|---|---|---|---|---|---|
| | W | L | PF | PA | W | L | PF | PA |
| *North Texas | 7 | 0 | 251 | 153 | 7 | 5 | 309 | 358 |
| *Troy | 5 | 2 | 197 | 96 | 7 | 5 | 286 | 200 |
| New Mexico St | 4 | 3 | 187 | 182 | 6 | 5 | 273 | 355 |
| LA-Monroe | 4 | 3 | 153 | 172 | 5 | 6 | 211 | 303 |
| Middle Tenn. St. | 4 | 4 | 202 | 190 | 5 | 6 | 269 | 293 |
| Arkansas St. | 3 | 4 | 136 | 185 | 3 | 8 | 215 | 365 |
| LA-Lafayette | 2 | 5 | 145 | 167 | 4 | 7 | 242 | 272 |
| Utah St. | 2 | 5 | 124 | 181 | 3 | 8 | 184 | 333 |
| Idaho | 2 | 5 | 154 | 218 | 3 | 9 | 245 | 473 |

**Bowls (0-2):** North Texas (lost New Orleans); Troy (lost Silicon Valley).

## Southeastern Conference

| Eastern | Conference | | | | Overall | | |
|---|---|---|---|---|---|---|---|
| | W | L | PF | PA | W | L | PF | PA |
| *Tennessee | 7 | 1 | 215 | 199 | 10 | 3 | 378 | 295 |
| *Georgia | 6 | 2 | 231 | 133 | 10 | 2 | 335 | 198 |
| *Florida | 4 | 4 | 251 | 187 | 7 | 5 | 382 | 253 |
| South Carolina | 4 | 4 | 185 | 190 | 6 | 5 | 243 | 229 |
| Kentucky | 1 | 7 | 106 | 253 | 2 | 9 | 173 | 341 |
| Vanderbilt | 1 | 7 | 133 | 213 | 2 | 9 | 212 | 286 |

| Western | Conference | | | | Overall | | |
|---|---|---|---|---|---|---|---|
| | W | L | PF | PA | W | L | PF | PA |
| *Auburn | 8 | 0 | 247 | 96 | 13 | 0 | 417 | 147 |
| *LSU | 6 | 2 | 220 | 131 | 9 | 3 | 344 | 205 |
| Arkansas | 3 | 5 | 196 | 215 | 5 | 6 | 328 | 270 |
| *Alabama | 3 | 5 | 152 | 149 | 6 | 6 | 295 | 189 |
| Mississippi | 3 | 5 | 142 | 200 | 4 | 7 | 215 | 278 |
| Mississippi St. | 2 | 6 | 125 | 237 | 3 | 8 | 173 | 280 |

**SEC championship game:** Auburn 38, Tennessee 28 (Dec. 4, 2004).

**Bowls (3-3):** Auburn (won Sugar); Tennessee (won Cotton); Georgia (won Outback); LSU (lost Capital One); Alabama (lost Music City); Florida (lost Peach).

**Note:** Mississippi St. was not eligible for the the SEC title.

## Western Athletic Conference

| | Conference | | | | Overall | | |
|---|---|---|---|---|---|---|---|
| | W | L | PF | PA | W | L | PF | PA |
| *Boise St. | 8 | 0 | 401 | 196 | 11 | 1 | 587 | 308 |
| *UTEP | 6 | 2 | 315 | 227 | 8 | 4 | 429 | 301 |
| *Fresno St. | 5 | 3 | 338 | 165 | 9 | 3 | 482 | 253 |
| La. Tech | 5 | 3 | 260 | 220 | 6 | 6 | 308 | 382 |
| *Hawaii | 4 | 4 | 238 | 324 | 8 | 5 | 467 | 499 |
| Nevada | 3 | 5 | 236 | 318 | 5 | 7 | 356 | 413 |
| Tulsa | 3 | 5 | 272 | 303 | 4 | 8 | 345 | 398 |
| SMU | 3 | 5 | 182 | 290 | 3 | 8 | 202 | 420 |
| Rice | 2 | 6 | 243 | 321 | 3 | 8 | 279 | 377 |
| San Jose St. | 1 | 7 | 256 | 377 | 2 | 9 | 312 | 469 |

**Bowls (2-2):** Boise St. (lost Liberty); UTEP (lost Houston); Fresno St. (won MPC Computers); Hawaii (won Hawaii).

## NCAA Division I-A individual Leaders

### Total Offense

| | | Rushing | | | | Passing | | Total Offense | | | |
|---|---|---|---|---|---|---|---|---|---|---|---|
| | Cl | Car | Gain | Loss | Net | Att | Yds | Plays | Yds | YdsPP | YdsPG |
| Sonny Cumbie, Texas Tech | Sr. | 52 | 49 | 216 | -167 | 642 | 4742 | 694 | 4575 | 6.59 | 381.3 |
| Omar Jacobs, Bowling Green | So. | 95 | 415 | 115 | 300 | 462 | 4002 | 557 | 4302 | 7.72 | 358.5 |
| Timmy Chang, Hawaii | Sr. | 37 | 123 | 108 | 15 | 602 | 4258 | 639 | 4273 | 6.69 | 328.7 |
| Joshua Cribbs, Kent St. | Sr. | 170 | 1151 | 258 | 893 | 335 | 2215 | 505 | 3108 | 6.15 | 310.8 |
| Alex Smith, Utah | Jr. | 135 | 774 | 143 | 631 | 317 | 2952 | 452 | 3583 | 7.93 | 298.6 |
| Matt Bohnet, Eastern Mich. | Jr. | 100 | 562 | 138 | 424 | 434 | 2807 | 534 | 3231 | 6.05 | 293.7 |
| Reggie McNeal, Texas A&M | Jr. | 151 | 932 | 214 | 718 | 344 | 2791 | 495 | 3509 | 7.09 | 292.4 |
| Kyle Orton, Purdue | Sr. | 80 | 284 | 172 | 112 | 389 | 3090 | 469 | 3202 | 6.83 | 291.1 |
| Derek Anderson, Oregon St. | Sr. | 75 | 147 | 299 | -152 | 515 | 3615 | 590 | 3463 | 5.87 | 288.6 |

### All-Purpose Yards

| | Cl | Gm | Rush | Rec | PR | KOR | Total Yds | YdsPG |
|---|---|---|---|---|---|---|---|---|
| Darren Sproles, Kansas St. | Sr. | 11 | 1318 | 223 | 34 | 492 | 2067 | 187.91 |
| DeAngelo Williams, Memphis | Jr. | 12 | 1948 | 210 | 0 | 72 | 2230 | 185.83 |
| Gattett Wolfe, Northern Illinois | So. | 11 | 1656 | 117 | 0 | 231 | 2004 | 182.18 |
| Jamario Thomas, North Texas | Fr. | 10 | 1801 | 14 | 0 | 0 | 1815 | 181.50 |
| Reggie Bush, USC | So. | 13 | 908 | 509 | 376 | 537 | 2330 | 179.23 |
| J.J. Arrington, California | Sr. | 12 | 2018 | 121 | 0 | 0 | 2139 | 178.25 |
| Cedric Benson, Texas | Sr. | 12 | 1834 | 179 | 0 | 0 | 2013 | 167.75 |
| Andre Hall, South Florida | Jr. | 11 | 1357 | 149 | 0 | 332 | 1838 | 167.09 |
| Jerry Seymour, Central Michigan | So. | 11 | 1284 | 413 | 0 | 105 | 1802 | 163.82 |

Louisville
**Stefan Lefors**
Passing Efficiency

Marshall
**Jonathan Goddard**
Sacks

North Texas
**Jamario Thomas**
Rushing

Ball St.
**Dante Ridgeway**
Receptions

## Passing Efficiency
(Minimum 15 attempts per game)

| | Cl | Gm | Att | Cmp | Cmp Pct | Int | Int Pct | Yds | Yds/Att | TD | TD Pct | Rating Points |
|---|---|---|---|---|---|---|---|---|---|---|---|---|
| Stefan Lefors, Louisville | Sr. | 12 | 257 | 189 | 73.54 | 3 | 1.17 | 2596 | 10.10 | 20 | 7.78 | 181.7 |
| Alex Smith, Utah | Jr. | 12 | 317 | 214 | 67.51 | 4 | 1.26 | 2952 | 9.31 | 32 | 10.09 | 176.5 |
| Jason Campbell, Auburn | Sr. | 13 | 270 | 188 | 69.63 | 7 | 2.59 | 2700 | 10.00 | 20 | 7.41 | 172.9 |
| Omar Jacobs, Bowling Green | So. | 12 | 462 | 309 | 66.88 | 4 | 0.87 | 4002 | 8.66 | 41 | 8.87 | 167.2 |
| Bruce Gradkowski, Toldeo | Jr. | 13 | 399 | 280 | 70.18 | 8 | 2.01 | 3518 | 8.82 | 27 | 6.77 | 162.6 |
| Jason White, Oklahoma | Sr. | 13 | 390 | 255 | 65.38 | 9 | 2.31 | 3205 | 8.22 | 35 | 8.97 | 159.4 |
| Matt Leinart, USC | Jr. | 13 | 412 | 269 | 65.29 | 6 | 1.46 | 3322 | 8.06 | 33 | 8.01 | 156.5 |
| Aaron Rodgers, California | Jr. | 12 | 316 | 209 | 66.14 | 8 | 2.53 | 2566 | 8.12 | 24 | 7.59 | 154.3 |
| Lester Ricard, Tulane | So. | 9 | 231 | 143 | 61.90 | 9 | 3.90 | 1881 | 8.14 | 21 | 9.09 | 152.5 |
| Kyle Orton, Purdue | Sr. | 11 | 389 | 236 | 60.67 | 5 | 1.29 | 3090 | 7.94 | 31 | 7.97 | 151.1 |
| Buck Pierce, New Mexico St. | Sr. | 11 | 285 | 191 | 67.02 | 5 | 1.75 | 2253 | 7.91 | 16 | 5.61 | 148.4 |
| David Greene, Georgia | Sr. | 12 | 299 | 175 | 58.53 | 4 | 1.34 | 2508 | 8.39 | 20 | 6.69 | 148.4 |
| Jared Zabransky, Boise St. | So. | 12 | 327 | 206 | 63.00 | 12 | 3.67 | 2927 | 8.95 | 16 | 4.89 | 147.0 |
| Darrell Hackney, UAB | Jr. | 12 | 358 | 197 | 55.03 | 8 | 2.23 | 3070 | 8.58 | 26 | 7.26 | 146.6 |

## Rushing

| | Cl | Car | Yds | TD | YdsPG |
|---|---|---|---|---|---|
| Jamario Thomas, N. Texas | Fr. | 285 | 1801 | 17 | 180.10 |
| J.J. Arrington, California | Sr. | 289 | 2018 | 15 | 167.17 |
| DeAngelo Williams, Memphis | Jr. | 313 | 1948 | 22 | 162.33 |
| Cedric Benson, Texas | Sr. | | | | |
| Garrett Wolfe, No. Illinois | So. | 256 | 1656 | 18 | 150.55 |
| Adrian Peterson, Oklahoma | Fr. | 339 | 1925 | 15 | 148.08 |
| Ryan Moats, La. Tech | Jr. | 288 | 1774 | 18 | 147.83 |
| Vernand Morency, Okla St. | Jr. | 258 | 1474 | 12 | 134.00 |
| Andre Hall, South Fla. | Jr. | 210 | 1357 | 11 | 123.36 |
| Michael Hart, Michigan | Fr. | 282 | 1455 | 9 | 121.25 |

**Games:** All played 12, except Thomas (10), Wolfe, Morency, Hall (11) and Peterson (13).

## Field Goals

| | Cl | FG/Att | Pct | P/Gm |
|---|---|---|---|---|
| Mike Nugent, Ohio St. | Sr. | 24/27 | .889 | 2.00 |
| Tyler Jones, Boise St. | Sr. | 24/27 | .889 | 2.00 |
| Andrew Wellock, E. Michigan | So. | 21/23 | .913 | 1.91 |
| David Rayner, Michigan St. | Sr. | 22/31 | .710 | 1.83 |
| Jonathan Nichols, Mississippi | Sr. | 20/27 | .741 | 1.82 |
| Mason Crosby, Colorado | So. | 23/29 | .793 | 1.77 |
| Kyle Schlicher, Iowa | So. | 21/26 | .808 | 1.75 |
| Matt Nuzie, Connecticut | Jr. | 20/28 | .714 | 1.67 |
| Stephen Gostkowski, Memphis | So. | 20/24 | .833 | 1.67 |
| Brandon Pace, Va. Tech | So. | 21/27 | .778 | 1.62 |

**Games:** All played 12, except Wellock, Nichols (11), Crosby and Pace (13).

## Receptions

| | Cl | No | Yds | TD | P/Gm |
|---|---|---|---|---|---|
| Dante Ridgeway, Ball St. | Jr. | 105 | 1399 | 8 | 9.55 |
| Braylon Edwards, Michigan | Sr. | 97 | 1330 | 15 | 8.08 |
| Bobby Bernal-Wood, Idaho | Sr. | 96 | 938 | 3 | 8.00 |
| Chad Owens, Hawaii | Sr. | 102 | 1290 | 17 | 7.85 |
| Eric Deslauriers, E. Mich. | Jr. | 84 | 1257 | 13 | 7.64 |
| | Sr. | 91 | 1126 | 6 | 7.58 |
| Nichiren Flowers, Nevada | Jr. | 71 | | | |
| Taylor Stubblefield, Purdue | Sr. | 89 | 1095 | 16 | 7.42 |
| Tres Moses, Rutgers | Sr. | 81 | 1056 | 5 | 7.36 |
| Josh Davis, Marshall | Sr. | 86 | 914 | 7 | 7.17 |
| Mike Hass, Oregon St. | Jr. | 86 | 1379 | 7 | 7.17 |

**Games:** All played 12, except Ridgeway, Deslauriers, Moses (11) and Owens (13).

## Interceptions

| | Cl | No | Yds | TD | P/Gm |
|---|---|---|---|---|---|
| Chris Harris, La-Monroe | Sr. | 7 | 11 | 0 | 0.64 |
| Charles Gordon, Kansas | So. | 7 | 52 | 0 | 0.64 |
| Ko Simpson, South Carolina | Fr. | 6 | 94 | 1 | 0.55 |
| Brandon Payne, N. Mexico | Sr. | 6 | 69 | 0 | 0.50 |
| Morgan Scalley, Utah | Sr. | 6 | 79 | 0 | 0.50 |
| Kerry Rhodes, Louisville | Sr. | 6 | 56 | 1 | 0.50 |
| Ray Henderson, Boston Coll. | Jr. | 6 | 52 | 0 | 0.50 |
| Keon Newson, Bowl. Green | Sr. | 6 | 107 | 2 | 0.50 |
| Mitch Meeuwsen, Oregon St. | Sr. | 6 | 12 | 0 | 0.50 |
| Chris Royal, Marshall | Jr. | 6 | 103 | 1 | 0.50 |

**Games:** All played 12, except Harris, Gordon and Simpson (11).

## Scoring

### Non-Kickers

| | Cl | TD | Pts | P/Gm |
|---|---|---|---|---|
| DeAngelo Williams, Memphis | Jr. | 23 | 138 | 11.50 |
| Garrett Wolfe, Northern Ill. | So. | 21 | 126 | 11.45 |
| P.J. Pope, Bowling Green | Jr. | 21 | 126 | 10.50 |
| Jamario Thomas, North Texas | Fr. | 17 | 102 | 10.20 |
| Chad Owens, Hawaii | Sr. | 22 | 132 | 10.15 |
| Eric Shelton, Louisville | Jr. | 20 | 120 | 10.00 |
| Cedric Benson, Texas | Sr. | 20 | 120 | 10.00 |
| Ryan Moats, La. Tech | Jr. | 19 | 114 | 9.50 |
| Carlton Jones, Army | Jr. | 17 | 104 | 9.45 |
| Taurean Henderson, Tex. Tech | Jr. | 18 | 108 | 9.00 |
| Steve Savoy, Utah | So. | 17 | 102 | 8.50 |
| Wali Lundy, Virginia | Jr. | 17 | 102 | 8.50 |

**Games:** All played 12, except Wolfe, Jones (11), Thomas (10) and Owens (13).

### Kickers

| | FG/Att | PAT/Att | Pts | P/Gm |
|---|---|---|---|---|
| Tyler Jones, Boise St. | 24/27 | 69/70 | 141 | 11.75 |
| Arthur Carmody, Louisville | 12/15 | 77/77 | 113 | 9.42 |
| Shaun Suisham, B. Green | 14/20 | 69/69 | 111 | 9.25 |
| Stephen Gostkowski, Mem. | 20/24 | 48/49 | 108 | 9.00 |
| David Rayner, Mich. St. | 22/31 | 39/39 | 105 | 8.75 |
| Andrew Wellock, E. Mich. | 21/23 | 32/33 | 95 | 8.64 |
| Ryan Killeen, USC | 16/25 | 64/64 | 112 | 8.62 |
| Mike Nugent, Ohio St. | 24/27 | 30/30 | 102 | 8.50 |
| Chris Nendick, N. Illinois | 16/21 | 51/52 | 99 | 8.25 |
| Brandon Pace, Va. Tech | 21/27 | 43/44 | 106 | 8.15 |
| Matt Nuzie, Connecticut | 20/28 | 37/42 | 97 | 8.08 |
| Reagan Schneider, UTEP | 15/20 | 52/53 | 97 | 8.08 |

**Games:** All played 12, Wellock (11), Killeen and Pace (13).

### Sacks

| | Cl | No | Yds | P/Gm |
|---|---|---|---|---|
| Jonathan Goddard, Marshall | Sr. | 16 | 113 | 1.33 |
| Justin Parrish, Kent St. | Jr. | 14 | 86 | 1.27 |
| Ryan Riddle, California | Sr. | 14½ | 122 | 1.21 |

## Punting

(Minimum of 3.6 per game)

| | Cl | No | Yds | Avg |
|---|---|---|---|---|
| Brandon Fields, Michigan St. | Jr. | 50 | 2394 | 47.88 |
| John Torp, Colorado | Jr. | 72 | 3351 | 46.54 |
| Daniel Sepulveda, Baylor | So. | 62 | 2850 | 45.97 |
| Steve Weatherford, Illinois | Jr. | 57 | 2589 | 45.42 |
| Matt Payne, BYU | Sr. | 62 | 2808 | 45.29 |
| Joel Stelly, La-Monroe | Jr. | 62 | 2796 | 45.10 |
| Bryce Benekos, UTEP | Sr. | 62 | 2734 | 44.06 |
| Ryan Plackemeier, Wake Forest | Jr. | 64 | 2809 | 43.89 |
| Tom Malone, USC | Jr. | 49 | 2144 | 43.76 |

## Punt Returns

(Minimum of 1.2 per game)

| | Cl | No | Yds | TD | Avg |
|---|---|---|---|---|---|
| Ted Ginn Jr., Ohio St. | Fr. | 15 | 384 | 4 | 25.60 |
| Kevin Robinson, Utah St. | Fr. | 17 | 382 | 2 | 22.47 |
| Darrell Blackmon, N.C. State | Fr. | 12 | 214 | 1 | 17.83 |
| Travis Williams, E. Carolina | Fr. | 20 | 354 | 1 | 17.70 |
| Domenik Hixon, Akron | Jr. | 16 | 275 | 1 | 17.19 |
| Devin Hester, Miami-FL | Jr. | 20 | 324 | 2 | 16.20 |
| Dan Sheldon, N. Illinois | Sr. | 24 | 394 | 1 | 16.42 |
| Roscoe Parrish, Miami-FL | Jr. | 20 | 324 | 2 | 16.20 |
| Reggie Bush, USC | So. | 24 | 376 | 3 | 15.67 |

## Kickoff Returns

(Minimum of 1.2 per game)

| | Cl | No | Yds | TD | Avg |
|---|---|---|---|---|---|
| Justin Miller, Clemson | Jr. | 20 | 661 | 2 | 33.05 |
| Larry Taylor, Connecticut | Fr. | 12 | 376 | 1 | 31.33 |
| Ashlan Davis, Tulsa | Jr. | 37 | 1131 | 5 | 30.57 |
| Lance Bennett, Indiana | So. | 20 | 599 | 1 | 29.95 |
| John Eubanks, So. Miss. | Jr. | 21 | 618 | 1 | 29.43 |
| T.J. Rushing, Stanford | Jr. | 23 | 653 | 1 | 28.39 |
| Asante White, C. Michigan | Fr. | 12 | 336 | 0 | 28.00 |
| Will Blackmon, Boston Coll. | Jr. | 28 | 762 | 1 | 27.21 |
| Diamond Ferri, Syracuse | Sr. | 24 | 653 | 0 | 27.21 |

## NCAA Division I-A Team Leaders

### Scoring Offense

| | Gm | Record | Pts | Avg |
|---|---|---|---|---|
| Louisville | 12 | 11-1 | 597 | 49.75 |
| Boise St. | 12 | 11-1 | 587 | 48.92 |
| Utah | 12 | 12-0 | 544 | 45.33 |
| Bowling Green | 12 | 9-3 | 532 | 44.33 |
| Fresno St. | 12 | 9-3 | 482 | 40.17 |
| USC | 13 | 13-0 | 496 | 38.15 |
| California | 12 | 10-2 | 441 | 36.75 |
| Texas Tech | 12 | 8-4 | 434 | 36.17 |
| Hawaii | 13 | 8-5 | 467 | 35.92 |
| Memphis | 12 | 8-4 | 430 | 35.83 |

### Scoring Defense

| | Gm | Record | Pts | Avg |
|---|---|---|---|---|
| Auburn | 13 | 13-0 | 147 | 11.3 |
| Virginia Tech | 13 | 10-3 | 167 | 12.8 |
| USC | 13 | 13-0 | 169 | 13.0 |
| Florida St. | 12 | 9-3 | 169 | 14.1 |
| Penn St. | 11 | 4-7 | 168 | 15.3 |
| Wisconsin | 12 | 9-3 | 185 | 15.4 |
| Alabama | 12 | 6-6 | 189 | 15.8 |
| California | 12 | 10-2 | 192 | 16.0 |
| Georgia | 12 | 10-2 | 198 | 16.5 |
| Troy | 12 | 7-5 | 200 | 16.7 |

### Total Offense

| | Gm | Plays | Yds | Avg | TD | YdsPG |
|---|---|---|---|---|---|---|
| Louisville | 12 | 893 | 6468 | 7.24 | 80 | 539.00 |
| Bowling Green | 12 | 904 | 6076 | 6.72 | 69 | 506.33 |
| Utah | 12 | 869 | 5997 | 6.90 | 75 | 499.75 |
| Boise St. | 12 | 951 | 5912 | 6.22 | 74 | 492.67 |
| California | 12 | 840 | 5909 | 7.03 | 59 | 492.42 |
| Texas Tech | 12 | 944 | 5900 | 6.25 | 59 | 491.67 |
| Texas | 12 | 890 | 5573 | 6.26 | 55 | 464.42 |
| Oklahoma | 13 | 971 | 6007 | 6.19 | 61 | 462.08 |
| Memphis | 12 | 903 | 5524 | 6.12 | 53 | 460.33 |
| Michigan St. | 12 | 899 | 5520 | 6.14 | 41 | 460.00 |

**Note:** Touchdowns scored by rushing and passing only.

### Total Defense

| | Gm | Plays | Yds | Avg | TD | YdsPG |
|---|---|---|---|---|---|---|
| N.C. State | 11 | 701 | 2435 | 3.47 | 23 | 221.36 |
| Alabama | 12 | 726 | 2946 | 4.06 | 23 | 245.50 |
| LSU | 12 | 743 | 3083 | 4.15 | 25 | 256.92 |
| Virginia Tech | 13 | 794 | 3484 | 4.39 | 18 | 268.00 |
| Auburn | 13 | 780 | 3609 | 4.63 | 19 | 277.62 |
| USC | 13 | 851 | 3631 | 4.27 | 20 | 279.31 |
| Florida St. | 12 | 798 | 6406 | 4.27 | 18 | 283.83 |
| Georgia | 12 | 747 | 3467 | 4.64 | 23 | 288.92 |
| Wisconsin | 12 | 756 | 3495 | 4.62 | 22 | 291.25 |
| Penn St. | 11 | 753 | 3207 | 4.26 | 18 | 291.55 |

**Note:** Opponents' TDs scored by rushing and passing only.

## Single Game Highs
### INDIVIDUAL

#### Rushing Yards

| Yds | |
|-----|---|
| 337 | Kay-Jay Harris, WVU vs. E. Carolina (Sept. 4) |
| 325 | Garrett Wolfe, No. Illinois vs. E. Mich. (Nov. 20) |
| 322 | Maurice Drew, UCLA vs. Washington (Sept. 18) |

#### Total Offense

| Yds | |
|-----|---|
| 548 | Brett Basanez, Northwestern vs. TCU (Sept. 2) |
| 530 | Kyle Orton, Purdue vs. Indiana (Nov. 20) |
| 514 | Sonny Cumbie, Texas Tech vs. California (Dec. 30) |

#### Passing Yards

| Yds | |
|-----|---|
| 522 | Kyle Orton, Purdue vs. Indiana (Nov. 20) |
| 520 | Sonny Cumbie, Texas Tech vs. California (Dec. 30) |
| 513 | Brett Basanez, Northwestern vs. TCU (Sept. 2) |

#### Passes Completed

| No | |
|----|---|
| 44 | Sonny Cumbie, Texas Tech vs. N. Mexico (Sept. 11) |
| 44 | Sonny Cumbie, Texas Tech vs. Nebraska (Oct. 9) |

#### Receptions

| No | |
|----|---|
| 15 | Paris Warren, Utah vs. Pittsburgh (Jan. 1) |
| 15 | Josh Davis, Marshall vs. Akron (Nov. 5) |
| 15 | Taylor Stubblefield, Purdue vs. Iowa (Nov. 6) |

#### Receiving Yards

| Yds | |
|-----|---|
| 293 | Mike Hass, Oregon St. vs. Boise St. (Sept. 10) |
| 283 | Chad Owens, Hawaii vs. Michigan St. (Dec. 4) |

#### Touchdowns

| No | |
|----|---|
| 5 | Seven players tied. |

### TEAM

#### Total Offense Yards Gained

| Yds | |
|-----|---|
| 763 | Purdue vs. Indiana (Nov. 20) |
| 704 | Minnesota vs. Toledo (Sept. 4) |

#### Total Defense Yards Allowed

| Yds | |
|-----|---|
| 46 | Oklahoma vs. Colorado (Dec. 4) |
| 82 | Georgia Tech vs. Maryland (Oct. 9) |

## Annual Awards

### Players of the Year

Matt Leinart, USC, QB . . . . . . . . . . . .AP, Camp, Heisman
Jason White, Oklahoma, QB . . . . . . . . . . . . . .Maxwell

Payton Award (I-AA) . . .Lang Campbell, Wm. & Mary, QB
Hill Trophy (Div. II) . . .Chad Friehauf, Colorado-Mines, QB
Gagliardi Trophy (Div. III) . . .Rocky Myers, Wesley (Del.), S

### Position Players of the Year

O'Brien Award (Quarterback) . . . .Jason White, Oklahoma
Walker Award (Running Back) . . . .Cedric Benson, Texas
Biletnikoff Award (Receiver) . . .Braylon Edwards, Michigan
Outland Trophy (Int. Lineman) . . .Jammal Brown, Oklahoma
Lombardi Award (Lineman) . . . . . .David Pollack, Georgia
Butkus Award (Linebacker) . . . . . .Derrick Johnson, Texas
Thorpe Award (Def. Back) . . . . . . .Carlos Rogers, Auburn
Nagurski Award (Def. Player) . . . . .Derrick Johnson, Texas
Bednarik Award (Def. Player) . . . . .David Pollack, Georgia
Groza Award (Kicker) . . . . . . . . .Mike Nugent, Ohio St.
Ray Guy Award (Punter) . . . . .Daniel Sepulveda, Baylor
Mackey Award (Tight End) . . . . . . .Heath Miller, Virginia

### Coaches of the Year

Tommy Tuberville, Auburn . . . . . . . . . . . .AFCA, AP, Camp
Urban Meyer, Utah . . . . . . . . . . . . . . . . . . . . . . . .FWAA
Paul Johnson, Navy . . . . . . . . . . . . . . . . . . . . . . . .Dodd

### Heisman Trophy Vote

Presented since 1935 by the Downtown Athletic Club of New York City and named after former college coach and DAC athletic director John W. Heisman. Voting done by national media and former Heisman winners. Each ballot allows for three names (points based on 3 for 1st, 2 for 2nd and 1 for 3rd).

#### Top 10 Vote-Getters

| | Pos | 1st | 2nd | 3rd | Pts |
|---|-----|-----|-----|-----|-----|
| Matt Leinart, USC | QB | 267 | 211 | 102 | 1325 |
| Adrian Peterson, Oklahoma | RB | 154 | 180 | 175 | 997 |
| Jason White, Oklahoma | QB | 171 | 149 | 146 | 957 |
| Alex Smith, Utah | QB | 98 | 112 | 117 | 635 |
| Reggie Bush, USC | RB | 118 | 80 | 83 | 597 |
| Cedric Benson, Texas | RB | 12 | 41 | 69 | 187 |
| Jason Campbell, Auburn | QB | 21 | 24 | 51 | 162 |
| J.J. Arrington, California | RB | 10 | 33 | 19 | 115 |
| Aaron Rodgers, California | QB | 8 | 14 | 15 | 67 |
| Braylon Edwards, Michigan | WR | 3 | 13 | 27 | 62 |

## Consensus All-America Team

NCAA Division I-A players cited most frequently by the following selectors: AFCA, AP, and Walter Camp Foundation. (*) indicates unanimous selection. Holdover from the 2003 team is in **bold** type.

### Offense

| | Player | Class | Ht | Wt |
|---|--------|-------|-----|-----|
| WR | Braylon Edwards*, Michigan . . . .Sr. | | 6-3 | 208 |
| WR | Taylor Stubblefield, Purdue . . . . .Sr. | | 6-1 | 182 |
| TE | Heath Miller*, Virginia . . . . . . . . .Jr. | | 6-5 | 255 |
| C | Ben Wilkerson, LSU . . . . . . . . . . .Sr. | | 6-4 | 297 |
| OL | Jammal Brown*, Oklahoma . . . . . .Sr. | | 6-6 | 313 |
| OL | Michael Munoz, Tennessee . . . . . .Sr. | | 6-6 | 315 |
| OL | **Alex Barron***, Florida St. . . . .Sr. | | 6-6 | 308 |
| OL | Elton Brown*, Virginia . . . . . . . . .Sr. | | 6-6 | 338 |
| QB | Matt Leinart*, USC . . . . . . . . . . .Jr. | | 6-5 | 225 |
| RB | Adrian Peterson*, Oklahoma . . . .Fr. | | 6-2 | 210 |
| RB | Carnell Williams, Auburn . . . . . . .Sr. | | 5-11 | 210 |
| K | Mike Nugent, Iowa . . . . . . . . . . .Sr. | | 5-10 | 180 |

### Defense

| | Player | Class | Ht | Wt |
|---|--------|-------|-----|-----|
| DL | Erasmus James*, Wisconsin . . . . .Sr. | | 6-4 | 263 |
| DL | David Pollack*, Georgia . . . . . . .Sr. | | 6-3 | 261 |
| DL | Shaun Cody, USC . . . . . . . . . . . . .Sr. | | 6-4 | 295 |
| DL | Marcus Spears*, LSU . . . . . . . . . .Sr. | | 6-4 | 298 |
| LB | Derrick Johnson*, Texas . . . . . . .Sr. | | 6-4 | 235 |
| LB | Matt Grootegoed*, USC . . . . . . .Sr. | | 5-11 | 215 |
| LB | A.J. Hawk, Ohio St. . . . . . . . . . . .Jr. | | 6-2 | 238 |
| DB | Thomas Davis, Georgia . . . . . . . . .Jr. | | 6-1 | 230 |
| DB | Marlin Jackson, Michigan . . . . . . .Sr. | | 6-1 | 196 |
| DB | Antrel Rolle*, Miami-FL . . . . . . . .Sr. | | 6-1 | 202 |
| DB | Carlos Rogers, Auburn . . . . . . . . .Sr. | | 6-1 | 194 |
| P | Brandon Fields, Michigan St. . . . .Jr. | | 6-6 | 235 |

## Underclassmen who declared for the 2005 draft

Forty-nine players forfeited the remainder of their college eligibility and declared for the NFL draft in 2005. NFL teams drafted 37 underclassmen. Players listed in alphabetical order; first round selections in **bold** type.

| | Pos | Drafted by | Overall Pick |
|---|---|---|---|
| Marion Barber III, Minnesota | RB | Dallas | 109 |
| Darryl Blackstock, Virginia | LB | Arizona | 95 |
| Bryant Brown, Houston | LB | not drafted | - |
| Brandon Browner, Oregon St. | CB | not drafted | - |
| Josh Bullocks, Nebraska | S | New Orleans | 40 |
| Maurice Clarett, Ohio St. | RB | Denver | 101 |
| Channing Crowder, Florida | LB | Miami | 70 |
| **Thomas Davis**, Georgia | S | Carolina | 14 |
| Ciatrick Fason, Florida | RB | Minnesota | 114 |
| Frank Gore, Miami-FL | RB | San Francisco | 65 |
| Michael Hawkins, Oklahoma | DB | Green Bay | 167 |
| Jovan Haye, Vanderbilt | DE | Carolina | 189 |
| Chris Henry, West Virginia | WR | Cincinnati | 83 |
| Richie Incognito, Nebraska | C | St. Louis | 81 |
| Rashad Jeanty, C. Florida | DE | not drafted | - |
| **Adam Jones**, West Virginia | CB | Tennessee | 6 |
| A.J. Lindsay, Temple | DL | not drafted | - |
| Matt McCoy, San Diego St. | LB | Philadelphia | 63 |
| T.A. McLendon, N.C. State | RB | not drafted | - |
| Adrian McPherson, Florida St. | QB | New Orleans | 152 |
| **Shawne Merriman**, Maryland | DE | San Diego | 12 |
| **Heath Miller**, Virginia | TE | Pittsburgh | 30 |
| Justin Miller, Clemson | CB | N.Y. Jets | 57 |
| Ryan Moats, La. Tech | RB | Philadelphia | 77 |
| Vernand Morency, Oklahoma St. | RB | Houston | 73 |

| | Pos | Drafted by | Overall Pick |
|---|---|---|---|
| Dominique Morris, Vanderbilt | DB | not drafted | - |
| C.J. Mosley, Missouri | DT | Minnesota | 191 |
| Damien Nash, Missouri | RB | Tennessee | 142 |
| Alex Ofili, Michigan | DT | not drafted | - |
| Roscoe Parrish, Miami-FL | WR | Buffalo | 55 |
| Brodney Pool, Oklahoma | S | Cleveland | 34 |
| Dante Ridgeway, Ball St. | WR | St. Louis | 192 |
| **Aaron Rodgers**, California | QB | Green Bay | 24 |
| James Sanders, Fresno St. | DB | New England | 133 |
| Steve Savoy, Utah | QB | not drafted | - |
| Ernest Shazor, Michigan | S | not drafted | - |
| Eric Shelton, Louisville | RB | Carolina | 54 |
| **Alex Smith**, Utah | QB | San Francisco | 1 |
| **Chris Spencer**, Mississippi | C | Seattle | 26 |
| Matthew Tant, Vanderbilt | FB | not drafted | - |
| Lofa Tatupu, USC | LB | Seattle | 45 |
| Tyson Thompson, San Jose St. | RB | not drafted | - |
| Odell Thurman, Georgia | LB | Cincinnati | 48 |
| Justin Tuck, Notre Dame | DE | N.Y. Giants | 74 |
| Rian Wallace, Temple | LB | Pittsburgh | 166 |
| **Fabian Washington**, Neb. | CB | Oakland | 23 |
| Walter Washington, Temple | QB | not drafted | - |
| **Mike Williams**, USC | WR | Detroit | 10 |
| **Troy Williamson**, S. Carolina | WR | Minnesota | 7 |

## NCAA Division I-AA Final Standings

Standings based on conference games only; overall records include postseason games.

### Atlantic 10 Conference

| North | Conference | | | | Overall | | | |
|---|---|---|---|---|---|---|---|---|
| | W | L | PF | PA | W | L | PF | PA |
| *New Hampshire | .6 | 2 | 278 | 200 | 10 | 3 | 426 | 339 |
| Massachusetts | .4 | 4 | 191 | 207 | 5 | 5 | 279 | 256 |
| Northeastern | .4 | 4 | 246 | 207 | 5 | 6 | 355 | 276 |
| Hofstra | .3 | 5 | 272 | 241 | 5 | 6 | 401 | 303 |
| Maine | .3 | 5 | 254 | 262 | 5 | 6 | 321 | 296 |
| Rhode Island | .2 | 6 | 176 | 292 | 4 | 7 | 265 | 355 |

| South | Conference | | | | Overall | | | |
|---|---|---|---|---|---|---|---|---|
| | W | L | PF | PA | W | L | PF | PA |
| *James Madison | .7 | 1 | 201 | 125 | 13 | 2 | 421 | 268 |
| *William & Mary | .7 | 1 | 249 | 180 | 11 | 3 | 486 | 373 |
| *Delaware | .7 | 1 | 213 | 178 | 9 | 4 | 344 | 300 |
| Villanova | .3 | 5 | 272 | 205 | 6 | 5 | 330 | 248 |
| Richmond | .2 | 6 | 148 | 227 | 3 | 8 | 198 | 297 |
| Towson | .0 | 8 | 99 | 275 | 3 | 8 | 195 | 306 |

**Playoffs (8-3):** James Madison (4-0), William & Mary (2-1), Delaware (1-1), New Hampshire (1-1).

### Big Sky Conference

| | Conference | | | | Overall | | | |
|---|---|---|---|---|---|---|---|---|
| | W | L | PF | PA | W | L | PF | PA |
| *Montana | .6 | 1 | 253 | 171 | 12 | 3 | 535 | 339 |
| *Eastern Wash. | .6 | 1 | 308 | 149 | 9 | 4 | 488 | 323 |
| Portland St. | .4 | 3 | 207 | 161 | 7 | 4 | 335 | 223 |
| Montana St. | .4 | 3 | 222 | 195 | 6 | 5 | 296 | 285 |
| Northern Arizona | 3 | 4 | 169 | 210 | 4 | 7 | 244 | 314 |
| Idaho St. | .2 | 5 | 145 | 197 | 3 | 8 | 266 | 357 |
| Sacramento St. | .2 | 5 | 124 | 223 | 3 | 8 | 190 | 415 |
| Weber St. | .1 | 6 | 125 | 247 | 1 | 10 | 202 | 375 |

**Playoffs (4-2):** Montana (3-1), Eastern Wash. (1-1).

### Big South Conference

| | Conference | | | | Overall | | | |
|---|---|---|---|---|---|---|---|---|
| | W | L | PF | PA | W | L | PF | PA |
| Coastal Carolina | .4 | 0 | 141 | 67 | 10 | 1 | 413 | 176 |
| Liberty | .3 | 1 | 95 | 65 | 6 | 5 | 280 | 275 |
| Gardner-Webb | .2 | 2 | 74 | 65 | 5 | 6 | 282 | 335 |
| Charleston So. | .1 | 3 | 59 | 132 | 5 | 5 | 268 | 212 |
| VMI | .0 | 4 | 72 | 112 | 0 | 11 | 137 | 327 |

**Playoffs:** No teams invited.

### Gateway Football Conference

| | Conference | | | | Overall | | | |
|---|---|---|---|---|---|---|---|---|
| | W | L | PF | PA | W | L | PF | PA |
| *Southern Ill. | .7 | 0 | 308 | 88 | 10 | 2 | 511 | 158 |
| *Western Ky. | .6 | 1 | 199 | 124 | 9 | 3 | 350 | 227 |
| Northern Iowa | .5 | 2 | 245 | 130 | 7 | 4 | 351 | 198 |
| SW Missouri St. | 3 | 4 | 179 | 218 | 6 | 5 | 295 | 324 |
| Western Ill. | .2 | 5 | 138 | 275 | 4 | 7 | 311 | 409 |
| Illinois St. | .2 | 5 | 182 | 242 | 4 | 7 | 282 | 352 |
| Youngstown St. | .2 | 5 | 172 | 196 | 4 | 7 | 270 | 272 |
| Indiana St. | .2 | 5 | 172 | 196 | 4 | 7 | 243 | 415 |

**Playoffs (0-2):** Southern Ill. (0-1), Western Ky. (0-1).

### Great West Football Conference

| | Conference | | | | Overall | | | |
|---|---|---|---|---|---|---|---|---|
| | W | L | PF | PA | W | L | PF | PA |
| Cal Poly | .4 | 1 | 115 | 70 | 9 | 2 | 336 | 183 |
| UC Davis | .3 | 2 | 140 | 97 | 6 | 4 | 323 | 211 |
| North Dakota St. | .2 | 3 | 96 | 80 | 8 | 3 | 338 | 150 |
| Southern Utah | .2 | 3 | 87 | 125 | 6 | 5 | 294 | 248 |
| South Dakota St. | .2 | 3 | 87 | 125 | 6 | 5 | 294 | 248 |
| Northern Colorado | 2 | 3 | 84 | 95 | 2 | 9 | 186 | 294 |

**Playoffs:** No teams invited.

### Ivy League

| | Conference | | | | Overall | | | |
|---|---|---|---|---|---|---|---|---|
| | W | L | PF | PA | W | L | PF | PA |
| Harvard | .7 | 0 | 225 | 97 | 10 | 0 | 339 | 141 |
| Pennsylvania | .6 | 1 | 132 | 86 | 8 | 2 | 238 | 145 |
| Cornell | .4 | 3 | 141 | 135 | 4 | 6 | 167 | 179 |
| Brown | .3 | 4 | 145 | 154 | 6 | 4 | 227 | 207 |
| Princeton | .3 | 4 | 126 | 143 | 5 | 5 | 211 | 207 |
| Yale | .3 | 4 | 100 | 130 | 5 | 5 | 179 | 207 |
| Columbia | .1 | 6 | 99 | 171 | 1 | 9 | 140 | 265 |
| Dartmouth | .1 | 6 | 69 | 119 | 1 | 9 | 108 | 205 |

**Playoffs:** League does not play postseason games.

## NCAA Division I-AA Final Standings (Cont.)

### Metro Atlantic Athletic Conference

| | Conference | | | | Overall | | | |
|---|---|---|---|---|---|---|---|---|
| | W | L | PF | PA | W | L | PF | PA |
| Duquesne . . . . . . . .4 | 0 | 139 | 60 | 7 | 3 | 319 | 212 |
| Marist . . . . . . . . .3 | 1 | 107 | 76 | 3 | 6 | 163 | 262 |
| La Salle . . . . . . . .1 | 3 | 135 | 166 | 3 | 7 | 297 | 327 |
| St. Peter's . . . . . . .1 | 3 | 69 | 109 | 3 | 7 | 154 | 260 |
| Iona . . . . . . . . . . .1 | 3 | 93 | 132 | 2 | 8 | 182 | 349 |

**Playoffs:** No teams invited.

### Mid-Eastern Athletic Conference

| | Conference | | | | Overall | | | |
|---|---|---|---|---|---|---|---|---|
| | W | L | PF | PA | W | L | PF | PA |
| *Hampton . . . . . . .6 | 1 | 304 | 166 | 10 | 2 | 523 | 279 |
| S. Carolina St. . . .6 | 1 | 226 | 173 | 9 | 2 | 384 | 230 |
| Bethune-Cookman 4 | 3 | 222 | 119 | 6 | 4 | 330 | 209 |
| Delaware St. . . . . .4 | 3 | 168 | 177 | 4 | 7 | 204 | 352 |
| Howard . . . . . . .3 | 4 | 143 | 175 | 6 | 5 | 249 | 225 |
| Morgan St. . . . . .3 | 4 | 248 | 264 | 5 | 6 | 403 | 423 |
| N. Carolina A&T .1 | 6 | 129 | 213 | 3 | 8 | 180 | 303 |
| Norfolk St. . . . . .1 | 6 | 127 | 280 | 1 | 8 | 168 | 338 |

**Playoffs (0-1):** Hampton (0-1).

**Note:** Florida A&M spent 2004 as an independent and will rejoin the MEAC in 2005 after aborting plans to move up to Division 1-A.

### Northeast Conference

| | Conference | | | | Overall | | | |
|---|---|---|---|---|---|---|---|---|
| | W | L | PF | PA | W | L | PF | PA |
| Monmouth (N.J.) . .6 | 1 | 154 | 140 | 10 | 1 | 299 | 182 |
| Central Conn St. . .6 | 1 | 196 | 125 | 8 | 2 | 261 | 192 |
| Albany . . . . . . . .3 | 4 | 177 | 142 | 4 | 7 | 198 | 280 |
| Sacred Heart . . . .3 | 4 | 142 | 175 | 6 | 4 | 276 | 206 |
| Robert Morris . . .3 | 4 | 161 | 148 | 6 | 5 | 277 | 213 |
| Wagner . . . . . . .3 | 4 | 197 | 151 | 6 | 5 | 241 | 241 |
| Stony Brook . . . . .2 | 5 | 178 | 176 | 3 | 7 | 246 | 275 |
| St. Francis (Pa.) . . .1 | 6 | 136 | 224 | 3 | 8 | 207 | 322 |

**Playoffs:** No teams invited.

### Ohio Valley Conference

| | Conference | | | | Overall | | | |
|---|---|---|---|---|---|---|---|---|
| | W | L | PF | PA | W | L | PF | PA |
| *Jacksonville St. . .7 | 1 | 315 | 148 | 9 | 2 | 412 | 233 |
| Murray St. . . . . . .6 | 2 | 196 | 137 | 7 | 4 | 287 | 220 |
| Eastern Ky. . . . . .6 | 2 | 254 | 150 | 6 | 5 | 290 | 239 |
| Eastern Ill. . . . . . .4 | 4 | 199 | 227 | 5 | 6 | 291 | 323 |
| Tennessee Tech . .3 | 4 | 183 | 174 | 6 | 5 | 290 | 265 |
| Samford . . . . . . .3 | 5 | 233 | 266 | 4 | 7 | 284 | 359 |
| SE Missouri St. . . .3 | 5 | 216 | 269 | 3 | 8 | 256 | 404 |
| Tennessee St. . . . .3 | 5 | 187 | 233 | 4 | 7 | 278 | 311 |
| Tenn.-Martin . . . .1 | 7 | 118 | 297 | 2 | 9 | 173 | 394 |

**Playoffs (0-1):** Jacksonville St. (0-1).

### NCAA I-AA Independents

| | W | L | PF | PA |
|---|---|---|---|---|
| Florida Atlantic . . . . . . . . .9 | 3 | 299 | 207 |
| SE Louisiana . . . . . . . . . . .7 | 4 | 425 | 271 |
| Florida International . . . .3 | 7 | 261 | 325 |
| Florida A&M . . . . . . . . . . .3 | 8 | 253 | 408 |
| Savannah St. . . . . . . . . . . .2 | 8 | 194 | 414 |

**Playoffs:** No teams invited.

**Note:** Florida A&M spent 2004 as an independent and we rejoin the MEAC in 2005 after aborting plans to move up to Division 1-A.

### Patriot League

| | Conference | | | | Overall | | | |
|---|---|---|---|---|---|---|---|---|
| | W | L | PF | PA | W | L | PF | PA |
| *Lafayette . . . . . . .5 | 1 | 165 | 91 | 8 | 4 | 324 | 229 |
| *Lehigh . . . . . . . .5 | 1 | 183 | 91 | 9 | 3 | 345 | 193 |
| Bucknell . . . . . . .4 | 2 | 170 | 127 | 7 | 4 | 296 | 221 |
| Colgate . . . . . . . .4 | 2 | 157 | 117 | 7 | 4 | 261 | 225 |
| Fordham . . . . . . .2 | 4 | 160 | 158 | 5 | 6 | 288 | 270 |
| Holy Cross . . . . . .1 | 5 | 134 | 251 | 3 | 8 | 240 | 367 |
| Georgetown . . . .0 | 6 | 77 | 201 | 3 | 8 | 174 | 280 |

**Playoffs (0-2):** Lafayette (0-1), Lehigh (0-1).

### Pioneer Football League

| North | Conference | | | | Overall | | | |
|---|---|---|---|---|---|---|---|---|
| | W | L | PF | PA | W | L | PF | PA |
| Drake . . . . . . . . .4 | 0 | 134 | 60 | 10 | 2 | 365 | 200 |
| San Diego . . . . . .3 | 1 | 166 | 102 | 7 | 4 | 397 | 266 |
| Dayton . . . . . . . .2 | 2 | 128 | 68 | 7 | 3 | 325 | 140 |
| Valparaiso . . . . . .1 | 3 | 62 | 150 | 5 | 6 | 250 | 300 |
| Butler . . . . . . . . . .0 | 4 | 54 | 164 | 1 | 10 | 118 | 344 |

| South | Conference | | | | Overall | | | |
|---|---|---|---|---|---|---|---|---|
| | W | L | PF | PA | W | L | PF | PA |
| Morehead St. . . . .2 | 1 | 66 | 42 | 6 | 6 | 235 | 231 |
| Jacksonville . . . . .2 | 1 | 74 | 68 | 3 | 7 | 188 | 345 |
| Davidson . . . . . . .1 | 2 | 57 | 59 | 2 | 7 | 132 | 254 |
| Austin Peay . . . . . .1 | 2 | 48 | 76 | 2 | 9 | 161 | 313 |

**PFL Championship Game:** Drake 20, Morehead St. 17.
**Playoffs:** No teams invited.

### Southern Conference

| | Conference | | | | Overall | | | |
|---|---|---|---|---|---|---|---|---|
| | W | L | PF | PA | W | L | PF | PA |
| *Furman . . . . . . . .6 | 1 | 214 | 131 | 10 | 3 | 449 | 216 |
| *Ga. Southern . . . .5 | 1 | 313 | 104 | 9 | 3 | 564 | 221 |
| Wofford . . . . . . .4 | 3 | 191 | 190 | 8 | 3 | 339 | 247 |
| Appalachian St. . . .4 | 3 | 234 | 210 | 6 | 5 | 366 | 358 |
| W. Carolina . . . . .2 | 5 | 120 | 162 | 4 | 7 | 245 | 254 |
| The Citadel . . . . .2 | 5 | 120 | 189 | 3 | 7 | 162 | 250 |
| Elon . . . . . . . . . .2 | 5 | 100 | 194 | 3 | 8 | 196 | 287 |
| Chattanooga . . . .2 | 5 | 205 | 317 | 2 | 9 | 320 | 529 |

**Playoffs (1-2):** Furman (1-1), Georgia Southern (0-1).

### Southland Conference

| | Conference | | | | Overall | | | |
|---|---|---|---|---|---|---|---|---|
| | W | L | PF | PA | W | L | PF | PA |
| *Sam Houston St. .4 | 1 | 175 | 139 | 11 | 3 | 518 | 338 |
| *Northwestern St. .4 | 1 | 187 | 107 | 8 | 4 | 401 | 282 |
| Texas St. . . . . . . .3 | 2 | 122 | 124 | 5 | 6 | 283 | 285 |
| Nicholls St. . . . . . .2 | 3 | 112 | 140 | 5 | 5 | 233 | 237 |
| Stephen F. Austin .1 | 4 | 136 | 133 | 6 | 5 | 284 | 256 |
| McNeese St. . . . . .1 | 4 | 128 | 217 | 4 | 7 | 262 | 423 |

**Playoffs (2-2):** Sam Houston St. (2-1), N'western St. (0-1).

### Southwestern Athletic Conference

| Eastern | Conference | | | | Overall | | | |
|---|---|---|---|---|---|---|---|---|
| | W | L | PF | PA | W | L | PF | PA |
| Alabama St. . . . .6 | 1 | 260 | 120 | 10 | 2 | 407 | 228 |
| Alabama A&M . . .5 | 2 | 166 | 116 | 7 | 4 | 269 | 200 |
| Alcorn St. . . . . . .4 | 3 | 160 | 158 | 7 | 4 | 245 | 230 |
| Jackson St. . . . . . .3 | 4 | 138 | 185 | 4 | 7 | 242 | 300 |
| Miss. Valley St. . . .1 | 6 | 127 | 191 | 3 | 8 | 248 | 314 |

| Western | Conference | | | | Overall | | | |
|---|---|---|---|---|---|---|---|---|
| | W | L | PF | PA | W | L | PF | PA |
| Southern . . . . . . .6 | 1 | 226 | 128 | 8 | 4 | 369 | 265 |
| Ark.-Pine Bluff . . .5 | 2 | 229 | 132 | 6 | 3 | 291 | 193 |
| Grambling St. . . . .3 | 4 | 182 | 188 | 6 | 5 | 294 | 295 |
| Prairie View A&M .1 | 6 | 133 | 236 | 3 | 8 | 246 | 349 |
| Texas Southern . . .0 | 7 | 35 | 230 | 0 | 11 | 82 | 355 |

**SWAC Champ. Game:** Alabama St. 40, Southern 35.
**Playoffs:** No teams invited.

E. Washington
**Erik Meyer**
Passing Efficiency

Georgia Southern
**Chaz Williams**
Touchdowns

Tennessee St.
**Charles Anthony**
Rushing

Appalachian St.
**DaVon Fowlkes**
Receptions

## NCAA Division I-AA Leaders
### INDIVIDUAL
### Passing Efficiency

| | Cl | Gm | Att | Cmp | Cmp Pct | Int | Int Pct | Yds | Yds/ Att | TD | TD Pct | Rating Points |
|---|---|---|---|---|---|---|---|---|---|---|---|---|
| Erik Meyer, Eastern Wash. . . . . | Jr. | 13 | 382 | 259 | 67.80 | 9 | 2.36 | 3707 | 9.70 | 31 | 8.12 | 171.4 |
| Joel Sambursky, Southern Ill. . . . | Jr. | 12 | 234 | 142 | 60.68 | 5 | 2.14 | 2224 | 9.50 | 19 | 8.12 | 163.0 |
| Eric Sanders, Northern Iowa . . . . | Fr. | 9 | 150 | 95 | 63.33 | 5 | 3.33 | 1307 | 8.71 | 15 | 10.00 | 162.9 |
| Craig Ochs, Montana . . . . . . . | Sr. | 15 | 450 | 309 | 68.67 | 8 | 1.78 | 3807 | 8.46 | 33 | 7.33 | 160.4 |
| Lang Campbell, William & Mary | Sr. | 14 | 455 | 298 | 65.49 | 5 | 1.10 | 3988 | 8.76 | 30 | 6.59 | 158.7 |
| Richie Williams, Appalachian St. | Jr. | 10 | 350 | 234 | 66.86 | 10 | 2.86 | 3109 | 8.88 | 24 | 6.86 | 158.4 |
| Princeton Shepherd, Hampton . . | Jr. | 12 | 200 | 108 | 54.00 | 7 | 3.50 | 1890 | 9.45 | 18 | 9.00 | 156.1 |
| Dustin Long, Sam Houston St. . . . | Sr. | 14 | 531 | 333 | 62.71 | 18 | 3.39 | 4588 | 8.64 | 39 | 7.34 | 152.7 |
| Ingle Martin, Furman . . . . . . . | Jr. | 13 | 320 | 198 | 61.88 | 9 | 2.81 | 2792 | 8.73 | 22 | 6.88 | 152.2 |
| Mark Borda, Lehigh . . . . . . . . | Jr. | 12 | 330 | 205 | 62.12 | 6 | 1.82 | 2682 | 8.13 | 24 | 7.27 | 150.8 |
| Martin Hankins, SE Louisiana . . | So. | 11 | 540 | 357 | 66.11 | 12 | 2.22 | 4240 | 7.85 | 35 | 6.48 | 149.0 |
| Ricky Santos, New Hampshire . . | Fr. | 13 | 425 | 272 | 64.00 | 10 | 2.35 | 3318 | 7.81 | 31 | 7.29 | 148.9 |
| Shawn Brady, Northeastern . . . . | Sr. | 11 | 287 | 175 | 60.98 | 11 | 3.83 | 2486 | 8.66 | 17 | 5.92 | 145.6 |

### Total Offense

| | Cl | Rush | Pass | Yds | YdsPG |
|---|---|---|---|---|---|
| Martin Hankins, SE La. . . . . | So. | -19 | 4240 | 4221 | 383.7 |
| Travis Lulay, Montana St. . . | Jr. | 371 | 3485 | 3856 | 350.5 |
| Richie Williams, Appalach. St. | Jr. | 284 | 3109 | 3393 | 339.3 |
| Ramon Nelson, Samford . . . | Sr. | 799 | 2807 | 3606 | 327.8 |
| Dustin Long, Sam Houston St. | Sr. | -12 | 4588 | 4576 | 326.9 |
| Casey Rehrer, Southern Utah | Sr. | 593 | 2846 | 3439 | 312.6 |
| Bradshaw Littlejohn, Morgan St. | Sr. | 775 | 2643 | 3418 | 310.7 |
| Lang Campbell, Wm. & Mary | Sr. | 317 | 3988 | 4305 | 307.5 |
| Erik Meyer, Eastern Wash. . . | Jr. | 227 | 3707 | 3934 | 302.6 |
| Thomas Ricks, Southern . . . . | Sr. | 725 | 2798 | 3523 | 293.6 |

**Games:** All played 11, except Williams (10), Long and Campbell (14), Meyer (13) and Ricks (12).

### Rushing

| | Cl | Car | Yds | TD | YdsPG |
|---|---|---|---|---|---|
| Charles Anthony, Tennessee St. | Sr. | 306 | 1739 | 14 | 158.09 |
| Sean Mayers, St. Peter's . . . . | Jr. | 270 | 1546 | 8 | 154.60 |
| Ed Pricolo, Sacred Heart . . . | Jr. | 209 | 1339 | 14 | 148.78 |
| Jason Jackson, Morgan St. . . | Jr. | 202 | 1191 | 9 | 132.33 |
| Clifton Dawson, Harvard . . . | So. | 248 | 1302 | 17 | 130.20 |
| Scott Phaydavong, Drake . . . | Fr. | 234 | 1539/ | 9 | 128.25 |
| Nick Hartigan, Brown . . . . | Jr. | 323 | 1263 | 17 | 126.30 |
| Evan Harney, San Diego . . . | Jr. | 303 | 1334 | 18 | 121.27 |
| John Leverett, Davidson . . . . | Sr. | 208 | 1084 | 9 | 120.44 |
| Robert Carr, Yale . . . . . . . . . | Sr. | 252 | 1185 | 7 | 118.50 |

**Games:** All played 10, except Anthony, Harney (11), Pricolo, Jackson, Leverett (9) and Phaydavong (12).

### Receptions

| | Cl | No | Yds | TD | P/Gm |
|---|---|---|---|---|---|
| DaVon Fowlkes, Appalachian St. | Sr. | 103 | 1618 | 14 | 9.36 |
| Ralph Plumb, Yale . . . . . . . . . | Sr. | 79 | 939 | 5 | 7.90 |
| Felton Huggins, SE Louisiana . . | Jr. | 84 | 1313 | 13 | 7.64 |
| Luke Palko, St. Francis-PA . . . . | So. | 82 | 679 | 2 | 7.45 |
| A.J. Smith, Southern Utah . . . . | Sr. | 79 | 730 | 4 | 7.18 |
| David Ball, New Hampshire . . | So. | 86 | 1504 | 17 | 7.17 |
| Jarrod Fuller, Sam Houston St. . . | Sr. | 99 | 1383 | 8 | 7.07 |
| Dan Castles, Pennsylvania . . . . | Sr. | 70 | 966 | 8 | 7.00 |
| Fred Amey, Sacramento St. . . . . | Sr. | 76 | 1186 | 6 | 6.91 |
| Edward Gadson, Charleston So. | Fr. | 69 | 792 | 9 | 6.90 |

**Games:** All played 11, except Plumb, Castles, Gadson (10), Ball (12) and Fuller (14).

### Interceptions

| | Cl | No | Yds | TD | Int/Gm |
|---|---|---|---|---|---|
| Ahmad Treaudo, Southern . . . | Sr. | 9 | 166 | 1 | 0.82 |
| Shannon James, Massachusetts | Jr. | 8 | 110 | 0 | 0.73 |
| Thaddeus Kornegay, Fordham | Sr. | 8 | 103 | 0 | 0.73 |
| Onsha Whitaker, Murray St. . . | Sr. | 7 | -1 | 0 | 0.70 |
| Allante Harrison, Towson . . . . | Jr. | 7 | 128 | 2 | 0.64 |
| Darren Barnett, SW Mo. St. . . . | Jr. | 7 | 91 | 0 | 0.64 |
| Ken Chicoine, Cal Poly . . . . | So. | 7 | 157 | 1 | 0.64 |
| Nick Collins, Bethune-Cookman | Sr. | 6 | 108 | 1 | 0.60 |
| Antonio Thomas, W. Kentucky | Jr. | 7 | 15 | 0 | 0.58 |
| David Pittman, Northwestern St. | Jr. | 5 | 136 | 1 | 0.56 |
| Tommy Lee Brown, Nicholls St. . | Jr. | 5 | 19 | 0 | 0.56 |

**Games:** All played 11, except Whitaker and Collins (10), Thomas (12), Pittman and Brown (9).

## NCAA Division I-AA Leaders (Cont.)

### Scoring
(ranked by points per game)

#### Non-Kickers

| | Cl | TD | XPt | Pts | P/Gm |
|---|---|---|---|---|---|
| Chaz Williams, Ga. Southern | .Sr. | 25 | 0 | 152 | 12.67 |
| Clifton Dawson, Harvard | .So. | 18 | 0 | 108 | 10.80 |
| Oscar Bonds, Jacksonville St. | .Sr. | 19 | 0 | 114 | 10.36 |
| Evan Harney, San Diego | .Jr. | 19 | 0 | 114 | 10.36 |
| Nick Hartigan, Brown | .Jr. | 17 | 0 | 102 | 10.20 |
| Bradshaw Littlejohn, Morgan St. | .Sr. | 18 | 0 | 112 | 10.18 |
| Ed Pricolo, Sacred Heart | .Jr. | 15 | 0 | 90 | 10.00 |
| Eric Kimble, Eastern Wash. | .Jr. | 21 | 0 | 128 | 9.85 |

**Games:** All played 11, except Williams (12), Dawson, Hartigan (10), Picolo (9) and Kimble (13).

#### Kickers

| | FG/Att | PAT/Att | Pts | P/Gm |
|---|---|---|---|---|
| Craig Coffin, Southern Ill. | .13/15 | 66/66 | 105 | 8.75 |
| Andrew Paterini, Hampton | .16/22 | 56/63 | 104 | 8.67 |
| Chris Onorato, Hofstra | .15/20 | 48/49 | 93 | 8.45 |
| Brian Wingert, N. Iowa | .14/18 | 40/42 | 82 | 8.20 |
| Greg Kuehn, Wm. & Mary | 19/28 | 57/58 | 114 | 8.14 |
| Dan Carpenter, Montana | .18/29 | 62/62 | 122 | 8.13 |
| Lance Garner, Sam Hou. St. | 16/21 | 57/57 | 108 | 8.08 |
| Jason Resch, Dayton | .19/39 | 37/38 | 76 | 7.60 |

**Games:** All played 12, except Onorato (11), Wingert, Resch (10), Kuehn (14) and Carpenter (15).

### Field Goals

| | Cl | FG/Att | Pct | P/Gm |
|---|---|---|---|---|
| Joe Johnson, Weber St. | .Jr. | 17/22 | .773 | 1.55 |
| Kyle Hooper, Indiana St. | .So. | 16/20 | .800 | 1.45 |
| Brian Wingert, N. Iowa | .So. | 14/18 | .778 | 1.40 |
| Jon Scifres, SW Mo. St. | .Jr. | 15/15 | 1.000 | 1.36 |
| Chris Onorato, Hofstra | .Sr. | 15/20 | .750 | 1.36 |
| Greg Kuehn, Wm. & Mary | .Jr. | 19/28 | .679 | 1.36 |
| E.J. Cochrane, Montana St. | .Sr. | 12/22 | .545 | 1.33 |
| Andrew Paterini, Hampton | .So. | 16/22 | .727 | 1.33 |

**Games:** All played 11, except Wingert (10), Kuehn (14), Cochrane (9) and Paterini (12).

### Punt/Kickoff Leaders

| Punting | Cl | No | Yds | Avg |
|---|---|---|---|---|
| Paul Ernster, N. Arizona | .Sr. | 55 | 2631 | 47.84 |
| David Simonhoff, SE Mo. St. | .So. | 69 | 3174 | 46.00 |
| Ryan Hoffman, Illinois St. | .Jr. | 55 | 2413 | 43.87 |

| Punt Returns | Cl | No | Yds | TD | Avg |
|---|---|---|---|---|---|
| Craig Agee, Jacksonville St. | .So. | 18 | 369 | 2 | 20.50 |
| Eric Kimble, Eastern Wash. | .Jr. | 26 | 460 | 2 | 17.69 |
| Marquay McDanile, Hampton | Jr. | 26 | 440 | 2 | 16.92 |

| Kickoff Returns | Cl | No | Yds | TD | Avg |
|---|---|---|---|---|---|
| Corey Smith, Montana St. | .Jr. | 20 | 664 | 2 | 33.20 |
| Chris Crawford, Nicholls St. | .So. | 20 | 646 | 2 | 32.30 |
| Lewis Barr, Ga. Southern | .So. | 20 | 598 | 0 | 29.90 |

## TEAM

### Scoring Offense

| | Gm | Record | Pts | Avg |
|---|---|---|---|---|
| Georgia Southern | .12 | 9-3 | 564 | 47.00 |
| Hampton | .12 | 10-2 | 523 | 43.58 |
| Southern Illinois | .12 | 10-2 | 511 | 42.58 |
| Southeastern Louisiana | .11 | 7-4 | 425 | 38.64 |
| Coastal Carolina | .11 | 10-1 | 413 | 37.55 |
| Eastern Wash. | .13 | 9-4 | 488 | 37.54 |
| Jacksonville St. | .11 | 9-2 | 412 | 37.45 |
| Sam Houston St. | .14 | 11-3 | 518 | 37.00 |
| Alabama St. | .11 | 9-2 | 407 | 37.00 |
| Morgan St. | .11 | 5-6 | 403 | 36.64 |
| Hofstra | .11 | 5-6 | 401 | 36.45 |
| Arkansas-Pine Bluff | .8 | 5-3 | 291 | 36.38 |
| San Diego | .11 | 7-4 | 397 | 36.09 |
| Montana | .15 | 12-3 | 535 | 35.67 |
| South Carolina St. | .11 | 9-2 | 384 | 34.91 |
| William & Mary | .14 | 11-3 | 486 | 34.71 |

### Scoring Defense

| | Gm | Record | Pts | Avg |
|---|---|---|---|---|
| Southern Illinois | .12 | 10-2 | 158 | 13.2 |
| Harvard | .10 | 10-0 | 134 | 13.4 |
| Dayton | .10 | 7-3 | 140 | 14.0 |
| Pennsylvania | .10 | 8-2 | 145 | 14.5 |
| Coastal Carolina | .11 | 10-1 | 176 | 16.0 |
| Lehigh | .12 | 9-3 | 193 | 16.1 |
| Monmouth | .11 | 10-1 | 182 | 16.5 |
| Furman | .13 | 10-3 | 216 | 16.6 |
| Cal Poly | .11 | 9-2 | 183 | 16.6 |
| Drake | .12 | 10-2 | 200 | 16.7 |
| James Madison | .15 | 13-2 | 268 | 17.9 |
| Northern Iowa | .11 | 7-4 | 198 | 18.0 |
| Cornell | .10 | 4-6 | 181 | 18.1 |
| Alabama A&M | .11 | 7-4 | 200 | 18.2 |
| Georgia Southern | .12 | 9-3 | 221 | 18.4 |

### Total Offense

| | Record | Plays | Yds | Avg |
|---|---|---|---|---|
| Southeastern Louisiana | .7-4 | 896 | 5908 | 537.09 |
| Southern Illinois | .10-2 | 831 | 6032 | 502.67 |
| Georgia Southern | .9-3 | 896 | 5860 | 488.33 |
| Eastern Washington | .9-4 | 970 | 6181 | 475.46 |
| Sam Houston St. | .11-3 | 990 | 6600 | 471.43 |
| Morgan St. | .5-6 | 788 | 5039 | 458.09 |
| Furman | .10-3 | 926 | 5914 | 454.92 |
| Jacksonville St. | .9-2 | 780 | 4889 | 444.45 |
| San Diego | .7-4 | 833 | 4756 | 432.36 |
| William & Mary | .11-3 | 984 | 6044 | 431.71 |
| Montana St. | .6-5 | 862 | 4737 | 430.64 |
| Florida A&M | .3-8 | 861 | 4733 | 430.27 |
| Montana | .12-3 | 1058 | 6416 | 427.73 |
| South Carolina St. | .9-2 | 839 | 4683 | 425.73 |
| Appalachian St. | .6-5 | 781 | 4681 | 425.55 |
| Alabama St. | .9-2 | 863 | 5086 | 423.83 |

### Total Defense

| | Record | Plays | Yds | Avg |
|---|---|---|---|---|
| Dayton | .7-3 | 616 | 2631 | 263.10 |
| Northwestern St. | .8-4 | 732 | 3296 | 274.67 |
| Alabama A&M | .7-4 | 739 | 3035 | 275.91 |
| Georgia Southern | .9-3 | 741 | 3321 | 276.75 |
| Robert Morris | .6-5 | 690 | 3181 | 289.18 |
| Southern Utah | .6-5 | 735 | 3256 | 296.00 |
| Drake | .10-2 | 799 | 3586 | 298.83 |
| Howard | .6-5 | 733 | 3289 | 299.00 |
| Colgate | .7-4 | 679 | 3293 | 299.36 |
| Villanova | .6-5 | 752 | 3295 | 299.55 |
| Murray St. | .7-4 | 746 | 3310 | 300.91 |
| Western Carolina | .4-7 | 740 | 3321 | 301.91 |
| Southern Illinois | .10-2 | 814 | 3652 | 304.33 |
| Duquesne | .7-3 | 679 | 3046 | 304.60 |
| Northern Iowa | .7-4 | 703 | 3355 | 305.00 |
| Harvard | .10-0 | 680 | 3062 | 306.20 |

# NCAA Playoffs

## Division I-AA

### First Round (Nov. 27)

at Furman 49 . . . . . . . . . . . . . . . . . . . . Jacksonville St. 7
James Madison 14 . . . . . . . . . . . . . . . . . . . at Lehigh 13
at Delaware 28 . . . . . . . . . . . . . . . . . . . . . . Lafayette 14
at William & Mary 42 . . . . . . . . . . . . . . . . Hampton 35
New Hampshire 27 . . . . . . . . . . at Georgia Southern 23
at Montana 56 . . . . . . . . . . . . . . . . . . Northwestern St. 7
at Sam Houston St. 54 . . . . . . . . . . Western Kentucky 24
Eastern Washington 35 . . . . . . . . . at Southern Illinois 31

### Quarterfinals (Dec. 4)

James Madison 14 . . . . . . . . . . . . . . . . . . . at Furman 13
at William & Mary 44 . . . . . 2 OT . . . . . . Delaware 38
at Montana 47 . . . . . . . . . . . . . . . . . . New Hampshire 17
Sam Houston St. 35 . . . . . . . . at Eastern Washington 34

### Semifinals (Dec. 10-11)

James Madison 48 . . . . . . . . . . . . at William & Mary 34
at Montana 34 . . . . . . . . . . . . . . . . . . Sam Houston St. 13

### Championship Game

Dec. 17 at Chattanooga, Tenn. (Att: 16,771)

James Madison 31 . . . . . . . . . . . . . . . . . . . . . Montana 21
(13-2)                                              (12-3)

## Division II

### First Round (Nov. 13)

North Dakota 20 . . . . . . . . . 2OT . . . at St. Cloud St. 17
Grand Valley St. 16 . . . . . . . . . . . . . . . . Winona St. 13
at Colorado Mines 52 . . . . . . . . . . . Midwestern St. 33
at Texas A&M-Kingsville 40 . . . . . . . . . SE Oklahoma 30
at West Chester 35 . . . . . . . . . . . . . . . . . . C.W. Post 3
Edinboro 47 . . . . . . . . . . . . . . . . . . . . . at Bentley 44
at Arkansas Tech 24 . . . . . . . . . . . . . . . . Catawba 20
at Carson-Newman 35 . . . . . . . . . . . . Fayetteville St. 14

### Second Round (Nov. 20)

North Dakota 20 . . . . . . . . . . . . . . . at Michigan Tech 3
Grand Valley St. 10 . . . . . . . . . . . . . . . at Northwood 7
at Pittsburg St. 70 . . . . . . . . . . . . . . Colorado Mines 35
at NW Missouri St. 34 . . . . . . . . . Tex. A&M-Kingsville 30
West Chester 33 . . . . . . . . . . . . . . . at Shippensburg 28
at East Stroudsburg 36 . . . . . . . . . . . . . . . . Edinboro 32
at Albany St. (Ga.) 42 . . . . . . . . . . . . Arkansas Tech 24
at Valdosta St. 38 . . . . . . . . . . . . . . . Carson-Newman 12

### Quarterfinals (Nov. 27)

at North Dakota 19 . . . . . . . . . . . . Grand Valley St. 15
at Pittsburg St. 50 . . . . . . . . . . . . . . NW Missouri St. 36
West Chester 48 . . . . . . . . . . . . at East Stroudsburg 38
Valdosta St. 38 . . . . . . . . . . . . . . . . at Albany St. (Ga.) 24

### Semifinals (Dec. 4)

at Pittsburg St. 31 . . . . . . . . . . . . . . . . . North Dakota 19
at Valdosta St. 45 . . . . . . . . . . . . . . . . West Chester 21

### Championship Game

Dec. 11 at Florence, Ala. (Att: 8,604)

Valdosta St. 36 . . . . . . . . . . . . . . . . . . . Pittsburg St. 31
(13-1)                                              (14-1)

---

### Division I-AA, II and III Awards

#### Players of the Year

NCAA I-AA . . . . . . Lang Campbell, Wm. & Mary, QB
NCAA II . . . . . . . . Chad Friehauf, Colorado-Mines, QB
NCAA III . . . . . . . . . . . Rocky Myers, Wesley (Del.), S
NAIA . . . . . . . . . . . . Cory Jacquay, St. Francis, RB

---

## Division III

### First Round (Nov. 20)

at Wisconsin-La Crosse 37 . . . . . . . . . . St. Norbert 23
at Occidental 28 . . . . . . . . . . . . . . . . . Willamette 14
at Concordia-M'head 28 . . . . . . . . . . . . Wartburg 14
at Hobart 35 . . . . . . . . . . . . . . . . . . . . . . . Curry 16
at St. John Fisher 31 . . . . . . . . . . . . . Muhlenberg 3
at Delaware Valley 21 . . . . . . . . . . . . Shenandoah 17
Mary Hardin-Baylor 32 . . . . . . . . . . . Trinity (Tex.) 13
Chris. Newport 35 . . . . . . . . . . . . . . . at Salisbury 24
at Washington & Jefferson 55 . 2OT . . Bridgewater (Va.) 48
at Wheaton (Ill.) 31 . . . . . . . . . . . . . Mt. St. Joseph 7
Carthage 31 . . . . . . . . . . . . . . . . . . . . at Alma 28
at Wooster 41 . . . . . . . . . . . . . . . . . . . . . Aurora 34

### Second Round (Nov. 27)

at Linfield 52 . . . . . . . . . . . . . . . Wisconsin-La Crosse 14
Occidental 42 . . . . . . . . . . . . at Concordia-M'head 40
at Rowan 45 . . . . . . . . . . . . . . . . . . . . . . Hobart 14
at Delaware Valley 26 . . . . . . . . . . . St. John Fisher 20
Mary Hardin-Baylor 42 . . . . . . . at Hardin-Simmons 28
at Washington & Jefferson 24 . . . . . . . Chris. Newport 14
at Mount Union 27 . . . . . . . . . . . . . . Wheaton (Ill.) 6
Carthage 14 . . . . . . . . . . . . . . . . . . . . at Wooster 7

### Quarterfinals (Dec. 4)

at Linfield 56 . . . . . . . . . . . . . . . . . . . Occidental 27
at Rowan 56 . . . . . . . . . . . . . . . . Delaware Valley 7
Mary Hardin-Baylor 52 . . . . . at Washington & Jefferson 16
at Mount Union 38 . . . . . . . . . . . . . . . . . Carthage 20

### Semifinals (Dec. 11)

Mary Hardin-Baylor 38 . . . . . . . . . . . . at Mt. Union 24
at Linfield 52 . . . . . . . . . . . . . . . . . . . . . . . . Rowan 0

### Amos Alonzo Stagg Bowl

Dec. 18 at Salem, Va. (Att: 3,240)

Linfield 28 . . . . . . . . . . . . . . . Mary Hardin-Baylor 21
(13-0)                                              (13-2)

# NAIA Playoffs

## Division I

### First Round (Nov. 20)

at Carroll 24 . . . . . . . . . . . . . . . . . . . . . . . Mary 14
at Dickinson St. 30 . . . . . . . . . . . . . . . Montana Tech 13
MidAmerica Nazarene 21 . . . . . . . . . . at McKendree 20
at Georgetown 35 . . . . . . . . . . . Trinity International 21
Azusa Pacific 16 . . . . . . . . . . at NW Oklahoma St. 0
at Sioux Falls 72 . . . . . . . . . . . . . . . . . . . . . Tabor 11
at St. Francis (Ind.) 53 . . . . . . . . . . . Morningside 3
at Hastings 20 . . . . . . . . . . . . . . . . . . . . Lindenwood 19

### Quarterfinals (Nov. 27)

at St. Francis 48 . . . . . . . . . . . . . . . . . . . . Hastings 17
at Georgetown 46 . . . . . . . . MidAmerica Nazarene 27
at Carroll 56 . . . . . . . . . . . . . . . . . . . Dickinson St. 17
Azusa Pacific 24 . . . . . . . . . . . . . . . . . at Sioux Falls 0

### Semifinals (Dec. 4)

St. Francis 12 . . . . . . . . . . . . . . . . . . . . Georgetown 7
Carroll 14 . . . . . . . . . . . . . . . . . . . . . . Azusa Pacific 10

### Championship

Dec. 18 at Savannah, Tenn. (Att: 5,276)

Carroll 15 . . . . . . . . . . . . . . . . . St. Francis (Ind.) 13
(12-2)                                              (13-1)

# 1869-2005
# *Through the Years*

SPORTS ALMANAC

## National Champions

Over the last 132 years, there have been 25 major selectors of national champions by way of polls (11), mathematical rating systems (10) and historical research (4). The best-known and most widely circulated of these surveys, the Associated Press poll of sportswriters and broadcasters, first appeared during the 1936 season. Champions prior to 1936 have been determined by retro polls, ratings and historical research.

### The Early Years (1869-1935)

National champions based on the Dickinson mathematical system (DS) and three historical retro polls taken by the College Football Researchers Association (CFRA), the National Championship Foundation (NCF) and the Helms Athletic Foundation (HF). The CFRA and NCF polls start in 1869, college football's inaugural year, while the Helms poll begins in 1883, the first season the game adopted a point system for scoring. Frank Dickinson, an economics professor at Illinois, introduced his system in 1926 and retro-picked winners in 1924 and '25. Bowl game results were counted in the Helms selections, but not in the other three.

**Multiple champions:** Yale (18); Princeton (17); Harvard (9); Michigan (7); Notre Dame and Penn (4); Alabama, California, Cornell, Illinois, Pittsburgh and USC (3); Georgia Tech, Minnesota and Penn St. (2).

| Year | | Record | Year | | Record | Year | | Record |
|---|---|---|---|---|---|---|---|---|
| 1869 | Princeton | 1-1-0 | 1880 | Yale (CFRA) | 4-0-1 | 1891 | Yale | 13-0-0 |
| 1870 | Princeton | 1-0-0 | | & Princeton (NCF) | 4-0-1 | 1892 | Yale | 13-0-0 |
| 1871 | No games played | | 1881 | Yale | 5-0-1 | 1893 | Princeton | 11-0-0 |
| 1872 | Princeton | 1-0-0 | 1882 | Yale | 8-0-0 | 1894 | Yale | 16-0-0 |
| 1873 | Princeton | 1-0-0 | 1883 | Yale | 8-0-0 | 1895 | Penn | 14-0-0 |
| 1874 | Yale | 3-0-0 | 1884 | Yale | 8-0-1 | 1896 | Princeton (CFRA) | 10-0-1 |
| 1875 | Princeton (CFRA) | 2-0-0 | 1885 | Princeton | 9-0-0 | | & Lafayette (NCF) | 11-0-1 |
| | & Harvard (NCF) | 4-0-0 | 1886 | Yale | 9-0-1 | 1897 | Penn | 15-0-0 |
| 1876 | Yale | 3-0-0 | 1887 | Yale | 9-0-0 | 1898 | Harvard | 11-0-0 |
| 1877 | Yale | 3-0-1 | 1888 | Yale | 13-0-0 | 1899 | Princeton (CFRA) | 12-1-0 |
| 1878 | Princeton | 6-0-0 | 1889 | Princeton | 10-0-0 | | & Harvard (NCF, HF) | 10-0-1 |
| 1879 | Princeton | 4-0-1 | 1890 | Harvard | 11-0-0 | | | |

| Year | | Record | Bowl Game | Head Coach | Outstanding Player |
|---|---|---|---|---|---|
| 1900 | Yale | 12-0-0 | No bowl | Malcolm McBride | Perry Hale, HB |
| 1901 | Harvard (CFRA) | 12-0-0 | No bowl | Bill Reid | Bob Kernan, HB |
| | & Michigan (NCF, HF) | 11-0-0 | Won Rose | Hurry Up Yost | Neil Snow, E |
| 1902 | Michigan | 11-0-0 | No bowl | Hurry Up Yost | Boss Weeks, QB |
| 1903 | Princeton | 11-0-0 | No bowl | Art Hillebrand | John DeWitt, G |
| 1904 | Penn (CFRA, HF) | 12-0-0 | No bowl | Carl Williams | Andy Smith, FB |
| | & Michigan (NCF) | 10-0-0 | No bowl | Hurry Up Yost | Willie Heston, HB |
| 1905 | Chicago | 10-0-0 | No bowl | Amos Alonzo Stagg | Walter Eckersall, QB |
| 1906 | Princeton | 9-0-1 | No bowl | Bill Roper | Cap Wister, E |
| 1907 | Yale | 9-0-1 | No bowl | Bill Knox | Tad Jones, HB |
| 1908 | Penn (CFRA, HF) | 11-0-1 | No bowl | Sol Metzger | Hunter Scarlett, E |
| | & LSU (NCF) | 10-0-0 | No bowl | Edgar Wingard | Doc Fenton, QB |
| 1909 | Yale | 12-1-0 | No bowl | Howard Jones | Ted Coy, FB |
| 1910 | Harvard (CFRA, HF) | 8-0-1 | No bowl | Percy Haughton | Percy Wendell, HB |
| | & Pittsburgh (NCF) | 9-0-0 | No bowl | Joe Thompson | Ralph Galvin, C |
| 1911 | Princeton (CFRA, HF) | 8-0-2 | No bowl | Bill Roper | Sam White, E |
| | & Penn St. (NCF) | 8-0-1 | No bowl | Bill Hollenback | Dexter Very, E |
| 1912 | Harvard (CFRA, HF) | 9-0-0 | No bowl | Percy Haughton | Charley Brickley, HB |
| | & Penn St. (NCF) | 8-0-0 | No bowl | Bill Hollenback | Dexter Very, E |
| 1913 | Harvard | 9-0-0 | No bowl | Percy Haughton | Eddie Mahan, FB |
| 1914 | Army | 9-0-0 | No bowl | Charley Daly | John McEwan, C |
| 1915 | Cornell | 9-0-0 | No bowl | Al Sharpe | Charley Barrett, QB |
| 1916 | Pittsburgh | 8-0-0 | No bowl | Pop Warner | Bob Peck, C |
| 1917 | Georgia Tech | 9-0-0 | No bowl | John Heisman | Ev Strupper, HB |
| 1918 | Pittsburgh (CFRA, HF) | 4-1-0 | No bowl | Pop Warner | Tom Davies, HB |
| | & Michigan (NCF) | 5-0-0 | No bowl | Hurry Up Yost | Frank Steketee, FB |
| 1919 | Harvard (CFRA-tie, HF) | 9-0-1 | Won Rose | Bob Fisher | Eddie Casey, HB |
| | Illinois (CFRA-tie) | 6-1-0 | No bowl | Bob Zuppke | Chuck Carney, E |
| | & Notre Dame (NCF) | 9-0-0 | No bowl | Knute Rockne | George Gipp, HB |
| 1920 | California | 9-0-0 | Won Rose | Andy Smith | Dan McMillan, T |
| 1921 | California (CFRA) | 9-0-1 | Tied Rose | Andy Smith | Brick Muller, E |
| | & Cornell (NCF, HF) | 8-0-0 | No bowl | Gil Dobie | Eddie Kaw, HB |
| 1922 | Princeton (CFRA) | 8-0-0 | No bowl | Bill Roper | Herb Treat, T |
| | California (NCF) | 9-0-0 | No bowl | Andy Smith | Brick Muller, E |
| | & Cornell (HF) | 8-0-0 | No bowl | Gil Dobie | Eddie Kaw, HB |

| Year | | Record | Bowl Game | Head Coach | Outstanding Player |
|---|---|---|---|---|---|
| 1923 | **Illinois** (CFRA, HF) | 8-0-0 | No bowl | Bob Zuppke | Red Grange, HB |
| | & **Michigan** (NCF) | 8-0-0 | No bowl | Hurry Up Yost | Jack Blott, C |
| 1924 | **Notre Dame** | 10-0-0 | Won Rose | Knute Rockne | "The Four Horsemen"* |
| 1925 | **Alabama** (CFRA, HF) | 10-0-0 | Won Rose | Wallace Wade | Johnny Mack Brown, HB |
| | & **Dartmouth** (DS) | 8-0-0 | No bowl | Jesse Hawley | Swede Oberlander, HB |
| 1926 | **Alabama** (CFRA, HF) | 9-0-1 | Tied Rose | Wallace Wade | Hoyt Winslett, E |
| | & **Stanford** (DS) | 10-0-1 | Tied Rose | Pop Warner | Ted Shipkey, E |
| 1927 | **Yale** (CFRA) | 7-1-0 | No bowl | Tad Jones | Bill Webster, G |
| | & **Illinois** (NCF, HF, DS) | 7-0-1 | No bowl | Bob Zuppke | Bob Reitsch, C |
| 1928 | **Georgia Tech** (CFRA, NCF, HF) | 10-0-0 | Won Rose | Bill Alexander | Pete Pund, C |
| | & **USC** (DS) | 9-0-1 | No bowl | Howard Jones | Jesse Hibbs, T |
| 1929 | **Notre Dame** | 9-0-0 | No bowl | Knute Rockne | Frank Carideo, QB |
| 1930 | **Alabama** (CFRA) | 10-0-0 | Won Rose | Wallace Wade | Fred Sington, T |
| | & **Notre Dame** (NCF, HF, DS) | 10-0-0 | No bowl | Knute Rockne | Marchy Schwartz, HB |
| 1931 | **USC** | 10-1-0 | Won Rose | Howard Jones | John Baker, G |
| 1932 | **USC** (CFRA, NCF, HF) | 10-0-0 | Won Rose | Howard Jones | Ernie Smith, T |
| | & **Michigan** (DS) | 8-0-0 | No bowl | Harry Kipke | Harry Newman, QB |
| 1933 | **Michigan** | 8-0-0 | No bowl | Harry Kipke | Chuck Bernard, C |
| 1934 | **Minnesota** | 8-0-0 | No bowl | Bernie Bierman | Pug Lund, HB |
| 1935 | **Minnesota** (CFRA, NCF, HF) | 8-0-0 | No bowl | Bernie Bierman | Dick Smith, T |
| | & **SMU** (DS) | 12-1-0 | Lost Rose | Matty Bell | Bobby Wilson, HB |

*Notre Dame's Four Horsemen were Harry Stuhldreher (QB), Jim Crowley (HB), Don Miller (HB-P) and Elmer Layden (FB).

## The Media Poll Years (since 1936)

National champions according to seven media and coaches' polls: Associated Press (since 1936), United Press (1950-57), International News Service (1952-57), United Press International (1958-92), Football Writers Association of America (since 1954), National Football Foundation and Hall of Fame (since 1959) and USA Today/CNN (since 1991). In 1991, the American Football Coaches Association switched outlets for its poll from UPI to USA Today/CNN and then to USA Today/ESPN in 1997.

After 29 years of releasing its final Top 20 poll in early December, AP named its 1965 national champion following that season's bowl games. AP returned to a pre-bowls final vote in 1966 and '67, but has polled its writers and broadcasters after the bowl games since the 1968 season. The FWAA has selected its champion after the bowl games since the 1955 season, the NFF-Hall of Fame since 1971, UPI after 1974, USA Today/CNN 1991-96, and USA Today/ESPN since 1997.

The Associated Press changed the name of its national championship award from the AP trophy to the Bear Bryant Trophy after the legendary Alabama coach's death in 1983. The FootballWriters' trophy is called the Grantland Rice Award (after the celebrated sportswriter) and the NFF-Hall of Fame trophy is called the MacArthur Bowl (in honor of Gen. Douglas MacArthur).

**Multiple champions:** Notre Dame (9); Alabama, Ohio St., Oklahoma and USC (7); Miami-FL and Nebraska (5); Minnesota (4); Michigan St. and Texas (3); Army, Florida St., Georgia Tech, LSU, Michigan, Penn St., Pittsburgh and Tennessee (2).

| Year | | Record | Bowl Game | Head Coach | Outstanding Player |
|---|---|---|---|---|---|
| 1936 | **Minnesota** | 7-1-0 | No bowl | Bernie Bierman | Ed Widseth, T |
| 1937 | **Pittsburgh** | 9-0-1 | No bowl | Jock Sutherland | Marshall Goldberg, HB |
| 1938 | **TCU** | 11-0-0 | Won Sugar | Dutch Meyer | Davey O'Brien, QB |
| 1939 | **Texas A&M** | 11-0-0 | Won Sugar | Homer Norton | John Kimbrough, FB |
| 1940 | **Minnesota** | 8-0-0 | No Bowl | Bernie Bierman | George Franck, HB |
| 1941 | **Minnesota** | 8-0-0 | No bowl | Bernie Bierman | Bruce Smith, HB |
| 1942 | **Ohio St.** | 9-1-0 | No bowl | Paul Brown | Gene Fekete, FB |
| 1943 | **Notre Dame** | 9-1-0 | No bowl | Frank Leahy | Angelo Bertelli, QB |
| 1944 | **Army** | 9-0-0 | No bowl | Red Blaik | Glenn Davis, HB |
| 1945 | **Army** | 9-0-0 | No bowl | Red Blaik | Doc Blanchard, FB |
| 1946 | **Notre Dame** | 8-0-1 | No bowl | Frank Leahy | Johnny Lujack, QB |
| 1947 | **Notre Dame** | 9-0-0 | No bowl | Frank Leahy | Johnny Lujack, QB |
| 1948 | **Michigan** | 9-0-0 | No bowl | Bennie Oosterbaan | Dick Rifenburg, E |
| 1949 | **Notre Dame** | 10-0-0 | No bowl | Frank Leahy | Leon Hart, E |
| 1950 | **Oklahoma** | 10-1-0 | Lost Sugar | Bud Wilkinson | Leon Heath, FB |
| 1951 | **Tennessee** | 10-0-0 | Lost Sugar | Bob Neyland | Hank Lauricella, TB |
| 1952 | **Michigan St.** (AP, UP) | 9-0-0 | No bowl | Biggie Munn | Don McAuliffe, HB |
| | & **Georgia Tech** (INS) | 12-0-0 | Won Sugar | Bobby Dodd | Hal Miller, T |
| 1953 | **Maryland** | 10-1-0 | Lost Orange | Jim Tatum | Bernie Faloney, QB |
| 1954 | **Ohio St.** (AP, INS) | 10-0-0 | Won Rose | Woody Hayes | Howard Cassady, HB |
| | & **UCLA** (UP, FW) | 9-0-0 | No bowl | Red Sanders | Jack Ellena, T |
| 1955 | **Oklahoma** | 11-0-0 | Won Orange | Bud Wilkinson | Jerry Tubbs, C |
| 1956 | **Oklahoma** | 10-0-0 | No bowl | Bud Wilkinson | Tommy McDonald, HB |
| 1957 | **Auburn** (AP) | 10-0-0 | No bowl | Shug Jordan | Jimmy Phillips, E |
| | & **Ohio St.** (UP, FW, INS) | 9-1-0 | Won Rose | Woody Hayes | Bob White, FB |
| 1958 | **LSU** (AP, UPI) | 11-0-0 | Won Sugar | Paul Dietzel | Billy Cannon, HB |
| | & **Iowa** (FW) | 8-1-1 | Won Rose | Forest Evashevski | Randy Duncan, QB |
| 1959 | **Syracuse** | 11-0-0 | Won Cotton | Ben Schwartzwalder | Ernie Davis, HB |
| 1960 | **Minnesota** (AP, UPI, NFF) | 8-2-0 | Lost Rose | Murray Warmath | Tom Brown, G |
| | & **Mississippi** (FW) | 10-0-1 | Won Sugar | Johnny Vaught | Jake Gibbs, QB |
| 1961 | **Alabama** (AP, UPI, NFF) | 11-0-0 | Won Sugar | Bear Bryant | Billy Neighbors, T |
| | & **Ohio St.** (FW) | 8-0-1 | No bowl | Woody Hayes | Bob Ferguson, HB |
| 1962 | **USC** | 11-0-0 | Won Rose | John McKay | Hal Bedsole, E |
| 1963 | **Texas** | 11-0-0 | Won Cotton | Darrell Royal | Scott Appleton, T |

## National Champions (Cont.)

| Year | | Record | Bowl Game | Head Coach | Outstanding Player |
|---|---|---|---|---|---|
| 1964 | **Alabama** (AP, UPI), . . . . . . . . . .10-1-0 | | Lost Orange | Bear Bryant | Joe Namath, QB |
| | **Arkansas** (FW) . . . . . . . . . . . . . .11-0-0 | | Won Cotton | Frank Broyles | Ronnie Caveness, LB |
| | & **Notre Dame** (NFF) . . . . . . . . . . .9-1-0 | | No bowl | Ara Parseghian | John Huarte, QB |
| 1965 | **Alabama** (AP, FW-tie) . . . . . . . . . .9-1-1 | | Won Orange | Bear Bryant | Paul Crane, C |
| | & **Michigan St.** (UPI, NFF, FW-tie) .10-1-0 | | Lost Rose | Duffy Daugherty | George Webster, LB |
| 1966 | **Notre Dame** (AP, UPI, FW, NFF-tie) .9-0-1 | | No bowl | Ara Parseghian | Jim Lynch, LB |
| | & **Michigan St.** (NFF-tie) . . . . . . .9-0-1 | | No bowl | Duffy Daugherty | Bubba Smith, DE |
| 1967 | **USC** . . . . . . . . . . . . . . . . . . . . .10-1-0 | | Won Rose | John McKay | O.J. Simpson, HB |
| 1968 | **Ohio St.** . . . . . . . . . . . . . . . . . .10-0-0 | | Won Rose | Woody Hayes | Rex Kern, QB |
| 1969 | **Texas** . . . . . . . . . . . . . . . . . . . .11-0-0 | | Won Cotton | Darrell Royal | James Street, QB |
| 1970 | **Nebraska** (AP, FW) . . . . . . . . . .11-0-1 | | Won Orange | Bob Devaney | Jerry Tagge, QB |
| | **Texas** (UPI, NFF), . . . . . . . . . . . .10-1-0 | | Lost Cotton | Darrell Royal | Steve Worster, RB |
| | & **Ohio St.** (NFF-tie) . . . . . . . . . . .9-1-0 | | Lost Rose | Woody Hayes | Jim Stillwagon, MG |
| 1971 | **Nebraska** . . . . . . . . . . . . . . . . .13-0-0 | | Won Orange | Bob Devaney | Johnny Rodgers, WR |
| 1972 | **USC** . . . . . . . . . . . . . . . . . . . . .12-0-0 | | Won Rose | John McKay | Charles Young, TE |
| 1973 | **Notre Dame** (AP, FW, NFF) . . . . .11-0-0 | | Won Sugar | Ara Parseghian | Mike Townsend, DB |
| | & **Alabama** (UPI) . . . . . . . . . . . . .11-1-0 | | Lost Sugar | Bear Bryant | Buddy Brown, OT |
| 1974 | **Oklahoma** (AP) . . . . . . . . . . . . .11-0-0 | | No bowl | Barry Switzer | Joe Washington, RB |
| | & **USC** (UPI, FW, NFF) . . . . . . . . .10-1-1 | | Won Rose | John McKay | Anthony Davis, RB |
| 1975 | **Oklahoma** . . . . . . . . . . . . . . . .11-1-0 | | Won Orange | Barry Switzer | Lee Roy Selmon, DT |
| 1976 | **Pittsburgh** . . . . . . . . . . . . . . . .12-0-0 | | Won Sugar | Johnny Majors | Tony Dorsett, RB |
| 1977 | **Notre Dame** . . . . . . . . . . . . . . .11-1-0 | | Won Cotton | Dan Devine | Ross Browner, DE |
| 1978 | **Alabama** (AP, FW, NFF) . . . . . . .11-1-0 | | Won Sugar | Bear Bryant | Marty Lyons, DT |
| | & **USC** (UPI) . . . . . . . . . . . . . . . .12-1-0 | | Won Rose | John Robinson | Charles White, RB |
| 1979 | **Alabama** . . . . . . . . . . . . . . . . .12-0-0 | | Won Sugar | Bear Bryant | Jim Bunch, OT |
| 1980 | **Georgia** . . . . . . . . . . . . . . . . . .12-0-0 | | Won Sugar | Vince Dooley | Herschel Walker, RB |
| 1981 | **Clemson** . . . . . . . . . . . . . . . . . .12-0-0 | | Won Orange | Danny Ford | Jeff Davis, LB |
| 1982 | **Penn St.** . . . . . . . . . . . . . . . . . .11-1-0 | | Won Sugar | Joe Paterno | Todd Blackledge, QB |
| 1983 | **Miami-FL** . . . . . . . . . . . . . . . . .11-1-0 | | Won Orange | H. Schnellenberger | Bernie Kosar, QB |
| 1984 | **BYU** . . . . . . . . . . . . . . . . . . . . .13-0-0 | | Won Holiday | LaVell Edwards | Robbie Bosco, QB |
| 1985 | **Oklahoma** . . . . . . . . . . . . . . . .11-1-0 | | Won Orange | Barry Switzer | Brian Bosworth, LB |
| 1986 | **Penn St.** . . . . . . . . . . . . . . . . . .12-0-0 | | Won Fiesta | Joe Paterno | D.J. Dozier, RB |
| 1987 | **Miami-FL** . . . . . . . . . . . . . . . . .12-0-0 | | Won Orange | Jimmy Johnson | Steve Walsh, QB |
| 1988 | **Notre Dame** . . . . . . . . . . . . . . .12-0-0 | | Won Fiesta | Lou Holtz | Tony Rice, QB |
| 1989 | **Miami-FL** . . . . . . . . . . . . . . . . .11-1-0 | | Won Sugar | Dennis Erickson | Craig Erickson, QB |
| 1990 | **Colorado** (AP, FW, NFF) . . . . . . .11-1-1 | | Won Orange | Bill McCartney | Eric Bieniemy, RB |
| | & **Georgia Tech** (UP) . . . . . . . . .11-0-1 | | Won Citrus | Bobby Ross | Shawn Jones, QB |
| 1991 | **Miami-FL** (AP) . . . . . . . . . . . . . .12-0-0 | | Won Orange | Dennis Erickson | Gino Torretta, QB |
| | & **Washington** (USA, FW, NFF) . . .12-0-0 | | Won Rose | Don James | Steve Emtman, DT |
| 1992 | **Alabama** . . . . . . . . . . . . . . . . .13-0-0 | | Won Sugar | Gene Stallings | Eric Curry, DE |
| 1993 | **Florida St.** . . . . . . . . . . . . . . . .12-1-0 | | Won Orange | Bobby Bowden | Charlie Ward, QB |
| 1994 | **Nebraska** . . . . . . . . . . . . . . . . .13-0-0 | | Won Orange | Tom Osborne | Zach Wiegert, OT |
| 1995 | **Nebraska** . . . . . . . . . . . . . . . . .12-0-0 | | Won Fiesta | Tom Osborne | Tommie Frazier, QB |
| 1996 | **Florida** . . . . . . . . . . . . . . . . . . .12-1* | | Won Sugar | Steve Spurrier | Danny Wuerffel, QB |
| 1997 | **Michigan** (AP, FW, NFF) . . . . . . .12-0 | | Won Rose | Lloyd Carr | Charles Woodson, DB |
| | & **Nebraska** (ESPN/USA) . . . . . . .13-0 | | Won Orange | Tom Osborne | Ahman Green, RB |
| 1998 | **Tennessee** . . . . . . . . . . . . . . . . .13-0 | | Won Fiesta | Phillip Fulmer | Peerless Price, WR |
| 1999 | **Florida St.** . . . . . . . . . . . . . . . .12-0 | | Won Sugar | Bobby Bowden | Peter Warrick, WR |
| 2000 | **Oklahoma** . . . . . . . . . . . . . . . .13-0 | | Won Orange | Bob Stoops | Josh Heupel, QB |
| 2001 | **Miami-FL** . . . . . . . . . . . . . . . . .12-0 | | Won Rose | Larry Coker | Ken Dorsey, QB |
| 2002 | **Ohio St.** . . . . . . . . . . . . . . . . . .14-0 | | Won Fiesta | Jim Tressel | Craig Krenzler, QB |
| 2003 | **USC** (AP) . . . . . . . . . . . . . . . . . .12-1 | | Won Rose | Pete Carroll | Matt Leinart, QB |
| | & **LSU** (ESPN/USA) . . . . . . . . . . .13-1 | | Won Sugar | Nick Saban | Matt Mauck, QB |
| 2004 | **USC** . . . . . . . . . . . . . . . . . . . . .13-0 | | Won Orange | Pete Carroll | Matt Leinart, QB |

*The NCAA instituted overtime for regular season games in 1996.

## Number 1 vs. Number 2

Since the Associated Press writers poll started keeping track of such things in 1936, the No. 1 and No. 2 ranked teams in the country have met 34 times; 20 during the regular season and 14 in bowl games. Since the first showdown in 1943, the No. 1 team has beaten the No. 2 team 22 times, lost 10 and there have been two ties. Each showdown is listed below with the date, the match-up, each team's record going into the game, the final score, the stadium and site.

| Date | | Match-up | Stadium | Date | | Match-up | Stadium |
|---|---|---|---|---|---|---|---|
| Oct. 9 | #1 | Notre Dame (2-0) . . .35 | Michigan | Nov. 10 | #1 | Army (6-0) . . . . . . . .48 | Yankee |
| 1943 | #2 | Michigan (3-0) . . . . . .12 | (Ann Arbor) | 1945 | #2 | Notre Dame (5-0-1) . .0 | (New York) |
| Nov. 20 | #1 | Notre Dame (8-0) . . .14 | Notre Dame | Dec. 1 | #1 | Army (8-0) . . . . . . . .32 | Municipal |
| 1943 | #2 | Iowa Pre-Flight (8-0) . .13 | (South Bend) | 1945 | #2 | Navy (7-0-1) . . . . . . .13 | (Philadelphia) |
| Dec. 2 | #1 | Army (8-0) . . . . . . . .23 | Municipal | Nov. 9 | #1 | Army (7-0) . . . . . . . . .0 | Yankee |
| 1944 | #2 | Navy (6-2) . . . . . . . . .7 | (Baltimore) | 1946 | #2 | Notre Dame (5-0) . . . .0 | (New York) |

| Date | | Match-up | | Stadium |
|---|---|---|---|---|
| Jan. 1 | #1 | USC (10-0) | ...42 | ROSE BOWL |
| 1963 | #2 | Wisconsin (8-1) | ...37 | (Pasadena) |
| Oct. 12 | #1 | Texas (3-0) | ...28 | Cotton Bowl |
| 1963 | #2 | Oklahoma (2-0) | ...7 | (Dallas) |
| Jan. 1 | #1 | Texas (10-0) | ...28 | COTTON BOWL |
| 1964 | #2 | Navy (9-1) | ...6 | (Dallas) |
| Nov. 19 | #1 | Notre Dame (8-0) | ...10 | Spartan |
| 1966 | #2 | Michigan St. (9-0) | ...10 | (East Lansing) |
| Sept. 28 | #1 | Purdue (1-0) | ...37 | Notre Dame |
| 1968 | #2 | Notre Dame (1-0) | ...22 | (South Bend) |
| Jan. 1 | #1 | Ohio St. (9-0) | ...27 | ROSE BOWL |
| 1969 | #2 | USC (9-0-1) | ...16 | (Pasadena) |
| Dec. 6 | #1 | Texas (9-0) | ...15 | Razorback |
| 1969 | #2 | Arkansas (9-0) | ...14 | (Fayetteville) |
| Nov. 25 | #1 | Nebraska (10-0) | ...35 | Owen Field |
| 1971 | #2 | Oklahoma (9-0) | ...31 | (Norman) |
| Jan. 1 | #1 | Nebraska (12-0) | ...38 | ORANGE BOWL |
| 1972 | #2 | Alabama (11-0) | ...6 | (Miami) |
| Jan. 1 | #2 | Alabama (10-1) | ...14 | SUGAR BOWL |
| 1979 | #1 | Penn St. (11-0) | ...7 | (New Orleans) |
| Sept. 26 | #1 | USC (2-0) | ...28 | Coliseum |
| 1981 | #2 | Oklahoma (1-0) | ...24 | (Los Angeles) |
| Jan. 1 | #1 | Penn St. (10-1) | ...27 | SUGAR BOWL |
| 1983 | #1 | Georgia (11-0) | ...23 | (New Orleans) |
| Oct. 19 | #1 | Iowa (5-0) | ...12 | Kinnick |
| 1985 | #2 | Michigan (5-0) | ...10 | (Iowa City) |
| Sept. 27 | #2 | Miami-FL (3-0) | ...28 | Orange Bowl |
| 1986 | #1 | Oklahoma (2-0) | ...16 | (Miami) |
| Jan. 2 | #2 | Penn St. (11-0) | ...14 | FIESTA BOWL |
| 1987 | #1 | Miami-FL (11-0) | ...10 | (Tempe) |
| Nov. 21 | #2 | Oklahoma (10-0) | ...17 | Memorial |
| 1987 | #1 | Nebraska (10-0) | ...7 | (Lincoln) |
| Jan. 1 | #2 | Miami-FL (11-0) | ...20 | ORANGE BOWL |
| 1988 | #1 | Oklahoma (11-0) | ...14 | (Miami) |
| Nov. 26 | #1 | Notre Dame (10-0) | ...27 | Coliseum |
| 1988 | #2 | USC (10-0) | ...10 | (Los Angeles) |
| Sept. 16 | #1 | Notre Dame (1-0) | ...24 | Michigan |
| 1989 | #2 | Michigan (0-0) | ...19 | (Ann Arbor) |
| Nov. 16 | #2 | Miami-FL (8-0) | ...17 | Doak Campbell |
| 1991 | #1 | Florida St. (10-0) | ...16 | (Tallahassee) |
| Jan. 1 | #2 | Alabama (12-0) | ...34 | SUGAR BOWL |
| 1993 | #1 | Miami-FL (11-0) | ...13 | (New Orleans) |
| Nov. 13 | #2 | Notre Dame (9-0) | ...31 | Notre Dame |
| 1993 | #1 | Florida St. (9-0) | ...24 | (South Bend) |
| Jan. 1 | #1 | Florida St. (11-1) | ...18 | ORANGE BOWL |
| 1994 | #2 | Nebraska (11-0) | ...16 | (Miami) |
| Jan. 2 | #1 | Nebraska (11-0) | ...62 | FIESTA BOWL |
| 1996 | #2 | Florida (12-0) | ...24 | (Tempe) |
| Nov. 30 | #2 | Florida St. (10-0) | ...24 | Doak Campbell |
| 1996 | #1 | Florida (10-1) | ...21 | (Tallahassee) |
| Jan. 4 | #1 | Tennessee (12-0) | ...23 | FIESTA BOWL |
| 1999 | #2 | Florida St. (11-1) | ...16 | (Tempe) |
| Jan. 4 | #1 | Florida St. (11-0) | ...46 | SUGAR BOWL |
| 2000 | #2 | Virginia Tech (11-0) | .29 | (New Orleans) |
| Jan. 3 | #2 | Ohio St. (13-0) | ...31 | FIESTA BOWL |
| 2003 | #1 | Miami-FL (12-0) | .2OT 24 | (Tempe) |
| Jan. 4 | #1 | USC (12-0) | ...55 | ORANGE BOWL |
| 2005 | #2 | Oklahoma (12-0) | ...19 | (Miami) |

**Note:** Bowl games are listed in CAPITAL letters.

## Top 50 Rivalries

Top Division I-A and I-AA series records, including games through the 2004 season. All rivalries listed below are renewed annually with the following exception. **Nebraska-Oklahoma** now play only when matched up as part of the rotating Big 12 schedule. **The Citadel-VMI** did not play in 2004 but were scheduled to play in 2005.

RECENTLY DISCONTINUED SERIES: **LSU vs Tulane** in 2002 after 94 games (LSU ahead 65-22-7)*; **Penn State vs Pitt** in 2001 after 96 games (Penn State ahead 50-42-4)

| | Gm | Series Leader | | Gm | Series Leader |
|---|---|---|---|---|---|
| **Air Force-Army** | .39 | Air Force (26-12-1) | **Michigan-Michigan St.** | .97 | Michigan (64-28-5) |
| **Air Force-Navy** | .37 | Air Force (25-12-0) | **Michigan-Notre Dame** | .32 | Michigan (18-13-1) |
| **Alabama-Auburn** | .69 | Alabama (38-30-1) | **Michigan-Ohio St.** | .101 | Michigan (57-38-6) |
| **Alabama-Tennessee** | .87 | Alabama (43-37-7) | **Minnesota-Wisconsin** | .113 | Minnesota (58-47-8) |
| **Arizona-Arizona St.** | .78 | Arizona (44-33-1) | **Mississippi-Miss. St.** | .101 | Ole Miss (58-37-6) |
| **Army-Navy** | .105 | Tied (49-49-7) | **Missouri-Kansas** | .113 | Missouri (52-52-9) |
| **Auburn-Georgia** | .108 | Auburn (52-48-8) | **Nebraska-Oklahoma** | .81 | Oklahoma (40-38-3) |
| **California-Stanford** | .107 | Stanford (54-42-11) | **N. Mexico-N. Mexico St.** | .94 | New Mexico (61-28-5) |
| **The Citadel-VMI** | .63 | The Citadel (31-30-2) | **N. Carolina-N.C. State** | .94 | N. Carolina (61-27-6) |
| **Clemson-S. Carolina** | .102 | Clemson (62-36-4) | **Notre Dame-Purdue** | .76 | Notre Dame (50-24-2) |
| **Colorado-Nebraska** | .63 | Nebraska (44-17-2) | **Notre Dame-USC** | .76 | Notre Dame (42-29-5) |
| **Colo.-Wyoming** | .94 | Colorado St. (50-39-5) | **Oklahoma-Okla. St.** | .99 | Oklahoma (76-16-7) |
| **Duke-N. Carolina** | .90 | N. Carolina (51-36-4)* | **Oregon-Oregon St.** | .108 | Oregon (54-44-10) |
| **Florida-Florida St.** | .49 | Florida (28-19-2) | **Penn-Cornell** | .111 | Penn (65-41-5) |
| **Florida-Georgia** | .83 | Georgia (47-34-2) | **Pittsburgh-West Va** | .97 | Pitt (58-36-3) |
| **Florida St.-Miami,FL** | .49 | Miami (29-20-0) | **Princeton-Yale** | .127 | Yale (68-49-10) |
| **Georgia-Georgia Tech** | .99 | Georgia (56-38-5)* | **Purdue-Indiana** | .107 | Purdue (66-35-6) |
| **Grambling-Southern** | .53 | Southern (28-25-0) | **Richmond-Wm. & Mary** | .114 | Wm. & Mary (58-51-5) |
| **Harvard-Yale** | .121 | Yale (64-49-8) | **Tennessee-Vanderbilt** | .98 | Tennessee (67-26-5) |
| **Iowa-Iowa St.** | .52 | Iowa (35-17-0) | **Texas-Oklahoma** | .99 | Texas (56-38-5) |
| **Kansas-Kansas St.** | .102 | Kansas (62-35-5) | **Texas-Texas A&M** | .111 | Texas (72-34-5) |
| **Kentucky-Tennessee** | .100 | Tennessee (68-23-9) | **UCLA-USC** | .74 | USC (49-28-7) |
| **Lafayette-Lehigh** | .140 | Lafayette (73-62-5) | **Utah-BYU** | .80 | Utah (48-28-4)* |
| **LSU-Mississippi** | .93 | LSU (52-37-4) | **Utah-Utah St.** | .102 | Utah (69-29-4) |
| **Miami,OH-Cincinnati** | .109 | Miami (58-44-7) | **Washington-Wash. St.** | .97 | Washington (64-27-6) |

*Disputed series records: UNC claims lead of 52-35-4; Georgia claims lead of 56-36-5; Tulane claims LSU leads 62-23-7; Utah claims lead of 51-31-4

## Associated Press Final Polls

The Associated Press introduced its weekly college football poll of sportswriters (later, sportswriters and broadcasters) in 1936. The final AP poll was released at the end of the regular season until 1965, when bowl results were included for one year. After a two-year return to regular season games only, the final poll has come out after the bowls since 1968. Starting in 1989, the AP Poll has ranked 25 teams.

### 1936

Final poll released Nov. 30. Top 20 regular season results after that: **Dec. 5**–#8 Notre Dame tied USC, 13-13; #17 Tennessee tied Ole Miss, 0-0; #18 Arkansas over Texas, 6-0. **Dec. 12**–#16 TCU over #6 Santa Clara, 9-0.

| | | As of Nov. 30 | Head Coach | After Bowls |
|---|---|---|---|---|
| 1 | Minnesota | 7-1-0 | Bernie Bierman | same |
| 2 | LSU | 9-0-1 | Bernie Moore | 9-1-1 |
| 3 | Pittsburgh | 7-1-1 | Jock Sutherland | 8-1-1 |
| 4 | Alabama | 8-0-1 | Frank Thomas | same |
| 5 | Washington | 7-1-1 | Jimmy Phelan | 7-2-1 |
| 6 | Santa Clara | 7-0-0 | Buck Shaw | 8-1-0 |
| 7 | Northwestern | 7-1-0 | Pappy Waldorf | same |
| 8 | Notre Dame | 6-2-0 | Elmer Layden | 6-2-1 |
| 9 | Nebraska | 7-2-0 | Dana X. Bible | same |
| 10 | Penn | 7-1-0 | Harvey Harman | same |
| 11 | Duke | 9-1-0 | Wallace Wade | same |
| 12 | Yale | 7-1-0 | Ducky Pond | same |
| 13 | Dartmouth | 7-1-1 | Red Blaik | same |
| 14 | Duquesne | 7-2-0 | John Smith | 8-2-0 |
| 15 | Fordham | 5-1-2 | Jim Crowley | same |
| 16 | TCU | 7-2-2 | Dutch Meyer | 9-2-2 |
| 17 | Tennessee | 6-2-1 | Bob Neyland | 6-2-2 |
| 18 | Arkansas | 6-3-0 | Fred Thomsen | 7-3-0 |
| | Navy | 6-3-0 | Tom Hamilton | same |
| 20 | Marquette | 7-1-0 | Frank Murray | 7-2-0 |

### Key Bowl Games

**Sugar**–#6 Santa Clara over #2 LSU, 21-14; **Rose**–#3 Pitt over #5 Washington, 21-0; **Orange**–#14 Duquesne over Mississippi St., 13-12; **Cotton**–#16 TCU over #20 Marquette, 16-6.

### 1937

Final poll released Nov. 29. Top 20 regular season results after that: **Dec. 4**–#18 Rice over SMU, 15-7.

| | | As of Nov. 29 | Head Coach | After Bowls |
|---|---|---|---|---|
| 1 | Pittsburgh | 9-0-1 | Jock Sutherland | same |
| 2 | California | 9-0-1 | Stub Allison | 10-0-1 |
| 3 | Fordham | 7-0-1 | Jim Crowley | same |
| 4 | Alabama | 9-0-0 | Frank Thomas | 9-1-0 |
| 5 | Minnesota | 6-2-0 | Bernie Bierman | same |
| 6 | Villanova | 8-0-1 | Clipper Smith | same |
| 7 | Dartmouth | 7-0-2 | Red Blaik | same |
| 8 | LSU | 9-1-0 | Bernie Moore | 9-2-0 |
| 9 | Notre Dame | 6-2-1 | Elmer Layden | same |
| | Santa Clara | 8-0-0 | Buck Shaw | 9-0-0 |
| 11 | Nebraska | 6-1-2 | Biff Jones | same |
| 12 | Yale | 6-1-1 | Ducky Pond | same |
| 13 | Ohio St. | 6-2-0 | Francis Schmidt | same |
| 14 | Holy Cross | 8-0-2 | Eddie Anderson | same |
| | Arkansas | 6-2-2 | Fred Thomsen | same |
| 16 | TCU | 4-2-2 | Dutch Meyer | same |
| 17 | Colorado | 8-0-0 | Bunnie Oakes | 8-1-0 |
| 18 | Rice | 4-3-2 | Jimmy Kitts | 6-3-2 |
| 19 | North Carolina | 7-1-1 | Ray Wolf | same |
| 20 | Duke | 7-2-1 | Wallace Wade | same |

### Key Bowl Games

**Rose**–#2 Cal over #4 Alabama, 13-0; **Sugar**–#9 Santa Clara over #8 LSU, 6-0; **Cotton**–#18 Rice over #17 Colorado, 28-14; **Orange**–Auburn over Michigan St., 6-0.

### 1938

Final poll released Dec. 5. Top 20 regular season results after that: **Dec. 26**–#14 Cal over Georgia Tech, 13-7.

| | | As of Dec. 5 | Head Coach | After Bowls |
|---|---|---|---|---|
| 1 | TCU | 10-0-0 | Dutch Meyer | 11-0-0 |
| 2 | Tennessee | 10-0-0 | Bob Neyland | 11-0-0 |
| 3 | Duke | 9-0-0 | Wallace Wade | 9-1-0 |
| 4 | Oklahoma | 10-0-0 | Tom Stidham | 10-1-0 |
| 5 | Notre Dame | 8-1-0 | Elmer Layden | same |
| 6 | Carnegie Tech | 7-1-0 | Bill Kern | 7-2-0 |
| 7 | USC | 8-2-0 | Howard Jones | 9-2-0 |
| 8 | Pittsburgh | 8-2-0 | Jock Sutherland | same |
| 9 | Holy Cross | 8-1-0 | Eddie Anderson | same |
| 10 | Minnesota | 6-2-0 | Bernie Bierman | same |
| 11 | Texas Tech | 10-0-0 | Pete Cawthon | 10-1-0 |
| 12 | Cornell | 5-1-1 | Carl Snavely | same |
| 13 | Alabama | 7-1-1 | Frank Thomas | same |
| 14 | California | 9-1-0 | Stub Allison | 10-1-0 |
| 15 | Fordham | 6-1-2 | Jim Crowley | same |
| 16 | Michigan | 6-1-1 | Fritz Crisler | same |
| 17 | Northwestern | 4-2-2 | Pappy Waldorf | same |
| 18 | Villanova | 8-0-1 | Clipper Smith | same |
| 19 | Tulane | 7-2-1 | Red Dawson | same |
| 20 | Dartmouth | 7-2-0 | Red Blaik | same |

### Key Bowl Games

**Sugar**–#1 TCU over #6 Carnegie Tech, 15-7; **Orange**–#2 Tennessee over #4 Oklahoma, 17-0; **Rose**–#7 USC over #3 Duke, 7-3; **Cotton**–St. Mary's over #11 Texas Tech 20-13.

### 1939

Final poll released Dec. 11. Top 20 regular season results after that: None.

| | | As of Dec. 11 | Head Coach | After Bowls |
|---|---|---|---|---|
| 1 | Texas A&M | 10-0-0 | Homer Norton | 11-0-0 |
| 2 | Tennessee | 10-0-0 | Bob Neyland | 10-1-0 |
| 3 | USC | 7-0-2 | Howard Jones | 8-0-2 |
| 4 | Cornell | 8-0-0 | Carl Snavely | same |
| 5 | Tulane | 8-0-1 | Red Dawson | 8-1-1 |
| 6 | Missouri | 8-1-0 | Don Faurot | 8-2-0 |
| 7 | UCLA | 6-0-4 | Babe Horrell | same |
| 8 | Duke | 8-1-0 | Wallace Wade | same |
| 9 | Iowa | 6-1-1 | Eddie Anderson | same |
| 10 | Duquesne | 8-0-1 | Buff Donelli | same |
| 11 | Boston College | 9-1-0 | Frank Leahy | 9-2-0 |
| 12 | Clemson | 8-1-0 | Jess Neely | 9-1-0 |
| 13 | Notre Dame | 7-2-0 | Elmer Layden | same |
| 14 | Santa Clara | 5-1-3 | Buck Shaw | same |
| 15 | Ohio St. | 6-2-0 | Francis Schmidt | same |
| 16 | Georgia Tech | 7-2-0 | Bill Alexander | 8-2-0 |
| 17 | Fordham | 6-2-0 | Jim Crowley | same |
| 18 | Nebraska | 7-1-1 | Biff Jones | same |
| 19 | Oklahoma | 6-2-1 | Tom Stidham | same |
| 20 | Michigan | 6-2-0 | Fritz Crisler | same |

### Key Bowl Games

**Sugar**–#1 Texas A&M over #5 Tulane, 14-13; **Rose**–#3 USC over #2 Tennessee, 14-0; **Orange**–#16 Georgia Tech over #6 Missouri, 21-7; **Cotton**–#12 Clemson over #11 Boston College, 6-3.

## 1940

Final poll released Dec. 2. Top 20 regular season results after that: **Dec. 7**–#16 SMU over Rice, 7-6.

| | | As of Dec. 2 | Head Coach | After Bowls |
|---|---|---|---|---|
| 1 | Minnesota | 8-0-0 | Bernie Bierman | same |
| 2 | Stanford | 9-0-0 | Clark Shaughnessy | 10-0-0 |
| 3 | Michigan | 7-1-0 | Fritz Crisler | same |
| 4 | Tennessee | 10-0-0 | Bob Neyland | 10-1-0 |
| 5 | Boston College | 10-0-0 | Frank Leahy | 11-0-0 |
| 6 | Texas A&M | 8-1-0 | Homer Norton | 9-1-0 |
| 7 | Nebraska | 8-1-0 | Biff Jones | 8-2-0 |
| 8 | Northwestern | 6-2-0 | Pappy Waldorf | same |
| 9 | Mississippi St. | 9-0-1 | Allyn McKeen | 10-0-1 |
| 10 | Washington | 7-2-0 | Jimmy Phelan | same |
| 11 | Santa Clara | 6-1-1 | Buck Shaw | same |
| 12 | Fordham | 7-1-0 | Jim Crowley | 7-2-0 |
| 13 | Georgetown | 8-1-0 | Jack Hagerty | 8-2-0 |
| 14 | Penn | 6-1-1 | George Munger | same |
| 15 | Cornell | 6-2-0 | Carl Snavely | same |
| 16 | SMU | 7-1-1 | Matty Bell | 8-1-1 |
| 17 | Hardin-Simmons | 9-0-0 | Warren Woodson | same |
| 18 | Duke | 7-2-0 | Wallace Wade | same |
| 19 | Lafayette | 9-0-0 | Hooks Mylin | same |
| 20 – | | | | |

**Note:** Only 19 teams ranked.

### Key Bowl Games

**Rose**–#2 Stanford over #7 Nebraska, 21-13; **Sugar**– #5 Boston College over #4 Tennessee, 19-13; **Cotton**–#6 Texas A&M over #12 Fordham, 13-12; **Orange**–#9 Mississippi St. over #13 Georgetown, 14-7.

## 1941

Final poll released Dec. 1. Top 20 regular season results after that: **Dec. 6**–#4 Texas over Oregon, 71-7; #9 Texas A&M over #19 Washington St., 7-0; #16 Mississippi St. over San Francisco, 26-13.

| | | As of Dec. 1 | Head Coach | After Bowls |
|---|---|---|---|---|
| 1 | Minnesota | 8-0-0 | Bernie Bierman | same |
| 2 | Duke | 9-0-0 | Wallace Wade | 9-1-0 |
| 3 | Notre Dame | 8-0-1 | Frank Leahy | same |
| 4 | Texas | 7-1-1 | Dana X. Bible | 8-1-1 |
| 5 | Michigan | 6-1-1 | Fritz Crisler | same |
| 6 | Fordham | 7-1-0 | Jim Crowley | 8-1-0 |
| 7 | Missouri | 8-1-0 | Don Faurot | 8-2-0 |
| 8 | Duquesne | 8-0-0 | Buff Donelli | same |
| 9 | Texas A&M | 8-1-0 | Homer Norton | 9-2-0 |
| 10 | Navy | 7-1-1 | Swede Larson | same |
| 11 | Northwestern | 5-3-0 | Pappy Waldorf | same |
| 12 | Oregon St. | 7-2-0 | Lon Stiner | 8-2-0 |
| 13 | Ohio St. | 6-1-1 | Paul Brown | same |
| 14 | Georgia | 8-1-1 | Wally Butts | 9-1-1 |
| 15 | Penn | 7-1-1 | George Munger | same |
| 16 | Mississippi St. | 7-1-1 | Allyn McKeen | 8-1-1 |
| 17 | Mississippi | 6-2-1 | Harry Mehre | same |
| 18 | Tennessee | 8-2-0 | John Barnhill | same |
| 19 | Washington St. | 6-3-0 | Babe Hollingbery | 6-4-0 |
| 20 | Alabama | 8-2-0 | Frank Thomas | 9-2-0 |

**Note:** 1942 Rose Bowl moved to Durham, N.C., for one year after outbreak of World War II.

### Key Bowl Games

**Rose**–#12 Oregon St. over #2 Duke, 20-16; **Sugar**–#6 Fordham over #7 Missouri, 2-0; **Cotton**–#20 Alabama over #9 Texas A&M, 29-21; **Orange**–#14 Georgia over TCU, 40-26.

## 1942

Final poll released Nov. 30. Top 20 regular season results after that: **Dec. 5**–#6 Notre Dame tied Great Lakes Naval Station, 13-13; #13 UCLA over Idaho, 40-13; #14 William & Mary over Oklahoma, 14-7; #17 Washington St. lost to Texas A&M, 21-0; #18 Mississippi St. over San Francisco, 19-7. **Dec. 12**–#13 UCLA over USC, 14-7.

| | | As of Nov. 30 | Head Coach | After Bowls |
|---|---|---|---|---|
| 1 | Ohio St. | 9-1-0 | Paul Brown | same |
| 2 | Georgia | 10-1-0 | Wally Butts | 11-1-0 |
| 3 | Wisconsin | 8-1-1 | Harry Stuhldreher | same |
| 4 | Tulsa | 10-0-0 | Henry Frnka | 10-1-0 |
| 5 | Georgia Tech | 9-1-0 | Bill Alexander | 9-2-0 |
| 6 | Notre Dame | 7-2-1 | Frank Leahy | 7-2-2 |
| 7 | Tennessee | 8-1-1 | John Barnhill | 9-1-1 |
| 8 | Boston College | 8-1-0 | Denny Myers | 8-2-0 |
| 9 | Michigan | 7-3-0 | Fritz Crisler | same |
| 10 | Alabama | 7-3-0 | Frank Thomas | 8-3-0 |
| 11 | Texas | 8-2-0 | Dana X. Bible | 9-2-0 |
| 12 | Stanford | 6-4-0 | Marchy Schwartz | same |
| 13 | UCLA | 5-3-0 | Babe Horrell | 7-4-0 |
| 14 | William & Mary | 8-1-1 | Carl Voyles | 9-1-1 |
| 15 | Santa Clara | 7-2-0 | Buck Shaw | same |
| 16 | Auburn | 6-4-1 | Jack Meagher | same |
| 17 | Washington St. | 6-1-2 | Babe Hollingbery | 6-2-2 |
| 18 | Mississippi St. | 7-2-0 | Allyn McKeen | 8-2-0 |
| 19 | Minnesota | 5-4-0 | George Hauser | same |
| | Holy Cross | 5-4-1 | Ank Scanlon | same |
| | Penn St. | 6-1-1 | Bob Higgins | same |

### Key Bowl Games

**Rose**–#2 Georgia over #13 UCLA, 9-0; **Sugar**–#7 Tennessee over #4 Tulsa, 14-7; **Cotton**–#11 Texas over #5 Georgia Tech, 14-7; **Orange**–#10 Alabama over #8 Boston College, 37-21.

## 1943

Final poll released Nov. 29. Top 20 regular season results after that: **Dec. 11**–#10 March Field over #19 Pacific, 19-0.

| | | As of Nov. 29 | Head Coach | After Bowls |
|---|---|---|---|---|
| 1 | Notre Dame | 9-1-0 | Frank Leahy | same |
| 2 | Iowa Pre-Flight | 9-1-0 | Don Faurot | same |
| 3 | Michigan | 8-1-0 | Fritz Crisler | same |
| 4 | Navy | 8-1-0 | Billick Whelchel | same |
| 5 | Purdue | 9-0-0 | Elmer Burnham | same |
| 6 | Great Lakes Naval Station | 10-2-0 | Tony Hinkle | same |
| 7 | Duke | 8-1-0 | Eddie Cameron | same |
| 8 | DelMonte Pre-Flight | 7-1-0 | Bill Kern | same |
| 9 | Northwestern | 6-2-0 | Pappy Waldorf | same |
| 10 | March Field | 8-1-0 | Paul Schissler | 9-1-0 |
| 11 | Army | 7-2-1 | Red Blaik | same |
| 12 | Washington | 4-0-0 | Ralph Welch | 4-1-0 |
| 13 | Georgia Tech | 7-3-0 | Bill Alexander | 8-3-0 |
| 14 | Texas | 7-1-0 | Dana X. Bible | 7-1-1 |
| 15 | Tulsa | 6-0-1 | Henry Frnka | 6-1-1 |
| 16 | Dartmouth | 6-1-0 | Earl Brown | same |
| 17 | Bainbridge Navy Training School | 7-0-0 | Joe Maniaci | same |
| 18 | Colorado College | 7-0-0 | Hal White | same |
| 19 | Pacific | 7-1-0 | Amos A. Stagg | 7-2-0 |
| 20 | Penn | 6-2-1 | George Munger | same |

### Key Bowl Games

**Rose**–USC over #12 Washington, 29-0; **Sugar**–#13 Georgia Tech over #15 Tulsa, 20-18; **Cotton**–#14 Texas tied Randolph Field, 7-7; **Orange**–LSU over Texas A&M, 19-14.

## Associated Press Final Polls (Cont.)

### 1944

Final poll released Dec. 4. Top 20 regular season results after that: **Dec. 10**–#3 Randolph Field over #10 March Field, 20-7; #18 Fort Pierce over Kessler Field, 34-7; Morris Field over #20 Second Air Force, 14-7.

| | As of Dec. 4 | Head Coach | After Bowls |
|---|---|---|---|
| 1 Army | .9-0-0 | Red Blaik | same |
| 2 Ohio St. | .9-0-0 | Carroll Widdoes | same |
| 3 Randolph Field | .10-0-0 | Frank Tritico | 12-0-0 |
| 4 Navy | .6-3-0 | Oscar Hagberg | same |
| 5 Bainbridge Navy Training School | .10-0-0 | Joe Maniaci | same |
| 6 Iowa Pre-Flight | .10-1-0 | Jack Meagher | same |
| 7 USC | .7-0-2 | Jeff Cravath | 8-0-2 |
| 8 Michigan | .8-2-0 | Fritz Crisler | same |
| 9 Notre Dame | .8-2-0 | Ed McKeever | same |
| 10 March Field | .7-0-2 | Paul Schissler | 7-1-2 |
| 11 Duke | .5-4-0 | Eddie Cameron | 6-4-0 |
| 12 Tennessee | .7-0-1 | John Barnhill | 7-1-1 |
| 13 Georgia Tech | .8-2-0 | Bill Alexander | 8-3-0 |
| 14 Norman Pre-Flight | .6-0-0 | John Gregg | same |
| 15 Illinois | .5-4-1 | Ray Eliot | same |
| 16 El Toro Marines | .8-1-0 | Dick Hanley | same |
| 17 Great Lakes Naval Station | .9-2-1 | Paul Brown | same |
| 18 Fort Pierce | .8-0-0 | Hamp.Pool | 9-0-0 |
| 19 St. Mary's Pre-Flight | .4-4-0 | Jules Sikes | same |
| 20 Second Air Force | .10-2-1 | Bill Reese | 10-4-1 |

#### Key Bowl Games

**Treasury**–#3 Randolph Field over #20 Second Air Force, 13-6; **Rose**–#7 USC over #12 Tennessee, 25-0; **Sugar**–#11 Duke over Alabama, 29-26; **Orange**–Tulsa over #13 Georgia Tech, 26-12; **Cotton**–Oklahoma A&M over TCU, 34-0.

### 1945

Final poll released Dec. 3. Top 20 regular season results after that: None.

| | As of Dec. 3 | Head Coach | After Bowls |
|---|---|---|---|
| 1 Army | .9-0-0 | Red Blaik | same |
| 2 Alabama | .9-0-0 | Frank Thomas | 10-0-0 |
| 3 Navy | .7-1-1 | Oscar Hagberg | same |
| 4 Indiana | .9-0-1 | Bo McMillan | same |
| 5 Oklahoma A&M | .8-0-0 | Jim Lookabaugh | 9-0-0 |
| 6 Michigan | .7-3-0 | Fritz Crisler | same |
| 7 St. Mary's-CA | .7-1-0 | Jimmy Phelan | 7-2-0 |
| 8 Penn | .6-2-0 | George Munger | same |
| 9 Notre Dame | .7-2-1 | Hugh Devore | same |
| 10 Texas | .9-1-0 | Dana X. Bible | 10-1-0 |
| 11 USC | .7-3-0 | Jeff Cravath | 7-4-0 |
| 12 Ohio St. | .7-2-0 | Carroll Widdoes | same |
| 13 Duke | .6-2-0 | Eddie Cameron | same |
| 14 Tennessee | .8-1-0 | John Barnhill | same |
| 15 LSU | .7-2-0 | Bernie Moore | same |
| 16 Holy Cross | .8-1-0 | John DeGrosa | 8-2-0 |
| 17 Tulsa | .8-2-0 | Henry Frnka | 8-3-0 |
| 18 Georgia | .8-2-0 | Wally Butts | 9-2-0 |
| 19 Wake Forest | .4-3-1 | Peahead Walker | 5-3-1 |
| 20 Columbia | .8-1-0 | Lou Little | same |

#### Key Bowl Games

**Rose**–#2 Alabama over #11 USC, 34-14; **Sugar**–#5 Oklahoma A&M over #7 St. Mary's, 33-13; **Cotton**–#10 Texas over Missouri, 40-27; **Orange**–Miami-FL over #16 Holy Cross, 13-6.

### 1946

Final poll released Dec. 2. Top 20 regular season results after that: None.

| | As of Dec. 2 | Head Coach | After Bowls |
|---|---|---|---|
| 1 Notre Dame | .8-0-1 | Frank Leahy | same |
| 2 Army | .9-0-1 | Red Blaik | same |
| 3 Georgia | .10-0-0 | Wally Butts | 11-0-0 |
| 4 UCLA | .10-0-0 | Bert LaBrucherie | 10-1-0 |
| 5 Illinois | .7-2-0 | Ray Eliot | 8-2-0 |
| 6 Michigan | .6-2-1 | Fritz Crisler | same |
| 7 Tennessee | .9-1-0 | Bob Neyland | 9-2-0 |
| 8 LSU | .9-1-0 | Bernie Moore | 9-1-1 |
| 9 North Carolina | .8-1-1 | Carl Snavely | 8-2-1 |
| 10 Rice | .8-2-0 | Jess Neely | 9-2-0 |
| 11 Georgia Tech | .8-2-0 | Bobby Dodd | 9-2-0 |
| 12 Yale | .7-1-1 | Howard Odell | same |
| 13 Penn | .6-2-0 | George Munger | same |
| 14 Oklahoma | .7-3-0 | Jim Tatum | 8-3-0 |
| 15 Texas | .8-2-0 | Dana X. Bible | same |
| 16 Arkansas | .6-3-1 | John Barnhill | 6-3-2 |
| 17 Tulsa | .9-1-0 | J.O. Brothers | same |
| 18 N.C. State | .8-2-0 | Beattie Feathers | 8-3-0 |
| 19 Delaware | .9-0-0 | Bill Murray | 10-0-0 |
| 20 Indiana | .6-3-0 | Bo McMillan | same |

#### Key Bowl Games

**Sugar**–#3 Georgia over #9 N. Carolina, 20-10; **Rose**–#5 Illinois over #4 UCLA, 45-14; **Orange**–#10 Rice over #7 Tennessee, 8-0; **Cotton**–#8 LSU tied #16 Arkansas, 0-0.

### 1947

Final poll released Dec. 8. Top 20 regular season results after that: None.

| | As of Dec. 8 | Head Coach | After Bowls |
|---|---|---|---|
| 1 Notre Dame | .9-0-0 | Frank Leahy | same |
| 2 Michigan | .9-0-0 | Fritz Crisler | 10-0-0 |
| 3 SMU | .9-0-1 | Matty Bell | 9-0-2 |
| 4 Penn St. | .9-0-0 | Bob Higgins | 9-0-1 |
| 5 Texas | .9-1-0 | Blair Cherry | 10-1-0 |
| 6 Alabama | .8-2-0 | Red Drew | 8-3-0 |
| 7 Penn | .7-0-1 | George Munger | same |
| 8 USC | .7-1-1 | Jeff Cravath | 7-2-1 |
| 9 North Carolina | .8-2-0 | Carl Snavely | same |
| 10 Georgia Tech | .9-1-0 | Bobby Dodd | 10-1-0 |
| 11 Army | .5-2-2 | Red Blaik | same |
| 12 Kansas | .8-0-2 | George Sauer | 8-1-2 |
| 13 Mississippi | .8-2-0 | Johnny Vaught | 9-2-0 |
| 14 William & Mary | .9-1-0 | Rube McCray | 9-2-0 |
| 15 California | .9-1-0 | Pappy Waldorf | same |
| 16 Oklahoma | .7-2-1 | Bud Wilkinson | same |
| 17 N.C. State | .5-3-1 | Beattie Feathers | same |
| 18 Rice | .6-3-1 | Jess Neely | same |
| 19 Duke | .4-3-2 | Wallace Wade | same |
| 20 Columbia | .7-2-0 | Lou Little | same |

#### Key Bowl Games

**Rose**–#2 Michigan over #8 USC, 49-0; **Cotton**–#3 SMU tied #4 Penn St., 13-13; **Sugar**–#5 Texas over #6 Alabama, 27-7; **Orange**–#10 Georgia Tech over #12 Kansas, 20-14.

**Note:** An unprecedented "Who's No. 1?" poll was conducted by AP after the Rose Bowl game, pitting Notre Dame against Michigan. The Wolverines won the vote, 226-119, but AP ruled that the Irish would be the No. 1 team of record.

## 1948

Final poll released Nov. 29. Top 20 regular season results after that: **Dec. 3**–#12 Vanderbilt over Miami-FL, 33-6. **Dec. 4**–#2 Notre Dame tied USC, 14-14; #11 Clemson over The Citadel, 20-0.

| | | As of Nov. 29 | Head Coach | After Bowls |
|---|---|---|---|---|
| 1 | Michigan | 9-0-0 | Bennie Oosterbaan | same |
| 2 | Notre Dame | 9-0-0 | Frank Leahy | 9-0-1 |
| 3 | North Carolina | 9-0-1 | Carl Snavely | 9-1-1 |
| 4 | California | 10-0-0 | Pappy Waldorf | 10-1-0 |
| 5 | Oklahoma | 9-1-0 | Bud Wilkinson | 10-1-0 |
| 6 | Army | 8-0-1 | Red Blaik | same |
| 7 | Northwestern | 7-2-0 | Bob Voigts | 8-2-0 |
| 8 | Georgia | 9-1-0 | Wally Butts | 9-2-0 |
| 9 | Oregon | 9-1-0 | Jim Aiken | 9-2-0 |
| 10 | SMU | 8-1-1 | Matty Bell | 9-1-1 |
| 11 | Clemson | 9-0-0 | Frank Howard | 11-0-0 |
| 12 | Vanderbilt | 7-2-1 | Red Sanders | 8-2-1 |
| 13 | Tulane | 9-1-0 | Henry Frnka | same |
| 14 | Michigan St. | 6-2-2 | Biggie Munn | same |
| 15 | Mississippi | 8-1-0 | Johnny Vaught | same |
| 16 | Minnesota | 7-2-0 | Bernie Bierman | same |
| 17 | William & Mary | 6-2-2 | Rube McCray | 7-2-2 |
| 18 | Penn St. | 7-1-1 | Bob Higgins | same |
| 19 | Cornell | 8-1-0 | Lefty James | same |
| 20 | Wake Forest | 6-3-0 | Peahead Walker | 6-4-0 |

**Note:** Big Nine "no-repeat" rule kept Michigan from Rose Bowl.

### Key Bowl Games

**Sugar**–#5 Oklahoma over #3 North Carolina, 14-6; **Rose**–#7 Northwestern over #4 Cal, 20-14; **Orange**–Texas over #8 Georgia, 41-28; **Cotton**–#10 SMU over #9 Oregon, 21-13.

## 1949

Final poll released Nov. 28. Top 20 regular season results after that: **Dec. 2**–#14 Maryland over Miami-FL, 13-0. **Dec. 3**–#1 Notre Dame over SMU, 27-20; #10 Pacific over Hawaii, 75-0.

| | | As of Nov. 28 | Head Coach | After Bowls |
|---|---|---|---|---|
| 1 | Notre Dame | 9-0-0 | Frank Leahy | 10-0-0 |
| 2 | Oklahoma | 10-0-0 | Bud Wilkinson | 11-0-0 |
| 3 | California | 10-0-0 | Pappy Waldorf | 10-1-0 |
| 4 | Army | 9-0-0 | Red Blaik | same |
| 5 | Rice | 9-1-0 | Jess Neely | 10-1-0 |
| 6 | Ohio St. | 6-1-2 | Wes Fesler | 7-1-2 |
| 7 | Michigan | 6-2-1 | Bennie Oosterbaan | same |
| 8 | Minnesota | 7-2-0 | Bernie Bierman | same |
| 9 | LSU | 8-2-0 | Gaynell Tinsley | 8-3-0 |
| 10 | Pacific | 10-0-0 | Larry Siemering | 11-0-0 |
| 11 | Kentucky | 9-2-0 | Bear Bryant | 9-3-0 |
| 12 | Cornell | 8-1-0 | Lefty James | same |
| 13 | Villanova | 8-1-0 | Jim Leonard | same |
| 14 | Maryland | 7-1-0 | Jim Tatum | 9-1-0 |
| 15 | Santa Clara | 7-2-1 | Len Casanova | 8-2-1 |
| 16 | North Carolina | 7-3-0 | Carl Snavely | 7-4-0 |
| 17 | Tennessee | 7-2-1 | Bob Neyland | same |
| 18 | Princeton | 6-3-0 | Charlie Caldwell | same |
| 19 | Michigan St. | 6-3-0 | Biggie Munn | same |
| 20 | Missouri | 7-3-0 | Don Faurot | 7-4-0 |
| | Baylor | 8-2-0 | Bob Woodruff | same |

### Key Bowl Games

**Sugar**–#2 Oklahoma over #9 LSU, 35-0; **Rose**–#6 Ohio St. over #3 Cal, 17-14; **Cotton**–#5 Rice over #16 North Carolina, 27-13; **Orange**–#15 Santa Clara over #11 Kentucky, 21-13.

## 1950

Final poll released Nov. 27. Top 20 regular season results after that: **Nov. 30**–#3 Texas over Texas A&M, 17-0. **Dec. 1**–#15 Miami-FL over Missouri, 27–9. **Dec. 2**–#1 Oklahoma over Okla. A&M, 41-14; Navy over #2 Army, 14-2; #4 Tennessee over Vanderbilt, 43-0; #16 Alabama over Auburn, 34-0; #19 Tulsa over Houston, 28-21; #20 Tulane tied LSU, 14-14. **Dec. 9**–#3 Texas over LSU, 21-6.

| | | As of Nov. 27 | Head Coach | After Bowls |
|---|---|---|---|---|
| 1 | Oklahoma | 9-0-0 | Bud Wilkinson | 10-1-0 |
| 2 | Army | 8-0-0 | Red Blaik | 8-1-0 |
| 3 | Texas | 7-1-0 | Blair Cherry | 9-2-0 |
| 4 | Tennessee | 9-1-0 | Bob Neyland | 11-1-0 |
| 5 | California | 9-0-1 | Pappy Waldorf | 9-1-1 |
| 6 | Princeton | 9-0-0 | Charlie Caldwell | same |
| 7 | Kentucky | 10-1-0 | Bear Bryant | 11-1-0 |
| 8 | Michigan St. | 8-1-0 | Biggie Munn | same |
| 9 | Michigan | 5-3-1 | Bennie Oosterbaan | 6-3-1 |
| 10 | Clemson | 8-0-1 | Frank Howard | 9-0-1 |
| 11 | Washington | 8-2-0 | Howard Odell | same |
| 12 | Wyoming | 9-0-0 | Bowden Wyatt | 10-0-0 |
| 13 | Illinois | 7-2-0 | Ray Eliot | same |
| 14 | Ohio St. | 6-3-0 | Wes Fesler | same |
| 15 | Miami-FL | 8-0-1 | Andy Gustafson | 9-1-1 |
| 16 | Alabama | 8-2-0 | Red Drew | 9-2-0 |
| 17 | Nebraska | 6-2-1 | Bill Glassford | same |
| 18 | Wash. & Lee | 8-2-1 | George Barclay | 8-3-0 |
| 19 | Tulsa | 8-1-1 | J.O. Brothers | 9-1-1 |
| 20 | Tulane | 6-2-0 | Henry Frnka | 6-2-1 |

### Key Bowl Games

**Sugar**–#7 Kentucky over #1 Oklahoma, 13-7; **Cotton**–#4 Tennessee over #3 Texas, 20-14; **Rose**–#9 Michigan over #5 Cal, 14-6; **Orange**–#10 Clemson over #15 Miami-FL, 15-14.

## 1951

Final poll released Dec. 3. Top 20 regular season results after that: None.

| | | As of Dec. 3 | Head Coach | After Bowls |
|---|---|---|---|---|
| 1 | Tennessee | 10-0-0 | Bob Neyland | 10-1-0 |
| 2 | Michigan St. | 9-0-0 | Biggie Munn | same |
| 3 | Maryland | 9-0-0 | Jim Tatum | 10-0-0 |
| 4 | Illinois | 8-0-1 | Ray Eliot | 9-0-1 |
| 5 | Georgia Tech | 10-0-1 | Bobby Dodd | 11-0-1 |
| 6 | Princeton | 9-0-0 | Charlie Caldwell | same |
| 7 | Stanford | 9-1-0 | Chuck Taylor | 9-2-0 |
| 8 | Wisconsin | 7-1-1 | Ivy Williamson | same |
| 9 | Baylor | 8-1-1 | George Sauer | 8-2-1 |
| 10 | Oklahoma | 8-2-0 | Bud Wilkinson | same |
| 11 | TCU | 6-4-0 | Dutch Meyer | 6-5-0 |
| 12 | California | 8-2-0 | Pappy Waldorf | same |
| 13 | Virginia | 8-1-0 | Art Guepe | same |
| 14 | San Francisco | 9-0-0 | Joe Kuharich | same |
| 15 | Kentucky | 7-4-0 | Bear Bryant | 8-4-0 |
| 16 | Boston Univ. | 6-4-0 | Buff Donelli | same |
| 17 | UCLA | 5-3-1 | Red Sanders | same |
| 18 | Washington St. | 7-3-0 | Forest Evashevski | same |
| 19 | Holy Cross | 8-2-0 | Eddie Anderson | same |
| 20 | Clemson | 7-2-0 | Frank Howard | 7-3-0 |

### Key Bowl Games

**Sugar**–#3 Maryland over #1 Tennessee, 28-13; **Rose**–#4 Illinois over #7 Stanford, 40-7; **Orange**–#5 Georgia Tech over #9 Baylor, 17-14; **Cotton**–#15 Kentucky over #11 TCU, 20-7.

## Associated Press Final Polls (Cont.)

### 1952

Final poll released Dec. 1. Top 20 regular season results after that: **Dec. 6**–#15 Florida over #20 Kentucky, 27-20.

| | | As of Dec. 1 | Head Coach | After Bowls |
|---|---|---|---|---|
| 1 | Michigan St. | .9-0-0 | Biggie Munn | same |
| 2 | Georgia Tech | .11-0-0 | Bobby Dodd | 12-0-0 |
| 3 | Notre Dame | .7-2-1 | Frank Leahy | same |
| 4 | Oklahoma | .8-1-1 | Bud Wilkinson | same |
| 5 | USC | .9-1-0 | Jess Hill | 10-1-0 |
| 6 | UCLA | .8-1-0 | Red Sanders | same |
| 7 | Mississippi | .8-0-2 | Johnny Vaught | 8-1-2 |
| 8 | Tennessee | .8-1-1 | Bob Neyland | 8-2-1 |
| 9 | Alabama | .9-2-0 | Red Drew | 10-2-0 |
| 10 | Texas | .8-2-0 | Ed Price | 9-2-0 |
| 11 | Wisconsin | .6-2-1 | Ivy Williamson | 6-3-1 |
| 12 | Tulsa | .8-1-1 | J.O. Brothers | 8-2-1 |
| 13 | Maryland | .7-2-0 | Jim Tatum | same |
| 14 | Syracuse | .7-2-0 | Ben Schwartzwalder | 7-3-0 |
| 15 | Florida | .6-3-0 | Bob Woodruff | 8-3-0 |
| 16 | Duke | .8-2-0 | Bill Murray | same |
| 17 | Ohio St. | .6-3-0 | Woody Hayes | same |
| 18 | Purdue | .4-3-2 | Stu Holcomb | same |
| 19 | Princeton | .8-1-0 | Charlie Caldwell | same |
| 20 | Kentucky | .5-3-2 | Bear Bryant | 5-4-2 |

**Note:** Michigan St. would officially join Big Ten in 1953.

#### Key Bowl Games

**Sugar**–#2 Georgia Tech over #7 Ole Miss, 24-7; **Rose**–#5 USC over #11 Wisconsin, 7-0; **Cotton**–#10 Texas over #8 Tennessee, 16-0; **Orange**–#9 Alabama over #14 Syracuse, 61-6.

### 1953

Final poll released Nov. 30. Top 20 regular season results after that: **Dec. 5**–Notre Dame over SMU, 40-14.

| | | As of Nov. 30 | Head Coach | After Bowls |
|---|---|---|---|---|
| 1 | Maryland | .10-0-0 | Jim Tatum | 10-1-0 |
| 2 | Notre Dame | .8-0-1 | Frank Leahy | 9-0-1 |
| 3 | Michigan St. | .8-1-0 | Biggie Munn | 9-1-0 |
| 4 | Oklahoma | .8-1-1 | Bud Wilkinson | 9-1-1 |
| 5 | UCLA | .8-1-0 | Red Sanders | 8-2-0 |
| 6 | Rice | .8-2-0 | Jess Neely | 9-2-0 |
| 7 | Illinois | .7-1-1 | Ray Eliot | same |
| 8 | Georgia Tech | .8-2-1 | Bobby Dodd | 9-2-1 |
| 9 | Iowa | .5-3-1 | Forest Evashevski | same |
| 10 | West Virginia | .8-1-0 | Art Lewis | 8-2-0 |
| 11 | Texas | .7-3-0 | Ed Price | same |
| 12 | Texas Tech | .10-1-0 | DeWitt Weaver | 11-1-0 |
| 13 | Alabama | .6-2-3 | Red Drew | 6-3-3 |
| 14 | Army | .7-1-1 | Red Blaik | same |
| 15 | Wisconsin | .6-2-1 | Ivy Williamson | 6-3-0 |
| 16 | Kentucky | .7-2-1 | Bear Bryant | same |
| 17 | Auburn | .7-2-1 | Shug Jordan | 7-3-1 |
| 18 | Duke | .7-2-1 | Bill Murray | same |
| 19 | Stanford | .6-3-1 | Chuck Taylor | same |
| 20 | Michigan | .6-3-0 | Bennie Oosterbaan | same |

#### Key Bowl Games

**Orange**–#4 Oklahoma over #1 Maryland, 7-0; **Rose**–#3 Michigan St. over #5 UCLA, 28-20; **Cotton**–#6 Rice over #13 Alabama, 28-6; **Sugar**–#8 Georgia Tech over #10 West Virginia, 42-19.

### 1954

Final poll released Nov. 29. Top 20 regular season results after that: **Dec. 4**–#4 Notre Dame over SMU, 26-14.

| | | As of Nov. 29 | Head Coach | After Bowls |
|---|---|---|---|---|
| 1 | Ohio St. | .9-0-0 | Woody Hayes | 10-0-0 |
| 2 | UCLA | .9-0-0 | Red Sanders | same |
| 3 | Oklahoma | .10-0-0 | Bud Wilkinson | same |
| 4 | Notre Dame | .8-1-0 | Terry Brennan | 9-1-0 |
| 5 | Navy | .7-2-0 | Eddie Erdelatz | 8-2-0 |
| 6 | Mississippi | .9-1-0 | Johnny Vaught | 9-2-0 |
| 7 | Army | .7-2-0 | Red Blaik | same |
| 8 | Maryland | .7-2-1 | Jim Tatum | same |
| 9 | Wisconsin | .7-2-0 | Ivy Williamson | same |
| 10 | Arkansas | .8-2-0 | Bowden Wyatt | 8-3-0 |
| 11 | Miami-FL | .8-1-0 | Andy Gustafson | same |
| 12 | West Virginia | .8-1-0 | Art Lewis | same |
| 13 | Auburn | .7-3-0 | Shug Jordan | 8-3-0 |
| 14 | Duke | .7-2-1 | Bill Murray | 8-2-1 |
| 15 | Michigan | .6-3-0 | Bennie Oosterbaan | same |
| 16 | Virginia Tech | .8-0-1 | Frank Moseley | same |
| 17 | USC | .8-3-0 | Jess Hill | 8-4-0 |
| 18 | Baylor | .7-3-0 | George Sauer | 7-4-0 |
| 19 | Rice | .7-3-0 | Jess Neely | same |
| 20 | Penn St. | .7-2-0 | Rip Engle | same |

**Note:** PCC and Big Seven "no-repeat" rules kept UCLA and Oklahoma from Rose and Orange bowls, respectively.

#### Key Bowl Games

**Rose**–#1 Ohio St. over #17 USC, 20-7; **Sugar**–#5 Navy over #6 Ole Miss, 21-0; **Cotton**–Georgia Tech over #10 Arkansas, 14-6; **Orange**–#14 Duke over Nebraska, 34-7.

### 1955

Final poll released Nov. 28. Top 20 regular season results after that: None.

| | | As of Nov. 28 | Head Coach | After Bowls |
|---|---|---|---|---|
| 1 | Oklahoma | .10-0-0 | Bud Wilkinson | 11-0-0 |
| 2 | Michigan St. | .8-1-0 | Duffy Daugherty | 9-1-0 |
| 3 | Maryland | .10-0-0 | Jim Tatum | 10-1-0 |
| 4 | UCLA | .9-1-0 | Red Sanders | 9-2-0 |
| 5 | Ohio St. | .7-2-0 | Woody Hayes | same |
| 6 | TCU | .9-1-0 | Abe Martin | 9-2-0 |
| 7 | Georgia Tech | .8-1-1 | Bobby Dodd | 9-1-1 |
| 8 | Auburn | .8-1-1 | Shug Jordan | 8-2-1 |
| 9 | Notre Dame | .8-2-0 | Terry Brennan | same |
| 10 | Mississippi | .9-1-0 | Johnny Vaught | 10-1-0 |
| 11 | Pittsburgh | .7-3-0 | John Michelosen | 7-4-0 |
| 12 | Michigan | .7-2-0 | Bennie Oosterbaan | same |
| 13 | USC | .6-4-0 | Jess Hill | same |
| 14 | Miami-FL | .6-3-0 | Andy Gustafson | same |
| 15 | Miami-OH | .9-0-0 | Ara Parseghian | same |
| 16 | Stanford | .6-3-1 | Chuck Taylor | same |
| 17 | Texas A&M | .7-2-1 | Bear Bryant | same |
| 18 | Navy | .6-2-1 | Eddie Erdelatz | same |
| 19 | West Virginia | .8-2-0 | Art Lewis | same |
| 20 | Army | .6-3-0 | Red Blaik | same |

**Note:** Big Ten "no-repeat" rule kept Ohio St. from Rose Bowl.

#### Key Bowl Games

**Orange**–#1 Oklahoma over #3 Maryland, 20-6; **Rose**–#2 Michigan St. over #4 UCLA, 17-14; **Cotton**–#10 Ole Miss over #6 TCU, 14-13; **Sugar**–#7 Georgia Tech over #11 Pitt, 7-0; **Gator**–Vanderbilt over #8 Auburn, 25-13.

## 1956

Final poll released Dec. 3. Top 20 regular season results after that: **Dec. 8**–#13 Pitt over #6 Miami-FL, 14-7.

| | | As of Dec. 3 | Head Coach | After Bowls |
|---|---|---|---|---|
| 1 | Oklahoma | 10-0-0 | Bud Wilkinson | same |
| 2 | Tennessee | 10-0-0 | Bowden Wyatt | 10-1-0 |
| 3 | Iowa | 8-1-0 | Forest Evashevski | 9-1-0 |
| 4 | Georgia Tech | 9-1-0 | Bobby Dodd | 10-1-0 |
| 5 | Texas A&M | 9-0-1 | Bear Bryant | same |
| 6 | Miami-FL | 8-0-1 | Andy Gustafson | 8-1-1 |
| 7 | Michigan | 7-2-0 | Bennie Oosterbaan | same |
| 8 | Syracuse | 7-1-0 | Ben Schwartzwalder | 7-2-0 |
| 9 | Michigan St. | 7-2-0 | Duffy Daugherty | same |
| 10 | Oregon St. | 7-2-1 | Tommy Prothro | 7-3-1 |
| 11 | Baylor | 8-2-0 | Sam Boyd | 9-2-0 |
| 12 | Minnesota | 6-1-2 | Murray Warmath | same |
| 13 | Pittsburgh | 6-2-1 | John Michelosen | 7-3-1 |
| 14 | TCU | 7-3-0 | Abe Martin | 8-3-0 |
| 15 | Ohio St. | 6-3-0 | Woody Hayes | same |
| 16 | Navy | 6-1-2 | Eddie Erdelatz | same |
| 17 | G. Washington | 7-1-1 | Gene Sherman | 8-1-1 |
| 18 | USC | 8-2-0 | Jess Hill | same |
| 19 | Clemson | 7-1-2 | Frank Howard | 7-2-2 |
| 20 | Colorado | 7-2-1 | Dallas Ward | 8-2-1 |

**Note:** Big Seven "no-repeat" rule kept Oklahoma from Orange Bowl and Texas A&M was on probation.

### Key Bowl Games

**Sugar**–#11 Baylor over #2 Tennessee, 13-7; **Rose**–#3 Iowa over #10 Oregon St., 35-19; **Gator**–#4 Georgia Tech over #13 Pitt, 21-14; **Cotton**–#14 TCU over #8 Syracuse, 28-27; **Orange**–#20 Colorado over #19 Clemson, 27-21.

## 1957

Final poll released Dec. 2. Top 20 regular season results after that: **Dec. 7**–#10 Notre Dame over SMU, 54-21.

| | | As of Dec. 2 | Head Coach | After Bowls |
|---|---|---|---|---|
| 1 | Auburn | 10-0-0 | Shug Jordan | same |
| 2 | Ohio St. | 8-1-0 | Woody Hayes | 9-1-0 |
| 3 | Michigan St. | 8-1-0 | Duffy Daugherty | same |
| 4 | Oklahoma | 9-1-0 | Bud Wilkinson | 10-1-0 |
| 5 | Navy | 8-1-1 | Eddie Erdelatz | 9-1-1 |
| 6 | Iowa | 7-1-1 | Forest Evashevski | same |
| 7 | Mississippi | 8-1-1 | Johnny Vaught | 9-1-1 |
| 8 | Rice | 7-3-0 | Jess Neely | 7-4-0 |
| 9 | Texas A&M | 8-2-0 | Bear Bryant | 8-3-0 |
| 10 | Notre Dame | 6-3-0 | Terry Brennan | 7-3-0 |
| 11 | Texas | 6-3-1 | Darrell Royal | 6-4-1 |
| 12 | Arizona St. | 10-0-0 | Dan Devine | same |
| 13 | Tennessee | 7-3-0 | Bowden Wyatt | 8-3-0 |
| 14 | Mississippi St. | 6-2-1 | Wade Walker | same |
| 15 | N.C. State | 7-1-2 | Earle Edwards | same |
| 16 | Duke | 6-2-2 | Bill Murray | 6-3-2 |
| 17 | Florida | 6-2-1 | Bob Woodruff | same |
| 18 | Army | 7-2-0 | Red Blaik | same |
| 19 | Wisconsin | 6-3-0 | Milt Bruhn | same |
| 20 | VMI | 9-0-1 | John McKenna | same |

**Note:** Auburn on probation, ineligible for bowl game.

### Key Bowl Games

**Rose**–#2 Ohio St. over Oregon, 10-7; **Orange**–#4 Oklahoma over #16 Duke, 48-21; **Cotton**–#5 Navy over #8 Rice, 20-7; **Sugar**–#7 Ole Miss over #11 Texas, 39-7; **Gator**–#13 Tennessee over #9 Texas A&M, 3-0.

## 1958

Final poll released Dec. 1. Top 20 regular season results after that: None.

| | | As of Dec. 1 | Head Coach | After Bowls |
|---|---|---|---|---|
| 1 | LSU | 10-0-0 | Paul Dietzel | 11-0-0 |
| 2 | Iowa | 7-1-1 | Forest Evashevski | 8-1-1 |
| 3 | Army | 8-0-1 | Red Blaik | same |
| 4 | Auburn | 9-0-1 | Shug Jordan | same |
| 5 | Oklahoma | 9-1-0 | Bud Wilkinson | 10-1-0 |
| 6 | Air Force | 9-0-1 | Ben Martin | 9-0-2 |
| 7 | Wisconsin | 7-1-1 | Milt Bruhn | same |
| 8 | Ohio St. | 6-1-2 | Woody Hayes | same |
| 9 | Syracuse | 8-1-0 | Ben Schwartzwalder | 8-2-0 |
| 10 | TCU | 8-2-0 | Abe Martin | 8-2-1 |
| 11 | Mississippi | 8-2-0 | Johnny Vaught | 9-2-0 |
| 12 | Clemson | 8-2-0 | Frank Howard | 8-3-0 |
| 13 | Purdue | 6-1-2 | Jack Mollenkopf | same |
| 14 | Florida | 6-3-1 | Bob Woodruff | 6-4-1 |
| 15 | South Carolina | 7-3-0 | Warren Giese | same |
| 16 | California | 7-3-0 | Pete Elliott | 7-4-0 |
| 17 | Notre Dame | 6-4-0 | Terry Brennan | same |
| 18 | SMU | 6-4-0 | Bill Meek | same |
| 19 | Oklahoma St. | 7-3-0 | Cliff Speegle | 8-3-0 |
| 20 | Rutgers | 8-1-0 | John Stiegman | same |

### Key Bowl Games

**Sugar**–#1 LSU over #12 Clemson, 7-0; **Rose**–#2 Iowa over #16 Cal, 38-12; **Orange**–#5 Oklahoma over #9 Syracuse, 21-6; **Cotton**–#6 Air Force tied #10 TCU, 0-0.

## 1959

Final poll released Dec. 7. Top 20 regular season results after that: None.

| | | As of Dec. 7 | Head Coach | After Bowls |
|---|---|---|---|---|
| 1 | Syracuse | 10-0-0 | Ben Schwartzwalder | 11-0-0 |
| 2 | Mississippi | 9-1-0 | Johnny Vaught | 10-1-0 |
| 3 | LSU | 9-1-0 | Paul Dietzel | 9-2-0 |
| 4 | Texas | 9-1-0 | Darrell Royal | 9-2-0 |
| 5 | Georgia | 9-1-0 | Wally Butts | 10-1-0 |
| 6 | Wisconsin | 7-2-0 | Milt Bruhn | 7-3-0 |
| 7 | TCU | 8-2-0 | Abe Martin | 8-3-0 |
| 8 | Washington | 9-1-0 | Jim Owens | 10-1-0 |
| 9 | Arkansas | 8-2-0 | Frank Broyles | 9-2-0 |
| 10 | Alabama | 7-1-2 | Bear Bryant | 7-2-2 |
| 11 | Clemson | 8-2-0 | Frank Howard | 9-2-0 |
| 12 | Penn St. | 8-2-0 | Rip Engle | 9-2-0 |
| 13 | Illinois | 5-3-1 | Ray Eliot | same |
| 14 | USC | 8-2-0 | Don Clark | same |
| 15 | Oklahoma | 7-3-0 | Bud Wilkinson | same |
| 16 | Wyoming | 9-1-0 | Bob Devaney | same |
| 17 | Notre Dame | 5-5-0 | Joe Kuharich | same |
| 18 | Missouri | 6-4-0 | Dan Devine | 6-5-0 |
| 19 | Florida | 5-4-1 | Bob Woodruff | same |
| 20 | Pittsburgh | 6-4-0 | John Michelosen | same |

**Note:** Big Seven "no-repeat" rule kept Oklahoma from Orange Bowl.

### Key Bowl Games

**Cotton**–#1 Syracuse over #4 Texas, 23-14; **Sugar**–#2 Ole Miss over #3 LSU, 21-0; **Orange**–#5 Georgia over #18 Missouri, 14-0; **Rose**–#8 Washington over #6 Wisconsin, 44-8; **Bluebonnet**–#11 Clemson over #7 TCU, 23-7; **Gator**–#9 Arkansas over Georgia Tech, 14-7; **Liberty**–#12 Penn St. over #10 Alabama, 7-0.

## Associated Press Final Polls (Cont.)

### 1960

Final poll released Nov. 28. Top 20 regular season results after that: **Dec. 3**—UCLA over #10 Duke, 27-6.

| | As of Nov. 28 | Head Coach | After Bowls |
|---|---|---|---|
| 1 | Minnesota . . . . . .8-1-0 | Murray Warmath | 8-2-0 |
| 2 | Mississippi . . . . .9-0-1 | Johnny Vaught | 10-0-1 |
| 3 | Iowa . . . . . . . . .8-1-0 | Forest Evashevski | same |
| 4 | Navy . . . . . . . . .9-1-0 | Wayne Hardin | 9-2-0 |
| 5 | Missouri . . . . . . .9-1-0 | Dan Devine | 10-1-0 |
| 6 | Washington . . . . .9-1-0 | Jim Owens | 10-1-0 |
| 7 | Arkansas . . . . . . .8-2-0 | Frank Broyles | 8-3-0 |
| 8 | Ohio St. . . . . . . .7-2-0 | Woody Hayes | same |
| 9 | Alabama . . . . . . .8-1-1 | Bear Bryant | 8-1-2 |
| 10 | Duke . . . . . . . .7-2-0 | Bill Murray | 8-3-0 |
| 11 | Kansas . . . . . . .7-2-1 | Jack Mitchell | same |
| 12 | Baylor . . . . . . . .8-2-0 | John Bridgers | 8-3-0 |
| 13 | Auburn . . . . . . .8-2-0 | Shug Jordan | same |
| 14 | Yale . . . . . . . . .9-0-0 | Jordan Olivar | same |
| 15 | Michigan St. . . . .6-2-1 | Duffy Daugherty | same |
| 16 | Penn St. . . . . . . .6-3-0 | Rip Engle | 7-3-0 |
| 17 | New Mexico St. | 10-0-0 | Warren Woodson | 11-0-0 |
| 18 | Florida . . . . . . .8-2-0 | Ray Graves | 9-2-0 |
| 19 | Syracuse . . . . . .7-2-0 | Ben Schwartzwalder | same |
| | Purdue . . . . . . .4-4-1 | Jack Mollenkopf | same |

#### Key Bowl Games
**Rose**–#6 Washington over #1 Minnesota, 17-7; **Sugar**–#2 Ole Miss over Rice, 14-6; **Orange**–#5 Missouri over #4 Navy, 21-14; **Cotton**–#10 Duke over #7 Arkansas, 7-6; **Bluebonnet**–#9 Alabama tied Texas, 3-3.

### 1961

Final poll released Dec. 4. Top 20 regular season results after that: None.

| | As of Dec. 4 | Head Coach | After Bowls |
|---|---|---|---|
| 1 | Alabama . . . . . .10-0-0 | Bear Bryant | 11-0-0 |
| 2 | Ohio St. . . . . . . .8-0-1 | Woody Hayes | same |
| 3 | Texas . . . . . . . .9-1-0 | Darrell Royal | 10-1-0 |
| 4 | LSU . . . . . . . . .9-1-0 | Paul Dietzel | 10-1-0 |
| 5 | Mississippi . . . . .9-1-0 | Johnny Vaught | 9-2-0 |
| 6 | Minnesota . . . . .7-2-0 | Murray Warmath | 8-2-0 |
| 7 | Colorado . . . . . .9-1-0 | Sonny Grandelius | 9-2-0 |
| 8 | Michigan St. . . . .7-2-0 | Duffy Daugherty | same |
| 9 | Arkansas . . . . . .8-2-0 | Frank Broyles | 8-3-0 |
| 10 | Utah St. . . . . . .9-0-1 | John Ralston | 9-1-1 |
| 11 | Missouri . . . . . .7-2-1 | Dan Devine | same |
| 12 | Purdue . . . . . . .6-3-0 | Jack Mollenkopf | same |
| 13 | Georgia Tech . . .7-3-0 | Bobby Dodd | 7-4-0 |
| 14 | Syracuse . . . . . .7-3-0 | Ben Schwartzwalder | 8-3-0 |
| 15 | Rutgers . . . . . . .9-0-0 | John Bateman | same |
| 16 | UCLA . . . . . . . .7-3-0 | Bill Barnes | 7-4-0 |
| 17 | Rice . . . . . . . . .7-3-0 | Jess Neely | 7-4-0 |
| | Penn St. . . . . . . .7-3-0 | Rip Engle | 8-3-0 |
| | Arizona . . . . . . .8-1-1 | Jim LaRue | same |
| 20 | Duke . . . . . . . .7-3-0 | Bill Murray | same |

**Note:** Ohio St. faculty council turned down Rose Bowl invitation citing concern with OSU's overemphasis on sports.

#### Key Bowl Games
**Sugar**–#1 Alabama over #9 Arkansas, 10-3; **Cotton**–#3 Texas over #5 Ole Miss, 12-7; **Orange**–#4 LSU over #7 Colorado, 25-7; **Rose**–#6 Minnesota over #16 UCLA, 21-3; **Gotham**–Baylor over #10 Utah St., 24-9.

### 1962

Final poll released Dec. 3. Top 10 regular season results after that: None.

| | As of Dec. 3 | Head Coach | After Bowls |
|---|---|---|---|
| 1 | USC . . . . . . . . .10-0-0 | John McKay | 11-0-0 |
| 2 | Wisconsin . . . . . .8-1-0 | Milt Bruhn | 8-2-0 |
| 3 | Mississippi . . . . .9-0-0 | Johnny Vaught | 10-0-0 |
| 4 | Texas . . . . . . . .9-0-1 | Darrell Royal | 9-1-1 |
| 5 | Alabama . . . . . . .9-1-0 | Bear Bryant | 10-1-0 |
| 6 | Arkansas . . . . . . .9-1-0 | Frank Broyles | 9-2-0 |
| 7 | LSU . . . . . . . . .8-1-1 | Charlie McClendon | 9-1-1 |
| 8 | Oklahoma . . . . . .8-2-0 | Bud Wilkinson | 8-3-0 |
| 9 | Penn St. . . . . . . .9-1-0 | Rip Engle | 9-2-0 |
| 10 | Minnesota . . . . .6-2-1 | Murray Warmath | same |

#### Key Bowl Games
**Rose**–#1 USC over #2 Wisconsin, 42-37; **Sugar**–#3 Ole Miss over #6 Arkansas, 17-13; **Cotton**–#7 LSU over #4 Texas, 13-0; **Orange**–#5 Alabama over #8 Oklahoma, 17-0; **Gator**–Florida over #9 Penn St.,17-7.

### 1963

Final poll released Dec. 9. Top 10 regular season results after that: **Dec.14**–#8 Alabama over Miami-FL, 17-12.

| | As of Dec. 9 | Head Coach | After Bowls |
|---|---|---|---|
| 1 | Texas . . . . . . . .10-0-0 | Darrell Royal | 11-0-0 |
| 2 | Navy . . . . . . . . .9-1-0 | Wayne Hardin | 9-2-0 |
| 3 | Illinois . . . . . . . .7-1-1 | Pete Elliott | 8-1-1 |
| 4 | Pittsburgh . . . . . .9-1-0 | John Michelosen | same |
| 5 | Auburn . . . . . . . .9-1-0 | Shug Jordan | 9-2-0 |
| 6 | Nebraska . . . . . .9-1-0 | Bob Devaney | 10-1-0 |
| 7 | Mississippi . . . . .7-0-2 | Johnny Vaught | 7-1-2 |
| 8 | Alabama . . . . . . .7-2-0 | Bear Bryant | 9-2-0 |
| 9 | Michigan St. . . . .6-2-1 | Duffy Daugherty | same |
| 10 | Oklahoma . . . . . .8-2-0 | Bud Wilkinson | same |

#### Key Bowl Games
**Cotton**–#1 Texas over #2 Navy, 28-6; **Rose**–#3 Illinois over Washington, 17-7; **Orange**–#6 Nebraska over #5 Auburn, 13-7; **Sugar**–#8 Alabama over #7 Ole Miss, 12-7.

### 1964

Final poll released Nov. 30. Top 10 regular season results after that: **Dec. 5**–Florida over #7 LSU, 20-6.

| | As of Nov. 30 | Head Coach | After Bowls |
|---|---|---|---|
| 1 | Alabama . . . . . .10-0-0 | Bear Bryant | 10-1-0 |
| 2 | Arkansas . . . . . .10-0-0 | Frank Broyles | 11-0-0 |
| 3 | Notre Dame . . . .9-1-0 | Ara Parseghian | same |
| 4 | Michigan . . . . . .8-1-0 | Bump Elliott | 9-1-0 |
| 5 | Texas . . . . . . . .9-1-0 | Darrell Royal | 10-1-0 |
| 6 | Nebraska . . . . . .9-1-0 | Bob Devaney | 9-2-0 |
| 7 | LSU . . . . . . . . .7-1-1 | Charlie McClendon | 8-2-1 |
| 8 | Oregon St. . . . .8-2-0 | Tommy Prothro | 8-3-0 |
| 9 | Ohio St. . . . . . . .7-2-0 | Woody Hayes | same |
| 10 | USC . . . . . . . . .7-3-0 | John McKay | same |

#### Key Bowl Games
**Orange**–#5 Texas over #1 Alabama, 21-17; **Cotton**–#2 Arkansas over #6 Nebraska, 10-7; **Rose**–#4 Michigan over #8 Oregon St., 34-7; **Sugar**–#7 LSU over Syracuse, 13-10.

## 1965

Final poll taken after bowl games for the first time.

| | After Bowls | Head Coach | Regular Season |
|---|---|---|---|
| 1 Alabama | 9-1-1 | Bear Bryant | 8-1-1 |
| 2 Michigan St | 10-1-0 | Duffy Daugherty | 10-0-0 |
| 3 Arkansas | 10-1-0 | Frank Broyles | 10-0-0 |
| 4 UCLA | 8-2-1 | Tommy Prothro | 7-1-1 |
| 5 Nebraska | 10-1-0 | Bob Devaney | 10-0-0 |
| 6 Missouri | 8-2-1 | Dan Devine | 7-2-1 |
| 7 Tennessee | 8-1-2 | Doug Dickey | 6-1-2 |
| 8 LSU | 8-3-0 | Charlie McClendon | 7-3-0 |
| 9 Notre Dame | 7-2-1 | Ara Parseghian | same |
| 10 USC | 7-2-1 | John McKay | same |

### Key Bowl Games

Rankings below reflect final regular season poll, released Nov. 29. No bowls for then #8 USC or #9 Notre Dame.
**Rose**—#5 UCLA over #1 Michigan St., 14-12; **Cotton**—LSU over #2 Arkansas, 14-7; **Orange**—#4 Alabama over #3 Nebraska, 39-28; **Sugar**—#6 Missouri over Florida, 20-18; **Bluebonnet**—#7 Tennessee over Tulsa, 27-6; **Gator**—Georgia Tech over #10 Texas Tech, 31-21.

## 1966

Final poll released Dec. 5, returning to pre-bowl status. Top 10 regular season results after that: None.

| | As of Dec. 5 | Head Coach | After Bowls |
|---|---|---|---|
| 1 Notre Dame | 9-0-1 | Ara Parseghian | same |
| 2 Michigan St | 9-0-1 | Duffy Daugherty | same |
| 3 Alabama | 10-0-0 | Bear Bryant | 11-0-0 |
| 4 Georgia | 9-1-0 | Vince Dooley | 10-1-0 |
| 5 UCLA | 9-1-0 | Tommy Prothro | same |
| 6 Nebraska | 9-1-0 | Bob Devaney | 9-2-0 |
| 7 Purdue | 8-2-0 | Jack Mollenkopf | 9-2-0 |
| 8 Georgia Tech | 9-1-0 | Bobby Dodd | 9-2-0 |
| 9 Miami-FL | 7-2-1 | Charlie Tate | 8-2-1 |
| 10 SMU | 8-2-0 | Hayden Fry | 8-3-0 |

### Key Bowl Games

**Sugar**—#3 Alabama over #6 Nebraska, 34-7; **Cotton**—#4 Georgia over #10 SMU, 24-9; **Rose**—#7 Purdue over USC, 14-13; **Orange**—Florida over #8 Georgia Tech, 27-12; **Liberty**—#9 Miami-FL over Virginia Tech, 14-7.

## 1967

Final poll released Nov. 27. Top 10 regular season results after that: **Dec. 2**—#2 Tennessee over Vanderbilt, 41-14; #3 Oklahoma over Oklahoma St., 38-14; #8 Alabama over Auburn, 7-3.

| | As of Nov. 27 | Head Coach | After Bowls |
|---|---|---|---|
| 1 USC | 9-1-0 | John McKay | 10-1-0 |
| 2 Tennessee | 8-1-0 | Doug Dickey | 9-2-0 |
| 3 Oklahoma | 8-1-0 | Chuck Fairbanks | 10-1-0 |
| 4 Indiana | 9-1-0 | John Pont | 9-2-0 |
| 5 Notre Dame | 8-2-0 | Ara Parseghian | same |
| 6 Wyoming | 10-0-0 | Lloyd Eaton | 10-1-0 |
| 7 Oregon St. | 7-2-1 | Dee Andros | same |
| 8 Alabama | 7-1-1 | Bear Bryant | 8-2-1 |
| 9 Purdue | 8-2-0 | Jack Mollenkopf | same |
| 10 Penn St. | 8-2-0 | Joe Paterno | 8-2-1 |

### Key Bowl Games

**Rose**—#1 USC over #4 Indiana, 14-3; **Orange**—#3 Oklahoma over #2 Tennessee, 26-24; **Sugar**—LSU over #6 Wyoming, 20-13; **Cotton**—Texas A&M over #8 Alabama, 20-16; **Gator**—#10 Penn St. tied Florida St. 17-17.

## 1968

Final poll taken after bowl games for first time since close of 1965 season.

| | After Bowls | Head Coach | Regular Season |
|---|---|---|---|
| 1 Ohio St. | 10-0-0 | Woody Hayes | 9-0-0 |
| 2 Penn St. | 11-0-0 | Joe Paterno | 10-0-0 |
| 3 Texas | 9-1-1 | Darrell Royal | 8-1-1 |
| 4 USC | 9-1-1 | John McKay | 9-0-1 |
| 5 Notre Dame | 7-2-1 | Ara Parseghian | same |
| 6 Arkansas | 10-1-0 | Frank Broyles | 9-1-0 |
| 7 Kansas | 9-2-0 | Pepper Rodgers | 9-1-0 |
| 8 Georgia | 8-1-2 | Vince Dooley | 8-0-2 |
| 9 Missouri | 8-3-0 | Dan Devine | 7-3-0 |
| 10 Purdue | 8-2-0 | Jack Mollenkopf | same |
| 11 Oklahoma | 7-4-0 | Chuck Fairbanks | 7-3-0 |
| 12 Michigan | 8-2-0 | Bump Elliott | same |
| 13 Tennessee | 8-2-1 | Doug Dickey | 8-1-1 |
| 14 SMU | 8-3-0 | Hayden Fry | 7-3-0 |
| 15 Oregon St. | 7-3-0 | Dee Andros | same |
| 16 Auburn | 7-4-0 | Shug Jordan | 6-4-0 |
| 17 Alabama | 8-3-0 | Bear Bryant | 8-2-0 |
| 18 Houston | 6-2-2 | Bill Yeoman | same |
| 19 LSU | 8-3-0 | Charlie McClendon | 7-3-0 |
| 20 Ohio Univ | 10-1-0 | Bill Hess | 10-0-0 |

### Key Bowl Games

Rankings below reflect final regular season poll, released Dec. 2. No bowls for then #7 Notre Dame and # i 1 Pudue.
**Rose**—#1 Ohio St. over #2 USC, 27-16; **Orange**—#3 Penn St. over #6 Kansas, 15-14; **Sugar**—#9 Arkansas over #4 Georgia, 16-2; **Cotton**—#5 Texas over #8 Tennessee, 36-13; **Bluebonnet**—#20 SMU over #10 Oklahoma, 28-27; **Gator**—#16 Missouri over #12 Alabama, 35-10.

## 1969

Final poll taken after bowl games.

| | After Bowls | Head Coach | Regular Season |
|---|---|---|---|
| 1 Texas | 11-0-0 | Darrell Royal | 10-0-0 |
| 2 Penn St | 11-0-0 | Joe Paterno | 10-0-0 |
| 3 USC | 10-0-1 | John McKay | 9-0-1 |
| 4 Ohio St. | 8-1-0 | Woody Hayes | same |
| 5 Notre Dame | 8-2-1 | Ara Parseghian | 8-1-1 |
| 6 Missouri | 9-2-0 | Dan Devine | 9-1-0 |
| 7 Arkansas | 9-2-0 | Frank Broyles | 9-1-0 |
| 8 Mississippi | 8-3-0 | Johnny Vaught | 7-3-0 |
| 9 Michigan | 8-3-0 | Bo Schembechler | 8-2-0 |
| 10 LSU | 9-1-0 | Charlie McClendon | same |
| 11 Nebraska | 9-2-0 | Bob Devaney | 8-2-0 |
| 12 Houston | 9-2-0 | Bill Yeoman | 8-2-0 |
| 13 UCLA | 8-1-1 | Tommy Prothro | same |
| 14 Florida | 9-1-1 | Ray Graves | 8-1-1 |
| 15 Tennessee | 9-2-0 | Doug Dickey | 9-1-0 |
| 16 Colorado | 8-3-0 | Eddie Crowder | 7-3-0 |
| 17 West Virginia | 10-1-0 | Jim Carlen | 9-1-0 |
| 18 Purdue | 8-2-0 | Jack Mollenkopf | same |
| 19 Stanford | 7-2-1 | John Ralston | same |
| 20 Auburn | 8-3-0 | Shug Jordan | 8-2-0 |

### Key Bowl Games

Rankings below reflect final regular season poll, released Dec. 8. No bowls for then #4 Ohio St., #8 LSU and #10 UCLA.
**Cotton**—#1 Texas over #9 Notre Dame, 21-17; **Orange**—#2 Penn St. over #6 Missouri, 10-3; **Sugar**—#13 Ole Miss over #3 Arkansas, 27-22; **Rose**—#5 USC over #7 Michigan, 10-3.

## Associated Press Final Polls (Cont.)

### 1970

| | After Bowls | Head Coach | Regular Season |
|---|---|---|---|
| 1 | Nebraska .....11-0-1 | Bob Devaney | 10-0-1 |
| 2 | Notre Dame ...10-1-0 | Ara Parseghian | 9-0-1 |
| 3 | Texas .........10-1-0 | Darrell Royal | 10-0-0 |
| 4 | Tennessee .....11-1-0 | Bill Battle | 10-1-0 |
| 5 | Ohio St. .......9-1-0 | Woody Hayes | 9-0-0 |
| 6 | Arizona St. ....11-0-0 | Frank Kush | 10-0-0 |
| 7 | LSU ..........9-3-0 | Charlie McClendon | 9-2-0 |
| 8 | Stanford .......9-3-0 | John Ralston | 8-3-0 |
| 9 | Michigan ......9-1-0 | Bo Schembechler | same |
| 10 | Auburn ........9-2-0 | Shug Jordan | 8-2-0 |
| 11 | Arkansas ......9-2-0 | Frank Broyles | same |
| 12 | Toledo .......12-0-0 | Frank Lauterbur | 11-0-0 |
| 13 | Georgia Tech ..9-3-0 | Bud Carson | 8-3-0 |
| 14 | Dartmouth .....9-0-0 | Bob Blackman | same |
| 15 | USC ..........6-4-1 | John McKay | same |
| 16 | Air Force .....9-3-0 | Ben Martin | 9-2-0 |
| 17 | Tulane ........8-4-0 | Jim Pittman | 7-4-0 |
| 18 | Penn St. ......7-3-0 | Joe Paterno | same |
| 19 | Houston .......8-3-0 | Bill Yeoman | same |
| 20 | Oklahoma .....7-4-1 | Chuck Fairbanks | 7-4-0 |
| | Mississippi ....7-4-0 | Johnny Vaught | 7-3-0 |

#### Key Bowl Games
Rankings below reflect final regular season poll, released Dec. 7. No bowls for then #4 Arkansas and #7 Michigan.
**Cotton**–#6 Notre Dame over #1 Texas, 24-11; **Rose**–#12 Stanford over #2 Ohio St., 27-17; **Orange**–#3 Nebraska over #8 LSU, 17-12; **Sugar**–#5 Tennessee over #11 Air Force, 34-13; **Peach**–#9 Ariz. St. over N. Carolina, 48-26.

### 1972

| | After Bowls | Head Coach | Regular Season |
|---|---|---|---|
| 1 | USC .........12-0-0 | John McKay | 11-0-0 |
| 2 | Oklahoma .....11-1-0 | Chuck Fairbanks | 10-1-0 |
| 3 | Texas .........10-1-0 | Darrell Royal | 9-1-0 |
| 4 | Nebraska ......9-2-1 | Bob Devaney | 8-2-1 |
| 5 | Auburn ........10-1-0 | Shug Jordan | 9-1-0 |
| 6 | Michigan ......10-1-0 | Bo Schembechler | same |
| 7 | Alabama ......10-2-0 | Bear Bryant | 10-1-0 |
| 8 | Tennessee .....10-2-0 | Bill Battle | 9-2-0 |
| 9 | Ohio St. .......9-2-0 | Woody Hayes | 9-1-0 |
| 10 | Penn St. ......10-2-0 | Joe Paterno | 10-1-0 |
| 11 | LSU ..........9-2-1 | Charlie McClendon | 9-1-1 |
| 12 | North Carolina .11-1-0 | Bill Dooley | 10-1-0 |
| 13 | Arizona St. ....10-2-0 | Frank Kush | 9-2-0 |
| 14 | Notre Dame ....8-3-0 | Ara Parseghian | -8-2-0 |
| 15 | UCLA .........8-3-0 | Pepper Rodgers | same |
| 16 | Colorado ......8-4-0 | Eddie Crowder | 8-3-0 |
| 17 | N.C. State .....8-3-1 | Lou Holtz | 7-3-1 |
| 18 | Louisville .....9-1-0 | Lee Corso | same |
| 19 | Washington St. ..7-4-0 | Jim Sweeney | same |
| 20 | Georgia Tech ...7-4-1 | Bill Fulcher | 6-4-1 |

#### Key Bowl Games
Rankings below reflect final regular season poll, released Dec. 4. No bowl for then #8 Michigan.
**Rose**–#1 USC over #3 Ohio St., 42-17; **Sugar**–#2 Oklahoma over #5 Penn St., 14-0; **Cotton**–#7 Texas over #4 Alabama, 17-13; **Orange**–#9 Nebraska over #12 Notre Dame, 40-6; **Gator**–#6 Auburn over #13 Colorado, 24-3; **Bluebonnet**–#11 Tennessee over #10 LSU, 24-17.

### 1971

| | After Bowls | Head Coach | Regular Season |
|---|---|---|---|
| 1 | Nebraska .....13-0-0 | Bob Devaney | 12-0-0 |
| 2 | Oklahoma .....11-1-0 | Chuck Fairbanks | 10-1-0 |
| 3 | Colorado ......10-2-0 | Eddie Crowder | 9-2-0 |
| 4 | Alabama ......11-1-0 | Bear Bryant | 11-0-0 |
| 5 | Penn St. ......11-1-0 | Joe Paterno | 10-1-0 |
| 6 | Michigan ......11-1-0 | Bo Schembechler | 11-0-0 |
| 7 | Georgia ......11-1-0 | Vince Dooley | 10-1-0 |
| 8 | Arizona St. ....11-1-0 | Frank Kush | 10-1-0 |
| 9 | Tennessee .....10-2-0 | Bill Battle | 9-2-0 |
| 10 | Stanford .......9-3-0 | John Ralston | 8-3-0 |
| 11 | LSU ..........9-3-0 | Charlie McClendon | 8-3-0 |
| 12 | Auburn ........9-2-0 | Shug Jordan | 9-1-0 |
| 13 | Notre Dame ...8-2-0 | Ara Parseghian | same |
| 14 | Toledo .......12-0-0 | John Murphy | 11-0-0 |
| 15 | Mississippi ...10-2-0 | Billy Kinard | 9-2-0 |
| 16 | Arkansas ......8-3-1 | Frank Broyles | 8-2-1 |
| 17 | Houston .......9-3-0 | Bill Yeoman | 9-2-0 |
| 18 | Texas .........8-3-0 | Darrell Royal | 8-2-0 |
| 19 | Washington ....8-3-0 | Jim Owens | same |
| 20 | USC ..........6-4-1 | John McKay | same |

#### Key Bowl Games
Rankings below reflect final regular season poll, released Dec. 6.
**Orange**–#1 Nebraska over #2 Alabama, 38-6; **Sugar**–#3 Oklahoma over #5 Auburn, 40-22; **Rose**–#16 Stanford over #4 Michigan, 13-12; **Gator**–#6 Georgia over N. Carolina, 7-3; **Bluebonnet**–#7 Colorado over #15 Houston, 29-17; **Fiesta**–#8 Ariz. St. over Florida St., 45-38; **Cotton**–#10 Penn St. over #12 Texas, 30-6.

### 1973

| | After Bowls | Head Coach | Regular Season |
|---|---|---|---|
| 1 | Notre Dame ...11-0-0 | Ara Parseghian | 10-0-0 |
| 2 | Ohio St. .......10-0-1 | Woody Hayes | 9-0-1 |
| 3 | Oklahoma .....10-0-1 | Barry Switzer | same |
| 4 | Alabama ......11-1-0 | Bear Bryant | 11-0-0 |
| 5 | Penn St. ......12-0-0 | Joe Paterno | 11-0-0 |
| 6 | Michigan ......10-0-1 | Bo Schembechler | same |
| 7 | Nebraska ......9-2-1 | Tom Osborne | 8-2-1 |
| 8 | USC ..........9-2-1 | John McKay | 9-1-1 |
| 9 | Arizona St. ....11-1-0 | Frank Kush | 10-1-0 |
| | Houston .......11-1-0 | Bill Yeoman | 10-1-0 |
| 11 | Texas Tech ....11-1-0 | Jim Carlen | 10-1-0 |
| 12 | UCLA .........9-2-0 | Pepper Rodgers | same |
| 13 | LSU ..........9-3-0 | Charlie McClendon | 9-2-0 |
| 14 | Texas .........8-3-0 | Darrell Royal | 8-2-0 |
| 15 | Miami-OH .....11-0-0 | Bill Mallory | 10-0-0 |
| 16 | N.C. State .....9-3-0 | Lou Holtz | 8-3-0 |
| 17 | Missouri .......8-4-0 | Al Onofrio | 7-4-0 |
| 18 | Kansas ........7-4-1 | Don Fambrough | 7-3-1 |
| 19 | Tennessee .....8-4-0 | Bill Battle | 8-3-0 |
| 20 | Maryland ......8-4-0 | Jerry Claiborne | 8-3-0 |
| | Tulane ........9-3-0 | Bennie Ellender | 9-2-0 |

#### Key Bowl Games
Rankings below reflect final regular season poll, released Dec. 3. No bowls for then #2 Oklahoma (probation), #5 Michigan and #9 UCLA.
**Sugar**–#3 Notre Dame over #1 Alabama, 24-23; **Rose**–#4 Ohio St. over #7 USC, 42-21; **Orange**–#6 Penn St. over #13 LSU, 16-9; **Cotton**–#12 Nebraska over #8 Texas, 19-3; **Fiesta**–#10 Ariz. St. over Pitt, 28-7; **Bluebonnet**–#14 Houston over #17 Tulane, 47-7.

## 1974

| | | After Bowls | Head Coach | Regular Season |
|---|---|---|---|---|
| 1 | Oklahoma | 11-0-0 | Barry Switzer | same |
| 2 | USC | 10-1-1 | John McKay | 9-1-1 |
| 3 | Michigan | 10-1-0 | Bo Schembechler | same |
| 4 | Ohio St. | 10-2-0 | Woody Hayes | 10-1-0 |
| 5 | Alabama | 11-1-0 | Bear Bryant | 11-0-0 |
| 6 | Notre Dame | 10-2-0 | Ara Parseghian | 9-2-0 |
| 7 | Penn St. | 10-2-0 | Joe Paterno | 9-2-0 |
| 8 | Auburn | 10-2-0 | Shug Jordan | 9-2-0 |
| 9 | Nebraska | 9-3-0 | Tom Osborne | 8-3-0 |
| 10 | Miami-OH | 10-0-1 | Dick Crum | 9-0-1 |
| 11 | N.C. State | 9-2-1 | Lou Holtz | 9-2-0 |
| 12 | Michigan St. | 7-3-1 | Denny Stolz | same |
| 13 | Maryland | 8-4-0 | Jerry Claiborne | 8-3-0 |
| 14 | Baylor | 8-4-0 | Grant Teaff | 8-3-0 |
| 15 | Florida | 8-4-0 | Doug Dickey | 8-3-0 |
| 16 | Texas A&M | 8-3-0 | Emory Ballard | same |
| 17 | Mississippi St. | 9-3-0 | Bob Tyler | 8-3-0 |
| | Texas | 8-4-0 | Darrell Royal | 8-3-0 |
| 19 | Houston | 8-3-1 | Bill Yeoman | 8-3-0 |
| 20 | Tennessee | 7-3-2 | Bill Battle | 6-3-2 |

### Key Bowl Games

Rankings below reflect final regular season poll, released Dec. 2. No bowls for #1 Oklahoma (probation) and then #4 Michigan.

**Orange**–#9 Notre Dame over #2 Alabama, 13-11; **Rose**–#5 USC over #3 Ohio St., 18-17; **Gator**–#6 Auburn over #11 Texas, 27-3; **Cotton**–#7 Penn St. over #12 Baylor, 41-20; **Sugar**–#8 Nebraska over #18 Florida, 13-10; **Liberty**–Tennessee over #10 Maryland, 7-3.

## 1975

| | | After Bowls | Head Coach | Regular Season |
|---|---|---|---|---|
| 1 | Oklahoma | 11-1-0 | Barry Switzer | 10-1-0 |
| 2 | Arizona St. | 12-0-0 | Frank Kush | 11-0-0 |
| 3 | Alabama | 11-1-0 | Bear Bryant | 10-1-0 |
| 4 | Ohio St. | 11-1-0 | Woody Hayes | 11-0-0 |
| 5 | UCLA | 9-2-1 | Dick Vermeil | 8-2-1 |
| 6 | Texas | 10-2-0 | Darrell Royal | 9-2-0 |
| 7 | Arkansas | 10-2-0 | Frank Broyles | 9-2-0 |
| 8 | Michigan | 8-2-2 | Bo Schembechler | 8-1-2 |
| 9 | Nebraska | 10-2-0 | Tom Osborne | 10-1-0 |
| 10 | Penn St. | 9-3-0 | Joe Paterno | 9-2-0 |
| 11 | Texas A&M | 10-2-0 | Emory Bellard | 10-1-0 |
| 12 | Miami-OH | 11-1-0 | Dick Crum | 10-1-0 |
| 13 | Maryland | 9-2-1 | Jerry Claiborne | 8-2-1 |
| 14 | California | 8-3-0 | Mike White | same |
| 15 | Pittsburgh | 8-4-0 | Johnny Majors | 7-4-0 |
| 16 | Colorado | 9-3-0 | Bill Mallory | 9-2-0 |
| 17 | USC | 8-4-0 | John McKay | 7-4-0 |
| 18 | Arizona | 9-2-0 | Jim Young | same |
| 19 | Georgia | 9-3-0 | Vince Dooley | 9-2-0 |
| 20 | West Virginia | 9-3-0 | Bobby Bowden | 8-3-0 |

### Key Bowl Games

Rankings below reflect final regular season poll, released Dec. 1. Texas A&M was unbeaten and ranked 2nd in that poll, but lost to #18 Arkansas, 31-6, in its final regular season game on Dec. 6.

**Rose**–#11 UCLA over #1 Ohio St., 23-10; **Liberty**–#17 USC over #2 Texas A&M, 20-0; **Orange**–#3 Oklahoma over #5 Michigan, 14-6; **Sugar**–#4 Alabama over #8 Penn St., 13-6; **Fiesta**–#7 Ariz. St. over #6 Nebraska, 17-14; **Bluebonnet**–#9 Texas over #10 Colorado, 38-21; **Cotton**–#18 Arkansas over #12 Georgia, 31-10.

## 1976

| | | After Bowls | Head Coach | Regular Season |
|---|---|---|---|---|
| 1 | Pittsburgh | 12-0-0 | Johnny Majors | 11-0-0 |
| 2 | USC | 11-1-0 | John Robinson | 10-1-0 |
| 3 | Michigan | 10-2-0 | Bo Schembechler | 10-1-0 |
| 4 | Houston | 10-2-0 | Bill Yeoman | 9-2-0 |
| 5 | Oklahoma | 9-2-1 | Barry Switzer | 8-2-1 |
| 6 | Ohio St. | 9-2-1 | Woody Hayes | 8-2-1 |
| 7 | Texas A&M | 10-2-0 | Emory Bellard | 9-2-0 |
| 8 | Maryland | 11-1-0 | Jerry Claiborne | 11-0-0 |
| 9 | Nebraska | 9-3-1 | Tom Osborne | 8-3-1 |
| 10 | Georgia | 10-2-0 | Vince Dooley | 10-1-0 |
| 11 | Alabama | 9-3-0 | Bear Bryant | 8-3-0 |
| 12 | Notre Dame | 9-3-0 | Dan Devine | 8-3-0 |
| 13 | Texas Tech | 10-2-0 | Steve Sloan | 10-1-0 |
| 14 | Oklahoma St. | 9-3-0 | Jim Stanley | 8-3-0 |
| 15 | UCLA | 9-2-1 | Terry Donahue | 9-1-1 |
| 16 | Colorado | 8-4-0 | Bill Mallory | 8-3-0 |
| 17 | Rutgers | 11-0-0 | Frank Burns | same |
| 18 | Kentucky | 8-4-0 | Fran Curci | 7-4-0 |
| 19 | Iowa St. | 8-3-0 | Earle Bruce | same |
| 20 | Mississippi St. | 9-2-0 | Bob Tyler | same |

### Key Bowl Games

Rankings below reflect final regular season poll, released Nov. 29. No bowl for then #20 Miss. St. (probation).

**Sugar**–#1 Pitt over #5 Georgia, 27-3; **Rose**–#3 USC over #2 Michigan, 14-6; **Cotton**–#6 Houston over #4 Maryland, 30-21; **Liberty**–#16 Alabama over #7 UCLA, 36-6; **Fiesta**–#8 Oklahoma over Wyoming, 41-7; **Bluebonnet**–#13 Nebraska over #9 Texas Tech, 27-24; **Sun**–#10 Texas A&M over Florida, 37-14; **Orange**–#11 Ohio St. over #12 Colorado, 27-10.

## 1977

| | | After Bowls | Head Coach | Regular Season |
|---|---|---|---|---|
| 1 | Notre Dame | 11-1-0 | Dan Devine | 10-1-0 |
| 2 | Alabama | 11-1-0 | Bear Bryant | 10-1-0 |
| 3 | Arkansas | 11-1-0 | Lou Holtz | 10-1-0 |
| 4 | Texas | 11-1-0 | Fred Akers | 11-0-0 |
| 5 | Penn St. | 11-1-0 | Joe Paterno | 10-1-0 |
| 6 | Kentucky | 10-1-0 | Fran Curci | same |
| 7 | Oklahoma | 10-2-0 | Barry Switzer | 10-1-0 |
| 8 | Pittsburgh | 9-2-1 | Jackie Sherrill | 8-2-1 |
| 9 | Michigan | 10-2-0 | Bo Schembechler | 10-1-0 |
| 10 | Washington | 8-4-0 | Don James | 7-4-0 |
| 11 | Ohio St. | 9-3-0 | Woody Hayes | 9-2-0 |
| 12 | Nebraska | 9-3-0 | Tom Osborne | 8-3-0 |
| 13 | USC | 8-4-0 | John Robinson | 7-4-0 |
| 14 | Florida St. | 10-2-0 | Bobby Bowden | 9-2-0 |
| 15 | Stanford | 9-3-0 | Bill Walsh | 8-3-0 |
| 16 | San Diego St. | 10-1-0 | Claude Gilbert | same |
| 17 | North Carolina | 8-3-1 | Bill Dooley | 8-2-1 |
| 18 | Arizona St. | 9-3-0 | Frank Kush | 9-2-0 |
| 19 | Clemson | 8-3-1 | Charley Pell | 8-2-1 |
| 20 | BYU | 9-2-0 | LaVell Edwards | same |

### Key Bowl Games

Rankings below reflect final regular season poll, released Nov. 28. No bowl for then #7 Kentucky (probation).

**Cotton**–#5 Notre Dame over #1 Texas, 38-10; **Orange**–#6 Arkansas over #2 Oklahoma, 31-6; **Sugar**–#3 Alabama over #9 Ohio St., 35-6; **Rose**–#13 Washington over #4 Michigan, 27-20; **Fiesta**–#8 Penn St. over #15 Ariz. St., 42-30; **Gator**–#10 Pitt over #11 Clemson, 34-3.

## Associated Press Final Polls (Cont.)

### 1978

| | | | Head Coach | Regular Season |
|---|---|---|---|---|
| | | **After Bowls** | | |
| 1 | Alabama | 11-1-0 | Bear Bryant | 10-1-0 |
| 2 | USC | 12-1-0 | John Robinson | 11-1-0 |
| 3 | Oklahoma | 11-1-0 | Barry Switzer | 10-1-0 |
| 4 | Penn St. | 11-1-0 | Joe Paterno | 11-0-0 |
| 5 | Michigan | 10-2-0 | Bo Schembechler | 10-1-0 |
| 6 | Clemson | 11-1-0 | Charley Pell | 10-1-0 |
| 7 | Notre Dame | 9-3-0 | Dan Devine | 8-3-0 |
| 8 | Nebraska | 9-3-0 | Tom Osborne | 9-2-0 |
| 9 | Texas | 9-3-0 | Fred Akers | 8-3-0 |
| 10 | Houston | 9-3-0 | Bill Yeoman | 9-2-0 |
| 11 | Arkansas | 9-2-1 | Lou Holtz | 9-2-0 |
| 12 | Michigan St. | 8-3-0 | Darryl Rogers | same |
| 13 | Purdue | 9-2-1 | Jim Young | 8-2-1 |
| 14 | UCLA | 8-3-1 | Terry Donahue | 8-3-0 |
| 15 | Missouri | 8-4-0 | Warren Powers | 7-4-0 |
| 16 | Georgia | 9-2-1 | Vince Dooley | 9-1-1 |
| 17 | Stanford | 8-4-0 | Bill Walsh | 7-4-0 |
| 18 | N.C. State | 9-3-0 | Bo Rein | 8-3-0 |
| 19 | Texas A&M | 8-4-0 | Emory Bellard (4-2) & Tom Wilson (4-2) | 7-4-0 |
| 20 | Maryland | 9-3-0 | Jerry Claiborne | 9-2-0 |

#### Key Bowl Games

Rankings below reflect final regular season poll, released Dec. 4. No bowl for then #12 Michigan St. (probation).
**Sugar**–#2 Alabama over #1 Penn St., 14-7; **Rose**–#3 USC over #5 Michigan, 17-10; **Orange**–#4 Oklahoma over #6 Nebraska, 31-24; **Gator**–#7 Clemson over #20 Ohio St., 17-15; **Fiesta**–#8 Arkansas tied #15 UCLA, 10-10; **Cotton**–#10 Notre Dame over #9 Houston, 35-34.

### 1979

| | | | Head Coach | Regular Season |
|---|---|---|---|---|
| | | **After Bowls** | | |
| 1 | Alabama | 12-0-0 | Bear Bryant | 11-0-0 |
| 2 | USC | 11-0-1 | John Robinson | 10-0-1 |
| 3 | Oklahoma | 11-1-0 | Barry Switzer | 10-1-0 |
| 4 | Ohio St. | 11-1-0 | Earle Bruce | 11-0-0 |
| 5 | Houston | 11-1-0 | Bill Yeoman | 10-1-0 |
| 6 | Florida St. | 11-1-0 | Bobby Bowden | 11-0-0 |
| 7 | Pittsburgh | 11-1-0 | Jackie Sherrill | 10-1-0 |
| 8 | Arkansas | 10-2-0 | Lou Holtz | 10-1-0 |
| 9 | Nebraska | 10-2-0 | Tom Osborne | 10-1-0 |
| 10 | Purdue | 10-2-0 | Jim Young | 9-2-0 |
| 11 | Washington | 9-3-0 | Don James | 8-3-0 |
| 12 | Texas | 9-3-0 | Fred Akers | 9-2-0 |
| 13 | BYU | 11-1-0 | LaVell Edwards | 11-0-0 |
| 14 | Baylor | 8-4-0 | Grant Teaff | 7-4-0 |
| 15 | North Carolina | 8-3-1 | Dick Crum | 7-3-1 |
| 16 | Auburn | 8-3-0 | Doug Barfield | same |
| 17 | Temple | 10-2-0 | Wayne Hardin | 9-2-0 |
| 18 | Michigan | 8-4-0 | Bo Schembechler | 8-3-0 |
| 19 | Indiana | 8-4-0 | Lee Corso | 7-4-0 |
| 20 | Penn St. | 8-4-0 | Joe Paterno | 7-4-0 |

#### Key Bowl Games

Rankings below reflect final regular season poll, released Dec. 3. No bowl for then #17 Auburn (probation).
**Sugar**–#2 Alabama over #6 Arkansas, 24-9; **Rose**–#3 USC over #1 Ohio St., 17-16; **Orange**–#5 Oklahoma over #4 Florida St., 24-7; **Sun**–#13 Washington over #11 Texas, 14-7; **Cotton**–#8 Houston over #7 Nebraska, 17-14; **Fiesta**–#10 Pitt over Arizona, 16-10.

### 1980

| | | | Head Coach | Regular Season |
|---|---|---|---|---|
| | | **After Bowls** | | |
| 1 | Georgia | 12-0-0 | Vince Dooley | 11-0-0 |
| 2 | Pittsburgh | 11-1-0 | Jackie Sherrill | 10-1-0 |
| 3 | Oklahoma | 10-2-0 | Barry Switzer | 9-2-0 |
| 4 | Michigan | 10-2-0 | Bo Schembechler | 9-2-0 |
| 5 | Florida St. | 10-2-0 | Bobby Bowden | 10-1-0 |
| 6 | Alabama | 10-2-0 | Bear Bryant | 9-2-0 |
| 7 | Nebraska | 10-2-0 | Tom Osborne | 9-2-0 |
| 8 | Penn St. | 10-2-0 | Joe Paterno | 9-2-0 |
| 9 | Notre Dame | 9-2-1 | Dan Devine | 9-1-1 |
| 10 | North Carolina | 11-1-0 | Dick Crum | 10-1-0 |
| 11 | USC | 8-2-1 | John Robinson | same |
| 12 | BYU | 12-1-0 | LaVell Edwards | 11-1-0 |
| 13 | UCLA | 9-2-0 | Terry Donahue | same |
| 14 | Baylor | 10-2-0 | Grant Teaff | 10-1-0 |
| 15 | Ohio St. | 9-3-0 | Earle Bruce | 9-2-0 |
| 16 | Washington | 9-3-0 | Don James | 9-2-0 |
| 17 | Purdue | 9-3-0 | Jim Young | 8-3-0 |
| 18 | Miami-FL | 9-3-0 | H. Schnellenberger | 8-3-0 |
| 19 | Mississippi St. | 9-3-0 | Emory Bellard | 9-2-0 |
| 20 | SMU | 8-4-0 | Ron Meyer | 8-3-0 |

#### Key Bowl Games

Rankings below reflect final regular season poll, released Dec. 8.
**Sugar**–#1 Georgia over #7 Notre Dame, 17-10; **Orange**–#4 Oklahoma over #2 Florida St., 18-17; **Gator**–#3 Pitt over #18 S. Carolina, 37-9; **Rose**–#5 Michigan over #16 Washington, 23-6; **Cotton**–#9 Alabama over #6 Baylor, 30-2; **Sun**–#8 Nebraska over #17 Miss. St., 31-17; **Fiesta**–#10 Penn St. over #11 Ohio St., 31-19; **Bluebonnet**–#13 N. Carolina over Texas, 16-7.

### 1981

| | | | Head Coach | Regular Season |
|---|---|---|---|---|
| | | **After Bowls** | | |
| 1 | Clemson | 12-0-0 | Danny Ford | 11-0-0 |
| 2 | Texas | 10-1-1 | Fred Akers | 9-1-1 |
| 3 | Penn St. | 10-2-0 | Joe Paterno | 9-2-0 |
| 4 | Pittsburgh | 11-1-0 | Jackie Sherrill | 10-1-0 |
| 5 | SMU | 10-1-0 | Ron Meyer | same |
| 6 | Georgia | 10-2-0 | Vince Dooley | 10-1-0 |
| 7 | Alabama | 9-2-1 | Bear Bryant | 9-1-1 |
| 8 | Miami-FL | 9-2-0 | H. Schnellenberger | same |
| 9 | North Carolina | 10-2-0 | Dick Crum | 9-2-0 |
| 10 | Washington | 10-2-0 | Don James | 9-2-0 |
| 11 | Nebraska | 9-3-0 | Tom Osborne | 9-2-0 |
| 12 | Michigan | 9-3-0 | Bo Schembechler | 8-3-0 |
| 13 | BYU | 11-2-0 | LaVell Edwards | 10-2-0 |
| 14 | USC | 9-3-0 | John Robinson | 9-2-0 |
| 15 | Ohio St. | 9-3-0 | Earle Bruce | 8-3-0 |
| 16 | Arizona St. | 9-2-0 | Darryl Rogers | same |
| 17 | West Virginia | 9-3-0 | Don Nehlen | 8-3-0 |
| 18 | Iowa | 8-4-0 | Hayden Fry | 8-3-0 |
| 19 | Missouri | 8-4-0 | Warren Powers | 7-4-0 |
| 20 | Oklahoma | 7-4-1 | Barry Switzer | 6-4-1 |

#### Key Bowl Games

Rankings below reflect final regular season poll, released Nov. 30. No bowl for then #5 SMU (probation), #9 Miami-FL (probation), and #17 Ariz. St. (probation).
**Orange**–#1 Clemson over #4 Nebraska, 22-15; **Sugar**–#10 Pitt over #2 Georgia, 24-20; **Cotton**–#6 Texas over #3 Alabama, 14-12; **Fiesta**–#7 Penn St. over #8 USC, 26-10; **Gator**–#11 N. Carolina over Arkansas, 31-27; **Rose**–#12 Washington over #13 Iowa, 28-0.

## 1982

| | | After Bowls | Head Coach | Regular Season |
|---|---|---|---|---|
| 1 | Penn St. | 11-1-0 | Joe Paterno | 10-1-0 |
| 2 | SMU | 11-0-1 | Bobby Collins | 10-0-1 |
| 3 | Nebraska | 12-1-0 | Tom Osborne | 11-1-0 |
| 4 | Georgia | 11-1-0 | Vince Dooley | 11-0-0 |
| 5 | UCLA | 10-1-1 | Terry Donahue | 9-1-1 |
| 6 | Arizona St. | 10-2-0 | Darryl Rogers | 9-2-0 |
| 7 | Washington | 10-2-0 | Don James | 9-2-0 |
| 8 | Clemson | 9-1-1 | Danny Ford | same |
| 9 | Arkansas | 9-2-1 | Lou Holtz | 8-2-1 |
| 10 | Pittsburgh | 9-3-0 | Foge Fazio | 9-2-0 |
| 11 | LSU | 8-3-1 | Jerry Stovall | 8-2-1 |
| 12 | Ohio St. | 9-3-0 | Earle Bruce | 8-3-0 |
| 13 | Florida St. | 9-3-0 | Bobby Bowden | 8-3-0 |
| 14 | Auburn | 9-3-0 | Pat Dye | 8-3-0 |
| 15 | USC | 8-3-0 | John Robinson | same |
| 16 | Oklahoma | 8-4-0 | Barry Switzer | 8-3-0 |
| 17 | Texas | 9-3-0 | Fred Akers | 9-2-0 |
| 18 | North Carolina | 8-4-0 | Dick Crum | 7-4-0 |
| 19 | West Virginia | 9-3-0 | Don Nehlen | 9-2-0 |
| 20 | Maryland | 8-4-0 | Bobby Ross | 8-3-0 |

**Key Bowl Games**

Rankings below reflect final regular season poll, released Dec. 6. No bowl for then #7 Clemson (probation) and #15 USC (probation).

**Sugar**–#2 Penn St. over #1 Georgia, 27-23; **Orange**–#3 Nebraska over #13 LSU, 21-20; **Cotton**–#4 SMU over #6 Pitt, 7-3; **Rose**–#5 UCLA over #19 Michigan, 24-14; **Aloha**–#9 Washington over #16 Maryland, 21-20; **Fiesta**–#11 Ariz. St. over #12 Oklahoma, 32-21; **Bluebonnet**–#14 Arkansas over Florida, 28-24.

## 1983

| | | After Bowls | Head Coach | Regular Season |
|---|---|---|---|---|
| 1 | Miami-FL | 11-1-0 | H. Schnellenberger | 10-1-0 |
| 2 | Nebraska | 12-1-0 | Tom Osborne | 12-0-0 |
| 3 | Auburn | 11-1-0 | Pat Dye | 10-1-0 |
| 4 | Georgia | 10-1-1 | Vince Dooley | 9-1-1 |
| 5 | Texas | 11-1-0 | Fred Akers | 11-0-0 |
| 6 | Florida | 9-2-1 | Charley Pell | 8-2-1 |
| 7 | BYU | 11-1-0 | LaVell Edwards | 10-1-0 |
| 8 | Michigan | 9-3-0 | Bo Schembechler | 9-2-0 |
| 9 | Ohio St. | 9-3-0 | Earle Bruce | 8-3-0 |
| 10 | Illinois | 10-2-0 | Mike White | 10-1-0 |
| 11 | Clemson | 9-1-1 | Danny Ford | same |
| 12 | SMU | 10-2-0 | Bobby Collins | 10-1-0 |
| 13 | Air Force | 10-2-0 | Ken Hatfield | 9-2-0 |
| 14 | Iowa | 9-3-0 | Hayden Fry | 9-2-0 |
| 15 | Alabama | 8-4-0 | Ray Perkins | 7-4-0 |
| 16 | West Virginia | 9-3-0 | Don Nehlen | 8-3-0 |
| 17 | UCLA | 7-4-1 | Terry Donahue | 6-4-1 |
| 18 | Pittsburgh | 8-3-1 | Foge Fazio | 8-2-1 |
| 19 | Boston College | 9-3-0 | Jack Bicknell | 9-2-0 |
| 20 | East Carolina | 8-3-0 | Ed Emory | same |

**Key Bowl Games**

Rankings below reflect final regular season poll, released Dec. 5. No bowl for then #12 Clemson (probation).

**Orange**–#5 Miami-FL over #1 Nebraska, 31-30; **Cotton**–#7 Georgia over #2 Texas, 10-9; **Sugar**–#3 Auburn over #8 Michigan, 9-7; **Rose**–UCLA over #4 Illinois, 45-9; **Holiday**–#9 BYU over Missouri, 21-17; **Gator**–#11 Florida over #10 Iowa, 14-6; **Fiesta**–#14 Ohio St. over #15 Pitt, 28-23.

## 1984

| | | After Bowls | Head Coach | Regular Season |
|---|---|---|---|---|
| 1 | BYU | 13-0-0 | LaVell Edwards | 12-0-0 |
| 2 | Washington | 11-1-0 | Don James | 10-1-0 |
| 3 | Florida | 9-1-1 | Charley Pell (0-1-1) & Galen Hall (9-0) | same |
| 4 | Nebraska | 10-2-0 | Tom Osborne | 9-2-0 |
| 5 | Boston College | 10-2-0 | Jack Bicknell | 9-2-0 |
| 6 | Oklahoma | 9-2-1 | Barry Switzer | 9-1-1 |
| 7 | Oklahoma St. | 10-2-0 | Pat Jones | 9-2-0 |
| 8 | SMU | 10-2-0 | Bobby Collins | 9-2-0 |
| 9 | UCLA | 9-3-0 | Terry Donahue | 8-3-0 |
| 10 | USC | 9-3-0 | Ted Tollner | 8-3-0 |
| 11 | South Carolina | 10-2-0 | Joe Morrison | 10-1-0 |
| 12 | Maryland | 9-3-0 | Bobby Ross | 8-3-0 |
| 13 | Ohio St. | 9-3-0 | Earle Bruce | 9-2-0 |
| 14 | Auburn | 9-4-0 | Pat Dye | 8-4-0 |
| 15 | LSU | 8-3-1 | Bill Arnsparger | 8-2-1 |
| 16 | Iowa | 8-4-1 | Hayden Fry | 7-4-1 |
| 17 | Florida St. | 7-3-2 | Bobby Bowden | 7-3-1 |
| 18 | Miami-FL | 8-5-0 | Jimmy Johnson | 8-4-0 |
| 19 | Kentucky | 9-3-0 | Jerry Claiborne | 8-3-0 |
| 20 | Virginia | 8-2-2 | George Welsh | 7-2-2 |

**Key Bowl Games**

Rankings below reflect final regular season poll, released Dec. 3. No bowl for then #3 Florida (probation).

**Holiday**–#1 BYU over Michigan, 24-17; **Orange**–#4 Washington over #2 Oklahoma, 28-17; **Sugar**–#5 Nebraska over #11 LSU, 28-10; **Rose**–#18 USC over #6 Ohio St., 20-17; **Gator**–#9 Okla. St. over #7 S. Carolina, 21-14; **Cotton**–#8 BC over Houston, 45-28; **Aloha**–#10 SMU over #17 Notre Dame, 27-20.

## 1985

| | | After Bowls | Head Coach | Regular Season |
|---|---|---|---|---|
| 1 | Oklahoma | 11-1-0 | Barry Switzer | 10-1-0 |
| 2 | Michigan | 10-1-1 | Bo Schembechler | 9-1-1 |
| 3 | Penn St. | 11-1-0 | Joe Paterno | 11-0-0 |
| 4 | Tennessee | 9-1-2 | Johnny Majors | 8-1-2 |
| 5 | Florida | 9-1-1 | Galen Hall | same |
| 6 | Texas A&M | 10-2-0 | Jackie Sherrill | 9-2-0 |
| 7 | UCLA | 9-2-1 | Terry Donahue | 8-2-1 |
| 8 | Air Force | 12-1-0 | Fisher DeBerry | 11-1-0 |
| 9 | Miami-FL | 10-2-0 | Jimmy Johnson | 10-1-0 |
| 10 | Iowa | 10-2-0 | Hayden Fry | 10-1-0 |
| 11 | Nebraska | 9-3-0 | Tom Osborne | 9-2-0 |
| 12 | Arkansas | 10-2-0 | Ken Hatfield | 9-2-0 |
| 13 | Alabama | 9-2-1 | Ray Perkins | 8-2-1 |
| 14 | Ohio St. | 9-3-0 | Earle Bruce | 8-3-0 |
| 15 | Florida St. | 9-3-0 | Bobby Bowden | 8-3-0 |
| 16 | BYU | 11-3-0 | LaVell Edwards | 11-2-0 |
| 17 | Baylor | 9-3-0 | Grant Teaff | 8-3-0 |
| 18 | Maryland | 9-3-0 | Bobby Ross | 8-3-0 |
| 19 | Georgia Tech | 9-2-1 | Bill Curry | 8-2-1 |
| 20 | LSU | 9-2-1 | Bill Arnsparger | 9-1-1 |

**Key Bowl Games**

Rankings below reflect final regular season poll, released Dec. 9. No bowl for then #6 Florida (probation).

**Orange**–#3 Oklahoma over #1 Penn St., 25-10; **Sugar**–#8 Tennessee over #2 Miami-FL, 35-7; **Rose**–#13 UCLA over #4 Iowa, 45-28; **Fiesta**–#5 Michigan over #7 Nebraska, 27-23; **Bluebonnet**–#10 Air Force over Texas, 24-16; **Cotton**–#11 Texas A&M over #16 Auburn, 36-16.

## Associated Press Final Polls (Cont.)

### 1986

| | | | After Bowls | Head Coach | Regular Season |
|---|---|---|---|---|---|
| 1 | Penn St. | ....... | 12-0-0 | Joe Paterno | 11-0-0 |
| 2 | Miami-FL | ....... | 11-1-0 | Jimmy Johnson | 11-0-0 |
| 3 | Oklahoma | ....... | 11-1-0 | Barry Switzer | 10-1-0 |
| 4 | Arizona St. | .... | 10-1-1 | John Cooper | 9-1-1 |
| 5 | Nebraska | ....... | 10-2-0 | Tom Osborne | 9-2-0 |
| 6 | Auburn | ........ | 10-2-0 | Pat Dye | 9-2-0 |
| 7 | Ohio St. | ....... | 10-3-0 | Earle Bruce | 9-3-0 |
| 8 | Michigan | ....... | 11-2-0 | Bo Schembechler | 11-1-0 |
| 9 | Alabama | ....... | 10-3-0 | Ray Perkins | 9-3-0 |
| 10 | LSU | ......... | 9-3-0 | Bill Arnsparger | 9-2-0 |
| 11 | Arizona | ....... | 9-3-0 | Larry Smith | 8-3-0 |
| 12 | Baylor | ........ | 9-3-0 | Grant Teaff | 8-3-0 |
| 13 | Texas A&M | ..... | 9-3-0 | Jackie Sherrill | 9-2-0 |
| 14 | UCLA | ........ | 8-3-1 | Terry Donahue | 7-3-1 |
| 15 | Arkansas | ....... | 9-3-0 | Ken Hatfield | 9-2-0 |
| 16 | Iowa | ......... | 9-3-0 | Hayden Fry | 8-3-0 |
| 17 | Clemson | ....... | 8-2-2 | Danny Ford | 7-2-2 |
| 18 | Washington | .... | 8-3-1 | Don James | 8-2-1 |
| 19 | Boston College | . | 9-3-0 | Jack Bicknell | 8-3-0 |
| 20 | Virginia Tech | .... | 9-2-1 | Bill Dooley | 8-2-1 |

**Key Bowl Games**

Rankings below reflect final regular season poll, released Dec. 1.

**Fiesta**–#2 Penn St. over #1 Miami-FL, 14-10; **Orange**–#3 Oklahoma over #9 Arkansas, 42-8; **Rose**–#7 Ariz. St. over #4 Michigan, 22-15; **Sugar**–#6 Nebraska over #5 LSU, 30-15; **Cotton**–#11 Ohio St. over #8 Texas A&M, 28-12; **Citrus**–#10 Auburn over USC, 16-7; **Sun**–#13 Alabama over #12 Washington, 28-6.

### 1988

| | | | After Bowls | Head Coach | Regular Season |
|---|---|---|---|---|---|
| 1 | Notre Dame | ... | 12-0-0 | Lou Holtz | 11-0-0 |
| 2 | Miami-FL | ....... | 11-1-0 | Jimmy Johnson | 10-1-0 |
| 3 | Florida St. | ..... | 11-1-0 | Bobby Bowden | 10-1-0 |
| 4 | Michigan | ....... | 9-2-1 | Bo Schembechler | 8-2-1 |
| 5 | West Virginia | . | 11-1-0 | Don Nehlen | 11-0-0 |
| 6 | UCLA | ........ | 10-2-0 | Terry Donahue | 9-2-0 |
| 7 | USC | ......... | 10-2-0 | Larry Smith | 10-1-0 |
| 8 | Auburn | ........ | 10-2-0 | Pat Dye | 10-1-0 |
| 9 | Clemson | ....... | 10-2-0 | Danny Ford | 9-2-0 |
| 10 | Nebraska | ....... | 11-2-0 | Tom Osborne | 11-1-0 |
| 11 | Oklahoma St. | .. | 10-2-0 | Pat Jones | 9-2-0 |
| 12 | Arkansas | ....... | 10-2-0 | Ken Hatfield | 10-1-0 |
| 13 | Syracuse | ....... | 10-2-0 | Dick MacPherson | 9-2-0 |
| 14 | Oklahoma | ....... | 9-3-0 | Barry Switzer | 9-2-0 |
| 15 | Georgia | ....... | 9-3-0 | Vince Dooley | 8-3-0 |
| 16 | Washington St. | .. | 9-3-0 | Dennis Erickson | 8-3-0 |
| 17 | Alabama | ....... | 9-3-0 | Bill Curry | 8-3-0 |
| 18 | Houston | ....... | 9-3-0 | Jack Pardee | 9-2-0 |
| 19 | LSU | ......... | 8-4-0 | Mike Archer | 8-3-0 |
| 20 | Indiana | ....... | 8-3-1 | Bill Mallory | 7-3-1 |

**Key Bowl Games**

Rankings below reflect final regular season poll, released Dec. 5.

**Fiesta**–#1 Notre Dame over #3 West Va., 34-21; **Orange**–#2 Miami-FL over #6 Nebraska, 23-3; **Sugar**–#4 Florida St. over #7 Auburn, 13-7; **Rose**–#11 Michigan over #5 USC, 22-14; **Cotton**–#9 UCLA over #8 Arkansas, 17-3; **Citrus**–#13 Clemson over #10 Oklahoma, 13-6.

### 1987

| | | | After Bowls | Head Coach | Regular Season |
|---|---|---|---|---|---|
| 1 | Miami-FL | ....... | 12-0-0 | Jimmy Johnson | 11-0-0 |
| 2 | Florida St. | ..... | 11-1-0 | Bobby Bowden | 10-1-0 |
| 3 | Oklahoma | ....... | 11-1-0 | Barry Switzer | 11-0-0 |
| 4 | Syracuse | ....... | 11-0-1 | Dick MacPherson | 11-0-0 |
| 5 | LSU | ......... | 10-1-1 | Mike Archer | 9-1-1 |
| 6 | Nebraska | ....... | 10-2-0 | Tom Osborne | 9-1-1 |
| 7 | Auburn | ........ | 9-1-2 | Pat Dye | 9-1-1 |
| 8 | Michigan St. | .. | 9-2-1 | George Perles | 8-2-1 |
| 9 | UCLA | ........ | 10-2-0 | Terry Donahue | 9-2-0 |
| 10 | Texas A&M | .... | 10-2-0 | Jackie Sherrill | 9-2-0 |
| 11 | Oklahoma St. | .. | 10-2-0 | Pat Jones | 9-2-0 |
| 12 | Clemson | ....... | 10-2-0 | Danny Ford | 9-2-0 |
| 13 | Georgia | ....... | 9-3-0 | Vince Dooley | 8-3-0 |
| 14 | Tennessee | .... | 10-2-1 | Johnny Majors | 9-2-1 |
| 15 | South Carolina | . | 8-4-0 | Joe Morrison | 8-3-0 |
| 16 | Iowa | ......... | 10-3-0 | Hayden Fry | 9-3-0 |
| 17 | Notre Dame | .... | 8-4-0 | Lou Holtz | 8-3-0 |
| 18 | USC | ......... | 8-4-0 | Larry Smith | 8-3-0 |
| 19 | Michigan | ....... | 8-4-0 | Bo Schembechler | 7-4-0 |
| 20 | Arizona St. | ..... | 7-4-1 | John Cooper | 6-4-1 |

**Key Bowl Games**

Rankings below reflect final regular season poll, released Dec. 7.

**Orange**–#2 Miami-FL over #1 Oklahoma, 20-14; **Fiesta**–#3 Florida St. over #5 Nebraska, 31-28; **Sugar**–#4 Syracuse tied #6 Auburn, 16-16; **Gator**–#7 LSU over #9 S. Carolina, 30-13; **Rose**–#8 Mich. St. over #16 USC, 20-17; **Aloha**–#10 UCLA over Florida, 20-16; **Cotton**–#13 Texas A&M over #12 Notre Dame, 35-10.

### 1989

| | | | After Bowls | Head Coach | Regular Season |
|---|---|---|---|---|---|
| 1 | Miami-FL | ....... | 11-1-0 | Dennis Erickson | 10-1-0 |
| 2 | Notre Dame | .... | 12-1-0 | Lou Holtz | 11-1-0 |
| 3 | Florida St. | ..... | 10-2-0 | Bobby Bowden | 9-2-0 |
| 4 | Colorado | ....... | 11-1-0 | Bill McCartney | 11-0-0 |
| 5 | Tennessee | .... | 11-1-0 | Johnny Majors | 10-1-0 |
| 6 | Auburn | ........ | 10-2-0 | Pat Dye | 9-2-0 |
| 7 | Michigan | ....... | 10-2-0 | Bo Schembechler | 10-1-0 |
| 8 | USC | ......... | 9-2-1 | Larry Smith | 8-2-1 |
| 9 | Alabama | ....... | 10-2-0 | Bill Curry | 10-1-0 |
| 10 | Illinois | ....... | 10-2-0 | John Mackovic | 9-2-0 |
| 11 | Nebraska | ....... | 10-2-0 | Tom Osborne | 10-1-0 |
| 12 | Clemson | ....... | 10-2-0 | Danny Ford | 9-2-0 |
| 13 | Arkansas | ....... | 10-2-0 | Ken Hatfield | 10-1-0 |
| 14 | Houston | ....... | 9-2-0 | Jack Pardee | same |
| 15 | Penn St. | ....... | 8-3-1 | Joe Paterno | 7-3-1 |
| 16 | Michigan St. | .. | 8-4-0 | George Perles | 7-4-0 |
| 17 | Pittsburgh | .... | 8-3-1 | Mike Gottfried (7-3-1) & Paul Hackett (1-0) | 7-3-1 |
| 18 | Virginia | ....... | 10-3-0 | George Welsh | 10-2-0 |
| 19 | Texas Tech | ..... | 9-3-0 | Spike Dykes | 8-3-0 |
| 20 | Texas A&M | .... | 8-4-0 | R.C. Slocum | 8-3-0 |
| 21 | West Virginia | .. | 8-3-1 | Don Nehlen | 8-2-1 |
| 22 | BYU | ......... | 10-3-0 | LaVell Edwards | 10-2-0 |
| 23 | Washington | .... | 8-4-0 | Don James | 7-4-0 |
| 24 | Ohio St. | ....... | 8-4-0 | John Cooper | 8-3-0 |
| 25 | Arizona | ....... | 8-4-0 | Dick Tomey | 7-4-0 |

**Key Bowl Games**

Rankings below reflect final regular season poll, released Dec. 11. No bowl for then #13 Houston (probation).

**Orange**–#4 Notre Dame over #1 Colorado, 21-6; **Sugar**–#2 Miami-FL over #7 Alabama, 33-25; **Rose**–#12 USC over #3 Michigan, 17-10; **Fiesta**–#5 Florida St. over #6 Nebraska, 41-17; **Cotton**–#8 Tennessee over #10 Arkansas, 31-27; **Hall of Fame**–#9 Auburn over #21 Ohio St., 31-14; **Citrus**–#11 Illinois over #15 Virginia, 31-21.

## 1990

| | After Bowls | Head Coach | Regular Season |
|---|---|---|---|
| 1 Colorado | 11-1-1 | Bill McCartney | 10-1-1 |
| 2 Georgia Tech | 11-0-1 | Bobby Ross | 10-0-1 |
| 3 Miami-FL | 10-2-0 | Dennis Erickson | 9-2-0 |
| 4 Florida St. | 10-2-0 | Bobby Bowden | 9-2-0 |
| 5 Washington | 10-2-0 | Don James | 9-2-0 |
| 6 Notre Dame | 9-3-0 | Lou Holtz | 9-2-0 |
| 7 Michigan | 9-3-0 | Gary Moeller | 8-3-0 |
| 8 Tennessee | 9-2-2 | Johnny Majors | 8-2-2 |
| 9 Clemson | 10-2-0 | Ken Hatfield | 9-2-0 |
| 10 Houston | 10-1-0 | John Jenkins | same |
| 11 Penn St. | 9-3-0 | Joe Paterno | 9-2-0 |
| 12 Texas | 10-2-0 | David McWilliams | 10-1-0 |
| 13 Florida | 9-2-0 | Steve Spurrier | same |
| 14 Louisville | 10-1-1 | H. Schnellenberger | 9-1-1 |
| 15 Texas A&M | 9-3-1 | R.C. Slocum | 8-3-1 |
| 16 Michigan St. | 8-3-1 | George Perles | 7-3-1 |
| 17 Oklahoma | 8-3-0 | Gary Gibbs | same |
| 18 Iowa | 8-4-0 | Hayden Fry | 8-3-0 |
| 19 Auburn | 8-3-1 | Pat Dye | 7-3-1 |
| 20 USC | 8-4-1 | Larry Smith | 8-3-1 |
| 21 Mississippi | 9-3-0 | Billy Brewer | 9-2-0 |
| 22 BYU | 10-3-0 | LaVell Edwards | 10-2-0 |
| 23 Virginia | 8-4-0 | George Welsh | 8-3-0 |
| 24 Nebraska | 9-3-0 | Tom Osborne | 9-2-0 |
| 25 Illinois | 8-4-0 | John Mackovic | 8-3-0 |

### Key Bowl Games

Rankings below reflect final regular season poll, released Dec. 3. No bowl for then #9 Houston (probation), #11 Florida (probation) and #20 Oklahoma (probation).
**Orange**–#1 Colorado over #5 Notre Dame, 10-9; **Citrus**–#2 Ga. Tech over #19 Nebraska, 45-21; **Cotton**–#4 Miami-FL over #3 Texas, 46-3; **Blockbuster**–#6 Florida St. over #7 Penn St., 24-17; **Rose**–#8 Washington over #17 Iowa, 46-34; **Sugar**–#10 Tennessee over Virginia, 23-22; **Gator**–#12 Michigan over #15 Ole Miss, 35-3.

## 1991

| | After Bowls | Head Coach | Regular Season |
|---|---|---|---|
| 1 Miami-FL | 12-0-0 | Dennis Erickson | 11-0-0 |
| 2 Washington | 12-0-0 | Don James | 11-0-0 |
| 3 Penn St. | 11-2-0 | Joe Paterno | 10-2-0 |
| 4 Florida St. | 11-2-0 | Bobby Bowden | 10-2-0 |
| 5 Alabama | 11-1-0 | Gene Stallings | 10-1-0 |
| 6 Michigan | 10-2-0 | Gary Moeller | 10-1-0 |
| 7 Florida | 10-2-0 | Steve Spurrier | 10-1-0 |
| 8 California | 10-2-0 | Bruce Snyder | 9-2-0 |
| 9 East Carolina | 11-1-0 | Bill Lewis | 10-1-0 |
| 10 Iowa | 10-1-1 | Hayden Fry | 10-1-0 |
| 11 Syracuse | 10-2-0 | Paul Pasqualoni | 9-2-0 |
| 12 Texas A&M | 10-2-0 | R.C. Slocum | 10-1-0 |
| 13 Notre Dame | 10-3-0 | Lou Holtz | 9-3-0 |
| 14 Tennessee | 9-3-0 | Johnny Majors | 9-2-0 |
| 15 Nebraska | 9-2-1 | Tom Osborne | 9-1-1 |
| 16 Oklahoma | 9-3-0 | Gary Gibbs | 8-3-0 |
| 17 Georgia | 9-3-0 | Ray Goff | 8-3-0 |
| 18 Clemson | 9-2-1 | Ken Hatfield | 9-1-1 |
| 19 UCLA | 9-3-0 | Terry Donahue | 8-3-0 |
| 20 Colorado | 8-3-1 | Bill McCartney | 8-2-1 |
| 21 Tulsa | 10-2-0 | David Rader | 9-2-0 |
| 22 Stanford | 8-4-0 | Dennis Green | 8-3-0 |
| 23 BYU | 8-3-2 | LaVell Edwards | 8-3-1 |
| 24 N.C. State | 9-3-0 | Dick Sheridan | 9-2-0 |
| 25 Air Force | 10-3-0 | Fisher DeBerry | 9-3-0 |

### Key Bowl Games

Rankings below reflect final regular season poll, taken Dec. 2.
**Orange**–#1 Miami-FL over #11 Nebraska, 22-0; **Rose**–#2 Washington over #4 Michigan, 34-14; **Sugar**–#18 Notre Dame over #3 Florida St., 39-28; **Cotton**–#5 Florida St. over #9 Texas A&M, 10-2; **Fiesta**–#6 Penn St. over #10 Tennessee, 42-17; **Holiday**–#7 Iowa tied BYU, 13-13; **Blockbuster**–#8 Alabama over #15 Colorado, 30-25; **Citrus**–#14 California over #13 Clemson, 37-13.

## 1992

| | After Bowls | Head Coach | Regular Season |
|---|---|---|---|
| 1 Alabama | 13-0-0 | Gene Stallings | 12-0-0 |
| 2 Florida St. | 11-1-0 | Bobby Bowden | 10-1-0 |
| 3 Miami-FL | 11-1-0 | Dennis Erickson | 11-0-0 |
| 4 Notre Dame | 10-1-1 | Lou Holtz | 9-1-1 |
| 5 Michigan | 9-0-3 | Gary Moeller | 8-0-3 |
| 6 Syracuse | 10-2-0 | Paul Pasqualoni | 9-2-0 |
| 7 Texas A&M | 12-1-0 | R.C. Slocum | 12-0-0 |
| 8 Georgia | 10-2-0 | Ray Goff | 9-2-0 |
| 9 Stanford | 10-3-0 | Bill Walsh | 9-3-0 |
| 10 Florida | 9-4-0 | Steve Spurrier | 8-4-0 |
| 11 Washington | 9-3-0 | Don James | 9-2-0 |
| 12 Tennessee | 9-3-0 | Johnny Majors (5-3) & Phillip Fulmer (4-0) | 8-3-0 |
| 13 Colorado | 9-2-1 | Bill McCartney | 9-1-1 |
| 14 Nebraska | 9-3-0 | Tom Osborne | 9-2-0 |
| 15 Washington St. | 9-3-0 | Mike Price | 8-3-0 |
| 16 Mississippi | 9-3-0 | Billy Brewer | 8-3-0 |
| 17 N.C. State | 9-3-1 | Dick Sheridan | 9-2-1 |
| 18 Ohio St. | 8-3-1 | John Cooper | 8-2-1 |
| 19 North Carolina | 9-3-0 | Mack Brown | 8-3-0 |
| 20 Hawaii | 11-2-0 | Bob Wagner | 10-2-0 |
| 21 Boston College | 8-3-1 | Tom Coughlin | 8-2-1 |
| 22 Kansas | 8-4-0 | Glen Mason | 7-4-0 |
| 23 Mississippi St. | 7-5-0 | Jackie Sherrill | 7-4-0 |
| 24 Fresno St. | 9-4-0 | Jim Sweeney | 9-3-0 |
| 25 Wake Forest | 8-4-0 | Bill Dooley | 7-4-0 |

### Key Bowl Games

Rankings below reflect final regular season poll, taken Dec. 5.
**Sugar**–#2 Alabama over #1 Miami-FL, 34-13; **Orange**–#3 Florida St. over #11 Nebraska, 27-14; **Cotton**–#5 Notre Dame over #4 Texas A&M, 28-3; **Fiesta**–#6 Syracuse over #10 Colorado, 26-22; **Rose**–#7 Michigan over #9 Washington, 38-31; **Citrus**–#8 Georgia over #15 Ohio St., 21-14.

## 1993

| | After Bowls | Head Coach | Regular Season |
|---|---|---|---|
| 1 Florida St | 12-1-0 | Bobby Bowden | 11-1-0 |
| 2 Notre Dame | 11-1-0 | Lou Holtz | 10-1-0 |
| 3 Nebraska | 11-1-0 | Tom Osborne | 11-0-0 |
| 4 Auburn | 11-0-0 | Terry Bowden | 11-0-0 |
| 5 Florida | 11-2-0 | Steve Spurrier | 10-2-0 |
| 6 Wisconsin | 10-1-1 | Barry Alvarez | 9-1-1 |
| 7 West Virginia | 11-1-0 | Don Nehlen | 11-0-0 |
| 8 Penn St. | 10-2-0 | Joe Paterno | 9-2-0 |
| 9 Texas A&M | 10-2-0 | R.C. Slocum | 10-1-0 |
| 10 Arizona | 10-2-0 | Dick Tomey | 9-2-0 |
| 11 Ohio St | 10-1-1 | John Cooper | 9-1-1 |
| 12 Tennessee | 9-2-1 | Phillip Fulmer | 9-1-1 |
| 13 Boston College | 9-3-0 | Tom Coughlin | 8-3-0 |
| 14 Alabama | 9-3-1 | Gene Stallings | 8-3-1 |
| 15 Miami-FL | 9-3-0 | Dennis Erickson | 9-2-0 |
| 16 Colorado | 8-3-1 | Bill McCartney | 7-3-1 |
| 17 Oklahoma | 9-3-0 | Gary Gibbs | 8-3-0 |
| 18 UCLA | 8-4-0 | Terry Donahue | 8-3-0 |
| 19 North Carolina | 10-3-0 | Mack Brown | 10-2-0 |
| 20 Kansas St | 9-2-1 | Bill Snyder | 8-2-1 |
| 21 Michigan | 8-4-0 | Gary Moeller | 7-4-0 |
| 22 Va. Tech | 9-3-0 | Frank Beamer | 8-3-0 |
| 23 Clemson | 9-3-0 | Ken Hatfield (8-3) & Tommy West (1-0) | 8-3-0 |
| 24 Louisville | 9-3-0 | H. Schnellenberger | 8-3-0 |
| 25 California | 9-4-0 | Keith Gilbertson | 8-4-0 |

### Key Bowl Games

Rankings below reflect final regular season poll, taken Dec. 5. No bowl for then #5 Auburn (probation). **Orange**–#1 Florida St. over #2 Nebraska, 18-16; **Sugar**–#8 Florida over #3 West Virginia, 41-7; **Cotton**–#4 Notre Dame over #7 Texas A&M, 24-21; **Citrus**–#13 Penn St. over #6 Tennessee, 31-13; **Rose**–#9 Wisconsin over #14 UCLA, 21-16; **Fiesta**–#16 Arizona over #10 Miami-FL, 29-0.

## Associated Press Final Polls (Cont.)

### 1994

| | | After Bowls | Head Coach | Regular Season |
|---|---|---|---|---|
| 1 | Nebraska | 13-0-0 | Tom Osborne | 12-0-0 |
| 2 | Penn St | 12-0-0 | Joe Paterno | 11-0-0 |
| 3 | Colorado | 11-1-0 | Bill McCartney | 10-1-0 |
| 4 | Florida St | 10-1-1 | Bobby Bowden | 9-1-1 |
| 5 | Alabama | 12-1-0 | Gene Stallings | 11-1-0 |
| 6 | Miami-FL | 10-2-0 | Dennis Erickson | 10-1-0 |
| 7 | Florida | 10-2-1 | Steve Spurrier | 10-1-1 |
| 8 | Texas A&M | 10-0-1 | R.C. Slocum | same |
| 9 | Auburn | 9-1-1 | Terry Bowden | same |
| 10 | Utah | 10-2-0 | Ron McBride | 9-2-0 |
| 11 | Oregon | 9-4-0 | Rich Brooks | 9-3-0 |
| 12 | Michigan | 8-4-0 | Gary Moeller | 7-4-0 |
| 13 | USC | 8-3-1 | John Robinson | 7-3-1 |
| 14 | Ohio St | 9-4-0 | John Cooper | 9-3-0 |
| 15 | Virginia | 9-3-0 | George Welsh | 8-3-0 |
| 16 | Colorado St | 10-2-0 | Sonny Lubick | 10-1-0 |
| 17 | N.C. State | 9-3-0 | Mike O'Cain | 8-3-0 |
| 18 | BYU | 10-3-0 | LaVell Edwards | 9-3-0 |
| 19 | Kansas St | 9-3-0 | Bill Snyder | 9-2-0 |
| 20 | Arizona | 8-4-0 | Dick Tomey | 8-3-0 |
| 21 | Washington St | 8-4-0 | Mike Price | 7-4-0 |
| 22 | Tennessee | 8-4-0 | Phillip Fulmer | 7-4-0 |
| 23 | Boston College | 7-4-1 | Dan Henning | 6-4-1 |
| 24 | Mississippi St | 8-4-0 | Jackie Sherrill | 8-3-0 |
| 25 | Texas | 8-4-0 | John Mackovic | 7-4-0 |

#### Key Bowl Games

Rankings below reflect final regular season poll, taken Dec. 4. No bowls for then #8 Texas A&M (probation) and #9 Auburn (probation). **Orange**–#1 Nebraska over #3 Miami-FL, 24-17; **Rose**–#2 Penn St. over #12 Oregon, 38-20; **Fiesta**–#4 Colorado over Notre Dame, 41-24; **Sugar**–#7 Florida St. over #5 Florida, 23-17; **Citrus**–#6 Alabama over #13 Ohio St., 24-17; **Freedom**–#14 Utah over #15 Arizona, 16-13.

### 1995

| | | After Bowls | Head Coach | Regular Season |
|---|---|---|---|---|
| 1 | Nebraska | 12-0-0 | Tom Osborne | 11-0-0 |
| 2 | Florida | 12-1-0 | Steve Spurrier | 12-0-0 |
| 3 | Tennessee | 11-1-0 | Phillip Fulmer | 10-1-0 |
| 4 | Florida St | 10-2-0 | Bobby Bowden | 9-2-0 |
| 5 | Colorado | 10-2-0 | Rick Neuheisel | 9-2-0 |
| 6 | Ohio St | 11-2-0 | John Cooper | 11-1-0 |
| 7 | Kansas St | 10-2-0 | Bill Snyder | 9-2-0 |
| 8 | Northwestern | 10-2-0 | Gary Barnett | 10-1-0 |
| 9 | Kansas | 10-2-0 | Glen Mason | 9-2-0 |
| 10 | Va. Tech | 10-2-0 | Frank Beamer | 9-2-0 |
| 11 | Notre Dame | 9-3-0 | Lou Holtz | 9-2-0 |
| 12 | USC | 9-2-1 | John Robinson | 8-2-1 |
| 13 | Penn St | 9-3-0 | Joe Paterno | 8-3-0 |
| 14 | Texas | 10-2-1 | John Mackovic | 10-1-1 |
| 15 | Texas A&M | 9-3-0 | R.C. Slocum | 8-3-0 |
| 16 | Virginia | 9-4-0 | George Welsh | 8-4-0 |
| 17 | Michigan | 9-4-0 | Lloyd Carr | 9-3-0 |
| 18 | Oregon | 9-3-0 | Mike Bellotti | 9-2-0 |
| 19 | Syracuse | 9-3-0 | Paul Pasqualoni | 8-3-0 |
| 20 | Miami-FL | 8-3-0 | Butch Davis | same |
| 21 | Alabama | 8-3-0 | Gene Stallings | same |
| 22 | Auburn | 8-4-0 | Terry Bowden | 8-3-0 |
| 23 | Texas Tech | 9-3-0 | Spike Dykes | 8-3-0 |
| 24 | Toledo | 11-0-1 | Gary Pinkel | 10-0-1 |
| 25 | Iowa | 8-4-0 | Hayden Fry | 7-4-0 |

#### Key Bowl Games

Rankings below reflect final regular season poll, taken Dec. 3. No bowl for then #21 Ala. (probation) and #22 Miami-FL (probation). **Fiesta**–#1 Neb. over #2 Fla., 62-24; **Rose**–#17 USC over #3 Northwestern, 41-32; **Citrus**–#4t Tenn. over #4t Ohio St., 20-14; **Orange**–#8 Fla. St. over #6 N. Dame, 31-26; **Cotton**–#7 Colo. over #12 Oregon, 38-6; **Sugar**–#13 Va. Tech over #9 Texas, 28-10.

### 1996

| | | After Bowls | Head Coach | Regular Season |
|---|---|---|---|---|
| 1 | Florida | 12-1 | Steve Spurrier | 11-1 |
| 2 | Ohio St. | 11-1 | John Cooper | 10-1 |
| 3 | Florida St. | 11-1 | Bobby Bowden | 11-0 |
| 4 | Arizona St | 11-1 | Bruce Snyder | 11-0 |
| 5 | BYU | 14-1 | LaVell Edwards | 13-1 |
| 6 | Nebraska | 11-2 | Tom Osborne | 10-2 |
| 7 | Penn St. | 11-2 | Joe Paterno | 10-2 |
| 8 | Colorado | 10-2 | Rick Neuheisel | 9-2 |
| 9 | Tennessee | 10-2 | Phillip Fulmer | 9-2 |
| 10 | North Carolina | 10-2 | Mack Brown | 9-2 |
| 11 | Alabama | 10-3 | Gene Stallings | 9-3 |
| 12 | LSU | 10-2 | Gerry DiNardo | 9-2 |
| 13 | Virginia Tech | 10-2 | Frank Beamer | 10-1 |
| 14 | Miami-FL | 9-3 | Butch Davis | 8-3 |
| 15 | Northwestern | 9-3 | Gary Barnett | 9-2 |
| 16 | Washington | 9-3 | Jim Lambright | 9-2 |
| 17 | Kansas St. | 9-3 | Bill Snyder | 9-2 |
| 18 | Iowa | 9-3 | Hayden Fry | 8-3 |
| 19 | Notre Dame | 8-3 | Lou Holtz | same |
| 20 | Michigan | 8-4 | Lloyd Carr | 8-3 |
| 21 | Syracuse | 9-3 | Paul Pasqualoni | 8-3 |
| 22 | Wyoming | 10-2 | Joe Tiller | same |
| 23 | Texas | 8-5 | John Mackovic | 8-4 |
| 24 | Auburn | 8-4 | Terry Bowden | 7-4 |
| 25 | Army | 10-2 | Bob Sutton | 10-1 |

#### Key Bowl Games

Rankings below reflect final regular season poll, taken Dec. 8. No bowl for then #18 N. Dame and #22 Wyoming. **Sugar**–#3 Fla. over #1 Fla. St., 52-20; **Rose**–#4 Ohio St. over #2 Ariz. St., 20-17; **Fiesta**–#7 Penn St. over #20 Texas, 38-15; **Cotton**–#5 BYU over #14 Kansas St., 19-15; **Citrus**–#9 Tenn. over #11 Northwestern, 48-28; **Orange**–#6 Neb. over #10 Va. Tech, 41-21.

### 1997

| | | After Bowls | Head Coach | Regular Season |
|---|---|---|---|---|
| 1 | Michigan | 12-0 | Lloyd Carr | 11-0 |
| 2 | Nebraska | 13-0 | Tom Osborne | 12-0 |
| 3 | Florida St | 11-1 | Bobby Bowden | 10-1 |
| 4 | Florida | 10-2 | Steve Spurrier | 9-2 |
| 5 | UCLA | 10-2 | Bob Toledo | 9-2 |
| 6 | North Carolina | 11-1 | Mack Brown (10-1) & Carl Torbush (1-0) | 10-1 (11-1) (1-0) |
| 7 | Tennessee | 11-2 | Phillip Fulmer | 11-1 |
| 8 | Kansas St | 11-1 | Bill Snyder | 10-1 |
| 9 | Washington St. | 10-2 | Mike Price | 10-1 |
| 10 | Georgia | 10-2 | Jim Donnan | 9-2 |
| 11 | Auburn | 10-3 | Terry Bowden | 9-3 |
| 12 | Ohio St. | 10-3 | John Cooper | 10-2 |
| 13 | LSU | 9-3 | Gerry DiNardo | 8-3 |
| 14 | Arizona St. | 8-3 | Bruce Snyder | 7-3 |
| 15 | Purdue | 9-3 | Joe Tiller | 8-3 |
| 16 | Penn St. | 9-3 | Joe Paterno | 9-2 |
| 17 | Colorado St. | 11-2 | Sonny Lubick | 10-2 |
| 18 | Washington | 8-4 | Jim Lambright | 7-4 |
| 19 | So. Mississippi | 9-3 | Jeff Bower | 8-3 |
| 20 | Texas A&M | 9-4 | R.C. Slocum | 9-3 |
| 21 | Syracuse | 9-4 | Paul Pasqualoni | 9-3 |
| 22 | Mississippi | 8-4 | Tommy Tuberville | 7-4 |
| 23 | Missouri | 7-5 | Larry Smith | 6-5 |
| 24 | Oklahoma St. | 8-4 | Bobby Simmons | 8-3 |
| 25 | Georgia Tech | 7-5 | George O'Leary | 6-5 |

#### Key Bowl Games

Rankings below reflect final regular season poll, taken Dec. 7. **Rose**–#1 Michigan over #7 Washington St., 21-16; **Orange**–#2 Nebraska over #3 Tennessee, 42-17; **Sugar**–#4 Florida St. over #10 Ohio St., 31-14; **Gator**–#5 North Carolina over Virginia Tech, 42-3; **Cotton**–#9 UCLA over #19 Texas A&M, 29-23; **Citrus**–#8 Florida over #12 Penn St., 21-6; **Fiesta**–#9 Kansas St. over #14 Syracuse, 35-18.

## 1998

| | | After Bowls | Head Coach | Regular Season |
|---|---|---|---|---|
| 1 | Tennessee | 13-0 | Phillip Fulmer | 12-0 |
| 2 | Ohio St. | 11-1 | John Cooper | 10-1 |
| 3 | Florida St. | 11-2 | Bobby Bowden | 11-1 |
| 4 | Arizona | 12-1 | Dick Tomey | 11-1 |
| 5 | Florida | 10-2 | Steve Spurrier | 9-2 |
| 6 | Wisconsin | 11-1 | Barry Alvarez | 10-1 |
| 7 | Tulane | 12-0 | Tommy Bowden | 11-0 |
| 8 | UCLA | 10-2 | Bob Toledo | 10-1 |
| 9 | Georgia Tech | 10-2 | George O'Leary | 9-2 |
| 10 | Kansas St. | 11-2 | Bill Snyder | 11-1 |
| 11 | Texas A&M | 11-3 | R.C. Slocum | 11-2 |
| 12 | Michigan | 10-3 | Lloyd Carr | 9-3 |
| 13 | Air Force | 12-1 | Fisher DeBerry | 11-1 |
| 14 | Georgia | 9-3 | Jim Donnan | 8-3 |
| 15 | Texas | 9-3 | Mack Brown | 8-3 |
| 16 | Arkansas | 9-3 | Houston Nutt | 9-2 |
| 17 | Penn St. | 9-3 | Joe Paterno | 8-3 |
| 18 | Virginia | 9-3 | George Welsh | 9-2 |
| 19 | Nebraska | 9-4 | Frank Solich | 9-3 |
| 20 | Miami-FL | 9-3 | Butch Davis | 8-3 |
| 21 | Missouri | 8-4 | Larry Smith | 7-4 |
| 22 | Notre Dame | 9-3 | Bob Davie | 9-2 |
| 23 | Va. Tech | 9-3 | Frank Beamer | 8-3 |
| 24 | Purdue | 9-4 | Joe Tiller | 8-4 |
| 25 | Syracuse | 8-4 | Paul Pasqualoni | 8-3 |

### Key Bowl Games
Rankings below reflect final regular season poll, taken Dec. 6. **Fiesta**– #1 Tennessee over #2 Florida St., 23-16; **Sugar**–#3 Ohio St. over #8 Texas A&M, 24-14; **Orange**–#7 Florida over #18 Syracuse, 31-10; **Rose**–#9 Wisconsin over #6 UCLA, 38-31; **Holiday**–#5 Arizona over #14 Nebraska, 23-20; **Alamo**–Purdue over #4 Kansas St., 37-34.

## 1999

| | | After Bowls | Head Coach | Regular Season |
|---|---|---|---|---|
| 1 | Florida St. | 12-0 | Bobby Bowden | 11-0 |
| 2 | Va. Tech | 11-1 | Frank Beamer | 11-0 |
| 3 | Nebraska | 12-1 | Frank Solich | 11-1 |
| 4 | Wisconsin | 10-2 | Barry Alvarez | 9-2 |
| 5 | Michigan | 10-2 | Lloyd Carr | 9-2 |
| 6 | Kansas St. | 11-1 | Bill Snyder | 10-1 |
| 7 | Michigan St. | 10-2 | Nick Saban (9-2) & B. Williams (1-0) | 9-2 |
| 8 | Alabama | 10-3 | Mike DuBose | 10-2 |
| 9 | Tennessee | 9-3 | Phillip Fulmer | 8-3 |
| 10 | Marshall | 13-0 | Bob Pruett | 12-0 |
| 11 | Penn St. | 10-3 | Joe Paterno | 9-3 |
| 12 | Florida | 9-4 | Steve Spurrier | 9-3 |
| 13 | Mississippi St. | 10-2 | Jackie Sherrill | 9-2 |
| 14 | Southern Miss. | 9-3 | Jeff Bower | 8-3 |
| 15 | Miami-FL | 9-4 | Butch Davis | 8-4 |
| 16 | Georgia | 8-4 | Jim Donnan | 7-4 |
| 17 | Arkansas | 8-4 | Houston Nutt | 7-4 |
| 18 | Minnesota | 8-4 | Glen Mason | 8-3 |
| 19 | Oregon | 9-3 | Mike Bellotti | 8-3 |
| 20 | Georgia Tech | 8-4 | George O'Leary | 8-3 |
| 21 | Texas | 9-5 | Mack Brown | 9-4 |
| 22 | Mississippi | 8-4 | David Cutcliffe | 7-4 |
| 23 | Texas A&M | 8-4 | R.C. Slocum | 8-3 |
| 24 | Illinois | 8-4 | Ron Turner | 7-4 |
| 25 | Purdue | 7-5 | Joe Tiller | 7-4 |

### Key Bowl Games
Rankings below reflect final regular season poll, taken Dec. 5. **Sugar**–#1 Florida St. over #2 Va. Tech, 46-29; **Fiesta**–#3 Nebraska over #6 Tennessee, 31-21; **Rose**–#4 Wisconsin over #22 Stanford, 17-9; **Orange**–#8 Michigan over #5 Alabama, 35-34; **Holiday**–#7 Kansas St. over Washington, 24-20; **Citrus**–#9 Michigan St. over #10 Florida, 37-34.

## 2000

| | | After Bowls | Head Coach | Regular Season |
|---|---|---|---|---|
| 1 | Oklahoma | 13-0 | Bob Stoops | 12-0 |
| 2 | Miami-FL | 11-1 | Butch Davis | 10-1 |
| 3 | Washington | 11-1 | Rick Neuheisel | 10-1 |
| 4 | Oregon St. | 11-1 | Dennis Erickson | 10-1 |
| 5 | Florida St. | 11-2 | Bobby Bowden | 11-1 |
| 6 | Va. Tech | 11-1 | Frank Beamer | 10-1 |
| 7 | Oregon | 10-2 | Mike Bellotti | 9-2 |
| 8 | Nebraska | 10-2 | Frank Solich | 9-2 |
| 9 | Kansas St. | 11-3 | Bill Snyder | 10-3 |
| 10 | Florida | 10-3 | Steve Spurrier | 10-2 |
| 11 | Michigan | 9-3 | Lloyd Carr | 8-3 |
| 12 | Texas | 9-3 | Mack Brown | 9-2 |
| 13 | Purdue | 8-4 | Joe Tiller | 8-3 |
| 14 | Colorado St. | 10-2 | Sonny Lubick | 9-2 |
| 15 | Notre Dame | 9-3 | Bob Davie | 9-2 |
| 16 | Clemson | 9-3 | Tommy Bowden | 9-2 |
| 17 | Georgia Tech | 9-3 | George O'Leary | 9-2 |
| 18 | Auburn | 9-4 | Tommy Tuberville | 9-3 |
| 19 | South Carolina | 8-4 | Lou Holtz | 7-4 |
| 20 | Georgia | 8-4 | Jim Donnan | 7-4 |
| 21 | TCU | 10-2 | D. Franchione (10-1) & G. Patterson (0-1) | 10-1 |
| 22 | LSU | 8-4 | Nick Saban | 7-4 |
| 23 | Wisconsin | 9-4 | Barry Alvarez | 8-4 |
| 24 | Mississippi St. | 8-4 | Jackie Sherrill | 7-4 |
| 25 | Iowa St. | 9-3 | Dan McCarney | 8-3 |

### Key Bowl Games
Rankings below reflect final regular season poll, taken Dec. 4. **Orange**–#1 Oklahoma over #3 Florida St., 13-2; **Sugar**–#2 Miami-FL over #7 Florida, 37-20; **Rose**–#4 Washington over #14 Purdue, 34-24; **Fiesta**–#5 Oregon St. over #10 Notre Dame, 41-9; **Gator**–#6 Virginia Tech over #16 Clemson, 41-20; **Holiday**–#8 Oregon over #12 Texas, 35-30; **Alamo**–#9 Nebraska over #18 Northwestern, 66-17.

## 2001

| | | After Bowls | Head Coach | Regular Season |
|---|---|---|---|---|
| 1 | Miami-FL | 12-0 | Larry Coker | 11-0 |
| 2 | Oregon | 11-1 | Mike Bellotti | 10-1 |
| 3 | Florida | 10-2 | Steve Spurrier | 9-2 |
| 4 | Tennessee | 11-2 | Phillip Fulmer | 10-2 |
| 5 | Texas | 11-2 | Mack Brown | 10-2 |
| 6 | Oklahoma | 11-2 | Bob Stoops | 10-2 |
| 7 | LSU | 10-3 | Nick Saban | 9-3 |
| 8 | Nebraska | 11-2 | Frank Solich | 11-1 |
| 9 | Colorado | 10-3 | Gary Barnett | 10-2 |
| 10 | Washington St. | 10-2 | Mike Price | 9-2 |
| 11 | Maryland | 10-2 | Ralph Friedgen | 10-1 |
| 12 | Illinois | 10-2 | Ron Turner | 10-1 |
| 13 | South Carolina | 9-3 | Lou Holtz | 8-3 |
| 14 | Syracuse | 10-3 | Paul Pasqualoni | 9-3 |
| 15 | Florida St. | 8-4 | Bobby Bowden | 7-4 |
| 16 | Stanford | 9-3 | Tyrone Willingham | 9-2 |
| 17 | Louisville | 11-2 | John L. Smith | 10-2 |
| 18 | Va. Tech | 8-4 | Frank Beamer | 8-3 |
| 19 | Washington | 8-4 | Rick Neuheisel | 8-3 |
| 20 | Michigan | 8-4 | Lloyd Carr | 8-3 |
| 21 | Boston College | 8-4 | Tom O'Brien | 7-4 |
| 22 | Georgia | 8-4 | Mark Richt | 8-3 |
| 23 | Toledo | 10-2 | Tom Amstutz | 9-2 |
| 24 | Georgia Tech | 8-5 | George O'Leary (7-5) & Mac McWhorter (1-0) | 7-5 |
| 25 | BYU | 12-2 | Gary Crowton | 12-1 |

### Key Bowl Games
Rankings below reflect final regular season poll, taken Dec. 9. **Rose**–#1 Miami-FL over #4 Nebraska, 37-14; **Fiesta**–#2 Oregon over #3 Colorado, 38-16; **Orange**–#5 Florida over #6 Maryland, 56-23; **Sugar**–#12 LSU over #7 Illinois 47-34; **Citrus**–#8 Tennessee over #17 Michigan, 45-17; **Holiday**–#9 Texas over #21 Washington, 47-43; **Cotton**–#10 Oklahoma over Arkansas, 10-3;

## Associated Press Final Polls (Cont.)

### 2002

| | After Bowls | Head Coach | Regular Season |
|---|---|---|---|
| 1 | Ohio St. ....... 14-0 | Jim Tressel | 13-0 |
| 2 | Miami-FL ....... 12-1 | Larry Coker | 12-0 |
| 3 | Georgia ........ 13-1 | Mark Richt | 12-1 |
| 4 | USC ........... 11-2 | Pete Carroll | 10-2 |
| 5 | Oklahoma ...... 12-2 | Bob Stoops | 11-2 |
| 6 | Texas ......... 11-2 | Mack Brown | 10-2 |
| 7 | Kansas St. ..... 11-2 | Bill Snyder | 10-2 |
| 8 | Iowa .......... 11-2 | Kirk Ferentz | 11-1 |
| 9 | Michigan ...... 10-3 | Lloyd Carr | 9-3 |
| 10 | Washington St. .. 10-3 | Mike Price | 10-2 |
| 11 | Alabama ....... 10-3 | Dennis Franchione | 10-3 |
| 12 | N.C. State ..... 11-3 | Chuck Amato | 10-3 |
| 13 | Maryland ...... 11-3 | Ralph Friedgen | 10-3 |
| 14 | Auburn ........ 9-4 | Tommy Tuberville | 8-4 |
| 15 | Boise St. ...... 12-1 | Dan Hawkins | 11-1 |
| 16 | Penn St. ....... 9-4 | Joe Paterno | 9-2 |
| 17 | Notre Dame .... 10-3 | Tyrone Willingham | 10-2 |
| 18 | Va. Tech ...... 10-4 | Frank Beamer | 9-4 |
| 19 | Pittsburgh ..... 9-4 | Walt Harris | 8-4 |
| 20 | Colorado ...... 9-5 | Gary Barnett | 9-4 |
| 21 | Florida St. ..... 9-5 | Bobby Bowden | 9-4 |
| 22 | Virginia ....... 9-5 | Al Groh | 8-5 |
| 23 | TCU .......... 10-2 | Gary Patterson | 9-2 |
| 24 | Marshall ...... 11-2 | Bob Pruett | 10-2 |
| 25 | West Virginia ... 9-4 | Rich Rodriguez | 9-3 |

**Key Bowl Games**

Rankings below reflect final regular season poll, taken Dec. 8. No bowl for then #13 Alabama (probation).
**Fiesta**—#2 Ohio St. over #1 Miami-FL, 31-24 (2OT); **Orange**—#5 USC over #3 Iowa, 38-17; **Sugar**—#4 Georgia over #16 Florida St. 26-13; **Holiday**—#6 Kansas St. over Arizona St., 34-27; **Rose**—#8 Oklahoma over #7 Washington St., 34-14; **Cotton**—#9 Texas over LSU, 35-20; **Capital One**—#19 Auburn over #10 Penn St., 13-9;

### 2003

| | After Bowls | Head Coach | Regular Season |
|---|---|---|---|
| 1 | USC .......... 12-1 | Pete Carroll | 11-1 |
| 2 | LSU .......... 13-1 | Nick Saban | 12-1 |
| 3 | Oklahoma ..... 12-2 | Bob Stoops | 12-1 |
| 4 | Ohio State .... 11-2 | Jim Tressel | 10-2 |
| 5 | Miami-FL ..... 11-2 | Larry Coker | 10-2 |
| 6 | Michigan ..... 10-3 | Lloyd Carr | 11-1 |
| 7 | Georgia ...... 11-3 | Mark Richt | 10-3 |
| 8 | Iowa ......... 10-3 | Kirk Ferentz | 9-3 |
| 9 | Washington St. .. 10-3 | Bill Doba | 9-3 |
| 10 | Miami-OH ..... 13-1 | Terry Hoeppner | 12-1 |
| 11 | Florida St. .... 10-3 | Bobby Bowden | 10-2 |
| 12 | Texas ........ 10-3 | Mack Brown | 10-2 |
| 13 | Mississippi ... 10-3 | David Cutliffe | 9-3 |
| 14 | Kansas St. .... 11-4 | Bill Snyder | 11-3 |
| 15 | Tennessee .... 10-3 | Phillip Fulmer | 10-2 |
| 16 | Boise St. ..... 13-1 | Dan Hawkins | 12-1 |
| 17 | Maryland ..... 10-3 | Ralph Friedgen | 9-3 |
| 18 | Purdue ....... 9-4 | Joe Tiller | 9-3 |
| 19 | Nebraska ..... 10-3 | Frank Solich (9-3) & Bo Pelini (1-0) | 9-3 |
| 20 | Minnesota .... 10-3 | Glen Mason | 9-3 |
| 21 | Utah ......... 10-2 | Urban Meyer | 9-2 |
| 22 | Clemson ...... 9-4 | Tommy Bowden | 8-4 |
| 23 | Bowling Green .. 11-3 | Gregg Brandon | 10-3 |
| 24 | Florida ....... 8-5 | Ron Zook | 8-4 |
| 25 | TCU ......... 11-2 | Gary Patterson | 11-1 |

**Key Bowl Games**

Rankings below reflect final regular season poll, taken Dec. 7.
**Rose**—#1 USC over #4 Michigan, 28-14; **Sugar**—#2 LSU over #3 Oklahoma, 21-14; **Holiday**—#14 Washington St. over #5 Texas, 28-20; **Fiesta**—#6 Ohio St. over #10 Kansas St., 35-28; **Peach**—Clemson over #7 Tennessee, 27-14; **Orange**—#9 Miami-FL over #8 Florida St., 16-14.

### 2004

| | After Bowls | Head Coach | Regular Season |
|---|---|---|---|
| 1 | USC .......... 13-0 | Pete Carroll | 12-0 |
| 2 | Auburn ....... 13-0 | Tommy Tuberville | 12-0 |
| 3 | Oklahoma ..... 12-1 | Bob Stoops | 12-0 |
| 4 | Utah ......... 12-0 | Urban Meyer | 11-0 |
| 5 | Texas ........ 11-1 | Mack Brown | 10-1 |
| 6 | Louisville .... 11-1 | Bobby Petrino | 10-1 |
| 7 | Georgia ...... 10-2 | Mark Richt | 9-2 |
| 8 | Iowa ......... 10-2 | Kirk Ferentz | 9-2 |
| 9 | California .... 10-2 | Jeff Tedford | 10-1 |
| 10 | Virginia Tech .. 10-3 | Frank Beamer | 10-2 |
| 11 | Miami-FL ..... 9-3 | Larry Coker | 8-3 |
| 12 | Boise St. ..... 11-1 | Dan Hawkins | 11-0 |
| 13 | Tennessee .... 10-3 | Philip Fullmer | 9-3 |
| 14 | Michigan ..... 9-3 | Lloyd Carr | 8-3 |
| 15 | Florida St. .... 9-3 | Bobby Bowden | 8-3 |
| 16 | LSU .......... 9-3 | Nick Saban | 9-2 |
| 17 | Wisconsin .... 9-3 | Barry Alvarez | 9-2 |
| 18 | Texas Tech .... 8-4 | Mike Leach | 7-4 |
| 19 | Arizona St. ... 9-3 | Dirk Koetter | 8-3 |
| 20 | Ohio St. ...... 8-4 | Jim Tressel | 7-4 |
| 21 | Boston College .. 9-3 | Tom O'Brien | 8-3 |
| 22 | Fresno St. .... 9-3 | Pat Hill | 8-3 |
| 23 | Virginia ...... 8-4 | Al Groh | 8-3 |
| 24 | Navy ......... 10-2 | Paul Johnson | 9-2 |
| 25 | Pittsburgh .... 8-4 | Walt Harris | 8-3 |

**Key Bowl Games**

Rankings below reflect final regular season poll, taken Dec. 5.
**Orange**—#1 USC over #2 Oklahoma, 55-19; **Sugar**—#3 Auburn over #9 Virginia Tech, 16-13; **Holiday**—#23 Texas Tech over #4 California, 45-31; **Fiesta**—#5 Utah over #19 Pittsburgh, 35-7; **Rose**—#6 Texas over #13 Michigan, 38-37; **Liberty**—#7 Louisville over #10 Boise St., 44-40; **Outback**—#8 Georgia over #16 Wisconsin, 24-21.

### All-Time AP Top 20

The composite AP Top 20 from the 1936 season through the 2004 season, based on the final rankings of each year. The final AP poll has been taken after the bowl games in 1965 and since 1968. Team point totals are based on 20 points for all 1st place finishes, 19 for each 2nd, etc. Also listed are the number of times each team has been named national champion by AP and times ranked in the final Top 10 and Top 20.

| | | Pts | No.1 | Top 10 | Top 20 |
|---|---|---|---|---|---|
| 1 | Oklahoma | 645 | 7 | 34 | 46 |
| 2 | Notre Dame | 636 | 8 | 34 | 46 |
| | Michigan | 636 | 2 | 36 | 52 |
| 4 | Alabama | 574 | 6 | 31 | 43 |
| 5 | Ohio St | 556 | 4 | 26 | 44 |
| 6 | Nebraska | 548 | 4 | 29 | 42 |
| 7 | Texas | 471 | 2 | 22 | 37 |
| | USC | 471 | 5 | 23 | 39 |
| 9 | Tennessee | 464 | 2 | 22 | 39 |
| 10 | Penn St | 408 | 2 | 21 | 36 |
| 11 | Miami-FL | 355 | 5 | 17 | 28 |
| 12 | Florida St | 336 | 2 | 16 | 23 |
| 13 | UCLA | 322 | 0 | 16 | 29 |
| 14 | LSU | 315 | 1 | 16 | 28 |
| 15 | Auburn | 310 | 1 | 15 | 29 |
| 16 | Georgia | 308 | 1 | 17 | 27 |
| 17 | Arkansas | 267 | 0 | 13 | 25 |
| 18 | Florida | 257 | 1 | 13 | 22 |
| 19 | Michigan St | 252 | 1 | 13 | 20 |
| 20 | Washington | 222 | 0 | 11 | 21 |

## Bowl Games

From Jan. 1, 1902 through Jan. 4, 2004. Please note that the Bowl selection process is now dominated by the Bowl Championship Series (which includes the Fiesta, Orange, Rose and Sugar bowls) and the following non-BCS bowls' so called "automatic berths" are contingent upon several factors, including the leftovers from the BCS, Notre Dame's record and the record of their designated choices.

### Rose Bowl

**City:** Pasadena, Calif. **Stadium:** Rose Bowl. **Capacity:** 102,083. **Playing surface:** Grass. **First game:** Jan. 1, 1902. **Playing sites:** Tournament Park (1902, 1916-22), Rose Bowl (1923-41 and since 1943) and Duke Stadium in Durham, N.C. (1942, due to wartime restrictions following Japan's attack at Pearl Harbor on Dec. 7, 1941). **Corporate sponsors:** AT&T (1998-2002), Sony Playstation 2 (2003) and Citi (2004).

**Automatic berths:** Pacific Coast Conference champion vs. opponent selected by PCC (1924-45 seasons); Big Ten champion vs. Pac-10 champion (1946-97); Bowl Championship Series: Big Ten champion vs. Pac-10 champion, if available (1998-2000, 2002-05 seasons) and #1 vs. #2 in Jan. 2002 and Jan. 2006.

**Multiple wins:** USC (21); Michigan (8); Washington (7); Ohio St. (6); Stanford and UCLA (5); Alabama (4); Illinois, Michigan St. and Wisconsin (3); California and Iowa (2).

| Year | | |
|---|---|---|
| 1902* Michigan 49, Stanford 0 | 1946 Alabama 34, USC 14 | 1977 USC 14, Michigan 6 |
| 1916 Washington St. 14, Brown 0 | 1947 Illinois 45, UCLA 14 | 1978 Washington 27, Michigan 20 |
| 1917 Oregon 14, Penn 0 | 1948 Michigan 49, USC 0 | 1979 USC 17, Michigan 10 |
| 1918 Mare Island 19, Camp Lewis 7 | 1949 Northwestern 20, California 14 | 1980 USC 17, Ohio St. 16 |
| 1919 Great Lakes 17, Mare Island 0 | 1950 Ohio St. 17, California 14 | 1981 Michigan 23, Washington 6 |
| 1920 Harvard 7, Oregon 6 | 1951 Michigan 14, California 6 | 1982 Washington 28, Iowa 0 |
| 1921 California 28, Ohio St. 0 | 1952 Illinois 40, Stanford 7 | 1983 UCLA 24, Michigan 14 |
| 1922 0-0, California vs Wash. & Jeff. | 1953 USC 7, Wisconsin 0 | 1984 UCLA 45, Illinois 9 |
| 1923 USC 14, Penn St. 0 | 1954 Michigan St. 28, UCLA 20 | 1985 USC 20, Ohio St. 17 |
| 1924  14-14, Navy vs Washington | 1955 Ohio St. 20, USC 7 | 1986 UCLA 45, Iowa 28 |
| 1925 Notre Dame 27, Stanford 10 | 1956 Michigan St. 17, UCLA 14 | 1987 Arizona St. 22, Michigan 15 |
| 1926 Alabama 20, Washington 19 | 1957 Iowa 35, Oregon St. 19 | 1988 Michigan St. 20, USC 17 |
| 1927 7-7, Alabama vs Stanford | 1958 Ohio St. 10, Oregon 7 | 1989 Michigan 22, USC 14 |
| 1928 Stanford 7, Pittsburgh 6 | 1959 Iowa 38, California 12 | 1990 USC 17, Michigan 10 |
| 1929 Georgia Tech 8, California 7 | 1960 Washington 44, Wisconsin 8 | 1991 Washington 46, Iowa 34 |
| 1930 USC 47, Pittsburgh 14 | 1961 Washington 17, Minnesota 7 | 1992 Washington 34, Michigan 14 |
| 1931 Alabama 24, Washington St. 0 | 1962 Minnesota 21, UCLA 3 | 1993 Michigan 38, Washington 31 |
| 1932 USC 21, Tulane 12 | 1963 USC 42, Wisconsin 37 | 1994 Wisconsin 21, UCLA 16 |
| 1933 USC 35, Pittsburgh 0 | 1964 Illinois 17, Washington 7 | 1995 Penn St. 38, Oregon 20 |
| 1934 Columbia 7, Stanford 0 | 1965 Michigan 34, Oregon St. 7 | 1996 USC 41, Northwestern 32 |
| 1935 Alabama 29, Stanford 13 | 1966 UCLA 14, Michigan St. 12 | 1997 Ohio St. 20, Arizona St. 17 |
| 1936 Stanford 7, SMU 0 | 1967 Purdue 14, USC 13 | 1998 Michigan 21, Washington St. 16 |
| 1937 Pittsburgh 21, Washington 0 | 1968 USC 14, Indiana 3 | 1999 Wisconsin 38, UCLA 31 |
| 1938 California 13, Alabama 0 | 1969 Ohio St. 27, USC 16 | 2000 Wisconsin 17, Stanford 9 |
| 1939 USC 7, Duke 3 | 1970 USC 10, Michigan 3 | 2001 Washington 34, Purdue 24 |
| 1940 USC 14, Tennessee 0 | 1971 Stanford 27, Ohio St. 17 | 2002  Miami-FL 37, Nebraska 14 |
| 1941 Stanford 21, Nebraska 13 | 1972 Stanford 13, Michigan 12 | 2003 Oklahoma 34, Washington St. 14 |
| 1942 Oregon St. 20, Duke 16 | 1973 USC 42, Ohio St. 17 | 2004 USC 28, Michigan 14 |
| 1943 Georgia 9, UCLA 0 | 1974 Ohio St. 42, USC 21 | 2005 Texas 38, Michigan 37 |
| 1944 USC 29, Washington 0 | 1975 USC 18, Ohio St. 17 | * January game since 1902. |
| 1945 USC 25, Tennessee 0 | 1976 UCLA 23, Ohio St. 10 | |

### Fiesta Bowl

**City:** Tempe, Ariz. **Stadium:** Sun Devil. **Capacity:** 73,656. **Playing surface:** Grass. **First game:** Dec. 27, 1971. **Playing site:** Sun Devil Stadium (since 1971). **Corporate title sponsors:** Sunkist Citrus Growers (1986-91), IBM OS/2 (1993-95) and Frito-Lay Tostitos chips (since 1996).

**Automatic berths:** Western Athletic Conference champion vs. at-large opponent (1971-79 seasons); Two of first five picks from 8-team Bowl Coalition pool (1992-94). Bowl Alliance (#1 vs. #2 on Jan. 2, 1996; #3 vs. #5 on Jan. 1, 1997; and #4 vs. #6 on Dec. 31, 1997); Big 12 champion vs. next best team in pool (New Bowl Alliance 1995-1997 seasons); Bowl Championship Series: #1 vs. #2 on Jan. 4, 1999 and Jan., 2003 and Big 12 champion, if available, vs. at-large (1999-2001 and 2003-05 seasons).

**Multiple wins:** Penn St. (6); Arizona St. (5); Ohio St. (3); Florida St. and Nebraska (2).

| Year | | |
|---|---|---|
| 1971† Arizona St. 45, Florida St. 38 | 1984 Ohio St. 28, Pittsburgh 23 | 1996 Nebraska 62, Florida 24 |
| 1972 Arizona St. 49, Missouri 35 | 1985 UCLA 39, Miami-FL 37 | 1997 Penn St. 38, Texas 15 |
| 1973 Arizona St. 28, Pittsburgh 7 | 1986 Michigan 27, Nebraska 23 | 1997† Kansas St. 35, Syracuse 18 |
| 1974 Oklahoma 16, BYU 6 | 1987 Penn St. 14, Miami-FL 10 | 1999 Tennessee 23, Florida St. 16 |
| 1975 Arizona St. 17, Nebraska 14 | 1988 Florida St. 31, Nebraska 28 | 2000 Nebraska 31, Tennessee 21 |
| 1976 Oklahoma 41, Wyoming 7 | 1989 Notre Dame 34, West Va. 21 | 2001 Oregon St. 41, Notre Dame 9 |
| 1977 Penn St. 42, Arizona St. 30 | 1990 Florida St. 41, Nebraska 17 | 2002 Oregon 38, Colorado 16 |
| 1978 10-10, Arkansas vs UCLA | 1991 Louisville 34, Alabama 7 | 2003 Ohio St. 31, Miami-FL 24 (2OT) |
| 1979 Pittsburgh 16, Arizona 10 | 1992 Penn St. 42, Tennessee 17 | 2004 Ohio St. 35, Kansas St. 28 |
| 1980 Penn St. 31, Ohio St. 19 | 1993 Syracuse 26, Colorado 22 | 2005 Utah 35, Pittsburgh 7 |
| 1982* Penn St. 26, USC 10 | 1994 Arizona 29, Miami-FL 0 | †December game from 1971-80 and in |
| 1983 Arizona St. 32, Oklahoma 21 | 1995 Colorado 41, Notre Dame 24 | '97. |
| | | *January game since 1982. |

## Bowl Games (Cont.)
### Sugar Bowl

**City:** Atlanta, Ga. **Stadium:** Georgia Dome. **Capacity:** 71,228. **Playing surface:** Turf. **First game:** Jan. 1, 1935. **Playing sites:** Tulane Stadium (1935-74), Louisiana Superdome (1975-2005), Georgia Dome (2006). **Corporate title sponsors:** USF&G Financial Services (1987-95) and Nokia (starting in 1995).

**Automatic berths:** SEC champion vs. at-large opponent (1976-91 seasons); SEC champion vs. one of first five picks from 8-team Bowl Coalition pool (1992-94 seasons); #4 vs. #6 on Dec. 31, 1995; #1 vs. #2 on Jan. 2, 1997; and #3 vs. #5 on Jan. 1, 1998; Bowl Championship Series: SEC champion, if available, vs. at-large (1998-99, 2000-02, 2004-05 seasons) and #1 vs. #2 on Jan. 2, 2000 and Jan. 2004.

**Multiple wins:** Alabama (8); Mississippi (5); Florida St., Georgia Tech, LSU, Oklahoma and Tennessee (4); Georgia and Nebraska (3); Auburn, Florida, LSU, Miami-FL, Notre Dame, Pittsburgh, Santa Clara and TCU (2).

| Year | | Year | | Year | |
|---|---|---|---|---|---|
| 1935* | Tulane 20, Temple 14 | 1960 | Mississippi 21, LSU 0 | 1985 | Nebraska 28, LSU 10 |
| 1936 | TCU 3, LSU 2 | 1961 | Mississippi 14, Rice 6 | 1986 | Tennessee 35, Miami-FL 7 |
| 1937 | Santa Clara 21, LSU 14 | 1962 | Alabama 10, Arkansas 3 | 1987 | Nebraska 30, LSU 15 |
| 1938 | Santa Clara 6, LSU 0 | 1963 | Mississippi 17, Arkansas 13 | 1988 | 16-16, Syracuse vs Auburn |
| 1939 | TCU 15, Carnegie Tech 7 | 1964 | Alabama 12, Mississippi 7 | 1989 | Florida St. 13, Auburn 7 |
| | | 1965 | LSU 13, Syracuse 10 | | |
| 1940 | Texas A&M 14, Tulane 13 | 1966 | Missouri 20, Florida 18 | 1990 | Miami-FL 33, Alabama 25 |
| 1941 | Boston College 19, Tennessee 13 | 1967 | Alabama 34, Nebraska 7 | 1991 | Tennessee 23, Virginia 22 |
| 1942 | Fordham 2, Missouri 0 | 1968 | LSU 20, Wyoming 13 | 1992 | Notre Dame 39, Florida 28 |
| 1943 | Tennessee 14, Tulsa 7 | 1969 | Arkansas 16, Georgia 2 | 1993 | Alabama 34, Miami-FL 13 |
| 1944 | Georgia Tech 20, Tulsa 18 | | | 1994 | Florida 41, West Va. 7 |
| 1945 | Duke 29, Alabama 26 | 1970 | Mississippi 27, Arkansas 22 | 1995 | Florida St. 23, Florida 17 |
| 1946 | Okla. A&M 33, St.Mary's 13 | 1971 | Tennessee 34, Air Force 13 | 1995† | Va. Tech 28, Texas 10 |
| 1947 | Georgia 20, N. Carolina 10 | 1972 | Oklahoma 40, Auburn 22 | 1997 | Florida 52, Florida St. 20 |
| 1948 | Texas 27, Alabama 7 | 1972† | Oklahoma 14, Penn St. 0 | 1998 | Florida St. 31, Ohio St. 14 |
| 1949 | Oklahoma 14, N. Carolina 6 | 1973 | Notre Dame 24, Alabama 23 | 1999 | Ohio St. 24, Texas A&M 14 |
| | | 1974 | Nebraska 13, Florida 10 | | |
| 1950 | Oklahoma 35, LSU 0 | 1975 | Alabama 13, Penn St. 6 | 2000 | Florida St. 46, Va. Tech 29 |
| 1951 | Kentucky 13, Oklahoma 7 | 1977* | Pittsburgh 27, Georgia 3 | 2001 | Miami-FL 37, Florida 20 |
| 1952 | Maryland 28, Tennessee 13 | 1978 | Alabama 35, Ohio St. 6 | 2002 | LSU 47, Illinois 34 |
| 1953 | Georgia Tech 24, Mississippi 7 | 1979 | Alabama 14, Penn St. 7 | 2003 | Georgia 26, Florida St. 13 |
| 1954 | Georgia Tech 42, West Va. 19 | | | 2004 | LSU 21, Oklahoma 14 |
| 1955 | Navy 21, Mississippi 0 | 1980 | Alabama 24, Arkansas 9 | 2005 | Auburn 16, Va. Tech 13 |
| 1956 | Georgia Tech 7, Pittsburgh 0 | 1981 | Georgia 17, Notre Dame 10 | | |
| 1957 | Baylor 13, Tennessee 7 | 1982 | Pittsburgh 24, Georgia 20 | | |
| 1958 | Mississippi 39, Texas 7 | 1983 | Penn St. 27, Georgia 23 | | |
| 1959 | LSU 7, Clemson 0 | 1984 | Auburn 9, Michigan 7 | | |

\* January game from 1935-72 and since 1977 (except in 1995).
† Game played on Dec. 31 from 1972-75 and in 1995.

### Orange Bowl

**City:** Miami, Fla. **Stadium:** Dolphin. **Capacity:** 74,916. **Playing surface:** Grass. **First game:** Jan. 1, 1935. **Playing sites:** Orange Bowl (1935-95); Dolphin Stadium (since 1996). Dolphin Stadium was originally named Joe Robbie Stadium then was named Pro Player Stadium (1996-2004). **Corporate title sponsor:** Federal Express (since 1989).

**Automatic berths:** Big 8 champion vs. Atlantic Coast Conference champion (1953-57 seasons); Big 8 champion vs. at-large opponent (1958-63 seasons and 1975-91 seasons); Big 8 champion vs. one of first five picks from 8-team Bowl Coalition pool (1992-94 seasons); #3 vs. #5 on Jan. 1, 1996; #4 vs. #6 on Dec. 31, 1996; and #1 vs. #2 on Jan. 2, 1998 (New Bowl Alliance 1995-97 seasons); Bowl Championship Series: Big East or ACC champion, if available, vs. at-large (1998-99, 2001-03, 2005 seasons) and #1 vs. #2 on Jan. 3, 2001 and Jan. 2005.

**Multiple wins:** Oklahoma (12); Nebraska (8); Miami-FL (6); Alabama (4); Florida, Florida State, Georgia Tech and Penn St. (3); Clemson, Colorado, Georgia, LSU, Notre Dame, Texas and USC (2).

| Year | | Year | | Year | |
|---|---|---|---|---|---|
| 1935* | Bucknell 26, Miami-FL 0 | 1955 | Duke 34, Nebraska 7 | 1975 | Notre Dame 13, Alabama 11 |
| 1936 | Catholic U. 20, Mississippi 19 | 1956 | Oklahoma 20, Maryland 6 | 1976 | Oklahoma 14, Michigan 6 |
| 1937 | Duquesne 13, Mississippi St. 12 | 1957 | Colorado 27, Clemson 21 | 1977 | Ohio St. 27, Colorado 10 |
| 1938 | Auburn 6, Michigan St. 0 | 1958 | Oklahoma 48, Duke 21 | 1978 | Arkansas 31, Oklahoma 6 |
| 1939 | Tennessee 17, Oklahoma 0 | 1959 | Oklahoma 21, Syracuse 6 | 1979 | Oklahoma 31, Nebraska 24 |
| | | | | | |
| 1940 | Georgia Tech 21, Missouri 7 | 1960 | Georgia 14, Missouri 0 | 1980 | Oklahoma 24, Florida St. 7 |
| 1941 | Mississippi St. 14, Georgetown 7 | 1961 | Missouri 21, Navy 14 | 1981 | Oklahoma 18, Florida St. 17 |
| 1942 | Georgia 40, TCU 26 | 1962 | LSU 25, Colorado 7 | 1982 | Clemson 22, Nebraska 15 |
| 1943 | Alabama 37, Boston College 21 | 1963 | Alabama 17, Oklahoma 0 | 1983 | Nebraska 21, LSU 20 |
| 1944 | LSU 19, Texas A&M 14 | 1964 | Nebraska 13, Auburn 7 | 1984 | Miami-FL 31, Nebraska 30 |
| 1945 | Tulsa 26, Georgia Tech 12 | 1965† | Texas 21, Alabama 17 | 1985 | Washington 28, Oklahoma 17 |
| 1946 | Miami-FL 13, Holy Cross 6 | 1966 | Alabama 39, Nebraska 28 | 1986 | Oklahoma 25, Penn St. 10 |
| 1947 | Rice 8, Tennessee 0 | 1967 | Florida 27, Georgia Tech 12 | 1987 | Oklahoma 42, Arkansas 8 |
| 1948 | Georgia Tech 20, Kansas 14 | 1968 | Oklahoma 26, Tennessee 24 | 1988 | Miami-FL 20, Oklahoma 14 |
| 1949 | Texas 41, Georgia 28 | 1969 | Penn St. 15, Kansas 14 | 1989 | Miami-FL 23, Nebraska 3 |
| | | | | | |
| 1950 | Santa Clara 21, Kentucky 13 | 1970 | Penn St. 10, Missouri 3 | 1990 | Notre Dame, 21, Colorado 6 |
| 1951 | Clemson 15, Miami-FL 14 | 1971 | Nebraska 17, LSU 12 | 1991 | Colorado 10, Notre Dame 9 |
| 1952 | Georgia Tech 17, Baylor 14 | 1972 | Nebraska 38, Alabama 6 | 1992 | Miami-FL 22, Nebraska 0 |
| 1953 | Alabama 61, Syracuse 6 | 1973 | Nebraska 40, Notre Dame 6 | 1993 | Florida St. 27, Nebraska 14 |
| 1954 | Oklahoma 7, Maryland 0 | 1974 | Penn St. 16, LSU 9 | 1994 | Florida St. 18, Nebraska 16 |

| Year | | Year | | Year | |
|---|---|---|---|---|---|
| 1995 | Nebraska 24, Miami-FL 17 | 2000 | Michigan 35, Alabama 34 | 2005 | USC 55, Oklahoma 19 |
| 1996 | Florida St. 31, Notre Dame 26 | 2001 | Oklahoma 13, Florida St. 2 | * | January game 1935-1996 and since |
| 1996** | Nebraska 41, Virginia Tech 21 | 2002 | Florida 56, Maryland 23 | | '98. |
| 1998* | Nebraska 42, Tennessee 17 | 2003 | USC 38, Iowa 17 | ** | December game in 1996 |
| 1999 | Florida 31, Syracuse 10 | 2004 | Miami-FL 16, Florida St. 14 | † | Night game since 1965. |

## Cotton Bowl

**City:** Dallas, Tex. **Stadium:** Cotton Bowl. **Capacity:** 68,252. **Playing surface:** Grass. **First game:** Jan 1, 1937. **Playing sites:** Fair Park Stadium (1937) and Cotton Bowl (since 1938). **Corporate title sponsor:** Mobil Corporation (1988-95), SBC Communications Inc., previously Southwestern Bell, (since 1997).

**Automatic berths:** SWC champion vs. at-large opponent (1941-91 seasons); SWC champion vs. one of first five picks from 8-team Bowl Coalition pool (1992-1994 seasons); second pick from Big 12 vs. first choice of WAC champion or second pick from Pac-10 (1995-97 seasons); Big 12 vs. SEC (since 1998).

**Multiple wins:** Texas (11); Notre Dame (5); Texas A&M (4); Arkansas, Rice and Tennessee (3); Alabama, Georgia, Houston, LSU, Mississippi, Penn St., SMU, TCU and UCLA (2).

| Year | | Year | | Year | |
|---|---|---|---|---|---|
| 1937* | TCU 16, Marquette 6 | 1961 | Duke 7, Arkansas 6 | 1985 | Boston College 45, Houston 28 |
| 1938 | Rice 28, Colorado 14 | 1962 | Texas 12, Mississippi 7 | 1986 | Texas A&M 36, Auburn 16 |
| 1939 | St. Mary's 20, Texas Tech 13 | 1963 | LSU 13, Texas 0 | 1987 | Ohio St. 28, Texas A&M 12 |
| 1940 | Clemson 6, Boston College 3 | 1964 | Texas 28, Navy 6 | 1988 | Texas A&M 35, Notre Dame 10 |
| 1941 | Texas A&M 13, Fordham 12 | 1965 | Arkansas 10, Nebraska 7 | 1989 | UCLA 17, Arkansas 3 |
| 1942 | Alabama 29, Texas A&M 21 | 1966 | LSU 14, Arkansas 7 | 1990 | Tennessee 31, Arkansas 27 |
| 1943 | Texas 14, Georgia Tech 7 | 1966† | Georgia 24, SMU 9 | 1991 | Miami-FL 46, Texas 3 |
| 1944 | 7-7, Texas vs Randolph Field | 1968* | Texas A&M 20, Alabama 16 | 1992 | Florida St. 10, Texas A&M 2 |
| 1945 | Oklahoma A&M 34, TCU 0 | 1969 | Texas 36, Tennessee 13 | 1993 | Notre Dame 28, Texas A&M 3 |
| 1946 | Texas 40, Missouri 27 | 1970 | Texas 21, Notre Dame 17 | 1994 | Notre Dame 24, Texas A&M 21 |
| 1947 | 0-0, Arkansas vs LSU | 1971 | Notre Dame 24, Texas 11 | 1995 | USC 55, Texas Tech 14 |
| 1948 | 13-13, SMU vs Penn St. | 1972 | Penn St. 30, Texas 6 | 1996 | Colorado 38, Oregon 6 |
| 1949 | SMU 21, Oregon 13 | 1973 | Texas 17, Alabama 13 | 1997 | BYU 19, Kansas St. 15 |
| 1950 | Rice 27, N. Carolina 13 | 1974 | Nebraska 19, Texas 3 | 1998 | UCLA 29, Texas A&M 23 |
| 1951 | Tennessee 20, Texas 14 | 1975 | Penn St. 41, Baylor 20 | 1999 | Texas 38, Mississippi St. 11 |
| 1952 | Kentucky 20, TCU 7 | 1976 | Arkansas 31, Georgia 10 | 2000 | Arkansas 27, Texas 6 |
| 1953 | Texas 16, Tennessee 0 | 1977 | Houston 30, Maryland 21 | 2001 | Kansas St. 35, Tennessee 21 |
| 1954 | Rice 28, Alabama 6 | 1978 | Notre Dame 38, Texas 10 | 2002 | Oklahoma 10, Arkansas 3 |
| 1955 | Georgia Tech 14, Arkansas 6 | 1979 | Notre Dame 35, Houston 34 | 2003 | Texas 35, LSU 20 |
| 1956 | Mississippi 14, TCU 13 | 1980 | Houston 17, Nebraska 14 | 2004 | Mississippi 31, Oklahoma St. 28 |
| 1957 | TCU 28, Syracuse 27 | 1981 | Alabama 30, Baylor 2 | 2005 | Tennessee '38, Texas A&M 7 |
| 1958 | Navy 20, Rice 7 | 1982 | Texas 14, Alabama 12 | * | January game from 1937-66 and |
| 1959 | 0-0, TCU vs Air Force | 1983 | SMU 7, Pittsburgh 3 | | since 1968. |
| 1960 | Syracuse 23, Texas 14 | 1984 | Georgia 10, Texas 9 | † | Game played on Dec. 31, 1966. |

## Capital One Bowl

**City:** Orlando, Fla. **Stadium:** Florida Citrus Bowl. **Capacity:** 70,188. **Playing surface:** Grass. **First game:** Jan. 1, 1947. **Name change:** Tangerine Bowl (1947-82), Florida Citrus Bowl (1983-2002) and Capital One Bowl (since 2003). **Playing sites:** Tangerine Bowl (1947-72, 1974-82), Florida Field in Gainesville (1973), Orlando Stadium (1983-85) and Florida Citrus Bowl (since 1986). The Tangerine Bowl, Orlando Stadium and Florida Citrus Bowl are all the same stadium. **Corporate title sponsors:** Florida Department of Citrus (1983-2002), CompUSA (1992-99), Ourhouse.com (2000) and Capital One (since 2001).

**Automatic berths:** Championship game of Atlantic Coast Regional Conference (1964-67 seasons); Mid-American Conference champion vs. Southern Conference champion (1968-71 seasons); ACC champion vs. at-large opponent (1988-91 seasons); second pick from SEC, if available, vs. second pick from Big 10, if available (since 1992 season).

**Multiple wins:** Tennessee (4); Auburn, East Texas St., Miami-OH and Toledo (3); Catawba, Clemson, East Carolina, Florida, Georgia and Michigan (2).

| Year | | Year | | Year | |
|---|---|---|---|---|---|
| 1947* | Catawba 31, Maryville 6 | 1967 | Tenn-Martin 25, West Chester 8 | 1989 | Clemson 13, Oklahoma 6 |
| 1948 | Catawba 7, Marshall 0 | 1968 | Richmond 49, Ohio U. 42 | 1990 | Illinois 31, Virginia 21 |
| 1949 | 21-21, Murray St. vs Sul Ross St. | 1969 | Toledo 56, Davidson 33 | 1991 | Georgia Tech 45, Nebraska 21 |
| 1950 | St. Vincent 7, Emory & Henry 6 | 1970 | Toledo 40, Wm. & Mary 12 | 1992 | California 37, Clemson 13 |
| 1951 | M. Harvey 35, Emory & Henry 14 | 1971 | Toledo 28, Richmond 3 | 1993 | Georgia 21, Ohio St. 14 |
| 1952 | Stetson 35, Arkansas St. 20 | 1972 | Tampa 21, Kent St. 18 | 1994 | Penn St. 31, Tennessee 13 |
| 1953 | E. Texas St. 33, Tenn. Tech 0 | 1973 | Miami-OH 16, Florida 7 | 1995 | Alabama 24, Ohio St. 17 |
| 1954 | 7-7, E. Texas St. vs Arkansas St. | 1974 | Miami-OH 21, Georgia 10 | 1996 | Tennessee 20, Ohio St. 14 |
| 1955 | Neb.-Omaha 7, Eastern Ky. 6 | 1975 | Miami-OH 20, S. Carolina 7 | 1997 | Tennessee 48, Northwestern 28 |
| 1956 | 6-6, Juniata vs Missouri Valley | 1976 | Oklahoma 49, BYU 21 | 1998 | Florida 21, Penn St. 6 |
| 1957 | W. Texas St. 20, So. Miss. 13 | 1977 | Florida St. 40, Texas Tech 17 | 1999 | Michigan 45, Arkansas 31 |
| 1958 | E. Texas St. 10, So. Miss. 9 | 1978 | N.C. State 30, Pittsburgh 17 | 2000 | Michigan St. 37, Florida 34 |
| 1958† | E. Texas St. 26, Mo. Valley 7 | 1979 | LSU 34, Wake Forest 10 | 2001 | Michigan 31, Auburn 28 |
| 1960* | Mid. Tenn. 21, Presbyterian 12 | 1980 | Florida 35, Maryland 20 | 2002 | Tennessee 45, Michigan 17 |
| 1960† | Citadel 27, Tenn. Tech 0 | 1981 | Missouri 19, Southern Miss. 17 | 2003 | Auburn 13, Penn St. 9 |
| 1961 | Lamar 21, Middle Tenn. 14 | 1982 | Auburn 33, Boston College 26 | 2004 | Georgia 34, Purdue 27 OT |
| 1962 | Houston 49, Miami-OH 21 | 1983 | Tennessee 30, Maryland 23 | 2005 | Iowa 30, LSU 25 |
| 1963 | Western Ky. 27, Coast Guard 0 | 1984 | 17-17, Florida St. vs Georgia | | |
| 1964 | E. Carolina 14, Massachusetts 13 | 1985 | Ohio St. 10, BYU 7 | * | January game from 1947-58, in 1960 |
| 1965 | E. Carolina 31, Maine 0 | 1987* | Auburn 16, USC 7 | | and since 1987. |
| 1966 | Morgan St. 14, West Chester 6 | 1988 | Clemson 35, Penn St. 10 | † | December game in 1958, 1960-85. |

## Bowl Games (Cont.)
### Gator Bowl

**City:** Jacksonville, Fla. **Stadium:** ALLTEL Stadium. **Capacity:** 73,000. **Playing surface:** Grass. **First game:** Jan. 1, 1946. **Playing sites:** Gator Bowl (1946-93), Florida Field in Gainesville (1994) and New Gator Bowl (since 1995). Name was changed to ALLTEL Stadium in 1997. **Corporate title sponsors:** Mazda Motors of America, Inc. (1986-91), Outback Steakhouse, Inc. (1992-94) and Toyota Motor Co. (since 1995).

**Automatic berths:** Third pick from SEC vs. sixth pick from 8-team Bowl Coalition pool (1992-94 seasons); second pick from ACC, if available, vs. second pick from Big East or Notre Dame, if available (since 1995 season).

**Multiple wins:** Florida (6); Florida St. and North Carolina (5); Auburn, Clemson (4); Georgia Tech, Maryland and Tennessee (3); Georgia, Miami-FL, Oklahoma, Pittsburgh, and Texas Tech (2).

| Year | Year | Year |
|---|---|---|
| 1946* Wake Forest 26, S. Carolina 14 | 1967  17-17, Florida St. vs Penn St. | 1989† Clemson 27, West Va. 7 |
| 1947  Oklahoma 34, N.C. State 13 | 1968  Missouri 35, Alabama 10 | 1991* Michigan 35, Mississippi 3 |
| 1948  20-20, Maryland vs Georgia | 1969  Florida 14, Tennessee 13 | 1991† Oklahoma 48, Virginia 14 |
| 1949  Clemson 24, Missouri 23 | 1971* Auburn 35, Mississippi 28 | 1992  Florida 27, N.C. State 10 |
| 1950  Maryland 20, Missouri 7 | 1971† Georgia 7, N. Carolina 3 | 1993  Alabama 24, N. Carolina 10 |
| 1951  Wyoming 20, Wash. & Lee 7 | 1972  Auburn 24, Colorado 3 | 1994  Tennessee 45, Va. Tech 23 |
| 1952  Miami-FL 14, Clemson 0 | 1973  Texas Tech 28, Tennessee 19 | 1996* Syracuse 41, Clemson 0 |
| 1953  Florida 14, Tulsa 13 | 1974  Auburn 27, Texas 3 | 1997  N. Carolina 20, West Va. 13 |
| 1954  Texas Tech 35, Auburn 13 | 1975  Maryland 13, Florida 0 | 1998  N. Carolina 42, Va. Tech 3 |
| 1954† Auburn 33, Baylor 13 | 1976  Notre Dame 20, Penn St. 9 | 1999  Ga. Tech 35, Notre Dame 28 |
| 1955  Vanderbilt 25, Auburn 13 | 1977  Pittsburgh 34, Clemson 3 | 2000  Miami-FL 28, Ga. Tech 13 |
| 1956  Georgia Tech 21, Pittsburgh 14 | 1978  Clemson 17, Ohio St. 15 | 2001  Va. Tech 41, Clemson 20 |
| 1957  Tennessee 3, Texas A&M 0 | 1979  N. Carolina 17, Michigan 15 | 2002  Florida St. 30, Va. Tech 17 |
| 1958  Mississippi 7, Florida 3 | 1980  Pittsburgh 37, S. Carolina 9 | 2003  N.C. State 28, Notre Dame 6 |
| 1960* Arkansas 14, Georgia Tech 7 | 1981  N. Carolina 31, Arkansas 27 | 2004  Maryland 41, West Va. 7 |
| 1960† Florida 13, Baylor 12 | 1982  Florida St. 31, West Va. 12 | 2005  Florida St. 30, West Va. 18 |
| 1961  Penn St. 30, Georgia Tech 15 | 1983  Florida 14, Iowa 6 | * January game from 1946-54, 1960, |
| 1962  Florida 17, Penn St. 7 | 1984  Oklahoma St. 21, S. Carolina 14 | 1965, 1971, 1989, 1991 and since |
| 1963  N. Carolina 35, Air Force 0 | 1985  Florida St. 34, Oklahoma St. 23 | 1996. |
| 1965* Florida St. 36, Oklahoma 19 | 1986  Clemson 27, Stanford 21 | † December game from 1954-58, 1960- |
| 1965† Georgia Tech 31, Texas Tech 21 | 1987  LSU 30, S. Carolina 13 | 63, 1965-69, 1971-87, 1989 and |
| 1966  Tennessee 18, Syracuse 12 | 1989* Georgia 34, Michigan St. 27 | 1991-94. |

### Holiday Bowl

**City:** San Diego, Calif. **Stadium:** Qualcomm. **Capacity:** 71,000. **Playing surface:** Grass. **First game:** Dec. 22, 1978. **Playing site:** San Diego/Jack Murphy Stadium (since 1978). Name changed to Qualcomm Stadium in 1997. **Corporate title sponsors:** SeaWorld (1986-90), Thrifty Car Rental (1991-94), Chrysler-Plymouth Division of Chrysler Corp. (1995-97), U.S. Filter/Culligan Water Tech. (1998-2001) and Pacific Life Insurance Co. (since 2002).

**Automatic berths:** WAC champion vs. at-large opponent (1978-84, 1986-90 seasons); WAC champ vs. second pick from Big 10 (1991 season); WAC champ vs. third pick from Big 10 (1992-94 seasons); choice of WAC champion, if available, or second pick from Pac-10, if available vs. third pick from Big 12, if available (1995-99); second pick from Pac-10 vs. third pick from Big 12 (since 2000).

**Multiple wins:** BYU (4); Kansas St. (3) Iowa and Ohio St. (2).

| Year | Year | Year |
|---|---|---|
| 1978† Navy 23, BYU 16 | 1988  Oklahoma St. 62, Wyoming 14 | 1998  Arizona 23, Nebraska 20 |
| 1979  Indiana 38, BYU 37 | 1989  Penn St. 50, BYU 39 | 1999  Kansas St. 24, Washington 20 |
| 1980  BYU 46, SMU 45 | 1990  Texas A&M 65, BYU 14 | 2000  Oregon 35, Texas 30 |
| 1981  BYU 38, Washington St. 36 | 1991  13-13, Iowa vs BYU | 2001  Texas 47, Washington 43 |
| 1982  Ohio St. 47, BYU 17 | 1992  Hawaii 27, Illinois 17 | 2002  Kansas St. 34, Arizona St. 27 |
| 1983  BYU 21, Missouri 17 | 1993  Ohio St. 28, BYU 21 | 2003  Washington St. 28, Texas 20 |
| 1984  BYU 24, Michigan 17 | 1994  Michigan 24, Colo. 14 | 2004  Texas Tech 45, California 31 |
| 1985  Arkansas 18, Arizona St. 17 | 1995  Kansas St. 54, Colorado St. 21 | |
| 1986  Iowa 39, San Diego St. 38 | 1996  Colorado 33, Washington 21 | †December game since 1978. |
| 1987  Iowa 20, Wyoming 19 | 1997  Colorado St. 35, Missouri 24 | |

### Outback Bowl

**City:** Tampa, Fla. **Stadium:** Raymond James. **Capacity:** 66,005. **Playing surface:** Grass. **First game:** Dec. 23, 1986. **Name change:** Hall of Fame Bowl (1986-95) and Outback Bowl (since 1995). **Playing sites:** Tampa/Houlihan's Stadium (1986-98) and Raymond James Stadium (since 1999). **Corporate title sponsor:** Outback Steakhouse, Inc. (since 1995).

**Automatic berths:** Fourth pick from ACC vs. fourth pick from Big 10 (1993-94 seasons); third pick from Big 10, if available, vs. third pick from SEC, if available (1995-99); fourth pick from Big 10 vs. third pick from SEC (2000 season).

**Multiple wins:** Georgia and Michigan (3); Penn St., South Carolina and Syracuse (2).

| Year | Year | Year |
|---|---|---|
| 1986† Boston College 27, Georgia 24 | 1994  Michigan 42, N.C. State 7 | 2001  S. Carolina 24, Ohio St. 7 |
| 1988* Michigan 28, Alabama 24 | 1995  Wisconsin 34, Duke 20 | 2002  S. Carolina 31, Ohio St. 28 |
| 1989  Syracuse 23, LSU 10 | 1996  Penn St. 43, Auburn 14 | 2003  Michigan 38, Florida 30 |
| 1990  Auburn 31, Ohio St. 14 | 1997  Alabama 17, Michigan 14 | 2004  Iowa 37, Florida 17 |
| 1991  Clemson 30, Illinois 0 | 1998  Georgia 33, Wisconsin 6 | 2005  Georgia 24, Wisconsin 21 |
| 1992  Syracuse 24, Ohio St. 17 | 1999  Penn St. 26, Kentucky 14 | |
| 1993  Tennessee 38, Boston Col. 23 | 2000  Georgia 28, Purdue 25 | †December game in 1986. |
| | | *January game since 1988. |

## Peach Bowl

**City:** Atlanta, Ga. **Stadium:** Georgia Dome. **Capacity:** 71,228. **Playing surface:** Turf. **First game:** Dec. 30, 1968. **Playing sites:** Grant Field (1968-70), Atlanta-Fulton County Stadium (1971-92) and Georgia Dome (since 1993). **Corporate title sponsor:** Chick-fil-A (since 1998).

**Automatic berths:** Third pick from ACC vs. at-large opponent (1992 season); third pick from ACC vs. fourth pick from SEC (1993-94 seasons); third pick from ACC, if available, vs. fourth pick from SEC, if available (since 1995 season).

**Multiple wins:** N.C. State (4); LSU and West Virginia (3); Auburn, Georgia, Miami-FL, North Carolina and Virginia (2).

| Year | Year | Year |
|---|---|---|
| 1968† LSU 31, Florida St. 27 | 1982 Iowa 28, Tennessee 22 | 1996 LSU 10, Clemson 7 |
| 1969 West Va. 14, S. Carolina 3 | 1983 Florida St. 28, N. Carolina 3 | 1998* Auburn 21, Clemson 17 |
| 1970 Arizona St. 48, N. Carolina 26 | 1984 Virginia 27, Purdue 24 | 1998† Georgia 35, Virginia 33 |
| 1971 Mississippi 41, Georgia Tech 18 | 1985 Army 31, Illinois 29 | 1999 Mississippi St. 17, Clemson 7 |
| 1972 N.C. State 49, West Va. 13 | 1986 Va. Tech 25, N.C. State 24 | 2000 LSU 28, Ga. Tech 14 |
| 1973 Georgia 17, Maryland 16 | 1988* Tennessee 27, Indiana 22 | 2001 N. Carolina 16, Auburn 10 |
| 1974 6-6, Vanderbilt vs Texas Tech | 1988† N.C. State 28, Iowa 23 | 2002 Maryland 30, Tennessee 3 |
| 1975 West Va. 13, N.C. State 10 | 1989 Syracuse 19, Georgia 18 | 2004* Clemson 27, Tennessee 14 |
| 1976 Kentucky 21, N. Carolina 0 | 1990 Auburn 27, Indiana 23 | 2004† Miami-FL 27, Florida 10 |
| 1977 N.C. State 24, Iowa St. 14 | 1992* E. Carolina 37, N.C. State 34 | †December game from 1968-79, |
| 1978 Purdue 41, Georgia Tech 21 | 1993 N. Carolina 21, Miss. St. 17 | 1981-86, 1988-90, 1993, 1995, |
| 1979 Baylor 24, Clemson 18 | 1993† Clemson 14, Kentucky 13 | 1996, 1998, 1999-2002 and 2004. |
| 1981* Miami-FL 20, Va. Tech 10 | 1995* N.C. State 24, Miss. St. 24 | *January game in 1981, 1988, 1992- |
| 1981† West Va. 26, Florida 6 | 1995† Virginia 34, Georgia 27 | 93, 1995 and 1998 and 2004. |

## Alamo Bowl

**City:** San Antonio, Tex. **Stadium:** Alamodome. **Capacity:** 65,000. **Playing surface:** Turf. **First game:** Dec. 31, 1993. **Playing site:** Alamodome (since 1993). **Corporate title sponsor:** Builders Square (1993-98), Sylvania (1999-2001) and Mastercard (2004).

**Automatic berths:** third pick from SWC vs. fourth pick from Pac-10 (1993-94 seasons); fourth pick from Big 10, if available vs. fourth pick from Big 12, if available (1995-99 seasons); fourth pick from Big 12 vs. third pick from Big 10 (2000 season).

**Multiple wins:** Iowa and Purdue (2).

| Year | Year | Year |
|---|---|---|
| 1993† California 37, Iowa 3 | 1998 Purdue 37, Kansas St. 34 | 2003 Nebraska 17, Michigan St. 3 |
| 1994 Washington St. 10, Baylor 3 | 1999 Penn St. 24, Texas A&M 0 | 2004 Ohio St. 33, Oklahoma St. 7 |
| 1995 Texas A&M 22, Michigan 20 | 2000 Nebraska 66, Northwestern 17 | †December game since 1993. |
| 1996 Iowa 27, Texas Tech 0 | 2001 Iowa 19, Texas Tech 16 | |
| 1997 Purdue 33, Oklahoma St. 20 | 2002 Wisconsin 31, Colorado 28 (OT) | |

## Sun Bowl

**City:** El Paso, Tex. **Stadium:** Sun Bowl. **Capacity:** 52,000. **Playing surface:** Turf. **First game:** Jan. 1, 1936. **Name changes:** Sun Bowl (1936-85), John Hancock Sun Bowl (1986-88), John Hancock Bowl (1989-93) and Sun Bowl (since 1994). **Playing sites:** Kidd Field (1936-62) and Sun Bowl (since 1963). **Corporate title sponsors:** John Hancock Financial Services (1986-93), Norwest Bank (1996-98), Wells Fargo (1999-2003) and Vitalis (since 2004).

**Automatic berths:** Eighth pick from 8-team Bowl Coalition pool vs. at-large opponent (1992); Seventh and eighth picks from 8-team Bowl Coalition pool (1993-94 seasons); third pick from Pac-10, if available, vs. fifth pick from Big 10, if available (since 1995 season).

**Multiple wins:** Texas Western/UTEP (5); Alabama and Wyoming (3); Arizona St., Nebraska, New Mexico St., North Carolina, Oklahoma, Oregon, Pittsburgh, Southwestern, Stanford, Texas, West Texas St. and West Virginia (2).

| Year | Year | Year |
|---|---|---|
| 1936* 14-14, Hardin-Simmons vs New Mexico St. | 1958† Wyoming 14, Hardin-Simmons 6 | 1983 Alabama 28, SMU 7 |
| 1937 Hardin-Simmons 34, Texas Mines 6 | 1959 New Mexico 28, St. Texas 8 | 1984 Maryland 28, Tennessee 27 |
| 1938 West Va. 7, Texas Tech 6 | 1960 New Mexico St. 20, Utah St. 13 | 1985 13-13, Georgia vs Arizona |
| 1939 Utah 26, New Mexico 0 | 1961 Villanova 17, Wichita 9 | 1986 Alabama 28, Washington 6 |
| 1940 0-0, Catholic U. vs Arizona St. | 1962 West Texas 15, Ohio U. 14 | 1987 Oklahoma St. 35, West Va. 33 |
| 1941 W. Reserve 26, Arizona St. 13 | 1963 Oregon 21, SMU 14 | 1988 Alabama 29, Army 28 |
| 1942 Tulsa 6, Texas Tech 0 | 1964 Georgia 7, Texas Tech 0 | 1989 Pittsburgh 31, Texas A&M 28 |
| 1943 Second Air Force 13, Hardin-Simmons 7 | 1965 Texas Western 13, TCU 12 | 1990 Michigan St. 17, USC 16 |
| 1944 Southwestern 7, New Mexico 0 | 1966 Wyoming 28, Florida St. 20 | 1991 UCLA 6, Illinois 3 |
| 1945 Southwestern 35, U. of Mexico 0 | 1967 UTEP 14, Mississippi 7 | 1992 Baylor 20, Arizona 15 |
| 1946 New Mexico 34, Denver 24 | 1968 Auburn 34, Arizona 10 | 1993 Oklahoma 41, Texas Tech 10 |
| 1947 Cincinnati 18, Va. Tech 6 | 1969 Nebraska 45, Georgia 6 | 1994 Texas 35, N. Carolina 31 |
| 1948 Miami-OH 13, Texas Tech 12 | 1970 Georgia Tech 17, Texas Tech 9 | 1995 Iowa 38, Washington 18 |
| 1949 West Va. 21, Texas Mines 12 | 1971 LSU 33, Iowa St. 15 | 1996 Stanford 38, Michigan St. 0 |
| 1950 Tex. Western 33, Georgetown 20 | 1972 N. Carolina 32, Texas Tech 28 | 1997 Arizona St. 17, Iowa 7 |
| 1951 West Texas 14, Cincinnati 13 | 1973 Missouri 34, Auburn 17 | 1998 TCU 28, USC 19 |
| 1952 Texas Tech 25, Pacific 14 | 1974 Miss. 26, N. Carolina 24 | 1999 Oregon 24, Minnesota 20 |
| 1953 Pacific 26, Southern Miss. 7 | 1975 Pittsburgh 33, Kansas 19 | 2000 Wisconsin 21, UCLA 20 |
| 1954 Tex. Western 37, So. Miss. 14 | 1977* Texas A&M 37, Florida 14 | 2001 Washington St. 33, Purdue 27 |
| 1955 Tex. Western 47, Florida St. 20 | 1977† Stanford 24, LSU 14 | 2002 Purdue 34, Washington 24 |
| 1956 Wyoming 21, Texas Tech 14 | 1978 Texas 42, Maryland 0 | 2003 Minnesota 31, Oregon 30 |
| 1957 Geo. Wash. 13, Tex. Western 0 | 1979 Washington 14, Texas 7 | 2004 Arizona St. 27, Purdue 23 |
| 1958* Louisville 34, Drake 20 | 1980 Nebraska 31, Miss. St. 17 | *January game from 1936-58 and in 1977. |
| | 1981 Oklahoma 40, Houston 14 | †December game from 1958-75 and since 1977. |
| | 1982 N. Carolina 26, Texas 10 | |

## Bowl Games (Cont.)
### Insight Bowl

**City:** Phoenix, Ariz. **Stadium:** Bank One Ballpark. **Capacity:** 42,915. **Playing surface:** Grass. **First game:** Dec. 31, 1989. **Name change:** Copper Bowl (1989-1996), Insight.com Bowl (1997-2001) and Insight Bowl (since 2002). **Playing sites:** Arizona Stadium (1989-2000) and Bank One,Ballpark (since 2000). **Corporate title sponsors:** Domino's Pizza (1990-91), Weiser Lock (1992-1996) and Insight Enterprises (since 1997).

**Automatic berths:** Third pick from WAC vs. at-large opponent (1992 season); third pick from WAC vs. fourth pick from Big Eight (1993-94 seasons); second pick from WAC vs. sixth pick from Big 12 (1995-97); third pick from Big East or Notre Dame, if available vs. fifth pick from Big 12, if available (1998-2001); third pick from Big East or Notre Dame, if available vs. fourth pick from Big East (since 2002).

**Multiple wins:** Arizona and California (2).

| Year | | Year | | Year | |
|---|---|---|---|---|---|
| 1989† | Arizona 17, N.C. State 10 | 1995 | Texas Tech 55, Air Force 41 | 2001 | Syracuse 26, Kansas St. 3 |
| 1990 | California 17, Wyoming 15 | 1996 | Wisconsin 38, Utah 10 | 2002 | Pittsburgh 38, Oregon St. 13 |
| 1991 | Indiana 24, Baylor 0 | 1997 | Arizona 20, New Mexico 14 | 2003 | California 52, Virginia Tech 49 |
| 1992 | Washington St. 31, Utah 28 | 1998 | Missouri 34, W. Virginia 31 | 2004 | Oregon St. 38, Notre Dame 21 |
| 1993 | Kansas St. 52, Wyoming 17 | 1999 | Colorado 62, Boston College 28 | †December game since 1989. | |
| 1994 | BYU 31, Oklahoma 6 | 2000 | Iowa St. 37, Pittsburgh 29 | | |

### Liberty Bowl

**City:** Memphis, Tenn. **Stadium:** Liberty Bowl Memorial. **Capacity:** 62,380. **Playing surface:** Grass. **First game:** Dec. 19, 1959. **Playing sites:** Municipal Stadium in Philadelphia (1959-63), Convention Hall in Atlantic City, N.J. (1964), Memphis Memorial Stadium (1965-75) and Liberty Bowl Memorial Stadium (since 1976). Memphis Memorial Stadium renamed Liberty Bowl Memorial in 1976. **Corporate title sponsors:** St. Jude's Hospital (since 1993), AXA/Equitable (since 1997).

**Automatic berths:** Commander-in-Chief's Trophy winner (Army, Navy or Air Force) vs. at-large opponent (1989-92 seasons); none (1993 season); first pick from independent group of Cincinnati, East Carolina, Memphis, Southern Miss. and Tulane vs. at-large opponent (for 1994 and '95 seasons); Conference USA champion vs. fourth pick from the Big East (1996-97 seasons); Conference USA champion, if available, vs. fifth, sixth or seventh pick or at-large from SEC (1998-99 seasons); Mountain West champion vs. Conference USA champion, if available (since 2000).

**Multiple wins:** Mississippi (4); Penn St. and Tennessee (3); Air Force, Alabama, Louisville, N.C. State, Southern Miss., Syracuse and Tulane (2).

| Year | | Year | | Year | |
|---|---|---|---|---|---|
| 1959† | Penn St. 7, Alabama 0 | 1975 | USC 20, Texas A&M 0 | 1991 | Air Force 38, Mississippi St. 15 |
| 1960 | Penn St. 41, Oregon 12 | 1976 | Alabama 36, UCLA 6 | 1992 | Mississippi 13, Air Force 0 |
| 1961 | Syracuse 15, Miami-FL 14 | 1977 | Nebraska 21, N. Carolina 17 | 1993 | Louisville 18, Michigan St. 7 |
| 1962 | Oregon St. 6, Villanova 0 | 1978 | Missouri 20, LSU 15 | 1994 | Illinois 30, E. Carolina 0 |
| 1963 | Mississippi St. 16, N.C. State 12 | 1979 | Penn St. 9, Tulane 6 | 1995 | E. Carolina 19, Stanford 13 |
| 1964 | Utah 32, West Virginia 6 | 1980 | Purdue 28, Missouri 25 | 1996 | Syracuse 30, Houston 17 |
| 1965 | Mississippi 13, Auburn 7 | 1981 | Ohio St. 31, Navy 28 | 1997 | Southern Miss. 41, Pittsburgh 7 |
| 1966 | Miami-FL 14, Virginia Tech 7 | 1982 | Alabama 21, Illinois 15 | 1998 | Tulane 41, BYU 27 |
| 1967 | N.C. State 14, Georgia 7 | 1983 | Notre Dame 19, Boston Col. 18 | 1999 | Southern Miss. 23, Colorado St. 17 |
| 1968 | Mississippi 34, Virginia Tech 17 | 1984 | Auburn 21, Arkansas 15 | 2000 | Colorado St. 22, Louisville 17 |
| 1969 | Colorado 47, Alabama 33 | 1985 | Baylor 21, LSU 7 | 2001 | Louisville 28, BYU 10 |
| 1970 | Tulane 17, Colorado 3 | 1986 | Tennessee 21, Minnesota 14 | 2002 | TCU 17, Colorado St. 3 |
| 1971 | Tennessee 14, Arkansas 13 | 1987 | Georgia 20, Arkansas 17 | 2003 | Utah 17, Southern Miss. 0 |
| 1972 | Georgia Tech 31, Iowa St. 30 | 1988 | Indiana 34, S. Carolina 10 | 2004 | Louisville 44, Boise St. 40 |
| 1973 | N.C. State 31, Kansas 18 | 1989 | Mississippi 42, Air Force 29 | | |
| 1974 | Tennessee 7, Maryland 3 | 1990 | Air Force 23, Ohio St. 11 | † December game since 1959. | |

### Champs Sports Bowl

**City:** Orlando, Fla. **Stadium:** Florida Citrus. **Capacity:** 65,525. **Playing surface:** Grass. **First game:** Dec. 28, 1990. **Name change:** Blockbuster Bowl (1990-93), Carquest Bowl (1994-97), Micron PC Bowl (1998), MicronPC.com Bowl (1999-2000) and Tangerine Bowl (2001-03). The game was called the Sunshine Football Classic for a short time in the offseason after Carquest Auto Parts dropped its sponsorship and before Micron signed on. Also, this game should not be confused with the Tangerine Bowl that became the Citrus Bowl in 1982. **Playing sites:** Joe Robbie Stadium (1990-2000). Name changed to Pro Player Stadium in 1996. **Corporate title sponsors:** Blockbuster Video (1990-93), Carquest Auto Parts (1993-97), Micron Electronics (1998-2000) and Mazda (since 2002).

**Automatic berths:** Penn St. vs. seventh pick from 8-team Bowl Coalition pool (1992 season); third pick from Big East vs. fifth pick from SEC (1993-94 seasons); third pick from Big East vs. fifth pick from SEC (1995 season); third pick from Big East vs. fourth pick from ACC (1996-97 seasons); sixth pick from Big Ten, if available, vs. fourth pick from ACC, if available (1998-2000 seasons); fifth pick from ACC vs. fifth pick from Big East (2001).

**Multiple wins:** Georgia Tech, Miami-FL and N.C. State (2).

| Year | | Year | | Year | |
|---|---|---|---|---|---|
| 1990† | Florida St. 24, Penn St. 17 | 1997 | Ga. Tech 35, W. Virginia 30 | 2003 | N.C. State 56, Kansas 26 |
| 1991 | Alabama 30, Colorado 25 | 1998 | Miami-FL 46, N.C. State 23 | 2004 | Ga. Tech 51, Syracuse 14 |
| 1993* | Stanford 24, Penn St. 3 | 1999 | Illinois 63, Virginia 21 | †December game from 1990-91 and since 1995. | |
| 1994 | Boston College 31, Virginia 13 | 2000 | N.C. State 38, Minnesota 30 | *January game 1993-95. | |
| 1995 | S. Carolina 24, West Va. 21 | 2001 | Pittsburgh 34, N.C. State 19 | | |
| 1995† | N. Carolina 20, Arkansas 10 | 2002 | Texas Tech 55, Clemson 15 | | |
| 1996 | Miami-FL 31, Virginia 21 | | | | |

## MPC Computers Bowl

**City:** Boise, Idaho. **Stadium:** Bronco. **Capacity:** 30,000. **Playing surface:** Turf. **First game:** Dec. 29, 1997. **Playing sites:** Bronco Stadium (since 1997). **Corporate title sponsors:** World Sports Humanitarian Hall of Fame (since 1997) and Crucial.com (1999-2002), MPC Computers (since 2004).
   **Automatic berths:** Big West champion, if available, vs. at-large (1997-2002) WAC vs. ACC (since 2004).
   **Multiple wins:** Boise St. (3).

| Year | | Year | | Year | |
|---|---|---|---|---|---|
| 1997† | Cincinnati 35, Utah St. 19 | 2000 | Boise St. 38, UTEP 23 | 2004* | Georgia Tech 52, Tulsa 10 |
| 1998 | Idaho 42, Southern Miss. 35 | 2001 | Clemson 49, La. Tech 24 | 2004† | Fresno St. 37, Virginia 34 OT |
| 1999 | Boise St. 34, Louisville 31 | 2002 | Boise St. 34, Iowa St. 16 | | †December game 1997-2002 and '04. |
| | | | | | *January game in 2004 |

## Las Vegas Bowl

**City:** Las Vegas, Nev. **Stadium:** Sam Boyd. **Capacity:** 40,000. **Playing surface:** Turf. **First game:** Dec. 18, 1992. **Playing site:** Sam Boyd Stadium (since 1992). **Corporate title sponsors:** EA Sports (1999-2000) Sega Sports (2001-02).
   **Automatic berths:** Mid-American champion vs. Big West champion (1992-96 season); none (1997 season); second or third pick from WAC, if available vs. at-large (1998-2000), second pick from Mountain West vs. fifth pick from Pac-10 (since 2001).
   **Multiple wins:** Fresno St. (4); UNLV (3); Bowling Green, San Jose St., Toledo and Utah (2).

| Year | | Year | | Year | |
|---|---|---|---|---|---|
| 1981† | Toledo 27, San Jose St. 25 | 1991 | Bowling Green 28, Fresno St. 21 | 2001 | Utah 10, USC 6 |
| 1982 | Fresno St. 29, Bowling Green 28 | 1992 | Bowling Green 35, Nevada 34 | 2002 | UCLA 27, New Mexico 13 |
| 1983 | Northern Ill. 20, CS-Fullerton 13 | 1993 | Utah St. 42, Ball St. 33 | 2003 | Oregon St. 55, New Mexico 14 |
| 1984* | UNLV 30, Toledo 13 | 1994 | UNLV 52, C. Michigan 24 | 2004 | Wyoming 24, UCLA 21 |
| 1985 | Fresno St. 51, Bowling Green 7 | 1995 | Toledo 40, Nevada 37 (OT) | | †December game since 1981. |
| 1986 | San Jose St. 37, Miami-OH 7 | 1996 | Nevada 18, Ball St. 15 | | *Toledo later ruled winner of 1984 |
| 1987 | E. Michigan 30, San Jose St. 27 | 1997 | Oregon 41, Air Force 13 | | game by forfeit because UNLV used |
| 1988 | Fresno St. 35, W. Michigan 30 | 1998 | N. Carolina 20, San Diego St. 13 | | ineligible players. |
| 1989 | Fresno St. 27, Ball St. 6 | 1999 | Utah 17, Fresno St. 16 | | |
| 1990 | San Jose St. 48, C. Michigan 24 | 2000 | UNLV 31, Arkansas 14 | | |

**Note:** The MAC and Big West champs met in a bowl game from 1981 to 1996, originally in Fresno at the California Bowl (1981-88, 1992) and California Raisin Bowl (1989-91). The results from 1981-91 are included above.

## Independence Bowl

**City:** Shreveport, La. **Stadium:** Independence. **Capacity:** 50,832. **Playing surface:** Grass. **First game:** Dec. 13, 1976. **Playing site:** Independence Stadium (since 1976). **Corporate title sponsors:** Poulan/Weed Eater (1990-97), Sanford (1998-2000) and MainStay (since 2001). **Automatic berths:** Southland Conference champion vs. at-large opponent (1976-81 seasons); none (1982-95 seasons); fifth pick from SEC, if available, vs. at-large (1995-97 season); fifth, sixth or seventh pick from SEC, if available, vs. at-large (1998-99 season); sixth pick from Big 12 vs. SEC (since 2000 season).
   **Multiple wins:** Mississippi (3); Air Force, LSU and Southern Miss (2).

| Year | | Year | | Year | |
|---|---|---|---|---|---|
| 1976† | McNeese St. 20, Tulsa 16 | 1986 | Mississippi 20, Texas Tech 17 | 1996 | Auburn 32, Army 29 |
| 1977 | La. Tech 24, Louisville 14 | 1987 | Washington 24, Tulane 12 | 1997 | LSU 27, Notre Dame 9 |
| 1978 | E. Carolina 35, La. Tech 13 | 1988 | Southern Miss 38, UTEP 18 | 1998 | Mississippi 35, Texas Tech 18 |
| 1979 | Syracuse 31, McNeese St. 7 | 1989 | Oregon 27, Tulsa 24 | 1999 | Mississippi 27, Oklahoma 25 |
| 1980 | Southern Miss 16, McNeese St. 14 | 1990 | 34-34, La. Tech vs Maryland | 2000 | Mississippi 43, Texas A&M 41 |
| 1981 | Texas A&M 33, Oklahoma St. 16 | 1991 | Georgia 24, Arkansas 15 | 2001 | Alabama 14, Iowa St. 13 |
| 1982 | Wisconsin 14, Kansas St. 3 | 1992 | Wake Forest 39, Oregon 35 | 2002 | Mississippi 27, Nebraska 23 |
| 1983 | Air Force 9, Mississippi 3 | 1993 | Va. Tech 45, Indiana 20 | 2003 | Arkansas 27, Missouri 14 |
| 1984 | Air Force 23, Va. Tech 7 | 1994 | Virginia 20, TCU 10 | 2004 | Iowa St. 17, Miami-OH 13 |
| 1985 | Minnesota 20, Clemson 13 | 1995 | LSU 45, Michigan St. 26 | | †December game since 1976. |

## Motor City Bowl

**City:** Detroit, Mich. **Stadium:** Ford Field. **Capacity:** 65,000. **Playing surface:** Turf. **First game:** Dec. 26, 1997. **Playing site:** Pontiac Silverdome (1997-2001) and Ford Field (since 2002). **Corporate title sponsor:** Ford Division of Ford Motor Company (since 1997), Daimler Chrysler and General Motors (since 2002). **Automatic berths:** Mid-American champions vs at-large (1997-99 season); Mid-American champions vs. fourth pick from Conference USA (2000 season).
   **Multiple wins:** Marshall (3).

| Year | | Year | | Year | |
|---|---|---|---|---|---|
| 1997† | Mississippi 34, Marshall 31 | 2000 | Marshall 25, Cincinnati 14 | 2003 | Bowling Green 28, N'western 24 |
| 1998 | Marshall 48, Louisville 29 | 2001 | Toledo 23, Cincinnati 16 | 2004 | Connecticut 39, Toledo 10 |
| 1999 | Marshall 21, BYU 3 | 2002 | Boston College 51, Toledo 25 | | †December game since 1997. |

## Music City Bowl

**City:** Nashville, Tenn. **Stadium:** The Coliseum. **Capacity:** 67,000. **Playing surface:** Grass. **First game:** Dec. 29, 1998. **Playing sites:** Vanderbilt Stadium (1998) and Adelphia Coliseum (since 1999). **Corporate title sponsors:** American General (1998), HomePoint.com (1999-2000) and Gaylord Hotels (since 2002). **Automatic berths:** sixth choice from the SEC, if available, vs. at-large (1998-99 season); fourth pick from Big East, if available vs SEC (2000-01).
   **Multiple wins:** Minnesota (2).

| Year | | Year | | Year | |
|---|---|---|---|---|---|
| 1998† | Va. Tech 38, Alabama 7 | 2001 | Boston College 20, Georgia 16 | 2003 | Auburn 28, Wisconsin 14 |
| 1999 | Syracuse 20, Kentucky 13 | 2002 | Minnesota 29, Arkansas 14 | 2004 | Minnesota 20, Alabama 16 |
| 2000 | West Va. 49, Mississippi 38 | | | | †December game since 1998. |

## Bowl Games (Cont.)

### GMAC Bowl

**City:** Mobile, Ala. **Stadium:** Ladd-Peebles. **Capacity:** 40,646. **Playing surface:** Grass. **First game:** Dec. 22, 1999.
**Name change:** Mobile Bowl (1999-2000), GMAC Bowl (since 2001). **Playing sites:** Ladd-Peebles Stadium (since 1999).
**Corporate title sponsors:** GMAC Financial Services (since 2001). **Automatic berths:** WAC champions (if team is from the east) or second pick from WAC vs. second pick from Conference USA, if available (2000 season).
**Multiple wins:** Marshall (2).

| Year | | Year | | Year | |
|---|---|---|---|---|---|
| 1999† | TCU 28, E. Carolina 14 | 2002 | Marshall 38, Louisville 15 | 2004 | Bowling Green 52, Memphis 35 |
| 2000 | So. Miss 28, TCU 21 | 2003 | Miami-OH 49, Louisville 28 | | †December game since 1999. |
| 2001 | Marshall 64, East Carolina 61 | | | | |

### Houston Bowl

**City:** Houston, Tex. **Stadium:** Reliant. **Capacity:** 69,500. **Playing surface:** Turf. **First game:** Dec. 27, 2000. **Name change:** GalleryFurniture.com Bowl (2000-01), Houston Bowl (2002) and EV1.net Houston Bowl (since 2003). **Playing sites:** Astrodome (2000-2002), Reliant Stadium (since 2003). **Corporate title sponsors:** GalleryFurniture.com (2000-2002) and EV1 (since 2003). **Automatic berths:** Big 12 vs. Conference USA.

| Year | | Year | | Year | |
|---|---|---|---|---|---|
| 2000† | E. Carolina 40, Tex. Tech 27 | 2002 | Oklahoma St. 33, So. Miss. 23 | 2004 | Colorado 33, UTEP 28 |
| 2001 | Texas A&M 28, TCU 9 | 2003 | Texas Tech 38, Navy 14 | | †December game since 2000. |

### New Orleans Bowl

**City:** Lafayette, La. **Stadium:** Cajun Field. **Capacity:** 31,000. **Playing surface:** Grass. **First game:** Dec. 18, 2001.
**Playing sites:** Louisiana Superdome (2001-04), Cajun Field (2005). **Corporate title sponsors:** Wyndam Hotels (since 2004). **Automatic berths:** Sun Belt champion vs. Conference USA (since 2002).

| Year | | Year | | | |
|---|---|---|---|---|---|
| 2001† | Colorado St. 45, North Texas 20 | 2003 | Memphis 27, North Texas 17 | | |
| 2002 | North Texas 24, Cincinnati 19 | 2004 | So. Miss. 31, North Texas 10 | | †December game since 2001. |

### Emerald Bowl

**City:** San Francisco, Calif. **Stadium:** SBC Park. **Capacity:** 37,000. **Playing surface:** Grass. **First game:** Dec. 31, 2002. **Name change:** Diamond Walnut San Francisco Bowl (2002-03), Emerald Bowl (since 2004). **Playing sites:** SBC (formerly known as Pacific Bell) Park (since 2002). **Corporate title sponsors:** Diamond Walnut (2002-03), Emerald Nuts (since 2004). **Automatic berths:** Mountain West vs. Big East or Notre Dame (2002-03).

| Year | | Year | | | |
|---|---|---|---|---|---|
| 2002† | Virginia Tech 20, Air Force 13 | 2004 | Navy 34, New Mexico 19 | | |
| 2003 | Boston Col. 35, Colorado St. 21 | | | | †December game since 2002. |

### Meineke Car Care Bowl

**City:** Charlotte, N.C. **Stadium:** Bank of America. **Capacity:** 73,367. **Playing surface:** Grass. **First game:** Dec. 28, 2002. **Name change:** Continental Tire Bowl (2002-04), Meineke Car Care Bowl (starting in Dec. 2005). **Playing sites:** Bank of America (formerly known as Ericsson) Stadium (since 2002). **Corporate title sponsors:** Continental Tire North America (2002-04), Meineke Car Care (since 2005). **Automatic berths:** ACC vs. Big East or Notre Dame (since 2002).

| Year | | Year | | | |
|---|---|---|---|---|---|
| 2002† | Virginia 48, West Va. 22 | 2004 | Boston Col. 37, N. Carolina 24 | | |
| 2003 | Virginia 23, Pittsburgh 16 | | | | †December game since 2002. |

### Hawaii Bowl

**City:** Honolulu, Hi. **Stadium:** Aloha Bowl. **Capacity:** 50,000. **Playing surface:** Turf. **First game:** Dec. 25, 2002.
**Playing sites:** Aloha Bowl (since 2002). **Corporate title sponsors:** ConAgra Foods (2002) and Sheraton Hotels & Resorts (since 2003). **Automatic berths:** Hawaii (if bowl eligible) otherwise another WAC school vs. Conference USA (since 2002).
**Multiple wins:** Hawaii (2).

| Year | | Year | | | |
|---|---|---|---|---|---|
| 2002† | Tulane 36, Hawaii 28 | 2004 | Hawaii 59, UAB 40 | | |
| 2003 | Hawaii 54, Houston 48 3OT | | | | †December game since 2002. |

### Forth Worth Bowl

**City:** Fort Worth, Tex. **Stadium:** Amon Carter. **Capacity:** 46,000. **Playing surface:** Grass **First game:** Dec. 23, 2003. **Playing sites:** Amon Carter Stadium (since 2003). **Corporate title sponsors:** PlainsCapital Corp. (since 2003). **Automatic berths:** Big 12 vs. Conference USA (since 2003).

| Year | | | |
|---|---|---|---|
| 2003† | Bosie St. 34, TCU 31 | | |
| 2004 | Cincinnati 32, Marshall 14 | | †December game since 2003. |

---

### NCAA certifies 28 Bowl Games for 2005-06

Among those certified was the newly established *Poinsetta Bowl* to be played Dec . 22 in San Diego, Calif. between an at-large team and a team from the Mountain West Conference.

## Division I-A Teams

Schools classified as Division I-A for at least 10 years; through 2004 season (including bowl games).

### Top 25 Winning Percentage

| | | Yrs | Gm | W | L | T | Pct | Bowls App | Record | Bowl | 2004 Season Record |
|---|---|---|---|---|---|---|---|---|---|---|---|
| 1 | Michigan | 125 | 1153 | 842 | 275 | 36 | .746 | 36 | 18-18-0 | lost Rose | 9-3 |
| 2 | Notre Dame | 116 | 1107 | 802 | 263 | 42 | .743 | 26 | 13-13-0 | lost Insight | 6-6 |
| 3 | Oklahoma | 110 | 1087 | 749 | 285 | 53 | .713 | 38 | 23-14-1 | lost Orange | 12-1 |
| 4 | Texas | 112 | 1130 | 787 | 310 | 33 | .711 | 44 | 21-21-2 | won Rose | 11-1 |
| 5 | Alabama* | 110 | 1106 | 764 | 299 | 43 | .710 | 52 | 29-20-3 | lost Music City | 6-6 |
| 6 | Ohio St. | 115 | 1115 | 764 | 298 | 53 | .709 | 36 | 17-19-0 | won Alamo | 8-4 |
| 7 | Nebraska | 115 | 1143 | 786 | 317 | 40 | .705 | 42 | 21-21-0 | none | 5-5 |
| 8 | Tennessee* | 108 | 1103 | 746 | 305 | 52 | .700 | 45 | 24-21-0 | won Cotton | 10-3 |
| 9 | USC | 112 | 1071 | 720 | 297 | 54 | .697 | 43 | 28-15-0 | won Orange | 13-0 |
| 10 | Penn St. | 118 | 1139 | 760 | 338 | 41 | .685 | 37 | 23-12-2 | none | 4-7 |
| 11 | Florida St.* | 58 | 345 | 428 | 200 | 17 | .677 | 33 | 19-12-2 | won Gator | 9-3 |
| 12 | Georgia | 111 | 1109 | 683 | 372 | 54 | .640 | 40 | 22-15-3 | won Outback | 10-2 |
| 13 | Miami-OH* | 116 | 1024 | 632 | 348 | 44 | .639 | 9 | 6-3-0 | lost Independence | 8-5 |
| 14 | Miami-FL | 78 | 823 | 516 | 288 | 19 | .639 | 29 | 17-12-0 | won Peach | 9-3 |
| 15 | LSU* | 111 | 1077 | 658 | 372 | 47 | .633 | 36 | 17-18-1 | lost Capital One | 9-3 |
| 16 | Washington* | 115 | 1052 | 639 | 363 | 50 | .631 | 29 | 14-14-1 | none | 1-10 |
| 17 | Auburn* | 112 | 1073 | 647 | 379 | 47 | .625 | 31 | 17-12-2 | won Sugar | 13-0 |
| 18 | Arizona St. | 92 | 853 | 516 | 313 | 24 | .619 | 21 | 11-9-1 | won Sun | 9-3 |
| 19 | Florida | 98 | 1001 | 597 | 364 | 40 | .616 | 32 | 14-18-0 | lost Peach | 7-5 |
| 20 | Colorado* | 115 | 1075 | 643 | 396 | 36 | .615 | 26 | 12-14-0 | won Houston | 8-5 |
| 21 | Central Michigan | 104 | 895 | 526 | 333 | 36 | .608 | 2 | 0-2-0 | none | 4-7 |
| 22 | Texas A&M | 110 | 1091 | 634 | 409 | 48 | .603 | 28 | 13-15-0 | lost Cotton | 7-5 |
| 23 | Syracuse | 115 | 1147 | 664 | 434 | 49 | .600 | 22 | 12-9-1 | lost Champs Sports | 6-6 |
| 24 | Bowling Green | 86 | 809 | 459 | 298 | 52 | .600 | 7 | 4-3-0 | won GMAC | 9-3 |
| 25 | UCLA | 86 | 884 | 511 | 336 | 37 | .599 | 26 | 12-13-1 | lost Las Vegas | 6-6 |

*Includes games forfeited following rulings by the NCAA Executive Council and/or the Committee on Infractions.

### Top 50 Victories

| | | Wins | | | Wins | | | Wins |
|---|---|---|---|---|---|---|---|---|
| 1 | Michigan | 842 | 19 | West Virginia | 631 | 37 | Rutgers | 562 |
| 2 | Notre Dame | 802 | 20 | Georgia Tech | 630 | | Missouri | 562 |
| 3 | Texas | 787 | 21 | Pittsburgh | 628 | 39 | Utah | 559 |
| 4 | Nebraska | 786 | 22 | Army | 624 | 40 | Illinois | 545 |
| 5 | Alabama | 764 | | Arkansas | 624 | | Purdue | 545 |
| | Ohio St | 764 | 24 | North Carolina | 619 | 42 | Kentucky | 539 |
| 7 | Penn St | 760 | 25 | Minnesota | 616 | | Iowa | 539 |
| 8 | Oklahoma | 749 | 26 | Virginia Tech | 615 | 44 | Stanford | 537 |
| 9 | Tennessee | 746 | 27 | Clemson | 600 | 45 | Vanderbilt | 533 |
| 10 | USC | 720 | 28 | Navy | 599 | 46 | Kansas | 530 |
| 11 | Georgia | 683 | 29 | Florida | 597 | 47 | Central Michigan | 526 |
| 12 | Syracuse | 664 | 30 | Mississippi | 587 | 48 | Arizona | 522 |
| 13 | LSU | 658 | 31 | Virginia | 586 | | Oregon | 522 |
| 14 | Auburn | 647 | 32 | Michigan St | 585 | 50 | Louisiana Tech | 516 |
| 15 | Colorado | 643 | 33 | California | 584 | | Miami-FL | 516 |
| 16 | Washington | 639 | 34 | Maryland | 571 | | Arizona St. | 516 |
| 17 | Texas A&M | 634 | 35 | Boston College | 570 | | | |
| 18 | Miami-OH | 632 | 36 | Wisconsin | 565 | | | |

### Top 30 Bowl Appearances

| | | App | Record | | | App | Record | | | App | Record |
|---|---|---|---|---|---|---|---|---|---|---|---|
| 1 | Alabama | 52 | 29-20-3 | 12 | Arkansas | 34 | 11-20-3 | 23 | Notre Dame | 26 | 13-13-0 |
| 2 | Tennessee | 45 | 24-21-0 | 13 | Georgia Tech | 33 | 22-11-0 | | Colorado | 26 | 12-14-0 |
| 3 | Texas | 44 | 21-21-2 | | Florida St | 33 | 19-12-2 | | UCLA | 26 | 12-13-1 |
| 4 | USC | 43 | 28-15-0 | 15 | Florida | 32 | 14-18-0 | 26 | North Carolina | 25 | 12-13-0 |
| 5 | Nebraska | 42 | 21-21-0 | 16 | Mississippi | 31 | 19-12-0 | 27 | Pittsburgh | 24 | 10-14-0 |
| 6 | Georgia | 40 | 22-15-3 | | Auburn | 31 | 17-12-2 | | West Virginia | 24 | 9-15-0 |
| 7 | Oklahoma | 38 | 23-14-1 | 18 | Washington | 29 | 14-14-1 | 29 | BYU | 23 | 7-15-1 |
| 8 | Penn St | 37 | 23-12-2 | | Miami-FL | 29 | 17-12-0 | 30 | Missouri | 22 | 9-13-0 |
| 9 | LSU | 36 | 17-18-1 | 20 | Texas A&M | 28 | 13-15-0 | | N.C. State | 22 | 11-10-1 |
| | Ohio St | 36 | 17-19-0 | | Texas Tech | 28 | 8-19-1 | | Syracuse | 22 | 12-9-1 |
| | Michigan | 36 | 18-18-0 | 22 | Clemson | 27 | 14-13-0 | | | | |

## Major Conference Champions
### Atlantic Coast Conference

**Founded** in 1953 when charter members all left Southern Conference to form ACC. **Charter members** (7): Clemson, Duke, Maryland, North Carolina, N.C. State, South Carolina and Wake Forest. **Admitted later** (6): Virginia in 1953 (began play in '54), Georgia Tech in 1979 (began play in '83), Florida St. in 1990 (began play in '92), Boston College, Virginia Tech and Miami-FL in 2003 (Virginia Tech and Miami began play in '04, Boston College in '05). **Withdrew later** (1): South Carolina in 1971 (became an independent after '70 season).
**2005 playing membership** (12): Boston College, Clemson, Duke, Florida St., Georgia Tech, Maryland, Miami-FL, North Carolina, N.C. State, Virginia, Virginia Tech and Wake Forest.
   **Multiple titles:** Clemson (13); Florida St. (11); Maryland (9); Duke and N.C. State (7); North Carolina (5); Georgia Tech & Virginia (2).

| Year | | Year | | Year | | Year | |
|---|---|---|---|---|---|---|---|
| 1953 | Duke (4-0) & Maryland (3-0) | 1965 | Clemson (5-2) & N.C. State (5-2) | 1980 | North Carolina (6-0) | 1994 | Florida St. (8-0) |
| 1954 | Duke (4-0) | 1966 | Clemson (6-1) | 1981 | Clemson (6-0) | 1995 | Virginia (7-1) & Florida St. (7-1) |
| 1955 | Maryland (4-0) & Duke (4-0) | 1967 | Clemson (6-0) | 1982 | Clemson (6-0) | 1996 | Florida St. (8-0) |
| 1956 | Clemson (4-0-1) | 1968 | N.C. State (6-1) | 1983 | Clemson (7-0) † & Maryland (5-0) | 1997 | Florida St. (8-0) & Georgia Tech (7-1) |
| 1957 | N.C. State (5-0-1) | 1969 | South Carolina (6-0) | 1984 | Maryland (5-0) | 1998 | Florida St. (7-1) |
| 1958 | Clemson (5-1) | 1970 | Wake Forest (5-1) | 1985 | Maryland (6-0) | 1999 | Florida St. (8-0) |
| 1959 | Clemson (6-1) | 1971 | North Carolina (6-0) | 1986 | Clemson (5-1-1) | 2000 | Florida St. (8-0) |
| 1960 | Duke (5-1) | 1972 | North Carolina (6-0) | 1987 | Clemson (6-1) | 2001 | Maryland (7-1) |
| 1961 | Duke (5-1) | 1973 | N.C. State (6-0) | 1988 | Clemson (6-1) | 2002 | Florida St. (7-1) |
| 1962 | Duke (6-0) | 1974 | Maryland (6-0) | 1989 | Virginia (6-1) & Duke (6-1) | 2003 | Florida St. (7-1) |
| 1963 | North Carolina (6-1) & N.C. State (6-1) | 1975 | Maryland (5-0) | 1990 | Georgia Tech (6-0-1) | 2004 | Virginia Tech (7-1) |
| 1964 | N.C. State (5-2) | 1976 | Maryland (5-0) | 1991 | Clemson (6-0-1) | | †On probation, ineligible for championship. |
| | | 1977 | North Carolina (5-0-1) | 1992 | Florida St. (8-0) | | |
| | | 1978 | Clemson (6-0) | 1993 | Florida St. (8-0) | | |
| | | 1979 | N.C. State (5-1) | | | | |

### Big East Conference

**Founded** in 1991 when charter members gave up independent football status to form Big East. **Charter members** (8): Boston College, Miami-FL, Pittsburgh, Rutgers, Syracuse, Temple, Virginia Tech and West Virginia. **Admitted later** (4): Connecticut (a charter member in all other sports) in 2004; Cincinnati, Louisville and South Florida in 2003 (to begin play in '05). **Withdrew later** (4): Boston College, Miami-FL and Virginia Tech in 2003 (Miami and Va. Tech joined ACC for 2004 season, Boston College joined ACC in 2005). Temple became an independent following 2004 season
**2005 playing membership** (8): Cincinnati, Connecticut, Louisville, Pittsburgh, Rutgers, South Florida, Syracuse and West Virginia. **Conference champion:** Member schools needed two years to adjust their regular season schedules in order to begin round-robin conference play in 1993. In the meantime, the 1991 and '92 Big East titles went to the highest-ranked member in the final regular season *USA Today*/CNN coaches' poll.
   **Multiple titles:** Miami-FL (9); Syracuse (5); Virginia Tech and West Virginia (3).

| Year | | Year | | Year | | Year | |
|---|---|---|---|---|---|---|---|
| 1991 | Miami-FL (2-0, #1) & Syracuse (5-0, #16) | 1996 | Virginia Tech (6-1), Miami-FL (6-1) & Syracuse (6-1) | 2000 | Miami-FL (7-0) | 2004 | Boston College (4-2), Pittsburgh (4-2), Syracuse (4-2) & West Virginia (4-2) |
| 1992 | Miami-FL (4-0, #1) | 1997 | Syracuse (6-1) | 2001 | Miami-FL (7-0) | | |
| 1993 | West Virginia (7-0) | 1998 | Syracuse (6-1) | 2002 | Miami-FL (6-1) | | |
| 1994 | Miami-FL (7-0) | 1999 | Virginia Tech (7-0) | 2003 | Miami-FL (6-1) & West Virginia (6-1) | | |
| 1995 | Virginia Tech (6-1) & Miami-FL (6-1) | | | | | | |

### Big Ten Conference

**Originally founded** in 1895 as the Intercollegiate Conference of Faculty Representatives, better known as the Western Conference. **Charter members** (7): Chicago, Illinois, Michigan, Minnesota, Northwestern, Purdue and Wisconsin. **Admitted later** (5): Indiana and Iowa in 1899; Ohio St. in 1912; Michigan St. in 1950 (began play in '53); Penn St. in 1990 (began play in '93). **Withdrew later** (2): Michigan in 1907 (rejoined in '17); Chicago in 1940 (dropped football after '39 season). **Note:** Iowa belonged to both the Western and Missouri Valley conferences from 1907-10.
   Unofficially called the **Big Ten** from 1912 until Chicago's withdrawal in 1939, then the **Big Nine** from 1940 until Michigan St. began conference play in 1953. Formally named the **Big Ten** in 1984 and has kept the name even after adding Penn St. as its 11th member in 1990.
**2005 playing membership** (11): Illinois, Indiana, Iowa, Michigan, Michigan St., Minnesota, Northwestern, Ohio St., Penn St., Purdue and Wisconsin.
   **Multiple titles:** Michigan (42); Ohio St. (29); Minnesota (18); Illinois (15); Iowa and Wisconsin (11); Purdue and Northwestern (8); Chicago and Michigan St. (6); Indiana (2).

| Year | | Year | | Year | | Year | |
|---|---|---|---|---|---|---|---|
| 1896 | Wisconsin (2-0-1) | 1904 | Minnesota (3-0) & Michigan (2-0) | 1912 | Wisconsin (6-0) | 1921 | Iowa (5-0) |
| 1897 | Wisconsin (3-0) | 1905 | Chicago (7-0) | 1913 | Chicago (7-0) | 1922 | Iowa (5-0) & Michigan (4-0) |
| 1898 | Michigan (3-0) | 1906 | Wisconsin (3-0), Minnesota (2-0) & Michigan (1-0) | 1914 | Illinois (6-0) | 1923 | Illinois (5-0) & Michigan (4-0) |
| 1899 | Chicago (4-0) | 1907 | Chicago (4-0) | 1915 | Minnesota (3-0-1) & Illinois (3-0-2) | 1924 | Chicago (3-0-3) |
| 1900 | Iowa (3-0-1) & Minnesota (3-0-1) | 1908 | Chicago (5-0) | 1916 | Ohio St. (4-0) | 1925 | Michigan (5-1) |
| 1901 | Michigan (4-0) & Wisconsin (2-0) | 1909 | Minnesota (3-0) | 1917 | Ohio St. (4-0) | 1926 | Michigan (5-0) & Northwestern (5-0) |
| 1902 | Michigan (5-0) | 1910 | Illinois (4-0) & Minnesota (2-0) | 1918 | Illinois (4-0), Michigan (2-0) & Purdue (1-0) | 1927 | Illinois (5-0) & Minnesota (3-0-1) |
| 1903 | Michigan (3-0-1), Minnesota (3-0-1) & Northwestern (1-0-2) | 1911 | Minnesota (3-0-1) | 1919 | Illinois (6-1) | 1928 | Illinois (4-1) |
| | | | | 1920 | Ohio St. (5-0) | 1929 | Purdue (5-0) |

| Year | | Year | | Year | | Year | |
|---|---|---|---|---|---|---|---|
| 1930 | Michigan (5-0) & Northwestern (5-0) | 1950 | Michigan (4-1-1) | 1971 | Michigan (8-0) | 1990 | Iowa (6-2), Michigan (6-2), Michigan St. (6-2) & Illinois (6-2) |
| 1931 | Purdue (5-1), Michigan (5-1) & Northwestern (5-1) | 1951 | Illinois (5-0-1) | 1972 | Ohio St. (7-1) & Michigan (7-1) | 1991 | Michigan (8-.90) |
| | | 1952 | Wisconsin (4-1-1) & Purdue (4-1-1) | 1973 | Ohio St. (7-0-1) & Michigan (7-0-1) | 1992 | Michigan (6-0-2) |
| 1932 | Michigan (6-0) & Purdue (5-0-1) | 1953 | Michigan St. (5-1) & Illinois (5-1) | 1974 | Ohio St. (7-1) & Michigan (7-1) | 1993 | Wisconsin (6-1-1) & Ohio St. (6-1-1) |
| 1933 | Michigan (5-0-1) & Minnesota (2-0-4) | 1954 | Ohio St. (7-0) | 1975 | Ohio St. (8-0) | 1994 | Penn St. (8-0) |
| 1934 | Minnesota (5-0) | 1955 | Ohio St. (6-0) | 1976 | Michigan (7-1) & Ohio St. (7-1) | 1995 | Northwestern (8-0) |
| 1935 | Minnesota (5-0) & Ohio St. (5-0) | 1956 | Iowa (5-1) | 1977 | Michigan (7-1) & Ohio St. (7-1) | 1996 | Ohio St. (7-1) & Northwestern (7-1) |
| 1936 | Northwestern (6-0) | 1957 | Ohio St. (7-0) | 1978 | Michigan (7-1) & Michigan St. (7-1) | 1997 | Michigan (8-0) |
| 1937 | Minnesota (5-0) | 1958 | Iowa (5-1) | 1979 | Ohio St. (8-0) | 1998 | Ohio St. (7-1), Wisconsin (7-1) & Michigan (7-1) |
| 1938 | Minnesota (4-1) | 1959 | Wisconsin (5-2) | 1980 | Michigan (8-0) | 1999 | Wisconsin (7-1) |
| 1939 | Ohio St. (5-1) | 1960 | Minnesota (5-1) & Iowa (5-1) | 1981 | Iowa (6-2) & Ohio St. (6-2) | 2000 | Purdue (6-2), Michigan (6-2) & Northwestern (6-2) |
| 1940 | Minnesota (6-0) | 1961 | Ohio St. (6-0) | 1982 | Michigan (8-1) | 2001 | Illinois (7-1) |
| 1941 | Minnesota (5-0) | 1962 | Wisconsin (6-1) | 1983 | Illinois (9-0) | 2002 | Ohio St. (8-0) & Iowa (8-0) |
| 1942 | Ohio St. (5-1) | 1963 | Illinois (5-1-1) | 1984 | Ohio St. (7-2) | 2003 | Michigan (7-1) |
| 1943 | Purdue (6-0) & Michigan (6-0) | 1964 | Michigan (6-1) | 1985 | Iowa (7-1) | 2004 | Iowa (7-1) & Michigan (7-1) |
| 1944 | Ohio St. (6-0) | 1965 | Michigan St. (7-0) | 1986 | Michigan (7-1) & Ohio St. (7-1) | | |
| 1945 | Indiana (5-0-1) | 1966 | Michigan St. (7-0) | 1987 | Michigan St. (7-0-1) | | |
| 1946 | Illinois (6-1) | 1967 | Indiana (6-1), Purdue (6-1) & Minnesota (6-1) | 1988 | Michigan (7-0-1) | | |
| 1947 | Michigan (6-0) | 1968 | Ohio St. (7-0) | 1989 | Michigan (8-0) | | |
| 1948 | Michigan (6-0) | 1969 | Ohio St. (6-1) & Michigan (6-1) | | | | |
| 1949 | Ohio St. (4-1-1) & Michigan (4-1-1) | 1970 | Ohio St. (7-0) | | | | |

## Big Eight Conference (1907-1996)

**Originally founded** in 1907 as the Missouri Valley Intercollegiate Athletic Assn. **Charter members** (5): Iowa, Kansas, Missouri, Nebraska and Washington University of St. Louis. **Admitted later** (11): Drake and Iowa St. (then Ames College) in 1908; Kansas St. (then Kansas College of Applied Science and Agriculture) in 1913; Grinnell (Iowa) College in 1919; Oklahoma in 1920; Oklahoma A&M (now Oklahoma St.) in 1925; Colorado in 1947 (began play in '48).

**Withdrew later** (9): Iowa in 1911 (left for Big Ten after 1910 season), Colorado, Iowa St., Kansas, Kansas St. Missouri, Nebraska, Oklahoma and Oklahoma St. in 1996 (left for Big 12 after 1995 season); **Excluded later** (4): Drake, Grinnell, Oklahoma A&M and Washington-MO (left out when MVIAA cut membership to six teams in 1928).

Streamlined MVIAA unofficially called **Big Six** from 1928-47 with surviving members Iowa St., Kansas, Kansas St., Missouri, Nebraska and Oklahoma. Became the **Big Seven** after 1947 season when Colorado came over from the Skyline Conference, and then the **Big Eight** with the return of Oklahoma A&M in 1957. A&M, which resumed conference play in '60, became Oklahoma St. on July 10, 1957. The MVIAA was officially renamed the Big Eight in 1964. The league folded in 1996 when the existing members formed the newly created Big 12 along with four schools from the Southwest Conference.

**Multiple titles:** Nebraska (43); Oklahoma (34); Missouri (12); Colorado and Kansas (5); Iowa St. and Oklahoma St. (2).

| Year | | Year | | Year | | Year | |
|---|---|---|---|---|---|---|---|
| 1907 | Iowa (1-0) & Nebraska (1-0) | 1928 | Nebraska (4-0) | 1952 | Oklahoma (5-0-1) | 1976 | Colorado (5-2), Oklahoma (5-2) & Oklahoma St. (5-2) |
| 1908 | Kansas (4-0) | 1929 | Nebraska (3-0-2) | 1953 | Oklahoma (6-0) | | |
| 1909 | Missouri (4-0-1) | 1930 | Kansas (4-1) | 1954 | Oklahoma (6-0) | | |
| | | 1931 | Nebraska (5-0) | 1955 | Oklahoma (6-0) | | |
| 1910 | Nebraska (2-0) | 1932 | Nebraska (5-0) | 1956 | Oklahoma (6-0) | 1977 | Oklahoma (7-0) |
| 1911 | Iowa St. (2-0-1) & Nebraska (2-0-1) | 1933 | Nebraska (5-0) | 1957 | Oklahoma (6-0) | 1978 | Nebraska (6-1) & Oklahoma (6-1) |
| 1912 | Iowa St. (2-0) & Nebraska (2-0) | 1934 | Kansas St. (5-0) | 1958 | Oklahoma (6-0) | | |
| | | 1935 | Nebraska (4-0-1) | 1959 | Oklahoma (5-1) | 1979 | Oklahoma (7-0) |
| 1913 | Missouri (4-0) & Nebraska (3-0) | 1936 | Nebraska (5-0) | 1960 | Missouri (7-0) | 1980 | Oklahoma (7-0) |
| 1914 | Nebraska (3-0) | 1937 | Nebraska (3-0-2) | 1961 | Colorado (7-0) | 1981 | Nebraska (7-0) |
| 1915 | Nebraska (4-0) | 1938 | Oklahoma (5-0) | 1962 | Oklahoma (7-0) | 1982 | Nebraska (7-0) |
| 1916 | Nebraska (3-1) | 1939 | Missouri (5-0) | 1963 | Nebraska (7-0) | 1983 | Nebraska (7-0) |
| 1917 | Nebraska (2-0) | 1940 | Nebraska (5-0) | 1964 | Nebraska (6-1) | 1984 | Oklahoma (6-1) & Nebraska (6-1) |
| 1918 | Vacant (WW I) | 1941 | Missouri (5-0) | 1965 | Nebraska (7-0) | | |
| 1919 | Missouri (4-0-1) | 1942 | Missouri (4-0-1) | 1966 | Nebraska (6-1) | 1985 | Oklahoma (7-0) |
| 1920 | Oklahoma (4-0-1) | 1943 | Oklahoma (5-0) | 1967 | Oklahoma (7-0) | 1986 | Oklahoma (7-0) |
| 1921 | Nebraska (3-0) | 1944 | Oklahoma (4-0-1) | 1968 | Kansas (6-1) & Oklahoma (6-1) | 1987 | Oklahoma (7-0) |
| 1922 | Nebraska (5-0) | 1945 | Missouri (5-0) | | | 1988 | Nebraska (7-0) |
| 1923 | Nebraska (3-0-2) & Kansas (3-0-3) | 1946 | Oklahoma (4-1) & Kansas (4-1) | 1969 | Missouri (6-1) & Nebraska (6-1) | 1989 | Colorado (7-0) |
| 1924 | Missouri (5-1) | 1947 | Kansas (4-0-1) & Oklahoma (4-0-1) | 1970 | Nebraska (7-0) | 1990 | Colorado (7-0) |
| 1925 | Missouri (5-1) | 1948 | Oklahoma (5-0) | 1971 | Nebraska (7-0) | 1991 | Nebraska (6-0-1) & Colorado (6-0-1) |
| 1926 | Okla. A&M (3-0-1) | 1949 | Oklahoma (5-0) | 1972 | Nebraska (5-1-1)* | | |
| 1927 | Missouri (5-1) | 1950 | Oklahoma (6-0) | 1973 | Oklahoma (7-0) | 1992 | Nebraska (6-1) |
| | | 1951 | Oklahoma (6-0) | 1974 | Oklahoma (7-0) | 1993 | Nebraska (7-0) |
| | | | | 1975 | Nebraska (6-1) & Oklahoma (6-1) | 1994 | Nebraska (7-0) |
| | | | | | | 1995 | Nebraska (7-0) |

*Oklahoma (6-1) forfeited title in 1972 after a player was ruled ineligible.

## Major Conference Champions (Cont.)
### Big 12 Conference

**Originally founded** in 1996 by the former teams of the Big Eight and four schools from the Southwest Conference. The league stages a conference championship game between the two division winners on the first Saturday in December. **Playing sites:** Trans World Dome in St. Louis (1996, 1998), the Alamodome in San Antonio (1997, 1999), Arrowhead Stadium in Kansas City, Mo. (2000, 2003, 2004), Texas Stadium in Irving, Texas (2001) and Reliant Stadium in Houston, Texas (2002).

    **2004 playing membership:** (12) NORTH—Colorado, Iowa St., Kansas, Kansas St., Missouri and Nebraska; SOUTH—Baylor, Oklahoma, Oklahoma St., Texas, Texas A&M and Texas Tech.

    **Multiple titles:** Oklahoma (3), Nebraska (2).

| Year | | Year | | Year | |
|------|--|------|--|------|--|
| 1996 | Texas 37, Nebraska 27 | 1999 | Nebraska 22, Texas 6 | 2002 | Oklahoma 29, Colorado 7 |
| 1997 | Nebraska 54, Texas A&M 15 | 2000 | Oklahoma 27, Kansas St. 24 | 2003 | Kansas St. 35, Oklahoma 7 |
| 1998 | Texas A&M 36, Kansas St. 33 | 2001 | Colorado 39, Texas 37 | 2004 | Oklahoma 42, Colorado 3 |

### Big West Conference (1969-2000)

**Originally founded** in 1969 as Pacific Coast Athletic Assn. **Charter members** (7): CS-Los Angeles, Fresno St., Long Beach St., Pacific, San Diego St., San Jose St. and UC-Santa Barbara. **Admitted later** (12): CS-Fullerton in 1974; Utah St. in 1977 (began play in '78); UNLV in 1982; New Mexico St. in 1983 (began play in '84); Nevada in 1991 (began play in '92); Arkansas St., Louisiana Tech, Northern Illinois and SW Louisiana in 1992 (all four began play in football only in '93); Boise St., Idaho and North Texas in 1994 (all three began play in '96); Arkansas St. rejoined in 1999 (in football only). **Withdrew later** (14): CS-Los Angeles and UC-Santa Barbara in 1972 (both dropped football after '71 season); San Diego St. in 1975 (became an independent after '75 season); Fresno St. in 1991 (left for WAC after '91 season); Long Beach St. in 1991 (dropped football after '91 season); CS-Fullerton in 1992 (dropped football after '92 season); San Jose St. and UNLV in 1994 (left for WAC after '95 season); Pacific in 1995 (dropped football after '95 season); Arkansas St., Louisiana Tech, Northern Illinois and SW Louisiana in 1995 (all four returned to independent football status after '95 season); Nevada in 2000 (left for WAC after '99 season). **Conference renamed** Big West in 1988.

    **Multiple titles:** San Jose St. (8); Fresno St. (6); Nevada, San Diego St. and Utah St. (5); Long Beach St. (3); Boise St., CS-Fullerton and SW Louisiana (2).

| Year | | Year | | Year | |
|------|--|------|--|------|--|
| 1969 | San Diego St. (6-0) | 1982 | Fresno St. (6-0) | 1994 | UNLV (5-1), |
| 1970 | Long Beach St. (5-1) | 1983 | CS-Fullerton (5-1) | | Nevada (5-1), |
| | & San Diego St. (5-1) | 1984 | CS-Fullerton (6-1)† | | & SW Louisiana (5-1) |
| 1971 | Long Beach St. (5-1) | 1985 | Fresno St. (7-0) | 1995 | Nevada (5-0) |
| 1972 | San Diego St. (4-0) | 1986 | San Jose St. (7-0) | 1996 | Nevada (4-1) |
| 1973 | San Diego St. (3-0-1) | 1987 | San Jose St. (7-0) | | & Utah St. (4-1) |
| 1974 | San Diego St. (4-0) | 1988 | Fresno St. (7-0) | 1997 | Utah St. (4-1) |
| 1975 | San Jose St. (5-0) | 1989 | Fresno St. (7-0) | | & Nevada (4-1) |
| 1976 | San Jose St. (5-0) | 1990 | San Jose St. (7-0) | 1998 | Idaho (4-1) |
| 1977 | Fresno St. (4-0) | 1991 | Fresno St. (6-1) | 1999 | Boise St. (5-1) |
| 1978 | San Jose St. (4-1) | | & San Jose St. (6-1) | 2000 | Boise St. (5-0) |
| | & Utah St. (4-1)* | 1992 | Nevada (5-1) | *San Jose St. (4-0-1) forfeited share of |
| 1979 | Utah St. (4-0-1)* | 1993 | Utah St. (5-1) | 1979 title for using ineligible player. |
| 1980 | Long Beach St. (5-0) | | & SW Louisiana (5-1) | †UNLV (7-0) forfeited title in 1984 for |
| 1981 | San Jose St. (5-0) | | | use of ineligible players. |

### Conference USA

**Founded** in 1994 by six independent football schools which began play as a conference in 1996. **Charter members** (6): Cincinnati, Houston, Louisville, Memphis, Southern Mississippi and Tulane. **Admitted later** (11): East Carolina in 1997, Army in 1998, Univ. of Alabama-Birmingham in 1999, Texas Christian Univ. in 2001, South Florida in 2003, Central Florida, Marshall, Rice, SMU, Tulsa and UTEP in 2005. **Withdrew later** (5): Cincinnati, Louisville and South Florida are set to leave for the Big East in 2005; Army is going back to independent and TCU is going to the Mountain West in 2005.

    **2005 playing members** (12): Alabama-Birmingham, Central Florida, East Carolina, Houston, Marshall, Memphis, Rice, SMU, Southern Mississippi, Tulsa, Tulane and UTEP.

    **Multiple titles:** Southern Mississippi (4), Louisville (3).

| Year | | Year | | Year | |
|------|--|------|--|------|--|
| 1996 | Southern Mississippi (4-1) | 1999 | Southern Mississippi (6-0) | 2002 | TCU (6-2) |
| | & Houston (4-1) | 2000 | Louisville (6-1) | | & Cincinnati (6-2) |
| 1997 | Southern Mississippi (6-0) | 2001 | Louisville (6-1) | 2003 | Southern Mississippi (8-0) |
| 1998 | Tulane (6-0) | | | 2004 | Louisville (8-0) |

### Mid-American Conference

**Founded** in 1946. **Charter members** (6): Butler, Cincinnati, Miami-OH, Ohio University, Western Michigan and Western Reserve (Miami and WMU began play in '48). **Admitted later** (12): Kent St. (now Kent) and Toledo in 1951 (Toledo began play in '52); Bowling Green in 1952; Marshall in 1954; Central Michigan and Eastern Michigan in 1972 (CMU began play in '75 and EMU in '76); Ball St. and Northern Illinois in 1973 (both began play in '75); Akron in 1991 (began play in '92); Marshall and Northern Illinois in 1995 (both resumed play in '97); Buffalo in 1995 (resumed play in '99); Central Florida in 2002; Temple in 2007. **Withdrew later** (5): Butler in 1950 (left for the Indiana Collegiate Conference); Cincinnati in 1953 (went independent); Western Reserve (now Case Western) in 1955 (left for President's Athletic Conference); Marshall in 1969 (went independent) and again in 2005 (left for Conference USA); Northern Illinois in 1986 (went independent); Central Florida in 2005 (left for Conference USA).

    **2005 playing membership** (12): EAST—Akron, Bowling Green, Buffalo, Kent St., Miami-OH and Ohio University; WEST—Ball St., Central Michigan, Eastern Michigan, Northern Illinois, Toledo and Western Michigan.

    **Multiple titles:** Miami-OH (14); Bowling Green (10); Toledo (9); Ball St., Marshall and Ohio University (5); Central Michigan, Cincinnati (4); Western Michigan (2).

| Year | | Year | | Year | | Year | |
|---|---|---|---|---|---|---|---|
| 1947 | Cincinnati (3-1) | 1959 | Bowling Green (6-0) | 1970 | Toledo (5-0) | 1984 | Toledo (7-1-1) |
| 1948 | Miami-OH (4-0) | 1960 | Ohio Univ. (6-0) | 1971 | Toledo (5-0) | 1985 | Bowling Green (9-0) |
| 1949 | Cincinnati (4-0) | 1961 | Bowling Green (5-1) | 1972 | Kent St. (4-1) | 1986 | Miami-OH (6-2) |
| | | 1962 | Bowling Green (5-0-1) | 1973 | Miami-OH (5-0) | 1987 | Eastern Mich. (7-1) |
| 1950 | Miami-OH (4-0) | 1963 | Ohio Univ. (5-1) | 1974 | Miami-OH (5-0) | 1988 | Western Mich. (7-1) |
| 1951 | Cincinnati (3-0) | 1964 | Bowling Green (5-1) | 1975 | Miami-OH (6-0) | 1989 | Ball St. (6-1-1) |
| 1952 | Cincinnati (3-0) | 1965 | Bowling Green (5-1) | 1976 | Ball St. (4-1) | | |
| 1953 | Ohio Univ. (5-0-1) | | & Miami-OH (5-1) | 1977 | Miami-OH (5-0) | 1990 | Central Mich. (7-1) |
| | & Miami-OH (3-0-1) | 1966 | Miami-OH (5-1) | 1978 | Ball St. (8-0) | | & Toledo (7-1) |
| 1954 | Miami-OH (4-0) | | & Western Mich. (5-1) | 1979 | Central Mich. (8-0-1) | 1991 | Bowling Green (8-0) |
| 1955 | Miami-OH (5-0) | 1967 | Toledo (5-1) | | | 1992 | Bowling Green (8-0) |
| 1956 | Bowling Green (5-0-1) | | & Ohio Univ. (5-1) | 1980 | Central Mich. (7-2) | 1993 | Ball St. (7-0-1) |
| | & Miami-OH (4-0-1) | 1968 | Ohio Univ. (6-0) | 1981 | Toledo (8-1) | 1994 | Central Mich. (8-1) |
| 1957 | Miami-OH (5-0) | 1969 | Toledo (5-0) | 1982 | Bowling Green (7-2) | 1995 | Toledo (7-0-1) |
| 1958 | Miami-OH (5-0) | | | 1983 | Northern Ill. (8-1) | 1996 | Ball St. (7-1) |

## MAC Championship Game

After expanding to 12 teams and splitting into two divisions in 1997, the MAC began staging a conference championship game between the two division winners on the first Saturday in December. The game has been played at Marshall Stadium in Huntington, W.V. (1997-2000, 2002), Glass Bowl Stadium in Toledo, Ohio (2001), Doyt Perry Stadium in Bowling Green, Ohio (2003) and Ford Field in Detroit (2004-06).

| Year | | Year | | Year | |
|---|---|---|---|---|---|
| 1997 | Marshall 34, Toledo 13 | 2000 | Marshall 19, W. Michigan 14 | 2003 | Miami-OH 49, Bowl. Green 27 |
| 1998 | Marshall 23, Toledo 17 | 2001 | Toledo 41, Marshall 36 | 2004 | Toledo 35, Miami-OH 27 |
| 1999 | Marshall 34, W. Michigan 30 | 2002 | Marshall 49, Toledo 45 | | |

## Mountain West Conference

**Founded** in 1999. **Charter members** (8): Air Force, Brigham Young, Colorado St., New Mexico, Nevada-Las Vegas, San Diego St., Utah and Wyoming. **Admitted later** (1): TCU (from Conference USA) is set to join in 2005.
    **2005 playing membership** (9): Air Force, Brigham Young, Colorado St., New Mexico, Nevada-Las Vegas, San Diego St., TCU, Utah and Wyoming.
    **Multiple titles:** Colorado St. and Utah (3), BYU (2).

| Year | | Year | | Year | |
|---|---|---|---|---|---|
| 1999 | BYU (5-2), | 2000 | Colorado St. (6-1) | 2002 | Colorado St. (6-1) |
| | Colorado St. (5-2) | 2001 | BYU (7-0) | 2003 | Utah (6-1) |
| | & Utah (5-2) | | | 2004 | Utah (7-0) |

## Pacific-10 Conference

**Originally founded** in 1915 as Pacific Coast Conference. **Charter members** (4): California, Oregon, Oregon St. and Washington. **Admitted later** (6): Washington St. in 1917; Stanford in 1918; Idaho and USC (Southern Cal) in 1922; Montana in 1924; and UCLA in 1928. **Withdrew later** (1): Montana in 1950 (left for the Mountain States Conf.).
    The **PCC** dissolved in 1959 and the **AAWU** (Athletic Assn. of Western Universities) was founded. **Charter members** (5): California, Stanford, UCLA, USC and Washington. **Admitted later** (5):Washington St. in 1962; Oregon and Oregon St. in 1964; Arizona and Arizona St. in 1978. **Conference renamed** Pacific-8 in 1968 and Pacific-10 in 1978.
    **2005 playing membership** (10): Arizona, Arizona St., California, Oregon, Oregon St., Stanford, UCLA, USC, Washington and Washington St.
    **Multiple titles:** USC (34); UCLA (17); Washington (15); California (13); Stanford (12); Oregon (7); Oregon St. (5); Washington St. (4); Arizona St. (2).

| Year | | Year | | Year | | Year | |
|---|---|---|---|---|---|---|---|
| 1916 | Washington (3-0-1) | 1938 | USC (6-1) | 1960 | Washington (4-0) | 1986 | Arizona St. (5-1-1) |
| 1917 | Washington St. (3-0) | | & California (6-1) | 1961 | UCLA (3-1) | 1987 | USC (7-1) |
| 1918 | California (3-0) | 1939 | USC (5-0-2) | 1962 | UCLA (4-0) | | & UCLA (7-1) |
| 1919 | Oregon (2-1) | | & UCLA (5-0-3) | 1963 | Washington (4-1) | 1988 | USC (8-0) |
| | & Washington (2-1) | 1940 | Stanford (7-0) | 1964 | Oregon St. (3-1) | 1989 | USC (6-0-1) |
| 1920 | California (3-0) | 1941 | Oregon St. (7-2) | | & USC (3-1) | 1990 | Washington (7-1) |
| 1921 | California (5-0) | 1942 | UCLA (6-1) | 1965 | UCLA (4-0) | 1991 | Washington (8-0) |
| 1922 | California (3-0) | 1943 | USC (4-0) | 1966 | USC (4-1) | 1992 | Washington (6-2) |
| 1923 | California (5-0) | 1944 | USC (3-0-2) | 1967 | USC (6-1) | | & Stanford (6-2) |
| 1924 | Stanford (3-0-1) | 1945 | USC (5-1) | 1968 | USC (6-0) | 1993 | UCLA (6-2), |
| 1925 | Washington (5-0) | 1946 | UCLA (7-0) | 1969 | USC (6-0) | | Arizona (6-2) |
| 1926 | Stanford (4-0) | 1947 | USC (6-0) | 1970 | Stanford (6-1) | | & USC (6-2) |
| 1927 | USC (4-0-1) | 1948 | California (6-0) | 1971 | Stanford (6-1) | 1994 | Oregon (7-1) |
| | & Stanford (4-0-1) | | & Oregon (6-0) | 1972 | USC (7-0) | 1995 | USC (6-1-1) |
| 1928 | USC (4-0-1) | 1949 | California (6-0) | 1973 | USC (7-0) | | & Washington (6-1-1) |
| 1929 | USC (6-1) | 1950 | California (5-0-1) | 1974 | USC (6-0-1) | 1996 | Arizona St. (8-0) |
| 1930 | Washington St. (6-0) | 1951 | Stanford (6-1) | 1975 | UCLA (6-1) | 1997 | Washington St. (7-1) |
| 1931 | USC (7-0) | 1952 | USC (6-0) | | & California (6-1) | | & UCLA (7-1) |
| 1932 | USC (6-0) | 1953 | UCLA (6-1) | 1976 | USC (7-0) | 1998 | UCLA (8-0) |
| 1933 | Oregon (4-1) | 1954 | UCLA (6-0) | 1977 | Washington (6-1) | 1999 | Stanford (7-1) |
| | & Stanford (4-1) | 1955 | UCLA (6-0) | 1978 | USC (6-1) | 2000 | Washington (7-1), |
| 1934 | Stanford (5-0) | 1956 | Oregon St. (6-1-1) | 1979 | USC (6-0-1) | | Oregon St. (7-1) |
| 1935 | California (4-1), | 1957 | Oregon (6-2) | 1980 | Washington (6-1) | | & Oregon (7-1) |
| | Stanford (4-1) | | & Oregon St. (6-2) | 1981 | Washington (6-2) | 2001 | Oregon (7-1) |
| | & UCLA (4-1) | 1958 | California (6-1) | 1982 | UCLA (5-1-1) | 2002 | Washington St. (7-1) |
| 1936 | Washington (6-0-1) | 1959 | Washington (3-1), | 1983 | UCLA (6-1-1) | | & USC (7-1) |
| 1937 | California (6-0-1) | | USC (3-1) | 1984 | USC (7-1) | 2003 | USC (7-1) |
| | | | & UCLA (3-1) | 1985 | UCLA (6-2) | 2004 | USC (8-0) |

## Major Conference Champions (Cont.)

### Southwest Conference (1914-95)

**Founded** in 1914 as Southwest Intercollegiate Athletic Conference. **Charter members** (8): Arkansas, Baylor, Oklahoma, Oklahoma A&M (now Oklahoma St.), Rice, Southwestern, Texas and Texas A&M. **Admitted later** (5): SMU (Southern Methodist) in 1918; Phillips University in 1920; TCU (Texas Christian) in 1923; Texas Tech in 1956 (began play in '60); Houston in 1971 (began play in '76). **Withdrew later** (13): Southwestern in 1917 (went independent); Oklahoma in 1920 (left for Missouri Valley after '19 season); Phillips in 1921; Oklahoma A&M (now Oklahoma St.) in 1925 (left for Big Six); Arkansas in 1990 (left for SEC after '91 season); Baylor, Texas, Texas A&M and Texas Tech in 1994 (all four left for Big 12 after '95 season); Rice, SMU and TCU in 1994 (all three left for WAC after '95 season); Houston in 1994 (left for Conference USA after '95 season). Conference folded on June 30, 1996.

**Multiple titles:** Texas (25); Texas A&M (17); Arkansas (13); SMU (9); TCU (9); Rice (7); Baylor (5); Houston (4); Texas Tech (2).

| Year | | Year | | Year | | Year | |
|---|---|---|---|---|---|---|---|
| 1914 | No champion | 1940 | Texas A&M (5-1) | 1961 | Texas (6-1) | 1981 | SMU (7-1) |
| 1915 | Oklahoma (3-0) | 1941 | Texas A&M (5-1) | | & Arkansas (6-1) | 1982 | SMU (7-0-1) |
| 1916 | No champion | 1942 | Texas (5-1) | 1962 | Texas (6-0-1) | 1983 | Texas (8-0) |
| 1917 | Texas A&M (2-0) | 1943 | Texas (5-0) | 1963 | Texas (7-0) | 1984 | SMU (6-2) |
| 1918 | No champion | 1944 | TCU (3-1-1) | 1964 | Arkansas (7-0) | | & Houston (6-2) |
| 1919 | Texas A&M (4-0) | 1945 | Texas (5-1) | 1965 | Arkansas (7-0) | 1985 | Texas A&M (7-1) |
| 1920 | Texas (5-0) | 1946 | Rice (5-1) | 1966 | SMU (6-1) | 1986 | Texas A&M (7-1) |
| 1921 | Texas A&M (3-0-2) | | & Arkansas (5-1) | 1967 | Texas A&M (6-1) | 1987 | Texas A&M (6-1) |
| 1922 | Baylor (5-0) | 1947 | SMU (5-0-1) | 1968 | Arkansas (6-1) | 1988 | Arkansas (7-0) |
| 1923 | SMU (5-0) | 1948 | SMU (5-0-1) | | & Texas (6-1) | 1989 | Arkansas (7-1) |
| 1924 | Baylor (4-0-1) | 1949 | Rice (6-0) | 1969 | Texas (7-0) | 1990 | Texas (8-0) |
| 1925 | Texas A&M (4-1) | 1950 | Texas (6-0) | 1970 | Texas (7-0) | 1991 | Texas A&M (8-0) |
| 1926 | SMU (5-0) | 1951 | TCU (5-1) | 1971 | Texas (6-1) | 1992 | Texas A&M (7-0) |
| 1927 | Texas A&M (4-0-1) | 1952 | Texas (6-0) | 1972 | Texas (7-0) | 1993 | Texas A&M (7-0) |
| 1928 | Texas (5-1) | 1953 | Rice (5-1) | 1973 | Texas (7-0) | 1994 | Baylor, Rice, TCU, |
| 1929 | TCU (4-0-1) | | & Texas (5-1) | 1974 | Baylor (6-1) | | Texas and Texas Tech† |
| 1930 | Texas (4-1) | 1954 | Arkansas (5-1) | 1975 | Arkansas (6-1), | | (4-3) |
| 1931 | SMU (5-0-1) | 1955 | TCU (5-1) | | Texas (6-1) | 1995 | Texas (7-0) |
| 1932 | TCU (6-0) | 1956 | Texas A&M (6-0) | | & Texas A&M (6-1) | | |
| 1933 | Arkansas (4-1)* | 1957 | Rice (5-1) | 1976 | Houston (7-1) | *Arkansas (4-1) forced to |
| 1934 | Rice (5-1) | 1958 | TCU (5-1) | | & Texas Tech (7-1) | vacate 1933 title for use of |
| 1935 | SMU (6-0) | 1959 | Texas (5-1), | 1977 | Texas (8-0) | ineligible player. |
| 1936 | Arkansas (5-1) | | TCU (5-1) | 1978 | Houston (7-1) | †Texas A&M had the best |
| 1937 | Rice (4-1-1) | | & Arkansas (5-1) | 1979 | Houston (7-1) | record (6-0-1) in 1994 but |
| 1938 | TCU (6-0) | 1960 | Arkansas (6-1) | | & Arkansas (7-1) | was on probation and |
| 1939 | Texas A&M (6-0) | | | 1980 | Baylor (8-0) | therefore ineligible for the |
| | | | | | | Southwest championship. | |

### Southeastern Conference

**Founded** in 1933 when charter members all left Southern Conference to form SEC. **Charter members** (13): Alabama, Auburn, Florida, Georgia, Georgia Tech, Kentucky, LSU (Louisiana St.), Mississippi, Mississippi St., Sewanee, Tennessee, Tulane and Vanderbilt. **Admitted later** (2): Arkansas and South Carolina in 1990 (both began play in '92). **Withdrew later** (3): Sewanee in 1940; Georgia Tech in 1964; and Tulane in 1966.
**2005 playing membership** (12): Alabama, Arkansas, Auburn, Florida, Georgia, Kentucky, LSU, Mississippi, Mississippi St., South Carolina, Tennessee and Vanderbilt. **Note:** Conference title decided by championship game between Western and Eastern division winners since 1992.

**Multiple titles:** Alabama (21); Tennessee (13); Georgia (11); Florida and LSU (9); Auburn and Mississippi (6); Georgia Tech (5); Kentucky and Tulane (3).

| Year | | Year | | Year | | Year | |
|---|---|---|---|---|---|---|---|
| 1933 | Alabama (5-0-1) | 1948 | Georgia (6-0) | 1965 | Alabama (6-1-1) | 1981 | Georgia (6-0) |
| 1934 | Tulane (8-0) | 1949 | Tulane (5-1) | 1966 | Alabama (6-0) | | & Alabama (6-0) |
| | & Alabama (7-0) | 1950 | Kentucky (5-1) | | & Georgia (6-0) | 1982 | Georgia (6-0) |
| 1935 | LSU (5-0) | 1951 | Georgia Tech (7-0) | 1967 | Tennessee (6-0) | 1983 | Auburn (6-0) |
| 1936 | LSU (6-0) | | & Tennessee (5-0) | 1968 | Georgia (5-0-1) | 1984 | Florida (5-0-1)* |
| 1937 | Alabama (6-0) | 1952 | Georgia Tech (6-0) | 1969 | Tennessee (5-1) | 1985 | Florida (5-1)† |
| 1938 | Tennessee (7-0) | 1953 | Alabama (4-0-3) | 1970 | LSU (5-0) | | & Tennessee (5-1) |
| 1939 | Tennessee (6-0), | 1954 | Mississippi (5-1) | 1971 | Alabama (7-0) | 1986 | LSU (5-1) |
| | Georgia Tech (6-0) | 1955 | Mississippi (5-1) | 1972 | Alabama (7-1) | 1987 | Auburn (5-0-1) |
| | & Tulane (5-0) | 1956 | Tennessee (6-0) | 1973 | Alabama (8-0) | 1988 | Auburn (6-1) |
| 1940 | Tennessee (5-0) | 1957 | Auburn (7-0) | 1974 | Alabama (6-0) | | & LSU (6-1) |
| 1941 | Mississippi St. (4-0-1) | 1958 | LSU (6-0) | 1975 | Alabama (6-0) | 1989 | Alabama (6-1), |
| 1942 | Georgia (6-0) | 1959 | Georgia (7-0) | 1976 | Georgia (5-1) | | Tennessee (6-1) |
| 1943 | Georgia Tech (3-0) | 1960 | Mississippi (5-0-1) | | & Kentucky (5-1) | | & Auburn (6-1) |
| 1944 | Georgia Tech (4-0) | 1961 | Alabama (7-0) | 1977 | Alabama (7-0) | 1990 | Florida (6-1)† |
| 1945 | Alabama (6-0) | | & LSU (6-0) | | & Kentucky (6-0) | | & Tennessee (5-1-1) |
| 1946 | Georgia (5-0) | 1962 | Mississippi (6-0) | 1978 | Alabama (6-0) | 1991 | Florida (7-0) |
| | & Tennessee (5-0) | 1963 | Mississippi (5-0-1) | 1979 | Alabama (6-0) | *Title vacated. |
| 1947 | Mississippi (6-1) | 1964 | Alabama (8-0) | 1980 | Georgia (6-0) | †On probation, ineligible |
| | | | | | | for championship. | |

### SEC Championship Game

Since expanding to 12 teams and splitting into two divisions in 1992, the SEC has staged a conference championship game between the two division winners on the first Saturday in December. The game has been played at Legion Field in Birmingham, Ala., (1992-93) and the Georgia Dome in Atlanta (since 1994). The divisions: EAST— Florida, Georgia, Kentucky, South Carolina, Tennessee and Vanderbilt; WEST— Alabama, Arkansas, Auburn, LSU, Mississippi and Mississippi St.

| Year | | Year | | Year | |
|---|---|---|---|---|---|
| 1992 | Alabama 28, Florida 21 | 1997 | Tennessee 30, Auburn 29 | 2002 | Georgia 30, Arkansas 3 |
| 1993 | Florida 28, Alabama 23 | 1998 | Tennessee 24, Miss. St. 14 | 2003 | LSU 34, Georgia 13 |
| 1994 | Florida 24, Alabama 23 | 1999 | Alabama 34, Florida 7 | 2004 | Auburn 38, Tennessee 28 |
| 1995 | Florida 34, Arkansas 3 | 2000 | Florida 28, Auburn 6 | | |
| 1996 | Florida 45, Alabama 30 | 2001 | LSU 31, Tennessee 20 | | |

### Sun Belt Conference

**Founded** in 2001 when the Sun Belt Conference sponsored football for the first time. **Charter members** (7): Arkansas State, Idaho, Louisiana-Lafayette, Louisiana-Monroe, Middle Tennessee State, New Mexico State and North Texas. **Admitted later** (4): Utah St. in 2003, Troy St. in 2004, Florida Atlantic and Florida International in 2005. **Withdrew later** (3): Idaho, New Mexico St. and Utah St. in 2005 (left for WAC).
**2005 playing membership** (8): Arkansas State, Florida Atlantic, Florida International, Louisiana-Lafayette, Louisiana-Monroe, Middle Tennessee, North Texas and Troy
 **Multiple titles:** North Texas (4)

| Year | | Year | | Year | |
|---|---|---|---|---|---|
| 2001 | North Texas (5-1) & Mid. Tenn. St. (5-1) | 2002 | North Texas (6-0) | 2004 | North Texas (7-0) |
| | | 2003 | North Texas (7-0) | | |

### Western Athletic Conference

**Founded** in 1962 when charter members left the Skyline and Border conferences to form the WAC. **Charter members** (6): Arizona and Arizona St. from Border; BYU (Brigham Young), New Mexico, Utah and Wyoming from Skyline. **Admitted later** (18): Colorado St. and UTEP (Texas-El Paso) in 1967 (both began play in '68); San Diego St. in 1978; Hawaii in 1979; Air Force in 1980; Fresno St. in 1991 (began play in '92); Rice, San Jose St., SMU , TCU , Tulsa and UNLV in 1994 (all began play in '96); Nevada in 2000; Boise St. and Louisiana Tech in 2001; Idaho, New Mexico St. and Utah St. in 2005. **Withdrew later** (13): Arizona and Arizona St. in 1978 (left for Pac-10 after '77 season); Air Force, BYU, Colorado St., New Mexico, San Diego St., UNLV, Utah and Wyoming (left to form Mountain West conference in '99); TCU in 2000 (left for Conference USA after 2000 season); Rice, SMU, Tulsa and UTEP in 2005 (left for Conference USA).
**2005 playing membership** (9): Boise St., Fresno St., Hawaii, Idaho, Louisiana Tech, Nevada, New Mexico St., San Jose St., and Utah St.
 **Multiple titles:** BYU (19); Arizona St. and Wyoming (7); Air Force, Boise St., Fresno St., New Mexico and Colorado St. (3); Arizona, Hawaii, TCU and Utah (2).

| Year | | Year | | Year | | Year | |
|---|---|---|---|---|---|---|---|
| 1962 | New Mexico (2-1-1) | 1974 | BYU (6-0-1) | 1986 | San Diego St. (7-1) | 1995 | Colorado St. (6-2), Air Force (6-2), BYU (6-2) & Utah (6-2) |
| 1963 | New Mexico (3-1) | 1975 | Arizona St. (7-0) | 1987 | Wyoming (8-0) | | |
| 1964 | Utah (3-1), New Mexico (3-1) & Arizona (3-1) | 1976 | BYU (6-1) & Wyoming (6-1) | 1988 | Wyoming (8-0) | | |
| | | | | 1989 | BYU (7-1) | 1996-98 | See below |
| 1965 | BYU (4-1) | 1977 | Arizona St. (6-1) & BYU (6-1) | 1990 | BYU (7-1) | 1999 | Fresno St. (5-2), Hawaii (7-2) & TCU (7-2) |
| 1966 | Wyoming (5-0) | 1978 | BYU (5-1) | 1991 | BYU (7-0-1) | | |
| 1967 | Wyoming (5-0) | 1979 | BYU (7-0) | 1992 | Hawaii (6-2), BYU (6-2) & Fresno St. (6-2) | 2000 | TCU (7-1) & UTEP (7-1) |
| 1968 | Wyoming (6-1) | 1980 | BYU (6-1) | | | | |
| 1969 | Arizona St. (6-1) | 1981 | BYU (7-1) | | | 2001 | La. Tech (7-1) |
| 1970 | Arizona St. (7-0) | 1982 | BYU (7-1 | 1993 | BYU (6-2), Fresno St. (6-2) & Wyoming (6-2) | 2002 | Boise St. (8-0) |
| 1971 | Arizona St. (7-0) | 1983 | BYU (7-0) | | | 2003 | Boise St. (8-0) |
| 1972 | Arizona St. (5-1) | 1984 | BYU (8-0) | | | 2004 | Boise St. (8-0) |
| 1973 | Arizona St. (6-1) & Arizona (6-1) | 1985 | Air Force (7-1) & BYU (7-1) | 1994 | Colorado St. (7-1) | | |

### WAC Championship Game (1996-98)

In addition to expanding to 16 teams and splitting into two divisions in 1996, the WAC staged a conference championship game between the two division winners on the first Saturday in December at Sam Boyd Stadium in Las Vegas until eight teams split off and formed the Mountain West Conference in 1999. The divisions: PACIFIC—BYU, Fresno St., Hawaii, New Mexico, San Diego St., San Jose St., UTEP, Utah; MOUNTAIN—Air Force, Colorado St., Rice, SMU, TCU, Tulsa, UNLV, Wyoming.

| Year | | Year | | Year | |
|---|---|---|---|---|---|
| 1996 | BYU 28, Wyoming 25 (OT) | 1997 | Colorado St. 41, New Mexico 13 | 1998 | Air Force 20, BYU 13 |

## Annual NCAA Division I-A Leaders

Note that Oklahoma A&M is now Oklahoma St. and Texas Mines is now UTEP.

### Rushing

Individual championship decided on Rushing Yards (1937-69), and on Yards Per Game (since 1970).

**Multiple winners:** Troy Davis, Marshall Faulk, Art Luppino, Ed Marinaro, Rudy Mobley, Jim Pilot, O.J. Simpson, LaDainian Tomlinson and Ricky Williams (2).

| Year | | Car | Yards | Year | | Car | Yards | P/Gm |
|---|---|---|---|---|---|---|---|---|
| 1937 | Byron (Whizzer) White, Colorado | 181 | 1121 | 1970 | Ed Marinaro, Cornell | 285 | 1425 | 158.3 |
| 1938 | Len Eshmont, Fordham | 132 | 831 | 1971 | Ed Marinaro, Cornell | 356 | 1881 | 209.0 |
| 1939 | John Polanski, Wake Forest | 137 | 882 | 1972 | Pete VanValkenburg, BYU | 232 | 1386 | 138.6 |
| 1940 | Al Ghesquiere, Detroit | 146 | 957 | 1973 | Mark Kellar, Northern Ill | 291 | 1719 | 156.3 |
| 1941 | Frank Sinkwich, Georgia | 209 | 1103 | 1974 | Louie Giammona, Utah St. | 329 | 1534 | 153.4 |
| 1942 | Rudy Mobley, Hardin-Simmons | 187 | 1281 | 1975 | Ricky Bell, USC | 357 | 1875 | 170.5 |
| 1943 | Creighton Miller, Notre Dame | 151 | 911 | 1976 | Tony Dorsett, Pittsburgh | 338 | 1948 | 177.1 |
| 1944 | Red Williams, Minnesota | 136 | 911 | 1977 | Earl Campbell, Texas | 267 | 1744 | 158.5 |
| 1945 | Bob Fenimore, Oklahoma A&M | 142 | 1048 | 1978 | Billy Sims, Oklahoma | 231 | 1762 | 160.2 |
| 1946 | Rudy Mobley, Hardin-Simmons | 227 | 1262 | 1979 | Charles White, USC | 293 | 1803 | 180.3 |
| 1947 | Wilton Davis, Hardin-Simmons | 193 | 1173 | 1980 | George Rogers, S. Carolina | 297 | 1781 | 161.9 |
| 1948 | Fred Wendt, Texas Mines | 184 | 1570 | 1981 | Marcus Allen, USC | 403 | 2342 | 212.9 |
| 1949 | John Dottley, Ole Miss | 208 | 1312 | 1982 | Ernest Anderson, Okla. St. | 353 | 1877 | 170.6 |
| 1950 | Wilford White, Arizona St | 199 | 1502 | 1983 | Mike Rozier, Nebraska | 275 | 2148 | 179.0 |
| 1951 | Ollie Matson, San Francisco | 245 | 1566 | 1984 | Keith Byars, Ohio St. | 313 | 1655 | 150.5 |
| 1952 | Howie Waugh, Tulsa | 164 | 1372 | 1985 | Lorenzo White, Mich. St. | 386 | 1908 | 173.5 |
| 1953 | J.C. Caroline, Illinois | 194 | 1256 | 1986 | Paul Palmer, Temple | 346 | 1866 | 169.6 |
| 1954 | Art Luppino, Arizona | 179 | 1359 | 1987 | Ickey Woods, UNLV | 259 | 1658 | 150.7 |
| 1955 | Art Luppino, Arizona | 209 | 1313 | 1988 | Barry Sanders, Okla. St. | 344 | 2628 | 238.9 |
| 1956 | Jim Crawford, Wyoming | 200 | 1104 | 1989 | Anthony Thompson, Ind | 358 | 1793 | 163.0 |
| 1957 | Leon Burton, Arizona St | 117 | 1126 | 1990 | Gerald Hudson, Okla. St | 279 | 1642 | 149.3 |
| 1958 | Dick Bass, Pacific | 205 | 1361 | 1991 | Marshall Faulk, S. Diego St. | 201 | 1429 | 158.8 |
| 1959 | Pervis Atkins, New Mexico St | 130 | 971 | 1992 | Marshall Faulk, S. Diego St. | 265 | 1630 | 163.0 |
| 1960 | Bob Gaiters, New Mexico St | 197 | 1338 | 1993 | LeShon Johnson, No. Ill. | 327 | 1976 | 179.6 |
| 1961 | Jim Pilot, New Mexico St | 191 | 1278 | 1994 | Rashaan Salaam, Colorado | 298 | 2055 | 186.8 |
| 1962 | Jim Pilot, New Mexico St | 208 | 1247 | 1995 | Troy Davis, Iowa St. | 345 | 2010 | 182.7 |
| 1963 | Dave Casinelli, Memphis St | 219 | 1016 | 1996 | Troy Davis, Iowa St. | 402 | 2185 | 198.6 |
| 1964 | Brian Piccolo, Wake Forest | 252 | 1044 | 1997 | Ricky Williams, Texas | 279 | 1893 | 172.1 |
| 1965 | Mike Garrett, USC | 267 | 1440 | 1998 | Ricky Williams, Texas | 361 | 2124 | 193.1 |
| 1966 | Ray McDonald, Idaho | 259 | 1329 | 1999 | LaDainian Tomlinson, TCU | 268 | 1850 | 168.2 |
| 1967 | O.J. Simpson, USC | 266 | 1415 | 2000 | LaDainian Tomlinson, TCU | 369 | 2158 | 196.2 |
| 1968 | O.J. Simpson, USC | 355 | 1709 | 2001 | Chance Kretschmer, Nevada | 302 | 1732 | 157.5 |
| 1969 | Steve Owens, Oklahoma | 358 | 1523 | 2002 | Larry Johnson, Penn St. | 271 | 2087 | 160.5 |
| | | | | 2003 | Patrick Cobbs, No. Texas | 307 | 1680 | 152.7 |
| | | | | 2004 | Jamario Thomas, No. Texas | 285 | 1801 | 180.1 |

### All-Purpose Yardage

**Multiple winners:** Marcus Allen, Pervis Atkins, Ryan Benjamin, Troy Davis, Troy Edwards, Louie Giammona, Tom Harmon, Art Luppino, Napolean McCallum, O.J. Simpson, Charles White and Gary Wood (2).

| Year | | Yards | P/Gm | Year | | Yards | P/Gm |
|---|---|---|---|---|---|---|---|
| 1937 | Byron (Whizzer) White, Colorado | 1970 | 246.3 | 1957 | Overton Curtis, Utah St | 1608 | 160.8 |
| 1938 | Parker Hall, Ole Miss | 1420 | 129.1 | 1958 | Dick Bass, Pacific | 1878 | 187.8 |
| 1939 | Tom Harmon, Michigan | 1208 | 151.0 | 1959 | Pervis Atkins, New Mexico St | 1800 | 180.0 |
| 1940 | Tom Harmon, Michigan | 1312 | 164.0 | 1960 | Pervis Atkins, New Mexico St | 1613 | 161.3 |
| 1941 | Bill Dudley, Virginia | 1674 | 186.0 | 1961 | Jim Pilot, New Mexico St | 1606 | 160.6 |
| 1942 | Complete records not available | | | 1962 | Gary Wood, Cornell | 1395 | 155.0 |
| 1943 | Stan Koslowski, Holy Cross | 1411 | 176.4 | 1963 | Gary Wood, Cornell | 1508 | 167.6 |
| 1944 | Red Williams, Minnesota | 1467 | 163.0 | 1964 | Donny Anderson, Texas Tech | 1710 | 171.0 |
| 1945 | Bob Fenimore, Oklahoma A&M | 1577 | 197.1 | 1965 | Floyd Little, Syracuse | 1990 | 199.0 |
| 1946 | Rudy Mobley, Hardin-Simmons | 1765 | 176.5 | 1966 | Frank Quayle, Virginia | 1616 | 161.6 |
| 1947 | Wilton Davis, Hardin-Simmons | 1798 | 179.8 | 1967 | O.J. Simpson, USC | 1700 | 188.9 |
| 1948 | Lou Kusserow, Columbia | 1737 | 193.0 | 1968 | O.J. Simpson, USC | 1966 | 196.6 |
| 1949 | Johnny Papit, Virginia | 1611 | 179.0 | 1969 | Lynn Moore, Army | 1795 | 179.5 |
| 1950 | Wilford White, Arizona St. | 2065 | 206.5 | 1970 | Don McCauley, North Carolina | 2021 | 183.7 |
| 1951 | Ollie Matson, San Francisco | 2037 | 226.3 | 1971 | Ed Marinaro, Cornell | 1932 | 214.7 |
| 1952 | Billy Vessels, Oklahoma | 1512 | 151.2 | 1972 | Howard Stevens, Louisville | 2132 | 213.2 |
| 1953 | J.C. Caroline, Illinois | 1470 | 163.3 | 1973 | Willard Harrell, Pacific | 1777 | 177.7 |
| 1954 | Art Luppino, Arizona | 2193 | 219.3 | 1974 | Louie Giammona, Utah St | 1984 | 198.4 |
| 1955 | Jim Swink, TCU | 1702 | 170.2 | 1975 | Louie Giammona, Utah St | 2045 | 185.9 |
| | & Art Luppino, Arizona | 1702 | 170.2 | 1976 | Tony Dorsett, Pittsburgh | 2021 | 183.7 |
| 1956 | Jack Hill, Utah St | 1691 | 169.1 | 1977 | Earl Campbell, Texas | 1855 | 168.6 |
| | | | | 1978 | Charles White, USC | 2096 | 174.7 |

| Year | | Yards | P/Gm | Year | | Yards | P/Gm |
|---|---|---|---|---|---|---|---|
| 1979 | Charles White, USC | 1941 | 194.1 | 1994 | Rashaan Salaam, Colorado | 2349 | 213.5 |
| 1980 | Marcus Allen, USC | 1794 | 179.4 | 1995 | Troy Davis, Iowa St | 2466 | 224.2 |
| 1981 | Marcus Allen, USC | 2559 | 232.6 | 1996 | Troy Davis, Iowa St | 2364 | 214.9 |
| 1982 | Carl Monroe, Utah | 2036 | 185.1 | 1997 | Troy Edwards, La. Tech | 2144 | 194.9 |
| 1983 | Napoleon McCallum, Navy | 2385 | 216.8 | 1998 | Troy Edwards, La. Tech | 2784 | 232.0 |
| 1984 | Keith Byars, Ohio St | 2284 | 207.6 | 1999 | Trevor Insley, Nevada | 2176 | 197.8 |
| 1985 | Napoleon McCallum, Navy | 2330 | 211.8 | 2000 | Emmett White, Utah St. | 2628 | 238.9 |
| 1986 | Paul Palmer, Temple | 2633 | 239.4 | 2001 | Levron Williams, Indiana | 2201 | 200.1 |
| 1987 | Eric Wilkerson, Kent St | 2074 | 188.6 | 2002 | Larry Johnson, Penn St. | 2655 | 204.2 |
| 1988 | Barry Sanders, Oklahoma St. | 3250 | 295.5 | 2003 | DeAngelo Williams, Memphis | 2113 | 192.1 |
| 1989 | Mike Pringle, CS-Fullerton | 2690 | 244.6 | 2004 | Darren Sproles, Kansas St. | 2067 | 187.9 |
| 1990 | Glyn Milburn, Stanford | 2222 | 202.0 | | | | |
| 1991 | Ryan Benjamin, Pacific | 2995 | 249.6 | | | | |
| 1992 | Ryan Benjamin, Pacific | 2597 | 236.1 | | | | |
| 1993 | LeShon Johnson, Northern Ill. | 2082 | 189.3 | | | | |

## Total Offense

Individual championship decided on Total Yards (1937-69) and on Yards Per Game (since 1970).

**Multiple winners:** Tim Rattay (3); Johnny Bright, Bob Fenimore, Mike Maxwell and Jim McMahon (2).

| Year | | Plays | Yards | Year | | Plays | Yards | P/Gm |
|---|---|---|---|---|---|---|---|---|
| 1937 | Byron (Whizzer) White, Colorado | 224 | 1596 | 1970 | Pat Sullivan, Auburn | 333 | 2856 | 285.6 |
| 1938 | Davey O'Brien, TCU | 291 | 1847 | 1971 | Gary Huff, Florida St. | 386 | 2653 | 241.2 |
| 1939 | Kenny Washington, UCLA | 259 | 1370 | 1972 | Don Strock, Va. Tech | 480 | 3170 | 288.2 |
| 1940 | Johnny Knolla, Creighton | 298 | 1420 | 1973 | Jesse Freitas, San Diego St. | 410 | 2901 | 263.7 |
| 1941 | Bud Schwenk, Washington-MO | 354 | 1928 | 1974 | Steve Joachim, Temple | 331 | 2227 | 222.7 |
| 1942 | Frank Sinkwich, Georgia | 341 | 2187 | 1975 | Gene Swick, Toledo | 490 | 2706 | 246.0 |
| 1943 | Bob Hoernschemeyer, Indiana | 355 | 1648 | 1976 | Tommy Kramer, Rice | 562 | 3272 | 297.5 |
| 1944 | Bob Fenimore, Oklahoma A&M | 241 | 1758 | 1977 | Doug Williams, Gambling | 377 | 3229 | 293.5 |
| 1945 | Bob Fenimore, Oklahoma A&M | 203 | 1641 | 1978 | Mike Ford, SMU | 459 | 2957 | 268.8 |
| 1946 | Travis Bidwell, Auburn | 339 | 1715 | 1979 | Marc Wilson, BYU | 488 | 3580 | 325.5 |
| 1947 | Fred Enke, Arizona | 329 | 1941 | 1980 | Jim McMahon, BYU | 540 | 4627 | 385.6 |
| 1948 | Stan Heath, Nevada-Reno | 233 | 1992 | 1981 | Jim McMahon, BYU | 487 | 3458 | 345.8 |
| 1949 | Johnny Bright, Drake | 275 | 1950 | 1982 | Todd Dillon, Long Beach St | 585 | 3587 | 326.1 |
| 1950 | Johnny Bright, Drake | 320 | 2400 | 1983 | Steve Young, BYU | 531 | 4346 | 395.1 |
| 1951 | Dick Kazmaier, Princeton | 272 | 1827 | 1984 | Robbie Bosco, BYU | 543 | 3932 | 327.7 |
| 1952 | Ted Marchibroda, Detroit | 305 | 1813 | 1985 | Jim Everett, Purdue | 518 | 3589 | 326.3 |
| 1953 | Paul Larson, California | 262 | 1572 | 1986 | Mike Perez, San Jose St. | 425 | 2969 | 329.9 |
| 1954 | George Shaw, Oregon | 276 | 1536 | 1987 | Todd Santos, San Diego St. | 562 | 3688 | 307.3 |
| 1955 | George Welsh, Navy | 203 | 1348 | 1988 | Scott Mitchell, Utah | 589 | 4299 | 390.8 |
| 1956 | John Brodie, Stanford | 295 | 1642 | 1989 | Andre Ware, Houston | 628 | 4661 | 423.7 |
| 1957 | Bob Newman, Washington St | 263 | 1444 | 1990 | David Klingler, Houston | 704 | 5221 | 474.6 |
| 1958 | Dick Bass, Pacific | 218 | 1440 | 1991 | Ty Detmer, BYU | 478 | 4001 | 333.4 |
| 1959 | Dick Norman, Stanford | 319 | 2018 | 1992 | Jimmy Klingler, Houston | 544 | 3768 | 342.6 |
| 1960 | Billy Kilmer, UCLA | 292 | 1889 | 1993 | Chris Vargas, Nevada | 535 | 4332 | 393.8 |
| 1961 | Dave Hoppmann, Iowa St. | 320 | 1638 | 1994 | Mike Maxwell, Nevada | 477 | 3498 | 318.0 |
| 1962 | Terry Baker, Oregon St | 318 | 2276 | 1995 | Mike Maxwell, Nevada | 443 | 3623 | 402.6 |
| 1963 | George Mira, Miami-FL | 394 | 2318 | 1996 | Josh Wallwork, Wyoming | 525 | 4209 | 350.8 |
| 1964 | Jerry Rhome, Tulsa | 470 | 3128 | 1997 | Tim Rattay, La. Tech | 541 | 3968 | 360.7 |
| 1965 | Bill Anderson, Tulsa | 580 | 3343 | 1998 | Tim Rattay, La. Tech | 602 | 4840 | 403.3 |
| 1966 | Virgil Carter, BYU | 388 | 2545 | 1999 | Tim Rattay, La. Tech | 562 | 3810 | 381.0 |
| 1967 | Sal Olivas, New Mexico St. | 368 | 2184 | 2000 | Drew Brees, Purdue | 564 | 3939 | 358.1 |
| 1968 | Greg Cook Cincinnati | 507 | 3210 | 2001 | Rex Grossman, Florida | 429 | 3904 | 354.9 |
| 1969 | Dennis Shaw, San Diego St | 388 | 3197 | 2002 | Byron Leftwich, Marshall | 528 | 4267 | 355.6 |
| | | | | 2003 | B.J. Symons, Texas Tech | 798 | 5976 | 459.7 |
| | | | | 2004 | Sonny Cumbie, Texas Tech | 694 | 4575 | 381.3 |

## Sacks

Pass sacks have only been compiled by the NCAA since the 2000 season.

| Year | | Gms | Total | Year | | Gms | Total |
|---|---|---|---|---|---|---|---|
| 2000 | Michael Josiah, Louisville | 91 | 12½ | 2003 | Dave Ball, UCLA | 13 | 16½ |
| 2001 | Dwight Freeney, Syracuse | 12 | 17½ | | Kenechi Udeze, USC | 13 | 16½ |
| 2002 | Terrell Suggs, Arizona St. | 14 | 24 | | & D.D. Acholonu, Wash. St. | 13 | 16½ |
| | | | | 2004 | Jonathan Goddard, Marshall | 12 | 16 |

## Annual NCAA Division I-A Leaders (Cont.)
### Passing

Individual championship decided on Completions (1937-69), on Completions Per Game (1970-78) and on Passing Efficiency rating points (since 1979).

**Multiple winners:** Elvis Grbac, Don Heinrich, Jim McMahon, Davey O'Brien and Don Trull (2).

| Year | | Cmp | Pct | TD | Yds |
|---|---|---|---|---|---|
| 1937 | Davey O'Brien, TCU. | .94 | .402 | – | 969 |
| 1938 | Davey O'Brien, TCU. | .93 | .557 | – | 1457 |
| 1939 | Kay Eakin, Arkansas. | .78 | .404 | – | 962 |
| 1940 | Billy Sewell, Wash. St | .86 | .494 | – | 1023 |
| 1941 | Bud Schwenk, Wash.-MO | ..114 | .487 | – | 1457 |
| 1942 | Ray Evans, Kansas | .101 | .505 | – | 1117 |
| 1943 | Johnny Cook, Georgia. | .73 | .465 | – | 1007 |
| 1944 | Paul Rickards, Pittsburgh | .84 | .472 | – | 997 |
| 1945 | Al Dekdebrun, Cornell | .90 | .464 | – | 1227 |
| 1946 | Travis Tidwell, Auburn | .79 | .500 | 5 | 943 |
| 1947 | Charlie Conerly, Ole Miss | .133 | .571 | 18 | 1367 |
| 1948 | Stan Heath, Nev-Reno | .126 | .568 | 22 | 2005 |
| 1949 | Adrian Burk, Baylor | .110 | .576 | 14 | 1428 |
| 1950 | Don Heinrich, Washington | .134 | .606 | 14 | 1846 |
| 1951 | Don Klosterman, Loyola-CA | .159 | .505 | 9 | 1843 |
| 1952 | Don Heinrich, Washington | .137 | .507 | 13 | 1647 |
| 1953 | Bob Garrett, Stanford | .118 | .576 | 17 | 1637 |
| 1954 | Paul Larson, California | .125 | .641 | 10 | 1537 |
| 1955 | George Welsh, Navy. | .94 | .627 | 8 | 1319 |
| 1956 | John Brodie, Stanford | .139 | .579 | 12 | 1633 |
| 1957 | Ken Ford, H-Simmons | .115 | .561 | 14 | 1254 |
| 1958 | Buddy Humphrey, Baylor | .112 | .574 | 7 | 1316 |
| 1959 | Dick Norman, Stanford | .152 | .578 | 11 | 1963 |
| 1960 | Harold Stephens, H-Simm | .145 | .566 | 3 | 1254 |
| 1961 | Chon Gallegos, S. Jose St | .117 | .594 | 14 | 1480 |
| 1962 | Don Trull, Baylor | .125 | .546 | 11 | 1627 |
| 1963 | Don Trull, Baylor | .174 | .565 | 12 | 2157 |
| 1964 | Jerry Rhome, Tulsa | .224 | .687 | 32 | 2870 |
| 1965 | Bill Anderson, Tulsa | .296 | .582 | 30 | 3464 |
| 1966 | John Eckman, Wichita St | .195 | .426 | 7 | 2339 |
| 1967 | Terry Stone, N. Mexico | .160 | .476 | 9 | 1946 |
| 1968 | Chuck Hixson, SMU. | .265 | .566 | 21 | 3103 |
| 1969 | John Reaves, Florida | .222 | .561 | 24 | 2896 |

| Year | | Cmp | P/Gm | TD | Yds |
|---|---|---|---|---|---|
| 1970 | Sonny Sixkiller, Wash. | .186 | 18.6 | 15 | 2303 |
| 1971 | Brian Sipe, S. Diego St | .196 | 17.8 | 17 | 2532 |
| 1972 | Don Strock, Va. Tech | .228 | 20.7 | 16 | 3243 |
| 1973 | Jesse Freitas, S. Diego St. | .227 | 20.6 | 21 | 2993 |
| 1974 | Steve Bartkowski, Cal | .182 | 16.5 | 12 | 2580 |
| 1975 | Craig Penrose, S. Diego St. | .198 | 18.0 | 15 | 2660 |
| 1976 | Tommy Kramer, Rice. | .269 | 24.5 | 21 | 3317 |
| 1977 | Guy Benjamin, Stanford | .208 | 20.8 | 19 | 2521 |
| 1978 | Steve Dils, Stanford | .247 | 22.5 | 22 | 2943 |

| Year | | Cmp | TD | Yds | Rating |
|---|---|---|---|---|---|
| 1979 | Turk Schonert, Stanford | .148 | 19 | 1922 | 163.0 |
| 1980 | Jim McMahon, BYU | .284 | 47 | 4571 | 176.9 |
| 1981 | Jim McMahon, BYU | .272 | 30 | 3555 | 155.0 |
| 1982 | Tom Ramsey, UCLA. | .191 | 21 | 2824 | 153.5 |
| 1983 | Steve Young, BYU. | .306 | 33 | 3902 | 168.5 |
| 1984 | Doug Flutie, BC. | .233 | 27 | 3454 | 152.9 |
| 1985 | Jim Harbaugh, Michigan. | .139 | 18 | 1913 | 163.7 |
| 1986 | Vinny Testaverde, Miami-FL | .175 | 26 | 2557 | 165.8 |
| 1987 | Don McPherson, Syracuse. | .129 | 22 | 2341 | 164.3 |
| 1988 | Timm Rosenbach, Wash. St. | 199 | 23 | 2791 | 162.0 |
| 1989 | Ty Detmer, BYU | .265 | 32 | 4560 | 175.6 |
| 1990 | Shawn Moore, Virginia | .144 | 21 | 2262 | 160.7 |
| 1991 | Elvis Grbac, Michigan | .152 | 24 | 1955 | 169.0 |
| 1992 | Elvis Grbac, Michigan | .112 | 15 | 1465 | 154.2 |
| 1993 | Trent Dilfer, Fresno St. | .217 | 28 | 3276 | 173.1 |
| 1994 | Kerry Collins, Penn St. | .176 | 21 | 2679 | 172.9 |
| 1995 | Danny Wuerffel, Florida | .210 | 35 | 3266 | 178.4 |
| 1996 | Steve Sarkisian, BYU | .278 | 33 | 4027 | 173.6 |
| 1997 | Cade McNown, UCLA. | .173 | 22 | 2877 | 168.6 |
| 1998 | Shaun King, Tulane | .223 | 36 | 3232 | 183.3 |
| 1999 | Michael Vick, Va. Tech. | .90 | 12 | 1840 | 180.4 |
| 2000 | Bart Hendricks, Boise St. | .210 | 35 | 3364 | 170.6 |
| 2001 | Rex Grossman, Florida | .259 | 34 | 3896 | 170.8 |
| 2002 | Brad Banks, Iowa | .170 | 26 | 2573 | 157.1 |
| 2003 | Philip Rivers, N.C. State | .348 | 34 | 4491 | 170.5 |
| 2004 | Stefan Lefors, Louisville | .189 | 20 | 2596 | 181.7 |

### Receptions

Championship decided on Passes Caught (1937-69) and on Catches Per Game (since 1970). Touchdown totals unavailable in 1939 and 1941-45.

**Multiple winners:** Neil Armstrong, Hugh Campell, Manny Hazard, Reid Moseley, Jason Phillips, Howard Twilley and Alex Van Dyke (2).

| Year | | No | TD | Yds |
|---|---|---|---|---|
| 1937 | Jim Benton, Arkansas | .47 | 7 | 754 |
| 1938 | Sam Boyd, Baylor | .32 | 5 | 537 |
| 1939 | Ken Kavanaugh, LSU | .30 | – | 467 |
| 1940 | Eddie Bryant, Virginia | .30 | 2 | 222 |
| 1941 | Hank Stanton, Arizona | .50 | – | 820 |
| 1942 | Bill Rogers, Texas A&M | .39 | – | 432 |
| 1943 | Neil Armstrong, Okla. A&M | .39 | – | 317 |
| 1944 | Reid Moseley, Georgia | .32 | – | 506 |
| 1945 | Reid Moseley, Georgia | .31 | – | 662 |
| 1946 | Neil Armstrong, Okla. A&M | .32 | 1 | 479 |
| 1947 | Barney Poole, Ole Miss | .52 | 8 | 513 |
| 1948 | Red O'Quinn, Wake Forest | .39 | 7 | 605 |
| 1949 | Art Weiner, N. Carolina | .52 | 7 | 762 |
| 1950 | Gordon Cooper, Denver | .46 | 8 | 569 |
| 1951 | Dewey McConnell, Wyoming | ..47 | 9 | 725 |
| 1952 | Ed Brown, Fordham | .57 | 6 | 774 |
| 1953 | John Carson, Georgia | .45 | 4 | 663 |
| 1954 | Jim Hanifan, California | .44 | 7 | 569 |
| 1955 | Hank Burnine, Missouri | .44 | 2 | 594 |
| 1956 | Art Powell, San Jose St | .40 | 5 | 583 |
| 1957 | Stuart Vaughan, Utah | .53 | 5 | 756 |

| Year | | No | TD | Yds |
|---|---|---|---|---|
| 1958 | Dave Hibbert, Arizona | .61 | 4 | 606 |
| 1959 | Chris Burford, Stanford | .61 | 6 | 756 |
| 1960 | Hugh Campbell, Wash. St | .66 | 10 | 881 |
| 1961 | Hugh Campbell, Wash. St | .53 | 5 | 723 |
| 1962 | Vern Burke, Oregon St | .69 | 10 | 1007 |
| 1963 | Lawrence Elkins, Baylor | .70 | 8 | 873 |
| 1964 | Howard Twilley, Tulsa | .95 | 13 | 1178 |
| 1965 | Howard Twilley, Tulsa | .134 | 16 | 1779 |
| 1966 | Glenn Meltzer, Wichita St | .91 | 4 | 1115 |
| 1967 | Bob Goodridge, Vanderbilt | .79 | 6 | 1114 |
| 1968 | Ron Sellers, Florida St | .86 | 12 | 1496 |
| 1969 | Jerry Hendren, Idaho | .95 | 12 | 1452 |

| Year | | No | P/Gm | TD | Yds |
|---|---|---|---|---|---|
| 1970 | Mike Mikolayunas, Davidson | 87 | 8.7 | 8 | 1128 |
| 1971 | Tom Reynolds, San Diego St | .67 | 6.7 | 7 | 1070 |
| 1972 | Tom Forzani, Utah St | .85 | 7.7 | 8 | 1169 |
| 1973 | Jay Miller, BYU | .100 | 9.1 | 8 | 1181 |
| 1974 | D. McDonald, San Diego St | .86 | 7.8 | 7 | 1157 |
| 1975 | Bob Farnham, Brown | .56 | 6.2 | 2 | 701 |
| 1976 | Billy Ryckman, La. Tech | .77 | 7.0 | 10 | 1382 |
| 1977 | W. Tolleson, W. Carolina | .73 | 6.6 | 7 | 1101 |

| Year | | No | P/Gm | TD | Yds |
|---|---|---|---|---|---|
| 1978 | Dave Petzke, Northern Ill | 91 | 8.3 | 11 | 1217 |
| 1979 | Rick Beasley, Appalach. St | 74 | 6.7 | 12 | 1205 |
| 1980 | Dave Young, Purdue | 67 | 6.1 | 8 | 917 |
| 1981 | Pete Harvey, N. Texas St | 57 | 6.3 | 3 | 743 |
| 1982 | Vincent White, Stanford. | 68 | 6.8 | 8 | 677 |
| 1983 | Keith Edwards, Vanderbilt | 97 | 8.8 | 8 | 909 |
| 1984 | David Williams, Illinois | 101 | 9.2 | 8 | 1278 |
| 1985 | Rodney Carter, Purdue | 98 | 8.9 | 4 | 1099 |
| 1986 | Mark Templeton, L. Beach St | 99 | 9.0 | 2 | 688 |
| 1987 | Jason Phillips, Houston | 99 | 9.0 | 3 | 875 |
| 1988 | Jason Phillips, Houston | 108 | 9.8 | 15 | 1444 |
| 1989 | Manny Hazard, Houston | 142 | 12.9 | 22 | 1689 |
| 1990 | Manny Hazard, Houston | 78 | 7.8 | 9 | 946 |
| 1991 | Fred Gilbert, Houston | 106 | 9.6 | 7 | 957 |
| 1992 | Sherman Smith, Houston | 103 | 9.4 | 6 | 923 |
| 1993 | Chris Penn, Tulsa | 105 | 9.6 | 12 | 1578 |
| 1994 | Alex Van Dyke, Nevada | 98 | 8.9 | 10 | 1246 |
| 1995 | Alex Van Dyke, Nevada | 129 | 11.7 | 16 | 1854 |
| 1996 | Damond Wilkins, Nevada | 114 | 10.4 | 4 | 1121 |
| 1997 | Eugene Baker, Kent | 103 | 9.4 | 18 | 1549 |
| 1998 | Troy Edwards, La. Tech | 140 | 11.7 | 27 | 1996 |
| 1999 | Trevor Insley, Nevada | 134 | 12.2 | 13 | 2060 |
| 2000 | James Jordan, La. Tech | 109 | 9.1 | 4 | 1003 |
| 2001 | Kevin Curtis, Utah St. | 100 | 9.1 | 10 | 1531 |
| 2002 | Nate Burleson, Nevada | 138 | 11.5 | 12 | 1629 |
| 2003 | Lance Moore, Toledo | 103 | 8.6 | 9 | 1194 |
| 2004 | Dante Ridgeway, Ball St. | 105 | 9.6 | 8 | 1399 |

## Scoring

Championship decided on Total Points (1937-69) and on Points Per Game (since 1970).

**Multiple winners:** Tom Harmon and Billy Sims (2).

| Year | | TD | XP | FG | Pts | P/Gm |
|---|---|---|---|---|---|---|
| 1937 | Byron (Whizzer) White, Colo | 16 | 23 | 1 | 122 | |
| 1938 | Parker Hall, Ole Miss | 11 | 7 | 0 | 73 | |
| 1939 | Tom Harmon, Michigan | 14 | 15 | 1 | 102 | |
| 1940 | Tom Harmon, Michigan | 16 | 18 | 1 | 117 | |
| 1941 | Bill Dudley, Virginia | 18 | 23 | 1 | 134 | |
| 1942 | Bob Steuber, Missouri | 18 | 13 | 0 | 121 | |
| 1943 | Steve Van Buren, LSU | 14 | 14 | 0 | 98 | |
| 1944 | Glenn Davis, Army | 20 | 0 | 0 | 120 | |
| 1945 | Doc Blanchard, Army. | 19 | 1 | 0 | 115 | |
| 1946 | Gene Roberts, Tenn-Chatt. | 18 | 9 | 0 | 117 | |
| 1947 | Lou Gambino, Maryland | 16 | 0 | 0 | 96 | |
| 1948 | Fred Wendt, Texas Mines. | 20 | 32 | 0 | 152 | |
| 1949 | George Thomas, Oklahoma | 19 | 3 | 0 | 117 | |
| 1950 | Bobby Reynolds, Nebraska. | 22 | 25 | 0 | 157 | |
| 1951 | Ollie Matson, San Francisco | 21 | 0 | 0 | 126 | |
| 1952 | Jackie Parker, Miss. St. | 16 | 24 | 0 | 120 | |
| 1953 | Earl Lindley, Utah St. | 13 | 3 | 0 | 81 | |
| 1954 | Art Luppino, Arizona | 24 | 22 | 0 | 166 | |
| 1955 | Jim Swink, TCU | 20 | 5 | 0 | 125 | |
| 1956 | Clendon Thomas, Oklahoma. | 18 | 0 | 0 | 108 | |
| 1957 | Leon Burton, Ariz. St. | 16 | 0 | 0 | 96 | |
| 1958 | Dick Bass, Pacific | 18 | 8 | 0 | 116 | |
| 1959 | Pervis Atkins, N. Mexico St. | 17 | 5 | 0 | 107 | |
| 1960 | Bob Gaiters, N. Mexico St. | 23 | 7 | 0 | 145 | |
| 1961 | Jim Pilot, N. Mexico St. | 21 | 12 | 0 | 138 | |
| 1962 | Jerry Logan, W. Texas St | 13 | 32 | 0 | 110 | |
| 1963 | Cosmo Iacavazzi, Princeton | 14 | 0 | 0 | 84 | |
| | & Dave Casinelli, Memphis St. | 14 | 0 | 0 | 84 | |
| 1964 | Brian Piccolo, Wake Forest | 17 | 9 | 0 | 111 | |
| 1965 | Howard Twilley, Tulsa | 16 | 31 | 0 | 127 | |
| 1966 | Ken Hebert, Houston | 11 | 41 | 2 | 113 | |
| 1967 | Leroy Keyes, Purdue | 19 | 0 | 0 | 114 | |
| 1968 | Jim O'Brien, Cincinnati | 12 | 31 | 13 | 142 | |
| 1969 | Steve Owens, Oklahoma | 23 | 0 | 0 | 138 | |
| 1970 | Brian Bream, Air Force | 20 | 0 | 0 | 120 | 12.0 |
| | & Gary Kosins, Dayton | 18 | 0 | 0 | 108 | 12.0 |
| 1971 | Ed Marinaro, Cornell | 24 | 4 | 0 | 148 | 16.4 |
| 1972 | Harold Henson, Ohio St | 20 | 0 | 0 | 120 | 12.0 |
| 1973 | Jim Jennings, Rutgers | 21 | 2 | 0 | 128 | 11.6 |
| 1974 | Bill Marek, Wisconsin | 19 | 0 | 0 | 114 | 12.7 |
| 1975 | Pete Johnson, Ohio St | 25 | 0 | 0 | 150 | 13.6 |
| 1976 | Tony Dorsett, Pitt | 22 | 2 | 0 | 134 | 12.2 |
| 1977 | Earl Campbell, Texas | 19 | 0 | 0 | 114 | 10.4 |
| 1978 | Billy Sims, Oklahoma | 20 | 0 | 0 | 120 | 10.9 |
| 1979 | Billy Sims, Oklahoma | 22 | 0 | 0 | 132 | 12.0 |
| 1980 | Sammy Winder, So. Miss | 20 | 0 | 0 | 120 | 10.9 |
| 1981 | Marcus Allen, USC | 23 | 0 | 0 | 138 | 12.5 |
| 1982 | Greg Allen, Fla. St | 21 | 0 | 0 | 126 | 11.5 |
| 1983 | Mike Rozier, Nebraska | 29 | 0 | 0 | 174 | 14.5 |
| 1984 | Keith Byars, Ohio St | 24 | 0 | 0 | 144 | 13.1 |
| 1985 | Bernard White, B. Green. | 19 | 0 | 0 | 114 | 10.4 |
| 1986 | Steve Bartalo, Colo. St. | 19 | 0 | 0 | 114 | 10.4 |
| 1987 | Paul Hewitt, S. Diego St. | 24 | 0 | 0 | 144 | 12.0 |
| 1988 | Barry Sanders, Okla.St. | 39 | 0 | 0 | 234 | 21.3 |
| 1989 | Anthony Thompson, Ind | 25 | 4 | 0 | 154 | 14.0 |
| 1990 | Stacey Robinson, No. Ill. | 19 | 6 | 0 | 120 | 10.9 |
| 1991 | Marshall Faulk, S.D. St. | 23 | 2 | 0 | 140 | 15.6 |
| 1992 | Garrison Hearst, Georgia | 21 | 0 | 0 | 126 | 11.5 |
| 1993 | Bam Morris, Texas Tech | 22 | 2 | 0 | 134 | 12.2 |
| 1994 | Rashaan Salaam, Colo | 24 | 0 | 0 | 144 | 13.1 |
| 1995 | Eddie George, Ohio St. | 24 | 0 | 0 | 144 | 12.0 |
| 1996 | Corey Dillon, Washington | 23 | 0 | 0 | 138 | 12.6 |
| 1997 | Ricky Williams, Texas | 25 | 2 | 0 | 152 | 13.8 |
| 1998 | Troy Edwards, La. Tech | 31 | 2 | 0 | 188 | 15.7 |
| 1999 | Shaun Alexander, Alabama | 24 | 0 | 0 | 144 | 13.1 |
| 2000 | Lee Suggs, Va. Tech | 28 | 0 | 0 | 168 | 15.3 |
| 2001 | Luke Staley, BYU | 28 | 2 | 0 | 170 | 15.5 |
| 2002 | Brock Forsey, Boise St. | 32 | 0 | 0 | 192 | 14.8 |
| 2003 | Patrick Cobbs, No. Texas | 21 | 0 | 0 | 126 | 11.5 |
| 2004 | Tyler Jones, Boise St. | 0 | 69 | 24 | 141 | 11.8 |

DID YOU KNOW?

USC's Heisman-winning quarterback Matt Leinart threw an Orange Bowl-record five touchdown passes in the Trojans' blowout win over the Oklahoma Sooner in the 2005 BCS Championship Game. **Did you know**, that Iowa's Chuck Long holds the NCAA bowl game record with six touchdown passes for the Hawkeyes in the 1984 Freedom Bowl? Long also holds the unofficial record for the best name for a quarterback ever.

## All-Time NCAA Division I-A Leaders

Through the 2004 regular season. The NCAA does not recognize active players among career Per Game leaders.

### CAREER

#### Passing
(Minimum 500 Completions)

| Passing Efficiency | Years | Rating |
|---|---|---|
| 1 Ryan Dinwiddie, Boise St. | 2000-03 | 168.4 |
| 2 Danny Wuerffel, Florida | 1993-96 | 163.6 |
| 3 Ty Detmer, BYU | 1988-91 | 162.7 |
| 4 Steve Sarkisian, BYU | 1995-96 | 162.0 |
| 5 Billy Blanton, San Diego St. | 1993-96 | 157.1 |

| Yards Gained | Years | Yards |
|---|---|---|
| 1 Timmy Chang, Hawaii | 2000-04 | 17,072 |
| 2 Ty Detmer, BYU | 1988-91 | 15,031 |
| 3 Philip Rivers, N.C. State | 2000-03 | 13,484 |
| 4 Tim Rattay, La. Tech | 1997-99 | 12,746 |
| 5 Luke McCown, La. Tech | 2000-03 | 12,666 |

| Completions | Years | No |
|---|---|---|
| 1 Timmy Chang, Hawaii | 2000-04 | 1388 |
| 2 Kliff Kingsbury, Texas Tech | 1999-02 | 1231 |
| 3 Philip Rivers, N.C. State | 2000-03 | 1147 |
| 4 Chris Redman, Louisville | 1996-99 | 1031 |
| 5 Tim Rattay, La. Tech | 1997-99 | 1015 |

#### Receptions

| Catches | Years | No |
|---|---|---|
| 1 Taylor Stubblefield, Purdue | 2001-04 | 316 |
| 2 Josh Davis, Marshall | 2001-04 | 306 |
| 3 Arnold Jackson, Louisville | 1997-00 | 300 |
| 4 Trevor Insley, Nevada | 1996-99 | 298 |
| 5 Geoff Noisy, Nevada | 1995-98 | 295 |

| Catches Per Game | Years | No | P/Gm |
|---|---|---|---|
| 1 Manny Hazard, Houston | 1989-90 | 220 | 10.5 |
| 2 Alex Van Dyke, Nevada | 1994-95 | 227 | 10.3 |
| 3 Howard Twilley, Tulsa | 1963-65 | 261 | 10.0 |
| 4 Jason Phillips, Houston | 1987-88 | 207 | 9.4 |
| 5 Troy Edwards, La. Tech | 1996-98 | 280 | 8.2 |

| Yards Gained | Years | No | Yards |
|---|---|---|---|
| 1 Trevor Insley, Nevada | 1996-99 | 298 | 5005 |
| 2 Marcus Harris, Wyoming | 1993-96 | 259 | 4518 |
| 3 Rashaun Woods, Oklahoma St. | 2000-03 | 293 | 4412 |
| 4 Ryan Yarborough, Wyoming | 1990-93 | 229 | 4357 |
| 5 Troy Edwards, La. Tech | 1996-98 | 280 | 4352 |

### Rushing

| Yards Gained | Years | Yards |
|---|---|---|
| 1 Ron Dayne, Wisconsin | 1996-99 | 6397 |
| 2 Ricky Williams, Texas | 1995-98 | 6279 |
| 3 Tony Dorsett, Pittsburgh | 1973-76 | 6082 |
| 4 Charles White, USC | 1976-79 | 5598 |
| 5 Travis Prentice, Miami-OH | 1996-99 | 5596 |

| Yards Per Game | Years | Yards | P/Gm |
|---|---|---|---|
| 1 Ed Marinaro, Cornell | 1969-71 | 4715 | 174.6 |
| 2 O.J. Simpson, USC | 1967-68 | 3124 | 164.4 |
| 3 Herschel Walker, Georgia | 1980-82 | 5259 | 159.4 |
| 4 LeShon Johnson, No. Ill. | 1992-93 | 3314 | 150.6 |
| 5 Ron Dayne, Wisconsin | 1996-99 | 6397 | 148.8 |

### Total Offense

| Yards Gained | Years | Yards |
|---|---|---|
| 1 Timmy Chang, Hawaii | 2000-04 | 16,910 |
| 2 Ty Detmer, BYU | 1988-91 | 14,665 |
| 3 Philip Rivers, N.C. State | 2000-03 | 13,582 |
| 4 Luke McCown, La. Tech | 2000-03 | 12,731 |
| 5 Tim Rattay, La. Tech | 1997-99 | 12,618 |

| Yards Per Game | Years | Yards | P/Gm |
|---|---|---|---|
| 1 Tim Rattay, La. Tech | 1997-99 | 12,689 | 382.4 |
| 2 Chris Vargas, Nevada | 1992-93 | 6,417 | 320.9 |
| 3 Timmy Chang, Hawaii | 2000-04 | 16,910 | 319.1 |
| 4 Ty Detmer, BYU | 1988-91 | 14,665 | 318.8 |
| 5 Daunte Culpepper*, C. Fla. | 1996-98 | 10,344 | 313.5 |

*Culpepper played I-AA with Central Florida in 1995.

### All-Purpose Yardage

| Yards Gained | Years | Yards |
|---|---|---|
| 1 Ricky Williams, Texas | 1995-98 | 7206 |
| 2 Napoleon McCallum, Navy | 1981-85 | 7172 |
| 3 Darrin Nelson, Stanford | 1977-78, 80-81 | 6885 |
| 4 Kevin Faulk, LSU | 1995-98 | 6833 |
| 5 Darren Sproles, Kansas St. | 2001-04 | 6812 |

| Yards Per Game | Years | Yards | P/Gm |
|---|---|---|---|
| 1 Ryan Benjamin, Pacific | 1990-92 | 5706 | 237.8 |
| 2 Sheldon Canley, S. Jose St. | 1988-90 | 5146 | 205.8 |
| 3 Howard Stevens, Louisville | 1971-72 | 3873 | 193.7 |
| 4 O.J. Simpson, USC | 1967-68 | 3666 | 192.9 |
| 5 Alex Van Dyke, Nevada | 1994-95 | 4146 | 188.5 |

### Miscellaneous

| Punting Average* | Years | Avg |
|---|---|---|
| 1 Shane Lechler, Texas A&M | 1996-99 | 44.7 |
| 2 Bill Smith, Mississippi | 1983-86 | 44.3 |
| 3 Jim Arnold, Vanderbilt | 1979-82 | 43.9 |
| 4 Ralf Mojsiejenko, Michigan St. | 1981-84 | 43.6 |
| 5 Jim Miller, Mississippi | 1976-79 | 43.4 |

*Minimum 250 punts.

| Punting Return Average* | Years | Avg |
|---|---|---|
| 1 Jack Mitchell, Oklahoma | 1946-48 | 23.6 |
| 2 Gene Gibson, Cincinnati | 1949-50 | 20.5 |
| 3 Eddie Macon, Pacific | 1949-51 | 18.9 |
| 4 Jackie Robinson, UCLA | 1939-40 | 18.8 |
| 5 Dan Shelton, N. Illinois | 2001-04 | 17.9 |

*Minimum 1.2 punt returns per game and 30 career returns.

| Kickoff Return Average* | Years | Avg |
|---|---|---|
| 1 Anthony Davis, USC | 1972-74 | 35.1 |
| 2 Eric Booth, So. Miss. | 1994-97 | 32.4 |
| 3 Overton Curtis, Utah St | 1957-58 | 31.0 |
| 4 Fred Montgomery, New Mexico St. | 1991-92 | 30.5 |
| 5 Altie Taylor, Utah St. | 1966-68 | 29.3 |

*Minimum 1.2 kickoff returns per game and 30 career returns.

| Interceptions | Years | No |
|---|---|---|
| 1 Al Brosky, Illinois | 1950-52 | 29 |
| 2 John Provost, Holy Cross | 1972-74 | 27 |
| Martin Bayless, Bowling Green | 1980-83 | 27 |
| 4 Tom Curtis, Michigan | 1967-69 | 25 |
| Tony Thurman, Boston College | 1981-84 | 25 |
| Tracy Saul, Texas Tech. | 1989-92 | 25 |

| Blocked Kicks | Years | FG | XP | P | Tot |
|---|---|---|---|---|---|
| 1 James Ferebee, N. Mexico St. | 1978-81 | 8 | 6 | 5 | 19 |
| 2 Max McGeary, Baylor | 1977-80 | 6 | 4 | 6 | 16 |
| 3 James King, C. Michigan | 2001-04 | 2 | 10 |   | 13 |
| 4 Terrence Holt, N.C. State | 1999-02 | 8 | 0 | 4 | 12 |
| 5 Matt Harding, Hawaii | 1992-95 | 5 | 1 | 6 | 12 |

**Note:** The blocked kicks category is a combined total of blocked field goals (FG), extra points (XP) and punts (P).

> **Editor's Note:** The keeping of complete defensive statistics, except for blocked kicks (see above), had been inconsistent until recently, as a result the NCAA only tracks most defensive stats back to 2000 and due to the lack of historical context, those records have been omitted here.

## Scoring
### Non-kickers

| Points | Years | TD | Xpt | FG | Pts |
|---|---|---|---|---|---|
| 1 Travis Prentice, Miami-OH | 1996-99 | 78 | 0 | 0 | 468 |
| 2 Ricky Williams, Texas | 1995-98 | 75 | 2 | 0 | 452 |
| 3 Brock Forsey, Boise St. | 1999-02 | 68 | 0 | 0 | 408 |
| 4 Cedric Benson, Texas | 2001-04 | 67 | 1 | 0 | 404 |
| 5 Anthony Thompson, Ind. | 1986-89 | 65 | 4 | 0 | 394 |

| Points Per Game | Years | Pts | P/Gm |
|---|---|---|---|
| 1 Marshall Faulk, S. Diego St. | 1991-93 | 376 | 12.1 |
| 2 Ed Marinaro, Cornell. | 1969-71 | 318 | 11.8 |
| 3 Bill Burnett, Arkansas | 1968-70 | 294 | 11.3 |
| 4 Steve Owens, Oklahoma | 1967-69 | 336 | 11.2 |
| 5 Eddie Talboom, Wyoming | 1948-50 | 303 | 10.8 |

| Touchdowns Rushing | Years | No |
|---|---|---|
| 1 Travis Prentice, Miami-OH | 1996-99 | 73 |
| 2 Ricky Williams, Texas | 1995-98 | 72 |
| 3 Anthony Thompson, Indiana. | 1986-89 | 64 |
| Cedric Benson, Texas | 2001-04 | 64 |
| 5 Ron Dayne, Wisconsin | 1996-99 | 63 |

| Touchdowns Passing | Years | No |
|---|---|---|
| 1 Ty Detmer, BYU. | 1988-91 | 121 |
| 2 Timmy Chang, Hawaii | 2000-04 | 117 |
| 3 Tim Rattay, La. Tech | 1997-99 | 115 |
| 4 Danny Wuerffel, Florida | 1993-96 | 114 |
| 5 Chad Pennington, Marshall | 1997-99 | 100 |

| Touchdowns Catches | Years | No |
|---|---|---|
| 1 Troy Edwards, La. Tech | 1996-98 | 50 |
| 2 Darius Watts, Marshall | 2000-03 | 47 |
| 3 Aaron Turner, Pacific | 1989-92 | 43 |
| 4 Ryan Yarborough, Wyoming | 1990-93 | 42 |
| Rashaun Woods, Oklahoma St. | 2000-03 | 42 |

### Kickers

| Points | Years | FG | XP | Pts |
|---|---|---|---|---|
| 1 Roman Anderson, Hou | 1988-91 | 70 | 213 | 423 |
| 2 Billy Bennett, Georgia | 2000-03 | 87 | 110 | 409 |
| 3 Carlos Huerta, Mia-FL | 1988-91 | 73 | 178 | 397 |
| 4 Jason Elam, Hawaii | 1988-89, 91-92 | 79 | 158 | 395 |
| 5 Nick Novak, Maryland | 2001-04 | 80 | 153 | 393 |
| Derek Schmidt, Florida St. | 1984-87 | 73 | 174 | 393 |

| Field Goals | Years | No |
|---|---|---|
| 1 Billy Bennett, Georgia | 2000-03 | 87 |
| 2 Jeff Jaeger, Washington | 1983-86 | 80 |
| Nick Novak, Maryland | 2001-04 | 80 |
| 4 John Lee, UCLA | 1982-85 | 79 |
| Jason Elam, Hawaii | 1988-89, 91-92 | 79 |

## SINGLE SEASON

Note that starting with the 2002 season postseason and bowl games are included in single season records

### Rushing

| Yards Gained | Year | Gm | Car | Yards |
|---|---|---|---|---|
| Barry Sanders, Okla. St | 1988 | 11 | 344 | 2628 |
| Marcus Allen, USC | 1981 | 11 | 403 | 2342 |
| Troy Davis, Iowa St. | 1996 | 11 | 402 | 2185 |
| LaDainian Tomlinson, TCU | 2000 | 11 | 369 | 2158 |
| Mike Rozier, Nebraska | 1983 | 12 | 275 | 2148 |

| Yards Per Game | Year | Gm | Yards | P/Gm |
|---|---|---|---|---|
| Barry Sanders, Okla. St | 1988 | 11 | 2628 | 238.9 |
| Marcus Allen, USC | 1981 | 11 | 2342 | 212.9 |
| Ed Marinaro, Cornell. | 1971 | 9 | 1881 | 209.0 |
| Troy Davis, Iowa St. | 1996 | 11 | 2185 | 198.6 |
| LaDainian Tomlinson, TCU | 2000 | 11 | 2158 | 196.2 |

### Passing
(Minimum 15 Attempts Per Game)

| Passing Efficiency | Year | Rating |
|---|---|---|
| Shaun King, Tulane | 1998 | 183.3 |
| Stefan Lefors, Louisville | 2004 | 181.7 |
| Michael Vick, Va. Tech | 1999 | 180.4 |
| Danny Wuerffel, Florida | 1995 | 178.4 |
| Jim McMahon, BYU | 1980 | 176.9 |

| Yards Gained | Year | Yards |
|---|---|---|
| B.J. Symons, Texas Tech | 2003 | 5833 |
| Ty Detmer, BYU. | 1990 | 5188 |
| David Klingler, Houston. | 1990 | 5140 |
| Kliff Kingsbury, Texas Tech | 2002 | 5017 |
| Tim Rattay, La. Tech | 1998 | 4943 |

| Completions | Year | Att | No |
|---|---|---|---|
| Kliff Kingsbury, Texas Tech | 2002 | 712 | 479 |
| B.J. Symons, Texas Tech | 2003 | 719 | 470 |
| Tim Rattay, La. Tech | 1998 | 559 | 380 |
| David Klingler, Houston. | 1990 | 643 | 374 |
| Andre Ware, Houston | 1989 | 578 | 365 |

### Receptions

| Catches | Year | Gm | No |
|---|---|---|---|
| Manny Hazard, Houston | 1989 | 11 | 142 |
| Troy Edwards, La. Tech | 1998 | 12 | 140 |
| Nate Burleson, Nevada | 2002 | 12 | 138 |
| Howard Twilley, Tulsa | 1965 | 10 | 134 |
| Trevor Insley, Nevada | 1999 | 11 | 134 |

| Catches Per Game | Year | No | P/Gm |
|---|---|---|---|
| Howard Twilley, Tulsa | 1965 | 134 | 13.4 |
| Manny Hazard, Houston | 1989 | 142 | 12.9 |
| Trevor Insley, Nevada | 1999 | 134 | 12.2 |
| Alex Van Dyke, Nevada | 1995 | 129 | 11.7 |
| Troy Edwards, La. Tech | 1998 | 140 | 11.7 |

| Yards Gained | Year | No | Yards |
|---|---|---|---|
| Trevor Insley, Nevada | 1999 | 134 | 2060 |
| Troy Edwards, La. Tech | 1998 | 140 | 1996 |
| Alex Van Dyke, Nevada | 1995 | 129 | 1854 |
| J.R. Tolver, San Diego St. | 2002 | 128 | 1785 |
| Howard Twilley, Tulsa | 1965 | 134 | 1779 |
| Josh Reed, LSU | 2001 | 94 | 1740 |

### Total Offense

| Yards Gained | Year | Gm | Plays | Yards |
|---|---|---|---|---|
| B.J. Symons, Texas Tech | 2003 | 13 | 798 | 5976 |
| David Klingler, Houston. | 1990 | 11 | 704 | 5221 |
| Ty Detmer, BYU. | 1990 | 12 | 635 | 5022 |
| Kliff Kingsbury, Texas Tech | 2002 | 14 | 814 | 4903 |
| Tim Rattay, La. Tech | 1998 | 12 | 602 | 4840 |

| Yards Per Game | Year | Gm | Yards | P/Gm |
|---|---|---|---|---|
| David Klingler, Houston. | 1990 | 11 | 5221 | 474.6 |
| B.J. Symons, Texas Tech | 2003 | 13 | 5976 | 459.7 |
| Andre Ware, Houston | 1989 | 11 | 4661 | 423.7 |
| Ty Detmer, BYU. | 1990 | 12 | 5022 | 418.5 |
| Tim Rattay, La. Tech | 1998 | 12 | 4840 | 403.3 |

### All-Purpose Yardage

| Yards Gained | Year | Yards |
|---|---|---|
| Barry Sanders, Okla. St | 1988 | 3250 |
| Ryan Benjamin, Pacific | 1991 | 2995 |
| Troy Edwards, La. Tech | 1998 | 2784 |
| Darren Sproles, Kansas St. | 2003 | 2735 |
| Mike Pringle, CS-Fullerton. | 1989 | 2690 |

| Yards Per Game | Year | Yards | P/Gm |
|---|---|---|---|
| Barry Sanders, Okla. St | 1988 | 3250 | 295.5 |
| Ryan Benjamin, Pacific | 1991 | 2995 | 249.6 |
| Byron (Whizzer) White, Colo | 1937 | 1970 | 246.3 |
| Mike Pringle, CS-Fullerton | 1989 | 2690 | 244.6 |
| Paul Palmer, Temple | 1986 | 2633 | 239.4 |

## All-Time NCAA Division I-A Leaders (Cont.)
### SINGLE SEASON
#### Scoring

| Points | Year | TD | Xpt | FG | Pts |
|---|---|---|---|---|---|
| Barry Sanders, Okla. St | 1988 | 39 | 0 | 0 | 234 |
| Brock Forsey, Boise St. | 2002 | 32 | 0 | 0 | 192 |
| Troy Edwards, La. Tech | 1998 | 31 | 2 | 0 | 188 |
| Mike Rozier, Nebraska | 1983 | 29 | 0 | 0 | 174 |
| Lydell Mitchell, Penn St | 1971 | 29 | 0 | 0 | 174 |

| Points Per Game | Year | Pts | P/Gm |
|---|---|---|---|
| Barry Sanders, Okla. St | 1988 | 234 | 21.3 |
| Bobby Reynolds, Nebraska | 1950 | 157 | 17.4 |
| Art Luppino, Arizona | 1954 | 166 | 16.6 |
| Ed Marinaro, Cornell | 1971 | 148 | 16.4 |
| Lydell Mitchell, Penn St | 1971 | 174 | 15.8 |

| Touchdowns Rushing | Year | No |
|---|---|---|
| Barry Sanders, Okla. St | 1988 | 37 |
| Mike Rozier, Nebraska | 1983 | 29 |
| Willis McGahee, Miami-FL | 2002 | 28 |
| Ricky Williams, Texas | 1998 | 27 |
| Lee Suggs, Va. Tech | 2000 | 27 |
| Brock Forsey, Boise St. | 2002 | 26 |

| Touchdowns Passing | Year | No |
|---|---|---|
| David Klingler, Houston | 1990 | 54 |
| B.J. Symons, Texas Tech | 2003 | 52 |
| Jim McMahon, BYU | 1980 | 47 |
| Andre Ware, Houston | 1989 | 46 |
| Tim Rattay, La. Tech | 1998 | 46 |

| Touchdown Catches | Year | No |
|---|---|---|
| Troy Edwards, La. Tech | 1998 | 27 |
| Randy Moss, Marshall | 1997 | 25 |
| Manny Hazard, Houston | 1989 | 22 |
| Larry Fitzgerald, Pittsburgh | 2003 | 22 |
| Desmond Howard, Michigan | 1991 | 19 |
| Ashley Lelie, Hawaii | 2001 | 19 |

| Field Goals | Year | No |
|---|---|---|
| Billy Bennett, Georgia | 2003 | 31 |
| John Lee, UCLA | 1984 | 29 |
| Paul Woodside, West Virginia | 1982 | 28 |
| Luis Zendejas, Arizona St | 1983 | 28 |
| Nick Browne, TCU | 2003 | 28 |

### Miscellaneous

| Interceptions | Year | No |
|---|---|---|
| Al Worley, Washington | 1968 | 14 |
| George Shaw, Oregon | 1951 | 13 |
| Eight tied with 12 each. | | |

| Punting Average* | Year | Avg |
|---|---|---|
| Chad Kessler, LSU | 1997 | 50.3 |
| Reggie Roby, Iowa | 1981 | 49.8 |
| Kirk Wilson, UCLA | 1956 | 49.3 |
| Todd Sauerbrun, West Virginia | 1994 | 48.4 |
| Travis Dorsch, Purdue | 2001 | 48.4 |

*Qualifiers for championship.

| Punt Return Average* | Year | Avg |
|---|---|---|
| Bill Blackstock, Tennessee | 1951 | 25.9 |
| Ted Ginn Jr., Ohio St. | 2004 | 25.6 |
| George Sims, Baylor | 1948 | 25.0 |

*At least 1.2 returns per game.

| Kickoff Return Average* | Year | Avg |
|---|---|---|
| Paul Allen, BYU | 1961 | 40.1 |
| Tremain Mack, Miami-FL | 1996 | 39.5 |
| Leeland McElroy, Texas A&M. | 1993 | 39.3 |
| Forrest Hall, San Francisco | 1946 | 38.2 |
| Tony Ball, Tenn-Chattanooga | 1977 | 36.4 |

*At least 1.2 kickoff returns per game.

### SINGLE GAME

#### Rushing

| Yards Gained | Opponent | Year | Yds |
|---|---|---|---|
| LaDainian Tomlinson, TCU | UTEP | 1999 | 406 |
| Tony Sands, Kansas | Missouri | 1991 | 396 |
| Marshall Faulk, San Diego St | Pacific | 1991 | 386 |
| Troy Davis, Iowa St. | Missouri | 1996 | 378 |
| Anthony Thompson, Indiana | Wisconsin | 1989 | 377 |
| Robbie Mixon, C. Michigan | E. Michigan | 2002 | 377 |

#### Passing

| Yards Gained | Opponent | Year | Yds |
|---|---|---|---|
| David Klingler, Houston | Arizona St. | 1990 | 716 |
| Matt Vogler, TCU | Houston | 1990 | 690 |
| B.J. Symons, Texas Tech | Mississippi | 2003 | 661 |
| Brian Lindgren, Idaho | Mid. Tenn. St. | 2001 | 637 |
| Scott Mitchell, Utah | Air Force | 1988 | 631 |

| Completions | Opponent | Year | No |
|---|---|---|---|
| Drew Brees, Purdue | Wisconsin | 1998 | 55 |
| Rusty LaRue, Wake Forest | Duke | 1995 | 55 |
| Rusty LaRue, Wake Forest | N.C. St. | 1995 | 50 |
| Four tied with 49 each (including twice by Kliff Kingsbury). | | | |

#### Total Offense

| Yards Gained | Opponent | Year | Yds |
|---|---|---|---|
| David Klingler, Houston | Arizona St. | 1990 | 732 |
| Matt Vogler, TCU | Houston | 1990 | 696 |
| B.J. Symons, Texas Tech | Mississippi | 2003 | 681 |
| David Klingler, Houston | TCU | 1990 | 625 |
| Scott Mitchell, Utah | Air Force | 1988 | 625 |

#### Receiving

| Catches | Opponent | Year | No |
|---|---|---|---|
| Randy Gatewood, UNLV. | Idaho | 1994 | 23 |
| Jay Miller, BYU | New Mexico | 1973 | 22 |
| Troy Edwards, La. Tech | Nebraska | 1998 | 21 |
| Chris Daniels, Purdue. | Mich. St. | 1999 | 21 |
| Two tied with 20 each. | | | |

| Yards Gained | Opponent | Year | Yds |
|---|---|---|---|
| Troy Edwards, La. Tech | Nebraska | 1998 | 405 |
| Randy Gatewood, UNLV. | Idaho | 1994 | 363 |
| Chuck Hughes, UTEP* | N. Texas St. | 1965 | 349 |
| Nate Burleson, Nevada | San Jose St. | 2001 | 326 |
| Rick Eber, Tulsa | Idaho St. | 1967 | 322 |

*UTEP was Texas Western in 1965.

## Scoring

| Points | Opponent | Year | Pts |
|---|---|---|---|
| Howard Griffith, Illinois | So. Ill. | 1990 | 48 |
| Marshall Faulk, S. Diego St | Pacific | 1991 | 44 |
| Jim Brown, Syracuse | Colgate | 1956 | 43 |
| Showboat Boykin, Ole Miss | Miss. St. | 1951 | 42 |
| Fred Wendt, UTEP* | N. Mex. St. | 1948 | 42 |
| Rashaun Woods, Oklahoma St. | SMU | 2003 | 42 |

*UTEP was Texas Mines in 1948.

| Touchdowns Rushing | Opponent | Year | No |
|---|---|---|---|
| Howard Griffith, Illinois | So. Ill | 1990 | 8 |
| Showboat Boykin, Ole Miss | Miss. St. | 1951 | 7 |

**Note:** Griffith's TD runs (5-51-7-41-5-18-5-3).

| Touchdown Catches | Opponent | Year | No |
|---|---|---|---|
| Rashaun Woods, Oklahoma St. | SMU | 2003 | 7 |
| Tim Delaney, S. Diego St | N. Mex. St. | 1969 | 6 |

**Note:** Woods's TD catches (2-10-34-32-25-5-11).

| Touchdowns Passing | Opponent | Year | No |
|---|---|---|---|
| David Klingler, Houston | E.Wash. | 1990 | 11 |
| Dennis Shaw, San Diego St | N. Mex. St. | 1969 | 9 |

**Note:** Klingler's TD passes (5-48-29-7-3-7-40-8-7-8-51).

| Field Goals | Opponent | Year | No |
|---|---|---|---|
| Dale Klein, Nebraska | Missouri | 1985 | 7 |
| Mike Prindle, W. Michigan | Marshall | 1984 | 7 |

**Note:** Klein's FGs (32-22-43-44-29-43-43); Prindle's FGs (32-44-42-23-48-41-27).

| Extra Points (Kick) | Opponent | Year | No |
|---|---|---|---|
| Terry Leiweke, Houston | Tulsa | 1968 | 13 |
| Derek Mahoney, Fresno St | New Mexico | 1991 | 13 |

## Longest Plays (since 1941)

| Rushing | Opponent | Year | Yds |
|---|---|---|---|
| Gale Sayers, Kansas | Nebraska | 1963 | 99 |
| Max Anderson, Ariz. St | Wyoming | 1967 | 99 |
| Ralph Thompson, W. Texas St | Wich. St. | 1970 | 99 |
| Kelsey Finch, Tennessee | Florida | 1977 | 99 |
| Eric Vann, Kansas | Oklahoma | 1997 | 99 |

Eleven tied at 98 each.

| Passing | Opponent | Year | Yds |
|---|---|---|---|
| Fred Owens to Jack Ford, Portland | St. Mary's | 1947 | 99 |
| Bo Burris to Warren McVea, Houston | Wash. St. | 1966 | 99 |
| Colin Clapton to Eddie Jenkins, Holy Cross | Boston U. | 1970 | 99 |
| Terry Peel to Robert Ford, Houston | Syracuse | 1970 | 99 |
| Terry Peel to Robert Ford, Houston | S. Diego St. | 1972 | 99 |
| Cris Collinsworth to Derrick Gaffney, Florida | Rice | 1977 | 99 |
| Scott Ankrom to James Maness, TCU | Rice | 1984 | 99 |
| Gino Torretta to Horace Copeland, Miami-FL | Ark. | 1991 | 99 |

| Passing (cont.) | Opponent | Year | Yds |
|---|---|---|---|
| John Paci to Thomas Lewis, Indiana | Penn St. | 1993 | 99 |
| Troy DeGar to West Caswell, Tulsa | Oklahoma | 1996 | 99 |
| Drew Brees to Vinny Sutherland, Purdue | N'western | 1999 | 99 |
| Dan Urban to Justin McCariens, N. Ill | Ball St. | 2000 | 99 |
| Jason Johnson to Brandon Marshall, Ariz. | Idaho | 2001 | 99 |
| Jim Sorgi to Lee Evans, Wisconsin | Akron | 2003 | 99 |
| Dondrial Pinkins to Troy Williamson, South Carolina | Virginia | 2003 | 99 |

| Field Goals | Opponent | Year | Yds |
|---|---|---|---|
| Steve Little, Arkansas | Texas | 1977 | 67 |
| Russell Erxleben, Texas | Rice | 1977 | 67 |
| Joe Williams, Wichita St | So. Ill. | 1978 | 67 |
| Tony Franklin, Tex. A&M | Baylor | 1976 | 65 |
| Martin Gramatica, Kan. St. | No. Ill. | 1998 | 65 |

**Note:** Gramatica's FG is the only one listed above that was not off a tee and through the narrower (18'6") goal posts.

## Longest Division I Streaks

### Winning Streaks
(Including bowl games)

| No | | Seasons | Spoiler | Score |
|---|---|---|---|---|
| 47 | Oklahoma | 1953-57 | Notre Dame | 7-0 |
| 39 | Washington | 1908-14 | Oregon St. | 0-0 |
| 37 | Yale | 1890-93 | Princeton | 6-0 |
| 37 | Yale | 1887-89 | Princeton | 10-0 |
| 35 | Toledo | 1969-71 | Tampa | 21-0 |
| 34 | Miami-FL | 2000-02 | Ohio St. | 31-24* |
| 34 | Penn | 1894-96 | Lafayette | 6-4 |
| 31 | Oklahoma | 1948-50 | Kentucky | 13-7* |
| 31 | Pittsburgh | 1914-18 | Cleve. Naval | 10-9 |
| 31 | Penn | 1896-98 | Harvard | 10-0 |
| 30 | Texas | 1968-70 | Notre Dame | 24-11* |
| 29 | Miami-FL | 1990-93 | Alabama | 34-13 |
| 29 | Michigan | 1901-03 | Minnesota | 6-6 |

*Ohio St. beat Miami in 2003 Fiesta Bowl in double overtime. Kentucky beat Oklahoma in 1951 Sugar Bowl and Notre Dame beat Texas in 1971 Cotton Bowl.

### Unbeaten Streaks
(Including bowl games)

| No W-T | | Seasons | Spoiler | Score |
|---|---|---|---|---|
| 63 | 59-4 Washington | 1907-17 | California | 27-0 |
| 56 | 55-1 Michigan | 1901-05 | Chicago | 2-0 |
| 50 | 46-4 California | 1920-25 | Olympic Club | 15-0 |
| 48 | 47-1 Oklahoma | 1953-57 | N. Dame | 7-0 |
| 48 | 47-1 Yale | 1885-89 | Princeton | 10-0 |
| 47 | 45-2 Yale | 1879-85 | Princeton | 6-5 |
| 44 | 42-2 Yale | 1894-96 | Princeton | 24-6 |
| 42 | 39-3 Yale | 1904-08 | Harvard | 4-0 |
| 39 | 37-2 N. Dame | 1946-50 | Purdue | 28-14 |

### Losing Streaks

| No | | Seasons | Victim | Score |
|---|---|---|---|---|
| 80 | Prairie View | 1989-98 | Langston | 14-12 |
| 44 | Columbia | 1983-88 | Princeton | 16-14 |
| 34 | Northwestern | 1979-82 | No. Illinois | 31-6 |
| 28 | Virginia | 1958-60 | Wm. & Mary | 21-6 |
| 28 | Kansas St | 1944-48 | Arkansas St. | 37-6 |

**Note:** Virginia ended its losing streak in the opening game of the 1961 season.

## Annual Awards
## Heisman Trophy

Originally presented in 1935 as the DAC Trophy by the Downtown Athletic Club of New York City to the best college football player east of the Mississippi. In 1936, players across the country were eligible and the award was renamed the Heisman Trophy following the death of former college coach and DAC athletic director John W. Heisman.

**Multiple winner:** Archie Griffin (2).

**Winners in junior year** (13): Doc Blanchard (1945), Ty Detmer (1990); Archie Griffin (1974), Desmond Howard (1991), Vic Janowicz (1950), Rashaan Salaam (1994), Barry Sanders (1988), Billy Sims (1978), Roger Staubach (1963), Doak Walker (1948), Herschel Walker (1982), Andre Ware (1989) and Charles Woodson (1997).

**Winners on AP national champions** (10): Angelo Bertelli (Notre Dame, 1943); Doc Blanchard (Army, 1945); Tony Dorsett (Pittsburgh, 1976); Leon Hart (Notre Dame, 1949); Johnny Lujack (Notre Dame, 1947); Davey O'Brien (TCU, 1938); Bruce Smith (Minnesota, 1941); Charlie Ward (Florida St., 1993); Danny Wuerffel (Florida, 1996); and Charles Woodson (Michigan, 1997).

| Year | | Points |
|------|---|--------|
| 1935 | **Jay Berwanger,** Chicago, HB | .84 |
| | 2nd–Monk Meyer, Army, HB | .29 |
| | 3rd–Bill Shakespeare, Notre Dame, HB | .23 |
| | 4th–Pepper Constable, Princeton, FB | .20 |
| 1936 | **Larry Kelley,** Yale, E | .219 |
| | 2nd–Sam Francis, Nebraska, FB | .47 |
| | 3rd–Ray Buivid, Marquette, HB | .43 |
| | 4th–Sammy Baugh, TCU, HB | .39 |
| 1937 | **Clint Frank,** Yale, HB | .524 |
| | 2nd–Byron (Whizzer) White, Colo., HB | .264 |
| | 3rd–Marshall Goldberg, Pitt, HB | .211 |
| | 4th–Alex Wojciechowicz, Fordham, C | .85 |
| 1938 | **Davey O'Brien,** TCU, QB | .519 |
| | 2nd–Marshall Goldberg, Pitt, HB | .294 |
| | 3rd–Sid Luckman, Columbia, HB | .154 |
| | 4th–Bob MacLeod, Dartmouth, HB | .78 |
| 1939 | **Nile Kinnick,** Iowa, HB | .651 |
| | 2nd–Tom Harmon, Michigan, HB | .405 |
| | 3rd–Paul Christman, Missouri, QB | .391 |
| | 4th–George Cafego, Tennessee, QB | .296 |
| 1940 | **Tom Harmon,** Michigan, HB | .1303 |
| | 2nd–John Kimbrough, Texas A&M, FB | .841 |
| | 3rd–George Franck, Minnesota, HB | .102 |
| | 4th–Frankie Albert, Stanford, QB | .90 |
| 1941 | **Bruce Smith,** Minnesota, HB | .554 |
| | 2nd–Angelo Bertelli, Notre Dame, QB | .345 |
| | 3rd–Frankie Albert, Stanford, QB | .336 |
| | 4th–Frank Sinkwich, Georgia, HB | .249 |
| 1942 | **Frank Sinkwich,** Georgia, TB | .1059 |
| | 2nd–Paul Governali, Columbia, QB | .218 |
| | 3rd–Clint Castleberry, Ga. Tech, HB | .99 |
| | 4th–Mike Holovak, Boston College, FB | .95 |
| 1943 | **Angelo Bertelli,** Notre Dame, QB | .648 |
| | 2nd–Bob Odell, Penn, HB | .177 |
| | 3rd–Otto Graham, Northwestern, QB | .140 |
| | 4th–Creighton Miller, Notre Dame, HB | .134 |
| 1944 | **Les Horvath,** Ohio St., TB-QB | .412 |
| | 2nd–Glenn Davis, Army, HB | .287 |
| | 3rd–Doc Blanchard, Army, FB | .237 |
| | 4th–Don Whitmire, Navy, T | .115 |
| 1945 | **Doc Blanchard,** Army, FB | .860 |
| | 2nd–Glenn Davis, Army, HB | .638 |
| | 3rd–Bob Fenimore, Oklahoma A&M, HB | .187 |
| | 4th–Herman Wedemeyer, St. Mary's, HB | .152 |
| 1946 | **Glenn Davis,** Army, HB | .792 |
| | 2nd–Charlie Trippi, Georgia, HB | .435 |
| | 3rd–Johnny Lujack, Notre Dame, QB | .379 |
| | 4th–Doc Blanchard, Army, FB | .267 |
| 1947 | **Johnny Lujack,** Notre Dame, QB | .742 |
| | 2nd–Bob Chappuis, Michigan, HB | .555 |
| | 3rd–Doak Walker, SMU, HB | .196 |
| | 4th–Charlie Conerly, Mississippi, QB | .186 |
| 1948 | **Doak Walker,** SMU, HB | .778 |
| | 2nd–Charlie Justice, N. Carolina, HB | .443 |
| | 3rd–Chuck Bednarik, Penn, C | .336 |
| | 4th–Jackie Jensen, California, HB | .143 |
| 1949 | **Leon Hart,** Notre Dame, E | .995 |
| | 2nd–Charlie Justice, N. Carolina, HB | .272 |
| | 3rd–Doak Walker, SMU, HB | .229 |
| | 4th–Arnold Galiffa, Army QB | .196 |

| Year | | Points |
|------|---|--------|
| 1950 | **Vic Janowicz,** Ohio St., HB | .633 |
| | 2nd–Kyle Rote, SMU, HB | .280 |
| | 3rd–Reds Bagnell, Penn, HB | .231 |
| | 4th–Babe Parilli, Kentucky, QB | .214 |
| 1951 | **Dick Kazmaier,** Princeton, TB | .1777 |
| | 2nd–Hank Lauricella, Tennessee, HB | .424 |
| | 3rd–Babe Parilli, Kentucky, QB | .344 |
| | 4th–Bill McColl, Stanford, E | .313 |
| 1952 | **Billy Vessels,** Oklahoma, HB | .525 |
| | 2nd–Jack Scarbath, Maryland, QB | .367 |
| | 3rd–Paul Giel, Minnesota, HB | .329 |
| | 4th–Donn Moomaw, UCLA, C | .257 |
| 1953 | **Johnny Lattner,** Notre Dame, HB | .1850 |
| | 2nd–Paul Giel, Minnesota, HB | .1794 |
| | 3rd–Paul Cameron, UCLA, HB | .444 |
| | 4th–Bernie Faloney, Maryland, QB | .258 |
| 1954 | **Alan Ameche,** Wisconsin, FB | .1068 |
| | 2nd–Kurt Burris, Oklahoma, C | .838 |
| | 3rd–Howard Cassady, Ohio St., HB | .810 |
| | 4th–Ralph Guglielmi, Notre Dame, QB | .691 |
| 1955 | **Howard Cassady,** Ohio St., HB | .2219 |
| | 2nd–Jim Swink, TCU, HB | .742 |
| | 3rd–George Welsh, Navy, QB | .383 |
| | 4th–Earl Morrall, Michigan St., QB | .323 |
| 1956 | **Paul Hornung,** Notre Dame, QB | .1066 |
| | 2nd–Johnny Majors, Tennessee, HB | .994 |
| | 3rd–Tommy McDonald, Oklahoma, HB | .973 |
| | 4th–Jerry Tubbs, Oklahoma, C | .724 |
| 1957 | **John David Crow,** Texas A&M, HB | .1183 |
| | 2nd–Alex Karras, Iowa, T | .693 |
| | 3rd–Walt Kowalczyk, Mich. St., HB | .630 |
| | 4th–Lou Michaels, Kentucky, T | .330 |
| 1958 | **Pete Dawkins,** Army, HB | .1394 |
| | 2nd–Randy Duncan, Iowa, QB | .1021 |
| | 3rd–Billy Cannon, LSU, HB | .975 |
| | 4th–Bob White, Ohio St., FB | .365 |
| 1959 | **Billy Cannon,** LSU, HB | .1929 |
| | 2nd–Richie Lucas, Penn St., QB | .613 |
| | 3rd–Don Meredith, SMU, QB | .286 |
| | 4th–Bill Burrell, Illinois, G | .196 |
| 1960 | **Joe Bellino,** Navy, HB | .1793 |
| | 2nd–Tom Brown, Minnesota, G | .731 |
| | 3rd–Jake Gibbs, Mississippi, QB | .453 |
| | 4th–Ed Dyas, Auburn, HB | .319 |
| 1961 | **Ernie Davis,** Syracuse, HB | .824 |
| | 2nd–Bob Ferguson, Ohio St., HB | .771 |
| | 3rd–Jimmy Saxton, Texas, HB | .551 |
| | 4th–Sandy Stephens, Minnesota, QB | .543 |
| 1962 | **Terry Baker,** Oregon St., QB | .707 |
| | 2nd–Jerry Stovall, LSU, HB | .618 |
| | 3rd–Bobby Bell, Minnesota, T | .429 |
| | 4th–Lee Roy Jordan, Alabama, C | .321 |
| 1963 | **Roger Staubach,** Navy, QB | .1860 |
| | 2nd–Billy Lothridge, Ga. Tech, QB | .504 |
| | 3rd–Sherman Lewis, Mich. St., HB | .369 |
| | 4th–Don Trull, Baylor, QB | .253 |
| 1964 | **John Huarte,** Notre Dame, QB | .1026 |
| | 2nd–Jerry Rhome, Tulsa, QB | .952 |
| | 3rd–Dick Butkus, Illinois, C | .505 |
| | 4th–Bob Timberlake, Michigan, QB | .361 |

| Year | | Points |
|---|---|---|
| 1965 | **Mike Garrett,** USC, HB | .926 |
| | 2nd–Howard Twilley, Tulsa, E | .528 |
| | 3rd–Jim Grabowski, Illinois, FB | .481 |
| | 4th–Donny Anderson, Texas Tech, HB | .408 |
| 1966 | **Steve Spurrier,** Florida, QB | .1679 |
| | 2nd–Bob Griese, Purdue, QB | .816 |
| | 3rd–Nick Eddy, Notre Dame, HB | .456 |
| | 4th–Gary Beban, UCLA, QB | .318 |
| 1967 | **Gary Beban,** UCLA, QB | .1968 |
| | 2nd–O.J. Simpson, USC, HB | .1722 |
| | 3rd–Leroy Keyes, Purdue, HB | .1366 |
| | 4th–Larry Csonka, Syracuse, FB | .136 |
| 1968 | **O.J. Simpson,** USC, HB | .2853 |
| | 2nd–Leroy Keyes, Purdue, HB | .1103 |
| | 3rd–Terry Hanratty, Notre Dame, QB | .387 |
| | 4th–Ted Kwalick, Penn St., TE | .254 |
| 1969 | **Steve Owens,** Oklahoma, HB | .1488 |
| | 2nd–Mike Phipps, Purdue, QB | .1344 |
| | 3rd–Rex Kern, Ohio St., QB | .856 |
| | 4th–Archie Manning, Mississippi, QB | .582 |
| 1970 | **Jim Plunkett,** Stanford, QB | .2229 |
| | 2nd–Joe Theismann, Notre Dame, QB | .1410 |
| | 3rd–Archie Manning, Mississippi, QB | .849 |
| | 4th–Steve Worster, Texas, RB | 398 |
| 1971 | **Pat Sullivan,** Auburn, QB | .1597 |
| | 2nd–Ed Marinaro, Cornell, RB | .1445 |
| | 3rd–Greg Pruitt, Oklahoma, RB | .586 |
| | 4th–Johnny Musso, Alabama, RB | .365 |
| 1972 | **Johnny Rodgers,** Nebraska, FL | .1310 |
| | 2nd–Greg Pruitt, Oklahoma, RB | .966 |
| | 3rd–Rich Glover, Nebraska, MG | .652 |
| | 4th–Bert Jones, LSU, QB | .351 |
| 1973 | **John Cappelletti,** Penn St., RB | .1057 |
| | 2nd–John Hicks, Ohio St., OT | .524 |
| | 3rd–Roosevelt Leaks, Texas, RB | .482 |
| | 4th–David Jaynes, Kansas, QB | .394 |
| 1974 | **Archie Griffin,** Ohio St., RB | .1920 |
| | 2nd–Anthony Davis, USC, RB | .819 |
| | 3rd–Joe Washington, Oklahoma, RB | .661 |
| | 4th–Tom Clements, Notre Dame, QB | .244 |
| 1975 | **Archie Griffin,** Ohio St., RB | .1800 |
| | 2nd–Chuck Muncie, California, RB | .730 |
| | 3rd–Ricky Bell, USC, RB | .708 |
| | 4th–Tony Dorsett, Pitt, RB | .616 |
| 1976 | **Tony Dorsett,** Pittsburgh, RB | .2357 |
| | 2nd–Ricky Bell, USC, RB | .1346 |
| | 3rd–Rob Lytle, Michigan, RB | .413 |
| | 4th–Terry Miller, Oklahoma St., RB | .197 |
| 1977 | **Earl Campbell,** Texas, RB | .1547 |
| | 2nd–Terry Miller, Oklahoma St., RB | .812 |
| | 3rd–Ken MacAfee, Notre Dame, TE | .343 |
| | 4th–Doug Williams, Grambling, QB | .266 |
| 1978 | **Billy Sims,** Oklahoma, RB | .827 |
| | 2nd–Chuck Fusina, Penn St., QB | .750 |
| | 3rd–Rick Leach, Michigan, QB | .435 |
| | 4th–Charles White, USC, RB | .354 |
| 1979 | **Charles White,** USC, RB | .1695 |
| | 2nd–Billy Sims, Oklahoma, RB | .773 |
| | 3rd–Marc Wilson, BYU, QB | .589 |
| | 4th–Art Schlichter, Ohio St., QB | .251 |
| 1980 | **George Rogers,** South Carolina, RB | .1128 |
| | 2nd–Hugh Green, Pittsburgh, DE | .861 |
| | 3rd–Herschel Walker, Georgia, RB | .683 |
| | 4th–Mark Herrmann, Purdue, QB | .405 |
| 1981 | **Marcus Allen,** USC, RB | .1797 |
| | 2nd–Herschel Walker, Georgia, RB | .1199 |
| | 3rd–Jim McMahon, BYU, QB | .706 |
| | 4th–Dan Marino, Pitt, QB | .256 |
| 1982 | **Herschel Walker,** Georgia, RB | .1926 |
| | 2nd–John Elway, Stanford, QB | .1231 |
| | 3rd–Eric Dickerson, SMU, RB | .465 |
| | 4th–Anthony Carter, Michigan, WR | .142 |
| 1983 | **Mike Rozier,** Nebraska, RB | .1801 |
| | 2nd–Steve Young, BYU, QB | .1172 |
| | 3rd–Doug Flutie, Boston College, QB | .253 |
| | 4th–Turner Gill, Nebraska, QB | .190 |

| Year | | Points |
|---|---|---|
| 1984 | **Doug Flutie,** Boston College, QB | .2240 |
| | 2nd–Keith Byars, Ohio St., RB | .1251 |
| | 3rd–Robbie Bosco, BYU, QB | .443 |
| | 4th–Bernie Kosar, Miami-FL, QB | .320 |
| 1985 | **Bo Jackson,** Auburn, RB | .1509 |
| | 2nd–Chuck Long, Iowa, QB | .1464 |
| | 3rd–Robbie Bosco, BYU, QB | .459 |
| | 4th–Lorenzo White, Michigan St., RB | .391 |
| 1986 | **Vinny Testaverde,** Miami-FL, QB | .2213 |
| | 2nd–Paul Palmer, Temple, RB | .672 |
| | 3rd–Jim Harbaugh, Michigan, QB | .458 |
| | 4th–Brian Bosworth, Oklahoma, LB | .395 |
| 1987 | **Tim Brown,** Notre Dame, WR | .1442 |
| | 2nd–Don McPherson, Syracuse, QB | .831 |
| | 3rd–Gordie Lockbaum, Holy Cross, WR-DB | .657 |
| | 4th–Lorenzo White, Michigan St., RB | .632 |
| 1988 | **Barry Sanders,** Oklahoma St., RB | .1878 |
| | 2nd–Rodney Peete, USC, QB | .912 |
| | 3rd–Troy Aikman, UCLA, QB | .582 |
| | 4th–Steve Walsh, Miami-FL, QB | .341 |
| 1989 | **Andre Ware,** Houston, QB | .1073 |
| | 2nd–Anthony Thompson, Ind., RB | .1003 |
| | 3rd–Major Harris, West Va., QB | .709 |
| | 4th–Tony Rice, Notre Dame, QB | .523 |
| 1990 | **Ty Detmer,** BYU, QB | .1482 |
| | 2nd–Rocket Ismail, Notre Dame, FL | .1177 |
| | 3rd–Eric Bieniemy, Colorado, RB | .798 |
| | 4th–Shawn Moore, Virginia, QB | .465 |
| 1991 | **Desmond Howard,** Michigan, WR | .2077 |
| | 2nd–Casey Weldon, Florida St., QB | .503 |
| | 3rd–Ty Detmer, BYU, QB | .445 |
| | 4th–Steve Emtman, Washington, DT | .357 |
| 1992 | **Gino Torretta,** Miami-FL, QB | .1400 |
| | 2nd–Marshall Faulk, San Diego St., RB | .1080 |
| | 3rd–Garrison Hearst, Georgia, RB | .982 |
| | 4th–Marvin Jones, Florida St., LB | .392 |
| 1993 | **Charlie Ward,** Florida St., QB | .2310 |
| | 2nd–Heath Shuler, Tennessee, QB | .688 |
| | 3rd–David Palmer, Alabama, RB | .292 |
| | 4th–Marshall Faulk, S. Diego St., RB | .250 |
| 1994 | **Rashaan Salaam,** Colorado, RB | .1743 |
| | 2nd–Ki-Jana Carter, Penn St., RB | .901 |
| | 3rd–Steve McNair, Alcorn St., QB | .655 |
| | 4th–Kerry Collins, Penn St., QB | .639 |
| 1995 | **Eddie George,** Ohio St., RB | .1460 |
| | 2nd–Tommie Frazier, Nebraska, QB | .1196 |
| | 3rd–Danny Wuerffel, Florida, QB | .987 |
| | 4th–Darnell Autry, Northwestern, RB | .535 |
| 1996 | **Danny Wuerffel,** Florida, QB | .1363 |
| | 2nd–Troy Davis, Iowa St., RB | .1174 |
| | 3rd–Jake Plummer, Arizona St., QB | .685 |
| | 4th–Orlando Pace, Ohio St., OT | .599 |
| 1997 | **Charles Woodson,** Michigan, DB-WR | .1815 |
| | 2nd–Peyton Manning, Tennessee, QB | .1543 |
| | 3rd–Ryan Leaf, Washington St., QB | .861 |
| | 4th–Randy Moss, Marshall, WR | .253 |
| 1998 | **Ricky Williams,** Texas, RB | .2355 |
| | 2nd–Michael Bishop, Kansas St., QB | .792 |
| | 3rd–Cade McNown, UCLA, QB | .696 |
| | 4th–Tim Couch, Kentucky, QB | .527 |
| 1999 | **Ron Dayne,** Wisconsin, RB | .2042 |
| | 2nd–Joe Hamilton, Ga. Tech, QB | .994 |
| | 3rd–Michael Vick, Va. Tech, QB | .319 |
| | 4th–Drew Brees, Purdue, QB | .308 |
| 2000 | **Chris Weinke,** Florida St., QB | .1628 |
| | 2nd–Josh Heupel, Oklahoma, QB | .1552 |
| | 3rd–Drew Brees, Purdue, QB | .619 |
| | 4th–LaDainian Tomlinson, TCU, RB | .566 |
| 2001 | **Eric Crouch,** Nebraska, QB | .770 |
| | 2nd–Rex Grossman, Florida, QB | .708 |
| | 3rd–Ken Dorsey, Miami-FL, QB | .638 |
| | 4th–Joey Harrington, Oregon, QB | .364 |
| 2002 | **Carson Palmer,** USC, QB | .1328 |
| | 2nd–Brad Banks, Iowa, QB | .1095 |
| | 3rd–Larry Johnson, Penn St., RB | .726 |
| | 4th–Willis McGahee, Midmi-FL, RB | .660 |

## Annual Awards (Cont.)

2003 **Jason White**, Oklahoma, QB ..........1481
    2nd–Larry Fitzgerald, Pittsburgh, WR .....1353
    3rd–Eli Manning, Mississippi, QB .......710
    4th–Chris Perry, Michigan, RB ...........341

2004 **Matt Leinart**, USC, QB ..............1325
    2nd–Adrian Peterson, Oklahoma, RB ....997
    3rd–Jason White, Oklahoma, QB ........957
    4th–Alex Smith, Utah, QB .............635

## Maxwell Award

First presented in 1937 by the Maxwell Memorial Football Club of Philadelphia, the award is named after Robert (Tiny) Maxwell, a Philadelphia native who was a standout lineman at the University of Chicago at the turn of the century. Like the Heisman, the Maxwell is given to the outstanding college player in the nation. Both awards have gone to the same player in the same season 34 times. Those players are preceded by (#). Glenn Davis of Army and Doak Walker of SMU won both but in different years.

**Multiple winner:** Johnny Lattner (2).

| Year | | Year | | Year | |
|---|---|---|---|---|---|
| 1937 | #Clint Frank, Yale, HB | 1960 | #Joe Bellino, Navy, HB | 1983 | #Mike Rozier, Nebraska, RB |
| 1938 | #Davey O'Brien, TCU, QB | 1961 | Bob Ferguson, Ohio St., HB | 1984 | #Doug Flutie, Boston Col., QB |
| 1939 | #Nile Kinnick, Iowa, QB | 1962 | #Terry Baker, Oregon St., QB | 1985 | Chuck Long, Iowa, QB |
| 1940 | #Tom Harmon, Michigan, HB | 1963 | #Roger Staubach, Navy, QB | 1986 | #V. Testaverde, Miami-FL, QB |
| 1941 | Bill Dudley, Virginia, HB | 1964 | Glenn Ressler, Penn St., G | 1987 | Don McPherson, Syracuse, QB |
| 1942 | Paul Governali, Columbia, QB | 1965 | Tommy Nobis, Texas, LB | 1988 | #Barry Sanders, Okla. St., RB |
| 1943 | Bob Odell, Penn, HB | 1966 | Jim Lynch, Notre Dame, LB | 1989 | Anthony Thompson, Indiana, RB |
| 1944 | Glenn Davis, Army, HB | 1967 | #Gary Beban, UCLA, QB | 1990 | #Ty Detmer, BYU, QB |
| 1945 | #Doc Blanchard, Army, FB | 1968 | #O.J. Simpson, USC, HB | 1991 | #Desmond Howard, Mich., WR |
| 1946 | Charley Trippi, Georgia, HB | 1969 | Mike Reid, Penn St., DT | 1992 | #Gino Torretta, Miami-FL, QB |
| 1947 | Doak Walker, SMU, HB | 1970 | #Jim Plunkett, Stanford, QB | 1993 | #Charlie Ward, Florida St., QB |
| 1948 | Chuck Bednarik, Penn, C | 1971 | Ed Marinaro, Cornell, RB | 1994 | Kerry Collins, Penn St., QB |
| 1949 | #Leon Hart, Notre Dame, E | 1972 | Brad Van Pelt, Michigan St., DB | 1995 | #Eddie George, Ohio St., RB |
| 1950 | Reds Bagnell, Penn, HB | 1973 | #John Cappelletti, Penn St., RB | 1996 | #Danny Wuerffel, Florida, QB |
| 1951 | #Dick Kazmaier, Princeton, TB | 1974 | Steve Joachim, Temple, QB | 1997 | Peyton Manning, Tennessee, QB |
| 1952 | Johnny Lattner, Notre Dame, HB | 1975 | #Archie Griffin, Ohio St., RB | 1998 | #Ricky Williams, Texas, RB |
| 1953 | #Johnny Lattner, N. Dame, HB | 1976 | #Tony Dorsett, Pitt, RB | 1999 | #Ron Dayne, Wisconsin, RB |
| 1954 | Ron Beagle, Navy, E | 1977 | Ross Browner, Notre Dame, DE | 2000 | Drew Brees, Purdue, QB |
| 1955 | #Howard Cassady, Ohio St., HB | 1978 | Chuck Fusina, Penn St., QB | 2001 | Ken Dorsey, Miami-FL, QB |
| 1956 | Tommy McDonald, Okla., HB | 1979 | #Charles White, USC, RB | 2002 | Larry Johnson, Penn St., RB |
| 1957 | Bob Reifsnyder, Navy, T | 1980 | Hugh Green, Pitt, DE | 2003 | Eli Manning, Mississippi, QB |
| 1958 | #Pete Dawkins, Army, HB | 1981 | #Marcus Allen, USC, RB | 2004 | Jason White, Oklahoma, QB |
| 1959 | Rich Lucas, Penn St., QB | 1982 | #Herschel Walker, Georgia, RB | | |

## Outland Trophy

First presented in 1946 by the Football Writers Association of America, honoring the nation's outstanding interior lineman. The award is named after its benefactor, Dr. John H. Outland (Kansas, Class of 1898). Players listed in **bold** type helped lead their team to a national championship (according to AP).

**Multiple winner:** Dave Rimington (2). **Winners in junior year:** Ross Browner (1976), Steve Emtman (1991), Rien Long (2002), Orlando Pace (1996) and Rimington (1981).

| Year | | Year | | Year | |
|---|---|---|---|---|---|
| 1946 | **George Connor,** N. Dame, T | 1966 | Loyd Phillips, Arkansas, T | 1986 | Jason Buck, BYU, DT |
| 1947 | Joe Steffy, Army, G | 1967 | **Ron Yary,** USC, T | 1987 | Chad Hennings, Air Force, DT |
| 1948 | Bill Fischer, Notre Dame, G | 1968 | Bill Stanfill, Georgia, T | 1988 | Tracy Rocker, Auburn, DT |
| 1949 | Ed Bagdon, Michigan St., G | 1969 | Mike Reid, Penn St., DT | 1989 | Mohammed Elewonibi, BYU, G |
| 1950 | Bob Gain, Kentucky, T | 1970 | Jim Stillwagon, Ohio St., MG | 1990 | Russell Maryland, Miami-FL, NT |
| 1951 | Jim Weatherall, Oklahoma, T | 1971 | **Larry Jacobson,** Neb., DT | 1991 | Steve Emtman, Washington, DT |
| 1952 | Dick Modzelewski, Maryland, T | 1972 | Rich Glover, Nebraska, MG | 1992 | Will Shields, Nebraska, G |
| 1953 | J.D. Roberts, Oklahoma, G | 1973 | John Hicks, Ohio St., OT | 1993 | Rob Waldrop, Arizona, NG |
| 1954 | Bill Brooks, Arkansas, G | 1974 | Randy White, Maryland, DT | 1994 | **Zach Wiegert,** Nebraska, OT |
| 1955 | Calvin Jones, Iowa, G | 1975 | **Lee Roy Selmon,** Okla., DT | 1995 | Jonathan Ogden, UCLA, OT |
| 1956 | Jim Parker, Ohio St., G | 1976 | Ross Browner, Notre Dame, DE | 1996 | Orlando Pace, Ohio St., OT |
| 1957 | Alex Karras, Iowa, T | 1977 | Brad Shearer, Texas, DT | 1997 | Aaron Taylor, Nebraska, G |
| 1958 | Zeke Smith, Auburn, G | 1978 | Greg Roberts, Oklahoma, G | 1998 | Kris Farris, UCLA, OT |
| 1959 | Mike McGee, Duke, T | 1979 | Jim Richter, N.C. State, C | 1999 | Chris Samuels, Alabama, OT |
| 1960 | **Tom Brown,** Minnesota, G | 1980 | Mark May, Pittsburgh, OT | 2000 | John Henderson, Tennessee, DT |
| 1961 | Merlin Olsen, Utah St., T | 1981 | Dave Rimington, Nebraska, C | 2001 | **Bryant McKinnie,** Miami-FL, OT |
| 1962 | Bobby Bell, Minnesota, T | 1982 | Dave Rimington, Nebraska, C | 2002 | Rien Long, Washington St., DT |
| 1963 | **Scott Appleton,** Texas, T | 1983 | Dean Steinkuhler, Nebraska, G | 2003 | Robert Gallery, Iowa, OT |
| 1964 | Steve DeLong, Tennessee, T | 1984 | Bruce Smith, Virginia Tech, DT | 2004 | Jammal Brown, Oklahoma, OT |
| 1965 | Tommy Nobis, Texas, G | 1985 | Mike Ruth, Boston College, NG | | |

## Butkus Award

First presented in 1985 by the Downtown Athletic Club of Orlando, Fla., to honor the nation's outstanding linebacker. The award is named after Dick Butkus, two-time consensus All-America at Illinois and six-time All-Pro with the Chicago Bears.

**Multiple winner:** Brian Bosworth (2).

| Year | | Year | | Year | |
|------|--|------|--|------|--|
| 1985 | Brian Bosworth, Oklahoma | 1992 | Marvin Jones, Florida St. | 1999 | LaVar Arrington, Penn St. |
| 1986 | Brian Bosworth, Oklahoma | 1993 | Trev Alberts, Nebraska | 2000 | Dan Morgan, Miami-FL |
| 1987 | Paul McGowan, Florida St. | 1994 | Dana Howard, Illinois | 2001 | Rocky Calmus, Oklahoma |
| 1988 | Derrick Thomas, Alabama | 1995 | Kevin Hardy, Illinois | 2002 | E.J. Henderson, Maryland |
| 1989 | Percy Snow, Michigan St. | 1996 | Matt Russell, Colorado | 2003 | Teddy Lehman, Oklahoma |
| 1990 | Alfred Williams, Colorado | 1997 | Andy Katzenmoyer, Ohio St. | 2004 | Derrick Johnson, Texas |
| 1991 | Erick Anderson, Michigan | 1998 | Chris Claiborne, USC | | |

## Lombardi Award

First presented in 1970 by the Rotary Club of Houston, honoring the nation's best lineman. The award is named after pro football coach Vince Lombardi, who, as a guard, was a member of the famous "Seven Blocks of Granite" at Fordham in the 1930s. The Lombardi and Outland awards have gone to the same player in the same year ten times. Those players are preceded by (#). Ross Browner of Notre Dame won both, but in different years.

**Multiple winner:** Orlando Pace (2).

| Year | | Year | | Year | |
|------|--|------|--|------|--|
| 1970 | #Jim Stillwagon, Ohio St., MG | 1982 | #Dave Rimington, Neb., C | 1994 | Warren Sapp, Miami-FL, DT |
| 1971 | Walt Patulski, Notre Dame, DE | 1983 | #Dean Steinkuhler, Neb., G | 1995 | Orlando Pace, Ohio St., OT |
| 1972 | #Rich Glover, Nebraska, MG | 1984 | Tony Degrate, Texas, DT | 1996 | #Orlando Pace, Ohio St., OT |
| 1973 | #John Hicks, Ohio St., OT | 1985 | Tony Casillas, Oklahoma, NG | 1997 | Grant Wistrom, Nebraska, DE |
| 1974 | #Randy White, Maryland, DT | 1986 | Cornelius Bennett, Alabama, LB | 1998 | Dat Nguyen, Tex. A&M, LB |
| 1975 | #Lee Roy Selmon, Okla., DT | 1987 | Chris Spielman, Ohio St., LB | 1999 | Corey Moore, Va. Tech, DE |
| 1976 | Wilson Whitley, Houston, DT | 1988 | #Tracy Rocker, Auburn, DT | 2000 | Jamal Reynolds, Florida St., DE |
| 1977 | Ross Browner, Notre Dame, DE | 1989 | Percy Snow, Michigan St., LB | 2001 | Julius Peppers, N. Carolina, DE |
| 1978 | Bruce Clark, Penn St., DT | 1990 | Chris Zorich, Notre Dame, NT | 2002 | Terrell Suggs, Arizona St., DE |
| 1979 | Brad Budde, USC, G | 1991 | #Steve Emtman, Wash., DT | 2003 | Tommie Harris, Oklahoma, DT |
| 1980 | Hugh Green, Pitt, DE | 1992 | Marvin Jones, Florida St., LB | 2004 | David Pollack, Georgia, DE |
| 1981 | Kenneth Sims, Texas, DT | 1993 | Aaron Taylor, Notre Dame, OT | | |

## O'Brien Quarterback Award

First presented in 1977 as the O'Brien Memorial Trophy, the award went to the outstanding player in the Southwest. In 1981, however, the Davey O'Brien Educational and Charitable Trust of Ft. Worth renamed the prize the O'Brien National Quarterback Award and now honors the nation's best quarterback. The award is named after 1938 Heisman Trophy-winning QB Davey O'Brien of Texas Christian.

**Multiple winners:** Ty Detmer, Mike Singletary, Jason White and Danny Wuerffel (2).

### Memorial Trophy

| Year | | Year | | Year | |
|------|--|------|--|------|--|
| 1977 | Earl Campbell, Texas, RB | 1979 | Mike Singletary, Baylor, LB | 1980 | Mike Singletary, Baylor, LB |
| 1978 | Billy Sims, Oklahoma, RB | | | | |

### National QB Award

| Year | | Year | | Year | |
|------|--|------|--|------|--|
| 1981 | Jim McMahon, BYU | 1989 | Andre Ware, Houston | 1997 | Peyton Manning, Tennessee |
| 1982 | Todd Blackledge, Penn St. | 1990 | Ty Detmer, BYU | 1998 | Michael Bishop, Kansas St. |
| 1983 | Steve Young, BYU | 1991 | Ty Detmer, BYU | 1999 | Joe Hamilton, Ga. Tech |
| 1984 | Doug Flutie, Boston College | 1992 | Gino Torretta, Miami-FL | 2000 | Chris Weinke, Florida St. |
| 1985 | Chuck Long, Iowa | 1993 | Charlie Ward, Florida St. | 2001 | Eric Crouch, Nebraska |
| 1986 | Vinny Testaverde, Miami, FL | 1994 | Kerry Collins, Penn St. | 2002 | Brad Banks, Iowa |
| 1987 | Don McPherson, Syracuse | 1995 | Danny Wuerffel, Florida | 2003 | Jason White, Oklahoma |
| 1988 | Troy Aikman, UCLA | 1996 | Danny Wuerffel, Florida | 2004 | Jason White, Oklahoma |

## Thorpe Award

First presented in 1986 by the Jim Thorpe Athletic Club of Oklahoma City to honor the nation's outstanding defensive back. The award is named after Jim Thorpe–Olympic champion and two-time consensus All-America halfback at Carlisle.

| Year | | Year | | Year | |
|------|--|------|--|------|--|
| 1986 | Thomas Everett, Baylor | 1992 | Deon Figures, Colorado | 1999 | Tyrone Carter, Minnesota |
| 1987 | Bennie Blades, Miami-FL | 1993 | Antonio Langham, Alabama | 2000 | Jamar Fletcher, Wisconsin |
| | & Rickey Dixon, Oklahoma | 1994 | Chris Hudson, Colorado | 2001 | Roy Williams, Oklahoma |
| 1988 | Deion Sanders, Florida St. | 1995 | Greg Myers, Colorado St. | 2002 | Terence Newman, Kansas St. |
| 1989 | Mike Carrier, USC | 1996 | Lawrence Wright, Florida | 2003 | Derrick Strait, Oklahoma |
| 1990 | Darryl Lewis, Arizona | 1997 | Charles Woodson, Michigan | 2004 | Carlos Rogers, Auburn |
| 1991 | Terrell Buckley, Florida St. | 1998 | Antoine Winfield, Ohio St. | | |

## All-Time Winningest Division I-A Coaches

Minimum of 10 years in Division I-A through 2004 season. Regular season and bowl games included. Coaches active in 2004 in **bold** type.

### Top 25 Winning Percentage

| | | Yrs | W | L | T | Pct |
|---|---|---|---|---|---|---|
| 1 | Knute Rockne | 13 | 105 | 12 | 5 | .881 |
| 2 | Frank Leahy | 13 | 107 | 13 | 9 | .864 |
| 3 | George Woodruff | 12 | 142 | 25 | 2 | .846 |
| 4 | Barry Switzer | 16 | 157 | 29 | 4 | .837 |
| 5 | Tom Osborne | 25 | 255 | 49 | 3 | .836 |
| 6 | Percy Haughton | 13 | 96 | 17 | 6 | .832 |
| 7 | Bob Neyland | 21 | 173 | 31 | 12 | .829 |
| 8 | Hurry Up Yost | 29 | 196 | 36 | 12 | .828 |
| 9 | Bud Wilkinson | 17 | 145 | 29 | 4 | .826 |
| 10 | Jock Sutherland | 20 | 144 | 28 | 14 | .812 |
| 11 | Bob Devaney | 16 | 136 | 30 | 7 | .806 |
| 12 | **Phillip Fulmer** | 13 | 123 | 31 | 0 | .799 |
| 13 | Frank Thomas | 19 | 141 | 33 | 9 | .795 |
| 14 | Henry Williams | 23 | 141 | 34 | 12 | .786 |
| 15 | Gil Dobie | 33 | 180 | 45 | 15 | .781 |
| 16 | Bear Bryant | 38 | 323 | 85 | 17 | .780 |
| 17 | Fred Folsom | 19 | 106 | 28 | 6 | .779 |
| 18 | Steve Spurrier | 15 | 142 | 40 | 2 | .777 |
| 19 | **Bobby Bowden** | 39 | 351 | 100 | 4 | .776 |
| 20 | Bo Schembechler | 27 | 234 | 65 | 8 | .775 |
| 21 | Fritz Crisler | 18 | 116 | 32 | 9 | .768 |
| 22 | Charley Moran | 18 | 122 | 33 | 12 | .766 |
| 23 | **Lloyd Carr** | 10 | 95 | 29 | 0 | .766 |
| 24 | Wallace Wade | 24 | 171 | 49 | 10 | .765 |
| 25 | Frank Kush | 22 | 176 | 54 | 1 | .764 |

### Top 25 Victories

| | | Yrs | W | L | T | Pct |
|---|---|---|---|---|---|---|
| 1 | **Bobby Bowden** | 39 | 351 | 100 | 4 | .776 |
| 2 | **Joe Paterno** | 39 | 343 | 116 | 3 | .746 |
| 3 | Bear Bryant | 38 | 323 | 85 | 17 | .780 |
| 4 | Pop Warner | 44 | 319 | 106 | 32 | .733 |
| 5 | Amos Alonzo Stagg | 57 | 314 | 199 | 35 | .605 |
| 6 | LaVell Edwards | 29 | 257 | 101 | 3 | .722 |
| 7 | Tom Osborne | 25 | 255 | 49 | 3 | .836 |
| 8 | **Lou Holtz** | 33 | 249 | 132 | 7 | .651 |
| 9 | Woody Hayes | 33 | 238 | 72 | 10 | .759 |
| 10 | Bo Schembechler | 27 | 234 | 65 | 8 | .775 |
| 11 | Hayden Fry | 37 | 232 | 178 | 10 | .564 |
| 12 | Jess Neely | 40 | 207 | 176 | 19 | .539 |
| 13 | Warren Woodson | 31 | 203 | 95 | 14 | .673 |
| 14 | Don Nehlen | 30 | 202 | 128 | 8 | .609 |
| 15 | Vince Dooley | 25 | 201 | 77 | 10 | .715 |
| | Eddie Anderson | 39 | 201 | 128 | 15 | .606 |
| 17 | Jim Sweeney | 32 | 200 | 154 | 4 | .564 |
| 18 | Dana X. Bible | 33 | 198 | 72 | 23 | .715 |
| 19 | Dan McGugin | 30 | 197 | 55 | 19 | .762 |
| 20 | Hurry Up Yost | 29 | 196 | 36 | 12 | .828 |
| 21 | Howard Jones | 29 | 194 | 64 | 21 | .733 |
| 22 | John Cooper | 24 | 192 | 84 | 6 | .691 |
| 23 | Johnny Vaught | 25 | 190 | 61 | 12 | .745 |
| 24 | George Welsh | 28 | 189 | 132 | 4 | .588 |
| 25 | John Heisman | 36 | 185 | 70 | 17 | .711 |
| | Johnny Majors | 29 | 185 | 137 | 10 | .572 |

**Note:** John Gagliardi of Division III St. John's (Minn.) became the all-time leader in college football coaching wins in 2003 (passing Grambling's Eddie Robinson at 408 wins), finishing the year with a career record of 414-114-11 over 52 seasons at St. John's and three seasons at Montana's Carroll College.

### Where They Coached

**Anderson**–Loras (1922-24), DePaul (1925-31), Holy Cross (1933-38), Iowa (1939-42), Holy Cross (1950-64); **Bible**– Mississippi College (1913-15), LSU (1916), Texas A&M (1917,1919-28), Nebraska (1929-36), Texas (1937-46); **Bowden**–Samford (1959-62), West Virginia (1970-75), Florida St. (1976–); **Bryant**–Maryland (1945), Kentucky (1946-53), Texas A&M (1954-57), Alabama (1958-82); **Carr**–Michigan (1995–); **Cooper**–Tulsa (1977-84), Arizona St. (1985-87), Ohio St. (1988-2000); **Crisler**–Minnesota (1930-31), Princeton (1932-37), Michigan (1938-47); **Devaney**–Wyoming (1957-61), Nebraska (1962-72); **Dobie**–North Dakota St. (1906-07), Washington (1908-16), Navy (1917-19), Cornell (1920-35), Boston College (1936- 38); **V. Dooley**–Georgia (1964-88); **Edwards**–BYU (1972-2000); **Folsom**–Colorado (1895-99, 1901-02), Dartmouth (1903-06), Colorado (1908-15); **Fry**–SMU (1962-72), North Texas (1973-78), Iowa (1979-98); **Fulmer**–Tennessee (1992–).

**Haughton**–Cornell (1899-1900), Harvard (1908-16), Columbia (1923-24); **Hayes**–Denison (1946-48), Miami-OH (1949-50), Ohio St. (1951-78); **Heisman**–Oberlin (1892), Akron (1893), Oberlin (1894), Auburn (1895-99), Clemson (1900-03), Georgia Tech (1904-19), Penn (1920-22), Washington & Jefferson (1923), Rice (1924-27); **Holtz**–William & Mary (1969-71), N.C. State (1972-75), Arkansas (1977-83), Minnesota (1984-85), Notre Dame (1986-96), South Carolina (1999-2004); **Jones**–Syracuse (1908), Yale (1909), Ohio St. (1910), Yale (1913), Iowa (1916-23), Duke (1924), USC (1925- 40); **Kush**–Arizona St. (1958-79); **Leahy**–Boston College (1939-40), Notre Dame (1941-43, 1946-53); **Majors**–Iowa St. (1968-72), Pittsburgh (1973-76, 93-96), Tennessee (1977-92); **Moran**–Texas A&M (1909-14), Centre (1919-23), Bucknell (1924-26), Catawba (1930-33).

**Neely**–Rhodes (1924-27), Clemson (1931-39), Rice (1940-66); **Nehlen**–Bowling Green (1968-76), West Virginia (1980-2000); **Neyland**–Tennessee (1926-34, 1936-40, 1946-52); **Osborne**–Nebraska (1973-97); **Paterno**–Penn St. (1966–); Rockne–Notre Dame (1918-30); **Schembechler**–Miami-OH (1963-68), Michigan (1969-89); **Spurrier**–Duke (1987-89), Florida (1990-2001); **Stagg**–Springfield College (1890-91), Chicago (1892-1932), Pacific (1933-46); **Sutherland**–Lafayette (1919-23), Pittsburgh (1924-38); **Sweeney**–Montana St. (1963-67), Washington St. (1968-75), Fresno St. (1976-96); **Switzer**–Oklahoma (1973-88).

**Thomas**–Chattanooga (1925-28), Alabama (1931-42, 1944-46); **Vaught**–Mississippi (1947-70); **Wade**–Alabama (1923-30), Duke (1931-41, 1946-50); **Warner**–Georgia (1895-96), Cornell (1897-98), Carlisle (1899-1903), Cornell (1904-06), Carlisle (1907-13), Pittsburgh (1915-23), Stanford (1924-32), Temple (1933-38); **Welsh**–Navy (1973-81), Virginia (1982-2000); **Wilkinson**–Oklahoma (1947-63); **Williams**–Army (1891), Minnesota (1900-21); **Woodruff**–Penn (1892-1901), Illinois (1903), Carlisle (1905); **Woodson**–Central Arkansas (1935-39), Hardin-Simmons (1941-42, 1946-51), Arizona (1952-56), New Mexico St. (1958-67), Trinity-TX (1972-73); **Yost**–Ohio Wesleyan (1897), Nebraska (1898), Kansas (1899), Stanford (1900), Michigan (1901-23, 1925-26).

## All-Time Winningest Division I-A Coaches (Cont.)

### All-Time Bowl Appearances
Coaches active in 2004 in **bold** type.

| | | App | W | L | T |
|---|---|---|---|---|---|
| 1 | **Joe Paterno** | 31 | 20 | 10 | 1 |
| 2 | Bear Bryant | 29 | 15 | 12 | 2 |
| 3 | **Bobby Bowden** | 28 | 19 | 8 | 1 |
| 4 | Tom Osborne | 25 | 12 | 13 | 0 |
| 5 | LaVell Edwards | 22 | 7 | 14 | 1 |
| | **Lou Holtz** | 22 | 12 | 8 | 2 |
| 7 | Vince Dooley | 20 | 8 | 10 | 2 |
| 8 | Johnny Vaught | 18 | 10 | 8 | 0 |
| 9 | Hayden Fry | 17 | 7 | 9 | 1 |
| | Bo Schembechler | 17 | 5 | 12 | 0 |
| 11 | Johnny Majors | 16 | 9 | 7 | 0 |
| | Darrell Royal | 16 | 8 | 7 | 1 |
| 13 | Don James | 15 | 10 | 5 | 0 |
| | George Welsh | 15 | 5 | 10 | 0 |
| 15 | John Cooper | 14 | 5 | 9 | 0 |
| | Jackie Sherrill | 14 | 8 | 6 | 0 |
| 17 | Seven coaches tied at 13. | | | | |

### Active Coaches' Victories
(Minimum 5 years in Division I-A.)

| | | Yrs | W | L | T | Pct |
|---|---|---|---|---|---|---|
| 1 | Bobby Bowden, Fla. St | 39 | **351** | 100 | 4 | .776 |
| 2 | Joe Paterno, Penn St | 39 | **343** | 116 | 3 | .746 |
| 3 | Frank Beamer, Va. Tech | 24 | **177** | 100 | 4 | .637 |
| 4 | Ken Hatfield, Rice | 25 | **167** | 130 | 4 | .561 |
| 5 | Dennis Franchione, Tex. A&M | 21 | **166** | 87 | 2 | .655 |
| 6 | Fisher DeBerry, Air Force | 21 | **161** | 94 | 1 | .631 |
| 7 | Dick Tomey, San Jose St. | 24 | **158** | 110 | 7 | .587 |
| 8 | Mack Brown, Texas | 21 | **156** | 93 | 1 | .626 |
| 9 | Steve Spurrier, So. Carolina | 15 | **142** | 40 | 2 | .777 |
| 10 | Mike Price, UTEP | 23 | **137** | 126 | 0 | .521 |
| 11 | Bill Snyder, Kansas St. | 16 | **131** | 62 | 1 | .678 |
| 12 | John L. Smith, Michigan St. | 16 | **123** | 72 | 0 | .631 |
| | Phillip Fulmer, Tennessee | 13 | **123** | 31 | 0 | .799 |
| 14 | Sonny Lubick, Colorado St. | 16 | **116** | 70 | 0 | .624 |
| 15 | Glen Mason, Minnesota | 19 | **110** | 109 | 1 | .502 |
| 16 | Barry Alvarez, Wisconsin | 15 | **108** | 70 | 4 | .604 |
| 17 | Bobby Wallace, Temple | 17 | **101** | 96 | 1 | .513 |
| | Mike Bellotti, Oregon | 15 | **101** | 65 | 2 | .601 |
| | Joe Tiller, Purdue | 14 | **101** | 67 | 1 | .598 |
| 20 | Rich Brooks, Kentucky | 20 | **97** | 126 | 0 | .435 |

## AFCA Coach of the Year
First presented in 1935 by the American Football Coaches Association.

**Multiple winners:** Joe Paterno (4), Bear Bryant (3), John McKay and Darrell Royal (2).

| Year | | Year | | Year | |
|---|---|---|---|---|---|
| 1935 | Pappy Waldorf, Northwestern | 1960 | Murray Warmath, Minnesota | 1983 | Ken Hatfield, Air Force |
| 1936 | Dick Harlow, Harvard | 1961 | Bear Bryant, Alabama | 1984 | LaVell Edwards, BYU |
| 1937 | Hooks Mylin, Lafayette | 1962 | John McKay, USC | 1985 | Fisher DeBerry, Air Force |
| 1938 | Bill Kern, Carnegie Tech | 1963 | Darrell Royal, Texas | 1986 | Joe Paterno, Penn St. |
| 1939 | Eddie Anderson, Iowa | 1964 | Frank Broyles, Arkansas | 1987 | Dick MacPherson, Syracuse |
| 1940 | Clark Shaughnessy, Stanford | | & Ara Parseghian, Notre Dame | 1988 | Don Nehlen, West Virginia |
| 1941 | Frank Leahy, Notre Dame | 1965 | Tommy Prothro, UCLA | 1989 | Bill McCartney, Colorado |
| 1942 | Bill Alexander, Georgia Tech | 1966 | Tom Cahill, Army | 1990 | Bobby Ross, Georgia Tech |
| 1943 | Amos Alonzo Stagg, Pacific | 1967 | John Pont, Indiana | 1991 | Bill Lewis, East Carolina |
| 1944 | Carroll Widdoes, Ohio St. | 1968 | Joe Paterno, Penn St. | 1992 | Gene Stallings, Alabama |
| 1945 | Bo McMillin, Indiana | 1969 | Bo Schembechler, Michigan | 1993 | Barry Alvarez, Wisconsin |
| 1946 | Red Blaik, Army | 1970 | Charlie McClendon, LSU | 1994 | Tom Osborne, Nebraska |
| 1947 | Fritz Crisler, Michigan | | & Darrell Royal, Texas | 1995 | Gary Barnett, Northwestern |
| 1948 | Bennie Oosterbaan, Michigan | 1971 | Bear Bryant, Alabama | 1996 | Bruce Snyder, Arizona St. |
| 1949 | Bud Wilkinson, Oklahoma | 1972 | John McKay, USC | 1997 | Lloyd Carr, Michigan |
| 1950 | Charlie Caldwell, Princeton | 1973 | Bear Bryant, Alabama | 1998 | Phillip Fulmer, Tennessee |
| 1951 | Chuck Taylor, Stanford | 1974 | Grant Teaff, Baylor | 1999 | Frank Beamer, Va. Tech |
| 1952 | Biggie Munn, Michigan St. | 1975 | Frank Kush, Arizona St. | 2000 | Bob Stoops, Oklahoma |
| 1953 | Jim Tatum, Maryland | 1976 | Johnny Majors, Pittsburgh | 2001 | Ralph Friedgen, Maryland |
| 1954 | Red Sanders, UCLA | 1977 | Don James, Washington | | & Larry Coker, Miami-FL |
| 1955 | Duffy Daugherty, Michigan St. | 1978 | Joe Paterno, Penn St. | 2002 | Jim Tressel, Ohio St. |
| 1956 | Bowden Wyatt, Tennessee | 1979 | Earle Bruce, Ohio St. | 2003 | Pete Carrol, USC |
| 1957 | Woody Hayes, Ohio St. | 1980 | Vince Dooley, Georgia | 2004 | Tommy Tuberville, Auburn |
| 1958 | Paul Dietzel, LSU | 1981 | Danny Ford, Clemson | | |
| 1959 | Ben Schwartzwalder, Syracuse | 1982 | Joe Paterno, Penn St. | | |

## FWAA Coach of the Year
First presented in 1957 by the Football Writers Association of America. The FWAA and AFCA awards have both gone to the same coach in the same season 32 times. Those double winners are preceded by (#).

**Multiple winners:** Woody Hayes and Joe Paterno (3); Lou Holtz, Johnny Majors and John McKay (2).

| Year | | Year | | Year | |
|---|---|---|---|---|---|
| 1957 | #Woody Hayes, Ohio St. | 1966 | #Tom Cahill, Army | 1975 | Woody Hayes, Ohio St. |
| 1958 | #Paul Dietzel, LSU | 1967 | #John Pont, Indiana | 1976 | #Johnny Majors, Pitt |
| 1959 | #Ben Schwartzwalder, Syracuse | 1968 | Woody Hayes, Ohio St. | 1977 | Lou Holtz, Arkansas |
| 1960 | #Murray Warmath, Minnesota | 1969 | #Bo Schembechler, Michigan | 1978 | #Joe Paterno, Penn St. |
| 1961 | Darrell Royal, Texas | 1970 | Alex Agase, Northwestern | 1979 | #Earle Bruce, Ohio St. |
| 1962 | #John McKay, USC | 1971 | Bob Devaney, Nebraska | 1980 | #Vince Dooley, Georgia |
| 1963 | #Darrell Royal, Texas | 1972 | #John McKay, USC | 1981 | #Danny Ford, Clemson |
| 1964 | #Ara Parseghian, Notre Dame | 1973 | Johnny Majors, Pitt | 1982 | #Joe Paterno, Penn St. |
| 1965 | Duffy Daugherty, Michigan St. | 1974 | #Grant Teaff, Baylor | 1983 | Howard Schnellenberger, Miami-FL |

| Year | | Year | | Year | |
|------|--|------|--|------|--|
| 1984 | #LaVell Edwards, BYU | 1991 | Don James, Washington | 1998 | #Phillip Fulmer, Tennessee |
| 1985 | #Fisher DeBerry, Air Force | 1992 | #Gene Stallings, Alabama | 1999 | #Frank Beamer, Va. Tech |
| 1986 | #Joe Paterno, Penn St. | 1993 | Terry Bowden, Auburn | 2000 | #Bob Stoops, Oklahoma |
| 1987 | #Dick MacPherson, Syracuse | 1994 | Rich Brooks, Oregon | 2001 | #Ralph Friedgen, Maryland |
| 1988 | Lou Holtz, Notre Dame | 1995 | #Gary Barnett, Northwestern | 2002 | #Jim Tressel, Ohio St. |
| 1989 | #Bill McCartney, Colorado | 1996 | #Bruce Snyder, Arizona St. | 2003 | Nick Saban, LSU |
| 1990 | #Bobby Ross, Georgia Tech | 1997 | Mike Price, Washington St. | 2004 | Urban Meyer, Utah |

## All-Time NCAA Division I-AA Leaders
### CAREER

#### Total Offense

**Yards Gained**

| | | Years | Yards |
|--|--|-------|-------|
| 1 | Steve McNair, Alcorn St. | 1991-94 | 16,823 |
| 2 | Marcus Brady, CS-Northridge | 1998-01 | 13,095 |
| 3 | Willie Totten, Miss. Valley | 1982-85 | 13,007 |
| 4 | Robert Kent, Jackson St. | 2000-03 | 12,538 |
| 5 | Jamie Martin, Weber St. | 1989-92 | 12,287 |

**Yards per Game**

| | | Years | Yards | P/Gm |
|--|--|-------|-------|------|
| 1 | Steve McNair, Alcorn St. | 1991-94 | 16,823 | 400.5 |
| 2 | Neil Lomax, Portland St. | 1978-80 | 11,647 | 352.9 |
| 3 | Aaron Flowers, CS-N'ridge | 1996-97 | 6,754 | 337.7 |
| 4 | David Macchi, Valparaiso | 2002-03 | 7,628 | 331.7 |
| 5 | Chris Sanders, Chatt. | 1999-00 | 7,247 | 329.4 |

#### Passing
(Minimum 300 Completions)

**Passing Efficiency**

| | | Years | Rating |
|--|--|-------|--------|
| 1 | Shawn Knight, William & Mary | 1991-94 | 170.8 |
| 2 | Dave Dickenson, Montana | 1992-95 | 166.3 |
| 3 | Drew Miller, Montana | 1999-00 | 160.5 |
| 4 | Eric Rasmussen, San Diego | 2001-03 | 160.1 |
| 5 | Lang Campbell, William & Mary | 2001-04 | 156.6 |

**Yards Gained**

| | | Years | Yards |
|--|--|-------|-------|
| 1 | Steve McNair, Alcorn St. | 1991-94 | 14,496 |
| 2 | Willie Totten, Miss. Valley | 1982-85 | 12,711 |
| 3 | Marcus Brady, CS-Northridge | 1998-01 | 12,479 |
| 4 | Jamie Martin, Weber St. | 1989-92 | 12,207 |
| 5 | Robert Kent, Jackson St. | 2000-03 | 11,784 |

#### Receiving

**Catches**

| | | Years | No |
|--|--|-------|-----|
| 1 | Jacquay Nunnally, Fla. A&M | 1997-00 | 317 |
| 2 | Stephen Campbell, Brown | 1997-00 | 305 |
| 3 | Jerry Rice, Miss. Valley | 1981-84 | 301 |
| 4 | Javarus Dudley, Fordham | 2000-03 | 295 |
| 5 | Chas Gessner, Brown | 1999-02 | 292 |

**Yards Gained**

| | | Years | No | Yards |
|--|--|-------|-----|-------|
| 1 | Jerry Rice, Miss. Valley | 1981-84 | 301 | 4693 |
| 2 | Jacquay Nunnally, Fla. A&M | 1997-00 | 317 | 4239 |
| 3 | Javarus Dudley, Fordham | 2000-03 | 295 | 4197 |
| 4 | Fred Amey, Sacramento St. | 2001-04 | 248 | 4049 |
| 5 | Rich Musinski, Wm. & Mary | 2000-03 | 219 | 4017 |

#### All-Purpose Yardage

**Yards per Game**

| | | Years | Yards | P/Gm |
|--|--|-------|-------|------|
| 1 | B. Westbrook, Villanova | 1997-98,00-01 | 9512 | 216.2 |
| 2 | Jerry Azumah, N. Hampshire | 1995-98 | 9376 | 204.3 |
| 3 | Arnold Mickens, Butler | 1994-95 | 3947 | 197.4 |
| 4 | Tim Hall, Robert Morris | 1994-95 | 3701 | 194.8 |
| 5 | Reggie Greene, Siena | 1994-97 | 6959 | 193.3 |

#### Rushing

**Yards Gained**

| | | Years | Yards |
|--|--|-------|-------|
| 1 | Adrian Peterson, Ga. So. | 1998-01 | 6559 |
| 2 | Charles Roberts, CS-Sac. | 1997-00 | 6553 |
| 3 | Jerry Azumah, N. Hampshire | 1995-98 | 6193 |
| 4 | Matt Cannon, S. Utah | 1997-00 | 5489 |
| 5 | Reggie Greene, Siena | 1994-97 | 5415 |

**Yards per Game**

| | | Years | Yards | P/Gm |
|--|--|-------|-------|------|
| 1 | Arnold Mickens, Butler | 1994-95 | 3813 | 190.7 |
| 2 | Adrian Peterson, Ga. So. | 1998-01 | 6559 | 156.2 |
| 3 | Aaron Stecker, W. Ill. | 1997-98 | 3081 | 154.1 |
| 4 | Tim Hall, Robert Morris | 1994-95 | 2908 | 153.1 |
| 5 | Jerry Azumah, N. Hampshire | 1995-98 | 6193 | 151.0 |

#### Miscellaneous

**Interceptions**

| | | Years | No |
|--|--|-------|-----|
| 1 | Rashean Mathis, Bethune-Cookman | 1999-02 | 31 |
| 2 | Dave Murphy, Holy Cross | 1986-89 | 28 |
| | Leigh Bodde, Duquesne | 1999-02 | 28 |
| 4 | Cedric Walker, S.F. Austin | 1990-93 | 25 |
| 5 | Three tied at 24. | | |

**Punting Average** (min. 150 punts)

| | | Years | Avg |
|--|--|-------|-----|
| 1 | Mark Gould, Northern Ariz. | 2000-03 | 44.8 |
| 2 | Pumpy Tudors, Tenn.-Chatt. | 1989-91 | 44.4 |
| 3 | Case de Brujin, Idaho St. | 1978-81 | 43.7 |
| 4 | Mike Scifres, Western Illinois | 1999-02 | 43.6 |
| 5 | Terry Belden, Northern Ariz. | 1990-93 | 43.4 |

**Note:** Northeastern's Tyler Grogan holds the I-AA record for longest punt with a 93-yarder against Villanova in 2001.

**Punt Return Average***

| | | Years | Avg |
|--|--|-------|-----|
| 1 | Willie Ware, Miss. Valley | 1982-85 | 16.4 |
| 2 | Buck Phillips, Western Ill. | 1994-95 | 16.4 |
| 3 | Tim Egerton, Delaware St. | 1986-89 | 16.1 |
| 4 | Mark Orlando, Towson St. | 1991-94 | 15.7 |
| 5 | Joseph Jefferson, Western Ky. | 1998-01 | 15.3 |

**Kickoff Return Average***

| | | Years | Avg |
|--|--|-------|-----|
| 1 | Lamont Brightful, E. Wash. | 1998-01 | 30.0 |
| 2 | Troy Brown, Marshall | 1991-92 | 29.7 |
| 3 | Charles Swann, Indiana St. | 1989-91 | 29.3 |
| 4 | Craig Richardson, Eastern Wash. | 1983-86 | 28.5 |
| 5 | Ramondo North, N.C. A&T | 1998-00 | 28.3 |

*(Minimum 1.2 returns per game)

**Blocked Kicks**

| | | Years | FG | XP | P | Tot |
|--|--|-------|----|----|----|-----|
| 1 | Leonard Smith, McNeese St. | 1980-82 | 10 | 4 | 3 | 17 |
| 2 | Trey Woods, Sam Houston St. | 1992-95 | 2 | 2 | 8 | 12 |
| 3 | Ryan Crawford, Davidson | 1997-00 | 5 | 0 | 7 | 12 |
| 4 | Bryan Cox, W. Illinois | 1987-90 | 4 | 5 | 1 | 10 |
| 5 | Tim Hauck, Montana | 1987-89 | 2 | 7 | 0 | 9 |

**Note:** The blocked kicks category is a combined total of blocked field goals (FG), extra points (XP) and punts (P).

### Scoring
#### Non-Kickers

**Points**

| | | Years | TD | XP | Pts |
|--|--|-------|----|----|-----|
| 1 | B. Westbrook, Villanova | 1997-98,00-01 | 89 | 10 | 544 |
| 2 | Adrian Peterson, Ga. Southern | 1998-01 | 87 | 2 | 524 |
| 3 | Matt Cannon, S. Utah | 1997-00 | 69 | 6 | 420 |
| 4 | Jerry Azumah, New Hampshire | 1995-98 | 69 | 4 | 418 |
| 5 | David Dinkins, Morehead St. | 1997-00 | 63 | 6 | 384 |

**Touchdowns Passing**

| | | Years | No |
|--|--|-------|-----|
| 1 | Willie Totten, Miss. Valley | 1982-85 | 139 |
| 2 | Steve McNair, Alcorn St. | 1991-94 | 119 |
| 3 | Marcus Brady, CS-Northridge | 1998-01 | 109 |
| 4 | Robert Kent, Jackson St. | 2000-03 | 104 |
| 5 | Niel Loebig, Duquesne | 2001-04 | 103 |

**Touchdowns Rushing**

| | | Years | No |
|--|--|-------|-----|
| 1 | Adrian Peterson, Ga. Southern | 1998-01 | 84 |
| 2 | Matt Cannon, S. Utah | 1997-00 | 69 |
| 3 | David Dinkins, Morehead St. | 1997-00 | 63 |
| 4 | Jerry Azumah, New Hampshire | 1995-98 | 60 |
| 5 | Charles Roberts, CS-Sacramento | 1997-00 | 56 |

**Touchdown Catches**

| | | Years | No |
|--|--|-------|-----|
| 1 | Jerry Rice, Miss. Valley | 1981-84 | 50 |
| 2 | Rennie Benn, Lehigh | 1982-85 | 44 |
| 3 | Dedric Ward, N. Iowa | 1993-96 | 41 |
| 4 | Rob Giancola, Valparaiso | 2001-04 | 40 |
| 5 | Sean Morey, Brown | 1995-98 | 39 |
| | Gharun Hester, Georgetown | 1997-00 | 39 |

## All-Time NCAA Division I-AA Leaders (Cont.)

### Kickers

| | Points | Years | FG | XP | Pts | | Field Goals | Years | No |
|---|---|---|---|---|---|---|---|---|---|
| 1 | Chris Snyder, Montana | 2000-03 | 70 | 182 | 394 | 1 | Marty Zendejas, Nevada | 1984-87 | 72 |
| 2 | Marty Zendejas, Nevada | 1984-87 | 72 | 169 | 385 | 2 | Kirk Roach, Western Carolina | 1984-87 | 71 |
| 3 | Justin Langan, W. Illinois | 2001-04 | 53 | 174 | 335 | 3 | Tony Zendejas, Nevada | 1981-83 | 70 |
| 4 | Dave Ettinger, Hofstra | 1994-97 | 62 | 140 | 326 | | Chris Snyder, Montana | 2000-03 | 70 |
| 5 | Brian Morgan, Grambling | 2001-04 | 50 | 174 | 324 | 5 | Scott Shields, Weber St. | 1995-98 | 67 |

**Note:** Chris Snyder's point total includes 1 2-point conversion. Scott Shields's point total includes 2 touchdowns.

**Note:** South Florida's Bill Gramatica, Arkansas State's Scott Roper and Georgia Southern's Tim Foley share the 1-AA record for longest field goal at 63 yards.

### Payton Award

First presented in 1987 by the Sports Network and Division I-AA sports information directors to honor the nation's outstanding Division I-AA player. The award is named after Walter Payton, the NFL's all-time leading rusher who was an All-America running back at Jackson St.

| Year | | Year | | Year | |
|---|---|---|---|---|---|
| 1987 | Kenny Gamble, Colgate, RB | 1993 | Doug Nussmeier, Idaho, QB | 1999 | Adrian Peterson, Ga. Southern, RB |
| 1988 | Dave Meggett, Towson St., RB | 1994 | Steve McNair, Alcorn St., QB | 2000 | Louis Ivory, Furman, RB |
| 1989 | John Friesz, Idaho, QB | 1995 | Dave Dickenson, Montana, QB | 2001 | Brian Westbrook, Villanova, RB |
| 1990 | Walter Dean, Grambling, RB | 1996 | Archie Amerson, N. Arizona, RB | 2002 | Tony Romo, Eastern Illinois, QB |
| 1991 | Jamie Martin, Weber St., QB | 1997 | Brian Finneran, Villanova, WR | 2003 | Jamaal Branch, Colgate, RB |
| 1992 | Michael Payton, Marshall, QB | 1998 | Jerry Azumah, N. Hampshire, RB | 2004 | Lang Campbell, Wm & Mary, QB |

## All-Time NCAA Division I-AA Winningest Programs

Includes record at a senior college only, minimum of 20 seasons of competition. Bowl and playoff games are included in the overall records but only 1-AA playoff games (since they began in 1978) are included in the W-L column under 1-AA playoffs.

### Top 20 Winning Percentage

| | | Yrs | Gm | W | L | T | Pct. | 1-AA Playoffs W-L | Titles |
|---|---|---|---|---|---|---|---|---|---|
| 1 | Georgia Southern | 23 | 300 | 227 | 72 | 1 | .758 | 38-9 | 6 |
| 2 | Yale | 132 | 1201 | 826 | 320 | 55 | .711 | 0-0 | 0 |
| 3 | Grambling St. | 62 | 669 | 466 | 188 | 15 | .708 | 9-7 | 0 |
| 4 | Florida A&M | 72 | 738 | 506 | 274 | 18 | .698 | 5-6 | 1 |
| 5 | Tennessee St. | 77 | 729 | 482 | 217 | 30 | .682 | 2-5 | 0 |
| 6 | Princeton | 135 | 1153 | 756 | 347 | 50 | .678 | 0-0 | 0 |
| 7 | Harvard | 130 | 1182 | 767 | 365 | 50 | .670 | 0-0 | 0 |
| 8 | Southern | 83 | 818 | 508 | 285 | 25 | .636 | 0-0 | 0 |
| 9 | Pennsylvania | 128 | 1253 | 776 | 435 | 42 | .636 | 0-0 | 0 |
| 10 | Jackson St. | 59 | 611 | 382 | 216 | 13 | .636 | 0-12 | 0 |
| 11 | Eastern Kentucky | 81 | 812 | 499 | 286 | 27 | .631 | 16-15 | 2 |
| 12 | Fordham | 106 | 1184 | 720 | 411 | 53 | .630 | 1-1 | 0 |
| 13 | Dayton | 97 | 927 | 570 | 329 | 26 | .629 | 0-0 | 0 |
| 14 | McNeese St. | 54 | 591 | 361 | 216 | 14 | .621 | 11-10 | 0 |
| 15 | Appalachian St. | 75 | 795 | 478 | 288 | 29 | .619 | 8-12 | 0 |
| 16 | Dartmouth | 123 | 1069 | 636 | 387 | 46 | .616 | 0-0 | 0 |
| 17 | S. Carolina St. | 77 | 723 | 431 | 265 | 27 | .615 | 2-2 | 0 |
| 18 | Hofstra | 64 | 626 | 378 | 237 | 11 | .613 | 2-5 | 0 |
| 19 | Albany | 32 | 322 | 196 | 126 | 0 | .609 | 0-0 | 0 |
| 20 | Delaware | 1113 | 1035 | 607 | 384 | 44 | .608 | 16-12 | 1 |

### Top 50 Victories

| | | Wins | | | Wins | | | Wins |
|---|---|---|---|---|---|---|---|---|
| 1 | Yale | 826 | 18 | Villanova | 520 | | Western Ill. | 458 |
| 2 | Pennsylvania | 776 | 19 | Furman | 518 | | Maine | 458 |
| 3 | Harvard | 767 | 20 | Butler | 514 | 37 | Georgetown | 453 |
| 4 | Princeton | 756 | 21 | Southern | 508 | 38 | Howard | 449 |
| 5 | Fordham | 720 | 22 | Florida A&M | 506 | 39 | VMI | 443 |
| 6 | Dartmouth | 636 | 23 | William & Mary | 504 | 40 | Texas St.-San Marcos | 442 |
| 7 | Lafayette | 612 | 24 | Massachusetts | 502 | 41 | Richmond | 440 |
| 8 | Delaware | 607 | 25 | E. Kentucky | 499 | 42 | Elon | 438 |
| 9 | Lehigh | 601 | 26 | W. Kentucky | 489 | 43 | The Citadel | 431 |
| 10 | Cornell | 597 | 27 | Hampton | 485 | | Idaho St. | 431 |
| 11 | Dayton | 570 | 28 | Tennessee St. | 482 | | S. Carolina St. | 431 |
| 12 | Colgate | 559 | 29 | Appalachian St. | 478 | 46 | Eastern Ill. | 430 |
| 13 | Holy Cross | 556 | 30 | Northwestern St. | 472 | 47 | Wofford | 429 |
| 14 | N. Iowa | 553 | 31 | Montana | 471 | 48 | Murray St. | 427 |
| 15 | Bucknell | 544 | 32 | Grambling St. | 466 | 49 | E. Washington | 423 |
| 16 | Brown | 540 | 33 | New Hampshire | 464 | 50 | Alabama St. | 418 |
| 17 | Drake | 522 | 34 | Chattanooga | 458 | | | |

## Top 10 Playoff Game Appearances

Ranked by NCAA Division 1-AA playoff games played from 1978-2004. CH refers to championships won.

| | | Years | Games | Record | CH | | | Years | Games | Record | CH |
|---|---|---|---|---|---|---|---|---|---|---|---|
| 1 | Georgia Southern | 15 | **47** | 38-9 | 6 | 6 | Delaware | 13 | **28** | 16-12 | 1 |
| 2 | Montana | 15 | **35** | 22-13 | 2 | 7 | Furman | 13 | **27** | 15-12 | 1 |
| 3 | Eastern Ky. | 17 | **31** | 16-15 | 2 | 8 | Northern Iowa | 11 | **23** | 12-11 | 0 |
| 4 | Marshall* | 8 | **29** | 23-6 | 2 | | McNeese St. | 11 | **22** | 11-11 | 0 |
| | Youngstown St. | 10 | **29** | 23-6 | 4 | 10 | Appalachian St. | 12 | **20** | 8-12 | 0 |

*Marshall moved up to I-A in 1997.

## Active Division I-AA Coaches

Minimum of five years as a Division I-A and/or Division I-AA through 2004 season.

### Top 10 Winning Percentage

| | | Yrs | W | L | T | Pct |
|---|---|---|---|---|---|---|
| 1 | Mike Kelly, Dayton | 24 | 222 | 46 | 1 | **.827** |
| 2 | Al Bagnoli, Pennsylvania | 23 | 180 | 53 | 0 | **.773** |
| 3 | Pete Richardson, Southern | 17 | 146 | 52 | 1 | **.736** |
| 4 | Dick Biddle, Colgate | 9 | 76 | 31 | 0 | **.710** |
| 5 | Joe Taylor, Hampton | 22 | 172 | 70 | 4 | **.707** |
| 6 | Tommy Tate, McNeese St. | 5 | 43 | 19 | 0 | **.694** |
| 7 | Kevin Higgins, Citadel | 7 | 56 | 25 | 1 | **.689** |
| 8 | Walt Hameline, Wagner | 24 | 169 | 81 | 2 | **.675** |
| 9 | Alvin Wyatt, Bet-Cookman | 8 | 60 | 29 | 0 | **.674** |
| 10 | Joe Walton, Robert Morris | 11 | 73 | 37 | 1 | **.662** |

### Top 10 Victories

| | | Yrs | W | L | T | Pct |
|---|---|---|---|---|---|---|
| 1 | Mike Kelly, Dayton | 24 | **222** | 46 | 1 | .827 |
| 2 | Robert Ford, Albany | 36 | **205** | 148 | 1 | .581 |
| 3 | Al Bagnoli, Pennsylvania | 23 | **180** | 53 | 0 | .773 |
| 4 | Joe Taylor, Hampton | 22 | **172** | 70 | 4 | .707 |
| 5 | Jimmye Laycock, Wm. & Mary | 25 | **170** | 113 | 2 | .600 |
| 6 | Walt Hameline, Wagner | 24 | **169** | 81 | 2 | .675 |
| 7 | Andy Talley, Villanova | 25 | **162** | 104 | 2 | .608 |
| 8 | Rob Ash, Drake | 25 | **161** | 93 | 5 | .631 |
| 9 | Jerry Moore, Appalachian St. | 23 | **155** | 112 | 2 | .580 |
| 10 | Pete Richardson, Southern | 17 | **146** | 52 | 1 | .736 |

**Note:** Eddie Robinson of Grambling State (1941-42, 1945-97) retired following the 1997 season as the all-time NCAA leader in coaching wins with a 408-165-15 record and a .707 winning percentage over 55 seasons.

## Division I-AA Coach of the Year

First presented in 1983 by the American Football Coaches Association.

**Multiple winners:** Mark Duffner, Paul Johnson and Erk Russell (2).

| Year | | Year | | Year | |
|---|---|---|---|---|---|
| 1983 | Rey Dempsey, Southern Ill. | 1991 | Mark Duffner, Holy Cross | 1999 | Paul Johnson, Ga. Southern |
| 1984 | Dave Arnold, Montana St. | 1992 | Charlie Taafe, Citadel | 2000 | Paul Johnson, Ga. Southern |
| 1985 | Dick Sheridan, Furman | 1993 | Dan Allen, Boston Univ. | 2001 | Bobby Johnson, Furman |
| 1986 | Erk Russell, Ga. Southern | 1994 | Jim Tressel, Youngstown St. | 2002 | Jack Harbaugh, E. Kentucky |
| 1987 | Mark Duffner, Holy Cross | 1995 | Don Read, Montana | 2003 | Dick Biddle, Colgate |
| 1988 | Jimmy Satterfield, Furman | 1996 | Ray Tellier, Columbia | 2004 | Mickey Matthews, James Madison |
| 1989 | Erk Russell, Ga. Southern | 1997 | Andy Talley, Villanova | | |
| 1990 | Tim Stowers, Ga. Southern | 1998 | Mark Whipple, Massachusetts | | |

## NCAA Playoffs

### Division I-AA

Established in 1978 as a four-team playoff. Tournament field increased to eight teams in 1981, 12 teams in 1982 and 16 teams in 1986. Automatic berths are awarded to champions of the Big Sky, Gateway, Mid-Eastern Athletic, Ohio Valley, Patriot, Southern, Southland and Atlantic 10 conferences.

**Multiple winners:** Georgia Southern (6); Youngstown St. (4); Eastern Kentucky, Marshall and Montana (2).

| Year | Winner | Score | Loser | Year | Winner | Score | Loser |
|---|---|---|---|---|---|---|---|
| 1978 | Florida A&M | 35-28 | Massachusetts | 1992 | Marshall | 31-28 | Youngstown St. |
| 1979 | Eastern Kentucky | 30-7 | Lehigh, PA | 1993 | Youngstown St. | 17-5 | Marshall |
| 1980 | Boise St., ID | 31-29 | Eastern Kentucky | 1994 | Youngstown St. | 28-14 | Boise St. |
| 1981 | Idaho St. | 34-23 | Eastern Kentucky | 1995 | Montana | 22-20 | Marshall |
| 1982 | Eastern Kentucky | 17-14 | Delaware | 1996 | Marshall | 49-29 | Montana |
| 1983 | Southern Illinois | 43-7 | Western Carolina | 1997 | Youngstown St. | 10-9 | McNeese St. |
| 1984 | Montana St. | 19-6 | Louisiana Tech | 1998 | Massachusetts | 55-43 | Georgia Southern |
| 1985 | Georgia Southern | 44-42 | Furman, SC | 1999 | Georgia Southern | 59-24 | Youngstown St. |
| 1986 | Georgia Southern | 48-21 | Arkansas St. | 2000 | Georgia Southern | 27-25 | Montana |
| 1987 | NE Louisiana | 43-42 | Marshall, WV | 2001 | Montana | 13-6 | Furman |
| 1988 | Furman, SC | 17-12 | Georgia Southern | 2002 | Western Kentucky | 34-14 | McNeese St. |
| 1989 | Georgia Southern | 37-34 | S.F. Austin St. | 2003 | Delaware | 40-0 | Colgate |
| 1990 | Georgia Southern | 36-13 | Nevada-Reno | 2004 | James Madison | 31-21 | Montana |
| 1991 | Youngstown St., OH | 25-17 | Marshall | | | | |

## Division II

Established in 1973 as an eight-team playoff. Tournament field increased to 16 teams in 1988. From 1964-72, eight qualifying NCAA College Division member institutions competed in four regional bowl games, but there was no tournament and no national championship until 1973.

**Multiple winners:** North Dakota St. (5); North Alabama (3); Grand Valley St., Northern Colorado, Northwest Missouri St., Southwest Texas St. and Troy St. (2).

| Year | Winner | Score | Loser | Year | Winner | Score | Loser |
|---|---|---|---|---|---|---|---|
| 1973 | Louisiana Tech | 34-0 | Western Kentucky | 1990 | North Dakota St. | 51-11 | Indiana, PA |
| 1974 | Central Michigan | 54-14 | Delaware | 1991 | Pittsburg St., KS | 23-6 | Jacksonville St., AL |
| 1975 | Northern Michigan. | 16-14 | Western Kentucky | 1992 | Jacksonville St., AL | 17-13 | Pittsburg St., KS |
| 1976 | Montana St. | 24-13 | Akron, OH | 1993 | North Alabama | 41-34 | Indiana, PA |
| 1977 | Lehigh, PA. | 33-0 | Jacksonville St., AL | 1994 | North Alabama | 16-10 | Tex. A&M (Kings.) |
| 1978 | Eastern Illinois | 10-9 | Delaware | 1995 | North Alabama | 22-7 | Pittsburg St., KS |
| 1979 | Delaware | 38-21 | Youngstown St., OH | 1996 | Northern Colorado | 23-14 | Carson-Newman |
| 1980 | Cal Poly-SLO | 21-13 | Eastern Illinois | 1997 | Northern Colorado | 51-0 | New Haven |
| 1981 | SW Texas St. | 42-13 | North Dakota St. | 1998 | NW Missouri St. | 24-6 | Carson-Newman |
| 1982 | SW Texas St. | 34-9 | UC-Davis | 1999 | NW Missouri St. | 58-52* | Carson-Newman |
| 1983 | North Dakota St. | 41-21 | Central St., OH | 2000 | Delta St., MS | 63-34 | Bloomsburg, PA |
| 1984 | Troy St., AL | 18-17 | North Dakota St. | 2001 | North Dakota | 17-14 | Grand Valley St. |
| 1985 | North Dakota St. | 35-7 | North Alabama | 2002 | Grand Valley St., OH | 31-24 | Valdosta St., GA |
| 1986 | North Dakota St. | 27-7 | South Dakota | 2003 | Grand Valley St., OH | 10-3 | North Dakota |
| 1987 | Troy St., AL | 31-17 | Portland St., OR | 2004 | Valdosta St., GA | 36-31 | Pittsburg St., KS |
| 1988 | North Dakota St | 35-21 | Portland St., OR | *Four overtimes | | | |
| 1989 | Mississippi Col. | 3-0 | Jacksonville St., AL | | | | |

## Hill Trophy

First presented in 1986 by the Harlon Hill Awards Committee in Florence, Ala., to honor the nation's outstanding Division II player. The award is named after three-time NFL All-Pro Harlon Hill, who played college ball at North Alabama.

**Multiple winners:** Johnny Bailey (3), Dusty Bonner (2).

| Year | | Year | | Year | |
|---|---|---|---|---|---|
| 1986 | Jeff Bentrim, N. Dakota St., QB | 1993 | Roger Graham, New Haven, RB | 2000 | Dusty Bonner, Valdosta St., QB |
| 1987 | Johnny Bailey, Texas A&I, RB | 1994 | Chris Hatcher, Valdosta St., QB | 2001 | Dusty Bonner, Valdosta St., QB |
| 1988 | Johnny Bailey, Texas A&I, RB | 1995 | Ronald McKinnon, N. Alabama, LB | 2002 | Curt Anes, Grand Valley St., QB |
| 1989 | Johnny Bailey, Texas A&I, RB | 1996 | Jarrett Anderson, Truman St., RB | 2003 | Will Hall, N. Alabama, QB |
| 1990 | Chris Simdorn, N. Dakota St., QB | 1997 | Irv Sigler, Bloomsburg, RB | 2004 | Chad Friehauf, Colo-Mines, QB |
| 1991 | Ronnie West, Pittsburg St., WR | 1998 | Brian Shay, Emporia St., RB | | |
| 1992 | Ronald Moore, Pittsburg St., RB | 1999 | Corte McGuffet, N. Colo., QB | | |

## Division III

Established in 1973 as a four-team playoff. Tournament field increased to eight teams in 1975, 16 teams in 1985 and 28 teams in 1999. From 1969-72, four qualifying NCAA College Division member institutions competed in two regional bowl games, but there was no tournament and no national championship until 1973. (*) denotes overtime.

**Multiple winners:** Mt. Union (7); Augustana (4); Ithaca (3); Dayton, St. John's, Widener, WI-La Crosse and Wittenberg (2).

| Year | Winner | Score | Loser | Year | Winner | Score | Loser |
|---|---|---|---|---|---|---|---|
| 1973 | Wittenberg, OH | 41-0 | Juniata, PA | 1990 | Allegheny, PA | 21-14* | Lycoming, PA |
| 1974 | Central, IA | 10-8 | Ithaca, NY | 1991 | Ithaca, NY | 34-20 | Dayton, OH |
| 1975 | Wittenberg, OH | 28-0 | Ithaca, NY | 1992 | WI-La Crosse | 16-12 | Wash. & Jeff., PA |
| 1976 | St. John's, MN | 31-28 | Towson St., MD | 1993 | Mt. Union, OH | 34-24 | Rowan, NJ |
| 1977 | Widener, PA | 39-36 | Wabash, IN | 1994 | Albion, MI | 38-15 | Wash. & Jeff. |
| 1978 | Baldwin-Wallace | 24-10 | Wittenberg, OH | 1995 | WI-La Crosse | 36-7 | Rowan, NJ |
| 1979 | Ithaca, NY | 14-10 | Wittenberg, OH | 1996 | Mt. Union, OH | 56-24 | Rowan, NJ |
| 1980 | Dayton, OH | 63-0 | Ithaca, NY | 1997 | Mt. Union, OH | 61-12 | Lycoming |
| 1981 | Widener, PA | 17-10 | Dayton, OH | 1998 | Mt. Union, OH | 44-24 | Rowan, NJ |
| 1982 | West Georgia | 14-0 | Augustana, IL | 1999 | Pacific Lutheran | 42-13 | Rowan, NJ |
| 1983 | Augustana, IL | 21-17 | Union, NY | 2000 | Mt. Union, OH | 10-7 | St. John's, MN |
| 1984 | Augustana, IL | 21-12 | Central, IA | 2001 | Mt. Union, OH | 30-27 | Bridgewater, VA |
| 1985 | Augustana, IL | 20-7 | Ithaca | 2002 | Mt. Union, OH | 48-7 | Trinity, TX |
| 1986 | Augustana, IL | 31-3 | Salisbury St., MD | 2003 | St. John's, MN | 24-6 | Mt. Union, OH |
| 1987 | Wagner, NY | 19-3 | Dayton, OH | 2004 | Linfield | 28-21 | Mary Hardin-Baylor |
| 1988 | Ithaca, NY | 39-24 | Central, IA | | | | |
| 1989 | Dayton, OH | 17-7 | Union, NY | | | | |

## Gagliardi Trophy

First presented in 1993 by the St. John's (Minn.) University J-Club, to honor the nation's outstanding Division III player. The award is named after John Gagliardi, St. John's legendary head coach, one of only two (Eddie Robinson) coaches in college football history with 400 wins.

| Year | | Year | | Year | |
|---|---|---|---|---|---|
| 1993 | Jim Ballard, Mt. Union, QB | 1998 | Scott Hvistendahl, | 2002 | Dan Pugh, Mt. Union, RB |
| 1994 | Carey Bender, Coe, RB | | Augsburg, WR/P | 2003 | Blake Elliott, St. John's, WR |
| 1995 | Chris Palmer, St. John's, WR | 1999 | Danny Ragsdale, Redlands, QB | 2004 | Rocky Myers, Wesley, S |
| 1996 | Lon Erickson, Ill. Wesleyan, QB | 2000 | Chad Johnson, Pac. Luth., QB | | |
| 1997 | Bill Borchert, Mt. Union, QB | 2001 | Chuck Moore, Mt. Union, RB | | |

## NAIA Playoffs

### Division I

Established in 1956 as two-team playoff. Tournament field increased to four teams in 1958, eight teams in 1978 and 16 teams in 1987 before cutting back to eight teams in 1989. NAIA went back to a single division 16-team playoff in 1997. The title game has ended in a tie four times (1956, '64, '84 and '85). Note that Northeastern St., OK was called NE Oklahoma in 1958.

**Multiple winners:** Texas A&I (7); Carson-Newman (5); Carroll-MT, Central Arkansas and Central St-OH (3); Abilene Christian, Central St-OK, Elon, Georgetown-KY, Northeastern St-OK, Pittsburg St. and St. John's-MN (2).

| Year | Winner | Score | Loser | Year | Winner | Score | Loser |
|---|---|---|---|---|---|---|---|
| 1956 | Montana St. | 0-0 | St. Joseph's, IN | 1982 | Central St., OK | 14-11 | Mesa, CO |
| 1957 | Pittsburg St., KS | 27-26 | Hillsdale, MI | 1983 | Car-Newman, TN | 36-28 | Mesa, CO |
| 1958 | NE Oklahoma | 19-13 | Northern Arizona | 1984 | Car-Newman, TN | 19-19 | Central Arkansas |
| 1959 | Texas A&I | 20-7 | Lenoir-Rhyne, NC | 1985 | Hillsdale, MI | 10-10 | Central Arkansas |
| 1960 | Lenoir-Rhyne, NC | 15-14 | Humboldt St., CA | 1986 | Car-Newman, TN | 17-0 | Cameron, OK |
| 1961 | Pittsburg St., KS | 12-7 | Linfield, OR | 1987 | Cameron, OK | 30-2 | Car-Newman, TN |
| 1962 | Central St., OK | 28-13 | Lenoir-Rhyne, NC | 1988 | Car-Newman, TN | 56-21 | Adams St., CO |
| 1963 | St. John's, MN | 33-27 | Prairie View, TX | 1989 | Car-Newman, TN | 34-20 | Emporia St., KS |
| 1964 | Concordia, MN | 7-7 | Sam Houston, TX | 1990 | Central St., OH | 38-16 | Mesa, CO |
| 1965 | St. John's, MN | 33-0 | Linfield, OR | 1991 | Central Arkansas | 19-16 | Central St., OH |
| 1966 | Waynesburg, PA | 42-21 | WI-Whitewater | 1992 | Central St., OH | 19-16 | Gardner-Webb, NC |
| 1967 | Fairmont St., WV | 28-21 | Eastern Wash. | 1993 | E. Central, OK | 49-35 | Glenville St., WV |
| 1968 | Troy St., AL. | 43-35 | Texas A&I | 1994 | N'eastern St., OK | 13-12 | Ark-Pine Bluff |
| 1969 | Texas A&I | 32-7 | Concordia, MN | 1995 | Central St., OK | 37-7 | N'eastern St., OK |
| 1970 | Texas A&I | 48-7 | Wofford, SC | 1996 | SW Oklahoma St. | 33-31 | Montana Tech |
| 1971 | Livingston, AL | 14-12 | Arkansas Tech | 1997 | Findlay, OH | 14-7 | Willamette, ORE |
| 1972 | East Texas St. | 21-18 | Car-Newman, TN | 1998 | Azusa Pacific, CA | 17-14 | Olivet Nazarene, IL |
| 1973 | Abilene Christian. | 42-14 | Elon, NC | 1999 | NW Oklahoma St. | 34-26 | Georgetown, KY |
| 1974 | Texas A&I | 34-23 | Henderson St., AR | 2000 | Georgetown, KY | 20-0 | NW Oklahoma St. |
| 1975 | Texas A&I | 37-0 | Salem, WV | 2001 | Georgetown, KY | 49-27 | Sioux Falls, S.D. |
| 1976 | Texas A&I | 26-0 | Central Arkansas | 2002 | Carroll, MT | 28-7 | Georgetown, KY |
| 1977 | Abilene Christian | 24-7 | SW Oklahoma | 2003 | Carroll, MT | 41-28 | NW Oklahoma St. |
| 1978 | Angelo St., TX | 34-14 | Elon, NC | 2004 | Carroll, MT | 15-13 | St. Francis, IN |
| 1979 | Texas A&I | 20-14 | Central St., OK | | | | |
| 1980 | Elon, NC | 17-10 | NE Oklahoma | | | | |
| 1981 | Elon, NC | 3-0 | Pittsburg St., KS | | | | |

### Division II

Established in 1970 as four-team playoff. Tournament field increased to eight teams in 1978 and 16 teams in 1987. NAIA went back to a single division playoff in 1997. The title game has ended in a tie twice (1981 and '87).

**Multiple winners:** Westminster (6); Findlay, Linfield and Pacific Lutheran (3); Concordia-MN, Northwestern-IA and Texas Lutheran (2).

| Year | Winner | Score | Loser | Year | Winner | Score | Loser |
|---|---|---|---|---|---|---|---|
| 1970 | Westminster, PA | 21-16 | Anderson, IN | 1984 | Linfield, OR | 33-22 | Northwestern, IA |
| 1971 | Calif. Lutheran | 20-14 | Westminster, PA | 1985 | WI-La Crosse | 24-7 | Pacific Lutheran |
| 1972 | Missouri Southern | 21-14 | Northwestern, IA | 1986 | Linfield, OR | 17-0 | Baker, KS |
| 1973 | Northwestern, IA | 10-3 | Glenville St., WV | 1987 | Pacific Lutheran | 16-16 | WI-Stevens Pt.* |
| 1974 | Texas Lutheran | 42-0 | Missouri Valley | 1988 | Westminster, PA | 21-14 | WI-La Crosse |
| 1975 | Texas Lutheran | 34-8 | Calif. Lutheran | 1989 | Westminster, PA | 51-30 | WI-La Crosse |
| 1976 | Westminster, PA | 20-13 | Redlands, CA | 1990 | Peru St., NE | 17-7 | Westminster, PA |
| 1977 | Westminster, PA | 17-9 | Calif. Lutheran | 1991 | Georgetown, KY | 28-20 | Pacific Lutheran |
| 1978 | Concordia, MN | 7-0 | Findlay, OH | 1992 | Findlay, OH | 26-13 | Linfield, OR |
| 1979 | Findlay, OH | 51-6 | Northwestern, IA | 1993 | Pacific Lutheran | 50-20 | Westminster, PA |
| 1980 | Pacific Lutheran | 38-10 | Wilmington, OH | 1994 | Westminster, PA | 27-7 | Pacific Lutheran |
| 1981 | Austin College, TX | 24-24 | Concordia, MN | 1995 | Findlay, OH | 21-21 | Central Wash. |
| 1982 | Linfield, OR | 33-15 | Wm. Jewell, MO | 1996 | Sioux Falls, S.D. | 47-25 | W. Washington |
| 1983 | Northwestern, IA | 25-21 | Pacific Lutheran | | | | |

*Wisconsin-Stevens Point forfeited its entire 1987 schedule due to its use of an ineligible player.

# Pro Football

**Peyton Manning** *tossed a record 49 TD passes in 2004 and the Colts finished 12-4.*

# Coming in Threes

*Brady, Belichick and Co. win ring number three with a 24-21 win over the Eagles in Super Bowl XXXIX.*

**Chris Berman**
*is the host of ESPN's NFL Prime Time.*

Patriots win Super Bowl by three. Again.

For the third time in four years, Bill Belichick and the New England Patriots raised the Vince Lombardi Trophy via the margin of a field goal, this time holding off the game Philadelphia Eagles, 24-21, in Super Bowl XXXIX at Jacksonville's ALLTEL Stadium. By doing so, the Pats cemented their place in history as one of the league's great teams.

The hero of the game was speedy Deion Branch, who tied a Super Bowl record by catching 11 passes from quarterback Tom Brady en route to MVP honors. But Branch wasn't the only wide receiver who made news that day as Philadelphia's Terrell Owens caught nine passes for 122 yards, roughly six weeks after suffering a severe leg injury that threatened to sideline him indefinitely. His performance would become part of Super Bowl lore.

Still, it was another season of championship football from the Patriots, whose run through these playoffs was classic. They held the league's highest-scoring team, the Colts, to a season-low three points in the Divisional Playoffs. Then they scored 41 points in the AFC title game victory over the Steelers, who had led the NFL in fewest points allowed. The win over the Eagles capped a second consecutive 17-2 season, highlighted by an NFL-record 21-game overall winning streak which spanned the last two years.

As for the two biggest non-Patriot headlines in 2004, we go back to Philadelphia and Owens, whose arrival in the City of Brotherly Love was eventful, to say the least. But so was his impact on the field as he set a team record with 14 touchdown receptions (in as many games) and helped quarterback Donovan McNabb enjoy the most productive season of his Pro Bowl-laden career.

AP/Wide World Photos

***Rodney Harrison*** *celebrates his second interception of Donovan McNabb late in Super Bowl XXXIX to seal the Patriots 24-21 win and their third championship in four years.*

It was hard not to marvel at the play of quarterback Peyton Manning, who captured league MVP honors for the second straight year as the Colts scored 522 points, the fifth-highest total ever. The prolific signal-caller set a new NFL record, throwing for 49 touchdowns, while wideouts Marvin Harrison, Reggie Wayne and Brandon Stokley became the first teammates to each catch 10 or more touchdown passes in the same season.

Age was served before beauty in the form of 31-year-old Jets running back Curtis Martin, who surprised many by saying he felt he could gain 1,500 yards. He more than lived up to those words by amassing a career-high 1,697 yards and becoming the oldest player to lead the NFL in rushing. He and Steelers' running back Jerome Bettis, he of the one-yard touchdown blasts early in the season, enjoyed eye-opening years that likely cemented their future induction into the Pro Football Hall of Fame.

There was the arrival of rookie quarterback Ben Roethlisberger, who not only provided Steelers' fans with a new sandwich but reeled off a tasty 14 straight wins (including a 34-20 win over New England on Halloween that ended the Patriots' 21-game overall winning streak) before he and his team fell

AP/Wide World Photos

*Outspoken **Terrell Owens** made a courageous return to the Eagles in Super Bowl XXXIX, following a Week 15 ankle injury. He caught nine balls for 122 yards but the Eagles came up just short.*

short in the AFC Championship Game. But there was also the disappearance of running back Ricky Williams, who decided that he no longer wanted to play professional football. His absence was a key factor in the Dolphins' forgettable 4-12 season.

There were other notable storylines as well. The defending NFC champion Panthers got off to a 1-7 start before staging a near-miraculous comeback and nearly reaching the postseason. Vikings' quarterback Daunte Culpepper threw for 4,717 yards and 39 scores, both amongst the best performances in league history. And the San Diego Chargers were the surprise team of the entire league, going from 4-12 in 2003 to 12-4 and making their first playoff appearance since 1995.

But once again, it was the savvy Patriots, who responded to all challenges and obstacles, that proved to be the team to beat. From the astute acquisition of running back Corey Dillon to the season-ending injury of veteran corner Ty Law at midseason. From the inspiring play of linebacker Tedy Bruschi and the defense to the reliable foot of kicker Adam Vinatieri. Not to mention the poise of quarterback Tom Brady. Simply put, Belichick and Co. now deserve to be ranked amongst the most revered of teams.

*continued on page 220* ▶

# The Ten Biggest Stories
# of the Year in Pro Football

**10** The defense rests! On November 28, the Cincinnati Bengals beat the Cleveland Browns, 58-48, in the second-highest scoring game of all-time. The 106 total points is behind only the Redskins' 72-41 win over the Giants in 1966. Four weeks earlier, the Chiefs and Colts put up 1,095 yards in the Chiefs 45-35 win, the third-highest yardage total in NFL history.

**9** Those that live by the foot shall die by the foot. In Week 1 of the playoffs, the Jets beat the Chargers, 20-17, in overtime after San Diego kicker Nate Kaeding's 40-yard field goal miss. A week later it is the Jets on the losing end of a 20-17 overtime game with Pittsburgh after Doug Brien misses two field goals in the final two minutes of regulation.

**8** While 31-year-old Curtis Martin leads the league in rushing, it is a new crop of young running backs that take the league by storm in the second half of the season. Willis McGahee (Buffalo), Julius Jones (Dallas) and Kevin Jones (Detroit) are all brilliant late in the year, giving their teams reason for excitement in 2005.

**7** Michael Vick shows his usual flashes of brilliance and Warrick Dunn rushes for over 1,000 yards as the Falcons (under new coach Jim Mora) advance to the NFC Championship Game.

**6** Still stung by the loss of Ricky Williams, who went AWOL in the off-season, the Dolphins fall from 10-6 to 4-12 in the span of a year.

**5** LaDainian Tomlinson, Antonio Gates, a rejuvenated Drew Brees and an inspired defense carries the Chargers to a 12-4 record (after a 4-12 mark the year before) and their first playoff appearance since the 1995-96 season.

**4** After Tommy Maddox is injured in a Week 2 loss against the Ravens, the Steelers season appears in jeopardy. Not so fast. Rookie Ben Roethlisberger more than ably takes over, guiding the team to a 14-0 mark the rest of the way and into the AFC Championship Game.

**3** Indianapolis quarterback Peyton Manning has the best regular season ever by an NFL quarterback, throwing for 49 touchdowns to break Dan Marino's 20-year-old record, and a 121.1 passer rating, shattering the former mark of 112.8.

**2** Terrell Owens energizes Donovan McNabb and the Eagles offense as Philly finishes 13-3 and, despite Owens missing the first two weeks of the playoffs with an injury, finally gets past the NFC Championship Game. Owens returns for the Super Bowl and catches nine passes for 122 yards.

**1** The New England Patriots win their third Super Bowl in the last four years with a 24-21 victory over the Eagles. Deion Branch grabs 11 of Tom Brady's passes to win the MVP award. The Pats finish 14-2 for the second consecutive year and break a league record with 21 consecutive wins (18 regular season) over the past two years.

So how do these Patriots compare to the 1960s Packers, '70s Steelers, '80s 49ers and '90s Cowboys? Let the debate begin. The Pats' repeat was just the eighth in the Super Bowl era, and only Dallas can also claim three Lombardi Trophies in a four-year span. Are the Pats truly a dynasty? It's safe to say that the answer to that question would become a whole lot clearer should Belichick and the Patriots add a third straight title in 2005-06.

## Worst to First

The San Diego Chargers and Atlanta Falcons went from last place in their respective divisions in 2003 to first place in 2004. It's the third time since 2001 that not just one team, but two, went from worst to first.

| Year | Team | Division | Record |
|------|------|----------|--------|
| 2004 | San Diego | AFC West | 4-12 to 12-4 |
| | Atlanta | NFC South | 5-11 to 11-5 |
| 2003 | Kansas City | AFC West | 8-8 to 13-3 |
| | Carolina | NFC South | 7-9 to 11-5 |
| 2001 | New Eng.* | AFC East | 5-11 to 11-5 |
| | Chicago | NFC Centr. | 5-11 to 13-3 |

*Super Bowl champions

## Put Me In, Coach

Green Bay's Brett Favre has started behind the center in every Packers game since 1992. His 210 consecutive starts (through Week 5 of the 2005 NFL season) is far and away the tops on the all-time list for quarterbacks.

| | Years | Starts |
|------|-------|--------|
| Brett Favre, GB | 1992– | 210 |
| Peyton Manning, Ind. | 1998– | 118 |
| Ron Jaworski, Phi. | 1977-84 | 116 |
| Joe Ferguson, Buf. | 1977-84 | 107 |
| Dan Marino, Mia. | 1987-93 | 95 |
| Roman Gabriel, Rams | 1965-72 | 89 |

(through Week 6, Oct. 17, 2005)

## My Favorite Martin

The Jets' Curtis Martin ran for a career-high 1,697 yards in 2004 to become the oldest running back in NFL history to lead the league in rushing.

| | Year | Yards | Age |
|------|------|-------|-----|
| Curtis Martin, NYJ | 2004 | 1,697 | 31 yrs, 26 days |
| Marion Motley, Cle. | 1950 | 810 | 30 yrs, 188 days |
| Charles White, Rams | 1987 | 1,374 | 29 yrs, 339 days |
| Jim Brown, Cle. | 1965 | 1,544 | 29 yrs, 305 days |
| Floyd Little, Den. | 1971 | 1,133 | 29 yrs, 168 days |

**Source**: *NFL Media*

# 2004-2005
# *Season in Review*

SPORTS ALMANAC

## Final NFL Standings

Division champions (*) and wild card playoff qualifiers (†) are noted; division champions with two best records received first round byes. Number of seasons listed after each head coach refers to latest tenure with club through 2004 season.

## American Football Conference

### East Division

| | W | L | T | PF | PA | vs Div | vs AFC |
|---|---|---|---|---|---|---|---|
| *New England | 14 | 2 | 0 | 437 | 260 | 5-1 | 10-2 |
| †NY Jets | 10 | 6 | 0 | 333 | 261 | 3-3 | 7-5 |
| Buffalo | 9 | 7 | 0 | 395 | 284 | 3-3 | 5-7 |
| Miami | 4 | 12 | 0 | 275 | 354 | 1-5 | 2-10 |

**2004 Head Coaches: NE**—Bill Belichick (5th season); **NY**—Herman Edwards (4th); **Buf**—Mike Mularkey (1st); **Mia**—Dave Wannstedt (5th; 1-8) resigned on Nov. 9 and was replaced by def. coordinator Jim Bates (3-4).

**2003 Standings:** 1. New England (14-2); 2. Miami (10-6); 3. Buffalo (6-10); 4. NY Jets (6-10).

### North Division

| | W | L | T | PF | PA | vs Div | vs AFC |
|---|---|---|---|---|---|---|---|
| *Pittsburgh | 15 | 1 | 0 | 372 | 251 | 5-1 | 11-1 |
| Baltimore | 9 | 7 | 0 | 317 | 268 | 3-3 | 6-6 |
| Cincinnati | 8 | 8 | 0 | 374 | 372 | 2-4 | 4-8 |
| Cleveland | 4 | 12 | 0 | 276 | 390 | 2-4 | 3-9 |

**2004 Head Coaches: Pit**—Bill Cowher (13th season); **Bal**—Brian Billick (6th); **Cin**—Marvin Lewis (2nd); **Cle**—Butch Davis (4th, 3-8) resigned on Nov. 30 and was replaced by off. coordinator Terry Robiskie (1-4).

**2003 Standings:** 1. Baltimore (10-6); 2. Cincinnati (8-8); 3. Pittsburgh (6-10); 4. Cleveland (5-11).

### South Division

| | W | L | T | PF | PA | vs Div | vs AFC |
|---|---|---|---|---|---|---|---|
| *Indianapolis | 12 | 4 | 0 | 522 | 351 | 5-1 | 9-3 |
| Jacksonville | 9 | 7 | 0 | 261 | 280 | 2-4 | 6-6 |
| Houston | 7 | 9 | 0 | 309 | 339 | 4-2 | 6-6 |
| Tennessee | 5 | 11 | 0 | 344 | 439 | 1-5 | 3-9 |

**2004 Head Coaches: Ind**—Tony Dungy (3rd season); **Jax**—Jack Del Rio (2nd); **Hou**—Dom Capers (3rd); **Ten**—Jeff Fisher (11th).

**2003 Standings:** 1. Indianapolis (12-4); 2. Tennessee (12-4); 3. Jacksonville (5-11); 4. Houston (5-11).

### West Division

| | W | L | T | PF | PA | vs Div | vs AFC |
|---|---|---|---|---|---|---|---|
| *San Diego | 12 | 4 | 0 | 446 | 313 | 5-1 | 9-3 |
| †Denver | 10 | 6 | 0 | 381 | 304 | 3-3 | 7-5 |
| Kansas City | 7 | 9 | 0 | 483 | 435 | 3-3 | 6-6 |
| Oakland | 5 | 11 | 0 | 320 | 442 | 1-5 | 3-9 |

**2004 Head Coaches: SD**—Marty Schottenheimer (3rd season); **Den**—Mike Shanahan (10th); **KC**—Dick Vermeil (4th); **Oak**—Norv Turner (1st).

**2003 Standings:** 1. Kansas City (13-3); 2. Denver (10-6); 3. Oakland (4-12); 4. San Diego (4-12).

## National Football Conference

### East Division

| | W | L | T | PF | PA | vs Div | vs NFC |
|---|---|---|---|---|---|---|---|
| *Philadelphia | 13 | 3 | 0 | 386 | 260 | 6-0 | 11-1 |
| NY Giants | 6 | 10 | 0 | 303 | 347 | 3-3 | 5-7 |
| Dallas | 6 | 10 | 0 | 293 | 405 | 2-4 | 5-7 |
| Washington | 6 | 10 | 0 | 240 | 265 | 1-5 | 6-6 |

**2004 Head Coaches: Phi**—Andy Reid (6th season); **NY**—Tom Coughlin (1st); **Dal**—Bill Parcells (2nd); **Wash**—Joe Gibbs (1st).

**2003 Standings:** 1. Philadelphia (12-4); 2. Dallas (10-6); 3. Washington (5-11); 4. NY Giants (4-12).

### North Division

| | W | L | T | PF | PA | vs Div | vs NFC |
|---|---|---|---|---|---|---|---|
| *Green Bay | 10 | 6 | 0 | 424 | 380 | 5-1 | 9-3 |
| †Minnesota | 8 | 8 | 0 | 405 | 395 | 3-3 | 5-7 |
| Detroit | 6 | 10 | 0 | 296 | 350 | 2-4 | 5-7 |
| Chicago | 5 | 11 | 0 | 231 | 331 | 2-4 | 4-8 |

**2004 Head Coaches: GB**—Mike Sherman (5th season); **Min**—Mike Tice (4th); **Det**—Steve Mariucci (2nd); **Chi**—Lovie Smith (1st).

**2003 Standings:** 1. Green Bay (10-6); 2. Minnesota (9-7); 3. Chicago (7-9); 4. Detroit (5-11).

### South Division

| | W | L | T | PF | PA | vs Div | vs NFC |
|---|---|---|---|---|---|---|---|
| *Atlanta | 11 | 5 | 0 | 340 | 337 | 4-2 | 8-4 |
| New Orleans | 8 | 8 | 0 | 348 | 405 | 3-3 | 6-6 |
| Carolina | 7 | 9 | 0 | 355 | 339 | 3-3 | 6-6 |
| Tampa Bay | 5 | 11 | 0 | 301 | 304 | 2-4 | 4-8 |

**2004 Head Coaches: Atl**—Jim Mora Jr. (1st season); **NO**—Jim Haslett (5th); **Car**—John Fox (3rd); **TB**—Jon Gruden (2nd).

**2003 Standings:** 1. Carolina (11-5); 2. New Orleans (8-8); 3. Tampa Bay (7-9); 4. Atlanta (5-11).

### West Division

| | W | L | T | PF | PA | vs Div | vs NFC |
|---|---|---|---|---|---|---|---|
| *Seattle | 9 | 7 | 0 | 371 | 373 | 3-3 | 8-4 |
| †St. Louis | 8 | 8 | 0 | 319 | 392 | 5-1 | 7-5 |
| Arizona | 6 | 10 | 0 | 284 | 322 | 2-4 | 5-7 |
| San Francisco | 2 | 14 | 0 | 259 | 452 | 2-4 | 1-5 |

**2004 Head Coaches: Sea**—Mike Holmgren (6th season); **St.L**—Mike Martz (5th); **Ariz**—Dennis Green (1st); **SF**—Dennis Erickson (2nd).

**2003 Standings:** 1. St. Louis (12-4); 2. Seattle (10-6); 3. San Francisco (7-9); 4. Arizona (4-12).

**Note:** St. Louis (8-8) qualified for a wildcard berth over Minnesota (8-8) and New Orleans (8-8) due to a better conference record. Minnesota qualified over New Orleans due to its 38-31 win over the Saints on Oct. 17.

## NFL Regular Season Individual Leaders
(* indicates rookies)

### Passing Efficiency
(Minimum of 224 attempts)

| AFC | Att | Cmp | Cmp Pct | Yds | Yds/ Att | TD | Long | Int | Sack/Lost | Rating Points |
|---|---|---|---|---|---|---|---|---|---|---|
| Peyton Manning, Ind | 497 | 336 | 67.6 | 4557 | 9.17 | 49 | 80-td | 10 | 13/101 | 121.1 |
| Drew Brees, SD | 400 | 262 | 65.5 | 3159 | 7.90 | 27 | 79-td | 7 | 18/131 | 104.8 |
| Ben Roethlisberger*, Pit | 295 | 196 | 66.4 | 2621 | 8.88 | 17 | 58 | 11 | 30/213 | 98.1 |
| Trent Green, KC | 556 | 369 | 66.4 | 4591 | 8.26 | 27 | 70-td | 17 | 32/227 | 98.2 |
| Tom Brady, NE | 474 | 288 | 60.8 | 3692 | 7.79 | 28 | 50 | 14 | 26/162 | 92.6 |
| Chad Pennington, NYJ | 370 | 242 | 65.4 | 2673 | 7.22 | 16 | 48 | 9 | 18/103 | 91.0 |
| Billy Volek, Ten | 357 | 218 | 61.1 | 2486 | 6.96 | 18 | 48-td | 10 | 30/216 | 87.1 |
| Jake Plummer, Den | 521 | 303 | 58.2 | 4089 | 7.85 | 27 | 85-td | 20 | 15/90 | 84.5 |
| David Carr, Hou | 466 | 285 | 61.2 | 3531 | 7.58 | 16 | 69 | 14 | 49/301 | 83.5 |
| Byron Leftwich, Jax | 441 | 267 | 60.5 | 2941 | 6.67 | 15 | 65 | 10 | 25/114 | 82.2 |
| Carson Palmer, Cin | 432 | 263 | 60.9 | 2897 | 6.71 | 18 | 76-td | 18 | 25/178 | 77.3 |
| Jeff Garcia, Cle. | 252 | 144 | 57.1 | 1731 | 6.87 | 10 | 99-td | 9 | 24/99 | 76.7 |
| Drew Bledsoe, Buf | 450 | 256 | 56.9 | 2932 | 6.52 | 20 | 69-td | 16 | 37/215 | 76.6 |
| Kerry Collins, Oak | 513 | 289 | 56.3 | 3495 | 6.81 | 21 | 63 | 20 | 25/144 | 74.8 |
| Kyle Boller, Bal | 464 | 258 | 55.6 | 2559 | 5.52 | 13 | 57-td | 11 | 35/247 | 70.9 |

| NFC | Att | Cmp | Cmp Pct | Yds | Yds/ Att | TD | Long | Int | Sack/Lost | Rating Points |
|---|---|---|---|---|---|---|---|---|---|---|
| Daunte Culpepper, Min | 548 | 379 | 69.2 | 4717 | 8.61 | 39 | 82-td | 11 | 46/238 | 110.9 |
| Donovan McNabb, Phi | 469 | 300 | 64.0 | 3875 | 8.26 | 31 | 80 | 8 | 32/192 | 104.7 |
| Brian Griese, TB | 336 | 233 | 69.3 | 2632 | 7.83 | 20 | 68 | 12 | 26/169 | 97.5 |
| Marc Bulger, St.L. | 485 | 321 | 66.2 | 3964 | 8.17 | 21 | 56 | 14 | 41/302 | 93.7 |
| Brett Favre, GB | 540 | 346 | 64.1 | 4088 | 7.57 | 30 | 79-td | 17 | 12/93 | 92.4 |
| Jake Delhomme, Car | 533 | 310 | 58.2 | 3886 | 7.29 | 29 | 63 | 15 | 33/246 | 87.3 |
| Kurt Warner, NYG | 277 | 174 | 62.8 | 2054 | 7.42 | 6 | 62-td | 4 | 39/196 | 86.5 |
| Matt Hasselbeck, Sea | 474 | 279 | 58.9 | 3382 | 7.14 | 22 | 60 | 15 | 30/155 | 83.1 |
| Aaron Brooks, NO | 542 | 309 | 57.0 | 3810 | 7.03 | 21 | 57 | 16 | 41/223 | 79.5 |
| Tim Rattay, SF | 325 | 198 | 60.9 | 2169 | 6.67 | 10 | 65 | 10 | 37/211 | 78.1 |
| Michael Vick, Atl. | 321 | 181 | 56.4 | 2313 | 7.21 | 14 | 62 | 12 | 46/266 | 78.1 |
| Joey Harrington, Det | 489 | 274 | 56.0 | 3047 | 6.23 | 19 | 62 | 12 | 36/196 | 77.5 |
| Vinny Testaverde, Dal | 495 | 297 | 60.0 | 3532 | 7.14 | 17 | 53 | 20 | 34/182 | 76.4 |
| Patrick Ramsey, Wash | 272 | 169 | 62.1 | 1665 | 6.12 | 10 | 51 | 11 | 23/137 | 74.8 |
| Josh McCown, Ari | 408 | 233 | 57.1 | 2511 | 6.15 | 11 | 48 | 10 | 31/263 | 74.1 |

### Receptions

| AFC | No | Yds | Avg | Long | TD |
|---|---|---|---|---|---|
| Tony Gonzalez, KC | 102 | 1258 | 12.3 | 32 | 7 |
| Derrick Mason, Ten | 96 | 1168 | 12.2 | 37-td | 7 |
| Chad Johnson, Cin. | 95 | 1274 | 13.4 | 53-td | 9 |
| Eric Moulds, Buf | 88 | 1043 | 11.9 | 49 | 5 |
| Marvin Harrison, Ind | 86 | 1113 | 12.9 | 59 | 15 |
| Antonio Gates, SD | 81 | 964 | 11.9 | 72-td | 13 |
| Drew Bennett, Ten | 80 | 1247 | 15.6 | 48-td | 11 |
| Hines Ward, Pit | 80 | 1004 | 12.6 | 58 | 4 |
| Rod Smith, Den | 79 | 1144 | 14.5 | 85-td | 7 |
| Andre Johnson, Hou | 79 | 1142 | 14.5 | 54-td | 6 |
| Reggie Wayne, Ind | 77 | 1210 | 15.7 | 71-td | 12 |
| Jimmy Smith, Jax | 74 | 1172 | 15.8 | 65 | 6 |
| T.J. Houshmandzadeh, Cin | 73 | 978 | 13.4 | 62 | 4 |
| Randy McMichael, Mia | 73 | 791 | 10.8 | 42-td | 4 |

| NFC | No | Yds | Avg | Long | TD |
|---|---|---|---|---|---|
| Joe Horn, NO | 94 | 1399 | 14.9 | 57 | 11 |
| Torry Holt, St.L. | 94 | 1372 | 14.6 | 75-td | 10 |
| Muhsin Muhammad, Car | 93 | 1405 | 15.1 | 51 | 16 |
| Laveranues Coles, Wash. | 90 | 950 | 10.6 | 45 | 1 |
| Javon Walker, GB | 89 | 1382 | 15.5 | 79-td | 12 |
| Isaac Bruce, St.L | 89 | 1292 | 14.5 | 54 | 6 |
| Darrell Jackson, Sea | 87 | 1199 | 13.8 | 56-td | 7 |
| Jason Witten, Dal | 87 | 980 | 11.3 | 42-td | 6 |
| Donald Driver, GB | 84 | 1208 | 14.4 | 50 | 9 |
| Eric Johnson, SF. | 82 | 825 | 10.1 | 25 | 2 |
| Michael Clayton*, TB | 80 | 1193 | 14.9 | 75-td | 7 |
| Terrell Owens, Phi | 77 | 1200 | 15.6 | 59-td | 14 |
| Brian Westbrook, Phi | 73 | 703 | 9.6 | 50 | 6 |
| Jermaine Wiggins, Min | 71 | 705 | 9.9 | 39 | 4 |

### Rushing Yards

| AFC | Att | Yds | Avg | Long | TD |
|---|---|---|---|---|---|
| Curtis Martin, NYJ | 371 | 1697 | 4.6 | 25-td | 12 |
| Corey Dillon, NE | 345 | 1635 | 4.7 | 44 | 12 |
| Edgerrin James, Ind. | 334 | 1548 | 4.6 | 40 | 9 |
| Rudi Johnson, Cin | 361 | 1454 | 4.0 | 52 | 12 |
| LaDainian Tomlinson, SD | 339 | 1335 | 3.9 | 42 | 17 |
| Reuben Droughns, Den | 275 | 1240 | 4.5 | 51-td | 6 |
| Fred Taylor, Jax | 260 | 1224 | 4.7 | 46 | 2 |
| Domanick Davis, Hou | 302 | 1188 | 3.9 | 44 | 13 |
| Willis McGahee, Buf | 284 | 1128 | 4.0 | 41 | 13 |
| Chris Brown, Ten | 220 | 1067 | 4.9 | 52 | 6 |
| Jamal Lewis, Bal | 235 | 1006 | 4.3 | 75-td | 7 |
| Jerome Bettis, Pit | 250 | 941 | 3.8 | 29 | 13 |
| Priest Holmes, KC | 196 | 892 | 4.6 | 33-td | 14 |
| Duce Staley, Pit. | 192 | 830 | 4.3 | 38 | 1 |

| NFC | Att | Yds | Avg | Long | TD |
|---|---|---|---|---|---|
| Shaun Alexander, Sea | 353 | 1696 | 4.8 | 44 | 16 |
| Tiki Barber, NYG | 322 | 1518 | 4.7 | 72-td | 13 |
| Clinton Portis, Wash. | 343 | 1315 | 3.8 | 64-td | 5 |
| Ahman Green, GB | 259 | 1163 | 4.5 | 90-td | 7 |
| Kevin Jones*, Det | 241 | 1133 | 4.7 | 74 | 5 |
| Warrick Dunn, Atl | 265 | 1106 | 4.2 | 60 | 9 |
| Deuce McAllister, NO | 269 | 1074 | 4.0 | 71 | 9 |
| Thomas Jones, Chi | 240 | 948 | 4.0 | 54 | 7 |
| Emmitt Smith, Ari | 267 | 937 | 3.5 | 29-td | 9 |
| Michael Pittman, TB | 219 | 926 | 4.2 | 78-td | 7 |
| Michael Vick, Atl. | 120 | 902 | 7.5 | 58 | 3 |
| Kevan Barlow, SF. | 244 | 822 | 3.4 | 60 | 7 |
| Nick Goings, Car | 217 | 821 | 3.8 | 57-td | 6 |
| Julius Jones*, Dal. | 197 | 819 | 4.2 | 53 | 7 |

Indianapolis Colts
**Peyton Manning**
Passing

Kansas City Chiefs
**Tony Gonzalez**
Receptions

Seattle Seahawks
**Shaun Alexander**
Touchdowns

Baltimore Ravens
**Ed Reed**
Interceptions

## All-Purpose Yardage

| AFC | Rush | Rec | Ret | Total | NFC | Rush | Rec | Ret | Total |
|---|---|---|---|---|---|---|---|---|---|
| Dante Hall, KC | 56 | 230 | 1950 | 2236 | Tiki Barber, NYG | 1518 | 578 | 0 | 2096 |
| Edgerrin James, Ind | 1548 | 483 | 0 | 2031 | Shaun Alexander, Sea | 1696 | 170 | 0 | 1866 |
| Curtis Martin, NYJ | 1697 | 245 | 0 | 1942 | Michael Lewis, NO | 0 | 127 | 1597 | 1724 |
| Wes Welker*, SD-Mia | 0 | 0 | 1879 | 1879 | Allen Rossum, Atl | 0 | 0 | 1707 | 1707 |
| B.J. Sams*, Bal | 19 | 2 | 1826 | 1847 | Clinton Portis, Wash | 1315 | 235 | 0 | 1550 |
| Reuben Droughns, Den | 1240 | 241 | 344 | 1825 | Brian Westbrook, Phi | 812 | 703 | 14 | 1529 |
| Domanick Davis, Hou | 1188 | 588 | 0 | 1776 | Ahman Green, GB | 1163 | 275 | 0 | 1438 |
| LaDainian Tomlinson, SD | 1335 | 441 | 0 | 1776 | Muhsin Muhammad, Car | 15 | 1405 | 0 | 1420 |
| Corey Dillon, NE | 1635 | 103 | 0 | 1738 | Eddie Drummond, Det | 9 | 0 | 1408 | 1417 |
| Doug Gabriel, Oak | 7 | 551 | 1147 | 1705 | Warrick Dunn, Atl | 1106 | 294 | 0 | 1400 |
| J.J. Moses, Hou | 0 | 0 | 1612 | 1612 | Joe Horn, NO | 0 | 1399 | 0 | 1399 |
| Fred Taylor, Jax | 1224 | 345 | 0 | 1569 | Javon Walker, GB | 0 | 1382 | 0 | 1382 |
| Rudi Johnson, Cin | 1454 | 84 | 0 | 1538 | Thomas Jones, Chi | 948 | 427 | 0 | 1375 |
| Antwaan Randle El, Pit | 34 | 601 | 874 | 1509 | Torry Holt, St.L | 0 | 1372 | 0 | 1372 |
| Dominic Rhodes, Ind | 254 | 24 | 1188 | 1466 | Nate Burleson, Min | 49 | 1006 | 265 | 1320 |

**Ret** column indicates all kickoff, punt, fumble and interception returns.

## Scoring

### Touchdowns

| AFC | TD | Rush | Rec | Ret | Pts |
|---|---|---|---|---|---|
| LaDainian Tomlinson, SD | 18 | 17 | 1 | 0 | 108 |
| Marvin Harrison, Ind | 15 | 0 | 15 | 0 | 90 |
| Priest Holmes, KC | 15 | 14 | 1 | 0 | 90 |
| Domanick Davis, Hou | 14 | 13 | 1 | 0 | 84 |
| Curtis Martin, NYJ | 14 | 12 | 2 | 0 | 84 |
| Corey Dillon, NE | 13 | 12 | 1 | 0 | 80† |
| Jerome Bettis, Pit | 13 | 13 | 0 | 0 | 78 |
| Antonio Gates, SD | 13 | 0 | 13 | 0 | 78 |
| Willis McGahee, Buf | 13 | 13 | 0 | 0 | 78 |
| Rudi Johnson, Cin | 12 | 12 | 0 | 0 | 72 |
| Reggie Wayne, Ind | 12 | 0 | 12 | 0 | 72 |
| Drew Bennett, Ten | 11 | 0 | 11 | 0 | 66 |
| Larry Johnson, KC | 11 | 9 | 2 | 0 | 66 |

† Two-point conversions: Dillon (1).

| NFC | TD | Rush | Rec | Ret | Pts |
|---|---|---|---|---|---|
| Shaun Alexander, Sea | 20 | 16 | 4 | 0 | 120 |
| Muhsin Muhammad, Car | 16 | 0 | 16 | 0 | 96 |
| Tiki Barber, NYG | 15 | 13 | 2 | 0 | 90 |
| Terrell Owens, Phi | 14 | 0 | 14 | 0 | 84 |
| Randy Moss, Min | 13 | 0 | 13 | 0 | 78 |
| Javon Walker, GB | 12 | 0 | 12 | 0 | 72 |
| Joe Horn, NO | 11 | 0 | 11 | 0 | 68† |
| Nate Burleson, Min | 10 | 0 | 9 | 1 | 62† |
| Torry Holt, St.L | 10 | 0 | 10 | 0 | 60 |
| Michael Pittman, TB | 10 | 7 | 3 | 0 | 60 |
| Donald Driver, GB | 9 | 0 | 9 | 0 | 56† |

Four tied with 9 TD for 54 pts.

† Two-point conversions: Horn, Burleson and Driver (1).

### Kickers

| AFC | PAT | FG | Long | Pts |
|---|---|---|---|---|
| Adam Vinatieri, NE | 48/48 | 31/33 | 48 | 141 |
| Jason Elam, Den | 42/42 | 29/34 | 52 | 129 |
| Jeff Reed, Pit | 40/40 | 28/33 | 51 | 124 |
| Shayne Graham, Cin | 41/41 | 27/31 | 53 | 122 |
| Mike Vanderjagt, Ind | 59/60 | 20/25 | 47 | 119 |
| Rian Lindell, Buf | 45/45 | 24/28 | 43 | 117 |
| Matt Stover, Bal | 30/30 | 29/32 | 50 | 117 |
| Nate Kaeding*, SD | 54/55 | 20/25 | 53 | 114 |
| Lawrence Tynes, KC | 58/60 | 17/23 | 50 | 109 |
| Sebastian Janikowski, Oak | 31/32 | 25/28 | 52 | 106 |
| Doug Brien, NYJ | 33/34 | 24/29 | 53 | 105 |
| Phil Dawson, Cle | 28/28 | 24/29 | 50 | 100 |
| Josh Scobee*, Jax | 21/21 | 24/31 | 53 | 93 |
| Gary Anderson, Ten | 37/37 | 17/22 | 45 | 88 |

| NFC | PAT | FG | Long | Pts |
|---|---|---|---|---|
| David Akers, Phi | 41/42 | 27/32 | 51 | 122 |
| Ryan Longwell, GB | 48/48 | 24/28 | 53 | 120 |
| Josh Brown, Sea | 40/40 | 23/25 | 54 | 109 |
| John Carney, NO | 38/38 | 22/27 | 53 | 104 |
| Jason Hanson, Det | 28/28 | 24/28 | 48 | 100 |
| Morten Andersen, Min | 45/45 | 18/22 | 48 | 99 |
| Steve Christie, NYG | 33/33 | 22/28 | 53 | 99 |
| Jay Feely, Atl | 40/40 | 18/23 | 47 | 94 |
| Neil Rackers, Ari | 28/28 | 22/29 | 55 | 94 |
| Billy Cundiff, Dal | 31/31 | 20/26 | 49 | 91 |
| Jeff Wilkins, St.L | 32/32 | 19/24 | 53 | 89 |
| John Kasay, Car | 27/28 | 19/22 | 54 | 84 |
| Todd Peterson, SF | 23/23 | 18/22 | 51 | 77 |

# NFL Regular Season Individual Leaders (Cont.)

## Sacks

| AFC | No |
|---|---|
| Dwight Freeney, Ind. | 16.0 |
| Shaun Ellis, NYJ | 11.0 |
| Reggie Hayward, Den | 10.5 |
| Robert Mathis, Ind | 10.5 |
| Terrell Suggs, Bal. | 10.5 |

| NFC | No |
|---|---|
| Bertrand Berry, Ari | 14.5 |
| Kabeer Gbaja-Biamila, GB | 13.5 |
| Patrick Kerney, Atl | 13.0 |
| Simeon Rice, TB | 12.0 |

Three tied with 11.5 sacks each.

## Interceptions

| AFC | No | Yds | Long | TD |
|---|---|---|---|---|
| Ed Reed, Bal | 9 | 358 | 106-td | 1 |
| Tory James, Cin | 8 | 66 | 23 | 0 |
| Dunta Robinson*, Hou | 6 | 146 | 61 | 0 |
| Andre Dyson, Ten | 6 | 135 | 44 | 0 |
| Nate Clements, Buf | 6 | 77 | 35 | 1 |

| NFC | No | Yds | Long | TD |
|---|---|---|---|---|
| Ken Lucas, Sea | 6 | 46 | 25 | 1 |
| Chris Gamble*, Car | 6 | 15 | 13 | 0 |

Seven tied with 5 int's each.

## Punting

| AFC | No | Yds | Lg | Avg | In20 |
|---|---|---|---|---|---|
| Shane Lechler, Oak | 73 | 3409 | 67 | 46.7 | 22 |
| Hunter Smith, Ind | 54 | 2443 | 62 | 45.2 | 21 |
| Brian Moorman, Buf | 77 | 3325 | 80 | 43.2 | 17 |
| Mike Scifres, SD | 69 | 2974 | 60 | 43.1 | 29 |
| Chris Gardocki, Pit | 67 | 2879 | 61 | 43.0 | 24 |

| NFC | No | Yds | Lg | Avg | In20 |
|---|---|---|---|---|---|
| Tom Tupa, Wash | 103 | 4544 | 61 | 44.1 | 30 |
| Todd Sauerbrun, Car | 76 | 3351 | 65 | 44.1 | 25 |
| Mitch Berger, NO | 85 | 3704 | 63 | 43.6 | 28 |
| Sean Landeta, St.L | 40 | 1733 | 63 | 43.3 | 9 |
| Scott Player, Ari | 98 | 4230 | 57 | 43.2 | 32 |

## Punt Returns
(Minimum of 20 returns)

| AFC | No | Yds | Avg | Long | TD |
|---|---|---|---|---|---|
| Dennis Northcutt, Cle | 36 | 432 | 12.0 | 44 | 0 |
| Wes Welker*, SD-Mia | 43 | 464 | 10.8 | 71 | 0 |
| B.J. Sams*, Bal | 55 | 575 | 10.5 | 78-td | 2 |
| Rod Smith, Den | 22 | 223 | 10.1 | 30 | 0 |
| Dante Hall, KC | 23 | 232 | 10.1 | 46 | 0 |

| NFC | No | Yds | Avg | Long | TD |
|---|---|---|---|---|---|
| Eddie Drummond, Det | 24 | 316 | 13.2 | 83-td | 2 |
| Allen Rossum, Atl | 37 | 457 | 12.4 | 75-td | 1 |
| Michael Lewis, NO | 34 | 382 | 11.2 | 53 | 0 |
| R.W. McQuarters, Chi | 44 | 435 | 9.9 | 75-td | 1 |
| Lance Frazier*, Dal | 24 | 229 | 9.5 | 55 | 0 |

## Kickoff Returns
(Minimum of 20 returns)

| AFC | No | Yds | Avg | Long | TD |
|---|---|---|---|---|---|
| Terrence McGee, Buf | 52 | 1370 | 26.3 | 104-td | 3 |
| Dante Hall, KC | 68 | 1718 | 25.3 | 97-td | 2 |
| Antwaan Randle El, Pit | 21 | 527 | 25.1 | 41 | 0 |
| Bethel Johnson, NE | 41 | 1016 | 24.8 | 93-td | 1 |
| Dominic Rhodes, Ind | 48 | 1188 | 24.8 | 88-td | 1 |

| NFC | No | Yds | Avg | Long | TD |
|---|---|---|---|---|---|
| Willie Ponder, NYG | 36 | 967 | 26.9 | 91-td | 1 |
| Eddie Drummond, Det | 41 | 1092 | 26.6 | 99-td | 2 |
| Torrie Cox, TB | 33 | 866 | 26.2 | 59 | 0 |
| Robert Ferguson, GB | 21 | 526 | 25.0 | 71 | 0 |
| Jamal Robertson, SF-Car | 31 | 740 | 23.9 | 49 | 0 |

# Single Game Highs

## Passing Yards

| AFC | Cmp/Att | Yds | TD |
|---|---|---|---|
| Jake Plummer, Den vs. Atl (10/31) | 31/55 | 499 | 4 |
| Billy Volek, Ten vs. Oak (12/19) | 40/60 | 492 | 4 |
| Peyton Manning, Ind vs. KC (10/31) | 25/44 | 472 | 5 |
| Billy Volek, Ten vs. KC (12/13) | 29/43 | 426 | 4 |
| Peyton Manning, Ind vs. Ten (12/5) | 25/33 | 425 | 3 |

| NFC | Cmp/Att | Yds | TD |
|---|---|---|---|
| Donovan McNabb, Phi vs. GB (12/5) | 32/43 | 464 | 5 |
| Marc Bulger, St.L vs. NYJ (1/2, OT) | 29/39 | 450 | 3 |
| Marc Bulger, St.L vs. GB (11/29) | 35/53 | 448 | 2 |
| Daunte Culpepper, Min vs. NO (10/17) | 26/37 | 425 | 5 |
| Tim Rattay, SF vs. Ari (10/10, OT) | 38/57 | 417 | 2 |

## Rushing Yards

| AFC | Car | Yds | TD |
|---|---|---|---|
| Edgerrin James, Ind vs. Chi (11/21) | 23 | 204 | 1 |
| Rudi Johnson, Cin vs. Cle (11/28) | 26 | 202 | 2 |
| Curtis Martin, NYJ vs. Cin (9/12) | 29 | 196 | 1 |
| Reuben Droughns, Den vs. Car (10/10) | 30 | 193 | 0 |
| Derrick Blaylock, KC vs. NO (11/14) | 33 | 186 | 1 |
| Jamal Lewis, Bal vs. Cin (9/26) | 18 | 186 | 1 |

| NFC | Car | Yds | TD |
|---|---|---|---|
| Julius Jones*, Dal vs. Sea (12/6) | 30 | 198 | 3 |
| Kevin Jones*, Det vs. Ari (12/5) | 26 | 196 | 1 |
| Shaun Alexander, Sea vs. Car (10/31) | 32 | 195 | 1 |
| Tiki Barber, NYG vs. GB (10/3) | 23 | 182 | 1 |
| Najeh Davenport, GB vs. St.L (11/29) | 19 | 178 | 1 |

## Receiving Yards

| AFC | Ct | Yds | TD |
|---|---|---|---|
| Drew Bennett, Ten vs. KC (12/13) | 12 | 233 | 3 |
| Rod Smith, Den vs. Atl (10/31) | 9 | 208 | 1 |
| Reggie Wayne, Ind vs. GB (9/26) | 11 | 184 | 1 |
| T.J. Houshmandzadeh, Cin vs. Bal (12/5) | 10 | 171 | 1 |
| Andre Johnson, Hou vs. Min (10/10, OT) | 12 | 170 | 2 |

| NFC | Ct | Yds | TD |
|---|---|---|---|
| Javon Walker, GB vs. Ind (9/26) | 11 | 200 | 3 |
| Muhsin Muhammad, Car vs. NO (12/5) | 10 | 179 | 1 |
| Isaac Bruce, St.L vs. GB (11/29) | 9 | 170 | 1 |
| Rod Gardner, Wash vs. Dal (9/27) | 10 | 167 | 2 |
| Joe Horn, NO vs. KC (11/14) | 5 | 167 | 1 |

## NFL Bests

**Longest Field Goal**
55 yds . . . . . . . . . . . . . . Neil Rackers, Ari vs. Sea (10/24)
**Longest Run from Scrimmage**
90 yds . . . . . . Ahman Green, GB vs. Dal (10/24) TD
**Longest Pass Play**
99 yds . . . J. Garcia to A. Davis, Cle vs. Cin (10/17) TD
**Longest Interception Return**
106 yds . . . . . . . . . . . . . Ed Reed, Bal vs Cle (11/17) TD
**Longest Punt Return**
91 yds . . . . . . . . Nate Burleson, Min vs. Ind (11/18) TD
**Longest Kickoff Return**
104 yds . . . . . . . . Terrence McGee, Buf vs. Mia (12/5) TD

## NFL Regular Season Team Leaders

### Offense

| | Points | | Yardage | | | |
|---|---|---|---|---|---|---|
| **AFC** | **For** | **Avg** | **Rush** | **Pass** | **Total** | **Avg** |
| Kansas City | 483 | 30.2 | 2289 | 4406 | 6695 | 418.4 |
| Indianapolis | 522 | 32.6 | 1852 | 4623 | 6475 | 404.7 |
| Denver | 381 | 23.8 | 2333 | 3999 | 6332 | 395.8 |
| New England | 437 | 27.3 | 2134 | 3588 | 5722 | 357.6 |
| San Diego | 446 | 27.9 | 2185 | 3357 | 5542 | 346.4 |
| Tennessee | 344 | 21.5 | 1871 | 3616 | 5487 | 342.9 |
| NY Jets | 333 | 20.8 | 2388 | 3050 | 5438 | 339.9 |
| Pittsburgh | 372 | 23.3 | 2464 | 2720 | 5184 | 324.0 |
| Oakland | 320 | 20.0 | 1295 | 3858 | 5153 | 322.1 |
| Cincinnati | 374 | 23.4 | 1839 | 3301 | 5140 | 321.3 |
| Houston | 309 | 19.3 | 1882 | 3246 | 5128 | 320.5 |
| Jacksonville | 261 | 16.3 | 1850 | 3159 | 5009 | 313.1 |
| Buffalo | 395 | 24.7 | 1874 | 2817 | 4691 | 293.2 |
| Cleveland | 276 | 17.3 | 1657 | 2824 | 4481 | 280.1 |
| Miami | 275 | 17.2 | 1339 | 3065 | 4404 | 275.3 |
| Baltimore | 317 | 19.8 | 2063 | 2312 | 4375 | 273.4 |

| | Points | | Yardage | | | |
|---|---|---|---|---|---|---|
| **NFC** | **For** | **Avg** | **Rush** | **Pass** | **Total** | **Avg** |
| Green Bay | 424 | 26.5 | 1908 | 4449 | 6357 | 397.3 |
| Minnesota | 405 | 25.3 | 1823 | 4516 | 6339 | 396.2 |
| St. Louis | 319 | 19.9 | 1624 | 4253 | 5877 | 367.3 |
| Seattle | 371 | 23.2 | 2095 | 3539 | 5634 | 352.1 |
| Philadelphia | 386 | 24.1 | 1639 | 3979 | 5618 | 351.1 |
| Carolina | 355 | 22.2 | 1582 | 3643 | 5225 | 326.6 |
| Dallas | 293 | 18.3 | 1769 | 3428 | 5197 | 324.8 |
| New Orleans | 348 | 21.8 | 1606 | 3587 | 5193 | 324.6 |
| Atlanta | 340 | 21.3 | 2672 | 2412 | 5084 | 317.8 |
| Tampa Bay | 301 | 18.8 | 1489 | 3474 | 4963 | 310.2 |
| NY Giants | 303 | 18.9 | 1904 | 2818 | 4722 | 295.1 |
| Detroit | 296 | 18.5 | 1777 | 2916 | 4693 | 293.3 |
| San Francisco | 259 | 16.2 | 1449 | 3136 | 4585 | 286.6 |
| Arizona | 284 | 17.8 | 1668 | 2882 | 4550 | 284.4 |
| Washington | 240 | 15.0 | 1765 | 2632 | 4397 | 274.8 |
| Chicago | 231 | 14.4 | 1624 | 2192 | 3816 | 238.5 |

### Defense

| | Points | | Yardage | | | |
|---|---|---|---|---|---|---|
| **AFC** | **Opp** | **Avg** | **Rush** | **Pass** | **Total** | **Avg** |
| Pittsburgh | 251 | 15.7 | 1299 | 2835 | 4134 | 258.4 |
| Buffalo | 284 | 17.8 | 1604 | 2624 | 4228 | 264.3 |
| Denver | 304 | 19.0 | 1512 | 2947 | 4459 | 278.7 |
| Baltimore | 268 | 16.8 | 1681 | 3122 | 4803 | 300.2 |
| NY Jets | 261 | 16.3 | 1566 | 3312 | 4878 | 304.9 |
| Miami | 354 | 22.1 | 2302 | 2592 | 4894 | 305.9 |
| New England | 260 | 16.3 | 1572 | 3400 | 4972 | 310.8 |
| Jacksonville | 280 | 17.5 | 1777 | 3357 | 5134 | 320.9 |
| Cleveland | 390 | 24.4 | 2314 | 2901 | 5215 | 325.9 |
| San Diego | 313 | 19.6 | 1307 | 4053 | 5360 | 335.0 |
| Cincinnati | 372 | 23.3 | 2062 | 3303 | 5365 | 335.3 |
| Houston | 339 | 21.2 | 1843 | 3615 | 5458 | 341.1 |
| Tennessee | 439 | 27.4 | 1917 | 3807 | 5724 | 357.8 |
| Indianapolis | 351 | 21.9 | 2037 | 3892 | 5929 | 370.6 |
| Oakland | 442 | 27.6 | 2012 | 3924 | 5936 | 371.0 |
| Kansas City | 435 | 27.2 | 1834 | 4203 | 6037 | 377.3 |

| | Points | | Yardage | | | |
|---|---|---|---|---|---|---|
| **NFC** | **Opp** | **Avg** | **Rush** | **Pass** | **Total** | **Avg** |
| Washington | 265 | 16.6 | 1304 | 2977 | 4281 | 267.6 |
| Tampa Bay | 304 | 19.0 | 1973 | 2579 | 4552 | 284.5 |
| Philadelphia | 260 | 16.3 | 1903 | 3212 | 5115 | 319.7 |
| Arizona | 322 | 20.1 | 2105 | 3036 | 5141 | 321.3 |
| NY Giants | 347 | 21.7 | 2157 | 3030 | 5187 | 324.2 |
| Atlanta | 337 | 21.1 | 1681 | 3526 | 5207 | 325.4 |
| Dallas | 405 | 25.3 | 1764 | 3521 | 5285 | 330.3 |
| St. Louis | 392 | 24.5 | 2179 | 3174 | 5353 | 334.6 |
| Carolina | 339 | 21.2 | 1904 | 3478 | 5382 | 336.4 |
| Chicago | 331 | 20.7 | 2050 | 3340 | 5390 | 336.9 |
| Detroit | 350 | 21.9 | 1887 | 3514 | 5401 | 337.6 |
| San Francisco | 452 | 28.3 | 1995 | 3486 | 5481 | 342.6 |
| Green Bay | 380 | 23.8 | 1878 | 3663 | 5541 | 346.3 |
| Seattle | 373 | 23.3 | 2031 | 3590 | 5621 | 351.3 |
| Minnesota | 395 | 24.7 | 2006 | 3896 | 5902 | 368.9 |
| New Orleans | 405 | 25.3 | 2253 | 3888 | 6141 | 383.8 |

## Overall Club Rankings

Combined AFC and NFC rankings by yards gained on offense and yards given up on defense. Teams are ranked by offense, with AFC teams in *italics*. (†) indicates tied for position.

| | Offense | | | Defense | | |
|---|---|---|---|---|---|---|
| | **Rush** | **Pass** | **Rank** | **Rush** | **Pass** | **Rank** |
| *Kansas City* | 5 | 4 | **1** | 12 | 32 | 31 |
| *Indianapolis* | 15 | 1 | **2** | 24 | 28 | 29 |
| Green Bay | 10 | 3 | **3** | 14 | 25 | 25 |
| Minnesota | 18 | 2 | **4** | 21 | 29 | 28 |
| *Denver* | 4 | 6 | **5** | 4 | 6 | 4 |
| St. Louis | 25t | 5 | **6** | 29 | 11 | 17 |
| *New England* | 7 | 11 | **7** | 6 | 17 | 9 |
| Seattle | 8 | 13 | **8** | 23 | 23 | 26 |
| Philadelphia | 24 | 7 | **9** | 16 | 12 | 10 |
| *San Diego* | 6 | 16 | **10** | 3 | 31 | 18 |
| *Tennessee* | 14 | 10 | **11** | 18 | 26 | 27 |
| *NY Jets* | 3 | 22 | **12** | 5 | 14 | 7 |
| Carolina | 28 | 9 | **13** | 17 | 18 | 20 |
| Dallas | 20 | 15 | **14** | 10 | 21 | 16 |
| New Orleans | 27 | 12 | **15** | 30 | 27 | 32 |
| *Pittsburgh* | 2 | 28 | **16** | 1 | 4 | 1 |

| | Offense | | | Defense | | |
|---|---|---|---|---|---|---|
| | **Rush** | **Pass** | **Rank** | **Rush** | **Pass** | **Rank** |
| *Oakland* | 32 | 8 | **17** | 22 | 30 | 30 |
| *Cincinnati* | 17 | 17 | **18** | 26 | 13 | 19 |
| *Houston* | 12 | 18 | **19** | 13 | 24 | 23 |
| Atlanta | 1 | 30 | **20** | 8t | 22 | 14 |
| *Jacksonville* | 16 | 19 | **21** | 11 | 16 | 11 |
| Tampa Bay | 29 | 14 | **22** | 19 | 1 | 5 |
| NY Giants | 11 | 26 | **23** | 28 | 8 | 13 |
| Detroit | 19 | 23 | **24** | 15 | 20 | 22 |
| *Buffalo* | 13 | 27 | **25** | 7 | 3 | 2 |
| San Francisco | 30 | 20 | **26** | 20 | 19 | 24 |
| Arizona | 22 | 24 | **27** | 27 | 9 | 12 |
| *Cleveland* | 23 | 25 | **28** | 32 | 5 | 15 |
| *Miami* | 31 | 21 | **29** | 31 | 2 | 8 |
| Washington | 21 | 29 | **30** | 2 | 7 | 3 |
| *Baltimore* | 9 | 31 | **31** | 8t | 10 | 6 |
| Chicago | 25t | 32 | **32** | 25 | 15 | 21 |

## AFC Team by Team Results

(*) indicates overtime game.

### Baltimore Ravens (9-7)

| | |
|---|---|
| at Cleveland | L, 3-20 |
| Pittsburgh | W, 30-13 |
| at Cincinnati | W, 23-9 |
| Kansas City | L, 24-27 |
| at Washington | W, 17-10 |
| OPEN· | — |
| Buffalo | W, 20-6 |
| at Philadelphia | L, 10-15 |
| Cleveland | W, 27-13 |
| at NY Jets | W, 20-17* |
| Dallas | W, 30-10 |
| at New England | L, 3-24 |
| Cincinnati | L, 26-27 |
| NY Giants | W, 37-14 |
| at Indianapolis | L, 10-20 |
| at Pittsburgh | L, 7-20 |
| Miami | W, 30-23 |

### Buffalo Bills (9-7)

| | |
|---|---|
| Jacksonville | L, 10-13 |
| at Oakland | L, 10-13 |
| OPEN | — |
| New England | L, 17-31 |
| at NY Jets | L, 14-16 |
| Miami | W, 20-13 |
| at Baltimore | L, 6-20 |
| Arizona | W, 38-14 |
| NY Jets | W, 22-17 |
| at New England | L, 6-29 |
| St. Louis | W, 37-17 |
| at Seattle | W, 38-9 |
| at Miami | W, 42-32 |
| Cleveland | W, 37-7 |
| at Cincinnati | W, 33-17 |
| at San Francisco | W, 41-7 |
| Pittsburgh | L, 24-29 |

### Cincinnati Bengals (8-8)

| | |
|---|---|
| at NY Jets | L, 24-31 |
| Miami | W, 16-13 |
| Baltimore | L, 9-23 |
| at Pittsburgh | L, 17-28 |
| OPEN | — |
| at Cleveland | L, 17-34 |
| Denver | W, 23-10 |
| at Tennessee | L, 20-27 |
| Dallas | W, 26-3 |
| at Washington | W, 17-10 |
| Pittsburgh | L, 14-19 |
| Cleveland | W, 58-48 |
| at Baltimore | W, 27-26 |
| at New England | L, 28-35 |
| Buffalo | L, 17-33 |
| NY Giants | W, 23-22 |
| at Philadelphia | W, 38-10 |

### Cleveland Browns (4-12)

| | |
|---|---|
| Baltimore | W, 20-3 |
| at Dallas | L, 12-19 |
| at NY Giants | L, 10-27 |
| Washington | W, 17-13 |
| at Pittsburgh | L, 23-34 |
| Cincinnati | W, 34-17 |
| Philadelphia | L, 31-34* |
| OPEN | — |
| at Baltimore | L, 13-27 |
| Pittsburgh | L, 10-24 |
| NY Jets | L, 7-10 |
| at Cincinnati | L, 48-58 |
| New England | L, 15-42 |
| at Buffalo | L, 7-37 |
| San Diego | L, 0-21 |
| at Miami | L, 7-10 |
| at Houston | W, 22-14 |

### Denver Broncos (10-6)

| | |
|---|---|
| Kansas City | W, 34-24 |
| at Jacksonville | L, 6-7 |
| San Diego | W, 23-13 |
| at Tampa Bay | W, 16-13 |
| Carolina | W, 20-17 |
| at Oakland | W, 31-3 |
| at Cincinnati | L, 10-23 |
| Atlanta | L, 28-41 |
| Houston | W, 31-13 |
| OPEN | — |
| at New Orleans | W, 34-13 |
| Oakland | L, 24-25 |
| at San Diego | L, 17-20 |
| Miami | W, 20-17 |
| at Kansas City | L, 17-45 |
| at Tennessee | W, 37-16 |
| Indianapolis | W, 33-14 |

### Houston Texans (7-9)

| | |
|---|---|
| San Diego | L, 20-27 |
| at Detroit | L, 16-28 |
| at Kansas City | W, 24-21 |
| Oakland | W, 30-17 |
| Minnesota | L, 28-34* |
| at Tennessee | W, 20-10 |
| OPEN | — |
| Jacksonville | W, 20-6 |
| at Denver | L, 13-31 |
| at Indianapolis | L, 14-49 |
| Green Bay | L, 13-16 |
| Tennessee | W, 31-21 |
| at NY Jets | L, 7-29 |
| Indianapolis | L, 14-23 |
| at Chicago | W, 24-5 |
| at Jacksonville | W, 21-0 |
| Cleveland | L, 14-22 |

### Indianapolis Colts (12-4)

| | |
|---|---|
| at New England | L, 24-27 |
| at Tennessee | W, 31-17 |
| Green Bay | W, 45-31 |
| at Jacksonville | W, 24-17 |
| Oakland | W, 35-14 |
| OPEN | — |
| Jacksonville | L, 24-27 |
| at Kansas City | L, 35-45 |
| Minnesota | W, 31-28 |
| Houston | W, 49-14 |
| at Chicago | W, 41-10 |
| at Detroit | W, 41-9 |
| Tennessee | W, 51-24 |
| at Houston | W, 23-14 |
| Baltimore | W, 20-10 |
| San Diego | W, 34-31* |
| at Denver | L, 14-33 |

### Jacksonville Jaguars (9-7)

| | |
|---|---|
| at Buffalo | W, 13-10 |
| Denver | W, 7-6 |
| at Tennessee | W, 15-12 |
| Indianapolis | L, 17-24 |
| at San Diego | L, 21-34 |
| Kansas City | W, 22-16 |
| at Indianapolis | W, 27-24 |
| at Houston | L, 6-20 |
| OPEN | — |
| Detroit | W, 23-17* |
| Tennessee | L, 15-18 |
| at Minnesota | L, 16-27 |
| Pittsburgh | L, 16-17 |
| Chicago | W, 22-3 |
| at Green Bay | W, 28-25 |
| Houston | L, 0-21 |
| at Oakland | W, 13-6 |

### Kansas City Chiefs (7-9)

| | |
|---|---|
| at Denver | L, 24-34 |
| Carolina | L, 17-28 |
| Houston | L, 21-24 |
| at Baltimore | W, 27-24 |
| OPEN | — |
| at Jacksonville | L, 16-22 |
| Atlanta | W, 56-10 |
| Indianapolis | W, 45-35 |
| at Tampa Bay | L, 31-34 |
| at New Orleans | L, 20-27 |
| New England | L, 19-27 |
| San Diego | L, 31-34 |
| at Oakland | W, 34-27 |
| at Tennessee | W, 49-38 |
| Denver | W, 45-17 |
| Oakland | W, 31-30 |
| at San Diego | L, 17-24 |

### Miami Dolphins (4-12)

| | |
|---|---|
| Tennessee | L, 7-17 |
| at Cincinnati | L, 13-16 |
| Pittsburgh | L, 3-13 |
| NY Jets | L, 9-17 |
| at New England | L, 10-24 |
| at Buffalo | L, 13-20 |
| St. Louis | W, 31-14 |
| at NY Jets | L, 14-41 |
| Arizona | L, 23-24 |
| OPEN | — |
| at Seattle | L, 17-24 |
| at San Fran. | W, 24-17 |
| Buffalo | L, 32-42 |
| at Denver | L, 17-20 |
| New England | W, 29-28 |
| Cleveland | W, 10-7 |
| at Baltimore | L, 23-30 |

### New England Patriots (14-2)

| | |
|---|---|
| Indianapolis | W, 27-24 |
| at Arizona | W, 23-12 |
| OPEN | — |
| at Buffalo | W, 31-17 |
| Miami | W, 24-10 |
| Seattle | W, 30-20 |
| NY Jets | W, 13-7 |
| at Pittsburgh | L, 20-34 |
| at St. Louis | W, 40-22 |
| Buffalo | W, 29-6 |
| at Kansas City | W, 27-19 |
| Baltimore | W, 24-3 |
| at Cleveland | W, 42-15 |
| Cincinnati | W, 35-28 |
| at Miami | L, 28-29 |
| at NY Jets | W, 23-7 |
| San Francisco | W, 21-7 |

### New York Jets (10-6)

| | |
|---|---|
| Cincinnati | W, 31-24 |
| at San Diego | W, 34-28 |
| OPEN | — |
| at Miami | W, 17-9 |
| Buffalo | W, 16-14 |
| San Francisco | W, 22-14 |
| at New England | L, 7-13 |
| Miami | W, 41-14 |
| at Buffalo | L, 17-22 |
| Baltimore | L, 17-20* |
| at Cleveland | W, 10-7 |
| at Arizona | W, 13-3 |
| Houston | W, 29-7 |
| at Pittsburgh | L, 6-17 |
| Seattle | W, 37-14 |
| New England | L, 7-23 |
| at St. Louis | L, 29-32* |

### Oakland Raiders (5-11)

| | |
|---|---|
| at Pittsburgh | L, 21-24 |
| Buffalo | W, 13-10 |
| Tampa Bay | W, 30-20 |
| at Houston | L, 17-30 |
| at Indianapolis | L, 14-35 |
| Denver | L, 3-31 |
| New Orleans | L, 26-31 |
| at San Diego | L, 14-42 |
| at Carolina | W, 27-24 |
| OPEN | — |
| San Diego | L, 17-23 |
| at Denver | W, 25-24 |
| Kansas City | L, 27-34 |
| at Atlanta | L, 10-35 |
| Tennessee | W, 40-35 |
| at Kansas City | L, 30-31 |
| Jacksonville | L, 6-13 |

### Pittsburgh Steelers (15-1)

| | |
|---|---|
| Oakland | W, 24-21 |
| at Baltimore | L, 13-30 |
| at Miami | W, 13-3 |
| Cincinnati | W, 28-17 |
| Cleveland | W, 34-23 |
| at Dallas | W, 24-20 |
| OPEN | — |
| New England | W, 34-20 |
| Philadelphia | W, 27-3 |
| at Cleveland | W, 24-10 |
| at Cincinnati | W, 19-14 |
| Washington | W, 16-7 |
| at Jacksonville | W, 17-16 |
| NY Jets | W, 17-6 |
| at NY Giants | W, 33-30 |
| Baltimore | W, 20-7 |
| at Buffalo | W, 29-24 |

### San Diego Chargers (12-4)

| | |
|---|---|
| at Houston | W, 27-20 |
| NY Jets | L, 28-34 |
| at Denver | L, 13-23 |
| Tennessee | W, 38-17 |
| Jacksonville | W, 34-21 |
| at Atlanta | L, 20-21 |
| at Carolina | W, 17-6 |
| Oakland | W, 42-14 |
| New Orleans | W, 43-17 |
| OPEN | — |
| at Oakland | W, 23-17 |
| at Kansas City | W, 34-31 |
| Denver | W, 20-17 |
| Tampa Bay | W, 31-24 |
| at Cleveland | W, 21-0 |
| at Indianapolis | L, 31-34* |
| Kansas City | W, 24-17 |

### Tennessee Titans (5-11)

| | |
|---|---|
| at Miami | W, 17-7 |
| Indianapolis | L, 17-31 |
| Jacksonville | L, 12-15 |
| at San Diego | L, 17-38 |
| at Green Bay | W, 48-27 |
| Houston | L, 10-20 |
| at Minnesota | L, 3-20 |
| Cincinnati | W, 27-20 |
| OPEN | — |
| Chicago | L, 17-19* |
| at Jacksonville | W, 18-15 |
| at Houston | L, 21-31 |
| at Indianapolis | L, 24-51 |
| Kansas City | L, 38-49 |
| at Oakland | L, 35-40 |
| Denver | L, 16-37 |
| Detroit | W, 24-19 |

## NFC Team by Team Results

(*) indicates overtime game

### Arizona Cardinals (6-10)

| | |
|---|---|
| at St. Louis | L, 10-17 |
| New England | L, 12-23 |
| at Atlanta | L, 3-6 |
| New Orleans | W, 34-10 |
| at San Francisco | L, 28-31* |
| OPEN | — |
| Seattle | W, 25-17 |
| at Buffalo | L, 14-38 |
| at Miami | W, 24-23 |
| NY Giants | W, 17-14 |
| at Carolina | L, 10-35 |
| NY Jets | L, 3-13 |
| at Detroit | L, 12-26 |
| San Francisco | L, 28-31* |
| St. Louis | W, 31-7 |
| at Seattle | L, 21-24 |
| Tampa Bay | W, 12-7 |

### Atlanta Falcons (11-5)

| | |
|---|---|
| at San Fran. | W, 21-19 |
| St. Louis | W, 34-17 |
| Arizona | W, 6-3 |
| at Carolina | W, 27-10 |
| Detroit | L, 10-17 |
| San Diego | W, 21-20 |
| at Kansas City | L, 10-56 |
| at Denver | W, 41-28 |
| OPEN | — |
| Tampa Bay | W, 24-14 |
| at NY Giants | W, 14-10 |
| New Orleans | W, 24-21 |
| at Tampa Bay | L, 0-27 |
| Oakland | W, 35-10 |
| Carolina | W, 34-31* |
| at New Orleans | L, 13-26 |
| at Seattle | L, 26-28 |

### Carolina Panthers (7-9)

| | |
|---|---|
| Green Bay | L, 14-24 |
| at Kansas City | W, 28-17 |
| OPEN | — |
| Atlanta | L, 10-27 |
| at Denver | L, 17-20 |
| at Philadelphia | L, 8-30 |
| San Diego | L, 6-17 |
| at Seattle | L, 17-23 |
| Oakland | L, 24-27 |
| at San Fran. | W, 37-27 |
| Arizona | W, 35-10 |
| Tampa Bay | W, 21-14 |
| at New Orleans | W, 32-21 |
| St. Louis | W, 20-7 |
| at Atlanta | L, 31-34* |
| at Tampa Bay | W, 37-20 |
| New Orleans | L, 18-21 |

### Chicago Bears (5-11)

| | |
|---|---|
| Detroit | L, 16-20 |
| at Green Bay | W, 21-10 |
| at Minnesota | L, 22-27 |
| Philadelphia | L, 9-19 |
| OPEN | — |
| Washington | L, 10-13 |
| at Tampa Bay | L, 7-19 |
| San Francisco | W, 23-13 |
| at NY Giants | W, 28-21 |
| at Tennessee | W, 19-17* |
| Indianapolis | L, 10-41 |
| at Dallas | L, 7-21 |
| Minnesota | W, 24-14 |
| at Jacksonville | L, 3-22 |
| Houston | L, 5-24 |
| at Detroit | L, 13-19 |
| Green Bay | L, 14-31 |

### Dallas Cowboys (6-10)

| | |
|---|---|
| at Minnesota | L, 17-35 |
| Cleveland | W, 19-12 |
| at Washington | W, 21-18 |
| OPEN | — |
| NY Giants | L, 10-26 |
| Pittsburgh | L, 20-24 |
| at Green Bay | L, 20-41 |
| Detroit | W, 31-21 |
| at Cincinnati | L, 3-26 |
| Philadelphia | L, 21-49 |
| at Baltimore | L, 10-30 |
| Chicago | W, 21-7 |
| at Seattle | W, 43-39 |
| New Orleans | L, 13-27 |
| at Philadelphia | L, 7-12 |
| Washington | W, 13-10 |
| at NY Giants | L, 24-28 |

### Detroit Lions (6-10)

| | |
|---|---|
| at Chicago | W, 20-16 |
| Houston | W, 28-16 |
| Philadelphia | L, 13-30 |
| OPEN | — |
| at Atlanta | W, 17-10 |
| Green Bay | L, 10-38 |
| at NY Giants | W, 28-13 |
| at Dallas | L, 21-31 |
| Washington | L, 10-17 |
| at Jacksonville | L, 17-23* |
| at Minnesota | L, 19-22 |
| Indianapolis | L, 9-41 |
| Arizona | W, 26-12 |
| at Green Bay | L, 13-16 |
| Minnesota | W, 27-28 |
| Chicago | W, 19-13 |
| at Tennessee | L, 19-24 |

### Green Bay Packers (10-6)

| | |
|---|---|
| at Carolina | W, 24-14 |
| Chicago | L, 10-21 |
| at Indianapolis | L, 31-45 |
| NY Giants | L, 7-14 |
| Tennessee | W, 27-48 |
| at Detroit | W, 38-10 |
| Dallas | W, 41-20 |
| at Washington | W, 28-14 |
| OPEN | — |
| Minnesota | W, 34-31 |
| at Houston | W, 16-13 |
| St. Louis | W, 45-17 |
| at Philadelphia | L, 17-47 |
| Detroit | W, 16-13 |
| Jacksonville | L, 25-28 |
| at Minnesota | W, 34-31 |
| at Chicago | W, 31-14 |

### Minnesota Vikings (8-8)

| | |
|---|---|
| Dallas | W, 35-17 |
| at Philadelphia | L, 16-27 |
| Chicago | W, 27-22 |
| OPEN | — |
| at Houston | W, 34-28* |
| at New Orleans | W, 38-31 |
| Tennessee | W, 20-3 |
| NY Giants | L, 13-34 |
| at Indianapolis | L, 28-31 |
| at Green Bay | L, 31-34 |
| Detroit | W, 22-19 |
| Jacksonville | W, 27-16 |
| at Chicago | L, 14-24 |
| Seattle | L, 23-27 |
| at Detroit | W, 28-27 |
| Green Bay | L, 31-34 |
| at Washington | L, 18-21 |

## NFC Team by Team Results (Cont.)

### New Orleans Saints (8-8)

| | |
|---|---|
| Seattle | L, 7-21 |
| San Francisco | W, 30-27 |
| at St. Louis | W, 28-25* |
| at Arizona | L, 10-34 |
| Tampa Bay | L, 17-20 |
| Minnesota | L, 31-38 |
| at Oakland | W, 31-26 |
| OPEN | — |
| at San Diego | L, 17-43 |
| Kansas City | W, 27-20 |
| Denver | L, 13-34 |
| at Atlanta | L, 21-24 |
| Carolina | L, 21-32 |
| at Dallas | W, 27-13 |
| at Tampa Bay | W, 21-17 |
| Atlanta | W, 26-13 |
| at Carolina | W, 21-18 |

### New York Giants (6-10)

| | |
|---|---|
| at Philadelphia | L, 17-31 |
| Washington | W, 20-14 |
| Cleveland | W, 27-10 |
| at Green Bay | W, 14-7 |
| at Dallas | W, 26-10 |
| OPEN | — |
| Detroit | L, 13-28 |
| at Minnesota | W, 34-13 |
| Chicago | L, 21-28 |
| at Arizona | L, 14-17 |
| Atlanta | L, 10-14 |
| Philadelphia | L, 6-27 |
| at Washington | L, 7-31 |
| at Baltimore | L, 14-37 |
| Pittsburgh | L, 30-33 |
| Dallas | W, 28-24 |

### Philadelphia Eagles (13-3)

| | |
|---|---|
| NY Giants | W, 31-17 |
| Minnesota | W, 27-16 |
| at Detroit | W, 30-13 |
| at Chicago | W, 19-9 |
| OPEN | — |
| Carolina | W, 30-8 |
| at Cleveland | W, 34-31* |
| Baltimore | W, 15-10 |
| at Pittsburgh | L, 3-27 |
| at Dallas | W, 49-21 |
| Washington | W, 28-6 |
| at NY Giants | W, 27-6 |
| Green Bay | W, 47-17 |
| at Washington | W, 17-14 |
| Dallas | W, 12-7 |
| at St. Louis | L, 7-20 |
| Cincinnati | L, 10-38 |

### St. Louis Rams (8-8)

| | |
|---|---|
| Arizona | W, 17-10 |
| at Atlanta | L, 17-34 |
| New Orleans | L, 25-28* |
| at San Fran. | W, 24-14 |
| at Seattle | W, 33-27* |
| Tampa Bay | W, 28-21 |
| at Miami | L, 14-31 |
| OPEN | — |
| New England | L, 22-40 |
| Seattle | W, 23-12 |
| at Buffalo | L, 17-37 |
| at Green Bay | L, 17-45 |
| San Francisco | W, 16-6 |
| at Carolina | L, 7-20 |
| at Arizona | L, 7-31 |
| Philadelphia | W, 20-7 |
| NY Jets | W, 32-29* |

### San Francisco 49ers (2-14)

| | |
|---|---|
| Atlanta | L, 19-21 |
| at New Orleans | L, 27-30 |
| at Seattle | L, 0-34 |
| St. Louis | L, 14-24 |
| Arizona | W, 31-28* |
| at NY Jets | L, 14-22 |
| OPEN | — |
| at Chicago | L, 13-23 |
| Seattle | L, 27-42 |
| Carolina | L, 27-37 |
| at Tampa Bay | L, 3-35 |
| Miami | L, 17-24 |
| at St. Louis | L, 6-16 |
| at Arizona | W, 31-28* |
| Washington | L, 16-26 |
| Buffalo | L, 7-41 |
| at New England | L, 7-21 |

### Seattle Seahawks (9-7)

| | |
|---|---|
| at New Orleans | W, 21-7 |
| at Tampa Bay | W, 10-6 |
| San Francisco | W, 34-0 |
| OPEN | — |
| St. Louis | L, 27-33* |
| at New England | L, 20-30 |
| at Arizona | L, 17-25 |
| Carolina | W, 23-17 |
| at San Fran. | W, 42-27 |
| at St. Louis | L, 12-23 |
| Miami | W, 24-17 |
| Buffalo | L, 9-38 |
| Dallas | L, 39-43 |
| at Minnesota | W, 27-23 |
| at NY Jets | L, 14-37 |
| Arizona | W, 24-21 |
| Atlanta | W, 28-26 |

### Tampa Bay Buccaneers (5-11)

| | |
|---|---|
| at Washington | L, 10-16 |
| Seattle | L, 6-10 |
| at Oakland | L, 20-30 |
| Denver | L, 13-16 |
| at New Orleans | W, 20-17 |
| at St. Louis | L, 21-28 |
| Chicago | W, 19-7 |
| OPEN | — |
| Kansas City | W, 34-31 |
| at Atlanta | L, 14-24 |
| San Francisco | W, 35-3 |
| at Carolina | L, 14-21 |
| Atlanta | W, 27-0 |
| at San Diego | L, 24-31 |
| New Orleans | L, 17-21 |
| Carolina | L, 20-37 |
| at Arizona | L, 7-12 |

### Washington Redskins (6-10)

| | |
|---|---|
| Tampa Bay | W, 16-10 |
| at NY Giants | L, 14-20 |
| Dallas | L, 18-21 |
| at Cleveland | L, 13-17 |
| Baltimore | L, 10-17 |
| at Chicago | W, 13-10 |
| OPEN | — |
| Green Bay | L, 14-28 |
| at Detroit | W, 17-10 |
| Cincinnati | L, 10-17 |
| at Philadelphia | L, 6-28 |
| at Pittsburgh | L, 7-16 |
| NY Giants | W, 31-7 |
| Philadelphia | L, 14-17 |
| at San Fran. | W, 26-16 |
| at Dallas | L, 10-13 |
| Minnesota | W, 21-18 |

## Takeaways/Giveaways

| AFC | Takeaways | | | Giveaways | | | Net Diff | NFC | Takeaways | | | Giveaways | | | Net Diff |
|---|---|---|---|---|---|---|---|---|---|---|---|---|---|---|---|
| | Int | Fum | Total | Int | Fum | Total | | | Int | Fum | Total | Int | Fum | Total | |
| Indianapolis | 19 | 17 | 36 | 10 | 7 | 17 | +19 | Carolina | 26 | 12 | 38 | 15 | 11 | 26 | +12 |
| NY Jets | 19 | 14 | 33 | 11 | 5 | 16 | +17 | Seattle | 23 | 12 | 35 | 18 | 9 | 27 | +8 |
| San Diego | 23 | 10 | 33 | 8 | 10 | 18 | +15 | New Orleans | 13 | 20 | 33 | 16 | 10 | 26 | +7 |
| Baltimore | 21 | 13 | 34 | 11 | 12 | 23 | +11 | Philadelphia | 17 | 11 | 28 | 11 | 11 | 22 | +6 |
| Pittsburgh | 19 | 13 | 32 | 13 | 8 | 21 | +11 | Detroit | 14 | 10 | 24 | 13 | 7 | 20 | +4 |
| Buffalo | 24 | 15 | 39 | 17 | 12 | 29 | +10 | NY Giants | 14 | 14 | 28 | 13 | 11 | 24 | +4 |
| New England | 20 | 16 | 36 | 14 | 13 | 27 | +9 | Atlanta | 19 | 13 | 32 | 16 | 14 | 30 | +2 |
| Jacksonville | 16 | 12 | 28 | 11 | 11 | 22 | +6 | Arizona | 15 | 15 | 30 | 18 | 11 | 29 | +1 |
| Houston | 22 | 8 | 30 | 14 | 11 | 25 | +5 | Minnesota | 11 | 11 | 22 | 12 | 9 | 21 | +1 |
| Cincinnati | 20 | 16 | 36 | 22 | 10 | 32 | +4 | Washington | 18 | 8 | 26 | 17 | 10 | 27 | -1 |
| Tennessee | 18 | 12 | 30 | 19 | 12 | 31 | -1 | Chicago | 17 | 12 | 29 | 16 | 21 | 37 | -8 |
| Kansas City | 13 | 8 | 21 | 17 | 10 | 27 | -6 | Tampa Bay | 16 | 11 | 27 | 18 | 18 | 36 | -9 |
| Denver | 12 | 8 | 20 | 20 | 9 | 29 | -9 | Green Bay | 8 | 7 | 15 | 19 | 10 | 29 | -14 |
| Cleveland | 15 | 13 | 28 | 21 | 19 | 40 | -12 | Dallas | 13 | 9 | 22 | 23 | 14 | 37 | -15 |
| Miami | 15 | 10 | 25 | 26 | 16 | 42 | -17 | San Francisco | 9 | 12 | 21 | 21 | 19 | 40 | -19 |
| Oakland | 9 | 9 | 18 | 22 | 13 | 35 | -17 | St. Louis | 6 | 9 | 15 | 22 | 17 | 39 | -24 |
| TOTALS | 285 | 194 | 479 | 256 | 178 | 434 | +45 | TOTALS | 239 | 186 | 425 | 268 | 202 | 470 | -45 |

## AFC Team by Team Statistics

Players with more than one team during the regular season are listed with club they ended season with; (*) indicates rookies.

### Baltimore Ravens

| Passing (5 Att) | Att | Cmp | Pct | Yds | TD | Rate |
|---|---|---|---|---|---|---|
| Kyle Boller | 464 | 258 | 55.6 | 2559 | 13 | 70.9 |

**Interceptions:** Boller 11.

| Top Receivers | No | Yds | Avg | Long | TD |
|---|---|---|---|---|---|
| Kevin Johnson | 35 | 373 | 10.7 | 35 | 1 |
| Travis Taylor | 34 | 421 | 12.4 | 47 | 0 |
| Chester Taylor | 30 | 184 | 6.1 | 23 | 0 |
| Todd Heap | 27 | 303 | 11.2 | 37 | 3 |
| Randy Hymes | 26 | 323 | 12.4 | 57-td | 2 |
| Daniel Wilcox | 25 | 219 | 8.8 | 20 | 1 |

| Top Rushers | Car | Yds | Avg | Long | TD |
|---|---|---|---|---|---|
| Jamal Lewis | 235 | 1006 | 4.3 | 75-td | 7 |
| Chester Taylor | 160 | 714 | 4.5 | 47 | 2 |
| Kyle Boller | 53 | 189 | 3.6 | 19 | 1 |
| Jamel White | 27 | 82 | 3.0 | 16 | 0 |
| TB | 13 | 20 | 1.5 | 10 | 0 |
| BAL | 14 | 62 | 4.4 | 16 | 0 |

**Signed:** free agent White (Nov. 24).

| Most Touchdowns | TD | Run | Rec | Ret | Pts |
|---|---|---|---|---|---|
| Jamal Lewis | 7 | 7 | 0 | 0 | 42 |
| Clarence Moore* | 4 | 0 | 4 | 0 | 26 |
| Todd Heap | 3 | 0 | 3 | 0 | 18 |
| B.J. Sams* | 3 | 1 | 0 | 2 | 18 |

**2-Pt. Conversions:** (1-3) Moore.

| Kicking | PAT/Att | FG/Att | Lg | Pts |
|---|---|---|---|---|
| Matt Stover | 30/30 | 29/32 | 50 | 117 |

| Punts (10 or more) | No | Yds | Long | Avg | In20 |
|---|---|---|---|---|---|
| Dave Zastudil | 73 | 2948 | 61 | 40.4 | 26 |

**Signed:** free agent Nick Murphy (Nov. 17). **Released:** Murphy on Dec. 21 (see KC).

| Most Interceptions | | Most Sacks | |
|---|---|---|---|
| Ed Reed | 9 | Terrell Suggs | 10.5 |

### Buffalo Bills

| Passing (5 Att) | Att | Cmp | Pct | Yds | TD | Rate |
|---|---|---|---|---|---|---|
| Drew Bledsoe | 450 | 256 | 56.9 | 2932 | 20 | 76.6 |
| J.P. Losman* | 5 | 3 | 60.0 | 32 | 0 | 39.2 |

**Interceptions:** Bledsoe 16, Losman 1.

| Top Receivers | No | Yds | Avg | Long | TD |
|---|---|---|---|---|---|
| Eric Moulds | 88 | 1043 | 11.9 | 49 | 5 |
| Lee Evans* | 48 | 843 | 17.6 | 69 | 9 |
| Willis McGahee | 22 | 169 | 7.7 | 16 | 0 |
| Mark Campbell | 17 | 203 | 11.9 | 27 | 5 |
| Daimon Shelton | 17 | 114 | 6.7 | 24 | 0 |
| Josh Reed | 16 | 153 | 9.6 | 20 | 0 |

| Top Rushers | Car | Yds | Avg | Long | TD |
|---|---|---|---|---|---|
| Willis McGahee | 284 | 1128 | 4.0 | 41 | 13 |
| Travis Henry | 94 | 326 | 3.5 | 19 | 0 |
| Shaud Williams* | 42 | 167 | 4.0 | 27-td | 2 |
| Lee Evans* | 5 | 85 | 17.0 | 14 | 0 |

| Most Touchdowns | TD | Run | Rec | Ret | Pts |
|---|---|---|---|---|---|
| Willis McGahee | 13 | 13 | 0 | 0 | 78 |
| Lee Evans* | 9 | 0 | 9 | 0 | 54 |
| Mark Campbell | 5 | 0 | 5 | 0 | 30 |
| Eric Moulds | 5 | 0 | 5 | 0 | 30 |
| Terrence McGee | 3 | 0 | 0 | 3 | 18 |

**2-Pt. Conversions:** (0-1).

| Kicking | PAT/Att | FG/Att | Lg | Pts |
|---|---|---|---|---|
| Rian Lindell | 45/45 | 24/28 | 43 | 117 |

| Punts (10 or more) | No | Yds | Long | Avg | In20 |
|---|---|---|---|---|---|
| Brian Moorman | 77 | 3325 | 80 | 43.2 | 17 |

| Most Interceptions | | Most Sacks | |
|---|---|---|---|
| Nate Clements | 6 | Aaron Schobel | 8.0 |

### Cincinnati Bengals

| Passing (5 Att) | Att | Cmp | Pct | Yds | TD | Rate |
|---|---|---|---|---|---|---|
| Carson Palmer | 432 | 263 | 60.9 | 2897 | 18 | 77.3 |
| Jon Kitna | 104 | 61 | 58.7 | 623 | 5 | 75.9 |

**Interceptions:** Palmer 18, Kitna 4.

| Top Receivers | No | Yds | Avg | Long | TD |
|---|---|---|---|---|---|
| Chad Johnson | 95 | 1274 | 13.4 | 53-td | 9 |
| T.J. Houshmandzadeh | 73 | 978 | 13.4 | 62 | 4 |
| Kelley Washington | 31 | 378 | 12.2 | 28 | 3 |
| Kenny Watson | 25 | 171 | 6.8 | 21 | 1 |
| Matt Schobel | 21 | 201 | 9.6 | 76-td | 4 |
| Jeremi Johnson | 16 | 53 | 3.3 | 9 | 1 |

| Top Rushers | Car | Yds | Avg | Long | TD |
|---|---|---|---|---|---|
| Rudi Johnson | 361 | 1454 | 4.0 | 52 | 12 |
| Kenny Watson | 26 | 161 | 6.2 | 25 | 0 |
| T.J. Houshmandzadeh | 6 | 51 | 8.5 | 16 | 0 |
| Carson Palmer | 18 | 47 | 2.6 | 14 | 1 |

| Most Touchdowns | TD | Run | Rec | Ret | Pts |
|---|---|---|---|---|---|
| Rudi Johnson | 12 | 12 | 0 | 0 | 72 |
| Chad Johnson | 9 | 0 | 9 | 0 | 54 |
| T.J. Houshmandzadeh | 4 | 0 | 4 | 0 | 24 |
| Matt Schobel | 4 | 0 | 4 | 0 | 24 |
| Kelley Washington | 3 | 0 | 3 | 0 | 18 |

**2-Pt. Conversions:** (0-1).

| Kicking | PAT/Att | FG/Att | Lg | Pts |
|---|---|---|---|---|
| Shayne Graham | 41/41 | 27/31 | 53 | 122 |

| Punts (10 or more) | No | Yds | Long | Avg | In20 |
|---|---|---|---|---|---|
| Kyle Larson* | 83 | 3499 | 66 | 42.2 | 21 |

| Most Interceptions | | Most Sacks | |
|---|---|---|---|
| Tory James | 8 | Justin Smith | 8.0 |

### Cleveland Browns

| Passing (5 Att) | Att | Cmp | Pct | Yds | TD | Rate |
|---|---|---|---|---|---|---|
| Jeff Garcia | 252 | 144 | 57.1 | 1731 | 10 | 76.7 |
| Luke McCown* | 98 | 48 | 49.0 | 608 | 4 | 52.6 |
| Kelly Holcomb | 87 | 59 | 67.8 | 737 | 7 | 96.8 |

**Interceptions:** Garcia 9, McCown 7, Holcomb 5.

| Top Receivers | No | Yds | Avg | Long | TD |
|---|---|---|---|---|---|
| Antonio Bryant | 58 | 812 | 14.0 | 55-td | 4 |
| DAL | 16 | 266 | 16.6 | 48 | 0 |
| CLE | 42 | 546 | 13.0 | 55-td | 4 |
| Dennis Northcutt | 55 | 806 | 14.7 | 58-td | 2 |
| Steve Heiden | 28 | 287 | 10.3 | 30 | 5 |
| Aaron Shea | 26 | 252 | 9.7 | 35 | 4 |

**Acquired:** Bryant from Dal. for WR Quincy Morgan (Oct. 19).

| Top Rushers | Car | Yds | Avg | Long | TD |
|---|---|---|---|---|---|
| Lee Suggs | 199 | 744 | 3.7 | 39 | 2 |
| William Green | 163 | 585 | 3.6 | 46 | 2 |
| Jeff Garcia | 35 | 169 | 4.8 | 21 | 2 |

**Waived:** James Jackson on Nov. 16 (see GB).

| Most Touchdowns | TD | Run | Rec | Ret | Pts |
|---|---|---|---|---|---|
| Steve Heiden | 5 | 0 | 5 | 0 | 32 |
| Antonio Bryant | 4 | 0 | 4 | 0 | 24 |
| DAL | 4 | 0 | 4 | 0 | 24 |
| CLE | 0 | 0 | 0 | 0 | 0 |
| Aaron Shea | 4 | 0 | 4 | 0 | 24 |

**2-Pt. Conversions:** (1-1) Heiden.

| Kicking | PAT/Att | FG/Att | Lg | Pts |
|---|---|---|---|---|
| Phil Dawson | 28/28 | 24/29 | 50 | 100 |

| Punts (10 or more) | No | Yds | Long | Avg | In20 |
|---|---|---|---|---|---|
| Derrick Frost | 85 | 3404 | 54 | 40.0 | 24 |

| Most Interceptions | | Most Sacks | |
|---|---|---|---|
| Anthony Henry | 4 | Ebenezer Ekuban | 8.0 |

## Denver Broncos

| Passing (5 Att) | Att | Cmp | Pct | Yds | TD | Rate |
|---|---|---|---|---|---|---|
| Jake Plummer | .521 | 303 | 58.2 | 4089 | 27 | 84.5 |

**Interceptions:** Plummer 20.

| Top Receivers | No | Yds | Avg | Long | TD |
|---|---|---|---|---|---|
| Rod Smith | .79 | 1144 | 14.5 | 85-td | 7 |
| Ashley Lelie | .54 | 1084 | 20.1 | 58 | 7 |
| Jeb Putzier | .36 | 572 | 15.9 | 39 | 2 |
| Reuben Droughns | .32 | 241 | 7.5 | 23-td | 2 |
| Darius Watts* | .31 | 385 | 12.4 | 28 | 1 |
| Dwayne Carswell | .22 | 198 | 9.0 | 20 | 1 |

| Top Rushers | Car | Yds | Avg | Long | TD |
|---|---|---|---|---|---|
| Reuben Droughns | .275 | 1240 | 4.5 | 51-td | 6 |
| Tatum Bell* | .75 | 396 | 5.3 | 29 | 3 |
| Quentin Griffin | .85 | 311 | 3.7 | 47-td | 2 |
| Jake Plummer | .62 | 202 | 3.3 | 22 | 1 |
| Garrison Hearst | .20 | 81 | 4.1 | 11 | 1 |

| Most Touchdowns | TD | Run | Rec | Ret | Pts |
|---|---|---|---|---|---|
| Reuben Droughns | .8 | 6 | 2 | 0 | 48 |
| Ashley Lelie | .7 | 0 | 7 | 0 | 42 |
| Rod Smith | .7 | 0 | 7 | 0 | 42 |
| Patrick Hape | .4 | 0 | 4 | 0 | 24 |
| Tatum Bell* | .3 | 3 | 0 | 0 | 18 |
| Quentin Griffin | .3 | 2 | 1 | 0 | 18 |

**2-Pt. Conversions:** (0-0).

| Kicking | PAT/Att | FG/Att | Lg | Pts |
|---|---|---|---|---|
| Jason Elam | .42/42 | 29/34 | 52 | 129 |

| Punts (10 or more) | No | Yds | Long | Avg | In20 |
|---|---|---|---|---|---|
| Micah Knorr | .54 | 2243 | 66 | 41.5 | 12 |
| Jason Baker | .24 | 931 | 52 | 38.8 | 10 |
| KC | .9 | 340 | 52 | 37.8 | 3 |
| DEN | .15 | 591 | 48 | 39.4 | 7 |

**Waived:** Knorr (Dec. 10). **Claimed:** Baker off waivers from Ind. (Dec. 10).

| Most Interceptions | | Most Sacks | |
|---|---|---|---|
| Champ Bailey | .3 | Reggie Hayward | .10.5 |

## Houston Texans

| Passing (5 Att) | Att | Cmp | Pct | Yds | TD | Rate |
|---|---|---|---|---|---|---|
| David Carr | .466 | 285 | 61.2 | 3531 | 16 | 83.5 |

**Interceptions:** Carr 14.

| Top Receivers | No | Yds | Avg | Long | TD |
|---|---|---|---|---|---|
| Andre Johnson | .79 | 1142 | 14.5 | 54-td | 6 |
| Domanick Davis | .68 | 588 | 8.6 | 38 | 1 |
| Jabar Gaffney | .41 | 632 | 15.4 | 69 | 2 |
| Derick Armstrong | .29 | 415 | 14.3 | 44 | 1 |
| Corey Bradford | .27 | 399 | 14.8 | 47 | 3 |
| Billy Miller | .17 | 178 | 10.5 | 27 | 1 |

| Top Rushers | Car | Yds | Avg | Long | TD |
|---|---|---|---|---|---|
| Domanick Davis | .302 | 1188 | 3.9 | 44 | 13 |
| David Carr | .73 | 299 | 4.1 | 24 | 0 |
| Jonathan Wells | .82 | 299 | 3.6 | 14 | 3 |
| Tony Hollings | .11 | 47 | 4.3 | 13 | 0 |

| Most Touchdowns | TD | Run | Rec | Ret | Pts |
|---|---|---|---|---|---|
| Domanick Davis | .14 | 13 | 1 | 0 | 84 |
| Andre Johnson | .6 | 0 | 6 | 0 | 36 |
| Jonathan Wells | .5 | 3 | 2 | 0 | 32 |
| Corey Bradford | .3 | 0 | 3 | 0 | 18 |
| Jabar Gaffney | .2 | 0 | 2 | 0 | 12 |

**2-Pt. Conversions:** (1-3) Wells.

| Kicking | PAT/Att | FG/Att | Lg | Pts |
|---|---|---|---|---|
| Kris Brown | .34/34 | 17/24 | 50 | 85 |

| Punts (10 or more) | No | Yds | Long | Avg | In20 |
|---|---|---|---|---|---|
| Chad Stanley | .73 | 3009 | 57 | 41.2 | 19 |

| Most Interceptions | | Most Sacks | |
|---|---|---|---|
| Dunta Robinson* | .6 | Kailee Wong | .5.5 |

## Indianapolis Colts

| Passing (5 Att) | Att | Cmp | Pct | Yds | TD | Rate |
|---|---|---|---|---|---|---|
| Peyton Manning | .497 | 336 | 67.6 | 4557 | 49 | 121.1 |
| Jim Sorgi | .29 | 17 | 58.6 | 175 | 2 | 99.1 |

**Interceptions:** Manning 10.

| Top Receivers | No | Yds | Avg | Long | TD |
|---|---|---|---|---|---|
| Marvin Harrison | .86 | 1113 | 12.9 | 59 | 15 |
| Reggie Wayne | .77 | 1210 | 15.7 | 71-td | 12 |
| Brandon Stokley | .68 | 1077 | 15.8 | 69-td | 10 |
| Edgerrin James | .51 | 483 | 9.5 | 56 | 0 |
| Marcus Pollard | .29 | 309 | 10.7 | 31 | 6 |
| Dallas Clark | .25 | 423 | 16.9 | 80-td | 5 |

| Top Rushers | Car | Yds | Avg | Long | TD |
|---|---|---|---|---|---|
| Edgerrin James | .334 | 1548 | 4.6 | 40 | 9 |
| Dominic Rhodes | .53 | 254 | 4.8 | 55 | 1 |
| Peyton Manning | .25 | 38 | 1.5 | 19 | 0 |

| Most Touchdowns | TD | Run | Rec | Ret | Pts |
|---|---|---|---|---|---|
| Marvin Harrison | .15 | 0 | 15 | 0 | 90 |
| Reggie Wayne | .12 | 0 | 12 | 0 | 72 |
| Brandon Stokley | .10 | 0 | 10 | 0 | 60 |
| Edgerrin James | .9 | 9 | 0 | 0 | 54 |
| Marcus Pollard | .6 | 0 | 6 | 0 | 36 |
| Dallas Clark | .5 | 0 | 5 | 0 | 30 |

**2-Pt. Conversions:** (1-1) James.

| Kicking | PAT/Att | FG/Att | Lg | Pts |
|---|---|---|---|---|
| Mike Vanderjagt | .59/60 | 20/25 | 47 | 119 |
| Martin Gramatica | .21/22 | 11/19 | 53 | 54 |
| TB | .21/22 | 11/19 | 53 | 54 |

**Signed:** free agent Matt Bryant (Oct. 8); free agent Gramatica (Dec. 8). **Waived:** Bryant on Oct. 12 (see Mia.).

| Punts (10 or more) | No | Yds | Long | Avg | In20 |
|---|---|---|---|---|---|
| Hunter Smith | .54 | 2443 | 62 | 45.2 | 21 |

| Most Interceptions | | Most Sacks | |
|---|---|---|---|
| Jason David* | .4 | Dwight Freeney | .16.0 |

## Jacksonville Jaguars

| Passing (15 Att) | Att | Cmp | Pct | Yds | TD | Rate |
|---|---|---|---|---|---|---|
| Byron Leftwich | .441 | 267 | 60.5 | 2941 | 15 | 82.2 |
| David Garrard | .72 | 38 | 52.8 | 374 | 2 | 71.2 |

**Interceptions:** Leftwich 10, Garrard 1.

| Top Receivers | No | Yds | Avg | Long | TD |
|---|---|---|---|---|---|
| Jimmy Smith | .74 | 1172 | 15.8 | 65 | 6 |
| Troy Edwards | .50 | 533 | 10.7 | 36 | 1 |
| Fred Taylor | .36 | 345 | 9.6 | 64-td | 1 |
| LaBrandon Toefield | .28 | 151 | 5.4 | 16 | 1 |
| Reggie Williams* | .27 | 268 | 9.9 | 26 | 1 |
| Ernest Wilford | .19 | 271 | 14.3 | 46 | 2 |

**Claimed:** Johnson off waivers from Cle. (Nov. 12).

| Top Rushers | Car | Yds | Avg | Long | TD |
|---|---|---|---|---|---|
| Fred Taylor | .260 | 1224 | 4.7 | 46 | 2 |
| LaBrandon Toefield | .51 | 169 | 3.3 | 16 | 0 |
| Greg Jones* | .62 | 162 | 2.6 | 12 | 3 |
| Byron Leftwich | .39 | 148 | 3.8 | 17 | 2 |

| Most Touchdowns | TD | Run | Rec | Ret | Pts |
|---|---|---|---|---|---|
| Jimmy Smith | .6 | 0 | 6 | 0 | 36 |
| Greg Jones* | .3 | 3 | 0 | 0 | 18 |
| Fred Taylor | .3 | 2 | 1 | 0 | 18 |

**2-Pt. Conversions:** (4-4) Williams 2, Wilford and Brian Jones 1.

| Kicking | PAT/Att | FG/Att | Lg | Pts |
|---|---|---|---|---|
| Josh Scobee* | .21/21 | 24/31 | 53 | 93 |

| Punts (10 or more) | No | Yds | Long | Avg | In20 |
|---|---|---|---|---|---|
| Chris Hanson | .84 | 3592 | 69 | 42.8 | 28 |

| Most Interceptions | | Most Sacks | |
|---|---|---|---|
| Rashean Mathis | .5 | Greg Favors | .5.5 |
| Donovin Darius | .5 | John Henderson | .5.5 |

## Kansas City Chiefs

| Passing (5 Att) | Att | Cmp | Pct | Yds | TD | Rate |
|---|---|---|---|---|---|---|
| Trent Green | .556 | 369 | 66.4 | 4591 | 27 | 95.2 |
| Todd Collins | .5 | 1 | 20.0 | 42 | 0 | 62.1 |

**Interceptions:** Green 17.

| Top Receivers | No | Yds | Avg | Long | TD |
|---|---|---|---|---|---|
| Tony Gonzalez | .102 | 1258 | 12.3 | 32 | 7 |
| Eddie Kennison | .62 | 1086 | 17.5 | 70-td | 8 |
| Johnnie Morton | .55 | 795 | 14.5 | 52 | 3 |
| Derrick Blaylock | .25 | 246 | 9.8 | 30 | 1 |
| Dante Hall | .25 | 230 | 9.2 | 22 | 0 |

| Top Rushers | Car | Yds | Avg | Long | TD |
|---|---|---|---|---|---|
| Priest Holmes | 196 | 892 | 4.6 | 33-td | 14 |
| Larry Johnson | 120 | 581 | 4.8 | 46-td | 9 |
| Derrick Blaylock | 118 | 539 | 4.6 | 24 | 8 |

| Most Touchdowns | TD | Run | Rec | Ret | Pts |
|---|---|---|---|---|---|
| Priest Holmes | .15 | 14 | 1 | 0 | 90 |
| Larry Johnson | .11 | 9 | 2 | 0 | 66 |
| Derrick Blaylock | .9 | 8 | 1 | 0 | 54 |
| Eddie Kennison | .8 | 0 | 8 | 0 | 50 |
| Tony Gonzalez | .7 | 0 | 7 | 0 | 42 |

**2-Pt. Conversions:** (1-2) Kennison.

| Kicking | PAT/Att | FG/Att | Lg | Pts |
|---|---|---|---|---|
| Lawrence Tynes | .58/60 | 17/23 | 50 | 109 |

| Punts (10 or more) | No | Yds | Long | Avg | In20 |
|---|---|---|---|---|---|
| Steve Cheek* | .42 | 1643 | 55 | 39.1 | 8 |
| Nick Murphy* | .22 | 966 | 58 | 43.9 | 7 |
| BAL | .18 | 777 | 54 | 43.2 | 6 |
| KC | .4 | 189 | 58 | 47.3 | 1 |

**Signed:** Jason Baker (Sept. 25); Murphy (Dec. 21).
**Waived:** Cheek (Sept. 25); Baker on Oct. 5 (see Den.).

| Most Interceptions | | Most Sacks | |
|---|---|---|---|
| Greg Wesley | .4 | Jared Allen* | .9.0 |
| Eric Warfield | .4 | | |

## Miami Dolphins

| Passing (5 Att) | Att | Cmp | Pct | Yds | TD | Rate |
|---|---|---|---|---|---|---|
| A.J. Feeley | .356 | 191 | 53.7 | 1893 | 11 | 61.7 |
| Jay Fiedler | .190 | 101 | 53.2 | 1186 | 7 | 67.1 |
| Sage Rosenfels | .39 | 16 | 41.0 | 264 | 1 | 41.0 |

**Interceptions:** Feeley 15, Fiedler 8, Rosenfels 3.

| Top Receivers | No | Yds | Avg | Long | TD |
|---|---|---|---|---|---|
| Randy McMichael | .73 | 791 | 10.8 | 42-td | 4 |
| Chris Chambers | .69 | 898 | 13.0 | 76-td | 7 |
| Marty Booker | .50 | 638 | 12.8 | 45 | 1 |
| Derrius Thompson | .23 | 359 | 15.6 | 36 | 4 |

| Top Rushers | Car | Yds | Avg | Long | TD |
|---|---|---|---|---|---|
| Sammy Morris | .132 | 523 | 4.0 | 35-td | 6 |
| Travis Minor | .109 | 388 | 3.6 | 34 | 3 |
| Leonard Henry | .46 | 141 | 3.1 | 53 | 0 |

| Most Touchdowns | TD | Run | Rec | Ret | Pts |
|---|---|---|---|---|---|
| Chris Chambers | .7 | 0 | 7 | 0 | 44 |
| Sammy Morris | .6 | 6 | 0 | 0 | 36 |
| Randy McMichael | .4 | 0 | 4 | 0 | 26 |
| Derrius Thompson | .4 | 0 | 4 | 0 | 24 |

**2-Pt. Conversions:** (2-4) Chambers, McMichael.

| Kicking (Top Scorers) | PAT/Att | FG/Att | Lg | Pts |
|---|---|---|---|---|
| Olindo Mare | .18/18 | 12/16 | 51 | 54 |
| Matt Bryant | .12/12 | 3/4 | 47 | 21 |
| IND | .5/5 | 0/1 | — | 5 |
| MIA | .7/7 | 3/3 | 47 | 16 |

**Signed:** Bryant (Oct. 13); Bill Gramatica (Nov. 6).
**Waived:** Gramatica (Nov. 10).

| Punts (10 or more) | No | Yds | Long | Avg | In20 |
|---|---|---|---|---|---|
| Matt Turk | .98 | 4088 | 67 | 41.7 | 29 |

| Most Interceptions | Most Sacks | |
|---|---|---|
| Three tied with 4 int's each. | Jason Taylor | .9.5 |

## New England Patriots

| Passing (5 Att) | Att | Cmp | Pct | Yds | TD | Rate |
|---|---|---|---|---|---|---|
| Tom Brady | .474 | 288 | 60.8 | 3692 | 28 | 92.6 |
| Rohan Davey | .10 | 4 | 40.0 | 54 | 0 | 57.9 |

**Interceptions:** Brady 14.

| Top Receivers | No | Yds | Avg | Long | TD |
|---|---|---|---|---|---|
| David Givens | .56 | 874 | 15.6 | 50 | 3 |
| David Patten | .44 | 800 | 18.2 | 48-td | 7 |
| Deion Branch | .35 | 454 | 13.0 | 26-td | 4 |
| Daniel Graham | .30 | 364 | 12.1 | 48 | 7 |
| Patrick Pass | .28 | 215 | 7.7 | 22 | 0 |
| Kevin Faulk | .26 | 248 | 9.5 | 31-td | 1 |
| Troy Brown | .17 | 184 | 10.8 | 22 | 1 |

| Top Rushers | Car | Yds | Avg | Long | TD |
|---|---|---|---|---|---|
| Corey Dillon | .345 | 1635 | 4.7 | 44 | 12 |
| Kevin Faulk | .54 | 255 | 4.7 | 20 | 2 |
| Patrick Pass | .39 | 141 | 3.6 | 19 | 0 |
| Cedric Cobbs* | .22 | 50 | 2.3 | 13 | 0 |

| Most Touchdowns | TD | Run | Rec | Ret | Pts |
|---|---|---|---|---|---|
| Corey Dillon | .13 | 12 | 1 | 0 | 80 |
| Daniel Graham | .7 | 0 | 7 | 0 | 42 |
| David Patten | .7 | 0 | 7 | 0 | 42 |
| Deion Branch | .4 | 0 | 4 | 0 | 24 |
| Kevin Faulk | .3 | 2 | 1 | 0 | 18 |
| David Givens | .3 | 0 | 3 | 0 | 18 |

**2-Pt. Conversions:** (1-1) Dillon.

| Kicking | PAT/Att | FG/Att | Lg | Pts |
|---|---|---|---|---|
| Adam Vinatieri | .48/48 | 31/33 | 48 | 141 |

| Punts (10 or more) | No | Yds | Long | Avg | In20 |
|---|---|---|---|---|---|
| Josh Miller | .56 | 2350 | 69 | 42.0 | 19 |

| Most Interceptions | Most Sacks | |
|---|---|---|
| Eugene Wilson | .4 | Willie McGinest | .9.5 |

## New York Jets

| Passing (5 Att) | Att | Cmp | Pct | Yds | TD | Rate |
|---|---|---|---|---|---|---|
| Chad Pennington | .370 | 242 | 65.4 | 2673 | 16 | 91.0 |
| Quincy Carter | .58 | 35 | 60.3 | 498 | 3 | 98.2 |
| Brooks Bollinger | .9 | 5 | 55.6 | 60 | 0 | 76.2 |

**Interceptions:** Pennington 9, Carter and LaMont Jordan 1.

| Top Receivers | No | Yds | Avg | Long | TD |
|---|---|---|---|---|---|
| Justin McCareins | .56 | 770 | 13.8 | 43 | 4 |
| Santana Moss | .45 | 838 | 18.6 | 69-td | 5 |
| Jerald Sowell | .45 | 342 | 7.6 | 34 | 1 |
| Curtis Martin | .41 | 245 | 6.0 | 22 | 2 |
| Wayne Chrebet | .31 | 397 | 12.8 | 35-td | 1 |
| Chris Baker | .18 | 182 | 10.1 | 23 | 4 |
| LaMont Jordan | .15 | 112 | 7.5 | 25 | 0 |

| Top Rushers | No | Yds | Avg | Long | TD |
|---|---|---|---|---|---|
| Curtis Martin | .371 | 1697 | 4.6 | 25-td | 12 |
| LaMont Jordan | .93 | 479 | 5.2 | 33 | 2 |
| Chad Pennington | .34 | 126 | 3.7 | 16 | 1 |

| Most Touchdowns | TD | Run | Rec | Ret | Pts |
|---|---|---|---|---|---|
| Curtis Martin | .14 | 12 | 2 | 0 | 84 |
| Santana Moss | .5 | 0 | 5 | 0 | 30 |
| Chris Baker | .4 | 0 | 4 | 0 | 24 |
| Justin McCareins | .4 | 0 | 4 | 0 | 24 |
| Donnie Abraham | .2 | 0 | 0 | 2 | 12 |
| LaMont Jordan | .2 | 2 | 0 | 0 | 12 |

**2-Pt. Conversions:** (0-4)

| Kicking | PAT/Att | FG/Att | Lg | Pts |
|---|---|---|---|---|
| Doug Brien | .33/34 | 24/29 | 53 | 105 |

| Punts (10 or more) | No | Yds | Long | Avg | In20 |
|---|---|---|---|---|---|
| Toby Gowin | .80 | 3057 | 58 | 38.2 | 22 |

| Most Interceptions | Most Sacks | |
|---|---|---|
| Erik Coleman* | .4 | Shaun Ellis | .11.0 |

## Oakland Raiders

**Passing** (5 Att)

| | Att | Cmp | Pct | Yds | TD | Rate |
|---|---|---|---|---|---|---|
| Kerry Collins | .513 | 289 | 56.3 | 3495 | 21 | 74.8 |
| Rich Gannon | .68 | 41 | 60.3 | 524 | 3 | 86.9 |

**Interceptions:** Collins 20, Gannon 2.

**Top Receivers**

| | No | Yds | Avg | Long | TD |
|---|---|---|---|---|---|
| Jerry Porter | .64 | 998 | 15.6 | 52 | 9 |
| Ronald Curry | .50 | 679 | 13.6 | 63 | 6 |
| Amos Zereoue | .39 | 284 | 7.3 | 13 | 0 |
| Doug Gabriel | .33 | 551 | 16.7 | 58-td | 2 |
| J.R. Redmond | .32 | 233 | 7.3 | 22 | 0 |
| Doug Jolley | .27 | 313 | 11.6 | 34-td | 2 |

**Top Rushers**

| | Car | Yds | Avg | Long | TD |
|---|---|---|---|---|---|
| Amos Zereoue | .112 | 425 | 3.8 | 55-td | 4 |
| Tyrone Wheatley | .85 | 327 | 3.8 | 60 | 4 |
| Zack Crockett | .48 | 232 | 4.8 | 47 | 2 |
| Justin Fargas | .35 | 126 | 3.6 | 15 | 1 |
| J.R. Redmond | .21 | 119 | 5.7 | 18 | 0 |

**Most Touchdowns**

| | TD | Run | Rec | Ret | Pts |
|---|---|---|---|---|---|
| Jerry Porter | .9 | 0 | 9 | 0 | 54 |
| Ronald Curry | .6 | 0 | 6 | 0 | 36 |
| Tyrone Wheatley | .4 | 4 | 0 | 0 | 24 |
| Amos Zereoue | .3 | 3 | 0 | 0 | 18 |

Five tied with 2 TD each.

**2-Pt. Conversions:** (1-3) Alvis Whitted.

**Kicking**

| | PAT/Att | FG/Att | Lg | Pts |
|---|---|---|---|---|
| Sebastian Janikowski | .31/32 | 25/28 | 52 | 106 |

**Punts** (10 or more)

| | No | Yds | Long | Avg | In20 |
|---|---|---|---|---|---|
| Shane Lechler | .73 | 3409 | 67 | 46.7 | 22 |

**Most Interceptions**
Phillip Buchanon . . . . . .3

**Most Sacks**
Tommy Kelly* . . . . . . .4.0

## Pittsburgh Steelers

**Passing** (5 Att)

| | Att | Cmp | Pct | Yds | TD | Rate |
|---|---|---|---|---|---|---|
| Ben Roethlisberger* | 295 | 196 | 66.4 | 2621 | 17 | 98.1 |
| Tommy Maddox | .60 | 30 | 50.0 | 329 | 1 | 58.3 |

**Interceptions:** Roethlisberger 11, Maddox 2.

**Top Receivers**

| | No | Yds | Avg | Long | TD |
|---|---|---|---|---|---|
| Hines Ward | .80 | 1004 | 12.6 | 58 | 4 |
| Antwaan Randle El | .43 | 601 | 14.0 | 39 | 3 |
| Plaxico Burress | .35 | 698 | 19.9 | 48 | 5 |
| Verron Haynes | .18 | 142 | 7.9 | 26 | 2 |
| Dan Kreider | .10 | 75 | 7.5 | 13 | 1 |
| Lee Mays | .9 | 137 | 15.2 | 46 | 0 |
| Jerame Tuman | .9 | 89 | 9.9 | 26 | 3 |

**Top Rushers**

| | Car | Yds | Avg | Long | TD |
|---|---|---|---|---|---|
| Jerome Bettis | .250 | 941 | 3.8 | 29 | 13 |
| Duce Staley | .192 | 830 | 4.3 | 38 | 1 |
| Verron Haynes | .55 | 272 | 4.9 | 18 | 0 |
| Willie Parker* | .32 | 186 | 5.8 | 58 | 0 |
| Ben Roethlisberger* | .56 | 144 | 2.6 | 20 | 1 |

**Most Touchdowns**

| | TD | Run | Rec | Ret | Pts |
|---|---|---|---|---|---|
| Jerome Bettis | .13 | 13 | 0 | 0 | 78 |
| Plaxico Burress | .5 | 0 | 5 | 0 | 30 |
| Hines Ward | .5 | 1 | 4 | 0 | 30 |
| Antwaan Randle El | .3 | 0 | 3 | 0 | 18 |
| Jerame Tuman | .3 | 0 | 3 | 0 | 18 |

Two tied with 2 TD each.

**2-Pt. Conversions:** (0-1).

**Kicking**

| | PAT/Att | FG/Att | Lg | Pts |
|---|---|---|---|---|
| Jeff Reed | .40/40 | 28/33 | 51 | 124 |

**Punts** (10 or more)

| | No | Yds | Long | Avg | In20 |
|---|---|---|---|---|---|
| Chris Gardocki | .67 | 2879 | 61 | 43.0 | 24 |

**Most Interceptions**
Troy Polamalu . . . . . . .5

**Most Sacks**
Aaron Smith . . . . . . .8.0

## San Diego Chargers

**Passing** (5 Att)

| | Att | Cmp | Pct | Yds | TD | Rate |
|---|---|---|---|---|---|---|
| Drew Brees | .400 | 262 | 65.5 | 3159 | 27 | 104.8 |
| Doug Flutie | .38 | 20 | 52.6 | 276 | 1 | 85.0 |
| Philip Rivers* | .8 | 5 | 62.5 | 33 | 1 | 110.9 |

**Interceptions:** Brees 7, Mike Scifres 1.

**Top Receivers**

| | No | Yds | Avg | Long | TD |
|---|---|---|---|---|---|
| Antonio Gates | .81 | 964 | 11.9 | 72-td | 13 |
| LaDainian Tomlinson | .53 | 441 | 8.3 | 74-td | 1 |
| Eric Parker | .47 | 690 | 14.7 | 79-td | 4 |
| Keenan McCardell | .31 | 393 | 12.7 | 31 | 1 |
| Reche Caldwell | .18 | 310 | 17.2 | 58-td | 3 |

**Acquired:** McCardell from TB for 2005 3rd and 6th round picks (Oct. 19).

**Top Rushers**

| | No | Yds | Avg | Long | TD |
|---|---|---|---|---|---|
| LaDainian Tomlinson | .339 | 1335 | 3.9 | 42 | 17 |
| Jesse Chatman | .65 | 392 | 6.0 | 52 | 3 |
| Michael Turner* | .20 | 104 | 5.2 | 30 | 0 |
| Drew Brees | .53 | 85 | 1.6 | 22 | 2 |

**Most Touchdowns**

| | TD | Run | Rec | Ret | Pts |
|---|---|---|---|---|---|
| LaDainian Tomlinson | .18 | 17 | 1 | 0 | 108 |
| Antonio Gates | .13 | 0 | 13 | 0 | 78 |
| Eric Parker | .4 | 0 | 4 | 0 | 24 |
| Reche Caldwell | .3 | 0 | 3 | 0 | 18 |
| Jesse Chatman | .3 | 3 | 0 | 0 | 18 |

**2-Pt. Conversions:** (0-0).

**Kicking**

| | PAT/Att | FG/Att | Lg | Pts |
|---|---|---|---|---|
| Nate Kaeding* | .54/55 | 20/25 | 53 | 114 |

**Punts** (10 or more)

| | No | Yds | Long | Avg | In20 |
|---|---|---|---|---|---|
| Mike Scifres | .69 | 2974 | 60 | 43.1 | 29 |

**Most Interceptions**
Donnie Edwards . . . . . .5

**Most Sacks**
Steve Foley . . . . . . . .10.0

## Tennessee Titans

**Passing** (5 Att)

| | Att | Cmp | Pct | Yds | TD | Rate |
|---|---|---|---|---|---|---|
| Billy Volek | .357 | 218 | 61.1 | 2486 | 18 | 87.1 |
| Steve McNair | .215 | 129 | 60.0 | 1343 | 8 | 73.1 |
| Doug Johnson | .12 | 6 | 50.0 | 68 | 0 | 67.4 |

**Interceptions:** Volek 10, McNair 9.

**Top Receivers**

| | No | Yds | Avg | Long | TD |
|---|---|---|---|---|---|
| Derrick Mason | .96 | 1168 | 12.2 | 37-td | 7 |
| Drew Bennett | .80 | 1247 | 15.6 | 48-td | 11 |
| Ben Troupe* | .33 | 329 | 10.0 | 33 | 1 |
| Erron Kinney | .25 | 193 | 7.7 | 21 | 3 |
| Shad Meier | .25 | 127 | 5.1 | 29 | 2 |

**Top Rushers**

| | Car | Yds | Avg | Long | TD |
|---|---|---|---|---|---|
| Chris Brown | .220 | 1067 | 4.9 | 52 | 6 |
| Antowain Smith | .137 | 509 | 3.7 | 43 | 4 |
| Steve McNair | .23 | 128 | 5.6 | 23 | 1 |
| Robert Holcombe | .17 | 62 | 3.6 | 20 | 0 |

**Most Touchdowns**

| | TD | Run | Rec | Ret | Pts |
|---|---|---|---|---|---|
| Drew Bennett | .11 | 0 | 11 | 0 | 66 |
| Derrick Mason | .7 | 0 | 7 | 0 | 42 |
| Chris Brown | .6 | 6 | 0 | 0 | 36 |
| Antowain Smith | .4 | 4 | 0 | 0 | 24 |
| Erron Kinney | .3 | 0 | 3 | 0 | 18 |

**2-Pt. Conversions:** (1-2) McNair.

**Kicking**

| | PAT/Att | FG/Att | Lg | Pts |
|---|---|---|---|---|
| Gary Anderson | .37/37 | 17/22 | 45 | 88 |
| Craig Hentrich | .0/0 | 1/3 | — | 3 |

**Signed:** Aaron Elling (Sept. 10); Anderson (Sept. 14). **Released:** Elling on Sept. 14 (see Min.).

**Punts** (10 or more)

| | No | Yds | Long | Avg | In20 |
|---|---|---|---|---|---|
| Craig Hentrich | .73 | 3117 | 64 | 42.7 | 20 |

**Most Interceptions**
Andre Dyson . . . . . . .6

**Most Sacks**
Kevin Carter . . . . . . . .6.0

## NFC Team by Team Statistics

Players with more than one team during the regular season are listed with club they ended season with; (*) indicates rookies.

### Arizona Cardinals

| Passing (5 Att) | Att | Cmp | Pct | Yds | TD | Rate |
|---|---|---|---|---|---|---|
| Josh McCown | 408 | 233 | 57.1 | 2511 | 11 | 74.1 |
| Shaun King | 84 | 47 | 56.0 | 502 | 1 | 57.7 |
| John Navarre* | 40 | 18 | 45.0 | 168 | 1 | 25.8 |

**Interceptions:** McCown 10, King and Navarre 4.

| Top Receivers | No | Yds | Avg | Long | TD |
|---|---|---|---|---|---|
| Larry Fitzgerald* | 58 | 780 | 13.4 | 48 | 8 |
| Anquan Boldin | 56 | 623 | 11.1 | 31-td | 1 |
| Bryant Johnson | 49 | 537 | 11.0 | 40 | 1 |
| Freddie Jones | 45 | 426 | 9.5 | 40 | 2 |
| Obafemi Ayanbadejo | 19 | 171 | 9.0 | 21-td | 1 |
| Karl Williams | 18 | 197 | 10.9 | 33 | 0 |
| Josh Scobey | 18 | 191 | 10.6 | 42 | 0 |

| Top Rushers | Car | Yds | Avg | Long | TD |
|---|---|---|---|---|---|
| Emmitt Smith | 267 | 937 | 3.5 | 29-td | 9 |
| Troy Hambrick | 63 | 283 | 4.5 | 62 | 1 |
| Obafemi Ayanbadejo | 30 | 122 | 4.1 | 23 | 3 |
| Josh McCown | 36 | 112 | 3.1 | 12 | 2 |

| Most Touchdowns | TD | Run | Rec | Ret | Pts |
|---|---|---|---|---|---|
| Emmitt Smith | 9 | 9 | 0 | 0 | 54 |
| Larry Fitzgerald* | 8 | 0 | 8 | 0 | 48 |
| Obafemi Ayanbadejo | 4 | 3 | 1 | 0 | 24 |

Three tied with 2 TD each.

**2-Pt. Conversions:** (1-3) McCown.

| Kicking | PAT/Att | FG/Att | Lg | Pts |
|---|---|---|---|---|
| Neil Rackers | 28/28 | 22/29 | 55 | 94 |

| Punts (10 or more) | No | Yds | Long | Avg | In20 |
|---|---|---|---|---|---|
| Scott Player | 98 | 4230 | 57 | 43.2 | 32 |

| Most Interceptions | | Most Sacks | |
|---|---|---|---|
| David Macklin | 4 | Bertrand Berry | 14.5 |

### Atlanta Falcons

| Passing (5 Att) | Att | Cmp | Pct | Yds | TD | Rate |
|---|---|---|---|---|---|---|
| Michael Vick | 321 | 181 | 56.4 | 2313 | 14 | 78.1 |
| Matt Schaub* | 70 | 33 | 47.1 | 330 | 1 | 42.0 |

**Interceptions:** Vick 12, Schaub 3.

| Top Receivers | No | Yds | Avg | Long | TD |
|---|---|---|---|---|---|
| Alge Crumpler | 47 | 774 | 16.1 | 49-td | 6 |
| Peerless Price | 45 | 575 | 12.8 | 50 | 3 |
| Dez White | 30 | 370 | 12.3 | 54 | 2 |
| Warrick Dunn | 29 | 294 | 10.1 | 59 | 0 |
| Brian Finneran | 23 | 258 | 11.2 | 26 | 2 |
| Justin Griffith | 22 | 220 | 10.0 | 62 | 1 |

| Top Rushers | Car | Yds | Avg | Long | TD |
|---|---|---|---|---|---|
| Warrick Dunn | 265 | 1106 | 4.2 | 60 | 9 |
| Michael Vick | 120 | 902 | 7.5 | 58 | 3 |
| T.J. Duckett | 104 | 509 | 4.9 | 35 | 8 |
| Justin Griffith | 9 | 39 | 4.3 | 10 | 0 |

| Most Touchdowns | TD | Run | Rec | Ret | Pts |
|---|---|---|---|---|---|
| Warrick Dunn | 9 | 9 | 0 | 0 | 54 |
| T.J. Duckett | 8 | 8 | 0 | 0 | 48 |
| Alge Crumpler | 6 | 0 | 6 | 0 | 36 |
| Peerless Price | 3 | 0 | 3 | 0 | 18 |
| Michael Vick | 3 | 3 | 0 | 0 | 18 |

Three tied with 2 TD each.

**2-Pt. Conversions:** (0-1).

| Kicking | PAT/Att | FG/Att | Lg | Pts |
|---|---|---|---|---|
| Jay Feely | 40/40 | 18/23 | 47 | 94 |

| Punts (10 or more) | No | Yds | Long | Avg | In20 |
|---|---|---|---|---|---|
| Chris Mohr | 76 | 3082 | 56 | 40.6 | 19 |

| Most Interceptions | | Most Sacks | |
|---|---|---|---|
| Aaron Beasley | 4 | Patrick Kerney | 13.0 |

### Carolina Panthers

| Passing (5 Att) | Att | Cmp | Pct | Yds | TD | Rate |
|---|---|---|---|---|---|---|
| Jake Delhomme | 533 | 310 | 58.2 | 3886 | 29 | 87.3 |

**Interceptions:** Delhomme 15.

| Top Receivers | No | Yds | Avg | Long | TD |
|---|---|---|---|---|---|
| Muhsin Muhammad | 93 | 1405 | 15.1 | 51 | 16 |
| Keary Colbert* | 47 | 754 | 16.0 | 63 | 5 |
| Nick Goings | 45 | 394 | 8.8 | 37 | 1 |
| Ricky Proehl | 34 | 497 | 14.6 | 34 | 0 |
| Kris Mangum | 34 | 323 | 9.5 | 26 | 3 |
| Brad Hoover | 21 | 161 | 7.7 | 34 | 2 |

| Top Rushers | Car | Yds | Avg | Long | TD |
|---|---|---|---|---|---|
| Nick Goings | 217 | 821 | 3.8 | 57-td | 6 |
| DeShaun Foster | 59 | 255 | 4.3 | 71 | 2 |
| Brad Hoover | 68 | 246 | 3.6 | 16 | 0 |
| Stephen Davis | 24 | 92 | 3.8 | 12 | 0 |

| Most Touchdowns | TD | Run | Rec | Ret | Pts |
|---|---|---|---|---|---|
| Muhsin Muhammad | 16 | 0 | 16 | 0 | 96 |
| Nick Goings | 7 | 6 | 1 | 0 | 42 |
| Keary Colbert* | 5 | 0 | 5 | 0 | 32 |
| Kris Mangum | 3 | 0 | 3 | 0 | 18 |

Four tied with 2 each.

**2-Pt. Conversions:** (2-2) Colbert, Mike Seidman.

| Kicking | PAT/Att | FG/Att | Lg | Pts |
|---|---|---|---|---|
| John Kasay | 27/28 | 19/22 | 54 | 84 |
| Todd Sauerbrun | 4/4 | 1/1 | 34 | 7 |

**Signed:** Jeff Chandler (Nov. 17). **Released:** Chandler on Dec. 1 (see Wash.).

| Punts (10 or more) | No | Yds | Long | Avg | In20 |
|---|---|---|---|---|---|
| Todd Sauerbrun | 76 | 3351 | 65 | 44.1 | 25 |

| Most Interceptions | | Most Sacks | |
|---|---|---|---|
| Chris Gamble* | 6 | Julius Peppers | 11.0 |

### Chicago Bears

| Passing (5 Att) | Att | Cmp | Pct | Yds | TD | Rate |
|---|---|---|---|---|---|---|
| Chad Hutchinson | 161 | 92 | 57.1 | 903 | 4 | 73.6 |
| Craig Krenzel* | 127 | 59 | 46.5 | 718 | 3 | 52.5 |
| Jonathan Quinn | 98 | 51 | 52.0 | 413 | 1 | 53.7 |
| Rex Grossman | 84 | 47 | 56.0 | 607 | 1 | 67.9 |

**Interceptions:** Krenzel 6, Hutchinson, Quinn and Grossman 3, Paul Edinger 1.

| Top Receivers | No | Yds | Avg | Long | TD |
|---|---|---|---|---|---|
| Thomas Jones | 56 | 427 | 7.6 | 45 | 0 |
| David Terrell | 42 | 699 | 16.6 | 63 | 1 |
| Bobby Wade | 42 | 481 | 11.5 | 40 | 0 |
| Desmond Clark | 24 | 282 | 11.8 | 31 | 1 |
| Anthony Thomas | 17 | 132 | 7.8 | 30 | 0 |
| Bernard Berrian* | 15 | 225 | 15.0 | 49-td | 2 |

| Top Rushers | Car | Yds | Avg | Long | TD |
|---|---|---|---|---|---|
| Thomas Jones | 240 | 948 | 4.0 | 54 | 7 |
| Anthony Thomas | 122 | 404 | 3.3 | 41-td | 2 |
| Bobby Wade | 12 | 76 | 6.3 | 14 | 0 |
| Rex Grossman | 11 | 48 | 4.4 | 8 | 1 |

| Most Touchdowns | TD | Run | Rec | Ret | Pts |
|---|---|---|---|---|---|
| Thomas Jones | 7 | 7 | 0 | 0 | 42 |

Five tied with 2 TD each.

**2-Pt. Conversions:** (1-4) Krenzel.

| Kicking | PAT/Att | FG/Att | Lg | Pts |
|---|---|---|---|---|
| Paul Edinger | 22/22 | 15/24 | 53 | 67 |

| Punts (10 or more) | No | Yds | Long | Avg | In20 |
|---|---|---|---|---|---|
| Brad Maynard | 108 | 4638 | 58 | 42.9 | 34 |

| Most Interceptions | | Most Sacks | |
|---|---|---|---|
| Nathan Vasher* | 5 | Alex Brown | 6.0 |

## Dallas Cowboys

**Passing** (5 Att)

| | Att | Cmp | Pct | Yds | TD | Rate |
|---|---|---|---|---|---|---|
| Vinny Testaverde | .495 | 297 | 60.0 | 3532 | 17 | 76.4 |
| Drew Henson* | .18 | 10 | 55.6 | 78 | 1 | 61.8 |

**Interceptions:** Testaverde 20, Henson, Keyshawn Johnson and Patrick Crayton 1.

**Top Receivers**

| | No | Yds | Avg | Long | TD |
|---|---|---|---|---|---|
| Jason Witten | .87 | 980 | 11.3 | 42-td | 6 |
| Keyshawn Johnson | .70 | 981 | 14.0 | 39 | 6 |
| Quincy Morgan | .31 | 404 | 13.0 | 53 | 3 |
| CLE | .9 | 144 | 16.0 | 46-td | 3 |
| DAL | .22 | 260 | 11.8 | 53 | 0 |
| Richie Anderson | .26 | 207 | 8.0 | 28 | 0 |
| Terry Glenn | .24 | 400 | 16.7 | 48 | 2 |

**Acquired:** Morgan from Cle. for WR Antonio Bryant (Oct. 19).

**Top Rushers**

| | Car | Yds | Avg | Long | TD |
|---|---|---|---|---|---|
| Julius Jones* | .197 | 819 | 4.2 | 53 | 7 |
| Eddie George | .132 | 432 | 3.3 | 24 | 4 |
| Richie Anderson | .57 | 246 | 4.3 | 27 | 1 |
| ReShard Lee* | .27 | 128 | 4.7 | 14 | 1 |

**Most Touchdowns**

| | TD | Run | Rec | Ret | Pts |
|---|---|---|---|---|---|
| Julius Jones* | .7 | 7 | 0 | 0 | 42 |
| Jason Witten | .6 | 0 | 6 | 0 | 38 |
| Keyshawn Johnson | .6 | 0 | 6 | 0 | 36 |
| Eddie George | .4 | 4 | 0 | 0 | 24 |
| Terry Glenn | .2 | 0 | 2 | 0 | 12 |
| Jeff Robinson | .2 | 0 | 2 | 0 | 12 |

**2-Pt. Conversions:** (1-2) Witten.

**Kicking**

| | PAT/Att | FG/Att | Lg | Pts |
|---|---|---|---|---|
| Billy Cundiff | .31/31 | 20/26 | 49 | 91 |

**Punts** (10 or more)

| | No | Yds | Long | Avg | In20 |
|---|---|---|---|---|---|
| Mat McBriar* | .75 | 3182 | 68 | 42.4 | 22 |

**Most Interceptions**    **Most Sacks**
Terence Newman .....4    Greg Ellis ..........9.0

## Detroit Lions

**Passing** (5 Att)

| | Att | Cmp | Pct | Yds | TD | Rate |
|---|---|---|---|---|---|---|
| Joey Harrington | .489 | 274 | 56.0 | 3047 | 19 | 77.5 |
| Mike McMahon | .15 | 11 | 73.3 | 77 | 0 | 56.8 |

**Interceptions:** Harrington 12, McMahon 1.

**Top Receivers**

| | No | Yds | Avg | Long | TD |
|---|---|---|---|---|---|
| Roy Williams* | .54 | 817 | 15.1 | 46 | 8 |
| Shawn Bryson | .44 | 322 | 7.3 | 30 | 0 |
| Stephen Alexander | .41 | 377 | 9.2 | 30 | 1 |
| Az-Zahir Hakim | .31 | 533 | 17.2 | 39-td | 3 |
| Tai Streets | .28 | 260 | 9.3 | 22 | 1 |
| Kevin Jones* | .28 | 180 | 6.4 | 34 | 1 |
| Reggie Swinton | .18 | 213 | 11.8 | 28 | 1 |

**Top Rushers**

| | Car | Yds | Avg | Long | TD |
|---|---|---|---|---|---|
| Kevin Jones* | .241 | 1133 | 4.7 | 74 | 5 |
| Shawn Bryson | .50 | 264 | 5.3 | 28 | 0 |
| Joey Harrington | .48 | 175 | 3.6 | 17 | 0 |
| Artose Pinner | .57 | 174 | 3.1 | 14 | 2 |

**Most Touchdowns**

| | TD | Run | Rec | Ret | Pts |
|---|---|---|---|---|---|
| Roy Williams* | .8 | 0 | 8 | 0 | 48 |
| Kevin Jones* | .6 | 5 | 1 | 0 | 36 |
| Eddie Drummond | .4 | 0 | 0 | 4 | 24 |
| Az-Zahir Hakim | .3 | 0 | 3 | 0 | 18 |
| Cory Schlesinger | .3 | 0 | 3 | 0 | 18 |

**2-Pt. Conversions:** (1-4) Streets.

**Kicking**

| | PAT/Att | FG/Att | Lg | Pts |
|---|---|---|---|---|
| Jason Hanson | .28/28 | 24/28 | 48 | 100 |

**Punts** (10 or more)

| | No | Yds | Long | Avg | In20 |
|---|---|---|---|---|---|
| Nick Harris | .92 | 3765 | 60 | 40.9 | 32 |

**Most Interceptions**    **Most Sacks**
Dre' Bly ..........4    James Hall ........11.5

## Green Bay Packers

**Passing** (5 Att)

| | Att | Cmp | Pct | Yds | TD | Rate |
|---|---|---|---|---|---|---|
| Brett Favre | .540 | 346 | 64.1 | 4088 | 30 | 92.4 |
| Craig Nall | .33 | 23 | 69.7 | 314 | 4 | 139.4 |
| Doug Pederson | .23 | 11 | 47.8 | 120 | 0 | 27.4 |

**Interceptions:** Favre 17, Pederson 2.

**Top Receivers**

| | No | Yds | Avg | Long | TD |
|---|---|---|---|---|---|
| Javon Walker | .89 | 1382 | 15.5 | 79-td | 12 |
| Donald Driver | .84 | 1208 | 14.4 | 50 | 9 |
| Ahman Green | .40 | 275 | 6.9 | 48 | 1 |
| Tony Fisher | .38 | 277 | 7.3 | 25 | 2 |
| Bubba Franks | .34 | 361 | 10.6 | 29 | 7 |
| William Henderson | .34 | 239 | 7.0 | 38-td | 1 |

**Top Rushers**

| | Car | Yds | Avg | Long | TD |
|---|---|---|---|---|---|
| Ahman Green | .259 | 1163 | 4.5 | 90-td | 7 |
| Najeh Davenport | .71 | 359 | 5.1 | 40-td | 2 |
| Tony Fisher | .65 | 224 | 3.4 | 24 | 0 |

**Most Touchdowns**

| | TD | Run | Rec | Ret | Pts |
|---|---|---|---|---|---|
| Javon Walker | .12 | 0 | 12 | 0 | 72 |
| Donald Driver | .9 | 0 | 9 | 0 | 56 |
| Ahman Green | .8 | 7 | 1 | 0 | 48 |
| Bubba Franks | .7 | 0 | 7 | 0 | 42 |
| William Henderson | .3 | 0 | 3 | 0 | 18 |
| Darren Sharper | .3 | 0 | 0 | 3 | 18 |

**2-Pt. Conversions:** (2-2) Driver, Ferguson.

**Kicking**

| | PAT/Att | FG/Att | Lg | Pts |
|---|---|---|---|---|
| Ryan Longwell | .48/48 | 24/28 | 53 | 120 |

**Punts** (10 or more)

| | No | Yds | Long | Avg | In20 |
|---|---|---|---|---|---|
| Bryan Barker | .66 | 2644 | 64 | 40.1 | 16 |

**Most Interceptions**    **Most Sacks**
Darren Sharper ......4    Kabeer Gbaja-
   Biamila ..........13.5

## Minnesota Vikings

**Passing** (5 Att)

| | Att | Cmp | Pct | Yds | TD | Rate |
|---|---|---|---|---|---|---|
| Daunte Culpepper | .548 | 379 | 69.2 | 4717 | 39 | 110.9 |

**Interceptions:** Culpepper 11, Moss 1.

**Top Receivers**

| | No | Yds | Avg | Long | TD |
|---|---|---|---|---|---|
| Jermaine Wiggins | .71 | 705 | 9.9 | 39 | 4 |
| Nate Burleson | .68 | 1006 | 14.8 | 68-td | 9 |
| Randy Moss | .49 | 767 | 15.7 | 82-td | 13 |
| Marcus Robinson | .47 | 657 | 14.0 | 50-td | 8 |
| Onterrio Smith | .36 | 394 | 10.9 | 63-td | 2 |
| Mewelde Moore* | .27 | 238 | 8.8 | 26 | 0 |

**Top Rushers**

| | Car | Yds | Avg | Long | TD |
|---|---|---|---|---|---|
| Onterrio Smith | .124 | 544 | 4.4 | 38 | 2 |
| Daunte Culpepper | .88 | 406 | 4.6 | 16 | 2 |
| Mewelde Moore* | .65 | 379 | 5.8 | 33 | 0 |
| Michael Bennett | .70 | 276 | 3.9 | 25 | 1 |

**Most Touchdowns**

| | TD | Run | Rec | Ret | Pts |
|---|---|---|---|---|---|
| Randy Moss | .13 | 0 | 13 | 0 | 78 |
| Nate Burleson | .10 | 0 | 9 | 1 | 62 |
| Marcus Robinson | .8 | 0 | 8 | 0 | 48 |
| Onterrio Smith | .4 | 2 | 2 | 0 | 26 |
| Jermaine Wiggins | .4 | 0 | 4 | 0 | 24 |
| Moe Williams | .4 | 3 | 1 | 0 | 24 |

**2-Pt. Conversions:** (3-4) Burleson, Culpepper and Smith.

**Kicking**

| | PAT/Att | FG/Att | Lg | Pts |
|---|---|---|---|---|
| Morten Andersen | .45/45 | 18/22 | 48 | 99 |
| Aaron Elling | .2/2 | 1/2 | 22 | 5 |
| TEN | .2/2 | 1/2 | 22 | 5 |

**Signed:** Elling (Sept. 17).

**Punts** (10 or more)

| | No | Yds | Long | Avg | In20 |
|---|---|---|---|---|---|
| Darren Bennett | .57 | 2240 | 61 | 39.3 | 18 |

**Most Interceptions**    **Most Sacks**
Antoine Winfield ......3    Kevin Williams ......11.5

## New Orleans Saints

| Passing (5 Att) | Att | Cmp | Pct | Yds | TD | Rate |
|---|---|---|---|---|---|---|
| Aaron Brooks | .542 | 309 | 57.0 | 3810 | 21 | 79.5 |

**Interceptions:** Brooks 16.

| Top Receivers | No | Yds | Avg | Long | TD |
|---|---|---|---|---|---|
| Joe Horn | .94 | 1399 | 14.9 | 57 | 11 |
| Donte' Stallworth | .58 | 767 | 13.2 | 45 | 5 |
| Jerome Pathon | .34 | 581 | 17.1 | 38 | 1 |
| Deuce McAllister | .34 | 228 | 6.7 | 20 | 0 |
| Boo Williams | .33 | 362 | 11.0 | 22 | 2 |
| Aaron Stecker | .29 | 174 | 6.0 | 26 | 0 |
| Ernie Conwell | .10 | 102 | 10.2 | 28 | 1 |

| Top Rushers | Car | Yds | Avg | Long | TD |
|---|---|---|---|---|---|
| Deuce McAllister | .269 | 1074 | 4.0 | 71 | 9 |
| Aaron Stecker | .58 | 244 | 4.2 | 42-td | 2 |
| Aaron Brooks | .58 | 173 | 3.0 | 15 | 4 |
| Fred McAfee | .2 | 54 | 27.0 | 53 | 0 |

| Most Touchdowns | TD | Run | Rec | Ret | Pts |
|---|---|---|---|---|---|
| Joe Horn | .11 | 0 | 11 | 0 | 68 |
| Deuce McAllister | .9 | 9 | 0 | 0 | 54 |
| Donte' Stallworth | .5 | 0 | 5 | 0 | 30 |
| Aaron Brooks | .4 | 4 | 0 | 0 | 24 |
| Aaron Stecker | .3 | 2 | 0 | 1 | 18 |
| Boo Williams | .2 | 0 | 2 | 0 | 12 |

**2-Pt. Conversions:** (1-2) Horn.

| Kicking | PAT/Att | FG/Att | Lg | Pts |
|---|---|---|---|---|
| John Carney | .38/38 | 22/27 | 53 | 104 |

| Punts (10 or more) | No | Yds | Long | Avg | In20 |
|---|---|---|---|---|---|
| Mitch Berger | .85 | 3704 | 63 | 43.6 | 28 |

| Most Interceptions | | Most Sacks | |
|---|---|---|---|
| Mike McKenzie | .5 | Darren Howard | .11.0 |

**Acquired:** DB McKenzie from GB for QB J.T. O'Sullivan and a 2005 2nd-round pick (Oct. 4).

## New York Giants

| Passing (5 Att) | Att | Cmp | Pct | Yds | TD | Rate |
|---|---|---|---|---|---|---|
| Kurt Warner | .277 | 174 | 62.8 | 2054 | 6 | 86.5 |
| Eli Manning* | .197 | 95 | 48.2 | 1043 | 6 | 55.4 |

**Interceptions:** Manning 9, Warner 4.

| Top Receivers | No | Yds | Avg | Long | TD |
|---|---|---|---|---|---|
| Jeremy Shockey | .61 | 666 | 10.9 | 38 | 6 |
| Tiki Barber | .52 | 578 | 11.1 | 62-td | 2 |
| Amani Toomer | .51 | 747 | 14.6 | 48 | 0 |
| Ike Hilliard | .49 | 437 | 8.9 | 43 | 0 |
| Jim Finn | .15 | 112 | 7.5 | 15 | 0 |
| Tim Carter | .12 | 182 | 15.2 | 38-td | 1 |
| David Tyree | .10 | 155 | 15.5 | 49 | 1 |

| Top Rushers | Car | Yds | Avg | Long | TD |
|---|---|---|---|---|---|
| Tiki Barber | .322 | 1518 | 4.7 | 72-td | 13 |
| Ron Dayne | .52 | 179 | 3.4 | 15 | 1 |
| Mike Cloud | .21 | 90 | 4.3 | 26 | 3 |
| Eli Manning | .6 | 35 | 5.8 | 15 | 0 |

| Most Touchdowns | TD | Run | Rec | Ret | Pts |
|---|---|---|---|---|---|
| Tiki Barber | .15 | 13 | 2 | 0 | 90 |
| Jeremy Shockey | .6 | 0 | 6 | 0 | 36 |
| Mike Cloud | .3 | 3 | 0 | 0 | 18 |

Ten tied with 1 TD each.

**2-Pt. Conversions:** (0-1).

| Kicking | PAT/Att | FG/Att | Lg | Pts |
|---|---|---|---|---|
| Steve Christie | .33/33 | 22/28 | 53 | 99 |

| Punts (10 or more) | No | Yds | Long | Avg | In20 |
|---|---|---|---|---|---|
| Jeff Feagles | .74 | 3069 | 55 | 41.5 | 23 |

| Most Interceptions | | Most Sacks | |
|---|---|---|---|
| Gibril Wilson* | .3 | Osi Umenyiora | .7.0 |
| Brent Alexander | .3 | | |

## Philadelphia Eagles

| Passing (5 Att) | Att | Cmp | Pct | Yds | TD | Rate |
|---|---|---|---|---|---|---|
| Donovan McNabb | 469 | 300 | 64.0 | 3875 | 31 | 104.7 |
| Koy Detmer | .40 | 18 | 45.0 | 207 | 0 | 40.3 |
| Jeff Blake | .37 | 18 | 48.6 | 126 | 1 | 54.6 |

**Interceptions:** McNabb 8, Detmer 2, Blake 1.

| Top Receivers | No | Yds | Avg | Long | TD |
|---|---|---|---|---|---|
| Terrell Owens | .77 | 1200 | 15.6 | 59-td | 14 |
| Brian Westbrook | .73 | 703 | 9.6 | 50 | 6 |
| Todd Pinkston | .36 | 676 | 18.8 | 80 | 1 |
| L.J. Smith | .34 | 377 | 11.1 | 31 | 5 |
| Chad Lewis | .29 | 267 | 9.2 | 21 | 3 |
| Freddie Mitchell | .22 | 377 | 17.1 | 60 | 2 |
| Greg Lewis | .17 | 183 | 10.8 | 25 | 0 |

| Top Rushers | Car | Yds | Avg | Long | TD |
|---|---|---|---|---|---|
| Brian Westbrook | .177 | 812 | 4.6 | 50 | 3 |
| Dorsey Levens | .94 | 410 | 4.4 | 45 | 4 |
| Donovan McNabb | .41 | 220 | 5.4 | 28 | 3 |
| Reno Mahe | .23 | 91 | 4.0 | 22 | 0 |

| Most Touchdowns | TD | Run | Rec | Ret | Pts |
|---|---|---|---|---|---|
| Terrell Owens | .14 | 0 | 14 | 0 | 84 |
| Brian Westbrook | .9 | 3 | 6 | 0 | 54 |
| L.J. Smith | .5 | 0 | 5 | 0 | 30 |
| Dorsey Levens | .4 | 4 | 0 | 0 | 24 |
| Chad Lewis | .3 | 0 | 3 | 0 | 18 |
| Donovan McNabb | .3 | 3 | 0 | 0 | 18 |

**2-Pt. Conversions:** (0-2).

| Kicking | PAT/Att | FG/Att | Lg | Pts |
|---|---|---|---|---|
| David Akers | .41/42 | 27/32 | 51 | 122 |

| Punts (15 or more) | No | Yds | Long | Avg | In20 |
|---|---|---|---|---|---|
| Dirk Johnson | .72 | 3032 | 62 | 42.1 | 20 |

| Most Interceptions | | Most Sacks | |
|---|---|---|---|
| Lito Sheppard | .5 | Jevon Kearse | .7.5 |

## St. Louis Rams

| Passing (5 Att) | Att | Cmp | Pct | Yds | TD | Rate |
|---|---|---|---|---|---|---|
| Marc Bulger | .485 | 321 | 66.2 | 3964 | 21 | 93.7 |
| Chris Chandler | .62 | 35 | 56.5 | 463 | 2 | 51.4 |
| Jamie Martin | .30 | 16 | 53.3 | 188 | 0 | 72.6 |

**Interceptions:** Bulger 14, Chandler 8.

| Top Receivers | No | Yds | Avg | Long | TD |
|---|---|---|---|---|---|
| Torry Holt | .94 | 1372 | 14.6 | 75-td | 10 |
| Isaac Bruce | .89 | 1292 | 14.5 | 56 | 6 |
| Marshall Faulk | .50 | 310 | 6.2 | 25 | 1 |
| Shaun McDonald | .37 | 494 | 13.4 | 52-td | 3 |
| Kevin Curtis | .32 | 421 | 13.2 | 41-td | 2 |
| Steven Jackson* | .19 | 189 | 9.9 | 28 | 0 |

| Top Rushers | Car | Yds | Avg | Long | TD |
|---|---|---|---|---|---|
| Marshall Faulk | .195 | 774 | 4.0 | 40 | 3 |
| Steven Jackson* | .134 | 673 | 5.0 | 48 | 4 |
| Marc Bulger | .19 | 89 | 4.7 | 19-td | 3 |

| Most Touchdowns | TD | Run | Rec | Ret | Pts |
|---|---|---|---|---|---|
| Torry Holt | .10 | 0 | 10 | 0 | 60 |
| Isaac Bruce | .6 | 0 | 6 | 0 | 36 |
| Marshall Faulk | .4 | 3 | 1 | 0 | 28 |
| Steven Jackson* | .4 | 4 | 0 | 0 | 26 |

Two tied with 3 TD each.

**2-Pt. Conversions:** (4-4) Faulk 2, Curtis and Jackson 1.

| Kicking | PAT/Att | FG/Att | Lg | Pts |
|---|---|---|---|---|
| Jeff Wilkins | .32/32 | 19/24 | 53 | 89 |

| Punts (10 or more) | No | Yds | Long | Avg | In20 |
|---|---|---|---|---|---|
| Sean Landeta | .40 | 1733 | 63 | 43.3 | 9 |
| Kevin Stemke | .28 | 1115 | 56 | 39.8 | 12 |

**Released:** Landeta (Nov. 26). **Signed:** Stemke (Nov. 26).

| Most Interceptions | | Most Sacks | |
|---|---|---|---|
| Jerametrius Butler | .5 | Bryce Fisher | .8.5 |

## San Francisco 49ers

| Passing (5 Att) | Att | Cmp | Pct | Yds | TD | Rate |
| --- | --- | --- | --- | --- | --- | --- |
| Tim Rattay | .325 | 198 | 60.9 | 2169 | 10 | 78.1 |
| Ken Dorsey | .226 | 123 | 54.4 | 1231 | 6 | 62.4 |
| Cody Pickett* | .10 | 4 | 40.0 | 55 | 0 | 18.8 |

**Interceptions:** Rattay 10, Dorsey 9, Pickett 2.

| Top Receivers | No | Yds | Avg | Long | TD |
| --- | --- | --- | --- | --- | --- |
| Eric Johnson | .82 | 825 | 10.1 | 25 | 2 |
| Cedrick Wilson | .47 | 641 | 13.6 | 39 | 3 |
| Brandon Lloyd | .43 | 565 | 13.1 | 52 | 6 |
| Curtis Conway | .38 | 403 | 10.6 | 37 | 3 |
| Kevan Barlow | .35 | 212 | 6.1 | 15 | 0 |
| Terry Jackson | .21 | 139 | 6.6 | 22 | 0 |

| Top Rushers | Car | Yds | Avg | Long | TD |
| --- | --- | --- | --- | --- | --- |
| Kevan Barlow | .244 | 822 | 3.4 | 60 | 7 |
| Maurice Hicks | .96 | 362 | 3.8 | 35 | 2 |
| Terry Jackson | .26 | 101 | 3.9 | 13 | 0 |
| Tim Rattay | .12 | 55 | 4.6 | 15 | 0 |

| Most Touchdowns | TD | Run | Rec | Ret | Pts |
| --- | --- | --- | --- | --- | --- |
| Kevan Barlow | .7 | 7 | 0 | 0 | 42 |
| Brandon Lloyd | .6 | 0 | 6 | 0 | 38 |
| Curtis Conway | .3 | 0 | 3 | 0 | 20 |
| Cedrick Wilson | .3 | 0 | 3 | 0 | 18 |

**2-Pt. Conversions:** (3-6) Conway, Lloyd, Rattay.

| Kicking | PAT/Att | FG/Att | Lg | Pts |
| --- | --- | --- | --- | --- |
| Todd Peterson | .23/23 | 18/22 | 51 | 77 |

| Punts (10 or more) | No | Yds | Long | Avg | In20 |
| --- | --- | --- | --- | --- | --- |
| Andy Lee* | .96 | 3990 | 81 | 41.6 | 25 |

| Most Interceptions | | Most Sacks | |
| --- | --- | --- | --- |
| Tony Parrish | .4 | John Engelberger | .6.0 |

## Seattle Seahawks

| Passing (5 Att) | Att | Cmp | Pct | Yds | TD | Rate |
| --- | --- | --- | --- | --- | --- | --- |
| Matt Hasselbeck | .474 | 279 | 58.9 | 3382 | 22 | 83.1 |
| Trent Dilfer | .58 | 25 | 43.1 | 333 | 1 | 46.1 |

**Interceptions:** Hasselbeck 15, Dilfer 3.

| Top Receivers | No | Yds | Avg | Long | TD |
| --- | --- | --- | --- | --- | --- |
| Darrell Jackson | .87 | 1199 | 13.8 | 56-td | 7 |
| Bobby Engram | .36 | 499 | 13.9 | 60 | 2 |
| Koren Robinson | .31 | 495 | 16.0 | 33 | 2 |
| Jerramy Stevens | .31 | 349 | 11.3 | 32 | 3 |
| Jerry Rice | .30 | 429 | 14.3 | 56 | 3 |
| OAK | .5 | 67 | 13.4 | 18 | 0 |
| SEA | .25 | 362 | 14.5 | 56 | 3 |

**Acquired:** Rice from Oak for a 2005 7th-round pick (Oct. 19).

| Top Rushers | Car | Yds | Avg | Long | TD |
| --- | --- | --- | --- | --- | --- |
| Shaun Alexander | .353 | 1696 | 4.8 | 44 | 16 |
| Mack Strong | .36 | 131 | 3.6 | 11 | 0 |
| Maurice Morris | .30 | 126 | 4.2 | 12 | 0 |
| Matt Hasselbeck | .27 | 90 | 3.3 | 19 | 1 |

| Most Touchdowns | TD | Run | Rec | Ret | Pts |
| --- | --- | --- | --- | --- | --- |
| Shaun Alexander | .20 | 16 | 4 | 0 | 120 |
| Darrell Jackson | .7 | 0 | 7 | 0 | 44 |
| Jerramy Stevens | .3 | 0 | 3 | 0 | 20 |
| Jerry Rice | .3 | 0 | 3 | 0 | 18 |
| SEA | .3 | 0 | 3 | 0 | 18 |

**2-Pt. Conversions:** (2-3) Jackson, Stevens.

| Kicking | PAT/Att | FG/Att | Lg | Pts |
| --- | --- | --- | --- | --- |
| Josh Brown | .40/40 | 23/25 | 54 | 109 |

| Punts (10 or more) | No | Yds | Long | Avg | In20 |
| --- | --- | --- | --- | --- | --- |
| Donnie Jones* | .26 | 988 | 51 | 38.0 | 6 |
| Tom Rouen | .26 | 1093 | 60 | 42.0 | 10 |
| Ken Walter | .24 | 920 | 50 | 38.3 | 4 |

**Signed:** Walter (Nov. 24). **Released:** Jones (Nov. 24).

| Most Interceptions | | Most Sacks | |
| --- | --- | --- | --- |
| Ken Lucas | .6 | Chike Okeafor | .8.5 |

## Tampa Bay Buccaneers

| Passing (5 Att) | Att | Cmp | Pct | Yds | TD | Rate |
| --- | --- | --- | --- | --- | --- | --- |
| Brian Griese | .336 | 233 | 69.3 | 2632 | 20 | 97.5 |
| Brad Johnson | .103 | 65 | 63.1 | 674 | 3 | 79.5 |
| Chris Simms | .73 | 42 | 57.5 | 467 | 1 | 64.1 |

**Interceptions:** Griese 12, Johnson and Simms 3.

| Top Receivers | No | Yds | Avg | Long | TD |
| --- | --- | --- | --- | --- | --- |
| Michael Clayton* | .80 | 1193 | 14.9 | 75-td | 7 |
| Michael Pittman | .41 | 391 | 9.5 | 68 | 3 |
| Ken Dilger | .39 | 345 | 8.8 | 45-td | 3 |
| Joey Galloway | .33 | 416 | 12.6 | 36-td | 5 |
| Mike Alstott | .29 | 202 | 7.0 | 20 | 0 |
| Joe Jurevicius | .27 | 333 | 12.3 | 42-td | 2 |

| Top Rushers | Car | Yds | Avg | Long | TD |
| --- | --- | --- | --- | --- | --- |
| Michael Pittman | .219 | 926 | 4.2 | 78-td | 7 |
| Mike Alstott | .67 | 230 | 3.4 | 32 | 2 |
| Charlie Garner | .30 | 111 | 3.7 | 25 | 0 |

| Most Touchdowns | TD | Run | Rec | Ret | Pts |
| --- | --- | --- | --- | --- | --- |
| Michael Pittman | .10 | 7 | 3 | 0 | 60 |
| Michael Clayton* | .7 | 0 | 7 | 0 | 42 |
| Joey Galloway | .6 | 0 | 5 | 1 | 36 |
| Ken Dilger | .3 | 0 | 3 | 0 | 20 |

**2-Pt. Conversions:** (1-4) Dilger.

| Kicking | PAT/Att | FG/Att | Lg | Pts |
| --- | --- | --- | --- | --- |
| Jay Taylor* | .11/11 | 4/5 | 50 | 23 |

**Signed:** Taylor (Nov. 30). **Released:** Martin Gramatica on Nov. 30 (see Ind.).

| Punts (10 or more) | No | Yds | Long | Avg | In20 |
| --- | --- | --- | --- | --- | --- |
| Josh Bidwell | .82 | 3472 | 60 | 42.3 | 23 |

| Most Interceptions | | Most Sacks | |
| --- | --- | --- | --- |
| Brian Kelly | .4 | Simeon Rice | .12.0 |

## Washington Redskins

| Passing (5 Att) | Att | Cmp | Pct | Yds | TD | Rate |
| --- | --- | --- | --- | --- | --- | --- |
| Patrick Ramsey | .272 | 169 | 62.1 | 1665 | 10 | 74.8 |
| Mark Brunell | .237 | 118 | 49.8 | 1194 | 7 | 63.9 |

**Interceptions:** Ramsey 11, Brunell 6.

| Top Receivers | No | Yds | Avg | Long | TD |
| --- | --- | --- | --- | --- | --- |
| Laveranues Coles | .90 | 950 | 10.6 | 45 | 1 |
| Rod Gardner | .51 | 650 | 12.7 | 51 | 5 |
| Clinton Portis | .40 | 235 | 5.9 | 18 | 2 |
| Chris Cooley* | .37 | 314 | 8.5 | 31 | 6 |
| James Thrash | .17 | 203 | 11.9 | 31 | 0 |

| Top Rushers | Car | Yds | Avg | Long | TD |
| --- | --- | --- | --- | --- | --- |
| Clinton Portis | .343 | 1315 | 3.8 | 64-td | 5 |
| Ladell Betts | .90 | 371 | 4.1 | 27 | 1 |
| Mark Brunell | .19 | 62 | 3.3 | 21 | 0 |

| Most Touchdowns | TD | Run | Rec | Ret | Pts |
| --- | --- | --- | --- | --- | --- |
| Clinton Portis | .7 | 5 | 2 | 0 | 42 |
| Chris Cooley* | .6 | 0 | 6 | 0 | 36 |
| Rod Gardner | .5 | 0 | 5 | 0 | 30 |
| Robert Royal | .4 | 0 | 4 | 0 | 24 |

**2-Pt. Conversions:** (1-1) Taylor Jacobs.

| Kicking | PAT/Att | FG/Att | Lg | Pts |
| --- | --- | --- | --- | --- |
| John Hall | .13/13 | 8/11 | 46 | 37 |
| Jeff Chandler | .14/14 | 5/8 | 49 | 29 |
| CAR | .8/8 | 0/2 | — | 8 |
| WASH | .6/6 | 5/6 | 49 | 21 |
| Ola Kimrin* | .6/6 | 6/10 | 41 | 24 |

**Signed:** Kimrin (Oct. 16); Chandler (Dec. 15). **Waived:** Kimrin (Nov. 26).

| Punts (10 or more) | No | Yds | Long | Avg | In20 |
| --- | --- | --- | --- | --- | --- |
| Tom Tupa | .103 | 4544 | 61 | 44.1 | 30 |

| Most Interceptions | | Most Sacks | |
| --- | --- | --- | --- |
| Shawn Springs | .5 | Cornelius Griffin | .6.0 |
| | | Shawn Springs | .6.0 |

# NFL Playoffs

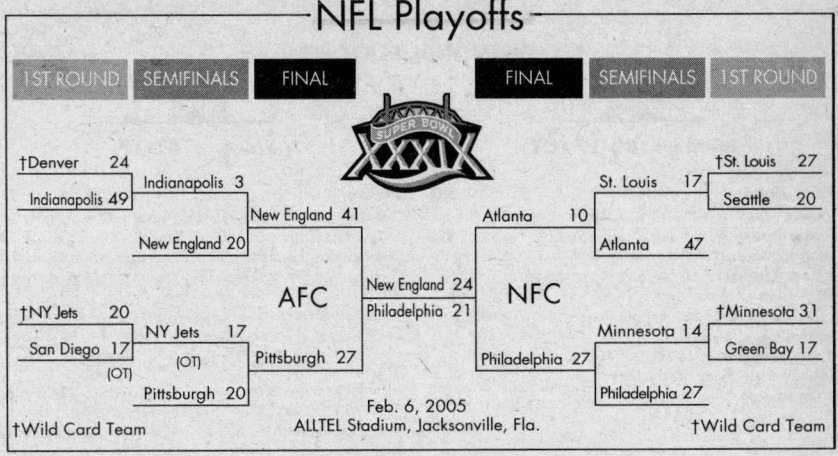

| 1ST ROUND | SEMIFINALS | FINAL | | FINAL | SEMIFINALS | 1ST ROUND |

†Denver 24
Indianapolis 49

Indianapolis 3

New England 41

New England 20

AFC

New England 24
Philadelphia 21

†NY Jets 20
San Diego 17
(OT)

NY Jets 17
(OT)

Pittsburgh 27

Pittsburgh 20

SUPER BOWL XXXIX

Atlanta 10

NFC

Atlanta 47

St. Louis 17

Minnesota 14

Philadelphia 27

Philadelphia 27

†St. Louis 27
Seattle 20

†Minnesota 31
Green Bay 17

†Wild Card Team

Feb. 6, 2005
ALLTEL Stadium, Jacksonville, Fla.

†Wild Card Team

## Playoff Game Summaries

Team records listed in parentheses indicate records before game.

### WILD CARD ROUND

**AFC**

### Jets, 20-17 (OT)

**NY Jets** (10-6) .......... 0  7  10  0  3— **20**
**San Diego** (12-4) ....... 0  7  0  10  0— **17**
**Date**—Jan. 8. **Att**—67,536. **Time**—3:49.

**2nd Quarter:** SD—Keenan McCardell 26-yd pass from Drew Brees (Nate Kaeding kick), 9:26; NYJ—Anthony Becht 13-yd pass from Chad Pennington (Doug Brien kick), 2:54.

**3rd Quarter:** NYJ—Santana Moss 47-yd pass from Pennington (Brien kick), 10:29; NYJ—Brien 42-yd FG, 1:23.

**4th Quarter:** SD—Kaeding 35-yd FG, 10:43; SD—Antonio Gates 1-yd pass from Brees (Kaeding kick), 0:11.

**Overtime:** NYJ—Brien 28-yd FG, 0:05.

### Colts, 49-24

**Denver** (10-6) ............. 0  3  14  7— **24**
**Indianapolis** (12-4) ....... 14  21  0  14— **49**
**Date**—Jan. 9. **Att**—56,609. **Time**—3:06.

**1st Quarter:** IND—James Mungro 2-yd pass from Peyton Manning (Mike Vanderjagt kick), 7:23; IND—Edgerrin James 1-yd run (Vanderjagt kick), 0:38.

**2nd Quarter:** IND—Dallas Clark 19-yd pass from Manning (Vanderjagt kick), 8:11; DEN—Jason Elam 33-yd FG, 5:19; IND—Reggie Wayne 35-yd pass from Manning (Vanderjagt kick), 4:29; IND—Manning 1-yd run (Vanderjagt kick), 0:06.

**3rd Quarter:** DEN—Rod Smith 9-yd pass from Jake Plummer (Elam kick), 9:01; DEN—Jeb Putzier 35-yd pass from Plummer (Elam kick), 1:10.

**4th Quarter:** IND—Wayne 43-yd pass from Manning (Vanderjagt kick), 12:48; DEN—Tatum Bell 1-yd run (Elam kick), 7:45; IND—Dominic Rhodes 2-yd run (Vanderjagt kick), 2:02.

**NFC**

### Rams, 27-20

**St. Louis** (8-8) ............. 7  7  3  10— **27**
**Seattle** (9-7) .............. 3  7  3  7— **20**
**Date**—Jan. 8. **Att**—65,397. **Time**—3:17.

**1st Quarter:** ST.L—Torry Holt 15-yd pass from Marc Bulger (Jeff Wilikns kick), 11:33; SEA—Josh Brown 47-yd FG, 2:05.

**2nd Quarter:** ST.L—Marshall Faulk 1-yd run (Wilkins kick), 13:32; SEA—Bobby Engram 19-yd pass from Matt Hasselbeck (Brown kick), 8:18.

**3rd Quarter:** SEA—Brown 30-yd FG, 8:52; ST.L—Wilkins 38-yd FG, 2:35.

**4th Quarter:** SEA—Darrell Jackson 23-yd pass from Hasselbeck (Brown kick), 13:43; ST.L—Wilkins 27-yd FG, 8:07; ST.L—Cam Cleeland 17-yd pass from Bulger (Wilkins kick), 2:11.

### Vikings, 31-17

**Minnesota** (8-8) ........... 17  7  0  7— **31**
**Green Bay** (10-6) ........... 3  7  0  7— **17**
**Date**—Jan. 9. **Att**—71,075. **Time**—3:00.

**1st Quarter:** MIN—Moe Williams 68-yd pass from Daunte Culpepper (Morten Andersen kick), 13:20; MIN—Randy Moss 20-yd pass from Culpepper (Andersen kick), 9:50; MIN—Andersen 35-yd FG, 6:06; GB—Ryan Longwell 43-yd FG, 2:42.

**2nd Quarter:** GB—Bubba Franks 4-yd pass from Brett Favre (Longwell kick), 10:24; MIN—Nate Burleson 19-yd pass from Culpepper (Andersen kick), 6:33.

**4th Quarter:** GB—Najeh Davenport 1-yd run (Longwell kick), 13:37; MIN—Moss 34-yd pass from Culpepper (Andersen kick), 10:18.

## NFL Playoffs (Cont.)
### DIVISIONAL PLAYOFFS

**AFC**

### Steelers, 20-17 (OT)

**NY Jets** (11-6) . . . . . . . . . 0  10  7  0  0— **17**
**Pittsburgh** (15-1) . . . . . 10  0  0  7  3— **20**
**Date**—Jan. 15. **Att**—64,915. **Time**—3:25.

**1st Quarter:** PIT—Jeff Reed 45-yd FG, 5:18; PIT—Jerome Bettis 3-yd run (Reed kick), 1:58.

**2nd Quarter:** NYJ—Doug Brien 42-yd FG, 10:33; NYJ—Santana Moss 75-yd punt return (Brien kick), 3:00.

**3rd Quarter:** NYJ—Reggie Tongue 86-yd interception return (Brien kick), 3:52.

**4th Quarter:** PIT—Hines Ward 4-yd pass from Ben Roethlisberger (Reed kick), 6:00.

**Overtime:** PIT—Reed 33-yd FG, 3:56.

### Patriots, 20-3

**Indianapolis** (13-4) . . . . . . . . 0  3  0  0— **3**
**New England** (14-2) . . . . . . . 0  6  7  7— **20**
**Date**—Jan. 16. **Att**—68,756. **Time**—2:55.

**2nd Quarter:** NE—Adam Vinatieri 24-yd FG, 10:40; NE—Vinatieri 31-yd FG, 7:56; IND—Mike Vanderjagt 23-yd FG, 0:00.

**3rd Quarter:** NE—David Givens 5-yd pass from Tom Brady (Vinatieri kick), 1:30.

**4th Quarter:** NE—Brady 1-yd run (Vinatieri kick), 7:10.

**NFC**

### Falcons, 47-17

**St. Louis** (9-8) . . . . . . . . . . . . . 7  10  0  0— **17**
**Atlanta** (11-5) . . . . . . . . . . . . 14  14  10  9— **47**
**Date**—Jan. 15. **Att**—70,709. **Time**—2:59.

**1st Quarter:** ATL—Alge Crumpler 18-yd pass from Michael Vick (Jay Feely kick), 12:00; ST.L—Kevin Curtis 57-yd pass from Marc Bulger (Jeff Wilkins kick), 9:14; ATL—Warrick Dunn 62-yd run (Feely kick), 7:52.

**2nd Quarter:** ATL—Dunn 19-yd run (Feely kick), 9:58; ST.L—Torry Holt 28-yd pass from Bulger (Wilkins kick), 5:26; ATL—Allen Rossum 68-yd punt return (Feely kick), 0:59; ST.L—Wilkins 55-yd FG, 0:00.

**3rd Quarter:** ATL—Peerless Price 6-yd pass from Vick (Feely kick), 10:05; ATL—Feely 38-yd FG, 5:54.

**4th Quarter:** ATL—Bulger tackled in end zone by Brady Smith for safety, 11:39; ATL—T.J. Duckett 4-yd run (Feely kick), 1:54.

### Eagles, 27-14

**Minnesota** (9-8) . . . . . . . . . . . 0  7  0  7— **14**
**Philadelphia** (13-3) . . . . . . . . 7  14  0  6— **27**
**Date**—Jan. 16. **Att**—67,722. **Time**—3:14.

**1st Quarter:** PHI—Freddie Mitchell 2-yd pass from Donovan McNabb (David Akers kick), 6:18.

**2nd Quarter:** PHI—Brian Westbrook 7-yd pass from McNabb (Akers kick), 14:16; MIN—Daunte Culpepper 7-yd run (Morten Andersen), 10:37; PHI—Mitchell recovered fumble in end zone (Akers kick), 10:08.

**4th Quarter:** PHI—Akers 21-yd FG, 13:20; PHI—Akers 23-yd FG, 6:39; MIN—Marcus Robinson 32-yd pass from Culpepper (Andersen kick), 1:59.

## CONFERENCE CHAMPIONSHIPS

**AFC**

### Patriots, 41-27

**New England** (15-2) . . . . . . . 10  14  7  10— **41**
**Pittsburgh** (16-1) . . . . . . . . . . 3  0  14  10— **27**
**Date**—Jan. 23. **Att**—65,242. **Time**—3:09.

**1st Quarter:** NE—Adam Vinatieri 48-yd FG, 11:20; NE—Deion Branch 60-yd pass from Tom Brady (Vinatieri kick), 6:49; PIT—Jeff Reed 43-yd FG, 1:22.

**2nd Quarter:** NE—David Givens 9-yd pass from Brady (Vinatieri kick), 7:08; NE—Rodney Harrison 87-yd interception return (Vinatieri kick), 2:14.

**3rd Quarter:** PIT—Jerome Bettis 5-yd run (Reed kick), 10:54; NE—Corey Dillon 25-yd run (Vinatieri kick), 7:27; PIT—Hines Ward 30-yd pass from Ben Roethlisberger (Reed kick), 2:35.

**4th Quarter:** PIT—Reed 20-yd FG, 13:29; NE—Vinatieri 31-yd FG, 8:03; NE—Branch 23-yd run (Vinatieri kick), 2:23; PIT—Plaxico Burress 7-yd pass from Roethlisberger (Reed kick), 0:52.

**NFC**

### Eagles, 27-10

**Atlanta** (12-5) . . . . . . . . . . . . . 0  10  0  0— **10**
**Philadelphia** (14-3) . . . . . . . . 7  7  6  7— **27**
**Date**—Jan. 23. **Att**—67,717. **Time**—3:00.

**1st Quarter:** PHI—Dorsey Levens 4-yd run (David Akers kick), 4:16.

**2nd Quarter:** ATL—Jay Feely 23-yd FG, 10:19; PHI—Chad Lewis 3-yd pass from Donovan McNabb (Akers kick), 4:58; ATL—Warrick Dunn 10-yd run (Feely kick), 2:02.

**3rd Quarter:** PHI—Akers 31-yd FG, 8:55; PHI—Akers 34-yd FG, 2:00.

**4th Quarter:** PHI—Lewis 2-yd pass from McNabb (Akers), 3:21.

## Super Bowl XXXIX

Sunday, Feb. 6, 2005 at ALLTEL Stadium in Jacksonville, Florida

**New England** (16-2) . . . . . . . .0   7   7   10— **24**
**Philadelphia** (15-3) . . . . . . . .0   7   7   7— **21**

**2nd Quarter: PHI**—L.J. Smith 6-yd pass from Donovan McNabb (David Akers kick), 9:55. Drive: 81 yards in 9 plays. Key play: Todd Pinkston 40-yd pass from McNabb to NE 17. **NE**—David Givens 4-yd pass from Tom Brady (Adam Vinatieri kick), 1:10. Drive: 37 yards in 7 plays. Key play: Troy Brown 12-yd pass from Brady to PHI 7.

**3rd Quarter: NE**—Mike Vrabel 2-yd pass from Brady (Vinatieri kick), 11:04. Drive: 69 yards in 9 plays. Key play: Deion Branch 27-yd pass from Brady to PHI 38. **PHI**—Brian Westbrook 10-yd pass from McNabb (Akers kick), 3:35. Drive: 74 yards in 10 plays. Key play: Westbrook 15-yd pass from McNabb to PHI 41.

**4th Quarter: NE**—Corey Dillon 2-yd run (Vinatieri kick), 13:44. Drive: 66 yards in 9 plays. Key play: Kevin Faulk 14-yd pass from Brady to PHI 2. **NE**—Vinatieri 22-yd FG, 8:40. Drive: 43 yards in 8 plays. Key play: Branch 19-yd pass from Brady plus 15-yd roughing the passer penalty to PHI 16. **PHI**—Greg Lewis 30-yd pass from McNabb (Akers kick), 1:48. Drive: 79 yards in 13 plays.

**Favorite:** Patriots by 7   **Attendance:** 78,125
**Time:** 3:38   **TV Rating:** 41.1/62 share (FOX)

**Officials:** Terry McAulay (referee), Carl Paganelli (umpire), Gary Slaughter (HL), Mark Steinkerchner (LJ), Rick Patterson (SJ), Tom Sifferman (FJ), Tony Steratore (BJ), Al Hynes (Rep.).

| Most Valuable Player |
|---|
| Deion Branch, New England, WR |
| 11 catches for 133 yards |

## Team Statistics

|  | Patriots | Eagles |
|---|---|---|
| First downs | 21 | 24 |
| Rushing | 6 | 4 |
| Passing | 14 | 18 |
| Penalty | 1 | 2 |
| 3rd down efficiency | 4/12 | 9/16 |
| 4th down efficiency | 0/0 | 0/0 |
| Total offense (net yards) | 331 | 369 |
| Plays | 63 | 72 |
| Average gain | 5.3 | 5.1 |
| Rushes/yards | 28/112 | 17/45 |
| Yards per rush | 4.0 | 2.6 |
| Passing yards (net) | 219 | 324 |
| Times sacked/yards lost | 2/17 | 4/33 |
| Passing yards (gross) | 236 | 357 |
| Completions/attempts | 23/33 | 30/51 |
| Yards per pass play | 6.3 | 5.9 |
| Times intercepted | 0 | 3 |
| Return yardage | 92 | 133 |
| Punt returns/yards | 4/26 | 3/19 |
| Kickoff returns/yards | 3/61 | 5/114 |
| Interceptions/yards | 3/5 | 0/0 |
| Fumbles/lost | 1/1 | 2/1 |
| Penalties/yards | 7/47 | 3/35 |
| Punts/average | 7/45.1 | 5/42.8 |
| Punts blocked | 0 | 0 |
| Field Goals made/attempted | 1/1 | 0/0 |
| Time of possession | 31:37 | 28:23 |

## Individual Statistics

### New England Patriots

| Passing | Att | Cmp | Pct. | Yds | TD | Int | Rate |
|---|---|---|---|---|---|---|---|
| Tom Brady | 33 | 23 | 69.7 | 236 | 2 | 0 | 110.2 |

| Receiving | No | Yds | Avg | Long | TD |
|---|---|---|---|---|---|
| Deion Branch | 11 | 133 | 12.1 | 27 | 0 |
| Corey Dillon | 3 | 31 | 10.3 | 16 | 0 |
| David Givens | 3 | 19 | 6.3 | 13 | 1 |
| Kevin Faulk | 2 | 27 | 13.5 | 14 | 0 |
| Troy Brown | 2 | 17 | 8.5 | 12 | 0 |
| Daniel Graham | 1 | 7 | 7.0 | 7 | 0 |
| Mike Vrabel | 1 | 2 | 2.0 | 2-td | 1 |
| TOTAL | 23 | 236 | 10.3 | 27 | 2 |

| Rushing | Car | Yds | Avg | Long | TD |
|---|---|---|---|---|---|
| Corey Dillon | 18 | 75 | 4.2 | 25 | 1 |
| Kevin Faulk | 8 | 38 | 4.8 | 12 | 0 |
| Patrick Pass | 1 | 0 | 0.0 | 0 | 0 |
| Tom Brady | 1 | -1 | -1.0 | -1 | 0 |
| TOTAL | 28 | 112 | 4.0 | 25 | 1 |

| Field Goals | 20-29 | 30-39 | 40-49 | 50-59 | Total |
|---|---|---|---|---|---|
| Adam Vinatieri | 1-1 | 0-0 | 0-0 | 0-0 | 1-1 |

| Punting | No | Yds | Avg | Long | In20 | Blk |
|---|---|---|---|---|---|---|
| Josh Miller | 7 | 316 | 45.1 | 50 | 3 | 0 |

| Punt Returns | Ret | Yds | Avg | Long | FC | TD |
|---|---|---|---|---|---|---|
| Troy Brown | 3 | 12 | 4.0 | 8 | 1 | 0 |
| Bethel Johnson | 1 | 14 | 14.0 | 14 | 0 | 0 |

| Kickoff Returns | Ret | Yds | Avg | Long | FC | TD |
|---|---|---|---|---|---|---|
| Bethel Johnson | 2 | 44 | 22.0 | 26 | 0 | 0 |
| Patrick Pass | 1 | 17 | 17.0 | 17 | 0 | 0 |

| Interceptions | No | Yds | Avg | Long | TD |
|---|---|---|---|---|---|
| Rodney Harrison | 2 | 5 | 2.5 | 6 | 0 |
| Tedy Bruschi | 1 | 0 | 0.0 | 0 | 0 |

**Sacks**        **Most Tackles** (solo)
Four tied with 1.0 each.    Randall Gay . . . . . . . . .11

### Philadelphia Eagles

| Passing | Att | Cmp | Pct. | Yds | TD | Int | Rate |
|---|---|---|---|---|---|---|---|
| D. McNabb | 51 | 30 | 58.8 | 357 | 3 | 3 | 75.4 |

| Receiving | No | Yds | Avg | Long | TD |
|---|---|---|---|---|---|
| Terrell Owens | 9 | 122 | 13.6 | 36 | 0 |
| Brian Westbrook | 7 | 60 | 8.6 | 15 | 1 |
| Todd Pinkston | 4 | 82 | 20.5 | 40 | 0 |
| Greg Lewis | 4 | 53 | 13.3 | 30-td | 1 |
| L.J. Smith | 4 | 27 | 6.8 | 9 | 1 |
| Freddie Mitchell | 1 | 11 | 11.0 | 11 | 0 |
| Josh Parry | 1 | 2 | 2.0 | 2 | 0 |
| TOTAL | 30 | 357 | 11.9 | 40 | 3 |

| Rushing | Car | Yds | Avg | Long | TD |
|---|---|---|---|---|---|
| Brian Westbrook | 15 | 44 | 2.9 | 22 | 0 |
| Dorsey Levens | 1 | 1 | 1.0 | 1 | 0 |
| Donovan McNabb | 1 | 0 | 0.0 | 0 | 0 |
| TOTAL | 17 | 45 | 2.6 | 22 | 0 |

| Field Goals | 20-29 | 30-39 | 40-49 | 50-59 | Total |
|---|---|---|---|---|---|
| none | | | | | |

| Punting | No | Yds | Avg | Long | In20 | Blk |
|---|---|---|---|---|---|---|
| Dirk Johnson | 5 | 214 | 42.8 | 52 | 1 | 0 |

| Punt Returns | Ret | Yds | Avg | Long | FC | TD |
|---|---|---|---|---|---|---|
| Brian Westbrook | 3 | 19 | 6.3 | 10 | 0 | 0 |
| Lito Sheppard | 0 | 0 | 0.0 | 0 | 2 | 0 |

| Kickoff Returns | Ret | Yds | Avg | Long | FC | TD |
|---|---|---|---|---|---|---|
| J.R. Reed | 4 | 82 | 20.5 | 26 | 0 | 0 |
| Roderick Hood | 1 | 32 | 32.0 | 32 | 0 | 0 |

| Interceptions | No | Yds | Avg | Long | TD |
|---|---|---|---|---|---|
| none | | | | | |

**Sacks**        **Most Tackles** (solo)
Derrick Burgess . . . . . . .1.0    Michael Lewis . . . . . . . .5
Team . . . . . . . . . . . . . .1.0

## Super Bowl Finalists' Playoff Statistics

### New England Patriots (3-0)

| Passing (5 att) | Att | Cmp | Pct. | Yds | TD | Rating |
|---|---|---|---|---|---|---|
| Tom Brady | .81 | 55 | 67.9 | 587 | 5 | 109.4 |

**Interceptions:** none.

| Top Receivers | No | Yds | Avg | Long | TD |
|---|---|---|---|---|---|
| Deion Branch | 16 | 264 | 16.5 | 60-td | 1 |
| David Givens | 12 | 104 | 8.7 | 18 | 3 |
| Corey Dillon | 9 | 53 | 5.9 | 16 | 0 |
| Troy Brown | 5 | 41 | 8.2 | 12 | 0 |
| Kevin Faulk | 3 | 38 | 12.7 | 14 | 0 |
| Daniel Graham | 3 | 16 | 5.3 | 10 | 0 |

| Top Rushers | Car | Yds | Avg | Long | TD |
|---|---|---|---|---|---|
| Corey Dillon | 65 | 292 | 4.5 | 42 | 2 |
| Kevin Faulk | 22 | 114 | 5.2 | 17 | 0 |

| Touchdowns | TD | Run | Rec | Ret | Pts |
|---|---|---|---|---|---|
| David Givens | 3 | 0 | 3 | 0 | 18 |
| Deion Branch | 2 | 1 | 1 | 0 | 12 |
| Corey Dillon | 2 | 2 | 0 | 0 | 12 |

Three tied with 1 TD each.
**2-Pt. Conversions:** (0-0).

| Kicking | PAT/Att | FG/Att | Lg | Pts |
|---|---|---|---|---|
| Adam Vinatieri | 10/10 | 5/5 | 48 | 25 |

| Punts | No | Yds | Avg | Long | In20 |
|---|---|---|---|---|---|
| Josh Miller | 16 | 672 | 42.0 | 52 | 6 |

| Interceptions | | Sacks | |
|---|---|---|---|
| Rodney Harrison | 4 | Mike Vrabel | 2.0 |
| Eugene Wilson | 2 | Four tied with 1.0 each. | |
| Tedy Bruschi | 1 | | |

### Philadelphia Eagles (2-1)

| Passing (5 att) | Att | Cmp | Pct. | Yds | TD | Rating |
|---|---|---|---|---|---|---|
| Donovan McNabb | .110 | 68 | 61.8 | 823 | 7 | 94.6 |

**Interceptions:** McNabb 3.

| Top Receivers | No | Yds | Avg | Long | TD |
|---|---|---|---|---|---|
| Brian Westbrook | 17 | 146 | 8.6 | 24 | 2 |
| Terrell Owens | 9 | 122 | 13.6 | 36 | 0 |
| L.J. Smith | 9 | 100 | 11.1 | 21 | 1 |
| Greg Lewis | 8 | 182 | 22.8 | 52 | 1 |
| Todd Pinkston | 8 | 141 | 17.6 | 40 | 0 |
| Freddie Mitchell | 8 | 96 | 12.0 | 30 | 1 |

| Top Rushers | Car | Yds | Avg | Long | TD |
|---|---|---|---|---|---|
| Brian Westbrook | 43 | 210 | 4.9 | 36 | 0 |
| Dorsey Levens | 17 | 55 | 3.2 | 11 | 1 |

| Touchdowns | TD | Run | Rec | Ret | Pts |
|---|---|---|---|---|---|
| Chad Lewis | 2 | 0 | 2 | 0 | 12 |
| Freddie Mitchell | 2 | 0 | 1 | 1 | 12 |
| Brian Westbrook | 2 | 0 | 2 | 0 | 12 |

Three tied with 1 TD each.
**2-Pt. Conversions:** (0-0).

| Kicking | PAT/Att | FG/Att | Lg | Pts |
|---|---|---|---|---|
| David Akers | 9/9 | 4/4 | 34 | 21 |

| Punts | No | Yds | Avg | Long | In20 |
|---|---|---|---|---|---|
| Dirk Johnson | 11 | 441 | 40.1 | 52 | 2 |

| Interceptions | | Sacks | |
|---|---|---|---|
| Jeremiah Trotter | 1 | Derrick Burgess | 3.0 |
| Brian Dawkins | 1 | Jevon Kearse | 2.0 |
| Ike Reese | 1 | Brian Dawkins | 1.0 |
| | | Hollis Thomas | 1.0 |
| | | Two tied with 0.5 each. | |

## NFL Playoff Leaders

### Passing Efficiency

(Minimum of 25 attempts)

| | Gm | Att | Cmp | Cmp% | Yards | Avg Gain | TD | TD% | Int | Int% | Rating |
|---|---|---|---|---|---|---|---|---|---|---|---|
| Tom Brady, NE | 3 | 81 | 55 | 67.9 | 587 | 7.25 | 5 | 6.2 | 0 | 0.0 | 109.4 |
| Peyton Manning, Ind | 2 | 75 | 54 | 72.0 | 696 | 9.28 | 4 | 5.3 | 2 | 2.7 | 107.4 |
| Jake Plummer, Den | 1 | 34 | 24 | 70.6 | 284 | 8.35 | 2 | 5.9 | 1 | 2.9 | 103.1 |
| Drew Brees, SD | 1 | 42 | 31 | 73.8 | 319 | 7.60 | 2 | 4.8 | 1 | 2.4 | 101.2 |
| Marc Bulger, St.L | 2 | 67 | 41 | 61.2 | 612 | 9.13 | 4 | 6.0 | 2 | 3.0 | 98.6 |

### Receptions

| | No | Yds | Avg | Long | TD |
|---|---|---|---|---|---|
| Brian Westbrook, Phi | 17 | 146 | 8.6 | 24 | 2 |
| Deion Branch, NE | 16 | 264 | 16.5 | 60-td | 1 |
| Hines Ward, Pit | 15 | 214 | 14.3 | 30-td | 2 |
| Reggie Wayne, Ind. | 13 | 256 | 19.7 | 49 | 2 |
| Justin McCareins, NYJ | 13 | 169 | 13.0 | 30 | 0 |

### Rushing

| | No | Yds | Avg | Long | TD |
|---|---|---|---|---|---|
| Corey Dillon, NE | 65 | 292 | 4.5 | 42 | 2 |
| Brian Westbrook, Phi | 43 | 210 | 4.9 | 36 | 0 |
| Warrick Dunn, Atl. | 32 | 201 | 6.3 | 62-td | 3 |
| Jerome Bettis, Pit. | 44 | 165 | 3.8 | 25 | 2 |
| Michael Vick, Atl | 12 | 145 | 12.1 | 47 | 0 |

### Touchdowns

| | TD | Rush | Rec | Ret | Pts |
|---|---|---|---|---|---|
| David Givens, NE | 3 | 0 | 3 | 0 | 18 |
| Warrick Dunn, Atl | 3 | 3 | 0 | 0 | 18 |

Eleven tied with 2 TD each for 12 pts.

### Kicking

| | PAT | FG | Long | Pts |
|---|---|---|---|---|
| Adam Vinatieri, NE | 10/10 | 5/5 | 48 | 25 |
| David Akers, Phi | 9/9 | 4/4 | 34 | 21 |
| Jeff Reed, Pit | 5/5 | 4/4 | 45 | 17 |
| Jeff Wilkins, St.L | 5/5 | 3/3 | 55 | 14 |
| Doug Brien, NYJ | 4/4 | 3/6 | 42 | 13 |
| Jay Feely, Atl | 7/7 | 2/2 | 38 | 13 |

### Interceptions

| | No | Yds | Long | TD |
|---|---|---|---|---|
| Rodney Harrison, NE | 4 | 101 | 87-td | 1 |
| Reggie Tongue, NYJ | 2 | 108 | 86-td | 1 |
| Eugene Wilson, NE | 2 | 0 | 0 | 0 |

Fifteen tied with 1 each.

### Sacks

| | No |
|---|---|
| Derrick Burgess, Phi | 3.0 |

Seven tied with 2.0 each.

## NFL Pro Bowl

55th NFL Pro Bowl Game and 35th AFC-NFC contest (AFC leads series,18-17). **Date:** Feb. 13, 2005 at Aloha Stadium in Honolulu. **Coaches:** Jim Mora Jr., Atl. (NFC) and Bill Cowher, Pit. (AFC). **Most Valuable Player:** QB Peyton Manning, Ind. (6 for 10 for 130 yards and three TD passes). **Attendance:** 50,225. **TV Rating:** 4.2 (ESPN). **Time:** 3:09.

| | | | | | |
|---|---|---|---|---|---|
| NFC | . . . . . . . . . . . . . .0 | 10 | 14 | 3— | **27** |
| AFC | . . . . . . . . . . . . . .14 | 14 | 0 | 10— | **38** |

**1st Quarter: AFC**—Marvin Harrison 62-yd pass from Peyton Manning (Adam Vinatieri kick), 8:33; **AFC**—Hines Ward 41-yd pass from Manning (Vinatieri kick), 2:49.

**2nd Quarter: NFC**—Brian Westbrook 12-yd run (David Akers kick), 12:09; **AFC**—Ward 39-yd kickoff return for TD (Vinatieri kick), 12:01; **AFC**—Antonio Gates 12-yd pass from Manning (Vinatieri kick), 5:50; **NFC**—Akers 33-yd FG, 1:41.

**3rd Quarter: NFC**—Torry Holt 27-yd pass from Michael Vick (Akers kick), 11:11; **NFC**—Vick 3-yd run (Akers kick), 3:53.

**4th Quarter: AFC**—Vinatieri 44-yd FG, 14:14; **NFC**—Akers 29-yd FG, 9:04; **AFC**—LaDainian Tomlinson 4-yd run (Vinatieri kick), 5:15.

### STARTING LINEUPS

As voted on by NFL players, coaches and fans. (*) denotes injured and unable to play.

#### National Conference

| Pos | Offense | Pos | Defense |
|---|---|---|---|
| WR | Terrell Owens*, Phi. | E | Bertrand Berry, Ari. |
| WR | M. Muhammad, Car. | E | Julius Peppers, Car. |
| TE | Alge Crumpler, Atl. | T | La'Roi Glover, Dal. |
| T | Walter Jones, Sea. | T | Kevin Williams, Min. |
| T | Orlando Pace, St.L | LB | Keith Brooking, Atl. |
| G | Larry Allen, Dal. | LB | Derrick Brooks*, TB |
| G | Marco Rivera, GB | LB | Dan Morgan, Car. |
| C | Olin Kreutz, Chi. | CB | Lito Sheppard, Phi. |
| QB | Donovan McNabb, Phi. | CB | Ronde Barber, TB |
| RB | Shaun Alexander*, Sea. | SS | Michael Lewis, Phi. |
| FB | William Henderson, GB | FS | Brian Dawkins, Phi. |
| K | David Akers, Phi. | P | Mitch Berger, NO |
| KR | Eddie Drummond*, Det. | ST | Ike Reese, Phi. |

##### Reserves

**Offense: WR**—Javon Walker, GB and Joe Horn, NO; **TE**—Jason Witten, Dal.; **T**—Tra Thomas*, Phi.; **G**—Steve Hutchinson, Sea.; **C**—Matt Birk, Min.; **QB**—Daunte Culpepper, Min. and Michael Vick, Atl.; **RB**—Tiki Barber, NYG and Ahman Green, GB.

**Defense: E**—Patrick Kerney, Atl.; **T**—Shaun Rogers, Det.; **LB**—Marcus Washington, Wash. and Jeremiah Trotter, Phi.; **CB**—Dre' Bly, Det.; **FS**—Roy Williams, Dal.

**Need Player:** Long snapper Brian Jennings, SF.

**Replacements:** OFFENSE—WR Torry Holt, St.L for Owens; RB Brian Westbrook, Phi. for Alexander; KR Allen Rossum, Atl. for Drummond; T Flozell Adams, Dal. for Thomas (Note: Adams' equipment never arrived in Hawaii so he was unable to play). DEFENSE—LB Mark Fields, Car. for Brooks.

#### American Conference

| Pos | Offense | Pos | Defense |
|---|---|---|---|
| WR | Marvin Harrison, Ind. | E | John Abraham*, NYJ |
| WR | Chad Johnson, Cin. | E | Dwight Freeney, Ind. |
| TE | Antonio Gates, SD | T | Richard Seymour*, NE |
| T | Willie Roaf*, KC | T | Marcus Stroud, Jax. |
| T | Jonathan Ogden, Bal. | LB | Takeo Spikes, Buf. |
| G | Alan Faneca, Pit. | LB | Terrell Suggs, Bal. |
| G | Will Shields, KC | LB | Ray Lewis*, Bal. |
| C | Kevin Mawae, NYJ | CB | Champ Bailey, Den. |
| QB | Peyton Manning, Ind. | CB | Chris McAlister*, Bal. |
| RB | Edgerrin James*, Ind. | SS | Ed Reed, Bal. |
| FB | Tony Richardson, KC | FS | John Lynch, Den. |
| K | Adam Vinatieri, NE | P | Shane Lechler, Oak. |
| KR | Terrence McGee, Buf. | ST | Larry Izzo, NE |

##### Reserves

**Offense: WR**—Andre Johnson, Hou. and Hines Ward, Pit.; **TE**—Tony Gonzalez, KC; **T**—Willie Anderson*, Cin.; **G**—Brian Waters, KC; **C**—Jeff Hartings, Pit.; **QB**—Tom Brady, NE and Drew Brees, SD; **RB**—LaDainian Tomlinson, SD and Curtis Martin*, NYJ.

**Defense: E**—Jason Taylor, Mia.; **T**—Sam Adams, Buf.; **LB**—James Farrior, Pit. and Joey Porter, Pit.; **CB**—Tory James, Cin.; **SS**—Troy Polamalu, Pit.

**Need Player:** Long snapper Kendall Gammon, KC.

**Replacements:** OFFENSE—T Marvel Smith, Pit. for Roaf; T Tarik Glenn, Ind. for Anderson; RB Jerome Bettis, Pit. for Corey Dillon, NE, who had originally replaced James; RB Rudi Johnson, Cin. for Martin. DEFENSE—E Aaron Smith, Pit. for Abraham; T John Henderson, Jax. for Seymour; LB Tedy Bruschi, NE for Lewis; CB Nate Clements, Buf. for McAlister.

---

## Annual Awards

The NFL does not sanction any of the major postseason awards for players and coaches, but many are given out. Among the presenters for the 2004 regular season were AP, The Maxwell Football Club of Philadelphia (Bert Bell Award for player; Greasy Neale Award for coach), *The Sporting News* and the Pro Football Writers of America/*Pro Football Weekly*.

### Most Valuable Player

Peyton Manning, Indianapolis, QB . . .AP, *TSN*, Bell, PFWA

### Offensive Player of the Year

Peyton Manning, Indianapolis, QB . . . . . . . . . .AP, PFWA

### Defensive Player of the Year

Ed Reed, Baltimore, CB . . . . . . . . . . . . . . . . .AP, PFWA

### Comeback Players of the Year

Drew Brees, San Diego, QB . . . . . . . . . . . . . . . . .AP
Willis McGahee, Buffalo, RB . . . . . . . . . . . . . . . .PFWA

### Rookies of the Year

| NFL | Ben Roethlisberger, Pittsburgh, QB . *TSN*, PFWA |
|---|---|
| Offense | Ben Roethlisberger, Pittsburgh, QB . . .AP, PFWA |
| Defense | Jonathan Vilma, NY Jets, LB . . . . . . . . . . .AP |
| | & Dunta Robinson, Houston, CB . . . . . . .PFWA |

### Coaches of the Year

Marty Schottenheimer, San Diego . . . . . .AP, Neale, PFWA
Bill Cowher, Pittsburgh . . . . . . . . . . . . . . . . . . . . .*TSN*

## 2004 All-NFL Team

The 2004 All-NFL team combining the All-Pro selections of the Associated Press, *The Sporting News (TSN)* and the Pro Football Writers of America/*Pro Football Weekly* (PFWA). Holdovers from the 2003 All-NFL Team in **bold** type.

### Offense

| Pos | Player | Selectors |
|---|---|---|
| WR— | Terrell Owens, Philadelphia | AP, *TSN*, PFWA |
| WR— | Muhsin Muhammad, Carolina | AP, PFWA |
| WR— | **Marvin Harrison**, Indianapolis | *TSN* |
| TE— | Antonio Gates, San Diego | AP, *TSN*, PFWA |
| T— | **Willie Roaf**, Kansas City | AP, PFWA |
| T— | Willie Anderson, Cincinnati | AP |
| T— | Walter Jones, Seattle | AP, *TSN*, PFWA |
| T— | **Orlando Pace**, St. Louis | *TSN* |
| G— | Alan Faneca, Pittsburgh | AP, *TSN*, PFWA |
| G— | Brian Waters, Kansas City | AP, *TSN*, PFWA |
| C— | Jeff Hartings, Pittsburgh | AP, *TSN* |
| C— | Kevin Mawae, NY Jets | PFWA |
| QB— | **Peyton Manning**, Indianapolis | AP, *TSN*, PFWA |
| RB— | Curtis Martin, NY Jets | AP, *TSN*, PFWA |
| RB— | LaDainian Tomlinson, San Diego | AP |
| RB— | Edgerrin James, Indianapolis | *TSN* |
| RB— | Shaun Alexander, Seattle | PFWA |
| FB— | William Henderson, Green Bay | AP |

### Defense

| Pos | Player | Selectors |
|---|---|---|
| DE— | Dwight Freeney, Indianapolis | AP, *TSN*, PFWA |
| DE— | Julius Peppers, Carolina | AP, *TSN*, PFWA |
| DT— | Kevin Williams, Minnesota | AP, *TSN*, PFWA |
| DT— | **Richard Seymour**, New Eng. | AP, *TSN*, PFWA |
| LB— | James Farrior, Pittsburgh | AP, *TSN*, PFWA |
| LB— | **Ray Lewis**, Baltimore | AP, *TSN* |
| LB— | **Derrick Brooks**, Tampa Bay | AP, PFWA |
| LB— | Takeo Spikes, Buffalo | AP, *TSN*, PFWA |
| CB— | Lito Sheppard, Philadelphia | AP, PFWA |
| CB— | Ronde Barber, Tampa Bay | AP |
| CB— | **Champ Bailey**, Denver | AP, *TSN*, PFWA |
| CB— | **Chris McAlister**, Baltimore | *TSN* |
| S— | Brian Dawkins, Philadelphia | AP, *TSN*, PFWA |
| S— | **Ed Reed**, Baltimore | AP, *TSN*, PFWA |

### Specialists

| Pos | Player | Selectors |
|---|---|---|
| K— | Adam Vinatieri, New England | AP, *TSN*, PFWA |
| P— | **Shane Lechler**, Oakland | AP, *TSN*, PFWA |
| KR/PR— | Eddie Drummond, Detroit | AP, *TSN*, PFWA |
| KR— | Terrence McGee, Buffalo | *TSN*, PFWA |
| ST— | Larry Izzo, New England | PFWA |

## 2005 College Draft

First and second round selections at the 70th annual NFL College Draft held April 23-24, 2005, at the Javits Convention Center in New York City. Eighteen underclassmen were among the first 64 players chosen and are listed in capital LETTERS.

### First Round

| No | Team | Player | Pos |
|---|---|---|---|
| 1 | San Francisco | ALEX SMITH, Utah | QB |
| 2 | Miami | Ronnie Brown, Auburn | RB |
| 3 | Cleveland | Braylon Edwards, Michigan | WR |
| 4 | Chicago | Cedric Benson, Texas | RB |
| 5 | Tampa Bay | Carnell Williams, Auburn | RB |
| 6 | Tennessee | ADAM JONES, West Virginia | CB |
| 7 | **a**-Minnesota | TROY WILLIAMSON, S. Carolina | WR |
| 8 | Arizona | Antrel Rolle, Miami-FL | CB |
| 9 | Washington | Carlos Rogers, Auburn | CB |
| 10 | Detroit | MIKE WILLIAMS, USC | WR |
| 11 | Dallas | Demarcus Ware, Troy | LB |
| 12 | **b**-San Diego | SHAWNE MERRIMAN, Maryland | DE |
| 13 | **c**-New Orleans | Jammal Brown, Oklahoma | OT |
| 14 | Carolina | THOMAS DAVIS, Georgia | FS |
| 15 | Kansas City | Derrick Johnson, Texas | LB |
| 16 | **d**-Houston | Travis Johnson, Florida St. | DT |
| 17 | Cincinnati | David Pollack, Georgia | DE |
| 18 | Minnesota | Erasmus James, Wisconsin | DE |
| 19 | St. Louis | Alex Barron, Florida St. | OT |
| 20 | **e**-Dallas | Marcus Spears, LSU | DE |
| 21 | Jacksonville | Matt Jones, Arkansas | TE |
| 22 | Baltimore | Mark Clayton, Oklahoma | WR |
| 23 | **f**-Oakland | FABIAN WASHINGTON, Nebraska | CB |
| 24 | Green Bay | AARON RODGERS, California | QB |
| 25 | **g**-Washington | Jason Campbell, Auburn | QB |
| 26 | **h**-Seattle | CHRIS SPENCER, Mississippi | C |
| 27 | Atlanta | Sharod White, UAB | WR |
| 28 | San Diego | Luis Castillo, Northwestern | DT |
| 29 | Indianapolis | Marlin Jackson, Michigan | CB |
| 30 | Pittsburgh | HEATH MILLER, Virginia | TE |
| 31 | Philadelphia | Mike Patterson, USC | DT |
| 32 | New England | Logan Mankins, Fresno St. | G |

### Second Round

| No | Team | Player | Pos |
|---|---|---|---|
| 33 | San Francisco | David Baas, Michigan | G |
| 34 | Cleveland | BRODNEY POOL, Oklahoma | FS |
| 35 | **i**-Philadelphia | Reggie Brown, Georgia | WR |
| 36 | Tampa Bay | Barrett Ruud, Nebraska | LB |
| 37 | **j**-Detroit | Shaun Cody, USC | DT |
| 38 | Oakland | Stanford Routt, Houston | CB |
| 39 | Chicago | Mark Bradley, Oklahoma | WR |
| 40 | **k**-New Orleans | JOSH BULLOCKS, Nebraska | FS |
| 41 | **l**-Tennessee | Michael Roos, Eastern Wash. | OT |
| 42 | Dallas | Kevin Burnett, Tennessee | LB |
| 43 | NY Giants | Corey Webster, LSU | CB |
| 44 | Arizona | J.J. Arrington, California | RB |
| 45 | **m**-Seattle | LOFA TATUPU, USC | LB |
| 46 | **n**-Miami | Matt Roth, Iowa | DE |
| 47 | **o**-NY Jets | Mike Nugent, Ohio St. | K |
| 48 | Cincinnati | ODELL THURMAN, Georgia | LB |
| 49 | Minnesota | Marcus Johnson, Mississippi | G |
| 50 | St. Louis | Ron Bartell, Howard | CB |
| 51 | **p**-Green Bay | Nick Collins, Bethune-Cookman | CB |
| 52 | Jacksonville | Khalif Barnes, Washington | OT |
| 53 | Baltimore | Dan Cody, Oklahoma | DE |
| 54 | **q**-Carolina | ERIC SHELTON, Louisville | RB |
| 55 | Buffalo | ROSCOE PARRISH, Miami-FL | WR |
| 56 | Denver | Darrent Williams, Oklahoma St. | CB |
| 57 | NY Jets | JUSTIN MILLER, Clemson | CB |
| 58 | Green Bay | Terrence Murphy, Texas A&M | WR |
| 59 | Atlanta | Jonathan Babineaux, Iowa | DT |
| 60 | Indianapolis | Kelvin Hayden, Illinois | CB |
| 61 | San Diego | Vincent Jackson, Northern Colorado | WR |
| 62 | Pittsburgh | Bryant McFadden, Florida St. | CB |
| 63 | Philadelphia | MATT McCOY, San Diego St. | LB |
| 64 | **r**-Baltimore | Adam Terry, Syracuse | OT |

**a**-from Oak.; **b**-from NYG; **c**-from Hou.; **d**-from NO; **e**-from Buf.; **f**-from Sea.; **g**-from Den.; **h**-from Oak. via NYJ; **i**-from Mia.; **j**-from Ten.; **k**-from Wash.; **l**-from Det.; **m**-from Car.; **n**-from KC; **o**-from Oak. via Hou.; **p**-from NO; **q**-from Sea.; **r**-from NE.

# NFL Europe

## Final 2005 Standings

| | W | L | T | Pct. | PF | PA |
|---|---|---|---|---|---|---|
| *Berlin | 7 | 3 | 0 | .700 | 241 | 191 |
| *Amsterdam | 6 | 4 | 0 | .600 | 265 | 207 |
| Cologne | 6 | 4 | 0 | .600 | 188 | 212 |
| Hamburg | 5 | 5 | 0 | .500 | 213 | 196 |
| Frankfurt | 3 | 7 | 0 | .300 | 163 | 246 |
| Scotland | 2 | 8 | 0 | .200 | 128 | 197 |

*The teams with the top two records after the regular season advance directly to the World Bowl.

**Note:** Amsterdam advances over Cologne due to a 2-0 head-to-head record.

### World Bowl XIII
June 11, 2005 at LTU Arena,
Dusseldorf, Germany (Att: 35,134)

**Amsterdam** (6-4) . . . . . . . 7  10   7   3— **27**
**Berlin** (7-3) . . . . . . . . . . 0   7   0  14— **21**

**MVP:** Kurt Kittner, Amsterdam, QB (15-28 for 239 yards and 2 TD passes)

## Regular Season Individual Leaders
Team listed in parentheses indicates player's NFL affiliation, if any.

### Passing Efficiency
(Min. 140 pass attempts)

| | Att | Cmp | Cmp Pct | Yds | Yds/ Att | TD | TDPct | Long | Int | IntPct | Rating |
|---|---|---|---|---|---|---|---|---|---|---|---|
| Dave Ragone, Ber (Hou) | 251 | 158 | 62.9 | 1746 | 6.96 | 13 | 5.2 | 70-td | 2 | 0.8 | 97.5 |
| Kevin Eakin, Fra (NYJ) | 180 | 105 | 58.3 | 1299 | 7.22 | 11 | 6.1 | 38 | 5 | 2.8 | 89.6 |
| Scott McBrien, Rhe (GB) | 217 | 116 | 53.5 | 1722 | 7.94 | 13 | 6.0 | 73-td | 12 | 5.5 | 76.6 |
| Casey Bramlet, Ham (CIN) | 212 | 131 | 61.8 | 1463 | 6.90 | 7 | 3.3 | 40-td | 10 | 4.7 | 73.7 |
| Kevin Thompson, Col (Buf) | 234 | 126 | 53.8 | 1561 | 6.67 | 8 | 3.4 | 75-td | 10 | 4.3 | 68.3 |

### Scoring

| Touchdowns | TD | Rus | Rec | Ret | Pts |
|---|---|---|---|---|---|
| Ruvell Martin, Ams (SD) | 12 | 0 | 12 | 0 | 72 |
| Jarrett Payton, Ams (Ten) | 7 | 7 | 0 | 0 | 42 |
| Little John Flowers, Ber (NYJ) | 7 | 7 | 0 | 0 | 42 |
| Keylon Kincade, Col (Dal) | 6 | 5 | 1 | 0 | 36 |
| Four tied with 5 TD each. | | | | | |

| Kicking | PAT | FG/FGA | Lg | Pts |
|---|---|---|---|---|
| Todd France, Ham (TB) | 17/17 | 24/34 | 54 | 91 |
| Chris Snyder, Ams (Hou) | 29/30 | 16/23 | 41 | 77 |
| Kevin Miller, Ber (Sea) | 24/25 | 17/21 | 48 | 75 |
| Jimmy Kibble, Col | 17/19 | 15/22 | 48 | 62 |
| Nicholas Setta, Rhe (Chi) | 22/22 | 13/18 | 48 | 61 |

### Rushing

| | Car | Yards | Avg | Long | TD |
|---|---|---|---|---|---|
| Joe Smith, Rhe (Ten) | 223 | 1026 | 4.6 | 59 | 5 |
| Kory Chapman, Col (NE) | 126 | 718 | 5.7 | 42-td | 5 |
| Jonathan Smith, Ams (KC) | 147 | 711 | 4.8 | 56-td | 2 |
| Jarrett Payton, Ams (Ten) | 104 | 578 | 5.6 | 53 | 7 |
| Ahmaad Galloway, Fra (SD) | 141 | 516 | 3.7 | 31 | 1 |

### Receptions

| | No | Yards | Avg | Long | TD |
|---|---|---|---|---|---|
| Aaron Boone, Ber (Car) | 43 | 582 | 13.5 | 47 | 5 |
| Chris Collins, Ham (Pit) | 42 | 458 | 10.9 | 24 | 0 |
| Ruvell Martin, Ams (SD) | 37 | 679 | 18.4 | 60-td | 12 |
| Scott McCready, Ham | 37 | 474 | 12.8 | 35 | 1 |
| Mark Anelli, Fra (Atl) | 36 | 395 | 11.0 | 28 | 3 |

### Punting

| | No | Yards | Avg | Long | In20 |
|---|---|---|---|---|---|
| Travis Dorsch, Rhe (Min) | 44 | 1870 | 42.5 | 60 | 11 |
| Ryan Dutton, Ams (Sea) | 35 | 1461 | 41.7 | 51 | 12 |
| Cody Scates, Col (Hou) | 28 | 1136 | 40.6 | 57 | 4 |

### Sacks

| | No |
|---|---|
| Greg White, Col (Chi) | 7.0 |
| Antonio Smith, Ham (Ari) | 6.0 |
| Isaac Hilton, Ber (Car) | 5.0 |
| Seante Williams, Fra (GB) | 5.0 |
| Ivory McCoy, Ham | 4.5 |
| Bryan Save, Col (TB) | 4.5 |

### Interceptions

| | No | Yds | Long | TD |
|---|---|---|---|---|
| B.J. Tucker, Ams (Sea) | 5 | 72 | 43-td | 2 |
| Shawn Mayer, Ham (Atl) | 5 | 48 | 25 | 0 |
| Willie Ford, Ber (Ind) | 4 | 22 | 11 | 0 |
| Jermaine Mays, Ber (Ind) | 4 | 130 | 100-td | 1 |
| Scott Connot, Ams (KC) | 4 | 22 | 18 | 0 |
| Lamont Brightful, Fra (NYG) | 4 | 108 | 44 | 0 |

### All-NFL Europe League Team
The All-NFL Europe League Team as selected by NFL Europe coaches, media and fans.

| | Offense | | Defense |
|---|---|---|---|
| QB | Dave Ragone, Ber. | DE | Antonio Smith, Ham. |
| RB | Jarrett Payton, Ams. | DT | Tim McGill, Ham. |
| WR | Ruvell Martin, Ams. | DT | Aaron Hunt, Ham. |
| WR | Cedric James, Rhe. | DE | Greg White, Col. |
| WR | Aaron Boone, Ber. | LB | Rich Scanlon, Ber. |
| TE | Bobby Blizzard, Ham. | LB | Nick McNeil, Ham. |
| T | Tony Pape, Ber. | LB | Bobby Brooks, Col. |
| G | Dante Ellington, Ber. | CB | B.J. Tucker, Ams. |
| C | Ben Claxton, Ber. | S | Scott Connot, Ams. |
| G | C. Setterstrom, Ams. | S | Shawn Mayer, Ham. |
| T | Tyson Clabo, Ham. | CB | Blue Adams, Rhe. |

**Special Teams**
| | |
|---|---|
| K | Todd France, Ham. |
| P | Travis Dorsch, Rhe. |
| Spec. | Lamont Brightful, Fra. |

### Annual Awards
Offensive MVP . . . . . . Dave Ragone, Berlin (Hou), QB
Defensive MVP . . . . . . . . Rich Scanlon, Berlin (KC), LB
Coach of the Year . . . . . . . . Bart Andrus, Amsterdam

## Canadian Football League
### Final 2004 Standings

Division champions (*) and playoff qualifiers (†) are noted. Wins are worth two points in the standings, ties are worth one point.

### East Division

| | W | L | T | Pts | PF | PA |
|---|---|---|---|---|---|---|
| *Montreal | 14 | 4 | 0 | 28 | 584 | 371 |
| †Toronto | 10 | 7 | 1 | 21 | 422 | 414 |
| †Hamilton | 9 | 8 | 1 | 19 | 455 | 542 |
| Ottawa | 5 | 13 | 0 | 10 | 401 | 560 |

### West Division

| | W | L | T | Pts | PF | PA |
|---|---|---|---|---|---|---|
| *British Columbia | 13 | 5 | 0 | 26 | 584 | 436 |
| †Edmonton | 9 | 9 | 0 | 18 | 532 | 472 |
| †Saskatchewan | 9 | 9 | 0 | 18 | 476 | 444 |
| Winnipeg | 7 | 11 | 0 | 14 | 448 | 507 |
| Calgary | 4 | 14 | 0 | 8 | 396 | 552 |

### Playoffs
#### Division Semifinals (Nov. 5 & 7)
**East:** at Toronto 24 . . . . . . . . . . . . . . . .Hamilton 6
**West:** Saskatchewan 14 . . . . . . . . . . . . .at Edmonton 6

#### Division Finals (Nov. 13)
**East:** Toronto 26 . . . . . . . . . . . . . . . .at Montreal 18
**West:** at British Columbia 27 . . . . .Saskatchewan 25 (OT)

### 92nd Grey Cup Championship
November 21, 2004
at Frank Clair Stadium in Ottawa
(Att: 51,242)

| | | | | | | |
|---|---|---|---|---|---|---|
| **Toronto** | . . . . . . . . . . . . . . . | 0 | 17 | 7 | 3— | **27** |
| **British Columbia** | . . . . . | 7 | 3 | 3 | 6— | **19** |

**MVP:** Damon Allen, Toronto, QB (23 of 34 for 299 yards and 1 TD, plus 2 rushing TD)

## Regular Season Individual Leaders
### Passing Yards

| | Att | Cmp | Cmp Pct | Yds | Yds/ Att | TD | TD Pct | Int | IntPct | Rating |
|---|---|---|---|---|---|---|---|---|---|---|
| Anthony Calvillo, Mon | 690 | 431 | 62.5 | 6041 | 8.8 | 31 | 4.5 | 15 | 2.2 | 96.5 |
| Jason Maas, Edm | 549 | 361 | 65.8 | 5270 | 9.6 | 31 | 5.6 | 14 | 2.6 | 105.1 |
| Casey Printers, B.C. | 494 | 325 | 65.8 | 5088 | 10.3 | 35 | 7.1 | 10 | 2.0 | 115.0 |
| Danny McManus, Ham | 590 | 331 | 56.1 | 5034 | 8.5 | 29 | 4.9 | 30 | 5.1 | 79.6 |
| Henry Burris, Sask | 544 | 322 | 59.2 | 4267 | 7.8 | 23 | 4.2 | 18 | 3.3 | 84.4 |

### Scoring

| Touchdowns | TD | Rus | Rec | Ret | Pts |
|---|---|---|---|---|---|
| Geroy Simon, B.C. | 14 | 0 | 14 | 0 | 84 |
| Charles Roberts, Win | 13 | 8 | 5 | 0 | 78 |
| Derrel Mitchell, Edm | 12 | 1 | 10 | 1 | 72 |
| Autry Denson, Mon | 12 | 9 | 3 | 0 | 72 |
| Kenton Keith, Sask | 11 | 9 | 2 | 0 | 66 |
| Jason Tucker, Edm | 11 | 0 | 11 | 0 | 66 |

| Kicking | PAT | FG | S* | Pts |
|---|---|---|---|---|
| Sean Fleming, Edm | 57/57 | 37/47 | 12 | 180 |
| Matt Kellett, Mon | 51/51 | 37/49 | 12 | 174 |
| Paul McCallum, Sask | 47/47 | 39/53 | 8 | 172 |
| Duncan O'Mahony, B.C. | 64/65 | 33/45 | 9 | 172 |
| Troy Westwood, Win | 41/41 | 39/50 | 8 | 166 |
| *Singles (or Rouges) | | | | |

### Rushing

| | Car | Yards | Avg | TD |
|---|---|---|---|---|
| Troy Davis, Ham | 324 | 1628 | 5.0 | 10 |
| Charles Roberts, Win | 300 | 1522 | 5.1 | 8 |
| Kenton Keith, Sask | 190 | 1154 | 6.1 | 9 |
| Mike Pringle, Edm | 259 | 1141 | 4.4 | 8 |
| Antonio Warren, B.C. | 219 | 1136 | 5.2 | 5 |

### All-CFL Team

| Offense | | Defense | |
|---|---|---|---|
| WR | Jason Tucker, Edm. | E | Tim Cheatwood, Ham. |
| WR | DJ Flick, Ham. | E | Anwar Stewart, Mon. |
| T | Uzooma Okeke, Mon. | T | Noah Cantor, Tor. |
| T | Gene Makowsky, Sask. | T | Nate Davis, Sask. |
| G | Paul Lambert, Mon. | LB | John Grace, Calg. |
| G | Andrew Greene, Sask. | LB | Kevin Eiben, Tor. |
| C | Bryan Chiu, Mon. | LB | Barrin Simpson, B.C. |
| QB | Casey Printers, B.C. | CB | Malcolm Frank, Edm. |
| RB | Troy Davis, Ham. | CB | Almondo Curry, Mon. |
| RB | Charles Roberts, Win. | DB | Eddie Davis, Sask. |
| SB | Ben Cahoon, Mon. | DB | Clifford Ivory, Tor. |
| SB | Geroy Simon, B.C. | S | Orlondo Steinauer, Tor. |

| Specialists | | | |
|---|---|---|---|
| PK | Sean Fleming, Edm. | P | Noel Prefontaine, Tor. |
| Special Teams | Keith Stokes, Win. | | |

### Receptions

| | No | Yards | Avg | TD |
|---|---|---|---|---|
| Geroy Simon, B.C. | 103 | 1750 | 17.0 | 14 |
| Ben Cahoon, Mon | 93 | 1183 | 12.7 | 6 |
| Jason Clermont, B.C. | 83 | 1220 | 14.7 | 7 |
| Jermaine Copeland, Mon | 83 | 1154 | 13.9 | 10 |
| Kwame Cavil, Mon | 78 | 1090 | 14.0 | 7 |
| Terry Vaughn, Edm | 78 | 1062 | 13.6 | 2 |

## Most Outstanding Awards

| | |
|---|---|
| Player . . . . . . . . . . . . . . . . . .Casey Printers, B.C., QB | Rookie . . . . . . . . . . . . . . .Nikolas Lewis, Calgary, WR |
| Canadian . . . . . . . . . . . . . .Jason Clermont, B.C., SB | Special Teams . . . . . . . . .Keith Stokes, Winnipeg, WR |
| Offensive Lineman . .Gene Makowsky, Saskatchewan, OT | Coach (Annis Stukus award) . . .Greg Marshall, Hamilton |
| Defensive Player . . . . . . . .Anwar Stewart, Montreal, DE | Tom Pate Award (Sportsmanship) . .Barron Miles, Mon., DB |

# Arena Football
## Final 2005 Standings

Division champions (*) and playoff qualifiers (†) are noted; top eight teams advance to the playoffs.

### American Conference
#### Central Division

|  | W | L | T | Pct. | PF | PA |
|---|---|---|---|---|---|---|
| *Colorado | 10 | 6 | 0 | .625 | 873 | 869 |
| †Chicago | 9 | 7 | 0 | .563 | 786 | 764 |
| Nashville | 6 | 9 | 1 | .406 | 668 | 715 |
| Grand Rapids | 4 | 12 | 0 | .250 | 761 | 932 |

#### Western Division

|  | W | L | T | Pct. | PF | PA |
|---|---|---|---|---|---|---|
| *Los Angeles | 10 | 6 | 0 | .625 | 861 | 813 |
| †San Jose | 9 | 7 | 0 | .563 | 945 | 821 |
| Las Vegas | 8 | 8 | 0 | .500 | 790 | 781 |
| Arizona | 7 | 9 | 0 | .438 | 816 | 793 |

### National Conference
#### Eastern Division

|  | W | L | T | Pct. | PF | PA |
|---|---|---|---|---|---|---|
| *New York | 10 | 6 | 0 | .625 | 862 | 798 |
| †Dallas | 8 | 7 | 1 | .531 | 888 | 825 |
| Philadelphia | 6 | 10 | 0 | .375 | 852 | 905 |
| Columbus | 2 | 14 | 0 | .125 | 718 | 908 |

#### Southern Division

|  | W | L | T | Pct. | PF | PA |
|---|---|---|---|---|---|---|
| *Georgia | 11 | 5 | 0 | .688 | 818 | 745 |
| †Tampa Bay | 10 | 6 | 0 | .625 | 836 | 779 |
| †Orlando | 10 | 6 | 0 | .625 | 800 | 755 |
| New Orleans | 9 | 7 | 0 | .563 | 835 | 787 |
| Austin | 6 | 10 | 0 | .375 | 774 | 893 |

## Annual Awards

Ironman of the Year . . . Kevin Ingram, Los Angeles, WR/DB
Offensive Player of the Year   Damian Harrell, Colorado, OS
Defensive Player of the Year  . Silas Demary, Los Angeles, DB
Lineman of the Year  . . . . Silas Demary, Los Angeles, OL/DL
Rookie of the Year . . . . . . . . . Troy Bergeron, Georgia, OS
Coach of the Year  . . . . . . . . . . . . . Doug Plank, Georgia

### ArenaBowl XIX

June 12, 2005 at the Thomas & Mack Center, Las Vegas
(Att: 10,822)

| | | | | | |
|---|---|---|---|---|---|
| **Georgia** | 7 | 13 | 7 | 21— | **48** |
| **Colorado** | 10 | 14 | 7 | 20— | **51** |

**MVP:** Off—Willis Marshall, Col., WR (4 rushes for 12 yds
and 3TDs; 6 receptions for 111 yds and 1 TD)

Def—Ahmad Hawkins, Col., DB (1 int; 1 fumble rec)

# arenafootball2
## Final 2005 Standings

Division champions (*) and playoff qualifiers (†) are noted; division champions received first round byes.

### American Conference
#### East Division

|  | W | L | T | Pct. | PF | PA |
|---|---|---|---|---|---|---|
| *Manchester | 12 | 4 | 0 | .750 | 805 | 686 |
| †Louisville | 11 | 5 | 0 | .688 | 890 | 826 |
| †Wilkes-Barre/Scranton | 9 | 7 | 0 | .562 | 790 | 738 |
| †Green Bay | 9 | 7 | 0 | .562 | 802 | 756 |
| Albany | 4 | 12 | 0 | .250 | 819 | 889 |

#### South Division

|  | W | L | T | Pct. | PF | PA |
|---|---|---|---|---|---|---|
| *Florida | 14 | 2 | 0 | .875 | 722 | 637 |
| †Macon | 8 | 8 | 0 | .500 | 777 | 754 |
| Arkansas | 5 | 11 | 0 | .312 | 704 | 828 |
| South Georgia | 3 | 13 | 0 | .188 | 698 | 840 |
| Birmingham | 2 | 14 | 0 | .125 | 702 | 893 |

### National Conference
#### Midwest Division

|  | W | L | T | Pct. | PF | PA |
|---|---|---|---|---|---|---|
| *Memphis | 13 | 3 | 0 | .812 | 892 | 601 |
| †Oklahoma | 10 | 6 | 0 | .625 | 868 | 757 |
| †Quad | 9 | 7 | 0 | .562 | 776 | 806 |
| †Amarillo | 8 | 8 | 0 | .500 | 892 | 887 |
| Bossier | 3 | 13 | 0 | .188 | 676 | 908 |

#### West Division

|  | W | L | T | Pct. | PF | PA |
|---|---|---|---|---|---|---|
| *Tulsa | 11 | 5 | 0 | .688 | 890 | 782 |
| †Rio Grande | 10 | 6 | 0 | .625 | 797 | 835 |
| Central Valley | 8 | 8 | 0 | .500 | 872 | 824 |
| Bakersfield | 6 | 10 | 0 | .375 | 647 | 665 |
| San Diego | 5 | 11 | 0 | .312 | 806 | 913 |

## Annual Awards

Ironman of the Year . . . Marquis Floyd, Rio Grande, WR/DB
Offensive Player of the Year . . . . Matt Sauk, Louisville, QB
Defensive Player of the Year  . Dahnel Singfield, Memphis, DS
Lineman of the Year . . . . . . . Khreem Smith, Memphis, DL
Rookie of the Year  . . . . Donovan Morgan, Tulsa, WR/DB
Coach of the Year  . . . . . . . . . . . Danton Barto, Memphis

### ArenaCup 2005

Aug. 27, 2005 at the CenturyTel Center in Bossier City, La.
(Att: 6,236)

| | | | | | |
|---|---|---|---|---|---|
| **Louisville** | 14 | 7 | 0 | 20— | **41** |
| **Memphis** | 13 | 14 | 9 | 27— | **63** |

**MVP:** Off—Kevin Prentiss, Mem., OS (9 rec., 124 yds,
4 TDs)

Def—Terrance Quattlebaum, Mem., DB
(2 interceptions, 4.5 tackles)

# 1920-2005
# *Through the Years*

SPORTS ALMANAC

## The Super Bowl

The first AFL-NFL World Championship Game, as it was originally called, was played seven months after the two leagues agreed to merge in June of 1966. It became the Super Bowl (complete with roman numerals) by the third game, in 1969. The Super Bowl winner has been presented the Vince Lombardi Trophy since 1971. Lombardi, whose Green Bay teams won the first two title games, died in 1970. NFL champions (1966-69) and NFC champions (since 1970) are listed in CAPITAL letters.

**Multiple winners:** Dallas and San Francisco (5); Pittsburgh (4); Green Bay, New England, Oakland-LA Raiders and Washington (3); Denver, Miami and NY Giants (2).

| Bowl | Date | Winner | Head Coach | Score | Loser | Head Coach | Site |
|------|------|--------|------------|-------|-------|------------|------|
| I | 1/15/67 | GREEN BAY | Vince Lombardi | 35-10 | Kansas City | Hank Stram | Los Angeles |
| II | 1/14/68 | GREEN BAY | Vince Lombardi | 33-14 | Oakland | John Rauch | Miami |
| III | 1/12/69 | NY Jets | Weeb Ewbank | 16-7 | BALT. COLTS | Don Shula | Miami |
| IV | 1/11/70 | Kansas City | Hank Stram | 23-7 | MINNESOTA | Bud Grant | New Orleans |
| V | 1/17/71 | Balt. Colts | Don McCafferty | 16-13 | DALLAS | Tom Landry | Miami |
| VI | 1/16/72 | DALLAS | Tom Landry | 24-3 | Miami | Don Shula | New Orleans |
| VII | 1/14/73 | Miami | Don Shula | 14-7 | WASHINGTON | George Allen | Los Angeles |
| VIII | 1/13/74 | Miami | Don Shula | 24-7 | MINNESOTA | Bud Grant | Houston |
| IX | 1/12/75 | Pittsburgh | Chuck Noll | 16-6 | MINNESOTA | Bud Grant | New Orleans |
| X | 1/18/76 | Pittsburgh | Chuck Noll | 21-17 | DALLAS | Tom Landry | Miami |
| XI | 1/9/77 | Oakland | John Madden | 32-14 | MINNESOTA | Bud Grant | Pasadena |
| XII | 1/15/78 | DALLAS | Tom Landry | 27-10 | Denver | Red Miller | New Orleans |
| XIII | 1/21/79 | Pittsburgh | Chuck Noll | 35-31 | DALLAS | Tom Landry | Miami |
| XIV | 1/20/80 | Pittsburgh | Chuck Noll | 31-19 | LA RAMS | Ray Malavasi | Pasadena |
| XV | 1/25/81 | Oakland | Tom Flores | 27-10 | PHILADELPHIA | Dick Vermeil | New Orleans |
| XVI | 1/24/82 | SAN FRANCISCO | Bill Walsh | 26-21 | Cincinnati | Forrest Gregg | Pontiac, MI |
| XVII | 1/30/83 | WASHINGTON | Joe Gibbs | 27-17 | Miami | Don Shula | Pasadena |
| XVIII | 1/22/84 | LA Raiders | Tom Flores | 38-9 | WASHINGTON | Joe Gibbs | Tampa |
| XIX | 1/20/85 | SAN FRANCISCO | Bill Walsh | 38-16 | Miami | Don Shula | Stanford |
| XX | 1/26/86 | CHICAGO | Mike Ditka | 46-10 | New England | Raymond Berry | New Orleans |
| XXI | 1/25/87 | NY GIANTS | Bill Parcells | 39-20 | Denver | Dan Reeves | Pasadena |
| XXII | 1/31/88 | WASHINGTON | Joe Gibbs | 42-10 | Denver | Dan Reeves | San Diego |
| XXIII | 1/22/89 | SAN FRANCISCO | Bill Walsh | 20-16 | Cincinnati | Sam Wyche | Miami |
| XXIV | 1/28/90 | SAN FRANCISCO | George Seifert | 55-10 | Denver | Dan Reeves | New Orleans |
| XXV | 1/27/91 | NY GIANTS | Bill Parcells | 20-19 | Buffalo | Marv Levy | Tampa |
| XXVI | 1/26/92 | WASHINGTON | Joe Gibbs | 37-24 | Buffalo | Marv Levy | Minneapolis |
| XXVII | 1/31/93 | DALLAS | Jimmy Johnson | 52-17 | Buffalo | Marv Levy | Pasadena |
| XXVIII | 1/30/94 | DALLAS | Jimmy Johnson | 30-13 | Buffalo | Marv Levy | Atlanta |
| XXIX | 1/29/95 | SAN FRANCISCO | George Seifert | 49-26 | San Diego | Bobby Ross | Miami |
| XXX | 1/28/96 | DALLAS | Barry Switzer | 27-17 | Pittsburgh | Bill Cowher | Tempe, AZ |
| XXXI | 1/26/97 | GREEN BAY | Mike Holmgren | 35-21 | New England | Bill Parcells | New Orleans |
| XXXII | 1/25/98 | Denver | Mike Shanahan | 31-24 | GREEN BAY | Mike Holmgren | San Diego |
| XXXIII | 1/31/99 | Denver | Mike Shanahan | 34-19 | ATLANTA | Dan Reeves | Miami |
| XXXIV | 1/30/00 | ST.L RAMS | Dick Vermeil | 23-16 | Tennessee | Jeff Fisher | Atlanta |
| XXXV | 1/28/01 | Balt. Ravens | Brian Billick | 34-7 | NY GIANTS | Jim Fassel | Tampa |
| XXXVI | 2/3/02 | New England | Bill Belichick | 20-17 | ST.L RAMS | Mike Martz | New Orleans |
| XXXVII | 1/26/03 | TAMPA BAY | Jon Gruden | 48-21 | Oakland | Bill Callahan | San Diego |
| XXXVIII | 2/1/04 | New England | Bill Belichick | 32-29 | CAROLINA | John Fox | Houston |
| XXXIX | 2/6/05 | New England | Bill Belichick | 24-21 | PHILADELPHIA | Andy Reid | Jacksonville |

*Super Bowl XXXIX was televised in 222 countries and broadcast in 31 different languages: Arabic, Basque, Cantonese, Catalan, Danish, English, Farsi, Faroese, Filipino, Finnish, French, Galician, German, Greek, Greenlandic, Hindu, Hungarian, Icelandic, Italian, Japanese, Korean, Mandarin Chinese, Norwegian, Polish, Portuguese, Romanian, Russian, Serbian, Spanish, Swedish and Thai.*

## Super Bowl Appearances

| App | | W | L | Pct | PF | PA | App | | W | L | Pct | PF | PA |
|---|---|---|---|---|---|---|---|---|---|---|---|---|---|
| 8 | Dallas | 5 | 3 | .625 | 221 | 132 | 2 | Baltimore Colts | 1 | 1 | .500 | 23 | 29 |
| 6 | Denver | 2 | 4 | .333 | 115 | 206 | 2 | Kansas City | 1 | 1 | .500 | 33 | 42 |
| 5 | San Francisco | 5 | 0 | 1.000 | 188 | 89 | 2 | Cincinnati | 0 | 2 | .000 | 37 | 46 |
| 5 | Pittsburgh | 4 | 1 | .800 | 120 | 100 | 2 | Philadelphia | 0 | 2 | .000 | 31 | 51 |
| 5 | New England | 3 | 2 | .600 | 107 | 148 | 1 | Baltimore Ravens | 1 | 0 | 1.000 | 34 | 7 |
| 5 | Oak/LA Raiders | 3 | 2 | .600 | 132 | 114 | 1 | Chicago | 1 | 0 | 1.000 | 46 | 10 |
| 5 | Washington | 3 | 2 | .600 | 122 | 103 | 1 | NY Jets | 1 | 0 | 1.000 | 16 | 7 |
| 5 | Miami | 2 | 3 | .400 | 74 | 103 | 1 | Tampa Bay | 1 | 0 | 1.000 | 48 | 21 |
| 4 | Green Bay | 3 | 1 | .750 | 127 | 76 | 1 | Atlanta | 0 | 1 | .000 | 19 | 34 |
| 4 | Buffalo | 0 | 4 | .000 | 73 | 139 | 1 | Carolina | 0 | 1 | .000 | 29 | 32 |
| 4 | Minnesota | 0 | 4 | .000 | 34 | 95 | 1 | San Diego | 0 | 1 | .000 | 26 | 49 |
| 3 | NY Giants | 2 | 1 | .667 | 66 | 73 | 1 | Tennessee | 0 | 1 | .000 | 16 | 23 |
| 3 | LA/St.L Rams | 1 | 2 | .333 | 59 | 67 | | | | | | | |

## Pete Rozelle Award (MVP)

The Most Valuable Player in the Super Bowl. Currently selected by a panel made up of national pro football writers and broadcasters chosen by the NFL (80 percent) and fans voting via the internet and text message (20 percent). Presented by *Sport* magazine from 1967-89 and by the NFL since 1990. Named after former NFL commissioner Pete Rozelle in 1990. Winner who did not play for Super Bowl champion is in **bold** type.

**Multiple winners:** Joe Montana (3); Terry Bradshaw, Tom Brady and Bart Starr (2).

| Bowl | | Bowl | | Bowl | |
|---|---|---|---|---|---|
| I | Bart Starr, Green Bay, QB | XIV | Terry Bradshaw, Pittsburgh, QB | XXVIII | Emmitt Smith, Dallas, RB |
| II | Bart Starr, Green Bay, QB | XV | Jim Plunkett, Oakland, QB | XXIX | Steve Young, San Fran., QB |
| III | Joe Namath, NY Jets, QB | XVI | Joe Montana, San Francisco, QB | XXX | Larry Brown, Dallas, CB |
| IV | Len Dawson, Kansas City, QB | XVII | John Riggins, Washington, RB | XXXI | Desmond Howard, Gr. Bay, KR |
| V | Chuck Howley, Dallas, LB | XVIII | Marcus Allen, LA Raiders, RB | XXXII | Terrell Davis, Denver, RB |
| VI | Roger Staubach, Dallas, QB | XIX | Joe Montana, San Francisco, QB | XXXIII | John Elway, Denver, QB |
| VII | Jake Scott, Miami, S | XX | Richard Dent, Chicago, DE | XXXIV | Kurt Warner, St. Louis, QB |
| VIII | Larry Csonka, Miami, RB | XXI | Phil Simms, NY Giants, QB | XXXV | Ray Lewis, Baltimore, LB |
| IX | Franco Harris, Pittsburgh, RB | XXII | Doug Williams, Washington, QB | XXXVI | Tom Brady, New England, QB |
| X | Lynn Swann, Pittsburgh, WR | XXIII | Jerry Rice, San Francisco, WR | XXXVII | Dexter Jackson, Tampa Bay, S |
| XI | Fred Biletnikoff, Oakland, WR | XXIV | Joe Montana, San Francisco, QB | XXXVIII | Tom Brady, New England, QB |
| XII | Harvey Martin, Dallas, DE & Randy White, Dallas, DT | XXV | Ottis Anderson, NY Giants, RB | XXXIX | Deion Branch, New England, WR |
| XIII | Terry Bradshaw, Pittsburgh, QB | XXVI | Mark Rypien, Washington, QB | | |
| | | XXVII | Troy Aikman, Dallas, QB | | |

## All-Time Super Bowl Leaders

Through 2005; participants in Super Bowl XXXIX in **bold** type.

### CAREER
### Passing Efficiency

| | (Minimum 25 passing attempts) | Gm | Att | Cmp | Cmp% | Yards | Avg Gain | TD | TD% | Int | Int% | Rating |
|---|---|---|---|---|---|---|---|---|---|---|---|---|
| 1 | Phil Simms, NYG | 1 | 25 | 22 | 88.0 | 268 | 10.72 | 3 | 12.0 | 0 | 0.0 | 150.9 |
| 2 | Steve Young, SF | 2 | 39 | 26 | 66.7 | 345 | 8.85 | 6 | 15.4 | 0 | 0.0 | 134.1 |
| 3 | Doug Williams, Wash. | 1 | 29 | 18 | 62.1 | 340 | 11.72 | 4 | 13.8 | 1 | 3.4 | 128.1 |
| 4 | Joe Montana, SF | 4 | 122 | 83 | 68.0 | 1142 | 9.36 | 11 | 9.0 | 0 | 0.0 | 127.8 |
| 5 | Jim Plunkett, Raiders | 2 | 46 | 29 | 63.0 | 433 | 9.41 | 4 | 8.7 | 0 | 0.0 | 122.8 |
| 6 | Jake Delhomme, Car. | 1 | 33 | 16 | 48.5 | 323 | 9.79 | 3 | 9.1 | 0 | 0.0 | 113.6 |
| 7 | Terry Bradshaw, Pit. | 4 | 84 | 49 | 58.3 | 932 | 11.10 | 9 | 10.7 | 4 | 4.8 | 112.8 |
| 8 | Troy Aikman, Dal | 3 | 80 | 56 | 70.0 | 689 | 8.61 | 5 | 6.3 | 1 | 1.3 | 111.9 |
| 9 | Bart Starr, GB | 2 | 47 | 29 | 61.7 | 452 | 9.62 | 3 | 6.4 | 1 | 2.1 | 106.0 |
| 10 | **Tom Brady**, NE | 3 | 108 | 71 | 65.7 | 735 | 6.81 | 6 | 5.6 | 1 | 0.9 | 99.9 |

Ratings based on performance standards established for completion percentage, average gain, touchdown percentage and interception percentage. Quarterbacks are allocated points according to how their statistics measure up to those standards.

### Passing Yards

| | | Gm | Att | Cmp | Pct | Yds |
|---|---|---|---|---|---|---|
| 1 | Joe Montana, SF | 4 | 122 | 83 | 68.0 | 1142 |
| 2 | John Elway, Den | 5 | 152 | 76 | 50.0 | 1128 |
| 3 | Terry Bradshaw, Pit | 4 | 84 | 49 | 58.3 | 932 |
| 4 | Jim Kelly, Buf | 4 | 145 | 81 | 55.9 | 829 |
| 5 | Kurt Warner, St.L | 2 | 89 | 52 | 58.4 | 779 |
| 6 | **Tom Brady**, NE | 3 | 108 | 71 | 65.7 | 735 |
| 7 | Roger Staubach, Dal | 4 | 98 | 61 | 62.2 | 734 |
| 8 | Troy Aikman, Dal | 3 | 80 | 56 | 70.0 | 689 |
| 9 | Brett Favre, GB | 2 | 69 | 39 | 56.5 | 502 |
| 10 | Fran Tarkenton, Min | 3 | 89 | 46 | 51.7 | 489 |

### Receptions

| | | Gm | No | Yds | Avg | TD |
|---|---|---|---|---|---|---|
| 1 | Jerry Rice, SF-Oak | 4 | 33 | 589 | 17.8 | 8 |
| 2 | Andre Reed, Buf | 4 | 27 | 323 | 12.0 | 0 |
| 3 | **Deion Branch**, NE | 2 | 21 | 276 | 13.1 | 1 |
| 4 | Roger Craig, SF | 3 | 20 | 212 | 10.6 | 2 |
| | Thurman Thomas, Buf | 4 | 20 | 144 | 7.2 | 0 |
| 6 | Jay Novacek, Dal | 3 | 17 | 148 | 8.7 | 2 |
| 7 | Lynn Swann, Pit | 4 | 16 | 364 | 22.8 | 3 |
| | Michael Irvin, Dal | 3 | 16 | 256 | 16.0 | 2 |
| | **Troy Brown**, NE | 3 | 16 | 182 | 11.4 | 0 |
| 10 | Chuck Foreman, Min | 3 | 15 | 139 | 9.3 | 0 |

## All-Time Super Bowl Leaders (Cont.)

### Rushing

| | | Gm | Car | Yds | Avg | TD |
|---|---|---|---|---|---|---|
| 1 | Franco Harris, Pit | 4 | 101 | 354 | 3.5 | 4 |
| 2 | Larry Csonka, Mia | 3 | 57 | 297 | 5.2 | 2 |
| 3 | Emmitt Smith, Dal | 3 | 70 | 289 | 4.1 | 5 |
| 4 | Terrell Davis, Den | 2 | 55 | 259 | 4.7 | 3 |
| 5 | John Riggins, Wash | 2 | 64 | 230 | 3.6 | 2 |
| 6 | Timmy Smith, Wash | 1 | 22 | 204 | 9.3 | 2 |
| | Thurman Thomas, Buf | 4 | 52 | 204 | 3.9 | 4 |
| 8 | Roger Craig, SF | 3 | 52 | 201 | 3.9 | 2 |
| 9 | Marcus Allen, Raiders | 1 | 20 | 191 | 9.5 | 2 |
| 10 | Antowain Smith, NE | 2 | 44 | 175 | 4.0 | 1 |

### All-Purpose Yards

| | | Gm | Rush | Rec | Ret | Total |
|---|---|---|---|---|---|---|
| 1 | Jerry Rice, SF-Oak | 4 | 15 | 589 | 0 | 604 |
| 2 | Franco Harris, Pit | 4 | 354 | 114 | 0 | 468 |
| 3 | Roger Craig, SF | 3 | 201 | 212 | 0 | 413 |
| 4 | Lynn Swann, Pit | 4 | -7 | 364 | 34 | 391 |
| 5 | Thurman Thomas, Buf | 4 | 204 | 144 | 0 | 348 |
| 6 | Emmitt Smith, Dal | 3 | 289 | 56 | 0 | 345 |
| 7 | Antonio Freeman, GB | 2 | 0 | 231 | 104 | 335 |
| 8 | Andre Reed, Buf | 4 | 0 | 323 | 0 | 323 |
| 9 | Terrell Davis, Den | 2 | 259 | 58 | 0 | 317 |
| 10 | Larry Csonka, Mia | 3 | 297 | 17 | 0 | 314 |

### Scoring

#### Points

| | | Gm | TD | FG | PAT | Pts |
|---|---|---|---|---|---|---|
| 1 | Jerry Rice, SF-Oak | 4 | 8 | 0 | 0 | 48 |
| 2 | Emmitt Smith, Dal | 3 | 5 | 0 | 0 | 30 |
| 3 | Roger Craig, SF | 3 | 4 | 0 | 0 | 24 |
| | Franco Harris, Pit | 4 | 4 | 0 | 0 | 24 |
| | Thurman Thomas, Buf | 4 | 4 | 0 | 0 | 24 |
| | John Elway, Den | 5 | 4 | 0 | 0 | 24 |
| 7 | **Adam Vinatieri**, NE | 4 | 0 | 4 | 11 | 23 |
| 8 | Ray Wersching, SF | 2 | 0 | 5 | 7 | 22 |
| 9 | Don Chandler, GB | 2 | 0 | 4 | 8 | 20 |
| 10 | Six tied with 18 pts. each. | | | | | |

### Punt Returns

| (Minimum 4 Returns) | | Gm | No | Yds | Avg. | TD |
|---|---|---|---|---|---|---|
| 1 | John Taylor, SF | 3 | 6 | 94 | 15.7 | 0 |
| 2 | Desmond Howard, GB | 1 | 6 | 90 | 15.0 | 0 |
| 3 | Dave Meggett, NYG-NE | 2 | 6 | 67 | 11.2 | 0 |
| 4 | Neal Colzie, Raiders | 1 | 4 | 43 | 10.8 | 0 |
| 5 | Dana McLemore, SF | 1 | 5 | 51 | 10.2 | 0 |

### Kickoff Returns

| (Minimum 4 Returns) | | Gm | No | Yds | Avg. | TD |
|---|---|---|---|---|---|---|
| 1 | Tim Dwight, Atl | 1 | 5 | 210 | 42.0 | 1 |
| 2 | Desmond Howard, GB | 1 | 4 | 154 | 38.5 | 1 |
| 3 | Fulton Walker, Mia | 2 | 8 | 283 | 35.4 | 1 |
| 4 | Andre Coleman, SD | 1 | 8 | 242 | 30.3 | 1 |
| 5 | Larry Anderson, Pit | 2 | 8 | 207 | 25.9 | 0 |

### Touchdowns

| | | Gm | Rush | Rec | Ret | TD |
|---|---|---|---|---|---|---|
| 1 | Jerry Rice, SF-Oak | 4 | 0 | 8 | 0 | 8 |
| 2 | Emmitt Smith, Dal | 3 | 5 | 0 | 0 | 5 |
| 3 | Roger Craig, SF | 3 | 2 | 2 | 0 | 4 |
| | Franco Harris, Pit | 4 | 4 | 0 | 0 | 4 |
| | John Elway, Den | 5 | 4 | 0 | 0 | 4 |
| | Thurman Thomas, Buf | 4 | 4 | 0 | 0 | 4 |
| 7 | Cliff Branch, Raiders | 3 | 0 | 3 | 0 | 3 |
| | John Stallworth, Pit | 4 | 0 | 3 | 0 | 3 |
| | Lynn Swann, Pit | 4 | 0 | 3 | 0 | 3 |
| | Ricky Watters, SF | 1 | 1 | 2 | 0 | 3 |
| | Terrell Davis, Den | 2 | 3 | 0 | 0 | 3 |
| | Antonio Freeman, GB | 2 | 0 | 3 | 0 | 3 |

### Interceptions

| | | Gm | No | Yds | TD |
|---|---|---|---|---|---|
| 1 | Larry Brown, Dal | 3 | 3 | 77 | 0 |
| | Chuck Howley, Dal | 2 | 3 | 63 | 0 |
| | Rod Martin, Raiders | 2 | 3 | 44 | 0 |
| 4 | Thirteen tied with 2 each. | | | | |

### Sacks

| | | Gm | No |
|---|---|---|---|
| 1 | Charles Haley, SF-Dal | 5 | 4.5 |
| 2 | Reggie White, GB | 2 | 3.0 |
| | Leonard Marshall, NYG | 2 | 3.0 |
| | Danny Stubbs, SF | 2 | 3.0 |
| | **Mike Vrabel**, NE | 3 | 3.0 |
| | Jeff Wright, Buf | 4 | 3.0 |
| | **Tedy Bruschi**, NE | 4 | 3.0 |
| | **Willie McGinest**, NE | 4 | 3.0 |
| 9 | Dexter Manley, Wash | 3 | 2.5 |

**Note:** The NFL did not begin officially compiling sacks until 1982.

### Punting

| (Minimum 10 Punts) | | Gm | No | Yds | Avg. |
|---|---|---|---|---|---|
| 1 | Jerrel Wilson, KC | 2 | 11 | 511 | 46.5 |
| 2 | Tom Tupa, NE-TB | 2 | 12 | 516 | 43.0 |
| | Kyle Richardson, Bal | 1 | 10 | 430 | 43.0 |
| 4 | Ray Guy, Raiders | 3 | 14 | 587 | 41.9 |
| 5 | Larry Seiple, Mia | 3 | 15 | 620 | 41.3 |

### SINGLE GAME

### Passing

| Yards Gained | Year | Att/Cmp | Yds |
|---|---|---|---|
| 1 Kurt Warner, St.L vs Ten | 2000 | 45/24 | 414 |
| 2 Kurt Warner, St.L vs NE | 2002 | 44/28 | 365 |
| 3 Joe Montana, SF vs Cin | 1989 | 36/23 | 357 |
|   **Donovan McNabb**, Phi vs NE | 2005 | 51/30 | 357 |
| 5 Tom Brady, NE vs Car | 2004 | 48/32 | 354 |
| 6 Doug Williams, Wash vs Den | 1988 | 29/18 | 340 |
| 7 John Elway, Den vs Atl | 1999 | 29/18 | 336 |
| 8 Joe Montana, SF vs Mia | 1985 | 35/24 | 331 |
| 9 Steve Young, SF vs SD | 1995 | 36/24 | 325 |
| 10 Jake Delhomme, Car vs NE | 2004 | 33/16 | 323 |

| Touchdown Passes | Year | TD | Int |
|---|---|---|---|
| 1 Steve Young, SF vs SD | 1995 | 6 | 0 |
| 2 Joe Montana, SF vs Den | 1990 | 5 | 0 |
| 3 Terry Bradshaw, Pit vs Dal | 1979 | 4 | 1 |
|   Doug Williams, Wash vs Den | 1988 | 4 | 1 |
|   Troy Aikman, Dal vs Buf | 1993 | 4 | 0 |
| 6 Roger Staubach, Dal vs Pit | 1979 | 3 | 1 |
|   Jim Plunkett, Raiders vs Phi | 1981 | 3 | 0 |
|   Joe Montana, SF vs Mia | 1985 | 3 | 0 |
|   Phil Simms, NYG vs Den | 1987 | 3 | 0 |
|   Brett Favre, GB vs Den | 1998 | 3 | 1 |
|   Jake Delhomme, Car vs NE | 2004 | 3 | 0 |
|   Tom Brady, NE vs Car | 2004 | 3 | 1 |
|   **Donovan McNabb**, Phi vs NE | 2005 | 3 | 3 |

## Receiving

| Catches | Year | No | Yds | TD |
|---|---|---|---|---|
| 1 Dan Ross, Cin vs SF | 1982 | 11 | 104 | 2 |
| Jerry Rice, SF vs Cin | 1989 | 11 | 215 | 1 |
| **Deion Branch**, NE vs Phi | 2005 | 11 | 133 | 0 |
| 4 Tony Nathan, Mia vs SF | 1985 | 10 | 83 | 0 |
| Jerry Rice, SF vs SD | 1995 | 10 | 149 | 3 |
| Andre Hastings, Pit vs Dal | 1996 | 10 | 98 | 0 |
| Deion Branch, NE vs Car | 2004 | 10 | 143 | 1 |

| Yards Gained | Year | No | Yds | TD |
|---|---|---|---|---|
| 1 Jerry Rice, SF vs Cin | 1989 | 11 | 215 | 1 |
| 2 Ricky Sanders, Wash vs Den | 1988 | 9 | 193 | 2 |
| 3 Isaac Bruce, St.L vs Ten | 2000 | 6 | 162 | 1 |
| 4 Lynn Swann, Pit vs Dal | 1976 | 4 | 161 | 1 |
| 5 Andre Reed, Buf vs Dal | 1993 | 8 | 152 | 0 |
| Rod Smith, Den vs Atl | 1999 | 5 | 152 | 1 |

## Rushing

| Yards Gained | Year | Car | Yds | TD |
|---|---|---|---|---|
| 1 Timmy Smith, Wash vs Den | 1988 | 22 | 204 | 2 |
| 2 Marcus Allen, Raiders vs Wash | 1984 | 20 | 191 | 2 |
| 3 John Riggins, Wash vs Mia | 1983 | 38 | 166 | 1 |
| 4 Franco Harris, Pit vs Min | 1975 | 34 | 158 | 1 |
| 5 Terrell Davis, Den vs GB | 1998 | 30 | 157 | 3 |
| 6 Larry Csonka, Mia vs Min | 1974 | 33 | 145 | 2 |
| 7 Clarence Davis, Raiders vs Min. | 1977 | 16 | 137 | 0 |
| 8 Thurman Thomas, Buf vs NYG | 1991 | 15 | 135 | 1 |
| 9 Emmitt Smith, Dal vs Buf | 1994 | 30 | 132 | 2 |
| 10 Michael Pittman, TB vs Oak | 2003 | 29 | 124 | 0 |

## All-Purpose Yards

| Yards Gained | Year | Run | Rec | Tot |
|---|---|---|---|---|
| 1 Desmond Howard, GB vs NE | 1997 | 0 | 0 | 244 |
| 2 Andre Coleman, SD vs SF | 1995 | 0 | 0 | 242 |
| 3 Ricky Sanders, Wash vs Den | 1988 | 193 | -4 | 235 |
| 4 Antonio Freeman, GB vs Den | 1998 | 0 | 126 | 230 |
| 5 Jerry Rice, SF vs Cin | 1989 | 5 | 215 | 220 |
| 6 Tim Dwight, Atl vs Den | 1999 | 5 | 0 | 215 |
| 7 Timmy Smith, Wash vs Den | 1988 | 204 | 9 | 213 |
| 8 Marcus Allen, Raiders vs Wash | 1984 | 191 | 18 | 209 |
| 9 Stephen Starring, NE vs Chi | 1986 | 0 | 39 | 192 |
| 10 Fulton Walker, Mia vs Wash | 1983 | 0 | 0 | 190 |
| Thurman Thomas, Buf vs NYG | 1991 | 135 | 55 | 190 |

**Return Yardage:** Howard 244, Coleman 242, Sanders 46, Freeman 104, Dwight 210, Starring 153, Walker 190.

## Scoring

| Points | Year | TD | FG | PAT | Pts |
|---|---|---|---|---|---|
| 1 Roger Craig, SF vs Mia | 1985 | 3 | 0 | 0 | 18 |
| Jerry Rice, SF vs Den | 1990 | 3 | 0 | 0 | 18 |
| Jerry-Rice, SF vs SD | 1995 | 3 | 0 | 0 | 18 |
| Ricky Watters, SF vs SD | 1995 | 3 | 0 | 0 | 18 |
| Terrell Davis, Den vs GB | 1998 | 3 | 0 | 0 | 18 |

| Touchdowns | Year | TD | Rush | Rec |
|---|---|---|---|---|
| 1 Roger Craig, SF vs Mia | 1985 | 3 | 1 | 2 |
| Jerry Rice, SF vs Den | 1990 | 3 | 0 | 3 |
| Jerry Rice, SF vs SD | 1995 | 3 | 0 | 3 |
| Ricky Watters, SF vs SD | 1995 | 3 | 1 | 2 |
| Terrell Davis, Den vs GB | 1998 | 3 | 3 | 0 |

## Interceptions

| | Year | No | Yds | TD |
|---|---|---|---|---|
| 1 Rod Martin, Raiders vs Phi | 1981 | 3 | 44 | 0 |
| Eleven tied with 2 each. | | | | |

## Punting

| (Minimum 4 punts) | Year | No | Yds | Avg |
|---|---|---|---|---|
| 1 Bryan Wagner, SD vs SF | 1995 | 4 | 195 | 48.8 |
| 2 Jerrel Wilson, KC vs Min | 1970 | 4 | 194 | 48.5 |
| 3 Jim Miller, SF vs Cin | 1982 | 4 | 185 | 46.3 |
| 4 Jerrel Wilson, KC vs GB | 1967 | 7 | 317 | 45.3 |
| 5 **Josh Miller**, NE vs Phi | 2005 | 7 | 316 | 45.1 |

## Punt Returns

| (Minimum 3 returns) | Year | No | Yds | Avg |
|---|---|---|---|---|
| 1 John Taylor, SF vs Cin | 1989 | 3 | 56 | 18.7 |
| 2 Desmond Howard, GB vs NE | 1997 | 6 | 90 | 15.0 |
| 3 John Taylor, SF vs Den | 1990 | 3 | 38 | 12.7 |
| 4 Kelvin Martin, Dal vs Buf | 1993 | 3 | 35 | 11.7 |
| 5 Lynn Swann, Pit vs Min | 1975 | 3 | 34 | 11.3 |
| Jermaine Lewis, Bal vs NYG | 2001 | 3 | 34 | 11.3 |

## Kickoff Returns

| (Minimum 3 returns) | Year | No | Yds | Avg |
|---|---|---|---|---|
| 1 Fulton Walker, Mia vs Wash | 1983 | 4 | 190 | 47.5 |
| 2 Tim Dwight, Atl vs Den | 1999 | 5 | 210 | 42.0 |
| 3 Desmond Howard, GB vs NE | 1997 | 4 | 154 | 38.5 |
| 4 Larry Anderson, Pit vs Rams | 1980 | 5 | 162 | 32.4 |
| 5 Rick Upchurch, Den vs Dal | 1978 | 3 | 94 | 31.3 |

## Super Bowl Playoffs

The Super Bowl forced the NFL to set up pro football's first guaranteed multiple-game playoff format. Over the years, the NFL-AFL merger, the creation of two conferences comprised of four divisions each and the proliferation of wild card entries has seen the postseason field grow from four teams (1966), to six (1967-68), to eight (1969-77), to 10 (1978-81, 1983-89), to the present 12 (since 1990). In 1968, there was a special playoff between Oakland and Kansas City which were both 12-2 and tied for first in the AFL's Western Division. In 1982, when a 57-day players' strike shortened the regular season to just nine games, playoff berths were extended to 16 teams (eight from each conference) and a 15-game tournament was played.

Note that in the following year-by-year summary, records of finalists include all games leading up to the Super Bowl; (*) indicates non-division winners or wild card teams.

### 1966 SEASON

#### AFL Playoffs

Championship . . . . . . . . . . . . Kansas City 31, at Buffalo 7

#### NFL Playoffs

Championship . . . . . . . . . . . . Green Bay 34, at Dallas 27

#### Super Bowl I

Jan. 15, 1967
Memorial Coliseum, Los Angeles
Favorite: Packers by 14—Attendance: 61,946

**Kansas City** (12-2-1) . . . . . . . . . . . 0  10  0  0 —**10**
**Green Bay** (13-2) . . . . . . . . . . . . . . 7  7  14  7 —**35**
**MVP:** Green Bay QB Bart Starr (16 for 23, 250 yds, 2 TD)

### 1967 SEASON

#### AFL Playoffs

Championship . . . . . . . . . . . . at Oakland 40, Houston 7

#### NFL Playoffs

Eastern Conference . . . . . . . . at Dallas 52, Cleveland 14
Western Conference . . . . . . . at Green Bay 28, LA Rams 7
Championship . . . . . . . . . . . . at Green Bay 21, Dallas 17

#### Super Bowl II

Jan. 14, 1968    Orange Bowl, Miami
Favorite: Packers by 13½—Attendance: 75,546

**Green Bay** (11-4-1) . . . . . . . . . . . . 3  13  10  7 —**33**
**Oakland** (14-1) . . . . . . . . . . . . . . . 0  7  0  7 —**14**
**MVP:** Green Bay QB Bart Starr (13 for 24, 202 yds, 1 TD)

## Super Bowl Playoffs (Cont.)

### 1968 SEASON

#### AFL Playoffs

Western Div. Playoff . . . . . .at Oakland 41, Kansas City 6
AFL Championship . . . . . . . . . .at NY Jets 27, Oakland 23

#### NFL Playoffs

Eastern Conference . . . . . . . . .at Cleveland 31, Dallas 20
Western Conference . . . . . .at Baltimore 24, Minnesota 14
NFL Championship . . . . . . . . .Baltimore 34, at Cleveland 0

#### Super Bowl III

Jan. 12, 1969     Orange Bowl, Miami
Favorite: Colts by 18—Attendance: 75,389

**NY Jets** (12-3) . . . . . . . . . . .0   7   6   3 — **16**
**Baltimore** (15-1) . . . . . . . . . .0   0   0   7 — **7**
**MVP:** NY Jets QB Joe Namath (17 for 28, 206 yds)

### 1969 SEASON

#### AFL Playoffs

Inter-Division . . . . . . . . . . .*Kansas City 13, at NY Jets 6
                       at Oakland 56, *Houston 7
AFL Championship . . . . . . .Kansas City 17, at Oakland 7

#### NFL Playoffs

Eastern Conference . . . . . . . .Cleveland 38, at Dallas 14
Western Conference . . . . . . .at Minnesota 23, LA Rams 20
NFL Championship . . . . . . .at Minnesota 27, Cleveland 7

#### Super Bowl IV

Jan. 11, 1970
Tulane Stadium, New Orleans
Favorite: Vikings by 12—Attendance: 80,562

**Minnesota** (14-2) . . . . . . . . . . .0   0   7   0 — **7**
**Kansas City** (13-3) . . . . . . . . .3  13   7   0 — **23**
**MVP:** KC QB Len Dawson (12 for 17, 142 yds, 1 TD, 1Int)

### 1970 SEASON

#### AFC Playoffs

First Round . . . . . . . . . . . . . .at Baltimore 17, Cincinnati 0
                     at Oakland 21,*Miami 14
Championship . . . . . . . . . .at Baltimore 27, Oakland 17

#### NFC Playoffs

First Round. . . . . . . . . . . . . . . . . .at Dallas 5, *Detroit 0
                San Francisco 17, at Minnesota 14
Championship . . . . . . . . . .Dallas 17, at San Francisco 10

#### Super Bowl V

Jan. 17, 1971     Orange Bowl, Miami
Favorite: Cowboys by 2½—Attendance: 79,204

**Baltimore** (13-2-1) . . . . . . . . . .0   6   0  10 — **16**
**Dallas** (12-4) . . . . . . . . . . . . . .3  10   0   0 — **13**
**MVP:** Dallas LB Chuck Howley (2 interceptions for 22 yds)·

### 1971 SEASON

#### AFC Playoffs

First Round . . . . . . . . . .Miami 27, at Kansas City 24 (OT)
                  *Baltimore 20, at Cleveland 3
Championship . . . . . . . . . . . . .at Miami 21, Baltimore 0

#### NFC Playoffs

First Round . . . . . . . . . . . . . .Dallas 20, at Minnesota 12
               at San Francisco 24,*Washington 20
Championship . . . . . . . . . .at Dallas 14, San Francisco 3

#### Super Bowl VI

Jan. 16, 1972
Tulane Stadium, New Orleans
Favorite: Cowboys by 6—Attendance: 81,023

**Dallas** (13-3) . . . . . . . . . . . . . .3   7   7   7 — **24**
**Miami** (12-3-1) . . . . . . . . . . . . .0   3   0   0 — **3**
**MVP:** Dallas QB Roger Staubach (12 for 19, 119 yds, 2 TD)

### 1972 SEASON

#### AFC Playoffs

First Round . . . . . . . . . . . . .at Pittsburgh 13, Oakland 7
                     at Miami 20, *Cleveland 14
Championship . . . . . . . . . . . .Miami 21, at Pittsburgh 17

#### NFC Playoffs

First Round . . . . . . . . . . .*Dallas 30, at San Francisco 28
               at Washington 16, Green Bay 3
Championship . . . . . . . . .at Washington 26, Dallas 3

#### Super Bowl VII

Jan. 14, 1973
Memorial Coliseum, Los Angeles
Favorite: Redskins by 1½—Attendance: 90,182

**Miami** (16-0) . . . . . . . . . . . . . .7   7   0   0 — **14**
**Washington** (13-3) . . . . . . . . . .0   0   0   7 — **7**
**MVP:** Miami safety Jake Scott (2 Interceptions for 63 yds)

### 1973 SEASON

#### AFC Playoffs

First Round . . . . . . . . . . . . .at Oakland 33, *Pittsburgh 14
                   at Miami 34, Cincinnati 16
Championship . . . . . . . . . .at Miami 27, Oakland 10

#### NFC Playoffs

First Round . . . . . . . . . .at Minnesota 27, *Washington 20
                   at Dallas 27, LA Rams 16
Championship . . . . . . . . . .Minnesota 27, at Dallas 10

#### Super Bowl VIII

Jan. 13, 1974
Rice Stadium, Houston
Favorite: Dolphins by 6½—Attendance: 71,882

**Minnesota** (14-2) . . . . . . . . . . .0   0   0   7 — **7**
**Miami** (12-4) . . . . . . . . . . . . . .14   3   7   0 — **24**
**MVP:** Miami FB Larry Csonka (33 carries, 145 yds, 2 TD)

### 1974 SEASON

#### AFC Playoffs

First Round . . . . . . . . . . . . . .at Oakland 28, Miami 26
                  at Pittsburgh 32, *Buffalo 14
Championship . . . . . . . . . .Pittsburgh 24, at Oakland 13

#### NFC Playoffs

First Round . . . . . . . . . . . .at Minnesota 30, St. Louis 14
              at LA Rams 19, *Washington 10
Championship . . . . . . . . . .at Minnesota 14, LA Rams 10

#### Super Bowl IX

Jan. 12, 1975
Tulane Stadium, New Orleans
Favorite: Steelers by 3—Attendance: 80,997

**Pittsburgh** (12-3-1) . . . . . . . . . .0   2   7   7 — **16**
**Minnesota** (12-4) . . . . . . . . . . .0   0   0   6 — **6**
**MVP:** Pittsburgh RB Franco Harris (34 carries, 158 yds, 1 TD)

## 1975 SEASON

### AFC Playoffs

First Round . . . . . . . . . . .at Pittsburgh 28, Baltimore 10
at Oakland 31, *Cincinnati 28
Championship . . . . . . . . .at Pittsburgh 16, Oakland 10

### NFC Playoffs

First Round . . . . . . . . . . .at LA Rams 35, St. Louis 23
*Dallas 17, at Minnesota 14
Championship . . . . . . . . . . . .Dallas 37, at LA Rams 7

### Super Bowl X

Jan. 18, 1976    Orange Bowl, Miami
Favorite: Steelers by 6½—Attendance: 80,187

**Dallas** (12-4) . . . . . . . . . . . . . . .7    3    0    7 — **17**
**Pittsburgh** (14-2) . . . . . . . . . . . .7    0    0   14 — **21**
**MVP:** Pittsburgh WR Lynn Swann (4 catches, 161 yds, 1 TD)

## 1976 SEASON

### AFC Playoffs

First Round . . . . . . . . . .at Oakland 24, *New England 21
Pittsburgh 40, at Baltimore 14
Championship . . . . . . . . . .at Oakland 24, Pittsburgh 7

### NFC Playoffs

First Round . . . . . . . . .at Minnesota 35, *Washington 20
LA Rams 14, at Dallas 12
Championship . . . . . . . . .at Minnesota 24, LA Rams 13

### Super Bowl XI

Jan. 9, 1977    Rose Bowl, Pasadena
Favorite: Raiders by 4½—Attendance: 103,438

**Oakland** (15-1) . . . . . . . . . . . . . . .0   16    3   13 — **32**
**Minnesota** (13-2-1) . . . . . . . . . . .0    0    7   14 — **14**
**MVP:** Oakland WR Fred Biletnikoff (4 catches, 79 yds)

## 1977 SEASON

### AFC Playoffs

First Round . . . . . . . . . . . . .at Denver 34, Pittsburgh 21
*Oakland 37, at Baltimore 31 (OT)
Championship . . . . . . . . . . .at Denver 20, Oakland 17

### NFC Playoffs

First Round . . . . . . . . . . . .at Dallas 37, *Chicago 7
Minnesota 14, at LA Rams 7
Championship . . . . . . . . . .at Dallas 23, Minnesota 6

### Super Bowl XII

Jan. 15, 1978
Louisiana Superdome, New Orleans
Favorite: Cowboys by 6—Attendance: 75,583

**Dallas** (14-2) . . . . . . . . . . . . . .10    3    7    7 — **27**
**Denver** (14-2) . . . . . . . . . . . . . . .0    0   10    0 — **10**
**MVPs:** Dallas DE Harvey Martin and DT Randy White
(Cowboys' defense forced 8 turnovers)

## 1978 SEASON

### AFC Playoffs

First Round . . . . . . . . . . . . . .*Houston 17, at *Miami 9
Second Round . . . . . . . .Houston 31, at New England 14
at Pittsburgh 33, Denver 10
Championship . . . . . . . . . .at Pittsburgh 34, Houston 5

### NFC Playoffs

First Round . . . . . . . . . .at *Atlanta 14, *Philadelphia 13
Second Round . . . . . . . . . .at Dallas 27, Atlanta 20
at LA Rams 34, Minnesota 10
Championship . . . . . . . . . . . . . .Dallas 28, at LA Rams 0

### Super Bowl XIII

Jan. 21, 1979
Orange Bowl, Miami
Favorite by 4—Attendance: 79,484

**Pittsburgh** (16-2) . . . . . . . . . . . .7   14    0   14 — **35**
**Dallas** (14-4) . . . . . . . . . . . . . . . .7    7    3   14 — **31**
**MVP:** Pit. QB Terry Bradshaw (17 for 30, 318 yds, 4 TD)

## 1979 SEASON

### AFC Playoffs

First Round . . . . . . . . . . . . .at *Houston 13, *Denver 7
Second Round . . . . . . . . . .Houston 17, at San Diego 14
at Pittsburgh 34, Miami 14
Championship . . . . . . . . . .at Pittsburgh 27, Houston 13

### NFC Playoffs

First Round . . . . . . .at *Philadelphia 27, *Chicago 17
Second Round . . . . . .at Tampa Bay 24, Philadelphia 17
LA Rams 21, at Dallas 19
Championship . . . . . . . . . . . .LA Rams 9, at Tampa Bay 0

### Super Bowl XIV

Jan. 20, 1980    Rose Bowl, Pasadena
Favorite: Steelers by 10½—Attendance: 103,985

**LA Rams** (11-7) . . . . . . . . . . . . . .7    6    6    0 — **19**
**Pittsburgh** (14-4) . . . . . . . . . . . .3    7    7   14 — **31**
**MVP:** Pit. QB Terry Bradshaw (14 for 21, 309 yds, 2 TD)

## 1980 SEASON

### AFC Playoffs

First Round . . . . . . . . . . . . .at *Oakland 27, *Houston 7
Second Round . . . . . . . . . .at San Diego 20, Buffalo 14
Oakland 14, at Cleveland 12
Championship . . . . . . . . .Oakland 34, at San Diego 27

### NFC Playoffs

First Round . . . . . . . . . . . .at *Dallas 34, *LA Rams 13
Second Round . . . . . . . .at Philadelphia 31, Minnesota 16
Dallas 30, at Atlanta 27
Championship . . . . . . . . .at Philadelphia 20, Dallas 7

### Super Bowl XV

Jan. 25, 1981
Louisiana Superdome, New Orleans
Favorite: Eagles by 3—Attendance: 76,135

**Oakland** (14-5) . . . . . . . . . . . . . .14    0   10    3 — **27**
**Philadelphia** (14-4) . . . . . . . . . . .0    3    0    7 — **10**
**MVP:** Oakland QB Jim Plunkett (13 for 21, 261 yds, 3 TD)

## 1981 SEASON

### AFC Playoffs

First Round . . . . . . . . . . . . .*Buffalo 31, at *NY Jets 27
Second Round . . . . . . . .San Diego 41, at Miami 38 (OT)
at Cincinnati 28, Buffalo 21
Championship . . . . . . . . .at Cincinnati 27, San Diego 7

### NFC Playoffs

First Round . . . . . . . .*NY Giants 27, at *Philadelphia 21
Second Round . . . . . . . . . .at Dallas 38, Tampa Bay 0
at San Francisco 38, NY Giants 24
Championship . . . . . . . . .at San Francisco 28, Dallas 27

### Super Bowl XVI

Jan. 24, 1982
Pontiac Silverdome, Pontiac, Mich.
Favorite: Pick 'em—Attendance: 81,270

**San Francisco** (15-3) . . . . . . . . .7   13    0    6 — **26**
**Cincinnati** (14-4) . . . . . . . . . . . .0    0    7   14 — **21**
**MVP:** San Francisco QB Joe Montana (14 for 22, 157
yds, 1 TD; 6 carries, 18 yds, 1 TD)

## Super Bowl Playoffs (Cont.)

### 1982 SEASON

A 57-day players' strike shortened the regular season from 16 games to nine. The playoff format was changed to a 16-team tournament open to the top eight teams in each conference.

#### AFC Playoffs

First Round . . . . . . . . . . .at LA Raiders 27, Cleveland 10
at Miami 28, New England 3
NY Jets 44, at Cincinnati 17
San Diego 31, at Pittsburgh 28
Second Round . . . . . . . . . .NY Jets 17, at LA Raiders 14
at Miami 34, San Diego 13
Championship . . . . . . . . . . . .at Miami 14, NY Jets 0

#### NFC Playoffs

First Round . . . . . . . . . . . . .at Washington 31, Detroit 7
at Dallas 30, Tampa Bay 17
at Green Bay 41, St. Louis 16
at Minnesota 30, Atlanta 24
Second Round . . . . . . . . .at Washington 21, Minnesota 7
at Dallas 37, Green Bay 26
Championship . . . . . . . . . .at Washington 31, Dallas 17

### Super Bowl XVII

Jan. 30, 1983
Rose Bowl, Pasadena
Favorite: Dolphins by 3—Attendance: 103,667

**Miami** (10-2) . . . . . . . . . . . . . . . .7  10  0  0 — **17**
**Washington** (11-1) . . . . . . . . . .0  10  3  14 — **27**
**MVP:** Washington RB John Riggins (38 carries, 166 yds, 1 TD; 1 catch, 15 yds)

### 1983 SEASON

#### AFC Playoffs

First Round . . . . . . . . . . . . . .at *Seattle 31, *Denver 7
Second Round . . . . . . . . . . . . .Seattle 27, at Miami 20
at LA Raiders 38, Pittsburgh 10
Championship . . . . . . . . . . .at LA Raiders 30, Seattle 14

#### NFC Playoffs

First Round . . . . . . . . . . . . . .*LA Rams 24, at *Dallas 17
Second Round . . . . . . . . . .at San Francisco 24, Detroit 23
at Washington 51, LA Rams 7
Championship . . . . . .at Washington 24, San Francisco 21

### Super Bowl XVIII

Jan. 22, 1984
Tampa Stadium, Tampa
Favorite: Redskins by 3—Attendance: 72,920

**Washington** (16-2) . . . . . . . . . . .0  3  6  0 — **9**
**LA Raiders** (14-4) . . . . . . . . . . .7  14  14  3 — **38**
**MVP:** LA Raiders RB Marcus Allen (20 carries, 191 yds, 2 TD; 2 catches, 18 yds)

#### Most Popular Playing Sites

Stadiums hosting more than one Super Bowl.

| No | | Years |
|----|----|----|
| 6 | Superdome (N. Orleans) | 1978, 81, 86, 90, 97, 2002 |
| 5 | Orange Bowl (Miami) | 1968-69, 71, 76, 79 |
| 5 | Rose Bowl (Pasadena) | 1977, 80, 83, 87, 93 |
| 3 | Tulane Stadium (N. Orleans) | 1970, 72, 75 |
| 3 | Joe Robbie/Pro Player Stadium (Miami) | 1989, 95, 99 |
| 3 | Jack Murphy/Qualcomm Stadium (San Diego) | 1988, 98, 2003 |
| 2 | LA Memorial Coliseum | 1967, 73 |
| 2 | Tampa Stadium | 1984, 91 |
| 2 | Georgia Dome (Atlanta) | 1994, 2000 |

### 1984 SEASON

#### AFC Playoffs

First Round . . . . . . . . . . . .at *Seattle 13, *LA Raiders 7
Second Round . . . . . . . . . . . . .at Miami 31, Seattle 10
Pittsburgh 24, at Denver 17
Championship . . . . . . . . . .at Miami 45, Pittsburgh 28

#### NFC Playoffs

First Round . . . . . . . . . . .*NY Giants 16, at *LA Rams 13
Second Round . . . . . . .at San Francisco 21, NY Giants 10
Chicago 23, at Washington 19
Championship . . . . . . . .at San Francisco 23, Chicago 0

### Super Bowl XIX

Jan. 20, 1985
Stanford Stadium, Stanford, Calif.
Favorite: 49ers by 3—Attendance: 84,059

**Miami** (16-2) . . . . . . . . . . . . .10  6  0  0 — **16**
**San Francisco** (17-1) . . . . . . . .7  21  10  0 — **38**
**MVP:** San Francisco QB Joe Montana (24 for 35, 331 yds, 2 TD; 5 carries, 59 yards, 1 TD)

### 1985 SEASON

#### AFC Playoffs

First Round . . . . . . . . . .*New England 26, at *NY Jets 14
Second Round . . . . . . . . . . .at Miami 24, Cleveland 21
New England 27, at LA Raiders 20
Championship . . . . . . . . . .New England 31, at Miami 14

#### NFC Playoffs

First Round . . . . . . .at *NY Giants 17, *San Francisco 3
Second Round . . . . . . . . . . . .at LA Rams 20, Dallas 0
at Chicago 21, NY Giants 0
Championship . . . . . . . . . .at Chicago 24, LA Rams 0

### Super Bowl XX

Jan. 26, 1986
Louisiana Superdome, New Orleans
Favorite: Bears by 10—Attendance: 73,818

**Chicago Bears** (17-1) . . . . . . . .13  10  21  2 — **46**
**New England** (14-5) . . . . . . . . . .3  0  0  7 — **10**
**MVP:** Chicago DE Richard Dent (Bears defense: 7 sacks, 2 turnovers, 1 safety and gave up just 123 total yards)

### 1986 SEASON

#### AFC Playoffs

First Round . . . . . . . . . . .at *NY Jets 35, *Kansas City 15
Second Round . . . . . . .at Cleveland 23, NY Jets 20 (OT)
at Denver 22, New England 17
Championship . . . . . . .Denver 23, at Cleveland 20 (OT)

#### NFC Playoffs

First Round . . . . . . . . . . .at *Washington 19, *LA Rams 7
Second Round . . . . . . . . .Washington 27, at Chicago 13
at NY Giants 49, San Francisco 3
Championship . . . . . . . .at NY Giants 17, Washington 0

### Super Bowl XXI

Jan. 25, 1987
Rose Bowl, Pasadena
Favorite: Giants by 9½—Attendance: 101,063

**Denver** (13-5) . . . . . . . . . . . . .10  0  0  10 — **20**
**NY Giants** (16-2) . . . . . . . . . . . .7  2  17  13 — **39**
**MVP:** NY Giants QB Phil Simms (22 for 25, 268 yds, 3 TD; 3 carries, 25 yds)

## 1987 SEASON

A 24-day players' strike shortened the regular season to 15 games with replacement teams playing for three weeks.

### AFC Playoffs

First Round . . . . . . . . . .at *Houston 23, *Seattle 20 (OT)
Second Round . . . . . . .at Cleveland 38, Indianapolis 21
                                          at Denver 34, Houston 10
Championship . . . . . . . . . .at Denver 38, Cleveland 33

### NFC Playoffs

First Round . . . . . . .*Minnesota 44, at *New Orleans 10
Second Round . . . . . .Minnesota 36, at San Francisco 24
                                  Washington 21, at Chicago 17
Championship . . . . . . .at Washington 17, Minnesota 10

### Super Bowl XXII

Jan. 31, 1988
San Diego/Jack Murphy Stadium
Favorite: Broncos by 3½—Attendance: 73,302

| | | | | | |
|---|---|---|---|---|---|
| **Washington** (13-4) | . . . . . . . . . .0 | 35 | 0 | 7 | **—42** |
| **Denver** (12-4-1) | . . . . . . . . . . .10 | 0 | 0 | 0 | **—10** |

**MVP:** Washington QB Doug Williams (18 for 29, 340 yds, 4 TD, 1 Int)

## 1988 SEASON

### AFC Playoffs

First Round . . . . . . . . . . . .*Houston 24, at *Cleveland 23
Second Round . . . . . . . . . . .at Buffalo 17, Houston 10
                                          at Cincinnati 21, Seattle 13
Championship . . . . . . . . .at Cincinnati 21, Buffalo 10

### NFC Playoffs

First Round . . . . . . . . . .at *Minnesota 28, *LA Rams 17
Second Round . . . . . . .at San Francisco 34, Minnesota 9
                                  at Chicago 20, Philadelphia 12
Championship . . . . . . . .San Francisco 28, at Chicago 3

### Super Bowl XXIII

Jan. 22, 1989
Joe Robbie Stadium, Miami
Favorite: 49ers by 7—Attendance: 75,129

| | | | | | |
|---|---|---|---|---|---|
| **Cincinnati** (14-4) | . . . . . . . . . .0 | 3 | 10 | 3 | **— 16** |
| **San Francisco** (12-6) | . . . . . . . . . .3 | 0 | 3 | 14 | **— 20** |

**MVP:** San Francisco WR Jerry Rice (11 catches, 215 yds, 1 TD; 1 carry, 5 yds)

## 1989 SEASON

### AFC Playoffs

First Round . . . . . . . . . . .*Pittsburgh 26, at *Houston 23
Second Round . . . . . . . . . . .at Cleveland 34, Buffalo 30
                                          at Denver 24, Pittsburgh 23
Championship . . . . . . . . . .at Denver 37, Cleveland 21

### NFC Playoffs

First Round . . . . . . . . . . .*LA Rams 21, at *Philadelphia 7
Second Round . . . . . . . .LA Rams 19, NY Giants 13 (OT)
                                  at San Francisco 41, Minnesota 13
Championship . . . . . . . .at San Francisco 30, LA Rams 3

### Super Bowl XXIV

Jan. 28, 1990
Louisiana Superdome, New Orleans
Favorite: 49ers by 12½—Attendance: 72,919

| | | | | | |
|---|---|---|---|---|---|
| **San Francisco** (17-2) | . . . . . . . .13 | 14 | 14 | 14 | **— 55** |
| **Denver** (13-6) | . . . . . . . . . . . . .3 | 0 | 7 | 0 | **— 10** |

**MVP:** San Francisco QB Joe Montana (22 for 29, 297 yds, 5 TD)

## 1990 SEASON

### AFC Playoffs

First Round . . . . . . . . . . .at *Miami 17, *Kansas City 16
                                  at Cincinnati 41, *Houston 14
Second Round . . . . . . . . . . . .at Buffalo 44, Miami 34
                                  at LA Raiders 20, Cincinnati 10
Championship . . . . . . . . . . . .at Buffalo 51, LA Raiders 3

### NFC Playoffs

First Round . . . . . . . .*Washington 20, at *Philadelphia 6
                                  at Chicago 16, *New Orleans 6
Second Round . . . . . .at San Francisco 28, Washington 10
                                  at NY Giants 31, Chicago 3
Championship . . . . . . .NY Giants 15, at San Francisco 13

### Super Bowl XXV

Jan. 27, 1991
Tampa Stadium, Tampa
Favorite: Bills by 7—Attendance: 73,813

| | | | | | |
|---|---|---|---|---|---|
| **Buffalo** (15-4) | . . . . . . . . . . . . . .3 | 9 | 0 | 7 | **—19** |
| **NY Giants** (16-3) | . . . . . . . . . . .3 | 7 | 7 | 3 | **—20** |

**MVP:** NY Giants RB Ottis Anderson (21 carries, 102 yds, 1 TD; 1 catch, 7 yds)

## 1991 SEASON

### AFC Playoffs

First Round . . . . . . . . . .at *Kansas City 10, *LA Raiders 6
                                  at Houston 17, *NY Jets 10
Second Round . . . . . . . . . . .at Denver 26, Houston 24
                                  at Buffalo 37, Kansas City 14
Championship . . . . . . . . . . . .at Buffalo 10, Denver 7

### NFC Playoffs

First Round . . . . . . . . . . .*Atlanta 27, at New Orleans 20
                                  *Dallas 17, at *Chicago 13
Second Round . . . . . . . . . . .at Washington 24, Atlanta 7
                                  at Detroit 38, Dallas 6
Championship . . . . . . . .at Washington 41, Detroit 10

### Super Bowl XXVI

Jan. 26, 1992
Hubert Humphrey Metrodome, Minneapolis
Favorite: Redskins by 7—Attendance: 63,130

| | | | | | |
|---|---|---|---|---|---|
| **Washington** (16-2) | . . . . . . . . . . .0 | 17 | 14 | 6 | **— 37** |
| **Buffalo** (15-3) | . . . . . . . . . . .0 | 0 | 10 | 14 | **— 24** |

**MVP:** Washington QB Mark Rypien (18 for 33, 292 yds, 2 TD, 1 Int)

## 1992 SEASON

### AFC Playoffs

First Round . . . . . . . . . .at *Buffalo 41, *Houston 38 (OT)
                                  at San Diego 17, *Kansas City 0
Second Round . . . . . . . . . . .Buffalo 24, at Pittsburgh 3
                                  at Miami 31, San Diego 0
Championship . . . . . . . . . .Buffalo 29, at Miami 10

### NFC Playoffs

First Round . . . . . . . . . . .*Washington 24, at Minnesota 7
                                  *Philadelphia 36, at *New Orleans 20
Second Round . . . . .at San Francisco 20, Washington 13
                                  at Dallas 34, Philadelphia 10
Championship . . . . . . . . .Dallas 30, at San Francisco 20

### Super Bowl XXVII

Jan. 31, 1993
Rose Bowl, Pasadena
Favorite: Cowboys by 7—Attendance: 98,374

| | | | | | |
|---|---|---|---|---|---|
| **Buffalo** (14-5) | . . . . . . . . . . . .7 | 3 | 7 | 0 | **— 17** |
| **Dallas** (15-3) | . . . . . . . . . . .14 | 14 | 3 | 21 | **— 52** |

**MVP:** Dallas QB Troy Aikman (22 for 30, 273 yds, 4 TD)

## Super Bowl Playoffs (Cont.)

### 1993 SEASON

#### AFC Playoffs

First Round . . . . . . .at Kansas City 27, *Pittsburgh 24 (OT)
at *LA Raiders 42, *Denver 24
Second Round . . . . . . . . . .at Buffalo 29, LA Raiders 23
Kansas City 28, at Houston 20
Championship . . . . . . . . . .at Buffalo 30, Kansas City 13

#### NFC Playoffs

First Round . . . . . . . . . . . .*Green Bay 28, at Detroit 24
at *NY Giants 17, *Minnesota 10
Second Round . . . . . . .at San Francisco 44, NY Giants 3
at Dallas 27, Green Bay 17
Championship . . . . . . . . . .at Dallas 38, San Francisco 21

#### Super Bowl XXVIII
Jan. 30, 1994
Georgia Dome, Atlanta
Favorite: Cowboys by 10½—Attendance: 72,817

| | | | | | |
|---|---|---|---|---|---|
| **Dallas** (15-4) . . . . . . . . . . . . . .6 | 0 | 14 | 10 | — | **30** |
| **Buffalo** (14-5) . . . . . . . . . . . . . .3 | 10 | 0 | 0 | — | **13** |

**MVP:** Dallas RB Emmitt Smith (30 carries, 132 yds, 2 TDs; 4 catches, 26 yds)

### 1994 SEASON

#### AFC Playoffs

First Round . . . . . . . . . . . .at Miami 27, *Kansas City 17
at *Cleveland 20, *New England 13
Second Round . . . . . . . . . . .at Pittsburgh 29, Cleveland 9
at San Diego 22, Miami 21
Championship . . . . . . . . .San Diego 17, at Pittsburgh 13

#### NFC Playoffs

First Round . . . . . . . . . . .at *Green Bay 16, *Detroit 12
*Chicago 25, at Minnesota 18
Second Round . . . . . . .at San Francisco 44, Chicago 15
at Dallas 35, Green Bay 9
Championship . . . . . . . .at San Francisco 38, Dallas 28

#### Super Bowl XXIX
Jan. 29, 1995
Joe Robbie Stadium, Miami
Favorite: 49ers by 18 —Attendance: 74,107

| | | | | | |
|---|---|---|---|---|---|
| **San Diego** (13-5) . . . . . . . . . . . .7 | 3 | 8 | 8 | — | **26** |
| **San Francisco** (15-3) . . . . . . . . . .14 | 14 | 14 | 7 | — | **49** |

**MVP:** San Francisco QB Steve Young (24 for 36, 325 yds, 6 TD)

### 1995 SEASON

#### AFC Playoffs

First Round . . . . . . . . . . . . . . .at Buffalo 37, *Miami 22
*Indianapolis 35, at *San Diego 20
Second Round . . . . . . . . . .at Pittsburgh 40, Buffalo 21
Indianapolis 10, at Kansas City 7
Championship . . . . . . . .at Pittsburgh 20, Indianapolis 16

#### NFC Playoffs

First Round . . . . . . . . . .at *Philadelphia 58, *Detroit 37
at Green Bay 37, *Atlanta 20
Second Round . . . . . .Green Bay 27, at San Francisco 17
at Dallas 30, Philadelphia 11
Championship . . . . . . .at Dallas 38, Green Bay 27

#### Super Bowl XXX
Jan. 28, 1996
Sun Devil Stadium, Tempe, Ariz.
Favorite: Cowboys by 13½—Attendance: 76,347

| | | | | | |
|---|---|---|---|---|---|
| **Dallas** (14-4) . . . . . . . . . . .10 | 3 | 7 | 7 | — | **27** |
| **Pittsburgh** (13-5) . . . . . . . . . . .0 | 7 | 0 | 10 | — | **17** |

**MVP:** Dallas CB Larry Brown (2 interceptions for 77 yds)

### 1996 SEASON

#### AFC Playoffs

First Round . . . . . . . . . . . .*Jacksonville 30, at *Buffalo 27
at Pittsburgh 42, *Indianapolis 14
Second Round . . . . . . . .Jacksonville 30, at Denver 27
at New England 28, Pittsburgh 3
Championship . . . . . . .at New England 20, Jacksonville 6

#### NFC Playoffs

First Round . . . . . . . . . . . . .at Dallas 40, *Minnesota 15
at *San Francisco 14, *Philadelphia 0
Second Round . . . . . . .at Green Bay 35, San Francisco 14
at Carolina 26, Dallas 17
Championship . . . . . . . . . .at Green Bay 30, Carolina 13

#### Super Bowl XXXI
Jan. 26, 1997
Louisiana Superdome, New Orleans
Favorite: Packers by 14—Attendance: 72,301

| | | | | | |
|---|---|---|---|---|---|
| **New England** (13-5) . . . . . . . . .14 | 0 | 7 | 0 | — | **21** |
| **Green Bay** (15-3) . . . . . . . . . . .10 | 17 | 8 | 0 | — | **35** |

**MVP:** Green Bay KR Desmond Howard (4 kickoff returns for 154 yds and 1 TD, also 6 punt returns for 90 yds)

### 1997 SEASON

#### AFC Playoffs

First Round . . . . . . . . . .at *Denver 42, *Jacksonville 17
at New England 17, *Miami 3
Second Round . . . . . . . . . .at Pittsburgh 7, New England 6
Denver 14, at Kansas City 10
Championship . . . . . . . . . . . .Denver 24, at Pittsburgh 21

#### NFC Playoffs

First Round . . . . . . . . . . .*Minnesota 23, at NY Giants 22
at *Tampa Bay 20, *Detroit 7
Second Round . . . . . . .at San Francisco 38, Minnesota 22
at Green Bay 21, Tampa Bay 7
Championship . . . . . . .Green Bay 23, at San Francisco 10

#### Super Bowl XXXII
Jan. 25, 1998
Qualcomm Stadium, San Diego
Favorite: Packers by 11½—Attendance: 68,912

| | | | | | |
|---|---|---|---|---|---|
| **Green Bay** (15-3) . . . . . . . . . . . . .7 | 7 | 3 | 7 | — | **24** |
| **Denver** (15-4) . . . . . . . . . . . . . .7 | 10 | 7 | 7 | — | **31** |

**MVP:** Denver RB Terrell Davis (30 carries, 157 yds, 3 TD)

### 1998 SEASON

#### AFC Playoffs

First Round . . . . . . . . . . . . . . .at *Miami 24, *Buffalo 17
at Jacksonville 25, *New England 10
Second Round . . . . . . . . . . .at NY Jets 34, Jacksonville 24
at Denver 38, Miami 3
Championship . . . . . . . . .at Denver 23, NY Jets 10

#### NFC Playoffs

First Round . . . . . . .at *San Francisco 30, *Green Bay 27
*Arizona 20, at Dallas 7
Second Round . . . . . . . . .at Atlanta 20, San Francisco 18
at Minnesota 41, Arizona 21
Championship . . . . . . . .Atlanta 30, at Minnesota 27 (OT)

#### Super Bowl XXXIII
Jan. 31, 1999
Pro Player Stadium, Miami
Favorite: Broncos by 7½—Attendance: 74,803

| | | | | | |
|---|---|---|---|---|---|
| **Denver** (16-2) . . . . . . . . . . . . . .7 | 10 | 0 | 17 | — | **34** |
| **Atlanta** (16-2) . . . . . . . . . . . . . .3 | 3 | 0 | 13 | — | **19** |

**MVP:** Denver QB John Elway (18 for 29, 336 yds, 1 TD, 1 Int and 1 rushing TD)

## 1999 SEASON

### AFC Playoffs

First Round . . . . . . . . . . . .at *Tennessee 22, *Buffalo 16
*Miami 20, at Seattle 17
Second Round . . . . . . . . . .at Jacksonville 62, Miami 7
Tennessee 19, at Indianapolis 16
Championship . . . . . . . .Tennessee 33, at Jacksonville 14

### NFC Playoffs

First Round . . . . . . . . . . . .at Washington 27, *Detroit 13
at *Minnesota 27, *Dallas 10
Second Round . . . . . . . .at Tampa Bay 14, Washington 13
at St. Louis 49, Minnesota 37
Championship . . . . . . . . . .at St. Louis 11, Tampa Bay 6

### Super Bowl XXXIV
Jan. 30, 2000
Georgia Dome, Atlanta
Favorite: Rams by 7—Attendance: 72,625

| | | | | | |
|---|---|---|---|---|---|
| **St. Louis** (15-3) | 3 | 6 | 7 | 7 | **23** |
| **Tennessee** (16-3) | 0 | 0 | 6 | 10 | **16** |

**MVP:** St. Louis QB Kurt Warner (24 for 45, 414 yds, 2 TD)

## 2000 SEASON

### AFC Playoffs

First Round . . . . . . . .at Miami 23, *Indianapolis 17 (OT)
at *Baltimore 21, *Denver 3
Second Round . . . . . . . . . . . .at Oakland 27, Miami 0
Baltimore 24, at Tennessee 10
Championship . . . . . . . . . . .Baltimore 16, at Oakland 3

### NFC Playoffs

First Round . . . . . . . . .at New Orleans 31, *St. Louis 28
at *Philadelphia 21, *Tampa Bay 3
Second Round . . . . . . .at Minnesota 34, New Orleans 16
at NY Giants 20, Philadelphia 10
Championship . . . . . . . .at NY Giants 41, Minnesota 0

### Super Bowl XXXV
Jan. 28, 2001
Raymond James Stadium, Tampa
Favorite: Ravens by 3—Attendance: 71,921

| | | | | | |
|---|---|---|---|---|---|
| **Baltimore** (15-4) | 7 | 3 | 14 | 10 | **34** |
| **NY Giants** (14-4) | 0 | 0 | 7 | 0 | **7** |

**MVP:** Baltimore LB Ray Lewis (5 tackles, 4 passes defended)

## 2001 SEASON

### AFC Playoffs

First Round . . . . . . . . . . . .at Oakland 38, *NY Jets 24
*Baltimore 20, at *Miami 3
Second Round . . . .at New England 16, Oakland 13 (OT)
at Pittsburgh 27, Baltimore 10
Championship . . . .New England 24, at Pittsburgh 17

### NFC Playoffs

First Round . . . . . . . . .at Philadelphia 31, *Tampa Bay 9
at *Green Bay 25, *San Francisco 15
Second Round . . . . . . . .Philadelphia 33, at Chicago 19
at St. Louis 45, Green Bay 17
Championship . . . . . . . .at St. Louis 29, Philadelphia 24

### Super Bowl XXXVI
Feb. 3, 2002
Louisiana Superdome, New Orleans
Favorite: Rams by 14—Attendance: 72,922

| | | | | | |
|---|---|---|---|---|---|
| **St. Louis** (16-2) | 3 | 0 | 0 | 14 | **17** |
| **New England** (13-5) | 0 | 14 | 3 | 3 | **20** |

**MVP:** New England QB Tom Brady (16 for 27, 145 yds, 1 TD)

## 2002 SEASON

### AFC Playoffs

First Round . . . . . . . . . .at NY Jets 41, *Indianapolis 0
at Pittsburgh 36, *Cleveland 33
Second Round . . . .at Tennessee 34, Pittsburgh 31 (OT)
at Oakland 30, NY Jets 10
Championship . . . .at Oakland 41, Tennessee 24

### NFC Playoffs

First Round . . . . . . . . . . .*Atlanta 27, at Green Bay 7
at San Francisco 39, *NY Giants 38
Second Round . . . . . . . . .at Philadelphia 20, Atlanta 6
at Tampa Bay 31, San Francisco 6
Championship . . . .Tampa Bay 27, at Philadelphia 10

### Super Bowl XXXVII
Jan. 26, 2003
Qualcomm Stadium, San Diego
Favorite: Raiders by 3½—Attendance: 67,603

| | | | | | |
|---|---|---|---|---|---|
| **Oakland** (13-5) | 3 | 0 | 6 | 12 | **21** |
| **Tampa Bay** (14-4) | 3 | 17 | 14 | 14 | **48** |

**MVP:** Tampa Bay S Dexter Jackson (2 interceptions for 34 yards)

## 2003 SEASON

### AFC Playoffs

First Round . . . . . . . . . . .*Tennessee 20, at Baltimore 17
at Indianapolis 41, *Denver 10
Second Round . . . . . .at New England 17, Tennessee 14
Indianapolis 38, at Kansas City 31
Championship . . . .at New England 24, Indianapolis 14

### NFC Playoffs

First Round . . . . . . . . . . . .at Carolina 29, *Dallas 10
at Green Bay 33, Seattle 27 (OT)
Second Round . . . . . .Carolina 29, at St. Louis 23 (2OT)
at Philadelphia 20, Green Bay 17 (OT)
Championship . . . . . . . .Carolina 14, at Philadelphia 3

### Super Bowl XXXVIII
Feb. 1, 2004
Reliant Stadium, Houston
Favorite: Patriots by 7—Attendance: 71,525

| | | | | | |
|---|---|---|---|---|---|
| **Carolina** (14-5) | 0 | 10 | 0 | 19 | **29** |
| **New England** (16-2) | 0 | 14 | 0 | 18 | **32** |

**MVP:** New England QB Tom Brady (32 for 48, 354 yds, 3 TD, 1 Int)

## 2004 SEASON

### AFC Playoffs

First Round . . . . . . . .*NY Jets 20, at San Diego 17 (OT)
at Indianapolis 49, *Denver 24
Second Round . . . . . .at Pittsburgh 20, NY Jets 17 (OT)
at New England 20, Indianapolis 3
Championship . . . . . .New England 41, at Pittsburgh 27

### NFC Playoffs

First Round . . . . . . . . . . . .*St. Louis 27, at Seattle 20
*Minnesota 31, at Green Bay 17
Second Round . . . . . . . . . .at Atlanta 47, St. Louis 17
at Philadelphia 27, Minnesota 14
Championship . . . . . . . .at Philadelphia 27, Atlanta 10

### Super Bowl XXXIX
Feb. 6, 2005
ALLTEL Stadium, Jacksonville
Favorite: Patriots by 7—Attendance: 78,125

| | | | | | |
|---|---|---|---|---|---|
| **New England** (16-2) | 0 | 7 | 7 | 10 | **24** |
| **Philadelphia** (15-3) | 0 | 7 | 7 | 7 | **21** |

**MVP:** New England WR Deion Branch (11 catches, 133 yds)

## Before the Super Bowl

The first NFL champion was the Akron Pros in 1920, when the league was called the American Professional Football Association (APFA) and the title went to the team with the best regular season record. The APFA changed its name to the National Football League in 1922.

The first playoff game with the championship at stake came in 1932, when the Chicago Bears (6-1-6) and Portsmouth (Ohio) Spartans (6-1-4) ended the regular season tied for first place. The Bears won the subsequent playoff, 9-0. Due to a snowstorm and cold weather, the game was moved from Wrigley Field to an improvised 80-yard dirt field at Chicago Stadium, making it the first indoor title game as well.

The NFL Championship Game decided the league title until the NFL merged with the AFL and the first Super Bowl was played following the 1966 season.

## NFL Champions, 1920-32

Winning player-coaches noted by position.

**Multiple winners:** Canton-Cleveland Bulldogs and Green Bay (3); Chicago Staleys/Bears (2).

| Year | Champion | Head Coach | Year | Champion | Head Coach |
|------|----------|------------|------|----------|------------|
| 1920 | Akron Pros | Fritz Pollard, HB & Elgie Tobin, QB | 1927 | New York Giants | Earl Potteiger, QB |
| | | | 1928 | Providence Steam Roller | Jimmy Conzelman, HB |
| 1921 | Chicago Staleys | George Halas, E | 1929 | Green Bay Packers | Curly Lambeau, QB |
| 1922 | Canton Bulldogs | Guy Chamberlin, E | 1930 | Green Bay Packers | Curly Lambeau |
| 1923 | Canton Bulldogs | Guy Chamberlin, E | 1931 | Green Bay Packers | Curly Lambeau |
| 1924 | Cleveland Bulldogs | Guy Chamberlin, E | 1932 | Chicago Bears | Ralph Jones |
| 1925 | Chicago Cardinals | Norm Barry | (Bears beat Portsmouth-OH in playoff, 9-0) | | |
| 1926 | Frankford Yellow Jackets | Guy Chamberlin, E | | | |

## NFL-NFC Championship Game

NFL Championship games from 1933-69 and NFC Championship games since the completion of the NFL-AFL merger following the 1969 season.

**Multiple winners:** Green Bay (10); Dallas (8); Chicago Bears and Washington (7); NY Giants (6); San Francisco, Cle-LA-St.L Rams and Philadelphia (5); Cleveland Browns, Detroit and Minnesota (4); Baltimore Colts (3).

| Season | Winner | Head Coach | Score | Loser | Head Coach | Site |
|--------|--------|------------|-------|-------|------------|------|
| 1933 | Chicago Bears | George Halas | 23-21 | New York | Steve Owen | Chicago |
| 1934 | New York | Steve Owen | 30-13 | Chicago Bears | George Halas | New York |
| 1935 | Detroit | Potsy Clark | 26-7 | New York | Steve Owen | Detroit |
| 1936 | Green Bay | Curly Lambeau | 21-6 | Boston Redskins | Ray Flaherty | New York |
| 1937 | Washington Redskins | Ray Flaherty | 28-21 | Chicago Bears | George Halas | Chicago |
| 1938 | New York | Steve Owen | 23-17 | Green Bay | Curly Lambeau | New York |
| 1939 | Green Bay | Curly Lambeau | 27-0 | New York | Steve Owen | Milwaukee |
| 1940 | Chicago Bears | George Halas | 73-0 | Washington | Ray Flaherty | Washington |
| 1941 | Chicago Bears | George Halas | 37-9 | New York | Steve Owen | Chicago |
| 1942 | Washington | Ray Flaherty | 14-6 | Chicago Bears | Hunk Anderson & Luke Johnsos | Washington |
| 1943 | Chicago Bears | Hunk Anderson & Luke Johnsos | 41-21 | Washington | Arthur Bergman | Chicago |
| 1944 | Green Bay | Curly Lambeau | 14-7 | New York | Steve Owen | New York |
| 1945 | Cleveland Rams | Adam Walsh | 15-14 | Washington | Dudley DeGroot | Cleveland |
| 1946 | Chicago Bears | George Halas | 24-14 | New York | Steve Owen | New York |
| 1947 | Chicago Cardinals | Jimmy Conzelman | 28-21 | Philadelphia | Greasy Neale | Chicago |
| 1948 | Philadelphia | Greasy Neale | 7-0 | Chicago Cardinals | Jimmy Conzelman | Philadelphia |
| 1949 | Philadelphia | Greasy Neale | 14-0 | Los Angeles Rams | Clark Shaughnessy | Los Angeles |
| 1950 | Cleveland Browns | Paul Brown | 30-28 | Los Angeles | Joe Stydahar | Cleveland |
| 1951 | Los Angeles | Joe Stydahar | 24-17 | Cleveland | Paul Brown | Los Angeles |
| 1952 | Detroit | Buddy Parker | 17-7 | Cleveland | Paul Brown | Cleveland |
| 1953 | Detroit | Buddy Parker | 17-16 | Cleveland | Paul Brown | Detroit |
| 1954 | Cleveland | Paul Brown | 56-10 | Detroit | Buddy Parker | Cleveland |
| 1955 | Cleveland | Paul Brown | 38-14 | Los Angeles | Sid Gillman | Los Angeles |
| 1956 | New York | Jim Lee Howell | 47-7 | Chicago Bears | Paddy Driscoll | New York |
| 1957 | Detroit | George Wilson | 59-14 | Cleveland | Paul Brown | Detroit |
| 1958 | Balt. Colts | Weeb Ewbank | 23-17* | New York | Jim Lee Howell | New York |
| 1959 | Balt. Colts | Weeb Ewbank | 31-16 | New York | Jim Lee Howell | Baltimore |
| 1960 | Philadelphia | Buck Shaw | 17-13 | Green Bay | Vince Lombardi | Philadelphia |
| 1961 | Green Bay | Vince Lombardi | 37-0 | New York | Allie Sherman | Green Bay |
| 1962 | Green Bay | Vince Lombardi | 16-7 | New York | Allie Sherman | New York |
| 1963 | Chicago | George Halas | 14-10 | New York | Allie Sherman | Chicago |
| 1964 | Cleveland | Blanton Collier | 27-0 | Balt. Colts | Don Shula | Cleveland |
| 1965 | Green Bay | Vince Lombardi | 23-12 | Cleveland | Blanton Collier | Green Bay |
| 1966 | Green Bay | Vince Lombardi | 34-27 | Dallas | Tom Landry | Dallas |
| 1967 | Green Bay | Vince Lombardi | 21-17 | Dallas | Tom Landry | Green Bay |

| Season | Winner | Head Coach | Score | Loser | Head Coach | Site |
|--------|--------|-----------|-------|-------|-----------|------|
| 1968 | Balt. Colts | Don Shula | 34-0 | Cleveland | Blanton Collier | Cleveland |
| 1969 | Minnesota | Bud Grant | 27-7 | Cleveland | Blanton Collier | Minnesota |
| 1970 | Dallas | Tom Landry | 17-10 | San Francisco | Dick Nolan | San Francisco |
| 1971 | Dallas | Tom Landry | 14-3 | SanFrancisco | Dick Nolan | Dallas |
| 1972 | Washington | George Allen | 26-3 | Dallas | Tom Landry | Washington |
| 1973 | Minnesota | Bud Grant | 27-10 | Dallas | Tom Landry | Dallas |
| 1974 | Minnesota | Bud Grant | 14-10 | Los Angeles | Chuck Knox | Minnesota |
| 1975 | Dallas | Tom Landry | 37-7 | Los Angeles | Chuck Knox | Los Angeles |
| 1976 | Minnesota | Bud Grant | 24-13 | Los Angeles | Chuck Knox | Minnesota |
| 1977 | Dallas | Tom Landry | 23-6 | Minnesota | Bud Grant | Dallas |
| 1978 | Dallas | Tom Landry | 28-0 | Los Angeles | Ray Malavasi | Los Angele |
| 1979 | Los Angeles | Ray Malavasi | 9-0 | Tampa Bay | John McKay | Tampa Bay |
| 1980 | Philadelphia | Dick Vermeil | 20-7 | Dallas | Tom Landry | Philadelphia |
| 1981 | San Francisco | Bill Walsh | 28-27 | Dallas | Tom Landry | San Francisco |
| 1982 | Washington | Joe Gibbs | 31-17 | Dallas | Tom Landry | Washington |
| 1983 | Washington | Joe Gibbs | 24-21 | San Francisco | Bill Walsh | Washington |
| 1984 | San Francisco | Bill Walsh | 23-0 | Chicago | Mike Ditka | San Francisco |
| 1985 | Chicago | Mike Ditka | 24-0 | Los Angeles | John Robinson | Chicago |
| 1986 | New York | Bill Parcells | 17-0 | Washington | Joe Gibbs | New York |
| 1987 | Washington | Joe Gibbs | 17-10 | Minnesota | Jerry Burns | Washington |
| 1988 | San Francisco | Bill Walsh | 28-3 | Chicago | Mike Ditka | Chicago |
| 1989 | San Francisco | George Seifert | 30-3 | Los Angeles | John Robinson | San Francisco |
| 1990 | New York | Bill Parcells | 15-13 | San Francisco | George Seifert | San Francisco |
| 1991 | Washington | Joe Gibbs | 41-10 | Detroit | Wayne Fontes | Washington |
| 1992 | Dallas | Jimmy Johnson | 30-20 | San Francisco | George Seifert | San Francisco |
| 1993 | Dallas | Jimmy Johnson | 38-21 | San Francisco | George Seifert | Dallas |
| 1994 | San Francisco | George Seifert | 38-28 | Dallas | Barry Switzer | San Francisco |
| 1995 | Dallas | Barry Switzer | 38-27 | Green Bay | Mike Holmgren | Dallas |
| 1996 | Green Bay | Mike Holmgren | 30-13 | Carolina | Dom Capers | Green Bay |
| 1997 | Green Bay | Mike Holmgren | 23-10 | San Francisco | Steve Mariucci | San Francisco |
| 1998 | Atlanta | Dan Reeves | 30-27* | Minnesota | Dennis Green | Minnesota |
| 1999 | St. Louis | Dick Vermeil | 11-6 | Tampa Bay | Tony Dungy | St. Louis |
| 2000 | New York | Jim Fassel | 41-0 | Minnesota | Dennis Green | New York |
| 2001 | St. Louis | Mike Martz | 29-24 | Philadelphia | Andy Reid | St. Louis |
| 2002 | Tampa Bay | Jon Gruden | 27-10 | Philadelphia | Andy Reid | Philadelphia |
| 2003 | Carolina | John Fox | 14-3 | Philadelphia | Andy Reid | Philadelphia |
| 2004 | Philadelphia | Andy Reid | 27-10 | Atlanta | Jim Mora Jr. | Philadelphia |

*Sudden death overtime

## NFL-NFC Championship Game Appearances

| App | | W | L | Pct | PF | PA | App | | W | L | Pct | PF | PA |
|-----|---|---|---|-----|----|----|-----|---|---|---|-----|----|----|
| 17 | NY Giants | 6 | 11 | .353 | 281 | 322 | 9 | Philadelphia | 5 | 4 | .556 | 143 | 128 |
| 16 | Dallas Cowboys | 8 | 8 | .500 | 361 | 319 | 8 | Minnesota | 4 | 4 | .500 | 135 | 151 |
| 14 | Cle-LA-St.L Rams | 5 | 9 | .357 | 163 | 300 | 6 | Detroit | 4 | 2 | .667 | 139 | 141 |
| 13 | Green Bay Packers | 10 | 3 | .769 | 303 | 177 | 4 | Baltimore Colts | 3 | 1 | .750 | 88 | 60 |
| 13 | Chicago Bears | 7 | 6 | .538 | 286 | 245 | 3 | Tampa Bay | 1 | 2 | .333 | 33 | 30 |
| 12 | Boston-Wash. Redskins | 7 | 5 | .583 | 222 | 255 | 2 | Chicago Cardinals | 1 | 1 | .500 | 28 | 28 |
| 12 | San Francisco | 5 | 7 | .417 | 245 | 222 | 2 | Carolina | 1 | 1 | .500 | 27 | 33 |
| 11 | Cleveland Browns | 4 | 7 | .364 | 224 | 253 | 2 | Atlanta | 1 | 1 | .500 | 40 | 54 |

## AFL-AFC Championship Game

AFL Championship games from 1960-69 and AFC Championship games since the completion of the NFL-AFL merger following the 1969 season.

**Multiple winners**: Buffalo and Denver (6); Miami, Oakland-LA Raiders, New England and Pittsburgh (5); Dallas Texans-KC Chiefs and Houston Oilers-Tennessee Titans (3); Cincinnati and San Diego (2).

| Season | Winner | Head Coach | Score | Loser | Head Coach | Site |
|--------|--------|-----------|-------|-------|-----------|------|
| 1960 | Houston | Lou Rymkus | 24-16 | LA Chargers | Sid Gillman | Houston |
| 1961 | Houston | Wally Lemm | 10-3 | SD Chargers | Sid Gillman | San Diego |
| 1962 | Dallas | Hank Stram | 20-17* | Houston | Pop Ivy | Houston |
| 1963 | San Diego | Sid Gillman | 51-10 | Boston Patriots | Mike Holovak | San Diego |
| 1964 | Buffalo | Lou Saban | 20-7 | SanDiego | Sid Gillman | Buffalo |
| 1965 | Buffalo | Lou Saban | 23-0 | San Diego | Sid Gillman | San Diego |
| 1966 | Kansas City | Hank Stram | 31-7 | Buffalo | Joe Collier | Buffalo |
| 1967 | Oakland | John Rauch | 40-7 | Houston | Wally Lemm | Oakland |
| 1968 | NY Jets | Weeb Ewbank | 27-23 | Oakland | John Rauch | New York |
| 1969 | Kansas City | Hank Stram | 17-7 | Oakland | John Madden | Oakland |
| 1970 | Balt. Colts | Don McCafferty | 27-17 | Oakland | John Madden | Baltimore |
| 1971 | Miami | Don Shula | 21-0 | Balt. Colts | Don McCafferty | Miami |
| 1972 | Miami | Don Shula | 21-17 | Pittsburgh | Chuck Noll | Pittsburgh |

## AFL-AFC Championship Game (Cont.)

| Season | Winner | Head Coach | Score | Loser | Head Coach | Site |
|---|---|---|---|---|---|---|
| 1973 | Miami | Don Shula | 27-10 | Oakland | John Madden | Miami |
| 1974 | Pittsburgh | Chuck Noll | 24-13 | Oakland | John Madden | Oakland |
| 1975 | Pittsburgh | Chuck Noll | 16-10 | Oakland | John Madden | Pittsburgh |
| 1976 | Oakland | John Madden | 24-7 | Pittsburgh | Chuck Noll | Oakland |
| 1977 | Denver | Red Miller | 20-17 | Oakland | John Madden | Denver |
| 1978 | Pittsburgh | Chuck Noll | 34-5 | Houston | Bum Phillips | Pittsburgh |
| 1979 | Pittsburgh | Chuck Noll | 27-13 | Houston | Bum Phillips | Pittsburgh |
| 1980 | Oakland | Tom Flores | 34-27 | San Diego | Don Coryell | San Diego |
| 1981 | Cincinnati | Forrest Gregg | 27-7 | San Diego | Don Coryell | Cincinnati |
| 1982 | Miami | Don Shula | 14-0 | NY Jets | Walt Michaels | Miami |
| 1983 | LA Raiders | Tom Flores | 30-14 | Seattle | Chuck Knox | Los Angeles |
| 1984 | Miami | Don Shula | 45-28 | Pittsburgh | Chuck Noll | Miami |
| 1985 | New England | Raymond Berry | 31-14 | Miami | Don Shula | Miami |
| 1986 | Denver | Dan Reeves | 23-20* | Cleveland | Marty Schottenheimer | Cleveland |
| 1987 | Denver | Dan Reeves | 38-33 | Cleveland | Marty Schottenheimer | Denver |
| 1988 | Cincinnati | Sam Wyche | 21-10 | Buffalo | Marv Levy | Cincinnati |
| 1989 | Denver | Dan Reeves | 37-21 | Cleveland | Bud Carson | Denver |
| 1990 | Buffalo | Marv Levy | 51-3 | LA Raiders | Art Shell | Buffalo |
| 1991 | Buffalo | Marv Levy | 10-7 | Denver | Dan Reeves | Buffalo |
| 1992 | Buffalo | Marv Levy | 29-10 | Miami | Don Shula | Miami |
| 1993 | Buffalo | Marv Levy | 30-13 | Kansas City | Marty Schottenheimer | Buffalo |
| 1994 | San Diego | Bobby Ross | 17-13 | Pittsburgh | Bill Cowher | Pittsburgh |
| 1995 | Pittsburgh | Bill Cowher | 20-16 | Indianapolis | Ted Marchibroda | Pittsburgh |
| 1996 | New England | Bill Parcells | 20-6 | Jacksonville | Tom Coughlin | New England |
| 1997 | Denver | Mike Shanahan | 24-21 | Pittsburgh | Bill Cowher | Pittsburgh |
| 1998 | Denver | Mike Shanahan | 23-10 | NY Jets | Bill Parcells | Denver |
| 1999 | Tennessee | Jeff Fisher | 33-14 | Jacksonville | Tom Coughlin | Jacksonville |
| 2000 | Balt. Ravens | Brian Billick | 16-3 | Oakland | Jon Gruden | Oakland |
| 2001 | New England | Bill Belichick | 24-17 | Pittsburgh | Bill Cowher | Pittsburgh |
| 2002 | Oakland | Bill Callahan | 41-24 | Tennessee | Jeff Fisher | Oakland |
| 2003 | New England | Bill Belichick | 24-14 | Indianapolis | Tony Dungy | New England |
| 2004 | New England | Bill Belichick | 41-27 | Pittsburgh | Bill Cowher | Pittsburgh |

*Sudden death overtime

### AFL-AFC Championship Game Appearances

| App | | W | L | Pct | PF | PA | App | | W | L | Pct | PF | PA |
|---|---|---|---|---|---|---|---|---|---|---|---|---|---|
| 14 | Oakland-LA Raiders | 5 | 9 | .357 | 272 | 304 | 4 | Dallas Texans/KC Chiefs | 3 | 1 | .750 | 81 | 61 |
| 11 | Pittsburgh | 5 | 6 | .455 | 224 | 212 | 4 | Baltimore-Indy Colts | 1 | 3 | .250 | 57 | 82 |
| 8 | Buffalo | 6 | 2 | .750 | 180 | 92 | 3 | NY Jets | 1 | 2 | .333 | 37 | 60 |
| 8 | Houston Oilers/Ten. Titans | 3 | 5 | .375 | 133 | 195 | 3 | Cleveland | 0 | 3 | .000 | 74 | 98 |
| 8 | LA-San Diego Chargers | 2 | 6 | .250 | 128 | 161 | 2 | Cincinnati | 2 | 0 | 1.000 | 48 | 17 |
| 7 | Denver | 6 | 1 | .857 | 172 | 132 | 2 | Jacksonville | 0 | 2 | .000 | 20 | 53 |
| 7 | Miami | 5 | 2 | .714 | 152 | 115 | 1 | Baltimore Ravens | 1 | 0 | 1.000 | 16 | 3 |
| 6 | Boston-NE Patriots | 5 | 1 | .833 | 150 | 129 | 1 | Seattle | 0 | 1 | .000 | 14 | 30 |

## NFL Divisional Champions

The NFL adopted divisional play for the first time in 1967, splitting both conferences into two four-team divisions—the Capitol and Century divisions in the East and the Central and Coastal divisions in the West. A merger with the AFL in 1970 increased NFL membership to 26 teams and made it necessary for realignment. Two 13-team conferences—the AFC and NFC—were formed by moving established NFL clubs in Baltimore, Cleveland and Pittsburgh to the AFC and rearranging both conferences into Eastern, Central and Western divisions. Expansion has since increased the league to 32 teams (beginning in 2002) with four NFC divisions and four AFC divisions, all with four teams each.

Division champions are listed below; teams that went on to win the Super Bowl are in **bold** type. Note that in the 1980 season, Oakland won the Super Bowl as a wild card team, as did Denver in 1997 and Baltimore in 2000; and in 1982, the players' strike shortened the regular season to nine games and eliminated divisional play for one season.

**Multiple champions** (since 1970): **AFC**—Pittsburgh (17); Miami and Oakland-LA Raiders (12); Denver (9); Baltimore-Indianapolis Colts (8); Buffalo and New England (7); Cleveland and San Diego (6); Cincinnati and Kansas City (5); Houston Oilers-Tennessee Titans (4); Jacksonville, NY Jets and Seattle (2). **NFC**—San Francisco (17); Dallas (15); Minnesota (14); LA-St. Louis Rams (11); Chicago and Green Bay (7); Philadelphia and Washington (6); NY Giants (5); Tampa Bay (4); Atlanta and Detroit (3); Carolina, New Orleans and St. Louis Cardinals (2).

| | American Football League | | | National Football League | |
|---|---|---|---|---|---|
| Season | East | West | Season | East | West |
| 1966 | Buffalo | Kansas City | 1966 | Dallas | **Green Bay** |

| Season | East | West | Season | Capitol | Century | Central | Coastal |
|---|---|---|---|---|---|---|---|
| 1967 | Houston | Oakland | 1967 | Dallas | Cleveland | **Green Bay** | LA Rams |
| 1968 | **NY Jets** | Oakland | 1968 | Dallas | Cleveland | Minnesota | Baltimore |
| 1969 | NY Jets | Oakland | 1969 | Dallas | Cleveland | Minnesota | LA Rams |

**Note:** Kansas City, an AFL second-place team, won the Super Bowl in the 1969 season.

### American Football Conference

| Season | East | Central | West |
|---|---|---|---|
| 1970 | **Balt. Colts** | Cincinnati | Oakland |
| 1971 | Miami | Cleveland | Kansas City |
| 1972 | **Miami** | Pittsburgh | Oakland |
| 1973 | **Miami** | Cincinnati | Oakland |
| 1974 | Miami | **Pittsburgh** | Oakland |
| 1975 | Balt.Colts | **Pittsburgh** | Oakland |
| 1976 | Balt.Colts | Pittsburgh | **Oakland** |
| 1977 | Balt.Colts | Pittsburgh | Denver |
| 1978 | New England | **Pittsburgh** | Denver |
| 1979 | Miami | **Pittsburgh** | San Diego |
| 1980 | Buffalo | Cleveland | San Diego |
| 1981 | Miami | Cincinnati | San Diego |
| 1982 | — | — | — |
| 1983 | Miami | Pittsburgh | **LA Raiders** |
| 1984 | Miami | Pittsburgh | Denver |
| 1985 | Miami | Cleveland | LA Raiders |
| 1986 | New England | Cleveland | Denver |
| 1987 | Indianapolis | Cleveland | Denver |
| 1988 | Buffalo | Cincinnati | Seattle |
| 1989 | Buffalo | Cleveland | Denver |
| 1990 | Buffalo | Cincinnati | LA Raiders |
| 1991 | Buffalo | Houston | Denver |
| 1992 | Miami | Pittsburgh | San Diego |
| 1993 | Buffalo | Houston | Kansas City |
| 1994 | Miami | Pittsburgh | San Diego |
| 1995 | Buffalo | Pittsburgh | Kansas City |
| 1996 | New England | Pittsburgh | Denver |
| 1997 | New England | Pittsburgh | Kansas City |
| 1998 | NY Jets | Jacksonville | **Denver** |
| 1999 | Indianapolis | Jacksonville | Seattle |
| 2000 | Miami | Tennessee | Oakland |
| 2001 | **New England** | Pittsburgh | Oakland |

| Season | East | North | South | West |
|---|---|---|---|---|
| 2002 | NY Jets | Pittsburgh | Tennessee | Oakland |
| 2003 | **New Eng.** | Baltimore | Indianapolis | Kansas City |
| 2004 | **New Eng.** | Pittsburgh | Indianapolis | San Diego |

### National Football Conference

| Season | East | Central | West |
|---|---|---|---|
| 1970 | Dallas | Minnesota | San Francisco |
| 1971 | **Dallas** | Minnesota | San Francisco |
| 1972 | Washington | Green Bay | San Francisco |
| 1973 | Dallas | Minnesota | LA Rams |
| 1974 | St. Louis | Minnesota | LA Rams |
| 1975 | St. Louis | Minnesota | LA Rams |
| 1976 | Dallas | Minnesota | LA Rams |
| 1977 | **Dallas** | Minnesota | LA Rams |
| 1978 | Dallas | Minnesota | LA Rams |
| 1979 | Dallas | Tampa Bay | LA Rams |
| 1980 | Philadelphia | Minnesota | Atlanta |
| 1981 | Dallas | Tampa Bay | **San Francisco** |
| 1982 | — | — | — |
| 1983 | Washington | Detroit | San Francisco |
| 1984 | Washington | Chicago | **San Francisco** |
| 1985 | Dallas | **Chicago** | LA Rams |
| 1986 | **NY Giants** | Chicago | San Francisco |
| 1987 | **Washington** | Chicago | San Francisco |
| 1988 | Philadelphia | Chicago | **San Francisco** |
| 1989 | NY Giants | Minnesota | **San Francisco** |
| 1990 | **NY Giants** | Chicago | San Francisco |
| 1991 | **Washington** | Detroit | New Orleans |
| 1992 | **Dallas** | Minnesota | San Francisco |
| 1993 | **Dallas** | Detroit | San Francisco |
| 1994 | Dallas | Minnesota | **San Francisco** |
| 1995 | **Dallas** | Green Bay | San Francisco |
| 1996 | Dallas | **Green Bay** | Carolina |
| 1997 | NY Giants | Green Bay | San Francisco |
| 1998 | Dallas | Minnesota | Atlanta |
| 1999 | Washington | Tampa Bay | **St. Louis** |
| 2000 | NY Giants | Minnesota | New Orleans |
| 2001 | Philadelphia | Chicago | St. Louis |

| Season | East | North | South | West |
|---|---|---|---|---|
| 2002 | Philadelphia | Green Bay | **Tampa Bay** | San Fran. |
| 2003 | Philadelphia | Green Bay | Carolina | St. Louis |
| 2004 | Philadelphia | Green Bay | Atlanta | Seattle |

## Overall Postseason Games

The postseason records of all NFL teams, ranked by number of playoff games participated in from 1933 through the 2004-05 postseason.

| Gm | | W | L | Pct | PF | PA |
|---|---|---|---|---|---|---|
| 54 | Dallas Cowboys | 32 | 22 | .593 | 1281 | 1008 |
| 43 | Oakland-LA Raiders | 25 | 18 | .581 | 1028 | 797 |
| 43 | Cle-LA-St.L Rams | 19 | 24 | .442 | 770 | 944 |
| 42 | San Francisco 49ers | 25 | 17 | .595 | 1044 | 853 |
| 42 | Pittsburgh Steelers | 24 | 18 | .571 | 959 | 866 |
| 42 | Minnesota Vikings | 18 | 24 | .429 | 824 | 957 |
| 39 | Miami Dolphins | 20 | 19 | .513 | 780 | 848 |
| 38 | Green Bay Packers | 24 | 14 | .632 | 888 | 723 |
| 37 | Boston-Wash. Redskins | 22 | 15 | .595 | 778 | 642 |
| 37 | New York Giants | 16 | 21 | .432 | 647 | 699 |
| 32 | Philadelphia Eagles | 16 | 16 | .500 | 606 | 561 |
| 31 | Houston Oilers/Ten. Titans | 14 | 17 | .452 | 563 | 732 |
| 31 | Cleveland Browns | 11 | 20 | .355 | 629 | 728 |
| 30 | Denver Broncos | 16 | 14 | .533 | 650 | 747 |
| 29 | Buffalo Bills | 14 | 15 | .483 | 681 | 658 |
| 29 | Chicago Bears | 14 | 15 | .483 | 598 | 585 |
| 28 | Balt-Indianapolis Colts | 13 | 15 | .464 | 538 | 581 |
| 26 | Boston-NE Patriots | 16 | 10 | .615 | 528 | 512 |
| 20 | Dallas Texans/KC Chiefs | 8 | 12 | .400 | 332 | 422 |
| 19 | LA-San Diego Chargers | 7 | 12 | .368 | 349 | 448 |
| 18 | New York Jets | 8 | 10 | .444 | 372 | 352 |
| 17 | Detroit Lions | 7 | 10 | .412 | 365 | 404 |
| 14 | Atlanta Falcons | 6 | 8 | .429 | 298 | 331 |
| 13 | Tampa Bay Buccaneers | 6 | 7 | .462 | 206 | 238 |
| 12 | Cincinnati Bengals | 5 | 7 | .417 | 246 | 257 |
| 10 | Seattle Seahawks | 3 | 7 | .300 | 192 | 219 |
| 8 | Jacksonville Jaguars | 4 | 4 | .500 | 208 | 200 |
| 7 | Baltimore Ravens | 5 | 2 | .714 | 142 | 73 |
| 7 | Chi-St.L.-Ari. Cardinals | 2 | 5 | .286 | 122 | 182 |
| 6 | Carolina Panthers | 4 | 2 | .667 | 140 | 115 |
| 6 | New Orleans Saints | 1 | 5 | .167 | 103 | 185 |

## Champions of Leagues That No Longer Exist

No professional league in American sports has had to contend with more pretenders to the throne than the NFL. Eight times in nine decades, a rival league has risen up to challenge the NFL and seven of them went under in less than five seasons. Only the fourth American Football League (1960-69) succeeded, forcing the older league to sue for peace and a full partnership in 1966.

Of the seven leagues that didn't make it, only the All-America Football Conference (1946-49) lives on—the Cleveland Browns and San Francisco 49ers joined the NFL after the AAFC folded in 1949. The champions of leagues past are listed below.

### American Football League I

| Year | | Head Coach |
|------|------|------|
| 1926 | Philadelphia Quakers (8-2) | Bob Folwell |

**Note:** Philadelphia was challenged to a postseason game by the 7th place New York Giants (8-4-1) of the NFL. The Giants won, 31-0, in a snowstorm.

### American Football League II

| Year | | Head Coach |
|------|------|------|
| 1936 | Boston Shamrocks (8-3) | |
| 1937 | Los Angeles Bulldogs (9-0) | Gus Henderson |

**Note:** Boston was scheduled to play 2nd place Cleveland (5-2-2) in the '36 championship game, but the Shamrock players refused to participate because they were owed pay for past games.

### American Football League III

| Year | | Head Coach |
|------|------|------|
| 1940 | Columbus Bullies (8-1-1) | Phil Bucklew |
| 1941 | Columbus Bullies (5-1-2) | Phil Bucklew |

### All-America Football Conference

| Year | Winner | Head Coach | Score | Loser | Head Coach | Site |
|------|--------|------------|-------|-------|------------|------|
| 1946 | Cleveland Browns | Paul Brown | 14-9 | NY Yankees | Ray Flaherty | Cleveland |
| 1947 | Cleveland Browns | Paul Brown | 14-3 | NY Yankees | Ray Flaherty | New York |
| 1948 | Cleveland Browns | Paul Brown | 49-7 | Buffalo Bills | Red Dawson | Cleveland |
| 1949 | Cleveland Browns | Paul Brown | 21-7 | S.F. 49ers | Buck Shaw | Cleveland |

### World Football League

| Year | Winner | Head Coach | Score | Loser | Head Coach | Site |
|------|--------|------------|-------|-------|------------|------|
| 1974 | Birmingham Americans | Jack Gotta | 22-21 | Florida Blazers | Jack Pardee | Birmingham |

### United States Football League

| Year | Winner | Head Coach | Score | Loser | Head Coach | Site |
|------|--------|------------|-------|-------|------------|------|
| 1983 | Michigan Panthers | Jim Stanley | 24-22 | Philadelphia Stars | Jim Mora | Denver |
| 1984 | Philadelphia Stars | Jim Mora | 23-3 | Arizona Wranglers | George Allen | Tampa |
| 1985 | Baltimore Stars | Jim Mora | 28-24 | Oakland Invaders | Charlie Sumner | E. Rutherford |

### XFL

| Year | Winner | Head Coach | Score | Loser | Head Coach | Site |
|------|--------|------------|-------|-------|------------|------|
| 2001 | Los Angeles Xtreme | Al Luginbill | 38-6 | San Fran. Demons | Jim Skipper | Los Angeles |

### Defunct Leagues

**AFL I** (1926): Boston Bulldogs, Brooklyn Horseman, Chicago Bulls, Cleveland Panthers, Los Angeles Wildcats, New York Yankees, Newark Bears, Philadelphia Quakers, Rock Island Independents.

**AFL II** (1936-37): Boston Shamrocks (1936-37); Brooklyn Tigers (1936); Cincinnati Bengals (1937); Cleveland Rams (1936); Los Angeles Bulldogs (1937); New York Yankees (1936-37); Pittsburgh Americans (1936-37); Rochester Tigers (1936-37).

**AFL III** (1940-41): Boston Bears (1940); Buffalo Indians (1940-41); Cincinnati Bengals (1940-41); Columbus Bullies (1940-41); Milwaukee Chiefs (1940-41); New York Yankees (1940) renamed Americans (1941).

**AAFC** (1946-49): Brooklyn Dodgers (1946-48) merged to become Brooklyn-New York Yankees (1949); Buffalo Bisons (1946) renamed Bills (1947-49); Chicago Rockets (1946-48) renamed Hornets (1949); Cleveland Browns (1946-49); Los Angeles Dons (1946-49); Miami Seahawks (1946) became Baltimore Colts (1947-49); New York Yankees (1946-48) merged to become Brooklyn-New York Yankees (1949); San Francisco 49ers (1946-49).

**WFL** (1974-75): Birmingham Americans (1974) renamed Vulcans (1975); Chicago Fire (1974) renamed Winds (1975); Detroit Wheels (1974); Florida Blazers (1974) became San Antonio Wings (1975); The Hawaiians (1974-75); Houston Texans (1974) became Shreveport (La.) Steamer (1974-75); Jacksonville Sharks (1974) renamed Express (1975); Memphis Southmen (1974) also known as Grizzlies (1975); New York Stars (1974) became Charlotte Hornets (1974-75); Philadelphia Bell (1974-75); Portland Storm (1974) renamed Thunder (1975); Southern California Sun (1974-75).

**USFL** (1983-85): Arizona Wranglers (1983-84) merged with Oklahoma to become Arizona Outlaws (1985); Birmingham Stallions (1983-85); Boston Breakers (1983) became New Orleans Breakers (1984) and then Portland Breakers (1985); Chicago Blitz (1983-84); Denver Gold (1983-85); Houston Gamblers (1984-85); Jacksonville Bulls (1984-85); Los Angeles Express (1983-85); Memphis Showboats (1984-85);

Michigan Panthers (1983-84) merged with Oakland (1985); New Jersey Generals (1983-85); Oakland Invaders (1983-85); Oklahoma Outlaws (1984) merged with Arizona to become Arizona Outlaws (1985); Philadelphia Stars (1983-84) became Baltimore Stars (1985); Pittsburgh Maulers (1984); San Antonio Gunslingers (1984-85); Tampa Bay Bandits (1983-85); Washington Federals (1983-84) became Orlando Renegades (1985).

**XFL** (2001): Birmingham Thunderbolts, Chicago Enforcers, Las Vegas Outlaws, Los Angeles Xtreme, Memphis Maniax, New York New Jersey Hitmen, Orlando Rage, San Francisco Demons.

## NFL Pro Bowl

A postseason All-Star game between the new league champion and a team of professional all-stars was added to the NFL schedule in 1939. In the first game at Wrigley Field in Los Angeles, the NY Giants beat a team made up of players from NFL teams and two independent clubs in Los Angeles (the LA Bulldogs and Hollywood Stars). An all-NFL All-Star team provided the opposition over the next four seasons, but the game was cancelled in 1943.

The Pro Bowl was revived in 1951 as a contest between conference all-star teams: American vs National (1951-53), Eastern vs Western (1954-70), and AFC vs NFC (since 1971). The AFC leads the current series, 18-17.

The MVP trophy was named the Dan McGuire Award in 1984 after the late SF 49ers publicist and *Honolulu Advertiser* sports columnist.

| Year | Winner | Score | Loser | | Year | Winner | MVP |
|------|--------|-------|-------|---|------|--------|-----|
| 1939 | NY Giants | 13-10 | All-Stars | | 1971 | NFC, 27-6 | Back—Mel Renfro, Dal. |
| 1940 | Green Bay | 16-7 | All-Stars | | | | Line—Fred Carr, GB |
| 1940 | Chicago Bears | 28-14 | All-Stars | | 1972 | AFC, 26-13 | Off—Jan Stenerud, KC |
| 1942 | Chicago Bears | 35-24 | All-Stars | | | | Def—Willie Lanier, KC |
| 1942 | All-Stars | 17-14 | Washington | | 1973 | AFC, 33-28 | O.J. Simpson, Buf., RB |
| 1943-50 | | No game | | | 1974 | AFC, 15-13 | Garo Yepremian, Mia., PK |
| | | | | | 1975 | NFC, 17-10 | James Harris, LA Rams, QB |

| Year | Winner | MVP | | Year | Winner | MVP |
|------|--------|-----|---|------|--------|-----|
| 1951 | American, 28-27 | Otto Graham, Cle., QB | | 1976 | NFC, 23-20 | Billy Johnson, Hou., KR |
| 1952 | National, 30-13 | Dan Towler, LA Rams, HB | | 1977 | AFC, 24-14 | Mel Blount, Pit., CB |
| 1953 | National, 27-7 | Don Doll, Det., DB | | 1978 | NFC, 14-13 | Walter Payton, Chi., RB |
| 1954 | East, 20-9 | Chuck Bednarik, Phi., LB | | 1979 | NFC, 13-7 | Ahmad Rashad, Min., WR |
| 1955 | West, 26-19 | Billy Wilson, SF, E | | | | |
| 1956 | East, 31-30 | Ollie Matson, Cards, HB | | 1980 | NFC, 37-27 | Chuck Muncie, NO, RB |
| 1957 | West, 19-10 | Back—Bert Rechichar, Bal. | | 1981 | NFC, 21-7 | Eddie Murray, Det., PK |
| | | Line—Ernie Stautner, Pit. | | 1982 | AFC, 16-13 | Kellen Winslow, SD, WR |
| 1958 | West, 26-7 | Back—Hugh McElhenny, SF | | | | & Lee Roy Selmon, TB, DE |
| | | Line—Gene Brito, Wash. | | 1983 | NFC, 20-19 | Dan Fouts, SD, QB |
| 1959 | East, 28-21 | Back—Frank Gifford, NY | | | | & John Jefferson, GB, WR |
| | | Line—Doug Atkins, Chi. | | 1984 | NFC, 45-3 | Joe Theismann, Wash., QB |
| 1960 | West, 38-21 | Back—Johnny Unitas, Bal. | | 1985 | AFC, 22-14 | Mark Gastineau, NYJ, DE |
| | | Line—Big Daddy Lipscomb, Pit. | | 1986 | NFC, 28-24 | Phil Simms, NYG, QB |
| 1961 | West, 35-31 | Back—Johnny Unitas, Bal. | | 1987 | AFC, 10-6 | Reggie White, Phi., DE |
| | | Line—Sam Huff, NY | | 1988 | AFC, 15-6 | Bruce Smith, Buf., DE |
| 1962 | West, 31-30 | Back—Jim Brown, Cle. | | 1989 | NFC, 34-3 | Randall Cunningham, Phi., QB |
| | | Line—Henry Jordan, GB | | | | |
| 1963 | East, 30-20 | Back—Jim Brown, Cle. | | 1990 | NFC, 27-21 | Jerry Gray, LA Rams, CB |
| | | Line—Big Daddy Lipscomb, Pit. | | 1991 | AFC, 23-21 | Jim Kelly, Buf., QB |
| 1964 | West, 31-17 | Back—Johnny Unitas, Bal. | | 1992 | NFC, 21-15 | Michael Irvin, Dal., WR |
| | | Line—Gino Marchetti, Bal. | | 1993 | AFC, 23-20 (OT) | Steve Tasker, Buf., Sp. Teams |
| 1965 | West, 34-14 | Back—Fran Tarkenton, Min. | | 1994 | NFC, 17-3 | Andre Rison, Atl., WR |
| | | Line—Terry Barr, Det. | | 1995 | AFC, 41-13 | Marshall Faulk, Ind., RB |
| 1966 | East, 36-7 | Back—Jim Brown, Cle. | | 1996 | NFC, 20-13 | Jerry Rice, SF, WR |
| | | Line—Dale Meinhart, St. L. | | 1997 | AFC, 26-23 (OT) | Mark Brunell, Jax, QB |
| 1967 | East, 20-10 | Back—Gale Sayers, Chi. | | 1998 | AFC, 29-24 | Warren Moon, Sea., QB |
| | | Line—Floyd Peters, Phi. | | 1999 | AFC, 23-10 | Ty Law, NE, CB |
| 1968 | West, 38-20 | Back—Gale Sayers, Chi. | | | | & Keyshawn Johnson, NYJ, WR |
| | | Line—Dave Robinson, GB | | | | |
| 1969 | West, 10-7 | Back—Roman Gabriel, LA Rams | | 2000 | NFC, 51-31 | Randy Moss, Min., WR |
| | | Line—Merlin Olsen, LA Rams | | 2001 | AFC, 38-17 | Rich Gannon, Oak., QB |
| 1970 | West, 16-13 | Back—Gale Sayers, Chi. | | 2002 | AFC, 38-30 | Rich Gannon, Oak., QB |
| | | Line—George Andrie, Dal. | | 2003 | AFC, 45-20 | Ricky Williams, Mia., RB |
| | | | | 2004 | NFC, 55-52 | Marc Bulger, St.L, QB |
| | | | | 2005 | AFC, 38-27 | Peyton Manning, Ind., QB |

**Playing sites:** Wrigley Field in Los Angeles (1939); Gilmore Stadium in Los Angeles (1940–both games); Polo Grounds in New York (Jan., 1942); Shibe Park in Philadelphia (Dec., 1942); Memorial Coliseum in Los Angeles (1951-72 and 1979); Texas Stadium in Irving, TX (1973); Arrowhead Stadium in Kansas City (1974); Orange Bowl in Miami (1975); Superdome in New Orleans (1976); Kingdome in Seattle (1977); Tampa Stadium in Tampa (1978) and Aloha Stadium in Honolulu (since 1980).

## AFL All-Star Game

The AFL did not play an All-Star game after its first season in 1960 but did stage All-Star games from 1962-70. All-Star teams from the Eastern and Western divisions played each other every year except 1966 with the West winning the series, 6-2. In 1966, the league champion Buffalo Bills met an elite squad made up of the best players from the league's other eight clubs and lost, 30-19.

| Year | Winner | MVP | | Year | Winner | MVP |
|------|--------|-----|---|------|--------|-----|
| 1962 | West, 47-27 | Cotton Davidson, Oak., QB | | 1967 | East, 30-23 | Off—Babe Parilli, Bos. |
| 1963 | West, 21-14 | Off—Curtis McClinton, Dal. | | | | Def—Verlon Biggs, NY |
| | | Def—Earl Faison, SD | | 1968 | East, 25-24 | Off—Joe Namath, NY |
| 1964 | West, 27-24 | Off—Keith Lincoln, SD | | | | & Don Maynard, NY |
| | | Def—Archie Matsos, Oak. | | | | Def—Speedy Duncan, SD |
| 1965 | West, 38-14 | Off—Keith Lincoln, SD | | 1969 | West, 38-25 | Off—Len Dawson, KC |
| | | Def—Willie Brown, Den. | | | | Def—George Webster, Hou. |
| 1966 | All-Stars 30 | Off—Joe Namath, NY | | 1970 | West, 26-3 | John Hadl, SD, QB |
| | Buffalo 19 | Def—Frank Buncom, SD | | | | |

**Playing sites:** Balboa Stadium in San Diego (1962-64); Jeppesen Stadium in Houston (1965); Rice Stadium in Houston (1966); Oakland Coliseum (1967); Gator Bowl in Jacksonville (1968-69) and Astrodome in Houston (1970).

## NFL Franchise Origins

Here is what the current 32 teams in the National Football League have to show for the years they have put in as members of the American Professional Football Association (APFA), the NFL, the All-America Football Conference (AAFC) and the American Football League (AFL). Years given for league titles indicate seasons championships were won.

## American Football Conference

| | First Season | League Titles | Franchise Stops |
|---|---|---|---|
| **Baltimore Ravens** | 1996 (NFL) | 1 Super Bowl (2000) | • Baltimore (1996—) |
| **Buffalo Bills** | 1960 (AFL) | 2 AFL (1964-65) | • Buffalo (1960-72) Orchard Park, NY (1973—) |
| **Cincinnati Bengals** | 1968 (AFL) | None | • Cincinnati (1968—) |
| **Cleveland Browns** | 1946 (AAFC) | 4 AAFC (1946-49) 4 NFL (1950,54-55,64) | • Cleveland (1946-95, 99—) |
| **Denver Broncos** | 1960 (AFL) | 2 Super Bowls (1997-98) | • Denver (1960—) |
| **Houston Texans** | 2002 (NFL) | None | • Houston (2002—) |
| **Indianapolis Colts** | 1953 (NFL) | 3 NFL (1958-59,68) 1 Super Bowl (1970) | • Baltimore (1953-83) Indianapolis (1984—) |
| **Jacksonville Jaguars** | 1995 (NFL) | | • Jacksonville, FL (1995—) |
| **Kansas City Chiefs** | 1960 (AFL) | 3 AFL (1962,66,69) 1 Super Bowl (1969) | • Dallas (1960-62) Kansas City (1963—) |
| **Miami Dolphins** | 1966 (AFL) | 2 Super Bowls (1972-73) | • Miami (1966—) |
| **New England Patriots** | 1960 (AFL) | 3 Super Bowls (2001,03-04) | • Boston (1960-70) Foxboro, MA (1971—) |
| **New York Jets** | 1960 (AFL) | 1 AFL (1968) 1 Super Bowl (1968) | • New York (1960-83) E. Rutherford, NJ (1984—) |
| **Oakland Raiders** | 1960 (AFL) | 1 AFL (1967) 3 Super Bowls (1976,80,83) | • Oakland (1960-81, 1995—) Los Angeles (1982-94) |
| **Pittsburgh Steelers** | 1933 (NFL) | 4 Super Bowls (1974-75,78-79) | • Pittsburgh (1933—) |
| **San Diego Chargers** | 1960 (AFL) | 1 AFL (1963) | • Los Angeles (1960) San Diego (1961—) |
| **Tennessee Titans** | 1960 (AFL) | 2 AFL (1960-61) | • Houston (1960-96) Memphis (1997) Nashville (1998—) |

## National Football Conference

| | First Season | League Titles | Franchise Stops |
|---|---|---|---|
| **Arizona Cardinals** | 1920 (APFA) | 2 NFL (1925,47) | • Chicago (1920-59) St. Louis (1960-87) Tempe, AZ (1988—) |
| **Atlanta Falcons** | 1966 (NFL) | None | • Atlanta (1966—) |
| **Carolina Panthers** | 1995 (NFL) | None | • Clemson, SC (1995) Charlotte, NC (1996—) |
| **Chicago Bears** | 1920 (APFA) | 8 NFL (1921, 32-33,40-41,43,46,63) 1 Super Bowl (1985) | • Decatur, IL (1920) Chicago (1921—) |
| **Dallas Cowboys** | 1960 (NFL) | 5 Super Bowls (1971,77,92-93,95) | • Dallas (1960-70) Irving, TX (1971—) |
| **Detroit Lions** | 1930 (NFL) | 4 NFL (1935,52-53,57) | • Portsmouth, OH (1980-33) Detroit (1934-74, 2002—) Pontiac, MI (1975-2001) |
| **Green Bay Packers** | 1921 (APFA) | 11 NFL (1929-31,36,39,44,61-62,65-67) 3 Super Bowls (1966-67,96) | • Green Bay (1921—) |
| **Minnesota Vikings** | 1961 (NFL) | 1 NFL (1969) | • Bloomington, MN (1961-81) Minneapolis, MN (1982—) |
| **New Orleans Saints** | 1967 (NFL) | None | • New Orleans (1967—) |
| **New York Giants** | 1925 (NFL) | 4 NFL (1927,34,38,56) 2 Super Bowls (1986,90) | • New York (1925-73,75) New Haven, CT (1973-74) E. Rutherford, NJ (1976—) |
| **Philadelphia Eagles** | 1933 (NFL) | 3 NFL (1948-49,60) | • Philadelphia (1933—) |
| **St. Louis Rams** | 1937 (NFL) | 2 NFL (1945,51) 1 Super Bowl (1999) | • Cleveland (1937-45) Los Angeles (1946-79) Anaheim (1980-94) St. Louis (1995—) |
| **San Francisco 49ers** | 1946 (AAFC) | 5 Super Bowls (1981,84,88-89,94) | • San Francisco (1946—) |
| **Seattle Seahawks** | 1976 (NFL) | None | • Seattle (1976—) |
| **Tampa Bay Buccaneers** | 1976 (NFL) | 1 Super Bowl (2002) | • Tampa, FL (1976—) |
| **Washington Redskins** | 1932 (NFL) | 2 NFL (1937,42) 3 Super Bowls (1982,87,91) | • Boston (1932-36) Washington, DC (1937-96) Raljon, MD (1997—) |

## The Growth of the NFL

Of the 14 franchises that comprised the American Professional Football Association in 1920, only two remain—the Arizona Cardinals (then the Chicago Cardinals) and the Chicago Bears (originally the Decatur-IL Staleys). Green Bay joined the APFC in 1921 and the league changed its name to the NFL in 1922. Since then, 54 NFL clubs have come and gone, six rival leagues have expired and two other leagues have been swallowed up.

The NFL merged with the **All-America Football Conference** (1946-49) following the 1949 season and adopted three of its seven clubs—the Baltimore Colts, Cleveland Browns and San Francisco 49ers. The four remaining AAFC teams—the Brooklyn/NY Yankees, Buffalo Bills, Chicago Hornets and Los Angeles Dons—did not survive. After the 1950 season, the financially troubled Colts were sold back to the NFL. The league folded the team and added its players to the 1951 college draft pool. A new Baltimore franchise, also named the Colts, joined the NFL in 1953.

The formation of the **American Football League** (1960-69) was announced in 1959 with ownership lined up in eight cities—Boston, Buffalo, Dallas, Denver, Houston, Los Angeles, Minneapolis and New York. Set to begin play in the autumn of 1960, the AFL was stunned early that year when Minneapolis withdrew to accept an offer to join the NFL as an expansion team in 1961. The new league responded by choosing Oakland to replace Minneapolis and inherit the departed team's draft picks. Since no AFL team actually played in Minneapolis, it is not considered the original home of the Oakland Raiders.

In 1966, the NFL and AFL agreed to a merger that resulted in the first Super Bowl (originally called the AFL-NFL World Championship Game) following the '66 league playoffs. In 1970, the now 10-member AFL officially joined the NFL, forming a 26-team league made up of two conferences of three divisions each. In 2002, the 32-team league was realigned into two conferences of four divisions each.

## Expansion/Merger Timetable

For teams currently in NFL.

**1921**–Green Bay Packers; **1925**–New York Giants; **1930**–Portsmouth-OH Spartans (now Detroit Lions); **1932**–Boston Braves (now Washington Redskins); **1933**–Philadelphia Eagles and Pittsburgh Pirates (now Steelers); **1937**–Cleveland Rams (now St. Louis); **1950**–added AAFC's Cleveland Browns and San Francisco 49ers; **1953**–Baltimore Colts (now Indianapolis).

**1960**–Dallas Cowboys; **1961**–Minnesota Vikings; **1966**–Atlanta Falcons; **1967**–New Orleans Saints; **1970**–added AFL's Boston Patriots (now New England), Buffalo Bills, Cincinnati Bengals (1968 expansion team), Denver Broncos, Houston Oilers (now Tennessee Titans), Kansas City Chiefs, Miami Dolphins (1966 expansion team), New York Jets, Oakland Raiders and San Diego Chargers (the AFL-NFL merger divided the league into two 13-team conferences with old-line NFL clubs Baltimore, Cleveland and Pittsburgh moving to the AFC); **1976**–Seattle Seahawks and Tampa Bay Buccaneers (Seattle was originally in the NFC West and Tampa Bay in the AFC West, but were switched to AFC West and NFC Central, respectively, in 1977); **1995**–Carolina Panthers and Jacksonville Jaguars; **1996**—Cleveland Browns move to Baltimore and become Ravens. City of Cleveland retains rights to team name, colors and all memorabilia; **1999**–Cleveland Browns return to the NFL. **2002**–Houston Texans. Seattle moves back to the NFC West.

## City and Nickname Changes

**1921**—Decatur Staleys move to Chicago; **1922**—Chicago Staleys renamed Bears; **1933**—Boston Braves renamed Redskins; **1937**—Boston Redskins move to Washington; **1934**—Portsmouth (Ohio) Spartans move to Detroit and become Lions; **1941**—Pittsburgh Pirates renamed Steelers; **1943**—Philadelphia and Pittsburgh merge for one season and become Phil-Pitt, or the "Steagles"; **1944**—Chicago Cardinals and Pittsburgh merge for one season and become Card-Pitt; **1946**—Cleveland Rams move to Los Angeles.

**1960**—Chicago Cardinals move to St. Louis; **1961**—Los Angeles Chargers (AFL) move to San Diego; **1963**—New York Titans (AFL) renamed Jets and Dallas Texans (AFL) move to Kansas City and become Chiefs; **1971**—Boston Patriots become New England Patriots; **1982**—Oakland Raiders move to Los Angeles; **1984**—Baltimore Colts move to Indianapolis; **1988**—St. Louis Cardinals move to Phoenix; **1994**—Phoenix Cardinals become Arizona Cardinals; **1995**—L.A. Rams move to St. Louis and L.A. Raiders move back to Oakland; **1996**—Cleveland Browns move to Baltimore and become Ravens. City of Cleveland retains rights to team name, colors and all memorabilia; **1997**—Houston Oilers move to Memphis and become Tennessee Oilers; **1998**—Tennessee Oilers move to Nashville; **1999**—Tennessee Oilers renamed Titans.

---

## Defunct NFL Teams

Teams that once played in the APFA and NFL, but no longer exist.

**Akron-OH**–Pros (1920-25) and Indians (1926); **Baltimore**–Colts (1950); **Boston**–Bulldogs (1926) and Yanks (1944-48); **Brooklyn**–Lions (1926), Dodgers (1930-43) and Tigers (1944); **Buffalo**–All-Americans (1920-23), Bisons (1924-25), Rangers (1926), Bisons (1927,1929); **Canton-OH**–Bulldogs (1920-23,1925-26); **Chicago**–Tigers (1920); **Cincinnati**–Celts (1921) and Reds (1933-34); **Cleveland**–Tigers (1920), Indians (1921), Indians (1923), Bulldogs (1924-25,1927) and Indians (1931); **Columbus-OH**–Panhandles (1920-22) and Tigers (1923-26); **Dallas**–Texans (1952); **Dayton-OH**–Triangles (1920-29).

**Detroit**–Heralds (1920-21), Panthers (1925-26) and Wolverines (1928); **Duluth-MN**–Kelleys (1923-25) and Eskimos (1926-27); **Evansville-IN**–Crimson Giants (1921-22); **Frankford-PA**–Yellow Jackets (1924-31); **Hammond-IN**–Pros (1920-26); **Hartford**–Blues (1926); **Kansas City**–Blues (1924) and Cowboys (1925-26); **Kenosha-WI** Maroons (1924); **Los Angeles**–Buccaneers (1926); **Louisville**–Brecks (1921-23) and Colonels (1926); **Marion-OH**–Oorang Indians (1922-23); **Milwaukee**–Badgers (1922-26); **Minneapolis**–Marines (1922-24) and Red Jackets (1929-30); **Muncie-IN**–Flyers (1920-21).

**New York**–Giants (1921), Yankees (1927-28), Bulldogs (1949) and Yankees (1950-51); **Newark-NJ**–Tornadoes (1930); **Orange-NJ**–Tornadoes (1929); **Pottsville-PA**–Maroons (1925-28); **Providence-RI**–Steam Roller (1925-31); **Racine-WI**–Legion (1922-24) and Tornadoes (1926); **Rochester-NY**–Jeffersons (1920-25); **Rock Island-IL**–Independents (1920-26); **Staten Island-NY**–Stapletons (1929-32); **St. Louis**–All-Stars (1923) and Gunners (1934); **Toledo-OH**–Maroons (1922-23); **Tonawanda-NY**–Kardex (1921), also called Lumbermen; **Washington**–Senators (1921).

## Annual NFL Leaders

Individual leaders in NFL (1932-69), NFC (since 1970), AFL (1960-69) and AFC (since 1970).

### Passing

Since 1932, the NFL has used several formulas to determine passing leadership, from Total Yards alone (1932-37), to the current rating system—adopted in 1973—that takes Completions, Completion Percentage, Yards Gained, TD Passes, Interceptions, Interception Percentage and other factors into account. The quarterbacks listed below all led the league according to the system in use at the time.

#### NFL-NFC

**Multiple winners:** Sammy Baugh and Steve Young (6); Joe Montana and Roger Staubach (5); Arnie Herber, Sonny Jurgensen, Bart Starr and Norm Van Brocklin (3); Daunte Culpepper, Ed Danowski, Otto Graham, Cecil Isbell, Milt Plum, Kurt Warner and Bob Waterfield (2).

| Year | | Att | Cmp | Yds | TD | Year | | Att | Cmp | Yds | TD |
|---|---|---|---|---|---|---|---|---|---|---|---|
| 1932 | Arnie Herber, GB | 101 | 37 | 639 | 9 | 1968 | Earl Morrall, Bal | 317 | 182 | 2909 | 26 |
| 1933 | Harry Newman, NY | 136 | 53 | 973 | 11 | 1969 | Sonny Jurgensen, Wash | 442 | 274 | 3102 | 22 |
| 1934 | Arnie Herber, GB | 115 | 42 | 799 | 8 | 1970 | John Brodie, SF | 378 | 223 | 2941 | 24 |
| 1935 | Ed Danowski, NY | 113 | 57 | 794 | 10 | 1971 | Roger Staubach, Dal | 211 | 126 | 1882 | 15 |
| 1936 | Arnie Herber, GB | 173 | 77 | 1239 | 11 | 1972 | Norm Snead, NY | 325 | 196 | 2307 | 17 |
| 1937 | Sammy Baugh, Wash | 171 | 81 | 1127 | 8 | 1973 | Roger Staubach, Dal | 286 | 179 | 2428 | 23 |
| 1938 | Ed Danowski, NY | 129 | 70 | 848 | 7 | 1974 | Sonny Jurgensen, Wash | 167 | 107 | 1185 | 11 |
| 1939 | Parker Hall, Cle. Rams | 208 | 106 | 1227 | 9 | 1975 | Fran Tarkenton, Min | 425 | 273 | 2994 | 25 |
| 1940 | Sammy Baugh, Wash | 177 | 111 | 1367 | 12 | 1976 | James Harris, LA | 158 | 91 | 1460 | 8 |
| 1941 | Cecil Isbell, GB | 206 | 117 | 1479 | 15 | 1977 | Roger Staubach, Dal | 361 | 210 | 2620 | 18 |
| 1942 | Cecil Isbell, GB | 268 | 146 | 2021 | 24 | 1978 | Roger Staubach, Dal | 413 | 231 | 3190 | 25 |
| 1943 | Sammy Baugh, Wash | 239 | 133 | 1754 | 23 | 1979 | Roger Staubach, Dal | 461 | 267 | 3586 | 27 |
| 1944 | Frank Filchock, Wash | 147 | 84 | 1139 | 13 | 1980 | Ron Jaworski, Phi | 451 | 257 | 3529 | 27 |
| 1945 | Sammy Baugh, Wash | 182 | 128 | 1669 | 11 | 1981 | Joe Montana, SF | 488 | 311 | 3565 | 19 |
| | & Sid Luckman, Chi. Bears | 217 | 117 | 1725 | 14 | 1982 | Joe Theismann, Wash | 252 | 161 | 2033 | 13 |
| 1946 | Bob Waterfield, LA | 251 | 127 | 1747 | 18 | 1983 | Steve Bartkowski, Atl | 432 | 274 | 3167 | 22 |
| 1947 | Sammy Baugh, Wash | 354 | 210 | 2938 | 25 | 1984 | Joe Montana, SF | 432 | 279 | 3630 | 28 |
| 1948 | Tommy Thompson, Phi | 246 | 141 | 1965 | 25 | 1985 | Joe Montana, SF | 494 | 303 | 3653 | 27 |
| 1949 | Sammy Baugh, Wash | 255 | 145 | 1903 | 18 | 1986 | Tommy Kramer, Min | 372 | 208 | 3000 | 24 |
| 1950 | Norm Van Brocklin, LA | 233 | 127 | 2061 | 18 | 1987 | Joe Montana, SF | 398 | 266 | 3054 | 31 |
| 1951 | Bob Waterfield, LA | 176 | 88 | 1566 | 13 | 1988 | Wade Wilson, Min | 332 | 204 | 2746 | 15 |
| 1952 | Norm Van Brocklin, LA | 205 | 113 | 1736 | 14 | 1989 | Don Majkowski, GB | 599 | 353 | 4318 | 27 |
| 1953 | Otto Graham, Cle | 258 | 167 | 2722 | 11 | 1990 | Joe Montana, SF | 520 | 321 | 3944 | 26 |
| 1954 | Norm Van Brocklin, LA | 260 | 139 | 2637 | 13 | 1991 | Steve Young, SF | 279 | 180 | 2517 | 17 |
| 1955 | Otto Graham, Cle | 185 | 98 | 1721 | 15 | 1992 | Steve Young, SF | 402 | 268 | 3465 | 25 |
| 1956 | Ed Brown, Chi. Bears | 168 | 96 | 1667 | 11 | 1993 | Steve Young, SF | 462 | 314 | 4023 | 29 |
| 1957 | Tommy O'Connell, Cle | 110 | 63 | 1229 | 9 | 1994 | Steve Young, SF | 461 | 324 | 3969 | 35 |
| 1958 | Eddie LeBaron, Wash | 145 | 79 | 1365 | 11 | 1995 | Brett Favre, GB | 570 | 359 | 4413 | 38 |
| 1959 | Charlie Conerly, NY | 194 | 113 | 1706 | 14 | 1996 | Steve Young, SF | 316 | 214 | 2410 | 14 |
| 1960 | Milt Plum, Cle | 250 | 151 | 2297 | 21 | 1997 | Steve Young, SF | 356 | 241 | 3029 | 19 |
| 1961 | Milt Plum, Cle | 302 | 177 | 2416 | 16 | 1998 | Randall Cunningham, Min | 425 | 259 | 3704 | 34 |
| 1962 | Bart Starr, GB | 285 | 178 | 2438 | 12 | 1999 | Kurt Warner, St.L | 499 | 325 | 4353 | 41 |
| 1963 | Y.A. Tittle, NY | 367 | 221 | 3145 | 36 | 2000 | Trent Green, St.L | 240 | 145 | 2063 | 16 |
| 1964 | Bart Starr, GB | 272 | 163 | 2144 | 15 | 2001 | Kurt Warner, St.L | 546 | 375 | 4830 | 36 |
| 1965 | Rudy Bukich, Chi | 312 | 176 | 2641 | 20 | 2002 | Brad Johnson, TB | 451 | 281 | 3049 | 22 |
| 1966 | Bart Starr, GB | 251 | 156 | 2257 | 14 | 2003 | Daunte Culpepper, Min | 454 | 295 | 3479 | 25 |
| 1967 | Sonny Jurgensen, Wash | 508 | 288 | 3747 | 31 | 2004 | Daunte Culpepper, Min | 548 | 379 | 4717 | 39 |

#### AFL-AFC

**Multiple winners:** Dan Marino (5); Ken Anderson and Len Dawson (4); Bob Griese, Daryle Lamonica, Peyton Manning, Warren Moon and Ken Stabler (2).

| Year | | Att | Cmp | Yds | TD | Year | | Att | Cmp | Yds | TD |
|---|---|---|---|---|---|---|---|---|---|---|---|
| 1960 | Jack Kemp, LA | 406 | 211 | 3018 | 20 | 1983 | Dan Marino, Mia | 296 | 173 | 2210 | 20 |
| 1961 | George Blanda, Hou | 362 | 187 | 3330 | 36 | 1984 | Dan Marino, Mia | 564 | 362 | 5084 | 48 |
| 1962 | Len Dawson, Dal | 310 | 189 | 2759 | 29 | 1985 | Ken O'Brien, NY | 488 | 297 | 3888 | 25 |
| 1963 | Tobin Rote, SD | 286 | 170 | 2510 | 20 | 1986 | Dan Marino, Mia | 623 | 378 | 4746 | 44 |
| 1964 | Len Dawson, KC | 354 | 199 | 2879 | 30 | 1987 | Bernie Kosar, Cle | 389 | 241 | 3033 | 22 |
| 1965 | John Hadl, SD | 348 | 174 | 2798 | 20 | 1988 | Boomer Esiason, Cin | 388 | 223 | 3572 | 28 |
| 1966 | Len Dawson, KC | 284 | 159 | 2527 | 26 | 1989 | Dan Marino, Mia | 550 | 308 | 3997 | 24 |
| 1967 | Daryle Lamonica, Oak | 425 | 220 | 3228 | 30 | 1990 | Warren Moon, Hou | 584 | 362 | 4689 | 33 |
| 1968 | Len Dawson, KC | 224 | 131 | 2109 | 17 | 1991 | Jim Kelly, Buf | 474 | 304 | 3844 | 33 |
| 1969 | Greg Cook, Cin | 197 | 106 | 1854 | 15 | 1992 | Warren Moon, Hou | 346 | 224 | 2521 | 18 |
| 1970 | Daryle Lamonica, Oak | 356 | 179 | 2516 | 22 | 1993 | John Elway, Den | 551 | 348 | 4030 | 25 |
| 1971 | Bob Griese, Mia | 263 | 145 | 2089 | 19 | 1994 | Dan Marino, Mia | 615 | 385 | 4453 | 30 |
| 1972 | Earl Morrall, Mia | 150 | 83 | 1360 | 11 | 1995 | Jim Harbaugh, Ind | 314 | 200 | 2575 | 17 |
| 1973 | Ken Stabler, Oak | 260 | 163 | 1997 | 14 | 1996 | John Elway, Den | 466 | 287 | 3328 | 26 |
| 1974 | Ken Anderson, Cin | 328 | 213 | 2667 | 18 | 1997 | Mark Brunell, Jax | 435 | 264 | 3281 | 18 |
| 1975 | Ken Anderson, Cin | 377 | 228 | 3169 | 21 | 1998 | Vinny Testaverde, NYJ | 421 | 259 | 3256 | 29 |
| 1976 | Ken Stabler, Oak | 291 | 194 | 2737 | 27 | 1999 | Peyton Manning, Ind | 533 | 331 | 4135 | 26 |
| 1977 | Bob Griese, Mia | 307 | 180 | 2252 | 22 | 2000 | Brian Griese, Den | 336 | 216 | 2688 | 19 |
| 1978 | Terry Bradshaw, Pit | 368 | 207 | 2915 | 28 | 2001 | Rich Gannon, Oak | 549 | 361 | 3828 | 27 |
| 1979 | Dan Fouts, SD | 530 | 332 | 4082 | 24 | 2002 | Chad Pennington, NYJ | 399 | 275 | 3120 | 22 |
| 1980 | Brian Sipe, Cle | 554 | 337 | 4132 | 30 | 2003 | Steve McNair, Ten | 400 | 250 | 3215 | 24 |
| 1981 | Ken Anderson, Cin | 479 | 300 | 3753 | 29 | 2004 | Peyton Manning, Ind | 497 | 336 | 4557 | 49 |
| 1982 | Ken Anderson, Cin | 309 | 218 | 2495 | 12 | | | | | | |

## Receptions
### NFL-NFC

**Multiple winners:** Don Hutson (8); Raymond Berry, Tom Fears, Pete Pihos, Jerry Rice, Sterling Sharpe and Billy Wilson (3); Dwight Clark, Torry Holt, Herman Moore, Muhsin Muhammad, Ahmad Rashad and Charley Taylor (2).

| Year | | No | Yds | Avg | TD |
|---|---|---|---|---|---|
| 1932 | Ray Flaherty, NY | 21 | 350 | 16.7 | 3 |
| 1933 | Shipwreck Kelly, Bklyn | 22 | 246 | 11.2 | 3 |
| 1934 | Joe Carter, Phi | 16 | 238 | 14.9 | 4 |
| | & Red Badgro, NY | 16 | 206 | 12.9 | 1 |
| 1935 | Tod Goodwin, NY | 26 | 432 | 16.6 | 4 |
| 1936 | Don Hutson, GB | 34 | 536 | 15.8 | 8 |
| 1937 | Don Hutson, GB | 41 | 552 | 13.5 | 7 |
| 1938 | Gaynell Tinsley, Chi. Cards | 41 | 516 | 12.6 | 1 |
| 1939 | Don Hutson, GB | 34 | 846 | 24.9 | 6 |
| 1940 | Don Looney, Phi | 58 | 707 | 12.2 | 4 |
| 1941 | Don Hutson, GB | 58 | 739 | 12.7 | 10 |
| 1942 | Don Hutson, GB | 74 | 1211 | 16.4 | 17 |
| 1943 | Don Hutson, GB | 47 | 776 | 16.5 | 11 |
| 1944 | Don Hutson, GB | 58 | 866 | 14.9 | 9 |
| 1945 | Don Hutson, GB | 47 | 834 | 17.7 | 9 |
| 1946 | Jim Benton, LA | 63 | 981 | 15.6 | 6 |
| 1947 | Jim Keane, Chi. Bears | 64 | 910 | 14.2 | 10 |
| 1948 | Tom Fears, LA | 51 | 698 | 13.7 | 4 |
| 1949 | Tom Fears, LA | 77 | 1013 | 13.2 | 9 |
| 1950 | Tom Fears, LA | 84 | 1116 | 13.3 | 7 |
| 1951 | Elroy Hirsch, LA | 66 | 1495 | 22.7 | 17 |
| 1952 | Mac Speedie, Cle | 62 | 911 | 14.7 | 5 |
| 1953 | Pete Pihos, Phi | 63 | 1049 | 16.7 | 10 |
| 1954 | Pete Pihos, Phi | 60 | 872 | 14.5 | 10 |
| | & Billy Wilson, SF | 60 | 830 | 13.8 | 5 |
| 1955 | Pete Pihos, Phi | 62 | 864 | 13.9 | 7 |
| 1956 | Billy Wilson, SF | 60 | 889 | 14.8 | 5 |
| 1957 | Billy Wilson, SF | 52 | 757 | 14.6 | 6 |
| 1958 | Raymond Berry, Bal | 56 | 794 | 14.2 | 9 |
| | & Pete Retzlaff, Phi | 56 | 766 | 13.7 | 2 |
| 1959 | Raymond Berry, Bal | 66 | 959 | 14.5 | 14 |
| 1960 | Raymond Berry, Bal | 74 | 1298 | 17.5 | 10 |
| 1961 | Red Phillips, LA | 78 | 1092 | 14.0 | 5 |
| 1962 | Bobby Mitchell, Wash | 72 | 1384 | 19.2 | 11 |
| 1963 | Bobby Joe Conrad, St.L | 73 | 967 | 13.2 | 10 |
| 1964 | Johnny Morris, Chi. Bears | 93 | 1200 | 12.9 | 10 |
| 1965 | Dave Parks, SF | 80 | 1344 | 16.8 | 12 |
| 1966 | Charley Taylor, Wash | 72 | 1119 | 15.5 | 12 |
| 1967 | Charley Taylor, Wash | 70 | 990 | 14.1 | 9 |
| 1968 | Clifton McNeil, SF | 71 | 994 | 14.0 | 7 |
| 1969 | Dan Abramowicz, NO | 73 | 1015 | 13.9 | 7 |
| 1970 | Dick Gordon, Chi | 71 | 1026 | 14.5 | 13 |
| 1971 | Bob Tucker, NY | 59 | 791 | 13.4 | 4 |
| 1972 | Harold Jackson, Phi | 62 | 1048 | 16.9 | 4 |
| 1973 | Harold Carmichael, Phi | 67 | 1116 | 16.7 | 9 |
| 1974 | Charles Young, Phi | 63 | 696 | 11.0 | 3 |
| 1975 | Chuck Foreman, Min | 73 | 691 | 9.5 | 9 |
| 1976 | Drew Pearson, Dal | 58 | 806 | 13.9 | 6 |
| 1977 | Ahmad Rashad, Min | 51 | 681 | 13.4 | 2 |
| 1978 | Rickey Young, Min | 88 | 704 | 8.0 | 5 |
| 1979 | Ahmad Rashad, Min | 80 | 1156 | 14.5 | 9 |
| 1980 | Earl Cooper, SF | 83 | 567 | 6.8 | 4 |
| 1981 | Dwight Clark, SF | 85 | 1105 | 13.0 | 4 |
| 1982 | Dwight Clark, SF | 60 | 913 | 12.2 | 5 |
| 1983 | Roy Green, St.L | 78 | 1227 | 15.7 | 14 |
| | Charlie Brown, Wash | 78 | 1225 | 15.7 | 8 |
| | & Earnest Gray, NY | 78 | 1139 | 14.6 | 5 |
| 1984 | Art Monk, Wash | 106 | 1372 | 12.9 | 7 |
| 1985 | Roger Craig, SF | 92 | 1016 | 11.0 | 6 |
| 1986 | Jerry Rice, SF | 86 | 1570 | 18.3 | 15 |
| 1987 | J.T. Smith, St.L | 91 | 1117 | 12.3 | 8 |
| 1988 | Henry Ellard, LA | 86 | 1414 | 16.4 | 10 |
| 1989 | Sterling Sharpe, GB | 90 | 1423 | 15.8 | 12 |
| 1990 | Jerry Rice, SF | 100 | 1502 | 15.0 | 13 |
| 1991 | Michael Irvin, Dal | 93 | 1523 | 16.4 | 8 |
| 1992 | Sterling Sharpe, GB | 108 | 1461 | 13.5 | 13 |
| 1993 | Sterling Sharpe, GB | 112 | 1274 | 11.4 | 11 |
| 1994 | Cris Carter, Min | 122 | 1256 | 10.3 | 7 |
| 1995 | Herman Moore, Det | 123 | 1686 | 13.7 | 14 |
| 1996 | Jerry Rice, SF | 108 | 1254 | 11.6 | 8 |
| 1997 | Herman Moore, Det | 104 | 1293 | 12.4 | 8 |
| 1998 | Frank Sanders, Ari | 89 | 1145 | 12.9 | 3 |
| 1999 | Muhsin Muhammad, Car | 96 | 1253 | 13.1 | 8 |
| 2000 | Muhsin Muhammad, Car | 102 | 1183 | 11.6 | 6 |
| 2001 | Keyshawn Johnson, TB | 106 | 1266 | 11.9 | 1 |
| 2002 | Randy Moss, Min | 106 | 1347 | 12.7 | 7 |
| 2003 | Torry Holt, St.L | 117 | 1696 | 14.5 | 12 |
| 2004 | Joe Horn, NO | 94 | 1399 | 14.9 | 11 |
| | & Torry Holt, St.L | 94 | 1372 | 14.6 | 10 |

### AFL-AFC

**Multiple winners:** Lionel Taylor (5); Lance Alworth, Haywood Jeffires, Lydell Mitchell and Kellen Winslow (3); Fred Biletnikoff, Todd Christensen, Marvin Harrison, Carl Pickens and Al Toon (2).

| Year | | No | Yds | Avg | TD |
|---|---|---|---|---|---|
| 1960 | Lionel Taylor, Den | 92 | 1235 | 13.4 | 12 |
| 1961 | Lionel Taylor, Den | 100 | 1176 | 11.8 | 4 |
| 1962 | Lionel Taylor, Den | 77 | 908 | 11.8 | 4 |
| 1963 | Lionel Taylor, Den | 78 | 1101 | 14.1 | 10 |
| 1964 | Charley Hennigan, Hou | 101 | 1546 | 15.3 | 8 |
| 1965 | Lionel Taylor, Den | 85 | 1131 | 13.3 | 6 |
| 1966 | Lance Alworth, SD | 73 | 1383 | 18.9 | 13 |
| 1967 | George Sauer, NY | 75 | 1189 | 15.9 | 6 |
| 1968 | Lance Alworth, SD | 68 | 1312 | 19.3 | 10 |
| 1969 | Lance Alworth, SD | 64 | 1003 | 15.7 | 4 |
| 1970 | Marlin Briscoe, Buf | 57 | 1036 | 18.2 | 8 |
| 1971 | Fred Biletnikoff, Oak | 61 | 929 | 15.2 | 9 |
| 1972 | Fred Biletnikoff, Oak | 58 | 802 | 13.8 | 7 |
| 1973 | Fred Willis, Hou | 57 | 371 | 6.5 | 1 |
| 1974 | Lydell Mitchell, Bal | 72 | 544 | 7.6 | 2 |
| 1975 | Reggie Rucker, Cle | 60 | 770 | 12.8 | 3 |
| | & Lydell Mitchell, Bal | 60 | 544 | 9.1 | 4 |
| 1976 | MacArthur Lane, KC | 66 | 686 | 10.4 | 1 |
| 1977 | Lydell Mitchell, Bal | 71 | 620 | 8.7 | 4 |
| 1978 | Steve Largent, Sea | 71 | 1168 | 16.5 | 8 |
| 1979 | Joe Washington, Bal | 82 | 750 | 9.1 | 3 |
| 1980 | Kellen Winslow, SD | 89 | 1290 | 14.5 | 9 |
| 1981 | Kellen Winslow, SD | 88 | 1075 | 12.2 | 10 |
| 1982 | Kellen Winslow, SD | 54 | 721 | 13.4 | 6 |
| 1983 | Todd Christensen, LA | 92 | 1247 | 13.6 | 12 |
| 1984 | Ozzie Newsome, Cle | 89 | 1001 | 11.2 | 5 |
| 1985 | Lionel James, SD | 86 | 1027 | 11.9 | 6 |
| 1986 | Todd Christensen, LA | 95 | 1153 | 12.1 | 8 |
| 1987 | Al Toon, NY | 68 | 976 | 14.4 | 5 |
| 1988 | Al Toon, NY | 93 | 1067 | 11.5 | 5 |
| 1989 | Andre Reed, Buf | 88 | 1312 | 14.9 | 9 |
| 1990 | Haywood Jeffires, Hou | 74 | 1048 | 14.2 | 8 |
| | & Drew Hill, Hou | 74 | 1019 | 13.8 | 5 |
| 1991 | Haywood Jeffires, Hou | 100 | 1181 | 11.8 | 7 |
| 1992 | Haywood Jeffires, Hou | 90 | 913 | 10.1 | 7 |
| 1993 | Reggie Langhorne, Ind | 85 | 1038 | 12.2 | 3 |
| 1994 | Ben Coates, NE | 96 | 1174 | 12.2 | 7 |
| 1995 | Carl Pickens, Cin | 99 | 1234 | 12.5 | 17 |
| 1996 | Carl Pickens, Cin | 100 | 1180 | 11.8 | 12 |
| 1997 | Tim Brown, Oak | 104 | 1408 | 13.5 | 5 |
| 1998 | O.J. McDuffie, Mia | 90 | 1050 | 11.7 | 7 |
| 1999 | Jimmy Smith, Jax | 116 | 1636 | 14.1 | 6 |
| 2000 | Marvin Harrison, Ind | 102 | 1413 | 13.9 | 14 |
| 2001 | Rod Smith, Den | 113 | 1343 | 11.9 | 11 |
| 2002 | Marvin Harrison, Ind | 143 | 1722 | 12.0 | 11 |
| 2003 | LaDainian Tomlinson, SD | 100 | 725 | 7.3 | 4 |
| 2004 | Tony Gonzalez, KC | 102 | 1258 | 12.3 | 7 |

## Rushing
### NFL-NFC

**Multiple winners:** Jim Brown (8); Walter Payton and Barry Sanders (5); Emmitt Smith and Steve Van Buren (4); Eric Dickerson (3); Cliff Battles, John Brockington, Larry Brown, Bill Dudley, Leroy Kelly, Bill Paschal, Joe Perry, Gale Sayers, Stephen Davis and Whizzer White (2).

| Year | | Car | Yds | Avg | TD | Year | | Car | Yds | Avg | TD |
|------|---|-----|-----|-----|----|----|---|-----|-----|-----|----|
| 1932 | Cliff Battles, Bos | 148 | 576 | 3.9 | 3 | 1969 | Gale Sayers, Chi | 236 | 1032 | 4.4 | 8 |
| 1933 | Jim Musick, Bos | 173 | 809 | 4.7 | 5 | 1970 | Larry Brown, Wash | 237 | 1125 | 4.7 | 5 |
| 1934 | Beattie Feathers, Chi. Bears | 119 | 1004 | 8.4 | 8 | 1971 | John Brockington, GB | 216 | 1105 | 5.1 | 4 |
| 1935 | Doug Russell, Chi. Cards | 140 | 499 | 3.6 | 0 | 1972 | Larry Brown, Wash | 285 | 1216 | 4.3 | 8 |
| 1936 | Tuffy Leemans, NY | 206 | 830 | 4.0 | 2 | 1973 | John Brockington, GB | 265 | 1144 | 4.3 | 3 |
| 1937 | Cliff Battles, Wash | 216 | 874 | 4.0 | 5 | 1974 | Lawrence McCutcheon, LA | 236 | 1109 | 4.7 | 3 |
| 1938 | Whizzer White, Pit | 152 | 567 | 3.7 | 4 | 1975 | Jim Otis, St.L | 269 | 1076 | 4.0 | 5 |
| 1939 | Bill Osmanski, Chi. Bears | 121 | 699 | 5.8 | 7 | 1976 | Walter Payton, Chi | 311 | 1390 | 4.5 | 13 |
| 1940 | Whizzer White, Det | 146 | 514 | 3.5 | 5 | 1977 | Walter Payton, Chi | 339 | 1852 | 5.5 | 14 |
| 1941 | Pug Manders, Bklyn | 111 | 486 | 4.4 | 5 | 1978 | Walter Payton, Chi | 333 | 1395 | 4.2 | 11 |
| 1942 | Bill Dudley, Pit | 162 | 696 | 4.3 | 5 | 1979 | Walter Payton, Chi | 369 | 1610 | 4.4 | 14 |
| 1943 | Bill Paschal, NY | 147 | 572 | 3.9 | 10 | 1980 | Walter Payton, Chi | 317 | 1460 | 4.6 | 6 |
| 1944 | Bill Paschal, NY | 196 | 737 | 3.8 | 9 | 1981 | George Rogers, NO | 378 | 1674 | 4.4 | 13 |
| 1945 | Steve Van Buren, Phi | 143 | 832 | 5.8 | 15 | 1982 | Tony Dorsett, Dal | 177 | 745 | 4.2 | 5 |
| 1946 | Bill Dudley, Pit | 146 | 604 | 4.1 | 3 | 1983 | Eric Dickerson, LA | 390 | 1808 | 4.6 | 18 |
| 1947 | Steve Van Buren, Phi | 217 | 1008 | 4.6 | 13 | 1984 | Eric Dickerson, LA | 379 | 2105 | 5.6 | 14 |
| 1948 | Steve Van Buren, Phi | 201 | 945 | 4.7 | 10 | 1985 | Gerald Riggs, Atl | 397 | 1719 | 4.3 | 10 |
| 1949 | Steve Van Buren, Phi | 263 | 1146 | 4.4 | 11 | 1986 | Eric Dickerson, LA | 404 | 1821 | 4.5 | 11 |
| 1950 | Marion Motley, Cle | 140 | 810 | 5.8 | 3 | 1987 | Charles White, LA | 324 | 1374 | 4.2 | 11 |
| 1951 | Eddie Price, NY Giants | 271 | 971 | 3.6 | 7 | 1988 | Herschel Walker, Dal | 361 | 1514 | 4.2 | 5 |
| 1952 | Dan Towler, LA | 156 | 894 | 5.7 | 10 | 1989 | Barry Sanders, Det | 280 | 1470 | 5.3 | 14 |
| 1953 | Joe Perry, SF | 192 | 1018 | 5.3 | 10 | 1990 | Barry Sanders, Det | 255 | 1304 | 5.1 | 13 |
| 1954 | Joe Perry, SF | 173 | 1049 | 6.1 | 8 | 1991 | Emmitt Smith, Dal | 365 | 1563 | 4.3 | 12 |
| 1955 | Alan Ameche, Bal | 213 | 961 | 4.5 | 9 | 1992 | Emmitt Smith, Dal | 373 | 1713 | 4.6 | 18 |
| 1956 | Rick Casares, Chi. Bears | 234 | 1126 | 4.8 | 12 | 1993 | Emmitt Smith, Dal | 283 | 1486 | 5.3 | 9 |
| 1957 | Jim Brown, Cle | 202 | 942 | 4.7 | 9 | 1994 | Barry Sanders, Det | 331 | 1883 | 5.7 | 7 |
| 1958 | Jim Brown, Cle | 257 | 1527 | 5.9 | 17 | 1995 | Emmitt Smith, Dal | 377 | 1773 | 4.7 | 25 |
| 1959 | Jim Brown, Cle | 290 | 1329 | 4.6 | 14 | 1996 | Barry Sanders, Det | 307 | 1553 | 5.1 | 11 |
| 1960 | Jim Brown, Cle | 215 | 1257 | 5.8 | 9 | 1997 | Barry Sanders, Det | 335 | 2053 | 6.1 | 11 |
| 1961 | Jim Brown, Cle | 305 | 1408 | 4.6 | 8 | 1998 | Jamal Anderson, Atl | 410 | 1846 | 4.5 | 14 |
| 1962 | Jim Taylor, GB | 272 | 1474 | 5.4 | 19 | 1999 | Stephen Davis, Wash | 290 | 1405 | 4.8 | 17 |
| 1963 | Jim Brown, Cle | 291 | 1863 | 6.4 | 12 | 2000 | Robert Smith, Min | 295 | 1521 | 5.2 | 7 |
| 1964 | Jim Brown, Cle | 280 | 1446 | 5.2 | 7 | 2001 | Stephen Davis, Wash | 356 | 1432 | 4.0 | 5 |
| 1965 | Jim Brown, Cle | 289 | 1544 | 5.3 | 17 | 2002 | Deuce McAllister, NO | 325 | 1388 | 4.3 | 13 |
| 1966 | Gale Sayers, Chi | 229 | 1231 | 5.4 | 8 | 2003 | Ahman Green, GB | 355 | 1883 | 5.3 | 15 |
| 1967 | Leroy Kelly, Cle | 235 | 1205 | 5.1 | 11 | 2004 | Shaun Alexander, Sea | 353 | 1696 | 4.8 | 16 |
| 1968 | Leroy Kelly, Cle | 248 | 1239 | 5.0 | 16 | | | | | | |

**Note:** Jim Brown led the NFL in rushing eight of his nine years in the league. The one season he didn't win (1962) he finished fourth (996 yds) behind Jim Taylor, John Henry Johnson of Pittsburgh (1,141 yds) and Dick Bass of the LA Rams (1,033 yds).

### AFL-AFC

**Multiple winners:** Earl Campbell and O.J. Simpson (4); Terrell Davis and Thurman Thomas (3); Eric Dickerson, Cookie Gilchrist, Edgerrin James, Floyd Little, Curtis Martin, Jim Nance and Curt Warner (2).

| Year | | Car | Yds | Avg | TD | Year | | Car | Yds | Avg | TD |
|------|---|-----|-----|-----|----|----|---|-----|-----|-----|----|
| 1960 | Abner Haynes, Dal | 157 | 875 | 5.6 | 9 | 1983 | Curt Warner, Sea | 335 | 1449 | 4.3 | 13 |
| 1961 | Billy Cannon, Hou | 200 | 948 | 4.7 | 6 | 1984 | Earnest Jackson, SD | 296 | 1179 | 4.0 | 8 |
| 1962 | Cookie Gilchrist, Buf | 214 | 1096 | 5.1 | 13 | 1985 | Marcus Allen, LA | 380 | 1759 | 4.6 | 11 |
| 1963 | Clem Daniels, Oak | 215 | 1099 | 5.1 | 3 | 1986 | Curt Warner, Sea | 319 | 1481 | 4.6 | 13 |
| 1964 | Cookie Gilchrist, Buf | 230 | 981 | 4.3 | 6 | 1987 | Eric Dickerson, Ind | 223 | 1011 | 4.5 | 5 |
| 1965 | Paul Lowe, SD | 222 | 1121 | 5.0 | 7 | 1988 | Eric Dickerson, Ind | 388 | 1659 | 4.3 | 14 |
| 1966 | Jim Nance, Bos | 299 | 1458 | 4.9 | 11 | 1989 | Christian Okoye, KC | 370 | 1480 | 4.0 | 12 |
| 1967 | Jim Nance, Bos | 269 | 1216 | 4.5 | 7 | 1990 | Thurman Thomas, Buf | 271 | 1297 | 4.8 | 11 |
| 1968 | Paul Robinson, Cin | 238 | 1023 | 4.3 | 8 | 1991 | Thurman Thomas, Buf | 288 | 1407 | 4.9 | 7 |
| 1969 | Dickie Post, SD | 182 | 873 | 4.8 | 6 | 1992 | Barry Foster, Pit | 390 | 1690 | 4.3 | 11 |
| 1970 | Floyd Little, Den | 209 | 901 | 4.3 | 3 | 1993 | Thurman Thomas, Buf | 355 | 1315 | 3.7 | 6 |
| 1971 | Floyd Little, Den | 284 | 1133 | 4.0 | 6 | 1994 | Chris Warren, Sea | 333 | 1545 | 4.6 | 9 |
| 1972 | O.J. Simpson, Buf | 292 | 1251 | 4.3 | 6 | 1995 | Curtis Martin, NE | 368 | 1487 | 4.0 | 14 |
| 1973 | O.J. Simpson, Buf | 332 | 2003 | 6.0 | 12 | 1996 | Terrell Davis, Den | 345 | 1538 | 4.5 | 13 |
| 1974 | Otis Armstrong, Den | 263 | 1407 | 5.3 | 9 | 1997 | Terrell Davis, Den | 369 | 1750 | 4.7 | 15 |
| 1975 | O.J. Simpson, Buf | 329 | 1817 | 5.5 | 16 | 1998 | Terrell Davis, Den | 392 | 2008 | 5.1 | 21 |
| 1976 | O.J. Simpson, Buf | 290 | 1503 | 5.2 | 8 | 1999 | Edgerrin James, Ind | 369 | 1553 | 4.2 | 13 |
| 1977 | Mark van Eeghen, Oak | 324 | 1273 | 3.9 | 7 | 2000 | Edgerrin James, Ind | 387 | 1709 | 4.4 | 13 |
| 1978 | Earl Campbell, Hou | 302 | 1450 | 4.8 | 13 | 2001 | Priest Holmes, KC | 327 | 1555 | 4.8 | 8 |
| 1979 | Earl Campbell, Hou | 368 | 1697 | 4.6 | 19 | 2002 | Ricky Williams, Mia | 383 | 1853 | 4.8 | 16 |
| 1980 | Earl Campbell, Hou | 373 | 1934 | 5.2 | 13 | 2003 | Jamal Lewis, Bal | 387 | 2066 | 5.3 | 14 |
| 1981 | Earl Campbell, Hou | 361 | 1376 | 3.8 | 10 | 2004 | Curtis Martin, NYJ | 371 | 1697 | 4.6 | 12 |
| 1982 | Freeman McNeil, NY | 151 | 786 | 5.2 | 6 | | | | | | |

**Note:** Eric Dickerson was traded to Indianapolis from the NFC's LA Rams during the 1987 season. In three games with the Rams, he carried the ball 60 times for 277 yds, a 4.6 avg and 1 TD. His official AFC statistics above came in nine games with the Colts.

## Scoring
### NFL-NFC

**Multiple winners:** Don Hutson (5); Dutch Clark, Pat Harder, Paul Hornung, Chip Lohmiller and Mark Moseley (3); Kevin Butler, Mike Cofer, Fred Cox, Marshall Faulk, Jack Manders, Chester Marcol, Eddie Murray, Emmitt Smith, Gordy Soltau, Jeff Wilkins and Doak Walker (2).

| Year | | TD | FG | PAT | Pts | Year | | TD | FG | PAT | Pts |
|---|---|---|---|---|---|---|---|---|---|---|---|
| 1932 | Dutch Clark, Portsmouth | 6 | 3 | 10 | 55 | 1969 | Fred Cox, Min | 0 | 26 | 43 | 121 |
| 1933 | Glenn Presnell, Portsmouth | 6 | 6 | 10 | 64 | 1970 | Fred Cox, Min | 0 | 30 | 35 | 125 |
| | & Ken Strong, NY | 6 | 5 | 13 | 64 | 1971 | Curt Knight, Wash | 0 | 29 | 27 | 114 |
| 1934 | Jack Manders, Chi. Bears | 3 | 10 | 31 | 79 | 1972 | Chester Marcol, GB | 0 | 33 | 29 | 128 |
| 1935 | Dutch Clark, Det | 6 | 1 | 16 | 55 | 1973 | David Ray, LA | 0 | 30 | 40 | 130 |
| 1936 | Dutch Clark, Det | 7 | 4 | 19 | 73 | 1974 | Chester Marcol, GB | 0 | 25 | 19 | 94 |
| 1937 | Jack Manders, Chi. Bears | 5 | 8 | 15 | 69 | 1975 | Chuck Foreman, Min | 22 | 0 | 0 | 132 |
| 1938 | Clarke Hinkle, GB | 7 | 3 | 7 | 58 | 1976 | Mark Moseley, Wash | 0 | 22 | 31 | 97 |
| 1939 | Andy Farkas, Wash | 11 | 0 | 2 | 68 | 1977 | Walter Payton, Chi | 16 | 0 | 0 | 96 |
| 1940 | Don Hutson, GB | 7 | 0 | 15 | 57 | 1978 | Frank Corral, LA | 0 | 29 | 31 | 118 |
| 1941 | Don Hutson, GB | 12 | 1 | 20 | 95 | 1979 | Mark Moseley, Wash | 0 | 25 | 39 | 114 |
| 1942 | Don Hutson, GB | 17 | 1 | 33 | 138 | 1980 | Eddie Murray, Det | 0 | 27 | 35 | 116 |
| 1943 | Don Hutson, GB | 12 | 3 | 26 | 117 | 1981 | Rafael Septien, Dal | 0 | 27 | 40 | 121 |
| 1944 | Don Hutson, GB | 9 | 0 | 31 | 85 | | & Eddie Murray, Det | 0 | 25 | 46 | 121 |
| 1945 | Steve Van Buren, Phi | 18 | 0 | 2 | 110 | 1982 | Wendell Tyler, LA | 13 | 0 | 0 | 78 |
| 1946 | Ted Fritsch, GB | 10 | 9 | 13 | 100 | 1983 | Mark Moseley, Wash | 0 | 33 | 62 | 161 |
| 1947 | Pat Harder, Chi. Cards | 7 | 7 | 39 | 102 | 1984 | Ray Wersching, SF | 0 | 25 | 56 | 131 |
| 1948 | Pat Harder, Chi. Cards | 6 | 7 | 53 | 110 | 1985 | Kevin Butler, Chi | 0 | 31 | 51 | 144 |
| 1949 | Gene Roberts, NY Giants | 17 | 0 | 0 | 102 | 1986 | Kevin Butler, Chi | 0 | 28 | 36 | 120 |
| | & Pat Harder, Chi. Cards | 8 | 3 | 45 | 102 | 1987 | Jerry Rice, SF | 23 | 0 | 0 | 138 |
| 1950 | Doak Walker, Det | 11 | 8 | 38 | 128 | 1988 | Mike Cofer, SF | 0 | 27 | 40 | 121 |
| 1951 | Elroy Hirsch, LA | 17 | 0 | 0 | 102 | 1989 | Mike Cofer, SF | 0 | 29 | 49 | 136 |
| 1952 | Gordy Soltau, SF | 7 | 6 | 34 | 94 | 1990 | Chip Lohmiller, Wash | 0 | 30 | 41 | 131 |
| 1953 | Gordy Soltau, SF | 6 | 10 | 48 | 114 | 1991 | Chip Lohmiller, Wash | 0 | 31 | 56 | 149 |
| 1954 | Bobby Walston, Phi | 11 | 4 | 36 | 114 | 1992 | Chip Lohmiller, Wash | 0 | 30 | 30 | 120 |
| 1955 | Doak Walker, Det | 7 | 9 | 27 | 96 | | & Morten Andersen, NO | 0 | 29 | 33 | 120 |
| 1956 | Bobby Layne, Det | 5 | 12 | 33 | 99 | 1993 | Jason Hanson, Det | 0 | 34 | 28 | 130 |
| 1957 | Sam Baker, Wash | 1 | 14 | 29 | 77 | 1994 | Emmitt Smith, Dal | 22 | 0 | 0 | 132 |
| | & Lou Groza, Cle | 0 | 15 | 32 | 77 | | & Fuad Reveiz, Min | 0 | 34 | 30 | 132 |
| 1958 | Jim Brown, Cle | 18 | 0 | 0 | 108 | 1995 | Emmitt Smith, Dal | 25 | 0 | 0 | 150 |
| 1959 | Paul Hornung, GB | 7 | 7 | 31 | 94 | 1996 | John Kasay, Car. | 0 | 37 | 34 | 145 |
| 1960 | Paul Hornung, GB | 15 | 15 | 41 | 176 | 1997 | Richie Cunningham, Dal | 0 | 34 | 24 | 126 |
| 1961 | Paul Hornung, GB | 10 | 15 | 41 | 146 | 1998 | Gary Anderson, Min | 0 | 35 | 59 | 164 |
| 1962 | Jim Taylor, GB | 19 | 0 | 0 | 114 | 1999 | Jeff Wilkins, St.L | 0 | 20 | 64 | 124 |
| 1963 | Don Chandler, NY | 0 | 18 | 52 | 106 | 2000 | Marshall Faulk, St.L | 26 | 0 | 4 | 160 |
| 1964 | Lenny Moore, Bal | 20 | 0 | 0 | 120 | 2001 | Marshall Faulk, St.L | 21 | 0 | 2 | 128 |
| 1965 | Gale Sayers, Chi | 22 | 0 | 0 | 132 | 2002 | Jay Feely, Atl | 0 | 32 | 42 | 138 |
| 1966 | Bruce Gossett, LA | 0 | 28 | 29 | 113 | 2003 | Jeff Wilkins, St.L | 0 | 39 | 46 | 163 |
| 1967 | Jim Bakken, St.L | 0 | 27 | 36 | 117 | 2004 | David Akers, Phi | 0 | 27 | 41 | 122 |
| 1968 | Leroy Kelly, Cle | 20 | 0 | 0 | 120 | | | | | | |

### AFL-AFC

**Multiple winners:** Gino Cappelletti (5); Gary Anderson (3); Jim Breech, Roy Gerela, Priest Holmes, Gene Mingo, Nick Lowery, John Smith, Pete Stoyanovich, Jim Turner and Mike Vanderjagt (2).

| Year | | TD | FG | PAT | Pts | Year | | TD | FG | PAT | Pts |
|---|---|---|---|---|---|---|---|---|---|---|---|
| 1960 | Gene Mingo, Den | 6 | 18 | 33 | 123 | 1982 | Marcus Allen, LA | 14 | 0 | 0 | 84 |
| 1961 | Gino Cappelletti,Bos | 8 | 17 | 48 | 147 | 1983 | Gary Anderson, Pit | 0 | 27 | 38 | 119 |
| 1962 | Gene Mingo, Den | 4 | 27 | 32 | 137 | 1984 | Gary Anderson, Pit | 0 | 24 | 45 | 117 |
| 1963 | Gino Cappelletti, Bos | 2 | 22 | 35 | 113 | 1985 | Gary Anderson, Pit | 0 | 33 | 40 | 139 |
| 1964 | Gino Cappelletti, Bos | 7 | 25 | 36 | 155 | 1986 | Tony Franklin, NE | 0 | 32 | 44 | 140 |
| 1965 | Gino Cappelletti, Bos | 9 | 17 | 27 | 132 | 1987 | Jim Breech, Cin | 0 | 24 | 25 | 97 |
| 1966 | Gino Cappelletti, Bos | 6 | 16 | 35 | 119 | 1988 | Scott Norwood, Buf | 0 | 32 | 33 | 129 |
| 1967 | George Blanda, Oak | 0 | 20 | 56 | 116 | 1989 | David Treadwell, Den | 0 | 27 | 39 | 120 |
| 1968 | Jim Turner, NY | 0 | 34 | 43 | 145 | 1990 | Nick Lowery, KC | 0 | 34 | 37 | 139 |
| 1969 | Jim Turner, NY | 0 | 32 | 33 | 129 | 1991 | Pete Stoyanovich, Mia | 0 | 31 | 28 | 121 |
| 1970 | Jan Stenerud, KC | 0 | 30 | 26 | 116 | 1992 | Pete Stoyanovich, Mia | 0 | 30 | 34 | 124 |
| 1971 | Garo Yepremian, Mia | 0 | 28 | 33 | 117 | 1993 | Jeff Jaeger, LA | 0 | 35 | 27 | 132 |
| 1972 | Bobby Howfield, NY | 0 | 27 | 40 | 121 | 1994 | John Carney, SD | 0 | 34 | 33 | 135 |
| 1973 | Roy Gerela, Pit | 0 | 29 | 36 | 123 | 1995 | Norm Johnson, Pit | 0 | 34 | 39 | 141 |
| 1974 | Roy Gerela, Pit | 0 | 20 | 33 | 93 | 1996 | Cary Blanchard, Ind | 0 | 36 | 27 | 135 |
| 1975 | O.J. Simpson, Buf | 23 | 0 | 0 | 138 | 1997 | Mike Hollis, Jax | 0 | 31 | 41 | 134 |
| 1976 | Toni Linhart, Bal | 0 | 20 | 49 | 109 | 1998 | Steve Christie, Buf | 0 | 33 | 41 | 140 |
| 1977 | Errol Mann, Oak | 0 | 20 | 39 | 99 | 1999 | Mike Vanderjagt, Ind | 0 | 34 | 43 | 145 |
| 1978 | Pat Leahy, NY | 0 | 22 | 41 | 107 | 2000 | Matt Stover, Bal | 0 | 35 | 30 | 135 |
| 1979 | John Smith, NE | 0 | 23 | 46 | 115 | 2001 | Mike Vanderjagt, Ind | 0 | 28 | 41 | 125 |
| 1980 | John Smith, NE | 0 | 26 | 51 | 129 | 2002 | Priest Holmes, KC | 24 | 0 | 0 | 144 |
| 1981 | Nick Lowery, KC | 0 | 26 | 37 | 115 | 2003 | Priest Holmes, KC | 27 | 0 | 0 | 162 |
| | & Jim Breech, Cin | 0 | 22 | 49 | 115 | 2004 | Adam Vinatieri, NE | 0 | 31 | 48 | 141 |

## All-Time NFL Leaders
Through 2004 regular season.

### CAREER
Players active in 2004 in **bold** type.

### Passing Efficiency

Ratings based on performance standards established for completion percentage, average gain, touchdown percentage and interception percentage. Quarterbacks are allocated points according to how their statistics measure up to those standards. Minimum 1500 passing attempts.

| | | Yrs | Att | Cmp | Cmp% | Yards | Avg Gain | TD | TD% | Int | Int% | Rating |
|---|---|---|---|---|---|---|---|---|---|---|---|---|
| 1 | Steve Young | 15 | 4149 | 2667 | 64.3 | 33,124 | 7.98 | 232 | 5.6 | 107 | 2.6 | 96.8 |
| 2 | **Kurt Warner** | 7 | 1965 | 1295 | 65.9 | 16,501 | 8.40 | 108 | 5.5 | 69 | 3.5 | 95.7 |
| 3 | **Daunte Culpepper** | 6 | 2391 | 1539 | 64.4 | 18,598 | 7.78 | 129 | 5.4 | 74 | 3.1 | 93.2 |
| 4 | **Peyton Manning** | 7 | 3880 | 2464 | 63.5 | 29,442 | 7.59 | 216 | 5.6 | 120 | 3.1 | 92.3 |
| 5 | Joe Montana | 15 | 5391 | 3409 | 63.2 | 40,551 | 7.52 | 273 | 5.1 | 139 | 2.6 | 92.3 |
| 6 | Trent Green | 7 | 2822 | 1705 | 60.4 | 21,607 | 7.66 | 133 | 4.7 | 82 | 2.9 | 87.9 |
| 7 | **Tom Brady** | 5 | 2018 | 1243 | 61.6 | 13,925 | 6.90 | 97 | 4.8 | 52 | 2.6 | 87.5 |
| 8 | **Brett Favre** | 14 | 7004 | 4306 | 61.5 | 49,734 | 7.10 | 376 | 5.4 | 226 | 3.2 | 87.4 |
| 9 | **Jeff Garcia** | 6 | 2612 | 1593 | 61.0 | 18,139 | 6.94 | 123 | 4.7 | 65 | 2.5 | 87.2 |
| 10 | Dan Marino | 17 | 8358 | 4967 | 59.4 | 61,361 | 7.34 | 420 | 5.0 | 252 | 3.0 | 86.4 |
| 11 | **Brian Griese** | 7 | 2144 | 1351 | 63.0 | 15,208 | 7.09 | 96 | 4.5 | 71 | 3.3 | 85.3 |
| 12 | **Rich Gannon** | 16 | 4206 | 2533 | 60.2 | 28,743 | 6.83 | 180 | 4.3 | 104 | 2.5 | 84.7 |
| 13 | Jim Kelly | 11 | 4779 | 2874 | 60.1 | 35,467 | 7.42 | 237 | 5.0 | 175 | 3.7 | 84.4 |
| 14 | **Brad Johnson** | 13 | 3504 | 2166 | 61.8 | 23,913 | 6.82 | 143 | 4.1 | 98 | 2.8 | 84.0 |
| 15 | **Donovan McNabb** | 6 | 2586 | 1507 | 58.3 | 16,926 | 6.55 | 118 | 4.6 | 57 | 2.2 | 83.9 |
| 16 | **Mark Brunell** | 11 | 3880 | 2314 | 59.6 | 26,987 | 6.96 | 151 | 3.9 | 92 | 2.4 | 83.9 |
| 17 | **Matt Hasselbeck** | 6 | 1756 | 1048 | 59.7 | 12,466 | 7.10 | 72 | 4.1 | 48 | 2.7 | 83.7 |
| 18 | Roger Staubach | 11 | 2958 | 1685 | 57.0 | 22,700 | 7.67 | 153 | 5.2 | 109 | 3.7 | 83.4 |
| 19 | **Steve McNair** | 10 | 3395 | 2013 | 59.3 | 23,980 | 7.06 | 140 | 4.1 | 92 | 2.7 | 83.4 |
| 20 | Neil Lomax | 8 | 3153 | 1817 | 57.6 | 22,771 | 7.22 | 136 | 4.3 | 90 | 2.9 | 82.7 |
| 21 | Sonny Jurgensen | 18 | 4262 | 2433 | 57.1 | 32,224 | 7.56 | 255 | 6.0 | 189 | 4.4 | 82.6 |
| 22 | Len Dawson | 19 | 3741 | 2136 | 57.1 | 28,711 | 7.67 | 239 | 6.4 | 183 | 4.9 | 82.6 |
| 23 | Ken Anderson | 16 | 4475 | 2654 | 59.3 | 32,838 | 7.34 | 197 | 4.4 | 160 | 3.6 | 81.9 |
| 24 | Bernie Kosar | 12 | 3365 | 1994 | 59.3 | 23,301 | 6.92 | 124 | 3.7 | 87 | 2.6 | 81.8 |
| 25 | Neil O'Donnell | 14 | 3229 | 1865 | 57.8 | 21,690 | 6.72 | 120 | 3.7 | 68 | 2.1 | 81.8 |

**Note:** The NFL does not recognize records from the All-American Football Conference (1946-49). If it did, **Otto Graham** would rank 10th (after Garcia) with the following stats: 10 Yrs; 2,626 Att; 1,464 Comp; 55.8 Comp Pct; 23,584 Yards; 8.98 Avg Gain; 174 TD; 6.6 TD Pct; 135 Int; 5.1 Int Pct; and 86.6 Rating Pts.

### Touchdown Passes

| | | No |
|---|---|---|
| 1 | Dan Marino | 420 |
| 2 | **Brett Favre** | 376 |
| 3 | Fran Tarkenton | 342 |
| 4 | John Elway | 300 |
| 5 | Warren Moon | 291 |
| 6 | Johnny Unitas | 290 |
| 7 | Joe Montana | 273 |
| 8 | **Vinny Testaverde** | 268 |
| 9 | Dave Krieg | 261 |
| 10 | Sonny Jurgensen | 255 |
| 11 | Dan Fouts | 254 |
| 12 | Boomer Esiason | 247 |
| 13 | John Hadl | 244 |
| 14 | Len Dawson | 239 |
| 15 | Jim Kelly | 237 |

| | | No |
|---|---|---|
| 16 | George Blanda | 236 |
| 17 | Steve Young | 232 |
| 18 | **Drew Bledsoe** | 221 |
| 19 | **Peyton Manning** | 216 |
| 20 | John Brodie | 214 |
| 21 | Terry Bradshaw | 212 |
| | Y.A. Tittle | 212 |
| 23 | Jim Hart | 209 |
| 24 | Randall Cunningham | 207 |
| 25 | Jim Everett | 203 |
| 26 | Roman Gabriel | 201 |
| 27 | Phil Simms | 199 |
| 28 | Ken Anderson | 197 |
| 29 | Joe Ferguson | 196 |
| | Bobby Layne | 196 |

| | | No |
|---|---|---|
| | Norm Snead | 196 |
| | Steve DeBerg | 196 |
| 33 | Ken Stabler | 194 |
| 34 | Bob Griese | 192 |
| 35 | Sammy Baugh | 187 |
| 36 | Craig Morton | 183 |
| 37 | Steve Grogan | 182 |
| 38 | **Rich Gannon** | 180 |
| 39 | Ron Jaworski | 179 |
| 40 | Babe Parilli | 178 |
| 41 | Charlie Conerly | 173 |
| | Joe Namath | 173 |
| | Norm Van Brocklin | 173 |
| 44 | Charley Johnson | 170 |
| | **Chris Chandler** | 170 |

**Note:** The NFL does not recognize records from the All-American Football Conference (1946-49). If it did, **Y.A. Tittle** would move up from 21st to 14th (after Hadl) with 242 TDs and **Otto Graham** would rank 41st (after Parilli) with 174 TDs.

### Passes Intercepted

| | | No |
|---|---|---|
| 1 | George Blanda | 277 |
| 2 | John Hadl | 268 |
| 3 | Fran Tarkenton | 266 |
| 4 | Norm Snead | 257 |
| 5 | **Vinny Testaverde** | 255 |
| 6 | Johnny Unitas | 253 |
| 7 | Dan Marino | 252 |
| 8 | Jim Hart | 247 |
| 9 | Bobby Layne | 245 |

| | | No |
|---|---|---|
| 10 | Dan Fouts | 242 |
| 11 | Warren Moon | 233 |
| 12 | John Elway | 226 |
| | **Brett Favre** | 226 |
| 14 | John Brodie | 224 |
| 15 | Ken Stabler | 222 |
| 16 | Y.A. Tittle | 221 |
| 17 | Joe Namath | 220 |
| | Babe Parilli | 220 |

| | | No |
|---|---|---|
| 19 | Terry Bradshaw | 210 |
| 20 | Joe Ferguson | 209 |
| 21 | Steve Grogan | 208 |
| 22 | Steve DeBerg | 204 |
| 23 | Sammy Baugh | 203 |
| 24 | Dave Krieg | 199 |
| 25 | Jim Plunkett | 198 |

## Passing Yards

| | | Yrs | Att | Comp | Pct | Yards |
|---|---|---|---|---|---|---|
| 1 | Dan Marino | 17 | 8358 | 4967 | 59.4 | 61,361 |
| 2 | John Elway | 16 | 7250 | 4123 | 56.9 | 51,475 |
| 3 | **Brett Favre** | 14 | 7004 | 4306 | 61.5 | 49,734 |
| 4 | Warren Moon | 17 | 6823 | 3988 | 58.5 | 49,325 |
| 5 | Fran Tarkenton | 18 | 6467 | 3686 | 57.0 | 47,003 |
| 6 | **Vinny Testaverde** | 18 | 6420 | 3631 | 56.6 | 44,475 |
| 7 | Dan Fouts | 15 | 5604 | 3297 | 58.8 | 43,040 |
| 8 | Joe Montana | 15 | 5391 | 3409 | 63.2 | 40,551 |
| 9 | Johnny Unitas | 18 | 5186 | 2830 | 54.6 | 40,239 |
| 10 | **Drew Bledsoe** | 12 | 6049 | 3449 | 57.0 | 39,808 |
| 11 | Dave Krieg | 19 | 5311 | 3105 | 58.5 | 38,147 |
| 12 | Boomer Esiason | 14 | 5205 | 2969 | 57.0 | 37,920 |
| 13 | Jim Kelly | 11 | 4779 | 2874 | 60.1 | 35,467 |
| 14 | Jim Everett | 12 | 4923 | 2841 | 57.7 | 34,837 |
| 15 | Jim Hart | 19 | 5076 | 2593 | 51.1 | 34,665 |
| 16 | Steve DeBerg | 17 | 5024 | 2874 | 57.2 | 34,241 |
| 17 | John Hadl | 16 | 4687 | 2363 | 50.4 | 33,503 |
| 18 | Phil Simms | 14 | 4647 | 2576 | 55.4 | 33,462 |
| 19 | Steve Young | 15 | 4149 | 2667 | 64.3 | 33,124 |
| 20 | Troy Aikman | 12 | 4715 | 2898 | 61.5 | 32,942 |
| 21 | Ken Anderson | 16 | 4475 | 2654 | 59.3 | 32,838 |
| 22 | Sonny Jurgensen | 18 | 4262 | 2433 | 57.1 | 32,224 |
| 23 | John Brodie | 17 | 4491 | 2469 | 55.0 | 31,548 |
| 24 | Norm Snead | 15 | 4353 | 2276 | 52.3 | 30,797 |
| 25 | Randall Cunningham | 17 | 4289 | 2429 | 56.6 | 29,979 |

**Note:** The NFL does not recognize records from the All-American Football Conference (1946-49). If it did, **Y.A. Tittle** would rank 20th (after Young) with the following stats: 17 Yrs; 4,395 Att; 2,427 Comp; 55.2 Pct; and 33,070 Yards.

## Receptions

| | | Yrs | No | Yards | Avg | TD |
|---|---|---|---|---|---|---|
| 1 | **Jerry Rice** | 20 | 1549 | 22,895 | 14.8 | 197 |
| 2 | Cris Carter | 16 | 1101 | 13,899 | 12.6 | 130 |
| 3 | **Tim Brown** | 17 | 1094 | 14,934 | 13.7 | 100 |
| 4 | Andre Reed | 16 | 951 | 13,198 | 13.9 | 87 |
| 5 | Art Monk | 16 | 940 | 12,721 | 13.5 | 68 |
| 6 | Irving Fryar | 17 | 851 | 12,785 | 15.0 | 84 |
| 7 | **Marvin Harrison** | 9 | 845 | 11,185 | 13.2 | 98 |
| 8 | Larry Centers | 14 | 827 | 6,797 | 8.2 | 28 |
| 9 | Steve Largent | 14 | 819 | 13,089 | 16.0 | 100 |
| 10 | Shannon Sharpe | 14 | 815 | 10,060 | 12.3 | 62 |
| 11 | Henry Ellard | 16 | 814 | 13,777 | 16.9 | 65 |
| 12 | **Jimmy Smith** | 11 | 792 | 11,264 | 14.2 | 61 |
| 13 | **Isaac Bruce** | 11 | 777 | 11,753 | 15.1 | 74 |
| 14 | James Lofton | 16 | 764 | 14,004 | 18.3 | 75 |
| 15 | **Keenan McCardell** | 13 | 755 | 9,763 | 12.9 | 53 |
| 16 | Charlie Joiner | 18 | 750 | 12,146 | 16.2 | 65 |
| | Michael Irvin | 12 | 750 | 11,904 | 15.9 | 65 |
| 18 | Andre Rison | 12 | 743 | 10,205 | 13.7 | 84 |
| 19 | **Marshall Faulk** | 11 | 723 | 6,584 | 9.1 | 35 |
| 20 | **Rod Smith** | 10 | 712 | 9,772 | 13.7 | 59 |
| 21 | Gary Clark | 11 | 699 | 10,856 | 15.5 | 65 |
| 22 | Terance Mathis | 13 | 689 | 8,809 | 12.8 | 63 |
| 23 | **Keyshawn Johnson** | 9 | 673 | 8,917 | 13.2 | 54 |
| 24 | Herman Moore | 12 | 670 | 9,174 | 13.7 | 62 |
| 25 | **Terrell Owens** | 9 | 669 | 9,772 | 14.6 | 95 |

## Rushing

| | | Yrs | Car | Yards | Avg | TD |
|---|---|---|---|---|---|---|
| 1 | **Emmitt Smith** | 15 | 4409 | 18,355 | 4.2 | 164 |
| 2 | Walter Payton | 13 | 3838 | 16,726 | 4.4 | 110 |
| 3 | Barry Sanders | 10 | 3062 | 15,269 | 5.0 | 99 |
| 4 | **Curtis Martin** | 10 | 3298 | 13,366 | 4.1 | 85 |
| 5 | **Jerome Bettis** | 12 | 3369 | 13,294 | 4.0 | 82 |
| 6 | Eric Dickerson | 11 | 2996 | 13,259 | 4.4 | 90 |
| 7 | Tony Dorsett | 12 | 2936 | 12,739 | 4.3 | 77 |
| 8 | Jim Brown | 9 | 2359 | 12,312 | 5.2 | 106 |
| 9 | Marcus Allen | 16 | 3022 | 12,243 | 4.1 | 123 |
| 10 | Franco Harris | 13 | 2949 | 12,120 | 4.1 | 91 |
| 11 | Thurman Thomas | 13 | 2877 | 12,074 | 4.2 | 65 |
| 12 | **Marshall Faulk** | 11 | 2771 | 11,987 | 4.3 | 100 |
| 13 | John Riggins | 14 | 2916 | 11,352 | 3.9 | 104 |
| 14 | O.J. Simpson | 11 | 2404 | 11,236 | 4.7 | 61 |
| 15 | Ricky Watters | 10 | 2622 | 10,643 | 4.1 | 78 |
| 16 | **Eddie George** | 9 | 2865 | 10,441 | 3.6 | 68 |
| 17 | Ottis Anderson | 14 | 2562 | 10,273 | 4.0 | 81 |
| 18 | **Corey Dillon** | 8 | 2210 | 9,696 | 4.4 | 57 |
| 19 | Earl Campbell | 8 | 2187 | 9,407 | 4.3 | 74 |
| 20 | Terry Allen | 10 | 2152 | 8,614 | 4.0 | 73 |
| 21 | Jim Taylor | 10 | 1941 | 8,597 | 4.4 | 83 |
| 22 | Joe Perry | 14 | 1737 | 8,378 | 4.8 | 53 |
| 23 | Earnest Byner | 14 | 2095 | 8,261 | 3.9 | 56 |
| 24 | Herschel Walker | 12 | 1954 | 8,225 | 4.2 | 61 |
| 25 | Roger Craig | 11 | 1991 | 8,189 | 4.1 | 56 |

**Note:** The NFL does not recognize records from the All-American Football Conference (1946-49). If it did, **Joe Perry** would move up from 22nd to 18th (after Anderson) with the following stats: 16 Yrs; 1,929 Att; 9,723 Yards; 5.0 Avg; and 71 TD.

## All-Purpose Yards

| | | Rush | Rec | Ret | Total |
|---|---|---|---|---|---|
| 1 | **Jerry Rice** | 645 | 22,895 | 6 | 23,546 |
| 2 | Brian Mitchell | 1,967 | 2,336 | 19,027 | 23,330 |
| 3 | Walter Payton | 16,726 | 4,538 | 539 | 21,803 |
| 4 | **Emmitt Smith** | 18,355 | 3,224 | -15 | 21,564 |
| 5 | **Tim Brown** | 190 | 14,934 | 4,558 | 19,682 |
| 6 | **Marshall Faulk** | 11,987 | 6,584 | 36 | 18,607 |
| 7 | Barry Sanders | 15,269 | 2,921 | 118 | 18,308 |
| 8 | Herschel Walker | 8,225 | 4,859 | 5,084 | 18,168 |
| 9 | Marcus Allen | 12,243 | 5,411 | -6 | 17,648 |
| 10 | Eric Metcalf | 2,392 | 5,572 | 9,266 | 17,230 |
| 11 | **Curtis Martin** | 13,366 | 3,211 | -9 | 16,568 |
| 12 | Thurman Thomas | 12,074 | 4,458 | 0 | 16,532 |
| 13 | Tony Dorsett | 12,739 | 3,554 | 33 | 16,326 |
| 14 | Henry Ellard | 50 | 13,777 | 1,891 | 15,718 |
| 15 | Irving Fryar | 242 | 12,785 | 2,567 | 15,594 |
| 16 | Jim Brown | 12,312 | 2,499 | 648 | 15,459 |
| 17 | Eric Dickerson | 13,259 | 2,137 | 15 | 15,411 |
| 18 | Glyn Milburn | 817 | 1,322 | 12,772 | 14,911 |
| 19 | James Brooks | 7,962 | 3,621 | 3,327 | 14,910 |
| 20 | Ricky Watters | 10,643 | 4,248 | 0 | 14,891 |
| 21 | **Jerome Bettis** | 13,294 | 1,409 | 2 | 14,705 |
| 22 | Franco Harris | 12,120 | 2,287 | 215 | 14,622 |
| 23 | O.J. Simpson | 11,236 | 2,142 | 990 | 14,368 |
| 24 | James Lofton | 246 | 14,004 | 27 | 14,277 |
| 25 | Cris Carter | 41 | 13,899 | 244 | 14,184 |

**Years played:** Allen (16), Bettis (12), Brooks (12), J. Brown (9), T. Brown (17), Carter (16), Dickerson (11), Dorsett (12), Ellard (16), Faulk (11), Fryar (17), Harris (13), Lofton (16), Martin (10), Metcalf (13), Milburn (9), Mitchell (14), Payton (13), Rice (20), Sanders (10), Simpson (11), Smith (15), Thomas (13), Walker (12) and Watters (10).

## All-Time NFL Leaders (Cont.)
### Scoring

### Points

| | | Yrs | TD | FG | PAT | Total |
|---|---|---|---|---|---|---|
| 1 | **Gary Anderson** | .23 | 0 | 538 | 820 | 2434 |
| 2 | **Morten Andersen** | .23 | 0 | 520 | 798 | 2358 |
| 3 | George Blanda | .26 | 9 | 335 | 943 | 2002 |
| 4 | Norm Johnson | .18 | 0 | 366 | 638 | 1736 |
| 5 | Nick Lowery | .18 | 0 | 383 | 562 | 1711 |
| 6 | Jan Stenerud | .19 | 0 | 373 | 580 | 1699 |
| 7 | Eddie Murray | .19 | 0 | 352 | 538 | 1594 |
| 8 | Al Del Greco | .17 | 0 | 347 | 543 | 1584 |
| 9 | **John Carney** | .17 | 0 | 365 | 442 | 1537 |
| 10 | **Matt Stover** | .14 | 0 | 350 | 431 | 1481 |
| 11 | **Steve Christie** | .15 | 0 | 336 | 468 | 1476 |
| 12 | Pat Leahy | .18 | 0 | 304 | 558 | 1470 |
| 13 | **Jason Elam** | .12 | 0 | 317 | 491 | 1442 |
| 14 | Jim Turner | .16 | 1 | 304 | 521 | 1439 |
| 15 | Matt Bahr | .17 | 0 | 300 | 522 | 1422 |
| 16 | Mark Moseley | .16 | 0 | 300 | 482 | 1382 |
| 17 | Jim Bakken | .17 | 0 | 282 | 534 | 1380 |
| 18 | Fred Cox | .15 | 0 | 282 | 519 | 1365 |
| 19 | Lou Groza | .17 | 0 | 234 | 641 | 1349 |
| 20 | **Jason Hanson** | .13 | 0 | 308 | 412 | 1336 |
| 21 | **Jerry Rice** | .20 | 208 | 0 | 0 | 1256† |
| 22 | Jim Breech | .14 | 0 | 243 | 517 | 1246 |
| 23 | Pete Stoyanovich | .12 | 0 | 272 | 420 | 1236 |
| 24 | Chris Bahr | .14 | 0 | 241 | 490 | 1213 |
| 25 | Kevin Butler | .13 | 0 | 265 | 413 | 1208 |

†Rice's total includes four 2-point conversions.
**Note:** The NFL does not recognize records from the All-American Football Conference (1946-49). If it did, **Lou Groza** would move up from 19th to 7th (after Stenerud) with the following stats: 21 Yrs; 1 TD; 264 FG, 810 PAT; 1,608 Pts.

### Interceptions

| | | Yrs | No | Yards | TD |
|---|---|---|---|---|---|
| 1 | Paul Krause | .16 | 81 | 1185 | 3 |
| 2 | Emlen Tunnell | .14 | 79 | 1282 | 4 |
| 3 | Rod Woodson | .17 | 71 | 1483 | 12 |
| 4 | Dick (Night Train) Lane | .14 | 68 | 1207 | 5 |
| 5 | Ken Riley | .15 | 65 | 596 | 5 |

### Sacks

| | | Yrs | No |
|---|---|---|---|
| 1 | Bruce Smith | .19 | 200.0 |
| 2 | Reggie White | .15 | 198.0 |
| 3 | Kevin Greene | .15 | 160.0 |
| 4 | Chris Doleman | .15 | 150.5 |
| 5 | Richard Dent | .15 | 137.5 |
| | John Randle | .14 | 137.5 |

**Note:** The NFL did not begin officially compiling sacks until 1982. Deacon Jones, who played with the Rams, Chargers and Redskins from 1961-74, is often credited with 173.5 sacks. Jack Youngblood and Alan Page are unofficially credited with 150.5 and 148, respectively. Also, Lawrence Taylor has 142 career sacks if you count his rookie year of 1981, the year before sacks became an official stat.

### Safeties

| | | Yrs | No |
|---|---|---|---|
| 1 | Ted Hendricks | .15 | 4 |
| | Doug English | .10 | 4 |
| 3 | Seventeen players tied with 3 each. | | |

### Touchdowns

| | | Yrs | Rush | Rec | Ret | Total |
|---|---|---|---|---|---|---|
| 1 | **Jerry Rice** | .20 | 10 | 197 | 1 | 208 |
| 2 | Emmitt Smith | .15 | 164 | 11 | 0 | 175 |
| 3 | Marcus Allen | .16 | 123 | 21 | 1 | 145 |
| 4 | **Marshall Faulk** | .11 | 100 | 35 | 0 | 135 |
| 5 | Cris Carter | .16 | 0 | 130 | 1 | 131 |
| 6 | Jim Brown | .9 | 106 | 20 | 0 | 126 |
| 7 | Walter Payton | .13 | 110 | 15 | 0 | 125 |
| 8 | John Riggins | .14 | 104 | 12 | 0 | 116 |
| 9 | Lenny Moore | .12 | 63 | 48 | 2 | 113 |
| 10 | Barry Sanders | .10 | 99 | 10 | 0 | 109 |
| 11 | Don Hutson | .11 | 3 | 99 | 3 | 105 |
| | **Tim Brown** | .17 | 1 | 100 | 4 | 105 |
| 13 | Steve Largent | .14 | 1 | 100 | 0 | 101 |
| 14 | Franco Harris | .13 | 91 | 9 | 0 | 100 |
| 15 | **Marvin Harrison** | .9 | 0 | 98 | 0 | 98 |
| 16 | **Terrell Owens** | .9 | 2 | 95 | 0 | 97 |
| 17 | Eric Dickerson | .11 | 90 | 6 | 0 | 96 |
| 18 | **Curtis Martin** | .10 | 85 | 10 | 0 | 95 |
| 19 | Jim Taylor | .10 | 83 | 10 | 0 | 93 |
| 20 | Tony Dorsett | .12 | 77 | 13 | 1 | 91 |
| | Bobby Mitchell | .11 | 18 | 65 | 8 | 91 |
| | **Randy Moss** | .7 | 0 | 90 | 1 | 91 |
| | Ricky Watters | .10 | 78 | 13 | 0 | 91 |
| 24 | Leroy Kelly | .10 | 74 | 13 | 3 | 90 |
| | Charley Taylor | .13 | 11 | 79 | 0 | 90 |

### Kickoff Returns
Minimum 75 returns.

| | | Yrs | No | Yards | Avg | TD |
|---|---|---|---|---|---|---|
| 1 | Gale Sayers | .7 | 91 | 2781 | 30.6 | 6 |
| 2 | Lynn Chandnois | .7 | 92 | 2720 | 29.6 | 3 |
| 3 | Abe Woodson | .9 | 193 | 5538 | 28.7 | 5 |
| 4 | Buddy Young | .6 | 90 | 2514 | 27.9 | 2 |
| 5 | Travis Williams | .5 | 102 | 2801 | 27.5 | 6 |

### Punting
Minimum 300 punts.

| | | Yrs | No | Yards | Avg |
|---|---|---|---|---|---|
| 1 | **Shane Lechler** | .5 | 360 | 16,522 | 45.9 |
| 2 | Sammy Baugh | .16 | 338 | 15,245 | 45.1 |
| 3 | Tommy Davis | .11 | 511 | 22,833 | 44.7 |
| 4 | Yale Lary | .11 | 503 | 22,279 | 44.3 |
| 5 | **Todd Sauerbrun** | .10 | 760 | 33,433 | 44.0 |

### Punt Returns
Minimum 75 returns.

| | | Yrs | No | Yards | Avg | TD |
|---|---|---|---|---|---|---|
| 1 | George McAfee | .8 | 112 | 1431 | 12.8 | 2 |
| 2 | Jack Christiansen | .8 | 85 | 1084 | 12.8 | 8 |
| 3 | Claude Gibson | .5 | 110 | 1381 | 12.6 | 3 |
| 4 | Bill Dudley | .9 | 124 | 1515 | 12.2 | 3 |
| 5 | Rick Upchurch | .9 | 248 | 3008 | 12.1 | 8 |

### Long-Playing Records

#### Seasons

| | | No |
|---|---|---|
| 1 | George Blanda, QB-K | .26 |
| 2 | **Gary Anderson**, K | .23 |
| | **Morten Andersen**, K | .23 |
| 4 | Earl Morrall, QB | .21 |
| 5 | Five tied with 20 each. | |

#### Games

| | | No |
|---|---|---|
| 1 | **Morten Andersen**, K | .354 |
| 2 | **Gary Anderson**, K | .353 |
| 3 | George Blanda, QB-K | .340 |
| 4 | **Jerry Rice**, WR | .303 |
| 5 | Bruce Matthews, OL | .296 |

#### Consecutive Games

| | | No |
|---|---|---|
| 1 | Jim Marshall, DE | .282 |
| 2 | **Jeff Feagles**, P | .272 |
| 3 | **Morten Andersen**, K | .248 |
| 4 | Bill Romanowski, LB | .243 |
| 5 | Mick Tingelhoff, C | .240 |

## SINGLE SEASON
### Passing

| Yards Gained | Year | Att | Cmp | Pct | Yds | Efficiency | Year | Att/Cmp | TD | Rtg |
|---|---|---|---|---|---|---|---|---|---|---|
| Dan Marino, Mia | 1984 | 564 | 362 | 64.2 | 5084 | **Peyton Manning**, Ind | 2004 | 497/336 | 49 | 121.1 |
| Kurt Warner, St.L | 2001 | 546 | 375 | 68.7 | 4830 | Steve Young, SF | 1994 | 461/324 | 35 | 112.8 |
| Dan Fouts, SD | 1981 | 609 | 360 | 59.1 | 4802 | Joe Montana, SF | 1989 | 386/271 | 26 | 112.4 |
| Dan Marino, Mia | 1986 | 623 | 378 | 60.7 | 4746 | **Daunte Culpepper**, Min | 2004 | 548/379 | 39 | 110.9 |
| **Daunte Culpepper**, Min | 2004 | 548 | 379 | 69.2 | 4717 | Milt Plum, Cle | 1960 | 250/151 | 21 | 110.4 |
| Dan Fouts, SD | 1980 | 589 | 348 | 59.1 | 4715 | Sammy Baugh, Wash | 1945 | 182/128 | 11 | 109.9 |
| Warren Moon, Hou | 1991 | 655 | 404 | 61.7 | 4690 | Kurt Warner, St.L | 1999 | 499/325 | 41 | 109.2 |
| Rich Gannon, Oak | 2002 | 618 | 418 | 67.6 | 4689 | Dan Marino, Mia | 1984 | 564/362 | 48 | 108.9 |
| Warren Moon, Hou | 1990 | 584 | 362 | 62.0 | 4689 | Sid Luckman, Chi. Bears | 1943 | 202/110 | 28 | 107.5 |
| Neil Lomax, St.L | 1984 | 560 | 345 | 61.6 | 4614 | Steve Young, SF | 1992 | 402/268 | 25 | 107.0 |

### Receptions

| Catches | Year | No | Yds |
|---|---|---|---|
| Marvin Harrison, Ind | 2002 | 143 | 1722 |
| Herman Moore, Det | 1995 | 123 | 1686 |
| Jerry Rice, SF | 1995 | 122 | 1848 |
| Cris Carter, Min | 1995 | 122 | 1371 |
| Cris Carter, Min | 1994 | 122 | 1256 |
| Isaac Bruce, St.L | 1995 | 119 | 1781 |
| Torry Holt, St.L | 2003 | 117 | 1696 |
| Jimmy Smith, Jax | 1999 | 116 | 1636 |
| Marvin Harrison, Ind | 1999 | 115 | 1663 |
| Rod Smith, Den | 2001 | 113 | 1343 |
| Hines Ward, Pit | 2002 | 112 | 1329 |
| Jimmy Smith, Jax | 2001 | 112 | 1373 |
| Jerry Rice, SF | 1994 | 112 | 1499 |
| Sterling Sharpe, GB | 1993 | 112 | 1274 |

### Rushing

| Yards Gained | Year | Car | Yds | Avg |
|---|---|---|---|---|
| Eric Dickerson, LA Rams | 1984 | 379 | 2105 | 5.6 |
| Jamal Lewis, Bal. | 2003 | 387 | 2066 | 5.3 |
| Barry Sanders, Det | 1997 | 335 | 2053 | 6.1 |
| Terrell Davis, Den | 1998 | 392 | 2008 | 5.1 |
| O.J. Simpson, Buf | 1973 | 332 | 2003 | 6.0 |
| Earl Campbell, Hou | 1980 | 373 | 1934 | 5.2 |
| Barry Sanders, Det | 1994 | 331 | 1883 | 5.7 |
| Ahman Green, GB | 2003 | 355 | 1883 | 5.3 |
| Jim Brown, Cle | 1963 | 291 | 1863 | 6.4 |
| Ricky Williams, Mia | 2002 | 383 | 1853 | 4.8 |
| Walter Payton, Chi | 1977 | 339 | 1852 | 5.5 |
| Jamal Anderson, Atl | 1998 | 410 | 1846 | 4.5 |
| Eric Dickerson, LA Rams | 1986 | 404 | 1821 | 4.5 |
| O.J. Simpson, Buf | 1975 | 329 | 1817 | 5.5 |

### Scoring

| Points | Year | TD | PAT | FG | Pts |
|---|---|---|---|---|---|
| Paul Hornung, GB | 1960 | 15 | 41 | 15 | 176 |
| Gary Anderson, Min | 1998 | 0 | 59 | 35 | 164 |
| Jeff Wilkins, St.L | 2003 | 0 | 46 | 39 | 163 |
| Priest Holmes, KC | 2003 | 27 | 0 | 0 | 162 |
| Mark Moseley, Wash | 1983 | 0 | 62 | 33 | 161 |
| Marshall Faulk, St.L | 2000 | 26 | 4 | 0 | 160 |
| Mike Vanderjagt, Ind | 2003 | 0 | 46 | 37 | 157 |
| Gino Cappelletti, Bos | 1964 | 7 | 38 | 25 | 155 |
| Emmitt Smith, Dal | 1995 | 25 | 0 | 0 | 150 |
| Chip Lohmiller, Wash | 1991 | 0 | 56 | 31 | 149 |
| Gino Cappelletti, Bos | 1961 | 8 | 48 | 17 | 147 |
| Paul Hornung, GB | 1961 | 10 | 41 | 15 | 146 |
| Jim Turner, Jets | 1968 | 0 | 43 | 34 | 145 |
| John Kasay, Car. | 1996 | 0 | 34 | 37 | 145 |
| Mike Vanderjagt, Ind | 1999 | 0 | 43 | 34 | 145 |

| Touchdowns | Year | Rush | Rec | Ret | Total |
|---|---|---|---|---|---|
| Priest Holmes, KC | 2003 | 27 | 0 | 0 | 27 |
| Marshall Faulk, St.L | 2000 | 18 | 8 | 0 | 26 |
| Emmitt Smith, Dal | 1995 | 25 | 0 | 0 | 25 |
| John Riggins, Wash | 1983 | 24 | 0 | 0 | 24 |
| Priest Holmes, KC | 2002 | 21 | 3 | 0 | 24 |
| Terrell Davis, Den | 1998 | 21 | 2 | 0 | 23 |
| O.J. Simpson, Buf | 1975 | 16 | 7 | 0 | 23 |
| Jerry Rice, SF | 1987 | 1 | 22 | 0 | 23 |
| Gale Sayers, Chi | 1966 | 14 | 6 | 2 | 22 |
| Chuck Foreman, Min | 1975 | 13 | 9 | 0 | 22 |
| Emmitt Smith, Dal | 1994 | 21 | 1 | 0 | 22 |
| Jim Brown, Cle | 1965 | 17 | 4 | 0 | 21 |
| Joe Morris, NY Giants | 1985 | 21 | 0 | 0 | 21 |
| Terry Allen, Wash | 1996 | 21 | 0 | 0 | 21 |
| Marshall Faulk, St.L | 2001 | 12 | 9 | 0 | 21 |

**Note:** The NFL regular season schedule grew from 12 games (1947-60) to 14 (1961-77) to 16 (1978-present). The AFL regular season schedule was always 14 games (1960-69).

### Touchdowns Passing

| | Year | No |
|---|---|---|
| **Peyton Manning**, Indianapolis | 2004 | 49 |
| Dan Marino, Miami | 1984 | 48 |
| Dan Marino, Miami | 1986 | 44 |
| Kurt Warner, St. Louis | 1999 | 41 |
| Brett Favre, Green Bay | 1996 | 39 |
| **Daunte Culpepper**, Minnesota | 2004 | 39 |
| Brett Favre, Green Bay | 1995 | 38 |
| George Blanda, Houston | 1961 | 36 |
| Y.A. Tittle, NY Giants | 1963 | 36 |
| Steve Young, San Francisco | 1998 | 36 |
| Steve Beuerlein, Carolina | 1999 | 36 |
| Kurt Warner, St. Louis | 2001 | 36 |
| Brett Favre, Green Bay | 1997 | 35 |
| Steve Young, San Francisco | 1994 | 35 |

### Touchdowns Receiving

| | Year | No |
|---|---|---|
| Jerry Rice, San Francisco | 1987 | 22 |
| Mark Clayton, Miami | 1984 | 18 |
| Sterling Sharpe, Green Bay | 1994 | 18 |
| Don Hutson, Green Bay | 1942 | 17 |
| Elroy (Crazylegs) Hirsch, LA Rams | 1951 | 17 |
| Bill Groman, Houston | 1961 | 17 |
| Jerry Rice, San Francisco | 1989 | 17 |
| Cris Carter, Minnesota | 1995 | 17 |
| Carl Pickens, Cincinnati | 1995 | 17 |
| Randy Moss, Minnesota | 1998 | 17 |
| Randy Moss, Minnesota | 2003 | 17 |
| Art Powell, Oakland | 1963 | 16 |
| Terrell Owens, SF | 2001 | 16 |
| **Muhsin Muhammad**, Carolina | 2004 | 16 |

## All-Time NFL Leaders (Cont.)

### Touchdowns Rushing

| | Year | No |
|---|---|---|
| Priest Holmes, Kansas City | 2003 | 27 |
| Emmitt Smith, Dallas | 1995 | 25 |
| John Riggins, Washington | 1983 | 24 |
| Joe Morris, NY Giants | 1985 | 21 |
| Emmitt Smith, Dallas | 1994 | 21 |
| Terry Allen, Washington | 1996 | 21 |
| Terrell Davis, Denver | 1998 | 21 |
| Priest Holmes, Kansas City | 2002 | 21 |
| Jim Taylor, Green Bay | 1962 | 19 |
| Earl Campbell, Houston | 1979 | 19 |
| Chuck Muncie, San Diego | 1981 | 19 |

### Field Goals

| | Year | Att | No |
|---|---|---|---|
| Jeff Wilkins, St. Louis | 2003 | 42 | 39 |
| Olindo Mare, Miami | 1999 | 46 | 39 |
| Mike Vanderjagt, Indianapolis | 2003 | 37 | 37 |
| John Kasay, Carolina | 1996 | 45 | 37 |
| Cary Blanchard, Indianapolis | 1996 | 40 | 36 |
| Al Del Greco, Tennessee | 1998 | 39 | 36 |
| Ali Haji-Sheikh, NY Giants | 1983 | 42 | 35 |
| Jeff Jaeger, LA Raiders | 1993 | 44 | 35 |
| Gary Anderson, Minnesota | 1998 | 35 | 35 |
| Matt Stover, Baltimore | 2000 | 39 | 35 |
| Ten tied with 34 FG each. | | | |

### Interceptions

| | Year | No |
|---|---|---|
| Dick (Night Train) Lane, Detroit | 1952 | 14 |
| Dan Sandifer, Washington | 1948 | 13 |
| Spec Sanders, NY Yanks | 1950 | 13 |
| Lester Hayes, Oakland | 1980 | 13 |
| Nine tied with 12 each. | | |

### Punting

| Qualifiers | Year | Avg |
|---|---|---|
| Sammy Baugh, Washington | 1940 | 51.4 |
| Yale Lary, Detroit | 1963 | 48.9 |
| Sammy Baugh, Washington | 1941 | 48.7 |
| Yale Lary, Detroit | 1961 | 48.4 |
| Sammy Baugh, Washington | 1942 | 48.2 |

### Kickoff Returns

| | Year | Avg |
|---|---|---|
| Travis Williams, Green Bay | 1967 | 41.1 |
| Gale Sayers, Chicago Bears | 1967 | 37.7 |
| Ollie Matson, Chicago Cards | 1958 | 35.5 |
| Jim Duncan, Baltimore Colts | 1970 | 35.4 |
| Lynn Chandnois, Pittsburgh | 1952 | 35.2 |

### Punt Returns

| | Year | Avg |
|---|---|---|
| Herb Rich, Baltimore | 1950 | 23.0 |
| Jack Christiansen, Detroit | 1952 | 21.5 |
| Dick Christy, NY Titans | 1961 | 21.3 |
| Bob Hayes, Dallas | 1968 | 20.8 |
| Claude Young, NY Yanks | 1951 | 19.3 |

### Sacks

| | Year | No | | Year | No |
|---|---|---|---|---|---|
| Michael Strahan, NY Giants | 2001 | 22.5 | Chris Doleman, Minnesota | 1989 | 21 |
| Mark Gastineau, NY Jets | 1984 | 22 | Lawrence Taylor, NY Giants | 1986 | 20.5 |
| Reggie White, Philadelphia | 1987 | 21 | Derrick Thomas, Kansas City | 1990 | 20 |

**Note:** The NFL did not begin officially compiling sacks until 1982. Cincinnati's Coy Bacon is widely, although not officially, credited with 26 sacks during the 1976 season.

## SINGLE GAME

### Passing

| Yards Gained | Date | Yds |
|---|---|---|
| Norm Van Brocklin, LA vs NY Yanks | 9/28/51 | 554 |
| Warren Moon, Hou vs KC | 12/16/90 | 527 |
| Boomer Esiason, Ariz vs Wash. | 11/10/96 | 522 |
| Dan Marino, Mia vs NYJ | 10/23/88 | 521 |
| Phil Simms, NYG vs Cin | 10/13/85 | 513 |

| Completions | Date | No |
|---|---|---|
| Drew Bledsoe, NE vs Min | 11/13/94 | 45 |
| Rich Gannon, Oak vs Pit | 9/15/02 | 43 |
| Richard Todd, NYJ vs SF | 9/21/80 | 42 |
| Vinny Testaverde, NYJ vs Sea | 12/6/98 | 42 |
| Warren Moon, Hou vs Dal | 11/10/91 | 41 |
| Four tied with 40 each. | | |

### Receiving

| Catches | Date | No |
|---|---|---|
| Terrell Owens, SF vs Chi | 12/17/00 | 20 |
| Tom Fears, LA vs GB | 12/3/50 | 18 |
| Clark Gaines, NYJ vs SF | 9/21/80 | 17 |
| Four tied with 16 each. | | |

| Yards Gained | Date | Yds |
|---|---|---|
| Flipper Anderson, LA Rams vs NO | 11/26/89 | 336 |
| Stephone Paige, KC vs SD | 12/22/85 | 309 |
| Jim Benton, Cle vs Det | 11/22/45 | 303 |
| Cloyce Box, Det vs Bal | 12/3/50 | 302 |
| Jimmy Smith, Jax vs Bal | 9/10/00 | 291 |
| Jerry Rice, SF vs Det | 9/25/95 | 289 |

### Rushing

| Yards Gained | Date | Yds |
|---|---|---|
| Jamal Lewis, Bal vs Cle | 9/14/03 | 295 |
| Corey Dillon, Cin vs Den | 10/22/00 | 278 |
| Walter Payton, Chi vs Min | 11/20/77 | 275 |
| O.J. Simpson, Buf vs Det | 11/25/76 | 273 |
| Shaun Alexander, Sea vs Oak | 11/11/01 | 266 |
| Mike Anderson, Den vs NO | 12/3/00 | 251 |
| O.J. Simpson, Buf vs NE | 9/16/73 | 250 |
| Willie Ellison, LA Rams vs NO | 12/5/71 | 247 |

### All-Purpose Yards

| | Date | Yds |
|---|---|---|
| Glyn Milburn, Den vs Sea | 12/10/95 | 404 |
| Billy Cannon, Hou vs NY Titans | 12/10/61 | 373 |
| Michael Lewis, NO vs Wash | 10/13/02 | 356 |
| Tyrone Hughes, NO vs LA Rams | 10/23/94 | 347 |
| Lionel James, SD vs Raiders | 11/10/85 | 345 |
| Timmy Brown, Phi vs S.L | 12/16/62 | 341 |
| Gale Sayers, Chi vs Min | 12/18/66 | 339 |
| Gale Sayers, Chi vs SF | 12/12/65 | 336 |
| Flipper Anderson, LA Rams vs NO | 11/26/89 | 336 |

# Scoring

## Points

| | Date | Pts |
|---|---|---|
| Ernie Nevers, Chi. Cards vs Chi. Bears | 11/28/29 | 40 |
| Dub Jones, Cle vs Chi. Bears | 11/25/51 | 36 |
| Gale Sayers, Chi vs SF | 12/12/65 | 36 |
| Paul Hornung, GB vs Bal | 10/8/61 | 33 |
| Bob Shaw, Chi. Cards vs Bal | 10/2/50 | 30 |
| Jim Brown, Cle vs Bal | 11/1/59 | 30 |
| Abner Haynes, Dal. Texans vs Oak | 11/26/61 | 30 |
| Billy Cannon, Hou vs NY Titans | 12/10/61 | 30 |
| Cookie Gilchrist, Buf vs NY Jets | 12/8/63 | 30 |
| Kellen Winslow, SD vs Oak | 11/22/81 | 30 |
| Jerry Rice, SF vs Atl | 10/14/90 | 30 |
| James Stewart, Jax vs Phi. | 10/12/97 | 30 |
| Shaun Alexander, Sea vs Min. | 9/29/02 | 30 |
| Clinton Portis, Den vs KC | 12/7/03 | 30 |

**Note:** Nevers celebrated Thanksgiving, 1929, by scoring all of the Chicago Cardinals' points on six rushing TDs and four PATs. The Cards beat Red Grange and the Chicago Bears, 40-6.

## Touchdowns Passing

| | Date | No |
|---|---|---|
| Sid Luckman, Chi. Bears vs NYG | 11/14/43 | 7 |
| Adrian Burk, Phi vs Wash | 10/17/54 | 7 |
| George Blanda, Hou vs NY Titans | 11/19/61 | 7 |
| Y.A. Tittle, NYG vs Wash | 10/28/62 | 7 |
| Joe Kapp, Min vs Bal | 9/28/69 | 7 |

## Touchdowns Receiving

| | Date | No |
|---|---|---|
| Bob Shaw, Chi. Cards vs Bal | 10/2/50 | 5 |
| Kellen Winslow, SD vs Oak | 11/22/81 | 5 |
| Jerry Rice, SF vs Atl | 10/14/90 | 5 |

## Touchdowns Rushing

| | Date | No |
|---|---|---|
| Ernie Nevers, Chi. Cards vs Chi. Bears | 11/28/29 | 6 |
| Jim Brown, Cle vs Bal | 11/1/59 | 5 |
| Cookie Gilchrist, Buf vs NY Jets | 12/8/63 | 5 |
| James Stewart, Jax vs Phi. | 10/12/97 | 5 |
| Clinton Portis, Den vs KC | 12/7/03 | 5 |

## Field Goals

| | Date | No |
|---|---|---|
| Jim Bakken, St.L vs Pit | 9/24/67 | 7 |
| Rich Karlis, Min vs LA Rams | 11/5/89 | 7 |
| Chris Boniol, Dal vs GB | 11/18/96 | 7 |
| Billy Cundiff, Dal vs NYG | 9/15/03 | 7 |

**Note:** Bakken was 7-for-9, Cundiff was 7-for-8, Boniol and Karlis were 7-for-7.

## Extra Point Kicks

| | Date | No |
|---|---|---|
| Pat Harder, Cards vs NYG | 10/17/48 | 9 |
| Bob Waterfield, LA Rams vs Bal | 10/22/50 | 9 |
| Charlie Gogolak, Wash vs NYG | 11/27/66 | 9 |

## Interceptions

| | No |
|---|---|
| By 18 players | 4 |

## Sacks

| | Date | No |
|---|---|---|
| Derrick Thomas, KC vs Sea | 11/11/90 | 7.0 |
| Fred Dean, SF vs NO | 11/13/83 | 6.0 |
| Derrick Thomas, KC vs Oak | 9/6/98 | 6.0 |
| William Gay, Det vs TB | 9/4/83 | 5.5 |

# Longest Plays

## Passing (all for TDs)

| | Date | Yds |
|---|---|---|
| Frank Filchock to Andy Farkas, Wash vs Pit | 10/15/39 | 99 |
| George Izo to Bobby Mitchell, Wash vs Cle | 9/15/63 | 99 |
| Karl Sweetan to Pat Studstill, Det vs Bal | 10/16/66 | 99 |
| Sonny Jurgensen to Gerry Allen, Wash vs Chi | 9/15/68 | 99 |
| Jim Plunkett to Cliff Branch, LA Raiders vs Wash | 10/2/83 | 99 |
| Ron Jaworski to Mike Quick, Phi vs Atl | 11/10/85 | 99 |
| Stan Humphries to Tony Martin, SD vs Sea | 9/18/94 | 99 |
| Brett Favre to Robert Brooks, GB vs Chi | 9/11/95 | 99 |
| Trent Green to Marc Boerigter, KC vs SD | 12/22/02 | 99 |
| **Jeff Garcia** to **Andre Davis**, Cle vs Cin | 10/17/04 | 99 |

## Runs from Scrimmage (all for TDs)

| | Date | Yds |
|---|---|---|
| Tony Dorsett, Dal vs Min | 1/3/83 | 99 |
| Ahman Green, GB vs Den | 12/28/03 | 98 |
| Andy Uram, GB vs Chi. Cards | 10/8/39 | 97 |
| Bob Gage, Pit vs Bears | 12/4/49 | 97 |

Four players tied with 96-yd rushes.

## Punts

| | Date | Yds |
|---|---|---|
| Steve O'Neal, NYJ vs Den | 9/21/69 | 98 |
| Joe Lintzenich, Chi. Bears vs NYG | 11/15/31 | 94 |
| Shawn McCarthy, NE vs Buf | 11/3/91 | 93 |

## Field Goals

| | Date | Yds |
|---|---|---|
| Tom Dempsey, NO vs Det | 11/8/70 | 63 |
| Jason Elam, Den vs Jax | 10/25/98 | 63 |
| Steve Cox, Cle vs Cin | 10/21/84 | 60 |
| Morten Andersen, NO vs Chi | 10/27/91 | 60 |
| Tony Franklin, Phi vs Dal | 11/12/79 | 59 |
| Pete Stoyanovich, Mia vs NYJ | 11/12/89 | 59 |
| Steve Christie, Buf vs Mia | 9/26/93 | 59 |
| Morten Andersen, Atl vs SF | 12/24/95 | 59 |

## Punt Returns (all for TDs)

| | Date | Yds |
|---|---|---|
| Robert Bailey, Rams vs NO | 10/23/94 | 103 |
| Gil LeFebvre, Cin vs Bklyn | 12/3/33 | 98 |
| Charlie West, Min vs Wash | 11/3/68 | 98 |
| Dennis Morgan, Dal vs St.L | 10/13/74 | 98 |
| Terance Mathis, NYJ vs Dal | 11/4/90 | 98 |
| Greg Pruitt, LA Raiders vs Wash. | 10/2/83 | 97 |

## Kickoff Returns (all for TDs)

| | Date | Yds |
|---|---|---|
| Al Carmichael, GB vs Chi. Bears | 10/7/56 | 106 |
| Noland Smith, KC vs Den | 12/17/67 | 106 |
| Roy Green, St.L vs Dal | 10/21/79 | 106 |

## Interception Returns (all for TDs)

| | Date | Yds |
|---|---|---|
| **Ed Reed**, Bal vs Cle | 11/17/04 | 106 |
| James Willis (14 yds) lateral to Troy Vincent (90 yds), Phi vs Dal | 11/3/96 | 104 |
| Vencie Glenn, SD vs Den | 11/29/87 | 103 |
| Louis Oliver, Mia vs Buf | 10/4/92 | 103 |

Seven players tied with 102-yd returns.

**Note:** On 9/30/02 Baltimore's Chris McAlister returned a missed FG 107 yards, the longest play in NFL history.

## Chicago College All-Star Game

On Aug. 31, 1934, a year after sponsoring Major League Baseball's first All-Star Game, *Chicago Tribune* sports editor Arch Ward presented the first Chicago College All-Star Game at Soldier Field. A crowd of 79,432 turned out to see an all-star team of graduated college seniors battle the 1933 NFL champion Chicago Bears to a scoreless tie. The preseason game was played at Soldier Field and pitted the College All-Stars against the defending NFL champions (1933-1966) or Super Bowl champions (1967-75) every year except 1935 until it was cancelled in 1977. The NFL champs won the series, 31-9-1.

| Year | | | Year | | | Year | | |
|------|---|---|------|---|---|------|---|---|
| 1934 | Chi. Bears 0, All-Stars 0 | | 1949 | Philadelphia 38, All-Stars 0 | | 1964 | Chi. Bears 28, All-Stars 17 | |
| 1935 | Chi. Bears 5, All-Stars 0 | | 1950 | All-Stars 17, Philadelphia 7 | | 1965 | Cleveland 24, All-Stars 16 | |
| 1936 | Detroit 7, All-Stars 0 | | 1951 | Cleveland 33, All-Stars 0 | | 1966 | Green Bay 38, All-Stars 0 | |
| 1937 | All-Stars 6, Green Bay 0 | | 1952 | LA Rams 10, All-Stars 7 | | 1967 | Green Bay 27, All-Stars 0 | |
| 1938 | All-Stars 28, Washington 16 | | 1953 | Detroit 24, All-Stars 10 | | 1968 | Green Bay 34, All-Stars 17 | |
| 1939 | NY Giants 9, All-Stars 0 | | 1954 | Detroit 31, All-Stars 6 | | 1969 | NY Jets 26, All-Stars 24 | |
| 1940 | Green Bay 45, All-Stars 28 | | 1955 | All-Stars 30, Cleveland 27 | | 1970 | Kansas City 24, All-Stars 3 | |
| 1941 | Chi. Bears 37, All-Stars 13 | | 1956 | Cleveland 26, All-Stars 0 | | 1971 | Baltimore 24, All-Stars 17 | |
| 1942 | Chi. Bears 21, All-Stars 0 | | 1957 | NY Giants 22, All-Stars 12 | | 1972 | Dallas 20, All-Stars 7 | |
| 1943 | All-Stars 27, Washington 7 | | 1958 | All-Stars 35, Detroit 19 | | 1973 | Miami 14, All-Stars 3 | |
| 1944 | Chi. Bears 24, All-Stars 21 | | 1959 | Baltimore 29, All-Stars 0 | | 1974 | No Game (NFLPA Strike) | |
| 1945 | Green Bay 19, All-Stars 7 | | 1960 | Baltimore 32, All-Stars 7 | | 1975 | Pittsburgh 21, All-Stars 14 | |
| 1946 | All-Stars 16, LA Rams 0 | | 1961 | Philadelphia 28, All-Stars 14 | | 1976 | Pittsburgh 24, All-Stars 0* | |
| 1947 | All-Stars 16, Chi. Bears 0 | | 1962 | Green Bay 42, All-Stars 20 | | | | |
| 1948 | Chi. Cards 28, All-Stars 0 | | 1963 | All-Stars 20, Green Bay 17 | | | | |

*Downpour flooded field, game called with 1:22 left in 3rd quarter.

## Number One Draft Choices

In an effort to blunt the dominance of the Chicago Bears and New York Giants in the 1930s and distribute talent more evenly throughout the league, the NFL established the college draft in 1936. The first player chosen in the first draft was Jay Berwanger, who was also college football's first Heisman Trophy winner. In all, 17 Heisman winners have also been the NFL's No. 1 draft choice. They are noted in **bold** type. The American Football League (formed in 1960) held its own draft for six years before agreeing to merge with the NFL and select players in a common draft starting in 1967.

| Year | Team | |
|------|------|---|
| 1936 | Philadelphia | **Jay Berwanger**, HB, Chicago |
| 1937 | Philadelphia | Sam Francis, FB, Nebraska |
| 1938 | Cleveland Rams | Corbett Davis, FB, Indiana |
| 1939 | Chicago Bears | Ki Aldrich, C, TCU |
| 1940 | Chicago Cards | George Cafego, HB, Tennessee |
| 1941 | Chicago Bears | **Tom Harmon**, HB, Michigan |
| 1942 | Pittsburgh | Bill Dudley, HB, Virginia |
| 1943 | Detroit | **Frank Sinkwich**, HB, Georgia |
| 1944 | Boston Yanks | **Angelo Bertelli**, QB, N. Dame |
| 1945 | Chicago Cards | Charley Trippi, HB, Georgia |
| 1946 | Boston Yanks | Frank Dancewicz, QB, N. Dame |
| 1947 | Chicago Bears | Bob Fenimore, HB, Okla. A&M |
| 1948 | Washington | Harry Gilmer, QB, Alabama |
| 1949 | Philadelphia | Chuck Bednarik, C, Penn |
| 1950 | Detroit | **Leon Hart**, E, Notre Dame |
| 1951 | NY Giants | Kyle Rote, HB, SMU |
| 1952 | LA Rams | Bill Wade, QB, Vanderbilt |
| 1953 | San Francisco | Harry Babcock, E, Georgia |
| 1954 | Cleveland | Bobby Garrett, QB, Stanford |
| 1955 | Baltimore | George Shaw, QB, Oregon |
| 1956 | Pittsburgh | Gary Glick, DB, Colo. A&M |
| 1957 | Green Bay | **Paul Hornung**, QB, N. Dame |
| 1958 | Chicago Cards | King Hill, QB, Rice |
| 1959 | Green Bay | Randy Duncan, QB, Iowa |
| 1960 | NFL–LA Rams | **Billy Cannon**, HB, LSU |
| | AFL–No choice | |
| 1961 | NFL–Minnesota | Tommy Mason, HB, Tulane |
| | AFL–Buffalo | Ken Rice, G, Auburn |
| 1962 | NFL–Washington | **Ernie Davis**, HB, Syracuse |
| | AFL–Oakland | Roman Gabriel, QB, N.C. State |
| 1963 | NFL–LA Rams | **Terry Baker**, QB, Oregon St. |
| | AFL–Kan.City | Buck Buchanan, DT, Grambling |
| 1964 | NFL–San Fran | Dave Parks, E, Texas Tech |
| | AFL–Boston | Jack Concannon, QB, Boston Col. |
| 1965 | NFL–NY Giants | Tucker Frederickson, FB, Auburn |
| | AFL–Houston | Lawrence Elkins, E, Baylor |
| 1966 | NFL–Atlanta | Tommy Nobis, LB, Texas |
| | AFL–Miami | Jim Grabowski, FB, Illinois |
| 1967 | Baltimore | Bubba Smith, DT, Michigan St. |

| Year | Team | |
|------|------|---|
| 1968 | Minnesota | Ron Yary, T, USC |
| 1969 | Buffalo | **O.J. Simpson**, RB, USC |
| 1970 | Pittsburgh | Terry Bradshaw, QB, La.Tech |
| 1971 | New England | **Jim Plunkett**, QB, Stanford |
| 1972 | Buffalo | Walt Patulski, DE, Notre Dame |
| 1973 | Houston | John Matuszak, DE, Tampa |
| 1974 | Dallas | Ed (Too Tall) Jones, DE, Tenn. St. |
| 1975 | Atlanta | Steve Bartkowski, QB, Calif. |
| 1976 | Tampa Bay | Lee Roy Selmon, DE, Oklahoma |
| 1977 | Tampa Bay | Ricky Bell, RB, USC |
| 1978 | Houston | **Earl Campbell**, RB, Texas |
| 1979 | Buffalo | Tom Cousineau, LB, Ohio St. |
| 1980 | Detroit | **Billy Sims**, RB, Oklahoma |
| 1981 | New Orleans | **George Rogers**, RB, S. Carolina |
| 1982 | New England | Kenneth Sims, DT, Texas |
| 1983 | Baltimore | John Elway, QB, Stanford |
| 1984 | New England | Irving Fryar, WR, Nebraska |
| 1985 | Buffalo | Bruce Smith, DE, Va. Tech |
| 1986 | Tampa Bay | **Bo Jackson**, RB, Auburn |
| 1987 | Tampa Bay | **V. Testaverde**, QB, Miami-FL |
| 1988 | Atlanta | Aundray Bruce, LB, Auburn |
| 1989 | Dallas | Troy Aikman, QB, UCLA |
| 1990 | Indianapolis | Jeff George, QB, Illinois |
| 1991 | Dallas | Russell Maryland, DT, Miami-FL |
| 1992 | Indianapolis | Steve Emtman, DT, Washington |
| 1993 | New England | Drew Bledsoe, QB, Washington St. |
| 1994 | Cincinnati | Dan Wilkinson, DT, Ohio St. |
| 1995 | Cincinnati | Ki-Jana Carter, RB, Penn St. |
| 1996 | NY Jets | Keyshawn Johnson, WR, USC |
| 1997 | St. Louis | Orlando Pace, OT, Ohio St. |
| 1998 | Indianapolis | Peyton Manning, QB, Tennessee |
| 1999 | Cleveland | Tim Couch, QB, Kentucky |
| 2000 | Cleveland | Courtney Brown, DE, Penn St. |
| 2001 | Atlanta | Michael Vick, QB, Va. Tech |
| 2002 | Houston | David Carr, QB, Fresno St. |
| 2003 | Cincinnati | **Carson Palmer**, QB, USC |
| 2004 | San Diego | Eli Manning, QB, Mississippi |
| 2005 | San Francisco | Alex Smith, QB, Utah |

AP/Wide World Photos
**Don Shula**

NFL Media
**Joe Gibbs**

NFL Media
**Bill Cowher**

NFL Media
**Dick Vermeil**

## All-Time Winningest NFL Coaches

NFL career victories through the 2004 season. Career, regular season and playoff records are noted along with NFL, AFL and Super Bowl titles won. Coaches active during 2004 season in **bold** type.

| | | Yrs | W | L | T | Pct | W | L | T | Pct | W | L | Pct. | League Titles |
|---|---|---|---|---|---|---|---|---|---|---|---|---|---|---|
| | | | **Career** | | | | **Regular Season** | | | | **Playoffs** | | | |
| 1 | Don Shula | 33 | **347** | 173 | 6 | .665 | 328 | 156 | 6 | .676 | 19 | 17 | .528 | 2 Super Bowls and 1 NFL |
| 2 | George Halas | 40 | **324** | 151 | 31 | .671 | 318 | 148 | 31 | .671 | 6 | 3 | .667 | 5 NFL |
| 3 | Tom Landry | 29 | **270** | 178 | 6 | .601 | 250 | 162 | 6 | .605 | 20 | 16 | .556 | 2 Super Bowls |
| 4 | Curly Lambeau | 33 | **229** | 134 | 22 | .623 | 226 | 132 | 22 | .624 | 3 | 2 | .600 | 6 NFL |
| 5 | Chuck Noll | 23 | **209** | 156 | 1 | .572 | 193 | 148 | 1 | .566 | 16 | 8 | .667 | 4 Super Bowls |
| 6 | Dan Reeves | 23 | **201** | 174 | 2 | .536 | 190 | 165 | 2 | .535 | 11 | 9 | .550 | —None— |
| 7 | Chuck Knox | 22 | **193** | 158 | 1 | .550 | 186 | 147 | 1 | .558 | 7 | 11 | .389 | —None— |
| 8 | **M. Schottenheimer** | 19 | **182** | 129 | 1 | .585 | 177 | 117 | 1 | .602 | 5 | 12 | .294 | —None— |
| 9 | Paul Brown | 21 | **170** | 108 | 6 | .609 | 166 | 100 | 6 | .621 | 4 | 8 | .333 | 3 NFL |
| 10 | Bud Grant | 18 | **168** | 108 | 5 | .607 | 158 | 96 | 5 | .620 | 10 | 12 | .455 | 1 NFL |
| 11 | **Bill Parcells** | 17 | **165** | 123 | 1 | .573 | 154 | 116 | 1 | .570 | 11 | 7 | .611 | 2 Super Bowls |
| 12 | Marv Levy | 17 | **154** | 120 | 0 | .562 | 143 | 112 | 0 | .561 | 11 | 8 | .579 | —None— |
| 13 | Steve Owen | 23 | **153** | 108 | 17 | .581 | 151 | 100 | 17 | .595 | 2 | 8 | .200 | 2 NFL |
| 14 | **Joe Gibbs** | 13 | **146** | 75 | 0 | .661 | 130 | 70 | 0 | .650 | 16 | 5 | .762 | 3 Super Bowls |
| 15 | **Bill Cowher** | 13 | **138** | 86 | 1 | .616 | 130 | 77 | 1 | .627 | 8 | 9 | .471 | —None— |
| 16 | Hank Stram | 17 | **136** | 100 | 10 | .573 | 131 | 97 | 10 | .571 | 5 | 3 | .625 | 1 Super Bowl and 3 AFL |
| 17 | **Mike Holmgren** | 13 | **134** | 91 | 0 | .596 | 125 | 83 | 0 | .601 | 9 | 8 | .529 | 1 Super Bowl |
| | Weeb Ewbank | 20 | **134** | 130 | 7 | .507 | 130 | 129 | 7 | .502 | 4 | 1 | .800 | 1 Super Bowl, 2 NFL, and 1 AFL |
| 19 | Mike Ditka | 14 | **127** | 101 | 0 | .557 | 121 | 95 | 0 | .560 | 6 | 6 | .500 | 1 Super Bowl |
| 20 | Jim Mora | 15 | **125** | 112 | 0 | .527 | 125 | 106 | 0 | .541 | 0 | 6 | .000 | —None— |
| 21 | George Seifert | 11 | **124** | 67 | 0 | .649 | 114 | 62 | 0 | .648 | 10 | 5 | .667 | 2 Super Bowls |
| 22 | Sid Gillman | 18 | **123** | 104 | 7 | .541 | 122 | 99 | 7 | .550 | 1 | 5 | .167 | 1 AFL |
| 23 | George Allen | 12 | **118** | 54 | 5 | .681 | 116 | 47 | 5 | .705 | 2 | 7 | .222 | —None— |
| 24 | **Mike Shanahan** | 12 | **116** | 75 | 0 | .607 | 109 | 71 | 0 | .606 | 7 | 4 | .636 | 2 Super Bowls |
| | **Dick Vermeil** | 14 | **116** | 108 | 0 | .518 | 110 | 103 | 0 | .516 | 6 | 5 | .545 | 1 Super Bowl |

**Notes:** The NFL does not recognize records from the All-American Football Conference (1946-49). If it did, **Paul Brown** (52-4-3 in four AAFC seasons) would move up from 9th to 5th on the all-time list with the following career stats— 25 Yrs; 222 Wins; 112 Losses; 9 Ties; .660 Pct; 9-8 playoff record; and 4 AAFC titles.

The NFL also considers the Playoff Bowl or "Runner-up Bowl" (officially: the Bert Bell Benefit Bowl) as a postseason exhibition game. The Playoff Bowl was contested every year from 1960-69 in Miami between Eastern and Western Conference second place teams. While the games did not count, six of the coaches above went to the Playoff Bowl at least once and came away with the following records— Allen (2-0), Brown (0-1), Grant (0-1), Landry (1-2) and Shula (2-0).

## Where They Coached

**Allen**—LA Rams (1966-70), Washington (1971-77); **Brown**—Cleveland (1950-62), Cincinnati (1968-75); **Cowher**—Pittsburgh (1992—); **Ditka**— Chicago (1982-92), New Orleans (1997-99); **Ewbank**—Baltimore (1954-62), NY Jets (1963-73); **Gibbs**—Washington (1981-92, 2004—); **Gillman**—LA Rams (1955-59), LA-San Diego Chargers (1960-69), Houston (1973-74); **Grant**—Minnesota (1967-83,1985); **Halas**—Chicago Bears (1920-29,33-42,46-55,58-67).

**Holmgren**—Green Bay (1992-98), Seattle (1999—); **Knox**— LA Rams (1973-77, 1992-94); Buffalo (1978-82), Seattle (1983-91); **Lambeau**— Green Bay (1921-49), Chicago Cards (1950-51), Washington (1952-53); **Landry**—Dallas (1960-88); **Levy**— Kansas City (1978-82), Buffalo (1986-97); **Mora**—New Orleans (1986-1995), Indianapolis (1998-2001); **Noll**—Pittsburgh (1969-91).

**Owen**—NY Giants (1931-53); **Parcells**— NY Giants (1983-90), New England (1993-97), NY Jets (1997-99), Dallas (2003—); **Reeves**— Denver (1981-92), NY Giants (1993-96), Atlanta (1997-2003); **Schottenheimer**—Cleveland (1984-88), Kansas City (1989-98), Washington (2001), San Diego (2002—); **Seifert**—San Francisco (1989-96), Carolina (1999-2001); **Shanahan**—LA Raiders (1988-89), Denver (1995—); **Shula**—Baltimore (1963-69), Miami (1970-95); **Stram**—Dallas-Kansas City (1960-74), New Orleans (1976-77); **Vermeil**—Philadelphia (1976-82); St. Louis (1997-99); Kansas City (2001—).

## Top Winning Percentages

Minimum of 85 NFL victories, including playoffs.

| | | Yrs | W | L | T | Pct |
|---|---|---|---|---|---|---|
| 1 | Vince Lombardi | 10 | 105 | 35 | 6 | **.740** |
| 2 | John Madden | 10 | 112 | 39 | 7 | **.731** |
| 3 | George Allen | 12 | 118 | 54 | 5 | **.681** |
| 4 | George Halas | 40 | 324 | 151 | 31 | **.671** |
| 5 | Don Shula | 33 | 347 | 173 | 6 | **.665** |
| 6 | **Joe Gibbs** | 13 | 146 | 75 | 0 | **.661** |
| 7 | George Seifert | 11 | 124 | 67 | 0 | **.649** |
| 8 | Curly Lambeau | 33 | 229 | 134 | 22 | **.623** |
| 9 | Bill Walsh | 10 | 102 | 63 | 1 | **.617** |
| 10 | **Bill Cowher** | 13 | 138 | 86 | 1 | **.616** |
| 11 | Paul Brown | 21 | 170 | 108 | 6 | **.609** |
| 12 | **Mike Shanahan** | 12 | 116 | 75 | 0 | **.607** |
| 13 | Bud Grant | 18 | 168 | 108 | 5 | **.607** |
| 14 | Tom Landry | 29 | 270 | 178 | 6 | **.601** |
| 15 | **Tony Dungy** | 9 | 93 | 63 | 0 | **.596** |
| 16 | **Mike Holmgren** | 13 | 134 | 91 | 0 | **.596** |
| 17 | **Marty Schottenheimer** | 19 | 182 | 129 | 1 | **.585** |
| 18 | Steve Owen | 23 | 153 | 108 | 17 | **.581** |
| 19 | Buddy Parker | 15 | 107 | 76 | 9 | **.581** |
| 20 | **Bill Belichick** | 10 | 99 | 72 | 0 | **.579** |
| 21 | Hank Stram | 17 | 136 | 100 | 10 | **.573** |
| 22 | **Bill Parcells** | 17 | 165 | 123 | 1 | **.573** |
| 23 | Chuck Noll | 23 | 209 | 156 | 1 | **.572** |
| 24 | **Dennis Green** | 11 | 107 | 80 | 0 | **.572** |
| 25 | Jimmy Johnson | 9 | 89 | 68 | 0 | **.567** |

**Note:** If AAFC records are included, **Paul Brown** moves from 12th to 7th with a percentage of .660 (25 yrs, 222-112-9) and **Buck Shaw** would be 11th at .619 (8 yrs, 91-55-5).

## Active Coaches' Victories

Through 2004 season, including playoffs.

| | | Yrs | W | L | T | Pct |
|---|---|---|---|---|---|---|
| 1 | Marty Schottenheimer, SD | 19 | **182** | 129 | 1 | .585 |
| 2 | Bill Parcells, Dallas | 17 | **165** | 123 | 1 | .573 |
| 3 | Joe Gibbs, Washington | 13 | **146** | 75 | 0 | .661 |
| 4 | Bill Cowher, Pittsburgh | 13 | **138** | 86 | 1 | .616 |
| 5 | Mike Holmgren, Seattle | 13 | **134** | 91 | 0 | .596 |
| 6 | Mike Shanahan, Denver | 12 | **116** | 75 | 0 | .607 |
| | Dick Vermeil, KC | 14 | **116** | 108 | 0 | .518 |
| 8 | Dennis Green, Arizona | 11 | **107** | 80 | 0 | .572 |
| 9 | Bill Belichick, New England | 10 | **99** | 72 | 0 | .579 |
| 10 | Jeff Fisher, Tennessee | 11 | **98** | 77 | 0 | .560 |
| 11 | Tony Dungy, Indianapolis | 9 | **93** | 63 | 0 | .596 |
| 12 | Tom Coughlin, NY Giants | 9 | **78** | 74 | 0 | .513 |
| 13 | Andy Reid, Philadelphia | 6 | **71** | 37 | 0 | .657 |
| | Steve Mariucci, Detroit | 8 | **71** | 64 | 0 | .526 |
| 15 | Jon Gruden, Tampa Bay | 7 | **67** | 52 | 0 | .563 |
| 16 | Brian Billick, Baltimore | 6 | **61** | 42 | 0 | .592 |
| 17 | Mike Sherman, Green Bay | 5 | **55** | 31 | 0 | .640 |
| | Norv Turner, Oakland | 8 | **55** | 71 | 1 | .437 |
| 19 | Mike Martz, St. Louis | 5 | **54** | 33 | 0 | .621 |
| 20 | Dom Capers, Houston | 7 | **47** | 67 | 0 | .412 |
| 21 | Jim Haslett, New Orleans | 5 | **43** | 39 | 0 | .524 |
| 22 | Herman Edwards, NY Jets | 4 | **37** | 32 | 0 | .536 |
| 23 | John Fox, Carolina | 3 | **28** | 24 | 0 | .538 |
| 24 | Mike Tice, Minnesota | 4 | **24** | 27 | 0 | .471 |
| 25 | Marvin Lewis, Cincinnati | 2 | **16** | 16 | 0 | .500 |
| 26 | Jack Del Rio, Jacksonville | 2 | **14** | 18 | 0 | .438 |
| 27 | Jim Mora Jr., Atlanta | 1 | **12** | 6 | 0 | .667 |
| 28 | Mike Mularkey, Buffalo | 1 | **9** | 7 | 0 | .563 |
| 29 | Lovie Smith, Chicago | 1 | **5** | 11 | 0 | .313 |
| 30 | Romeo Crennel, Cleveland | 0 | **0** | 0 | 0 | .000 |
| | Mike Nolan, San Fran. | 0 | **0** | 0 | 0 | .000 |
| | Nick Saban, Miami | 0 | **0** | 0 | 0 | .000 |

## Annual Awards
### Most Valuable Player

Currently, the NFL does not sanction an official MVP award. It awarded the Joe F. Carr Trophy (Carr was NFL president from 1921-39) to the league MVP from 1938 to 1946. Since then, four principal MVP awards have been given out throughout the years and are noted below: UPI (1953-69), AP (since 1957), the Maxwell Club of Philadelphia's Bert Bell Trophy (since 1959) and the Pro Football Writers Assn. (since 1976). UPI switched to AFC and NFC Player of the Year awards in 1970 and then discontinued its awards in 1997.

**Multiple winners** (more than one season): Jim Brown (4); Randall Cunningham, Brett Favre, Johnny Unitas and Y.A. Tittle (3); Earl Campbell, Marshall Faulk, Rich Gannon, Otto Graham, Don Hutson, Peyton Manning, Joe Montana, Walter Payton, Barry Sanders, Ken Stabler, Joe Theismann, Kurt Warner and Steve Young (2).

| Year | Awards |
|---|---|
| 1938 Mel Hein, NY Giants, C | Carr |
| 1939 Parker Hall, Cleveland Rams, HB | Carr |
| 1940 Ace Parker, Brooklyn, HB | Carr |
| 1941 Don Hutson, Green Bay, E | Carr |
| 1942 Don Hutson, Green Bay, E | Carr |
| 1943 Sid Luckman, Chicago Bears, QB | Carr |
| 1944 Frank Sinkwich, Detroit, HB | Carr |
| 1945 Bob Waterfield, Cleveland Rams, QB | Carr |
| 1946 Bill Dudley, Pittsburgh, HB | Carr |
| 1947-52 No award | |
| 1953 Otto Graham, Cleveland Browns, QB | UPI |
| 1954 Joe Perry, San Francisco, FB | UPI |
| 1955 Otto Graham, Cleveland, QB | UPI |
| 1956 Frank Gifford, NY Giants, HB | UPI |
| 1957 Y.A. Tittle, San Francisco, QB | UPI |
| & Jim Brown, Cleveland, FB | AP |
| 1958 Jim Brown, Cleveland, FB | UPI |
| & Gino Marchetti, Baltimore, DE | AP |
| 1959 Johnny Unitas, Baltimore, QB | UPI, Bell |
| & Charley Conerly, NY Giants, QB | AP |
| 1960 Norm Van Brocklin, Phi., QB | UPI, AP (tie), Bell |
| & Joe Schmidt, Detroit, LB | AP (tie) |
| 1961 Paul Hornung, Green Bay, HB | UPI, AP, Bell |
| 1962 Y.A. Tittle, NY Giants, QB | UPI |
| Jim Taylor, Green Bay, FB | AP |
| & Andy Robustelli, NY Giants, DE | Bell |
| 1963 Jim Brown, Cleveland, FB | UPI, Bell |
| & Y.A. Tittle, NY Giants, QB | AP |
| 1964 Johnny Unitas, Baltimore, QB | UPI, AP, Bell |
| 1965 Jim Brown, Cleveland, FB | UPI, AP |
| & Pete Retzlaff, Philadelphia, TE | Bell |
| 1966 Bart Starr, Green Bay, QB | UPI, AP |
| & Don Meredith, Dallas, QB | Bell |
| 1967 Johnny Unitas, Baltimore, QB | UPI, AP, Bell |
| 1968 Earl Morrall, Baltimore, QB | UPI, AP |
| & Leroy Kelly, Cleveland, RB | Bell |
| 1969 Roman Gabriel, LA Rams, QB | UPI, AP, Bell |
| 1970 John Brodie, San Francisco, QB | AP |
| & George Blanda, Oakland, QB-PK | Bell |
| 1971 Alan Page, Minnesota, DT | AP |
| & Roger Staubach, Dallas, QB | Bell |
| 1972 Larry Brown, Washington, RB | AP, Bell |
| 1973 O.J. Simpson, Buffalo, RB | AP, Bell |
| 1974 Ken Stabler, Oakland, QB | AP |
| & Merlin Olsen, LA Rams, DT | Bell |
| 1975 Fran Tarkenton, Minnesota, QB | AP, Bell |
| 1976 Bert Jones, Baltimore, QB | AP, PFWA |
| & Ken Stabler, Oakland, QB | Bell |
| 1977 Walter Payton, Chicago, RB | AP, PFWA |
| & Bob Griese, Miami, QB | Bell |
| 1978 Terry Bradshaw, Pittsburgh, QB | AP, Bell |
| & Earl Campbell, Houston, RB | PFWA |
| 1979 Earl Campbell, Houston, RB | AP, Bell, PFWA |
| 1980 Brian Sipe, Cleveland, QB | AP, PFWA |
| & Ron Jaworski, Philadelphia, QB | Bell |
| 1981 Ken Anderson, Cincinnati, QB | AP, Bell, PFWA |

| Year | Awards | Year | Awards |
|------|--------|------|--------|
| 1982 Mark Moseley, Washington, PK | AP | 1993 Emmitt Smith, Dallas, RB | AP, Bell, PFWA |
| Joe Theismann, Washington, QB | Bell | 1994 Steve Young, San Francisco, QB | AP, Bell, PFWA |
| & Dan Fouts, San Diego, QB | PFWA | 1995 Brett Favre, Green Bay, QB | AP, Bell, PFWA |
| 1983 Joe Theismann, Washington, QB | AP, PFWA | 1996 Brett Favre, Green Bay, QB | AP, Bell, PFWA |
| & John Riggins, Washington, RB | Bell | 1997 Barry Sanders, Detroit, RB | AP (tie), Bell, PFWA |
| 1984 Dan Marino, Miami, QB | AP, Bell, PFWA | & Brett Favre, Green Bay, QB | AP (tie) |
| 1985 Marcus Allen, LA Raiders, RB | AP, PFWA | 1998 Terrell Davis, Denver, RB | AP, PFWA |
| & Walter Payton, Chicago, RB | Bell | & Randall Cunningham, Minnesota, QB | Bell |
| 1986 Lawrence Taylor, NY Giants, LB | AP, Bell, PFWA | 1999 Kurt Warner, St. Louis, QB | AP, Bell, PFWA |
| 1987 Jerry Rice, San Francisco, WR | Bell, PFWA | 2000 Marshall Faulk, St. Louis, RB | AP, PFWA |
| & John Elway, Denver, QB | AP | & Rich Gannon, Oakland, QB | Bell |
| 1988 Boomer Esiason, Cincinnati, QB | AP, PFWA | 2001 Kurt Warner, St. Louis, QB | AP |
| Randall Cunningham, Phila., QB | Bell | & Marshall Faulk, St. Louis, RB | Bell, PFWA |
| 1989 Joe Montana, San Francisco, QB | AP, Bell, PFWA | 2002 Rich Gannon, Oakland, QB | AP, Bell, PFWA |
| 1990 Randall Cunningham, Phila., QB | Bell, PFWA | 2003 Peyton Manning, Indianapolis, QB | AP (tie), Bell |
| & Joe Montana, San Francisco, QB | AP | Steve McNair, Tennessee, QB | AP (tie) |
| 1991 Thurman Thomas, Buffalo, RB | AP, PFWA | & Jamal Lewis, Baltimore, RB | PFWA |
| & Barry Sanders, Detroit, RB | Bell | 2004 Peyton Manning, Indianapolis, QB | AP, Bell, PFWA |
| 1992 Steve Young, San Francisco, QB | AP, Bell, PFWA | | |

## AP Offensive Player of the Year

Selected by The Associated Press in balloting by a nationwide media panel. Given out since 1972. Rookie winners are in **bold** type.
**Multiple winners:** Earl Campbell and Marshall Faulk (3); Terrell Davis, Jerry Rice and Barry Sanders (2).

| Year | | Pos | Year | | Pos | Year | | Pos |
|------|--|-----|------|--|-----|------|--|-----|
| 1972 Larry Brown, Was | | RB | 1983 Joe Theismann, Was | | QB | 1994 Barry Sanders, Det | | RB |
| 1973 O.J. Simpson, Buf | | RB | 1984 Dan Marino, Mia | | QB | 1995 Brett Favre, GB | | QB |
| 1974 Ken Stabler, Oak | | QB | 1985 Marcus Allen, Raiders | | RB | 1996 Terrell Davis, Den | | RB |
| 1975 Fran Tarkenton, Min | | QB | 1986 Eric Dickerson, Rams | | RB | 1997 Barry Sanders, Det | | RB |
| 1976 Bert Jones, Bal | | QB | 1987 Jerry Rice, SF | | WR | 1998 Terrell Davis, Den | | RB |
| 1977 Walter Payton, Chi | | RB | 1988 Roger Craig, SF | | RB | 1999 Marshall Faulk, St.L | | RB |
| 1978 **Earl Campbell**, Hou | | RB | 1989 Joe Montana, SF | | QB | 2000 Marshall Faulk, St.L | | RB |
| 1979 Earl Campbell, Hou | | RB | 1990 Warren Moon, Hou | | QB | 2001 Marshall Faulk, St.L | | RB |
| 1980 Earl Campbell, Hou | | RB | 1991 Thurman Thomas, Buf | | RB | 2002 Priest Holmes, KC | | RB |
| 1981 Ken Anderson, Cin | | QB | 1992 Steve Young, SF | | QB | 2003 Jamal Lewis, Bal | | RB |
| 1982 Dan Fouts, SD | | QB | 1993 Jerry Rice, SF | | WR | 2004 Peyton Manning, Ind | | QB |

## AP Defensive Player of the Year

Selected by The Associated Press in balloting by a nationwide media panel. Given out since 1971. Rookie winners are in **bold** type.
**Multiple winners:** Lawrence Taylor (3); Joe Greene, Ray Lewis, Mike Singletary, Bruce Smith and Reggie White (2).

| Year | | Pos | Year | | Pos | Year | | Pos |
|------|--|-----|------|--|-----|------|--|-----|
| 1971 Alan Page, Min | | DT | 1983 Doug Betters, Mia | | DE | 1995 Bryce Paup, Buf | | LB |
| 1972 Joe Greene, Pit | | DT | 1984 Kenny Easley, Sea | | S | 1996 Bruce Smith, Buf | | DE |
| 1973 Dick Anderson, Mia | | S | 1985 Mike Singletary, Chi | | LB | 1997 Dana Stubblefield, SF | | DT |
| 1974 Joe Greene, Pit | | DT | 1986 Lawrence Taylor, NYG | | LB | 1998 Reggie White, GB | | DE |
| 1975 Mel Blount, Pit | | CB | 1987 Reggie White, Phi | | DE | 1999 Warren Sapp, TB | | DT |
| 1976 Jack Lambert, Pit | | LB | 1988 Mike Singletary, Chi | | LB | 2000 Ray Lewis, Bal | | LB |
| 1977 Harvey Martin, Dal | | DE | 1989 Keith Millard, Min | | DT | 2001 Michael Strahan, NYG | | DE |
| 1978 Randy Gradishar, Den | | LB | 1990 Bruce Smith, Buf | | DE | 2002 Derrick Brooks, TB | | LB |
| 1979 Lee Roy Selmon, TB | | DE | 1991 Pat Swilling, NO | | LB | 2003 Ray Lewis, Bal | | LB |
| 1980 Lester Hayes, Oak | | CB | 1992 Cortez Kennedy, Sea | | DT | 2004 Ed Reed, Bal | | CB |
| 1981 **Lawrence Taylor**, NYG | | LB | 1993 Rod Woodson, Pit | | CB | | | |
| 1982 Lawrence Taylor, NYG | | LB | 1994 Deion Sanders, SF | | CB | | | |

## UPI NFC Player of the Year

Given out by UPI from 1970-96. Offensive and defensive players honored since 1983. Rookie winners are in **bold** type.
**Multiple winners:** Eric Dickerson, Reggie White and Mike Singletary (3); Brett Favre, Charles Haley, Walter Payton, Lawrence Taylor and Steve Young (2).

| Year | | Pos | Year | | Pos | Year | | Pos |
|------|--|-----|------|--|-----|------|--|-----|
| 1970 John Brodie, SF | | QB | 1984 Off–Eric Dickerson, Rams | | RB | 1991 Off–Mark Rypien, Was | | QB |
| 1971 Alan Page, Min | | DT | Def–Mike Singletary, Chi | | LB | Def–Reggie White, Phi | | DE |
| 1972 Larry Brown, Was | | RB | 1985 Off–Walter Payton, Chi | | RB | 1992 Off–Steve Young, SF | | QB |
| 1973 John Hadl, Rams | | QB | Def–Mike Singletary, Chi | | LB | Def–Chris Doleman, Min | | DE |
| 1974 Jim Hart, St.L | | QB | 1986 Off–Eric Dickerson, Rams | | RB | 1993 Off–Emmitt Smith, Dal | | RB |
| 1975 Fran Tarkenton, Min | | QB | Def–Lawrence Taylor, NYG | | LB | Def–Eric Allen, Phi | | CB |
| 1976 Chuck Foreman, Min | | RB | 1987 Off–Jerry Rice, SF | | WR | 1994 Off–Steve Young, SF | | QB |
| 1977 Walter Payton, Chi | | RB | Def–Reggie White, Phi | | DE | Def–Charles Haley, Dal | | DE |
| 1978 Archie Manning, NO | | QB | 1988 Off–Roger Craig, SF | | RB | 1995 Off–Brett Favre, GB | | QB |
| 1979 Ottis Anderson, St.L | | RB | Def–Mike Singletary, Chi | | LB | Def–Reggie White, GB | | DE |
| 1980 Ron Jaworski, Phi | | QB | 1989 Off–Joe Montana, SF | | QB | 1996 Off–Brett Favre, GB | | QB |
| 1981 Tony Dorsett, Dal | | RB | Def–Keith Millard, Min | | DT | Def–Kevin Greene, Car | | LB |
| 1982 Mark Moseley, Was | | PK | 1990 Off–Randall Cunningham,Phi.| | QB | 1997 Award discontinued. | | |
| 1983 Off–Eric Dickerson, Rams | | RB | Def–Charles Haley, SF | | LB | | | |
| Def–Lawrence Taylor, NYG | | LB | | | | | | |

## Annual Awards (Cont.)
### UPI AFL-AFC Player of the Year

Presented by UPI to the top player in the AFL (1960-69) and AFC (1970-96). Offensive and defensive players have been honored since 1983. Rookie winners are in **bold** type.
**Multiple winners:** Bruce Smith (4); O.J. Simpson (3); Cornelius Bennett, George Blanda, John Elway, Dan Fouts, Daryle Lamonica, Dan Marino and Curt Warner (2).

| Year | Pos | Year | Pos | Year | Pos |
|---|---|---|---|---|---|
| 1960 **Abner Haynes**, Dal | HB | 1978 **Earl Campbell**, Hou | RB | 1989 Off–Christian Okoye, KC | RB |
| 1961 George Blanda, Hou | QB | 1979 Dan Fouts, SD | QB | Def–Michael Dean Perry,Cle | NT |
| 1962 Cookie Gilchrist, Buf | FB | 1980 Brian Sipe, Cle | QB | 1990 Off-Warren Moon, Hou | QB |
| 1963 Lance Alworth, SD | FL | 1981 Ken Anderson, Cin | QB | Def–Bruce Smith,Buf | DE |
| 1964 Gino Cappelletti, Bos | FL-PK | 1982 Dan Fouts, SD | QB | 1991 Off–Thurman Thomas, Buf | RB |
| 1965 Paul Lowe, SD | HB | 1983 Off–**Curt Warner**, Sea | RB | Def–Cornelius Bennett, Buf | LB |
| 1966 Jim Nance, Bos | FB | Def–Rod Martin, Raiders | LB | 1992 Off–Barry Foster, Pit | RB |
| 1967 Daryle Lamonica, Raiders | QB | 1984 Off–Dan Marino, Mia | QB | Def–Junior Seau, SD | LB |
| 1968 Joe Namath, NYJ | QB | Def–Mark Gastineau, NYJ | DE | 1993 Off–John Elway, Den | QB |
| 1969 Daryle Lamonica, Raiders | QB | 1985 Off–Marcus Allen, Raiders | RB | Def–Rod Woodson, Pit | CB |
| 1970 George Blanda, Raiders | QB-PK | Def–Andre Tippett, NE | LB | 1994 Off–Dan Marino, Mia | QB |
| 1971 Otis Taylor, KC | WR | 1986 Off–Curt Warner, Sea | RB | Def–Greg Lloyd, Pit | LB |
| 1972 O.J. Simpson, Buf | RB | Def–Rulon Jones, Den | DE | 1995 Off–Jim Harbaugh, Ind | QB |
| 1973 O.J. Simpson, Buf | RB | 1987 Off–John Elway, Den | QB | Def–Bryce Paup, Buf | LB |
| 1974 Ken Stabler, Raiders | QB | Def–Bruce Smith, Buf | DE | 1996 Off–Terrell Davis, Den | RB |
| 1975 O.J. Simpson, Buf | RB | 1988 Off–Boomer Esiason, Cin | QB | Def–Bruce Smith, Buf | DE |
| 1976 Bert Jones, Bal | QB | Def–Bruce Smith, Buf | DE | 1997 Award discontinued. | |
| 1977 Craig Morton, Den | QB | & Cornelius Bennett, Buf | LB | | |

### UPI NFL-NFC Rookie of the Year

Presented by UPI to the top rookie in the NFL (1955-69) and NFC (1970-96). Players who were the overall first pick in the NFL draft are in **bold** type.

| Year | Pos | Year | Pos | Year | Pos |
|---|---|---|---|---|---|
| 1955 Alan Ameche, Bal | FB | 1970 Bruce Taylor, SF | DB | 1985 Jerry Rice, SF | WR |
| 1956 Lenny Moore, Bal | HB | 1971 John Brockington, GB | RB | 1986 Reuben Mayes, NO | RB |
| 1957 Jim Brown, Cle | FB | 1972 Chester Marcol, GB | PK | 1987 Robert Awalt, St.L | TE |
| 1958 Jimmy Orr, Pit | FL | 1973 Charle Young, Phi | TE | 1988 Keith Jackson, Phi | TE |
| 1959 Boyd Dowler, GB | FL | 1974 John Hicks, NY | G | 1989 Barry Sanders, Det | RB |
| 1960 Gail Cogdill, Det | FL | 1975 Mike Thomas, Wash | RB | 1990 Mark Carrier, Chi | S |
| 1961 Mike Ditka, Chi | TE | 1976 Sammy White, Min | WR | 1991 Lawrence Dawsey, TB | WR |
| 1962 Ronnie Bull, Chi | FB | 1977 Tony Dorsett, Dal | RB | 1992 Robert Jones, Dal | LB |
| 1963 Paul Flatley, Min | FL | 1978 Bubba Baker, Det | DE | 1993 Jerome Bettis, LA | RB |
| 1964 Charley Taylor, Wash | HB | 1979 Ottis Anderson, St.L | RB | 1994 Bryant Young, SF | DT |
| 1965 Gale Sayers, Chi | HB | 1980 **Billy Sims**, Det | RB | 1995 Rashaan Salaam, Chi | RB |
| 1966 Johnny Roland, St.L | HB | 1981 **George Rogers**, NO | RB | 1996 Simeon Rice, Ari. | DE |
| 1967 Mel Farr, Det | RB | 1982 Jim McMahon, Chi | QB | 1997 Award discontinued. | |
| 1968 Earl McCullough, Det | FL | 1983 Eric Dickerson, LA | RB | | |
| 1969 Calvin Hill, Dal | RB | 1984 Paul McFadden, Phi | PK | | |

### UPI AFL-AFC Rookie of the Year

Presented by UPI to the top rookie in the AFL (1960-69) and AFC (1970-96). Players who were the overall first pick in the AFL or NFL draft are in **bold** type.

| Year | Pos | Year | Pos | Year | Pos |
|---|---|---|---|---|---|
| 1960 Abner Haynes, Dal | HB | 1973 Bobbie Clark, Cin | RB | 1986 Leslie O'Neal, SD | DE |
| 1961 Earl Faison, SD | DE | 1974 Don Woods, SD | RB | 1987 Shane Conlan, Buf | LB |
| 1962 Curtis McClinton, Dal | FB | 1975 Robert Brazile, Hou | LB | 1988 John Stephens, NE | RB |
| 1963 Billy Joe, Den | FB | 1976 Mike Haynes, NE | DB | 1989 Derrick Thomas, KC | LB |
| 1964 Matt Snell, NY | FB | 1977 A.J. Duhe, Mia | DE | 1990 Richmond Webb, Mia | OT |
| 1965 Joe Namath, NY | QB | 1978 **Earl Campbell**, Hou | RB | 1991 Mike Croel, Den | LB |
| 1966 Bobby Burnett, Buf | HB | 1979 Jerry Butler, Buf | WR | 1992 Dale Carter, KC | CB |
| 1967 George Webster, Hou | LB | 1980 Joe Cribbs, Buf | RB | 1993 Rick Mirer, Sea | QB |
| 1968 Paul Robinson, Cin | RB | 1981 Joe Delaney, KC | RB | 1994 Marshall Faulk, Ind | RB |
| 1969 Greg Cook, Cin | QB | 1982 Marcus Allen, LA | RB | 1995 Curtis Martin, NE | RB |
| 1970 Dennis Shaw, Buf | QB | 1983 Curt Warner, Sea | RB | 1996 Terry Glenn, NE | WR |
| 1971 **Jim Plunkett**, NE | QB | 1984 Louis Lipps, Pit | WR | 1997 Award discontinued. | |
| 1972 Franco Harris, Pit | RB | 1985 Kevin Mack, Cle | RB | | |

## AP Offensive Rookie of the Year

Selected by The Associated Press in balloting by a nationwide media panel. Given out since 1967.

| Year | Pos | Year | Pos | Year | Pos |
|------|-----|------|-----|------|-----|
| 1967 Mel Farr, Det | RB | 1980 Billy Sims, Det | RB | 1993 Jerome Bettis, Rams | RB |
| 1968 Earl McCullouch, Det | OE | 1981 George Rogers, NO | RB | 1994 Marshall Faulk, Ind | RB |
| 1969 Calvin Hill, Dal | RB | 1982 Marcus Allen, Raiders | RB | 1995 Curtis Martin, NE | RB |
| 1970 Dennis Shaw, Buf | QB | 1983 Eric Dickerson, Rams | RB | 1996 Eddie George, Hou | RB |
| 1971 John Brockington, GB | RB | 1984 Louis Lipps, Pit | WR | 1997 Warrick Dunn, TB | RB |
| 1972 Franco Harris, Pit | RB | 1985 Eddie Brown, Cin | WR | 1998 Randy Moss, Min | WR |
| 1973 Chuck Foreman, Min | RB | 1986 Reuben Mayes, NO | RB | 1999 Edgerrin James, Ind | RB |
| 1974 Don Woods, SD | RB | 1987 Troy Stradford, Mia | RB | 2000 Mike Anderson, Den | RB |
| 1975 Mike Thomas, Was | RB | 1988 John Stephens, NE | RB | 2001 Anthony Thomas, Chi | RB |
| 1976 Sammy White, Min | WR | 1989 Barry Sanders, Det | RB | 2002 Clinton Portis, Den | RB |
| 1977 Tony Dorsett, Dal | RB | 1990 Emmitt Smith, Dal | RB | 2003 Anquan Boldin, Ari | WR |
| 1978 Earl Campbell, Hou | RB | 1991 Leonard Russell, NE | RB | 2004 Ben Roethlisberger, Pit | QB |
| 1979 Ottis Anderson, St.L | RB | 1992 Carl Pickens, Cin | WR | | |

## AP Defensive Rookie of the Year

Selected by The Associated Press in balloting by a nationwide media panel. Given out since 1967.

| Year | Pos | Year | Pos | Year | Pos |
|------|-----|------|-----|------|-----|
| 1967 Lem Barney, Det | CB | 1980 Buddy Curry, Atl | LB | 1992 Dale Carter, KC | CB |
| 1968 Claude Humphrey, Atl | DE | & Al Richardson, Atl | LB | 1993 Dana Stubblefield, SF | DT |
| 1969 Joe Greene, Pit | DT | 1981 Lawrence Taylor, NYG | LB | 1994 Tim Bowens, Mia | DT |
| 1970 Bruce Taylor, SF | CB | 1982 Chip Banks, Cle | LB | 1995 Hugh Douglas, NYJ | DE |
| 1971 Isiah Robertson, Rams | LB | 1983 Vernon Maxwell, Bal | LB | 1996 Simeon Rice, Ari | DE |
| 1972 Willie Buchanon, GB | CB | 1984 Bill Maas, KC | DT | 1997 Peter Boulware, Bal | LB |
| 1973 Wally Chambers, Chi | DT | 1985 Duane Bickett, Ind | LB | 1998 Charles Woodson, Raiders | CB |
| 1974 Jack Lambert, Pit | LB | 1986 Leslie O'Neal, SD | DE | 1999 Jevon Kearse, Ten | DE |
| 1975 Robert Brazile, Hou | LB | 1987 Shane Conlan, Buf | LB | 2000 Brian Urlacher, Chi | LB |
| 1976 Mike Haynes, NE | CB | 1988 Erik McMillan, NYJ | S | 2001 Kendrell Bell, Pit | LB |
| 1977 A.J. Duhe, Mia | DE | 1989 Derrick Thomas, KC | LB | 2002 Julius Peppers, Car | DE |
| 1978 Al Baker, Det | DE | 1990 Mark Carrier, Chi | S | 2003 Terrell Suggs, Bal | LB |
| 1979 Jim Haslett, Buf | LB | 1991 Mike Croel, Den | LB | 2004 Jonathan Vilma, NYJ | LB |

## Coach of the Year

Presented by UPI to the top coach in the AFL-NFL (1955-69) and AFC-NFC (1970-96). In 1997, the UPI awards were discontinued. Awards beginning in 1997 are the consensus selections from presenters such as AP, the Maxwell Football Club of Philadelphia, *The Sporting News* and the Pro Football Writers Association. Records indicate the team's change in record from the previous season.

**Multiple winners:** Dan Reeves (4); Paul Brown, Chuck Knox, Marty Schottenheimer and Don Shula (3); George Allen, Leeman Bennett, Mike Ditka, George Halas, Tom Landry, Marv Levy, Bill Parcells, Jack Pardee, Sam Rutigliano, Lou Saban, Allie Sherman, Dick Vermeil and Bill Walsh (2).

| Year | Improvement | Year | Improvement |
|------|-------------|------|-------------|
| 1955 NFL–Joe Kuharich, Washington | 3-9 to 8-4 | 1970 NFC–Alex Webster, New York | 6-8 to 9-5 |
| 1956 NFL–Buddy Parker, Detroit | 3-9 to 9-3 | AFC–Paul Brown, Cincinnati | 4-9-1 to 8-6 |
| 1957 NFL–Paul Brown, Cleveland | 5-7 to 9-2-1 | 1971 NFC–George Allen, Washington | 6-8 to 9-4-1 |
| 1958 NFL–Weeb Ewbank, Baltimore | 7-5 to 9-3 | AFC–Don Shula, Miami | 10-4 to 10-3-1 |
| 1959 NFL–Vince Lombardi, Green Bay | 1-10-1 to 7-5 | 1972 NFC–Dan Devine, Green Bay | 4-8-2 to 10-4 |
| 1960 NFL–Buck Shaw, Philadelphia | 7-5 to 10-2 | AFC–Chuck Noll, Pittsburgh | 6-8 to 11-3 |
| AFL–Lou Rymkus, Houston | 10-4 | 1973 NFC–Chuck Knox, Los Angeles | 6-7-1 to 12-2 |
| 1961 NFL–Allie Sherman, New York | 6-4-2 to 10-3-1 | AFC–John Ralston, Denver | 5-9 to 7-5-2 |
| AFL–Wally Lemm, Houston | 10-4 to 10-3-1 | 1974 NFC–Don Coryell, St. Louis | 4-9-1 to 10-4 |
| 1962 NFL–Allie Sherman, New York | 10-3-1 to 12-2 | AFC–Sid Gillman, Houston | 1-13 to 7-7 |
| AFL–Jack Faulkner, Denver | 3-11 to 7-7 | 1975 NFC–Tom Landry, Dallas | 8-6 to 10-4 |
| 1963 NFL–George Halas, Chicago | 9-5 to 11-1-2 | AFC–Ted Marchibroda, Baltimore | 2-12 to 10-4 |
| AFL–Al Davis, Oakland | 1-13 to 10-4 | 1976 NFC–Jack Pardee, Chicago | 4-10 to 7-7 |
| 1964 NFL–Don Shula, Baltimore | 8-6 to 12-2 | AFC–Chuck Fairbanks, New England | 3-11 to 11-3 |
| AFL–Lou Saban, Buffalo | 7-6-1 to 12-2 | 1977 NFC–Leeman Bennett, Atlanta | 4-10 to 7-7 |
| 1965 NFL–George Halas, Chicago | 5-9 to 9-5 | AFC–Red Miller, Denver | 9-5 to 12-2 |
| AFL–Lou Saban, Buffalo | 12-2 to 10-3-1 | 1978 NFC–Dick Vermeil, Philadelphia | 5-9 to 9-7 |
| 1966 NFL–Tom Landry, Dallas | 7-7 to 10-3-1 | AFC–Walt Michaels, New York | 3-11 to 8-8 |
| AFL–Mike Holovak, Boston | 4-8-2 to 8-4-2 | 1979 NFC–Jack Pardee, Washington | 8-8 to 10-6 |
| 1967 NFL–George Allen, Los Angeles | 8-6 to 11-1-2 | AFC–Sam Rutigliano, Cleveland | 8-8 to 9-7 |
| AFL–John Rauch, Oakland | 8-5-1 to 13-1 | 1980 NFC–Leeman Bennett, Atlanta | 6-10 to 12-4 |
| 1968 NFL–Don Shula, Baltimore | 11-1-2 to 13-1 | AFC–Sam Rutigliano, Cleveland | 9-7 to 11-5 |
| AFL–Hank Stram, Kansas City | 9-5 to 12-2 | 1981 NFC–Bill Walsh, San Francisco | 6-10 to 13-3 |
| 1969 NFL–Bud Grant, Minnesota | 8-6 to 12-2 | AFC–Forrest Gregg, Cincinnati | 6-10 to 12-4 |
| AFL–Paul Brown, Cincinnati | 3-11 to 4-9-1 | 1982 NFC–Joe Gibbs, Washington | 8-8 to 8-1 |
| | | AFC–Tom Flores, Los Angeles | 7-9 to 8-1 |

## Annual Awards (Cont.)

| Year | | Improvement |
|---|---|---|
| 1983 | NFC–John Robinson, Los Angeles | 2-7 to 9-7 |
| | AFC–Chuck Knox, Seattle | 4-5 to 9-7 |
| 1984 | NFC–Bill Walsh, San Francisco | 10-6 to 15-1 |
| | AFC–Chuck Knox, Seattle | 9-7 to 12-4 |
| 1985 | NFC–Mike Ditka, Chicago | 10-6 to 15-1 |
| | AFC–Raymond Berry, New England | 9-7 to 11-5 |
| 1986 | NFC–Bill Parcells, New York | 10-6 to 14-2 |
| | AFC–Marty Schottenheimer, Cleveland | 8-8 to 12-4 |
| 1987 | NFC–Jim Mora, New Orleans | 7-9 to 12-3 |
| | AFC–Ron Meyer, Indianapolis | 3-13 to 9-6 |
| 1988 | NFC–Mike Ditka, Chicago | 11-4 to 12-4 |
| | AFC–Marv Levy, Buffalo | 7-8 to 12-4 |
| 1989 | NFC–Lindy Infante, Green Bay | 4-12 to 10-6 |
| | AFC–Dan Reeves, Denver | 8-8 to 11-5 |
| 1990 | NFC–Jimmy Johnson, Dallas | 1-15 to 7-9 |
| | AFC–Art Shell, Los Angeles | 8-8 to 12-4 |
| 1991 | NFC–Wayne Fontes, Detroit | 6-10 to 12-4 |
| | AFC–Dan Reeves, Denver | 5-11 to 12-4 |

| Year | | Improvement |
|---|---|---|
| 1992 | NFC–Dennis Green, Minnesota | 8-8 to 11-5 |
| | AFC–Bobby Ross, San Diego | 4-12 to 11-5 |
| 1993 | NFC–Dan Reeves, New York | 6-10 to 11-5 |
| | AFC–Marv Levy, Buffalo | 11-5 to 12-4 |
| 1994 | NFC–Dave Wannstedt, Chicago | 7-9 to 9-7 |
| | AFC–Bill Parcells, New England | 5-11 to 10-6 |
| 1995 | NFC–Ray Rhodes, Philadelphia | 7-9 to 10-6 |
| | AFC–Marty Schottenheimer, Kansas City | 9-7 to 13-3 |
| 1996 | NFC–Dom Capers, Carolina | 7-9 to 12-4 |
| | AFC–Tom Coughlin, Jacksonville | 4-12 to 9-7 |
| 1997 | NFL–Jim Fassel, NY Giants | 6-10 to 10-5-1 |
| 1998 | NFL–Dan Reeves, Atlanta | 7-9 to 14-2 |
| 1999 | NFL–Dick Vermeil, St. Louis | 4-12 to 13-3 |
| 2000 | NFL–Jim Haslett, New Orleans | 3-13 to 10-6 |
| 2001 | NFL–Dick Jauron, Chicago | 5-11 to 13-3 |
| 2002 | NFL–Andy Reid, Philadelphia | 11-5 to 12-4 |
| 2003 | NFL–Bill Belichick, New England | 9-7 to 14-2 |
| 2004 | NFL–Marty Schottenheimer, San Diego | 4-12 to 12-4 |

## CANADIAN FOOTBALL

## The Grey Cup

Earl Grey, the Governor-General of Canada (1904-11), donated a trophy in 1909 for the Rugby Football Championship of Canada. The trophy, which later became known as the Grey Cup, was originally open to competition for teams registered with the Canada Rugby Union. Since 1954, the Cup has gone to the champion of the Canadian Football League (CFL).

**Overall multiple winners:** Toronto Argonauts (15); Edmonton Eskimos (12); Winnipeg Blue Bombers (9); Hamilton Tiger-Cats (8); Ottawa Rough Riders (7); Calgary Stampeders, Hamilton Tigers and Montreal Alouettes (5); B.C. Lions and University of Toronto (4); Queen's University (3); Ottawa Senators, Sarnia Imperials, Saskatchewan Roughriders and Toronto Balmy Beach (2).

**CFL multiple winners** (since 1954): Edmonton (12); Hamilton and Winnipeg (7); Ottawa and Toronto (5); B.C. Lions, Calgary and Montreal (4); Saskatchewan (2).

**Year Cup Final**
1909 Univ. of Toronto 26, Toronto Parkdale 6
1910 Univ. of Toronto 16, Hamilton Tigers 7
1911 Univ. of Toronto 14, Toronto Argonauts 7
1912 Hamilton Alerts 11, Toronto Argonauts 4
1913 Hamilton Tigers 44, Toronto Parkdale 2
1914 Toronto Argonauts 14, Univ. of Toronto 2
1915 Hamilton Tigers 13, Toronto Rowing 7
1916-19 Not held (WWI)

1920 Univ. of Toronto 16, Toronto Argonauts 3
1921 Toronto Argonauts 23, Edmonton Eskimos 0
1922 Queens Univ. 13, Edmonton Elks 1
1923 Queens Univ. 54, Regina Roughriders 0
1924 Queens Univ. 11, Toronto Balmy Beach 3
1925 Ottawa Senators 24, Winnipeg Tigers 1
1926 Ottawa Senators 10, Univ. of Toronto 7
1927 Toronto Balmy Beach 9, Hamilton Tigers 6
1928 Hamilton Tigers 30, Regina Roughriders 0
1929 Hamilton Tigers 14, Regina Roughriders 3

1930 Toronto Balmy Beach 11, Regina Roughriders 6
1931 Montreal AAA 22, Regina Roughriders 0
1932 Hamilton Tigers 25, Regina Roughriders 6
1933 Toronto Argonauts 4, Sarnia Imperials 3

**Year Cup Final**
1934 Sarnia Imperials 20, Regina Roughriders 12
1935 Winnipeg 'Pegs 18, Hamilton Tigers 12
1936 Sarnia Imperials 26, Ottawa Rough Riders 20
1937 Toronto Argonauts 4, Winnipeg Blue Bombers 3
1938 Toronto Argonauts 30, Winnipeg Blue Bombers 7
1939 Winnipeg Blue Bombers 8, Ottawa Rough Riders 7

1940 Gm 1: Ottawa Rough Riders 8, Toronto B-Beach 2
      Gm 2: Toronto Rough Riders 12, Toronto B-Beach 5
1941 Winnipeg Blue Bombers 18, Ottawa Rough Riders 16
1942 Toronto RACF 8, Winnipeg RACF 5
1943 Hamilton Wildcats 23, Winnipeg RACF 14
1944 Montreal HMCS 7, Hamilton Wildcats 6
1945 Toronto Argonauts 35, Winnipeg Blue Bombers 0
1946 Toronto Argonauts 28, Winnipeg Blue Bombers 6
1947 Toronto Argonauts 10, Winnipeg Blue Bombers 9
1948 Calgary Stampeders 12, Ottawa Rough Riders 7
1949 Montreal Alouettes 28, Calgary Stampeders 15

1950 Toronto Argonauts 13, Winnipeg Blue Bombers 0
1951 Ottawa Rough Riders 21, Saskatch. Roughriders 14
1952 Toronto Argonauts 21, Edmonton Eskimos 11
1953 Hamilton Tiger-Cats 12, Winnipeg Blue Bombers 6

| Year | Winner | Head Coach | Score | Loser | Head Coach | Site |
|---|---|---|---|---|---|---|
| 1954 | Edmonton | Frank (Pop) Ivy | 26-25 | Montreal | Doug Walker | Toronto |
| 1955 | Edmonton | Frank (Pop) Ivy | 34-19 | Montreal | Doug Walker | Vancouver |
| 1956 | Edmonton | Frank (Pop) Ivy | 50-27 | Montreal | Doug Walker | Toronto |
| 1957 | Hamilton | Jim Trimble | 32-7 | Winnipeg | Bud Grant | Toronto |
| 1958 | Winnipeg | Bud Grant | 35-28 | Hamilton | Jim Trimble | Vancouver |
| 1959 | Winnipeg | Bud Grant | 21-7 | Hamilton | Jim Trimble | Toronto |
| 1960 | Ottawa | Frank Clair | 16-6 | Edmonton | Eagle Keys | Vancouver |
| 1961 | Winnipeg | Bud Grant | 21-14 (OT) | Hamilton | Jim Trimble | Toronto |
| 1962 | Winnipeg | Bud Grant | 28-27 * | Hamilton | Jim Trimble | Toronto |

| Year | Winner | Head Coach | Score | Loser | Head Coach | Site |
|------|--------|------------|-------|-------|------------|------|
| 1963 | Hamilton | Ralph Sazio | 21-10 | B.C. Lions | Dave Skrien | Vancouver |
| 1964 | B.C. Lions | Dave Skrien | 34-24 | Hamilton | Ralph Sazio | Toronto |
| 1965 | Hamilton | Ralph Sazio | 22-16 | Winnipeg | Bud Grant | Toronto |
| 1966 | Saskatchewan | Eagle Keys | 29-14 | Ottawa | Frank Clair | Vancouver |
| 1967 | Hamilton | Ralph Sazio | 24-1 | Saskatchewan | Eagle Keys | Ottawa |
| 1968 | Ottawa | Frank Clair | 24-21 | Calgary | Jerry Williams | Toronto |
| 1969 | Ottawa | Frank Clair | 29-11 | Saskatchewan | Eagle Keys | Montreal |
| 1970 | Montreal | Sam Etcheverry | 23-10 | Calgary | Jim Duncan | Toronto |
| 1971 | Calgary | Jim Duncan | 14-11 | Toronto | Leo Cahill | Vancouver |
| 1972 | Hamilton | Jerry Williams | 13-10 | Saskatchewan | Dave Skrien | Hamilton |
| 1973 | Ottawa | Jack Gotta | 22-18 | Edmonton | Ray Jauch | Toronto |
| 1974 | Montreal | Marv Levy | 20-7 | Edmonton | Ray Jauch | Vancouver |
| 1975 | Edmonton | Ray Jauch | 9-8 | Montreal | Marv Levy | Calgary |
| 1976 | Ottawa | George Brancato | 23-20 | Saskatchewan | John Payne | Toronto |
| 1977 | Montreal | Marv Levy | 41-6 | Edmonton | Hugh Campbell | Montreal |
| 1978 | Edmonton | Hugh Campbell | 20-13 | Montreal | Joe Scannella | Toronto |
| 1979 | Edmonton | Hugh Campbell | 17-9 | Montreal | Joe Scannella | Montreal |
| 1980 | Edmonton | Hugh Campbell | 48-10 | Hamilton | John Payne | Toronto |
| 1981 | Edmonton | Hugh Campbell | 26-23 | Ottawa | George Brancato | Montreal |
| 1982 | Edmonton | Hugh Campbell | 32-16 | Toronto | Bob O'Billovich | Toronto |
| 1983 | Toronto | Bob O'Billovich | 18-17 | B.C. Lions | Don Matthews | Vancouver |
| 1984 | Winnipeg | Cal Murphy | 47-17 | Hamilton | Al Bruno | Edmonton |
| 1985 | B.C. Lions | Don Matthews | 37-24 | Hamilton | Al Bruno | Montreal |
| 1986 | Hamilton | Al Bruno | 39-15 | Edmonton | Jack Parker | Vancouver |
| 1987 | Edmonton | Joe Faragalli | 38-36 | Toronto | Bob O'Billovich | Vancouver |
| 1988 | Winnipeg | Mike Riley | 22-21 | B.C. Lions | Larry Donovan | Ottawa |
| 1989 | Saskatchewan | John Gregory | 43-40 | Hamilton | Al Bruno | Toronto |
| 1990 | Winnipeg | Mike Riley | 50-11 | Edmonton | Joe Faragalli | Vancouver |
| 1991 | Toronto | Adam Rita | 36-21 | Calgary | Wally Buono | Winnipeg |
| 1992 | Calgary | Wally Buono | 24-10 | Winnipeg | Urban Bowman | Toronto |
| 1993 | Edmonton | Ron Lancaster | 33-23 | Winnipeg | Cal Murphy | Calgary |
| 1994 | B.C. Lions | Dave Ritchie | 26-23 | Baltimore | Don Matthews | Vancouver |
| 1995 | Baltimore | Don Matthews | 37-20 | Calgary | Wally Buono | Regina |
| 1996 | Toronto | Don Matthews | 43-37 | Edmonton | Ron Lancaster | Hamilton |
| 1997 | Toronto | Don Matthews | 47-23 | Saskatchewan | Jim Daley | Edmonton |
| 1998 | Calgary | Wally Buono | 26-24 | Hamilton | Ron Lancaster | Winnipeg |
| 1999 | Hamilton | Ron Lancaster | 32-21 | Calgary | Wally Buono | Vancouver |
| 2000 | B.C. Lions | Steve Buratto | 28-26 | Montreal | Charlie Taaffe | Calgary |
| 2001 | Calgary | Wally Buono | 27-19 | Winnipeg | Dave Ritchie | Montreal |
| 2002 | Montreal | Don Matthews | 25-16 | Edmonton | Tom Higgins | Edmonton |
| 2003 | Edmonton | Tom Higgins | 34-22 | Montreal | Don Matthews | Regina |
| 2004 | Toronto | Mike Clemons | 27-19 | B.C. Lions | Wally Buono | Ottawa |

*Halted by fog in 4th quarter, final 9:29 played the following day.

## CFL Most Outstanding Player

Regular season Player of the Year as selected by The Football Reporters of Canada since 1953.
**Multiple winners:** Doug Flutie (6); Russ Jackson and Jackie Parker (3); Dieter Brock, Ron Lancaster and Mike Pringle (2).

**Year**
1953 Billy Vessels, Edmonton, RB
1954 Sam Etcheverry, Montreal, QB
1955 Pat Abbruzzi, Montreal, RB
1956 Hal Patterson, Montreal, E-DB
1957 Jackie Parker, Edmonton, RB
1958 Jackie Parker, Edmonton, QB
1959 Johnny Bright, Edmonton, RB
1960 Jackie Parker, Edmonton, QB
1961 Bernie Faloney, Hamilton, QB
1962 George Dixon, Montreal, RB
1963 Russ Jackson, Ottawa, QB
1964 Lovell Coleman, Calgary, RB
1965 George Reed, Saskatchewan, RB
1966 Russ Jackson, Ottawa, QB
1967 Peter Liske, Calgary, QB
1968 Bill Symons, Toronto, RB
1969 Russ Jackson, Ottawa, QB
1970 Ron Lancaster, Saskatch., QB

**Year**
1971 Don Jonas, Winnipeg, QB
1972 Garney Henley, Hamilton, WR
1973 Geo. McGowan, Edmonton, WR
1974 Tom Wilkinson, Edmonton, QB
1975 Willie Burden, Calgary, RB
1976 Ron Lancaster, Saskatch., QB
1977 Jimmy Edwards, Hamilton, RB
1978 Tony Gabriel, Ottawa, TE
1979 David Green, Montreal, RB
1980 Dieter Brock, Winnipeg, QB
1981 Dieter Brock, Winnipeg, QB
1982 Condredge Holloway, Tor., QB
1983 Warren Moon, Edmonton, QB
1984 Willard Reaves, Winnipeg, RB
1985 Merv Fernandez, B.C. Lions, WR
1986 James Murphy, Winnipeg, WR
1987 Tom Clements, Winnipeg, QB
1988 David Williams, B.C. Lions, WR

**Year**
1989 Tracy Ham, Edmonton, QB
1990 Mike Clemons, Toronto, RB
1991 Doug Flutie, B.C. Lions, QB
1992 Doug Flutie, Calgary, QB
1993 Doug Flutie, Calgary, QB
1994 Doug Flutie, Calgary, QB
1995 Mike Pringle, Baltimore, RB
1996 Doug Flutie, Toronto, QB
1997 Doug Flutie, Toronto, QB
1998 Mike Pringle, Montreal, RB
1999 Danny McManus, Hamilton, QB
2000 Dave Dickenson, Calgary, QB
2001 Khari Jones, Winnipeg, QB
2002 Milt Stegall, Winnipeg, SB
2003 Anthony Calvillo, Montreal, QB
2004 Casey Printers, B.C. Lions, QB

## NFL EUROPE

The World League of American Football was formed in 1991 with hopes of expanding the popularity of the NFL to overseas markets. Funded by the NFL, the inaugural league in 1991 consisted of three European teams (London, Barcelona and Frankfurt), and seven North American teams (New York/New Jersey, Orlando, Montreal, Raleigh-Durham, Birmingham, Sacramento and San Antonio). The second season used the same format with Columbus, Ohio, replacing Raleigh-Durham.

In the fall of 1992, the NFL and WLAF Board of Directors voted to restructure the league to include more European teams. Play was subsequently suspended. In 1993, NFL clubs approved a six-team European-only league to resume play in 1995 with teams in Amsterdam, Barcelona, Frankfurt, London, Rhein and Scotland. In January 1998, the name of the league was changed to NFL Europe. In 1999, Berlin was added and London was disbanded. In 2004, Cologne was added and Barcelona was disbanded. In 2004, Hamburg was added and Scotland was disbanded.

### The World Bowl

**Multiple Winners:** Frankfurt (3); Berlin and Rhein (2).

| Bowl | Year | Winner | Head Coach | Score | Loser | Head Coach | Site |
|------|------|--------|------------|-------|-------|------------|------|
| I | 1991 | London | Larry Kennan | 21-0 | Barcelona | Jack Bicknell | London |
| II | 1992 | Sacramento | Kay Stephenson | 21-17 | Orlando | Galen Hall | Montreal |
| III | 1995 | Frankfurt | Ernie Stautner | 26-22 | Amsterdam | Al Luginbill | Amsterdam |
| IV | 1996 | Scotland | Jim Criner | 32-27 | Frankfurt | Ernie Stautner | Edinburgh, Scot. |
| V | 1997 | Barcelona | Jack Bicknell | 38-24 | Rhein | Galen Hall | Barcelona |
| VI | 1998 | Rhein | Galen Hall | 34-10 | Frankfurt | Dick Curl | Frankfurt |
| VII | 1999 | Frankfurt | Dick Curl | 38-24 | Barcelona | Jack Bicknell | Dusseldorf |
| VIII | 2000 | Rhein | Galen Hall | 13-10 | Scotland | Jim Criner | Frankfurt |
| IX | 2001 | Berlin | Peter Vaas | 24-17 | Barcelona | Jack Bicknell | Amsterdam |
| X | 2002 | Berlin | Peter Vaas | 26-20 | Rhein | Pete Kuharchek | Dusseldorf |
| XI | 2003 | Frankfurt | Doug Graber | 35-16 | Rhein | Pete Kuharchek | Glasgow |
| XII | 2004 | Berlin | Rick Lantz | 30-24 | Frankfurt | Mike Jones | Gelsenkirchen, Ger. |
| XIII | 2005 | Amsterdam | Bart Andrus | 27-21 | Berlin | Rick Lantz | Dusseldorf |

### World Bowl MVP

| Year | | |
|------|------|------|
| 1991 Dan Crossman, London, S | 1998 Jim Arellanes, Rhein, QB | 2003 Jonas Lewis, Frankfurt, RB |
| 1992 Davis Archer, Sacramento, QB | 1999 Andy McCullough, Frankfurt, WR | 2004 Eric McCoo, Berlin, RB |
| 1995 Paul Justin, Frankfurt, QB | 2000 Aaron Stecker, Scotland, RB | 2005 Kurt Kittner, Amsterdam, QB |
| 1996 Yo Murphy, Scotland, WR | 2001 Jonathan Quinn, Berlin, QB | |
| 1997 Jon Kitna, Barcelona, QB | 2002 Dane Looker, Berlin, WR | |

## ARENA FOOTBALL

The Arena Football League debuted in June of 1987 with four teams in Chicago, Denver, Pittsburgh and Washington D.C. Currently there are 18 teams in the league (including expansion Utah in 2006), divided into two conferences and four divisions.

### ArenaBowl

**Multiple Winners:** Tampa Bay (5); Detroit (4); Arizona, Orlando and San Jose (2).

| Bowl | Year | Winner | Head Coach | Score | Loser | Head Coach | Site |
|------|------|--------|------------|-------|-------|------------|------|
| I | 1987 | Denver | Tim Marcum | 45-16 | Pittsburgh | Joe Haering | Pittsburgh |
| II | 1988 | Detroit | Tim Marcum | 24-13 | Chicago | Perry Moss | Chicago |
| III | 1989 | Detroit | Tim Marcum | 39-26 | Pittsburgh | Joe Haering | Detroit |
| IV | 1990 | Detroit | Perry Moss | 51-27 | Dallas | Ernie Stautner | Detroit |
| V | 1991 | Tampa Bay | Fran Curci | 48-42 | Detroit | Tim Marcum | Detroit |
| VI | 1992 | Detroit | Tim Marcum | 56-38 | Orlando | Perry Moss | Orlando |
| VII | 1993 | Tampa Bay | Lary Kuharich | 51-31 | Detroit | Tim Marcum | Detroit |
| VIII | 1994 | Arizona | Danny White | 36-31 | Orlando | Perry Moss | Orlando |
| IX | 1995 | Tampa Bay | Tim Marcum | 48-35 | Orlando | Perry Moss | St. Petersburg |
| X | 1996 | Tampa Bay | Tim Marcum | 42-38 | Iowa | John Gregory | Des Moines |
| XI | 1997 | Arizona | Danny White | 55-33 | Iowa | John Gregory | Phoenix |
| XII | 1998 | Orlando | Jay Gruden | 62-31 | Tampa Bay | Tim Marcum | Tampa |
| XIII | 1999 | Albany | Mike Dailey | 59-48 | Orlando | Jay Gruden | Albany |
| XIV | 2000 | Orlando | Jay Gruden | 41-38 | Nashville | Pat Sperduto | Orlando |
| XV | 2001 | Grand Rapids | Michael Trigg | 64-42 | Nashville | Pat Sperduto | Grand Rapids |
| XVI | 2002 | San Jose | Darren Arbet | 52-14 | Arizona | Danny White | San Jose |
| XVII | 2003 | Tampa Bay | Tim Marcum | 43-29 | Arizona | Danny White | Tampa |
| XVIII | 2004 | San Jose | Darren Arbet | 69-62 | Arizona | Danny White | Phoenix |
| XIX | 2005 | Colorado | Mike Dailey | 51-48 | Georgia | Doug Plank | Las Vegas |

### ArenaBowl MVP

**Multiple Winners:** George LaFrance (3); Stevie Thomas (2).

| Year | | |
|------|------|------|
| 1987 Gary Mullen, Denver, WR | 1994 Sherdrick Bonner, Arizona, QB | 2001 Terrill Shaw, Grand Rapids, OS |
| 1988 Steve Griffin, Detroit, WR/DB | 1995 George LaFrance, Tampa Bay, OS | 2002 John Dutton, San Jose, QB |
| 1989 George LaFrance, Det., WR/DB | 1996 Stevie Thomas, TB, WR/LB | 2003 Lawrence Samuels, TB, WR/LB |
| 1990 Art Schlichter, Detroit, QB | 1997 Donnie Davis, Arizona, QB | 2004 Off–Mark Grieb, San Jose, QB |
| 1991 Stevie Thomas, TB, WR/LB | 1998 Rick Hamilton, Orlando, FB/LB |     Def–Ricky Parker, Arizona, DS |
| 1992 George LaFrance, Detroit, OS | 1999 Eddie Brown, Albany, OS | 2005 Off–Willis Marshall, Col., WR |
| 1993 Jay Gruden, Tampa Bay, QB | 2000 Connell Maynor, Orlando, QB |     Def–Ahmad Hawkins, Col., DB |

# College Basketball

*Roy Williams* and *Sean May* led the way on North Carolina's national title run in 2005.

# Where have you been all my life?

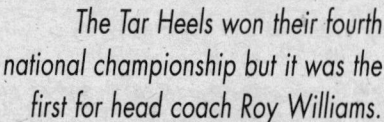

*The Tar Heels won their fourth national championship but it was the first for head coach Roy Williams.*

**Andy Katz**
*covers college basketball for ESPN.com*

Sometimes you're just lucky to witness one of the defining moments in a season.

Watching North Carolina head coach Roy Williams run into the stands in St. Louis, searching for his wife, Wanda, who has been loyal and privately passionate about her husband's teams over the years, and his two children, Scott and Kimberly, was the one image that will remain from the 2004-05 season.

Williams hadn't gone through a tragedy or anything that dramatic to get to this point. But he had endured plenty of professional heartache, coaching one of the best teams in the country in 1997 at Kansas, only to fall to Arizona in the Sweet 16. He had coached the Jayhawks to the Final Four in 1991, '93, 2002 and 2003, the last time getting within one possession of the title in a loss to Syracuse.

With all that history, you could say, he was due. Getting the title at North Carolina, the only job that could ever get him to leave Lawrence, was a bonus.

Despite his special attachment to the University of Kansas, where he coached for 15 years, his first love was and remains North Carolina after getting his start under Tar Heel legend Dean Smith. Still, getting a title for Jayhawk Nation, his second home, would have been just about as sweet as the one he earned for the Tar Heels in 2005.

Illinois coach Bruce Weber, who will go down as having one of the best seasons in recent memory, with or without a title, even felt for Williams. Following the game, Weber said Williams had been someone he had cheered for to win a title. Certainly, he added, he didn't want him to win one against the Illini, but he couldn't be too upset to lose to Williams.

Williams, who had been in Weber's spot in 1991 and 2003, ran to catch Weber walking off the court after the game to congratulate him on his season. He said he had been there before and knew what the long walk to the locker room had felt like.

After the title victory, Williams said of his family, "I wanted to be with her

AP/Wide World Photos

*Having players like **Raymond Felton** and **Sean May** gave **Roy Williams** plenty of reasons to smile—all the way to St. Louis in 2005.*

[Wanda] and Scott and Kimberly, because coaching is very difficult in some ways, because we make so many sacrifices away from the family and I just wanted them to be with me."

It was honest. Williams is one of the most organized, thorough and overall driven coaches in the game. He manages his time better than most. Somehow, he has found enough time to spend with his family in an all-inclusive and always intense job.

Getting the Tar Heels to the title was hardly a walk. First of all, he truly wrestled with the idea of leaving Kansas and replacing his former assistant Matt Doherty in Chapel Hill. Furthermore, the first season, which ended in a second-round loss in the NCAAs against Texas, was hardly a

smooth transition. He had to get the veteran players to buy into his concepts while also massaging the egos of the heralded underclassmen. He had his battles with top-scorer Rashad McCants but the two had their epiphany and realized that they needed each other to win a title.

Year two was hardly a breather, but moments like the losses at Wake Forest and Duke, hardened this team. The group only lost four times all year, and one of them was the season opener against Santa Clara with point guard Raymond Felton suspended for the game for playing in an unsanctioned summer league game.

Despite the trials of the regular season, the Tar Heels cruised through the first two games in the NCAA

AP/Wide World Photos

*Illinois guard **Dee Brown** pointed the way for the Fighting Illini to a wire-to-wire run as the nation's top-ranked team and an NCAA record-tying 37 wins in 2005.*

Tournament, crushing Oakland and Iowa State before Villanova gave the Tar Heels a legitimate scare, losing by just a point in the Sweet 16. Then Wisconsin wasn't a walkover either in a six-point Carolina win in the Elite Eight.

But at the Final Four, Michigan State couldn't hang with the Tar Heels in the second half of their national semifinal meeting and Illinois ultimately couldn't climb all the way out of a big hole in a five-point loss in the national championship game.

Williams was able to manage McCants, maximize Felton and Sean May, work in Marvin Williams (ultimately the second pick in the NBA draft) and balance the egos of seniors Jawad Williams, Melvin Scott and

Jackie Manuel, who had to accept changing roles.

The coaching was masterful in a season that should be remembered for the way a team of studs came together to win a title. Williams wouldn't be any less of a coach had he not won the national championship, but he wouldn't have had quite the opportunity to publicly thank his wife and two children for their devotion to him and his career.

This was the right time to see Williams' raw emotion. This wasn't a scheduled news conference where he got teared up over something. This was genuine. This was about his family, both his immediate and extended North Carolina kin that are now woven together for years to come.

# Dick Vitale's Ten Biggest Stories of the Year in College Basketball

**10 Andrew Bogut.** The Utah Utes' awesome Aussie wins Player of the Year honors, averaging 20 points and 12 rebounds a game. Bogut declares for the draft and the Milwaukee Bucks make the sophomore center the first overall pick in the 2005 NBA draft.

**9 Boston College's sensational, scintillating start.** The Eagles begin the season with 20 straight victories before finally falling to Notre Dame, 68-65, in South Bend on Feb. 8. BC was ranked No. 4 when the streak ended, its highest ever mark in the AP Poll. Notre Dame seems to have a knack for ending long win streaks, having stopped several famous ones, including UCLA's NCAA record 88-game win streak in 1974.

**8 Duke wins the ACC tourney** and earns a top-seed in the NCAA tournament despite being short-handed most of the season, because of injuries to Shavlik Randolph and Sean Dockery and NBA defections. Coach K does another amazing job, guiding the Blue Devils to 27 wins before losing in the Sweet 16 to the Final Four-bound Michigan State Spartans.

**7 Wisconsin-Milwaukee stuns Boston College** to reach the Sweet 16. After upsetting Alabama in the first round, the 12th-seeded Panthers eliminate four-seed BC, head coach Bruce Pearl's alma mater, in the second round of the NCAAs. Wisconsin-Milwaukee's terrific tourney run ends with a loss to top-ranked Illinois.

**6 Some legendary winning college coaches make the Hall.** Syracuse's longtime leader Jim Boeheim, Connecticut coach Jim Calhoun and former LSU women's coach Sue Gunter are all deservingly inducted into the Basketball Hall of Fame in Springfield, Mass. as part of the Class of 2005.

**5 A couple of NCAA Tournament first round shockers.** The 14th-seeded Bucknell Bisons surprise three-seed Kansas, 64-63, earning the Patriot League its first ever NCAA tournament win in 14 tries. In the other early round jaw-dropper, the America East champion and 13th-seeded Vermont Catamounts and retiring coach Tom Brennan upset the Big East champion and fourth-seeded Syracuse Orangemen, 60-57.

**4** **Louisville makes the Final Four** for the first time since 1986 when Denny Crum and Pervis Ellison took them to a second national title. Head coach Rick Pitino returns the Cardinals to the highest level of college basketball, finishing the season with a Conference USA title and a 33-5 record after losing to top-ranked Illinois in the national semifinals.

**3** **Illinois' super season.** Consensus Coach of the Year Bruce Weber's Fighting Illini nearly go undefeated in the regular season but fall at the buzzer to Ohio State. The team still earns a No. 1 seed and reaches the Final Four but loses to North Carolina in the national championship game. Illinois finishes with a record-tying 37 wins.

**2** **The greatest Elite Eight weekend ever.** Three of the four regional finals go to overtime and all four games are decided by single digits. Michigan State advances to the Final Four by beating Kentucky, 94-88, in the first double-overtime regional final in nearly 40 years. North Carolina battles to beat Wisconsin, 88-82, and Louisville rallies from 20 points down to win, 93-85, in overtime against Kevin Pittsnoggle and West Virginia. Maybe most impressive is Illinois' improbable comeback from a 15-point deficit with just four minutes left to force overtime and stun Arizona, 90-89.

**1** **Roy Williams finally cuts the nets down** as UNC edges Illinois, 75-70, giving the veteran coach his first national championship after three trips to the NCAA title game. On his 21st birthday junior center Sean May dominates inside, finishing with a game-high 26 points and 10 rebounds to bring a second national title to the family, matching the one his father Scott May won with the Indiana Hoosiers in 1976.

Baylor women's basketball coach Kim Mulkey-Robertson made history in 2005 becoming the first person to win an NCAA women's basketball championship as a player (Louisiana Tech) and a coach with Baylor's 84-62 victory against Michigan St. **Did you know** that previously, Dean Smith (Kansas & North Carolina) and Bob Knight (Ohio State & Indiana) were the only people to win national titles as players and coaches?

# 2004-2005
# Season in Review

SPORTS ALMANAC

## Final Regular Season AP Men's Top 25 Poll
Taken **before** start of NCAA tournament.

The sportswriters & broadcasters poll: first place votes in parentheses; records through Monday, March 14, 2005; total points (based on 25 for 1st, 24 for 2nd, etc.); record in NCAA tourney and team lost to; head coach (career years and record including 2005 postseason), and preseason ranking. Teams in **bold** type went on to reach NCAA Final Four.

| | | Mar. 14 Record | Points | NCAA Recap | Head Coach | Preseason Rank |
|---|---|---|---|---|---|---|
| 1 | **Illinois** (72) | 32-1 | 1800 | 5-1 (North Carolina) | Bruce Weber (7 yrs: 166-63) | 5 |
| 2 | **North Carolina** | 27-4 | 1676 | 6-0 | Roy Williams (17 yrs: 470-116) | 4 |
| 3 | Duke | 25-5 | 1671 | 2-1 (Michigan St.) | Mike Krzyzewski (30 yrs: 721-246) | 11 |
| 4 | **Louisville** | 29-4 | 1495 | 4-1 (Illinois) | Rick Pitino (19 yrs: 449-159) | 14 |
| 5 | Wake Forest | 26-5 | 1457 | 1-1 (West Virginia) | Skip Prosser (12 yrs: 259-113) | 2 |
| 6 | Oklahoma St. | 24-6 | 1393 | 2-1 (Arizona) | Eddie Sutton (35 yrs: 781-299) | 7 |
| 7 | Kentucky | 25-5 | 1342 | 3-1 (Michigan St.) | Tubby Smith (14 yrs: 343-120) | 9 |
| 8 | Washington | 27-5 | 1318 | 2-1 (Louisville) | Lorenzo Romar (9 yrs: 151-123) | 22 |
| 9 | Arizona | 27-6 | 1133 | 3-1 (Illinois) | Lute Olson (32 yrs: 740-257) | 10 |
| 10 | Gonzaga | 25-4 | 1122 | 1-1 (Texas Tech) | Mark Few (6 yrs: 159-37) | 10 |
| 11 | Syracuse | 27-6 | 1072 | 0-1 (Vermont) | Jim Boeheim (29 yrs: 703-241) | 6 |
| 12 | Kansas | 23-6 | 1049 | 0-1 (Bucknell) | Bill Self (12 yrs: 257-121) | 1 |
| 13 | Connecticut | 22-7 | 949 | 1-1 (N.C. State) | Jim Calhoun (33 yrs: 703-310) | 8 |
| 14 | Boston College | 24-4 | 878 | 1-1 (WI-Milwaukee) | Al Skinner (17 yrs: 285-246) | NR |
| 15 | **Michigan St.** | 22-6 | 690 | 4-1 (North Carolina) | Tom Izzo (10 yrs: 233-97) | 13 |
| 16 | Florida | 23-7 | 651 | 1-1 (Villanova) | Billy Donovan (11 yrs: 227-113) | 23 |
| 17 | Oklahoma | 24-7 | 605 | 1-1 (Utah) | Kelvin Sampson (22 yrs: 436-247) | NR |
| 18 | Utah | 27-5 | 599 | 2-1 (Kentucky) | Ray Giacoletti (8 yrs: 146-89) | NR |
| 19 | Villanova | 22-7 | 494 | 2-1 (North Carolina) | Jay Wright (11 yrs: 198-139) | NR |
| 20 | Wisconsin | 22-8 | 384 | 3-1 (North Carolina) | Bo Ryan (21 yrs: 476-140) | 21 |
| 21 | Alabama | 24-7 | 376 | 0-1 (Wisconsin) | Mark Gottfried (10 yrs: 211-107) | 18 |
| 22 | Pacific | 26-3 | 349 | 1-1 (Washington) | Bob Thomason (21 yrs: 365-244) | NR |
| 23 | Cincinnati | 24-7 | 163 | 1-1 (Kentucky) | Bob Huggins (24 yrs: 567-199) | 18 |
| 24 | Texas Tech | 20-10 | 143 | 2-1 (West Virginia) | Bob Knight (39 yrs: 854-333) | NR |
| 25 | Georgia Tech | 19-11 | 132 | 1-1 (Louisville) | Paul Hewitt (7 yrs: 162-93) | 3 |

**Others receiving votes:** 26. **Pittsburgh** (20-8) 124 points; 27. **LSU** (20-9) 79; **West Virginia** (21-10) 51; 28. **Nevada** (24-6) 48; 29. **Charlotte** (21-7) 44; 30. **Southern Illinois** (26-7) 28; 31. **New Mexico** (26-6) 22; 32. **Wisc-Milwaukee** (24-5) 16; 33. **Old Dominion** (28-5) 8; 34. **Creighton** (23-10) 7; 35. **Vermont** (24-6) 6; 36. **Stanford** (18-12) 4; 37. **UTEP** (27-7); 39. **Utah St.** (24-7) 3; 40. **Bucknell** (22-9), **Ohio** (21-10), **Winthrop** (27-5) 2; 43. **George Washington** (22-7), **Iowa** (21-11), **Minnesota** (21-10), **N.C. State** (19-13), **Penn** (20-8), **St. Mary's-CA** (25-8) and **UCLA** (18-10) 1.

## NCAA Men's Division I Tournament Seeds

| | ALBUQUERQUE | | AUSTIN | | CHICAGO | | SYRACUSE |
|---|---|---|---|---|---|---|---|
| 1 | Washington (27-5) | 1 | Duke (25-5) | 1 | Illinois (32-1) | 1 | North Carolina (27-4) |
| 2 | Wake Forest (26-5) | 2 | Kentucky (25-5) | 2 | Oklahoma St. (24-6) | 2 | Connecticut (22-7) |
| 3 | Gonzaga (25-4) | 3 | Oklahoma (24-7) | 3 | Arizona (27-6) | 3 | Kansas (23-6) |
| 4 | Louisville (29-4) | 4 | Syracuse (27-6) | 4 | Boston College (24-4) | 4 | Florida (23-7) |
| 5 | Georgia Tech (19-11) | 5 | Michigan St. (22-6) | 5 | Alabama (24-7) | 5 | Villanova (22-7) |
| 6 | Texas Tech (20-10) | 6 | Utah (27-5) | 6 | LSU (20-9) | 6 | Wisconsin (22-8) |
| 7 | West Virginia (21-10) | 7 | Cincinnati (24-7) | 7 | Southern Illinois (26-7) | 7 | Charlotte (21-7) |
| 8 | Pacific (26-3) | 8 | Stanford (18-12) | 8 | Texas (20-10) | 8 | Minnesota (21-10) |
| 9 | Pittsburgh (20-8) | 9 | Mississippi St. (22-10) | 9 | Nevada (24-6) | 9 | Iowa St. (18-11) |
| 10 | Creighton (23-10) | 10 | Iowa (21-11) | 10 | St. Mary's-CA (25-8) | 10 | N.C. State (19-13) |
| 11 | UCLA (18-10) | 11 | UTEP (27-7) | 11 | UAB (21-10) | 11 | Northern Iowa (21-10) |
| 12 | Geo. Washington (22-7) | 12 | Old Dominion (28-5) | 12 | Wisc-Milwaukee (24-5) | 12 | New Mexico (26-6) |
| 13 | LA-Lafayette (20-10) | 13 | Vermont (24-6) | 13 | Pennsylvania (20-8) | 13 | Ohio (21-10) |
| 14 | Winthrop (27-5) | 14 | Niagara (20-9) | 14 | Utah St. (24-7) | 14 | Bucknell (22-9) |
| 15 | Chattanooga (20-10) | 15 | Eastern Kentucky (22-8) | 15 | SE Louisiana (24-8) | 15 | Central Florida (24-8) |
| 16 | Montana (18-12) | 16 | Delaware St. (19-13) | 16 | Fairleigh Dickinson (20-12) | 16 | Oakland* (13-18) |

*Oakland defeated Alabama A&M, 79-69, in the NCAA Tournament "opening-round" play-in game at Dayton, Ohio for a berth in the field of 64.

# 2005 NCAA Tournament Men's Division

| 1st ROUND March 17-18 | 2nd ROUND March 19-20 | SWEET 16 March 24 | ELITE EIGHT March 26 | FINAL FOUR April 2 | NATIONAL CHAMPIONSHIP | FINAL FOUR April 2 | ELITE EIGHT March 27 | SWEET 16 March 25 | 2nd ROUND March 19-20 | 1st ROUND March 17-18 |
|---|---|---|---|---|---|---|---|---|---|---|

**CHICAGO**

- (1) Illinois 67
- (16) FDU 55
- (8) Texas 57
- (9) Nevada 61
- (5) Alabama 73
- (12) WI-Milw. 83
- (13) Boston Coll. 85
- (13) Penn. 75
- (6) LSU 68
- (11) UAB 82
- (3) Arizona 66
- (14) Utah St. 53
- (7) Southern Ill. 65
- (2) St. Mary's 56
- (10) Oklahoma St. 63
- (15) SW La. 50

Illinois 71 / Nevada 59 → Illinois 77
WI-Milwaukee 83 / Boston College 75 → WI-Milwaukee 63
UAB 63 / Arizona 85 → Arizona 79
Southern Ill. 77 / Oklahoma St. 85 → Oklahoma St. 78

Illinois (ot) 90 / Arizona 89 → Illinois 72

**ALBUQUERQUE**

- (1) Washington 88
- (16) Montana 77
- (8) Pacific 79
- (9) Pittsburgh 71
- (5) Ga. Tech 80
- (12) Geo. Wash. 68
- (4) Louisville 68
- (13) LA-Lafayette 62
- (6) Texas Tech 78
- (11) UCLA 66
- (3) Gonzaga 74
- (14) Winthrop 64
- (7) West Virginia 63
- (10) Creighton 61
- (2) Wake Forest 70
- (15) Chattanooga 54

Washington 97 / Pacific 79 → Washington 79
Ga. Tech 54 / Louisville 76 → Louisville 93
Texas Tech 71 / Gonzaga 69 → Texas Tech 60
West Virginia (2ot) 111 / Wake Forest 105 → West Virginia 65

Louisville (ot) 93 / West Virginia 85 → Louisville 57

**National Championship**
No. Carolina 75
Illinois 70
Edward Jones Dome
St. Louis, Missouri
Monday, April 4, 2005

**SYRACUSE**

- (1) North Carolina 96
- (16) Oakland 68
- (8) Minnesota 53
- (9) Iowa St. 64
- (5) Villanova 55
- (12) New Mexico 47
- (4) Florida 67
- (13) Ohio 62
- (6) Wisconsin 57
- (11) No. Iowa 52
- (3) Kansas 63
- (14) Bucknell 64
- (7) Charlotte 63
- (10) N.C. State 75
- (2) Connecticut 77
- (15) C. Florida 71

North Carolina 92 / Iowa St. 65 → North Carolina 67
Villanova 76 / Florida 65 → Villanova 66
Wisconsin 71 / Bucknell 62 → Wisconsin 65
N.C. State 65 / Connecticut 62 → N.C. State 56

North Carolina 88 / Wisconsin 82 → North Carolina 87

**AUSTIN**

Play-in Game to
Syracuse (16) seed
Oakland 79
Alabama A&M 69

- (1) Duke 57
- (16) Delware St. 46
- (9) Stanford 70
- (9) Mississippi St. 93
- (5) Michigan St. 89
- (12) Old Dom. 81
- (4) Syracuse 57
- (13) Vermont (ot) 60
- (6) Utah 60
- (11) UTEP 54
- (14) Oklahoma 84
- (14) Niagara 67
- (7) Cincinnati 76
- (10) Iowa 64
- (2) Kentucky 72
- (15) Eastern Ky. 64

Duke 63 / Mississippi St. 55 → Duke 68
Michigan St. 72 / Vermont 61 → Michigan St. 78
Utah 67 / Oklahoma 58 → Utah 52
Cincinnati 60 / Kentucky 69 → Kentucky 67

Michigan St. (2ot) 94 / Kentucky 88 → Michigan St. 71

**NCAA FINAL FOUR St. Louis 2005**

## NCAA Men's Championship Game

67th NCAA Division I Championship Game. **Date:** Monday, April 4, at the Edward Jones Dome in St. Louis. **Coaches:** Roy Williams of North Carolina and Bruce Weber of Illinois. **Favorite:** North Carolina by 2½.
**Attendance:** 47,262; **Officials:** Ed Corbett, John Cahill, Verne Harris. **TV Rating:** 15.0/23 share (CBS).

### North Carolina 75

| | Min | FG M-A | FT M-A | Pts | Reb O-T | A | PF |
|---|---|---|---|---|---|---|---|
| Raymond Felton | 35 | 4-9 | 5-6 | 17 | 0-3 | 7 | 4 |
| Sean May | 34 | 10-11 | 6-8 | 26 | 2-10 | 2 | 1 |
| Rashad McCants | 31 | 6-15 | 0-0 | 14 | 1-2 | 1 | 0 |
| Jawad Williams | 22 | 3-6 | 0-0 | 9 | 1-5 | 0 | 1 |
| Jackie Manuel | 18 | 0-1 | 0-2 | 0 | 0-3 | 2 | 4 |
| Marvin Williams | 24 | 4-8 | 0-1 | 8 | 3-5 | 0 | 2 |
| David Noel | 20 | 0-0 | 1-2 | 1 | 1-3 | 0 | 0 |
| Melvin Scott | 13 | 0-2 | 0-0 | 0 | 0-2 | 0 | 0 |
| Reyshawn Terry | 2 | 0-0 | 0-0 | 0 | 0-0 | 0 | 0 |
| Quentin Thomas | 1 | 0-0 | 0-0 | 0 | 0-1 | 0 | 1 |
| TOTALS | 200 | 27-52 | 12-19 | 75 | 8-34 | 12 | 13 |

**Three-point FG:** 9-16 (Felton 4-5, J. Williams 3-4, McCants 2-2, M Williams 0-1, Scott 0-1); **Blocked Shots:** 2 (J. Williams, May); **Turnovers:** 10 (Manuel 4, Felton 2, McCants 2, J. Williams 2, May, Thomas); **Steals:** 4 (Felton 2, J. Williams, McCants); **Percentages:** 2-Pt FG (.500), 3-Pt FG (.563), Total FG (.519), Free Throws (.632).

### Illinois 70

| | Min | FG M-A | FT M-A | Pts | Reb O-T | A | PF |
|---|---|---|---|---|---|---|---|
| James Augustine | 9 | 0-3 | 0-0 | 0 | 1-2 | 0 | 5 |
| Roger Powell Jr. | 38 | 4-10 | 0-0 | 9 | 8-14 | 1 | 2 |
| Luther Head | 37 | 8-21 | 1-5 | 21 | 1-5 | 3 | 1 |
| Deron Williams | 40 | 7-16 | 0-2 | 17 | 0-4 | 7 | 4 |
| Dee Brown | 38 | 4-10 | 2-2 | 12 | 0-4 | 7 | 1 |
| Rich McBride | 2 | 0-0 | 0-0 | 0 | 0-0 | 0 | 0 |
| Warren Carter | 5 | 0-1 | 0-0 | 0 | 1-1 | 0 | 1 |
| Nick Smith | 1 | 0-0 | 0-0 | 0 | 0-0 | 0 | 0 |
| Jack Ingram | 30 | 4-9 | 2-2 | 11 | 5-7 | 0 | 4 |
| TOTALS | 200 | 27-70 | 4-6 | 70 | 16-37 | 18 | 18 |

**Three-point FGs:** 12-40 (Ingram 1-3, Head 5-16, Powell 1-2, Brown 2-8, Williams 3-10, Carter 0-1); **Blocked Shots:** 1 (Head); **Turnovers:** 8 (Head 4, Powell 2, Augustine, Williams); **Steals:** 8 (Brown 3, Head 2, Powell, Williams, Carter). **Percentages:** 2-Pt FG (.500), 3-Pt FG (.300), Total FG (.386), Free Throws (.667).

| | | | |
|---|---|---|---|
| **North Carolina** (ACC) | 40 | 35 — | **75** |
| **Illinois** (Big Ten) | 27 | 43 — | **70** |

## Final ESPN/USA Today Coaches' Poll

Taken **after** NCAA Tournament.

Voted on by a panel of 31 Division I head coaches following the NCAA tournament: first place votes in parentheses with total points (based on 25 for 1st, 24 for 2nd, etc.). Schools on major probation are ineligible to be ranked.

| | | W-L | Pts | Before NCAAs W-L | Rank |
|---|---|---|---|---|---|
| 1 | North Carolina (31) | 33-4 | 775 | 27-4 | 3 |
| 2 | Illinois | 37-2 | 744 | 32-1 | 1 |
| 3 | Louisville | 33-5 | 704 | 29-4 | 15 |
| 4 | Michigan St. | 26-7 | 676 | 22-6 | 15 |
| 5 | Kentucky | 28-6 | 637 | 25-5 | 5 |
| 6 | Arizona | 30-7 | 612 | 27-6 | 9 |
| 7 | Duke | 27-6 | 560 | 25-5 | 2 |
| 8 | Oklahoma St. | 26-7 | 515 | 24-6 | 8 |
| 9 | Washington | 29-6 | 511 | 27-5 | 7 |
| 10 | Wisconsin | 25-9 | 489 | 22-8 | 19 |
| 11 | Wake Forest | 27-6 | 399 | 26-5 | 6 |
| 12 | West Virginia | 24-11 | 364 | 21-10 | NR |
| 13 | Villanova | 24-8 | 355 | 22-7 | 22 |
| 14 | Utah | 29-6 | 333 | 27-5 | 17 |
| 15 | Kansas | 23-7 | 253 | 23-6 | 10 |
| 16 | Texas Tech | 22-11 | 251 | 20-10 | 24 |
| 17 | Connecticut | 23-8 | 249 | 22-7 | 14 |
| 18 | Gonzaga | 26-5 | 239 | 25-4 | 11 |
| 19 | Boston College | 25-5 | 234 | 24-4 | 12 |
| 20 | Oklahoma | 25-8 | 218 | 24-7 | 16 |
| 21 | Syracuse | 27-7 | 179 | 27-6 | 13 |
| 22 | N.C. State | 21-14 | 137 | 19-13 | NR |
| 23 | Wisc-Milwaukee | 26-6 | 123 | 24-5 | NR |
| 24 | Florida | 24-8 | 118 | 23-7 | 18 |
| 25 | Cincinnati | 25-8 | 96 | 24-7 | 23 |

**Others receiving votes:** 26. **Pacific** (84 pts); 27. **Georgia Tech** (45); 28. **Alabama** (45); 29. **Vermont** (34); 30. **South Carolina** (12); 31. **Texas** (11); 32. **Southern Illinois**, **Minnesota** and **Iowa** (10); 35. **Saint Joseph's** (9); 36. **Bucknell** (8); 37. **Nevada** (7); 38. **UAB** (5); 39. **Pittsburgh** and **Iowa St.** (4); 41. **New Mexico** (3); 42. **Charlotte** (2); 43. **Memphis** (1).

## THE FINAL FOUR

at the Alamodome in San Antonio. (April 2-4, 2005).

### Semifinal — Game One

Chicago Regional champ Illinois vs. Albuquerque Regional champ Louisville; Saturday, Apr. 2 (5:07 p.m. tipoff). **Coaches:** Bruce Weber, Illinois and Rick Pitino, Louisville. **Favorite:** Illinois by 3.

| | | | |
|---|---|---|---|
| **Louisville** (C-USA) | 28 | 29 — | **57** |
| **Illinois** (Big Ten) | 31 | 41 — | **72** |

**High scorers** — Ellis Myles, Louisville (17) and Roger Powell Jr. and Luther Head, Illinois (20); **Att** — 47,754; **TV rating** — 10.0/20 share (CBS).

### Semifinal — Game Two

Syracuse Regional champion North Carolina vs. Austin Regional champion Michigan St.; Saturday, Apr. 2 (7:47 p.m. tipoff). **Coaches:** Tom Izzo, Michigan St. and Roy Williams, North Carolina. **Favorite:** North Carolina by 5.

| | | | |
|---|---|---|---|
| **Michigan St.** (Big Ten) | 38 | 33 — | **71** |
| **North Carolina** (ACC) | 33 | 54 — | **87** |

**High scorers** — Sean May, North Carolina (22) and Maurice Ager, Michigan (24); **Att** — 47,754; **TV rating** — 10.9/19 share (CBS).

### Most Outstanding Player

Sean May, North Carolina junior center.
SEMIFINAL — 31 minutes, 22 points, 7 rebounds, 3 assists, 1 block; FINAL — 34 minutes, 26 points, 10 rebounds, 2 assists, 1 block.

### All-Final Four Team

Sean May, junior guard Raymond Felton and junior guard/forward Rashad McCants of North Carolina and senior guard Luther Head and junior guard Deron Williams of Illinois.

## NCAA Finalists' Tournament and Season Statistics
At least 10 games played during the overall season.

### Illinois (37-2)

| | NCAA Tournament | | | | | | Overall Season | | | | | |
| | | | | —Per Game— | | | | | | —Per Game— | | |
| | Gm | FG % | TPts | Pts | Reb | Ast | Gm | FG % | TPts | Pts | Reb | Ast |
|---|---|---|---|---|---|---|---|---|---|---|---|---|
| Luther Head | 6 | .385 | 100 | 16.7 | 3.3 | 4.0 | 39 | .463 | 622 | 15.9 | 4.0 | 3.8 |
| Deron Williams | 6 | .471 | 88 | 14.7 | 3.5 | 8.3 | 39 | .433 | 489 | 12.5 | 3.6 | 6.8 |
| Dee Brown | 6 | .450 | 77 | 12.8 | 3.2 | 4.5 | 39 | .499 | 518 | 13.3 | 2.7 | 4.5 |
| Roger Powell Jr. | 6 | .500 | 67 | 11.2 | 6.5 | 0.8 | 39 | .549 | 467 | 12.0 | 5.7 | 0.4 |
| James Augustine | 6 | .571 | 55 | 9.2 | 9.0 | 0.2 | 39 | .621 | 392 | 10.1 | 7.6 | 1.1 |
| Jack Ingram | 6 | .541 | 46 | 7.7 | 3.8 | 0.5 | 39 | .473 | 174 | 4.5 | 2.7 | 0.4 |
| Nick Smith | 5 | .375 | 6 | 1.2 | 0.4 | 0.3 | 38 | .406 | 127 | 3.3 | 2.1 | 0.6 |
| Warren Carter | 6 | .333 | 5 | 0.8 | 0.8 | 0.3 | 33 | .516 | 74 | 2.2 | 1.8 | 0.2 |
| Rich McBride | 6 | .167 | 3 | 0.5 | 0.5 | 0.0 | 38 | .323 | 98 | 2.6 | 1.3 | 0.8 |
| Shaun Pruitt | 1 | — | 0 | 0.0 | 0.0 | 0.0 | 21 | .385 | 29 | 1.4 | 0.9 | 0.0 |
| Fred Nkedmi | 0 | — | 0 | 0.0 | 0.0 | 0.0 | 18 | .600 | 12 | 0.7 | 0.3 | 0.1 |
| ILLINOIS | 6 | .457 | 447 | 74.5 | 34.0 | 19.0 | 39 | .484 | 3002 | 77.0 | 34.3 | 18.6 |
| OPPONENTS | 6 | .433 | 398 | 66.3 | 34.3 | 12.7 | 39 | .415 | 2382 | 61.1 | 31.3 | 12.4 |

**Three-pointers:** NCAA TOURNAMENT—Head (23-58), Brown (14-41), Williams (11-34), Powell (5-11), Ingram (3-7), McBride (1-6), Carter (0-1), Team (57-158 for .361 pct.); OVERALL—Head (116-283), Brown (99-228), Williams (68-187), McBride (27-87), Powell (20-52), Ingram (9-23), Smith (4-11), Carter (1-6), Team 344-877 for .392 pct.).

### North Carolina (33-4)

| | NCAA Tournament | | | | | | Overall Season | | | | | |
| | | | | —Per Game— | | | | | | —Per Game— | | |
| | Gm | FG % | TPts | Pts | Reb | Ast | Gm | FG % | TPts | Pts | Reb | Ast |
|---|---|---|---|---|---|---|---|---|---|---|---|---|
| Sean May | 6 | .667 | 134 | 22.3 | 10.7 | 1.8 | 37 | .567 | 647 | 17.5 | 10.7 | 1.7 |
| Rashad McCants | 6 | .486 | 102 | 17.0 | 3.2 | 2.7 | 33 | .489 | 528 | 16.0 | 3.0 | 2.7 |
| Jawad Williams | 6 | .488 | 47 | 7.8 | 3.8 | 0.7 | 37 | .541 | 483 | 13.1 | 4.0 | 1.4 |
| Raymond Felton | 6 | .426 | 82 | 13.7 | 5.8 | 6.8 | 36 | .455 | 464 | 12.9 | 4.3 | 6.9 |
| Marvin Williams | 6 | .500 | 72 | 12.0 | 7.3 | 0.5 | 36 | .506 | 407 | 11.3 | 6.6 | 0.7 |
| Jackie Manuel | 6 | .500 | 22 | 3.7 | 2.7 | 1.2 | 37 | .490 | 204 | 5.5 | 2.8 | 1.5 |
| Melvin Scott | 6 | .429 | 23 | 3.8 | 1.3 | 1.5 | 37 | .377 | 188 | 5.1 | 1.4 | 1.1 |
| David Noel | 6 | .375 | 7 | 1.2 | 2.3 | 1.2 | 37 | .548 | 143 | 3.9 | 2.6 | 1.5 |
| Reyshawn Terry | 4 | .750 | 7 | 1.8 | 0.3 | 0.0 | 32 | .542 | 73 | 2.3 | 0.7 | 0.2 |
| Jesse Holley | 3 | .333 | 2 | 0.7 | 1.3 | 0.3 | 10 | .400 | 13 | 1.3 | 0.4 | 0.2 |
| Wes Miller | 3 | .333 | 4 | 1.3 | 0.3 | 0.3 | 24 | .300 | 26 | 1.1 | 0.2 | 0.5 |
| Byron Sanders | 2 | .500 | 2 | 1.0 | 0.0 | 0.0 | 26 | .455 | 22 | -0.8 | 0.9 | 0.3 |
| Quentin Thomas | 6 | .000 | 0 | 0.0 | 0.7 | 1.2 | 37 | .455 | 28 | 0.8 | 0.8 | 1.3 |
| C.J. Hooker | 3 | — | 0 | 0.0 | 0.3 | 0.0 | 25 | .471 | 18 | 0.7 | 0.5 | 0.1 |
| Charlie Everett | 3 | — | 1 | 0.3 | 0.0 | 0.0 | 22 | .625 | 12 | 0.5 | 0.2 | 0.1 |
| NORTH CAROLINA | 6 | .508 | 505 | 84.2 | 33.3 | 17.0 | 37 | .499 | 3257 | 88.0 | 40.5 | 19.1 |
| OPPONENTS | 6 | .393 | 422 | 70.3 | 32.3 | 14.8 | 37 | .401 | 2600 | 70.3 | 33.0 | 13.5 |

**Three-pointers:** NCAA TOURNAMENT— McCants (15-30), Felton (15-34), J. Williams (6-17), Scott (5-12), M. Williams (5-12), Terry (1-2), Miller (1-3), Manuel (0-2), Noel (0-2), Holley (0-1) Team (48-115 for .417 pct.); OVERALL— McCants (71-168), Felton (70-159), M. Scott (45-126), J. Williams (40-105), M. Williams (19-44), Terry (12-20), Noel (7-20), Manuel (5-18), Miller (5-16), Holley (1-4), Thomas (1-3), Everett (1-1), May (0-3), Team (277-687 for .403 pct.).

### Illinois' Schedule

**Reg. Season**
**(29-1)**

| | | |
|---|---|---|
| W | Delaware St. | .87-67 |
| W | Florida A&M | .91-60 |
| W | Oakland | .85-54 |
| W | Gonzaga | .89-72 |
| W | Wake Forest | .91-73 |
| W | Arkansas | .72-60 |
| W | Chicago St. | .78-59 |
| W | at Georgetown | .74-59 |
| W | Oregon | .83-66 |
| W | Valparaiso | .93-56 |
| W | Missouri | .70-64 |
| W | Longwood | .105-79 |
| W | Northwestern St. | .69-51 |
| W | Cincinnati | .67-45 |
| W | Ohio St. | .84-65 |
| W | at Purdue | .68-59 |
| W | Penn St. | .90-64 |
| W | at Northwestern | .78-66 |
| W | Iowa | .73-68 |
| W | at Wisconsin | .75-65 |
| W | Minnesota | .89-66 |
| W | at Michigan St. | .81-68 |
| W | Indiana | .60-47 |
| W | at Michigan | .57-51 |
| W | Wisconsin | .70-59 |
| W | at Penn St. | .83-63 |
| W | at Iowa | .75-65 |
| W | Northwestern | .84-48 |
| W | Purdue | .84-50 |
| L | at Ohio St. | .64-65 |

**Big Ten Tourney**
**(3-0)**

| | | |
|---|---|---|
| W | Northwestern | .68-51 |
| W | Minnesota | .64-56 |
| W | Wisconsin | .54-43 |

**NCAA Tourney**
**(5-1)**

| | | |
|---|---|---|
| W | Fairleigh Dickinson | 67-55 |
| W | Nevada | .71-59 |
| W | WI-Milwaukee | .77-63 |
| W | Arizona | .90-89 |
| W | Louisville | .72-57 |
| L | North Carolina | .70-75 |

### North Carolina's Schedule

**Reg. Season**
**(26-3)**

| | | |
|---|---|---|
| L | Santa Clara | .66-77 |
| W | BYU | .86-50 |
| W | Tennessee | .94-81 |
| W | Iowa | .106-92 |
| W | USC | .97-65 |
| W | at Indiana | .70-63 |
| W | Kentucky | .91-78 |
| W | Loyola | .109-60 |
| W | at Virginia Tech | .85-51 |
| W | Vermont | .93-65 |
| W | NC-Wilmington | .96-75 |
| W | at Cleveland St. | .107-64 |
| W | William & Mary | 105-66 |
| W | Maryland | .109-75 |
| W | Georgia Tech | .91-69 |
| L | at Wake Forest | .82-95 |
| W | at Clemson | .77-58 |
| W | Miami-FL | .87-67 |
| W | at Virginia | .110-76 |
| W | N.C. State | .95-71 |
| W | at Florida St. | .81-60 |
| L | at Duke | .70-71 |
| W | at Connecticut | .77-70 |
| W | Virginia | .85-61 |
| W | Clemson | .88-56 |
| W | at N.C. State | .81-71 |
| W | at Maryland | .85-83 |
| W | Florida St. | .91-76 |
| W | Duke | .75-73 |

**ACC Tourney**
**(1-1)**

| | | |
|---|---|---|
| W | Clemson | .88-81 |
| L | Georgia Tech | .75-78 |

**NCAA Tourney**
**(6-0)**

| | | |
|---|---|---|
| W | Oakland | .96-68 |
| W | Iowa St. | .92-65 |
| W | Villanova | .67-66 |
| W | Wisconsin | .88-82 |
| W | Michigan St. | .87-71 |
| W | Illinois | .75-70 |

# Final NCAA Men's Division I Standings

Conference records include regular season games only. Overall records include all postseason tournament games.

## America East Conference

| Team | Conference W | L | Pct | Overall W | L | Pct |
|---|---|---|---|---|---|---|
| *Vermont | 16 | 2 | .889 | 25 | 7 | .781 |
| †Northeastern | 15 | 3 | .833 | 21 | 10 | .677 |
| †Boston University | 14 | 4 | .778 | 20 | 9 | .690 |
| Albany | 9 | 9 | .500 | 13 | 15 | .464 |
| Binghamton | 8 | 10 | .444 | 12 | 17 | .414 |
| Maine | 8 | 10 | .444 | 14 | 15 | .483 |
| Stony Brook | 6 | 12 | .333 | 12 | 17 | .414 |
| New Hampshire | 5 | 13 | .278 | 9 | 19 | .321 |
| UMBC | 5 | 13 | .278 | 11 | 18 | .379 |
| Hartford | 4 | 14 | .222 | 8 | 20 | .286 |

**Conf. Tourney Final:** Vermont 80, Northeastern 57.
**\*NCAA Tourney (1-1):** Vermont (1-1).
**†NIT (0-2):** Northeastern (0-1), Boston University (0-1).

## Atlantic Coast Conference

| Team | Conference W | L | Pct | Overall W | L | Pct |
|---|---|---|---|---|---|---|
| *North Carolina | 14 | 2 | .875 | 33 | 4 | .892 |
| *Wake Forest | 13 | 3 | .813 | 27 | 6 | .818 |
| *Duke | 11 | 5 | .688 | 27 | 6 | .818 |
| †Virginia Tech | 8 | 8 | .500 | 16 | 14 | .533 |
| *Georgia Tech | 8 | 8 | .500 | 20 | 12 | .625 |
| †Miami-FL | 7 | 9 | .438 | 16 | 13 | .552 |
| *N.C. State | 7 | 9 | .483 | 21 | 14 | .600 |
| †Maryland | 7 | 9 | .438 | 19 | 13 | .594 |
| †Clemson | 5 | 11 | .313 | 16 | 16 | .500 |
| Florida St | 4 | 12 | .250 | 12 | 19 | .387 |
| Virginia | 4 | 12 | .250 | 14 | 15 | .483 |

**Conf. Tourney Final:** Duke 69, Georgia Tech 64.

**\*NCAA Tourney (12-4):** North Carolina (6-0), Wake Forest (1-1), Duke (2-1), N.C. State (2-1), Georgia Tech (1-1).
**†NIT (4-4):** Virginia Tech (1-1), Miami-FL (0-1), Maryland (3-1), Clemson (0-1).

## Atlantic Sun Conference

| Team | Conference W | L | Pct | Overall W | L | Pct |
|---|---|---|---|---|---|---|
| Gardner-Webb | 13 | 7 | .650 | 18 | 12 | .600 |
| *Central Florida | 13 | 7 | .650 | 24 | 9 | .727 |
| Belmont | 12 | 8 | .600 | 14 | 16 | .467 |
| Jacksonville | 11 | 9 | .550 | 16 | 13 | .552 |
| Lipscomb | 11 | 9 | .550 | 12 | 15 | .571 |
| Georgia St. | 11 | 9 | .550 | 14 | 15 | .483 |
| Mercer | 11 | 9 | .550 | 12 | 15 | .571 |
| Troy | 10 | 10 | .500 | 12 | 18 | .400 |
| Florida Atlantic | 10 | 10 | .500 | 10 | 17 | .370 |
| Stetson | 8 | 12 | .400 | 10 | 17 | .370 |
| Campbell | 0 | 20 | .000 | 2 | 25 | .074 |

**Conf. Tourney Final:** C. Florida 63, Gardner-Webb 54.
**\*NCAA Tourney (0-1):** Central Florida (0-1).

## Atlantic 10 Conference

| East | Conference W | L | Pct | Overall W | L | Pct |
|---|---|---|---|---|---|---|
| †St. Joseph's | 14 | 2 | .875 | 24 | 12 | .667 |
| †Temple | 11 | 5 | .688 | 16 | 14 | .533 |
| Massachusetts | 9 | 7 | .562 | 16 | 12 | .571 |
| Fordham | 8 | 8 | .500 | 13 | 16 | .448 |
| Rhode Island | 4 | 12 | .250 | 6 | 22 | .214 |
| St. Bonaventure | 1 | 15 | .062 | 2 | 26 | .071 |
| **West** | **W** | **L** | **Pct** | **W** | **L** | **Pct** |
| *Geo. Washington | 11 | 5 | .688 | 22 | 8 | .733 |
| Dayton | 10 | 6 | .625 | 18 | 11 | .621 |
| Xavier | 10 | 6 | .625 | 17 | 12 | .586 |
| Richmond | 8 | 8 | .500 | 14 | 15 | .483 |
| La Salle | 5 | 11 | .312 | 10 | 19 | .345 |
| Duquesne | 5 | 11 | .312 | 8 | 22 | .267 |

**Conf. Tourney Final:** G. Washington 76, St. Joseph's 67.
**\*NCAA Tourney (0-1):** G. Washington (0-1).
**†NIT (5-2):** St. Joseph's (5-1), Temple (0-1).

## Big East Conference

| East | Conference W | L | Pct | Overall W | L | Pct |
|---|---|---|---|---|---|---|
| *Boston College | 13 | 3 | .813 | 25 | 5 | .833 |
| *Connecticut | 13 | 3 | .813 | 23 | 8 | .742 |
| *Syracuse | 11 | 5 | .688 | 27 | 7 | .794 |
| *Villanova | 11 | 5 | .688 | 24 | 8 | .750 |
| *Pittsburgh | 10 | 6 | .625 | 20 | 9 | .690 |
| †Notre Dame | 9 | 7 | .563 | 17 | 12 | .586 |
| †Georgetown | 8 | 8 | .500 | 19 | 13 | .594 |
| *West Virginia | 8 | 8 | .500 | 24 | 11 | .686 |
| Providence | 4 | 12 | .250 | 14 | 17 | .452 |
| Seton Hall | 4 | 12 | .250 | 12 | 16 | .429 |
| St. John's | 3 | 13 | .188 | 9 | 18 | .333 |
| Rutgers | 2 | 14 | .125 | 10 | 19 | .345 |

**Conf. Tourney Final:** Syracuse 68, West Virginia 59.
**\*NCAA Tourney (7-6):** Boston College (1-1), Connecticut (1-1), Pittsburgh (0-1), Syracuse (0-1), Villanova (2-1), West Virginia (3-1).
**†NIT (2-2):** Georgetown (2-1), Notre Dame (0-1).

## Big Sky Conference

| Team | Conference W | L | Pct | Overall W | L | Pct |
|---|---|---|---|---|---|---|
| Portland St. | 11 | 3 | .786 | 19 | 9 | .679 |
| *Montana | 9 | 5 | .643 | 18 | 13 | .581 |
| Montana St | 9 | 5 | .643 | 14 | 14 | .500 |
| Sacramento St. | 8 | 6 | .571 | 12 | 16 | .429 |
| Weber St | 7 | 7 | .500 | 14 | 16 | .467 |
| Eastern Washington | 5 | 9 | .357 | 8 | 20 | .286 |
| Northern Arizona | 4 | 10 | .286 | 11 | 17 | .393 |
| Idaho St | 3 | 11 | .214 | 9 | 18 | .333 |

**Conf. Tourney Final:** Montana 63, Weber St. 61.
**\*NCAA Tourney (0-1):** Montana (0-1).

## Big South Conference

| Team | Conference W | L | Pct | Overall W | L | Pct |
|---|---|---|---|---|---|---|
| *Winthrop | 15 | 1 | .938 | 27 | 6 | .818 |
| Liberty | 11 | 5 | .688 | 13 | 15 | .464 |
| NC-Asheville | 8 | 8 | .500 | 11 | 17 | .393 |
| Birmingham-Southern | 7 | 9 | .438 | 16 | 14 | .533 |
| Radford | 7 | 9 | .438 | 12 | 16 | .429 |
| High Point | 7 | 9 | .438 | 13 | 18 | .419 |
| Charleston Southern | 7 | 9 | .438 | 13 | 17 | .433 |
| Coastal Carolina | 7 | 9 | .438 | 10 | 19 | .345 |
| VMI | 3 | 13 | .188 | 9 | 18 | .333 |

**Conf. Tourney Final:** Winthrop 68, Charleston Southern 46.
**\*NCAA Tourney (0-1):** Winthrop (0-1).

## Big Ten Conference

| Team | Conference W | L | Pct | Overall W | L | Pct |
|---|---|---|---|---|---|---|
| *Illinois | 15 | 1 | .938 | 37 | 2 | .948 |
| *Michigan St | 13 | 3 | .812 | 26 | 7 | .788 |
| *Wisconsin | 11 | 5 | .688 | 25 | 9 | .735 |
| *Minnesota | 10 | 6 | .625 | 21 | 11 | .656 |
| †Indiana | 10 | 6 | .625 | 15 | 14 | .517 |
| Ohio St | 8 | 8 | .500 | 20 | 12 | .625 |
| *Iowa | 7 | 9 | .438 | 21 | 12 | .636 |
| Northwestern | 6 | 10 | .375 | 15 | 16 | .484 |
| Michigan | 4 | 12 | .250 | 13 | 18 | .419 |
| Purdue | 3 | 13 | .188 | 7 | 21 | .250 |
| Penn St | 1 | 15 | .063 | 7 | 23 | .233 |

**Conf. Tourney Final:** Illinois 54, Wisconsin 43.
**\*NCAA Tourney (12-5):** Illinois (5-1), Michigan St. (4-1), Wisconsin (3-1), Minnesota (0-1), Iowa (0-1).
**†NIT (0-1):** Indiana (0-1).

## Final NCAA Men's Division I Standings (Cont.)

### Big 12 Conference

| Team | Conference W | L | Pct | Overall W | L | Pct |
|---|---|---|---|---|---|---|
| *Oklahoma | 12 | 4 | .750 | 25 | 8 | .758 |
| *Kansas | 12 | 4 | .750 | 23 | 7 | .767 |
| *Oklahoma St. | 11 | 5 | .688 | 26 | 7 | .788 |
| *Texas Tech | 10 | 6 | .625 | 22 | 11 | .667 |
| *Iowa St. | 9 | 7 | .563 | 19 | 12 | .613 |
| *Texas | 9 | 7 | .563 | 20 | 11 | .645 |
| †Texas A&M | 8 | 8 | .500 | 21 | 10 | .677 |
| †Missouri | 7 | 9 | .438 | 16 | 17 | .485 |
| Nebraska | 7 | 9 | .438 | 14 | 14 | .500 |
| Kansas St | 6 | 10 | .375 | 17 | 12 | .586 |
| Colorado | 4 | 12 | .250 | 14 | 16 | .467 |
| Baylor | 1 | 15 | .063 | 9 | 19 | .321 |

**Conf. Tourney Final:** Oklahoma St. 72, Texas Tech 68.
**\*NCAA Tourney (6-6):** Oklahoma (1-1), Kansas (0-1), Oklahoma St. (2-1), Texas Tech (2-1), Iowa St. (1-1), Texas (0-1).
**†NIT (2-2):** Texas A&M (2-1), Missouri (0-1).

### Big West Conference

| Team | Conference W | L | Pct | Overall W | L | Pct |
|---|---|---|---|---|---|---|
| *Pacific | 18 | 0 | 1.000 | 27 | 4 | .871 |
| *Utah St | 13 | 5 | .722 | 24 | 8 | .750 |
| †Cal St.-Fullerton | 12 | 6 | .667 | 21 | 11 | .656 |
| Cal St.-Northridge | 12 | 6 | .667 | 18 | 13 | .581 |
| UC-Irvine | 8 | 10 | .444 | 16 | 13 | .552 |
| Long Beach St | 7 | 11 | .389 | 10 | 20 | .333 |
| UC-Santa Barbara | 7 | 11 | .389 | 11 | 18 | .379 |
| Idaho | 6 | 12 | .333 | 8 | 22 | .267 |
| UC-Riverside | 4 | 14 | .222 | 9 | 19 | .321 |
| Cal Poly | 3 | 13 | .167 | 5 | 22 | .185 |

**Conf. Tourney Final:** Utah St. 65, Pacific 52.
**\*NCAA Tourney (1-2):** Pacific (1-1), Utah St. (0-1).
**†NIT (2-1):** Cal St.-Fullerton (2-1).

### Colonial Athletic Association

| Team | Conference W | L | Pct | Overall W | L | Pct |
|---|---|---|---|---|---|---|
| *Old Dominion | 15 | 3 | .833 | 28 | 6 | .824 |
| NC-Wilmington | 13 | 5 | .722 | 19 | 10 | .655 |
| †Va. Commonwealth | 13 | 5 | .722 | 19 | 13 | .594 |
| †Hofstra | 12 | 6 | .667 | 21 | 9 | .700 |
| †Drexel | 12 | 6 | .667 | 17 | 12 | .586 |
| George Mason | 10 | 8 | .556 | 16 | 13 | .552 |
| Delaware | 7 | 11 | .389 | 11 | 20 | .355 |
| William & Mary | 3 | 15 | .167 | 8 | 21 | .276 |
| James Madison | 3 | 15 | .167 | 6 | 22 | .214 |
| Towson | 2 | 16 | .111 | 5 | 24 | .172 |

**Conf. Tourney Final:** Old Dominion 73, Virginia Commonwealth 66 OT.
**\*NCAA Tourney (0-1):** Old Dominion (0-1).
**†NIT (0-3):** Va. Commonwealth (0-1), Hofstra (0-1), Drexel (0-1).

#### Division I Independents

| Team | Overall W | L | Pct |
|---|---|---|---|
| Texas A&M-Corpus Christi | 20 | 8 | .714 |
| Utah Valley St. | 16 | 12 | .571 |
| Texas-Pan American | 12 | 16 | .429 |
| UC-Davis | 11 | 17 | .393 |
| Northern Colorado | 8 | 21 | .276 |
| IPFW | 7 | 22 | .241 |
| Longwood | 1 | 30 | .032 |
| Savannah St. | 0 | 28 | .000 |

### Conference USA

| Team | Conference W | L | Pct | Overall W | L | Pct |
|---|---|---|---|---|---|---|
| *Louisville | 14 | 2 | .875 | 33 | 5 | .868 |
| *Charlotte | 12 | 4 | .750 | 21 | 8 | .724 |
| *Cincinnati | 12 | 4 | .750 | 25 | 8 | .757 |
| *Ala-Birmingham | 10 | 6 | .625 | 22 | 11 | .667 |
| †DePaul | 10 | 6 | .625 | 20 | 11 | .645 |
| †Houston | 9 | 7 | .563 | 18 | 14 | .563 |
| †Memphis | 9 | 7 | .563 | 22 | 16 | .579 |
| †Texas Christian | 8 | 8 | .500 | 21 | 14 | .600 |
| †Marquette | 7 | 9 | .437 | 19 | 12 | .613 |
| Saint Louis | 6 | 10 | .375 | 9 | 21 | .300 |
| So. Florida | 5 | 11 | .313 | 14 | 16 | .467 |
| Tulane | 4 | 12 | .250 | 10 | 18 | .357 |
| East Carolina | 4 | 12 | .250 | 9 | 19 | .321 |
| So. Mississippi | 2 | 14 | .125 | 11 | 17 | .393 |

**Conf. Tourney Final:** Louisville 75, Memphis 74.
**\*NCAA Tourney (6-4):** Louisville (4-1), Charlotte (0-1), Cincinnati (1-1), Ala-Birmingham (1-1).
**†NIT (6-5):** DePaul (1-1), Houston (0-1), Memphis (3-1), Texas Christian (2-1), Marquette (0-1).

### Horizon League

| Team | Conference W | L | Pct | Overall W | L | Pct |
|---|---|---|---|---|---|---|
| *WI-Milwaukee | 14 | 2 | .875 | 26 | 6 | .813 |
| WI-Green Bay | 10 | 6 | .625 | 17 | 11 | .607 |
| Detroit | 9 | 7 | .563 | 14 | 16 | .467 |
| Illinois-Chicago | 8 | 8 | .500 | 15 | 14 | .517 |
| Wright St | 8 | 8 | .500 | 15 | 15 | .500 |
| Loyola-IL | 8 | 8 | .500 | 13 | 17 | .433 |
| Butler | 7 | 9 | .438 | 13 | 15 | .464 |
| Cleveland St. | 6 | 10 | .375 | 9 | 17 | .346 |
| Youngstown St. | 2 | 14 | .125 | 5 | 23 | .179 |

**Conf. Tourney Final:** WI-Milwaukee 59, Detroit 58.
**\*NCAA Tourney (2-1):** WI-Milwaukee (2-1).

### Ivy League

| Team | Conference W | L | Pct | Overall W | L | Pct |
|---|---|---|---|---|---|---|
| *Pennsylvania | 13 | 1 | .929 | 20 | 9 | .690 |
| Cornell | 8 | 6 | .571 | 13 | 14 | .481 |
| Harvard | 7 | 7 | .500 | 12 | 15 | .444 |
| Yale | 7 | 7 | .500 | 12 | 15 | .444 |
| Dartmouth | 7 | 7 | .500 | 10 | 17 | .370 |
| Princeton | 6 | 8 | .429 | 15 | 13 | .536 |
| Brown | 5 | 9 | .357 | 12 | 16 | .429 |
| Columbia | 3 | 11 | .214 | 12 | 15 | .444 |

**Conf. Tourney Final:** Ivy League has no tournament.
**\*NCAA Tourney (0-1):** Penn (0-1).

### Metro Atlantic Athletic Conference

| Team | Conference W | L | Pct | Overall W | L | Pct |
|---|---|---|---|---|---|---|
| *Niagara | 13 | 5 | .722 | 20 | 10 | .667 |
| Rider | 13 | 5 | .722 | 19 | 11 | .633 |
| Fairfield | 11 | 7 | .611 | 15 | 15 | .500 |
| Saint Peter's | 10 | 8 | .556 | 15 | 13 | .536 |
| Iona | 9 | 9 | .500 | 15 | 16 | .484 |
| Manhattan | 9 | 9 | .500 | 15 | 14 | .517 |
| Canisius | 8 | 10 | .444 | 11 | 18 | .379 |
| Marist | 8 | 10 | .444 | 11 | 17 | .393 |
| Loyola | 5 | 13 | .278 | 6 | 22 | .214 |
| Siena | 4 | 14 | .222 | 6 | 24 | .200 |

**Conf. Tourney Final:** Niagara 81, Rider 59.
**\*NCAA Tourney (0-1):** Niagara (0-1).

## Mid-American Conference

| East | Conference | | | Overall | | |
|------|---|---|---|---|---|---|
| | W | L | Pct | W | L | Pct |
| †Miami-OH | 12 | 6 | .667 | 19 | 11 | .633 |
| †Buffalo | 11 | 7 | .611 | 23 | 10 | .697 |
| *Ohio | 11 | 7 | .611 | 21 | 11 | .656 |
| Akron | 11 | 7 | .611 | 19 | 10 | .655 |
| †Kent St. | 11 | 7 | .611 | 20 | 13 | .606 |
| Marshall | 3 | 15 | .167 | 6 | 22 | .214 |
| **West** | W | L | Pct | W | L | Pct |
| †Western Mich | 11 | 7 | .611 | 20 | 13 | .606 |
| Toledo | 11 | 7 | .611 | 16 | 13 | .552 |
| Bowling Green | 10 | 8 | .555 | 18 | 11 | .621 |
| Ball St. | 10 | 8 | .556 | 15 | 13 | .536 |
| N. Illinois | 7 | 11 | .389 | 11 | 17 | .393 |
| Eastern Mich | 5 | 13 | .278 | 12 | 18 | .400 |
| Central Mich | 4 | 14 | .222 | 10 | 18 | .357 |

**Conf. Tourney Final:** Ohio 80, Buffalo 79 OT.
***NCAA Tourney (0-1):** Ohio (0-1).
**†NIT (2-4):** Miami-OH (0-1), Buffalo (1-1), Kent St. (0-1), Western Mich. (1-1).

## Mid-Continent Conference

| Team | Conference | | | Overall | | |
|------|---|---|---|---|---|---|
| | W | L | Pct | W | L | Pct |
| †Oral Roberts | 13 | 3 | .813 | 25 | 8 | .758 |
| Missouri-KC | 12 | 4 | .750 | 16 | 12 | .571 |
| Valparaiso | 10 | 6 | .625 | 15 | 16 | .484 |
| IUPUI | 9 | 7 | .563 | 15 | 16 | .484 |
| Western Illinois | 7 | 9 | .438 | 11 | 17 | .393 |
| Chicago St. | 7 | 9 | .438 | 9 | 19 | .321 |
| *Oakland | 7 | 9 | .438 | 13 | 19 | .406 |
| Southern Utah | 6 | 10 | .375 | 13 | 15 | .464 |
| Centenary | 1 | 15 | .062 | 3 | 24 | .111 |

**Conf. Tourney Final:** Oakland 61, Oral Roberts 60.
***NCAA Tourney (1-1):** Oakland (1-1).
**†NIT (0-1):** Oral Roberts (0-1).

## Mid-Eastern Athletic Conference

| Team | Conference | | | Overall | | |
|------|---|---|---|---|---|---|
| | W | L | Pct | W | L | Pct |
| *Delaware St. | 14 | 4 | .779 | 19 | 14 | .576 |
| Hampton | 13 | 5 | .722 | 17 | 13 | .567 |
| Coppin St. | 13 | 5 | .722 | 14 | 15 | .483 |
| S.C. State | 11 | 7 | .611 | 19 | 12 | .613 |
| Norfolk St. | 11 | 7 | .611 | 13 | 14 | .481 |
| Morgan St. | 11 | 7 | .611 | 14 | 16 | .467 |
| Florida A&M | 10 | 8 | .556 | 14 | 15 | .483 |
| Bethune-Cookman | 8 | 10 | .444 | 13 | 17 | .433 |
| N. Carolina A&T | 5 | 13 | .278 | 6 | 24 | .200 |
| Howard | 2 | 15 | .118 | 5 | 23 | .179 |
| MD-Eastern Shore | 1 | 17 | .055 | 2 | 26 | .071 |

**Conf. Tourney Final:** Delaware St. 55, Hampton 53.
***NCAA Tourney (0-1):** Delaware St. (0-1).

## Missouri Valley Conference

| Team | Conference | | | Overall | | |
|------|---|---|---|---|---|---|
| | W | L | Pct | W | L | Pct |
| *Southern Illinois | 15 | 3 | .833 | 27 | 8 | .771 |
| †Wichita St. | 12 | 6 | .667 | 22 | 10 | .688 |
| *Creighton | 11 | 7 | .611 | 23 | 11 | .676 |
| †Northern Iowa | 11 | 7 | .611 | 21 | 11 | .656 |
| †SW Missouri St. | 10 | 8 | .556 | 19 | 13 | .594 |
| Illinois St. | 8 | 10 | .444 | 17 | 13 | .567 |
| Drake | 7 | 11 | .389 | 13 | 16 | .448 |
| Bradley | 6 | 12 | .333 | 13 | 15 | .464 |
| Evansville | 5 | 13 | .278 | 11 | 17 | .393 |
| Indiana St. | 5 | 13 | .278 | 11 | 20 | .355 |

**Conf. Tourney Final:** Creighton 75, SW Mo. St. 57.
***NCAA Tourney (1-3):** Creighton (0-1), So. Illinois (1-1), Northern Iowa (0-1).
**†NIT (3-2):** Wichita St. (2-1), SW Mo. St, (1-1).

## Mountain West Conference

| Team | Conference | | | Overall | | |
|------|---|---|---|---|---|---|
| | W | L | Pct | W | L | Pct |
| *Utah | 13 | 1 | .929 | 29 | 6 | .829 |
| *New Mexico | 10 | 4 | .714 | 26 | 7 | .788 |
| Air Force | 9 | 5 | .643 | 18 | 12 | .600 |
| †UNLV | 7 | 7 | .500 | 17 | 14 | .548 |
| Wyoming | 7 | 7 | .500 | 15 | 13 | .536 |
| San Diego St. | 4 | 10 | .286 | 11 | 18 | .379 |
| Colorado St. | 3 | 11 | .214 | 11 | 17 | .393 |
| BYU | 3 | 11 | .214 | 9 | 21 | .300 |

**Conf. Tourney Final:** New Mexico 60, Utah 56.
***NCAA Tourney (2-2):** Utah (2-1), New Mexico (0-1).
**†NIT (1-1):** UNLV (1-1).

## Northeast Conference

| Team | Conference | | | Overall | | |
|------|---|---|---|---|---|---|
| | W | L | Pct | W | L | Pct |
| Monmouth | 14 | 4 | .778 | 16 | 13 | .552 |
| *Fairleigh Dickinson | 13 | 5 | .722 | 20 | 13 | .606 |
| Robert Morris | 11 | 7 | .611 | 14 | 15 | .483 |
| St. Francis-PA | 10 | 8 | .556 | 15 | 13 | .536 |
| LIU Brooklyn | 10 | 8 | .556 | 14 | 15 | .483 |
| Wagner | 10 | 8 | .556 | 13 | 17 | .433 |
| St. Francis-NY | 9 | 9 | .500 | 13 | 15 | .464 |
| Central Connecticut St. | 8 | 10 | .444 | 12 | 16 | .429 |
| Quinnipiac | 6 | 12 | .333 | 10 | 17 | .370 |
| Mt. St. Mary's | 5 | 13 | .278 | 7 | 20 | .259 |
| Sacred Heart | 3 | 15 | .167 | 4 | 23 | .148 |

**Conf. Tourney Final:** Fairleigh Dickinson 58, Wagner 52.
***NCAA Tourney (0-1):** Fairleigh Dickinson (0-1).

## Ohio Valley Conference

| Team | Conference | | | Overall | | |
|------|---|---|---|---|---|---|
| | W | L | Pct | W | L | Pct |
| Tennessee Tech | 12 | 4 | .750 | 18 | 11 | .621 |
| *Eastern Kentucky | 11 | 5 | .688 | 22 | 9 | .710 |
| Murray St | 11 | 5 | .688 | 17 | 11 | .607 |
| Samford | 10 | 6 | .625 | 15 | 13 | .536 |
| SE Missouri St | 9 | 7 | .563 | 15 | 14 | .517 |
| Tennessee St | 9 | 7 | .563 | 14 | 17 | .452 |
| Austin Peay | 9 | 7 | .563 | 13 | 19 | .406 |
| Eastern Illinois | 7 | 9 | .438 | 12–16 | | .429 |
| Morehead St | 5 | 11 | .313 | 11 | 16 | .407 |
| Tennessee-Martin | 3 | 13 | .188 | 6 | 21 | .222 |
| Jacksonville St. | 2 | 14 | .125 | 7 | 22 | .241 |

**Conf. Tourney Final:** Eastern Kentucky 52, Austin Peay 46.
***NCAA Tourney (0-1):** Eastern Kentucky (0-1).

## Pacific-10 Conference

| Team | Conference | | | Overall | | |
|------|---|---|---|---|---|---|
| | W | L | Pct | W | L | Pct |
| *Arizona | 15 | 3 | .833 | 30 | 7 | .811 |
| *Washington | 14 | 4 | .777 | 29 | 6 | .829 |
| *UCLA | 11 | 7 | .611 | 18 | 11 | .621 |
| *Stanford | 11 | 7 | .611 | 18 | 13 | .581 |
| †Oregon St | 8 | 10 | .444 | 17 | 15 | .531 |
| †Arizona St | 7 | 11 | .389 | 18 | 14 | .563 |
| Washington St | 7 | 11 | .389 | 12 | 16 | .429 |
| Oregon | 6 | 12 | .333 | 14 | 13 | .519 |
| California | 6 | 12 | .333 | 13 | 16 | .448 |
| USC | 5 | 13 | .278 | 12 | 17 | .414 |

**Conf. Tourney Final:** Washington 81, Arizona 72.
***NCAA Tourney (5-4):** Arizona (3-1), Washington (2-1), UCLA (0-1), Stanford (0-1).
**†NIT (0-2):** Oregon St. (0-1), Arizona St. (0-1).

## Final NCAA Men's Division I Standings (Cont.)

### Patriot League

| | Conference | | | Overall | | |
|---|---|---|---|---|---|---|
| Team | W | L | Pct | W | L | Pct |
| †Holy Cross | 13 | 1 | .929 | 25 | 7 | .781 |
| *Bucknell | 10 | 4 | .714 | 23 | 10 | .697 |
| American | 8 | 6 | .571 | 16 | 12 | .571 |
| Lehigh | 7 | 7 | .500 | 14 | 15 | .483 |
| Colgate | 7 | 7 | .500 | 12 | 16 | .429 |
| Navy | 5 | 9 | .357 | 9 | 19 | .321 |
| Lafayette | 5 | 9 | .357 | 9 | 19 | .321 |
| Army | 1 | 13 | .071 | 3 | 24 | .111 |

**Conf. Tourney Final:** Bucknell 61, Holy Cross 57.
***NCAA Tourney (1-1):** Bucknell (1-1).
**†NIT (1-1):** Holy Cross (1-1).

### Southeastern Conference

| | Conference | | | Overall | | |
|---|---|---|---|---|---|---|
| Eastern Div. | W | L | Pct | W | L | Pct |
| *Kentucky | 14 | 2 | .875 | 28 | 6 | .824 |
| *Florida | 12 | 4 | .750 | 24 | 8 | .750 |
| †Vanderbilt | 8 | 8 | .500 | 20 | 14 | .588 |
| †South Carolina | 7 | 9 | .438 | 20 | 13 | .606 |
| Tennessee | 6 | 10 | .375 | 14 | 17 | .452 |
| Georgia | 2 | 14 | .125 | 8 | 20 | .286 |

| | Conference | | | Overall | | |
|---|---|---|---|---|---|---|
| Western Div. | W | L | Pct | W | L | Pct |
| *Alabama | 12 | 4 | .750 | 24 | 8 | .750 |
| *LSU | 12 | 4 | .750 | 20 | 10 | .667 |
| *Mississippi St | 9 | 7 | .563 | 23 | 11 | .676 |
| Arkansas | 6 | 10 | .375 | 18 | 12 | .600 |
| Mississippi | 4 | 12 | .250 | 14 | 17 | .452 |
| Auburn | 4 | 12 | .250 | 14 | 17 | .452 |

**Conf. Tourney Final:** Florida 70, Kentucky 53.
***NCAA Tourney (5-5):** Kentucky (3-1), Florida (1-1), Alabama (0-1), LSU (0-1), Mississippi St. (1-1).
**†NIT (7-1):** Vanderbilt (2-1), South Carolina (5-0).

### Southern Conference

| | Conference | | | Overall | | |
|---|---|---|---|---|---|---|
| North Div. | W | L | Pct | W | L | Pct |
| *Chattanooga | 10 | 6 | .625 | 20 | 11 | .645 |
| Appalachian St. | 9 | 7 | .563 | 18 | 12 | .600 |
| NC-Greensboro | 9 | 7 | .563 | 18 | 12 | .600 |
| Elon | 5 | 11 | .313 | 8 | 23 | .258 |
| East Tennessee St. | 4 | 12 | .250 | 10 | 19 | .345 |
| W. Carolina | 3 | 13 | .188 | 8 | 22 | .267 |

| | Conference | | | Overall | | |
|---|---|---|---|---|---|---|
| South Div. | W | L | Pct | W | L | Pct |
| †Davidson | 16 | 0 | 1.000 | 23 | 9 | .719 |
| College of Charleston | 10 | 6 | .625 | 18 | 10 | .643 |
| Georgia Southern | 10 | 6 | .625 | 18 | 13 | .581 |
| Furman | 9 | 7 | .563 | 16 | 13 | .552 |
| Wofford | 7 | 9 | .438 | 14 | 14 | .500 |
| The Citadel | 4 | 12 | .250 | 12 | 16 | .429 |

**Conf. Tourney Final:** Chattanooga 66, NC-Greensboro 62
***NCAA Tourney (0-1):** Chattanooga (0-1).
**†NIT (2-1):** Davidson (2-1).

---

**Best in Show**

Conferences with the most wins in the 2005 NCAA tournament. Number of tourney teams in parenthesis.

| Conference | W-L | Pct. |
|---|---|---|
| ACC (5) | 12-4 | .750 |
| Big Ten (5) | 12-5 | .706 |
| Big East (6) | 7-6 | .538 |
| Conference USA (4) | 6-4 | .600 |
| Big 12 (6) | 6-6 | .500 |

---

### Southland Conference

| | Conference | | | Overall | | |
|---|---|---|---|---|---|---|
| Team | W | L | Pct | W | L | Pct |
| *SE Louisiana | 13 | 3 | .813 | 24 | 9 | .727 |
| Northwestern St. | 13 | 3 | .813 | 21 | 12 | .636 |
| Sam Houston St. | 11 | 5 | .688 | 18 | 12 | .600 |
| Texas-San Antonio | 10 | 6 | .625 | 15 | 13 | .536 |
| Lamar | 9 | 7 | .563 | 18 | 11 | .621 |
| Texas St. | 8 | 8 | .500 | 14 | 14 | .500 |
| McNeese St. | 8 | 8 | .500 | 13 | 15 | .464 |
| Texas-Arlington | 7 | 9 | .438 | 13 | 15 | .464 |
| Stephen F. Austin | 6 | 10 | .375 | 12 | 15 | .444 |
| Louisiana-Monroe | 2 | 14 | .125 | 8 | 19 | .296 |
| Nicholls St. | 1 | 15 | .063 | 6 | 21 | .222 |

**Conf. Tourney Final:** SE Louisiana 49, Northwestern St. 42.
***NCAA Tourney (0-1):** SE Louisiana (0-1).

### Southwestern Athletic Conference

| | Conference | | | Overall | | |
|---|---|---|---|---|---|---|
| Team | W | L | Pct | W | L | Pct |
| *Alabama A&M | 12 | 6 | .667 | 18 | 14 | .563 |
| Grambling St. | 11 | 7 | .611 | 14 | 12 | .538 |
| Alabama St. | 11 | 7 | .611 | 15 | 15 | .500 |
| Miss. Valley St | 11 | 7 | .611 | 13 | 15 | .464 |
| Southern | 10 | 8 | .556 | 14 | 15 | .483 |
| Jackson St. | 10 | 8 | .556 | 15 | 17 | .469 |
| Texas Southern | 9 | 9 | .500 | 11 | 15 | .423 |
| Alcorn St. | 6 | 12 | .333 | 7 | 22 | .247 |
| Ark-Pine Bluff | 5 | 13 | .278 | 7 | 21 | .250 |
| Prairie View A&M | 5 | 13 | .278 | 5 | 23 | .179 |

**Conf. Tourney Final:** Alabama A&M 72, Alabama St. 53.
***NCAA Tourney (0-1):** Alabama A&M (0-1).

### Sun Belt Conference

| | Conference | | | Overall | | |
|---|---|---|---|---|---|---|
| East Div. | W | L | Pct | W | L | Pct |
| Arkansas-Little Rock | 10 | 4 | .714 | 18 | 10 | .643 |
| †Western Kentucky | 9 | 5 | .643 | 21 | 8 | .724 |
| Middle Tennessee | 7 | 7 | .500 | 19 | 12 | .613 |
| Arkansas St | 7 | 7 | .500 | 16 | 13 | .552 |
| Florida International | 4 | 10 | .286 | 13 | 17 | .433 |

| | Conference | | | Overall | | |
|---|---|---|---|---|---|---|
| West Div. | W | L | Pct | W | L | Pct |
| †Denver | 12 | 3 | .800 | 20 | 10 | .667 |
| *Louisiana-Lafayette | 11 | 4 | .733 | 20 | 11 | .645 |
| New Orleans | 7 | 8 | .467 | 13 | 17 | .433 |
| North Texas | 6 | 9 | .400 | 14 | 14 | .500 |
| South Alabama | 6 | 9 | .400 | 10 | 18 | .357 |
| New Mexico St. | 1 | 14 | .067 | 6 | 21 | .200 |

**Conf. Tourney Final:** Louisiana-Lafayette 88, Denver 69.
***NCAA Tourney (0-1):** Louisiana-Lafayette (0-1).
**†NIT (1-2):** Western Kentucky (1-1), Denver (0-1).

### West Coast Conference

| | Conference | | | Overall | | |
|---|---|---|---|---|---|---|
| Team | W | L | Pct | W | L | Pct |
| *Gonzaga | 12 | 2 | .857 | 26 | 5 | .839 |
| *St. Mary's-CA | 11 | 3 | .786 | 25 | 9 | .735 |
| San Diego | 7 | 7 | .500 | 16 | 13 | .552 |
| Santa Clara | 7 | 7 | .500 | 15 | 16 | .484 |
| Pepperdine | 6 | 8 | .429 | 17 | 14 | .548 |
| †San Francisco | 6 | 8 | .429 | 17 | 14 | .548 |
| Portland | 4 | 10 | .286 | 15 | 15 | .500 |
| Loyola Marymount | 3 | 11 | .214 | 11 | 17 | .393 |

**Conf. Tourney Final:** Gonzaga 80, St. Mary's 67.
***NCAA Tourney (1-2):** Gonzaga (1-1), St. Mary's (0-1).
**†NIT (1-1):** San Francisco (1-1).

## Western Athletic Conference

| Team | Conference W | L | Pct | Overall W | L | Pct |
|------|---|---|-----|---|---|-----|
| *Nevada | 16 | 2 | .889 | 25 | 7 | .781 |
| *UTEP | 14 | 4 | .778 | 27 | 8 | .771 |
| †Rice | 12 | 6 | .667 | 19 | 12 | .613 |
| Fresno St. | 9 | 9 | .500 | 16 | 14 | .533 |
| Louisiana Tech | 9 | 9 | .500 | 14 | 15 | .483 |
| SMU | 9 | 9 | .500 | 14 | 14 | .500 |
| Hawaii | 7 | 11 | .389 | 16 | 13 | .552 |
| Boise St. | 6 | 12 | .333 | 16 | 18 | .471 |
| Tulsa | 5 | 13 | .277 | 9 | 20 | .310 |
| San Jose St | 3 | 15 | .167 | 6 | 23 | .207 |

**Conf. Tourney Final:** UTEP 91, Boise St. 76.
*NCAA Tourney (1-2): Nevada (1-1), UTEP (0-1).
†NIT (0-1): Rice (0-1).

### NCAA Major Conference Merry-Go-Round

The division 1 college basketball landscape will look a lot different for the 2005-06 season. The **ACC** officially welcomes Boston College to the fold, a year after Miami and Virginia Tech joined. The **Big East** will add former **Conference USA** members Cincinnati, DePaul, Louisville, Marquette and South Florida to fill the void. In fact with the loss of TCU to the **Mountain West** and Charlotte and Saint Louis to the **A-10**, more than half of the C-USA are jumping ship. To refill their bare cupboards C-USA raids the **WAC** pantry and two other conferences to add Marshall, Rice, SMU, Tulsa, UTEP and Central Florida. As a result, the WAC welcomes New Mexico St. (Sun Belt), Idaho (Big West) and Utah St. (Big West).

## Annual Awards

### Player of the Year

Andrew Bogut, Utah, C/F . . . . . . .AP, Wooden, Naismith, USBWA, NABC

J.J. Redick, Duke, G . . . . . . . . . . . . . . . . . . . . . . . .Rupp

### Wooden Award Voting

Presented since 1977 by the Los Angeles Athletic Club and named after the former Purdue All-America and UCLA coach John Wooden. Voting done by 1,047-member panel of national media; candidates must have a cumulative college grade point average of 2.0 (out of 4.0) and be making progress toward graduation.

| | | Cl | Pos | Pts |
|---|---|---|---|---|
| 1 | Andrew Bogut, Utah | So. | C/F | 4314 |
| 2 | J.J. Redick, Duke | Jr. | G | 3552 |
| 3 | Dee Brown, Illinois | Jr. | G | 3003 |
| 4 | Sean May, North Carolina | Jr. | F | 2806 |
| 5 | Wayne Simien, Kansas | Sr. | F | 2707 |
| 6 | Chris Paul, Wake Forest | So. | G | 2659 |
| 7 | Salim Stoudamire, Arizona | Sr. | G | 2395 |
| 8 | Hakim Warrick, Syracuse | Sr. | F | 2257 |
| 9 | Francisco Garcia, Louisville | Jr. | F | 1178 |
| 10 | Deron Williams, Illinois | Jr. | G | 1016 |

### Defensive Player of the Year

Formerly the Henry Iba Award, for defensive skills, sportsmanship and dedication; first presented by the Rotary Club of River Oaks in Houston in 1987 and named after the late Oklahoma State and U.S. Olympic team coach. Voting done by the National Association of Basketball Coaches.

Shelden Williams, Duke, F

### Div. II and III Awards

Awarded by the National Association of Basketball Coaches.

**Players of the Year**
Div. II . . . . . . . . . . . . .Mark Worthington, Metro. St.
Div. III . . . . . . . . . . . Jason Kalsow, WI-Stevens Point
**Coaches of the Year**
Div. II . . . . . . . . . . . . .Dave Robbins, Virginia Union
Div. III . . . . . . . . . . . . Jeff Gamber, York College (PA)

### Coach of the Year

Bruce Weber, Illinois . . . . . .AP, NABC, Naismith, USBWA

### Consensus All-America Teams

The NCAA Division I players cited most frequently by the following All-America selectors: Associated Press, U.S. Basketball Writers, National Association of Basketball Coaches and Wooden Award Committee. (*) indicates unanimous first team selection. There were no holdovers from the 2003-04 first team.

#### First Team

| | Class | Hgt | Pos |
|---|---|---|---|
| Andrew Bogut*, Utah | So. | 7-0 | C/F |
| Wayne Simien*, Kansas | Sr. | 6-9 | F |
| J.J. Redick*, Duke | Jr. | 6-4 | G |
| Chris Paul, Wake Forest | So. | 6-0 | G |
| Dee Brown, Illinois | Jr. | 6-0 | G |

#### Second Team

| | Class | Hgt | Pos |
|---|---|---|---|
| Hakim Warrick, Syracuse | Sr. | 6-8 | F |
| Ike Diogu, Arizona St. | Jr. | 6-8 | F |
| Luther Head, Illinois | Sr. | 6-3 | G |
| Salim Stoudamire, Arizona | Sr. | 6-1 | G |
| Sean May, North Carolina | Jr. | 6-9 | F |

#### Third Team

| | Class | Hgt | Pos |
|---|---|---|---|
| Francisco Garcia, Louisville | Jr. | 6-7 | F |
| Deron Williams, Illinois | Jr. | 6-3 | G |
| Joey Graham, Oklahoma St. | Sr. | 6-7 | F |
| Nate Robinson, Washington | Jr. | 5-9 | G |
| Rashad McCants, North Carolina | Jr. | 6-4 | F/G |

**Also mentioned:** Craig Smith (Boston College), Shelden Williams (Duke) and Raymond Felton (North Carolina).

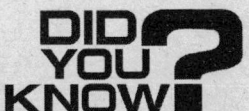

*In 2005, Illinois became just the sixth team since 1979 to be undefeated on March 1, joining last year's Stanford and St. Joseph's teams and the 1991 UNLV, 1981 Oregon State, and 1979 Indiana State squads. Did you know, none of those six teams won the national championship?*

## NCAA Men's Division I Leaders

Includes games through NCAA and NIT tourneys.

### INDIVIDUAL

#### Scoring

| | Cl | Gm | FG% | 3FG/Att | FT% | Reb | Ast | Stl | Blk | Pts | Avg | Hi |
|---|---|---|---|---|---|---|---|---|---|---|---|---|
| Keydren Clark, St. Peter's | Jr. | 28 | .406 | 109/297 | .835 | 116 | 115 | 93 | 6 | 721 | 25.8 | 43 |
| Taylor Coppenrath, Vermont | Sr. | 31 | .517 | 9/33 | .766 | 277 | 60 | 38 | 21 | 777 | 25.1 | 43 |
| Juan Mendez, Niagara | Sr. | 30 | .471 | 39/128 | .815 | 319 | 39 | 37 | 63 | 705 | 23.5 | 39 |
| Rob Monroe, Quinnipiac | Sr. | 26 | .409 | 72/206 | .859 | 83 | 170 | 35 | 0 | 589 | 22.7 | 41 |
| Bo McCalebb, New Orleans | So. | 30 | .480 | 25/96 | .567 | 129 | 110 | 55 | 5 | 679 | 22.6 | 35 |
| Ike Diogu, Arizona St. | Jr. | 32 | .575 | 18/45 | .797 | 312 | 43 | 18 | 75 | 724 | 22.6 | 39 |
| Tim Smith, E. Tenn. St. | Sr. | 29 | .423 | 59/155 | .756 | 123 | 123 | 63 | 0 | 645 | 22.2 | 41 |
| Jose Juan Barea, Northeastern | Jr. | 30 | .419 | 68/212 | .784 | 129 | 218 | 53 | 0 | 665 | 22.2 | 41 |
| J.J. Redick, Duke | Jr. | 33 | .408 | 121/300 | .938 | 108 | 86 | 35 | 2 | 721 | 21.8 | 38 |
| Ryan Gomes, Providence | Sr. | 31 | .496 | 52/137 | .770 | 255 | 100 | 47 | 5 | 670 | 21.6 | 37 |
| Darshan Luckey, St. Francis-PA | Sr. | 28 | .473 | 39/98 | .827 | 147 | 36 | 39 | 9 | 602 | 21.5 | 39 |
| Hakim Warrick, Syracuse | Sr. | 34 | .548 | 9/31 | .681 | 294 | 50 | 33 | 27 | 726 | 21.4 | 36 |
| Daryll Hill, St. John's | So. | 27 | .419 | 51/143 | .764 | 88 | 95 | 48 | 10 | 560 | 20.7 | 33 |
| Nick Fazekas, Nevada | So. | 32 | .502 | 33/101 | .789 | 301 | 30 | 20 | 51 | 662 | 20.7 | 33 |
| Michael Harris, Rice | Sr. | 31 | .608 | 7/29 | .800 | 363 | 39 | 40 | 37 | 639 | 20.6 | 31 |
| Seamus Boxley, Portland St. | Sr. | 28 | .592 | 13/36 | .680 | 228 | 69 | 21 | 39 | 576 | 20.6 | 32 |
| Omar Thomas, UTEP | Sr. | 35 | .512 | 13/32 | .845 | 233 | 51 | 57 | 12 | 716 | 20.5 | 33 |
| Paul Millsap, Louisiana Tech | So. | 29 | .575 | 0/1 | .601 | 360 | 29 | 33 | 55 | 593 | 20.4 | 31 |
| Andrew Bogut, Utah | So. | 35 | .620 | 9/25 | .692 | 427 | 82 | 34 | 65 | 715 | 20.4 | 33 |
| Wayne Simien, Kansas | Sr. | 26 | .552 | 4/14 | .816 | 287 | 36 | 15 | 16 | 528 | 20.3 | 32 |

#### Rebounding

| | Cl | Gm | No | Avg |
|---|---|---|---|---|
| Paul Millsap, Louisiana Tech | So. | 29 | 360 | 12.4 |
| Andrew Bogut, Utah | So. | 35 | 427 | 12.2 |
| Lance Allred, Weber St. | Sr. | 29 | 348 | 12.0 |
| Michael Harris, Rice | Sr. | 31 | 363 | 11.7 |
| Dwayne Jones, St. Joseph's | Jr. | 36 | 418 | 11.6 |
| Shelden Williams, Duke | Jr. | 33 | 369 | 11.2 |
| Wayne Simien, Kansas | Sr. | 26 | 287 | 11.0 |
| Lawrence Roberts, Mississippi St. | Sr. | 32 | 351 | 11.0 |
| Sean May, North Carolina | Jr. | 37 | 397 | 10.7 |
| Juan Mendez, Niagara | Sr. | 30 | 319 | 10.6 |
| Harding Nana, Delaware | Jr. | 31 | 322 | 10.4 |
| Corey Rouse, E. Carolina | Jr. | 28 | 285 | 10.2 |
| Micheal Sneed, Texas Southern | Sr. | 25 | 252 | 10.1 |
| Ivan Almonte, Florida International | Jr. | 30 | 297 | 9.9 |
| Aaron Johnson, Penn St. | Jr. | 30 | 297 | 9.9 |
| Ike Diogu, Arizona St. | Jr. | 32 | 312 | 9.8 |
| Carlton Aaron, UMKC | Sr. | 28 | 271 | 9.7 |
| Terrence Leather, South Florida | Sr. | 29 | 277 | 9.6 |
| Danny Horace, Miami-OH | Sr. | 30 | 286 | 9.5 |
| Ronny Turiaf, Gonzaga | Sr. | 31 | 295 | 9.5 |

#### Assists

| | Cl | Gm | No | Avg |
|---|---|---|---|---|
| Damitrius Coleman, Mercer | Jr. | 28 | 224 | 8.0 |
| Will Funn, Portland St. | Sr. | 28 | 224 | 8.0 |
| Marcus Williams, Connecticut | So. | 31 | 243 | 7.8 |
| Walker Russell, Jacksonville St. | Jr. | 29 | 211 | 7.3 |
| Jose Juan Barea, Northeastern | Jr. | 30 | 218 | 7.3 |
| Aaron Miles, Kansas | Sr. | 30 | 216 | 7.2 |
| Filberto Rivera, UTEP | Sr. | 32 | 229 | 7.2 |
| Javier Mendiburu, WI-Green Bay | Sr. | 26 | 184 | 7.1 |
| Garrett Farha, St. Francis-PA | Jr. | 28 | 194 | 6.9 |
| Raymond Felton, North Carolina | Jr. | 36 | 249 | 6.9 |
| Deron Williams, Illinois | Jr. | 39 | 264 | 6.8 |
| Chris Thomas, Notre Dame | Sr. | 29 | 195 | 6.7 |
| Chris Paul, Wake Forest | So. | 32 | 212 | 6.6 |
| Rob Monroe, Quinnipiac | Sr. | 26 | 170 | 6.5 |
| Mike Slattery, Delaware | Sr. | 26 | 168 | 6.5 |
| Will Conroy, Washington | Sr. | 34 | 219 | 6.4 |
| Rodney Billups, Denver | Sr. | 31 | 199 | 6.4 |
| Alvin Cruz, Niagara | Sr. | 30 | 191 | 6.4 |
| Jared Jordan, Marist | So. | 27 | 169 | 6.3 |
| Matt Witt, Eastern Ky. | Jr. | 31 | 194 | 6.3 |

#### Field Goal Percentage

Minimum 5 Field Goals made per game.

| | Cl | Gm | FG | FGA | Pct |
|---|---|---|---|---|---|
| Bruce Brown, Hampton | Sr. | 30 | 178 | 269 | 66.2 |
| Nate Harris, Utah St. | Jr. | 32 | 172 | 264 | 65.2 |
| Eric Williams, Wake Forest | Jr. | 33 | 201 | 319 | 63.0 |
| Chad McKnight, Morehead St. | Sr. | 27 | 155 | 246 | 63.0 |
| Aaron Andrews, Morgan St. | Sr. | 28 | 140 | 224 | 62.5 |
| Michael Haney, Eastern Ky. | Sr. | 31 | 174 | 279 | 62.4 |
| Kyle Hines, NC-Greensboro | Fr. | 30 | 175 | 282 | 62.1 |
| Andrew Bogut, Utah | So. | 35 | 281 | 453 | 62.0 |
| Carl Landry, Purdue | Jr. | 25 | 160 | 259 | 61.8 |
| Quincy Davis, Tulane | Sr. | 28 | 153 | 250 | 61.2 |
| Michael Harris, Rice | Sr. | 31 | 240 | 395 | 60.8 |
| Matt Nelson, Colorado St. | Sr. | 27 | 153 | 253 | 60.5 |
| Spencer Nelson, Utah St. | Sr. | 32 | 174 | 290 | 60.0 |
| Jason Osborne, St. Francis-PA | Sr. | 28 | 149 | 249 | 59.8 |
| Steven Thomas, TX-Arlington | Jr. | 28 | 153 | 258 | 59.3 |

#### Free Throw Percentage

Minimum 2.5 Free Throws made per game.

| | Cl | Gm | FT | FTA | Pct |
|---|---|---|---|---|---|
| Blake Ahearn, SW Mo. St. | So. | 32 | 90 | 95 | 94.7 |
| J.J. Redick, Duke | Jr. | 33 | 196 | 209 | 93.8 |
| Vince Greene, Illinois St. | Sr. | 28 | 81 | 88 | 92.0 |
| Salim Stoudamire, Arizona | Sr. | 36 | 122 | 134 | 91.0 |
| Jamaal Hilliard, Lafayette | So. | 28 | 91 | 100 | 91.0 |
| Chris McCray, Maryland | Jr. | 31 | 102 | 113 | 90.3 |
| Derek Raivio, Gonzaga | So. | 31 | 102 | 113 | 90.3 |
| Anthony Roberson, Florida | Jr. | 32 | 81 | 90 | 90.0 |
| David Doubley, Pacific | Sr. | 31 | 94 | 105 | 89.5 |
| Jerry Johnson, Rider | Sr. | 30 | 107 | 120 | 89.2 |
| Chris Thomas, Notre Dame | Sr. | 29 | 98 | 110 | 89.1 |
| Kevin Bettencourt, Bucknell | Jr. | 33 | 95 | 107 | 88.8 |
| Joey Graham, Oklahoma St. | Sr. | 33 | 157 | 177 | 88.7 |
| Terrell Stovall, Weber St. | Jr. | 29 | 86 | 97 | 88.7 |
| Matt Rohde, WI-Green Bay | Sr. | 28 | 72 | 82 | 87.8 |

St. Peter's
**Keydren Clark**
Scoring

Louisiana Tech
**Paul Millsap**
Rebounds

Portland St.
**Will Funn**
Assists

Fairfield
**Deng Gai**
Blocks

## 3-Pt Field Goal Percentage
Minimum 2.5 Three-Point FGs made per game.

|  | Cl | Gm | FG | FGA | Pct |
|---|---|---|---|---|---|
| Salim Stoudamire, Arizona | Sr. | 36 | 120 | 238 | 50.4 |
| Will Whittington, Marist | So. | 28 | 97 | 197 | 49.2 |
| Dennis Trammell, Ball St. | Sr. | 23 | 59 | 122 | 48.4 |
| Chris Lofton, Tennessee | Fr. | 31 | 93 | 200 | 46.5 |
| Drake Diener, DePaul | Sr. | 31 | 85 | 184 | 46.2 |
| Steve Novak, Marquette | Jr. | 31 | 89 | 193 | 46.1 |
| John Reimold, Bowling Green | Sr. | 29 | 79 | 173 | 45.7 |
| Troy DeVries, New Mexico | Sr. | 33 | 93 | 206 | 45.1 |
| Taquan Dean, Louisville | Jr. | 37 | 122 | 273 | 44.7 |
| J. Robert Merritt, Samford | Jr. | 28 | 85 | 193 | 44.0 |
| Ross Schraeder, UC-Irvine | Jr. | 29 | 79 | 180 | 43.9 |

## 3-Pt Field Goals Per Game

|  | Cl | Gm | No | Avg |
|---|---|---|---|---|
| Brendan Plavich, Charlotte | Sr. | 29 | 114 | 3.9 |
| Keydren Clark, St. Peter's | Jr. | 28 | 109 | 3.9 |
| Pat Carroll, St. Joseph's | Sr. | 35 | 135 | 3.9 |
| T.J. Sorrentine, Vermont | Sr. | 31 | 116 | 3.7 |
| J.J. Redick, Duke | Jr. | 33 | 121 | 3.7 |
| Will Whittington, Marist | So. | 28 | 97 | 3.5 |
| Jerry Johnson, Rider | Sr. | 30 | 102 | 3.4 |
| Ed McCants, WI-Milwaukee | Sr. | 32 | 107 | 3.3 |
| Salim Stoudamire, Arizona | Sr. | 36 | 120 | 3.3 |
| Taquan Dean, Louisville | Jr. | 37 | 122 | 3.3 |
| Erik Benzel, Denver | Sr. | 31 | 101 | 3.3 |

## Blocked Shots

|  | Cl | Gm | No | Avg |
|---|---|---|---|---|
| Deng Gai, Fairfield | Sr. | 30 | 165 | 5.5 |
| Shawn James, Northeastern | Fr. | 25 | 136 | 5.4 |
| Shelden Williams, Duke | Jr. | 33 | 122 | 3.7 |
| Kyle Hines, NC-Greensboro | Fr. | 30 | 106 | 3.5 |
| Dwayne Jones, St. Joseph's | Jr. | 36 | 109 | 3.0 |
| Yemi Nicholson, Denver | Jr. | 31 | 92 | 3.0 |
| Chaz Crawford, Drexel | So. | 29 | 86 | 3.0 |
| Anthony King, Miami-FL | So. | 29 | 86 | 3.0 |
| Ronald Alexander, Miss. Valley St. | Jr. | 28 | 82 | 3.0 |
| Josh Boone, Connecticut | So. | 31 | 90 | 2.9 |
| Justin Williams, Wyoming | Jr. | 28 | 81 | 2.9 |
| Elgrace Wilborn, Western Ky. | Jr. | 29 | 83 | 2.9 |

## Steals

|  | Cl | Gm | No | Avg |
|---|---|---|---|---|
| Obie Trotter, Alabama A&M | Jr. | 32 | 125 | 3.9 |
| Chakowby Hicks, Norfolk St. | Sr. | 27 | 91 | 3.4 |
| Keydren Clark, St. Peter's | Jr. | 28 | 93 | 3.3 |
| Hosea Butler, Miss. Valley St. | Jr. | 28 | 91 | 3.3 |
| Eddie Basden, Charlotte | Sr. | 29 | 93 | 3.2 |
| Ibrahim Jaaber, Pennsylvania | So. | 29 | 85 | 2.9 |
| DaShawn Freeman, Sacramento St. | Jr. | 28 | 82 | 2.9 |
| Kevin Hamilton, Holy Cross | Jr. | 32 | 92 | 2.9 |
| Damitrius Coleman, Mercer | Jr. | 28 | 80 | 2.9 |
| Mardy Collins, Temple | Jr. | 30 | 85 | 2.8 |
| Dainmon Gonner, SE Mo. St. | Sr. | 27 | 74 | 2.7 |

## Single Game Highs

### Points

| No | | Opponent | Date |
|---|---|---|---|
| 45 | Joe Knight, Lehigh | Colgate | Mar. 4 |
| 43 | Elton Nesbitt, Ga. Southern | Chattanooga | Jan. 17 |
| 43 | Keydren Clark, St. Peter's | Charleston | Dec. 30 |
| 41 | Jose Juan Barea, Northeastern | Stony Brook | Mar. 5 |
| 41 | Jay Straight, Wyoming | Colorado St. | Feb. 26 |
| 41 | Rob Monroe, Quinnipiac | Longwood | Jan. 2 |

### Rebounds

| No | | Opponent | Date |
|---|---|---|---|
| 25 | Paul Millsap, La. Tech | Boise St. | Feb. 12 |
| 24 | Sean May, North Carolina | Duke | Mar. 6 |
| 24 | Michael Harris, Rice | Hawaii | Feb. 27 |
| 24 | Aaron Johnson, Penn St. | W. Carolina | Nov. 15 |

### Assists

| No | | Opponent | Date |
|---|---|---|---|
| 18 | Filberto Rivera, UTEP | La. Tech | Feb. 25 |
| 18 | Ronald Steele, Alabama | E. Tenn. St. | Dec. 1 |

### Blocks

| No | | Opponent | Date |
|---|---|---|---|
| 13 | Deng Gai, Fairfield | Siena | Jan. 22 |
| 13 | Anthony King, Miami-FL | Fla. Atlantic | Nov. 29 |
| 11 | Shawn James, Northeastern | Albany | Feb. 27 |
| 11 | Mustafa Al-Sayyad, Fresno St. | Buffalo | Feb. 19 |
| 11 | Shawn James, Northeastern | Iona | Dec. 30 |

### Steals

| No | | Opponent | Date |
|---|---|---|---|
| 10 | Doron Perkin, Santa Clara | San Diego | Feb. 24 |
| 10 | Louis Ford, Howard | MD-Eastern Shore | Dec. 6 |
| 9 | Obie Trotter, Ala. A&M | Jackson St. | Mar. 5 |
| 9 | Bryan Hopkins, SMU | San Jose St. | Feb. 20 |
| 9 | Mardy Collins, Temple | South Carolina | Nov. 27 |

### 3-point FGs

| No | | Opponent | Date |
|---|---|---|---|
| 11 | Elton Nesbitt, Ga. Southern | Chattanooga | Jan. 17 |
| 10 | Joe Knight, Lehigh | Colgate | Mar. 4 |
| 10 | Elton Nesbitt, Ga. Southern | The Citadel | Feb. 14 |

## NCAA Men's Division I Leaders (Cont.)
### TEAM

### Scoring Offense

| | Gm | W-L | Pts | Avg |
|---|---|---|---|---|
| North Carolina | .37 | 33-4 | 3257 | 88.0 |
| Washington | .35 | 29-6 | 3026 | 86.5 |
| Wake Forest | .33 | 27-6 | 2801 | 84.9 |
| Niagara | .30 | 20-10 | 2537 | 84.6 |
| Maryland | .32 | 19-13 | 2620 | 81.9 |
| Ga. Southern | .31 | 18-13 | 2506 | 80.8 |
| Louisville | .38 | 33-5 | 3066 | 80.7 |
| Lamar | .29 | 18-11 | 2338 | 80.6 |
| Mercer | .28 | 16-12 | 2242 | 80.1 |
| Arizona | .37 | 30-7 | 2948 | 79.7 |
| Gonzaga | .31 | 26-5 | 2454 | 79.2 |
| St. Peter's | .28 | 15-13 | 2200 | 78.6 |

### Scoring Defense

| | Gm | W-L | Pts | Avg |
|---|---|---|---|---|
| Air Force | .30 | 18-12 | 1629 | 54.3 |
| Princeton | .28 | 15-13 | 1521 | 54.3 |
| Boston University | .29 | 20-9 | 1616 | 55.7 |
| Southeastern La. | .33 | 24-9 | 1842 | 55.8 |
| Holy Cross | .32 | 25-7 | 1817 | 56.8 |
| Washington St. | .28 | 12-16 | 1594 | 56.9 |
| Utah | .35 | 29-6 | 2005 | 57.3 |
| Utah St. | .32 | 24-8 | 1848 | 57.8 |
| St. Joseph's | .36 | 24-12 | 2110 | 58.6 |
| Bucknell | .33 | 23-10 | 1946 | 59.0 |
| Winthrop | .33 | 27-6 | 1961 | 59.4 |
| Wisconsin | .34 | 25-9 | 2047 | 60.2 |

### Scoring Margin

| | Off | Def | Mar |
|---|---|---|---|
| North Carolina | .88.0 | 70.3 | 17.8 |
| Louisville | .80.7 | 64.1 | 16.6 |
| Illinois | .77.0 | 61.1 | 15.9 |
| Utah St. | .72.3 | 57.8 | 14.6 |
| Oklahoma St. | .78.3 | 65.2 | 13.1 |
| Florida | .76.2 | 63.1 | 13.1 |
| Michigan St. | .78.5 | 65.4 | 13.1 |
| Duke | .78.2 | 65.2 | 13.0 |
| Washington | .86.5 | 74.2 | 12.3 |
| Oklahoma | .75.2 | 63.3 | 11.9 |
| Cincinnati | .75.9 | 64.3 | 11.2 |
| New Mexico | .75.5 | 64.3 | 11.2 |

### Won-Lost Percentage

| | W | L | Pct |
|---|---|---|---|
| Illinois | .37 | 2 | 94.9 |
| North Carolina | .33 | 4 | 89.2 |
| Pacific | .27 | 4 | 87.1 |
| Louisville | .33 | 5 | 86.8 |
| Gonzaga | .26 | 5 | 83.9 |
| Boston College | .25 | 5 | 83.3 |
| Utah | .29 | 6 | 82.9 |
| Washington | .29 | 6 | 82.9 |
| Kentucky | .28 | 6 | 82.4 |
| Old Dominion | .28 | 6 | 82.4 |
| Winthrop | .27 | 6 | 81.8 |
| Duke | .27 | 6 | 81.8 |

### Field Goal Percentage

| | FG | FGA | Pct |
|---|---|---|---|
| Utah St. | .851 | 1621 | 52.5 |
| Utah | .837 | 1628 | 51.4 |
| Samford | .616 | 1224 | 50.3 |
| Gonzaga | .856 | 1702 | 50.3 |
| North Carolina | 1128 | 2260 | 49.9 |
| Oklahoma St. | .911 | 1833 | 49.7 |
| Pacific | .794 | 1598 | 49.7 |
| Texas A&M-CC | .768 | 1553 | 49.5 |
| New Mexico | .855 | 1733 | 49.3 |
| Portland St. | .708 | 1440 | 49.2 |
| Wake Forest | .965 | 1966 | 49.1 |
| Bowling Green | .718 | 1471 | 48.8 |

### Field Goal Percentage Defense

| | FG | FGA | Pct |
|---|---|---|---|
| Boston University | .588 | 1584 | 37.1 |
| Cincinnati | .749 | 2008 | 37.3 |
| Connecticut | .761 | 2011 | 37.8 |
| Memphis | .827 | 2155 | 38.4 |
| Kansas | .663 | 1712 | 38.7 |
| Nevada | .727 | 1872 | 38.8 |
| Holy Cross | .604 | 1554 | 38.9 |
| Louisville | .823 | 2116 | 38.9 |
| Sam Houston St. | .676 | 1738 | 38.9 |
| Syracuse | .760 | 1950 | 39.0 |
| Duke | .783 | 2006 | 39.0 |
| Norfolk St. | .584 | 1496 | 39.0 |

### Rebound Margin

| | Off | Def | Mar |
|---|---|---|---|
| Connecticut | .45.5 | 34.3 | 11.3 |
| Chattanooga | .41.4 | 30.6 | 10.8 |
| Utah | .34.1 | 23.6 | 10.5 |
| Pittsburgh | .38.0 | 29.5 | 8.6 |
| Mississippi St. | .40.9 | 32.4 | 8.5 |
| Gonzaga | .38.4 | 30.4 | 8.0 |
| Nevada | .39.7 | 32.1 | 7.6 |
| North Carolina | .40.5 | 33.0 | 7.5 |
| Wake Forest | .39.8 | 32.8 | 7.1 |
| Niagara | .40.7 | 33.8 | 6.9 |
| Michigan St. | .36.3 | 29.5 | 6.8 |
| Utah St. | .34.2 | 27.6 | 6.6 |

### Free Throw Percentage

| | FT | FTA | Pct |
|---|---|---|---|
| UTEP | .606 | 765 | 79.2 |
| Oklahoma St. | .521 | 668 | 78.0 |
| Michigan St. | .543 | 699 | 77.7 |
| Arizona | .541 | 697 | 77.6 |
| Monmouth | .420 | 545 | 77.1 |
| Army | .296 | 385 | 76.9 |
| Duquesne | .360 | 471 | 76.4 |
| Morehead St. | .386 | 507 | 76.1 |
| Niagara | .601 | 791 | 76.0 |
| Texas Tech | .526 | 696 | 75.6 |
| Rider | .427 | 566 | 75.4 |
| San Diego | .469 | 625 | 75.0 |

## 3-point FG Percentage

| | 3PT | 3PTA | Pct |
|---|---|---|---|
| Oklahoma St. | .240 | 564 | 42.6 |
| Samford | .247 | 590 | 41.9 |
| Valparaiso | .207 | 498 | 41.6 |
| Creighton | .293 | 707 | 41.4 |
| Southern Utah | .218 | 536 | 40.7 |
| San Diego | .211 | 519 | 40.7 |
| North Carolina | .277 | 687 | 40.3 |
| Arizona | .253 | 630 | 40.2 |
| Wake Forest | .251 | 629 | 39.9 |
| Louisville | .361 | 906 | 39.6 |
| Texas A&M-CC | .166 | 419 | 39.6 |
| Alabama | .249 | 632 | 39.4 |

## 3-point FG Made Per Game

| | Gm | No | Avg |
|---|---|---|---|
| Troy | .30 | 338 | 11.3 |
| Belmont | .30 | 292 | 9.7 |
| Louisville | .38 | 361 | 9.5 |
| Vanderbilt | .34 | 322 | 9.5 |
| Furman | .29 | 267 | 9.2 |
| West Virginia | .35 | 319 | 9.1 |
| Niagara | .30 | 270 | 9.0 |
| Davidson | .32 | 286 | 8.9 |
| Air Force | .30 | 266 | 8.9 |
| Georgia St. | .29 | 257 | 8.9 |
| Samford | .28 | 247 | 8.8 |
| Illinois | .39 | 344 | 8.8 |

## Assists Per Game

| | Gm | No | Avg |
|---|---|---|---|
| North Carolina | .37 | 706 | 19.1 |
| Washington | .35 | 660 | 18.9 |
| Illinois | .39 | 727 | 18.6 |
| Texas A&M-CC | .28 | 514 | 18.4 |
| Sam Houson St. | .30 | 535 | 17.8 |
| Boston College | .30 | 527 | 17.6 |
| Oral Roberts | .33 | 574 | 17.4 |
| Utah St. | .32 | 549 | 17.2 |
| Connecticut | .31 | 531 | 17.1 |
| Michigan St. | .33 | 565 | 17.1 |
| Mercer | .28 | 477 | 17.0 |
| Hawaii | .29 | 492 | 17.0 |

## Blocks Per Game

| | Gm | No | Avg |
|---|---|---|---|
| Connecticut | .31 | 275 | 8.9 |
| Cincinnati | .33 | 225 | 6.8 |
| Duke | .33 | 220 | 6.7 |
| Northeastern | .31 | 202 | 6.5 |
| Fairfield | .30 | 192 | 6.4 |
| Maryland | .32 | 200 | 6.3 |
| Iona | .31 | 187 | 6.0 |
| Providence | .31 | 187 | 6.0 |
| NC-Greensboro | .30 | 178 | 5.9 |
| Tulsa | .29 | 165 | 5.7 |
| Jacksonville | .29 | 162 | 5.6 |
| Villanova | .32 | 178 | 5.6 |

## Underclassmen in NBA Draft

Forty-nine collegiate and high school players and 11 international players (not included below) forfeited their college eligibility and declared for the 2005 NBA Draft which took place at Madison Square Garden in New York City on June 28. Fifty American and International players (including Illinois' All-American Dee Brown), who initially declared themselves eligible for the 2005 NBA Draft withdrew their names before the June 21 deadline. First round selections in **bold** type.

| | Cl | Drafted by | Overall Pick |
|---|---|---|---|
| Alex Acker, Pepperdine | Jr. | Detroit | 60 |
| Deji Akindele, Chicago St. | So. | not drafted | - |
| Keleena Azubuike, Kentucky | Jr. | not drafted | - |
| Sean Banks, Memphis | So. | not drafted | - |
| Brandon Bass, LSU | So. | New Orleans | 33 |
| Jermaine Bell, Indian Hills CC | Fr. | not drafted | - |
| Andray Blatche, S. Kent Prep | HS | not drafted | - |
| **Andrew Bogut**, Utah | So. | Milwaukee | 1 |
| Curtis Brown Jr., Beach HS | HS | not drafted | - |
| **Andrew Bynum**, St. Joseph's | HS | LA Lakers | 10 |
| **Ike Diogu**, Arizona St. | Jr. | Golden St. | 9 |
| Monta Ellis, Lanier HS | HS | Golden St. | 40 |
| Olu Famutimi, Arkansas | Jr. | not drafted | - |
| **Raymond Felton**, N. Carolina | Jr. | Charlotte | 5 |
| Anderson Ferreira, Chipola C | So. | not drafted | - |
| **Francisco Garcia**, Louisville | Jr. | Sacramento | 23 |
| John Gilchrist, Maryland | Jr. | not drafted | - |
| **Gerald Green**, Gulf Shores | HS | Boston | 18 |
| **Jarrett Jack**, Georgia Tech | Jr. | Denver* | 22 |
| Amir Johnson, Westchester, CA | HS | Detroit | 56 |
| Dwayne Jones, St. Joseph's | Jr. | not drafted | - |
| **Linas Kleiza**, Missouri | So. | Portland* | 27 |
| Julius Lamptey, Garden City CC | Fr. | not drafted | - |
| Kyle Luckett, South Side, IN | HS | not drafted | - |
| Darshan Luckey, St. Francis-PA | Jr. | not drafted | - |
| **Sean May**, North Carolina | Jr. | Charlotte | 13 |
| **Rashard McCants**, N. Carolina | Jr. | Minnesota | 14 |
| C.J. Miles, Skyline, TX | HS | Utah | 34 |
| J.R. Morris, Seton Hall | Jr. | not drafted | - |
| Randolph Morris, Kentucky | Fr. | not drafted | - |
| **Chris Paul**, Wake Forest | So. | New Orleans | 4 |
| Pierre Pierce, Iowa | Jr. | not drafted | - |
| Shavlik Randolph, Duke | Jr. | not drafted | - |
| Anthony Roberson, Florida | Jr. | not drafted | - |
| **Nate Robinson**, Washington | Jr. | Phoenix* | 21 |
| Ray Rose, Olivet Nazarene | Jr. | not drafted | - |
| Ricky Sanchez, IMG Academy | HS | Portland* | 35 |
| Chris Taft, Pittsburgh | So. | Pittsburgh | 42 |
| **Charlie Villanueva**, UConn | So. | Toronto | 7 |
| Tiras Wade, LA-Lafayette | Jr. | not drafted | - |
| Von Wafer, Florida St. | So. | LA Lakers | 39 |
| Matt Walsh, Florida | Jr. | not drafted | - |
| **Martell Webster**, Seattle Prep | HS | Portland | 6 |
| **Deron Williams**, Illinois | Jr. | Utah | 3 |
| Louis Williams, SW Gwinnett | HS | Philadelphia | 45 |
| **Marvin Williams**, N. Carolina | Fr. | Atlanta | 2 |
| Kennedy Winston, Alabama | Jr. | not drafted | - |
| **Antoine Wright**, Texas A&M | Jr. | New Jersey | 15 |
| Bracey Wright, Indiana | Jr. | Minnesota | 47 |

*traded on draft day.

There were four North Carolina Tar Heels (Marvin Williams, Raymond Felton, Sean May and Rashard McCants) selected in the first round of the 2005 NBA Draft. **Did you know**, that only one other team has had four first-rounders in one draft? The Duke Blue Devils did it in 1999 with Elton Brand (1st), Trajan Langdon (11), Corey Maggette (13) and William Avery (14). In both instances all four players were taken by the 14th overall pick.

## Other 2005 Men's Tournaments

### NIT Tournament

The 68th annual National Invitation Tournament had a 40-team field. First four rounds played on home courts of higher seeded teams. Semifinal and Championship games played Mar 29-31 at Madison Square Garden in New York City.

#### Opening Round

| | |
|---|---|
| Davidson 77 | at Va. Commonwealth 62 |
| CS-Fullerton 85 | at Oregon St. 83 |
| at SW Missouri St. 105 | Rice 82 |
| at San Francisco 69 | Denver 67 |
| at Western Ky. 88 .........OT | Kent St. 80 |
| at Wichita St. 85 | Houston 69 |
| at Buffalo 81 ..........OT | Drexel 76 |
| at St. Joseph's 53 | Hofstra 44 |

#### 1st Round

| | |
|---|---|
| Western Michigan 54 | at Marquette 40 |
| Holy Cross 78 | at Notre Dame 73 |
| at South Carolina 69 | Miami-FL 63 |
| at Virginia Tech 60 | Temple 50 |
| DePaul 75 | at Missouri 70 |
| TCU 60 | at Miami-OH 58 |
| at Georgetown 64 | Boston University 34 |
| Vanderbilt 67 | at Indiana 60 |
| at Texas A&M 82 | Clemson 74 |
| at Maryland 85 | Oral Roberts 72 |
| at Memphis 90 | Northeastern 65 |
| at UNLV 89 | Arizona St. 78 |
| CS-Fullerton 85 | at San Francisco 69 |
| at St. Joseph's 55 | Buffalo 50 |
| Davidson 82 | at SW Missouri St. 71 |
| at Wichita St. 84 | Western Ky. 81 |

#### 2nd Round

| | |
|---|---|
| at Memphis 83 | Virginia Tech 62 |
| Texas A&M 75 | at DePaul 72 |
| TCU 78 ..........OT ...at Western Michigan 76 | |
| at St. Joseph's 68 | Holy Cross 60 |
| at Vanderbilt 65 | Wichita St. 63 |
| at Georgetown 74 | CS-Fullerton 57 |
| at South Carolina 77 | UNLV 66 |
| at Maryland 78 | Davidson 63 |

#### Quarterfinals

| | |
|---|---|
| St. Joseph's 58 | at Texas A&M 51 |
| at Memphis 81 | Vanderbilt 68 |
| at South Carolina 69 | Georgetown 66 |
| at Maryland 85 | TCU 73 |

#### Semifinals

| | |
|---|---|
| St. Joseph's 70 | Memphis 58 |
| South Carolina 75 | Maryland 67 |

#### Championship

| | |
|---|---|
| South Carolina 60 | St. Joseph's 57 |

---

### Tournament MVPs

**NIT**

Carlos Powell, South Carolina forward

**NCAA Division II**

Antwan Walton, Virginia Union forward

**NCAA Division III**

Jason Kalsow, WI-Stevens Point forward

**NAIA Division I**

Brandon Cole, John Brown guard

**NAIA Division II**

Robert Whaley, Walsh center

---

### NCAA Division II

The eight regional winners of the 48-team field: NORTHEAST—Bryant (23-8); EAST—Mount Olive (29-4); SOUTH ATLANTIC—Virginia Union (27-4); SOUTH—Lynn (28-5); SOUTH CENTRAL—Tarleton St. (24-8); GREAT LAKES—Findlay (30-3); NORTH CENTRAL—Metro St. (29-3); WEST—Cal Poly Pomona (24-6).

The Elite Eight was played March 23-26, at Grand Forks, North Dakota. There was no Third Place game.

#### Quarterfinals

| | |
|---|---|
| Bryant 84 | Mount Olive 69 |
| Tarleton St. 58 | Cal Poly Pomona 56 |
| Lynn 75 | Findlay 66 |
| Virginia Union 78 | Metro St. 63 |

#### Semifinals

| | |
|---|---|
| Bryant 60 | Tarleton St. 55 |
| Virginia Union 76 | Lynn 61 |

#### Championship

| | |
|---|---|
| Virginia Union 63 | Bryant 58 |

### NCAA Division III

The four regional winners of the 48-team field: WI-Stevens Point (27-3), York (27-3), Rochester (24-4), Calvin (26-6).

The Final Four was played March 18-19, at Salem Civic Center in Salem, Va.

#### Semifinals

| | |
|---|---|
| WI-Stevens Point 81 | York 58 |
| Rochester 65 | Calvin 62 |

#### Third Place

| | |
|---|---|
| Calvin 98 | York 84 |

#### Championship

| | |
|---|---|
| WI-Stevens Point 73 | Rochester 49 |

### NAIA Division I

The quarterfinalists, in alphabetical order, after two rounds of the 32-team NAIA tournament: Azusa Pacific, Calif. (28-9); Biola, Calif. (28-8); Carroll, Mont. (28-6); Georgetown, Ky. (28-6); John Brown, Ark. (22-11); Mountain St., W.V. (31-4); Robert Morris, Ill. (29-4); St. Xavier, Ill. (30-7).

All tournament games played, March 19-22, at the Municipal Auditorium, Kansas City, Mo. There was no Third Place game.

**Quarterfinals:** Azusa Pacific def. Mountain St. 82-66; Robert Morris def. Georgetown, 99-87; Carroll def. St. Xavier, 67-57; John Brown def. Biola, 58-56.

**Semifinals:** Azusa Pacific def. Robert Morris, 96-88; John Brown def. Carroll, 73-60.

**Championship:** John Brown def. Azusa Pacific, 65-55.

### NAIA Division II

The quarterfinalists, in alphabetical order, after two rounds of the 32-team NAIA tournament: Cedarville, Ohio (28-9), Concordia, Neb. (31-5); Cornerstone, Mich. (28-10); Indiana Tech (26-8); Oregon Tech. (28-9); Northwestern, Iowa (29-4); Southern Oregon (22-10); Walsh, Ohio (25-8).

All tournament games played, March 12-15, at Keeter Gymnasium in Point Lookout, Missouri. There was no Third Place game.

**Quarterfinals:** Concordia def. Cornerstone, 71-68; Cedarville def. Southern Oregon, 66-64; Oreon Tech def. Indiana Tech, 78-63; Walsh def. Northwestern, 68-61.

**Semifinals:** Concordia def. Cedarville, 62-56; Walsh def. Oregon Tech, 77-70.

**Championship:** Walsh def. Concordia, 81-70.

## Final Regular Season AP Women's Top 25 Poll

Taken **before** start of NCAA tournament.

The sportswriters & broadcasters poll: first place votes in parentheses; records through Sunday, March 13, 2005; total points (based on 25 for 1st, 24 for 2nd, etc.); record in NCAA tourney and team lost to; head coach (career years and career record including 2005 postseason), and preseason ranking. Teams in **bold** type went on to reach the NCAA Final Four.

| | | Mar. 13 Record | Points | NCAA Recap | | Head Coach | Preseason Rank |
|---|---|---|---|---|---|---|---|
| 1 | Stanford (29) | 29-2 | 1091 | 3-1 | (Michigan St.) | Tara VanDerveer (26 yrs: 634-171) | 7 |
| 2 | LSU (11) | 29-2 | 1073 | 4-1 | (Baylor) | Pokey Chatman (1 yr: 33-3) | 3 |
| 3 | **Tennessee** (1) | 26-4 | 1029 | 4-1 | (Michigan St.) | Pat Summitt (31 yrs: 882-172) | 1 |
| 4 | North Carolina (2) | 27-3 | 983 | 3-1 | (Baylor) | Sylvia Hatchell (30 yrs: 684-266) | 9 |
| 5 | **Baylor** (2) | 27-3 | 944 | 6-0 | | Kim Mulkey-Robertson (5 yrs: 131-38) | 8 |
| 6 | **Michigan St.** | 28-3 | 929 | 5-1 | (Baylor) | Joanne P. McCallie (13 yrs: 268-129) | 15 |
| 7 | Duke | 28-4 | 836 | 3-1 | (LSU) | Gail Goestenkors (13 yrs: 333-93) | 6 |
| 8 | Ohio St. | 28-4 | 818 | 2-1 | (Rutgers) | Jim Foster (27 yrs: 577-250) | 10 |
| 9 | Rutgers | 25-6 | 734 | 3-1 | (Tennessee) | C. Vivian Stringer (33 yrs: 723-246) | 17 |
| 10 | Connecticut | 23-7 | 730 | 2-1 | (Stanford) | Geno Auriemma (20 yrs: 557-111) | 4 |
| 11 | Notre Dame | 26-5 | 657 | 1-1 | (Arizona St.) | Muffett McGraw (23 yrs: 499-196) | 10 |
| 12 | Minnesota | 24-7 | 610 | 2-1 | (Baylor) | Pam Borton (7 yrs: 145-53) | 14 |
| 13 | Texas | 21-8 | 580 | 1-1 | (Georgia) | Jody Conradt (36 yrs: 859-278) | 2 |
| 14 | Texas Tech | 22-7 | 515 | 2-1 | (Tennessee) | Marsha Sharp (23 yrs: 556-175) | 12 |
| 15 | Temple | 27-3 | 488 | 1-1 | (Rutgers) | Dawn Staley (5 yrs: 102-50) | NR |
| 16 | Kansas St. | 23-7 | 465 | 1-1 | (Vanderbilt) | Deb Patterson (9 yrs: 175-106) | 19 |
| 17 | DePaul | 25-4 | 415 | 1-1 | (Liberty) | Doug Bruno (19 yrs: 348-210) | 20 |
| 18 | Vanderbilt | 22-7 | 324 | 2-1 | (Michigan St.) | Melanie Balcomb (12 yrs: 235-131) | 13 |
| 19 | Iowa St. | 23-6 | 294 | 0-1 | (Utah) | Bill Fennelly (17 yrs: 381-150) | NR |
| 20 | Georgia | 22-9 | 208 | 2-1 | (Duke) | Andy Landers (26 yrs: 634-199) | 5 |
| 21 | N.C. State | 21-7 | 198 | 0-1 | (Mid. Tenn. St.) | Kay Yow (34 yrs: 674-308) | NR |
| 22 | Penn St. | 19-10 | 176 | 0-1 | (Liberty) | Rene Portland (29 yrs: 668-233) | 21 |
| 23 | TCU | 23-9 | 117 | 0-1 | (Oregon) | Jeff Mittie (13 yrs: 283-120) | NR |
| 24 | Wisconsin-Green Bay | 27-3 | 116 | 0-1 | (Maryland) | Kevin Borseth (18 yrs: 389-147) | NR |
| 25 | Boston College | 19-9 | 66 | 1-1 | (Duke) | Cathy Inglese (19 yrs: 338-213) | 18 |

**Others receiving votes:** 26. **New Mexico** (26-4, 59 points); 27. **Arizona St.** (22-9, 53); 28. **Maryland** (21-9, 42); 29. **Virginia** (20-10, 22); 30. **Gonzaga** (27-3, 13); 31 **George Washington** (22-8, 8); 32. **Utah** (25-7, 7); 33. **Oregon** (20-9, 4); 34. **Louisville** (22-8, 2) and **USC** (19-10, 2), 36. **Oklahoma** (17-12, 1).

## NCAA Women's Division I Tournament Seeds

| | TEMPE | | KANSAS CITY | | CHATTANOOGA | | PHILADELPHIA |
|---|---|---|---|---|---|---|---|
| 1 | North Carolina (27-3) | 1 | Michigan St. (28-3) | 1 | LSU (29-2) | 1 | Tennessee (26-4) |
| 2 | Baylor (27-3) | 2 | Stanford (29-2) | 2 | Duke (28-4) | 2 | Ohio St. (28-4) |
| 3 | Minnesota (24-7) | 3 | Connecticut (23-7) | 3 | Texas (21-8) | 3 | Rutgers (25-6) |
| 4 | Notre Dame (26-5) | 4 | Kansas St. (23-7) | 4 | Penn St. (19-10) | 4 | Texas Tech (22-7) |
| 5 | Arizona St. (22-9) | 5 | Vanderbilt (22-7) | 5 | DePaul (25-4) | 5 | N.C. State (21-7) |
| 6 | Virginia (20-10) | 6 | Florida St. (23-7) | 6 | Georgia (22-9) | 6 | Temple (27-3) |
| 7 | TCU (23-9) | 7 | Iowa St. (23-6) | 7 | Boston College (19-9) | 7 | Maryland (21-9) |
| 8 | Mississippi (19-10) | 8 | USC (19-10) | 8 | Oklahoma (17-12) | 8 | New Mexico (26-4) |
| 9 | G. Washington (22-8) | 9 | Louisville (22-8) | 9 | Arizona (19-11) | 9 | Purdue (16-12) |
| 10 | Oregon (20-9) | 10 | Utah (25-7) | 10 | Houston (21-8) | 10 | WI-Green Bay (27-3) |
| 11 | Old Dominion (22-8) | 11 | Richmond (23-7) | 11 | Rice (24-8) | 11 | Louisiana Tech (20-9) |
| 12 | Eastern Ky. (23-7) | 12 | Montana (22-7) | 12 | Virginia Tech (17-11) | 12 | Mid. Tennessee St. (23-3) |
| 13 | UC-Santa Barbara (21-8) | 13 | Bowling Green (23-7) | 13 | Liberty (24-6) | 13 | Texas-Arlington (21-9) |
| 14 | St. Francis-PA (21-9) | 14 | Dartmouth (17-10) | 14 | Oral Roberts (22-8) | 14 | Hartford (22-8) |
| 15 | Illinois St. (13-17) | 15 | Santa Clara (17-13) | 15 | Canisius (21-9) | 15 | Holy Cross (20-10) |
| 16 | Coppin St. (23-7) | 16 | Alcorn St. (21-8) | 16 | Stetson (17-13) | 16 | Western Carolina (18-13) |

# 2005 NCAA Tournament Women's Division

Column rounds: 1st ROUND March 19-20 | 2nd ROUND March 21-22 | SWEET 16 March 26 | ELITE EIGHT March 28 | FINAL FOUR April 3 | NATIONAL CHAMPIONSHIP | FINAL FOUR April 3 | ELITE EIGHT March 28 | SWEET 16 March 26 | 2nd ROUND March 21-22 | 1st ROUND March 19-20

## Tennessee / Philadelphia Region

1st Round:
- (1) Tennessee 94
- (16) W. Carolina 43
- (8) New Mexico 56
- (9) Purdue 68
- (5) N.C. State 58
- (12) Mid. Tenn. 60
- (4) Texas Tech 69
- (13) TX-Arlington 49
- (6) Temple 66
- (11) La. Tech 61
- (3) Rutgers 62
- (14) Hartford 37
- (7) Maryland 65
- (10) WI-GB 55
- (2) Ohio St. 86
- (15) Holy Cross 45

2nd Round: Tennessee 75 / Purdue 54 | Mid. Tenn. 69 / Texas Tech 80 | Temple 54 / Rutgers 61 | Maryland 65 / Ohio St. 75

Sweet 16 (Philadelphia): Tennessee 75 / Texas Tech 59 | Rutgers 64 / Ohio St. 58

Elite Eight: Tennessee 59 / Rutgers 49

Final Four: **Tennessee 64**

## Michigan St. / Kansas City Region

1st Round:
- (1) Michigan St. 73
- (16) Alcorn St. 41
- (8) USC 65
- (9) Louisville 49
- (5) Vanderbilt 67
- (12) Montana 44
- (4) Kansas St. 70
- (13) Bowl. Green 60
- (6) Florida St. 87
- (11) Richmond 54
- (3) Connecticut 95
- (14) Dartmouth 47
- (7) Iowa St. 61
- (10) Utah 73
- (2) Stanford 94
- (15) Santa Clara 57

2nd Round: Michigan St. 61 / USC 59 | Vanderbilt 63 / Kansas St. 60 | Florida St. 52 / Connecticut 70 | Utah 62 / Stanford 88

Sweet 16 (Kansas City): Michigan St. 76 / Vanderbilt 64 | Connecticut 69 / Stanford 76

Elite Eight: Michigan St. 76 / Stanford 69

Final Four: **Michigan St. 68**

## LSU / Chattanooga Region

1st Round:
- (1) LSU 70
- (16) Stetson 36
- (8) Oklahoma 69
- (9) Arizona 72
- (5) DePaul 79
- (12) Va. Tech 78
- (4) Penn St. 78
- (13) Liberty 70
- (6) Georgia 75
- (11) Rice 49
- (3) Texas 64
- (14) Oral Roberts 47
- (7) Boston Coll. 65
- (10) Houston 43
- (2) Duke 80
- (15) Canisius 48

2nd Round: LSU 76 / Arizona 43 | DePaul 79 / Liberty 88 | Georgia 70 / Texas 68 | Boston College 65 / Duke 70

Sweet 16 (Chattanooga): LSU 90 / Liberty 48 | Georgia 57 / Duke 63

Elite Eight (Chattanooga): LSU 59 / Duke 49

Final Four: **LSU 57**

## North Carolina / Tempe Region

1st Round:
- (1) N. Carolina 97
- (16) Coppin St. 62
- (8) Mississippi 57
- (9) Geo. Wash. 60
- (5) Arizona St. 87
- (12) Eastern Ky. 65
- (4) Notre Dame 61
- (13) UCSB 51
- (6) Virginia 79
- (11) ODU 57
- (3) Minnesota 64
- (14) St. Francis-PA 33
- (7) TCU 55
- (10) Oregon 58
- (2) Baylor 91
- (15) Illinois St. 70

2nd Round: N. Carolina 71 / G. Washington 47 | Arizona St. 70 / Notre Dame 61 | Virginia 58 / Minnesota 73 | Oregon 46 / Baylor 69

Sweet 16 (Tempe): North Carolina 79 / Arizona St. 72 | Minnesota 57 / Baylor 64

Elite Eight (Tempe): North Carolina 63 / Baylor 72

Final Four: **Baylor 68**

## National Championship

**Baylor 84, Michigan St. 62**

RCA Dome
Indianapolis, Indiana
Tuesday, April 5, 2005

## NCAA Championship Game

### Baylor 84

| | Min | FG M-A | FT M-A | Pts | Reb O-T | A | PF |
|---|---|---|---|---|---|---|---|
| Sophia Young | 36 | 10-19 | 6-9 | 26 | 4-9 | 4 | 1 |
| Steffanie Blackmon | 35 | 8-19 | 6-8 | 22 | 2-7 | 1 | 2 |
| Chelsea Whitaker | 32 | 0-2 | 0-1 | 0 | 3-5 | 6 | 1 |
| Chameka Scott | 18 | 3-3 | 0-0 | 7 | 1-4 | 3 | 0 |
| Abiola Wabara | 10 | 0-1 | 0-0 | 0 | 0-2 | 1 | 1 |
| Emily Niemann | 33 | 6-10 | 2-2 | 19 | 1-3 | 1 | 1 |
| LaToya Wyatt | 20 | 3-5 | 2-4 | 8 | 1-6 | 0 | 4 |
| Angela Tisdale | 8 | 0-2 | 2-2 | 2 | 0-1 | 1 | 2 |
| Melanie Hamerly | 2 | 0-0 | 0-0 | 0 | 0-0 | 0 | 0 |
| Chanelle Fox | 2 | 0-0 | 0-0 | 0 | 0-2 | 0 | 0 |
| Monique Jones | 1 | 0-0 | 0-0 | 0 | 0-0 | 0 | 0 |
| Jordan Davis | 1 | 0-0 | 0-0 | 0 | 0-0 | 0 | 0 |
| Victoria Jones | 1 | 0-0 | 0-0 | 0 | 0-0 | 0 | 0 |
| Chisa Ononiwu | 1 | 0-0 | 0-0 | 0 | 0-0 | 0 | 0 |
| TOTALS | 200 | 30-61 | 18-26 | 84 | 12-38 | 17 | 12 |

**Three-point FG:** 6-12 (Niemann 5-8, Scott 1-1, Wabara 0-1, Wyatt 0-1, Tisdale 0-1); **Blocked Shots:** 0; **Turnovers:** 12 (Young 3, Blackmon 2, Scott 2, Tisdale 2, Whitaker, Wabara, Wyatt); **Steals:** 8 (Whitaker 2, Wabara 2, Blackmon, Scott, Niemann, Ononiwu); **Percentages:** 2-Pt FG (.490); 3-Pt FG (.500); Total FG (.492); Free Throws (.692).

### Michigan St. 62

| | Min | FG M-A | FT M-A | Pts | Reb O-T | A | PF |
|---|---|---|---|---|---|---|---|
| Kristin Haynie | 37 | 7-14 | 3-5 | 17 | 0-1 | 5 | 4 |
| Lindsay Bowen | 37 | 5-14 | 8-10 | 20 | 1-3 | 1 | 0 |
| Kelli Roehrig | 30 | 3-8 | 2-2 | 8 | 0-5 | 0 | 3 |
| Victoria Lucas-Perry | 25 | 3-6 | 0-0 | 7 | 0-2 | 0 | 3 |
| Myisha Bannister | 1 | 0-0 | 0-0 | 0 | 0-0 | 0 | 0 |
| Liz Shimek | 37 | 3-6 | 0-0 | 7 | 0-5 | 2 | 3 |
| Rene Haynes | 19 | 0-3 | 1-2 | 1 | 0-2 | 1 | 2 |
| Laura Hall | 9 | 1-2 | 0-0 | 2 | 0-1 | 0 | 2 |
| Katrina Grantham | 3 | 0-0 | 0-0 | 0 | 0-0 | 0 | 2 |
| Maggie Dwyer | 1 | 0-0 | 0-0 | 0 | 1-1 | 0 | 0 |
| Melanie Small | 1 | 0-0 | 0-0 | 0 | 0-0 | 0 | 0 |
| TOTALS | 200 | 22-53 | 14-19 | 62 | 2-20 | 9 | 19 |

**Three-point FG:** 4-18 (Bowen 2-9, Lucas-Perry 1-3, Shimek 1-2, Haynie 0-3, Haynes 0-1); **Blocked Shots:** 5 (Roehrig 3, Shimek, Hall); **Turnovers:** 12 (Shimek 4, Bowen 2, Haynes 2, Haynie, Roehrig, Lucas-Perry, Dwyer); **Steals:** 8 (Haynie 5, Bowen 2, Lucas-Perry); **Percentages:** 2-Pt FG (.514); 3-Pt FG (.222); Total FG (.415); Free Throws (.737).

**Baylor** (Big 12) .............37  47— **84**
**Michigan St.** (Big Ten) .......25  37— **62**

**Technical Fouls:** None. **Attendance:** 28,937.

## Final *ESPN/USA Today* Coaches' Poll

Taken **after** NCAA tournament.
Voted on by panel of 40 women's coaches and media following the NCAA tournament: first place votes in parentheses.

| | Pts | | | Pts |
|---|---|---|---|---|
| 1 Baylor (40) | 1,000 | | 14 Vanderbilt | .433 |
| 2 Michigan St. | .950 | | 15 Notre Dame | .393 |
| 3 LSU | .913 | | 16 Arizona St. | .391 |
| 4 Tennesse | .891 | | 17 Texas | .379 |
| 5 Stanford | .813 | | 18 Temple | .352 |
| 6 North Carolina | .756 | | 19 Kansas St. | .312 |
| 7 Rutgers | .747 | | 20 DePaul | .242 |
| 8 Duke | .724 | | 21 Liberty | .214 |
| 9 Ohio St. | .656 | | 22 USC | .91 |
| 10 Connecticut | .610 | | 23 Boston College | .84 |
| 11 Minnesota | .589 | | 24 Maryland | .82 |
| 12 Texas Tech | .527 | | 25 Iowa St. | .79 |
| 13 Georgia | .444 | | | |

## Annual Awards

### Player of the Year

Seimone Augustus, LSU ....AP, Wade, Wooden, Naismith, USBWA, Broderick

### Coaches of the Year

Pokey Chatman, LSU ........USBWA, WBCA, Naismith
Joanne McCallie, Michigan St. ..................AP

### Consensus All-America Team

The NCAA Division I players cited most frequently by the Associated Press, US Basketball Writers Association and the Women's Basketball Coaches Association. There were no holdovers from 2003-04 All-America first team; (*) indicates unanimous first team selection.

#### First Team

| | Class | Hgt | Pos |
|---|---|---|---|
| Seimone Augustus*, LSU | Jr. | 6-1 | G |
| Kendra Wecker*, Kansas St. | Sr. | 6-2 | F |
| Monique Currie*, Duke | Jr. | 6-0 | G/F |
| Jessica Davenport*, Ohio St. | So. | 6-5 | C |
| Sandora Irvin*, Texas Christian | Sr. | 6-3 | F |

#### Second Team

| | Class | Hgt | Pos |
|---|---|---|---|
| Sophia Young, Baylor | Jr. | 6-1 | F |
| Janel McCarville, Minnesota | Sr. | 6-2 | C |
| Candice Wiggins, Stanford | Fr. | 5-11 | G |
| Tan White, Mississippi St. | Sr. | 5-7 | G |
| Temeka Johnson, LSU | Sr. | 5-3 | G |

**Players also named:** Jacqueline Batteast, Notre Dame; Tiffany Jackson, Texas; Ivory Latta, North Carolina; Khara Smith, DePaul; Tanisha Wright, Penn St.; Steffanie Blackmon, Baylor.

## NCAA Women's Division I Leaders
Includes games through NCAA and NIT tourneys.

### INDIVIDUAL

#### Scoring

| | Cl | Gm | Pts | Avg |
|---|---|---|---|---|
| Tan White, Mississippi St. | Sr. | 29 | 681 | 23.5 |
| Emily Faurholt, Idaho | Jr. | 30 | 697 | 23.2 |
| Tori Talbert, Texas St. | Sr. | 25 | 560 | 22.4 |
| Tamara James, Miami-FL | Jr. | 29 | 647 | 22.3 |
| Beth Swink, St. Francis-PA | Sr. | 31 | 688 | 22.2 |
| Rolanda Monroe, Southern U. | Sr. | 30 | 640 | 21.3 |
| Kendra Wecker, Kansas St. | Sr. | 29 | 609 | 21.0 |
| Reka Cserny, Harvard | Jr. | 27 | 564 | 20.9 |
| Tara Boothe, Xavier | Jr. | 32 | 659 | 20.6 |
| Seimone Augustus, LSU | Jr. | 36 | 724 | 20.1 |
| Sugiery Monsac, Robert Morris | Jr. | 30 | 602 | 20.1 |
| Jenni Lingor, Missouri St. | Sr. | 33 | 660 | 20.0 |
| Sandora Irvin, TCU | Sr. | 33 | 657 | 19.9 |
| Tiffani Mayes, E. Tenn. St. | Sr. | 29 | 571 | 19.7 |
| Emily Christian, Tenn. Tech | Jr. | 29 | 566 | 19.5 |
| Meg Bulger, West Virginia | So. | 34 | 663 | 19.5 |
| Kristen Mann, UC-Santa Barbara | Sr. | 29 | 565 | 19.5 |
| Jessica Davenport, Ohio St. | So. | 35 | 677 | 19.3 |
| Crystal Kelly, Western Ky. | Fr. | 30 | 579 | 19.3 |
| Tanisha Wright, Penn St. | Sr. | 30 | 578 | 19.3 |

#### Assists

| | Cl | Gm | No | Avg |
|---|---|---|---|---|
| Yolanda Paige, West Virginia | Sr. | 34 | 297 | 8.7 |
| Temeka Johnson, LSU | Sr. | 36 | 278 | 7.7 |
| Erin Grant, Texas Tech | Jr. | 31 | 218 | 7.0 |
| Corrie Mizusawa, Oregon | Sr. | 30 | 209 | 7.0 |
| Anesia Smith, Maryland | Sr. | 32 | 214 | 6.7 |
| Shona Thorburn, Utah | Sr. | 34 | 221 | 6.5 |
| Carolyn Kieger, Marquette | Jr. | 30 | 185 | 6.2 |
| Erica McGlaston, San Jose St. | Sr. | 30 | 185 | 6.2 |
| Shannon Mathews, Gonzaga | Sr. | 32 | 197 | 6.2 |
| Anedra Gilmore, South Florida | Jr. | 31 | 190 | 6.1 |
| Lynsey Monaco, Montana | Sr. | 28 | 169 | 6.0 |
| Dee Davis, Vanderbilt | So. | 32 | 192 | 6.0 |
| Erika Ford, E. Michigan | Jr. | 31 | 186 | 6.0 |
| Lyndsey Medders, Iowa St. | So. | 30 | 180 | 6.0 |
| Nikki Blue, UCLA | Jr. | 27 | 162 | 6.0 |

#### Rebounding

| | Cl | Gm | No | Avg |
|---|---|---|---|---|
| Sancho Lyttle, Houston | Sr. | 30 | 362 | 12.1 |
| Sandora Irvin, TCU | Sr. | 33 | 390 | 11.8 |
| Nakeya Downing, SE Louisiana | Sr. | 27 | 318 | 11.8 |
| Kahra Smith, DePaul | Jr. | 31 | 364 | 11.7 |
| Sugiery Monsac, Robert Morris | Jr. | 30 | 348 | 11.6 |
| Kemie Nkele, UC-Riverside | Fr. | 28 | 321 | 11.5 |
| Evena Morency, South Carolina St. | Sr. | 29 | 321 | 11.1 |
| Kristy Brown, Stetson | Sr. | 31 | 334 | 10.8 |
| Jen Perugini, Youngstown St. | Sr. | 27 | 288 | 10.7 |
| Jennifer Fleischer, Penn | Jr. | 27 | 287 | 10.6 |
| Crystal Langhorne, Maryland | Fr. | 32 | 340 | 10.6 |
| Jackie Ododa, TX-Corpus Christi | Sr. | 30 | 317 | 10.6 |
| Janel McCarville, Minnesota | Sr. | 32 | 338 | 10.6 |
| Shameka Smith, Gardner-Webb | So. | 27 | 282 | 10.4 |
| Lizanne Murphy, Hofstra | So. | 29 | 302 | 10.4 |

#### Blocked Shots

| | Cl | Gm | No | Avg |
|---|---|---|---|---|
| Marita Payne, Auburn | Jr. | 28 | 141 | 5.0 |
| Ashley Sparkman, Northwestern St. | Sr. | 27 | 132 | 4.9 |
| Sandora Irvin, TCU | Sr. | 33 | 150 | 4.5 |
| Cassie Hager, Northern Iowa | Jr. | 31 | 135 | 4.4 |
| Brooke McAfee, IUPUI | Jr. | 28 | 105 | 3.8 |
| Alison Bales, Duke | So. | 36 | 134 | 3.7 |

#### Steals

| | Cl | Gm | No | Avg |
|---|---|---|---|---|
| Kristen Boone, NC-Greensboro | Fr. | 28 | 121 | 4.3 |
| Leilani Mitchell, Idaho | So. | 30 | 118 | 3.9 |
| Melanie Boeglin, Indiana St. | Jr. | 32 | 123 | 3.8 |
| Stephanie Raymond, Northern Ill. | So. | 28 | 107 | 3.8 |
| Kyle DeHaven, William & Mary | So. | 27 | 100 | 3.7 |
| Lisa Willis, UCLA | Jr. | 28 | 102 | 3.6 |

#### High-Point Games

| Pts | | Opponent | Date |
|---|---|---|---|
| 47 | Tan White, Mississippi St. | Vanderbilt | Feb. 3 |
| 45 | Jennifer Gardner, W. Caro. | Ga. Southern | Mar. 5 |

### TEAM

#### Scoring Offense

| | Gm | W-L | Pts | Avg |
|---|---|---|---|---|
| DePaul | 31 | 26-5 | 2563 | 82.7 |
| North Carolina | 34 | 30-4 | 2701 | 79.4 |
| Western Ky. | 30 | 20-10 | 2354 | 78.5 |
| Stanford | 35 | 32-3 | 2724 | 77.8 |
| Vanderbilt | 32 | 24-8 | 2480 | 77.5 |
| Duke | 36 | 31-5 | 2737 | 76.0 |
| Indiana St. | 32 | 23-9 | 2432 | 76.0 |
| Iowa St. | 30 | 23-7 | 2273 | 75.8 |
| Baylor | 36 | 33-3 | 2673 | 74.3 |
| Missouri St. | 33 | 25-8 | 2449 | 74.2 |

#### High-Point Games

| Pts | | Opponent | Date |
|---|---|---|---|
| 118 | DePaul | Northwestern | Nov. 27 |
| 116 | Central Michigan | Tri-State | Nov. 19 |
| 115 | Bowling Green | IPFW | Nov. 19 |
| 113 | N.C. A&T | Morgan St. | Feb. 7 |
| 113 | Iowa St. | IPFW | Nov. 29 |

#### Scoring Defense

| | Gm | W-L | Pts | Avg |
|---|---|---|---|---|
| Delaware St. | 28 | 16-12 | 1389 | 49.6 |
| Rutgers | 35 | 28-7 | 1794 | 51.3 |
| Connecticut | 33 | 25-8 | 1696 | 51.4 |
| Marist | 29 | 22-7 | 1494 | 51.5 |
| LSU | 36 | 33-3 | 1886 | 52.4 |
| Villanova | 31 | 19-12 | 1635 | 52.7 |
| Ohio St. | 35 | 30-5 | 1848 | 52.8 |
| New Mexico | 31 | 26-5 | 1641 | 52.9 |
| Hartford | 31 | 22-9 | 1641 | 52.9 |
| Western Illinois | 28 | 19-9 | 1486 | 53.1 |

#### Scoring Margin

| | Off | Def | Mar |
|---|---|---|---|
| Stanford | 77.8 | 56.0 | 21.9 |
| North Carolina | 79.4 | 59.0 | 20.4 |
| Duke | 76.0 | 56.0 | 20.0 |
| DePaul | 82.7 | 62.7 | 20.0 |
| Ohio St. | 72.6 | 52.8 | 19.8 |
| LSU | 71.9 | 52.4 | 19.5 |
| Connecticut | 70.6 | 51.4 | 19.2 |
| Vanderbilt | 77.5 | 59.6 | 17.9 |
| Texas Tech | 71.7 | 55.3 | 16.4 |
| Wisconsin-Green Bay | 72.0 | 55.6 | 16.4 |

# 1901-2005
# Through the Years

ESPN SPORTS ALMANAC

## National Champions and NCAA Final Four

The Helms Foundation of Los Angeles, under the direction of founder Bill Schroeder, selected national college basketball champions from 1942-82 and researched retroactive picks from 1901-41. The first NIT tournament and then the NCAA tournament have settled the national championship since 1938, but there are four years (1939, '40, '44 and '54) where the Helms selections differ. In 1939, Helms picked undefeated LIU-Brooklyn (24-0), winners of the NIT. In 1940, Helms picked USC (20-3) although they were beaten by Kansas in the West Regionals of the NCAA tourney. In 1944, Helms picked unbeaten Army (15-0). Army did not lift its policy barring postseason play until the 1961 NIT. In 1954, Helms chose unbeaten Kentucky (25-0), even though Kentucky refused its NCAA bid after seniors Cliff Hagan, Frank Ramsey and Lou Tsioropoulos were declared ineligible.

**Multiple champions (1901-37):** Chicago, Columbia and Wisconsin (3); Kansas, Minnesota, Notre Dame, Penn, Pittsburgh, Syracuse and Yale (2).

**Multiple champions (since 1938):** UCLA (11); Kentucky (7); Indiana (5); North Carolina (4); Duke (3); Cincinnati, Connecticut, Kansas, Louisville, Michigan St., N.C. State, Oklahoma A&M (now Oklahoma St.) and San Francisco (2).

| Year | Champion | Record | Head Coach | Outstanding Player |
|---|---|---|---|---|
| 1901 | Yale | 10-4 | No coach | G.M. Clark, F |
| 1902 | Minnesota | 11-0 | Louis Cooke | W.C. Deering, F |
| 1903 | Yale | 15-1 | W.H. Murphy | R.B. Hyatt, F |
| 1904 | Columbia | 17-1 | No coach | Harry Fisher, F |
| 1905 | Columbia | 19-1 | No coach | Harry Fisher, F |
| 1906 | Dartmouth | 16-2 | No coach | George Grebenstein, F |
| 1907 | Chicago | 22-2 | Joseph Raycroft | John Schommer, C |
| 1908 | Chicago | 21-2 | Joseph Raycroft | John Schommer, C |
| 1909 | Chicago | 12-0 | Joseph Raycroft | John Schommer, C |
| 1910 | Columbia | 11-1 | Harry Fisher | Ted Kiendl, F |
| 1911 | St. John's-NY | 14-0 | Claude Allen | John Keenan, F/C |
| 1912 | Wisconsin | 15-0 | Doc Meanwell | Otto Stangel, F |
| 1913 | Navy | 9-0 | Louis Wenzell | Laurence Wild, F |
| 1914 | Wisconsin | 15-0 | Doc Meanwell | Gene Van Gent, C |
| 1915 | Illinois | 16-0 | Ralph Jones | Ray Woods, G |
| 1916 | Wisconsin | 20-1 | Doc Meanwell | George Levis, F |
| 1917 | Washington St | 25-1 | Doc Bohler | Roy Bohler, G |
| 1918 | Syracuse | 16-1 | Edmund Dollard | Joe Schwarzer, G |
| 1919 | Minnesota | 13-0 | Louis Cooke | Arnold Oss, F |
| 1920 | Penn | 22-1 | Lon Jourdet | George Sweeney, F |
| 1921 | Penn | 21-2 | Edward McNichol | Danny McNichol, G |
| 1922 | Kansas | 16-2 | Phog Allen | Paul Endacott, G |
| 1923 | Kansas | 17-1 | Phog Allen | Paul Endacott, G |
| 1924 | North Carolina | 25-0 | Bo Shepard | Jack Cobb, F |
| 1925 | Princeton | 21-2 | Al Wittmer | Art Loeb, G |
| 1926 | Syracuse | 19-1 | Lew Andreas | Vic Hanson, F |
| 1927 | Notre Dame | 19-1 | George Keogan | John Nyikos, C |
| 1928 | Pittsburgh | 21-0 | Doc Carlson | Chuck Hyatt, F |
| 1929 | Montana St. | 36-2 | Schubert Dyche | John (Cat) Thompson, F |
| 1930 | Pittsburgh | 23-2 | Doc Carlson | Chuck Hyatt, F |
| 1931 | Northwestern | 16-1 | Dutch Lonborg | Joe Reiff, C |
| 1932 | Purdue | 17-1 | Piggy Lambert | John Wooden, G |
| 1933 | Kentucky | 20-3 | Adolph Rupp | Forest Sale, F |
| 1934 | Wyoming | 26-3 | Willard Witte | Les Witte, G |
| 1935 | NYU | 19-1 | Howard Cann | Sid Gross, F |
| 1936 | Notre Dame | 22-2-1 | George Keogan | John Moir, F |
| 1937 | Stanford | 25-2 | John Bunn | Hank Luisetti, F |

| Year | Champion | Record | Winner | Head Coach | Outstanding Player |
|---|---|---|---|---|---|
| 1938 | Temple | 23-2 | NIT | James Usilton | Meyer Bloom, G |

| Year | Champion | Runner-up | Score | Final Two | Third Place | |
|---|---|---|---|---|---|---|
| 1939 | Oregon | Ohio St. | 46-33 | @ Evanston, IL | Oklahoma | Villanova |
| 1940 | Indiana | Kansas | 60-42 | @ Kansas City | Duquesne | USC |
| 1941 | Wisconsin | Washington St. | 39-34 | @ Kansas City | Arkansas | Pittsburgh |
| 1942 | Stanford | Dartmouth | 53-38 | @ Kansas City | Colorado | Kentucky |
| 1943 | Wyoming | Georgetown | 46-34 | @ New York | DePaul | Texas |
| 1944 | Utah | Dartmouth | 42-40 (OT) | @ New York | Iowa St. | Ohio St. |
| 1945 | Oklahoma A&M | NYU | 49-45 | @ New York | Arkansas | Ohio St. |

## NCAA Final Four (Cont.)

| Year | Champion | Runner-up | Score | Final Two | Third Place | Fourth Place |
|---|---|---|---|---|---|---|
| 1946 | Oklahoma A&M | North Carolina | 43-40 | @ New York | Ohio St. | California |
| 1947 | Holy Cross | Oklahoma | 58-47 | @ New York | Texas | CCNY |
| 1948 | Kentucky | Baylor | 58-42 | @ New York | Holy Cross | Kansas St. |
| 1949 | Kentucky | Oklahoma A&M | 46-36 | @ Seattle | Illinois | Oregon St. |
| 1950 | CCNY | Bradley | 71-68 | @ New York | N.C. State | Baylor |
| 1951 | Kentucky | Kansas St. | 68-58 | @ Minneapolis | Illinois | Oklahoma A&M |

| Year | Champion | Runner-up | Score | Third Place | Fourth Place | Final Four |
|---|---|---|---|---|---|---|
| 1952 | Kansas | St. John's | 80-63 | Illinois | Santa Clara | @ Seattle |
| 1953 | Indiana | Kansas | 69-68 | Washington | LSU | @ Kansas City |
| 1954 | La Salle | Bradley | 92-76 | Penn St. | USC | @ Kansas City |
| 1955 | San Francisco | La Salle | 77-63 | Colorado | Iowa | @ Kansas City |
| 1956 | San Francisco | Iowa | 83-71 | Temple | SMU | @ Evanston, IL |
| 1957 | North Carolina | Kansas | 54-53 (3OT) | San Francisco | Michigan St. | @ Kansas City |
| 1958 | Kentucky | Seattle | 84-72 | Temple | Kansas St. | @ Louisville |
| 1959 | California | West Virginia | 71-70 | Cincinnati | Louisville | @ Louisville |
| 1960 | Ohio St. | California | 75-55 | Cincinnati | NYU | @ San Francisco |
| 1961 | Cincinnati | Ohio St. | 70-65 (OT) | St. Joseph's-PA | Utah | @ Kansas City |
| 1962 | Cincinnati | Ohio St. | 71-59 | Wake Forest | UCLA | @ Louisville |
| 1963 | Loyola-IL | Cincinnati | 60-58 (OT) | Duke | Oregon St. | @ Louisville |
| 1964 | UCLA | Duke | 98-83 | Michigan | Kansas St. | @ Kansas City |
| 1965 | UCLA | Michigan | 91-80 | Princeton | Wichita St. | @ Portland, OR |
| 1966 | Texas Western | Kentucky | 72-65 | Duke | Utah | @ College Park, MD |
| 1967 | UCLA | Dayton | 79-64 | Houston | North Carolina | @ Louisville |
| 1968 | UCLA | North Carolina | 78-55 | Ohio St. | Houston | @ Los Angeles |
| 1969 | UCLA | Purdue | 92-72 | Drake | North Carolina | @ Louisville |
| 1970 | UCLA | Jacksonville | 80-69 | New Mexico St. | St. Bonaventure | @ College Park, MD |
| 1971 | UCLA | Villanova | 68-62 | Western Ky. | Kansas | @ Houston |
| 1972 | UCLA | Florida St. | 81-76 | North Carolina | Louisville | @ Los Angeles |
| 1973 | UCLA | Memphis St. | 87-66 | Indiana | Providence | @ St. Louis |
| 1974 | N.C. State | Marquette | 76-64 | UCLA | Kansas | @ Greensboro, NC |
| 1975 | UCLA | Kentucky | 92-85 | Louisville | Syracuse | @ San Diego |
| 1976 | Indiana | Michigan | 86-68 | UCLA | Rutgers | @ Philadelphia |
| 1977 | Marquette | North Carolina | 67-59 | UNLV | NC-Charlotte | @ Atlanta |
| 1978 | Kentucky | Duke | 94-88 | Arkansas | Notre Dame | @ St. Louis |
| 1979 | Michigan St. | Indiana St. | 75-64 | DePaul | Penn | @ Salt Lake City |
| 1980 | Louisville | UCLA | 59-54 | Purdue | Iowa | @ Indianapolis |
| 1981 | Indiana | North Carolina | 63-50 | Virginia | LSU | @ Philadelphia |

| Year | Champion | Runner-up | Score | ——Third Place—— | | Final Four |
|---|---|---|---|---|---|---|
| 1982 | North Carolina | Georgetown | 63-62 | Houston | Louisville | @ New Orleans |
| 1983 | N.C. State | Houston | 54-52 | Georgia | Louisville | @ Albuquerque |
| 1984 | Georgetown | Houston | 84-75 | Kentucky | Virginia | @ Seattle |
| 1985 | Villanova | Georgetown | 66-64 | Memphis St. | St. John's | @ Lexington |
| 1986 | Louisville | Duke | 72-69 | Kansas | LSU | @ Dallas |
| 1987 | Indiana | Syracuse | 74-73 | Providence | UNLV | @ New Orleans |
| 1988 | Kansas | Oklahoma | 83-79 | Arizona | Duke | @ Kansas City |
| 1989 | Michigan | Seton Hall | 80-79 (OT) | Duke | Illinois | @ Seattle |
| 1990 | UNLV | Duke | 103-73 | Arkansas | Georgia Tech | @ Denver |
| 1991 | Duke | Kansas | 72-65 | North Carolina | UNLV | @ Indianapolis |
| 1992 | Duke | Michigan | 71-51 | Cincinnati | Indiana | @ Minneapolis |
| 1993 | North Carolina | Michigan | 77-71 | Kansas | Kentucky | @ New Orleans |
| 1994 | Arkansas | Duke | 76-72 | Arizona | Florida | @ Charlotte |
| 1995 | UCLA | Arkansas | 89-78 | North Carolina | Oklahoma St. | @ Seattle |
| 1996 | Kentucky | Syracuse | 76-67 | UMass | Mississippi St. | @ E. Rutherford, NJ |
| 1997 | Arizona | Kentucky | 84-79 (OT) | Minnesota | North Carolina | @ Indianapolis |
| 1998 | Kentucky | Utah | 78-69 | Stanford | North Carolina | @ San Antonio |
| 1999 | Connecticut | Duke | 77-74 | Michigan St. | Ohio St. | @ St. Petersburg, FL |
| 2000 | Michigan St. | Florida | 89-76 | Wisconsin | North Carolina | @ Indianapolis |
| 2001 | Duke | Arizona | 82-72 | Michigan St. | Maryland | @ Minneapolis |
| 2002 | Maryland | Indiana | 64-52 | Oklahoma | Kansas | @ Atlanta |
| 2003 | Syracuse | Kansas | 81-78 | Marquette | Texas | @ New Orleans |
| 2004 | Connecticut | Georgia Tech | 82-73 | Duke | Oklahoma St. | @ San Antonio |
| 2005 | North Carolina | Illinois | 75-70 | Michigan St. | Louisville | @ San Antonio |

**Note:** Six teams have had their standing in the Final Four vacated for using ineligible players: 1961–St. Joseph's-PA (3rd place); 1971–Villanova (Runner-up) and Western Kentucky (3rd); 1980–UCLA (Runner-up); 1985–Memphis St. (3rd); 1996–UMass (3rd).

## Most Outstanding Player

A Most Outstanding Player has been selected every year of the NCAA tournament. Winners who did not play for the tournament champion are listed in **bold** type. The 1939 and 1951 winners are unofficial and not recognized by the NCAA. Statistics listed are for Final Four games only.

**Multiple winners:** Lew Alcindor (3); Alex Groza, Bob Kurland, Jerry Lucas and Bill Walton (2).

| Year | | Gm | FGM | Pct | 3PTM | 3PTA | FTM | Pct | Reb | Ast | Blk | Stl | PPG |
|------|---|----|-----|-----|------|------|-----|-----|-----|-----|-----|-----|-----|
| 1939 | **Jimmy Hull**, Ohio St. | 2 | 15 | — | — | — | 10 | .833 | — | — | — | — | 20.0 |
| 1940 | Marv Huffman, Indiana | 2 | 7 | — | — | — | 4 | — | — | — | — | — | 9.0 |
| 1941 | John Kotz, Wisconsin | 2 | 8 | — | — | — | 6 | — | — | — | — | — | 11.0 |
| 1942 | Howie Dallmar, Stanford | 2 | 8 | — | — | — | 4 | .667 | — | — | — | — | 10.0 |
| 1943 | Kenny Sailors, Wyoming | 2 | 10 | — | — | — | 8 | .727 | — | — | — | — | 14.0 |
| 1944 | Arnie Ferrin, Utah | 2 | 11 | — | — | — | 6 | — | — | — | — | — | 14.0 |
| 1945 | Bob Kurland, Okla. A&M | 2 | 16 | — | — | — | 5 | — | — | — | — | — | 18.5 |
| 1946 | Bob Kurland, Okla. A&M | 2 | 21 | — | — | — | 10 | .667 | — | — | — | — | 26.0 |
| 1947 | George Kaftan, Holy Cross | 2 | 18 | — | — | — | 12 | .706 | — | — | — | — | 24.0 |
| 1948 | Alex Groza, Kentucky | 2 | 16 | — | — | — | 5 | — | — | — | — | — | 18.5 |
| 1949 | Alex Groza, Kentucky | 2 | 19 | — | — | — | 14 | — | — | — | — | — | 26.0 |
| 1950 | Irwin Dambrot, CCNY | 2 | 12 | .429 | — | — | 4 | .500 | — | — | — | — | 14.0 |
| 1951 | Bill Spivey, Kentucky | 2 | 20 | .400 | — | — | 10 | .625 | 37 | — | — | — | 25.0 |
| 1952 | Clyde Lovellette, Kansas | 2 | 24 | — | — | — | 18 | — | — | — | — | — | 33.0 |
| 1953 | **B.H. Born**, Kansas | 2 | 17 | — | — | — | 17 | — | — | — | — | — | 25.5 |
| 1954 | Tom Gola, La Salle | 2 | 12 | — | — | — | 14 | — | — | — | — | — | 19.0 |
| 1955 | Bill Russell, San Francisco | 2 | 19 | — | — | — | 9 | — | — | — | — | — | 23.5 |
| 1956 | **Hal Lear**, Temple | 2 | 32 | — | — | — | 16 | — | — | — | — | — | 40.0 |
| 1957 | **Wilt Chamberlain**, Kansas | 2 | 18 | .514 | — | — | 19 | .704 | 25 | — | — | — | 32.5 |
| 1958 | **Elgin Baylor**, Seattle | 2 | 18 | .340 | — | — | 12 | .750 | 41 | — | — | — | 24.0 |
| 1959 | **Jerry West**, West Virginia | 2 | 22 | .667 | — | — | 22 | .688 | 25 | — | — | — | 33.0 |
| 1960 | Jerry Lucas, Ohio St. | 2 | 16 | .667 | — | — | 3 | 1.000 | 23 | — | — | — | 17.5 |
| 1961 | **Jerry Lucas**, Ohio St. | 2 | 20 | .714 | — | — | 16 | .941 | 25 | — | — | — | 28.0 |
| 1962 | Paul Hogue, Cincinnati | 2 | 23 | .639 | — | — | 12 | .632 | 38 | — | — | — | 29.0 |
| 1963 | **Art Heyman**, Duke | 2 | 18 | .409 | — | — | 15 | .682 | 19 | — | — | — | 25.5 |
| 1964 | Walt Hazzard, UCLA | 2 | 11 | .550 | — | — | 8 | .667 | 10 | — | — | — | 15.0 |
| 1965 | **Bill Bradley**, Princeton | 2 | 34 | .630 | — | — | 19 | .950 | 24 | — | — | — | 43.5 |
| 1966 | **Jerry Chambers**, Utah | 2 | 25 | .532 | — | — | 20 | .833 | 35 | — | — | — | 35.0 |
| 1967 | Lew Alcindor, UCLA | 2 | 14 | .609 | — | — | 11 | .458 | 38 | — | — | — | 19.5 |
| 1968 | Lew Alcindor, UCLA | 2 | 22 | .629 | — | — | 9 | .900 | 34 | — | — | — | 26.5 |
| 1969 | Lew Alcindor, UCLA | 2 | 23 | .676 | — | — | 16 | .640 | 41 | — | — | — | 31.0 |
| 1970 | Sidney Wicks, UCLA | 2 | 15 | .714 | — | — | 9 | .600 | 34 | — | — | — | 19.5 |
| 1971 | **Howard Porter**, Villanova | 2 | 20 | .488 | — | — | 7 | .778 | 24 | — | — | — | 23.5 |
| 1972 | Bill Walton, UCLA | 2 | 20 | .690 | — | — | 17 | .739 | 41 | — | — | — | 28.5 |
| 1973 | Bill Walton, UCLA | 2 | 28 | .824 | — | — | 2 | .400 | 30 | — | — | — | 29.0 |
| 1974 | David Thompson, N.C. State | 2 | 19 | .514 | — | — | 11 | .786 | 17 | — | — | — | 24.5 |
| 1975 | Richard Washington, UCLA | 2 | 23 | .548 | — | — | 8 | .727 | 20 | — | — | — | 27.0 |
| 1976 | Kent Benson, Indiana | 2 | 17 | .500 | — | — | 7 | .636 | 18 | — | — | — | 20.5 |
| 1977 | Butch Lee, Marquette | 2 | 11 | .344 | — | — | 8 | 1.000 | 6 | 2 | 1 | 1 | 15.0 |
| 1978 | Jack Givens, Kentucky | 2 | 28 | .651 | — | — | 8 | .667 | 17 | 4 | 1 | 3 | 32.0 |
| 1979 | Magic Johnson, Michigan St. | 2 | 17 | .680 | — | — | 19 | .864 | 17 | 3 | 0 | 2 | 26.5 |
| 1980 | Darrell Griffith, Louisville | 2 | 23 | .622 | — | — | 11 | .688 | 7 | 15 | 0 | 2 | 28.5 |
| 1981 | Isiah Thomas, Indiana | 2 | 14 | .560 | — | — | 9 | .818 | 4 | 9 | 3 | 4 | 18.5 |
| 1982 | James Worthy, N. Carolina | 2 | 20 | .741 | — | — | 2 | .286 | 8 | 9 | 0 | 4 | 21.0 |
| 1983 | **Akeem Olajuwon**, Houston | 2 | 16 | .552 | — | — | 9 | .643 | 40 | 3 | 2 | 5 | 20.5 |
| 1984 | Patrick Ewing, Georgetown | 2 | 8 | .571 | — | — | 2 | 1.000 | 18 | 1 | 15 | 1 | 9.0 |
| 1985 | Ed Pinckney, Villanova | 2 | 8 | .571 | — | — | 12 | .750 | 15 | 6 | 3 | 0 | 14.0 |
| 1986 | Pervis Ellison, Louisville | 2 | 15 | .600 | — | — | 6 | .750 | 24 | 2 | 3 | 1 | 18.0 |
| 1987 | Keith Smart, Indiana | 2 | 14 | .636 | — | — | 7 | .778 | 7 | 7 | 0 | 2 | 17.5 |
| 1988 | Danny Manning, Kansas | 2 | 25 | .556 | 0 | 1 | 6 | .667 | 17 | 4 | 8 | 9 | 28.0 |
| 1989 | Glen Rice, Michigan | 2 | 24 | .490 | 7 | 16 | 4 | 1.000 | 16 | 1 | 0 | 3 | 29.5 |
| 1990 | Anderson Hunt, UNLV | 2 | 19 | .613 | 9 | 16 | 2 | .500 | 4 | 9 | 1 | 1 | 24.5 |
| 1991 | Christian Laettner, Duke | 2 | 12 | .545 | 1 | 1 | 21 | .913 | 17 | 2 | 1 | 2 | 23.0 |
| 1992 | Bobby Hurley, Duke | 2 | 10 | .417 | 7 | 12 | 8 | .800 | 3 | 11 | 0 | 3 | 17.5 |
| 1993 | Donald Williams, N. Carolina | 2 | 15 | .652 | 10 | 14 | 10 | 1.000 | 4 | 1 | 0 | 2 | 25.0 |
| 1994 | Corliss Williamson, Arkansas | 2 | 21 | .500 | 0 | 0 | 10 | .714 | 21 | 8 | 3 | 4 | 26.0 |
| 1995 | Ed O'Bannon, UCLA | 2 | 16 | .457 | 3 | 8 | 10 | .769 | 25 | 3 | 1 | 7 | 22.5 |
| 1996 | Tony Delk, Kentucky | 2 | 15 | .417 | 8 | 16 | 6 | .546 | 9 | 2 | 3 | 2 | 22.0 |
| 1997 | Miles Simon, Arizona | 2 | 17 | .459 | 3 | 10 | 17 | .773 | 8 | 6 | 0 | 1 | 27.0 |
| 1998 | Jeff Sheppard, Kentucky | 2 | 16 | .552 | 4 | 10 | 7 | .778 | 10 | 7 | 0 | 4 | 21.5 |
| 1999 | Richard Hamilton, Connecticut | 2 | 20 | .513 | 3 | 7 | 8 | .727 | 12 | 4 | 1 | 2 | 25.5 |
| 2000 | Mateen Cleaves, Michigan St. | 2 | 8 | .444 | 3 | 4 | 10 | .833 | 6 | 5 | 0 | 2 | 14.5 |
| 2001 | Shane Battier, Duke | 2 | 13 | .464 | 5 | 12 | 12 | .706 | 19 | 8 | 6 | 2 | 21.5 |
| 2002 | Juan Dixon, Maryland | 2 | 16 | .593 | 7 | 15 | 12 | .800 | 8 | 5 | 0 | 7 | 25.5 |
| 2003 | Carmelo Anthony, Syracuse | 2 | 19 | .543 | 6 | 9 | 9 | .818 | 24 | 8 | 0 | 4 | 26.5 |
| 2004 | Emeka Okafor, Connecticut | 2 | 17 | .654 | 0 | 0 | 8 | .533 | 22 | 2 | 4 | 1 | 21.0 |
| 2005 | Sean May, North Carolina | 2 | 19 | .655 | 0 | 0 | 10 | .714 | 17 | 5 | 2 | 1 | 24.0 |

## Final Four All-Decade Teams

To celebrate the 50th anniversary of the NCAA tournament in 1989, five All-Decade teams were selected by a blue ribbon panel of coaches and administrators. An All-Time Final Four team was also chosen. Selections were actually made prior to the 1988 tournament.

**Selection panel:** Vic Bubas, Denny Crum, Wayne Duke, Dave Gavitt, Joe B. Hall, Jud Heathcote, Hank Iba, Pete Newell, Dean Smith, John Thompson and John Wooden.

### All-Time Team

| | Years |
|---|---|
| Lew Alcindor, UCLA | 1967-69 |
| Larry Bird, Indiana St. | 1979 |
| Wilt Chamberlain, Kansas | 1957 |
| Magic Johnson, Mich. St | 1979 |
| Michael Jordan, N. Carolina | 1982 |

### All-1950s

| | Years |
|---|---|
| Elgin Baylor, Seattle | 1958 |
| Wilt Chamberlain, Kansas | 1957 |
| Tom Gola, La Salle | 1954 |
| K.C. Jones, San Francisco | 1955 |
| Clyde Lovellette, Kansas | 1952 |
| Oscar Robertson, Cinn. | 1959-60 |
| Guy Rodgers, Temple | 1958 |
| Lennie Rosenbluth, N. Carolina | 1957 |
| Bill Russell, San Francisco | 1955-56 |
| Jerry West, West Virginia | 1959 |

### All-1970s

| | Years |
|---|---|
| Kent Benson, Indiana | 1976 |
| Larry Bird, Indiana St | 1979 |
| Jack Givens, Kentucky | 1978 |
| Magic Johnson, Mich. St | 1979 |
| Marques Johnson, UCLA | 1975-76 |
| Scott May, Indiana | 1976 |
| David Thompson, N.C. State | 1974 |
| Bill Walton, UCLA | 1972-74 |
| Sidney Wicks, UCLA | 1969-71 |
| Keith Wilkes, UCLA | 1972-74 |

### All-1940s

| | Years |
|---|---|
| Ralph Beard, Kentucky | 1948-49 |
| Howie Dallmar, Stanford | 1942 |
| Dwight Eddleman, Illinois | 1949 |
| Arnie Ferrin, Utah | 1944 |
| Alex Groza, Kentucky | 1948-49 |
| George Kaftan, Holy Cross | 1947 |
| Bob Kurland, Okla. A&M | 1945-46 |
| Jim Pollard, Stanford | 1942 |
| Kenny Sailors, Wyoming | 1943 |
| Gerry Tucker, Oklahoma | 1947 |

### All-1960s

| | Years |
|---|---|
| Lew Alcindor, UCLA | 1967-69 |
| Bill Bradley, Princeton | 1965 |
| Gail Goodrich, UCLA | 1964-65 |
| John Havlicek, Ohio St | 1961-62 |
| Elvin Hayes, Houston | 1967 |
| Walt Hazzard, UCLA | 1964 |
| Jerry Lucas, Ohio St | 1960-61 |
| Jeff Mullins, Duke | 1964 |
| Cazzie Russell, Michigan | 1965 |
| Charlie Scott, N. Carolina | 1968-69 |

### All-1980s

| | Years |
|---|---|
| Steve Alford, Indiana | 1987 |
| Johnny Dawkins, Duke | 1986 |
| Patrick Ewing, Georgetown | 1982-84 |
| Darrell Griffith, Louisville | 1980 |
| Michael Jordan, N. Carolina | 1982 |
| Rodney McCray, Louisville | 1980 |
| Akeem Olajuwon, Houston | 1983-84 |
| Ed Pinckney, Villanova | 1985 |
| Isiah Thomas, Indiana | 1981 |
| James Worthy, N. Carolina | 1982 |

**Note:** Lew Alcindor later changed his name to Kareem Abdul-Jabbar; Keith Wilkes later changed his first name to Jamaal; and Akeem Olajuwon later changed the spelling of his first name to Hakeem.

## Seeds at the Final Four

NCAA champions in **bold** type.

| Year | Seeds (Total) | Teams |
|---|---|---|
| 1979 | 1,2,2,9 (14) | Indiana St., **Mich. St.**, DePaul, Penn. |
| 1980 | 2,5,6,8 (21) | **Louisville**, Iowa, Purdue, UCLA |
| 1981 | 1,1,2,3 (7) | Virginia, LSU, N. Carolina, **Indiana** |
| 1982 | 1,1,3,6 (11) | **N. Carolina**, Georgetown, Louisville, Houston |
| 1983 | 1,1,4,6 (12) | Houston, Louisville, Georgia, **N.C. State** |
| 1984 | 1,1,2,7 (11) | Kentucky, **Georgetown**, Houston, Virginia |
| 1985 | 1,1,2,8 (12) | St. John's, Georgetown, Memphis, **Villanova** |
| 1986 | 1,1,2,11 (15) | Duke, Kansas, **Louisville**, LSU |
| 1987 | 1,1,2,6 (10) | UNLV, **Indiana**, Syracuse, Providence |
| 1988 | 1,1,2,6 (10) | Arizona, Oklahoma, Duke, **Kansas** |
| 1989 | 1,2,3,3 (9) | Illinois, Duke, Seton Hall, **Michigan** |
| 1990 | 1,3,4,4 (12) | **UNLV**, Duke, Ga. Tech, Arkansas |
| 1991 | 1,2,2,3 (7) | UNLV, N. Carolina, **Duke**, Kansas |
| 1992 | 1,2,4,6 (13) | **Duke**, Indiana, Cincinnati, Michigan |
| 1993 | 1,1,1,2 (5) | **N. Carolina**, Kentucky, Michigan, Kansas |
| 1994 | 1,2,2,3 (8) | **Arkansas**, Arizona, Duke, Florida |
| 1995 | 1,2,2,4 (9) | **UCLA**, Arkansas, N. Carolina, Okla. St. |
| 1996 | 1,1,4,5 (11) | **Kentucky**, UMass, Syracuse, Miss. St. |
| 1997 | 1,1,1,4 (7) | Kentucky, N. Carolina, Minnesota, **Arizona** |
| 1998 | 1,2,3,3 (9) | N. Carolina, **Kentucky**, Stanford, Utah |
| 1999 | 1,1,1,4 (7) | **Connecticut**, Duke, Mich. St., Ohio St. |
| 2000 | 1,5,8,8 (22) | **Michigan St.**, Florida, Wisconsin, N. Carolina |
| 2001 | 1,1,2,3 (7) | **Duke**, Mich. St., Arizona, Maryland |
| 2002 | 1,1,2,5 (9) | **Maryland**, Kansas, Oklahoma, Indiana |
| 2003 | 1,2,3,3 (9) | Texas, Kansas, **Syracuse**, Marquette |
| 2004 | 1,2,2,3 (8) | Duke, **Connecticut**, Oklahoma St., Georgia Tech |
| 2005 | 1,1,4,5 (11) | **N. Carolina**, Illinois, Louisville, Mich. St. |

**Note:** teams were not seeded before 1979.

## All-Time Seeds Records

All-time records of NCAA tournament seeds since tourney began seeding teams in 1979. Records are through the 2005 NCAA Tournament. Note that 1st refers to championships. 2nd refers to runners-up and FF refers to Final Four appearances not including 1st and 2nd place finishes.

| Seed | W | L | Pct. | 1st | 2nd | FF |
|---|---|---|---|---|---|---|
| 1 | 330 | 95 | .776 | 14 | 10 | 21 |
| 2 | 239 | 102 | .701 | 6 | 6 | 11 |
| 3 | 172 | 105 | .621 | 3 | 5 | 5 |
| 4 | 149 | 107 | .582 | 1 | 1 | 7 |
| 5 | 128 | 109 | .540 | 0 | 2 | 3 |
| 6 | 146 | 106 | .579 | 2 | 1 | 3 |
| 7 | 91 | 108 | .457 | 0 | 0 | 1 |
| 8 | 82 | 107 | .434 | 1 | 1 | 2 |
| 9 | 63 | 109 | .366 | 0 | 0 | 1 |
| 10 | 74 | 108 | .407 | 0 | 0 | 0 |
| 11 | 44 | 104 | .297 | 0 | 0 | 1 |
| 12 | 45 | 104 | .302 | 0 | 0 | 0 |
| 13 | 20 | 84 | .192 | 0 | 0 | 0 |
| 14 | 16 | 84 | .160 | 0 | 0 | 0 |
| 15 | 4 | 84 | .045 | 0 | 0 | 0 |
| 16 | 0 | 84 | .000 | 0 | 0 | 0 |

## Collegiate Commissioners Association Tournament

The Collegiate Commissioners Association staged an eight-team tournament for teams that didn't make the NCAA tournament in 1974 and '75.

**Most Valuable Players:** 1974–Kent Benson, Indiana: 1975–Bob Elliot, Arizona.

| Year | Winner | Score | Loser | Site |
|---|---|---|---|---|
| 1974 | Indiana | 85-60 | USC | St. Louis |
| 1975 | Drake | 83-76 | Arizona | Louisville |

## NCAA Tournament Appearances

| App | | W-L | F4 | Championships | App | | W-L | F4 | Championships |
|---|---|---|---|---|---|---|---|---|---|
| 47 | Kentucky | .98-42 | 13 | 7 (1948-49, 51, 58, 78, 96, 98) | 23 | Oklahoma | .31-23 | 4 | None |
| 39 | UCLA | .85-32 | 15 | 11 (1964-65,67-73,75,95) | 23 | Texas | .25-26 | 3 | None |
| 37 | N. Carolina | .88-35 | 16 | 4 (1957,82,93, 2005) | 22 | Kansas St. | .27-26 | 4 | None |
| 33 | Kansas | .68-33 | 11 | 2 (1952,88) | 22 | Georgetown | .38-21 | 4 | 1 (1984) |
| 32 | Indiana | .58-27 | 8 | 5 (1940,53,76,81,87) | 22 | Ohio St. | .37-21 | 9 | 1 (1960) |
| 32 | Louisville | .53-34 | 8 | 2 (1980,86) | 22 | DePaul | .21-25 | 2 | None |
| 30 | Syracuse | .48-30 | 4 | 1 (2003) | 22 | Oklahoma St. | .37-21 | 6 | 2 (1945-46) |
| 29 | Duke | .83-26 | 14 | 3 (1991-92, 2001) | 21 | Missouri | .18-21 | 0 | None |
| 27 | St. John's | .27-29 | 2 | None | 21 | BYU | .11-24 | 0 | None |
| 27 | Notre Dame | .29-31 | 1 | None | 21 | Maryland | .35-20 | 2 | 1 (2002) |
| 26 | Arkansas | .39-26 | 6 | 1 (1994) | 21 | Iowa | .27-23 | 3 | None |
| 26 | Connecticut | .39-25 | 2 | 2 (1999, 2004) | 21 | Pennsylvania | .13-23 | 1 | None |
| 26 | Villanova | .39-26 | 3 | 1 (1985) | 21 | N.C. State | .31-20 | 3 | 2 (1974,83) |
| 26 | Utah | .35-29 | 4 | 1 (1944) | 20 | Michigan | .41-19 | 6 | 1 (1989) |
| 25 | Temple | .31-25 | 2 | None | 20 | Purdue | .27-20 | 2 | None |
| 25 | Illinois | .37-25 | 5 | None | 20 | Wake Forest | .27-20 | 1 | None |
| 24 | Arizona | .40-23 | 3 | 1 (1997) | 19 | West Virginia | .16-19 | 1 | None |
| 24 | Cincinnati | .40-23 | 6 | 2 (1961-62) | 19 | Western Ky. | .15-20 | 1 | None |
| 23 | Marquette | .32-24 | 3 | 1 (1977) | 19 | Michigan St. | .40-18 | 7 | 1 (1989) |
| 23 | Princeton | .13-27 | 1 | None | | | | | |

**Note:** Although all NCAA tournament appearances are included above, the NCAA has officially voided the records of Villanova (4-1) and Western Ky. (4-1) in 1971; UCLA (5-1) in 1980 and again (0-1) in 1999; Oregon St. (2-3) from 1980-82; DePaul (6-4) from 1986-89; N.C. State (0-2) from 1987-88; Kentucky (2-1) and Maryland (1-1) in 1988; Missouri (3-1) in 1994; Connecticut (2-1) and Purdue (1-1) in 1996; Arizona (0-1) in 1999.

## All-Time NCAA Division I Tournament Leaders

Through 2005; minimum of six games; **Last** column indicates final year played.

### CAREER

#### Scoring

| | Points | Yrs | Last | Gm | Pts |
|---|---|---|---|---|---|
| 1 | Christian Laettner, Duke | 4 | 1992 | 23 | 407 |
| 2 | Elvin Hayes, Houston | 3 | 1968 | 13 | 358 |
| 3 | Danny Manning, Kansas | 4 | 1988 | 16 | 328 |
| 4 | Oscar Robertson, Cincinnati | 3 | 1960 | 10 | 324 |
| 5 | Glen Rice, Michigan | 4 | 1989 | 13 | 308 |
| 6 | Lew Alcindor, UCLA | 3 | 1969 | 12 | 304 |
| 7 | Bill Bradley, Princeton | 3 | 1965 | 9 | 303 |
| | Corliss Williamson, Arkansas | 3 | 1995 | 15 | 303 |
| 9 | Juan Dixon, Maryland | 4 | 2002 | 16 | 294 |
| 10 | Austin Carr, Notre Dame | 3 | 1971 | 7 | 289 |

| | Average | Yrs | Last | Pts | Avg |
|---|---|---|---|---|---|
| 1 | Austin Carr, Notre Dame | 3 | 1971 | 289 | 41.3 |
| 2 | Bill Bradley, Princeton | 3 | 1965 | 303 | 33.7 |
| 3 | Oscar Robertson, Cincinnati | 3 | 1960 | 324 | 32.4 |
| 4 | Jerry West, West Virginia | 3 | 1960 | 275 | 30.6 |
| 5 | Bob Pettit, LSU | 2 | 1954 | 183 | 30.5 |
| 6 | Dan Issel, Kentucky | 3 | 1970 | 176 | 29.3 |
| | Jim McDaniels, Western Ky | 2 | 1971 | 176 | 29.3 |
| 8 | Dwight Lamar, SW Louisiana | 2 | 1973 | 175 | 29.2 |
| 9 | Bo Kimble, Loyola-CA | 3 | 1990 | 204 | 29.1 |
| 10 | David Robinson, Navy | 3 | 1987 | 200 | 28.6 |

#### 3-Pt Field Goals

| | Total | Yrs | Last | Gm | No |
|---|---|---|---|---|---|
| 1 | Bobby Hurley, Duke | 4 | 1993 | 20 | 42 |
| 2 | Tony Delk, Kentucky | 4 | 1996 | 17 | 40 |
| 3 | Jeff Fryer, Loyola-CA | 3 | 1990 | 7 | 38 |
| | Donald Williams, North Carolina | 4 | 1995 | 15 | 38 |
| | Juan Dixon, Maryland | 4 | 2002 | 16 | 38 |

#### Rebounds

| | Total | Yrs | Last | Gm | No |
|---|---|---|---|---|---|
| 1 | Elvin Hayes, Houston | 3 | 1968 | 13 | 222 |
| 2 | Lew Alcindor, UCLA | 3 | 1969 | 12 | 201 |
| 3 | Jerry Lucas, Ohio St. | 3 | 1962 | 12 | 197 |
| 4 | Nick Collison, Kansas | 4 | 2003 | 16 | 181 |
| 5 | Bill Walton, UCLA | 3 | 1974 | 12 | 176 |
| 6 | Christian Laettner, Duke | 4 | 1992 | 23 | 169 |
| 7 | Tim Duncan, Wake Forest | 4 | 1997 | 11 | 165 |
| 8 | Paul Hogue, Cincinnati | 3 | 1962 | 12 | 160 |
| 9 | Sam Lacey, New Mexico St. | 3 | 1970 | 11 | 157 |
| 10 | Derrick Coleman, Syracuse | 4 | 1990 | 14 | 155 |

| | Average | Yrs | Last | Reb | Avg |
|---|---|---|---|---|---|
| 1 | Johnny Green, Michigan St. | 2 | 1959 | 118 | 19.7 |
| 2 | Artis Gilmore, Jacksonville | 2 | 1971 | 115 | 19.2 |
| 3 | Paul Silas, Creighton | 3 | 1964 | 111 | 18.5 |
| 4 | Len Chappell, Wake Forest | 2 | 1962 | 137 | 17.1 |
| 5 | Elvin Hayes, Houston | 3 | 1968 | 222 | 17.1 |
| 6 | Lew Alcindor, UCLA | 3 | 1969 | 201 | 16.8 |
| 7 | Jerry Lucas, Ohio St. | 3 | 1962 | 197 | 16.4 |
| 8 | Tim Duncan, Wake Forest | 4 | 1997 | 165 | 15.0 |
| 9 | Bill Walton, UCLA | 3 | 1974 | 176 | 14.7 |
| 10 | Sam Lacey, New Mexico St. | 3 | 1970 | 157 | 14.3 |

#### Assists

| | Total | Yrs | Last | Gm | No |
|---|---|---|---|---|---|
| 1 | Bobby Hurley, Duke | 4 | 1993 | 20 | 145 |
| 2 | Ed Cota, N. Caroina | 4 | 2000 | 16 | 118 |
| | Sherman Douglas, Syracuse | 4 | 1989 | 14 | 106 |
| | Greg Anthony, UNLV | 3 | 1991 | 15 | 100 |
| | Aaron Miles, Kansas | 3 | 2004 | 15 | 100 |

### SINGLE TOURNAMENT

#### Scoring

| | Points | Year | Gm | Pts |
|---|---|---|---|---|
| 1 | Glen Rice, Michigan | 1989 | 6 | 184 |
| 2 | Bill Bradley, Princeton | 1965 | 5 | 177 |
| 3 | Elvin Hayes, Houston | 1968 | 5 | 167 |
| 4 | Danny Manning, Kansas | 1988 | 6 | 163 |
| 5 | Hal Lear, Temple | 1956 | 5 | 160 |
| | Jerry West, West Virginia | 1959 | 5 | 160 |

| | Average | Year | Gm | Pts | Avg |
|---|---|---|---|---|---|
| 1 | Austin Carr, Notre Dame | 1970 | 3 | 158 | 52.7 |
| 2 | Austin Carr, Notre Dame | 1971 | 3 | 125 | 41.7 |
| 3 | Jerry Chambers, Utah | 1966 | 4 | 143 | 35.8 |
| | Bo Kimble, Loyola-CA | 1990 | 4 | 143 | 35.8 |
| 5 | Bill Bradley, Princeton | 1965 | 5 | 177 | 35.4 |
| 6 | Clyde Lovellette, Kansas | 1952 | 4 | 141 | 35.3 |

### Rebounds

| | Total | Year | Gm | No | Avg |
|---|---|---|---|---|---|
| 1 | Elvin Hayes, Houston | 1968 | 5 | **97** | 19.4 |
| 2 | Artis Gilmore, Jacksonville | 1970 | 5 | **93** | 18.6 |
| 3 | Elgin Baylor, Seattle | 1958 | 5 | **91** | 18.2 |
| 4 | Sam Lacey, New Mexico St. | 1970 | 5 | **90** | 18.0 |
| 5 | Clarence Glover, Western Ky | 1971 | 5 | **89** | 17.8 |
| 6 | Len Chappell, Wake Forest | 1962 | 5 | **86** | 17.2 |

### Assists

| | Total | Year | Gm | No | Avg |
|---|---|---|---|---|---|
| 1 | Mark Wade, UNLV | 1987 | 5 | **61** | 12.2 |
| 2 | Rumeal Robinson, Michigan | 1989 | 6 | **56** | 9.3 |
| 3 | T.J. Ford, Texas | 2003 | 5 | **51** | 10.2 |
| 4 | Sherman Douglas, Syracuse | 1987 | 6 | **49** | 8.2 |
| 5 | Bobby Hurley, Duke | 1992 | 6 | **47** | 7.8 |
| 6 | Lazarus Sims, Syracuse | 1996 | 6 | **46** | 7.7 |

## SINGLE GAME

### Scoring

| | Points | Year | Pts |
|---|---|---|---|
| 1 | Austin Carr, Notre Dame vs Ohio Univ | 1970 | 61 |
| 2 | Bill Bradley, Princeton vs Wichita St. | 1965 | 58 |
| 3 | Oscar Robertson, Cincinnati vs Arkansas | 1958 | 56 |
| 4 | Austin Carr, Notre Dame vs Kentucky | 1970 | 52 |
| | Austin Carr, Notre Dame vs TCU | 1971 | 52 |
| 6 | David Robinson, Navy vs Michigan | 1987 | 50 |
| 7 | Elvin Hayes, Houston vs Loyola-IL | 1968 | 49 |
| 8 | Hal Lear, Temple vs SMU | 1956 | 48 |
| 9 | Austin Carr, Notre Dame vs Houston | 1971 | 47 |
| 10 | Dave Corzine, DePaul vs Louisville | 1978 | 46 |
| 11 | Bob Houbregs, Washington vs Seattle | 1953 | 45 |
| | Austin Carr, Notre Dame vs Iowa | 1970 | 45 |
| | Bo Kimble, Loyola-CA vs New Mexico St. | 1990 | 45 |
| 14 | Seven players tied with 44 each. | | |

### Rebounds

| | Total | Year | No |
|---|---|---|---|
| 1 | Fred Cohen, Temple vs UConn | 1956 | 34 |
| 2 | Nate Thurmond, Bowl. Green vs Miss. St. | 1963 | 31 |
| 3 | Jerry Lucas, Ohio St. vs Kentucky | 1961 | 30 |
| 4 | Toby Kimball, UConn vs St. Joseph's-PA | 1965 | 29 |
| 5 | Elvin Hayes, Houston vs Pacific | 1966 | 28 |
| 6 | Four players tied with 27 each. | | |

### Assists

| | Total | Year | No |
|---|---|---|---|
| 1 | Mark Wade, UNLV vs Indiana | 1987 | 18 |
| 2 | Sam Crawford, N. Mexico St. vs Nebraska | 1993 | 16 |
| 3 | Kenny Patterson, DePaul vs Syracuse | 1985 | 15 |
| | Keith Smart, Indiana vs Auburn | 1987 | 15 |
| | Pepe Sanchez, Temple vs. Lafayette | 2000 | 15 |

## SINGLE FINAL FOUR GAME

Letters in the **Year** column indicate the following: C for Consolation Game, F for Final and S for Semifinal.

### Scoring

| | Points | Year | Pts |
|---|---|---|---|
| 1 | Bill Bradley, Princeton vs Wichita St | 1965-C | 58 |
| 2 | Hal Lear, Temple vs SMU | 1956-C | 48 |
| 3 | Bill Walton, UCLA vs Memphis St | 1973-F | 44 |
| 4 | Bob Houbregs, Washington vs LSU | 1953-C | 42 |
| | Jack Egan, St. Joseph's-PA vs Utah | 1961-C | 42* |
| | Gail Goodrich, UCLA vs Michigan | 1965-C | 42 |
| 7 | Jack Givens, Kentucky vs Duke | 1978-F | 41 |
| 8 | Oscar Robertson, Cincinnati vs L'ville | 1959-C | 39 |
| | Al Wood, N. Carolina vs Virginia | 1981-S | 39 |
| 10 | Jerry West, West Va. vs Louisville | 1959-S | 38 |
| | Jerry Chambers, Utah vs Texas Western | 1966-S | 38 |
| | Freddie Banks, UNLV vs Indiana | 1987-S | 38 |
| | *Four overtimes. | | |

### 3-Pt Field Goals

| | Total | Year | No |
|---|---|---|---|
| 1 | Freddie Banks, UNLV vs. Indiana | 1987-S | 10 |
| 2 | Four players tied with 7 each. | | |

### Rebounds

| | Total | Year | No |
|---|---|---|---|
| 1 | Bill Russell, San Francisco vs Iowa | 1956-F | 27 |
| 2 | Elvin Hayes, Houston vs UCLA | 1967-S | 24 |
| 3 | Bill Russell, San Francisco vs SMU | 1956-S | 23 |
| 4 | Elgin Baylor, Seattle vs Kansas St. | 1958-S | 22 |
| | Tom Sanders, NYU vs Ohio St. | 1960-S | 22 |
| | Larry Kenon, Memphis vs Providence | 1973-S | 22 |
| | Akeem Olajuwon, Houston vs Louisville | 1983-S | 22 |
| 8 | Bill Spivey, Kentucky vs Kansas St. | 1951-C | 21 |
| | Lew Alcindor, UCLA vs Drake | 1969-C | 21 |
| | Artis Gilmore, Jacksonville vs St. Bonav. | 1970-S | 21 |
| | Bill Walton, UCLA vs Louisville | 1972-S | 21 |
| | Nick Collison, Kansas vs Syracuse | 2003-C | 21 |

### Assists

| | Total | Year | No |
|---|---|---|---|
| 1 | Mark Wade, UNLV vs Indiana | 1987-S | 18 |
| 2 | T.J. Ford, Texas vs. Syracuse | 2003-C | 13 |
| 3 | Rumeal Robinson, Michigan vs Illinois | 1989-S | 12 |
| | Edgar Padilla, UMass vs. Ky. | 1996-S | 12 |
| 5 | Michael Jackson, G'town vs St. John's | 1985-S | 11 |
| | Milt Wagner, Louisville vs LSU | 1986-S | 11 |
| | Rumeal Robinson, Mich. vs Seton Hall | 1989-F | 11* |
| | Steve Blake, Maryland vs. Kansas | 2002-S | 11 |
| | *Overtime. | | |

### Blocked Shots

| | Total | Year | No |
|---|---|---|---|
| 1 | Danny Manning, Kansas vs Duke | 1988-S | 6 |
| | Marcus Camby, UMass vs Kentucky | 1996-S | 6 |
| 3 | Six players tied with 4 each. | | |

### Steals

| | Total | Year | No |
|---|---|---|---|
| 1 | Tommy Amaker, Duke vs. Louisville | 1986-C | 7 |
| | Mookie Blaylock, Oklahoma vs. Kansas | 1988-C | 7 |
| 3 | Gilbert Arenas, Arizona vs. Michigan St. | 2001-S | 6 |

### Triple Doubles

| | Total | Year | No |
|---|---|---|---|
| 1 | Oscar Robertson, Cincinnati vs. Louisville | 1959-C | 1 |
| | Magic Johnson, Mich. St. vs. Penn | 1979-S | 1 |

**Note:** Robertson had 39 pts, 17 rebs and 10 asts; Johnson had 29 pts, 10 rebs, 10 asts

## Most Popular Final Four Sites

The NCAA has staged its Men's Division I championship—the Final Two (1939-51) and Final Four (since 1952)—at 33 different arenas and indoor stadiums in 27 different cities. The following facilities have all hosted the event more than twice.

| No | Arena | Years |
|---|---|---|
| 9 | Municipal Auditorium (KC) | 1940-42, 53-55, 57, 61, 64 |
| 7 | Madison Sq. Garden (NYC) | 1943-48, 50 |
| 6 | Freedom Hall (Louisville) | 1958-59, 62-63, 67, 69 |
| 4 | Superdome (New Orleans) | 1982, 87, 93, 2003 |
| 3 | Kingdome (Seattle) | 1984, 89, 95 |
| | RCA Dome (Indianapolis) | 1991, 97, 2000 |

## NIT Championship

The National Invitation Tournament began under the sponsorship of the Metropolitan New York Basketball Writers Association in 1938. The NIT is now administered by the Metropolitan Intercollegiate Basketball Association. All championship games have been played at Madison Square Garden.

**Multiple winners:** St. John's (6); Bradley (4); Michigan (3); BYU, Dayton, Kentucky, LIU-Brooklyn, Minnesota, Providence, Temple, Tulsa, Virginia and Virginia Tech (2).

| Year | Winner | Score | Loser | Year | Winner | Score | Loser |
|------|--------|-------|-------|------|--------|-------|-------|
| 1938 | Temple | 60-36 | Colorado | 1972 | Maryland | 100-69 | Niagara |
| 1939 | LIU-Brooklyn | 44-32 | Loyola-IL | 1973 | Virginia Tech | 92-91 (OT) | Notre Dame |
| 1940 | Colorado | 51-40 | Duquesne | 1974 | Purdue | 97-81 | Utah |
| 1941 | LIU-Brooklyn | 56-42 | Ohio Univ. | 1975 | Princeton | 80-69 | Providence |
| 1942 | West Virginia | 47-45 | Western Ky. | 1976 | Kentucky | 71-67 | NC-Charlotte |
| 1943 | St. John's | 48-27 | Toledo | 1977 | St. Bonaventure | 94-91 | Houston |
| 1944 | St. John's | 47-39 | DePaul | 1978 | Texas | 101-93 | N.C. State |
| 1945 | DePaul | 71-54 | Bowling Green | 1979 | Indiana | 53-52 | Purdue |
| 1946 | Kentucky | 46-45 | Rhode Island | 1980 | Virginia | 58-55 | Minnesota |
| 1947 | Utah | 49-45 | Kentucky | 1981 | Tulsa | 86-84 (OT) | Syracuse |
| 1948 | Saint Louis | 65-52 | NYU | 1982 | Bradley | 67-58 | Purdue |
| 1949 | San Francisco | 48-47 | Loyola-IL | 1983 | Fresno St. | 69-60 | DePaul |
| 1950 | CCNY | 69-61 | Bradley | 1984 | Michigan | 83-63 | Notre Dame |
| 1951 | BYU | 62-43 | Dayton | 1985 | UCLA | 65-62 | Indiana |
| 1952 | La Salle | 75-64 | Dayton | 1986 | Ohio St. | 73-63 | Wyoming |
| 1953 | Seton Hall | 58-46 | St. John's | 1987 | Southern Miss. | 84-80 | La Salle |
| 1954 | Holy Cross | 71-62 | Duquesne | 1988 | Connecticut | 72-67 | Ohio St. |
| 1955 | Duquesne | 70-58 | Dayton | 1989 | St. John's | 73-65 | Saint Louis |
| 1956 | Louisville | 93-80 | Dayton | 1990 | Vanderbilt | 74-72 | Saint Louis |
| 1957 | Bradley | 84-83 | Memphis St. | 1991 | Stanford | 78-72 | Oklahoma |
| 1958 | Xavier-OH | 78-74 (OT) | Dayton | 1992 | Virginia | 81-76 (OT) | Notre Dame |
| 1959 | St. John's | 76-71 (OT) | Bradley | 1993 | Minnesota | 62-61 | Georgetown |
| 1960 | Bradley | 88-72 | Providence | 1994 | Villanova | 80-73 | Vanderbilt |
| 1961 | Providence | 62-59 | Saint Louis | 1995 | Virginia Tech | 65-64 (OT) | Marquette |
| 1962 | Dayton | 73-67 | St. John's | 1996 | Nebraska | 60-56 | St. Joseph's |
| 1963 | Providence | 81-66 | Canisius | 1997 | Michigan | 82-72 | Florida St. |
| 1964 | Bradley | 86-54 | New Mexico | 1998 | Minnesota | 79-72 | Penn St. |
| 1965 | St. John's | 55-51 | Villanova | 1999 | California | 61-60 | Clemson |
| 1966 | BYU | 97-84 | NYU | 2000 | Wake Forest | 71-61 | Notre Dame |
| 1967 | Southern Illinois | 71-56 | Marquette | 2001 | Tulsa | 79-60 | Alabama |
| 1968 | Dayton | 61-48 | Kansas | 2002 | Memphis | 72-62 | South Carolina |
| 1969 | Temple | 89-76 | Boston Coll. | 2003 | St. John's | 70-67 | Georgetown |
| 1970 | Marquette | 65-53 | St. John's | 2004 | Michigan | 62-55 | Rutgers |
| 1971 | North Carolina | 84-66 | Georgia Tech | 2005 | South Carolina | 60-57 | St. Joseph's |

## Most Valuable Player

A Most Valuable Player has been selected every year of the NIT tournament. Winners who did not play for the tournament champion are listed in **bold** type. Note the all-time team listed below was selected by a media panel on Mar. 15, 1997.

**Multiple winners:** None. However, Tom Gola of La Salle is the only player to be named MVP in the NIT (1952) and Most Outstanding Player of the NCAA tournament (1954).

**Year**
1938 Don Shields, Temple
1939 **Bill Lloyd**, St. John's
1940 Bob Doll, Colorado
1941 **Frank Baumholtz**, Ohio U.
1942 Rudy Baric, West Virginia
1943 Harry Boykoff, St. John's
1944 Bill Kotsores, St. John's
1945 George Mikan, DePaul
1946 **Ernie Calverley**, Rhode Island
1947 Vern Gardner, Utah
1948 Ed Macauley, Saint Louis
1949 Don Lofgan, San Francisco
1950 Ed Warner, CCNY
1951 Roland Minson, BYU
1952 Tom Gola, La Salle
& Norm Grekin, La Salle
1953 Walter Dukes, Seton Hall
1954 Togo Palazzi, Holy Cross
1955 **Maurice Stokes**, St. Francis-PA
1956 Charlie Tyra, Louisville
1957 **Win Wilfong**, Memphis St.
1958 Hank Stein, Xavier-OH
1959 Tony Jackson, St. John's
1960 **Lenny Wilkens**, Providence
1961 Vinny Ernst, Providence
1962 Bill Chmielewski, Dayton
1963 Ray Flynn, Providence

**Year**
1964 Lavern Tart, Bradley
1965 Ken McIntyre, St. John's
1966 **Bill Melchionni**, Villanova
1967 Walt Frazier, So. Illinois
1968 Don May, Dayton
1969 **Terry Driscoll**, Boston College
1970 Dean Meminger, Marquette
1971 Bill Chamberlain, N. Carolina
1972 Tom McMillen, Maryland
1973 **John Shumate**, Notre Dame
1974 **Mike Sojourner**, Utah
1975 **Ron Lee**, Oregon
1976 **Cedric Maxwell**, NC-Charlotte
1977 Greg Sanders, St. Bonaventure
1978 Ron Baxter, Texas
& Jim Krivacs, Texas
1979 Clarence Carter, Indiana
& Ray Tolbert, Indiana
1980 Ralph Sampson, Virginia
1981 Greg Stewart, Tulsa
1982 Mitchell Anderson, Bradley
1983 Ron Anderson, Fresno St.
1984 Tim McCormick, Michigan
1985 Reggie Miller, UCLA
1986 Brad Sellers, Ohio St.
1987 Randolph Keys, So. Miss.
1988 Phil Gamble, Connecticut

**Year**
1989 Jayson Williams, St. John's
1990 Scott Draud, Vanderbilt
1991 Adam Keefe, Stanford
1992 Bryant Stith, Virginia
1993 Voshon Lenard, Minnesota
1994 **Doremus Bennerman**, Siena
1995 Shawn Smith, Va. Tech
1996 Erick Strickland, Nebraska
1997 Robert Traylor, Michigan
1998 Kevin Clark, Minnesota
1999 Sean Lampley, California
2000 Robert O'Kelley, Wake Forest
2001 Marcus Hill, Tulsa
2002 Dajuan Wagner, Memphis
2003 Marcus Hatten, St. John's
2004 Daniel Horton, Michigan
2005 Carlos Powell, South Carolina

### All-Time NIT Team

Walt Frazier, S. Illinois
George Mikan, DePaul
Tom Gola, La Salle
Maurice Stokes, St. Francis-PA
Ralph Beard, Kentucky

## All-Time Winningest Division I Teams
### Top 25 Winning Percentage

Division I schools with best winning percentages through 2004-05 season (including tournament games). Years in Division I only; minimum 20 years. NCAA tournament columns indicate years in tournament, record and number of championships.

| | | First Year | Yrs | Games | Won | Lost | Tied | Pct | NCAA Tourney Yrs | W-L | Titles |
|---|---|---|---|---|---|---|---|---|---|---|---|
| 1 | Kentucky | 1903 | 102 | 2488 | 1904 | 583 | 1 | .765 | 47 | 98-42 | 7 |
| 2 | North Carolina | 1911 | 95 | 2541 | 1860 | 681 | 0 | .732 | 37 | 88-35 | 4 |
| 3 | UNLV | 1959 | 47 | 1353 | 963 | 390 | 0 | .712 | 14 | 30-13 | 1 |
| 4 | Kansas | 1899 | 107 | 2617 | 1848 | 769 | 0 | .706 | 33 | 68-33 | 2 |
| 5 | Duke | 1906 | 100 | 2551 | 1764 | 787 | 0 | .691 | 29 | 83-26 | 3 |
| 6 | UCLA | 1920 | 86 | 2249 | 1548 | 701 | 0 | .688 | 39 | 85-32 | 11 |
| 7 | Syracuse | 1901 | 104 | 2416 | 1657 | 759 | 0 | .686 | 30 | 48-30 | 1 |
| 8 | St. John's | 1908 | 98 | 2479 | 1677 | 802 | 0 | .676 | 27 | 27-29 | 0 |
| 9 | Western Kentucky | 1915 | 86 | 2246 | 1502 | 744 | 0 | .669 | 19 | 15-20 | 0 |
| 10 | Utah | 1909 | 97 | 2369 | 1570 | 799 | 0 | .663 | 26 | 35-29 | 1 |
| 11 | Illinois | 1906 | 100 | 2325 | 1520 | 805 | 0 | .654 | 25 | 37-25 | 0 |
| 12 | Louisville | 1912 | 91 | 2277 | 1484 | 793 | 0 | .652 | 32 | 53-34 | 2 |
| 13 | Arizona | 1905 | 100 | 2293 | 1488 | 805 | 0 | .649 | 24 | 40-23 | 1 |
| 14 | Indiana | 1901 | 105 | 2423 | 1570 | 853 | 0 | .648 | 32 | 58-27 | 5 |
| 15 | Arkansas | 1924 | 82 | 2177 | 1407 | 770 | 0 | .646 | 26 | 39-26 | 1 |
| 16 | Chattanooga | 1978 | 28 | 836 | 540 | 296 | 0 | .646 | 9 | 3-9 | 0 |
| 17 | Temple | 1895 | 109 | 2541 | 1639 | 902 | 0 | .645 | 25 | 31-25 | 0 |
| 18 | Notre Dame | 1898 | 100 | 2429 | 1565 | 863 | 1 | .645 | 27 | 29-31 | 0 |
| 19 | Pennsylvania | 1897 | 105 | 2489 | 1592 | 895 | 2 | .640 | 21 | 13-23 | 0 |
| 20 | Weber St. | 1963 | 43 | 12288 | 785 | 443 | 0 | .639 | 13 | 6-14 | 0 |
| 21 | DePaul | 1924 | 82 | 2037 | 1300 | 737 | 0 | .638 | 22 | 21-25 | 0 |
| 22 | Cincinnati | 1902 | 104 | 2340 | 1490 | 850 | 0 | .637 | 24 | 40-23 | 2 |
| 23 | Murray St. | 1926 | 80 | 2079 | 1319 | 761 | 0 | .634 | 12 | 1-12 | 0 |
| 24 | Connecticut | 1901 | 102 | 2204 | 1397 | 807 | 0 | .634 | 26 | 39-25 | 2 |
| 25 | Villanova | 1921 | 85 | 2216 | 1403 | 813 | 0 | .633 | 26 | 39-26 | 1 |

### Top 35 All-Time Victories

Division I schools with most victories through 2004-05 (including postseason tournaments). Minimum 20 years in Division I.

| | | Wins | | | Wins | | | Wins | | | Wins |
|---|---|---|---|---|---|---|---|---|---|---|---|
| 1 | Kentucky | 1904 | | Utah | 1570 | 19 | Arizona | 1488 | 28 | Alabama | 1409 |
| 2 | North Carolina | 1860 | 11 | Notre Dame | 1565 | 20 | Louisville | 1484 | | Ohio St | 1409 |
| 3 | Kansas | 1848 | 12 | UCLA | 1548 | 21 | Purdue | 1482 | 30 | Arkansas | 1407 |
| 4 | Duke | 1764 | 13 | Oregon St. | 1546 | 22 | BYU | 1481 | 31 | Villanova | 1403 |
| 5 | St. John's | 1677 | 14 | Illinois | 1520 | 23 | Texas | 1477 | 32 | St. Joseph's | 1402 |
| 6 | Syracuse | 1657 | 15 | Princeton | 1510 | 24 | N.C. State | 1461 | 33 | Connecticut | 1397 |
| 7 | Temple | 1639 | 16 | Washington | 1503 | 25 | West Virginia | 1452 | 34 | Oklahoma St. | 1396 |
| 8 | Penn | 1592 | 17 | Western Ky. | 1502 | 26 | Bradley | 1451 | 35 | Iowa | 1395 |
| 9 | Indiana | 1570 | 18 | Cincinnati | 1490 | 27 | Oklahoma | 1410 | | | |

### Top 25 Single-Season Victories

Division I schools with most victories in a season through 2004-05 (including postseason tournaments). NCAA champions in **bold** type.

| | | Year W-L | | | Year W-L |
|---|---|---|---|---|---|
| 1 | UNLV | 1987 37-2 | 16 | UNLV | 1991 34-1 |
| | Duke | 1999 37-2 | | **Connecticut** | 1999 34-2 |
| | Illinois | 2005 37-2 | | Duke | 1992 34-2 |
| | Duke | 1986 37-3 | | **Kentucky** | 1996 34-2 |
| 5 | **Kentucky** | 1948 36-3 | | Kansas | 1997 34-2 |
| 6 | Massachusetts | 1996 35-2 | | Kentucky | 1947 34-3 |
| | Georgetown | 1985 35-3 | | **Georgetown** | 1984 34-3 |
| | Arizona | 1988 35-3 | | Arkansas | 1991 34-4 |
| | **Duke** | 2001 35-4 | | **N. Carolina** | 1993 34-4 |
| | Kansas | 1986 35-4 | | N. Carolina | 1998 34-4 |
| | Kansas | 1998 35-4 | | | |
| | **Kentucky** | 1998 35-4 | | | |
| | Oklahoma | 1988 35-4 | | | |
| | **UNLV** | 1990 35-5 | | | |
| | Kentucky | 1997 35-5 | | | |

*NCAA later stripped UMass of its four 1996 tournament victories after learning that center Marcus Camby accepted gifts from an agent.

### Division I Winning Streaks
#### Full Season
(including tournaments)

| No | | Seasons | Broken by | Score |
|---|---|---|---|---|
| 88 | UCLA | 1971-74 | Notre Dame | 71-70 |
| 60 | San Francisco | 1955-57 | Illinois | 62-33 |
| 47 | UCLA | 1966-68 | Houston | 71-69 |
| 45 | UNLV | 1990-91 | Duke | 79-77 |
| 44 | Texas | 1913-17 | Rice | 24-18 |
| 43 | Seton Hall | 1939-41 | LIU-Bklyn | 49-26 |
| 43 | LIU-Brooklyn | 1935-37 | Stanford | 45-31 |
| 41 | UCLA | 1968-69 | USC | 46-44 |
| 39 | Marquette | 1970-71 | Ohio St. | 60-59 |
| 37 | Cincinnati | 1962-63 | Wichita St. | 65-64 |
| 37 | North Carolina | 1957-58 | West Virginia | 75-64 |

#### Home Court

| No | | Seasons | Broken By | Score |
|---|---|---|---|---|
| 129 | Kentucky | 1943-55 | Georgia Tech | 59-58 |
| 99 | St. Bonaventure | 1948-61 | Detroit | 77-70 |
| 98 | UCLA | 1970-76 | Oregon | 65-45 |
| 86 | Cincinnati | 1957-64 | Kansas | 51-47 |
| 81 | Arizona | 1945-51 | Kansas St. | 76-57 |
| 81 | Marquette | 1967-73 | Notre Dame | 71-69 |
| 80 | Lamar | 1978-84 | Louisiana Tech | 68-65 |

## Associated Press Final Polls
### Taken before NCAA, NIT and Collegiate Commissioner's Association (1974-75) tournaments.

The Associated Press introduced its weekly college basketball poll of sportswriters (later, sportswriters and broadcasters) during the 1948-49 season.

Since the NCAA Division I tournament has determined the national champion since 1939, the final AP poll ranks the nation's best teams through the regular season and conference tournaments.

Except for four seasons (see AP Post-Tournament Final Polls), the final AP poll has been released prior to the NCAA and NIT tournaments and has gone from a Top 10 (1949 and 1963-67) to a Top 20 (1950-62 and 1968-89) to a Top 25 (since 1990). Tournament champions are in **bold** type.

### 1949

| | | Before Tourns | Head Coach | Final Record |
|---|---|---|---|---|
| 1 | **Kentucky** | 29-1 | Adolph Rupp | 32-2 |
| 2 | Oklahoma A&M | 21-4 | Hank Iba | 23-5 |
| 3 | Saint Louis | 22-3 | Eddie Hickey | 22-4 |
| 4 | Illinois | 19-3 | Harry Combes | 21-4 |
| 5 | Western Ky. | 25-3 | Ed Diddle | 25-4 |
| 6 | Minnesota | 18-3 | Ozzie Cowles | same |
| 7 | Bradley | 25-6 | Forddy Anderson | 27-8 |
| 8 | **San Francisco** | 21-5 | Pete Newell | 25-5 |
| 9 | Tulane | 24-4 | Cliff Wells | same |
| 10 | Bowling Green | 21-6 | Harold Anderson | 24-7 |

**NCAA Final Four** (at Edmundson Pavilion, Seattle): **Third Place**–Illinois 57, Oregon St. 53. **Championship**–Kentucky 46, Oklahoma A&M 36.

**NIT Final Four** (at Madison Square Garden): **Semifinals**–San Francisco 49, Bowling Green 39; Loyola-IL 55, Bradley 50. **Third Place**–Bowling Green 82, Bradley 77. **Championship**–San Francisco 48, Loyola-IL 47.

### 1950

| | | Before Tourns | Head Coach | Final Record |
|---|---|---|---|---|
| 1 | Bradley | 28-3 | Forddy Anderson | 32-5 |
| 2 | Ohio St. | 21-3 | Tippy Dye | 22-4 |
| 3 | Kentucky | 25-4 | Adolph Rupp | 25-5 |
| 4 | Holy Cross | 27-2 | Buster Sheary | 27-4 |
| 5 | N.C. State | 25-5 | Everett Case | 27-6 |
| 6 | Duquesne | 22-5 | Dudey Moore | 23-6 |
| 7 | UCLA | 24-5 | John Wooden | 24-7 |
| 8 | Western Ky. | 24-5 | Ed Diddle | 25-6 |
| 9 | St. John's | 23-4 | Frank McGuire | 24-5 |
| 10 | La Salle | 20-3 | Ken Loeffler | 21-4 |
| 11 | Villanova | 25-4 | Al Severance | same |
| 12 | San Francisco | 19-6 | Pete Newell | 19-7 |
| 13 | LIU-Brooklyn | 20-4 | Clair Bee | 20-5 |
| 14 | Kansas St. | 17-7 | Jack Gardner | same |
| 15 | Arizona | 26-4 | Fred Enke | 26-5 |
| 16 | Wisconsin | 17-5 | Bud Foster | same |
| 17 | San Jose St. | 21-7 | Walter McPherson | same |
| 18 | Washington St. | 19-13 | Jack Friel | same |
| 19 | Kansas | 14-11 | Phog Allen | same |
| 20 | Indiana | 17-5 | Branch McCracken | same |

**Note:** Unranked **CCNY**, coached by Nat Holman, won both the NCAAs and NIT. The Beavers entered the postseason at 17-5 and had a final record of 24-5.

**NCAA Final Four** (at Madison Square Garden): **Third Place**–N. Carolina St. 53, Baylor 41. **Championship**–CCNY 71, Bradley 68.

**NIT Final Four** (at Madison Square Garden): **Semifinals**–Bradley 83, St. John's 72; CCNY 62, Duquesne 52. **Third Place**–St. John's 69, Duquesne 67 (OT). **Championship**–CCNY 69, Bradley 61.

### 1951

| | | Before Tourns | Head Coach | Final Record |
|---|---|---|---|---|
| 1 | **Kentucky** | 28-2 | Adolph Rupp | 32-2 |
| 2 | Oklahoma A&M | 27-4 | Hank Iba | 29-6 |
| 3 | Columbia | 22-0 | Lou Rossini | 22-1 |
| 4 | Kansas St. | 22-3 | Jack Gardner | 25-4 |
| 5 | Illinois | 19-4 | Harry Combes | 22-5 |
| 6 | Bradley | 32-6 | Forddy Anderson | same |
| 7 | Indiana | 19-3 | Branch McCracken | same |
| 8 | N.C. State | 29-4 | Everett Case | 30-7 |
| 9 | St. John's | 22-3 | Frank McGuire | 26-5 |
| 10 | Saint Louis | 21-7 | Eddie Hickey | 22-8 |
| 11 | **BYU** | 22-8 | Stan Watts | 26-10 |
| 12 | Arizona | 24-4 | Fred Enke | 24-6 |
| 13 | Dayton | 24-4 | Tom Blackburn | 27-5 |
| 14 | Toledo | 23-8 | Jerry Bush | same |
| 15 | Washington | 22-5 | Tippy Dye | 24-6 |
| 16 | Murray St. | 21-6 | Harlan Hodges | same |
| 17 | Cincinnati | 18-3 | John Wiethe | 18-4 |
| 18 | Siena | 19-8 | Dan Cunha | same |
| 19 | USC | 21-6 | Forrest Twogood | same |
| 20 | Villanova | 25-6 | Al Severance | 25-7 |

**NCAA Final Four** (at Williams Arena, Minneapolis): **Third Place**–Illinois 61, Oklahoma St. 46. **Championship**–Kentucky 68, Kansas St. 58.

**NIT Final Four** (at Madison Sq. Garden): **Semifinals**–Dayton 69, St. John's 62 (OT); BYU 69, Seton Hall 59. **Third Place**–St. John's 70, Seton Hall 68 (2 OT). **Championship**–BYU 62, Dayton 43.

### 1952

| | | Before Tourns | Head Coach | Final Record |
|---|---|---|---|---|
| 1 | Kentucky | 28-2 | Adolph Rupp | 29-3 |
| 2 | Illinois | 19-3 | Harry Combes | 22-4 |
| 3 | Kansas St. | 19-5 | Jack Gardner | same |
| 4 | Duquesne | 21-1 | Dudey Moore | 23-4 |
| 5 | Saint Louis | 22-6 | Eddie Hickey | 23-8 |
| 6 | Washington | 25-6 | Tippy Dye | same |
| 7 | Iowa | 19-3 | Bucky O'Connor | same |
| 8 | **Kansas** | 24-3 | Phog Allen | 28-3 |
| 9 | West Virginia | 23-4 | Red Brown | same |
| 10 | St. John's | 22-3 | Frank McGuire | 25-5 |
| 11 | Dayton | 24-3 | Tom Blackburn | 28-5 |
| 12 | Duke | 24-6 | Harold Bradley | same |
| 13 | Holy Cross | 23-3 | Buster Sheary | 24-4 |
| 14 | Seton Hall | 25-2 | Honey Russell | 25-3 |
| 15 | St. Bonaventure | 19-5 | Ed Melvin | 21-6 |
| 16 | Wyoming | 27-6 | Everett Shelton | 28-7 |
| 17 | Louisville | 20-5 | Peck Hickman | 20-6 |
| 18 | Seattle | 29-7 | Al Brightman | 29-8 |
| 19 | UCLA | 19-10 | John Wooden | 19-12 |
| 20 | SW Texas St. | 30-1 | Milton Jowers | same |

**Note:** Unranked La Salle, coached by Ken Loeffler, won the NIT. The Explorers entered the postseason at 21-7 and had a final record of 25-7.

**NCAA Final Four** (at Edmundson Pavilion, Seattle): **Semifinals**–St. John's 61, Illinois 59; Kansas 74, Santa Clara 59. **Third Place**–Illinois 67, Santa Clara 64. **Championship**–Kansas 80, St. John's 63.

**NIT Final Four** (at Madison Sq. Garden): **Semifinals**–La Salle 59, Duquesne 46; Dayton 69, St. Bonaventure 62. **Third Place**–St. Bonaventure 48, Duquesne 34. **Championship**–La Salle 75, Dayton 64.

## Associated Press Final Polls (Cont.)

### 1953

| | | Head Coach | Final Record |
|---|---|---|---|
| | | Before Tourns | |
| 1 | **Indiana** . . . . . .18-3 | Branch McCracken | 23-3 |
| 2 | La Salle . . . . . .25-2 | Ken Loeffler | 25-3 |
| 3 | **Seton Hall** . . . .28-2 | Honey Russell | 31-2 |
| 4 | Washington . . . .27-2 | Tippy Dye | 30-3 |
| 5 | LSU . . . . . . . .22-1 | Harry Rabenhorst | 24-3 |
| 6 | Kansas . . . . . . .16-5 | Phog Allen | 19-6 |
| 7 | Oklahoma A&M .22-6 | Hank Iba | 23-7 |
| | Kansas St. . . . . .17-4 | Jack Gardner | same |
| 9 | Western Ky. . . . .25-5 | Ed Diddle | 25-6 |
| 10 | Illinois . . . . . . .18-4 | Harry Combes | same |
| 11 | Oklahoma City .18-4 | Doyle Parrick | 18-6 |
| 12 | N.C. State . . . . .26-6 | Everett Case | same |
| 13 | Notre Dame . . . .17-4 | John Jordan | 19-5 |
| 14 | Louisville . . . . . .21-5 | Peck Hickman | 22-6 |
| | Seattle . . . . . . .27-3 | Al Brightman | 29-4 |
| 16 | Miami-OH . . . . .17-5 | Bill Rohr | 17-6 |
| 17 | Eastern Ky. . . . . .16-8 | Paul McBrayer | 16-9 |
| 18 | Duquesne . . . . .18-7 | Dudey Moore | 21-8 |
| | Navy . . . . . . . .16-4 | Ben Carnevale | 16-5 |
| 20 | Holy Cross . . . . .18-5 | Buster Sheary | 20-6 |

**NCAA Final Four** (at Municipal Auditorium, Kansas City): **Semifinals**–Indiana 80, LSU 67; Kansas 79, Washington 53. **Third Place**–Washington 88, LSU 69. **Championship**–Indiana 69, Kansas 68.
**NIT Final Four** (at Madison Sq. Garden): **Semifinals**–Seton Hall 74, Manhattan 56; St. John's 64, Duquesne 55. **Third Place**–Duquesne 81, Manhattan 67. **Championship**–Seton Hall 58, St. John's 46.

### 1955

| | | Head Coach | Final Record |
|---|---|---|---|
| | | Before Tourns | |
| 1 | **San Francisco** .23-1 | Phil Woolpert | 28-1 |
| 2 | Kentucky . . . . . .22-2 | Adolph Rupp | 23-3 |
| 3 | La Salle . . . . . . .22-4 | Ken Loeffler | 26-5 |
| 4 | N.C. State . . . . .28-4 | Everett Case | same |
| 5 | Iowa . . . . . . . .17-5 | Bucky O'Connor | 19-7 |
| 6 | **Duquesne** . . . .19-4 | Dudey Moore | 22-4 |
| 7 | Utah . . . . . . . .23-3 | Jack Gardner | 24-4 |
| 8 | Marquette . . . . .22-2 | Jack Nagle | 24-3 |
| 9 | Dayton . . . . . . .23-3 | Tom Blackburn | 25-4 |
| 10 | Oregon St. . . . . .21-7 | Slats Gill | 22-8 |
| 11 | Minnesota . . . . .15-7 | Ozzie Cowles | same |
| 12 | Alabama . . . . . .19-5 | Johnny Dee | same |
| 13 | UCLA . . . . . . . .21-5 | John Wooden | same |
| 14 | G. Washington . .24-6 | Bill Reinhart | same |
| 15 | Colorado . . . . . .16-5 | Bebe Lee | 19-6 |
| 16 | Tulsa . . . . . . . .20-6 | Clarence Iba | 21-7 |
| 17 | Vanderbilt . . . . .16-6 | Bob Polk | same |
| 18 | Illinois . . . . . . .17-5 | Harry Combes | same |
| 19 | West Virginia . . .19-10 | Fred Schaus | 19-11 |
| 20 | Saint Louis . . . . .19-7 | Eddie Hickey | 20-8 |

**NCAA Final Four** (at Municipal Auditorium, Kansas City): **Semifinals**–La Salle 76, Iowa 73; San Francisco 62, Colorado 50. **Third Place**–Colorado 75, Iowa 74. **Championship**–San Francisco 77, La Salle 63.
**NIT Final Four** (at Madison Square Garden): **Semifinals**–Dayton 79, St. Francis-PA 73 (OT); Duquesne 65, Cincinnati 51. **Third Place**–Cincinnati 96, St. Francis-PA 91 (OT). **Championship**–Duquesne 70, Dayton 58.

### 1954

| | | Head Coach | Final Record |
|---|---|---|---|
| | | Before Tourns | |
| 1 | Kentucky . . . . . .25-0 | Adolph Rupp | same* |
| 2 | Indiana . . . . . . .19-3 | Branch McCracken | 20-4 |
| 3 | Duquesne . . . . .24-2 | Dudey Moore | 26-3 |
| 4 | Western Ky. . . . .28-1 | Ed Diddle | 29-3 |
| 5 | Oklahoma A&M .23-4 | Hank Iba | 24-5 |
| 6 | Notre Dame . . . .20-2 | John Jordan | 22-3 |
| 7 | Kansas . . . . . . .16-5 | Phog Allen | same |
| 8 | **Holy Cross** . . . .23-2 | Buster Sheary | 26-2 |
| 9 | LSU . . . . . . . . .21-3 | Harry Rabenhorst | 21-5 |
| 10 | **La Salle** . . . . . .21-4 | Ken Loeffler | 26-4 |
| 11 | Iowa . . . . . . . .17-5 | Bucky O'Connor | same |
| 12 | Duke . . . . . . . .22-6 | Harold Bradley | same |
| 13 | Colorado A&M .22-5 | Bill Strannigan | 22-7 |
| 14 | Illinois . . . . . . .17-5 | Harry Combes | same |
| 15 | Wichita . . . . . . .27-3 | Ralph Miller | 27-4 |
| 16 | Seattle . . . . . . .26-1 | Al Brightman | 26-2 |
| 17 | N.C. State . . . . .26-6 | Everett Case | 28-7 |
| 18 | Dayton . . . . . . .24-6 | Tom Blackburn | 25-7 |
| | Minnesota . . . . .17-5 | Ozzie Cowles | same |
| 20 | Oregon St. . . . . .19-10 | Slats Gill | same |
| | UCLA . . . . . . . .18-7 | John Wooden | same |
| | USC . . . . . . . .17-12 | Forrest Twogood | 19-14 |

*Kentucky turned down invitation to NCAA tournament after NCAA declared seniors Cliff Hagan, Frank Ramsey and Lou Tsioropoulos ineligible for postseason play.
**NCAA Final Four** (at Municipal Auditorium, Kansas City): **Semifinals**–La Salle 69, Penn St. 54; Bradley 74, USC 72. **Third Place**–Penn St. 70, USC 61. **Championship**–La Salle 92, Bradley 76.
**NIT Final Four** (at Madison Square Garden): **Semifinals**–Duquesne 66, Niagara 51; Holy Cross 75, Western Ky. 69. **Third Place**–Niagara 71, Western Ky. 65. **Championship**–Holy Cross 71, Duquesne 62.

### 1956

| | | Head Coach | Final Record |
|---|---|---|---|
| | | Before Tourns | |
| 1 | **San Francisco** .25-0 | Phil Woolpert | 29-0 |
| 2 | N.C. State . . . . .24-3 | Everett Case | 24-4 |
| 3 | Dayton . . . . . . .23-3 | Tom Blackburn | 25-4 |
| 4 | Iowa . . . . . . . .17-5 | Bucky O'Connor | 20-6 |
| 5 | Alabama . . . . . .21-3 | Johnny Dee | same |
| 6 | **Louisville** . . . . .23-3 | Peck Hickman | 26-3 |
| 7 | SMU . . . . . . . .22-2 | Doc Hayes | 25-4 |
| 8 | UCLA . . . . . . . .21-5 | John Wooden | 22-6 |
| 9 | Kentucky . . . . . .19-5 | Adolph Rupp | 20-6 |
| 10 | Illinois . . . . . . .18-4 | Harry Combes | same |
| 11 | Oklahoma City .18-6 | Abe Lemons | 20-7 |
| 12 | Vanderbilt . . . . .19-4 | Bob Polk | same |
| 13 | North Carolina .18-5 | Frank McGuire | same |
| 14 | Holy Cross . . . . .22-4 | Roy Leenig | 22-5 |
| 15 | Temple . . . . . . .23-3 | Harry Litwack | 27-4 |
| 16 | Wake Forest . . . .19-9 | Murray Greason | same |
| 17 | Duke . . . . . . . .19-7 | Harold Bradley | same |
| 18 | Utah . . . . . . . .21-5 | Jack Gardner | 22-6 |
| 19 | Oklahoma A&M .18-8 | Hank Iba | 18-9 |
| 20 | West Virginia . . .21-8 | Fred Schaus | 21-9 |

**NCAA Final Four** (at McGaw Hall, Evanston, IL): **Semifinals**–Iowa 83, Temple 76; San Francisco 76, SMU 68. **Third Place**–Temple 90, SMU 81. **Championship**–San Francisco 83, Iowa 71.
**NIT Final Four** (at Madison Square Garden): **Semifinals**–Dayton 89, St. Francis-NY 58; Louisville 89, St. Joseph's-PA 79. **Third Place**–St. Joseph's-PA 93, St. Francis-NY 82. **Championship**–Louisville 93, Dayton 80.

## 1957

| | | Before Tourns | Head Coach | Final Record |
|---|---|---|---|---|
| 1 | **N. Carolina** | .27-0 | Frank McGuire | 32-0 |
| 2 | Kansas | .21-2 | Dick Harp | 24-3 |
| 3 | Kentucky | .22-4 | Adolph Rupp | 23-5 |
| 4 | SMU | .21-3 | Doc Hayes | 22-4 |
| 5 | Seattle | .24-2 | John Castellani | 24-3 |
| 6 | Louisville | .21-5 | Peck Hickman | same |
| 7 | West Va. | .25-4 | Fred Schaus | 25-5 |
| 8 | Vanderbilt | .17-5 | Bob Polk | same |
| 9 | Oklahoma City | .17-8 | Abe Lemons | 19-9 |
| 10 | Saint Louis | .19-7 | Eddie Hickey | 19-9 |
| 11 | Michigan St. | .14-8 | Forddy Anderson | 16-10 |
| 12 | Memphis St. | .21-5 | Bob Vanatta | 24-6 |
| 13 | California | .20-4 | Pete Newell | 21-5 |
| 14 | UCLA | .22-4 | John Wooden | same |
| 15 | Mississippi St. | .17-8 | Babe McCarthy | same |
| 16 | Idaho St. | .24-2 | John Grayson | 25-4 |
| 17 | Notre Dame | .18-7 | John Jordan | 20-8 |
| 18 | Wake Forest | .19-9 | Murray Greason | same |
| 19 | Canisius | .20-5 | Joe Curran | 22-6 |
| 20 | Oklahoma A&M | .17-9 | Hank Iba | same |

**Note:** Unranked **Bradley**, coached by Chuck Orsborn, won the NIT. The Braves entered the tourney at 19-7 and had a final record of 22-7.
**NCAA Final Four** (at Municipal Auditorium, Kansas City): **Semifinals**–North Carolina 74, Michigan St. 70 (3 OT); Kansas 80, San Francisco 56. **Third Place**–San Francisco 67, Michigan St. 60. **Championship**–North Carolina 54, Kansas 53 (3 OT).
**NIT Final Four** (at Madison Square Garden): **Semifinals**–Memphis St. 80, St. Bonaventure 78; Bradley 78, Temple 66. **Third Place**–Temple 67, St. Bonaventure 50. **Championship**–Bradley 84, Memphis St. 83.

## 1958

| | | Before Tourns | Head Coach | Final Record |
|---|---|---|---|---|
| 1 | West Virginia | .26-1 | Fred Schaus | 26-2 |
| 2 | Cincinnati | .24-2 | George Smith | 25-3 |
| 3 | Kansas St. | .20-3 | Tex Winter | 22-5 |
| 4 | San Francisco | .24-1 | Phil Woolpert | 25-2 |
| 5 | Temple | .22-2 | Harry Litwack | 27-3 |
| 6 | Maryland | .20-6 | Bud Millikan | 22-7 |
| 7 | Kansas | .18-5 | Dick Harp | same |
| 8 | Notre Dame | .22-4 | John Jordan | 24-5 |
| 9 | **Kentucky** | .19-6 | Adolph Rupp | 23-6 |
| 10 | Duke | .18-7 | Harold Bradley | same |
| 11 | Dayton | .23-3 | Tom Blackburn | 25-4 |
| 12 | Indiana | .12-10 | Branch McCracken | 13-11 |
| 13 | North Carolina | .19-7 | Frank McGuire | same |
| 14 | Bradley | .20-6 | Chuck Orsborn | 20-7 |
| 15 | Mississippi St. | .20-5 | Babe McCarthy | same |
| 16 | Auburn | .16-6 | Joel Eaves | same |
| 17 | Michigan St. | .16-6 | Forddy Anderson | same |
| 18 | Seattle | .20-6 | John Castellani | 24-7 |
| 19 | Oklahoma St. | .19-7 | Hank Iba | 21-8 |
| 20 | N.C. State | .18-6 | Everett Case | same |

**Note:** Unranked **Xavier-OH**, coached by Jim McCafferty, won the NIT. The Musketeers entered the tourney at 15-11 and had a final record of 19-11.
**NCAA Final Four** (at Freedom Hall, Louisville): **Semifinals**–Kentucky 61, Temple 60; Seattle 73, Kansas St. 51. **Third Place**–Temple 67, Kansas St. 57. **Championship**–Kentucky 84, Seattle 72.
**NIT Final Four** (at Madison Square Garden): **Semifinals**–Dayton 80, St. John's 56; Xavier-OH 72, St. Bonaventure 53. **Third Place**–St. Bonaventure 84, St. John's 69. **Championship**–Xavier-OH 78, Dayton 74 (OT).

## 1959

| | | Before Tourns | Head Coach | Final Record |
|---|---|---|---|---|
| 1 | Kansas St. | .24-1 | Tex Winter | 25-2 |
| 2 | Kentucky | .23-2 | Adolph Rupp | 24-3 |
| 3 | Mississippi St. | .24-1 | Babe McCarthy | same* |
| 4 | Bradley | .23-3 | Chuck Orsborn | 25-4 |
| 5 | Cincinnati | .23-3 | George Smith | 26-4 |
| 6 | N.C. State | .22-4 | Everett Case | same |
| 7 | Michigan St. | .18-3 | Forddy Anderson | 19-4 |
| 8 | Auburn | .20-2 | Joel Eaves | same |
| 9 | North Carolina | .20-4 | Frank McGuire | 20-5 |
| 10 | West Virginia | .25-4 | Fred Schaus | 29-5 |
| 11 | **California** | .21-4 | Pete Newell | 25-4 |
| 12 | Saint Louis | .20-5 | John Benington | 20-6 |
| 13 | Seattle | .23-6 | Vince Cazzetta | same |
| 14 | St. Joseph's-PA | .22-3 | Jack Ramsay | 22-5 |
| 15 | St. Mary's-CA | .18-5 | Jim Weaver | 19-6 |
| 16 | TCU | .19-5 | Buster Brannon | 20-6 |
| 17 | Oklahoma City | .20-6 | Abe Lemons | 20-7 |
| 18 | Utah | .21-5 | Jack Gardner | 21-7 |
| 19 | St. Bonaventure | .20-2 | Eddie Donovan | 20-3 |
| 20 | Marquette | .22-4 | Eddie Hickey | 23-6 |

*Mississippi St. turned down invitation to NCAA tournament because it was an integrated event.
**Note:** Unranked **St. John's**, coached by Joe Lapchick, won the NIT. The Redmen entered the tourney at 16-6 and had a final record of 20-6.
**NCAA Final Four** (at Freedom Hall, Louisville): **Semifinals**–West Virginia 94, Louisville 79; California 64, Cincinnati 58. **Third Place**–Cincinnati 98, Louisville 85. **Championship**–California 71, West Virginia 70.
**NIT Final Four** (at Madison Square Garden): **Semifinals**–Bradley 59, NYU 57; St. John's 76, Providence 55. **Third Place**–NYU 71, Providence 57. **Championship**–St. John's 76, Bradley 71 (OT).

## 1960

| | | Before Tourns | Head Coach | Final Record |
|---|---|---|---|---|
| 1 | Cincinnati | .25-1 | George Smith | 28-2 |
| 2 | California | .24-1 | Pete Newell | 28-2 |
| 3 | **Ohio St.** | .21-3 | Fred Taylor | 25-3 |
| 4 | **Bradley** | .24-2 | Chuck Orsborn | 27-2 |
| 5 | West Virginia | .24-4 | Fred Schaus | 26-5 |
| 6 | Utah | .24-2 | Jack Gardner | 26-3 |
| 7 | Indiana | .20-4 | Branch McCracken | same |
| 8 | Utah St. | .22-4 | Cecil Baker | 24-5 |
| 9 | St. Bonaventure | .19-3 | Eddie Donovan | 21-5 |
| 10 | Miami-FL | .23-3 | Bruce Hale | 23-4 |
| 11 | Auburn | .19-3 | Joel Eaves | same |
| 12 | NYU | .19-4 | Lou Rossini | 22-5 |
| 13 | Georgia Tech | .21-5 | Whack Hyder | 22-6 |
| 14 | Providence | .21-4 | Joe Mullaney | 24-5 |
| 15 | Saint Louis | .19-7 | John Benington | 19-8 |
| 16 | Holy Cross | .20-5 | Roy Leenig | 20-6 |
| 17 | Villanova | .19-5 | Al Severance | 20-6 |
| 18 | Duke | .15-10 | Vic Bubas | 17-11 |
| 19 | Wake Forest | .21-7 | Bones McKinney | same |
| 20 | St. John's | .17-7 | Joe Lapchick | 17-8 |

**NCAA Final Four** (at the Cow Palace, San Fran.): **Semifinals**–Ohio St. 76, NYU 54; California 77, Cincinnati 69. **Third Place**–Cincinnati 95, NYU 71. **Championship**–Ohio St. 75, California 55.
**NIT Final Four** (at Madison Square Garden): **Semifinals**–Bradley 82, St. Bonaventure 71; Providence 68, Utah St. 62. **Third Place**–Utah St. 99, St. Bonaventure 93. **Championship**–Bradley 88, Providence 72.

## Associated Press Final Polls (Cont.)

### 1961

| | | Before Tourns | Head Coach | Final Record |
|---|---|---|---|---|
| 1 | Ohio St. | .24-0 | Fred Taylor | 27-1 |
| 2 | **Cincinnati** | .23-3 | Ed Jucker | 27-3 |
| 3 | St. Bonaventure | .22-3 | Eddie Donovan | 24-4 |
| 4 | Kansas St. | .22-3 | Tex Winter | 23-4 |
| 5 | North Carolina | .19-4 | Frank McGuire | same |
| 6 | Bradley | .21-5 | Chuck Orsborn | same |
| 7 | USC | .20-6 | Forrest Twogood | 21-8 |
| 8 | Iowa | .18-6 | S. Scheuerman | same |
| 9 | West Virginia | .23-4 | George King | same |
| 10 | Duke | .22-6 | Vic Bubas | same |
| 11 | Utah | .21-6 | Jack Gardner | 23-8 |
| 12 | Texas Tech | .14-9 | Polk Robison | 15-10 |
| 13 | Niagara | .16-4 | Taps Gallagher | 16-5 |
| 14 | Memphis St. | .20-2 | Bob Vanatta | 20-3 |
| 15 | Wake Forest | .17-10 | Bones McKinney | 19-11 |
| 16 | St. John's | .20-4 | Joe Lapchick | 20-5 |
| 17 | St. Joseph's-PA | .22-4 | Jack Ramsay | 25-5 |
| 18 | Drake | .19-7 | Maury John | same |
| 19 | Holy Cross | .19-4 | Roy Leenig | 22-5 |
| 20 | Kentucky | .18-8 | Adolph Rupp | 19-9 |

**Note:** Unranked **Providence**, coached by Joe Mullaney, won the NIT. The Friars entered the tourney at 20-5 and had a final record of 24-5.

**NCAA Final Four** (at Municipal Auditorium, Kansas City): **Semifinals**–Ohio St. 95, St. Joseph's-PA 69; Cincinnati 82, Utah 67. **Third Place**–St. Joseph's-PA 127, Utah 120 (4 OT). **Championship**–Cincinnati 70, Ohio St. 65 (OT).

**NIT Final Four** (at Madison Square Garden) **Semifinals**–St. Louis 67, Dayton 60; Providence 90, Holy Cross 83 (OT). **Third Place**–Holy Cross 85, Dayton 67. **Championship**–Providence 62, St. Louis 59.

### 1962

| | | Before Tourns | Head Coach | Final Record |
|---|---|---|---|---|
| 1 | Ohio St. | .23-1 | Fred Taylor | 26-2 |
| 2 | **Cincinnati** | .25-2 | Ed Jucker | 29-2 |
| 3 | Kentucky | .22-2 | Adolph Rupp | 23-3 |
| 4 | Mississippi St. | .19-6 | Babe McCarthy | same |
| 5 | Bradley | .21-6 | Chuck Orsborn | 21-7 |
| 6 | Kansas St. | .22-3 | Tex Winter | same |
| 7 | Utah | .23-3 | Jack Gardner | same |
| 8 | Bowling Green | .21-3 | Harold Anderson | same |
| 9 | Colorado | .18-6 | Sox Walseth | 19-7 |
| 10 | Duke | .20-5 | Vic Bubas | same |
| 11 | Loyola-IL | .21-3 | George Ireland | 23-4 |
| 12 | St. John's | .19-4 | Joe Lapchick | 21-5 |
| 13 | Wake Forest | .18-8 | Bones McKinney | 22-9 |
| 14 | Oregon St. | .22-4 | Slats Gill | 24-5 |
| 15 | West Virginia | .24-5 | George King | 24-6 |
| 16 | Arizona St. | .23-3 | Ned Wulk | 23-4 |
| 17 | Duquesne | .20-5 | Red Manning | 22-7 |
| 18 | Utah St. | .21-5 | Ladell Andersen | 22-7 |
| 19 | UCLA | .16-9 | John Wooden | 18-11 |
| 20 | Villanova | .19-6 | Jack Kraft | 21-7 |

**Note:** Unranked **Dayton**, coached by Tom Blackburn, won the NIT. The Flyers entered the tourney at 20-6 and had a final record of 24-6.

**NCAA Final Four** (at Freedom Hall, Louisville): **Semifinals**–Ohio St. 84, Wake Forest 68; Cincinnati 72, UCLA 70. **Third Place**–Wake Forest 82, UCLA 80. **Championship**–Cincinnati 71, Ohio St. 59.

**NIT Final Four** (at Madison Square Garden): **Semifinals**–Dayton 98, Loyola-IL 82; St. John's 76, Duquesne 65. **Third Place**–Loyola-IL 95, Duquesne 84. **Championship**–Dayton 73, St. John's 67.

### 1963

AP ranked only 10 teams from the 1962-63 season through 1967-68.

| | | Before Tourns | Head Coach | Final Record |
|---|---|---|---|---|
| 1 | Cincinnati | .23-1 | Ed Jucker | 26-2 |
| 2 | Duke | .24-2 | Vic Bubas | 27-3 |
| 3 | **Loyola-IL** | .24-2 | George Ireland | 29-2 |
| 4 | Arizona St. | .24-2 | Ned Wulk | 26-3 |
| 5 | Wichita | .19-7 | Ralph Miller | 19-8 |
| 6 | Mississippi St. | .21-5 | Babe McCarthy | 22-6 |
| 7 | Ohio St. | .20-4 | Fred Taylor | same |
| 8 | Illinois | .19-5 | Harry Combes | 20-6 |
| 9 | NYU | .17-3 | Lou Rossini | 18-5 |
| 10 | Colorado | .18-6 | Sox Walseth | 19-7 |

**Note:** Unranked **Providence**, coached by Joe Mullaney, won the NIT. The Friars entered the tourney at 21-4 and had a final record of 24-4.

**NCAA Final Four** (at Freedom Hall, Louisville): **Semifinals**–Loyola-IL 94, Duke 75; Cincinnati 80, Oregon St. 46. **Third Place**–Duke 85, Oregon St. 63. **Championship**–Loyola-IL 60, Cincinnati 58 (OT).

**NIT Final Four** (at Madison Square Garden): **Semifinals**–Providence 70, Marquette 64; Canisius 61, Villanova 46. **Third Place**–Marquette 66, Villanova 58. **Championship**–Providence 81, Canisius 66.

### 1964

AP ranked only 10 teams from the 1962-63 season through 1967-68.

| | | Before Tourns | Head Coach | Final Record |
|---|---|---|---|---|
| 1 | **UCLA** | .26-0 | John Wooden | 30-0 |
| 2 | Michigan | .20-4 | Dave Strack | 23-5 |
| 3 | Duke | .23-4 | Vic Bubas | 26-5 |
| 4 | Kentucky | .21-4 | Adolph Rupp | 21-6 |
| 5 | Wichita St. | .22-5 | Ralph Miller | 23-6 |
| 6 | Oregon St. | .25-3 | Slats Gill | 25-4 |
| 7 | Villanova | .22-3 | Jack Kraft | 24-4 |
| 8 | Loyola-IL | .20-5 | George Ireland | 22-6 |
| 9 | DePaul | .21-3 | Ray Meyer | 21-4 |
| 10 | Davidson | .22-4 | Lefty Driesell | same |

**Note:** Unranked **Bradley**, coached by Chuck Orsborn, won the NIT. The Braves entered the tourney at 20-6 and finished with a record of 23-6.

**NCAA Final Four** (at Municipal Auditorium, Kansas City): **Semifinals**–Duke 91, Michigan 80; UCLA 90, Kansas St. 84. **Third Place**–Michigan 100, Kansas St. 90. **Championship**–UCLA 98, Duke 83.

**NIT Final Four** (at Madison Square Garden): **Semifinals**–New Mexico 72, NYU 65; Bradley 67, Army 52. **Third Place**–Army 60, NYU 59. **Championship**–Bradley 86, New Mexico 54.

---

## Undefeated National Champions

Seven NCAA seasons have ended with an undefeated national champion. UCLA has accomplished the feat four times.

| Year | | W-L |
|---|---|---|
| 1956 | San Francisco | .29-0 |
| 1957 | North Carolina | .32-0 |
| 1964 | UCLA | .30-0 |
| 1967 | UCLA | .30-0 |
| 1972 | UCLA | .30-0 |
| 1973 | UCLA | .30-0 |
| 1976 | Indiana | .32-0 |

### 1965

AP ranked only 10 teams from the 1962-63 season through 1967-68.

| | | Before Tourns | Head Coach | Final Record |
|---|---|---|---|---|
| 1 | Michigan | 21-3 | Dave Strack | 24-4 |
| 2 | **UCLA** | 24-2 | John Wooden | 28-2 |
| 3 | St. Joseph's-PA | 25-1 | Jack Ramsay | 26-3 |
| 4 | Providence | 22-1 | Joe Mullaney | 24-2 |
| 5 | Vanderbilt | 23-3 | Roy Skinner | 24-4 |
| 6 | Davidson | 24-2 | Lefty Driesell | same |
| 7 | Minnesota | 19-5 | John Kundla | same |
| 8 | Villanova | 21-4 | Jack Kraft | 23-5 |
| 9 | BYU | 21-5 | Stan Watts | 21-7 |
| 10 | Duke | 20-5 | Vic Bubas | same |

**Note:** Unranked **St. John's,** coached by Joe Lapchick, won the NIT. The Redmen entered the tourney at 17-8 and finished with a record of 21-8.
**NCAA Final Four** (at Memorial Coliseum, Portland, OR): **Semifinals**–Michigan 93, Princeton 76; UCLA 108, Wichita St. 89. **Third Place**–Princeton 118, Wichita St. 82. **Championship**–UCLA 91, Michigan 80.
**NIT Final Four** (at Madison Square Garden): **Semifinals**–Villanova 91, NYU 69; St. John's 67, Army 60. **Third Place**–Army 75, NYU 74. **Championship**– St. John's 55, Villanova 51.

### 1966

AP ranked only 10 teams from the 1962-63 season through 1967-68.

| | | Before Tourns | Head Coach | Final Record |
|---|---|---|---|---|
| 1 | Kentucky | 24-1 | Adolph Rupp | 27-2 |
| 2 | Duke | 23-3 | Vic Bubas | 26-4 |
| 3 | **Texas Western** | 23-1 | Don Haskins | 28-1 |
| 4 | Kansas | 22-3 | Ted Owens | 23-4 |
| 5 | St. Joseph's-PA | 21-4 | Jack Ramsay | 24-5 |
| 6 | Loyola-IL | 22-2 | George Ireland | 22-3 |
| 7 | Cincinnati | 21-5 | Tay Baker | 21-7 |
| 8 | Vanderbilt | 22-4 | Roy Skinner | same |
| 9 | Michigan | 17-7 | Dave Strack | 18-8 |
| 10 | Western Ky. | 23-2 | Johnny Oldham | 25-3 |

**Note:** Unranked **BYU,** coached by Stan Watts, won the NIT. The Cougars entered the tourney at 17-5 and had a final record of 20-5.
**NCAA Final Four** (at Cole Fieldhouse, College Park, MD): **Semifinals**–Kentucky 83, Duke 79; Texas Western 85, Utah 78. **Third Place**–Duke 79, Utah 77. **Championship**–Texas Western 72, Kentucky 65.
**NIT Final Four** (at Madison Square Garden): **Semifinals**–BYU 66, Army 60; NYU 69, Villanova 63. **Third Place**–Villanova 76, Army 65. **Championship**–BYU 97, NYU 84.

### 1967

AP ranked only 10 teams from the 1962-63 season through 1967-68.

| | | Before Tourns | Head Coach | Final Record |
|---|---|---|---|---|
| 1 | **UCLA** | 26-0 | John Wooden | 30-0 |
| 2 | Louisville | 23-3 | Peck Hickman | 23-5 |
| 3 | Kansas | 22-3 | Ted Owens | 23-4 |
| 4 | North Carolina | 24-4 | Dean Smith | 26-6 |
| 5 | Princeton | 23-2 | B. van Breda Kolff | 25-3 |
| 6 | Western Ky. | 23-2 | Johnny Oldham | 23-3 |
| 7 | Houston | 23-3 | Guy Lewis | 27-4 |
| 8 | Tennessee | 21-5 | Ray Mears | 21-7 |
| 9 | Boston College | 19-2 | Bob Cousy | 21-3 |
| 10 | Texas Western | 20-5 | Don Haskins | 22-6 |

**Note:** Unranked **Southern Illinois,** coached by Jack Hartman, won the NIT. The Salukis entered the tourney at 20-2 and had a final record of 24-2.
**NCAA Final Four** (at Freedom Hall, Louisville): **Semifinals**–Dayton 76, N. Carolina 62; UCLA 73, Houston 58. **Third Place**–Houston 84, N. Carolina 62. **Championship**–UCLA 79, Dayton 64.
**NIT Final Four** (at Madison Square Garden): **Semifinals**–Marquette 83, Marshall 78; Southern Ill. 79, Rutgers 70. **Third Place**–Rutgers 93, Marshall 76. **Championship**–Southern Ill. 71, Marquette 56.

### 1968

AP ranked only 10 teams from the 1962-63 season through 1967-68.

| | | Before Tourns | Head Coach | Final Record |
|---|---|---|---|---|
| 1 | Houston | 28-0 | Guy Lewis | 31-2 |
| 2 | **UCLA** | 25-1 | John Wooden | 29-1 |
| 3 | St. Bonaventure | 22-0 | Larry Weise | 23-2 |
| 4 | North Carolina | 25-3 | Dean Smith | 28-4 |
| 5 | Kentucky | 21-4 | Adolph Rupp | 22-5 |
| 6 | New Mexico | 23-3 | Bob King | 23-5 |
| 7 | Columbia | 21-4 | Jack Rohan | 23-5 |
| 8 | Davidson | 22-4 | Lefty Driesell | 24-5 |
| 9 | Louisville | 20-6 | John Dromo | 21-7 |
| 10 | Duke | 21-5 | Vic Bubas | 22-6 |

**Note:** Unranked **Dayton,** coached by Don Donoher, won the NIT. The Flyers entered the tourney at 17-9 and had a final record of 21-9.
**NCAA Final Four** (at the Sports Arena, Los Angeles): **Semifinals**–N. Carolina 80, Ohio St. 66; UCLA 101, Houston 69. **Third Place**–Ohio St. 89, Houston 85. **Championship**–UCLA 78, N. Carolina 55.
**NIT Final Four** (at Madison Square Garden): **Semifinals**–Dayton 76, Notre Dame 74 (OT); Kansas 58, St. Peter's 46. **Third Place**–Notre Dame 81, St.Peter's 78. **Championship**–Dayton 61, Kansas 48.

## All-Time AP Top 20

The composite AP Top 20 from the 1948-49 season through 2004-05, based on the final regular season rankings of each year. The final AP poll has been taken before the NCAA and NIT tournaments each season since 1949 except in 1953 and '54 and again in 1974 and '75 when the final poll came out after the postseason. Team point totals are based on 20 points for all 1st place finishes, 19 for each 2nd, etc. Also listed are the number of times ranked No.1 by AP going into the tournaments, and times ranked in the pre-tournament Top 10 and Top 20.

| | | Pts | No.1 | Top 10 | Top 20 | | | Pts | No.1 | Top10 | Top 20 |
|---|---|---|---|---|---|---|---|---|---|---|---|
| 1 | Kentucky | 672 | 8 | 38 | 45 | 11 | Michigan | 200 | 2 | 10 | 15 |
| 2 | North Carolina | 532 | 5 | 29 | 38 | 12 | Notre Dame | 190 | 0 | 12 | 18 |
| 3 | Duke | 462 | 6 | 26 | 35 | 13 | Marquette | 187 | 0 | 12 | 17 |
| 4 | UCLA | 449 | 7 | 22 | 35 | 14 | N.C. State | 182 | 1 | 9 | 17 |
| 5 | Kansas | 369 | 1 | 19 | 29 | 15 | Syracuse | 179 | 0 | 9 | 20 |
| 6 | Indiana | 293 | 4 | 16 | 24 | 16 | Ohio St | 176 | 2 | 10 | 13 |
| 7 | Cincinnati | 259 | 2 | 13 | 19 | 17 | UNLV | 173 | 2 | 8 | 13 |
| 8 | Louisville | 257 | 0 | 12 | 24 | 18 | Arkansas | 166 | 0 | 9 | 15 |
| 9 | Arizona | 245 | 1 | 12 | 20 | 19 | Maryland | 160 | 0 | 8 | 17 |
| 10 | Illinois | 227 | 1 | 10 | 23 | 20 | Oklahoma | 157 | 1 | 7 | 13 |

## Associated Press Final Polls (Cont.)

### 1969

| | | Before Tourns | Head Coach | Final Record |
|---|---|---|---|---|
| 1 | UCLA | 25-1 | John Wooden | 29-1 |
| 2 | La Salle | 23-1 | Tom Gola | same* |
| 3 | Santa Clara | 26-1 | Dick Garibaldi | 27-2 |
| 4 | North Carolina | 27-1 | Dean Smith | 27-5 |
| 5 | Davidson | 24-2 | Lefty Driesell | 26-3 |
| 6 | Purdue | 20-4 | George King | 23-5 |
| 7 | Kentucky | 22-4 | Adolph Rupp | 23-5 |
| 8 | St. John's | 22-4 | Lou Carnesecca | 23-6 |
| 9 | Duquesne | 19-4 | Red Manning | 21-5 |
| 10 | Villanova | 21-4 | Jack Kraft | 21-5 |
| 11 | Drake | 23-4 | Maury John | 26-5 |
| 12 | New Mexico St. | 23-3 | Lou Henson | 24-5 |
| 13 | South Carolina | 20-6 | Frank McGuire | 21-7 |
| 14 | Marquette | 22-4 | Al McGuire | 24-5 |
| 15 | Louisville | 20-5 | John Dromo | 21-6 |
| 16 | Boston College | 21-3 | Bob Cousy | 24-4 |
| 17 | Notre Dame | 20-6 | Johnny Dee | 20-7 |
| 18 | Colorado | 20-6 | Sox Walseth | 21-7 |
| 19 | Kansas | 20-6 | Ted Owens | 20-7 |
| 20 | Illinois | 19-5 | Harvey Schmidt | same |

*On probation

**Note:** Unranked **Temple**, coached by Harry Litwack, won the NIT. The Owls entered the tourney at 18-8 and finished with a record of 22-8.

**NCAA Final Four** (at Freedom Hall, Louisville): **Semifinals**–Purdue 92, N. Carolina 65; UCLA 85, Drake 82. **Third Place**–Drake 104, N. Carolina 84. **Championship**–UCLA 92, Purdue 72.

**NIT Final Four** (at Madison Square Garden): **Semifinals**–Temple 63, Tennessee 58; Boston College 73, Army 61. **Third Place**–Tennessee 64, Army 52. **Championship**–Temple 89, Boston College 76.

### 1971

| | | Before Tourns | Head Coach | Final Record |
|---|---|---|---|---|
| 1 | UCLA | 25-1 | John Wooden | 29-1 |
| 2 | Marquette | 26-0 | Al McGuire | 28-1 |
| 3 | Penn | 26-0 | Dick Harter | 28-1 |
| 4 | Kansas | 25-1 | Ted Owens | 27-3 |
| 5 | USC | 24-2 | Bob Boyd | 24-2 |
| 6 | South Carolina | 23-4 | Frank McGuire | 23-6 |
| 7 | Western Ky. | 20-5 | John Oldham | 24-6 |
| 8 | Kentucky | 22-4 | Adolph Rupp | 22-6 |
| 9 | Fordham | 25-1 | Digger Phelps | 26-3 |
| 10 | Ohio St. | 19-5 | Fred Taylor | 20-6 |
| 11 | Jacksonville | 22-3 | Tom Wasdin | 22-4 |
| 12 | Notre Dame | 19-7 | Johnny Dee | 20-9 |
| 13 | N. Carolina | 22-6 | Dean Smith | 26-6 |
| 14 | Houston | 20-6 | Guy Lewis | 22-7 |
| 15 | Duquesne | 21-3 | Red Manning | 21-4 |
| 16 | Long Beach St. | 21-4 | Jerry Tarkanian | 23-5 |
| 17 | Tennessee | 20-6 | Ray Mears | 21-7 |
| 18 | Villanova | 19-5 | Jack Kraft | 23-6 |
| 19 | Drake | 20-7 | Maury John | 21-8 |
| 20 | BYU | 18-9 | Stan Watts | 18-11 |

**NCAA Final Four** (at the Astrodome, Houston): **Semifinals**–Villanova 92, Western Ky. 89 (2 OT); UCLA 68, Kansas 60. **Third Place**–Western Ky. 77, Kansas 75. **Championship**–UCLA 68, Villanova 62.

**NIT Final Four** (at Madison Square Garden): **Semifinals**–N. Carolina 73, Duke 69; Ga.Tech 76, St. Bonaventure 71 (2 OT). **Third Place**–St. Bonaventure 92, Duke 88 (OT). **Championship**–N. Carolina 84, Ga. Tech 66.

### 1970

| | | Before Tourns | Head Coach | Final Record |
|---|---|---|---|---|
| 1 | Kentucky | 25-1 | Adolph Rupp | 26-2 |
| 2 | UCLA | 24-2 | John Wooden | 28-2 |
| 3 | St. Bonaventure | 22-1 | Larry Weise | 25-3 |
| 4 | Jacksonville | 23-1 | Joe Williams | 27-2 |
| 5 | New Mexico St. | 23-2 | Lou Henson | 27-3 |
| 6 | South Carolina | 25-3 | Frank McGuire | 25-3 |
| 7 | Iowa | 19-4 | Ralph Miller | 20-5 |
| 8 | Marquette | 22-3 | Al McGuire | 26-3 |
| 9 | Notre Dame | 20-6 | Johnny Dee | 21-8 |
| 10 | N.C. State | 22-6 | Norm Sloan | 23-7 |
| 11 | Florida St. | 23-3 | Hugh Durham | 23-3 |
| 12 | Houston | 24-3 | Guy Lewis | 25-5 |
| 13 | Penn | 25-1 | Dick Harter | 25-2 |
| 14 | Drake | 21-6 | Maury John | 22-7 |
| 15 | Davidson | 22-4 | Terry Holland | 22-5 |
| 16 | Utah St. | 20-6 | Ladell Andersen | 22-7 |
| 17 | Niagara | 21-5 | Frank Layden | 22-7 |
| 18 | Western Ky. | 22-2 | John Oldham | 22-3 |
| 19 | Long Beach St. | 23-3 | Jerry Tarkanian | 24-5 |
| 20 | USC | 18-8 | Bob Boyd | 18-8 |

**NCAA Final Four** (at Cole Fieldhouse, College Park, MD): **Semifinals**–Jacksonville 91, St. Bonaventure 83; UCLA 93, New Mexico St. 77. **Third Place**–N. Mexico St. 79, St. Bonaventure 73. **Championship**–UCLA 80, Jacksonville 69.

**NIT Final Four** (at Madison Square Garden): **Semifinals**–St. John's 60, Army 59; Marquette 101, LSU 79. **Third Place**–Army 75, LSU 68. **Championship**–Marquette 65, St. John's 53.

### 1972

| | | Before Tourns | Head Coach | Final Record |
|---|---|---|---|---|
| 1 | UCLA | 26-0 | John Wooden | 30-0 |
| 2 | North Carolina | 23-4 | Dean Smith | 26-5 |
| 3 | Penn | 23-2 | Chuck Daly | 25-3 |
| 4 | Louisville | 23-4 | Denny Crum | 26-5 |
| 5 | Long Beach St. | 23-3 | Jerry Tarkanian | 25-4 |
| 6 | South Carolina | 22-4 | Frank McGuire | 24-5 |
| 7 | Marquette | 24-2 | Al McGuire | 25-4 |
| 8 | SW Louisiana | 23-3 | Beryl Shipley | 25-4 |
| 9 | BYU | 21-4 | Stan Watts | 21-5 |
| 10 | Florida St. | 23-5 | Hugh Durham | 27-6 |
| 11 | Minnesota | 17-6 | Bill Musselman | 18-7 |
| 12 | Marshall | 22-3 | Carl Tacy | 23-4 |
| 13 | Memphis St. | 21-6 | Gene Bartow | 21-7 |
| 14 | Maryland | 23-5 | Lefty Driesell | 27-5 |
| 15 | Villanova | 19-6 | Jack Kraft | 20-8 |
| 16 | Oral Roberts | 25-1 | Ken Trickey | 26-2 |
| 17 | Indiana | 17-7 | Bob Knight | 17-8 |
| 18 | Kentucky | 20-6 | Adolph Rupp | 21-7 |
| 19 | Ohio St. | 18-6 | Fred Taylor | same |
| 20 | Virginia | 21-6 | Bill Gibson | 21-7 |

**NCAA Final Four** (at the Sports Arena, Los Angeles): **Semifinals**–Florida St. 79, N. Carolina 75; UCLA 96, Louisville 77. **Third Place**–N. Carolina 105, Louisville 91. **Championship**–UCLA 81, Florida St. 76.

**NIT Final Four** (at Madison Square Garden): **Semifinals**–Maryland 91, Jacksonville 77; Niagara 69, St. John's 67. **Third Place**–Jacksonville 83, St. John's 80. **Championship**–Maryland 100, Niagara 69.

## 1973

| | | Head Coach | Final Record |
|---|---|---|---|
| | | **Before Tourns** | |
| 1 | **UCLA** ........26-0 | John Wooden | 30-0 |
| 2 | N.C. State ....27-0 | Norm Sloan | same* |
| 3 | Long Beach St. ..24-2 | Jerry Tarkanian | 26-3 |
| 4 | Providence ....24-2 | Dave Gavitt | 27-4 |
| 5 | Marquette ....23-3 | Al McGuire | 25-4 |
| 6 | Indiana ......19-5 | Bob Knight | 22-6 |
| 7 | SW Louisiana ..23-2 | Beryl Shipley | 24-5 |
| 8 | Maryland ....22-6 | Lefty Driesell | 23-7 |
| 9 | Kansas St. ....22-4 | Jack Hartman | 23-5 |
| 10 | Minnesota ....20-4 | Bill Musselman | 21-5 |
| 11 | North Carolina ..22-7 | Dean Smith | 25-8 |
| 12 | Memphis St. ....21-5 | Gene Bartow | 24-6 |
| 13 | Houston ......23-3 | Guy Lewis | 23-4 |
| 14 | Syracuse ......22-4 | Roy Danforth | 24-5 |
| 15 | Missouri ......21-5 | Norm Stewart | 21-6 |
| 16 | Arizona St. ....18-7 | Ned Wulk | 19-9 |
| 17 | Kentucky ......19-7 | Joe B. Hall | 20-8 |
| 18 | Penn .........20-5 | Chuck Daly | 21-7 |
| 19 | Austin Peay ....21-5 | Lake Kelly | 22-7 |
| 20 | San Francisco ...22-4 | Bob Gaillard | 23-5 |

*N.C. State was ineligible for NCAA tournament for using improper methods to recruit David Thompson.
**Note:** Unranked **Virginia Tech**, coached by Don DeVoe, won the NIT. The Hokies entered the tourney at 18-5 and finished with a record of 22-5.
**NCAA Final Four** (at The Arena, St. Louis): **Semifinals**—Memphis St. 98, Providence 85; UCLA 70, Indiana 59. **Third Place**—Indiana 97, Providence 79. **Championship**—UCLA 87, Memphis St. 66.
**NIT Final Four** (at Madison Square Garden): **Semifinals**—Va. Tech 74, Alabama 73; Notre Dame 78, N. Carolina 71. **Third Place**—N. Carolina 88, Alabama 69. **Championship**—Va. Tech 92, Notre Dame 91 (OT).

## 1974

| | | Head Coach | Final Record |
|---|---|---|---|
| | | **Before Tourns** | |
| 1 | **N.C. State** ....26-1 | Norm Sloan | 30-1 |
| 2 | UCLA ........23-3 | John Wooden | 26-4 |
| 3 | Notre Dame ...24-2 | Digger Phelps | 26-3 |
| 4 | Maryland .....23-5 | Lefty Driesell | same |
| 5 | Providence ....26-3 | Dave Gavitt | 28-4 |
| 6 | Vanderbilt ....23-3 | Roy Skinner | 23-5 |
| 7 | Marquette ....22-4 | Al McGuire | 26-5 |
| 8 | North Carolina ..22-5 | Dean Smith | 22-6 |
| 9 | Long Beach St. ..24-2 | Lute Olson | same |
| 10 | **Indiana** ......20-5 | Bob Knight | 23-5 |
| 11 | Alabama .....22-4 | C.M. Newton | same |
| 12 | Michigan .....21-4 | Johnny Orr | 22-5 |
| 13 | Pittsburgh ....23-3 | Buzz Ridl | 25-4 |
| 14 | Kansas........21-5 | Ted Owens | 23-7 |
| 15 | USC .........22-4 | Bob Boyd | 24-5 |
| 16 | Louisville ....21-6 | Denny Crum | 21-7 |
| 17 | New Mexico ...21-6 | Norm Ellenberger | 22-7 |
| 18 | South Carolina ..22-4 | Frank McGuire | 22-5 |
| 19 | Creighton .....22-6 | Eddie Sutton | 23-7 |
| 20 | Dayton ......19-7 | Don Donoher | 20-9 |

**NCAA Final Four** (at Greensboro, NC, Coliseum): **Semifinals**—N.C. State 80, UCLA 77 (2 OT); Marquette 64, Kansas 51. **Third Place**—UCLA 78, Kansas 61. **Championship**—N.C. State 76, Marquette 64.
**NIT Final Four** (at Madison Square Garden): **Semifinals**—Purdue 78, Jacksonville 63; Utah 117, Boston Col. 93. **Third Place**—Boston Col. 87, Jacksonville 77. **Championship**—Purdue 87, Utah 81.
**CCA Final Four** (at The Arena, St. Louis): **Semifinals**—Indiana 73, Toledo 72; USC 74, Bradley 73. **Championship**—Indiana 85, USC 60.

## 1975

| | | Head Coach | Final Record |
|---|---|---|---|
| | | **Before Tourns** | |
| 1 | Indiana ......29-0 | Bob Knight | 31-1 |
| 2 | **UCLA** ........23-3 | John Wooden | 28-3 |
| 3 | Louisville ....24-2 | Denny Crum | 28-3 |
| 4 | Maryland .....22-4 | Lefty Driesell | 24-5 |
| 5 | Kentucky .....22-4 | Joe B. Hall | 26-5 |
| 6 | North Carolina ..21-7 | Dean Smith | 23-8 |
| 7 | Arizona St. ....23-3 | Ned Wulk | 25-4 |
| 8 | N.C.State ....22-6 | Norm Sloan | 22-6 |
| 9 | Notre Dame ...18-8 | Digger Phelps | 19-10 |
| 10 | Marquette ....23-3 | Al McGuire | 23-4 |
| 11 | Alabama .....22-4 | C.M. Newton | 22-5 |
| 12 | Cincinnati ....21-5 | Gale Catlett | 23-6 |
| 13 | Oregon St.....18-10 | Ralph Miller | 19-12 |
| 14 | **Drake** ......16-10 | Bob Ortegel | 19-10 |
| 15 | Penn ........23-4 | Chuck Daly | 23-5 |
| 16 | UNLV ........22-4 | Jerry Tarkanian | 24-5 |
| 17 | Kansas St. ....18-8 | Jack Hartman | 20-9 |
| 18 | USC .........18-7 | Bob Boyd | 18-8 |
| 19 | Centenary ....25-4 | Larry Little | same |
| 20 | Syracuse .....20-7 | Roy Danforth | 23-9 |

**NCAA Final Four** (at San Diego Sports Arena): **Semifinals**—Kentucky 95, Syracuse 79; UCLA 75, Louisville 74 (OT). **Third Place**—Louisville 96, Syracuse 88 (OT). **Championship**—UCLA 92, Kentucky 85.
**NIT Championship** (at Madison Sq. Garden): Princeton 80, Providence 69. No Top 20 teams played in NIT.
**CCA Championship** (at Freedom Hall, Louisville): Drake 83, Arizona 76. No.14 Drake and No.18 USC were only Top 20 teams in CCA.

## 1976

| | | Head Coach | Final Record |
|---|---|---|---|
| | | **Before Tourns** | |
| 1 | **Indiana** ......27-0 | Bob Knight | 32-0 |
| 2 | Marquette ....25-1 | Al McGuire | 27-2 |
| 3 | UNLV .........28-1 | Jerry Tarkanian | 29-2 |
| 4 | Rutgers .......28-0 | Tom Young | 31-2 |
| 5 | UCLA ........24-3 | Gene Bartow | 28-4 |
| 6 | Alabama .....22-4 | C.M. Newton | 23-5 |
| 7 | Notre Dame ...22-5 | Digger Phelps | 23-6 |
| 8 | North Carolina ..25-3 | Dean Smith | 25-4 |
| 9 | Michigan .....21-6 | Johnny Orr | 25-7 |
| 10 | Western Mich. ..24-2 | Eldon Miller | 25-3 |
| 11 | Maryland .....22-6 | Lefty Driesell | same |
| 12 | Cincinnati ....25-5 | Gale Catlett | 25-6 |
| 13 | Tennessee ....21-5 | Ray Mears | 21-6 |
| 14 | Missouri ......24-4 | Norm Stewart | 26-5 |
| 15 | Arizona ......22-8 | Fred Snowden | 24-9 |
| 16 | Texas Tech ....24-5 | Gerald Myers | 25-6 |
| 17 | DePaul ......19-8 | Ray Meyer | 20-9 |
| 18 | Virginia .....18-11 | Terry Holland | 18-12 |
| 19 | Centenary ....22-5 | Larry Little | same |
| 20 | Pepperdine ...21-5 | Gary Colson | 22-6 |

**NCAA Final Four** (at the Spectrum, Phila.); **Semifinals**—Michigan 86, Rutgers 70; Indiana 65, UCLA 51. **Third Place**—UCLA 106, Rutgers 92. **Championship**—Indiana 86, Michigan 68.
**NIT Championship** (at Madison Square Garden): Kentucky 71, NC-Charlotte 67. No Top 20 teams played in NIT.

## Associated Press Final Polls (Cont.)

### 1977

| | | Before Tourns | Head Coach | Final Record |
|---|---|---|---|---|
| 1 | Michigan | 24-3 | Johnny Orr | 26-4 |
| 2 | UCLA | 24-3 | Gene Bartow | 25-4 |
| 3 | Kentucky | 24-3 | Joe B. Hall | 26-4 |
| 4 | UNLV | 25-2 | Jerry Tarkanian | 29-3 |
| 5 | North Carolina | 24-4 | Dean Smith | 28-5 |
| 6 | Syracuse | 25-3 | Jim Boeheim | 26-4 |
| 7 | **Marquette** | 20-7 | Al McGuire | 25-7 |
| 8 | San Francisco | 29-1 | Bob Gaillard | 29-2 |
| 9 | Wake Forest | 20-7 | Carl Tacy | 22-8 |
| 10 | Notre Dame | 21-6 | Digger Phelps | 22-7 |
| 11 | Alabama | 23-4 | C.M. Newton | 25-6 |
| 12 | Detroit | 24-3 | Dick Vitale | 25-4 |
| 13 | Minnesota | 24-3 | Jim Dutcher | same* |
| 14 | Utah | 22-6 | Jerry Pimm | 23-7 |
| 15 | Tennessee | 22-5 | Ray Mears | 22-6 |
| 16 | Kansas St. | 23-6 | Jack Hartman | 24-7 |
| 17 | NC-Charlotte | 25-3 | Lee Rose | 28-5 |
| 18 | Arkansas | 26-1 | Eddie Sutton | 26-2 |
| 19 | Louisville | 21-6 | Denny Crum | 21-7 |
| 20 | VMI | 25-3 | Charlie Schmaus | 26-4 |

*On probation

**NCAA Final Four** (at the Omni, Atlanta): **Semifinals**–Marquette 51, NC-Charlotte, 49; N. Carolina 84, UNLV 83. **Third Place**–UNLV 106, NC-Charlotte 94. **Championship**–Marquette 67, N. Carolina 59.
**NIT Championship** (at Madison Square Garden): St. Bonaventure 94, Houston 91. No.11 Alabama was only Top 20 team in NIT.

### 1979

| | | Before Tourns | Head Coach | Final Record |
|---|---|---|---|---|
| 1 | Indiana St. | 29-0 | Bill Hodges | 33-1 |
| 2 | UCLA | 23-4 | Gary Cunningham | 25-5 |
| 3 | **Michigan St.** | 21-6 | Jud Heathcote | 26-6 |
| 4 | Notre Dame | 22-5 | Digger Phelps | 24-6 |
| 5 | Arkansas | 23-4 | Eddie Sutton | 25-5 |
| 6 | DePaul | 22-5 | Ray Meyer | 26-6 |
| 7 | LSU | 22-5 | Dale Brown | 23-6 |
| 8 | Syracuse | 25-3 | Jim Boeheim | 26-4 |
| 9 | North Carolina | 23-5 | Dean Smith | 23-6 |
| 10 | Marquette | 21-6 | Hank Raymonds | 22-7 |
| 11 | Duke | 22-7 | Bill Foster | 22-8 |
| 12 | San Francisco | 21-6 | Dan Belluomini | 22-7 |
| 13 | Louisville | 23-7 | Denny Crum | 24-8 |
| 14 | Penn | 21-5 | Bob Weinhauer | 25-7 |
| 15 | Purdue | 23-7 | Lee Rose | 27-8 |
| 16 | Oklahoma | 20-9 | Dave Bliss | 21-10 |
| 17 | St. John's | 18-10 | Lou Carnesecca | 21-11 |
| 18 | Rutgers | 21-8 | Tom Young | 22-9 |
| 19 | Toledo | 21-6 | Bob Nichols | 22-7 |
| 20 | Iowa | 20-7 | Lute Olson | 20-8 |

**NCAA Final Four** (at Special Events Center, Salt Lake City): **Semifinals**–Michigan St. 101, Penn 67; Indiana St. 76, DePaul 74; **Third Place**–DePaul 96, Penn 93; **Championship**–Michigan St. 75, Indiana St. 64.
**NIT Championship** (at Madison Square Garden): Indiana 53, Purdue 52. No. 15 Purdue was the only Top 20 team in NIT.

### 1978

| | | Before Tourns | Head Coach | Final Record |
|---|---|---|---|---|
| 1 | **Kentucky** | 25-2 | Joe B. Hall | 30-2 |
| 2 | UCLA | 24-2 | Gary Cunningham | 25-3 |
| 3 | DePaul | 25-2 | Ray Meyer | 27-3 |
| 4 | Michigan St. | 23-4 | Jud Heathcote | 25-5 |
| 5 | Arkansas | 28-3 | Eddie Sutton | 32-3 |
| 6 | Notre Dame | 20-6 | Digger Phelps | 23-8 |
| 7 | Duke | 23-6 | Bill Foster | 27-7 |
| 8 | Marquette | 24-3 | Hank Raymonds | 24-4 |
| 9 | Louisville | 22-6 | Denny Crum | 23-7 |
| 10 | Kansas | 24-4 | Ted Owens | 24-5 |
| 11 | San Francisco | 22-5 | Bob Gaillard | 23-6 |
| 12 | New Mexico | 24-3 | Norm Ellenberger | 24-4 |
| 13 | Indiana | 20-7 | Bob Knight | 21-8 |
| 14 | Utah | 22-5 | Jerry Pimm | 23-6 |
| 15 | Florida St. | 23-5 | Hugh Durham | 23-6 |
| 16 | North Carolina | 23-7 | Dean Smith | 23-8 |
| 17 | **Texas** | 22-5 | Abe Lemons | 26-5 |
| 18 | Detroit | 24-3 | Dave Gaines | 25-4 |
| 19 | Miami-OH | 18-8 | Darrell Hedric | 19-9 |
| 20 | Penn | 19-7 | Bob Weinhauer | 20-8 |

**NCAA Final Four** (at the Checkerdome, St. Louis): **Semifinals**–Kentucky 64, Arkansas 59; Duke 90, Notre Dame 86. **Third Place**–Arkansas 71, Notre Dame 69. **Championship**–Kentucky 94, Duke 88.
**NIT Championship** (at Madison Square Garden): Texas 101, N.C. State 93. No. 17 Texas and No. 18 Detroit were only Top 20 teams in NIT.

### 1980

| | | Before Tourns | Head Coach | Final Record |
|---|---|---|---|---|
| 1 | DePaul | 26-1 | Ray Meyer | 26-2 |
| 2 | **Louisville** | 28-3 | Denny Crum | 33-3 |
| 3 | LSU | 24-5 | Dale Brown | 26-6 |
| 4 | Kentucky | 28-5 | Joe B. Hall | 29-6 |
| 5 | Oregon St. | 26-3 | Ralph Miller | 26-4 |
| 6 | Syracuse | 25-3 | Jim Boeheim | 26-4 |
| 7 | Indiana | 20-7 | Bob Knight | 21-8 |
| 8 | Maryland | 23-6 | Lefty Driesell | 24-7 |
| 9 | Notre Dame | 20-7 | Digger Phelps | 20-8 |
| 10 | Ohio St. | 24-5 | Eldon Miller | 21-8 |
| 11 | Georgetown | 24-5 | John Thompson | 26-6 |
| 12 | BYU | 24-4 | Frank Arnold | 24-5 |
| 13 | St. John's | 24-4 | Lou Carnesecca | 24-5 |
| 14 | Duke | 22-8 | Bill Foster | 24-9 |
| 15 | North Carolina | 21-7 | Dean Smith | 21-8 |
| 16 | Missouri | 23-5 | Norm Stewart | 25-6 |
| 17 | Weber St. | 26-2 | Neil McCarthy | 26-3 |
| 18 | Arizona St. | 21-6 | Ned Wulk | 22-7 |
| 19 | Iona | 28-4 | Jim Valvano | 29-5 |
| 20 | Purdue | 19-9 | Lee Rose | 23-10 |

**NCAA Final Four** (at Market Square Arena, Indianapolis): **Semifinals**–Louisville 80, Iowa 72; UCLA 67, Purdue 62; **Championship**–Louisville 59, UCLA 54.
**NIT Championship** (at Madison Square Garden): Virginia 58, Minnesota 55. No Top 20 teams played in NIT.

## 1981

| | | Before Tourns | Head Coach | Final Record |
|---|---|---|---|---|
| 1 | DePaul | 27-1 | Ray Meyer | 27-2 |
| 2 | Oregon St. | 26-1 | Ralph Miller | 26-2 |
| 3 | Arizona St. | 24-3 | Ned Wulk | 24-4 |
| 4 | LSU | 28-3 | Dale Brown | 31-5 |
| 5 | Virginia | 25-3 | Terry Holland | 29-4 |
| 6 | North Carolina | 25-7 | Dean Smith | 29-8 |
| 7 | Notre Dame | 22-5 | Digger Phelps | 23-6 |
| 8 | Kentucky | 22-5 | Joe B. Hall | 22-6 |
| 9 | **Indiana** | 21-9 | Bob Knight | 26-9 |
| 10 | UCLA | 20-6 | Larry Brown | 20-7 |
| 11 | Wake Forest | 22-6 | Carl Tacy | 22-7 |
| 12 | Louisville | 21-8 | Denny Crum | 21-9 |
| 13 | Iowa | 21-6 | Lute Olson | 21-7 |
| 14 | Utah | 24-4 | Jerry Pimm | 25-5 |
| 15 | Tennessee | 20-7 | Don DeVoe | 21-8 |
| 16 | BYU | 22-6 | Frank Arnold | 25-7 |
| 17 | Wyoming | 23-5 | Jim Brandenburg | 24-6 |
| 18 | Maryland | 20-9 | Lefty Driesell | 21-10 |
| 19 | Illinois | 20-7 | Lou Henson | 21-8 |
| 20 | Arkansas | 22-7 | Eddie Sutton | 24-8 |

**NCAA Final Four** (at the Spectrum, Phila.): **Semifinals**–N. Carolina 78, Virginia 65; Indiana 67, LSU 49. **Third Place**–Virginia 78, LSU 74. **Championship**–Indiana 63, N. Carolina 50.

**NIT Championship** (at Madison Square Garden): Tulsa 86, Syracuse 84. Top 20 teams played in NIT.

## 1982

| | | Before Tourns | Head Coach | Final Record |
|---|---|---|---|---|
| 1 | **N. Carolina** | 27-2 | Dean Smith | 32-2 |
| 2 | DePaul | 26-1 | Ray Meyer | 26-2 |
| 3 | Virginia | 29-3 | Terry Holland | 30-4 |
| 4 | Oregon St. | 23-4 | Ralph Miller | 25-5 |
| 5 | Missouri | 26-3 | Norm Stewart | 27-4 |
| 6 | Georgetown | 26-6 | John Thompson | 30-7 |
| 7 | Minnesota | 22-5 | Jim Dutcher | 23-6 |
| 8 | Idaho | 26-2 | Don Monson | 27-3 |
| 9 | Memphis St. | 23-4 | Dana Kirk | 24-5 |
| 10 | Tulsa | 24-5 | Nolan Richardson | 24-6 |
| 11 | Fresno St. | 26-2 | Boyd Grant | 27-3 |
| 12 | Arkansas | 23-5 | Eddie Sutton | 23-6 |
| 13 | Alabama | 23-6 | Wimp Sanderson | 24-7 |
| 14 | West Virginia | 26-3 | Gale Catlett | 27-4 |
| 15 | Kentucky | 22-7 | Joe B. Hall | 22-8 |
| 16 | Iowa | 20-7 | Lute Olson | 21-8 |
| 17 | Ala-Birmingham | 23-5 | Gene Bartow | 25-6 |
| 18 | Wake Forest | 20-8 | Carl Tacy | 21-9 |
| 19 | UCLA | 21-6 | Larry Farmer | 21-6 |
| 20 | Louisville | 20-9 | Denny Crum | 23-10 |

**NCAA Final Four** (at the Superdome, New Orleans): **Semifinals**–N. Carolina 68, Houston 63; Georgetown 50, Louisville 46. **Championship**–N. Carolina 63, Georgetown 62.

**NIT Championship** (at Madison Square Garden): Bradley 67, Purdue 58. No Top 20 teams played in NIT.

## 1983

| | | Before Tourns | Head Coach | Final Record |
|---|---|---|---|---|
| 1 | Houston | 27-2 | Guy Lewis | 31-3 |
| 2 | Louisville | 29-3 | Denny Crum | 32-4 |
| 3 | St. John's | 27-4 | Lou Carnesecca | 28-5 |
| 4 | Virginia | 27-4 | Terry Holland | 29-5 |
| 5 | Indiana | 23-5 | Bob Knight | 24-6 |
| 6 | UNLV | 28-2 | Jerry Tarkanian | 28-3 |
| 7 | UCLA | 23-5 | Larry Farmer | 23-6 |
| 8 | North Carolina | 26-7 | Dean Smith | 28-8 |
| 9 | Arkansas | 25-3 | Eddie Sutton | 26-4 |
| 10 | Missouri | 26-7 | Norm Stewart | 26-8 |
| 11 | Boston College | 24-6 | Gary Williams | 25-7 |
| 12 | Kentucky | 22-7 | Joe B. Hall | 23-8 |
| 13 | Villanova | 22-7 | Rollie Massimino | 24-8 |
| 14 | Wichita St. | 25-3 | Gene Smithson | same* |
| 15 | Tenn-Chatt. | 26-3 | Murray Arnold | 26-4 |
| 16 | **N.C. State** | 20-10 | Jim Valvano | 26-10 |
| 17 | Memphis St. | 22-7 | Dana Kirk | 23-8 |
| 18 | Georgia | 21-9 | Hugh Durham | 24-10 |
| 19 | Oklahoma St. | 24-6 | Paul Hansen | 24-7 |
| 20 | Georgetown | 21-9 | John Thompson | 22-10 |

*On probation

**NCAA Final Four** (at The Pit, Albuquerque, NM): **Semifinals**–N.C. State 67, Georgia 60; Houston 94, Louisville 81. **Championship**–N.C. State 54, Houston 52.

**NIT Championship** (at Madison Square Garden): Fresno St. 69, DePaul 60. No Top 20 teams played in NIT.

## 1984

| | | Before Tourns | Head Coach | Final Record |
|---|---|---|---|---|
| 1 | North Carolina | 27-2 | Dean Smith | 28-3 |
| 2 | **Georgetown** | 29-3 | John Thompson | 34-3 |
| 3 | Kentucky | 26-4 | Joe B. Hall | 29-5 |
| 4 | DePaul | 26-2 | Ray Meyer | 27-3 |
| 5 | Houston | 28-4 | Guy Lewis | 32-5 |
| 6 | Illinois | 24-4 | Lou Henson | 26-5 |
| 7 | Oklahoma | 29-4 | Billy Tubbs | 29-5 |
| 8 | Arkansas | 25-6 | Eddie Sutton | 25-7 |
| 9 | UTEP | 27-3 | Don Haskins | 27-4 |
| 10 | Purdue | 22-6 | Gene Keady | 22-7 |
| 11 | Maryland | 23-7 | Lefty Driesell | 24-8 |
| 12 | Tulsa | 27-3 | Nolan Richardson | 27-4 |
| 13 | UNLV | 27-5 | Jerry Tarkanian | 29-6 |
| 14 | Duke | 24-9 | Mike Krzyzewski | 24-10 |
| 15 | Washington | 22-6 | Marv Harshman | 24-7 |
| 16 | Memphis St. | 24-6 | Dana Kirk | 26-7 |
| 17 | Oregon St. | 22-6 | Ralph Miller | 22-7 |
| 18 | Syracuse | 22-8 | Jim Boeheim | 23-9 |
| 19 | Wake Forest | 21-8 | Carl Tacy | 23-9 |
| 20 | Temple | 25-4 | John Chaney | 26-5 |

**NCAA Final Four** (at the Kingdome, Seattle): **Semifinals**–Houston 49, Virginia 47 (OT); Georgetown 53, Kentucky 40. **Championship**–Georgetown 84, Houston 75.

**NIT Championship** (at Madison Square Garden): Michigan 83, Notre Dame 63. No Top 20 teams played in NIT.

## Highest-Rated College Games on TV

The dozen highest-rated college basketball games seen on U.S. television have been NCAA tournament championship games, led by the 1979 Michigan State-Indiana State final that featured Magic Johnson and Larry Bird.

Listed below are the finalists (winning team first), date of game, TV network, and TV rating and audience share (according to Nielson Media Research).

| | | Date | Net | Rtg/Sh |
|---|---|---|---|---|
| 1 | Michigan St.-Indiana St. | 3/26/79 | NBC | 24.1/38 |
| 2 | Villanova-Georgetown | 4/1/85 | CBS | 23.3/33 |
| 3 | Duke-Michigan | 4/6/92 | CBS | 22.7/35 |
| 4 | N.C. State-Houston | 4/4/83 | CBS | 22.3/32 |
| 5 | N. Carolina-Michigan | 4/5/93 | CBS | 22.2/34 |
| 6 | Arkansas-Duke | 4/4/94 | CBS | 21.6/33 |

| | | Date | Net | Rtg/Sh |
|---|---|---|---|---|
| 7 | N. Carolina-Georgetown | 3/29/82 | CBS | 21.6/31 |
| 8 | UCLA-Kentucky | 3/31/75 | NBC | 21.3/33 |
| 9 | Michigan-Seton Hall | 4/3/89 | CBS | 21.3/33 |
| 10 | Louisville-Duke | 3/31/86 | CBS | 20.7/31 |
| 11 | Indiana-N. Carolina | 3/30/81 | NBC | 20.7/29 |
| 12 | UCLA-Memphis St. | 3/26/73 | NBC | 20.5/32 |

## Associated Press Final Polls (Cont.)

### 1985

| | | | Before Tourns | Head Coach | Final Record |
|---|---|---|---|---|---|
| 1 | Georgetown | . . . | .30-2 | John Thompson | 35-3 |
| 2 | Michigan | . . . . . | .25-3 | Bill Frieder | 26-4 |
| 3 | St. John's | . . . . . | .27-3 | Lou Carnesecca | 31-4 |
| 4 | Oklahoma | . . . . | .28-5 | Billy Tubbs | 31-6 |
| 5 | Memphis St. | . . . | .27-3 | Dana Kirk | 31-4 |
| 6 | Georgia Tech | . . | .24-7 | Bobby Cremins | 27-8 |
| 7 | North Carolina | . . | .24-8 | Dean Smith | 27-9 |
| 8 | Louisiana Tech | . . | .27-2 | Andy Russo | 29-3 |
| 9 | UNLV | . . . . . . . | .27-3 | Jerry Tarkanian | 28-4 |
| 10 | Duke | . . . . . . | .22-7 | Mike Krzyzewski | 23-8 |
| 11 | VCU | . . . . . | .25-5 | J.D. Barnett | 26-6 |
| 12 | Illinois | . . . . . | .24-8 | Lou Henson | 26-9 |
| 13 | Kansas | . . . . . | .25-7 | Larry Brown | 26-8 |
| 14 | Loyola-IL | . . . . | .25-5 | Gene Sullivan | 27-6 |
| 15 | Syracuse | . . . . | .21-8 | Jim Boeheim | 22-9 |
| 16 | N.C. State | . . . . | .20-9 | Jim Valvano | 23-10 |
| 17 | Texas Tech | . . . | .23-7 | Gerald Myers | 23-8 |
| 18 | Tulsa | . . . . . . . | .23-7 | Nolan Richardson | 23-8 |
| 19 | Georgia | . . . . . | .21-8 | Hugh Durham | 22-9 |
| 20 | LSU | . . . . . . . . | .19-9 | Dale Brown | 19-10 |

**Note:** Unranked **Villanova**, coached by Rollie Massimino, won the NCAAs. The Wildcats entered the tourney at 19-10 and had a final record of 25-10.

**NCAA Final Four** (at Rupp Arena, Lexington, KY): **Semifinals–** Georgetown 77, St. John's 59; Villanova 52, Memphis St. 45. **Championship–**Villanova 66, Georgetown 64.

**NIT Championship** (at Madison Square Garden): UCLA 65, Indiana 62. No Top 20 teams played in NIT.

### 1987

| | | | Before Tourns | Head Coach | Final Record |
|---|---|---|---|---|---|
| 1 | UNLV | . . . . . . . . | .33-1 | Jerry Tarkanian | 37-2 |
| 2 | North Carolina | . . | .29-3 | Dean Smith | 32-4 |
| 3 | **Indiana** | . . . . . | .24-4 | Bob Knight | 30-4 |
| 4 | Georgetown | . . . | .26-4 | John Thompson | 29-5 |
| 5 | DePaul | . . . . . | .26-2 | Joey Meyer | 28-3 |
| 6 | Iowa | . . . . . . . | .27-4 | Tom Davis | 30-5 |
| 7 | Purdue | . . . . . | .24-4 | Gene Keady | 25-5 |
| 8 | Temple | . . . . . | .31-3 | John Chaney | 32-4 |
| 9 | Alabama | . . . . | .26-4 | Wimp Sanderson | 28-5 |
| 10 | Syracuse | . . . . | .26-6 | Jim Boeheim | 31-7 |
| 11 | Illinois | . . . . . | .23-7 | Lou Henson | 23-8 |
| 12 | Pittsburgh | . . . | .24-7 | Paul Evans | 25-8 |
| 13 | Clemson | . . . . | .25-5 | Cliff Ellis | 25-6 |
| 14 | Missouri | . . . . | .24-9 | Norm Stewart | 24-10 |
| 15 | UCLA | . . . . . . | .24-6 | Walt Hazzard | 25-7 |
| 16 | New Orleans | . . | .25-3 | Benny Dees | 26-4 |
| 17 | Duke | . . . . . . | .22-8 | Mike Krzyzewski | 24-9 |
| 18 | Notre Dame | . . . | .22-7 | Digger Phelps | 24-8 |
| 19 | TCU | . . . . . . | .23-6 | Jim Killingsworth | 24-7 |
| 20 | Kansas | . . . . . . | .23-10 | Larry Brown | 25-11 |

**NCAA Final Four** (at the Superdome, New Orleans): **Semifinals–**Syracuse 77, Providence 63; Indiana 97, UNLV 93. **Championship–**Indiana 74, Syracuse 73.

**NIT Championship** (at Madison Square Garden): Southern Miss. 84, La Salle 80. No Top 20 teams played in NIT.

### 1986

| | | | Before Tourns | Head Coach | Final Record |
|---|---|---|---|---|---|
| 1 | Duke | . . . . . . . . | .32-2 | Mike Krzyzewski | 37-3 |
| 2 | Kansas | . . . . . | .31-3 | Larry Brown | 35-4 |
| 3 | Kentucky | . . . . | .29-3 | Eddie Sutton | 32-4 |
| 4 | St. John's | . . . . | .30-4 | Lou Carnesecca | 31-5 |
| 5 | Michigan | . . . . | .27-4 | Bill Frieder | 28-5 |
| 6 | Georgia Tech | . . | .25-6 | Bobby Cremins | 27-7 |
| 7 | **Louisville** | . . . | .26-7 | Denny Crum | 32-7 |
| 8 | North Carolina | . . | .26-5 | Dean Smith | 28-6 |
| 9 | Syracuse | . . . . | .25-5 | Jim Boeheim | 26-6 |
| 10 | Notre Dame | . . . | .23-5 | Digger Phelps | 23-6 |
| 11 | UNLV | . . . . . . | .31-4 | Jerry Tarkanian | 33-5 |
| 12 | Memphis St. | . . . | .27-5 | Dana Kirk | 28-6 |
| 13 | Georgetown | . . . | .23-7 | John Thompson | 24-8 |
| 14 | Bradley | . . . . . | .31-2 | Dick Versace | 32-3 |
| 15 | Oklahoma | . . . | .25-8 | Billy Tubbs | 26-9 |
| 16 | Indiana | . . . . . | .21-7 | Bob Knight | 21-8 |
| 17 | Navy | . . . . . . | .27-4 | Paul Evans | 30-5 |
| 18 | Michigan St. | . . . | .21-7 | Jud Heathcote | 23-8 |
| 19 | Illinois | . . . . . | .21-9 | Lou Henson | 22-10 |
| 20 | UTEP | . . . . . . | .27-5 | Don Haskins | 27-6 |

**NCAA Final Four** (at Reunion Arena, Dallas): **Semifinals–**Duke 71, Kansas 67; Louisville 88, LSU 77. **Championship–**Louisville 72, Duke 69.

**NIT Championship** (at Madison Square Garden): Ohio St. 73, Wyoming 63. No Top 20 teams played in NIT.

### 1988

| | | | Before Tourns | Head Coach | Final Record |
|---|---|---|---|---|---|
| 1 | Temple | . . . . . . | .29-1 | John Chaney | 32-2 |
| 2 | Arizona | . . . . . | .31-2 | Lute Olson | 35-3 |
| 3 | Purdue | . . . . . | .27-3 | Gene Keady | 29-4 |
| 4 | Oklahoma | . . . | .30-3 | Billy Tubbs | 35-4 |
| 5 | Duke | . . . . . . | .24-6 | Mike Krzyzewski | 28-7 |
| 6 | Kentucky | . . . . | .25-5 | Eddie Sutton | 27-6 |
| 7 | North Carolina | . . | .24-6 | Dean Smith | 27-7 |
| 8 | Pittsburgh | . . . | .23-6 | Paul Evans | 24-7 |
| 9 | Syracuse | . . . . | .25-8 | Jim Boeheim | 26-9 |
| 10 | Michigan | . . . . | .24-7 | Bill Frieder | 26-8 |
| 11 | Bradley | . . . . . | .26-4 | Stan Albeck | 26-5 |
| 12 | UNLV | . . . . . . | .27-5 | Jerry Tarkanian | 28-6 |
| 13 | Wyoming | . . . . | .26-5 | Benny Dees | 26-6 |
| 14 | N.C. State | . . . . | .24-7 | Jim Valvano | 24-8 |
| 15 | Loyola-CA | . . . | .27-3 | Paul Westhead | 28-4 |
| 16 | Illinois | . . . . . | .22-9 | Lou Henson | 23-10 |
| 17 | Iowa | . . . . . . . | .22-9 | Tom Davis | 24-10 |
| 18 | Xavier-OH | . . . . | .26-3 | Pete Gillen | 26-4 |
| 19 | BYU | . . . . . | .25-5 | Ladell Andersen | 26-6 |
| 20 | Kansas St. | . . . . | .22-8 | Lon Kruger | 25-9 |

**Note:** Unranked **Kansas**, coached by Larry Brown, won the NCAAs. The Jayhawks entered the tourney at 21-11 and had a final record of 27-11.

**NCAA Final Four** (at Kemper Arena, Kansas City): **Semifinals–**Kansas 66, Duke 59; Oklahoma 86, Arizona 78. **Championship–**Kansas 83, Oklahoma 79.

**NIT Championship** (at Madison Square Garden): Connecticut 72, Ohio St. 67. No Top 20 teams played in NIT.

## 1989

| | Team | Before Tourns | Head Coach | Final Record |
|---|---|---|---|---|
| 1 | Arizona | 27-3 | Lute Olson | 29-4 |
| 2 | Georgetown | 26-4 | John Thompson | 29-5 |
| 3 | Illinois | 27-4 | Lou Henson | 31-5 |
| 4 | Oklahoma | 28-5 | Billy Tubbs | 30-6 |
| 5 | North Carolina | 27-7 | Dean Smith | 29-8 |
| 6 | Missouri | 27-7 | Norm Stewart & Rich Daly* | 29-8 |
| 7 | Syracuse | 27-7 | Jim Boeheim | 30-8 |
| 8 | Indiana | 25-7 | Bob Knight | 27-8 |
| 9 | Duke | 24-7 | Mike Krzyzewski | 28-8 |
| 10 | **Michigan** | 24-7 | Bill Frieder (24-7) & Steve Fisher (6-0) | 30-7 |
| 11 | Seton Hall | 26-6 | P.J. Carlesimo | 31-7 |
| 12 | Louisville | 22-8 | Denny Crum | 24-9 |
| 13 | Stanford | 26-6 | Mike Montgomery | 26-7 |
| 14 | Iowa | 22-9 | Tom Davis | 23-10 |
| 15 | UNLV | 26-7 | Jerry Tarkanian | 29-8 |
| 16 | Florida St. | 22-7 | Pat Kennedy | 22-8 |
| 17 | West Virginia | 25-4 | Gale Catlett | 26-5 |
| 18 | Ball State | 28-2 | Rick Majerus | 29-3 |
| 19 | N.C. State | 20-8 | Jim Valvano | 22-9 |
| 20 | Alabama | 23-7 | Wimp Sanderson | 23-8 |

**NCAA Final Four** (at The Kingdome, Seattle): **Semifinals**–Seton Hall 95, Duke 78; Michigan 83, Illinois 81. **Championship**–Michigan 80, Seton Hall 79 (OT). **NIT Championship** (at Madison Square Garden): St. John's 73, St. Louis 65. No Top 20 teams played in NIT.
*Norm Stewart's assistant Rich Daly temporarily took over for his ailing boss (Daly coached the final 14 games of the season) but returned to his role as an assistant when Stewart recovered before the start of the following season.

## 1991

| | Team | Before Tourns | Head Coach | Final Record |
|---|---|---|---|---|
| 1 | UNLV | 30-0 | Jerry Tarkanian | 34-1 |
| 2 | Arkansas | 31-3 | Nolan Richardson | 34-4 |
| 3 | Indiana | 27-4 | Bob Knight | 29-5 |
| 4 | North Carolina | 25-5 | Dean Smith | 29-6 |
| 5 | Ohio St. | 25-3 | Randy Ayers | 27-4 |
| 6 | **Duke** | 26-7 | Mike Krzyzewski | 32-7 |
| 7 | Syracuse | 26-5 | Jim Boeheim | 26-6 |
| 8 | Arizona | 26-6 | Lute Olson | 28-7 |
| 9 | Kentucky | 22-6 | Rick Pitino | same* |
| 10 | Utah | 28-3 | Rick Majerus | 30-4 |
| 11 | Nebraska | 26-7 | Danny Nee | 26-8 |
| 12 | Kansas | 22-7 | Roy Williams | 27-8 |
| 13 | Seton Hall | 22-8 | P.J. Carlesimo | 25-9 |
| 14 | Oklahoma St. | 22-7 | Eddie Sutton | 24-8 |
| 15 | New Mexico St. | 23-5 | Neil McCarthy | 23-6 |
| 16 | UCLA | 23-5 | Jim Harrick | 23-9 |
| 17 | E.Tennessee St. | 28-4 | Alan LaForce | 28-5 |
| 18 | Princeton | 24-2 | Pete Carril | 24-3 |
| 19 | Alabama | 21-9 | Wimp Sanderson | 23-10 |
| 20 | St. John's | 20-8 | Lou Carnesecca | 23-9 |
| 21 | Mississippi St. | 20-8 | Richard Williams | 20-9 |
| 22 | LSU | 20-9 | Dale Brown | 20-10 |
| 23 | Texas | 22-8 | Tom Penders | 23-9 |
| 24 | DePaul | 20-8 | Joey Meyer | 20-9 |
| 25 | Southern Miss. | 21-7 | M.K. Turk | 21-8 |

*On probation
**NCAA Final Four** (at the Hoosier Dome, Indianapolis): **Semifinals**–Kansas 79, North Carolina 73; Duke 79, UNLV 77. **Championship**–Duke 72, Kansas 65. **NIT Championship** (at Madison Square Garden): Stanford 78, Oklahoma 72. No Top 25 teams played in NIT.

## 1990

| | Team | Before Tourns | Head Coach | Final Record |
|---|---|---|---|---|
| 1 | Oklahoma | 26-4 | Billy Tubbs | 27-5 |
| 2 | **UNLV** | 29-5 | Jerry Tarkanian | 35-5 |
| 3 | Connecticut | 28-5 | Jim Calhoun | 31-6 |
| 4 | Michigan St. | 26-5 | Jud Heathcote | 28-6 |
| 5 | Kansas | 29-4 | Roy Williams | 30-5 |
| 6 | Syracuse | 24-6 | Jim Boeheim | 26-7 |
| 7 | Arkansas | 26-4 | Nolan Richardson | 30-5 |
| 8 | Georgetown | 23-6 | John Thompson | 24-7 |
| 9 | Georgia Tech | 24-6 | Bobby Cremins | 28-7 |
| 10 | Purdue | 21-7 | Gene Keady | 22-8 |
| 11 | Missouri | 26-5 | Norm Stewart | 26-6 |
| 12 | La Salle | 29-1 | Speedy Morris | 30-2 |
| 13 | Michigan | 22-7 | Steve Fisher | 23-8 |
| 14 | Arizona | 24-6 | Lute Olson | 25-7 |
| 15 | Duke | 24-8 | Mike Krzyzewski | 29-9 |
| 16 | Louisville | 26-7 | Denny Crum | 27-8 |
| 17 | Clemson | 24-8 | Cliff Ellis | 26-9 |
| 18 | Illinois | 21-7 | Lou Henson | 21-8 |
| 19 | LSU | 22-8 | Dale Brown | 23-9 |
| 20 | Minnesota | 20-8 | Clem Haskins | 23-9 |
| 21 | Loyola-CA | 23-5 | Paul Westhead | 26-6 |
| 22 | Oregon St. | 22-6 | Jim Anderson | 22-7 |
| 23 | Alabama | 24-8 | Wimp Sanderson | 26-9 |
| 24 | New Mexico St. | 26-4 | Neil McCarthy | 26-5 |
| 25 | Xavier-OH | 26-4 | Pete Gillen | 28-5 |

**NCAA Final Four** (at McNichols Sports Arena, Denver): **Semifinals**–Duke 97, Arkansas 83; UNLV 90, Georgia Tech 81. **Championship**–UNLV 103, Duke 73. **NIT Championship** (at Madison Square Garden): Vanderbilt 74, St.Louis 72. No Top 25 teams played in NIT.

## 1992

| | Team | Before Tourns | Head Coach | Final Record |
|---|---|---|---|---|
| 1 | **Duke** | 28-2 | Mike Krzyzewski | 34-2 |
| 2 | Kansas | 26-4 | Roy Williams | 27-5 |
| 3 | Ohio St. | 23-5 | Randy Ayers | 26-6 |
| 4 | UCLA | 25-4 | Jim Harrick | 28-5 |
| 5 | Indiana | 23-6 | Bob Knight | 27-7 |
| 6 | Kentucky | 26-6 | Rick Pitino | 29-7 |
| 7 | UNLV | 26-2 | Jerry Tarkanian | same* |
| 8 | USC | 23-5 | George Raveling | 24-6 |
| 9 | Arkansas | 25-7 | Nolan Richardson | 26-8 |
| 10 | Arizona | 24-6 | Lute Olson | 24-7 |
| 11 | Oklahoma St. | 26-7 | Eddie Sutton | 28-8 |
| 12 | Cincinnati | 25-4 | Bob Huggins | 29-5 |
| 13 | Alabama | 25-8 | Wimp Sanderson | 26-9 |
| 14 | Michigan St. | 21-7 | Jud Heathcote | 22-8 |
| 15 | Michigan | 20-8 | Steve Fisher | 25-9 |
| 16 | Missouri | 20-8 | Norm Stewart | 21-9 |
| 17 | Massachusetts | 28-4 | John Calipari | 30-5 |
| 18 | North Carolina | 21-9 | Dean Smith | 23-10 |
| 19 | Seton Hall | 21-8 | P.J. Carlesimo | 23-9 |
| 20 | Florida St. | 20-9 | Pat Kennedy | 22-10 |
| 21 | Syracuse | 21-9 | Jim Boeheim | 22-10 |
| 22 | Georgetown | 21-9 | John Thompson | 22-10 |
| 23 | Oklahoma | 21-8 | Billy Tubbs | 21-9 |
| 24 | DePaul | 20-9 | Joey Meyer | 20-9 |
| 25 | LSU | 20-9 | Dale Brown | 21-10 |

*On probation
**NCAA Final Four** (at the Metrodome, Minneapolis): **Semifinals**–Michigan 76, Cincinnati 72; Duke 81, Indiana 78. **Championship**–Duke 71, Michigan 51. **NIT Championship** (at Madison Square Garden): Virginia 81, Notre Dame 76 (OT). No Top 25 teams played in NIT.

## Associated Press Final Polls (Cont.)

### 1993

| | | Before Tourns | Head Coach | Final Record |
|---|---|---|---|---|
| 1 | Indiana | 28-3 | Bob Knight | 31-4 |
| 2 | Kentucky | 26-3 | Rick Pitino | 30-4 |
| 3 | Michigan | 26-4 | Steve Fisher | 31-5 |
| 4 | N. Carolina | 28-4 | Dean Smith | 34-4 |
| 5 | Arizona | 24-3 | Lute Olson | 24-4 |
| 6 | Seton Hall | 27-6 | P.J. Carlesimo | 28-7 |
| 7 | Cincinnati | 24-4 | Bob Huggins | 27-5 |
| 8 | Vanderbilt | 26-5 | Eddie Fogler | 28-6 |
| 9 | Kansas | 25-6 | Roy Williams | 29-7 |
| 10 | Duke | 23-7 | Mike Krzyzewski | 24-8 |
| 11 | Florida St. | 22-9 | Pat Kennedy | 25-10 |
| 12 | Arkansas | 20-8 | Nolan Richardson | 22-9 |
| 13 | Iowa | 22-8 | Tom Davis | 23-9 |
| 14 | Massachusetts | 23-6 | John Calipari | 24-7 |
| 15 | Louisville | 20-8 | Denny Crum | 22-9 |
| 16 | Wake Forest | 19-8 | Dave Odom | 21-9 |
| 17 | New Orleans | 26-3 | Tim Floyd | 26-4 |
| 18 | Georgia Tech | 19-10 | Bobby Cremins | 19-11 |
| 19 | Utah | 23-6 | Rick Majerus | 24-7 |
| 20 | Western Ky. | 24-5 | Ralph Willard | 26-6 |
| 21 | New Mexico | 24-6 | Dave Bliss | 24-7 |
| 22 | Purdue | 18-9 | Gene Keady | 18-10 |
| 23 | Oklahoma St. | 19-8 | Eddie Sutton | 20-9 |
| 24 | New Mexico St. | 25-7 | Neil McCarthy | 26-8 |
| 25 | UNLV | 21-7 | Rollie Massimino | 21-8 |

**NCAA Final Four** (at the Superdome, New Orleans): **Semifinals**–North Carolina 78, Kansas 68; Michigan 81, Kentucky 78 (OT). **Championship**–North Carolina 77, Michigan 71.

**NIT Championship** (at Madison Square Garden): Minnesota 62, Georgetown 61. No. 25 UNLV was the only Top 25 team that played in the NIT.

### 1994

| | | Before Tourns | Head Coach | Final Record |
|---|---|---|---|---|
| 1 | North Carolina | 27-6 | Dean Smith | 28-7 |
| 2 | Arkansas | 25-3 | Nolan Richardson | 31-3 |
| 3 | Purdue | 26-4 | Gene Keady | 29-5 |
| 4 | Connecticut | 27-4 | Jim Calhoun | 29-5 |
| 5 | Missouri | 25-3 | Norm Stewart | 28-4 |
| 6 | Duke | 23-5 | Mike Krzyzewski | 28-6 |
| 7 | Kentucky | 26-6 | Rick Pitino | 27-7 |
| 8 | Massachusetts | 27-6 | John Calipari | 28-7 |
| 9 | Arizona | 25-5 | Lute Olson | 29-6 |
| 10 | Louisville | 26-5 | Denny Crum | 28-6 |
| 11 | Michigan | 21-7 | Steve Fisher | 24-8 |
| 12 | Temple | 22-7 | John Chaney | 23-8 |
| 13 | Kansas | 25-7 | Roy Williams | 27-8 |
| 14 | Florida | 25-7 | Lon Kruger | 29-8 |
| 15 | Syracuse | 21-6 | Jim Boeheim | 23-7 |
| 16 | California | 22-7 | Todd Bozeman | 22-8 |
| 17 | UCLA | 21-6 | Jim Harrick | 21-7 |
| 18 | Indiana | 19-8 | Bob Knight | 21-9 |
| 19 | Oklahoma St. | 23-9 | Eddie Sutton | 24-10 |
| 20 | Texas | 25-7 | Tom Penders | 26-8 |
| 21 | Marquette | 22-8 | Kevin O'Neill | 24-9 |
| 22 | Nebraska | 20-9 | Danny Nee | 20-10 |
| 23 | Minnesota | 20-11 | Clem Haskins | 21-12 |
| 24 | Saint Louis | 23-5 | Charlie Spoonhour | 23-6 |
| 25 | Cincinnati | 22-9 | Bob Huggins | 22-10 |

**NCAA Final Four** (at the Charlotte Coliseum): **Semifinals**– Arkansas 91, Arizona 82; Duke 70, Florida 65. **Championship**– Arkansas 76, Duke 72.

**NIT Championship** (at Madison Square Garden): Villanova 80, Vanderbilt 73. No top 25 teams played in NIT.

### 1995

| | | Before Tourns | Head Coach | Final Record |
|---|---|---|---|---|
| 1 | UCLA | 25-2 | Jim Harrick | 31-2 |
| 2 | Kentucky | 25-4 | Rick Pitino | 28-5 |
| 3 | Wake Forest | 24-5 | Dave Odom | 26-6 |
| 4 | North Carolina | 24-5 | Dean Smith | 28-6 |
| 5 | Kansas | 23-5 | Roy Williams | 25-6 |
| 6 | Arkansas | 27-6 | Nolan Richardson | 32-7 |
| 7 | Massachusetts | 26-4 | John Calipari | 26-5 |
| 8 | Connecticut | 25-4 | Jim Calhoun | 28-5 |
| 9 | Villanova | 25-7 | Steve Lappas | 25-8 |
| 10 | Maryland | 24-7 | Gary Williams | 26-8 |
| 11 | Michigan St. | 22-5 | Jud Heathcote | 22-6 |
| 12 | Purdue | 24-6 | Gene Keady | 25-7 |
| 13 | Virginia | 22-8 | Jeff Jones | 25-9 |
| 14 | Oklahoma St. | 23-9 | Eddie Sutton | 27-10 |
| 15 | Arizona | 23-7 | Lute Olson | 23-8 |
| 16 | Arizona St. | 22-8 | Bill Frieder | 24-9 |
| 17 | Oklahoma | 23-8 | Kelvin Sampson | 23-9 |
| 18 | Mississippi St. | 20-7 | Richard Williams | 22-8 |
| 19 | Utah | 27-5 | Rick Majerus | 28-6 |
| 20 | Alabama | 22-9 | David Hobbs | 23-10 |
| 21 | Western Ky. | 26-3 | Matt Kilcullen | 27-4 |
| 22 | Georgetown | 19-9 | John Thompson | 21-10 |
| 23 | Missouri | 19-8 | Norm Stewart | 20-9 |
| 24 | Iowa St. | 22-10 | Tim Floyd | 23-11 |
| 25 | Syracuse | 19-9 | Jim Boeheim | 20-10 |

**NCAA Final Four** (at the Kingdome, Seattle): **Semifinals**– UCLA 74, Oklahoma St. 61; Arkansas 75, North Carolina 68. **Championship**–UCLA 89, Arkansas 78.

**NIT Championship** (at Madison Square Garden):Virginia Tech 65, Marquette 64 (OT). No top 25 teams played in NIT.

### 1996

| | | Before Tourns | Head Coach | Final Record |
|---|---|---|---|---|
| 1 | Massachusetts | 31-1 | John Calipari | 35-2 |
| 2 | Kentucky | 28-2 | Rick Pitino | 34-2 |
| 3 | Connecticut | 30-2 | Jim Calhoun | 32-3 |
| 4 | Georgetown | 26-7 | John Thompson | 29-8 |
| 5 | Kansas | 26-4 | Roy Williams | 29-5 |
| 6 | Purdue | 25-5 | Gene Keady | 26-6 |
| 7 | Cincinnati | 25-4 | Bob Huggins | 28-5 |
| 8 | Texas Tech | 28-1 | James Dickey | 30-2 |
| 9 | Wake Forest | 23-5 | Dave Odom | 26-6 |
| 10 | Villanova | 25-6 | Steve Lappas | 26-7 |
| 11 | Arizona | 24-6 | Lute Olson | 26-7 |
| 12 | Utah | 25-6 | Rick Majerus | 27-7 |
| 13 | Georgia Tech | 22-11 | Bobby Cremins | 24-12 |
| 14 | UCLA | 23-7 | Jim Harrick | 23-8 |
| 15 | Syracuse | 24-8 | Jim Boeheim | 29-9 |
| 16 | Memphis | 22-7 | Larry Finch | 22-8 |
| 17 | Iowa St. | 23-8 | Tim Floyd | 24-9 |
| 18 | Penn St. | 21-6 | Jerry Dunn | 21-7 |
| 19 | Mississippi St. | 22-7 | Richard Williams | 26-8 |
| 20 | Marquette | 22-7 | Mike Deane | 23-8 |
| 21 | Iowa | 22-8 | Tom Davis | 23-9 |
| 22 | Virginia Tech | 22-5 | Bill Foster | 23-6 |
| 23 | New Mexico | 27-4 | Dave Bliss | 28-5 |
| 24 | Louisville | 20-11 | Denny Crum | 22-12 |
| 25 | North Carolina | 20-10 | Dean Smith | 21-11 |

**NCAA Final Four** (at the Meadowlands, E. Rutherford, N.J.): **Semifinals**– Kentucky 81, Massachusetts 74; Syracuse 77, Mississippi St. 69. **Championship**– Kentucky 76, Syracuse 67.

**NIT Championship** (at Madison Square Garden): Nebraska 60, St. Joseph's 56. No top 25 teams played in NIT.

### 1997

| | | Before Tourns | Head Coach | Final Record |
|---|---|---|---|---|
| 1 | Kansas | 32-1 | Roy Williams | 34-2 |
| 2 | Utah | 26-3 | Rick Majerus | 29-4 |
| 3 | Minnesota | 27-3 | Clem Haskins | 31-4 |
| 4 | North Carolina | 24-6 | Dean Smith | 28-7 |
| 5 | Kentucky | 30-4 | Rick Pitino | 35-5 |
| 6 | South Carolina | 24-7 | Eddie Fogler | 24-8 |
| 7 | UCLA | 21-7 | Steve Lavin | 24-8 |
| 8 | Duke | 23-8 | Mike Krzyzewski | 24-9 |
| 9 | Wake Forest | 23-6 | Dave Odom | 24-7 |
| 10 | Cincinnati | 25-7 | Bob Huggins | 26-8 |
| 11 | New Mexico | 24-7 | Dave Bliss | 25-8 |
| 12 | St. Joseph's | 24-6 | Phil Martelli | 26-7 |
| 13 | Xavier | 22-5 | Skip Prosser | 23-6 |
| 14 | Clemson | 21-9 | Rick Barnes | 23-10 |
| 15 | **Arizona** | 19-9 | Lute Olson | 25-9 |
| 16 | Charleston | 28-2 | John Kresse | 29-3 |
| 17 | Georgia | 24-8 | Tubby Smith | 24-9 |
| 18 | Iowa St. | 20-8 | Tim Floyd | 22-9 |
| 19 | Illinois | 21-9 | Lon Kruger | 22-10 |
| 20 | Villanova | 23-9 | Steve Lappas | 24-10 |
| 21 | Stanford | 20-7 | Mike Montgomery | 22-8 |
| 22 | Maryland | 21-10 | Gary Williams | 21-11 |
| 23 | Boston College | 21-8 | Jim O'Brien | 22-9 |
| 24 | Colorado | 21-9 | Ricardo Patton | 22-10 |
| 25 | Louisville | 23-8 | Denny Crum | 26-9 |

**NCAA Final Four** (at the RCA Dome, Indianapolis): **Semifinals**– Kentucky 78, Minnesota 69; Arizona 66, North Carolina 58. **Championship**– Arizona 84, Kentucky 79 (OT).
**NIT Championship** (at Madison Square Garden): Michigan 82, Florida St. 72. No top 25 teams played in NIT.

### 1998

| | | Before Tourns | Head Coach | Final Record |
|---|---|---|---|---|
| 1 | North Carolina | 30-3 | Bill Guthridge | 34-4 |
| 2 | Kansas | 34-3 | Roy Williams | 35-4 |
| 3 | Duke | 29-3 | Mike Krzyzewski | 32-4 |
| 4 | Arizona | 27-4 | Lute Olson | 30-5 |
| 5 | **Kentucky** | 29-4 | Tubby Smith | 35-4 |
| 6 | Connecticut | 29-4 | Jim Calhoun | 32-5 |
| 7 | Utah | 25-3 | Rick Majerus | 30-4 |
| 8 | Princeton | 26-1 | Bill Carmody | 27-2 |
| 9 | Cincinnati | 26-5 | Bob Huggins | 27-6 |
| 10 | Stanford | 26-4 | Mike Montgomery | 30-5 |
| 11 | Purdue | 26-7 | Gene Keady | 28-8 |
| 12 | Michigan | 24-8 | Brian Ellerbe | 25-9 |
| 13 | Mississippi | 22-6 | Rob Evans | 22-7 |
| 14 | South Carolina | 23-7 | Eddie Fogler | 23-8 |
| 15 | TCU | 27-5 | Billy Tubbs | 27-6 |
| 16 | Michigan St. | 20-7 | Tom Izzo | 22-8 |
| 17 | Arkansas | 23-8 | Nolan Richardson | 24-9 |
| 18 | New Mexico | 23-7 | Dave Bliss | 24-8 |
| 19 | UCLA | 22-8 | Steve Lavin | 24-9 |
| 20 | Maryland | 19-10 | Gary Williams | 21-11 |
| 21 | Syracuse | 24-8 | Jim Boeheim | 26-9 |
| 22 | Illinois | 22-9 | Lon Kruger | 23-10 |
| 23 | Xavier | 22-7 | Skip Prosser | 22-8 |
| 24 | Temple | 21-8 | John Chaney | 21-9 |
| 25 | Murray St. | 29-3 | Mark Gottfried | 29-4 |

**NCAA Final Four** (at the Alamodome, San Antonio): **Semifinals**– Kentucky 86, Stanford 85 (OT); Utah 65, North Carolina 59. **Championship**– Kentucky 78, Utah 69.
**NIT Championship** (at Madison Square Garden): Minnesota 79, Penn St. 72. No top 25 teams played in NIT.

---

## AP Post-Tournament Final Polls

The final AP Top 20 poll has been released after the NCAA tournament and NIT four times– in 1953 and '54 and again in 1974 and '75. Those four polls are listed below; teams that were not included in the last regular season polls are in *CAPITAL* italic letters.

### 1953

| | | Final Record |
|---|---|---|
| 1 | Indiana | 23-3 |
| 2 | Seton Hall | 31-2 |
| 3 | Kansas | 19-6 |
| 4 | Washington | 30-3 |
| 5 | LSU | 24-3 |
| 6 | La Salle | 25-3 |
| 7 | *ST. JOHN'S* | 17-6 |
| 8 | Okla. A&M | 23-7 |
| 9 | Duquesne | 21-8 |
| 10 | Notre Dame | 19-5 |
| 11 | Illinois | 18-4 |
| 12 | Kansas St. | 17-4 |
| 13 | Holy Cross | 20-6 |
| 14 | Seattle | 29-4 |
| 15 | *WAKE FOREST* | 22-7 |
| 16 | *SANTA CLARA* | 20-7 |
| 17 | Western Ky. | 25-6 |
| 18 | N.C. State | 26-6 |
| 19 | *DEPAUL* | 19-9 |
| 20 | *SW MISSOURI* | 24-4 |

### 1954

| | | Final Record |
|---|---|---|
| 1 | Kentucky | 25-0 |
| 2 | La Salle | 26-4 |
| 3 | Holy Cross | 26-2 |
| 4 | Indiana | 20-4 |
| 5 | Duquesne | 26-3 |
| 6 | Notre Dame | 22-3 |
| 7 | *BRADLEY* | 19-13 |
| 8 | Western Ky. | 29-3 |
| 9 | *PENN ST.* | 18-6 |
| 10 | Okla. A&M | 24-5 |
| 11 | USC | 19-14 |
| 12 | *GEO. WASH.* | 23-3 |
| 13 | Iowa | 17-5 |
| 14 | LSU | 21-5 |
| 15 | Duke | 22-6 |
| 16 | *NIAGARA* | 24-6 |
| 17 | Seattle | 26-2 |
| 18 | Kansas | 16-5 |
| 19 | Illinois | 17-5 |
| 20 | *MARYLAND* | 23-7 |

### 1974

| | | Final Record |
|---|---|---|
| 1 | N.C. State | 30-1 |
| 2 | UCLA | 26-4 |
| 3 | Marquette | 26-5 |
| 4 | Maryland | 23-5 |
| 5 | Notre Dame | 26-3 |
| 6 | Michigan | 22-5 |
| 7 | Kansas | 23-7 |
| 8 | Providence | 28-4 |
| 9 | Indiana | 23-5 |
| 10 | Long Beach St. | 24-2 |
| 11 | *PURDUE* | 22-8 |
| 12 | North Carolina | 22-6 |
| 13 | Vanderbilt | 23-5 |
| 14 | Alabama | 22-4 |
| 15 | *UTAH* | 22-8 |
| 16 | Pittsburgh | 25-4 |
| 17 | USC | 24-5 |
| 18 | *ORAL ROBERTS* | 23-6 |
| 19 | South Carolina | 22-5 |
| 20 | Dayton | 20-9 |

### 1975

| | | Final Record |
|---|---|---|
| 1 | UCLA | 28-3 |
| 2 | Kentucky | 26-5 |
| 3 | Indiana | 31-1 |
| 4 | Louisville | 28-3 |
| 5 | Maryland | 24-5 |
| 6 | Syracuse | 23-9 |
| 7 | N.C. State | 22-6 |
| 8 | Arizona St. | 25-4 |
| 9 | North Carolina | 23-8 |
| 10 | Alabama | 22-5 |
| 11 | Marquette | 23-4 |
| 12 | *PRINCETON* | 22-8 |
| 13 | Cincinnati | 23-6 |
| 14 | Notre Dame | 19-10 |
| 15 | Kansas St. | 20-9 |
| 16 | Drake | 19-10 |
| 17 | UNLV | 24-5 |
| 18 | Oregon St. | 19-12 |
| 19 | *MICHIGAN* | 19-8 |
| 20 | Penn | 23-5 |

### Pre-Tournament Records

**1953**– St. John's (Al DeStefano, 14-5); Wake Forest (Murray Greason, 21-6); Santa Clara (Bob Feerick, 18-6); DePaul (Ray Meyer, 18-7); SW Missouri St. (Bob Vanatta, 19-4 before NAIA tourney). **1954**– Bradley (Forddy Anderson, 15-12); Penn St. (Elmer Gross, 14-5); George Washington (Bill Reinhart, 23-2); Niagara (Taps Gallagher, 22-5); Maryland (Bud Millikan, 23-7). **1974**– Purdue (Fred Schaus, 18-8); Utah (Bill Foster, 19-7); Oral Roberts (Ken Trickey, 21-5). **1975**– Princeton (Pete Carril, 18-8); Michigan (Johnny Orr, 19-7).

## Associated Press Final Polls (Cont.)

### 1999

| | | Before Tourns | Head Coach | Final Record |
|---|---|---|---|---|
| 1 | Duke | 32-1 | Mike Krzyzewski | 37-2 |
| 2 | Michigan St. | 29-4 | Tom Izzo | 33-5 |
| 3 | **Connecticut** | 28-2 | Jim Calhoun | 34-2 |
| 4 | Auburn | 27-3 | Cliff Ellis | 29-4 |
| 5 | Maryland | 26-5 | Gary Williams | 28-6 |
| 6 | Utah | 27-4 | Rick Majerus | 28-5 |
| 7 | Stanford | 25-6 | Mike Montgomery | 26-7 |
| 8 | Kentucky | 25-8 | Tubby Smith | 28-9 |
| 9 | St. John's | 25-8 | Mike Jarvis | 28-9 |
| 10 | Miami-FL | 22-6 | Leonard Hamilton | 23-7 |
| 11 | Cincinnati | 26-5 | Bob Huggins | 27-6 |
| 12 | Arizona | 22-6 | Lute Olson | 22-7 |
| 13 | North Carolina | 24-9 | Bill Guthridge | 24-10 |
| 14 | Ohio St. | 23-8 | Jim O'Brien | 27-9 |
| 15 | UCLA | 22-8 | Steve Lavin | 22-9 |
| 16 | College of Charleston | 28-2 | John Kresse | 28-3 |
| 17 | Arkansas | 22-10 | Nolan Richardson | 23-11 |
| 18 | Wisconsin | 22-9 | Dick Bennett | 22-10 |
| 19 | Indiana | 22-10 | Bobby Knight | 23-11 |
| 20 | Tennessee | 20-8 | Jerry Green | 21-9 |
| 21 | Iowa | 18-9 | Tom Davis | 20-10 |
| 22 | Kansas | 22-9 | Roy Williams | 23-10 |
| 23 | Florida | 20-8 | Billy Donovan | 22-9 |
| 24 | NC-Charlotte | 22-10 | Bob Lutz | 23-11 |
| 25 | New Mexico | 24-8 | Dave Bliss | 25-9 |

**NCAA Final Four** (at the Tropicana Field, St. Petersburg): **Semifinals**– Duke 68, Michigan St. 62; Connecticut 64, Ohio St. 58. **Championship**– Connecticut 77, Duke 74.

**NIT Championship** (at Madison Square Garden): California 61, Clemson 60. No top 25 teams played in NIT.

### 2000

| | | Before Tourns | Head Coach | Final Record |
|---|---|---|---|---|
| 1 | Duke | 27-4 | Mike Krzyzewski | 29-5 |
| 2 | **Michigan St.** | 26-7 | Tom Izzo | 32-7 |
| 3 | Stanford | 26-3 | Mike Montgomery | 27-4 |
| 4 | Arizona | 26-6 | Lute Olson | 27-7 |
| 5 | Temple | 26-5 | John Chaney | 27-6 |
| 6 | Iowa St. | 29-4 | Larry Eustachy | 32-5 |
| 7 | Cincinnati | 28-3 | Bob Huggins | 29-4 |
| 8 | Ohio St. | 22-6 | Jim O'Brien | 23-7 |
| 9 | St. John's | 24-7 | Mike Jarvis | 25-8 |
| 10 | LSU | 26-5 | John Brady | 28-6 |
| 11 | Tennessee | 24-6 | Jerry Green | 26-7 |
| 12 | Oklahoma | 26-6 | Kelvin Sampson | 27-7 |
| 13 | Florida | 24-7 | Billy Donovan | 29-8 |
| 14 | Oklahoma St. | 24-6 | Eddie Sutton | 27-7 |
| 15 | Texas | 23-8 | Rick Barnes | 24-9 |
| 16 | Syracuse | 26-6 | Jim Boeheim | 26-6 |
| 17 | Maryland | 24-9 | Gary Williams | 25-10 |
| 18 | Tulsa | 29-4 | Bill Self | 32-5 |
| 19 | Kentucky | 22-9 | Tubby Smith | 23-10 |
| 20 | Connecticut | 24-9 | Jim Calhoun | 25-10 |
| 21 | Illinois | 21-9 | Lon Kruger | 22-10 |
| 22 | Indiana | 20-8 | Bobby Knight | 20-9 |
| 23 | Miami-FL | 21-10 | Leonard Hamilton | 23-11 |
| 24 | Auburn | 23-9 | Cliff Ellis | 24-10 |
| 25 | Purdue | 21-9 | Gene Keady | 24-10 |

**NCAA Final Four** (at the RCA Dome, Indianapolis): **Semifinals**– Michigan St. 53, Wisconsin 41; Florida 71, North Carolina 59. **Championship**– Michigan St. 89, Florida 76.

**NIT Championship** (at Madison Square Garden): Wake Forest 71, Notre Dame 61. No top 25 teams played in NIT.

### 2001

| | | Before Tourns | Head Coach | Final Record |
|---|---|---|---|---|
| 1 | **Duke** | 29-4 | Mike Krzyzewski | 35-4 |
| 2 | Stanford | 28-2 | Mike Montgomery | 31-3 |
| 3 | Michigan St. | 24-4 | Tom Izzo | 28-5 |
| 4 | Illinois | 24-7 | Bill Self | 27-8 |
| 5 | Arizona | 23-7 | Lute Olson | 28-8 |
| 6 | North Carolina | 25-6 | Matt Doherty | 26-7 |
| 7 | Boston College | 26-4 | Al Skinner | 27-5 |
| 8 | Florida | 23-6 | Billy Donovan | 24-7 |
| 9 | Kentucky | 22-9 | Tubby Smith | 24-10 |
| 10 | Iowa St. | 25-5 | Larry Eustachy | 25-6 |
| 11 | Maryland | 21-10 | Gary Williams | 25-11 |
| 12 | Kansas | 24-6 | Roy Williams | 26-7 |
| 13 | Oklahoma | 26-6 | Kelvin Sampson | 26-7 |
| 14 | Mississippi | 25-7 | Rod Barnes | 27-8 |
| 15 | UCLA | 21-8 | Steve Lavin | 23-9 |
| 16 | Virginia | 20-8 | Pete Gillen | 20-9 |
| 17 | Syracuse | 24-8 | Jim Boeheim | 25-9 |
| 18 | Texas | 25-8 | Rick Barnes | 25-9 |
| 19 | Notre Dame | 19-9 | Mike Brey | 20-10 |
| 20 | Indiana | 21-12 | Mike Davis | 21-13 |
| 21 | Georgetown | 23-7 | Craig Esherick | 25-8 |
| 22 | St. Joseph's | 25-6 | Phil Martelli | 26-7 |
| 23 | Wake Forest | 19-10 | Dave Odom | 19-11 |
| 24 | Iowa | 22-11 | Steve Alford | 23-12 |
| 25 | Wisconsin | 18-10 | Dick Bennett (2-1) & Brad Soderberg (16-10) | 18-11 |

**NCAA Final Four** (at the HHH Metrodome, Minneapolis): **Semifinals**–Duke 95, Maryland 84; Arizona 80, Michigan St. 61. **Championship**–Duke 82, Arizona 72.

**NIT Championship** (at Madison Square Garden): Tulsa 79, Alabama 60. No top 25 teams played in NIT.

### 2002

| | | Before Tourns | Head Coach | Final Record |
|---|---|---|---|---|
| 1 | Duke | 29-3 | Mike Krzyzewski | 32-4 |
| 2 | Kansas | 29-3 | Roy Williams | 33-4 |
| 3 | Oklahoma | 27-4 | Kelvin Sampson | 31-5 |
| 4 | **Maryland** | 26-4 | Gary Williams | 32-4 |
| 5 | Cincinnati | 30-3 | Bob Huggins | 31-4 |
| 6 | Gonzaga | 29-3 | Mark Few | 29-4 |
| 7 | Arizona | 22-9 | Lute Olson | 24-10 |
| 8 | Alabama | 26-7 | Mark Gottfried | 27-8 |
| 9 | Pittsburgh | 27-5 | Ben Howland | 29-6 |
| 10 | Connecticut | 24-6 | Jim Calhoun | 27-7 |
| 11 | Oregon | 23-8 | Ernie Kent | 26-9 |
| 12 | Marquette | 26-6 | Tom Crean | 26-7 |
| 13 | Illinois | 24-8 | Bill Self | 26-9 |
| 14 | Ohio St. | 23-7 | Jim O'Brien | 24-8 |
| 15 | Florida | 22-8 | Billy Donovan | 22-9 |
| 16 | Kentucky | 20-9 | Tubby Smith | 22-10 |
| 17 | Mississippi St. | 26-7 | Rick Stansbury | 27-8 |
| 18 | USC | 22-9 | Henry Bibby | 22-10 |
| 19 | Western Ky. | 28-3 | Dennis Felton | 28-4 |
| 20 | Oklahoma St. | 23-8 | Eddie Sutton | 23-9 |
| 21 | Miami-FL | 24-7 | Perry Clark | 24-8 |
| 22 | Xavier | 25-5 | Thad Matta | 26-6 |
| 23 | Georgia | 21-9 | Jim Harrick | 22-10 |
| 24 | Stanford | 19-9 | Mike Montgomery | 20-10 |
| 25 | Hawaii | 27-5 | Riley Wallace | 27-6 |

**NCAA Final Four** (at the Georgia Dome, Atlanta): **Semifinals**–Maryland 97, Kansas 88; Indiana 73, Oklahoma 64. **Championship**–Maryland 64, Indiana 52.

**NIT Championship** (at Madison Square Garden): Memphis 72, South Carolina 62. No top 25 teams played in NIT.

## 2003

| | | Head Coach | Final Record |
|---|---|---|---|
| | | Before Tourns | |
| 1 | Kentucky | 29-3 | Tubby Smith | 32-4 |
| 2 | Arizona | 25-3 | Lute Olson | 28-4 |
| 3 | Oklahoma | 24-6 | Kelvin Sampson | 27-7 |
| 4 | Pittsburgh | 26-4 | Ben Howland | 28-5 |
| 5 | Texas | 22-6 | Rick Barnes | 26-7 |
| 6 | Kansas | 25-7 | Roy Williams | 30-8 |
| 7 | Duke | 24-6 | Mike Krzyzewski | 26-7 |
| 8 | Wake Forest | 24-5 | Skip Prosser | 25-6 |
| 9 | Marquette | 23-5 | Tom Crean | 27-6 |
| 10 | Florida | 24-7 | Billy Donovan | 25-8 |
| 11 | Illinois | 24-6 | Bill Self | 25-7 |
| 12 | Xavier | 25-5 | Thad Matta | 26-6 |
| 13 | **Syracuse** | 24-5 | Jim Boeheim | 30-5 |
| 14 | Louisville | 24-6 | Rick Pitino | 25-7 |
| 15 | Creighton | 29-4 | Dana Altman | 29-5 |
| 16 | Dayton | 25-5 | Oliver Purnell | 25-6 |
| 17 | Maryland | 19-9 | Gary Williams | 21-10 |
| 18 | Stanford | 23-8 | Mike Montgomery | 23-9 |
| 19 | Memphis | 23-6 | John Calipari | 23-7 |
| 20 | Mississippi St. | 21-9 | Rick Stansbury | 21-10 |
| 21 | Wisconsin | 22-7 | Bo Ryan | 24-8 |
| 22 | Notre Dame | 22-9 | Mike Brey | 24-10 |
| 23 | Connecticut | 21-9 | Jim Calhoun | 23-10 |
| 24 | Missouri | 21-10 | Quin Snyder | 22-11 |
| 25 | Georgia | 19-8 | Jim Harrick | same* |

*Georgia chose not to participate in any postseason tournaments due to an investigation into academic fraud.

**NCAA Final Four** (at the Superdome, New Orleans):
**Semifinals**–Syracuse 95, Texas 84; Kansas 94, Marquette 61. **Championship**–Syracuse 81, Kansas 78.

**NIT Championship** (at Madison Square Garden): St. John's 70, Georgetown 67. No top 25 teams played in NIT.

## 2004

| | | Before Tourns | Head Coach | Final Record |
|---|---|---|---|---|
| 1 | Stanford | 29-1 | Mike Montgomery | 30-2 |
| 2 | Kentucky | 26-4 | Tubby Smith | 27-5 |
| 3 | Gonzaga | 27-2 | Mark Few | 28-3 |
| 4 | Oklahoma St. | 27-3 | Eddie Sutton | 31-4 |
| 5 | St. Joseph's | 27-1 | Phil Martelli | 30-2 |
| 6 | Duke | 27-5 | Mike Krzyzewski | 31-6 |
| 7 | Connecticut | 27-6 | Jim Calhoun | 33-6 |
| 8 | Mississippi St. | 25-3 | Rick Stansbury | 26-4 |
| 9 | Pittsburgh | 29-4 | Jamie Dixon | 31-5 |
| 10 | Wisconsin | 24-6 | Bo Ryan | 25-7 |
| 11 | Cincinnati | 24-6 | Bob Huggins | 25-7 |
| 12 | Texas | 23-7 | Rick Barnes | 25-8 |
| 13 | illinois | 24-6 | Bruce Weber | 26-7 |
| 14 | Georgia Tech | 23-9 | Paul Hewitt | 28-10 |
| 15 | N.C. State | 20-9 | Herb Sendek | 21-10 |
| 16 | Kansas | 21-8 | Bill Self | 24-9 |
| 17 | Wake Forest | 19-9 | Skip Prosser | 21-10 |
| 18 | North Carolina | 18-10 | Roy Williams | 19-11 |
| 19 | Maryland | 19-11 | Gary Williams | 20-12 |
| 20 | Syracuse | 21-7 | Jim Boeheim | 23-8 |
| 21 | Providence | 20-8 | Tim Welsh | 20-9 |
| 22 | Arizona | 20-9 | Lute Olson | 20-10 |
| 23 | So. Illinois | 25-4 | Matt Painter | 25-5 |
| 24 | Memphis | 21-7 | John Calipari | 22-8 |
| 25 | Boston College | 23-9 | Al Skinner | 24-10 |
| | Utah St. | 25-3 | Stew Morrill | 25-4 |

**NCAA Final Four** (at the Alamodome, San Antonio):
**Semifinals**–Georgia Tech 67, Oklahoma St. 65; Connecticut 79, Duke 78. **Championship**–Connecticut 82, Georgia Tech 73.

**NIT Championship** (at Madison Square Garden): Michigan 62, Rutgers 55. No. 25 Utah St. was the only Top 25 team that played in the NIT.

## 2005

| | | Before Tourns | Head Coach | Final Record |
|---|---|---|---|---|
| 1 | Illinois | 32-1 | Bruce Weber | 37-2 |
| 2 | North Carolina | 27-4 | Roy Williams | 33-4 |
| 3 | Duke | 25-5 | Mike Krzyzewski | 27-6 |
| 4 | Louisville | 29-4 | Rick Pitino | 33-5 |
| 5 | Wake Forest | 26-5 | Skip Prosser | 27-6 |
| 6 | Oklahoma St. | 24-6 | Eddie Sutton | 26-7 |
| 7 | Kentucky | 25-5 | Tubby Smith | 28-6 |
| 8 | Washington | 27-5 | Lorenzo Romar | 29-6 |
| 9 | Arizona | 27-6 | Lute Olson | 30-7 |
| 10 | Gonzaga | 25-4 | Mark Few | 26-5 |
| 11 | Syracuse | 27-6 | Jim Boeheim | 27-7 |
| 12 | Kansas | 23-6 | Bill Self | 23-7 |
| 13 | Connecticut | 22-7 | Jim Calhoun | 23-8 |
| 14 | Boston College | 24-4 | Al Skinner | 25-5 |
| 15 | Michigan St. | 22-6 | Tom Izzo | 26-7 |
| 16 | Florida | 23-7 | Billy Donovan | 24-8 |
| 17 | Oklahoma | 24-7 | Kelvin Sampson | 25-8 |
| 18 | Utah | 27-5 | Ray Giacoletti | 29-6 |
| 19 | Villanova | 22-7 | Jay Wright | 24-8 |
| 20 | Wisconsin | 22-8 | Bo Ryan | 25-9 |
| 21 | Alabama | 24-7 | Mark Gottfried | 24-8 |
| 22 | Pacific | 26-3 | Bob Thomason | 27-4 |
| 23 | Cincinnati | 24-7 | Bob Huggins | 25-8 |
| 24 | Texas Tech | 20-10 | Bob Knight | 22-11 |
| 25 | Georgia Tech | 19-11 | Paul Hewitt | 20-12 |

**NCAA Final Four** (at the Edward Jones Dome, St. Louis):
**Semifinals**–Illinois 72, Louisville 57; North Carolina 87, Michigan St. 71. **Championship**–North Carolina 75, Illinois 70.

**NIT Championship** (at Madison Square Garden): South Carolina 60, St. Joseph's 57. No top 25 teams played in NIT.

## The Red Cross Benefit Games, 1943-45

For three seasons during World War II, the NCAA and NIT champions met in a benefit game at Madison Square Garden in New York to raise money for the Red Cross. The NCAA champs won all three games.

| Year | Winner | Score | Loser |
|---|---|---|---|
| 1943 | Wyoming (NCAA) | 52-47 | St. John's (NIT) |
| 1944 | Utah (NCAA) | 43-36 | St. John's (NIT) |
| 1945 | Oklahoma A&M (NCAA) | 52-44 | DePaul (NIT) |

## Teams in Both NCAA and NIT

Fourteen teams played in both the NCAA and NIT tournaments from 1940-52. Colorado (1940), Utah (1944), Kentucky (1949) and BYU (1951) won one of the titles, while CCNY won two in 1950, beating Bradley in both championship games.

| Year | | NIT | NCAA |
|---|---|---|---|
| 1940 | Colorado | **Won Final** | Lost 1st Rd |
| | Duquesne | Lost Final | Lost 2nd Rd |
| 1944 | Utah | Lost 1st Rd | **Won Final** |
| 1949 | Kentucky | Lost 2nd Rd | **Won Final** |
| 1950 | CCNY | **Won Final** | **Won Final** |
| | Bradley | Lost Final | Lost Final |
| 1951 | BYU | **Won Final** | Lost 2nd Rd |
| | St. John's | Lost 3rd Rd | Lost 2nd Rd |
| | N.C. State | Lost 2nd Rd | Lost 2nd Rd |
| | Arizona | Lost 2nd Rd | Lost 1st Rd |
| 1952 | St. John's | Lost 2nd Rd | Lost Final |
| | Dayton | Lost Final | Lost 1st Rd |
| | Duquesne | Lost 3rd Rd | Lost 2nd Rd |

## Annual NCAA Division I Leaders
### Scoring

The NCAA did not begin keeping individual scoring records until the 1947-48 season. All averages include postseason games where applicable.

**Multiple winners:** Pete Maravich and Oscar Robertson (3); Keydren Clark, Darrell Floyd, Charles Jones, Harry Kelly, Frank Selvy and Freeman Williams (2).

| Year | | Gm | Pts | Avg | Year | | Gm | Pts | Avg |
|---|---|---|---|---|---|---|---|---|---|
| 1948 | Murray Wier, Iowa | 19 | 399 | 21.0 | 1977 | Freeman Williams, Portland St. | 26 | 1010 | 38.8 |
| 1949 | Tony Lavelli, Yale | 30 | 671 | 22.4 | 1978 | Freeman Williams, Portland St. | 27 | 969 | 35.9 |
| 1950 | Paul Arizin, Villanova | 29 | 735 | 25.3 | 1979 | Lawrence Butler, Idaho St | 27 | 812 | 30.1 |
| 1951 | Bill Mlkvy, Temple | 25 | 731 | 29.2 | 1980 | Tony Murphy, Southern-BR | 29 | 932 | 32.1 |
| 1952 | Clyde Lovellette, Kansas | 28 | 795 | 28.4 | 1981 | Zam Fredrick, S. Carolina | 27 | 781 | 28.9 |
| 1953 | Frank Selvy, Furman | 25 | 738 | 29.5 | 1982 | Harry Kelly, Texas Southern | 29 | 862 | 29.7 |
| 1954 | Frank Selvy, Furman | 29 | 1209 | 41.7 | 1983 | Harry Kelly, Texas Southern | 29 | 835 | 28.8 |
| 1955 | Darrell Floyd, Furman | 25 | 897 | 35.9 | 1984 | Joe Jakubick, Akron | 27 | 814 | 30.1 |
| 1956 | Darrell Floyd, Furman | 28 | 946 | 33.8 | 1985 | Xavier McDaniel, Wichita St | 31 | 844 | 27.2 |
| 1957 | Grady Wallace, S. Carolina | 29 | 906 | 31.2 | 1986 | Terrance Bailey, Wagner | 29 | 854 | 29.4 |
| 1958 | Oscar Robertson, Cincinnati | 28 | 984 | 35.1 | 1987 | Kevin Houston, Army | 29 | 953 | 32.9 |
| 1959 | Oscar Robertson, Cincinnati | 30 | 978 | 32.6 | 1988 | Hersey Hawkins, Bradley | 31 | 1125 | 36.3 |
| 1960 | Oscar Robertson, Cincinnati | 30 | 1011 | 33.7 | 1989 | Hank Gathers, Loyola-CA | 31 | 1015 | 32.7 |
| 1961 | Frank Burgess, Gonzaga | 26 | 842 | 32.4 | 1990 | Bo Kimble, Loyola-CA | 32 | 1131 | 35.3 |
| 1962 | Billy McGill, Utah | 26 | 1009 | 38.8 | 1991 | Kevin Bradshaw, US Int'l | 28 | 1054 | 37.6 |
| 1963 | Nick Werkman, Seton Hall | 22 | 650 | 29.5 | 1992 | Brett Roberts, Morehead St | 29 | 815 | 28.1 |
| 1964 | Howie Komives, Bowling Green | 23 | 844 | 36.7 | 1993 | Greg Guy, Texas-Pan Am | 19 | 556 | 29.3 |
| 1965 | Rick Barry, Miami-FL | 26 | 973 | 37.4 | 1994 | Glenn Robinson, Purdue | 34 | 1030 | 30.3 |
| 1966 | Dave Schellhase, Purdue | 24 | 781 | 32.5 | 1995 | Kurt Thomas, TCU | 27 | 781 | 28.9 |
| 1967 | Jimmy Walker, Providence | 28 | 851 | 30.4 | 1996 | Kevin Granger, Texas Southern | 24 | 648 | 27.0 |
| 1968 | Pete Maravich, LSU | 26 | 1138 | 43.8 | 1997 | Charles Jones, LIU-Brooklyn | 30 | 903 | 30.1 |
| 1969 | Pete Maravich, LSU | 26 | 1148 | 44.2 | 1998 | Charles Jones, LIU-Brooklyn | 30 | 869 | 29.0 |
| 1970 | Pete Maravich, LSU | 31 | 1381 | 44.5 | 1999 | Alvin Young, Niagara | 29 | 728 | 25.1 |
| 1971 | Johnny Neumann, Ole Miss | 23 | 923 | 40.1 | 2000 | Courtney Alexander, Fresno St. | 27 | 669 | 24.8 |
| 1972 | Dwight Lamar, SW La | 29 | 1054 | 36.3 | 2001 | Ronnie McCollum, Centenary | 27 | 787 | 29.1 |
| 1973 | Bird Averitt, Pepperdine | 25 | 848 | 33.9 | 2002 | Jason Conley, VMI | 28 | 820 | 29.3 |
| 1974 | Larry Fogle, Canisius | 25 | 835 | 33.4 | 2003 | Ruben Douglas, New Mexico | 28 | 783 | 28.0 |
| 1975 | Bob McCurdy, Richmond | 26 | 855 | 32.9 | 2004 | Keydren Clark, St. Peter's | 29 | 775 | 26.7 |
| 1976 | Marshall Rodgers, Texas-Pan Am | 25 | 919 | 36.8 | 2005 | Keydren Clark, St. Peter's | 28 | 721 | 25.8 |

### Rebounds

The NCAA did not begin keeping individual rebounding records until the 1950-51 season. From 1956-62, the championship was decided on highest percentage of recoveries out of all rebounds made by both teams in all games. All averages include postseason games where applicable.

**Multiple winners:** Artis Gilmore, Jerry Lucas, Xavier McDaniel, Paul Millsap, Kermit Washington and Leroy Wright (2).

| Year | | Gm | No | Avg | Year | | Gm | No | Avg |
|---|---|---|---|---|---|---|---|---|---|
| 1951 | Ernie Beck, Penn | 27 | 556 | 20.6 | 1979 | Monti Davis, Tennessee St. | 26 | 421 | 16.2 |
| 1952 | Bill Hannon, Army | 17 | 355 | 20.9 | 1980 | Larry Smith, Alcorn State | 26 | 392 | 15.1 |
| 1953 | Ed Conlin, Fordham | 26 | 612 | 23.5 | 1981 | Darryl Watson, Miss. Valley St. | 27 | 379 | 14.0 |
| 1954 | Art Quimby, Connecticut | 26 | 588 | 22.6 | 1982 | LaSalle Thompson, Texas | 27 | 365 | 13.5 |
| 1955 | Charlie Slack, Marshall | 21 | 538 | 25.6 | 1983 | Xavier McDaniel, Wichita St. | 28 | 403 | 14.4 |
| 1956 | Joe Holup, G. Washington | 26 | 604 | 25.6 | 1984 | Akeem Olajuwon, Houston | 37 | 500 | 13.5 |
| 1957 | Elgin Baylor, Seattle | 25 | 508 | 23.5 | 1985 | Xavier McDaniel, Wichita St. | 31 | 460 | 14.8 |
| 1958 | Alex Ellis, Niagara | 25 | 536 | 26.2 | 1986 | David Robinson, Navy | 35 | 455 | 13.0 |
| 1959 | Leroy Wright, Pacific | 26 | 652 | 23.8 | 1987 | Jerome Lane, Pittsburgh | 33 | 444 | 13.5 |
| 1960 | Leroy Wright, Pacific | 17 | 380 | 23.4 | 1988 | Kenny Miller, Loyola-IL | 29 | 395 | 13.6 |
| 1961 | Jerry Lucas, Ohio St. | 27 | 470 | 19.8 | 1989 | Hank Gathers, Loyola-CA | 31 | 426 | 13.7 |
| 1962 | Jerry Lucas, Ohio St. | 28 | 499 | 21.1 | 1990 | Anthony Bonner, St. Louis | 33 | 456 | 13.8 |
| 1963 | Paul Silas, Creighton | 27 | 557 | 20.6 | 1991 | Shaquille O'Neal, LSU | 28 | 411 | 14.7 |
| 1964 | Bob Pelkington, Xavier-OH | 26 | 567 | 21.8 | 1992 | Popeye Jones, Murray St. | 30 | 431 | 14.4 |
| 1965 | Toby Kimball, Connecticut | 23 | 483 | 21.0 | 1993 | Warren Kidd, Mid. Tenn. St. | 26 | 386 | 14.8 |
| 1966 | Jim Ware, Oklahoma City | 29 | 607 | 20.9 | 1994 | Jerome Lambert, Baylor | 24 | 355 | 14.8 |
| 1967 | Dick Cunningham, Murray St. | 22 | 479 | 21.8 | 1995 | Kurt Thomas, TCU | 27 | 393 | 14.6 |
| 1968 | Neal Walk, Florida | 25 | 494 | 19.8 | 1996 | Marcus Mann, Miss. Valley St. | 29 | 394 | 13.6 |
| 1969 | Spencer Haywood, Detroit | 22 | 472 | 21.5 | 1997 | Tim Duncan, Wake Forest | 31 | 457 | 14.7 |
| 1970 | Artis Gilmore, Jacksonville | 28 | 621 | 22.2 | 1998 | Ryan Perryman, Dayton | 33 | 412 | 12.5 |
| 1971 | Artis Gilmore, Jacksonville | 26 | 603 | 23.2 | 1999 | Ian McGinnis, Dartmouth | 26 | 317 | 12.2 |
| 1972 | Kermit Washington, American | 23 | 455 | 19.8 | 2000 | Darren Phillip, Fairfield | 29 | 405 | 14.0 |
| 1973 | Kermit Washington, American | 22 | 439 | 20.0 | 2001 | Chris Marcus, Western Ky. | 31 | 374 | 12.1 |
| 1974 | Marvin Barnes, Providence | 32 | 597 | 18.7 | 2002 | Jeremy Bishop, Quinnipiac | 29 | 347 | 12.0 |
| 1975 | John Irving, Hofstra | 21 | 323 | 15.4 | 2003 | Brandon Hunter, Ohio | 30 | 378 | 12.6 |
| 1976 | Sam Pellom, Buffalo | 26 | 420 | 16.2 | 2004 | Paul Millsap, Louisiana Tech | 30 | 374 | 12.5 |
| 1977 | Glenn Mosley, Seton Hall | 29 | 473 | 16.3 | 2005 | Paul Millsap, Louisiana Tech | 29 | 360 | 12.4 |
| 1978 | Ken Williams, N. Texas | 28 | 411 | 14.7 | | | | | |

**Note:** Only three players have ever led the NCAA in scoring and rebounding in the same season: Xavier McDaniel of Wichita St. (1985), Hank Gathers of Loyola-Marymount (1989) and Kurt Thomas of TCU (1995).

## Assists

The NCAA did not begin keeping individual assist records until the 1983-84 season. All averages include postseason games where applicable.

**Multiple winner:** Avery Johnson (2).

| Year | | Gm | No | Avg |
|---|---|---|---|---|
| 1984 | Craig Lathen, IL-Chicago | 29 | 274 | 9.45 |
| 1985 | Rob Weingard, Hofstra | 24 | 228 | 9.50 |
| 1986 | Mark Jackson, St. John's | 36 | 328 | 9.11 |
| 1987 | Avery Johnson, Southern-BR | 31 | 333 | 10.74 |
| 1988 | Avery Johnson, Southern-BR | 30 | 399 | 13.30 |
| 1989 | Glenn Williams, Holy Cross | 28 | 278 | 9.93 |
| 1990 | Todd Lehmann, Drexel | 28 | 260 | 9.29 |
| 1991 | Chris Corchiani, N.C. State | 31 | 299 | 9.65 |
| 1992 | Van Usher, Tennessee Tech | 29 | 254 | 8.76 |
| 1993 | Sam Crawford, N. Mexico St | 34 | 310 | 9.12 |
| 1994 | Jason Kidd, California | 30 | 272 | 9.06 |
| 1995 | Nelson Haggerty, Baylor | 28 | 284 | 10.14 |
| 1996 | Raimonds Miglinieks, UC-Irvine | 27 | 230 | 8.52 |
| 1997 | Kenny Mitchell, Dartmouth | 26 | 203 | 7.81 |
| 1998 | Ahlon Lewis, Arizona St. | 32 | 294 | 9.19 |
| 1999 | Doug Gottlieb, Oklahoma St. | 34 | 299 | 8.79 |
| 2000 | Mark Dickel, UNLV | 31 | 280 | 9.03 |
| 2001 | Markus Carr, CS-Northridge | 32 | 286 | 8.94 |
| 2002 | T.J. Ford, Texas | 33 | 273 | 8.27 |
| 2003 | Martell Bailey, Illinois-Chicago | 30 | 244 | 8.13 |
| 2004 | Greg Day, Troy St. | 31 | 256 | 8.26 |
| 2005 | Damitrius Coleman, Mercer | 28 | 224 | 8.00 |
| | & Will Funn, Portland St. | 28 | 224 | 8.00 |

## Blocked Shots

The NCAA did not begin keeping individual blocked shots records until the 1985-86 season. All averages include postseason games where applicable.

**Multiple winners:** Keith Closs, David Robinson and Tarvis Williams (2).

| Year | | Gm | No | Avg |
|---|---|---|---|---|
| 1986 | David Robinson, Navy | 35 | 207 | 5.91 |
| 1987 | David Robinson, Navy | 32 | 144 | 4.50 |
| 1988 | Rodney Blake, St. Joe's-PA | 29 | 116 | 4.00 |
| 1989 | Alonzo Mourning, G'town | 34 | 169 | 4.97 |
| 1990 | Kenny Green, Rhode Island | 26 | 124 | 4.77 |
| 1991 | Shawn Bradley, BYU | 34 | 177 | 5.21 |
| 1992 | Shaquille O'Neal, LSU | 30 | 157 | 5.23 |
| 1993 | Theo Ratliff, Wyoming | 28 | 124 | 4.43 |
| 1994 | Grady Livingston, Howard | 26 | 115 | 4.42 |
| 1995 | Keith Closs, Cen. Conn. St. | 26 | 139 | 5.35 |
| 1996 | Keith Closs, Cen. Conn. St. | 28 | 178 | 6.36 |
| 1997 | Adonal Foyle, Colgate | 28 | 180 | 6.43 |
| 1998 | Jerome James, Florida A&M | 27 | 125 | 4.63 |
| 1999 | Tarvis Williams, Hampton | 27 | 135 | 5.00 |
| 2000 | Ken Johnson, Ohio St. | 30 | 161 | 5.37 |
| 2001 | Tarvis Williams, Hampton | 32 | 147 | 4.59 |
| 2002 | Wojciech Myrda, La-Monroe | 32 | 172 | 5.38 |
| 2003 | Emeka Okafor, Connecticut | 33 | 156 | 4.73 |
| 2004 | Anwar Ferguson, Houston | 27 | 111 | 4.11 |
| 2005 | Deng Gai, Fairfield | 30 | 165 | 5.50 |

## All-Time NCAA Division I Individual Leaders

Through 2004-05; includes regular season and tournament games; **Last** column indicates final year played.

### CAREER

### Scoring

| | Points | Yrs | Last | Gm | Pts |
|---|---|---|---|---|---|
| 1 | Pete Maravich, LSU | 3 | 1970 | 83 | 3667 |
| 2 | Freeman Williams, Port. St. | 4 | 1978 | 106 | 3249 |
| 3 | Lionel Simmons, La Salle | 4 | 1990 | 131 | 3217 |
| 4 | Alphonso Ford, Miss. Val. St. | 4 | 1993 | 109 | 3165 |
| 5 | Harry Kelly, Texas Southern | 4 | 1983 | 110 | 3066 |
| 6 | Hersey Hawkins, Bradley | 4 | 1988 | 125 | 3008 |
| 7 | Oscar Robertson, Cincinnati | 3 | 1960 | 88 | 2973 |
| 8 | Danny Manning, Kansas | 4 | 1988 | 147 | 2951 |
| 9 | Alfredrick Hughes, Loyola-IL | 4 | 1985 | 120 | 2914 |
| 10 | Elvin Hayes, Houston | 3 | 1968 | 93 | 2884 |
| 11 | Larry Bird, Indiana St. | 3 | 1979 | 94 | 2850 |
| 12 | Otis Birdsong, Houston | 4 | 1977 | 116 | 2832 |
| 13 | Kevin Bradshaw, Beth-Cook/US Int'l | 4 | 1991 | 111 | 2804 |
| 14 | Allan Houston, Tennessee | 4 | 1993 | 128 | 2801 |
| 15 | Hank Gathers, USC/Loyola-CA | 4 | 1990 | 117 | 2723 |
| 16 | Reggie Lewis, Northeastern | 4 | 1987 | 122 | 2708 |
| 17 | Daren Queenan, Lehigh | 4 | 1988 | 118 | 2703 |
| 18 | Byron Larkin, Xavier-OH | 4 | 1988 | 121 | 2696 |
| 19 | David Robinson, Navy | 4 | 1987 | 127 | 2669 |
| 20 | Wayman Tisdale, Oklahoma | 3 | 1985 | 104 | 2661 |

| | Average | Yrs | Last | Pts | Avg |
|---|---|---|---|---|---|
| 1 | Pete Maravich, LSU | 3 | 1970 | 3667 | 44.2 |
| 2 | Austin Carr, Notre Dame | 3 | 1971 | 2560 | 34.6 |
| 3 | Oscar Robertson, Cinn | 3 | 1960 | 2973 | 33.8 |
| 4 | Calvin Murphy, Niagara | 3 | 1970 | 2548 | 33.1 |
| 5 | Dwight Lamar, SW La | 2 | 1973 | 1862 | 32.7 |
| 6 | Frank Selvy, Furman | 3 | 1954 | 2538 | 32.5 |
| 7 | Rick Mount, Purdue | 3 | 1970 | 2323 | 32.3 |
| 8 | Darrell Floyd, Furman | 3 | 1956 | 2281 | 32.1 |
| 9 | Nick Werkman, Seton Hall | 3 | 1964 | 2273 | 32.0 |
| 10 | Willie Humes, Idaho St. | 2 | 1971 | 1510 | 31.5 |
| 11 | William Averitt, Pepperdine | 2 | 1973 | 1541 | 31.4 |
| 12 | Elgin Baylor, Idaho/Seattle | 3 | 1958 | 2500 | 31.3 |
| 13 | Elvin Hayes, Houston | 3 | 1968 | 2884 | 31.0 |
| 14 | Freeman Williams, Port. St. | 4 | 1979 | 3249 | 30.7 |
| 15 | Larry Bird, Indiana St. | 3 | 1979 | 2850 | 30.3 |
| 16 | Bill Bradley, Princeton | 3 | 1965 | 2503 | 30.2 |
| 17 | Rich Fuqua, Oral Roberts | 2 | 1973 | 1617 | 29.9 |
| 18 | Wilt Chamberlain, Kansas | 2 | 1958 | 1433 | 29.9 |
| 19 | Rick Barry, Miami-FL | 3 | 1965 | 2298 | 29.8 |
| 20 | Doug Collins, Illinois St. | 3 | 1973 | 2240 | 29.1 |

| | Field Goal Pct. | Yrs | Last | FG | FGA | Pct |
|---|---|---|---|---|---|---|
| 1 | Steve Johnson, Ore. St. | 4 | 1981 | 828 | 1222 | .678 |
| 2 | Michael Bradley, Kentucky/ Villanova | 3 | 2001 | 441 | 651 | .677 |
| 3 | Murray Brown, Fla. St. | 4 | 1980 | 566 | 847 | .668 |
| 4 | Lee Campbell, M.Tenn St./ SW Mo.St. | 3 | 1990 | 411 | 618 | .665 |
| 5 | Warren Kidd, M.Tenn.St. | 3 | 1993 | 496 | 747 | .664 |
| 6 | Todd MacCulloch, Wash. | 4 | 1999 | 702 | 1058 | .664 |
| 7 | Joe Senser, West Chester | 4 | 1979 | 476 | 719 | .662 |
| 8 | Kevin Magee, UC-Irvine | 2 | 1982 | 552 | 841 | .656 |
| 9 | Orlando Phillips, Pepperdine | 2 | 1983 | 404 | 618 | .654 |
| 10 | Bill Walton, UCLA | 3 | 1974 | 747 | 1147 | .651 |

**Note:** minimum 400 FGs made and an average of four per game.

| | Free Throw Pct. | Yrs | Last | FT | FTA | Pct |
|---|---|---|---|---|---|---|
| 1 | Gary Buchanan, Villanova | 4 | 2003 | 324 | 355 | .913 |
| 2 | Greg Starrick, Ky/So.Ill | 4 | 1972 | 341 | 375 | .909 |
| 3 | Jack Moore, Nebraska | 4 | 1982 | 446 | 495 | .901 |
| 4 | Steve Henson, Kansas St. | 4 | 1990 | 361 | 401 | .900 |
| 5 | Steve Alford, Indiana | 4 | 1987 | 535 | 596 | .898 |
| 6 | Bob Lloyd, Rutgers | 3 | 1967 | 543 | 605 | .898 |
| 7 | Jim Barton, Dartmouth | 4 | 1989 | 394 | 440 | .895 |
| 8 | Tommy Boyer, Arkansas | 3 | 1963 | 315 | 353 | .892 |
| 9 | Kyle Korver, Creighton | 4 | 2003 | 312 | 350 | .891 |
| 10 | Brent Jolly, Tenn. Tech | 4 | 2003 | 347 | 391 | .887 |

**Note:** minimum 300 FTs made and an average of 2.5 per game.

## All-Time NCAA Division I Individual Leaders (Cont.)
### Rebounds

| Total (before 1973) | Yrs | Last | Gm | No |
|---|---|---|---|---|
| 1 Tom Gola, La Salle | 4 | 1955 | 118 | 2201 |
| 2 Joe Holup, G. Washington | 4 | 1956 | 104 | 2030 |
| 3 Charlie Slack, Marshall | 4 | 1956 | 88 | 1916 |
| 4 Ed Conlin, Fordham | 4 | 1955 | 102 | 1884 |
| 5 Dickie Hemric, Wake Forest | 4 | 1955 | 104 | 1802 |
| 6 Paul Silas, Creighton | 3 | 1964 | 81 | 1751 |
| 7 Art Quimby, Connecticut | 4 | 1955 | 80 | 1716 |
| 8 Jerry Harper, Alabama | 4 | 1956 | 93 | 1688 |
| 9 Jeff Cohen, Wm. & Mary | 4 | 1961 | 103 | 1679 |
| 10 Steve Hamilton, Morehead St. | 4 | 1958 | 102 | 1675 |

| Total (since 1973) | Yrs | Last | Gm | No |
|---|---|---|---|---|
| 1 Tim Duncan, Wake Forest | 4 | 1997 | 128 | 1570 |
| 2 Derrick Coleman, Syracuse | 4 | 1990 | 143 | 1537 |
| 3 Malik Rose, Drexel | 4 | 1996 | 120 | 1514 |
| 4 Ralph Sampson, Virginia | 4 | 1983 | 132 | 1511 |
| 5 Pete Padgett, Nevada-Reno | 4 | 1976 | 104 | 1464 |
| 6 Lionel Simmons, La Salle | 4 | 1990 | 131 | 1429 |
| 7 Anthony Bonner, St. Louis | 4 | 1990 | 133 | 1424 |
| 8 Tyrone Hill, Xavier-OH | 4 | 1990 | 126 | 1380 |
| 9 Popeye Jones, Murray St. | 4 | 1992 | 123 | 1374 |
| 10 Michael Brooks, La Salle | 4 | 1980 | 114 | 1372 |

| Average (before 1973) | Yrs | Last | No | Avg |
|---|---|---|---|---|
| 1 Artis Gilmore, Jacksonville | 2 | 1971 | 1224 | 22.7 |
| 2 Charlie Slack, Marshall | 4 | 1956 | 1916 | 21.8 |
| 3 Paul Silas, Creighton | 3 | 1964 | 1751 | 21.6 |
| 4 Leroy Wright, Pacific | 3 | 1960 | 1442 | 21.5 |
| 5 Art Quimby, Connecticut | 4 | 1955 | 1716 | 21.5 |

**Note:** minimum 800 rebounds.

| Average (since 1973) | Yrs | Last | No | Avg |
|---|---|---|---|---|
| 1 Glenn Mosley, Seton Hall | 4 | 1977 | 1263 | 15.2 |
| 2 Bill Campion, Manhattan | 3 | 1975 | 1070 | 14.2 |
| 3 Pete Padgett, Nevada-Reno | 4 | 1976 | 1464 | 14.1 |
| 4 Bob Warner, Maine | 4 | 1976 | 1304 | 13.6 |
| 5 Shaquille O'Neal, LSU | 3 | 1992 | 1217 | 13.5 |

**Note:** minimum 650 rebounds.

### Assists

| Total | Yrs | Last | Gm | No |
|---|---|---|---|---|
| 1 Bobby Hurley, Duke | 4 | 1993 | 140 | 1076 |
| 2 Chris Corchiani, N.C. State | 4 | 1991 | 124 | 1038 |
| 3 Ed Cota, N. Carolina | 4 | 2000 | 138 | 1030 |
| 4 Keith Jennings, E. Tenn. St. | 4 | 1991 | 127 | 983 |
| 5 Steve Blake, Maryland | 4 | 2003 | 138 | 972 |
| 6 Sherman Douglas, Syracuse | 4 | 1989 | 138 | 960 |
| 7 Tony Miller, Marquette | 4 | 1995 | 123 | 956 |
| 8 Greg Anthony, Portland/UNLV | 4 | 1991 | 138 | 950 |
| 9 Doug Gottlieb, ND/Okla St. | 4 | 2000 | 124 | 947 |
| 10 Gary Payton, Oregon St. | 4 | 1990 | 120 | 938 |

| Average | Yrs | Last | No | Avg |
|---|---|---|---|---|
| 1 Avery Johnson, Southern | 2 | 1988 | 732 | 12.00 |
| 2 Sam Crawford, N. Mexico St. | 2 | 1993 | 592 | 8.84 |
| 3 Mark Wade, Okla/UNLV | 3 | 1987 | 693 | 8.77 |
| 4 Chris Corchiani, N.C. State | 4 | 1991 | 1038 | 8.37 |
| 5 Taurence Chisholm, Delaware | 4 | 1988 | 877 | 7.97 |
| 6 Van Usher, Tennessee Tech | 3 | 1992 | 676 | 7.95 |
| 7 Anthony Manuel, Bradley | 3 | 1989 | 855 | 7.92 |
| 8 Chico Fletcher, Ark. St. | 4 | 2000 | 893 | 7.83 |
| 9 Gary Payton, Oregon St. | 4 | 1990 | 938 | 7.82 |
| 10 Orlando Smart, San Francisco | 4 | 1994 | 902 | 7.78 |

**Note:** minimum 550 assists.

### Blocked Shots

| Average | Yrs | Last | No | Avg |
|---|---|---|---|---|
| 1 Keith Closs, Cen. Conn. St. | 2 | 1996 | 317 | 5.87 |
| 2 Adonal Foyle, Colgate | 3 | 1997 | 492 | 5.66 |
| 3 David Robinson, Navy | 2 | 1987 | 351 | 5.24 |
| 4 Wojciech Mydra, LA-Monroe | 4 | 2002 | 535 | 4.65 |
| 5 Shaquille O'Neal, LSU | 3 | 1992 | 412 | 4.58 |

**Note:** minimum 225 blocked shots.

### Steals

| Average | Yrs | Last | No | Avg |
|---|---|---|---|---|
| 1 Desmond Cambridge, Ala. A&M | 3 | 2002 | 330 | 3.93 |
| 2 Mookie Blaylock, Oklahoma | 2 | 1989 | 281 | 3.80 |
| 3 Ronn McMahon, Eastern Wash | 3 | 1990 | 225 | 3.52 |
| 4 Eric Murdock, Providence | 4 | 1991 | 376 | 3.21 |
| 5 Van Usher, Tennessee Tech | 3 | 1992 | 270 | 3.18 |

**Note:** minimum 225 steals.

### 3-PT Field Goals

| 3-Pt Field Goals Made | Yrs | Last | Gm | 3FG |
|---|---|---|---|---|
| 1 Curtis Staples, Virginia | 4 | 1998 | 122 | 413 |
| 2 Keith Veney, Lamar/Marshall | 4 | 1997 | 111 | 409 |
| 3 Doug Day, Radford | 4 | 1993 | 117 | 401 |
| 4 Michael Watson, Missouri-KC | 4 | 2004 | 117 | 391 |
| 5 Ronnie Schmitz, Missouri-KC | 4 | 1993 | 112 | 378 |

| 3-Pt Field Goals/Game | Yrs | Last | 3FG | Avg |
|---|---|---|---|---|
| 1 Timothy Pollard, Miss. Vall | 2 | 1989 | 256 | 4.57 |
| 2 Sydney Grider, LA-Lafayette | 2 | 1990 | 253 | 4.36 |
| 3 Brian Merriweather, TX-Pan Am | 3 | 2001 | 332 | 3.95 |
| 4 Josh Heard, Tenn. Tech | 2 | 2000 | 210 | 3.82 |
| 5 Kareem Townes, La Salle | 3 | 1995 | 300 | 3.70 |

| 3-Pt Field Goal Pct. | Yrs | Last | 3FG | Att | Pct |
|---|---|---|---|---|---|
| 1 Tony Bennett, Wisc-GB | 4 | 1992 | 290 | 584 | .497 |
| 2 David Olson, Eastern Ill. | 4 | 1992 | 262 | 562 | .466 |
| 3 Ross Land, N. Arizona | 4 | 2000 | 308 | 664 | .464 |
| 4 Dan Dickau, Washington/ Gonzaga | 4 | 2002 | 215 | 465 | .462 |
| 5 Sean Jackson, Ohio/ Princeton | 4 | 1992 | 243 | 528 | .460 |

**Note:** minimum 200 3FGs made and an average of two per game.

## SINGLE SEASON
### Scoring

| Points | Year | Gm | Pts |
|---|---|---|---|
| 1 Pete Maravich, LSU | 1970 | 31 | 1381 |
| 2 Elvin Hayes, Houston | 1968 | 33 | 1214 |
| 3 Frank Selvy, Furman | 1954 | 29 | 1209 |
| 4 Pete Maravich, LSU | 1969 | 26 | 1148 |
| 5 Pete Maravich, LSU | 1968 | 26 | 1138 |
| 6 Bo Kimble, Loyola-CA | 1990 | 32 | 1131 |
| 7 Hersey Hawkins, Bradley | 1988 | 31 | 1125 |
| 8 Austin Carr, Notre Dame | 1970 | 29 | 1106 |
| 9 Austin Carr, Notre Dame | 1971 | 29 | 1101 |
| 10 Otis Birdsong, Houston | 1977 | 36 | 1090 |

| Average | Year | Gm | Pts | Avg |
|---|---|---|---|---|
| 1 Pete Maravich, LSU | 1970 | 31 | 1381 | 44.5 |
| 2 Pete Maravich, LSU | 1969 | 26 | 1148 | 44.2 |
| 3 Pete Maravich, LSU | 1968 | 26 | 1138 | 43.8 |
| 4 Frank Selvy, Furman | 1954 | 29 | 1209 | 41.7 |
| 5 Johnny Neumann, Ole Miss | 1971 | 23 | 923 | 40.1 |
| 6 Freeman Williams, Port. St. | 1977 | 26 | 1010 | 38.8 |
| 7 Billy McGill, Utah | 1962 | 26 | 1009 | 38.8 |
| 8 Calvin Murphy, Niagara | 1968 | 24 | 916 | 38.2 |
| 9 Austin Carr, Notre Dame | 1970 | 29 | 1106 | 38.1 |
| 10 Austin Carr, Notre Dame | 1971 | 29 | 1101 | 38.0 |

### Field Goal Pct.

| | | Year | FG | FGA | Pct |
|---|---|---|---|---|---|
| 1 | Steve Johnson, Oregon St. | 1981 | 235 | 315 | .746 |
| 2 | Dwayne Davis, Florida | 1989 | 179 | 248 | .722 |
| 3 | Keith Walker, Utica | 1985 | 154 | 216 | .713 |
| 4 | Steve Johnson, Oregon St. | 1980 | 211 | 297 | .710 |
| 5 | Adam Mark, Belmont | 2002 | 150 | 212 | .708 |

### Free Throw Pct.

| | | Year | FT | FTA | Pct |
|---|---|---|---|---|---|
| 1 | Blake Ahearn, SW Mo. St. | 2004 | 117 | 120 | .975 |
| 2 | Craig Collins, Penn St. | 1985 | 94 | 98 | .959 |
| 3 | J.J. Redick, Duke | 2004 | 143 | 150 | .953 |
| 4 | Rod Foster, UCLA | 1982 | 95 | 100 | .950 |
| 5 | Clay McKnight, Pacific | 2000 | 74 | 78 | .949 |

### 3-Pt Field Goal Pct.

| | | Year | 3FG | Att | Pct |
|---|---|---|---|---|---|
| 1 | Glenn Tropf, Holy Cross | 1988 | 52 | 82 | .634 |
| 2 | Sean Wightman, W. Mich | 1992 | 48 | 76 | .632 |
| 3 | Keith Jennings, E. Tenn. St. | 1991 | 84 | 142 | .592 |
| 4 | Dave Calloway, Monmouth | 1989 | 48 | 82 | .585 |
| 5 | Steve Kerr, Arizona | 1988 | 114 | 199 | .573 |

### Assists

| | Average | Year | Gm | No | Avg |
|---|---|---|---|---|---|
| 1 | Avery Johnson, Southern-BR | 1988 | 30 | 399 | 13.3 |
| 2 | Anthony Manuel, Bradley | 1988 | 31 | 373 | 12.0 |
| 3 | Avery Johnson, Southern-BR | 1987 | 31 | 333 | 10.7 |
| 4 | Mark Wade, UNLV | 1987 | 38 | 406 | 10.7 |
| 5 | Nelson Haggerty, Baylor | 1995 | 28 | 284 | 10.1 |
| 6 | Glenn Williams, Holy Cross | 1989 | 28 | 278 | 9.9 |
| 7 | Chris Corchiani, N.C. State | 1991 | 31 | 299 | 9.7 |
| 8 | Tony Fairley, Charleston-So. | 1987 | 28 | 270 | 9.6 |
| 9 | Tyrone Bogues, Wake Forest | 1987 | 29 | 276 | 9.5 |
| 10 | Ron Weingard, Hofstra | 1985 | 24 | 228 | 9.5 |

### Rebounds

| | Average (before 1973) | Year | Gm | No | Avg |
|---|---|---|---|---|---|
| 1 | Charlie Slack, Marshall | 1955 | 21 | 538 | 25.6 |
| 2 | Leroy Wright, Pacific | 1959 | 26 | 652 | 25.1 |
| 3 | Art Quimby, Connecticut | 1955 | 25 | 611 | 24.4 |
| 4 | Charlie Slack, Marshall | 1956 | 22 | 520 | 23.6 |
| 5 | Ed Conlin, Fordham | 1953 | 26 | 612 | 23.5 |

| | Average (since 1973) | Year | Gm | No | Avg |
|---|---|---|---|---|---|
| 1 | Kermit Washington, American | 1973 | 25 | 511 | 20.4 |
| 2 | Marvin Barnes, Providence | 1973 | 30 | 571 | 19.0 |
| 3 | Marvin Barnes, Providence | 1974 | 32 | 597 | 18.7 |
| 4 | Pete Padgett, Nevada | 1973 | 26 | 462 | 17.8 |
| 5 | Jim Bradley, Northern Ill | 1973 | 24 | 426 | 17.8 |

### Blocked Shots

| | Average | Year | Gm | No | Avg |
|---|---|---|---|---|---|
| 1 | Adonal Foyle, Colgate | 1997 | 28 | 180 | 6.42 |
| 2 | Keith Closs, Cen. Conn. St. | 1996 | 28 | 178 | 6.36 |
| 3 | David Robinson, Navy | 1986 | 35 | 207 | 5.91 |
| 4 | Deng Gair, Fairfield | 2005 | 30 | 165 | 5.50 |
| 5 | Shawn James, Northeastern | 2005 | 25 | 136 | 5.44 |

### Steals

| | Average | Year | Gm | No | Avg |
|---|---|---|---|---|---|
| 1 | Desmond Cambridge, Ala. A&M | 2002 | 29 | 160 | 5.52 |
| 2 | Darron Brittman, Chicago St. | 1986 | 28 | 139 | 4.96 |
| 3 | Aldwin Ware, Florida A&M | 1988 | 29 | 142 | 4.90 |
| 4 | John Linehan, Providence | 2002 | 31 | 139 | 4.48 |
| 5 | Ronn McMahon, East Wash | 1990 | 29 | 130 | 4.48 |

## SINGLE GAME

### Scoring

| | Points vs Div. I Team | Year | Pts |
|---|---|---|---|
| 1 | Kevin Bradshaw, US Int'l vs Loyola-CA | 1991 | 72 |
| 2 | Pete Maravich, LSU vs Alabama | 1970 | 69 |
| 3 | Calvin Murphy, Niagara vs Syracuse | 1969 | 68 |
| 4 | Jay Handlan, Wash. & Lee vs Furman | 1951 | 66 |
| | Pete Maravich, LSU vs Tulane | 1969 | 66 |
| | Anthony Roberts, Oral Rbts vs N.C. A&T | 1977 | 66 |
| 7 | Anthony Roberts, Oral Rbts vs Ore | 1977 | 65 |
| | Scott Haffner, Evansville vs Dayton | 1989 | 65 |
| 9 | Pete Maravich, LSU vs Kentucky | 1970 | 64 |
| 10 | Johnny Neumann, Ole Miss vs LSU | 1971 | 63 |
| | Hersey Hawkins, Bradley vs Detroit | 1988 | 63 |

| | Points vs Non-Div. I Team | Year | Pts |
|---|---|---|---|
| 1 | Frank Selvy, Furman vs Newberry | 1954 | 100 |
| 2 | Paul Arizin, Villanova vs Phi. NAMC | 1949 | 85 |
| 3 | Freeman Williams, Port. St. vs Rocky Mt | 1978 | 81 |
| 4 | Bill Mlkvy, Temple vs Wilkes | 1951 | 73 |
| 5 | Freeman Williams, Port. St. vs So. Ore | 1977 | 71 |
| 6 | Darrell Floyd, Furman vs Morehead St. | 1955 | 67 |

**Note:** Bevo Francis of Division II Rio Grande (Ohio) scored an overall collegiate record 113 points against Hillsdale in 1954. He also scored 84 against Alliance and 82 against Bluffton that same season.

### 3-Pt Field Goals

| | | Year | No |
|---|---|---|---|
| 1 | Keith Veney, Marshall vs Morehead St. | 1996 | 15 |
| 2 | Dave Jamerson, Ohio U. vs Charleston | 1989 | 14 |
| | Askia Jones, Kansas St. vs Fresno St. | 1994 | 14 |
| | Ronald Blackshear, Marshall vs. Akron | 2002 | 14 |
| 5 | Gary Bossert, Niagara vs Siena | 1987 | 12 |
| | Darrin Fitzgerald, Butler vs Detroit | 1987 | 12 |
| | Al Dillard, Arkansas vs Delaware St. | 1993 | 12 |
| | Mitch Taylor, South-BR vs La. Christian | 1995 | 12 |
| | David McMahan, Winthrop vs C. Carolina | 1996 | 12 |
| | Clarence Gilbert, Missouri vs Colorado | 2002 | 12 |
| | Terrence Woods, Fla. A&M vs Coppin St. | 2003 | 12 |

### Assists

| | | Year | No |
|---|---|---|---|
| 1 | Tony Fairley, Baptist vs Armstrong St. | 1987 | 22 |
| | Avery Johnson, Southern-BR vs TX-South | 1988 | 22 |
| | Sherman Douglas, Syracuse vs Providence | 1989 | 22 |
| 4 | Mark Wade, UNLV vs Navy | 1986 | 21 |
| | Kelvin Scarborough, N. Mexico vs Hawaii | 1987 | 21 |
| | Anthony Manuel, Bradley vs UC-Irvine | 1987 | 21 |
| | Avery Johnson, Southern-BR vs Ala. St. | 1988 | 21 |

### Rebounds

| | Total (before 1973) | Year | No |
|---|---|---|---|
| 1 | Bill Chambers, Wm. & Mary vs Virginia | 1953 | 51 |
| 2 | Charlie Slack, Marshall vs M. Harvey | 1954 | 43 |
| 3 | Tom Heinsohn, Holy Cross vs BC | 1955 | 42 |
| 4 | Art Quimby, UConn vs BU | 1955 | 40 |
| 5 | Three players tied with 39 each. | | |

| | Total (since 1973) | Year | No |
|---|---|---|---|
| 1 | Larry Abney, Fresno St. vs SMU | 2000 | 35 |
| 2 | David Vaughn, Oral Roberts vs Brandeis | 1973 | 34 |
| 3 | Robert Parish, Centenary vs So. Miss | 1973 | 33 |
| 4 | Durand Macklin, LSU vs Tulane | 1976 | 32 |
| | Jervaughn Scales, South-BR vs Grambling | 1994 | 32 |

### Blocked Shots

| | | Year | No |
|---|---|---|---|
| 1 | David Robinson, Navy vs NC-Wilmington | 1986 | 14 |
| | Shawn Bradley, BYU vs Eastern Ky | 1990 | 14 |
| | Roy Rogers, Alabama vs Georgia | 1996 | 14 |
| | Loren Woods, Arizona vs Oregon | 2000 | 14 |
| 5 | Seven players tied with 13 each. | | |

### Steals

| | | Year | No |
|---|---|---|---|
| 1 | Mookie Blaylock, Oklahoma vs Centenary | 1987 | 13 |
| | Mookie Blaylock, Oklahoma vs Loyola-CA | 1988 | 13 |
| 3 | Kenny Robertson, Cleve. St. vs Wagner | 1988 | 12 |
| | Terry Evans, Oklahoma vs Florida A&M | 1993 | 12 |
| | Richard Duncan, Mid. Tenn St. vs E. Ky. | 1999 | 12 |
| | Greedy Daniels, TCU vs Ark-Pine Bluff | 2001 | 12 |
| | Jehiel Lewis, Navy vs Bucknell | 2002 | 12 |

## Players of the Year and Top Draft Picks

Consensus College Players of the Year and first overall selections in NBA draft since the abolition of the NBA's territorial draft in 1966. Top draft picks who became Rookie of the Year are in **bold** type; (*) indicates top draft pick chosen as junior, (**) indicates top draft pick chosen as sophomore, (†) indicates top draft pick chosen as a high school senior. Only five players have been the unanimous college player of the year, the first overall pick in the NBA draft and then the NBA Rookie of the year.

| Year | Player of the Year | Top Draft Pick |
|------|--------------------|----------------|
| 1966 | Cazzie Russell, Mich. | Cazzie Russell, NY |
| 1967 | Lew Alcindor, UCLA | Jimmy Walker, Det. |
| 1968 | Elvin Hayes, Houston | Elvin Hayes, SD |
| 1969 | Lew Alcindor, UCLA | **Lew Alcindor**, Mil. |
| 1970 | Pete Maravich, LSU | Bob Lanier, Det. |
| 1971 | Sidney Wicks, UCLA | Austin Carr, Cle. |
| 1972 | Bill Walton, UCLA | LaRue Martin, Por. |
| 1973 | Bill Walton, UCLA | Doug Collins, Phi. |
| 1974 | Bill Walton, UCLA | Bill Walton, Por. |
| 1975 | David Thompson, N.C. St. | David Thompson, Atl. |
| 1976 | Scott May, Indiana | John Lucas, Hou. |
| 1977 | Marques Johnson, UCLA | Kent Benson, Ind. |
| 1978 | Butch Lee, Marquette | |
| | & Phil Ford, N. Caro. | Mychal Thompson, Por. |
| 1979 | Larry Bird, Indiana St. | **Magic Johnson**, LAL** |
| 1980 | Mark Aguirre, DePaul | Joe Barry Carroll, G. St. |
| 1981 | Ralph Sampson, Va. | |
| | & Danny Ainge, BYU | Mark Aguirre, Dal. |
| 1982 | Ralph Sampson, Va. | James Worthy, LAL* |
| 1983 | Ralph Sampson, Va. | **Ralph Sampson**, Hou. |
| 1984 | Michael Jordan, N. Caro. | Akeem Olajuwon, Hou. |
| 1985 | Patrick Ewing, Georgetown | |
| | & Chris Mullin, St. John's | **Patrick Ewing**, NY |
| 1986 | Walter Berry, St. John's | Brad Daugherty, Cle. |
| 1987 | David Robinson, Navy | **David Robinson**, SA |
| 1988 | Hersey Hawkins, Bradley | |
| | & Danny Manning, Kan. | Danny Manning, LAC |

| Year | Player of the Year | Top Draft Pick |
|------|--------------------|----------------|
| 1989 | Sean Elliott, Arizona | |
| | & Danny Ferry, Duke | Pervis Ellison, Sac. |
| 1990 | Lionel Simmons, La Salle | **Derrick Coleman**, NJ |
| 1991 | Larry Johnson, UNLV | |
| | & Shaquille O'Neal, LSU | **Larry Johnson**, Cha. |
| 1992 | Christian Laettner, Duke | **Shaquille O'Neal**, Orl.* |
| 1993 | Calbert Cheaney, Ind. | **Chris Webber**, Orl.** |
| 1994 | Glenn Robinson, Purdue | Glenn Robinson, Mil.* |
| 1995 | Ed O'Bannon, UCLA | |
| | & Joe Smith, Maryland | Joe Smith, G. St.** |
| 1996 | Marcus Camby, UMass | **Allen Iverson**, Phi.** |
| 1997 | Tim Duncan, Wake Forest | **Tim Duncan**, SA |
| 1998 | Antawn Jamison, N. Caro. | M. Olowokandi, LAC |
| 1999 | Elton Brand, Duke | **Elton Brand**, Chi.** |
| 2000 | Kenyon Martin, Cincinnati | Kenyon Martin, NJ |
| 2001 | Shane Battier, Duke | |
| | & Jason Williams, Duke | Kwame Brown, Wash.† |
| 2002 | Jason Williams, Duke | |
| | & Drew Gooden, Kansas | Yao Ming, Hou. |
| 2003 | T.J. Ford, Texas | |
| | & David West, Xavier | **LeBron James**, Cle.† |
| 2004 | Jameer Nelson, St. Joseph's | |
| | & Emeka Okafor, UConn | Dwight Howard, Orl.† |
| 2005 | Andrew Bogut, Utah | Andrew Bogut, Mil.** |

## Annual Awards

UPI picked the first national Division I Player of the Year in 1955. Since then, the U.S. Basketball Writers Assn. (1959), the Associated Press Player of the Year (1961), the Atlanta Tip-Off Club (1969), the National Assn. of Basketball Coaches (1975), and the LA Athletic Club's John Wooden Award (1977) have joined in. UPI discontinued its award in 1997. Since 1977, the first year all the following awards were given out, the same player has won all of them in the same season 14 times: Marques Johnson in 1977, Larry Bird in 1979, Ralph Sampson in both 1982 and '83, Michael Jordan in 1984, David Robinson in 1987, Lionel Simmons in 1990, Calbert Cheaney in 1993, Glenn Robinson in 1994, Tim Duncan in 1997, Antawn Jamison in 1998, Elton Brand in 1999, Kenyon Martin in 2000 and Andrew Bogut in 2005.

## Wooden Award

Voted on by a panel of coaches, sportswriters and broadcasters and first presented in 1977 by the Los Angeles Athletic Club in the name of former Purdue All-American and UCLA coach John Wooden. Unlike the other five player of the year awards, candidates for the Wooden must have a minimum grade point average of 2.00 (out of 4.00).

**Multiple winner:** Ralph Sampson (2).

| Year | Year | Year |
|------|------|------|
| 1977 Marques Johnson, UCLA | 1987 David Robinson, Navy | 1997 Tim Duncan, Wake Forest |
| 1978 Phil Ford, North Carolina | 1988 Danny Manning, Kansas | 1998 Antawn Jamison, N. Carolina |
| 1979 Larry Bird, Indiana St. | 1989 Sean Elliott, Arizona | 1999 Elton Brand, Duke |
| 1980 Darrell Griffith, Louisville | 1990 Lionel Simmons, La Salle | 2000 Kenyon Martin, Cincinnati |
| 1981 Danny Ainge, BYU | 1991 Larry Johnson, UNLV | 2001 Shane Battier, Duke |
| 1982 Ralph Sampson, Virginia | 1992 Christian Laettner, Duke | 2002 Jason Williams, Duke |
| 1983 Ralph Sampson, Virginia | 1993 Calbert Cheaney, Indiana | 2003 T.J. Ford, Texas |
| 1984 Michael Jordan, N. Carolina | 1994 Glenn Robinson, Purdue | 2004 Jameer Nelson, St. Joseph's |
| 1985 Chris Mullin, St. John's | 1995 Ed O'Bannon, UCLA | 2005 Andrew Bogut, Utah |
| 1986 Walter Berry St. John's | 1996 Marcus Camby, UMass | |

## United Press International

Voted on by a panel of UPI college basketball writers and first presented in 1955.

**Multiple winners:** Oscar Robertson, Ralph Sampson and Bill Walton (3); Lew Alcindor and Jerry Lucas (2).

| Year | Year | Year |
|------|------|------|
| 1955 Tom Gola, La Salle | 1963 Art Heyman, Duke | 1971 Austin Carr, Notre Dame |
| 1956 Bill Russell, San Francisco | 1964 Gary Bradds, Ohio St. | 1972 Bill Walton, UCLA |
| 1957 Chet Forte, Columbia | 1965 Bill Bradley, Princeton | 1973 Bill Walton, UCLA |
| 1958 Oscar Robertson, Cincinnati | 1966 Cazzie Russell, Michigan | 1974 Bill Walton, UCLA |
| 1959 Oscar Robertson, Cincinnati | 1967 Lew Alcindor, UCLA | 1975 David Thompson, N.C. State |
| 1960 Oscar Robertson, Cincinnati | 1968 Elvin Hayes, Houston | 1976 Scott May, Indiana |
| 1961 Jerry Lucas, Ohio St. | 1969 Lew Alcindor, UCLA | 1977 Marques Johnson, UCLA |
| 1962 Jerry Lucas, Ohio St. | 1970 Pete Maravich, LSU | 1978 Butch Lee, Marquette |

| Year | Year | Year |
|---|---|---|
| 1979 Larry Bird, Indiana St. | 1986 Walter Berry, St. John's | 1993 Calbert Cheaney, Indiana |
| 1980 Mark Aguirre, DePaul | 1987 David Robinson, Navy | 1994 Glenn Robinson, Purdue |
| 1981 Ralph Sampson, Virginia | 1988 Hersey Hawkins, Bradley | 1995 Joe Smith, Maryland |
| 1982 Ralph Sampson, Virginia | 1989 Danny Ferry, Duke | 1996 Ray Allen, UConn |
| 1983 Ralph Sampson, Virginia | 1990 Lionel Simmons, La Salle | 1997 award discontinued |
| 1984 Michael Jordan, N. Carolina | 1991 Shaquille O'Neal, LSU | |
| 1985 Chris Mullin, St. John's | 1992 Jim Jackson, Ohio St. | |

## U.S. Basketball Writers Association

Voted on by the USBWA and first presented in 1959.
**Multiple winners:** Ralph Sampson and Bill Walton (3); Lew Alcindor, Jerry Lucas and Oscar Robertson (2).

| Year | Year | Year |
|---|---|---|
| 1959 Oscar Robertson, Cincinnati | 1975 David Thompson, N.C. State | 1991 Larry Johnson, UNLV |
| 1960 Oscar Robertson, Cincinnati | 1976 Adrian Dantley, Notre Dame | 1992 Christian Laettner, Duke |
| 1961 Jerry Lucas, Ohio St. | 1977 Marques Johnson, UCLA | 1993 Calbert Cheaney, Indiana |
| 1962 Jerry Lucas, Ohio St. | 1978 Phil Ford, North Carolina | 1994 Glenn Robinson, Purdue |
| 1963 Art Heyman, Duke | 1979 Larry Bird, Indiana St. | 1995 Ed O'Bannon, UCLA |
| 1964 Walt Hazzard, UCLA | 1980 Mark Aguirre, DePaul | 1996 Marcus Camby, UMass |
| 1965 Bill Bradley, Princeton | 1981 Ralph Sampson, Virginia | 1997 Tim Duncan, Wake Forest |
| 1966 Cazzie Russell, Michigan | 1982 Ralph Sampson, Virginia | 1998 Antawn Jamison, N. Carolina |
| 1967 Lew Alcindor, UCLA | 1983 Ralph Sampson, Virginia | 1999 Elton Brand, Duke |
| 1968 Elvin Hayes, Houston | 1984 Michael Jordan, N. Carolina | 2000 Kenyon Martin, Cincinnati |
| 1969 Lew Alcindor, UCLA | 1985 Chris Mullin, St. John's | 2001 Shane Battier, Duke |
| 1970 Pete Maravich, LSU | 1986 Walter Berry, St. John's | 2002 Jason Williams, Duke |
| 1971 Sidney Wicks, UCLA | 1987 David Robinson, Navy | 2003 David West, Xavier |
| 1972 Bill Walton, UCLA | 1988 Hersey Hawkins, Bradley | 2004 Jameer Nelson, St. Joseph's |
| 1973 Bill Walton, UCLA | 1989 Danny Ferry, Duke | 2005 Andrew Bogut, Utah |
| 1974 Bill Walton, UCLA | 1990 Lionel Simmons, La Salle | |

## Associated Press Player of the Year

Voted on by AP sportswriters and broadcasters.
**Multiple winners:** Ralph Sampson (3); Lew Alcindor, Jerry Lucas, David Thompson and Bill Walton (2).

| Year | Year | Year |
|---|---|---|
| 1961 Jerry Lucas, Ohio St. | 1976 Scott May, Indiana | 1991 Shaquille O'Neal, LSU |
| 1962 Jerry Lucas, Ohio St. | 1977 Marques Johnson, UCLA | 1992 Christian Laettner, Duke |
| 1963 Art Heyman, Duke | 1978 Butch Lee, Marquette | 1993 Calbert Cheaney, Indiana |
| 1964 Gary Bradds, Ohio St. | 1979 Larry Bird, Indiana St. | 1994 Glenn Robinson, Purdue |
| 1965 Bill Bradley, Princeton | 1980 Mark Aguirre, DePaul | 1995 Joe Smith, Maryland |
| 1966 Cazzie Russell, Michigan | 1981 Ralph Sampson, Virginia | 1996 Marcus Camby, UMass |
| 1967 Lew Alcindor, UCLA | 1982 Ralph Sampson, Virginia | 1997 Tim Duncan, Wake Forest |
| 1968 Elvin Hayes, Houston | 1983 Ralph Sampson, Virginia | 1998 Antawn Jamison, N. Carolina |
| 1969 Lew Alcindor, UCLA | 1984 Michael Jordan, N. Carolina | 1999 Elton Brand, Duke |
| 1970 Pete Maravich, LSU | 1985 Patrick Ewing, Georgetown | 2000 Kenyon Martin, Cincinnati |
| 1971 Austin Carr, Notre Dame | 1986 Walter Berry, St. John's | 2001 Shane Battier, Duke |
| 1972 Bill Walton, UCLA | 1987 David Robinson, Navy | 2002 Jason Williams, Duke |
| 1973 Bill Walton, UCLA | 1988 Hersey Hawkins, Bradley | 2003 David West, Xavier |
| 1974 David Thompson, N.C. State | 1989 Sean Elliott, Arizona | 2004 Jameer Nelson, St. Joseph's |
| 1975 David Thompson, N.C. State | 1990 Lionel Simmons, La Salle | 2005 Andrew Bogut, Utah |

## Naismith Award

Voted on by a panel of coaches, sportswriters and broadcasters and first presented in 1969 by the Atlanta Tip-Off Club in 1969 in the name of the inventor of basketball, Dr. James Naismith.
**Multiple winners:** Ralph Sampson and Bill Walton (3).

| Year | Year | Year |
|---|---|---|
| 1969 Lew Alcindor, UCLA | 1982 Ralph Sampson, Virginia | 1995 Joe Smith, Maryland |
| 1970 Pete Maravich, LSU | 1983 Ralph Sampson, Virginia | 1996 Marcus Camby, UMass |
| 1971 Austin Carr, Notre Dame | 1984 Michael Jordan, N. Carolina | 1997 Tim Duncan, Wake Forest |
| 1972 Bill Walton, UCLA | 1985 Patrick Ewing, Georgetown | 1998 Antawn Jamison, N. Carolina |
| 1973 Bill Walton, UCLA | 1986 Johnny Dawkins, Duke | 1999 Elton Brand, Duke |
| 1974 Bill Walton, UCLA | 1987 David Robinson, Navy | 2000 Kenyon Martin, Cincinnati |
| 1975 David Thompson, N.C. State | 1988 Danny Manning, Kansas | 2001 Shane Battier, Duke |
| 1976 Scott May, Indiana | 1989 Danny Ferry, Duke | 2002 Jason Williams, Duke |
| 1977 Marques Johnson, UCLA | 1990 Lionel Simmons, La Salle | 2003 T.J. Ford, Texas |
| 1978 Butch Lee, Marquette | 1991 Larry Johnson, UNLV | 2004 Jameer Nelson, St. Joseph's |
| 1979 Larry Bird, Indiana St. | 1992 Christian Laettner, Duke | 2005 Andrew Bogut, Utah |
| 1980 Mark Aguirre, DePaul | 1993 Calbert Cheaney, Indiana | |
| 1981 Ralph Sampson, Virginia | 1994 Glenn Robinson, Purdue | |

## National Association of Basketball Coaches

Voted on by the National Assn. of Basketball Coaches and presented by the Eastman Kodak Co. from 1975-94.
**Multiple winners:** Ralph Sampson and Jason Williams (2).

| Year | Year | Year |
|---|---|---|
| 1975 David Thompson, N.C. State | 1986 Walter Berry, St. John's | 1997 Tim Duncan, Wake Forest |
| 1976 Scott May, Indiana | 1987 David Robinson, Navy | 1998 Antawn Jamison, N. Carolina |
| 1977 Marques Johnson, UCLA | 1988 Danny Manning, Kansas | 1999 Elton Brand, Duke |
| 1978 Phil Ford, North Carolina | 1989 Sean Elliott, Arizona | 2000 Kenyon Martin, Cincinnati |
| 1979 Larry Bird, Indiana St. | 1990 Lionel Simmons, La Salle | 2001 Jason Williams, Duke |
| 1980 Michael Brooks, La Salle | 1991 Larry Johnson, UNLV | 2002 Jason Williams, Duke |
| 1981 Danny Ainge, BYU | 1992 Christian Laettner, Duke | & Drew Gooden, Kansas |
| 1982 Ralph Sampson, Virginia | 1993 Calbert Cheaney, Indiana | 2003 Nick Collison, Kansas |
| 1983 Ralph Sampson, Virginia | 1994 Glenn Robinson, Purdue | 2004 Jameer Nelson, St. Joseph's |
| 1984 Michael Jordan, N. Carolina | 1995 Shawn Respert, Mich. St. | & Emeka Okafor, Connecticut |
| 1985 Patrick Ewing, Georgetown | 1996 Marcus Camby, UMass | 2005 Andrew Bogut, Utah |

## All-Time Winningest Division I Coaches

Minimum of 10 seasons as Division I head coach; regular season and tournament games included; coaches active during 2004-05 in **bold** type.

### Top 30 Winning Percentage

| | | Yrs | W | L | Pct |
|---|---|---|---|---|---|
| 1 | Clair Bee | .21 | 412 | 87 | **.826** |
| 2 | Adolph Rupp | .41 | 876 | 190 | **.822** |
| 3 | John Wooden | .29 | 664 | 162 | **.804** |
| 4 | **Roy Williams** | .17 | 470 | 116 | **.802** |
| 5 | John Kresse | .23 | 560 | 143 | **.797** |
| 6 | Jerry Tarkanian | .31 | 778 | 202 | **.794** |
| 7 | Dean Smith | .36 | 879 | 254 | **.776** |
| 8 | Harry Fisher | .13 | 147 | 44 | **.770** |
| 9 | Frank Keaney | .27 | 387 | 117 | **.768** |
| 10 | George Keogan | .24 | 385 | 117 | **.767** |
| 11 | Jack Ramsay | .11 | 231 | 71 | **.765** |
| 12 | Vic Bubas | .10 | 213 | 67 | **.761** |
| 13 | Chick Davies | .21 | 314 | 106 | **.748** |
| 14 | Ray Mears | .21 | 399 | 135 | **.747** |
| 15 | **Mike Krzyzewski** | .30 | 721 | 246 | **.746** |
| 16 | **Jim Boeheim** | .29 | 703 | 241 | **.745** |
| 17 | **Lute Olson** | .32 | 740 | 257 | **.742** |
| 18 | Rick Majerus | .20 | 431 | 151 | **.741** |
| 19 | **Tubby Smith** | .14 | 343 | 120 | **.740** |
| 20 | **Bob Huggins** | .24 | 567 | 199 | **.740** |
| 21 | Al McGuire | .20 | 405 | 143 | **.739** |
| 22 | Everett Case | .18 | 376 | 133 | **.739** |
| 23 | Phog Allen | .48 | 746 | 264 | **.739** |
| 24 | **Rick Pitino** | .19 | 449 | 159 | **.738** |
| 25 | Walter Meanwell | .22 | 280 | 101 | **.735** |
| 26 | Lew Andreas | .25 | 355 | 134 | **.726** |
| 27 | Lou Carnesecca | .24 | 526 | 200 | **.725** |
| 28 | Fred Schaus | .12 | 251 | 96 | **.723** |
| 29 | **Eddie Sutton** | .35 | 781 | 299 | **.723** |
| 30 | Cam Henderson | .35 | 630 | 243 | **.722** |

### Top 30 Victories

| | | Yrs | W | L | Pct |
|---|---|---|---|---|---|
| 1 | Dean Smith | .36 | 879 | 254 | .776 |
| 2 | Adolph Rupp | .41 | **876** | 190 | .822 |
| 3 | **Bob Knight** | .39 | **854** | 333 | .719 |
| 4 | Jim Phelan | .49 | **830** | 524 | .613 |
| 5 | **Eddie Sutton** | .35 | **781** | 299 | .723 |
| 6 | Lou Henson | .41 | **779** | 408 | .656 |
| 7 | Lefty Driesell | .41 | **786** | 394 | .666 |
| 8 | Jerry Tarkanian | .31 | **778** | 202 | .794 |
| 9 | Hank Iba | .41 | **767** | 338 | .694 |
| 10 | Ed Diddle | .42 | **759** | 302 | .715 |
| 11 | Phog Allen | .48 | **746** | 264 | .739 |
| 12 | **Lute Olson** | .32 | **740** | 257 | .742 |
| 13 | Norm Stewart | .38 | **731** | 375 | .661 |
| 14 | **John Chaney** | .33 | **724** | 297 | .709 |
| | Ray Meyer | .42 | **724** | 354 | .672 |
| 16 | **Mike Krzyzewski** | .30 | **721** | 246 | .746 |
| 17 | Don Haskins | .38 | **719** | 353 | .671 |
| 18 | **Jim Calhoun** | .33 | **703** | 310 | .694 |
| | **Jim Boeheim** | .29 | **703** | 241 | .745 |
| 20 | Denny Crum | .30 | **675** | 295 | .696 |
| 21 | John Wooden | .29 | **664** | 162 | .804 |
| 22 | Ralph Miller | .38 | **657** | 382 | .632 |
| 23 | Marv Harshman | .40 | **654** | 449 | .593 |
| 24 | Gene Bartow | .34 | **647** | 353 | .647 |
| 25 | **Hugh Durham** | .37 | **633** | 429 | .596 |
| 26 | Cam Henderson | .35 | **630** | 243 | .722 |
| 27 | Norm Sloan | .37 | **624** | 393 | .614 |
| | **Billy Tubbs** | .30 | **624** | 326 | .657 |
| 29 | Slats Gill | .36 | **599** | 392 | .604 |
| 30 | Abe Lemons | .34 | **597** | 344 | .634 |

**Note: Clarence (Bighouse) Gaines** of Division II Winston-Salem St. (1947-93) retired after the 1992-93 season to finish his 47-year career ranked No. 3 on the all-time NCAA list of all coaches regardless of division. His record is 828-446 with a .650 winning percentage.

## Where They Coached

**Allen**–Baker (1906-08), Kansas (1908-09), Haskell (1909), Central Mo. St. (1913-19), Kansas (1920-56); **Andreas**–Syracuse (1925-43; 45-50); **Bartow**–Central Mo. St. (1962-64), Valparaiso (1965-70), Memphis St. (1971-74), Illinois (1975), UCLA (1976-77), UAB (1979-96); **Bee**–Rider (1929-31), LIU-Brooklyn (1932-45, 46-51); **Boeheim**–Syracuse (1977–); **Bubas**–Duke (1960-69); **Calhoun**–Northeastern (1973-86), Connecticut (1987–); **Carnesecca**–St. John's (1966-70, 74-92); **Case**–N.C. State (1947-64); **Chaney**–Cheyney St. (1973-82), Temple (1983–); **Crum**–Louisville (1972-01); **Davies**–Duquesne (1925-43, 47-48); **Diddle**–Western Ky. (1923-64); **Driesell**–Davidson (1961-69), Maryland (1970-86), J. Madison (1989-97), Georgia St. (1997-2003); **Durham**–Florida St. (1967-78), Georgia (1979-95), Jacksonville (1999-05); **Fisher**–Columbia (1907-16), Army (1922-23, 25). **Gill**–Oregon St. (1929-64); **Harshman**–Pacific Lutheran (1946-58), Wash. St. (1959-71), Washington (1972-85); **Haskins**–UTEP (1962-99); **Henderson**–Muskingum (1920-22), Davis & Elkins (1923-35), Marshall (1936-55); **Henson**–Hardin-Simmons (1963-66), N. Mexico St. (1967-75), Illinois (1976-96), N. Mexico St. (1997-05); **Huggins**–Walsh (1981-83), Akron (1985-89), Cincinnati (1990–); **Iba**–NW Missouri St. (1930-33), Colorado (1934), Oklahoma St. (1935-70); **Keaney**–Rhode Island (1921-48); **Keogan**–St. Louis (1916), Allegheny (1919), Valparaiso (1920-21), Notre Dame (1924-43); **Knight**–Army (1966-71), Indiana (1972-00), Texas Tech (2001–); **Kresse**–Charleston (1979-2002); **Krzyzewski**–Army (1976-80), Duke (1981–).
**Lemons**–Okla. City (1956-73), Pan American (1974-76), Texas (1977-82), Okla. City (1984-90); **Majerus**–Marquette

(1984-86), Ball St. (1988-89), Utah (1991–); **McGuire**–Belmont Abbey (1958-64), Marquette (1965-77); **Meanwell**–Wisconsin (1912-17, 21-34), Missouri (1918-20); **Mears**–Wittenberg (1957-62), Tennessee (1963-77); **Meyer**–DePaul (1943-84); **Miller**–Wichita St. (1952-64), Iowa (1965-70), Oregon St. (1971-89); **Olson**–Long Beach St. (1974), Iowa (1975-83), Arizona (1984–); **Phelan**– Mount St. Mary's (1955-2003); **Pitino**–Boston Univ. (1979-83), Providence (1986-87), Kentucky (1989-97), Louisville (2001–).

**Ramsay**–St. Joseph's-PA (1956-66); **Rupp**–Kentucky (1931-72); **Schaus**–West Va. (1955-60), Purdue (1973-78); **Sloan**–Presbyterian (1952-55), Citadel (1957-60), Florida (1961-66), N.C. State (1967-80), Florida (1981-89); **D. Smith**–North Carolina (1962-97); **T. Smith**–Tulsa (1992-95), Georgia (1996-97), Kentucky (1998–); **Stewart**–No. Iowa (1962-67), Missouri (1968-99); **Sutton**–Creighton (1970-74), Arkansas (1975-85), Kentucky (1986-89), Oklahoma St. (1991–); **Tarkanian**–Long Beach St. (1969-73), UNLV (1974-92), Fresno St. (1995-2002); **Tubbs**–Southwestern (1971-73), Lamar (1976-80, 2003–), Oklahoma (1981-94), TCU (1995-2002); **Williams**–Kansas (1989-2003), North Carolina (2003–); **Wooden**–Indiana St. (1947-48), UCLA (1949-75).

## Most NCAA Tournaments

Through 2005; listed are number of appearances, overall tournament record, times reaching Final Four, and number of NCAA championships. (*) denotes that actual records are different from official NCAA records.

| App | | W-L | F4 | Championships |
|-----|-----|-----|-----|-----|
| 27 | Dean Smith | 65-27 | 11 | 2 (1982, 93) |
| 26 | **Bob Knight** | 44-22 | 5 | 3 (1976, 81, 87) |
| 26 | **Lute Olson**\* | 45-26 | 5 | 1 (1997) |
| 26 | **Eddie Sutton**\* | 39-26 | 2 | None |
| 24 | **Jim Boeheim** | 40-23 | 3 | 1 (2003) |
| 23 | Denny Crum | 42-23 | 6 | 2 (1980, 86) |
| 21 | **Mike Krzyzewski** | 66-18 | 9 | 3 (1991-92, 2001) |
| 20 | Adolph Rupp | 30-18 | 6 | 4 (1948-49, 51, 58) |
| 20 | John Thompson | 34-19 | 3 | 1 (1984) |
| 19 | **Lou Henson** | 19-20 | 2 | None |
| 18 | Lou Carnesecca | 17-20 | 1 | None |
| 18 | Jerry Tarkanian | 38-18 | 4 | 1 (1990) |
| 18 | **Gene Keady**\* | 19-18 | 0 | None |
| 18 | **Jim Calhoun**\* | 38-16 | 2 | 2 (1999, 2004) |
| 17 | **John Chaney** | 23-17 | 0 | None |
| 16 | John Wooden | 47-10 | 12 | 10 (1964-65, 67-73, 75) |
| 16 | Norm Stewart\* | 12-16 | 0 | None |
| 16 | Nolan Richardson | 26-15 | 3 | 1 (1994) |
| 16 | Jim Harrick | 18-15 | 1 | 1 (1995) |
| 16 | **Roy Williams** | 41-15 | 5 | 1 (2005) |
| 15 | Digger Phelps | 17-17 | 1 | None |
| 15 | **Bob Huggins** | 20-14 | 1 | None |
| 14 | Don Haskins | 14-13 | 1 | 1 (1966) |
| 14 | Guy Lewis | 26-18 | 5 | None |
| 14 | **Gary Williams** | 26-13 | 2 | 1 (2002) |

## Active Coaches' Victories

Minimum five seasons in Division I.

| | | Yrs | W | L | Pct |
|-----|-----|-----|-----|-----|-----|
| 1 | Bob Knight, Texas Tech | 39 | 854 | 333 | .719 |
| 2 | Eddie Sutton, Okla. St. | 35 | 781 | 299 | .723 |
| 3 | Lute Olson, Arizona | 32 | 740 | 257 | .742 |
| 4 | John Chaney, Temple | 33 | 724 | 297 | .709 |
| 5 | Mike Krzyzewski, Duke | 30 | 721 | 246 | .746 |
| 6 | Jim Calhoun, UConn | 33 | 703 | 310 | .694 |
| | Jim Boeheim, Syracuse | 29 | 703 | 241 | .745 |
| 8 | Billy Tubbs, Lamar | 30 | 624 | 326 | .657 |
| 9 | Tom Davis, Drake | 30 | 568 | 322 | .638 |
| 10 | Tom Penders, Houston | 31 | 545 | 375 | .592 |
| 11 | Gary Williams, Maryland | 27 | 541 | 306 | .639 |
| 12 | Homer Drew, Valparaiso | 28 | 538 | 335 | .616 |
| 13 | Ben Braun, California | 28 | 503 | 353 | .588 |
| 14 | Pat Douglass, UC-Irvine | 24 | 498 | 226 | .688 |
| 15 | Bo Ryan, Wisconsin | 21 | 476 | 140 | .773 |
| 16 | Rick Byrd, Belmont | 24 | 473 | 273 | .634 |
| 17 | Roy Williams, North Carolina | 17 | 470 | 116 | .802 |
| 18 | Rick Pitino, Louisville | 19 | 449 | 159 | .738 |
| 19 | Kelvin Sampson, Oklahoma | 22 | 436 | 247 | .638 |
| 20 | John Beilein, West Virginia | 23 | 427 | 255 | .626 |
| 21 | Dick Bennett, Washington St. | 23 | 426 | 235 | .644 |
| 22 | Pat Kennedy, Towson | 25 | 421 | 335 | .557 |
| 23 | Dave Bike, Sacred Heart | 27 | 416 | 370 | .529 |
| 24 | Danny Nee, Duquesne | 25 | 406 | 358 | .531 |
| 25 | Don Maestri, Troy | 23 | 394 | 265 | .598 |
| 26 | Stew Morrill, Utah St. | 19 | 385 | 192 | .667 |
| 27 | L. Vann Pettaway, Ala. A&M | 19 | 384 | 181 | .680 |
| 28 | Mike Deane, Wagner | 21 | 368 | 253 | .593 |
| 29 | Gary Garner, SE Missouri St. | 22 | 366 | 276 | .570 |
| 30 | Rick Barnes, Texas | 18 | 363 | 203 | .641 |

## Annual Awards

UPI picked the first national Division I Coach of the Year in 1955. Since then, the U.S. Basketball Writers Assn. (1959), AP (1967), the National Assn. of Basketball Coaches (1969), and the Atlanta Tip-Off Club (1987) have joined in. Since 1987, the first year all five awards were given out, no coach has won all of them in the same season.

## United Press International

Voted on by a panel of UPI college basketball writers and first presented in 1955.

**Multiple winners:** John Wooden (6); Bob Knight, Ray Meyer, Adolph Rupp, Norm Stewart, Fred Taylor and Phil Woolpert (2).

| Year | Year | Year |
|-----|-----|-----|
| 1955 Phil Woolpert, San Francisco | 1970 John Wooden, UCLA | 1985 Lou Carnesecca, St. John's |
| 1956 Phil Woolpert, San Francisco | 1971 Al McGuire, Marquette | 1986 Mike Krzyzewski, Duke |
| 1957 Frank McGuire, North Carolina | 1972 John Wooden, UCLA | 1987 John Thompson, Georgetown |
| 1958 Tex Winter, Kansas St. | 1973 John Wooden, UCLA | 1988 John Chaney, Temple |
| 1959 Adolph Rupp, Kentucky | 1974 Digger Phelps, Notre Dame | 1989 Bob Knight, Indiana |
| 1960 Pete Newell, California | 1975 Bob Knight, Indiana | 1990 Jim Calhoun, Connecticut |
| 1961 Fred Taylor, Ohio St. | 1976 Tom Young, Rutgers | 1991 Rick Majerus, Utah |
| 1962 Fred Taylor, Ohio St. | 1977 Bob Gaillard, San Francisco | 1992 Perry Clark, Tulane |
| 1963 Ed Jucker, Cincinnati | 1978 Eddie Sutton, Arkansas | 1993 Eddie Fogler, Vanderbilt |
| 1964 John Wooden, UCLA | 1979 Bill Hodges, Indiana St. | 1994 Norm Stewart, Missouri |
| 1965 Dave Strack, Michigan | 1980 Ray Meyer, DePaul | 1995 Leonard Hamilton, Miami-FL |
| 1966 Adolph Rupp, Kentucky | 1981 Ralph Miller, Oregon St. | 1996 Gene Keady, Purdue |
| 1967 John Wooden, UCLA | 1982 Norm Stewart, Missouri | 1997 award discontinued |
| 1968 Guy Lewis, Houston | 1983 Jerry Tarkanian, UNLV | |
| 1969 John Wooden, UCLA | 1984 Ray Meyer, DePaul | |

## Annual Awards (Cont.)
### U.S. Basketball Writers Association
Voted on by the USBWA and first presented in 1959.
**Multiple winners:** John Wooden (5); Bob Knight (3); Lou Carnesecca, John Chaney, Ray Meyer and Fred Taylor (2).

| Year | Year | Year |
|---|---|---|
| 1959 Eddie Hickey, Marquette | 1975 Bob Knight, Indiana | 1991 Randy Ayers, Ohio St. |
| 1960 Pete Newell, California | 1976 Bob Knight, Indiana | 1992 Perry Clark, Tulane |
| 1961 Fred Taylor, Ohio St. | 1977 Eddie Sutton, Arkansas | 1993 Eddie Fogler, Vanderbilt |
| 1962 Fred Taylor, Ohio St. | 1978 Ray Meyer, DePaul | 1994 Charlie Spoonhour, St. Louis |
| 1963 Ed Jucker, Cincinnati | 1979 Dean Smith, North Carolina | 1995 Kelvin Sampson, Oklahoma |
| 1964 John Wooden, UCLA | 1980 Ray Meyer, DePaul | 1996 Gene Keady, Purdue |
| 1965 Butch van Breda Kolff, Princeton | 1981 Ralph Miller, Oregon St. | 1997 Clem Haskins, Minnesota |
| 1966 Adolph Rupp, Kentucky | 1982 John Thompson, Georgetown | 1998 Tom Izzo, Michigan St. |
| 1967 John Wooden, UCLA | 1983 Lou Carnesecca, St. John's | 1999 Cliff Ellis, Auburn |
| 1968 Guy Lewis, Houston | 1984 Gene Keady, Purdue | 2000 Larry Eustachy, Iowa St. |
| 1969 Maury John, Drake | 1985 Lou Carnesecca, St. John's | 2001 Al Skinner, Boston College |
| 1970 John Wooden, UCLA | 1986 Dick Versace, Bradley | 2002 Ben Howland, Pittsburgh |
| 1971 Al McGuire, Marquette | 1987 John Chaney, Temple | 2003 Tubby Smith, Kentucky |
| 1972 John Wooden, UCLA | 1988 John Chaney, Temple | 2004 Phil Martelli, St. Joseph's |
| 1973 John Wooden, UCLA | 1989 Bob Knight, Indiana | 2005 Bruce Weber, Illinois |
| 1974 Norm Sloan, N.C. State | 1990 Roy Williams, Kansas | |

### Associated Press
Voted on by AP sportswriters and broadcasters and first presented in 1967.
**Multiple winners:** John Wooden (5); Bob Knight (3); Guy Lewis, Ray Meyer, Ralph Miller and Eddie Sutton (2).

| Year | Year | Year |
|---|---|---|
| 1967 John Wooden, UCLA | 1980 Ray Meyer, DePaul | 1993 Eddie Fogler, Vanderbilt |
| 1968 Guy Lewis, Houston | 1981 Ralph Miller, Oregon St. | 1994 Norm Stewart, Missouri |
| 1969 John Wooden, UCLA | 1982 Ralph Miller, Oregon St. | 1995 Kelvin Sampson, Oklahoma |
| 1970 John Wooden, UCLA | 1983 Guy Lewis, Houston | 1996 Gene Keady, Purdue |
| 1971 Al McGuire, Marquette | 1984 Ray Meyer, DePaul | 1997 Clem Haskins, Minnesota |
| 1972 John Wooden, UCLA | 1985 Bill Frieder, Michigan | 1998 Tom Izzo, Michigan St. |
| 1973 John Wooden, UCLA | 1986 Eddie Sutton, Kentucky | 1999 Cliff Ellis, Auburn |
| 1974 Norm Sloan, N.C. State | 1987 Tom Davis, Iowa | 2000 Larry Eustachy, Iowa St. |
| 1975 Bob Knight, Indiana | 1988 John Chaney, Temple | 2001 Matt Doherty, North Carolina |
| 1976 Bob Knight, Indiana | 1989 Bob Knight, Indiana | 2002 Ben Howland, Pittsburgh |
| 1977 Bob Gaillard, San Francisco | 1990 Jim Calhoun, Connecticut | 2003 Tubby Smith, Kentucky |
| 1978 Eddie Sutton, Arkansas | 1991 Randy Ayers, Ohio St. | 2004 Phil Martelli, St. Joseph's |
| 1979 Bill Hodges, Indiana St. | 1992 Roy Williams, Kansas | 2005 Bruce Weber, Illinois |

### National Association of Basketball Coaches
Voted on by NABC membership and first presented in 1969.
**Multiple winners:** John Wooden (3); Gene Keady and Mike Krzyzewski (2).

| Year | Year | Year |
|---|---|---|
| 1969 John Wooden, UCLA | 1982 Don Monson, Idaho | 1996 John Calipari, UMass |
| 1970 John Wooden, UCLA | 1983 Lou Carnesecca, St. John's | 1997 Clem Haskins, Minnesota |
| 1971 Jack Kraft, Villanova | 1984 Marv Harshman, Washington | 1998 Bill Guthridge, N. Carolina |
| 1972 John Wooden, UCLA | 1985 John Thompson, Georgetown | 1999 Mike Krzyzewski, Duke |
| 1973 Gene Bartow, Memphis St. | 1986 Eddie Sutton, Kentucky |    & Jim O'Brien, Ohio St. |
| 1974 Al McGuire, Marquette | 1987 Rick Pitino, Providence | 2000 Gene Keady, Purdue |
| 1975 Bob Knight, Indiana | 1988 John Chaney, Temple | 2001 Tom Izzo, Michigan St. |
| 1976 Johnny Orr, Michigan | 1989 P.J. Carlesimo, Seton Hall | 2002 Kelvin Sampson, Oklahoma |
| 1977 Dean Smith, North Carolina | 1990 Jud Heathcote, Michigan St. | 2003 Tubby Smith, Kentucky |
| 1978 Bill Foster, Duke | 1991 Mike Krzyzewski, Duke | 2004 Phil Martelli, St. Joseph's |
|    & Abe Lemons, Texas | 1992 George Raveling, USC |    & Mike Montgomery, Stanford |
| 1979 Ray Meyer, DePaul | 1993 Eddie Fogler, Vanderbilt | 2005 Bruce Weber, Illinois |
| 1980 Lute Olson, Iowa | 1994 Nolan Richardson, Arkansas | |
| 1981 Ralph Miller, Oregon St. |    & Gene Keady, Purdue | |
|    & Jack Hartman, Kansas St. | 1995 Jim Harrick, UCLA | |

### Naismith Award
Voted on by a panel of coaches, sportswriters and broadcasters and first presented by the Atlanta Tip-Off Club in 1987 in the name of the inventor of basketball, Dr. James Naismith.
**Multiple winner:** Mike Krzyzewski (3).

| Year | Year | Year |
|---|---|---|
| 1987 Bob Knight, Indiana | 1994 Nolan Richardson, Arkansas | 2001 Rod Barnes, Mississippi |
| 1988 Larry Brown, Kansas | 1995 Jim Harrick, UCLA | 2002 Ben Howland, Pittsburgh |
| 1989 Mike Krzyzewski, Duke | 1996 John Calipari, UMass | 2003 Tubby Smith, Kentucky |
| 1990 Bobby Cremins, Georgia Tech | 1997 Roy Williams, Kansas | 2004 Phil Martelli, St. Joseph's |
| 1991 Randy Ayers, Ohio St. | 1998 Bill Guthridge, N. Carolina | 2005 Bruce Weber, Illinois |
| 1992 Mike Krzyzewski, Duke | 1999 Mike Krzyzewski, Duke | |
| 1993 Dean Smith, North Carolina | 2000 Mike Montgomery, Stanford | |

## Player of the Year and NBA MVP

College Players of the Year who have gone on to win the NBA's Most Valuable Player award:

**Bill Russell** COLLEGE–San Francisco (1956); PROS–Boston Celtics (1958, 1961, 1962, 1963 and 1965).
**Oscar Robertson** COLLEGE–Cincinnati (1958, 1959 and 1960); PROS–Cincinnati Royals (1964).
**Kareem Abdul-Jabbar** COLLEGE–UCLA (1967 and 1969); PROS–Milwaukee Bucks (1971, 1972 and 1974) and LA Lakers (1976, 1977 and 1980).
**Bill Walton** COLLEGE–UCLA (1972, 1973 and 1974); PROS–Portland Trail Blazers (1978).
**Larry Bird** COLLEGE–Indiana St. (1979); PROS–Boston Celtics (1984, 1985, and 1986).
**Michael Jordan** COLLEGE–North Carolina (1984); PROS–Chicago Bulls (1988, 1991, 1992, 1996 and 1998).
**David Robinson** COLLEGE–Navy (1987); PROS–San Antonio Spurs (1995).
**Shaquille O'Neal** COLLEGE–LSU (1991); PROS–LA Lakers (2000).
**Tim Duncan** COLLEGE–Wake Forest (1997); PROS–San Antonio Spurs (2002, 2003).

## Other Men's Champions

The NCAA has sanctioned national championship tournaments for Division II since 1957 and Division III since 1975. The NAIA sanctioned a single tournament from 1937-91, then split into two divisions in 1992.

### NCAA Div. II Finals

**Multiple winners:** Kentucky Wesleyan (8); Evansville (5); CS-Bakersfield and Virginia Union (3); Metropolitan State, North Alabama (2).

| Year | Winner | Score | Loser | Year | Winner | Score | Loser |
|---|---|---|---|---|---|---|---|
| 1957 | Wheaton, IL | 89-65 | Ky. Wesleyan | 1982 | Dist. of Columbia | 73-63 | Florida Southern |
| 1958 | South Dakota | 75-53 | St. Michael's, VT | 1983 | Wright St., OH | 92-73 | Dist. of Columbia |
| 1959 | Evansville, IN | 83-67 | SW Missouri St. | 1984 | Central Mo. St. | 81-77 | St. Augustine's, NC |
| 1960 | Evansville | 90-69 | Chapman, CA | 1985 | Jacksonville St. | 74-73 | South Dakota St. |
| 1961 | Wittenberg, OH | 42-38 | SE Missouri St. | 1986 | Sacred Heart, CT | 93-87 | SE Missouri St. |
| 1962 | Mt. St. Mary's, MD | 58-57* | CS-Sacramento | 1987 | Ky. Wesleyan | 92-74 | Gannon, PA |
| 1963 | South Dakota St. | 42-40 | Wittenberg, OH | 1988 | Lowell, MA | 75-72 | AK-Anchorage |
| 1964 | Evansville | 72-59 | Akron, OH | 1989 | N.C. Central | 73-46 | SE Missouri St. |
| 1965 | Evansville | 85-82* | Southern Illinois | 1990 | Ky. Wesleyan | 93-79 | CS-Bakersfield |
| 1966 | Ky. Wesleyan | 54-51 | Southern Illinois | 1991 | North Alabama | 79-72 | Bridgeport, CT |
| 1967 | Winston-Salem, NC | 77-74 | SW Missouri St. | 1992 | Virginia Union | 100-75 | Bridgeport |
| 1968 | Ky. Wesleyan | 63-52 | Indiana St. | 1993 | CS-Bakersfield | 85-72 | Troy St., AL |
| 1969 | Ky. Wesleyan | 75-71 | SW Missouri St. | 1994 | CS-Bakersfield | 92-86 | Southern Ind. |
| 1970 | Phila. Textile | 76-65 | Tennessee St. | 1995 | Southern Indiana | 71-63 | UC-Riverside |
| 1971 | Evansville | 97-82 | Old Dominion, VA | 1996 | Fort Hays St. | 70-63 | N. Kentucky |
| 1972 | Roanoke, VA | 84-72 | Akron, OH | 1997 | CS-Bakersfield | 57-56 | N. Kentucky |
| 1973 | Ky. Wesleyan | 78-76* | Tennessee St. | 1998 | UC-Davis | 83-77 | Ky. Wesleyan |
| 1974 | Morgan St., MD | 67-52 | SW Missouri St. | 1999 | Ky. Wesleyan | 75-60 | Metropolitan St. |
| 1975 | Old Dominion | 76-74 | New Orleans | 2000 | Metropolitan St. | 97-79 | Ky. Wesleyan |
| 1976 | Puget Sound, WA | 83-74 | Tennessee-Chatt. | 2001 | Ky. Wesleyan | 72-63 | Washburn, KS |
| 1977 | Tennessee-Chatt. | 71-62 | Randolph-Macon | 2002 | Metropolitan St. | 80-72 | Ky. Wesleyan |
| 1978 | Cheyney, PA | 47-40 | WI-Green Bay | 2003 | Northeastern St., OK | 75-64 | Ky. Wesleyan |
| 1979 | North Alabama | 64-50 | WI-Green Bay | 2004 | Kennesaw St., GA | 84-59 | Southern Indiana |
| 1980 | Virginia Union | 80-74 | New York Tech | 2005 | Virginia Union | 63-58 | Bryant |
| 1981 | Florida Southern | 73-68 | Mt. St. Mary's, MD | | *Overtime | | |

### NCAA Div. III Finals

**Multiple winners:** North Park (5); WI-Platteville (4); Calvin, Potsdam St., Scranton, WI-Stevens Point and WI-Whitewater (2).

| Year | Winner | Score | Loser | Year | Winner | Score | Loser |
|---|---|---|---|---|---|---|---|
| 1975 | LeMoyne-Owen, TN | 57-54 | Glassboro St., NJ | 1991 | WI-Platteville | 81-74 | Franklin Marshall |
| 1976 | Scranton, PA | 60-57 | Wittenberg, OH | 1992 | Calvin, MI | 62-49 | Rochester, NY |
| 1977 | Wittenberg, OH | 79-66 | Oneonta St., NY | 1993 | Ohio Northern | 71-68 | Augustana, IL |
| 1978 | North Park, IL | 69-57 | Widener, PA | 1994 | Lebanon Valley, PA | 66-59* | NYU |
| 1979 | North Park, IL | 66-62 | Potsdam St., NY | 1995 | WI-Platteville | 69-55 | Manchester, IN |
| 1980 | North Park, IL | 83-76 | Upsala, NJ | 1996 | Rowan, NJ | 100-93 | Hope, MI |
| 1981 | Potsdam St., NY | 67-65* | Augustana, IL | 1997 | Illinois Wesleyan | 89-86 | Neb-Wesleyan |
| 1982 | Wabash, IN | 83-62 | Potsdam St., NY | 1998 | WI-Platteville | 69-56 | Hope, MI |
| 1983 | Scranton, PA | 64-63 | Wittenberg, OH | 1999 | WI-Platteville | 76-75** | Hampden-Sydney |
| 1984 | WI-Whitewater | 103-86 | Clark, MA | 2000 | Calvin, MI | 79-74 | WI-Eau Claire |
| 1985 | North Park, IL | 72-71 | Potsdam St., NY | 2001 | Catholic, DC | 76-62 | Wm. Paterson |
| 1986 | Potsdam St., NY | 76-73 | LeMoyne-Owen, TN | 2002 | Otterbein | 102-83 | Elizabethtown |
| 1987 | North Park, IL | 106-100 | Clark, MA | 2003 | Williams, MA | 67-65 | Gustavus Adolphus |
| 1988 | Ohio Wesleyan | 92-70 | Scranton, PA | 2004 | WI-Stevens Point | 84-82 | Williams |
| 1989 | WI-Whitewater | 94-86 | Trenton St., NJ | 2005 | WI-Stevens Point | 73-49 | Rochester |
| 1990 | Rochester, NY | 43-42 | DePauw, IN | | *Overtime | | |
| | | | | | **Double overtime | | |

## NAIA Finals, 1937-91

**Multiple winners:** Grand Canyon, Hamline, Kentucky St. and Tennessee St. (3); Central Missouri, Central St., Fort Hays St. and SW Missouri St. (2).

| Year | Winner | Score | Loser | Year | Winner | Score | Loser |
|------|--------|-------|-------|------|--------|-------|-------|
| 1937 | Central Missouri | 35-24 | Morningside, IA | 1975 | Grand Canyon, AZ | 65-54 | M'western St., TX |
| 1938 | Central Missouri | 45-30 | Roanoke, VA | 1976 | Coppin St., MD | 96-91 | Henderson St., AR |
| 1939 | Southwestern, KS | 32-31 | San Diego St. | 1977 | Texas Southern | 71-44 | Campbell, NC |
| 1940 | Tarkio, MO | 52-31 | San Diego St. | 1978 | Grand Canyon | 79-75 | Kearney St., NE |
| 1941 | San Diego St. | 36-32 | Murray St., KY | 1979 | Drury, MO | 60-54 | Henderson St., AR |
| 1942 | Hamline, MN | 33-31 | SE Oklahoma | 1980 | Cameron, OK | 84-77 | Alabama St. |
| 1943 | SE Missouri St. | 34-32 | NW Missouri St. | 1981 | Beth. Nazarene, OK | 86-85* | Al-Huntsville |
| 1944 | Not held | | | 1982 | SC-Spartanburg | 51-38 | Biola, CA |
| 1945 | Loyola-LA | 49-36 | Pepperdine, CA | 1983 | Charleston, SC | 57-53 | WV-Wesleyan |
| 1946 | Southern Illinois | 49-40 | Indiana St. | 1984 | Fort Hays St., KS | 48-46* | WI-Stevens Pt. |
| 1947 | Marshall, WV | 73-59 | Mankato St., MN | 1985 | Fort Hays St. | 82-80* | Wayland Bapt., TX |
| 1948 | Louisville, KY | 82-70 | Indiana St. | 1986 | David Lipscomb, TN | 67-54 | AR-Monticello |
| 1949 | Hamline, MN | 57-46 | Regis, CO | 1987 | Washburn, KS | 79-77 | West Virginia St. |
| 1950 | Indiana St. | 61-47 | East Central, OK | 1988 | Grand Canyon | 88-86* | Auburn-Montg, AL |
| 1951 | Hamline, MN | 69-61 | Millikin, IL | 1989 | St.Mary's, TX | 61-58 | East Central, OK |
| 1952 | SW Missouri St. | 73-64 | Murray St., KY | 1990 | Birm-Southern, AL | 88-80 | WI-Eau Claire |
| 1953 | SW Missouri St. | 79-71 | Hamline, MN | 1991 | Oklahoma City | 77-74 | Central Arkansas |
| 1954 | St.Benedict's, KS | 62-56 | Western Illinois | *Overtime | | | |
| 1955 | East Texas St. | 71-54 | SE Oklahoma | | | | |
| 1956 | McNeese St., LA | 60-55 | Texas Southern | | | | |
| 1957 | Tennessee St. | 92-73 | SE Oklahoma | | | | |
| 1958 | Tennessee St. | 85-73 | Western Illinois | | | | |
| 1959 | Tennessee St. | 97-87 | Pacific-Luth., WA | | | | |
| 1960 | SW Texas St. | 66-44 | Westminster, PA | | | | |
| 1961 | Grambling, LA | 95-75 | Georgetown, KY | | | | |
| 1962 | Prairie View, TX | 62-53 | Westminster, PA | | | | |
| 1963 | Pan American, TX | 73-62 | Western Carolina | | | | |
| 1964 | Rockhurst, MO | 66-56 | Pan American, TX | | | | |
| 1965 | Central St., OH | 85-51 | Oklahoma Baptist | | | | |
| 1966 | Oklahoma Baptist | 88-59 | Georgia Southern | | | | |
| 1967 | St.Benedict's, KS | 71-65 | Oklahoma Baptist | | | | |
| 1968 | Central St., OH | 51-48 | Fairmont St., WV | | | | |
| 1969 | Eastern N. Mex | 99-76 | MD-Eastern Shore | | | | |
| 1970 | Kentucky St. | 79-71 | Central Wash. | | | | |
| 1971 | Kentucky St. | 102-82 | Eastern Michigan | | | | |
| 1972 | Kentucky St. | 71-62 | WI-Eau Claire | | | | |
| 1973 | Guilford, NC | 99-96 | MD-Eastern Shore | | | | |
| 1974 | West Georgia | 97-79 | Alcorn St., MS | | | | |

### NAIA Div. I Finals

NAIA split tournament into two divisions in 1992.

**Multiple winners:** Life, GA and Oklahoma City (3).

| Year | Winner | Score | Loser |
|------|--------|-------|-------|
| 1992 | Oklahoma City | 82-73* | Central Arkansas |
| 1993 | Hawaii Pacific | 88-83 | Okla. Baptist |
| 1994 | Oklahoma City | 99-81 | Life, GA |
| 1995 | Birm-Southern | 92-76 | Pfeiffer, NC |
| 1996 | Oklahoma City | 86-80 | Georgetown, KY |
| 1997 | Life, GA | 73-64 | Okla. Baptist |
| 1998 | Georgetown, KY | 83-69 | So. Nazarene |
| 1999 | Life, GA | 63-60 | Mobile, AL |
| 2000 | Life, GA | 61-59 | Georgetown, KY |
| 2001 | Faulkner, AL | 63-59 | Science & Arts, OK |
| 2002 | Science & Arts, OK | 96-79 | Okla. Baptist |
| 2003 | Concordia, CA | 88-84* | Mountain St., WV |
| 2004 | Mountain St., WV | 74-70 | Concordia, CA |
| 2005 | John Brown | 65-55 | Azusa Pacific |
| *Overtime | | | |

### NAIA Div. II Finals

NAIA split tournament into two divisions in 1992.

**Multiple winners:** Bethel, IN (3); Northwestern, IA (2).

| Year | Winner | Score | Loser | Year | Winner | Score | Loser |
|------|--------|-------|-------|------|--------|-------|-------|
| 1992 | Grace, IN | 85-79* | Northwestern, IA | 2000 | Embry-Riddle, FL | 75-63 | Ozarks, MO |
| 1993 | Williamette, OR | 63-56 | Northern St., SD | 2001 | Northwestern, IA | 82-78 | Mid. Am. |
| 1994 | Eureka, IL | 98-95* | Northern St. | | | | Nazarene, KS |
| 1995 | Bethel, IN | 103-95* | NW Nazarene, ID | 2002 | Evangel, MO | 84-61 | Robert Morris, IL |
| 1996 | Albertson, ID | 81-72* | Whitworth, WA | 2003 | Northwestern, IA | 77-57 | Bethany, KS |
| 1997 | Bethel, IN | 95-94 | Siena Heights, MI | 2004 | Oregon Tech | 81-72 | Bellevue, NE |
| 1998 | Bethel, IN | 89-87 | Oregon Tech | 2005 | Walsh, OH | 81-70 | Concordia, NE |
| 1999 | Cornerstone, MI | 113-109 | Bethel | *Overtime | | | |

## WOMEN

### NCAA Final Four

Replaced the Association of Intercollegiate Athletics for Women (AIAW) tournament in 1982 as the official playoff for the national championship.

**Multiple winners:** Tennessee (6); Connecticut (5); Louisiana Tech, Stanford and USC (2)

| Year | Champion | Head Coach | Score | Runner-up | | Third Place |
|------|----------|-----------|-------|-----------|---|-------------|
| 1982 | Louisiana Tech | Sonya Hogg | 76-62 | Cheyney | Maryland | Tennessee |
| 1983 | USC | Linda Sharp | 69-67 | Louisiana Tech | Georgia | Old Dominion |
| 1984 | USC | Linda Sharp | 72-61 | Tennessee | Cheyney | Louisiana Tech |
| 1985 | Old Dominion | Marianne Stanley | 70-65 | Georgia | NE Louisiana | Western Ky. |
| 1986 | Texas | Jody Conradt | 97-81 | USC | Tennessee | Western Ky. |
| 1987 | Tennessee | Pat Summitt | 67-44 | Louisiana Tech | Long Beach St. | Texas |
| 1988 | Louisiana Tech | Leon Barmore | 56-54 | Auburn | Long Beach St. | Tennessee |
| 1989 | Tennessee | Pat Summitt | 76-60 | Auburn | Louisiana Tech | Maryland |
| 1990 | Stanford | Tara VanDerveer | 88-81 | Auburn | Louisiana Tech | Virginia |
| 1991 | Tennessee | Pat Summitt | 70-67 (OT) | Virginia | Connecticut | Stanford |

| Year | Champion | Head Coach | Score | Runner-up | —Third Place— | |
|------|----------|------------|-------|-----------|-----------|---|
| 1992 | Stanford | Tara VanDerveer | 78-62 | Western Kentucky | SW Missouri St. | Virginia |
| 1993 | Texas Tech | Marsha Sharp | 84-82 | Ohio St. | Iowa | Vanderbilt |
| 1994 | N. Carolina | Sylvia Hatchell | 60-59 | Louisiana Tech | Alabama | Purdue |
| 1995 | Connecticut | Geno Auriemma | 70-64 | Tennessee | Georgia | Stanford |
| 1996 | Tennessee | Pat Summitt | 83-65 | Georgia | Connecticut | Stanford |
| 1997 | Tennessee | Pat Summitt | 68-59 | Old Dominion | Stanford | Notre Dame |
| 1998 | Tennessee | Pat Summitt | 93-75 | Louisiana Tech | Arkansas | N.C. State |
| 1999 | Purdue | Carolyn Peck | 62-45 | Duke | Louisiana Tech | Georgia |
| 2000 | Connecticut | Geno Auriemma | 71-52 | Tennessee | Penn St. | Rutgers |
| 2001 | Notre Dame | Muffet McGraw | 68-66 | Purdue | Connecticut | SW Missouri St. |
| 2002 | Connecticut | Geno Auriemma | 82-70 | Oklahoma | Tennessee | Duke |
| 2003 | Connecticut | Geno Auriemma | 73-68 | Tennessee | Texas | Duke |
| 2004 | Connecticut | Geno Auriemma | 70-61 | Tennessee | LSU | Minnesota |
| 2005 | Baylor | Kim Mulkey-Robertson | 84-62 | Michigan St. | LSU | Tennessee |

**Final Four sites: 1982** (Norfolk, Va.), **1983** (Norfolk, Va.), **1984** (Los Angeles), **1985** (Austin), **1986** (Lexington), **1987** (Austin), **1988** (Tacoma), **1989** (Tacoma), **1990** (Knoxville), **1991** (New Orleans), **1992** (Los Angeles), **1993** (Atlanta), **1994** (Richmond), **1995** (Minneapolis), **1996** (Charlotte), **1997** (Cincinnati), **1998** (Kansas City), **1999** (San Jose), **2000** (Philadelphia), **2001** (St. Louis), **2002** (San Antonio), **2003** (Atlanta), **2004** (New Orleans), **2005** (Indianapolis), **2006** (Boston), **2007** (Cleveland), **2008** (Tampa), **2009** (St. Louis), **2010** (San Antonio).

## Most Outstanding Player

A Most Outstanding Player has been selected every year of the NCAA tournament. Winner who did not play for the tournament champion is listed in **bold**, type.

**Multiple winners:** Chamique Holdsclaw, Cheryl Miller and Diana Taurasi (2).

**Year**
1982 Janice Lawrence, La. Tech
1983 Cheryl Miller, USC
1984 Cheryl Miller, USC
1985 Tracy Claxton, Old Dominion
1986 Clarissa Davis, Texas
1987 Tonya Edwards, Tennessee
1988 Erica Westbrooks, La. Tech
1989 Bridgette Gordon, Tennessee

**Year**
1990 Jennifer Azzi, Stanford
1991 **Dawn Staley**, Virginia
1992 Molly Goodenbour, Stanford
1993 Sheryl Swoopes, Texas Tech
1994 Charlotte Smith, N. Carolina
1995 Rebecca Lobo, Connecticut
1996 Michelle Marciniak, Tennessee
1997 Chamique Holdsclaw, Tenn.

**Year**
1998 Chamique Holdsclaw, Tenn.
1999 Ukari Figgs, Purdue
2000 Shea Ralph, Connecticut
2001 Ruth Riley, Notre Dame
2002 Swin Cash, Connecticut
2003 Diana Taurasi, Connecticut
2004 Diana Taurasi, Connecticut
2005 Sophia Young, Baylor

## All-Time NCAA Division I Tournament Leaders

Through 2004-05; minimum of six games; **Last** column indicates final year played.

### CAREER

#### Scoring

| | Total Points | Yrs | Last | Pts | Avg |
|---|--------------|-----|------|-----|-----|
| 1 | Chamique Holdsclaw, Tennessee | 4 | 1999 | **479** | 21.8 |
| 2 | Diana Taurasi, Connecticut | 4 | 2004 | **428** | 18.6 |
| 3 | Bridgette Gordon, Tenn | 4 | 1989 | **388** | 21.6 |
| 4 | Alana Beard, Duke | 4 | 2004 | **352** | 18.5 |
| 5 | Cheryl Miller, USC | 4 | 1986 | **333** | 20.8 |
| 6 | Katie Douglas, Purdue | 4 | 2001 | **318** | 14.4 |
| 7 | Janice Lawrence, La. Tech | 3 | 1984 | **312** | 22.3 |
| 8 | Penny Toler, San Diego St/ Long Beach St | 4 | 1989 | **291** | 22.4 |
| 9 | Ruth Riley, Notre Dame | 4 | 2001 | **276** | 19.7 |
| 10 | Dawn Staley, Virginia | 4 | 1992 | **274** | 18.3 |
| 11 | Tamika Cathcings, Tennessee | 3 | 2000 | **269** | 16.8 |
| 12 | Cindy Brown, Long Beach St | 4 | 1987 | **263** | 21.9 |
| | Venus Lacy, La. Tech | 3 | 1990 | **263** | 18.8 |
| 14 | Clarissa Davis, Texas | 3 | 1989 | **261** | 21.8 |
| 15 | Sue Bird, Connecticut | 3 | 2002 | **260** | 15.3 |

#### Rebounds

| | Total Rebounds | Yrs | Last | No | Avg |
|---|----------------|-----|------|-----|-----|
| 1 | Chamique Holdsclaw, Tennessee | 4 | 1999 | **196** | 8.9 |
| 2 | Cheryl Miller, USC | 4 | 1986 | **170** | 10.6 |
| 3 | Sheila Frost, Tennessee | 4 | 1989 | **162** | 9.0 |
| 4 | Val Whiting, Stanford | 4 | 1993 | **161** | 10.1 |
| 5 | Venus Lacy, La. Tech | 3 | 1990 | **148** | 10.6 |
| 6 | Bridgette Gordon, Tennessee | 4 | 1989 | **142** | 7.9 |
| | Tamika Catchings, Tennessee | 3 | 2000 | **142** | 7.9 |
| 8 | Kirsten Cummings, Long Beach St. | 4 | 1985 | **136** | 10.5 |
| 9 | Swin Cash, Connecticut | 4 | 2002 | **133** | 6.7 |
| 10 | Gwen Jackson, Tennessee | 4 | 2003 | **133** | 6.7 |
| 11 | Nora Lewis, La. Tech | 3 | 1989 | **130** | 9.3 |
| 12 | Pam McGee, USC | 3 | 1984 | **127** | 9.8 |
| 13 | Daedra Charles, Tennessee | 3 | 1991 | **125** | 9.6 |
| 14 | Paula McGee, USC | 3 | 1984 | **125** | 9.6 |
| 15 | Charlotte Smith, UNC | 4 | 1995 | **125** | 10.4 |

### SINGLE GAME

#### Scoring

| | | Year | Pts |
|---|---|------|-----|
| 1 | Lorri Bauman, Drake vs Maryland | 1982 | 50 |
| 2 | Sheryl Swoopes, Texas Tech vs Ohio St | 1993 | 47 |
| 3 | Barbara Kennedy, Clemson vs Penn St | 1982 | 43 |
| 4 | Jackie Stiles, SW Mo. St. vs. Duke | 2001 | 41 |
| 5 | LaTaunya Pollard, L. Beach St. vs Howard | 1982 | 40 |
| | Cindy Brown, L. Beach St. vs Ohio St | 1987 | 40 |
| | Tamika Whitmore, Memphis vs. YSU | 1998 | 40 |
| | Tara Mitchem, SW Mo. St. vs. Toledo | 2001 | 40 |

#### Rebounds

| | | Year | No |
|---|---|------|-----|
| 1 | Cheryl Taylor, Tenn. Tech vs Georgia | 1985 | 23 |
| | Charlotte Smith, N. Car. vs La. Tech | 1994 | 23 |
| 3 | Daedra Charles, Tenn. vs SW Missouri | 1991 | 22 |

#### Assists

| | | Year | No |
|---|---|------|-----|
| 1 | Anne Troyan, Penn St. vs. N.C. State | 1983 | 19 |
| 2 | Tasha Pointer, Rutgers vs. S.F. Austin | 2001 | 18 |
| 3 | Three tied at 17 each. | | |

## Associated Press Final Top 10 Polls

The Associated Press weekly women's college basketball poll was begun by Mel Greenberg of *The Philadelphia Inquirer* during the 1976-77 season. Although the poll was started as a Top 20 in 1977 and was expanded to a Top 25 in 1990, only the Top 10 from each poll are listed below due to space constraints. The Association of Intercollegiate Athletics for Women (AIAW) Tournament determined the Division I national champion from 1972-81. The NCAA began its women's Division I tournament in 1982. The final AP Polls were taken before the NCAA tournament. Eventual national champions are in **bold** type.

### 1977
1 **Delta St.**
2 Immaculata
3 St. Joseph's-PA
4 CS-Fullerton
5 Tennessee
6 Tennessee Tech
7 Wayland Baptist
8 Montclair St.
9 S.F. Austin St.
10 N.C. State

### 1978
1 Tennessee
2 Wayland Baptist
3 N.C. State
4 Montclair St.
5 **UCLA**
6 Maryland
7 Queens-NY
8 Valdosta St.
9 Delta St.
10 LSU

### 1979
1 **Old Dominion**
2 Louisiana Tech
3 Tennessee
4 Texas
5 S.F. Austin St.
6 UCLA
7 Rutgers
8 Maryland
9 Cheyney
10 Wayland Baptist

### 1980
1 **Old Dominion**
2 Tennessee
3 Louisiana Tech
4 South Carolina
5 S.F. Austin St.
6 Maryland
7 Texas
8 Rutgers
9 Long Beach St.
10 N.C. State

### 1981
1 **Louisiana Tech**
2 Tennessee
3 Old Dominion
4 USC
5 Cheyney
6 Long Beach St.
7 UCLA
8 Maryland
9 Rutgers
10 Kansas

### 1982
1 **Louisiana Tech**
2 Cheyney
3 Maryland
4 Tennessee
5 Texas
6 USC
7 Old Dominion
8 Rutgers
9 Long Beach St.
10 Penn St.

### 1983
1 **USC**
2 Louisiana Tech
3 Texas
4 Old Dominion
5 Cheyney
6 Long Beach St.
7 Maryland
8 Penn St.
9 Georgia
10 Tennessee

### 1984
1 Texas
2 Louisiana Tech
3 Georgia
4 Old Dominion
5 **USC**
6 Long Beach St.
7 Kansas St.
8 LSU
9 Cheyney
10 Mississippi

### 1985
1 Texas
2 NE Louisiana
3 Long Beach St.
4 Louisiana Tech
5 **Old Dominion**
6 Mississippi
7 Ohio St.
8 Georgia
9 Penn St.
10 Auburn

### 1986
1 **Texas**
2 Georgia
3 USC
4 Louisiana Tech
5 Western Ky.
6 Virginia
7 Auburn
8 Long Beach St.
9 LSU
10 Rutgers

### 1987
1 Texas
2 Auburn
3 Louisiana Tech
4 Long Beach St.
5 Rutgers
6 Georgia
7 **Tennessee**
8 Mississippi
9 Iowa
10 Ohio St.

### 1988
1 Tennessee
2 Iowa
3 Auburn
4 Texas
5 **Louisiana Tech**
6 Ohio St.
7 Long Beach St.
8 Rutgers
9 Maryland
10 Virginia

### 1989
1 **Tennessee**
2 Auburn
3 Louisiana Tech
4 Stanford
5 Maryland
6 Texas
7 Long Beach St.
8 Iowa
9 Colorado
10 Georgia

### 1990
1 Louisiana Tech
2 **Stanford**
3 Washington
4 Tennessee
5 UNLV
6 S.F. Austin St.
7 Georgia
8 Texas
9 Auburn
10 Iowa

### 1991
1 Penn St.
2 Virginia
3 Georgia
4 **Tennessee**
5 Purdue
6 Auburn
7 N.C. State
8 LSU
9 Arkansas
10 Western Ky.

### 1992
1 Virginia
2 Tennessee
3 **Stanford**
4 S.F. Austin St.
5 Mississippi
6 Miami-FL
7 Iowa
8 Maryland
9 Penn St.
10 SW Missouri St.

### 1993
1 Vanderbilt
2 Tennessee
3 Ohio St.
4 Iowa
5 **Texas Tech**
6 Stanford
7 Auburn
8 Penn St.
9 Virginia
10 Colorado

### 1994
1 Tennessee
2 Penn St.
3 Connecticut
4 **North Carolina**
5 Colorado
6 Louisiana Tech
7 USC
8 Purdue
9 Texas Tech
10 Virginia

### 1995
1 **Connecticut**
2 Colorado
3 Tennessee
4 Stanford
5 Texas Tech
6 Vanderbilt
7 Penn St.
8 Louisiana Tech
9 Western Ky.
10 Virginia

### 1996
1 Louisiana Tech
2 Connecticut
3 Stanford
4 **Tennessee**
5 Georgia
6 Old Dominion
7 Iowa
8 Penn St.
9 Texas Tech
10 Alabama

### 1997
1 Connecticut
2 Old Dominion
3 Stanford
4 North Carolina
5 Louisiana Tech
6 Georgia
7 Florida
8 Alabama
9 LSU
10 **Tennessee**

### 1998
1 **Tennessee**
2 Old Dominion
3 Connecticut
4 Louisiana Tech
5 Stanford
6 Texas Tech
7 North Carolina
8 Duke
9 Arizona
10 N.C. State

### 1999
1 **Purdue**
2 Tennessee
3 Louisiana Tech
4 Colorado St.
5 Old Dominion
6 Connecticut
7 Rutgers
8 Notre Dame
9 Texas Tech
10 Duke

### 2000
1 **Connecticut**
2 Tennessee
3 Louisiana Tech
4 Georgia
5 Notre Dame
6 Penn St.
7 Iowa St.
8 Rutgers
9 UC-Santa Barbara
10 Duke

### 2001
1 Connecticut
2 **Notre Dame**
3 Tennessee
4 Georgia
5 Duke
6 Louisiana Tech
7 Oklahoma
8 Iowa St.
9 Purdue
10 Vanderbilt

### 2002
1 **Connecticut**
2 Oklahoma
3 Duke
4 Vanderbilt
5 Stanford
6 Tennessee
7 Baylor
8 Louisiana Tech
9 Purdue
10 Iowa St.

### 2003
1 **Connecticut**
2 Duke
3 LSU
4 Tennessee
5 Texas
6 Louisiana Tech
7 Texas Tech
8 Kansas St.
9 Stanford
10 Purdue

### 2004
1 Duke
2 Tennessee
3 Purdue
4 Texas
5 Penn St.
6 **Connecticut**
7 Louisiana Tech
8 Kansas St.
9 Houston
10 Stanford

### 2005
1 Stanford
2 LSU
3 Tennessee
4 North Carolina
5 **Baylor**
6 Michigan St.
7 Duke
8 Ohio St.
9 Rutgers
10 Connecticut

## All-Time AP Top 10

The composite AP Top 10 from the 1976-77 season through 2004-05, based on the final regular season rankings of each year. Team points are based on 10 points for all 1st place finishes, 9 for each 2nd, etc. Also listed are the number of times ranked No. 1 by AP going into the tournaments, and times ranked in the pre-tournament Top 10.

| | | Pts | No.1 | Top 10 | | | Pts | No.1 | Top 10 |
|---|---|---|---|---|---|---|---|---|---|
| 1 | Tennessee | 206 | 5 | 27 | 6 | Stanford | 77 | 1 | 12 |
| 2 | Louisiana Tech | 173 | 4 | 24 | 7 | Georgia | 72 | 0 | 13 |
| 3 | Connecticut | 96 | 6 | 12 | 8 | Penn St. | 52 | 1 | 11 |
| 4 | Texas | 93 | 4 | 18 | 9 | Long Beach St. | 45 | 0 | 10 |
| 5 | Old Dominion | 81 | 2 | 11 | 10 | Auburn | 42 | 0 | 8 |
| | | | | | | Duke | 42 | 1 | 8 |

## All-Time Winningest Division I Teams

Division I schools with best winning percentages (with a minimum of 350 victories) and most victories through 2004-05 (including postseason tournaments). Although official NCAA women's basketball records didn't begin until the 1981-82 season, results from previous seasons are included below.

### Top 15 Winning Percentage

| | | Yrs | W | L | Pct |
|---|---|---|---|---|---|
| 1 | Louisiana Tech | 31 | 873 | 149 | .854 |
| 2 | Tennessee | 60 | 975 | 229 | .810 |
| 3 | Texas | 31 | 790 | 243 | .765 |
| 4 | Old Dominion | 36 | 795 | 264 | .751 |
| 5 | Montana | 31 | 655 | 229 | .741 |
| 6 | Stephen F. Austin St. | 33 | 750 | 276 | .731 |
| 7 | Utah | 31 | 648 | 249 | .722 |
| 8 | Stanford | 31 | 661 | 255 | .722 |
| 9 | Penn St. | 41 | 711 | 281 | .717 |
| 10 | Texas Tech | 30 | 689 | 285 | .707 |
| 11 | Connecticut | 31 | 649 | 273 | .704 |
| 12 | Auburn | 34 | 675 | 285 | .703 |
| 13 | Georgia | 32 | 671 | 284 | .703 |
| 14 | Maine | 30 | 571 | 242 | .702 |
| 15 | Rutgers | 31 | 648 | 276 | .701 |

### Top 15 Victories

| | | Yrs | W | L | Pct |
|---|---|---|---|---|---|
| 1 | Tennessee | 60 | 975 | 229 | .810 |
| 2 | Louisiana Tech | 31 | 873 | 149 | .854 |
| 3 | Old Dominion | 36 | 795 | 264 | .751 |
| 4 | Texas | 31 | 790 | 243 | .765 |
| 5 | James Madison | 83 | 757 | 440 | .632 |
| 6 | Stephen F. Austin St. | 33 | 750 | 276 | .731 |
| 7 | Tennessee Tech | 35 | 748 | 320 | .700 |
| 8 | Long Beach St. | 43 | 740 | 339 | .686 |
| 9 | Penn St. | 41 | 711 | 281 | .717 |
| | Richmond | 85 | 711 | 476 | .599 |
| 11 | Ohio St. | 40 | 696 | 325 | .682 |
| 12 | Western Kentucky | 43 | 693 | 342 | .670 |
| 13 | Texas Tech | 30 | 689 | 285 | .707 |
| 14 | Kansas St. | 37 | 678 | 406 | .625 |
| 15 | Auburn | 34 | 675 | 285 | .703 |

## Annual NCAA Division I Leaders

All averages include postseason games

### Scoring

**Multiple winners:** Cindy Blodgett, Andrea Congreaves and Jackie Stiles (2).

| Year | | Gm | Pts | Avg |
|---|---|---|---|---|
| 1982 | Barbara Kennedy, Clemson | 31 | 908 | 29.3 |
| 1983 | LaTaunya Pollard, L. Beach St | 31 | 907 | 29.3 |
| 1984 | Deborah Temple, Delta St | 28 | 873 | 31.2 |
| 1985 | Anucha Browne, Northwestern | 28 | 855 | 30.5 |
| 1986 | Wanda Ford, Drake | 30 | 919 | 30.6 |
| 1987 | Tresa Spaulding, BYU | 28 | 810 | 28.9 |
| 1988 | LeChandra LeDay, Grambling | 28 | 850 | 30.4 |
| 1989 | Patricia Hoskins, Miss. Valley | 27 | 908 | 33.6 |
| 1990 | Kim Perrot, SW Louisiana | 28 | 839 | 30.0 |
| 1991 | Jan Jensen, Drake | 30 | 888 | 29.6 |
| 1992 | Andrea Congreaves, Mercer | 28 | 925 | 33.0 |
| 1993 | Andrea Congreaves, Mercer | 26 | 805 | 31.0 |
| 1994 | Kristy Ryan, CS-Sacramento | 26 | 727 | 28.0 |
| 1995 | Koko Lahanas, CS-Fullerton | 29 | 778 | 26.8 |
| 1996 | Cindy Blodgett, Maine | 32 | 889 | 27.8 |
| 1997 | Cindy Blodgett, Maine | 30 | 810 | 27.0 |
| 1998 | Allison Feaster, Harvard | 28 | 797 | 28.5 |
| 1999 | Tamika Whitmore, Memphis | 32 | 843 | 26.3 |
| 2000 | Jackie Stiles, SW Missouri St. | 32 | 890 | 27.8 |
| 2001 | Jackie Stiles, SW Missouri St. | 35 | 1062 | 30.3 |
| 2002 | Kelly Mazzante, Penn St. | 35 | 872 | 24.9 |
| 2003 | Chandi Jones, Houston | 28 | 770 | 27.5 |
| 2004 | Emily Faurholt, Idaho | 29 | 737 | 25.4 |
| 2005 | Tan White, Mississippi St. | 29 | 681 | 23.5 |

### Rebounds

**Multiple winner:** Patricia Hoskins (2).

| Year | | Gm | No | Avg |
|---|---|---|---|---|
| 1982 | Anne Donovan, Old Dominion | 28 | 412 | 14.7 |
| 1983 | Deborah Mitchell, Miss. Col | 28 | 447 | 16.0 |
| 1984 | Joy Kellog, Oklahoma City | 23 | 373 | 16.2 |
| 1985 | Rosina Pearson, Beth-Cookman | 26 | 480 | 18.5 |
| 1986 | Wanda Ford, Drake | 30 | 506 | 16.9 |
| 1987 | Patricia Hoskins, Miss. Valley St. | 28 | 476 | 17.0 |
| 1988 | Katie Beck, East Tenn. St. | 25 | 441 | 17.6 |
| 1989 | Patricia Hoskins, Miss. Valley St. | 27 | 440 | 16.3 |
| 1990 | Pam Hudson, Northwestern St | 29 | 438 | 15.1 |
| 1991 | Tarcha Hollis, Grambling | 29 | 443 | 15.3 |
| 1992 | Christy Greis, Evansville | 28 | 383 | 13.7 |
| 1993 | Ann Barry, Nevada | 25 | 355 | 14.2 |
| 1994 | DeShawne Blocker, E. Tenn. St. | 26 | 450 | 17.3 |
| 1995 | Tera Sheriff, Jackson St | 29 | 401 | 13.8 |
| 1996 | Dana Wynne, Seton Hall | 29 | 372 | 12.8 |
| 1997 | Etolia Mitchell, Georgia St. | 25 | 330 | 13.2 |
| 1998 | Alisha Hill, Howard | 30 | 397 | 13.2 |
| 1999 | Monica Logan, UMBC | 27 | 364 | 13.5 |
| 2000 | Malveata Johnson, N.C. A&T | 27 | 363 | 13.4 |
| 2001 | Andrea Gardner, Howard | 31 | 439 | 14.2 |
| 2002 | Mandi Carver, Idaho St. | 27 | 336 | 12.4 |
| 2003 | Jennifer Butler, Massachusetts | 28 | 412 | 14.7 |
| 2004 | Ashlee Kelly, Quinnipiac | 29 | 392 | 13.5 |
| 2005 | Sancho Lyttle, Houston | 30 | 362 | 12.1 |

**Note:** Wanda Ford (1986) and Patricia Hoskins (1989) each led the country in scoring and rebounds in the same year.

## All-Time NCAA Division I Individual Leaders

Through 2004-05; includes regular season and tournament games; Official NCAA women's basketball records began with 1981-82 season. Players who competed earlier than that are not included below; **Last** column indicates final year played.

### CAREER

#### Scoring
Average

| | Average | Yrs | Last | Pts | Avg |
|---|---|---|---|---|---|
| 1 | Patricia Hoskins, Miss. Valley St. | .4 | 1989 | 3122 | 28.4 |
| 2 | Sandra Hodge, New Orleans | .4 | 1984 | 2860 | 26.7 |
| 3 | Jackie Stiles, SW Mo. St. | .4 | 2001 | 3206 | 26.1 |
| 4 | Lorri Bauman, Drake | .4 | 1984 | 3115 | 26.0 |
| 5 | Andrea Congreaves, Mercer | .4 | 1993 | 2796 | 25.9 |
| 6 | Cindy Blodgett, Maine | .4 | 1998 | 3005 | 25.5 |
| 7 | Valorie Whiteside, Aplach St. | .4 | 1988 | 2944 | 25.4 |
| 8 | Joyce Walker, LSU | .4 | 1984 | 2906 | 24.8 |
| 9 | Tarcha Hollis, Grambling | .4 | 1991 | 2058 | 24.2 |
| 10 | Korie Hlede, Duquesne | .4 | 1998 | 2631 | 24.1 |

#### Rebounds
Average

| | Average | Yrs | Last | Reb | Avg |
|---|---|---|---|---|---|
| 1 | Wanda Ford, Drake | .4 | 1986 | 1887 | 16.1 |
| 2 | Patricia Hoskins, Miss. Valley St. | .4 | 1989 | 1662 | 15.1 |
| 3 | Tarcha Hollis, Grambling | .4 | 1991 | 1185 | 13.9 |
| 4 | Katie Beck, East Tenn. St. | .4 | 1988 | 1404 | 13.4 |
| 5 | Marilyn Stephens, Temple | .4 | 1984 | 1519 | 13.0 |
| 6 | Natalie Williams, UCLA | .4 | 1994 | 1137 | 12.8 |
| 7 | Cheryl Taylor, Tenn. Tech | .4 | 1987 | 1532 | 12.8 |
| 8 | DeShawne Blocker, E. Tenn. St. | .4 | 1995 | 1361 | 12.7 |
| 9 | Olivia Bradley, West Virginia | .4 | 1985 | 1484 | 12.7 |
| 10 | Judy Mosley, Hawaii | .4 | 1990 | 1441 | 12.6 |

### SINGLE SEASON

#### Scoring
Average

| | Average | Year | Gm | Pts | Avg |
|---|---|---|---|---|---|
| 1 | Patricia Hoskins, Miss.Valley St. | 1989 | 27 | 908 | 33.6 |
| 2 | Andrea Congreaves, Mercer | 1992 | 28 | 925 | 33.0 |
| 3 | Deborah Temple, Delta St. | 1984 | 28 | 873 | 31.2 |
| 4 | Andrea Congreaves, Mercer | 1993 | 26 | 805 | 31.0 |
| 5 | Wanda Ford, Drake | 1986 | 30 | 919 | 30.6 |
| 6 | Anucha Browne, Northwestern | 1985 | 28 | 855 | 30.5 |
| 7 | LeChandra LeDay, Grambling | 1988 | 28 | 850 | 30.4 |
| 8 | Jackie Stiles, SW Mo. St. | 2001 | 35 | 1062 | 30.3 |
| 9 | Kim Perrot, SW Louisiana | 1990 | 28 | 841 | 30.0 |
| 10 | Tina Hutchinson, San Diego St. | 1984 | 30 | 898 | 29.9 |

### SINGLE GAME

#### Scoring

| | | Year | Pts |
|---|---|---|---|
| 1 | Cindy Brown, Long Beach St. vs San Jose St. | 1987 | 60 |
| 2 | Lorri Bauman, Drake vs SW Missouri St. | 1984 | 58 |
| | Kim Perrot, SW La. vs SE La | 1990 | 58 |
| 4 | Jackie Stiles, SW Mo. St. vs Evansville | 2000 | 56 |
| 5 | Patricia Hoskins, Miss.Valley St. vs South-BR | 1989 | 55 |
| | Patricia Hoskins, Miss.Valley St. vs Ala. St. | 1989 | 55 |
| 7 | Wanda Ford, Drake vs SW Missouri St. | 1986 | 54 |
| | Anjinea Hopson, Grambling vs Jackson St. | 1994 | 54 |
| | Mary Lowry, Baylor vs Texas | 1994 | 54 |
| 10 | Chris Starr, Nevada vs CS-Sacramento | 1983 | 53 |
| | Felisha Edwards, NE La. vs Southern Miss | 1991 | 53 |
| | Sheryl Swoopes, Texas Tech vs Texas | 1993 | 53 |

## All-Time Winningest Division I Coaches

Minimum of 10 seasons as Division I head coach; regular season and tournament games included.

### Top 10 Winning Percentage

| | | Yrs | W | L | Pct |
|---|---|---|---|---|---|
| 1 | Leon Barmore, La. Tech | 20 | 576 | 87 | .869 |
| 2 | **Pat Summitt**, Tennessee | 31 | 882 | 172 | .837 |
| 3 | **Geno Auriemma**, Connecticut | 19 | 532 | 103 | .834 |
| 4 | **Tara VanDerveer**, Stanford | .26 | 634 | 171 | .788 |
| 5 | **Gail Goestenkors**, Duke | .13 | 333 | 93 | .782 |
| 6 | Bill Sheahan, Mt. St. Mary's | .17 | 372 | 104 | .782 |
| 7 | **Robin Selvig**, Montana | .27 | 624 | 180 | .776 |
| 8 | **Andy Landers**, Georgia | .26 | 634 | 199 | .761 |
| 9 | **Marsha Sharp**, Texas Tech | .23 | 556 | 175 | .761 |
| 10 | **Jody Conradt**, Texas | .36 | 869 | 278 | .758 |

### Top 10 Victories

| | | Yrs | W | L | Pct |
|---|---|---|---|---|---|
| 1 | **Pat Summitt**, Tennessee | .31 | 882 | 172 | .837 |
| 2 | **Jody Conradt**, Texas | .36 | 869 | 278 | .758 |
| 3 | **C. Vivian Stringer**, Rutgers | .33 | 723 | 246 | .746 |
| 4 | **Sylvia Hatchell**, N. Carolina | .30 | 684 | 266 | .720 |
| 5 | Sue Gunter, LSU | .33 | 681 | 300 | .694 |
| 6 | **Kay Yow**, N.C. State | .34 | 674 | 308 | .686 |
| 7 | **Rene Portland**, Penn St. | .29 | 668 | 233 | .741 |
| 8 | **Theresa Grentz**, Illinois | .31 | 636 | 284 | .691 |
| 9 | **Andy Landers**, Georgia | .26 | 634 | 199 | .761 |
| 10 | **Tara VanDerveer**, Stanford | .26 | 634 | 171 | .788 |

**Note:** active coaches in **bold** type and listed with current teams. Retired coached listed with last team coached.

## Annual Awards

The Broderick Award was first given out to the Women's Division I or Large School Player of the Year in 1977. Since then, the National Assn. for Girls and Women in Sports (1978), the Women's Basketball Coaches Assn. (1983), the Atlanta Tip-Off Club (1983) and the Associated Press (1995) have joined in.

Since 1983, the first year as many as four awards were given out, the same player has won all of them in the same season twice: Cheryl Miller of USC in 1985 and Rebecca Lobo of Connecticut in 1995.

### Associated Press

Voted on by AP sportswriters and broadcasters and first presented in 1995.

**Multiple winner:** Chamique Holdsclaw (2).

| Year | Year | Year |
|---|---|---|
| 1995 Rebecca Lobo, Connecticut | 1999 Chamique Holdsclaw, Tennessee | 2003 Diana Taurasi, Connecticut |
| 1996 Jennifer Rizzotti, Connecticut | 2000 Tamika Catchings, Tennessee | 2004 Alana Beard, Duke |
| 1997 Kara Wolters, Connecticut | 2001 Ruth Riley, Notre Dame | 2005 Seimone Augustus, LSU |
| 1998 Chamique Holdsclaw, Tennessee | 2002 Sue Bird, Connecticut | |

### Broderick Award

Voted on by a national panel of women's collegiate athletic directors and first presented by the late Thomas Broderick, an athletic outfitter, in 1977. Honda has presented the award since 1987. Basketball Player of the Year is one of 10 nominated for Collegiate Woman Athlete of the Year; (*) indicates player also won Athlete of the Year.

**Multiple winners:** Chamique Holdsclaw, Nancy Lieberman, Cheryl Miller, Dawn Staley and Diana Taurasi (2).

| Year | Year | Year |
|---|---|---|
| 1977 Lucy Harris, Delta St.* | 1979 Nancy Lieberman, Old Dominion* | 1981 Lynette Woodard, Kansas |
| 1978 Ann Meyers, UCLA* | 1980 Nancy Lieberman, Old Dominion* | 1982 Pam Kelly, La. Tech |

| Year | Year | Year |
|---|---|---|
| 1983 Anne Donovan, Old Dominion | 1991 Dawn Staley, Virginia | 1999 Stephanie White-McCarty, Purdue |
| 1984 Cheryl Miller, USC* | 1992 Dawn Staley, Virginia | 2000 Shea Ralph, Connecticut |
| 1985 Cheryl Miller, USC | 1993 Sheryl Swoopes, Texas Tech | 2001 Jackie Stiles, SW Missouri St.* |
| 1986 Kamie Ethridge, Texas* | 1994 Lisa Leslie, USC | 2002 Sue Bird, Connecticut |
| 1987 Katrina McClain, Georgia | 1995 Rebecca Lobo, Connecticut | 2003 Diana Taurasi, Connecticut |
| 1988 Teresa Weatherspoon, La. Tech* | 1996 Jennifer Rizzotti, Connecticut | 2004 Diana Taurasi, Connecticut |
| 1989 Bridgette Gordon, Tennessee | 1997 Chamique Holdsclaw, Tennessee | 2005 Seimone Augustus, LSU |
| 1990 Jennifer Azzi, Stanford | 1998 Chamique Holdsclaw,Tennessee* | |

## Wade Trophy

Originally voted on by the National Assn. for Girls and Women in Sports (NAGWS) and awarded for academics and community service as well as player performance. First presented in 1978 in the name of former Delta St. coach Lily Margaret Wade. Since 2002, the trophy has been awarded to the Women's Basketball Coaches Association player of the year.
   **Multiple winner:** Nancy Lieberman (2).

| Year | Year | Year |
|---|---|---|
| 1978 Carol Blazejowski, Montclair St. | 1988 Teresa Weatherspoon, La. Tech | 1998 Ticha Penicheiro, Old Dominion |
| 1979 Nancy Lieberman, Old Dominion | 1989 Clarissa Davis, Texas | 1999 Stephanie White-McCarty, Purdue |
| 1980 Nancy Lieberman, Old Dominion | 1990 Jennifer Azzi, Stanford | 2000 Edwina Brown, Texas |
| 1981 Lynette Woodard, Kansas | 1991 Daedra Charles, Tennessee | 2001 Jackie Stiles, SW Missouri St. |
| 1982 Pam Kelly, La. Tech | 1992 Susan Robinson, Penn St. | 2002 Sue Bird, Connecticut |
| 1983 LaTaunya Pollard, L. Beach St. | 1993 Karen Jennings, Nebraska | 2003 Diana Taurasi, Connecticut |
| 1984 Janice Lawrence, La. Tech | 1994 Carol Ann Shudlick, Minnesota | 2004 Alana Beard, Duke |
| 1985 Cheryl Miller, USC | 1995 Rebecca Lobo, Connecticut | 2005 Seimone Augustus, LSU |
| 1986 Kamie Ethridge, Texas | 1996 Jennifer Rizzotti, Connecticut | |
| 1987 Shelly Pennefather, Villanova | 1997 DeLisha Milton, Florida | |

## Naismith Trophy

Voted on by a panel of coaches, sportswriters and broadcasters and first presented in 1983 by the Atlanta Tip-Off Club in the name of the inventor of basketball, Dr. James Naismith.
   **Multiple winners:** Cheryl Miller (3); Clarissa Davis, Chamique Holdsclaw, Dawn Staley and Diana Taurasi (2).

| Year | Year | Year |
|---|---|---|
| 1983 Anne Donovan, Old Dominion | 1991 Dawn Staley, Virgina | 1999 Chamique Holdsclaw, Tennessee |
| 1984 Cheryl Miller, USC | 1992 Dawn Staley, Virginia | 2000 Tamika Catchings, Tennessee |
| 1985 Cheryl Miller, USC | 1993 Sheryl Swoopes, Texas Tech | 2001 Ruth Riley, Notre Dame |
| 1986 Cheryl Miller, USC | 1994 Lisa Leslie, USC | 2002 Sue Bird, Connecticut |
| 1987 Clarissa Davis, Texas | 1995 Rebecca Lobo, Connecticut | 2003 Diana Taurasi, Connecticut |
| 1988 Sue Wicks, Rutgers | 1996 Saudia Roundtree, Georgia | 2004 Diana Taurasi, Connecticut |
| 1989 Clarissa Davis, Texas | 1997 Kate Starbird, Stanford | 2005 Seimone Augustus, LSU |
| 1990 Jennifer Azzi, Stanford | 1998 Chamique Holdsclaw, Tennessee | |

## Women's Basketball Coaches Association

Voted on by the WBCA and first presented by Champion athletic outfitters in 1983.
   **Multiple winners:** Chamique Holdsclaw, Cheryl Miller and Dawn Staley (2).

| Year | Year | Year |
|---|---|---|
| 1983 Anne Donovan, Old Dominion | 1990 Venus Lacy, La. Tech | 1997 Kate Starbird, Stanford |
| 1984 Janice Lawrence, La. Tech | 1991 Dawn Staley, Virgina | 1998 Chamique Holdsclaw, Tennessee |
| 1985 Cheryl Miller, USC | 1992 Dawn Staley, Virginia | 1999 Chamique Holdsclaw, Tennessee |
| 1986 Cheryl Miller, USC | 1993 Sheryl Swoopes, Texas Tech | 2000 Tamika Catchings, Tennessee |
| 1987 Katrina McClain, Georgia | 1994 Lisa Leslie, USC | 2001 Ruth Riley, Notre Dame |
| 1988 Michelle Edwards, Iowa | 1995 Rebecca Lobo, Connecticut | 2002 merged with Wade Trophy |
| 1989 Clarissa Davis, Texas | 1996 Saudia Roundtree, Georgia | |

## Wooden Award

Voted on by a panel of coaches, sportswriters and broadcasters and first presented in 2004 by the Los Angeles Athletic Club in the name of former Purdue All-American and UCLA coach John Wooden. Unlike the other player of the year awards, candidates for the Wooden must have a minimum grade point average of 2.00 (out of 4.00).

| Year | Year |
|---|---|
| 2004 Alana Beard, Duke | 2005 Seimone Augustus, LSU |

## Coach of the Year Award

Voted on by the Women's Basketball Coaches Assn. and first presented by Converse athletic outfitters in 1983.
   **Multiple winners:** Geno Auriemma and Pat Summitt (3), Jody Conradt, Rene Portland and Vivian Stringer (2).

| Year | Year | Year |
|---|---|---|
| 1983 Pat Summitt, Tennessee | 1991 Rene Portland, Penn St. | 1999 Carolyn Peck, Purdue |
| 1984 Jody Conradt, Texas | 1992 Ferne Labati, Miami-FL | 2000 Geno Auriemma, Connecticut |
| 1985 Jim Foster, St. Joseph's-PA | 1993 Vivian Stringer, Iowa | 2001 Muffet McGraw, Notre Dame |
| 1986 Jody Conradt, Texas | 1994 Marsha Sharp, Texas Tech | 2002 Geno Auriemma, Connecticut |
| 1987 Theresa Grentz, Rutgers | 1995 Pat Summitt, Tennessee | 2003 Gail Goestenkors, Duke |
| 1988 Vivian Stringer, Iowa | 1996 Leon Barmore, La. Tech | 2004 Rene Portland, Penn St. |
| 1989 Tara VanDerveer, Stanford | 1997 Geno Auriemma, Connecticut | 2005 Pokey Chatman, LSU |
| 1990 Kay Yow, N.C. State | 1998 Pat Summitt, Tennessee | |

## Other Women's Champions

The NCAA has sanctioned national championship tournaments for Division II and Division III since 1982. The NAIA sanctioned a single tournament from 1981-91, then split in to two divisions in 1992.

### NCAA Div. II Finals

**Multiple winners:** North Dakota St. and Cal Poly Pomona (5); Delta St. and North Dakota (3).

| Year | Winner | Score | Loser |
|------|--------|-------|-------|
| 1982 | Cal Poly Pomona | 93-74 | Tuskegee, AL |
| 1983 | Virginia Union | 73-60 | Cal Poly Pomona |
| 1984 | Central Mo.St. | 80-73 | Virginia Union |
| 1985 | Cal Poly Pomona | 80-69 | Central Mo.St. |
| 1986 | Cal Poly Pomona | 70-63 | North Dakota St. |
| 1987 | New Haven, CT | 77-75 | Cal Poly Pomona |
| 1988 | Hampton, VA | 65-48 | West Texas St. |
| 1989 | Delta St., MS | 88-58 | Cal Poly Pomona |
| 1990 | Delta St., MS | 77-43 | Bentley, MA |
| 1991 | North Dakota St. | 81-74 | SE Missouri St. |
| 1992 | Delta St., MS | 65-63 | North Dakota St. |
| 1993 | North Dakota St. | 95-63 | Delta St. |
| 1994 | North Dakota St. | 89-56 | CS-San Bernadino |
| 1995 | North Dakota St. | 98-85 | Portland St. |
| 1996 | North Dakota St. | 104-78 | Shippensburg, PA |
| 1997 | North Dakota | 94-78 | S. Indiana |
| 1998 | North Dakota | 92-76 | Emporia St. |
| 1999 | North Dakota | 80-63 | Arkansas Tech |
| 2000 | Northern Kentucky | 71-62 | North Dakota St. |
| 2001 | Cal Poly Pomona | 87-80* | North Dakota St. |
| 2002 | Cal Poly Pomona | 74-62 | SE Oklahoma St. |
| 2003 | South Dakota St. | 65-60 | Northern Kentucky |
| 2004 | California, PA | 75-72 | Drury |
| 2005 | Washburn | 70-53 | Seattle Pacific |

*Overtime

### NCAA Div. III Finals

**Multiple winners:** Washington (4); Capital, Elizabethtown and WI-Stevens Point (2).

| Year | Winner | Score | Loser |
|------|--------|-------|-------|
| 1982 | Elizabethtown, PA | 67-66* | NC-Greensboro |
| 1983 | North Central, IL | 83-71 | Elizabethtown, PA |
| 1984 | Rust College, MS | 51-49 | Elizabethtown, PA |
| 1985 | Scranton, PA | 68-59 | New Rochelle, NY |
| 1986 | Salem St., MA | 89-85 | Bishop, TX |
| 1987 | WI-Stevens Pt. | 81-74 | Concordia, MN |
| 1988 | Concordia, MN | 65-57 | St. John Fisher, NY |
| 1989 | Elizabethtown, PA | 66-65 | CS-Stanislaus |
| 1990 | Hope, MI | 65-63 | St. John Fisher |
| 1991 | St. Thomas, MN | 73-55 | Muskingum, OH |
| 1992 | Alma, MI | 79-75 | Moravian, PA |
| 1993 | Central Iowa | 71-63 | Capital, OH |
| 1994 | Capital, OH | 82-63 | Washington, MO |
| 1995 | Capital, OH | 59-55 | WI-Oshkosh |
| 1996 | WI-Oshkosh | 66-50 | Mt. Union, OH |
| 1997 | NYU | 72-70 | WI-Eau Claire |
| 1998 | Washington, MO | 77-69 | So. Maine |
| 1999 | Washington, MO | 74-65 | Col.of St. Benedict, MN |
| 2000 | Washington, MO | 79-33 | So. Maine |
| 2001 | Washington, MO | 67-45 | Messiah, PA |
| 2002 | WI-Stevens Pt. | 67-65 | St. Lawrence, NY |
| 2003 | Trinity, TX | 60-58 | E. Connecticut St. |
| 2004 | Wilmington | 59-53 | Bowdoin |
| 2005 | Millikin | 70-50 | Randolph-Macon |

*Overtime

### NAIA Finals

**Multiple winners:** One tournament–SW Oklahoma (4); Div. I tourney–Southern Nazarene (6), Oklahoma City (4); Arkansas Tech and Union (2); Div. II tourney–Hastings, Morningside, Northern St. and Western Oregon (2).

| Year | Winner | Score | Loser | Year | Winner | Score | Loser |
|------|--------|-------|-------|------|--------|-------|-------|
| 1981 | Kentucky St. | 73-67 | Texas Southern | 1997 | I– So. Nazarene | 78-73 | Union, TN |
| 1982 | SW Oklahoma | 80-45 | Mo. Southern | | II– NW Nazarene | 64-46 | Black Hills St., SD |
| 1983 | SW Oklahoma | 80-68 | AL-Huntsville | 1998 | I– Union, TN | 73-70 | So. Nazarene |
| 1984 | NC-Asheville | 72-70* | Portland, OR | | II– Walsh, OH | 73-66 | Mary Hardin-Baylor |
| 1985 | SW Oklahoma | 55-54 | Saginaw Val., MI | 1999 | I– Oklahoma City | 72-55 | Simon Fraser, B.C. |
| 1986 | Francis Marion, SC | 75-65 | Wayland Baptist, TX | | II– Shawnee St., OH | 80-65 | St. Francis, IN |
| 1987 | SW Oklahoma | 60-58 | North Georgia | 2000 | I– Oklahoma City | 64-55 | Simon Fraser, B.C. |
| 1988 | Oklahoma City | 113-95 | Claflin, SC | | II– Mary, N.D. | 59-49 | Northwestern, IA |
| 1989 | So. Nazarene, OK | 98-96 | Claflin, SC | 2001 | I– Oklahoma City | 69-52 | Auburn |
| 1990 | SW Oklahoma | 82-75 | AR-Monticello | | | | Montgomery, AL |
| 1991 | Ft. Hays St., KS | 57-53 | SW Oklahoma | | II– Northwestern, IA | 77-50 | Albertson, ID |
| 1992 | I– Arkansas Tech | 84-68 | Wayland Baptist, TX | 2002 | I– Oklahoma City | 82-73 | So. Nazarene |
| | II– Northern St., SD | 73-56 | Tarleton St., TX | | II– Hastings, NE | 73-69 | Cornerstone, MI. |
| 1993 | I– Arkansas Tech | 76-75 | Union, TN | 2003 | I– So. Nazarene | 71-70 | Oklahoma City |
| | II– No. Montana | 71-68 | Northern St., SD | | II– Hastings, NE | 59-53 | Dakota Wesleyan |
| 1994 | I– So. Nazarene | 97-74 | David Lipscomb, TN | 2004 | I– So. Nazarene | 77-61 | Oklahoma City |
| | II– Northern St., SD | 48-45 | Western Oregon | | II– Morningside | 70-62 | Mary, N.D. |
| 1995 | I– So. Nazarene | 78-77 | SE Oklahoma | 2005 | I– Union, TN | 67-63 | Oklahoma City |
| | II– Western Oregon | 75-67 | NW Nazarene, ID | | II– Morningside | 75-65 | Cedarville, OH |
| 1996 | I– So. Nazarene | 80-79 | SE Oklahoma | | | | |
| | II– Western Oregon | 80-77 | Huron, SD | | | | |

*Overtime

### AIAW Finals

The Association of Intercollegiate Athletics for Women Large College tournament determined the women's national champion for 10 years until supplanted by the NCAA.

In 1982, most Division I teams entered the first NCAA tournament rather than the last one staged by the AIAW.

| Year | Winner | Score | Loser | Year | Winner | Score | Loser |
|------|--------|-------|-------|------|--------|-------|-------|
| 1972 | Immaculata, PA | 52-48 | West Chester, PA | 1978 | UCLA | 90-74 | Maryland |
| 1973 | Immaculata, PA | 59-52 | Queens College, NY | 1979 | Old Dominion | 75-65 | Louisiana Tech |
| 1974 | Immaculata, PA | 68-53 | Mississippi College | 1980 | Old Dominion | 68-53 | Tennessee |
| 1975 | Delta St., MS | 90-81 | Immaculata, PA | 1981 | Louisiana Tech | 79-59 | Tennessee |
| 1976 | Delta St., MS | 69-64 | Immaculata, PA | 1982 | Rutgers | 83-77 | Texas |
| 1977 | Delta St., MS | 68-55 | LSU | | | | |

# Professional Basketball

**Tim Duncan** won a third NBA championship and a third Finals MVP award with the Spurs in 2005.

# The Five-Million Dollar Ban

*Indiana's Ron Artest loses his cool and most of his paycheck in an ugly incident that mars a year to remember in the NBA.*

**Jerry Bembry**
*is the NBA Editor for ESPN The Magazine.*

Two players, Ron Artest and Ben Wallace, exchange shoves during an early season game. One fan tosses a beverage with incredible precision, striking Artest in the face. Dozens of players and fans become "involved" in the stands. And millions watch perhaps the ugliest incident in U.S. sports history either live or on the replays that are broadcast over and over and over again.

When we think back to the NBA regular season we should recall how Tim Duncan joined MJ, Magic and Shaq as the only players to win the MVP of the Finals at least three times. How Shaq's moving to Florida made the AmericanAirlines Arena one of the premier hotspots in and around South Beach. How a team with a long-haired point guard (Steve Nash) and a short-on-experience center (Amare Stoudemire) helped welcome the fast-break back to basketball and record the highest scoring team average in a decade.

And how Reggie Miller and Karl Malone both said goodbye.

But unfortunately, the indelible image imprinted in our brain from this season will be Artest running into the stands at The Palace in Auburn Hills and the ugly melee that followed in the nationally televised game. In all, nine players lost 142 games to suspensions at the cost of over $12 million in lost wages — the most severe penalties in NBA history.

"The line is drawn," NBA commissioner David Stern said in handing down the punishment. "And my guess is that it won't happen again."

Maybe one day we will be able to let those vivid images go, and remember the 2004-05 season not for its worst moments, but for its best.

Moments like Duncan, shaking off two subpar performances in Games 5 and 6 of the Finals to record a solid effort in Game 7 — earning that chance to raise a third career Finals MVP trophy.

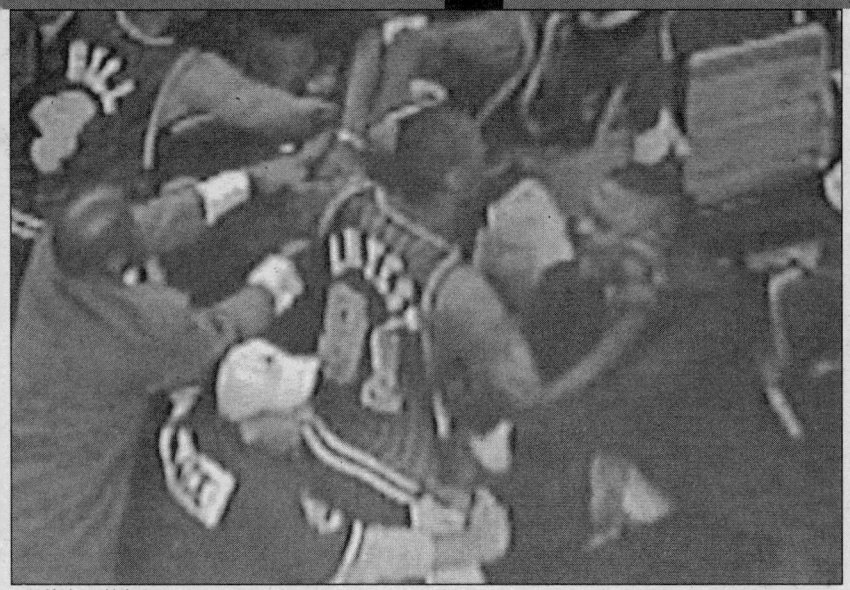

AP/Wide World Photos

*The November 2004 **Pacers-Pistons-Palace Brawl** was a low point in league history. The Pacers **Ron Artest** was suspended for the remainder of the season for his role in the fracas.*

Moments like Stoudemire torching the Spurs, averaging 37 points and dominating Duncan in the Western Conference Finals. So what that the Suns, the best team in the regular season, didn't advance to the Finals? With Nash, voted the league's Most Valuable Player, running the show in Phoenix, the Suns were the greatest show in basketball.

Moments like the Kobe/Shaq reunion in December, which gave the league television ratings so huge (the highest since the Chicago Bulls and Michael Jordan played on Christmas in 1998), that it decided to have the former running mates hook up again on the holiday for the 2005-06 season (maybe we'll witness a little acknowledgment next time).

And moments like Reggie Miller's final game in Indiana, a 27-point effort that had the fans at Conseco Fieldhouse standing and applauding in the final seconds, chanting in unison "one more year, one more year, one more year." Combatants in December, even the Pistons players walked to halfcourt to applaud Miller as Detroit head coach Larry Brown called consecutive timeouts so that the clutch shooting guard could soak in the moment.

"Words can never express how I feel about the city and fans," Miller said afterward.

***Kobe Bryant*** *and* ***Shaquille O'Neal*** *were on opposite sides for the 2004-05 NBA season. Shaq's Heat got the best of Kobe's Lakers in overtime of their first meeting on Christmas Day, 2004.*

When we recall the special moments of the 2004-05 season we'll think back to the final moments of Game 5 of the NBA Finals, when Rasheed Wallace left San Antonio's Robert Horry, of all people, open for the final shot.

Horry simply did what he does: he knocked down yet another game-winning clutch shot. In an April 2002 column on ESPN.com I wrote these words about Horry:

"When Horry's career is over, no one will ever equate him with legendary clutch performers Larry Bird, Michael Jordan, Jerry West or Clyde Frazier. But don't laugh as I say this: Robert Horry, a 6-foot-10 power forward, has established himself as one of the top clutch 3-point shooters in NBA history."

Who could have known at the time, that the best of Horry was yet to come.

So, you see, the 2004-05 season was indeed special. Heck, if I had a couple of more pages I easily could have filled them with heaping words of praise for the likes of Dwyane Wade, LeBron James and Manu Ginobili.

Some might look back at the season and remember what was ugly. It will be hard not to. Those will be forever etched in our brains.

But those great moments? Those are the ones that I will try to remember.

# Jerry Bembry's Ten Biggest Stories of the Year in Pro Basketball

**10** **Welcome Back.** Prior to last season, the Chicago Bulls hadn't been to the playoffs since their 1998 title run led by Michael Jordan. Prior to last season, the Washington Wizards hadn't tasted the playoffs since 1997. When the 2005 playoffs arrived, it was Washington taking on Chicago— a nice return for a couple of cities that, until 2005, had not had much to cheer.

**9** **Welcome Back.** Grant Hill, coming back from multiple surgeries on his ankle that limited him to 47 games over three seasons, averages 19.7 points in 67 games for Orlando. Miami's reserve center Alonzo Mourning, several years removed from a kidney transplant, actually looks spry in backing up Shaq and helping the Heat to a deep playoff run.

**8** **Final Farewell.** The Pacers' Reggie Miller was one of the best clutch shooters the game has ever known. Longtime Utah Jazz fixture Karl Malone just might be the best power forward ever. Both call it a career last season, assuring that in the near future they will be visiting Springfield, Massachusetts for a Hall of Fame Weekend in their honor.

**7** **Wounded Wolves.** We all assumed, with Shaq down in South Beach, that the Timberwolves—one year removed from the Western Conference Finals—would be ready for that next step forward. And weren't we all shocked when that step took Minnesota from the high of a Western Conference-best 58 wins in 2003-04 to failing to make the playoffs.

**6** **Rising Suns.** At the end of the 2003-04 regular season the Phoenix Suns' 29 wins (sixth fewest in the NBA) kept them near the league's cellar. One year later the Suns—with the newly aquired Steve Nash and rising star Amare Stoudemire emerging as the latest iteration of Stockton-to-Malone— scored a league-best 110.4 points per game, elevating the team to the league's elite.

**5** **Power Shift.** Phil Jackson getting a reported $8 million a year to recoach the Lakers and Larry Brown estimated $10-12 million to lead the New York Knicks. There's no doubt Jackson and Brown are difference makers and the size of their paychecks alone will allow their voices to carry just a little bit more weight in the lockerroom.

**4** **Dreams Postponed.** No more will high school gymnasiums look like an NBA GM meeting with the new collective bargaining agreement making it mandatory for players entering the draft to be 19 years old and a full year removed from high school hoops.

**3** **New Kings in Town.** After a tough seven-game series against the Pistons, the Spurs win their third title in seven seasons and once again put a spotlight on international ball as their top three players hail from the Virgin Islands (Tim Duncan), Argentina (Manu Ginobili) and France (Tony Parker).

**2** **Renewing Acquaintances.** Together, Shaq and Kobe won three championship rings in Los Angeles. Together again, but in different uniforms, their first meeting on Christmas Day, 2004, was the most hyped and anticipated game of the 2004-05 season—and surprisingly lived up to the build-up. Shaq's Heat edged Kobe's Lakers, 104-102, in overtime. Shaq fouled out in the fourth quarter but his new wingman, Dwyane Wade, stepped up down the stretch. Kobe scored a season-high 42 points, but had nine turnovers and missed a potential game-winning 3-pointer at the buzzer in OT.

**1** **Friday Night Fights.** When the smoke of the November brawl between the Pacers and Pistons (and some of their fans) finally cleared nine players were suspended for a combined total of 142 games. The biggest loser: Ron Artest, whose 72-game suspension cost him close to $5 million in salary.

## INSIDE the numbers

### Keeping them in Suspense

When Ron Artest was suspended for the rest of the season following his role in the melee that erupted near the end of the Pistons-Pacers game on Nov. 19, 2004, he jumped to the top of the list of the longest non-drug related suspensions in league history.

| Gm | Player, Team | Year |
|----|--------------|------|
| 72 | Ron Artest, Pacers | 2004 |
| 68 | Latrell Sprewell, Golden St. | 1997 |
| 30 | Stephen Jackson, Pacers | 2004 |
| 26 | Kermit Washington, Lakers | 1977 |
| 25 | Jermaine O'Neal, Pacers | 2004 |
| 11 | Dennis Rodman, Bulls | 1997 |
| 10 | Vernon Maxwell, Rockets | 1995 |

### Phoenix Rising

The Suns and free agent signee Steve Nash won 62 regular-season games in 2004-05 a year after Phoenix won just 29 games, achieving one of the greatest single-season turnarounds in NBA history.

| Gms | Team | Improvement | Year |
|-----|------|-------------|------|
| +36 | Spurs | 20-62 to 56-26 | 1997-98 |
| +35 | Spurs | 21-61 to 56-26 | 1989-90 |
| +33 | Suns | 29-53 to 62-20 | 2004-05 |
| +32 | Celtics | 29-53 to 61-21 | 1979-80 |
| +29 | Bucks | 27-55 to 56-26 | 1969-70 |

**Note:** The Lakers had 36 more wins in 1999-2000 (67-15) than 1998-99 (31-19) but they had only played 50 games the previous year due to the lockout.

# 2004-2005
# *Season in Review*

ESPN
SPORTS ALMANAC

## Final NBA Standings

Division champions (*) and playoff qualifiers (†) are noted. Number of seasons listed after each head coach refers to current tenure with club.

### Western Conference

| Northwest Div. | W | L | Pct | GB | Per Game For | Opp |
|---|---|---|---|---|---|---|
| *Seattle | 52 | 30 | .634 | — | 98.9 | 96.6 |
| †Denver | 49 | 33 | .598 | 3 | 99.5 | 97.5 |
| Minnesota | 44 | 38 | .537 | 8 | 96.8 | 95.3 |
| Portland | 27 | 55 | .329 | 25 | 92.9 | 96.9 |
| Utah | 26 | 56 | .317 | 26 | 93.0 | 97.3 |

**Head Coaches: Sea**—Nate McMillan (5th season); **Den**—Jeff Bzdelik (3rd, 13-15) was fired Dec. 28, 2004 and replaced on an interim basis by asst. Michael Cooper (4-10), then by George Karl (32-8) on Jan. 27, 2005; **Min**—Phil Saunders (10th, 25-26) was fired and replaced by GM Kevin McHale (19-12); **Port**—Maurice Cheeks (4th, 22-33) was fired Mar. 2, 2005 and replaced on an interim basis by personnel director Kevin Pritchard (5-22); **Utah**—Jerry Sloan (17th).

| Pacific Div. | W | L | Pct | GB | Per Game For | Opp |
|---|---|---|---|---|---|---|
| *Phoenix | 62 | 30 | .756 | — | 110.4 | 103.3 |
| †Sacramento | 50 | 32 | .610 | 12 | 103.7 | 101.6 |
| LA Clippers | 37 | 45 | .451 | 25 | 95.7 | 96.4 |
| LA Lakers | 34 | 48 | .415 | 28 | 98.7 | 101.7 |
| Golden St. | 34 | 48 | .415 | 28 | 98.7 | 100.9 |

**Head Coaches: Pho**—Mike D'Antoni (2nd season); **Sac**—Rick Adelman (7th); **LAC**—Mike Dunleavy (2nd); **LAL**—Rudy Tomjanovich (1st, 24-19) resigned Feb. 2, 2005 and was replaced on an interim basis by asst. Frank Hamblen (10-29); **G.St.**—Mike Montgomery (1st).

| Southwest Div. | W | L | Pct | GB | Per Game For | Opp |
|---|---|---|---|---|---|---|
| *San Antonio | 59 | 23 | .720 | — | 96.2 | 88.4 |
| †Dallas | 58 | 24 | .707 | 1 | 102.5 | 96.8 |
| †Houston | 51 | 31 | .622 | 8 | 95.1 | 91.0 |
| †Memphis | 45 | 37 | .549 | 14 | 93.4 | 91.1 |
| New Orleans | 18 | 64 | .220 | 41 | 88.4 | 95.5 |

**Head Coaches: SA**—Gregg Popovich (9th season); **Dal**—Don Nelson (8th, 42-22) resigned Mar. 19, 2005 and was replaced by asst. Avery Johnson (16-2); **Hou**—Jeff Van Gundy (2nd); **Mem**—Hubie Brown (3rd, 5-7) resigned on Nov. 25, 2004 and was replaced on an interim basis by asst. Lionel Hollins (0-4) who was replaced by Mike Fratello (40-26) on Dec. 2, 2004; **NO**—Byron Scott (1st).

### Eastern Conference

| Atlantic Div. | W | L | Pct | GB | Per Game For | Opp |
|---|---|---|---|---|---|---|
| *Boston | 45 | 37 | .549 | — | 101.3 | 100.4 |
| †Philadelphia | 43 | 39 | .524 | 2 | 99.1 | 99.9 |
| †New Jersey | 42 | 40 | .512 | 3 | 91.4 | 92.9 |
| Toronto | 33 | 49 | .402 | 12 | 99.7 | 101.4 |
| New York | 33 | 49 | .402 | 12 | 97.3 | 99.7 |

**Head Coaches: Bos**—Doc Rivers (1st season); **Phi**—Jim O'Brien (1st); **NJ**—Lawrence Frank (2nd); **Tor**—Sam Mitchell (1st); **NY**—Lenny Wilkens (2nd, 17-22) resigned on Jan. 22, 2005 and was replaced on an interim basis by asst. Herb Williams (16-27).

| Central Div. | W | L | Pct | GB | Per Game For | Opp |
|---|---|---|---|---|---|---|
| *Detroit | 54 | 28 | .659 | — | 93.3 | 89.5 |
| †Chicago | 47 | 35 | .573 | 7 | 94.5 | 93.4 |
| †Indiana | 44 | 38 | .537 | 10 | 93.0 | 92.2 |
| Cleveland | 42 | 40 | .512 | 12 | 96.5 | 95.7 |
| Milwaukee | 30 | 52 | .366 | 24 | 97.2 | 100.2 |

**Head Coaches: Det**—Larry Brown (2nd season); **Chi**—Scott Skiles (2nd); **Ind**—Rick Carlisle (2nd); **Cle**—Paul Silas (2nd 34-30) was fired on Mar. 21, 2005 and replaced on an interim basis by asst. Brendan Malone (8-10); **Mil**—Terry Porter (2nd).

| Southeast Div. | W | L | Pct | GB | Per Game For | Opp |
|---|---|---|---|---|---|---|
| *Miami | 59 | 23 | .720 | — | 101.5 | 95.0 |
| †Washington | 45 | 37 | .549 | 14 | 100.5 | 100.8 |
| Orlando | 36 | 46 | .439 | 23 | 99.5 | 101.8 |
| Charlotte | 18 | 64 | .220 | 41 | 94.3 | 100.2 |
| Atlanta | 13 | 69 | .159 | 46 | 92.7 | 102.5 |

**Head Coaches: Mia**—Stan Van Gundy (2nd season); **Wash**—Eddie Jordan (2nd); **Orl**—Johnny Davis (2nd, 31-33) was fired on Mar. 17 and replaced on an interim basis by asst. Chris Jent (5-13). **Cha**—Bernie Bickerstaff (1st). **Atl**—Mike Woodson (1st).

## Overall Conference Standings

Sixteen teams—eight from each conference—qualify for the NBA Playoffs; (*) indicates division champions.

### Western Conference

| | | W | L | Home | Away | Conf | Div |
|---|---|---|---|---|---|---|---|
| 1 | Phoenix* | 62 | 20 | 31-10 | 31-10 | 38-14 | 12-4 |
| 2 | San Antonio* | 59 | 23 | 38-3 | 21-20 | 36-16 | 10-6 |
| 3 | Seattle* | 52 | 30 | 26-15 | 31-21 | 11-5 | 11-5 |
| 4 | Dallas | 58 | 24 | 29-12 | 29-12 | 35-17 | 11-5 |
| 5 | Houston | 51 | 31 | 26-15 | 25-16 | 33-19 | 10-6 |
| 6 | Sacramento | 50 | 32 | 30-11 | 20-21 | 28-24 | 10-6 |
| 7 | Denver | 49 | 33 | 31-10 | 18-23 | 28-24 | 9-7 |
| 8 | Memphis | 45 | 37 | 26-15 | 19-22 | 27-25 | 7-9 |
| | Minnesota | 44 | 38 | 24-17 | 20-21 | 30-22 | 10-6 |
| | LA Clippers | 37 | 45 | 27-14 | 10-31 | 20-32 | 6-10 |
| | LA Lakers | 34 | 48 | 22-19 | 12-29 | 21-31 | 6-10 |
| | Golden St. | 34 | 48 | 20-21 | 14-27 | 20-32 | 6-10 |
| | Portland | 27 | 55 | 18-23 | 9-32 | 13-39 | 4-12 |
| | Utah | 26 | 56 | 18-23 | 8-33 | 20-32 | 6-10 |
| | New Orleans | 18 | 64 | 11-30 | 7-34 | 10-42 | 2-14 |

### Eastern Conference

| | | W | L | Home | Away | Conf | Div |
|---|---|---|---|---|---|---|---|
| 1 | Miami* | 59 | 23 | 35-6 | 24-17 | 41-11 | 15-1 |
| 2 | Detroit* | 54 | 28 | 32-9 | 22-19 | 35-17 | 8-8 |
| 3 | Boston* | 45 | 37 | 27-14 | 18-23 | 30-22 | 8-8 |
| 4 | Chicago | 47 | 35 | 27-14 | 20-21 | 32-20 | 8-8 |
| 5 | Washington | 45 | 37 | 29-12 | 16-25 | 28-24 | 10-6 |
| 6 | Indiana | 44 | 38 | 25-16 | 19-22 | 29-23 | 9-7 |
| 7 | Philadelphia | 43 | 39 | 25-16 | 18-23 | 33-19 | 8-8 |
| 8 | New Jersey | 42 | 40 | 24-17 | 18-23 | 31-21 | 11-5 |
| | Cleveland | 42 | 40 | 29-12 | 13-28 | 26-26 | 7-9 |
| | Orlando | 36 | 46 | 24-17 | 12-29 | 21-31 | 6-10 |
| | Toronto | 33 | 49 | 22-19 | 11-30 | 20-32 | 7-9 |
| | New York | 33 | 49 | 22-19 | 11-30 | 21-31 | 6-10 |
| | Milwaukee | 30 | 52 | 23-18 | 7-34 | 24-28 | 8-8 |
| | Charlotte | 18 | 64 | 14-27 | 4-37 | 11-41 | 7-9 |
| | Atlanta | 13 | 69 | 9-32 | 4-37 | 8-44 | 2-14 |

# 2005 NBA All-Star Game

## East, 125-115

54th NBA All-Star Game. **Date:** Feb. 15, at the Pepsi Center in Denver; **Coaches:** Stan Van Gundy, Miami (East) and Gregg Popovich, San Antonio (West); **MVP:** Allen Iverson, East (15 points, 9 assists, 5 steals); Starters chosen by fan vote, (Houston's Yao Ming was the leading vote-getter receiving a record 2,558,278 votes); bench chosen by conference coaches' vote.

## Western Conference

| Pos | Starters | Min | FG M-A | Pts | Reb | A |
|-----|----------|-----|--------|-----|-----|---|
| G | Kobe Bryant, LAL | 29 | 7-14 | 16 | 6 | 7 |
| G | Tracy McGrady, Hou | 24 | 4-13 | 8 | 5 | 5 |
| F | Tim Duncan, SA | 16 | 7-10 | 15 | 9 | 2 |
| F | Kevin Garnett, Min | 16 | 5-8 | 10 | 3 | 2 |
| C | Yao Ming, Hou | 22 | 5-9 | 11 | 8 | 5 |
| **Bench** | | | | | | |
| G | Ray Allen, Sea | 23 | 6-16 | 17 | 4 | 1 |
| G | Manu Ginobili, SA | 22 | 3-6 | 8 | 3 | 1 |
| F | Dirk Nowitzki, Dal | 21 | 4-10 | 10 | 7 | 2 |
| F | Amare Stoudemire, Pho | 20 | 3-11 | 6 | 9 | 2 |
| G | Steve Nash, Pho | 17 | 1-2 | 2 | 0 | 6 |
| F | Shawn Marion, Pho | 16 | 5-7 | 10 | 3 | 4 |
| F | Rashard Lewis, Sea | 14 | 1-7 | 2 | 4 | 1 |
| | TOTALS | 240 | 51-113 | 115 | 61 | 38 |

**Three-Point FG:** 9-29 (Allen 5-11, Bryant 2-5, Duncan 1-1, Nowitzki 1-3, McGrady 0-4, Ginobili 0-2, Nash 0-1, Lewis 0-2); **Free Throws:** 4-11 (Ginobili 2-2, Nowitzki 1-2, Ming 1-2, Duncan 0-1, Garnett 0-1, Marion 0-1, Stoudemire 0-2); **Percentages:** FG (.451), Three-Pt. FG (.310), Free Throws (.364); **Turnovers:** 25 (Bryant 4, McGrady 3, Ginobili 3, Nowitzki 3, Nash 3, Duncan 2, Garnett 2, Ming, Allena, Stoudemire, Marion, Lewis); **Steals:** 13 (Nowitzki 4, Bryant 3, McGrady 3, Ginobili, Stoudemire, Lewis); **Blocked Shots:** 9 (Nowitzki 4, McGrady 2, Bryant, Ming, Ginobili); **Fouls:** 19 (Bryant 5, Ginobili 3, Garnett 2, Allen 2, Stoudemire 2, Lewis 2, McGrady, Ming, Nowitzki); **Team Rebounds:** 8.

## Eastern Conference

| Pos | Starters | Min | FG M-A | Pts | Reb | A |
|-----|----------|-----|--------|-----|-----|---|
| G | Allen Iverson, Phi | 32 | 4-13 | 15 | 4 | 9 |
| G | LeBron James, Cle | 31 | 6-13 | 13 | 8 | 6 |
| F | Grant Hill, Orl | 18 | 3-6 | 6 | 3 | 2 |
| F | Vince Carter, Tor | 18 | 4-8 | 11 | 3 | 1 |
| C | Shaquille O'Neal, Mia | 25 | 6-11 | 12 | 6 | 1 |
| **Bench** | | | | | | |
| G | Dwyane Wade, Mia | 23 | 6-13 | 14 | 3 | 1 |
| F | Jermaine O'Neal, Ind | 19 | 6-10 | 15 | 5 | 1 |
| C | Zydrunas Ilgauskas, Cle | 17 | 5-8 | 12 | 7 | 1 |
| C | Ben Wallace, Det | 15 | 3-7 | 6 | 7 | 0 |
| G | Gilbert Arenas, Wash. | 15 | 3-11 | 7 | 2 | 2 |
| G | Paul Pierce, Bos | 14 | 4-7 | 9 | 3 | 3 |
| F | Antawn Jamison, Wash | 13 | 2-5 | 5 | 4 | 1 |
| | TOTALS | 240 | 52-112 | 125 | 55 | 28 |

**Three-Point FG:** 6-17 (Carter 3-5, Jamison 1-1, Arenas 1-3, James 1-4, S. O'Neal 0-1, Wade 0-1, Pierce 0-2); **Free Throws:** 15-20 (Iverson 7-7, J. O'Neal 3-4, Wade 2-2, Ilgauskas 2-2, Pierce 1-1, S. O'Neal 0-3, James 0-1); **Percentages:** FG (.464), Three-Pt. FG (.353), Free Throws (.750); **Turnovers:** 18 (Iverson 3, James 3, Carter 2, Wallace 2, Hill, Wade, J. O'Neal, Ilgauskas); **Steals:** 16 (Iverson 5, S. O'Neal 3, Wade 2, James 2, Pierce 2, Hill, J. O'Neal); **Blocked Shots:** 7 (S. O'Neal 3, Ilgauskas 2, Wade, J. O'Neal); **Fouls:** 13 (S. O'Neal 2, Wade 2, Ilgauskas 2, Wallace 2, Hill, J. O'Neal, Arenas); **Team Rebounds:** 10.

**Halftime—** East, 61-59; **Third Quarter—** East, 95-89; **Technical Fouls—** none; **Officials—** #41 Ken Mauer, #35 Jack Nies, #22 Bill Spooner; **Attendance—** 18,227; **TV Rating—** 4.9 (TNT).

| | 1 | 2 | 3 | 4 | F |
|-----|---|---|---|---|---|
| East | 27 | 34 | 34 | 30 | 125 |
| West | 33 | 26 | 30 | 26 | 115 |

# NBA 3-point Shootout

Six players are invited to compete in the annual three-point shooting contest held during All-Star Weekend, since 1986. Each shooter has 60 seconds to shoot the 25 balls in five racks outside the three-point line. Each ball is worth one point, except the last ball in each rack, which is worth two points. Highest scores advance. First prize: $25,000.

| First Round | Pts |
|-------------|-----|
| Quentin Richardson, Phoenix | 14 |
| Voshon Lenard, Denver | 14 |
| Kyle Korver, Philadelphia | 14 |

| Failed to advance | Pts |
|-------------------|-----|
| Ray Lewis, Seattle | 13 |
| Joe Johnson, Phoenix | 8 |
| Vladimir Radmanovic, Seattle | 8 |

| Finals | Pts |
|--------|-----|
| Quentin Richardson | 19 |
| Kyle Korver | 18 |
| Voshon Lenard | 16 |

# Slam Dunk Contest

The Dunk contest was held annually from 1984-97 before being replaced by the 2Ball competition. It made its return in 2000. The competitors are selected based on "the creativity and artistry they have displayed in dunking" over the course of the season. The dunks are judged by five judges on a scale from six to ten. The top two scorers from the first round advance to the final round and attempt two dunks. The combined score of the two dunks determines the winner. First prize: $25,000.

| First Round | Pts |
|-------------|-----|
| Josh Smith, Atlanta | 95 |
| Amare Stoudemire, Phoenix | 95 |

| Failed to advance | Pts |
|-------------------|-----|
| J.R. Smith, New Orleans | 95 |
| Chris Anderson, New Orleans | 77 |

| Finals | Score |
|--------|-------|
| Josh Smith def. Amare Stoudemire | 100-87 |

In 2006, the **NBA All-Star Weekend** will return to Houston, Texas for the first time since 1989. The NBA announced that the 2007 All-Star Game is headed to **Las Vegas, Nevada.** As part of the deal casinos have agreed not to take any bets on the game. It will be the first time the event will be held in a non-NBA city. It may not be the last, however, as NBA Commissioner David Stern has said that the league is considering holding the 2008 or 2009 game in **Paris.**

NBA ALL-STAR
*Las Vegas*
2007

Philadelphia
**Allen Iverson**
Scoring

Minnesota
**Kevin Garnett**
Rebounding

Miami
**Shaquille O'Neal**
Field Goal Pct.

Phoenix
**Steve Nash**
Assists

## NBA Regular Season Individual Leaders

### Scoring
(*indicates rookie)

| | Gm | Min | FG | FG% | 3pt/Att | FT | FT% | Reb | Ast | Stl | Blk | Pts | Avg | Hi |
|---|---|---|---|---|---|---|---|---|---|---|---|---|---|---|
| Allen Iverson, Phi | 75 | 3174 | 771 | 42.4 | 104/338 | 656 | 83.5 | 299 | 596 | 180 | 9 | 2302 | **30.7** | 60 |
| Kobe Bryant, LAL | 66 | 2689 | 573 | 43.3 | 131/387 | 542 | 81.6 | 392 | 398 | 86 | 53 | 1812 | **27.6** | 48 |
| LeBron James, Cle | 80 | 3388 | 795 | 47.2 | 108/308 | 477 | 75.0 | 588 | 577 | 177 | 52 | 2175 | **27.2** | 56 |
| Dirk Nowitzki, Dal | 78 | 3020 | 663 | 45.9 | 91/228 | 615 | 86.9 | 757 | 240 | 97 | 119 | 2032 | **26.1** | 53 |
| Amare Stoudemire, Pho | 80 | 2889 | 747 | 55.9 | 3/16 | 583 | 73.3 | 713 | 131 | 77 | 130 | 2080 | **26.0** | 50 |
| Tracy McGrady, Hou | 78 | 3182 | 715 | 43.1 | 142/435 | 431 | 77.4 | 484 | 448 | 135 | 52 | 2003 | **25.7** | 48 |
| Gilbert Arenas, Wash | 80 | 3274 | 656 | 42.4 | 205/562 | 521 | 81.4 | 378 | 411 | 139 | 23 | 2038 | **25.5** | 44 |
| Vince Carter, Tor-NJ | 77 | 2828 | 696 | 45.2 | 127/313 | 367 | 79.8 | 401 | 327 | 109 | 48 | 1886 | **24.5** | 45 |
| Dwyane Wade, Mia | 77 | 2974 | 630 | 47.8 | 13/45 | 581 | 76.2 | 397 | 520 | 121 | 82 | 1854 | **24.1** | 48 |
| Ray Allen, Sea | 78 | 3064 | 640 | 42.8 | 209/556 | 378 | 88.3 | 347 | 289 | 84 | 5 | 1867 | **23.9** | 40 |
| Michael Redd, Milw | 75 | 2848 | 625 | 44.1 | 104/293 | 369 | 85.4 | 312 | 172 | 63 | 8 | 1723 | **23.0** | 39 |
| Shaquille O'Neal, Mia | 73 | 2492 | 658 | 60.1 | 0/0 | 353 | 46.1 | 760 | 200 | 36 | 171 | 1669 | **22.9** | 40 |
| Corey Maggette, LAC | 66 | 2436 | 425 | 43.1 | 51/168 | 563 | 85.7 | 394 | 225 | 70 | 8 | 1464 | **22.2** | 38 |
| Kevin Garnett, Min | 82 | 3121 | 683 | 50.2 | 6/25 | 445 | 81.1 | 1108 | 466 | 121 | 112 | 1817 | **22.2** | 47 |
| Larry Hughes, Wash | 61 | 2358 | 467 | 43.0 | 59/209 | 352 | 77.7 | 382 | 285 | 176 | 18 | 1345 | **22.0** | 33 |
| Stephon Marbury, NY | 82 | 3281 | 604 | 46.2 | 115/325 | 458 | 83.4 | 248 | 668 | 122 | 6 | 1781 | **21.7** | 45 |
| Jason Richardson, G.St. | 72 | 2724 | 610 | 44.6 | 125/370 | 214 | 69.3 | 424 | 281 | 105 | 32 | 1559 | **21.7** | 42 |
| Paul Pierce, Bos | 82 | 2960 | 556 | 45.5 | 108/292 | 549 | 82.2 | 539 | 348 | 133 | 39 | 1769 | **21.6** | 38 |
| Steve Francis, Orl | 78 | 2978 | 563 | 42.3 | 38/127 | 499 | 82.3 | 450 | 547 | 112 | 28 | 1663 | **21.3** | 39 |
| Carmelo Anthony, Den | 75 | 2608 | 530 | 43.1 | 111/372 | 456 | 79.6 | 285 | 194 | 68 | 30 | 1558 | **20.8** | 36 |
| Rashard Lewis, Sea | 71* | 2697 | 532 | 46.2 | 173/432 | 220 | 77.7 | 388 | 94 | 75 | 62 | 1457 | **20.5** | 37 |
| Tim Duncan, SA | 66 | 2203 | 517 | 49.6 | 3/9 | 305 | 67.0 | 732 | 179 | 45 | 174 | 1342 | **20.3** | 39 |
| Peja Stojakovic, Sac | 66 | 2534 | 451 | 44.4 | 174/433 | 253 | 92.0 | 285 | 138 | 79 | 12 | 1329 | **20.1** | 38 |
| Elton Brand, LAC | 81 | 3001 | 629 | 50.3 | 0/3 | 364 | 75.2 | 770 | 208 | 62 | 169 | 1622 | **20.0** | 36 |
| Grant Hill, Orl | 67 | 2338 | 517 | .509 | 3/13 | 280 | 82.1 | 318 | 220 | 97 | 28 | 1317 | **19.7** | 39 |
| Mike Bibby, Sac | 80 | 3084 | 560 | 44.3 | 131/364 | 320 | 77.5 | 332 | 541 | 124 | 30 | 1571 | **19.6** | 40 |
| Antawn Jamison, Wash | 68 | 2605 | 519 | 43.7 | 71/208 | 225 | 76.0 | 519 | 154 | 55 | 16 | 1334 | **19.6** | 35 |
| Chris Webber, Sac-Phi | 67 | 2370 | 555 | 43.3 | 15/44 | 181 | 79.4 | 612 | 318 | 94 | 53 | 1306 | **19.5** | 41 |
| Shawn Marion, Pho | 81 | 3146 | 613 | 47.6 | 114/341 | 229 | 83.3 | 915 | 154 | 163 | 119 | 1569 | **19.4** | 37 |
| Antoine Walker, Atl-Bos | 77 | 2955 | 581 | 42.2 | 110/341 | 201 | 53.9 | 695 | 265 | 89 | 58 | 1473 | **19.1** | 36 |

### Rebounds

| | Gm | Off | Def | Tot | Avg |
|---|---|---|---|---|---|
| Kevin Garnett, Min | 82 | 247 | 861 | 1108 | 13.5 |
| Ben Wallace, Det | 74 | 292 | 610 | 902 | 12.2 |
| Shawn Marion, Pho | 81 | 235 | 680 | 915 | 11.3 |
| Tim Duncan, SA | 66 | 202 | 530 | 732 | 11.1 |
| Emeka Okafor*, Cha | 73 | 275 | 520 | 795 | 10.9 |
| Troy Murphy, G.St. | 70 | 251 | 505 | 756 | 10.8 |
| Shaquille O'Neal, Mia | 73 | 253 | 507 | 760 | 10.4 |
| Kurt Thomas, NY | 80 | 170 | 661 | 831 | 10.4 |
| Dwight Howard*, Orl | 82 | 287 | 536 | 823 | 10.0 |
| Marcus Camby, Den | 66 | 131 | 530 | 661 | 10.0 |
| Dirk Nowitzki, Dal | 78 | 86 | 661 | 757 | 9.7 |
| Tyson Chandler, Chi | 80 | 261 | 514 | 775 | 9.7 |
| Elton Brand, LAC | 81 | 296 | 474 | 770 | 9.5 |
| Reggie Evans, Sea | 79 | 254 | 482 | 736 | 9.3 |
| Drew Gooden, Cle | 82 | 207 | 546 | 753 | 9.2 |

### Assists

| | Gm | Ast | Avg |
|---|---|---|---|
| Steve Nash, Dal | 75 | 861 | 11.5 |
| Brevin Knight, Cha | 66 | 591 | 9.0 |
| Jason Kidd, NJ | 66 | 545 | 8.3 |
| Stephon Marbury, NY | 82 | 668 | 8.1 |
| Allen Iverson, Phi | 75 | 596 | 7.9 |
| LeBron James, Cle | 80 | 577 | 7.2 |
| Steve Francis, Orl | 78 | 547 | 7.0 |
| Andre Miller, Den | 82 | 569 | 6.9 |
| Mike Bibby, Sac | 80 | 541 | 6.8 |
| Dwyane Wade, Mia | 77 | 520 | 6.8 |
| Rafer Alston, Tor | 80 | 514 | 6.4 |
| Kirk Hinrich, Chi | 77 | 494 | 6.4 |
| Tony Parker, SA | 80 | 491 | 6.1 |
| Gary Payton, Bos | 77 | 469 | 6.1 |
| Maurice Williams, Milw | 80 | 484 | 6.1 |

### Field Goal Pct.

| | Gm | FG | Att | Pct |
|---|---|---|---|---|
| Shaquille O'Neal, Mia | .73 | 658 | 1095 | .601 |
| Amare Stoudemire, Pho | .80 | 747 | 1336 | .559 |
| Yao Ming, Hou | .80 | 538 | 975 | .552 |
| Udonis Haslem, Mia | .80 | 346 | 641 | .540 |
| Eddy Curry, Chi | .63 | 393 | 730 | .538 |
| Ruben Patterson, Port | .70 | 319 | 601 | .531 |
| Mark Blount, Bos | .82 | 327 | 618 | .529 |
| Brad Miller, Sac | .56 | 319 | 609 | .524 |
| Carlos Boozer, Utah | .51 | 361 | 693 | .521 |
| Dwight Howard*, Orl | .82 | 352 | 677 | .520 |

### Free Throw Pct.

| | Gm | FT | Att | Pct |
|---|---|---|---|---|
| Reggie Miller, Ind | .66 | 250 | 268 | .933 |
| Earl Boykins, Den | .82 | 279 | 303 | .921 |
| Peja Stojakovic, Sac | .66 | 253 | 275 | .920 |
| Damon Stoudamire, Port | .81 | 182 | 199 | .915 |
| Chauncey Billups, Det | .80 | 343 | 382 | .898 |
| Steve Nash, Pho | .75 | 211 | 238 | .887 |
| Luke Ridnour, Sea | .82 | 159 | 180 | .883 |
| Ray Allen, Sea | .78 | 163 | 184 | .883 |
| Austin Croshere, Ind | .73 | 226 | 256 | .883 |
| Danny Fortson, Sea | .62 | 227 | 258 | .880 |

### 3-Point Field Goal Pct.

| | Gm | 3FG | Att | Pct |
|---|---|---|---|---|
| Fred Hoiberg, Minn | .76 | 70 | 145 | .483 |
| Joe Johnson, Pho | .82 | 177 | 370 | .478 |
| Cuttino Mobley, Sac | .66 | 150 | 342 | .439 |
| Mike Miller, Mem | .76 | 140 | 323 | .433 |
| Damon Jones, Mia | .82 | 225 | 521 | .432 |
| Steve Nash, Pho | .75 | 94 | 218 | .431 |
| Jon Barry, Atl-Hou | .69 | 71 | 165 | .430 |
| Chauncey Billups, Det | .80 | 165 | 387 | .426 |
| Eric Piatkowski, Chi | .68 | 57 | 134 | .425 |
| Jason Terry, Dal | .80 | 103 | 245 | .420 |

### High-Point Games

| | Opp | Date | FG-FT-Pts |
|---|---|---|---|
| Allen Iverson, Phi | vs Orl | 2/12/05 | 17-24—60 |
| LeBron James, Cle | at Tor | 3/20/05 | 18-14—56 |
| Jermaine O'Neal, Ind | vs Milw | 1/4/05 | 18-19—55 |
| Allen Iverson, Phi | at Milw | 12/18/04 | 17-16—54 |
| Damon Stoudamire, Port | at NO | 1/14/05 | 20- 6—54 |
| Dirk Nowitzki, Dal | vs Hou | 12/2/04 | 15-22—53 |
| Allen Iverson, Phi | vs Utah | 12/20/04 | 18-11—51 |
| Amare Stoudemire, Pho | vs Port | 1/2/05 | 20-10—50 |

Five players tied with 48-point games, including Allen Iverson, who did it twice.

### Personal Fouls

| | |
|---|---|
| Jason Collins, NJ | .322 |
| Zydrunas Ilgauskas, Cle | .313 |
| Kurt Thomas, NY | .310 |
| Yao Ming, Hou | .298 |
| Nenad Krstic*, NJ | .280 |
| Jerome James, Sea | .279 |
| Amare Stoudemire, Pho | .278 |
| Steve Francis, Orl | .273 |

### Triple Doubles

| | |
|---|---|
| Jason Kidd, NJ | .8 |
| Kobe Bryant, LAL | .5 |
| LeBron James, Cle | .4 |
| Chris Webber, Phi | .4 |
| Paul Pierce, Bos | .2 |
| Damon Stoudamire, Port | .2 |
| Seven players tied | .1 |

### Blocked Shots

| | Gm | Blk | Avg |
|---|---|---|---|
| Andrei Kirilenko, Utah | .41 | 136 | 3.32 |
| Marcus Camby, Den | .66 | 199 | 3.02 |
| Tim Duncan, SA | .66 | 174 | 2.64 |
| Theo Ratliff, Port | .63 | 158 | 2.51 |
| Ben Wallace, Det | .74 | 176 | 2.38 |
| Shaquille O'Neal, Mia | .73 | 171 | 2.34 |
| Joel Przybilla, Port | .76 | 163 | 2.14 |
| Zydrunas Ilgauskas, Cle | .78 | 165 | 2.12 |
| Elton Brand, LAC | .81 | 169 | 2.09 |

### Steals

| | Gm | Stl | Avg |
|---|---|---|---|
| Larry Hughes, Wash | .61 | 176 | 2.89 |
| Allen Iverson, Phi | .75 | 180 | 2.40 |
| LeBron James, Cle | .80 | 177 | 2.21 |
| Shawn Marion, Pho | .81 | 163 | 2.01 |
| Brevin Knight, Cha | .66 | 131 | 1.98 |
| Jason Kidd, NJ | .77 | 123 | 1.86 |
| Speedy Claxton, G.St.-NO | .62 | 109 | 1.76 |
| Gilbert Arenas, Wash | .80 | 139 | 1.74 |
| Tracy McGrady, Hou | .78 | 135 | 1.73 |
| Andre Iguodala, Phi | .82 | 138 | 1.68 |

### Rookie Leaders

**Scoring**

| | Gm | FG | FT | Pts | Avg |
|---|---|---|---|---|---|
| Emeka Okafor, Cha | .73 | 448 | 209 | 1105 | 15.1 |
| Ben Gordon, Chi | .82 | 434 | 233 | 1235 | 15.1 |
| Dwight Howard, Orl | .82 | 352 | 277 | 981 | 12.0 |
| Luol Deng, Chi | .61 | 280 | 120 | 711 | 11.7 |
| J.R. Smith, NO | .76 | 295 | 111 | 782 | 10.3 |

**Field Goal Pct.**

| | Gm | FG | Att | Pct |
|---|---|---|---|---|
| Nick Collison, Sea | .82 | 190 | 354 | .537 |
| Matt Bonner, Tor | .82 | 247 | 463 | .533 |
| Al Jefferson, Bos | .71 | 195 | 369 | .528 |
| Dwight Howard, Orl | .82 | 352 | 677 | .520 |
| Nenad Krstic, NJ | .75 | 281 | 570 | .493 |

**Rebounds**

| | Gm | Off | Def | Tot | Avg |
|---|---|---|---|---|---|
| Emeka Okafor, Cha | .73 | 275 | 520 | 795 | 10.9 |
| Dwight Howard, Orl | .82 | 287 | 536 | 823 | 10.0 |
| Josh Smith, Atl | .74 | 147 | 310 | 457 | 6.2 |
| Josh Childress, Atl | .80 | 195 | 287 | 482 | 6.0 |
| Andre Iguodala, Phi | .82 | 89 | 375 | 464 | 5.7 |

**Assists**

| | Gm | No | Avg |
|---|---|---|---|
| Chris Duhon, Chi | .82 | 398 | 4.9 |
| Sebastian Telfair, Port | .68 | 224 | 3.3 |
| Andre Iguodala, Phi | .82 | 246 | 3.0 |
| Jameer Nelson, Orl | .79 | 237 | 3.0 |
| Devin Harris, Dal | .76 | 169 | 2.2 |
| Luol Deng, Chi | .61 | 135 | 2.2 |

### Disqualifications

| | |
|---|---|
| Jason Collins, NJ | .14 |
| Danny Fortson, Sea | .12 |
| Kirk Hinrich, Chi | .9 |
| Richard Hamilton, Det | .8 |
| Yao Ming, Hou | .8 |
| Speedy Claxton, NO | .7 |
| Zydrunas Ilgauskas, Cle | .7 |
| Nenad Krstic, NJ | .7 |

### Minutes Played

| | |
|---|---|
| LeBron James, Cle | .3388 |
| Stephon Marbury, NY | .3281 |
| Gilbert Arenas, Wash | .3274 |
| Joe Johnson, Pho | .3240 |
| Tracy McGrady, Hou | .3182 |
| Allen Iverson, Phi | .3174 |
| Shawn Marion, Pho | .3146 |
| Kevin Garnett, Min | .3121 |

### Turnovers

| | |
|---|---|
| Allen Iverson, Phi | .344 |
| Dwyane Wade, Mia | .321 |
| Steve Francis, Orl | .317 |
| Kobe Bryant, LAL | .270 |
| LeBron James, Cle | .262 |
| Antoine Walker, Atl-Bos | .253 |
| Steve Nash, Pho | .245 |
| Gilbert Arenas, Wash | .242 |

### Technical Fouls

| | |
|---|---|
| Rasheed Wallace, Det | .27 |
| Danny Fortson, Sea | .23 |
| Steve Francis, Orl | .22 |
| Kenyon Martin, Den | .17 |
| Amare Stoudemire, Pho | .15 |
| Antoine Walker, Atl-Bos | .15 |
| Kelvin Cato, Orl | .15 |
| Three players tied | .14 |

# Team by Team Statistics

Players who competed for more than one team during the regular season are listed with their final club; (*) indicates rookies.

## Atlanta Hawks

| | Gm | FG% | Tpts | PPG | RPG | APG |
|---|---|---|---|---|---|---|
| Al Harrington | 66 | .459 | 1158 | 17.5 | 7.0 | 3.2 |
| Tony Delk | 56 | .416 | 667 | 11.9 | 2.3 | 1.9 |
| Tyronn Lue | 70 | .451 | 787 | 11.2 | 2.1 | 4.6 |
| Josh Childress* | 80 | .470 | 807 | 10.1 | 6.0 | 1.9 |
| Josh Smith* | 74 | .455 | 715 | 9.7 | 6.2 | 1.7 |
| Predrag Drobnjak | 71 | .438 | 597 | 8.4 | 3.4 | 0.7 |
| Jason Collier | 70 | .463 | 402 | 5.7 | 2.6 | 0.3 |
| Obinna Ekezie | 42 | .434 | 230 | 5.5 | 4.3 | 0.3 |
| Tom Gugliotta | 47 | .411 | 239 | 5.1 | 4.1 | 1.4 |
| Boris Diaw | 66 | .422 | 314 | 4.8 | 2.6 | 2.3 |
| Royal Ivey* | 62 | .429 | 220 | 3.5 | 1.4 | 1.7 |
| Donta Smith* | 38 | .389 | 127 | 3.3 | 1.4 | 1.0 |
| Kevin Willis | 29 | .389 | 87 | 3.0 | 2.6 | 0.3 |
| James Thomas | 11 | .600 | 26 | 2.4 | 3.4 | 0.4 |
| Michael Stewart | 12 | .524 | 25 | 2.1 | 3.3 | 0.4 |
| Anthony Miller | 2 | .667 | 4 | 2.0 | 0.5 | 0.5 |
| Jelani McCoy | 10 | .538 | 15 | 1.5 | 2.1 | 0.0 |

**Triple Doubles:** none. **3-pt FG leader:** Delk (72). **Steals leader:** Harrington (85). **Blocks leader:** Smith (144).
**Signed:** C/F McCoy (Nov. 8); C Ekezie (Jan. 10); F Thomas (Apr. 9). **Acquired:** G Lue from Houston for G Jon Barry (Dec. 23); F Gugliotta, F Stewart, G Gary Payton and a first round pick from Boston for F Antoine Walker (Feb. 24).

## Boston Celtics

| | Gm | FG% | Tpts | PPG | RPG | APG |
|---|---|---|---|---|---|---|
| Paul Pierce | 82 | .455 | 1769 | 21.6 | 6.6 | 4.2 |
| Antoine Walker | 77 | .422 | 1473 | 19.1 | 9.0 | 3.4 |
| Ricky Davis | 82 | .462 | 1309 | 16.0 | 3.0 | 3.0 |
| Gary Payton | 77 | .468 | 873 | 11.3 | 3.1 | 6.1 |
| Raef LaFrentz | 80 | .496 | 884 | 11.1 | 3.0 | 3.0 |
| Mark Blount | 82 | .468 | 771 | 9.4 | 4.8 | 1.6 |
| Al Jefferson* | 71 | .528 | 475 | 6.7 | 4.4 | 0.3 |
| Tony Allen* | 77 | .475 | 492 | 6.4 | 2.9 | 0.8 |
| Marcus Banks | 81 | .402 | 372 | 4.6 | 1.7 | 1.4 |
| Delonte West* | 39 | .426 | 175 | 4.5 | 1.7 | 1.4 |
| Kendrick Perkins | 60 | .471 | 149 | 2.5 | 2.9 | 0.4 |
| Justin Reed* | 23 | .517 | 41 | 1.8 | 0.7 | 0.4 |

**Triple Doubles:** Pierce (2). **3-pt FG leader:** Walker (110). **Steals leaders:** Pierce (133). **Blocks leader:** LaFrentz (99).
**Acquired:** F Walker from Atlanta for G Payton, F Tom Gugliotta, F Michael Stewart and a first round pick (Feb. 24). **Signed:** G Payton (Mar. 4).

## Charlotte Bobcats

| | Gm | FG% | Tpts | PPG | RPG | APG |
|---|---|---|---|---|---|---|
| Emeka Okafor | 73 | .447 | 1105 | 15.1 | 10.9 | 0.9 |
| Primoz Brezec | 72 | .512 | 938 | 13.0 | 7.4 | 1.2 |
| Gerald Wallace | 70 | .449 | 780 | 11.1 | 5.5 | 2.0 |
| Brevin Knight | 66 | .422 | 666 | 10.1 | 2.6 | 9.0 |
| Keith Bogans | 74 | .381 | 714 | 9.6 | 3.1 | 1.8 |
| Jason Hart | 74 | .449 | 706 | 9.5 | 2.7 | 5.0 |
| Matt Carroll | 25 | .389 | 224 | 9.0 | 2.4 | 0.7 |
| Jason Kapono | 81 | .401 | 688 | 8.5 | 2.0 | 0.8 |
| Kareem Rush | 48 | .387 | 402 | 8.4 | 1.9 | 1.4 |
| Melvin Ely | 79 | .432 | 576 | 7.3 | 4.1 | 1.0 |
| Malik Allen | 36 | .475 | 194 | 5.4 | 2.8 | 0.5 |
| Tamar Slay | 8 | .333 | 28 | 3.5 | 1.8 | 0.4 |
| Jamal Sampson | 23 | .452 | 79 | 3.4 | 5.3 | 0.3 |
| Theron Smith | 33 | .324 | 105 | 3.2 | 3.5 | 0.8 |
| Cory Alexander | 16 | .327 | 49 | 3.1 | 1.8 | 2.3 |
| Bernard Robinson* | 31 | .444 | 93 | 3.0 | 1.5 | 1.0 |
| Jahidi White | 17 | .432 | 42 | 2.5 | 2.0 | 0.1 |

**Triple Doubles:** none. **3-pt FG leader:** Kapono (80). **Steals leaders:** Knight (131). **Blocks leader:** Okafor (125).
**Signed:** G Carroll (Feb. 23); G Alexander (Feb. 28).
**Acquired:** G Rush from Lakers for two second round picks (Dec. 6). F Allen from Miami for G Steve Smith (Feb. 24).

## Chicago Bulls

| | Gm | FG% | Tpts | PPG | RPG | APG |
|---|---|---|---|---|---|---|
| Eddy Curry | 63 | .538 | 1235 | 16.1 | 5.4 | 0.6 |
| Kirk Hinrich | 77 | .398 | 1206 | 15.7 | 3.9 | 6.4 |
| Ben Gordon* | 82 | .411 | 1235 | 15.1 | 2.6 | 2.0 |
| Luol Deng* | 61 | .434 | 1012 | 11.7 | 5.3 | 2.2 |
| Andres Nocioni* | 81 | .401 | 677 | 8.4 | 4.8 | 1.5 |
| Tyson Chandler | 80 | .494 | 640 | 8.0 | 9.7 | 0.8 |
| Othella Harrington | 70 | .512 | 561 | 8.0 | 4.2 | 0.8 |
| Antonio Davis | 72 | .461 | 501 | 7.0 | 5.9 | 1.1 |
| Jannero Pargo | 32 | .385 | 204 | 6.4 | 1.5 | 2.4 |
| Chris Duhon* | 82 | .352 | 487 | 5.9 | 2.6 | 4.9 |
| Eric Piatkowski | 68 | .430 | 324 | 4.8 | 1.2 | 0.8 |
| Lawrence Funderburke | 2 | .500 | 9 | 4.5 | 1.5 | 0.0 |
| Adrian Griffin | 69 | .360 | 151 | 2.2 | 2.1 | 0.8 |
| Jared Reiner | 19 | .333 | 21 | 1.1 | 2.0 | 0.1 |
| Frank Williams | 9 | .150 | 6 | 0.7 | 0.7 | 1.2 |

**Triple Doubles:** none. **3-pt FG leader:** Hinrich (145). **Steals leader:** Hinrich (122). **Blocks leader:** Chandler (141).
**Signed:** F Funderburke (Apr. 18).

## Cleveland Cavaliers

| | Gm | FG% | Tpts | PPG | RPG | APG |
|---|---|---|---|---|---|---|
| LeBron James | 80 | .472 | 2175 | 27.2 | 7.4 | 7.2 |
| Zydrunas Ilgauskas | 78 | .468 | 1320 | 16.9 | 8.6 | 1.3 |
| Drew Gooden | 82 | .492 | 1184 | 14.4 | 9.2 | 1.6 |
| Jeff McInnis | 76 | .412 | 975 | 12.8 | 2.1 | 5.1 |
| Jiri Welsch | 71 | .402 | 461 | 6.5 | 2.4 | 1.5 |
| Ira Newble | 74 | .429 | 438 | 5.9 | 3.0 | 1.2 |
| Robert Traylor | 74 | .444 | 409 | 5.5 | 4.5 | 0.8 |
| Anderson Varejao* | 65 | .435 | 266 | 4.9 | 4.8 | 0.5 |
| Aleksandar Pavlovic | 65 | .435 | 314 | 4.8 | 1.1 | 0.8 |
| Lucious Harris | 73 | .395 | 313 | 4.3 | 1.7 | 0.7 |
| Eric Snow | 81 | .382 | 322 | 4.0 | 1.9 | 3.9 |
| Dajuan Wagner | 11 | .327 | 44 | 4.0 | 0.2 | 1.2 |
| Luke Jackson* | 10 | .370 | 29 | 2.9 | 0.6 | 0.3 |
| Scott Williams | 19 | .293 | 33 | 1.7 | 1.6 | 0.4 |
| Jerome Moiso | 20 | .500 | 28 | 1.4 | 1.9 | 0.1 |
| DeSagana Diop | 39 | .290 | 40 | 1.0 | 1.8 | 0.4 |

**Triple Doubles:** James (4). **3-pt FG leader:** James (108). **Steals leader:** James (177). **Blocks leader:** Ilgauskas (165).
**Signed:** F/C Moiso (Feb. 1). **Acquired:** G/F Welsch from Boston for a first round pick (Feb. 24).

## Dallas Mavericks

| | Gm | FG% | Tpts | PPG | RPG | APG |
|---|---|---|---|---|---|---|
| Dirk Nowitzki | 78 | .459 | 2032 | 26.1 | 9.7 | 3.1 |
| Michael Finley | 64 | .427 | 1003 | 15.7 | 4.1 | 2.6 |
| Jerry Stackhouse | 56 | .414 | 833 | 14.9 | 3.3 | 2.3 |
| Josh Howard | 76 | .475 | 958 | 12.6 | 6.4 | 1.4 |
| Jason Terry | 80 | .501 | 993 | 12.4 | 2.4 | 5.4 |
| Keith Van Horn | 62 | .456 | 696 | 11.2 | 4.7 | 1.2 |
| Erick Dampier | 59 | .550 | 542 | 9.2 | 8.5 | 0.9 |
| Marquis Daniels | 60 | .437 | 545 | 9.1 | 3.6 | 2.1 |
| Devin Harris* | 76 | .429 | 436 | 5.7 | 1.3 | 2.2 |
| Darrell Armstrong | 66 | .321 | 264 | 4.0 | 1.7 | 2.7 |
| Alan Henderson | 52 | .494 | 180 | 3.5 | 4.5 | 0.3 |
| Shawn Bradley | 77 | .452 | 211 | 2.7 | 2.8 | 0.2 |
| Didier Illunga-Mbenga | 15 | .429 | 15 | 1.0 | 0.5 | 0.0 |
| Pavel Podkolzin | 5 | .000 | 1 | 0.2 | 0.4 | 0.0 |

**Triple Doubles:** none. **3-pt FG leader:** Finley (116). **Steals leader:** Howard (116). **Blocks leader:** Nowitzki (119).
**Signed:** F Henderson (Mar. 1). **Acquired:** G Armstrong from New Orleans for G Dan Dickau and a second round pick (Dec. 3); F Van Horn from Milwaukee for C Calvin Booth and F Alan Henderson (Feb. 24).

## Denver Nuggets

| | Gm | FG% | Tpts | PPG | RPG | APG |
|---|---|---|---|---|---|---|
| Carmelo Anthony | .75 | .431 | 1558 | 20.8 | 5.7 | 2.6 |
| Kenyon Martin | .70 | .490 | 1087 | 15.5 | 7.3 | 2.4 |
| Andre Miller | .82 | .477 | 1113 | 13.6 | 4.1 | 6.9 |
| Earl Boykins | .82 | .413 | 1015 | 12.4 | 1.7 | 4.5 |
| Marcus Camby | .66 | .465 | 683 | 10.3 | 10.0 | 2.3 |
| Voshon Lenard | .3 | .385 | 29 | 9.7 | 2.0 | 2.0 |
| Nene | .55 | .503 | 528 | 9.6 | 5.9 | 1.5 |
| DerMarr Johnson | .71 | .499 | 503 | 7.1 | 2.1 | 1.1 |
| Wesley Person | .41 | .473 | 264 | 6.4 | 2.0 | 1.0 |
| Greg Buckner | .70 | .528 | 432 | 6.2 | 3.0 | 1.9 |
| Eduardo Najera | .68 | .450 | 354 | 5.2 | 3.6 | 1.0 |
| Byron Russell | .70 | .307 | 307 | 4.4 | 2.5 | 1.0 |
| Francisco Elson | .67 | .468 | 248 | 3.7 | 3.0 | 0.5 |
| Luis Flores* | .16 | .483 | 35 | 2.2 | 0.2 | 0.7 |
| Mark Pope | .9 | .333 | 4 | 0.4 | 0.9 | 0.1 |

**Triple Doubles:** none. **3-pt FG leader:** Boykins and Russell (56). **Steals leader:** Miller (121). **Blocks leader:** Camby (199).
**Acquired:** F Najera, G Flores and a first round pick from Golden State for F Rodney White and F Nikoloz Tskitishvili (Feb. 24).
**Signed:** C/F Pope (Feb. 15); G Person (Mar. 3).

## Detroit Pistons

| | Gm | FG% | Tpts | PPG | RPG | APG |
|---|---|---|---|---|---|---|
| Richard Hamilton | .76 | .440 | 1424 | 18.7 | 3.9 | 4.9 |
| Chauncey Billups | .80 | .442 | 1316 | 16.5 | 3.4 | 5.8 |
| Tayshaun Prince | .82 | .487 | 1206 | 14.7 | 5.3 | 3.0 |
| Rasheed Wallace | .79 | .440 | 1145 | 14.5 | 8.2 | 1.8 |
| Ben Wallace | .74 | .453 | 721 | 9.7 | 12.2 | 1.7 |
| Antonio McDyess | .77 | .513 | 740 | 9.6 | 6.3 | 0.9 |
| Carlos Arroyo | .70 | .389 | 461 | 6.6 | 1.5 | 4.0 |
| Carlos Delfino | .30 | .359 | 116 | 3.9 | 1.8 | 1.3 |
| Lindsey Hunter | .76 | .358 | 285 | 3.8 | 1.6 | 1.7 |
| Ronald Dupree | .47 | .481 | 152 | 3.2 | 2.0 | 0.5 |
| Elden Campbell | .40 | .317 | 120 | 3.0 | 2.3 | 0.5 |
| Horace Jenkins | .15 | .333 | 42 | 2.8 | 0.6 | 0.6 |
| Darko Milicic | .37 | .329 | 67 | 1.8 | 1.2 | 0.2 |
| Derrick Coleman | .5 | .214 | 9 | 1.8 | 3.0 | 0.0 |
| Darvin Ham | .47 | .459 | 46 | 1.0 | 0.7 | 0.1 |

**Triple Doubles:** none. **3-pt FG leader:** Billups (165). **Steals leader:** Wallace (106). **Blocks leader:** Wallace (176).
**Acquired:** G Arroyo from Utah for C Campbell and a first round pick. (Jan. 21).
**Signed:** C Campbell (Mar. 4).

## Golden St. Warriors

| | Gm | FG% | Tpts | PPG | RPG | APG |
|---|---|---|---|---|---|---|
| Jason Richardson | .72 | .446 | 1559 | 21.7 | 5.9 | 3.9 |
| Baron Davis | .46 | .387 | 885 | 19.2 | 3.8 | 7.9 |
| Troy Murphy | .70 | .414 | 1076 | 15.4 | 10.8 | 1.4 |
| Mike Dunleavy | .79 | .451 | 1057 | 13.4 | 5.5 | 2.6 |
| Derek Fisher | .74 | .393 | 877 | 11.9 | 2.9 | 4.1 |
| Mickael Pietrus | .67 | .427 | 636 | 9.5 | 2.8 | 1.2 |
| Zarko Cabarkapa | .40 | .486 | 238 | 6.0 | 2.6 | 0.6 |
| Rodney White | .58 | .419 | 293 | 5.1 | 1.5 | 0.8 |
| Adonal Foyle | .78 | .502 | 352 | 4.5 | 5.5 | 0.7 |
| Calbert Cheaney | .55 | .426 | 250 | 4.5 | 2.3 | 1.2 |
| Andris Biedrins* | .30 | .577 | 109 | 3.6 | 3.9 | 0.4 |
| Ansu Sesay | .16 | .405 | 49 | 3.1 | 2.4 | 0.8 |
| Nikoloz Tskitishvili | .35 | .297 | 50 | 1.4 | 1.2 | 0.3 |

**Triple Doubles:** Davis (1). **3-pt FG leader:** Richardson (125). **Steals leader:** Richardson (105). **Blocks leader:** Foyle (159).
**Acquired:** F/C Cabarkapa from Phoenix for two second round picks (Jan. 3). G Davis from New Orleans for G Speedy Claxton and C Dale Davis (Feb. 24). F White and F Tskitishvili from Denver for F Eduardo Najera, G Luis Flores and a first round pick. (Feb. 24).

## Houston Rockets

| | Gm | FG% | Tpts | PPG | RPG | APG |
|---|---|---|---|---|---|---|
| Tracy McGrady | .78 | .431 | 2003 | 25.7 | 6.2 | 5.7 |
| Yao Ming | .80 | .552 | 1465 | 18.3 | 8.4 | 0.8 |
| David Wesley | .80 | .398 | 948 | 11.9 | 2.9 | 3.3 |
| Mike James | .74 | .441 | 871 | 11.8 | 2.8 | 3.6 |
| Bob Sura | .61 | .427 | 626 | 10.3 | 5.5 | 5.2 |
| Juwan Howard | .61 | .451 | 585 | 9.6 | 5.7 | 1.5 |
| Jon Barry | .69 | .438 | 455 | 6.6 | 2.3 | 2.4 |
| Charlie Ward | .14 | .312 | 75 | 5.4 | 2.8 | 3.1 |
| Scott Padgett | .66 | .421 | 275 | 4.2 | 2.8 | 0.8 |
| Dikembe Mutombo | .80 | .498 | 322 | 4.0 | 5.3 | 0.1 |
| C. Weatherspoon | .40 | .412 | 123 | 3.1 | 3.1 | 0.4 |
| Rod Strickland | .16 | .209 | 28 | 1.8 | 1.7 | 2.4 |
| Ryan Bowen | .46 | .423 | 111 | 1.7 | 1.2 | 0.3 |
| Moochie Norris | .38 | .321 | 90 | 2.4 | 1.2 | 1.0 |
| Vin Baker | .27 | .310 | 35 | 1.3 | 1.4 | 0.4 |
| Torraye Braggs | .7 | .429 | 6 | 0.9 | 1.7 | 0.0 |
| Brandin Knight | .1 | 1.000 | 0 | 0.0 | 0.0 | 1.0 |

**Triple Doubles:** none. **3-pt FG leader:** McGrady (142).
**Steals leader:** McGrady (135). **Blocks leader:** Ming (160).
**Acquired:** G Barry from Atl. for G Tyronn Lue (Dec. 23). G Wesley from N. Orleans for F Jim Jackson, F Bostjan Nachbar (Dec. 28). G James and F Zendon Hamilton from Milw. for G Reece Gaines and two second round picks (Feb. 24). F Baker, G Norris and 2nd round pick from N.Y. for F Maurice Taylor (Feb. 24). **Signed:** G Knight (Jan. 16); G Strickland (Jan. 19).

## Indiana Pacers

| | Gm | FG% | Tpts | PPG | RPG | APG |
|---|---|---|---|---|---|---|
| Ron Artest | .7 | .496 | 172 | 24.6 | 6.4 | 3.1 |
| Jermaine O'Neal | .44 | .452 | 1068 | 24.3 | 8.8 | 1.9 |
| Stephen Jackson | .51 | .403 | 953 | 18.7 | 4.9 | 2.3 |
| Jamaal Tinsley | .40 | .418 | 616 | 15.4 | 4.0 | 6.4 |
| Reggie Miller | .66 | .437 | 974 | 14.8 | 2.4 | 2.2 |
| Fred Jones | .77 | .425 | 813 | 10.6 | 3.1 | 2.5 |
| Austin Croshere | .73 | .378 | 647 | 8.9 | 5.1 | 1.3 |
| Anthony Johnson | .63 | .445 | 532 | 8.4 | 2.8 | 4.8 |
| Jeff Foster | .61 | .519 | 426 | 7.0 | 9.0 | 0.7 |
| David Harrison* | .43 | .576 | 264 | 6.1 | 3.1 | 0.3 |
| Jonathan Bender | .7 | .400 | 36 | 5.1 | 2.0 | 0.6 |
| James Jones | .75 | .396 | 371 | 4.9 | 2.3 | 0.8 |
| Dale Davis | .61 | .479 | 284 | 4.7 | 6.1 | 0.8 |
| Scot Pollard | .49 | .473 | 191 | 3.9 | 4.2 | 0.4 |
| Eddie Gill | .73 | .335 | 269 | 3.7 | 1.5 | 1.1 |
| Marcus Haislip | .9 | .342 | 32 | 3.6 | 1.7 | 0.3 |
| Tremaine Fowlkes | .8 | .529 | 19 | 2.4 | 1.0 | 0.0 |
| Britton Johnsen | .6 | .273 | 12 | 2.0 | 1.7 | 0.7 |
| Michael Curry | .18 | .448 | 30 | 1.7 | 1.5 | 0.8 |
| John Edwards | .25 | .367 | 29 | 1.2 | 0.8 | 0.1 |

**Triple Doubles:** none. **3-pt FG leader:** Jackson (103). **Steals leader:** Tinsley (81). **Blocks leader:** O'Neal (88). **Signed:** Haislip (Dec. 1); Curry (Dec. 13); C Davis (Mar. 4).

## Los Angeles Clippers

| | Gm | FG% | Tpts | PPG | RPG | APG |
|---|---|---|---|---|---|---|
| Corey Maggette | .66 | .431 | 1464 | 22.2 | 6.0 | 3.4 |
| Elton Brand | .81 | .503 | 1622 | 20.0 | 9.5 | 2.6 |
| Bobby Simmons | .75 | .466 | 1229 | 16.4 | 5.9 | 2.7 |
| Marko Jaric | .50 | .414 | 493 | 9.9 | 3.2 | 6.1 |
| Chris Kaman | .63 | .497 | 572 | 9.1 | 6.7 | 1.2 |
| Chris Wilcox | .54 | .514 | 426 | 7.9 | 4.2 | 0.7 |
| Shaun Livingston* | .30 | .414 | 222 | 7.4 | 3.0 | 5.0 |
| Kerry Kittles | .11 | .384 | 69 | 6.3 | 2.9 | 1.8 |
| Zeljko Rebraca | .58 | .568 | 339 | 5.8 | 3.2 | 0.4 |
| Rick Brunson | .80 | .376 | 437 | 5.5 | 2.3 | 5.1 |
| Mikki Moore | .74 | .502 | 396 | 5.4 | 3.3 | 0.6 |
| Quinton Ross | .78 | .432 | 397 | 5.1 | 2.7 | 1.4 |
| Kenny Anderson | .43 | .423 | 203 | 4.7 | 2.0 | 2.4 |
| Darrick Martin | .11 | .320 | 42 | 3.8 | 0.9 | 2.5 |
| Lionel Chalmers* | .36 | .336 | 111 | 3.1 | 1.0 | 1.4 |
| Mamdou N'diaye | .11 | .400 | 20 | 1.8 | 1.6 | 0.1 |
| Kirk Penney | .4 | .333 | 2 | 0.5 | 0.3 | 0.3 |

**Triple Doubles:** none. **3-pt FG leader:** Jaric (56). **Steals leader:** Simmons (106). **Blocks leader:** Brand (169). **Claimed:** G Anderson off waivers (Feb. 28). **Signed:** G Penney (Dec. 26).

## Los Angeles Lakers

| | Gm | FG% | Tpts | PPG | RPG | APG |
|---|---|---|---|---|---|---|
| Kobe Bryant | .66 | .433 | 1819 | 27.6 | 5.9 | 6.0 |
| Caron Butler | .77 | .445 | 1195 | 15.5 | 5.8 | 1.9 |
| Lamar Odom | .64 | .473 | 975 | 15.2 | 10.2 | 3.7 |
| Chucky Atkins | .82 | .426 | 1115 | 13.6 | 2.4 | 4.4 |
| Chris Mihm | .75 | .507 | 735 | 9.8 | 6.7 | 0.7 |
| Jumaine Jones | .76 | .432 | 577 | 7.6 | 5.2 | 0.9 |
| Devean George | .15 | .356 | 110 | 7.3 | 3.5 | 0.9 |
| Brian Cook | .72 | .417 | 458 | 6.4 | 3.0 | 0.5 |
| Tierre Brown | .76 | .356 | 333 | 4.4 | 1.2 | 2.0 |
| Brian Grant | .69 | .493 | 263 | 3.8 | 3.7 | 0.5 |
| Slava Medvedenko | .43 | .455 | 165 | 3.8 | 1.8 | 0.3 |
| Luke Walton | .61 | .411 | 198 | 3.2 | 2.3 | 1.5 |
| Sasha Vujacic* | .35 | .282 | 101 | 2.9 | 1.8 | 1.5 |
| Tony Bobbitt* | .2 | .400 | 5 | 2.5 | 1.5 | 0.0 |
| Vlade Divac | .15 | .419 | 34 | 2.3 | 2.1 | 1.3 |

**Triple Doubles:** Bryant (5). **3-pt FG leader:** Atkins (176).
**Steals leader:** Butler (110). **Blocks leader:** Mihm (108).
**Signed:** G Bobbit (Dec. 6)

## Memphis Grizzlies

| | Gm | FG% | Tpts | PPG | RPG | APG |
|---|---|---|---|---|---|---|
| Pau Gasol | .56 | .514 | 997 | 17.8 | 7.3 | 2.4 |
| Mike Miller | .76 | .505 | 1022 | 13.4 | 3.9 | 2.9 |
| Bonzi Wells | .69 | .441 | 721 | 10.4 | 3.3 | 1.2 |
| Stromile Swift | .60 | .449 | 604 | 10.1 | 4.6 | 0.7 |
| Jason Williams | .71 | .413 | 719 | 10.1 | 1.7 | 5.6 |
| Shane Battier | .80 | .442 | 792 | 9.9 | 5.2 | 1.6 |
| Lorenzen Wright | .80 | .469 | 771 | 9.6 | 7.7 | 1.1 |
| Brian Cardinal | .58 | .370 | 522 | 9.0 | 3.9 | 2.0 |
| James Posey | .50 | .357 | 405 | 8.1 | 4.4 | 1.8 |
| Earl Watson | .80 | .426 | 615 | 7.7 | 2.1 | 4.5 |
| Dahntay Jones | .52 | .437 | 233 | 4.5 | 1.3 | 0.4 |
| Antonio Burks | .24 | .467 | 73 | 3.0 | 0.5 | 1.2 |
| Ryan Humphrey | .35 | .408 | 102 | 2.9 | 2.5 | 0.2 |
| Jake Tsakalidis | .31 | .500 | 78 | 2.5 | 1.8 | 0.3 |
| Andre Emmett | .8 | .447 | 7 | 0.9 | 0.3 | 0.0 |

**Triple Doubles:** none. **3-pt FG leader:** Miller (140).
**Steals leader:** Battier (91). **Blocks leader:** Gasol (93).

## Miami Heat

| | Gm | FG% | Tpts | PPG | RPG | APG |
|---|---|---|---|---|---|---|
| Dwyane Wade | .77 | .478 | 1854 | 24.1 | 5.2 | 6.8 |
| Shaquille O'Neal | .73 | .601 | 1669 | 22.9 | 10.4 | 2.7 |
| Eddie Jones | .80 | .428 | 1018 | 12.7 | 5.1 | 2.7 |
| Damon Jones | .82 | .456 | 955 | 11.6 | 2.8 | 4.3 |
| Udonis Haslem | .80 | .540 | 870 | 10.9 | 9.1 | 1.4 |
| Alonzo Mourning | .37 | .472 | 282 | 7.6 | 5.4 | 0.5 |
| Rasual Butler | .65 | .399 | 420 | 6.5 | 2.3 | 1.0 |
| Steve Smith | .50 | .411 | 314 | 6.3 | 1.3 | 1.4 |
| Christian Laettner | .49 | .582 | 260 | 5.3 | 2.7 | 0.8 |
| Keyon Dooling | .78 | .403 | 382 | 5.2 | 1.2 | 1.8 |
| Michael Doleac | .80 | .447 | 321 | 4.0 | 3.2 | 0.6 |
| Shandon Anderson | .66 | .452 | 255 | 3.9 | 2.9 | 1.1 |
| Qyntel Woods | .3 | .273 | 10 | 3.3 | 2.0 | 0.0 |
| Dorell Wright* | .3 | .273 | 7 | 2.3 | 0.3 | 1.0 |
| Wang Zhizhi | .20 | .472 | 43 | 2.2 | 0.9 | 0.3 |

**Triple Doubles:** Wade (1). **3-pt FG leader:** D. Jones (225).

**Steals leader:** Wade (121). **Blocks leader:** O'Neal (171).

**Signed:** G/F Anderson (Nov. 14); F Woods (Jan. 26); M Mourning (Mar. 1).
**Acquired:** G Smith from Charlotte for F Malik Allen (Feb. 24).

## Milwaukee Bucks

| | Gm | FG% | Tpts | PPG | RPG | APG |
|---|---|---|---|---|---|---|
| Michael Redd | .75 | .441 | 1723 | 23.0 | 4.2 | 2.3 |
| Desmond Mason | .80 | .443 | 1377 | 17.2 | 3.9 | 2.7 |
| Joe Smith | .74 | .514 | 813 | 11.0 | 7.3 | 0.9 |
| Maurice Williams | .80 | .438 | 814 | 10.2 | 3.1 | 6.1 |
| Dan Gadzuric | .81 | .539 | 593 | 7.3 | 8.3 | 0.4 |
| Marcus Fizer | .54 | .455 | 336 | 6.2 | 3.2 | 1.2 |
| Zaza Pachulia | .74 | .452 | 458 | 6.2 | 5.1 | 0.8 |
| Kendall Gill | .14 | .400 | 85 | 6.1 | 2.6 | 1.9 |
| Toni Kukoc | .53 | .410 | 296 | 5.6 | 3.0 | 3.0 |
| Anthony Goldwire | .33 | .419 | 172 | 5.2 | 1.8 | 2.4 |
| Erick Strickland | .62 | .375 | 301 | 4.9 | 1.7 | 1.9 |
| Calvin Booth | .51 | .454 | 124 | 2.4 | 2.1 | 0.2 |
| Daniel Santiago | .11 | .333 | 22 | 2.0 | 1.7 | 0.1 |
| Reece Gaines | .21 | .340 | 41 | 2.0 | 0.7 | 0.3 |

**Triple Doubles:** none. **3-pt FG leader:** Redd (104).
**Steals leader:** Williams (74). **Blocks leader:** Gadzuric (106).
**Signed:** G Gill (Dec. 6); G Goldwire (Mar. 7).
**Acquired:** C Booth, F Alan Henderson and cash from Dallas for F Keith Van Horn (Feb. 24). G Gaines and two second round picks from Houston for G Mike James and F Zendon Hamilton (Feb. 24).

## Minnesota Timberwolves

| | Gm | FG% | Tpts | PPG | RPG | APG |
|---|---|---|---|---|---|---|
| Kevin Garnett | .82 | .502 | 1817 | 22.2 | 13.5 | 5.7 |
| Wally Szczerbiak | .81 | .506 | 1253 | 15.5 | 3.7 | 2.4 |
| Ndubi Ebi | .2 | .524 | 27 | 13.5 | 8.0 | 0.5 |
| Sam Cassell | .59 | .464 | 799 | 13.5 | 2.7 | 5.1 |
| Latrell Sprewell | .80 | .414 | 1021 | 12.8 | 3.2 | 2.2 |
| Troy Hudson | .79 | .401 | 691 | 8.7 | 1.3 | 3.6 |
| Eddie Griffin | .70 | .387 | 527 | 7.5 | 6.5 | 0.8 |
| Trenton Hassell | .82 | .474 | 541 | 6.6 | 2.7 | 1.6 |
| Michael Olowokandi | .62 | .456 | 368 | 5.9 | 5.2 | 0.5 |
| Fred Hoiberg | .76 | .489 | 437 | 5.8 | 2.4 | 1.1 |
| Anthony Carter | .66 | .407 | 181 | 2.7 | 1.0 | 2.4 |
| John Thomas | .44 | .488 | 111 | 2.5 | 2.2 | 0.4 |
| Mark Madsen | .41 | .515 | 88 | 2.1 | 3.1 | 0.4 |
| Ervin Johnson | .46 | .519 | 73 | 1.6 | 2.5 | 0.1 |

**Triple Doubles:** Garnett (1). **3-pt FG leader:** Hudson (89). **Steals leader:** Garnett (121). **Blocks leader:** Griffin (118).
**Signed:** F Thomas (Jan. 10).

## New Jersey Nets

| | Gm | FG% | Tpts | PPG | RPG | APG |
|---|---|---|---|---|---|---|
| Vince Carter | .77 | .452 | 1886 | 24.5 | 5.2 | 4.2 |
| Richard Jefferson | .33 | .422 | 733 | 22.2 | 7.3 | 4.0 |
| Jason Kidd | .66 | .398 | 951 | 14.4 | 7.4 | 8.3 |
| Nenad Krstic* | .75 | .493 | 747 | 10.0 | 5.3 | 1.0 |
| Ron Mercer | .18 | .411 | 137 | 7.6 | 2.2 | 1.1 |
| Clifford Robinson | .71 | .386 | 533 | 7.5 | 2.9 | 1.5 |
| Rodney Buford | .64 | .382 | 445 | 7.0 | 3.0 | 1.0 |
| Travis Best | .76 | .420 | 514 | 6.8 | 1.4 | 1.9 |
| Jason Collins | .80 | .412 | 511 | 6.4 | 6.1 | 1.3 |
| Brian Scalabrine | .54 | .398 | 339 | 6.3 | 4.5 | 1.6 |
| Jacque Vaughn | .71 | .449 | 373 | 5.3 | 1.5 | 1.9 |
| Zoran Planinic | .43 | .448 | 217 | 5.0 | 1.6 | 1.0 |
| Jabari Smith | .45 | .419 | 166 | 3.7 | 2.5 | 0.8 |
| Billy Thomas | .25 | .362 | 92 | 3.7 | 1.4 | 0.7 |
| Donnell Harvey | .3 | 1.000 | 8 | 2.7 | 2.3 | 0.3 |
| Kaniel Dickens | .11 | .429 | 13 | 1.2 | 0.8 | 0.1 |
| Awvee Storey | .9 | .300 | 8 | 0.9 | 0.6 | 0.1 |

**Triple Doubles:** Kidd (8). **3-pt FG leader:** Kidd (129).
**Steals leader:** Kidd (123). **Blocks leaders:** Collins (71).
**Acquired:** F Carter from Toronto for C Alonzo Mourning, F Aaron Williams, F Eric Williams and two first round picks (Dec. 17); F Robinson from Golden St. for two second round picks (Feb. 14). **Signed:** F Dickens (Dec. 8); G Thomas (Jan. 20); F Harvey (Feb. 1).

### New Orleans Hornets

| | Gm | FG% | Tpts | PPG | RPG | APG |
|---|---|---|---|---|---|---|
| Lee Nailon | .68 | .478 | 963 | 14.2 | 4.4 | 1.6 |
| Dan Dickau | .71 | .405 | 887 | 12.5 | 2.5 | 4.9 |
| Jamaal Magloire | .23 | .432 | 270 | 11.7 | 8.9 | 1.3 |
| Speedy Claxton | .62 | .421 | 712 | 11.5 | 3.0 | 6.0 |
| P.J. Brown | .82 | .446 | 886 | 10.8 | 9.0 | 2.2 |
| J.R. Smith* | .76 | .394 | 782 | 10.3 | 2.0 | 1.9 |
| Chris Andersen | .67 | .534 | 513 | 7.7 | 6.1 | 1.1 |
| Bostjan Nachbar | .71 | .392 | 494 | 7.0 | 2.6 | 1.0 |
| Casey Jacobsen | .84 | .404 | 547 | 6.5 | 2.0 | 1.3 |
| David West | .30 | .436 | 186 | 6.2 | 4.3 | 0.8 |
| Junior Harrington | .29 | .360 | 163 | 5.6 | 2.2 | 2.1 |
| Alex Garcia | .8 | .346 | 44 | 5.5 | 1.9 | 2.3 |
| Jackson Vroman* | .46 | .412 | 212 | 4.6 | 3.8 | 0.9 |
| Matt Freije | .23 | .291 | 93 | 4.0 | 2.7 | 0.9 |
| George Lynch | .44 | .360 | 164 | 3.7 | 4.0 | 2.0 |
| Maciej Lampe | .37 | .371 | 115 | 3.1 | 2.4 | 0.3 |
| Corsley Edwards | .10 | .323 | 27 | 2.7 | 2.5 | 0.3 |
| Lonny Baxter | .4 | .273 | 6 | 1.5 | 2.0 | 0.0 |

**Triple Doubles:** none. **3-pt FG leader:** Dickau (85). **Steals leader:** Claxton (109). **Blocks leader:** Andersen (100). **Signed:** F Baxter (Dec. 12); F Edwards (Jan. 5); G Harrington (Jan. 28). **Acquired:** G Dickau from Dallas for G Darrell Armstrong (Dec. 3); G Jim Jackson, F Nachbar from Houston for G David Wesley (Dec. 27); G/F Jacobsen, F/C Vroman and F/C Lampe from Phoenix for G Jim Jackson and a second round pick (Jan. 21); F Dale Davis and G Claxton from Golden State for G Baron Davis (Feb. 24).

### New York Knicks

| | Gm | FG% | Tpts | PPG | RPG | APG |
|---|---|---|---|---|---|---|
| Stephon Marbury | .82 | .462 | 1781 | 21.7 | 3.0 | 8.1 |
| Jamal Crawford | .70 | .398 | 1241 | 17.7 | 2.9 | 4.3 |
| Tim Thomas | .71 | .439 | 851 | 12.0 | 3.3 | 1.5 |
| Allan Houston | .20 | .415 | 237 | 11.9 | 1.2 | 2.1 |
| Kurt Thomas | .80 | .471 | 916 | 11.5 | 10.4 | 2.0 |
| Michael Sweetney | .77 | .531 | 650 | 8.4 | 5.4 | 0.6 |
| Anfernee Hardaway | .37 | .423 | 269 | 7.3 | 2.4 | 2.0 |
| Maurice Taylor | .65 | .455 | 472 | 7.3 | 4.0 | 1.0 |
| Malik Rose | .76 | .449 | 534 | 7.0 | 4.5 | 0.8 |
| Trevor Ariza* | .80 | .442 | 468 | 5.9 | 3.0 | 1.1 |
| Jerome Williams | .79 | .502 | 359 | 4.5 | 3.6 | 0.5 |
| Jackie Butler | .3 | 1.000 | 10 | 3.3 | 0.0 | 0.0 |
| Jermaine Jackson | .21 | .515 | 42 | 2.0 | 1.1 | 1.1 |
| Jamison Brewer | .18 | .297 | 31 | 1.7 | 1.2 | 0.7 |
| Bruno Sundov | .21 | .297 | 25 | 1.2 | 0.6 | 0.1 |

**Triple Doubles:** none. **3-pt FG leader:** Crawford (185). **Steals leader:** Marbury (122) **Blocks leader:** K.Thomas (79). **Acquired:** F Rose and two first round picks from San Antonio for F/C Nazr Mohammed and G Jamison Brewer (Feb. 24); F Taylor from Houston for G Moochie Norris, F Vin Baker and a second round pick (Feb. 24). **Signed:** C Butler (Feb. 27); G Jackson (Jan. 28).

### Orlando Magic

| | Gm | FG% | Tpts | PPG | RPG | APG |
|---|---|---|---|---|---|---|
| Steve Francis | .78 | .423 | 1663 | 21.3 | 5.8 | 7.0 |
| Grant Hill | .67 | .509 | 1317 | 19.7 | 4.7 | 3.3 |
| Hedo Turkoglu | .67 | .419 | 937 | 14.0 | 3.5 | 2.3 |
| Dwight Howard | .82 | .520 | 981 | 12.0 | 10.0 | 0.9 |
| Jameer Nelson* | .79 | .455 | 689 | 8.7 | 2.4 | 3.3 |
| Kelvin Cato | .62 | .539 | 432 | 7.0 | 6.7 | 0.6 |
| Doug Christie | .52 | .392 | 345 | 6.6 | 3.4 | 3.8 |
| Tony Battie | .81 | .460 | 394 | 4.9 | 5.6 | 0.5 |
| Pat Garrity | .71 | .402 | 324 | 4.6 | 1.7 | 0.4 |
| Stacey Augmon | .55 | .407 | 193 | 3.5 | 1.8 | 0.7 |
| Andre Barrett | .38 | .363 | 118 | 3.1 | 1.1 | 1.8 |
| Brandon Hunter | .31 | .507 | 95 | 3.1 | 2.2 | 0.1 |
| Mario Kasun | .45 | .480 | 118 | 2.6 | 2.8 | 0.2 |
| Mark Jones | .10 | .290 | 23 | 2.3 | 1.3 | 0.6 |
| Andrew DeClercq | .8 | .444 | 9 | 1.1 | 1.3 | 0.0 |

**Triple Doubles:** none. **3-pt FG leader:** Turkoglu (93). **Steals leader:** Francis (112). **Blocks leader:** Howard (136). **Acquired:** G Christie from Sacramento for G Cuttino Mobley and F Michael Bradley (Jan. 10). **Signed:** G Jones (Mar. 23); G Barrett (Mar. 31).

### Philadelphia 76ers

| | Gm | FG% | Tpts | PPG | RPG | APG |
|---|---|---|---|---|---|---|
| Allen Iverson | .75 | .424 | 2302 | 30.7 | 4.0 | 7.9 |
| Chris Webber | .67 | .433 | 1306 | 19.5 | 9.1 | 4.7 |
| Marc Jackson | .81 | .465 | 969 | 12.0 | 5.0 | 1.0 |
| Kyle Korver | .82 | .418 | 942 | 11.5 | 4.6 | 2.2 |
| Andre Iguodala* | .82 | .493 | 741 | 9.0 | 5.7 | 3.0 |
| Samuel Dalembert | .72 | .524 | 589 | 8.2 | 7.5 | 0.5 |
| Willie Green | .57 | .366 | 437 | 7.7 | 2.3 | 1.8 |
| Rodney Rogers | .58 | .382 | 444 | 7.7 | 4.2 | 1.5 |
| John Salmons | .58 | .405 | 236 | 4.1 | 2.1 | 2.0 |
| Josh Davis | .42 | .378 | 117 | 2.8 | 1.9 | 0.3 |
| Aaron McKie | .68 | .430 | 152 | 2.2 | 2.5 | 1.5 |
| Michael Bradley | .18 | .625 | 33 | 1.8 | 1.6 | 0.3 |
| Kedrick Brown | .8 | .333 | 12 | 1.5 | 1.4 | 0.5 |
| Kevin Ollie | .26 | .355 | 28 | 1.1 | 0.7 | 0.7 |

**Triple Doubles:** Webber (4) and Iguodala (1). **3-pt FG leader:** Korver (226). **Steals leader:** Iverson (180). **Blocks leader:** Dalembert (121). **Acquired:** F Webber, F Bradley and F Matt Barnes from Sacramento for F Kenny Thomas, F Corliss Williamson and F/C Brian Skinner. (Feb. 23); F Rogers and F Jamal Mashburn from New Orleans from F Glenn Robinson. (Feb. 24).

### Phoenix Suns

| | Gm | FG% | Tpts | PPG | RPG | APG |
|---|---|---|---|---|---|---|
| Amare Stoudemire | .80 | .559 | 2080 | 26.0 | 8.9 | 1.6 |
| Shawn Marion | .81 | .476 | 1569 | 19.4 | 11.3 | 1.9 |
| Joe Johnson | .82 | .461 | 1400 | 17.1 | 5.1 | 3.5 |
| Steve Nash | .75 | .502 | 1165 | 15.5 | 3.3 | 11.5 |
| Quentin Richardson | .79 | .389 | 1176 | 14.9 | 6.1 | 2.0 |
| Jim Jackson | .64 | .426 | 672 | 10.5 | 4.2 | 2.9 |
| Leandro Barbosa | .63 | .475 | 442 | 7.0 | 2.1 | 2.0 |
| Steven Hunter | .76 | .614 | 348 | 4.6 | 3.0 | 0.2 |
| Walter McCarty | .72 | .404 | 260 | 3.6 | 1.9 | 0.5 |
| Smush Parker | .16 | .419 | 48 | 3.0 | 0.8 | 0.9 |
| Jake Voskuhl | .38 | .458 | 80 | 2.1 | 2.4 | 0.4 |
| Yuta Tabuse | .4 | .167 | 7 | 1.8 | 1.0 | 0.8 |
| Paul Shirley | .9 | .455 | 12 | 1.3 | 0.2 | 0.3 |
| Bo Outlaw | .39 | .353 | 29 | 0.7 | 1.4 | 0.3 |

**Triple Doubles:** Nash (1). **3-pt FG leader:** Richardson (226). **Steals leader:** Marion (163). **Blocks leader:** Stoudemire (130). **Signed:** G Parker (Jan. 19); F Shirley (Jan. 23). **Acquired:** G Jackson and a second round pick from New Orleans for G/F Casey Jacbosen, F/C Jackson Vroman and F/C Maciej Lampe (Jan. 21); F McCarty from Boston for a second round pick (Feb. 8).

### Portland Trail Blazers

| | Gm | FG% | Tpts | PPG | RPG | APG |
|---|---|---|---|---|---|---|
| Zach Randolph | .46 | .448 | 871 | 18.9 | 9.6 | 1.9 |
| Shareef Abdur-Rahim | .54 | .503 | 909 | 16.8 | 7.3 | 2.1 |
| Damon Stoudamire | .81 | .392 | 1277 | 15.8 | 3.8 | 5.7 |
| Darius Miles | .63 | .482 | 809 | 12.8 | 4.7 | 2.0 |
| Ruben Patterson | .70 | .531 | 809 | 11.6 | 3.9 | 2.0 |
| Nick Van Exel | .53 | .381 | 586 | 11.1 | 3.0 | 4.3 |
| Derek Anderson | .47 | .389 | 432 | 9.2 | 2.7 | 3.0 |
| Sebastian Telfair* | .68 | .393 | 460 | 6.8 | 1.5 | 3.3 |
| Joel Przybilla | .76 | .598 | 488 | 6.4 | 7.7 | 1.0 |
| Travis Outlaw | .59 | .498 | 319 | 5.4 | 2.1 | 0.6 |
| Theo Ratliff | .63 | .447 | 304 | 4.8 | 5.3 | 0.5 |
| Viktor Khryapa | .32 | .435 | 135 | 4.2 | 3.4 | 0.8 |
| Richie Frahm | .43 | .400 | 164 | 3.8 | 1.4 | 0.7 |
| Ha Seung-Jin* | .19 | .435 | 26 | 1.4 | 0.9 | 0.1 |
| Geno Carlisle | .6 | .667 | 8 | 1.3 | 0.2 | 0.2 |
| Maurice Baker | .5 | .000 | 0 | 0.0 | 0.4 | 0.2 |

**Triple Doubles:** Stoudamire (2). **3-pt FG leader:** Stoudamire (181). **Steals leader:** Patterson (106). **Blocks leader:** Przybilla (158). **Signed:** C Seung-jin (Dec. 27).

## Sacramento Kings

| | Gm | FG% | Tpts | PPG | RPG | APG |
|---|---|---|---|---|---|---|
| Peja Stojakovic | 66 | .444 | 1329 | 20.1 | 4.3 | 2.1 |
| Mike Bibby | 80 | .443 | 1571 | 19.6 | 4.2 | 6.8 |
| Cuttino Mobley | 66 | .438 | 1134 | 17.2 | 3.5 | 2.8 |
| Brad Miller | 56 | .524 | 876 | 15.6 | 9.3 | 3.9 |
| Kenny Thomas | 73 | .470 | 908 | 12.4 | 7.3 | 2.1 |
| Bobby Jackson | 25 | .427 | 301 | 12.0 | 3.4 | 2.4 |
| Corliss Williamson | 72 | .467 | 741 | 10.3 | 3.6 | 1.1 |
| Darius Songaila | 81 | .527 | 608 | 7.5 | 4.2 | 1.4 |
| Brian Skinner | 49 | .507 | 233 | 4.8 | 5.7 | 0.9 |
| Maurice Evans | 65 | .442 | 416 | 6.4 | 3.1 | 0.7 |
| Eddie House | 68 | .451 | 397 | 5.8 | 1.2 | 1.4 |
| Kevin Martin* | 45 | .385 | 131 | 2.9 | 1.3 | 0.5 |
| Greg Ostertag | 56 | .440 | 87 | 1.6 | 3.0 | 0.7 |
| Erik Daniels | 21 | .333 | 13 | 0.6 | 0.9 | 0.2 |

**Triple Doubles:** Bibby (1). **3-pt FG leader:** Stojakovic (174). **Steals leader:** Bibby (124). **Blocks leader:** Miller (68).
**Acquired:** G Mobley and F Michael Bradley from Orlando for G Doug Christie (Jan. 10); F Thomas, F Williamson and F/C Skinner from Philadelphia for F Chris Webber, F Michael Bradley and F Matt Barnes (Feb. 23).

## San Antonio Spurs

| | Gm | FG% | Tpts | PPG | RPG | APG |
|---|---|---|---|---|---|---|
| Tim Duncan | 66 | .496 | 1342 | 20.3 | 11.1 | 2.7 |
| Tony Parker | 80 | .482 | 1331 | 16.6 | 3.7 | 6.1 |
| Manu Ginobili | 74 | .471 | 1186 | 16.0 | 4.4 | 3.9 |
| Glenn Robinson | 9 | .442 | 90 | 10.0 | 2.7 | 0.9 |
| Nazr Mohammed | 77 | .480 | 731 | 9.5 | 7.6 | 0.4 |
| Bruce Bowen | 82 | .420 | 675 | 8.2 | 3.5 | 1.5 |
| Brent Barry | 81 | .423 | 601 | 7.4 | 2.3 | 2.2 |
| Devin Brown | 67 | .423 | 494 | 7.4 | 2.6 | 1.4 |
| Robery Horry | 75 | .419 | 451 | 6.0 | 3.6 | 1.1 |
| Beno Udrih* | 80 | .444 | 471 | 5.9 | 1.0 | 1.9 |
| Rasho Nesterovic | 70 | .460 | 410 | 5.9 | 6.6 | 1.0 |
| Dion Glover | 7 | .364 | 25 | 3.6 | 1.6 | 0.6 |
| Sean Marks | 23 | .338 | 76 | 3.3 | 2.4 | 0.3 |
| Tony Massenburg | 61 | .407 | 196 | 3.2 | 2.7 | 0.2 |
| Mike Wilks | 48 | .416 | 81 | 1.7 | 0.5 | 0.7 |
| Linton Johnson III | 2 | .000 | 0 | 0.0 | 1.5 | 0.0 |

**Triple Doubles:** none. **3-pt FG leader:** Bowen (102). **Steals leader:** Ginobili (119). **Blocks leader:** Duncan (174).
**Acquired:** F/C Mohammed and G Jamison Brewer from New York for F Malik Rose and two first round picks (Feb. 24).
**Signed:** G Glover (Mar. 17); F Robinson (Apr. 4).

## Seattle Supersonics

| | Gm | FG% | Tpts | PPG | RPG | APG |
|---|---|---|---|---|---|---|
| Ray Allen | 78 | .428 | 1867 | 23.9 | 4.4 | 3.7 |
| Rashard Lewis | 71 | .462 | 1457 | 20.5 | 5.5 | 1.3 |
| Vladimir Radmanovic | 63 | .409 | 741 | 11.8 | 4.6 | 1.4 |
| Antonio Daniels | 75 | .438 | 843 | 11.2 | 2.3 | 4.1 |
| Luke Ridnour | 82 | .405 | 824 | 10.0 | 2.5 | 5.9 |
| Danny Fortson | 62 | .522 | 463 | 7.5 | 5.6 | 0.1 |
| Ronald Murray | 49 | .361 | 345 | 7.0 | 2.0 | 1.3 |
| Damien Wilkins | 29 | .435 | 163 | 6.3 | 2.3 | 0.9 |
| Nick Collison* | 82 | .537 | 463 | 5.6 | 4.6 | 0.4 |
| Reggie Evans | 79 | .476 | 387 | 4.9 | 9.3 | 0.7 |
| Jerome James | 80 | .509 | 395 | 4.9 | 3.0 | 0.2 |
| Vitaly Potapenko | 33 | .517 | 117 | 3.5 | 2.4 | 0.3 |
| Robert Swift* | 16 | .455 | 15 | 0.9 | 0.3 | 0.1 |
| Mateen Cleaves | 14 | .357 | 13 | 0.9 | 0.4 | 0.5 |
| Ibrahim Kutluay | 5 | .000 | 0 | 0.0 | 0.2 | 0.0 |

**Triple Doubles:** none. **3-pt FG leader:** Allen (209). **Steals leader:** Ridnour (94). **Blocks leader:** James (111).

## Toronto Raptors

| | Gm | FG% | Tpts | PPG | RPG | APG |
|---|---|---|---|---|---|---|
| Jalen Rose | 81 | .455 | 1495 | 18.5 | 3.4 | 2.6 |
| Chris Bosh | 81 | .471 | 1361 | 16.8 | 8.9 | 1.9 |
| Rafer Alston | 80 | .414 | 1136 | 14.2 | 3.5 | 6.4 |
| Morris Peterson | 82 | .420 | 1029 | 12.5 | 4.1 | 2.1 |
| Donyell Marshall | 65 | .443 | 747 | 11.5 | 6.6 | 1.2 |
| Eric Williams | 55 | .430 | 424 | 7.7 | 3.1 | 1.7 |
| Matt Bonner | 82 | .533 | 589 | 7.2 | 3.5 | 0.6 |
| Lamond Murray | 62 | .426 | 371 | 6.0 | 2.6 | 0.8 |
| Milt Palacio | 80 | .446 | 467 | 5.8 | 1.7 | 3.5 |
| Omar Cook | 5 | .417 | 23 | 4.6 | 1.4 | 4.4 |
| Loren Woods | 45 | .433 | 176 | 3.9 | 4.9 | 0.4 |
| Rafael Araujo* | 59 | .434 | 196 | 3.3 | 3.1 | 0.3 |
| Pape Sow* | 27 | .397 | 62 | 2.3 | 2.1 | 0.1 |
| Aaron Williams | 42 | .460 | 73 | 1.7 | 1.4 | 0.2 |

**Triple Doubles:** none. **3-pt FG leader:** Marshall (151). **Steals leader:** Alston (118). **Blocks leader:** Bosh (113).
**Acquired:** C Alonzo Mourning, F A. Williams, F E. Williams and two first round picks from New Jersey for F Vince Carter.
**Signed:** G Cook (Apr. 9).

## Utah Jazz

| | Gm | FG% | Tpts | PPG | RPG | APG |
|---|---|---|---|---|---|---|
| Carlos Boozer | 51 | .521 | 909 | 17.8 | 9.0 | 2.8 |
| Andrei Kirilenko | 41 | .493 | 640 | 15.6 | 6.2 | 3.2 |
| Matt Harpring | 78 | .489 | 1090 | 14.0 | 6.2 | 1.8 |
| Mehmet Okur | 82 | .468 | 1054 | 12.9 | 7.5 | 2.0 |
| Raja Bell | 63 | .454 | 772 | 12.3 | 3.2 | 1.4 |
| Gordan Giricek | 81 | .448 | 715 | 8.8 | 2.2 | 1.7 |
| Keith McLeod | 53 | .350 | 416 | 7.8 | 2.1 | 4.5 |
| Howard Eisley | 74 | .398 | 415 | 5.6 | 1.2 | 3.4 |
| Raul Lopez | 31 | .422 | 200 | 5.2 | 1.3 | 4.0 |
| Kirk Snyder | 68 | .372 | 338 | 5.0 | 1.8 | 0.5 |
| Ben Handlogten | 21 | .518 | 95 | 4.5 | 3.1 | 0.6 |
| Jarron Collins | 50 | .414 | 213 | 4.3 | 3.3 | 1.2 |
| Kris Humphries* | 67 | .404 | 278 | 4.1 | 2.9 | 0.6 |
| Randy Livingston | 17 | .423 | 64 | 3.8 | 0.7 | 2.6 |
| Curtis Borchardt | 67 | .430 | 200 | 3.0 | 3.0 | 0.7 |
| Aleksandar Radojevic | 12 | .316 | 19 | 1.6 | 2.3 | 0.5 |

**Triple Doubles:** none. **3-pt FG leader:** Bell (54). **Steals leader:** Harpring (70). **Blocks leader:** Kirilenko (136).
**Signed:** G Livingston (Mar. 3); C Handlogten (Mar. 29).

## Washington Wizards

| | Gm | FG% | Tpts | PPG | RPG | APG |
|---|---|---|---|---|---|---|
| Gilbert Arenas | 80 | .431 | 2038 | 25.5 | 4.7 | 5.1 |
| Larry Hughes | 61 | .430 | 1345 | 22.0 | 6.3 | 4.7 |
| Antawn Jamison | 68 | .437 | 1334 | 19.6 | 7.6 | 2.3 |
| Jarvis Hayes | 54 | .389 | 553 | 10.2 | 4.2 | 1.7 |
| Brendan Haywood | 68 | .560 | 637 | 9.4 | 6.8 | 0.8 |
| Juan Dixon | 63 | .416 | 507 | 8.0 | 1.9 | 1.8 |
| Etan Thomas | 47 | .502 | 332 | 7.1 | 5.2 | 0.4 |
| Kwame Brown | 42 | .460 | 292 | 7.0 | 4.9 | 0.9 |
| Jared Jeffries | 77 | .468 | 523 | 6.8 | 4.9 | 2.0 |
| Steve Blake | 44 | .328 | 191 | 4.3 | 1.6 | 1.6 |
| Damone Brown | 14 | .371 | 54 | 3.9 | 2.0 | 1.0 |
| Anthony Peeler | 40 | .373 | 153 | 3.8 | 1.6 | 1.4 |
| Laron Profit | 42 | .438 | 136 | 3.2 | 1.8 | 0.9 |
| Peter Ramos* | 6 | .500 | 11 | 1.8 | 0.7 | 0.0 |
| Samaki Walker | 14 | .355 | 24 | 1.7 | 1.3 | 0.3 |
| Michael Ruffin | 79 | .414 | 111 | 1.4 | 4.2 | 0.8 |

**Triple Doubles:** Hughes (1). **3-pt FG leader:** Arenas (205). **Steals leader:** Hughes (176). **Blocks leader:** Haywood (114).
**Signed:** F D. Brown (Mar. 19).

# NBA Regular Season Team Leaders

## OFFENSE

### —Per Game—

| WEST | Pts | Reb | Ast | FG% | 3Pt% | FT% |
|---|---|---|---|---|---|---|
| Phoenix | 110.4 | 44.1 | 23.5 | .477 | .393 | .748 |
| Sacramento | 103.7 | 42.4 | 24.5 | .459 | .374 | .787 |
| Dallas | 102.5 | 42.9 | 19.6 | .457 | .364 | .789 |
| Denver | 99.5 | 42.0 | 23.9 | .459 | .340 | .763 |
| Seattle | 98.9 | 40.9 | 18.1 | .444 | .365 | .790 |
| LA Lakers | 98.7 | 43.2 | 20.4 | .437 | .355 | .777 |
| Golden St. | 98.7 | 42.7 | 22.1 | .430 | .352 | .722 |
| Minnesota | 96.8 | 43.0 | 23.4 | .459 | .345 | .796 |
| San Antonio | 96.2 | 42.4 | 21.6 | .453 | .363 | .724 |
| LA Clippers | 95.7 | 41.9 | 23.2 | .459 | .345 | .778 |
| Houston | 95.1 | 42.4 | 21.1 | .443 | .364 | .781 |
| Memphis | 93.4 | 39.0 | 20.9 | .447 | .357 | .754 |
| Utah | 93.0 | 40.1 | 22.3 | .449 | .328 | .757 |
| Portland | 92.9 | 41.1 | 21.0 | .451 | .362 | .725 |
| New Orleans | 88.4 | 40.2 | 21.0 | .415 | .315 | .766 |

### —Per Game—

| EAST | Pts | Reb | Ast | FG% | 3Pt% | FT% |
|---|---|---|---|---|---|---|
| Miami | 101.5 | 43.0 | 21.8 | .486 | .377 | .672 |
| Boston | 101.3 | 40.8 | 22.1 | .468 | .349 | .764 |
| Washington | 100.5 | 42.8 | 19.1 | .437 | 343 | .725 |
| Toronto | 99.7 | 40.1 | 20.4 | .444 | .385 | .774 |
| Orlando | 99.5 | 43.7 | 19.3 | .454 | .349 | .759 |
| Philadelphia | 99.1 | 42.0 | 20.9 | .437 | .348 | .789 |
| New York | 97.3 | 41.0 | 20.3 | .451 | .356 | .767 |
| Milwaukee | 97.2 | 43.1 | 21.0 | .450 | .351 | .772 |
| Cleveland | 96.5 | 42.3 | 22.6 | .447 | .332 | .752 |
| Chicago | 94.5 | 43.8 | 21.3 | .432 | .357 | .750 |
| Charlotte | 94.3 | 41.7 | 21.9 | .432 | .363 | .709 |
| Detroit | 93.3 | 43.4 | 21.8 | .444 | .345 | .739 |
| Indiana | 93.0 | 40.1 | 18.2 | .434 | .344 | .792 |
| Atlanta | 92.7 | 41.9 | 19.7 | .441 | .312 | .711 |
| New Jersey | 91.4 | 39.5 | 21.6 | .429 | .362 | .763 |

## DEFENSE

### —Per Game—

| WEST | Pts | Reb | Ast | FG% | 3Pt% | FT% |
|---|---|---|---|---|---|---|
| San Antonio | 88.4 | 40.2 | 16.9 | .426 | .367 | .768 |
| Houston | 91.0 | 40.7 | 20.7 | .423 | .338 | .742 |
| Memphis | 91.1 | 41.2 | 19.9 | .432 | .351 | .771 |
| Minnesota | 95.3 | 41.4 | 21.7 | .438 | .363 | .752 |
| New Orleans | 95.5 | 41.9 | 21.2 | .452 | .367 | .775 |
| LA Clippers | 96.5 | 39.5 | 21.1 | .444 | .368 | .762 |
| Seattle | 96.6 | 37.9 | 20.7 | .459 | .357 | .749 |
| Dallas | 96.8 | 43.2 | 20.9 | .438 | .338 | .754 |
| Portland | 96.9 | 42.2 | 23.5 | .447 | .343 | .755 |
| Utah | 97.3 | 37.7 | 19.4 | .458 | .375 | .764 |
| Denver | 97.5 | 41.7 | 21.7 | .447 | .345 | .746 |
| Golden State | 100.9 | 46.7 | 22.7 | .458 | .363 | .745 |
| Sacramento | 101.6 | 44.3 | 21.5 | .459 | .357 | .738 |
| LA Lakers | 101.7 | 42.4 | 24.4 | .453 | .361 | .780 |
| Phoenix | 103.3 | 46.1 | 21.2 | .445 | .335 | .744 |

### —Per Game—

| EAST | Pts | Reb | Ast | FG% | 3Pt% | FT% |
|---|---|---|---|---|---|---|
| New Jersey | 91.4 | 41.2 | 20.3 | .439 | .368 | .744 |
| Atlanta | 92.7 | 41.3 | 22.0 | .476 | .379 | .770 |
| Indiana | 93.0 | 41.3 | 18.8 | .440 | .365 | .743 |
| Detroit | 93.3 | 39.6 | 19.7 | .430 | .338 | .751 |
| Charlotte | 94.3 | 43.2 | 21.6 | .463 | .361 | .767 |
| Chicago | 94.5 | 42.7 | 20.9 | .422 | .334 | .744 |
| Cleveland | 96.5 | 39.8 | 21.2 | .452 | .376 | .750 |
| Milwaukee | 97.2 | 40.8 | 23.8 | .464 | .343 | .771 |
| New York | 97.3 | 41.7 | 20.7 | .465 | .364 | .756 |
| Philadelphia | 99.1 | 44.1 | 22.9 | .443 | .362 | .767 |
| Orlando | 99.7 | 42.1 | 21.3 | .451 | .343 | .754 |
| Toronto | 99.7 | 45.3 | 22.1 | .467 | .356 | .744 |
| Washington | 100.5 | 43.0 | 23.0 | .459 | .364 | .762 |
| Boston | 101.3 | 42.3 | 22.7 | .444 | .356 | .753 |
| Miami | 101.5 | 40.5 | 19.8 | .427 | .348 | .760 |

# Playoff Series Summaries

## WESTERN CONFERENCE

### FIRST ROUND (Best of 7)

#### (1) **Phoenix Suns** 4, (8) **Memphis Grizzlies** 0

| Date | Winner | Home Court |
|---|---|---|
| Apr. 24 | Suns, 114-103 | at Phoenix |
| Apr. 27 | Suns, 108-103 | at Phoenix |
| Apr. 29 | Suns, 110-90 | at Memphis |
| May 1 | Suns, 123-115 | at Memphis |

#### (2) **San Antonio Spurs** 4, (7) **Denver Nuggets** 1

| Date | Winner | Home Court |
|---|---|---|
| Apr. 24 | Nuggets, 93-87 | at San Antonio |
| Apr. 27 | Spurs, 104-76 | at San Antonio |
| Apr. 30 | Spurs, 86-78 | at Denver |
| May 2 | Spurs, 126-115 OT | at Denver |
| May 4 | Spurs, 99-89 | at San Antonio |

#### (3) **Seattle Supersonics** 4, (6) **Sacramento Kings** 1

| Date | Winner | Home Court |
|---|---|---|
| Apr. 23 | Supersonics 87-82 | at Seattle |
| Apr. 26 | Supersonics, 105-93 | at Seattle |
| Apr. 29 | Kings, 116-104 | at Sacramento |
| May 1 | Supersonics, 115-102 | at Sacramento |
| May 3 | Supersonics, 122-118 | at Seattle |

#### (4) **Dallas Mavericks** 4, (5) **Houston Rockets** 3

| Date | Winner | Home Court |
|---|---|---|
| Apr. 23 | Rockets, 98-86 | at Dallas |
| Apr. 25 | Rockets, 113-111 | at Dallas |
| Apr. 28 | Mavericks, 106-102 | at Houston |
| Apr. 30 | Mavericks, 97-93 | at Houston |
| May 2 | Mavericks, 103-100 | at Dallas |
| May 5 | Rockets, 101-83 | at Houston |
| May 7 | Mavericks, 116-76 | at Dallas |

### SEMIFINALS (Best of 7)

#### (1) **Phoenix Suns** 4, (4) **Dallas Mavericks** 2

| Date | Winner | Home Court |
|---|---|---|
| May 9 | Suns, 127-102 | at Phoenix |
| May 11 | Mavericks, 108-106 | at Phoenix |
| May 13 | Suns, 119-102 | at Dallas |
| May 15 | Mavericks, 119-109 | at Dallas |
| May 18 | Suns, 114-108 | at Phoenix |
| May 20 | Suns, 130-126 | at Dallas |

#### (2) **San Antonio Spurs** 4, (3) **Seattle Supersonics** 2

| Date | Winner | Home Court |
|---|---|---|
| May 8 | Spurs, 103-81 | at San Antonio |
| May 10 | Spurs, 108-91 | at San Antonio |
| May 12 | Supersonics, 92-91 | at Seattle |
| May 15 | Supersonics, 101-89 | at Seattle |
| May 17 | Spurs, 103-90 | at San Antonio |
| May 19 | Spurs, 98-96 | at Seattle |

### CHAMPIONSHIP (Best of 7)

#### (2) **San Antonio Spurs** 4, (1) **Phoenix Suns** 1

| Date | Winner | Home Court |
|---|---|---|
| May 22 | Spurs, 121-114 | at Phoenix |
| May 24 | Spurs, 111-108 | at Phoenix |
| May 28 | Spurs, 102-92 | at San Antonio |
| May 30 | Suns, 111-106 | at San Antonio |
| June 1 | Spurs, 101-95 | at Phoenix |

# 2005 NBA PLAYOFFS

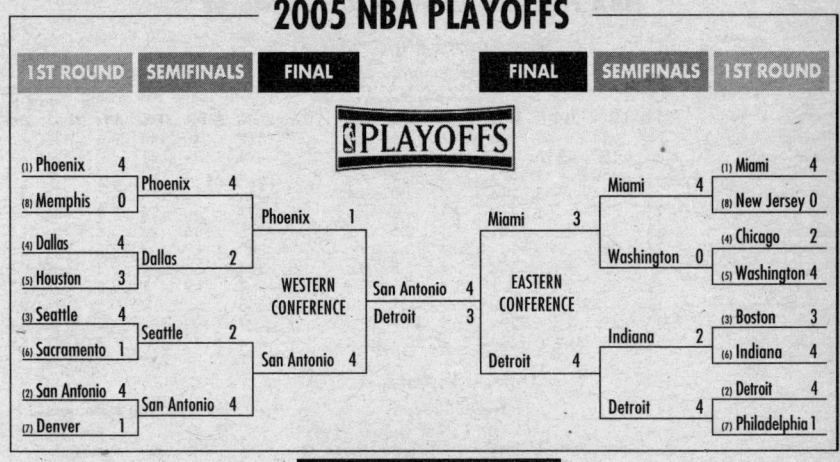

| 1ST ROUND | SEMIFINALS | FINAL | | FINAL | SEMIFINALS | 1ST ROUND |

**PLAYOFFS**

**(1) Phoenix 4**
**(8) Memphis 0**
Phoenix 4
**(4) Dallas 4**
**(5) Houston 3**
Dallas 2
Phoenix 1
**WESTERN CONFERENCE**
San Antonio 4
**(3) Seattle 4**
**(6) Sacramento 1**
Seattle 4
**(2) San Antonio 4**
**(7) Denver 1**
San Antonio 4
San Antonio 4

Miami 3
Detroit 3
Detroit 4

**EASTERN CONFERENCE**

Miami 3
**EASTERN CONFERENCE**
Detroit 4
Miami 4
Washington 0
Indiana 2
Detroit 4
**(1) Miami 4**
**(8) New Jersey 0**
**(4) Chicago 2**
**(5) Washington 4**
**(3) Boston 3**
**(6) Indiana 4**
**(2) Detroit 4**
**(7) Philadelphia 1**

## EASTERN CONFERENCE

### FIRST ROUND (Best of 7)

#### (1) Miami Heat 4, (8) New Jersey Nets 0

| Date | Winner | Home Court |
|---|---|---|
| Apr. 24 | Heat, 116-98 | at Miami |
| Apr. 26 | Heat, 104-87 | at Miami |
| Apr. 28 | Heat, 108-105 2OT | at New Jersey |
| May 1 | Heat, 110-97 | at New Jersey |

#### (6) Indiana Pacers 4, (3) Boston Celtics 3

| Date | Winner | Home Court |
|---|---|---|
| Apr. 23 | Celtics, 102-82 | at Boston |
| Apr. 25 | Pacers, 82-79 | at Boston |
| Apr. 28 | Pacers, 99-76 | at Indiana |
| Apr. 30 | Celtics, 110-79 | at Indiana |
| May 3 | Pacers, 90-85 | at Boston |
| May 5 | Celtics, 92-89 OT | at Indiana |
| May 7 | Pacers, 97-70 | at Boston |

#### (2) Detroit Pistons 4, (7) Philadelphia 76ers 1

| Date | Winner | Home Court |
|---|---|---|
| Apr. 23 | Pistons, 106-85 | at Detroit |
| Apr. 26 | Pistons, 99-84 | at Detroit |
| Apr. 29 | 76ers, 115-104 | at Philadelphia |
| May 1 | Pistons, 97-92 OT | at Philadelphia |
| May 3 | Pistons, 88-78 | at Detroit |

#### (5) Washington Wizards 4, (4) Chicago Bulls 2

| Date | Winner | Home Court |
|---|---|---|
| Apr. 24 | Bulls, 103-94 | at Chicago |
| Apr. 27 | Bulls, 113-103 | at Chicago |
| Apr. 30 | Wizards, 117-99 | at Washington |
| May 2 | Wizards, 106-99 | at Washington |
| May 4 | Wizards, 112-110 | at Chicago |
| May 6 | Wizards, 94-91 | at Washington |

### SEMIFINALS (Best of 7)

#### (1) Miami Heat 4, (5) Washington Wizards 0

| Date | Winner | Home Court |
|---|---|---|
| May 8 | Heat, 105-86 | at Miami |
| May 10 | Heat, 108-102 | at Miami |
| May 12 | Heat, 102-95 | at Washington |
| May 14 | Heat, 99-95 | at Washington |

#### (2) Detroit Pistons 4, (6) Indiana Pacers 2

| Date | Winner | Home Court |
|---|---|---|
| May 9 | Pistons, 96-81 | at Detroit |
| May 11 | Pacers, 92-83 | at Detroit |
| May 13 | Pacers, 79-74 | at Indiana |
| May 15 | Pistons, 89-76 | at Indiana |
| May 17 | Pistons, 86-67 | at Detroit |
| May 19 | Pistons, 88-79 | at Indiana |

### CHAMPIONSHIP (Best of 7)

#### (2) Detroit Pistons 4, (1) Miami Heat 3

| Date | Winner | Home Court |
|---|---|---|
| May 23 | Pistons, 90-81 | at Miami |
| May 25 | Heat, 92-86 | at Miami |
| May 29 | Heat, 113-104 | at Detroit |
| May 31 | Pistons, 106-96 | at Detroit |
| June 2 | Heat, 88-76 | at Miami |
| June 4 | Pistons, 91-66 | at Detroit |
| June 6 | Pistons, 88-82 | at Miami |

### NBA FINALS (Best of 7)

| | W-L | Avg. | Leading Scorer |
|---|---|---|---|
| San Antonio | 4-3 | 84.9 | Duncan (20.6) |
| Detroit | 3-4 | 86.7 | Billups (20.4) |

| Date | Winner | Home Court |
|---|---|---|
| June 9 | Spurs, 84-69 | at San Antonio |
| June 12 | Spurs, 97-76 | at San Antonio |
| June 14 | Pistons, 96-79 | at Detroit |
| June 16 | Pistons, 102-71 | at Detroit |
| June 19 | Spurs, 96-95 OT | at Detroit |
| June 21 | Pistons, 95-86 | at San Antonio |
| June 23 | Spurs, 81-74 | at San Antonio |

### Finals MVP
Tim Duncan, San Antonio, C
20.6 ppg, 14.1 rpg, 2.1 apg, 2.1 bpg

## NBA Finalists' Composite Box Scores

### San Antonio Spurs (16-7)

| | | Overall Playoffs | | | —Per Game— | | | | | Finals vs. Detroit | | | —Per Game— | | |
|---|---|---|---|---|---|---|---|---|---|---|---|---|---|---|---|
| | Gm | FG% | 3PT-A | TPts | Pts | Reb | Ast | | Gm | FG% | 3PT-A | TPts | Pts | Reb | Ast |
| Tim Duncan | .23 | .464 | 1-5 | 542 | 23.6 | 12.4 | 2.7 | | 7 | .419 | 0-0 | 144 | 20.6 | 14.1 | 2.1 |
| Manu Ginobili | .23 | .507 | 42-96 | 479 | 20.8 | 0.8 | 5.0 | | 7 | .494 | 12-31 | 131 | 18.7 | 5.9 | 4.0 |
| Tony Parker | .23 | .454 | 9-48 | 396 | 17.2 | 0.6 | 2.3 | | 7 | .458 | 2-14 | 97 | 13.9 | 2.4 | 3.4 |
| Robert Horry | .23 | .448 | 38-85 | 214 | 9.3 | 2.0 | 3.4 | | 7 | .444 | 15-31 | 74 | 10.6 | 4.9 | 2.1 |
| Nazr Mohammed | .23 | .528 | 1-1 | 163 | 7.1 | 3.3 | 3.4 | | 7 | .433 | 0-0 | 34 | 4.9 | 6.0 | 0.0 |
| Brent Barry | .23 | .457 | 28-66 | 141 | 6.1 | 0.6 | 1.9 | | 7 | .407 | 6-16 | 32 | 4.6 | 2.1 | 1.6 |
| Bruce Bowen | .23 | .359 | 29-67 | 132 | 5.7 | 0.4 | 2.5 | | 7 | .380 | 13-29 | 55 | 7.9 | 2.7 | 2.0 |
| Beno Udrih | .21 | .359 | 10-37 | 78 | 3.7 | 0.2 | 0.6 | | 5 | .364 | 2-4 | 12 | 2.4 | 1.0 | 0.8 |
| Devin Brown | .12 | .350 | 3-7 | 21 | 1.8 | 0.1 | 0.5 | | 6 | .364 | 1-2 | 11 | 1.8 | 1.0 | 0.5 |
| Rasho Nesterovic | .15 | .417 | 0-0 | 10 | 0.7 | 0.7 | 1.0 | | 4 | .500 | 0-0 | 2 | 0.5 | 2.0 | 0.3 |
| SPURS | .23 | .454 | 164-422 | 2229 | 96.9 | 42.1 | 18.4 | | 7 | .429 | 51-128 | 594 | 84.9 | 41.7 | 16.4 |
| OPPONENTS | .23 | .449 | 81-270 | 2129 | 92.6 | 39.3 | 16.4 | | 7 | .434 | 18-75 | 607 | 86.7 | 41.0 | 18.6 |

### Detroit Pistons (15-10)

| | | Overall Playoffs | | | Per Game | | | | | Finals vs. San Antonio | | | Per Game | | |
|---|---|---|---|---|---|---|---|---|---|---|---|---|---|---|---|
| | Gm | FG% | 3PT-A | TPts | Pts | Reb | Ast | | Gm | FG% | 3PT-A | TPts | Pts | Reb | Ast |
| Richard Hamilton | .25 | .453 | 10-34 | 501 | 20.0 | 4.3 | 4.3 | | 7 | .386 | 1-6 | 117 | 16.7 | 5.3 | 2.6 |
| Chauncey Billups | .25 | .428 | 44-126 | 467 | 18.7 | 4.3 | 6.5 | | 7 | .434 | 11-37 | 143 | 20.4 | 5.0 | 6.3 |
| Rasheed Wallace | .25 | .439 | 29-86 | 341 | 13.6 | 6.9 | 1.3 | | 7 | .438 | 5-17 | 76 | 10.9 | 5.6 | 1.9 |
| Tayshaun Prince | .25 | .433 | 22-60 | 336 | 13.4 | 6.3 | 3.3 | | 7 | .382 | 1-9 | 71 | 10.1 | 4.9 | 2.6 |
| Ben Wallace | .25 | .481 | 0-4 | 251 | 10.3 | 11.3 | 1.0 | | 7 | .569 | 0-0 | 75 | 10.7 | 10.3 | 1.0 |
| Antonio McDyess | .25 | .486 | 0-0 | 201 | 8.0 | 5.9 | 0.4 | | 7 | .508 | 0-0 | 71 | 10.1 | 7.3 | 1.0 |
| Lindsey Hunter | .25 | .319 | 8-36 | 96 | 3.8 | 1.6 | 1.6 | | 7 | .381 | 0-6 | 39 | 5.6 | 1.9 | 2.7 |
| Carlos Arroyo | .19 | .356 | 0-1 | 40 | 2.1 | 0.5 | 2.1 | | 5 | .500 | 0-0 | 11 | 2.2 | 0.2 | 0.6 |
| Darko Milicic | .9 | .286 | 0-0 | 5 | 0.6 | 0.4 | 0.1 | | 3 | .333 | 0-0 | 2 | 0.7 | 0.7 | 0.0 |
| Ronald Dupree | .14 | .286 | 0-0 | 4 | 0.3 | 0.4 | 0.0 | | 5 | .000 | 0-0 | 0 | 0.0 | 0.0 | 0.0 |
| PISTONS | .25 | .437 | 113-347 | 2258 | 90.3 | 42.3 | 20.5 | | 7 | .434 | 18-75 | 607 | 86.7 | 41.0 | 18.6 |
| OPPONENTS | .25 | .433 | 134-413 | 2140 | 85.6 | 39.2 | 17.2 | | 7 | .429 | 51-128 | 594 | 84.9 | 41.7 | 16.4 |

## NBA Playoff Leaders

### Scoring Average

| | Gm | FG | FT | Pts | Avg |
|---|---|---|---|---|---|
| Allen Iverson, Phi | .5 | 59 | 26 | 156 | 31.2 |
| Tracy McGrady, Hou | .7 | 78 | 42 | 215 | 30.7 |
| Amare Stoudamire, Pho | .15 | 153 | 143 | 449 | 29.9 |
| Dwyane Wade, Mia | .14 | 136 | 111 | 384 | 27.4 |
| Vince Carter, NJ | .4 | 35 | 31 | 107 | 26.8 |
| Ray Allen, Sea | .11 | 102 | 56 | 291 | 26.5 |
| Steve Nash, Pho | .15 | 140 | 57 | 358 | 23.9 |
| Dirk Nowitzki, Dal | .13 | 103 | 92 | 308 | 23.7 |
| Gilbert Arenas, Wash. | .10 | 73 | 72 | 236 | 23.6 |
| Tim Duncan, SA | .23 | 197 | 147 | 542 | 23.6 |

### Total Points

| | Gm | FG | FT | Pts | Avg |
|---|---|---|---|---|---|
| Tim Duncan, SA | .23 | 197 | 147 | **542** | 23.6 |
| Richard Hamilton, Det | .25 | 198 | 95 | 501 | 20.0 |
| Manu Ginobili, SA | .23 | 145 | 147 | 479 | 20.8 |
| Chauncey Billups, Det | .25 | 145 | 133 | 467 | 18.7 |
| Amare Stoudamire, Pho | .15 | 153 | 143 | 449 | 29.9 |

### Rebounds

| | Gm | Off | Def | Tot | Avg |
|---|---|---|---|---|---|
| Samuel Dalembert, Phi | .5 | 18 | 46 | 64 | 12.8 |
| Tim Duncan, SA | .23 | 87 | 199 | 286 | 12.4 |
| Shawn Marion, Pho | .15 | 46 | 131 | 177 | 11.8 |
| Ben Wallace, Det | .25 | 95 | 187 | 282 | 11.3 |
| Marcus Camby, Den | .5 | 4 | 52 | 56 | 11.2 |
| Amare Stoudamire, Pho | .15 | 60 | 100 | 160 | 10.7 |
| Dirk Nowitzki, Dal | .13 | 25 | 106 | 131 | 10.1 |

### Assists

| | Gm | No | Avg |
|---|---|---|---|
| Steve Nash, Pho | .15 | 170 | 11.3 |
| Allen Iverson, Phi | .5 | 50 | 10.0 |
| Jason Kidd, NJ | .4 | 29 | 7.3 |
| Tracy McGrady, Hou | .7 | 47 | 6.7 |
| Dwyane Wade, Mia | .14 | 93 | 6.6 |
| Mike Bibby, Sac | .5 | 33* | 6.6 |

### Final Playoff Standings

ranked by victories

| | Gm | W | L | Pct | Per Game For | Opp |
|---|---|---|---|---|---|---|
| San Antonio | .23 | 16 | 7 | .696 | 96.9 | 92.6 |
| Detroit | .25 | 15 | 10 | .600 | 90.3 | 85.6 |
| Miami | .15 | 11 | 4 | .733 | 98.0 | 93.7 |
| Phoenix | .15 | 9 | 6 | .600 | 112.0 | 107.8 |
| Seattle | .11 | 6 | 5 | .545 | 98.5 | 100.3 |
| Dallas | .13 | 6 | 7 | .462 | 105.2 | 106.8 |
| Indiana | .13 | 6 | 7 | .462 | 84.0 | 86.9 |
| Washington | .10 | 4 | 6 | .400 | 100.4 | 102.9 |
| Boston | .7 | 3 | 4 | .429 | 87.7 | 88.3 |
| Houston | .7 | 3 | 4 | .429 | 97.6 | 100.3 |
| Chicago | .6 | 2 | 4 | .333 | 102.5 | 104.3 |
| Sacramento | .5 | 1 | 4 | .200 | 102.2 | 106.6 |
| Denver | .5 | 1 | 4 | .200 | 90.2 | 100.4 |
| Philadelphia | .5 | 1 | 4 | .200 | 90.8 | 98.8 |
| New Jersey | .4 | 0 | 4 | .000 | 96.8 | 109.5 |
| Memphis | .4 | 0 | 4 | .000 | 102.8 | 113.8 |

# Annual Awards

## Most Valuable Player

The Maurice Podoloff Trophy; voting by 127-member panel of local and national pro basketball writers and broadcasters. Each ballot has five entries; points awarded on 10-7-5-3-1 basis.

|  | 1st | 2nd | 3rd | 4th | 5th | Pts |
|---|---|---|---|---|---|---|
| Steve Nash, Phoenix | 65 | 54 | 7 | 1 | 0 | 1066 |
| Shaquille O'Neal, Miami | 58 | 61 | 3 | 3 | 1 | 1032 |
| Dirk Nowitzki, Dallas | 0 | 4 | 43 | 30 | 16 | 349 |
| Tim Duncan, San Antonio | 1 | 0 | 40 | 33 | 19 | 328 |
| Allen Iverson, Philadelphia | 2 | 4 | 20 | 23 | 23 | 240 |
| LeBron James, Cleveland | 0 | 0 | 7 | 11 | 25 | 93 |
| Tracy McGrady, Houston | 0 | 1 | 1 | 8 | 8 | 44 |
| Dwyane Wade, Miami | 0 | 2 | 2 | 1 | 16 | 43 |
| Ray Allen, Seattle | 0 | 0 | 2 | 8 | 7 | 41 |
| Amare Stoudemire, Phoenix | 1 | 1 | 1 | 5 | 4 | 41 |
| Kevin Garnett, Minnesota | 0 | 0 | 1 | 2 | 4 | 15 |
| Vince Carter, New Jersey | 0 | 0 | 0 | 1 | 0 | 3 |
| Marcus Camby, Denver | 0 | 0 | 0 | 0 | 1 | 1 |
| P.J. Brown, New Orleans | 0 | 0 | 0 | 0 | 1 | 1 |
| Shawn Marion, Phoenix | 0 | 0 | 0 | 0 | 1 | 1 |

## All-NBA Teams

Voting by a 124-member panel of local and national pro basketball writers and broadcasters. Each ballot has entries for three teams; points awarded on 5-3-1 basis. First Team repeaters from 2003-04 are in **bold** type.

| Pos | First Team | 1st | Pts |
|---|---|---|---|
| F | **Tim Duncan**, San Antonio | 95 | 553 |
| F | Dirk Nowitzki, Dallas | 75 | 510 |
| C | **Shaquille O'Neal**, Miami | 122 | 616 |
| G | Allen Iverson, Philadelphia | 69 | 498 |
| G | Steve Nash, Phoenix | 118 | 606 |

| Pos | Second Team | 1st | Pts |
|---|---|---|---|
| F | LeBron James, Cleveland | 45 | 421 |
| F | Kevin Garnett, Minnesota | 34 | 408 |
| F | Amare Stoudemire, Phoenix | 9 | 367 |
| G | Dwyane Wade, Miami | 35 | 417 |
| G | Ray Allen, Seattle | 1 | 177 |

| Pos | Third Team | 1st | Pts |
|---|---|---|---|
| F | Tracy McGrady, Houston | 15 | 264 |
| F | Shawn Marion, Phoenix | 0 | 134 |
| C | Ben Wallace, Detroit | 0 | 105 |
| G | Kobe Bryant, LA Lakers | 1 | 108 |
| G | Gilbert Arenas, Washington | 1 | 104 |

**Other players receiving votes:** Yao Ming, Hou., 82; Vince Carter, NJ, 63; Jason Kidd, NJ, 16; Paul Pierce, Bos., 15; Marcus Camby, Den., 14; Rashard Lewis, Sea., 13; Manu Ginobili, SA, 12; Zydrunas Ilgauskas, Cle., 11; Jermaine O'Neal, Ind., 8; Tony Parker, SA, 7; Mike Bibby, Sac., 6; Elton Brand, LAC, 6; Grant Hill, Orl., 6; Carmelo Anthony, Den., 5; Antawn Jamison, Was., 5; Richard Hamilton, Det., 3; Tayshaun Prince, Det., 3; Chauncey Billups, Det., 2; Chris Bosh, Tor., 2; Stephon Marbury, NY, 2; Reggie Miller, Ind., 2; Michael Redd, Milw., 2; Larry Hughes, Wash., 1; Corey Maggette, LAC, 1; Kenyon Martin, Denv., 1; Brad Miller, Sac.; Peja Stojakovic, Sac., 1.

## Rookie of the Year

The Eddie Gottlieb Trophy; voting by 126-member panel of local and national pro basketball writers and broadcasters. Each ballot has entries for three players; points awarded on 5-3-1 basis.

|  | 1st | 2nd | 3rd | Pts |
|---|---|---|---|---|
| Emeka Okafor, Charlotte | 77 | 40 | 9 | 514 |
| Ben Gordon, Chicago | 43 | 73 | 9 | 443 |
| Dwight Howard, Orlando | 6 | 11 | 98 | 161 |
| Andre Iguodala, Philadelphia | 0 | 2 | 8 | 14 |
| Luol Deng, Chicago | 0 | 0 | 1 | 1 |
| J.R. Smith, New Orleans | 0 | 0 | 1 | 1 |

## All-Defensive Teams

Voting by NBA head coaches. Each ballot has entries for two teams; two points given for 1st team, one for 2nd. Coaches cannot vote for own players. First Team repeaters from 2003-04 are in **bold** type.

| Pos | First Team | 1st | Pts |
|---|---|---|---|
| F | Tim Duncan, San Antonio | 16 | 39 |
| F | **Kevin Garnett**, Minnesota | 19 | 48 |
| C | **Ben Wallace**, Detroit | 23 | 51 |
| G | **Bruce Bowen**, San Antonio | 23 | 48 |
| G | Larry Hughes, Washington | 9 | 22 |

| Pos | Second Team | 1st | Pts |
|---|---|---|---|
| F | Andrei Kirilenko, Utah | 5 | 17 |
| F | Tayshaun Prince, Detroit | 6 | 21 |
| C | Marcus Camby, Denver | 6 | 21 |
| G | Chauncey Billups, Detroit | 8 | 17 |
| G | Jason Kidd, New Jersey | 4 | 16 |
| G | Dwyane Wade, Miami | 6 | 16 |

## Coach of the Year

The Red Auerbach Trophy; voting by 126-member panel of local and national pro basketball writers and broadcasters.

|  | 1st | 2nd | 3rd | Pts |
|---|---|---|---|---|
| Mike D'Antoni, Phoenix | 41 | 34 | 19 | 326 |
| Rick Carlisle, Indiana | 26 | 29 | 24 | 241 |
| Nate McMillan, Seattle | 30 | 22 | 18 | 234 |
| Scott Skiles, Chicago | 18 | 24 | 37 | 199 |
| George Karl, Denver | 10 | 10 | 17 | 97 |
| Stan Van Gundy, Miami | 1 | 3 | 4 | 18 |
| Eddie Jordan, Washington | 0 | 3 | 5 | 14 |
| Gregg Popovich, San Antonio | 0 | 1 | 0 | 3 |
| Mike Fratello, Memphis | 0 | 0 | 2 | 2 |

## All-Rookie Team

Voting by NBA's 30 head coaches, who cannot vote for players on their team. Each ballot has entries for two five-man teams, regardless of position. Coaches are not permitted to vote for players on their own team. two points given for 1st team, one for 2nd. First team votes in parentheses.

| First Team | College | Pts |
|---|---|---|
| Dwight Howard, Orlando (29) | — | 58 |
| Emeka Okafor, Charlotte (29) | Connecticut | 58 |
| Ben Gordon, Chicago (29) | Connecticut | 58 |
| Andre Iguodala, Philadelphia (27) | Arizona | 56 |
| Luol Deng, Chicago (11) | Duke | 33 |

| Second Team | College | Pts |
|---|---|---|
| Nenad Krsitc, New Jersey (7) | — | 30 |
| Josh Smith, Atlanta (3) | — | 22 |
| Josh Childress, Atlanta (4) | Stanford | 21 |
| Jameer Nelson, Orlando (1) | St. Joseph's | 20 |
| Al Jefferson, Boston (2) | — | 17 |

# J. Walter Kennedy Citizenship Award

The award, named for the NBA's second commissioner, is presented annually by the Professional Basketball Writers Association to honor an NBA player or coach "for outstanding community service and commitment to serve and give of his time outside the arena." The five finalists this season were Snow, Adonal Foyle of the Golden State Warriors, Richard Hamilton of the Detroit Pistons and Shaquille O'Neal of the Miami Heat.

**Eric Snow, Cleveland**

## Sixth-Man Award

Voted on by a 125-member panel of local and national pro basketball writers and broadcasters. Each ballot has entries for three players; points awarded on 5-3-1 basis.

| | 1st | 2nd | 3rd | Pts |
|---|---|---|---|---|
| Ben Gordon, Chicago | .88 | 22 | 7 | 513 |
| Ricky Davis, Boston | .17 | 49 | 25 | 257 |
| Earl Boykins, Denver | .11 | 22 | 34 | 155 |
| Jerry Stackhouse, Dallas | .6 | 14 | 23 | 95 |
| Vladimir Radmanovic, Seattle | .2 | 8 | 7 | 41 |
| Wally Szczerbiak, Minnesota | .1 | 2 | 11 | 22 |
| Antonio McDyess, Detroit | .0 | 2 | 5 | 11 |
| Antonio Daniels, Seattle | .0 | 2 | 4 | 10 |
| Donyell Marshall, Toronto | .0 | 1 | 4 | 7 |
| Jim Jackson, Phoenix | .0 | 1 | 1 | 4 |

## Most Improved Player Award

Voted on by a 123-member panel of local and national pro basketball writers and broadcasters. Each ballot has entries for three players; points awarded on 5-3-1 basis.

| | 1st | 2nd | 3rd | Pts |
|---|---|---|---|---|
| Bobby Simmons, LA Clippers | .59 | 23 | 20 | 384 |
| Dwyane Wade, Miami | .15 | 16 | 6 | 129 |
| Tayshaun Prince, Detroit | .14 | 9 | 10 | 107 |
| Primoz Brezec, Charlotte | .5 | 10 | 20 | 75 |
| Dan Dickau, New Orleans | .5 | 9 | 16 | 68 |
| LeBron James, Cleveland | .4 | 10 | 7 | 57 |
| Amare Stoudemire, Phoenix | .5 | 6 | 3 | 46 |
| Joel Przybilla, Portland | .1 | 5 | 8 | 28 |
| Larry Hughes, Washington | 1. | 7 | 2 | 28 |
| Chris Bosh, Toronto | .1 | 2 | 7 | 21 |

## Defensive Player of the Year Award

Voted on by a 125-member panel of local and national pro basketball writers and broadcasters.

| | 1st | 2nd | 3rd | Pts |
|---|---|---|---|---|
| Ben Wallace, Detroit | .45 | 30 | 24 | 339 |
| Bruce Bowen, San Antonio | .33 | 22 | 16 | 247 |
| Marcus Camby, Denver | .19 | 19 | 16 | 168 |
| Tim Duncan, San Antonio | .6 | 13 | 12 | 81 |
| Shawn Marion, Phoenix | .5 | 7 | 11 | 57 |
| Larry Hughes, Washington | .3 | 9 | 11 | 53 |
| Tayshaun Prince, Detroit | .6 | 4 | 4 | 46 |
| Shaquille O'Neal, Miami | .3 | 5 | 2 | 32 |
| Kevin Garnett, Minnesota | .4 | 2 | 4 | 30 |
| Andrei Kirilenko, Utah | .1 | 5 | 5 | 25 |

## Sportsmanship Award

Each of the 30 NBA teams nominated one player from their roster "who best represents the ideals of sportsmanship on the court," then a panel made up of former NBA players Tommy Heinsohn, Eddie Johnson, Steve Mix, Kelly Tripucka and Stu Lantz selected the six divisional winners from the pool of nominees. The award winner is chosen from the divisional winners in vote by a panel of local and national pro basketball writers and broadcasters. The winner receives the Joe Dumars Trophy, named for the Detroit Pistons guard who won the inaugural sportsmanship award in 1996.

| | 1st | 2nd | 3rd | 4th | 5th | 6th | Pts |
|---|---|---|---|---|---|---|---|
| Grant Hill, Orl | 134 | 78 | 58 | 27 | 15 | 16 | 2778 |
| Steve Nash, Pho | 63 | 79 | 86 | 49 | 34 | 17 | 2370 |
| Shane Battier, Mem | 36 | 65 | 69 | 73 | 37 | 48 | 1988 |
| Andrei Kirilenko, Utah | 38 | 36 | 45 | 69 | 73 | 68 | 1689 |
| Jacque Vaughn, NJ | 33 | 47 | 41 | 58 | 87 | 61 | 1685 |
| Austin Croshere, Ind | 24 | 23 | 29 | 52 | 82 | 118 | 1298 |

## 2005 College Draft

First and second round picks at the 59th annual NBA Draft held June 28, 2005 held in New York City at the Theatre at Madison Square Garden. The order of the first 14 positions were determined by a Draft Lottery held May 24, in Secaucus, N.J. Positions 15 through 30 reflect regular season records in reverse order. College seniors selected are noted in CAPITAL letters.

### First Round

| | Team | | Pos |
|---|---|---|---|
| 1 | Milwaukee | Andrew Bogut, Utah | C |
| 2 | Atlanta | Marvin Williams, North Carolina | F |
| 3 | Utah | Deron Williams, Illinois | G |
| 4 | New Orleans | Chris Paul, Wake Forest | G |
| 5 | Charlotte | Raymond Felton, North Carolina | G |
| 6 | Portland | Martell Webster, Seattle Prep | G/F |
| 7 | Toronto | Charlie Villanueva, Connecticut | F |
| 8 | New York | CHANNING FRYE, Arizona | C |
| 9 | Golden State | Ike Diogu, Arizona St. | F |
| 10 | LA Lakers | Andrew Bynum, St. Joseph (NJ) HS | C |
| 11 | Orlando | Fran Vazquez, Spain | F/C |
| 12 | LA Clippers | Yaroslav Korolev, CSKA Moscow | F |
| 13 | Charlotte | Sean May, North Carolina | F |
| 14 | Minnesota | Rashad McCants, North Carolina | G |
| 15 | New Jersey | Antoine Wright, Texas A&M | G/F |
| 16 | Toronto | Joey Graham, Oklahoma St. | F |
| 17 | Indiana | Danny Granger, New Mexico | F |
| 18 | Boston | Gerald Green, Gulf Shores Acad. | F |
| 19 | Memphis | HAKIM WARRICK, Syracuse | F |
| 20 | Denver | JULIUS HODGE, N.C. State | G |
| 21 | Phoenix | Nate Robinson, Washington | G |
| 22 | Denver | Jarret Jack, Georgia Tech | G |
| 23 | Sacramento | Francisco Garcia, Louisville | G/F |
| 24 | Houston | LUTHER HEAD, Illinois | G |
| 25 | Seattle | Johan Petro, France | C |
| 26 | Detroit | JASON MAXWELL, Cincinnati | F |
| 27 | Portland | Linas Kleiza, Missouri | F |
| 28 | San Antonio | Ian Mahinmi, France | F |
| 29 | Miami | WAYNE SIMIEN, Kansas | F |
| 30 | New York | DAVID LEE, Florida | F |

### Second Round

| | Team | | Pos |
|---|---|---|---|
| 31 | Atlanta | SALIM STOUDAMIRE, Arizona | G |
| 32 | LA Clippers | DANIEL EWING, Duke | G |
| 33 | New Orleans | Brandon Bass, LSU | F |
| 34 | Utah | C.J. Miles, Skyline (TX) HS | G |
| 35 | Portland | Ricky Sanchez, IMG Academy | F |
| 36 | Milwaukee | Ersan Ilyasova, Turkey | F |
| 37 | LA Lakers | RONNY TURIAF, Gonzaga | F |
| 38 | Orlando | TRAVIS DIENER, Marquette | G |
| 39 | LA Lakers | Von Wafer, Florida St. | G |
| 40 | Golden St. | Monta Ellis, Lanier (MS) HS | G |
| 41 | Toronto | Roko Ujic, Croatia | G |
| 42 | Golden St. | Christ Taft, Pittsburgh | F |
| 43 | New Jersey | Mile Ilic, Serbia & Montenegro | C |
| 44 | Orlando | Martynas Andriuskevicius, Lithuania | C |
| 45 | Philadelphia | Louis Williams, S. Gwinnett (GA) HS | G |
| 46 | Indiana | Erazem Lorbek, Italy | F |
| 47 | Minnesota | Bracey Wright, Indiana | G |
| 48 | Seattle | Mickael Galebale, France | F |
| 49 | Washington | Andray Blatche, South Kent Prep | F |
| 50 | Boston | Ryan Gomes, Providence | F |
| 51 | Utah | Robert Whaley, Walsh U. | F |
| 52 | Denver | Axel Hervelle, Belgium | F |
| 53 | Boston | Orien Green, LA-Lafayete | G |
| 54 | New York | Dijon Thompson, UCLA | G/F |
| 55 | Seattle | Lawrence Roberts, Mississippi St. | F |
| 56 | Detroit | Amir Johnson, Westchester (CA) HS | F |
| 57 | Phoenix | Marcin Gortat, Poland | F/C |
| 58 | Toronto | Uros Slokar, Slovenia | F |
| 59 | Atlanta | Cenk Akyol, Turkey | G |
| 60 | Detroit | Alex Acker, Pepperdine | G |

## Continental Basketball Association
### Final Standings

QW refers to quarters won. Teams get 3 points for a win, 1 point for each quarter won and ½ point for any quarters tied. (*) denotes playoff qualifiers.

| Eastern | W | L | Home | Away | QW | Pts | Avg |
|---|---|---|---|---|---|---|---|
| *Great Lakes Storm | .28 | 20 | 17-7 | 11-13 | 105.5 | 189.5 | 3.9 |
| *Rockford Lightning | .26 | 22 | 18-6 | 8-16 | 100.5 | 178.5 | 3.7 |
| Michgan Mayhem | .18 | 30 | 12-12 | 6-18 | 81.5 | 135.5 | 2.8 |
| Gary Steelheads | .17 | 31 | 13-11 | 4-20 | 84.5 | 135.5 | 2.8 |

| Western | W | L | Home | Away | QW | Pts | Avg |
|---|---|---|---|---|---|---|---|
| *Dakota Wizards | .32 | 16 | 18-16 | 14-10 | 101.5 | 197.5 | 4.1 |
| *Sioux Falls Skyforce | .31 | 17 | 19-5 | 12-12 | 101.0 | 194.0 | 4.0 |
| Idaho Stampede | .23 | 25 | 16-8 | 7-14 | 99.0 | 168.0 | 3.5 |
| Yakima Sun Kings | .17 | 31 | 10-14 | 7-17 | 94.5 | 145.5 | 3.0 |

## Playoffs

### Semifinals
(best of five)

#### EASTERN CONFERENCE
**Rockford vs. Great Lakes**

Mar. 15 at Great Lakes 130 . . OT . . . . . Rockford 127
Mar. 17 at Great Lakes 121 . . . . . . . . . . Rockford 112
Mar. 19 at Rockford 137 . . . . . . . . . Great Lakes 122
Mar. 20 at Rockford 115 . . OT . . .Great Lakes 114
Mar. 22 Rockford 105 . . . . . . . . .at Great Lakes 104
Rockford wins series, 3 games to 2

#### WESTERN CONFERENCE
**Dakota vs. Sioux Falls**

Mar. 16 at Dakota 132 . . . . . . . . . .Sioux Falls 116
Mar. 18 Sioux Falls 107 . . . . . . . . . .at Dakota 105
Mar. 20 at Sioux Falls 133 . . . . . . . . . .Dakota 129
Mar. 22 Dakota 121 . . . . . . . . . .at Sioux Falls 118
Mar. 24 Sioux Falls 102 . . . . . . . . . .at Dakota 97
Sioux Falls wins series, 3 games to 2

### CBA Finals
(best of five)

**Rockford vs. Sioux Falls**

Mar. 28 at Sioux Falls 119 . . . . . . . . . .Rockford 112
Mar. 29 at Sioux Falls 150 . . . . . . . . . .Rockford 132
Mar. 31 at Rockford 116 . . . . . . . . . .Sioux Falls 107
Apr. 2 Sioux Falls 135 . . . . . . . . . .at Rockford 126
Sioux Falls wins series, 3 games to 1

**Playoff MVP:** Corsley Edwards, Sioux Falls
(21.1 ppg, 12.4 rpg)

### CBA Annual Awards

**Most Valuable Player** . . . . . . .Sam Clancy, Idaho
**Newcomer of the Year** . . . . .Billy Thomas, Dakota
**Rookie of the Year** . . . .Jackie Butler, Great Lakes
**Def. Player of the Year** . . . . .Sam Clancy, Idaho
**Coach of the Year** . . . .Russ Bergman, Great Lakes

## CBA Regular Season Individual Leaders

### Scoring

| | Gm | Pts | Avg |
|---|---|---|---|
| Sam Mack, Michigan | .31 | 682 | 22.0 |
| Ezra Williams, Great Lakes | .28 | 586 | 20.9 |
| Billy Thomas, Dakota | .24 | 500 | 20.8 |
| Mark Jones, Great Lakes | .41 | 852 | 20.8 |
| David Graves, Gary | .48 | 945 | 19.7 |
| Marshall Phillips, Rockford | .40 | 776 | 19.4 |
| Stais Boseman, Rockford | .45 | 861 | 19.1 |
| Sam Clancy, Idaho | .48 | 918 | 19.1 |

### Rebounding

| | Gm | Reb | Avg |
|---|---|---|---|
| Charles Gaines, Michigan | .44 | 502 | 11.4 |
| Sam Clancy, Idaho | .48 | 520 | 10.8 |
| Jackie Butler, Great Lakes | .41 | 439 | 10.7 |
| Derek Hood, Yakima | .31 | 308 | 9.9 |
| Lonnie Jones, Gary | .30 | 260 | 8.7 |
| Carlos Daniel, Yakima | .40 | 310 | 7.8 |
| Daniel Watts, Gary | .25 | 188 | 7.5 |
| Noel Felix, Yakima | .30 | 222 | 7.4 |

### Field Goal Pct.

| | FGM | FGA | Pct |
|---|---|---|---|
| Lawrence Nelson, Gary | .91 | 150 | .607 |
| Sidney Holmes, Rockford | .61 | 102 | .598 |
| Charles Gaines, Michigan | .296 | 511 | .579 |
| Lonnie Jones, Gary | .154 | 266 | .579 |
| Patrick Okafor, Idaho | .145 | 255 | .569 |
| Brant Bailey, Rockford | .191 | 346 | .552 |
| Darrin Hancock, Gary | .157 | 285 | .551 |
| Shawn Daniels, Dakota | .193 | 352 | .548 |

### Assists

| | Gm | Ast | Avg |
|---|---|---|---|
| Jemeil Rich, Gary | .42 | 409 | 9.7 |
| Randy Livingston, Sioux Falls | .40 | 336 | 8.4 |
| Taliek Brown, Idaho | .42 | 304 | 7.2 |
| Darrick Martin, Michigan | .30 | 214 | 7.1 |
| Maurice Baker, Dakota | .34 | 237 | 7.0 |
| Cliff Hawkins, Yakima | .27 | 166 | 6.1 |
| Stais Boseman, Rockford | .45 | 232 | 5.2 |
| Trevor Huffman, Great Lakes | .35 | 175 | 5.0 |

### Steals

| | Gm | Stl | Avg |
|---|---|---|---|
| Jemeil Rich, Gary | .42 | 117 | 2.8 |
| Ezra Williams, Great Lakes | .28 | 65 | 2.3 |
| Marshall Phillips, Rockford | .40 | 88 | 2.2 |
| Ronnie Fields, Rockford | .26 | 54 | 2.1 |
| Randy Livingston, Sioux Falls | .40 | 82 | 2.1 |
| Billy Thomas, Dakota | .34 | 47 | 2.0 |
| Maurice Baker, Dakota | .34 | 66 | 1.9 |
| Stais Boseman, Rockford | .45 | 86 | 1.9 |

### Free Throw Pct.

| | FTM | FTA | Pct |
|---|---|---|---|
| Darrick Martin, Michigan | .100 | 109 | .917 |
| Andre McCollum, Yakima | .47 | 53 | .887 |
| Sam Mack, Michigan | .109 | 126 | .865 |
| DeSean Hadley, Sioux Falls | .245 | 285 | .860 |
| Ezra Williams, Great Lakes | .139 | 162 | .858 |
| Melvin Sanders, Dakota | .159 | 186 | .855 |
| David Jackson, Sioux Falls | .72 | 86 | .837 |
| David Bailey, Sioux Falls | .138 | 165 | .836 |

## National Basketball Association Development League

The newly redubbed D-League is a feeder league founded by the NBA in 2001. (*) denotes playoff qualifiers.

### 2005 Final Standings

| | W | L | Pct | GB |
|---|---|---|---|---|
| *Columbus Riverdragons | 30 | 18 | .625 | — |
| *Asheville Altitude | 27 | 21 | .563 | 3 |
| *Huntsville Flight | 27 | 21 | .563 | 3 |
| *Roanoke Dazzle | 26 | 22 | .542 | 4 |
| Fayetteville Patriots | 17 | 31 | .354 | 13 |
| Florida Flame | 17 | 31 | .354 | 13 |

**Head Coaches:** Columbus—Jeff Malone (3rd season); Asheville—Joey Meyer (4th); Huntsville—Ralph Lewis (3rd); Roanoke—Kent Davison (4th); Fayetteville—Mike Brown (1st); Florida—Dennis Johnson (1st).

## Regular Season Individual Leaders

### Scoring

| | Gm | Pts | Avg |
|---|---|---|---|
| Isiah Victor, Roanoke | 41 | 801 | 19.5 |
| David Young, Fayetteville | 45 | 831 | 18.5 |
| Ron Slay, Asheville | 48 | 819 | 17.1 |
| Kirk Haston, Florida | 46 | 754 | 16.4 |
| Damone Brown, Huntsville | 32 | 510 | 15.9 |
| Tang Hamilton, Fayetteville | 42 | 662 | 15.8 |
| Ramel Curry, Columbus | 25 | 375 | 15.0 |
| Terrence Shannon, Asheville | 40 | 592 | 14.8 |
| Carl English, Florida | 48 | 699 | 14.6 |
| Mike King, Fayetteville | 44 | 622 | 14.1 |

### Rebounds

| | Gm | Reb | Avg |
|---|---|---|---|
| James Thomas, Roanoke | 36 | 480 | 13.3 |
| Rodney Bias, Huntsville | 43 | 556 | 12.9 |
| Hiram Fuller, Florida | 41 | 347 | 8.5 |
| Kirk Haston, Florida | 46 | 363 | 7.9 |
| Ruben Boumtje, Fayetteville | 38 | 284 | 7.5 |

### Assists

| | Gm | Ast | Avg |
|---|---|---|---|
| Omar Cook, Fayetteville | 44 | 380 | 8.6 |
| Derrick Zimmerman, Columbus | 48 | 271 | 5.6 |
| Jason Miskiri, Huntsville | 40 | 223 | 5.6 |
| Kevin Braswell, Columbus | 27 | 137 | 5.1 |
| Marcus Moore, Florida | 45 | 211 | 4.7 |

### Steals

| | Gm | Stl | Avg |
|---|---|---|---|
| Omar Cook, Fayetteville | 44 | 92 | 2.1 |
| Leonard Stokes, Asheville | 42 | 78 | 1.9 |
| Derrick Zimmerman, Columbus | 48 | 89 | 1.9 |
| Jason Miskiri, Huntsville | 40 | 59 | 1.5 |
| Mike Kings, Fayetteville | 44 | 56 | 1.3 |

### Field Goal Pct.

| | FG | FGA | Pct |
|---|---|---|---|
| Rodney Bias, Huntsville | 140 | 228 | .614 |
| Sean Finn, Florida | 65 | 111 | .586 |
| Tony Kitchings, Asheville | 170 | 304 | .559 |
| James Thomas, Roanoke | 165 | 312 | .529 |
| Tang Hamilton, Fayetteville | 268 | 508 | .528 |

### Blocks

| | Gm | Blk | Avg |
|---|---|---|---|
| Cedric Suitt, Asheville | 32 | 69 | 2.2 |
| Mike Benton, Columbus | 48 | 98 | 2.0 |
| Ousmane Cisse, Fayetteville | 48 | 85 | 1.8 |
| Casey Sanders, Roanoke | 31 | 53 | 1.7 |
| Hiram Fuller, Florida | 48 | 68 | 1.7 |

### Playoffs

#### Semifinals

Apr. 16 at Asheville, N.C.

| | 1 | 2 | 3 | 4 | F |
|---|---|---|---|---|---|
| Huntsville Flight | 21 | 20 | 27 | 18 | – 86 |
| Asheville Altitude | 24 | 19 | 22 | 25 | – 90 |

Apr. 17 at Columbus, Ga.

| | 1 | 2 | 3 | 4 | F |
|---|---|---|---|---|---|
| Roanoke Dazzle | 11 | 18 | 23 | 37 | – 89 |
| Columbus Riverdragons | 26 | 27 | 15 | 28 | – 96 |

---

#### Final

Apr. 23 at Columbus, Ga.    Attendance: 5,156

| | 1 | 2 | 3 | 4 | F |
|---|---|---|---|---|---|
| Asheville Altitude | 18 | 25 | 18 | 29 | – 90 |
| Columbus Riverdragons | 21 | 14 | 22 | 10 | – 67 |

---

### Annual Awards

**Most Valuable Player** . . . . . . . .Matt Carroll, Roanoke
**Rookie of the Year** . . . . . . . . James Thomas, Roanoke
**Defensive Player of the Year** Derrick Zimmerman, Col.

#### All-NBDL First Team

There were no holdovers from 2003-04 first team.

| Pos | | Team |
|---|---|---|
| F | Isiah Victor | Roanoke |
| F | Kirk Hanson | Florida |
| C | Hiram Fuller | Florida |
| G | Matt Carroll | Roanoke |
| G | Cory Alexander | Roanoke |

#### All-NBDL Second Team

| Pos | | Team |
|---|---|---|
| F | James Thomas | Roanoke |
| F | Ron Slay | Asheville |
| F | Damone Brown | Huntsville |
| C | Omar Cook | Fayetteville |
| G | Derrick Zimmerman | Columbus |
| G | David Young | Fayetteville |

---

### Changes come to D-League

The NBA Development League, has dropped the acronym NBDL and officially adopted the previously informal nickname "D-League." The league also announced plans to relocate three teams to larger markets and add two new franchises. The D-League will begin the 2005-06 season with eight teams with plans to expand to 15 prior to the 2006-07 season. The Huntsville Flight will move to New Mexico and be known as the **Albuquerque Thunderbirds**. The Columbus (Ga.) Riverdragons will go to Austin, Texas, and be renamed the **Austin Toros**. The two-time defending champion Asheville Altitude will move to Tulsa, Okla. and become the **Tulsa 66ers**. The teams relocating will inherit the 2004-05 season-ending rosters and will be able to protect up to four players each. Little Rock's **Arkansas RimRockers**, the 2005 champions of the American Basketball Association, were invited to join the D-League while the **Fort Worth** (Texas) **Flyers** are a new expansion franchise. Four of the teams (Austin, Fort Worth, Albuquerque and Tulsa) are owned by a private ownership group led by former Indiana Pacers GM David Kahn and including tennis star **Andre Agassi**. The NBA recently assigned team-by-team affiliations with the D-League clubs (see list on p. 389) and players (and coaches) will occasionally be sent down and called up depending on NBA team needs.

# Women's National Basketball Association
## 2005 WNBA Final Standings

Conference champions (*) and playoff qualifiers (†) are noted. GB refers to Games Behind leader. Number of seasons listed after each head coach refers to current tenure with club.

### Eastern Conference

|  | W | L | Pct | GB | Home | Road |
|---|---|---|---|---|---|---|
| *Connecticut | .26 | 8 | .765 | – | 14-3 | 12-5 |
| †Indiana | .21 | 13 | .618 | 5 | 14-3 | 7-10 |
| †New York | .18 | 16 | .529 | 8 | 10-7 | 8-9 |
| †Detroit | .16 | 18 | .471 | 10 | 12-5 | 4-13 |
| Washington | .16 | 18 | .471 | 10 | 9-11 | 10-7 |
| Charlotte | ..6 | 28 | .176 | 20 | 5-12 | 1-16 |

**Head Coaches: Conn**– Mike Thibault (3rd season); **nd**–Brian Winters (2nd); **NY**–Pat Coyle (2nd); **Det**–Bill Laimbeer (4th); **Wash**–Richie Adubato (1st); **Cha**–Trudi Lacey (3rd, 3-21) was replaced by Tyrone "Muggsy" Bogues (3-7) on Aug. 3, 2005.

**2004 Standings:** 1. Connecticut (18-16); 2. New York (18-16); 3. Detroit (17-17); 4. Washington (17-17); 5. Charlotte (16-18); 6. Indiana (15-19).

**WNBA GROWS:** The expansion Chicago Sky will become the WNBA's 14th team in 2006 and play in the Eastern Conference.

### Western Conference

|  | W | L | Pct | GB | Home | Road |
|---|---|---|---|---|---|---|
| *Sacramento | .25 | 9 | .735 | – | 15-2 | 10-7 |
| †Seattle | .20 | 14 | .588 | 5 | 14-3 | 6-11 |
| †Houston | .19 | 15 | .559 | 6 | 11-6 | 8-9 |
| †Los Angeles | .17 | 17 | .500 | 8 | 11-6 | 6-11 |
| Phoenix | .16 | 18 | .471 | 9 | 11-6 | 5-12 |
| Minnesota | .14 | 20 | .412 | 11 | 11-6 | 3-14 |
| San Antonio | .7 | 27 | .206 | 18 | 5-12 | 2-15 |

**Head Coaches: Sac**–John Whisenant (3rd season); **Sea**–Anne Donovan (3rd); **Hou**–Van Chancellor (9th); **LA**–Henry Bibby (1st, 13-15) was fired and replaced by assistant Joe "Jellybean" Bryant (4-2) on Aug. 18, 2005; **Pho**–Carrie Graf (2nd); **Minn**–Suzie McConnell Serio (3rd); **SA**–Dan Hughes (1st).

**2004 Standings:** 1. Los Angeles (25-9); 2. Seattle (20-14); 3. Sacramento (18-16); 4. Minnesota (18-16); 5. Phoenix (17-17); 6. Houston (13-21); 7. San Antonio (9-25).

## WNBA Regular Season Individual Leaders

### Scoring

|  | Gm | Pts | Avg |
|---|---|---|---|
| Sheryl Swoopes, Houston | .33 | 614 | 18.6 |
| Lauren Jackson, Seattle | .34 | 597 | 17.6 |
| Chamique Holdsclaw, Los Angeles | .33 | 561 | 17.0 |
| Diana Taurasi, Phoenix | .33 | 527 | 16.0 |
| Deanna Nolan, Detroit | .33 | 524 | 15.9 |
| Nykesha Sales, Connecticut | .34 | 532 | 15.6 |
| Lisa Leslie, Los Angeles | .34 | 512 | 15.2 |
| Tamika Catchings, Indiana | .34 | 501 | 14.7 |
| Alana Beard, Washington | .30 | 422 | 14.1 |
| Becky Hammon, New York | .34 | 473 | 13.9 |
| Taj McWilliams-Franklin, Connecitcut | .34 | 471 | 13.9 |
| Yolanda Griffith, Sacramento | .34 | 469 | 13.8 |
| Ann Wauters, New York | .28 | 383 | 13.7 |
| Tangela Smith, Charlotte | .31 | 421 | 13.6 |
| Penny Taylor, Phoenix | .29 | 382 | 13.2 |
| Anna DeForge, Phoenix | .33 | 433 | 13.1 |

### Field Goal Pct.

|  | FGM | FGA | Pct |
|---|---|---|---|
| Michelle Snow, Houston | .152 | 276 | .551 |
| Ann Wauters, New York | .151 | 279 | .541 |
| DeMya Walker, Sacramento | .125 | 234 | .534 |
| Janell Burse, Seattle | .127 | 243 | .523 |
| Wendy Palmer-Daniel, San Antonio | .125 | 242 | .517 |
| Tammy Sutton-Brown, Charlotte | .111 | 218 | .509 |
| Taj McWilliams-Franklin, Connecticut | .180 | 364 | .495 |
| Kamila Vodichkova, Phoenix | .127 | 257 | .494 |
| Chasity Melvin, Washington | .150 | 305 | .492 |
| Yolanda Griffith, Sacramento | .173 | 357 | .485 |
| Asjha Jones, Connecticut | .133 | 275 | .484 |
| Chamique Holdsclaw, Los Angeles | .216 | 450 | .480 |

### Steals

|  | Gm | Stl | Avg |
|---|---|---|---|
| Tamika Catchings, Indiana | .34 | 90 | 2.65 |
| Sheryl Swoopes, Houston | .33 | 66 | 2.00 |
| Lisa Leslie, Los Angeles | .34 | 67 | 1.97 |
| Tully Bevilaqua, Indiana | .34 | 60 | 1.94 |
| Nykesha Sales, Connecticut | .34 | 61 | 1.79 |
| Becky Hammon, New York | .34 | 60 | 1.76 |
| DeLisha Milton-Jones, Washington | .33 | 57 | 1.73 |

### Rebounds

|  | Gm | Reb | Avg |
|---|---|---|---|
| Cheryl Ford, Detroit | .33 | 322 | 9.8 |
| Lauren Jackson, Seattle | .34 | 313 | 9.2 |
| Tamika Catchings, Indiana | .34 | 264 | 7.8 |
| Lisa Leslie, Los Angeles | .34 | 248 | 7.3 |
| Taj McWilliams-Franklin, Connecticut | .34 | 248 | 7.3 |
| Kamila Vodichkova, Phoenix | .28 | 196 | 7.0 |
| Elena Baranova, New York | .33 | 227 | 6.9 |
| Michelle Snow, Houston | .33 | 225 | 6.8 |
| Chamique Holdsclaw, Los Angeles | .33 | 223 | 6.8 |
| Ann Wauters, New York | .28 | 184 | 6.6 |
| Yolanda Griffith, Sacramento | .34 | 223 | 6.6 |
| Margo Dydek, Connecticut | .31 | 195 | 6.3 |
| Janell Burse, Seattle | .34 | 199 | 5.9 |
| Chasity Melvin, Washington | .34 | 199 | 5.9 |
| Nicole Ohlde, Minnesota | .34 | 194 | 5.7 |
| Wendy Palmer-Daniel, San Antonio | .34 | 193 | 5.7 |

### Assists

|  | Gm | Ast | Avg |
|---|---|---|---|
| Sue Bird, Seattle | .30 | 176 | 5.9 |
| Temeka Johnson, Washington | .34 | 177 | 5.2 |
| Lindsay Whalen, Connecticut | .34 | 172 | 5.1 |
| Shannon Johnson, San Antonio | .34 | 158 | 4.6 |
| Diana Taurasi, Phoenix | .33 | 150 | 4.5 |
| Dawn Staley, Houston | .33 | 149 | 4.5 |
| Ticha Penicheiro, Sacramento | .34 | 149 | 4.4 |
| Becky Hammon, New York | .34 | 146 | 4.3 |
| Sheryl Swoopes, Houston | .33 | 141 | 4.3 |
| Tamika Catchings, Indiana | .34 | 143 | 4.2 |
| Deanna Nolan, Detroit | .33 | 121 | 3.7 |
| Penny Taylor, Phoenix | .29 | 94 | 3.2 |

### Blocks

|  | Gm | Blk | Avg |
|---|---|---|---|
| Margo Dydek, Connecticut | .31 | 71 | 2.29 |
| Vanessa Hayden, Minnesota | .31 | 68 | 2.19 |
| Lisa Leslie, Los Angeles | .34 | 71 | 2.09 |
| Lauren Jackson, Seattle | .34 | 67 | 1.97 |
| Ruth Riley, Detroit | .33 | 46 | 1.39 |
| Cheryl Ford, Detroit | .33 | 46 | 1.39 |
| Elena Baranova, New York | .33 | 46 | 1.39 |

## WNBA Playoffs
### First Round (Best of 3)

### East

**Connecticut vs. Detroit**

Aug. 31  Connecticut 73 . . . . . . . . . . . . . .at Detroit 62
Sept. 2  at Connecticut 75 . . . . . . . . . . . . .Detroit 67

Connecticut Sun win series, 2-0

**Indiana vs. New York**

Aug. 30  Indiana 63 . . . . . . . . . . . . . .at New York 51
Sept. 1  at Indiana 58 . . . . . . . . . . . . . .New York 50

Indiana Fever win series, 2-0

### West

**Sacramento vs. Los Angeles**

Aug. 31  Sacramento 75 . . . . . . . . . . .at Los Angeles 72
Sept. 2  at Sacramento 81 . . . . . . . . . .Los Angeles 63

Sacramento Monarchs win series, 2-0

**Seattle vs. Houston**

Aug. 30  Seattle 75 . . . . . . . . . . . . . . . .at Houston 67
Sept. 1  Houston 67 . . . . . . . . . . . . . . .at Seattle 64
Sept. 3  Houston 75 . . . . . . . . . . . . . . .at Seattle 58

Houston Comets win series, 2-1

### Conference Finals (Best of 3)

#### East

**Connecticut vs. Indiana**

Sept. 8  Connecticut 73 . . . . . . . . . . . . . .at Indiana 68
Sept. 10  at Connecticut 77 . . . .OT . . . . . . .Indiana 67

Connecticut Sun win series, 2-0

#### West

**Sacramento vs. Houston**

Sept. 8  Sacramento 73 . . . . . . . . . . . . . .at Houston 69
Sept. 10  at Sacramento 74 . . . . . . . . . . . .Houston 65

Sacramento Monarchs win series, 2-0

### Championship Series (Best of 5)

**Connecticut vs. Sacramento**

Sacramento wins series, 3 games to 1

| | W-L | Avg | Leading Scorer |
|---|---|---|---|
| Sacramento Monarchs | .3-1 | 66.8 | Griffith (18.5 ppg) |
| Connecticut Sun | .1-3 | 64.0 | Sales (17.3 ppg) |

| Date | Winner | Home Court |
|---|---|---|
| Sept. 14 . . . . . . . .Monarchs, 69-65 | | at Connecticut |
| Sept. 15 . . . . . . . . . .Sun, 77-70 OT | | at Connecticut |
| Sept. 18 . . . . . . . .Monarchs, 66-55 | | at Sacramento |
| Sept. 20 . . . . . . . .Monarchs, 62-59 | | at Sacramento |

**Finals MVP:** Yolanda Griffith, Sacramento, C (18.5 ppg, 9.8 rpg, 1.2 apg)

### Annual Awards

**Most Valuable Player** . . . . .Sheryl Swoopes, Hou.
**Rookie of the Year** . . . . . .Temeka Johnson, Wash.
**Most Improved** . . . . . . . . . .Nicole Powell, Sac.
**Def. Player of the Year** . . .Tamika Catchings, Ind.
**Coach of the Year** . . . . . . .John Whisenant, Sac.
**Kim Perrot Sportsmanship**
   **Award** . . . . . . . . .Taj McWilliams-Franklin, Conn.

### All-WNBA First Team

Holdovers from 2003-04 team are in **bold** type.

| Pos | Team |
|---|---|
| F | Sheryl Swoopes, Houston |
| F | **Lauren Jackson**, Seattle |
| C | Yolanda Griffith, Sacramento |
| G | Deanna Nolan, Detroit |
| G | **Sue Bird**, Seattle |

### 2005 WNBA Draft
#### First Round

| Pick | Team | Player, College, Pos |
|---|---|---|
| 1 | Charlotte | Janel McCarville, Minnesota, C |
| 2 | Indiana | Tan White, Mississippi St., G |
| 3 | Phoenix | Sandora Irvin, TCU, F |
| 4 | San Antonio | Kendra Wecker, Kansas St., F |
| 5 | Houston | Sancho Lyttle, Houston, C |
| 6 | Washington | Temeka Johnson, LSU, G |
| 7 | Detroit | Kara Braxton, Georgia, F |
| 8 | Connecticut | Katie Feenstra*, Liberty, C |
| 9 | Sacramento | Kristin Haynie, Michigan St., G |
| 10 | New York | Loree Moore, Tennessee, G |
| 11 | Minnesota | Kristen Mann, UC-Santa Barbara, F |
| 12 | Seattle | Tanisha Wright, Penn St., G |
| 13 | Detroit | Dionnah Jackson, Oklahoma, F |

*Feenstra's draft rights were traded to San Antonio for C Margo Dydek.

### All-WNBA First Team

*Sheryl Swoopes*
**Houston**

*Lauren Jackson*
**Seattle**

*Yolanda Griffith*
**Sacramento**

*Deanna Nolan*
**Detroit**

*Sue Bird*
**Seattle**

# 1938-2005
# Through the Years

SPORTS ALMANAC

## The NBA Finals

Although the National Basketball Association traces its first championship back to the 1946-47 season, the league was then called the Basketball Association of America (BAA). It did not become the NBA until after the 1948-49 season when the BAA and the National Basketball League (NBL) agreed to merge.

In the chart below, the Eastern finalists (representing the NBA Eastern Division from 1947-70, and the NBA Eastern Conference since 1971) are listed in CAPITAL letters. Also, each NBA champion's wins and losses are noted in parentheses after the series score.

**Multiple winners:** Boston (16); Minneapolis-LA Lakers (14); Chicago Bulls (6); Detroit, Phi-SF-Golden St. Warriors, San Antonio and Syracuse Nationals-Phi. 76ers (3); Houston, New York (2).

| Year | Winner | Head Coach | Series | Loser | Head Coach |
|------|--------|-----------|--------|-------|-----------|
| 1947 | PHILADELPHIA WARRIORS | Eddie Gottlieb | 4-1 (WWWLW) | Chicago Stags | Harold Olsen |
| 1948 | Baltimore Bullets | Buddy Jeannette | 4-2 (LWWWLW) | PHILA. WARRIORS | Eddie Gottlieb |
| 1949 | Minneapolis Lakers | John Kundla | 4-2 (WWWLLW) | WASH. CAPITOLS | Red Auerbach |
| 1950 | Minneapolis Lakers | John Kundla | 4-2 (WLWWLW) | SYRACUSE | Al Cervi |
| 1951 | Rochester | Les Harrison | 4-3 (WWWLLLW) | NEW YORK | Joe Lapchick |
| 1952 | Minneapolis Lakers | John Kundla | 4-3 (WLWLWLW) | NEW YORK | Joe Lapchick |
| 1953 | Minneapolis Lakers | John Kundla | 4-1 (LWWWW) | NEW YORK | Joe Lapchick |
| 1954 | Minneapolis Lakers | John Kundla | 4-3 (WLWLWLW) | SYRACUSE | Al Cervi |
| 1955 | SYRACUSE | Al Cervi | 4-3 (WWLLLWW) | Ft. Wayne Pistons | Charley Eckman |
| 1956 | PHILADELPHIA WARRIORS | George Senesky | 4-1 (WLWWW) | Ft. Wayne Pistons | Charley Eckman |
| 1957 | BOSTON | Red Auerbach | 4-3 (WLWLWLW) | St. Louis Hawks | Alex Hannum |
| 1958 | St. Louis Hawks | Alex Hannum | 4-2 (WLWLWW) | BOSTON | Red Auerbach |
| 1959 | BOSTON | Red Auerbach | 4-0 | Mpls. Lakers | John Kundla |
| 1960 | BOSTON | Red Auerbach | 4-3 (WLWLWLW) | St. Louis Hawks | Ed Macauley |
| 1961 | BOSTON | Red Auerbach | 4-1 (WWLWW) | St. Louis Hawks | Paul Seymour |
| 1962 | BOSTON | Red Auerbach | 4-3 (WLLWLWW) | LA Lakers | Fred Schaus |
| 1963 | BOSTON | Red Auerbach | 4-2 (WLWLWW) | LA Lakers | Fred Schaus |
| 1964 | BOSTON | Red Auerbach | 4-1 (WWLWW) | SF Warriors | Alex Hannum |
| 1965 | BOSTON | Red Auerbach | 4-1 (WWLWW) | LA Lakers | Fred Schaus |
| 1966 | BOSTON | Red Auerbach | 4-3 (WWLWLLW) | LA Lakers | Fred Schaus |
| 1967 | PHILADELPHIA 76ERS | Alex Hannum | 4-2 (WWLWLW) | SF Warriors | Bill Sharman |
| 1968 | BOSTON | Bill Russell | 4-2 (WLWLWW) | LA Lakers | B.van Breda Kolff |
| 1969 | BOSTON | Bill Russell | 4-3 (LLWWLWW) | LA Lakers | B.van Breda Kolff |
| 1970 | NEW YORK | Red Holzman | 4-3 (WLWLWLW) | LA Lakers | Joe Mullaney |
| 1971 | Milwaukee | Larry Costello | 4-0 | BALT. BULLETS | Gene Shue |
| 1972 | LA Lakers | Bill Sharman | 4-1 (LWWWW) | NEW YORK | Red Holzman |
| 1973 | NEW YORK | Red Holzman | 4-1 (LWWWW) | LA Lakers | Bill Sharman |
| 1974 | BOSTON | Tommy Heinsohn | 4-3 (WLWLWLW) | Milwaukee | Larry Costello |
| 1975 | Golden St. Warriors | Al Attles | 4-0 | WASH. BULLETS | K.C. Jones |
| 1976 | BOSTON | Tommy Heinsohn | 4-2 (WWLLWW) | Phoenix | John MacLeod |
| 1977 | Portland | Jack Ramsay | 4-2 (LLWWWW) | PHILA. 76ERS | Gene Shue |
| 1978 | WASHINGTON BULLETS | Dick Motta | 4-3 (LWLWLWW) | Seattle | Lenny Wilkens |
| 1979 | Seattle | Lenny Wilkens | 4-1 (LWWWW) | WASH. BULLETS | Dick Motta |
| 1980 | LA Lakers | Paul Westhead | 4-2 (WLWLWW) | PHILA. 76ERS | Billy Cunningham |
| 1981 | BOSTON | Bill Fitch | 4-2 (WLWLWW) | Houston | Del Harris |
| 1982 | LA Lakers | Pat Riley | 4-2 (WLWWLW) | PHILA. 76ERS | Billy Cunningham |
| 1983 | PHILADELPHIA 76ERS | Billy Cunningham | 4-0 | LA Lakers | Pat Riley |
| 1984 | BOSTON | K.C. Jones | 4-3 (LWLWWLW) | LA Lakers | Pat Riley |
| 1985 | LA Lakers | Pat Riley | 4-2 (LWWLWW) | BOSTON | K.C. Jones |
| 1986 | BOSTON | K.C. Jones | 4-2 (WWLWLW) | Houston | Bill Fitch |
| 1987 | LA Lakers | Pat Riley | 4-2 (WWLWLW) | BOSTON | K.C. Jones |
| 1988 | LA Lakers | Pat Riley | 4-3 (LWWLLWW) | DETROIT PISTONS | Chuck Daly |
| 1989 | DETROIT | Chuck Daly | 4-0 | LA Lakers | Pat Riley |
| 1990 | DETROIT | Chuck Daly | 4-1 (WLWWW) | Portland | Rick Adelman |
| 1991 | CHICAGO | Phil Jackson | 4-1 (LWWWW) | LA Lakers | Mike Dunleavy |
| 1992 | CHICAGO | Phil Jackson | 4-2 (WLWWLW) | Portland | Rick Adelman |
| 1993 | CHICAGO | Phil Jackson | 4-2 (WWLWLW) | Phoenix | Paul Westphal |
| 1994 | Houston | Rudy Tomjanovich | 4-3 (WLWLLWW) | NEW YORK | Pat Riley |
| 1995 | Houston | Rudy Tomjanovich | 4-0 | ORLANDO | Brian Hill |
| 1996 | CHICAGO | Phil Jackson | 4-2 (WWWLLW) | Seattle | George Karl |
| 1997 | CHICAGO | Phil Jackson | 4-2 (WWLLWW) | Utah | Jerry Sloan |

## The NBA Finals (Cont.)

| Year | Winner | Head Coach | Series | Loser | Head Coach |
|------|--------|-----------|--------|-------|-----------|
| 1998 | CHICAGO | Phil Jackson | 4-2 (LWWWLW) | Utah | Jerry Sloan |
| 1999 | San Antonio | Gregg Popovich | 4-1 (WWLWW) | NEW YORK | Jeff Van Gundy |
| 2000 | LA Lakers | Phil Jackson | 4-2 (WLWLW) | INDIANA | Larry Bird |
| 2001 | LA Lakers | Phil Jackson | 4-1 (LWWWW) | PHILA. 76ERS | Larry Brown |
| 2002 | LA Lakers | Phil Jackson | 4-0 | NEW JERSEY | Byron Scott |
| 2003 | San Antonio | Gregg Popovich | 4-2 (WLWLWW) | NEW JERSEY | Byron Scott |
| 2004 | DETROIT | Larry Brown | 4-1 (WLWWW) | LA Lakers | Phil Jackson |
| 2005 | San Antonio | Gregg Popovich | 4-3 (WWLLWLW) | DETROIT | Larry Brown |

**Note:** Four finalists were led by player-coaches: **1948**—Buddy Jeannette (guard) of Baltimore; **1950**—Al Cervi (guard) of Syracuse; **1968**—Bill Russell (center) of Boston; **1969**—Bill Russell (center) of Boston.

## Most Valuable Player

Winner who did not play for the NBA champion is in **bold** type.

**Multiple winners:** Michael Jordan (6); Tim Duncan, Magic Johnson and Shaquille O'Neal (3); Kareem Abdul-Jabbar, Larry Bird, Hakeem Olajuwon and Willis Reed (2).

| Year | Year | Year |
|------|------|------|
| 1969 **Jerry West**, LA Lakers, G | 1982 Magic Johnson, LA Lakers, G | 1995 Hakeem Olajuwon, Houston, C |
| 1970 Willis Reed, New York, C | 1983 Moses Malone, Philadelphia, C | 1996 Michael Jordan, Chicago, G |
| 1971 Lew Alcindor, Milwaukee, C | 1984 Larry Bird, Boston, F | 1997 Michael Jordan, Chicago, G |
| 1972 Wilt Chamberlain, LA Lakers, C | 1985 K. Abdul-Jabbar, LA Lakers, C | 1998 Michael Jordan, Chicago, G |
| 1973 Willis Reed, New York, C | 1986 Larry Bird, Boston, F | 1999 Tim Duncan, San Antonio, F/C |
| 1974 John Havlicek, Boston, F | 1987 Magic Johnson, LA Lakers, G | 2000 Shaquille O'Neal, LA Lakers, C |
| 1975 Rick Barry, Golden State, F | 1988 James Worthy, LA Lakers, F | 2001 Shaquille O'Neal, LA Lakers, C |
| 1976 Jo Jo White, Boston, G | 1989 Joe Dumars, Detroit, G | 2002 Shaquille O'Neal, LA Lakers, C |
| 1977 Bill Walton, Portland, C | 1990 Isiah Thomas, Detroit, G | 2003 Tim Duncan, San Antonio, F/C |
| 1978 Wes Unseld, Washington, C | 1991 Michael Jordan, Chicago, G | 2004 Chauncey Billups, Detroit, G |
| 1979 Dennis Johnson, Seattle, G | 1992 Michael Jordan, Chicago, G | 2005 Tim Duncan, San Antonio, F/C |
| 1980 Magic Johnson, LA Lakers, G/C | 1993 Michael Jordan, Chicago, G | |
| 1981 Cedric Maxwell, Boston, F | 1994 Hakeem Olajuwon, Houston, C | |

**Note:** Lew Alcindor changed his name to Kareem Abdul-Jabbar after the 1970-71 season.

## All-Time NBA Playoff Leaders

Through the 2005 playoffs.

### CAREER

Years listed indicate number of playoff appearances. Players active in 2005 in **bold** type. DNP indicates player that was active in 2005 but did not participate in playoffs.

### Points

| | Yrs | Gm | Pts | Avg |
|---|-----|----|----|-----|
| 1 Michael Jordan | 13 | 179 | **5987** | 33.4 |
| 2 Kareem Abdul-Jabbar | 18 | 237 | **5762** | 24.3 |
| 3 Karl Malone | 19 | 193 | **4761** | 24.7 |
| 4 **Shaquille O'Neal** | 12 | 171 | **4546** | 26.6 |
| 5 Jerry West | 13 | 153 | **4457** | 29.1 |
| 6 Larry Bird | 12 | 164 | **3897** | 23.8 |
| 7 John Havlicek | 13 | 172 | **3776** | 22.0 |
| 8 Hakeem Olajuwon | 15 | 145 | **3755** | 25.9 |
| 9 Magic Johnson | 13 | 190 | **3701** | 19.5 |
| 10 Elgin Baylor | 12 | 134 | **3623** | 27.0 |
| 11 Scottie Pippen | 16 | 208 | **3642** | 17.5 |
| 12 Wilt Chamberlain | 13 | 160 | **3607** | 22.5 |
| 13 Kevin McHale | 13 | 169 | **3182** | 18.8 |
| 14 Dennis Johnson | 13 | 180 | **3116** | 17.3 |
| 15 Julius Erving | 11 | 141 | **3088** | 21.9 |
| 16 James Worthy | 9 | 143 | **3022** | 21.1 |
| 17 Clyde Drexler | 15 | 145 | **2963** | 20.4 |
| 18 Sam Jones | 12 | 154 | **2909** | 18.9 |
| 19 Charles Barkley | 13 | 123 | **2833** | 23.0 |
| 20 Robert Parish | 16 | 184 | **2820** | 15.3 |

### Scoring Average

Minimum of 25 games or 700 points.

| | Yrs | Gm | Pts | Avg |
|---|-----|----|----|-----|
| 1 Michael Jordan | 13 | 179 | 5987 | 33.4 |
| 2 **Allen Iverson** | 6 | 62 | 1899 | 30.6 |
| 3 Jerry West | 13 | 153 | 4457 | 29.1 |
| 4 Elgin Baylor | 12 | 134 | 3623 | 27.0 |
| 5 George Gervin | 9 | 59 | 1592 | 27.0 |
| 6 **Shaquille O'Neal** | 12 | 171 | 4546 | 26.6 |
| 7 Hakeem Olajuwon | 15 | 145 | 3755 | 25.9 |
| 8 Dominique Wilkins | 9 | 55 | 1421 | 25.8 |
| 9 Bob Pettit | 9 | 88 | 2240 | 25.5 |
| 10 **Dirk Nowitzki** | 7 | 53 | 1332 | 25.1 |
| 11 Rick Barry | 7 | 74 | 1833 | 24.8 |
| 12 Karl Malone | 19 | 193 | 4761 | 24.7 |
| 13 **Paul Pierce** | 4 | 37 | 908 | 24.5 |
| 14 Bernard King | 5 | 28 | 687 | 24.5 |
| 15 Alex English | 10 | 68 | 1661 | 24.4 |
| 16 Kareem Abdul-Jabbar | 18 | 237 | 5762 | 24.3 |
| 17 Paul Arizin | 8 | 49 | 1186 | 24.2 |
| 18 **Tim Duncan** | 7 | 105 | 2502 | 23.8 |
| 19 Larry Bird | 12 | 164 | 3897 | 23.8 |
| 20 George Mikan | 9 | 91 | 2141 | 23.5 |

### Field Goals

| | Yrs | FG | Att | Pct |
|---|-----|----|----|-----|
| 1 Kareem Abdul-Jabbar | 18 | **2356** | 4422 | .533 |
| 2 Michael Jordan | 13 | **2188** | 4497 | .487 |
| 3 **Shaquille O'Neal** | 12 | **1759** | 3132 | .562 |
| 4 Karl Malone | 19 | **1743** | 3768 | .463 |
| 5 Jerry West | 13 | **1622** | 3460 | .469 |
| 6 Hakeem Olajuwon | 12 | **1504** | 2847 | .528 |
| 7 Larry Bird | 12 | **1458** | 3090 | .472 |
| 8 John Havlicek | 13 | **1451** | 3329 | .436 |
| 9 Wilt Chamberlain | 13 | **1425** | 2728 | .522 |
| 10 Elgin Baylor | 12 | **1388** | 3161 | .439 |

### Free Throws

| | Yrs | FT | Att | Pct |
|---|-----|----|----|-----|
| 1 Michael Jordan | 13 | **1463** | 1766 | .828 |
| 2 Karl Malone | 19 | **1269** | 1725 | .736 |
| 3 Jerry West | 13 | **1213** | 1507 | .805 |
| 4 Kareem Abdul-Jabbar | 18 | **1050** | 1419 | .740 |
| 5 Magic Johnson | 12 | **1040** | 1241 | .838 |
| 6 **Shaquille O'Neal** | 12 | **1028** | 1995 | .515 |
| 7 Larry Bird | 12 | **901** | 1012 | .891 |
| 8 John Havlicek | 13 | **874** | 1046 | .836 |
| 9 Elgin Baylor | 12 | **847** | 1101 | .769 |
| 10 Scottie Pippen | 16 | **772** | 1067 | .724 |

## Assists

| | | Yrs | Gm | No | Avg |
|---|---|---|---|---|---|
| 1 | Magic Johnson | 13 | 190 | **2346** | 12.3 |
| 2 | John Stockton | 19 | 182 | **1839** | 10.1 |
| 3 | Larry Bird | 12 | 164 | **1062** | 6.5 |
| 4 | Scottie Pippen | 16 | 208 | **1048** | 5.0 |
| 5 | Michael Jordan | 13 | 179 | **1022** | 5.7 |

## Rebounds

| | | Yrs | Gm | No | Avg |
|---|---|---|---|---|---|
| 1 | Bill Russell | 13 | 165 | **4104** | 24.9 |
| 2 | Wilt Chamberlain | 13 | 160 | **3913** | 24.5 |
| 3 | Kareem Abdul-Jabbar | 18 | 237 | **2481** | 10.5 |
| 4 | **Shaquille O'Neal** | 12 | 171 | **2142** | 12.5 |
| 5 | Karl Malone | 19 | 193 | **2062** | 10.7 |

## Appearances

| | No | | No |
|---|---|---|---|
| Karl Malone | 19 | Sam Perkins | 15 |
| John Stockton | 19 | Jerome Kersey | 15 |
| Kareem Abdul-Jabbar | 18 | Tree Rollins | 15 |
| Robert Parish | 16 | Charles Oakley | 15 |
| Scottie Pippen | 16 | Dolph Schayes | 15 |
| Terry Porter | 16 | Clyde Drexler | 15 |

## Games Played

| | No | | No |
|---|---|---|---|
| K. Abdul-Jabbar | 237 | Dennis Johnson | 180 |
| Scottie Pippen | 208 | Michael Jordan | 179 |
| Danny Ainge | 193 | John Havlicek | 172 |
| Karl Malone | 193 | **Shaquille O'Neal** | 171 |
| Magic Johnson | 190 | Kevin McHale | 169 |
| Robert Parish | 184 | Michael Cooper | 168 |
| Byron Scott | 183 | Bill Russell | 165 |
| John Stockton | 182 | Larry Bird | 164 |

## SINGLE GAME

### Points

| | Date | FG-FT–Pts |
|---|---|---|
| Michael Jordan, Chi at Bos* | 4/20/86 | 22-19-63 |
| Elgin Baylor, LA at Bos | 4/14/62 | 22-17-61 |
| Wilt Chamberlain, Phi vs Syr | 3/22/62 | 22-12-56 |
| Michael Jordan, Chi at Mia | 4/29/92 | 20-16-56 |
| Charles Barkley, Pho vs G.St. | 5/4/94 | 23-7-56 |
| Rick Barry, SF vs Phi | 4/18/67 | 22-11-55 |
| Michael Jordan, Chi vs Cle | 5/1/88 | 24-7-55 |
| Michael Jordan, Chi vs Pho | 4/16/93 | 21-13-55 |
| Michael Jordan, Chi vs Wash | 4/27/97 | 22-10-55 |

*Double overtime.

### Field Goals

| | Date | FG | Att |
|---|---|---|---|
| Wilt Chamberlain, Phi vs Syr | 3/14/60 | 24 | 42 |
| John Havlicek, Bos vs Atl | 4/1/73 | 24 | 36 |
| Michael Jordan, Chi vs Cle | 5/1/88 | 24 | 45 |

Eight tied with 22 each.

### Miscellaneous

**3-Pt Field Goals**

| | Date | No |
|---|---|---|
| Rex Chapman, Pho at Sea | 4/25/97 | 9 |
| Dan Majerle, Pho vs Sea | 6/1/93 | 8 |
| Allen Iverson, Phi vs Tor | 5/16/01 | 8 |

Nine tied with 7 each.

**Assists**

| | Date | No |
|---|---|---|
| Magic Johnson, LA vs Pho | 5/15/84 | 24 |
| John Stockton, Utah at LA Lakers | 5/17/88 | 24 |
| Magic Johnson, LA Lakers at Port | 5/3/85 | 23 |
| John Stockton, Utah vs Port | 4/25/96 | 23 |
| Doc Rivers, Atl vs Bos | 5/16/88 | 22 |

Four tied with 21 each.

**Rebounds**

| | Date | No |
|---|---|---|
| Wilt Chamberlain, Phi vs Bos | 4/5/67 | 41 |
| Bill Russell, Bos vs Phi | 3/23/58 | 40 |
| Bill Russell, Bos vs St.L | 3/29/60 | 40 |
| Bill Russell, Bos vs LA* | 4/18/62 | 40 |

Three tied with 39 each.
*Overtime.

## Appearances in NBA Finals

Standings of all NBA teams that have reached the NBA Finals since 1947.

| App | | Titles | Last Won |
|---|---|---|---|
| 28 | Minneapolis-LA Lakers | 14 | 2002 |
| 19 | Boston Celtics | 16 | 1986 |
| 9 | Syracuse Nats-Phila. 76ers | 3 | 1983 |
| 8 | New York Knicks | 2 | 1973 |
| 7 | Ft. Wayne-Detroit Pistons | 3 | 2004 |
| 6 | Chicago Bulls | 6 | 1998 |
| 6 | Phila-SF-Golden St. Warriors | 3 | 1975 |
| 4 | Houston Rockets | 2 | 1995 |
| 4 | St. Louis Hawks | 1 | 1958 |
| 4 | Baltimore-Washington Bullets | 1 | 1978 |
| 3 | San Antonio Spurs | 3 | 2005 |
| 3 | Portland Trail Blazers | 1 | 1977 |
| 3 | Seattle SuperSonics | 1 | 1979 |
| 2 | Milwaukee Bucks | 1 | 1971 |
| 2 | New Jersey Nets | 0 | — |
| 2 | Phoenix Suns | 0 | — |
| 2 | Utah Jazz | 0 | — |
| 1 | Baltimore Bullets | 1 | 1948 |
| 1 | Rochester Royals | 1 | 1951 |
| 1 | Chicago Stags | 0 | — |
| 1 | Orlando Magic | 0 | — |
| 1 | Washington Capitols | 0 | — |
| 1 | Indiana Pacers | 0 | — |

**Change of address:** The St. Louis Hawks now play in Atlanta and the Rochester Royals are now the Sacramento Kings.
**Teams now defunct:** Baltimore Bullets (1947-55), Chicago Stags (1946-50) and Washington Capitols (1946-51).

## NBA FINALS

### Points

| Series | | Year | Pts |
|---|---|---|---|
| 4-Gm | Shaquille O'Neal, LAL vs NJ | 2002 | 145 |
| 5-Gm | Allen Iverson, Phi vs LAL | 2001 | 178 |
| 6-Gm | Michael Jordan, Chi vs Pho | 1993 | 246 |
| 7-Gm | Elgin Baylor, LA vs Bos | 1962 | 284 |

### Field Goals

| Series | | Year | No |
|---|---|---|---|
| 4-Gm | Hakeem Olajuwon, Hou vs Orl | 1995 | 56 |
| 5-Gm | Allen Iverson, Phi vs LAL | 2001 | 66 |
| 6-Gm | Michael Jordan, Chi vs Pho | 1993 | 101 |
| 7-Gm | Elgin Baylor, LA vs Bos | 1962 | 101 |

### Assists

| Series | | Year | No |
|---|---|---|---|
| 4-Gm | Bob Cousy, Bos vs Mpls | 1959 | 51 |
| 5-Gm | Magic Johnson, LAL vs Chi | 1991 | 62 |
| 6-Gm | Magic Johnson, LAL vs Bos | 1985 | 84 |
| 7-Gm | Magic Johnson, LA vs Bos | 1984 | 95 |

### Rebounds

| Series | | Year | No |
|---|---|---|---|
| 4-Gm | Bill Russell, Bos vs Mpls | 1959 | 118 |
| 5-Gm | Bill Russell, Bos vs St.L | 1961 | 144 |
| 6-Gm | Wilt Chamberlain, Phi vs SF | 1967 | 171 |
| 7-Gm | Bill Russell, Bos vs LA | 1962 | 189 |

## The National Basketball League

The NBL started with 13 previously independent teams in 1937-38 and although GE, Firestone and Goodyear were gone by late 1942, ran 12 years before merging with the three-year-old Basketball Association of America in 1949 to form the NBA.
**Multiple champions:** Akron Firestone Non-Skids, Fort Wayne Zollner Pistons, Oshkosh All-Stars (2).

| Year | Winner | Series | Loser | Year | Winner | Series | Loser |
|------|--------|--------|-------|------|--------|--------|-------|
| 1938 | Goodyear Wingfoots | 2-1 | Oshkosh All-Stars | 1944 | Ft. Wayne Pistons | 3-0 | Sheboygan Redskins |
| 1939 | Firestone Non-Skids | 3-2 | Oshkosh All-Stars | 1945 | Ft. Wayne Pistons | 3-2 | Sheboygan Redskins |
| 1940 | Firestone Non-Skids | 3-2 | Oshkosh All-Stars | 1946 | Rochester Royals | 3-0 | Sheboygan Redskins |
| 1941 | Oshkosh All-Stars | 3-0 | Sheboygan Redskins | 1947 | Chicago Gears | 3-2 | Rochester Royals |
| 1942 | Oshkosh All-Stars | 2-1 | Ft. Wayne Pistons | 1948 | Minneapolis Lakers | 3-1 | Rochester Royals |
| 1943 | Sheboygan Redskins | 2-1 | Ft. Wayne Pistons | 1949 | Anderson Packers | 3-0 | Oshkosh All-Stars |

## NBA All-Star Game

The NBA staged its first All-Star Game before 10,094 at Boston Garden on March 2, 1951. From that year on, the game has matched the best players in the East against the best in the West. Winning coaches are listed first. East leads series, 33-19.

**Multiple MVP winners:** Bob Pettit (4); Michael Jordan and Oscar Robertson (3); Bob Cousy, Julius Erving, Allen Iverson, Magic Johnson, Karl Malone, Shaquille O'Neal and Isiah Thomas (2).

| Year | | Host | Coaches | Most Valuable Player |
|------|--|------|---------|----------------------|
| 1951 | East 111, West 94 | Boston | Joe Lapchick, John Kundla | Ed Macauley, Boston |
| 1952 | East 108, West 91 | Boston | Al Cervi, John Kundla | Paul Arizin, Philadelphia |
| 1953 | West 79, East 75 | Ft. Wayne | John Kundla, Joe Lapchick | George Mikan, Minneapolis |
| 1954 | East 98, West 93 (OT) | New York | Joe Lapchick, John Kundla | Bob Cousy, Boston |
| 1955 | East 100, West 91 | New York | Al Cervi, Charley Eckman | Bill Sharman, Boston |
| 1956 | West 108, East 94 | Rochester | Charley Eckman, George Senesky | Bob Pettit, St. Louis |
| 1957 | East 109, West 97 | Boston | Red Auerbach, Bobby Wanzer | Bob Cousy, Boston |
| 1958 | East 130, West 118 | St. Louis | Red Auerbach, Alex Hannum | Bob Pettit, St. Louis |
| 1959 | West 124, East 108 | Detroit | Ed Macauley, Red Auerbach | Bob Pettit, St. Louis |
|      |                    |         |                          | & Elgin Baylor, Minneapolis |
| 1960 | East 125, West 115 | Philadelphia | Red Auerbach, Ed Macauley | Wilt Chamberlain, Philadelphia |
| 1961 | West 153, East 131 | Syracuse | Paul Seymour, Red Auerbach | Oscar Robertson, Cincinnati |
| 1962 | West 150, East 130 | St. Louis | Fred Schaus, Red Auerbach | Bob Pettit, St. Louis |
| 1963 | East 115, West 108 | Los Angeles | Red Auerbach, Fred Schaus | Bill Russell, Boston |
| 1964 | East 111, West 107 | Boston | Red Auerbach, Fred Schaus | Oscar Robertson, Cincinnati |
| 1965 | East 124, West 123 | St. Louis | Red Auerbach, Alex Hannum | Jerry Lucas, Cincinnati |
| 1966 | East 137, West 94 | Cincinnati | Red Auerbach, Fred Schaus | Adrian Smith, Cincinnati |
| 1967 | West 135, East 120 | San Francisco | Fred Schaus, Red Auerbach | Rick Barry, San Francisco |
| 1968 | East 144, West 124 | New York | Alex Hannum, Bill Sharman | Hal Greer, Philadelphia |
| 1969 | East 123, West 112 | Baltimore | Gene Shue, Richie Guerin | Oscar Robertson, Cincinnati |
| 1970 | East 142, West 135 | Philadelphia | Red Holzman, Richie Guerin | Willis Reed, New York |
| 1971 | West 108, East 107 | San Diego | Larry Costello, Red Holzman | Lenny Wilkens, Seattle |
| 1972 | West 112, East 110 | Los Angeles | Bill Sharman, Tom Heinsohn | Jerry West, Los Angeles |
| 1973 | East 104, West 84 | Chicago | Tom Heinsohn, Bill Sharman | Dave Cowens, Boston |
| 1974 | West 134, East 123 | Seattle | Larry Costello, Tom Heinsohn | Bob Lanier, Detroit |
| 1975 | East 108, West 102 | Phoenix | K.C. Jones, Al Attles | Walt Frazier, New York |
| 1976 | East 123, West 109 | Philadelphia | Tom Heinsohn, Al Attles | Dave Bing, Washington |
| 1977 | West 125, East 124 | Milwaukee | Larry Brown, Gene Shue | Julius Erving, Philadelphia |
| 1978 | East 133, West 125 | Atlanta | Billy Cunningham, Jack Ramsay | Randy Smith, Buffalo |
| 1979 | West 134, East 129 | Detroit | Lenny Wilkens, Dick Motta | David Thompson, Denver |
| 1980 | East 144, West 136 (OT) | Washington | Billy Cunningham, Lenny Wilkens | George Gervin, San Antonio |
| 1981 | East 123, West 120 | Cleveland | Billy Cunningham, John MacLeod | Nate Archibald, Boston |
| 1982 | East 120, West 118 | New Jersey | Bill Fitch, Pat Riley | Larry Bird, Boston |
| 1983 | East 132, West 123 | Los Angeles | Billy Cunningham, Pat Riley | Julius Erving, Philadelphia |
| 1984 | East 154, West 145 (OT) | Denver | K.C. Jones, Frank Layden | Isiah Thomas, Detroit |
| 1985 | West 140, East 129 | Indiana | Pat Riley, K.C. Jones | Ralph Sampson, Houston |
| 1986 | East 139, West 132 | Dallas | K.C. Jones, Pat Riley | Isiah Thomas, Detroit |
| 1987 | West 154, East 149 (OT) | Seattle | Pat Riley, K.C. Jones | Tom Chambers, Seattle |
| 1988 | East 138, West 133 | Chicago | Mike Fratello, Pat Riley | Michael Jordan, Chicago |
| 1989 | West 143, East 134 | Houston | Pat Riley, Lenny Wilkens | Karl Malone, Utah |
| 1990 | East 130, West 113 | Miami | Chuck Daly, Pat Riley | Magic Johnson, LA Lakers |
| 1991 | East 116, West 114 | Charlotte | Chris Ford, Rick Adelman | Charles Barkley, Philadelphia |
| 1992 | West 153, East 113 | Orlando | Don Nelson, Phil Jackson | Magic Johnson, LA Lakers |
| 1993 | West 135, East 132 (OT) | Salt Lake City | Paul Westphal, Pat Riley | Karl Malone, Utah |
|      |                    |         |                          | & John Stockton, Utah |
| 1994 | East 127, West 118 | Minneapolis | Lenny Wilkens, George Karl | Scottie Pippen, Chicago |
| 1995 | West 139, East 112 | Phoenix | Paul Westphal, Brian Hill | Mitch Richmond, Sacramento |
| 1996 | East 129, West 118 | San Antonio | Phil Jackson, George Karl | Michael Jordan, Chicago |
| 1997 | East 132, West 120 | Cleveland | Doug Collins, Rudy Tomjanovich | Glen Rice, Charlotte |
| 1998 | East 135, West 114 | New York | Larry Bird, George Karl | Michael Jordan, Chicago |
| 1999 | Not held—due to lockout | | | |
| 2000 | West 137, East 126 | Oakland | Phil Jackson, Jeff Van Gundy | Tim Duncan, San Antonio |
|      |                    |         |                          | & Shaquille O'Neal, LA Lakers |
| 2001 | East 111, West 110 | Washington | Larry Brown, Rick Adelman | Allen Iverson, Philadelphia |
| 2002 | West 135, East 120 | Philadelphia | Don Nelson, Byron Scott | Kobe Bryant, LA Lakers |
| 2003 | West 155, East 145 (2 OT) | Atlanta | Rick Adelman, Isiah Thomas | Kevin Garnett, Minnesota |
| 2004 | West 136, East 132 | Los Angeles | Flip Saunders, Rick Carlisle | Shaquille O'Neal, LA Lakers |
| 2005 | East 125, West 115 | Denver | Stan Van Gundy, Gregg Popovich | Allen Iverson, Philadelphia |

## NBA Franchise Origins

Here is what the current 30 teams in the National Basketball Association have to show for the years they have put in as members of the National Basketball League (NBL), Basketball Association of America (BAA), the NBA, and the American Basketball Association (ABA). League titles are noted by year won.

## Western Conference

| | First Season | League Titles | Franchise Stops |
|---|---|---|---|
| **Dallas Mavericks** | 1980-81 (NBA) | None | •Dallas (1980– ) |
| **Denver Nuggets** | 1967-68 (ABA) | None | •Denver (1967– ) |
| **Golden St. Warriors** | 1946-47 (BAA) | 1 BAA (1947) | •Philadelphia (1946-62) |
| | | 2 NBA (1956, 75) | San Francisco (1962-71) |
| | | | Oakland (1971– ) |
| **Houston Rockets** | 1967-68 (NBA) | 2 NBA (1994-95) | •San Diego (1967-71) |
| | | | Houston (1971– ) |
| **Los Angeles Clippers** | 1970-71 (NBA) | None | •Buffalo (1970-78) |
| | | | San Diego (1978-84) |
| | | | Los Angeles (1984– ) |
| **Los Angeles Lakers** | 1947-48 (NBL) | 1 NBL (1948) | •Minneapolis (1947-60) |
| | | 1 BAA (1949) | Los Angeles (1960-67) |
| | | 14 NBA (1950,52-54,72, | Inglewood, CA (1967-99) |
| | | 80,82,85,87-88,00-02) | Los Angeles (1999– ) |
| **Memphis Grizzlies** | 1995-96 (NBA) | None | •Vancouver (1995-01) |
| | | | Memphis, TN (2001– ) |
| **Minnesota Timberwolves** | 1989-90 (NBA) | None | •Minneapolis (1989– ) |
| **New Orleans Hornets** | 1988-89 (NBA) | None | •Charlotte (1988-2002) |
| | | | New Orleans (2002– ) |
| **Phoenix Suns** | 1968-69 (NBA) | None | •Phoenix (1968– ) |
| **Portland Trail Blazers** | 1970-71 (NBA) | 1 NBA (1977) | •Portland (1970– ) |
| **Sacramento Kings** | 1945-46 (NBL) | 1 NBL (1946) | •Rochester, NY (1945-58) |
| | | 1 NBA (1951) | Cincinnati (1958-72) |
| | | | KC-Omaha (1972-75) |
| | | | Kansas City (1975-85) |
| | | | Sacramento (1985– ) |
| **San Antonio Spurs** | 1967-68 (ABA) | 3 NBA (1999, 2003, 05) | •Dallas (1967-73) |
| | | | San Antonio (1973– ) |
| **Seattle SuperSonics** | 1967-68 (NBA) | 1 NBA (1979) | •Seattle (1967– ) |
| **Utah Jazz** | 1974-75 (NBA) | None | •New Orleans (1974-79) |
| | | | Salt Lake City (1979– ) |

## Eastern Conference

| | First Season | League Titles | Franchise Stops |
|---|---|---|---|
| **Atlanta Hawks** | 1946-47 (NBL) | 1 NBA (1958) | •Tri-Cities (1946-51) |
| | | | Milwaukee (1951-55) |
| | | | St. Louis (1955-68) |
| | | | Atlanta (1968– ) |
| **Boston Celtics** | 1946-47 (BAA) | 16 NBA (1957,59-66,68-69 | •Boston (1946– ) |
| | | 74,76,81,84,86) | |
| **Charlotte Bobcats** | 2004-05 (NBA) | None | •Charlotte (2004– ) |
| **Chicago Bulls** | 1966-67 (NBA) | 6 NBA (1991-93,96-98) | •Chicago (1966– ) |
| **Cleveland Cavaliers** | 1970-71 (NBA) | None | •Cleveland (1970-74) |
| | | | Richfield, OH (1974-94) |
| | | | Cleveland (1994– ) |
| **Detroit Pistons** | 1941-42 (NBL) | 2 NBL (1944-45) | •Ft. Wayne, IN (1941-57) |
| | | 3 NBA (1989-90, 2004) | Detroit (1957-78) |
| | | | Pontiac, MI (1978-88) |
| | | | Auburn Hills, MI (1988– ) |
| **Indiana Pacers** | 1967-68 (ABA) | 3 ABA (1970,72-73) | •Indianapolis (1967– ) |
| **Miami Heat** | 1988-89 (NBA) | None | •Miami (1988– ) |
| **Milwaukee Bucks** | 1968-69 (NBA) | 1 NBA (1971) | •Milwaukee (1968– ) |
| **New Jersey Nets** | 1967-68 (ABA) | 2 ABA (1974,76) | •Teaneck, NJ (1967-68) |
| | | | Commack, NY (1968-69) |
| | | | W. Hempstead, NY (1969-71) |
| | | | Uniondale, NY (1971-77) |
| | | | Piscataway, NJ (1977-81) |
| | | | E. Rutherford, NJ (1981– ) |
| **New York Knicks** | 1946-47 (BAA) | 2 NBA (1970,73) | •New York (1946– ) |
| **Orlando Magic** | 1989-90 (NBA) | None | •Orlando, FL (1989– ) |
| **Philadelphia 76ers** | 1949-50 (NBA) | 3 NBA (1955,67,83) | •Syracuse (1949-63) |
| | | | Philadelphia (1963– ) |
| **Toronto Raptors** | 1995-96 (NBA) | None | •Toronto (1995– ) |
| **Washington Wizards** | 1961-62 (NBA) | 1 NBA (1978) | •Chicago (1961-63) |
| | | | Baltimore (1963-73) |
| | | | Landover, MD (1973– ) |

**Note:** The Tri-Cities Blackhawks represented Moline and Rock Island, Ill., and Davenport, Iowa.

## The Growth of the NBA

Of the 11 franchises that comprised the Basketball Association of America (BAA) at the start of the 1946-47 season, only three remain—the Boston Celtics, New York Knickerbockers and Golden State Warriors (originally Philadelphia Warriors).

Just before the start of the 1948-49 season, four teams from the more established **National Basketball League** (NBL)—the Ft. Wayne Pistons (now Detroit), Indianapolis Jets, Minneapolis Lakers (now Los Angeles) and Rochester Royals (now Sacramento Kings)—joined the BAA.

A year later, the six remaining NBL franchises—Anderson (Ind.), Denver, Sheboygan (Wisc.), the Syracuse Nationals (now Philadelphia 76ers), Tri-Cities Blackhawks (now Atlanta Hawks) and Waterloo (Iowa)—joined along with the new Indianapolis Olympians and the BAA became the 17-team **National Basketball Association**.

The NBA was down to 10 teams by the 1950-51 season and slipped to eight by 1954-55 with Boston, New York, Philadelphia and Syracuse in the Eastern Division, and Ft. Wayne, Milwaukee (formerly Tri-Cities), Minneapolis and Rochester in the West.

By 1960, five of those surviving eight teams had moved to other cities but by the end of the decade the NBA was a 14-team league. It also had a rival, the **American Basketball Association**, which began play in 1967 with a red, white and blue ball, a three-point line and 11 teams. After a nine-year run, the ABA merged four clubs—the Denver Nuggets, Indiana Pacers, New York Nets and San Antonio Spurs—with the NBA following the 1975-76 season. The NBA adopted the three-point shot in 1979-80.

## Expansion/Merger Timetable

For teams currently in NBA.

**1948**—Added NBL's Ft. Wayne Pistons (now Detroit), Minneapolis Lakers (now Los Angeles) and Rochester Royals (now Sacramento Kings); **1949**—Syracuse Nationals (now Philadelphia 76ers) and Tri-Cities Blackhawks (now Atlanta Hawks).
**1961**—Chicago Packers (now Washington Wizards); **1966**—Chicago Bulls; **1967**—San Diego Rockets (now Houston) and Seattle SuperSonics; **1968**—Milwaukee Bucks and Phoenix Suns.
**1970**—Buffalo Braves (now Los Angeles Clippers), Cleveland Cavaliers and Portland Trail Blazers; **1974**—New Orleans Jazz (now Utah); **1976**—added ABA's Denver Nuggets, Indiana Pacers, New York Nets (now New Jersey) and San Antonio Spurs.
**1980**—Dallas Mavericks; **1988**—Charlotte Hornets and Miami Heat; **1989**—Minnesota Timberwolves and Orlando Magic.
**1995**—Toronto Raptors and Vancouver Grizzlies (Now Memphis).
**2004**—Charlotte Bobcats.

## City and Nickname Changes

**1951**—Tri-Cities Blackhawks, who divided home games between Moline and Rock Island, Ill., and Davenport, Iowa, move to Milwaukee and become the Hawks; **1955**—Milwaukee Hawks move to St. Louis; **1957**—Ft. Wayne Pistons move to Detroit, while Rochester Royals move to Cincinnati.
**1960**—Minneapolis Lakers move to Los Angeles; **1962**—Chicago Packers renamed Zephyrs, while Philadelphia Warriors move to San Francisco; **1963**—Chicago Zephyrs move to Baltimore and become Bullets, while Syracuse Nationals move to Philadelphia and become 76ers; **1968**—St. Louis Hawks move to Atlanta.
**1971**—San Diego Rockets move to Houston, while San Francisco Warriors move to Oakland and become Golden State Warriors; **1972**—Cincinnati Royals move to Midwest, divide home games between Kansas City, Mo., and Omaha, Neb., and become Kings; **1973**—Baltimore Bullets move to Landover, Md., outside Washington and become Capital Bullets; **1974**—Capital Bullets renamed Washington Bullets; **1975**—KC-Omaha Kings settle in Kansas City; **1977**—New York Nets move from Uniondale, N.Y., to Piscataway, N.J. (later East Rutherford) and become New Jersey Nets; **1978**—Buffalo Braves move to San Diego and become Clippers; **1979**—New Orleans Jazz move to Salt Lake City and become Utah Jazz.
**1984**—San Diego Clippers move to Los Angeles; **1985**—Kansas City Kings move to Sacramento.
**1997**—Washington Bullets become Washington Wizards.
**2001**—Vancouver Grizzlies move to Memphis, Tenn.; **2002**—Charlotte Hornets move to New Orleans.

---

## Defunct NBA Teams

Teams that once played in the BAA and NBA, but no longer exist.
**Anderson (Ind.)**—Packers (1949-50); **Baltimore**—Bullets (1947-55); **Chicago**—Stags (1946-50); **Cleveland**—Rebels (1946-47); **Denver**—Nuggets (1949-50); **Detroit**—Falcons (1946-47); **Indianapolis**—Jets (1948-49) and Olympians (1949-53); **Pittsburgh**—Ironmen (1946-47); **Providence**—Steamrollers (1946-49); **St. Louis**—Bombers (1946-50); **Sheboygan (Wisc.)**—Redskins (1949-50); **Toronto**—Huskies (1946-47); **Washington**—Capitols (1946-51); **Waterloo (Iowa)**—Hawks (1949-50).

---

## ABA Teams (1967-76)

**Anaheim**—Amigos (1967-68, moved to LA); **Baltimore**—Claws (1975, never played); **Carolina**—Cougars (1969-74, moved to St. Louis); **Dallas**—Chaparrals (1967-73, called Texas Chaparrals in 1970-71, moved to San Antonio); **Denver**—Rockets (1967-76, renamed Nuggets in 1974-76); **Miami**—Floridians (1968-72, called simply Floridians from 1970-72).
**Houston**—Mavericks (1967-69, moved to North Carolina); **Indiana**—Pacers (1967-76); **Kentucky**—Colonels (1967-76); **Los Angeles**—Stars (1968-70, moved to Utah); **Memphis**—Pros (1970-75, renamed Tams in 1972 and Sounds in 1974, moved to Baltimore); **Minnesota**—Muskies (1967-68, moved to Miami) and Pipers (1968-69, moved back to Pittsburgh); **New Jersey**—Americans (1967-68, moved to New York).
**New Orleans**—Buccaneers (1967-70, moved to Memphis); **New York**—Nets (1968-76); **Oakland**—Oaks (1967-69, moved to Washington); **Pittsburgh**—Pipers (1967-68, moved to Minnesota), Pipers (1969-72, renamed Condors in 1970); **St. Louis**—Spirits of St. Louis (1974-76); **San Antonio**—Spurs (1973-76); **San Diego**—Conquistadors (1972-75, renamed Sails in 1975); **Utah**—Stars (1970-75); **Virginia**—Squires (1970-76); **Washington**—Caps (1969-70, moved to Virginia).

## Annual NBA Leaders
### Scoring

Decided by total points from 1947-69, and per game average since 1970. A lockout in 1999 shortened the regular season to 50 games.

**Multiple winners:** Michael Jordan (10); Wilt Chamberlain (7); George Gervin and Allen Iverson (4); Neil Johnston, Bob McAdoo and George Mikan (3); Kareem Abdul-Jabbar, Paul Arizin, Adrian Dantley, Tracy McGrady, Shaquille O'Neal and Bob Pettit (2).

| Year | | Gm | Pts | Avg | Year | | Gm | Pts | Avg |
|---|---|---|---|---|---|---|---|---|---|
| 1947 | Joe Fulks, Phi | .60 | 1389 | 23.2 | 1977 | Pete Maravich, NO | .73 | 2273 | 31.1 |
| 1948 | Max Zaslofsky, Chi | .48 | 1007 | 21.0 | 1978 | George Gervin, SA | .82 | 2232 | 27.2 |
| 1949 | George Mikan, Mpls | .60 | 1698 | 28.3 | 1979 | George Gervin, SA | .80 | 2365 | 29.6 |
| 1950 | George Mikan, Mpls | .68 | 1865 | 27.4 | 1980 | George Gervin, SA | .78 | 2585 | 33.1 |
| 1951 | George Mikan, Mpls | .68 | 1932 | 28.4 | 1981 | Adrian Dantley, Utah | .80 | 2452 | 30.7 |
| 1952 | Paul Arizin, Phi | .66 | 1674 | 25.4 | 1982 | George Gervin, SA | .79 | 2551 | 32.3 |
| 1953 | Neil Johnston, Phi | .70 | 1564 | 22.3 | 1983 | Alex English, Den | .82 | 2326 | 28.4 |
| 1954 | Neil Johnston, Phi | .72 | 1759 | 24.4 | 1984 | Adrian Dantley, Utah | .79 | 2418 | 30.6 |
| 1955 | Neil Johnston, Phi | .72 | 1631 | 22.7 | 1985 | Bernard King, NY | .55 | 1809 | 32.9 |
| 1956 | Bob Pettit, St.L | .72 | 1849 | 25.7 | 1986 | Dominique Wilkins, Atl | .78 | 2366 | 30.3 |
| 1957 | Paul Arizin, Phi | .71 | 1817 | 25.6 | 1987 | Michael Jordan, Chi | .82 | 3041 | 37.1 |
| 1958 | George Yardley, Det | .72 | 2001 | 27.8 | 1988 | Michael Jordan, Chi | .82 | 2868 | 35.0 |
| 1959 | Bob Pettit, St.L | .72 | 2105 | 29.2 | 1989 | Michael Jordan, Chi | .81 | 2633 | 32.5 |
| 1960 | Wilt Chamberlain, Phi | .72 | 2707 | 37.6 | 1990 | Michael Jordan, Chi | .82 | 2753 | 33.6 |
| 1961 | Wilt Chamberlain, Phi | .79 | 3033 | 38.4 | 1991 | Michael Jordan, Chi | .82 | 2580 | 31.5 |
| 1962 | Wilt Chamberlain, Phi | .80 | 4029 | 50.4 | 1992 | Michael Jordan, Chi | .80 | 2404 | 30.1 |
| 1963 | Wilt Chamberlain, SF | .80 | 3586 | 44.8 | 1993 | Michael Jordan, Chi | .78 | 2541 | 32.6 |
| 1964 | Wilt Chamberlain, SF | .80 | 2948 | 36.9 | 1994 | David Robinson, SA | .80 | 2383 | 29.8 |
| 1965 | Wilt Chamberlain, SF-Phi | .73 | 2534 | 34.7 | 1995 | Shaquille O'Neal, Orl | .79 | 2315 | 29.3 |
| 1966 | Wilt Chamberlain, Phi | .79 | 2649 | 33.5 | 1996 | Michael Jordan, Chi | .82 | 2491 | 30.4 |
| 1967 | Rick Barry, SF | .78 | 2775 | 35.6 | 1997 | Michael Jordan, Chi | .82 | 2431 | 29.7 |
| 1968 | Dave Bing, Det | .79 | 2142 | 27.1 | 1998 | Michael Jordan, Chi | .82 | 2357 | 28.7 |
| 1969 | Elvin Hayes, SD | .82 | 2327 | 28.4 | 1999 | Allen Iverson, Phi | .48 | 1284 | 26.8 |
| 1970 | Jerry West, LA | .74 | 2309 | 31.2 | 2000 | Shaquille O'Neal, LAL | .79 | 2344 | 29.7 |
| 1971 | Lew Alcindor, Mil | .82 | 2596 | 31.7 | 2001 | Allen Iverson, Phi | .71 | 2207 | 31.1 |
| 1972 | Kareem Abdul-Jabbar, Mil | .81 | 2822 | 34.8 | 2002 | Allen Iverson, Phi | .60 | 1883 | 31.4 |
| 1973 | Nate Archibald, KC-Omaha | .80 | 2719 | 34.0 | 2003 | Tracy McGrady, Orl | .75 | 2407 | 32.1 |
| 1974 | Bob McAdoo, Buf | .74 | 2261 | 30.6 | 2004 | Tracy McGrady, Orl | .67 | 1878 | 28.0 |
| 1975 | Bob McAdoo, Buf | .82 | 2831 | 34.5 | 2005 | Allen Iverson, Phi | .75 | 2302 | 30.7 |
| 1976 | Bob McAdoo, Buf | .78 | 2427 | 31.1 | | | | | |

**Note:** Lew Alcindor changed his name to Kareem Abdul-Jabbar after the 1970-71 season.

### Rebounds

Decided by total rebounds from 1951-69 and per game average since 1970.
**Multiple winners:** Wilt Chamberlain (11); Dennis Rodman (7); Moses Malone (6); Bill Russell (4); Kevin Garnett, Elvin Hayes, Dikembe Mutombo, Hakeem Olajuwon and Ben Wallace (2).

| Year | | Gm | No | Avg | Year | | Gm | No | Avg |
|---|---|---|---|---|---|---|---|---|---|
| 1951 | Dolph Schayes, Syr | .66 | 1080 | 16.4 | 1970 | Elvin Hayes, SD | .82 | 1386 | 16.9 |
| 1952 | Larry Foust, Ft. Wayne | .66 | 880 | 13.3 | 1971 | Wilt Chamberlain, LA | .82 | 1493 | 18.2 |
| | & Mel Hutchins, Mil | .66 | 880 | 13.3 | 1972 | Wilt Chamberlain, LA | .82 | 1572 | 19.2 |
| 1953 | George Mikan, Mpls | .70 | 1007 | 14.4 | 1973 | Wilt Chamberlain, LA | .82 | 1526 | 18.6 |
| 1954 | Harry Gallatin, NY | .72 | 1098 | 15.3 | 1974 | Elvin Hayes, Cap* | .81 | 1463 | 18.1 |
| 1955 | Neil Johnston, Phi | .72 | 1085 | 15.1 | 1975 | Wes Unseld, Wash | .73 | 1077 | 14.8 |
| 1956 | Bob Pettit, St.L | .72 | 1164 | 16.2 | 1976 | Kareem Abdul-Jabbar, LA | .82 | 1383 | 16.9 |
| 1957 | Maurice Stokes, Roch | .72 | 1256 | 17.4 | 1977 | Bill Walton, Port | .65 | 934 | 14.4 |
| 1958 | Bill Russell, Bos | .69 | 1564 | 22.7 | 1978 | Len Robinson, NO | .82 | 1288 | 15.7 |
| 1959 | Bill Russell, Bos | .70 | 1612 | 23.0 | 1979 | Moses Malone, Hou | .82 | 1444 | 17.6 |
| 1960 | Wilt Chamberlain, Phi | .72 | 1941 | 27.0 | 1980 | Swen Nater, SD | .81 | 1216 | 15.0 |
| 1961 | Wilt Chamberlain, Phi | .79 | 2149 | 27.2 | 1981 | Moses Malone, Hou | .80 | 1180 | 14.8 |
| 1962 | Wilt Chamberlain, Phi | .80 | 2052 | 25.7 | 1982 | Moses Malone, Hou | .81 | 1188 | 14.7 |
| 1963 | Wilt Chamberlain, SF | .80 | 1946 | 24.3 | 1983 | Moses Malone, Phi | .78 | 1194 | 15.3 |
| 1964 | Bill Russell, Bos | .78 | 1930 | 24.7 | 1984 | Moses Malone, Phi | .71 | 950 | 13.4 |
| 1965 | Bill Russell, Bos | .78 | 1878 | 24.1 | 1985 | Moses Malone, Phi | .79 | 1031 | 13.1 |
| 1966 | Wilt Chamberlain, Phi | .79 | 1943 | 24.6 | 1986 | Bill Laimbeer, Det | .82 | 1075 | 13.1 |
| 1967 | Wilt Chamberlain, Phi | .81 | 1957 | 24.2 | 1987 | Charles Barkley, Phi | .68 | 994 | 14.6 |
| 1968 | Wilt Chamberlain, Phi | .82 | 1952 | 23.8 | 1988 | Michael Cage, LAC | .72 | 938 | 13.0 |
| 1969 | Wilt Chamberlain, LA | .81 | 1712 | 21.1 | 1989 | Hakeem Olajuwon, Hou | .82 | 1105 | 13.5 |

*The Baltimore Bullets moved to Landover, Md. in 1973-74 and became first the Capital Bullets, then the Washington Bullets in 1974-75.

## Rebounds (Cont.)

| Year | Player | | | | Year | Player | | | |
|------|--------|--|--|--|------|--------|--|--|--|
| 1990 | Hakeem Olajuwon, Hou | .82 | 1149 | 14.0 | 1998 | Dennis Rodman, Chi | .80 | 1201 | 15.0 |
| 1991 | David Robinson, SA | .82 | 1063 | 13.0 | 1999 | Chris Webber, Sac | .42 | 545 | 13.0 |
| 1992 | Dennis Rodman, Det | .82 | 1530 | 18.7 | 2000 | Dikembe Mutombo, Atl | .82 | 1157 | 14.1 |
| 1993 | Dennis Rodman, Det | .62 | 1232 | 18.3 | 2001 | Dikembe Mutombo, Atl-Phi | .75 | 1015 | 13.5 |
| 1994 | Dennis Rodman, SA | .79 | 1132 | 17.3 | 2002 | Ben Wallace, Det | .80 | 1039 | 13.0 |
| 1995 | Dennis Rodman, SA | .49 | 823 | 16.8 | 2003 | Ben Wallace, Det | .73 | 1126 | 15.4 |
| 1996 | Dennis Rodman, Chi | .64 | 952 | 14.9 | 2004 | Kevin Garnett, Min | .82 | 1139 | 13.9 |
| 1997 | Dennis Rodman, Chi | .55 | 883 | 16.1 | 2005 | Kevin Garnett, Min | .82 | 1108 | 13.5 |

## Assists

Decided by total assists from 1952-69 and per game average since 1970.

**Multiple winners:** John Stockton (9); Bob Cousy (8); Oscar Robertson (6); Jason Kidd (5); Magic Johnson and Kevin Porter (4); Andy Phillip and Guy Rodgers (2).

| Year | | No | Year | | No | Year | | APG |
|------|--|-----|------|--|-----|------|--|-----|
| 1947 | Ernie Calverley, Prov | 202 | 1967 | Guy Rodgers, Chi | 908 | 1987 | Magic Johnson, LAL | 12.2 |
| 1948 | Howie Dallmar, Phi | 120 | 1968 | Wilt Chamberlain, Phi | 702 | 1988 | John Stockton, Utah | 13.8 |
| 1949 | Bob Davies, Roch | 321 | 1969 | Oscar Robertson, Cin | 772 | 1989 | John Stockton, Utah | 13.6 |
| 1950 | Dick McGuire, NY | 386 | 1970 | Lenny Wilkens, Sea | 9.1 | 1990 | John Stockton, Utah | 14.5 |
| 1951 | Andy Phillip, Phi | 414 | 1971 | Norm Van Lier, Chi | 10.1 | 1991 | John Stockton, Utah | 14.2 |
| 1952 | Andy Phillip, Phi | 539 | 1972 | Jerry West, LA | 9.7 | 1992 | John Stockton, Utah | 13.7 |
| 1953 | Bob Cousy, Bos | 547 | 1973 | Nate Archibald, KC-O | 11.4 | 1993 | John Stockton, Utah | 12.0 |
| 1954 | Bob Cousy, Bos | 518 | 1974 | Ernie DiGregorio, Buf | 8.2 | 1994 | John Stockton, Utah | 12.6 |
| 1955 | Bob Cousy, Bos | 557 | 1975 | Kevin Porter, Wash | 8.0 | 1995 | John Stockton, Utah | 12.3 |
| 1956 | Bob Cousy, Bos | 642 | 1976 | Slick Watts, Sea | 8.1 | 1996 | John Stockton, Utah | 11.2 |
| 1957 | Bob Cousy, Bos | 478 | 1977 | Don Buse, Ind | 8.5 | 1997 | Mark Jackson, Den-Ind | 11.4 |
| 1958 | Bob Cousy, Bos | 463 | 1978 | Kevin Porter, Det-NJ | 10.2 | 1998 | Rod Strickland, Wash | 10.5 |
| 1959 | Bob Cousy, Bos | 557 | 1979 | Kevin Porter, Det | 13.4 | 1999 | Jason Kidd, Pho | 10.8 |
| 1960 | Bob Cousy, Bos | 715 | 1980 | M.R. Richardson, NY | 10.1 | 2000 | Jason Kidd, Pho | 10.1 |
| 1961 | Oscar Robertson, Cin | 690 | 1981 | Kevin Porter, Wash | 9.1 | 2001 | Jason Kidd, Pho | 9.8 |
| 1962 | Oscar Robertson, Cin | 899 | 1982 | Johnny Moore, SA | 9.6 | 2002 | Andre Miller, Cle | 10.9 |
| 1963 | Guy Rodgers, SF | 825 | 1983 | Magic Johnson, LA | 10.5 | 2003 | Jason Kidd, NJ | 8.9 |
| 1964 | Oscar Robertson, Cin | 868 | 1984 | Magic Johnson, LA | 13.1 | 2004 | Jason Kidd, NJ | 9.2 |
| 1965 | Oscar Robertson, Cin | 861 | 1985 | Isiah Thomas, Det | 13.9 | 2005 | Steve Nash, Dal | 11.5 |
| 1966 | Oscar Robertson, Cin | 847 | 1986 | Magic Johnson, LAL | 12.6 | | | |

## Field Goal Percentage

**Multiple winners:** Wilt Chamberlain (9); Shaquille O'Neal (8); Artis Gilmore (4); Neil Johnston (3); Bob Feerick, Johnny Green, Alex Groza, Cedric Maxwell, Kevin McHale, Gheorghe Muresan, Kenny Sears and Buck Williams (2).

| Year | | Pct | Year | | Pct | Year | | Pct |
|------|--|-----|------|--|-----|------|--|-----|
| 1947 | Bob Feerick, Wash | .401 | 1967 | Wilt Chamberlain, Phi | .683 | 1987 | Kevin McHale, Bos | .604 |
| 1948 | Bob Feerick, Wash | .340 | 1968 | Wilt Chamberlain, Phi | .595 | 1988 | Kevin McHale, Bos | .604 |
| 1949 | Arnie Risen, Roch | .423 | 1969 | Wilt Chamberlain, LA | .583 | 1989 | Dennis Rodman, Det | .595 |
| 1950 | Alex Groza, Indpls | .478 | 1970 | Johnny Green, Cin | .559 | 1990 | Mark West, Pho | .625 |
| 1951 | Alex Groza, Indpls | .470 | 1971 | Johnny Green, Cin | .587 | 1991 | Buck Williams, Port | .602 |
| 1952 | Paul Arizin, Phi | .448 | 1972 | Wilt Chamberlain, LA | .649 | 1992 | Buck Williams, Port | .604 |
| 1953 | Neil Johnston, Phi | .452 | 1973 | Wilt Chamberlain, LA | .727 | 1993 | Cedric Ceballos, Pho | .576 |
| 1954 | Ed Macauley, Bos | .486 | 1974 | Bob McAdoo, Buf | .547 | 1994 | Shaquille O'Neal, Orl | .599 |
| 1955 | Larry Foust, Ft.W | .487 | 1975 | Don Nelson, Bos | .539 | 1995 | Chris Gatling, G.St | .633 |
| 1956 | Neil Johnston, Phi | .457 | 1976 | Wes Unseld, Wash | .561 | 1996 | Gheorghe Muresan, Wash | .584 |
| 1957 | Neil Johnston, Phi | .447 | 1977 | K. Abdul-Jabbar, LA | .579 | 1997 | Gheorghe Muresan, Wash | .604 |
| 1958 | Jack Twyman, Cin | .452 | 1978 | Bobby Jones, Den | .578 | 1998 | Shaquille O'Neal, LAL | .584 |
| 1959 | Kenny Sears, NY | .490 | 1979 | Cedric Maxwell, Bos | .584 | 1999 | Shaquille O'Neal, LAL | .576 |
| 1960 | Kenny Sears, NY | .477 | 1980 | Cedric Maxwell, Bos | .609 | 2000 | Shaquille O'Neal, LAL | .574 |
| 1961 | Wilt Chamberlain, Phi | .509 | 1981 | Artis Gilmore, Chi | .670 | 2001 | Shaquille O'Neal, LAL | .572 |
| 1962 | Walt Bellamy, Chi | .519 | 1982 | Artis Gilmore, Chi | .652 | 2002 | Shaquille O'Neal, LAL | .579 |
| 1963 | Wilt Chamberlain, SF | .528 | 1983 | Artis Gilmore, SA | .626 | 2003 | Eddy Curry, Chi | .585 |
| 1964 | Jerry Lucas, Cin | .527 | 1984 | Artis Gilmore, SA | .631 | 2004 | Shaquille O'Neal, LAL | .584 |
| 1965 | W. Chamberlain, SF-Phi | .510 | 1985 | James Donaldson, LAC | .637 | 2005 | Shaquille O'Neal, Mia | .601 |
| 1966 | Wilt Chamberlain, Phi | .540 | 1986 | Steve Johnson, SA | .632 | | | |

## Free Throw Percentage

**Multiple winners:** Bill Sharman (7); Rick Barry (6); Reggie Miller (5); Larry Bird (4); Mark Price and Dolph Schayes (3); Mahmoud Abdul-Rauf, Larry Costello, Ernie DiGregorio, Bob Feerick, Kyle Macy, Calvin Murphy, Oscar Robertson and Larry Siegfried (2).

| Year | | Pct | Year | | Pct | Year | | Pct |
|------|--|-----|------|--|-----|------|--|-----|
| 1947 | Fred Scolari, Wash | .811 | 1955 | Bill Sharman, Bos | .897 | 1963 | Larry Costello, Syr | .881 |
| 1948 | Bob Feerick, Wash | .788 | 1956 | Bill Sharman, Bos | .867 | 1964 | Oscar Robertson, Cin | .853 |
| 1949 | Bob Feerick, Wash | .859 | 1957 | Bill Sharman, Bos | .905 | 1965 | Larry Costello, Phi | .877 |
| 1950 | Max Zaslofsky, Chi | .843 | 1958 | Dolph Schayes, Syr | .904 | 1966 | Larry Siegfried, Bos | .881 |
| 1951 | Joe Fulks, Phi | .855 | 1959 | Bill Sharman, Bos | .932 | 1967 | Adrian Smith, Cin | .903 |
| 1952 | Bob Wanzer, Roch | .904 | 1960 | Dolph Schayes, Syr | .892 | 1968 | Oscar Robertson, Cin | .873 |
| 1953 | Bill Sharman, Bos | .850 | 1961 | Bill Sharman, Bos | .921 | 1969 | Larry Siegfried, NY | .864 |
| 1954 | Bill Sharman, Bos | .844 | 1962 | Dolph Schayes, Syr | .896 | 1970 | Flynn Robinson, Mil | .898 |

## Free Throw Percentage (Cont.)

| Year | | Pct | Year | | Pct | Year | | Pct |
|---|---|---|---|---|---|---|---|---|
| 1971 | Chet Walker, Chi | .859 | 1983 | Calvin Murphy, Hou | .920 | 1995 | Spud Webb, Sac. | .934 |
| 1972 | Jack Marin, Bal. | .894 | 1984 | Larry Bird, Bos | .888 | 1996 | M. Abdul-Rauf, Den | .930 |
| 1973 | Rick Barry, G.St. | .902 | 1985 | Kyle Macy, Pho. | .907 | 1997 | Mark Price, G.St. | .906 |
| 1974 | Ernie DiGregorio, Buf | .902 | 1986 | Larry Bird, Bos | .896 | 1998 | Chris Mullin, Ind. | .939 |
| 1975 | Rick Barry, G.St. | .904 | 1987 | Larry Bird, Bos | .910 | 1999 | Reggie Miller, Ind | .915 |
| 1976 | Rick Barry, G.St. | .923 | 1988 | Jack Sikma, Mil. | .922 | 2000 | Jeff Hornacek, Utah | .950 |
| 1977 | Ernie DiGregorio, Buf | .945 | 1989 | Magic Johnson, LAL | .911 | 2001 | Reggie Miller, Ind | .928 |
| 1978 | Rick Barry, G.St. | .924 | 1990 | Larry Bird, Bos | .930 | 2002 | Reggie Miller, Ind | .911 |
| 1979 | Rick Barry, Hou. | .947 | 1991 | Reggie Miller, Ind | .918 | 2003 | Allan Houston, NY | .919 |
| 1980 | Rick Barry, Hou. | .935 | 1992 | Mark Price, Cle. | .947 | 2004 | Predrag Stojakovic, Sac. | .927 |
| 1981 | Calvin Murphy, Hou | .958 | 1993 | Mark Price, Cle. | .948 | 2005 | Reggie Miller, Ind | .933 |
| 1982 | Kyle Macy, Pho. | .899 | 1994 | M. Abdul-Rauf, Den | .956 | | | |

## Three-Point Field Goal Percentage

**Multiple winners:** Craig Hodges, Steve Kerr (2)

| Year | | Pct | Year | | Pct | Year | | Pct |
|---|---|---|---|---|---|---|---|---|
| 1980 | Fred Brown, Sea | .443 | 1989 | Jon Sundvold, Mia. | .522 | 1998 | Dale Ellis, Sea. | .464 |
| 1981 | Brian Taylor, SD | .383 | 1990 | Steve Kerr, Cle | .507 | 1999 | Dell Curry, Milw | .476 |
| 1982 | Campy Russell, NY | .439 | 1991 | Jim Les, Sac | .461 | 2000 | Hubert Davis, Dal | .491 |
| 1983 | Mike Dunleavy, SA | .345 | 1992 | Dana Barros, Sea | .446 | 2001 | Brent Barry, Sea | .476 |
| 1984 | Darrell Griffith, Utah | .361 | 1993 | B.J. Armstrong, Chi | .453 | 2002 | Steve Smith, SA. | .472 |
| 1985 | Byron Scott, LAL | .433 | 1994 | Tracy Murray, Por | .459 | 2003 | Bruce Bowen, SA | .441 |
| 1986 | Craig Hodges, Milw | .451 | 1995 | Steve Kerr, Chi | .524 | 2004 | Anthony Peeler, Sac. | .482 |
| 1987 | Kiki Vandeweghe, Por | .481 | 1996 | Tim Legler, Wash. | .522 | 2005 | Fred Hoiberg, Min. | .483 |
| 1988 | Craig Hodges, Milw-Pho | .491 | 1997 | Glen Rice, Cha | .470 | | | |

## Blocked Shots

**Multiple winners:** Kareem Abdul-Jabbar and Mark Eaton (4); George Johnson, Dikembe Mutombo, Hakeem Olajuwon and Theo Ratliff (3); Manute Bol and Alonzo Mourning (2).

| Year | | Gm | No | Avg |
|---|---|---|---|---|
| 1974 | Elmore Smith, LA | 81 | 393 | 4.85 |
| 1975 | Kareem Abdul-Jabbar, Mil | 65 | 212 | 3.26 |
| 1976 | Kareem Abdul-Jabbar, LA | 82 | 338 | 4.12 |
| 1977 | Bill Walton, Port | 65 | 211 | 3.25 |
| 1978 | George Johnson, NJ | 81 | 274 | 3.38 |
| 1979 | Kareem Abdul-Jabbar, LA | 80 | 316 | 3.95 |
| 1980 | Kareem Abdul-Jabbar, LA | 82 | 280 | 3.41 |
| 1981 | George Johnson, SA | 82 | 278 | 3.39 |
| 1982 | George Johnson, SA | 75 | 234 | 3.12 |
| 1983 | Tree Rollins, Atl | 80 | 343 | 4.29 |
| 1984 | Mark Eaton, Utah | 82 | 351 | 4.28 |
| 1985 | Mark Eaton, Utah | 82 | 456 | 5.56 |
| 1986 | Manute Bol, Wash. | 80 | 397 | 4.96 |
| 1987 | Mark Eaton, Utah | 79 | 321 | 4.06 |
| 1988 | Mark Eaton, Utah | 82 | 304 | 3.71 |
| 1989 | Manute Bol, G.St. | 80 | 345 | 4.31 |
| 1990 | Akeem Olajuwon, Hou | 82 | 376 | 4.59 |
| 1991 | Hakeem Olajuwon, Hou | 56 | 221 | 3.95 |
| 1992 | David Robinson, SA | 68 | 305 | 4.49 |
| 1993 | Hakeem Olajuwon, Hou | 82 | 342 | 4.17 |
| 1994 | Dikembe Mutombo, Den | 82 | 336 | 4.10 |
| 1995 | Dikembe Mutombo, Den | 82 | 321 | 3.91 |
| 1996 | Dikembe Mutombo, Den | 74 | 332 | 4.49 |
| 1997 | Shawn Bradley, Dal-NJ | 73 | 248 | 3.40 |
| 1998 | Marcus Camby, Tor. | 63 | 230 | 3.65 |
| 1999 | Alonzo Mourning, Mia | 46 | 180 | 3.91 |
| 2000 | Alonzo Mourning, Mia | 79 | 294 | 3.72 |
| 2001 | Theo Ratliff, Phi-Atl | 50 | 187 | 3.74 |
| 2002 | Ben Wallace, Det | 80 | 278 | 3.48 |
| 2003 | Theo Ratliff, Atl | 81 | 262 | 3.23 |
| 2004 | Theo Ratliff, Atl-Port | 85 | 307 | 3.61 |
| 2005 | Andrei Kirilenko, Utah | 41 | 136 | 3.32 |

## Steals

**Multiple winners:** Allen Iverson, Michael Jordan, Micheal Ray Richardson and Alvin Robertson (3); Mookie Blaylock, Magic Johnson and John Stockton (2).

| Year | | Gm | No | Avg |
|---|---|---|---|---|
| 1974 | Larry Steele, Port | 81 | 217 | 2.68 |
| 1975 | Rick Barry, G.St. | 80 | 228 | 2.85 |
| 1976 | Slick Watts, Sea | 82 | 261 | 3.18 |
| 1977 | Don Buse, Ind | 81 | 281 | 3.47 |
| 1978 | Ron Lee, Pho | 82 | 225 | 2.74 |
| 1979 | M.L. Carr, Det | 80 | 197 | 2.46 |
| 1980 | Micheal Ray Richardson, NY | 82 | 265 | 3.23 |
| 1981 | Magic Johnson, LA | 37 | 127 | 3.43 |
| 1982 | Magic Johnson, LA | 78 | 208 | 2.67 |
| 1983 | Micheal Ray Richardson, G. ST-NJ | 64 | 182 | 2.84 |
| 1984 | Rickey Green, Utah | 81 | 215 | 2.65 |
| 1985 | Micheal Ray Richardson, NJ | 82 | 243 | 2.96 |
| 1986 | Alvin Robertson, SA | 82 | 301 | 3.67 |
| 1987 | Alvin Robertson, SA | 81 | 260 | 3.21 |
| 1988 | Michael Jordan, Chi | 82 | 259 | 3.16 |
| 1989 | John Stockton, Utah | 82 | 263 | 3.21 |
| 1990 | Michael Jordan, Chi | 82 | 227 | 2.77 |
| 1991 | Alvin Robertson, Chi | 81 | 246 | 3.04 |
| 1992 | John Stockton, Utah | 82 | 244 | 2.98 |
| 1993 | Michael Jordan, Chi | 78 | 221 | 2.83 |
| 1994 | Nate McMillan, Sea | 73 | 216 | 2.96 |
| 1995 | Scottie Pippen, Chi | 79 | 232 | 2.94 |
| 1996 | Gary Payton, Sea | 81 | 231 | 2.85 |
| 1997 | Mookie Blaylock, Atl | 78 | 212 | 2.72 |
| 1998 | Mookie Blaylock, Atl. | 70 | 183 | 2.61 |
| 1999 | Kendall Gill, NJ | 50 | 134 | 2.68 |
| 2000 | Eddie Jones, Cha | 72 | 192 | 2.67 |
| 2001 | Allen Iverson, Phi. | 71 | 178 | 2.51 |
| 2002 | Allen Iverson, Phi. | 60 | 168 | 2.80 |
| 2003 | Allen Iverson, Phi | 82 | 225 | 2.74 |
| 2004 | Baron Davis, NO | 67 | 158 | 2.36 |
| 2005 | Larry Hughes, Wash | 61 | 176 | 2.89 |

**Note:** Akeem Olajuwon changed the spelling of his first name to Hakeem during the 1990-91 season.

# All-Time NBA Regular Season Leaders
Through the 2004-05 regular season.
## CAREER
Players active in 2004-05 in **bold** type.

### Points

| | | Yrs | Gm | Pts | Avg |
|---|---|---|---|---|---|
| 1 | Kareem Abdul-Jabbar | 20 | 1560 | **38,387** | 24.6 |
| 2 | Karl Malone | 19 | 1476 | **36,928** | 25.0 |
| 3 | Michael Jordan | 15 | 1072 | **32,292** | 30.1 |
| 4 | Wilt Chamberlain | 14 | 1045 | **31,419** | 30.1 |
| 5 | Moses Malone | 19 | 1329 | **27,409** | 20.6 |
| 6 | Elvin Hayes | 16 | 1303 | **27,313** | 21.0 |
| 7 | Hakeem Olajuwon | 18 | 1238 | **26,946** | 21.8 |
| 8 | Oscar Robertson | 14 | 1040 | **26,710** | 25.7 |
| 9 | Dominique Wilkins | 15 | 1074 | **26,668** | 24.8 |
| 10 | John Havlicek | 16 | 1270 | **26,395** | 20.8 |
| 11 | Alex English | 15 | 1193 | **25,613** | 21.5 |
| 12 | **Reggie Miller** | 18 | 1389 | **25,279** | 18.2 |
| 13 | Jerry West | 14 | 932 | **25,192** | 27.0 |
| 14 | Patrick Ewing | 17 | 1183 | **24,815** | 21.0 |
| 15 | Charles Barkley | 16 | 1073 | **23,757** | 22.1 |
| | **Shaquille O'Neal** | 13 | 882 | **23,757** | 26.7 |
| 17 | Robert Parish | 21 | 1611 | **23,334** | 14.5 |
| 18 | Adrian Dantley | 15 | 955 | **23,177** | 24.3 |
| 19 | Elgin Baylor | 14 | 846 | **23,149** | 27.4 |
| 20 | Clyde Drexler | 15 | 1086 | **22,195** | 20.4 |
| 21 | Larry Bird | 13 | 897 | **21,791** | 24.3 |
| 22 | Hal Greer | 15 | 1122 | **21,586** | 19.2 |
| 23 | Walt Bellamy | 14 | 1043 | **20,941** | 20.1 |
| 24 | Bob Pettit | 11 | 792 | **20,880** | 26.4 |
| 25 | **Gary Payton** | 16 | 1186 | **20,829** | 17.6 |
| 26 | David Robinson | 14 | 987 | **20,790** | 21.1 |
| 27 | George Gervin | 10 | 791 | **20,708** | 26.2 |
| 28 | Mitch Richmond | 14 | 976 | **20,497** | 21.0 |
| 29 | Tom Chambers | 16 | 1107 | **20,049** | 18.1 |
| 30 | John Stockton | 19 | 1504 | **19,711** | 13.1 |

### Scoring Average
Minimum of 400 games or 10,000 points.

| | | Yrs | Gm | Pts | Avg |
|---|---|---|---|---|---|
| 1 | Michael Jordan | 15 | 1072 | 32,292 | 30.1 |
| 2 | Wilt Chamberlain | 14 | 1045 | 31,419 | 30.1 |
| 3 | **Allen Iverson** | 9 | 610 | 16,738 | 27.4 |
| 4 | Elgin Baylor | 14 | 846 | 23,149 | 27.4 |
| 5 | Jerry West | 14 | 932 | 25,192 | 27.0 |
| 6 | **Shaquille O'Neal** | 13 | 882 | 23,757 | 26.7 |
| 7 | Bob Pettit | 11 | 792 | 20,880 | 26.4 |
| 8 | George Gervin | 10 | 791 | 20,708 | 26.2 |
| 9 | Oscar Robertson | 14 | 1040 | 26,710 | 25.7 |
| 10 | Karl Malone | 19 | 1476 | 36,928 | 25.0 |
| 11 | Dominique Wilkins | 15 | 1074 | 26,668 | 24.8 |
| 12 | Kareem Abdul-Jabbar | 20 | 1560 | 38,387 | 24.6 |
| 13 | Larry Bird | 13 | 897 | 21,791 | 24.3 |
| 14 | Adrian Dantley | 15 | 955 | 23,177 | 24.3 |
| 15 | Pete Maravich | 10 | 658 | 15,948 | 24.2 |
| 16 | **Vince Carter** | 7 | 460 | 10,989 | 23.9 |
| 17 | Rick Barry | 10 | 794 | 18,395 | 23.2 |
| 18 | **Paul Pierce** | 7 | 526 | 12,086 | 23.0 |
| 19 | Paul Arizin | 10 | 713 | 16,266 | 22.8 |
| 20 | George Mikan | 9 | 520 | 11,764 | 22.6 |
| 21 | **Tim Duncan** | 8 | 586 | 13,204 | 22.5 |
| 22 | Bernard King | 14 | 874 | 19,655 | 22.5 |
| 23 | **Kobe Bryant** | 9 | 627 | 14,034 | 22.4 |
| 24 | David Thompson | 8 | 509 | 11,264 | 22.1 |
| 25 | Charles Barkley | 16 | 1073 | 23,757 | 22.1 |
| 26 | Bob McAdoo | 14 | 852 | 18,787 | 22.1 |
| 27 | Julius Erving | 11 | 836 | 18,364 | 22.0 |
| 28 | **Tracy McGrady** | 8 | 565 | 12,423 | 22.0 |
| 29 | Geoff Petrie | 6 | 446 | 9,732 | 21.8 |
| 30 | **Chris Webber** | 12 | 686 | 14,945 | 21.8 |

### Assists

| | | Yrs | Gm | No | Avg |
|---|---|---|---|---|---|
| 1 | John Stockton | 19 | 1504 | **15,806** | 10.5 |
| 2 | Mark Jackson | 17 | 1296 | **10,334** | 8.0 |
| 3 | Magic Johnson | 13 | 906 | **10,141** | 11.2 |
| 4 | Oscar Robertson | 14 | 1040 | **9,887** | 9.5 |
| 5 | Isiah Thomas | 13 | 979 | **9,061** | 9.3 |
| 6 | **Gary Payton** | 15 | 1186 | **8,508** | 7.2 |
| 7 | **Rod Strickland** | 17 | 1094 | **7,987** | 7.3 |
| 8 | Maurice Cheeks | 15 | 1101 | **7,392** | 6.7 |
| 9 | **Jason Kidd** | 11 | 786 | **7,283** | 9.3 |
| 10 | Lenny Wilkens | 15 | 1077 | **7,211** | 6.7 |
| 11 | Terry Porter | 17 | 1274 | **7,160** | 5.6 |
| 12 | Tim Hardaway | 13 | 867 | **7,095** | 8.2 |

### Rebounds

| | | Yrs | Gm | No | Avg |
|---|---|---|---|---|---|
| 1 | Wilt Chamberlain | 14 | 1045 | **23,924** | 22.9 |
| 2 | Bill Russell | 13 | 963 | **21,620** | 22.5 |
| 3 | Kareem Abdul-Jabbar | 20 | 1560 | **17,440** | 11.2 |
| 4 | Elvin Hayes | 16 | 1303 | **16,279** | 12.5 |
| 5 | Moses Malone | 19 | 1329 | **16,212** | 12.2 |
| 6 | Karl Malone | 19 | 1476 | **14,968** | 10.1 |
| 7 | Robert Parish | 21 | 1611 | **14,715** | 9.1 |
| 8 | Nate Thurmond | 14 | 964 | **14,464** | 15.0 |
| 9 | Walt Bellamy | 14 | 1043 | **14,241** | 13.7 |
| 10 | Wes Unseld | 13 | 984 | **13,769** | 14.0 |
| 11 | Hakeem Olajuwon | 18 | 1238 | **13,748** | 11.1 |
| 12 | Buck Williams | 17 | 1307 | **13,017** | 10.0 |

**Note:** If rebounds accumulated in the ABA are included, consider the following totals: Moses Malone (17,834) and Artis Gilmore (16,330).

### Steals

| | | Yrs | Gm | No |
|---|---|---|---|---|
| 1 | John Stockton | 19 | 1504 | 3265 |
| 2 | Michael Jordan | 15 | 1072 | 2514 |
| 3 | **Gary Payton** | 15 | 1186 | 2331 |
| 4 | Maurice Cheeks | 15 | 1101 | 2310 |
| 5 | Scottie Pippen | 17 | 1178 | 2307 |

**Note:** Steals have only been an official stat since the 1973-74 season.

### Blocked Shots

| | | Yrs | Gm | No |
|---|---|---|---|---|
| 1 | Hakeem Olajuwon | 18 | 1238 | 3830 |
| 2 | Kareem Abdul-Jabbar | 20 | 1560 | 3189 |
| 3 | **Dikembe Mutombo** | 14 | 1009 | 3097 |
| 4 | Mark Eaton | 11 | 875 | 3064 |
| 5 | David Robinson | 14 | 987 | 2954 |

**Note:** Blocked shots have only been an official stat since the 1973-74 season. Also, note that if ABA records are included, consider the following block totals: Artis Gilmore (3,178).

### Games Played

| | | Yrs | Career | Gm |
|---|---|---|---|---|
| 1 | Robert Parish | 21 | 1976-97 | 1611 |
| 2 | Kareem Abdul-Jabbar | 20 | 1970-89 | 1560 |
| 3 | John Stockton | 19 | 1984-03 | 1504 |
| 4 | Karl Malone | 19 | 1985-04 | 1476 |
| 5 | **Kevin Willis** | 19 | 1985— | 1419 |

**Note:** If ABA records are included, consider the following game totals: Moses Malone (1,455).

### Field Goals

| | | Yrs | FG | Att | Pct |
|---|---|---|---|---|---|
| 1 | Kareem Abdul-Jabbar | .20 | **15,837** | 28,307 | .559 |
| 2 | Karl Malone | .19 | **13,528** | 26,210 | .516 |
| 3 | Wilt Chamberlain | .14 | **12,681** | 23,497 | .540 |
| | Michael Jordan | .15 | **12,681** | 24,537 | .497 |
| 5 | Elvin Hayes | .16 | **10,976** | 24,272 | .452 |
| 6 | Hakeem Olajuwon | .18 | **10,749** | 20,991 | .512 |
| 7 | Alex English | .15 | **10,659** | 21,036 | .507 |
| 8 | John Havlicek | .16 | **10,513** | 23,930 | .439 |
| 9 | Dominique Wilkins | .15 | **9,963** | 21,589 | .461 |
| 10 | Patrick Ewing | .17 | **9,702** | 19,241 | .504 |
| 11 | Robert Parish | .21 | **9,508** | 17,914 | .537 |
| | Oscar Robertson | .14 | **9,508** | 19,620 | .485 |

**Note:** If field goals made in the ABA are included, consider these NBA-ABA totals: Julius Erving (11,818), Dan Issel (10,431), George Gervin (10,368), Moses Malone (10,277) and Rick Barry (9,695).

### Free Throws

| | | Yrs | FT | Att | Pct |
|---|---|---|---|---|---|
| 1 | Karl Malone | .19 | **9787** | 13,188 | .742 |
| 2 | Moses Malone | .19 | **8531** | 11,090 | .769 |
| 3 | Oscar Robertson | .14 | **7694** | 9,185 | .838 |
| 4 | Michael Jordan | .15 | **7327** | 8,772 | .835 |
| 5 | Jerry West | .14 | **7160** | 8,801 | .814 |
| 6 | Dolph Schayes | .16 | **6979** | 8,273 | .844 |
| 7 | Adrian Dantley | .15 | **6832** | 8,351 | .818 |
| 8 | Kareem Abdul-Jabbar | .20 | **6712** | 9,304 | .721 |
| 9 | Charles Barkley | .16 | **6349** | 8,643 | .734 |
| 10 | **Reggie Miller** | .18 | **6237** | 7,026 | .888 |
| 11 | Bob Pettit | .11 | **6182** | 8,119 | .761 |
| 12 | Wilt Chamberlain | .14 | **6057** | 11,862 | .511 |

**Note:** If free throws made in the ABA are included, consider these totals: Moses Malone (9,018), Dan Issel (6,591), and Julius Erving (6,256).

### Free Throw Percentage

| | | Yrs | FT | Att | Pct |
|---|---|---|---|---|---|
| 1 | Mark Price | .12 | 2135 | 2362 | .904 |
| 2 | Rick Barry | .10 | 3818 | 4243 | .900 |
| 3 | **Steve Nash** | .9 | 1469 | 1647 | .892 |
| 4 | Calvin Murphy | .13 | 3445 | 3864 | .892 |
| 5 | **Peja Stojakovic** | .7 | 1626 | 1826 | .890 |

**Note:** If ABA records are included, consider the following free throw percentage: Rick Barry (5713-6397 for .893)

### 3-Pt Field Goal Pct.

(minimum 250 3-pt FGs made)

| | | Yrs | Gm | Pct | 3FGM |
|---|---|---|---|---|---|
| 1 | Steve Kerr | .15 | 910 | **.454** | 726 |
| 2 | Hubert Davis | .12 | 685 | **.441** | 728 |
| 3 | Drazen Petrovic | .4 | 290 | **.437** | 255 |
| 4 | Tim Legler | .10 | 310 | **.431** | 260 |
| 5 | B.J. Armstrong | .11 | 747 | **.425** | 436 |

### 3-Pt Field Goals Made

| | | Yrs | Gm | Pct | 3FGM |
|---|---|---|---|---|---|
| 1 | **Reggie Miller** | .18 | 1389 | .395 | 2560 |
| 2 | Dale Ellis | .17 | 1209 | .403 | 1719 |
| 3 | Glen Rice | .15 | 1000 | .400 | 1559 |
| 4 | Tim Hardaway | .14 | 867 | .355 | 1542 |
| 5 | **Ray Allen** | .9 | 657 | .397 | 1486 |

### Minutes Played

| | | Gm | MPG | Min |
|---|---|---|---|---|
| 1 | Kareem Abdul-Jabbar | .1560 | 36.8 | 57,446 |
| 2 | Karl Malone | .1476 | 37.2 | 54,852 |
| 3 | Elvin Hayes | .1303 | 38.4 | 50,000 |
| 4 | Wilt Chamberlain | .1045 | 45.8 | 47,859 |
| 5 | John Stockton | .1504 | 31.8 | 47,764 |

### Triple-Doubles

| | | Yrs | Gm | No |
|---|---|---|---|---|
| 1 | Oscar Robertson | .14 | 1040 | 181 |
| 2 | Magic Johnson | .13 | 906 | 138 |
| 3 | Wilt Chamberlain | .14 | 1045 | 78 |
| 4 | **Jason Kidd** | .11 | 786 | 67 |
| 5 | Larry Bird | .13 | 897 | 59 |

**Note:** The triple-double totals of Oscar Robertson and Wilt Chamberlain do not include games in which they may have recorded a triple-double with double-digit blocks and/or steals, since those stats have only be official since the 1973-74 season.

### Personal Fouls

| | | Yrs | Gm | Fouls | DQ |
|---|---|---|---|---|---|
| 1 | Kareem Abdul-Jabbar | .20 | 1560 | **4657** | 48 |
| 2 | Karl Malone | .19 | 1476 | **4578** | 28 |
| 3 | Robert Parish | .21 | 1611 | **4443** | 86 |
| 4 | Charles Oakley | .19 | 1282 | **4421** | 63 |
| 5 | Hakeem Olajuwon | .18 | 1238 | **4383** | 80 |

**Note:** If ABA records are included, consider the following personal foul totals: Artis Gilmore (4,529) and Caldwell Jones (4,436).

### Disqualifications

| | | Yrs | Gm | No |
|---|---|---|---|---|
| 1 | Vern Mikkelsen | .10 | 699 | 127 |
| 2 | Walter Dukes | .8 | 553 | 121 |
| 3 | Shawn Kemp | .14 | 1051 | 115 |
| 4 | Charlie Share | .8 | 555 | 105 |
| 5 | Paul Arizin | .10 | 713 | 101 |

## NBA-ABA Top 20
### Points

All-Time combined regular season scoring leaders, including ABA service (1968-76). NBA players with ABA experience are listed in CAPITAL letters. Players active during 2004-05 are in **bold** type.

| | | Yrs | Pts | Avg |
|---|---|---|---|---|
| 1 | Kareem Abdul-Jabbar | .20 | **38,387** | 24.6 |
| 2 | Karl Malone | .19 | **36,928** | 25.0 |
| 3 | Wilt Chamberlain | .14 | **31,419** | 30.1 |
| 4 | Michael Jordan | .15 | **32,292** | 30.1 |
| 5 | JULIUS ERVING | .16 | **30,026** | 24.2 |
| 6 | MOSES MALONE | .21 | **29,580** | 20.3 |
| 7 | DAN ISSEL | .15 | **27,482** | 22.6 |
| 8 | Elvin Hayes | .16 | **27,313** | 21.0 |
| 9 | Hakeem Olajuwon | .18 | **26,946** | 21.8 |
| 10 | Oscar Robertson | .14 | **26,710** | 25.7 |
| 11 | Dominique Wilkins | .15 | **26,668** | 24.8 |
| 12 | GEORGE GERVIN | .14 | **26,595** | 25.1 |
| 13 | John Havlicek | .16 | **26,395** | 20.8 |
| 14 | Alex English | .15 | **25,613** | 21.5 |
| 15 | RICK BARRY | .14 | **25,279** | 24.8 |
| | **Reggie Miller** | .18 | **25,279** | 18.2 |
| 17 | Jerry West | .14 | **25,192** | 27.0 |
| 18 | ARTIS GILMORE | .17 | **24,941** | 18.8 |
| 19 | Patrick Ewing | .17 | **24,815** | 21.0 |
| 20 | Charles Barkley | .16 | **23,757** | 22.1 |
| | **Shaquille O'Neal** | .13 | **23,757** | 26.7 |

**ABA Totals:** BARRY (4 yrs, 226 gm, 6884 pts, 30.5 avg); ERVING (5 yrs, 407 gm, 11,662 pts, 28.7 avg); GERVIN (4 yrs, 269 gm, 5887 pts, 21.9 avg); GILMORE (5 yrs, 420 gm, 9362 pts, 22.3 avg); ISSEL (6 yrs, 500 gm, 12,823 pts, 25.6 avg); MALONE (2 yrs, 126 gm, 2171 pts, 17.2 avg).

## All-Time NBA Regular Season Leaders (Cont.)

### SINGLE SEASON

#### Scoring Average

| | | Season | Avg |
|---|---|---|---|
| 1 | Wilt Chamberlain, Phi | 1961-62 | 50.4 |
| 2 | Wilt Chamberlain, SF | 1962-63 | 44.8 |
| 3 | Wilt Chamberlain, Phi | 1960-61 | 38.4 |
| 4 | Elgin Baylor, LA | 1961-62 | 38.3 |
| 5 | Wilt Chamberlain, Phi | 1959-60 | 37.6 |
| 6 | Michael Jordan, Chi | 1986-87 | 37.1 |
| 7 | Wilt Chamberlain, SF | 1963-64 | 36.9 |
| 8 | Rick Barry, SF | 1966-67 | 35.6 |
| 9 | Michael Jordan, Chi | 1987-88 | 35.0 |
| 10 | Elgin Baylor, LA | 1960-61 | 34.8 |
| | Kareem Abdul-Jabbar, Mil | 1971-72 | 34.8 |

#### Field Goal Pct.

| | | Season | Pct |
|---|---|---|---|
| 1 | Wilt Chamberlain, LA | 1972-73 | .727 |
| 2 | Wilt Chamberlain, SF | 1966-67 | .683 |
| 3 | Artis Gilmore, Chi | 1980-81 | .670 |
| 4 | Artis Gilmore, Chi | 1981-82 | .652 |
| 5 | Wilt Chamberlain, LA | 1971-72 | .649 |

#### Free Throw Pct.

| | | Season | Pct |
|---|---|---|---|
| 1 | Calvin Murphy, Hou | 1980-81 | .958 |
| 2 | Mahmoud Abdul-Rauf, Den. | 1993-94 | .956 |
| 3 | Mark Price, Cle | 1992-93 | .948 |
| 4 | Mark Price, Cle | 1991-92 | .947 |
| | Rick Barry, Hou | 1978-79 | .947 |

#### 3-Pt Field Goal Pct.

| | | Season | Pct |
|---|---|---|---|
| 1 | Steve Kerr, Chi | 1994-95 | .524 |
| 2 | Jon Sundvold, Mia | 1988-89 | .522 |
| 3 | Tim Legler, Wash | 1995-96 | .522 |
| 4 | Steve Kerr, Chi | 1995-96 | .515 |
| 5 | Detlef Schrempf, Sea | 1994-95 | .514 |

#### Assists

| | | Season | Avg |
|---|---|---|---|
| 1 | John Stockton, Utah | 1989-90 | 14.5 |
| 2 | John Stockton, Utah | 1990-91 | 14.2 |
| 3 | Isiah Thomas, Det | 1984-85 | 13.9 |
| 4 | John Stockton, Utah | 1987-88 | 13.8 |
| 5 | John Stockton, Utah | 1991-92 | 13.7 |
| 6 | John Stockton, Utah | 1988-89 | 13.6 |
| 7 | Kevin Porter, Det | 1978-79 | 13.4 |
| 8 | Magic Johnson, LAL | 1983-84 | 13.1 |
| 9 | Magic Johnson, LAL | 1988-89 | 12.8 |
| 10 | Magic Johnson, LAL | 1984-85 | 12.6 |
| | John Stockton, Utah | 1993-94 | 12.6 |

#### Rebounds

| | | Season | Avg |
|---|---|---|---|
| 1 | Wilt Chamberlain, Phi | 1960-61 | 27.2 |
| 2 | Wilt Chamberlain, Phi | 1959-60 | 27.0 |
| 3 | Wilt Chamberlain, Phi | 1961-62 | 25.7 |
| 4 | Bill Russell, Bos | 1963-64 | 24.7 |
| 5 | Wilt Chamberlain, Phi | 1965-66 | 24.6 |

#### Blocked Shots

| | | Season | Avg |
|---|---|---|---|
| 1 | Mark Eaton, Utah | 1984-85 | 5.56 |
| 2 | Manute Bol, Wash | 1985-86 | 4.96 |
| 3 | Elmore Smith, LA | 1973-74 | 4.85 |
| 4 | Mark Eaton, Utah | 1985-86 | 4.61 |
| 5 | Hakeem Olajuwon, Hou | 1989-90 | 4.59 |

#### Steals

| | | Season | Avg |
|---|---|---|---|
| 1 | Alvin Robertson, SA | 1985-86 | 3.67 |
| 2 | Don Buse, Ind | 1976-77 | 3.47 |
| 3 | Magic Johnson, LAL | 1980-81 | 3.43 |
| 4 | Micheal Ray Richardson, NY | 1979-80 | 3.23 |
| 5 | Alvin Robertson, SA | 1986-87 | 3.21 |

### SINGLE GAME

#### Points

| | Date | FG-FT | Pts |
|---|---|---|---|
| Wilt Chamberlain, Phi vs NY | 3/2/62 | 36-28– | 100 |
| Wilt Chamberlain, Phi vs LA*** | 12/8/61 | 31-16– | 78 |
| Wilt Chamberlain, Phi vs Chi | 1/13/62 | 29-15– | 73 |
| Wilt Chamberlain, SF at NY | 11/16/62 | 29-15– | 73 |
| David Thompson, Den at Det | 4/9/78 | 28-17– | 73 |
| Wilt Chamberlain, SF at LA | 11/3/62 | 29-14– | 72 |
| Elgin Baylor, LA at NY | 11/15/60 | 28-15– | 71 |
| David Robinson, SA at LAC | 4/24/94 | 26-18– | 71 |
| Wilt Chamberlain, SF at Syr | 3/10/63 | 27-16– | 70 |
| Michael Jordan, Chi at Cle* | 3/28/90 | 23-21– | 69 |
| Wilt Chamberlain, Phi at Chi | 12/16/67 | 30- 8– | 68 |
| Pete Maravich, NO vs NYK | 2/25/77 | 26-16– | 68 |
| Wilt Chamberlain, Phi vs NY | 3/9/61 | 27-13– | 67 |
| Wilt Chamberlain, Phi at St. L | 2/17/62 | 26-15– | 67 |
| Wilt Chamberlain, Phi vs NY | 2/25/62 | 25-17– | 67 |
| Wilt Chamberlain, SF vs LA | 1/11/63 | 28-11– | 67 |
| Wilt Chamberlain, LA vs Pho | 2/9/69 | 29- 8– | 66 |
| Wilt Chamberlain, Phi at Cin | 2/13/62 | 24-17– | 65 |
| Wilt Chamberlain, Phi at St. L | 2/27/62 | 25-15– | 65 |
| Wilt Chamberlain, Phi vs LA | 2/7/66 | 28- 9– | 65 |
| Elgin Baylor, Mpls vs Bos | 11/8/59 | 25-14– | 64 |
| Rick Barry, G.St. vs Port | 3/26/74 | 30- 4– | 64 |
| Michael Jordan, Chi vs Orl | 1/16/93 | 27- 9– | 64 |

*Overtime
***Triple overtime.
**Note:** Wilt Chamberlain's 100-point game vs New York was played at Hershey, Penn.

#### Field Goals

| | Date | FG | Att |
|---|---|---|---|
| Wilt Chamberlain, Phi vs NY | 3/2/62 | 36 | 63 |
| Wilt Chamberlain, Phi vs LA*** | 12/8/61 | 31 | 62 |
| Wilt Chamberlain, Phi at Chi | 12/16/67 | 30 | 40 |
| Rick Barry, G.St. vs Port | 2/26/74 | 30 | 45 |
| Wilt Chamberlain made 29 four times. | | | |

***Triple overtime.

#### Free Throws

| | Date | FT | Att |
|---|---|---|---|
| Wilt Chamberlain, Phi vs NY | 3/2/62 | 28 | 32 |
| Adrian Dantley, Utah vs Hou | 1/4/84 | 28 | 29 |
| Adrian Dantley, Utah vs Den | 11/25/83 | 27 | 31 |
| Adrian Dantley, Utah vs Dal | 10/31/80 | 26 | 29 |
| Michael Jordan, Chi vs NJ | 2/26/87 | 26 | 27 |

#### 3-Pt Field Goals

| | Date | No |
|---|---|---|
| Kobe Bryant, LAL vs Sea | 1/7/03 | 12 |
| Dennis Scott, Orl vs Atl | 4/18/96 | 11 |
| Ray Allen, Milw vs Char | 4/14/02 | 10 |
| Brian Shaw, Mia at Mil | 4/8/93 | 10 |
| Joe Dumars, Det vs Min | 11/8/94 | 10 |
| George McCloud, Dal vs Pho | 12/16/95 | 10* |

Many tied with 9 each
* Overtime

## Assists

| | Date | No |
|---|---|---|
| Scott Skiles, Orl vs Den | 12/30/90 | 30 |
| Kevin Porter, NJ vs Hou | 2/24/78 | 29 |
| Bob Cousy, Bos vs Mpls | 2/27/59 | 28 |
| Guy Rodgers, SF vs St.L | 3/14/63 | 28 |
| John Stockton, Utah vs SA | 1/15/91 | 28 |

## Rebounds

| | Date | No |
|---|---|---|
| Wilt Chamberlain, Phi vs Bos | 11/24/60 | 55 |
| Bill Russell, Bos vs Syr | 2/5/60 | 51 |
| Bill Russell, Bos vs Phi | 11/16/57 | 49 |
| Bill Russell, Bos vs Det | 3/11/65 | 49 |
| Wilt Chamberlain, Phi vs Syr | 2/6/60 | 45 |
| Wilt Chamberlain, Phi vs LA | 1/21/61 | 45 |

## Blocked Shots

| | Date | No |
|---|---|---|
| Elmore Smith, LA vs Port | 10/28/73 | 17 |
| Manute Bol, Wash vs Atl | 1/25/86 | 15 |
| Manute Bol, Wash vs Ind | 2/26/87 | 15 |
| Shaquille O'Neal, Orl at NJ | 11/20/93 | 15 |

## Steals

| | Date | No |
|---|---|---|
| Larry Kenon, San Antonio at KC | 12/26/76 | 11 |
| Kendall Gill, NJ vs Mia. | 4/3/99 | 11 |
| 14 different players tied with 10 each, including Alvin Robertson, who had 10 steals in a game four times. | | |

## All-Time Winningest NBA Coaches

Top 25 NBA career victories through the 2004-05 season. Career, regular season and playoff records are noted along with NBA titles won. Coaches active during 2004-05 season in **bold** type.

| | | Career | | | | Regular Season | | | Playoffs | | | |
|---|---|---|---|---|---|---|---|---|---|---|---|---|
| | | Yrs | W | L | Pct | W | L | Pct | W | L | Pct | NBA Titles |
| 1 | **Lenny Wilkens** | 32 | **1412** | 1253 | .530 | 1332 | 1155 | .536 | 80 | 98 | .449 | 1 (1979) |
| 2 | Pat Riley | 21 | **1265** | 669 | .654 | 1110 | 569 | .661 | 155 | 100 | .608 | 4 (1982,85,87-88) |
| 3 | **Don Nelson** | 27 | **1260** | 965 | .566 | 1190 | 880 | .575 | 70 | 85 | .452 | None |
| 4 | **Larry Brown** | 22 | **1087** | 830 | .567 | 987 | 741 | .571 | 100 | 89 | .529 | 1 (2004) |
| 5 | Red Auerbach | 20 | **1037** | 548 | .654 | 938 | 479 | .662 | 99 | 69 | .589 | 9 (1957, 59-66) |
| 6 | **Jerry Sloan** | 20 | **1021** | 697 | .594 | 943 | 617 | .604 | 78 | 80 | .494 | None |
| 7 | Phil Jackson | 14 | **1007** | 385 | .723 | 832 | 316 | .725 | 175 | 69 | .717 | 9 (1991-93,96-98,00-02) |
| 8 | Bill Fitch | 25 | **999** | 1160 | .463 | 944 | 1106 | .460 | 55 | 54 | .505 | 1 (1981) |
| 9 | Dick Motta | 25 | **991** | 1087 | .477 | 935 | 1017 | .479 | 56 | 70 | .444 | 1 (1978) |
| 10 | Jack Ramsay | 21 | **908** | 841 | .519 | 864 | 783 | .525 | 44 | 58 | .431 | 1 (1977) |
| 11 | Cotton Fitzsimmons | 21 | **867** | 824 | .513 | 832 | 775 | .518 | 35 | 49 | .417 | None |
| 12 | Gene Shue | 22 | **814** | 908 | .473 | 784 | 861 | .477 | 30 | 47 | .390 | None |
| 13 | **George Karl** | 17 | **800** | 578 | .581 | 740 | 507 | .593 | 60 | 71 | .458 | None |
| 14 | **Rick Adelman** | 15 | **776** | 535 | .592 | 708 | 443 | .615 | 68 | 64 | .515 | None |
| 15 | Red Holzman | 18 | **754** | 652 | .536 | 696 | 604 | .535 | 58 | 48 | .547 | 2 (1970, 73) |
| | John MacLeod | 18 | **754** | 711 | .515 | 707 | 657 | .518 | 47 | 54 | .465 | None |
| 17 | Chuck Daly | 14 | **713** | 488 | .594 | 638 | 437 | .593 | 75 | 51 | .595 | 2 (1989-90) |
| 18 | Doug Moe | 15 | **661** | 579 | .533 | 628 | 529 | .543 | 33 | 50 | .398 | None |
| 19 | K.C. Jones | 10 | **603** | 309 | .661 | 522 | 252 | .674 | 81 | 57 | .587 | 2 (1984,86) |
| 20 | Del Harris | 14 | **594** | 507 | .540 | 556 | 457 | .549 | 38 | 50 | .432 | None |
| 21 | **Mike Fratello** | 15 | **632** | 529 | .544 | 612 | 491 | .555 | 20 | 38 | .345 | None |
| 22 | Al Attles | 14 | **588** | 548 | .518 | 557 | 518 | .518 | 31 | 30 | .508 | 1 (1975) |
| 23 | **Rudy Tomjanovich** | 13 | **578** | 455 | .560 | 527 | 416 | .559 | 51 | 39 | .567 | 2 (1994-95) |
| 24 | **Gregg Popovich** | 9 | **524** | 274 | .657 | 455 | 233 | .661 | 69 | 41 | .627 | 3 (1999, 2003, 05) |
| 25 | Billy Cunningham | 8 | **520** | 235 | .689 | 454 | 196 | .698 | 66 | 39 | .629 | 1 (1983) |

**Note:** The NBA does not recognize records from the National Basketball League (1937-49), the American Basketball League (1961-62) or the American Basketball Assn. (1968-76), so the following NBL, ABL and ABA overall coaching records are not included above: NBL—**John Kundla** (51-19 and a title in 1 year). ABA—**Larry Brown** (249-129 in 4 yrs), **Alex Hannum** (194-164 and one title in 4 yrs), **K.C. Jones** (30-58 in 1 yr); **Kevin Loughery** (189-95 and one title in 3 yrs).

## Where They Coached

**Adelman**—Portland (1988-94), Golden State (1995-97), Sacramento (1998–); **Attles**—Golden St. (1970-80,80-83); **Auerbach**—Washington (1946-49), Tri-Cities (1949-50), Boston (1950-66); **Brown**—Denver (1976-79), New Jersey (1981-83), San Antonio (1988-92), LA Clippers (1992-93), Indiana (1993-97), Philadelphia (1997-2003), Detroit (2003-05), New York (2005–); **Cunningham**—Philadelphia (1977-85); **Daly**—Cleveland (1981-82), Detroit (1983-92), New Jersey (1992-94), Orlando (1997-99); **Fitch**—Cleveland (1970-79), Boston (1979-83), Houston (1983-88), New Jersey (1989-92), LA Clippers (1994-98); **Fitzsimmons**—Phoenix (1970-72), Atlanta (1972-76), Buffalo (1977-78), Kansas City (1978-84), San Antonio (1984-86), Phoenix (1988-92, 95-96); **Fratello**—Atlanta (1980-90), Cleveland (1993-99), Memphis (2004–).

**Harris**—Houston (1979-83), Milwaukee (1987-92), LA Lakers (1994-99); **Holzman**—Milwaukee-St. Louis Hawks (1954-57), NY Knicks (1968-77,78-82); **Jackson**—Chicago (1989-98), LA Lakers (1999-2004); **Jones**—Washington (1973-76), Boston (1983-88), Seattle (1990-92); **Karl**—Cleveland (1984-86); Golden St. (1986-88), Seattle (1991-98), Milwaukee (1999-2003), Denver (2004–); **MacLeod**—Phoenix (1973-87), Dallas (1987-89), NY Knicks (1990-91); **Moe**—San Antonio (1976-80), Denver (1981-90), Philadelphia (1992-93).

**Motta**—Chicago (1968-76), Washington (1976-80), Dallas (1980-87), Sacramento (1990-91), Dallas (1994-96), Denver (1997); **Nelson**—Milwaukee (1976-87), Golden St. (1988-95), New York (1995-96), Dallas (1997-2005); **Popovich**—San Antonio (1996–); **Ramsay**—Philadelphia (1968-72), Buffalo (1972-76), Portland (1976-86), Indiana (1986-89); **Riley**—LA Lakers (1981-90), New York (1991-95), Miami (1995-2003); **Shue**—Baltimore (1967-73), Philadelphia (1973-77), San Diego Clippers (1978-80), Washington (1980-86), LA Clippers (1987-89); **Sloan**—Chicago (1979-82), Utah (1988–); **Tomjanovich**—Houston (1991-2003), LA Lakers (2004-05); **Wilkens**—Seattle (1969-72), Portland (1974-76), Seattle (1977-85), Cleveland (1986-93), Atlanta (1993-2000), Toronto (2000-03), New York (2004-05).

## All-Time Winningest NBA Coaches (Cont.)

### Top Winning Percentages

Minimum of 350 victories, including playoffs; coaches active during 2004-05 season in **bold** type.

| | | Yrs | W | L | Pct |
|---|---|---|---|---|---|
| 1 | Phil Jackson . . . . . . . . . . . . | 14 | 1007 | 385 | **.723** |
| 2 | Billy Cunningham . . . . . . . . . | 8 | 520 | 235 | **.689** |
| 3 | K.C. Jones . . . . . . . . . . . . | 10 | 603 | 309 | **.661** |
| 4 | **Gregg Popovich** . . . . . . . . . | 9 | 524 | 274 | **.657** |
| 5 | Red Auerbach . . . . . . . . . . . | 20 | 1037 | 548 | **.654** |
| 6 | Pat Riley . . . . . . . . . . . . . . | 21 | 1265 | 669 | **.654** |
| 7 | Tommy Heinsohn . . . . . . . . | 9 | 474 | 296 | **.616** |
| 8 | **Jerry Sloan** . . . . . . . . . . . . | 20 | 1021 | 697 | **.594** |
| 9 | Chuck Daly . . . . . . . . . . . . | 14 | 713 | 488 | **.594** |
| 10 | **Rick Adelman** . . . . . . . . . . | 15 | 776 | 535 | **.592** |
| 11 | Larry Costello . . . . . . . . . . | 10 | 467 | 323 | **.591** |
| 12 | John Kundla . . . . . . . . . . . | 11 | 485 | 338 | **.589** |
| 13 | **George Karl** . . . . . . . . . . . | 17 | 800 | 578 | **.581** |
| 14 | Bill Sharman . . . . . . . . . . . | 7 | 368 | 267 | **.580** |
| 15 | **Jeff Van Gundy** . . . . . . . . . | 9 | 385 | 280 | **.579** |
| 16 | Al Cervi . . . . . . . . . . . . . | 9 | 359 | 267 | **.573** |
| 17 | **Larry Brown** . . . . . . . . . . . | 22 | 1087 | 830 | **.567** |
| 18 | **Don Nelson** . . . . . . . . . . . | 27 | 1260 | 965 | **.566** |
| 19 | Joe Lapchick . . . . . . . . . . . | 9 | 356 | 277 | **.562** |
| 20 | **Rudy Tomjanovich** . . . . . . | 13 | 578 | 455 | **.560** |
| 21 | **Phil "Flip" Saunders** . . . . | 10 | 428 | 356 | **.546** |
| 22 | **Mike Fratello** . . . . . . . . . . | 15 | 632 | 529 | **.544** |
| 23 | Bill Russell . . . . . . . . . . . . | 8 | 375 | 317 | **.542** |
| 24 | Del Harris . . . . . . . . . . . . . | 14 | 594 | 507 | **.540** |
| 25 | Alex Hannum . . . . . . . . . . | 12 | 518 | 446 | **.537** |
| 26 | Red Holzman . . . . . . . . . . | 18 | 754 | 652 | **.536** |
| 27 | Doug Moe . . . . . . . . . . . . | 15 | 661 | 579 | **.533** |
| 28 | **Lenny Wilkens** . . . . . . . . . | 32 | 1412 | 1253 | **.530** |
| 29 | Richie Guerin . . . . . . . . . . | 8 | 353 | 325 | **.521** |
| 30 | Jack Ramsay . . . . . . . . . . . | 21 | 908 | 841 | **.519** |

### Active Coaches' Victories

Through 2004-05 season, including playoffs.

| | | Yrs | W | L | Pct |
|---|---|---|---|---|---|
| 1 | Larry Brown, New York . . . . . | 22 | **1087** | 830 | .567 |
| 2 | Jerry Sloan, Utah . . . . . . . . . | 20 | **1021** | 697 | .594 |
| 3 | Phil Jackson, LA Lakers . . . . . | 14 | **1007** | 385 | .723 |
| 4 | George Karl, Denver . . . . . . . | 17 | **800** | 578 | .581 |
| 5 | Rick Adelman, Sacramento . . | 15 | **776** | 535 | .592 |
| 6 | Mike Fratello, Memphis . . . . . | 15 | **632** | 529 | .544 |
| 7 | Gregg Popovich, San Antonio . | 9 | **524** | 274 | .657 |
| 8 | Mike Dunleavy Sr., LA Clippers | 13 | **494** | 517 | .489 |
| 9 | Phil Saunders, Detroit . . . . . . | 10 | **428** | 356 | .546 |
| 10 | Jeff Van Gundy, Houston . . . . | 9 | **385** | 280 | .579 |
| 11 | Bernie Bickerstaff, Charlotte . . | 11 | **368** | 433 | .459 |
| 12 | Brian Hill, Orlando . . . . . . . . | 7 | **240** | 245 | .495 |
| 13 | Rick Carlisle, Indiana . . . . . . | 4 | **233** | 151 | .607 |
| 14 | Doc Rivers, Boston . . . . . . . . | 6 | **224** | 219 | .506 |
| 15 | Nate McMillan, Portland . . . . | 5 | **220** | 191 | .535 |
| 16 | Bob Weiss, Seattle . . . . . . . . | 6 | **212** | 291 | .421 |
| 17 | Byron Scott, New Orleans . . . | 6 | **192** | 218 | .469 |
| 18 | Scott Skiles, Chicago . . . . . . | 5 | **189** | 173 | .522 |
| 19 | Maurice Cheeks, Philadelphia . | 4 | **165** | 146 | .531 |
| 20 | Stan Van Gundy, Miami . . . . . | 2 | **118** | 74 | .615 |
| 21 | Eddie Jordan, Washington . . . | 4 | **107** | 164 | .395 |
| 22 | Mike D'Antoni, Phoenix . . . . . | 3 | **106** | 102 | .510 |
| 23 | Lawrence Frank, New Jersey . . | 2 | **74** | 63 | .540 |
| 24 | Terry Stotts, Milwaukee . . . . . | 2 | **52** | 85 | .380 |
| 25 | Mike Montgomery, Golden St. . | 1 | **34** | 48 | .415 |
| 26 | Sam Mitchell, Toronto . . . . . . | 1 | **33** | 49 | .402 |
| 27 | Avery Johnson, Dallas . . . . . . | 1 | **22** | 9 | .710 |
| 28 | Mike Woodson, Atlanta . . . . . | 1 | **13** | 69 | .159 |
| 29 | Mike Brown, Cleveland . . . . . | 0 | **0** | 0 | — |
| | Dwayne Casey, Minnesota . . . | 0 | **0** | 0 | — |

## Annual Awards
### Most Valuable Player

The Maurice Podoloff Trophy for regular season MVP. Named after the first commissioner (then president) of the NBA. Winners first selected by the NBA players (1956-80) then a national panel of pro basketball writers and broadcasters (since 1981). Winners' scoring averages are provided; (*) indicates led league.

**Multiple winners:** Kareem Abdul-Jabbar (6); Michael Jordan and Bill Russell (5); Wilt Chamberlain (4); Larry Bird, Magic Johnson and Moses Malone (3); Tim Duncan, Karl Malone and Bob Pettit (2).

| Year | | Avg | Year | | Avg |
|---|---|---|---|---|---|
| 1956 | Bob Pettit, St. Louis, F . . . . . . . . . . . . . . . . . | 25.7* | 1982 | Moses Malone, Houston, C . . . . . . . . . . . | 31.1 |
| 1957 | Bob Cousy, Boston, G . . . . . . . . . . . . . . . . | 20.6 | 1983 | Moses Malone, Philadelphia, C . . . . . . . . | 24.5 |
| 1958 | Bill Russell, Boston, C . . . . . . . . . . . . . . . | 16.6 | 1984 | Larry Bird, Boston, F . . . . . . . . . . . . . . . | 24.2 |
| 1959 | Bob Pettit, St. Louis, F . . . . . . . . . . . . . . | 29.2* | 1985 | Larry Bird, Boston, F . . . . . . . . . . . . . . . | 28.7 |
| 1960 | Wilt Chamberlain, Philadelphia, C . . . . . . | 37.6* | 1986 | Larry Bird, Boston, F . . . . . . . . . . . . . . . | 25.8 |
| 1961 | Bill Russell, Boston, C . . . . . . . . . . . . . . . | 16.9 | 1987 | Magic Johnson, LAL, G . . . . . . . . . . . . . | 23.9 |
| 1962 | Bill Russell, Boston, C . . . . . . . . . . . . . . . | 18.9 | 1988 | Michael Jordan, Chicago, G . . . . . . . . . . | 35.0* |
| 1963 | Bill Russell, Boston, C . . . . . . . . . . . . . . . | 16.8 | 1989 | Magic Johnson, LAL, G . . . . . . . . . . . . . | 22.5 |
| 1964 | Oscar Robertson, Cincinnati, G . . . . . . . . | 31.4 | 1990 | Magic Johnson, LAL, G . . . . . . . . . . . . . | 22.3 |
| 1965 | Bill Russell, Boston, C . . . . . . . . . . . . . . . | 14.1 | 1991 | Michael Jordan, Chicago, G . . . . . . . . . . | 31.5* |
| 1966 | Wilt Chamberlain, Philadelphia, C . . . . . . | 33.5* | 1992 | Michael Jordan, Chicago, G . . . . . . . . . . | 30.1* |
| 1967 | Wilt Chamberlain, Philadelphia, C . . . . . . | 24.1 | 1993 | Charles Barkley, Phoenix, F . . . . . . . . . . | 25.6 |
| 1968 | Wilt Chamberlain, Philadelphia, C . . . . . . | 24.3 | 1994 | Hakeem Olajuwon, Houston, C . . . . . . . . | 27.3 |
| 1969 | Wes Unseld, Baltimore, C . . . . . . . . . . . . | 13.8 | 1995 | David Robinson, San Antonio, C . . . . . . . | 27.6 |
| 1970 | Willis Reed, New York, C . . . . . . . . . . . . | 21.7 | 1996 | Michael Jordan, Chicago, G . . . . . . . . . . | 30.4* |
| 1971 | Lew Alcindor, Milwaukee, C . . . . . . . . . . | 31.7* | 1997 | Karl Malone, Utah, F . . . . . . . . . . . . . . | 27.4 |
| 1972 | Kareem Abdul-Jabbar, Milwaukee, C . . . . | 34.8* | 1998 | Michael Jordan, Chicago, G . . . . . . . . . . | 28.7* |
| 1973 | Dave Cowens, Boston, C . . . . . . . . . . . . | 20.5 | 1999 | Karl Malone, Utah, F . . . . . . . . . . . . . . | 23.8 |
| 1974 | Kareem Abdul-Jabbar, Milwaukee, C . . . . | 27.0 | 2000 | Shaquille O'Neal, LAL, C . . . . . . . . . . . . | 29.7* |
| 1975 | Bob McAdoo, Buffalo, F . . . . . . . . . . . . | 34.5* | 2001 | Allen Iverson, Philadelphia, G . . . . . . . . | 31.1* |
| 1976 | Kareem Abdul-Jabbar, LA, C . . . . . . . . . . | 27.7 | 2002 | Tim Duncan, San Antonio, F/C . . . . . . . . | 25.5 |
| 1977 | Kareem Abdul-Jabbar, LA, C . . . . . . . . . . | 26.2 | 2003 | Tim Duncan, San Antonio, F/C . . . . . . . . | 23.3 |
| 1978 | Bill Walton, Portland, C . . . . . . . . . . . . . | 18.9 | 2004 | Kevin Garnett, Minnesota, F . . . . . . . . . | 24.2 |
| 1979 | Moses Malone, Houston, C . . . . . . . . . . | 24.8 | 2005 | Steve Nash, Phoenix, G . . . . . . . . . . . . | 15.5 |
| 1980 | Kareem Abdul-Jabbar, LA, C . . . . . . . . . . | 24.8 | | | |
| 1981 | Julius Erving, Philadelphia, F . . . . . . . . . | 24.6 | | | |

**Note:** Lew Alcindor changed his name to Kareem Abdul-Jabbar after the 1970-71 season.

## Rookie of the Year

The Eddie Gottlieb Trophy for outstanding rookie of the regular season. Named after the pro basketball pioneer and owner-coach of the first NBA champion Philadelphia Warriors. Winners selected by a national panel of pro basketball writers and broadcasters. Winners' scoring averages provided; (*) indicates led league; winners who were also named MVP are in **bold** type.

| Year | | Avg | Year | | Avg |
|------|---|-----|------|---|-----|
| 1953 | Don Meineke, Ft. Wayne, F | 10.8 | 1980 | Larry Bird, Boston, F | 21.3 |
| 1954 | Ray Felix, Baltimore, C | 17.6 | 1981 | Darrell Griffith, Utah, G | 20.6 |
| 1955 | Bob Pettit, Milwaukee Hawks, F | 20.4 | 1982 | Buck Williams, New Jersey, F | 15.5 |
| 1956 | Maurice Stokes, Rochester, F/C | 16.8 | 1983 | Terry Cummings, San Diego, F | 23.7 |
| 1957 | Tommy Heinsohn, Boston, F | 16.2 | 1984 | Ralph Sampson, Houston, C | 21.0 |
| 1958 | Woody Sauldsberry, Philadelphia, F/C | 12.8 | 1985 | Michael Jordan, Chicago, G | 28.2 |
| 1959 | Elgin Baylor, Minneapolis, F | 24.9 | 1986 | Patrick Ewing, New York, C | 20.0 |
| 1960 | **Wilt Chamberlain**, Philadelphia, C | 37.6* | 1987 | Chuck Person, Indiana, F | 18.8 |
| 1961 | Oscar Robertson, Cincinnati, G | 30.5 | 1988 | Mark Jackson, New York, G | 13.6 |
| 1962 | Walt Bellamy, Chicago Packers, C | 31.6 | 1989 | Mitch Richmond, Golden St., G | 22.0 |
| 1963 | Terry Dischinger, Chicago Zephyrs, F | 25.5 | 1990 | David Robinson, San Antonio, C | 24.3 |
| 1964 | Jerry Lucas, Cincinnati, F/C | 17.7 | 1991 | Derrick Coleman, New Jersey, F | 18.4 |
| 1965 | Willis Reed, New York, C | 19.5 | 1992 | Larry Johnson, Charlotte, F | 19.2 |
| 1966 | Rick Barry, San Francisco, F | 25.7 | 1993 | Shaquille O'Neal, Orlando, C | 23.4 |
| 1967 | Dave Bing, Detroit, G | 20.0 | 1994 | Chris Webber, Golden St., F | 17.5 |
| 1968 | Earl Monroe, Baltimore, G | 24.3 | 1995 | Grant Hill, Detroit, F | 19.9 |
| 1969 | **Wes Unseld**, Baltimore, C | 13.8 | | & Jason Kidd, Dallas, G | 11.7 |
| 1970 | Lew Alcindor, Milwaukee Bucks, C | 28.8 | 1996 | Damon Stoudamire, Toronto, G | 19.0 |
| 1971 | Dave Cowens, Boston, C | 17.0 | 1997 | Allen Iverson, Philadelphia, G | 23.5 |
| | & Geoff Petrie, Portland, G | 24.8 | 1998 | Tim Duncan, San Antonio, F/C | 21.6 |
| 1972 | Sidney Wicks, Portland, F | 24.5 | 1999 | Vince Carter, Toronto, F | 18.3 |
| 1973 | Bob McAdoo, Buffalo, C/F | 18.0 | 2000 | Elton Brand, Chicago, F | 20.1 |
| 1974 | Ernie DiGregorio, Buffalo, G | 15.2 | | & Steve Francis, Houston, G | 18.0 |
| 1975 | Keith Wilkes, Golden St., F | 14.2 | 2001 | Mike Miller, Orlando, G/F | 11.9 |
| 1976 | Alvan Adams, Phoenix, C | 19.0 | 2002 | Pau Gasol, Memphis, F | 17.6 |
| 1977 | Adrian Dantley, Buffalo, F | 20.3 | 2003 | Amare Stoudemire, Phoenix, F | 13.5 |
| 1978 | Walter Davis, Phoenix, G | 24.2 | 2004 | LeBron James, Cleveland, F | 20.9 |
| 1979 | Phil Ford, Kansas City, G | 15.9 | 2005 | Emeka Okafor, Charlotte, C | 15.1 |

**Note:** The Chicago Packers changed their name to the Zephyrs after 1961-62 season. Also, Lew Alcindor changed his name to Kareem Abdul-Jabbar after the 1970-71 season.

## Number One Draft Choices

Overall first choices in the NBA draft since the abolition of the territorial draft in 1966. Players who became Rookie of the Year are in **bold** type. The draft lottery began in 1985.

| Year | | Overall 1st Pick | Year | | Overall 1st Pick |
|------|---|------------------|------|---|------------------|
| 1966 | New York | Cazzie Russell, Michigan | 1986 | Cleveland | Brad Daugherty, N. Carolina |
| 1967 | Detroit | Jimmy Walker, Providence | 1987 | San Antonio | **David Robinson**, Navy |
| 1968 | San Diego | Elvin Hayes, Houston | 1988 | LA Clippers | Danny Manning, Kansas |
| 1969 | Milwaukee | **Lew Alcindor**, UCLA | 1989 | Sacramento | Pervis Ellison, Louisville |
| 1970 | Detroit | Bob Lanier, St. Bonaventure | 1990 | New Jersey | **Derrick Coleman**, Syracuse |
| 1971 | Cleveland | Austin Carr, Notre Dame | 1991 | Charlotte | **Larry Johnson**, UNLV |
| 1972 | Portland | LaRue Martin, Loyola-Chicago | 1992 | Orlando | **Shaquille O'Neal**, LSU |
| 1973 | Philadelphia | Doug Collins, Illinois St. | 1993 | Orlando | **Chris Webber**, Michigan |
| 1974 | Portland | Bill Walton, UCLA | 1994 | Milwaukee | Glenn Robinson, Purdue |
| 1975 | Atlanta | David Thompson, N.C. State | 1995 | Golden St. | Joe Smith, Maryland |
| 1976 | Houston | John Lucas, Maryland | 1996 | Philadelphia | **Allen Iverson**, Georgetown |
| 1977 | Milwaukee | Kent Benson, Indiana | 1997 | San Antonio | **Tim Duncan**, Wake Forest |
| 1978 | Portland | Mychal Thompson, Minnesota | 1998 | LA Clippers | Michael Olowokandi, Pacific |
| 1979 | LA Lakers | Magic Johnson, Michigan St. | 1999 | Chicago | **Elton Brand**, Duke |
| 1980 | Golden St | Joe Barry Carroll, Purdue | 2000 | New Jersey | Kenyon Martin, Cincinnati |
| 1981 | Dallas | Mark Aguirre, DePaul | 2001 | Washington | Kwame Brown, Glynn Acad. |
| 1982 | LA Lakers | James Worthy, N. Carolina | 2002 | Houston | Yao Ming, China |
| 1983 | Houston | **Ralph Sampson**, Virginia | 2003 | Cleveland | **LeBron James**, St. Vincent/St. Mary |
| 1984 | Houston | Akeem Olajuwon, Houston | 2004 | Orlando | Dwight Howard, SW Atlanta Christ. |
| 1985 | New York | **Patrick Ewing**, Georgetown | 2005 | Milwaukee | Andrew Bogut, Utah |

**Note:** Lew Alcindor changed his name to Kareem Abdul-Jabbar after the 1970-71 season; Akeem Olajuwon changed his first name to Hakeem in 1991; in 1975 David Thompson signed with Denver of the ABA and did not play for Atlanta; David Robinson joined NBA for 1989-90 season after fulfilling military obligation.

## Sixth Man Award

Awarded to the Best Player Off the Bench for the regular season. Winners selected by a national panel of pro basketball writers and broadcasters.

**Multiple winners:** Kevin McHale, Ricky Pierce and Detlef Schrempf (2).

| Year | | Year | | Year | |
|------|--|------|--|------|--|
| 1983 | Bobby Jones, Phi., F | 1991 | Detlef Schrempf, Ind., F | 1999 | Darrell Armstrong, Orl., G |
| 1984 | Kevin McHale, Bos., F | 1992 | Detlef Schrempf, Ind., F | 2000 | Rodney Rogers, Pho., F |
| 1985 | Kevin McHale, Bos., F | 1993 | Cliff Robinson, Port., F | 2001 | Aaron McKie, Phi., G |
| 1986 | Bill Walton, Bos., F/C | 1994 | Dell Curry, Char., G | 2002 | Corliss Williamson, Det., F |
| 1987 | Ricky Pierce, Mil., G/F | 1995 | Anthony Mason, NY, F | 2003 | Bobby Jackson, Sac., G |
| 1988 | Roy Tarpley, Dal., F | 1996 | Toni Kukoc, Chi., F | 2004 | Antawn Jamison, Dal., F |
| 1989 | Eddie Johnson, Pho., F | 1997 | John Starks, NY, G | 2005 | Ben Gordon, Chicago, G |
| 1990 | Ricky Pierce, Mil., G/F | 1998 | Danny Manning, Pho., F | | |

## Defensive Player of the Year

Awarded to the Best Defensive Player for the regular season. Winners selected by a national panel of pro basketball writers and broadcasters.

**Multiple winners:** Dikembe Mutombo (4); Ben Wallace (3); Mark Eaton, Sidney Moncrief, Alonzo Mourning, Hakeem Olajuwon and Dennis Rodman (2).

| Year | | Year | | Year | |
|------|--|------|--|------|--|
| 1983 | Sidney Moncrief, Mil., G | 1991 | Dennis Rodman, Det., F | 1999 | Alonzo Mourning, Mia., C |
| 1984 | Sidney Moncrief, Mil., G | 1992 | David Robinson, SA, C | 2000 | Alonzo Mourning, Mia., C |
| 1985 | Mark Eaton, Utah, C | 1993 | Hakeem Olajuwon, Hou., C | 2001 | Dikembe Mutombo, Atl.-Phi., C |
| 1986 | Alvin Robertson, SA, G | 1994 | Hakeem Olajuwon, Hou., C | 2002 | Ben Wallace, Det., C/F |
| 1987 | Michael Cooper, LAL, F | 1995 | Dikembe Mutombo, Den., C | 2003 | Ben Wallace, Det., C/F |
| 1988 | Michael Jordan, Chi., G | 1996 | Gary Payton, Sea., G | 2004 | Ron Artest, Ind., F |
| 1989 | Mark Eaton, Utah, C | 1997 | Dikembe Mutombo, Atl., C | 2005 | Ben Wallace, Det., C/F |
| 1990 | Dennis Rodman, Det., F | 1998 | Dikembe Mutombo, Atl., C | | |

## Most Improved Player

Awarded to the Most Improved Player for the regular season. Winners selected by a national panel of pro basketball writers and broadcasters.

| Year | | Year | | Year | |
|------|--|------|--|------|--|
| 1986 | Alvin Robertson, SA, G | 1993 | Mahmoud Abdul-Rauf, Den., G | 2000 | Jalen Rose, Ind., G |
| 1987 | Dale Ellis, Sea., G | 1994 | Don Maclean, Wash., F | 2001 | Tracy McGrady, Orl., F |
| 1988 | Kevin Duckworth, Port., C | 1995 | Dana Barros, Phi., G | 2002 | Jermaine O'Neal, Ind., F |
| 1989 | Kevin Johnson, Pho., G | 1996 | Gheorghe Muresan, Wash., C | 2003 | Gilbert Arenas, G.St., G |
| 1990 | Rony Seikaly, Mia., C | 1997 | Isaac Austin, Miami, C | 2004 | Zach Randolph, Port., F |
| 1991 | Scott Skiles, Orl., G | 1998 | Alan Henderson, Atl., F | 2005 | Bobby Simmons, LAC, F |
| 1992 | Pervis Ellison, Wash., C | 1999 | Darrell Armstrong, Orl., G | | |

## Coach of the Year

The Red Auerbach Trophy for outstanding coach of the year. Renamed in 1967 for the former Boston coach who led the Celtics to nine NBA titles. Winners selected by a national panel of pro basketball writers and broadcasters. Previous season and winning season records are provided; (*) indicates division title.

**Multiple winners:** Don Nelson and Pat Riley (3); Hubie Brown, Bill Fitch, Cotton Fitzsimmons and Gene Shue (2).

| Year | | Improvement | | Year | | Improvement | |
|------|--|------|--|------|--|------|--|
| 1963 | Harry Gallatin, St. L | .29-51 | to 48-32 | 1985 | Don Nelson, Mil | .50-32* | to 59-23* |
| 1964 | Alex Hannum, SF | .31-49 | to 48-32* | 1986 | Mike Fratello, Atl | .34-48 | to 50-32 |
| 1965 | Red Auerbach, Bos | .59-21* | to 61-18* | 1987 | Mike Schuler, Port | .40-42 | to 49-33 |
| 1966 | Dolph Schayes, Phi | .40-40 | to 55-25* | 1988 | Doug Moe, Den | .37-45 | to 54-28* |
| 1967 | Johnny Kerr, Chi | Expan. | to 33-48 | 1989 | Cotton Fitzsimmons, Pho | .28-54 | to 55-27 |
| 1968 | Richie Guerin, St. L | .39-42 | to 56-26* | 1990 | Pat Riley, LA Lakers | .57-25* | to 63-19* |
| 1969 | Gene Shue, Balt | .36-46 | to 57-25* | 1991 | Don Chaney, Hou | .41-41 | to 52-30 |
| 1970 | Red Holzman, NY | .54-28 | to 60-22* | 1992 | Don Nelson, GS | .44-38 | to 55-27 |
| 1971 | Dick Motta, Chi | .39-43 | to 51-31 | 1993 | Pat Riley, NY | .51-31 | to 60-22 |
| 1972 | Bill Sharman, LA | .48-34* | to 69-13* | 1994 | Lenny Wilkens, Atl | .43-39 | to 57-25* |
| 1973 | Tommy Heinsohn, Bos | .56-26* | to 68-14* | 1995 | Del Harris, LA Lakers | .33-49 | to 48-34 |
| 1974 | Ray Scott, Det | .40-42 | to 52-30 | 1996 | Phil Jackson, Chi | .47-35 | to 72-10* |
| 1975 | Phil Johnson, KC-Omaha | .33-49 | to 44-38 | 1997 | Pat Riley, Mia | .42-40 | to 61-21 |
| 1976 | Bill Fitch, Cle | .40-42 | to 49-33* | 1998 | Larry Bird, Ind | .39-43 | to 58-24 |
| 1977 | Tom Nissalke, Hou | .40-42 | to 49-33* | 1999 | Mike Dunleavy, Port. | .46-36 | to 35-15* |
| 1978 | Hubie Brown, Atl | .31-51 | to 41-41 | 2000 | Doc Rivers, Orlando | .33-17 | to 41-41 |
| 1979 | Cotton Fitzsimmons, KC | .31-51 | to 48-34* | 2001 | Larry Brown, Phila. | .49-33 | to 56-26* |
| 1980 | Bill Fitch, Bos | .29-53 | to 61-21* | 2002 | Rick Carlisle, Det | .32-50 | to 50-32* |
| 1981 | Jack McKinney, Ind | .37-45 | to 44-38 | 2003 | Gregg Popovich, SA | .58-24* | to 60-22* |
| 1982 | Gene Shue, Wash | .39-43 | to 43-39 | 2004 | Hubie Brown, Mem. | .28-54 | to 50-32 |
| 1983 | Don Nelson, Mil | .55-27* | to 51-31* | 2005 | Mike D'Antoni, Pho | .29-53 | to 62-30* |
| 1984 | Frank Layden, Utah | .30-52 | to 45-37* | | | | |

## NBA's 50 Greatest Players

In October 1996, as part of its 50th anniversary celebration, the NBA named the 50 greatest players in league history. The voting was done by a league-approved panel of media, former players and coaches, current and former general managers and team executives. The players are listed alphabetically along with the dates of their professional careers and positions. Shaquille O'Neal, the only player active in 2004-05, is in **bold** type.

| Player | Pos | Player | Pos | Player | Pos |
|---|---|---|---|---|---|
| Kareem Abdul-Jabbar, 1969-89 | C | George Gervin, 1972-86 | G | Robert Parish, 1976-97 | C |
| Nate Archibald, 1970-84 | G | Hal Greer, 1958-73 | G | Bob Pettit, 1954-65 | F/C |
| Paul Arizin, 1950-61 | F/G | John Havlicek, 1962-78 | F/G | Scottie Pippen, 1987-2005 | F |
| Charles Barkley, 1984-00 | F | Elvin Hayes, 1968-84 | F/C | Willis Reed, 1964-74 | C |
| Rick Barry, 1965-80 | F | Magic Johnson, 1979-91, 96 | G | Oscar Robertson, 1960-74 | G |
| Elgin Baylor, 1958-72 | F | Sam Jones, 1957-69 | G | David Robinson, 1989-2003 | C |
| Dave Bing, 1966-78 | G | Michael Jordan, 1984-93, | G | Bill Russell, 1956-69 | C |
| Larry Bird, 1979-92 | F | 95-98, 01-03 | | Dolph Schayes, 1948-64 | F/C |
| Wilt Chamberlain, 1959-73 | C | Jerry Lucas, 1963-74 | F/C | Bill Sharman, 1950-61 | G |
| Bob Cousy, 1950-63, 69-70 | G | Karl Malone, 1985-2005 | F | John Stockton, 1984-2003 | G |
| Dave Cowens, 1970-80, 1982-83 | C | Moses Malone, 1974-95 | C | Isiah Thomas, 1981-94 | G |
| Billy Cunningham, 1965-76 | G | Pete Maravich, 1970-80 | G | Nate Thurmond, 1963-77 | C/F |
| Dave DeBusschere, 1962-74 | F | Kevin McHale, 1980-93 | F | Wes Unseld, 1968-81 | C/F |
| Clyde Drexler, 1983-98 | G | George Mikan, 1946-54, 55-56 | C | Bill Walton, 1974-88 | C |
| Julius Erving, 1971-87 | F | Earl Monroe, 1967-80 | G | Jerry West, 1960-74 | G |
| Patrick Ewing, 1985-2002 | C | Hakeem Olajuwon, 1984-2002 | C | Lenny Wilkens, 1960-75 | G |
| Walt Frazier, 1967-80 | G | **Shaquille O'Neal**, 1992— | C | James Worthy, 1982-94 | F |

**Note:** Rick Barry, Billy Cunningham, Julius Erving, George Gervin and Moses Malone all played part of their pro careers in the ABA.

## NBA's 10 Greatest Coaches

In December 1996, as part of its 50th anniversary celebration, the NBA named the 10 greatest coaches in league history. The voting was done by a league-approved panel of media. The coaches are listed alphabetically along with the dates of their professional coaching careers and overall records, including playoff games, and number of NBA titles won. Active coaches are in **bold** type.

| Coach | W | L | Pct. | Titles | Coach | W | L | Pct. | Titles |
|---|---|---|---|---|---|---|---|---|---|
| Red Auerbach, 1946-66 | 1037 | 548 | .654 | 9 | John Kundla, 1947-59 | .485 | 338 | .589 | 5 |
| Chuck Daly, 1981-94, 97-99 | .713 | 488 | .594 | 2 | Don Nelson, 1976-96, 97-2005 | 1260 | 965 | .566 | 0 |
| Bill Fitch, 1970-98 | .999 | 1160 | .463 | 1 | Jack Ramsay, 1968-89 | .908 | 841 | .519 | 1 |
| Red Holzman, 1953-82 | .754 | 652 | .536 | 2 | Pat Riley, 1981-2003 | 1265 | .669 | .654 | 4 |
| **Phil Jackson**, 1989-98, 99-04, 05— | 1007 | 385 | .723 | 9 | Lenny Wilkens, 1969-2005 | 1412 | 1253 | .530 | 1 |
| | | | | | TOTALS | 9840 | 7299 | .574 | 34 |

## World Championships

The World Basketball Championships for men and women have been played regularly at four-year intervals (give or take a year) since 1970. The men's tournament began in 1950 and the women's in 1953. The Federation Internationale de Basketball Amateur (FIBA), which governs the World and Olympic tournaments, was founded in 1932. FIBA first allowed professional players from the NBA to participate in 1994. A team of collegians represented the USA in 1998.

### Men

**Multiple wins:** Yugoslavia (5); Soviet Union and USA (3); Brazil (2).

| Year | |
|---|---|
| 1950 | **Argentina**, United States, Chile |
| 1954 | **United States**, Brazil, Philippines |
| 1959 | **Brazil**, United States, Chile |
| 1963 | **Brazil**, Yugoslavia, Soviet Union |
| 1967 | **Soviet Union**, Yugoslavia, Brazil |
| 1970 | **Yugoslavia**, Brazil, Soviet Union |
| 1974 | **Soviet Union**, Yugoslavia, United States |
| 1978 | **Yugoslavia**, Soviet Union, Brazil |
| 1982 | **Soviet Union**, United States, Yugoslavia |
| 1986 | **United States**, Soviet Union, Yugoslavia |
| 1990 | **Yugoslavia**, Soviet Union, United States |
| 1994 | **United States**, Russia, Croatia |
| 1998 | **Yugoslavia**, Russia, United States |
| 2002 | **Yugoslavia**, Argentina, Germany |
| 2006 | at Japan |
| 2010 | at Turkey |

### Women

**Multiple wins:** USA (7); Soviet Union (6).

| Year | |
|---|---|
| 1953 | **United States**, Chile, France |
| 1957 | **United States**, Soviet Union, Czechoslovakia |
| 1959 | **Soviet Union**, Bulgaria, Czechoslovakia |
| 1964 | **Soviet Union**, Czechoslovakia, Bulgaria |
| 1967 | **Soviet Union**, South Korea, Czechoslovakia |
| 1971 | **Soviet Union**, Czechoslovakia, Brazil |
| 1975 | **Soviet Union**, Japan, Czechoslovakia |
| 1979 | **United States**, South Korea, Canada |
| 1983 | **Soviet Union**, United States, China |
| 1986 | **United States**, Soviet Union, Canada |
| 1990 | **United States**, Yugoslavia, Cuba |
| 1994 | **Brazil**, China, United States |
| 1998 | **United States**, Russia, Australia |
| 2002 | **United States**, Russia, Australia |
| 2006 | at Brazil |
| 2010 | TBD |

## American Basketball Association
### ABA Finals

The original American Basketball Assn. began play in 1967-68 as a 10-team rival of the 21-year-old NBA. The ABA, which introduced the three-point basket, a multi-colored ball and the All-Star Game Slam Dunk Contest, lasted nine seasons before folding following the 1975-76 season. Four ABA teams–Denver, Indiana, New York and San Antonio–survived to enter the NBA in 1976-77. The NBA also adopted the three-point basket (in 1979-80) and the All-Star Game Slam Dunk Contest. The older league, however, refused to take in the ABA ball.

**Multiple winners:** Indiana (3); New York (2).

| Year | Winner | Head Coach | Series | Loser | Head Coach |
|------|--------|-----------|--------|-------|-----------|
| 1968 | Pittsburgh Pipers | Vince Cazzetta | 4-3 (WLLWLWW) | New Orleans Bucs | Babe McCarthy |
| 1969 | Oakland Oaks | Alex Hannum | 4-1 (WLWWW) | Indiana Pacers | Bob Leonard |
| 1970 | Indiana Pacers | Bob Leonard | 4-2 (WWLWLW) | Los Angeles Stars | Bill Sharman |
| 1971 | Utah Stars | Bill Sharman | 4-3 (WWLLWLW) | Kentucky Colonels | Frank Ramsey |
| 1972 | Indiana Pacers | Bob Leonard | 4-2 (WLWLWW) | New York Nets | Lou Carnesecca |
| 1973 | Indiana Pacers | Bob Leonard | 4-3 (WLLWWLW) | Kentucky Colonels | Joe Mullaney |
| 1974 | New York Nets | Kevin Loughery | 4-1 (WWWLW) | Utah Stars | Joe Mullaney |
| 1975 | Kentucky Colonels | Hubie Brown | 4-1 (WWWLW) | Indiana Pacers | Bob Leonard |
| 1976 | New York Nets | Kevin Loughery | 4-2 (WLWWWLW) | Denver Nuggets | Larry Brown |

### Most Valuable Player

Winners' scoring averages provided; (*) indicates led league.

**Multiple winners:** Julius Erving (3); Mel Daniels (2).

| Year | | Avg |
|------|--|-----|
| 1968 | Connie Hawkins, Pittsburgh, C | 26.8* |
| 1969 | Mel Daniels, Indiana, C | 24.0 |
| 1970 | Spencer Haywood, Denver, C | 30.0* |
| 1971 | Mel Daniels, Indiana, C | 21.0 |
| 1972 | Artis Gilmore, Kentucky, C | 23.8 |
| 1973 | Billy Cunningham, Carolina, F | 24.1 |
| 1974 | Julius Erving, New York, F | 27.4* |
| 1975 | George McGinnis, Indiana, F | 29.8* |
| | & Julius Erving, New York, F | 27.9 |
| 1976 | Julius Erving, New York, F | 29.3* |

### Rookie of the Year

Winners' scoring averages provided; (*) indicates led league. Rookies who were also named Most Valuable Player are in **bold** type.

| Year | | Avg |
|------|--|-----|
| 1968 | Mel Daniels, Minnesota, C | 22.2 |
| 1969 | Warren Armstrong, Oakland, G | 21.5 |
| 1970 | **Spencer Haywood**, Denver, C | 30.0* |
| 1971 | Dan Issel, Kentucky, C | 29.8* |
| | & Charlie Scott, Virginia, G | 27.1 |
| 1972 | **Artis Gilmore**, Kentucky, C | 23.8 |
| 1973 | Brian Taylor, New York, G | 15.3 |
| 1974 | Swen Nater, Virginia-SA, C | 14.1 |
| 1975 | Marvin Barnes, St. Louis, C | 24.0 |
| 1976 | David Thompson, Denver, F | 26.0 |

**Note:** Warren Armstrong changed his name to Warren Jabali after the 1970-71 season.

### Coach of the Year

Previous season and winning season records are provided; (*) indicates division title.

**Multiple winner:** Larry Brown (3).

| Year | | | Improvement |
|------|--|--|-------------|
| 1968 | Vince Cazzetta, Pittsburgh | | 54-24* |
| 1969 | Alex Hannum, Oakland | 22-56 to | 60-18* |
| 1970 | Joe Belmont, Denver | 44-34 to | 51-33* |
| | & Bill Sharman, LA Stars | 33-45 to | 43-41 |
| 1971 | Al Bianchi, Virginia | 44-40 to | 55-29* |
| 1972 | Tom Nissalke, Dallas | 30-54 to | 42-42 |
| 1973 | Larry Brown, Carolina | 35-49 to | 57-27* |
| 1974 | Babe McCarthy, Kentucky | 56-28 to | 53-31 |
| | & Joe Mullaney, Utah | 55-29* to | 51-33* |
| 1975 | Larry Brown, Denver | 37-47 to | 65-19* |
| 1976 | Larry Brown, Denver | 65-19* to | 60-24* |

### Scoring Leaders

Scoring championship decided by per game point average every season.

**Multiple winner:** Julius Erving (3).

| Year | | Gm | Avg | Pts |
|------|--|----|-----|-----|
| 1968 | Connie Hawkins, Pittsburgh | 70 | 1875 | 26.8 |
| 1969 | Rick Barry, Oakland | 35 | 1190 | 34.0 |
| 1970 | Spencer Haywood, Denver | 84 | 2519 | 30.0 |
| 1971 | Dan Issel, Kentucky | 83 | 2480 | 29.8 |
| 1972 | Charlie Scott, Virginia | 73 | 2524 | 34.6 |
| 1973 | Julius Erving, Virginia | 71 | 2268 | 31.9 |
| 1974 | Julius Erving, New York | 84 | 2299 | 27.4 |
| 1975 | George McGinnis, Indiana | 79 | 2353 | 29.8 |
| 1976 | Julius Erving, New York | 84 | 2462 | 29.3 |

### ABA All-Star Game

The ABA All-Star Game was an Eastern Division vs. Western Division contest from 1968-75. League membership had dropped to seven teams by 1976, the ABA's last season, so the team in first place at the break (Denver) played an All-Star team made up from the other six clubs.

**Series:** East won 5, West 3 and Denver 1.

| Year | Result | Host | Coaches | Most Valuable Player |
|------|--------|------|---------|---------------------|
| 1968 | East 126, West 120 | Indiana | Jim Pollard, Babe McCarthy | Larry Brown, New Orleans |
| 1969 | West 133, East 127 | Louisville | Alex Hannum, Gene Rhodes | John Beasley, Dallas |
| 1970 | West 128, East 98 | Indiana | Babe McCarthy, Bob Leonard | Spencer Haywood, Denver |
| 1971 | East 126, West 122 | Carolina | Al Bianchi, Bill Sharman | Mel Daniels, Indiana |
| 1972 | East 142, West 115 | Louisville | Joe Mullaney, Ladell Andersen | Dan Issel, Kentucky |
| 1973 | West 123, East 111 | Utah | Ladell Andersen, Larry Brown | Warren Jabali, Denver |
| 1974 | East 128, West 112 | Virginia | Babe McCarthy, Joe Mullaney | Artis Gilmore, Kentucky |
| 1975 | East 151, West 124 | San Antonio | Kevin Loughery, Larry Brown | Freddie Lewis, St. Louis |
| 1976 | Denver 144, ABA 138 | Denver | Larry Brown, Kevin Loughery | David Thompson, Denver |

## Continental Basketball Association

Originally named the Eastern Pennsylvania Basketball League when it formed on April 23, 1946, the league changed names several times before becoming known as the Eastern Basketball Association. In 1978, the EBA was redubbed the CBA. The CBA suspended operations following the 2000 season but reorganized for the 2001-02 season.

**Multiple champions:** Allentown and Wilkes-Barre (8); Scranton, Tampa Bay, Williamsport and Yakima (3); Albany, Dakota, La Crosse, Pottsville, Rochester, Sioux Falls and Wilmington (2).

### League Champions

| Year | | Year | | Year | | Year | |
|---|---|---|---|---|---|---|---|
| 1947 | Wilkes-Barre Barons | 1964 | Camden Bullets | 1979 | Rochester Zeniths | 1995 | Yakima Sun Kings |
| 1948 | Reading Keys | 1965 | Allentown Jets | 1980 | Anchorage Northern | 1996 | Sioux Falls Skyforce |
| 1949 | Pottsville Packers | 1966 | Wilmington Blue | | Knights | 1997 | Oklahoma City |
| 1950 | Williamsport Billies | | Bombers | 1981 | Rochester Zeniths | | Calvary |
| 1951 | Sunbury Mercuries | 1967 | Wilmington Blue | 1982 | Lancaster Lightning | 1998 | Quad City Thunder |
| 1952 | Pottsville Packers | | Bombers | 1983 | Detroit Spirits | 1999 | Connecticut Pride |
| 1953 | Williamsport Billies | 1968 | Allentown Jets | 1984 | Albany Patroons | 2000 | Yakima Sun Kings |
| 1954 | Williamsport Billies | 1969 | Wilkes-Barre Barons | 1985 | Tampa Bay Thrillers | 2001 | suspended play |
| 1955 | Wilkes-Barre Barons | 1970 | Allentown Jets | 1986 | Tampa Bay Thrillers | 2002 | Dakota Wizards |
| 1956 | Wilkes-Barre Barons | 1971 | Scranton Apollos | 1987 | Rapid City Thrillers* | 2003 | Yakima Sun Kings |
| 1957 | Scranton Miners | 1972 | Allentown Jets | 1988 | Albany Patroons | 2004 | Dakota Wizards |
| 1958 | Wilkes-Barre Barons | 1973 | Wilkes-Barre Barons | 1989 | Tulsa Fast Breakers | 2005 | Sioux Falls Skyforce |
| 1959 | Wilkes-Barre Barons | 1974 | Hartford Capitols | 1990 | La Crosse Catbirds | | |
| 1960 | Easton Madisons | 1975 | Allentown Jets | 1991 | Wichita Falls Texans | *The Tampa Bay Thrillers | |
| 1961 | Baltimore Bullets | 1976 | Allentown Jets | 1992 | La Crosse Catbirds | moved to Rapid City, S.D. at | |
| 1962 | Allentown Jets | 1977 | Scranton Apollos | 1993 | Omaha Racers | the end of the 1987 regular | |
| 1963 | Allentown Jets | 1978 | Wilkes-Barre Barons | 1994 | Quad City Thunder | season. | |

## National Basketball Association Development League

"The D League" was founded in 2001 as an eight-team player and coach development league owned and operated by the NBA. Until recently, the individual teams did not have a direct relationship with NBA clubs but occasionally players and coaches were called up to the NBA. The NBDL champion was determined in a best-of-three championship series for the first two seasons of the league before changing the format to a single-game playoff in 2004.

The North Charleston Lowgators dropped the North from their name following the 2003 season and the franchise moved to Fort Myers, Florida following the 2004 season and became the first privately-owned team in the league. The league contracted to six teams for the 2004 season when the Greenville Groove and Mobile Revelers each ceased operations. In 2005, the league dropped the NBDL acronym and officially adopted the name D-League. Also three teams relocated and two new teams entered the league to bring the total number of franchises to eight.

In 2005, the NBA announced that each D-League team would now be affiliated with a several NBA teams, more of a true minor league system. Here are the team assignments: FAYETTEVILLE—Charlotte Bobcats, NY Knicks, Detroit Pistons; AUSTIN—Denver Nuggets, San Antonio Spurs, Houston Rockets, LA Clippers; FORT WORTH—Golden State Warriors, LA Lakers, Dallas Mavericks, Portland Trail Blazers; ARKANSAS—Atlanta Hawks, Cleveland Cavaliers, Memphis Grizzlies, Toronto Raptors; FLORIDA—Miami Heat, Orlando Magic, Boston Celtics, Minnesota Timberwolves; TULSA—New Orleans Hornets, Indiana Pacers, Milwaukee Bucks, Chicago Bulls; ALBUQUERQUE—Utah Jazz, Phoenix Suns, Sacramento Kings, Seattle SuperSonics; ROANOKE—NJ Nets, Philadelphia 76ers, Washington Wizards.

### League Champions

**Multiple champions:** Asheville (2).

| Year | Champions | Head Coach | Score | Runners-up | Head Coach |
|---|---|---|---|---|---|
| 2002 | Greenville Groove | Milton Barnes | 2-0 | No. Charleston Lowgators | Alex English |
| 2003 | Mobile Revelers | Sam Vincent | 2-1 (WLW) | Fayetteville Patriots | Jeff Capel |
| 2004 | Asheville Altitude | Joey Meyer | 108-106 OT | Huntsville Flight | Ralph Lewis |
| 2005 | Asheville Altitude | Joey Meyer | 90-67 | Columbus Riverdragons | Jeff Malone |

### Annual Awards

#### Most Valuable Player

Winner's scoring averages provided; (*) indicates led league.

| Year | | PPG |
|---|---|---|
| 2002 | Ansu Sesay, Greenville, F | 16.5 |
| 2003 | Devin Brown, Fayetteville, G | 16.9 |
| 2004 | Tierre Brown, Charleston, G | 18.6 |
| 2005 | Matt Carroll, Roanoke, G | 20.1* |

#### Rookie of the Year

| Year | |
|---|---|
| 2002 | Fred House, N. Charleston |
| 2003 | Devin Brown, Fayetteville |
| 2004 | Desmond Penigar, Asheville |
| 2005 | James Thomas, Roanoke |

#### Scoring Champion

Scoring championship decided by per game point average every season.

| Year | | PPG |
|---|---|---|
| 2002 | Isaac Fontaine, Mobile | 17.4 |
| 2003 | Nate Johnson, Columbus | 19.5 |
| 2004 | Desmond Penigar, Asheville | 19.6 |
| 2005 | Isiah Victor, Roanoke | 19.5 |

**Note:** Matt Carroll was leading the league in scoring in 2005 but was called up to the NBA's Charlotte Bobcats so he did not win the league scoring title.

#### Defensive Player of the Year

| Year | |
|---|---|
| 2002 | Jeff Myers, Greenville |
| 2003 | Mikki Moore, Roanoke |
| 2004 | Karim Shabazz, Charleston |
| 2005 | Derrick Zimmerman, Columbus |

# WOMEN
## Women's National Basketball Association

The WNBA, owned and operated by the NBA, began play in 1997 as an eight-team summer league. The league added two teams prior to its second season (1998), then added two more teams before its third season in 1999. Four additional teams were added before the 2000 season, bringing the total number of teams to 16. Prior to the 2003 season two franchises were relocated and two were contracted and one franchise folded before the 2004 season. One team (Chicago Sky) was added for the 2006 season. The WNBA champion was determined by a single-game playoff in the league's 1997 inaugural season, before going to a best-of-three championship series in 1998 and a best-of-five championship series starting in 2005.

**Multiple winners:** Houston (4); Los Angeles (2).

| Year | Champions | Head Coach | Series | Runners-up | Head Coach |
|------|-----------|-----------|--------|------------|-----------|
| 1997 | Houston Comets | Van Chancellor | 65-51 | New York Liberty | Nancy Darsch |
| 1998 | Houston Comets | Van Chancellor | 2-1 (LWW) | Phoenix Mercury | Cheryl Miller |
| 1999 | Houston Comets | Van Chancellor | 2-1 (WLW) | New York Liberty | Richie Adubato |
| 2000 | Houston Comets | Van Chancellor | 2-0 | New York Liberty | Richie Adubato |
| 2001 | Los Angeles Sparks | Michael Cooper | 2-0 | Charlotte Sting | Anne Donovan |
| 2002 | Los Angeles Sparks | Michael Cooper | 2-0 | New York Liberty | Richie Adubato |
| 2003 | Detroit Shock | Bill Laimbeer | 2-1 (LWW) | Los Angeles Sparks | Michael Cooper |
| 2004 | Seattle Storm | Anne Donovan | 2-1 (LWW) | Connecticut Sun | Mike Thibault |
| 2005 | Sacramento Monarchs | John Whisenant | 3-1 (WLWW) | Connecticut Sun | Mike Thibault |

**Championship MVPs:** 1997-Cynthia Cooper, Houston; 1998-Cynthia Cooper, Houston; 1999-Cynthia Cooper, Houston; 2000-Cynthia Cooper, Houston; 2001-Lisa Leslie, Los Angeles; 2002-Lisa Leslie, Los Angeles; 2003-Ruth Riley, Detroit; 2004-Betty Lennox, Seattle; 2005-Yolanda Griffith, Sacramento.

## Annual Awards

### Most Valuable Player

Winner's scoring averages provided; (*) indicates led league.

**Multiple winners:** Sheryl Swoopes (3); Cynthia Cooper and Lisa Leslie (2).

| Year | | Avg |
|------|--|-----|
| 1997 | Cynthia Cooper, Houston | 22.2* |
| 1998 | Cynthia Cooper, Houston | 22.7* |
| 1999 | Yolanda Griffith, Sacramento | 18.8 |
| 2000 | Sheryl Swoopes, Houston | 20.7* |
| 2001 | Lisa Leslie, Los Angeles | 19.5 |
| 2002 | Sheryl Swoopes, Houston | 18.5 |
| 2003 | Lauren Jackson, Seattle | 21.2* |
| 2004 | Lisa Leslie, Los Angeles | 17.6 |
| 2005 | Sheryl Swoopes, Houston | 18.6* |

### Coach of the Year

Previous season and winning season's record are provided; (*) indicates division title.

**Multiple winner:** Van Chancellor (3).

| Year | | Improvement |
|------|--|-------------|
| 1997 | Van Chancellor, Houston | 18-10* |
| 1998 | Van Chancellor, Houston | 18-10 to 27-3* |
| 1999 | Van Chancellor, Houston | 27-3 to 26-6* |
| 2000 | Michael Cooper, Los Angeles | 20-12 to 28-4* |
| 2001 | Dan Hughes, Cleveland | 17-15 to 22-10* |
| 2002 | Marianne Stanley, Washington | 10-22 to 17-15 |
| 2003 | Bill Laimbeer, Detroit | 9-23 to 25-9* |
| 2004 | Suzie McConnell Serio, Minn. | 18-16 to 18-16 |
| 2005 | John Whisenant, Sacramento | 18-16 to 25-9* |

### Rookie of the Year

| Year | | Year | |
|------|--|------|--|
| 1998 | Tracy Reid, Cha | 2002 | Tamika Catchings, Ind |
| 1999 | Chamique Holdsclaw, Was | 2003 | Cheryl Ford, Det |
| | | 2004 | Diana Taurasi, Pho |
| 2000 | Betty Lennox, Min | 2005 | Temeka Johnson, Was |
| 2001 | Jackie Stiles, Port | | |

### Defensive Player of the Year

**Multiple winners:** Sheryl Swoopes (3); Teresa Weatherspoon (2).

| Year | | Year | |
|------|--|------|--|
| 1997 | Teresa Weatherspoon, NY | 2001 | Debbie Black, Mia |
| | | 2002 | Sheryl Swoopes, Hou |
| 1998 | Teresa Weatherspoon, NY | 2003 | Sheryl Swoopes, Hou |
| 1999 | Yolanda Griffith, Sac | 2004 | Lisa Leslie, LA |
| 2000 | Sheryl Swoopes, Hou | 2005 | Tamika Catchings, Ind |

### WNBA Number One Draft Picks

| Year | Overall First Pick |
|------|--------------------|
| 1997 | Utah Starzz | Dena Head |
| 1998 | Utah Starzz | Margo Dydek |
| 1999 | Washington Mystics | Chamique Holdsclaw |
| 2000 | Cleveland Rockers | Ann Wauters |
| 2001 | Seattle Storm | Lauren Jackson |
| 2002 | Seattle Storm | Sue Bird |
| 2003 | Cleveland Rockers | LaToya Thomas |
| 2004 | Phoenix Mercury | Diana Taurasi |
| 2005 | Charlotte Sting | Janel McCarville |

# American Basketball League (1997-98)
## League Champions

The American Basketball League began play in 1996 as an eight-team league. Before the 1997-98 season the league added an expansion franchise in Long Beach, Calif. while the Richmond Rage was relocated to Philadelphia. In the spring of 1998, the league announced plans to dissolve an original franchise, the Atlanta Glory, and expand to Chicago and Nashville before the 1998-99 season, increasing the league's size to 10 teams. The ABL finals was a best of five series. Each ABL champion's wins and losses are noted in parentheses after the series score. The ABL folded before the 1999 season.

| Year | Champions | Head Coach | Series | Runners-up | Head Coach |
|------|-----------|-----------|--------|------------|-----------|
| 1997 | Columbus Quest | Brian Agler | 3-2 (WLLWW) | Richmond Rage | Lisa Boyer |
| 1998 | Columbus Quest | Brian Agler | 3-2 (LLWWW) | Long Beach StingRays | Maura McHugh |

### Most Valuable Player

Winner's scoring averages provided; (*) indicates led league.

| Year | | Avg |
|------|--|-----|
| 1997 | Nikki McCray, Columbus | 19.9 |
| 1998 | Natalie Williams, Portland | 21.9* |

### Coach of the Year

Previous season and winning season's record are provided; (*) indicates division title.

| Year | | Improvement |
|------|--|-------------|
| 1997 | Brian Agler, Columbus | 31-9* |
| 1998 | Lin Dunn, Portland | 14-26 to 27-17 |

# Hockey

Players and owners couldn't find a way to come to an agreement in time to save the 2004-05 NHL season.

# Season on Ice

*The NHL locks its doors in 2004-05 and begins the slow process of making ammends with fans.*

**Michael Morrison**
*is co-editor of the ESPN Sports Almanac.*

So was it all worth it? In 2004 NHL owners, citing unacceptable financial losses, locked out players and in the process canceled an entire major professional sports season for the first time in history.

The NHL's financial model was clearly flawed, with player salaries accounting for 75 percent of the league's two billion dollar revenues. By comparison, NFL player salaries account for 64 percent of revenues, MLB 63 percent and the NBA 57 percent.

The NHL said it suffered losses of $224 million during the 2003-04 season, and financial guru Arthur Leavitt (hired by the league) claimed the league lost $273 million in 2002-03, with only 11 of the 30 teams turning profits.

Granted, it was free-spending owners that doled out exorbitant salaries in the first place. But regardless of fault, the owners knew they needed a new economic system — and the expiration of the collective bargaining agreement on Sept. 15, 2004 was their chance to get it. At midnight, the lockout began. The two sides met several times throughout the fall and early winter with neither budging.

And then the Players' Union showed its first sign of weakness. On Feb. 14, Union head Bob Goodenow agreed to a salary cap, something he said he'd never do under any circumstances. The Union offered a $49 million cap. The league countered with $40 million. And they could find no middle ground.

Two days later the season was canceled.

"This might be the worst day in the history of the NHL," said Brian Burke, the former general manager of the Vancouver Canucks. "The Rocket Richard riot, the flu epidemic...nothing compares to this."

Later that week, reports surfaced that Wayne Gretzky (part owner of Phoenix Coyotes) and Mario Lemieux (owner/player for Pittsburgh Penguins) had met with the sides as a last-ditch effort to save the season, but even in the presence of two living legends, the talks proved fruitless.

AP/Wide World Photos

*On-ice battles in 2004-05 were replaced by boardroom meetings and public sniping between Commissioner **Gary Bettman**, left, and Players' Assosiation head **Bob Goodenow**.*

The Union's offer of a cap, however, proved to Commissioner Gary Bettman and the owners which side had the leverage. And if that didn't do it, telling quotes from outspoken winger Jeremy Roenick did.

"To be totally honest, I really don't care what the deal is anymore. All I care about is getting the game back on the ice."

In mid-July, Roenick got his wish. After ten consecutive days of talks, including 24 straight hours, a deal was struck.

The salary cap would be set at $39 million (less than what the league offered in February) with salaries ranging between 54 and 57 percent of league revenues. As Roenick bluntly put it, "we got our [bleeps] kicked."

Nevertheless, hockey was back — with a myriad of rule changes (see next page for more details), a new TV deal with a snazzy ad campaign and the introduction of a tie-breaking shootout, all with hopes of wooing fans. Long-awaited teenage wunderkind Sidney Crosby takes over as the new face of the league and looks to somehow fill the void left by newly-retired future hall of famers Mark Messier, Ron Francis, Scott Stevens and Al MacInnis.

All of these rule changes and the new financial system could very well make the game better and the league stronger well into the future. Sadly, it comes at the expense of a lost season – and countless lost fans.

## What's New for the NHL in 2005-06?

1. **Hockey will be played in 2005-06.**
   No explanation needed.
2. **Invigorated NHL shield (below)**
   The new shield uses upward-reading letters to project a vibrant, optimistic image, yet maintains the time-honored shape.

**Source:** NHL

3. **Numerous rule changes**
   Multiple rule changes will be in effect to showcase the skills of the league's most talented players. These include the removal of the red line, smaller goalie equipment, expanded offensive zones, and...
4. **Shootouts to guarantee a winner.**
   A breakaway shootout will decide a game's winner if the score is still tied following a four-on-four, five-minute sudden death OT.
5. **Rivalry-based schedule**
   To create a greater number of compelling matchups and stronger division rivalries.
6. **Aggressive broadcast initiatives**
   New TV deals with OLN and NBC and more cameras and microphones designed to bring the fans closer to the game.
7. **Olympic break**
   The league will suspend play in Feb. in order to let NHLers play for their countries in Turin.

## 2005 NHL Draft

First round selections at the 43rd annual NHL Entry Draft held July 30, 2005, at the Westin Hotel in Ottawa. A draft drawing held July 22 in New York City determined the order of the first round. The drawing was weighted to benefit teams that neither qualified for the playoffs during the previous three seasons, nor were awarded the first overall selection in any of the past four entry drafts.

### First Round

| | Team | Player, Last Team | Pos |
|---|---|---|---|
| 1 | Pittsburgh | Sidney Crosby, Rimouski (QMJHL) | C |
| 2 | Anaheim | Bobby Ryan, Owen Sound (OHL) | R |
| 3 | Carolina | Jack Johnson, U.S. Nat'l U-18 | D |
| 4 | Minnesota | Benoit Pouliot, Sudbury (OHL) | L |
| 5 | Montreal | Carey Price, Tri-City (WHL) | G |
| 6 | Columbus | Gilbert Brule, Vancouver (WHL) | C |
| 7 | Chicago | Jack Skille, U.S. Nat'l U-18 | R |
| 8 | **a-**San Jose | Devin Setoguchi, Saskatoon (WHL) | R |
| 9 | Ottawa | Brian Lee, Moorhead, Minn. (HS) | D |
| 10 | Vancouver | Luc Bourdon, Val D'or (QMJHL) | D |
| 11 | Los Angeles | Anze Kopitar, Sodertalje Jr. (SWE) | C |
| 12 | **b-**NY Rangers | Marc Staal, Sudbury (OHL) | D |
| 13 | Buffalo | Marek Zagrapan, Chicoutimi (QMJHL) | C |
| 14 | Washington | Sasha Pokulok, Cornell (ECAC) | D |
| 15 | NY Islanders | Ryan O'Marra, Erie (OHL) | C |
| 16 | **c-**Atlanta | Alex Bourret, Lewiston (QMJHL) | R |
| 17 | Phoenix | Martin Hanzal, Budejovice Jr. (CZE) | C |
| 18 | Nashville | Ryan Parent, Guelph (OHL) | D |
| 19 | Detroit | Jakub Kindl, Kitchener (OHL) | D |
| 20 | **d-**Florida | Kenndal McArdle, Moose Jaw (WHL) | L |
| 21 | Toronto | Tuukka Rask, Ilves Jr. (FIN) | G |
| 22 | Boston | Matt Lashoff, Kitchener (OHL) | D |
| 23 | New Jersey | Nicklas Bergfors, Sodertalje Jr. (SWE) | W |
| 24 | St. Louis | T.J. Oshie, Warroad, Minn. (HS) | C |
| 25 | Edmonton | Andrew Cogliano, St. Michael's (OPJHL) | C |
| 26 | Calgary | Matt Pelech, Sarnia (OHL) | D |
| 27 | **e-**Washington | Joe Finley, Sioux Falls (USHL) | D |
| 28 | Dallas | Matt Niskanen, Virginia, Minn. (HS) | D |
| 29 | **f-**Philadelphia | Steve Downie, Windsor (OHL) | R |
| 30 | Tampa Bay | Vladimir Mihalik, Presov (SVK) | D |

**Acquired picks: a-**from Atl.; **b-**from SJ; **c-**from NYR; **d-**from Phi.; **e-**from Col.; **f-**from Fla.

AP/Wide World Photos

The Penguins, and for that matter the entire NHL, have high hopes for teenage phenom and top pick **Sidney Crosby.** He is shown here yukking it up on "The Tonight Show With Jay Leno."

# 2004-2005
# *Season in Review*

SPORTS ALMANAC

## MINOR LEAGUE HOCKEY

### American Hockey League

Division champions (*) and playoff qualifiers (†) are noted. **OTL** denotes any game that was tied at the end of regulation and lost during a five-minute overtime period. If the game is tied after the overtime period, a shootout ensues with each team getting five attempts to score on a breakaway from the red line. Shootout Losses are listed as **SOL**. Teams are awarded two points for a win (regulation, overtime or shootout), one point for an OTL or SOL, and zero points for a regulation loss.

## Eastern Conference
### Atlantic Division

| Team (Affiliate) | W | L | OTL | SOL | Pts |
|---|---|---|---|---|---|
| *Manchester (LA) | 51 | 21 | 4 | 4 | 110 |
| †Hartford (NYR) | 50 | 24 | 3 | 3 | 106 |
| †Lowell (Car/Calg) | 47 | 27 | 1 | 5 | 100 |
| †Providence (Bos) | 40 | 30 | 3 | 7 | 90 |
| Worcester (St.L) | 39 | 34 | 4 | 3 | 85 |
| Portland (Wash) | 34 | 34 | 6 | 6 | 80 |
| Springfield (TB) | 24 | 47 | 6 | 3 | 57 |

### East Division

| Team (Affiliate) | W | L | OTL | SOL | Pts |
|---|---|---|---|---|---|
| *Binghamton (Ott) | 47 | 21 | 5 | 7 | 106 |
| †Philadelphia (Phi) | 48 | 25 | 3 | 4 | 103 |
| †Norfolk (Chi) | 43 | 30 | 1* | 6 | 93 |
| †Wilkes-Barre/Scran. (Pit) | 39 | 27 | 7 | 7 | 92 |
| Hershey (Col) | 39 | 37 | 2 | 2 | 82 |
| Bridgeport (NYI) | 37 | 38 | 4 | 1 | 79 |
| Albany (NJ) | 29 | 38 | 7 | 6 | 71 |

## Western Conference
### North Division

| Team (Affiliate) | W | L | OTL | SOL | Pts |
|---|---|---|---|---|---|
| *Rochester (Buf) | 51 | 19 | 4 | 6 | 112 |
| †St. John's (Tor) | 46 | 28 | 1 | 5 | 98 |
| †Manitoba (Van) | 44 | 26 | 3 | 7 | 98 |
| †Hamilton (Mon/Dal) | 38 | 29 | 7 | 6 | 89 |
| Syracuse (Clb) | 36 | 33 | 7 | 4 | 83 |
| Edmonton (Edm) | 32 | 33 | 4 | 11 | 79 |
| Cleveland (SJ) | 35 | 37 | 2 | 6 | 78 |

### West Division

| Team (Affiliate) | W | L | OTL | SOL | Pts |
|---|---|---|---|---|---|
| *Chicago (Atl) | 49 | 24 | 5 | 2 | 105 |
| †Milwaukee (Nash) | 47 | 24 | 4 | 5 | 103 |
| †Cincinnati (Ana) | 44 | 31 | 1 | 4 | 93 |
| †Houston (Min/Dal) | 40 | 28 | 6 | 6 | 92 |
| Grand Rapids (Det) | 41 | 35 | 2 | 2 | 86 |
| San Antonio (Fla) | 27 | 45 | 3 | 5 | 62 |
| Utah (Pho) | 23 | 50 | 2 | 5 | 53 |

## Scoring Leaders

| | Gm | G | A | Pts | PM |
|---|---|---|---|---|---|
| Jason Spezza, Bing | 80 | 32 | 85 | 117 | 50 |
| Mike Cammalleri, Mch | 79 | 46 | 63 | 109 | 60 |
| David Ling, St.J | 80 | 28 | 60 | 88 | 152 |
| Kyle Wellwood, St.J | 80 | 38 | 49 | 87 | 20 |
| Simon Gamache, Mil | 80 | 29 | 57 | 86 | 93 |
| Peter Sarno, Mtb | 80 | 16 | 66 | 82 | 53 |
| Andy Hilbert, Pro | 79 | 37 | 42 | 79 | 83 |
| Chris Taylor, Roch | 79 | 21 | 58 | 79 | 50 |
| Denis Hamel, Bing | 80 | 39 | 39 | 78 | 75 |
| Eric Staal, Low | 77 | 26 | 51 | 77 | 88 |
| Chuck Kobasew, Low | 79 | 38 | 37 | 75 | 110 |
| Brad Boyes, Pro | 80 | 33 | 42 | 75 | 58 |
| Dustin Brown, Mch | 79 | 29 | 45 | 74 | 96 |
| Antoine Vermette, Bing | 78 | 28 | 45 | 73 | 36 |
| Eric Perrin, Her | 80 | 24 | 49 | 73 | 46 |

## Goaltending Leaders

| (At least 1590 minutes) | GP | GAA | Sv% | Record |
|---|---|---|---|---|
| Steve Valiquette, Har | 35 | 1.77 | .935 | 19-11-1 |
| Jason LaBarbera, Har | 53 | 1.84 | .934 | 31-16-2 |
| Adam Hauser, Mch | 32 | 1.93 | .933 | 19-11-0 |
| Cam Ward, Low | 50 | 1.99 | .937 | 27-17-3 |
| Josh Harding, Hou | 42 | 2.01 | .930 | 21-16-3 |

**Note:** *Record* is listed in wins, losses and shootout losses.

## Calder Cup Finals

| | W-L | GF | Leading Scorers |
|---|---|---|---|
| Philadelphia | 4-0 | 10 | Patrick Sharp (4-2-6) |
| Chicago | 0-4 | 4 | Steve Maltais (2-1-3) |

| Date | Winner | Home Ice |
|---|---|---|
| June 2 | Philadelphia, 1-0 | at Chicago |
| June 4 | Philadelphia, 2-1 (2OT) | at Chicago |
| June 8 | Philadelphia, 2-1 | at Philadelphia |
| June 10 | Philadelphia, 5-2 | at Philadelphia |

### Playoff MVP

Antero Niittymaki, Philadelphia, G
15-5, 1.75 GAA, .943 save pct., 3 ShO

## Other Minor League Champions

### ECHL

Trenton 4 .......................... Florida 2

### Central Hockey League

Colorado 4 ...................... Laredo, TX 1

## COLLEGE HOCKEY

## NCAA Men's Division I

Final regular season standings; overall records, including all postseason tournament games, in parentheses.

### Atlantic Hockey

|  | W | L | T | Pts | GF | GA |
|---|---|---|---|---|---|---|
| Quinnipiac (21-13-3) . . . .16 | 6 | 2 | 34 | 96 | 64 |
| *Mercyhurst (18-16-4) . . . .14 | 7 | 3 | 31 | 86 | 64 |
| Canisius (16-15-4) . . . . . .14 | 7 | 3 | 31 | 76 | 62 |
| Holy Cross (16-14-6) . . . .12 | 7 | 5 | 29 | 76 | 60 |
| Sacred Heart (13-21-1) . .13 | 10 | 1 | 27 | 76 | 73 |
| Connecticut (11-23-3) . . .10 | 12 | 2 | 22 | 64 | 71 |
| Bentley (8-20-6) . . . . . . . .6 | 13 | 5 | 17 | 65 | 83 |
| Army (7-21-3) . . . . . . . . .5 | 16 | 3 | 13 | 47 | 71 |
| American Int'l (4-23-4) . . .4 | 16 | 4 | 12 | 50 | 88 |

**Conf. Tourney Final:** Mercyhurst 3, Quinnipiac 2 (OT).
***NCAA Tourney (0-1):** Mercyhurst (0-1).

### Central Collegiate Hockey Assn.

|  | W | L | T | Pts | GF | GA |
|---|---|---|---|---|---|---|
| *Michigan (31-8-3) . . . . . . .23 | 3 | 2 | 48 | 128 | 70 |
| *Ohio State (27-11-4) . . . . . .21 | 5 | 2 | 44 | 100 | 62 |
| N. Michigan (22-11-7) . . . . .17 | 7 | 4 | 38 | 82 | 57 |
| Nebraska-Omaha (19-16-4) .13 | 11 | 4 | 30 | 101 | 84 |
| Bowling Green (16-16-4) . . .13 | 12 | 3 | 29 | 92 | 87 |
| Michigan State (20-17-4) . . .12 | 13 | 3 | 27 | 87 | 74 |
| Miami-OH (15-18-5) . . . . . .11 | 13 | 4 | 26 | 80 | 76 |
| Alaska-Fairbanks (17-16-4) . .11 | 14 | 3 | 25 | 74 | 99 |
| Lake Superior (9-22-7) . . . . .8 | 14 | 6 | 22 | 64 | 84 |
| W. Michigan (14-21-2) . . . . . .8 | 18 | 2 | 18 | 78 | 112 |
| Ferris State (13-22-4) . . . . . .7 | 17 | 4 | 18 | 73 | 97 |
| Notre Dame (5-27-6) . . . . . . .3 | 20 | 5 | 11 | 48 | 105 |

**Conf. Tourney Final:** Michigan 4, Ohio State 2.
***NCAA Tourney (1-2):** Michigan (1-1), Ohio State (0-1).

### College Hockey America

|  | W | L | T | Pts | GF | GA |
|---|---|---|---|---|---|---|
| *Bemidji State (23-13-1) . . .16 | 4 | 0 | 32 | 69 | 45 |
| Alab.-Huntsville (18-10-4) .14 | 5 | 1 | 29 | 71 | 43 |
| Niagara (15-19-2) . . . . . . .9 | 9 | 2 | 20 | 61 | 62 |
| Wayne State (14-17-4) . . . .7 | 9 | 4 | 18 | 55 | 54 |
| Air Force (13-18-2) . . . . . .5 | 14 | 1 | 11 | 41 | 64 |
| Robert Morris (8-21-4) . . . .4 | 14 | 2 | 10 | 35 | 64 |

**Conf. Tourney Final:** Bemidji State 3, Alab.-Huntsville 0.
***NCAA Tourney (0-1):** Bemidji State (0-1).

### ECAC Hockey League

|  | W | L | T | Pts | GF | GA |
|---|---|---|---|---|---|---|
| *Cornell (27-5-3) . . . . . . . .18 | 2 | 2 | 38 | 70 | 26 |
| *Harvard (21-10-3) . . . . . .15 | 5 | 2 | 32 | 71 | 38 |
| *Colgate (25-11-3) . . . . . .14 | 5 | 3 | 31 | 55 | 38 |
| Vermont (14-14-4) . . . . . .13 | 6 | 3 | 29 | 66 | 37 |
| Dartmouth (20-13-2) . . . . .14 | 8 | 0 | 28 | 74 | 49 |
| Brown (16-14-3) . . . . . . . .9 | 11 | 2 | 20 | 54 | 60 |
| St. Lawrence (17-19-2) . . . .9 | 12 | 1 | 19 | 70 | 73 |
| Union (13-22-2) . . . . . . . . .8 | 13 | 1 | 17 | 43 | 72 |
| Clarkson (13-23-3) . . . . . . .7 | 13 | 2 | 16 | 44 | 66 |
| Princeton (8-20-3) . . . . . . .6 | 14 | 2 | 14 | 59 | 81 |
| Rensselaer (14-22-2) . . . . .6 | 15 | 1 | 13 | 46 | 73 |
| Yale (5-25-2) . . . . . . . . . . .3 | 18 | 1 | 7 | 50 | 89 |

**Conf. Tourney Final:** Cornell 3, Harvard 1.
***NCAA Tourney (1-3):** Cornell (1-1), Harvard (0-1),
Colgate (0-1).

### Hockey East Association

|  | W | L | T | Pts | GF | GA |
|---|---|---|---|---|---|---|
| *Boston College (26-7-7) . .14 | 3 | 7 | 35 | 78 | 47 |
| *Boston University (23-14-4) 15 | 5 | 4 | 34 | 76 | 54 |
| *New Hampshire (26-11-5) 15 | 5 | 4 | 34 | 90 | 59 |
| *Maine (20-13-7) . . . . . . . .13 | 6 | 5 | 31 | 75 | 47 |
| UMass-Lowell (20-12-4) . .11 | 10 | 3 | 25 | 76 | 66 |
| Northeastern (15-18-5) . . .10 | 10 | 4 | 24 | 66 | 58 |
| Providence (12-21-4) . . . . .6 | 14 | 4 | 16 | 54 | 73 |
| Massachusetts (13-23-2) . .6 | 16 | 2 | 14 | 48 | 96 |
| Merrimack (8-26-2) . . . . . .1 | 22 | 1 | 3 | 41 | 104 |

**Conf. Tourney Final:** Boston College 3, New Hampshire 1.
***NCAA Tourney (2-4):** Boston College (1-1), Boston
University (0-1), New Hampshire (1-1), Maine (0-1).

### Western Collegiate Hockey Assn.

|  | W | L | T | Pts | GF | GA |
|---|---|---|---|---|---|---|
| *Denver (32-9-2) . . . . . . . . .19 | 7 | 2 | 40 | 114 | 81 |
| *Colorado College (31-9-3) .19 | 7 | 2 | 40 | 98 | 66 |
| *Minnesota (28-15-1) . . . . . .17 | 10 | 1 | 35 | 105 | 80 |
| *Wisconsin (23-14-4) . . . . . .16 | 9 | 3 | 35 | 94 | 64 |
| *North Dakota (25-15-5) . . .13 | 12 | 3 | 29 | 71 | 67 |
| Minnesota Duluth (15-17-6) .11 | 13 | 4 | 26 | 90 | 89 |
| Alaska-Anchorage (12-19-6) .9 | 15 | 4 | 22 | 72 | 102 |
| Minnesota State (13-19-6) . .8 | 16 | 4 | 20 | 82 | 109 |
| St. Cloud State (14-23-3) . . .8 | 19 | 1 | 17 | 66 | 100 |
| Michigan Tech (8-25-4) . . . .7 | 19 | 2 | 16 | 64 | 98 |

**Conf. Tourney Final:** Denver 1, Colorado College 0.
***NCAA Tourney (11-4):** Denver (4-0), Colorado College
(2-1), Minnesota (2-1), Wisconsin (0-1), North Dakota (3-1).

---

### USCHO.com/CSTV
### Division I Men's Poll

Taken **before** the NCAA tournament

Final weekly regular season poll compiled by U.S. College Hockey Online and taken March 21, before the start of the NCAA tournament. Voting panel consists of 28 Division I coaches and 12 beat writers from across the country. Poll is published weekly by the Associated Press. First place votes are in parentheses. Teams in **bold** type went on to reach the NCAA Frozen Four.

|  |  |  | League | W | L | T | Pts |
|---|---|---|---|---|---|---|---|
| 1 | **Denver** (17) | . . . . . . . . | WCHA | 28 | 9 | 2 | 569 |
| 2 | Boston College (7) | . . . . . . . | HEA | 25 | 6 | 7 | 520 |
| 3 | **Colorado College** (6) | . | WCHA | 29 | 8 | 3 | 517 |
| 4 | Cornell (8) | . . . . . . . . . . | ECAC | 26 | 4 | 3 | 503 |
| 5 | Michigan (1) | . . . . . . . . . | CCHA | 30 | 7 | 3 | 473 |
| 6 | New Hampshire | . . . . . . | HEA | 25 | 10 | 5 | 362 |
| 7 | **Minnesota** | . . . . . . . . . | WCHA | 26 | 14 | 1 | 336 |
| 8 | Harvard | . . . . . . . . . . . . | ECAC | 21 | 9 | 3 | 296 |
| 9 | Ohio State | . . . . . . . . . | CCHA | 27 | 10 | 4 | 269 |
| 10 | **North Dakota** (1) | . . . | WCHA | 24 | 15 | 5 | 250 |
| 11 | Boston University | . . . . . | HEA | 23 | 13 | 4 | 212 |
| 12 | Maine | . . . . . . . . . . . . | HEA | 20 | 12 | 7 | 172 |
| 13 | Wisconsin | . . . . . . . . . | WCHA | 23 | 13 | 4 | 155 |
| 14 | Colgate | . . . . . . . . . . . | ECAC | 25 | 10 | 3 | 103 |
| 15 | Dartmouth | . . . . . . . . | ECAC | 20 | 13 | 2 | 17 |

**Also receiving votes:** Northern Michigan (12 pts), Vermont (10), UMass-Lowell (7), Bemidji State (6), Alaska-Fairbanks and Mercyhurst (4), Michigan State (3).

## Scoring Leaders

Including postseason games; minimum 20 games.

| | Cl | Gm | G | A | Pts | Avg |
|---|---|---|---|---|---|---|
| Marty Sertich, Colorado Col. | Jr. | 43 | 27 | 37 | 64 | **1.49** |
| Brett Sterling, Colorado Col. | Jr. | 43 | 34 | 29 | 63 | **1.47** |
| Colin Murphy, Mich. Tech | .Sr. | 37 | 11 | 42 | 53 | **1.43** |
| T.J. Hensick, Michigan | .So. | 39 | 23 | 32 | 55 | **1.41** |
| Jeff Tambellini, Michigan | .Jr. | 42 | 24 | 33 | 57 | **1.36** |
| Brent Walton, Western Mich. | .Sr. | 37 | 21 | 29 | 50 | **1.35** |
| Sean Collins, UNH | .Sr. | 42 | 19 | 37 | 56 | **1.33** |
| Patrick Eaves, Boston Col. | .Jr. | 36 | 19 | 29 | 48 | **1.33** |
| Jared Ross, Ala.-Huntsville | .Sr. | 30 | 22 | 18 | 40 | **1.33** |
| Gabe Gauthier, Denver | .Jr. | 43 | 26 | 31 | 57 | **1.33** |
| Preston Callander, UNH | .Sr. | 42 | 25 | 29 | 54 | **1.29** |
| Barret Ehgoetz, Niagara | .Sr. | 36 | 16 | 30 | 46 | **1.28** |
| Jason Guerriero, Northeastern | .Sr. | 38 | 17 | 31 | 48 | **1.26** |
| Bruce Mulherin, Ala.-Huntsville | .Jr. | 31 | 24 | 15 | 39 | **1.26** |
| Scott Parse, Neb.-Omaha | .So. | 39 | 19 | 30 | 49 | **1.26** |
| Matt Moulson, Cornell | .Sr. | 34 | 22 | 20 | 42 | **1.26** |
| Scott Mifsud, Vermont | .Sr. | 39 | 21 | 27 | 48 | **1.23** |
| Lee Stempniak, Dartmouth | .Sr. | 35 | 14 | 29 | 43 | **1.23** |
| Reid Cashman, Quinnipiac | .So. | 37 | 13 | 32 | 45 | **1.22** |
| Jeff Legue, Ferris State | .Sr. | 37 | 24 | 20 | 44 | **1.19** |

## Goaltending Leaders

Including postseason games; minimum 15 games.

| | Cl | Record | Sv% | GAA |
|---|---|---|---|---|
| David McKee, Cornell | .So. | 27-5-3 | .947 | **1.24** |
| Dov Grumet-Morris, Harvard | .Sr. | 19-9-3 | .947 | **1.63** |
| Matti Kaltiainen, Boston Col. | .Sr. | 12-6-3 | .922 | **1.80** |
| Matt Climie, Bemidji St. | .Fr. | 12-5-1 | .916 | **1.80** |
| Steve Silverthorn, Colgate | .Sr. | 24-10-3 | .922 | **1.88** |
| Cory Schneider, Boston Col. | .Fr. | 13-1-4 | .916 | **1.91** |
| Jimmy Howard, Maine | .Jr. | 19-13-7 | .924 | **1.92** |
| Joe Fallon, Vermont | .Fr. | 17-10-4 | .921 | **1.96** |
| John Curry, Boston Univ. | .So. | 18-10-3 | .923 | **1.97** |
| Tuomas Tarkki, N. Mich. | .Sr. | 20-8-5 | .930 | **2.07** |

## Division I All-America

First team CCM Division I All-Americans as chosen by the American Hockey Coaches Association. Holdover from the 2003-04 All-America team is in **bold** type.

### East Team

| Pos | | Yr | Hgt | Wgt |
|---|---|---|---|---|
| G | David McKee, Cornell | .So. | 6-1 | 180 |
| D | **Andrew Alberts**, Boston College | .Sr. | 6-4 | 215 |
| D | Noah Welch, Harvard | .Sr. | 6-4 | 212 |
| F | Sean Collins, New Hampshire | .Sr. | 5-9 | 170 |
| F | Patrick Eaves, Boston College | .Jr. | 6-0 | 185 |
| F | Jason Guerriero, Northeastern | .Sr. | 5-8 | 180 |

### West Team

| Pos | | Yr | Hgt | Wgt |
|---|---|---|---|---|
| G | Curtis McElhinney, Colorado Col. | .Sr. | 6-3 | 200 |
| D | Matt Carle, Denver | .So. | 6-0 | 200 |
| D | Mark Stuart, Colorado College | .Jr. | 6-2 | 218 |
| F | T.J. Hensick, Michigan | .So. | 5-10 | 187 |
| F | Marty Sertich, Colorado College | .Jr. | 5-9 | 163 |
| F | Brett Sterling, Colorado College | .Jr. | 5-8 | 170 |

## Hobey Baker Award

For College Hockey Player of the Year. Voting is done by a 25-member panel of college hockey personnel, national media, and pro scouts, plus a one percent fan vote.

**Winner:** Marty Sertich, Colorado College . . . Jr. | **Cl Pos** F

Other nine finalists, as selected by the nation's 58 Division I coaches, along with an on-line vote (listed alphabetically):

  Reid Cashman, Quinnipiac, So., D
  Patrick Eaves, Boston College, Jr., F
  Dov Grumet-Morris, Harvard, Sr., G
  T.J. Hensick, Michigan, So., F
* David McKee, Cornell, So., G
  Colin Murphy, Michigan Tech, Sr., F
  Jordan Sigalet, Bowling Green, Sr., G
* Brett Sterling, Colorado College, Jr., F
  Tuomas Tarkki, Northern Michigan, Sr. G

* Top-3 finalist

## NCAA Division I Tournament

Regional seeds in parentheses

### East Regional

Held in Worcester, Mass., March 25-26.

#### First Round

(1) Boston College 5 . . . . . . . . . . . . . . .(4) Mercyhurst 4
(2) North Dakota 4 . . . . . . . . . . . .(3) Boston University 0

#### Second Round

North Dakota 6 . . . . . . . . . . . . . . . . .Boston College 3

### Northeast Regional

Held in Amherst, Mass., March 26-27.

#### First Round

(1) Denver 4 . . . . . . . . . .OT . . . . . . .(4) Bemidji State 3
(2) New Hampshire 3 . . . .OT . . . . . . . . .(3) Harvard 2

#### Second Round

Denver 4 . . . . . . . . . . . . . . . . . . . . .New Hampshire 2

### West Regional

Held in Minneapolis, Minn., March 26-27.

#### First Round

(1) Minnesota 1 . . . . . . . .OT . . . . . . . . . . . .(4) Maine 0
(2) Cornell 3 . . . . . . . . . . . . . . . . . . . .(3) Ohio State 2

#### Second Round

Minnesota 2 . . . . . . . . . .OT . . . . . . . . . . . .Cornell 1

### Midwest Regional

Held in Grand Rapids, Mich., March 25-26.

#### First Round

(1) Colorado College 6 . . . . . . . . . . . . . . (4) Colgate 5
(2) Michigan 4 . . . . . . . . . . . . . . . . . .(3) Wisconsin 1

#### Second Round

Colorado College 4 . . . . . . . . . . . . . . . . .Michigan 3

## U.S. Division I Men's College Hockey (Cont.)

AP/Wide World Photos

*Denver's entire team mobs goaltender **Peter Mannino** after the Pioneers sewed up their second straight NCAA Division I men's title with a 4-1 win over North Dakota in Columbus.*

### The Frozen Four

Held at the Schottenstein Center in Columbus, Ohio, April 7 and April 9. Single elimination; no consolation game.

### Semifinals

Denver 6 . . . . . . . . . . . . . . . . Colorado College 2
North Dakota 4 . . . . . . . . . . . . . . . . . Minnesota 2

### Championship Game

Denver 4 . . . . . . . . . . . . . . . . . North Dakota 1

### Most Outstanding Player

Peter Mannino, Denver freshman goalie: SEMIFINAL—43 shots, 41 saves; FINAL—45 shots, 44 saves.

### All-Tournament Team

| Pos. | Player | School |
| --- | --- | --- |
| Forward | Gabe Gauthier | Denver |
| Forward | Travis Zajac | North Dakota |
| Forward | Paul Stastny | Denver |
| Defense | Matt Carle | Denver |
| Defense | Brett Skinner | Denver |
| Goaltender | Peter Mannino | Denver |

### Future Sites

| | | |
| --- | --- | --- |
| 2006 | Bradley Center | Milwaukee, Wis. |
| 2007 | Savvis Center | St. Louis, Mo. |
| 2008 | Pepsi Center | Denver, Colo. |

### Championship Game Box

Denver, 4-1

| | 1 | 2 | 3 | Tot |
| --- | --- | --- | --- | --- |
| North Dakota (WCHA) . . . . . . . . | 1 | 0 | 0 | —1 |
| Denver (WCHA) . . . . . . . . . . . . . | 1 | 1 | 2 | —4 |

#### 1st Period

DEN—Jeff Drummond 16 (Kevin Ulanski, Gabe Gauthier), 6:15; **UND**—Travis Zajac 20 (Nick Fuher, Drew Stafford), 9:52 (pp).

#### 2nd Period

DEN—Paul Stastny 16 (Ulanski, Matt Laatsch), 10:08 (pp).

#### 3rd Period

DEN—Stastny 17 (Matt Carle, Brett Skinner), 8:19 (pp); DEN—Gauthier 26 (Skinner, Stastny), 19:23 (en).

**Shots on Goal:** North Dakota—10-12-23—45; Denver—7-11-6-24. **Power plays:** North Dakota 1-7; Denver 2-6.

**Goalies:** North Dakota—Jordan Parise (23 shots, 20 saves); Denver—Peter Mannino (45 shots, 44 saves).

**Officials:** Steve Piotrowski (referee); Kevin Langseth and Paul Tunison (linesmen).

**Attendance:** 17,155. **Time:** 2:37.

## NCAA Division III Men's Tournament

Single elimination. First round games held on campus sites of higher seed. Semifinals and Championship Game held at Kenyon Arena in Middlebury, Vt.

### First Round
March 9

St. Thomas (Minn.) 4 . . . . . . . . . . . .at St. John's (Minn.) 1

### Second Round
March 12

St. Thomas (Minn.) 3 . . . . . . . . . .at St. Norbert (Wis.) 2
Trinity (Conn.) 4 . . . . . . . . . . . .at Geneseo St. (N.Y.) 0
at Middlebury (Vt.) 6 . . . . . . . . . . . . . . .Curry (Mass.) 0
New England College 4 . . . . . . .Manhattanville (N.Y.) 2

### Semifinals
March 18

St. Thomas 4 . . . . . . . . . . . . . . . . . . . . . .Trinity 1
Middlebury 5 . . . . . . . . . . . . .New England College 2

### Championship Game
March 19

Middlebury 5 . . . . . . . . . . . . . . . . . . . . .St. Thomas 0

**Records of semifinalists:** Middlebury (23-4-3); St. Thomas (20-6-5); NE College (18-12-0); Trinity (21-4-2).

# Women's College Hockey

## NCAA Division I

### Regionals

at Minnesota 6 . . . . . . . . . . . . . . . . . .Providence 1
St. Lawrence 3 . . . . . . . . .OT . . . .at Minnesota Duluth 2
at Dartmouth 4 . . . . . . . . . . . . . . . . . .Wisconsin 3
at Harvard 5 . . . . . . . . . .3OT . . . . . . . . .Mercyhurst 4

### The Frozen Four

Held at the Whittemore Center in Durham, N.H., March 25 and March 27. Single elimination.

#### Semifinals

Minnesota 7 . . . . . . . . . . . . . . . . . . . . . .Dartmouth 2
Harvard 4 . . . . . . . . . . . . . . . . . . . . . .St. Lawrence 1

#### Third Place

St. Lawrence 5 . . . . . . . . . . . . . . . . . . . . .Dartmouth 1

#### Championship

Minnesota 4 . . . . . . . . . . . . . . . . . . . . . . .Harvard 3

**Frozen Four Most Outstanding Player:** Natalie Darwitz, Minnesota junior forward: SEMIFINAL—2 goals, 3 assists; FINAL—1 goal, 3 assists.

### All-Tournament Team

| Pos. | Player | School |
|------|--------|--------|
| Forward | Natalie Darwitz | Minnesota |
| Forward | Krissy Wendell | Minnesota |
| Forward | Sarah Vaillancourt | Harvard |
| Defense | Lyndsay Wall | Minnesota |
| Defense | Caitlin Cahow | Harvard |
| Goaltender | Ali Boe | Harvard |

## NCAA Division III Championship

First round games held on campus sites of higher seed. Semifinals, Championship and Third Place games held March 18-19 at the Murray Athletic Center in Pineville, N.Y.

### First Round

at Plattsburgh St. (N.Y) 9 . . . . . . . . . . . .Bowdoin (Me.) 4
at Middlebury (Vt.) 3 . . . . .OT . . .Manhattanville (N.Y.) 2
Gustavus Adolphus (Minn.) 3 . . . . .Wis.-Stevens Point 0

### Semifinals

Elmira (N.Y.) 4 . . . . . . . . . . . . . . . . .Plattsburgh St. 3
Middlebury 7 . . . . . . . . . . . . . . .Gustavus Adolphus 3

### Third Place

Gustavus Adolphus 3 . . . . . . . . . . . . .Plattsburgh St. 1

### Championship

Middlebury 4 . . . . . . . . . . . . . . . . . . . . . . .Elmira 3

### Championship Game Box

Minnesota, 4-3

| | 1 | 2 | 3 | Tot |
|------|---|---|---|-----|
| **Harvard** (ECAC) . . . . . . . . . . . . | 0 | 2 | 1 | **—3** |
| **Minnesota** (WCHA) . . . . . . . . . . | 1 | 2 | 1 | **—4** |

#### 1st Period

**MIN**—Krissy Wendell 43 (Natalie Darwitz), 17:24.

#### 2nd Period

**HAR**—Jennifer Sifers 6 (Carrie Schroyer), 0:46; **MIN**—Lyndsay Wall 14 (Darwitz, Kelly Stephens), 7:58 (pp); **HAR**—Sarah Vaillancourt 25 (Nicole Corriero, Julie Chu), 10:33 (pp); **MIN**—Ashley Albrecht 4 (Wendell, Darwitz), 18:02.

#### 3rd Period

**HAR**—Caitlin Cahow 6 (Chu, Vaillancourt), 13:54 (pp); **MIN**—Darwitz 42 (Stephens), 18:52.

**Shots on Goal:** Harvard—9-12-5–26; Minnesota—6-14-4–24. **Power plays:** Harvard 2-5; Minnesota 1-3.

**Goalies:** Harvard—Alie Boe (24 shots, 20 saves); Minnesota—Jody Horak (26 shots, 23 saves).

**Officials:** Ed Boyle (referee); Pat Silva and Kelli O'Brian (linesmen).

**Attendance:** 2,056. **Time:** 2:17.

### Patty Kazmaier Award

Awarded by the USA Hockey Foundation to the women's college hockey player of the Year. Voting is done by a 13-member panel of national media, varsity college coaches, and one USA Hockey member.

| | Cl | Pos |
|---|----|----|
| **Winner:** Krissy Wendell, Minnesota . . . . . . . | Jr. | F |

Other nine finalists, as selected by the nation's Division I coaches (listed alphabetically):

   Julie Chu, Harvard, Jr., F
   Desi Clark, Mercyhurst, Sr., G
   Nicole Corriero, Harvard, Sr. F
\*  Natalie Darwitz, Minnesota, Jr., F
   Molly Engstrom, Wisconsin, Sr., D
   Carla McLeod, Wisconsin, Sr., D
\*  Caroline Ouellette, Minnesota Duluth, Sr. F
   Cherie Piper, Dartmouth, Jr., F
   Rebecca Russell, St. Lawrence, Sr., F

\* Top-3 finalist

## WORLD HOCKEY CHAMPIONSHIPS

### MEN

The 2005 IIHF World Hockey Championship held in Vienna and Innsbruck, Austria from April 30 through May 15. Top three teams (*) in each group after preliminary round-robin advance to the second round. Fourth-place teams play in a consolation round. Top four teams (*) from each group of the second round advance to the quarterfinals.

### Preliminary Round Robin Standings

| Group A | W-L-T | Pts | GF | GA |
|---|---|---|---|---|
| *Slovakia | 2-0-1 | 5 | 13 | 5 |
| *Russia | 2-0-1 | 5 | 9 | 5 |
| *Belarus | 1-2-0 | 2 | 6 | 4 |
| Austria | 0-3-0 | 0 | 3 | 17 |

| Group B | W-L-T | Pts | GF | GA |
|---|---|---|---|---|
| *Canada | 3-0-0 | 6 | 17 | 5 |
| *United States | 2-1-0 | 4 | 11 | 4 |
| *Latvia | 1-2-0 | 2 | 8 | 10 |
| Slovenia | 0-3-0 | 0 | 1 | 18 |

| Group C | W-L-T | Pts | GF | GA |
|---|---|---|---|---|
| *Sweden | 3-0-0 | 6 | 15 | 3 |
| *Finland | 2-1-0 | 4 | 7 | 7 |
| *Ukraine | 1-2-0 | 2 | 5 | 8 |
| Denmark | 0-3-0 | 0 | 2 | 11 |

| Group D | W-L-T | Pts | GF | GA |
|---|---|---|---|---|
| *Czech Republic | 3-0-0 | 6 | 6 | 1 |
| *Switzerland | 2-1-0 | 4 | 8 | 5 |
| *Kazakhstan | 1-2-0 | 2 | 3 | 4 |
| Germany | 0-3-0 | 0 | 2 | 9 |

### Second Round

| Group E | W-L-T | Pts | GF | GA |
|---|---|---|---|---|
| *Russia | 3-0-2 | 8 | 13 | 8 |
| *Czech Republic | 4-1-0 | 8 | 15 | 5 |
| *Slovakia | 3-1-1 | 7 | 12 | 11 |
| *Switzerland | 2-2-1 | 5 | 9 | 10 |
| Belarus | 1-4-0 | 2 | 4 | 11 |
| Kazakhstan | 0-5-0 | 0 | 3 | 11 |

| Group F | W-L-T | Pts | GF | GA |
|---|---|---|---|---|
| *Sweden | 4-1-0 | 8 | 23 | 13 |
| *Canada | 3-1-1 | 7 | 18 | 14 |
| *United States | 2-1-2 | 6 | 14 | 10 |
| *Finland | 1-1-3 | 5 | 12 | 13 |
| Latvia | 1-3-1 | 3 | 9 | 18 |
| Ukraine | 0-4-1 | 1 | 5 | 13 |

### Quarterfinals

| | | |
|---|---|---|
| Czech Republic 3 | ShO | United States 2 |
| Canada 5 | | Slovakia 4 |
| Russia 4 | ShO | Finland 3 |
| Sweden 2 | | Switzerland 1 |

### Semifinals

| | | |
|---|---|---|
| Canada 4 | | Russia 3 |
| Czech Republic 3 | OT | Sweden 2 |

**Bronze Medal Game:** Russia 6 . . . . . . . . . .Sweden 3
**Gold Medal Game:** Czech Republic 3 . . . . .Canada 0

### Scoring Leaders

| | Gm | G | A | Pts | PM |
|---|---|---|---|---|---|
| Joe Thornton, Canada | 9 | 6 | 10 | 16 | 4 |
| Rick Nash, Canada | 9 | 9 | 6 | 15 | 8 |
| Simon Gagne, Canada | 9 | 3 | 7 | 10 | 0 |
| Zigmund Palffy, Slovakia | 7 | 5 | 4 | 9 | 10 |
| Daniel Sedin, Sweden | 9 | 5 | 4 | 9 | 2 |
| Daniel Alfredsson, Sweden | 9 | 3 | 6 | 9 | 6 |
| Jaromir Jagr, Czech Republic | 8 | 2 | 7 | 9 | 2 |

| Tournament MVP: | Joe Thornton, Canada |
|---|---|
| Best Forward: | Alexei Kovalev, Russia |
| Best Defenseman: | Wade Redden, Canada |
| Best Goaltender: | Tomas Vokoun, Czech Republic |

### WOMEN

The 2005 IIHF World Womens Hockey Championship held in Linkoping and Norrkoping, Sweden, April 2-9. Top two teams (*) in each group after preliminary round-robin advance to the medal round.

### Preliminary Round Robin Standings

| Group A | W-L-T | Pts | GF | GA |
|---|---|---|---|---|
| *Canada | 3-0-0 | 6 | 35 | 0 |
| *Sweden | 2-1-0 | 4 | 8 | 12 |
| Russia | 0-2-1 | 1 | 3 | 17 |
| Kazakhstan | 0-2-1 | 1 | 3 | 20 |

| Group B | W-L-T | Pts | GF | GA |
|---|---|---|---|---|
| *United States | 3-0-0 | 6 | 23 | 3 |
| *Finland | 2-1-0 | 4 | 11 | 10 |
| China | 0-2-1 | 1 | 6 | 16 |
| Germany | 0-2-1 | 1 | 4 | 15 |

| Tournament MVP: | Krissy Wendell, USA |
|---|---|
| Best Forward: | Jayna Hefford, Canada |
| Best Defenseman: | Angela Ruggiero, USA |
| Best Goaltender: | Chanda Gunn, USA |

### Semifinals

| | | |
|---|---|---|
| Canada 3 | | Finland 0 |
| United States 4 | | Sweden 1 |

**Bronze Medal Game:** Sweden 5 . . . . . . . . .Finland 2
**Gold Medal Game:** United States 1 . . . . .Canada 0
(USA wins a shootout, 3-1)

### Scoring Leaders

| | Gm | G | A | Pts | PM |
|---|---|---|---|---|---|
| Krissy Wendell, USA | 5 | 4 | 5 | 9 | 0 |
| Jayna Hefford, Canada | 5 | 6 | 2 | 8 | 0 |
| Hayley Wickenheiser, Canada | 5 | 5 | 3 | 8 | 6 |
| Sarah Vaillancourt, Canada | 5 | 3 | 5 | 8 | 2 |
| Caroline Ouellette, Canada | 5 | 2 | 6 | 8 | 0 |
| Kelly Stephens, USA | 5 | 3 | 4 | 7 | 16 |
| Jennifer Botterill, Canada | 5 | 1 | 6 | 7 | 4 |

# 1893-2005
# *Through the Years*

SPORTS ALMANAC

## The Stanley Cup

The Stanley Cup was originally donated to the Canadian Amateur Hockey Association by Sir Frederick Arthur Stanley, Lord Stanley of Preston and 16th Earl of Derby, who had become interested in the sport while Governor General of Canada from 1888 to 1893. Stanley wanted the trophy to be a challenge cup, contested for each year by the best amateur hockey teams in Canada.

In 1893, the Cup was presented without a challenge to the AHA champion Montreal Amateur Athletic Association team. Every year since, however, there has been a playoff. In 1914, Cup trustees limited the field challenging for the trophy to the champion of the eastern professional National Hockey Association (NHA, organized in 1910) and the western professional Pacific Coast Hockey Association (PCHA, organized in 1912).

The NHA disbanded in 1917 and the National Hockey League (NHL) was formed. From 1918 to 1926, the NHL and PCHA champions played for the Cup with the Western Canada Hockey League (WCHL) champion joining in a three-way challenge in 1923 and '24. The PCHA disbanded in 1924, while the WCHL became the Western Hockey League (WHL) for the 1925-26 season and folded the following year. The NHL playoffs have decided the winner of the Stanley Cup ever since.

## Champions, 1893-1917

**Multiple winners:** Montreal Victorias and Montreal Wanderers (4); Montreal Amateur Athletic Association and Ottawa Silver Seven (3); Montreal Shamrocks, Ottawa Senators, Quebec Bulldogs and Winnipeg Victorias (2).

| Year | | Year | | Year | |
|------|------|------|------|------|------|
| 1893 | Montreal AAA | 1901 | Winnipeg Victorias | 1909 | Ottawa Senators |
| 1894 | Montreal AAA | 1902 | Montreal AAA | 1910 | Montreal Wanderers |
| 1895 | Montreal Victorias | 1903 | Ottawa Silver Seven | 1911 | Ottawa Senators |
| 1896 | (Feb.) Winnipeg Victorias | 1904 | Ottawa Silver Seven | 1912 | Quebec Bulldogs |
| | (Dec.) Montreal Victorias | 1905 | Ottawa Silver Seven | 1913 | Quebec Bulldogs |
| 1897 | Montreal Victorias | 1906 | Montreal Wanderers | 1914 | Toronto Blueshirts (NHA) |
| 1898 | Montreal Victorias | 1907 | (Jan.) Kenora Thistles | 1915 | Vancouver Millionaires (PCHA) |
| 1899 | Montreal Shamrocks | | (Mar.) Montreal Wanderers | 1916 | Montreal Canadiens (NHA) |
| 1900 | Montreal Shamrocks | 1908 | Montreal Wanderers | 1917 | Seattle Metropolitans (PCHA) |

## Champions Since 1918

**Multiple winners:** Montreal Canadiens (23); Toronto Arenas-St. Pats-Maple Leafs (13); Detroit Red Wings (10); Boston Bruins and Edmonton Oilers (5); NY Islanders, NY Rangers and Ottawa Senators (4); Chicago Blackhawks and New Jersey Devils (3); Colorado Avalanche, Montreal Maroons, Philadelphia Flyers and Pittsburgh Penguins (2).

| Year | Winner | Head Coach | Series | Loser | Head Coach |
|------|--------|-----------|--------|-------|-----------|
| 1918 | Toronto Arenas | Dick Carroll | 3-2 (WLWLW) | Vancouver (PCHA) | Frank Patrick |
| 1919 | No Decision* | | | | |
| 1920 | Ottawa | Pete Green | 3-2 (WWLLW) | Seattle (PCHA) | Pete Muldoon |
| 1921 | Ottawa | Pete Green | 3-2 (LWWLW) | Vancouver (PCHA) | Frank Patrick |
| 1922 | Toronto St. Pats | Eddie Powers | 3-2 (LWLWW) | Vancouver (PCHA) | Frank Patrick |
| 1923 | Ottawa | Pete Green | 3-1 (WLWW) | Vancouver (PCHA) | Frank Patrick |
| | | | 2-0 | Edmonton (WCHL) | K.C. McKenzie |
| 1924 | Montreal | Leo Dandurand | 2-0 | Vancouver (PCHA) | Frank Patrick |
| | | | 2-0 | Calgary (WCHL) | Eddie Oatman |
| 1925 | Victoria (WCHL) | Lester Patrick | 3-1 (WWLW) | Montreal | Leo Dandurand |
| 1926 | Montreal Maroons | Eddie Gerard | 3-1 (WWLW) | Victoria (WHL) | Lester Patrick |
| 1927 | Ottawa | Dave Gill | 2-0-2 (TWTW) | Boston | Art Ross |
| 1928 | NY Rangers | Lester Patrick | 3-2 (LWLWW) | Montreal Maroons | Eddie Gerard |
| 1929 | Boston | Cy Denneny | 2-0 | NY Rangers | Lester Patrick |
| 1930 | Montreal | Cecil Hart | 2-0 | Boston | Art Ross |
| 1931 | Montreal | Cecil Hart | 3-2 (WLLWW) | Chicago | Art Duncan |
| 1932 | Toronto | Dick Irvin | 3-0 | NY Rangers | Lester Patrick |
| 1933 | NY Rangers | Lester Patrick | 3-1 (WWLW) | Toronto | Dick Irvin |
| 1934 | Chicago | Tommy Gorman | 3-1 (WWLW) | Detroit | Jack Adams |
| 1935 | Montreal Maroons | Tommy Gorman | 3-0 | Toronto | Dick Irvin |
| 1936 | Detroit | Jack Adams | 3-1 (WWLW) | Toronto | Dick Irvin |
| 1937 | Detroit | Jack Adams | 3-2 (LWLWW) | NY Rangers | Lester Patrick |
| 1938 | Chicago | Bill Stewart | 3-1 (WLWW) | Toronto | Dick Irvin |
| 1939 | Boston | Art Ross | 4-1 (WLWWW) | Toronto | Dick Irvin |

* The 1919 finals were cancelled after five games due to an influenza epidemic with Montreal and Seattle (PCHA) tied at 2-2-1.

## The Stanley Cup (Cont.)

| Year | Winner | Head Coach | Series | Loser | Head Coach |
|------|--------|-----------|--------|-------|-----------|
| 1940 | NY Rangers | Frank Boucher | 4-2 (WWLLWW) | Toronto | Dick Irvin |
| 1941 | Boston | Cooney Weiland | 4-0 | Detroit | Jack Adams |
| 1942 | Toronto | Hap Day | 4-3 (LLLWWWW) | Detroit | Jack Adams |
| 1943 | Detroit | Ebbie Goodfellow | 4-0 | Boston | Art Ross |
| 1944 | Montreal | Dick Irvin | 4-0 | Chicago | Paul Thompson |
| 1945 | Toronto | Hap Day | 4-3 (WWWWLLLW) | Detroit | Jack Adams |
| 1946 | Montreal | Dick Irvin | 4-1 (WWWLW) | Boston | Dit Clapper |
| 1947 | Toronto | Hap Day | 4-2 (LWWWLW) | Montreal | Dick Irvin |
| 1948 | Toronto | Hap Day | 4-0 | Detroit | Tommy Ivan |
| 1949 | Toronto | Hap Day | 4-0 | Detroit | Tommy Ivan |
| 1950 | Detroit | Tommy Ivan | 4-3 (WLWLLWW) | NY Rangers | Lynn Patrick |
| 1951 | Toronto | Joe Primeau | 4-1 (WLWWW) | Montreal | Dick Irvin |
| 1952 | Detroit | Tommy Ivan | 4-0 | Montreal | Dick Irvin |
| 1953 | Montreal | Dick Irvin | 4-1 (WLWWW) | Boston | Lynn Patrick |
| 1954 | Detroit | Tommy Ivan | 4-3 (WLWWLLW) | Montreal | Dick Irvin |
| 1955 | Detroit | Jimmy Skinner | 4-3 (WWLLWLW) | Montreal | Dick Irvin |
| 1956 | Montreal | Toe Blake | 4-1 (WWLWW) | Detroit | Jimmy Skinner |
| 1957 | Montreal | Toe Blake | 4-1 (WWWLW) | Boston | Milt Schmidt |
| 1958 | Montreal | Toe Blake | 4-2 (WLWLWW) | Boston | Milt Schmidt |
| 1959 | Montreal | Toe Blake | 4-1 (WWLWW) | Toronto | Punch Imlach |
| 1960 | Montreal | Toe Blake | 4-0 | Toronto | Punch Imlach |
| 1961 | Chicago | Rudy Pilous | 4-2 (WLWLWW) | Detroit | Sid Abel |
| 1962 | Toronto | Punch Imlach | 4-2 (WWLLWW) | Chicago | Rudy Pilous |
| 1963 | Toronto | Punch Imlach | 4-1 (WWLWW) | Detroit | Sid Abel |
| 1964 | Toronto | Punch Imlach | 4-3 (WLLWLWW) | Detroit | Sid Abel |
| 1965 | Montreal | Toe Blake | 4-3 (WWLLWLW) | Chicago | Billy Reay |
| 1966 | Montreal | Toe Blake | 4-2 (LLWWWW) | Detroit | Sid Abel |
| 1967 | Toronto | Punch Imlach | 4-2 (LWWLWW) | Montreal | Toe Blake |
| 1968 | Montreal | Toe Blake | 4-0 | St. Louis | Scotty Bowman |
| 1969 | Montreal | Claude Ruel | 4-0 | St. Louis | Scotty Bowman |
| 1970 | Boston | Harry Sinden | 4-0 | St. Louis | Scotty Bowman |
| 1971 | Montreal | Al MacNeil | 4-3 (LLWWLWW) | Chicago | Billy Reay |
| 1972 | Boston | Tom Johnson | 4-2 (WWWLWLW) | NY Rangers | Emile Francis |
| 1973 | Montreal | Scotty Bowman | 4-2 (WWLWLW) | Chicago | Billy Reay |
| 1974 | Philadelphia | Fred Shero | 4-2 (LWWLWW) | Boston | Bep Guidolin |
| 1975 | Philadelphia | Fred Shero | 4-2 (WWLLWW) | Buffalo | Floyd Smith |
| 1976 | Montreal | Scotty Bowman | 4-0 | Philadelphia | Fred Shero |
| 1977 | Montreal | Scotty Bowman | 4-0 | Boston | Don Cherry |
| 1978 | Montreal | Scotty Bowman | 4-2 (WWLLWW) | Boston | Don Cherry |
| 1979 | Montreal | Scotty Bowman | 4-1 (LWWWW) | NY Rangers | Fred Shero |
| 1980 | NY Islanders | Al Arbour | 4-2 (WLWLWW) | Philadelphia | Pat Quinn |
| 1981 | NY Islanders | Al Arbour | 4-1 (WWWLW) | Minnesota | Glen Sonmor |
| 1982 | NY Islanders | Al Arbour | 4-0 | Vancouver | Roger Neilson |
| 1983 | NY Islanders | Al Arbour | 4-0 | Edmonton | Glen Sather |
| 1984 | Edmonton | Glen Sather | 4-1 (WLWWW) | NY Islanders | Al Arbour |
| 1985 | Edmonton | Glen Sather | 4-1 (LWWWW) | Philadelphia | Mike Keenan |
| 1986 | Montreal | Jean Perron | 4-1 (WLWWW) | Calgary | Bob Johnson |
| 1987 | Edmonton | Glen Sather | 4-3 (WWLWLLW) | Philadelphia | Mike Keenan |
| 1988 | Edmonton | Glen Sather | 4-0 | Boston | Terry O'Reilly |
| 1989 | Calgary | Terry Crisp | 4-2 (WLLLWW) | Montreal | Pat Burns |
| 1990 | Edmonton | John Muckler | 4-1 (WWLWW) | Boston | Mike Milbury |
| 1991 | Pittsburgh | Bob Johnson | 4-2 (LWLWWW) | Minnesota | Bob Gainey |
| 1992 | Pittsburgh | Scotty Bowman | 4-0 | Chicago | Mike Keenan |
| 1993 | Montreal | Jacques Demers | 4-1 (LWWWW) | Los Angeles | Barry Melrose |
| 1994 | NY Rangers | Mike Keenan | 4-3 (LWWWLLW) | Vancouver | Pat Quinn |
| 1995 | New Jersey | Jacques Lemaire | 4-0 | Detroit | Scotty Bowman |
| 1996 | Colorado | Marc Crawford | 4-0 | Florida | Doug MacLean |
| 1997 | Detroit | Scotty Bowman | 4-0 | Philadelphia | Terry Murray |
| 1998 | Detroit | Scotty Bowman | 4-0 | Washington | Ron Wilson |
| 1999 | Dallas | Ken Hitchcock | 4-2 (LWWLWW) | Buffalo | Lindy Ruff |
| 2000 | New Jersey | Larry Robinson | 4-2 (WLWWLW) | Dallas | Ken Hitchcock |
| 2001 | Colorado | Bob Hartley | 4-3 (WLWLLWW) | New Jersey | Larry Robinson |
| 2002 | Detroit | Scotty Bowman | 4-1 (LWWWW) | Carolina | Paul Maurice |
| 2003 | New Jersey | Pat Burns | 4-3 (WWLLWLW) | Anaheim | Mike Babcock |
| 2004 | Tampa Bay | John Tortorella | 4-3 (LWLWLWW) | Calgary | Darryl Sutter |
| 2005 | Not held* | | | | |

* The lack of a labor agreement between the owners and NHLPA, and the ensuing owners' lockout, canceled the 2004-05 season.

## M.J. O'Brien Trophy

Donated by Canadian mining magnate M.J. O'Brien, whose son Ambrose founded the National Hockey Association in 1910. Originally presented to the NHA champion until the league's demise in 1917, the trophy then passed to the NHL champion through 1927. It was awarded to the NHL's Canadian Division winner from 1927-38 and the Stanley Cup runner-up from 1939-50 before being retired in 1950.

NHA winners included the Montreal Wanderers (1910), original Ottawa Senators (1911 and '15), Quebec Bulldogs (1912 and '13), Toronto Blueshirts (1914) and Montreal Canadiens (1916 and '17).

## Conn Smythe Trophy

The Most Valuable Player of the Stanley Cup Playoffs, as selected by the Pro Hockey Writers Association. Presented since 1965 by Maple Leaf Gardens Limited in the name of the former Toronto coach, GM and owner, Conn Smythe. Winners who did not play for the Cup champion are in **bold** type.

**Multiple winners:** Patrick Roy (3); Wayne Gretzky, Mario Lemieux, Bobby Orr and Bernie Parent (2).

| Year | | Year | | Year | |
|---|---|---|---|---|---|
| 1965 | Jean Beliveau, Mon., C | 1979 | Bob Gainey, Mon., LW | 1993 | Patrick Roy, Mon., G |
| 1966 | **Roger Crozier**, Det., G | 1980 | Bryan Trottier, NYI, C | 1994 | Brian Leetch, NYR, D |
| 1967 | Dave Keon, Tor., C | 1981 | Butch Goring, NYI, C | 1995 | Claude Lemieux, NJ, RW |
| 1968 | **Glenn Hall**, St.L., G | 1982 | Mike Bossy, NYI, RW | 1996 | Joe Sakic, Col., C |
| 1969 | Serge Savard, Mon., D | 1983 | Billy Smith, NYI, G | 1997 | Mike Vernon, Det., G |
| 1970 | Bobby Orr, Bos., D | 1984 | Mark Messier, Edm., LW | 1998 | Steve Yzerman, Det., C |
| 1971 | Ken Dryden, Mon., G | 1985 | Wayne Gretzky, Edm., C | 1999 | Joe Nieuwendyk, Dal., C |
| 1972 | Bobby Orr, Bos., D | 1986 | Patrick Roy, Mon., G | 2000 | Scott Stevens, NJ, D |
| 1973 | Yvan Cournoyer, Mon., RW | 1987 | **Ron Hextall**, Phi., G | 2001 | Patrick Roy, Col., G |
| 1974 | Bernie Parent, Phi., G | 1988 | Wayne Gretzky, Edm., C | 2002 | Nicklas Lidstrom, Det., D |
| 1975 | Bernie Parent, Phi., G | 1989 | Al MacInnis, Calg., D | 2003 | **J-S Giguere**, Ana., G |
| 1976 | **Reggie Leach**, Phi., RW | 1990 | Bill Ranford, Edm., G | 2004 | Brad Richards, TB, C |
| 1977 | Guy Lafleur, Mon., RW | 1991 | Mario Lemieux, Pit., C | 2005 | Not awarded |
| 1978 | Larry Robinson, Mon., D | 1992 | Mario Lemieux, Pit., C | | |

**Note:** Ken Dryden (1971) and Patrick Roy (1986) are the only players to win as rookies.

## All-Time Stanley Cup Playoff Leaders

### CAREER

Stanley Cup Playoff leaders through 2005. Years listed indicate number of playoff appearances. Players active in 2003-04 are in **bold** type; (DNP) indicates player that was active in 2003-04 but did not participate in playoffs.

### Scoring

#### Points

| | | Yrs | Gm | G | A | Pts |
|---|---|---|---|---|---|---|
| 1 | Wayne Gretzky | 16 | 208 | 122 | 260 | 382 |
| 2 | **Mark Messier** (DNP) | 17 | 236 | 109 | 186 | 295 |
| 3 | Jari Kurri | 14 | 200 | 106 | 127 | 233 |
| 4 | Glenn Anderson | 15 | 225 | 93 | 121 | 214 |
| 5 | Paul Coffey | 16 | 194 | 59 | 137 | 196 |
| 6 | **Brett Hull** | 19 | 202 | 103 | 87 | 190 |
| 7 | Doug Gilmour | 17 | 182 | 60 | 128 | 188 |
| 8 | Bryan Trottier | 17 | 221 | 71 | 113 | 184 |
| 9 | **Steve Yzerman** | 19 | 192 | 70 | 111 | 181 |
| 10 | Ray Bourque | 21 | 214 | 41 | 139 | 180 |
| 11 | Jean Beliveau | 17 | 162 | 79 | 97 | 176 |
| 12 | Denis Savard | 16 | 169 | 66 | 109 | 175 |
| 13 | **Mario Lemieux** (DNP) | 8 | 107 | 76 | 96 | 172 |
| 14 | **Joe Sakic** | 11 | 153 | 78 | 91 | 169 |
| 15 | Denis Potvin | 14 | 185 | 56 | 108 | 164 |
| 16 | **Sergei Fedorov** (DNP) | 13 | 162 | 50 | 113 | 163 |
| 17 | Mike Bossy | 10 | 129 | 85 | 75 | 160 |
| | Gordie Howe | 20 | 157 | 68 | 92 | 160 |
| | Bobby Smith | 13 | 184 | 64 | 96 | 160 |
| | **Al MacInnis** (DNP) | 19 | 177 | 39 | 121 | 160 |
| 21 | Claude Lemieux | 17 | 233 | 80 | 78 | 158 |
| 22 | **Adam Oates** (DNP) | 15 | 163 | 42 | 114 | 156 |
| 23 | **Jaromir Jagr** (DNP) | 12 | 146 | 67 | 87 | 154 |
| | **Peter Forsberg** | 10 | 133 | 57 | 97 | 154 |
| 25 | Larry Murphy | 20 | 215 | 37 | 115 | 152 |

#### Goals

| | | Yrs | Gm | G |
|---|---|---|---|---|
| 1 | Wayne Gretzky | 16 | 208 | 122 |
| 2 | **Mark Messier** (DNP) | 17 | 236 | 109 |
| 3 | Jari Kurri | 15 | 200 | 106 |
| 4 | **Brett Hull** | 19 | 202 | 103 |
| 5 | Glenn Anderson | 15 | 225 | 93 |
| 6 | Mike Bossy | 10 | 129 | 85 |
| 7 | Maurice Richard | 15 | 133 | 82 |
| 8 | Claude Lemieux | 17 | 233 | 80 |
| 9 | Jean Beliveau | 17 | 162 | 79 |
| 10 | **Joe Sakic** | 11 | 153 | 78 |

#### Assists

| | | Yrs | Gm | A |
|---|---|---|---|---|
| 1 | Wayne Gretzky | 16 | 208 | 260 |
| 2 | **Mark Messier** (DNP) | 17 | 236 | 186 |
| 3 | Ray Bourque | 21 | 214 | 139 |
| 4 | Paul Coffey | 16 | 194 | 137 |
| 5 | Doug Gilmour | 17 | 182 | 128 |
| 6 | Jari Kurri | 15 | 200 | 127 |
| 7 | Glenn Anderson | 15 | 225 | 121 |
| | **Al MacInnis** (DNP) | 19 | 177 | 121 |
| 9 | Larry Robinson | 20 | 227 | 116 |
| 10 | Larry Murphy | 20 | 215 | 115 |

# The Stanley Cup (Cont.)

## Goaltending
### Wins

| | | Gm | W-L | Pct | GAA |
|---|---|---|---|---|---|
| 1 | Patrick Roy | 247 | 151-94 | .616 | 2.30 |
| 2 | Grant Fuhr | 150 | 92-50 | .648 | 2.92 |
| 3 | Billy Smith | 132 | 88-36 | .710 | 2.73 |
| | **Ed Belfour** | 161 | 88-68 | .564 | 2.17 |
| 5 | **Martin Brodeur** | 144 | 84-60 | .583 | 1.87 |
| 6 | Ken Dryden | 112 | 80-32 | .714 | 2.40 |
| 7 | Mike Vernon | 138 | 77-56 | .579 | 2.68 |
| 8 | Jacques Plante | 112 | 71-37 | .657 | 2.17 |
| 9 | Andy Moog | 132 | 68-57 | .544 | 3.04 |
| 10 | **Curtis Joseph** | 131 | 62-66 | .484 | 2.44 |

### Shutouts

| | | Gm | GAA | No |
|---|---|---|---|---|
| 1 | Patrick Roy | 247 | 2.30 | 23 |
| 2 | **Martin Brodeur** | 144 | 1.87 | 20 |
| 3 | **Curtis Joseph** | 131 | 2.44 | 16 |
| 4 | Clint Benedict | 48 | 1.80 | 15 |
| | Jacques Plante | 112 | 2.17 | 15 |

## Goals Against Average
Minimum of 50 games played

| | | Gm | Min | GA | GAA |
|---|---|---|---|---|---|
| 1 | **Martin Brodeur** | 144 | 9000 | 280 | 1.87 |
| 2 | George Hainsworth | 52 | 3486 | 112 | 1.93 |
| 3 | Turk Broda | 101 | 6389 | 211 | 1.98 |
| 4 | **Dominik Hasek** (DNP) | 97 | 5972 | 202 | 2.03 |
| 5 | Jacques Plante | 112 | 6652 | 240 | 2.16 |
| 6 | **Ed Belfour** | 161 | 9945 | 359 | 2.17 |
| 7 | **Chris Osgood** | 87 | 5085 | 190 | 2.24 |
| 8 | **Nikolai Khabibulin** | 57 | 3464 | 131 | 2.27 |
| 9 | Patrick Roy | 247 | 15209 | 584 | 2.30 |
| 10 | Ken Dryden | 112 | 6846 | 274 | 2.40 |

**Note:** Clint Benedict had an average of 1.80 but played in only 48 games.

## Games Played

| | | Yrs | Gm |
|---|---|---|---|
| 1 | Patrick Roy, Mon-Col | 17 | 247 |
| 2 | **Ed Belfour**, Chi-Dal-Tor | 13 | 161 |
| 3 | Grant Fuhr, Edm-Buf-St.L | 14 | 150 |
| 4 | **Martin Brodeur**, New Jersey | 11 | 144 |
| 5 | Mike Vernon, Calg-Det-SJ-Fla | 14 | 138 |

## Appearances in Cup Finals
Standings of all teams that have reached the Stanley Cup championship round, since 1918.

| App | | Cups | Last Won |
|---|---|---|---|
| 32 | Montreal Canadiens | 23 * | 1993 |
| 22 | Detroit Red Wings | 10 | 2002 |
| 21 | Toronto Maple Leafs | 13 † | 1967 |
| 17 | Boston Bruins | 5 | 1972 |
| 10 | New York Rangers | 4 | 1994 |
| 10 | Chicago Blackhawks | 3 | 1961 |
| 7 | Philadelphia Flyers | 2 | 1975 |
| 6 | Edmonton Oilers | 5 | 1990 |
| 5 | New York Islanders | 4 | 1983 |
| 5 | Vancouver Millionaires (PCHA) | 0 | — |
| 4 | (original) Ottawa Senators | 4 | 1927 |
| 4 | Minnesota/Dallas (North) Stars | 1 | 1999 |
| 4 | New Jersey Devils | 3 | 2003 |
| 3 | Montreal Maroons | 2 | 1935 |
| 3 | Calgary Flames | 1 | 1989 |
| 3 | St. Louis Blues | 0 | — |
| 2 | Colorado Avalanche | 2 | 2001 |
| 2 | Pittsburgh Penguins | 2 | 1992 |
| 2 | Victoria Cougars (WCHL-WHL) | 1 | 1925 |
| 2 | Buffalo Sabres | 0 | — |
| 2 | Seattle Metropolitans (PCHA) | 0 | — |
| 2 | Vancouver Canucks | 0 | — |
| 1 | Tampa Bay Lightning | 1 | 2004 |
| 1 | Mighty Ducks of Anaheim | 0 | — |
| 1 | Calgary Tigers (WCHL) | 0 | — |
| 1 | Carolina Hurricanes | 0 | — |
| 1 | Edmonton Eskimos (WCHL) | 0 | — |
| 1 | Florida Panthers | 0 | — |
| 1 | Los Angeles Kings | 0 | — |
| 1 | Washington Capitals | 0 | — |

*Les Canadiens also won the Cup in 1916 for a total of 24. Also, their final with Seattle in 1919 was cancelled due to an influenza epidemic that claimed the life of the Habs' Joe Hall.
†Toronto has won the Cup under three nicknames—Arenas (1918), St. Pats (1922) and Maple Leafs (1932,42,45,47-49,51,62-64,67).

**Teams now defunct** (7): Calgary Tigers, Edmonton Eskimos, Montreal Maroons, (original) Ottawa Senators, Seattle, Vancouver Millionaires and Victoria. Edmonton (1923) and Calgary (1924) represented the WCHL and later the WHL, while Vancouver (1918,1921-24) and Seattle (1919-20) played out of the PCHA.

## Miscellaneous
### Championships

| | | Yrs | Cups |
|---|---|---|---|
| 1 | Henri Richard, Montreal | 18 | 11 |
| 2 | Yvan Cournoyer, Montreal | 15 | 10 |
| | Jean Beliveau, Montreal | 17 | 10 |
| 4 | Claude Provost, Montreal | 14 | 9 |
| 5 | Jacques Lemaire, Montreal | 11 | 8 |
| | Maurice Richard, Montreal | 15 | 8 |
| | Red Kelly, Detroit-Toronto | 19 | 8 |

### Years in Playoffs

| | | Yrs | Gm |
|---|---|---|---|
| 1 | Ray Bourque, Boston-Colorado | 21 | 214 |
| 2 | Gordie Howe, Detroit-Hartford | 20 | 157 |
| | Larry Robinson, Montreal-Los Angeles | 20 | 227 |
| | Larry Murphy, LA-Wash-Min-Pit-Tor-Det | 20 | 215 |
| | **Scott Stevens**, Wash-St.L-NJ (DNP) | 20 | 233 |
| | **Chris Chelios**, Mon-Chi-Det | 20 | 222 |

### Games Played

| | | Yrs | Gm |
|---|---|---|---|
| 1 | **Mark Messier**, Edm-NYR-Van (DNP) | 17 | 236 |
| 2 | Claude Lemieux, Mon-NJ-Col-Pho-Dal | 17 | 233 |
| | **Scott Stevens**, Wash-St.L-NJ (DNP) | 20 | 233 |
| 4 | Guy Carbonneau, Mon-St.L-Dal | 17 | 231 |
| 5 | Larry Robinson, Montreal-Los Angeles | 20 | 227 |

### Penalty Minutes

| | | Yrs | Gm | Min |
|---|---|---|---|---|
| 1 | Dale Hunter, Que-Wash-Col | 18 | 186 | 729 |
| 2 | Chris Nilan, Mon-NYR-Bos-Mon | 12 | 111 | 541 |
| 3 | Claude Lemieux, Mon-NJ-Col-Pho-Dal | 17 | 233 | 529 |
| 4 | Rick Tocchet, Phi-Pit-Bos-Pho | 13 | 145 | 471 |
| 5 | Willi Plett, Atl-Calg-Min-Bos | 10 | 83 | 466 |

## Five Longest Playoff Overtime Games

The 5 longest overtime games in Stanley Cup history. Note the following Series initials: SF (semifinals), CQF (conference quarterfinal), CSF (conference semifinal), DSF (division semifinal), QF (quarterfinal) and Final (Cup final). Series winners are in **bold** type; (*) indicates deciding game of series.

| | | OTs | Elapsed Time | Goal Scorer | Date | Series | Location |
|---|---|---|---|---|---|---|---|
| 1 | **Detroit** 1, Montreal Maroons 0 | .6 | 176:30 | Mud Bruneteau | 3/24/36 | SF, Gm 1 | Montreal |
| 2 | **Toronto** 1, Boston 0 | .6 | 164:46 | Ken Doraty | 4/3/33 | SF, Gm 5 | Toronto |
| 3 | **Philadelphia** 2, Pittsburgh 1 | .5 | 152:01 | Keith Primeau | 5/4/00 | CSF, Gm 4 | Pittsburgh |
| 4 | **Anaheim** 4, Dallas 3 | .5 | 140:48 | Petr Sykora | 4/24/03 | CSF, Gm 1 | Dallas |
| 5 | **Pittsburgh** 3 Washington 2 | .4 | 139:15 | Petr Nedved | 4/24/96 | CQF, Gm 4 | Washington |

## SINGLE SEASON

### Points

| | | Year | Gm | G | A | Pts |
|---|---|---|---|---|---|---|
| 1 | Wayne Gretzky, Edm | 1985 | 18 | 17 | 30 | 47 |
| 2 | Mario Lemieux, Pit | 1991 | 23 | 16 | 28 | 44 |
| 3 | Wayne Gretzky, Edm | 1988 | 19 | 12 | 31 | 43 |
| 4 | Wayne Gretzky, LA | 1993 | 24 | 15 | 25 | 40 |
| 5 | Wayne Gretzky, Edm | 1983 | 16 | 12 | 26 | 38 |
| 6 | Paul Coffey, Edm | 1985 | 18 | 12 | 25 | 37 |
| 7 | Mike Bossy, NYI | 1981 | 18 | 17 | 18 | 35 |
| | Wayne Gretzky, Edm | 1984 | 19 | 13 | 22 | 35 |
| | Doug Gilmour, Tor | 1993 | 21 | 10 | 25 | 35 |
| 10 | Six tied with 34 each. | | | | | |

### Goals

| | | Year | Gm | No |
|---|---|---|---|---|
| 1 | Reggie Leach, Philadelphia | 1976 | 16 | 19 |
| | Jari Kurri, Edmonton | 1985 | 18 | 19 |
| 3 | Joe Sakic, Colorado | 1996 | 22 | 18 |
| 4 | Seven tied with 17 each, incl. 3 times by Mike Bossy. | | | |

### Assists

| | | Year | Gm | No |
|---|---|---|---|---|
| 1 | Wayne Gretzky, Edmonton | 1988 | 19 | 31 |
| 2 | Wayne Gretzky, Edmonton | 1985 | 18 | 30 |
| 3 | Wayne Gretzky, Edmonton | 1987 | 21 | 29 |
| 4 | Mario Lemieux, Pittsburgh | 1991 | 23 | 28 |
| 5 | Wayne Gretzky, Edmonton | 1983 | 16 | 26 |

## Goaltending

### Wins

1  Sixteen tied with 16 each.

### Shutouts

| | | Year | Gm | No |
|---|---|---|---|---|
| 1 | Martin Brodeur, New Jersey | 2003 | 24 | 7 |
| 2 | Dominik Hasek, Detroit | 2002 | 23 | 6 |
| 3 | J-S Giguere, Anaheim | 2003 | 21 | 5 |
| | Nikolai Khabibulin, Tampa Bay | 2004 | 23 | 5 |
| | Miikka Kiprusoff, Calgary | 2004 | 26 | 5 |

### Goals Against Average

| | (Min. 8 games played) | Year | Gm | Min | GA | GAA |
|---|---|---|---|---|---|---|
| 1 | Terry Sawchuk, Det | 1952 | 8 | 480 | 5 | 0.63 |
| 2 | Clint Benedict, Mon-M | 1928 | 9 | 555 | 8 | 0.89 |
| 3 | Turk Broda, Tor | 1951 | 9 | 509 | 9 | 1.06 |
| 4 | Dave Kerr, NYR | 1937 | 9 | 553 | 10 | 1.11 |
| 5 | Jacques Plante, Mon | 1960 | 8 | 489 | 11 | 1.35 |

**Note:** Average determined by games played through 1942-43 season and by minutes played since then.

## SINGLE SERIES

### Points

| | Year | Rd | G-A—Pts |
|---|---|---|---|
| Rick Middleton, Bos vs Buf | 1983 | DF | 5-14—19 |
| Wayne Gretzky, Edm vs Chi | 1985 | CF | 4-14—18 |
| Mario Lemieux, Pit vs Wash | 1992 | DSF | 7-10—17 |
| Barry Pederson, Bos vs Buf | 1983 | DF | 7-9—16 |
| Doug Gilmour, Tor vs SJ | 1994 | CSF | 3-13—16 |

### Goals

| | Year | Rd | No |
|---|---|---|---|
| Jari Kurri, Edm vs Chi | 1985 | CF | 12 |
| Newsy Lalonde, Mon vs Ott | 1919 | SF* | 11 |
| Tim Kerr, Phi vs Pit | 1989 | DF | 10 |
| Five tied with 9 each. | | | |

*NHL final prior to Stanley Cup series with Seattle (PCHA).

### Assists

| | Year | Rd | No |
|---|---|---|---|
| Rick Middleton, Bos vs Buf | 1983 | DF | 14 |
| Wayne Gretzky, Edm vs Chi | 1985 | CF | 14 |
| Wayne Gretzky, Edm vs LA | 1987 | DSF | 13 |
| Doug Gilmour, Tor vs SJ | 1994 | CSF | 13 |
| Four tied with 11 each. | | | |

## SINGLE GAME

### Points

| | Date | G | A | Pts |
|---|---|---|---|---|
| Patrik Sundstrom, NJ vs Wash | 4/22/88 | 3 | 5 | 8 |
| Mario Lemieux, Pit vs Phi | 4/25/89 | 5 | 3 | 8 |
| Wayne Gretzky, Edm at Calg | 4/17/83 | 4 | 3 | 7 |
| Wayne Gretzky, Edm at Win | 4/25/85 | 3 | 4 | 7 |
| Wayne Gretzky, Edm vs LA | 4/9/87 | 1 | 6 | 7 |

### Goals

| | Date | No |
|---|---|---|
| Newsy Lalonde, Mon vs Ott | 3/1/19 | 5 |
| Maurice Richard, Mon vs Tor | 3/23/44 | 5 |
| Darryl Sittler, Tor vs Phi | 4/22/76 | 5 |
| Reggie Leach, Phi vs Bos | 5/6/76 | 5 |
| Mario Lemieux, Pit vs Phi | 4/25/89 | 5 |

### Assists

| | Date | No |
|---|---|---|
| Mikko Leinonen, NYR vs Phi | 4/8/82 | 6 |
| Wayne Gretzky, Edm vs LA | 4/9/87 | 6 |
| 11 tied with 5 each. | | |

## NHL All-Star Game

Three benefit NHL All-Star Games were staged in the 1930s for forward Ace Bailey and the families of Howie Morenz and Babe Siebert. Bailey, of Toronto, suffered a fractured skull on a career-ending check by Boston's Eddie Shore. Morenz, the Montreal Canadiens' legend, died of a heart attack at 35 after a severely broken leg ended his career. Siebert, who played with both Montreal teams, drowned at age 35.

The All-Star Game was revived at the start of the 1947-48 season as an annual exhibition match between the defending Stanley Cup champion and all-stars from the league's other five teams. The format has changed several times since then. The game was moved to midseason in 1966-67 and became an East vs. West contest in 1968-69. The Eastern (East, 1968-1974; Wales, 1975-93) Conference leads the series 19-8-1. From 1998-2002, the East-West format was abandoned for one pitting North America vs. the rest of the world (N. America leads that series 3-2). In 2003 the game returned to East vs. West.

## NHL All-Star Game (Cont.)
### Benefit Games

| Date | Occasion | | Host | Coaches |
|------|----------|--|------|---------|
| 2/14/34 | Ace Bailey Benefit | Toronto 7, All-Stars 3 | Toronto | Dick Irvin, Lester Patrick |
| 11/3/37 | Howie Morenz Memorial | All-Stars 6, Montreals* 5 | Montreal | Jack Adams, Cecil Hart |
| 10/29/39 | Babe Seibert Memorial | All-Stars 5, Canadiens 3 | Montreal | Art Ross, Pit Lepine |

*Combined squad of Montreal Canadiens and Montreal Maroons.

### All-Star Games

**Multiple MVP winners:** Wayne Gretzky and Mario Lemieux (3); Bobby Hull and Frank Mahovlich (2).

| Year | | Host | Coaches | Most Valuable Player |
|------|--|------|---------|----------------------|
| 1947 | All-Stars 4, Toronto 3 | Toronto | Dick Irvin, Hap Day | No award |
| 1948 | All-Stars 3, Toronto 1 | Chicago | Tommy Ivan, Hap Day | No award |
| 1949 | All-Stars 3, Toronto 1 | Toronto | Tommy Ivan, Hap Day | No award |
| 1950 | Detroit 7, All-Stars 1 | Detroit | Tommy Ivan, Lynn Patrick | No award |
| 1951 | 1st Team 2, 2nd Team 2 | Toronto | Joe Primeau, Hap Day | No award |
| 1952 | 1st Team 1, 2nd Team 1 | Detroit | Tommy Ivan, Dick Irvin | No award |
| 1953 | All-Stars 3, Montreal 1 | Montreal | Lynn Patrick, Dick Irvin | No award |
| 1954 | All-Stars 2, Detroit 2 | Detroit | King Clancy, Jim Skinner | No award |
| 1955 | Detroit 3, All-Stars 1 | Detroit | Jim Skinner, Dick Irvin | No award |
| 1956 | All-Stars 1, Montreal 1 | Montreal | Jim Skinner, Toe Blake | No award |
| 1957 | All-Stars 5, Montreal 3 | Montreal | Milt Schmidt, Toe Blake | No award |
| 1958 | Montreal 6, All-Stars 3 | Montreal | Toe Blake, Milt Schmidt | No award |
| 1959 | Montreal 6, All-Stars 1 | Montreal | Toe Blake, Punch Imlach | No award |
| 1960 | All-Stars 2, Montreal 1 | Montreal | Punch Imlach, Toe Blake | No award |
| 1961 | All-Stars 3, Chicago 1 | Chicago | Sid Abel, Rudy Pilous | No award |
| 1962 | Toronto 4, All-Stars 1 | Toronto | Punch Imlach, Rudy Pilous | Eddie Shack, Tor., RW |
| 1963 | All-Stars 3, Toronto 3 | Toronto | Sid Abel, Punch Imlach | Frank Mahovlich, Tor., LW |
| 1964 | All-Stars 3, Toronto 2 | Toronto | Sid Abel, Punch Imlach | Jean Beliveau, Mon., C |
| 1965 | All-Stars 5, Montreal 2 | Montreal | Billy Reay, Toe Blake | Gordie Howe, Det., RW |
| 1966 | No game (see below) | | | |
| 1967 | Montreal 3, All-Stars 0 | Montreal | Toe Blake, Sid Abel | Henri Richard, Mon., C |
| 1968 | Toronto 4, All-Stars 3 | Toronto | Punch Imlach, Toe Blake | Bruce Gamble, Tor., G |
| 1969 | West 3, East 3 | Montreal | Scotty Bowman, Toe Blake | Frank Mahovlich, Det., LW |
| 1970 | East 4, West 1 | St. Louis | Claude Ruel, Scotty Bowman | Bobby Hull, Chi., LW |
| 1971 | West 2, East 1 | Boston | Scotty Bowman, Harry Sinden | Bobby Hull, Chi., LW |
| 1972 | East 3, West 2 | Minnesota | Al MacNeil, Billy Reay | Bobby Orr, Bos., D |
| 1973 | East 5, West 4 | NY Rangers | Tom Johnson, Billy Reay | Greg Polis, Pit., LW |
| 1974 | West 6, East 4 | Chicago | Billy Reay, Scotty Bowman | Garry Unger, St.L., C |
| 1975 | Wales 7, Campbell 1 | Montreal | Bep Guidolin, Fred Shero | Syl Apps Jr., Pit., C |
| 1976 | Wales 7, Campbell 5 | Philadelphia | Floyd Smith, Fred Shero | Peter Mahovlich, Mon., C |
| 1977 | Wales 4, Campbell 3 | Vancouver | Scotty Bowman, Fred Shero | Rick Martin, Buf., LW |
| 1978 | Wales 3, Campbell 2 (OT) | Buffalo | Scotty Bowman, Fred Shero | Billy Smith, NYI, G |
| 1979 | No game (see below) | | | |
| 1980 | Wales 6, Campbell 3 | Detroit | Scotty Bowman, Al Arbour | Reggie Leach, Phi., RW |
| 1981 | Campbell 4, Wales 1 | Los Angeles | Pat Quinn, Scotty Bowman | Mike Liut, St.L., G |
| 1982 | Wales 4, Campbell 2 | Washington | Al Arbour, Glen Sonmor | Mike Bossy, NYI, RW |
| 1983 | Campbell 9, Wales 3 | NY Islanders | Roger Neilson, Al Arbour | Wayne Gretzky, Edm., C |
| 1984 | Wales 7, Campbell 6 | New Jersey | Al Arbour, Glen Sather | Don Maloney, NYR, LW |
| 1985 | Wales 6, Campbell 4 | Calgary | Al Arbour, Glen Sather | Mario Lemieux, Pit., C |
| 1986 | Wales 4, Campbell 3 (OT) | Hartford | Mike Keenan, Glen Sather | Grant Fuhr, Edm., G |
| 1987 | No game (see below) | | | |
| 1988 | Wales 6, Campbell 5 (OT) | St. Louis | Mike Keenan, Glen Sather | Mario Lemieux, Pit., C |
| 1989 | Campbell 9, Wales 5 | Edmonton | Glen Sather, Terry O'Reilly | Wayne Gretzky, LA, C |
| 1990 | Wales 12, Campbell 7 | Pittsburgh | Pat Burns, Terry Crisp | Mario Lemieux, Pit., C |
| 1991 | Campbell 11, Wales 5 | Chicago | John Muckler, Mike Milbury | Vincent Damphousse, Tor., LW |
| 1992 | Campbell 10, Wales 6 | Philadelphia | Bob Gainey, Scotty Bowman | Brett Hull, St.L., RW |
| 1993 | Wales 16, Campbell 6 | Montreal | Scotty Bowman, Mike Keenan | Mike Gartner, NYR, RW |
| 1994 | East 9, West 8 | NY Rangers | Jacques Demers, Barry Melrose | Mike Richter, NYR, G |
| 1995 | No game (see below) | | | |
| 1996 | East 5, West 4 | Boston | Doug MacLean, Scotty Bowman | Ray Bourque, Bos., D |
| 1997 | East 11, West 7 | San Jose | Doug MacLean, Ken Hitchcock | Mark Recchi, Mon., RW |
| 1998 | North America 8, World 7 | Vancouver | Jacques Lemaire, Ken Hitchcock | Teemu Selanne, Ana., RW |
| 1999 | North America 8, World 6 | Tampa | Ken Hitchcock, Lindy Ruff | Wayne Gretzky, NYR, C |
| 2000 | World 9, North America 4 | Toronto | Scotty Bowman, Pat Quinn | Pavel Bure, Fla., RW |
| 2001 | North America 14, World 12 | Denver | Joel Quenneville, Jacques Martin | Bill Guerin, Bos., RW |
| 2002 | World 8, North America 5 | Los Angeles | Scotty Bowman, Pat Quinn | Eric Daze, Chi., LW |
| 2003 | West 6, East 5 (OT)† | Florida | Marc Crawford, Jacques Martin | Dany Heatley, Atl., RW |
| 2004 | East 6, West 4 | Minnesota | Pat Quinn, Dave Lewis | Joe Sakic, Col., C |
| 2005 | No game (see below) | | | |

†After a five-minute scoreless overtime, the game was settled by a shootout. The West outscored the East, 3-1.

**No All-Star Game:** in 1966 (moved from start of season to mid-season); in 1979 (replaced by Challenge Cup series with USSR); in 1987 (replaced by Rendez-Vous '87 series with USSR); in 1995 (canceled when NHL lockout shortened season to 48 games); and in 2005 (NHL lockout canceled the entire season).

## NHL Franchise Origins

Here is what the current 30 teams in the National Hockey League have to show for the years they have put in as members of the NHL, the early National Hockey Association (NHA) and the more recent World Hockey Association (WHA). League titles and Stanley Cup championships are noted by year won. The Stanley Cup has automatically gone to the NHL champion since the 1926-27 season. Following the 1992-93 season, the NHL renamed the Clarence Campbell Conference the Western Conference, while the Prince of Wales Conference became the Eastern Conference.

### Western Conference

| | First Season | League Titles | Franchise Stops |
|---|---|---|---|
| **Anaheim, Mighty Ducks of** | 1993-94 (NHL) | None | •Anaheim, CA (1993— ) |
| **Calgary Flames** | 1972-73 (NHL) | 1 Cup (1989) | •Atlanta (1972-80) |
| | | | Calgary (1980— ) |
| **Chicago Blackhawks** | 1926-27 (NHL) | 3 Cups (1934,38,61) | •Chicago (1926— ) |
| **Colorado Avalanche** | 1972-73 (WHA) | 1 WHA (1977) | •Quebec City (1972-95) |
| | | 2 Cups (1996, 2001) | Denver (1995— ) |
| **Columbus Blue Jackets** | 2000-01 (NHL) | None | •Columbus, OH (2000— ) |
| **Dallas Stars** | 1967-68 (NHL) | 1 Cup (1999) | •Bloomington, MN (1967-93) |
| | | | Dallas (1993—) |
| **Detroit Red Wings** | 1926-27 (NHL) | 10 Cups (1936-37,43,50,52,54-55,97,98, 2002) | •Detroit (1926— ) |
| **Edmonton Oilers** | 1972-73 (WHA) | 5 Cups (1984-85,87-88,90) | •Edmonton (1972— ) |
| **Los Angeles Kings** | 1967-68 (NHL) | None | •Inglewood, CA (1967-99) |
| | | | Los Angeles (1999— ) |
| **Minnesota Wild** | 2000-01 (NHL) | None | •St. Paul, MN (2000— ) |
| **Nashville Predators** | 1998-99 (NHL) | None | •Nashville, TN (1998— ) |
| **Phoenix Coyotes** | 1972-73 (WHA) | 3 WHA (1976, 78-79) | •Winnipeg (1972-96) |
| | | | Phoenix (1996—) |
| **St. Louis Blues** | 1967-68 (NHL) | None | •St. Louis (1967— ) |
| **San Jose Sharks** | 1991-92 (NHL) | None | •San Francisco (1991-93) |
| | | | San Jose (1993—) |
| **Vancouver Canucks** | 1970-71 (NHL) | None | •Vancouver (1970—) |

### Eastern Conference

| | First Season | League Titles | Franchise Stops |
|---|---|---|---|
| **Atlanta Thrashers** | 1999-00 (NHL) | None | •Atlanta (1999— ) |
| **Boston Bruins** | 1924-25 (NHL) | 5 Cups (1929,39,41,70,72) | •Boston (1924— ) |
| **Buffalo Sabres** | 1970-71 (NHL) | None | •Buffalo (1970— ) |
| **Carolina Hurricanes** | 1972-73 (WHA) | 1 WHA (1973) | •Boston (1972-74) |
| | | | W. Springfield, MA (1974-75) |
| | | | Hartford, CT (1975-78) |
| | | | Springfield, MA (1978-80) |
| | | | Hartford (1980-97 ) |
| | | | Greensboro, NC (1997-99) |
| | | | Raleigh, NC (1999—) |
| **Florida Panthers** | 1993-94 (NHL) | None | •Miami (1993-98) |
| | | | Sunrise, FL (1998— ) |
| **Montreal Canadiens** | 1909-10 (NHA) | 2 NHA (1916-17) | •Montreal (1909— ) |
| | | 2 NHL (1924-25) | |
| | | 24 Cups (1916,24,30-31,44,46,53,56-60,65-66,68-69,71,73,76-79,86,93) | |
| **New Jersey Devils** | 1974-75 (NHL) | 3 Cups (1995, 2000,03) | •Kansas City (1974-76) |
| | | | Denver (1976-82) |
| | | | E. Rutherford, NJ (1982— ) |
| **New York Islanders** | 1972-73 (NHL) | 4 Cups (1980-83) | •Uniondale, NY (1972— ) |
| **New York Rangers** | 1926-27 (NHL) | 4 Cups (1928,33,40,94) | •New York (1926— ) |
| **Ottawa Senators** | 1992-93 (NHL) | None | •Ottawa (1992-1996) |
| | | | Kanata, Ont. (1996— ) |
| **Philadelphia Flyers** | 1967-68 (NHL) | 2 Cups (1974-75) | •Philadelphia (1967— ) |
| **Pittsburgh Penguins** | 1967-68 (NHL) | 2 Cups (1991-92) | •Pittsburgh (1967— ) |
| **Tampa Bay Lightning** | 1992-93 (NHL) | 1 Cup (2004) | •Tampa, FL (1992-93 ) |
| | | | St. Petersburg, FL (1993-96) |
| | | | Tampa, FL (1996— ) |
| **Toronto Maple Leafs** | 1916-17 (NHA) | 2 NHL (1918,22) | •Toronto (1916— ) |
| | | 13 Cups (1918,22,32,42,45,47-49,51,62-64,67) | |
| **Washington Capitals** | 1974-75 (NHL) | None | •Landover, MD (1974-97 ) |
| | | | Washington, D.C. (1997— ) |

**Note:** The Hartford Civic Center roof collapsed after a snowstorm in January 1978, forcing the Whalers to move their home games to Springfield, Mass., for two years.

# The Growth of the NHL

Of the four franchises that comprised the National Hockey League (NHL) at the start of the 1917-18 season, only two remain—the Montreal Canadiens and the Toronto Maple Leafs (originally the Toronto Arenas). From 1919-26, eight new teams joined the league, but only four—the Boston Bruins, Chicago Blackhawks (originally Black Hawks), Detroit Red Wings (originally Cougars) and New York Rangers—survived.

It was 41 years before the NHL expanded again, doubling in size for the 1967-68 season with new teams in Bloomington (Minn.), Los Angeles, Oakland, Philadelphia, Pittsburgh and St. Louis. The league had 16 clubs by the start of the 1972-73 season, but it also had a rival in the **World Hockey Association,** which debuted that year with 12 teams.

The NHL added two more teams in 1974 and merged the struggling Cleveland Barons (originally the Oakland Seals) and Minnesota North Stars in 1978, before absorbing four WHA clubs—the Edmonton Oilers, Hartford Whalers, Quebec Nordiques and Winnipeg Jets—in time for the 1979-80 season. Seven expansion teams joined the league in the 1990s, with two more being added in 2000 to make it an even 30.

## Expansion/Merger Timetable

For teams currently in NHL.

**1919**—Quebec Bulldogs finally take the ice after sitting out NHL's first two seasons; **1924**—Boston Bruins and Montreal Maroons; **1925**—New York Americans and Pittsburgh Pirates; **1926**—Chicago Black Hawks (now Blackhawks), Detroit Cougars (now Red Wings) and New York Rangers; **1932**—Ottawa Senators return after sitting out 1931-32 season.

**1967**—California-Oakland Seals (later Cleveland Barons), Los Angeles Kings, Minnesota North Stars, Philadelphia Flyers, Pittsburgh Penguins and St. Louis Blues.

**1970**—Buffalo Sabres and Vancouver Canucks; **1972**—Atlanta Flames (now Calgary) and New York Islanders; **1974**—Kansas City Scouts (now New Jersey Devils) and Washington Capitals; **1978**—Cleveland Barons merge with Minnesota North Stars (now Dallas Stars) and team remains in Minnesota; **1979**—added WHA's Edmonton Oilers, Hartford Whalers (now Carolina Hurricanes), Quebec Nordiques (now Colorado Avalanche) and Winnipeg Jets (now Phoenix Coyotes).

**1991**—San Jose Sharks; **1992**—Ottawa Senators and Tampa Bay Lightning; **1993**—Mighty Ducks of Anaheim and Florida Panthers; **1998**—Nashville Predators; **1999**—Atlanta Thrashers.

**2000**—Columbus Blue Jackets and Minnesota Wild.

## City and Nickname Changes

**1919**—Toronto Arenas renamed St. Pats; **1920**—Quebec Bulldogs move to Hamilton and become Tigers (will fold in 1925); **1926**—Toronto St. Pats renamed Maple Leafs; **1929**—Detroit Cougars renamed Falcons.

**1930**—Pittsburgh Pirates move to Philadelphia and become Quakers (will fold in 1931); **1932**—Detroit Falcons renamed Red Wings; **1934**—Ottawa Senators move to St. Louis and become Eagles (will fold in 1935); **1941**—New York Americans renamed Brooklyn Americans (will fold in 1942).

**1967**—California Seals renamed Oakland Seals three months into first season; **1970**—Oakland Seals renamed California Golden Seals; **1975**—California Golden Seals renamed Seals; **1976**—California Seals move to Cleveland and become Barons, while Kansas City Scouts move to Denver and become Colorado Rockies; **1978**—Cleveland Barons merge with Minnesota North Stars and become Minnesota North Stars.

**1980**—Atlanta Flames move to Calgary; **1982**—Colorado Rockies move to East Rutherford, N.J., and become New Jersey Devils; **1986**—Chicago Black Hawks renamed Blackhawks; **1993**—Minnesota North Stars move to Dallas and become Stars. **1995**—Quebec Nordiques move to Denver and become Colorado Avalanche; **1996**—Winnipeg Jets move to Phoenix and become Coyotes; **1997**—Hartford Whalers move to Greensboro, N.C. and become Carolina Hurricanes; **1999**—Carolina Hurricanes move to Raleigh, N.C.

## Defunct NHL Teams

Teams that once played in the NHL, but no longer exist.

**Brooklyn**—Americans (1941-42, formerly NY Americans from 1925-41); **Cleveland**—Barons (1976-78, originally California-Oakland Seals from 1967-76); **Hamilton (Ont.)**—Tigers (1920-25, originally Quebec Bulldogs from 1919-20); **Montreal**—Maroons (1924-38) and Wanderers (1917-18); **New York**—Americans (1925-41, later Brooklyn Americans for 1941-42); **Oakland**—Seals (1967-76, also known as California Seals and Golden Seals and later Cleveland Barons from 1976-78); **Ottawa**—Senators (1917-31 and 1932-34, later St. Louis Eagles for 1934-35); **Philadelphia**—Quakers (1930-31, originally Pittsburgh Pirates from 1925-30); **Pittsburgh**—Pirates (1925-30, later Philadelphia Quakers for 1930-31); **Quebec**—Bulldogs (1919-20, later Hamilton Tigers from 1920-25); **St. Louis**—Eagles (1934-35), originally Ottawa Senators (1917-31 and 1932-34).

## WHA Teams (1972-79)

**Baltimore**—Blades (1975); **Birmingham**—Bulls (1976-78); **Calgary**—Cowboys (1975-77); **Chicago**—Cougars (1972-75); **Cincinnati**—Stingers (1975-79); **Cleveland**—Crusaders (1972-76, moved to Minnesota); **Denver**—Spurs (1975-76, moved to Ottawa); **Edmonton**—Oilers (1972-79, originally called Alberta Oilers in 1972-73); **Houston**—Aeros (1972-78); **Indianapolis**—Racers (1974-78).

**Los Angeles**—Sharks (1972-74, moved to Michigan); **Michigan**—Stags (1974-75, moved to Baltimore); **Minnesota**—Fighting Saints (1972-76) and New Fighting Saints (1976-77); **New England**—Whalers (1972-79, played in Boston from 1972-74, West Springfield, MA from 1974-75, Hartford from 1975-78 and Springfield, MA in 1979); **New Jersey**—Knights (1973-74, moved to San Diego); **New York**—Raiders (1972-73, renamed Golden Blades in 1973, moved to New Jersey).

**Ottawa**—Nationals (1972-73, moved to Toronto) and Civics (1976); **Philadelphia**—Blazers (1972-73, moved to Vancouver); **Phoenix**—Roadrunners (1974-77); **Quebec**—Nordiques (1972-79); **San Diego**—Mariners (1974-77); **Toronto**—Toros (1973-76, moved to Birmingham, AL); **Vancouver**—Blazers (1973-75, moved to Calgary); **Winnipeg**—Jets (1972-79).

## Annual NHL Leaders
### Art Ross Trophy (Scoring)

Given to the player who leads the league in points scored and named after the former Boston Bruins general manager-coach. First presented in 1948, names of prior leading scorers have been added retroactively. A tie for the scoring championship is broken three ways: 1. total goals; 2. fewest games played; 3. first goal scored.

**Multiple winners:** Wayne Gretzky (10); Gordie Howe and Mario Lemieux (6); Phil Esposito and Jaromir Jagr (5); Stan Mikita (4); Bobby Hull and Guy Lafleur (3); Max Bentley, Charlie Conacher, Bill Cook, Babe Dye, Bernie Geoffrion, Elmer Lach, Newsy Lalonde, Joe Malone, Dickie Moore, Howie Morenz, Bobby Orr and Sweeney Schriner (2).

| Year | | Gm | G | A | Pts | Year | | Gm | G | A | Pts |
|------|--|----|---|---|-----|------|--|----|---|---|-----|
| 1918 | Joe Malone, Mon | 20 | 44 | 0 | 44 | 1962 | Bobby Hull, Chi. | 70 | 50 | 34 | 84 |
| 1919 | Newsy Lalonde, Mon | 17 | 23 | 9 | 32 | 1963 | Gordie Howe, Det | 70 | 38 | 48 | 86 |
| 1920 | Joe Malone, Que | 24 | 39 | 6 | 45 | 1964 | Stan Mikita, Chi | 70 | 39 | 50 | 89 |
| 1921 | Newsy Lalonde, Mon | 24 | 33 | 8 | 41 | 1965 | Stan Mikita, Chi | 70 | 28 | 59 | 87 |
| 1922 | Punch Broadbent, Ott | 24 | 32 | 14 | 46 | 1966 | Bobby Hull, Chi | 65 | 54 | 43 | 97 |
| 1923 | Babe Dye, Tor | 22 | 26 | 11 | 37 | 1967 | Stan Mikita, Chi | 70 | 35 | 62 | 97 |
| 1924 | Cy Denneny, Ott | 21 | 22 | 1 | 23 | 1968 | Stan Mikita, Chi | 72 | 40 | 47 | 87 |
| 1925 | Babe Dye, Tor | 29 | 38 | 6 | 44 | 1969 | Phil Esposito, Bos | 74 | 49 | 77 | 126 |
| 1926 | Nels Stewart, Maroons | 36 | 34 | 8 | 42 | 1970 | Bobby Orr, Bos | 76 | 33 | 87 | 120 |
| 1927 | Bill Cook, NYR | 44 | 33 | 4 | 37 | 1971 | Phil Esposito, Bos | 78 | 76 | 76 | 152 |
| 1928 | Howie Morenz, Mon. | 43 | 33 | 18 | 51 | 1972 | Phil Esposito, Bos | 76 | 66 | 67 | 133 |
| 1929 | Ace Bailey, Tor | 44 | 22 | 10 | 32 | 1973 | Phil Esposito, Bos | 78 | 55 | 75 | 130 |
| 1930 | Cooney Weiland, Bos | 44 | 43 | 30 | 73 | 1974 | Phil Esposito, Bos | 78 | 68 | 77 | 145 |
| 1931 | Howie Morenz, Mon. | 39 | 28 | 23 | 51 | 1975 | Bobby Orr, Bos | 80 | 46 | 89 | 135 |
| 1932 | Busher Jackson, Tor. | 48 | 28 | 25 | 53 | 1976 | Guy Lafleur, Mon | 80 | 56 | 69 | 125 |
| 1933 | Bill Cook, NYR | 48 | 28 | 22 | 50 | 1977 | Guy Lafleur, Mon | 80 | 56 | 80 | 136 |
| 1934 | Charlie Conacher, Tor | 42 | 32 | 20 | 52 | 1978 | Guy Lafleur, Mon | 79 | 60 | 72 | 132 |
| 1935 | Charlie Conacher, Tor | 47 | 36 | 21 | 57 | 1979 | Bryan Trottier, NYI | 76 | 47 | 87 | 134 |
| 1936 | Sweeney Weiland, NYA | 48 | 19 | 26 | 45 | 1980 | Marcel Dionne, LA | 80 | 53 | 84 | 137 |
| 1937 | Sweeney Schriner, NYA | 48 | 21 | 25 | 46 | 1981 | Wayne Gretzky, Edm | 80 | 55 | 109 | 164 |
| 1938 | Gordie Drillon, Tor | 48 | 26 | 26 | 52 | 1982 | Wayne Gretzky, Edm | 80 | 92 | 120 | 212 |
| 1939 | Toe Blake, Mon | 48 | 24 | 23 | 47 | 1983 | Wayne Gretzky, Edm | 80 | 71 | 125 | 196 |
| 1940 | Milt Schmidt, Bos | 48 | 22 | 30 | 52 | 1984 | Wayne Gretzky, Edm | 74 | 87 | 118 | 205 |
| 1941 | Bill Cowley, Bos | 46 | 17 | 45 | 62 | 1985 | Wayne Gretzky, Edm | 80 | 73 | 135 | 208 |
| 1942 | Bryan Hextall, NYR | 48 | 24 | 32 | 56 | 1986 | Wayne Gretzky, Edm | 80 | 52 | 163 | 215 |
| 1943 | Doug Bentley, Chi | 50 | 33 | 40 | 73 | 1987 | Wayne Gretzky, Edm | 79 | 62 | 121 | 183 |
| 1944 | Herbie Cain, Bos | 48 | 36 | 46 | 82 | 1988 | Mario Lemieux, Pit | 77 | 70 | 98 | 168 |
| 1945 | Elmer Lach, Mon | 50 | 26 | 54 | 80 | 1989 | Mario Lemieux, Pit | 76 | 85 | 114 | 199 |
| 1946 | Max Bentley, Chi | 47 | 31 | 30 | 61 | 1990 | Wayne Gretzky, LA | 73 | 40 | 102 | 142 |
| 1947 | Max Bentley, Chi | 60 | 29 | 43 | 72 | 1991 | Wayne Gretzky, LA | 78 | 41 | 122 | 163 |
| 1948 | Elmer Lach, Mon | 60 | 30 | 31 | 61 | 1992 | Mario Lemieux, Pit. | 64 | 44 | 87 | 131 |
| 1949 | Roy Conacher, Chi | 60 | 26 | 42 | 68 | 1993 | Mario Lemieux, Pit | 60 | 69 | 91 | 160 |
| 1950 | Ted Lindsay, Det | 69 | 23 | 55 | 78 | 1994 | Wayne Gretzky, LA | 81 | 38 | 92 | 130 |
| 1951 | Gordie Howe, Det | 70 | 43 | 43 | 86 | 1995 | Jaromir Jagr, Pit | 48 | 32 | 38 | 70 |
| 1952 | Gordie Howe, Det | 70 | 47 | 39 | 86 | 1996 | Mario Lemieux, Pit | 70 | 69 | 92 | 161 |
| 1953 | Gordie Howe, Det | 70 | 49 | 46 | 95 | 1997 | Mario Lemieux, Pit | 76 | 50 | 72 | 122 |
| 1954 | Gordie Howe, Det | 70 | 33 | 48 | 81 | 1998 | Jaromir Jagr, Pit | 77 | 35 | 67 | 102 |
| 1955 | Bernie Geoffrion, Mon | 70 | 38 | 37 | 75 | 1999 | Jaromir Jagr, Pit | 81 | 44 | 83 | 127 |
| 1956 | Jean Beliveau, Mon. | 70 | 47 | 41 | 88 | 2000 | Jaromir Jagr, Pit | 63 | 42 | 54 | 96 |
| 1957 | Gordie Howe, Det | 70 | 44 | 45 | 89 | 2001 | Jaromir Jagr, Pit | 81 | 52 | 69 | 121 |
| 1958 | Dickie Moore, Mon. | 70 | 36 | 48 | 84 | 2002 | Jarome Iginla, Calg. | 82 | 52 | 44 | 96 |
| 1959 | Dickie Moore, Mon. | 70 | 41 | 55 | 96 | 2003 | Peter Forsberg, Col. | 75 | 29 | 77 | 106 |
| 1960 | Bobby Hull, Chi | 70 | 39 | 42 | 81 | 2004 | Martin St. Louis, TB | 82 | 38 | 56 | 94 |
| 1961 | Bernie Geoffrion, Mon | 64 | 50 | 45 | 95 | | | | | | |

**Note:** The three times players have tied for total points in one season the player with more goals has won the trophy. In 1961-62, Hull outscored Andy Bathgate of NY Rangers, 50 goals to 28. In 1979-80, Dionne outscored Wayne Gretzky of Edmonton, 53-51. In 1995, Jagr outscored Eric Lindros of Philadelphia, 32-29.

## Goals

**Multiple winners:** Bobby Hull (7); Phil Esposito (6); Charlie Conacher, Wayne Gretzky, Gordie Howe and Maurice Richard (5); Bill Cooke, Babe Dye, Brett Hull, Mario Lemieux, Pavel Bure and Teemu Selanne (3); Jean Beliveau, Doug Bentley, Peter Bondra, Mike Bossy, Bernie Geoffrion, Bryan Hextall, Jarome Iginla, Joe Malone and Nels Stewart (2).

| Year | | No | Year | | No | Year | | No |
|------|--|----|------|--|----|------|--|----|
| 1918 | Joe Malone, Mon | 44 | 1927 | Bill Cook, NYR | 33 | 1936 | Charlie Conacher, Tor | 23 |
| 1919 | Odie Cleghorn, Mon | 23 | 1928 | Howie Morenz, Mon | 33 | | & Bill Thoms, Tor | 23 |
| | & Newsy Lalonde, Mon | 23 | 1929 | Ace Bailey, Tor. | 22 | 1937 | Larry Aurie, Det | 23 |
| 1920 | Joe Malone, Que | 39 | 1930 | Cooney Weiland, Bos. | 43 | | & Nels Stewart, Bos-NYA | 23 |
| 1921 | Babe Dye, Ham-Tor. | 35 | 1931 | Charlie Conacher, Tor. | 31 | 1938 | Gordie Drillon, Tor | 26 |
| 1922 | Punch Broadbent, Ott | 32 | 1932 | Charlie Conacher, Tor. | 34 | 1939 | Roy Conacher, Bos. | 26 |
| 1923 | Babe Dye, Tor | 26 | | & Bill Cook, NYR. | 34 | 1940 | Bryan Hextall, NYR | 24 |
| 1924 | Cy Denneny, Ott | 22 | 1933 | Bill Cook, NYR. | 28 | 1941 | Bryan Hextall, NYR | 26 |
| 1925 | Babe Dye, Tor | 38 | 1934 | Charlie Conacher, Tor. | 32 | 1942 | Lynn Patrick, NYR. | 32 |
| 1926 | Nels Stewart, Maroons | 34 | 1935 | Charlie Conacher, Tor. | 36 | 1943 | Doug Bentley, Chi. | 33 |

## Annual NHL Leaders (Cont.)

| Year | | No | Year | | No | Year | | No |
|---|---|---|---|---|---|---|---|---|
| 1944 | Doug Bentley, Chi | 38 | 1965 | Norm Ullman, Tor | 42 | 1986 | Jari Kurri, Edm | 68* |
| 1945 | Maurice Richard, Mon | 50 | 1966 | Bobby Hull, Chi | 54 | 1987 | Wayne Gretzky, Edm | 62 |
| 1946 | Gaye Stewart, Tor | 37 | 1967 | Bobby Hull, Chi | 52 | 1988 | Mario Lemieux, Pit | 70 |
| 1947 | Maurice Richard, Mon | 45 | 1968 | Bobby Hull, Chi | 44 | 1989 | Mario Lemieux, Pit | 85 |
| 1948 | Ted Lindsay, Det | 33 | 1969 | Bobby Hull, Chi | 58 | 1990 | Brett Hull, St.L | 72 |
| 1949 | Sid Abel, Det | 28 | 1970 | Phil Esposito, Bos | 43 | 1991 | Brett Hull, St.L | 86 |
| 1950 | Maurice Richard, Mon | 43 | 1971 | Phil Esposito, Bos | 76 | 1992 | Brett Hull, St.L | 70 |
| 1951 | Gordie Howe, Det | 43 | 1972 | Phil Esposito, Bos | 66 | 1993 | Alexander Mogilny, Buf | 76 |
| 1952 | Gordie Howe, Det | 47 | 1973 | Phil Esposito, Bos | 55 | | & Teemu Selanne, Win | 76 |
| 1953 | Gordie Howe, Det | 49 | 1974 | Phil Esposito, Bos | 68 | 1994 | Pavel Bure, Van | 60 |
| 1954 | Maurice Richard, Mon | 37 | 1975 | Phil Esposito, Bos | 61 | 1995 | Peter Bondra, Wash | 34 |
| 1955 | Bernie Geoffrion, Mon | 38 | 1976 | Reggie Leach, Phi | 61 | 1996 | Mario Lemieux, Pit | 69 |
| | & Maurice Richard, Mon | 38 | 1977 | Steve Shutt, Mon | 60 | 1997 | Keith Tkachuk, Pho | 52 |
| 1956 | Jean Beliveau, Mon | 47 | 1978 | Guy Lafleur, Mon | 60 | 1998 | Teemu Selanne, Ana | 52 |
| 1957 | Gordie Howe, Det | 44 | 1979 | Mike Bossy, NYI | 69 | | & Peter Bondra, Wash | 52 |
| 1958 | Dickie Moore, Mon | 36 | 1980 | Danny Gare, Buf | 56 | 1999 | Teemu Selanne, Ana | 47 |
| 1959 | Jean Beliveau, Mon | 45 | | Charlie Simmer, LA | 56 | 2000 | Pavel Bure, Fla | 58 |
| 1960 | Bronco Horvath, Bos | 39 | | & Blaine Stoughton, Hart | 56 | 2001 | Pavel Bure, Fla | 59 |
| | & Bobby Hull, Chi | 39 | 1981 | Mike Bossy, NYI | 68 | 2002 | Jarome Iginla, Calg | 52 |
| 1961 | Bernie Geoffrion, Mon | 50 | 1982 | Wayne Gretzky, Edm | 92 | 2003 | Milan Hejduk, Col | 50 |
| 1962 | Bobby Hull, Chi | 50 | 1983 | Wayne Gretzky, Edm | 71 | 2004 | Jarome Iginla, Calg | 41 |
| 1963 | Gordie Howe, Det | 38 | 1984 | Wayne Gretzky, Edm | 87 | | Ilya Kovalchuk, Atl | 41 |
| 1964 | Bobby Hull, Chi | 43 | 1985 | Wayne Gretzky, Edm | 73 | | & Rick Nash, Clb | 41 |

## Assists

**Multiple winners:** Wayne Gretzky (16); Bobby Orr (5); Adam Oates, Frank Boucher, Bill Cowley, Phil Esposito, Gordie Howe, Jaromir Jagr, Elmer Lach, Mario Lemieux, Stan Mikita and Joe Primeau (3); Syl Apps, Andy Bathgate, Jean Beliveau, Doug Bentley, Art Chapman, Bobby Clarke, Ron Francis, Ted Lindsay, Bert Olmstead, Henri Richard and Bryan Trottier (2).

| Year | | No | Year | | No | Year | | No |
|---|---|---|---|---|---|---|---|---|
| 1918 | No official records kept. | | 1949 | Doug Bentley, Chi | 43 | 1979 | Bryan Trottier, NYI | 87 |
| 1919 | Newsy Lalonde, Mon | 9 | 1950 | Ted Lindsay, Det | 55 | 1980 | Wayne Gretzky, Edm | 86 |
| 1920 | Corbett Denneny, Tor | 12 | 1951 | Gordie Howe, Det | 43 | 1981 | Wayne Gretzky, Edm | 109 |
| 1921 | Louis Berlinquette, Mon | 9 | | & Teeder Kennedy, Tor | 43 | 1982 | Wayne Gretzky, Edm | 120 |
| | Harry Cameron, Tor | 9 | 1952 | Elmer Lach, Mon | 50 | 1983 | Wayne Gretzky, Edm | 125 |
| | & Joe Matte, Ham | 9 | 1953 | Gordie Howe, Det | 46 | 1984 | Wayne Gretzky, Edm | 118 |
| 1922 | Punch Broadbent, Ott | 14 | 1954 | Gordie Howe, Det | 48 | 1985 | Wayne Gretzky, Edm | 135 |
| | & Leo Reise, Ham | 14 | 1955 | Bert Olmstead, Mon | 48 | 1986 | Wayne Gretzky, Edm | 163 |
| 1923 | Ed Bouchard, Ham | 12 | 1956 | Bert Olmstead, Mon | 56 | 1987 | Wayne Gretzky, Edm | 121 |
| 1924 | King Clancy, Ott | 8 | 1957 | Ted Lindsay, Det | 55 | 1988 | Wayne Gretzky, Edm | 109 |
| 1925 | Cy Denneny, Ott | 15 | 1958 | Henri Richard, Mon | 52 | 1989 | Wayne Gretzky, LA | 114 |
| 1926 | Frank Nighbor, Ott | 13 | 1959 | Dickie Moore, Mon | 55 | | & Mario Lemieux, Pit | 114 |
| 1927 | Dick Irvin, Chi | 18 | 1960 | Don McKenney, Bos | 49 | 1990 | Wayne Gretzky, LA | 102 |
| 1928 | Howie Morenz, Mon | 18 | 1961 | Jean Beliveau, Mon | 58 | 1991 | Wayne Gretzky, LA | 122 |
| 1929 | Frank Boucher, NYR | 16 | 1962 | Andy Bathgate, NYR | 56 | 1992 | Wayne Gretzky, LA | 90 |
| 1930 | Frank Boucher, NYR | 36 | 1963 | Henri Richard, Mon | 50 | 1993 | Adam Oates, Bos | 97 |
| 1931 | Joe Primeau, Tor | 32 | 1964 | Andy Bathgate, NYR-Tor | 58 | 1994 | Wayne Gretzky, LA | 92 |
| 1932 | Joe Primeau, Tor | 37 | 1965 | Stan Mikita, Chi | 59 | 1995 | Ron Francis, Pit | 48 |
| 1933 | Frank Boucher, NYR | 28 | 1966 | Jean Beliveau, Mon | 48 | 1996 | Ron Francis, Pit | 92 |
| 1934 | Joe Primeau, Tor | 32 | | Stan Mikita, Chi | 48 | | & Mario Lemieux, Pit | 92 |
| 1935 | Art Chapman, NYA | 34 | | & Bobby Rousseau, Mon | 48 | 1997 | Mario Lemieux, Pit | 72 |
| 1936 | Art Chapman, NYA | 28 | 1967 | Stan Mikita, Chi | 62 | | & Wayne Gretzky, NYR | 72 |
| 1937 | Syl Apps, Tor | 29 | 1968 | Phil Esposito, Bos | 49 | 1998 | Jaromir Jagr, Pit | 67 |
| 1938 | Syl Apps, Tor | 29 | 1969 | Phil Esposito, Bos | 77 | | & Wayne Gretzky, NYR | 67 |
| 1939 | Bill Cowley, Bos | 34 | 1970 | Bobby Orr, Bos | 87 | 1999 | Jaromir Jagr, Pit | 83 |
| 1940 | Milt Schmidt, Bos | 30 | 1971 | Bobby Orr, Bos | 102 | 2000 | Mark Recchi, Phi | 63 |
| 1941 | Bill Cowley, Bos | 45 | 1972 | Bobby Orr, Bos | 80 | 2001 | Jaromir Jagr, Pit | 69 |
| 1942 | Phil Watson, NYR | 37 | 1973 | Phil Esposito, Bos | 75 | | & Adam Oates, Wash | 69 |
| 1943 | Bill Cowley, Bos | 45 | 1974 | Bobby Orr, Bos | 90 | 2002 | Adam Oates, Wash-Phi | 64 |
| 1944 | Clint Smith, Chi | 49 | 1975 | Bobby Clarke, Phi | 89 | 2003 | Peter Forsberg, Col | 77 |
| 1945 | Elmer Lach, Mon | 54 | | & Bobby Orr, Bos | 89 | 2004 | Scott Gomez, NJ | 56 |
| 1946 | Elmer Lach, Mon | 34 | 1976 | Bobby Clarke, Phi | 89 | | & Martin St. Louis, TB | 56 |
| 1947 | Billy Taylor, Det | 46 | 1977 | Guy Lafleur, Mon | 80 | | | |
| 1948 | Doug Bentley, Chi | 37 | 1978 | Bryan Trottier, NYI | 77 | | | |

## Goals Against Average

Average determined by games played through 1942-43 season and by minutes played since then. Minimum of 15 games from 1917-18 season through 1925-26; minimum of 25 games since 1926-27 season. Not to be confused with the Vezina Trophy. Goaltenders who posted the season's lowest goals against average, but did not win the Vezina are in **bold** type.

**Multiple winners:** Jacques Plante (9); Clint Benedict and Bill Durnan (6); Johnny Bower, Ken Dryden and Tiny Thompson (4); Patrick Roy and Georges Vezina (3); Ed Belfour, Frankie Brimsek, Turk Broda, George Hainsworth, Dominik Hasek, Harry Lumley, Bernie Parent, Pete Peeters, Terry Sawchuk and Marty Turco (2).

| Year | | GAA | Year | | GAA | Year | | GAA |
|---|---|---|---|---|---|---|---|---|
| 1918 | Georges Vezina, Mon | 3.82 | 1947 | Bill Durnan, Mon | 2.30 | 1976 | Ken Dryden, Mon | 2.03 |
| 1919 | Clint Benedict, Ott | 2.94 | 1948 | Turk Broda, Tor | 2.38 | 1977 | Bunny Larocque, Mon | 2.09 |
| 1920 | Clint Benedict, Ott | 2.67 | 1949 | Bill Durnan, Mon | 2.10 | 1978 | Ken Dryden, Mon | 2.05 |
| 1921 | Clint Benedict, Ott | 3.13 | 1950 | Bill Durnan, Mon | 2.20 | 1979 | Ken Dryden, Mon | 2.30 |
| 1922 | Clint Benedict, Ott | 3.50 | 1951 | Al Rollins, Tor | 1.77 | 1980 | Bob Sauve, Buf | 2.36 |
| 1923 | Clint Benedict, Ott | 2.25 | 1952 | Terry Sawchuk, Det | 1.90 | 1981 | Richard Sevigny, Mon | 2.40 |
| 1924 | Georges Vezina, Mon | 2.00 | 1953 | Terry Sawchuk, Det | 1.90 | 1982 | **Denis Herron,** Mon | 2.64 |
| 1925 | Georges Vezina, Mon | 1.87 | 1954 | Harry Lumley, Tor | 1.86 | 1983 | Pete Peeters, Bos | 2.36 |
| 1926 | Alex Connell, Ott | 1.17 | 1955 | **Harry Lumley,** Tor | 1.94 | 1984 | **Pat Riggin,** Wash | 2.66 |
| 1927 | **Clint Benedict,** Mon-M | 1.51 | 1956 | Jacques Plante, Mon | 1.86 | 1985 | **Tom Barrasso,** Buf | 2.66 |
| 1928 | Geo. Hainsworth, Mon | 1.09 | 1957 | Jacques Plante, Mon | 2.02 | 1986 | **Bob Froese,** Phi | 2.55 |
| 1929 | Geo. Hainsworth, Mon | 0.98 | 1958 | Jacques Plante, Mon | 2.11 | 1987 | **Brian Hayward,** Mon | 2.81 |
| 1930 | Tiny Thompson, Bos | 2.23 | 1959 | Jacques Plante, Mon | 2.16 | 1988 | **Pete Peeters,** Wash | 2.78 |
| 1931 | Roy Worters, NYA | 1.68 | 1960 | Jacques Plante, Mon | 2.54 | 1989 | Patrick Roy, Mon | 2.47 |
| 1932 | Chuck Gardiner, Chi | 1.92 | 1961 | Johnny Bower, Tor | 2.50 | | | |
| 1933 | Tiny Thompson, Bos | 1.83 | 1962 | Jacques Plante, Mon | 2.37 | 1990 | **Mike Liut,** Hart-Wash | 2.53 |
| 1934 | **Wilf Cude,** Det-Mon | 1.57 | 1963 | **Jacques Plante,** Mon | 2.49 | 1991 | Ed Belfour, Chi | 2.47 |
| 1935 | Lorne Chabot, Chi | 1.83 | 1964 | **Johnny Bower,** Tor | 2.11 | 1992 | Patrick Roy, Mon | 2.36 |
| 1936 | Tiny Thompson, Bos | 1.71 | 1965 | Johnny Bower, Tor | 2.38 | 1993 | **Felix Potvin,** Tor | 2.50 |
| 1937 | Norm Smith, Det | 2.13 | 1966 | **Johnny Bower,** Tor | 2.25 | 1994 | Dominik Hasek, Buf | 1.95 |
| 1938 | Tiny Thompson, Bos | 1.85 | 1967 | Glenn Hall, Chi | 2.38 | 1995 | Dominik Hasek, Buf | 2.11 |
| 1939 | Frankie Brimsek, Bos | 1.58 | 1968 | Gump Worsley, Mon | 1.98 | 1996 | **Ron Hextall,** Phi | 2.17 |
| 1940 | Dave Kerr, NYR | 1.60 | 1969 | Jacques Plante, St.L. | 1.96 | 1997 | **Martin Brodeur,** NJ | 1.88 |
| 1941 | Turk Broda, Tor | 2.06 | 1970 | **Ernie Wakely,** St.L. | 2.11 | 1998 | **Ed Belfour,** Dal | 1.88 |
| 1942 | Frankie Brimsek, Bos | 2.45 | 1971 | **Jacques Plante,** Tor | 1.88 | 1999 | **Ron Tugnutt,** Ott | 1.79 |
| 1943 | John Mowers, Det | 2.47 | 1972 | Tony Esposito, Chi | 1.77 | 2000 | **Brian Boucher,** Phi | 1.91 |
| 1944 | Bill Durnan, Mon | 2.18 | 1973 | Ken Dryden, Mon | 2.26 | 2001 | **Marty Turco,** Dal | 1.90 |
| 1945 | Bill Durnan, Mon | 2.42 | 1974 | Bernie Parent, Phi | 1.89 | 2002 | **Patrick Roy,** Col | 1.94 |
| 1946 | Bill Durnan, Mon | 2.60 | 1975 | Bernie Parent, Phi | 2.03 | 2003 | **Marty Turco,** Dal | 1.72 |
| | | | | | | 2004 | **Miikka Kiprusoff,** Calg | 1.69 |

## Penalty Minutes

**Multiple winners:** Red Horner (8); Gus Mortson and Dave Schultz (4); Bert Corbeau, Lou Fontinato and Tiger Williams (3); Matthew Barnaby, Billy Boucher, Carl Brewer, Red Dutton, Pat Egan, Bill Ezinicki, Joe Hall, Tim Hunter, Keith Magnuson, Chris Nilan, Jimmy Orlando and Rob Ray (2).

| Year | | Min | Year | | Min | Year | | Min |
|---|---|---|---|---|---|---|---|---|
| 1918 | Joe Hall, Mon | 60 | 1947 | Gus Mortson, Tor | 133 | 1976 | Steve Durbano, Pit-KC | 370 |
| 1919 | Joe Hall, Mon | 85 | 1948 | Bill Barilko, Tor | 147 | 1977 | Tiger Williams, Tor | 338 |
| 1920 | Cully Wilson, Tor | 79 | 1949 | Bill Ezinicki, Tor | 145 | 1978 | Dave Schultz, LA-Pit | 405 |
| 1921 | Bert Corbeau, Mon | 86 | 1950 | Bill Ezinicki, Tor | 144 | 1979 | Tiger Williams, Tor | 298 |
| 1922 | Sprague Cleghorn, Mon | 63 | 1951 | Gus Mortson, Tor | 142 | 1980 | Jimmy Mann, Win | 287 |
| 1923 | Billy Boucher, Mon | 52 | 1952 | Gus Kyle, Bos | 127 | 1981 | Tiger Williams, Van | 343 |
| 1924 | Bert Corbeau, Tor | 55 | 1953 | Maurice Richard, Mon | 112 | 1982 | Paul Baxter, Pit | 409 |
| 1925 | Billy Boucher, Mon | 92 | 1954 | Gus Mortson, Chi | 132 | 1983 | Randy Holt, Wash | 275 |
| 1926 | Bert Corbeau, Tor | 121 | 1955 | Fern Flaman, Bos | 150 | 1984 | Chris Nilan, Mon | 338 |
| 1927 | Nels Stewart, Mon-M | 133 | 1956 | Lou Fontinato, NYR | 202 | 1985 | Chris Nilan, Mon | 358 |
| 1928 | Eddie Shore, Bos | 165 | 1957 | Gus Mortson, Chi | 147 | 1986 | Joey Kocur, Det | 377 |
| 1929 | Red Dutton, Mon-M | 139 | 1958 | Lou Fontinato, NYR | 152 | 1987 | Tim Hunter, Calg | 361 |
| 1930 | Joe Lamb, Ott | 119 | 1959 | Ted Lindsay, Chi | 184 | 1988 | Bob Probert, Det | 398 |
| 1931 | Harvey Rockburn, Det | 118 | 1960 | Carl Brewer, Tor | 150 | 1989 | Tim Hunter, Calg | 375 |
| 1932 | Red Dutton, NYA | 107 | 1961 | Pierre Pilote, Chi | 165 | | | |
| 1933 | Red Horner, Tor | 144 | 1962 | Lou Fontinato, Mon | 167 | 1990 | Basil McRae, Min | 351 |
| 1934 | Red Horner, Tor | 146 | 1963 | Howie Young, Det | 273 | 1991 | Rob Ray, Buf | 350 |
| 1935 | Red Horner, Tor | 125 | 1964 | Vic Hadfield, NYR | 151 | 1992 | Mike Peluso, Chi | 408 |
| 1936 | Red Horner, Tor | 167 | 1965 | Carl Brewer, Tor | 177 | 1993 | Marty McSorley, LA | 399 |
| 1937 | Red Horner, Tor | 124 | 1966 | Reg Fleming, Bos-NYR | 166 | 1994 | Tie Domi, Win | 347 |
| 1938 | Red Horner, Tor | 82 | 1967 | John Ferguson, Mon | 177 | 1995 | Enrico Ciccone, TB | 225 |
| 1939 | Red Horner, Tor | 85 | 1968 | Barclay Plager, St.L. | 153 | 1996 | Matthew Barnaby, Buf. | 335 |
| 1940 | Red Horner, Tor | 87 | 1969 | Forbes Kennedy, Phi-Tor | 219 | 1997 | Gino Odjick, Van. | 371 |
| 1941 | Jimmy Orlando, Det | 99 | 1970 | Keith Magnuson, Chi | 213 | 1998 | Donald Brashear, Van. | 372 |
| 1942 | Pat Egan, NYA | 124 | 1971 | Keith Magnuson, Chi | 291 | 1999 | Rob Ray, Buf | 261 |
| 1943 | Jimmy Orlando, Det | 99 | 1972 | Bryan Watson, Pit | 212 | 2000 | Denny Lambert, Atl | 219 |
| 1944 | Mike McMahon, Mon | 98 | 1973 | Dave Schultz, Phi | 259 | 2001 | Matthew Barnaby, Pit-TB | 265 |
| 1945 | Pat Egan, Bos | 86 | 1974 | Dave Schultz, Phi | 348 | 2002 | Peter Worrell, Fla | 354 |
| 1946 | Jack Stewart, Det | 73 | 1975 | Dave Schultz, Phi | 472 | 2003 | Jody Shelley, Clb | 249 |
| | | | | | | 2004 | Sean Avery, LA | 261 |

## All-Time NHL Regular Season Leaders

Through 2004 regular season.

### CAREER

Players active during 2004 season in **bold** type.

### Points

| | | Yrs | Gm | G | A | Pts |
|---|---|---|---|---|---|---|
| 1 | Wayne Gretzky | 20 | 1487 | 894 | 1963 | 2857 |
| 2 | **Mark Messier** | 25 | 1756 | 694 | 1193 | 1887 |
| 3 | Gordie Howe | 26 | 1767 | 801 | 1049 | 1850 |
| 4 | **Ron Francis** | 23 | 1731 | 549 | 1249 | 1798 |
| 5 | Marcel Dionne | 18 | 1348 | 731 | 1040 | 1771 |
| 6 | **Steve Yzerman** | 21 | 1453 | 678 | 1043 | 1721 |
| 7 | **Mario Lemieux** | 16 | 889 | 683 | 1018 | 1701 |
| 8 | Phil Esposito | 18 | 1282 | 717 | 873 | 1590 |
| 9 | Ray Bourque | 22 | 1612 | 410 | 1169 | 1579 |
| 10 | Paul Coffey | 21 | 1409 | 396 | 1135 | 1531 |
| 11 | Stan Mikita | 22 | 1394 | 541 | 926 | 1467 |
| 12 | Bryan Trottier | 18 | 1279 | 524 | 901 | 1425 |
| 13 | **Adam Oates** | 19 | 1337 | 341 | 1079 | 1420 |
| 14 | Doug Gilmour | 20 | 1474 | 450 | 964 | 1414 |
| 15 | Dale Hawerchuk | 16 | 1188 | 518 | 891 | 1409 |
| 16 | **Joe Sakic** | 16 | 1155 | 542 | 860 | 1402 |
| 17 | Jari Kurri | 17 | 1251 | 601 | 797 | 1398 |
| 18 | **Brett Hull** | 19 | 1264 | 741 | 649 | 1390 |
| 19 | **Luc Robitaille** | 18 | 1366 | 653 | 717 | 1370 |
| 20 | John Bucyk | 23 | 1540 | 556 | 813 | 1369 |
| 21 | Guy Lafleur | 17 | 1126 | 560 | 793 | 1353 |
| 22 | Denis Savard | 17 | 1196 | 473 | 865 | 1338 |
| 23 | Mike Gartner | 19 | 1432 | 708 | 627 | 1335 |
| 24 | Gilbert Perreault | 17 | 1191 | 512 | 814 | 1326 |
| 25 | Dave Andreychuk | 22 | 1597 | 634 | 686 | 1320 |
| 26 | **Jaromir Jagr** | 14 | 1027 | 537 | 772 | 1309 |
| 27 | Alex Delvecchio | 24 | 1549 | 456 | 825 | 1281 |
| 28 | Pierre Turgeon | 17 | 1215 | 495 | 779 | 1274 |
| | **Al MacInnis** | 23 | 1416 | 340 | 934 | 1274 |
| 30 | Jean Ratelle | 21 | 1281 | 491 | 776 | 1267 |

### Goals

| | | Yrs | Gm | No |
|---|---|---|---|---|
| 1 | Wayne Gretzky | 20 | 1487 | 894 |
| 2 | Gordie Howe | 26 | 1767 | 801 |
| 3 | **Brett Hull** | 19 | 1264 | 741 |
| 4 | Marcel Dionne | 18 | 1348 | 731 |
| 5 | Phil Esposito | 18 | 1282 | 717 |
| 6 | Mike Gartner | 19 | 1432 | 708 |
| 7 | **Mark Messier** | 25 | 1756 | 694 |
| 8 | **Mario Lemieux** | 16 | 889 | 683 |
| 9 | **Steve Yzerman** | 21 | 1453 | 678 |
| 10 | **Luc Robitaille** | 18 | 1366 | 653 |
| 11 | **Dave Andreychuk** | 22 | 1597 | 634 |
| 12 | Bobby Hull | 16 | 1063 | 610 |
| 13 | Dino Ciccarelli | 19 | 1232 | 608 |
| 14 | Jari Kurri | 17 | 1251 | 601 |
| 15 | Mike Bossy | 10 | 752 | 573 |
| 16 | Guy Lafleur | 17 | 1126 | 560 |
| 17 | **Brendan Shanahan** | 17 | 1268 | 558 |
| 18 | John Bucyk | 23 | 1540 | 556 |
| 19 | **Ron Francis** | 23 | 1731 | 549 |
| 20 | Michel Goulet | 15 | 1089 | 548 |
| 21 | Maurice Richard | 18 | 978 | 544 |
| 22 | **Joe Sakic** | 16 | 1155 | 542 |
| 23 | Stan Mikita | 22 | 1394 | 541 |
| 24 | **Jaromir Jagr** | 14 | 1027 | 537 |
| 25 | **Joe Nieuwendyk** | 18 | 1177 | 533 |
| | Frank Mahovlich | 18 | 1181 | 533 |
| 27 | Bryan Trottier | 18 | 1279 | 524 |
| 28 | Pat Verbeek | 20 | 1424 | 522 |
| 29 | Dale Hawerchuk | 16 | 1188 | 518 |
| 30 | Gilbert Perreault | 17 | 1191 | 512 |

### Assists

| | | Yrs | Gm | No |
|---|---|---|---|---|
| 1 | Wayne Gretzky | 20 | 1487 | 1963 |
| 2 | **Ron Francis** | 23 | 1731 | 1249 |
| 3 | **Mark Messier** | 25 | 1756 | 1193 |
| 4 | Ray Bourque | 22 | 1612 | 1169 |
| 5 | Paul Coffey | 21 | 1409 | 1135 |
| 6 | **Adam Oates** | 19 | 1337 | 1079 |
| 7 | Gordie Howe | 26 | 1767 | 1049 |
| 8 | **Steve Yzerman** | 21 | 1453 | 1043 |
| 9 | Marcel Dionne | 18 | 1348 | 1040 |
| 10 | **Mario Lemieux** | 16 | 889 | 1018 |
| 11 | Doug Gilmour | 20 | 1474 | 964 |
| 12 | **Al MacInnis** | 23 | 1416 | 934 |
| 13 | Larry Murphy | 21 | 1615 | 929 |
| 14 | Stan Mikita | 22 | 1394 | 926 |
| 15 | Bryan Trottier | 18 | 1279 | 901 |
| 16 | Phil Housley | 21 | 1495 | 894 |
| 17 | Dale Hawerchuk | 16 | 1188 | 891 |
| 18 | Phil Esposito | 18 | 1281 | 873 |
| 19 | Denis Savard | 17 | 1196 | 865 |
| 20 | **Joe Sakic** | 16 | 1155 | 860 |

### Penalty Minutes

| | | Yrs | Gm | Min |
|---|---|---|---|---|
| 1 | Tiger Williams | 14 | 962 | 3966 |
| 2 | Dale Hunter | 19 | 1407 | 3565 |
| 3 | **Tie Domi** | 15 | 943 | 3406 |
| 4 | Marty McSorley | 17 | 961 | 3381 |
| 5 | Bob Probert | 16 | 935 | 3300 |
| 6 | **Rob Ray** | 15 | 900 | 3207 |
| 7 | Craig Berube | 17 | 1054 | 3149 |
| 8 | Tim Hunter | 16 | 815 | 3146 |
| 9 | Chris Nilan | 13 | 688 | 3043 |
| 10 | Rick Tocchet | 18 | 1144 | 2972 |
| 11 | Pat Verbeek | 20 | 1424 | 2905 |
| 12 | Dave Manson | 16 | 1103 | 2792 |
| 13 | **Scott Stevens** | 22 | 1635 | 2785 |
| 14 | **Chris Chelios** | 21 | 1395 | 2695 |
| 15 | Willi Plett | 12 | 834 | 2572 |

### NHL-WHA Top 10

All-time regular season scoring leaders, including games played in World Hockey Association (1972-79). NHL players with WHA experience are listed in CAPITAL letters. Players active during 2004 are in **bold** type.

#### Points

| | | Yrs | G | A | Pts |
|---|---|---|---|---|---|
| 1 | WAYNE GRETZKY | 21 | 940 | 2027 | 2967 |
| 2 | GORDIE HOWE | 32 | 975 | 1383 | 2358 |
| 3 | **MARK MESSIER** | 26 | 695 | 1203 | 1898 |
| 4 | BOBBY HULL | 23 | 913 | 895 | 1808 |
| 5 | **Ron Francis** | 23 | 549 | 1249 | 1798 |
| 6 | Marcel Dionne | 18 | 731 | 1040 | 1771 |
| 7 | **Steve Yzerman** | 21 | 678 | 1043 | 1721 |
| 8 | **Mario Lemieux** | 16 | 683 | 1018 | 1701 |
| 9 | Phil Esposito | 18 | 717 | 873 | 1590 |
| 10 | Ray Bourque | 22 | 410 | 1169 | 1579 |

**WHA Totals:** GRETZKY (1 yr, 80 gm, 46-64—110); HOWE (6 yrs, 419 gm, 174-334—508); MESSIER (1 yr, 52 gm, 1-10—11); HULL (7 yrs, 411 gm, 303-335—638).

## Years Played

| | | Yrs | Career | Gm |
|---|---|---|---|---|
| 1 | Gordie Howe | 26 | 1946-71, 79-80 | 1767 |
| 2 | **Mark Messier** | 25 | 1979- | 1756 |
| 3 | Alex Delvecchio | 24 | 1950-74 | 1549 |
| | Tim Horton | 24 | 1949-50, 51-74 | 1446 |
| 5 | Ron Francis | 23 | 1981- | 1731 |
| | John Bucyk | 23 | 1955-78 | 1540 |
| | **Al MacInnis** | 23 | 1982- | 1416 |
| 8 | Scott Stevens | 22 | 1982- | 1635 |
| | Ray Bourque | 22 | 1979-2001 | 1612 |
| | **Dave Andreychuk** | 22 | 1982- | 1597 |
| | Stan Mikita | 22 | 1958-80 | 1394 |
| | Doug Mohns | 22 | 1953-75 | 1390 |
| | Dean Prentice | 22 | 1952-74 | 1378 |
| 14 | Fifteen tied with 21 years each. | | | |

**Note:** Combined NHL-WHA years played: Howe (32); Messier (26); Howell (24); Bobby Hull (23); Norm Ullman, Eric Nesterenko, Frank Mahovlich and Dave Keon (22).

## Games Played

| | | Yrs | Career | Gm |
|---|---|---|---|---|
| 1 | Gordie Howe | 26 | 1946-71, 79-80 | 1767 |
| 2 | **Mark Messier** | 25 | 1979- | 1756 |
| 3 | Ron Francis | 23 | 1981- | 1731 |
| 4 | **Scott Stevens** | 22 | 1982- | 1635 |
| 5 | Larry Murphy | 21 | 1980-2001 | 1615 |
| 6 | Ray Bourque | 22 | 1979-2001 | 1612 |
| 7 | **Dave Andreychuk** | 22 | 1982- | 1597 |
| 8 | Alex Delvecchio | 24 | 1950-74 | 1549 |
| 9 | John Bucyk | 23 | 1955-78 | 1540 |
| 10 | Phil Housley | 21 | 1982-2003 | 1495 |
| 11 | Wayne Gretzky | 20 | 1979-99 | 1487 |
| 12 | Doug Gilmour | 20 | 1983-2003 | 1474 |
| 13 | **Steve Yzerman** | 21 | 1983- | 1453 |
| 14 | Tim Horton | 24 | 1949-50, 51-74 | 1446 |
| 15 | Mike Gartner | 19 | 1979-98 | 1432 |

**Note:** Combined NHL-WHA games played: Howe (2,186), Messier (1808), Dave Keon (1,597), Harry Howell (1,581), Gretzky (1,567), Norm Ullman (1,554), Gartner (1,510) and Bobby Hull (1,474).

## Goaltending

### Wins

| | | Yrs | Gm | W | L | T | Pct |
|---|---|---|---|---|---|---|---|
| 1 | Patrick Roy | 19 | 1029 | **551** | 315 | 131 | .618 |
| 2 | Terry Sawchuk | 21 | 971 | **447** | 330 | 172 | .562 |
| 3 | **Ed Belfour** | 16 | 856 | **435** | 281 | 111 | .593 |
| 4 | Jacques Plante | 18 | 837 | **434** | 247 | 146 | .614 |
| 5 | Tony Esposito | 16 | 886 | **423** | 306 | 152 | .566 |
| 6 | Glenn Hall | 18 | 906 | **407** | 326 | 163 | .545 |
| 7 | **Martin Brodeur** | 12 | 740 | **403** | 217 | 105 | .628 |
| | Grant Fuhr | 19 | 868 | **403** | 295 | 114 | .567 |
| 9 | **Curtis Joseph** | 15 | 798 | **396** | 289 | 90 | .569 |
| 10 | Mike Vernon | 19 | 781 | **385** | 273 | 92 | .575 |
| 11 | John Vanbiesbrouck | 20 | 882 | **374** | 346 | 119 | .517 |
| 12 | Andy Moog | 18 | 713 | **372** | 209 | 88 | .622 |
| 13 | Tom Barrasso | 19 | 777 | **369** | 277 | 86 | .563 |
| 14 | Rogie Vachon | 16 | 795 | **355** | 291 | 127 | .541 |
| 15 | Gump Worsley | 21 | 861 | **335** | 352 | 150 | .490 |
| 16 | Harry Lumley | 16 | 804 | **330** | 329 | 143 | .501 |
| 17 | Chris Osgood | 11 | 568 | **305** | 177 | 66 | .617 |
| | Billy Smith | 18 | 680 | **305** | 233 | 105 | .556 |
| 19 | **Sean Burke** | 16 | 762 | **304** | 321 | 101 | .488 |
| 20 | Turk Broda | 12 | 629 | **302** | 224 | 101 | .562 |

### Losses

| | | Yrs | Gm | W | L | T | Pct |
|---|---|---|---|---|---|---|---|
| 1 | Gump Worsley | 21 | 861 | 335 | **352** | 150 | .490 |
| 2 | Gilles Meloche | 18 | 788 | 270 | **351** | 131 | .446 |
| 3 | John Vanbiesbrouck | 20 | 882 | 374 | **346** | 119 | .517 |
| 4 | Terry Sawchuk | 21 | 971 | 447 | **330** | 172 | .562 |
| 5 | Harry Lumley | 16 | 804 | 330 | **329** | 143 | .501 |

### Shutouts

| | | Yrs | Games | No |
|---|---|---|---|---|
| 1 | Terry Sawchuk | 21 | 971 | 103 |
| 2 | George Hainsworth | 11 | 465 | 94 |
| 3 | Glenn Hall | 18 | 906 | 84 |
| 4 | Jacques Plante | 18 | 837 | 82 |
| 5 | Alex Connell | 12 | 417 | 81 |
| | Tiny Thompson | 12 | 553 | 81 |
| 7 | Tony Esposito | 16 | 886 | 76 |
| 8 | **Ed Belfour** | 16 | 856 | 75 |
| | **Martin Brodeur** | 12 | 740 | 75 |
| 10 | Lorne Chabot | 11 | 411 | 73 |
| 11 | Harry Lumley | 16 | 804 | 71 |
| 12 | Roy Worters | 12 | 484 | 66 |
| | Patrick Roy | 19 | 1029 | 66 |
| 14 | **Dominik Hasek** | 13 | 595 | 63 |
| 15 | Turk Broda | 14 | 629 | 62 |

### Goals Against Average

Minimum of 300 games played.

#### Before 1950

| | | Gm | Min | GA | GAA |
|---|---|---|---|---|---|
| 1 | George Hainsworth | 465 | 29,415 | 937 | 1.91 |
| 2 | Alex Connell | 417 | 26,050 | 830 | 1.91 |
| 3 | Chuck Gardiner | 316 | 19,687 | 664 | 2.02 |
| 4 | Lorne Chabot | 411 | 25,307 | 860 | 2.04 |
| 5 | Tiny Thompson | 553 | 34,175 | 1183 | 2.08 |

#### Since 1950

| | | Gm | Min | GA | GAA |
|---|---|---|---|---|---|
| 1 | **Martin Brodeur** | 740 | 43,511 | 1573 | 2.17 |
| 2 | **Dominik Hasek** | 595 | 34,562 | 1284 | 2.23 |
| 3 | Ken Dryden | 397 | 23,352 | 870 | 2.24 |
| 4 | **Roman Turek** | 328 | 19,095 | 734 | 2.31 |
| 5 | Jacques Plante | 837 | 49,533 | 1965 | 2.38 |
| 6 | Patrick Lalime | 322 | 18,553 | 738 | 2.39 |
| 7 | **Ed Belfour** | 856 | 49,509 | 2006 | 2.43 |
| 8 | **Chris Osgood** | 568 | 32,604 | 1324 | 2.44 |
| 9 | Glen Hall | 906 | 53,484 | 2222 | 2.49 |
| 10 | Terry Sawchuk | 971 | 57,194 | 2389 | 2.51 |

### NHL-WHA Top 10

All-time regular season wins leaders, including games played in World Hockey Association (1972-79). NHL goaltenders with WHA experience are listed in CAPITAL letters. Players active during 2004 are in bold type.

#### Wins

| | | Yrs | W | L | T | Pct |
|---|---|---|---|---|---|---|
| 1 | Patrick Roy | 19 | **551** | 315 | 131 | .618 |
| 2 | JACQUES PLANTE | 19 | **449** | 261 | 147 | .610 |
| 3 | Terry Sawchuk | 21 | **447** | 330 | 172 | .562 |
| 4 | **Ed Belfour** | 16 | **435** | 281 | 111 | .593 |
| 5 | Tony Esposito | 16 | **423** | 306 | 152 | .566 |
| 6 | Glenn Hall | 18 | **407** | 326 | 163 | .545 |
| 7 | **Martin Brodeur** | 12 | **403** | 217 | 105 | .628 |
| | Grant Fuhr | 19 | **403** | 295 | 114 | .567 |
| 9 | **Curtis Joseph** | 15 | **396** | 289 | 90 | .569 |
| 10 | Mike Vernon | 19 | **385** | 273 | 92 | .575 |

**WHA Totals:** PLANTE (1 yr, 31 gm, 15-14-1).

## All-Time NHL Regular Season Leaders (Cont.)
### SINGLE SEASON

### Scoring
#### Points

| | | Season | G | A | Pts |
|---|---|---|---|---|---|
| 1 | Wayne Gretzky, Edm | 1985-86 | 52 | 163 | 215 |
| 2 | Wayne Gretzky, Edm | 1981-82 | 92 | 120 | 212 |
| 3 | Wayne Gretzky, Edm | 1984-85 | 73 | 135 | 208 |
| 4 | Wayne Gretzky, Edm | 1983-84 | 87 | 118 | 205 |
| 5 | Mario Lemieux, Pit | 1988-89 | 85 | 114 | 199 |
| 6 | Wayne Gretzky, Edm | 1982-83 | 71 | 125 | 196 |
| 7 | Wayne Gretzky, Edm | 1986-87 | 62 | 121 | 183 |
| 8 | Mario Lemieux, Pit | 1987-88 | 70 | 98 | 168 |
| | Wayne Gretzky, LA | 1988-89 | 54 | 114 | 168 |
| 10 | Wayne Gretzky, Edm | 1980-81 | 55 | 109 | 164 |
| 11 | Wayne Gretzky, LA | 1990-91 | 41 | 122 | 163 |
| 12 | Mario Lemieux, Pit | 1995-96 | 69 | 92 | 161 |
| 13 | Mario Lemieux, Pit | 1992-93 | 69 | 91 | 160 |
| 14 | Steve Yzerman, Det | 1988-89 | 65 | 90 | 155 |
| 15 | Phil Esposito, Bos | 1970-71 | 76 | 76 | 152 |
| 16 | Bernie Nicholls, LA | 1988-89 | 70 | 80 | 150 |
| 17 | Jaromir Jagr, Pit | 1995-96 | 62 | 87 | 149 |
| | Wayne Gretzky, Edm | 1987-88 | 40 | 109 | 149 |
| 19 | Pat LaFontaine, Buf | 1992-93 | 53 | 95 | 148 |
| 20 | Mike Bossy, NYI | 1981-82 | 64 | 83 | 147 |

**WHA 150 points or more:** 154—Marc Tardif, Que. (1977-78).

#### Goals

| | | Season | Gm | No |
|---|---|---|---|---|
| 1 | Wayne Gretzky, Edm | 1981-82 | 80 | 92 |
| 2 | Wayne Gretzky, Edm | 1983-84 | 74 | 87 |
| 3 | Brett Hull, St.L | 1990-91 | 78 | 86 |
| 4 | Mario Lemieux, Pit | 1988-89 | 76 | 85 |
| 5 | Alexander Mogilny, Buf. | 1992-93 | 77 | 76 |
| | Phil Esposito, Bos | 1970-71 | 78 | 76 |
| | Teemu Selanne, Win | 1992-93 | 84 | 76 |
| 8 | Wayne Gretzky, Edm | 1984-85 | 80 | 73 |
| 9 | Brett Hull, St.L | 1989-90 | 80 | 72 |
| 10 | Jari Kurri, Edm | 1984-85 | 73 | 71 |
| | Wayne Gretzky, Edm | 1982-83 | 80 | 71 |
| 12 | Brett Hull, St.L | 1991-92 | 73 | 70 |
| | Mario Lemieux, Pit | 1987-88 | 77 | 70 |
| | Bernie Nicholls, LA | 1988-89 | 79 | 70 |
| 15 | Mario Lemieux, Pit | 1992-93 | 60 | 69 |
| | Mario Lemieux, Pit | 1995-96 | 70 | 69 |
| | Mike Bossy, NYI | 1978-79 | 80 | 69 |
| 18 | Phil Esposito, Bos | 1973-74 | 78 | 68 |
| | Jari Kurri, Edm | 1985-86 | 78 | 68 |
| | Mike Bossy, NYI | 1980-81 | 79 | 68 |

**WHA 70 goals or more:** 77—Bobby Hull, Win. (1974-75); 75—Real Cloutier, Que. (1978-79); 71—Marc Tardif, Que. (1975-76); 70—Anders Hedberg, Win. (1976-77).

#### Assists

| | | Season | Gm | No |
|---|---|---|---|---|
| 1 | Wayne Gretzky, Edm | 1985-86 | 80 | 163 |
| 2 | Wayne Gretzky, Edm | 1984-85 | 80 | 135 |
| 3 | Wayne Gretzky, Edm | 1982-83 | 80 | 125 |
| 4 | Wayne Gretzky, LA | 1990-91 | 78 | 122 |
| 5 | Wayne Gretzky, Edm | 1986-87 | 79 | 121 |
| 6 | Wayne Gretzky, Edm | 1981-82 | 80 | 120 |
| 7 | Wayne Gretzky, Edm | 1983-84 | 74 | 118 |
| 8 | Mario Lemieux, Pit | 1988-89 | 76 | 114 |
| | Wayne Gretzky, LA | 1988-89 | 78 | 114 |
| 10 | Wayne Gretzky, Edm | 1987-88 | 64 | 109 |
| | Wayne Gretzky, Edm | 1980-81 | 80 | 109 |
| 12 | Wayne Gretzky, LA | 1989-90 | 73 | 102 |
| | Bobby Orr, Bos | 1970-71 | 78 | 102 |
| 14 | Mario Lemieux, Pit | 1987-88 | 77 | 98 |
| 15 | Adam Oates, Bos | 1992-93 | 84 | 97 |

**WHA 95 assists or more:** 106—Andre Lacroix, San Diego (1974-75).

### Goaltending
#### Wins

| | | Season | Record |
|---|---|---|---|
| 1 | Bernie Parent, Phi | 1973-74 | 47-13-12 |
| 2 | Bernie Parent, Phi | 1974-75 | 44-14-9 |
| | Terry Sawchuk, Det | 1950-51 | 44-13-13 |
| | Terry Sawchuk, Det | 1951-52 | 44-14-12 |
| 5 | Martin Brodeur, NJ | 1999-00 | 43-20-8 |
| | Martin Brodeur, NJ | 1997-98 | 43-17-8 |
| | Tom Barrasso, Pit | 1992-93 | 43-14-5 |
| | Ed Belfour, Chi | 1990-91 | 43-19-7 |
| 9 | Jacques Plante, Mon | 1955-56 | 42-12-10 |
| | Jacques Plante, Mon | 1961-62 | 42-14-14 |
| | Ken Dryden, Mon | 1975-76 | 42-10-8 |
| | Mike Richter, NYR | 1993-94 | 42-12-6 |
| | Roman Turek, St.L | 1999-00 | 42-15-9 |
| | Martin Brodeur, NJ | 2000-01 | 42-17-11 |

**Most WHA wins in one season:** 44—Richard Brodeur, Que. (1975-76).

#### Losses

| | | Season | Record |
|---|---|---|---|
| 1 | Gary Smith, Cal | 1970-71 | 19-48-4 |
| 2 | Al Rollins, Chi | 1953-54 | 12-47-7 |
| 3 | Peter Sidorkiewicz, Ott | 1992-93 | 8-46-3 |
| 4 | Harry Lumley, Chi | 1951-52 | 17-44-9 |
| 5 | Three tied with 41 losses each. | | |

**Most WHA losses in one season:** 36—Don McLeod, Van. (1974-75) and Andy Brown, Ind. (1974-75).

#### Shutouts

| | | Season | Gm | No |
|---|---|---|---|---|
| 1 | George Hainsworth, Mon | 1928-29 | 44 | 22 |
| 2 | Alex Connell, Ott | 1925-26 | 36 | 15 |
| | Alex Connell, Ott | 1927-28 | 44 | 15 |
| | Hal Winkler, Bos | 1927-28 | 44 | 15 |
| | Tony Esposito, Chi | 1969-70 | 63 | 15 |

**Most WHA shutouts in one season:** 5—Gerry Cheevers, Cle. (1972-73) and Joe Daly, Win. (1975-76).

#### Goals Against Average
##### Before 1950

| | | Season | Gm | GAA |
|---|---|---|---|---|
| 1 | George Hainsworth, Mon | 1928-29 | 44 | 0.98 |
| 2 | George Hainsworth, Mon | 1927-28 | 44 | 1.09 |
| 3 | Alex Connell, Ott | 1925-26 | 36 | 1.17 |
| 4 | Tiny Thompson, Bos | 1928-29 | 44 | 1.18 |
| 5 | Roy Worters, NY Americans | 1928-29 | 38 | 1.21 |

##### Since 1950

| | | Season | Gm | GAA |
|---|---|---|---|---|
| 1 | Miikka Kiprusoff, Calg | 2003-04 | 38 | 1.69 |
| 2 | Marty Turco, Dal | 2002-03 | 55 | 1.72 |
| 3 | Tony Esposito, Chi | 1971-72 | 48 | 1.77 |
| 4 | Al Rollins, Tor | 1950-51 | 40 | 1.77 |
| 5 | Ron Tugnutt, Ott | 1998-99 | 43 | 1.79 |

#### Penalty Minutes

| | | Season | PM |
|---|---|---|---|
| 1 | Dave Schultz, Phi | 1974-75 | 472 |
| 2 | Paul Baxter, Pit | 1981-82 | 409 |
| 3 | Mike Peluso, Chi | 1991-92 | 408 |
| 4 | Dave Schultz, LA-Pit | 1977-78 | 405 |
| 5 | Marty McSorley, LA | 1992-93 | 399 |
| 6 | Bob Probert, Det | 1987-88 | 398 |
| 7 | Basil McRae, Min | 1987-88 | 382 |
| 8 | Joey Kocur, Det | 1985-86 | 377 |
| 9 | Tim Hunter, Calg | 1988-89 | 375 |
| 10 | Donald Brashear, Van | 1997-98 | 372 |

**WHA 355 minutes or more:** 365—Curt Brackenbury, Min-Que. (1975-76).

## SINGLE GAME

### Points

| | Date | G-A—Pts |
|---|---|---|
| Darryl Sittler, Tor vs Bos | 2/7/76 | 6-4— 10 |
| Maurice Richard, Mon vs Det | 12/28/44 | 5-3— 8 |
| Bert Olmstead, Mon vs Chi | 1/9/54 | 4-4— 8 |
| Tom Bladon, Phi vs Cle | 12/11/77 | 4-4— 8 |
| Bryan Trottier, NYI vs NYR | 12/23/78 | 5-3— 8 |
| Peter Stastny, Que at Wash | 2/22/81 | 4-4— 8 |
| Anton Stastny, Que at Wash | 2/22/81 | 3-5— 8 |
| Wayne Gretzky, Edm vs NJ | 11/19/83 | 3-5— 8 |
| Wayne Gretzky, Edm vs Min | 1/4/84 | 4-4— 8 |
| Paul Coffey, Edm vs Det | 3/14/86 | 2-6— 8 |
| Mario Lemieux, Pit vs St.L | 10/15/88 | 2-6— 8 |
| Bernie Nicholls, LA vs Tor | 12/1/88 | 2-6— 8 |
| Mario Lemieux, Pit vs NJ | 12/31/88 | 5-3— 8 |

### Goals

| | Date | No |
|---|---|---|
| Joe Malone, Que vs Tor | 1/31/20 | 7 |
| Newsy Lalonde, Mon vs Tor | 1/10/20 | 6 |
| Joe Malone, Que vs Ott | 3/10/20 | 6 |
| Corb Denneny, Tor vs Ham | 1/26/21 | 6 |
| Cy Denneny, Ott vs Ham | 3/7/21 | 6 |
| Syd Howe, Det vs NYR | 2/3/44 | 6 |
| Red Berenson, St.L at Phi | 11/7/68 | 6 |
| Darryl Sittler, Tor vs Bos | 2/7/76 | 6 |

### Assists

| | Date | No |
|---|---|---|
| Billy Taylor, Det at Chi | 3/16/47 | 7 |
| Wayne Gretzky, Edm vs Wash | 2/15/80 | 7 |
| Wayne Gretzky, Edm at Chi | 12/11/85 | 7 |
| Wayne Gretzky, Edm vs Que | 2/14/86 | 7 |
| 24 players tied with 6 each. | | |

### Penalty Minutes

| | Date | Min |
|---|---|---|
| Randy Holt, LA at Phi | 3/11/79 | 67 |
| Brad Smith, Tor vs Det | 11/15/86 | 57 |
| Reed Low, St.L at Calg | 2/28/02 | 57 |
| Frank Bathe, Phi vs LA | 3/11/79 | 55 |
| Reed Low, St.L at Det | 12/31/02 | 53 |
| Russ Anderson, Pit vs Edm | 1/19/80 | 51 |

### Penalties

| | Date | No |
|---|---|---|
| Chris Nilan, Bos vs Har | 3/31/91 | 10* |
| Nine tied with 9 each. | | |

* Nilan accumulated six minors, two majors, one 10-minute misconduct and one game misconduct.

## All-Time Winningest NHL Coaches

Top 20 NHL career victories through the 2003-04 season. Career, regular season and playoff records are noted along with NHL titles won. Coaches active during 2003-04 season in **bold** type. **Note:** In the following tables, overtime losses are considered losses.

| | | Career | | | | Regular Season | | | | Playoffs | | | |
|---|---|---|---|---|---|---|---|---|---|---|---|---|---|
| | | Yrs | W | L | T | Pct | W | L | T | Pct | W | L | T | Pct | Stanley Cups |
| 1 | Scotty Bowman | 30 | **1467** | 714 | 313 | .651 | 1244 | 584 | 313 | .654 | 223 | 130 | 0 | .632 | 9 (1973, 76-79, 92, 97-98, 2002) |
| 2 | Al Arbour | 22 | **904** | 663 | 248 | .566 | 781 | 577 | 248 | .564 | 123 | 86 | 0 | .589 | 4 (1980-83) |
| 3 | Dick Irvin | 26 | **790** | 609 | 228 | .556 | 690 | 521 | 226 | .559 | 100 | 88 | 2 | .532 | 4 (1932,44,46,53) |
| 4 | **Pat Quinn** | 18 | **710** | 555 | 154 | .555 | 616 | 466 | 154 | .561 | 94 | 89 | 0 | .514 | None |
| 5 | **Mike Keenan** | 18 | **675** | 560 | 147 | .542 | 584 | 491 | 147 | .538 | 91 | 69 | 0 | .569 | 1 (1994) |
| 6 | Billy Reay | 16 | **599** | 445 | 175 | .563 | 542 | 385 | 175 | .571 | 57 | 60 | 0 | .487 | None |
| 7 | **Glen Sather** | 13 | **586** | 351 | 122 | .611 | 497 | 314 | 121 | .598 | 89 | 37 | 1 | .705 | 4 (1984-85,87-88) |
| 8 | Toe Blake | 13 | **582** | 292 | 159 | .640 | 500 | 255 | 159 | .634 | 82 | 37 | 0 | .689 | 8 (1956-60,65-66,68) |
| 9 | **Pat Burns** | 14 | **579** | 438 | 151 | .560 | 501 | 367 | 151 | .566 | 78 | 71 | 0 | .523 | 1 (2003) |
| 10 | Bryan Murray | 14 | **547** | 457 | 131 | .540 | 513 | 413 | 131 | .547 | 34 | 44 | 0 | .436 | None |
| 11 | Roger Neilson | 17 | **511** | 436 | 159 | .540 | 460 | 381 | 159 | .540 | 51 | 55 | 0 | .481 | None |
| 12 | **Brian Sutter** | 13 | **479** | 477 | 140 | .501 | 451 | 437 | 140 | .507 | 28 | 40 | 0 | .412 | None |
| 13 | Jack Adams | 21 | **465** | 442 | 162 | .511 | 413 | 390 | 161 | .512 | 52 | 52 | 1 | .500 | 3 (1936-37, 43) |
| 14 | Jacques Demers | 14 | **464** | 510 | 130 | .479 | 409 | 467 | 130 | .471 | 55 | 43 | 0 | .561 | 1 (1993) |
| 15 | Fred Shero | 10 | **451** | 272 | 119 | .606 | 390 | 225 | 119 | .612 | 61 | 47 | 0 | .565 | 2 (1974-75) |
| 16 | **Jacques Martin** | 11 | **445** | 373 | 119 | .538 | 407 | 326 | 119 | .548 | 38 | 47 | 0 | .447 | None |
| 17 | Punch Imlach | 15 | **439** | 384 | 148 | .528 | 395 | 336 | 148 | .534 | 44 | 48 | 0 | .478 | 4 (1962-64,67) |
| 18 | Emile Francis | 13 | **433** | 326 | 112 | .561 | 393 | 273 | 112 | .577 | 40 | 53 | 0 | .430 | None |
| 19 | **Jacques Lemaire** | 11 | **427** | 353 | 124 | .541 | 370 | 309 | 124 | .538 | 57 | 44 | 0 | .564 | 1 (1995) |
| 20 | **Ken Hitchcock** | 9 | **426** | 264 | 88 | .604 | 362 | 217 | 88 | .609 | 64 | 47 | 0 | .577 | 1 (1999) |

### Where They Coached

**Adams**—Toronto (1922-23), Detroit (1927-47); **Arbour**—St. Louis (1970-73), NY Islanders (1973-86,88-94); **Blake**—Montreal (1955-68); **Bowman**—St. Louis (1967-71), Montreal (1971-79), Buffalo (1979-87), Pittsburgh (1991-93), Detroit (1993-2002); **Burns**—Montreal (1988-92), Toronto (1992-96), Boston (1997-2000), New Jersey (2002– ); **Demers**—Quebec (1979-80), St. Louis (1983-86), Detroit (1986-90), Montreal (1992-95), Tampa Bay (1997-99); **Francis**—NY Rangers (1965-75), St. Louis (1976-77,81-83).

**Hitchcock**—Dallas (1996-2002), Philadelphia (2002– ); **Imlach**—Toronto (1958-69), Buffalo (1970-72), Toronto (1979-81); **Irvin**—Chicago (1930-31,55-56), Toronto (1931-40), Montreal (1940-55); **Keenan**—Philadelphia (1984-88), Chicago (1988-92), NY Rangers (1993-94), St. Louis (1994-96), Vancouver (1997-99), Boston (2000-01), Florida (2001-03); **Lemaire**—Montreal (1984-85), New Jersey (1993-98), Minnesota (2000– ); **Martin**—St. Louis (1986-88), Ottawa (1995-2004), Florida (2004– ); **Murray**—Washington (1982-90), Detroit (1990-93), Florida (1997-98), Anaheim (2001-02), Ottawa (2004– ).

**Neilson**—Toronto (1977-79), Buffalo (1979-81), Vancouver (1982-83), Los Angeles (1984), NY Rangers (1989-93), Florida (1993-95), Philadelphia (1998-00), Ottawa (2002); **Quinn**—Philadelphia (1978-82), Los Angeles (1984-87), Vancouver (1990-94, 96), Toronto (1998– ); **Reay**—Toronto (1957-59), Chicago (1963-77); **Sather**—Edmonton (1979-89, 93-94), NY Rangers (2003-04); **Shero**—Philadelphia (1971-78), NY Rangers (1978-81); **Sutter**—St. Louis (1988-92), Boston (1992-95), Calgary (1997-2000), Chicago (2001– ).

## Top Winning Percentages

Minimum of 275 victories, including playoffs.

| | | Yrs | W | L | T | Pct. |
|---|---|---|---|---|---|---|
| 1 | Scotty Bowman | 30 | 1467 | 714 | 313 | .651 |
| 2 | Toe Blake | 13 | 582 | 292 | 159 | .640 |
| 3 | Glen Sather | 13 | 586 | 351 | 122 | .611 |
| 4 | Fred Shero | 10 | 451 | 272 | 119 | .606 |
| 5 | Ken Hitchcock | 9 | 426 | 264 | 88 | .604 |
| 6 | Don Cherry | 6 | 281 | 177 | 77 | .597 |
| 7 | Tommy Ivan | 9 | 324 | 205 | 111 | .593 |
| 8 | Bob Hartley | 6 | 294 | 205 | 61 | .579 |
| 9 | Joel Quenneville | 8 | 341 | 243 | 77 | .574 |
| 10 | Al Arbour | 22 | 904 | 663 | 248 | .566 |
| 11 | Billy Reay | 16 | 599 | 445 | 175 | .563 |
| 12 | Marc Crawford | 10 | 412 | 309 | 103 | .563 |
| 13 | Emile Francis | 13 | 433 | 326 | 112 | .561 |
| 14 | Pat Burns | 14 | 579 | 438 | 151 | .560 |
| 15 | Hap Day | 10 | 308 | 237 | 81 | .557 |
| 16 | Dick Irvin | 26 | 790 | 609 | 228 | .556 |
| 17 | Pat Quinn | 18 | 710 | 555 | 154 | .555 |
| 18 | Lester Patrick | 13 | 312 | 242 | 115 | .552 |
| 19 | Art Ross | 18 | 393 | 310 | 95 | .552 |
| 20 | Bob Johnson | 6 | 275 | 223 | 58 | .547 |
| 21 | Terry Murray | 11 | 406 | 331 | 89 | .545 |
| 22 | Mike Keenan | 18 | 675 | 560 | 147 | .542 |
| 23 | Jacques Lemaire | 11 | 427 | 353 | 124 | .541 |
| 24 | Bryan Murray | 14 | 547 | 457 | 131 | .540 |
| 25 | Jacques Martin | 11 | 445 | 373 | 119 | .538 |
| 26 | Roger Neilson | 16 | 511 | 436 | 159 | .534 |
| 27 | Punch Imlach | 15 | 439 | 384 | 148 | .528 |
| 28 | Darryl Sutter | 10 | 407 | 364 | 101 | .525 |
| 29 | Terry Crisp | 9 | 310 | 286 | 78 | .518 |
| 30 | Lindy Ruff | 7 | 285 | 265 | 78 | .516 |

## Active Coaches' Victories

Records through 2003-04 season, including playoffs.

| | | Yrs | W | L | T | Pct. |
|---|---|---|---|---|---|---|
| 1 | Pat Quinn, Tor. | 18 | 710 | 555 | 154 | .555 |
| 2 | Bryan Murray, Ott. | 14 | 547 | 457 | 131 | .540 |
| 3 | Jacques Martin, Fla. | 11 | 445 | 373 | 119 | .538 |
| 4 | Jacques Lemaire, Min. | 11 | 427 | 353 | 124 | .541 |
| 5 | Ken Hitchcock, Phi. | 9 | 426 | 264 | 88 | .604 |
| 6 | Marc Crawford, Van. | 10 | 412 | 309 | 103 | .563 |
| 7 | Darryl Sutter, Calg. | 10 | 407 | 364 | 101 | .525 |
| 8 | Ron Wilson, SJ | 11 | 403 | 401 | 101 | .501 |
| 9 | Joel Quenneville, Col | 8 | 341 | 243 | 77 | .574 |
| 10 | Bob Hartley, Atl. | 6 | 294 | 205 | 61 | .579 |
| 11 | Lindy Ruff, Buf. | 7 | 285 | 265 | 78 | .516 |
| 12 | Larry Robinson, NJ | 7 | 226 | 231 | 64 | .495 |
| 13 | Andy Murray, LA | 5 | 188 | 188 | 58 | .500 |
| 14 | Barry Trotz, Nash. | 6 | 185 | 253 | 60 | .432 |
| 15 | Craig MacTavish, Edm. | 4 | 153 | 140 | 47 | .519 |
| 16 | John Tortorella, TB | 5 | 142 | 148 | 37 | .491 |
| 17 | Peter Laviolette, Car. | 3 | 101 | 102 | 25 | .498 |
| 18 | Dave Tippett, Dal. | 2 | 94 | 59 | 28 | .597 |
| 19 | Mike Babcock, Det. | 2 | 84 | 82 | 19 | .505 |
| 20 | Claude Julien, Mon. | 2 | 57 | 62 | 10 | .481 |
| 21 | Mike Sullivan, Bos. | 1 | 44 | 30 | 15 | .579 |
| | Tom Renney, NYR | 3 | 44 | 68 | 9 | .401 |
| 23 | Steve Stirling, NYI | 1 | 39 | 37 | 11 | .511 |
| 24 | Ed Olczyk, Pit. | 1 | 23 | 51 | 8 | .329 |
| 25 | Gerard Gallant, Clb. | 1 | 16 | 25 | 4 | .400 |
| 26 | Glen Hanlon, Wash. | 1 | 15 | 30 | 9 | .361 |
| 27 | Mike Kitchen, St.L | 1 | 11 | 11 | 4 | .500 |
| 28 | Randy Carlyle, Ana. | 0 | 0 | 0 | 0 | .000 |
| | Wayne Gretzky, Pho. | 0 | 0 | 0 | 0 | .000 |
| | Trent Yawney, Chi. | 0 | 0 | 0 | 0 | .000 |

## Annual Awards

Note that due to the owners' lockout and cancellation of the 2004-05 season, no awards were given out in 2005.

### Hart Memorial Trophy

Awarded to the player "adjudged to be the most valuable to his team" and named after Cecil Hart, the former manager-coach of the Montreal Canadiens. Winners selected by Pro Hockey Writers Assn. (PHWA). Winners' scoring statistics or goaltender W-L records and goals against average are provided; (*) indicates led or tied for league lead.

**Multiple winners:** Wayne Gretzky (9); Gordie Howe (6); Eddie Shore (4); Bobby Clarke, Mario Lemieux, Howie Morenz and Bobby Orr (3); Jean Beliveau, Bill Cowley, Phil Esposito, Dominik Hasek, Bobby Hull, Guy Lafleur, Mark Messier, Stan Mikita and Nels Stewart (2).

| Year | | G | A | Pts |
|---|---|---|---|---|
| 1924 | Frank Nighbor, Ottawa, C | 10 | 3 | 13 |
| 1925 | Billy Burch, Hamilton, C | 20 | 4 | 24 |
| 1926 | Nels Stewart, Maroons, C | 34 | 8 | 42* |
| 1927 | Herb Gardiner, Mon., D | 6 | 6 | 12 |
| 1928 | Howie Morenz, Mon., C | 33 | 18 | 51 |
| 1929 | Roy Worters, NYA, G | 16-13-9; | | 1.21 |
| 1930 | Nels Stewart, Maroons, C | 39 | 16 | 55 |
| 1931 | Howie Morenz, Mon., C | 28 | 23 | 51* |
| 1932 | Howie Morenz, Mon., C | 24 | 25 | 49 |
| 1933 | Eddie Shore, Bos., D | 8 | 27 | 35 |
| 1934 | Aurel Joliat, Mon., LW | 22 | 15 | 37 |
| 1935 | Eddie Shore, Bos., D | 7 | 26 | 33 |
| 1936 | Eddie Shore, Bos., D | 3 | 16 | 19 |
| 1937 | Babe Siebert, Mon., D | 8 | 20 | 28 |
| 1938 | Eddie Shore, Bos., D | 3 | 14 | 17 |
| 1939 | Toe Blake, Mon., LW | 24 | 23 | 47* |
| 1940 | Ebbie Goodfellow, Det., D | 11 | 17 | 28 |
| 1941 | Bill Cowley, Bos., C | 17 | 45 | 62* |
| 1942 | Tommy Anderson, NYA, D | 12 | 29 | 41 |
| 1943 | Bill Cowley, Bos., C | 27 | 45 | 72 |
| 1944 | Babe Pratt, Tor., D | 17 | 40 | 57 |
| 1945 | Elmer Lach, Mon., C | 26 | 54 | 80* |
| 1946 | Max Bentley, Chi., C | 31 | 30 | 61* |
| 1947 | Maurice Richard, Mon., RW | 45 | 26 | 71 |
| 1948 | Buddy O'Connor, NYR, C | 24 | 36 | 60 |
| 1949 | Sid Abel, Det., C | 28 | 26 | 54 |
| 1950 | Chuck Rayner, NYR, G | 28-30-11; | | 2.62 |
| 1951 | Milt Schmidt, Bos., C | 22 | 39 | 61 |
| 1952 | Gordie Howe, Det., RW | 47 | 39 | 86* |
| 1953 | Gordie Howe, Det., RW | 49 | 46 | 95* |
| 1954 | Al Rollins, Chi., G | 12-47-7; | | 3.23 |
| 1955 | Ted Kennedy, Tor., C | 10 | 42 | 52 |
| 1956 | Jean Beliveau, Mon., C | 47 | 41 | 88 |
| 1957 | Gordie Howe, Det., RW | 44 | 45 | 89* |
| 1958 | Gordie Howe, Det., RW | 33 | 44 | 77 |
| 1959 | Andy Bathgate, NYR, RW | 40 | 48 | 88 |
| 1960 | Gordie Howe, Det., RW | 28 | 45 | 73 |
| 1961 | Bernie Geoffrion, Mon., RW | 50 | 45 | 95* |
| 1962 | Jacques Plante, Mon., G | 42-14-14; | | 2.37* |
| 1963 | Gordie Howe, Det., RW | 38 | 48 | 86* |
| 1964 | Jean Beliveau, Mon., C | 28 | 50 | 78 |
| 1965 | Bobby Hull, Chi., LW | 39 | 32 | 71 |
| 1966 | Bobby Hull, Chi., LW | 54 | 43 | 97* |
| 1967 | Stan Mikita, Chi., C | 35 | 62 | 97* |
| 1968 | Stan Mikita, Chi., C | 40 | 47 | 87* |
| 1969 | Phil Esposito, Bos., C | 49 | 77 | 126* |
| 1970 | Bobby Orr, Bos., D | 33 | 87 | 120* |
| 1971 | Bobby Orr, Bos., D | 37 | 102 | 139 |
| 1972 | Bobby Orr, Bos., D | 37 | 80 | 117 |
| 1973 | Bobby Clarke, Phi., C | 37 | 67 | 104 |
| 1974 | Phil Esposito, Bos., C | 68 | 77 | 145* |
| 1975 | Bobby Clarke, Phi., C | 27 | 89 | 116 |
| 1976 | Bobby Clarke, Phi., C | 30 | 89 | 119 |
| 1977 | Guy Lafleur, Mon., RW | 56 | 80 | 136* |

| Year | | G | A | Pts | Year | | G | A | Pts |
|---|---|---|---|---|---|---|---|---|---|
| 1978 | Guy Lafleur, Mon., RW | 60 | 72 | 132* | 1992 | Mark Messier, NYR, C | 35 | 72 | 107 |
| 1979 | Bryan Trottier, NYI., C | 47 | 87 | 134* | 1993 | Mario Lemieux, Pit., C | 69 | 91 | 160* |
| 1980 | Wayne Gretzky, Edm., C | 51 | 86 | 137* | 1994 | Sergei Fedorov, Det., C | 56 | 64 | 120 |
| 1981 | Wayne Gretzky, Edm., C | 55 | 109 | 164* | 1995 | Eric Lindros, Phi., C | 29 | 41 | 70* |
| 1982 | Wayne Gretzky, Edm., C | 92 | 120 | 212* | 1996 | Mario Lemieux, Pit., C | 69 | 92 | 161* |
| 1983 | Wayne Gretzky, Edm., C | 71 | 125 | 196* | 1997 | Dominik Hasek, Buf., G | 37-20-10; | | 2.27 |
| 1984 | Wayne Gretzky, Edm., C | 87 | 118 | 205* | 1998 | Dominik Hasek, Buf., G | 33-23-13; | | 2.09 |
| 1985 | Wayne Gretzky, Edm., C | 73 | 135 | 208* | 1999 | Jaromir Jagr, Pit., RW | 44 | 83 | 127* |
| 1986 | Wayne Gretzky, Edm., C | 52 | 163 | 215* | 2000 | Chris Pronger, St.L, D | 14 | 48 | 62 |
| 1987 | Wayne Gretzky, Edm., C | 62 | 121 | 183* | 2001 | Joe Sakic, Col., C | 54 | 64 | 118 |
| 1988 | Mario Lemieux, Pit., C | 70 | 98 | 168* | 2002 | Jose Theodore, Mon., G | 30-24-10; | | 2.11 |
| 1989 | Wayne Gretzky, LA, C | 54 | 114 | 168 | 2003 | Peter Forsberg, Col., C | 29 | 77 | 106* |
| 1990 | Mark Messier, Edm., C | 45 | 84 | 129 | 2004 | Martin St. Louis, TB, RW | 38 | 56 | 94* |
| 1991 | Brett Hull, St. L., RW | 86 | 45 | 131 | | | | | |

## Calder Memorial Trophy

Awarded to the most outstanding rookie of the year and named after Frank Calder, the late NHL president (1917-43). Since the 1990-91 season, all eligible candidates must not have attained their 26th birthday by Sept. 15 of their rookie year. Winners selected by PHWA. Winners' scoring statistics or goaltender W-L record & goals against average are provided.

| Year | | G | A | Pts | Year | | G | A | Pts |
|---|---|---|---|---|---|---|---|---|---|
| 1933 | Carl Voss, NYR-Det., C | 8 | 15 | 23 | 1969 | Danny Grant, Min., LW | 34 | 31 | 65 |
| 1934 | Russ Blinco, Maroons, C | 14 | 9 | 23 | 1970 | Tony Esposito, Chi., G | 38-17-8; | | 2.17 |
| 1935 | Sweeney Schriner, NYA, LW | 18 | 22 | 40 | 1971 | Gilbert Perreault, Buf., C | 38 | 34 | 72 |
| 1936 | Mike Karakas, Chi., G | 21-19-8; | | 1.92 | 1972 | Ken Dryden, Mon., G | 39-8-15; | | 2.24 |
| 1937 | Syl Apps, Tor., C | 16 | 29 | 45 | 1973 | Steve Vickers, NYR, LW | 30 | 23 | 53 |
| 1938 | Cully Dahlstrom, Chi., C | 10 | 9 | 19 | 1974 | Denis Potvin, NYI, D | 17 | 37 | 54 |
| 1939 | Frankie Brimsek, Bos., G | 33-9-1; | | 1.58 | 1975 | Eric Vail, Atl., LW | 39 | 21 | 60 |
| 1940 | Kilby MacDonald, NYR, LW | 15 | 13 | 28 | 1976 | Bryan Trottier, NYI, C | 32 | 63 | 95 |
| 1941 | John Quilty, Mon., C | 18 | 16 | 34 | 1977 | Willi Plett, Atl., RW | 33 | 23 | 56 |
| 1942 | Knobby Warwick, NYR, RW | 16 | 17 | 33 | 1978 | Mike Bossy, NYI, RW | 53 | 38 | 91 |
| 1943 | Gaye Stewart, Tor., LW | 24 | 23 | 47 | 1979 | Bobby Smith, Min., C | 30 | 44 | 74 |
| 1944 | Gus Bodnar, Tor., C | 22 | 40 | 62 | 1980 | Ray Bourque, Bos., D | 17 | 48 | 65 |
| 1945 | Frank McCool, Tor., G | 24-22-4; | | 3.22 | 1981 | Peter Stastny, Que., C | 39 | 70 | 109 |
| 1946 | Edgar Laprade, NYR, C | 15 | 19 | 34 | 1982 | Dale Hawerchuk, Win., C | 45 | 58 | 103 |
| 1947 | Howie Meeker, Tor., RW | 27 | 18 | 45 | 1983 | Steve Larmer, Chi., RW | 43 | 47 | 90 |
| 1948 | Jim McFadden, Det., C | 24 | 24 | 48 | 1984 | Tom Barrasso, Buf., G | 26-12-3; | | 2.84 |
| 1949 | Penny Lund, NYR, RW | 14 | 16 | 30 | 1985 | Mario Lemieux, Pit., C | 43 | 57 | 100 |
| 1950 | Jack Gelineau, Bos., G | 22-30-15; | | 3.28 | 1986 | Gary Suter, Calg., D | 18 | 50 | 68 |
| 1951 | Terry Sawchuk, Det., G | 44-13-13; | | 1.99 | 1987 | Luc Robitaille, LA, LW | 45 | 39 | 84 |
| 1952 | Bernie Geoffrion, Mon., RW | 30 | 24 | 54 | 1988 | Joe Nieuwendyk, Calg., C | 51 | 41 | 92 |
| 1953 | Gump Worsley, NYR, G | 13-29-8; | | 3.06 | 1989 | Brian Leetch, NYR, D | 23 | 48 | 71 |
| 1954 | Camille Henry, NYR, LW | 24 | 15 | 39 | 1990 | Sergei Makarov, Calg., RW | 24 | 62 | 86 |
| 1955 | Ed Litzenberger, Mon-Chi., RW | 23 | 28 | 51 | 1991 | Ed Belfour, Chi., G | 43-19-7; | | 2.47 |
| 1956 | Glenn Hall, Det., G | 30-24-16; | | 2.11 | 1992 | Pavel Bure, Van., RW | 34 | 26 | 60 |
| 1957 | Larry Regan, Bos., RW | 14 | 19 | 33 | 1993 | Teemu Selanne, Win., RW | 76 | 56 | 132 |
| 1958 | Frank Mahovlich, Tor., LW | 20 | 16 | 36 | 1994 | Martin Brodeur, NJ, G | 27-11-8; | | 2.40 |
| 1959 | Ralph Backstrom, Mon., C | 18 | 22 | 40 | 1995 | Peter Forsberg, Que., C | 15 | 35 | 50 |
| 1960 | Billy Hay, Chi., C | 18 | 37 | 55 | 1996 | Daniel Alfredsson, Ott., RW | 26 | 35 | 61 |
| 1961 | Dave Keon, Tor., C | 20 | 25 | 45 | 1997 | Bryan Berard, NYI, D | 8 | 40 | 48 |
| 1962 | Bobby Rousseau, Mon., RW | 21 | 24 | 45 | 1998 | Sergei Samsonov, Bos., LW | 22 | 25 | 47 |
| 1963 | Kent Douglas, Tor., D | 7 | 15 | 22 | 1999 | Chris Drury, Col., C | 20 | 24 | 44 |
| 1964 | Jacques Laperriere, Mon., D | 2 | 28 | 30 | 2000 | Scott Gomez, NJ, C | 19 | 51 | 70 |
| 1965 | Roger Crozier, Det., G | 40-23-7; | | 2.42 | 2001 | Evgeni Nabokov, SJ, G | 32-21-7; | | 2.19 |
| 1966 | Brit Selby, Tor., LW | 14 | 13 | 27 | 2002 | Dany Heatley, Atl., RW | 26 | 41 | 67 |
| 1967 | Bobby Orr, Bos., D | 13 | 28 | 41 | 2003 | Barret Jackman, St.L, D | 3 | 16 | 19 |
| 1968 | Derek Sanderson, Bos., C | 24 | 25 | 49 | 2004 | Andrew Raycroft, Bos., G | 29-18-9; | | 2.05 |

## Vezina Trophy

From 1927-80, given to the principal goaltender(s) on the team allowing the fewest goals during the regular season. Trophy named after 1920's goalie Georges Vezina of the Montreal Canadiens, who died of tuberculosis in 1926. Since the 1980-81 season, the trophy has been awarded to the most outstanding goaltender of the year as selected by the league's general managers.

**Multiple Winners:** Jacques Plante (7, one of them shared); Bill Durnan and Dominik Hasek (6); Ken Dryden (5, three shared); Bunny Larocque (4, all shared); Terry Sawchuk (4, one shared); Tiny Thompson (4); Tony Esposito (3, one shared); George Hainsworth (3); Glenn Hall (3, two shared); Patrick Roy (3); Ed Belfour (2); Johnny Bower (2, one shared); Frankie Brimsek (2); Turk Broda (2); Martin Brodeur (2); Chuck Gardiner (2); Charlie Hodge (2, one shared); Bernie Parent (2, one shared); Gump Worsley (2, both shared).

| Year | | Record | GAA | Year | | Record | GAA |
|---|---|---|---|---|---|---|---|
| 1927 | George Hainsworth, Mon | 28-14-2 | 1.52 | 1931 | Roy Worters, NYA | 18-16-10 | 1.68 |
| 1928 | George Hainsworth, Mon | 26-11-7 | 1.09 | 1932 | Chuck Gardiner, Chi | 18-19-11 | 1.92 |
| 1929 | George Hainsworth, Mon | 22-7-15 | 0.98 | 1933 | Tiny Thompson, Bos | 25-15-8 | 1.83 |
| 1930 | Tiny Thompson, Bos | 38-5-1 | 2.23 | 1934 | Chuck Gardiner, Chi | 20-17-11 | 1.73 |

## Annual Awards (Cont.)

| Year | | Record | GAA |
|------|---|--------|-----|
| 1935 | Lorne Chabot, Chi | 26-17-5 | 1.83 |
| 1936 | Tiny Thompson, Bos | 22-20-6 | 1.71 |
| 1937 | Norm Smith, Det | 25-14-9 | 2.13 |
| 1938 | Tiny Thompson, Bos | 30-11-7 | 1.85 |
| 1939 | Frankie Brimsek, Bos. | 33-9-1 | 1.58 |
| 1940 | Dave Kerr, NYR | 27-11-10 | 1.60 |
| 1941 | Turk Broda, Tor | 28-14-6 | 2.06 |
| 1942 | Frankie Brimsek, Bos. | 24-17-6 | 2.45 |
| 1943 | John Mowers, Det | 25-14-11 | 2.47 |
| 1944 | Bill Durnan, Mon | 38-5-7 | 2.18 |
| 1945 | Bill Durnan, Mon | 38-8-4 | 2.42 |
| 1946 | Bill Durnan, Mon | 24-11-5 | 2.60 |
| 1947 | Bill Durnan, Mon | 34-16-10 | 2.30 |
| 1948 | Turk Broda, Tor | 32-15-13 | 2.38 |
| 1949 | Bill Durnan, Mon | 28-23-9 | 2.10 |
| 1950 | Bill Durnan, Mon | 26-21-17 | 2.20 |
| 1951 | Al Rollins, Tor. | 27-5-8 | 1.77 |
| 1952 | Terry Sawchuk, Det. | 44-14-12 | 1.90 |
| 1953 | Terry Sawchuk, Det. | 32-15-16 | 1.90 |
| 1954 | Harry Lumley, Tor | 32-24-13 | 1.86 |
| 1955 | Terry Sawchuk, Det. | 40-17-11 | 1.96 |
| 1956 | Jacques Plante, Mon. | 42-12-10 | 1.86 |
| 1957 | Jacques Plante, Mon. | 31-18-12 | 2.02 |
| 1958 | Jacques Plante, Mon. | 34-14-8 | 2.11 |
| 1959 | Jacques Plante, Mon. | 38-16-13 | 2.16 |
| 1960 | Jacques Plante, Mon. | 40-17-12 | 2.54 |
| 1961 | Johnny Bower, Tor | 33-15-10 | 2.50 |
| 1962 | Jacques Plante, Mon. | 42-14-14 | 2.37 |
| 1963 | Glenn Hall, Chi | 30-20-16 | 2.55 |
| 1964 | Charlie Hodge, Mon | 33-18-11 | 2.26 |
| 1965 | Johnny Bower, Tor | 13-13-8 | 2.38 |
| | & Terry Sawchuk, Tor | 17-13-6 | 2.56 |
| 1966 | Gump Worsley, Mon | 29-14-6 | 2.36 |
| | & Charlie Hodge, Mon. | 12-7-2 | 2.58 |
| 1967 | Glenn Hall, Chi | 19-5-5 | 2.38 |
| | & Denis Dejordy, Chi | 22-12-7 | 2.46 |
| 1968 | Gump Worsley, Mon | 19-9-8 | 1.98 |
| | & Rogie Vachon, Mon | 23-13-2 | 2.48 |
| 1969 | Jacques Plante, St.L | 18-12-6 | 1.96 |
| | & Glenn Hall, St.L | 19-12-8 | 2.17 |
| 1970 | Tony Esposito, Chi | 38-17-8 | 2.17 |
| 1971 | Ed Giacomin, NYR | 27-10-7 | 2.16 |
| | & Gilles Villemure, NYR | 22-8-4 | 2.30 |

| Year | | Record | GAA |
|------|---|--------|-----|
| 1972 | Tony Esposito, Chi | 31-10-6 | 1.77 |
| | & Gary Smith, Chi | 14-5-6 | 2.42 |
| 1973 | Ken Dryden, Mon | 33-7-13 | 2.26 |
| 1974 | (Tie) Bernie Parent, Phi | 47-13-12 | 1.89 |
| | Tony Esposito, Chi | 34-14-21 | 2.04 |
| 1975 | Bernie Parent, Phi. | 44-14-10 | 2.03 |
| 1976 | Ken Dryden, Mon | 42-10-8 | 2.03 |
| 1977 | Ken Dryden, Mon | 41-6-8 | 2.14 |
| | & Bunny Larocque, Mon | 19-2-4 | 2.09 |
| 1978 | Ken Dryden, Mon | 37-7-7 | 2.05 |
| | & Bunny Larocque, Mon. | 22-3-4 | 2.67 |
| 1979 | Ken Dryden, Mon | 30-10-7 | 2.30 |
| | & Bunny Larocque, Mon. | 22-7-4 | 2.84 |
| 1980 | Bob Sauve, Buf | 20-8-4 | 2.36 |
| | & Don Edwards, Buf. | 27-9-12 | 2.57 |
| 1981 | Richard Sevigny, Mon. | 20-4-3 | 2.40 |
| | Denis Herron, Mon. | 6-9-6 | 3.50 |
| | & Bunny Larocque, Mon. | 16-9-3 | 3.03 |
| 1982 | Billy Smith, NYI | 32-9-4 | 2.97 |
| 1983 | Pete Peeters, Bos | 40-11-9 | 2.36 |
| 1984 | Tom Barrasso, Buf. | 26-12-3 | 2.84 |
| 1985 | Pelle Lindbergh, Phi | 40-17-7 | 3.02 |
| 1986 | John Vanbiesbrouck, NYR | 31-21-5 | 3.32 |
| 1987 | Ron Hextall, Phi. | 37-21-6 | 3.00 |
| 1988 | Grant Fuhr, Edm. | 40-24-9 | 3.43 |
| 1989 | Patrick Roy, Mon | 33-5-6 | 2.47 |
| 1990 | Patrick Roy, Mon | 31-16-5 | 2.53 |
| 1991 | Ed Belfour, Chi. | 43-19-7 | 2.47 |
| 1992 | Patrick Roy, Mon. | 36-22-8 | 2.36 |
| 1993 | Ed Belfour, Chi. | 41-18-11 | 2.59 |
| 1994 | Dominik Hasek, Buf | 30-20-6 | 1.95 |
| 1995 | Dominik Hasek, Buf | 19-14-7 | 2.11 |
| 1996 | Jim Carey, Wash | 35-24-9 | 2.26 |
| 1997 | Dominik Hasek, Buf | 37-20-10 | 2.27 |
| 1998 | Dominik Hasek, Buf | 33-23-13 | 2.09 |
| 1999 | Dominik Hasek, Buf | 30-18-14 | 1.87 |
| 2000 | Olaf Kolzig, Wash | 41-20-11 | 2.24 |
| 2001 | Dominik Hasek, Buf | 37-24-4 | 2.11 |
| 2002 | Jose Theodore, Mon. | 30-24-10 | 2.11 |
| 2003 | Martin Brodeur, NJ. | 41-23-9 | 2.02 |
| 2004 | Martin Brodeur, NJ. | 38-26-11 | 2.03 |

## Lady Byng Memorial Trophy

Awarded to the player "adjudged to have exhibited the best type of sportsmanship and gentlemanly conduct combined with a high standard of playing ability" and named after Lady Evelyn Byng, the wife of former Canadian Governor General (1921-26) Baron Byng of Vimy. Winners selected by PHWA.

**Multiple winners:** Frank Boucher (7); Wayne Gretzky (5); Red Kelly (4); Bobby Bauer, Mike Bossy, Alex Delvecchio and Ron Francis (3); Johnny Bucyk, Marcel Dionne, Paul Kariya, Dave Keon, Stan Mikita, Joey Mullen, Frank Nighbor, Jean Ratelle, Clint Smith and Sid Smith (2).

| Year | | Year | | Year | |
|------|---|------|---|------|---|
| 1925 | Frank Nighbor, Ott., C | 1943 | Max Bentley, Chi., C | 1961 | Red Kelly, Tor., D |
| 1926 | Frank Nighbor, Ott., C | 1944 | Clint Smith, Chi., C | 1962 | Dave Keon, Tor., C |
| 1927 | Billy Burch, NYA, C | 1945 | Bill Mosienko, Chi., RW | 1963 | Dave Keon, Tor., C |
| 1928 | Frank Boucher, NYR, C | 1946 | Toe Blake, Mon., LW | 1964 | Ken Wharram, Chi., RW |
| 1929 | Frank Boucher, NYR, C | 1947 | Bobby Bauer, Bos., RW | 1965 | Bobby Hull, Chi., LW |
| 1930 | Frank Boucher, NYR, C | 1948 | Buddy O'Connor, NYR, C | 1966 | Alex Delvecchio, Det., LW |
| 1931 | Frank Boucher, NYR, C | 1949 | Bill Quackenbush, Det., D | 1967 | Stan Mikita, Chi., C |
| 1932 | Joe Primeau, Tor., C | 1950 | Edgar Laprade, NYR, C | 1968 | Stan Mikita, Chi., C |
| 1933 | Frank Boucher, NYR, C | 1951 | Red Kelly, Det., D | 1969 | Alex Delvecchio, Det., LW |
| 1934 | Frank Boucher, NYR, C | 1952 | Sid Smith, Tor., LW | | |
| 1935 | Frank Boucher, NYR, C | 1953 | Red Kelly, Det., D | 1970 | Phil Goyette, St.L., C |
| 1936 | Doc Romnes, Chi., F | 1954 | Red Kelly, Det., D | 1971 | Johnny Bucyk, Bos., LW |
| 1937 | Marty Barry, Det., C | 1955 | Sid Smith, Tor., LW | 1972 | Jean Ratelle, NYR, C |
| 1938 | Gordie Drillon, Tor., RW | 1956 | Earl Reibel, Det., C | 1973 | Gilbert Perreault, Buf., C |
| 1939 | Clint Smith, NYR, C | 1957 | Andy Hebenton, NYR, RW | 1974 | Johnny Bucyk, Bos., LW |
| 1940 | Bobby Bauer, Bos., RW | 1958 | Camille Henry, NYR, LW | 1975 | Marcel Dionne, Det., C |
| 1941 | Bobby Bauer, Bos., RW | 1959 | Alex Delvecchio, Det., LW | 1976 | Jean Ratelle, NY-Bos., C |
| 1942 | Syl Apps, Tor., C | 1960 | Don McKenney, Bos., C | 1977 | Marcel Dionne, LA, C |
| | | | | 1978 | Butch Goring, LA, C |

| Year | Year | Year |
|------|------|------|
| 1979 Bob MacMillan, Atl., RW | 1988 Mats Naslund, Mon., LW | 1997 Paul Kariya, Ana., LW |
| 1980 Wayne Gretzky, Edm., C | 1989 Joey Mullen, Calg., RW | 1998 Ron Francis, Pit., C |
| 1981 Rick Kehoe, Pit., RW | 1990 Brett Hull, St.L., RW | 1999 Wayne Gretzky, NYR, C |
| 1982 Rick Middleton, Bos., RW | 1991 Wayne Gretzky, LA, C | 2000 Pavol Demitra, St.L, RW |
| 1983 Mike Bossy, NYI, RW | 1992 Wayne Gretzky, LA, C | 2001 Joe Sakic, Col., C |
| 1984 Mike Bossy, NYI, RW | 1993 Pierre Turgeon, NYI, C | 2002 Ron Francis, Car., C |
| 1985 Jari Kurri, Edm., RW | 1994 Wayne Gretzky, LA, C | 2003 Alexander Mogilny, Tor., RW |
| 1986 Mike Bossy, NYI, RW | 1995 Ron Francis, Pit., C | 2004 Brad Richards, TB, C |
| 1987 Joey Mullen, Calg., RW | 1996 Paul Kariya, Ana., LW | |

**Note:** Bill Quackenbush and Red Kelly are the only defensemen to win the Lady Byng.

## James Norris Memorial Trophy

Awarded to the most outstanding defenseman of the year and named after James Norris, the late Detroit Red Wings owner-president. Winners selected by PHWA.

**Multiple winners:** Bobby Orr (8); Doug Harvey (7); Ray Bourque (5); Chris Chelios, Paul Coffey, Nicklas Lidstrom, Pierre Pilote and Denis Potvin (3); Rod Langway, Brian Leetch and Larry Robinson (2).

| Year | Year | Year |
|------|------|------|
| 1954 Red Kelly, Detroit | 1971 Bobby Orr, Boston | 1988 Ray Bourque, Boston |
| 1955 Doug Harvey, Montreal | 1972 Bobby Orr, Boston | 1989 Chris Chelios, Montreal |
| 1956 Doug Harvey, Montreal | 1973 Bobby Orr, Boston | 1990 Ray Bourque, Boston |
| 1957 Doug Harvey, Montreal | 1974 Bobby Orr, Boston | 1991 Ray Bourque, Boston |
| 1958 Doug Harvey, Montreal | 1975 Bobby Orr, Boston | 1992 Brian Leetch, NY Rangers |
| 1959 Tom Johnson, Montreal | 1976 Denis Potvin, NY Islanders | 1993 Chris Chelios, Chicago |
| 1960 Doug Harvey, Montreal | 1977 Larry Robinson, Montreal | 1994 Ray Bourque, Boston |
| 1961 Doug Harvey, Montreal | 1978 Denis Potvin, NY Islanders | 1995 Paul Coffey, Detroit |
| 1962 Doug Harvey, NY Rangers | 1979 Denis Potvin, NY Islanders | 1996 Chris Chelios, Chicago |
| 1963 Pierre Pilote, Chicago | 1980 Larry Robinson, Montreal | 1997 Brian Leetch, NY Rangers |
| 1964 Pierre Pilote, Chicago | 1981 Randy Carlyle, Pittsburgh | 1998 Rob Blake, Los Angeles |
| 1965 Pierre Pilote, Chicago | 1982 Doug Wilson, Chicago | 1999 Al MacInnis, St. Louis |
| 1966 Jacques Laperriere, Montreal | 1983 Rod Langway, Washington | 2000 Chris Pronger, St. Louis |
| 1967 Harry Howell, NY Rangers | 1984 Rod Langway, Washington | 2001 Nicklas Lidstrom, Detroit |
| 1968 Bobby Orr, Boston | 1985 Paul Coffey, Edmonton | 2002 Nicklas Lidstrom, Detroit |
| 1969 Bobby Orr, Boston | 1986 Paul Coffey, Edmonton | 2003 Nicklas Lidstrom, Detroit |
| 1970 Bobby Orr, Boston | 1987 Ray Bourque, Boston | 2004 Scott Niedermayer, NJ |

## Frank Selke Trophy

Awarded to the outstanding defensive forward of the year and named after the late Montreal Canadiens general manager. Winners selected by the PHWA.

**Multiple winners:** Bob Gainey (4); Guy Carbonneau and Jere Lehtinen (3); Sergei Fedorov and Michael Peca (2).

| Year | Year | Year |
|------|------|------|
| 1978 Bob Gainey, Mon., LW | 1987 Dave Poulin, Phi., C | 1996 Sergei Fedorov, Det., C |
| 1979 Bob Gainey, Mon., LW | 1988 Guy Carbonneau, Mon., C | 1997 Michael Peca, Buf., C |
| 1980 Bob Gainey, Mon., LW | 1989 Guy Carbonneau, Mon., C | 1998 Jere Lehtinen, Dal., RW |
| 1981 Bob Gainey, Mon., LW | 1990 Rick Meagher, St.L., C | 1999 Jere Lehtinen, Dal., RW |
| 1982 Steve Kasper, Bos., C | 1991 Dirk Graham, Chi., RW | 2000 Steve Yzerman, Det., C |
| 1983 Bobby Clarke, Phi., C | 1992 Guy Carbonneau, Mon., C | 2001 John Madden, NJ, LW |
| 1984 Doug Jarvis, Wash., C | 1993 Doug Gilmour, Tor., C | 2002 Michael Peca, NYI, C |
| 1985 Craig Ramsay, Buf., LW | 1994 Sergei Fedorov, Det., C | 2003 Jere Lehtinen, Dal., RW |
| 1986 Troy Murray, Chi., C | 1995 Ron Francis, Pit., C | 2004 Kris Draper, Det., C |

## Jack Adams Award

Awarded to the coach "adjudged to have contributed the most to his team's success" and named after the late Detroit Red Wings coach and general manager. Winners selected by NHL Broadcasters' Assn.; (*) indicates division champion.

**Multiple winners:** Pat Burns (3); Scotty Bowman, Jacques Demers and Pat Quinn (2).

| Year | Improvement | | Year | Improvement | |
|------|------|------|------|------|------|
| 1974 Fred Shero, Phi. | 37-30-11 | to 50-16-12* | 1990 Bob Murdoch, Win | 26-42-12 | to 37-32-11 |
| 1975 Bob Pulford, LA | 41-14-23 | to 37-35-8 | 1991 Brian Sutter, St.L | 37-34-9 | to 47-22-11 |
| 1976 Don Cherry, Bos | 40-26-14 | to 48-15-17* | 1992 Pat Quinn, Van | 28-43-9 | to 42-26-12* |
| 1977 Scotty Bowman, Mon | 58-11-11* | to 60-8-12* | 1993 Pat Burns, Tor | 30-43-7 | to 44-29-11 |
| 1978 Bobby Kromm, Det | 6-55-9 | to 32-34-14 | 1994 Jacques Lemaire, NJ | 40-37-7 | to 47-25-12 |
| 1979 Al Arbour, NYI | 48-17-15* | to 51-15-14* | 1995 Marc Crawford, Que | 34-42-8 | to 30-13-5* |
| 1980 Pat Quinn, Phi | 40-25-15 | to 48-12-20* | 1996 Scotty Bowman, Det | 33-11-4* | to 62-13-7* |
| 1981 Red Berenson, St.L | 34-34-12 | to 45-18-17* | 1997 Ted Nolan, Buf | 33-42-7 | to 40-30-12* |
| 1982 Tom Watt, Win | 9-57-14 | to 33-33-14 | 1998 Pat Burns, Bos | 26-47-9 | to 39-30-13 |
| 1983 Orval Tessier, Chi | 30-38-12 | to 47-23-10 | 1999 Jacques Martin, Ott | 34-33-15 | to 44-23-15* |
| 1984 Bryan Murray, Wash | 39-25-16 | to 48-27-5 | 2000 Joel Quenneville, St.L. | 37-32-13 | to 51-20-11* |
| 1985 Mike Keenan, Phi | 44-26-10 | to 53-20-7* | 2001 Bill Barber, Phi | 45-25-12 | to 43-25-11-3 |
| 1986 Glen Sather, Edm | 49-20-11* | to 56-17-7* | 2002 Bob Francis, Pho | 35-27-17-3 | to 40-27-9-6 |
| 1987 Jacques Demers, Det | 17-57-6 | to 34-36-10 | 2003 Jacques Lemaire, Minn. | 26-35-12-9 | to 42-29-10-1 |
| 1988 Jacques Demers, Det | 34-36-10 | to 41-28-11* | 2004 John Tortorella, TB | 36-25-16-5 | to 46-22-8-6* |
| 1989 Pat Burns, Mon | 45-22-13 | to 53-18- 9* | | | |

## Annual Awards (Cont.)
### Lester B. Pearson Award

Awarded to the season's most outstanding player and named after the former diplomat, Nobel Peace Prize winner and Canadian prime minister. Winners selected by the NHL Players Association.

**Multiple winners:** Wayne Gretzky (5); Mario Lemieux (4); Guy Lafleur (3); Marcel Dionne, Phil Esposito, Dominik Hasek, Jaromir Jagr and Mark Messier (2).

| Year | | Year | | Year | |
|------|---|------|---|------|---|
| 1971 | Phil Esposito, Bos., C | 1983 | Wayne Gretzky, Edm., C | 1995 | Eric Lindros, Phi., C |
| 1972 | Jean Ratelle, NYR, C | 1984 | Wayne Gretzky, Edm., C | 1996 | Mario Lemieux, Pit., C |
| 1973 | Bobby Clarke, Phi., C | 1985 | Wayne Gretzky, Edm., C | 1997 | Dominik Hasek, Buf., G |
| 1974 | Phil Esposito, Bos., C | 1986 | Mario Lemieux, Pit., C | 1998 | Dominik Hasek, Buf., G |
| 1975 | Bobby Orr, Bos., D | 1987 | Wayne Gretzky, Edm., C | 1999 | Jaromir Jagr, Pit., RW |
| 1976 | Guy Lafleur, Mon., RW | 1988 | Mario Lemieux, Pit., C | 2000 | Jaromir Jagr, Pit., RW |
| 1977 | Guy Lafleur, Mon., RW | 1989 | Steve Yzerman, Det., C | 2001 | Joe Sakic, Col., C |
| 1978 | Guy Lafleur, Mon., RW | 1990 | Mark Messier, Edm., C | 2002 | Jarome Iginla, Calg., RW |
| 1979 | Marcel Dionne, LA, C | 1991 | Brett Hull, St.L., RW | 2003 | Markus Naslund, Van., LW |
| 1980 | Marcel Dionne, LA, C | 1992 | Mark Messier, NYR, C | 2004 | Martin St. Louis, TB, RW |
| 1981 | Mike Liut, St.L., C | 1993 | Mario Lemieux, Pit., C | | |
| 1982 | Wayne Gretzky, Edm., C | 1994 | Sergei Fedorov, Det., C | | |

### King Clancy Memorial Trophy

Awarded to the player who "best exemplifies leadership on and off the ice and who has made a noteworthy humanitarian contribution to his community" and named after former player, coach, official and executive Frank "King" Clancy. Presented by the NHL's Board of Governors.

| Year | | Year | | Year | |
|------|---|------|---|------|---|
| 1988 | Lanny McDonald, Calg., RW | 1994 | Adam Graves, NYR, LW | 2000 | Curtis Joseph, Tor., G |
| 1989 | Bryan Trottier, NYI, C | 1995 | Joe Nieuwendyk, Calg., C | 2001 | Shjon Podein, Col., LW |
| 1990 | Kevin Lowe, Edm., D | 1996 | Kris King, Win., LW | 2002 | Ron Francis, Car., C |
| 1991 | Dave Taylor, LA, RW | 1997 | Trevor Linden, Van., C | 2003 | Brendan Shanahan, Det., LW |
| 1992 | Ray Bourque, Bos., D | 1998 | Kelly Chase, St.L, RW | 2004 | Jarome Iginla, Calg., RW |
| 1993 | Dave Poulin, Bos., C | 1999 | Rob Ray, Buf., RW | | |

### Bill Masterton Trophy

Awarded to the player who "best exemplifies the qualities of perseverance, sportsmanship and dedication to hockey" and named after the 29-year-old rookie center of the Minnesota North Stars who died of a head injury sustained in a 1968 NHL game. Presented by the PHWA.

| Year | | Year | | Year | |
|------|---|------|---|------|---|
| 1968 | Claude Provost, Mon., RW | 1981 | Blake Dunlop, St.L., C | 1994 | Cam Neely, Bos., RW |
| 1969 | Ted Hampson, Oak., C | 1982 | Chico Resch, Colo., G | 1995 | Pat LaFontaine, Buf., C |
| 1970 | Pit Martin, Chi., C | 1983 | Lanny McDonald, Calg., RW | 1996 | Gary Roberts, Calg., LW |
| 1971 | Jean Ratelle, NYR, C | 1984 | Brad Park, Det., D | 1997 | Tony Granato, SJ, LW |
| 1972 | Bobby Clarke, Phi., C | 1985 | Anders Hedberg, NYR, RW | 1998 | Vincent Lecavalier, TB, C |
| 1973 | Lowell MacDonald, Pit., RW | 1986 | Charlie Simmer, Bos., LW | 1998 | Jamie McLennan, St.L, G |
| 1974 | Henri Richard, Mon., C | 1987 | Doug Jarvis, Hart., C | 1999 | John Cullen, TB, C |
| 1975 | Don Luce, Buf., C | 1988 | Bob Bourne, LA, C | 2000 | Ken Daneyko, NJ, D |
| 1976 | Rod Gilbert, NYR, RW | 1989 | Tim Kerr, Phi., C | 2001 | Adam Graves, NYR, LW |
| 1977 | Ed Westfall, NYI, RW | 1990 | Gord Kluzak, Bos., D | 2002 | Saku Koivu, Mon., C |
| 1978 | Butch Goring, LA, C | 1991 | Dave Taylor, LA, RW | 2003 | Steve Yzerman, Det., C |
| 1979 | Serge Savard, Mon., D | 1992 | Mark Fitzpatrick, NYI, G | 2004 | Bryan Berard, Chi., D |
| 1980 | Al MacAdam, Min., RW | 1993 | Mario Lemieux, Pit., C | | |

## Number One Draft Choices

Overall first choices in the NHL draft since the league staged its first universal amateur draft in 1969. Players are listed with team that selected them; those who became Rookie of the Year are in **bold** type.

| Year | | Year | | Year | |
|------|---|------|---|------|---|
| 1969 | Rejean Houle, Mon., LW | 1982 | Gord Kluzak, Bos., D | 1995 | **Bryan Berard,** Ott., D |
| 1970 | **Gilbert Perreault,** Buf., C | 1983 | Brian Lawton, Min., C | 1996 | Chris Phillips, Ott., D |
| 1971 | Guy Lafleur, Mon., RW | 1984 | **Mario Lemieux,** Pit., C | 1997 | Joe Thornton, Bos., C |
| 1972 | Billy Harris, NYI, RW | 1985 | Wendel Clark, Tor., LW/D | 1998 | Vincent Lecavalier, TB, C |
| 1973 | **Denis Potvin,** NYI, D | 1986 | Joe Murphy, Det., C | 1999 | Patrik Stefan, Atl., C |
| 1974 | Greg Joly, Wash., D | 1987 | Pierre Turgeon, Buf., C | 2000 | Rick DiPietro, NYI, G |
| 1975 | Mel Bridgman, Phi., C | 1988 | Mike Modano, Min., C | 2001 | Ilya Kovalchuk, Atl., RW |
| 1976 | Rick Green, Wash., D | 1989 | Mats Sundin, Que., RW | 2002 | Rick Nash, Clb., LW |
| 1977 | Dale McCourt, Det., C | 1990 | Owen Nolan, Que., RW | 2003 | Marc-Andre Fleury, Pit., G |
| 1978 | **Bobby Smith,** Min., C | 1991 | Eric Lindros, Que., C | 2004 | Alexander Ovechkin, Wash., LW |
| 1979 | Rob Ramage, Colo., D | 1992 | Roman Hamrlik, TB, D | | |
| 1980 | Doug Wickenheiser, Mon., C | 1993 | Alexandre Daigle, Ott., C | 2005 | Sidney Crosby, Pit., C |
| 1981 | **Dale Hawerchuk,** Win., C | 1994 | Ed Jovanovski, Fla., D | | |

## World Hockey Association

### WHA Finals

The World Hockey Association began play in 1972-73 as a 12-team rival of the 56-year-old NHL. The WHA played for the AVCO World Trophy in its seven playoff finals (Avco Financial Services underwrote the playoffs).

**Multiple winners:** Winnipeg (3); Houston (2).

| Year | Winner | Head Coach | Series | Loser | Head Coach |
|------|--------|-----------|--------|-------|-----------|
| 1973 | New England Whalers | Jack Kelley | 4-1 (WWLWW) | Winnipeg Jets | Bobby Hull |
| 1974 | Houston Aeros | Bill Dineen | 4-0 | Chicago Cougars | Pat Stapleton |
| 1975 | Houston Aeros | Bill Dineen | 4-0 | Quebec Nordiques | Jean-Guy Gendron |
| 1976 | Winnipeg Jets | Bobby Kromm | 4-0 | Houston Aeros | Bill Dineen |
| 1977 | Quebec Nordiques | Marc Boileau | 4-3 (LWLWWLW) | Winnipeg Jets | Bobby Kromm |
| 1978 | Winnipeg Jets | Larry Hillman | 4-0 | NE Whalers | Harry Neale |
| 1979 | Winnipeg Jets | Larry Hillman | 4-2 (WWLWLW) | Edmonton Oilers | Glen Sather |

**Playoff MVPs—1973**—No award; **1974**—No award; **1975**—Ron Grahame, Houston, G; **1976**—Ulf Nilsson, Winnipeg, C; **1977**—Serg Bernier, Quebec, C; **1978**—Bobby Guindon, Winnipeg, C; **1979**—Rich Preston, Winnipeg, RW.

### Most Valuable Player

(Gordie Howe Trophy, 1976-79)

| Year | | G | A | Pts |
|------|---|---|---|-----|
| 1973 | Bobby Hull, Win., LW | 51 | 52 | 103 |
| 1974 | Gordie Howe, Hou., RW | 31 | 69 | 100 |
| 1975 | Bobby Hull, Win., LW | 77 | 65 | 142 |
| 1976 | Marc Tardif, Que., LW | 71 | 77 | 148 |
| 1977 | Robbie Ftorek, Pho., C | 46 | 71 | 117 |
| 1978 | Marc Tardif, Que., LW | 65 | 89 | 154 |
| 1979 | Dave Dryden, Edm., G | 41-17-2; 2.89 | | |

### Scoring Leaders

| Year | | Gm | G | A | Pts |
|------|---|----|---|---|-----|
| 1973 | Andre Lacroix, Phi | 78 | 50 | 74 | 124 |
| 1974 | Mike Walton, Min | 78 | 57 | 60 | 117 |
| 1975 | Andre Lacroix, S. Diego | 78 | 41 | 106 | 147 |
| 1976 | Marc Tardif, Que | 81 | 71 | 77 | 148 |
| 1977 | Real Cloutier, Que | 76 | 66 | 75 | 141 |
| 1978 | Marc Tardif, Que | 78 | 65 | 89 | 154 |
| 1979 | Real Cloutier, Que | 77 | 75 | 54 | 129 |

**Note:** In 1979, 18 year-old Rookie of the Year Wayne Gretzky finished third in scoring (46-64—110).

### Rookie of the Year

| Year | | G | A | Pts |
|------|---|---|---|-----|
| 1973 | Terry Caffery, N. Eng., C | 39 | 61 | 100 |
| 1974 | Mark Howe, Hou., LW | 38 | 41 | 79 |
| 1975 | Anders Hedberg, Win., RW | 53 | 47 | 100 |
| 1976 | Mark Napier, Tor., RW | 43 | 50 | 93 |
| 1977 | George Lyle, N. Eng., LW | 39 | 33 | 72 |
| 1978 | Kent Nilsson, Win., C | 42 | 65 | 107 |
| 1979 | Wayne Gretzky, Ind.-Edm., C | 46 | 64 | 110 |

### Best Goaltender

| Year | | Record | GAA |
|------|---|--------|-----|
| 1973 | Gerry Cheevers, Cleveland | 32-20-0 | 2.84 |
| 1974 | Don McLeod, Houston | 33-13-3 | 2.56 |
| 1975 | Ron Grahame, Houston | 33-10-0 | 3.03 |
| 1976 | Michel Dion, Indianapolis | 14-15-1 | 2.74 |
| 1977 | Ron Grahame, Houston | 27-10-2 | 2.74 |
| 1978 | Al Smith, New England | 30-20-3 | 3.22 |
| 1979 | Dave Dryden, Edmonton | 41-17-2 | 2.89 |

### Best Defenseman

| Year | |
|------|---|
| 1973 | J.C. Tremblay, Quebec |
| 1974 | Pat Stapleton, Chicago |
| 1975 | J.C. Tremblay, Quebec |
| 1976 | Paul Shmyr, Cleveland |
| 1977 | Ron Plumb, Cincinnati |
| 1978 | Lars-Erik Sjoberg, Winnipeg |
| 1979 | Rick Ley, New England |

### Coach of the Year

| Year | | | Improvement |
|------|---|---|-------------|
| 1973 | Jack Kelley, N. Eng | | 46-30-2* |
| 1974 | Billy Harris, Tor | 35-39-4 to | 41-33-4 |
| 1975 | Sandy Hucul, Pho | Expan. to | 39-31-8 |
| 1976 | Bobby Kromm, Win | 38-35-5 to | 52-27-2* |
| 1977 | Bill Dineen, Hou | 53-27-0 * to | 50-24-6* |
| 1978 | Bill Dineen, Hou | 50-24-6 * to | 42-34-4 |
| 1979 | John Brophy, Birm | 36-41-3 to | 32-42-6 |

*Won Division.

### WHA All-Star Game

The WHA All-Star Game was an Eastern Division vs Western Division contest from 1973-75. In 1976, the league's five Canadian-based teams played the nine teams in the US. Over the final three seasons—East played West in 1977; AVCO Cup champion Quebec played a WHA All-Star team in 1978; and in 1979, a full WHA All-Star team played a three-game series with Moscow Dynamo of the Soviet Union.

| Year | Result | Host | Coaches | Most Valuable Player |
|------|--------|------|---------|---------------------|
| 1973 | East 6, West 2 | Quebec | Jack Kelley, Bobby Hull | Wayne Carleton, Ottawa |
| 1974 | East 8, West 4 | St. Paul, MN | Jack Kelley, Bobby Hull | Mike Walton, Minnesota |
| 1975 | West 6, East 4 | Edmonton | Bill Dineen, Ron Ryan | Rejean Houle, Quebec |
| 1976 | Canada 6, USA 1 | Cleveland | Jean-Guy Gendron, Bill Dineen | Can—Real Cloutier, Que. USA—Paul Shmyr, Cleve. |
| 1977 | East 4, West 2 | Hartford | Jacques Demers, Bobby Kromm | East—L. Levasseur, Min. West—W. Lindstrom, Win. |
| 1978 | Quebec 5, WHA 4 | Quebec | Marc Boileau, Bill Dineen | Quebec—Marc Tardif WHA—Mark Howe, NE |
| 1979 | WHA def. Moscow Dynamo 3 games to none (4-2, 4-2, 4-3) | Edmonton | Larry Hillman, P. Iburtovich | No awards |

# World Championship
## Men

The World Hockey Championship tournament has been played regularly since 1930. The International Ice Hockey Federation (IIHF), which governs both the World and Winter Olympic tournaments, considers the Olympic champions from 1920-68 to also be the World champions. However the IIHF has not recognized an Olympic champion as World champion since 1968. The IIHF has sanctioned separate World Championships in Olympic years four times—in 1972, 1976, 1992 and 2002. The world championship is officially vacant for the three Olympic years from 1980-88.

**Multiple winners:** Soviet Union/Russia and Canada (23); Sweden (7); Czechoslovakia (6) Czech Republic (5), USA (2).

| Year | | Year | | Year | | Year | |
|---|---|---|---|---|---|---|---|
| 1920 | Canada | 1952 | Canada | 1971 | Soviet Union | 1990 | Soviet Union |
| 1924 | Canada | 1953 | Sweden | 1972 | Czechoslovakia | 1991 | Sweden |
| 1928 | Canada | 1954 | Soviet Union | 1973 | Soviet Union | 1992 | Sweden |
| 1930 | Canada | 1955 | Canada | 1974 | Soviet Union | 1993 | Russia |
| 1931 | Canada | 1956 | Soviet Union | 1975 | Soviet Union | 1994 | Canada |
| 1932 | Canada | 1957 | Sweden | 1976 | Czechoslovakia | 1995 | Finland |
| 1933 | United States | 1958 | Canada | 1977 | Czechoslovakia | 1996 | Czech Republic |
| 1934 | Canada | 1959 | Canada | 1978 | Czechoslovakia | 1997 | Canada |
| 1935 | Canada | 1960 | United States | 1979 | Soviet Union | 1998 | Sweden |
| 1936 | Great Britain | 1961 | Canada | 1980 | Not held | 1999 | Czech Republic |
| 1937 | Canada | 1962 | Sweden | 1981 | Soviet Union | 2000 | Czech Republic |
| 1938 | Canada | 1963 | Soviet Union | 1982 | Soviet Union | 2001 | Czech Republic |
| 1939 | Canada | 1964 | Soviet Union | 1983 | Soviet Union | 2002 | Slovakia |
| 1940-46 | Not held | 1965 | Soviet Union | 1984 | Not held | 2003 | Canada |
| 1947 | Czechoslovakia | 1966 | Soviet Union | 1985 | Czechoslovakia | 2004 | Canada |
| 1948 | Canada | 1967 | Soviet Union | 1986 | Soviet Union | 2005 | Czech Republic |
| 1949 | Czechoslovakia | 1968 | Soviet Union | 1987 | Sweden | | |
| 1950 | Canada | 1969 | Soviet Union | 1988 | Not held | | |
| 1951 | Canada | 1970 | Soviet Union | 1989 | Soviet Union | | |

## Women

The women's World Hockey Championship tournament is governed by the International Ice Hockey Federation (IIHF).

**Multiple winners:** Canada (8).

| Year | | Year | | Year | | Year | | Year | |
|---|---|---|---|---|---|---|---|---|---|
| 1990 | Canada | 1994 | Canada | 1999 | Canada | 2001 | Canada | 2005 | United States |
| 1992 | Canada | 1997 | Canada | 2000 | Canada | 2004 | Canada | | |

# Canada vs. USSR Summits

The first competition between the Soviet National Team and the NHL took place Sept. 2-28, 1972. A team of NHL All-Stars emerged as the winner of the heralded 8-game series, but just barely—winning with a record of 4-3-1 after trailing 1-3-1.

Two years later a WHA All-Star team played the Soviet Nationals and could win only one game and tie three others in eight contests. Two other Canada vs USSR series took place during NHL All-Star breaks: the three-game Challenge Cup at New York in 1979, and the two-game Rendez-Vous '87 in Quebec City in 1987.

The NHL All-Stars played the USSR in a three-game Challenge Cup series in 1979.

## 1972 Team Canada vs. USSR
NHL All-Stars vs Soviet National Team.

| Date | City | Result | Goaltenders |
|---|---|---|---|
| 9/2 | Montreal | USSR, 7-3 | Tretiak/Dryden |
| 9/4 | Toronto | Canada, 4-1 | Esposito/Tretiak |
| 9/6 | Winnipeg | Tie, 4-4 | Tretiak/Esposito |
| 9/8 | Vancouver | USSR, 5-3 | Tretiak/Dryden |
| 9/22 | Moscow | USSR, 5-4 | Tretiak/Esposito |
| 9/24 | Moscow | Canada,3-2 | Dryden/Tretiak |
| 9/26 | Moscow | Canada, 4-3 | Esposito/Tretiak |
| 9/28 | Moscow | Canada, 6-5 | Dryden/Tretiak |

### Standings

| | W | L | T | Pts | GF | GA |
|---|---|---|---|---|---|---|
| Team Canada (NHL) | 4 | 3 | 1 | 9 | 32 | 32 |
| Soviet Union | 3 | 4 | 1 | 7 | 32 | 32 |

### Leading Scorers

**1.** Phil Esposito, Canada, (7-6—13); **2.** Aleksandr Yakushev, USSR (7-4—11); **3.** Paul Henderson, Canada (7-2—9); **4.** Boris Shadrin, USSR (3.5—8); **5.** Valeri Kharlamov, USSR (3-4—7) and Vladimir Petrov, USSR (3-4—7).

## 1979 Challenge Cup Series
NHL All-Stars vs Soviet National Team

| Date | City | Result | Goaltenders |
|---|---|---|---|
| 2/8 | New York | NHL, 4-2 | K. Dryden/Tretiak |
| 2/10 | New York | USSR, 5-4 | Tretiak/K. Dryden |
| 2/11 | New York | USSR, 6-0 | Myshkin/Cheevers |

## 1974 Team Canada vs. USSR
WHA All-Stars vs Soviet National Team.

| Date | City | Result | Goaltenders |
|---|---|---|---|
| 9/17 | Quebec City | Tie, 3-3 | Tretiak/Cheevers |
| 9/19 | Toronto | Canada, 4-1 | Cheevers/Tretiak |
| 9/21 | Winnipeg | USSR, 8-5 | Tretiak/McLeod |
| 9/23 | Vancouver | Tie, 5-5 | Tretiak/Cheevers |
| 10/1 | Moscow | USSR, 3-2 | Tretiak/Cheevers |
| 10/3 | Moscow | USSR, 5-2 | Tretiak/Cheevers |
| 10/5 | Moscow | Tie, 4-4 | Cheevers/Tretiak |
| 10/6 | Moscow | USSR, 3-2 | Sidelinkov/Cheevers |

### Standings

| | W | L | T | Pts | GF | GA |
|---|---|---|---|---|---|---|
| Soviet Union | 4 | 1 | 3 | 11 | 32 | 27 |
| Team Canada (WHA) | 1 | 4 | 3 | 5 | 27 | 32 |

### Leading Scorers

**1.** Bobby Hull, Canada (7-2—9); **2.** Aleksandr Yakushev, USSR (6-2—8), Ralph Backstrom, Canada (4-4—8) and Valeri Kharlamov, USSR (2-6—8); **5.** Gordie Howe, Canada (3-4—7), Andre Lacroix, Canada (1-6—7) and Vladimi Petrov, USSR (1-6—7).

## Rendez-Vous '87
NHL All-Stars vs Soviet National Team

| Date | City | Result | Goaltenders |
|---|---|---|---|
| 2/11 | Quebec | NHL, 4-3 | Fuhr/Belosheykhin |
| 2/13 | Quebec | USSR, 5-3 | Belosheykhin/Fuhr |

## The Canada Cup

After organizing the historic 8-game Team Canada-Soviet Union series of 1972, NHL Players Association executive director Alan Eagleson and the NHL created the Canada Cup in 1976. For the first time, the best players from the world's six major hockey powers—Canada, Czechoslovakia, Finland, Russia, Sweden and the USA—competed together in one tournament.

### 1976
#### Round Robin Standings

|  | W | L | T | Pts | GF | GA |
|---|---|---|---|---|---|---|
| Canada | 4 | 1 | 0 | 8 | 22 | 6 |
| Czechoslovakia | 3 | 1 | 1 | 7 | 19 | 9 |
| Soviet Union | 2 | 2 | 1 | 5 | 23 | 14 |
| Sweden | 2 | 2 | 1 | 5 | 16 | 18 |
| United States | 1 | 3 | 1 | 3 | 14 | 21 |
| Finland | 1 | 4 | 0 | 2 | 16 | 42 |

#### Finals (Best of 3)

| Date | City | Score |
|---|---|---|
| 9/13 | Toronto | Canada 6, Czechoslovakia 0 |
| 9/15 | Montreal | Canada 5, Czechoslovakia 4 (OT) |

**Note:** Darryl Sittler scored the winning goal for Canada at 11:33 in overtime to clinch the Cup, 2 games to none.

#### Leading Scorers

**1.** Victor Hluktov, USSR (5-4—9), Bobby Orr, Canada (2-7—9) and Denis Potvin, Canada (1-8—9); **4.** Bobby Hull, Canada (5-3—8) and Milan Novy, Czechoslovakia (5-3—8).

#### Team MVPs

Canada—Rogie Vachon     Sweden—Borje Salming
Czech.—Milan Novy     USA—Robbie Ftorek
USSR—Alexandr Maltsev     Finland—Matti Hagman
**Tournament MVP**—Bobby Orr, Canada

### 1981
#### Round Robin Standings

|  | W | L | T | Pts | GF | GA |
|---|---|---|---|---|---|---|
| Canada | 4 | 0 | 1 | 9 | 32 | 13 |
| Soviet Union | 3 | 1 | 1 | 7 | 20 | 13 |
| Czechoslovakia | 2 | 1 | 2 | 6 | 21 | 13 |
| United States | 2 | 2 | 1 | 5 | 17 | 19 |
| Sweden | 1 | 4 | 0 | 2 | 13 | 20 |
| Finland | 0 | 4 | 1 | 1 | 6 | 31 |

#### Semifinals

| Date | City | Score |
|---|---|---|
| 9/11 | Ottawa | USSR 4, Czechoslovakia 1 |
| 9/11 | Montreal | Canada 4, United States 1 |

#### Finals

| Date | City | Score |
|---|---|---|
| 9/13 | Montreal | USSR 8, Canada 1 |

#### Leading Scorers

**1.** Wayne Gretzky, Canada (5-7—12); **2.** Mike Bossy, Canada (8-3—11), Bryan Trottier, Canada (3-8—11), Guy Lafleur, Canada (2-9—11), Alexei Kasatonov, USSR (1-10—11).

#### All-Star Team

**Goal**—Vladislav Tretiak, USSR; **Defense**—Arnold Kadlec, Czech. and Alexei Kasatonov, USSR; **Forwards**—Mike Bossy, Canada, Gil Perreault, Canada, and Sergei Shepelev, USSR. **Tournament MVP**—Tretiak.

### 1984
#### Round Robin Standings

|  | W | L | T | Pts | GF | GA |
|---|---|---|---|---|---|---|
| Soviet Union | 5 | 0 | 0 | 10 | 22 | 7 |
| United States | 3 | 1 | 1 | 7 | 21 | 13 |
| Sweden | 3 | 2 | 0 | 6 | 15 | 16 |
| Canada | 2 | 2 | 1 | 5 | 23 | 18 |
| West Germany | 0 | 4 | 1 | 1 | 13 | 29 |
| Czechoslovakia | 0 | 4 | 1 | 1 | 10 | 21 |

#### Semifinals

| Date | City | Score |
|---|---|---|
| 9/12 | Edmonton | Sweden 9, United States 2 |
| 9/15 | Montreal | Canada 3, USSR 2 (OT) |

**Note:** Mike Bossy scored the winning goal for Canada at 12:29 in overtime.

#### Finals (Best of 3)

| Date | City | Score |
|---|---|---|
| 9/16 | Calgary | Canada 5, Sweden 2 |
| 9/18 | Edmonton | Canada 6, Sweden 5 |

#### Leading Scorers

**1.** Wayne Gretzky, Canada (5-7—12); **2.** Michel Goulet, Canada (5-6—11), Kent Nilsson, Sweden (3-8—11), Paul Coffey, Canada (3-8—11); **5.** Hakan Loob, Sweden (6-4—10).

#### All-Star Team

**Goal**—Vladimir Myshkin, USSR; **Defense**—Paul Coffey, Canada and Rod Langway, USA; **Forwards**—Wayne Gretzky, Canada, John Tonelli, Canada, and Sergei Makarov, USSR. **Tournament MVP**—Tonelli.

### 1987
#### Round Robin Standings

|  | W | L | T | Pts | GF | GA |
|---|---|---|---|---|---|---|
| Canada | 3 | 0 | 2 | 8 | 19 | 13 |
| Soviet Union | 3 | 1 | 1 | 7 | 22 | 13 |
| Sweden | 3 | 2 | 0 | 6 | 17 | 14 |
| Czechoslovakia | 2 | 2 | 1 | 5 | 12 | 15 |
| United States | 2 | 3 | 0 | 4 | 13 | 14 |
| Finland | 0 | 5 | 0 | 0 | 9 | 23 |

#### Semifinals

| Date | City | Score |
|---|---|---|
| 9/8 | Hamilton | USSR 4, Sweden 2 |
| 9/9 | Montreal | Canada 5, Czechoslovakia 3 |

#### Finals (Best of 3)

| Date | City | Score |
|---|---|---|
| 9/11 | Montreal | USSR 6, Canada 5 (OT) |
| 9/13 | Hamilton | Canada 6, USSR 5 (2 OT) |
| 9/15 | Hamilton | Canada 6, USSR 5 |

**Note:** In Game 1, Alexander Semak of USSR scored at 5:33 in overtime. In Game 2, Mario Lemieux of Canada scored at 10:01 in the second overtime period. Lemieux also won Game 3 on a goal with 1:26 left in regulation time.

#### Leading Scorers

**1.** Wayne Gretzky, Canada (3-18—21); **2.** Mario Lemieux, Canada (11-7—18); **3.** Sergei Makarov, USSR (7-8—15); **4.** Vladimir Krutov, USSR (7-7—14); **5.** Viacheslav Bykov, USSR (2-7—9); **6.** Ray Bourque, Canada (2-6—8).

#### All-Star Team

**Goal**—Grant Fuhr, Canada; **Defense**—Ray Bourque, Canada and Viacheslav Fetisov, USSR; **Forwards**—Wayne Gretzky, Canada, Mario Lemieux, Canada, and Vladimir Krutov, USSR. **Tournament MVP**—Gretzky.

## 1991

### Round Robin Standings

|  | W | L | T | Pts | GF | GA |
|---|---|---|---|---|---|---|
| Canada | 3 | 0 | 2 | 8 | 21 | 11 |
| United States | 4 | 1 | 0 | 8 | 19 | 15 |
| Finland | 2 | 2 | 1 | 5 | 10 | 13 |
| Sweden | 2 | 3 | 0 | 4 | 13 | 17 |
| Soviet Union | 1 | 3 | 1 | 3 | 14 | 14 |
| Czechoslovakia | 1 | 4 | 0 | 2 | 11 | 18 |

### Semifinals

| Date | City | Score |
|---|---|---|
| 9/11 | Hamilton | United States 7, Finland 3 |
| 9/12 | Toronto | Canada 4, Sweden 0 |

### Finals (Best of 3)

| Date | City | Score |
|---|---|---|
| 9/14 | Montreal | Canada 4, United States 1 |
| 9/16 | Hamilton | Canada 4, United States 2 |

#### Leading Scorers

**1.** Wayne Gretzky, Canada (4-8—12); **2.** Steve Larmer, Canada (6-5—11); **3.** Brett Hull, USA (2-7—9); **4.** Mike Modano, USA (2-7—9); **5.** Mark Messier, Canada (2-6—8).

#### All-Star Team

**Goal**—Bill Ranford, Canada; **Defense**—Al MacInnis, Canada and Chris Chelios, USA; **Forwards**—Wayne Gretzky, Canada, Jeremy Roenick, USA and Mats Sundin, Sweden. **Tournament MVP**—Bill Ranford.

## The World Cup

Formed jointly by the NHL and the NHL Players Association in cooperation with the International Ice Hockey Federation. The inaugural World Cup held games in nine different cities throughout North America and Europe, the most ever by a single international hockey tournament.

## 1996

### Round Robin Standings

| European Pool | W | L | T | Pts | GF | GA |
|---|---|---|---|---|---|---|
| Sweden | 3 | 0 | 0 | 6 | 14 | 3 |
| Finland | 2 | 1 | 0 | 4 | 17 | 11 |
| Germany | 1 | 2 | 0 | 2 | 11 | 15 |
| Czech Republic | 0 | 3 | 0 | 0 | 4 | 17 |

| North American Pool | W | L | T | Pts | GF | GA |
|---|---|---|---|---|---|---|
| United States | 3 | 0 | 0 | 6 | 19 | 8 |
| Canada | 2 | 1 | 0 | 4 | 11 | 10 |
| Russia | 1 | 2 | 0 | 2 | 12 | 14 |
| Slovakia | 0 | 3 | 0 | 0 | 10 | 18 |

### Semifinals

| Date | City | Score |
|---|---|---|
| 9/7 | Philadelphia | Canada 3, Sweden 2 (OT) |
| 9/8 | Ottawa | United States 5, Russia 2 |

### Finals (Best of 3)

| Date | City | Score |
|---|---|---|
| 9/10 | Philadelphia | Canada 4, United States 3 (OT) |
| 9/12 | Montreal | United States 5, Canada 2 |
| 9/14 | Montreal | United States 5, Canada 2 |

#### Leading Scorers

**1.** Brett Hull, USA (7-4—11); **2.** John LeClair, USA (6-4—10); **3.** Mats Sundin, Sweden (4-3—7); Wayne Gretzky, Canada (3-4—7); Doug Weight, USA (3-4—7); Paul Coffey, Canada (0-7—7); Brian Leetch, USA (0-7—7).

#### All-Tournament Team

**Goal**—Mike Richter, USA; **Defense**—Calle Johansson, Sweden and Chris Chelios, USA; **Forwards**—Brett Hull, USA; John LeClair, USA and Mats Sundin, Sweden. **Tournament MVP**—Mike Richter, USA.

## 2004

### Round Robin Standings

| European Pool | W | L | T | Pts | GF | GA |
|---|---|---|---|---|---|---|
| Finland | 2 | 0 | 1 | 5 | 11 | 4 |
| Sweden | 2 | 0 | 1 | 5 | 13 | 9 |
| Czech Republic | 1 | 2 | 0 | 2 | 10 | 10 |
| Germany | 0 | 3 | 0 | 0 | 4 | 15 |

| North American Pool | W | L | T | Pts | GF | GA |
|---|---|---|---|---|---|---|
| Canada | 3 | 0 | 0 | 6 | 10 | 3 |
| Russia | 2 | 1 | 0 | 4 | 9 | 6 |
| United States | 1 | 2 | 0 | 2 | 5 | 6 |
| Slovakia | 0 | 3 | 0 | 0 | 4 | 13 |

### Semifinals

| Date | City | Score |
|---|---|---|
| 9/10 | St. Paul, Minn. | Finland 2, United States 1 |
| 9/11 | Toronto | Canada 4, Czech Rep. 3 (OT) |

### Championship Game

| Date | City | Score |
|---|---|---|
| 9/14 | Toronto | Canada 3, Finland 2 |

#### Leading Scorers

**1.** Fredrik Modin, Sweden (4-4—8); **2.** Vincent Lecavalier, Canada (2-5—7); **3.** Keith Tkachuk, USA (5-1—6); Joe Sakic, Canada (4-2—6); Martin Havlat, Czech Republic (3-3—6); Kimmo Timonen, Finland (1-5—6); Joe Thornton, Canada (1-5—6); Mike Modano, USA (0-6—6); Daniel Alfredsson, Sweden (0-6—6).

#### All-Tournament Team

**Goal**—Martin Brodeur, Canada; **Defense**—Kimmo Timonen, Finland and Adam Foote, Canada; **Forwards**—Vincent Lecavalier, Canada; Saku Koivu, Finland and Fredrik Modin, Sweden. **Tournament MVP**—Vincent Lecavalier, Canada.

## U.S. DIVISION I COLLEGE HOCKEY

### NCAA Men's Frozen Four

The NCAA Division I hockey tournament began in 1948 and was played at the Broadmoor Ice Palace in Colorado Springs from 1948-57. Since 1958, the tournament has moved around the country, stopping for consecutive years only at Boston Garden from 1972-74. Consolation games to determine third place were played from 1949-89 and discontinued in 1990.

**Multiple winners:** Michigan (9); North Dakota and Denver (7); Minnesota and Wisconsin (5); Boston University (4); Lake Superior St. and Michigan Tech (3); Boston College, Colorado College, Cornell, Maine, Michigan St. and RPI (2).

| Year | Champion | Head Coach | Score | Runner-up | Third Place | | |
|------|----------|-----------|-------|-----------|-------------|---|---|
| 1948 | Michigan | Vic Heyliger | 8-4 | Dartmouth | Colorado College and Boston College | | |

| Year | Champion | Head Coach | Score | Runner-up | Third Place | Score | Fourth Place |
|------|----------|-----------|-------|-----------|-------------|-------|--------------|
| 1949 | Boston College | Snooks Kelley | 4-3 | Dartmouth | Michigan | 10-4 | Colorado Col. |
| 1950 | Colorado College | Cheddy Thompson | 13-4 | Boston Univ. | Michigan | 10-6 | Boston College |
| 1951 | Michigan | Vic Heyliger | 7-1 | Brown | Boston Univ. | 7-4 | Colorado College |
| 1952 | Michigan | Vic Heyliger | 4-1 | Colorado Col. | Yale | 4-1 | St. Lawrence |
| 1953 | Michigan | Vic Heyliger | 7-3 | Minnesota | RPI | 6-3 | Boston Univ. |
| 1954 | RPI | Ned Harkness | 5-4 * | Minnesota | Michigan | 7-2 | Boston College |
| 1955 | Michigan | Vic Heyliger | 5-3 | Colorado Col. | Harvard | 6-3 | St. Lawrence |
| 1956 | Michigan | Vic Heyliger | 7-5 | Michigan Tech | St. Lawrence | 6-2 | Boston College |
| 1957 | Colorado College | Tom Bedecki | 13-6 | Michigan | Clarkson | 2-1† | Harvard |
| 1958 | Denver | Murray Armstrong | 6-2 | North Dakota | Clarkson | 5-1 | Harvard |
| 1959 | North Dakota | Bob May | 4-3 * | Michigan St. | Boston College | 7-6† | St. Lawrence |
| 1960 | Denver | Murray Armstrong | 5-3 | Michigan Tech | Boston Univ. | 7-6 | St. Lawrence |
| 1961 | Denver | Murray Armstrong | 12-2 | St. Lawrence | Minnesota | 4-3 | RPI |
| 1962 | Michigan Tech | John MacInnes | 7-1 | Clarkson | Michigan | 5-1 | St. Lawrence |
| 1963 | North Dakota | Barry Thorndycraft | 6-5 | Denver | Clarkson | 5-3 | Boston College |
| 1964 | Michigan | Allen Renfrew | 6-3 | Denver | RPI | 2-1 | Providence |
| 1965 | Michigan Tech | John MacInnes | 8-2 | Boston College | North Dakota | 9-5 | Brown |
| 1966 | Michigan St. | Amo Bessone | 6-1 | Clarkson | Denver | 4-3 | Boston Univ. |
| 1967 | Cornell | Ned Harkness | 4-1 | Boston Univ. | Michigan St. | 6-1 | North Dakota |
| 1968 | Denver | Murray Armstrong | 4-0 | North Dakota | Cornell | 6-1 | Boston College |
| 1969 | Denver | Murray Armstrong | 4-3 | Cornell | Harvard | 6-5† | Michigan Tech |
| 1970 | Cornell | Ned Harkness | 6-4 | Clarkson | Wisconsin | 6-5 | Michigan Tech |
| 1971 | Boston Univ. | Jack Kelley | 4-2 | Minnesota | Denver | 1-0 | Harvard |
| 1972 | Boston Univ. | Jack Kelley | 4-0 | Cornell | Wisconsin | 5-2 | Denver |
| 1973 | Wisconsin | Bob Johnson | 4-2 | Denver | Boston College | 3-1 | Cornell |
| 1974 | Minnesota | Herb Brooks | 4-2 | Michigan Tech | Boston Univ. | 7-5 | Harvard |
| 1975 | Michigan Tech | John MacInnes | 6-1 | Minnesota | Boston Univ. | 10-5 | Harvard |
| 1976 | Minnesota | Herb Brooks | 6-4 | Michigan Tech | Brown | 8-7 | Boston Univ. |
| 1977 | Wisconsin | Bob Johnson | 6-5 * | Michigan | Boston Univ. | 6-5 | N. Hampshire |
| 1978 | Boston Univ. | Jack Parker | 5-3 | Boston College | Bowl. Green | 4-3 | Wisconsin |
| 1979 | Minnesota | Herb Brooks | 4-3 | North Dakota | Dartmouth | 7-3 | N. Hampshire |
| 1980 | North Dakota | Gino Gasparini | 5-2 | N. Michigan | Dartmouth | 8-4 | Cornell |
| 1981 | Wisconsin | Bob Johnson | 6-3 | Minnesota | Mich. Tech | 5-2 | N. Michigan |
| 1982 | North Dakota | Gino Gasparini | 5-2 | Wisconsin | Northeastern | 10-4 | N. Hampshire |
| 1983 | Wisconsin | Jeff Sauer | 6-2 | Harvard | Providence | 4-3 | Minnesota |
| 1984 | Bowling Green | Jerry York | 5-4 * | Minn-Duluth | North Dakota | 6-5† | Michigan St. |
| 1985 | RPI | Mike Addesa | 2-1 | Providence | Minn. Duluth | 7-6† | Boston College |
| 1986 | Michigan St. | Ron Mason | 6-5 | Harvard | Minnesota | 6-4 | Denver |
| 1987 | North Dakota | Gino Gasparini | 5-3 | Michigan St. | Minnesota | 6-3 | Harvard |
| 1988 | Lake Superior St. | Frank Anzalone | 4-3 * | St. Lawrence | Maine | 5-2 | Minnesota |
| 1989 | Harvard | Billy Cleary | 4-3 * | Minnesota | Michigan St. | 7-4 | Maine |

| Year | Champion | Head Coach | Score | Runner-up | Third Place |
|------|----------|-----------|-------|-----------|-------------|
| 1990 | Wisconsin | Jeff Sauer | 7-3 | Colgate | Boston College and Boston Univ. |
| 1991 | Northern Michigan | Rick Comley | 8-7 * | Boston Univ. | Maine and Clarkson |
| 1992 | Lake Superior St. | Jeff Jackson | 5-3 | Wisconsin | Michigan and Michigan St. |
| 1993 | Maine | Shawn Walsh | 5-4 | Lake Superior St. | Boston Univ. and Michigan |
| 1994 | Lake Superior St. | Jeff Jackson | 9-1 | Boston Univ. | Harvard and Minnesota |
| 1995 | Boston Univ. | Jack Parker | 6-2 | Maine | Michigan and Minnesota |
| 1996 | Michigan | Red Berenson | 3-2 * | Colorado Col. | Vermont and Boston Univ. |
| 1997 | North Dakota | Dean Blais | 6-4 | Boston Univ. | Colorado College and Michigan |
| 1998 | Michigan | Red Berenson | 3-2 * | Boston College | New Hampshire and Ohio St. |
| 1999 | Maine | Shawn Walsh | 3-2 * | New Hampshire | Boston College and Michigan St. |
| 2000 | North Dakota | Dean Blais | 4-2 | Boston College | St. Lawrence and Maine |
| 2001 | Boston College | Jerry York | 3-2 * | North Dakota | Michigan and Michigan St. |
| 2002 | Minnesota | Don Lucia | 4-3 * | Maine | Michigan and New Hampshire |
| 2003 | Minnesota | Don Lucia | 5-1 | New Hampshire | Michigan and Cornell |
| 2004 | Denver | George Gwozdecky | 1-0 | Maine | Minnesota Duluth and Boston College |
| 2005 | Denver | George Gwozdecky | 4-1 | North Dakota | Colorado College and Minnesota |

**\*Championship game overtime goals: 1954**—1:54; **1959**—4:22; **1977**—0: 23; **1984**—7:11 in 4th OT; **1988**—4:46; **1989**—4:16; **1991**—1:57 in 3rd OT; **1996**—3:35; **1998**—10:50; **2001**—4:43; **2002**—16:58.

†Consolation game overtimes ended in 1st OT except in 1957, '59, and '69, which all ended in 2nd OT.

**Note:** Runners-up Denver (1973) and Wisconsin (1992) had participation voided by the NCAA for using ineligible players.

## U.S. Division I College Hockey (Cont.)

### Tournament Most Outstanding Player

The Most Outstanding Players of each NCAA Div. I tournament since 1948. Winners of the award who did not play for the tournament champion are in **bold** type. In 1960, three players, none on the winning team, shared the award.

**Multiple winners:** Lou Angotti and Marc Behrend (2).

| Year | Year | Year |
|---|---|---|
| 1948 **Joe Riley,** Dartmouth, F | 1966 Gaye Cooley, Mich. St., G | 1986 Mike Donnelly, Mich. St., F |
| 1949 **Dick Desmond,** Dart., G | 1967 Walt Stanowski, Cornell, D | 1987 Tony Hrkac, N. Dakota, F |
| 1950 **Ralph Bevins,** Boston U., G | 1968 Gerry Powers, Denver, G | 1988 Bruce Hoffort, Lk. Superior, G |
| 1951 **Ed Whiston,** Brown, G | 1969 Keith Magnuson, Denver, D | 1989 Ted Donato, Harvard, F |
| 1952 **Ken Kinsley,** Colo. Col., G | 1970 Dan Lodboa, Cornell, D | 1990 Chris Tancill, Wisconsin, F |
| 1953 John Matchefts, Mich., F | 1971 Dan Brady, Boston U., G | 1991 Scott Beattie, No. Mich., F |
| 1954 Abbie Moore, RPI, F | 1972 Tim Regan, Boston U., G | 1992 Paul Constantin, Lk. Superior, F |
| 1955 **Phil Hilton,** Colo. Col., D | 1973 Dean Talafous, Wisc., F | 1993 Jim Montgomery, Maine, F |
| 1956 Lorne Howes, Mich., G | 1974 Brad Shelstad, Minn., G | 1994 Sean Tallaire, Lk. Superior, F |
| 1957 Bob McCusker, Colo. Col., F | 1975 Jim Warden, Mich. Tech, G | 1995 Chris O'Sullivan, Boston U., F |
| 1958 Murray Massier, Denver, F | 1976 Tom Vannelli, Minn., F | 1996 Brendan Morrison, Michigan, F |
| 1959 Reg Morelli, N. Dakota, F | 1977 Julian Baretta, Wisc., G | 1997 Matt Henderson, N. Dakota, F |
| 1960 **Lou Angotti,** Mich. Tech, F; | 1978 Jack O'Callahan, Boston U., D | 1998 Marty Turco, Michigan, G |
| **Bob Marquis,** Boston U., F; | 1979 Steve Janaszak, Minn., G | 1999 Alfie Michaud, Maine, G |
| & **Barry Urbanski,** BU, G | 1980 Doug Smail, N. Dakota, F | 2000 Lee Goren, N. Dakota, F |
| 1961 Bill Masterton, Denver, F | 1981 Marc Behrend, Wisc., G | 2001 Chuck Kobasew, Boston College, F |
| 1962 Lou Angotti, Mich. Tech, F | 1982 Phil Sykes, N. Dakota, F | 2002 Grant Potulny, Minnesota, F |
| 1963 Al McLean, N. Dakota, F | 1983 Marc Behrend, Wisc., G | 2003 Thomas Vanek, Minnesota, F |
| 1964 Bob Gray, Michigan, G | 1984 Gary Kruzich, Bowl. Green, G | 2004 Adam Berkhoel, Denver, G |
| 1965 Gary Milroy, Mich. Tech, F | 1985 **Chris Terreri,** Prov., G | 2005 Peter Mannino, Denver, G |

### Hobey Baker Award

College hockey's Player of the Year award; voted on by a national panel of sportswriters, broadcasters, college coaches and pro scouts (plus a fan vote beginning in 2003). First presented in 1981 by the Decathlon Athletic Club of Bloomington, Minn., in the name of the Princeton collegiate hockey and football star who was killed in a plane crash.

| Year | Year | Year |
|---|---|---|
| 1981 Neal Broten, Minnesota, F | 1990 Kip Miller, Michigan St., F | 1999 Jason Krog, UNH, F |
| 1982 George McPhee, Bowl. Green, F | 1991 Dave Emma, Boston College, F | 2000 Mike Mottau, Boston College, D |
| 1983 Mark Fusco, Harvard, D | 1992 Scott Pellerin, Maine, F | 2001 Ryan Miller, Michigan St., G |
| 1984 Tom Kurvers, Minn. Duluth, D | 1993 Paul Kariya, Maine, F | 2002 Jordan Leopold, Minnesota, D |
| 1985 Bill Watson, Minn. Duluth, F | 1994 Chris Marinucci, Minn. Duluth, F | 2003 Peter Sejna, Colorado Coll., F |
| 1986 Scott Fusco, Harvard, F | 1995 Brian Holzinger, Bowl. Green, F | 2004 Junior Lessard, Minn. Duluth, F |
| 1987 Tony Hrkac, North Dakota, F | 1996 Brian Bonin, Minnesota, F | 2005 Marty Sertich, Colorado Coll., F |
| 1988 Robb Stauber, Minnesota, G | 1997 Brendan Morrison, Michigan, F | |
| 1989 Lane MacDonald, Harvard, F | 1998 Chris Drury, Boston U., F | |

## NCAA Women's Frozen Four

Women's college hockey was officially introduced as an NCAA Division I sport in 2000-01.

**Multiple winner:** Minnesota-Duluth (3); Minnesota (2).

| Year | Champion | Head Coach | Score | Runner-up | Third Place | Score | Fourth Place |
|---|---|---|---|---|---|---|---|
| 2001 | Minnesota Duluth | Shannon Miller | 4-2 | St. Lawrence | Harvard | 3-2 | Dartmouth |
| 2002 | Minnesota Duluth | Shannon Miller | 3-2 | Brown | (tie) Niagara and Minnesota, 2-2 | | |
| 2003 | Minnesota Duluth | Shannon Miller | 4-3* | Harvard | Dartmouth | 4-2 | Minnesota |
| 2004 | Minnesota | Laura Halldorson | 6-2 | Harvard | St. Lawrence | 2-1 | Dartmouth |
| 2005 | Minnesota | Laura Halldorson | 4-3 | Harvard | St. Lawrence | 5-1 | Dartmouth |

**\*Championship game overtime goal: 2003**—4:19 in 2nd OT.

### Tournament Most Outstanding Player

The Most Outstanding Players of each NCAA Women's Division I tournament since 2001. Winner of the award who did not play for the tournament champion are in **bold** type.

| Year | Year | Year |
|---|---|---|
| 2001 Maria Rooth, Minn. Duluth, F | 2003 Caroline Ouellette, Minn. Duluth, F | 2005 Natalie Darwitz, Minnesota, F |
| 2002 **Kristy Zamora,** Brown, F | 2004 Krissy Wendell, Minnesota, F | |

### Patty Kazmaier Award

Awarded annually to the women's Division I player who displays the highest standards of personal and team excellence during the season; voted on by a 13-member panel of national media, college coaches and one USA Hockey member. First presented in 1998, in the name of the Princeton collegiate hockey and lacrosse star who died in 1990 of a rare blood disease.

**Multiple winner:** Jennifer Botterill (2).

| Year | Year | Year |
|---|---|---|
| 1998 Brandy Fisher, New Hampshire, F | 2001 Jennifer Botterill, Harvard, F | 2004 Angela Ruggiero, Harvard, D |
| 1999 A.J. Mleczko, Harvard, F | 2002 Brooke Whitney, Northeastern, F | 2005 Krissy Wendell, Minnesota, F |
| 2000 Ali Brewer, Brown, G | 2003 Jennifer Botterill, Harvard, F | |

# College Sports

*Illinois' controversial* **Chief Illiniwek** *performs at halftime of an Illini hoops game.*

AP/Wide World Photos

# Mascot Matters

*The NCAA's new policy on Native American nicknames and imagery sent 18 schools scrambling.*

**Michael Morrison**
*is co-editor of the ESPN Sports Almanac.*

After years of meetings, interviews and research, the NCAA Executive Committee put the proverbial hammer down on schools with Native American nicknames in 2005. Not surprisingly, their actions led to confusion, shouting matches and well...more meetings, interviews and research.

Early in the year, the Executive Committee (made up of select NCAA chancellors and presidents) distributed self-evaluations to 33 schools that were judged to have potentially offensive Native American nicknames and/or mascots.

The evaluations included the origin and history of the nickname; how decisions are made about the mascot; attempts to value diversity and sportsmanship; and perhaps most importantly, correspondence between the institution and local Native American tribes. Or to put another way, what do the namesake tribes formally think about the school's use of their name, culture and imagery?

At their August 4 meeting, the Executive Committee issued their ruling – 14 schools "passed" their self-exams, 18 "failed" and one received an extension (see accompanying box on page 430 for complete list). For the 18 that failed, action would be swift and severe.

The schools in question must remove any hostile or abusive references on uniforms or other paraphernalia during any of the 88 NCAA championships.

Additionally, if these schools don't make appropriate changes by Feb. 1, 2006, they will be prohibited from hosting any NCAA championship event, unless they had already been selected to do so. Even then, however, those schools would be required to take "reasonable steps" to cover up any Native American references before the games can begin.

The inevitable question is — why are these nicknames and mascots hostile and abusive during the championships season but not during the regular season?

Committee chairman Walter Harrison (president of the University of Hartford) explains, "Colleges and universities may adopt any mascots they wish, as that is an

AP/Wide World Photos

*In August, Florida State was removed from the list of 18 schools deemed to have "hostile and abusive" nicknames. Mascot* **Chief Osceola** *poses here with center David Castillo.*

institutional matter. But as a national association, we believe that mascots, nicknames or images deemed hostile or abusive in terms of race, ethnicity or national origin should not be visible at the championship events that we administer."

All 18 schools on the *wanted* list were given the opportunity to appeal. And appeal they did. First up in the process was Florida State, who has been using "Seminole" as its nickname with the consent of the Seminole Tribe of Florida since 1947. The image of a student dressed as Chief Osceola riding onto the field on a horse and thrusting a flaming spear into the ground has become synonymous with Florida State football.

In June the Seminole Tribe of Florida passed a resolution supporting the school's use of the nickname and tribal images. So most FSU supporters, and president T.K. Wetherell were stunned that their school even made the list.

"That the NCAA would now label our close bond with the Seminole Tribe of Florida as culturally 'hostile and abusive' is both outrageous and insulting," Wetherell said.

NCAA Vice President for Diversity and Inclusion Charlotte Westerhaus argued, "other Seminole Tribes are not supportive."

In the end, the Seminole Tribe of Oklahoma shifted its position, paving the

AP/Wide World Photos

*Utah won its appeal to continue using its nickname with no NCAA postseason implications.*

way for a slam-dunk Florida State win. Officially the school won its appeal because "the staff committee noted the unique relationship between the university and the Seminole Tribe of Florida."

The following week, Central Michigan and Utah were removed from the list of 18 for the same reason — "the relationship between the universities and the Saginaw Chippewa Indian Tribe of Michigan and the Northern Ute Indian Tribe, respectively."

The case of North Dakota was a little more complex because the Fighting Sioux had three namesake tribes instead of just one. And of those three, two opposed the nickname and imagery and one had made

*continued on page 432* ▶

## Listworthy

Thirty-three schools performed mandatory self-evaluations in early 2005 in order to clarify their position on the continued use of Native American mascots, nicknames and imagery.

Of those 33, 14 either removed all references to Native American culture or were judged to have never had such references:

Cal State Stanislaus Warriors
Lycoming Warriors
Winona State Warriors
Hawaii-Manoa Warriors/Wahine
Eastern Connecticut State Warriors
East Stroudsburg Warriors
Husson College Eagles (formerly Braves)
Merrimack College Warriors
SE Missouri St. Redhawks (formerly Indians)
West Georgia Braves (until end of '05)
Stonehill Skyhawks (formerly Chieftains)
San Diego State Aztecs
Wisconsin Lutheran Warriors
† North Carolina-Pembroke Braves

† over 20 percent of the student body is of Native American descent.

Eighteen were subject to the NCAA's new policies:

Alcorn State Braves
Arkansas State Indians
Bradley Braves
\* Central Michigan Chippewas
Carthage College Redmen
Catawba College Indians
Chowan College Braves
\* Florida State Seminoles
Illinois Illini
Indiana (Penn.) Indians
Louisiana-Monroe Indians
McMurry Indians
Midwestern State Indians
Mississippi College Choctaws
Newberry College Indians
North Dakota Fighting Sioux
SE Oklahoma State Savages
\* Utah Utes

\* Later removed following an appeal to the Executive Committee (as of Sept. 30, 2005).

One school was granted an extension:
William & Mary Tribe

# The Ten Biggest Stories of the Year in College Sports

**10** Michigan freshman Samantha Findlay blasts a three-run home run in the 10th inning of the NCAA Division I softball championship game to lead her team to a 4-1 win over UCLA. The Wolverines are the first school east of the Mississippi River to win the title.

**9** The Georgia Lady Bulldogs become the first team in NCAA history to win all five relays at the Division I Swimming and Diving Championship. They also take four individual titles in cruising to their fourth title.

**8** The NCAA Executive Committee gives President Myles Brand a vote of confidence, electing to extend his contract by two years. Brand's contract now runs through Dec. 31, 2009 and can be extended on an annual basis thereafter.

**7** The highly successful Oklahoma State wrestling team wins its 33rd NCAA Division I championship and three-peats for the first time since 1956. The Cowboys crown an NCAA record-tying five individual champions and score a school-record 153 points. Michigan places second, 70 points behind.

**6** Stanford wins its 11th consecutive Directors' Cup as the NCAA's best overall Division I program. Grand Valley St., Mich. (Division II) and Williams, Mass. (Division III) also repeat while Azusa Pacific, CA wins its first NAIA title.

**5** The annual NCAA report on graduation rates shows a three percentage point increase in the rate at which Division I-A football players earn their degrees (from 54 to 57 percent). Overall, student athletes graduate at a 62 percent rate, as compared to 60 for the entire student body.

**4** Florida's Kerron Clement breaks Michael Johnson's 400-meter indoor world record at the NCAA Division I men's track and field championship. Clement runs a 44.57 to better Johnson's 44.63 set in 1995. Three months later he successfully defends his 400-m hurdles crown at the outdoor championships.

**3** Hurricanes Katrina and Rita inflict significant damage to numerous athletic facilities in New Orleans and all along the Gulf Coast, causing in some instances the cancellation of entire seasons. Tulane cancels its first semester of classes, but the school's athletic teams continue to compete.

**2** After several years of haggling and lawsuits, the NCAA purchases the rights to the preseason and postseason men's NIT from the Metropolitan Intercollegiate Basketball Association (MIBA) for $56.5 million.

**1** The NCAA does its part to eliminate what it believes are "hostile and abusive" Native American nicknames and mascots during postseason play. Eighteen schools are cited as having unacceptable imagery. By late September, three are already cleared via appeals.

statements both favoring and objecting to the use.

On Sept. 28, North Dakota's appeal was denied. President Charles Kupchella immediately announced plans for another appeal, followed by possible legal action. The University will, however, still be allowed to host the West Regional of the NCAA Division I Hockey Championship in late March, 2006 without making alterations to the 2,000 Sioux logos in Ralph Engelstad Arena. According to the NCAA's Bernard Franklin, "it just wasn't reasonable to cover up or remove all of the Native American imagery in the arena." After that, however, no more NCAA championships are allowed in the unless alterations are made.

"I can get really cynical and say it's OK to be hostile and abusive for another six months," said Kupchella.

And so it goes. By the end of September, appeals from several of the 14 schools still on the list were either in the works or expected. The NCAA has taken its share of heat from critics who claim the organization is overly bureaucratic and sticking its nose where it doesn't belong. But for many Native Americans, or for that matter anyone who view tomahawk chops, war chants and cartoon logos with oversized teeth and red faces as derogatory, this is at least a step in the right direction — a step that was long overdue.

## Perfecto!

Ten teams were undefeated champions in 2005. They are listed below along with their record:

| Sport | Team | Record |
|---|---|---|
| D-III Field Hockey | Salisbury, MD | 22-0 |
| D-III Football | Linfield, OR | 13-0 |
| D-I M Lacrosse | Johns Hopkins | 16-0 |
| D-III M Lacrosse | Salisbury, MD | 20-0 |
| D-II M Soccer | Seattle | 22-0-1 |
| D-II W Lacrosse | Stonehill, MA | 21-0 |
| D-II W Tennis | Armstrong Atl. | 30-0 |
| Nat. W Water Polo | UCLA | 33-0 |

**Source**: NCAA News

## Streaking

Kenyon, OH has won an astounding 26 consecutive Division III NCAA men's swimming and diving championships, far and away the longest current championship streak.

| Team | Consec. Titles |
|---|---|
| Kenyon D-III M Swimming/Diving | 26 |
| Methodist, NC D-III W Golf | 8 |
| Wis-La Crosse D-III M Indoor T&F | 5 |
| Truman, MO D-II W Swimming/Diving | 5 |
| Abilene Christian D-II M Outdoor T&F | 4 |
| Auburn M Swimming/Diving | 4 |

**Source**: NCAA News

# NCAA Schools & Champions

SPORTS ALMANAC

## NCAA Division I-A Football Schools
### 2005 Season
Conferences and coaches as of Sept. 30, 2005.

**Joining ACC in 2005:** BOSTON COLLEGE from Big East.
**Joining Big East in 2005:** CINCINNATI, LOUISVILLE and SOUTH FLORIDA from Conference USA.
**Joining Conference USA in 2005:** MARSHALL and CENTRAL FLORIDA from Mid-American; RICE, SMU, TULSA and UTEP from the WAC.
**Joining Mountain West in 2005:** TCU from Conference USA.
**Joining Sun Belt in 2005:** FLORIDA ATLANTIC and FLORIDA INTERNATIONAL from I-AA Independent (2004 transition).
**Joining WAC in 2005:** IDAHO, NEW MEXICO STATE and UTAH ST from Sun Belt.
**To I-A Independent from conferences in 2005:** TEMPLE from Big East and ARMY from Conference USA.
**Joining Mid-American in 2007:** TEMPLE from I-A Independent (affiliate member in 2005 & 2006).

| | Nickname | Conference | Head Coach | Location | Colors |
|---|---|---|---|---|---|
| Air Force | Falcons | Mountain West | Fisher DeBerry | Colo. Springs, CO | Blue/Silver |
| Akron | Zips | Mid-American | J.D. Brookhart | Akron, OH | Blue/Gold |
| Alabama | Crimson Tide | SEC-West | Mike Shula | Tuscaloosa, AL | Crimson/White |
| Arizona | Wildcats | Pac-10 | Mike Stoops | Tucson, AZ | Cardinal/Navy |
| Arizona St. | Sun Devils | Pac-10 | Dirk Koetter | Tempe, AZ | Maroon/Gold |
| Arkansas | Razorbacks | SEC-West | Houston Nutt | Fayetteville, AR | Cardinal/White |
| Arkansas St. | Indians | Sun Belt | Steve Roberts | State Univ., AR | Scarlet/Black |
| Army | Cadets, Black Knights | Independent | Bobby Ross | West Point, NY | Black/Gold/Gray |
| Auburn | Tigers | SEC-West | Tommy Tuberville | Auburn, AL | Orange/Blue |
| Ball St. | Cardinals | Mid-American | Brady Hoke | Muncie, IN | Cardinal/White |
| Baylor | Bears | Big 12 | Guy Morriss | Waco, TX | Green/Gold |
| Boise St. | Broncos | WAC | Dan Hawkins | Boise, ID | Orange/Blue |
| Boston College | Eagles | ACC | Tom O'Brien | Chestnut Hill, MA | Maroon/Gold |
| Bowling Green | Falcons | Mid-American | Gregg Brandon | Bowling Green, OH | Orange/Brown |
| Brigham Young | Cougars | Mountain West | Bronco Mendenhall | Provo, UT | Blue/White/Tan |
| Buffalo | Bulls | Mid-American | Jim Hofher | Buffalo, NY | Royal Blue/White |
| California | Golden Bears | Pac-10 | Jeff Tedford | Berkeley, CA | Blue/Gold |
| Central Florida | Golden Knights | USA | George O'Leary | Orlando, FL | Black/Gold |
| Central Michigan | Chippewas | Mid-American | Brian Kelly | Mt. Pleasant, MI | Maroon/Gold |
| Cincinnati | Bearcats | Big East | Mark Dantonio | Cincinnati, OH | Red/Black |
| Clemson | Tigers | ACC | Tommy Bowden | Clemson, SC | Purple/Orange |
| Colorado | Buffaloes | Big 12 | Gary Barnett | Boulder, CO | Silver/Gold/Black |
| Colorado St. | Rams | Mountain West | Sonny Lubick | Ft. Collins, CO | Green/Gold |
| Connecticut | Huskies | Big East | Randy Edsall | Storrs, CT | Blue/White |
| Duke | Blue Devils | ACC | Ted Roof | Durham, NC | Royal Blue/White |
| East Carolina | Pirates | USA | Skip Holtz | Greenville, NC | Purple/Gold |
| Eastern Michigan | Eagles | Mid-American | Jeff Genyk | Ypsilanti, MI | Green/White |
| Florida | Gators | SEC-East | Urban Meyer | Gainesville, FL | Orange/Blue |
| Florida Atlantic | Owls | Sun Belt | H. Schnellenberger | Boca Raton, FL | Blue/Red |
| Florida Int'l | Golden Panthers | Sun Belt | Don Strock | Miami, FL | Blue/Gold |
| Florida St. | Seminoles | ACC | Bobby Bowden | Tallahassee, FL | Garnet/Gold |
| Fresno St. | Bulldogs | WAC | Pat Hill | Fresno, CA | Red/Blue |
| Georgia | Bulldogs | SEC-East | Mark Richt | Athens, GA | Red/Black |
| Georgia Tech | Yellow Jackets | ACC | Chan Gailey | Atlanta, GA | Old Gold/White |
| Hawaii | Warriors | WAC | June Jones | Honolulu, HI | Green/White |
| Houston | Cougars | USA | Art Briles | Houston, TX | Scarlet/White |
| Idaho | Vandals | WAC | Nick Holt | Moscow, ID | Silver/Gold |
| Illinois | Fighting Illini | Big Ten | Ron Zook | Champaign, IL | Orange/Blue |
| Indiana | Hoosiers | Big Ten | Terry Hoeppner | Bloomington, IN | Cream/Crimson |
| Iowa | Hawkeyes | Big Ten | Kirk Ferentz | Iowa City, IA | Old Gold/Black |
| Iowa St. | Cyclones | Big 12 | Dan McCarney | Ames, IA | Cardinal/Gold |
| Kansas | Jayhawks | Big 12 | Mark Mangino | Lawrence, KS | Crimson/Blue |
| Kansas St. | Wildcats | Big 12 | Bill Snyder | Manhattan, KS | Purple/White |
| Kent St. | Golden Flashes | Mid-American | Doug Martin | Kent, OH | Navy Blue/Gold |
| Kentucky | Wildcats | SEC-East | Rich Brooks | Lexington, KY | Blue/White |
| LSU | Fighting Tigers | SEC-West | Les Miles | Baton Rouge, LA | Purple/Gold |
| LA-Lafayette | Ragin' Cajuns | Sun Belt | Rickey Bustle | Lafayette, LA | Vermilion/White |

| | Nickname | Conference | Head Coach | Location | Colors |
|---|---|---|---|---|---|
| **LA-Monroe** | Indians | Sun Belt | Charlie Weatherbie | Monroe, LA | Maroon/Gold |
| **Louisiana Tech** | Bulldogs | WAC | Jack Bicknell III | Ruston, LA | Red/Blue |
| **Louisville** | Cardinals | Big East | Bob Petrino | Louisville, KY | Red/Black/White |
| **Marshall** | Thundering Herd | USA | Mark Snyder | Huntington, WV | Green/White |
| **Maryland** | Terrapins, Terps | ACC | Ralph Friedgen | College Park, MD | Red/White/Black/Gold |
| **Memphis** | Tigers | USA | Tommy West | Memphis, TN | Blue/Gray |
| **Miami-FL** | Hurricanes | ACC | Larry Coker | Coral Gables, FL | Orange/Grn./Wt. |
| **Miami-OH** | RedHawks | Mid-American | Shane Montgomery | Oxford, OH | Red/White |
| **Michigan** | Wolverines | Big Ten | Lloyd Carr | Ann Arbor, MI | Maize/Blue |
| **Michigan St.** | Spartans | Big Ten | John L. Smith | E. Lansing, MI | Green/White |
| **Middle Tennessee** | Blue Raiders | Sun Belt | Andy McCollum | Murfreesboro, TN | Royal Blue/White |
| **Minnesota** | Golden Gophers | Big Ten | Glen Mason | Minneapolis, MN | Maroon/Gold |
| **Mississippi** | Ole Miss, Rebels | SEC-West | Ed Orgeron | Oxford, MS | Cardinal/Navy Bl. |
| **Mississippi St.** | Bulldogs | SEC-West | Sylvester Croom | Starkville, MS | Maroon/White |
| **Missouri** | Tigers | Big 12 | Gary Pinkel | Columbia, MO | Old Gold/Black |
| **Navy** | Midshipmen | Independent | Paul Johnson | Annapolis, MD | Navy Blue/Gold |
| **Nebraska** | Cornhuskers | Big 12 | Bill Callahan | Lincoln, NE | Scarlet/Cream |
| **Nevada** | Wolf Pack | WAC | Chris Ault | Reno, NV | Silver/Blue |
| **New Mexico** | Lobos | Mountain West | Rocky Long | Albuquerque, NM | Cherry/Silver |
| **New Mexico St.** | Aggies | WAC | Hal Mumme | Las Cruces, NM | Crimson/White |
| **North Carolina** | Tar Heels | ACC | John Bunting | Chapel Hill, NC | Carolina Blue/Wt. |
| **North Carolina St.** | Wolfpack | ACC | Chuck Amato | Raleigh, NC | Red/White |
| **North Texas** | Mean Green | Sun Belt | Darrell Dickey | Denton, TX | Green/White |
| **Northern Illinois** | Huskies | Mid-American | Joe Novak | DeKalb, IL | Cardinal/Black |
| **Northwestern** | Wildcats | Big Ten | Randy Walker | Evanston, IL | Purple/White |
| **Notre Dame** | Fighting Irish | Independent | Charlie Weis | Notre Dame, IN | Gold/Blue |
| **Ohio University** | Bobcats | Mid-American | Frank Solich | Athens, OH | Hunter Green/Wt. |
| **Ohio St.** | Buckeyes | Big Ten | Jim Tressel | Columbus, OH | Scarlet/Gray |
| **Oklahoma** | Sooners | Big 12 | Bob Stoops | Norman, OK | Crimson/Cream |
| **Oklahoma St.** | Cowboys | Big 12 | Mike Gundy | Stillwater, OK | Orange/Black |
| **Oregon** | Ducks | Pac-10 | Mike Bellotti | Eugene, OR | Green/Yellow |
| **Oregon St.** | Beavers | Pac-10 | Mike Riley | Corvallis, OR | Orange/Black |
| **Penn St.** | Nittany Lions | Big Ten | Joe Paterno | University Park, PA | Blue/White |
| **Pittsburgh** | Panthers | Big East | Dave Wannstedt | Pittsburgh, PA | Blue/Gold |
| **Purdue** | Boilermakers | Big Ten | Joe Tiller | W. Lafayette, IN | Old Gold/Black |
| **Rice** | Owls | USA | Ken Hatfield | Houston, TX | Blue/Gray |
| **Rutgers** | Scarlet Knights | Big East | Greg Schiano | New Brunswick, NJ | Scarlet |
| **San Diego St.** | Aztecs | Mountain West | Tom Craft | San Diego, CA | Scarlet/Black |
| **San Jose St.** | Spartans | WAC | Dick Tomey | San Jose, CA | Gold/White/Blue |
| **South Carolina** | Gamecocks | SEC-East | Steve Spurrier | Columbia, SC | Garnet/Black |
| **South Florida** | Bulls | Big East | Jim Leavitt | Tampa, FL | Green/Gold |
| **SMU** | Mustangs | USA | Phil Bennett | Dallas, TX | Red/Blue |
| **Southern Miss.** | Golden Eagles | USA | Jeff Bower | Hattiesburg, MS | Black/Gold |
| **Stanford** | Cardinal | Pac-10 | Walt Harris | Stanford, CA | Cardinal/White |
| **Syracuse** | Orange | Big East | Greg Robinson | Syracuse, NY | Orange |
| **Temple** | Owls | Independent | Bobby Wallace | Philadelphia, PA | Cherry/White |
| **Tennessee** | Volunteers | SEC-East | Phillip Fulmer | Knoxville, TN | Orange/White |
| **Texas** | Longhorns | Big 12 | Mack Brown | Austin, TX | Burnt Orange/Wt. |
| **Texas A&M** | Aggies | Big 12 | Dennis Franchione | College Station, TX | Maroon/White |
| **TCU** | Horned Frogs | Mountain West | Gary Patterson | Ft. Worth, TX | Purple/White |
| **Texas Tech** | Red Raiders | Big 12 | Mike Leach | Lubbock, TX | Scarlet/Black |
| **Toledo** | Rockets | Mid-American | Tom Amstutz | Toledo, OH | Blue/Gold |
| **Troy** | Trojans | Sun Belt | Larry Blakeney | Troy, AL | Cardinal/Slvr./Blk. |
| **Tulane** | Green Wave | USA | Chris Scelfo | New Orleans, LA | Olive Grn./Sky Bl. |
| **Tulsa** | Golden Hurricane | USA | Steve Kragthorpe | Tulsa, OK | Blue/Gold/Crimson |
| **UAB** | Blazers | USA | Watson Brown | Birmingham, AL | Green/Gold |
| **UCLA** | Bruins | Pac-10 | Karl Dorrell | Los Angeles, CA | Blue/Gold |
| **UNLV** | Rebels | Mountain West | Mike Sanford | Las Vegas, NV | Scarlet/Gray |
| **USC** | Trojans | Pac-10 | Pete Carroll | Los Angeles, CA | Cardinal/Gold |
| **Utah** | Utes | Mountain West | Kyle Whittingham | Salt Lake City, UT | Crimson/White |
| **Utah St.** | Aggies | WAC | Brent Guy | Logan, UT | Navy Blue/White |
| **UTEP** | Miners | USA | Mike Price | El Paso, TX | Orange/Blue/Silver |
| **Vanderbilt** | Commodores | SEC-East | Bobby Johnson | Nashville, TN | Black/Gold |
| **Virginia** | Cavaliers | ACC | Al Groh | Charlottesville, VA | Orange/Blue |
| **Virginia Tech** | Hokies, Gobblers | ACC | Frank Beamer | Blacksburg, VA | Orange/Maroon |
| **Wake Forest** | Demon Deacons | ACC | Jim Grobe | Winston-Salem, NC | Old Gold/Black |
| **Washington** | Huskies | Pac-10 | Tyrone Willingham | Seattle, WA | Purple/Gold |
| **Washington St.** | Cougars | Pac-10 | Bill Doba | Pullman, WA | Crimson/Gray |
| **West Virginia** | Mountaineers | Big East | Rich Rodriguez | Morgantown, WV | Old Gold/Blue |
| **Western Michigan** | Broncos | Mid-American | Bill Cubit | Kalamazoo, MI | Brown/Gold |
| **Wisconsin** | Badgers | Big Ten | Barry Alvarez | Madison, WI | Cardinal/White |
| **Wyoming** | Cowboys | Mountain West | Joe Glenn | Laramie, WY | Brown/Gold |

## NCAA Division I-AA Football Schools
### 2005 Season
Conferences and coaches as of Sept. 30, 2005.

**Joining Southland in 2005:** SOUTHEASTERN LOUISIANA from Independent.

**Joining Mid-Eastern in 2005:** FLORIDA A&M from Independent (former Mid-Eastern member spent 2004 as an Independent after an aborted move to Division I-A).

**Joining Big Sky in 2006:** NORTHERN COLORADO from Great West.

**Joining Ohio Valley in 2007:** AUSTIN PEAY ST. from Pioneer (program will leave Pioneer League after the 2005 season and spend 2006 as a I-AA Independent).

**New Conference in 2007:** Colonial Athletic Association (12 teams) — DELAWARE, HOFSTRA, JAMES MADISON, MAINE, MASSACHUSETTS, NEW HAMPSHIRE, NORTHEASTERN, RHODE ISLAND, RICHMOND, TOWSON, VILLANOVA and WILLIAM & MARY from Atlantic 10 (conference will no longer sponsor football).

| | Nickname | Conference | Head Coach | Location | Colors |
|---|---|---|---|---|---|
| **Alabama A&M** | Bulldogs | SWAC | Anthony Jones | Huntsville, AL | Maroon/White |
| **Alabama St.** | Hornets | SWAC | Charles Coe | Montgomery, AL | Black/Gold |
| **Albany** | Great Danes | Northeast | Bob Ford | Albany, NY | Purple/Gold |
| **Alcorn St.** | Braves | SWAC | Johnny Thomas | Lorman, MS | Purple/Gold |
| **Appalachian St.** | Mountaineers | Southern | Jerry Moore | Boone, NC | Black/Gold |
| **Ark.-Pine Bluff** | Golden Lions | SWAC | Mo Forte | Pine Bluff, AR | Black/Gold |
| **Austin Peay St.** | Governors | Pioneer | Carroll McCray | Clarksville, TN | Red/White |
| **Bethune-Cookman** | Wildcats | Mid-Eastern | Alvin Wyatt | Daytona Beach, FL | Maroon/Gold |
| **Brown** | Bears | Ivy | Phil Estes | Providence, RI | Brown/Red/White |
| **Bucknell** | Bison | Patriot | Tim Landis | Lewisburg, PA | Orange/Blue |
| **Butler** | Bulldogs | Pioneer | Kit Cartwright | Indianapolis, IN | Blue/White |
| **Cal Poly** | Mustangs | Great West | Rich Ellerson | San Luis Obispo, CA | Green/Gold |
| **Central Conn. St.** | Blue Devils | Northeast | Tom Masella | New Britain, CT | Blue/White |
| **Charleston So.** | Buccaneers | Big South | Jay Mills | Charleston, SC | Blue/Gold |
| **Chattanooga** | Mocs | Southern | Rodney Allison | Chattanooga, TN | Navy Blue/Old Gold |
| **The Citadel** | Bulldogs | Southern | Kevin Higgins | Charleston, SC | Blue/White |
| **Coastal Carolina** | Chanticleers | Big South | David Bennett | Conway, SC | Green/Bronze/Black |
| **Colgate** | Raiders | Patriot | Dick Biddle | Hamilton, NY | Maroon/White/Gray |
| **Columbia** | Lions | Ivy | Bob Shoop | New York, NY | Lt. Blue/White |
| **Cornell** | Big Red | Ivy | Jim Knowles | Ithaca, NY | Carnelian/White |
| **Dartmouth** | Big Green | Ivy | Buddy Teevens | Hanover, NH | Green/White |
| **Davidson** | Wildcats | Pioneer | Tripp Merritt | Davidson, NC | Red/Black |
| **Dayton** | Flyers | Pioneer | Mike Kelly | Dayton, OH | Red/Blue |
| **Delaware** | Blue Hens | Atlantic 10 | K.C. Keeler | Newark, DE | Blue/Gold |
| **Delaware St.** | Hornets | Mid-Eastern | Al Lavan | Dover, DE | Red/Blue |
| **Drake** | Bulldogs | Pioneer | Rob Ash | Des Moines, IA | Blue/White |
| **Duquesne** | Dukes | Metro Atlantic | Jerry Schmitt | Pittsburgh, PA | Red/Blue |
| **Eastern Illinois** | Panthers | Ohio Valley | Bob Spoo | Charleston, IL | Blue/Gray |
| **Eastern Kentucky** | Colonels | Ohio Valley | Danny Hope | Richmond, KY | Maroon/White |
| **Eastern Washington** | Eagles | Big Sky | Paul Wulff | Cheney, WA | Red/White |
| **Elon** | Phoenix | Southern | Paul Hamilton | Elon, NC | Maroon/Gold |
| **Florida A&M** | Rattlers | Mid-Eastern | Rubin Carter | Tallahassee, FL | Orange/Green |
| **Fordham** | Rams | Patriot | Ed Foley | Bronx, NY | Maroon/White |
| **Furman** | Paladins | Southern | Bobby Lamb | Greenville, SC | Purple/White |
| **Gardner-Webb** | Bulldogs | Big South | Steve Patton | Boiling Springs, NC | Scarlet/Black |
| **Georgetown** | Hoyas | Patriot | Bob Benson | Washington, DC | Blue/Gray |
| **Georgia Southern** | Eagles | Southern | Mike Sewak | Statesboro, GA | Blue/White |
| **Grambling St.** | Tigers | SWAC | Melvin Spears | Grambling, LA | Black/Gold |
| **Hampton** | Pirates | Mid-Eastern | Joe Taylor | Hampton, VA | Royal Blue/White |
| **Harvard** | Crimson | Ivy | Tim Murphy | Cambridge, MA | Crimson/Black/White |
| **Hofstra** | Pride | Atlantic 10 | Joe Gardi | Hempstead, NY | Gold/White/Blue |
| **Holy Cross** | Crusaders | Patriot | Tom Gilmore | Worcester, MA | Royal Purple |
| **Howard** | Bison | Mid-Eastern | Rayford T. Petty | Washington, DC | Blue/Wt./Red |
| **Idaho St.** | Bengals | Big Sky | Larry Lewis | Pocatello, ID | Orange/Black |
| **Illinois St.** | Redbirds | Gateway | Denver Johnson | Normal, IL | Red/White |
| **Indiana St.** | Sycamores | Gateway | Lou West | Terre Haute, IN | Royal Blue/White |
| **Iona** | Gaels | Metro Atlantic | Fred Mariani | New Rochelle, NY | Maroon/Gold |
| **Jackson St.** | Tigers | SWAC | James Bell | Jackson, MS | Blue/White |
| **Jacksonville** | Dolphins | Pioneer | Steve Gilbert | Jacksonville, FL | Green/White |
| **Jacksonville St.** | Gamecocks | Ohio Valley | Jack Crowe | Jacksonville, AL | Red/White |
| **James Madison** | Dukes | Atlantic 10 | Mickey Matthews | Harrisonburg, VA | Purple/Gold |
| **Lafayette** | Leopards | Patriot | Frank Tavani | Easton, PA | Maroon/White |
| **La Salle** | Explorers | Metro Atlantic | Phil Longo | Philadelphia, PA | Blue/Gold |
| **Lehigh** | Mountain Hawks | Patriot | Pete Lembo | Bethlehem, PA | Brown/White |

| | Nickname | Conference | Head Coach | Location | Colors |
|---|---|---|---|---|---|
| Liberty | Flames | Big South | Ken Karcher | Lynchburg, VA | Red/White/Blue |
| Maine | Black Bears | Atlantic 10 | Jack Cosgrove | Orono, ME | Blue/White |
| Marist | Red Foxes | Metro Atlantic | Jim Parady | Poughkeepsie, NY | Red/White |
| Massachusetts | Minutemen | Atlantic 10 | Don Brown | Amherst, MA | Maroon/White |
| McNeese St. | Cowboys | Southland | Tommy Tate | Lake Charles, LA | Blue/Gold |
| Miss. Valley St. | Delta Devils | SWAC | Willie Totten | Itta Bena, MS | Green/White |
| Missouri St. | Bears | Gateway | Randy Ball | Springfield, MO | Maroon/White |
| Monmouth | Hawks | Northeast | Kevin Callahan | W. Long Branch, NJ | Royal Blue/White |
| Montana | Grizzlies | Big Sky | Bobby Hauck | Missoula, MT | Maroon/Silver |
| Montana St. | Bobcats | Big Sky | Mike Kramer | Bozeman, MT | Blue/Gold |
| Morehead St. | Eagles | Pioneer | Matt Ballard | Morehead, KY | Blue/Gold |
| Morgan St. | Bears | Mid-Eastern | Donald Hill-Eley | Baltimore, MD | Blue/Orange |
| Murray St. | Racers | Ohio Valley | Joe Pannunzio | Murray, KY | Blue/Gold |
| New Hampshire | Wildcats | Atlantic 10 | Sean McDonnell | Durham, NH | Blue/White |
| Nicholls St. | Colonels | Southland | Jay Thomas | Thibodaux, LA | Red/Gray |
| Norfolk State | Spartans | Mid-Eastern | Pete Adrian | Norfolk, VA | Green/Gold |
| North Carolina A&T | Aggies | Mid-Eastern | George Small | Greensboro, NC | Blue/Gold |
| North Dakota St. | Bison | Great West | Craig Bohl | Fargo, ND | Green/Yellow |
| Northeastern | Huskies | Atlantic 10 | Rocky Hager | Boston, MA | Red/Black |
| Northern Arizona | Lumberjacks | Big Sky | Jerome Souers | Flagstaff, AZ | Blue/Gold |
| Northern Colorado | Bears | Great West | O. Kay Dalton | Greeley, CO | Blue/Gold |
| Northern Iowa | Panthers | Gateway | Mark Farley | Cedar Falls, IA | Purple/Old Gold |
| Northwestern St. | Demons | Southland | Scott Stoker | Natchitoches, LA | Purple/White |
| Pennsylvania | Quakers | Ivy | Al Bagnoli | Philadelphia, PA | Red/Blue |
| Portland St. | Vikings | Big Sky | Tim Walsh | Portland, OR | Green/White |
| Prairie View A&M | Panthers | SWAC | Henry Frazier | Prairie View, TX | Purple/Gold |
| Princeton | Tigers | Ivy | Roger Hughes | Princeton, NJ | Orange/Black |
| Rhode Island | Rams | Atlantic 10 | Tim Stowers | Kingston, RI | Light Blue/Navy/Wt. |
| Richmond | Spiders | Atlantic 10 | Dave Clawson | Richmond, VA | Red/Blue |
| Robert Morris | Colonials | Northeast | Joe Walton | Moon Township, PA | Blue/White |
| Sacramento St. | Hornets | Big Sky | Steve Mooshagian | Sacramento, CA | Green/Gold |
| Sacred Heart | Pioneers | Northeast | Paul Gorham | Fairfield, CT | Scarlet/White |
| St. Francis-PA | Red Flash | Northeast | Dave Opfar | Loretto, PA | Red/White |
| Saint Peter's | Peacocks | Metro Atlantic | Chris Taylor | Jersey City, NJ | Blue/White |
| Sam Houston St. | Bearkats | Southland | Todd Whitten | Huntsville, TX | Orange/White |
| Samford | Bulldogs | Ohio Valley | Bill Gray | Birmingham, AL | Crimson/Blue |
| San Diego | Toreros | Pioneer | Jim Harbaugh | San Diego, CA | Lt. Blue/Navy |
| Savannah St. | Tigers | Independent | Richard Basil | Savannah, GA | Orange/Blue |
| South Carolina St. | Bulldogs | Mid-Eastern | Oliver Pough | Orangeburg, SC | Garnet/Blue |
| South Dakota St. | Jackrabbits | Great West | John Stiegelmeier | Brookings, SD | Yellow/Blue |
| SE Missouri St. | Redhawks | Ohio Valley | Tim Billings | Cape Girardeau, MO | Red/Black |
| Southeastern Louisiana | Lions | Southland | Dennis Roland | Hammond, LA | Green/Gold |
| Southern-BR | Jaguars | SWAC | Pete Richardson | Baton Rouge, LA | Blue/Gold |
| Southern Illinois | Salukis | Gateway | Jerry Kill | Cardondale, IL | Maroon/White |
| Southern Utah | Thunderbirds | Great West | Wes Meier | Cedar City, UT | Scarlet/White |
| S.F. Austin St. | Lumberjacks | Southland | Robert McFarland | Nacogdoches, TX | Purple/White |
| Stony Brook | Seawolves | Northeast | Sam Kornhauser | Stony Brook, NY | Scarlet/Gray |
| Tennessee-Martin | Skyhawks | Ohio Valley | Matt Griffin | Martin, TN | Orange/White/Blue |
| Tennessee St. | Tigers | Ohio Valley | James Webster | Nashville, TN | Blue/White |
| Tennessee Tech | Golden Eagles | Ohio Valley | Mike Hennigan | Cookeville, TN | Purple/Gold |
| Texas Southern | Tigers | SWAC | Steve Wilson | Houston, TX | Maroon/Gray |
| Texas St. | Bobcats | Southland | David Bailiff | San Marcos, TX | Maroon/Gold |
| Towson | Tigers | Atlantic 10 | Gordy Combs | Towson, MD | Gold/White |
| UC-Davis | Aggies | Great West | Bob Biggs | Davis, CA | Yale Blue/Gold |
| Valparaiso | Crusaders | Pioneer | Stacy Adams | Valparaiso, IN | Brown/Gold |
| Villanova | Wildcats | Atlantic 10 | Andy Talley | Villanova, PA | Blue/White |
| VMI | Keydets | Big South | Cal McCombs | Lexington, VA | Red/White/Yellow |
| Wagner | Seahawks | Northeast | Walt Hameline | Staten Island, NY | Green/White |
| Weber St. | Wildcats | Big Sky | Ron McBride | Ogden, UT | Royal Purple/White |
| Western Carolina | Catamounts | Southern | Kent Briggs | Cullowhee, NC | Purple/Gold |
| Western Illinois | Leathernecks | Gateway | Don Patterson | Macomb, IL | Purple/Gold |
| Western Kentucky | Hilltoppers | Gateway | David Elson | Bowling Green, KY | Red/White |
| William & Mary | Tribe | Atlantic 10 | Jimmye Laycock | Williamsburg, VA | Green/Gold/Silver |
| Wofford | Terriers | Southern | Mike Ayers | Spartanburg, SC | Old Gold/Black |
| Yale | Bulldogs, Elis | Ivy | Jack Siedlecki | New Haven, CT | Yale Blue/White |
| Youngstown St. | Penguins | Gateway | Jon Heacock | Youngstown, OH | Red/White |

## NCAA Division I Basketball Schools
### 2005-2006 Season
Conferences and coaches as of Sept. 30, 2005.

**Joining ACC in 2005-06:** BOSTON COLLEGE from Big East.
**Joining Atlantic Sun in 2005-06:** EAST TENNESSEE STATE from Southern; NORTH FLORIDA and KENNESAW ST. from Div. II.
**Joining Atlantic 10 in 2005-06:** CHARLOTTE and SAINT LOUIS from Conference USA.
**Joining Big East in 2005-06:** CINCINNATI, DEPAUL, LOUISVILLE, MARQUETTE and SOUTH FLORIDA from C-USA.
**Joining Colonial Athletic Association in 2005-06:** GEORGIA STATE from Atlantic Sun; NORTHEASTERN from America East.
**Joining Conference USA in 2005-06:** MARSHALL from Mid-American; RICE, SMU, TULSA and UTEP from the WAC; CENTRAL FLORIDA from Atlantic Sun.
**Joining Mountain West in 2005-06:** TCU from Conference USA.
**Joining Sun Belt in 2005-06:** TROY from Atlantic Sun.
**Joining WAC in 2005-06:** NEW MEXICO ST. from Sun Belt; IDAHO and UTAH STATE from Big West.
**Joining Big Sky in 2006-07:** NORTHERN COLORADO from Independent.
**Joining Southland in 2006-07:** TEXAS A&M-CORPUS CHRISTI from Independent.
**Joining Sun Belt in 2006-07:** FLORIDA ATLANTIC from Atlantic Sun; LA-MONROE from Southland.
**Joining Big West in 2007-08:** UC-Davis from Independent.

| | Nickname | Conference | Head Coach | Location | Colors |
|---|---|---|---|---|---|
| Air Force | Falcons | Mountain West | Jeff Bzdelik | Colo. Springs, CO | Blue/Silver |
| Akron | Zips | Mid-American | Keith Dambrot | Akron, OH | Blue/Gold |
| Alabama | Crimson Tide | SEC-West | Mark Gottfried | Tuscaloosa, AL | Crimson/White |
| Alabama A&M | Bulldogs | SWAC | Vann Pettaway | Huntsville, AL | Maroon/White |
| Alabama St. | Hornets | SWAC | Lewis Jackson | Montgomery, AL | Black/Gold |
| Albany | Great Danes | America East | Will Brown | Albany, NY | Purple/Gold |
| Alcorn St. | Braves | SWAC | Samuel West | Lorman, MS | Purple/Gold |
| American | Eagles | Patriot | Jeff Jones | Washington, DC | Red/Blue |
| Appalachian St. | Mountaineers | Southern | Houston Fancher | Boone, NC | Black/Gold |
| Arizona | Wildcats | Pac-10 | Lute Olson | Tucson, AZ | Cardinal/Navy |
| Arizona St. | Sun Devils | Pac-10 | Rob Evans | Tempe, AZ | Maroon/Gold |
| Arkansas | Razorbacks | SEC-West | Stan Heath | Fayetteville, AR | Cardinal/White |
| Ark.-Little Rock | Trojans | Sun Belt | Steve Shields | Little Rock, AR | Silver/Black/Maroon |
| Ark.-Pine Bluff | Golden Lions | SWAC | Van Holt | Pine Bluff, AR | Black/Gold |
| Arkansas St. | Indians | Sun Belt | Dickey Nutt | State Univ., AR | Scarlet/Black |
| Army | Black Knights | Patriot | Jim Crews | West Point, NY | Black/Gold/Gray |
| Auburn | Tigers | SEC-West | Jeff Lebo | Auburn, AL | Orange/Blue |
| Austin Peay St. | Governors | Ohio Valley | Dave Loos | Clarksville, TN | Red/White |
| Ball St. | Cardinals | Mid-American | Tim Buckley | Muncie, IN | Cardinal/White |
| Baylor | Bears | Big 12 | Scott Drew | Waco, TX | Green/Gold |
| Belmont | Bruins | Atlantic Sun | Rick Byrd | Nashville, TN | Navy Blue/Red |
| Bethune-Cookman | Wildcats | Mid-Eastern | Clifford Reed | Daytona Beach, FL | Maroon/Gold |
| Binghamton | Bearcats | America East | Al Walker | Binghamton, NY | Green/Black/White |
| Birmingham Southern | Panthers | Big South | Duane Reboul | Birmingham, AL | Black/Gold |
| Boise St. | Broncos | WAC | Greg Graham | Boise, ID | Orange/Blue |
| Boston College | Eagles | ACC | Al Skinner | Chestnut Hill, MA | Maroon/Gold |
| Boston University | Terriers | America East | Dennis Wolff | Boston, MA | Scarlet/White |
| Bowling Green | Falcons | Mid-American | Dan Dakich | Bowling Green, OH | Orange/Brown |
| Bradley | Braves | Mo. Valley | Jim Les | Peoria, IL | Red/White |
| Brigham Young | Cougars | Mountain West | Dave Rose | Provo, UT | Blue/White/Tan |
| Brown | Bears | Ivy | Glen Miller | Providence, RI | Brown/Cardinal/White |
| Bucknell | Bison | Patriot | Pat Flannery | Lewisburg, PA | Orange/Blue |
| Buffalo | Bulls | Mid-American | R. Witherspoon | Buffalo, NY | Royal Blue/White |
| Butler | Bulldogs | Horizon | Todd Lickliter | Indianapolis, IN | Blue/White |
| California | Golden Bears | Pac-10 | Ben Braun | Berkeley, CA | Blue/Gold |
| Cal Poly | Mustangs | Big West | Kevin Bromley | San Luis Obispo, CA | Green/Gold |
| CS-Fullerton | Titans | Big West | Bob Burton | Fullerton, CA | Blue/Orange/White |
| CS-Northridge | Matadors | Big West | Bobby Braswell | Northridge, CA | Red/White/Black |
| Campbell | Camels | Atlantic Sun | Robbie Laing | Buies Creek, NC | Orange/Black |
| Canisius | Golden Griffins | Metro Atlantic | Mike MacDonald | Buffalo, NY | Blue/Gold |
| Centenary | Gents, Gentlemen | Mid-Continent | Rob Flaska | Shreveport, LA | Maroon/White |
| Central Conn. St. | Blue Devils | Northeast | Howie Dickenman | New Britain, CT | Blue/White |
| Central Florida | Golden Knights | USA | Kirk Speraw | Orlando, FL | Black/Gold |
| Central Michigan | Chippewas | Mid-American | Jay Smith | Mt. Pleasant, MI | Maroon/Gold |
| Charleston So. | Buccaneers | Big South | Barclay Radebaugh | Charleston, SC | Blue/Gold |
| Charlotte | 49ers | Atlantic 10 | Bobby Lutz | Charlotte, NC | Green/White |
| Chattanooga | Mocs | Southern | John Shulman | Chattanooga, TN | Navy Blue/Old Gold |
| Chicago St. | Cougars | Mid-Continent | Kevin Jones | Chicago, IL | Green/White |
| Cincinnati | Bearcats | Big East | Andy Kennedy | Cincinnati, OH | Red/Black |
| The Citadel | Bulldogs | Southern | Pat Dennis | Charleston, SC | Blue/White |
| Clemson | Tigers | ACC | Oliver Purnell | Clemson, SC | Purple/Orange |
| Cleveland St. | Vikings | Horizon | Mike Garland | Cleveland, OH | Forest Green/White |

## NCAA Division I Basketball Schools (Cont.)

| | Nickname | Conference | Head Coach | Location | Colors |
|---|---|---|---|---|---|
| Coastal Carolina | Chanticleers | Big South | Buzz Peterson | Conway, SC | Green/Bronze/Black |
| Colgate | Raiders | Patriot | Emmett Davis | Hamilton, NY | Maroon/Gray/White |
| College of Charleston | Cougars | Southern | Tom Herrion | Charleston, SC | Maroon/White |
| Colorado | Buffaloes | Big 12 | Ricardo Patton | Boulder, CO | Silver/Gold/Black |
| Colorado St. | Rams | Mountain West | Dale Layer | Ft. Collins, CO | Green/Gold |
| Columbia | Lions | Ivy | Joseph Jones | New York, NY | Lt. Blue/White |
| Connecticut | Huskies | Big East | Jim Calhoun | Storrs, CT | Blue/White |
| Coppin St. | Eagles | Mid-Eastern | Ron Mitchell | Baltimore, MD | Royal Blue/Gold |
| Cornell | Big Red | Ivy | Steve Donahue | Ithaca, NY | Carnelian/White |
| Creighton | Bluejays | Mo. Valley | Dana Altman | Omaha, NE | Blue/White |
| Dartmouth | Big Green | Ivy | Terry Dunn | Hanover, NH | Green/White |
| Davidson | Wildcats | Southern | Bob McKillop | Davidson, NC | Red/Black |
| Dayton | Flyers | Atlantic 10 | Brian Gregory | Dayton, OH | Red/Blue |
| Delaware | Fightin' Blue Hens | Colonial | David Henderson | Newark, DE | Blue/Gold |
| Delaware St. | Hornets | Mid-Eastern | Greg Jackson | Dover, DE | Red/Columbia Blue |
| Denver | Pioneers | Sun Belt | Terry Carroll | Denver, CO | Crimson/Gold |
| DePaul | Blue Demons | Big East | Jerry Wainwright | Chicago, IL | Scarlet/Blue |
| Detroit Mercy | Titans | Horizon | Perry Watson | Detroit, MI | Red/White/Blue |
| Drake | Bulldogs | Mo. Valley | Tom Davis | Des Moines, IA | Blue/White |
| Drexel | Dragons | Colonial | Bruiser Flint | Philadelphia, PA | Navy Blue/Gold |
| Duke | Blue Devils | ACC | Mike Krzyzewski | Durham, NC | Royal Blue/White |
| Duquesne | Dukes | Atlantic 10 | Danny Nee | Pittsburgh, PA | Red/Blue |
| East Carolina | Pirates | USA | Ricky Stokes | Greenville, NC | Purple/Gold |
| East Tenn. St. | Buccaneers | Atlantic Sun | Murry Bartow | Johnson City, TN | Blue/Gold |
| Eastern Illinois | Panthers | Ohio Valley | Mike Miller | Charleston, IL | Blue/Gray |
| Eastern Kentucky | Colonels | Ohio Valley | Jeff Neubauer | Richmond, KY | Maroon/White |
| Eastern Michigan | Eagles | Mid-American | Charles Ramsey | Ypsilanti, MI | Green/White |
| Eastern Washington | Eagles | Big Sky | Mike Burns | Cheney, WA | Red/White |
| Elon | Phoenix | Southern | Ernie Nestor | Elon, NC | Maroon/Gold |
| Evansville | Aces | Mo. Valley | Steve Merfeld | Evansville, IN | Purple/White |
| Fairfield | Stags | Metro Atlantic | Tim O'Toole | Fairfield, CT | Cardinal Red |
| Fairleigh Dickinson | Knights | Northeast | Tom Green | Teaneck, NJ | Maroon/Blue |
| Florida | Gators | SEC-East | Billy Donovan | Gainesville, FL | Orange/Blue |
| Florida A&M | Rattlers | Mid-Eastern | Mike Gillespie | Tallahassee, FL | Orange/Green |
| Florida Atlantic | Owls | Atlantic Sun | Matt Doherty | Boca Raton, FL | Blue/Red |
| Florida Int'l | Golden Panthers | Sun Belt | Sergio Rouco | Miami, FL | Blue/Gold |
| Florida St. | Seminoles | ACC | Leonard Hamilton | Tallahassee, FL | Garnet/Gold |
| Fordham | Rams | Atlantic 10 | Dereck Whittenburg | Bronx, NY | Maroon/White |
| Fresno St. | Bulldogs | WAC | Steve Cleveland | Fresno, CA | Red/Blue |
| Furman | Paladins | Southern | Larry Davis | Greenville, SC | Purple/White |
| Gardner-Webb | Bulldogs | Atlantic Sun | Rick Scruggs | Boiling Springs, NC | Scarlet/Black |
| George Mason | Patriots | Colonial | Jim Larranaga | Fairfax, VA | Green/Gold |
| George Washington | Colonials | Atlantic 10 | Karl Hobbs | Washington, DC | Buff/Blue |
| Georgetown | Hoyas | Big East | John Thompson III | Washington, DC | Blue/Gray |
| Georgia | Bulldogs, 'Dawgs | SEC-East | Dennis Felton | Athens, GA | Red/Black |
| Georgia Southern | Eagles | Southern | Jeff Price | Statesboro, GA | Blue/White |
| Georgia St. | Panthers | Colonial | Michael Perry | Atlanta, GA | Roy. Blue/White |
| Georgia Tech | Yellow Jackets | ACC | Paul Hewitt | Atlanta, GA | Old Gold/White |
| Gonzaga | Bulldogs, Zags | West Coast | Mark Few | Spokane, WA | Blue/White/Red |
| Grambling St. | Tigers | SWAC | Larry Wright | Grambling, LA | Black/Gold |
| Hampton | Pirates | Mid-Eastern | Bobby Collins | Hampton, VA | Royal Blue/White |
| Hartford | Hawks | America East | Larry Harrison | W. Hartford, CT | Scarlet/White |
| Harvard | Crimson | Ivy | Frank Sullivan | Cambridge, MA | Crimson/Black/White |
| Hawaii | Rainbow Warriors | WAC | Riley Wallace | Honolulu, HI | Green/White |
| High Point | Panthers | Big South | Bart Lundy | High Point, NC | Purple/White |
| Hofstra | Pride | Colonial | Tom Pecora | Hempstead, NY | Blue/Gold/White |
| Holy Cross | Crusaders | Patriot | Ralph Willard | Worcester, MA | Royal Purple |
| Houston | Cougars | USA | Tom Penders | Houston, TX | Scarlet/White |
| Howard | Bison | Mid-Eastern | Gil Jackson | Washington, DC | Blue/White/Red |
| Idaho | Vandals | WAC | Leonard Perry | Moscow, ID | Silver/Gold |
| Idaho St. | Bengals | Big Sky | Doug Oliver | Pocatello, ID | Orange/Black |
| Illinois | Fighting Illini | Big Ten | Bruce Weber | Champaign, IL | Orange/Blue |
| Illinois-Chicago | Flames | Horizon | Jim Collins | Chicago, IL | Navy Blue/Red |
| Illinois St. | Redbirds | Mo. Valley | Porter Moser | Normal, IL | Red/White |
| Indiana | Hoosiers | Big Ten | Mike Davis | Bloomington, IN | Cream/Crimson |
| IPFW | Mastodons | Independent | Dane Fife | Fort Wayne, IN | Royal Blue/White |
| IUPUI | Jaguars | Mid-Continent | Ron Hunter | Indianapolis, IN | Red/Gold |
| Indiana St. | Sycamores | Mo. Valley | Royce Waltman | Terre Haute, IN | Blue/White |
| Iona | Gaels | Metro Atlantic | Jeff Ruland | New Rochelle, NY | Maroon/Gold |
| Iowa | Hawkeyes | Big Ten | Steve Alford | Iowa City, IA | Old Gold/Black |

| | Nickname | Conference | Head Coach | Location | Colors |
|---|---|---|---|---|---|
| Iowa St. | Cyclones | Big 12 | Wayne Morgan | Ames, IA | Cardinal/Gold |
| Jackson St. | Tigers | SWAC | Tevester Anderson | Jackson, MS | Blue/White |
| Jacksonville | Dolphins | Atlantic Sun | Cliff Warren | Jacksonville, FL | Green/White |
| Jacksonville St. | Gamecocks | Ohio Valley | Mike LaPlante | Jacksonville, AL | Red/White |
| James Madison | Dukes | Colonial | Dean Keener | Harrisonburg, VA | Purple/Gold |
| Kansas | Jayhawks | Big 12 | Bill Self. | Lawrence, KS | Crimson/Blue |
| Kansas St. | Wildcats | Big 12 | Jim Wooldridge | Manhattan, KS | Purple/White |
| Kennesaw St. | Owls | Atlantic Sun | Tony Ingle | Kennesaw, GA | Black/Gold |
| Kent St. | Golden Flashes | Mid-American | Jim Christian | Kent, OH | Navy Blue/Gold |
| Kentucky | Wildcats | SEC-East | Tubby Smith | Lexington, KY | Blue/White |
| La Salle | Explorers | Atlantic 10 | John Giannini | Philadelphia, PA | Blue/Gold |
| Lafayette | Leopards | Patriot | Fran O'Hanlon | Easton, PA | Maroon/White |
| Lamar | Cardinals | Southland | Billy Tubbs | Beaumont, TX | Red/White |
| Lehigh | Mountain Hawks | Patriot | Bill Taylor | Bethlehem, PA | Brown/White |
| Liberty | Flames | Big South | Randy Dunton | Lynchburg, VA | Red/White/Blue |
| Lipscomb | Bisons | Atlantic Sun | Scott Sanderson | Nashville, TN | Purple/Gold |
| Long Beach St. | 49ers | Big West | Larry Reynolds | Long Beach, CA | Black/Gold |
| Long Island | Blackbirds | Northeast | Jim Ferry | Brooklyn, NY | Black/Silver/Blue |
| Longwood | Lancers | Independent | Mike Gillian | Farmville, VA | Blue/White |
| LSU | Fighting Tigers | SEC-West | John Brady | Baton Rouge, LA | Purple/Gold |
| LA-Lafayette | Ragin' Cajuns | Sun Belt | Robert Lee | Lafayette, LA | Vermilion/White |
| LA-Monroe | Indians | Southland | Orlando Early | Monroe, LA | Maroon/Gold |
| Louisiana Tech | Bulldogs | WAC | Keith Richard | Ruston, LA | Red/Blue |
| Louisville | Cardinals | Big East | Rick Pitino | Louisville, KY | Red/Black/White |
| Loyola Chicago | Ramblers | Horizon | Jim Whitesell | Chicago, IL | Maroon/Gold |
| Loyola Maryland | Greyhounds | Metro Atlantic | Jimmy Patsos | Baltimore, MD | Green/Gray |
| Loyola Marymount | Lions | West Coast | Rodney Tention | Los Angeles, CA | Crimson/Blue |
| Maine | Black Bears | America East | Ted Woodward | Orono, ME | Blue/White |
| Manhattan | Jaspers | Metro Atlantic | Bobby Gonzalez | Riverdale, NY | Kelly Green/White |
| Marist | Red Foxes | Metro Atlantic | Matt Brady | Poughkeepsie, NY | Red/White |
| Marquette | Golden Eagles | Big East | Tom Crean | Milwaukee, WI | Blue/Gold |
| Marshall | Thundering Herd | USA | Ron Jirsa | Huntington, WV | Green/White |
| Maryland | Terrapins, Terps | ACC | Gary Williams | College Park, MD | Red/Wt./Black/Gold |
| MD-Balt. County | Retrievers | America East | Randy Monroe | Baltimore, MD | Black/Gold/Red |
| MD-Eastern Shore | Hawks | Mid-Eastern | Larry Lessett | Princess Anne, MD | Maroon/Gray |
| Massachusetts | Minutemen | Atlantic 10 | Travis Ford | Amherst, MA | Maroon/White |
| McNeese St. | Cowboys | Southland | Tic Price | Lake Charles, LA | Blue/Gold |
| Memphis | Tigers | USA | John Calipari | Memphis, TN | Blue/Gray |
| Mercer | Bears | Atlantic Sun | Mark Slonaker | Macon, GA | Orange/Black |
| Miami-FL | Hurricanes | ACC | Frank Haith | Coral Gables, FL | Orange/Grn./White |
| Miami-OH | RedHawks | Mid-American | Charlie Coles | Oxford, OH | Red/White |
| Michigan | Wolverines | Big Ten | Tommy Amaker | Ann Arbor, MI | Maize/Blue |
| Michigan St. | Spartans | Big Ten | Tom Izzo | East Lansing, MI | Green/White |
| Middle Tennessee | Blue Raiders | Sun Belt | Kermit Davis Jr. | Murfreesboro, TN | Royal Blue/White |
| Minnesota | Golden Gophers | Big Ten | Dan Monson | Minneapolis, MN | Maroon/Gold |
| Mississippi | Ole Miss, Rebels | SEC-West | Rod Barnes | Oxford, MS | Cardinal/Navy Blue |
| Mississippi St. | Bulldogs | SEC-West | Rick Stansbury | Starkville, MS | Maroon/White |
| Miss. Valley St. | Delta Devils | SWAC | James Green | Itta Bena, MS | Green/White |
| Missouri | Tigers | Big 12 | Quin Snyder | Columbia, MO | Old Gold/Black |
| Missouri St. | Bears | Mo. Valley | Barry Hinson | Springfield, MO | Maroon/White |
| Missouri-KC | Kangaroos | Mid-Continent | Rich Zvosec | Kansas City, MO | Blue/Gold |
| Monmouth | Hawks | Northeast | Dave Calloway | W. Long Branch, NJ | Midnight Blue/White |
| Montana | Grizzlies | Big Sky | Larry Krystkowiak | Missoula, MT | Copper/Silver/Gold |
| Montana St. | Bobcats | Big Sky | Mick Durham | Bozeman, MT | Blue/Gold |
| Morehead St. | Eagles | Ohio Valley | Kyle Macy | Morehead, KY | Blue/Gold |
| Morgan St. | Bears | Mid-Eastern | Butch Beard | Baltimore, MD | Blue/Orange |
| Mt. St. Mary's | Mountaineers | Northeast | Milan Brown | Emmitsburg, MD | Blue/White |
| Murray St. | Racers | Ohio Valley | Mick Cronin | Murray, KY | Blue/Gold |
| Navy | Midshipmen | Patriot | Billy Lange | Annapolis, MD | Navy Blue/Gold |
| Nebraska | Cornhuskers | Big 12 | Barry Collier | Lincoln, NE | Scarlet/Cream |
| Nevada | Wolf Pack | WAC | Mark Fox | Reno, NV | Silver/Blue |
| New Hampshire | Wildcats | America East | Bill Herrion | Durham, NH | Blue/White |
| New Mexico | Lobos | Mountain West | Ritchie McKay | Albuquerque, NM | Cherry/Silver |
| New Mexico St. | Aggies | WAC | Reggie Theus | Las Cruces, NM | Crimson/White |
| New Orleans | Privateers | Sun Belt | Monte Towe | New Orleans, LA | Royal Blue/Silver |
| Niagara | Purple Eagles | Metro Atlantic | Joe Mihalich | Lewiston, NY | Purple/White/Gold |
| Nicholls St. | Colonels | Southland | J.P. Piper | Thibodaux, LA | Red/Gray |
| Norfolk State | Spartans | Mid-Eastern | Dwight Freeman | Norfolk, VA | Green/Gold |
| North Carolina | Tar Heels | ACC | Roy Williams | Chapel Hill, NC | Carolina Blue/Wht. |
| North Carolina A&T | Aggies | Mid-Eastern | Jerry Eaves | Greensboro, NC | Blue/Gold |
| North Carolina St. | Wolfpack | ACC | Herb Sendek | Raleigh, NC | Red/White |

## NCAA Division I Basketball Schools (Cont.)

| | Nickname | Conference | Head Coach | Location | Colors |
|---|---|---|---|---|---|
| NC-Asheville | Bulldogs | Big South | Eddie Biedenbach | Asheville, NC | Royal Blue/White |
| NC-Greensboro | Spartans | Southern | Mike Dement | Greensboro, NC | Gold/White/Navy |
| NC-Wilmington | Seahawks | Colonial | Brad Brownell | Wilmington, NC | Green/Gold/Navy |
| North Dakota St. | Bison | Independent | Tim Miles | Fargo, ND | Yellow/Green |
| North Florida | Ospreys | Atlantic Sun | Matt Kilcullen | Jacksonville, FL | Navy Blue/Gray |
| North Texas | Mean Green | Sun Belt | Johnny Jones | Denton, TX | Green/White |
| Northeastern | Huskies | Colonial | Ron Everhart | Boston, MA | Red/Black |
| Northern Arizona | Lumberjacks | Big Sky | Mike Adras | Flagstaff, AZ | Blue/Gold |
| Northern Colorado | Bears | Independent | Craig Rasmuson | Greeley, CO | Blue/Gold |
| Northern Illinois | Huskies | Mid-American | Rob Judson | DeKalb, IL | Cardinal/Black |
| Northern Iowa | Panthers | Mo. Valley | Greg McDermott | Cedar Falls, IA | Purple/Old Gold |
| Northwestern | Wildcats | Big Ten | Bill Carmody | Evanston, IL | Purple/White |
| Northwestern St. | Demons | Southland | Mike McConathy | Natchitoches, LA | Purple/Orange/Wt. |
| Notre Dame | Fighting Irish | Big East | Mike Brey | Notre Dame, IN | Gold/Blue |
| Oakland-MI | Golden Grizzlies | Mid-Continent | Greg Kampe | Rochester, MI | Black/Gold |
| Ohio University | Bobcats | Mid-American | Tim O'Shea | Athens, OH | Hunter Green/White |
| Ohio St. | Buckeyes | Big Ten | Thad Matta | Columbus, OH | Scarlet/Gray |
| Oklahoma | Sooners | Big 12 | Kelvin Sampson | Norman, OK | Crimson/Cream |
| Oklahoma St. | Cowboys | Big 12 | Eddie Sutton | Stillwater, OK | Orange/Black |
| Old Dominion | Monarchs | Colonial | Blaine Taylor | Norfolk, VA | Slate Blue/Silver |
| Oral Roberts | Golden Eagles | Mid-Continent | Scott Sutton | Tulsa, OK | Navy Blue/White |
| Oregon | Ducks | Pac-10 | Ernie Kent | Eugene, OR | Green/Yellow |
| Oregon St. | Beavers | Pac-10 | Jay John | Corvallis, OR | Orange/Black |
| Pacific | Tigers | Big West | Bob Thomason | Stockton, CA | Orange/Black |
| Pennsylvania | Quakers | Ivy | Fran Dunphy | Philadelphia, PA | Red/Blue |
| Penn St. | Nittany Lions | Big Ten | Ed DeChellis | University Park, PA | Blue/White |
| Pepperdine | Waves | West Coast | Paul Westphal | Malibu, CA | Blue/Orange |
| Pittsburgh | Panthers | Big East | Jamie Dixon | Pittsburgh, PA | Gold/Blue |
| Portland | Pilots | West Coast | Mike Holton | Portland, OR | Purple/White |
| Portland St. | Vikings | Big Sky | Ken Bone | Portland, OR | Green/White |
| Prairie View A&M | Panthers | SWAC | Darrell Hawkins | Prairie View, TX | Purple/Gold |
| Princeton | Tigers | Ivy | Joe Scott | Princeton, NJ | Orange/Black |
| Providence | Friars | Big East | Tim Welsh | Providence, RI | Black/White |
| Purdue | Boilermakers | Big Ten | Matt Painter | W. Lafayette, IN | Old Gold/Black |
| Quinnipiac | Bobcats | Northeast | Joe DeSantis | Hamden, CT | Navy/Gold |
| Radford | Highlanders | Big South | Byron Samuels | Radford, VA | Blue/Red/Green/Wt. |
| Rhode Island | Rams | Atlantic 10 | Jim Baron | Kingston, RI | Lt. Blue/White/Navy |
| Rice | Owls | USA | Willis Wilson | Houston, TX | Blue/Gray |
| Richmond | Spiders | Atlantic 10 | Chris Mooney | Richmond, VA | Red/Blue |
| Rider | Broncs | Metro Atlantic | Tommy Dempsey | Lawrenceville, NJ | Cranberry/White |
| Robert Morris | Colonials | Northeast | Mark Schmidt | Moon Township, PA | Blue/Red/White |
| Rutgers | Scarlet Knights | Big East | Gary Waters | New Brunswick, NJ | Scarlet |
| Sacramento St. | Hornets | Big Sky | Jerome Jenkins | Sacramento, CA | Green/Gold |
| Sacred Heart | Pioneers | Northeast | Dave Bike | Fairfield, CT | Scarlet/White |
| St. Bonaventure | Bonnies | Atlantic 10 | Anthony Solomon | St. Bonaventure, NY | Brown/White |
| St. Francis-NY | Terriers | Northeast | Brian Nash | Brooklyn, NY | Red/Blue |
| St. Francis-PA | Red Flash | Northeast | Bobby Jones | Loretto, PA | Red/White |
| St. John's | Red Storm | Big East | Norm Roberts | Jamaica, NY | Red/White |
| Saint Joseph's | Hawks | Atlantic 10 | Phil Martelli | Philadelphia, PA | Crimson/Gray |
| Saint Louis | Billikens | Atlantic 10 | Brad Soderberg | St. Louis, MO | Blue/White |
| Saint Mary's-CA | Gaels | West Coast | Randy Bennett | Moraga, CA | Red/Blue |
| Saint Peter's | Peacocks | Metro Atlantic | Bob Leckie | Jersey City, NJ | Blue/White |
| Sam Houston St. | Bearkats | Southland | Bob Marlin | Huntsville, TX | Orange/White |
| Samford | Bulldogs | Ohio Valley | Jimmy Tillette | Birmingham, AL | Red/Blue |
| San Diego | Toreros | West Coast | Brad Holland | San Diego, CA | Lt. Blue/Navy |
| San Diego St. | Aztecs | Mountain West | Steve Fisher | San Diego, CA | Scarlet/Black |
| San Francisco | Dons | West Coast | Jessie Evans | San Francisco, CA | Green/Gold |
| San Jose St. | Spartans | WAC | George Nessman | San Jose, CA | Gold/White/Blue |
| Santa Clara | Broncos | West Coast | Dick Davey | Santa Clara, CA | Bronco Red/White |
| Savannah St. | Tigers | Independent | Horace Broadnax | Savannah, GA | Orange/Blue |
| Seton Hall | Pirates | Big East | Louis Orr | South Orange, NJ | Blue/White |
| Siena | Saints | Metro Atlantic | Fran McCaffery | Loudonville, NY | Green/Gold |
| South Alabama | Jaguars | Sun Belt | John Pelphrey | Mobile, AL | Red/White/Blue |
| South Carolina | Gamecocks | SEC-East | Dave Odom | Columbia, SC | Garnet/Black |
| South Carolina St. | Bulldogs | Mid-Eastern | Benjamin Betts Jr. | Orangeburg, SC | Garnet/Blue |
| South Dakota St. | Jackrabbits | Independent | Scott Nagy | Brookings, SD | Yellow/Blue |
| South Florida | Bulls | Big East | Robert McCullum | Tampa, FL | Green/Gold |
| SE Missouri St. | Redhawks | Ohio Valley | Gary Garner | Cape Girardeau, MO | Red/Black |
| Southeastern Louisiana | Lions | Southland | Jim Yarbrough Jr. | Hammond, LA | Green/Gold |
| Southern-BR | Jaguars | SWAC | Rob Spivery | Baton Rouge, LA | Blue/Gold |

| | Nickname | Conference | Head Coach | Location | Colors |
|---|---|---|---|---|---|
| Southern Illinois | Salukis | Mo. Valley | Chris Lowery | Carbondale, IL | Maroon/White |
| SMU | Mustangs | USA | Jimmy Tubbs | Dallas, TX | Red/Blue |
| Southern Miss | Golden Eagles | USA | Larry Eustachy | Hattiesburg, MS | Black/Gold |
| Southern Utah | Thunderbirds | Mid-Continent | Bill Evans | Cedar City, UT | Scarlet/White |
| Stanford | Cardinal | Pac-10 | Trent Johnson | Stanford, CA | Cardinal/White |
| S.F. Austin St. | Lumberjacks | Southland | Danny Kaspar | Nacogdoches, TX | Purple/White |
| Stetson | Hatters | Atlantic Sun | Derek Waugh | DeLand, FL | Green/White |
| Stony Brook | Seawolves | America East | Steve Pikiell | Stony Brook, NY | Scarlet/Gray |
| Syracuse | Orange | Big East | Jim Boeheim | Syracuse, NY | Orange |
| Temple | Owls | Atlantic 10 | John Chaney | Philadelphia, PA | Cherry/White |
| Tennessee | Volunteers | SEC-East | Bruce Pearl | Knoxville, TN | Orange/White |
| Tenn-Martin | Skyhawks | Ohio Valley | Bret Campbell | Martin, TN | Orange/Wt./Blue |
| Tennessee St. | Tigers | Ohio Valley | Cy Alexander | Nashville, TN | Blue/White |
| Tennessee Tech | Golden Eagles | Ohio Valley | Mike Sutton | Cookeville, TN | Purple/Gold |
| Texas | Longhorns | Big 12 | Rick Barnes | Austin, TX | Burnt Orange/White |
| Texas A&M | Aggies | Big 12 | Billy Gillispie | College Station, TX | Maroon/White |
| TX A&M Corpus-Christi | Islanders | Independent | Ronnie Arrow | Corpus Christi, TX | Blue/Green/Silver |
| TCU | Horned Frogs | Mountain West | Neil Dougherty | Ft. Worth, TX | Purple/White |
| Texas Southern | Tigers | SWAC | Ronnie Courtney | Houston, TX | Maroon/Gray |
| Texas St. | Bobcats | Southland | Dennis Nutt | San Marcos, TX | Maroon/Gold |
| Texas Tech | Red Raiders | Big 12 | Bob Knight | Lubbock, TX | Scarlet/Black |
| TX-Arlington | Mavericks | Southland | Eddie McCarter | Arlington, TX | Royal Blue/White |
| TX-Pan American | Broncs | Independent | Robert Davenport | Edinburg, TX | Green/White |
| TX-San Antonio | Roadrunners | Southland | Tim Carter | San Antonio, TX | Orange/Navy/White |
| Toledo | Rockets | Mid-American | Stan Joplin | Toledo, OH | Blue/Gold |
| Towson | Tigers | Colonial | Pat Kennedy | Towson, MD | Gold/White/Black |
| Troy | Trojans | Sun Belt | Don Maestri | Troy, AL | Cardinal/Silver/Black |
| Tulane | Green Wave | USA | Dave Dickerson | New Orleans, LA | Olive Grn./Sky Blue |
| Tulsa | Golden Hurricane | USA | Doug Wojcik | Tulsa, OK | Blue/Gold/Crimson |
| UAB | Blazers | USA | Mike Anderson | Birmingham, AL | Green/Gold |
| UC-Irvine | Anteaters | Big West | Pat Douglass | Irvine, CA | Blue/Gold |
| UCLA | Bruins | Pac-10 | Ben Howland | Los Angeles, CA | Blue/Gold |
| UC-Davis | Aggies | Independent | Gary Stewart | Davis, CA | Yale Blue/Gold |
| UC-Riverside | Highlanders | Big West | David Spencer | Riverside, CA | Blue/Gold |
| UC-Santa Barbara | Gauchos | Big West | Bob Williams | Santa Barbara, CA | Blue/Gold |
| UNLV | Runnin' Rebels | Mountain West | Lon Kruger | Las Vegas, NV | Scarlet/Gray |
| USC | Trojans | Pac-10 | Tim Floyd | Los Angeles, CA | Cardinal/Gold |
| Utah | Utes, Runnin' Utes | Mountain West | Ray Giacoletti | Salt Lake City, UT | Crimson/White |
| Utah St. | Aggies | WAC | Stew Morrill | Logan, UT | Navy Blue/White |
| Utah Valley St. | Wolverines | Independent | Dick Hunsaker | Orem, UT | Green/Gold/White |
| UTEP | Miners | USA | Doc Sadler | El Paso, TX | Orange/Blue/Silver |
| Valparaiso | Crusaders | Mid-Continent | Homer Drew | Valparaiso, IN | Brown/Gold |
| Vanderbilt | Commodores | SEC-East | Kevin Stallings | Nashville, TN | Black/Gold |
| Vermont | Catamounts | America East | Mike Lonergan | Burlington, VT | Green/Gold |
| Villanova | Wildcats | Big East | Jay Wright | Villanova, PA | Blue/White |
| Virginia | Cavaliers | ACC | Dave Leitao | Charlottesville, VA | Orange/Blue |
| VCU | Rams | Colonial | Jeff Capel III | Richmond, VA | Black/Gold |
| VMI | Keydets | Big South | Duggar Baucom | Lexington, VA | Red/White/Yellow |
| Virginia Tech | Hokies, Gobblers | ACC | Seth Greenberg | Blacksburg, VA | Orange/Maroon |
| Wagner | Seahawks | Northeast | Mike Deane | Staten Island, NY | Green/White |
| Wake Forest | Demon Deacons | ACC | Skip Prosser | Winston-Salem, NC | Old Gold/Black |
| Washington | Huskies | Pac-10 | Lorenzo Romar | Seattle, WA | Purple/Gold |
| Washington St. | Cougars | Pac-10 | Dick Bennett | Pullman, WA | Crimson/Gray |
| Weber St. | Wildcats | Big Sky | Joe Cravens | Ogden, UT | Purple/White |
| West Virginia | Mountaineers | Big East | John Beilein | Morgantown, WV | Old Gold/Blue |
| Western Carolina | Catamounts | Southern | Larry Hunter | Cullowhee, NC | Purple/Gold |
| Western Illinois | Leathernecks | Mid-Continent | Derek Thomas | Macomb, IL | Purple/Gold |
| Western Kentucky | Hilltoppers | Sun Belt | Darrin Horn | Bowling Green, KY | Red/White |
| Western Michigan | Broncos | Mid-American | Steve Hawkins | Kalamazoo, MI | Brown/Gold |
| Wichita St. | Shockers | Mo. Valley | Mark Turgeon | Wichita, KS | Yellow/Black |
| William & Mary | Tribe | Colonial | Tony Shaver | Williamsburg, VA | Green/Gold/Silver |
| Winthrop | Eagles | Big South | Gregg Marshall | Rock Hill, SC | Garnet/Gold |
| Wisconsin | Badgers | Big Ten | Bo Ryan | Madison, WI | Cardinal/White |
| WI-Green Bay | Phoenix | Horizon | Tod Kowalczyk | Green Bay, WI | Green/White/Red |
| WI-Milwaukee | Panthers | Horizon | Rob Jeter | Milwaukee, WI | Black/Gold |
| Wofford | Terriers | Southern | Mike Young | Spartanburg, SC | Old Gold/Black |
| Wright St. | Raiders | Horizon | Paul Biancardi | Dayton, OH | Green/Gold |
| Wyoming | Cowboys | Mountain West | Steve McClain | Laramie, WY | Brown/Gold |
| Xavier | Musketeers | Atlantic 10 | Sean Miller | Cincinnati, OH | Blue/Gray/White |
| Yale | Bulldogs, Elis | Ivy | James Jones | New Haven, CT | Yale Blue/White |
| Youngstown St. | Penguins | Horizon | Jerry Slocum | Youngstown, OH | Red/White |

Notre Dame
**Charlie Weis**
Patriots to Notre Dame

South Carolina
**Steve Spurrier**
South Carolina

Florida Atlantic
**Matt Doherty**
Florida Atlantic

Virginia
**Dave Leitao**
DePaul to Virginia

## Coaching Changes

New head coaches were named at 23 Division 1-A and 13 Division 1-AA football schools while 48 Division 1 basketball schools changed head coaches during or after the 2004-05 season. Coaching changes listed below are as of September 30, 2005.

### Division I-A Football

| | Old Coach | Record | Why Left? | New Coach | Old Job |
|---|---|---|---|---|---|
| **Brigham Young** | Gary Crowton | 5-6 | resigned | Bronco Mendenhall | Def. coord., Brigham Young |
| **East Carolina** | John Thompson | 2-9 | resigned | Skip Holtz | QB coach, South Carolina |
| **Florida** | Ron Zook | 7-5 † | fired | Urban Meyer | Coach, Utah |
| **Illinois** | Ron Turner | 3-8 | fired | Ron Zook | Coach, Florida |
| **Indiana** | Gerry DiNardo | 3-8 | fired | Terry Hoeppner | Coach, Miami-OH |
| **LSU** | Nick Saban | 9-3 | to NFL Miami* | Les Miles | Coach, Oklahoma St. |
| **Marshall** | Bob Pruett | 6-6 | retired | Mark Snyder | Def. coord., Ohio St. |
| **Miami-OH** | Terry Hoeppner | 8-5 | to Indiana* | Shane Montgomery | Off. coord., Miami-OH |
| **Mississippi** | David Cutcliffe | 4-7 | fired | Ed Orgeron | Asst., USC |
| **New Mexico St.** | Tony Samuel | 5-6 | fired | Hal Mumme | Coach, Southeastern La. |
| **Notre Dame** | Tyrone Willingham | 6-6@ | fired | Charlie Weis | Off. coord., NFL New Eng. |
| **Ohio** | Brian Knorr | 4-7 | fired | Frank Solich | Former coach, Nebraska |
| **Oklahoma St.** | Les Miles | 7-5 | to LSU* | Mike Gundy | Off. coord., Oklahoma St. |
| **Pittsburgh** | Walt Harris | 8-4 | to Stanford* | Dave Wannstedt | Former coach, NFL Miami |
| **San Jose St.** | Fitz Hill | 2-9 | resigned | Dick Tomey | Asst., Texas |
| **South Carolina** | Lou Holtz | 6-5 | retired | Steve Spurrier | Former coach, NFL Wash. |
| **Stanford** | Buddy Teevens | 4-7 | fired | Walt Harris | Coach, Pittsburgh |
| **Syracuse** | Paul Pasqualoni | 6-6 | fired | Greg Robinson | Co-def. coord., Texas |
| **UNLV** | John Robinson | 2-9 | retired | Mike Sanford | Off. coord., Utah |
| **Utah** | Urban Meyer | 12-0 | to Florida* | Kyle Whittingham | Def. coord., Utah |
| **Utah St.** | Mick Dennehy | 3-8 | fired | Brent Guy | Def. coord., Arizona St. |
| **Washington** | Keith Gilbertson | 1-10 | resigned | Tyrone Willingham | Coach, Notre Dame |
| **Western Michigan** | Gary Darnell | 1-10 | fired | Bill Cubit | Off. coord., Stanford |

\* as head coach    \*\* as assistant coach

† Zook (7-4) was fired on Oct. 25, 2004 after a 4-3 start and was allowed to finish out the regular season. He was replaced for the Peach Bowl by defensive coordinator Charlie Strong (0-1).

@ Willingham (6-5) was fired on Nov. 30, 2004 and replaced by defensive coordinator Kent Baer (0-1) for the Insight Bowl.

### Division I-AA Football

| | Old Coach | Record | Why Left? | New Coach | Old Job |
|---|---|---|---|---|---|
| **The Citadel** | John Zernhelt | 3-7 | to NFL NY Jets** | Kevin Higgins | Asst., NFL Detroit |
| **Dartmouth** | John Lyons | 1-9 | fired | Buddy Teevens | Coach, Stanford |
| **Davidson** | Mike Toop | 2-7 | to U.S. Merchant Marine Academy* | Tripp Merritt | Def. coord., Bucknell |
| **Duquesne** | Greg Gattuso | 7-3 | to Pittsburgh** | Jerry Schmitt | Coach, D-III Westminster |
| **Florida A&M** | Billy Joe | 3-8 | fired | Rubin Carter | Asst., Temple |
| **Indiana St.** | Tim McGuire | 4-7 | fired | Lou West | Def. coord., Toledo |
| **Norfolk St.** | Willie Gillus | 1-8 | fired | Pete Adrian | Def. coord., Beth.-Cookman |
| **Sam Houston St.** | Ron Randleman | 11-3 | retired | Todd Whitten | Coach, D-II Tarleton St. |
| **Southeastern La.** | Hal Mumme | 7-4 | to New Mexico St.* | Dennis Roland | Coach, N. Gwinnett (Ga.) HS |
| **Stephen F. Austin** | Mike Santiago | 6-5 | fired | Robert McFarland | Asst., East Carolina |
| **Tennessee St.** | James Reese | 4-7 | fired | James Webster | Asst., North Carolina |
| **Valparaiso** | Tom Horne | 5-6 | resigned | Stacy Adams | Off. coord., Valparaiso |
| **Weber St.** | Jerry Graybeal | 1-10 | resigned | Ron McBride | Asst., Kentucky |

\* as head coach    \*\* as assistant coach

## Division I Basketball

| | Old Coach | Record | Why Left? | New Coach | Old Job |
|---|---|---|---|---|---|
| **Air Force** | Chris Mooney | 18-12 | to Richmond* | Jeff Bzdelik | Former coach, NBA Denver |
| **Alabama St.** | Rob Spivery | 15-15 | to Southern-BR* | Lewis Jackson | Asst., Alabama St. |
| **Brigham Young** | Steve Cleveland | 9-21 | to Fresno St.* | Dave Rose | Asst., Brigham Young |
| **Centenary** | Kevin Johnson | 3-24 | resigned | Rob Flaska | Asst., Arkansas |
| **Charleston So.** | Jim Platt | 13-17 | to Army** | Barclay Radebaugh | Asst., Miami-FL |
| **Cincinnati** | Bob Huggins | 25-8 | resigned | $ Andy Kennedy | Asst., Cincinnati |
| **Coastal Carolina** | Pete Strickland | 10-19 | fired | Buzz Peterson | Coach, Tennessee |
| **DePaul** | Dave Leitao | 20-11 | to Virginia* | Jerry Wainwright | Coach, Richmond |
| **East Carolina** | Bill Herrion | 9-19 | resigned | Ricky Stokes | Asst., South Carolina |
| **Eastern Illinois** | Rick Samuels | 12-16 | fired | Mike Miller | Asst., Kansas St. |
| **Eastern Kentucky** | Travis Ford | 22-9 | to Massachusetts* | Jeff Neubauer | Asst., West Virginia |
| **Eastern Michigan** | Jim Boone | 12-18 | fired | Charles Ramsey | Asst., Michigan |
| **Florida Atlantic** | Sidney Green | 10-17 | fired | Matt Doherty | Former coach, N. Carolina |
| **Fresno St.** | Ray Lopes | 16-14 | resigned | Steve Cleveland | Coach, Brigham Young |
| **Howard** | Frankie Allen | 5-23 | fired | Gil Jackson | Asst., Pennsylvania |
| **IPFW** | Doug Noll | 7-22 † | fired | Dane Fife | Asst., Indiana |
| **Jacksonville** | Hugh Durham | 16-13 | retired | Cliff Warren | Asst., Georgia Tech |
| **LA-Monroe** | Mike Vining | 8-19 | resigned | Orlando Early | Asst., Alabama |
| **Loyola Marymount** | Steve Aggers | 11-17 | fired | Rodney Tention | Asst., Arizona |
| **Massachusetts** | Steve Lappas | 16-12 | fired | Travis Ford | Coach, Eastern Kentucky |
| **Miss. Valley St.** | Lafayette Stribling | 13-15 | retired | James Green | Fmr. coach, Southern Miss |
| **New Hampshire** | Phil Rowe | 9-19 | resigned | Bill Herrion | Coach, East Carolina |
| **New Mexico St.** | Lou Henson | 6-24@ | retired | Reggie Theus | Asst., Louisville |
| **Nicholls St.** | Ricky Blanton | 6-21# | resigned | J.P. Piper | Asst., Nicholls St. |
| **NC-Greensboro** | Fran McCaffery | 18-12 | to Siena* | Mike Dement | Former coach, SMU |
| **Portland St.** | Heath Schroyer | 19-9 | to Fresno St.** | Ken Bone | Asst., Washington |
| **Prairie View A&M** | Jerry Francis | 5-23 | resigned | $ Darrell Hawkins | Asst., Prairie View A&M |
| **Purdue** | Gene Keady | 7-21 | retired | Matt Painter | Asst., Purdue |
| **Richmond** | Jerry Wainwright | 14-15 | to DePaul* | Chris Mooney | Coach, Air Force |
| **Rider** | Don Harnum | 19-11 | resigned to AD | $ Tommy Dempsey | Asst., Rider |
| **St. Francis-NY** | Ron Ganulin | 13-15 | fired | Brian Nash | Asst., Seton Hall |
| **San Jose St.** | Phil Johnson | 6-23 | resigned | George Nessman | Asst., California |
| **Savannah St.** | Ed Daniels | 0-28 | fired | Horace Broadnax | Fmr coach, Beth.-Cookman |
| **Siena** | Rob Lanier | 6-24 | fired | Fran McCaffery | Coach, NC-Greensboro |
| **Southeastern La.** | Billy Kennedy | 24-9 | to Miami-FL** | Jim Yarbrough Jr. | Coach, D-II Valdosta St. |
| **Southern-BR** | Michael Grant | 14-15 | resigned | Rob Spivery | Coach, Alabama St. |
| **Stony Brook** | Nick Macarchuk | 12-17 | resigned | Steve Pikiell | Asst., George Washington |
| **Tennessee** | Buzz Peterson | 14-17 | fired | Bruce Pearl | Coach, WI-Milwaukee |
| **Tulane** | Shawn Finney | 10-18 | fired | Dave Dickerson | Asst., Maryland |
| **Tulsa** | John Phillips | 9-20+ | resigned | Doug Wojcik | Asst., Michigan St. |
| **UC-Riverside** | John Masi | 9-19 | fired | David Spencer | Academic coord., UCR |
| **USC** | Henry Bibby | 12-17% | fired | Tim Floyd | Fmr coach, NBA N. Orleans |
| **Vermont** | Tom Brennan | 25-7 | retired | Mike Lonergan | Asst., Maryland |
| **Virginia** | Pete Gillen | 14-15 | resigned | Dave Leitao | Coach, DePaul |
| **VMI** | Bart Bellairs | 9-18 | fired | Duggar Baucom | Coach, D-II Tusculum |
| **Western Carolina** | Steve Shurina | 8-22 | fired | Larry Hunter | Asst., N.C. State |
| **WI-Milwaukee** | Bruce Pearl | 26-7 | to Tennessee* | Rob Jeter | Asst., Wisconsin |
| **Youngstown St.** | John Robic | 5-23 | fired | Jerry Slocum | Coach, D-II Gannon |

\* as head coach
\*\* as assistant coach
$ on an interim basis

† Noll (3-13) was fired on Jan. 13 and replaced on an interim basis by assistant Joe Pechota (4-9).
@ Health issues prevented Henson from coaching in 2004-05. Assistant Tony Stubblefield served as acting head coach for the entire season. Henson retired from coaching on January 21.
# Blanton resigned on Oct. 18, 2004 and was replaced by Piper before the season began.
+ Phillips (2-5) resigned on Dec. 24, 2004 and was a replaced for the remainder of the season by assistant Alvin "Pooh" Williamson (7-15).
% Bibby (2-2) was fired on Dec. 6, 2004 and replaced for the remainder of the season by assistant Jim Saia (10-15). Former Utah coach Rick Majerus accepted the job on Dec. 15, then resigned three days later due to health issues.

## 2004-05 Directors' Cup

Sponsored by the United States Sports Academy (USSA). Developed as a joint effort between the National Association of Collegiate Directors of Athletics (NACDA) and USA Today. Introduced in 1993-94 to honor the nation's best overall NCAA Division I athletic department (combining men's and women's sports). Winners in NCAA Division II and III and NAIA were named for the first time following the 1995-96 season.

Standings are computed by NACDA with points awarded for each Div. I school's finish in 20 sports (top 10 scoring sports for both men and women). Div. II schools are awarded points in 14 sports (top 7 scoring sports for both men and women). Div III schools are awarded points in 18 sports (top 9 scoring sports for both men and women). NAIA schools are awarded points in 12 sports (top 6 scoring sports for both men and women). National champions in each sport earn 100 points, while 2nd through 64th-place finishers earn decreasing points depending on the size of the tournament field. Division I-A football points are based on the final ESPN/USA Today Coaches' Top 25 poll. Listed below are team conferences (for Div. I only), combined Final Four finishes (1st through 4th place) for men's and women's programs, overall points in **bold** type, and the previous year's ranking (for Div. I only).

**Multiple winners:** Stanford (11); Williams, MA (9); Simon Fraser, BC and UC-Davis (6); Grand Valley St., MI and Lindenwood, MO (2).

### Division I

| | | Conf | 1-2-3-4 | Pts | 03-04 Rank | | | Conf | 1-2-3-4 | Pts | 03-04 Rank |
|---|---|---|---|---|---|---|---|---|---|---|---|
| 1 | Stanford | Pac-10 | 2-3-0-0 | **1238.75** | 1 | 14 | Washington | Pac-10 | 0-0-2-0 | **797.25** | 8 |
| 2 | Texas | Big 12 | 2-1-1-1 | **1074** | 10 | 15 | California | Pac-10 | 1-0-0-1 | **792.5** | 9 |
| 3 | UCLA | Pac-10 | 3-5-0-1 | **1067** | 3 | 16 | Notre Dame | Big East | 2-0-0-1 | **788** | 19 |
| 4 | Michigan | Big Ten | 1-1-0-0 | **1064.25** | 2 | 17 | Auburn | SEC | 1-2-1-1 | **781** | 23 |
| 5 | Duke | ACC | 1-3-2-0 | **1021.25** | 18 | 18 | Arizona | Pac-10 | 0-0-2-0 | **739** | 12 |
| 6 | Florida | SEC | 0-4-2-1 | **979.25** | 6 | 19 | Wisconsin | Big Ten | 0-1-1-0 | **686.75** | 26 |
| 7 | Georgia | SEC | 3-0-0-0 | **970** | 5 | 20 | Penn St. | Big Ten | 0-0-1-2 | **657.25** | 13 |
| 8 | Tennessee | SEC | 0-0-1-1 | **960.25** | 14 | 21 | Nebraska | Big 12 | 1-0-1-1 | **649.25** | 32 |
| 9 | North Carolina | ACC | 1-0-0-0 | **940.5** | 7 | 22 | Minnesota | Big Ten | 1-1-1-0 | **622.75** | 20 |
| 10 | USC | Pac-10 | 1-0-2-0 | **902.25** | 21 | 23 | LSU | SEC | 0-0-2-0 | **614.5** | 11 |
| 11 | Arizona St. | Pac-10 | 0-0-1-0 | **838.25** | 17 | 24 | Oklahoma | Big 12 | 1-0-2-0 | **571.25** | 15 |
| 12 | Ohio St. | Big Ten | 0-2-1-1 | **834.25** | 4 | 25 | Baylor | Big 12 | 1-1-1-0 | **570.5** | 47 |
| 13 | Virginia | ACC | 0-2-1-0 | **808.5** | 30 | | | | | | |

### Division II

| | | 1-2-3-4 | Pts | | | 1-2-3-4 | Pts |
|---|---|---|---|---|---|---|---|
| 1 | Grand Valley St., MI | 0-1-0-2 | **801** | 14 | Indiana, PA | 0-0-1-0 | **431.5** |
| 2 | Nebraska-Omaha | 1-0-1-0 | **607** | 15 | Northwood, MI | 0-0-0-0 | **425.5** |
| 3 | Cal State-Chico | 0-0-0-1 | **588.5** | 16 | Drury, MO | 1-1-0-0 | **422** |
| 4 | North Dakota | 0-1-2-0 | **584** | 17 | Adams St., CO | 1-3-0-1 | **420** |
| 5 | Cal State-Bakersfield | 0-2-0-2 | **561** | 18 | Indianapolis | 0-0-0-0 | **410.5** |
| 6 | UC San Diego | 0-0-1-1 | **556.5** | 19 | North Florida | 0-2-0-0 | **398** |
| 7 | Central Missouri St. | 0-1-1-0 | **533.5** | 20 | Nebraska Kearney | 0-0-1-0 | **389.75** |
| 8 | Truman St., MO | 1-1-0-0 | **527.5** | 21 | Ferris St., MI | 0-0-0-1 | **387.5** |
| 9 | Abilene Christian, TX | 2-1-2-0 | **514** | 22 | St. Cloud St., MN | 0-0-0-0 | **382** |
| 10 | Minnesota St. Mankato | 0-0-1-0 | **487** | 23 | West Chester, PA | 0-1-1-1 | **381.5** |
| 11 | South Dakota | 0-0-0-0 | **486.25** | 24 | Western St., CO | 1-0-1-0 | **379.5** |
| 12 | Lynn, FL | 1-0-0-0 | **449** | 25 | Wayne St., MI | 0-0-0-0 | **367.25** |
| 13 | Florida Southern | 1-0-1-0 | **445.5** | | | | |

### Division III

| | | 1-2-3-4 | Pts | | | 1-2-3-4 | Pts |
|---|---|---|---|---|---|---|---|
| 1 | Williams, MA | 1-0-0-3 | **1068.25** | 14 | Ithaca, NY | 1-0-0-1 | **512.25** |
| 2 | Middlebury, VT | 2-4-1-1 | **900** | 15 | Springfield, MA | 0-0-0-0 | **485** |
| 3 | Washington, MO | 0-1-1-0 | **675.75** | 16 | Redlands, CA | 0-1-0-0 | **458.5** |
| 4 | Trinity, TX | 0-0-0-0 | **672** | 17 | Gustavus Adolphus, MN | 0-0-1-1 | **442** |
| 5 | Wisconsin Stevens Point | 1-0-0-0 | **646.75** | 18 | Denison, OH | 0-0-1-0 | **399** |
| 6 | Calvin, MI | 1-1-1-0 | **617** | 19 | Bowdoin, ME | 0-0-0-0 | **390.5** |
| 7 | Wisconsin La Crosse | 1-1-1-1 | **600.5** | 20 | Messiah, PA | 1-0-2-0 | **380** |
| 8 | Emory, GA | 2-1-1-0 | **594** | 21 | Mary Washington, VA | 0-0-0-0 | **371.5** |
| 9 | Amherst, MA | 0-0-2-0 | **593.5** | 22 | Johns Hopkins, MD | 1-0-1-0 | **363.25** |
| 10 | New Jersey | 1-0-0-1 | **584** | 23 | Wisconsin Whitewater | 1-0-0-0 | **360.25** |
| 11 | Salisbury, MD | 2-2-1-0 | **570.5** | 24 | St. Thomas, MN | 1-1-0-0 | **356** |
| 12 | Wartburg, IA | 1-2-0-1 | **553.5** | 25 | Wheaton, IL | 1-0-0-0 | **355.5** |
| 13 | Cortland St., NY | 0-1-0-0 | **530.5** | | | | |

## NAIA

| | | 1-2-3-4 | Pts | | | 1-2-3-4 | Pts |
|---|---|---|---|---|---|---|---|
| 1 | Azusa Pacific, CA | 1-1-2-2 | **881** | 14 | Cedarville, OH | 0-1-1-0 | **476.25** |
| 2 | Lindenwood, MO | 3-0-2-0 | **699** | 15 | Olivet Nazarene, IL | 0-0-0-0 | **456.75** |
| 3 | Simon Fraser, BC | 4-1-1-1 | **684** | 16 | Jamestown, ND | 0-0-0-0 | **452.5** |
| 4 | Pt. Loma Nazarene, CA | 0-0-1-1 | **618** | 17 | McKendree, IL | 0-1-0-0 | **451.5** |
| 5 | Mary, ND | 0-0-0-0 | **572.75** | 18 | Savannah Art & Design, GA | 0-0-0-0 | **445.5** |
| 6 | Lindsey Wilson, KY | 1-0-1-0 | **550.25** | 19 | Vanguard, CA | 0-0-1-0 | **425** |
| 7 | Oklahoma City | 2-1-1-0 | **542** | 20 | Indiana Wesleyan | 0-0-0-0 | **422.5** |
| 8 | Berry, GA | 0-0-1-0 | **527** | 21 | Lewis Clark St., ID | 0-0-1-0 | **417.5** |
| 9 | Concordia, NE | 0-2-1-0 | **523.25** | 22 | Flagler, FL | 0-0-0-0 | **410** |
| 10 | Oklahoma Baptist | 1-1-1-1 | **513** | 23 | Dickinson St., ND | 1-0-0-0 | **404.5** |
| 11 | Embry Riddle, FL | 0-1-2-0 | **512.5** | 24 | British Columbia | 0-1-1-1 | **402.5** |
| 12 | Concordia, CA | 0-0-1-0 | **504.5** | 25 | Malone, OH | 0-0-0-1 | **396** |
| 13 | Cumberland, KY | 0-0-2-0 | **494** | | | | |

## NCAA Division I Schools on Probation

As of Sept. 30, 2005, there were 28 Division I member institutions serving NCAA probations.

| School | Sport | Yrs | Penalty To End | School | Sport | Yrs | Penalty To End |
|---|---|---|---|---|---|---|---|
| Chicago St. | W Basketball | 2 | 12/16/05 | Washington | Football | 2 | 2/9/07 |
| Marshall | Football | 4 | 12/20/05 | Gardner-Webb | Baseball | 3 | 3/3/07 |
| | & M Basketball | 4 | 12/20/05 | | M & W Basketball | 3 | 3/3/07 |
| California | Football | 5 | 3/7/06 | | M Soccer | 3 | 3/3/07 |
| Arkansas | Football | 3 | 4/15/06 | | & W Track | 3 | 3/3/07 |
| | & M Basketball | 3 | 4/15/06 | Michigan | M Basketball | 4 | 5/6/07 |
| Auburn | M Basketball | 2 | 4/26/06 | CS-Northridge | M Basketball | 3 | 6/1/07 |
| Oregon | Football | 2 | 6/22/06 | St. Bonaventure | M Basketball | 3 | 7/17/07 |
| Villanova | M Basketball | 2 | 7/7/06 | TCU | M & W Indoor | 2 | 9/21/07 |
| Utah | M Basketball | 3 | 7/29/06 | | M & W Outdoor | 2 | 9/21/07 |
| Jacksonville | M Soccer | 5 | 8/29/06 | Missouri | M Basketball | 3 | 11/10/07 |
| | & W Rowing | 5 | 8/29/06 | Texas St.-San Marcos | Numerous | 3 | 3/9/08 |
| Wisconsin | M Basketball | 5 | 9/30/06 | Georgia | M Basketball | 4 | 4/16/08 |
| | & Football | 5 | 9/30/06 | Stony Brook | Numerous | 3 | 4/20/08 |
| Minnesota | W Basketball | 4 | 10/22/06 | Florida International | Football | 3 | 8/23/08 |
| | & M Basketball | 6 | 10/22/06 | Mississippi St. | Football | 4 | 10/25/08 |
| Tennessee St. | M Basketball | 3 | 10/23/06 | Nicholls St. | M Basketball | 4 | 5/8/09 |
| Fresno St. | M & W Basketball | 4 | 12/3/06 | | Football | 4 | 5/8/09 |
| | & M & W Soccer | 4 | 12/3/06 | Baylor | M Basketball | 5 | 6/22/10 |
| Alabama | Football | 5 | 1/31/07 | | Football | 5 | 6/22/10 |

### Remaining postseason and TV sanctions

**2005-2006 postseason bans:** TCU men's and women's indoor and outdoor track (team participation).
**2005-2006 television bans:** None.

## NCAA Graduation Rates Match All-Time High

The following table compares graduation rates of NCAA Division I student athletes with the entire student body in those schools. Years given denote the year in which students entered college. Rates are based on students who enrolled as freshmen, received an athletics scholarship and graduated in six years or less. All figures are percentages.

Source: NCAA Graduation-Rates Report, 2004.

| | 1992 | 1993 | 1994 | 1995 | 1996 | 1997 |
|---|---|---|---|---|---|---|
| All Student Athletes | 58 | 58 | 58 | 60 | 62 | 62 |
| Entire Student Body | 56 | 56 | 56 | 58 | 59 | 60 |
| Male Student Athletes | 52 | 51 | 51 | 54 | 55 | 55 |
| Male Student Body | 54 | 54 | 54 | 56 | 56 | 57 |
| Female Student Athletes | 68 | 68 | 69 | 69 | 70 | 70 |
| Female Student Body | 59 | 59 | 59 | 61 | 62 | 63 |
| Div. I-A Football Players | 51 | 48 | 51 | 53 | 54 | 57 |
| Male Basketball Players | 41 | 42 | 40 | 43 | 44 | 44 |
| Female Basketball Players | 62 | 63 | 65 | 65 | 66 | 64 |

## 2004-05 NCAA Team Champions

The NCAA administers 88 championships in 23 sports (not including Division I-A football). In 2004-2005, 75 different schools won titles (including I-A football champ USC) and 12 won multiple titles, led by Georgia and UCLA with three each.

**Multiple winners: Three**—GEORGIA (National Div. women's gymnastics, Div. I women's swimming & diving, Div. I men's golf); UCLA (National Div. men's and women's water polo, Div. I men's tennis).

**Two**—ABILENE CHRISTIAN (Div. II men's indoor and outdoor track); ARKANSAS (Div. I men's indoor and outdoor track); COLORADO (Div. I men's and women's cross country); DENVER (Div. I men's ice hockey, National Div. skiing); EMORY (Div. III women's swimming & diving, Div. III women's tennis); MIDDLEBURY, VT (Div. III men's and women's ice hockey); NOTRE DAME (Div. I women's soccer, National Div. fencing); SALISBURY, MD (Div. III field hockey, Div. III men's lacrosse); STANFORD (Div. I women's volleyball. Div. I women's tennis); TEXAS (Div. I baseball, Div. I women's outdoor track).

Overall titles in parentheses; (*) indicates defending champions.

## FALL

### Cross Country
#### Men

| Div. | Winner | Runner-Up | Score |
|---|---|---|---|
| I | Colorado | (2) Wisconsin | 90-94 |
| II | Western St., CO | (6) Adams St., CO* | 39-76 |
| III | Calvin, MI | (3) North Central, IL | 107-137 |

#### Women

| Div. | Winner | Runner-Up | Score |
|---|---|---|---|
| I | Colorado | (2) Stanford | 63-144 |
| II | Adams St., CO* | (10) Edinboro, PA | 31-101 |
| III | Williams, MA | (2) Middlebury, VT* | 110-129 |

### Field Hockey

| Div. | Winner | Runner-Up | Score |
|---|---|---|---|
| I | Wake Forest* | (3) Duke | 3-0 |
| II | Bloomsburg, PA* | (12) Bentley, MA | 3-2 (OT) |
| III | Salisbury, MD | (3) Middlebury, VT | 6-3 |

### Football

| Div. | Winner | Runner-Up | Score |
|---|---|---|---|
| I-A | USC | (10) Oklahoma | 55-19 |
| I-AA | James Madison | (1) Montana | 31-21 |
| II | Valdosta St., GA | (1) Pittsburg St., KS | 36-31 |
| III | Linfield, OR | (1) Mary Hardin-Baylor | 28-21 |

**Note:** There is no official Div. I-A playoff. USC defeated Oklahoma in the BCS Championship Game (Orange Bowl).

### Soccer
#### Men

| Div. | Winner | Runner-Up | Score |
|---|---|---|---|
| I | Indiana* | (7) UC Santa Barbara | 2-1 (PK) |
| II | Seattle | (1) So. Illinois-Edwardsville | 2-1 |
| III | Messiah, PA | (3) UC Santa Cruz | 4-0 |

#### Women

| Div. | Winner | Runner-Up | Score |
|---|---|---|---|
| I | Notre Dame | (2) UCLA | 2-1 (PK) |
| II | Metro St., CO | (1) Adelphi, NY | 3-2 |
| III | Wheaton, IL | (1) Puget Sound, WA | 2-1 (PK) |

**Note:** (PK) denotes penalty kick shootout.

### Volleyball
#### Women

| Div. | Winner | Runner-Up | Score |
|---|---|---|---|
| I | Stanford | (6) Minnesota | 3-0 |
| II | Barry, FL | (3) Truman St., MO | 3-1 |
| III | Juniata, PA | (1) Washington, MO* | 3-0 |

### Water Polo
#### Men

| Div. | Winner | Runner-Up | Score |
|---|---|---|---|
| National | UCLA | (8) Stanford | 10-9 (2OT) |

## WINTER

### Basketball
#### Men

| Div. | Winner | Runner-Up | Score |
|---|---|---|---|
| I | North Carolina | (4) Illinois | 75-70 |
| II | Virginia Union | (3) Bryant, RI | 63-58 |
| III | Wis.-Stevens Point* | (2) Rochester, NY | 73-49 |

#### Women

| Div. | Winner | Runner-Up | Score |
|---|---|---|---|
| I | Baylor | (1) Michigan St. | 84-62 |
| II | Washburn, KS | (1) Seattle Pacific | 70-53 |
| III | Millikin, IL | (1) Randolph-Macon, VA | 70-50 |

### Bowling
#### Women

| Div. | Winner | Runner-Up | Score |
|---|---|---|---|
| National | Nebraska | (2) Central Missouri St. | 4-2 |

**Note:** Women's bowling became an official NCAA sport in 2003-04.

### Fencing

| Div. | Winner | Runner-Up | Score |
|---|---|---|---|
| Combined | Notre Dame | (7) Ohio St.* | 173-171 |

### Gymnastics

| Div. | Winner | Runner-Up | Margin |
|---|---|---|---|
| Men | Oklahoma | (6) Ohio St. | by .225 |
| Women | Georgia | (6) Alabama | by .425 |

### Ice Hockey
#### Men

| Div. | Winner | Runner-Up | Score |
|---|---|---|---|
| I | Denver* | (7) North Dakota | 4-1 |
| III | Middlebury, VT* | (7) St. Thomas, MN | 5-0 |

#### Women

| Div. | Winner | Runner-Up | Score |
|---|---|---|---|
| I | Minnesota* | (2) Harvard | 4-3 |
| III | Middlebury, VT* | (2) Elmira, NY | 4-3 |

### Rifle

| Div. | Winner | Runner-Up | Score |
|---|---|---|---|
| Combined | Army | (1) Jacksonville St. | 4659-4658 |

### Skiing

| Div. | Winner | Runner-Up | Score |
|---|---|---|---|
| Combined | Denver | (18) Vermont | 622.5-575 |

### Swimming & Diving
#### Men

| Div. | Winner | Runner-Up | Score |
|---|---|---|---|
| I | Auburn* | (5) Stanford | 491-414 |
| II | Drury, MO | (3) CS-Bakersfield* | 726-480 |
| III | Kenyon, OH* | (26) Emory, GA | 556.5-404.5 |

### Women

| Div. | Winner | | Runner-Up | Score |
|---|---|---|---|---|
| I | Georgia | (4) | Auburn* | 609.5-492 |
| II | Truman St., MO* | (5) | Drury, MO | 579.5-530 |
| III | Emory, GA | (1) | Kenyon, OH* | 399.5-313 |

## Indoor Track
### Men

| Div. | Winner | | Runner-Up | Score |
|---|---|---|---|---|
| I | Arkansas | (18) | Florida | 56-46 |
| II | Abilene Christian* | (12) | Adams St., CO | 84-46 |
| III | Wis.-La Crosse* | (12) | Lincoln, PA | 53-38 |

### Women

| Div. | Winner | | Runner-Up | Score |
|---|---|---|---|---|
| I | Tennessee | (1) | Florida | 46-36 |
| II | St. Augustine's, NC | (5) | Abilene Christian | 53-48.5 |
| III | Wis.-Oshkosh* | (5) | Wartburg, IA | 36-32 |

## Wrestling
### Men

| Div. | Winner | | Runner-Up | Score |
|---|---|---|---|---|
| I | Oklahoma St.* | (33) | Michigan | 153-83 |
| II | Nebraska-Omaha* | (7) | Augustana, SD | 109.5-101 |
| III | Augsburg, MN | (9) | Wartburg, IA* | 162-104.5 |

## SPRING
### Baseball

| Div. | Winner | | Runner-Up | Score |
|---|---|---|---|---|
| I | Texas | (6) | Florida | 4-2, 6-2 |
| II | Florida Southern | (9) | North Florida | 12-9 |
| III | Wis.-Whitewater | (1) | Cortland St., NY | 11-4 |

**Note:** The Division I Championship Series is best-of-three.

## Golf
### Men

| Div. | Winner | | Runner-Up | Score |
|---|---|---|---|---|
| I | Georgia | (2) | Georgia Tech | 1135-1146 |
| II | S. Carolina-Aiken* | (2) | Armstrong Atlantic | 1158-1163 |
| III | Guilford, NC | (2) | Redlands, CA | 1174-1199 |

### Women

| Div. | Winner | | Runner-Up | Score |
|---|---|---|---|---|
| I | Duke | (3) | UCLA* | 1170-1175 |
| II | Rollins, FL* | (3) | Grand Valley St. | 1185-1220 |
| III | Methodist, NC* | (9) | Mary Hardin-Baylor | 1272-1284 |

## Lacrosse
### Men

| Div. | Winner | | Runner-Up | Score |
|---|---|---|---|---|
| I | Johns Hopkins | (8) | Duke | 9-8 |
| II | NY Inst. of Technology | (3) | Limestone, SC | 14-13 (OT) |
| III | Salisbury, MD* | (6) | Middlebury, VT | 11-10 |

### Women

| Div. | Winner | | Runner-Up | Score |
|---|---|---|---|---|
| I | Northwestern | (1) | Virginia* | 13-10 |
| II | Stonehill, MA | (2) | West Chester, PA | 13-10 |
| III | Colll. of New Jersey | (11) | Salisbury, MD | 9-7 |

## Rowing
### Women

| Div. | Winner | | Runner-Up | Score |
|---|---|---|---|---|
| I | California | (1) | Virginia | 67-63 |
| II | Western Washington | (1) | Mercyhurst, PA* | 20-12 |
| III | Ithaca, NY* | (2) | Smith, MA | 10-10† |

† While Ithaca and Smith tied with 10 pts., Ithaca was awarded the championship based on a higher finish in the Varsity Eights final.

## Softball

| Div. | Winner | | Runner-Up | Score |
|---|---|---|---|---|
| I | Michigan | (1) | UCLA* | 4-1 (10 inn.) |
| II | Lynn, FL | (1) | Kennesaw St., GA | 5-3 |
| III | St. Thomas, MN* | (2) | Salisbury, MD | 9-3 |

## Tennis
Note that both Div. II tournaments were team-only.

### Men

| Div. | Winner | | Runner-Up | Score |
|---|---|---|---|---|
| I | UCLA | (16) | Baylor* | 4-3 |
| II | West Florida* | (2) | North Florida | 5-0 |
| III | UC Santa Cruz | (5) | Middlebury, VT* | 4-1 |

### Women

| Div. | Winner | | Runner-Up | Score |
|---|---|---|---|---|
| I | Stanford* | (14) | Texas | 4-0 |
| II | Armstrong Atlantic | (3) | BYU-Hawaii* | 5-3 |
| III | Emory, GA* | (4) | Washington & Lee, VA | 5-3 |

## Outdoor Track
### Men

| Div. | Winner | | Runner-Up | Score |
|---|---|---|---|---|
| I | Arkansas* | (12) | Florida | 60-49 |
| II | Abilene Christian* | (15) | Adams St., CO | 109-84 |
| III | Lincoln, PA | (7) | Wis.-La Crosse* | 69-66.5 |

### Women

| Div. | Winner | | Runner-Up | Score |
|---|---|---|---|---|
| I | Texas | (4) | UCLA* & S. Carolina | 55-48 |
| II | Lincoln, MO* | (3) | CS-Bakersfield | 108-53 |
| III | Wartburg, IA | (1) | Calvin, MI & Wis-Oshkosh* | 43-42 |

## Volleyball
### Men

| Div. | Winner | | Runner-Up | Score |
|---|---|---|---|---|
| National | Pepperdine | (5) | UCLA | 3-2 |

## Water Polo
### Women

| Div. | Winner | | Runner-Up | Score |
|---|---|---|---|---|
| National | UCLA | (3) | Stanford | 3-2 |

## All-Time Team Champions
### Division I - Top Ten

Combined NCAA Division I men's, women's and coed team champions through spring 2005.

| | School | Men's | Women's | Coed | Total |
|---|---|---|---|---|---|
| 1 | UCLA | 69 | 28 | 0 | 97 |
| 2 | Stanford | 57 | 33 | 0 | 90 |
| 3 | USC | 72 | 11 | 0 | 83 |
| 4 | Oklahoma St. | 46 | 0 | 0 | 46 |
| 5 | Arkansas | 42 | 0 | 0 | 42 |
| 6 | LSU | 16 | 24 | 0 | 40 |
| 7 | Texas | 17 | 21 | 0 | 38 |
| 8 | Michigan | 30 | 2 | 0 | 32 |
| 9 | North Carolina | 9 | 22 | 0 | 31 |
| 10 | Penn State | 17 | 4 | 9 | 30 |

**Note:** Totals above do not reflect Division I-A football championships, which are not conducted by the NCAA. Coed championships include rifle, skiing and fencing (since 1990).

**Source:** NCAA

Providence
**Kim Smith**
Cross Country

Penn St.
**Luis Vargas**
Gymnastics

Arkansas
**Wallace Spearmon**
Track & Field

Dartmouth
**David Chodounsky**
Skiing

## 2004-05 Division I Individual Champions
Repeat champions in **bold** type.

### FALL

### Cross Country

| Men (10,000 meters) | Time |
|---|---|
| 1 Simon Bairu, Wisconsin | 30:37.7 |
| 2 Matt Gonzales, New Mexico | 30:40.9 |
| 3 Josphat Boit, Arkansas | 30:41.8 |

| Women (6,000 meters) | Time |
|---|---|
| 1 Kim Smith, Providence | 20:08.5 |
| 2 Renee Metivier, Colorado | 20:26.4 |
| 3 Caroline Bierbaum, Columbia | 20:30.7 |

### WINTER

### Fencing
#### Men

| Event | | Score |
|---|---|---|
| Foil | **Boaz Ellis**, Ohio St. | 15-8 |
| Epee | Mical Sobieraj, Notre Dame | 15-13 |
| Sabre | Sergey Isayenko, St. John's | 15-12 |

#### Women

| Event | | Score |
|---|---|---|
| Foil | Emily Cross, Harvard | 15-7 |
| Epee | **Anna Garina**, Wayne St. | 15-6 |
| Sabre | Emily Jacobson, Columbia | 15-11 |

### Gymnastics
#### Men

| Event | | Points |
|---|---|---|
| All-Around | **Luis Vargas**, Penn St. | 57.175 |
| Floor Exercise | **Graham Ackerman**, California | 9.600 |
| Pommel Horse | Luis Vargas, Penn St. | 9.787 |
| Rings | David Henderson, Oklahoma | 9.700 |
| Vault | Michael Reavis, Iowa | 9.550 |
| Parallel Bars | Justin Spring, Illinois | 9.737 |
| High Bar | Ronald Ferris, Ohio St. | 9.762 |

#### Women

| Event | | Points |
|---|---|---|
| All-Around | Tasha Schwikert, UCLA | 39.725 |
| Vault | Kristen Maloney, UCLA | 9.9375 |
| Uneven Bars | Terin Humphrey, Alabama | 9.9375 |
| Balance Beam | Kristen Maloney, UCLA | 9.9375 |
| Floor Exercise | **Courtney Bumpers**, UNC | 10.0000 |

### Rifle
### Combined
Number in parentheses denotes inner tens.
#### Smallbore

| | | Points |
|---|---|---|
| 1 | **Matthew Rawlings**, AK-Fairbanks | 686.5 |
| 2 | Jamie Beyerle, AK-Fairbanks | 686.5 |
| 3 | Kristina Fehlings, Nebraska | 685.2 |

**Note:** Rawlings defeated Beyerle in a "shootoff," 9.3-6.9.

#### Air Rifle

| | | Points |
|---|---|---|
| 1 | Beth Tidmore, Memphis | 694.2 |
| 2 | Andrea Franzen, Nebraska | 689.4 |
| 3 | Matthew Rawlings, AK-Fairbanks | 688.4 |

### Skiing
#### Men

| Event | | Time |
|---|---|---|
| Slalom | David Chodounsky, Dartmouth | 1:18.12 |
| Giant Slalom | Greg Hardy, Vermont | 1:45.49 |
| 10-k Classic | Rene Reisshauer, Denver | 30:49.1 |
| 20-k Freestyle | Rene Reisshauer, Denver | 55:57.3 |

#### Women

| Event | | Time |
|---|---|---|
| Slalom | Megan Hughes, Middlebury | 1:25.39 |
| Giant Slalom | Jamie Kingsbury, Vermont | 1:55.03 |
| 5-k Classic | Mandy Kaempf, AK-Anchorage | 17:19.3 |
| 15-k Freestyle | Mandy Kaempf, AK-Anchorage | 46:18.8 |

### Wrestling

| Wgt | Champion | Runner-Up |
|---|---|---|
| 125 | Joe Dubuque, Indiana | K. Ott, Illinois |
| 133 | Travis Lee, Cornell | S. Bunch, Edinboro |
| 141 | Teyon Ware, Oklahoma | N. Gallick, Iowa St. |
| 149 | Zack Esposito, Okla. St. | P. Simpson, Army |
| 157 | Ryan Bertin, Michigan | J. Johnston, Iowa |
| 165 | Johny Hendricks, Okla. St. | M. Perry, Iowa |
| 174 | **Chris Pendleton**, Okla. St. | B. Askren, Missouri |
| 184 | **Greg Jones**, W. Virginia | T. Baier, Cornell |
| 197 | Jake Rosholt, Okla. St. | S. Stender, N. Iowa |
| Hvy | Steve Mocco, Okla. St. | C. Konrad, Minnesota |

Auburn
**Kirsty Coventry**
Swimming

Florida
**Kerron Clement**
Track & Field

Duke
**Anna Grzebien**
Golf

Baylor
**Zuzana Zemenova**
Tennis

## Swimming & Diving
(*) indicates meet record.

### Men

| Event (yards) | | Time |
|---|---|---|
| 50 free | **Fred Bousquet**, Auburn | 18.90 |
| 100 free | Duje Draganja, California | 41.49* |
| 200 free | Simon Burnett, Arizona | 1:33.28 |
| 500 free | Peter Vanderkaay, Michigan | 4:09.82 |
| 1650 free | Larsen Jensen, USC | 14:32.01 |
| 100 back | Matt Grevers, Northwestern | 45.62 |
| 200 back | Ryan Lochte, Florida | 1:38.37* |
| 100 breast | Gary Marshall, Stanford | 52.68 |
| 200 breast | Vladislav Polyakov, Alabama | 1:53.93 |
| 100 butterfly | Duje Draganja, California | 45.39 |
| 200 butterfly | Davis Tarwater, Michigan | 1:42.30 |
| 200 IM | Ryan Lochte, Florida | 1:41.71* |
| 400 IM | Ous Mellouli, USC | 3:39.19 |
| 200 free relay | California | 1:15.78* |
| 400 free relay | California | 2:47.70* |
| 800 free relay | Florida | 6:16.53* |
| 200 medley relay | California | 1:25.30 |
| 400 medley relay | Stanford | 3:06.45 |

| Diving | | Points |
|---|---|---|
| 1-meter | Joona Puhakka, Arizona St. | 421.05 |
| 3-meter | **Joona Puhakka**, Arizona St. | 645.20 |
| Platform | Matthew Bricker, Auburn | 604.35 |

### Women

| Event (yards) | | Time |
|---|---|---|
| 50 free | **Kara Lynn Joyce**, Georgia | 21.97 |
| 100 free | **Kara Lynn Joyce**, Georgia | 47.50 |
| 200 free | **Margaret Hoelzer**, Auburn | 1:44.60 |
| 500 free | Emily Mason, Arizona | 4:37.11 |
| 1650 free | Flavia Rigamonti, SMU | 15:46.84 |
| 100 back | Marshi Smith, Arizona | 52.82 |
| 200 back | **Kirsty Coventry**, Auburn | 1:50.54 |
| 100 breast | Caroline Bruce, Stanford | 59.55 |
| 200 breast | Caroline Bruce, Stanford | 2:08.67 |
| 100 butterfly | Mary DeScenza, Georgia | 52.11 |
| 200 butterfly | **Mary DeScenza**, Georgia | 1:54.19 |
| 200 IM | Kirsty Coventry, Auburn | 1:54.37 |
| 400 IM | Kirsty Coventry, Auburn | 4:04.48 |
| 200 free relay | Georgia | 1:28.10* |
| 400 free relay | Georgia | 3:13.56* |
| 800 free relay | Georgia | 7:01.03* |
| 200 medley relay | Georgia | 1:37.81 |
| 400 medley relay | Georgia | 3:33.89 |

| Diving | | Points |
|---|---|---|
| 1-meter | Qiong Jie Huang, Hawaii | 327.00 |
| 3-meter | Blythe Hartley, USC | 586.15 |
| Platform | Cassandra Cardinell, Indiana | 501.45 |

## Indoor Track
(*) indicates meet record. (†) indicates world record.

### Men

| Event | | Time |
|---|---|---|
| 60 meters | **DaBryan Blanton**, Oklahoma | 6.58 |
| 200 meters | Wallace Spearmon, Arkansas | 20.10* |
| 400 meters | Kerron Clement, Florida | 44.57† |
| 800 meters | Kevin Hicks, Florida A&M | 1:46.97 |
| Mile | Nick Willis, Michigan | 4:00.69 |
| 3000 meters | Chris Solinsky, Wisconsin | 7:53.59 |
| 5000 meters | Ian Dobson, Stanford | 13:43.36 |
| 60-m hurdles | **Antwon Hicks**, Mississippi | 7.64 |
| 4x400-m relay | Florida | 3:03.51* |
| Distance medley relay | **Michigan** | 9:30.82 |

| Event | | Hgt/Dist |
|---|---|---|
| High Jump | Jesse Williams, USC | 7-5 |
| Pole Vault | Tommy Skipper, Oregon | 18-4½ |
| Long Jump | Aarik Wilson, Indiana | 26-9¾ |
| Triple Jump | Aarik Wilson, Indiana | 55-6¼ |
| Shot Put | Edis Elkasevic, Auburn | 64-7¼ |
| 35-lb Throw | Spyridon Jullien, Virginia Tech | 76-0¾ |
| Heptathlon | Maurice Smith, Auburn | 6004 pts. |

### Women

| Event | | Time |
|---|---|---|
| 60 meters | Fana Ashby, Auburn | 7.18 |
| 200 meters | Tremedia Brice, Texas Southern | 22.90 |
| 400 meters | Tiandra Ponteen, Florida | 50.91 |
| 800 meters | Aneita Denton, Arkansas | 2:03.65 |
| Mile | Anne Shadle, Nebraska | 4:38.23 |
| 3000 meters | Renee Metivier, Colorado | 9:22.81 |
| 5000 meters | Ida Nilsson, N. Arizona | 15:50.20 |
| 60-m hurdles | Virginia Powell, USC | 7.97 |
| 4x400-m relay | South Carolina | 3:30.01 |
| Distance medley relay | Michigan | 11:08.24 |

| Event | | Hgt/Dist |
|---|---|---|
| High Jump | **Chaunte Howard**, Georgia Tech | 6-3½ |
| Pole Vault | Amy Linnen, Kansas | 14-1¼ |
| Long Jump | Tianna Madison, Tennessee | 22-3 |
| Triple Jump | Gisele Oliveira, Clemson | 45-1¾ |
| Shot Put | Kimberli Barrett, Miami | 59-4¾ |
| 20-lb Throw | **Candice Scott**, Florida | 79-3¾* |
| Pentathlon | Ashley Selig, Nebraska | 4327 pts. |

## SPRING
## Golf
### Men

| | | Total |
|---|---|---|
| 1 | James Lepp, Washington | 70-67-76-63—276* |
| 2 | Michael Putnam, Pepperdine | 67-67-73-69—276 |
| 3 | Roberto Castro, Georgia Tech. | 69-68-71-71—279 |

* Lepp defeated Putnam in a 3-hole playoff.

## Golf (cont.)
### Women

| | | Total |
|---|---|---|
| 1 | Anna Grzebien, Duke | .73-75-65-73—286 |
| 2 | Leah Wigger, Virginia | .73-72-73-69—287 |
| 3 | Amie Cochran, UCLA | .71-79-70-68—288 |
| | & Brittany Lang, Duke | .74-75-68-71—288 |

## Tennis
### Men

**Singles—** Benedikt Dorsch (Baylor) def. Pierrik Ysern (San Diego), 6-2, 7-6(6).
**Doubles—** John Isner & Antonio Ruiz (Georgia) def. Mark Growcott & Ken Skupski (LSU), 7-6(4), 7-5.

### Women

**Singles—** Zuzana Zemenova (Baylor) def. Audra Cohen (Northwestern), 4-6, 6-2, 7-5.
**Doubles—** Alice Barnes & Erin Burdette (Stanford) def. Amber Liu & Anne Yelsey (Stanford), 6-3, 6-4.

## Outdoor Track
(*) indicates meet record
### Men

| Event | | Time |
|---|---|---|
| 100 meters | Walter Dix, Florida St. | 10.21 |
| 200 meters | **Wallace Spearmon**, Arkansas | 19.91 |
| 400 meters | Darold Williamson, Baylor | 44.51 |
| 800 meters | Dmitrijs Milkevics, Nebraska | 1:44.74 |
| 1500 meters | Leonel Manzano, Texas | 3:37.13 |
| 5000 meters | Ryan Hall, Stanford | 13:22.32 |
| 10,000 meters | Robert Cheseret, Arizona | 28:20.11 |
| 110-m hurdles | **Josh Walker**, Florida | 13.39 |
| 400-m hurdles | **Kerron Clement**, Florida | 47.56* |
| 3000-m steeple | Mircea Bogdan, UTEP | 8:27.29 |
| 4x100-m relay | Arkansas | 38.49 |
| 4x400-m relay | LSU | 2:59.59* |

| Event | | Hgt/Dist |
|---|---|---|
| High Jump | Jesse Williams, USC | 7-6 |
| Pole Vault | Robison Pratt, BYU | 18-0½ |
| Long Jump | Fabrice Lapierre, Texas A&M | 26-9 |
| Triple Jump | Rodrigo Mendes, BYU | 55-11 |
| Shot Put | Edis Elkasevic, Auburn | 68-6 |
| Discus | Michael Robertson, Stanford | 202-5 |
| Javelin | **Gabriel Wallin**, Boise St. | 258-5 |
| Hammer | Spyridon Jullien, Virginia Tech | 231-1 |
| Decathlon | Trey Hardee, Texas | 7881 pts. |

### Women

| Event | | Time |
|---|---|---|
| 100 meters | Marshevet Hooker, Texas | 11.16 |
| 200 meters | Sherri-Ann Brooks, Fla. Int'l. | 22.85 |
| 400 meters | Monique Henderson, UCLA | 50.10* |
| 800 meters | Aneita Denton, Arkansas | 2:02.84 |
| 1500 meters | Anne Shadle, Nebraska | 4:11.37 |
| 5000 meters | Megan Metcalfe, W. Virginia | 16:31.88 |
| 10,000 meters | Sara Slattery, Colorado | 33:02.21 |
| 100-m hurdles | Virginia Powell, USC | 12.80 |
| 400-m hurdles | Shauna Smith, Wyoming | 54.32 |
| 3000-m steeple | Victoria Mitchell, Butler | 9:54.32 |
| 4x100-m relay | Texas | 42.87 |
| 4x400-m relay | Texas | 3:27.13 |

| Event | | Hgt/Dist |
|---|---|---|
| High Jump | Sharon Day, Cal Poly-SLO | 6-4 |
| Pole Vault | Kate Soma, Washington | 14-1¼ |
| Long Jump | Tianna Madison, Tennessee | 21-10¼ |
| Triple Jump | Candice Baucham, UCLA | 46-2* |
| Shot Put | Kimberli Barrett, Miami-FL | 59-8½ |
| Discus | Beth Mallory, Alabama | 194-9 |
| Javelin | Dana Pounds, Air Force | 185-4 |
| Hammer | Loree Smith, Colorado St. | 224-8 |
| Heptathlon | Lela V. Nelson, Eastern Michigan | 5878 pts. |

## Championships
## Most Outstanding Players
### Men

| | |
|---|---|
| Baseball | David Maroul, Texas |
| Basketball | Sean May, North Carolina |
| Cross Country | Simon Bairu, Wisconsin* |
| Golf | James Lepp, Washington* |
| Gymnastics | Luis Vargas, Penn St.* |
| Ice Hockey | Peter Mannino, Denver |
| Lacrosse | Jesse Schwartzman, Johns Hopkins |
| Rifle (coed) | Matt Rawlings, AK-Fairbanks |
| Soccer: Offense | Drew McAthy, UC Santa Barbara |
| Soccer: Defense | Jay Nolly, Indiana |
| Swimming | Ryan Lochte, Florida |
| & Diving | Joona Puhakka, Arizona St. |
| Tennis | Benedikt Dorsch, Baylor* |
| Track: Indoor | Aarik Wilson, Indiana† |
| Track: Outdoor | Wallace Spearmon, Arkansas† |
| Volleyball | Sean Rooney, Pepperdine |
| Water Polo | Brett Ormsby, UCLA |
| Wrestling | Greg Jones, West Virginia |

### Women

| | |
|---|---|
| Basketball | Sophia Young, Baylor |
| Bowling | Amanda Burgoyne, Nebraska |
| Cross Country | Kim Smith, Providence* |
| Golf | Anna Grzebien, Duke* |
| Gymnastics | Tasha Schwikert, UCLA* |
| Ice Hockey | Natalie Darwitz, Minnesota |
| Lacrosse | Kristen Kjellman, Northwestern |
| Soccer: Offense | Katie Thorlakson, Notre Dame |
| Soccer: Defense | Erika Bohn, Notre Dame |
| Softball | Samantha Findlay, Michigan |
| Swimming | Kirsty Coventry, Auburn |
| & Diving | Blythe Hartley, USC |
| Tennis | Zuzana Zemenova, Baylor* |
| Track: Indoor | Fana Ashby, Auburn† |
| Track: Outdoor | Marshevet Hooker, Texas† |
| Volleyball | Ogonna Nnamani, Stanford |
| Water Polo | Natalie Golda, UCLA |

(*) indicates won individual or all-around NCAA championship; There were no official Outstanding Players in fencing, field hockey, I-AA football, rowing and skiing. (†) Outstanding players in indoor and outdoor track are the individuals earning the most points in the Championships.

## 2004-05 NAIA Team Champions
Total NAIA titles in parentheses.

### FALL

**Cross Country:** MEN'S–Virginia Intermont (1); WOMEN'S–Simon Fraser, BC (7). **Football:** MEN'S– Carroll, MT (3). **Soccer:** MEN'S–Lindenwood, MO (1); WOMEN'S–Lindsey Wilson, KY (1). **Volleyball:** WOMENS–California Baptist (1).

### WINTER

**Basketball:** MEN'S–Division I: John Brown, AR (1) and Division II: Walsh, OH (1); WOMEN'S–Division I: Union, TN (2) and Division II: Morningside, IA (2). **Swimming & Diving:** MEN'S–Simon Fraser, BC (17); WOMEN'S– California Baptist (1). **Indoor Track:** MEN'S–Lindenwood, MO (2); WOMEN'S–Oklahoma Baptist (1). **Wrestling:** MEN'S–Lindenwood, MO (2).

### SPRING

**Baseball:** MEN'S–Oklahoma City (1). **Golf:** MEN'S–Johnson & Wales, FL (1); WOMEN'S–Oklahoma City (1). **Softball:** WOMEN'S–Simon Fraser, BC (3). **Tennis:** MEN'S–Azusa Pacific, CA (1); WOMEN'S–Auburn-Montgomery (6). **Outdoor Track:** MEN'S–Dickinson St., ND (2); WOMEN'S–Simon Fraser, BC (2).

## Annual NCAA Division I Team Champions

Men's and women's NCAA Division I team champions from cross country to wrestling. Also see team champions for baseball, basketball, bowling, football, golf, ice hockey, soccer and tennis in the appropriate chapters throughout the almanac. See pages 448-450 for the list of 2004-05 individual champions.

## CROSS COUNTRY

### Men

With two runners in the top five and five in the top 35, Colorado raced to its second Division I men's cross country title in the last four years. Brent Vaughn and Bret Schoolmeester placed fourth and fifth, respectively, to lead the Buffaloes to victory. Colorado finished with 90 points to edge Wisconsin (94). Arkansas placed a distant third with 202 points. Wisconsin's Simon Bairu claimed the individual title, completing the 10K course in 30:38. (*Terre Haute, IN; Nov. 22, 2004.*)

**Multiple winners:** Arkansas (11); Michigan St. (8); UTEP (7); Oregon, Stanford and Villanova (4); Drake, Indiana, Penn St. and Wisconsin (3); Colorado, Iowa St., San Jose St. and Western Michigan (2).

| Year | | Year | | Year | | Year | | Year | |
|------|--|------|--|------|--|------|--|------|--|
| 1938 | Indiana | 1951 | Syracuse | 1965 | Western Mich. | 1979 | UTEP | 1993 | Arkansas |
| 1939 | Michigan St. | 1952 | Michigan St. | 1966 | Villanova | 1980 | UTEP | 1994 | Iowa St. |
| 1940 | Indiana | 1953 | Kansas | 1967 | Villanova | 1981 | UTEP | 1995 | Arkansas |
| 1941 | Rhode Island | 1954 | Oklahoma St. | 1968 | Villanova | 1982 | Wisconsin | 1996 | Stanford |
| 1942 | Indiana | 1955 | Michigan St. | 1969 | UTEP | 1983 | Vacated | 1997 | Stanford |
| | & Penn St. | 1956 | Michigan St. | 1970 | Villanova | 1984 | Arkansas | 1998 | Arkansas |
| 1943 | Not held | 1957 | Notre Dame | 1971 | Oregon | 1985 | Wisconsin | 1999 | Arkansas |
| 1944 | Drake | 1958 | Michigan St. | 1972 | Tennessee | 1986 | Arkansas | 2000 | Arkansas |
| 1945 | Drake | 1959 | Michigan St. | 1973 | Oregon | 1987 | Arkansas | 2001 | Colorado |
| 1946 | Drake | 1960 | Houston | 1974 | Oregon | 1988 | Wisconsin | 2002 | Stanford |
| 1947 | Penn St. | 1961 | Oregon St. | 1975 | UTEP | 1989 | Iowa St. | 2003 | Stanford |
| 1948 | Michigan St. | 1962 | San Jose St. | 1976 | UTEP | 1990 | Arkansas | 2004 | Colorado |
| 1949 | Michigan St. | 1963 | San Jose St. | 1977 | Oregon | 1991 | Arkansas | | |
| 1950 | Penn St. | 1964 | Western Mich. | 1978 | UTEP | 1992 | Arkansas | | |

### Women

Paced by Renee Metivier's second-place finish, Colorado ran away with their second title in five years at the 2004 Division I Cross Country Championship. Liza Pasciuto placed ninth, followed closely by teammate Christine Bolf in 10th as the Buffaloes amassed a total of 63 points. Duke was runner-up with 144 points, while Providence's 164 points was good for third. Providence's indoor and outdoor champ Kim Smith took the overall individual title. (*Terre Haute, IN; Nov. 22, 2004.*)

**Multiple winners:** Villanova (7); BYU (4); Colorado, Oregon, Stanford, Virginia and Wisconsin (2).

| Year | | Year | | Year | | Year | | Year | |
|------|--|------|--|------|--|------|--|------|--|
| 1981 | Virginia | 1986 | Texas | 1991 | Villanova | 1996 | Stanford | 2001 | BYU |
| 1982 | Virginia | 1987 | Oregon | 1992 | Villanova | 1997 | BYU | 2002 | BYU |
| 1983 | Oregon | 1988 | Kentucky | 1993 | Villanova | 1998 | Villanova | 2003 | Stanford |
| 1984 | Wisconsin | 1989 | Villanova | 1994 | Villanova | 1999 | BYU | 2004 | Colorado |
| 1985 | Wisconsin | 1990 | Villanova | 1995 | Providence | 2000 | Colorado | | |

## FENCING

### Men & Women

While men's epeeist Mical Sobieraj claimed Notre Dame's only individual championship, it was the dominant Irish women who led a stunning comeback for the school's seventh overall team fencing national championship. Women's epeeist Amy Orlando, sabre Mariel Zagunis and three-time NCAA foil champ Alicja Kryczalo all recorded second-place finishes as Notre Dame overcame a late 24-point deficit to edge runner-up Ohio State, 173-171. (*Houston, TX; Mar. 17-20, 2005.*)

**Multiple winners:** Penn St. (9); Notre Dame (3); Columbia/Barnard (2). **Note:** Prior to 1990, men and women held separate championships. Men's multiple winners included: NYU (12); Columbia (11); Wayne St. (7); Navy, Notre Dame and Penn (3); Illinois (2). Women's multiple winners included: Wayne St. (3); Yale (2).

| Year | | Year | | Year | | Year | |
|------|--|------|--|------|--|------|--|
| 1990 | Penn St. | 1994 | Notre Dame | 1998 | Penn St. | 2002 | Penn St. |
| 1991 | Penn St. | 1995 | Penn St. | 1999 | Penn St. | 2003 | Notre Dame |
| 1992 | Columbia/Barnard | 1996 | Penn St. | 2000 | Penn St. | 2004 | Ohio St. |
| 1993 | Columbia/Barnard | 1997 | Penn St. | 2001 | St. John's | 2005 | Notre Dame |

## FIELD HOCKEY

### Women

Tamar Meijer netted two goals, Kelly Wood added the third and the stellar Wake Forest defense took care of the rest as the Deacons defeated Duke, 3-0, to register their third consecutive NCAA field hockey title. It was the second straight year the two ACC rivals met in the championship game. Wake's Kristina Gagliardi needed just two saves to record her second consecutive shutout of the 2004 tournament. (*Winston-Salem, NC; Nov. 20, 2004.*)

**Multiple winners:** Old Dominion (9); North Carolina (4); Maryland and Wake Forest (3); Connecticut (2).

| Year | | Year | | Year | | Year | | Year | |
|------|--|------|--|------|--|------|--|------|--|
| 1981 | Connecticut | 1986 | Iowa | 1991 | Old Dominion | 1996 | North Carolina | 2001 | Michigan |
| 1982 | Old Dominion | 1987 | Maryland | 1992 | Old Dominion | 1997 | North Carolina | 2002 | Wake Forest |
| 1983 | Old Dominion | 1988 | Old Dominion | 1993 | Maryland | 1998 | Old Dominion | 2003 | Wake Forest |
| 1984 | Old Dominion | 1989 | North Carolina | 1994 | J. Madison | 1999 | Maryland | 2004 | Wake Forest |
| 1985 | Connecticut | 1990 | Old Dominion | 1995 | North Carolina | 2000 | Old Dominion | | |

## Annual NCAA Division I Team Champions (Cont.)

### GYMNASTICS

### Men

Oklahoma edged Ohio State by a mere .225 to capture its sixth NCAA men's gymnastics title and third in the last four years. The Sooners' final performer, freshman Jonathan Horton, scored a clutch 9.5 in the rings competition to deliver the championship. Oklahoma accumulated a school-record 222.675 points to beat runner-up Ohio State (225.450), Illinois (223.750) and defending champ Penn State (222.400). *(West Point, NY; Apr. 7-9, 2005.)*

**Multiple winners:** Penn St. (11); Illinois (9); Nebraska (8); Oklahoma (6); California and So. Illinois (4); Iowa St., Michigan, Ohio St. and Stanford (3); Florida St and UCLA (2).

| Year | Year | Year | Year | Year |
|---|---|---|---|---|
| 1938 Chicago | 1957 Penn St. | 1970 Michigan | 1983 Nebraska | 1998 California |
| 1939 Illinois | 1958 Michigan St. | & Michigan (T) | 1984 UCLA | 1999 Michigan |
| 1940 Illinois | & Illinois | 1971 Iowa St. | 1985 Ohio St. | 2000 Penn St. |
| 1941 Illinois | 1959 Penn St. | 1972 So. Illinois | 1986 Arizona St. | 2001 Ohio St. |
| 1942 Illinois | 1960 Penn St. | 1973 Iowa St. | 1987 UCLA | 2002 Oklahoma |
| 1943-47 Not held | 1961 Penn St. | 1974 Iowa St. | 1988 Nebraska | 2003 Oklahoma |
| 1948 Penn St. | 1962 USC | 1975 California | 1989 Illinois | 2004 Penn St. |
| 1949 Temple | 1963 Michigan | 1976 Penn St. | 1990 Nebraska | 2005 Oklahoma |
| 1950 Illinois | 1964 So. Illinois | 1977 Indiana St. | 1991 Oklahoma | |
| 1951 Florida St. | 1965 Penn St. | & Oklahoma | 1992 Stanford | (T) indicates won tram- |
| 1952 Florida St. | 1966 So. Illinois | 1978 Oklahoma | 1993 Stanford | poline competition |
| 1953 Penn St. | 1967 So. Illinois | 1979 Nebraska | 1994 Nebraska | (1969-70). |
| 1954 Penn St. | 1968 California | 1980 Nebraska | 1995 Stanford | |
| 1955 Illinois | 1969 Iowa | 1981 Nebraska | 1996 Ohio St. | |
| 1956 Illinois | & Michigan (T) | 1982 Nebraska | 1997 California | |

### Women

Suzanne Yoculan's well-balanced Georgia squad overcame a late surge by Alabama to win its sixth NCAA women's gymnastics title and first since 1999. The Bulldogs, led by freshman Katie Heenan with an all-around score of 39.725, amassed 197.825 points to beat Alabama (197.400) and Utah (197.275). Alabama junior Ashley Miles scored two perfect tens on the floor and vault to pace the Crimson Tide. *(Auburn, AL; Apr. 21-23, 2005.)*

**Multiple winners:** Utah (9); Georgia (6); UCLA (5); Alabama (4).

| Year | Year | Year | Year | Year |
|---|---|---|---|---|
| 1982 Utah | 1987 Georgia | 1992 Utah | 1997 UCLA | 2002 Alabama |
| 1983 Utah | 1988 Alabama | 1993 Georgia | 1998 Georgia | 2003 UCLA |
| 1984 Utah | 1989 Georgia | 1994 Utah | 1999 Georgia | 2004 UCLA |
| 1985 Utah | 1990 Utah | 1995 Utah | 2000 UCLA | 2005 Georgia |
| 1986 Utah | 1991 Alabama | 1996 Alabama | 2001 UCLA | |

### LACROSSE

### Men

Sophomore Jake Byrne scored with 13:35 remaining to lift Johns Hopkins to a 9-8 victory over Duke in the NCAA Division I men's lacrosse championship game. It is the eighth overall title for the Blue Jays and their first in 18 years. Goaltender Jesse Schwartzman shut out the high-powered Duke offense during the fourth quarter and was named the tournament's most outstanding player. The victory completed a perfect 16-0 season for Johns Hopkins as they became just the third team in men's history to accomplish that feat. A record crowd of 44,920 watched the affair. *(Philadelphia, PA; May 30, 2005.)*

**Multiple winners:** Syracuse and Johns Hopkins (8); Princeton (6); North Carolina (4); Cornell and Virginia (3); Maryland (2).

| Year | Year | Year | Year | Year |
|---|---|---|---|---|
| 1971 Cornell | 1978 Johns Hopkins | 1985 Johns Hopkins | 1992 Princeton | 1999 Virginia |
| 1972 Virginia | 1979 Johns Hopkins | 1986 North Carolina | 1993 Syracuse | 2000 Syracuse |
| 1973 Maryland | 1980 Johns Hopkins | 1987 Johns Hopkins | 1994 Princeton | 2001 Princeton |
| 1974 Johns Hopkins | 1981 North Carolina | 1988 Syracuse | 1995 Syracuse | 2002 Syracuse |
| 1975 Maryland | 1982 North Carolina | 1989 Syracuse | 1996 Princeton | 2003 Virginia |
| 1976 Cornell | 1983 Syracuse | 1990 Syracuse* | 1997 Princeton | 2004 Syracuse |
| 1977 Cornell | 1984 Johns Hopkins | 1991 North Carolina | 1998 Princeton | 2005 Johns Hopkins |

*Title was later vacated due to action by the NCAA Committee on Infractions.

### Women

Northwestern upended defending champ Virginia, 13-10, in the NCAA Division I women's lacrosse championship game for its first lacrosse title, and first team championship in any sport since 1941. Kristen Kjellman scored a team-high five goals in the title game and was awarded tournament MVP honors for her efforts. Sarah Albrecht added three goals while goaltender Ashley Gersuk registered eight saves to anchor the Wildcats defense. Northwestern ended its season with a perfect 21-0 mark. Cary Chasney scored a championship game record-tying six goals for Virginia (17-5). *(Annapolis, MD; May 22, 2005.)*

**Multiple winners:** Maryland (9); Princeton and Virginia (3); Penn St. and Temple (2).

| Year | Year | Year | Year | Year |
|---|---|---|---|---|
| 1982 Massachusetts | 1987 Penn St. | 1992 Maryland | 1997 Maryland | 2002 Princeton |
| 1983 Delaware | 1988 Temple | 1993 Virginia | 1998 Maryland | 2003 Princeton |
| 1984 Temple | 1989 Penn St. | 1994 Princeton | 1999 Maryland | 2004 Virginia |
| 1985 New Hampshire | 1990 Harvard | 1995 Maryland | 2000 Maryland | 2005 Northwestern |
| 1986 Maryland | 1991 Virginia | 1996 Maryland | 2001 Maryland | |

## RIFLE
### Men & Women

The U.S. Military Academy at West Point ended Alaska-Fairbanks' six-year reign, winning its first team title in any sport in over 50 years at the NCAA Rifle Championships. Just four points separated the tournament's top four teams as Army (4659 pts.) edged Jacksonville State (4658), Nebraska (4657) and Alaska-Fairbanks (4656). The defending champ Nanooks won the smallbore competition but fell on day two due to a poor air rifle performance. (*Colorado Springs, CO; Mar. 11-12, 2005.*)

**Multiple winners:** West Virginia (13); Alaska-Fairbanks (7); Tennessee Tech (3); Murray St. (2).

| Year | | Year | | Year | | Year | | Year | |
|------|--|------|--|------|--|------|--|------|--|
| 1980 | Tenn. Tech | 1986 | West Virginia | 1992 | West Virginia | 1998 | West Virginia | 2004 | AK-Fairbanks |
| 1981 | Tenn. Tech | 1987 | Murray St. | 1993 | West Virginia | 1999 | AK-Fairbanks | 2005 | Army |
| 1982 | Tenn. Tech | 1988 | West Virginia | 1994 | AK-Fairbanks | 2000 | AK-Fairbanks | | |
| 1983 | West Virginia | 1989 | West Virginia | 1995 | West Virginia | 2001 | AK-Fairbanks | | |
| 1984 | West Virginia | 1990 | West Virginia | 1996 | West Virginia | 2002 | AK-Fairbanks | | |
| 1985 | Murray St. | 1991 | West Virginia | 1997 | West Virginia | 2003 | AK-Fairbanks | | |

## ROWING
### NCAA Championships
#### Women

Trailing Virginia by five points heading into the Varsity Eights, California put on a late surge to win its first NCAA women's rowing title. The Bears crossed the finish line in 6:20.74 to edge Princeton (6:22.80), Harvard (6:23.86) and Virginia (6:24.22). The win gave Cal a total of 67 points to best runner-up Virginia and defending champ Brown (49). Virginia had previously won both the Varsity Fours and the Second Varsity Eights. (*Rancho Cordova, CA; May 27-29, 2005.*)

**Multiple winners:** Brown (4); Washington (3).

| Year | Overall winner | Varsity Eights | Year | Overall winner | Varsity Eights |
|------|----------------|----------------|------|----------------|----------------|
| 1997 | Washington | Washington | 2002 | Brown | Washington |
| 1998 | Washington | Washington | 2003 | Harvard | Harvard |
| 1999 | Brown | Brown | 2004 | Brown | Brown |
| 2000 | Brown | Brown | 2005 | California | California |
| 2001 | Washington | Washington | | | |

## Intercollegiate Rowing Association Regatta
### VARSITY EIGHTS
#### Men

Harvard captured its third straight Varsity Eights title and third straight Ten Eyck trophy, crossing the finish line in 5:31.68, ahead of runner-up Princeton (5:32.94) and third place California (5:35.90). (*Cooper River, Camden, NJ; June 2-4, 2005.*)

The IRA was formed in 1895 by several Northeastern colleges after Harvard and Yale quit the Rowing Association (established in 1871) to stage an annual race of their own. Since then the IRA Regatta has been contested over courses of varying lengths in Poughkeepsie, N.Y., Marietta, Ohio, Syracuse, N.Y. and Camden, N.J.

**Distances:** 4 miles (1895-97,1899-1916,1925-41); 3 miles (1898,1921-24,1947-49,1952-63,1965-67); 2 miles (1920,1950-51); 2000 meters (1964, since 1968).

**Multiple winners:** Cornell (24); California (14); Navy (13); Washington (11); Penn (9); Brown and Wisconsin (7); Syracuse (6); Columbia (4); Harvard and Princeton (3); Northeastern (2).

| Year | | Year | | Year | | Year | | Year | |
|------|--|------|--|------|--|------|--|------|--|
| 1895 | Columbia | 1917-19 | Not held | 1941 | Washington | 1967 | Penn | 1989 | Penn |
| 1896 | Cornell | 1920 | Syracuse | 1942-46 | Not held | 1968 | Penn | 1990 | Wisconsin |
| 1897 | Cornell | 1921 | Navy | 1947 | Navy | 1969 | Penn | 1991 | Northeastern |
| 1898 | Penn | 1922 | Navy | 1948 | Washington | 1970 | Washington | 1992 | Dartmouth, |
| 1899 | Penn | 1923 | Washington | 1949 | California | 1971 | Cornell | | Navy & Penn† |
| 1900 | Penn | 1924 | Washington | 1950 | Washington | 1972 | Penn | 1993 | Brown |
| 1901 | Cornell | 1925 | Navy | 1951 | Wisconsin | 1973 | Wisconsin | 1994 | Brown |
| 1902 | Cornell | 1926 | Washington | 1952 | Navy | 1974 | Wisconsin | 1995 | Brown |
| 1903 | Cornell | 1927 | Columbia | 1953 | Navy | 1975 | Wisconsin | 1996 | Princeton |
| 1904 | Syracuse | 1928 | California | 1954 | Navy* | 1976 | California | 1997 | Washington |
| 1905 | Cornell | 1929 | Columbia | 1955 | Cornell | 1977 | Cornell | 1998 | Princeton |
| 1906 | Cornell | 1930 | Cornell | 1956 | Cornell | 1978 | Syracuse | 1999 | California |
| 1907 | Cornell | 1931 | Navy | 1957 | Cornell | 1979 | Brown | 2000 | California |
| 1908 | Syracuse | 1932 | California | 1958 | Cornell | 1980 | Navy | 2001 | California |
| 1909 | Cornell | 1933 | Not held | 1959 | Wisconsin | 1981 | Cornell | 2002 | California |
| 1910 | Cornell | 1934 | California | 1960 | California | 1982 | Cornell | 2003 | Harvard |
| 1911 | Cornell | 1935 | California | 1961 | California | 1983 | Brown | 2004 | Harvard |
| 1912 | Cornell | 1936 | Washington | 1962 | Cornell | 1984 | Navy | 2005 | Harvard |
| 1913 | Syracuse | 1937 | Washington | 1963 | Cornell | 1985 | Princeton | | |
| 1914 | Columbia | 1938 | Navy | 1964 | California | 1986 | Brown | | |
| 1915 | Cornell | 1939 | California | 1965 | Navy | 1987 | Brown | | |
| 1916 | Syracuse | 1940 | Washington | 1966 | Wisconsin | 1988 | Northeastern | | |

*In 1954, Navy was disqualified because of an ineligible coxswain; no trophies were given.
†First dead heat in history of IRA Regatta.

## Annual NCAA Division I Team Champions (Cont.)

## National Rowing Championship
### VARSITY EIGHTS
#### Men

National championship raced annually from 1982-96 in Bantam, Ohio over a 2,000-meter course on Lake Harsha. Winner received the Herschede Cup. Regatta discontinued in 1997.
**Multiple winners:** Harvard (6); Brown (3); Wisconsin (2).

| Year | Champion | Time | Runner-up | Time | Year | Champion | Time | Runner-up | Time |
|------|----------|------|-----------|------|------|----------|------|-----------|------|
| 1982 | Yale | 5:50.8 | Cornell | 5:54.15 | 1990 | Wisconsin | 5:52.5 | Harvard | 5:56.84 |
| 1983 | Harvard | 5:59.6 | Washington | 6:00.0 | 1991 | Penn | 5:58.21 | Northeastern | 5:58.48 |
| 1984 | Washington | 5:51.1 | Yale | 5:55.6 | 1992 | Harvard | 5:33.97 | Dartmouth | 5:34.28 |
| 1985 | Harvard | 5:44.4 | Princeton | 5:44.87 | 1993 | Brown | 5:54.15 | Penn | 5:56.98 |
| 1986 | Wisconsin | 5:57.8 | Brown | 5:59.9 | 1994 | Brown | 5:24.52 | Harvard | 5:25.83 |
| 1987 | Harvard | 5:35.17 | Brown | 5:35.63 | 1995 | Brown | 5:23.40 | Princeton | 5:25.83 |
| 1988 | Harvard | 5:35.98 | Northeastern | 5:37.07 | 1996 | Princeton | 5:57.47 | Penn | 6:03.28 |
| 1989 | Harvard | 5:36.6 | Washington | 5:38.93 | 1997 | discontinued | | | |

#### Women

National championship held over various distances at 10 different venues from 1979-96. Distances– 1000 meters (1979-81); 1500 meters (1982-83); 1000 meters (1984); 1750 meters (1985); 2000 meters (1986-88, 1991-96); 1852 meters (1989-90). Winner received the Ferguson Bowl. Regatta discontinued in 1997.
**Multiple winners:** Washington (7); Princeton (4); Boston University (2).

| Year | Champion | Time | Runner-up | Time | Year | Champion | Time | Runner-up | Time |
|------|----------|------|-----------|------|------|----------|------|-----------|------|
| 1979 | Yale | 3:06 | California | 3:08.6 | 1988 | Washington | 6:41.0 | Yale | 6:42.37 |
| 1980 | California | 3:05.4 | Oregon St. | 3:05.8 | 1989 | Cornell | 5:34.9 | Wisconsin | 5:37.5 |
| 1981 | Washington | 3:20.6 | Yale | 3:22.9 | 1991 | Boston Univ. | 7:03.2 | Cornell | 7:06.21 |
| 1982 | Washington | 4:56.4 | Wisconsin | 4:59.83 | 1992 | Boston Univ. | 6:28.79 | Cornell | 6:32.79 |
| 1983 | Washington | 4:57.5 | Dartmouth | 5:03.02 | 1993 | Princeton | 6:40.75 | Washington | 6:43.86 |
| 1984 | Washington | 3:29.48 | Radcliffe | 3:31.08 | 1994 | Princeton | 6:11.38 | Yale | 6:14.46 |
| 1985 | Washington | 5:28.4 | Wisconsin | 5:32.0 | 1995 | Princeton | 6:11.98 | Washington | 6:12.69 |
| 1986 | Wisconsin | 6:53.28 | Radcliffe | 6:53.34 | 1996 | Brown | 6:45.7 | Princeton | 6:49.3 |
| 1987 | Washington | 6:33.8 | Yale | 6:37.4 | 1997 | discontinued | | | |

### The Harvard-Yale Regatta

Harvard made it six in a row and 19 of the last 21 by defeating Yale at the 140th running of the Harvard/Yale Regatta on June 11, 2005. The win gave the Harvard crew is third consecutive undefeated season. Harvard's Varsity Eights squad finished the four-mile course on the Thames River in New London, Conn. in 19:20.4, almost 40 seconds ahead of the Elis (20:00.0). Harvard was also victorious in the freshman race, while Yale's Second Varsity squad recorded a 20-second victory. The Harvard/Yale Regatta is the nation's oldest intercollegiate sporting event. Harvard holds an 87-53 series edge.

## SKIING
### Men & Women

After a two-year hiatus, Denver regained its championship form at the 2005 NCAA Skiing National Championships for its 18th title. The Pioneers amassed a total of 622.5 points to crush the rest of the field at Trapp Family Lodge. Host Vermont placed second, 47.5 points behind with 575 while Utah finished third with 545. Rene Reisshauer led Denver with two individual titles in the men's Nordic events, taking the 10-k Classic, then following with a dominating performance in the 20-k Freestyle, finishing 51 seconds ahead of his closest competitor. Alaska-Anchorage's Mandy Kaempf was the meet's other double champ, winning the women's 5-k Classic and 15-k Freestyle. (Stowe, VT; March 9-12, 2005.)
**Multiple winners:** Denver (18); Colorado (15); Utah (10); Vermont (5); Dartmouth and Wyoming (2).

| Year | | Year | | Year | | Year | | Year | |
|------|--|------|--|------|--|------|--|------|--|
| 1954 | Denver | 1965 | Denver | 1976 | Colorado | 1986 | Utah | 1997 | Utah |
| 1955 | Denver | 1966 | Denver | | & Dartmouth | 1987 | Utah | 1998 | Colorado |
| 1956 | Denver | 1967 | Denver | 1977 | Colorado | 1988 | Utah | 1999 | Colorado |
| 1957 | Denver | 1968 | Wyoming | 1978 | Colorado | 1989 | Vermont | 2000 | Denver |
| 1958 | Dartmouth | 1969 | Denver | 1979 | Colorado | 1990 | Vermont | 2001 | Denver |
| 1959 | Colorado | 1970 | Denver | 1980 | Vermont | 1991 | Colorado | 2002 | Denver |
| 1960 | Colorado | 1971 | Denver | 1981 | Utah | 1992 | Vermont | 2003 | Utah |
| 1961 | Denver | 1972 | Colorado | 1982 | Colorado | 1993 | Utah | 2004 | New Mexico |
| 1962 | Denver | 1973 | Colorado | 1983 | Utah | 1994 | Vermont | 2005 | Denver |
| 1963 | Denver | 1974 | Colorado | 1984 | Utah | 1995 | Colorado | | |
| 1964 | Denver | 1975 | Colorado | 1985 | Wyoming | 1996 | Utah | | |

## SOFTBALL

### Women

Freshman Samantha Findlay blasted a 10th-inning, three-run homer over the left field wall to give Michigan a 4-1 victory over two-time defending champ UCLA and its first NCAA softball title. It is the first NCAA Division I softball championship for any school east of the Mississippi River. The two evenly matched teams had split the first two games of the best-of-three series with UCLA grabbing Game 1, 5-0, and Michigan winning Game 2, 5-2.

UCLA first baseman Lisa Dodd gave the Bruins an early 1-0 lead with a solo shot in the bottom of the second. Findlay singled in the tying run in the top of the sixth and the score stayed knotted at one until her heroics in the top of the tenth. With three hits in the final game (five overall in the best-of-three series), she became the first freshman positional player to earn World Series most outstanding player honors. Wolverine hurler Jennifer Ritter pitched a complete game for the victory while UCLA's Anjelica Selden was the hard-luck loser, also throwing all 10 innings and striking out ten Michigan batters. (*Oklahoma City, OK; June 2-8, 2005.*)

**Multiple winners:** UCLA (10); Arizona (6); Texas A&M (2).

| Year | Year | Year | Year | Year |
|------|------|------|------|------|
| 1982 UCLA | 1987 Texas A&M | 1992 UCLA | 1997 Arizona | 2002 California |
| 1983 Texas A&M | 1988 UCLA | 1993 Arizona | 1998 Fresno St. | 2003 UCLA |
| 1984 UCLA | 1989 UCLA | 1994 Arizona | 1999 UCLA | 2004 UCLA |
| 1985 UCLA | 1990 UCLA | 1995 UCLA* | 2000 Oklahoma | 2005 Michigan |
| 1986 CS-Fullerton | 1991 Arizona | 1996 Arizona | 2001 Arizona | |

*Title was later vacated due to action by the NCAA Committee on Infractions.

## SWIMMING & DIVING

### Men

The Auburn Tigers proved unbeatable once again, scoring 491 points at the NCAA Division I Men's Swimming and Diving Championships to win their third consecutive title and fifth overall. Stanford finished runner-up with 414 points while Arizona placed third with 388. The well-balanced Auburn squad reached its lofty total with just two individual victories. Fred Bousquet won the 50-yard freestyle for the third straight year in 18.90 after previously setting a new NCAA record in the prelims with a dazzling 18.74. Diver Matthew Bricker was Auburn's other individual titlist with an impressive victory in the platform dive. California's Duje Draganja had a spectacular meet, winning both the 100-yard butterfly, then following that with an NCAA record 41.49 in the 100-yard freestyle. Florida ace Ryan Lochte set an NCAA and American record in the 200-yard individual medley (1:41.71) and earned swimmer of the meet honors. (*Minneapolis, MN; Mar. 24-26, 2005.*)

**Multiple winners:** Michigan and Ohio St. (11); Texas and USC (9); Stanford (8); Indiana (6); Auburn (5); Yale (4); California and Florida (2).

| Year | Year | Year | Year | Year |
|------|------|------|------|------|
| 1937 Michigan | 1951 Yale | 1965 USC | 1979 California | 1993 Stanford |
| 1938 Michigan | 1952 Ohio St. | 1966 USC | 1980 California | 1994 Stanford |
| 1939 Michigan | 1953 Yale | 1967 Stanford | 1981 Texas | 1995 Michigan |
| 1940 Michigan | 1954 Ohio St. | 1968 Indiana | 1982 UCLA | 1996 Texas |
| 1941 Michigan | 1955 Ohio St. | 1969 Indiana | 1983 Florida | 1997 Auburn |
| 1942 Yale | 1956 Ohio St. | 1970 Indiana | 1984 Florida | 1998 Stanford |
| 1943 Ohio St. | 1957 Michigan | 1971 Indiana | 1985 Stanford | 1999 Auburn |
| 1944 Yale | 1958 Michigan | 1972 Indiana | 1986 Stanford | 2000 Texas |
| 1945 Ohio St. | 1959 Michigan | 1973 Indiana | 1987 Stanford | 2001 Texas |
| 1946 Ohio St. | 1960 USC | 1974 USC | 1988 Texas | 2002 Texas |
| 1947 Ohio St. | 1961 Michigan | 1975 USC | 1989 Texas | 2003 Auburn |
| 1948 Michigan | 1962 Ohio St. | 1976 USC | 1990 Texas | 2004 Auburn |
| 1949 Ohio St. | 1963 USC | 1977 USC | 1991 Texas | 2005 Auburn |
| 1950 Ohio St. | 1964 USC | 1978 Tennessee | 1992 Stanford | |

### Women

Georgia became the first team in NCAA history to win all five team relay events and powered to a dominant victory at the Division I Women's Swimming and Diving Championships. It is the fourth overall title for the Bulldogs, who finished with 609.5 points, followed by three-time defending champ Auburn (492) and Arizona (440). In addition to its unprecedented relay success, Georgia also received two individual titles each from Kara Lynn Joyce (50- and 100-yard free) and Mary DeScenza (100- and 200-yard butterfly). Auburn's Kirsty Coventry was the meet's only triple winner as she successfully defended her title in the 200-yard backstroke and added titles in the 200- and 400-yard individual medley. Her Tiger teammate Margaret Hoelzer repeated in the 200-yard freestyle. (*West LaFayette, IN; Mar. 17-19, 2005.*)

**Multiple winners:** Stanford (8); Texas (7); Georgia (4); Auburn (3).

| Year | Year | Year | Year | Year |
|------|------|------|------|------|
| 1982 Florida | 1987 Texas | 1992 Stanford | 1997 USC | 2002 Auburn |
| 1983 Stanford | 1988 Texas | 1993 Stanford | 1998 Stanford | 2003 Auburn |
| 1984 Texas | 1989 Stanford | 1994 Stanford | 1999 Georgia | 2004 Auburn |
| 1985 Texas | 1990 Texas | 1995 Stanford | 2000 Georgia | 2005 Georgia |
| 1986 Texas | 1991 Texas | 1996 Stanford | 2001 Georgia | |

## Annual NCAA Division I Team Champions (Cont.)

### INDOOR TRACK

#### Men

One night after the costly disqualification of its distance medley relay squad, Arkansas roared back to win its record 18th NCAA men's Division I indoor track and field title. Speedster Wallace Spearmon recorded the Razorbacks' only individual title with a new American record (20.10) in the 200-meter dash. Arkansas wrapped up the title even before the meet's final event, the 4x400-meter relay, accumulating a total of 56 points to best runner-up Florida (46) and Wisconsin (43). Indiana's Aarik Wilson was the meet's only individual double winner with victories in the long jump and triple jump. Florida's Kerron Clement broke Michael Johnson's ten-year old record (44.63) in the 400-meter dash with a scorching 44.57, then anchored Florida to victory in the 4x400. *(Fayetteville, AR; Mar. 11-12, 2005.)*

**Multiple winners:** Arkansas (18); UTEP (7); Kansas and Villanova (3); LSU and USC (2).

| Year | Year | Year | Year | Year |
|---|---|---|---|---|
| 1965 Missouri | 1974 UTEP | 1983 SMU | 1992 Arkansas | 2001 LSU |
| 1966 Kansas | 1975 UTEP | 1984 Arkansas | 1993 Arkansas | 2002 Tennessee |
| 1967 USC | 1976 UTEP | 1985 Arkansas | 1994 Arkansas | 2003 Arkansas |
| 1968 Villanova | 1977 Washington St. | 1986 Arkansas | 1995 Arkansas | 2004 LSU |
| 1969 Kansas | 1978 UTEP | 1987 Arkansas | 1996 George Mason | 2005 Arkansas |
| 1970 Kansas | 1979 Villanova | 1988 Arkansas | 1997 Arkansas | |
| 1971 Villanova | 1980 UTEP | 1989 Arkansas | 1998 Arkansas | |
| 1972 USC | 1981 UTEP | 1990 Arkansas | 1999 Arkansas | |
| 1973 Manhattan | 1982 UTEP | 1991 Arkansas | 2000 Arkansas | |

#### Women

Buoyed by 17 points in the 60-meter dash, the Tennessee Lady Vols won their first non-basketball NCAA title in the school's history at the Division I Women's Track and Field Championships. Tennessee recorded 46 points, ahead of runner-up Florida (36) and Miami-FL (32). While Auburn's Fana Ashby won the 60-meter dash in 7.18, Tennessee's Toyin Olupona, Tianna Madison and Courtney Champion finished second, third and sixth, respectively, to lift their team to victory. Madison was Tennessee's only individual titlist with her 22-3 leap in the long jump. The Lady Vols clinched the title with a second-place showing in the final event, the 4x400-m relay. *(Fayetteville, AR; Mar. 11-12, 2005.)*

**Multiple winners:** LSU (11); Texas (5); Nebraska and UCLA (2).

| Year | Year | Year | Year | Year |
|---|---|---|---|---|
| 1983 Nebraska | 1988 Texas | 1993 LSU | 1998 Texas | 2003 LSU |
| 1984 Nebraska | 1989 LSU | 1994 LSU | 1999 Texas | 2004 LSU |
| 1985 Florida St. | 1990 Texas | 1995 LSU | 2000 UCLA | 2005 Tennessee |
| 1986 Texas | 1991 LSU | 1996 LSU | 2001 UCLA | |
| 1987 LSU | 1992 Florida | 1997 LSU | 2002 LSU | |

### OUTDOOR TRACK

#### Men

Surprise, surprise! Arkansas won its third straight title, its 11th in the last 14 years and 12th overall at the NCAA Division I Men's Outdoor Track and Field Championships. The Razorbacks finished with 60 points, followed by Florida (49) and LSU (36). Sophomore sprinter Wallace Spearmon won the 200-meter title in 19.93 while teammate Tyson Gay placed third (20.16). The duo also led Arkansas to victory in the 4x100-meter relay. Meet and collegiate records were set by LSU's 4x400-meter relay team (2:59.59) and Florida phenom Kerron Clement, who followed up his world record 400-meter dash performance in the Indoor Championships with a 47.56 in the 400-m hurdles. *(Sacramento, CA; June 8-11, 2005.)*

**Multiple winners:** USC (26); Arkansas (12); UCLA (8); UTEP (6); Illinois and Oregon (5); LSU and Stanford (4); Kansas and Tennessee (3); SMU (2).

| Year | Year | Year | Year | Year |
|---|---|---|---|---|
| 1921 Illinois | 1939 USC | 1957 Villanova | 1974 Tennessee | 1992 Arkansas |
| 1922 California | 1940 USC | 1958 USC | 1975 UTEP | 1993 Arkansas |
| 1923 Michigan | 1941 USC | 1959 Kansas | 1976 USC | 1994 Arkansas |
| 1924 Not held | 1942 USC | | 1977 Arizona St. | 1995 Arkansas |
| 1925 Stanford* | 1943 USC | 1960 Kansas | 1978 UCLA & UTEP | 1996 Arkansas |
| 1926 USC* | 1944 Illinois | 1961 USC | 1979 UTEP | 1997 Arkansas |
| 1927 Illinois* | 1945 Navy | 1962 Oregon | | 1998 Arkansas |
| 1928 Stanford | 1946 Illinois | 1963 USC | 1980 UTEP | 1999 Arkansas |
| 1929 Ohio St. | 1947 Illinois | 1964 Oregon | 1981 UTEP | |
| | 1948 Minnesota | 1965 Oregon & USC | 1982 UTEP | 2000 Stanford |
| 1930 USC | 1949 USC | 1966 UCLA | 1983 SMU | 2001 Tennessee |
| 1931 USC | | 1967 USC | 1984 Oregon | 2002 LSU |
| 1932 Indiana | 1950 USC | 1968 USC | 1985 Arkansas | 2003 Arkansas |
| 1933 LSU | 1951 USC | 1969 San Jose St. | 1986 SMU | 2004 Arkansas |
| 1934 Stanford | 1952 USC | | 1987 UCLA | 2005 Arkansas |
| 1935 USC | 1953 USC | 1970 BYU, Kansas | 1988 UCLA | |
| 1936 USC | 1954 USC | & Oregon | 1989 LSU | |
| 1937 USC | 1955 USC | 1971 UCLA | | |
| 1938 USC | 1956 UCLA | 1972 UCLA | 1990 LSU | |
| | | 1973 UCLA | 1991 Tennessee | |

(*) indicates unofficial championship.

AP/Wide World Photos

*Texas sprinter **Marshevet Hooker** edges ahead of Tennessee's Cleo Tyson, left, to win the 100-meter dash title at the NCAA Championships in Sacramento.*

## Women

Coach Bev Kearney's Texas squad won its first title since 1999 and fourth overall at the NCAA Division I Women's Outdoor Track and Field Championships. The Longhorns amassed 55 points to get by UCLA and South Carolina, who tied for second with 48. Sophomore Marshevet Hooker won the 100-meter dash and also anchored Texas' 4x100-meter relay team to victory in 42.87. The championship was still on the line heading into the meet's final event, the 4x400-meter relay. Texas trailed UCLA by three points and was five points ahead of South Carolina but when the foursome of Sheretta Jones, Melaine Walker, LaTashia Kerr and Jerrika Chapple broke the tape first, the championship was theirs.

Two UCLA Bruins broke meet records as Monique Henderson ran a 50.10 in the 400-meters and Candice Baucham set a new mark (46-2) in the triple jump. (*Sacramento, CA; June 8-11, 2005.*)

**Multiple winners:** LSU (13); Texas (4); UCLA (3).

| Year | Year | Year | Year | Year |
|---|---|---|---|---|
| 1982 UCLA | 1987 LSU | 1992 LSU | 1997 LSU | 2002 South Carolina |
| 1983 UCLA | 1988 LSU | 1993 LSU | 1998 Texas | 2003 LSU |
| 1984 Florida St. | 1989 LSU | 1994 LSU | 1999 UCLA | 2004 UCLA |
| 1985 Oregon | 1990 LSU | 1995 LSU | 2000 LSU | 2005 Texas |
| 1986 Texas | 1991 LSU | 1996 LSU | 2001 USC | |

## VOLLEYBALL

### Men

Top-seeded Pepperdine won a thrilling, come-from-behind five-game match over host UCLA for its fifth overall men's national volleyball title and first since 1992. UCLA had never lost an NCAA tournament match on its home floor until Pepperdine's 30-23, 23-30, 24-30, 30-25, 15-10 victory. The tournament's most outstanding player, Sean Rooney, led Pepperdine with 26 kills, six block assists and eight digs. Teammate Jon Parfitt added 18 kills and seven digs while UCLA was led by Jonathan Acosta, who recorded 29 kills and a .523 attack percentage. (*Los Angeles, CA; May 5, 2005.*)

**Multiple winners:** UCLA (18); Pepperdine (5); USC (4); BYU (3).

| Year | Year | Year | Year | |
|---|---|---|---|---|
| 1970 UCLA | 1979 UCLA | 1988 USC | 1997 Stanford | *Division II |
| 1971 UCLA | 1980 USC | 1989 UCLA | 1998 UCLA | †Title was later vacat- |
| 1972 UCLA | 1981 UCLA | 1990 USC | 1999 BYU | ed due to action by |
| 1973 San Diego St. | 1982 UCLA | 1991 Long Beach St. | 2000 UCLA | the NCAA Committee |
| 1974 UCLA | 1983 UCLA | 1992 Pepperdine | 2001 BYU | on Infractions. |
| 1975 UCLA | 1984 UCLA | 1993 UCLA | 2002 Hawaii† | |
| 1976 UCLA | 1985 Pepperdine | 1994 Penn St. | 2003 Lewis, IL* | |
| 1977 USC | 1986 Pepperdine | 1995 UCLA | 2004 BYU | |
| 1978 Pepperdine | 1987 UCLA | 1996 UCLA | 2005 Pepperdine | |

## Annual NCAA Division I Team Champions (Cont.)
### Women

Stanford captured its sixth NCAA women's volleyball title with a three-game sweep of Minnesota, 30-23, 30-27, 30-21. Senior Ogonna Nnamani was overpowering for the Cardinal as she blasted 29 kills and hit .562 for the match. She totaled an NCAA tournament-record 165 kills during her team's 21 games and was named most outstanding player. Cardinal setter Bryn Kehoe dished out 48 assists while Minnesota's Erin Martin and Trisha Bratford recorded 13 kills each to lead the Gophers. (*Long Beach, CA; Dec. 18, 2004.*)

**Multiple winners:** Stanford (6); Hawaii, Long Beach St., UCLA and USC (3); Nebraska and Pacific (2).

| Year | | Year | | Year | | Year | | Year | |
|------|--|------|--|------|--|------|--|------|--|
| 1981 | USC | 1986 | Pacific | 1991 | UCLA | 1996 | Stanford | 2001 | Stanford |
| 1982 | Hawaii | 1987 | Hawaii | 1992 | Stanford | 1997 | Stanford | 2002 | USC |
| 1983 | Hawaii | 1988 | Texas | 1993 | Long Beach St. | 1998 | Long Beach St. | 2003 | USC |
| 1984 | UCLA | 1989 | Long Beach St. | 1994 | Stanford | 1999 | Penn St. | 2004 | Stanford |
| 1985 | Pacific | 1990 | UCLA | 1995 | Nebraska | 2000 | Nebraska | | |

## WATER POLO
### Men

Sophomore Logan Powell netted the game winner with 13 seconds left in double overtime as the UCLA Bruins edged host Stanford, 10-9, in the NCAA men's water polo championship game. It is the eighth title for UCLA and first since 2000. Down by two goals with under a minute to play in regulation, Stanford struck for two goals within 30 seconds to send the game into overtime. Senior attacker Brett Ormsby tallied two goals and was named Final Four MVP. (*Stanford, CA; Dec. 5, 2004.*)

**Multiple winners:** California (11); Stanford (10); UCLA (8); UC-Irvine (3); USC (2).

| Year | | Year | | Year | | Year | | Year | |
|------|--|------|--|------|--|------|--|------|--|
| 1969 | UCLA | 1977 | California | 1985 | Stanford | 1993 | Stanford | 2001 | Stanford |
| 1970 | UC-Irvine | 1978 | Stanford | 1986 | Stanford | 1994 | Stanford | 2002 | Stanford |
| 1971 | UCLA | 1979 | UC-S. Barbara | 1987 | California | 1995 | UCLA | 2003 | USC |
| 1972 | UCLA | 1980 | Stanford | 1988 | California | 1996 | UCLA | 2004 | UCLA |
| 1973 | California | 1981 | Stanford | 1989 | UC-Irvine | 1997 | Pepperdine | | |
| 1974 | California | 1982 | UC-Irvine | 1990 | California | 1998 | USC | | |
| 1975 | California | 1983 | California | 1991 | California | 1999 | UCLA | | |
| 1976 | Stanford | 1984 | California | 1992 | California | 2000 | UCLA | | |

### Women

Undefeated UCLA won its third NCAA women's water polo title with a 3-2 victory over Stanford in the championship game. The Bruins carried a 2-0 lead into halftime behind goals by Natalie Golda and Brittany Rowe, but Cardinal senior Hannah Luber closed the gap early in the third quarter. Rowe's second made it a two-goal lead early in the fourth and while Stanford's Katie Hansen scored with four minutes remaining in the game, the Cardinal could get no closer. (*Ann Arbor, MI; May 15, 2005.*)

**Multiple winner:** UCLA (3).

| Year | | Year | | Year | | Year | | Year | |
|------|--|------|--|------|--|------|--|------|--|
| 2001 | UCLA | 2002 | Stanford | 2003 | UCLA | 2004 | USC | 2005 | UCLA |

## WRESTLING
### Men

With five individual champions and a school-record 153 points, Oklahoma State cruised to its third consecutive NCAA Division I wrestling title and 33rd overall. The Cowboys were so dominant, they actually clinched the team title after Day 2 of the three-day event. Zack Esposito (149 pounds), Johny Hendricks (165), Chris Pendleton (174), Jake Rosholt (197) and heavyweight Steve Mocco were the school's five individual titlists, tying an NCAA record. (*St. Louis, MO; Mar. 17-19, 2005.*)

**Multiple winners:** Oklahoma St. (33); Iowa (20); Iowa St. (8); Oklahoma (7); Minnesota (2).

| Year | | Year | | Year | | Year | | Year | |
|------|--|------|--|------|--|------|--|------|--|
| 1928 | Okla. A&M* | 1943-45 | Not held | 1961 | Okla. St. | 1977 | Iowa St. | 1993 | Iowa |
| 1929 | Okla. A&M | 1946 | Okla. A&M | 1962 | Okla. St. | 1978 | Iowa | 1994 | Okla. St. |
| 1930 | Okla. A&M | 1947 | Cornell Col. | 1963 | Oklahoma | 1979 | Iowa | 1995 | Iowa |
| 1931 | Okla. A&M* | 1948 | Okla. A&M | 1964 | Okla. St. | 1980 | Iowa | 1996 | Iowa |
| 1932 | Indiana* | 1949 | Okla. A&M | 1965 | Iowa St. | 1981 | Iowa | 1997 | Iowa |
| 1933 | Okla. A&M* | 1950 | Northern Iowa | 1966 | Okla. St. | 1982 | Iowa | 1998 | Iowa |
| | & Iowa St.* | 1951 | Oklahoma | 1967 | Michigan St. | 1983 | Iowa | 1999 | Iowa |
| 1934 | Okla. A&M | 1952 | Oklahoma | 1968 | Okla. St. | 1984 | Iowa | 2000 | Iowa |
| 1935 | Okla. A&M | 1953 | Penn St. | 1969 | Iowa St. | 1985 | Iowa | 2001 | Minnesota |
| 1936 | Oklahoma | 1954 | Okla. A&M | 1970 | Iowa St. | 1986 | Iowa | 2002 | Minnesota |
| 1937 | Okla. A&M | 1955 | Okla. A&M | 1971 | Okla. St. | 1987 | Iowa St. | 2003 | Okla. St. |
| 1938 | Okla. A&M | 1956 | Okla. A&M | 1972 | Iowa St. | 1988 | Arizona St. | 2004 | Okla. St. |
| 1939 | Okla. A&M | 1957 | Oklahoma | 1973 | Iowa St. | 1989 | Okla. St. | 2005 | Okla. St. |
| 1940 | Okla. A&M | 1958 | Okla. St. | 1974 | Oklahoma | 1990 | Okla. St. | | |
| 1941 | Okla. A&M | 1959 | Okla. St. | 1975 | Iowa | 1991 | Iowa | | |
| 1942 | Okla. A&M | 1960 | Oklahoma | 1976 | Iowa | 1992 | Iowa | | |

(*) indicates unofficial champions. **Note:** Oklahoma A&M became Oklahoma St. in 1958.

# Halls of Fame & Awards

Legendary Dolphins quarterback **Dan Marino** was busted up in Canton, Ohio in 2005.

## BASEBALL

### National Baseball Hall of Fame & Museum

Established in 1935 by Major League Baseball to celebrate the game's 100th anniversary. **Address:** 25 Main Street, Cooperstown, NY 13326. **Telephone:** (607) 547-7200. **Web:** www.baseballhalloffame.org

**Eligibility:** In August 2001, the Hall of Fame announced changes in the way players are elected via the Veterans Committee. The voting done by Baseball Writers' Association of America remains unchanged. Nominated players must have played at least parts of 10 seasons in the major leagues and be retired for at least five. Certain nominated players not elected by the writers can become eligible via the Veterans Committee. The new Veterans Committee will be comprised of all living Hall of Famers (currently 60 people) as well as all living winners of the Ford Frick (14) and J.G. Taylor Spink (13) Awards and three members of the old 15-member Veterans Committee with unexpired terms. There was no Veterans Committee vote in 2002. Beginning in 2003 the new Veterans Committee votes every two years on former players and every four years on managers, umpires and executives. Previously, the committee voted annually.

Also, the eligibility of all players that had been dropped from the ballots for not receiving five percent of the vote was restored and those players can now be immediately considered by the new Veterans Committee. The players on baseball's ineligible list are still excluded from consideration. Pete Rose is the only living ex-player on that list.

**Class of 2005** (2): BBWAA vote— **Wade Boggs**, Boston (1982-92), New York Yankees (1993-97), Tampa Bay (1998-99); **Ryne Sanberg**, Philadelphia (1981), Chicago Cubs (1982-94, 97).

**2005 Top 10 vote-getters** (516 BBWAA ballots cast, 387 needed to elect): 1. **Wade Boggs** (474), 2. **Ryne Sandberg** (393), 3. **Bruce Sutter** (344), 4. **Jim Rice** (307), 5. **Rich Gossage** (285), 6. **Andre Dawson** (270), 7. **Bert Blyleven** (211), 8. **Lee Smith** (200), 9. **Jack Morris** (172), 10. **Tommy John** (123).

**Elected first year on ballot** (40): Hank Aaron, Ernie Banks, Johnny Bench, Wade Boggs, George Brett, Lou Brock, Rod Carew, Steve Carlton, Ty Cobb, Dennis Eckersley, Bob Feller, Bob Gibson, Reggie Jackson, Walter Johnson, Al Kaline, Sandy Koufax, Mickey Mantle, Christy Mathewson, Willie Mays, Willie McCovey, Paul Molitor, Joe Morgan, Eddie Murray, Stan Musial, Jim Palmer, Kirby Puckett, Brooks Robinson, Frank Robinson, Jackie Robinson, Babe Ruth, Nolan Ryan, Mike Schmidt, Tom Seaver, Ozzie Smith, Warren Spahn, Willie Stargell, Honus Wagner, Ted Williams, Dave Winfield, Carl Yastrzemski and Robin Yount.

Members are listed with years of induction; (+) indicates deceased members.

### Catchers

| | | | | | | |
|---|---|---|---|---|---|---|
| | Bench, Johnny | 1989 | + | Cochrane, Mickey | 1947 | + Hartnett, Gabby ...... 1955 |
| | Berra, Yogi | 1972 | + | Dickey, Bill | 1954 | + Lombardi, Ernie ...... 1986 |
| + | Bresnahan, Roger | 1945 | + | Ewing, Buck | 1939 | + Schalk, Ray ......... 1955 |
| + | Campanella, Roy | 1969 | + | Ferrell, Rick | 1984 | |
| | Carter, Gary | 2003 | | Fisk, Carlton | 2000 | |

### 1st Basemen

| | | | | | | |
|---|---|---|---|---|---|---|
| + | Anson, Cap | 1939 | + | Connor, Roger | 1976 | McCovey, Willie ..... 1986 |
| + | Beckley, Jake | 1971 | + | Foxx, Jimmie | 1951 | + Mize, Johnny ....... 1981 |
| + | Bottomley, Jim | 1974 | + | Gehrig, Lou | 1939 | Murray, Eddie ...... 2003 |
| + | Brouthers, Dan | 1945 | + | Greenberg, Hank | 1956 | Perez, Tony ......... 2000 |
| | Cepeda, Orlando | 1999 | + | Kelly, George | 1973 | + Sisler, George ...... 1939 |
| + | Chance, Frank | 1946 | | Killebrew, Harmon | 1984 | + Terry, Bill .......... 1954 |

### 2nd Basemen

| | | | | | | |
|---|---|---|---|---|---|---|
| | Carew, Rod | 1991 | + | Herman, Billy | 1975 | + Robinson, Jackie ... 1962 |
| + | Collins, Eddie | 1939 | + | Hornsby, Rogers | 1942 | Sandberg, Ryne ... 2005 |
| | Doerr, Bobby | 1986 | + | Lajoie, Nap | 1937 | Schoendienst, Red .. 1989 |
| + | Evers, Johnny | 1946 | + | Lazzeri, Tony | 1991 | |
| + | Fox, Nellie | 1997 | | Mazeroski, Bill | 2001 | **Designated Hitters** |
| + | Frisch, Frankie | 1947 | + | McPhee, Bid | 2000 | Molitor, Paul ....... 2004 |
| + | Gehringer, Charlie | 1949 | | Morgan, Joe | 1990 | |

### Shortstops

| | | | | | | |
|---|---|---|---|---|---|---|
| | Aparicio, Luis | 1984 | + | Jackson, Travis | 1982 | + Tinker, Joe ......... 1946 |
| + | Appling, Luke | 1964 | + | Jennings, Hugh | 1945 | + Vaughan, Arky ...... 1985 |
| + | Bancroft, Dave | 1971 | + | Maranville, Rabbit | 1954 | + Wagner, Honus ..... 1936 |
| | Banks, Ernie | 1977 | + | Reese, Pee Wee | 1984 | + Wallace, Bobby ..... 1953 |
| + | Boudreau, Lou | 1970 | | Rizzuto, Phil | 1994 | + Ward, Monte ........ 1964 |
| + | Cronin, Joe | 1956 | + | Sewell, Joe | 1977 | Yount, Robin ....... 1999 |
| + | Davis, George | 1998 | | Smith, Ozzie | 2002 | |

### 3rd Basemen

| | | | | | | |
|---|---|---|---|---|---|---|
| + | Baker, Frank | 1955 | | Kell, George | 1983 | Schmidt, Mike ...... 1995 |
| | Boggs, Wade | 2005 | + | Lindstrom, Fred | 1976 | + Traynor, Pie ........ 1948 |
| | Brett, George | 1999 | + | Mathews, Eddie | 1978 | |
| + | Collins, Jimmy | 1945 | | Robinson, Brooks | 1983 | |

### Center Fielders

| | | | | | | |
|---|---|---|---|---|---|---|
| + | Ashburn, Richie | 1995 | + | Doby, Larry | 1998 | + Roush, Edd ......... 1962 |
| + | Averill, Earl | 1975 | + | Duffy, Hugh | 1945 | Snider, Duke ....... 1980 |
| + | Carey, Max | 1961 | + | Hamilton, Billy | 1961 | + Speaker, Tris ....... 1937 |
| + | Cobb, Ty | 1936 | + | Mantle, Mickey | 1974 | + Waner, Lloyd ....... 1967 |
| + | Combs, Earle | 1970 | | Mays, Willie | 1979 | + Wilson, Hack ....... 1979 |
| + | DiMaggio, Joe | 1955 | | Puckett, Kirby | 2001 | |

## Left Fielders

| | | |
|---|---|---|
| Brock, Lou . . . . . . . . . . . .1985 | + Kelley, Joe . . . . . . . . . . . .1971 | + Simmons, Al . . . . . . . . . .1953 |
| + Burkett, Jesse . . . . . . . . .1946 | Kiner, Ralph . . . . . . . . . .1975 | + Stargell, Willie · · · · · · · ·1988 |
| + Clarke, Fred . . . . . . . . . .1945 | + Manush, Heinie . . . . . . . .1964 | + Wheat, Zack . . . . . . . . . .1959 |
| + Delahanty, Ed . . . . . . . . .1945 | + Medwick, Joe . . . . . . . . .1968 | Williams, Billy . . . . . . . . .1987 |
| + Goslin, Goose . . . . . . . . .1968 | Musial, Stan . . . . . . . . . .1969 | + Williams, Ted . . . . . . . . .1966 |
| + Hafey, Chick . . . . . . . . . .1971 | + O'Rourke, Jim . . . . . . . . .1945 | Yastrzemski, Carl . . . . . . .1989 |

## Right Fielders

| | | |
|---|---|---|
| Aaron, Hank . . . . . . . . . .1982 | Kaline, Al . . . . . . . . . . . .1980 | + Ruth, Babe . . . . . . . . . . .1936 |
| + Clemente, Roberto . . . . . .1973 | + Keeler, Willie . . . . . . . . .1939 | + Slaughter, Enos . . . . . . . .1985 |
| + Crawford, Sam . . . . . . . .1957 | + Kelly, King . . . . . . . . . . .1945 | + Thompson, Sam . . . . . . . .1974 |
| + Cuyler, Kiki . . . . . . . . . .1968 | + Klein, Chuck . . . . . . . . . .1980 | + Waner, Paul . . . . . . . . . .1952 |
| + Flick, Elmer . . . . . . . . . .1963 | + McCarthy, Tommy . . . . . .1946 | Winfield, Dave . . . . . . . . .2001 |
| + Heilmann, Harry . . . . . . .1952 | + Ott, Mel . . . . . . . . . . . .1951 | + Youngs, Ross . . . . . . . . .1972 |
| + Hooper, Harry . . . . . . . .1971 | + Rice, Sam . . . . . . . . . . .1963 | |
| Jackson, Reggie . . . . . . . .1993 | Robinson, Frank . . . . . . . .1982 | |

## Pitchers

| | | |
|---|---|---|
| + Alexander, Grover . . . . . .1938 | + Dean, Dizzy . . . . . . . . . .1953 | Gibson, Bob . . . . . . . . . .1981 |
| + Bender, Chief . . . . . . . . .1953 | + Drysdale, Don . . . . . . . . .1984 | + Gomez, Lefty . . . . . . . . .1972 |
| + Brown, Mordecai . . . . . . .1949 | Eckersley, Dennis . . . . . . .2004 | + Grimes, Burleigh . . . . . . .1964 |
| Bunning, Jim . . . . . . . . . .1996 | + Faber, Red . . . . . . . . . . .1964 | + Grove, Lefty . . . . . . . . . .1947 |
| Carlton, Steve . . . . . . . . .1994 | Feller, Bob . . . . . . . . . . .1962 | + Haines, Jess . . . . . . . . . .1970 |
| + Chesbro, Jack . . . . . . . . .1946 | Fingers, Rollie . . . . . . . . .1992 | + Hoyt, Waite . . . . . . . . . .1969 |
| + Clarkson, John . . . . . . . .1963 | Ford, Whitey . . . . . . . . . .1974 | |
| + Coveleski, Stan . . . . . . . .1969 | + Galvin, Pud . . . . . . . . . .1965 | |

---

## Major League Baseball's All-Time Team — 1969 and 1997

The Baseball Writers' Association of America originally selected an all-time team as part of major league baseball's 100th anniversary, announcing the outcome of its vote on July 21, 1969. Vote totals were not released. Another vote was released when a panel of 36 BWAA members picked an all-time team for the *Classic Sports Network* just before the 1997 All-Star Game. This time vote totals were given, the single outfield category was divided into three (left, center and right) and two recently popularized positions—the designated hitter and relief pitcher—were added. In the most recent vote two points were awarded for first-place votes and one point for second place. Point totals follow the names with the number of first-place votes in parentheses. All-time team members are listed in **bold** type

### 1969 Vote

C  **Mickey Cochrane**, Bill Dickey, Roy Campanella
1B  **Lou Gehrig**, George Sisler, Stan Musial
2B  **Rogers Hornsby**, Charlie Gehringer, Eddie Collins
SS  **Honus Wagner**, Joe Cronin, Ernie Banks
3B  **Pie Traynor**, Brooks Robinson, Jackie Robinson
OF  **Babe Ruth**, **Ty Cobb**, **Joe DiMaggio**, Ted Williams, Tris Speaker, Willie Mays

RHP  **Walter Johnson**, Christy Mathewson, Cy Young
LHP  **Lefty Grove**, Sandy Koufax, Carl Hubbell
Mgr.  **John McGraw**, Casey Stengel, Joe McCarthy

1969 Vote All-Time Outstanding Player: **Ruth**, Cobb, Wagner, DiMaggio

### 1997 Vote

C  **Johnny Bench** (24) 52; Yogi Berra (4) 22; Roy Campanella (4) 17; Mickey Cochrane (1) 5; Bill Dickey (1) 4; Gabby Hartnett (1) 3; Carlton Fisk 2.
1B  **Lou Gehrig** (31) 661/2; Jimmie Foxx (3) 19; George Sisler (2) 8; Willie McCovey 6; Hank Greenberg 21/2; Stan Musial, Eddie Murray, Mark McGwire and Frank Thomas 1.
2B  **Rogers Hornsby** (17) 44; Joe Morgan (6) 23; Jackie Robinson (6) 15; Charley Gehringer (4) and Napoleon Lajoie (3) 11; Eddie Collins (1) 3; Rod Carew 2; Ryne Sandberg 1.
SS  **Honus Wagner** (23) 55; Cal Ripken Jr. (6) 24; Ozzie Smith (5) 16; Ernie Banks (1) 8; Lou Boudreau and Luke Appling 1.
3B  **Mike Schmidt** (21) 50; Brooks Robinson (13) 37; Eddie Mathews (6) 29; George Brett (1) 8; Pete Rose (1) 2; Frank Baker, Al Rosen and Wade Boggs 1.
LF  **Ted Williams** (32) 68; Stan Musial (4) 36; Pete Rose, Ralph Kiner, Rickey Henderson and Barry Bonds 1.
CF  **Willie Mays** (25) 57; Ty Cobb (7) 22; Joe DiMaggio (3) 17; Mickey Mantle (1) 10; Tris Speaker 2.
RF  **Babe Ruth** (31) 67; Hank Aaron (5) 36; Frank Robinson 2; Al Kaline, Roberto Clemente and Tony Gwynn 1.

DH  **Paul Molitor** (22) 48; Harold Baines (3) 12; Don Baylor (1) 10; Edgar Martinez (2) 9; Ty Cobb (2) 6; Hal McRae (1) 5; Mickey Mantle (1) and Dave Parker (1) 3; Joe DiMaggio (1) 2; Lee May, Frank Robinson and Tony Oliva 1.
RHP  **Walter Johnson** (9) 30; Cy Young (12) 25; Christy Mathewson (5) 18; Bob Feller (4) 10; Bob Gibson (2) 9; Nolan Ryan (2) 7; Tom Seaver (1) 3; Greg Maddux, Grover Cleveland Alexander and Juan Marichal 2.
LHP  **Sandy Koufax** (11) 32; Warren Spahn (11) 28; Lefty Grove (8) 25; Steve Carlton (4) 12; Carl Hubbell 6; Whitey Ford (1) 3; Eddie Plank (1) 2.
RP  **Dennis Eckersley** (16) 40; Rollie Fingers (9) 29; Lee Smith (4) 13; Hoyt Wilhelm (3) 10; Rich Gossage (3) 9; Bruce Sutter (1) 6, Dan Quisenberry 1.
Mgr.  **Casey Stengel** (6) 22; Joe McCarthy (6) 18; Connie Mack (7) 17; John McGraw (6) 14; Sparky Anderson (3) 11; Leo Durocher (2) 6; Dick Williams (1) 4; Billy Martin (1) 3; Al Lopez (1), Ned Hanlon (1), Whitey Herzog (1), Earl Weaver and Bobby Cox 2; Tony La Russa 1.

## Baseball (Cont.)

+ Hubbell, Carl .........1947
+ Hunter, Catfish ........1987
+ Jenkins, Ferguson ......1991
+ Johnson, Walter ........1936
+ Joss, Addie ...........1978
+ Keefe, Tim ...........1964
  Koufax, Sandy ........1972
+ Lemon, Bob ..........1976
+ Lyons, Ted ...........1955
  Marichal, Juan ........1983
+ Marquard, Rube .......1971
+ Mathewson, Christy .....1936
+ McGinnity, Joe ........1946

  Niekro, Phil ..........1997
+ Newhouser, Hal .......1992
+ Nichols, Kid ..........1949
  Palmer, Jim ..........1990
+ Pennock, Herb ........1948
  Perry, Gaylord ........1991
+ Plank, Eddie ..........1946
+ Radbourne, Old Hoss ...1939
+ Rixey, Eppa ..........1963
  Roberts, Robin ........1976
+ Ruffing, Red ..........1967
+ Rusie, Amos ..........1977
  Ryan, Nolan ..........1999

  Seaver, Tom ..........1992
+ Spahn, Warren ........1973
  Sutton, Don ..........1998
+ Vance, Dazzy .........1955
+ Waddell, Rube ........1946
+ Walsh, Ed ...........1946
+ Welch, Mickey ........1973
+ Wilhelm, Hoyt ........1985
+ Willis, Vic ...........1995
+ Wynn, Early ..........1972
+ Young, Cy ...........1937

### Managers

+ Alston, Walter ........1983
  Anderson, Sparky .....2000
+ Durocher, Leo ........1994
+ Hanlon, Ned ..........1996
+ Harris, Bucky .........1975
+ Huggins, Miller ........1964

  Lasorda, Tommy .......1997
  Lopez, Al ............1977
+ Mack, Connie .........1937
+ McCarthy, Joe ........1957
+ McGraw, John .........1937
+ McKechnie, Bill .......1962

+ Robinson, Wilbert ......1945
+ Selee, Frank ..........1999
+ Stengel, Casey ........1966
  Weaver, Earl ..........1996

### Umpires

+ Barlick, Al ...........1989
+ Chylak, Nestor ........1999
+ Conlan, Jocko ........1974

+ Connolly, Tom .........1953
+ Evans, Billy ..........1973
+ Hubbard, Cal .........1976

+ Klem, Bill ...........1953
+ McGowan, Bill ........1992

### From Negro Leagues

+ Bell, Cool Papa (OF) .....1974
+ Charleston, Oscar (1B-OF) .1976
+ Dandridge, Ray (3B) .....1987
+ Day, Leon (P-OF-2B) .....1995
+ Dihigo, Martin (P-OF) ....1977
+ Foster, Rube (P-Mgr) .....1981

+ Foster, Willie (P) ........1996
+ Gibson, Josh (C) ........1972
  Irvin, Monte (OF) ........1973
+ Johnson, Judy (3B) ......1975
+ Leonard, Buck (1B) ......1972
+ Lloyd, Pop (SS) ........1977

+ Paige, Satchel (P) .......1971
+ Rogan, Wilber (P) .......1998
+ Smith, Hilton ..........2001
+ Stearnes, Turkey (OF) ....2000
+ Wells, Willie (SS) .......1997
+ Williams, Joe (P) .......1999

### Pioneers and Executives

+ Barrow, Ed ...........1953
+ Bulkeley, Morgan .......1937
+ Cartwright, Alexander ....1938
+ Chadwick, Henry .......1938
+ Chandler, Happy .......1982
+ Comiskey, Charles ......1939
+ Cummings, Candy ......1939
+ Frick, Ford ...........1970

+ Giles, Warren .........1979
+ Griffith, Clark .........1946
+ Harridge, Will .........1972
+ Hulbert, William .......1995
+ Johnson, Ban .........1937
+ Landis, Kenesaw .......1944
+ MacPhail, Larry .......1978
  MacPhail, Lee .........1998

+ Rickey, Branch ........1967
+ Spalding, Al ..........1939
+ Veeck, Bill ...........1991
+ Weiss, George .........1971
+ Wright, George ........1937
+ Wright, Harry .........1953
+ Yawkey, Tom .........1980

### Ford Frick Award

First presented in 1978 by the Hall of Fame for meritorious contributions by baseball broadcasters. Named in honor of the late newspaper reporter, broadcaster, National League president and commissioner, the Frick Award does not constitute induction into the Hall of Fame.

| Year | | Year | | Year | |
|---|---|---|---|---|---|
| 1978 | Mel Allen & Red Barber | 1988 | Lindsey Nelson | 1998 | Jaime Jarrin |
| 1979 | Bob Elson | 1989 | Harry Caray | 1999 | Arch McDonald |
| 1980 | Russ Hodges | 1990 | Byrum Saam | 2000 | Marty Brennaman |
| 1981 | Ernie Harwell | 1991 | Joe Garagiola | 2001 | Felo Ramirez |
| 1982 | Vin Scully | 1992 | Milo Hamilton | 2002 | Harry Kalas |
| 1983 | Jack Brickhouse | 1993 | Chuck Thompson | 2003 | Bob Uecker |
| 1984 | Curt Gowdy | 1994 | Bob Murphy | 2004 | Lon Simmons |
| 1985 | Buck Canel | 1995 | Bob Wolff | 2005 | Jerry Coleman |
| 1986 | Bob Prince | 1996 | Herb Carneal | | |
| 1987 | Jack Buck | 1997 | Jimmy Dudley | | |

### J.G. Taylor Spink Award

First presented in 1962 by the Baseball Writers' Association of America for meritorious contributions by members of the BBWAA. Named in honor of the late publisher of The Sporting News, the Spink Award does not constitute induction into the Hall of Fame. Winners are honored in the year following their selection.

| Year | | Year | | Year | |
|---|---|---|---|---|---|
| 1962 | J.G. Taylor Spink | 1971 | Frank Graham | 1977 | Gordon Cobbledick |
| 1963 | Ring Lardner | 1972 | Dan Daniel, Fred Lieb | | & Edgar Munzel |
| 1964 | Hugh Fullerton | | & J. Roy Stockton | 1978 | Tim Murnane & Dick Young |
| 1965 | Charley Dryden | 1973 | Warren Brown, John | 1979 | Bob Broeg & Tommy Holmes |
| 1966 | Grantland Rice | | Drebinger & John F. Kieran | 1980 | Joe Reichler & Milt Richman |
| 1967 | Damon Runyon | 1974 | John Carmichael | 1981 | Bob Addie & Allen Lewis |
| 1968 | H.G. Salsinger | | & James Isaminger | 1982 | Si Burick |
| 1969 | Sid Mercer | 1975 | Tom Meany & Shirley Povich | 1983 | Ken Smith |
| 1970 | Heywood C. Broun | 1976 | Harold Kaese & Red Smith | 1984 | Joe McGuff |

| Year | | Year | | Year | |
|---|---|---|---|---|---|
| 1985 | Earl Lawson | 1992 | Leonard Koppett | 1998 | Bob Stevens |
| 1986 | Jack Lang | | & Buzz Saidt | 1999 | Hal Lebovitz |
| 1987 | Jim Murray | 1993 | John Wendell Smith | 2000 | Ross Newhan |
| 1988 | Bob Hunter & Ray Kelly | 1994 | No award | 2001 | Joe Falls |
| 1989 | Jerome Holtzman | 1995 | Joseph Durso | 2002 | Hal McCoy |
| 1990 | Phil Collier | 1996 | Charley Feeney | 2003 | Murray Chass |
| 1991 | Ritter Collett | 1997 | Sam Lacy | 2004 | Peter Gammons |

## BASKETBALL

### Naismith Memorial Basketball Hall of Fame

Established in 1949 by the National Association of Basketball Coaches in memory of the sport's inventor, Dr. James Naismith. Original Hall opened in 1968 and a renovated version of the Hall opened in 1985. A completely new building opened Sept. 28, 2002. **Address:** 1000 West Columbus Avenue, Springfield, MA 01105. **Telephone:** (413) 781-6500. **Web:** www.hoophall.com.

**Eligibility:** Nominated players and referees must be retired for five years, coaches must have coached 25 years or be retired for five, and contributors must have already completed their noteworthy service to the game. Voting done by 24-member honors committee made up of media representatives, Hall of Fame members and trustees. Any nominee not elected after five years becomes eligible for consideration by the Veterans' Committee after a five-year wait.

**Class of 2005** (5): COACH—**Jim Boeheim, Jim Calhoun, Sue Gunter**; CONTRIBUTOR—**Hubie Brown**; INTERNATIONAL—**Hortencia Marcari**.

**2005 finalists** (nominated but not elected): PLAYERS—Maurice Cheeks, Adrian Dantley, Joe Dumars, Dennis Johnson, Bernard King, Chet Walker and Dominique Wilkins. COACH—Van Chancellor. VETERANS—John Isaacs and John Kerr. INTERNATIONAL—Sandro Gamba.

**Note: John Wooden, Lenny Wilkens** and **Bill Sharman** are the only members to be inducted as both a player and a coach.

Members are listed with years of induction; (+) indicates deceased members.

## Men

| | | | | | |
|---|---|---|---|---|---|
| Abdul-Jabbar, Kareem | ..1995 | Greer, Hal | ..1981 | Monroe, Earl | ..1990 |
| Archibald, Nate | ..1991 | + Gruenig, Robert | ..1963 | Murphy, Calvin | ..1993 |
| Arizin, Paul | ..1977 | Hagan, Cliff | ..1977 | + Murphy, Charles (Stretch) | 1960 |
| + Barlow, Thomas (Babe) | ..1980 | Hanson, Victor | ..1960 | + Page, Harlan (Pat) | ..1962 |
| Barry, Rick | ..1987 | Havlicek, John | ..1983 | Parish, Robert | ..2003 |
| Baylor, Elgin | ..1976 | Hawkins, Connie | ..1992 | + Petrovic, Drazen | ..2002 |
| + Beckman, John | ..1972 | Hayes, Elvin | ..1990 | Pettit, Bob | ..1970 |
| Bellamy, Walt | ..1993 | Haynes, Marques | ..1998 | + Phillip, Andy | ..1961 |
| Belov, Sergei | ..1992 | Heinsohn, Tom | ..1986 | + Pollard, Jim | ..1977 |
| Bing, Dave | ..1990 | + Holman, Nat | ..1964 | Ramsey, Frank | ..1981 |
| Bird, Larry | ..1998 | Houbregs, Bob | ..1987 | Reed, Willis | ..1981 |
| + Borgmann, Bennie | ..1961 | Howell, Bailey | ..1997 | Risen, Arnie | ..1998 |
| Bradley, Bill | ..1982 | + Hyatt, Chuck | ..1959 | Robertson, Oscar | ..1979 |
| + Brennan, Joe | ..1974 | Issel, Dan | ..1993 | + Roosma, John | ..1961 |
| Cervi, Al | ..1984 | + Jeannette, Buddy | ..1994 | Russell, Bill | ..1974 |
| + Chamberlain, Wilt | ..1978 | Johnson, Bill (Skinny) | ..1976 | + Russell, John (Honey) | ..1964 |
| + Cooper, Charles (Tarzan) | 1976 | Johnson, Earvin (Magic) | ..2002 | Schayes, Dolph | ..1972 |
| + Cosic, Kresimir | ..1996 | + Johnston, Neil | ..1990 | + Schmidt, Ernest J | ..1973 |
| Cousy, Bob | ..1970 | Jones, K. C | ..1989 | + Schommer, John | ..1959 |
| Cowens, Dave | ..1991 | Jones, Sam | ..1983 | + Sedran, Barney | ..1962 |
| Cunningham, Billy | ..1986 | + Krause, Edward (Moose) | ..1975 | Sharman, Bill | ..1975 |
| + Davies, Bob | ..1969 | Kurland, Bob | ..1961 | + Steinmetz, Christian | ..1961 |
| + DeBernardi, Forrest | ..1961 | Lanier, Bob | ..1992 | Thomas, Isiah | ..2000 |
| + DeBusschere, Dave | ..1982 | + Lapchick, Joe | ..1966 | Thompson, David | ..1996 |
| + Dehnert, Dutch | ..1968 | Lovellette, Clyde | ..1988 | + Thompson, John (Cat) | ..1962 |
| Drexler, Clyde | ..2004 | Lucas, Jerry | ..1979 | Thurmond, Nate | ..1984 |
| + Endacott, Paul | ..1971 | Luisetti, Hank | ..1959 | Twyman, Jack | ..1982 |
| English, Alex | ..1997 | Macauley, Ed | ..1960 | Unseld, Wes | ..1988 |
| Erving, Julius (Dr. J) | ..1993 | Malone, Moses | ..2001 | Vandivier, Robert (Fuzzy) | 1974 |
| + Foster, Bud | ..1964 | + Maravich, Pete | ..1987 | + Wachter, Ed | ..1961 |
| Frazier, Walt | ..1987 | Martin, Slater | ..1981 | Walton, Bill | ..1993 |
| + Friedman, Marty | ..1971 | McAdoo, Bob | ..2000 | Wanzer, Bobby | ..1987 |
| + Fulks, Joe | ..1977 | + McCracken, Branch | ..1960 | West, Jerry | ..1979 |
| + Gale, Laddie | ..1976 | + McCracken, Jack | ..1962 | Wilkens, Lenny | ..1989 |
| Gallatin, Harry | ..1991 | + McDermott, Bobby | ..1988 | Wooden, John | ..1960 |
| + Gates, William (Pop) | ..1989 | McGuire, Dick | ..1993 | Worthy, James | ..2003 |
| Gervin, George | ..1996 | McHale, Kevin | ..1999 | + Yardley, George | ..1996 |
| Gola, Tom | ..1975 | + Mikan, George | ..1959 | | |
| Goodrich, Gail | ..1996 | Mikkelsen, Vern | ..1995 | | |

## Women

| | | | | | |
|---|---|---|---|---|---|
| Blazejowski, Carol | ..1994 | Harris-Stewart, Lucia | ..1992 | Miller, Cheryl | ..1995 |
| Crawford, Joan | ..1997 | Lieberman, Nancy | ..1996 | Semenova, Uljana | ..1993 |
| Curry, Denise | ..1997 | Marcari, Hortencia | ..2005 | White, Nera | ..1992 |
| Donovan, Anne | ..1995 | Meyers, Ann | ..1993 | Woodard, Lynette | ..2004 |

# Basketball (Cont.)

## Teams

| | | |
|---|---|---|
| Buffalo Germans . . . . . . . .1961 | Harlem Globetrotters . . . . .2002 | Original Celtics . . . . . . . . .1959 |
| First Team . . . . . . . . . . . .1959 | New York Renaissance . . . .1963 | |

## Referees

| | | |
|---|---|---|
| + Enright, Jim . . . . . . . . . . . .1978 | + Leith, Lloyd . . . . . . . . . . .1982 | + Shirley, J. Dallas . . . . . . . .1979 |
| + Hepbron, George . . . . . . .1960 | + Mihalik, Red . . . . . . . . . . .1986 | + Strom, Earl . . . . . . . . . . .1995 |
| + Hoyt, George . . . . . . . . . .1961 | + Nucatola, John . . . . . . . . .1977 | + Tobey, Dave . . . . . . . . . . .1961 |
| + Kennedy, Pat . . . . . . . . . .1959 | + Quigley, Ernest (Quig) . . . .1961 | + Walsh, David . . . . . . . . . .1961 |

## Coaches

| | | |
|---|---|---|
| + Allen, Forrest (Phog) . . . . .1959 | + Gill, Amory (Slats) . . . . . .1967 | Meyer, Ray . . . . . . . . . . .1978 |
| + Anderson, Harold (Andy) . .1984 | + Gomelsky, Aleksandr . . . . .1995 | + Miller, Ralph . . . . . . . . . .1988 |
| Auerbach, Red . . . . . . . . .1968 | + Gunter, Sue . . . . . . . . . . .2005 | Moore, Billie . . . . . . . . . .1999 |
| Barmore, Leon . . . . . . . . .2003 | + Hannum, Alex . . . . . . . . . .1998 | Newell, Pete . . . . . . . . . .1978 |
| + Barry, Sam . . . . . . . . . . . .1978 | Harshman, Marv . . . . . . . .1984 | + Nikolic, Aleksandar . . . . . .1998 |
| + Blood, Ernest (Prof) . . . . . .1960 | Haskins, Don . . . . . . . . . .1997 | Olson, Lute . . . . . . . . . . .2002 |
| Boeheim, Jim . . . . . . . . . .2005 | + Hickey, Eddie . . . . . . . . . .1978 | Ramsay, Jack . . . . . . . . . .1992 |
| Brown, Larry . . . . . . . . . .2002 | + Hobson, Howard (Hobby) . .1965 | Rubini, Cesare . . . . . . . . .1994 |
| Calhoun, Jim . . . . . . . . . .2005 | + Holzman, Red . . . . . . . . . .1986 | + Rupp, Adolph . . . . . . . . . .1968 |
| + Cann, Howard . . . . . . . . . .1967 | + Iba, Hank . . . . . . . . . . . . .1968 | + Sachs, Leonard . . . . . . . . .1961 |
| + Carlson, Henry (Doc) . . . . .1959 | + Julian, Alvin (Doggie) . . . . .1967 | Sharman, Bill . . . . . . . . . .2004 |
| Carnesecca, Lou . . . . . . . .1992 | + Keaney, Frank . . . . . . . . . .1960 | + Shelton, Everett . . . . . . . .1979 |
| Carnevale, Ben . . . . . . . . .1969 | + Keogan, George . . . . . . . .1961 | Smith, Dean . . . . . . . . . . .1982 |
| Carril, Pete . . . . . . . . . . . .1997 | Knight, Bob . . . . . . . . . . .1991 | Summitt, Pat . . . . . . . . . .2000 |
| + Case, Everett . . . . . . . . . .1981 | Krzyzewski, Mike . . . . . . .2001 | + Taylor, Fred . . . . . . . . . . .1986 |
| Chaney, John . . . . . . . . . .2001 | Kundla, John . . . . . . . . . .1995 | Thompson, John . . . . . . . .1999 |
| Conradt, Jody . . . . . . . . . .1998 | + Lambert, Ward (Piggy) . . . .1960 | + Wade, Margaret . . . . . . . .1984 |
| Crum, Denny . . . . . . . . . .1994 | + Litwack, Harry . . . . . . . . .1975 | Watts, Stan . . . . . . . . . . .1985 |
| Daly, Chuck . . . . . . . . . . .1994 | + Loeffler, Ken . . . . . . . . . .1964 | Wilkens, Lenny . . . . . . . . .1998 |
| + Dean, Everett . . . . . . . . . .1966 | + Lonborg, Dutch . . . . . . . . .1972 | Wooden, John . . . . . . . . .1972 |
| + Diaz-Miguel, Antonio . . . . .1997 | + McCutchan, Arad . . . . . . . .1980 | + Woolpert, Phil . . . . . . . . . .1992 |
| + Diddle, Ed . . . . . . . . . . . .1971 | + McGuire, Al . . . . . . . . . . .1992 | Wootten, Morgan . . . . . . .2000 |
| + Drake, Bruce . . . . . . . . . .1972 | + McGuire, Frank . . . . . . . . .1976 | Yow, Kay . . . . . . . . . . . . .2002 |
| Gaines, Clarence (Bighouse) .1981 | + McLendon, John . . . . . . . .1978 | |
| + Gardner, Jack . . . . . . . . . .1983 | + Meanwell, Walter (Doc) . . .1959 | |

## Contributors

| | | |
|---|---|---|
| + Abbott, Senda Berenson . . .1984 | + Hepp, Ferenc . . . . . . . . . .1980 | + Porter, Henry (H.V.) . . . . . .1960 |
| + Bee, Clair . . . . . . . . . . . . .1967 | + Hickox, Ed . . . . . . . . . . . .1959 | + Reid, William A . . . . . . . . .1963 |
| + Biasone, Danny . . . . . . . . .2000 | + Hinkle, Tony . . . . . . . . . . .1965 | + Ripley, Elmer . . . . . . . . . .1972 |
| Brown, Hubie . . . . . . . . . .2005 | + Irish, Ned . . . . . . . . . . . . .1964 | + St. John, Lynn W . . . . . . . .1962 |
| + Brown, Walter A . . . . . . . .1965 | + Jones, R. William . . . . . . . .1964 | + Saperstein, Abe . . . . . . . .1970 |
| + Bunn, John . . . . . . . . . . . .1964 | + Kennedy, Walter . . . . . . . .1980 | + Schabinger, Arthur . . . . . .1961 |
| Colangelo, Jerry . . . . . . . .2004 | Lemon, Meadowlark . . . . .2003 | + Stagg, Amos Alonzo . . . . .1959 |
| Douglas, Bob . . . . . . . . . .1971 | + Liston, Emil (Liz) . . . . . . . .1974 | Stankovic, Boris . . . . . . . .1991 |
| + Duer, Al . . . . . . . . . . . . . .1981 | + Mokray, Bill . . . . . . . . . . .1965 | + Steitz, Ed . . . . . . . . . . . . .1983 |
| Embry, Wayne . . . . . . . . .1999 | + Morgan, Ralph . . . . . . . . .1959 | + Taylor, Chuck . . . . . . . . . .1968 |
| + Fagan, Clifford B . . . . . . . .1983 | + Morgenweck, Frank (Pop) . .1962 | + Teague, Bertha . . . . . . . . .1984 |
| + Fisher, Harry . . . . . . . . . . .1973 | + Naismith, James . . . . . . . .1959 | + Tower, Oswald . . . . . . . . .1959 |
| Fleisher, Larry . . . . . . . . . .1991 | Newton, Charles M. . . . . .2000 | + Trester, Arthur (A.L.) . . . . . .1961 |
| + Gottlieb, Eddie . . . . . . . . .1971 | + O'Brien, John J. (Jack) . . . . .1961 | + Wells, Cliff . . . . . . . . . . . .1971 |
| + Gulick, Luther . . . . . . . . . .1959 | + O'Brien, Larry . . . . . . . . . .1991 | + Wilke, Lou . . . . . . . . . . . .1982 |
| + Harrison, Les . . . . . . . . . . .1979 | + Olsen, Harold G . . . . . . . .1959 | + Zollner, Fred . . . . . . . . . . .1999 |
| + Hearn, Francis (Chick) . . . .2003 | + Podoloff, Maurice . . . . . . .1973 | |

## Curt Gowdy Award

First presented in 1990 by the Hall of Fame Board of Trustees for meritorious contributions by the media. Named in honor of the former NBC sportscaster, the Gowdy Award does not constitute induction into the Hall of Fame.

| Year | | Year | | Year | |
|---|---|---|---|---|---|
| 1990 | Curt Gowdy & Dick Herbert | 1997 | Marv Albert & Bob Ryan | 2003 | Sid Hartman |
| 1991 | Dave Dorr & Marty Glickman | 1998 | Dick Vitale, Larry Donald | | & Hot Rod Hundley |
| 1992 | Sam Goldaper & Chick Hearn | | & Dick Weiss | 2004 | Phil Jasner & Max Falkenstien |
| 1993 | Leonard Lewin & Johnny Most | 1999 | Smith Barrier & Bob Costas | 2005 | Jack McCallum & |
| 1994 | Leonard Koppett | 2000 | Dave Kindred & Hubie Brown | | Bill Campbell |
| | & Cawood Ledford | 2001 | Dick Stockton | | |
| 1995 | Dick Enberg & Bob Hammel | | & Curry Kirkpatrick | | |
| 1996 | Billy Packer & Bob Hentzen | 2002 | Jim Nantz & Jim O'Connell | | |

## BOWLING

# International Bowling Hall of Fame & Museum

The National Bowling Hall is one museum with separate wings for honorees of the American Bowling Congress (ABC), Professional Bowlers' Association (PBA), Women's International Bowling Congress (WIBC) and Professional Women Bowlers Association (PWBA). In 2005 the ABC and WIBC merged, becoming the United States Bowling Congress. There are plans to merge the respective wings in the hall of fame and there will be no future inductions under the banner of the ABC or WIBC. **Address:** 111 Stadium Plaza, St. Louis, MO 63102. **Telephone:** (314) 231-6340. **Web:** www.bowlingmuseum.com

## Professional Bowlers Association

Established in 1975. **Eligibility:** The criteria was revamped in 2002. Nominees must now be retired from full-time competition on the PBA Tour for a minimum of at least five years, or reached the age of 50, and must have won a minimum of 10 PBA Tour titles or two major titles.

**Class of 2004** (2): MERITORIOUS SERVICE—**Matt Fiorito** and **Mort Luby Jr.**.

Members are listed with years of induction; (+) indicates deceased members.

### Performance

| | | |
|---|---|---|
| + Allen, Bill . . . . . . . . . . . .1983 | + Fazio, Buzz . . . . . . . . . . .1976 | Roth, Mark . . . . . . . . . .1987 |
| + Anthony, Earl . . . . . . . . .1986 | Ferraro, Dave . . . . . . . . .1997 | Salvino, Carmen . . . . . . .1975 |
| Aulby, Mike . . . . . . . . . .1996 | + Godman, Jim . . . . . . . . .1987 | Semiz, Teata . . . . . . . . .1998 |
| Berardi, Joe . . . . . . . . . .1990 | Hardwick, Billy . . . . . . . .1977 | Smith, Harry . . . . . . . . .1975 |
| Bluth, Ray . . . . . . . . . . .1975 | Holman, Marshall . . . . . .1990 | Soutar, Dave . . . . . . . . .1979 |
| Bohn, Parker III . . . . . . . .2000 | Hudson, Tommy . . . . . . .1989 | Stefanich, Jim . . . . . . . .1980 |
| Buckley, Roy . . . . . . . . . .1992 | Husted, Dave . . . . . . . . .1996 | Voss, Brian . . . . . . . . . .1994 |
| Burton, Nelson Jr . . . . . . .1979 | Johnson, Don . . . . . . . . .1977 | Webb, Wayne . . . . . . . .1993 |
| Carter, Don . . . . . . . . . .1975 | Laub, Larry . . . . . . . . . .1985 | + Weber, Dick . . . . . . . . .1975 |
| Colwell, Paul . . . . . . . . .1991 | Monacelli, Amleto . . . . . .1997 | Weber, Pete . . . . . . . . .1998 |
| Cook, Steve . . . . . . . . . .1993 | Ozio, David . . . . . . . . . .1995 | + Welu, Billy . . . . . . . . . .1975 |
| Davis, Dave . . . . . . . . . .1978 | Pappas, George . . . . . . .1986 | Williams, Mark . . . . . . . .1999 |
| Dickinson, Gary . . . . . . . .1988 | Petraglia, John . . . . . . . .1982 | Williams, Walter Ray Jr. . . .1995 |
| Durbin, Mike . . . . . . . . .1984 | Ritger, Dick . . . . . . . . . .1978 | Zahn, Wayne . . . . . . . . .1981 |

### Veterans

| | | |
|---|---|---|
| Allison, Glenn . . . . . . . . .1984 | + Joseph, Joe . . . . . . . . . .1985 | Schlegel, Ernie . . . . . . . .1997 |
| Asher, Barry . . . . . . . . . .1988 | Limongello, Mike . . . . . . .1994 | + St. John, Jim . . . . . . . . .1989 |
| Baker, Tom . . . . . . . . . . .1999 | Marzich, Andy . . . . . . . .1990 | Strampe, Bob . . . . . . . . .1987 |
| Foremsky, Skee . . . . . . . .1992 | McCune, Don . . . . . . . . .1991 | |
| Guenther, Johnny . . . . . . .1986 | McGrath, Mike . . . . . . . .1988 | |

### Meritorious Service

| | | |
|---|---|---|
| + Antenora, Joe . . . . . . . . .1993 | + Fitzgerald, Jim . . . . . . . .2000 | Nakano, Keijiro . . . . . . . .1999 |
| Archibald, John . . . . . . . .1989 | + Frantz, Lou . . . . . . . . . .1978 | Pezzano, Chuck . . . . . . . .1975 |
| Clemens, Chuck . . . . . . . .1994 | Golden, Harry . . . . . . . .1983 | Reichert, Jack . . . . . . . . .1992 |
| + Elias, Eddie . . . . . . . . . .1976 | Hoffman, Ted Jr . . . . . . . .1985 | + Richards, Joe . . . . . . . . .1976 |
| Esposito, Frank . . . . . . . .1975 | Jowdy, John . . . . . . . . . .1988 | + Schenkel, Chris . . . . . . . .1976 |
| Evans, Dick . . . . . . . . . .1986 | Kelley, Joe . . . . . . . . . . .1989 | Stitzlein, Lorraine . . . . . . .1980 |
| Fiorito, Matt . . . . . . . . . .2004 | Lichstein, Larry . . . . . . . .1996 | Thompson, Al . . . . . . . . .1991 |
| Firestone, Raymond . . . . . .1987 | Luby, Mort Jr. . . . . . . . . .2004 | Zeller, Roger . . . . . . . . .1995 |
| Fisher, E.A. (Bud) . . . . . . .1984 | + Nagy, Steve . . . . . . . . . .1977 | |

## American Bowling Congress

Established in 1941 and open to professional and amateur bowlers. **Eligibility:** Nominated bowlers must have competed in at least 20 years of ABC tournaments. Voting done by 170-member panel made up of ABC officials, Hall of Fame members and media representatives..

**Class of 2005** (4): PERFORMANCE—**Bob Chamberlain, Todd Savoy** and **Walter Ray Williams Jr.**. MERITORIOUS SERVICE—**Steve James**.

Members are listed with years of induction; (+) indicates deceased members.

### Performance

| | | |
|---|---|---|
| Allison, Glenn . . . . . . . . .1979 | + Brosius, Eddie . . . . . . . . .1976 | + Crimmins, Johnny . . . . . . .1962 |
| + Anthony, Earl . . . . . . . . .1986 | + Bujack, Fred . . . . . . . . . .1967 | Davis, Dave . . . . . . . . . .1990 |
| Asher, Barry . . . . . . . . . .1998 | Bunetta, Bill . . . . . . . . . .1968 | + Daw, Charlie . . . . . . . . . .1941 |
| + Asplund, Harold . . . . . . . .1978 | Burton, Nelson Jr . . . . . . .1981 | + Day, Ned . . . . . . . . . . . .1952 |
| Aulby, Mike . . . . . . . . . .2001 | + Burton, Nelson Sr . . . . . . .1964 | Dickinson, Gary . . . . . . . .1992 |
| Baer, Gordy . . . . . . . . . .1987 | + Campi, Lou . . . . . . . . . .1968 | Duke, Norm . . . . . . . . . .2002 |
| Beach, Bill . . . . . . . . . . .1991 | + Carlson, Adolph . . . . . . . .1941 | + Easter, Sarge . . . . . . . . . .1963 |
| + Benkovic, Frank . . . . . . . .1958 | Carter, Don . . . . . . . . . .1970 | Ellis, Don . . . . . . . . . . . .1981 |
| Berlin, Mike . . . . . . . . . .1994 | + Caruana, Frank . . . . . . . .1977 | + Falcaro, Joe . . . . . . . . . .1968 |
| + Billick, George . . . . . . . . .1982 | + Cassio, Marty . . . . . . . . .1972 | + Faragalli, Lindy . . . . . . . .1968 |
| + Blouin, Jimmy . . . . . . . . .1953 | + Castellano, Graz . . . . . . . .1976 | + Fazio, Buzz . . . . . . . . . .1963 |
| Bluth, Ray . . . . . . . . . . .1973 | Chamberlain, Bob . . . . . .2005 | Fehr, Steve . . . . . . . . . .1993 |
| + Bodis, Joe . . . . . . . . . . .1941 | + Clause, Hank . . . . . . . . .1980 | + Gersonde, Russ . . . . . . . .1968 |
| + Bomar, Buddy . . . . . . . . .1966 | Cohn, Alfred . . . . . . . . . .1985 | + Gibson, Therm . . . . . . . .1965 |
| Bower, Gary . . . . . . . . . .2001 | Colwell, Paul . . . . . . . . .1999 | + Godman, Jim . . . . . . . . .1987 |
| + Brandt, Allie . . . . . . . . . .1960 | Couture, Pete . . . . . . . . .2004 | Goike, Robert . . . . . . . . .1996 |

## Bowling (Cont.)

| | | |
|---|---|---|
| + Golembiewski, Billy | 1979 | |
| Griffo, Greg | 1995 | |
| Guenther, Johnny | 1988 | |
| Hanson, Bob | 2004 | |
| Hardwick, Billy | 1985 | |
| Hart, Bob | 1994 | |
| + Hennessey, Tom | 1976 | |
| Hoover, Dick | 1974 | |
| Horn, Bud | 1992 | |
| Howard, George | 1986 | |
| Jackson, Eddie | 1988 | |
| + Jackson, Lowell | 2003 | |
| + Johnson, Don | 1982 | |
| Johnson, Earl | 1987 | |
| + Joseph, Joe | 1969 | |
| + Jouglard, Lee | 1979 | |
| + Kartheiser, Frank | 1967 | |
| + Kawolics, Ed | 1968 | |
| + Kissoff, Joe | 1976 | |
| + Klares, John | 1982 | |
| + Knox, Billy | 1954 | |
| + Koster, John | 1941 | |
| + Krems, Eddie | 1973 | |
| Kristof, Joe | 1968 | |
| + Krumske, Paul | 1968 | |
| + Lange, Herb | 1941 | |
| + Lauman, Hank | 1976 | |
| Lewis, Mark | 2004 | |
| Lillard, Bill | 1972 | |
| Lindemann, Tony | 1979 | |
| + Lindsey, Mort | 1941 | |

| | | |
|---|---|---|
| + Lippe, Harry | 1989 | |
| Lubanski, Ed | 1971 | |
| + Lucci, Vince Sr | 1978 | |
| + Marino, Hank | 1941 | |
| + Martino, John | 1969 | |
| Marzich, Andy | 1993 | |
| McGrath, Mike | 1993 | |
| + McMahon, Junie | 1967 | |
| + Meisel, Darold | 1998 | |
| + Mercurio, Skang | 1967 | |
| Meyers, Norm | 1984 | |
| + Nagy, Steve | 1963 | |
| + Norris, Joe | 1954 | |
| + O'Donnell, Chuck | 1968 | |
| Pappas, George | 1989 | |
| + Patterson, Pat | 1974 | |
| + Powell, John (Junior) | 2000 | |
| Ritger, Dick | 1984 | |
| + Rogoznica, Andy | 1993 | |
| Salvino, Carmen | 1979 | |
| Savoy, Todd | 2005 | |
| Schissler, Les | 1991 | |
| Schlegel, Ernie | 1997 | |
| Schroeder, Jim | 1990 | |
| + Schwoegler, Connie | 1968 | |
| Scudder, Don | 1999 | |
| Semiz, Teata | 1991 | |
| + Sielaff, Lou | 1968 | |
| + Sinke, Joe | 1977 | |
| + Sixty, Billy | 1961 | |
| Smith, Harry | 1978 | |

| | | |
|---|---|---|
| + Smith, Jimmy | 1941 | |
| Soutar, Dave | 1985 | |
| + Sparando, Tony | 1968 | |
| Spigner, Bill | 2001 | |
| + Spinella, Barney | 1968 | |
| + Steers, Harry | 1941 | |
| Stefanich, Jim | 1983 | |
| + Stein, Otto Jr | 1971 | |
| Stoudt, Bud | 1991 | |
| Strampe, Bob | 1977 | |
| + Thoma, Sykes | 1971 | |
| Toft, Rod | 1991 | |
| + Totsky, Mike | 1996 | |
| Tountas, Pete | 1989 | |
| Tucker, Bill | 1988 | |
| Tuttle, Tommy | 1995 | |
| + Varipapa, Andy | 1957 | |
| + Ward, Walter | 1959 | |
| + Weber, Dick | 1970 | |
| Weber, Pete | 2002 | |
| + Welu, Billy | 1975 | |
| Wilcox, John | 1999 | |
| Williams, Walter Ray Jr. | 2005 | |
| + Wilman, Joe | 1951 | |
| + Wolf, Phil | 1961 | |
| Wonders, Rich | 1990 | |
| + Young, George | 1959 | |
| Zahn, Wayne | 1980 | |
| Zikes, Les | 1983 | |
| + Zunker, Gil | 1941 | |

### Pioneers

| | | |
|---|---|---|
| + Allen, Lafayette Jr. | 1994 | |
| + Briell, Frank | 1996 | |
| + Carow, Rev. Charles | 1995 | |
| + Celestine, Sydney | 1993 | |
| + Curtis, Thomas | 1993 | |
| + de Freitas, Eric | 1994 | |

| | | |
|---|---|---|
| + Hall, William Sr. | 1994 | |
| Hirashima, Hiroto | 1995 | |
| + Karpf, Samuel | 1993 | |
| + Moore, Henry | 1996 | |
| + Pasdeloup, Frank | 1993 | |
| + Rhodman, Bill | 1997 | |

| | | |
|---|---|---|
| + Satow, Masao | 1994 | |
| + Schutte, Louis | 1993 | |
| Shimada, Fuzzy | 1997 | |
| + Stein, Louis | 1997 | |
| + Thompson, William V. | 1993 | |
| + Timm, Dr. Henry | 1993 | |

### Meritorious Service

| | | |
|---|---|---|
| + Allen, Harold | 1966 | |
| Archibald, John | 1996 | |
| + Baker, Frank | 1975 | |
| + Baumgarten, Elmer | 1963 | |
| + Bellisimo, Lou | 1986 | |
| + Bensinger, Bob | 1969 | |
| Borden, Fred | 2002 | |
| + Chase, LeRoy | 1972 | |
| + Coker, John | 1980 | |
| + Collier, Chuck | 1963 | |
| + Cruchon, Steve | 1983 | |
| + Ditzen, Walt | 1973 | |
| + Dobs, Darold | 1999 | |
| + Doehrman, Bill | 1968 | |
| + Elias, Eddie | 1985 | |
| Esposito, Frank | 1997 | |
| Evans, Dick | 1992 | |

| | | |
|---|---|---|
| + Franklin, Bill | 1992 | |
| + Hagerty, Jack | 1963 | |
| + Hattstrom, H.A. (Doc) | 1980 | |
| + Hermann, Cornelius | 1968 | |
| + Howley, Pete | 1941 | |
| James, Steve | 2005 | |
| Jensen, Mark | 2002 | |
| Jowdy, John | 2001 | |
| + Kennedy, Bob | 1981 | |
| + Langtry, Abe | 1963 | |
| + Levine, Sam | 1971 | |
| + Luby, David | 1969 | |
| Luby, Mort Jr. | 1988 | |
| + Luby, Mort Sr. | 1974 | |
| Matzelle, Al | 1995 | |
| + McCullough, Howard | 1971 | |
| Mormando, Nick | 2003 | |

| | | |
|---|---|---|
| + Patterson, Morehead | 1985 | |
| + Petersen, Louie | 1963 | |
| Pezzano, Chuck | 1982 | |
| Picchietti, Remo | 1993 | |
| Pluckhahn, Bruce | 1989 | |
| + Raymer, Milt | 1972 | |
| + Reed, Elmer | 1978 | |
| Reichert, Jack | 1998 | |
| Rudo, Milt | 1984 | |
| Schenkel, Chris | 1988 | |
| Skelton, Max | 2002 | |
| + Sweeney, Dennis | 1974 | |
| Tessman, Roger | 1994 | |
| + Thum, Joe | 1980 | |
| Weinstein, Sam | 1970 | |
| + Whitney, Eli | 1975 | |
| + Wolf, Fred | 1976 | |

## Women's International Bowling Congress

Established in 1953. **Eligibility:** Performance nominees must have won at least one WIBC Championship Tournament title, a WIBC Queens tournament title or an international competition title and have bowled in at least 15 national WIBC Championship Tournaments (unless injury or illness cut career short).

**Class of 2005** (2): PERFORMANCE—**Anne Marie Duggan**; MERITORIOUS SERVICE—**Sylvia Broyles**.

Members are listed with years of induction; (+) indicates deceased members.

### Performance

| | | |
|---|---|---|
| Abel, Joy | 1984 | |
| Adamek, Donna | 1996 | |
| Ann, Patty | 1995 | |
| Bolt, Mae | 1978 | |
| Bouvia, Gloria | 1987 | |
| Boxberger, Loa | 1984 | |

| | | |
|---|---|---|
| Buckner, Pam | 1990 | |
| + Burling, Catherine | 1958 | |
| + Burns, Nina | 1977 | |
| Cantaline, Anita | 1979 | |
| Carter, LaVerne | 1977 | |
| Carter, Paula | 1994 | |

| | | |
|---|---|---|
| Coburn, Doris | 1976 | |
| Coburn-Carroll, Cindy | 1998 | |
| Costello, Pat | 1986 | |
| Costello, Patty | 1989 | |
| Daniels, Cheryl | 2002 | |
| Dryer, Pat | 1978 | |

Duggan, Anne Marie . . . . .2005
Duval, Helen . . . . . . . . . .1970
+ Fellmeth, Catherine . . . . .1970
Fiebig, Cora . . . . . . . . . .2004
Fothergill, Dotty . . . . . . . .1980
+ Fulton, Louise . . . . . . . . .2001
+ Fritz, Deane . . . . . . . . . .1966
Garms, Shirley . . . . . . . . .1971
Gianulias, Nikki . . . . . . . .1997
+ Gloor, Olga . . . . . . . . . .1976
Gonzalez, Ashie . . . . . . . .1998
Graham, Linda . . . . . . . . .1992
Graham, Mary Lou . . . . . .1989
+ Greenwald, Goldie . . . . . .1953
Grinfelds, Vesma . . . . . . . .1991
+ Harman, Janet . . . . . . . . .1985
Hartrick, Stella . . . . . . . . .1972
+ Hatch, Grayce . . . . . . . . .1953
Havlish, Jean . . . . . . . . . .1987
+ Hoffman, Martha . . . . . . .1979
Holm, Joan . . . . . . . . . . .1974
+ Humphreys, Birdie . . . . . .1979
Ignizio, Millie Martorella . . .1975
Jacobson, D.D . . . . . . . . .1981
+ Jaeger, Emma . . . . . . . . .1953

Johnson, Tish . . . . . . . . . .2002
Kelly, Annese . . . . . . . . . .1985
Kelly, Linda . . . . . . . . . . .2003
+ Knechtges, Doris . . . . . . .1983
Kuczynski, Betty . . . . . . . .1981
Ladewig, Marion . . . . . . . .1964
+ Matthews, Merle . . . . . . . .1974
+ McCutcheon, Floretta . . . . .1956
Merrick, Marge . . . . . . . . .1980
+ Mikiel, Val . . . . . . . . . . .1979
Miller-Mackey, Dana . . . . .2000
Miller, Carol . . . . . . . . . .1997
+ Miller, Dorothy . . . . . . . .1954
Mivelaz, Betty . . . . . . . . .1991
Mohacsi, Mary . . . . . . . . .1994
Morris, Betty . . . . . . . . . .1983
Naccarato, Jeanne . . . . . . .1999
Nichols, Lorrie Koch . . . . . .1989
Norman, Carol . . . . . . . . .2001
Norman, Edie Jo . . . . . . . .1993
Norton, Virginia . . . . . . . .1988
Notaro, Phyllis . . . . . . . . .1979
Ortner, Bev . . . . . . . . . . .1972
+ Powers, Connie . . . . . . . .1973
Reichley, Susie . . . . . . . . .2000

Rickard, Robbie . . . . . . . . .1994
+ Robinson, Leona . . . . . . .1969
Romeo, Robin . . . . . . . . .1995
+ Rump, Anita . . . . . . . . . .1962
+ Ruschmeyer, Addie . . . . . .1961
+ Ryan, Esther . . . . . . . . . .1963
+ Sablatnik, Ethel . . . . . . . .1979
Sandelin, Lucy . . . . . . . . .1999
+ Schulte, Myrtle . . . . . . . . .1965
+ Shablis, Helen . . . . . . . . .1977
Sill, Aleta . . . . . . . . . . . .1996
+ Simon, Violet (Billy) . . . . . .1960
+ Small, Tess . . . . . . . . . . .1971
+ Smith, Grace . . . . . . . . . .1968
Soutar, Judy . . . . . . . . . .1976
+ Stockdale, Louise . . . . . . .1953
Toepfer, Elvira . . . . . . . . .1976
+ Twyford, Sally . . . . . . . . .1964
Wagner, Lisa . . . . . . . . . .2000
+ Warmbier, Marie . . . . . . .1953
Wene-Martin, Sylvia . . . . . .1966
Wilkinson, Dorothy . . . . . . .1990
+ Winandy, Cecelia . . . . . . .1975
Zimmerman, Donna . . . . . .1982

## Meritorious Service

+ Baetz, Helen . . . . . . . . . .1977
+ Baker, Helen . . . . . . . . . .1989
+ Banker, Gladys . . . . . . . . .1994
+ Bayley, Clover . . . . . . . . .1992
Bennie, Bernice . . . . . . . . .2003
+ Berger, Winifred . . . . . . . .1976
+ Bohlen, Philena . . . . . . . .1955
Borschuk, Lo . . . . . . . . . .1988
+ Botkin, Freda . . . . . . . . . .1986
Broyles, Sylvia . . . . . . . . .2005
+ Chapman, Emily . . . . . . . .1957
Chapman, Nancy . . . . . . . .2002
+ Crowe, Alberta . . . . . . . . .1982
Deitch, Joyce . . . . . . . . . .2003
+ Dornblaser, Gertrude . . . . .1979
Duffy, Agnes . . . . . . . . . .1987
Finke, Gertrude . . . . . . . . .1990
+ Fisk, Rae . . . . . . . . . . . .1983

+ Haas, Dorothy . . . . . . . . .1977
Hagin, Elaine . . . . . . . . . .2000
+ Herold, Mitzi . . . . . . . . . .1998
+ Higley, Margaret . . . . . . . .1969
+ Hochstadter, Bee . . . . . . . .1967
+ Kay, Nora . . . . . . . . . . . .1964
Keller, Pearl . . . . . . . . . . .1999
+ Kelly, Ellen . . . . . . . . . . .1979
Kelone, Theresa . . . . . . . . .1978
+ Knepprath, Jeannette . . . . .1963
+ Lasher, Iolia . . . . . . . . . .1967
+ Marrs, Mabel . . . . . . . . . .1979
+ McBride, Bertha . . . . . . . .1968
McLeary, Hazel . . . . . . . . .2000
+ Menne, Catherine . . . . . . .1979
Mitchell, Flora . . . . . . . . . .1996
Morton, Clara . . . . . . . . . .2001
+ Mraz, Jo . . . . . . . . . . . .1959

O'Connor, Billie . . . . . . . . .1992
+ Phaler, Emma . . . . . . . . . .1965
+ Porter, Cora . . . . . . . . . . .1986
+ Quin, Zoe . . . . . . . . . . . .1979
+ Rishling, Gertrude . . . . . . .1972
Robinson, Jeanette . . . . . . .2000
Rowe, Dorothy . . . . . . . . . .2004
Simone, Anne . . . . . . . . . .1991
Sloan, Catherine . . . . . . . .1985
+ Speck, Berdie . . . . . . . . . .1966
Spitalnick, Mildred . . . . . . .1994
+ Spring, Alma . . . . . . . . . .1979
+ Switzer, Pearl . . . . . . . . . .1973
+ Todd, Trudy . . . . . . . . . . .1993
+ Veatch, Georgia . . . . . . . .1974
+ White, Mildred . . . . . . . . .1975
+ Wood, Ann . . . . . . . . . . .1970

## Professional Women Bowlers Hall of Fame

Established in 1995 by the Ladies Pro Bowlers Tour. The LPBT has since been renamed the Professional Women Bowlers Association and the PWBA Hall of Fame has since been folded into the International Bowling Hall of Fame. The PWBA has not inducted any new members since 2003.

**Eligibility:** Nominees in performance category must have at least five titles from organizations including All-Star, World Invitational, LPBT, WPBA, PWBA, TPA and LPBA.

Members are listed with year of induction; (+) indicates deceased member.

### Performance

Adamek, Donna . . . . . . . .1995
Coburn-Carroll, Cindy . . . . .1997
Costello, Pat . . . . . . . . . .1997
Costello, Patty . . . . . . . . .1995
Duggan, Anne Marie . . . . .2003
Fothergill, Dotty . . . . . . . .1995
Gianulias, Nikki . . . . . . . .1996

Grinfelds, Vesma . . . . . . . .1997
Johnson, Tish . . . . . . . . . .1998
Ladewig, Marion . . . . . . . .1995
Martorella, Millie . . . . . . . .1995
Miller-Mackie, Dana . . . . . .2002
Morris, Betty . . . . . . . . . .1995
Naccarato, Jeanne . . . . . . .2002

Nichols, Lorrie . . . . . . . . . .1996
Norton, Virginia . . . . . . . .2003
Romeo, Robin . . . . . . . . .1996
Sill, Aleta . . . . . . . . . . . .1998
Wagner, Lisa . . . . . . . . . .1996

### Pioneers

Able, Joy . . . . . . . . . . . .1998
Boxberger, Loa . . . . . . . . .1997
Carter, LaVerne . . . . . . . . .1995

Coburn, Doris . . . . . . . . . .1996
Duval, Helen . . . . . . . . . .1995
Garms, Shirley . . . . . . . . .1995

Ortner, Bev . . . . . . . . . . .1998
Soutar, Judy . . . . . . . . . .1997
Zimmerman, Donna . . . . . .1996

### Builders

+ Buehler, Janet . . . . . . . .1996
Keller, Pearl . . . . . . . . . .1997

Robinson, Jeanette . . . . . . .1996
Sommer Jr., John . . . . . . . .1997

+ Veatch, Georgia . . . . . . .1995

## BOXING

### International Boxing Hall of Fame

Established in 1984 and opened in 1989. **Address:** 1 Hall of Fame Drive, Canastota, NY 13032. **Telephone:** (315) 697-7095. **Web:** www.ibhof.com.

**Eligibility:** All nominees must be retired for five years. Voting done by 142-member panel made up of Boxing Writers' Association members and world-wide boxing historians.

**Class of 2005** (15): MODERN ERA—**Bobby Chacon, Duilio Loi, Barry McGuigan, Terry Norris.** OLD TIMERS—**Eugene Criqui, Joe Lynch, Charles "Bud" Taylor, Marcel Thil.** PIONEER—**Jack Randall**; NON-PARTICIPANTS—**Bill Cayton, Don Fraser, Lope Sarreal;** OBSERVERS—**Jersey Jones, Harry Mullan, Bert Sugar.**

Members are listed with year of induction; (+) indicates deceased member.

### Modern Era

| | |
|---|---|
| Ali, Muhammad | 1990 |
| + Angott, Sammy | 1998 |
| + Apostoli, Fred | 2003 |
| Arguello, Alexis | 1992 |
| + Armstrong, Henry | 1990 |
| Basilio, Carmen | 1990 |
| Benitez, Wilfredo | 1996 |
| Benvenuti, Nino | 1992 |
| + Berg, Jackie (Kid) | 1994 |
| Bivins, Jimmy | 1999 |
| + Brown, Joe | 1996 |
| Buchanan, Ken | 2000 |
| + Burley, Charley | 1992 |
| Canto, Miguel | 1998 |
| + Carter, Jimmy | 2000 |
| + Cerdan, Marcel | 1991 |
| Cervantes, Antonio | 1998 |
| Chacon, Bobby | 2005 |
| Chandler, Jeff | 2000 |
| + Charles, Ezzard | 1990 |
| Cokes, Curtis | 2003 |
| + Conn, Billy | 1990 |
| Cuevas, Pipino | 2002 |
| + Elorde, Gabriel (Flash) | 1993 |
| Fenech, Jeff | 2002 |
| Foreman, George | 2003 |
| Foster, Bob | 1990 |
| Frazier, Joe | 1990 |
| Fullmer, Gene | 1991 |
| Galaxy, Khaosai | 1999 |
| + Galindez, Victor | 2002 |
| Gavilan, Kid | 1990 |
| Giardello, Joey | 1993 |
| Gomez, Wilfredo | 1995 |
| + Graham, Billy | 1992 |
| + Graziano, Rocky | 1991 |
| Griffith, Emile | 1990 |
| Hagler, Marvelous Marvin | 1993 |
| Harada, Masahiko (Fighting) | 1995 |
| Jack, Beau | 1991 |
| + Jenkins, Lew | 1999 |
| Jofre, Eder | 1992 |
| Johansson, Ingemar | 2002 |
| Johnson, Harold | 1993 |
| Laguna, Ismael | 2001 |
| LaMotta, Jake | 1990 |
| Leonard, Sugar Ray | 1997 |
| + Liston, Sonny | 1991 |
| + Locche, Nicolino | 2003 |
| Loi, Duilio | 2005 |
| + Louis, Joe | 1990 |
| + Marciano, Rocky | 1990 |
| + Maxim, Joey | 1994 |
| McCallum, Mike | 2003 |
| McGuigan, Barry | 2005 |
| + Montgomery, Bob | 1995 |
| + Monzon, Carlos | 1990 |
| + Moore, Archie | 1990 |
| Muhammad, Matthew Saad | 1998 |
| Napoles, Jose | 1990 |
| Nelson, Azumah | 2004 |
| Norris, Terry | 2005 |
| Norton, Ken | 1992 |
| Olivares, Ruben | 1991 |
| + Olson, Carl (Bobo) | 2000 |
| Ortiz, Carlos | 1991 |
| + Ortiz, Manuel | 1996 |
| Palomino, Carlos | 2004 |
| Papp, Laszlo | 2001 |
| + Pastrano, Willie | 2001 |
| Patterson, Floyd | 1991 |
| Pedroza, Eusebio | 1999 |
| Pep, Willie | 1990 |
| + Perez, Pascual | 1995 |
| Pryor, Aaron | 1996 |
| Qawi, Dwight Muhammad | 2004 |
| Ramos, Ultiminio | 2001 |
| + Robinson, Sugar Ray | 1990 |
| + Rodriguez, Luis | 1997 |
| + Saddler, Sandy | 1990 |
| + Saldivar, Vicente | 1999 |
| + Sanchez, Salvador | 1991 |
| + Schmeling, Max | 1992 |
| Spinks, Michael | 1994 |
| + Tiger, Dick | 1991 |
| Torres, Jose | 1997 |
| + Turpin, Randy | 2001 |
| + Walcott, Jersey Joe | 1990 |
| + Williams, Ike | 1990 |
| + Wright, Chalky | 1997 |
| + Zale, Tony | 1991 |
| Zaragoza, Daniel | 2004 |
| + Zarate, Carlos | 1994 |
| + Zivic, Fritzie | 1993 |

### Old-Timers

| | |
|---|---|
| + Ambers, Lou | 1992 |
| + Arizmendi, Baby | 2004 |
| + Attell, Abe | 1990 |
| + Baer, Max | 1995 |
| + Barry, Jimmy | 2000 |
| + Bass, Benny | 2002 |
| + Battalino, Battling | 2003 |
| + Berlenbach, Paul | 2001 |
| + Braddock, Jim | 2001 |
| + Britton, Jack | 1990 |
| + Brown, Aaron (Dixie Kid) | 2002 |
| + Brown, Panama Al | 1992 |
| + Burns, Tommy | 1996 |
| + Canzoneri, Tony | 1990 |
| + Carpentier, Georges | 1991 |
| + Chocolate, Kid | 1991 |
| + Choynski, Joe | 1998 |
| + Corbett, James J. | 1990 |
| + Corbett III, Young | 2004 |
| + Coulon, Johnny | 1999 |
| + Criqui, Eugene | 2005 |
| + Darcy, Les | 1993 |
| + Delaney, Jack | 1996 |
| + Dempsey, Jack | 1990 |
| + Dempsey, Jack (Nonpareil) | 1992 |
| + Dillon, Jack | 1995 |
| + Dixon, George | 1990 |
| + Driscoll, Jim | 1990 |
| + Dundee, Johnny | 1991 |
| + Escobar, Sixto | 2002 |
| + Fields, Jackie | 2004 |
| + Fitzsimmons, Bob | 1990 |
| + Flowers, Theodore (Tiger) | 1993 |
| + Gans, Joe | 1990 |
| + Genaro, Frankie | 1998 |
| + Gibbons, Mike | 1992 |
| + Gibbons, Tommy | 1993 |
| + Greb, Harry | 1990 |
| + Griffo, Young | 1991 |
| + Harris, Harry | 2002 |
| + Herman, Pete | 1997 |
| + Jackson, Peter | 1990 |
| + Jeanette, Joe | 1997 |
| + Jeffries, James J | 1990 |
| + Johnson, Jack | 1990 |
| + Kaplan, Louis (Kid) | 2003 |
| + Ketchel, Stanley | 1990 |
| + Kilbane, Johnny | 1995 |
| + LaBarba, Fidel | 1996 |
| + Langford, Sam | 1990 |
| + Lavigne, George (Kid) | 1998 |
| + Leonard, Benny | 1990 |
| + Levinsky, Battling | 2000 |
| + Lewis, John Henry | 1994 |
| + Lewis, Ted (Kid) | 1992 |
| + Loughran, Tommy | 1991 |
| + Lynch, Benny | 1998 |
| + Lynch, Joe | 2005 |
| + Mandell, Sammy | 1998 |
| + McAuliffe, Jack | 1995 |
| + McCoy, Charles (Kid) | 1991 |
| + McFarland, Packey | 1992 |
| + McGovern, Terry | 1990 |
| + McLarnin, Jimmy | 1991 |
| + McVey, Sam | 1999 |
| + Miller, Freddie | 1997 |
| + Mitchell, Charley | 2002 |
| + Moran, Owen | 2002 |
| + Nelson, Battling | 1992 |
| + O'Brien, Philadelphia Jack | 1994 |
| + Papke, Billy | 2001 |
| + Petrolle, Billy | 2000 |
| + Ritchie, Willie | 2004 |
| + Rosenbloom, Maxie | 1993 |
| + Ross, Barney | 1990 |
| + Ryan, Tommy | 1991 |
| + Sharkey, Jack | 1994 |
| + Sharkey, Tom | 2003 |
| + Steele, Freddie | 1999 |
| + Stribling, Young | 1996 |
| + Taylor, Charles (Bud) | 2005 |

+ Tendler, Lew . . . . . . . . . . .1999
+ Thil, Marcel . . . . . . . . . . . .2005
+ Tunney, Gene . . . . . . . . . .1990
+ Villa, Pancho . . . . . . . . . . .1994
+ Walcott, Joe (Barbados) . . .1991

+ Walker, Mickey . . . . . . . . .1990
+ Welsh, Freddie . . . . . . . . .1997
+ Wilde, Jimmy . . . . . . . . . .1990
+ Willard, Jess . . . . . . . . . . .2003
+ Williams, Kid . . . . . . . . . .1996

+ Wills, Harry . . . . . . . . . . . .1992
+ Wolgast, Ad . . . . . . . . . . .2000
+ Wolgast, Midget . . . . . . . .2001

## Pioneers

+ Aaron, Barney . . . . . . . . . .2001
+ Baldwin, Caleb . . . . . . . . .2003
+ Belcher, Jem . . . . . . . . . . .1992
+ Brain, Ben . . . . . . . . . . . . .1994
+ Broughton, Jack . . . . . . . . .1990
+ Burke, James (Deaf) . . . . . .1992
+ Chambers, Arthur . . . . . . . .2000
+ Cribb, Tom . . . . . . . . . . . .1991
+ Donovan, Prof. Mike . . . . . .1998
+ Duffy, Paddy . . . . . . . . . . .1994
+ Goss, Joe . . . . . . . . . . . . .2003

+ Edwards, Billy . . . . . . . . . .2004
+ Figg, James . . . . . . . . . . .1992
+ Heenan, John C. . . . . . . . .2002
+ Jackson, Gentleman John . .1992
+ Johnson, Tom . . . . . . . . . .1995
+ King, Tom . . . . . . . . . . . .1992
+ Langham, Nat . . . . . . . . . .1992
+ Mace, Jem . . . . . . . . . . . .1990
+ Mendoza, Daniel . . . . . . . .1990
+ Molineaux, Tom . . . . . . . . .1997
+ Morrissey, John . . . . . . . . .1996

+ Pearce, Henry . . . . . . . . . .1993
+ Randall, Jack . . . . . . . . . . .2005
+ Richmond, Bill . . . . . . . . . .1999
+ Sam, Dutch . . . . . . . . . . . .1997
+ Sam, Young Dutch . . . . . . .2002
+ Sayers, Tom . . . . . . . . . . .1990
+ Spring, Tom . . . . . . . . . . .1992
+ Sullivan, John L . . . . . . . . .1990
+ Thompson, William . . . . . . .1991
+ Ward, Jem . . . . . . . . . . . .1995

## Non-Participants

+ Andrews, Thomas S . . . . . .1992
+ Arcel, Ray . . . . . . . . . . . . .1991
    Arum, Bob . . . . . . . . . . . .1999
+ Ballarati, Giuseppe . . . . . .1999
    Benton, George . . . . . . . . .2001
+ Blackburn, Jack . . . . . . . . .1992
+ Brady, William A. . . . . . . . .1998
+ Branchini, Umberto . . . . . . .2004
    Brenner, Teddy . . . . . . . . .1993
+ Cayton, Bill . . . . . . . . . . . .2005
+ Chambers, John Graham . . .1990
    Chargin, Don . . . . . . . . . .2001
    Christodolou, Stanley . . . . .2004
    Clancy, Gil . . . . . . . . . . . .1993
+ Coffroth, James W. . . . . . . .1991
+ Cohen, Irving . . . . . . . . . .2002
+ D'Amato, Cus. . . . . . . . . . .1995
    Dickson, Jeff . . . . . . . . . . .2000
+ Donovan, Arthur . . . . . . . .1993
    Duff, Mickey . . . . . . . . . . .1999
    Dundee, Angelo . . . . . . . .1992
+ Dundee, Chris . . . . . . . . . .1994
+ Dunphy, Don . . . . . . - . . . .1993

+ Duva, Dan . . . . . . . . . . . .2003
    Duva, Lou . . . . . . . . . . . .1998
+ Eaton, Aileen . . . . . . . . . .2002
+ Egan, Pierce . . . . . . . . . . .1991
+ Fleischer, Nat . . . . . . . . . .1990
+ Fox, Richard K. . . . . . . . . .1997
+ Fragetta, Dewey . . . . . . . .2003
    Fraser, Don . . . . . . . . . . . .2005
+ Futch, Eddie . . . . . . . . . . .1994
+ Goldman, Charley . . . . . . .1992
+ Goldstein, Ruby . . . . . . . . .1994
    Goodman, Murray . . . . . . .1999
+ Humphreys, Joe . . . . . . . . .1997
+ Ichinose, Sam . . . . . . . . . .2001
+ Jacobs, Jimmy . . . . . . . . . .1993
+ Jacobs, Mike . . . . . . . . . . .1990
+ Johnston, Jimmy . . . . . . . .1999
+ Kearns, Jack (Doc) . . . . . . .1990
    King, Don . . . . . . . . . . . . .1997
    Lectoure, Tito . . . . . . . . . .2000
+ Liebling, A.J . . . . . . . . . . .1992
+ Lonsdale, Lord . . . . . . . . . .1990
+ Markson, Harry . . . . . . . . .1992

    Mercante, Arthur . . . . . . . .1995
+ Morgan, Dan . . . . . . . . . . .2000
+ Muldoon, William . . . . . . . .1996
    Odd, Gilbert . . . . . . . . . . .1995
+ O'Rourke, Tom . . . . . . . . .1999
+ Parker, Dan . . . . . . . . . . . .1996
+ Parnassus, George . . . . . . .1991
    Peltz, J. Russell . . . . . . . . .2004
+ Queensberry, Marquis of . .1990
+ Rickard, Tex . . . . . . . . . . .1990
+ Rudd, Irving . . . . . . . . . . .1999
+ Sarreal Lope . . . . . . . . . . .2005
+ Siler, George . . . . . . . . . . .1995
+ Silverman, Sam . . . . . . . . .2002
+ Solomons, Jack . . . . . . . . .1995
    Steward, Emanuel . . . . . . .1996
+ Taub, Sam . . . . . . . . . . . .1994
+ Taylor, Herman . . . . . . . . .1998
+ Viscusi, Lou . . . . . . . . . . . .2004
+ Walker, James J. (Jimmy) . .1992
+ Weill, Al . . . . . . . . . . . . . .2003

## Observers

+ Bromberg, Lester . . . . . . . .2001
+ Cannon, Jimmy . . . . . . . . .2002
+ Citro, Ralph . . . . . . . . . . .2001
    Fiske, Jack . . . . . . . . . . . .2003
    Gallo, Bill . . . . . . . . . . . . .2001

    Gutteridge, Reg . . . . . . . . .2002
    Heinz, W.C. . . . . . . . . . . .2004
+ Jones, Jersey . . . . . . . . . . .2005
+ Mullan, Harry . . . . . . . . . .2005
+ Nagler, Barney . . . . . . . . . .2004

+ Runyon, Damon . . . . . . . . .2002
    Schulberg, Budd . . . . . . . .2003
    Sugar, Bert . . . . . . . . . . . .2005

---

## Old *Ring* Hall Members Not in Int'l. Boxing Hall

Nat Fleischer, the late founder and editor-in-chief of *The Ring*, established his magazine's Boxing Hall of Fame in 1954, but it was abandoned after the 1987 inductions. One hundred and thirty members of the old *Ring* Hall have been elected to the International Hall since 1989. The 24 boxers and one sportswriter who have yet to be elected to the International Hall are listed below with their year of induction into the *Ring* Hall.

### Modern Group

+ Garcia, Ceferino . . . . . . . .1977

+ Lesnevich, Gus . . . . . . . . .1973

+ Shirai, Yoshio . . . . . . . . . .1977

### Old-Timers

+ Britt, Jimmy . . . . . . . . . . .1976
+ Chaney, George (K.O.) . . .1974
+ Corbett, Young II . . . . . . . .1965

+ Houck, Leo . . . . . . . . . . . .1969
+ Jeffra, Harry . . . . . . . . . . .1982
+ Klaus, Frank . . . . . . . . . . .1974

+ Maher, Peter . . . . . . . . . . .1978
+ Root, Jack . . . . . . . . . . . . .1961
+ Smith, Jeff . . . . . . . . . . . .1969

### Pioneers

+ Chandler, Tom . . . . . . . . . .1972
+ Clark, Nobby . . . . . . . . . .1971
+ Collyer, Sam . . . . . . . . . . .1964
+ Donnelly, Dan . . . . . . . . . .1960
+ Gully, John . . . . . . . . . . . .1959

+ Hyer, Jacob . . . . . . . . . . .1968
+ Hyer, Tom . . . . . . . . . . . .1954
+ Jackling, Thomas . . . . . . . .1985
+ Kilrain, Jack . . . . . . . . . . .1965
+ Price, Ned . . . . . . . . . . . .1962

+ Ryan, Paddy . . . . . . . . . . .1973

### Non-Participant

+ Daniel, Dan (sportswriter) . .1977

---

### FOOTBALL

## College Football Hall of Fame

Established in 1955 by the National Football Foundation. **Address:** 111 South St. Joseph St., South Bend, IN 46601. **Telephone:** (574) 235-9999. **Web:** www.collegefootball.org

**Eligibility:** Nominated players must be out of college 10 years and a first team All-America pick by a major selector during their careers; coaches must be retired three years. Voting done by 12-member panel of athletic directors, conference and bowl officials and media representatives. The first year representatives from NCAA Div. I-AA, II, and III, and the NAIA were eligible for induction was 1996.

**Class of 2005** (19): LARGE COLLEGE—LB **Cornelius Bennett**, Alabama (1983-86); DB **Tom Curtis**, Michigan (1967-69); RB **Anthony Davis**, USC (1972-74); OT **Keith Dorney**, Penn St. (1975-78); E **Jim Houston**, Ohio St. (1957-59); QB **John Huarte**, Notre Dame (1962-64); FB **Roosevelt Leaks**, Texas (1972-74); OT **Mark May**, Pittsburgh (1977-80); RB **Joe Washington**, Oklahoma (1972-75); DT **Paul Wiggin**, Stanford (1954-56); WR **David Williams**, Illinois (1983-85). COACHES—**Pat Dye**, East Carolina (1974-79), Wyoming (1980), Auburn (1981-92); **Don Nehlen**, Bowling Green (1968-76), West Virginia (1980-2000). SMALL COLLEGE—WR **Mike Barber**, Marshall (1985-88); QB **Kirk Baumgartner**, WI-Stevens Point (1986-89); RB **Leo Lewis**, Lincoln (1951-54); QB **Willie Totten**, Mississippi Valley St. (1982-85). SMALL COLLEGE COACHES—**Roger Harring**, Wisconsin-La Crosse (1969-99); **Frosty Westering**, Parsons-IA (1962-63), Lea College-MN (1966-71), Pacific Lutheran-WA (1972-2003).

**Note: Bobby Dodd** and **Amos Alonzo Stagg** are the only members to be honored as both players and coaches.

Players are listed with *final year they played* in college and coaches are listed with year of induction; (+) indicates deceased members.

## Players

+ Abell, Earl-Colgate . . . . . . .1915
  Agase, Alex-Purdue/Ill . . . .1946
+ Agganis, Harry-Boston U . .1952
  Albert, Frank-Stanford . . . . .1941
+ Aldrich, Ki-TCU . . . . . . . . . .1938
+ Aldrich, Malcolm-Yale . . . . .1921
+ Alexander, Joe-Syracuse . . .1920
  Allen, Marcus-USC . . . . . . . .1981
  Alworth, Lance-Arkansas . . .1961
+ Ameche, Alan-Wisconsin . . .1954
+ Ames, Knowlton-Princeton . .1889
+ Amling, Warren-Ohio St . . . .1946
  Anderson, Bob P.-Army . . . .1959
  Anderson, Dick-Colorado . . .1967
  Anderson, Donny-Tex.Tech . .1965
+ Anderson, Hunk-N.Dame . . .1921
  Arnett, Jon-USC . . . . . . . . . .1956
  Atkins, Doug-Tennessee . . . .1952
  Babich, Bob-Miami-OH . . . .1968
+ Bacon, Everett-Wesleyan . . .1912
+ Bagnell, Reds-Penn . . . . . . .1950
+ Baker, Hobey-Princeton . . . .1913
+ Baker, John-USC . . . . . . . . .1931
+ Baker, Moon-N'western . . . .1926
  Baker, Terry-Oregon St . . . .1962
+ Ballin, Harold-Princeton . . . .1914
+ Banker, Bill-Tulane . . . . . . . .1929
  Banonis, Vince-Detroit . . . . .1941
+ Barnes, Stan-California . . . . .1921
+ Barrett, Charles-Cornell . . . .1915
+ Baston, Bert-Minnesota . . . . .1916
+ Battles, Cliff-WV Wesleyan .1931
  Baugh, Sammy-TCU . . . . . . .1936
  Baughan, Maxie-Ga.Tech . . .1959
+ Bausch, James-Wichita/
  Kansas . . . . . . . . . . . . . . .1930
  Beagle, Ron-Navy . . . . . . . .1955
  Beasley, Terry-Auburn . . . . .1971
  Beban, Gary-UCLA . . . . . . . .1967
  Bechtol, Hub-Tex.Tech/Texas 1946
  Beck, Ray-Ga. Tech . . . . . . .1951
+ Beckett, John-Oregon . . . . . .1916
  Bednarik, Chuck-Penn . . . . .1948
  Behm, Forrest-Nebraska . . . .1940
  Bell, Bobby-Minnesota . . . . .1962
  Bell, Ricky-USC . . . . . . . . . .1976
  Bellino, Joe-Navy . . . . . . . . .1960
  Below, Marty-Wisconsin . . . .1923
+ Benbrook, Al-Michigan . . . . .1910

  Bennett, Cornelius-Alabama 1986
+ Berry, Charlie-Lafayette . . . .1924
+ Bertelli, Angelo-N.Dame . . . .1943
+ Berwanger, Jay-Chicago . . . .1935
+ Bettencourt, L.-St.Mary's . . .1927
  Biletnikoff, Fred-Fla.St. . . . . .1964
  Blanchard, Doc-Army . . . . . .1946
+ Blozis, Al-Georgetown . . . . .1941
  Bock, Ed-Iowa St . . . . . . . . .1938
+ Bomar, Lynn-Vanderbilt . . . .1924
+ Bomeisler, Bo-Yale . . . . . . . .1912
+ Booth, Albie-Yale . . . . . . . . .1931
+ Borries, Fred-Navy . . . . . . . .1934
+ Bosley, Bruce-West Va . . . . .1955
+ Bosseler, Don-Miami,FL . . . .1956
  Bottari, Vic-California . . . . . .1938
  Bowden, Murry-Dartmouth . .1970
+ Boynton, Ben-Williams . . . . .1920
+ Brewer, Charles-Harvard . . . .1895
+ Bright, Johnny-Drake . . . . . .1951
  Brodie, John-Stanford . . . . . .1956
+ Brooke, George-Penn . . . . . .1895
  Brosky, Al-Illinois . . . . . . . . .1952
  Brown, Bob-Nebraska . . . . . .1963
  Brown, Geo-Navy/S.Diego St . .1947
+ Brown, Gordon-Yale . . . . . . .1900
  Brown, Jim-Syracuse . . . . . . .1956
+ Brown, John, Jr.-Navy . . . . . .1913
+ Brown, Johnny Mack-Ala . . .1925
+ Brown, Tay-USC . . . . . . . . . .1932
  Brown, Tom-Minnesota . . . . .1960
  Browner, Ross-Notre Dame . .1977
  Budde, Brad-USC . . . . . . . . .1979
+ Bunker, Paul-Army . . . . . . . .1902
  Burford, Chris-Stanford . . . . .1959
+ Burris, Kurt-Oklahoma . . . . .1954
  Burton, Ron-N'western . . . . .1959
  Butkus, Dick-Illinois . . . . . . .1964
  Butler, Kevin-Georgia . . . . . .1984
+ Butler, Robert-Wisconsin . . . .1913
+ Cafego, George-Tenn . . . . . .1939
+ Cagle, Red-SWLa/Army . . . .1929
+ Cain, John-Alabama . . . . . . .1932
  Cameron, Ed-Wash.& Lee . .1924
+ Campbell, David-Harvard . . .1901
  Campbell, Earl-Texas . . . . . .1977
+ Cannon, Jack-N.Dame . . . . .1929
  Cappelletti, John-Penn St . . .1973
+ Carideo, Frank-N.Dame . . . .1930

+ Carney, Charles-Illinois . . . .1921
  Caroline, J.C.-Illinois . . . . . .1954
+ Carpenter, Bill-Army . . . . . . .1959
+ Carpenter, Hunter-No. Carolina/
  Virginia Tech . . . . . . . . . .1905
  Carroll, Chas.-Washington . .1928
  Carter, Anthony-Michigan . . .1982
  Casanova, Tommy-LSU . . . . .1971
+ Casey, Edward-Harvard . . . .1919
  Casillas, Tony-Oklahoma . . .1985
+ Cassady, Howard-Ohio St . . .1955
+ Chamberlin, Guy-Neb.Wesleyan/
  Nebraska . . . . . . . . . . . . .1915
  Chapman, Sam-California . . .1937
  Chappuis, Bob-Michigan . . . .1947
+ Christman, Paul-Missouri . . . .1940
+ Clark, Dutch-Colo. Col. . . . . .1929
  Cleary, Paul-USC . . . . . . . . .1947
+ Clevenger, Zora-Indiana . . . .1903
  Cloud, Jack-Wm. & Mary . . .1949
+ Cochran, Gary-Princeton . . . .1897
+ Cody, Josh-Vanderbilt . . . . . .1919
  Coleman, Don-Mich.St . . . . .1951
+ Conerly, Charlie-Miss . . . . . .1947
  Connor, George-HC/ND . . . .1947
+ Corbin, William-Yale . . . . . . .1888
  Corbus, William-Stanford . . .1933
  Covert, Jimbo-Pittsburgh . . . .1983
+ Cowan, Hector-Princeton . . . .1889
+ Coy, Edward (Ted)-Yale . . . .1909
+ Crawford, Fred-Duke . . . . . . .1933
  Crow, John David-Tex.A&M .1957
+ Crowley, Jim-Notre Dame . . .1924
  Csonka, Larry-Syracuse . . . . .1967
  Curtis, Tom-Michigan . . . . . .1969
+ Cutter, Slade-Navy . . . . . . . .1934
+ Czarobski, Ziggie-N.Dame . .1947
  Dale, Carroll-Va.Tech . . . . . .1959
+ Dalrymple, Gerald-Tulane . . .1931
+ Dalton, John-Navy . . . . . . . .1911
+ Daly, Chas.-Harvard/Army . .1902
+ Daniell, Averell-Pitt . . . . . . . .1936
  Daniell, James-Ohio St . . . . .1941
+ Davies, Tom-Pittsburgh . . . . .1921
  Davis, Anthony-USC . . . . . . .1974
+ Davis, Ernie-Syracuse . . . . . .1961
+ Davis, Glenn-Army . . . . . . . .1946
+ Davis, Robert-Ga.Tech . . . . . .1947
  Dawkins, Pete-Army . . . . . . .1958

DeLong, Steve-Tennessee . . .1964
+ DeRogatis, Al-Duke . . . . . .1948
+ DesJardien, Paul-Chicago -. .1914
+ Devine, Aubrey-Iowa . . . . . .1921
+ DeWitt, John-Princeton . . . . .1903
Dial, Buddy-Rice . . . . . . . .1958
Dicus, Chuck-Arkansas . . . . .1970
Dierdorf, Dan-Michigan . . . . .1970
Ditka, Mike-Pittsburgh . . . . .1960
Dobbs, Glenn-Tulsa . . . . . . .1942
+ Dodd, Bobby-Tennessee . . . .1930
Donan, Holland-Princeton . . .1950
+ Donchess, Joseph-Pitt . . . . .1929
Dorney, Keith-Penn St. . . . . .1978
Dorsett, Tony-Pitt . . . . . . . .1976
+ Dougherty, Nathan-Tenn . . . .1909
Dove, Bob-Notre Dame . . . . .1942
Drahos, Nick-Cornell . . . . . .1940
+ Driscoll, Paddy-N'western . . .1917
+ Drury, Morley-USC . . . . . . .1927
Duden, Dick-Navy . . . . . . . .1945
Dudley, Bill-Virginia . . . . . . .1941
Duncan, Randy-Iowa . . . . . .1958
Easley, Kenny-UCLA . . . . . .1980
+ Eckersall, Walter-Chicago . . .1906
+ Edwards, Turk-Wash.St . . . . .1931
+ Edwards, Wm.-Princeton . . . .1899
+ Eichenlaub, Ray-N.Dame . . . .1914
Eisenhauer, Steve-Navy . . . .1953
Elkins, Larry-Baylor . . . . . . .1964
Elliott, Bump-Mich/Purdue . . .1947
Elliott, Pete-Michigan . . . . . .1948
Elmendorf, Dave-Tex. A&M . .1970
Elway, John-Stanford . . . . . .1982
Emanuel, Frank-Tennessee . . .1965
+ Evans, Ray-Kansas . . . . . . .1947
+ Exendine, Albert-Carlisle . . . .1907
Falaschi, Nello-S.Clara . . . . .1936
Fears, Tom-S.Clara/UCLA . . .1947
+ Feathers, Beattie-Tenn . . . . .1933
Fenimore, Bob-Okla.St . . . . .1946
+ Fenton, Doc-Mansfield/LSU . .1909
Ferguson, Bob-Ohio St. . . . . .1961
+ Ferraro, John-USC . . . . . . .1947
Fesler, Wes-Ohio St . . . . . . .1930
+ Fincher, Bill-Ga.Tech . . . . . .1920
Fischer, Bill-Notre Dame . . . .1948
+ Fish, Hamilton-Harvard . . . .1909
+ Fisher, Robert-Harvard . . . . .1911
+ Flowers, Buck-Davidson/
Ga.Tech . . . . . . . . . . . . .1920
Flowers, Charlie-Ole Miss. . . .1959
+ Fortmann Danny-Colgate . . . .1935
Fralic, Bill-Pittsburgh . . . . . .1984
+ Francis, Sam-Nebraska . . . . .1936
Franck, George-Minnesota . . .1940
Franco, Ed-Fordham . . . . . .1937
+ Frank, Clint-Yale . . . . . . . . .1937
Franz, Rodney-California . . . .1949
Frederickson, Tucker-Auburn 1964
+ Friedman, Benny-Michigan . . .1926
Gabriel, Roman-N.C. State . . .1961
Gain, Bob-Kentucky . . . . . .1950
+ Galiffa, Arnold-Army . . . . . .1949
Gallarneau, Hugh-Stanford . . .1940
+ Garbisch, Edgar-W.& J./Army .1924
Garrett, Mike-USC . . . . . . .1965
+ Gelbert, Charles-Penn . . . . .1896
+ Geyer, Forest-Oklahoma . . . .1915
Gibbs, Jake-Miss . . . . . . . .1960
+ Giel, Paul-Minnesota . . . . . .1953
Gifford, Frank-USC . . . . . . .1951
Gilbert, Chris-Texas . . . . . . .1968

+ Gilbert, Walter-Auburn . . . .1936
Gilmer, Harry-Alabama . . . .1947
+ Gipp, George-N.Dame . . . .1920
+ Gladchuk, Chet-Boston Col .1940
Glass, Bill-Baylor . . . . . . . .1956
Glover, Rich-Nebraska . . . .1972
Goldberg, Marshall-Pitt . . . .1938
Goodreault, Gene-BC . . . . .1940
+ Gordon, Walter-Calif . . . . .1918
+ Governali, Paul-Columbia . .1942
Grabowski, Jim-Illinois . . . .1965
Gradishar, Randy-Ohio St. . .1973
Graham, Otto-N'western . . .1943
+ Grange, Red-Illinois . . . . . .1925
+ Grayson, Bobby-Stanford . .1935
Green, Hugh-Pitt . . . . . . . .1980
+ Green, Jack-Tulane/Army . . .1945
Green, Tim-Syracuse . . . . .1985
Greene, Joe-N.Texas St . . . .1968
Griese, Bob-Purdue . . . . . .1966
Griffin, Archie-Ohio St . . . .1975
Groom, Jerry-Notre Dame . .1950
+ Gulick, Merle-Toledo/Hobart .1929
Guglielmi, Ralph-N.Dame . .1954
Guy, Ray-SMU . . . . . . . . .1972
+ Guyon, Joe-Carlisle/Ga.Tech 1918
Hadl, John-Kansas . . . . . . .1961
+ Hale, Edwin-Miss.College . .1921
Hall, Parker-Miss . . . . . . . .1938
Ham, Jack-Penn St . . . . . . .1970
+ Hamilton, Bob-Stanford . . . .1935
+ Hamilton, Tom-Navy . . . . .1926
Hannah, John-Alabama . . . .1972
+ Hanson, Vic-Syracuse . . . .1926
+ Harder, Pat-Wisconsin . . . .1942
+ Hardwick, Tack-Harvard . . .1914
+ Hare, T.Truxton-Penn . . . . .1900
+ Harley, Chick-Ohio St . . . .1919
+ Harmon, Tom-Michigan . . . .1940
+ Harpster, Howard-Carnegie .1928
Harris, Wayne-Arkansas . . .1960
+ Hart, Edward-Princeton . . . .1911
+ Hart, Leon-Notre Dame . . . .1949
Hartman, Bill-Georgia . . . . .1937
Haynes, Michael-Arizona St .1975
+ Hazel, Homer-Rutgers . . . .1924
Hazeltine, Matt-Calif . . . . .1954
+ Healey, Ed-H. Cross/Dart. . .1916
+ Heffelfinger, Pudge-Yale . . .1891
+ Hein, Mel-Washington St . . .1930
+ Heinrich, Don-Washington . .1952
Hendricks, Ted-Miami,FL . . .1968
+ Henry, Pete-Wash&Jeff . . . .1919
+ Herschberger, C.-Chicago . .1898
+ Herwig, Robert-Calif . . . . .1937
+ Heston, Willie-SJ St./Mich . .1904
+ Hickman, Herman-Tenn . . . .1931
+ Hickok, William-Yale . . . . .1894
Hicks, John-Ohio State . . . .1973
Hill, Dan-Duke . . . . . . . . .1938
+ Hillebrand, Art-Princeton . . .1899
+ Hinkey, Frank-Yale . . . . . . .1894
Hinkle, Carl-Vanderbilt . . . .1937
Hinkle, Clarke-Bucknell . . . .1931
Hirsch, Elroy-Wisc./Mich . . .1943
+ Hitchcock, James-Auburn . .1932
Hoage, Terry-Georgia . . . . .1983
Hoffmann, Frank-N.Dame . . .1931
+ Hogan, James J.-Yale . . . . .1904
+ Holland, Brud-Cornell . . . . .1938
+ Holleder, Don-Army . . . . . .1955
+ Hollenback, Bill-Penn . . . . .1908
Holovak, Mike-Boston Col . .1942

Holub, E.J.-Texas Tech . . . .1960
Hornung, Paul-N.Dame . . . .1956
+ Horrell, Edwin-California . . .1924
+ Horvath, Les-Ohio St. . . . . .1944
Houston, Jim-Ohio St. . . . . .1959
+ Howe, Arthur-Yale . . . . . . .1911
+ Howell, Dixie-Alabama . . . .1934
Huarte, John-Notre Dame . . .1964
+ Hubbard, Cal-Centenary/
Geneva . . . . . . . . . . . . .1926
+ Hubbard, John-Amherst . . . .1906
+ Hubert, Pooley-Ala. . . . . . .1925
Huff, Sam-West Virginia . . . .1955
Humble, Weldon-SWLa/Rice 1946
Hunley, Ricky-Arizona . . . . .1983
+ Hunt, Joe-Texas A&M . . . . .1927
Huntington, Ellery-Colgate . .1913
+ Hutson, Don-Alabama . . . . .1934
Iacavazzi, Cosmo-Princeton .1964
+ Ingram, Jonas-Navy . . . . . .1906
+ Isbell, Cecil-Purdue . . . . . .1937
+ Jablonsky, J.-Army/Wash-MO 1933
Jackson, Bo-Auburn . . . . . .1985
Jackson, Keith-Oklahoma . . .1987
+ Janowicz, Vic-Ohio St . . . . .1951
Jefferson, John-Arizona St. . .1977
+ Jenkins, Darold-Missouri . . .1941
+ Jensen, Jackie-California . . .1948
+ Joesting, Herbert-Minn . . . .1927
+ Johnson, Bob-Tennessee . . .1967
+ Johnson, Jimmie-Carlisle/
Northwestern . . . . . . . . .1905
Johnson, Ron-Michigan . . . .1968
+ Jones, Calvin-Iowa . . . . . . .1955
+ Jones, Gomer-Ohio St . . . . .1935
Jones, Stan-Maryland . . . . .1953
Jordan, Lee Roy-Alabama . . .1962
+ Juhan, Frank-U.of South . . .1910
Justice, Charlie-N.Car . . . . .1949
+ Kaer, Mort-USC . . . . . . . .1926
Kapp, Joe-California . . . . . .1958
Karras, Alex-Iowa . . . . . . .1957
Kavanaugh, Ken-LSU . . . . .1939
+ Kaw, Edgar-Cornell . . . . . .1922
Kazmaier, Dick-Princeton . . .1951
+ Keck, Stan-Princeton . . . . .1921
+ Kelley, Larry-Yale . . . . . . .1936
+ Kelly, Wild Bill-Montana . . . .1926
Kenna, Doug-Army . . . . . . .1944
+ Kerr, George-Boston Col . . .1940
+ Ketcham, Henry-Yale . . . . .1913
Keyes, Leroy-Purdue . . . . . .1968
+ Killinger, Glenn-Penn St . . . .1921
Kilmer, Billy-UCLA . . . . . . .1960
+ Kilpatrick, John-Yale . . . . . .1910
Kimbrough, John-Tex A&M . .1940
+ Kinard, Bruiser-Mississippi . .1937
Kinard, Terry-Clemson . . . . .1982
Kiner, Steve-Tennessee . . . .1969
+ King, Phil-Princeton . . . . . .1893
+ Kinnick, Nile-Iowa . . . . . . .1939
+ Kipke, Harry-Michigan . . . . .1923
+ Kitzmiller, John-Oregon . . . .1930
+ Koch, Barton-Baylor . . . . . .1930
+ Koppisch, Walt-Columbia . . .1924
Kramer, Ron-Michigan . . . . .1956
Kroll, Alex-Yale/Rutgers . . . .1961
Krueger, Charlie-Tex. A&M . .1957
Kutner, Malcolm-Texas . . . .1941
Kwalick, Ted-Penn St . . . . .1968
+ Lach, Steve-Duke . . . . . . . .1941
+ Lane, Myles-Dartmouth . . . .1927
Lattner, Johnny-N.Dame . . . .1953

## College Football Hall of Fame (Cont.)

Scott, Clyde-Navy/Arkansas .1948
Scott, Richard-Navy . . . . . .1947
Scott, Tom-Virginia . . . . . . .1952
+ Seibels, Henry-Sewanee . .1900
Sellers, Ron-Florida St . . . .1968
Selmon, Lee Roy-Okla . . . . .1975
Sewell, Harley-Texas . . . . .1952
+ Shakespeare, Bill-N.Dame .1935
Shell, Donnie-S.Carolina St. .1998
+ Shelton, Murray-Cornell . .1915
+ Shevlin, Tom-Yale . . . . . . .1905
+ Shively, Bernie-Illinois . . . .1926
+ Simons, Monk-Tulane . . . . .1934
Simpson, O.J.-USC . . . . . .1968
Sims, Billy-Oklahoma . . . . .1979
Singletary, Mike-Baylor . . . .1980
Sington, Fred-Alabama . . . .1930
+ Sinkwich, Frank-Georgia . .1942
Sisemore, Jerry-Texas . . . . .1972
+ Sitko, Emil-Notre Dame . . .1949
+ Skladany, Joe-Pittsburgh . .1933
+ Slater, Duke-Iowa . . . . . . .1921
Smith, Billy Ray-Arkansas . .1982
+ Smith, Bruce-Minnesota . . .1941
Smith, Bubba-Michigan St . .1966
+ Smith, Clipper-N.Dame . . . .1927
+ Smith, Ernie-USC . . . . . . . .1932
Smith, Harry-USC . . . . . . . .1939
Smith, Jim Ray-Baylor . . . . .1954
Smith, Riley-Alabama . . . . .1935
+ Smith, Vernon-Georgia . . . .1931
+ Snow, Neil-Michigan . . . . . .1901
Spani, Gary-Kansas St. . . . .1977
Sparlis, Al-UCLA . . . . . . . . .1945
+ Spears, Clarence-Knox/Dart 1915
Spears, W.D.-Vanderbilt . . .1927
+ Sprackling, Wm.-Brown . . . .1911
+ Sprague, Bud-Army/Texas .1928
Spurrier, Steve-Florida . . . .1966
Stafford, Harrison-Texas . . .1932
+ Stagg, Amos Alonzo-Yale . .1889
Stanfill, Bill-Georgia . . . . . .1968
+ Starcevich, Max-Wash . . . .1936
Staubach, Roger-Navy . . . . .1964
+ Steffen, Walter-Chicago . . .1908
Steffy, Joe-Tenn/Army . . . .1947
+ Stein, Herbert-Pitt . . . . . . .1921
Steuber, Bob-Missouri/
  DePauw . . . . . . . . . . . . . .1943
+ Stevens, Mal-Washburn/Yale 1923
+ Stevenson, Vincent-Penn . .1905
Stillwagon, Jim-Ohio St. . . .1970
+ Stinchcomb, Pete-Ohio St. .1920
+ Strom, Brock-Air Force . . . .1959
+ Strong, Ken-NYU . . . . . . . .1928
+ Strupper, Ev-Ga.Tech . . . . .1917

+ Stuhldreher, Harry-N.Dame .1924
+ Sturhahn, Herb-Yale . . . . . .1926
+ Stydahar, Joe-West Va . . . .1935
+ Suffridge, Bob-Tennessee . .1940
+ Suhey, Steve-Penn St . . . . .1947
Sullivan, Pat-Auburn . . . . . .1971
+ Sundstrom, Frank-Cornell . .1923
Swann, Lynn-USC . . . . . . . .1973
+ Swanson, Clarence-Neb . . .1921
+ Swiacki, Bill-Columbia/HC .1947
Swink, Jim-TCU . . . . . . . . . .1956
+ Talboom, Eddie-Wyoming . .1950
Taliafarro, Geo.-Indiana . . .1948
Tarkenton, Fran-Georgia . . .1960
Tatum, Jack-Ohio St. . . . . . .1970
+ Tavener, John-Indiana . . . . .1944
+ Taylor, Chuck-Stanford . . . .1942
Theismann, Joe-Notre Dame 1970
Thomas, Aurelius-Ohio St . .1957
+ Thompson, Joe-Geneva/
  Pittsburgh . . . . . . . . . . . .1906
+ Thorne, Samuel-Yale . . . . . .1895
+ Thorpe, Jim-Carlisle . . . . . .1912
+ Ticknor, Ben-Harvard . . . . .1930
+ Tigert, John-Vanderbilt . . . .1903
+ Tinsley, Gaynell-LSU . . . . . .1936
+ Tipton, Eric-Duke . . . . . . . .1938
+ Tonnemaker, Clayton-Minn .1949
+ Torrey, Bob-Pennsylvania . .1905
+ Travis, Brick-Tarkio/Missouri 1920
+ Trippi, Charley-Georgia . . . .1946
+ Tryon, Edward-Colgate . . . .1925
Tubbs, Jerry-Oklahoma . . . .1956
Turner, Bulldog-H.Simmons .1939
Twilley, Howard-Tulsa . . . . .1965
+ Utay, Joe-Texas A&M . . . . .1907
+ Van Brocklin, Norm-Ore . . .1948
Van Pelt, Brad-Michigan St. .1972
+ Van Sickel, Dale-Florida . . .1929
+ Van Surdam, H.-Wesleyan . .1905
+ Very, Dexter-Penn St . . . . . .1912
+ Vessels, Billy-Oklahoma . . . .1952
+ Vick, Ernie-Michigan . . . . . .1921
+ Wagner, Hube-Pittsburgh . .1913
+ Walker, Doak-SMU . . . . . . . .1949
Walker, Herschel-Georgia . .1982
+ Wallace, Bill-Rice . . . . . . . .1935
+ Walsh, Adam-N.Dame . . . .1924
+ Warburton, Cotton, USC . . .1934
Ward, Bob-Maryland . . . . . .1951
Ware, Andre-Houston . . . . .1989
+ Warner, William-Cornell . . .1902
Washington, Joe-Oklahoma 1975
+ Washington, Kenny-UCLA . .1939
+ Weatherall, Jim-Okla. . . . . .1951
Webster, George-Mich. St . .1966

+ Wedemeyer, H.-St. Mary's .1947
+ Weekes, Harold-Columbia .1902
Wehrli, Roger-Missouri . . . .1968
Weiner, Art-N. Carolina . . .1949
+ Weir, Ed-Nebraska . . . . . . .1925
+ Welch, Gus-Carlisle . . . . . . .1914
+ Weller, John-Princeton . . . .1935
+ Wendell, Percy-Harvard . . .1912
+ West, Belford-Colgate . . . . .1919
+ Westfall, Bob-Michigan . . . .1941
+ Weyand, Babe-Army . . . . . .1915
+ Wharton, Buck-Penn . . . . . .1896
+ Wheeler, Arthur-Princeton .1894
+ White, Byron-Colorado . . . .1937
White, Charles-USC . . . . . .1979
White, Danny-Ariz. St. . . . .1973
+ White, Ed-Cal.Berkeley . . . .1968
White, Randy-Maryland . . . .1974
+ White, Reggie-Tennessee . .1983
Whitmire, Don-Navy/Ala . .1944
+ Wickhorst, Frank-Navy . . . .1926
Widseth, Ed-Minnesota . . .1936
Wiggin, Paul-Stanford . . . . .1956
+ Wildung, Dick-Minnesota . .1942
Williams, Bob-N. Dame . . .1950
Williams, David-Illinois . . . .1985
Williams, Froggie-Rice . . . . .1949
Willis, Bill-Ohio St . . . . . . .1944
+ Wilson, Bobby-SMU . . . . . . .1935
+ Wilson, George-Lafayette . .1928
+ Wilson, George-Wash . . . . .1925
+ Wilson, Harry-Army/Penn St .1927
Wilson, Marc-BYU . . . . . . . .1979
Wilson, Mike-Lafayette . . . .1928
Winslow, Kellen-Missouri . .1978
+ Wistert, Albert-Michigan . . .1942
Wistert, Alvin-Michigan . . . .1949
+ Wistert, Whitey-Michigan . .1933
+ Wojciechowicz, Alex-Fordham 1937
+ Wood, Barry-Harvard . . . . .1931
+ Wyatt, Andy-Bucknell/
  Chicago . . . . . . . . . . . . . .1894
+ Wyatt, Bowden-Tenn . . . . .1938
+ Wyckoff, Clint-Cornell . . . . .1895
+ Yarr, Tommy-N.Dame . . . . .1931
Yary, Ron-USC . . . . . . . . . . .1967
+ Yoder, Lloyd-Carnegie . . . . .1926
Young, Charles-USC . . . . . . .1972
+ Young, Claude-Illinois . . . . .1946
+ Young, Harry-Wash.& Lee . .1916
+ Young, Steve-Brigham Young .1983
+ Young, Waddy-Okla . . . . . .1938
Youngblood, Jack-Florida . .1970
+ Younger, Tank-Grambling . .1948
Zarnas, Gustave-Ohio St. . .1937

## Coaches

+ Aillet, Joe . . . . . . . . . . . . .1989
+ Alexander, Bill . . . . . . . . .1951
+ Anderson, Ed . . . . . . . . . .1971
+ Armstrong, Ike . . . . . . . . .1957
+ Bachman, Charlie . . . . . .1978
+ Banks, Earl . . . . . . . . . . . .1992
+ Baujan, Harry . . . . . . . . . .1990
+ Bell, Matty . . . . . . . . . . . .1955
+ Bezdek, Hugo . . . . . . . . . .1954
+ Bible, Dana X . . . . . . . . . .1951
+ Bierman, Bernie . . . . . . . .1955
Blackman, Bob . . . . . . . .1987
+ Blaik, Earl (Red) . . . . . . .1965
Broyles, Frank . . . . . . . . .1983

Bruce, Earle . . . . . . . . . .2002
+ Bryant, Paul (Bear) . . . . . .1986
+ Butts, Wally . . . . . . . . . .1997
+ Caldwell, Charlie . . . . . . .1961
+ Camp, Walter . . . . . . . . .1951
Casanova, Len . . . . . . . .1977
+ Cavanaugh, Frank . . . . .1954
+ Claiborne, Jerry . . . . . . .1999
+ Colman, Dick . . . . . . . . .1990
Coryell, Don . . . . . . . . . .1999
+ Cozza, Carmen . . . . . . . .2002
+ Crisler, Fritz . . . . . . . . . .1954
+ Daugherty, Duffy . . . . . .1984
+ Devaney, Bob . . . . . . . . .1981

+ Devine, Dan . . . . . . . . . . .1985
Dickey, Doug . . . . . . . . . . .2003
+ Dobie, Gil . . . . . . . . . . . .1951
+ Dodd, Bobby . . . . . . . . . .1993
+ Donahue, Tom . . . . . . . .2000
+ Donohue, Michael . . . . .1951
Dooley, Vince . . . . . . . . . .1994
+ Dorais, Gus . . . . . . . . . . .1954
Dye, Pat . . . . . . . . . . . . .2005
+ Edwards, Bill . . . . . . . . . .1986
Edwards, LaVell . . . . . . .2004
+ Engle, Rip . . . . . . . . . . . .1973
Evashevski, Forest . . . . .2000
Faurot, Don . . . . . . . . . . .1961

## College Football Hall of Fame (Cont.)
### Coaches (Cont.)

Fry, Hayden . . . . . . . . . . .2003
+ Gaither, Jake . . . . . . . . . .1973
Gillman, Sid . . . . . . . . . . .1989
+ Godfrey, Ernest . . . . . . . .1972
Graves, Ray . . . . . . . . . . .1990
+ Gustafson, Andy . . . . . . . .1985
+ Hall, Edward . . . . . . . . . .1951
+ Harding, Jack . . . . . . . . .1980
+ Harlow, Richard . . . . . . . .1954
+ Harman, Harvey . . . . . . .1981
+ Harper, Jesse . . . . . . . . .1971
+ Haughton, Percy . . . . . . .1951
+ Hayes, Woody . . . . . . . . .1983
+ Heisman, John W . . . . . . .1954
+ Higgins, Robert . . . . . . . .1954
+ Hollingberry, Babe . . . . . .1979
+ Howard, Frank . . . . . . . . .1989
+ Ingram, Bill . . . . . . . . . . .1973
James, Don . . . . . . . . . . .1997
+ Jennings, Morley . . . . . . .1973
+ Jones, Biff . . . . . . . . . . . .1954
+ Jones, Howard . . . . . . . . .1951
+ Jones, Tad . . . . . . . . . . .1958
+ Jordan, Lloyd . . . . . . . . . .1978
+ Jordan, Ralph (Shug) . . . . .1982
+ Kerr, Andy . . . . . . . . . . .1951
Kush, Frank . . . . . . . . . . .1995
+ Leahy, Frank . . . . . . . . . .1970
+ Little, George . . . . . . . . . .1955
+ Little, Lou . . . . . . . .* . . .1960
+ Madigan, Slip . . . . . . . . .1974
Maurer, Dave . . . . . . . . .1991
+ McClendon, Charley . . . . .1986
+ McCracken, Herb . . . . . . .1973

+ McGugin, Dan . . . . . . . . .1951
+ McKay, John . . . . . . . . . .1988
+ McKeen, Allyn . . . . . . . . .1991
+ McLaughry, Tuss . . . . . . .1962
+ Merritt, John . . . . . . . . . .1994
+ Meyer, Dutch . . . . . . . . . .1956
+ Mollenkopf, Jack . . . . . . .1988
+ Moore, Bernie . . . . . . . . .1954
+ Moore, Scrappy . . . . . . . .1980
+ Morrison, Ray . . . . . . . . .1954
+ Munger, George . . . . . . . .1976
+ Munn, Clarence (Biggie) . . .1959
+ Murray, Bill . . . . . . . . . . .1974
+ Murray, Frank . . . . . . . . .1983
+ Mylin, Ed (Hooks) . . . . . . .1974
+ Neale, Earle (Greasy) . . . . .1967
+ Neely, Jess . . . . . . . . . . .1971
Nehlen, Don . . . . . . . . . .2005
+ Nelson, David . . . . . . . . .1987
+ Neyland, Robert . . . . . . . .1956
+ Norton, Homer . . . . . . . . .1971
+ O'Neill, Frank (Buck) . . . . .1951
+ Osborne, Tom . . . . . . . . .1998
+ Owen, Bennie . . . . . . . . .1951
Parseghian, Ara . . . . . . . .1980
+ Perry, Doyt . . . . . . . . . . .1988
+ Phelan, Jimmy . . . . . . . . .1973
+ Prothro, Tommy . . . . . . . .1991
Ralston, John . . . . . . . . . .1992
+ Robinson, E.N. . . . . . . . . .1955
+ Rockne, Knute . . . . . . . . .1951
+ Romney, Dick . . . . . . . . .1954
+ Roper, Bill . . . . . . . . . . .1951
Royal, Darrell . . . . . . . . .1983

+ Sanders, Henry (Red) . . . . .1996
+ Sanford, George . . . . . . . .1971
Schembechler, Bo . . . . . . .1993
+ Schmidt, Francis . . . . . . . .1971
+ Schwartzwalder, Ben . . . . .1982
+ Shaughnessy, Clark . . . . . .1968
+ Shaw, Buck . . . . . . . . . . .1972
+ Smith, Andy . . . . . . . . . .1951
+ Snavely, Carl . . . . . . . . . .1965
+ Stagg, Amos Alonzo . . . . .1951
+ Sutherland, Jock . . . . . . . .1951
Switzer, Barry . . . . . . . . .2001
+ Tatum, Jim . . . . . . . . . . .1984
Teaff, Grant . . . . . . . . . .2001
+ Thomas, Frank . . . . . . . . .1951
+ Vann, Thad . . . . . . . . . . .1987
Vaught, Johnny . . . . . . . .1979
+ Wade, Wallace . . . . . . . . .1955
+ Waldorf, Lynn (Pappy) . . . .1966
+ Warner, Glenn (Pop) . . . . .1951
Welsh, George . . . . . . . . .2004
+ Wieman, E.E. (Tad) . . . . . .1956
+ Wilce, John . . . . . . . . . . .1954
+ Wilkinson, Bud . . . . . . . . .1969
+ Williams, Henry . . . . . . . .1951
+ Woodruff, George . . . . . . .1963
+ Woodson, Warren . . . . . . .1989
+ Wyatt, Bowden . . . . . . . .1997
Yeoman, Bill . . . . . . . . . .2001
+ Yost, Fielding (Hurry Up) . . .1951
Young, Jim . . . . . . . . . . .1999
+ Zuppke, Bob . . . . . . . . . .1951

## Small College
### Players

Bailey, Johnny-Texas A&I . . .1989
Barber, Mike-Marshall . . . . .1988
Baumgartner, Kirk-
  WI-Stevens Point . . . . . . .1989
Bentrim, Jeff-N.Dakota St. . . .1986
+ Blazine, Tony-Ill Wesleyan . .1934
Bork, George-N. Illinois . . . .1963
Bradshaw, Terry-La. Tech . . .1969
Bruner, Teel-Centre KY . . . .1985
+ Buchanon, Buck-Grambling . .1962
Calip, Brad-E. Central . . . . .1984
Carson, Harry, S.C. State . . .1975
Cason, Rod, Angelo St. . . . .1971
Cichy, Joe-N.Dakota St. . . . .1970
Cooper, Bill-Muskinghum . . .1960
Crawford, Brad-Franklin . . . .1977
Davis, Harold-Wesminster . . .1956
Deery, Tom-Widener . . . . . .1981
+ Delaney, Joe-N'western St. . .1980
Dement, Kenneth-SE Mo St. . .1954
Den Herder, Vern-Central IA .1970
Dryer, Fred-San Diego St. . . .1968
Dudek, Joe-Plymouth St. . . . .1985

Floyd, George-E. Kentucky . .1981
Galimore, Willie-Fla. A&M . . .1956
Gamble, Kenny-Colgate . . . .1987
Green, Charlie-Wittenberg . . .1964
Green, Darrell-Texas A&I . . . .1982
Grinnell, Williams-Tufts . . . . .1934
Haslett, Jim-Indiana, PA . . . .1978
Hawkins, Frank-Nevada . . . .1980
Henley, Garney-Huron . . . . .1959
Holt, Pierce-Angelo St. . . . . .1987
+ Hunt, Jackie-Marshall . . . . .1941
Johnson, Billy-Widener . . . . .1973
Johnson, Gary-Grambling . . .1974
Lanier, Willie-Morgan St. . . . .1966
LeClair, Jim-North Dakota . . .1971
Lewis, Leo-Lincoln . . . . . . . .1954
Lockbaum, Gordie-Holy Cross 1987
Lomax, Neil-Portland . . . . . .1980
McGriff, Tyrone-Jackson St. . .1974
Montgomery, Wilbert-
  Abilene Christian . . . . . . .1976
Nix, Dwayne-Texas A&I . . . .1968
O'Brien, Ken-UC Davis . . . . .1982

+ Payton, Walter-Jackson St. . .1974
Pugh, Larrry-Westminster . . . .1964
Reasons, Gary-N'western St. .1983
Redell, Bill-Occidental . . . . .1963
Reppert, Scott-Lawrence . . . .1982
Richardson, Willie-Jackson St. 1962
Ritchie, Richard-Texas A&I . . .1976
+ Roberts, Calvin-
  Gustavus Adolphus . . . . .1952
Ross, Dan-Northeastern . . . .1978
Scott, Freddie-Amherst . . . . .1973
Shell, Donnie-S.C. State . . . .1973
+ Stevenson, Ben-Tuskegee . . .1930
Stromberg, Bill-Johns Hopkins 1981
Taylor, Bruce-Boston U. . . . . .1969
Thomsen, Lynn-Augustana . . .1986
Totten, Willie-Miss. Valley St. .1985
Trautman, Randy-Boise St. . . .1964
Williams, Doug-Grambling . . .1977
Youngblood, Jim-Tenn. Tech .1972
Younger, Paul-Grambling . . . .1948

### Coaches

Ault, Chris . . . . . . . . . . . .2002
Beck, Tom . . . . . . . . . . . .2004
+ Burry, Harold . . . . . . . . . .1996
Butterfield, Jim . . . . . . . . .1997
Casem, Marino . . . . . . . . .2003
Fusco, Joe . . . . . . . . . . . .2001

Harring, Roger . . . . . . . . .2005
Hoerneman, Paul . . . . . . . .1997
Huerta, Marcelino . . . . . . .2002
Keade, Bob . . . . . . . . . . .1998
Kidd, Roy . . . . . . . . . . . .2003
Klausing, Chuck . . . . . . . .1998

Martinelli, Fred . . . . . . . . .1993
Mudra, Darrell . . . . . . . . .2000
+ Mumford, Ace . . . . . . . . .2001
Nicks, Billy . . . . . . . . . . . .1999
Raymond, Tubby . . . . . . . .2003
Reade, Bob . . . . . . . . . . .1998

### Small College Coaches (Cont.)

Robinson, Eddie G. . . . . . .1997
+ Richard, Charlie . . . . . . .2004
Rutschman, Ad . . . . . . . .1998
Schipper, Ron . . . . . . . . .2000

Sherman, Edgar . . . . . . . .1996
Sochor, James . . . . . . . . .1999
+ Steinke, Gilbert . . . . . . . .1996
Strahm, Dick . . . . . . . . . .2004

+ Tressel, Lee . . . . . . . . . . .1996
Waters, Frank . . . . . . . . .2000
Westering, Frosty . . . . . . .2005

## Pro Football Hall of Fame

Established in 1963 by National Football League to commemorate the sport's professional origins. **Address:** 2121 George Halas Drive NW, Canton, OH 44708. **Telephone:** (330) 456-8207. **Web:** www.profootballhof.com

**Eligibility:** Nominated players must be retired five years, coaches must be retired, and contributors can still be active. Voting done by 39-member panel made up of media representatives from all 31 NFL cities (two from New York), one PFWA representative and six selectors-at-large.

**Class of 2005** (4): PLAYERS—QB **Benny Friedman**, Cleveland Bulldogs (1927), Detroit Wolverines (1928), NY Giants (1929-31), Brooklyn Dodgers (1932-34); QB **Dan Marino**, Miami (1983-99); RB **Fritz Pollard**, Akron Pros/Indians (1919-21, 1925-26), Milwaukee Badgers (1922), Hammond Pros (1923, 25), Gilberton Cadamounts (1923-24), Providence Steam Roller (1925) and QB **Steve Young**, Tampa Bay (1985-86) and San Francisco (1987-99).

### Quarterbacks

Baugh, Sammy . . . . . . . . .1963
Blanda, George (also PK) . .1981
Bradshaw, Terry . . . . . . . .1989
+ Clark, Dutch . . . . . . . . . .1963
+ Conzelman, Jimmy . . . . . .1964
Dawson, Len . . . . . . . . . .1987
+ Driscoll, Paddy . . . . . . . .1965
Elway, John . . . . . . . . . .2004
Fouts, Dan . . . . . . . . . . .1993
+ Friedman, Benny . . . . . . .2005

+ Graham, Otto . . . . . . . . .1965
Griese, Bob . . . . . . . . . .1990
+ Herber, Arnie . . . . . . . . .1966
Jurgensen, Sonny . . . . . . .1983
Kelly, Jim . . . . . . . . . . . .2002
+ Layne, Bobby . . . . . . . . .1967
+ Luckman, Sid . . . . . . . . .1965
Marino, Dan . . . . . . . . . .2005
Montana, Joe . . . . . . . . .2000
Namath, Joe . . . . . . . . . .1985

Parker, Clarence (Ace) . . . .1972
Starr, Bart . . . . . . . . . . .1977
Staubach, Roger . . . . . . . .1985
Tarkenton, Fran . . . . . . . .1986
Tittle, Y.A. . . . . . . . . . . .1971
+ Unitas, Johnny . . . . . . . .1979
+ Van Brocklin, Norm . . . . .1971
+ Waterfield, Bob . . . . . . . .1965
Young, Steve . . . . . . . . . .2005

### Running Backs

Allen, Marcus . . . . . . . . . .2003
+ Battles, Cliff . . . . . . . . . .1968
Brown, Jim . . . . . . . . . . .1971
Campbell, Earl . . . . . . . . .1991
Canadeo, Tony . . . . . . . . .1974
Csonka, Larry . . . . . . . . . .1987
Dickerson, Eric . . . . . . . . .1999
Dorsett, Tony . . . . . . . . . .1994
Dudley, Bill . . . . . . . . . . .1966
Gifford, Frank . . . . . . . . . .1977
+ Grange, Red . . . . . . . . . .1963
+ Guyon, Joe . . . . . . . . . . .1966
Harris, Franco . . . . . . . . .1990

+ Hinkle, Clarke . . . . . . . . .1964
Hornung, Paul . . . . . . . . .1986
Johnson, John Henry . . . . .1987
Kelly, Leroy . . . . . . . . . . .1994
+ Leemans, Tuffy . . . . . . . .1978
Matson, Ollie . . . . . . . . . .1972
McAfee, George . . . . . . . .1966
McElhenny, Hugh . . . . . . .1970
+ McNally, Johnny (Blood) . . .1963
Moore, Lenny . . . . . . . . . .1975
+ Motley, Marion . . . . . . . .1968
+ Nagurski, Bronko . . . . . . .1963
+ Nevers, Ernie . . . . . . . . .1963

+ Payton, Walter . . . . . . . .1993
Perry, Joe . . . . . . . . . . . .1969
+ Pollard, Fritz . . . . . . . . . .2005
Riggins, John . . . . . . . . . .1992
Sanders, Barry . . . . . . . . .2004
Sayers, Gale . . . . . . . . . .1977
Simpson, O.J. . . . . . . . . .1985
+ Strong, Ken . . . . . . . . . .1967
Taylor, Jim . . . . . . . . . . .1976
+ Thorpe, Jim . . . . . . . . . .1963
Trippi, Charley . . . . . . . . .1968
Van Buren, Steve . . . . . . .1965
+ Walker, Doak . . . . . . . . .1986

### Ends & Wide Receivers

Alworth, Lance . . . . . . . . .1978
+ Badgro, Red . . . . . . . . . .1981
Berry, Raymond . . . . . . . .1973
Biletnikoff, Fred . . . . . . . .1988
Casper, Dave . . . . . . . . . .2002
+ Chamberlin, Guy . . . . . . .1965
Ditka, Mike . . . . . . . . . . .1988
+ Fears, Tom . . . . . . . . . . .1970
+ Hewitt, Bill . . . . . . . . . . .1971
Hirsch, Elroy (Crazylegs) . .1968

+ Hutson, Don . . . . . . . . . .1963
Joiner, Charlie . . . . . . . . .1996
Largent, Steve . . . . . . . . .1995
Lavelli, Dante . . . . . . . . . .1975
Lofton, James . . . . . . . . . .2003
Mackey, John . . . . . . . . . .1992
Maynard, Don . . . . . . . . .1987
McDonald, Tommy . . . . . .1998
+ Millner, Wayne . . . . . . . .1968
Mitchell, Bobby . . . . . . . .1983

Newsome, Ozzie . . . . . . . .1999
Pihos, Pete . . . . . . . . . . .1970
Smith, Jackie . . . . . . . . . .1994
Stallworth, John . . . . . . . .2002
Swann, Lynn . . . . . . . . . .2001
Taylor, Charley . . . . . . . . .1984
Warfield, Paul . . . . . . . . . .1983
Winslow, Kellen . . . . . . . .1995

### Offensive Linemen

Bednarik, Chuck (C-LB) . . . .1967
Brown, Bob (T) . . . . . . . . .2004
Brown, Roosevelt (T) . . . . .1975
DeLamielleure, Joe (G) . . . .2003
Dierdorf, Dan (T) . . . . . . . .1996
Gatski, Frank (C) . . . . . . . .1985
Gregg, Forrest (T-G) . . . . . .1977
+ Groza, Lou (T-PK) . . . . . . .1974
Hannah, John (G) . . . . . . .1991
Jones, Stan (T-G-DT) . . . . . .1991

Langer, Jim (C) . . . . . . . . .1987
Little, Larry (G) . . . . . . . . .1993
Mack, Tom (G) . . . . . . . . .1999
McCormack, Mike (T) . . . . .1984
Mix, Ron (T-G) . . . . . . . . .1979
Munchak, Mike (G) . . . . . .2001
Munoz, Anthony (T) . . . . . .1998
+ Musso, George (T-G) . . . . .1982
Otto, Jim (C) . . . . . . . . . .1980
Parker, Jim (G) . . . . . . . . .1973

Ringo, Jim (C) . . . . . . . . . .1981
St. Clair, Bob (T) . . . . . . . .1990
Shaw, Billy (G) . . . . . . . . .1999
Shell, Art (T) . . . . . . . . . .1989
Slater, Jackie (T) . . . . . . . .2001
Stephenson, Dwight (C) . . .1998
Upshaw, Gene (G) . . . . . . .1987
Yary, Ron (T) . . . . . . . . . .2001
+ Webster, Mike (C) . . . . . . .1997

## Linemen (pre-World War II)

+ Edwards, Turk (T) . . . . . . . .1969
+ Fortmann, Dan (G) . . . . . . .1985
+ Healey, Ed (T) . . . . . . . . .1964
+ Hein, Mel (C) . . . . . . . . .1963
+ Henry, Pete (T) . . . . . . . .1963

+ Hubbard, Cal (T) . . . . . . .1963
+ Kiesling, Walt (G) . . . . . . .1966
+ Kinard, Bruiser (T) . . . . . .1971
+ Lyman, Link (T) . . . . . . . .1964
+ Michalske, Mike (G) . . . . .1964

+ Musso, George (T-G) . . . . .1982
+ Stydahar, Joe (T) . . . . . . .1967
+ Trafton, George (C) . . . . . .1964
+ Turner, Bulldog (C) . . . . . .1966
+ Wojciechowicz, Alex (C) . .1968

## Defensive Linemen

Atkins, Doug . . . . . . . . . .1982
Bethea, Elvin . . . . . . . . . .2003
+ Buchanan, Buck . . . . . . . .1990
Creekmur, Lou . . . . . . . . .1996
Davis, Willie . . . . . . . . . .1981
Donovan, Art . . . . . . . . . .1968
Eller, Carl . . . . . . . . . . .2004
+ Ford, Len . . . . . . . . . . .1976
Greene, Joe . . . . . . . . . .1987

Hampton, Dan . . . . . . . . .2002
Jones, Deacon . . . . . . . . .1980
+ Jordan, Henry . . . . . . . . .1995
Lilly, Bob . . . . . . . . . . . .1980
Long, Howie . . . . . . . . . .2000
Marchetti, Gino . . . . . . . .1972
+ Nomellini, Leo . . . . . . . . .1969
Olsen, Merlin . . . . . . . . . .1982
Page, Alan . . . . . . . . . . .1988

Robustelli, Andy . . . . . . . .1971
Selmon, Lee Roy . . . . . . . .1995
Stautner, Ernie . . . . . . . . .1969
+ Weinmeister, Arnie . . . . . . .1984
White, Randy . . . . . . . . . .1994
Willis, Bill . . . . . . . . . . . .1977
Youngblood, Jack . . . . . . .2001

## Linebackers

Bell, Bobby . . . . . . . . . . .1983
Buoniconti, Nick . . . . . . . .2001
Butkus, Dick . . . . . . . . . .1979
Connor, George (DT-OT) . . .1975
+ George, Bill . . . . . . . . . .1974

Ham, Jack . . . . . . . . . . .1988
Hendricks, Ted . . . . . . . . .1990
Huff, Sam . . . . . . . . . . .1982
Lambert, Jack . . . . . . . . .1990
Lanier, Willie . . . . . . . . . .1986

+ Nitschke, Ray . . . . . . . . .1978
Schmidt, Joe . . . . . . . . . .1973
Singletary, Mike . . . . . . . .1998
Taylor, Lawrence . . . . . . . .1999
Wilcox, Dave . . . . . . . . . .2000

## Defensive Backs

Adderley, Herb . . . . . . . .1980
Barney, Lem . . . . . . . . . .1992
Blount, Mel . . . . . . . . . . .1989
Brown, Willie . . . . . . . . . .1984
+ Christiansen, Jack . . . . . . .1970
Haynes, Michael . . . . . . . .1997

Houston, Ken . . . . . . . . . .1986
Johnson, Jimmy . . . . . . . .1994
Krause, Paul . . . . . . . . . .1998
+ Lane, Dick (Night Train) . . .1974
Lary, Yale . . . . . . . . . . . .1979
Lott, Ronnie . . . . . . . . . .2000

Renfro, Mel . . . . . . . . . . .1996
+ Tunnell, Emlen . . . . . . . . .1967
Wilson, Larry . . . . . . . . . .1978
Wood, Willie . . . . . . . . . .1989

## Placekicker

Stenerud, Jan . . . . . . . . . .1991

## Coaches

+ Allen, George . . . . . . . . .2002
+ Brown, Paul . . . . . . . . . .1967
+ Ewbank, Weeb . . . . . . . .1978
+ Flaherty, Ray . . . . . . . . . .1976
Gibbs, Joe . . . . . . . . . . .1996
Gillman, Sid . . . . . . . . . .1983

Grant, Bud . . . . . . . . . . .1994
+ Halas, George . . . . . . . . .1963
+ Lambeau, Curly . . . . . . . .1963
+ Landry, Tom . . . . . . . . . .1990
Levy, Marv . . . . . . . . . . .2001
+ Lombardi, Vince . . . . . . . .1971

+ Neale, Earle (Greasy) . . . .1969
Noll, Chuck . . . . . . . . . .1993
+ Owen, Steve . . . . . . . . . .1966
Shula, Don . . . . . . . . . . .1997
Stram, Hank . . . . . . . . . .2003
Walsh, Bill . . . . . . . . . . .1993

## Contributors

+ Bell, Bert . . . . . . . . . . . .1963
+ Bidwill, Charles . . . . . . . .1967
+ Carr, Joe . . . . . . . . . . . .1963
Davis, Al . . . . . . . . . . . .1992
+ Finks, Jim . . . . . . . . . . .1995
+ Halas, George . . . . . . . . .1963

Hunt, Lamar . . . . . . . . . .1972
+ Mara, Tim . . . . . . . . . . .1963
Mara, Wellington . . . . . . . .1997
+ Marshall, George . . . . . . .1963
+ Ray, Hugh (Shorty) . . . . . .1966
+ Reeves, Dan . . . . . . . . . .1967

+ Rooney, Art . . . . . . . . . .1964
Rooney, Dan . . . . . . . . . .2000
+ Rozelle, Pete . . . . . . . . . .1985
Schramm, Tex . . . . . . . . .1991

---

## NFL's All-Time Team

Selected by the Pro Football Hall of Fame voters and released Aug. 1, 2000 as part of the NFL Century celebration.

### Offense

**Wide Receivers:** Don Hutson and Jerry Rice
**Tight End:** John Mackey
**Tackles:** Roosevelt Brown and Anthony Munoz
**Guards:** John Hannah and Jim Parker
**Center:** Mike Webster
**Quarterback:** Johnny Unitas
**Running Backs:** Jim Brown and Walter Payton

### Defense

**Ends:** Deacon Jones and Reggie White
**Tackles:** Joe Greene and Bob Lilly
**Linebackers:** Dick Butkus, Jack Ham and Lawrence Taylor
**Cornerbacks:** Mel Blount and Dick (Night Train) Lane
**Safeties:** Ronnie Lott and Larry Wilson

### Specialists

**Placekicker:** Jan Stenerud
**Punter:** Ray Guy
**Kick Returner:** Gale Sayers

**Punt Returner:** Deion Sanders
**Special Teams:** Steve Tasker

## GOLF

# World Golf Hall of Fame

The World Golf Hall of Fame opened its doors in 1998 at the World Golf Village outside of Jacksonville, Fla. **Address:** One World Golf Place, St. Augustine, FL 32092. **Telephone:** (904) 940-4000. **Web:** www.wghof.com/hof/hof.html **Eligibility:** Professionals have three avenues into the WGHF. A PGA Tour player qualifies for the ballot if he has at least 10 victories in approved tournaments, or at least two victories among The Players Championship, Masters, U.S. Open, British Open and PGA Championship, is at least 40 years old and has been a member of the Tour for 10 years. A senior PGA Tour player qualifies if he has been a Senior Tour member for five years and has 20 wins between the PGA Tour and Senior Tour or five wins among the PGA majors, the Players Championship and the senior majors (U.S. Senior Open, Tradition, PGA Seniors' Championship and Senior Players Championship). Final selections for both Veteran's (for players who played bulk of their career before 1974) and Lifetime Achievement Categories are made by the Executive Committee of the World Golf Hall of Fame, which includes leaders from the major golf organizations.

Any player qualifying for the LPGA Hall automatically qualifies for the WGHF. Until 1999, nominees must have had played 10 years on the LPGA tour and won 30 official events, including two major championships; 35 official events and one major; or 40 official events and no majors. The eligibility requirements were loosened somewhat in 1999. The new guidelines are based on a system which awards two points for winning a major and one point for winning other tournaments, the Vare trophy (for lowest scoring average) and the player of the year award. Players must win at least one major, Vare trophy, or player of the year award and accumulate a total of 27 points to be inducted. For players not eligible for either the PGA Tour or the LPGA Hall of Fame, a body of over 300 international golf writers and historians will vote each year.

Members are listed with year of induction; (+) indicates deceased members.

**Class of 2005** (6): MEN—**Vijay Singh** and **Willie Park Sr.**; WOMEN—**Karrie Webb** and **Ayako Okamoto**; CONTRIBUTORS—**Bernard Darwin** and **Alister MacKenzie**.

## Men

| | | |
|---|---|---|
| + Anderson, Willie .........1975 | Floyd, Ray ...........1989 | + Ouimet, Francis .........1974 |
| Aoki, Isao .............2004 | + Guldahl, Ralph .........1981 | Palmer, Arnold .........1974 |
| + Armour, Tommy .........1976 | + Hagen, Walter .........1974 | + Park, Willie Sr. ...: ....2005 |
| + Ball, John, Jr ...........1977 | + Hilton, Harold .........1978 | Player, Gary ...........1974 |
| Ballesteros, Seve .......1999 | + Hogan, Ben ...........1974 | Price, Nick ............2003 |
| + Barnes, Jim ...........1989 | Irwin, Hale ...........1992 | + Robertson, Allan .......2001 |
| Beman, Deane .........2000 | Jacklin, Tony ..........2002 | + Runyan, Paul .........1990 |
| Bolt, Tommy ...........2002 | Jacobs, John ..........2000 | + Sarazen, Gene .........1974 |
| Bonallack, Sir Michael ....2000 | + Jones, Bobby .........1974 | Sifford, Charlie .........2004 |
| + Boros, Julius ..........1982 | Kite, Tom .............2004 | Singh, Vijay ...........2005 |
| + Braid, James ..........1976 | Langer, Bernhard .......2002 | + Smith, Horton .........1990 |
| Burke, Jack Jr. .........2000 | + Little, Lawson .........1980 | + Snead, Sam ..........1974 |
| Casper, Billy ..........1978 | Littler, Gene ..........1990 | + Stewart, Payne .......2001 |
| Coles, Neil ............2000 | + Locke, Bobby .........1977 | + Taylor, John H ........1975 |
| + Cooper, Lighthorse Harry ..1992 | + Mangrum, Lloyd .......1998 | Thomson, Peter ........1988 |
| + Cotton, Sir Henry .......1980 | + Middlecoff, Cary .......1986 | + Travers, Jerry ........1976 |
| Crenshaw, Ben .........2002 | Miller, Johnny .........1996 | + Travis, Walter ........1979 |
| + Demaret, Jimmy .......1983 | + Morris, Tom Jr .........1975 | Trevino, Lee ...........1981 |
| De Vicenzo, Roberto .....1989 | + Morris, Tom Sr .........1976 | + Vardon, Harry .........1974 |
| + Diegel, Leo ...........2003 | Nelson, Byron .........1974 | Watson, Tom ..........1988 |
| + Evans, Chick ..........1975 | Nicklaus, Jack .........1974 | |
| Faldo, Nick ...........1997 | Norman, Greg .........2001 | |

## Women

| | | |
|---|---|---|
| Alcott, Amy ...........1999 | Inkster, Julie ..........2000 | Streit, Marlene Stewart ....2004 |
| Berg, Patty ...........1974 | Jameson, Betty ........1951 | Suggs, Louise .........1979 |
| Bradley, Pat ..........1986 | King, Betsy ...........1995 | + Vare, Glenna Collett .....1975 |
| Carner, JoAnne ........1985 | Lopez, Nancy .........1989 | Webb, Karrie ..........2005 |
| Caponi, Donna .........2001 | Mann, Carol ..........1977 | + Wethered, Joyce .......1975 |
| Daniel, Beth ..........1999 | Okamoto, Ayako ........2005 | Whitworth, Kathy .......1982 |
| Hagge, Marlene ........2002 | Rankin, Judy ..........2000 | Wright, Mickey .........1976 |
| Haynie, Sandra ........1977 | Rawls, Betsy ..........1987 | + Zaharias, Babe Didrikson ..1974 |
| Higuchi, Chako ........2003 | Sheehan, Patty ........1993 | |
| + Howe, Dorothy C.H ......1978 | Sorenstam, Annika ......2003 | |

## Contributors

| | | |
|---|---|---|
| Bell, Judy ............2001 | + Graffis, Herb ..........1977 | + Roberts, Clifford .......1978 |
| Campbell, William .......1990 | + Harlow, Robert ........1988 | Rodriguez, Chi Chi ......1992 |
| + Corcoran, Fred ........1975 | + Hope, Bob ...........1983 | + Ross, Donald .........1977 |
| + Crosby, Bing .........1978 | + Jones, Robert Trent .....1987 | + Solheim, Karsten .......2001 |
| + Darwin, Bernard .......2005 | + MacKenzie, Alister ......2005 | + Shore, Dinah .........1994 |
| + Dey, Joe ...........1975 | + Penick, Harvey ........2002 | + Tufts, Richard .........1992 |

## HOCKEY

# Hockey Hall of Fame

Established in 1945 by the National Hockey League and opened in 1961. **Address:** BCE Place, 30 Yonge Street, Toronto, Ontario, M5E 1X8. **Telephone:** (416) 360-7735. **Web:** www.hhof.com

**Eligibility:** Nominated players and referees must be retired three years. However that waiting period has now been waived 10 times. Players that have had the waiting period waived are indicated with an asterisk. Voting done by 18-member panel made up of pro and amateur hockey personalities and media representatives. A 15-member Veterans Committee that selected older players was eliminated in 2000.

**Class of 2005** (3): PLAYERS—LW **Valeri Kharlamov**, CSKA Moscow; RW **Cam Neely**, Vancouver (1983-86), Boston (1986-1996). BUILDER—**Murray Costello**, executive.

Members are listed with year of induction; (+) indicates deceased members.

## Forwards

| | | |
|---|---|---|
| + Abel, Sid . . . . . . . . . . . .1969 | Gartner, Mike . . . . . . . . .2001 | + Nighbor, Frank . . . . . . . .1947 |
| + Adams, Jack . . . . . . . . . .1959 | Geoffrion, Bernie . . . . . . .1972 | + Noble, Reg . . . . . . . . . .1962 |
| + Apps, Syl . . . . . . . . . . . .1961 | + Gerard, Eddie . . . . . . . . .1945 | + O'Connor, Buddy . . . . . . .1988 |
| Armstrong, George . . . .1975 | Gilbert, Rod . . . . . . . . . .1982 | + Oliver, Harry . . . . . . . . .1967 |
| + Bailey, Ace . . . . . . . . . . .1975 | Gillies, Clark . . . . . . . . .2002 | Olmstead, Bert . . . . . . . .1985 |
| + Bain, Dan . . . . . . . . . . . .1945 | + Gilmour, Billy . . . . . . . . .1962 | + Patrick, Lynn . . . . . . . . .1980 |
| + Baker, Hobey . . . . . . . . .1945 | Goulet, Michel . . . . . . . .1998 | Perreault, Gilbert . . . . . .1990 |
| Barber, Bill . . . . . . . . . .1990 | Gretzky, Wayne* . . . . . . .1999 | + Phillips, Tom . . . . . . . . .1945 |
| + Barry, Marty . . . . . . . . . .1965 | + Griffis, Si . . . . . . . . . . . .1950 | + Primeau, Joe . . . . . . . . .1963 |
| Bathgate, Andy . . . . . . .1978 | Hawerchuk, Dale . . . . . .2001 | Pulford, Bob . . . . . . . . . .1991 |
| + Bauer, Bobby . . . . . . . . .1996 | + Hay, George . . . . . . . . . .1958 | + Rankin, Frank . . . . . . . . .1961 |
| Beliveau, Jean* . . . . . . .1972 | + Hextall, Bryan . . . . . . . . .1969 | Ratelle, Jean . . . . . . . . .1985 |
| + Bentley, Doug . . . . . . . . .1964 | + Hooper, Tom . . . . . . . . . .1962 | + Richard, Henri . . . . . . . .1979 |
| + Bentley, Max . . . . . . . . . .1966 | + Howe, Gordie* . . . . . . . .1972 | + Richard, Maurice (Rocket)* .1961 |
| + Blake, Toe . . . . . . . . . . . .1966 | + Howe, Syd . . . . . . . . . . .1965 | + Richardson, George . . . . .1950 |
| Bossy, Mike . . . . . . . . . .1991 | Hull, Bobby . . . . . . . . . .1983 | + Roberts, Gordie . . . . . . .1971 |
| + Boucher, Frank . . . . . . . .1958 | + Hyland, Harry . . . . . . . . .1962 | + Russel, Blair . . . . . . . . . .1965 |
| + Bowie, Dubbie . . . . . . . .1945 | + Irvin, Dick . . . . . . . . . . . .1958 | + Russell, Ernie . . . . . . . . .1965 |
| + Broadbent, Punch . . . . . .1962 | + Jackson, Busher . . . . . . .1971 | + Ruttan, Jack . . . . . . . . . .1962 |
| Bucyk, John (Chief) . . . .1981 | + Joliat, Aurel . . . . . . . . . .1947 | Savard, Denis . . . . . . . .2000 |
| + Burch, Billy . . . . . . . . . . .1974 | + Keats, Duke . . . . . . . . . .1958 | + Scanlan, Fred . . . . . . . . .1965 |
| Clarke, Bobby . . . . . . . .1987 | Kennedy, Ted (Teeder) . .1966 | Schmidt, Milt . . . . . . . . .1961 |
| + Colville, Neil . . . . . . . . . .1967 | Keon, Dave . . . . . . . . . .1986 | + Schriner, Sweeney . . . . . .1962 |
| + Conacher, Charlie . . . . . .1961 | + Kharlamov, Valeri . . . . . .2005 | + Seibert, Oliver . . . . . . . . .1961 |
| Conacher, Roy . . . . . . . .1998 | Kurri, Jari . . . . . . . . . . .2001 | Shutt, Steve . . . . . . . . . .1993 |
| + Cook, Bill . . . . . . . . . . . .1952 | Lach, Elmer . . . . . . . . . .1966 | + Siebert, Babe . . . . . . . . .1964 |
| + Cook, Bun . . . . . . . . . . . .1995 | Lafleur, Guy . . . . . . . . . .1988 | Sittler, Darryl . . . . . . . . .1989 |
| Cournoyer, Yvan . . . . . .1982 | LaFontaine, Pat . . . . . . .2003 | + Smith, Alf . . . . . . . . . . . .1962 |
| + Cowley, Bill . . . . . . . . . . .1968 | + Lalonde, Newsy . . . . . . .1950 | Smith, Clint . . . . . . . . . .1991 |
| + Crawford, Rusty . . . . . . .1962 | Laprade, Edgar . . . . . . .1993 | + Smith, Hooley . . . . . . . . .1972 |
| + Darragh, Jack . . . . . . . . .1962 | Lemaire, Jacques . . . . . .1984 | + Smith, Tommy . . . . . . . . .1973 |
| + Davidson, Scotty . . . . . . .1950 | Lemieux, Mario* . . . . . . .1997 | + Stanley, Barney . . . . . . . .1962 |
| + Day, Hap . . . . . . . . . . . .1961 | + Lewis, Herbie . . . . . . . . .1989 | Stastny, Peter . . . . . . . .1998 |
| Delvecchio, Alex . . . . . .1977 | Lindsay, Ted* . . . . . . . . .1966 | + Stewart, Nels . . . . . . . . .1962 |
| + Denneny, Cy . . . . . . . . . .1959 | + MacKay, Mickey . . . . . . .1952 | + Stuart, Bruce . . . . . . . . .1961 |
| Dionne, Marcel . . . . . . .1992 | Mahovlich, Frank . . . . . .1981 | + Taylor, Fred (Cyclone) . . . .1947 |
| + Drillon, Gordie . . . . . . . .1975 | + Malone, Joe . . . . . . . . . .1950 | Trihey, Harry . . . . . . . . .1950 |
| + Drinkwater, Graham . . . . .1950 | + Marshall, Jack . . . . . . . . .1965 | Trottier, Bryan . . . . . . . .1997 |
| Dumart, Woody . . . . . . .1992 | + Maxwell, Fred . . . . . . . . .1962 | Ullman, Norm . . . . . . . .1982 |
| + Dunderdale, Tommy . . . . .1974 | McDonald, Lanny . . . . . .1992 | + Walker, Jack . . . . . . . . . .1960 |
| + Dye, Babe . . . . . . . . . . . .1970 | + McGee, Frank . . . . . . . . .1945 | + Walsh, Marty . . . . . . . . . .1962 |
| Esposito, Phil . . . . . . . . .1984 | + McGimsie, Billy . . . . . . . .1962 | + Watson, Harry (Whipper) . .1994 |
| + Farrell, Arthur . . . . . . . . .1965 | Mikita, Stan . . . . . . . . . .1983 | + Watson, Harry (Moose) . . .1962 |
| Federko, Bernie . . . . . . .2002 | Moore, Dickie . . . . . . . .1974 | + Weiland, Cooney . . . . . . .1971 |
| + Foyston, Frank . . . . . . . .1958 | + Morenz, Howie . . . . . . . .1945 | + Westwick, Harry (Rat) . . . .1962 |
| + Frederickson, Frank . . . . .1958 | + Mosienko, Bill . . . . . . . . .1965 | + Whitcroft, Fred . . . . . . . .1962 |
| Gainey, Bob . . . . . . . . . .1992 | Mullen, Joe . . . . . . . . . .2000 | |
| + Gardner, Jimmy . . . . . . .1962 | Neely, Cam . . . . . . . . . .2005 | |

## Referees & Linesmen

| | | |
|---|---|---|
| Armstrong, Neil . . . . . . .1991 | + Hayes, George . . . . . . . .1988 | + Smeaton, J. Cooper . . . . . .1961 |
| Ashley, John . . . . . . . . . .1981 | + Hewitson, Bobby . . . . . . .1963 | Storey, Red . . . . . . . . . .1967 |
| Chadwick, Bill . . . . . . . .1964 | + Ion, Mickey . . . . . . . . . .1961 | Udvari, Frank . . . . . . . . .1973 |
| D'Amico, John . . . . . . . .1993 | Pavelich, Matt . . . . . . . .1987 | van Hellemond, Andy . . . .1999 |
| + Elliott, Chaucer . . . . . . . .1961 | + Rodden, Mike . . . . . . . . .1962 | |

## Goaltenders

+ Benedict, Clint . . . . . . . . .1965
  Bower, Johnny . . . . . . . . .1976
+ Brimsek, Frankie . . . . . . . .1966
+ Broda, Turk . . . . . . . . . . .1967
  Cheevers, Gerry . . . . . . . .1985
+ Connell, Alex . . . . . . . . . .1958
  Dryden, Ken . . . . . . . . . . .1983
+ Durnan, Bill . . . . . . . . . . .1964
  Esposito, Tony . . . . . . . . .1988
  Fuhr, Grant . . . . . . . . . . .2003
+ Gardiner, Chuck . . . . . . . .1945

  Giacomin, Eddie . . . . . . . .1987
+ Hainsworth, George . . . . . .1961
  Hall, Glenn . . . . . . . . . . .1975
  Hern, Riley . . . . . . . . . . .1962
  Holmes, Hap . . . . . . . . . .1972
  Hutton, J.B. (Bouse) . . . . . .1962
+ Lehman, Hughie . . . . . . . .1958
+ LeSueur, Percy . . . . . . . . .1961
+ Lumley, Harry . . . . . . . . .1980
+ Moran, Paddy . . . . . . . . . .1958

  Parent, Bernie . . . . . . . . .1984
+ Plante, Jacques . . . . . . . . .1978
+ Rayner, Chuck . . . . . . . . .1973
+ Sawchuk, Terry* . . . . . . . .1971
  Smith, Billy . . . . . . . . . . .1993
+ Thompson, Tiny . . . . . . . .1959
  Tretiak, Vladislav . . . . . . . .1989
+ Vezina, Georges . . . . . . . .1945
  Worsley, Gump . . . . . . . . .1980
+ Worters, Roy . . . . . . . . . .1969

## Defensemen

  Boivin, Leo . . . . . . . . . . .1986
+ Boon, Dickie . . . . . . . . . .1952
  Bouchard, Butch . . . . . . . .1966
+ Boucher, George . . . . . . . .1960
+ Bourque, Ray . . . . . . . . . .2004
+ Cameron, Harry . . . . . . . .1962
+ Clancy, King . . . . . . . . . .1958
+ Clapper, Dit* . . . . . . . . . .1947
+ Cleghorn, Sprague . . . . . . .1958
  Coffey, Paul . . . . . . . . . . .2004
+ Conacher, Lionel . . . . . . . .1994
+ Coulter, Art . . . . . . . . . . .1974
+ Dutton, Red . . . . . . . . . . .1958
  Fetisov, Viacheslav . . . . . . .2001
  Flaman, Fernie . . . . . . . . .1990
  Gadsby, Bill . . . . . . . . . . .1970
  Gardiner, Herb . . . . . . . . .1958
+ Goheen, F.X. (Moose) . . . . .1952
+ Goodfellow, Ebbie . . . . . . .1963
+ Grant, Mike . . . . . . . . . . .1950

+ Green, Wilf (Shorty) . . . . . .1962
+ Hall, Joe . . . . . . . . . . . . .1961
+ Harvey, Doug . . . . . . . . . .1973
  Horner, Red . . . . . . . . . . .1965
+ Horton, Tim . . . . . . . . . . .1977
  Howell, Harry . . . . . . . . . .1979
+ Johnson, Ching . . . . . . . . .1958
+ Johnson, Ernie . . . . . . . . .1952
  Johnson, Tom . . . . . . . . . .1970
  Kelly, Red* . . . . . . . . . . .1969
  Langway, Rod . . . . . . . . . .2002
+ Laperriere, Jacques . . . . . .1987
  Lapointe, Guy . . . . . . . . . .1993
+ Laviolette, Jack . . . . . . . . .1962
+ Mantha, Sylvio . . . . . . . . .1960
+ McNamara, George . . . . . . .1958
  Murphy, Larry . . . . . . . . . .2004
  Orr, Bobby* . . . . . . . . . . .1979
  Park, Brad . . . . . . . . . . . .1988
+ Patrick, Lester . . . . . . . . . .1947

  Pilote, Pierre . . . . . . . . . .1975
+ Pitre, Didier . . . . . . . . . . .1962
  Potvin, Denis . . . . . . . . . .1991
+ Pratt, Babe . . . . . . . . . . .1966
  Pronovost, Marcel . . . . . . .1978
+ Pulford, Harvey . . . . . . . . .1945
+ Quackenbush, Bill . . . . . . . .1976
  Reardon, Kenny . . . . . . . . .1966
  Robinson, Larry . . . . . . . . .1995
+ Ross, Art . . . . . . . . . . . . .1945
  Salming, Borje . . . . . . . . . .1996
  Savard, Serge . . . . . . . . . .1986
+ Seibert, Earl . . . . . . . . . . .1963
+ Shore, Eddie . . . . . . . . . . .1947
+ Simpson, Joe . . . . . . . . . .1962
  Stanley, Allan . . . . . . . . . .1981
+ Stewart, Jack . . . . . . . . . .1964
+ Stuart, Hod . . . . . . . . . . .1945
+ Wilson, Gordon (Phat) . . . . .1962

## Builders

+ Adams, Charles . . . . . . . . .1960
+ Adams, Weston W. Sr . . . . .1972
+ Ahearn, Frank . . . . . . . . . .1962
+ Ahearne, J.F. (Bunny) . . . . .1977
+ Allan, Sir Montagu . . . . . . .1945
  Allen, Keith . . . . . . . . . . .1992
  Arbour, Al . . . . . . . . . . . .1996
+ Ballard, Harold . . . . . . . . .1977
+ Bauer, Fr. David . . . . . . . . .1989
+ Bickell, J.P. . . . . . . . . . . .1978
  Bowman, Scotty . . . . . . . . .1991
+ Brown, George . . . . . . . . .1961
+ Brown, Walter . . . . . . . . . .1962
+ Buckland, Frank . . . . . . . . .1975
  Bush, Walter . . . . . . . . . . .2000
  Butterfield, Jack . . . . . . . . .1980
+ Calder, Frank . . . . . . . . . .1945
+ Campbell, Angus . . . . . . . .1964
+ Campbell, Clarence . . . . . . .1966
+ Cattarinich, Joseph . . . . . . .1977
  Costello, Murray . . . . . . . .2005
+ Dandurand, Leo . . . . . . . . .1963
+ Dilio, Frank . . . . . . . . . . .1964
+ Dudley, George . . . . . . . . .1958
+ Dunn, James . . . . . . . . . . .1968
  Fletcher, Cliff . . . . . . . . . .2004
  Francis, Emile . . . . . . . . . .1982
+ Gibson, Jack . . . . . . . . . . .1976
+ Gorman, Tommy . . . . . . . .1963
+ Griffiths, Frank A. . . . . . . . .1993
+ Hanley, Bill . . . . . . . . . . .1986
+ Hay, Charles . . . . . . . . . . .1984
+ Hendy, Jim . . . . . . . . . . .1968

+ Hewitt, Foster . . . . . . . . . .1965
+ Hewitt, W.A. . . . . . . . . . . .1945
+ Hume, Fred . . . . . . . . . . .1962
  Ilitch, Mike . . . . . . . . . . .2003
+ Imlach, Punch . . . . . . . . . .1984
+ Ivan, Tommy . . . . . . . . . . .1964
+ Jennings, Bill . . . . . . . . . .1975
+ Johnson, Bob . . . . . . . . . .1992
+ Juckes, Gordon . . . . . . . . .1979
+ Kilpatrick, John . . . . . . . . .1960
  Kilrea, Brian . . . . . . . . . . .2003
+ Knox, Seymour III . . . . . . . .1993
+ Leader, Al . . . . . . . . . . . .1969
+ LeBel, Bob . . . . . . . . . . .1970
+ Lockhart, Tom . . . . . . . . . .1965
+ Loicq, Paul . . . . . . . . . . .1961
+ Mariucci, John . . . . . . . . . .1985
  Mathers, Frank . . . . . . . . .1992
+ McLaughlin, Frederic . . . . . .1963
+ Milford, Jake . . . . . . . . . .1984
+ Molson, Hartland . . . . . . . .1973
  Morrison, Ian (Scotty) . . . . .1999
+ Murray, Athol (Pere) . . . . . .1998
+ Nelson, Francis . . . . . . . . .1945
+ Neilson, Roger . . . . . . . . .2002
+ Norris, Bruce . . . . . . . . . .1969
+ Norris, James D . . . . . . . . .1962
+ Norris, James Sr . . . . . . . . .1958
+ Northey, William . . . . . . . .1945
+ O'Brien, J.A. . . . . . . . . . . .1962
  O'Neill, Brian . . . . . . . . . .1994
  Page, Fred . . . . . . . . . . . .1993
  Patrick, Craig . . . . . . . . . .2001

+ Patrick, Frank . . . . . . . . . .1958
+ Pickard, Allan . . . . . . . . . .1958
+ Pilous, Rudy . . . . . . . . . . .1985
  Poile, Bud . . . . . . . . . . . .1990
  Pollock, Sam . . . . . . . . . . .1978
+ Raymond, Donat . . . . . . . .1958
+ Robertson, John Ross . . . . . .1945
+ Robinson, Claude . . . . . . . .1945
+ Ross, Philip . . . . . . . . . . .1976
+ Sabetzki, Gunther . . . . . . . .1995
  Sather, Glen . . . . . . . . . . .1997
+ Selke, Frank . . . . . . . . . . .1960
  Sinden, Harry . . . . . . . . . .1983
+ Smith, Frank . . . . . . . . . . .1962
+ Smythe, Conn . . . . . . . . . .1958
  Snider, Ed . . . . . . . . . . . .1988
+ Stanley, Lord of Preston . . . .1945
+ Sutherland, James . . . . . . . .1945
+ Tarasov, Anatoli . . . . . . . . .1974
  Torrey, Bill . . . . . . . . . . . .1995
+ Turner, Lloyd . . . . . . . . . .1958
+ Tutt, William Thayer . . . . . . .1978
+ Voss, Carl . . . . . . . . . . . .1974
+ Waghorne, Fred . . . . . . . . .1961
+ Wirtz, Arthur . . . . . . . . . .1971
  Wirtz, Bill . . . . . . . . . . . .1976
  Ziegler, John . . . . . . . . . . .1987

**Note:** Alan Eagleson was inducted into the Hockey Hall of Fame in 1989 but resigned in 1998 after being found guilty of fraud.

## U.S. Hockey Hall of Fame

Established in 1968 by the Eveleth (Minn.) Civic Association Project H Committee and opened in 1973. **Address:** 801 Hat Trick Ave., P.O. Box 657, Eveleth, MN 55734. **Telephone:** (218) 744-5167. **Web:** www.ushockeyhall.com

**Eligibility:** Nominated players and referees must be American-born and retired five years; coaches must be American-born and must have coached predominantly American teams. Voting done by 12-member panel made up of Hall of Fame members and U.S. hockey officials.

**Class of 2005** (4): PLAYERS—**Keith Christiansen**, **Lane McDonald**, **Maurice Roberts** and **Murray Williamson**.

Members are listed with year of induction; (+) indicates deceased members.

### Players

| | | |
|---|---|---|
| + Abel, Clarence (Taffy) .....1973 | Fusco, Mark ..........2002 | Mayasich, John .........1976 |
| + Baker, Hobey ..........1973 | Fusco, Scott ..........2002 | McCartan, Jack ........1983 |
| Bartholome, Earl .........1977 | + Garrison, John .........1974 | Moe, Bill ..........1974 |
| + Bessone, Peter .........1978 | Garrity, Jack ..........1986 | Morrow, Ken ..........1995 |
| Blake, Bob ..........1985 | + Goheen, Frank (Moose) ...1973 | + Moseley, Fred .........1975 |
| Boucha, Henry .........1995 | Grant, Wally ..........1994 | Mullen, Joe ..........1998 |
| + Brimsek, Frankie .......1973 | + Harding, Austie .........1975 | + Murray, Hugh (Muzz) Sr ...1987 |
| Broten, Neal ..........2000 | Housley, Phil ..........2004 | + Nelson, Hub ..........1978 |
| Cavanagh, Joe .........1994 | Howe, Mark ..........2003 | + Nyrop, William D. .......1997 |
| + Chaisson, Ray .........1974 | Iglehart, Stewart .......1975 | Olson, Eddie ..........1977 |
| Chase, John ..........1973 | Ikola, Willard .........1990 | + Owen, George .........1973 |
| Christian, Bill ..........1984 | Johnson, Mark .........2004 | + Palmer, Winthrop .......1973 |
| Christian, Dave .........2001 | Johnson, Paul .........2001 | Paradise, Bob .........1989 |
| Christian, Roger .........1989 | Johnson, Virgil .........1974 | + Purpur, Clifford (Fido) ....1974 |
| Christiansen, Keith ......2005 | + Karakas, Mike .........1973 | Ramsey, Mike .........2001 |
| Cleary, Bill ..........1976 | Kirrane, Jack ..........1987 | Riley, Bill ..........1977 |
| Cleary, Bob ..........1981 | LaFontaine, Pat .........2003 | Riley, Joe ..........2002 |
| + Conroy, Tony .........1975 | + Lane, Myles ..........1973 | + Roberts, Maurice (Moe) ..2005 |
| Coppo, Paul ..........2004 | Langevin, Dave .........1993 | + Romnes, Elwin (Doc) .....1973 |
| Curran, Mike ..........1998 | Langway, Rod .........1999 | Rondeau, Dick .........1985 |
| + Dahlstrom, Carl (Cully) ...1973 | Larson, Reed ..........1996 | Sheehy, Timothy .......1997 |
| + Desjardins, Vic .........1974 | + Linder, Joe ..........1975 | Watson, Gordie .........1999 |
| + Desmond, Richard .......1988 | + LoPresti, Sam .........1973 | + Williams, Tom .........1981 |
| + Dill, Bob ..........1979 | MacDonald, Lane .......2005 | Williamson, Murray ......2005 |
| Dougherty, Richard ......2003 | + Mariucci, John .........1973 | + Winters, Frank (Coddy) ...1973 |
| + Everett, Doug .........1974 | Matchefts, John .........1991 | + Yackel, Ken ..........1986 |
| Ftorek, Robbie .........1991 | + Mather, Bruce .........1998 | |

### Coaches

| | | |
|---|---|---|
| + Almquist, Oscar .........1983 | Heyliger, Vic ..........1974 | Pleban, Connie .........1990 |
| Bessone, Amo .........1992 | + Holt Jr., Charles E. .......1997 | Ramsay, Mike .........2001 |
| + Brooks, Herb .........1990 | Ikola, Willard .........1990 | Riley, Jack ..........1979 |
| Ceglarski, Len .........1992 | + Jeremiah, Eddie .........1973 | + Ross, Larry ..........1988 |
| + Cunniff, John .........2003 | + Johnson, Bob .........1991 | + Thompson, Cliff .........1973 |
| + Fullerton, James .......1992 | Johnson, Paul .........2001 | + Stewart, Bill ..........1982 |
| Gambucci, Sergio ....... .1996 | Kelley, Jack ..........1993 | Watson, Sid ..........1999 |
| + Gordon, Malcolm .......1973 | + Kelly, John (Snooks) .....1974 | + Winsor, Ralph .........1973 |
| Harkness, Ned .........1994 | Nanne, Lou ..........1998 | Woog, Doug ..........2002 |

### Referee

Chadwick, Bill ..........1974

### Contributor

+ Schulz, Charles M. ......1993

### Administrators

| | | |
|---|---|---|
| + Brown, George .........1973 | + Jennings, Bill ..........1981 | Ridder, Bob ..........1976 |
| + Brown, Walter .........1973 | + Kahler, Nick ..........1980 | Trumble, Hal ..........1970 |
| Bush, Walter ..........1980 | + Lockhart, Tom .........1973 | + Tutt, Thayer ..........1973 |
| + Clark, Don ..........1978 | Marvin, Cal ..........1982 | Wirtz, Bill ..........1967 |
| Claypool, Jim ..........1995 | Palazzari, Doug .........2000 | + Wright, Lyle ..........1973 |
| + Gibson, J.L. (Doc) .......1973 | Patrick, Craig .........1996 | |
| Ilitch, Mike ..........2004 | Pleau, Larry ..........2000 | |

---

## Members of Both Hockey and U.S. Hockey Halls of Fame

| **Players** | **Coach** | | **Builders** |
|---|---|---|---|
| Hobey Baker | Bob Johnson | George Brown | Bill Jennings |
| Frankie Brimsek | | Walter Brown | Tom Lockhart |
| Frank (Moose) Goheen | **Referee** | Walter Bush | Craig Patrick |
| Pat LaFontaine | Bill Chadwick | Doc Gibson | Thayer Tutt |
| Rod Langway | | Mike Ilitch | Bill Wirtz |
| John Mariucci | | | |
| Joe Mullen | | | |

## HORSE RACING

### National Museum of Racing and Hall of Fame

Established in 1950 by the Saratoga Springs Racing Association and opened in 1955. **Address:** National Museum of Racing and Hall of Fame, 191 Union Ave., Saratoga Springs, NY 12866. **Telephone:** (518) 584-0400. **Web:** www.racingmuseum.org

**Eligibility:** Nominated horses must be retired five years; jockeys must be active at least 15 years; trainers must be active at least 25 years. Voting done by 125-member panel of horse racing media.

**Class of 2005** (4): JOCKEY—**Thomas Walsh**. TRAINER—**Sidney Watters Jr.** and **Nick Zito**. HORSES—**Lonesome Glory**.

Members are listed with year of induction; (+) indicates deceased members.

### Jockeys

| | | |
|---|---|---|
| + Adams, Frank (Dooley)* . . .1970 | + Garner, Andrew (Mack) . . . .1969 | Pincay, Laffit Jr. . . . . . . . . .1975 |
| + Adams, John . . . . . . . . . .1965 | + Garrison, Snapper . . . . . . . .1955 | + Purdy, Sam . . . . . . . . . . . .1970 |
| + Aitcheson, Joe Jr.* . . . . . . . .1978 | + Gomez, Avelino . . . . . . . . .1982 | + Reiff, John . . . . . . . . . . . .1956 |
| + Arcaro, Eddie . . . . . . . . . .1958 | + Griffin, Henry . . . . . . . . . .1956 | + Robertson, Alfred . . . . . . . .1971 |
| Atkinson, Ted . . . . . . . . . .1957 | + Guerin, Eric . . . . . . . . . . .1972 | Rotz, John L. . . . . . . . . . . .1983 |
| Baeza, Braulio . . . . . . . . . .1976 | Hartack, Bill . . . . . . . . . . .1959 | + Sande, Earl . . . . . . . . . . . .1955 |
| Bailey, Jerry . . . . . . . . . . .1995 | Hawley, Sandy . . . . . . . . . .1992 | + Shilling, Carroll . . . . . . . . .1970 |
| + Barbee, George . . . . . . . . .1996 | + Johnson, Albert . . . . . . . . .1971 | + Shoemaker, Bill . . . . . . . . .1958 |
| + Bassett, Carroll* . . . . . . . .1972 | + Knapp, Willie . . . . . . . . . .1969 | + Simms, Willie . . . . . . . . . .1977 |
| Baze, Russell . . . . . . . . . . .1999 | + Krone, Julie . . . . . . . . . . .2000 | + Sloan, Todhunter . . . . . . . .1955 |
| + Blum, Walter . . . . . . . . . .1987 | + Kummer, Clarence . . . . . . .1972 | Smith, Mike . . . . . . . . . . .2003 |
| + Bostwick, George H.* . . . . .1968 | + Kurtsinger, Charley . . . . . . .1967 | + Smithwick, A. Patrick* . . . . .1973 |
| + Boulmetis, Sam . . . . . . . . .1973 | + Loftus, Johnny . . . . . . . . .1959 | Stevens, Gary . . . . . . . . . .1997 |
| + Brooks, Steve . . . . . . . . . .1963 | Longden, Johnny . . . . . . . .1958 | + Stout, James . . . . . . . . . . .1968 |
| Brumfield, Don . . . . . . . . .1996 | Maher, Danny . . . . . . . . . .1955 | + Taral, Fred . . . . . . . . . . . .1955 |
| + Burns, Tommy . . . . . . . . . .1983 | + McAtee, Linus . . . . . . . . . .1956 | + Tuckerman, Bayard Jr.* . . . .1973 |
| + Butwell, Jimmy . . . . . . . . .1984 | McCarron, Chris . . . . . . . . .1989 | Turcotte, Ron . . . . . . . . . .1979 |
| + Byers, J.D. (Dolly) . . . . . . .1967 | + McCreary, Conn . . . . . . . . .1975 | + Turner, Nash . . . . . . . . . . .1955 |
| Cauthen, Steve . . . . . . . . . .1994 | + McKinney, Rigan . . . . . . . . .1968 | Ussery, Robert . . . . . . . . . .1980 |
| + Coltiletti, Frank . . . . . . . . .1970 | + McLaughlin, James . . . . . . .1955 | Vasquez, Jacinto . . . . . . . .1998 |
| + Cordero, Angel Jr. . . . . . . .1988 | + Miller, Walter . . . . . . . . . .1955 | Velasquez, Jorge . . . . . . . .1990 |
| + Crawford, Robert (Specs)* . .1973 | + Murphy, Isaac . . . . . . . . . .1955 | Walsh, Thomas* . . . . . . . .2005 |
| Day, Pat . . . . . . . . . . . . .1991 | + Neves, Ralph . . . . . . . . . .1960 | + Westrope, Jack . . . . . . . . .2002 |
| Delahoussaye, Eddie . . . . . .1993 | + Notter, Joe . . . . . . . . . . .1963 | + Woolf, George . . . . . . . . .1955 |
| Desormeaux, Kent . . . . . . .2004 | + O'Connor, Winnie . . . . . . . .1956 | + Workman, Raymond . . . . . .1956 |
| + Ensor, Lavelle (Buddy) . . . . .1962 | + Odom, George . . . . . . . . .1955 | Ycaza, Manuel . . . . . . . . .1977 |
| + Fator, Laverne . . . . . . . . . .1955 | + O'Neill, Frank . . . . . . . . . .1956 | *Steeplechase jockey |
| Fires, Earlie . . . . . . . . . . .2001 | + Parke, Ivan . . . . . . . . . . .1978 | |
| Fishback, Jerry* . . . . . . . . .1992 | + Patrick, Gil . . . . . . . . . . .1970 | |

### Harness Racing Museum & Hall of Fame

Established by the U.S. Harness Writers Association (USHWA) in 1958. **Address:** Trotting Horse Museum, 240 Main Street, P.O. Box 590, Goshen, NY 10924; **Telephone:** (845) 294-6330. **Web:** www.harnessmuseum.com

**Eligibility:** Open to all harness racing drivers, trainers and executives. Voting done by USHWA membership. There are 92 members of the Living Hall of Fame, but only the 49 drivers and trainer-drivers are listed below.

**Class of 2005** (1): TRAINER/DRIVERS—**Ron Pierce**

Members are listed with years of induction; (+) indicates deceased members.

### Trainer-Drivers

| | | |
|---|---|---|
| Abbatiello, Carmine . . . . .1986 | Filion, Herve . . . . . . . . . .1976 | O'Donnell, Bill . . . . . . . . .1991 |
| Abbatiello, Tony . . . . . . .1995 | + Garnsey, Glen . . . . . . . . .1983 | Patterson, John Sr . . . . . . .1994 |
| Ackerman, Doug . . . . . . .1995 | Galbraith, Clint . . . . . . . .1990 | Pierce, Ron . . . . . . . . . . .2005 |
| + Avery, Earle . . . . . . . . . .1975 | Gilmour, Buddy . . . . . . . .1990 | + Pownall, Harry . . . . . . . .1971 |
| + Baldwin, Ralph . . . . . . . .1972 | Harner, Levi . . . . . . . . . .1986 | Remmen, Ray . . . . . . . . .1998 |
| Beissinger, Howard . . . . . .1975 | Harvey, Harry M. . . . . . . .2002 | Riegle, Gene . . . . . . . . . .1992 |
| Bostwick, Dunbar . . . . . .1989 | + Haughton, Billy . . . . . . . .1969 | + Russell, Sanders . . . . . . . .1971 |
| + Cameron, Del . . . . . . . . .1975 | + Hodgins, Clint . . . . . . . . .1973 | + Shively, Bion . . . . . . . . . .1968 |
| Campbell, John . . . . . . . .1991 | Insko, Del . . . . . . . . . . .1981 | Sholty, George . . . . . . . . .1985 |
| + Chapman, John . . . . . . . .1980 | Kopas, Jack . . . . . . . . . .1996 | Simpson, John Sr . . . . . . . .1972 |
| Cruise, Jimmy . . . . . . . . .1987 | Lachance, Mike . . . . . . . .1996 | Simpson, John Jr. . . . . . . .2004 |
| Dancer, Stanley . . . . . . . .1970 | Lindstedt, Berndt . . . . . . .2003 | + Smart, Curly . . . . . . . . . .1970 |
| Dancer, Vernon . . . . . . . .2001 | Magee, Dave . . . . . . . . .2001 | Sylvester, Charles . . . . . . .1998 |
| Dennis, Jim . . . . . . . . . .2002 | Manzi, Catello . . . . . . . . .2002 | Waples, Keith . . . . . . . . .1987 |
| Doherty, James . . . . . . . .2003 | McIntosh, Robert . . . . . . .2003 | Waples, Ron . . . . . . . . . .1994 |
| + Ervin, Frank . . . . . . . . . .1969 | Miller, Del . . . . . . . . . . .1969 | |
| Farrington, Bob . . . . . . . .1980 | + O'Brien, Joe . . . . . . . . . .1971 | |

## Horse Racing (Cont.)
### Trainers

+ Barrera, Laz . . . . . . . . . . .1979
+ Bedwell, H. Guy . . . . . . . . .1971
+ Brown, Edward D. . . . . . . .1984
  Burch, Elliot . . . . . . . . . . . .1980
+ Burch, Preston M. . . . . . . . .1963
+ Burch, W.P. . . . . . . . . . . . .1955
+ Burlew, Fred . . . . . . . . . . .1973
+ Childs, Frank E. . . . . . . . . .1968
+ Clark, Henry . . . . . . . . . . .1982
+ Cocks, W. Burling . . . . . . . .1985
  Conway, James P. . . . . . . . .1996
  Croll, Jimmy . . . . . . . . . . .1994
  Delp, Bud . . . . . . . . . . . . .2002
  Drysdale, Neil . . . . . . . . . .2000
+ Duke, William . . . . . . . . . .1956
+ Feustel, Louis . . . . . . . . . .1964
+ Fitzsimmons, J. (Sunny Jim) .1958
  Frankel, Bobby . . . . . . . . . .1995
+ Gaver, John M. . . . . . . . . .1966
+ Healey, Thomas . . . . . . . . .1955
+ Hildreth, Samuel . . . . . . . .1955
+ Hine, Hubert (Sonny) . . . . .2003
+ Hirsch, Max . . . . . . . . . . . .1959
+ Hirsch, W.J. (Buddy) . . . . . .1982
+ Hitchcock, Thomas Sr. . . . . .1973
+ Hughes, Hollie . . . . . . . . . .1973
+ Hyland, John . . . . . . . . . . .1956

+ Jacobs, Hirsch . . . . . . . . . .1958
  Jerkens, H. Allen . . . . . . . .1975
  Johnson, Philip . . . . . . . . . .1997
+ Johnson, William R. . . . . . .1986
+ Jolley, LeRoy . . . . . . . . . . .1987
+ Jones, Ben A. . . . . . . . . . .1958
+ Jones, H.A. (Jimmy) . . . . . .1959
+ Joyner, Andrew . . . . . . . . .1955
  Kelly, Tom . . . . . . . . . . . . .1993
+ Laurin, Lucien . . . . . . . . . .1977
+ Lewis, J. Howard . . . . . . . .1969
+ Lukas, D. Wayne . . . . . . . .1999
+ Luro, Horatio . . . . . . . . . . .1980
  Mandella, Richard . . . . . . .2001
+ Madden, John . . . . . . . . . .1983
+ Maloney, Jim . . . . . . . . . . .1989
  Martin, Frank (Pancho) . . . .1981
  McAnally, Ron . . . . . . . . . .1990
+ McDaniel, Henry . . . . . . . .1956
  McGaughey, Shug . . . . . . .2004
+ Miller, MacKenzie . . . . . . .1987
+ Molter, William, Jr. . . . . . . .1960
  Mott, Bill . . . . . . . . . . . . . .1998
+ Mulholland, Winbert . . . . . .1967
+ Neloy, Eddie . . . . . . . . . . .1983
  Nerud, John . . . . . . . . . . . .1972
+ Parke, Burley . . . . . . . . . . .1986

+ Penna, Angel Sr. . . . . . . . .1988
+ Pincus, Jacob . . . . . . . . . .1988
+ Rogers, John . . . . . . . . . . .1955
+ Rowe, James Sr. . . . . . . . .1955
  Schulhofer, Scotty . . . . . . . .1992
  Sheppard, Jonathan . . . . . .1990
+ Smith, Robert A. . . . . . . . .1976
  Smith, Tom . . . . . . . . . . . .2001
+ Smithwick, Mike . . . . . . . .1976
+ Stephens, Woody . . . . . . . .1976
  Tenny, Mesh . . . . . . . . . . .1991
+ Thompson, H.J. . . . . . . . . .1969
+ Trotsek, Harry . . . . . . . . . .1984
  Van Berg, Jack . . . . . . . . .1985
+ Van Berg, Marion . . . . . . .1970
+ Veitch, Sylvester . . . . . . . . .1977
+ Walden, Robert . . . . . . . . .1970
  Walsh, Michael . . . . . . . . .1997
+ Ward, Sherrill . . . . . . . . . . .1978
  Watters, Sidney Jr. . . . . . . .2005
+ Whiteley, Frank Jr. . . . . . . .1978
+ Whittingham, Charlie . . . . .1974
+ Williamson, Ansel . . . . . . . .1998
  Winfrey, W.C. (Bill) . . . . . . .1971
  Zito, Nick . . . . . . . . . . . . .2005

### Horses
Year foaled in parentheses.

  A.P. Indy (1989) . . . . . . . .2000
+ Ack Ack (1966) . . . . . . . .1986
  Affectionately (1960) . . . . .1989
+ Affirmed (1975) . . . . . . . .1980
  All-Along (1979) . . . . . . . .1990
+ Alsab (1939) . . . . . . . . . .1976
+ Alydar (1975) . . . . . . . . . .1989
  Alysheba (1984) . . . . . . . .1993
+ American Eclipse (1814) . .1970
+ Armed (1941) . . . . . . . . .1963
+ Artful (1902) . . . . . . . . . .1956
+ Arts and Letters (1966) . . .1994
+ Assault (1943) . . . . . . . . .1964
+ Battleship (1927) . . . . . . . .1969
+ Bayakoa (1984) . . . . . . . .1998
+ Bed O'Roses (1947) . . . . .1976
+ Beldame (1901) . . . . . . . .1956
+ Ben Brush (1893) . . . . . . .1955
+ Bewitch (1945) . . . . . . . . .1977
+ Bimelech (1937) . . . . . . . .1990
+ Black Gold (1919) . . . . . .1989
+ Black Helen (1932) . . . . . .1991
+ Blue Larkspur (1926) . . . . .1957
+ Bold 'n Determined (1977) .1997
+ Bold Ruler (1954) . . . . . . .1973
+ Bon Nouvel (1960) . . . . . .1976
+ Boston (1833) . . . . . . . . . .1955
+ Broomstick (1901) . . . . . . .1956
+ Buckpasser (1963) . . . . . .1970
+ Busher (1942) . . . . . . . . . .1964
+ Bushranger (1930) . . . . . .1967
+ Cafe Prince (1970) . . . . . .1985
+ Carry Back (1958) . . . . . .1975
+ Cavalcade (1931) . . . . . . .1993
+ Challendon (1936) . . . . . .1977
+ Chris Evert (1971) . . . . . . .1988
+ Cicada (1959) . . . . . . . . .1967
  Cigar (1990) . . . . . . . . . . .2002
+ Citation (1945) . . . . . . . . .1959
+ Coaltown (1945) . . . . . . . .1983
+ Colin (1905) . . . . . . . . . . .1956
+ Commando (1898) . . . . . .1956
+ Count Fleet (1940) . . . . . . .1961

+ Crusader (1923) . . . . . . . .1995
+ Dahlia (1971) . . . . . . . . . .1981
+ Damascus (1964) . . . . . . .1974
  Dance Smartly (1989) . . . .2003
+ Dark Mirage (1965) . . . . .1974
+ Davona Dale (1976) . . . . .1985
+ Desert Vixen (1970) . . . . . .1979
+ Devil Diver (1939) . . . . . . .1980
+ Discovery (1931) . . . . . . . .1969
+ Domino (1891) . . . . . . . . .1955
+ Dr. Fager (1964) . . . . . . . .1971
  Easy Goer (1986) . . . . . . . .1997
+ Eight 30 (1936) . . . . . . . .1994
+ Elkridge (1938) . . . . . . . . .1966
+ Emperor of Norfolk (1885) .1988
+ Equipoise (1928) . . . . . . . .1957
+ Exceller (1973) . . . . . . . . .1999
+ Exterminator (1915) . . . . . .1957
+ Fairmount (1921) . . . . . . . .1985
+ Fair Play (1905) . . . . . . . .1956
+ Firenze (1885) . . . . . . . . . .1981
  Flatterer (1979) . . . . . . . . .1994
  Flawlessly (1989) . . . . . . . .2004
+ Foolish Pleasure (1972) . . .1995
+ Forego (1971) . . . . . . . . . .1979
+ Fort Marcy (1964) . . . . . . .1998
+ Gallant Bloom (1966) . . . .1977
+ Gallant Fox (1927) . . . . . .1957
+ Gallant Man (1954) . . . . .1987
+ Gallorette (1942) . . . . . . . .1962
+ Gamely (1964) . . . . . . . . .1980
  Genuine Risk (1977) . . . . . .1986
+ Good and Plenty (1900) . . .1956
+ Go For Wand (1987) . . . . .1996
+ Granville (1933) . . . . . . . . .1997
+ Grey Lag (1918) . . . . . . . .1957
+ Gun Bow (1960) . . . . . . . .1999
+ Hamburg (1895) . . . . . . . .1986
+ Hanover (1884) . . . . . . . . .1955
+ Henry of Navarre (1891) . .1985
+ Hill Prince (1947) . . . . . . . .1991
+ Hindoo (1878) . . . . . . . . .1955
  Holy Bull (1991) . . . . . . . .2001

+ Imp (1894) . . . . . . . . . . . .1965
+ Jay Trump (1957) . . . . . . .1971
  John Henry (1975) . . . . . . .1990
+ Johnstown (1936) . . . . . . .1992
+ Jolly Roger (1922) . . . . . . .1965
+ Kingston (1884) . . . . . . . . .1955
+ Kelso (1957) . . . . . . . . . . .1967
+ Kentucky (1861) . . . . . . . .1983
  Lady's Secret (1982) . . . . . .1992
+ La Prevoyante (1970) . . . . .1995
+ L'Escargot (1963) . . . . . . .1977
+ Lexington (1850) . . . . . . . .1955
  Lonesome Glory (1989) . . . .2005
+ Longfellow (1867) . . . . . . .1971
+ Luke Blackburn (1877) . . . .1956
+ Majestic Prince (1966) . . . .1988
+ Man o' War (1917) . . . . . .1957
  Maskette (1906) . . . . . . . . .2001
  Miesque (1984) . . . . . . . . .1999
+ Miss Woodford (1880) . . . .1967
+ Myrtlewood (1933) . . . . . .1979
+ Nashua (1952) . . . . . . . . .1965
+ Native Dancer (1950) . . . . .1963
+ Native Diver (1959) . . . . . .1978
+ Needles (1953) . . . . . . . . .2000
+ Neji (1950) . . . . . . . . . . . .1966
+ Noor (1945) . . . . . . . . . . .2002
+ Northern Dancer (1961) . . .1976
+ Oedipus (1941) . . . . . . . . .1978
+ Old Rosebud (1911) . . . . . .1968
+ Omaha (1932) . . . . . . . . .1965
+ Pan Zareta (1910) . . . . . . .1972
+ Parole (1873) . . . . . . . . . .1984
  Personal Ensign (1984) . . . .1993
  Paseana (1987) . . . . . . . . .2001
+ Peter Pan (1904) . . . . . . . .1956
  Precisionist (1983) . . . . . . .2003
  Princess Rooney (1980) . . . .1991
+ Real Delight (1949) . . . . . .1987
+ Regret (1912) . . . . . . . . . .1957
+ Reigh Count (1925) . . . . . .1978
  Riva Ridge (1969) . . . . . . .1998
+ Roamer (1911) . . . . . . . . .1981

+ Roseben (1901) . . . . . . . . 1956
+ Round Table (1954) . . . . . 1972
+ Ruffian (1972) . . . . . . . . . 1976
+ Ruthless (1864) . . . . . . . . 1975
+ Salvator (1886) . . . . . . . . 1955
+ Sarazen (1921) . . . . . . . . 1957
+ Seabiscuit (1933) . . . . . . . 1958
+ Searching (1952) . . . . . . . 1978
+ Seattle Slew (1974) . . . . . . 1981
+ Secretariat (1970) . . . . . . . 1974
Serena's Song (1992) . . . . 2002
+ Shuvee (1966) . . . . . . . . 1975
+ Silver Spoon (1956) . . . . . 1978

+ Sir Archy (1805) . . . . . . . 1955
+ Sir Barton (1916) . . . . . . . 1957
Skip Away (1993) . . . . . . 2004
Slew o' Gold (1980) . . . . . 1992
+ Sun Beau (1925) . . . . . . . 1996
+ Sunday Silence (1986) . . . . 1996
+ Stymie (1941) . . . . . . . . 1975
+ Susan's Girl (1969) . . . . . 1976
+ Swaps (1952) . . . . . . . . 1966
+ Sword Dancer (1956) . . . . 1977
+ Sysonby (1902) . . . . . . . 1956
+ Ta Wee (1966) . . . . . . . . 1994
+ Tim Tam (1955) . . . . . . . 1985

+ Tom Fool (1949) . . . . . . . 1960
+ Top Flight (1929) . . . . . . . 1966
+ Tosmah (1961) . . . . . . . . 1984
+ Twenty Grand (1928) . . . . 1957
+ Twilight Tear (1941) . . . . . 1963
+ War Admiral (1934) . . . . . 1958
+ Whirlaway (1938) . . . . . . 1959
+ Whisk Broom II (1907) . . . . 1979
Winning Colors (1985) . . . 2000
Zaccio (1976) . . . . . . . . 1990
+ Zev (1920) . . . . . . . . . . 1983

## Exemplars of Racing

+ Hanes, John W . . . . . . . . 1982
+ Jeffords, Walter M . . . . . . 1973

+ Mellon, Paul . . . . . . . . . 1989

Widener, George D . . . . . 1971

---

## MEDIA

## National Sportscasters and Sportswriters Hall of Fame

Established in 1959 by the National Sportscasters and Sportswriters Association. **Address:** 322 East Innes St., Salisbury, NC 28144. **Telephone:** (704) 633-4275. **Web:** www.nssahalloffame.com. **Eligibility:** Nominees must be active for at least 25 years. Voting done by NSSA membership and other media representatives.

**Class of 2005** (2): **Marty Brennaman** and **Sally Jenkins**.

Members are listed with year of induction; (+) indicates deceased members.

### Sportscasters

+ Allen, Mel . . . . . . . . . . . 1972
+ Barber, Walter (Red) . . . . . 1973
Brennaman, Marty . . . . . . 2005
+ Brickhouse, Jack . . . . . . . 1983
+ Buck, Jack . . . . . . . . . . 1990
+ Caray, Harry . . . . . . . . . 1989
+ Cosell, Howard . . . . . . . 1993
+ Dean, Dizzy . . . . . . . . . 1976
+ Dunphy, Don . . . . . . . . . 1986
+ Elson, Bob . . . . . . . . . . 1995
Enberg, Dick . . . . . . . . . 1996
Garagiola, Joe . . . . . . . . 2004

+ Glickman, Marty . . . . . . . 1992
Gowdy, Curt . . . . . . . . . 1981
Harwell, Ernie . . . . . . . . 1989
+ Hearn, Chick . . . . . . . . . 1997
Hodges, Russ . . . . . . . . 1975
+ Hoyt, Waite . . . . . . . . . 1987
+ Husing, Ted . . . . . . . . . 1963
Jackson, Keith . . . . . . . . 1995
+ McCarthy, Clem . . . . . . . 1970
McKay, Jim . . . . . . . . . . 1987
+ McNamee, Graham . . . . . 1964
Michaels, Al . . . . . . . . . 1998

Miller, Jon . . . . . . . . . . 1999
+ Murphy, Bob . . . . . . . . . 2002
+ Nelson, Lindsey . . . . . . . 1979
+ Prince, Bob . . . . . . . . . 1986
+ Schenkel, Chris . . . . . . . 1981
+ Scott, Ray . . . . . . . . . . 1982
Scully, Vin . . . . . . . . . . 1991
Simpson, Jim . . . . . . . . . 2000
+ Stern, Bill . . . . . . . . . . . 1974
Summerall, Pat . . . . . . . . 1994
Whitaker, Jack . . . . . . . . 2001
Wolff, Bob . . . . . . . . . . 2003

### Sportswriters

Anderson, Dave . . . . . . . 1990
Bisher, Furman . . . . . . . . 1989
Broeg, Bob . . . . . . . . . . 1997
+ Burick, Si . . . . . . . . . . . 1985
+ Cannon, Jimmy . . . . . . . 1986
+ Carmichael, John P. . . . . . 1994
Collins, Bud . . . . . . . . . 2002
+ Connor, Dick . . . . . . . . . 1992
+ Considine, Bob . . . . . . . . 1980
+ Daley, Arthur . . . . . . . . . 1976
Deford, Frank . . . . . . . . 1998
Durslag, Mel . . . . . . . . . 1995
+ Gould, Alan . . . . . . . . . 1990

+ Graham, Frank Sr. . . . . . . 1995
+ Grimsley, Will . . . . . . . . 1987
Heinz, W.C. . . . . . . . . . 2001
Holtzman, Jerome . . . . . . 2004
Izenberg, Jerry . . . . . . . . 2000
Jenkins, Dan . . . . . . . . . 1996
Jenkins, Sally . . . . . . . . . 2005
+ Kieran, John . . . . . . . . . 1971
+ Lardner, Ring . . . . . . . . . 1967
+ McDonough, Will . . . . . . 2003
+ Murphy, Jack . . . . . . . . . 1988
+ Murray, Jim . . . . . . . . . . 1978
Olderman, Murray . . . . . . 1993

+ Parker, Dan . . . . . . . . . . 1975
Pope, Edwin . . . . . . . . . 1994
+ Povich, Shirley . . . . . . . . 1984
+ Rice, Grantland . . . . . . . 1962
+ Runyon, Damon . . . . . . . 1964
Russell, Fred . . . . . . . . . 1988
Sherrod, Blackie . . . . . . . 1991
+ Smith, Walter (Red) . . . . . 1977
+ Spink, J.G. Taylor . . . . . . . 1969
+ Steadman, John . . . . . . . 1999
Vecsey, George . . . . . . . 2001
+ Ward, Arch . . . . . . . . . . 1973
+ Woodward, Stanley . . . . . 1974

---

## MOTORSPORTS

## Motorsports Hall of Fame of America

Established in 1989. **Mailing Address:** P.O. Box 194, Novi, MI 48376. **Telephone:** (248) 349-7223. **Web:** www.mshf.com. **Eligibility:** Nominees must be retired at least three years or engaged in their area of motorsports for at least 20 years. Areas include: open wheel, stock car, dragster, sports car, motorcycle, off road, power boat, air racing, land speed records, historic and at-large.

**Class of 2005** (9): DRIVERS—**Danny Foster** (powerboats), **Hurley Haywood** (sports cars), **Tommy Ivo** (drag racing), **Benny Parsons** (stock cars), **Tom Sneva** (open wheel), **Troy Ruttman** (open wheel), **Jay Springsteen** (motorcycles). CONTRIBUTORS—**John Holman** and **Ralph Moody**.

Members are listed with year of induction; (+) indicates deceased members.

### Drivers

Allison, Bobby . . . . . . . . 1992
Amato, Joe . . . . . . . . . . 2004
Andretti, Mario . . . . . . . . 1990
Arfons, Art . . . . . . . . . . 1991
+ Baker, Buck . . . . . . . . . 1998
+ Baker, Cannonball . . . . . . 1989

+ Bettenhausen, Tony . . . . . 1997
Brabham, Geoff . . . . . . . 2004
Breedlove, Craig . . . . . . . 1993
Bryan, Jimmy . . . . . . . . 1999
+ Campbell, Sir Malcolm . . . . 1994
+ Cantrell, Bill . . . . . . . . . 1992

+ Chenoweth, Dean . . . . . . 1991
+ Chevrolet, Gaston . . . . . . 2002
Chrisman, Art . . . . . . . . 1997
+ Clark, Jim . . . . . . . . . . 1990
+ Cook, Betty . . . . . . . . . 1996
+ Cooper, Earl . . . . . . . . . 2001

## Motorsports (Cont.)

Cunningham, Briggs ......1997
+ Davis, Jim ...........1997
D'Eath, Tom ..........2000
DeCoster, Roger .......1994
+ DePalma, Ralph .......1992
+ DePaolo, Peter .......1995
+ Donahue, Mark .......1990
+ Earnhardt, Dale ......2002
Fittipaldi, Emerson ....2001
Flock, Tim ...........1999
Follmer, George .......1999
Foster, Danny ........2005
Foyt, A.J. ...........1989
Garlits, Don .........1989
Glidden, Bob .........1994
+ Gregg, Peter .........2000
Gurney, Dan ..........1991
Hanauer, Chip ........1995
Hannah, Bob ..........2000
+ Hanks, Sam ..........2000
+ Harroun, Ray .........2000
Hart, C.J. ...........1999
Haywood, Hurley ......2005
Hill, Eddie ..........2002
Hill, Phil ...........1989
+ Hinnershitz, Tommy ...2003
+ Holbert, Al ..........1993
+ Horn, Ted ...........1993
+ Hulme, Denis .........1998
Ivo, Tommy ..........2005
Jarrett, Ned .........1997

Jenkins, Bill (Grumpy) ....1996
Johncock, Gordon .....2002
Johnson, Junior .......1991
Jones, Parnelli .......1992
Kalitta, Connie .......1992
Kenyon, Mel .........2003
+ Kurtis, Frank ........1999
Lawson, Eddie ........2002
Leonard, Joe .........1991
+ Lockhart, Frank ......1999
Lorenzen, Fred .......2001
+ McLaren, Bruce .......1995
Mann, Dick ..........1993
Markle, Bart .........1999
+ Mays, Rex ...........1995
McEwen, Tom .........2001
Mears, Rick ..........1998
+ Meyer, Louis .........1993
+ Miles, Ken ...........2001
+ Milton, Tommy ........1998
Muldowney, Shirley ....1990
+ Muncy, Bill ..........1989
+ Murphy, Jimmy ........1998
+ Musson, Ron ..........1993
Nickelson, Don .......1998
Nixon, Gary ..........2003
+ Nordskog, Bob ........1997
+ Oldfield, Barney ......1989
+ Ongais, Danny ........2000
Parks, Wally .........1993
Parsons, Benny .......2005

+ Parsons, Johnnie ......2004
Pearson, David .......1993
+ Petrali, Joe ..........1992
+ Petty, Lee ...........1996
Petty, Richard .......1989
Prudhomme, Don .......1991
Rahal, Bobby ........2004
Resweber, Carroll ....1998
Redman, Brian ........2002
+ Revson, Peter ........1996
+ Roberts, Fireball ......1995
Roberts, Kenny .......1990
Rutherford, Johnny ....1996
+ Ruttman, Troy ........2005
Seebold, Bill ........1999
+ Shaw, Wilbur .........1991
Slovak, Mira .........2001
Smith, Malcolm .......1996
Sneva, Tom ..........2005
Spencer, Freddie ......2001
Springsteen, Jay ......2005
+ Thompson, Mickey .....1990
Unser, Al ...........1991
Unser, Bobby ........1994
Vesco, Don ..........2004
+ Vukovich, Bill Sr .....1992
Waltrip, Darrell ......2003
Ward, Rodger ........1995
+ Wood, Gar ..........1990
Yarborough, Cale .....1994

## Contributors

+ Agajanian, J.C ........1992
Bignotti, George .......1993
+ Black, Keith .........1995
Bondurant, Bob .......2003
+ Brawner, Clint ........1998
Chapman, Colin .......1997
+ Chevrolet, Louis ......1995
+ Donovan, Ed .........2003
Duesenberg, Fred .....1997
Economaki, Chris .....1994
+ Ford, Henry .........1996

France, Bill Jr. ......2004
+ France, Bill Sr. ......1990
Glick, Shav ..........2004
Granatelli, Andy ......2001
Hall, Jim ...........1994
+ Holman, John ........2005
+ Hulman, Tony ........1991
+ Jones, Ted ..........2003
+ Kiekhaefer, Carl ......1998
Little, Bernie ........1994
+ Miller, Harry ........1999

+ Moody, Ralph ........2005
+ Offenhauser, Fred .....2002
Penske, Roger ........1995
+ Rickenbacker, Eddie ...1994
+ Rose, Mauri .........1996
Shelby, Carroll .......1992
Simpson, Bill ........2003
Watson, A.J. .........1996
Wood, Glen ..........2000
Wood, Leonard .......2000
+ Yunick, Smokey ......2000

# International Motorsports Hall of Fame

Established in 1990 by the International Motorsports Hall of Fame Commission. **Mailing Address:** P.O. Box 1018, Talladega, AL 35161. **Telephone:** (256) 362-5002. **Web:** www.motorsportshalloffame.com.

**Eligibility:** Nominees must be retired from their specialty in motorsports for five years. Voting done by 150-member panel made up of the world-wide auto racing media. Members are listed with year of induction; (+) indicates deceased members.

**Class of 2005** (5): DRIVERS—**Darrell Waltrip** (stock cars), **Joe Amato** (drag racing), **Bob Glidden** (drag racing), **Chip Hanauer** (hydroplane racing), **Nigel Mansell** (open wheel).

## Drivers

Allison, Bobby .........1993
Amato, Joe ..........2005
Andretti, Mario .......2000
+ Ascari, Alberto .......1992
+ Baker, Buck .........1990
Bonnett, Neil ........2001
+ Bettenhausen, Tony ...1991
Brabham, Jack .......1990
Bryan, Jimmy ........2001
+ Campbell, Sir Malcolm ..1990
+ Caracciola, Rudolph ...1998
+ Clark, Jim ..........1990
+ DePalma, Ralph ......1991
+ Donahue, Mark ......1990
+ Evans, Richie ........1996
+ Fangio, Juan Manuel ..1990
Farmer, Charles ......2004
Fittipaldi, Emerson ....2003
+ Flock, Tim ..........1991
Foyt, A.J. ..........2000

Glidden, Bob .........2005
+ Gregg, Peter .........1992
Gurney, Dan .........1990
Hailwood, Mike ......2001
+ Haley, Donald ........1996
Hanauer, Chip .......2005
+ Hill, Graham ........1990
Hill, Phil ..........1991
+ Holbert, Al .........1993
+ Hulme, Denis ........2002
Ickx, Jacky .........2002
+ Isaac, Bobby ........1996
Jarrett, Ned ........1991
Johncock, Gordon ....1999
Johnson, Junior ......1990
Jones, Parnelli ......1990
Kenyon, Mel ........2003
+ Kulwicki, Alan .......2002
Lauda, Niki .........1993
Lorenzen, Fred ......1991

+ Lund, Tiny ..........1994
Mansell, Nigel .......2005
+ Mays, Rex ..........1993
+ McLaren, Bruce ......1991
+ Meyer, Louis ........1992
Moss, Stirling .......1990
Muldowney, Shirley ...2004
+ Muncey, Bill ........2004
+ Nuvolari, Tazio ......1998
+ Oldfield, Barney ......1990
Parsons, Benny ......1994
Pearson, David .......1993
+ Petty, Lee ..........1990
Piquet, Nelson .......2000
Prudhomme, Don ......2000
Prost, Alain .........1999
Rahal, Bobby ........2004
+ Richmond, Tim .......2002
+ Roberts, Fireball ......1990
Roberts, Kenny ......1992

| | | |
|---|---|---|
| Rose, Mauri . . . . . . . . . .1994 | Stewart, Jackie . . . . . . . .1990 | + Vukovich, Bill . . . . . . . . .1991 |
| Rutherford, Johnny . . . . . .1996 | Surtees, John . . . . . . . . .1996 | Waltrip, Darrell . . . . . . . .2005 |
| Scott, Wendell . . . . . . . . .1999 | + Thomas, Herb . . . . . . . .1994 | Ward Rodger . . . . . . . . .1992 |
| + Senna, Ayrton . . . . . . . . .2000 | + Turner, Curtis . . . . . . . .1992 | + Weatherly, Joe . . . . . . . .1994 |
| + Shaw, Wilbur . . . . . . . . .1991 | Unser, Al Sr. . . . . . . . . .1998 | Wood, Glen . . . . . . . . . .2002 |
| Smith, Louise . . . . . . . . .1999 | Unser, Bobby . . . . . . . . .1990 | Yarborough, Cale . . . . . . .1993 |

## Contributors

| | | |
|---|---|---|
| Bignotti, George . . . . . . .1993 | France, Bill Jr. . . . . . . . .2004 | Parks, Wally . . . . . . . . .1992 |
| Breedlove, Craig . . . . . . .2000 | + France, Bill Sr . . . . . . . .1990 | Penske, Roger . . . . . . . .1998 |
| + Bugatti, Ettore . . . . . . . .2002 | Granatelli, Andy . . . . . . .1992 | + Porsche, Ferdinand . . . . . .1996 |
| + Chapman, Colin . . . . . . . .1994 | + Hulman, Tony . . . . . . . .1990 | + Rickenbacker, Eddie . . . . . .1992 |
| + Chevrolet, Louis . . . . . . . .1992 | Hyde, Harry . . . . . . . . .1999 | Shelby, Carroll . . . . . . . .1991 |
| + Cunningham, Briggs . . . . . .2003 | Marcum, John . . . . . . . .1994 | + Thompson, Mickey . . . . . . .1990 |
| + Ferrari, Enzo . . . . . . . . .1994 | + Matthews, Banjo . . . . . . .1998 | Watson, A.J. . . . . . . . . .2003 |
| + Ford, Henry . . . . . . . . .1993 | Moody, Ralph . . . . . . . .1994 | + Yunick, Smokey . . . . . . . .1990 |
| Fox, Ray . . . . . . . . . . . .2003 | + Offenhauser, Fred . . . . . .2001 | |

## OLYMPICS

## U.S. Olympic Hall of Fame

Established in 1983 by the United States Olympic Committee. **Mailing Address:** U.S. Olympic Committee, 1750 East Boulder Street, Colorado Springs, CO 80909. Plans for a permanent museum site have been suspended due to lack of funding. **Telephone:** (719) 866-4529. **Web:** www.usoc.org

**Eligibility:** Nominated athletes must be four years removed from their last Olympic competition. Voting for membership in the Hall was suspended in 1993 but resumed in 2004. Voting from 1983-92 was done by National Sportscasters and Sportswriters Association, Hall of Fame members and the USOC board members of directors. Beginning in 2004 the voting weight was divided among U.S. Olympians, select U.S. Olympic family/media and fans.

**Class of 2005:** The next inductions are scheduled for some time in 2006.

Members are listed with year of induction; (+) indicates deceased members.

### Teams

**1956 Basketball** Dick Boushka, Carl Cain, Chuck Darling, Bill Evans, Gib Ford, Burdy Haldorson, Bill Hougland, Bob Jeangerard, K.C. Jones, Bill Russell, Ron Tomsic, +Jim Walsh and coach +Gerald Tucker.

**1960 Basketball** Jay Arnette, Walt Bellamy, Bob Boozer, Terry Dischinger, Burdy Haldorson, Darrall Imhoff, Allen Kelley, +Lester Lane, Jerry Lucas, Oscar Robertson, Adrian Smith, Jerry West and coach Pete Newell.

**1964 Basketball** Jim Barnes, Bill Bradley, Larry Brown, Joe Caldwell, Mel Counts, Richard Davies, Walt Hazzard, Luke Jackson, John McCaffrey, Jeff Mullins, Jerry Shipp, George Wilson and coach +Hank Iba.

**1960 Ice Hockey** Billy Christian, Roger Christian, Billy Cleary, Bob Cleary, Gene Grazia, Paul Johnson, Jack Kirrane, John Mayasich, Jack McCartan, Bob McKay, Dick Meredith, Weldon Olson, Ed Owen, Rod Paavola, Larry Palmer, Dick Rodenheiser, +Tom Williams and coach Jack Riley.

**1980 Ice Hockey** Bill Baker, Neal Broten, Dave Christian, Steve Christoff, Jim Craig, Mike Eruzione, John Harrington, Steve Janaszak, Mark Johnson, Ken Morrow, Rob McClanahan, Jack O'Callahan, Mark Pavelich, Mike Ramsey, Buzz Schneider, Dave Silk, Eric Strobel, Bob Suter, Phil Verchota, Mark Wells and coach Herb Brooks.

**1996 Women's Soccer** Michelle Akers, Brandi Chastain, Amanda Cromwell, Joy Fawcett, Julie Foudy, Carin Gabarra, Mia Hamm, Mary Harvey, Kristine Lilly, Shannon MacMillan, Tiffeny Milbrett, Carla Overbeck, Cindy Parlow, Tiffany Roberts, Briana Scurry, Thori Staples Bryan, Tisha Venturini, Saskia Webber, Staci Wilson and coach Tony DiCicco.

### Alpine Skiing

Mahre, Phil . . . . . . . . . .1992

### Bobsled

+ Eagan, Eddie (see Boxing) .1983

### Boxing

Clay, Cassius* . . . . . . . .1983
+ Eagan, Eddie (see Bobsled) .1983
Foreman, George . . . . . .1990
Frazier, Joe . . . . . . . . . .1989
Leonard, Sugar Ray . . . . .1985
Patterson, Floyd . . . . . . .1987
*Clay changed name to Muhammad Ali in 1964.

### Cycling

Carpenter-Phinney, Connie .1992

### Diving

King, Miki . . . . . . . . . . .1992
Lee, Sammy . . . . . . . . . .1990
Louganis, Greg . . . . . . . .1985
McCormick, Pat . . . . . . .1985

### Gymnastics

Conner, Bart . . . . . . . . . .1991
Retton, Mary Lou . . . . . . .1985
Vidmar, Peter . . . . . . . . .1991

### Figure Skating

Albright, Tenley . . . . . . . .1988
Button, Dick . . . . . . . . . .1983
Fleming, Peggy . . . . . . . .1983
Hamill, Dorothy . . . . . . . .1991
Hamilton, Scott . . . . . . . .1990

### Rowing

+ Kelly, Jack Sr. . . . . . . . .1990

### Speed Skating

Blair, Bonnie . . . . . . . . . .2004
Heiden, Eric . . . . . . . . . .1983
Jansen, Dan . . . . . . . . . .2004

### Swimming

Babashoff, Shirley . . . . . .1987
Biondi, Matt . . . . . . . . . .2004
Caulkins, Tracy . . . . . . . .1990
+ Daniels, Charles . . . . . . .1988
de Varona, Donna . . . . . .1987
Evans, Janet . . . . . . . . . .2004
+ Kahanamoku, Duke . . . . . .1984
+ Madison, Helene . . . . . . .1992
Meyer, Debbie . . . . . . . .1986
Naber, John . . . . . . . . . .1984
Schollander, Don . . . . . . .1983
Spitz, Mark . . . . . . . . . . .1983
+ Weissmuller, Johnny . . . . .1983

### Track & Field

Beamon, Bob . . . . . . . . .1983
Boston, Ralph . . . . . . . . .1985
+ Calhoun, Lee . . . . . . . . .1991
Campbell, Milt . . . . . . . . .1992
Coachman, Alice . . . . . . .2004
+ Davenport, Willie . . . . . . .1991
Davis, Glenn . . . . . . . . . .1986
+ Didrikson, Babe . . . . . . . .1983
Dillard, Harrison . . . . . . . .1983
Evans, Lee . . . . . . . . . . .1989
+ Ewry, Ray . . . . . . . . . . .1983
Fosbury, Dick . . . . . . . . .1992
Jenner, Bruce . . . . . . . . .1986
Johnson, Rafer . . . . . . . . .1983
+ Joyner, Florence Griffith . . .2004
Joyner-Kersee, Jackie . . . .2004
+ Kraenzlein, Alvin . . . . . . .1985
Lewis, Carl . . . . . . . . . . .1985
Mathias, Bob . . . . . . . . . .1983
Mills, Billy . . . . . . . . . . . .1984
Morrow, Bobby . . . . . . . .1989
Moses, Edwin . . . . . . . . .1985
O'Brien, Parry . . . . . . . . .1984
Oerter, Al . . . . . . . . . . . .1983
+ Owens, Jesse . . . . . . . . . .1983
+ Paddock, Charley . . . . . . .1991

Richards, Bob . . . . . . . . . .1983
+ Rudolph, Wilma . . . . . . . .1983
+ Sheppard, Mel . . . . . .1989
Shorter, Frank . . . . . . . . .1984
+ Thorpe, Jim . . . . . . . . . .1983
Toomey, Bill . . . . . . . . . .1984
Tyus, Wyomia . . . . . . . . .1985
Whitfield, Mal . . . . . . . . .1988
+ Wykoff, Frank . . . . . . . . .1984

### Weight Lifting
+ Davis, John . . . . . . . . . . .1989
Kono, Tommy . . . . . . . . .1990

### Wrestling
Gable, Dan . . . . . . . . . . .1985

### Contributors
+ Arledge, Roone . . . . . . . .1989
+ Brundage, Avery . . . . . . .1983
+ Bushnell, Asa . . . . . . . . .1990

Greenspan, Bud . . . . . . . .2004
Hull, Col. Don . . . . . . . . .1992
+ Iba, Hank . . . . . . . . . . .1985
+ Kane, Robert . . . . . . . . .1986
+ Kelly, Jack Jr. . . . . . . . . .1992
McKay, Jim . . . . . . . . . .1988
Miller, Don . . . . . . . . . . .1984
+ Simon, William . . . . . . . .1991
Walker, LeRoy . . . . . . . . .1987

---

## SOCCER

# National Soccer Hall of Fame

Established in 1950 by the Philadelphia Oldtimers Association. First exhibit unveiled in Oneonta, NY in 1982. Moved into new Hall of Fame building in the summer of 1999. **Address:** 18 Stadium Circle, Oneonta, NY 13820. **Telephone:** (607) 432-3351. **Web:** www.soccerhall.org

**Eligibility:** Players must have been retired as a player for at least three years, but for no more than 10 years He or she must have played at least 20 full international games for the United States. He or she must have played at least five seasons in an American first-division professional league (NASL or MLS), and won the league championship, won the U.S. Open Cup or been a league all-star at least once. Other categories include Veterans (included under Players) and Builders. Voting done by a committee made up of Hall of Famers, U.S. Soccer officials and members of the national media.

**Class of 2005** (10): **Marcelo Balboa, Fernando Clavijo, Tom "Whitey" Fleming, John Harkes, Alex McNab, Johnny Nelson, Werner Nilsen, Tab Ramos, Frabie Salcedo** and **Hank Steinbrecher.**

Members are listed with home state and year of induction; (+) indicates deceased members.

## Players

Akers, Michelle . . . . . . . . .2004
Alberto, Carlos . . . . . . . .2003
Annis, Robert . . . . . . . . .1976
+ Auld, Andrew . . . . . . . . .1986
Bachmeier, Adolph . . . . . .2002
Bahr, Walter . . . . . . . . . .1976
Balboa, Marcelo . . . . . . .2005
+ Barr, George . . . . . . . . .1983
+ Beardsworth, Fred . . . . . .1965
Beckenbauer, Franz (Ger) . .1998
Bernabei, Ray . . . . . . . . .1978
Bogicevic, Vladislav (Yug) . .2002
+ Bookie, Michael . . . . . . .1986
Borghi, Frank . . . . . . . . .1976
+ Boulos, Frenchy . . . . . . . .1980
+ Brittan, Harold . . . . . . . .1951
+ Brown, David . . . . . . . . .1951
Brown, George . . . . . . . .1995
+ Brown, James . . . . . . . . .1986
Caligiuri, Paul . . . . . . . . .2004
+ Carenza, Joe . . . . . . . . .1982
+ Caraffi, Ralph . . . . . . . . .1959
Chacurian, Chico . . . . . . .1992
+ Chesney, Stan . . . . . . . . .1966
Child, Paul (Eng) . . . . . . .2003
Chinaglia, Giorgio (Italy) . .2000
Clavijo, Fernando . . . . . . .2005
+ Colombo, Charlie . . . . . . .1976
Coombes, Geoff . . . . . . . .1976
Craddock Jr., Robert . . . . .1976
Danilo, Paul . . . . . . . . . .1997
Davis, Rick . . . . . . . . . . .2001
+ Dick, Walter . . . . . . . . . .1989
Diorio, Nick . . . . . . . . . .1974
+ Donelli, Buff . . . . . . . . . .1954
+ Douglas, Jimmy . . . . . . . .1953
+ Duggan, Thomas . . . . . . .1951
+ Dunn, James . . . . . . . . . .1974
Ely, Alexander . . . . . . . . .1997
+ Ferguson, John . . . . . . . .1950
+ Fleming, Tom (Whitey) . . . .2005
+ Florie, Thomas . . . . . . . .1986

+ Fricker, Werner . . . . . . . .1992
+ Fryer, William J. . . . . . . .1951
Gabarra, Carin . . . . . . . .2000
+ Gaetjens, Joe . . . . . . . . .1976
+ Gallagher, James . . . . . . .1986
Gard, Gino . . . . . . . . . . .1976
+ Gentle, James . . . . . . . . .1986
Getzinger, Rudy . . . . . . . .1991
+ Glover, Teddy . . . . . . . . .1965
+ Gonsalves, Billy . . . . . . . .1950
Gormley, Bob . . . . . . . . .1989
+ Govier, Sheldon . . . . . . . .1950
Granitza, Karl-Heinz (Ger) .2003
Gryzik, Joe . . . . . . . . . . .1973
Harker, Al . . . . . . . . . . .1979
Harkes, John . . . . . . . . . .2005
Heinrichs, April . . . . . . . .1998
Higgins, Shannon . . . . . . .2002
Howard, Ted . . . . . . . . . .2003
Hynes, John . . . . . . . . . .1977
+ Japp, John . . . . . . . . . . .1953
Keough, Harry . . . . . . . .1976
Kropfelder, Nicholas . . . . .1996
+ Kunter, Rudy . . . . . . . . .1963
Lang, Millard . . . . . . . . .1950
Lenarduzzi, Bob (Can) . . . .2003
+ Looby, Bill . . . . . . . . . . .2001
+ Maca, Joe . . . . . . . . . . .1976
Mausser, Arnie . . . . . . . .2003
McBride, Pat . . . . . . . . . .1994
+ McGhee, Bart . . . . . . . . .1986
+ McGuire, John . . . . . . . .1951
+ McIlveney, Eddie . . . . . . .1976
McLaughlin, Bennie . . . . . .1977
+ McNab, Alex . . . . . . . . . .2005
+ Mieth, Werner . . . . . . . . .1974
+ Millar, Robert . . . . . . . . .1950
Monsen, Joe . . . . . . . . . .1994
Moore, Johnny . . . . . . . .1997
+ Moorehouse, George . . . . .1986
+ Morrison, Robert . . . . . . .1951
Murphy, Edward . . . . . . .1998

Nanoski, Jukey . . . . . . . .1993
+ Nelson, Johnny . . . . . . . .2005
+ Nilsen, Werner . . . . . . . .2005
Ntsoelengoe, Ace (S.Afr.) . .2003
+ O'Brien, Shamus . . . . . . .1990
Olaff, Gene . . . . . . . . . .1971
+ Oliver, Arnie . . . . . . . . . .1968
Oliver, Len . . . . . . . . . . .1996
Pariani, Gino . . . . . . . . .1976
+ Patenaude, Bert . . . . . . . .1971
Pel|fe (Brazil) . . . . . . . . .1993
Ramos, Tab . . . . . . . . . .2005
+ Ratican, Harry . . . . . . . .1950
+ Renzulli, Pete . . . . . . . . .1951
+ Roe, Jimmy . . . . . . . . . .1997
Roth, Werner . . . . . . . . .1989
Roy, Willy . . . . . . . . . . .1989
+ Ryan, Hun . . . . . . . . . . .1958
Salcedo Frabie . . . . . . . .2005
Schaller, Willy . . . . . . . . .1995
Slone, Philip . . . . . . . . . .1986
+ Souza, Ed . . . . . . . . . . .1976
Souza, Clarkie . . . . . . . . .1976
+ Spalding, Dick . . . . . . . . .1951
+ Stark, Archie . . . . . . . . . .1950
+ Swords, Thomas . . . . . . . .1951
+ Tintle, Joseph . . . . . . . . .1952
+ Tracey, Ralph . . . . . . . . .1986
+ Vaughn, Frank . . . . . . . . .1986
+ Wallace, Frank . . . . . . . .1976
+ Weir, Alex . . . . . . . . . . .1975
Willey, Alan (Eng) . . . . . . .2003
Wilson, Bruce (Can) . . . . . .2003
+ Wilson, Peter . . . . . . . . .1950
Wolanin, Adam . . . . . . . .1976
+ Wood, Alex . . . . . . . . . . .1986
Wynalda, Eric . . . . . . . . .2004
Zerhusen, Al . . . . . . . . . .1978

## Builders

| | | |
|---|---|---|
| Abronzino, Umberto . . . . .1971 | + Fowler, Peg . . . . . . . . . . . .1979 | + Netto, Fred . . . . . . . . . . . .1958 |
| Aimi, Milton . . . . . . . . . . . .1991 | + Garcia, Pete . . . . . . . . . . .1964 | Newman, Ron . . . . . . . . . .1992 |
| + Alonso, Julie . . . . . . . . . .1972 | + Giesler, Walter . . . . . . . . .1962 | + Niotis, D.J. . . . . . . . . . . . .1963 |
| + Andersen, William . . . . . .1956 | + Gould, David L. . . . . . . . . .1953 | + Palmer, William . . . . . . . .1952 |
| + Ardizzone, John . . . . . . . .1971 | + Greer, Don . . . . . . . . . . . .1985 | + Pearson, Eddie . . . . . . . . .1990 |
| + Armstrong, James . . . . . . .1952 | + Guelker, Bob . . . . . . . . . . .1980 | + Peel, Peter . . . . . . . . . . . .1951 |
| + Barriskill, Joe . . . . . . . . . .1953 | Guennel, Joe . . . . . . . . . .1980 | + Peters, Wally . . . . . . . . . .1967 |
| Berling, Clay . . . . . . . . . .1995 | + Healey, George . . . . . . . . .1951 | Phillipson, Don . . . . . . . . .1987 |
| + Best, John O. . . . . . . . . . . .1982 | Heilpern, Herb . . . . . . . . .1988 | + Piscopo, Giorgio . . . . . . . .1978 |
| + Booth, Joseph . . . . . . . . . .1952 | + Hemmings, William . . . . . .1961 | + Pomeroy, Edgar . . . . . . . .1955 |
| + Boxer, Matt . . . . . . . . . . . .1961 | Hermann, Robert . . . . . . .2001 | + Ramsden, Arnold . . . . . . .1957 |
| Bradley, Gordon (Eng) . . . .1996 | + Hudson, Maurice . . . . . . . .1966 | + Reese, Doc . . . . . . . . . . . .1957 |
| + Briggs, Lawrence E. . . . . . .1978 | Hunt, Lamar . . . . . . . . . . .1982 | Ringsdorf, Gene . . . . . . . .1979 |
| + Brock, John . . . . . . . . . . . .1950 | + Iglehart, Alfredda . . . . . . .1951 | Robbie, Elizabeth . . . . . . .2003 |
| + Brown, Andrew M. . . . . . . .1950 | + Jeffrey, William . . . . . . . . .1951 | + Robbie, Joe . . . . . . . . . . . .2003 |
| + Cahill, Thomas W . . . . . . . .1950 | + Johnston, Jack . . . . . . . . .1952 | Ross, Steve . . . . . . . . . . .2003 |
| + Chyzowych, Walter . . . . . . .1997 | + Kabanica, Mike . . . . . . . . .1987 | + Rottenberg, Jack . . . . . . . .1971 |
| + Coll, John . . . . . . . . . . . . . .1986 | Kehoe, Bob . . . . . . . . . . .1990 | + Sager, Tom . . . . . . . . . . . .1968 |
| + Collins, George M. . . . . . . .1951 | + Kelly, Frank . . . . . . . . . . . .1994 | Saunders, Harry . . . . . . . .1981 |
| Collins, Peter . . . . . . . . . .1998 | + Kempton, George . . . . . . .1950 | Schellscheidt, Mannie . . . .1990 |
| + Commander, Colin . . . . . . .1967 | + Klein, Paul . . . . . . . . . . . .1953 | + Schillinger, Emil . . . . . . . .1960 |
| + Cordery, Ted . . . . . . . . . . .1975 | + Kleinaitis, Al . . . . . . . . . . .1995 | + Schroeder, Elmer . . . . . . . .1951 |
| + Craddock, Robert . . . . . . . .1959 | + Kozma, Oscar . . . . . . . . . .1964 | + Schwarz, Erno . . . . . . . . . .1951 |
| + Craggs, Edmund . . . . . . . .1969 | + Kracher, Frank . . . . . . . . . .1983 | + Shields, Fred . . . . . . . . . . .1968 |
| Craggs, George . . . . . . . .1981 | Kraft, Granny . . . . . . . . . .1984 | + Single, Erwin . . . . . . . . . .1981 |
| + Cummings, Wilfred R. . . . . .1953 | + Kraus, Harry . . . . . . . . . . .1963 | + Smith, Alfred . . . . . . . . . .1951 |
| + Delach, Joseph . . . . . . . . .1973 | + Lamm, Kurt . . . . . . . . . . . .1979 | Smith, Patrick . . . . . . . . .1998 |
| DeLuca, Enzo . . . . . . . . . .1979 | Larson, Bert . . . . . . . . . . .1988 | Spath, Reinhold . . . . . . . .1997 |
| + Donaghy, Edward J. . . . . . .1951 | + Lewis, H. Edgar . . . . . . . . .1950 | + Steelink, Nicolaas . . . . . . .1971 |
| + Donnelly, George . . . . . . . .1989 | Lombardo, Joe . . . . . . . . .1984 | Steinbrecher, Hank . . . . . .2005 |
| + Dresmich, John W. . . . . . . .1968 | Long, Denny . . . . . . . . . . .1993 | Stern, Lee . . . . . . . . . . . .2003 |
| + Duff, Duncan . . . . . . . . . . .1972 | + MacEwan, John J. . . . . . . .1953 | + Steur, August . . . . . . . . . .1969 |
| + Edwards, Gene . . . . . . . . .1985 | + Magnozzi, Enzo . . . . . . . . .1977 | + Stewart, Douglas . . . . . . . .1950 |
| + Epperleim, Rudy . . . . . . . .1951 | + Maher, Jack . . . . . . . . . . .1970 | + Stone, Robert T . . . . . . . . .1971 |
| Ertegun, Ahmet . . . . . . . .2003 | + Manning, Dr. Randolf . . . . .1950 | Toye, Clive . . . . . . . . . . .2003 |
| Ertegun, Nesuhi . . . . . . . .2003 | + Marre, John . . . . . . . . . . .1953 | + Triner, Joseph . . . . . . . . . .1951 |
| + Fairfield, Harry . . . . . . . . .1951 | + McClay, Allan . . . . . . . . . .1971 | + Walder, Jimmy . . . . . . . . .1971 |
| Feibusch, Ernst . . . . . . . .1984 | + McGrath, Frank . . . . . . . . .1978 | + Washauer, Adolph . . . . . . .1977 |
| + Fernley, John A. . . . . . . . . .1951 | + McGuire, Jimmy . . . . . . . .1951 | + Webb, Tom . . . . . . . . . . . .1987 |
| + Ferro, Charles . . . . . . . . . .1958 | + McSkimming, Dent . . . . . . .1951 | + Weston, Victor . . . . . . . . .1956 |
| + Fishwick, George E. . . . . . .1974 | Merovich, Pete . . . . . . . . .1971 | + Woods, John W. . . . . . . . .1952 |
| + Flamhaft, Jack . . . . . . . . . .1964 | Miller, Al . . . . . . . . . . . . . .1995 | Woosnam, Phil . . . . . . . . .1997 |
| + Fleming, Harry G. . . . . . . .1967 | + Miller, Milton . . . . . . . . . .1971 | Yeagley, Jerry . . . . . . . . . .1989 |
| + Foulds, Pal . . . . . . . . . . . .1953 | + Mills, Jimmy . . . . . . . . . . .1954 | + Young, John . . . . . . . . . . .1958 |
| + Foulds, Sam . . . . . . . . . . .1969 | + Moore, James F. . . . . . . . .1971 | + Zampini, Dan . . . . . . . . . .1963 |
| + Fowler, Dan . . . . . . . . . . .1970 | + Morrissette, Bill . . . . . . . . .1967 | |

## SWIMMING

## International Swimming Hall of Fame

Established in 1965 by the U.S. College Coaches' Swim Forum. **Address:** One Hall of Fame Drive, Ft. Lauderdale, FL 33316. **Telephone:** (954) 462-6536. **Web:** www.ishof.org.

Categories for induction are: swimming, diving, water polo, synchronized swimming, coaching, pioneers and contributors. Coaches and contributors are not included in the following list. Only U.S. men and women listed below.

**Class of 2005** (2): U.S. MEN—**David Berkoff** and **Craig Wilson.**

Members are listed with year of induction; (+) indicates deceased members.

### U.S. Men

| | | |
|---|---|---|
| + Anderson, Miller . . . . . . . .1967 | Clark, Steve . . . . . . . . . . .1966 | + Farrell, Jeff . . . . . . . . . . . .1968 |
| Barrowman, Mike . . . . . .1997 | + Cleveland, Dick . . . . . . . . .1991 | + Fick, Peter . . . . . . . . . . . .1978 |
| Berkoff, David . . . . . . . . .2005 | Clotworthy, Robert . . . . . .1980 | + Flanagan, Ralph . . . . . . . .1978 |
| Biondi, Matt . . . . . . . . . .1997 | + Crabbe, Buster . . . . . . . . .1965 | Ford, Alan . . . . . . . . . . . .1966 |
| + Boggs, Phil . . . . . . . . . . . .1985 | + Daniels, Charlie . . . . . . . . .1965 | Furniss, Bruce . . . . . . . . .1987 |
| Breen, George . . . . . . . . .1975 | Degener, Dick . . . . . . . . .1971 | Gaines, Rowdy . . . . . . . . .1995 |
| + Browning, Skippy . . . . . . .1975 | DeMont, Rick . . . . . . . . . .1990 | Garton, Tim . . . . . . . . . . .1997 |
| Bruner, Mike . . . . . . . . . .1988 | Dempsey, Frank . . . . . . . .1996 | + Glancy, Harrison . . . . . . . .1990 |
| Burton, Mike . . . . . . . . . .1977 | + Desjardins, Pete . . . . . . . .1966 | Goodell, Brian . . . . . . . . .1986 |
| + Cann, Tedford . . . . . . . . .1967 | Dysdale, Taylor . . . . . . . .1994 | + Goodwin, Budd . . . . . . . . .1971 |
| Carey, Rick . . . . . . . . . . .1993 | Edgar, David . . . . . . . . . .1996 | Graef, Jed . . . . . . . . . . . .1988 |
| Clark, Earl . . . . . . . . . . . .1972 | + Faricy, John . . . . . . . . . . .1990 | Haines, George . . . . . . . .1977 |

Hall Sr., Gary . . . . . . . . .1981
+ Harlan, Bruce . . . . . . . . .1973
Harper, Don . . . . . . . . .1998
+ Hebner, Harry . . . . . . . .1968
+ Heidenreich, Jerry . . . . . .1992
Hencken, John . . . . . . . .1988
Hickcox, Charles . . . . . . .1976
Higgins, John . . . . . . . . .1971
+ Holiday, Harry . . . . . . . .1991
Hough, Richard . . . . . . . .1970
Irwin, Juno Stover . . . . . .1980
Graham, Johnston . . . . . .1998
Jager, Tom . . . . . . . . . .2001
Jastremski, Chet . . . . . . .1977
+ Kahanamoku, Duke . . . . .1965
+ Kealoha, Warren . . . . . . .1968
Kiefer, Adolph . . . . . . . .1965
Kinsella, John . . . . . . . . .1986
+ Kojac, George . . . . . . . .1968
Konno, Ford . . . . . . . . .1972
+ Kruger, Stubby . . . . . . . .1986
+ Kuehn, Louis . . . . . . . . .1988
+ Langer, Ludy . . . . . . . . .1988
+ Langner, G. Harold . . . . . .1995
Larson, Lance . . . . . . . . .1980
Laufer, Walter . . . . . . . .1973
Lee, Dr. Sammy . . . . . . . .1968
Lemmon, Kelley . . . . . . . .1999
+ LeMoyne, Harry . . . . . . . .1988
Lenzi, Mark . . . . . . . . . .2003
Louganis, Greg . . . . . . . .1993
Lundquist, Steve . . . . . . .1990

Mann, Thompson . . . . . . .1984
+ Martin, G. Harold . . . . . . .1999
McCormick, Pat . . . . . . . .1965
+ McDermott, Turk . . . . . . .1969
+ McGillivray, Perry . . . . . . .1981
McKee, Tim . . . . . . . . . .1998
McKenzie, Don . . . . . . . .1989
McKinney, Frank . . . . . . .1975
McLane, Jimmy . . . . . . . .1970
+ Medica, Jack . . . . . . . . .1966
Montgomery, Jim . . . . . . .1986
Morales, Pablo . . . . . . . .1998
Mulliken, Bill . . . . . . . . .1984
Naber, John . . . . . . . . . .1982
Nakama, Keo . . . . . . . . .1975
+ O'Connor, Wally . . . . . . .1966
Oyakawa, Yoshi . . . . . . . .1973
+ Patnik, Al . . . . . . . . . . .1969
Prew, William . . . . . . . . .1998
+ Riley, Mickey . . . . . . . . .1977
+ Ris, Wally . . . . . . . . . . .1966
Robie, Carl . . . . . . . . . .1976
Ross, Clarence . . . . . . . .1988
+ Ross, Norman . . . . . . . . .1967
Roth, Dick . . . . . . . . . . .1987
Rouse, Jeff . . . . . . . . . .2001
+ Ruddy Sr., Joe . . . . . . . .1986
Russell, Doug . . . . . . . . .1985
Saari, Roy . . . . . . . . . . .1976
+ Schaeffer, E. Carroll . . . . .1968
Scholes, Clarke . . . . . . . .1980
Schollander, Don . . . . . . .1965

Schroeder, Terry . . . . . . .2002
Shaw, Tim . . . . . . . . . . .1989
+ Sheldon, George . . . . . . .1989
Sitzberger, Ken . . . . . . . .1994
+ Skelton, Robert . . . . . . . .1988
Smith, Bill . . . . . . . . . . .1966
+ Smith, Dutch . . . . . . . . .1979
+ Smith, Jimmy . . . . . . . . .1992
Spitz, Mark . . . . . . . . . .1977
+ Stack, Allen . . . . . . . . . .1979
Stewart, Melvin . . . . . . . .2002
Stickles, Ted . . . . . . . . .1995
Stock, Tom . . . . . . . . . .1989
+ Swendsen, Clyde . . . . . . .1991
Taft, Ray . . . . . . . . . . . .1996
Tobian, Gary . . . . . . . . .1978
Troy, Mike . . . . . . . . . . .1971
Vande Weghe, Albert . . . . .1990
Vassallo, Jesse . . . . . . . .1997
+ Verdeur, Joe . . . . . . . . .1966
Vogel, Matt . . . . . . . . . .1996
+ Vollmer, Hal . . . . . . . . . .1990
+ Wayne, Marshall . . . . . . .1981
Webster, Bob . . . . . . . . .1970
+ Weissmuller, Johnny . . . . .1965
+ White, Al . . . . . . . . . . . .1965
Wilson, Craig . . . . . . . . .2005
Wiggins, Al . . . . . . . . . . .1994
Wrightson, Bernie . . . . . . .1984
Yorzyk, Bill . . . . . . . . . . .1971

## U.S. Women

Andersen, Teresa . . . . . . .1986
Atwood, Sue . . . . . . . . . .1992
Babashoff, Shirley . . . . . .1982
Babb-Sprague, Kristen . . . .1999
Ball, Catie . . . . . . . . . . .1976
+ Bauer, Sybil . . . . . . . . . .1967
Bean, Dawn Pawson . . . . .1996
Belote, Melissa . . . . . . . .1983
Bleibtrey, Ethelda . . . . . . .1967
+ Boyle, Charlotte . . . . . . . .1988
Bruner, Jayne Owen . . . . . .1998
Burke, Lynn . . . . . . . . . .1978
Bush, Lesley . . . . . . . . . .1986
Callen, Gloria . . . . . . . . .1984
Caretto, Patty . . . . . . . . .1987
Carr, Cathy . . . . . . . . . .1988
Caulkins, Tracy . . . . . . . .1990
+ Chadwick, Florence . . . . . .1970
Chandler, Jennifer . . . . . . .1987
Cohen, Tiffany . . . . . . . . .1996
+ Coleman, Georgia . . . . . . .1966
Cone, Carin . . . . . . . . . .1984
Costie, Candy . . . . . . . . .1995
Cox, Lynne . . . . . . . . . . .2000
Crlenkovich, Helen . . . . . . .1981
Curtis, Ann . . . . . . . . . . .1966
Daniel, Ellie . . . . . . . . . .1997
de Varona, Donna . . . . . . .1969
Dean, Penny . . . . . . . . . .1996
+ Dorfner, Olga . . . . . . . . .1970
Draves, Vickie . . . . . . . . .1969
Duenkel, Ginny . . . . . . . .1985
Dunbar, Barbara . . . . . . . .2000
Dyroen-Lancer, Becky . . . . .2004
Ederle, Gertrude . . . . . . . .1965
Ellis, Kathy . . . . . . . . . . .1991
Elsener, Patty . . . . . . . . .2002
Evans, Janet . . . . . . . . . .2001
Fauntz, Jane . . . . . . . . . .1991
Ferguson, Cathy . . . . . . . .1978

Finneran, Sharon . . . . . . .1985
+ Fulton, Patty Robinson . . . .2001
+ Galligan, Claire . . . . . . . .1970
+ Garatti-Seville, Eleanor . . . .1992
Gestring, Marjorie . . . . . . .1976
Gossick, Sue . . . . . . . . . .1988
+ Guest, Irene . . . . . . . . . .1990
Gundling, Buelah . . . . . . .1965
Hall, Kaye . . . . . . . . . . .1979
Henne, Jan . . . . . . . . . . .1979
Hogan, Peg . . . . . . . . . .2002
Hogshead, Nancy . . . . . . .1994
Holm, Eleanor . . . . . . . . .1966
Hunt-Newman, Virginia . . . .1993
Johnson, Gail . . . . . . . . .1983
Josephson, Karen . . . . . . .1997
Josephson, Sarah . . . . . . .1997
+ Kaufman, Beth . . . . . . . . .1967
+ Kight, Lenore . . . . . . . . .1981
King, Micki . . . . . . . . . . .1978
Kolb, Claudia . . . . . . . . .1975
+ Lackie, Ethel . . . . . . . . . .1969
+ Landon, Alice Lord . . . . . . .1993
Linehan, Kim . . . . . . . . . .1997
+ Madison, Helene . . . . . . . .1966
Mann, Shelly . . . . . . . . . .1966
McCormick, Kelly . . . . . . . .1999
McGrath, Margo . . . . . . . .1989
McKim, Josephine . . . . . . .1991
Meagher, Mary T. . . . . . . .1993
+ Meany, Helen . . . . . . . . .1971
Merlino, Maxine . . . . . . . .1999
Meyer, Debbie . . . . . . . . .1977
Mitchell, Betsy . . . . . . . . .1998
Mitchell, Michele . . . . . . . .1995
Moe, Karen . . . . . . . . . . .1992
Morris, Pam . . . . . . . . . .1965
Mueller, Ardeth . . . . . . . .1996
Neilson, Sandra . . . . . . . .1986
Neyer, Megan . . . . . . . . .1997

+ Norelius, Martha . . . . . . . .1967
Olsen, Zoe Ann . . . . . . . .1989
O'Rourke, Heidi . . . . . . . .1980
+ Osipowich, Albina . . . . . . .1986
Pedersen, Susan . . . . . . . .1995
Pinkston, Betty Becker . . . .1967
Pope, Paula Jean Meyers . .1979
Potter, Cynthia . . . . . . . . .1987
+ Poynton, Dorothy . . . . . . .1968
+ Rawls, Katherine . . . . . . . .1965
Redmond, Carol . . . . . . . .1989
Riggin, Aileen . . . . . . . . .1967
Roper, Gail . . . . . . . . . . .1997
Ross, Anne . . . . . . . . . . .1984
Rothhammer, Keena . . . . . .1991
Ruiz-Conforto, Tracie . . . . .1993
Ruuska, Sylvia . . . . . . . . .1976
Sanders, Summer . . . . . . .2002
Schuler, Carolyn . . . . . . . .1989
Seller, Peg . . . . . . . . . . .1988
+ Smith, Caroline . . . . . . . .1988
Steinseifer, Carrie . . . . . . .1999
Sterkel, Jill . . . . . . . . . . .2002
Stouder, Sharon . . . . . . . .1972
+ Toner, Vee . . . . . . . . . . .1995
Val, Laura . . . . . . . . . . . .2003
+ Vilen, Kay . . . . . . . . . . . .1978
Von Saltza, Chris . . . . . . . .1966
+ Wainwright, Helen . . . . . . .1972
Walker, Clara Lamore . . . . .1995
+ Watson, Lillian (Pokey) . . . .1984
Wayte, Mary . . . . . . . . . .2000
Wehselau, Mariechen . . . . .1989
Welshons, Kim . . . . . . . . .1988
Wichman, Sharon . . . . . . .1991
Williams, Esther . . . . . . . .1966
+ Woodbridge, Margaret . . . . .1989
Woodhead, Cynthia . . . . . .1994
Wyland, Wendy . . . . . . . .2001

## TENNIS

## International Tennis Hall of Fame

Originally the National Tennis Hall of Fame. Established in 1953 by James Van Alen and sanctioned by the U.S. Tennis Association in 1954. Renamed the International Tennis Hall of Fame in 1976. **Address:** 194 Bellevue Ave., Newport, RI 02840.
**Telephone:** (401) 849-3990. **Web:** www.tennisfame.com

**Eligibility:** Nominated players must be five years removed from being a "significant factor" in competitive tennis. Voting done by members of the international tennis media.

**Class of 2005** (4): **Jim Courier, Yannick Noah, Jana Novotna** and **Earl "Butch" Buchholz Jr.**.

Members are listed with year of induction; (+) indicates deceased members.

### Men

| | | |
|---|---|---|
| + Adee, George . . . . . . . . . .1964 | + Griffin, Clarence . . . . . . .1970 | + Pettitt, Tom . . . . . . . . . . .1982 |
| + Alexander, Fred . . . . . . .1961 | + Hackett, Harold . . . . . . .1961 | Pietrangeli, Nicola . . . .1986 |
| + Allison, Wilmer . . . . . . .1963 | Hewitt, Bob . . . . . . . . . .1992 | + Quist, Adrian . . . . . . . . .1984 |
| + Alonso, Manuel . . . . . . .1977 | + Hoad, Lew . . . . . . . . . .1980 | Ralston, Dennis . . . . . . .1987 |
| Anderson, Malcolm . . .2000 | + Hovey, Fred . . . . . . . . . .1974 | + Renshaw, Ernest . . . . . .1983 |
| + Ashe, Arthur . . . . . . . . . .1985 | + Hunt, Joe . . . . . . . . . . . .1966 | + Renshaw, William . . . . .1983 |
| + Austin, Bunny . . . . . . . . .1997 | + Hunter, Frank . . . . . . . .1961 | + Richards, Vincent . . . . .1961 |
| Becker, Boris . . . . . . . . .2003 | + Johnston, Bill . . . . . . . . .1958 | + Riggs, Bobby . . . . . . . . .1967 |
| + Behr, Karl . . . . . . . . . . . .1969 | + Jones, Perry . . . . . . . . . .1970 | Roche, Tony . . . . . . . . .1986 |
| Borg, Bjorn . . . . . . . . . .1987 | Kelleher, Robert . . . . . .2000 | Rose, Mervyn . . . . . . . .2001 |
| + Borotra, Jean . . . . . . . . .1976 | Kodes, Jan . . . . . . . . . .1990 | Rosewall, Ken . . . . . . . .1980 |
| + Bromwich, John . . . . . . .1984 | Kramer, Jack . . . . . . . . .1968 | Santana, Manuel . . . . .1984 |
| + Brookes, Norman . . . . . .1977 | + Lacoste, Rene . . . . . . . .1976 | Savitt, Dick . . . . . . . . . .1976 |
| + Brugnon, Jacques . . . . .1976 | + Larned, William . . . . . . .1956 | Schroeder, Ted . . . . . . .1966 |
| + Budge, Don . . . . . . . . . .1964 | Larsen, Art . . . . . . . . . .1969 | + Sears, Richard . . . . . . . .1955 |
| + Campbell, Oliver . . . . . .1955 | Laver, Rod . . . . . . . . . .1981 | Sedgman, Frank . . . . . .1979 |
| + Chace, Malcolm . . . . . .1961 | Lendl, Ivan . . . . . . . . . .2001 | Segura, Pancho . . . . . .1984 |
| + Clark, Clarence . . . . . . .1983 | + Lott, George . . . . . . . . . .1964 | Seixas, Vic . . . . . . . . . .1971 |
| + Clark, Joseph . . . . . . . . .1955 | Mako, Gene . . . . . . . . .1973 | + Shields, Frank . . . . . . . .1964 |
| + Clothier, William . . . . . .1956 | McEnroe, John . . . . . . .1999 | + Slocum, Henry . . . . . . . .1955 |
| + Cochet, Henri . . . . . . . .1976 | McGregor, Ken . . . . . . .1999 | Smith, Stan . . . . . . . . . .1987 |
| Connors, Jimmy . . . . . .1998 | + McKinley, Chuck . . . . . .1986 | Stolle, Fred . . . . . . . . . .1985 |
| Cooper, Ashley . . . . . . .1991 | + McLoughlin, Maurice . . .1957 | + Talbert, Bill . . . . . . . . . .1967 |
| Courier, Jim . . . . . . . . . .2005 | McMillan, Frew . . . . . . .1992 | + Tilden, Bill . . . . . . . . . . .1959 |
| + Crawford, Jack . . . . . . . .1979 | + McNeill, Don . . . . . . . . .1965 | Trabert, Tony . . . . . . . .1970 |
| + David, Herman . . . . . . . .1998 | Mulloy, Gardnar . . . . . .1972 | + Van Ryn, John . . . . . . . .1963 |
| + Doeg, John . . . . . . . . . . .1962 | + Murray, Lindley . . . . . . .1958 | Vilas, Guillermo . . . . . .1991 |
| Drobny, Jaroslav . . . . . .1983 | + Myrick, Julian . . . . . . . .1963 | + Vines, Ellsworth . . . . . .1962 |
| + Dwight, James . . . . . . . .1955 | Nastase, Ilie . . . . . . . . .1991 | + von Cramm, Gottfried . .1977 |
| Edberg, Stefan . . . . . . .2004 | Newcombe, John . . . . .1986 | + Ward, Holcombe . . . . . .1956 |
| Emerson, Roy . . . . . . . .1982 | + Nielsen, Arthur . . . . . . .1971 | + Washburn, Watson . . . . .1965 |
| + Etchebaster, Pierre . . . . .1978 | Noah, Yannick . . . . . . .2005 | + Whitman, Malcolm . . . .1955 |
| Falkenburg, Bob . . . . . .1974 | Olmedo, Alex . . . . . . . .1987 | Wilander, Mats . . . . . . .2002 |
| Fraser, Neale . . . . . . . . .1984 | + Osuna, Rafael . . . . . . . .1979 | + Wilding, Anthony . . . . . .1978 |
| + Garland, Chuck . . . . . . .1969 | + Parker, Frank . . . . . . . . .1966 | + Williams, Richard 2nd . .1957 |
| + Gonzales, Pancho . . . . .1968 | + Patterson, Gerald . . . . . .1989 | Wood, Sidney . . . . . . . .1964 |
| + Grant, Bryan (Bitsy) . . . .1972 | Patty, Budge . . . . . . . . .1977 | + Wrenn, Robert . . . . . . . .1955 |
| | + Perry, Fred . . . . . . . . . . .1975 | + Wright, Beals . . . . . . . . .1956 |

### Women

| | | |
|---|---|---|
| + Atkinson, Juliette . . . . . .1974 | + Gibson, Althea . . . . . . . .1971 | Novotna, Jana . . . . . . .2005 |
| Austin, Tracy . . . . . . . . .1992 | Goolagong Cawley, Evonne 1988 | Navratilova, Martina . . .2000 |
| + Barger-Wallach, Maud . .1958 | Graf, Steffi . . . . . . . . . .2004 | + Nuthall Shoemaker, Betty .1977 |
| Betz Addie, Pauline . . . .1965 | + Hansell, Ellen . . . . . . . .1965 | Osborne duPont, Margaret .1967 |
| + Bjurstedt Mallory, Molla .1958 | Hard, Darlene . . . . . . . .1973 | + Palfrey Danzig, Sarah . . . .1963 |
| Bowrey, Lesley Turner . . .1997 | Hart, Doris . . . . . . . . . .1969 | Richey, Nancy . . . . . . .2003 |
| Brough Clapp, Louise . . .1967 | Haydon Jones, Ann . . . .1985 | + Roosevelt, Ellen . . . . . . .1975 |
| + Browne, Mary . . . . . . . .1957 | Heldman, Gladys . . . . .1979 | + Round Little, Dorothy . . .1986 |
| Bueno, Maria . . . . . . . . .1978 | + Hotchkiss Wightman, Hazel 1957 | + Ryan, Elizabeth . . . . . . .1972 |
| + Cahill, Mabel . . . . . . . . .1976 | + Jacobs, Helen Hull . . . .1962 | + Sears, Eleanora . . . . . . .1968 |
| Casals, Rosie . . . . . . . . .1996 | King, Billie Jean . . . . . .1987 | Shriver, Pam . . . . . . . . .2002 |
| Cheney, Dorothy (Dodo) .2004 | + Lenglen, Suzanne . . . . . .1978 | Smith Court, Margaret . .1979 |
| + Connolly Brinker, Maureen 1968 | Mandlikova, Hana . . . . .1994 | + Sutton Bundy, May . . . . .1956 |
| + Dod, Charlotte (Lottie) . . .1983 | + Marble, Alice . . . . . . . .1964 | + Townsend Toulmin, Bertha .1974 |
| + Douglass Chambers, Dorothy 1981 | + McKane Godfree, Kitty . .1978 | Wade, Virginia . . . . . . .1989 |
| Dürr, Françoise . . . . . . .2003 | Moore, Elisabeth . . . . . .1971 | + Wagner, Marie . . . . . . . .1969 |
| Evert, Chris . . . . . . . . . .1995 | Mortimer Barrett, Angela 1993 | + Wills Moody Roark, Helen .1959 |
| Fry Irvin, Shirley . . . . . .1970 | | |

### Contributors

| | | |
|---|---|---|
| + Baker, Lawrence Sr . . . . .1975 | + Gustaf, V (King of Sweden) .1980 | + Outerbridge, Mary . . . . .1981 |
| Buchholz, Eral (Butch) . . . .2005 | + Hester, W.E. (Slew) . . . . .1981 | + Pell, Theodore . . . . . . . .1966 |
| + Chatrier, Philippe . . . . . .1992 | + Hopman, Harry . . . . . . .1978 | + Tingay, Lance . . . . . . . .1982 |
| Collins, Bud . . . . . . . . .1994 | Hunt, Lamar . . . . . . . . .1993 | + Tinling, Ted . . . . . . . . . .1986 |
| + Cullman, Joseph F. 3rd . .1990 | + Laney, Al . . . . . . . . . . . .1979 | Tobin, John . . . . . . . . . .2003 |
| + Danzig, Allison . . . . . . .1968 | Martin, Alastair . . . . . . .1973 | + Van Alen, James . . . . . . .1965 |
| + Davis, Dwight . . . . . . . .1956 | + Martin, William M. . . . . .1982 | + Wingfield, Walter Clopton .1997 |
| + Gray, David . . . . . . . . . .1985 | + Maskell, Dan . . . . . . . . .1996 | |

## TRACK & FIELD

# National Track & Field Hall of Fame

Established in 1974 by the The Athletics Congress (now USA Track & Field). Originally located in Charleston, WV, the Hall moved to Indianapolis in 1983 and opened at the Hoosier Dome (now RCA Dome) in 1986. The Hall moved to Manhattan and reopened at the 168th Street Armory in early 2004. **Address:** 216 Fort Washington Ave., New York, NY 10032. **Telephone:** (212) 923-1803, ext. 10. **Web:** www.trackhall.com.

**Eligibility:** Nominated athletes must be retired three years and coaches must have coached at least 20 years if retired or 35 years if still coaching. Voting done by 800-member panel made up of Hall of Fame and USA Track & Field officials, Hall of Fame members, current U.S. champions and members of the Track & Field Writers of America. The coaches and contributors are not listed below.

**Class of 2004** (10): MEN—**Mike Conley** (triple jump/long jump), **Jack Davis** (hurdles), **Otis Davis** (sprinter), **Michael Johnson** (sprinter), **Gerry Lindgren** (distance), **John Pennel** (pole vault). WOMEN—**Jackie Joyner-Kersee** (heptathlon) and **Joan Samuelson** (distance). Members are listed with year of induction; (+) indicates deceased members.

## Men

| | | |
|---|---|---|
| + Albritton, Dave ....1980 | + Hubbard, DeHart ......1979 | Pennel, John ..........2004 |
| Ashenfelter, Horace ...1975 | James, Larry .........2003 | + Prefontaine, Steve ....1976 |
| Banks, Willie ........1999 | Jenkins, Charlie .......1992 | Prinstein, Meyer ......2000 |
| + Bausch, James ........1979 | Jenner, Bruce ........1980 | + Ray, Joie ...........1976 |
| Beamon, Bob .........1977 | + Johnson, Cornelius .....1994 | + Rice, Greg ..........1977 |
| Beatty, Jim ..........1990 | Johnson, Michael ......2004 | Richards, Rev. Bob .....1975 |
| Bell, Earl ...........2002 | Johnson, Rafer ........1974 | Robinson, Arnie .......2000 |
| Bell, Greg ...........1988 | Jones, Hayes .........1976 | Rodgers, Bill .........1999 |
| + Boeckmann, Dee .......1976 | + Kelley, John A. ........1980 | + Rose, Ralph .........1976 |
| Boston, Ralph ........1974 | + Kiviat, Abel ..........1985 | Ryun, Jim ...........1980 |
| + Borican, Jonn ........2000 | + Kraenzlein, Alvin ......1974 | Salazar, Alberto ......2001 |
| Bragg, Don ..........1996 | Laird, Ron ...........1986 | + Scholz, Jackson ......1977 |
| + Calhoun, Lee .........1974 | Larrabee, Mike ........2003 | Schul, Bob ..........1991 |
| Campbell, Milt ........1989 | + Lash, Don ...........1995 | Scott, Steve .........2002 |
| Carlos, John .........2003 | + Laskau, Henry ........1997 | Seagren, Bob .........1986 |
| Carr, Henry ..........1997 | Lewis, Carl ..........2001 | + Sheppard, Mel ........1976 |
| + Clark, Ellery .........1991 | Lindgren, Gerry .......2004 | + Sheridan, Martin ......1988 |
| Conley, Mike .........2004 | Liquori, Marty ........1995 | Shorter, Frank ........1989 |
| Connolly, Harold ......1984 | Long, Dr. Dallas .......1996 | Silvester, Jay ........1998 |
| Courtney, Tom ........1978 | Marsh, Henry .........2001 | Sime, Dave ..........1981 |
| Cunningham, Glenn .....1974 | Mathias, Bob .........1974 | + Simpson, Robert ......1974 |
| + Curtis, William .......1979 | Matson, Randy ........1984 | Smith, Tommie ........1978 |
| + Davenport, Willie .....1982 | McCluskey, Joe ........1996 | + Stanfield, Andy .......1977 |
| Davis, Glenn .........1974 | + Meadows, Earle .......1996 | Steers, Les ..........1974 |
| Davis, Harold ........1974 | + Meredith, Ted ........1982 | Stones, Dwight ........1998 |
| Davis, Jack ..........2004 | + Metcalfe, Ralph .......1975 | + Taylor, Frederick Morgan ..2000 |
| Davis, Otis ..........2004 | + Milburn, Rod .........1993 | + Tewksbury, Dr. Walter ...1996 |
| Dillard, Harrison ......1974 | Mills, Billy ..........1976 | Thomas, John .........1985 |
| Dumas, Charles .......1990 | Moore, Charles ........1999 | + Thomson, Earl ........1977 |
| Evans, Lee ..........1983 | Moore, Tom ..........1988 | + Thorpe, Jim .........1975 |
| + Ewell, Barney ........1986 | Morrow, Bobby ........1975 | + Tolan, Eddie ........1982 |
| + Ewry, Ray ..........1974 | + Mortensen, Jess .......1992 | Toomey, Bill .........1975 |
| + Flanagan, John .......1975 | Moses, Edwin .........1994 | + Towns, Forrest (Spec) ...1976 |
| Fosbury, Dick .........1981 | + Myers, Lawrence .......1974 | Warmerdam, Cornelius ...1974 |
| Foster, Greg .........1998 | Myricks, Larry ........2001 | Whitfield, Mal ........1974 |
| + Gordien, Fortune ......1979 | Nehemiah, Renaldo .....1997 | Wilkins, Mac .........1993 |
| Greene, Charles .......1992 | O'Brien, Parry ........1974 | + Williams, Archie ......1992 |
| + Hahn, Archie ........1983 | Oerter, Al ...........1974 | Wohlhuter, Rick .......1990 |
| Hardin, Glenn ........1978 | + Osborn, Harold .......1974 | Woodruff, John ........1978 |
| + Hayes, Bob ..........1976 | + Owens, Jesse .........1974 | Wottle, Dave .........1982 |
| Held, Bud ...........1987 | + Paddock, Charlie ......1976 | + Wykoff, Frank ........1977 |
| Hines, Jim ..........1979 | Patton, Mel ..........1985 | Young, George ........1981 |
| + Houser, Bud .........1979 | + Peacock, Eulace ......1987 | Young, Larry .........2002 |

## Women

| | | |
|---|---|---|
| Ashford, Evelyn .......1997 | + Jackson, Nell ........1989 | Seidler, Maren ........2000 |
| Brisco, Valerie .......1995 | Joyner-Kersee, Jackie ...2004 | + Shiley Newhouse, Jean ..1993 |
| Cheeseborough, Chandra .2000 | Larrieu Smith, Francie ...1998 | Slaney, Mary .........2003 |
| Coachman, Alice .......1975 | Manning-Mims, Madeline ..1984 | + Stephens, Helen ......1975 |
| + Copeland, Lillian ......1994 | McDaniel, Mildred ......1983 | Torrence, Gwen ........2002 |
| + Didrikson, Babe .......1974 | McGuire, Edith ........1979 | Tyus, Wyomia .........1980 |
| + Faggs, Mae ..........1976 | Ritter, Louise ........1995 | + Walsh, Stella ........1975 |
| Ferrell, Barbara .......1988 | + Robinson, Betty .......1977 | Watson, Martha ........1987 |
| + Griffith Joyner, Florence ..1995 | + Rudolph, Wilma .......1974 | White, Willye .........1981 |
| + Hall Adams, Evelyne ....1988 | Samuelson, Joan .......2004 | |
| Heritage, Doris Brown ....1990 | Schmidt, Kate .........1994 | |

## WOMEN

# International Women's Sports Hall of Fame

Established in 1980 by the Women's Sports Foundation. **Address:** Women's Sports Foundation, Eisenhower Park, East Meadow, NY 11554. **Telephone:** (516) 542-4700.

**Eligibility:** Nominees' achievements and commitment to the development of women's sports must be internationally recognized. Athletes are elected in two categories—Pioneer (before 1960) and Contemporary (since 1960). Members are divided below by sport for the sake of easy reference; (*) indicates member inducted in Pioneer category. Coaching nominees must have coached at least 10 years. Members are listed with year of induction; (+) indicates deceased members.

**Class of 2004** (3): CONTEMPORARY—**Maria Esther Bueno** (tennis) and **Nancy Hogshead-Makar** (swimming); COACH—**Beverly Kearney** (track & field).

**Note: Charlotte Dod** is inducted for tennis, as well as archery and golf; **Marie Marvingt** is inducted for aviation, as well as mountaineering; **Eleanora Sears** is inducted for golf, as well as polo and squash.

### Alpine Skiing
| | |
|---|---|
| Cranz, Christl* | 1991 |
| + Golden Brosnihan, Diana | 1997 |
| Lawrence, Andrea Mead* | 1983 |
| Moser-Proell, Annemarie | 1982 |

### Auto Racing
| | |
|---|---|
| Guthrie, Janet | 1980 |

### Aviation
| | |
|---|---|
| + Coleman, Bessie* | 1992 |
| + Earhart, Amelia* | 1980 |
| + Marvingt, Marie* | 1987 |

### Badminton
| | |
|---|---|
| Hashman, Judy Devlin* | 1995 |

### Baseball
| | |
|---|---|
| Stone, Toni* | 1993 |

### Basketball
| | |
|---|---|
| Meyers, Ann | 1985 |
| Miller, Cheryl | 1991 |

### Bowling
| | |
|---|---|
| Ladewig, Marion* | 1984 |

### Cycling
| | |
|---|---|
| Carpenter Phinney, Connie | 1990 |

### Diving
| | |
|---|---|
| Gào, Min | 2003 |
| King, Micki | 1983 |
| McCormick, Pat* | 1984 |
| Riggin, Aileen* | 1988 |

### Equestrian
| | |
|---|---|
| Hartel, Lis | 1994 |

### Fencing
| | |
|---|---|
| Schacherer-Elek, Ilona* | 1989 |

### Figure Skating
| | |
|---|---|
| Albright, Tenley* | 1983 |
| + Blanchard, Theresa Weld* | 1989 |
| Fleming, Peggy | 1981 |
| Heiss Jenkins, Carol* | 1992 |
| + Henie, Sonja* | 1982 |
| Protopopov, Ludmila | 1992 |
| Rodnina, Irena | 1988 |
| Scott-King, Barbara Ann* | 1997 |
| Torvill, Jayne | 2002 |

### Golf
| | |
|---|---|
| Berg, Patty* | 1980 |
| Carner, JoAnne | 1987 |
| Haynie, Sandra | 1999 |
| Hicks, Betty* | 1995 |
| Jameson, Betty* | 1999 |
| Mann, Carol | 1982 |
| Rawls, Betsy* | 1986 |
| + Sears, Eleanora | 1984 |
| Suggs, Louise* | 1987 |
| + Vare, Glenna Collett* | 1981 |
| Whitworth, Kathy | 1984 |
| Wright, Mickey | 1981 |

### Golf/Track & Field
| | |
|---|---|
| + Zaharias, Babe Didrikson* | 1980 |

### Gymnastics
| | |
|---|---|
| Caslavska, Vera | 1991 |
| Comaneci, Nadia | 1990 |
| Korbut, Olga | 1982 |
| Latynina, Larysa* | 1985 |
| Retton, Mary Lou | 1993 |
| Tourischeva, Lyudmila | 1987 |

### Orienteering
| | |
|---|---|
| Kringstad, Annichen | 1995 |

### Shooting
| | |
|---|---|
| Murdock, Margaret | 1988 |

### Softball
| | |
|---|---|
| Joyce, Joan | 1989 |

### Speed Skating
| | |
|---|---|
| + Klein Outland, Kit* | 1993 |
| Young, Sheila | 1981 |

### Squash
| | |
|---|---|
| McKay, Heather* | 2003 |

### Swimming
| | |
|---|---|
| Caulkins, Tracy | 1986 |
| + Chadwick, Florence* | 1996 |
| Curtis Cuneo, Ann* | 1985 |
| de Varona, Donna | 1983 |
| Ederle, Gertrude* | 1980 |
| Fraser, Dawn | 1985 |
| Hogshead-Makar, Nancy | 2004 |
| Holm, Eleanor* | 1980 |
| Meagher, Mary T. | 1993 |
| Meyer-Reyes, Debbie | 1987 |
| Ruiz-Confronto, Tracie | 2001 |

### Tennis
| | |
|---|---|
| Bueno, Maria Esther* | 2004 |
| + Connolly, Maureen* | 1987 |
| + Dod, Charlotte (Lottie)* | 1986 |
| Evert, Chris | 1981 |
| + Gibson, Althea* | 1980 |
| Goolagong Cawley, Evonne | 1989 |
| + Hotchkiss Wightman, Hazel* | 1986 |
| King, Billie Jean | 1980 |
| + Lenglen, Suzanne* | 1984 |
| Navratilova, Martina | 1984 |
| Osbourne du Pont, Margaret* | 1998 |
| + Sears, Eleanora* | 1984 |
| Smith Court, Margaret | 1986 |

### Track & Field
| | |
|---|---|
| Ashford, Evelyn | 1997 |
| Blankers-Koen, Fanny* | 1982 |
| Brisco, Valerie | 2002 |
| Cheng, Chi | 1994 |
| Coachman Davis, Alice* | 1991 |
| Cuthbert, Betty* | 2002 |
| + Faggs Star, Aeriwentha Mae* | 1996 |
| + Griffith Joyner, Florence | 1998 |
| Joyner-Kersee, Jackie | 2003 |
| Manning Mims, Madeline | 1987 |
| Nelson, Marjorie Jackson* | 2001 |
| + Rudolph, Wilma | 1980 |
| Samuelson, Joan Benoit | 1999 |
| + Stephens, Helen* | 1983 |
| Strickland de la Hunty, Shirley* | 1998 |
| Szewinska, Irena | 1992 |
| Tyus, Wyomia | 1981 |
| Waitz, Grete | 1995 |
| White, Willye | 1988 |

### Volleyball
| | |
|---|---|
| + Hyman, Flo | 1986 |

### Water Skiing
| | |
|---|---|
| McGuire, Willa Worthington* | 1990 |

### Coaches
| | |
|---|---|
| + Applebee, Constance | 1991 |
| Backus, Sharron | 1993 |
| Carver, Chris | 2001 |
| Conradt, Judy | 1995 |
| Emery, Gail | 1997 |
| Franke, Nikki | 2002 |
| Green, Tina Sloan | 1999 |
| Grossfeld, Muriel | 1991 |
| Holum, Diana | 1996 |
| Jacket, Barbara | 1995 |
| + Jackson, Nell | 1990 |
| Kanakogi, Rusty | 1994 |
| Kearney, Beverly | 2004 |
| Summitt, Pat Head | 1990 |
| VanDerveer, Tara | 1998 |
| Vollstedt, Linda | 2003 |
| + Wade, Margaret | 1992 |

## RETIRED NUMBERS

# Major League Baseball

The New York Yankees have retired the most uniform numbers (14) in the major leagues; followed by the Brooklyn/Los Angeles Dodgers (10), the St. Louis Cardinals (9), the Chicago White Sox, the Pittsburgh Pirates and New York/San Francisco Giants (8). **Jackie Robinson** had his #42 retired by Major League Baseball in 1997. Players who were already wearing the number were allowed to continue to do so. Los Angeles had already retired Robinson's number so he's only listed with the Dodgers below. **Nolan Ryan** has had his number retired by three teams—#34 by Texas and Houston and #30 by California (now Los Angeles Angels of Anaheim). Six players and a manager have had their numbers retired by two teams: **Hank Aaron**—#44 by the Boston/Milwaukee/Atlanta Braves and the Milwaukee Brewers; **Rod Carew**—#29 by Minnesota and California (now Anaheim); **Rollie Fingers**—#34 by Milwaukee and Oakland; **Carlton Fisk**—#27 by Boston and #72 by the Chicago White Sox; **Reggie Jackson**— #9 by the Oakland Athletics and #44 by the New York Yankees; **Frank Robinson**—#20 by Cincinnati and Baltimore; **Casey Stengel**—#37 by the New York Yankees and New York Mets.

**Number retired in 2005** (5): CHICAGO CUBS—#23 worn by **Ryne Sandberg** (1982-97 with Cubs); CINCINNATI REDS—#10 worn by manager **Sparky Anderson** (1970-78 with Reds); HOUSTON ASTROS—#24 worn by **Jimmy Wynn** (1963-73 with Astros); OAKLAND ATHLETICS—#43 worn by **Dennis Eckersley** (1987-95 with A's); SAN FRANCISCO GIANTS—#36 worn by **Gaylord Perry** (1962-71 with Giants).

## American League

Two AL teams—the Seattle Mariners and the Toronto Blue Jays—have not retired any numbers. The Blue Jays have a "level of excellence" which includes Joe Carter (#29), Tony Fernandez (#1), Dave Stieb (#11), George Bell (#37), and Cito Gaston (#43). All numbers have been used in recent years, however.

### Baltimore Orioles
- 4 Earl Weaver
- 5 Brooks Robinson
- 8 Cal Ripken Jr.
- 20 Frank Robinson
- 22 Jim Palmer
- 33 Eddie Murray

### Boston Red Sox
- 1 Bobby Doerr
- 4 Joe Cronin
- 8 Carl Yastrzemski
- 9 Ted Williams
- 27 Carlton Fisk

### Chicago White Sox
- 2 Nellie Fox
- 3 Harold Baines
- 4 Luke Appling
- 9 Minnie Minoso
- 11 Luis Aparicio
- 16 Ted Lyons
- 19 Billy Pierce
- 72 Carlton Fisk

### Cleveland Indians
- 3 Earl Averill
- 5 Lou Boudreau
- 14 Larry Doby
- 18 Mel Harder
- 19 Bob Feller
- 21 Bob Lemon
- 455 Fans (# of consecutive sellouts)

### Detroit Tigers
- 2 Charlie Gehringer
- 5 Hank Greenberg
- 6 Al Kaline
- 16 Hal Newhouser
- 23 Willie Horton

### Kansas City Royals
- 5 George Brett
- 10 Dick Howser
- 20 Frank White

### LA Angels of Anaheim
- 11 Jim Fregosi
- 26 Gene Autry
- 29 Rod Carew
- 30 Nolan Ryan
- 50 Jimmie Reese

### Minnesota Twins
- 3 Harmon Killebrew
- 6 Tony Oliva
- 14 Kent Hrbek
- 29 Rod Carew
- 34 Kirby Puckett

### Oakland Athletics
- 9 Reggie Jackson
- 27 Catfish Hunter
- 34 Rollie Fingers
- 43 Dennis Eckersley

### New York Yankees
- 1 Billy Martin
- 3 Babe Ruth
- 4 Lou Gehrig
- 5 Joe DiMaggio
- 7 Mickey Mantle
- 8 Yogi Berra & Bill Dickey
- 9 Roger Maris
- 10 Phil Rizzuto
- 15 Thurman Munson
- 16 Whitey Ford
- 23 Don Mattingly
- 32 Elston Howard
- 37 Casey Stengel
- 44 Reggie Jackson
- 49 Ron Guidry

### Tampa Bay Devil Rays
- 12 Wade Boggs

### Texas Rangers
- 34 Nolan Ryan

## National League

Two NL teams—the Arizona Diamondbacks and Colorado Rockies—have not retired any numbers. San Francisco has honored former NY Giants Christy Mathewson and John McGraw even though they played before numbers were worn. As did the Philadelphia Phillies for Grover Cleveland Alexander and Chuck Klein.

### Atlanta Braves
- 3 Dale Murphy
- 21 Warren Spahn
- 35 Phil Niekro
- 41 Eddie Mathews
- 44 Hank Aaron

### Chicago Cubs
- 10 Ron Santo
- 14 Ernie Banks
- 23 Ryne Sandberg
- 26 Billy Williams

### Cincinnati Reds
- 1 Fred Hutchinson
- 5 Johnny Bench
- 8 Joe Morgan
- 10 Sparky Anderson
- 18 Ted Kluszewski
- 20 Frank Robinson
- 24 Tony Perez

### Florida Marlins
- 5 Carl Barger

### Houston Astros
- 24 Jimmy Wynn
- 25 Jose Cruz
- 32 Jim Umbricht
- 33 Mike Scott
- 34 Nolan Ryan
- 40 Don Wilson
- 49 Larry Dierker

### Los Angeles Dodgers
- 1 Pee Wee Reese
- 2 Tommy Lasorda
- 4 Duke Snider
- 19 Jim Gilliam
- 20 Don Sutton
- 24 Walter Alston
- 32 Sandy Koufax
- 39 Roy Campanella
- 42 Jackie Robinson
- 53 Don Drysdale

### Milwaukee Brewers
- 4 Paul Molitor
- 19 Robin Yount
- 34 Rollie Fingers
- 44 Hank Aaron

### New York Mets
- 14 Gil Hodges
- 37 Casey Stengel
- 41 Tom Seaver

### Philadelphia Phillies
- 1 Richie Ashburn
- 14 Jim Bunning
- 20 Mike Schmidt
- 32 Steve Carlton
- 36 Robin Roberts

### Pittsburgh Pirates
- 1 Billy Meyer
- 4 Ralph Kiner
- 8 Willie Stargell
- 9 Bill Mazeroski
- 20 Pie Traynor
- 21 Roberto Clemente
- 33 Honus Wagner
- 40 Danny Murtaugh

### San Diego Padres
- 6 Steve Garvey
- 19 Tony Gwynn
- 31 Dave Winfield
- 35 Randy Jones

### San Francisco Giants
- 3 Bill Terry
- 4 Mel Ott
- 11 Carl Hubbell
- 24 Willie Mays
- 27 Juan Marichal
- 30 Orlando Cepeda
- 36 Gaylord Perry
- 44 Willie McCovey

### St. Louis Cardinals
- 1 Ozzie Smith
- 2 Red Schoendienst
- 6 Stan Musial
- 9 Enos Slaughter
- 14 Ken Boyer
- 17 Dizzy Dean
- 20 Lou Brock
- 45 Bob Gibson
- 85 August (Gussie) Busch

### Washington Nationals
- 8 Gary Carter
- 10 Rusty Staub & Andre Dawson
- 30 Tim Raines

## National Basketball Association

Boston has retired the most numbers (21) in the NBA, followed by Portland (9); the Rochester/Cincinnati Royals/K.C./Sacramento Kings, Syracuse Nats/Philadelphia 76ers and New York Knicks (8); Detroit, Los Angeles Lakers, Milwaukee and Phoenix Suns have (7); Cleveland and New Jersey have (6). **Wilt Chamberlain** is the only player to have his number retired by three teams: #13 by the LA Lakers, Golden State and Philadelphia; Nine players have had their numbers retired by two teams: **Kareem Abdul-Jabbar**—#33 by LA Lakers and Milwaukee; **Charles Barkley**—#34 by Philadelphia and Phoenix; **Clyde Drexler**—#22 by Houston and Portland; **Julius Erving**—#6 by Philadelphia and #32 by New Jersey; **Michael Jordan**—#23 by Chicago and Miami (in his honor); **Bob Lanier**—#16 by Detroit and Milwaukee; **Pete Maravich**—#7 by Utah and New Orleans; **Oscar Robertson**—#1 by Milwaukee and #14 by Sacramento; **Nate Thurmond**—#42 by Cleveland and Golden State.

**Numbers retired in 2004-05** (2): SEATTLE—#1 worn by **Gus Williams** (1977-84 with Sonics), CHICAGO—#33 worn by **Scottie Pippen** (1987-98 with Bulls).

## Eastern Conference

Two Eastern teams—the Charlotte Bobcats and Toronto Raptors—have not retired any numbers.

### Atlanta Hawks
| | |
|---|---|
| 9 | Bob Pettit |
| 21 | Dominique Wilkins |
| 23 | Lou Hudson |

### Boston Celtics
| | |
|---|---|
| 1 | Walter A. Brown |
| 2 | Red Auerbach |
| 2 | Dennis Johnson |
| 6 | Bill Russell |
| 10 | Jo Jo White |
| 14 | Bob Cousy |
| 15 | Tom Heinsohn |
| 16 | Tom (Satch) Sanders |
| 17 | John Havlicek |
| 18 | Dave Cowens |
| 19 | Don Nelson |
| 21 | Bill Sharman |
| 22 | Ed Macauley |
| 23 | Frank Ramsey |
| 24 | Sam Jones |
| 25 | K.C. Jones |
| 31 | Cedric Maxwell |
| 32 | Kevin McHale |
| 33 | Larry Bird |
| 35 | Reggie Lewis |
| 00 | Robert Parish |
| **Loscy** | Jim Loscutoff (#18) |
| **Radio mic** | Johnny Most |

### Chicago Bulls
| | |
|---|---|
| 4 | Jerry Sloan |
| 10 | Bob Love |
| 23 | Michael Jordan |
| 33 | Scottie Pippen |

### Cleveland Cavaliers
| | |
|---|---|
| 7 | Bingo Smith |
| 22 | Larry Nance |
| 25 | Mark Price |
| 34 | Austin Carr |
| 42 | Nate Thurmond |
| 43 | Brad Daugherty |

### Detroit Pistons
| | |
|---|---|
| 2 | Chuck Daly |
| 4 | Joe Dumars |
| 11 | Isiah Thomas |
| 15 | Vinnie Johnson |
| 16 | Bob Lanier |
| 21 | Dave Bing |
| 40 | Bill Laimbeer |

### Indiana Pacers
| | |
|---|---|
| 30 | George McGinnis |
| 34 | Mel Daniels |
| 35 | Roger Brown |
| 529 | Bob "Slick" Leonard |

### Miami Heat
| | |
|---|---|
| 23 | Michael Jordan |

### Milwaukee Bucks
| | |
|---|---|
| 1 | Oscar Robertson |
| 2 | Junior Bridgeman |
| 4 | Sidney Moncrief |
| 14 | Jon McGlocklin |
| 16 | Bob Lanier |
| 32 | Brian Winters |
| 33 | Kareem Abdul-Jabbar |

### New York Knicks
| | |
|---|---|
| 10 | Walt Frazier |
| 12 | Dick Barnett |
| 15 | Dick McGuire & Earl Monroe |
| 19 | Willis Reed |
| 22 | Dave DeBusschere |
| 24 | Bill Bradley |
| 33 | Patrick Ewing |
| 613 | Red Holzman |

### New Jersey Nets
| | |
|---|---|
| 3 | Drazen Petrovic |
| 4 | Wendell Ladner |
| 23 | John Williamson |
| 25 | Bill Melchionni |
| 32 | Julius Erving |
| 52 | Buck Williams |

### Orlando Magic
| | |
|---|---|
| 6 | Fans ("Sixth Man") |

### Philadelphia 76ers
| | |
|---|---|
| 2 | Moses Malone |
| 6 | Julius Erving |
| 10 | Maurice Cheeks |
| 13 | Wilt Chamberlain |
| 15 | Hal Greer |
| 24 | Bobby Jones |
| 32 | Billy Cunningham |
| 34 | Charles Barkley |
| **P.A. mic** | Dave Zinkoff |

### Washington Wizards
| | |
|---|---|
| 11 | Elvin Hayes |
| 25 | Gus Johnson |
| 41 | Wes Unseld |

## Western Conference

Two Western teams—the Los Angeles Clippers and Memphis Grizzlies—have not retired any numbers.

### Dallas Mavericks
| | |
|---|---|
| 15 | Brad Davis |
| 22 | Rolando Blackman |

### Denver Nuggets
| | |
|---|---|
| 2 | Alex English |
| 33 | David Thompson |
| 40 | Byron Beck |
| 44 | Dan Issel |
| 432 | Doug Moe |

### Golden St. Warriors
| | |
|---|---|
| 13 | Wilt Chamberlain |
| 14 | Tom Meschery |
| 16 | Al Attles |
| 24 | Rick Barry |
| 42 | Nate Thurmond |

### Houston Rockets
| | |
|---|---|
| 22 | Clyde Drexler |
| 23 | Calvin Murphy |
| 24 | Moses Malone |
| 34 | Hakeem Olajuwon |
| 45 | Rudy Tomjanovich |

### Los Angeles Lakers
| | |
|---|---|
| 13 | Wilt Chamberlain |
| 22 | Elgin Baylor |
| 25 | Gail Goodrich |
| 32 | Magic Johnson |
| 33 | Kareem Abdul-Jabbar |
| 42 | James Worthy |
| 44 | Jerry West |
| **Radio mic** | Chick Hearn |

### Minn. Timberwolves
| | |
|---|---|
| 2 | Malik Sealy |

### New Orleans Hornets
| | |
|---|---|
| 7 | Pete Maravich |
| 13 | Bobby Phills |

### Phoenix Suns
| | |
|---|---|
| 5 | Dick Van Arsdale |
| 6 | Walter Davis |
| 7 | Kevin Johnson |
| 9 | Dan Majerle |
| 24 | Tom Chambers |
| 33 | Alvan Adams |
| 34 | Charles Barkley |
| 42 | Connie Hawkins |
| 44 | Paul Westphal |

### Portland Trail Blazers
| | |
|---|---|
| 1 | Larry Weinberg |
| 13 | Dave Twardzik |
| 15 | Larry Steele |
| 20 | Maurice Lucas |
| 22 | Clyde Drexler |
| 32 | Bill Walton |
| 36 | Lloyd Neal |
| 45 | Geoff Petrie |
| 77 | Jack Ramsay |

### Sacramento Kings
| | |
|---|---|
| 1 | Nate Archibald |
| 2 | Mitch Richmond |
| 6 | Fans ("Sixth Man") |
| 11 | Bob Davies |
| 12 | Maurice Stokes |
| 14 | Oscar Robertson |
| 27 | Jack Twyman |
| 44 | Sam Lacey |

### San Antonio Spurs
| | |
|---|---|
| 13 | James Silas |
| 44 | George Gervin |
| 50 | David Robinson |
| 00 | Johnny Moore |

### Seattle SuperSonics
| | |
|---|---|
| 1 | Gus Williams |
| 10 | Nate McMillan |
| 19 | Lenny Wilkens |
| 32 | Fred Brown |
| 43 | Jack Sikma |
| **Radio mic** | Bob Blackburn |

### Utah Jazz
| | |
|---|---|
| 1 | Frank Layden |
| 7 | Pete Maravich |
| 12 | John Stockton |
| 14 | Jeff Hornacek |
| 35 | Darrell Griffith |
| 53 | Mark Eaton |

## Retired Numbers (Cont.)
## National Football League

The Chicago Bears have retired the most uniform numbers (13) in the NFL; followed by the New York Giants (11); the Dallas Texans/Kansas City Chiefs, Boston-New England Patriots and San Francisco (8); the Baltimore-Indianapolis Colts (7); Detroit and Philadelphia (6); Cleveland (5). No player has ever had his number retired by more than one NFL team.

**Number retired in 2004-05** (3): CAROLINA—#51 worn by **Sam Mills** (1995-97 with Panthers); GREEN BAY—#92 worn by **Reggie White** (1993-98 with Packers); NY JETS—#73 worn by **Joe Klecko** (1977-87 with Jets); SAN DIEGO—#19 worn by **Lance Alworth** (1962-70 with Chargers).

### AFC

Four AFC teams—the Baltimore Ravens, Houston Texans, Jacksonville Jaguars and Oakland Raiders—have not retired any numbers.

| | | | |
|---|---|---|---|
| **Buffalo Bills** | **Indianapolis Colts** | **Miami Dolphins** | **New York Jets** |
| 12 Jim Kelly | 19 Johnny Unitas | 12 Bob Griese | 12 Joe Namath |
| **Cincinnati Bengals** | 22 Buddy Young | 13 Dan Marino | 13 Don Maynard |
| 54 Bob Johnson | 24 Lenny Moore | 39 Larry Csonka | 73 Joe Klecko |
| **Cleveland Browns** | 70 Art Donovan | **New England** | **Pittsburgh Steelers** |
| 14 Otto Graham | 77 Jim Parker | **Patriots** | 70 Ernie Stautner |
| 32 Jim Brown | 82 Raymond Berry | 20 Gino Cappelletti | **San Diego** |
| 45 Ernie Davis | 89 Gino Marchetti | 40 Mike Haynes | **Chargers** |
| 46 Don Fleming | **Kansas City Chiefs** | 56 Andre Tippett | 14 Dan Fouts |
| 76 Lou Groza | 3 Jan Stenerud | 57 Steve Nelson | 19 Lance Alworth |
| **Denver Broncos** | 16 Len Dawson | 73 John Hannah | **Tennessee Titans** |
| 7 John Elway | 28 Abner Haynes | 78 Bruce Armstrong | 34 Earl Campbell |
| 18 Frank Tripucka | 33 Stone Johnson | 79 Jim Lee Hunt | 43 Jim Norton |
| 44 Floyd Little | 36 Mack Lee Hill | 89 Bob Dee | 63 Mike Munchak |
| | 63 Willie Lanier | | 65 Elvin Bethea |
| | 78 Bobby Bell | | |
| | 86 Buck Buchanan | | |

### NFC

Dallas is the only NFC team that hasn't officially retired any numbers. The Falcons haven't issued uniform #10 (Steve Bartkowski) and #78 (Mike Kenn) since those players retired. The Cowboys have a "Ring of Honor" at Texas Stadium that includes 15 players, one coach and one president/GM—Troy Aikman, Tony Dorsett, Cliff Harris, Bob Hayes, Chuck Howley, Michael Irvin, Lee Roy Jordan, Tom Landry, Bob Lilly, Don Meredith, Don Perkins, Mel Renfro, Tex Schramm, Emmitt Smith, Roger Staubach, Randy White and Rayfield Wright.

| | | | |
|---|---|---|---|
| **Arizona Cardinals** | **Detroit Lions** | **New York Giants** | **St. Louis Rams** |
| 8 Larry Wilson | 7 Dutch Clark | 1 Ray Flaherty | 7 Bob Waterfield |
| 40 Pat Tillman | 22 Bobby Layne | 4 Tuffy Leemans | 29 Eric Dickerson |
| 77 Stan Mauldin | 37 Doak Walker | 7 Mel Hein | 74 Merlin Olsen |
| 88 J.V. Cain | 56 Joe Schmidt | 11 Phil Simms | 78 Jackie Slater |
| 99 Marshall Goldberg | 85 Chuck Hughes | 14 Y.A. Tittle | 85 Jack Youngblood |
| **Atlanta Falcons** | 88 Charlie Sanders | 16 Frank Gifford | **San Francisco** |
| 31 William Andrews | **Green Bay** | 32 Al Blozis | **49ers** |
| 57 Jeff Van Note | **Packers** | 40 Joe Morrison | 12 John Brodie |
| 60 Tommy Nobis | 3 Tony Canadeo | 42 Charlie Conerly | 16 Joe Montana |
| **Carolina Panthers** | 14 Don Hutson | 50 Ken Strong | 34 Joe Perry |
| 51 Sam Mills | 15 Bart Starr | 56 Lawrence Taylor | 37 Jimmy Johnson |
| **Chicago Bears** | 66 Ray Nitschke | **Philadelphia** | 39 Hugh McElhenny |
| 3 Bronko Nagurski | 92 Reggie White | **Eagles** | 42 Ronnie Lott |
| 5 George McAfee | **Minnesota Vikings** | 15 Steve Van Buren | 70 Charlie Krueger |
| 7 George Halas | 10 Fran Tarkenton | 40 Tom Brookshier | 73 Leo Nomellini |
| 28 Willie Galimore | 53 Mick Tingelhoff | 44 Pete Retzlaff | 79 Bob St. Clair |
| 34 Walter Payton | 70 Jim Marshall | 60 Chuck Bednarik | 87 Dwight Clark |
| 40 Gale Sayers | 77 Korey Stringer | 70 Al Wistert | **Seattle Seahawks** |
| 41 Brian Piccolo | 80 Cris Carter | 99 Jerome Brown | 12 Fans ("12th Man") |
| 42 Sid Luckman | 88 Alan Page | | 80 Steve Largent |
| 51 Dick Butkus | **New Orleans** | | **Tampa Bay Bucs** |
| 56 Bill Hewitt | **Saints** | | 63 Lee Roy Selmon |
| 61 Bill George | 31 Jim Taylor | | **Wash. Redskins** |
| 66 Bulldog Turner | 81 Doug Atkins | | 33 Sammy Baugh |
| 77 Red Grange | | | |

## National Hockey League

The Boston Bruins have retired the most uniform numbers (10) in the NHL; followed by Montreal (7); N.Y. Islanders (6); Chicago and Detroit (5). Following his retirement in 1999, the NHL announced that the league would retire **Wayne Gretzky**'s #99. Three other players have had their numbers retired by two teams: **Gordie Howe**—#9 by Detroit and Hartford; **Bobby Hull**—#9 by Chicago and Winnipeg (now Phoenix); and **Ray Bourque**—#77 by Boston and Colorado.

**Numbers retired in 2004-05** (2): EDMONTON—#7 worn by **Paul Coffey** (1980-87 with Oilers). **Note:** The NY Rangers announced plans to retire #11 for **Mark Messier** (1991-97, 2000-04 with Rangers) in Jan. 2006.

### Eastern Conference

Five Eastern teams—the Atlanta Thrashers, Carolina Hurricanes, Florida Panthers, New Jersey Devils and Tampa Bay Lightning—have not retired any numbers. The Hartford Whalers had retired three numbers: #2 Rick Ley, #9 Gordie Howe and #19 John McKenzie. Mario Lemieux's retired #66 with Pittsburgh has been temporarily unretired during his recent comeback.

**Boston Bruins**
2 Eddie Shore
3 Lionel Hitchman
4 Bobby Orr
5 Dit Clapper
7 Phil Esposito
8 Cam Neely
9 John Bucyk
15 Milt Schmidt
24 Terry O'Reilly
77 Ray Bourque

**Buffalo Sabres**
2 Tim Horton
7 Rick Martin
11 Gilbert Perreault
14 Rene Robert

**Montreal Canadiens**
1 Jacques Plante
2 Doug Harvey
4 Jean Beliveau
7 Howie Morenz
9 Maurice Richard
10 Guy Lafleur
16 Henri Richard

**New York Islanders**
5 Denis Potvin
9 Clark Gillies
19 Bryan Trottier
22 Mike Bossy
23 Bob Nystrom
31 Billy Smith

**New York Rangers**
1 Eddie Giacomin
7 Rod Gilbert
11 Mark Messier (2006)
35 Mike Richter

**Ottawa Senators**
8 Frank Finnigan

**Philadelphia Flyers**
1 Bernie Parent
4 Barry Ashbee
7 Bill Barber
16 Bobby Clarke

**Pittsburgh Penguins**
21 Michel Briere
66 Mario Lemieux

**Toronto Maple Leafs**
5 Bill Barilko
6 Ace Bailey

**Washington Capitals**
5 Rod Langway
7 Yvon Labre
32 Dale Hunter

### Western Conference

Four Western teams—the Columbus Blue Jackets, Mighty Ducks of Anaheim, Nashville Predators and San Jose Sharks—have not retired any numbers. Note, the Quebec Nordiques retired the numbers of J.C. Tremblay (3), Marc Tardif (8) and Michel Goulet (16) but these numbers have been worn since the team moved to Colorado. Detroit has not officially retired the numbers of Larry Aurie (6) and Vladimir Konstantinov (16) but has kept them "out of circulation." Similarly, St. Louis has not officially retired the number of Doug Wickenheiser (14) but has kept it out of circulation since his death in 1999.

**Calgary Flames**
9 Lanny McDonald

**Chicago Blackhawks**
1 Glenn Hall
9 Bobby Hull
18 Denis Savard
21 Stan Mikita
35 Tony Esposito

**Colorado Avalanche**
33 Patrick Roy
77 Ray Bourque

**Dallas Stars**
7 Neal Broten
8 Bill Goldsworthy
19 Bill Masterton

**Detroit Red Wings**
1 Terry Sawchuk
7 Ted Lindsay
9 Gordie Howe
10 Alex Delvecchio
12 Sid Abel

**Edmonton Oilers**
3 Al Hamilton
7 Paul Coffey
17 Jari Kurri
31 Grant Fuhr
99 Wayne Gretzky

**Los Angeles Kings**
16 Marcel Dionne
18 Dave Taylor
30 Rogie Vachon
99 Wayne Gretzky

**Minnesota Wild**
1 Fans

**Phoenix Coyotes**
9 Bobby Hull
25 Thomas Steen

**St. Louis Blues**
3 Bob Gassoff
8 Barclay Plager
11 Brian Sutter
24 Bernie Federko

**Vancouver Canucks**
12 Stan Smyl

---

### AWARDS

## Associated Press Athletes of the Year

Selected annually by AP newspaper sports editors since 1931.

### Male

Lance Armstrong won his sixth consecutive Tour de France and third straight AP Male Athlete of the Year Award in 2004. Armstrong broke the record for most Tour de France victories, and did so in dominating fashion, winning five stages and beating second-place Andreas Kloden of Germany by more than six minutes. Armstrong joins Michael Jordan as the only athletes to win the award three straight times.

The top 5 vote-getters (first place votes in parentheses): 1. **Lance Armstrong**, cycling (51), 312 pts; 2. **Peyton Manning**, football (17), 156 pts; 3. **Michael Phelps**, swimming (11), 124 pts; 4. **Curt Schilling**, baseball (17), 122 pts; 5. **Vijay Singh**, golf (9), 90 pts.

**Multiple winners:** Lance Armstrong, Michael Jordan and Tiger Woods (3); Don Budge, Sandy Koufax, Carl Lewis, Joe Montana and Byron Nelson (2).

| Year | | Year | | Year | |
|---|---|---|---|---|---|
| 1931 | **Pepper Martin**, baseball | 1941 | **Joe DiMaggio**, baseball | 1951 | **Dick Kazmaier**, col. football |
| 1932 | **Gene Sarazen**, golf | 1942 | **Frank Sinkwich**, col. football | 1952 | **Bob Mathias**, track |
| 1933 | **Carl Hubbell**, baseball | 1943 | **Gunder Haegg**, track | 1953 | **Ben Hogan**, golf |
| 1934 | **Dizzy Dean**, baseball | 1944 | **Byron Nelson**, golf | 1954 | **Willie Mays**, baseball |
| 1935 | **Joe Louis**, boxing | 1945 | **Byron Nelson**, golf | 1955 | **Hopalong Cassady**, col. football |
| 1936 | **Jesse Owens**, track | 1946 | **Glenn Davis**, college football | | |
| 1937 | **Don Budge**, tennis | 1947 | **Johnny Lujack**, col. football | 1956 | **Mickey Mantle**, baseball |
| 1938 | **Don Budge**, tennis | 1948 | **Lou Boudreau**, baseball | 1957 | **Ted Williams**, baseball |
| 1939 | **Nile Kinnick**, college football | 1949 | **Leon Hart**, college football | 1958 | **Herb Elliott**, track |
| 1940 | **Tom Harmon**, college football | 1950 | **Jim Konstanty**, baseball | 1959 | **Ingemar Johansson**, boxing |

## Awards (Cont.)

| Year | | Year | | Year | |
|---|---|---|---|---|---|
| 1960 | **Rafer Johnson**, track | 1975 | **Fred Lynn**, baseball | 1990 | **Joe Montana**, pro football |
| 1961 | **Roger Maris**, baseball | 1976 | **Bruce Jenner**, track | 1991 | **Michael Jordan**, pro basketball |
| 1962 | **Maury Wills**, baseball | 1977 | **Steve Cauthen**, horse racing | 1992 | **Michael Jordan**, pro basketball |
| 1963 | **Sandy Koufax**, baseball | 1978 | **Ron Guidry**, baseball | 1993 | **Michael Jordan**, pro basketball |
| 1964 | **Don Schollander**, swimming | 1979 | **Willie Stargell**, baseball | 1994 | **George Foreman**, boxing |
| 1965 | **Sandy Koufax**, baseball | 1980 | **U.S. Olympic hockey team** | 1995 | **Cal Ripken Jr.**, baseball |
| 1966 | **Frank Robinson**, baseball | 1981 | **John McEnroe**, tennis | 1996 | **Michael Johnson**, track |
| 1967 | **Carl Yastrzemski**, baseball | 1982 | **Wayne Gretzky**, hockey | 1997 | **Tiger Woods**, golf |
| 1968 | **Denny McLain**, baseball | 1983 | **Carl Lewis**, track | 1998 | **Mark McGwire**, baseball |
| 1969 | **Tom Seaver**, baseball | 1984 | **Carl Lewis**, track | 1999 | **Tiger Woods**, golf |
| 1970 | **George Blanda**, pro football | 1985 | **Dwight Gooden**, baseball | 2000 | **Tiger Woods**, golf |
| 1971 | **Lee Trevino**, golf | 1986 | **Larry Bird**, pro basketball | 2001 | **Barry Bonds**, baseball |
| 1972 | **Mark Spitz**, swimming | 1987 | **Ben Johnson**, track | 2002 | **Lance Armstrong**, cycling |
| 1973 | **O.J. Simpson**, pro football | 1988 | **Orel Hershiser**, baseball | 2003 | **Lance Armstrong**, cycling |
| 1974 | **Muhammad Ali**, boxing | 1989 | **Joe Montana**, pro football | 2004 | **Lance Armstrong**, cycling |

### Female

Golfer Annika Sorenstam won a major, 10 tournaments overall in just 20 starts and a fourth straight LPGA money title in 2004. The 34-year-old Swede also became the first female to win consecutive AP Athlete of Year awards since Monica Seles did it in 1992. UConn/WNBA star Diana Taurasi finished second to Sorenstam for the second year in a row.

The top 5 vote-getters (first place votes in parentheses): 1. **Annika Sorenstam**, golf (40) 263 pts; 2. **Diana Taurasi**, basketball (15), 154 pts; 3. **Maria Sharapova**, tennis (19), 152 pts; 4. **Carly Patterson**, gymnastics (10), 104 pts; 5. **Jennie Finch**, softball (11), 88 pts.

**Multiple winners:** Babe Didrikson Zaharias (6); Chris Evert (4); Patty Berg and Maureen Connolly (3); Tracy Austin, Althea Gibson, Billie Jean King, Nancy Lopez, Alice Marble, Martina Navratilova, Wilma Rudolph, Monica Seles, Annika Sorenstam, Kathy Whitworth and Mickey Wright (2).

| Year | | Year | | Year | |
|---|---|---|---|---|---|
| 1931 | **Helene Madison**, swimming | 1956 | **Pat McCormick**, diving | 1981 | **Tracy Austin**, tennis |
| 1932 | **Babe Didrikson**, track | 1957 | **Althea Gibson**, tennis | 1982 | **Mary Decker Tabb**, track |
| 1933 | **Helen Jacobs**, tennis | 1958 | **Althea Gibson**, tennis | 1983 | **Martina Navratilova**, tennis |
| 1934 | **Virginia Van Wie**, golf | 1959 | **Maria Bueno**, tennis | 1984 | **Mary Lou Retton**, gymnastics |
| 1935 | **Helen Wills Moody**, tennis | 1960 | **Wilma Rudolph**, track | 1985 | **Nancy Lopez**, golf |
| 1936 | **Helen Stephens**, track | 1961 | **Wilma Rudolph**, track | 1986 | **Martina Navratilova**, tennis |
| 1937 | **Katherine Rawls**, swimming | 1962 | **Dawn Fraser**, swimming | 1987 | **Jackie Joyner-Kersee**, track |
| 1938 | **Patty Berg**, golf | 1963 | **Mickey Wright**, golf | 1988 | **Florence Griffith Joyner**, track |
| 1939 | **Alice Marble**, tennis | 1964 | **Mickey Wright**, golf | 1989 | **Steffi Graf**, tennis |
| 1940 | **Alice Marble**, tennis | 1965 | **Kathy Whitworth**, golf | 1990 | **Beth Daniel**, golf |
| 1941 | **Betty Hicks Newell**, golf | 1966 | **Kathy Whitworth**, golf | 1991 | **Monica Seles**, tennis |
| 1942 | **Gloria Callen**, swimming | 1967 | **Billie Jean King**, tennis | 1992 | **Monica Seles**, tennis |
| 1943 | **Patty Berg**, golf | 1968 | **Peggy Fleming**, skating | 1993 | **Sheryl Swoopes**, basketball |
| 1944 | **Ann Curtis**, swimming | 1969 | **Debbie Meyer**, swimming | 1994 | **Bonnie Blair**, speed skating |
| 1945 | **Babe Didrikson Zaharias**, golf | 1970 | **Chi Cheng**, track | 1995 | **Rebecca Lobo**, col. basketball |
| 1946 | **Babe Didrikson Zaharias**, golf | 1971 | **Evonne Goolagong**, tennis | 1996 | **Amy Van Dyken**, swimming |
| 1947 | **Babe Didrikson Zaharias**, golf | 1972 | **Olga Korbut**, gymnastics | 1997 | **Martina Hingis**, tennis |
| 1948 | **Fanny Blankers-Koen**, track | 1973 | **Billie Jean King**, tennis | 1998 | **Se Ri Pak**, golf |
| 1949 | **Marlene Bauer**, golf | 1974 | **Chris Evert**, tennis | 1999 | **U.S. Soccer Team** |
| 1950 | **Babe Didrikson Zaharias**, golf | 1975 | **Chris Evert**, tennis | 2000 | **Marion Jones**, track |
| 1951 | **Maureen Connolly**, tennis | 1976 | **Nadia Comaneci**, gymnastics | 2001 | **Jennifer Capriati**, tennis |
| 1952 | **Maureen Connolly**, tennis | 1977 | **Chris Evert**, tennis | 2002 | **Serena Williams**, tennis |
| 1953 | **Maureen Connolly**, tennis | 1978 | **Nancy Lopez**, golf | 2003 | **Annika Sorenstam**, golf |
| 1954 | **Babe Didrikson Zaharias**, golf | 1979 | **Tracy Austin**, tennis | 2004 | **Annika Sorenstam**, golf |
| 1955 | **Patty Berg**, golf | 1980 | **Chris Evert Lloyd**, tennis | | |

## USOC Sportsman & Sportswoman of the Year

To the outstanding overall male and female athletes from within the U.S. Olympic Committee member organizations. Winners are chosen from nominees of the national governing bodies for Olympic and Pan American Games and affiliated organizations. Voting is done by members of the national media, USOC board of directors and Athletes' Advisory Council.

### Sportsman

**Multiple winners:** Lance Armstrong (4); Eric Heiden and Michael Johnson (3); Matt Biondi and Greg Louganis (2).

| Year | | Year | | Year | |
|---|---|---|---|---|---|
| 1974 | **Jim Bolding**, track | 1985 | **Willie Banks**, track | 1996 | **Michael Johnson**, track |
| 1975 | **Clint Jackson**, boxing | 1986 | **Matt Biondi**, swimming | 1997 | **Pete Sampras**, tennis |
| 1976 | **John Naber**, swimming | 1987 | **Greg Louganis**, diving | 1998 | **Jonny Moseley**, skiing |
| 1977 | **Eric Heiden**, speed skating | 1988 | **Matt Biondi**, swimming | 1999 | **Lance Armstrong**, cycling |
| 1978 | **Bruce Davidson**, equestrian | 1989 | **Roger Kingdom**, track | 2000 | **Rulon Gardner**, wrestling |
| 1979 | **Eric Heiden**, speed skating | 1990 | **John Smith**, wrestling | 2001 | **Lance Armstrong**, cycling |
| 1980 | **Eric Heiden**, speed skating | 1991 | **Carl Lewis**, track | 2002 | **Lance Armstrong**, cycling |
| 1981 | **Scott Hamilton**, fig. skating | 1992 | **Pablo Morales**, swimming | 2003 | **Lance Armstrong**, cycling |
| 1982 | **Greg Louganis**, diving | 1993 | **Michael Johnson**, track | 2004 | **Michael Phelps**, swimming |
| 1983 | **Rick McKinney**, archery | 1994 | **Dan Jansen**, speed skating | | |
| 1984 | **Edwin Moses**, track | 1995 | **Michael Johnson**, track | | |

## Sportswoman

**Multiple winners:** Bonnie Blair, Tracy Caulkins, Jackie Joyner-Kersee, Picabo Street and Sheila Young Ochowicz (2).

| Year | | Year | | Year | |
|------|---|------|---|------|---|
| 1974 | **Shirley Babashoff**, swimming | 1984 | **Tracy Caulkins**, swimming | 1995 | **Picabo Street**, skiing |
| 1975 | **Kathy Heddy**, swimming | 1985 | **Mary Decker Slaney**, track | 1996 | **Amy Van Dyken**, swimming |
| 1976 | **Sheila Young**, speedskating | 1986 | **Jackie Joyner-Kersee**, track | 1997 | **Tara Lipinski**, figure skating |
| 1977 | **Linda Fratianne**, fig. skating | 1987 | **Jackie Joyner-Kersee**, track | 1998 | **Picabo Street**, skiing |
| 1978 | **Tracy Caulkins**, swimming | 1988 | **Florence Griffith Joyner**, track | 1999 | **Jenny Thompson**, swimming |
| 1979 | **Sippy Woodhead**, swimming | 1989 | **Janet Evans**, swimming | 2000 | **Marion Jones**, track |
| 1980 | **Beth Heiden**, speed skating | 1990 | **Lynn Jennings**, track | 2001 | **Jennifer Capriati**, tennis |
| 1981 | **Sheila Ochowicz**, speed skating & cycling | 1991 | **Kim Zmeskal**, gymnastics | 2002 | **Sarah Hughes**, figure skating |
| | | 1992 | **Bonnie Blair**, speed skating | 2003 | **Michelle Kwan**, figure skating |
| 1982 | **Melanie Smith**, equestrian | 1993 | **Gail Devers**, track | 2004 | **Carly Patterson**, gymnastics |
| 1983 | **Tamara McKinney**, skiing | 1994 | **Bonnie Blair**, speed skating | | |

## UPI International Athletes of the Year

Selected annually by United Press International's European newspaper sports editors from 1974-95.

### Male

**Multiple winners:** Sebastian Coe, Alberto Juantorena and Carl Lewis (2).

| Year | | Year | | Year | |
|------|---|------|---|------|---|
| 1974 | **Muhammad Ali**, boxing | 1982 | **Daley Thompson**, track | 1990 | **Stefan Edberg**, tennis |
| 1975 | **Joao Oliveira**, track | 1983 | **Carl Lewis**, track | 1991 | **Sergei Bubka**, track |
| 1976 | **Alberto Juantorena**, track | 1984 | **Carl Lewis**, track | 1992 | **Kevin Young**, track |
| 1977 | **Alberto Juantorena**, track | 1985 | **Steve Cram**, track | 1993 | **Miguel Indurain**, cycling |
| 1978 | **Henry Rono**, track | 1986 | **Diego Maradona**, soccer | 1994 | **Johann Olav Koss**, speed skating |
| 1979 | **Sebastian Coe**, track | 1987 | **Ben Johnson**, track | | |
| 1980 | **Eric Heiden**, speed skating | 1988 | **Matt Biondi**, swimming | 1995 | **Jonathan Edwards**, track |
| 1981 | **Sebastian Coe**, track | 1989 | **Boris Becker**, tennis | 1996 | discontinued |

### Female

**Multiple winners:** Nadia Comaneci, Steffi Graf, Marita Koch and Monica Seles (2).

| Year | | Year | | Year | |
|------|---|------|---|------|---|
| 1974 | **Irena Szewinska**, track | 1982 | **Marita Koch**, track | 1990 | **Merlene Ottey**, track |
| 1975 | **Nadia Comaneci**, gymnastics | 1983 | **Jarmila Kratochvilova**, track | 1991 | **Monica Seles**, tennis |
| 1976 | **Nadia Comaneci**, gymnastics | 1984 | **Martina Navratilova**, tennis | 1992 | **Monica Seles**, tennis |
| 1977 | **Rosie Ackermann**, track | 1985 | **Mary Decker Slaney**, track | 1993 | **Wang Junxia**, track |
| 1978 | **Tracy Caulkins**, swimming | 1986 | **Heike Drechsler**, track | 1994 | **Le Jingyi**, swimming |
| 1979 | **Marita Koch**, track | 1987 | **Steffi Graf**, tennis | 1995 | **Gwen Torrence**, track |
| 1980 | **Hanni Wenzel**, alpine skiing | 1988 | **Florence Griffith Joyner**, track | 1996 | discontinued |
| 1981 | **Chris Evert Lloyd**, tennis | 1989 | **Steffi Graf**, tennis | | |

## American-International Athlete Trophy

Formerly known as the Jesse Owens International Trophy, the trophy has been presented annually by the International Amateur Athletic Association since 1981 and selected by a worldwide panel of electors.

**Multiple winners:** Lance Armstrong, Michael Johnson and Marion Jones (2).

| Year | | Year | | Year | |
|------|---|------|---|------|---|
| 1981 | **Eric Heiden**, speed skating | 1990 | **Roger Kingdom**, track | 1997 | **Michael Johnson**, track |
| 1982 | **Sebastian Coe**, track | 1991 | **Greg LeMond**, cycling | 1998 | **Haile Gebrselassie**, track |
| 1983 | **Mary Decker**, track | 1992 | **Mike Powell**, track | 1999 | **Marion Jones**, track |
| 1984 | **Edwin Moses**, track | 1993 | **Vitaly Scherbo**, gymnastics | 2000 | **Lance Armstrong**, cycling |
| 1985 | **Carl Lewis**, track | 1994 | **Wang Junxia**, track | 2001 | **Marion Jones**, track |
| 1986 | **Said Aouita**, track | 1995 | **Johann Olva Koss**, speed skating | 2002 | **Ian Thorpe**, swimming |
| 1987 | **Greg Louganis**, diving | | | 2003 | **Lance Armstrong**, cycling |
| 1988 | **Ben Johnson**, track | 1996 | **Michael Johnson**, track | 2004 | **Michael Phelps**, swimming |

## Honda-Broderick Cup

To the outstanding collegiate woman athlete of the year in NCAA competition. Winner is chosen from nominees in each of the NCAA's 10 competitive sports. Final voting is done by member athletic directors. Award is named after founder and sportswear manufacturer Thomas Broderick.

**Multiple winner:** Tracy Caulkins (2).

| Year | | Year | | |
|------|---|------|---|---|
| 1977 | **Lucy Harris**, Delta St . . . . . . . . . . . . .basketball | 1987 | **Mary T. Meagher**, California . . . . . .swimming | |
| 1978 | **Ann Meyers**, UCLA . . . . . . . . . . . . .basketball | 1988 | **Teresa Weatherspoon**, La. Tech . . . .basketball | |
| 1979 | **Nancy Lieberman**, Old Dominion . . .basketball | 1989 | **Vicki Huber**, Villanova . . . . . . . . . . . . .track | |
| 1980 | **Julie Shea**, N.C. State . . . . . . . . . .track & field | 1990 | **Suzy Favor**, Wisconsin . . . . . . . . . . . . .track | |
| 1981 | **Jill Sterkel**, Texas . . . . . . . . . . . . .swimming | 1991 | **Dawn Staley**, Virginia . . . . . . . . . .basketball | |
| 1982 | **Tracy Caulkins**, Florida . . . . . . . . .swimming | 1992 | **Missy Marlowe**, Utah . . . . . . . . .gymnastics | |
| 1983 | **Deitre Collins**, Hawaii . . . . . . . . . . .volleyball | 1993 | **Lisa Fernandez**, UCLA . . . . . . . . . . . .softball | |
| 1984 | **Tracy Caulkins**, Florida . . . . . . . . .swimming & **Cheryl Miller**, USC . . . . . . . . . . .basketball | 1994 | **Mia Hamm**, North Carolina . . . . . . . . . .soccer | |
| | | 1995 | **Rebecca Lobo**, UConn . . . . . . . . .basketball | |
| 1985 | **Jackie Joyner**, UCLA . . . . . . . . . .track & field | 1996 | **Jennifer Rizzotti**, UConn . . . . . . . .basketball | |
| 1986 | **Kamie Ethridge**, Texas . . . . . . . . .basketball | 1997 | **Cindy Daws**, Notre Dame . . . . . . . . . . .soccer | |

## Awards (Cont.)

| Year | | Year | |
|------|--|------|--|
| 1998 | **Chamique Holdsclaw**, Tennessee . . .basketball | 2002 | **Angela Williams**, USC . . . . . . . . . . . . .track |
| 1999 | **Misty May**, Long Beach St. . . . . . . . .volleyball | 2003 | **Natasha Watley**, UCLA . . . . . . . . . .softball |
| 2000 | **Cristina Teuscher**, Columbia . . . . . .swimming | 2004 | **Tara Kirk**, Stanford . . . . . . . . . . . . .swimming |
| 2001 | **Jackie Stiles**, SW Missouri St. . . . . . .basketball | 2005 | **Ogonna Nnamani**, Stanford . . . . . .volleyball |

## Flo Hyman Award

Presented annually since 1987 by the Women's Sports Foundation for "exemplifying dignity, spirit and commitment to excellence" and named in honor of the late captain of the 1984 U.S. Women's Volleyball team. Voting by WSF members.

| Year | | Year | | Year | |
|------|--|------|--|------|--|
| 1987 | **Martina Navratilova**, tennis | 1993 | **Lynette Woodard**, basketball | 1999 | **Bonnie Blair**, speed skating |
| 1988 | **Jackie Joyner-Kersee**, track | 1994 | **Patty Sheehan**, golf | 2000 | **Monica Seles**, tennis |
| 1989 | **Evelyn Ashford**, track | 1995 | **Mary Lou Retton**, gymnastics | 2001 | **Lisa Leslie**, basketball |
| 1990 | **Chris Evert**, tennis | 1996 | **Donna de Varona**, swimming | 2002 | **Dot Richardson**, softball |
| 1991 | **Diana Golden**, skiing | 1997 | **Billie Jean King**, tennis | 2003 | **Nawal El Moutawakel**, track |
| 1992 | **Nancy Lopez**, golf | 1998 | **Nadia Comaneci**, gymnastics | 2004 | **Kristi Yamaguchi**, fig. skating |

## James E. Sullivan Memorial Award

Presented annually by the Amateur Athletic Union since 1930. The Sullivan Award is named after the former AAU president and given to the athlete who, "by his or her performance, example and influence as an amateur, has done the most during the year to advance the cause of sportsmanship."

Olympic gymnast **Paul Hamm** won the 75th Sullivan Award. At the Athens Summer Games, Hamm came back from 12th place with only two events left to become the first American man to win the Olympic all-around gold medal. His gold medal was threatened after officials later discovered a silver medal-winning South Korean rival was incorrectly docked a tenth of a point in his second-to-last routine. But an appeal was denied, allowing Hamm to keep his gold. Vote totals were not released.

| Year | | Year | | Year | |
|------|--|------|--|------|--|
| 1930 | **Bobby Jones**, golf | 1956 | **Pat McCormick**, diving | 1982 | **Mary Decker**, track |
| 1931 | **Barney Berlinger**, track | 1957 | **Bobby Morrow**, track | 1983 | **Edwin Moses**, track |
| 1932 | **Jim Bausch**, track | 1958 | **Glenn Davis**, track | 1984 | **Greg Louganis**, diving |
| 1933 | **Glenn Cunningham**, track | 1959 | **Parry O'Brien**, track | 1985 | **Joan B. Samuelson**, track |
| 1934 | **Bill Bonthron**, track | 1960 | **Rafer Johnson**, track | 1986 | **Jackie Joyner-Kersee**, track |
| 1935 | **Lawson Little**, golf | 1961 | **Wilma Rudolph**, track | 1987 | **Jim Abbott**, baseball |
| 1936 | **Glenn Morris**, track | 1962 | **Jim Beatty**, track | 1988 | **Florence Griffith Joyner**, track |
| 1937 | **Don Budge**, tennis | 1963 | **John Pennel**, track | 1989 | **Janet Evans**, swimming |
| 1938 | **Don Lash**, track | 1964 | **Don Schollander**, swimming | 1990 | **John Smith**, wrestling |
| 1939 | **Joe Burk**, rowing | 1965 | **Bill Bradley**, basketball | 1991 | **Mike Powell**, track |
| 1940 | **Greg Rice**, track | 1966 | **Jim Ryun**, track | 1992 | **Bonnie Blair**, speed skating |
| 1941 | **Leslie MacMitchell**, track | 1967 | **Randy Matson**, track | 1993 | **Charlie Ward**, football |
| 1942 | **Cornelius Warmerdam**, track | 1968 | **Debbie Meyer**, swimming | 1994 | **Dan Jansen**, speed skating |
| 1943 | **Gilbert Dodds**, track | 1969 | **Bill Toomey**, track | 1995 | **Bruce Baumgartner**, wrestling |
| 1944 | **Ann Curtis**, swimming | 1970 | **John Kinsella**, swimming | 1996 | **Michael Johnson**, track |
| 1945 | **Doc Blanchard**, football | 1971 | **Mark Spitz**, swimming | 1997 | **Peyton Manning**, football |
| 1946 | **Arnold Tucker**, football | 1972 | **Frank Shorter**, track | 1998 | **Chamique Holdsclaw**, |
| 1947 | **John B. Kelly, Jr.**, rowing | 1973 | **Bill Walton**, basketball | | basketball |
| 1948 | **Bob Mathias**, track | 1974 | **Rich Wohlhuter**, track | 1999 | **Coco and Kelly Miller**, |
| 1949 | **Dick Button**, skating | 1975 | **Tim Shaw**, swimming | | basketball |
| 1950 | **Fred Wilt**, track | 1976 | **Bruce Jenner**, track | 2000 | **Rulon Gardner**, wrestling |
| 1951 | **Bob Richards**, track | 1977 | **John Naber**, swimming | 2001 | **Michelle Kwan**, figure skating |
| 1952 | **Horace Ashenfelter**, track | 1978 | **Tracy Caulkins**, swimming | 2002 | **Sarah Hughes**, figure skating |
| 1953 | **Sammy Lee**, diving | 1979 | **Kurt Thomas**, gymnastics | 2003 | **Michael Phelps**, swimming |
| 1954 | **Mal Whitfield**, track | 1980 | **Eric Heiden**, speed skating | 2004 | **Paul Hamm**, gymnastics |
| 1955 | **Harrison Dillard**, track | 1981 | **Carl Lewis**, track | | |

## ESPY Awards

The ESPY Awards, which represent the convergence of the sports and entertainment communities, were created by ESPN in 1993 and are given for Excellence in Sports Performance in more than 30 categories. ESPYs are awarded by a panel of sports executives, journalists and retired athletes whose decisions are based on the performances of the nominees during the year preceding the awards ceremony. Note that not all categories are listed below.

### Breakthrough Athlete

| Year | | Year | |
|------|--|------|--|
| 1993 | Gary Sheffield, San Diego Padres | 2000 | Kurt Warner, St. Louis Rams |
| 1994 | Mike Piazza, Los Angeles Dodgers | 2001 | Daunte Culpepper, Minnesota Vikings |
| 1995 | Jeff Bagwell, Houston Astros | 2002 | Tom Brady, New England Patriots |
| 1996 | Hideo Nomo, Los Angeles Dodgers | 2003 | Alfonso Soriano, New York Yankees |
| 1997 | Tiger Woods, golf | 2004 | LeBron James, Cleveland Cavaliers |
| 1998 | Nomar Garciaparra, Boston Red Sox | 2005 | Dwyane Wade, Miami Heat |
| 1999 | Randy Moss, Minnesota Vikings | | |

## Best Coach/Manager

| Year | |
| --- | --- |
| 1993 | Jimmy Johnson, Dallas Cowboys |
| 1994 | Jimmy Johnson, Dallas Cowboys |
| 1995 | George Siefert, San Francisco 49ers |
| 1996 | Gary Barnett, Northwestern |
| 1997 | Joe Torre, New York Yankees |
| 1998 | Jim Leyland, Florida Marlins |
| 1999 | Joe Torre, New York Yankees |
| 2000 | Joe Torre, New York Yankees |
| 2001 | Joe Torre, New York Yankees |
| 2002 | Phil Jackson, Los Angeles Lakers |
| 2003 | Jon Gruden, Tampa Bay Buccaneers |
| 2004 | Larry Brown, Detroit Pistons |
| 2005 | Bill Belichick, New England Patriots |

## Best Comeback Athlete

| Year | |
| --- | --- |
| 1993 | Dave Winfield, Toronto Blue Jays |
| 1994 | Mario Lemieux, Pittsburgh Penguins |
| 1995 | Dan Marino, Miami Dolphins |
| 1996 | Michael Jordan, Chicago Bulls |
| 1997 | Evander Holyfield, boxer |
| 1998 | Roger Clemens, Toronto Blue Jays |
| 1999 | Eric Davis, Baltimore Orioles |
| 2000 | Lance Armstrong, cycling |
| 2001 | Andres Galarraga, baseball |
| 2002 | Jennifer Capriati, tennis |
| 2003 | Tommy Maddox, Pittsburgh Steelers |
| 2004 | Bethany Hamilton, surfing |
| 2005 | Mark Fields, Carolina Panthers |

## Best Female Athlete

| Year | |
| --- | --- |
| 1993 | Monica Seles, tennis |
| 1994 | Julie Krone, jockey |
| 1995 | Bonnie Blair, speed skater |
| 1996 | Rebecca Lobo, basketball |
| 1997 | Amy Van Dyken, swimming |
| 1998 | Mia Hamm, soccer |
| 1999 | Chamique Holdsclaw, college basketball |
| 2000 | Mia Hamm, soccer |
| 2001 | Marion Jones, track |
| 2002 | Venus Williams, tennis |
| 2003 | Serena Williams, tennis |
| 2004 | Diana Taurasi, basketball |
| 2005 | Annika Sorenstam, golf |

## Best Male Athlete

| Year | |
| --- | --- |
| 1993 | Michael Jordan, Chicago Bulls |
| 1994 | Barry Bonds, San Francisco Giants |
| 1995 | Steve Young, San Francisco 49ers |
| 1996 | Cal Ripken, Baltimore Orioles |
| 1997 | Michael Johnson, Olympic sprinter |
| 1998 | Tiger Woods, golf |
| 1999 | Mark McGwire, St. Louis Cardinals |
| 2000 | Tiger Woods, golf |
| 2001 | Tiger Woods, golf |
| 2002 | Tiger Woods, golf |
| 2003 | Lance Armstrong, cycling |
| 2004 | Lance Armstrong, cycling |
| 2005 | Lance Armstrong, cycling |

## Outstanding Performance Under Pressure

| Year | |
| --- | --- |
| 1993 | Christian Laettner, Duke |
| 1994 | Joe Carter, Toronto Blue Jays |
| 1995 | Mark Messier, New York Rangers |
| 1996 | Martin Brodeur, New Jersey Devils |
| 1997 | Kerri Strug, Olympic gymnast |
| 1998 | Terrell Davis, Denver Broncos |
| 1999 | Mark O'Meara, golf |
| 2000 | discontinued |

## Best Team

| Year | |
| --- | --- |
| 1993 | Dallas Cowboys |
| 1994 | Toronto Blue Jays |
| 1995 | New York Rangers |
| 1996 | UConn women's hoops |
| 1997 | New York Yankees |
| 1998 | Denver Broncos |
| 1999 | New York Yankees |
| 2000 | U.S. Women's World Cup Soccer Team |
| 2001 | New York Yankees & Oklahoma football |
| 2002 | Los Angeles Lakers |
| 2003 | Anaheim Angels |
| 2004 | Detroit Pistons |
| 2005 | Boston Red Sox |

## Best Baseball Player

| Year | |
| --- | --- |
| 1993 | Dennis Eckersley, Oakland A's |
| 1994 | Barry Bonds, San Francisco Giants |
| 1995 | Jeff Bagwell, Houston Astros |
| 1996 | Greg Maddux, Atlanta Braves |
| 1997 | Ken Caminiti, San Diego Padres |
| 1998 | Larry Walker, Colorado Rockies |
| 1999 | Mark McGwire, St. Louis Cardinals |
| 2000 | Pedro Martinez, Boston Red Sox |
| 2001 | Pedro Martinez, Boston Red Sox |
| 2002 | Barry Bonds, San Francisco Giants |
| 2003 | Barry Bonds, San Francisco Giants |
| 2004 | Barry Bonds, San Francisco Giants |
| 2005 | Albert Pujols, St. Louis Cardinals |

## Best NFL Player

| Year | |
| --- | --- |
| 1993 | Emmitt Smith, Dallas Cowboys |
| 1994 | Emmitt Smith, Dallas Cowboys |
| 1995 | Barry Sanders, Detroit Lions |
| 1996 | Brett Favre, Green Bay Packers |
| 1997 | Brett Favre, Green Bay Packers |
| 1998 | Barry Sanders, Detroit Lions |
| 1999 | Terrell Davis, Denver Broncos |
| 2000 | Kurt Warner, St. Louis Rams |
| 2001 | Marshall Faulk, St. Louis Rams |
| 2002 | Marshall Faulk, St. Louis Rams |
| 2003 | Michael Vick, Atlanta Falcons |
| 2004 | Peyton Manning, Indianapolis Colts |
| 2005 | Peyton Manning, Indianapolis Colts |

## Best NBA Player

| Year | |
| --- | --- |
| 1993 | Michael Jordan, Chicago Bulls |
| 1994 | Charles Barkley, Phoenix Suns |
| 1995 | Hakeem Olajuwon, Houston Rockets |
| 1996 | Hakeem Olajuwon, Houston Rockets |
| 1997 | Michael Jordan, Chicago Bulls |
| 1998 | Michael Jordan, Chicago Bulls |
| 1999 | Michael Jordan, Chicago Bulls |
| 2000 | Tim Duncan, San Antonio Spurs |
| 2001 | Shaquille O'Neal, Los Angeles Lakers |
| 2002 | Shaquille O'Neal, Los Angeles Lakers |
| 2003 | Tim Duncan, San Antonio Spurs |
| 2004 | Kevin Garnett, Minnesota Timberwolves |
| 2005 | Steve Nash, Phoenix Suns |

## Best WNBA Player

| Year | |
| --- | --- |
| 1998 | Cynthia Cooper, Houston Comets |
| 1999 | Cynthia Cooper, Houston Comets |
| 2000 | Cynthia Cooper, Houston Comets |
| 2001 | Sheryl Swoopes, Houston Comets |
| 2002 | Lisa Leslie, Los Angeles Sparks |
| 2003 | Lisa Leslie, Los Angeles Sparks |
| 2004 | Lauren Jackson, Seattle Storm |
| 2005 | Lauren Jackson, Seattle Storm |

## Best NHL Player

| Year | |
|------|---|
| 1993 | Mario Lemieux, Pittsburgh Penguins |
| 1994 | Mario Lemieux, Pittsburgh Penguins |
| 1995 | Mark Messier, New York Rangers |
| 1996 | Eric Lindros, Philadelphia Flyers |
| 1997 | Joe Sakic, Colorado Avalanche |
| 1998 | Mario Lemieux, Pittsburgh Penguins |
| 1999 | Dominik Hasek, Buffalo Sabres |
| 2000 | Dominik Hasek, Buffalo Sabres |
| 2001 | Chris Pronger, St. Louis Blues |
| 2002 | Jarome Iginla, Calgary Flames |
| 2003 | Jean-Sebastien Giguere, Anaheim Mighty Ducks |
| 2004 | Jarome Iginla, Calgary Flames |
| 2005 | not awarded |

## Outstanding College Football Performer of the Year

| Year | |
|------|---|
| 1993 | Garrison Hearst, Georgia |
| 1994 | Charlie Ward, Florida State |
| 1995 | Rashaan Salaam, Colorado |
| 1996 | Eddie George, Ohio State |
| 1997 | Danny Wuerffel, Florida |
| 1998 | Peyton Manning, Tennessee |
| 1999 | Ricky Williams, Texas |
| 2000 | Michael Vick, Virginia Tech |
| 2001 | Chris Weinke, Florida State |
| 2002 | discontinued |

## Outstanding College Basketball Performer of the Year

| Year | |
|------|---|
| 1993 | Christian Laettner, Duke |
| 1994 | Bobby Hurley, Duke |
| 1995 | Grant Hill, Duke |
| 1996 | Ed O'Bannon, UCLA |
| 1997 | Tim Duncan, Wake Forest |
| 1998 | Keith Van Horn, Utah |
| 1999 | Antawn Jamison, North Carolina |
| 2000 | Elton Brand, Duke |
| 2001 | Kenyon Martin, Cincinnati |
| 2002 | discontinued |

## Outstanding Women's College Hoops Performer of the Year

| Year | |
|------|---|
| 1993 | Dawn Staley, Virginia |
| 1994 | Sheryl Swoopes, Texas Tech |
| 1995 | Charlotte Smith, North Carolina |
| 1996 | Rebecca Lobo, Connecticut |
| 1997 | Saudia Roundtree, Georgia |
| 1998 | Chamique Holdsclaw, Tennessee |
| 1999 | Chamique Holdsclaw, Tennessee |
| 2000 | Chamique Holdsclaw, Tennessee |
| 2001 | Tamika Catchings, Tennessee |
| 2002 | discontinued |

## Best Men's Tennis Player

| Year | | Year | |
|------|---|------|---|
| 1993 | Jim Courier | 2000 | Andre Agassi |
| 1994 | Pete Sampras | 2001 | Pete Sampras |
| 1995 | Pete Sampras | 2002 | Lleyton Hewitt |
| 1996 | Pete Sampras | 2003 | Andre Agassi |
| 1997 | Pete Sampras | 2004 | Andy Roddick |
| 1998 | Pete Sampras | 2005 | Roger Federer |
| 1999 | Pete Sampras | | |

## Best Women's Tennis Player

| Year | | Year | |
|------|---|------|---|
| 1993 | Monica Seles | 2000 | Lindsay Davenport |
| 1994 | Steffi Graf | 2001 | Venus Williams |
| 1995 | A. Sanchez Vicario | 2002 | Venus Williams |
| 1996 | Steffi Graf | 2002 | Venus Williams |
| 1997 | Steffi Graf | 2003 | Serena Williams |
| 1998 | Martina Hingis | 2004 | Serena Williams |
| 1999 | Lindsay Davenport | 2005 | Maria Sharapova |

## Best Men's Golfer

| Year | | Year | |
|------|---|------|---|
| 1993 | Fred Couples | 2000 | Tiger Woods |
| 1994 | Nick Price | 2001 | Tiger Woods |
| 1995 | Nick Price | 2002 | Tiger Woods |
| 1996 | Corey Pavin | 2003 | Tiger Woods |
| 1997 | Tom Lehman | 2004 | Phil Mickelson |
| 1998 | Tiger Woods | 2005 | Tiger Woods |
| 1999 | Mark O'Meara | | |

## Best Women's Golfer

| Year | | Year | |
|------|---|------|---|
| 1993 | Dottie Mochrie | 2000 | Julie Inkster |
| 1994 | Betsy King | 2001 | Karrie Webb |
| 1995 | Laura Davies | 2002 | Annika Sorenstam |
| 1996 | Annika Sorenstam | 2003 | Annika Sorenstam |
| 1997 | Karrie Webb | 2004 | Annika Sorenstam |
| 1998 | Annika Sorenstam | 2005 | not awarded |
| 1999 | Annika Sorenstam | | |

## Best Jockey

| Year | | Year | |
|------|---|------|---|
| 1994 | Mike Smith | 2000 | Chris Antley |
| 1995 | Chris McCarron | 2001 | Kent Desormeaux |
| 1996 | Jerry Bailey | 2002 | Victor Espinoza |
| 1997 | Jerry Bailey | 2003 | Jose Santos |
| 1998 | Gary Stevens | 2004 | Stewart Elliot |
| 1999 | Kent Desormeaux | 2005 | Jeremy Rose |

## Best Bowler

| Year | | Year | |
|------|---|------|---|
| 1995 | Norm Duke | 2001 | Walter Ray Williams |
| 1996 | Mike Aulby | 2002 | Pete Weber |
| 1997 | Bob Learn Jr. | 2003 | Walter Ray Williams |
| 1998 | Walter Ray Williams | 2004 | Pete Weber |
| 1999 | Walter Ray Williams | 2005 | Walter Ray Williams |
| 2000 | Parker Bohn III | | |

## Best Driver

| Year | | Year | |
|------|---|------|---|
| 1993 | Nigel Mansell | 2000 | Dale Jarrett |
| 1994 | Nigel Mansell | 2001 | Bobby Labonte |
| 1995 | Al Unser Jr. | 2002 | Michael Schumacher |
| 1996 | Jeff Gordon | 2003 | Tony Stewart |
| 1997 | Jimmy Vasser | 2004 | Dale Earnhardt Jr. |
| 1998 | Jeff Gordon | 2005 | Michael Schumacher |
| 1999 | Jeff Gordon | | |

## Best Men's Track Athlete

| Year | | Year | |
|------|---|------|---|
| 1993 | Kevin Young | 2000 | Michael Johnson |
| 1994 | Michael Johnson | 2001 | Maurice Greene |
| 1995 | Dennis Mitchell | 2002 | Maurice Greene |
| 1996 | Michael Johnson | 2003 | Tim Montgomery |
| 1997 | Michael Johnson | 2004 | Tom Pappas |
| 1998 | Wilson Kipketer | 2005 | not awarded |
| 1999 | Maurice Greene | | |

### Best Women's Track Athlete

| Year | | Year | |
|------|--|------|--|
| 1993 | Evelyn Ashford | 2000 | Marion Jones |
| 1994 | Gail Devers | 2001 | Marion Jones |
| 1995 | Gwen Torrence | 2002 | Marion Jones |
| 1996 | Kim Batten | 2003 | Gail Devers |
| 1997 | Marie-Jose Perec | 2004 | Gail Devers |
| 1998 | Marion Jones | 2005 | not awarded |
| 1999 | Marion Jones | | |

### Game of the Year

| Year | |
|------|--|
| 1996 | AFC championship between Colts and Steelers |
| 1997 | Rose Bowl, Ohio State edges Arizona St. |
| 1998 | Super Bowl XXXII, Broncos over Packers |
| 1999-2001 | not awarded |
| 2002 | World Series Game 7, Diamondbacks-Yankees |
| 2003 | Fiesta Bowl, Ohio State beat Miami-FL in OT |
| 2004 | Super Bowl XXXVIII, Patriots over Panthers |
| 2005 | ALCS Game 5, Red Sox beat Yankees |

### Best Play

| Year | |
|------|--|
| 2002 | Derek Jeter's throw in World Series Game 3. |
| 2003 | LSU's Hail Mary TD. |
| 2004 | New Orleans Saints' lateral |
| 2005 | Blake Hoffarber's last second 3-pointer from flat on his back. |

### Best Boxer

| Year | | Year | |
|------|--|------|--|
| 1993 | Riddick Bowe | 2000 | Roy Jones Jr. |
| 1994 | Evander Holyfield | 2001 | Felix Trinidad |
| 1995 | George Foreman | 2002 | Lennox Lewis |
| 1996 | Roy Jones Jr. | 2003 | Roy Jones Jr. |
| 1997 | Evander Holyfield | 2004 | Antonio Tarver |
| 1998 | Evander Holyfield | 2005 | Bernard Hopkins |
| 1999 | Oscar De La Hoya | | |

### Best Male College Athlete

| Year | |
|------|--|
| 2002 | Cael Sanderson, Iowa St. wrestling |
| 2003 | Carmelo Anthony, Syracuse basketball |
| 2004 | Emeka Okafor, UConn basketball |
| 2005 | Matt Leinart, USC football |

### Best Female College Athlete

| Year | |
|------|--|
| 2002 | Sue Bird, UConn basketball |
| 2003 | Diana Taurasi, UConn basketball |
| 2004 | Diana Taurasi, UConn basketball |
| 2005 | Cat Osterman, Texas softball |

### Best Male Soccer Player

| Year | |
|------|--|
| 2002 | Landon Donovan |
| 2003 | Ronaldo |
| 2004 | David Beckham |
| 2005 | Award combined with female category |

### Best Female Soccer Player

| Year | |
|------|--|
| 2002 | Tiffeny Milbrett |
| 2003 | Katia |
| 2004 | Mia Hamm |
| 2005 | Award combined with male category |

### Best Soccer Player

| Year | |
|------|--|
| 2005 | Mia Hamm |

### Best Outdoors Athlete

| Year | |
|------|--|
| 2002 | Kevin VanDam, fishing |
| 2003 | Jay Yelas, fishing |
| 2004 | Tina Bosworth, log rolling |
| 2005 | J.R. Salzman, lumberjack |

### Best Action Sports Athlete

| Year | |
|------|--|
| 2002 | Kelly Clark, snowboarding |
| 2003 | Shaun White, snowboarding |
| 2004 | Award split into female and male categories |

### Best Male Action Sports Athlete

| Year | |
|------|--|
| 2004 | Ryan Nyquist, bike |
| 2005 | Dave Mirra, bike stunt |

### Best Female Action Sports Athlete

| Year | |
|------|--|
| 2004 | Dallas Friday, wakeboarding |
| 2005 | Sofia Mulanovich, surfing |

### Best Male Athlete with a Disability

| Year | |
|------|--|
| 2005 | Marlon Shirley, track & field |

### Best Female Athlete with a Disability

| Year | |
|------|--|
| 2005 | Erin Popovich, swimming |

### Best Sports Movie

| Year | | Year | |
|------|--|------|--|
| 2002 | The Rookie | 2004 | Miracle |
| 2003 | Bend it like Beckham | 2005 | Friday Night Lights |

### Best Record-Breaking Performance

| Year | |
|------|--|
| 2001 | Pete Sampras, Grand Slam singles titles |
| 2002 | Tiger Woods, four straight Majors |
| 2003 | Emmitt Smith, NFL rushing record |
| 2004 | Eric Gagne, baseball consecutive saves |
| 2005 | Peyton Manning, NFL single-season TD passes |

### Best Upset

| Year | |
|------|--|
| 2004 | Pistons over Lakers in NBA Finals |
| 2005 | #14 Bucknell over #3 Kansas in NCAA tournament |

### Arthur Ashe Award for Courage

Presented since 1993 on the annual ESPN "ESPYs" telecast. Given to a member of the sports community who has exemplified the same courage, spirit and determination to help others despite personal hardship that characterized Arthur Ashe, the late tennis champion and humanitarian. Voting done by select 26-member committee of media and sports personalities.

| Year | | Year | | Year | |
|------|--|------|--|------|--|
| 1993 | **Jim Valvano**, basketball | 1999 | **Billie Jean King**, tennis | 2003 | **Pat Tillman**, football & **Kevin Tillman**, baseball |
| 1994 | **Steve Palermo**, baseball | 2000 | **Dave Sanders**, Columbine H.S. coach | | |
| 1995 | **Howard Cosell**, TV & radio | | | 2004 | **George Weah**, soccer |
| 1996 | **Loretta Clairborne**, special olympics | 2001 | **Cathy Freeman**, track | 2005 | **Emmanuel Ofosu Yeboah** & **Jim MacLaren**, disabled athletes |
| 1997 | **Muhammad Ali**, boxing | 2002 | **Todd Beamer, Mark Bingham, Tom Burnett** and **Jeremy Glick**, Flight 93 | | |
| 1998 | **Dean Smith**, college basketball | | | | |

## The Hickok Belt

Officially known as the S. Rae Hickok Professional Athlete of the Year Award and presented by the Kickik Manufacturing Co. of Arlington, Texas, from 1950-76. The trophy was a large belt of gold, diamonds and other jewels, reportedly worth $30,000 in 1976, the last year it was handed out. Voting was done by 270 newspaper sports editors from around the country.
**Multiple winner:** Sandy Koufax (2).

| Year | | Year | | Year | |
|---|---|---|---|---|---|
| 1950 | **Phil Rizzuto**, baseball | 1960 | **Arnold Palmer**, golf | 1970 | **Brooks Robinson**, baseball |
| 1951 | **Allie Reynolds**, baseball | 1961 | **Roger Maris**, baseball | 1971 | **Lee Trevino**, golf |
| 1952 | **Rocky Marciano**, boxing | 1962 | **Maury Wills**, baseball | 1972 | **Steve Carlton**, baseball |
| 1953 | **Ben Hogan**, golf | 1963 | **Sandy Koufax**, baseball | 1973 | **O.J. Simpson**, football |
| 1954 | **Willie Mays**, baseball | 1964 | **Jim Brown**, football | 1974 | **Muhammad Ali**, boxing |
| 1955 | **Otto Graham**, football | 1965 | **Sandy Koufax**, baseball | 1975 | **Pete Rose**, baseball |
| 1956 | **Mickey Mantle**, baseball | 1966 | **Frank Robinson**, baseball | 1976 | **Ken Stabler**, football |
| 1957 | **Carmen Basilio**, boxing | 1967 | **Carl Yastrzemski**, baseball | 1977 | Discontinued |
| 1958 | **Bob Turley**, baseball | 1968 | **Joe Namath**, football | | |
| 1959 | **Ingemar Johansson**, boxing | 1969 | **Tom Seaver**, baseball | | |

## ABC's "Wide World of Sports" Athlete of the Year

Selected annually by the producers of ABC Sports since 1962.
**Multiple winners:** Greg LeMond and Tiger Woods (2).

| Year | | Year | | Year | |
|---|---|---|---|---|---|
| 1962 | **Jim Beatty**, track | 1975 | **Jack Nicklaus**, golf | 1989 | **Greg LeMond**, cycling |
| 1963 | **Valery Brumel**, track | 1976 | **Nadia Comaneci**, gymnastics | 1990 | **Greg LeMond**, cycling |
| 1964 | **Don Schollander**, swimming | 1977 | **Steve Cauthen**, horse racing | 1991 | **Carl Lewis**, track |
| 1965 | **Jim Clark**, auto racing | 1978 | **Ron Guidry**, baseball | | & **Kim Zmeskal**, gymnastics |
| 1966 | **Jim Ryun**, track | 1979 | **Willie Stargell**, baseball | 1992 | **Bonnie Blair**, speed skating |
| 1967 | **Peggy Fleming**, figure skating | 1980 | **U.S. Olympic hockey team** | 1993 | **Evander Holyfield**, boxing |
| 1968 | **Bill Toomey**, track | 1981 | **Sugar Ray Leonard**, boxing | 1994 | **Al Unser Jr.**, auto racing |
| 1969 | **Mario Andretti**, auto racing | 1982 | **Wayne Gretzky**, hockey | 1995 | **Miguel Indurlfain**, cycling |
| 1970 | **Willis Reed**, basketball | 1983 | **Australia II**, yachting | 1996 | **Michael Johnson**, track |
| 1971 | **Lee Trevino**, golf | 1984 | **Edwin Moses**, track | 1997 | **Tiger Woods**, golf |
| 1972 | **Olga Korbut**, gymnastics | 1985 | **Pete Rose**, baseball | 1998 | **Mark McGwire**, baseball |
| 1973 | **O.J. Simpson**, football | 1986 | **Debi Thomas**, figure skating | 1999 | **Lance Armstrong**, cycling |
| | & **Jackie Stewart**, auto racing | 1987 | **Dennis Conner**, yachting | 2000 | **Tiger Woods**, golf |
| 1974 | **Muhammad Ali**, boxing | 1988 | **Greg Louganis**, diving | 2001 | discontinued |

## Presidential Medal of Freedom

Since President John F. Kennedy established the Medal of Freedom as America's highest civilian honor in 1963, only 12 sports figures have won the award. Note that (*) indicates the presentation was made posthumously.

| Year | | President | Year | | President |
|---|---|---|---|---|---|
| 1963 | **Bob Kiphuth**, swimming | Kennedy | 1991 | **Ted Williams**, baseball | G. Bush |
| 1976 | **Jesse Owens**, track & field | Ford | 1992 | **Richard Petty**, auto racing | G. Bush |
| 1977 | **Joe DiMaggio**, baseball | Ford | 1993 | **Arthur Ashe***, tennis | Clinton |
| 1983 | **Paul (Bear) Bryant***, football | Reagan | 2002 | **Hank Aaron**, baseball | G.W. Bush |
| 1984 | **Jackie Robinson***, baseball | Reagan | 2003 | **John Wooden**, basketball | G.W. Bush |
| 1986 | **Earl (Red) Blaik**, football | Reagan | 2004 | **Arnold Palmer**, golf | G.W. Bush |

## Congressional Gold Medal

Since the American Revolution, the U.S. Congress has commissioned gold medals as its highest expression of national appreciation for distinguished achievements and contributions. The medals are produced by the U.S. Mint. Each medal honors a particular individual, institution or event. Only four sports figure have won the award but note that track legend **Wilma Rudolph** has been nominated for, but not yet awarded, the Congressional gold medal.

| Year | | Year | |
|---|---|---|---|
| 1973 | **Roberto Clemente**, baseball | 1988 | **Jesse Owens**, track & field |
| 1982 | **Joe Louis**, boxing | 2005 | **Jackie Robinson**, baseball |

## *Time* Person of the Year

Since Charles Lindbergh was named *Time* magazine's first Man of the Year for 1927, two individuals with significant sports credentials have won the honor.

| Year | |
|---|---|
| 1984 | **Peter Ueberroth**, president of the Los Angeles Olympic Organizing Committee. |
| 1991 | **Ted Turner**, owner-president of Turner Broadcasting System, founder of CNN cable news network, owner of the Atlanta Braves (NL) and Atlanta Hawks (NBA), and former winning America's Cup skipper. |

## TROPHY CASE

From the first organized track meet at Olympia in 776 B.C., to the Athens Summer Olympics over 2,700 years later, championships have been officially recognized with prizes that are symbolically rich and eagerly pursued. Here are 15 of the most coveted trophies in America.

*(Illustrations by Lynn Mercer Michaud)*

### America's Cup

First presented by England's Royal Yacht Squadron to the winner of an invitational race around the Isle of Wight on Aug. 22, 1851 . . . originally called the Hundred Guinea Cup . . . renamed after the U.S. boat America, winner of the first race . . . made of sterling silver and designed by London jewelers R. & G. Garrard . . . measures 2 feet, 3 inches high and weighs 16 lbs . . . originally cost 100 guineas ($500), now valued at $250,000 . . . bell-shaped base added in 1958 . . . challenged for every three to four years . . . trophy held by yacht club sponsoring winning boat . . . Cup was badly damaged when a Maori protester repeatedly smashed it with a sledgehammer on March 14, 1997. It was sent back to the original maker and fully restored.

### Vince Lombardi Trophy

First presented at the AFL-NFL World Championship Game (now Super Bowl) on Jan. 15, 1967 . . . originally called the World Championship Game Trophy . . . renamed in 1971 in honor of former Green Bay Packers GM-coach and two-time Super Bowl winner Vince Lombardi, who died in 1970 as coach of Washington . . .made of sterling silver and designed by Tiffany & Co. of New York . . . measures 21 inches high and weighs 7 lbs (football depicted is regulation size) . . . valued at $12,500 . . . competed for annually . . . winning team keeps trophy.

### Olympic Gold Medal

First presented by International Olympic Committee in 1908 (until then winners received silver medals) . . . second and third place finishers also got medals of silver and bronze for first time in 1908 . . . each medal must be at least 2.4 inches in diameter and 0.12 inches thick . . . tthe gold medal is actually made of silver, but must be gilded with at least 6 grams (0.21 ounces) of pure gold . . . the medals for the 1996 Atlanta Games were designed by Malcolm Grear Designers and produced by Reed & Barton of Taunton, Mass . . 604 gold, 604 silver and 630 bronze medals were made . . . competed for every two years as Winter and Summer Games alternate . . . winners keep medals.

# Awards (Cont.)

## Stanley Cup

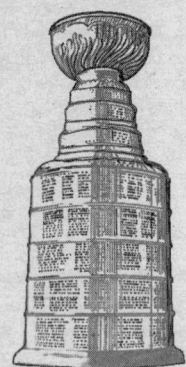

Donated by Lord Stanley of Preston, the Governor General of Canada and first presented in 1893 . . . original cup was made of sterling silver by an unknown London silversmith and measured 7 inches high with an 11½-inch diameter . . . in order to accommodate all the rosters of winning teams, the cup now measures 35½ inches high with a base 54 inches around and weighs 32 lbs . . . in order to add new names each year, bands on the trophy are often retired and displayed at the Hall of Fame . . . originally bought for 10 guineas ($48.67), it is now insured for $75,000 . . . actual cup retired to Hall of Fame and replaced in 1970 . . . presented to NHL playoff champion since 1918 . . . trophy loaned to winning team for one year.

## World Cup

First presented by the Federation Internationale de Football Association (FIFA) . . . originally called the World Cup Trophy . . . renamed the Jules Rimet Cup (after the then FIFA president) in 1946, but retired by Brazil after that country's third title in 1970 . . . new World Cup trophy created in 1974 . . . designed by Italian sculptor Silvio Gazzaniga and made of solid 18 carat gold with two malachite rings inlaid at the base . . . measures 14.2 inches high and weighs 11 lbs . . . insured for $200,000 (U.S.) . . . competed for every four years . . . winning team gets gold-plated replica.

## Commissioner's Trophy

First presented by the Commissioner of baseball to the winner of the 1967 World Series . . . also known as the World Championship Trophy . . . made of brass and gold plate with an ebony base and a baseball in the center made of pewter with a silver finish . . . designed by Balfour & Co. of Attleboro, Mass . . . 30 pennants represent 14 AL and 16 NL teams . . . measures 30 inches high and 36 inches around at the base and weighs 30 lbs . . . valued at $15,000 . . . competed for annually . . . winning team keeps trophy.

## Larry O'Brien Trophy

First presented in 1978 to winner of NBA Finals . . . originally called the Walter A. Brown Trophy after the league pioneer and Boston Celtics owner (an earlier NBA championship bowl was also named after Brown) . . . renamed in 1984 in honor of outgoing commissioner O'Brien, who served from 1975-84 . . . made of sterling silver with 24 carat gold overlay and designed by Tiffany & Co. of New York . . . measures 2 feet high and weighs 14½ lbs (basketball depicted is regulation size) . . . valued at $13,500 . . . competed for annually . . . winning team keeps trophy.

### Heisman Trophy

First presented in 1935 to the best college football player east of the Mississippi by the Downtown Athletic Club of New York . . . players across the entire country eligible since 1936 . . . originally called the DAC Trophy . . . renamed in 1936 following the death of DAC athletic director and former college coach John W. Heisman . . . made of bronze and designed by New York sculptor Frank Eliscu, it measures 13½ in. high, 6½ in. wide and 14 in. long at the base and weighs 25 lbs . . . valued at $2,000 . . . voting done by national media and former Heisman winners . . . trophy sponsor American Suzuki announced plans for limited fan voting starting in 1999 . . . awarded annually . . . winner keeps trophy.

### James E. Sullivan Memorial Award

First presented by the Amateur Athletic Union (AAU) in 1930 as a gold medal and given to the nation's outstanding amateur athlete . . . trophy given since 1933 . . . named after the amateur sports movement pioneer, who was a founder and past president of AAU and the director of the 1904 Olympic Games in St. Louis . . . made of bronze with a marble base, it measures 17½ in. high and 11 in. wide at the base and weighs 13½ lbs . . . valued at $2,500 . . . voting done by AAU and USOC officials, former winners and selected media . . . awarded annually . . . winner keeps trophy.

### Ryder Cup

Donated in 1927 by English seed merchant Samuel Ryder, who offered the gold cup for a biennial match between teams of golfing pros from Great Britain and the United States . . . the format changed in 1977 to include the best players on the European PGA Tour . . . made of 14 carat gold on a wood base and designed by Mappin and Webb of London . . . the golfer depicted on the top of the trophy is Ryder's friend and teaching pro Abe Mitchell . . . the cup measures 16 in. high and weighs 4 lbs . . . insured for $50,000 . . . competed for every two years at alternating European and U.S. sites . . . the cup is held by the PGA headquarters of the winning side.

### Davis Cup

Donated by American college student and U.S. doubles champion Dwight F. Davis in 1900 and presented by the International Tennis Federation (ITF) to the winner of the annual 16-team men's competition . . . officially called the International Lawn Tennis Challenge Trophy . . . made of sterling silver and designed by Shreve, Crump and Low of Boston, the cup has a matching tray (added in 1921) and a very heavy two-tiered base containing rosters of past winning teams . . . it stands 34½ in. high and 108 in. around at the base and weighs 400 lbs . . . insured for $150,000 . . . competed for annually . . . trophy loaned to winning country for one year.

### Borg-Warner Trophy

First presented by the Borg-Warner Automotive Co. of Chicago in 1936 to the winner of the Indianapolis 500 . . . replaced the Wheeler-Schebler Trophy which went to the 400-mile leader from 1911-32 . . . made of sterling silver with bas-relief sculptured heads of each winning driver and a gold bas-relief head of Tony Hulman, the owner of the Indy Speedway from 1945-77 . . . designed by Robert J. Hill and made by Gorham, Inc. of Rhode Island . . . measures 51½ in. high and weighs over 80 lbs . . . new base added in 1988 and the entire trophy restored in 1991 . . . competed for annually . . . insured for $1 million . . . trophy stays at Speedway Hall of Fame . . . winner gets a 14-in. high replica valued at $30,000.

### NCAA Championship Trophy

First presented in 1952 by the NCAA to all 1st, 2nd and 3rd place teams in sports with sanctioned tournaments . . . 1st place teams receive gold-plated awards, 2nd place award is silver-plated and 3rd is bronze . . . replaced silver cup given to championship teams from 1939-51 . . . made of walnut, the trophy stands 24¾ in. high, 14⅛ in. wide and 4½ in. deep at the base and weighs 15 lbs . . . designed by Medallic Art Co. of Danbury, Conn. and made by House of Usher of Kansas City since 1990 . . . valued at $500 . . . competed for annually . . . winning teams keep trophies.

### World Championship Belt

First presented in 1921 by the World Boxing Association, one of the three organizations (the World Boxing Council and International Boxing Federation are the others) generally accepted as sanctioning legitimate world championship fights . . . belt weighs 8 lbs. and is made of hand tanned leather . . . the outsized buckle measures 10½ in. high and 8 in. wide, is made of pewter with 24 carat gold plate and contains crystal and semi-precious stones . . . side panels of polished brass are for engraving title bout results . . . currently made by Champbelts by Ronn Scala in Pittsburgh . . . champions keep belts even if they lose their title.

### World Championship Ring

Rings decorated with gems and engraving date back to ancient Egypt where the wealthy wore heavy gold and silver rings to indicate social status . . . championship rings in sports serve much the same purpose, indicating the wearer is a champion . . . As an example, the Dallas Cowboys' ring for winning Superbowl XXX on Jan. 28, 1996 was designed by Diamond Cutters International of Houston . . . each ring is made of 14 carat yellow gold, weighs 48-51 penny weights and features five trimmed marquis diamonds interlocking in the shape of the Cowboys' star logo as well as five more marquis diamonds (for the team's five Super Bowl wins) on a bed of 51 smaller diamonds . . . rings were appraised at over $30,000 each.

# Who's Who

In Oxford, England on May 6, 1954, med student **Roger Bannister** became the first man in history to run a mile in under four minutes.

AP/Wide World Photos

# Sports Personalities
Nine hundred thirty-six entries dating back to the 19th century. Entries updated through Oct. 1, 2005.

**Hank Aaron** (b. Feb. 5, 1934): Baseball OF; led NL in HRs and RBI 4 times each and batting twice with Milwaukee and Atlanta Braves; MVP in 1957; played in 24 All-Star Games, all-time leader in HRs (755), RBI (2,297), total bases (6,856), 3rd in hits (3,771); won 3 Gold Gloves; executive with Braves.

**Kareem Abdul-Jabbar** (b. Lew Alcindor, Apr. 16, 1947): Basketball C; led UCLA to 3 NCAA titles (1967-69); Final 4 MOP 3 times; Player of Year twice; led Milwaukee (1) and LA Lakers (5) to 6 NBA titles; playoff MVP twice (1971,85), regular season MVP 6 times (1971-72,74,76-77,80); retired in 1989 after 20 seasons as all-time leader in over 20 categories.

**Andre Agassi** (b. Apr. 29, 1970): Tennis; 60 career tournament wins including the career grand slam; Wimbledon (1992), U.S. Open (1994,99), Australian Open (1995,2000,01,03), French Open (1999); helped U.S. win 2 Davis Cup finals (1990,92); regained the world No. 1 ranking in 1999 for the first time since 1996; made inspiring run to U.S. Open final in 2005 before falling to No. 1 Roger Federer.

**Troy Aikman** (b. Nov. 21, 1966): Football QB; consensus All-America at UCLA (1988); 1st overall pick in 1989 NFL Draft (by Dallas); led Cowboys to 3 Super Bowl titles (1992,93,95 seasons); MVP of Super Bowl XXVII.

**Marv Albert** (b. June 12, 1941): Radio-TV; NBC announcer and radio broadcaster for the New York Knicks, Rangers and Giants who pleaded guilty to a misdemeanor assault charge amid embarrassing allegations of his sex life. Rehired to MSG and Turner networks in 1998 and NBC in '99.

**Tenley Albright** (b. July 18, 1935): Figure skater; 2-time world champion (1953,55); won Olympic silver (1952) and gold (1956) medals; became a surgeon.

**Amy Alcott** (b. Feb. 22, 1956): Golfer; 29 career wins, including five majors; inducted into World Golf Hall of Fame in 1999.

**Grover Cleveland (Pete) Alexander** (b. Feb. 26, 1887, d. Nov. 4, 1950): Baseball RHP; won 20 or more games 9 times; 373 career wins and 90 shutouts.

**Muhammad Ali** (b. Cassius Clay, Jan. 17, 1942): Boxer; 1960 Olympic light heavyweight champion; 3-time world heavyweight champ (1964-67, 1974-78,1978-79); defeated Sonny Liston (1964), George Foreman (1974) and Leon Spinks (1978) for title; fought Joe Frazier in 3 memorable bouts (1971-75), winning twice; adopted Black Muslim faith in 1964 and changed name; stripped of title in 1967 after conviction for refusing induction into U.S. Army; verdict reversed by Supreme Court in 1971; career record of 56-5 with 37 KOs and 19 successful title defenses; lit the flaming cauldron to signal the beginning of the 1996 Summer Olympics in Atlanta.

**Forrest (Phog) Allen** (b. Nov. 18, 1885, d. Sept. 16, 1974): Basketball; college coach 48 years; directed Kansas to NCAA title (1952); 746 wins.

**Bobby Allison** (b. Dec. 3, 1937): Auto racer; 3-time winner of Daytona 500 (1978,82,88); NASCAR national champ in 1983; father of Davey.

**Davey Allison** (b. Feb. 25, 1961, d. July 13, 1993): Auto racer; stock car Rookie of Year (1987); winner of 19 NASCAR races, including 1992 Daytona 500; killed at age 32 in helicopter accident at Talladega Superspeedway; son of Bobby.

**Roberto Alomar** (b. Feb. 5, 1968): Baseball; 10-time Gold Glove second baseman; MVP of 1992 ALCS; became known well beyond baseball for spitting in the face of umpire John Hirschbeck during final weekend of 1996 season; named MVP of 1998 All-Star Game.

**Walter Alston** (b. Dec. 1, 1911, d. Oct. 1, 1984): Baseball; managed Brooklyn-LA Dodgers 23 years; won 7 pennants and 4 World Series (1955,59,63,65); retired after 1976 season with 2,063 wins (2,040 regular season and 23 postseason).

**Gary Anderson** (b. July 16, 1959): Football K; all-time leading scorer in NFL history; had perfect regular season in 1998 (59/59 PAT, 35/35 FG); held NFL record for consecutive FG made (40, broken by M. Vanderjagt's 42); led AFC in scoring 3 times (1983-85 with Steelers) and NFC once (1998 with Vikings).

**Sparky Anderson** (b. Feb. 22, 1934): Baseball; only manager to win World Series in each league—Cincinnati in NL (1975-76) and Detroit in AL (1984); 4th-ranked skipper on all-time career list with 2,228 wins (2,194 regular season and 34 postseason); inducted into the Baseball Hall of Fame in 2000.

**Mario Andretti** (b. Feb. 28, 1940): Auto racer; 4-time USAC-CART national champion (1965-66,69,84); only driver to win Daytona 500 (1967), Indy 500 (1969) and Formula One world title (1978); Indy 500 Rookie of Year (1965); retired after 1994 racing season ranked 1st in poles (67) and starts (407) and 2nd in wins (52) on all-time CART list; father of Michael and Jeff, uncle of John.

**Michael Andretti** (b. Oct. 5, 1962): Auto racer; 1991 CART national champion with single-season record 8 wins; Indy 500 Rookie of Year (1984); left IndyCar circuit for ill-fated Formula One try in 1993; returned to IndyCar in 1994; son of Mario.

**Earl Anthony** (b. Apr. 27, 1938, d. Aug. 14, 2001): Bowler; 6-time PBA Bowler of Year; 41 career titles; first to earn $100,000 in 1 season (1975); first to earn $1 million in career; won 10 Majors (2 Tournament of Champions, 6 PBA National Championships and 2 ABC Masters).

**Said Aouita** (b. Nov. 2, 1959): Moroccan runner; won gold (5000m) and bronze (800m) in 1984 Olympics; won 5000m at 1987 World Championships; formerly held 2 world records recognized by IAAF—2000m and 5000m.

**Luis Aparicio** (b. Apr. 29, 1934): Baseball SS; retired as all-time leader in most games, assists and double plays by shortstop; led AL in stolen bases 9 times (1956-64); 506 career steals.

**Al Arbour** (b. Nov. 1, 1932): Hockey; coached NY Islanders to 4 straight Stanley Cup titles (1980-83); retired after 1993-94 season; 2nd on all-time career list with 904 wins (781 regular season and 123 postseason); elected to Hockey Hall of Fame in 1996.

**Eddie Arcaro** (b. Feb. 19, 1916, d. Nov. 14, 1997): Jockey; 2-time Triple Crown winner (Whirlaway in 1941, Citation in '48); he won Kentucky Derby 5 times, Preakness and Belmont 6 times each.

**Roone Arledge** (b. July 8, 1931, d. Dec. 5, 2002): Sports TV pioneer; innovator of live events, anthology shows, Olympic coverage, "Monday Night Football" and "Wide World of Sports"; ran ABC Sports from 1968-86; ran ABC News from 1977-98.

**Henry Armstrong** (b. Dec. 12, 1912, d. Oct. 22, 1988): Boxer; held feather-, light- and welterweight titles simultaneously in 1938; pro record 152-21-8 with 100 KOs.

**Lance Armstrong** (b. Sept. 18, 1971): Cyclist; Texan who made cycling history becoming the first 6-time, then 7-time winner of the Tour de France (1999-2005); returned from treatment for testicular cancer to become the world's top cyclist; only the 2nd American winner (Greg Lemond) in the race's history; engaged to singer Sheryl Crowe.

**Arthur Ashe** (b. July 10, 1943, d. Feb. 6, 1993): Tennis; first black man to win U.S. Championship (1968) and Wimbledon (1975); 1st U.S. player to earn $100,000 in 1 year (1970); won Davis Cup as player (1968-70) and captain (1981-82); wrote black sports history, Hard Road to Glory; announced in 1992 that he was infected with AIDS virus during a blood transfusion during 1983 heart surgery; in 1997, the new home for the U.S. Open was named Arthur Ashe Stadium.

**Evelyn Ashford** (b. Apr. 15, 1957): Track & Field; winner of 4 Olympic gold medals—100m in 1984, and 4x100m in 1984, '88 and '92; also won silver medal in 100m in '88; member of 5 U.S. Olympic teams (1976-92); Inducted into Track and Field and Women's Sports Halls of Fame in 1997.

**Red Auerbach** (b. Sept. 20, 1917): Basketball; retired as winningest all-time coach (regular season and playoffs) in NBA history (now 5th); won 1,037 times in 20 years; as coach-GM, led Boston to a record 9 NBA titles, including 8 in a row (1959-66); also coached defunct Washington Capitols (1946-49); NBA Coach of the Year award named after him; retired as Celtics coach in 1966 and as GM in '84; club president from 1970 to 1997 and then again beginning in 2001.

**Tracy Austin** (b. Dec. 12, 1962): Tennis; youngest player to win U.S. Open (age 16 in 1979); won 2nd U.S. Open in '81; named AP Female Athlete of Year twice before she was 20; recurring neck and back injuries shortened career after 1983; youngest player ever inducted into Tennis Hall of Fame (age 29 in 1992).

**Paul Azinger** (b. Jan. 6, 1960): Golf; PGA Player of Year (1987); 12 career wins, including '93 PGA Championship; missed most of '94 season overcoming lymphoma (a form of cancer) in right shoulder blade; member of 4 U.S. Ryder Cup teams (1989,91,93,2002).

**Bob Baffert** (b. Jan. 13, 1953): Horse racing; 3-time Eclipse Award winner as outstanding trainer (1997-99); trained 3 Kentucky Derby winners (1997,98,02), 4 Preakness winners (1997,98,01,02) and 1 Belmont Stakes winner (2001); 4-time leading annual money leader for trainers (1998-01).

**Donovan Bailey** (b. Dec. 16, 1967): Track; Jamaican-born Canadian sprinter who set world record in the 100m (9.84) in gold medal-winning performance at 1996 Olympics which stood until '99; set indoor record in 50m (5.56) in 1996; member of Canadian 4x100 relay that won gold in 1996 Olympics.

**Oksana Baiul** (b. Feb. 26, 1977): Ukrainian figure skater; 1993 world champion at age 15; edged Nancy Kerrigan by a 5-4 judges' vote for 1994 Olympic gold medal.

**Hobey Baker** (b. Jan. 15, 1892, d. Dec. 21, 1918): Football and hockey star at Princeton (1911-14); member of college football and pro hockey Halls of Fame; college hockey Player of Year award named after him; killed in plane crash.

**Seve Ballesteros** (b. Apr. 9, 1957): Spanish golfer; has won British Open 3 times (1979,84,88) and Masters twice (1980,83); 3-time European Golfer of Year (1986,88,91); has led Europe to 5 Ryder Cup titles (1985,87,89,95,97).

**Ernie Banks** (b. Jan. 31, 1931): Baseball SS-1B; led NL in home runs and RBI twice each; 2-time MVP (1958-59) with Chicago Cubs; 512 career HRs.

**Roger Bannister** (b. Mar. 23, 1929): British runner; first to run mile in less than 4 minutes (3:59.4 on May 6, 1954).

**Walter (Red) Barber** (b. Feb. 17, 1908, d. Oct. 22, 1992): Radio-TV; renowned baseball play-by-play broadcaster for Cincinnati, Brooklyn and N.Y. Yankees from 1934-66; won Peabody Award for radio commentary in 1991.

**Charles Barkley** (b. Feb. 20, 1963): Basketball F; 5-time All-NBA 1st team with Philadelphia and Phoenix; U.S. Olympic Dream Team member in '92; NBA regular season MVP in 1993; currently a basketball announcer for TNT.

**Leon Barmore** (b. June 3, 1944): college basketball coach; respected coach of Louisiana Tech Lady Techsters; career win pct. of .869 (576-87, 20 yrs) is best all-time; won national championship with Louisiana Tech in 1988.

**Rick Barry** (b. Mar. 28, 1944): Basketball F; only player to lead both NBA and ABA in scoring; 5-time All-NBA 1st team; Finals MVP with Golden St. in 1975. Perfected the underhand foul shot.

**Sammy Baugh** (b. Mar. 17, 1914): Football QB-DB-P; led Washington to NFL titles in 1937 (his rookie year) and '42; led league in passing 6 times, punting 4 times and interceptions once.

**Elgin Baylor** (b. Sept. 16, 1934): Basketball F; MOP of Final 4 in 1958; led Minneapolis-LA Lakers to 8 NBA Finals; 10-time All-NBA 1st team (1959-65,67-69); LA Clippers' VP of basketball operations.

**Bob Beamon** (b. Aug. 29, 1946): Track & Field; won 1968 Olympic gold medal in long jump with world record (29-ft, 2½in.) that shattered old mark by nearly 2 feet; record finally broken by 2 inches in 1991 by Mike Powell.

**Franz Beckenbauer** (b. Sept. 11, 1945): Soccer; captain of West German World Cup champions in 1974 then coached West Germany to World Cup title in 1990; invented sweeper position; played in U.S. for NY Cosmos (1977-80,83)

**Boris Becker** (b. Nov. 22, 1967): German tennis player; 3-time Wimbledon champ (1985-86,89); youngest male (17) to win Wimbledon; led country to 1st Davis Cup win in 1988; has also won U.S. (1989) and Australian (1991,96) Opens.

**Chuck Bednarik** (b. May 1, 1925): Football C-LB; 2-time All-America at Penn and 7-time All-Pro with NFL Eagles as both center (1950) and linebacker (1951-56); missed only 3 games in 14 seasons; led Eagles to 1960 NFL title as a 35-year-old two-way player.

**Clair Bee** (b. Mar. 2, 1896, d. May 20, 1983): Basketball coach who led LIU to 2 undefeated seasons (1936,39) and 2 NIT titles (1939,41); his teams won 95 percent of their games between 1931-51, including 43 in a row from 1935-37; coached NBA Baltimore Bullets from 1952-54, but was only 34-116; contributions to game include 1-3-1 zone defense, 3-second rule and NBA 24-second clock.

**Bill Belichick** (b. Apr. 16, 1952): Football; long-time assistant to Bill Parcells who became head coach of N.E. Patriots in 2000 and went on to win 3 Super Bowls; best playoff record in NFL history (10-1).

**Jean Beliveau** (b. Aug. 31, 1931): Hockey C; led Montreal to 10 Stanley Cups in 17 playoffs; play-off MVP (1965); 2-time regular season MVP (1956,64).

**Bert Bell** (b. Feb. 25, 1895, d. Oct. 11, 1959): Football; team owner and 2nd NFL commissioner (1946-59); proposed college draft in 1935 and instituted TV blackout rule.

**James (Cool Papa) Bell** (b. May 17, 1903, d. Mar. 8, 1991): Baseball; member of the Negro Leagues; widely considered the fastest player ever to play baseball; also coached for the Kansas City Monarchs, teaching such players as Jackie Robinson; member of the National Baseball Hall of Fame.

**Deane Beman** (b. Apr. 22, 1938): Golf; 1st commissioner of PGA Tour (1974-94); introduced "stadium golf" and created The Players Championship; as player, won U.S. Amateur twice and British Amateur once; inducted into the World Golf Hall of Fame in 2000.

**Johnny Bench** (b. Dec. 7, 1947): Baseball C; led NL in HRs twice and RBI 3 times; 2-time regular season MVP (1970,72) with Cincinnati, World Series MVP in 1976; 389 career HRs.

**Patty Berg** (b. Feb. 13, 1918): Golfer; 60 career pro wins, including 15 majors; 3-time AP Female Athlete of Year (1938,43,55).

**Chris Berman** (b. May 10, 1955): Radio-TV; 6-time National Sportscaster of Year famous for his nicknames and jovial studio anchoring on ESPN; play-by-play man first year Brown University football team won the Ivy League (1976).

**Yogi Berra** (b. May 12, 1925): Baseball C; played on 10 World Series winners with NY Yankees; holds WS records for games played (75), at bats (259) and hits (71); 3-time AL MVP (1951,54-55); managed both Yankees (1964) and NY Mets (1973) to pennants.

**Jay Berwanger** (b. Mar. 19, 1914, d. June 26, 2002): Football HB; Univ. of Chicago star; won 1st Heisman Trophy in 1935; top selection in the 1st-ever NFL Draft (1936).

**Gary Bettman** (b. June 2, 1952): Hockey; former NBA executive, who was named first commissioner of NHL on Dec. 11, 1992; took office on Feb. 1, 1993; announced NHL lockout on Sept. 15, 2004.

**Abebe Bikila** (b. Aug. 7, 1932, d. Oct. 25, 1973): Ethiopian runner; 1st to win consecutive Olympic marathons (1960,64).

**Matt Biondi** (b. Oct. 8, 1965): Swimmer; won 7 medals in 1988 Olympics, including 5 gold (2 individual, 3 relay); won a total of 11 medals (8 gold, 2 silver and a bronze) in 3 Olympics (1984,88,92).

**Larry Bird** (b. Dec. 7, 1956): Basketball F; college Player of Year (1979) at Indiana St.; 1980 NBA Rookie of Year; 9-time All-NBA 1st team; 3-time regular season MVP (1984-86); led Boston to 3 NBA titles (1981,84, 86); 2-time Finals MVP (1984,86); U.S. Olympic Dream Team member in '92; inducted into Hall of Fame in 1998; in 1997, named coach of Indiana Pacers and won Coach of the Year honors in first season; led the Pacers to the NBA Finals in 2000 but lost in 6 games to the Lakers and retired; named president of basketball operations of Pacers in 2003.

**The Black Sox:** Eight Chicago White Sox players who were banned from baseball for life in 1921 for allegedly throwing the 1919 World Series— RHP Eddie Cicotte (1884-1969), OF Happy Felsch (1891-1964), 1B Chick Gandil (1887-1970), OF Shoeless Joe Jackson (1889-1951), INF Fred McMullin (1891-1952), SS Swede Risberg (1894-1975), 3B-SS Buck Weaver (1890-1956), and LHP Lefty Williams (1893-1959).

**Earl (Red) Blaik** (b. Feb. 15, 1897, d. May 6, 1989): Football; coached Army to consecutive national titles in 1944-45; 166 career wins and 3 Heisman winners (Blanchard, Davis, Dawkins).

**Bonnie Blair** (b. Mar. 18, 1964): Speed skater; only American woman to win 5 Olympic gold medals in Winter Games; won 500-meters in 1988, then 500m and 1,000m in both 1992 and '94; added 1,000m bronze in 1988; Sullivan Award winner (1992); retired on 31st birthday as reigning world sprint champ.

**Hector (Toe) Blake** (b. Aug. 21, 1912, d. May 17, 1995): Hockey LW; led Montreal to 2 Stanley Cups as a player and 8 more as coach; 1939 NHL MVP.

**Felix (Doc) Blanchard** (b. Dec. 11, 1924): Football FB; 3-time All-America; led Army to national titles in 1944-45; Glenn Davis' running mate; won Heisman Trophy and Sullivan Award in 1945.

**George Blanda** (b. Sept. 17, 1927): Football QB-PK; was pro football's all-time leading scorer (2,002 points) until 2000 when he was finally passed by kicker Gary Anderson; led Houston to 2 AFL titles (1960-61); played 26 pro seasons; retired at age 48.

**Fanny Blankers-Koen** (b. Apr. 26, 1918, d. Jan. 25, 2004): Dutch sprinter; 30-year-old mother of two, who won 4 gold medals (100m, 200m, 800m hurdles and 4x100m relay) at 1948 Olympics.

**Drew Bledsoe** (b. Feb. 14, 1972): Football QB; 1st overall pick in 1993 NFL draft (N.E. Patriots); one of only 10 QBs in NFL history with 40,000 career passing yards; traded to Buffalo before 2002 season; signed with Dallas in 2005.

**Jim Boeheim** (b. Nov. 17, 1944): Basketball; long-time coach at Syracuse; finally won 1st NCAA title in 2003; entered 2005-06 with career record of 703-241.

**Wade Boggs** (b. June 15, 1958): Baseball 3B; 5 AL batting titles (1983,85-88) with Boston Red Sox; 11-time All-Star; two Gold Gloves; later played with NY Yankees and Tampa Bay; got 3000th career hit with a home run Aug. 7, 1999 against Cleveland; inducted into Hall of Fame in 2005.

**Barry Bonds** (b. July 24, 1964): Baseball OF; set MLB single-season HR record in 2001 with 73; 7-time NL MVP, 2 with Pittsburgh (1990,92) and 5 with San Francisco (1993,2001-04); one of only 3 men with 40 HRs and 40 SBs in same season (1996); became the 3rd player to reach 700 career HRs in 2004 (had 708 through 2005 season); holds major league record for single season (2004) and career walks; hit .370 in 2002 at age 38; son of Bobby.

**Bjorn Borg** (b. June 6, 1956): Swedish tennis player; 2-time Player of Year (1979-80); won 6 French Opens and 5 straight Wimbledons (1976-80); led Sweden to 1st Davis Cup win in 1975; retired in 1983 at age 26; attempted unsuccessful comeback in 1991.

**Mike Bossy** (b. Jan. 22, 1957): Hockey RW; led NY Isles to 4 Stanley Cups; playoff MVP in 1982; 50 goals or more 9 straight years; 573 career goals.

**Ralph Boston** (b. May 9, 1939): Track & Field; medaled in 3 consecutive Olympic long jumps— gold (1960), silver (1964), bronze (1968).

**Ray Bourque** (b. Dec. 28, 1960): Hockey D; 12-time All-NHL 1st team; won 5 Norris Trophies (1987-88,1990-91,94) with Boston; '96 All-Star Game MVP; all-time leader for points and assists by a defenseman; won 2001 Stanley Cup with Colorado then retired; elected to Hall of Fame in 2004.

**Bobby Bowden** (b. Nov. 8, 1929): Football; coached Florida St. to 2 national titles (1993,99); entered 2005 season as all-time wins leader in college football history with 351 victories including a 19-8-1 bowl record in 39 years as coach at Samford, West Va. and FSU; father of Clemson head coach Tommy and former Auburn coach Terry.

**Riddick Bowe** (b. Aug. 10, 1967): Boxer; former undisputed heavyweight champ who fought career-defining trilogy with Evander Holyfield (1992-1995); won 1st meeting by decision, lost rematch in "Fan Man Fight," won last Holyfield fight by 8th-round KO.

**Scotty Bowman** (b. Sept. 18, 1933): Hockey coach; all-time winningest NHL coach in both regular season (1,244) and playoffs (223) over 30 seasons; coached a record nine Stanley Cup winners with Montreal (1973,76-79), Pittsburgh (1992) and Detroit (1997,98,2002); retired after 2001-02 season.

**Jack Brabham** (b. Apr. 2, 1926): Australian auto racer; 3-time Formula One champion (1959-60,66); 14 career wins; member of the Hall of Fame.

**James J. Braddock** (b. June 7, 1905, d. Nov. 29, 1974): Boxer; journeyman who won heavyweight belt in 10-1 upset of hard-hitting Max Baer in 1935.

**Bill Bradley** (b. July 28, 1943): Basketball F; 2-time All-America at Princeton; Player of the Year and Final 4 MOP in 1965; captain of gold medal-winning 1964 Olympic team; Sullivan Award winner (1965); led NY Knicks to 2 NBA titles (1970,73); U.S. Senator (D, N.J.) 1979-95; ran for President in 2000.

**Pat Bradley** (b. Mar. 24, 1951): Golfer; 2-time LPGA Player of Year (1986,91); won career LPGA grand slam, including 3 du Maurier Classics; inducted into the LPGA Hall of Fame on Jan. 18, 1992; among all-time LPGA money leaders and tournament winners (31); captained the 2000 U.S. Solheim Cup team.

**Terry Bradshaw** (b. Sept. 2, 1948): Football QB; led Pittsburgh to 4 Super Bowl titles (1975-76,79-80); 2-time Super Bowl MVP (1979-80) and regular season MVP in 1978; Fox TV studio analyst.

**Tom Brady** (b. Aug. 3, 1977): Football QB; 6th-round draft pick (Michigan) who became 3-time Super Bowl winner with N.E. Patriots, 2-time Super Bowl MVP.

**George Brett** (b. May 15, 1953): Baseball 3B-1B; AL batting champion in 3 different decades (1976,80,90); MVP in 1980; led KC to World Series title in 1985; retired after 1993 season with 3,154 hits and .305 average; inducted into Hall of Fame in 1999.

**Valerie Brisco-Hooks** (b. July 6, 1960): Track & Field; won three gold medals at the 1984 Olympics (200 meters, 400 meters and 4x100 relay); first athlete to ever win the 200 and 400 in the same Olympics.

**Lou Brock** (b. June 18, 1939): Baseball OF; former all-time stolen base leader (938); led NL in SBs 8 times; led St. Louis to 2 World Series titles (1964,67); 3,023 career hits.

**Herb Brooks** (b. Aug. 5, 1937, d. Aug. 11, 2003): Hockey; former U.S. Olympic player (1964,68) who coached 1980 "Miracle on Ice" team to gold medal and 2002 U.S. team to silver medal; coached Minnesota to 3 NCAA titles (1974,76,78); also coached 4 NHL teams.

**Jim Brown** (b. Feb. 17, 1936): Football FB; All-America at Syracuse (1956) and NFL Rookie of Year (1957); led NFL in rushing 8 times; 8-time All-Pro (1957-61,63-65); 3-time MVP (1958,63,65) with Cleveland; ran for 12,312 yards and scored 126 touchdowns in just 9 seasons; went to jail for 4 mos in 2002 after he was convicted of vandalizing his wife's car and refused court ordered counseling.

**Larry Brown** (b. Sept. 14, 1940): Basketball; played in ACC, AAU, 1964 Olympics and ABA; 3-time assist leader (1968-70) and 3-time Coach of Year (1973,75-76) in ABA; coached ABA's Carolina and Denver and NBA's Denver, N.J., San Antonio, LA Clippers, Indiana, Philadelphia, Detroit and N.Y. Knicks, winning the 2004 NBA title with Pistons; also coached UCLA to NCAA Final (1980), Kansas to NCAA title (1988) and the USA men's basketball team to a disappointing bronze medal in Athens in 2004.

**Mordecai (Three-Finger) Brown** (b. Oct. 18, 1876, d. Feb. 14, 1948): Baseball; nickname derived from injury in a childhood accident that left him with three digits on right hand; injury gave him a particularly nasty curve ball; won the decisive game of the the 1907 World Series as a Chicago Cub; in 1908, first pitcher to record 4 consecutive shutouts and finished at 29-9; career record of 239-130 with lifetime ERA of 2.06; member of Hall of Fame.

**Paul Brown** (b. Sept. 7, 1908, d. Aug. 5, 1991): Football innovator; coached Ohio St. to national title in 1942; in pros, directed Cleveland Browns to 4 straight AAFC titles (1946-49) and 3 NFL titles (1950,54-55); formed Cincinnati Bengals as head coach and part owner in 1968 (reached playoffs in '70).

**Valery Brumel** (b. Apr. 14, 1942, d. Jan. 26, 2003): Soviet high jumper; dominated event from 1961-64; broke world record 5 times; won silver in 1960 Olympics and gold in 1964; highest jump was 7-5¾.

**Avery Brundage** (b. Sept. 28, 1887, d. May 5, 1975): Amateur sports czar for over 40 years as president of AAU (1928-35), U.S. Olympic Committee (1929-53) and Int'l Olympic Committee (1952-72).

**Kobe Bryant** (b. Aug. 23, 1978): Basketball; G/F for the LA Lakers; graduated from Lower Merion (Penn.) HS and made the jump directly to the NBA; youngest player (18 yrs., 2 mos., 11 days) ever to appear in an NBA game; became the youngest all-star in NBA history in 1998 and scored a team-high 18 points; won 3 consecutive titles with the Lakers (2000,01,02); accused of rape in 2003 but charges were dropped in 2004.

**Paul (Bear) Bryant** (b. Sept. 11, 1913, d. Jan. 26, 1983): Football; coached at 4 colleges over 38 years; directed Alabama to 6 national titles (1961,64-65,73,78-79); retired as the winningest coach of all-time (323-85-17 record) finally passed by Joe Paterno in 2001; 15 bowl wins, including 8 Sugar Bowls.

**Sergey Bubka** (b. Dec. 4, 1963): Ukrainian pole vaulter; 1st man to clear 20 feet both indoors and out (1991); holder of indoor (20-2) and outdoor (20-1¾) world records as of Sept. 30, 2004; 6-time world champion (1983,87,91,93,95,97); won Olympic gold medal in 1988, but failed to clear any height in 1992 Games.

**Buck Buchanan** (b. Sept. 10, 1940, d. July 16, 1992): Football; played both ways in college at Grambling; first player chosen in the first AFL draft by the Dallas Texans who later became the KC Chiefs; missed one game in a 13-year pro career; played in six AFL All-Star games and two Pro Bowls at def. tackle; defensive star of the Chiefs team that won Super Bowl IV; later coached the New Orleans Saints and Cleveland Browns; member of Pro Football Hall of Fame.

**Jack Buck** (b. Aug. 21, 1924, d. June 18, 2002): Radio-TV; broadcast baseball games for St. Louis Cardinals from 1954-2001; CBS Radio voice for Monday Night Football (1978-96) and announcer for 1st televised AFL game in 1960; recipient of Baseball Hall of Fame's Ford Frick Award (1987) and Football Hall of Fame's Pete Rozelle Award (1996); received the Purple Heart in WWII; father of sportscaster Joe.

**Don Budge** (b. June 13, 1915, d. Jan. 26, 2000): Tennis; in 1938 became 1st player to win the Grand Slam— the French, Wimbledon, U.S. and Australian titles in 1 year; led U.S. to 2 Davis Cups (1937-38); turned pro in late '38.

**Maria Bueno** (b. Oct. 11, 1939): Brazilian tennis player; won 4 U.S. Championships (1959,63-64,66) and 3 Wimbledons (1959-60,64).

**Leroy Burrell** (b. Feb. 21, 1967): Track & Field; set former world record of 9.85 in 100 meters, July 6, 1994; previously held record (9.90) in 1991; member of 4 world record-breaking 4x100m relay teams.

**Susan Butcher** (b. Dec. 26, 1956): Sled Dog racer; 4-time winner of Iditarod Trail race (1986-88,90).

**Dick Butkus** (b. Dec. 9, 1942): Football LB; 2-time All-America at Illinois (1963-64); All-Pro 7 of 9 NFL seasons with Chicago Bears; worked with XFL in 2001.

**Dick Button** (b. July 18, 1929): Figure skater; 5-time world champion (1948-52); 2-time Olympic champ (1948,52); Sullivan Award winner (1949); won Emmy Award as Best Analyst for 1980-81 TV season.

**Walter Byers** (b. Mar. 13, 1922): College athletics; 1st exec. director of NCAA, serving from 1951-88.

**Frank Calder** (b. Nov. 17, 1877, d. Feb. 4, 1943): Hockey; 1st NHL president (1917-43); guided league through its formative years; NHL's Rookie of the Year award named after him.

**Jim Calhoun** (b. May 10, 1942): Basketball; has coached UConn to 2 NCAA titles (1999, 2004); inducted into Basketball Hall of Fame in 2005.

**Lee Calhoun** (b. Feb. 23, 1933, d. June 22, 1989): Track & Field; won consecutive Olympic gold medals in the 110m hurdles (1956,60).

**Walter Camp** (b. Apr. 7, 1859, d. Mar. 14, 1925): Football coach and innovator; established scrimmage line, center snap, downs, 11 players per side; selected 1st All-America team (1889).

**Roy Campanella** (b. Nov. 19, 1921, d. June 26, 1993): Baseball C; 3-time NL MVP (1951,53,55); led Brooklyn to 5 pennants and 1st World Series title (1955); career cut short when paralyzed in 1958 car crash.

**Clarence Campbell** (b. July 9, 1905, d. June 24, 1984): Hockey; 3rd NHL president (1946-77); league tripled in size from 6 to 18 teams during his tenure.

**Earl Campbell** (b. Mar. 29, 1955): Football RB; won Heisman Trophy in 1977; led NFL in rushing 3 times; 3-time All-Pro; 2-time MVP (1978-79) at Houston.

**John Campbell** (b. Apr. 8, 1955): Harness racing; 5-time winner of Hambletonian (1987,88,90,95,98); 3-time Driver of Year; first driver to go over $100 million in career winnings.

**Milt Campbell** (b. Dec. 9, 1933): Track & Field; won silver medal in 1952 Olympic decathlon and gold medal in '56.

**Jimmy Cannon** (b. 1910, d. Dec. 5, 1973): Tough, opinionated New York sportswriter and essayist who viewed sports as an extension of show business; protégé of Damon Runyon; covered World War II for Stars & Stripes.

**Jose Canseco** (b. July 2, 1964): Baseball OF/DH; 1986 AL ROY and 1988 MVP with the Oakland A's; became the 1st player in MLB history with 40 HRs and 40 steals in a season (1988); retired in 2003 with 462 career HRs; admitted steroid use in 2005 book.

**Tony Canzoneri** (b. Nov. 6, 1908, d. Dec. 9, 1959): Boxer; 2-time world lightweight champion (1930-33,35-36); pro record 141-24-10 with 44 KOs.

**Jennifer Capriati** (b. Mar. 29, 1976): Tennis; youngest Grand Slam semifinalist ever (age 14 in 1990 French Open); surprise gold medalist at 1992 Olympics; left Tour from 1994-96 due to personal problems including an arrest for marijuana possession; waged successful comeback, winning French Open (2001) and 2 Australian Opens (2001,02).

**Harry Caray** (b. Mar. 1, 1917, d. Feb. 18, 1998): Radio-TV; baseball play-by-play broadcaster for St. Louis Cardinals, Oakland, Chicago White Sox and Cubs 1945-98; father of sportscaster Skip and grandfather of sportscaster Chip.

**Rod Carew** (b. Oct. 1, 1945): Baseball 2B-1B; led AL in batting 7 times (1969,72-75,77-78) with Minnesota; MVP in 1977; had 3,053 career hits.

**Steve Carlton** (b. Dec. 22, 1944): Baseball LHP; won 20 or more games 6 times; 4-time Cy Young winner (1972,77,80,82) with Philadelphia; 329-244 career record; 4,136 career Ks.

**JoAnne Carner** (b. Apr. 4, 1939): Golfer; 5-time U.S. Amateur champion; 2-time U.S. Open champ; 3-time LPGA Player of Year (1974,81-82); 43 career wins.

**Cris Carter** (b. Nov. 25, 1965): Football; WR with Philadelphia (1987-89), Minnesota (1990-2001) and Miami (2002); twice caught 122 passes in a season (1994, '95), the first time establishing an NFL record for catches in a season that was beaten a year later; 2nd player to reach 1000 career catches.

**Don Carter** (b. July 29, 1926): Bowler; 6-time Bowler of Year (1953-54,57-58,60,62); voted Greatest of All-Time in 1970.

**Joe Carter** (b. Mar. 7, 1960): Baseball OF; 3-time All-America at Wichita St. (1979-81); won 1993 World Series for Toronto with 3-run HR in bottom of the 9th of Game 6.

**Alexander Cartwright** (b. Apr. 17, 1820, d. July 12, 1892): Baseball; engineer and draftsman who spread gospel of baseball from New York City to California gold fields; widely regarded as the father of modern game; his guidelines included setting 3 strikes for an out and 3 outs for each half inning.

**Billy Casper** (b. June 24, 1931): Golfer; 2-time PGA Player of Year (1966,70); has won U.S. Open (1959,66), Masters (1970), U.S. Senior Open (1983); compiled 51 PGA Tour wins and 9 on Senior Tour.

**Tracy Caulkins** (b. Jan. 11, 1963): Swimmer; won 3 gold medals (2 individual) at 1984 Olympics; set 5 world records and won 48 U.S. national titles from 1978-84; Sullivan Award winner (1978); 2-time Honda Broderick Cup winner (1982,84).

**Steve Cauthen** (b. May 1, 1960): Jockey; became youngest jockey (18) to win the Triple Crown with Affirmed in 1978; won a record $6.1 million in 1977, winning the Eclipse Award as the nation's top rider and the award for AP male athlete of the year.

**Evonne Goolagong Cawley** (b. July 31, 1951): Australian tennis player; won Australian Open 4 times, Wimbledon twice (1971,80), French once (1971).

**Florence Chadwick** (b. Nov. 9, 1917, d. Mar. 15, 1995): Dominant distance swimmer of 1950s; set English Channel records from France to England (1950) and England to France (1951 and '55).

**Wilt Chamberlain** (b. Aug. 21, 1936, d. Oct. 12, 1999): Basketball C; consensus All-America in 1957 and '58 at Kansas; Final Four MOP in 1957; led NBA in scoring 7 times and rebounding 11 times; 7-time All-NBA first team; 4-time MVP (1960,66-68) in Philadelphia; scored 100 points vs. NY Knicks in Hershey, Pa., Mar. 2, 1962; led 76ers (1967) and LA Lakers (1972) to NBA titles; Finals MVP in 1972.

**A.B. (Happy) Chandler** (b. July 14, 1898, d. June 15, 1991): Baseball; former Kentucky governor and U.S. Senator who succeeded Judge Landis as commissioner in 1945; backed Branch Rickey's move in 1947 to make Jackie Robinson 1st black player in major leagues; deemed too pro-player and ousted by owners in 1951.

**Michael Chang** (b. Feb. 22, 1972): Tennis; won the 1989 French Open, becoming the youngest men's champion of a grand slam event (17 years, 3 months.); went 11 consecutive years (1988-98) with at least one title; finished in top 10 in the ATP year-end rankings from 1992-97 (career high no. 2 in 1996).

**Julio Cesar Chavez** (b. July 12, 1962): Mexican boxer; world jr. welterweight champ (1989-94); also held titles as jr. lightweight (1984-87) and lightweight (1987-89); won over 100 bouts; 90-bout unbeaten streak ended 1/29/94 when Frankie Randall won title on split decision; Chavez won title back 4 months later.

**Linford Christie** (b. Apr. 2, 1960): British sprinter; won 100-meter gold medals at both 1992 Olympics (9.96) and '93 World Championships (9.87).

**Jim Clark** (b. Mar. 14, 1936, d. Apr. 7, 1968): Scottish auto racer; 2-time Formula One world champion (1963,65); won Indy 500 in 1965; killed in car crash.

**Bobby Clarke** (b. Aug. 13, 1949): Hockey C; led Philadelphia Flyers to consecutive Stanley Cups in 1974-75; 3-time regular season MVP (1973,75-76); currently Flyers GM.

**Ron Clarke** (b. Feb. 21, 1937): Australian runner; from 1963-70 set 17 world records in races from 2 miles to 20,000m; never won Olympic gold medal.

**Roger Clemens** (b. Aug. 4, 1962): Baseball RHP; twice fanned MLB record 20 batters in 9-inning game (April 29, 1986 & Sept. 18, 1996); won a record 7 Cy Young Awards with Boston (1986-87,91), Toronto (1997,98), N.Y. Yankees (2001) and Houston (2004); AL MVP in 1986; won 2 World Series with N.Y. (1999-2000); got 300th win in 2003; led majors in ERA in 2005 at age 43; 2nd to Nolan Ryan in career K's.

**Roberto Clemente** (b. Aug. 18, 1934, d. Dec. 31, 1972): Baseball OF; hit over .300 13 times with Pittsburgh; led NL in batting 4 times; World Series MVP in 1971; regular season MVP in 1966; had 3,000 career hits; killed in plane crash; MLB Man of the Year award is named for him.

**Alice Coachman** (b. Nov. 9, 1923): Track & Field; became the first black woman to win an Olympic gold medal with her win in the high jump in 1948 (London); broke the high school and college high jump records despite not wearing any shoes; member of the National Track & Field Hall of Fame.

**Ty Cobb** (b. Dec. 18, 1886, d. July 17, 1961): Baseball OF; all-time highest career batting average (.367); hit over .400 3 times; led AL in batting 12 times and stole bases 6 times with Detroit; MVP in 1911; had 4,191 career hits, 2,245 career runs and 892 steals; played 24 years (22 with Detroit, 2 with Philadelphia); nicknamed "The Georgia Peach"; part of Baseball Hall of Fame's inaugural class.

**Mickey Cochrane** (b. Apr. 6, 1903, d. June 28, 1962): Baseball C; led Philadelphia A's (1929-30) and Detroit (1935) to 3 World Series titles; 2-time AL MVP (1928,34).

**Sebastian Coe** (b. Sept. 29, 1956): British runner; won gold medal in 1500m and silver medal in 800m at both 1980 and '84 Olympics; long-time world record holder in 800m and 1000m; elected to Parliament as Conservative in 1992.

**Paul Coffey** (b. June 1, 1961): Hockey D; 3-time Norris Trophy winner; member of 4 Stanley Cup champions at Edmonton (1984-85,87) and Pittsburgh (1991); ranks 10th on NHL all-time scoring list; elected to Hall of Fame in 2004.

**Rocky Colavito** (b. August 10, 1933): Baseball OF; six-time all-star who hit 374 HRs over his 14-year career; hugely popular in Cleveland where he played from 1955-59 and then 1965-67; led the league in HRs in 1959 with 42 and RBI in 1965 with 108; hit four consecutive HRs in one game.

**Eddie Collins** (b. May 2, 1887, d. Mar. 25, 1951): Baseball 2B; led Philadelphia A's (1910-11) and Chicago White Sox (1917) to 3 World Series titles; AL MVP in 1914; had 3,311 career hits and 743 stolen bases.

**Nadia Comaneci** (b. Nov. 12, 1961): Romanian gymnast; first to record perfect 10 in Olympics; won 3 individual golds at 1976 Olympics and 2 more in '80.

**Lionel Conacher** (b. May 24, 1901, d. May 26, 1954): Canada's greatest all-around athlete; NHL hockey (2 Stanley Cups), CFL football (1 Grey Cup), minor league baseball, soccer, lacrosse, track, amateur boxing champion; member of Parliament (1949-54).

**Tony Conigliaro** (b. Jan. 7, 1945, d. Feb. 24, 1990): Baseball OF; youngest (20 years old) to lead the AL in HRs (32 in 1965); hit in the face with a fastball in 1967; came back to hit 36 HRs in 1970 but was never the same.

**Gene Conley** (b. Nov. 10, 1930): Baseball and Basketball; played for World Series and NBA champions with Milwaukee Braves (1957) and Boston Celtics (1959-61); losing pitcher in 1954 All-Star Game and winning pitcher in 1955 Game; 91-96 record in 11 seasons.

**Billy Conn** (b. Oct. 8, 1917, d. May 29, 1993): Boxer; Pittsburgh native and world light heavyweight champion from 1939-41; nearly upset heavyweight champ Joe Louis in 1941 title bout, but was knocked out in 13th round; pro record 63-11-1 with 14 KOs.

**Dennis Conner** (b. Sept. 16, 1942): Sailing; 3-time America's Cup-winning skipper aboard *Freedom* (1980), *Stars & Stripes* (1987) and the *Stars & Stripes* catamaran (1988); only American skipper to lose Cup, first in 1983 when *Australia II* beat *Liberty* and again in '95 when New Zealand's *Black Magic* swept Conner and his *Stars & Stripes* crew aboard the borrowed *Young America*.

**Maureen Connolly** (b. Sept. 17, 1934, d. June 21, 1969): Tennis; 1st woman to win Grand Slam (in 1953 at age 18); horse riding accident ended her career in '54 at age 19; won 3 Wimbledons (1952-54), 3 U.S. Opens (1951-53), 2 French Opens (1953-54) and 1 Australian Open (1953); 3-time AP Female Athlete of Year (1951-53).

**Jimmy Connors** (b. Sept. 2, 1952): Tennis; No.1 player in world 5 times (1974-78); won 5 U.S. Opens, 2 Wimbledons and 1 Australian; rose from No. 936 at the close of 1990 to U.S. Open semifinals in 1991 at age 39; NCAA singles champ (1971); all-time leader in pro singles titles (109) and matches won at U.S. Open (98) and Wimbledon (84).

**Jack Kent Cooke** (b. Oct. 25, 1912, d. April 6, 1997): Football; sole owner of NFL Washington Redskins from 1985-97; teams won 2 Super Bowls (1988,92); also owned NBA Lakers and NHL Kings in LA; built LA Forum for $12 million in 1967.

**Cynthia Cooper** (b. April 14, 1963): Women's basketball G; won two NCAA basketball titles at USC (1983-84); won gold medal with U.S. team in 1988; 2-time WNBA MVP and 4-time league champion with Houston Comets; coach of WNBA's Phoenix Mercury 2001-02.

**Angel Cordero Jr.** (b. Nov. 8, 1942): Jockey; retired third on all-time list with 7,057 wins in 38,646 starts; won Kentucky Derby 3 times (1974,76,85), Preakness twice and Belmont once; 2-time Eclipse Award winner (1982-83).

**Howard Cosell** (b. Mar. 25, 1920, d. Apr. 23, 1995): Radio-TV; former ABC commentator on *Monday Night Football* and *Wide World of Sports*, who energized TV sports journalism with abrasive "tell it like it is" style.

**Bob Costas** (b. Mar. 22, 1952): Radio-TV; NBC broadcaster who has been anchor for NBA, NFL and Olympics as well as baseball play-by-play man; 14-time Emmy winner as studio host/play-by-play and 8-time National Sportscaster of Year.

**James (Doc) Counsilman** (b. Dec. 28, 1920, d. Jan. 4, 2004): Swimming; coached Indiana men's swim team to 6 NCAA championships (1968-73); coached the 1964 and '76 U.S. men's Olympic teams that won a combined 21 of 24 gold medals; in 1979 became oldest person (59) to swim English Channel; retired in 1990 with dual meet record of 287-36-1.

**Fred Couples** (b. Oct. 3, 1959): Golfer; 2-time PGA Tour Player of the Year (1991,92); 15 Tour victories, including 1992 Masters.

**Jim Courier** (b. Aug. 17, 1970): Tennis; No. 1 player in world in 1992, won 2 Australian Opens (1992-93) and 2 French Opens (1991-92); played on 1992 Davis Cup winner; Nick Bollettieri Academy classmate of Andre Agassi; entered Hall of Fame in 2005.

**Margaret Smith Court** (b. July 16, 1942): Australian tennis player; won Grand Slam in both singles (1970) and mixed doubles (1963 with Ken Fletcher); record 24 Grand Slam singles titles—11 Australian, 5 U.S., 5 French and 3 Wimbledon.

**Bob Cousy** (b. Aug. 9, 1928): Basketball G; led NBA in assists 8 times; 10-time All-NBA 1st team; 1957 MVP; led Boston to 6 NBA titles (1957,59-63); elected to Hall of Fame in 1970, one of NBA's 50 Greatest Players.

**Buster Crabbe** (b. Feb. 7, 1908, d. Apr. 23, 1983): Swimmer; 2-time Olympic freestyle medalist with bronze in 1928 (1500m) and gold in '32 (400m); became movie star and King of Serials as Flash Gordon and Buck Rogers.

**Ben Crenshaw** (b. Jan. 11, 1952): Golfer; co-NCAA champion with Tom Kite in 1972; battled Graves' disease in mid-1980s; 19 career Tour victories; won Masters for second time in 1995 and dedicated it to 90-year-old mentor Harvey Penick, who had died a week earlier; captain of 1999 Ryder Cup team.

**Joe Cronin** (b. Oct. 12, 1906, d. Sept. 7, 1984): Baseball SS; hit over .300 and drove in over 100 runs 8 times each; player-manager in Washington and Boston (1933-47); AL president (1959-73).

**Larry Csonka** (b. Dec. 25, 1946): Football RB; powerful runner and blocker who gained 8,081 yards in 11 seasons in the AFL and NFL; won two consecutive Super Bowls with the Miami Dolphins (1973-74) and was named MVP in the latter, rushing for 145 yards and two TDs; member of the College and Pro Football Halls of Fame; rescued from storm-tossed vessel by Coast Guard in Bering Sea in 2005.

**Ann Curtis** (b. Mar. 6, 1926): Swimming; won 2 gold medals and 1 silver in 1948 Olympics; set 4 world and 18 U.S. records during career; 1st woman and swimmer to win Sullivan Award (1944).

**Betty Cuthbert** (b. Apr. 20, 1938): Australian runner; won gold medals in 100 and 200 meters and 4x100m relay at 1956 Olympics; also won 400m gold at 1964 Olympics.

**Bjorn Dählie** (b. June 19, 1967): Norwegian cross-country skier; winner of a record eight gold and 12 overall Winter Olympic medals from 1992-98.

**Chuck Daly** (b. July 20, 1930): Basketball; coached Detroit to two NBA titles (1989-90); also coached NBA "Dream Team" to gold medal in 1992 Olympics; retired in 1994 but returned in 1997 to coach Orlando Magic for two seasons.

**John Daly** (b. Apr. 28, 1966): Golfer; big hitter who was surprise winner of 1991 PGA Championship as unknown 25-year old; battled through personal troubles in 1994 to return in '95 and win 2nd major at British Open, beating Italy's Costantino Rocca in 4-hole playoff; won first PGA Tour event in nine years at 2004 Buick Invitational.

**Johnny Damon** (b. Nov. 5, 1973): Baseball CF; long-haired lead-off man for the 2005 World Series champion Boston Red Sox.

**Stanley Dancer** (b. July 25, 1927, d. Sept. 8, 2005): Harness racing; winner of 4 Hambletonians; trainer-driver of Triple Crown winners in trotting (Nevele Pride in 1968 and Super Bowl in '72) and pacing (Most Happy Fella in 1970).

**Beth Daniel** (b. Oct. 14, 1956): Golfer; 33 career wins, including 1 major; inducted into World Golf Hall of Fame in 1999.

**Alvin Dark** (b. Jan. 7, 1922): Baseball IF and MGR; hit .322 to win the NL Rookie of the Year award in 1948 with the Boston Braves; traded to the N.Y. Giants where he led the league in doubles (41) in 1951; won 994 games as a manager and led the Oakland A's to a World Series win in 1974.

**Tamas Darnyi** (b. June 3, 1967): Hungarian swimmer; 2-time double gold medal winner in 200m and 400m individual medley at 1988 and '92 Olympics; also won both events in 1986 and '91 world championships; set world records in both at '91 worlds; 1st swimmer to break 2 minutes in 200m IM (1:59:36).

**Lindsay Davenport** (b. June 8, 1976): Tennis player; became first American female ranked No. 1 in the world (1998) since Chris Evert in 1985; won U.S. Open (1998), Wimbledon (1999) and Australian Open (2000); won Olympic gold medal in 1996.

**Al Davis** (b. July 4, 1929): Football; GM-coach of Oakland 1963-66; helped force AFL-NFL merger as AFL commissioner in 1966; returned to Oakland as managing general partner and directed club to 3 Super Bowl wins (1977,81,84); defied fellow NFL owners and moved Raiders to LA in 1982; turned down owners' 1995 offer to build him a new stadium in LA and moved back to Oakland instead.

**Dwight Davis** (b. July 5, 1879, d. Nov. 28, 1945): Tennis; donor of Davis Cup; played for winning U.S. team in 1st two Cup finals (1900,02); won U.S. and Wimbledon doubles titles in 1901; Secretary of War (1925-29) under President Coolidge.

**Ernie Davis** (b. Dec. 14, 1939, d. May 18, 1963): Football; star running back at Syracuse University; first black player to win the Heisman Trophy in 1961; drafted by the Washington Redskins and traded to Cleveland but died the following year of leukemia before playing a pro game.

**Glenn Davis** (b. Dec. 26, 1924): Football HB; 3-time All-America; led Army to national titles in 1944-45; Doc Blanchard's running mate; won Heisman Trophy in 1946.

**John Davis** (b. Jan. 12, 1921, d. July 13, 1984): Weightlifting; 6-time world champion; 2-time Olympic super-heavyweight champ (1948,52); undefeated from 1938-53.

**Terrell Davis** (b. Oct. 28, 1972): Football RB; 1998 NFL MVP, rushing for a league-leading 2,008 yards (4th all-time); played for two Super Bowl winners in Denver (XXXII and XXXIII), earning MVP honors in the former with Super Bowl-record 3 rushing TDs.

**Pat Day** (b. Oct. 13, 1953): Jockey; 4-time Eclipse award winner; became all-time leader in earnings in 2002; 4th all-time with 8,804 career victories; won Kentucky Derby (1992), 5 Preakness (1985,90,94-96) and 3 Belmonts (1989,94,2000); inducted into Hall of Fame in 1991; retired in 2005.

**Ron Dayne** (b. Mar. 14, 1978): Football RB; NCAA Div. I-A all-time leading rusher, gaining 6,397 yards at Wisconsin (1996-99); 1999 Heisman Trophy winner; selected in 1st round (11th overall) of 2000 NFL draft by NY Giants.

**Dizzy Dean** (b. Jan. 16 1911, d. July 17, 1974): Baseball RHP; led NL in strikeouts and complete games 4 times; last NL pitcher to win 30 games (30-7 in 1934); MVP in 1934 with St. Louis; 150-83 record.

**Dave DeBusschere** (b. Oct. 16, 1940, d. May, 14, 2003): Basketball F; youngest coach in NBA history (24 in 1964); player-coach of Detroit Pistons (1964-67); played in 8 All-Star games; won 2 NBA titles as player with NY Knicks (1970, 73); ABA commissioner (1975-76); also pitched 2 seasons for Chicago White Sox (1962-63) with 3-4 record.

**Pierre de Coubertin** (b. Jan. 1, 1863, d. Sept. 2, 1937): French educator; father of the Modern Olympic Games; IOC president from 1896-1925.

**Anita DeFrantz** (b. Oct. 4, 1952): Olympics; attorney who became the International Olympic Committee's first female vice president in 1997; first woman to represent U.S. on IOC (elected in 1986); member of USOC Executive Committee; member of bronze medal U.S. women's eight-oared shell at Montreal in 1976.

**Oscar De La Hoya** (b. Feb. 4, 1973): Boxer; 1992 Olympic gold medallist (lightweight); has held world titles in 4 weight classes (lightweight, super lightweight, welterweight and jr. middleweight); was unbeaten until losing WBC Welterweight belt to Felix Trinidad in a majority decision in 1999; later moved to jr. middleweight and won WBA and WBC belts; TKO'd in 9th round by champ Bernard Hopkins in their undisputed middleweight title fight in September 2004.

**Cedric Dempsey** (b. Apr. 14, 1932): College sports; succeeded Dick Schultz as NCAA executive director (title later changed to president) in 1993 and served until the end of 2002; former athletic director at Pacific (1967-79), San Diego St. (1979), Houston (1979-82) and Arizona (1983-93).

**Jack Dempsey** (b. June 24, 1895, d. May 31, 1983): Boxer; world heavyweight champion from 1919-26; lost title to Gene Tunney, then lost "Long Count" rematch in 1927 when he floored Tunney in 7th round but failed to retreat to neutral corner; pro record 64-6-9 with 49 KOs.

**Bob Devaney** (b. April 13, 1915, d. May 9, 1997): Football; head coach at Wyoming from 1957-1961; from 1962 to 1972 built Nebraska into a college football power; won two consecutive national championships in 1970-71; won eight Big Eight Conference titles; later served as Nebraska's athletic director.

**Donna de Varona** (b. Apr. 26, 1947): Swimming; won gold medals in 400 IM and 400 freestyle relay at 1964 Olympics; set 18 world records during career; co-founder of Women's Sports Foundation in 1974.

**Gail Devers** (b. Nov. 19, 1966): Track & Field; won Olympic gold medal in 100 meters in 1992 and '96; world champion in 100 meters (1993) and 100-meter hurdles (1993,95,99); overcame thyroid disorder (Graves' disease) that sidelined her in 1989-90 and nearly resulted in having both feet amputated.

**Klaus Dibiasi** (b. Oct. 6, 1947): Italian diver; won 3 consecutive Olympic gold medals in platform event (1968,72,76).

**Eric Dickerson** (b. Sept. 2, 1960): Football RB; led NFL in rushing 4 times (1983-84,86,88); ran for single-season record 2,105 yards in 1984; NFC Rookie of Year in 1983; All-Pro 5 times; traded from LA Rams to Indianapolis (Oct. 31, 1987) in 3-team, 10-player deal (including draft picks) that also involved Buffalo; 4th on all-time career rushing list with 13,259 yards in 11 seasons.

**Harrison Dillard** (b. July 8, 1923): Track & Field; only man to win Olympic gold medals in both sprints (100m in 1948) and hurdles (110m in 1952).

**Joe DiMaggio** (b. Nov. 25, 1914, d. Mar. 8, 1999): Baseball OF; hit safely in 56 straight games (1941); led AL in batting, HRs and RBI twice each; 3-time MVP (1939,41,47); hit .325 with 361 HRs over 13 seasons; led NY Yankees to 10 World Series titles.

**Marcel Dionne** (b. Aug. 3, 1951): Hockey C; fifth on NHL's all-time points list (1,771) and fourth on goals list (731) through 2004; tied Wayne Gretzky for the league lead in points (137) in 1980; scored 50 goals in a season 6 times; won the Lady Byng Trophy for gentlemanly play in 1975 and 1977; member of the Hockey Hall of Fame.

**Mike Ditka** (b. Oct. 18, 1939): Football; All-America at Pitt (1960); NFL Rookie of Year (1961); 5-time Pro Bowl tight end for Chicago Bears; returned to Chicago as head coach in 1982 and won Super Bowl XX in 1986; left Bears in 1992 and worked as a broadcaster at NBC for four years; coached the New Orleans Saints from 1997-99; compiled 127-101-0 record in 14 seasons; currently an analyst on ESPN.

**Larry Doby** (b. Dec. 13, 1924, d. June 18, 2003): Baseball OF; first black player in the AL; joined the Cleveland Indians in July 1947, three months after Jackie Robinson entered the Majors with the NL's Brooklyn Dodgers; an all-star centerfielder from 1949-55; managed the Chicago White Sox in 1978, becoming the second black major league manager; inducted into the Hall of Fame in 1998.

**Charlotte (Lottie) Dod** (b. Sept. 24, 1871, d. June 27, 1960): British athlete; was 5-time Wimbledon singles champion (1887-88,91-93); youngest player ever to win Wimbledon (15 in 1887); archery silver medalist at 1908 Olympics; member of national field hockey team in 1899; British Amateur golf champ in 1904.

**Tony Dorsett** (b. Apr. 7, 1954): Football RB; won Heisman Trophy leading Pitt to national title in 1976; 3rd all-time in NCAA Div. I-A with 6,082 yards; led Dallas to Super Bowl title as NFC Rookie of Year (1977); NFC Player of Year (1981); rushed for 12,739 yards in 12 years.

**James (Buster) Douglas** (b. Apr. 7, 1960): Boxer; 42-1 shot who knocked out undefeated Mike Tyson in 10th round on Feb. 10, 1990 to win heavyweight title in Tokyo; 8½ months later, lost only title defense to Evander Holyfield by KO in 3rd round.

**Vicki Manalo Draves** (b. Dec. 31, 1924): Diver; First woman in olympic history to win gold medals in both platform diving and springboard diving; inducted into Int'l Swimming Hall of Fame in 1969.

**The Dream Team** Head coach Chuck Daly's "Best Ever" 12-man NBA All-Star squad that headlined the 1992 Summer Olympics in Barcelona and easily won the basketball gold medal; co-captained by Larry Bird and Magic Johnson, with veterans Charles Barkley, Clyde Drexler, Patrick Ewing, Michael Jordan, Karl Malone, Chris Mullin, Scottie Pippen, David Robinson, John Stockton and Duke's Christian Laettner.

**Heike Drechsler** (b. Dec. 16, 1964): German long jumper and sprinter; East German before reunification in 1991; set world long jump record (24-2¼) in 1988; won long jump gold medals at 1992 Olympics and 1983 and '93 World Championships; won silver medal in long jump and bronze medals in both 100- and 200-meter sprints at 1988 Olympics.

**Ken Dryden** (b. Aug. 8, 1947): Hockey G; led Montreal to 6 Stanley Cup titles; playoff MVP as rookie in 1971; won or shared 5 Vezina trophies; 2.24 career GAA.

**Don Drysdale** (b. July 23, 1936, d. July 3, 1993): Baseball RHP; led NL in strikeouts 3 times and games started 4 straight years; pitched record 6 shutouts in a row in 1968; won Cy Young (1962); had 209-166 record and hit 29 HRs in 14 years.

**Charley Dumas** (b. Feb. 12, 1937): U.S. high jumper; first man to clear 7 feet (7-0½) on June 29, 1956; won gold medal at 1956 Olympics.

**Tim Duncan** (b. Apr. 25, 1976): Basketball C/F; drafted first overall by San Antonio in 1997 NBA Draft; 7-footer who dominates on offense and defense; has won 3 NBA titles (1999, 2003, 2005) earning Finals MVP honors each time; 2-time NBA MVP (2002-03); 1997 College Player of the Year at Wake Forest; 1998 NBA Rookie of the Year.

**Margaret Osborne du Pont** (b. Mar. 4, 1918): Tennis; won 5 French, 7 Wimbledon and an unprecedented 25 U.S. national titles in singles, doubles and mixed doubles from 1941-62.

**Roberto Duran** (b. June 16, 1951): Panamanian boxer; one of only 6 fighters to hold 4 different world titles— lightweight (1972-79), welterweight (1980), junior middleweight (1983) and middleweight (1989-90); lost famous "No Mas" welterweight title bout when he quit in 8th round against Sugar Ray Leonard (1980); finally retired in 2002 at the age of 50 with a record of 104-16 (69 KOs).

**Leo Durocher** (b. July 27, 1905, d. Oct. 7, 1991): Baseball; managed in NL 24 years; won 2,015 games, including postseason; 3 pennants with Brooklyn (1941) and NY Giants (1951,54); won World Series in 1954.

**Eddie Eagan** (b. Apr. 26, 1898, d. June 14, 1967): Only athlete to win gold medals in both Summer and Winter Olympics (Boxing–1920, Bobsled–1932).

**Alan Eagleson** (b. Apr. 24, 1933): Hockey; Toronto lawyer, agent and 1st executive director of NHL Players Assn. (1967-90); midwived Team Canada vs. Soviet series (1972) and Canada Cup; charged with racketeering and defrauding NHLPA in indictment handed down by U.S. grand jury in 1994; was sentenced to 18 months in jail in Jan. 1998 after pleading guilty but only served 6 months; resigned from Hall of Fame in 1998.

**Dale Earnhardt** (b. Apr. 29, 1951, d. Feb. 18, 2001): Auto racer; 7-time NASCAR national champion (1980,86-87,90-91,93-94); Rookie of Year in 1979; was all-time NASCAR money leader with over $34 million won and 76 career wins when he died; finally won Daytona 500 in 1998 on 20th attempt; died in last lap crash at the 2001 Daytona 500.

**James Easton** (b. July 26, 1935): Olympics; archer and sporting goods manufacturer (Easton softball bats); one of 4 American delegates to the International Olympic Committee; president of International Archery Federation (FITA); member of LA Olympic Organizing Committee in 1984.

**Dennis Eckersley** (b. Oct. 3, 1954): Baseball P; began his career as a starter in 1975 with Cleveland; no-hit Angels in 1977; won 20 games in 1978 with Boston; moved to the bullpen after 12 seasons as a starter and became one of the best closers of all-time with Oakland; won 1992 AL Cy Young and MVP.

**Stefan Edberg** (b. Jan. 19, 1966): Swedish tennis player; 2-time No.1 player (1990-91); 2-time winner of Australian Open (1985,87), Wimbledon (1988,90) and U.S. Open (1991-92).

**Gertrude Ederle** (b. Oct. 23, 1906, d. Nov. 30, 2003): Swimmer; 1st woman to swim English Channel, breaking men's record by 2 hours in 1926; won 3 medals in 1924 Olympics.

**Krisztina Egerszegi** (b. Aug. 16, 1974): Hungarian swimmer; 3-time gold medal winner (100m and 200m backstroke and 400m IM) at 1992 Olympics; also won a gold (200m back) and silver (100m back) at 1988 Games; youngest (14) ever to win swimming gold. Won fifth gold medal (200m back) at '96 Games.

**Lee Elder** (b. July 14, 1934): Golf; in 1975, became the first black golfer to play in the Masters Tournament; also played in the 1977 Masters; member of the 1979 U.S. Ryder Cup team; played in South Africa's first integrated tournament in 1972.

**Todd Eldredge** (b. Aug. 28, 1971): Figure Skater; 6-time U.S. champion (1990,91,95,97,98,2002); 1996 World Champion; won U.S. titles at all three levels (novice, junior and senior); most decorated American figure skater without an Olympic medal.

**Bill Elliott** (b. Oct. 8, 1955): Auto racer; 2-time winner of Daytona 500 (1985,87); NASCAR national champ in 1988; 44 career NASCAR wins.

**Herb Elliott** (b. Feb. 25, 1938): Australian runner; undefeated from 1958-60; ran 17 sub-4:00 miles; 3 world records; won gold medal in 1500 meters at 1960 Olympics; retired at age 22.

**Ernie Els** (b. Oct. 17, 1969): Golfer; sweet swinging South African; 1994 PGA Tour Rookie of the Year and European Golfer of the Year; 2-time U.S. Open winner (1994,97); won 3rd major in 2002 British Open playoff; 15 PGA Tour wins.

**John Elway** (b. June 28, 1960): Football QB; All-American at Stanford; #1 overall pick in the famous quarterback draft of 1983; known for his last-minute, game-winning scoring drives; led Broncos to 3 Super Bowl losses before back-to-back wins in Super Bowl XXXII and XXXIII; 1987 NFL MVP; 4-time Pro Bowler; one of only three quarterbacks (Marino & Favre) to throw for over 50,000 yards.

**Roy Emerson** (b. Nov. 3, 1936): Australian tennis player; won 12 majors in singles— 6 Australian, 2 French, 2 Wimbledon and 2 U.S. from 1961-67.

**Kornelia Ender** (b. Oct. 25, 1958): East German swimmer; 1st woman to win 4 gold medals at one Olympics (1976), all in world-record time.

**Julius Erving** (b. Feb. 22, 1950): Basketball F; "Dr. J"; changed game in ABA, then NBA with his "above-the-rim" style of play; in ABA (1971-76): 3-time MVP, 2-time playoff MVP, led NY Nets to 2 titles (1974,76); in NBA (1976-87): 5-time All-NBA 1st team, MVP in 1981, led Phila. 76ers to 1983 NBA title.

**Phil Esposito** (b. Feb. 20, 1942): Hockey C; 1st NHL player to score 100 points in a season (126 in 1969); 6-time All-NHL 1st team with Boston (1969-74); 2-time MVP (1969,74); 5-time scoring champ; star of 1972 Canada-Soviet series; former president-GM of Tampa Bay Lightning.

**Janet Evans** (b. Aug. 28, 1971): Swimmer; won 3 individual gold medals (400m & 800m freestyle, 400m IM) at 1988 Olympics; 1989 Sullivan Award winner; won 1 gold (800m) and 1 silver (400m) at 1992 Olympics.

**Lee Evans** (b. Feb. 25, 1947): Track & Field; dominant quarter-miler in world from 1966-72; world record in 400m set at 1968 Olympics stood 20 years.

**Chris Evert** (b. Dec. 21, 1954): Tennis; No. 1 player in world 5 times (1975-77,80-81); won at least 1 Grand Slam singles title every year from 1974-86; 18 majors in all— 7 French, 6 U.S., 3 Wimbledon and 2 Australian; retired after 1989 season with 154 singles titles and $8,896,195 in career earnings.

**Weeb Ewbank** (b. May 6, 1907, d. Nov. 18, 1998): Football; only coach to win NFL and AFL titles; led Baltimore to 2 NFL titles (1958-59) and NY Jets to Super Bowl III win.

**Patrick Ewing** (b. Aug. 5, 1962): Basketball C; 3-time All-America; led Georgetown to 3 NCAA Finals and 1984 title; Final 4 MOP in '84; 1986 NBA Rookie of Year with New York; All-NBA (1990); on U.S. Olympic gold medal-winning teams in 1984 and '92; named one of the NBA's 50 Greatest Players.

**Ray Ewry** (b. Oct. 14, 1873, d. Sept. 29, 1937): Track & Field; won 10 gold medals (although 2 are not recognized by IOC) over 4 consecutive Olympics (1900,04,06,08); all events he won (Standing HJ, LJ and TJ) were discontinued in 1912.

**Nick Faldo** (b. July 18, 1957): British golfer; 3-time winner of British Open (1987,90,92) and Masters (1989, 90, 96); 3-time European Golfer of Year (1989-90,92); PGA Player of Year in 1990.

**Juan Manuel Fangio** (b. June 24, 1911, d. July 17, 1995): Argentine auto racer; 5-time Formula One world champion (1951,54-57); 24 career wins, retired in 1958.

**Marshall Faulk** (b. Feb. 26, 1973): Football RB; 3-time consensus All-America at San Diego St.; 2-time NCAA Div. I-A rushing leader (1991-92); 2nd overall pick (Indianapolis) of the 1994 NFL draft; traded to St.L Rams in 1999; 3-time AP Offensive Player of the Year (1999-2001); NFL MVP in 2000 (AP/PFWA) and 2001 (Bell/PFWA); set NFL single season record with 26 TDs in 2000 (broken by P. Holmes's 27 in 2003).

**Brett Favre** (b. Oct. 10, 1969): Football; Strong-armed Southern Miss. QB drafted in 1991 in the 2nd round (33rd overall) by Atlanta; traded to Green Bay in 1992; NFL's only 3-time league MVP (1995-97); 8-time Pro Bowl QB; led Packers to Super Bowl victory in 1997; holds NFL quarterback record for consecutive games started with over 200...and counting.

**Sergei Fedorov** (b. Dec. 13, 1969): Hockey C; first Russian to win NHL Hart Trophy as 1993-94 regular season MVP; 5-time All-Star and 3-time Stanley Cup winner (1997,98,2002) with Detroit.

**Donald Fehr** (b. July 18, 1948): Baseball labor leader; protégé of Marvin Miller; executive director and general counsel of Major League Players Assn. since 1983; led players in 1994 "salary cap" strike that lasted eight months and resulted in first cancellation of World Series since 1904.

**Bob Feller** (b. Nov. 3, 1918): Baseball RHP; Hall of Fame fire-baller who led AL in strikeouts 7 times and wins 6 times with Cleveland Indians; threw 3 no-hitters and major league record 12 one-hitters; 266-162 record; amassed 2,581 Ks despite missing four seasons to military service during WWII.

**Tom Ferguson** (b. Dec. 20, 1950): Rodeo; 6-time All-Around champion (1974-79); 1st cowboy to win $100,000 in one season (1978); 1st to win $1 million in career (1986).

**Herve Filion** (b. Feb. 1, 1940): Harness racing; 10-time Driver of Year; all-time leader in races won with 15,011 in 37 years.

**Rollie Fingers** (b. Aug. 25, 1946): Baseball RHP; mustachioed relief ace with 341 career saves; won AL MVP and Cy Young awards in 1981 with Milwaukee; World Series MVP in 1974 with Oakland; elected to Hall of Fame in 1992.

**Charles O. Finley** (b. Feb. 22, 1918, d. Feb. 19, 1997): Baseball owner; moved KC A's to Oakland in 1968; won 3 straight World Series from 1972-74; also owned teams in NHL and ABA.

**Bobby Fischer** (b. Mar. 9, 1943): Chess; at 15, became youngest international grandmaster in chess history; only American to hold world championship (1972-75); was stripped of title in 1975 after refusing to defend against Anatoly Karpov and became recluse; re-emerged to defeat old foe and former world champion Boris Spassky in 1992.

**Carlton Fisk** (b. Dec. 26, 1947): Baseball C; holds all-time major league record for games caught (2,229); also held HR record for catchers (351) until 2004 (Mike Piazza); AL Rookie of Year (1972) and 10-time All-Star; hit epic, 12th-inning Game 6 homer for Boston Red Sox in 1975 World Series; elected to the Hall of Fame in 2000.

**Emerson Fittipaldi** (b. Dec. 12, 1946): Brazilian auto racer; 2-time Formula One world champion (1972,74); 2-time winner of Indy 500 (1989,93); won overall IndyCar title in 1989.

**Bob Fitzsimmons** (b. May 26, 1863, d. Oct. 22, 1917): British boxer; held three world titles— middleweight (1881-97), heavyweight (1897-99) and light heavyweight (1903-05); pro record 40-11 with 32 KOs.

**James (Sunny Jim) Fitzsimmons** (b. July 23, 1874, d. Mar. 11, 1966): Horse racing; trained horses that won over 2,275 races, including 2 Triple Crown winners—Gallant Fox in 1930 and Omaha in '35.

**Jim Fixx** (b. Apr. 23, 1932, d. July 20, 1984): Running; author who popularized the sport of running; his 1977 bestseller *The Complete Book of Running*, is credited with helping start America's fitness revolution; ironically died of a heart attack while running.

**Larry Fleisher** (b. Sept. 26, 1930, d. May 4, 1989): Basketball; led NBA players union from 1961-89; increased average yearly salary from $9,400 in 1967 to $600,000 without a strike.

**Peggy Fleming** (b. July 27, 1948): Figure skating; 3-time world champion (1966-68); won Olympic gold medal in 1968.

**Curt Flood** (b. Jan. 18, 1938, d. Jan. 20, 1997): Baseball OF; played 15 years (1956-69,71) mainly with St. Louis; hit over .300 6 times with 7 Gold Gloves; refused trade to Phillies in 1969; lost challenge to baseball's reserve clause in Supreme Court in 1972 but his case helped bring free agency to MLB.

**Ray Floyd** (b. Sept. 14, 1942): Golfer; has 22 PGA victories in 4 decades; joined Senior PGA Tour in 1992 and has 14 Senior wins; has won Masters (1976), U.S. Open (1986), PGA twice (1969,82) and PGA Seniors Championship (1995); first player to win on PGA and Senior tours in same year (1992); member of 8 Ryder Cup teams and captain in 1989.

**Doug Flutie** (b. Oct. 23, 1962): Football QB; Boston College QB who threw famous 48-yard "Hail Mary" to defeat Miami on Nov. 23, 1984; 1984 Heisman Trophy winner; has played in USFL, NFL and CFL; 6-time CFL MVP with B.C. Lions (1991), Calgary (1992-94) and Toronto (1996-97); led Calgary (1992) and Toronto (1996-97) to Grey Cup titles.

**Whitey Ford** (b. Oct. 21, 1928): Baseball LHP; all-time leader in World Series wins (10); led AL in wins 3 times; won Cy Young and World Series MVP in 1961 with NY Yankees; 236-106 record.

**George Foreman** (b. Jan. 10, 1949): Boxer; Olympic heavyweight champ (1968); world heavyweight champ (1973-74, 94-95); lost title to Muhammad Ali (KO-8th) in '74; recaptured it on Nov. 5, 1994 at age 45 with a 10-round KO of WBA/IBF champ Michael Moorer, becoming the oldest man to win heavyweight crown; named AP Male Athlete of Year 20 years after losing title to Ali; stripped of WBA title in 1995 after declining to fight No. 1 contender; successfully defended title at age 46 against 26-year-old Axel Schulz in controversial maj. decision; gave up IBF title after refusing rematch with Schulz.

**Dick Fosbury** (b. Mar. 6, 1947): Track & Field; revolutionized high jump with back-first "Fosbury Flop"; won gold medal at 1968 Olympics.

**Greg Foster** (b. Aug. 4, 1958): Track & Field; 3-time winner of World Championship in 110-m hurdles (1983,87,91); won silver in 1984 Olympics; world indoor champion in 1991.

**The Four Horsemen** Senior backfield that led Notre Dame to national collegiate football championship in 1924; put together as sophomores by Irish coach Knute Rockne; immortalized by sportswriter Grantland Rice, whose report of the Oct. 19, 1924, Notre Dame-Army game began: "Outlined against a blue, gray October sky the Four Horsemen rode again..."; HB Jim Crowley (b. Sept. 10, 1902, d. Jan. 15, 1986), FB Elmer Layden (b. May 4, 1903, d. June 30, 1973), HB Don Miller (b. May 30, 1902, d. July 28, 1979) and QB Harry Stuhldreher (b. Oct. 14, 1901, d. Jan. 26, 1965).

**The Four Musketeers** French quartet that dominated men's tennis in 1920s and '30s, winning 8 straight French singles titles (1925-32), 6 Wimbledons in a row (1924-29) and 6 consecutive Davis Cups (1927-32)— Jean Borotra (b. Aug. 13, 1898, d. July 17, 1994), Jacques Brugnon (b. May 11, 1895, d. Mar. 20, 1978), Henri Cochet (b. Dec. 14, 1901, d. Apr. 1, 1987), Rene Lacoste (b. July 2, 1905, d. Oct. 13, 1996).

**Nellie Fox** (b. Dec. 25, 1927, d. Dec. 1, 1975): Baseball 2B; batted .306 in 1959 to win the AL MVP award with the pennant-winning Chicago White Sox; led the league in fielding percentage six times, hits four times and triples once; ended his 19-year career with 2,663 hits, 1,279 runs and .288 average.

**Jimmie Foxx** (b. Oct. 22, 1907, d. July 21, 1967): Baseball 1B; led AL in HRs 4 times and batting twice; won Triple Crown in 1933; 3-time MVP (1932-33,38) with Philadelphia and Boston; hit 30 HRs or more 12 years in a row; 534 career HRs.

**A.J. Foyt** (b. Jan. 16, 1935): Auto racer; 7-time USAC-CART national champion (1960-61,63-64, 67,75,79); 4-time Indy 500 winner (1961,64, 67,77); only driver in history to win Indy 500, Daytona 500 (1972) and 24 Hours of LeMans (1967 with Dan Gurney); retired in 1993 as all-time CART wins leader with 67.

**Bill France Sr.** (b. Sept. 26, 1909, d. June 7, 1992): Stock car pioneer and promoter; founded NASCAR in 1948; guided race circuit through formative years; built both Daytona (Fla.) Int'l Speedway and Talladega (Ala.) Superspeedway.

**Dawn Fraser** (b. Sept. 4, 1937): Australian swimmer; won gold medals in 100m freestyle at 3 consecutive Olympics (1956,60,64).

**Joe Frazier** (b. Jan. 12, 1944): Boxer; 1964 Olympic heavyweight champion; world heavyweight champ (1970-73); decisioned former champ Muhammad Ali in March 1971 in one of the most anticipated prizefights in history, fought Ali twice more, losing both times including the "Thrilla in Manila" in 1975; pro record 32-4-1 with 27 KOs.

**Walt Frazier** (b. March 29, 1945): Basketball G; won the NBA championship twice (1970 and 73) with the New York Knicks; stole spotlight from teammate Willis Reed in Game 7 of 1970 Finals vs. the Lakers with 36 points, 19 assists and 5 steals; averaged 18.9 PPG and 6.1 APG over his career; four-time all-NBA and a member of the Hall of Fame; nicknamed "Clyde" after well-dressed gangster Clyde Barrow.

**Cathy Freeman** (b. Feb. 16, 1973): Track & Field; Australian Aborigine who lit the cauldron at the start of the 2000 Olympic Games in Sydney and later won gold in the 400-meters on her home soil; 2-time world champion in the 400-meters (1997,99); won silver in 400 at the 1996 Olympics in Atlanta.

**Ford Frick** (b. Dec. 19, 1894, d. Apr. 8, 1978): Baseball; sportswriter and radio announcer who served as NL president (1934-51) and commissioner (1951-65); convinced record-keepers to list Roger Maris' and Babe Ruth's season records separately; major leagues moved to West Coast and expanded from 16 to 20 teams during his tenure.

**Frankie Frisch** (b. Sept. 9, 1898, d. Mar. 12, 1973): Baseball 2B; played on 8 NL pennant winners in 19 years with NY and St. Louis; hit .300 or better 11 years in a row (1921-31); MVP in 1931; player-manager from 1933-37.

**Dan Gable** (b. Oct. 25, 1948): Wrestling; career wrestling record of 118-1 (Larry Owings beat him in his final collegiate match) at Iowa St., where he was a 2-time NCAA champ (1968,69) and tourney MVP in 1969 (137 lbs); won gold medal (149 lbs) at 1972 Olympics; coached U.S. freestyle team in 1988; coached Iowa to 9 straight NCAA titles (1978-86) and 15 overall in 21 years.

**Eddie Gaedel** (b. June 8, 1925, d. June 18, 1961): Baseball PH; St. Louis Browns' 3-foot-7 player whose career lasted one at bat (he walked) on Aug 19, 1951; hired as a publicity stunt by eccentric owner Bill Veeck.

**Clarence (Big House) Gaines** (b. May 21, 1924): Basketball; retired as coach of Div. II Winston-Salem after 1992-93 season with 828-447 record in 47 years.

**Alonzo (Jake) Gaither** (b. Apr. 11, 1903, d. Feb. 18, 1994): Football; head coach at Florida A&M for 25 years; led Rattlers to 6 national black college titles; retired after 1969 season with record of 203-36-4 and a winning percentage of .844; coined phrase, "I like my boys agile, mobile and hostile."

**Rulon Gardner** (b. Aug. 16, 1971): Olympic wrestler; surprise winner of the super heavyweight Greco-Roman gold medal at the 2000 Sydney Games; beat unbeatable Russian legend Alexandre Kareline, 1-0; won 2000 Sullivan Award and USOC Sportsman of the Year Award; lost a toe to frostbite in 2002 but still took bronze medal in Athens (2004).

**Cito Gaston** (b. Mar. 17, 1944): Baseball; managed Toronto to consecutive World Series titles (1992-93); first black manager to win Series.

**Justin Gatlin** (b. Feb. 10, 1982): American sprinter; won 100m gold and 200m bronze at 2004 Summer Olympics in Athens; won 100m and 200m dashes at 2005 World Outdoor Championships.

**Lou Gehrig** (b. June 19, 1903, d. June 2, 1941): Baseball 1B; played in 2,130 consecutive games from 1925-39 a major league record until Cal Ripken Jr. surpassed it in 1995; led AL in RBI 5 times and HRs 3 times; drove in 100 runs or more 13 years in a row; 2-time MVP (1927,36); hit .340 with 493 HRs over 17 seasons; led NY Yankees to 6 World Series titles; died at age 37 of Amyotrophic Lateral Sclerosis (ALS), a rare and incurable disease of the nervous system now better known as Lou Gehrig's disease.

**Bernie Geoffrion** (b. Feb. 14, 1931): Hockey RW; credited with popularizing the slap shot, earning his nickname "Boom Boom"; scored 30 goals in 1952 to win the NHL's Calder Trophy (Rookie of the Year Award); won the MVP award (Hart) in 1955; became the second player in history to score 50 goals in one season; led the league in points in 1955 and 61; won 6 Stanley Cups with Montreal; member of the Hockey Hall of Fame.

**George Gervin** (b. April 27, 1952): Basketball G/F; joined the ABA in 1972 and came to the NBA with San Antonio in 1976; a five-time NBA all-star; led the league in scoring four times; scored 26,595 points with an average of 25.1 per game; known as the "Iceman" because of his cool style; elected to the Hall of Fame in 1996.

**A. Bartlett Giamatti** (b. Apr. 14, 1938, d. Sept. 1, 1989): Scholar and 7th commissioner of baseball; banned Pete Rose for life for betting on Major League games and associating with known gamblers; also served as president of Yale (1978-86) and National League (1986-89); father of character actor Paul.

**Joe Gibbs** (b. Nov. 25, 1940): Football; coached Washington to 3 Super Bowl titles in 12 seasons before retiring in 1993; owner of NASCAR racing team that won 1993 Daytona 500 and 2000 Winston Cup title; lured out of retirement to coach Redskins in 2004.

**Althea Gibson** (b. Aug. 25, 1927, d. Sept. 28, 2003): Tennis; won both Wimbledon and U.S. championships in 1957 and '58; 1st black to play in either tourney and 1st to win each title.

**Bob Gibson** (b. Nov. 9, 1935): Baseball RHP; won 20 or more games 5 times; won 2 NL Cy Youngs (1968,70); MVP in 1968; led St. Louis to 2 World Series titles (1964,67); his ERA of 1.12 in 1968 is the lowest for a starter since 1914; 251-174 record.

**Josh Gibson** (b. Dec. 21, 1911, d. Jan. 20, 1947): Baseball C; the "Babe Ruth of the Negro Leagues"; Satchel Paige's battery mate with Pittsburgh Crawfords. The Negro Leagues did not keep accurate records but Gibson hit 84 home runs in one season and his Baseball Hall of Fame plaque says he hit "almost 800" home runs in his 17-year career.

**Kirk Gibson** (b. May 28, 1957): Baseball OF; All-America flanker at Mich. St. in 1978; chose baseball career and was AL playoff MVP with Detroit in 1984 and NL regular season MVP with Los Angeles in 1988; hit famous pinch-hit home run against Oakland's Dennis Eckersley in Game 1 of the 1988 World Series to vault the Dodgers to the title.

**Frank Gifford** (b. Aug. 16, 1930): Football HB; 4-time All-Pro (1955-57,59); NFL MVP in 1956; led NY Giants to 3 NFL title games; longtime TV sportscaster, beginning career in 1958 while still a player; scandal struck the married Gifford after he was videotaped in a compromising position with a former stewardess in 1997.

**Sid Gillman** (b. Oct. 26, 1911, d. Jan. 3, 2003): Football innovator; coach elected to both College and Pro Football Halls of Fame; led college teams at Miami-OH and Cincinnati to combined 81-19-2 record from 1944-54; coached LA Rams (1955-59) in NFL, then led LA-San Diego Chargers to 5 Western titles and 1 league championship in first six years of AFL.

**George Gipp** (b. Feb. 18, 1895, d. Dec. 14, 1920): Football HB; died of throat infection 2 weeks before he made All-America at Notre Dame; rushed for 2,341 yards, scored 156 points and averaged 38 yards a punt in 4 years (1917-20); inspiration for Knute Rockne's "Win one for the Gipper" speech.

**Marc Girardelli** (b. July 18, 1963): Luxembourg Alpine skier; Austrian native who refused to join Austrian Ski Federation because he wanted to be coached by his father; won unprecedented 5th overall World Cup title in 1993; winless at Olympics, although he won 2 silver medals in 1992.

**Tom Glavine** (b. Mar. 26, 1966): Baseball LHP; led the majors in wins from 1991-95 with 91; NL Cy Young winner in 1991 and '98; seven-time All-Star and was the NL starter twice; World Series MVP with Atlanta in 1995.

**Tom Gola** (b. Jan. 13, 1933): Basketball F; 4-time All-America and 1955 Player of Year at La Salle; MOP in 1952 NIT and '54 NCAA Final 4, leading Explorers to both titles; won NBA title as rookie with Philadelphia Warriors in 1956; 4-time NBA All-Star.

**Marshall Goldberg** (b. Oct. 24, 1917): Football HB; 2-time consensus All-America at Pittsburgh (1937-38); led Pitt to national championship in 1937; played with NFL champion Chicago Cardinals 10 years later.

**Lefty Gomez** (b. Nov. 26, 1908, d. Feb. 17, 1989): Baseball LHP; 4-time 20-game winner with NY Yankees; holds World Series record for most wins (6) without a defeat; pitched on 5 world championship clubs in 1930s.

**Pancho Gonzales** (b. May 9, 1928, d. July 3, 1995): Tennis; won consecutive U.S. Championships in 1948-49 before turning pro at 21; dominated pro tour from 1950-61; in 1969 at age 41, played longest Wimbledon match ever (5:12), beating Charlie Pasarell 22-24,1-6,16-14,6-3,11-9.

**Bob Goodenow** (b. Oct. 29, 1952): Hockey; succeeded Alan Eagleson as executive director of NHL Players Assn. in 1990; led players out on 10-day strike (Apr. 1-10) in 1992, during 103-day owners' lockout in 1994-95 and lockout in 2004; resigned in 2005.

**Gail Goodrich** (b. April 23, 1943): Basketball G; starred at UCLA and won two national championships in 1964 and 1965 under legendary coach John Wooden's tutelage; won the NBA championship with the L.A. Lakers in 1972 and led the team in scoring (25.9 ppg); averaged 18.6 ppg over his 14-year career.

**Jeff Gordon** (b. Aug. 4, 1971): Auto racer; 1993 NASCAR Rookie of Year; 4-time Winston Cup champion (1995,97,98,2001); won inaugural Brickyard 400 in 1994; became youngest winner (25) of the Daytona 500 in 1997, won Daytona 500 again in 1999 and 2005; in 1998 he tied Richard Petty for the modern-era record for wins in a single season with 13; NASCAR's all-time leading money winner; has 72 Winston/Nextel Cup career wins as of Sept. 2005.

**Rich (Goose) Gossage** (b. July 5, 1951): Baseball RHP; Nine-time All-Star (1975-78, 80-82, 84-85); intimidating relief pitcher; Fireman of the Year in 1975 with White Sox and 1978 with Yankees; led AL in saves with 26 (1975), 27 (1978); 1,002 career appearances; 310 saves.

**Shane Gould** (b. Nov. 23, 1956): Australian swimmer; set world records in 5 different women's freestyle events between July 1971 and Jan. 1972; won 3 gold medals, a silver and bronze in 1972 Olympics then retired at age 16.

**Alf Goullet** (b. Apr. 5, 1891, d. Mar. 11, 1995): Cycling; Australian who gained fame and fortune early in century as premier performer on U.S. 6-day bike race circuit; won 8 annual races at Madison Square Garden with 6 different partners from 1913-23.

**Curt Gowdy** (b. July 31, 1919): Radio-TV; former radio voice of NY Yankees and then Boston Red Sox from 1949-66; TV play-by-play man for AFL, NFL and major league baseball; has broadcast World Series, All-Star Games, Rose Bowls, Super Bowls, Olympics and NCAA Final Fours for 3 networks; hosted "The American Sportsman."

**Steffi Graf** (b. June 14, 1969): German tennis player; won Grand Slam and Olympic gold medal in 1988 at age 19; won three of four majors in 1993, '95 and '96; won 22 Grand Slam singles titles— 7 at Wimbledon, 6 French, 5 U.S. and 4 Australian Opens, retired in 1999 as 3rd all-time with 107 career singles titles and as all-time tour leader in career earnings with over $21 million in prize money; married to fellow tennis great Andre Agassi.

**Otto Graham** (b. Dec. 6, 1921, d. Dec. 17, 2003): Football QB and basketball All-America at Northwestern; in pro ball, led Cleveland Browns to 7 league titles in 10 years, winning 4 AAFC championships (1946-49) and 3 NFL (1950,54-55); 5-time All-Pro; 2-time NFL MVP (1953,55).

**Cammi Granato** (b. Mar. 25, 1971): Hockey; American women's hockey pioneer; captain of U.S. team that won gold at the inaugural Olympic women's hockey competition in 1998 at Nagano; sister of NHL veteran Tony.

**Red Grange** (b. June 13, 1903, d. Jan. 28, 1991): Football HB; 3-time All-America at Illinois who brought 1st huge crowds to pro football when he signed with Chicago Bears in 1925; formed 1st AFL with manager-promoter C.C. Pyle in 1926, but league folded and he returned to Bears.

**Bud Grant** (b. May 20, 1927): Football and Basketball; only coach to win 100 games in both CFL and NFL and only member of both CFL and U.S. Pro Football Halls of Fame; led Winnipeg to 4 Grey Cup titles (1958-59,61-62) in 6 appearances, but his Minnesota Vikings lost all 4 Super Bowl attempts in 1970s; accumulated 122 CFL wins and 168 NFL wins; also All-Big Ten at Minnesota in both football and basketball in late 1940s; a 3-time CFL All-Star offensive end; also member of 1950 NBA champion Minneapolis Lakers.

**Rocky Graziano** (b. June 7, 1922, d. May 22, 1990): Boxer; world middleweight champion (1946-47); fought Tony Zale for title 3 times in 21 months, losing twice; pro record 67-10-6 with 52 KOs; movie "Somebody Up There Likes Me" based on his life.

**Hank Greenberg** (b. Jan. 1, 1911, d. Sept. 4, 1986): Baseball 1B/LF; slugging right-hander who led AL in HRs and RBI 4 times each; 2-time MVP (1935, 40) with Detroit; 331 career HRs, including 58 in 1938; elected to Hall of Fame in 1956.

**Joe Greene** (b. Sept. 24, 1946): Football DT; 5-time All-Pro (1972-74,77,79); led Pittsburgh to 4 Super Bowl titles in 1970s; nicknamed "Mean Joe."

**Maurice Greene** (b. July 23, 1974): Track & Field; world 100m champion in 1997, 99 and 2001 and 200m champion in 1999; former world record holder (9.79) in the 100m; won the gold medal in the 100m and 4x100m at the 2000 Sydney Olympics; took 100m bronze at 2004 Athens Olympics.

**Bud Greenspan** (b. Sept. 18, 1926): Filmmaker specializing in the Olympic Games; has won Emmy awards for 22-part "The Olympiad" (1976-77) and historical vignettes for ABC-TV's coverage of 1980 Winter Games; won 1994 Emmy award for edited special on Lillehammer Winter Olympics; won The Peabody Award in 1996 for his outstanding service in chronicling the Olympic Games.

**Wayne Gretzky** (b. Jan. 26, 1961): Hockey C; 10-time NHL scoring champion; 9-time regular season MVP (1979-87,89) and 9-time All-NHL first team; scored 200 points or more in a season 4 times; led Edmonton to 4 Stanley Cups (1984-85,87-88); 2-time playoff MVP (1985,88); traded to LA Kings (Aug. 9, 1988); broke Gordie Howe's all-time NHL goal scoring record of 801 on Mar. 23, 1994; all-time NHL leader in points (2857), goals (894) and assists (1963); also all-time Stanley Cup leader in points, goals and assists; spent the end of the 1996 season with the St. Louis Blues and then signed a free agent contract with the New York Rangers; retired in 1999 at age 38 with 61 NHL scoring records in 20 seasons; became part-owner of NHL's Coyotes in 2000 and stepped behind the bench as Coyotes head coach in 2005.

**Bob Griese** (b. Feb. 3, 1945): Football QB; 2-time All-Pro (1971,77); led Miami to undefeated season (17-0) in 1972 and consecutive Super Bowl titles (1973-74); father of Brian.

**Ken Griffey Jr.** (b. Nov. 21, 1969): Baseball OF; overall 1st pick of 1987 draft by Seattle; 10-time Gold Glove winner; 12-time All-Star; 1997 AL MVP; MVP of 1992 All-Star game at age 23; hit home runs in 8 consecutive games in 1993; son of Ken Sr. and in 1990 they became the first father-son combination to appear in the same major league lineup; traded to the Cincinnati Reds before the 2000 season but has been plagued with injuries; hit 35 homers in 2005 to reach 536 for his career.

**Archie Griffin** (b. Aug. 21, 1954): Football RB; only college player to win two Heisman Trophies (1974-75); rushed for 5,177 yards in career at Ohio St. and played in four straight Rose Bowls; drafted by Cincinnati Bengals and played 8 years in NFL.

**Emile Griffith** (b. Feb. 3, 1938): Boxer; world welterweight champion (1961,62-63,63-65); world middleweight champ (1966-67,67-68); pro record 85-24-2 with 23 KOs.

**Dick Groat** (b. Nov. 4, 1930): Basketball G and Baseball SS; 2-time basketball All-America at Duke and college Player of Year in 1951; won NL MVP award as shortstop with Pittsburgh in 1960; won World Series with Pirates (1960) and St. Louis (1964).

**Lefty Grove** (b. Mar. 6, 1900, d. May 23, 1975): Baseball LHP; won 20 or more games 8 times; led AL in ERA 9 times and strikeouts 7 times; 31-4 record and MVP in 1931 with Philadelphia; 300-141 record; real name: Robert Moses Grove.

**Lou Groza** (b. Jan. 25, 1924, d. Nov. 29, 2000): Football T-PK; 6-time All-Pro; played in 13 championship games for Cleveland from 1946-67; kicked winning field goal in 1950 NFL title game; 1,608 career points (1,349 in NFL).

**Janet Guthrie** (b. Mar. 7, 1938): Auto racer; in 1977, became 1st woman to race in Indianapolis 500; placed 9th at Indy in 1978.

**Tony Gwynn** (b. May 9, 1960): Baseball OF; 8-time NL batting champion (1984,87-89,94-97) with San Diego, 15-time All-Star; got 3,000th career hit Aug. 6, 1999 at Montreal; played basketball at San Diego St. leaving as school's all-time assist leader; drafted in 10th round of 1981 NBA draft by then San Diego Clippers; retired with 3,141 career hits.

**Harvey Haddix** (b. Sept. 18, 1925, d. Jan. 9, 1994): Baseball LHP; pitched 12 perfect innings for Pittsburgh, but lost to Milwaukee in the 13th, 1-0 (May 26, 1959); won Game 7 of 1960 World Series.

**Walter Hagen** (b. Dec. 21, 1892, d. Oct. 5, 1969): Pro golf pioneer; won 2 U.S. Opens (1914,19), 4 British Opens (1922,24,28-29), 5 PGA Championships (1921,24,26-27) & 5 Western Opens; 44 career PGA wins; 6-time U.S. Ryder Cup captain.

**Marvin Hagler** (b. May 23, 1954): Boxer; hard-punching world middleweight champion from 1980-87; enjoyed his nickname "Marvelous Marvin" so much he had his name legally changed; pro record of 62-3-2 with 52 KOs; retired after suffering 1987 upset loss to Sugar Ray Leonard.

**Mika Hakkinen** (b. Sept. 28, 1968): Finnish auto racer; won two consecutive Formula One world drivers championships in 1998 and '99; recorded eight wins in '98 and five in '99; 20 career F1 wins.

**George Halas** (b. Feb. 2, 1895, d. Oct. 31, 1983): Football pioneer; MVP in 1919 Rose Bowl; player-coach-owner of Chicago Bears from 1920-83; signed Red Grange in 1925; coached Bears for 40 seasons and won 8 NFL titles (1921,32-33,40-41,43,46,63); 2nd on all-time career list with 324 wins; elected to NFL Hall of Fame in 1963.

**Dorothy Hamill** (b. July 26, 1956): Figure skater; won Olympic gold medal and world championship in 1976; Ice Capades headliner from 1977-84; bought the financially-strapped Ice Capades in 1993 and sold it several years later.

**Scott Hamilton** (b. Aug. 28, 1958): Figure skater; 4-time world champion (1981-84); won gold medal at 1984 Olympics.

**Mia Hamm** (b. Mar. 17, 1972): Soccer F; all-time leading international scorer with 154 goals; member of 3 U.S. Olympic teams (1996,2000,04), and 4 U.S. World Cup teams (1991,95,99,2003); made the U.S. National Team at 15; a three-time collegiate All-American; led UNC to 4 national titles (1989,90, 92,93); Two-time FIFA Women's World Player of the Year (2001-02); married to baseball's Nomar Garciaparra.

**Tonya Harding** (b. Nov. 12, 1970): Figure skater; 1991 and 1994 U.S. women's champion; involved in plot hatched by ex-husband Jeff Gillooly to injure rival Nancy Kerrigan and keep her off Olympic team; won '94 U.S. title in Kerrigan's absence; denied any role in assault and sued USOC to keep her spot in Olympics; finished 8th at Lillehammer (Kerrigan recovered and won silver medal); pleaded guilty on Mar. 16 to conspiracy to hinder investigation; stripped of 1994 title by U.S. Figure Skating Association.

**Tom Harmon** (b. Sept. 28, 1919, d. Mar. 17, 1990): Football HB; 2-time All-America at Michigan; won Heisman Trophy in 1940; played with AFL NY Americans in 1941 and NFL LA Rams (1946-47);World War II fighter pilot who won Silver Star and Purple Heart; became radio-TV commentator.

**Franco Harris** (b. Mar. 7, 1950): Football RB; ran for over 1,000 yards in a season 8 times; rushed for 12,120 yards in 13 years; led Pittsburgh to 4 Super Bowl titles.

**Leon Hart** (b. Nov. 2, 1928, d. Sept. 24, 2002): Football E; only player to win 3 national championships in college and 3 more in the NFL; won his titles at Notre Dame (1946-47,49) and with Detroit Lions (1952-53,57); 3-time All-America and last lineman to win Heisman Trophy (1949); All-Pro on both offense and defense in 1951.

**Bill Hartack** (b. Dec. 9, 1932): Jockey; won Kentucky Derby 5 times (1957,60,62,64,69), Preakness 3 times (1956,64,69), and the Belmont once (1960).

**Doug Harvey** (b. Dec. 19, 1924, d. Dec. 26, 1989): Hockey D; 10-time All-NHL 1st team; won Norris Trophy 7 times (1955-58,60-62); led Montreal to 6 Stanley Cups.

**Dominik Hasek** (b. Jan. 29, 1965): Czech hockey goaltender; 2-time NHL MVP (1997,98) with Buffalo; 6-time Vezina Trophy winner (1994,95,97,98,99, 2001); led Czech Republic to Olympic gold medal in 1998 at Nagano; won Stanley Cup with Detroit in 2002.

**Billy Haughton** (b. Nov. 2, 1923, d. July 15, 1986): Harness racing; 4-time winner of Hambletonian; trainer-driver of one Pacing Triple Crown winner (1968); 4,910 career wins.

**João Havelange** (b. May 8, 1916): Soccer; Brazilian-born president of Federation Internationale de Football Assoc. (FIFA) 1974-98; also member of International Olympic Committee.

**John Havlicek** (b. Apr. 8, 1940): Basketball F; played in 3 NCAA Finals at Ohio St. (1960-62); led Boston to 8 NBA titles (1963-66,68-69,74,76); Finals MVP in 1974; 4-time All-NBA 1st team.

**Bob Hayes** (b. Dec. 20, 1942, d. Sept. 18, 2002): Track & Field and Football; won gold medal in 100m at 1964 Olympics; all-pro SE for Dallas in 1966; won Super Bowl with Cowboys in 1972; convicted of drug trafficking in 1979 and served 18 months of a 5-year sentence.

**Elvin Hayes** (b. Nov. 17, 1945): Basketball C; Known as "the Big E"; Overall number one pick of the 1968 NBA draft; three-time All-NBA first team (1975,77,79); 1978 Finals MVP; 12-time NBA all-star (1969-80); named to NBA's 50 Greatest Players; amassed 27,313 points and 16,279 rebounds; member of basketball Hall of Fame.

**Woody Hayes** (b. Feb. 14, 1913, d. Mar. 12, 1987): Football; coached Ohio St. to 6 national titles (1954,57,61,68,70) and 4 Rose Bowl victories; 238 career wins in 28 seasons at Denison, Miami-OH and OSU; his coaching career ended abruptly in 1978 after he attacked an opposing player on the sidelines.

**Thomas Hearns** (b. Oct. 18, 1958): Boxer; held world titles as welterweight, junior middleweight, middleweight and light heavyweight; four career losses came against Ray Leonard, Marvin Hagler and twice to Iran Barkley; pro record of 60-4-1, 46 KOs.

**Eric Heiden** (b. June 14, 1958): Speed skater; 3-time overall world champion (1977-79); won all 5 men's speed skating gold medals at 1980 Olympics, setting records in each; Sullivan Award winner (1980).

**Mel Hein** (b. Aug. 22, 1909, d. Jan. 31, 1992): Football C; NFL All-Pro 8 straight years (1933-40); MVP in 1938 with Giants; didn't miss a game in 15 years.

**John W. Heisman** (b. Oct. 23, 1869, d. Oct. 3, 1936): Football; coached at 9 colleges from 1892-1927; won 185 games; Director of Athletics at Downtown Athletic Club in NYC (1928-36); DAC named Heisman Trophy after him.

**Carol Heiss** (b. Jan. 20, 1940): Figure skater; 5-time world champion (1956-60); won Olympic silver medal in 1956 and gold in '60; married 1956 men's gold medalist Hayes Jenkins.

**Rickey Henderson** (b. Dec. 25, 1958): Baseball OF; AL playoff MVP (1989) and AL regular season MVP (1990); set single-season base stealing record of 130 in 1982; led AL in steals a record 12 times; broke Lou Brock's all-time record of 938 on May 1, 1991; holds all-time MLB records in runs (2295), stolen bases (1406), and HRs as leadoff batter (81).

**Sonja Henie** (b. Apr. 8, 1912, d. Oct. 12, 1969): Norwegian figure skater; 10-time world champion (1927-36); won 3 consecutive Olympic gold medals (1928,32,36); became movie star.

**Foster Hewitt** (b. Nov. 21, 1902, d. Apr. 21, 1985): Radio-TV; Canada's premier hockey play-by-play broadcaster from 1923-81; coined phrase, "He shoots, he scores!"

**Damon Hill** (b. Sept. 17, 1960): British auto racer; 1996 Formula 1 champion; 22 F1 wins places him 10th all-time; retired following 1999 season; son of Graham.

**Graham Hill** (b. Feb. 15, 1929, d. Nov. 29, 1975): British auto racer; 2-time Formula One world champion (1962,68); won Indy 500 in 1966; killed in plane crash; father of Damon.

**Phil Hill** (b. Apr. 20, 1927): Auto racer; first U.S. driver to win Formula One championship (1961); 3 career wins (1958-64).

**Sir Edmund Hillary** (b. July 20, 1919): New Zealand mountaineer; On May 29, 1953, along with Sherpa Tenzing Norgay, Hillary became the first to reach summitt of Mt. Everest, the world's highest peak.

**Martina Hingis** (b. Sept. 30, 1980): Swiss tennis player; in March 1997 at 16 years, 6 months, she became the youngest No. 1 ranked player since the ranking system began in 1975; won Wimbledon (1997), U.S. Open (1997) and 3 Australian Opens (1997,98,99); first woman to surpass the $3 million mark in earnings for one season (1997).

**Max Hirsch** (b. July 30, 1880, d. Apr. 3, 1969): Horse racing; trained 1,933 winners from 1908-68; won Triple Crown with Assault in 1946.

**Tommy Hitchcock** (b. Feb. 11, 1900, d. Apr. 19, 1944): Polo; world class player at 20; achieved 10-goal rating 18 times from 1922-40.

**Lew Hoad** (b. Nov. 23, 1934, d. July 3, 1994): Australian tennis player; 2-time Wimbledon winner (1956-57); won Australian, French and Wimbledon titles in 1956, but missed capturing Grand Slam at Forest Hills when beaten by Ken Rosewall in 4-set final.

**Gil Hodges** (b. Apr. 4, 1924, d. Apr. 2, 1972): Baseball 1B-Manager; tied Major League record with four home runs in one game on Aug 31, 1950; won three Gold Gloves (1957-59); drove in 100 runs in seven consecutive seasons (1949-55); hit 370 home runs and 1,274 RBIs lifetime; won 660 games as a manager (Senators and Mets).

**Ben Hogan** (b. Aug. 13, 1912, d. July 25, 1997): Golfer; 4-time PGA Player of Year; one of only five players to win all four Grand Slam titles (others are Nicklaus, Player, Sarazen and Woods); won 4 U.S. Opens, 2 Masters, 2 PGAs and 1 British Open between 1946-53; nearly killed in Feb. 2, 1949 car accident, but came back to win 1950 U.S. Open just 16 months later; one of only two players (Woods) to win three of the four current majors in one year when he won Masters, U.S. Open and British Open in 1953 at age 41; third on all-time list with 64 career wins.

**Chamique Holdsclaw** (b. Aug. 9, 1977): Basketball F; 2-time national player of the year, leading Tennessee to 3 straight national championships (1996-98); 1998 Sullivan Award winner; top selection by the Washington Mystics in the 1999 WNBA draft; 1999 WNBA Rookie of the Year.

**Eleanor Holm** (b. Dec. 6, 1913, d. Jan. 31, 2004): Swimmer; won gold medal in 100m backstroke at 1932 Olympics; thrown off '36 U.S. team for drinking champagne in public and shooting craps on boat to Germany.

**Nat Holman** (b. Oct. 18, 1896, d. Feb. 12, 1995): Basketball pioneer; played with Original Celtics (1920-28); coached CCNY to both NCAA and NIT titles in 1950 (a year later, several of his players were caught up in a point-shaving scandal); 423 career wins.

**Larry Holmes** (b. Nov. 3, 1949): Boxer; heavyweight champion (WBC or IBF) from 1978-85; beat Gerry Cooney on a 13th-round TKO in their 1982 mega-fight; successfully defended title 20 times before losing to Michael Spinks; returned from first retirement in 1988 and was KO'd in 4th by champ Mike Tyson; launched second comeback in 1991; fought and lost title bids against Evander Holyfield in '92 and Oliver McCall in '95; pro record of 69-6 and 44 KOs.

**Lou Holtz** (b. Jan. 6, 1937): Football; coached Notre Dame to national title in 1988; 2-time Coach of Year (1977,88); also coached NFL's NY Jets for 13 games (3-10) in 1976.

**Evander Holyfield** (b. Oct. 19, 1962): Boxer; only man in history to win (and lose) world heavyweight title 4 times; Wore belt off and on from 1990-2001; defeated former champ Mike Tyson in 1996 to win WBA belt; in 1997 rematch, Tyson was DQ'd for twice biting his ear; former undisputed cruiserweight world (1987-88) champ before moving to heavyweight.

**Red Holzman** (b. Aug. 10, 1920, d. Nov. 13, 1998): Basketball; played for NBL and NBA champions at Rochester (1946,51); coached NY Knicks to 2 NBA titles (1970,73); Coach of Year (1970); 754 career NBA wins.

**Bernard Hopkins** (b. Jan. 15, 1965): Boxer; became first undisputed world middleweight champion since Marvin Hagler when he upset undefeated Felix Trinidad with a 12th-round TKO in 2001 to unify belts; defended title for a division-record 20 times before finally losing belts on a split decision to Jermain Taylor in 2005.

**Rogers Hornsby** (b. Apr. 27, 1896, d. Jan. 5, 1963): Baseball 2B; hit .400 3 times, including .424 in 1924; led NL in batting 7 times; 2-time MVP (1925,29); career BA of .358 over 23 years is highest in NL.

**Paul Hornung** (b. Dec. 23, 1935): Football HB-PK; only Heisman Trophy winner to play for losing team (2-8 Notre Dame in 1956); 3-time NFL scoring leader (1959-61) at Green Bay; 176 points in 1960, an all-time record; MVP in 1961; suspended by NFL for 1963 season for betting on his own team.

**Gordie Howe** (b. Mar. 31, 1928): Hockey RW; played 32 seasons in NHL and WHA from 1946-80; led NHL in scoring 6 times; All-NHL 1st team 12 times; MVP 6 times in NHL (1952-53,57-58,60,63) with Detroit and once in WHA (1974) with Houston; ranks 2nd on all-time NHL list in goals (801) and 3rd in points (1,850); played with sons Mark and Marty at Houston (1973-77) and New England-Hartford (1977-80).

**Cal Hubbard** (b. Oct. 31, 1900, d. Oct. 17, 1977): Member of college football, pro football and baseball halls of fame; 9 years in NFL; 4-time All-Pro at end and tackle; AL umpire (1936-51).

**William DeHart Hubbard** (b. Nov. 25, 1903, d. June 23, 1976): Track & Field; won the long jump at the 1924 Olympics, becoming the first black athlete to win an Olympic gold medal in an individual event; set the long jump world record in 1925 (25-10¾) and tied the 100-yard dash record (9.6) in 1926.

**Carl Hubbell** (b. June 22, 1903, d. Nov. 21, 1988): Baseball LHP; led NL in wins and ERA 3 times each; 2-time MVP (1933,36) with NY Giants; fanned Ruth, Gehrig, Foxx, Simmons and Cronin in succession in 1934 All-Star Game; 253-154 career record.

**Sam Huff** (b. Oct. 4, 1934): Football LB; glamorized NFL's middle linebacker position with NY Giants from 1956-63; subject of "The Violent World of Sam Huff" TV special in 1961; helped club win 6 division titles and a world championship (1956).

**Miller Huggins** (b. Mar. 27, 1878, d. Sept. 25, 1929): Baseball; managed NY Yankees from 1918 until his death late in '29 season; led Yanks to 6 pennants and 3 World Series titles from 1921-28.

**Bobby Hull** (b. Jan. 3, 1939): Hockey LW; led NHL in scoring 3 times; 2-time MVP (1965-66) with Chicago; All-NHL first team 10 times; jumped to WHA in 1972, 2-time MVP there (1973,75) with Winnipeg; scored 913 goals in both leagues; father of Brett.

**Brett Hull** (b. Aug. 9, 1964): Hockey RW; NHL MVP in 1991 with St. Louis; holds single season RW scoring record with 86 goals; he and father Bobby have both won Hart (MVP), Lady Byng (sportsmanship) and All-Star Game MVP trophies; won Stanley Cup with Dallas in 1999 and Detroit in 2002.

**Lamar Hunt** (b. Aug. 2, 1932): Football/Soccer; Founder of the Kansas City Chiefs (formerly Dallas Texans); instrumental in forming the AFL in 1959 and merging the league with NFL in 1966; elected to the Pro Football Hall of Fame in 1972; AFC Championship trophy bear his name; investor/operator in Major League Soccer.

**Jim (Catfish) Hunter** (b. Apr. 8, 1946, d. Sept. 9, 1999): Baseball RHP; won 20 games or more 5 times (1971-75); played on 5 World Series winners with Oakland and NY Yankees; threw perfect game in 1968; won AL Cy Young Award in 1974; 224-166 career record.

**Ibrahim Hussein** (b. June 3, 1958): Kenyan distance runner; 3-time winner of Boston Marathon (1988,91-92) and 1st African runner to win in Boston; won New York Marathon in 1987.

**Don Hutson** (b. Jan. 31, 1913, d. June 24, 1997): Football E-PK; led NFL in receptions 8 times and interceptions once; 9-time All-Pro (1936,38-45) for Green Bay; 99 career TD catches.

**Flo Hyman** (b. July 31, 1954, d. Jan. 24, 1986): Volleyball; 3-time All-America spiker at Houston and captain of 1984 U.S. Women's Olympic team; died of heart attack caused by Marfan Syndrome during a match in Japan in 1986; namesake of award given out annually by the Women's Sports Foundation.

**Hank Iba** (b. Aug. 6, 1904, d. Jan. 15, 1993): Basketball; coached Oklahoma A&M to 2 straight NCAA titles (1945-46); 767 career wins in 41 years; coached U.S. Olympic team to 2 gold medals (1964,68), but lost to Soviets in controversial '72 final.

**Punch Imlach** (b. Mar. 15, 1918, d. Dec. 1, 1987): Hockey; directed Toronto to 4 Stanley Cups (1962-64,67) in 11 seasons as GM-coach.

**Miguel Induráin** (b. July 16, 1964): Spanish cyclist; won 5 straight Tour de Frances (1991-95), won gold in time trial at '96 Olympics; retired in 1997.

**Juli Inkster** (b. June 24, 1960): Golfer; 30 career LPGA victories; winner of 7 major LPGA titles and 3 consecutive U.S. Women's Amateur tournaments (1980-82); inducted into the World Golf Hall of Fame in 2000; LPGA Rookie of the Year in 1984.

**Hale Irwin** (b. June 3, 1945): Golfer; oldest player ever to win U.S. Open (45 in 1990); NCAA champion in 1967; 20 PGA victories, including 3 U.S. Opens (1974,79,90); 5-time Ryder Cup team member; joined Senior PGA Tour in 1995 and has already won 44 titles.

**Allen Iverson** (b. June 7, 1975): Basketball G; former Georgetown Hoya chosen first overall by the Philadelphia 76ers in the 1996 NBA Draft; NBA Rookie of the Year (1997); 3-time NBA scoring leader (2001-02,05) and steals leader (2001-02); voted regular season MVP in 2001 and led 76ers to NBA Finals.

**Bo Jackson** (b. Nov. 30, 1962): Baseball OF and Football RB; won Heisman Trophy in 1985 and MVP of baseball All-Star Game in 1989; starter for both baseball's KC Royals and NFL's LA Raiders in 1988 and '89; severely injured left hip Jan. 13, 1991, in NFL playoffs; waived by Royals but signed by Chicago White Sox in 1991; missed entire 1992 season recovering from hip surgery; played for White Sox in 1993 and California in '94 before retiring.

**Joe Jackson** (b. July 16, 1889, d. Dec. 5, 1951): Baseball OF; hit .300 or better 11 times; nicknamed "Shoeless Joe"; career average of .356, third highest all-time; was placed on MLB's ineligible list in 1921 following the Black Sox scandal in which he and 7 teammates were accused of fixing 1919 World Series.

**Phil Jackson** (b. Sept. 17, 1945): Basketball; NBA champion as reserve forward with New York in 1973 (injured when Knicks won in '70); coached Chicago to six NBA titles in eight years (1991-93, 96-98); coach of the year in 1996 and 97; returned to coach the LA Lakers in 1999 and won 3 more titles (2000,01,02); all-time leader in winning pct. for NBA coaches with 350 or more wins; left Lakers after 2004 Finals loss to Detroit but returned after one season; all-time NBA leader in playoff wins (175).

**Reggie Jackson** (b. May 18, 1946): Baseball OF; led AL in HRs 4 times; MVP in 1973; played on 5 World Series winners with Oakland and NY Yankees; 1977 Series MVP with 5 HRs; 563 career HRs; all-time strikeout leader (2,597); member of the Hall of Fame.

**Dr. Robert Jackson** (b. Aug. 6, 1932): Surgeon; revolutionized sports medicine by popularizing the use of arthroscopic surgery to treat injuries; learned technique from Japanese physician that allowed athletes to return quickly from potentially career-ending injuries.

**Helen Jacobs** (b. Aug. 6, 1908, d. June 2, 1997): Tennis; 4-time winner of U.S. Championship (1932-35); Wimbledon winner in 1936; lost 4 Wimbledon finals to arch-rival Helen Wills Moody.

**Jaromir Jagr** (b. Feb. 15, 1972): Czech Hockey RW; fifth overall pick by Pittsburgh (1990); NHL All-Rookie team (1991); NHL MVP (1999); Won Art Ross Trophy (1995,98,99,00,01); 7-time All-NHL First Team; NHL single season record for most points by a right wing (149); NHL single season record for most assists by a RW (87).

**LeBron James** (b. Dec. 30, 1984): Basketball; mega-hyped top overall pick in 2003 NBA Draft (Cleveland) straight out of high school; youngest-ever NBA Rookie of the Year (2004).

**Dan Jansen** (b. June 17, 1965): Speed skater; fell in 500m and 1,000m in 1988 Olympics just after sister Jane's death; placed 4th in 500m and didn't attempt 1,000m in 1992; fell in 500m at '94 Games, but finally won an Olympic medal with world record (1:12.43) effort in 1,000m, then took victory lap with baby daughter Jane in his arms; won 1994 Sullivan Award.

**Dale Jarrett** (b. Nov. 26, 1956): Auto racer; 1999 Winston Cup champion; 3-time Daytona 500 champion (1993,96,2000); son of driver Ned Jarrett.

**James J. Jeffries** (b. Apr. 15, 1875, d. Mar. 3, 1953): Boxer; world heavyweight champion (1899-1905); retired undefeated but came back to fight Jack Johnson in 1910 and lost (KO, 15th).

**David Jenkins** (b. June 29, 1936): Figure skater; brother of Hayes; 3-time world champion (1957-59); won gold medal at 1960 Olympics.

**Hayes Jenkins** (b. Mar. 23, 1933): Figure skater; 4-time world champion (1953-56); won gold medal at 1956 Olympics; married 1960 women's gold medalist Carol Heiss.

**Bruce Jenner** (b. Oct. 28, 1949): Track & Field; won gold medal in 1976 Olympic decathlon.

**Jackie Jensen** (b. Mar. 9, 1927, d. July 14, 1982): Football RB and Baseball OF; All-America at Cal in 1948; AL MVP with Boston Red Sox in 1958.

**Ben Johnson** (b. Dec. 30, 1961): Canadian sprinter; set 100m world record (9.83) at 1987 World Championships; won 100m at 1988 Olympics, but flunked drug test and forfeited gold medal; 1987 world record revoked in '89 for admitted steroid use; returned drug-free in 1991, but performed poorly; banned for life by IAAF in 1993 for testing positive again.

**Bob Johnson** (b. Mar. 4, 1931, d. Nov. 26, 1991): Hockey; coached Pittsburgh Penguins to 1st Stanley Cup title in 1991; led Wisconsin to 3 NCAA titles (1973,77,81); also coached 1976 U.S. Olympic team and NHL Calgary Flames (1982-87).

**Earvin (Magic) Johnson** (b. Aug. 14, 1959): Basketball G; led Michigan St. to NCAA title in 1979 and was Final 4 MOP; All-NBA 1st team 9 times; 3-time MVP (1987,89-90); led LA Lakers to 5 NBA titles; 3-time Finals MVP (1980, 82, 87); 3rd all-time in NBA assists with 10,141; retired on Nov. 7, 1991 after announcing he was HIV-positive; returned to score 25 points in 1992 NBA All-Star Game; U.S. Olympic Dream Team co-captain; announced NBA comeback then retired again before start of 1992-93 season; named head coach of Lakers on Mar. 23, 1994, but finished season at 5-11 and quit; later became minority owner of team; came back a final time and played 32 games during 1995-96 season.

**Jack Johnson** (b. Mar. 31, 1878, d. June 10, 1946): Boxer; controversial heavyweight champion (1908-15) and 1st black to hold title; defeated Tommy Burns for crown at age 30; fled to Europe in 1913 after Mann Act conviction; lost title to Jess Willard in Havana, but claimed to have taken a dive; pro record 78-8-12 with 45 KOs.

**Jimmy Johnson** (b. July 16, 1943): Football; All-SWC defensive lineman on Arkansas' 1964 national championship team; coached U. of Miami-FL to national title in 1987; college record of 81-34-3 in 10 years; hired by old pal Jerry Jones to succeed Tom Landry in 1989; went 1-15 in '89, then led Cowboys to consecutive Super Bowl victories (1993-94); quit in 1994 after feuding with Jones; replaced Don Shula as Miami Dolphins head coach from 1996-99.

**Judy Johnson** (b. Oct. 26, 1899, d. June 13, 1989): Baseball IF; one of the great stars of the Negro Leagues; a terrific fielding third baseman who regularly batted over .300; when baseball integrated Johnson's playing days were over but he coached and scouted for the Philadelphia Athletics, Boston Braves and Philadelphia Phillies; member of Hall of Fame.

**Junior Johnson** (b. June 28, 1931): Auto Racing; won Daytona 500 in 1960; also won 13 NASCAR races in 1965, including the Rebel 300 at Darlington; retired from racing to become a highly successful car owner; his first driver was Bobby Allison.

**Michael Johnson** (b. Sep. 13, 1967): Track & Field; Shattered world record in 200m (19.32) and set Olympic record in 400m (43.49) to become first man to win the gold in both races in the same Olympic Games at Atlanta in 1996; two-time world champion in 200 (1991,95) and four-time world champ in 400 (1993,95,97,99); set world record in 400m (43.18) at '99 world championships in Seville; won the 400 in Sydney in 2000 to become the only man to win the event in two consecutive Olympics; retired in 2001.

**Rafer Johnson** (b. Aug. 18, 1935): Track & Field; won silver medal in 1956 Olympic decathlon and gold medal in 1960.

**Randy Johnson** (b. Sept. 10, 1963): Baseball LHP; 6'10" flamethrower; struck out over 300 batters 6 times (1993,98,99,00,01,02); led AL in Ks 4 times (1992-95) and NL 5 times (1999-2002,04); struck out 20 batters in a game (5/8/01); 5-time Cy Young Award winner with Seattle and Arizona (AL-1995, NL-1999-2002); won 3 games and co-MVP honors (Curt Schilling) in 2001 World Series; became oldest in baseball history to pitch a perfect game at age 40; signed free-agent deal with N.Y. Yankees in 2005.

**Walter Johnson** (b. Nov. 6, 1887, d. Dec. 10, 1946): Baseball RHP; nicknamed "Big Train" Johnson had an overpowering fastball; won 20 games or more 10 straight years; led AL in ERA 5 times, wins 6 times and strikeouts 12 times; twice MVP (1913, 24) with Washington Senators; all-time leader in shutouts (110) and 2nd in wins (417); part of the Hall of Fame's inaugural class of 1936

**Ben A. Jones** (b. Dec. 31, 1882, d. June 13, 1961): Horse racing; Calumet Farm trainer (1939-47); saddled 6 Kentucky Derby champions, including 2 Triple Crown winners—Whirlaway in 1941 and Citation in '48.

**Bobby Jones** (b. Mar. 17, 1902, d. Dec. 18, 1971): Won U.S. and British Opens plus U.S. and British Amateurs in 1930 to become golf's only Grand Slam winner ever; between 1922-30, he won 4 U.S. Opens, 5 U.S. Amateurs, 3 British Opens, and 1 British Amateur for 13 Major titles in all, a record that stood until Jack Nicklaus broke it; played in 6 Walker Cups; designed Augusta National (with Alister Mackenzie) and founded Masters tournament in 1934.

**Deacon Jones** (b. Dec. 9, 1938): Football DE; 5-time All-Pro (1965-69) with LA Rams; unofficially 3rd all-time in NFL sacks with 173½ in 14 years; inducted into Pro Football Hall of Fame in 1980.

**Jerry Jones** (b. Oct. 13, 1942): Football; owner-GM of Dallas Cowboys; maverick who bought declining team (3-13) and Texas Stadium for $140 million in 1989; hired pal Jimmy Johnson to replace legendary coach Tom Landry; their partnership led to 2 Super Bowl titles (1993-94); when feud developed, he fired Johnson and hired Barry Switzer and won Super Bowl in 1996; hired proven winner Bill Parcells as head coach in 2003 following three losing seasons.

**Marion Jones** (b. Oct. 12, 1975): Track & Field; American sprinter who won 3 golds (100m, 200m, 4x100m) at 2000 Sydney Olympics; 5-time world champion: 100m (1997,99), 200m (2001), 4x100m (1997, 2001); voted Women's Athlete of the Year by *Track & Field News* in 1997,98 and 2000; 1999 Jesse Owens Award winner; 2000 AP and USOC Female Athlete of the Year.

**Roy Jones Jr.** (b. Jan. 16, 1969): Boxing; robbed of gold medal at 1988 Olympics on a scoring error; still voted Outstanding Boxer of the Games; won IBF middleweight crown, beating Bernard Hopkins in 1993; moved up to super middleweight and won IBF title from James Toney in 1994; moved up to light heavyweight, winning WBC (1997), WBA (1998) and IBF titles (1999); made temporary move to heavyweight in 2003 and decisioned John Ruiz for WBA belt; lost WBC light heavyweight belt to Antonio Tarver in a 2nd round KO in 2004; knocked out in comeback fight with Glen Johnson in 2004; fought Tarver for a 3rd time in 2005.

**Michael Jordan** (b. Feb. 17, 1963): Basketball G; College Player of Year with North Carolina in 1984; NBA Rookie of the Year (1985); led NBA in scoring 7 years in a row (1987-93) and also 1996-98; 10-time All-NBA 1st team; 5-time regular season MVP (1988,91-92,96,98) and 6-time MVP of NBA Finals (1991-93,96-98); 3-time AP Male Athlete of Year; led U.S. Olympic team to gold in 1984 and '92; retired with most sports world when he retired at age 30 on Oct. 6, 1993; signed as OF with Chi. White Sox and spent summer of '94 in AA with Birmingham; struggled with .204 average; made one of the most anticipated comebacks in sports history when he returned to the Bulls lineup on Mar. 19, 1995 but Bulls were eliminated by Orlando in 2nd round of playoffs later that season; led Bulls to NBA titles for the next 3 years for 6 titles in all (1991-93,96-98); retired in 1999; became pres. of Wash. Wizards before unretiring again in 2001 and returning to play with Wizards for 2 seasons.

**Florence Griffith Joyner** (b. Dec. 21, 1959, d. Sept. 21, 1998): Track & Field; world records in 100 and 200m in 1988; won 3 gold medals at '88 Olympics (100m, 200m, 4x100m relay); Sullivan Award winner (1988); retired in 1989; named as co-chairperson of President's Council on Physical Fitness and Sports in 1993; sister-in-law of Jackie Joyner-Kersee; died of suffocation during an epileptic seizure in 1998.

**Jackie Joyner-Kersee** (b. Mar. 3, 1962): Track & Field; 2-time world champion in both long jump (1987,91) and heptathlon (1987,93); won heptathlon gold medals at 1988 and '92 Olympics and LJ gold at '88 Games; also won Olympic silver (1984) in heptathlon and bronze (1992,96) in LJ; Sullivan Award winner (1986); only woman to receive *The Sporting News* Man of Year award.

**Alberto Juantorena** (b. Nov. 21, 1950): Cuban runner; won both 400m and 800m gold medals at 1976 Olympics.

**Sonny Jurgensen** (b. Aug. 23, 1934): Football QB; played 18 seasons with Philadelphia and Washington; led NFL in passing twice (1967,69); All-Pro in 1961; 255 career TD passes.

**Duke Kahanamoku** (b. Aug. 24, 1890, d. Jan. 22, 1968): Swimmer; won 3 gold medals and 2 silver over 3 Olympics (1912,20,24); also surfing pioneer.

**Al Kaline** (b. Dec. 19, 1934): Baseball; youngest player (at age 20) to win batting title (led AL with .340 in 1955); had 3,007 hits, 399 HRs in 22 years with Detroit.

**Paul Kariya** (b. Oct. 16, 1974): Hockey LW; first-ever selection of Anaheim (4th overall in 1993); led Maine to an NCAA Div. I national title in 1993; won Hobey Baker Award in 1993 as a freshman.

**Anatoly Karpov** (b. May 23, 1951): Chess; Soviet world champion from 1975-85; regained International Chess Federation (FIDE) championship in 1993 when countryman Garry Kasparov was stripped of title after forming new Professional Chess Association; held FIDE title until 1999.

**Garry Kasparov** (b. Apr. 13, 1963): Chess; Azerbaijani who became youngest player (22 years, 210 days) ever to win world championship as Soviet in 1985; defeated countryman Anatoly Karpov for title; split with International Chess Federation (FIDE) to form Professional Chess Association (PCA) in 1993; stripped of FIDE title in '93 but successfully defended PCA title against Briton Nigel Short; beat IBM supercomputer "Deep Blue" 4 games to 2 in 1996 much-publicized match in New York; lost rematch to computer in 1997; finally lost world title to Vladimir Kramnik in 2000.

**Mike Keenan** (b. Oct. 21, 1949): Hockey; coach who finally led NY Rangers to Stanley Cup title in 1994 after 53 unsuccessful years; ranked 5th all-time on NHL coaching wins list.

**Kipchoge (Kip) Keino** (b. Jan. 17, 1940): Kenyan runner; policeman who beat USA's Jim Ryun to win 1,500m gold medal at 1968 Olympics; won again in steeplechase at 1972 Summer Games; his success spawned long line of distance champions from Kenya.

**Johnny A. Kelley** (b. Sept. 6, 1907, d. Oct. 7, 2004): Distance runner; ran in his 61st and final Boston Marathon at age 84 in 1992, finishing in 5:58:36; won Boston twice (1935,45) and was 2nd seven times.

**Jim Kelly** (b. Feb. 14, 1960): Football QB; led Buffalo to four straight Super Bowls, and is only QB to lose four times; named to AFC Pro Bowl team 5 times; inducted into Pro Football Hall of Fame in 2002.

**Leroy Kelly** (b. May 20, 1942): Football; replaced Jim Brown in the Cleveland Browns backfield; in 1967, he led the NFL in rushing yards (1,205), rushing average (5.1 per carry) and rushing touchdowns (11).

**Walter Kennedy** (b. June 8, 1912, d. June 26, 1977): Basketball; 2nd NBA commissioner (1963-75), league doubled in size to 18 teams during his tenure.

**Nancy Kerrigan** (b. Oct. 13, 1969): Figure skating; 1993 U.S. women's champion and Olympic medalist in 1992 (bronze) and '94 (silver); victim of Jan. 6, 1994 assault at U.S. nationals in Detroit when Shane Stant clubbed her in right knee with metal baton after a practice session; conspiracy hatched by Jeff Gillooly, ex-husband of rival Tonya Harding; although unable to compete in nationals, she recovered and was granted berth on Olympic team; finished 2nd in Lillehammer to Oksana Baiul of Ukraine by a 5-4 judges' vote.

**Billy Kidd** (b. Apr. 13, 1943): Skiing; the first great American male Alpine skier; first American male to win an Olympic medal when he won a silver in the slalom and a bronze in the Alpine combined in 1964; competed respectably with the great Jean-Claude Killy; won the world Alpine combined event in 1970, which was the first world championship for an American male.

**Harmon Killebrew** (b. June 29, 1936): Baseball 3B-1B; led AL in HRs 6 times and RBI 3 times; MVP in 1969 with Minnesota; 573 career HRs.

**Jean-Claude Killy** (b. Aug. 30, 1943): French alpine skier; 2-time World Cup champion (1967-68); won 3 gold medals at 1968 Olympics in Grenoble; co-president of 1992 Winter Games in Albertville; president of coordination commission for 2006 Turin Games.

**Ralph Kiner** (b. Oct. 27, 1922): Baseball OF; led NL in home runs 7 straight years (1946-52) with Pittsburgh; 369 career HRs and 1,015 RBI in 10 seasons; long-time NY Mets announcer.

**Betsy King** (b. Aug. 13, 1955): Golfer; 2-time LPGA Player of Year (1984,89); 3-time winner of Dinah Shore (1987,90,97) and 2-time winner of U.S. Open (1989,90); 34 overall Tour wins; 1st player in LPGA history to break $5 million mark in career earnings; member of LPGA Hall of Fame.

**Billie Jean King** (b. Nov. 22, 1943): Tennis; women's rights pioneer; Wimbledon singles champ 6 times; U.S. champ 4 times; first woman athlete to earn $100,000 in one year (1971); beat 55-year-old Bobby Riggs 6-4,6-3,6-3, in "Battle of the Sexes" to win $100,000 at Astrodome in 1973; founded the Women's Sports Foundation in 1974; captained the U.S. Olympic team in 1996 and 2000.

**Don King** (b. Aug. 20, 1931): Boxing promoter; first major black promoter who has controlled heavyweight title off and on since 1978; first big promotion was Muhammad Ali's fight against George Foreman in 1974; former numbers operator who served 4 years for manslaughter (1967-70); acquitted of tax evasion and fraud in 1985; also promoted Larry Holmes, Mike Tyson, Evander Holyfield, Roberto Duran and Julio Cesar Chavez among others; has been accused of bilking his fighters out of money; famous for his gravity-defying hairstyle and his catchphrase "Only in America".

**Karch Kiraly** (b. Nov. 3, 1960): Volleyball; USA's preeminent volleyball player; led UCLA to three NCAA championships (1979,81,82); played on US national teams that won Olympic gold medals in 1984 and '88, world championships in '82 and '86; won the inaugural gold medal for Olympic beach volleyball with Kent Steffes in 1996.

**Tom Kite** (b. Dec. 9, 1949): Golfer; co-NCAA champion with Ben Crenshaw (1972); PGA Rookie of Year (1973); PGA Player of Year (1989); finally won 1st major with victory in 1992 U.S. Open at Pebble Beach; captain of 1997 US Ryder Cup team; 19 career PGA wins, played on the Senior tour since 2000.

**Gene Klein** (b. Jan. 29, 1921, d. Mar. 12, 1990): Horseman; won 3 Eclipse awards as top owner (1985-87); his filly Winning Colors won 1988 Kentucky Derby; also owned San Diego Chargers football team (1966-84).

**Bob Knight** (b. Oct. 25, 1940): Basketball; coached Indiana to 3 NCAA titles (1976,81,87); 3-time Coach of Year (1975-76,89); coached 1984 U.S. Olympic team to gold medal; his volatile temper finally cost him when he was fired from Indiana in Sept. 2000 after a string of unacceptable incidents that included choking one of his players; returned to coaching with Texas Tech in 2001; 3rd on all-time NCAA list with 854 wins in 39 years.

**Phil Knight** (b. Feb. 24, 1938): Founder and chairman of Nike, Inc., the multi-billion dollar shoe and fitness company founded in 1972 and based in Beaverton, Ore.; named "The Most Powerful Man in Sports" by *The Sporting News* in 1992.

**Bill Koch** (b. June 7, 1955): Cross country skiing; first highly accomplished American male in his sport; first American male to win a cross country Olympic medal when he took home a silver in the 30-kilometer race in 1976; in 1982, he was the first American male to win the Nordic World Cup.

**Tommy Kono** (b. June 27, 1930): weight lifter; won 2 olympic gold medals for U.S. (1952,56) and 1 silver (1960); all 3 medals were in different weight classes; set world records in four different classes; inducted into U.S. Olympic Hall of Fame in 1990.

**Olga Korbut** (b. May 16, 1955): Soviet gymnast; became the media darling of the 1972 Olympics in Munich by winning 3 gold medals (balance beam, floor exercise and team all-around); came back in the 1976 Olympics in Montreal and was a part of the USSR's gold medal winning all-around team; first to perform back somersault on balance beam; was inducted into the International Women's Sports Hall of Fame in 1982, the first gymnast to be inducted.

**Johann Olav Koss** (b. Oct. 29, 1968): Norwegian speed skater; won three gold medals at 1994 Olympics in Lillehammer with world records in the 1,500m, 5,000m and 10,000m; also won 1,500m gold and 10,000m silver in 1992 Games; retired shortly after '94 Olympics.

**Sandy Koufax** (b. Dec. 30, 1935): Baseball LHP; led NL in strikeouts 4 times and ERA 5 straight years; won 3 Cy Young Awards (1963,65,66) with LA Dodgers; MVP in 1963; 2-time World Series MVP (1963, 65); threw perfect game against Chicago Cubs (1-0, Sept. 9, 1965) and had 3 other no-hitters, 40 shutouts and 137 complete games in a career that ended prematurely due to an arm injury.

**Alvin Kraenzlein** (b. Dec. 12, 1876, d. Jan. 6, 1928): Track & Field; won 4 individual gold medals in 1900 Olympics (60m, long jump and the 110m and 200m hurdles).

**Jack Kramer** (b. Aug. 1, 1921): Tennis; Wimbledon singles champ 1947; U.S. champ 1946-47; promoter and Open pioneer.

**Lenny Krayzelburg** (b. Sept. 28, 1975): Swimmer; born in Ukraine but became American citizen in 1995; won gold for U.S. in the 100m and 200m backstrokes at the 2000 Sydney Games; was also part of U.S. team that set a world record in the 4x100m medley relay in Sydney.

**Ingrid Kristiansen** (b. Mar. 21, 1956): Norwegian runner; 2-time Boston Marathon winner (1986,89); won New York City Marathon in 1989; former world record holder in the marathon.

**Julie Krone** (b. July 24, 1963): Jockey; only woman to ride winner in a Triple Crown race when she took 1993 Belmont Stakes aboard Colonial Affair; retired in 1999 as all-time winningest female jockey with over 3,000 wins; became the first female jockey named to hall of fame in 2000; came out of retirement in 2002, winning 2003 Breeders Cup race aboard Halfbridled.

**Mike Krzyzewski** (b. Feb. 13, 1947): Basketball; has coached Duke to 10 Final Four appearances and 3 NCAA titles (1991-92,2001); has coached at Army (1976-80) and Duke (1981–); inducted into Hall of Fame in 2001.

**Bowie Kuhn** (b. Oct. 28, 1926): Baseball Commissioner; Elected commissioner on Feb. 4, 1969 and served until Sept. 30, 1984; kept Willie Mays and Mickey Mantle out of baseball for their employment with casinos; handed down one-year suspensions of several players for drug involvement; nixed Charlie Finley's sale of three players for $3.5 million; baseball enjoyed unprecedented attendance and television contracts during his reign.

**Alan Kulwicki** (b. Dec. 14, 1954, d. Apr. 1, 1993): Auto racer; 1992 NASCAR national champion; 1st college grad and Northerner to win title; NASCAR Rookie of Year in 1986; famous for driving car backwards on victory lap; killed at age 38 in plane crash near Bristol, Tenn.

**Michelle Kwan** (b. July 7, 1980): Figure Skater; 1998 Olympic silver medalist at Nagano and 2002 bronze medalist at Salt Lake City; 9-time U.S. Champion (1996,98-05) and 5-time World Champ (1996,98,00,01,03); holds U.S. record with 8 career overall medals at the World Championships (5 gold, 3 silver); was U.S. alternate to the Olympics in 1994 as a 13-year-old.

**Marion Ladewig** (b. Oct. 30, 1914): Bowler; named Woman Bowler of the Year 9 times (1950-54,57-59,63).

**Guy Lafleur** (b. Sept. 20, 1951): Hockey RW; led NHL in scoring 3 times (1976-78); 2-time MVP (1977-78), played for 5 Stanley Cup winners in Montreal; playoff MVP in 1977; returned to NHL as player in 1988 after election to Hall of Fame; retired again in 1991 with 560 goals and 1,353 points.

**Napoleon (Nap) Lajoie** (b. Sept. 5, 1874, d. Feb. 7, 1959): Baseball 2B; led AL in batting 3 times (1901,03-04); batted .422 in 1901; hit .339 for career with 3,251 hits.

**Jack Lambert** (b. July 8, 1952): Football LB; 6-time All-Pro (1975-76,79-82); led Pittsburgh to 4 Super Bowl titles.

**Kenesaw Mountain Landis** (b. Nov. 20, 1866, d. Nov. 25, 1944): U.S. District Court judge who became first baseball commissioner (1920-44); banned eight Chicago "Black Sox" from baseball for life for throwing 1919 World Series.

**Tom Landry** (b. Sept. 11, 1924, d. Feb. 12, 2000): Football; All-Pro DB for NY Giants (1954); coached Dallas for 29 years (1960-88); won 2 Super Bowls (1972,78); 3rd on NFL all-time list with 270 wins.

**Steve Largent** (b. Sept. 28, 1954): Football WR; retired in 1989 after 14 years in Seattle with then NFL records in passes caught (819) and TD passes caught (100); elected to U.S. House of Representatives (R, Okla.) in 1994 and Pro Football Hall of Fame in '95; ran for governor of Oklahoma in 2002 but suffered a narrow defeat.

**Don Larsen** (b. Aug. 7, 1929): Baseball RHP; NY Yankees hurler who pitched the only perfect game in World Series history— a 2-0 victory over Brooklyn in Game 5 of the 1956 Series (Oct. 8); Series MVP that year; had career record of 81-91 in 14 seasons with 6 clubs.

**Tommy Lasorda** (b. Sept. 22, 1927): Baseball; managed LA Dodgers to 2 World Series titles (1981,88) in 4 appearances; retired as manager during 1996 season with 1,599 regular-season wins in 21 years; named interim GM of Dodgers in 1998; member of Baseball Hall of Fame; managed gold-medal winning U.S. Olympic team in 2000 at Sydney.

**Larissa Latynina** (b. Dec. 27, 1934): Soviet gymnast; won total of 18 medals, (9 gold) in 3 Olympics (1956,60,64).

**Nikki Lauda** (b. Feb. 22, 1949): Austrian auto racer; 3-time world Formula One champion (1975, 77,84); 25 career wins from 1971-85.

**Rod Laver** (b. Aug. 9, 1938): Australian tennis player; undersized but big-hitting left-hander is only player to win Grand Slam twice (1962,69); Wimbledon champion 4 times; 1st to earn $1 million in career prize money, won 11 Grand Slam and 47 professional singles titles.

**Andrea Mead Lawrence** (b. Apr. 19, 1932): Alpine skier; won 2 gold medals at 1952 Olympics.

**Bobby Layne** (b. Dec. 19, 1926, d. Dec. 1, 1986): Football QB; college star at Texas; master of 2-minute offense; led Detroit to 4 divisional titles and 3 NFL championships in 1950s.

**Frank Leahy** (b. Aug. 27, 1908, d. June 21, 1973): Football; coached Notre Dame to four national titles (1943,46-47,49); career record of 107-13-9 for a winning pct. of .864.

**Sammy Lee** (b. Aug. 1, 1920): Diving; won Olympic gold medals for U.S. in the platform diving event in 1948 and 1952, the first male diver in history to win 2 golds in that event; Sullivan Award winner (1953); former doctor in U.S. Army; trained Greg Louganis.

**Brian Leetch** (b. Mar. 3, 1968): Hockey D; NHL Rookie of Year in 1989; won Norris Trophy as top defenseman in 1992; Conn Smythe Trophy winner as playoffs' MVP in 1994 when he helped lead NY Rangers to 1st Stanley Cup title in 54 years.

**Jacques Lemaire** (b. Sept. 7, 1945): Hockey C; member of 8 Stanley Cup champions in Montreal; scored 366 goals in 12 seasons; coached Canadiens (1983-85) and NJ Devils (1993-98), won 1995 Stanley Cup with New Jersey; returned to coaching with the expansion Minnesota Wild in 2000.

**Claude Lemieux** (b. July 16, 1965): Hockey RW; played on 4 Stanley Cup winners in Montreal (1986), New Jersey (1995, 2000) and Colorado (1996); playoff MVP in 1995 (N.J.) and 1996 (Colorado).

**Mario Lemieux** (b. Oct. 5, 1965): Hockey C; 6-time NHL scoring leader (1988-89,92,93,96,97); Rookie of Year (1985); 4-time All-NHL 1st team (1988-89,93,96); 3-time regular season MVP (1988,93,96); 3-time All-Star Game MVP; led Pittsburgh to consecutive Stanley Cup titles (1991 and '92) and was playoff MVP both years; won 1993 scoring title despite missing 24 games to undergo radiation treatments for Hodgkin's disease; missed 62 games during 1993-94 season and entire 1994-95 season due to back injuries and fatigue; returned in 1995-96 to lead NHL in scoring and win the MVP trophy; retired after 1996-97 season and inducted into the Hall of Fame; headed group of investors that bought bankrupt Penguins in 1999; made surprising return to the ice in 2001 as owner-player with Penguins.

**Greg LeMond** (b. June 26, 1961): American cyclist; 3-time Tour de France winner (1986,89-90); only non-European to win the event until Lance Armstrong in 1999; retired in Dec. 1994 after being diagnosed with a rare muscular disease known as mitochondrial myopathy.

**Ivan Lendl** (b. Mar. 7, 1960): Czech tennis player; No. 1 player in world 4 times (1985-87,89); won both French and U.S. Opens 3 times and Australian twice; owns 94 career tournament wins.

**Suzanne Lenglen** (b. May 24, 1899, d. July 4, 1938): French tennis player; dominated women's tennis from 1919-26; won both Wimbledon and French singles titles 6 times.

**Sugar Ray Leonard** (b. May 17, 1956): Boxer; light welterweight Olympic champ (1976); won world welterweight title in 1979 and 4 more titles; in 1987 he upset Marvin Hagler for the middleweight crown; retired and unretired several times, before ending his career for good in 1997 with record of 36-3-1 and 25 KOs following a TKO loss to Hector Camacho.

**Walter (Buck) Leonard** (b. Sept. 8, 1907, d. Nov. 27, 1997): Baseball 1B; won Negro League championship nine years in a row with the Homestead Grays; hit .391 in 1948 to lead the league; usually batted cleanup behind Josh Gibson; retired at the age of 48; member of the National Baseball Hall of Fame.

**Lisa Leslie** (b. July 7, 1972): Basketball C; 2-time WNBA Finals MVP (2001-02) with the champion Los Angeles Sparks; 2001 regular season MVP; 3-time WNBA All-Star Game MVP (1999,2001-02); 3-time Olympic gold medalist (1996,2000,2004); consensus National Player of the Year at USC (1994).

**Marv Levy** (b. Aug. 3, 1928): Football; coached Buffalo to four consecutive Super Bowls, but is one of two coaches who are 0-4 (Bud Grant is the other); won 50 games and two CFL Grey Cups with Montreal (1974,77).

**Bill Lewis** (b. Nov. 30, 1868, d. Jan. 1, 1949): Football; college star at Amherst College and then Harvard; first black player to be selected as an All-American (1892-93); also the first black admitted to the American Bar Association (1911); was U.S. Assistant Attorney General.

**Carl Lewis** (b. July 1, 1961): Track & Field; won 9 Olympic gold medals; 4 in 1984 (100m, 200m, 4x100m, LJ), 2 in '88 (100m, LJ), 2 in '92 (4x100m, LJ) and 1 in '96 (LJ); has record 8 World Championship titles and 9 medals in all; Sullivan Award winner (1981); two-time AP Athlete of the Year (1983-84); in 1991, set world record in 100m with a 9.86 (since broken).

**Lennox Lewis** (b. Sept. 2, 1965): British boxer; won 1988 Olympic super heavyweight gold medal for Canada; was awarded WBC heavyweight belt when Riddick Bowe tossed it in a London trash can in 1993; lost title in a 2nd round TKO loss to Oliver McCall; won rematch 3 years later when McCall suffered emotional breakdown in the ring; unified titles in his rematch with Evander Holyfield in Nov. 1999; lost belts in upset loss to Hasim Rahman in April 2001 but took them back 7 months later; recorded 8th-round KO of Mike Tyson in June 2002.

**Nancy Lieberman** (b. July 1, 1958): Basketball; 3-time All-America and 2-time Player of Year (1979-80); led Old Dominion to consecutive AIAW titles in 1979 and '80; played in defunct WPBL and WABA and became 1st woman to play in men's pro league (USBL) in 1986; played in the inaugural season of the WNBA for the Phoenix Mercury and served as coach/GM of Detroit Shock (1998-2000).

**Eric Lindros** (b. Feb. 28, 1973): Hockey C; No. 1 pick in 1991 NHL draft by Quebec but sat out 1991-92 season rather than play for Nordiques; traded to Philadelphia in 1992 for 6 players, 2 No. 1 picks and $15 million; elected Flyers captain at age 22; won Hart Trophy as NHL MVP in 1995; suffered series of concussions in 1999-00 and was traded to NY Rangers in 2001; signed by Toronto in 2005.

**Tara Lipinski** (b. June 10, 1982): Figure Skater; won the 1998 women's figure skating gold medal at the Olympics in Nagano, becoming the youngest in history (15 yrs., 7 mos.) to do so; she and Michelle Kwan gave the U.S. its first 1-2 finish in that event since 1956; 1997 U.S. and World champion; turned pro in April 1998.

**Sonny Liston** (b. May 8, 1932, d. Dec. 30, 1970): Boxer; heavyweight champion (1962-64), who knocked out Floyd Patterson twice in the first round, then lost title to Muhammad Ali (then Cassius Clay) in 1964; pro record of 50-4 with 39 KOs.

**Vince Lombardi** (b. June 11, 1913, d. Sept. 3, 1970): Football; coached Green Bay to 5 NFL titles; won first 2 Super Bowls (1967-68); died as NFL's all-time winningest coach with percentage of .740 (105-35-6); Super Bowl trophy named in his honor.

**Johnny Longden** (b. Feb. 14, 1907, d. Feb. 14, 2003): Jockey; first to win 6,000 races; rode Count Fleet to Triple Crown in 1943.

**Jeannie Longo** (b. Oct. 31, 1958): French cyclist; 12-time world cycling champion and 1996 olympic road race gold medallist.

**Nancy Lopez** (b. Jan. 6, 1957): Golfer; 4-time LPGA Player of the Year (1978-79,85,88); Rookie of Year (1977); 3-time winner of LPGA Championship; reached Hall of Fame by age 30 with 35 victories; 48 career wins.

**Donna Lopiano** (b. Sept. 11, 1946): Former basketball and softball star who was women's AD at Texas for 18 years before leaving to become executive director of Women's Sports Foundation in 1992.

**Greg Louganis** (b. Jan. 29, 1960): U.S. diver; widely considered the greatest diver in history; won platform and springboard gold medals at both 1984 and '88 Olympics; also won a silver medal at the 1976 Olympics at the age of 16; won five world championships and 47 U.S. National Diving titles; revealed on Feb. 22, 1995 that he has AIDS.

**Joe Louis** (b. May 13, 1914, d. Apr. 12, 1981): Boxer; world heavyweight champion from June 22, 1937 to Mar. 1, 1949; his reign of 11 years, 8 months longest in division history; successfully defended title 25 times; retired in 1949, but returned to lose title shot against successor Ezzard Charles in 1950 and then to Rocky Marciano in '51; pro record of 63-3 with 49 KOs.

**Sid Luckman** (b. Nov. 21, 1916, d. July 5, 1998): Football QB; 6-time All-Pro; led Chicago Bears to 4 NFL titles (1940-41,43,46); MVP in 1943.

**Hank Luisetti** (b. June 16, 1916, d. Dec. 17, 2002): Basketball F; 3-time All-America at Stanford (1936-38); revolutionized game with one-handed shot.

**Johnny Lujack** (b. Jan. 4, 1925): Football QB; led Notre Dame to three national titles (1943,46-47); won Heisman Trophy in 1947.

**Darrell Wayne Lukas** (b. Sept. 2, 1935): Horse racing; 4-time Eclipse-winning trainer who saddled Horses of Year Lady's Secret in 1988 and Criminal Type in 1990; first trainer to earn over $100 million in purses; led nation in earnings 14 times since 1983; Grindstone's Kentucky Derby win in 1996 gave him six Triple Crown wins in a row; has won Preakness 5 times, Kentucky Derby 4 times and Belmont 4 times; his most recent Triple Crown victory came in the 2000 Belmont with Commendable; leads all Breeders' Cup trainers with 16 victories.

**Gen. Douglas MacArthur** (b. Jan. 26, 1880, d. Apr. 5, 1964): Controversial U.S. general of World War II and Korea; president of U.S. Olympic Committee (1927-28); college football devotee, National Football Foundation MacArthur Bowl named after him.

**Connie Mack** (b. Dec. 22, 1862, d. Feb. 8, 1956): Baseball owner; managed Philadelphia A's until he was 87 (1901-50); all-time major league wins leader with 3,755, including World Series; won 9 AL pennants and 5 World Series (1910-11,13,29-30); also finished last 17 times.

**Andy MacPhail** (b. Apr. 5, 1953): Baseball; Chicago Cubs president/CEO who was GM of 2 World Series champions in Minnesota (1987,91); won first title at age 34; son of Lee, grandson of Larry.

**Larry MacPhail** (b. Feb. 3, 1890, d. Oct. 1, 1975): Baseball exec. and innovator; introduced major leagues to night games at Cincinnati (May 24, 1935); won pennant in Brooklyn (1941) and World Series with NY Yankees (1947); father of Lee, grandfather of Andy.

**Lee MacPhail** (b. Oct. 25, 1917): Baseball; AL president (1974-83); president of owners' Player Relations Committee (1984-85); also GM of Baltimore (1959-65) and NY Yankees (1967-74); son of Larry and father of Andy.

**Wendy Macpherson** (b. Jan. 28, 1968): Bowling; voted Bowler of the Decade for the 1990s; Major titles include the 1986 BPAA U.S. Open, 1988, 2000 and 2003 WIBC Queens and 1999 Sam's Town Invitational; annual PWBA money winner 4 times (1996, 97,99,2000).

**John Madden** (b. Apr. 10, 1936): Football and Radio-TV; won 112 games and a Super Bowl (1976 season) as coach of Oakland Raiders; has won 14 Emmy Awards since 1982 as NFL analyst; signed 4-year, $32 million deal with Fox in 1994— a richer contract than any NFL player at the time; joined Al Michaels in ABC's Monday Night Football booth in 2002 after 21 seasons alongside Pat Summerall.

**Greg Maddux** (b. Apr. 14, 1966): Baseball RHP; won unprecedented 4 straight NL Cy Young Awards with Cubs (1992) and Atlanta (1993-95); has led NL in ERA four times (1993-95,98); won 13th straight gold glove in 2002; only pitcher to win at least 15 games in 17 straight seasons (1988-2004); got his 300th win in 2004.

**Larry Mahan** (b. Nov. 21, 1943): Rodeo; 6-time All-Around world champion cowboy (1966-70,73).

**Phil Mahre** (b. May 10, 1957): Alpine skier; 3-time World Cup overall champ (1981-83); finished 1-2 with twin brother Steve in 1984 Olympic slalom.

**Karl Malone** (b. July 24, 1963): Basketball F; 11-time All-NBA 1st team (1989-99) with Utah; 2-time NBA MVP (1997,99); all-time NBA leader in free throws made (9,787), 2nd in career points (36,928) and field goals made (13,528); member of the 1992 and '96 Olympic gold medal teams; named one of the NBA's 50 greatest players.

**Moses Malone** (b. Mar. 23, 1955): Basketball C; signed with Utah of ABA out of high school at age 19; led NBA in rebounding 6 times; 4-time All-NBA 1st team; 3-time NBA MVP (1979,82-83); Finals MVP with Philadelphia in 1983; played in 21st pro season in 1994-95.

**Nigel Mansell** (b. Aug. 8, 1953): British auto racer; won 1992 Formula One driving championship with record 9 victories and 14 poles; quit Grand Prix circuit to race Indy cars in 1993; 1st rookie to win IndyCar title; 3rd driver to win IndyCar and F1 titles; returned to F1 after 1994 IndyCar season and won '94 Australian Grand Prix; left F1 again on May 23, 1995 with 31 wins and 32 poles in 15 years.

**Mickey Mantle** (b. Oct. 20, 1931, d. Aug. 13, 1995): Baseball CF; led AL in home runs 4 times; won Triple Crown in 1956; hit 52 HRs in 1956 and 54 in '61; 3-time MVP (1956-57,62); hit 536 career HRs; played in 12 World Series with NY Yankees and won 7 times; all-time World Series leader in HRs (18), RBI (40), runs (42) and strikeouts (54); inducted into Baseball Hall of Fame in 1974.

**Diego Maradona** (b. Oct. 30, 1960): Soccer F; captain and MVP of 1986 World Cup champion Argentina; also led national team to 1990 World Cup final; consensus Player of Decade in 1980s; led Napoli to 2 Italian League titles (1987,90) and UEFA Cup (1989); tested positive for cocaine and suspended 15 months by FIFA in 1991; returned to World Cup as Argentine captain in 1994, but was kicked out after two games when test found 5 banned substances in his urine.

**Pete Maravich** (b. June 27, 1947, d. Jan. 5, 1988): Basketball; NCAA scoring leader 3 times at LSU (1968-70); averaged NCAA-record 44.2 points a game over career; Player of Year in 1970; NBA scoring champ in '77 with New Orleans.

**Alice Marble** (b. Sept. 28, 1913, d. Dec. 13, 1990): Tennis; 4-time U.S. champion (1936,38-40); won Wimbledon in 1939; swept U.S. singles, doubles and mixed doubles from 1938-40.

**Gino Marchetti** (b. Jan. 2, 1927): Football DE; 8-time NFL All-Pro (1957-64) with Baltimore Colts.

**Rocky Marciano** (b. Sept. 1, 1923, d. Aug. 31, 1969): Boxer; heavyweight champion (1952-56); only heavyweight champ in history to retire undefeated; pro record of 49-0 with 43 KOs; killed in plane crash.

**Juan Marichal** (b. Oct. 20, 1938): Baseball RHP; won 21 or more games 6 times for S.F. Giants from 1963-69; ended 16-year career at 243-142.

**Dan Marino** (b. Sept. 15, 1961): Football QB; all-time NFL leader in career TD passes (420), passing yards (61,361), attempts (8,358) and completions (4,967); 4-time leading passer in AFC (1983-84,86,89); set NFL single-season records for TD passes (48) and passing yards (5,084) in 1984.

**Roger Maris** (b. Sept. 10, 1934, d. Dec. 14, 1985): Baseball OF; broke Babe Ruth's season HR record with 61 in 1961 and held record until 1998 (Mark McGwire); 2-time AL MVP (1960-61) with NY Yankees; 275 HRs in 12 years.

**Jim Marshall** (b. Dec. 30, 1937): Football; long-time Vikings DE and NFL ironman; played in an NFL-record 282 consecutive games (1960-1979); also famous for picking up a fumble and running 66 yards the wrong way into the opponent's (49ers) endzone.

**Billy Martin** (b. May 16, 1928, d. Dec. 25, 1989): Baseball; 5-time manager of NY Yankees; won 2 pennants and 1 World Series (1977); also managed Minnesota, Detroit, Texas and Oakland; played on 5 Yankee world champions in 1950s.

**Casey Martin** (b. June 2, 1972): Golfer; suffers from a birth defect in his right leg known as Klippel-Trenauney-Webber Syndrome; won lawsuit against the PGA Tour for the right to use a golf cart during competition under the Americans with Disabilities Act.

**Pedro Martinez** (b. Oct. 25, 1971): Baseball RHP; one of baseball's premier pitchers; won 1997 NL Cy Young award with Montreal; traded to Boston Red Sox in Nov. 1997; 2-time AL Cy Young Award winner with Boston (1999,2000); signed with NY Mets in 2005.

**Eddie Mathews** (b. Oct. 13, 1931, d. Feb. 18, 2001): Baseball 3B; led in HRs twice (1953,59); hit 30 or more home runs 9 straight years; 512 career HRs.

**Christy Mathewson** (b. Aug. 12, 1880, d. Oct. 7, 1925): Baseball RHP; won 22 or more games 12 straight years (1903-14); 373 career wins; pitched 3 shutouts in 1905 World Series.

**Bob Mathias** (b. Nov. 17, 1930): Track & Field; youngest winner of decathlon with gold medal in 1948 Olympics at age 17; first to repeat as decathlon champ in 1952; Sullivan Award winner (1948); 4-term member of U.S. Congress (R, Calif.) from 1967-74.

**Ollie Matson** (b. May 1, 1930): Football HB; All-America at San Francisco (1951); bronze medal winner in 400m at 1952 Olympics; 4-time All-Pro for NFL Chicago Cardinals (1954-57); traded to LA Rams for 9 players in 1959; accounted for 12,884 all-purpose yards and scored 73 TDs in 14 seasons.

**Don Mattingly** (b. Apr. 20, 1961): Baseball 1B; AL MVP (1985); won AL batting title in 1984 (.343); led majors in 145 RBI in 1985; led AL with 238 hits (major record) and 53 doubles in 1986; won 9 Gold Glove Awards at 1B (1985-89, 91-94).

**Willie Mays** (b. May 6, 1931): Baseball OF; nicknamed the "Say Hey Kid"; led NL in HRs and stolen bases 4 times each; 2-time MVP (1954,65) with NY-SF Giants; Hall of Famer who played in 24 All-Star Games, earning MVP honors twice (1963,68); 12-time Gold Glove winner; 660 HRs and 3,283 hits in career.

**Bill Mazeroski** (b. Sept. 5, 1936): Baseball 2B; career .260 hitter who won the 1960 World Series for Pittsburgh with a lead-off HR in the bottom of the 9th inning of Game 7; the pitcher was Ralph Terry of the NY Yankees, the count was 1-0 and the score was tied 9-9; also a sure-fielder, Maz won 8 Gold Gloves in 17 seasons.

**Bob McAdoo** (b. Sept. 25, 1951): Basketball F/C; 1972 Sporting News First Team All-American; NBA Rookie of the Year (1973); NBA MVP (1975); All-NBA First Team (1975); Led NBA in scoring three consecutive years (1974-76); 5-time All-Star (1974-78); two championships with LA Lakers (1982,85).

**Joe McCarthy** (b. Apr. 21, 1887, d. Jan. 13, 1978): Baseball; first manager to win pennants in both leagues (Chicago Cubs in 1929 and NY Yankees in 1932); greatest success came with Yankees when he won seven pennants and six World Series championships from 1936 to 1943; first manager to win four World Series in a row (1936-39); finished his career with the Boston Red Sox (1948-50); lifetime record of 2125-1333; member of Baseball Hall of Fame.

**Pat McCormick** (b. May 12, 1930): U.S. diver; won women's platform and springboard gold medals in both 1952 and '56 Olympics.

**Willie McCovey** (b. Jan. 10, 1938): Baseball 1B; led NL in HRs 3 times and RBI twice; MVP in 1969 with SF; 521 career HRs; indicted for tax evasion in July 1995, pled guilty; "McCovey Cove," the bay outside the rightfield fence at San Francisco's SBC Park is named for him.

**John McEnroe** (b. Feb. 16, 1959): Tennis; No.1 player in the world 4 times (1981-84); 4-time U.S. Open champ (1979-81,84); 3-time Wimbledon champ (1981,83-84); played on 5 Davis Cup winners (1978,79,81,82,92); won NCAA singles title (1978); finished career with 77 singles championships, 77 more in men's doubles (including 9 Grand Slam titles), and U.S. Davis Cup records for years played (13) and singles matches won (41).

**John McGraw** (b. Apr. 7, 1873, d. Feb. 25, 1934): Baseball; managed NY Giants to 9 NL pennants between 1905-24; won 3 World Series (1905,21-22); 2nd on all-time career list with 2,866 wins in 33 seasons (2,840 regular season and 26 World Series).

**Frank McGuire** (b. Nov. 8, 1916, d. Oct. 11, 1994): Basketball; winner of 731 games as high school, college and pro coach; won at least 100 games at 3 colleges— St. John's (103), North Carolina (164) and South Carolina (283); won 550 games in 30 college seasons; 1957 UNC team went 32-0 and beat Kansas 54-53 in triple OT to win NCAA title; coached NBA Philadelphia Warriors to 49-31 record in 1961-62 season, but refused to move with team to San Francisco.

**Mark McGwire** (b. Oct. 1, 1963): Baseball 1B; Sporting News college player of the year (1984); Member of 1984 U.S. Olympic baseball team; won AL Rookie of the Year and hit rookie-record 49 HRs in 1987; shattered Roger Maris' season home run record (61) in 1998 with St. Louis (70); followed that magical season with 65 HRs and 147 RBI in 1999.

**Jim McKay** (b. Sept. 24, 1921): Radio-TV; host and commentator of ABC's Olympic coverage and "Wide World of Sports" show since 1961; 12-time Emmy winner; also given Peabody Award in 1988 and Life Achievement Emmy in 1990; became part owner of Baltimore Orioles in 1993.

**Tamara McKinney** (b. Oct. 16, 1962): Skiing; first American woman to win overall Alpine World Cup championship (1983); won World Cup slalom (1984) and giant slalom titles twice (1981,83).

**Denny McLain** (b. Mar. 29, 1944): Baseball RHP; last pitcher to win 30 games (1968); 2-time Cy Young winner (1968-69) with Detroit; convicted of racketeering, extortion and drug possession in 1985, served 29 months of 25-year jail term, sentence overturned when court ruled he had not received a fair trial; he has faced subsequent legal troubles.

**Rick Mears** (b. Dec. 3, 1951): Auto racer; 3-time CART national champ (1979,81-82); 4-time winner of Indy 500 (1979,84,88,91) and only driver to win 6 Indy 500 poles; Indy 500 Rookie of Year (1978); retired in 1992 with 29 CART wins and 40 poles.

**Mark Messier** (b. Jan. 18, 1961): Hockey C; 2-time NHL MVP with Edmonton (1990) and NY Rangers (1992); captain of 1994 Rangers team that won 1st Stanley Cup since 1940; ranks 2nd in all-time play-off points, goals and assists; 2nd on all-time regular season points list (1,887); retired in 2005.

**Debbie Meyer** (b. Aug. 14, 1952): Swimmer; 1st swimmer to win 3 individual gold medals at one Olympics (1968).

**Ann Meyers** (b. Mar. 26, 1955): Basketball G; In 1974, became first high schooler to play for U.S. national team; 4-time All-American at UCLA (1976-79); member of 1976 U.S. Olympic team; Broderick Award and Cup winner (1978); Signed $50,000 no cut contract with NBA's Indiana Pacers (1980); married Dodger great Don Drysdale.

**George Mikan** (b. June 18, 1924, d. June 2, 2005): Basketball C; 3-time All-America (1944-46); led DePaul to NIT title (1945); led Minneapolis Lakers to 5 NBA titles in 6 years (1949-54); first commissioner of ABA (1967-69).

**Stan Mikita** (b. May 20, 1940): Hockey C; led NHL in scoring 4 times; won both MVP and Lady Byng awards in 1967 and '68 with Chicago.

**Bode Miller** (b. Oct. 12, 1977): Alpine Skier; won 2 silver medals at 2002 Winter Games; 2 golds, 1 silver at 2003 World Championships; 2nd overall in 2003 World Cup standings; 2004 Giant Slalom World Cup champion; 2005 Overall World Cup champ.

**Cheryl Miller** (b. Jan. 3, 1964): Basketball; 3-time College Player of Year (1984-86); led USC to NCAA title and U.S. to Olympic gold medal in 1984; coached USC to 44-14 record in 2 years; coached WNBA's Phoenix Mercury for 4 years; sister of NBA's Reggie.

**Del Miller** (b. July 5, 1913, d. Aug. 19, 1996): Harness racing; driver, trainer, owner, breeder, seller and track owner; drove to 2,441 wins from 1929-90.

**Marvin Miller** (b. Apr. 14, 1917): Baseball labor leader; executive director of Players' Assn. from 1966-82; increased average salary from $19,000 to over $240,000; led 13-day strike in 1972 and 50-day walkout in '81.

**Shannon Miller** (b. Mar. 10, 1977): Gymnast; won 5 medals in 1992 Olympics and 2 golds in '96 Games; All-Around world champion in 1993 and '94.

**Billy Mills** (b. June 30, 1938): Track & Field; Native American who was upset winner of 10,000m gold medal at 1964 Olympics.

**Bora Milutinovic** (b. Sept. 7, 1944): Soccer; Serbian who coached United States national team from 1991-95; led Mexico (1986), Costa Rica ('90), USA ('94) and Nigeria ('98) into the 2nd round of the World Cup.

**Tommy Moe** (b. Feb. 17, 1970): Alpine skier; won Downhill gold and Super-G silver at 1994 Winter Olympics; 1st U.S. man to win 2 Olympic alpine medals in one year.

**Paul Molitor** (b. Aug. 22, 1956): Baseball DH-1B; All-America SS at Minnesota in 1976; spent 15 years with Milwaukee, then 3 each with Toronto and Minnesota; led Blue Jays to 2nd straight World Series title as MVP (1993); hit .418 in 2 Series appearances (1982,93); holds World Series game record with 5 hits.

**Joe Montana** (b. June 11, 1956): Football QB; led Notre Dame to national title in 1977; led San Francisco to 4 Super Bowl titles in 1980s; only 3-time Super Bowl MVP; 2-time NFL MVP (1989-90); led NFL in passing 5 times; traded to K.C. in 1993; ranks 5th all-time in passing efficiency (92.3); 273 career TD passes and 40,551 passing yards; inducted into Pro Football Hall of Fame in 2000.

**Tim Montgomery** (b. Jan. 25, 1975): American sprinter; broke world record in 100m with a 9.78 on Sept. 14, 2002; failed to qualify for 2004 Olympics.

**Helen Wills Moody** (b. Oct. 6, 1905, d. Jan. 1, 1998): Tennis; won 8 Wimbledon singles titles, 7 U.S. and 4 French from 1923-38.

**Warren Moon** (b. Nov. 18, 1956): Football QB; MVP of 1978 Rose Bowl with Washington; MVP of CFL with Edmonton in 1983; led Eskimos to 5 consecutive Grey Cup titles (1978-82) and was playoff MVP twice (1980,82); entered NFL in 1984 and played for 4 different teams; picked for 9 Pro Bowls.

**Archie Moore** (b. Dec. 13, 1913, d. Dec. 9, 1998): Boxer; world light heavyweight champion (1952-60); pro record 199-26-8 with a record 145 KOs.

**Noureddine Morceli** (b. Feb. 28, 1970): Algerian runner; 3-time world champion at 1,500 meters (1991,93,95) and 1996 Olympic gold medal winner; former holder of world records in several middle distance events.

**Howie Morenz** (b. June 21, 1902, d. Mar. 8, 1937): Hockey C; 3-time NHL MVP (1928,31,32); led Montreal Canadiens to 3 Stanley Cups; voted Outstanding Player of the Half-Century in 1950.

**Joe Morgan** (b. Sept. 19, 1943): Baseball 2B; regular-season MVP both years he led Cincinnati to World Series titles (1975-76); 1,865 career walks; led NL in walks 4 times.

**Bobby Morrow** (b. Oct. 15, 1935): Track & Field; won 3 gold medals at 1956 Olympics (100m, 200m and 4x400m relay).

**Willie Mosconi** (b. June 27, 1913, d. Sept. 12, 1993): Pocket Billiards; 14-time world champion from 1941-57.

**Annemarie Moser-Pröll** (b. Mar. 27, 1953): Austrian alpine skier; won World Cup overall title 6 times (1971-75,79); all-time women's World Cup leader in career wins with 61; won Downhill in 1980 Olympics.

**Edwin Moses** (b. Aug. 31, 1955): Track & Field; won 400m hurdles at 1976 and '84 Olympics, bronze medal in '88; also winner of 122 consecutive races from 1977-87.

**Stirling Moss** (b. Sept. 17, 1929): Auto racer; won 194 of 466 career races and 16 Formula One events, but was never world champion.

**Marion Motley** (b. June 5, 1920, d. June 27, 1999): Football FB/LB; hard-charging runner who was all-time leading AAFC rusher; ran for over 4,700 yards and 31 TDs for Cleveland Browns (1946-53), leading the NFL in 1950; first black member of the Pro Football Hall of Fame.

**Shirley Muldowney** (b. June 19, 1940): Drag Racer; "Cha Cha"; women's racing pioneer; 3-time Winston drag racing Top Fuel champion (1977,80,82); recorded 18 career NHRA National Event Victories.

**Anthony Munoz** (b. Aug. 19, 1958): Football OT; drafted 3rd overall in 1980 out of USC; 11-time All-Pro with Cincinnati; member of NFL 75th Anniv. All-Time Team; elected to Hall of Fame in 1998.

**Calvin Murphy** (b. May 9, 1948): Basketball G; NBA All-Rookie team (1971); holds NBA single season free throw percentage (.958); third all-time career free throw pct. (.892); elected to Basketball Hall of Fame in 1992; though only 5'9" and 165 pounds, he is regarded as one of the best guards ever.

**Dale Murphy** (b. Mar. 12, 1956): Baseball OF; led NL in HRs and RBI twice; 2-time MVP (1982-83) with Atlanta; also played with Philadelphia and Colorado; retired in 1993 with 398 HRs.

**Jack Murphy** (b. Feb. 5, 1923, d. Sept. 24, 1980): Sports editor and columnist of The San Diego Union from 1951-80; instrumental in bringing AFL Chargers south from LA in 1961, landing Padres as NL expansion team in '69; and lobbying for San Diego stadium that would later bear his name.

**Eddie Murray** (b. Feb. 24, 1956): Baseball 1B-DH; AL Rookie of Year in 1977; became 20th player in history, but only 2nd switch hitter (after Pete Rose) to get 3,000 hits; one of only 4 men (Aaron, Mays and Palmeiro) with 500 HRs and 3,000 hits.

**Jim Murray** (b. Dec. 29, 1919, d. Aug. 16, 1998): Sports columnist for *LA Times* 1961-98; 14-time Sportswriter of the Year; won Pulitzer Prize for commentary in 1990.

**Ty Murray** (b. Oct. 11, 1969): Rodeo cowboy; 7-time All-Around world champion (1989-94,98); Rookie of Year in 1988; youngest (age 20) to win All-Around title; set single season earnings mark with $297,896 in 1993; career hampered by injury.

**Stan Musial** (b. Nov. 21, 1920): Baseball OF-1B; led NL in batting 7 times and RBI 2 times; 3-time MVP (1943,46,48) with St. Louis; played in 24 All-Star Games; had 3,630 career hits (4th all-time) and .331 average.

**John Naber** (b. Jan. 20, 1956): Swimmer; won 4 gold medals and a silver in 1976 Olympics.

**Bronko Nagurski** (b. Nov. 3, 1908, d. Jan. 7, 1990): Football FB-T; All-America at Minnesota (1929); All-Pro with Chicago Bears (1932-34); charter member of college and pro Halls of Fame.

**James Naismith** (b. Nov. 6, 1861, d. Nov. 28, 1939): Canadian physical education instructor who invented basketball in 1891 at the YMCA Training School (now Springfield College) in Springfield, Mass.

**Joe Namath** (b. May 31, 1943): Football QB; signed for unheard-of $400,000 as rookie with AFL's NY Jets in 1965; 2-time All-AFL (1968-69) and All-NFL (1972); led Jets to Super Bowl upset as MVP in '69 after making brash prediction of victory.

**Ilie Nastase** (b. July 19, 1946): Romanian tennis player; No.1 in the world twice (1972-73); won U.S. (1972) and French (1973) Opens; has since entered Romanian politics.

**Martina Navratilova** (b. Oct. 18, 1956): Tennis player; No.1 player in the world 7 times (1978-79,82-86); won her record 9th Wimbledon singles title in 1990; also won 4 U.S. Opens, 3 Australian and 2 French; in all, won 18 Grand Slam singles titles, 40 Grand Slam doubles titles; all-time leader among men and women in singles titles (167); 2nd all-time (Steffi Graf) on women's career money list with over $21 million; still active in limited competition; inducted into International Tennis Hall of Fame in 2000.

**Cosmas Ndeti** (b. Nov. 24, 1971): Kenyan distance runner; winner of three consecutive Boston Marathons (1993-95); set what is still the course record of 2:07:15 in 1994.

**Earle (Greasy) Neale** (b. Nov. 5, 1891, d. Nov. 2, 1973): Baseball and Football; hit .357 for Cincinnati in 1919 World Series; also played with pre-NFL Canton Bulldogs; later coached Philadelphia Eagles to 2 NFL titles (1948-49).

**Primo Nebiolo** (b. July 14, 1923, d. Nov. 7, 1999): Italian president of International Amateur Athletic Federation (IAAF) since 1981; also an at-large member of International Olympic Committee; regarded as dictatorial, but credited with elevating track & field to world class financial status.

**Byron Nelson** (b. Feb. 4, 1912): Golfer; 2-time winner of both Masters (1937,42) and PGA (1940,45); also U.S. Open champion in 1939; won 19 tournaments in 1945, including 11 in a row; also set all-time PGA stroke average with 68.33 strokes per round over 120 rounds in '45.

**Lindsey Nelson** (b. May 25, 1919, d. June 10, 1995): Radio-TV; all-purpose play-by-play broadcaster for CBS, NBC and others; 4-time Sportscaster of the Year (1959-62); voice of Cotton Bowl for 25 years and NY Mets from 1962-78; given Life Achievement Emmy Award in 1991.

**Ernie Nevers** (b. June 11, 1903, d. May 3, 1976): Football FB; earned 11 letters in four sports at Stanford; played pro football, baseball and basketball; scored 40 points for Chicago Cardinals in one NFL game (1929).

**Paula Newby-Fraser** (b. June 2, 1962): Zimbabwean triathlete; 8-time winner of Ironman Triathlon in Hawaii; established women's record of 8:55:28 in 1992.

**John Newcombe** (b. May 23, 1944): Australian tennis player; No.1 player in world 3 times (1967,70-71); won Wimbledon 3 times and U.S. and Australian championships twice each.

**Pete Newell** (b. Aug. 31, 1915): Basketball; coached at Univ. of San Francisco, Michigan St. and the Univ. of California; first coach to win NIT (San Francisco-1949), NCAA (California-1959) and Olympic gold medal (1960); later served as the general manager of the San Diego Rockets and LA Lakers in the NBA; member of Basketball Hall of Fame.

**Jack Nicklaus** (b. Jan. 21, 1940): Golfer; all-time leader in major tournament wins with 18— 6 Masters, 5 PGAs, 4 U.S. Opens and 3 British Opens; oldest player to win Masters (46 in 1986); PGA Player of Year 5 times (1967,72-73,75-76); named Golfer of the Century by PGA in 1988; 6-time Ryder Cup player and 2-time captain (1983,87); won NCAA title (1961) and 2 U.S. Amateurs (1959,61); 73 PGA Tour wins (2nd to Sam Snead's 82); fourth win in Tradition in 1996 gave him 8 majors on Senior PGA Tour; nicknamed "the Golden Bear."

**Chuck Noll** (b. Jan. 5, 1932): Football; coached Pittsburgh to 4 Super Bowl titles (1975-76,79-80); retired after 1991 season with 209 career wins (including playoffs) in 23 years.

**Greg Norman** (b. Feb. 10, 1955): Australian golfer; 73 tournament wins worldwide including 20 PGA Tour victories; 2-time British Open winner (1986,93); lost Masters by a stroke in both 1986 (to Jack Nicklaus) and '87 (to Larry Mize in sudden death); 1995 PGA Tour Player of the Year.

**James D. Norris** (b. Nov. 6, 1906, d. Feb. 25, 1966): Boxing promoter and NHL owner; president of International Boxing Club from 1949 until U.S. Supreme Court ordered its break-up (for anti-trust violations) in 1958; only NHL owner to win Stanley Cups in two cities: Detroit (1936-37,43) and Chicago (1961).

**Paavo Nurmi** (b. June 13, 1897, d. Oct. 2, 1973): Finnish runner; won 9 gold medals (6 individual) in 1920, '24 and '28 Olympics; from 1921-31 broke 23 world outdoor records in events ranging from 1,500 to 20,000 meters.

**Dan O'Brien** (b. July 18, 1966): Track & Field; Olympic decathlon gold medalist (1996); set former world record in decathlon (8,891 pts) in 1992, after shockingly failing to qualify for event at U.S. Olympic Trials; three-time gold medalist at World Championships (1991,93,95).

**Larry O'Brien** (b. July 7, 1917, d. Sept. 27, 1990): Basketball; former U.S. Postmaster General and 3rd NBA commissioner (1975-84), league absorbed 4 ABA teams and created salary cap during his term in office.

**Parry O'Brien** (b. Jan. 28, 1932): Track & Field; in 4 consecutive Olympics, won two gold medals, a silver and placed 4th in the shot put (1952-64).

**Al Oerter** (b. Sept. 19, 1936): Track & Field; his 4 discus gold medals in consecutive Olympics from 1956-68 is an unmatched Olympic record.

**Sadaharu Oh** (b. May 20, 1940): Baseball 1B; led Japan League in HRs 15 times; 9-time MVP for Tokyo Giants; hit 868 HRs in 22 years.

**Hakeem Olajuwon** (b. Jan. 21, 1963): Basketball C; Nigerian native who was All-America in 1984 and Final Four MOP in 1983 for Houston; overall 1st pick by Houston Rockets in 1984 NBA draft; led Rockets to back-to-back NBA titles (1994-95); regular season MVP (1994) and 2-time Finals MVP ('94-95); 6-time All-NBA 1st team (1987-89,93-95); all-time NBA blocks leader.

**Jose Maria Olazabal** (b. Feb. 5, 1966): Spanish golfer; has 28 worldwide victories including 2 Masters (1994,99); played on 6 European Ryder Cup teams.

**Barney Oldfield** (b. Jan. 29, 1878, d. Oct. 4, 1946): Auto racing pioneer; drove cars built by Henry Ford; first man to drive car a mile per minute (1903).

**Walter O'Malley** (b. Oct. 9, 1903, d. Aug. 9, 1979): Baseball owner; moved Brooklyn Dodgers to Los Angeles after 1957 season; won 4 World Series (1955,59,63,65).

**Shaquille O'Neal** (b. Mar. 6, 1972): Basketball C; 2-time All-America at LSU (1991-92); overall 1st pick (as a junior) by Orlando in 1992 NBA draft; Rookie of Year in 1993; 2-time NBA scoring leader (1995,2000); regular season MVP (2000) and 3-time NBA Finals MVP (2000,01,02); named one of the NBA's 50 Greatest Players; traded to Miami in 2004.

**Bobby Orr** (b. Mar. 20, 1948): Hockey D; league's only 8-time Norris Trophy winner as best defenseman (1968-75); credited with revolutionizing the position; 3-time Hart Trophy winner as NHL regular season MVP (1970-72); led NHL in scoring twice and assists 5 times; All-NHL 1st team 8 times; playoff MVP twice (1970,72) with Boston.

**Tom Osborne** (b. Feb. 23, 1937): Football; Nebraska head coach from 1973-97; career record of 255-49-3; his win pct. of .836 is fifth all-time; won national championships in 1994 and '95 and shared national title with Michigan in '97; elected to U.S. Congress (R., Neb.) in 2000.

**Mel Ott** (b. Mar. 2, 1909, d. Nov. 21, 1958): Baseball OF; joined NY Giants at age 16; led NL in HRs 6 times; had 511 HRs and 1,860 RBI in 22 years.

**Kristin Otto** (b. Feb. 7, 1966): East German swimmer; 1st woman to win 6 gold medals (4 individual) at one Olympics (1988).

**Francis Ouimet** (b. May 8, 1893, d. Sept. 3, 1967): Golfer; won 1913 U.S. Open as 20-year-old amateur playing on Brookline, Mass. course where he used to caddie; won U.S. Amateur twice; 8-time Walker Cup player.

**Steve Owen** (b. Apr. 21, 1898, d. May 17, 1964): Football; All-Pro guard (1927); coached NY Giants for 23 years (1931-53); won 153 career games and 2 NFL titles (1934,38).

**Jesse Owens** (b. Sept. 12, 1913, d. Mar. 31, 1980): Track & Field; set 4 world records in one afternoon competing for Ohio State at the Big Ten Championships (May 25, 1935); a year later, he soundly debunked Adolf Hitler's "master race" claims, winning 4 gold medals (100m, 200m, 4x100m relay and long jump) at 1936 Summer Olympics in Berlin.

**Alan Page** (b. Aug. 7, 1945): Football DE; All-America at Notre Dame in 1966 and member of two national championship teams; 6-time NFL All-Pro and 1971 Player of Year with Minnesota Vikings; later a lawyer who was elected to Minnesota Supreme Court in 1992.

**Satchel Paige** (b. July 7, 1906, d. June 6, 1982): Baseball RHP; pitched 55 career no-hitters over 20 seasons in Negro Leagues; entered major leagues with Cleveland in 1948 at age 42; had 28-31 record in 5 years; returned to AL at age 59 to start 1 game for Kansas City in 1965 (went 3 innings, gave up a hit and got a strikeout); elected to Baseball Hall of Fame in 1971.

**Se Ri Pak** (b. Sept. 28, 1977): Golfer; won two Majors as an LPGA rookie in 1998 (LPGA Championship and U.S. Open); youngest player to win the U.S. Open (20); won British Open in 2001 and added her 2nd LPGA Championship in 2002.

**Arnold Palmer** (b. Sept. 10, 1929): Golfer; winner of 4 Masters, 2 British Opens and a U.S. Open; 2-time PGA Player of Year (1960,62); 1st player to earn over $1 million in career (1968); annual PGA Tour money leader award named after him; 62 wins on PGA Tour and 10 more on Senior Tour; made 48 consecutive Masters starts.

**Jim Palmer** (b. Oct. 15, 1945): Baseball RHP; 3-time Cy Young Award winner (1973,75-76); won 20 or more games 8 times with Baltimore; elected to the Baseball Hall of Fame in 1990; 1991 comeback attempt at age 45 scrubbed in spring training.

**Bill Parcells** (b. Aug. 22, 1941): Football; coached NY Giants to 2 Super Bowl titles (1987,91); retired after 1990 season then returned in 1993 as coach of New England; took hapless Pats from 2-14 in 1992 to Super Bowl (loss to Green Bay) in 1997; left Patriots after Super Bowl to coach the New York Jets; coached 3 seasons with the Jets (1997-99), turning them from 1-15 doormat to AFC East champ in 2 years; retired again in 2000 but returned to the sidelines in 2003 as head coach of the Dallas Cowboys.

**Jack Pardee** (b. Apr. 19, 1936): Football; All-America LB at Texas A&M; All-Pro with LA Rams (1963) and Washington (1971); 2-time NFL Coach of Year (1976,79); won 87 games in 11 seasons; only man hired as head coach in NFL, WFL, USFL and CFL.

**Bernie Parent** (b. Apr. 3, 1945): Hockey G; led Philadelphia Flyers to 2 Stanley Cups as playoff MVP (1974,75); 2-time Vezina Trophy winner; posted 55 career shutouts and 2.55 GAA in 13 seasons.

**Joe Paterno** (b. Dec. 21, 1926): Football; passed Bear Bryant in 2001 as all-time wins leader in college football (since passed himself by Bobby Bowden); coached Penn St. to 343-116-3 record, 20-10-1 bowl record and 2 national titles (1982,86) in 39 years; also had three unbeaten teams that didn't finish No. 1; 4-time Coach of Year (1968,78,82,86).

**Craig Patrick** (b. May 20, 1946): Hockey; 3rd generation Patrick to have name inscribed on Stanley Cup; GM of 2-time Cup champion Pittsburgh Penguins (1991-92); also captain of 1969 NCAA champion at Denver; assistant coach-GM of 1980 gold medal-winning U.S. Olympic team; grandson of Lester.

**Lester Patrick** (b. Dec. 30, 1883, d. June 1, 1960): Hockey; pro hockey pioneer as player, coach and general manager for 43 years; led NY Rangers to Stanley Cups as coach (1928,33) and GM (1940); grandfather of Craig.

**Carly Patterson** (b. Feb. 4, 1988): American gymnast; Olympic all-around champ at Athens in 2004.

**Floyd Patterson** (b. Jan. 4, 1935): Boxer; Olympic middleweight champ in 1952; world heavyweight champion (1956-59,60-62); 1st to regain heavyweight crown; fought Ingemar Johansson 3 times in 22 months from 1959-61 and won last two; pro record 55-8-1 with 40 KOs.

**Walter Payton** (b. July 25, 1954, d. Nov. 1, 1999): Football RB; formerly NFL's all-time leading rusher with 16,726 yards (1984-2002, passed by Emmitt Smith); scored 125 career TDs; All-Pro 7 times with Chicago; led NFC in rushing 5 times (1976-80); league MVP in 1977 (AP & PFWA) and 1985 (Bell); won ring with Bears in Super Bowl XX; known as superb runner, receiver and blocker; nicknamed "Sweetness".

**Calvin Peete** (b. July 18, 1943): Golf; began playing golf at the age of 23; earned over $2 million in career earnings; selected to the U.S. Ryder Cup teams in 1983 and 1985.

**Pelé** (b. Oct. 23, 1940): Brazilian soccer F; given name— Edson Arantes do Nascimento; led Brazil to 3 World Cup titles (1958,62,70); came to U.S. in 1975 to play for NY Cosmos in NASL; scored 1,281 goals in 22 years including 12 goals in the World Cup; served as Brazil's minister of sport (1990-98); named IOC Athlete of the Century and FIFA's co-Player of the Century (along with Diego Maradona).

**Roger Penske** (b. Feb. 20, 1937): Auto racing; national sports car driving champion (1964); established racing team in 1961; co-founder of Championship Auto Racing Teams (CART); Penske Racing has won 13 Indianapolis 500s and 11 CART points titles; announced surprising move to IRL for 2002 season.

**Willie Pep** (b. Sept. 19, 1922): Boxer; 2-time world featherweight champion (1942-48,49-50); pro record 230-11-1 with 65 KOs.

**Marie-Jose Perec** (b. 1968): Track & Field; French sprinter who became 2nd woman to win the 200m and 400m events in the same Olympics (1996); her time in the 400 (48.25) set an Olympic record; also won the 400 in 1992 Games.

**Fred Perry** (b. May 18, 1909, d. Feb. 2, 1995): British tennis player; 3-time Wimbledon champ (1934-36); first player to win all four Grand Slam singles titles, though not in same year; last native to win All-England men's title.

**Gaylord Perry** (b. Sept. 15, 1938): Baseball RHP; was only pitcher to win Cy Young Award in both leagues until 1999 (Randy Johnson and Pedro Martinez); retired in 1983 with 314-265 record and 3,534 strikeouts over 22 years with 8 teams; brother Jim won 215 games for family total of 529.

**Bob Pettit** (b. Dec. 12, 1932): Basketball F; All-NBA 1st team 10 times (1955-64); 2-time MVP (1956,59) with St. Louis Hawks; first player to score 20,000 points.

**Richard Petty** (b. July 2, 1937): Auto racer; 7-time winner of Daytona 500; 7-time NASCAR national champ (1964,67,71-72,74-75,79); first stock car driver to win $1 million in career; all-time NASCAR leader in races won (200), poles (126) and wins in a single season (27 in 1967); son of Lee (55 career wins), father of Kyle (8 career wins), grandfather of Adam; nicknamed "The King".

**Michael Phelps** (b. June 30, 1985): American swimmer who attempted to break Mark Spitz's Olympic record of 7 gold medals in 2004 but "settled" for 6 golds and two bronzes in Athens.

**Mike Piazza** (b. Sept. 4, 1968): Baseball C; slugger who broke Carlton Fisk's MLB record for HRs by a catcher in 2004 with his 352nd; 11-time All-Star.

**Laffit Pincay Jr.** (b. Dec. 29, 1946): Jockey; 5-time Eclipse Award winner (1971,73-74,79,85); winner of 3 Belmonts and 1 Kentucky Derby (aboard Swale in 1984); retired as all-time winningest jockey with 9,531 career wins.

**Scottie Pippen** (b. Sept. 25, 1965): Basketball F; started on 6 NBA champions with Chicago (1991-93, 96-98); 3-time All-NBA first team (1994-96). Voted one of NBA's 50 Greatest Players.

**Uta Pippig** (b. Sept. 7, 1965): German marathoner; won three-straight Boston Marathons (1994,95,96); set a new course record in '94 (since broken in 2002).

**Nelson Piquet** (b. Aug. 17, 1952): Brazilian auto racer; 3-time Formula One world champion (1981,83, 87); left circuit in 1991 with 23 career wins.

**Rick Pitino** (b. Sept. 18, 1952): Basketball coach; won 1996 NCAA title at Kentucky; became coach and president of NBA's Celtics in 1997 but was unsuccessful, resigning in 2001; returned to college ranks with Louisville in 2005 became 1st to take 3 schools to the Final Four (Providence, Ky., Louisville).

**Jacques Plante** (b. Jan. 17, 1929, d. Feb. 27, 1986): Hockey G; led Montreal to 6 Stanley Cups (1953,56-60); won 7 Vezina Trophies; MVP in 1962; first goalie to regularly wear a mask; posted 82 shutouts with 2.38 GAA.

**Gary Player** (b. Nov. 1, 1936): South African golfer; 3-time winner of Masters (1961,74,78) and British Open (1959,68,74); one of only 5 players to win career Grand Slam (Hogan, Nicklaus, Sarazen and Woods); also won 2 PGAs, a U.S. Open and 2 U.S. Senior Opens.

**Jim Plunkett** (b. Dec. 5, 1947): Football QB; Heisman Trophy winner (Stanford) in 1970; AFL Rookie of the Year in 1971; led Oakland-LA Raiders to Super Bowl wins in 1981 and '84; MVP in '81.

**Maurice Podoloff** (b. Aug. 18, 1890, d. Nov. 24, 1985): Basketball; engineered merger of Basketball Assn. of America and National Basketball League into NBA in 1949; NBA commissioner (1949-63); league MVP trophy named after him.

**Fritz Pollard** (b. Jan. 27, 1894, d. May 11, 1986): Football; 1st black All-America RB (1916 at Brown); 1st black to play in Rose Bowl; 7-year NFL pro (1920-26); 1st black NFL coach, at Milwaukee and Hammond, Ind.

**Sam Pollock** (b. Dec. 15, 1925): Hockey GM; managed NHL Montreal Canadiens to 9 Stanley Cups in 14 years (1965-78).

**Denis Potvin** (b. Oct. 29, 1953): Hockey D; won Norris Trophy 3 times (1976,78-79); 5-time All-NHL 1st-team; led NY Islanders to 4 Stanley Cups.

**Asafa Powell** (b. Nov. 11, 1982): Track & Field; Jamaican sprinter who broke Tim Montgomery's 100m world record with a 9.77 on June 14, 2005.

**Mike Powell** (b. Nov. 10, 1963): Track & Field; broke Bob Beamon's 23-year-old long jump world record by 2 inches with leap of 29-ft., 4½ in. at the 1991 World Championships; Sullivan Award winner (1991); won long jump silver medals in 1988 and '92 Olympics; repeated as world champ in 1993.

**Steve Prefontaine** (b. Jan. 25, 1951, d. May 30, 1975): Track & Field; All-America distance runner at Oregon; first athlete to win same event at NCAA championships 4 straight years (5,000 meters from 1970-73); finished 4th in 5,000 at 1972 Munich Olympics; first athlete to endorse Nike running shoes; killed in a one-car accident.

**Nick Price** (b. Jan. 28, 1957): Zimbabwean golfer; PGA Tour Player of Year in 1993 and '94; became 1st since Nick Faldo in 1990 to win 2 Grand Slam titles in same year when he took British Open and PGA Championship in 1994; also won PGA in '92.

**Alain Prost** (b. Feb. 24, 1955): French auto racer; 4-time Formula One world champion (1985-86,89,93); sat out 1992 then returned to win title in 1993; retired after '93 season as all-time F1 wins leader with 51 (passed by Michael Schumacher in 2001).

**Kirby Puckett** (b. Mar. 14, 1961): Baseball OF; led Minnesota Twins to World Series titles in 1987 and '91; retired in 1996 due to an eye ailment with a batting title (1989), 2,304 hits and a .318 career average in 12 seasons; elected to Hall of Fame in 2001.

**C.C. Pyle** (b. 1882, d. Feb. 3, 1939): Promoter; known as "Cash and Carry"; hyped Red Grange's pro football debut by arranging 1925 barnstorming tour with Chicago Bears; had Grange bolt NFL for new AFL in 1926 (AFL folded in '27); also staged two transcontinental footraces (1928-29), known as "Bunion Derbies."

**Bobby Rahal** (b. Jan. 10, 1953): Auto racer; 3-time PPG Cup champ (1986,87,92); 24 career Indy-Car wins, including 1986 Indy 500; current IRL team owner with TV's David Letterman; acted as interim president-CEO of CART in 2000 but resigned to assume position with Jaguar Formula One team.

**Jack Ramsay** (b. Feb. 21, 1925): Basketball; coach who won 239 college games with St. Joe's-PA in 11 seasons and 906 NBA games (including playoffs) with 4 teams over 21 years; led Portland to 1977 NBA title; placed 3rd in 1961 Final Four (later vacated).

**Bill Rassmussen** (b. Oct. 15, 1932): Radio-TV; unemployed radio broadcaster who founded ESPN, the nation's first 24-hour all-sports cable-TV network, in 1978; bought out by Getty Oil in 1981.

**Willis Reed** (b. June 25, 1942): Basketball C; led NY Knicks to NBA titles in 1970 and '73, Finals MVP both years; 1970 regular season MVP. Voted one of NBA's 50 Greatest Players; fought off serious injury and limped onto court just prior to Game 7 of the 1970 Finals, his dramatic entrance helped inspire his team to victory over Wilt Chamberlain's Lakers.

**Pee Wee Reese** (b. July 23, 1918, d. Aug. 14, 1999): Baseball SS; member of Brooklyn/Los Angeles Dodgers from 1940-58; led NL in runs scored (132) in 1949 and stolen bases (30) in 1952; hit over .300 in a season once (.309 in 1954); led the NL in putouts four times; real name was Harold H. Reese.

**Mary Lou Retton** (b. Jan. 24, 1968): Gymnast; won gold medal in women's All-Around at the 1984 Olympics; also won 2 silvers and 2 bronzes.

**Manon Rheaume** (b. Feb. 24, 1972): Hockey G; started in goal in an exhibition game for Tampa Bay Lightning on Sept. 23, 1992 to become the only woman to play in an NHL game.

**Grantland Rice** (b. Nov. 1, 1880, d. July 13, 1954): First celebrated American sportswriter; chronicled the Golden Age of Sport in 1920s; immortalized Notre Dame's "Four Horsemen."

**Jerry Rice** (b. Oct. 13, 1962): Football WR; 2-time Div. I-AA All-America at Mississippi Valley St. (1983-84); won 3 Super Bowls with San Francisco (1989,90,95); 10-time All-Pro; regular season MVP in 1987 and Super Bowl MVP in 1989; all-time NFL leader in touchdowns (208), receptions (1549) and receiving yards (22,895); announced retirement in 2005 at age 42 after a 20-year NFL career.

**Henri Richard** (b. Feb. 29, 1936): Hockey C; leap year baby who played on more Stanley Cup championship teams (11) than anybody else; at 5-foot-7, known as the "Pocket Rocket"; brother of Maurice.

**Maurice Richard** (b. Aug. 4, 1921, d. May 27, 2000): Hockey RW; the "Rocket"; 8-time NHL 1st team All-Star; MVP in 1947; 1st to score 50 goals in one season (1944-45); 544 career goals; played on 8 Stanley Cup winners in Montreal.

**Bob Richards** (b. Feb. 2, 1926): Track & Field; pole vaulter, ordained minister and original *Wheaties* pitchman, remains only 2-time Olympic pole vault champ (1952,56).

**Nolan Richardson** (b. Dec. 27, 1941): Basketball; coached Arkansas to consecutive NCAA finals, beating Duke in 1994 and losing to UCLA in '95; school bought out his contract in 2002, ending his 17-year reign.

**Tex Rickard** (b. Jan. 2, 1870, d. Jan. 6, 1929): Promoter who handled boxing's first $1 million gate (Dempsey vs. Carpentier in 1921); built Madison Square Garden in 1925; founded NY Rangers as Garden tenant in 1926 and named NHL team after himself (Tex's Rangers); also built Boston Garden in 1928.

**Eddie Rickenbacker** (b. Oct. 8, 1890, d. July 23, 1973): Mechanic and auto racer; became America's top flying ace (22 kills) in World War I; owned Indianapolis Speedway (1927-45) and ran Eastern Air Lines (1938-59).

**Branch Rickey** (b. Dec. 20, 1881, d. Dec. 9, 1965): Baseball innovator; revolutionized game with creation of modern farm system while GM of St. Louis Cardinals (1917-42); integrated major leagues in 1947 as president-GM of Brooklyn Dodgers when he brought up Jackie Robinson (whom he had signed on Oct. 23, 1945); later GM of Pittsburgh Pirates.

**Leni Riefenstahl** (b. Aug. 22, 1902, d. Sept. 8, 2003): German filmmaker of 1930s; directed classic sports documentary "Olympia" on 1936 Berlin Summer Olympics; infamous, however, for also making 1934 Hitler propaganda film "Triumph of the Will."

**Roy Riegels** (b. Apr. 4, 1908, d. Mar. 26, 1993): Football; California center who picked up fumble in 2nd quarter of 1929 Rose Bowl and raced 70 yards in the wrong direction to set up a 2-point safety in 8-7 loss to Georgia Tech.

**Bobby Riggs** (b. Feb. 25, 1918, d. Oct. 25, 1995): Tennis; won Wimbledon once (1939) and U.S. title twice (1939,41); legendary hustler who made his biggest score in 1973 as 55-year-old male chauvinist challenging the best women players; beat No. 1 Margaret Court 6-2,6-1, but was thrashed by No. 2 Billie Jean King, 6-4,6-3,6-3 in nationally televised "Battle of the Sexes" on Sept. 20, before 30,492 at the Astrodome.

**Pat Riley** (b. Mar. 20, 1945): Basketball; coached LA Lakers to 4 of their 5 NBA titles in 1980s (1982,85,87-88); coached New York Knicks from 1991-95, then signed with Miami Heat as coach, team president and part-owner; 3-time Coach of Year (1990,93,97); 2nd on list of all-time coaching victories behind Lenny Wilkens.

**Cal Ripken Jr.** (b. Aug. 24, 1960): Baseball SS; broke Lou Gehrig's major league Iron Man record of 2,130 consecutive games played on Sept. 6, 1995; record streak began on May 30, 1982 and ended Sept. 19, 1998 after 2,632 games; 2-time AL MVP (1983,91) for Baltimore; AL Rookie of Year (1982); AL starter in All-Star Game from 1984-2001; 2-time All-Star Game MVP (1991,2001); holds record for career home runs by a shortstop.

**Phil Rizzuto** (b. Sept. 25, 1918): Baseball SS; nicknamed "the Scooter"; AL MVP with the Yankees in 1950; 5-time All-Star; retired in 1956 and became Yankees radio and television announcer; elected to the Hall of Fame in 1994.

**Oscar Robertson** (b. Nov. 24, 1938): Basketball G; 3-time College Player of Year (1958-60) at Cincinnati; led 1960 U.S. Olympic team to gold medal; NBA Rookie of Year (1961); 9-time All-NBA 1st team; MVP in 1964 with Cincinnati Royals; NBA champion in 1971 with Milwaukee Bucks; 6-time annual NBA assist leader; 4th in career assists with 9,887; 8th in career points with 26,710.

**Paul Robeson** (b. Apr. 8, 1898, d. Jan. 23, 1976): Black 4-sport star and 2-time football All-America (1917-18) at Rutgers; 3-year NFL pro; also scholar, lawyer, singer, actor and political activist; long-tainted by Communist sympathies, he was finally inducted into College Football Hall of Fame in 1995.

**Brooks Robinson** (b. May 18, 1937): Baseball 3B; led AL in fielding 12 times from 1960-72 with Baltimore; AL MVP in 1964; World Series MVP in 1970; 16 Gold Gloves; entered Hall of Fame in 1983.

**David Robinson** (b. Aug. 6, 1965): Basketball C; 1987 College Player of Year at Navy; overall 1st pick by San Antonio in 1987 NBA draft; served in military (1987-89); NBA Rookie of Year (1990) and MVP (1995); 2-time All-NBA 1st team (1991,92); led NBA in scoring in 1994; member of 1988, '92 and '96 U.S. Olympic teams; won 2 NBA titles (1999, 2003).

**Eddie Robinson** (b. Feb. 13, 1919): Football; head coach at Div. I-AA Grambling from 1941-97; retired as winningest coach in college history (408-165-15), since passed by St. John's-Minn. (Div. III) coach John Gagliardi; led Tigers to 8 national black college titles.

**Frank Robinson** (b. Aug. 31, 1935): Baseball OF; won MVP in NL (1961) and AL (1966); Triple Crown winner and World Series MVP in 1966 with Baltimore; 6th on all-time home run list with 586; 1st black manager in major leagues with Cleveland in 1975; has also managed in San Francisco, Baltimore and Montreal/Washington; served as the league's VP of on-field operations (2000-01).

**Jackie Robinson** (b. Jan. 31, 1919, d. Oct. 24, 1972): Baseball 1B-2B-3B; 4-sport athlete at UCLA (baseball, basketball, football and track); hit .387 with Kansas City Monarchs of Negro Leagues in 1945; signed by Brooklyn Dodgers' Branch Rickey on Oct. 23, 1945. Played in minors (Montreal) in 1946 and broke Major League Baseball's color line in 1947; Rookie of Year in 1947 and NL's MVP in 1949; hit .311 over 10 seasons. His #42 was retired by Major League Baseball in 1997.

**Sugar Ray Robinson** (b. May 3, 1921, d. Apr. 12, 1989): Boxer; arguably the greatest pound-for-pound prizefighter of all-time; world welterweight champion (1946-51); 5-time middleweight champ; retired at age 45 after 25 years in the ring; pro record 174-19-6 with 109 KOs.

**Knute Rockne** (b. Mar. 4, 1888, d. Mar. 31, 1931): Football; coached Notre Dame to 3 consensus national titles (1924,29,30), highest winning percentage in college history (.881) with record of 105-12-5 over 13 seasons; killed in plane crash.

**Bill Rodgers** (b. Dec. 23, 1947): Distance runner; won Boston and New York City marathons 4 times each from 1975-80.

**Dennis Rodman** (b. May 13, 1961): Basketball F; superb rebounder and defender; known for dyeing his hair various colors and for getting suspended regularly; in 1997, he was suspended for 11 games for kicking a cameraman; led NBA in rebounding 7 straight years (1992-98); member of 5 NBA champion teams with Detroit (1989,90) and Chicago (1996-98); 2-time defensive player of the year (1990-91).

**Irina Rodnina** (b. Sept. 12, 1949): Soviet figure skater; won 10 world championships and 3 Olympic gold medals in pairs competition from 1969-80.

**Alex Rodriguez** (b. July 27, 1975): Baseball 3B; led AL in hitting (.358) his first full season in the majors (1996); in 1998 became third player ever with 40 HRs and 40 steals in one season; signed a 10-year, $252mil deal (the biggest in U.S. sports history) with Texas in 2000, won AL MVP in 2003 but was traded to NY Yankees in 2004.

**Juan (Chi Chi) Rodriguez** (b. Oct. 23, 1935): Golfer; popular player with 8 PGA Tour victories and 22 Senior Tour wins; 1973 U.S. Ryder Cup team.

**Ronaldo** (b. Sept. 22, 1976): Brazilian soccer F; named to the Brazilian National Team when he was 17; 3-time FIFA World Player of the Year (1996,97,2002); European Player of the Year in 1997 and 2002; named 1998 World Cup MVP; led Brazil to World Cup title in 2002, scoring 8 times including both of Brazil's goals in its win over Germany in the final.

**Art Rooney** (b. Jan. 27, 1901, d. Aug. 25, 1988): Race track legend and pro football pioneer; bought Pittsburgh Steelers franchise in 1933 for $2,500; finally won NFL title with 1st of 4 Super Bowls in 1974 season.

**Theodore Roosevelt** (b. Oct. 27, 1858, d. Jan. 6, 1919): 26th President of the U.S.; physical fitness buff who boxed as undergraduate at Harvard; credited with presidential assist in forming of Intercollegiate Athletic Assn. (now NCAA) in 1905-06.

**Mauri Rose** (b. May 26, 1906, d. Jan. 1, 1981): Auto racer; 3-time winner of Indy 500 (1941,47-48).

**Murray Rose** (b. Jan. 6, 1939): Australian swimmer; won 3 gold medals at 1956 Olympics; added a gold, silver and bronze in 1960.

**Pete Rose** (b. Apr. 14, 1941): Baseball OF-IF; all-time hits leader with 4,256 and games leader with 3562; led NL in batting 3 times; regular-season MVP in 1973; World Series MVP in 1975; had 44-game hitting streak in '78; managed Cincinnati (1984-89); banned for life in 1989 for conduct detrimental to baseball (betting on baseball); convicted of tax evasion in 1990 and sentenced to 5 months in prison.

**Ken Rosewall** (b. Nov. 2, 1934): Tennis; won French and Australian singles titles at age 18; U.S. champ twice, but never won Wimbledon.

**Mark Roth** (b. Apr. 10, 1951): Bowler; 4-time PBA Player of Year (1977-79,84); has 34 tournament wins and over $1.6 million in career earnings; U.S. Open champ in 1984.

**Alan Rothenberg** (b. Apr. 10, 1939): Soccer; president of U.S. Soccer 1990-98; surprised European skeptics by directing hugely successful 1994 World Cup tournament; successfully got oft-delayed outdoor Major League Soccer off ground in 1996.

**Chad Rowan (Akebono)** (b. May 8, 1969): Sumo Wrestling; 6-foot-9, 510-pound naturalized Japanese citizen born in Hawaii; first foreign grand champion in sumo wrestling's 2,000-year history; retired in 2001.

**Patrick Roy** (b. Oct. 5, 1965): Hockey G; led Montreal to 2 Stanley Cup titles (1986,93) and won 3rd and 4th Cups with Colorado (1996,2001); 3-time playoff MVP (as rookie in 1986,93,2001); won Vezina Trophy 3 times (1989-90,92); led NHL in goals against average 3 times (1989,92,2002); all-time leader in career regular season wins (551) and playoff wins (151).

**Pete Rozelle** (b. Mar. 1, 1926, d. December 6, 1996): Football; NFL Commissioner from 1960-89; presided over growth of league from 12 to 28 teams, merger with AFL, creation of Super Bowl and advent of huge TV rights fees.

**Wilma Rudolph** (b. June 23, 1940, d. Nov. 12, 1994): Track & Field; won 3 gold medals (100m, 200m and 4x100m relay) at 1960 Olympics; also won relay silver in '56 Games at age 16; 2-time AP Athlete of Year (1960-61) and Sullivan Award winner in 1961; suffered from polio and wore leg braces until she was 9.

**John Ruiz** (b. Jan. 4, 1972): Boxer; defeated Evander Holyfield by decision in 2001 for the WBA heavyweight title; the first-ever Hispanic heavyweight champ; lost belt to Roy Jones Jr. on unanimous dec. in 2003.

**Damon Runyon** (b. Oct. 4, 1884, d. Dec. 10, 1946): Kansas native who gained fame as New York journalist, sports columnist and short-story writer; best known for 1932 story collection, "Guys and Dolls."

**Adolph Rupp** (b. Sept. 2, 1901, d. Dec. 10, 1977): Basketball; 2nd in all-time college coaching wins with 876; led Kentucky to 4 NCAA championships (1948-49,51,58) and 1 NIT title (1946).

**Bill Russell** (b. Feb. 12, 1934): Basketball C; won titles in college (with San Francisco in 1955,56), Olympics (1956) and pros; 5-time NBA MVP (1958,61,62,63,65); led Boston Celtics to an amazing 11 titles from 1957-69; 4-time NBA rebound leader (1958-59,64-65); 2nd on all-time rebound list with 21,620; became first black NBA (and major professional sports) head coach in 1966.

**Babe Ruth** (b. Feb. 6, 1895, d. Aug. 16, 1948): Baseball LHP-OF; two-time 20-game winner with Boston Red Sox (1916-17); had a 94-46 record with a 2.28 ERA, while he was 3-0 in the World Series with an ERA of 0.87; sold to New York Yankees for $100,000 in 1920; AL MVP in 1923; led AL in slugging average 13 times, HRs 12 times, RBI 6 times and batting once (.378 in 1924); hit 60 HRs in 1927 and at least 54 3 other times; ended career with Boston Braves in 1935 with 714 HRs, 2,211 RBI, 2,062 walks and a batting average of .342; remains all-time leader in slugging percentage (.690); member of the Hall of Fame's inaugural class of 1936.

**Johnny Rutherford** (b. Mar. 12, 1938): Auto racer; 3-time winner of Indy 500 (1974,76,80); CART national champion in 1980.

**Nolan Ryan** (b. Jan. 31, 1947): Baseball RHP; recorded 7 no-hitters against Kansas City and Detroit (1973), Minnesota (1974), Baltimore (1975), LA Dodgers (1981), Oakland A's (1990) and Toronto (1991 at age 44); 2-time 20-game winner (1973-74); 2-time NL leader in ERA (1981,87); led AL in strikeouts 9 times and NL twice in 27 years; retired after 1993 season with 324 wins, 292 losses and all-time records for strikeouts (5,714) and walks (2,795); never won Cy Young Award; had his number retired by three teams (California, Houston, Texas).

**Samuel Ryder** (b. Mar. 24, 1858, d. Jan. 2, 1936): Golf; English seed merchant who donated the Ryder Cup in 1927 for competition between pro golfers from Great Britain and the U.S.; made his fortune by coming up with idea of selling seeds in small packages.

**Toni Sailer** (b. Nov. 17, 1935): Austrian skier; 1st to win 3 alpine gold medals in Winter Olympics—taking downhill, slalom and giant slalom events in 1956.

**Alberto Salazar** (b. Aug. 7, 1958): Track and Field; set one world and six U.S. records during his career; broke 12-year-old record at New York Marathon in 1981 and broke Boston Marathon record in 1982; won three straight NY Marathons (1980-82); qualified for the 1980 and 1984 U.S. Olympic teams.

**Juan Antonio Samaranch** (b. July 17, 1920): president of International Olympic Committee (1980-2001); the native of Barcelona was re-elected in 1996 after IOC's move in '95 to bump membership age limit to 80; replaced by Belgian Jacques Rogge.

**Pete Sampras** (b. Aug. 12, 1971): Tennis; No.1 in world (1993-98); youngest ever U.S. Open men's champ (19 years, 28 days) in 1990; his win at 2002 U.S. Open was record 14th grand slam singles title; won 2 Australian Opens (1994,97), 7 Wimbledons (1993-95, 1997-2000) and 5 U.S. Opens (1990,93, 95-96,2002); career money leader on ATP Tour.

**Joan Benoit Samuelson** (b. May 16, 1957): Distance runner; won Boston Marathon twice (1979,83); won first women's Olympic marathon in 1984 Games; Sullivan Award recipient in 1985.

**Arantxa Sanchez-Vicario** (b. Dec. 18, 1971): Spanish tennis player; won 29 singles titles including 3 French Opens (1989,94,98) and 1 U.S. Open (1994); 6 doubles and 4 mixed doubles grand slam titles.

**Earl Sande** (b. Nov. 13, 1898, d. Aug. 19, 1968): Jockey; rode Gallant Fox to Triple Crown in 1930; won 5 Belmonts and 3 Kentucky Derbies.

**Barry Sanders** (b. July 16, 1968): Football RB; won 1988 Heisman Trophy as junior at Oklahoma St.; all-time NCAA single season leader in rushing (2,628 yards), scoring (234 points) and TDs (39); 4-time NFL rushing leader with Detroit Lions (1990,94,96,97); NFC Rookie of Year (1988); 2-time NFL Player of Year (1991,97); NFC MVP (1994); rushed for 2,053 yards in 1997; No. 3 all-time rusher (15,269 yds); abruptly retired just prior to 1999 season; inducted into Pro Football Hall of Fame in 2004.

**Deion Sanders** (b. Aug. 9, 1967): Baseball OF and Football DB-KR-WR; 2-time All-America at Florida St. in football (1987-88); 7-time NFL All-Pro CB with Atlanta, San Fran. and Dallas (1991-94,96-98); led majors in triples (14) with Braves in 1992 and hit .533 in World Series that year; played on 2 Super Bowl winners (SF in XXIX, and Dallas in XXX); first 2-way starter in NFL since 1962 (Chuck Bednarik); only athlete to play in both World Series and Super Bowl.

**Cael Sanderson** (b. June 20, 1979): Wrestling; first 4-time undefeated NCAA college wrestling champion (1999-2002); went 159-0 during 4-year career at Iowa State; 4-time NCAA Most Outstanding Wrestler; won gold medal at Athens Games in 2004.

**Abe Saperstein** (b. July 4, 1901, d. Mar. 15, 1966): Basketball; founded all-black, Harlem Globetrotters barnstorming team in 1927; coached sharpshooting comedians to 1940 world pro title in Chicago and established troupe as game's foremost goodwill ambassadors; also served as 1st commissioner of American Basketball League (1961-62).

**Gene Sarazen** (b. Feb. 27, 1902, d. May 13, 1999): Golfer; one of only five players to win all four Grand Slam titles (others are Hogan, Nicklaus, Player and Woods); won Masters, British Open, 2 U.S. Opens and 3 PGA titles between 1922-35; invented sand wedge in 1930.

**Glen Sather** (b. Sept. 2, 1943): Hockey; GM-coach of 4 Stanley Cup winners in Edmonton (1984-85,87-88) and GM-only for another in 1990; ranks 7th on all-time NHL coaching list with 586 wins (including playoffs); entered Hockey Hall of Fame in 1997; named Pres-GM of NY Rangers in 2000.

**Terry Sawchuk** (b. Dec. 28, 1929, d. May 31, 1970): Hockey G; recorded 103 shutouts in 21 NHL seasons; 4-time Vezina Trophy winner; played on 4 Stanley Cup winners at Detroit and Toronto; posted career 2.52 GAA.

**Gale Sayers** (b. May 30, 1943): Football HB; 2-time All-America at Kansas; NFL Rookie of Year (1965) and 5-time All-Pro with Chicago; scored then-record 22 TDs in rookie year; led league in rushing twice (1966,69).

**Chris Schenkel** (b. Aug. 21, 1923, d. Sept. 11, 2005): Radio-TV; 4-time Sportscaster of Year; easygoing baritone who covered basketball, bowling, football, golf and the Olympics for ABC and CBS; host of ABC's Pro Bowlers Tour for 33 years; received lifetime achievement Emmy Award in 1992.

**Vitaly Scherbo** (b. Jan. 13, 1972): Russian gymnast; winner of unprecedented 6 gold medals in gymnastics, including men's All-Around, for Unified Team in 1992 Olympics; also won 3 bronze in '96 Games.

**Curt Schilling** (b. Nov. 14, 1966): Baseball RHP; led majors in strikeouts twice (1997-98) with Philadelphia; 3-time 20-game winner with Arizona (2001-02,04); shared 2001 World Series MVP award with teammate Randy Johnson; traded to Boston and helped Red Sox end 86-year championship drought in 2004.

**Mike Schmidt** (b. Sept. 27, 1949): Baseball 3B; led NL in HRs 8 times; 3-time MVP (1980,81,86) with Philadelphia; 548 career HRs and 10 Gold Gloves; inducted into Hall of Fame in 1995.

**Don Schollander** (b. Apr. 30, 1946): Swimming; won 4 gold medals at 1964 Olympics, plus one gold and one silver in 1968; won Sullivan Award in 1964.

**Dick Schultz** (b. Sept. 5, 1929): Reform-minded executive director of NCAA from 1988-93; announced resignation on May 11, 1993 in wake of special investigator's report citing Univ. of Virginia with improper student-athlete loan program during Schultz's tenure as athletic director (1981-87); executive director of the USOC 1995-2000.

**Michael Schumacher** (b. Jan. 3, 1969): German auto racer; Formula One's all-time win leader with 84 grand prix victories (and counting); 7-time world champion (1994-95,2000-04); broke his own F1 single-season record with 13 wins in 2004.

**Bob Seagren** (b. Oct. 17, 1946): Track & Field; won gold medal in pole vault at 1968 Olympics; broke world outdoor record 5 times.

**Tom Seaver** (b. Nov. 17, 1944): Baseball RHP; won 3 Cy Young Awards (1969,73,75); led NL in K 5 times (1970,71,73,75,76); pitched no-hitter in 1978 for Cin.; had 311 wins, 3,640 strikeouts and 2.86 ERA over 20 years.

**Peter Seitz** (b. May 17, 1905, d. Oct. 17, 1983): Baseball arbitrator; ruled on Dec. 23, 1975 that players who perform for one season without a signed contract can become free agents; decision ushered in big money era for players.

**Monica Seles** (b. Dec. 2, 1973): Tennis; No. 1 in the world in 1991 and '92 after winning Australian, French and U.S. Opens both years; won 4 Australian, 3 French and 2 US Opens; winner of 30 singles titles in just 5 years before she was stabbed in the back by Steffi Graf fan Gunter Parche on Apr. 30, 1993 during match in Hamburg, Germany; spent remainder of 1993, all of '94 and most of '95 recovering; returned to tennis with win at the 1995 Canadian Open; won 1996 Australian Open; winner of 53 WTA tournaments.

**Bud Selig** (b. July 30, 1934): Baseball; Milwaukee car dealer who bought AL Seattle Pilots for $10.8 million in 1970 and moved team to Midwest; as de facto commissioner, he presided over 232-day players' strike that resulted in cancellation of World Series for first time since 1904; officially elected baseball's ninth commissioner on July 9, 1998; has overseen many changes in MLB including interleague play, wild card playoffs, and new steroid testing policy.

**Frank Selke** (b. May 7, 1893, d. July 3, 1985): Hockey; GM of 6 Stanley Cup champions in Montreal (1953,56-60); the annual NHL trophy for best defensive forward bears his name.

**Ayrton Senna** (b. Mar. 21, 1960, d. May 1, 1994): Brazilian auto racer; 3-time Formula One champion (1988,90-91); died as all-time F1 leader in poles (65) and 2nd in wins (41, currently in 3rd); killed in crash at Imola, Italy during '94 San Marino GP.

**Wilbur Shaw** (b. Oct. 13, 1902, d. Oct. 30, 1954): Auto racer; 3-time winner and 3-time runner-up of Indy 500 from 1933-1940.

**Patty Sheehan** (b. Oct. 27, 1956): Golfer; LPGA Player of Year in 1983; clinched entry into LPGA Hall of Fame with her 30th career win in 1993; her 6 major titles include 3 LPGA Champ. (1983-84,93), 2 U.S. Opens (1992,94) 1 Dinah Shore (1996).

**Bill Shoemaker** (b. Aug. 19, 1931, d. Oct. 12, 2003): Jockey; ranks second all-time in career wins with 8,833 (passed by Laffit Pincay Jr. in Dec. 1999); 3-time Eclipse Award winner as jockey (1981) and special award recipient (1976,81); won Belmont 5 times, Kentucky Derby 4 times and Preakness twice; oldest jockey to win Kentucky Derby (age 54, aboard Ferdinand in 1986); retired in 1990 to become trainer; paralyzed in 1991 auto accident but continued to train horses.

**Eddie Shore** (b. Nov. 25, 1902, d. Mar. 16, 1985): Hockey D; only NHL defenseman to win Hart Trophy as MVP 4 times (1933,35-36,38); led Boston Bruins to Stanley Cup titles in 1929 and '39; had 105 goals and 1,047 penalty minutes in 14 seasons.

**Frank Shorter** (b. Oct. 31, 1947): Track & Field; won gold medal in marathon at 1972 Olympics, 1st American to win in 64 years.

**Don Shula** (b. Jan. 4, 1930): Football; retired after 1995 season with an NFL-record 347 career wins (including playoffs) and a winning percentage of .665; took six teams to Super Bowl and won twice with Miami (VII, VIII); 4-time Coach of Year, twice with Baltimore (1964,68) and twice with Miami (1970-71); coached 1972 Dolphins to 17-0 record, the only undefeated team in NFL history.

**Charlie Sifford** (b. June 2, 1922): Golf; won the Hartford Open in 1967 with a final-round 64, becoming the first black player to win a PGA event; won the PGA Seniors Championship in 1975; amassed over $1 million in career earnings; published his autobiography "Just Let Me Play" in 1992.

**Al Simmons** (b. May 22, 1902, d. May 26, 1956): Baseball OF; led AL in batting twice (1930-31) with Philadelphia A's and knocked in 100 runs or more 11 straight years (1924-34).

**O.J. Simpson** (b. July 9, 1947): Football RB; won Heisman Trophy in 1968 at USC; ran for 2,003 yards in NFL in 1973; All-Pro 5 times; MVP in 1973; rushed for 11,236 career yards; TV analyst and actor after career ended; arrested June 17, 1994 as suspect in double murder of ex-wife Nicole Brown Simpson and her friend Ronald Goldman; acquitted on Oct. 3, 1995 by a Los Angeles jury in criminal trial but forced to make financial reparations after losing wrongful death suit.

**Vijay Singh** (b. Feb. 22, 1963): Fijian golfer; temporarily dethroned Tiger Woods as world's top-ranked player in 2004; has 28 career PGA Tour wins including 1998 and 2004 PGA championships and 2000 Masters; 2003-04 PGA Tour money leader.

**George Sisler** (b. Mar. 24, 1893, d. Mar. 26, 1973): Baseball 1B; hit over .400 twice (1920,22) and batted over .300 in 13 of his 15 seasons; his MLB record of 257 hits (1920) was finally broken by Seattle's Ichiro Suzuki (262) in 2004; played most of his career with the St. Louis Browns; inducted into Baseball Hall of Fame in 1939.

**Mary Decker Slaney** (b. Aug. 4, 1958): U.S. middle distance runner; has held 7 separate American track & field records from the 800 to 10,000 meters; won both 1,500 and 3,000 meters at 1983 World Championships in Helsinki, but no Olympic medals.

**Raisa Smetanina** (b. Feb. 29, 1952): Russian Nordic skier; all-time leading female Winter Olympics' medalist with 10 cross country medals (4 gold, 5 silver and a bronze) in 5 appearances (1976,80,84, 88,92) for USSR and Unified Team.

**Billy Smith** (b. Dec. 12, 1950): Hockey G; led NY Islanders to 4 consecutive Stanley Cups (1980-83); won Vezina Trophy in 1982; Stanley Cup MVP in 1983.

**Dean Smith** (b. Feb. 28, 1931): Basketball; No. 1 on all-time NCAA coaches victory list (879 wins); led North Carolina to 25 NCAA tournaments in 34 years, reaching Final Four 10 times and winning championship twice (1982,93); coached U.S. Olympic team to gold medal in 1976.

**Emmitt Smith** (b. May 15, 1969): Football RB; NFL's all-time leading rusher (18,355 yards); also holds all-time record for rushing TDs (164); 4-time NFL rushing leader (1991-93,95); 11 straight 1,000-yard seasons (1991-2001) with Dallas Cowboys; regular season and Super Bowl MVP in 1993; played on three Super Bowl champions (1993,94,96).

**John Smith** (b. Aug. 9, 1965): Wrestler; 2-time NCAA champion for Oklahoma St. at 134 lbs (1987-88) and Most Outstanding Wrestler of '88 championships; 3-time world champion; gold medal winner at 1988 and '92 Olympics at 137 lbs; won Sullivan Award (1990); coached Oklahoma St. to 1994 NCAA title and brother Pat was Most Outstanding Wrestler.

**Lee Smith** (b. Dec. 4, 1957): Baseball RHP; 3-time NL saves leader (1983,91-92); retired as all-time saves leader with 478 and an ERA of 3.03; 10 seasons with 30+ saves and 3 times saved over 40.

**Michelle Smith deBruin** (b. Apr. 7, 1969): Irish swimmer; won three gold medals at the 1996 Olympics; accused of using performance-enhancing drugs but passed all tests until she was suspended for 4 years by FINA in 1998 for tampering with a urine sample.

**Ozzie Smith** (b. Dec. 26, 1954): Baseball SS; won 13 straight Gold Gloves (1980-92); played in 12 straight All-Star Games (1981-92); MVP of 1985 NL playoffs; all-time MLB assist leader (8,375); inducted into Baseball Hall of Fame in 2002.

**Walter (Red) Smith** (b. Sept. 25, 1905, d. Jan. 15, 1982): Sportswriter for newspapers in Philadelphia and New York from 1936-82; won Pulitzer Prize for commentary in 1976.

**Conn Smythe** (b. Feb. 1, 1895, d. Nov. 18, 1980): Hockey pioneer; built Maple Leaf Gardens in 1931; managed Toronto to 7 Stanley Cups.

**Sam Snead** (b. May 27, 1912, d. May 23, 2002): Golfer; won both Masters and PGA 3 times and British Open once; runner-up in U.S. Open 4 times; PGA Player of Year in 1949; oldest player (52 years, 10 months) to win PGA event with Greater Greensboro Open title in 1965; all-time PGA Tour career victory leader with 82.

**Peter Snell** (b. Dec. 17, 1938): Track & Field; New Zealander who won gold medal in 800m at 1960 Olympics, then won both the 800m and 1,500m at 1964 Games.

**Duke Snider** (b. Sept. 19, 1926): Baseball OF; hit 40 or more home runs five straight seasons (1953-57); led the league in runs scored 1953-55; played in six World Series with the Dodgers and batted .286 with 11 home runs; nicknamed "Duke of Flatbush"; in 18 seasons hit 407 home runs, scored 1,259 runs and had 1,333 RBI.

**Annika Sorenstam** (b. Oct. 9, 1970): Swedish golfer; has won 9 women's majors; 7-time Rolex Player of the Year (1995,97-98, 2001-04); shot an LPGA-record 59 in round 2 of the 2001 Standard Register Ping; LPGA all-time leading money winner; in 2003 she became first woman in 58 years to play on men's PGA Tour (via a sponsor's exemption); shot 71-74 but missed the cut at the Colonial by 4 strokes.

**Sammy Sosa** (b. Nov. 12, 1968): Baseball OF; slugging Chicago Cub who surpassed Roger Maris' season home run record (61), just after Mark McGwire did in 1998 and finished the year with 66; followed that up with seasons of 63, 50 and 64 HRs; 1998 NL MVP; 7-time All-Star (1995,98-2002,2004); 588 career homers.

**Javier Sotomayor** (b. Oct. 13, 1967): Cuban high jumper; first man to clear 8 feet (8-0) on July 29, 1989; won gold medal at 1992 Olympics with jump of only 7-ft, 8-in.; broke world record with leap of 8-0½ in 1993; had a controversial drug suspension reduced, which allowed him to participate in 2000 Olympics; won the silver medal in Sydney with a leap of 7-7¼.

**Warren Spahn** (b. Apr. 23, 1921, d. Nov. 23, 2003): Baseball LHP; led NL in wins 8 times; won 20 or more games 13 times; Cy Young winner in 1957; most career wins (363) by a lefthander.

**Tris Speaker** (b. Apr. 4, 1888, d. Dec. 8, 1958): Baseball OF; all-time leader in outfield assists (449) and doubles (792); had .344 career BA and 3,515 hits.

**J.G. Taylor Spink** (b. Nov. 6, 1888, d. Dec. 7, 1962): Publisher of The Sporting News from 1914-62; BBWAA annual meritorious service award named after him.

**Leon Spinks** (b. July 11, 1953): Boxing; won heavyweight crown in split decision over Muhammad Ali in Feb. 1978; Ali regained title seven months later; won gold medal in light heavyweight division at 1976 Olympics; brother Michael won the heavyweight title in 1983; were the only brothers to hold world titles; known more for frequent traffic violations and lavish lifestyle than bouts late in career; filed for bankruptcy in 1986.

**Mark Spitz** (b. Feb. 10, 1950): American swimmer; set 23 world and 35 U.S. records; won all-time record 7 gold medals (4 individual, 3 relay) in 1972 Olympics; also won 4 medals (2 gold, a silver and a bronze) in 1968 Games for a total of 11; comeback attempt at age 41 foundered in 1991.

**Latrell Sprewell** (b. Sept. 8, 1970): Basketball G; former NBA All-Star who made headlines in 1997 after being suspended by the NBA for attacking Golden State Warriors head coach P.J. Carlesimo during a practice.

**Lyn St. James** (b. Mar. 13, 1947): Auto racer; one of just 3 women to qualify for the Indianapolis 500; best finish in the race came in 1992 when she came in 11th and won Indianapolis 500 Rookie of the Year.

**Amos Alonzo Stagg** (b. Aug. 16, 1862, d. Mar. 17, 1965): Football innovator; coached at U. of Chicago for 41 seasons and College of the Pacific for 14 more; 314-199-35 record; elected to both college football and basketball Halls of Fame.

**Willie Stargell** (b. Mar. 6, 1940, d. Apr. 9, 2001): Baseball OF-1B; "Pops"; led NL in home runs twice (1971,73); 475 career HRs; NL co-MVP and World Series MVP in 1979.

**Bart Starr** (b. Jan. 9, 1934): Football QB; led Green Bay to 5 NFL titles and 2 Super Bowl wins from 1961-67; regular season MVP in 1966; MVP of Super Bowls I and II.

**Roger Staubach** (b. Feb. 5, 1942): Football QB; Heisman Trophy winner as Navy junior in 1963; led Dallas to 2 Super Bowl titles (1972,78) and was Super Bowl MVP in 1972; 5-time leading passer in NFC (1971,73,77-79).

**George Steinbrenner** (b. July 4, 1930): Baseball; principal owner of NY Yankees since 1973; teams have won 10 pennants and 6 World Series (1977-78,96,98,99,00); has changed managers 21 times and GMs 11 times in 31 years; ordered by baseball commish Fay Vincent in 1990 to surrender control of club for dealings with small-time gambler; reinstated in 1993.

**Casey Stengel** (b. July 30, 1890, d. Sept. 29, 1975): Baseball; player for 14 years and manager for 25; outfielder and lifetime .284 hitter with 5 clubs (1912-25); guided NY Yankees to 10 AL pennants and 7 World Series titles from 1949-60; 1st NY Mets skipper from 1962-65.

**Ingemar Stenmark** (b. Mar. 18, 1956): Swedish alpine skier; 3-time World Cup overall champ (1976-78); posted 86 World Cup wins in 16 years; won 2 gold medals at 1980 Olympics.

**Helen Stephens** (b. Feb. 3, 1918, d. Jan. 17, 1994): Track & Field; set 3 world records in 100-yard dash and 4 more in 100 meters in 1935-36; won gold medals in 100 meters and 4x100-meter relay in 1936 Olympics; retired in 1937.

**Woody Stephens** (b. Sept. 1, 1913, d. Aug. 22, 1998): Horse racing; trainer who saddled an unprecedented 5 straight winners in Belmont Stakes (1982-86); also had two Kentucky Derby winners (1974,84) and one Preakness winner (1952); trained 1982 Horse of Year Conquistador Cielo; won Eclipse award as nation's top trainer in 1983.

**David Stern** (b. Sept. 22, 1942): Basketball; marketing expert and NBA commissioner since 1984; took office the year Michael Jordan turned pro; league has grown from 23 teams to 30 during his watch and opened offices worldwide; oversaw launch of WNBA in 1997.

**Teófilo Stevenson** (b. Mar. 29, 1952): Cuban boxer; won 3 consecutive gold medals as Olympic heavyweight (1972,76,80); was denied a chance to win a fourth when Cuba boycotted 1984 Los Angeles Games; did not turn pro.

**Jackie Stewart** (b. June 11, 1939): Auto racer; won 27 Formula One races and 3 world driving titles from 1965-73.

**John Stockton** (b. Mar 26, 1962): Basketball G; all-time NBA leader in every major assist category, including most in a season (1,164) and most in a career (15,806); also the NBA's all-time leader in steals (3,265); All-NBA team in '94 and '95; member of 1992 and '96 US Olympic basketball teams; 10-time All-Star; played 19 seasons with Utah Jazz—18 of them with Karl Malone—perfecting the pick and roll.

**Curtis Strange** (b. Jan. 30, 1955): Golfer; won consecutive U.S. Open titles (1988-89); 3-time leading money winner on PGA Tour (1985,87-88); first PGA player to win $1 million in one year (1988); captain of the 2002 U.S. Ryder Cup team.

**Picabo Street** (b. Apr. 3, 1971): Skiing; 2-time Olympic medalist, gold (Super G in 1998) and silver (downhill in 1994); her 1995 World Cup downhill series title first-ever by U.S. woman, she repeated the feat in 1996.

**Kerri Strug** (b. Nov. 19, 1977): Gymnastics; delivered the most dramatic moment of the 1996 Summer Olympics when she completed a vault (9.712) after spraining her ankle; the second vault helped assure the first all-around gold medal for a US Women's gymnastics team.

**Louise Suggs** (b. Sept. 7, 1923): Golfer; won 11 majors and 58 LPGA events overall from 1949-62.

**James E. Sullivan** (b. Nov. 18, 1862, d. Sept. 16, 1914): Track & Field; pioneer who founded Amateur Athletic Union (AAU) in 1888; director of St. Louis Olympic Games in 1904; AAU's annual Sullivan Award for performance and sportsmanship named after him.

**John L. Sullivan** (b. Oct. 15, 1858, d. Feb. 2, 1918): Boxer; nicknamed "The Boston Strong Boy"; world heavyweight champion (1882-92); last of bare-knuckle champions, beating Jake Kilrain after 75 rounds in 1889; was knocked out by "Gentleman" Jim Corbett in the 21st round in 1892, never fought again.

**Pat Summitt** (b. June 14, 1952): Basketball; women's basketball coach at Tennessee (1974—); entered 2005-06 season as all-time leader in career victories with 882; coached 1984 US women's basketball team to its first Olympic gold medal; has coached Lady Vols to 6 national championships (1987, 89,91,96,97,98); her Lady Vols have made 9 or last 11 Final Fours.

**Don Sutton** (b. April 2, 1945): Baseball RHP; won 324 games and tossed 58 shutouts in his 23-year career; recorded NL record five career 1-hitters; played with Dodgers, Astros, Brewers, Athletics, Angels and was a 4-time All-Star; elected to Hall of Fame in 1998.

**Ichiro Suzuki** (b. Oct. 22, 1973): Baseball OF; became the 2nd player (Fred Lynn) to win AL Rookie of the Year and MVP in same year (2001); 1st Japanese-born position player to play in MLB; won 7 consecutive Japanese batting titles (1994-2000) and has won two more in AL with Seattle (2001,04); broke George Sisler's 84-year-old hits record with 262 in 2004.

**Lynn Swann** (b. Mar. 7, 1952): Football WR; played nine seasons with Pittsburgh (1974-82); appeared in four Super Bowls and had 16 catches for 364 yards and three TDs; named MVP of Super Bowl X for 4 catch, 161 yard, 1 TD performance.

**Barry Switzer** (b. Oct. 5, 1937): Football; coached Oklahoma to 3 national titles (1974-75,85); 4th on all-time winning pct list at .837 (157-29-4); resigned in 1989 after OU was slapped with 3-year NCAA probation; hired as Dallas Cowboys head coach in 1994 and led team to victory in Super Bowl XXX in 1996.

**Sheryl Swoopes** (b. Mar. 25, 1971): Basketball; forward for WNBA's Houston Comets; 4-time WNBA regular season MVP (2000,02,03,05); Defensive Player of the Year in 2000, 3-time Olympic gold medalist (1996,2000,2004); led Texas Tech to Div. I NCAA championship in 1993; consensus National Player of the Year in 1993.

**Paul Tagliabue** (b. Nov. 24, 1940): Football; NFL attorney who was elected league's 4th commissioner in 1989; ushered in salary cap in 1994; the league has expanded from 28 teams to 32 in his tenure.

**Anatoli Tarasov** (b. 1918, d. June 23, 1995): Hockey; coached Soviet Union to 9 straight world championships and 3 Olympic gold medals (1964, 68,72).

**Jerry Tarkanian** (b. Aug. 30, 1930): Basketball; amassed 778 wins in 31 years at Long Beach St., UNLV and Fresno St.; led UNLV to 4 Final Fours and 1 national title (1990); fought battle with NCAA over purity of UNLV program; quit as coach after going 26-2 in 1991-92; fired after 20 games (9-11) as coach of NBA San Antonio Spurs in 1992.

**Fran Tarkenton** (b. Feb. 3, 1940): Football QB; scrambling two-time NFL All-Pro (1973,75); 1975 Player of the Year; threw for 47,003 yards and 342 TDs (both former NFL records) in 18 seasons with Vikings and N.Y. Giants; selected to 9 Pro Bowls; inducted into Pro Football Hall of Fame in 1986.

**Chuck Taylor** (b. June 24, 1901, d. June 23, 1969): Converse traveling salesman whose name came to grace the classic, high-top canvas basketball sneakers known as "Chucks"; over 750 million pairs have been sold since 1917; he also ran clinics worldwide and edited Converse Basketball Yearbook (1922-68).

**Lawrence Taylor** (b. Feb. 4, 1959): Football LB; All-America at North Carolina (1980); only defensive player in NFL history to be consensus Player of Year (1986); led N.Y. Giants to Super Bowl titles in 1986 and '90 seasons; played in 10 Pro Bowls (1981-90); retired after 1993 season with 132½ sacks; had several drug-related arrests in retirement; inducted into Hall of Fame in 1999.

**Marshall (Major) Taylor** (b. Nov. 26, 1878, d. June 21, 1932): Cyclist; Considered one of the first African-American sports heroes; held seven world cycling records at the turn of the century, racing mostly in Europe, Australia and New Zealand after being barred from many events in the U.S. due to racial prejudices; won the world one-mile championship in 1899.

**Gustavo Thoeni** (b. Feb. 28, 1951): Italian alpine skier; 4-time World Cup overall champion (1971-73,75); won giant slalom at 1972 Olympics.

**Isiah Thomas** (b. Apr. 30, 1961): Basketball; led Indiana to NCAA title as sophomore and Final 4 MOP in 1981; consensus All-America guard in '81; led Detroit to 2 NBA titles (1989,1990); NBA Finals MVP in 1990; 3-time All-NBA 1st team (1984-86); elected to Hall of Fame in 2000; currently president of the N.Y. Knicks.

**Thurman Thomas** (b. May 16, 1966): Football RB; 3-time AFC rushing leader (1990-91,93); 2-time All-Pro (1990-91); 1991 NFL Player of Year; led Buffalo to 4 straight Super Bowls (1991-94).

**Daley Thompson** (b. July 30, 1958): British Track & Field; won consecutive gold medals in decathlon at 1980 and '84 Olympics.

**Jenny Thompson** (b. Feb. 26, 1973): American swimmer; 8-time Olympic gold medalist (all in relays) and winner of 12 Olympic medals overall, more than any other American; competed in 5 Olympic Games (1988,92,96,2000,04) won 3 golds (4x100 free, 4x200 free, 4x100 medley) and 1 bronze (100m freestyle) at Sydney.

**John Thompson** (b. Sept. 2, 1941): Basketball; coached centers Patrick Ewing, Alonzo Mourning and Dikembe Mutombo at Georgetown; reached NCAA tourney final 3 out of 4 years with Ewing, winning title in 1984; also led Hoyas to 6 Big East tourney titles; coached 1988 U.S. Olympic team to bronze medal; retired abruptly during 1999 season with 27-year mark of 596-239.

**Bobby Thomson** (b. Oct. 25, 1923): Baseball OF; career .270 hitter who won the 1951 NL pennant for the NY Giants with a 1-out, 3-run HR in the bottom of the 9th inning of Game 3 of a best-of-3 playoff with Brooklyn; the pitcher was Ralph Branca, the count was 0-1 and the Dodgers were ahead 4-2; the Giants had trailed Brooklyn by 13½ games on Aug. 11.

**Ian Thorpe** (b. Oct. 13, 1982): Australian swimmer; 5-time gold medalist; won 400m free at Sydney Olympics (breaking his own world record) and silver in 200m free; won gold and broke the world record in the 4x100m and 4x200 free relays; won 200m free and 400m free Olympic gold at Athens in 2004; 2002 Jesse Owens Award winner.

**Jim Thorpe** (b. May 28, 1887, d. Mar. 28, 1953): Native American multi-sport superstar; 2-time All-America halfback at Carlisle; won both pentathlon and decathlon gold medals at 1912 Olympics; stripped of medals a month later for playing semi-pro baseball prior to Games (medals restored in 1982); played major league baseball (1913-19) and pro football (1920-26,28); became first president of NFL (then known as the APFA) in 1920; chosen "Athlete of the Half Century" by AP in 1950.

**Bill Tilden** (b. Feb. 10, 1893, d. June 5, 1953): Tennis; won 7 U.S. and 3 Wimbledon titles in 1920s; led U.S. to 7 straight Davis Cup victories (1920-26).

**Tinker to Evers to Chance** Chicago Cubs double play combination from 1903-10; immortalized in poem by New York sportswriter Franklin P. Adams—SS Joe Tinker (1880-1948), 2B Johnny Evers (1883-1947) and 1B Frank Chance (1877-1924); all 3 managed the Cubs and made the Hall of Fame.

**Y.A. Tittle** (b. Oct. 24, 1926): Football QB; Yelberton Abraham Tittle played 17 years in AAFC and NFL; All-Pro 4 times; league MVP with San Francisco (1957) and NY Giants (1962, 63); passed for 28,339 career yards.

**Alberto Tomba** (b. Dec. 19, 1966): Italian alpine skier; winner of 5 Olympic medals (3 gold, 2 silver); became 1st alpine skier to win gold medals in 2 consecutive Winter Games when he won the slalom and giant slalom in 1988 then repeated in the GS in '92; also won silvers in slalom in 1992 and '94.

**Dara Torres** (b. April 15, 1967): Swimmer; her 9 career Olympic medals (4G, 1S, 4B) are the 2nd-most for an American woman; took a 7-year hiatus before returning to the pool to win 5 medals in Sydney in 2000.

**Vladislav Tretiak** (b. Apr. 25, 1952): Hockey G; led USSR to Olympic gold medals in 1972 and '76; starred for Soviets against Team Canada in 1972, and again in 2 Canada Cups (1976,81).

**Lee Trevino** (b. Dec. 1, 1939): Golfer; 2-time winner of 3 majors—U.S. Open (1968, 71), British Open (1971-72) and PGA (1974,84); Player of Year once on PGA Tour (1971) and 3 times with Seniors (1990,92,94); 29 PGA Tour and 29 Senior Tour wins.

**Felix Trinidad** (b. Jan. 10, 1973): Puerto Rican boxer; former WBC/IBF welterweight champion; won WBC belt with a maj. dec. over Oscar De La Hoya in 1999; stepped up to jr. middleweight and won the WBA title from David Reid in 2000; moved to middleweight and suffered a 12th-round TKO to Bernard Hopkins in 2001 then retired; KO'd Ricardo Mayorga in 2004 comeback fight but was soundly defeated by Winky Wright in 2005.

**Bryan Trottier** (b. July 17, 1956): Hockey C; led NY Islanders to 4 straight Stanley Cups (1980-83); Rookie of Year (1976); scoring champion (134 points) and regular season MVP in 1979; playoff MVP (1980); added 5th and 6th Cups with Pittsburgh in 1991 and '92; entered Hockey Hall of Fame in 1997; head coach of NY Rangers in 2002, fired in 2003.

**Gene Tunney** (b. May 25, 1897, d. Nov. 7, 1978): Boxer; world heavyweight champion from 1926-28; beat 31-year-old champ Jack Dempsey in unanimous 10 round decision in 1926; beat him again in famous "long count" rematch in '27; quit while still champion in 1928 with 65-1-1 record and 47 KOs.

**Ted Turner** (b. Nov. 19, 1938): Sportsman and TV mogul; skippered Courageous to America's Cup win in 1977; one-time owner of MLB Atlanta Braves, NBA Hawks and NHL Thrashers; founder of CNN, TNT and TBS; founder of Goodwill Games; 1991 Time Man of Year.

**Mike Tyson** (b. June 30, 1966): Boxer; youngest (19) heavyweight champion ever (WBC in 1986); undisputed champ from 1987 until upset loss to 42-1 shot Buster Douglas on Feb. 10, 1990, in Tokyo; found guilty on Feb. 10, 1992, of raping 18-year-old Miss Black America contestant Desiree Washington in Indianapolis on July 19, 1991; sentenced to 6-year prison term; released May 9, 1995 after serving 3 years; reclaimed WBC and WBA belts with wins over Frank Bruno and Bruce Seldon in 1996; lost WBA title to Evander Holyfield in 1996; he bit Holyfield's ear twice during their 1997 WBA title rematch; was KO'd in 8th round by Lennox Lewis in 2002; despite earning $300m in his career, he filed for bankruptcy in 2003.

**Wyomia Tyus** (b. Aug. 29, 1945): Track & Field; 1st woman to win consecutive Olympic gold medals in 100m (1964-68).

**Peter Ueberroth** (b. Sept. 2, 1937): Organizer of 1984 Summer Olympics in LA; 1984 *Time* Man of Year; baseball commissioner from 1984-89; headed Rebuild Los Angeles for one year after 1992 riots; currently chairman of USOC.

**Johnny Unitas** (b. May 7, 1933, d. Sept. 11, 2002): Football QB; Big-game field general who led Baltimore Colts to 2 NFL titles (1958-59) and a Super Bowl win (1971); All-Pro 5 times; 3-time MVP (1959,64,67); selected to 10 Pro Bowls; passed for 40,239 career yards and 290 TDs.

**Al Unser Jr.** (b. Apr. 19, 1962): Auto racer; 2-time CART-IndyCar national champion (1990,94); 2-time Indy 500 winer (1992,94), giving Unser family 9 overall titles at the Brickyard; retired in 2004 with 31 CART wins in 19 years; left CART for Indy Racing League in 2000; son of Al and nephew of Bobby.

**Al Unser Sr.** (b. May 29, 1939): Auto racer; 3-time USAC-CART national champion (1970,83,85); 4-time winner of Indy 500 (1970,71,78,87); retired in 1994 with 39 wins; younger brother of Bobby and father of Al Jr.

**Bobby Unser** (b. Feb. 20, 1934): Auto racer; 2-time USAC-CART national champion (1968,74); 3-time winner of Indy 500 (1968,75,81); retired after 1981 season; fifth all-time with 35 career wins.

**Gene Upshaw** (b. Aug. 15, 1945): Football G; 2-time All-AFL and 3-time All-NFL selection with Oakland; helped lead Raiders to 2 Super Bowl titles in 1976 and '80 seasons; executive director of NFL Players Assn. since 1987; agreed to application of salary cap in 1994.

**Jim Valvano** (b. Mar. 10, 1946, d. Apr. 28, 1993): Basketball; coach at N.C. State whose team upset Houston to win national title in 1983; in 19 seasons as a coach appeared in 8 NCAA tournaments; twice voted ACC Coach of the Year; career record 346-212; AD at N.C. State (1986-89) when a recruiting and admissions scandal forced him out of the job; worked as a broadcaster for ESPN and ABC; died after a year-long battle with cancer; The V Foundation for cancer research is named for him.

**Norm Van Brocklin** (b. Mar. 15, 1926, d. May 2, 1983): Football QB-P; led NFL in passing 3 times and punting twice; led LA Rams (1951) and Philadelphia (1960) to NFL titles; MVP in 1960.

**Amy Van Dyken** (b. Feb. 17, 1973): Swimming; first American woman to win four gold medals in one Olympics (1996); won the individual 50m freestyle, 100m butterfly, and was on the US team for the 4x100 freestyle and 4x50 medley; won gold at Sydney in 2000 as part of the US 4x100 freestyle relay.

**Johnny Vander Meer** (b. Nov. 2, 1914, d. Oct. 6, 1997): Baseball LHP; only major leaguer to pitch consecutive no-hitters (June 11 & 15, 1938).

**Harold S. Vanderbilt** (b. July 6, 1884, d. July 4, 1970): Sportsman; successfully defended America's Cup 3 times (1930, 34,37); also invented contract bridge in 1926.

**Glenna Collett Vare** (b. June 20, 1903, d. Feb. 10, 1989): Golfer; won record 6 U.S. Women's Amateur titles from 1922-35; "the female Bobby Jones."

**Andy Varipapa** (b. Mar. 31, 1891, d. Aug. 25, 1984): Bowler; trick-shot artist; won consecutive All-Star match game titles (1947-48) at age 55 and 56.

**Bill Veeck** (b. Feb. 9, 1914, d. Jan. 2, 1986): Maverick baseball executive; owned AL teams in Cleveland, St. Louis and Chicago from 1946-80; introduced ballpark giveaways, exploding scoreboards, Wrigley Field's ivy-covered walls and midget Eddie Gaedel; won World Series with Indians (1948) and pennant with White Sox (1959).

**Jacques Villeneuve** (b. Apr. 9, 1971): Canadian auto racer; Indianapolis 500 runner-up and Indy-Car Rookie of Year in 1994; won 500 and IndyCar driving championship in 1995; jumped to Formula One racing in 1996 and won the F1 title in 1997.

**Fay Vincent** (b. May 29, 1938): Baseball; became 8th commissioner after death of A. Bartlett Giamatti in 1989; presided over World Series earthquake, owners' lockout and banishment of NY Yankees owner George Steinbrenner in his first year on the job; contentious relationship with owners resulted in his resignation on Sept. 7, 1992, four days after 18-9 "no confidence" vote.

**Lasse Viren** (b. July 22, 1949): Finnish runner; won gold medals at 5,000 and 10,000 meters in 1972 Munich Olympics; repeated 5,000/10,000 double in 1976 Games and added a fifth place finish in the marathon.

**Dick Vitale** (b. June 9, 1939): Broadcaster; Radio and television commentator for ESPN and ABC Sports known for his enthusiastic, almost spastic style; had successful college and pro basketball coaching career with the University of Detroit (1973-77) and the Detroit Pistons (1978-79).

**Lanny Wadkins** (b. Dec. 5, 1949): Golfer; member of 8 U.S. Ryder Cup teams and captain of 1995 team; 21 PGA Tour wins.

**Honus Wagner** (b. Feb. 24, 1874, d. Dec. 6, 1955): Baseball SS; hit .300 for 17 consecutive seasons (1897-1913) with Louisville and Pittsburgh; led NL in batting 8 times; ended career with 3,430 career hits, a .329 average and 722 stolen bases.

**Lisa Wagner** (b. May 19, 1961): Bowler; 4-time LPBT Player of Year (1983,86,88,93); 1980's Bowler of Decade; first woman to earn $100,000 in a season; winner of 32 pro titles.

**Grete Waitz** (b. Oct. 1, 1953): Norwegian runner; 9-time winner of New York City Marathon from 1978-88; won silver medal at 1984 Olympics.

**Jersey Joe Walcott** (b. Jan. 31, 1914, d. Feb. 27, 1994): Boxer; oldest heavyweight (37) to win the championship (until George Foreman beat his record in 1994); lost four championship bouts before knocking out Ezzard Charles in the seventh round in 1951; lost the title the following year to Rocky Marciano; won 50 bouts, 30 by knockout, lost 17 and fought one draw as a professional; later became sheriff of Camden County, NJ.

**Doak Walker** (b. Jan. 1, 1927, d. Sept. 27, 1998): Football HB; won Heisman Trophy as SMU junior in 1948; led Detroit to 2 NFL titles (1952-53); All-Pro 4 times in 6 years.

**Herschel Walker** (b. Mar. 3, 1962): Football RB; led Georgia to national title as freshman in 1980; won Heisman in 1982 then jumped to upstart USFL in '83; signed by Dallas Cowboys after USFL folded; led NFL in rushing in 1988; traded to Minnesota in 1989 for 5 players and 3 draft picks.

**Rusty Wallace** (b. Aug. 14, 1956): Auto racing; NASCAR Winston Cup champion in 1989 and runner-up in 1988, 1988 and 1993; recorded 55 victories and has won over $40 million in earnings in more than 25 years of racing.

**Bill Walsh** (b. Nov. 30, 1931): Football; Hall of Fame coach and GM of 3 Super Bowl winners with San Francisco (1982,85,89); retired after 1989 Super Bowl; returned to college coaching in 1992 for his second stint at Stanford; retired again after 1994 season; returned as 49er GM from 1999-2001.

**Bill Walton** (b. Nov. 5, 1952): Basketball C; 3-time College Player of Year (1972-74); led UCLA to 2 national titles (1972-73); led Portland to NBA title as MVP in 1977; regular season MVP in 1978; won 1986 NBA title with Boston.

**Darrell Waltrip** (b. Feb. 5, 1947): Auto racing; 3-time NASCAR Winston Cup champion (1981,82,85); 84 career Winston Cup wins and 59 poles.

**Arch Ward** (b. Dec. 27, 1896, d. July 9, 1955): Promoter and sports editor of *Chicago Tribune* from 1930-55; founder of baseball All-Star game (1933), Chicago College All-Star Football Game (1934) and the All-America Football Conference (1946-49).

**Charlie Ward** (b. Oct. 12, 1970): Football QB and Basketball G; 1993 Heisman winner with national champion Florida St.; won Sullivan Award (1993); 3-year starter for FSU basketball team; not taken in NFL draft (made it clear he was pursuing NBA career); 1st round pick of NY Knicks in 1994 NBA draft.

**Glenn (Pop) Warner** (b. Apr. 5, 1871, d. Sept. 7, 1954): Football innovator; coached at 7 colleges over 49 years; 319 career wins, fourth all-time; produced 47 All-Americas, including Jim Thorpe and Ernie Nevers.

**Kurt Warner** (b. June 22, 1971): Football QB; former Arena leaguer who led the St. Louis Rams to 2000 Super Bowl win; threw for a record 414 yards and was voted Super Bowl MVP; lost Super Bowl in 2002 with Rams; 2-time NFL MVP (1999,2001).

**Tom Watson** (b. Sept. 4, 1949): Golfer; 6-time PGA Player of the Year (1977-80,82,84); has won 5 British Opens, 2 Masters and a U.S. Open; 4-time Ryder Cup member and captain of 1993 team; 39 PGA tour wins.

**Earl Weaver** (b. Aug. 14, 1930): Baseball; managed the Baltimore Orioles to 6 Eastern Division titles, four AL pennants and a World Series victory in 1970; was ejected 91 times and suspended four times for outbursts against umpires; record of 1,480-1,060 from 1968-82 and 1985-86.

**Alan Webb** (b. Jan. 13, 1983): Track; on May 27, 2001 at the Prefontaine Classic, he ran a mile in 3:53.43 to break Jim Ryun's 36-year-old national high school record.

**Karrie Webb** (b. Dec. 21, 1974): Australian golfer; youngest woman (26) to win career Grand Slam; her win in the 2002 British Open made her the first player to win the "Super Grand Slam" (5 different majors) and gave her 6 major titles; 2-time Rolex Player of the Year (1999-2000); entered Hall of Fame in 2005.

**Dick Weber** (b. Dec. 23, 1929, d. Feb. 13, 2005): Bowler; 3-time PBA Bowler of the Year (1961,63,65); won 30 PBA titles in 4 decades; father of Pete.

**Pete Weber** (b. Aug. 21, 1962): Bowler; 2nd on all-time PBA money list; 1990 PBA Rookie of the Year; inducted into PBA Hall of Fame (1998); has 31 PBA titles; son of Dick.

**Johnny Weissmuller** (b. June 2, 1904, d. Jan. 20 1984): American swimmer; won 3 gold medals (100m free, 400m free, 4x200m free) at 1924 Olympics and 2 more at 1928 Games (100m free and 4x200m free); set 51 world records; became Hollywood's most famous Tarzan.

**Jerry West** (b. May 28, 1938): Basketball G; 2-time All-America and NCAA Final 4 MOP (1959) at West Virginia; led 1960 U.S. Olympic team to gold medal; 10-time All-NBA 1st-team; NBA finals MVP (1969); led LA Lakers to NBA title once as player (1972) and then 6 more times (1980,82,85,87,88,00) as an executive in various positions with the club; hired as President of Basketball Ops. by Memphis Grizzlies in 2002; his silhouette serves as the NBA's logo.

**Pernell Whitaker** (b. Jan. 2, 1964): Boxer; won Olympic gold medal as lightweight in 1984; won 4 world championships as lightweight, jr. welterweight, welterweight and jr. middleweight; outfought but failed to beat Julio Cesar Chavez when 1993 welterweight title defense ended in controversial draw; pro record of 41-3-1 (17 KOs); nicknamed "Sweet Pea".

**Bill White** (b. Jan. 28, 1934): Baseball; former NL president and highest ranking black executive in sports from 1989-94; as 1st baseman, won 7 Gold Gloves and hit .286 with 202 HRs in 13 seasons.

**Byron (Whizzer) White** (b. June 8, 1917, d. Apr. 15, 2002): Football; All-America HB at Colorado (1937); signed with Pittsburgh in 1938 for the then largest contract in pro history ($15,800); took Rhodes Scholarship in 1939; returned to NFL in 1940 to lead league in rushing and retired in 1941; named to U.S. Supreme Court by President Kennedy in 1962 and stepped down in 1993.

**Reggie White** (b. Dec. 19, 1961, d. Dec. 26, 2004): Football DE; consensus All-America in 1983 at Tennessee; 7-time All-NFL (1986-92) with Philadelphia; signed as free agent with Green Bay in 1993; made headlines in 1998 after making controversial public comments about gays and minorities; 2nd all-time in NFL sacks (198).

**Kathy Whitworth** (b. Sept. 27, 1939): Golf; 7-time LPGA Player of the Year (1966-69,71-73); won 6 majors; 88 tour wins, most on LPGA or PGA tour.

**Hoyt Wilhelm** (b. July 26, 1923, d. Aug. 23, 2002): Baseball RHP; Knuckleballer who is 4th all-time in games pitched (1,070) and 1st in games finished (651) and games won in relief (123); career ERA of 2.52 and 227 saves; 1st reliever inducted into Hall of Fame (1985); threw no-hitter vs. NY Yankees (1958); also hit lone HR of career in first major league at bat (1952); won Purple Heart at the Battle of the Bulge.

**Lenny Wilkens** (b. Oct. 28, 1937): Basketball; NBA's all-time winningest coach; MVP of 1960 NIT as Providence guard; played 15 years in NBA, including 4 as player-coach; 9-time All-Star and MVP of 1971 game; coached Seattle to 1979 NBA title; Coach of Year in 1994 with Atlanta; career record of 1412-1253 including playoffs with 7 NBA teams; coached USA basketball team to gold medal in 1996; member of the basketball hall of fame as player *and* coach.

**Dominique Wilkins** (b. Jan. 12, 1960): Basketball F; prolific scorer and ferocious dunker who led NBA in scoring (30.3 ppg) in 1986 with Atlanta; All-NBA 1st team in 1986; 2-time NBA slam dunk champion; nicknamed "The Human Highlight Film".

**Bud Wilkinson** (b. Apr. 23, 1916, d. Feb. 9, 1994): Football; played on 1936 national championship team at Minnesota; coached Oklahoma to 3 national titles (1950, 55, 56); won 4 Orange and 2 Sugar Bowls; teams had winning streaks of 47 (1953-57) and 31 (1948-50); retired after 1963 season with 145-29-4 record in 17 years; also coached St. Louis of NFL to 9-20 record from 1978-79.

**Ricky Williams** (b. May 21, 1977): Football RB; became all-time NCAA Div. I-A leader in rushing yards (6,279) and TDs (75) at Texas but has been passed in both categories; 1998 Heisman Trophy winner; Mike Ditka and New Orleans Saints traded their entire draft to take him fifth overall in 1999 NFL draft; traded to Miami Dolphins in 2002; stunned teammates when he retired suddenly just prior to 2004 season but returned in 2005.

**Serena Williams** (b. Sept. 26, 1981): Tennis; first African-American woman to win a Grand Slam title since Althea Gibson in 1958 by winning the 1999 U.S. Open; has 7 career Grand Slam titles: 2 Wimbledons (2002-03), French Open (2002), 2 U.S. Opens (1999,02) and 2 Australian Opens (2003,05); has won career doubles Grand Slam with Venus.

**Ted Williams** (b. Aug. 30, 1918, d. July 5, 2002): Baseball OF; led AL in batting 6 times, and HRs and RBI 4 times each; won Triple Crown twice (1942,47); 2-time MVP (1946,49); last player to bat .400 when he hit .406 in 1941; Marine Corps combat pilot who missed 3 full seasons during WWII (1943-45) and most of two others (1952-53) during Korean War; hit .344 lifetime with 521 HRs in 19 years with Boston Red Sox; also known as avid fisherman; furor erupted following his death when plans to keep his body frozen at a cryogenic lab were made public.

**Venus Williams** (b. June 17, 1980): Tennis; won 3 Wimbledon (2000,01,05) and 2 U.S. Open (2000, 01) singles titles; 2000 Olympic singles and doubles (with sister Serena) gold medalist; recorded fastest serve in WTA history with 127 mph blast in 1998; won career doubles grand slam with Serena.

**Walter Ray Williams Jr.** (b. Oct. 6, 1959): Bowling and Horseshoes; 6-time PBA Bowler of Year (1986,93,96,97,98,2003); all-time leading money winner on the PBA Tour; has 40 PBA titles; won 6 World Horseshoe Pitching titles.

**Hack Wilson** (b. Apr. 26, 1900, d. Nov. 23, 1948): Baseball; as a Chicago Cub, he produced one of baseball's most outstanding seasons in 1930 with 56 home runs, .356 batting average, 105 walks and, most amazingly, a major league record 191 RBIs that still stands; finished career with 1,461 hits, 244 homers, 1,062 RBIs; member of Baseball Hall of Fame.

**Dave Winfield** (b. Oct. 3, 1951): Baseball OF-DH; selected in 4 major sports league drafts in 1973—NFL, NBA, ABA, and MLB; chose baseball and played in 12 All-Star Games over 22-year career; at age 41, helped lead Toronto to World Series title in 1992; 3,110 hits and 465 HRs.

**Katarina Witt** (b. Dec. 3, 1965): East German figure skater; 4-time world champion (1984-85,87-88); won consecutive Olympic gold medals (1984,88).

**John Wooden** (b. Oct. 14, 1910): Basketball; College Player of Year at Purdue in 1932; coached UCLA to 88 straight wins (1971-74), 10 national titles (1964-65,67-73,75); inducted into the Hall of Fame as both player and coach; career college coaching record of 664-162 over 29 years.

**Tiger Woods** (b. Dec. 30, 1975): Golfer; 3-time winner of U.S. Amateur (1994-96); won 6 events and broke the single season money record in his 1st full season on PGA Tour; won 1997 Masters by a record 18-under par and 13 strokes; won 2nd major at 1999 PGA Championship; in 2000 won the U.S. Open at Pebble Beach by a record 15 strokes, the British Open by 8 strokes and the PGA Championship in a playoff; held all 4 Major titles simultaneously with his win at 2001 Masters; has since won 4 more majors: 2 Masters (2002,05), 2002 U.S. Open and 2005 British Open; all-time PGA Tour money leader; 1 of only 5 players to win all 4 Grand Slam titles (others are Hogan, Nicklaus, Player and Sarazen).

**Mickey Wright** (b. Feb. 14, 1935): Golfer; won 3 of 4 majors (LPGA, U.S. Open, Titleholders) in 1961; 4-time winner of both U.S. Open and LPGA titles; 82 career wins including 13 majors.

**Early Wynn** (b. Jan. 6, 1920, d. Mar. 4, 1999): Baseball RHP; won 20 games 5 times; Cy Young winner in 1959; 300-244 record in 23 years.

**Kristi Yamaguchi** (b. July 12, 1971): Figure Skating; finished second in the 1991 American nationals but won the world title that year; dominated the sport in 1992 by winning the national, world and Olympic titles and then turned professional.

**Cale Yarborough** (b. Mar. 27, 1940): Auto racer; 3-time NASCAR national champion (1976-78); 4-time winner of Daytona 500 (1968,77,83-84); 83 career NASCAR wins.

**Carl Yastrzemski** (b. Aug. 22, 1939): Baseball OF; led AL in batting 3 times; won Triple Crown and MVP in 1967; had 3,419 hits and 452 HRs in 23 years with Boston Red Sox; member of Hall of Fame.

**Cy Young** (b. Mar. 29, 1867, d. Nov. 4, 1955): Baseball RHP; all-time leader in wins (511), losses (313), complete games (751) and innings pitched (7,356); had career 2.63 ERA in 22 years (1890-1911); 30-game winner 5 times and 20-game winner 11 other times; threw three no-hitters and a perfect game (1904); annual AL and NL pitching awards named after him.

**Dick Young** (b. Oct. 17, 1917, d. Aug. 31, 1987): Confrontational sportswriter for 44 years with NY tabloids; as baseball beat writer and columnist, he led change from flowery prose to hard-nosed reporting.

**Sheila Young** (b. Oct. 14, 1950): Speed skater and cyclist; 1st U.S. athlete to win 3 medals at Winter Olympics (1976); won speed skating overall and sprint cycling world titles in 1976.

**Steve Young** (b. Oct. 11, 1961): Football QB; All-America at BYU (1983); NFL Player of Year (1992) with SF 49ers; only QB to lead NFL in passer rating 4 straight years (1991-94); rating of 112.8 in 1994 is highest ever; threw record 6 TD passes in MVP performance in Super Bowl XXIX; retired with NFL records for highest passer rating (96.8) and completion pct. (64.4); 232 career TD passes and 33,124 yards.

**Robin Yount** (b. Sept. 16, 1955): Baseball SS-OF; AL MVP at 2 positions—as SS in 1982 and OF in '89; retired after 1993 season with 3,142 hits, 251 HRs and a major-league-record 123 sacrifice flies after 20 seasons with Brewers; inducted into Hall of Fame in 1999.

**Steve Yzerman** (b. May 9, 1965): Hockey C; Captained the Detroit Red Wings to 3 Stanley Cup wins (1997-98,2002); won the Conn Smythe Trophy as the playoff MVP in 1998; one of only 14 NHL players to score more than 600 goals; 1,721 career points.

**Mario Zagalo** (b. Aug. 9, 1931): Soccer; Brazilian forward who is one of only two men (Franz Beckenbauer is the other) to serve as both captain (1962) and coach (1970,94) of World Cup champion.

**Babe Didrikson Zaharias** (b. June 26, 1911, d. Sept. 27, 1956): All-around athlete who was chosen AP Female Athlete of Year 6 times from 1932-54; won 2 gold medals (javelin and 80-meter hurdles) and a silver (high jump) at 1932 Olympics; played baseball and acquired the nickname "Babe" for her tape measure home runs; real first name was Mildred; took up golf in 1935 and went on to win 55 pro and amateur events; won 10 majors, including 3 U.S. Opens (1948,50,54); helped found LPGA in 1949; chosen female "Athlete of the Half Century" by AP in 1950; when asked if there was anything she didn't play, she replied, "Yeah, dolls."

**Tony Zale** (b. May 29, 1913, d. March 20, 1997): Boxer; 2-time world middleweight champion (1941-47,48); fought Rocky Graziano for title 3 times in 21 months in 1947-48, winning twice; pro record 67-18-2 with 44 KOs.

**Frank Zamboni** (b. Jan. 16, 1901, d. July 27, 1988): Mechanic, ice salesman and skating rink owner in Paramount, Calif.; invented ice-resurfacing machine in 1949; now there are few skating rinks without one as thousands have been sold in over 35 countries.

**Emil Zatopek** (b. Sept. 19, 1922, d. Nov. 22, 2000): Czech distance runner; winner of 1948 Olympic gold medal at 10,000 meters; 4 years later, won unprecedented Olympic triple crown (5,000 meters, 10,000 meters and marathon) at 1952 Games in Helsinki.

**Zinedine Zidane** (b. June 23, 1972): French soccer player; 2-time FIFA World Player of the Year (1998, 2000); led host nation France to 1998 World Cup title, scoring twice in final against Brazil; a record $64M transfer fee sent the midfielder from Juventus to Real Madrid in 2001.

**John Ziegler** (b. Feb. 9, 1934): Hockey; NHL president from 1977-92; negotiated settlement with rival WHA in 1979 that led to inviting four WHA teams (Edmonton, Hartford, Quebec and Winnipeg) to join NHL; stepped down June 12, 1992, 2 months after settling 10-day players' strike.

**Nick Zito** (b. Feb. 6, 1948): Horse racing; trainer who has saddled 2 Kentucky Derby winners (Strike the Gold in 1991 and Go for Gin in 1994), 1996 Preakness Stakes winner (Louis Quartoze) and 2004 Belmont Stakes winner (Birdstone).

**Pirmin Zurbriggen** (b. Feb. 4, 1963): Swiss alpine skier; 4-time World Cup overall champ (1984,87-88,90) and 3-time runner-up; 40 World Cup wins in 10 years; won gold and bronze medals at 1988 Olympics.

# Ballparks & Arenas

The damage caused by Hurricane Katrina has left the future of the **Louisiana Superdome** uncertain.

AP/Wide World Photos

# Coming Attractions

SPORTS ALMANAC

## 2005

### NBA BASKETBALL

**Charlotte** (East): The new Charlotte Bobcats Arena (title sponsor pending) opened Oct. 21, 2005 with a concert by the Rolling Stones. The new building is home to the NBA's Charlotte Bobcats, the WNBA's Charlotte Sting and the ECHL's Charlotte Checkers. The arena, which seats 18,500 (including 60 luxury suites) for NBA basketball and 14,100 for hockey, was built by the City of Charlotte and Mecklenburg County and cost approximately $265 million. The building is located in Center City Charlotte bounded by East Trade, Fifth and North Caldwell streets and the South Corridor Light Rail Line. The key feature inside the arena is its one-of-a-kind high-resolution LED scoreboard.

## 2006

### BASEBALL

**St. Louis** (NL): The Cardinals broke ground on the site of the new Busch Stadium (Anheuser-Busch Cos. Inc. is the title sponsor) on Dec. 19, 2003. The site is on the northern edge of the current Busch Stadium (Walnut Street) to the base of the elevated Interstate 40/64 highway (Poplar Street). The open-air, baseball-only park will offer a spectacular view of the Gateway Arch and St. Louis skyline. The seating capacity will be approximately 46,000. The estimated cost of the project, including a new Cardinals Hall of Fame and Museum, is $387.5 million. The new ballpark's opening is scheduled for April 2006. The ballpark will initially open at a reduced seating capacity but should be fully functional by midseason.

### NFL FOOTBALL

**Arizona** (NFC): Construction on a new home for the Arizona Cardinals and college football's annual Fiesta Bowl is well underway. The 63,000-seat (expandable to 75,000 for major events) stadium is located in Glendale, Ariz. (15 miles west of Phoenix) on a site on the Loop 101 (Agua Fria Freeway) south of Glendale Avenue and adjacent to the new home of the NHL's Coyotes. The stadium will have a partially retractable roof and wall and feature a natural grass field that can be rolled out into the parking lot to help it grow. The stadium will include 88 luxury suites and 7,000 club seats; the estimated cost of the complex is $450 million. The Cardinals' home opener is scheduled for September 2006.

## 2007

### NHL HOCKEY

**New Jersey** (East): After several starts and stops, the Devils signed an agreement to build a new 18,000-seat arena in Newark. Groundbreaking on the new construction was scheduled for Oct. 3, 2005. Funding from a new lease on Newark Airport will help pay for the project. The arena site is located in downtown Newark near Penn Station; estimated cost: $310 million of which the city will contribute $210 million. The arena will include 68 luxury suites and the earliest opening would be prior to the 2007-08 NHL season.

## 2008

### BASEBALL

**Washington** (NL): The latest plans call for a $440 million bond package that would pay for a new ballpark along the Anacostia River at South Capitol and M Streets for the relocated Washington Nationals (formerly known as the Montreal Expos). The proposal also includes a $13 million renovation of RFK Stadium, where the team will play for three seasons until the new park is ready. The home opener will likely be no earlier than 2008.

### NBA BASKETBALL

**New Jersey** (East): New Nets owner Bruce Ratner plans to move the team to Brooklyn and build a 19,000-seat, Frank Gehry-designed arena that will be part of a $3.5 billion office, residential and shopping complex. The plans got a boost in September 2005 when New York's Metropolitan Transportation Authority voted to sell an 8.3-acre parcel to Ratner for $100 million, $50 million less than another offer and $114.5 million less than the appraised value. The plans still face opposition from area residents and the arena is expected to be open for business no sooner than 2008. The entire project is expected to take 10 years to complete.

### NFL FOOTBALL

**Indianapolis** (AFC): A ceremonial groundbreaking took place on Sept. 20, 2005 on a new home for the Colts. Indiana Stadium (corporate title sponsor pending) will seat 63,000 and cost about $500 million. The new stadium will feature a retractable-roof and be located in the parking lot across South Street from the RCA Dome, which will continue to serve as the Colts' home until the new stadium is completed. That is scheduled to be in time for the 2008 season.

## 2009

### BASEBALL

**Florida** (NL): Discussions for a new ballpark for the Marlins between the team and local government are currently stalled with both sides saying the can't contribute any more money; plans currently call for a new retractable-roofed, 38,000-seat ballpark to be built in Miami-Dade County. The estimated cost is $450 million. The City of Miami and Miami-Dade County have reportedly promised $166 million in tourist taxes to the project and the team has committed $192 million, leaving the plan roughly $100 million short. No timetable has been set forth but the earliest home opener would likely be April 2009.

**Minnesota** (AL): The Twins are seeking legislative approval for a sales tax initiative that would be the primary funding source for a new ballpark in the Minneapolis Warehouse District. If approved by the state legislature, the .15 percent Hennepin County sales tax would pay for most of the proposed $360 million open-air ballpark, scheduled to open by 2009. The Twins announced they would contribute $125 million toward the construction of the ballpark. The new ballpark would seat 42,000 including 72 suites and 4,000 club seats. It would be located at the Rapid Park site behind the

AP/Wide World Photos

Following the 2005 St. Louis Cardinals season, demolition of **Busch Stadium** (right) will begin to make way for the new Busch Stadium (left) set to open in 2006. The last of the "cookie-cutter" stadiums, Busch opened in 1966

Target Center, which is located at the convergence of I-394 and I-94, the Hiawatha Light Rail line and the proposed Northstar Commuter Rail line

**New York** (AL): In 2005, New York Governor George Pataki and New York City Mayor Michael Bloomberg announced an agreement with the Yankees for an area revitalization plan that will include a new Yankee Stadium to be built just north of the existing facility in Macombs Dam and Mullaly Parks in time for the opening of the 2009 baseball season. The plan calls for a new waterfront park and esplanade along the Harlem River, major infrastructure improvements, and the construction of more than 5,000 new parking spaces. The Yankees agreed to privately finance the new $800 million facility with the city chipping in $135 million to replace parkland (and make the necessary infrastructure improvements) and the State on the hook for $70 million for the construction of new parking facilities. The new retro-styled park would have 50,800 seats, fewer than "The House that Ruth Built" but it would have a lot more luxury suites. The Yankees, which anticipate breaking ground by summer 2006, hired HOK Sport as their architect.

**Oakland** (AL): In August 2005, A's owner Lew Wolff announced plans for a new baseball-only stadium in Oakland. If built, the ballpark would be located just north of McAfee Coliseum. Plans call for the ballpark to be the smallest in Major League Baseball with an approximate seating capacity of 35,000. Above the seating area in left and center field would be a hotel or apartment buildings with views of the field. The ballpark is expected to cost between $300 and $400 million, with most of the money coming from the team. Meanwhile, the city of San Jose is reportedly attempting to lure the team away with a ballpark proposal of their own. The earliest opener would be April 2009.

## NFL FOOTBALL

**Dallas** (NFC): Plans for a new stadium for the Cowboys were unveiled in 2004. The 75,000-seat stadium would be located south of the Tom Landry Freeway, next door to the Texas Rangers' Ameriquest Field in Arlington. The retractable-roof stadium would be expandable to hold up to 90,000 fans and cost an estimated $650 million. The plan which would be partly financed through an increase in sales, hotel and car-rental taxes, was set to go to the voters on Nov. 2, 2004. Earliest home opener would be in the fall of 2009.

### Hurricane Sends Them Packing

Despite the incredible devastation that crippled the city of New Orleans in the wake of Hurricane Katrina in August 2005, many professional and college sports teams needed to take the field. Perhaps most acutely affected were the NFL's New Orleans Saints, whose homefield at the **Louisiana Superdome** was badly damaged and used to shelter storm and flood refugees.

The Saints were displaced, possibly permanently, and played their first "home" game on Sept. 19 at Giants Stadium in New Jersey, losing 27-10 to the Giants. The Saints played the rest of their 2005 home dates split between **LSU's Tiger Stadium** in Baton Rouge and San Antonio's Alamodome.

The future of the Superdome is uncertain. The roof developed sizeable holes during the hurricane and water leaked throughout the building. The building will need to be cleaned and decontaminated before an intelligent decision can be made about rehabbing the place. The NFL is making plans to find a home for the Saints for the 2006 season.

The NBA's New Orleans Hornets were forced to leave a storm-damaged New Orleans Arena and signed a deal to play 35 games of their 2005-06 schedule at Oklahoma City's Ford Center and play their six remaining home games at LSU's **Maravich Assembly Center**. The Arena is reportedly less damaged than the Superdome and could be back in business relatively soon.

The annual college bowl games in New Orleans—The BCS's Sugar Bowl and the lower tier New Orleans Bowl—also had to scramble to find new quarters. At press time, the new home for the 2006 Sugar Bowl was likely to be Atlanta's **Georgia Dome** but organizers were also looking at Tiger Stadium in an effort to keep the game in Louisiana. The New Orleans bowl, scheduled for Dec. 20, 2005, was looking to move to Cajun Field in Lafayette, La.

### Oh Yeah...

Plans are also in the works for new stadiums for the San Diego Chargers, San Francisco 49ers and New York Mets but all still face local approval. The N.Y. Giants and Jets announced plans for a joint venture to build a new 80,000-seat stadium in the Meadowlands.

# Home, Sweet Home

The home fields, home courts and home ice of the AL, NL, NBA, NFL, NHL, NCAA Division I-A college football and Division I basketball. Also included are MLS stadiums, Formula One, Champ Car, Indy Racing League and NASCAR auto racing tracks. Attendance figures for the 2004 NFL regular season and the 2004-05 NBA and NHL regular seasons are provided. See baseball chapter for 2005 AL and NL attendance figures.

## MAJOR LEAGUE BASEBALL

### American League

| | | Built | Capacity | LF | LCF | CF | RCF | RF | Field |
|---|---|---|---|---|---|---|---|---|---|
| Baltimore Orioles | Oriole Park at Camden Yards | 1992 | 48,190 | 337 | 376 | 406 | 391 | 320 | Grass |
| Boston Red Sox | Fenway Park | 1912 | 38,815 | 310 | 379 | 390* | 380 | 302 | Grass |
| Chicago White Sox | U.S. Cellular Field | 1991 | 41,000 | 330 | 377 | 400 | 372 | 335 | Grass |
| Cleveland Indians | Jacobs Field | 1994 | 43,068 | 325 | 370 | 405 | 375 | 325 | Grass |
| Detroit Tigers | Comerica Park | 2000 | 40,120 | 345 | 395 | 420 | 365 | 330 | Grass |
| Kansas City Royals | Kauffman Stadium | 1973 | 40,793 | 330 | 375 | 400 | 375 | 330 | Grass |
| Los Angeles Angels of Anaheim | Angel Stadium of Anaheim | 1966 | 45,030 | 365 | 387 | 400 | 370 | 365 | Grass |
| Minnesota Twins | Hubert H. Humphrey Metrodome | 1982 | 48,678 | 343 | 385 | 408 | 367 | 327 | Turf |
| New York Yankees | Yankee Stadium | 1923 | 57,478 | 318 | 399 | 408 | 385 | 314 | Grass |
| Oakland Athletics | McAfee Coliseum | 1966 | 43,662 | 330 | 367 | 400 | 367 | 330 | Grass |
| Seattle Mariners | SAFECO Field | 1999 | 47,116 | 331 | 390 | 405 | 387 | 327 | Grass |
| Tampa Bay Devil Rays | Tropicana Field | 1990 | 43,761 | 315 | 370 | 404 | 370 | 322 | Turf |
| Texas Rangers | Ameriquest Field in Arlington | 1994 | 49,115 | 332 | 390 | 400 | 381 | 325 | Grass |
| Toronto Blue Jays | Rogers Centre | 1989 | 50,516 | 328 | 375 | 400 | 375 | 328 | Turf |

*The straightaway center-field fence at Fenway Park is 390 feet from home plate but the deepest part of center-field, a.k.a. "the Triangle," is 420 feet away. The left-field fence, known as "the Green Monster," is 37 feet tall. Two hundred and seventy seats were added to the top of the wall in 2003 replacing the 23-foot screen that previously topped the Monster.

### National League

| | | Built | Capacity | LF | LCF | CF | RCF | RF | Field |
|---|---|---|---|---|---|---|---|---|---|
| Arizona Diamondbacks | Chase Field | 1998 | 49,033 | 330 | 376 | 407 | 376 | 334 | Grass |
| Atlanta Braves | Turner Field | 1996 | 50,091 | 335 | 380 | 401 | 390 | 330 | Grass |
| Chicago Cubs | Wrigley Field | 1914 | 39,111 | 355 | 368 | 400 | 368 | 353 | Grass |
| Cincinnati Reds | Great American Ball Park | 2003 | 42,059 | 328 | 379 | 404 | 370 | 325 | Grass |
| Colorado Rockies | Coors Field | 1995 | 50,449 | 347 | 390 | 415 | 375 | 350 | Grass |
| Florida Marlins | Dolphins Stadium | 1987 | 36,331 | 330 | 385 | 434 | 385 | 345 | Grass |
| Houston Astros | Minute Maid Park | 2000 | 40,950 | 315 | 362 | 436 | 373 | 326 | Grass |
| Los Angeles Dodgers | Dodger Stadium | 1962 | 56,000 | 330 | 385 | 395 | 385 | 330 | Grass |
| Milwaukee Brewers | Miller Park | 2001 | 42,400 | 340 | 374 | 400 | 378 | 345 | Grass |
| New York Mets | Shea Stadium | 1964 | 56,749 | 338 | 378 | 410 | 378 | 338 | Grass |
| Philadelphia Phillies | Citizens Bank Park | 2004 | 43,000 | 329 | 369 | 401* | 369 | 330 | Grass |
| Pittsburgh Pirates | PNC Park | 2001 | 37,898 | 326 | 368 | 399* | 375 | 324 | Grass |
| St. Louis Cardinals | Busch Stadium | 2006 | 46,000† | 336 | 390 | 400 | 390 | 335 | Grass |
| San Diego Padres | PETCO Park | 2004 | 46,000 | 334 | 367 | 396* | 387 | 322 | Grass |
| San Francisco Giants | SBC Park | 2000 | 41,467 | 339 | 364 | 399 | 421 | 309 | Grass |
| Washington Nationals | RFK Stadium | 1962 | 45,250 | 335 | 380 | 410 | 380 | 335 | Grass |

*The deepest part of PNC Park is 410 feet between straightaway center and left-center. The deepest part of Citizens Bank Park is 409 feet in part of left-center. The deepest part of PETCO Park is 411 feet in part of right-center.

†The new Busch Stadium will open at a reduced capacity, due to the site overlap with the to-be-demolished Busch Stadium but is scheduled to be operating at a full capacity of 46,000 by mid-season.

## Rank by Capacity

### AL
| | |
|---|---|
| New York | 57,478 |
| Toronto | 50,516 |
| Texas | 49,115 |
| Minnesota | 48,678 |
| Baltimore | 48,190 |
| Seattle | 47,116 |
| Los Angeles | 45,030 |
| Tampa Bay | 43,761 |
| Oakland | 43,662 |
| Cleveland | 43,068 |
| Chicago | 41,000 |
| Kansas City | 40,793 |
| Detroit | 40,120 |
| Boston | 34,892 |

### NL
| | |
|---|---|
| New York | 56,749 |
| Los Angeles | 56,000 |
| Colorado | 50,449 |
| Atlanta | 50,091 |
| Arizona | 49,033 |
| Montreal | 46,500 |
| St. Louis | 46,000 |
| San Diego | 46,000 |
| Philadelphia | 43,000 |
| Milwaukee | 42,400 |
| Cincinnati | 42,059 |
| San Francisco | 41,467 |
| Houston | 40,950 |
| Chicago | 39,111 |
| Pittsburgh | 37,898 |
| Florida | 36,331 |

## Rank by Age

### AL
| | |
|---|---|
| Boston | 1912 |
| New York | 1923 |
| Los Angeles | 1966 |
| Oakland | 1966 |
| Kansas City | 1973 |
| Minnesota | 1982 |
| Toronto | 1989 |
| Tampa Bay | 1990 |
| Chicago | 1991 |
| Baltimore | 1992 |
| Cleveland | 1994 |
| Texas | 1994 |
| Seattle | 1999 |
| Detroit | 2000 |

**Note:** New York's Yankee Stadium (AL) was rebuilt in 1976.

### NL
| | |
|---|---|
| Chicago | 1914 |
| Los Angeles | 1962 |
| New York | 1964 |
| Montreal | 1976 |
| Florida | 1987 |
| Atlanta | 1993 |
| Colorado | 1995 |
| Arizona | 1998 |
| Houston | 2000 |
| San Francisco | 2000 |
| Milwaukee | 2001 |
| Pittsburgh | 2001 |
| Cincinnati | 2003 |
| Philadelphia | 2004 |
| San Diego | 2004 |
| St. Louis | 2006 |

# Home Fields

Listed below are the principal home fields used through the years by current American and National League teams. The NL became a major league in 1876, the AL in 1901.

The capacity figures in the right-hand column indicate the largest seating capacity of the ballpark while the club played there. Capacity figures before 1915 (and the introduction of concrete grandstands) are sketchy at best and have been left blank.

## American League

### Baltimore Orioles

| | | |
|---|---|---|
| 1901 | Lloyd Street Grounds (Milwaukee) . . . | — |
| 1902–53 | Sportsman's Park II (St. Louis) . . . . . | 30,500 |
| 1954–91 | Memorial Stadium (Baltimore) . . . . . | 53,371 |
| 1992– | Oriole Park at Camden Yards . . . . . | 48,190 |

### Boston Red Sox

| | | |
|---|---|---|
| 1901–11 | Huntington Ave. Grounds . . . . . . . | — |
| 1912– | Fenway Park . . . . . . . . . . . . . . | 38,815 |
| | (1934 capacity—27,000) | |

### Chicago White Sox

| | | |
|---|---|---|
| 1901–10 | Southside Park . . . . . . . . . . . . | — |
| 1910–90 | Comiskey Park I . . . . . . . . . . . | 43,931 |
| 1991– | U.S. Cellular Field . . . . . . . . . . | 41,000 |
| | (2003 capacity—46,943) | |

### Cleveland Indians

| | | |
|---|---|---|
| 1901–09 | League Park I . . . . . . . . . . . . | — |
| 1910–46 | League Park II . . . . . . . . . . . | 21,414 |
| 1932–93 | Cleveland Stadium . . . . . . . . . | 74,483 |
| 1994– | Jacobs Field . . . . . . . . . . . . | 43,068 |

### Detroit Tigers

| | | |
|---|---|---|
| 1901–11 | Bennett Park . . . . . . . . . . . . | — |
| 1912–99 | Tiger Stadium . . . . . . . . . . . | 46,945 |
| 2000– | Comerica Park . . . . . . . . . . . | 40,120 |
| | (1912 capacity—23,000) | |

### Kansas City Royals

| | | |
|---|---|---|
| 1969–72 | Municipal Stadium . . . . . . . . . | 35,020 |
| 1973– | Kauffman Stadium . . . . . . . . . | 40,793 |
| | (1973 capacity—40,762) | |

### Los Angeles Angels of Anaheim

| | | |
|---|---|---|
| 1961 | Wrigley Field (Los Angeles) . . . . . | 20,457 |
| 1962-65 | Dodger Stadium . . . . . . . . . . | 56,000 |
| 1966– | Angel Stadium of Anaheim . . . . . | 45,030 |
| | (1966 capacity—43,250) | |

### Minnesota Twins

| | | |
|---|---|---|
| 1901-02 | American League Park (Washington, DC) | — |
| 1903-60 | Griffith Stadium . . . . . . . . . . | 27,410 |
| 1960-81 | Metropolitan Stadium | |
| | (Bloomington, MN) . . . . . . . | 45,919 |
| 1982– | HHH Metrodome (Minneapolis) . . . | 48,678 |
| | (1982 capacity—54,000) | |

### New York Yankees

| | | |
|---|---|---|
| 1901-02 | Oriole Park (Baltimore) . . . . . . . | — |
| 1903-12 | Hilltop Park (New York) . . . . . . | — |
| 1913-22 | Polo Grounds II . . . . . . . . . . | 38,000 |
| 1923-73 | Yankee Stadium I . . . . . . . . . | 67,224 |
| 1974-75 | Shea Stadium . . . . . . . . . . . | 55,101 |
| 1976– | Yankee Stadium II . . . . . . . . . | 57,478 |
| | (1976 capacity—57,145) | |

### Oakland Athletics

| | | |
|---|---|---|
| 1901-08 | Columbia Park (Philadelphia) . . . . | — |
| 1909-54 | Shibe Park . . . . . . . . . . . . . | 33,608 |
| 1955-67 | Municipal Stadium (Kansas City) . . | 35,020 |
| 1968– | McAfee Coliseum . . . . . . . . . | 43,662 |
| | (1968 capacity—48,621) | |

### Seattle Mariners

| | | |
|---|---|---|
| 1977-99 | The Kingdome . . . . . . . . . . . | 59,166 |
| 1999– | SAFECO Field . . . . . . . . . . . | 47,116 |

### Tampa Bay Devil Rays

| | | |
|---|---|---|
| 1990– | Tropicana Field . . . . . . . . . . | 43,761 |

### Texas Rangers

| | | |
|---|---|---|
| 1961 | Griffith Stadium (Washington, DC) . | 27,410 |
| 1962-71 | RFK Stadium . . . . . . . . . . . | 45,016 |
| 1972-93 | Arlington Stadium (Texas) . . . . . | 43,521 |
| 1994– | Ameriquest Field in Arlington . . . | 49,115 |

### Toronto Blue Jays

| | | |
|---|---|---|
| 1977-89 | Exhibition Stadium . . . . . . . . | 43,737 |
| 1989– | Rogers Centre . . . . . . . . . . | 50,516 |
| | (1989 capacity—49,500) | |

**Ballpark Name Changes:** ANAHEIM—**Angel Stadium of Anaheim**, originally Anaheim Stadium (1966-98), then Edison International Field of Anaheim (1998-2003); CHICAGO—**Comiskey Park I** originally White Sox Park (1910-12), then Comiskey Park in 1913, then White Sox Park again in 1962, then Comiskey Park again in 1976; **U.S. Cellular Field** originally Comiskey Park (1991-2002); CLEVELAND—**League Park** renamed Dunn Field in 1920, then League Park again in 1928; **Cleveland Stadium** originally Municipal Stadium (1932-74); DETROIT—**Tiger Stadium** originally Navin Field (1912-37), then Briggs Stadium (1938-60); KANSAS CITY—**Kauffman Stadium** originally Royals Stadium (1973-93); LOS ANGELES—**Dodger Stadium** referred to as Chavez Revine by AL while Angels played there (1962-65); OAKLAND—**McAfee Coliseum** originally Oakland Alameda Coliseum (1968-98), then Network Associates Coliseum (1998-2004); PHILADELPHIA—**Shibe Park** renamed Connie Mack Stadium in 1953; ST. LOUIS—**Sportsman's Park** renamed Busch Stadium in 1953; WASHINGTON—**Griffith Stadium** originally National Park (1892-1920), **RFK Stadium** originally D.C. Stadium (1961-68); TEXAS—**Ameriquest Field in Arlington** originally The Ballpark in Arlington (1994-2004); TORONTO—**Rogers Centre** originally Skydome (1989-2005).

## National League

### Arizona Diamondbacks

| | | |
|---|---|---|
| 1998– | Chase Field . . . . . . . . . . . . | 49,033 |

### Atlanta Braves

| | | |
|---|---|---|
| 1876–94 | South End Grounds I (Boston) . . . . | — |
| 1894–1914 | South End Grounds II . . . . . . . | — |
| 1915–52 | Braves Field . . . . . . . . . . . | 40,000 |
| 1953–65 | County Stadium (Milwaukee) . . . . | 43,394 |
| 1966–96 | Atlanta-Fulton County Stadium . . . | 52,769 |
| | (1966 capacity—50,000) | |
| 1997– | Turner Field . . . . . . . . . . . | 50,091 |

### Chicago Cubs

| | | |
|---|---|---|
| 1876–77 | State Street Grounds . . . . . . . . | — |
| 1878–84 | Lakefront Park . . . . . . . . . . . | — |
| 1885–91 | West Side Park . . . . . . . . . . . | — |
| 1891–93 | Brotherhood Park . . . . . . . . . | — |
| 1893–1915 | West Side Grounds . . . . . . . . . | — |
| 1916– | Wrigley Field . . . . . . . . . . . | 39,111 |
| | (1916 capacity—16,000) | |

### Cincinnati Reds

| | | |
|---|---|---|
| 1876–79 | Avenue Grounds . . . . . . . . . . | — |
| 1880 | Bank Street Grounds . . . . . . . . | — |
| 1890–1901 | Redland Field I . . . . . . . . . . | — |
| 1902–11 | Palace of the Fans . . . . . . . . . | — |
| 1912–70 | Crosley Field . . . . . . . . . . . | 29,603 |
| 1970–2002 | Cinergy Field . . . . . . . . . . . | 40,007 |
| | (1970 capacity—52,000) | |
| 2003– | Great American Ball Park . . . . . . | 42,059 |

## Major League Baseball (Cont.)

### Colorado Rockies
| | | |
|---|---|---|
| 1993–94 | Mile High Stadium (Denver) | 76,100 |
| 1995– | Coors Field | 50,449 |

### Florida Marlins
| | | |
|---|---|---|
| 1993– | Dolphins Stadium (Miami) | 36,331 |
| | (1993 capacity—47,662) | |

### Houston Astros
| | | |
|---|---|---|
| 1962–64 | Colt Stadium | 32,601 |
| 1965–99 | The Astrodome | 54,370 |
| | (1965 capacity—45,011) | |
| 2000– | Minute Maid Park | 40,950 |

### Los Angeles Dodgers
| | | |
|---|---|---|
| 1890 | Washington Park I (Brooklyn) | — |
| 1891–97 | Eastern Park | — |
| 1898–1912 | Washington Park II | — |
| 1913–55 | Ebbets Field | 31,497 |
| 1956–57 | Ebbets Field | 31,497 |
| | & Roosevelt Stadium (Jersey City) | 24,167 |
| 1958–61 | Memorial Coliseum (Los Angeles) | 93,600 |
| 1962– | Dodger Stadium | 56,000 |

### Milwaukee Brewers
| | | |
|---|---|---|
| 1969 | Sick's Stadium (Seattle) | 59,166 |
| 1970– | County Stadium (Milwaukee) | 53,192 |
| 2000 | (1970 capacity—46,620) | |
| 2001– | Miller Park | 42,400 |

### New York Mets
| | | |
|---|---|---|
| 1962–63 | Polo Grounds | 55,987 |
| 1964– | Shea Stadium | 56,749 |
| | (1964 capacity—55,101) | |

### Philadelphia Phillies
| | | |
|---|---|---|
| 1883–86 | Recreation Park | — |
| 1887–90 | Huntingdon Ave. Grounds | — |
| 1895–1938 | Baker Bowl | 18,800 |
| 1938–70 | Shibe Park | 33,608 |

### Philadelphia Phillies (Cont.)
| | | |
|---|---|---|
| 1971–2003 | Veterans Stadium | 62,418 |
| 2004– | Citizens Bank Park | 43,000 |

### Pittsburgh Pirates
| | | |
|---|---|---|
| 1887–90 | Recreation Park | — |
| 1891–1909 | Exposition Park | — |
| 1909–70 | Forbes Field | 35,000 |
| 1970–2000 | Three Rivers Stadium | 47,687 |
| | (1970 capacity—50,235) | |
| 2001– | PNC Park | 37,898 |

### St. Louis Cardinals
| | | |
|---|---|---|
| 1876–77 | Sportsman's Park I | — |
| 1885–86 | Vandeventer Lot | — |
| 1892–1920 | Robison Field | 18,000 |
| 1920–66 | Sportsman's Park II | 30,500 |
| 1966–2005 | Busch Stadium | 49,814 |
| 2006– | Busch Stadium II | 46,000 |

### San Diego Padres
| | | |
|---|---|---|
| 1969–2003 | Qualcomm Stadium | 66,083 |
| 2004– | PETCO Park | 46,000 |

### San Francisco Giants
| | | |
|---|---|---|
| 1876 | Union Grounds (Brooklyn) | — |
| 1883–88 | Polo Grounds I (New York) | — |
| 1889–90 | Manhattan Field | — |
| 1891–1957 | Polo Grounds II | 55,987 |
| 1958–59 | Seals Stadium (San Francisco) | 22,900 |
| 1960–99 | 3Com Park | 63,000 |
| | (1960 capacity—42,553) | |
| 2000– | SBC Park | 41,467 |

### Washington Nationals
| | | |
|---|---|---|
| 1969–76 | Jarry Park (Montreal) | 28,000 |
| 1977–2002 | Olympic Stadium | 46,500 |
| 2003–04 | Olympic Stadium | 46,500 |
| | & Hiram Bithon Stadium (San Juan) | 18,000 |
| 2005– | RFK Stadium (Washington D.C.) | 45,250 |

**Ballpark Name Changes:** ARIZONA—**Chase Field** originally named Bank One Ballpark (1998-2005); ATLANTA—**Atlanta-Fulton County Stadium** originally Atlanta Stadium (1966-74), **Turner Field** originally Centennial Olympic Stadium (1996); CHICAGO—**Wrigley Field** originally Weeghman Park (1914-17), then Cubs Park (1918-25); CINCINNATI—**Redland Field** originally League Park (1890-93), **Crosley Field** originally Redland Field II (1912-33) and **Cinergy Field** originally Riverfront Stadium (1970-96); FLORIDA—**Dolphins Stadium** originally Joe Robbie Stadium (1987-96), then Pro Player Stadium (1997-2004); HOUSTON—**Astrodome** originally Harris County Domed Stadium before it opened in 1965; **Enron Field** renamed Astros Field briefly and then Minute Maid Park in 2002; PHILADELPHIA—**Baker Field** originally Philadelphia Park (1895-1912), **Shibe Park** renamed Connie Mack Stadium in 1953; ST. LOUIS—**Robison Field** originally Vandeventer Lot, then League Park, then Cardinal Park all before becoming Robison Field in 1901, **Sportsman's Park** renamed Busch Stadium in 1953, and **Busch Stadium** originally Busch Memorial Stadium (1966-82); SAN DIEGO—**Qualcomm Stadium** originally San Diego Stadium (1967-81) and San Diego/Jack Murphy Stadium (1982-96); SAN FRANCISCO—**3Com Park** originally Candlestick Park (1960-95), **SBC Park** originally Pacific Bell Park (2000-03).

## NATIONAL BASKETBALL ASSOCIATION

### Western Conference

| | | Location | Built | Capacity |
|---|---|---|---|---|
| Dallas Mavericks | American Airlines Center | Dallas, Texas | 2001 | **19,200** |
| Denver Nuggets | Pepsi Center | Denver, Colo. | 1999 | **19,099** |
| Golden State Warriors | Oakland Arena | Oakland, Calif. | 1997 | **19,596** |
| Houston Rockets | Toyota Center | Houston, Texas | 2003 | **18,300** |
| Los Angeles Clippers | Staples Center | Los Angeles, Calif. | 1999 | **18,694** |
| Los Angeles Lakers | Staples Center | Los Angeles, Calif. | 1999 | **18,997** |
| Memphis Grizzlies | FedEx Forum | Memphis, Tenn. | 2004 | **18,400** |
| Minnesota Timberwolves | Target Center | Minneapolis, Minn. | 1990 | **19,006** |
| New Orleans Hornets* | Ford Center & Maravich Assembly Center | Oklahoma City, Okla. | 2002 | **19,675** |
| | | Baton Rouge, La. | 1971 | **14,164** |
| Phoenix Suns | America West Arena | Phoenix, Ariz. | 1992 | **19,023** |
| Portland Trail Blazers | Rose Garden | Portland, Ore. | 1995 | **19,980** |
| Sacramento Kings | ARCO Arena | Sacramento, Calif. | 1988 | **17,317** |
| San Antonio Spurs | SBC Center | San Antonio, Texas | 2002 | **18,500** |
| Seattle SuperSonics | KeyArena at Seattle Center | Seattle, Wash. | 1962 | **17,072** |
| Utah Jazz | Delta Center | Salt Lake City, Utah | 1991 | **19,911** |

*Due to the aftermath of Hurricane Katrina the New Orleans Hornets were forced out of New Orleans Arena and arranged to play 35 regular-season games at Oklahoma City's Ford Center and six games at LSU's Maravich Assembly Center.
**Notes:** Seattle's KeyArena was originally the Seattle Center Coliseum before being rebuilt in 1995; The Staples Center has different listed capacities for Clippers games and Lakers games because of different floor seating arrangements.

## Eastern Conference

| | | Location | Built | Capacity |
|---|---|---|---|---|
| Atlanta Hawks | Philips Arena | Atlanta, Ga. | 1999 | **19,445** |
| Boston Celtics | TD Banknorth Garden | Boston, Mass. | 1995 | **18,624** |
| Charlotte Bobcats | Charlotte Arena | Charlotte, N.C. | 2005 | **18,500** |
| Chicago Bulls | United Center | Chicago, Ill. | 1994 | **21,711** |
| Cleveland Cavaliers | The Quicken Loans Arena | Cleveland, Ohio | 1994 | **20,562** |
| Detroit Pistons | The Palace of Auburn Hills | Auburn Hills, Mich. | 1988 | **22,076** |
| Indiana Pacers | Conseco Fieldhouse | Indianapolis, Ind. | 1999 | **18,345** |
| Miami Heat | AmericanAirlines Arena | Miami, Fla. | 1999 | **16,500** |
| Milwaukee Bucks | Bradley Center | Milwaukee, Wisc. | 1988 | **18,717** |
| New Jersey Nets | Continental Airlines Arena | E. Rutherford, N.J. | 1981 | **20,049** |
| New York Knicks | Madison Square Garden | New York, N.Y. | 1968 | **19,763** |
| Orlando Magic | TD Waterhouse Centre | Orlando, Fla. | 1989 | **17,248** |
| Philadelphia 76ers | Wachovia Center | Philadelphia, Penn. | 1996 | **20,444** |
| Toronto Raptors | Air Canada Centre | Toronto, Ont. | 1999 | **19,800** |
| Washington Wizards | MCI Center | Washington, D.C. | 1997 | **20,674** |

## Rank by Capacity

| Western | | Eastern | |
|---|---|---|---|
| Portland | 19,980 | Detroit | 22,076 |
| Utah | 19,911 | Chicago | 21,711 |
| New Orleans | 19,675 | Washington | 20,674 |
| Golden State | 19,596 | Cleveland | 20,562 |
| Dallas | 19,200 | Philadelphia | 20,444 |
| Denver | 19,099 | New Jersey | 20,049 |
| Phoenix | 19,023 | Toronto | 19,800 |
| Minnesota | 19,006 | New York | 19,763 |
| LA Lakers | 18,997 | Atlanta | 19,445 |
| LA Clippers | 18,694 | Milwaukee | 18,717 |
| San Antonio | 18,500 | Boston | 18,624 |
| Memphis | 18,400 | Charlotte | 18,500 |
| Houston | 18,300 | Indiana | 18,345 |
| Sacramento | 17,317 | Orlando | 17,248 |
| Seattle | 17,072 | Miami | 16,500 |

## Rank by Age

| Western | | Eastern | |
|---|---|---|---|
| Seattle | 1962 | New York | 1968 |
| Sacramento | 1988 | New Jersey | 1981 |
| Minnesota | 1990 | Detroit | 1988 |
| Utah | 1991 | Milwaukee | 1988 |
| Phoenix | 1992 | Orlando | 1989 |
| Portland | 1995 | Chicago | 1994 |
| Golden St. | 1997 | Cleveland | 1994 |
| Denver | 1999 | Boston | 1995 |
| LA Clippers | 1999 | Philadelphia | 1996 |
| LA Lakers | 1999 | Washington | 1997 |
| Dallas | 2001 | Toronto | 1999 |
| San Antonio | 2002 | Atlanta | 1999 |
| New Orleans | 2002 | Indiana | 1999 |
| Houston | 2003 | Miami | 1999 |
| Memphis | 2004 | Charlotte | 2005 |

**Note:** The Seattle Center Coliseum was rebuilt and renamed KeyArena in 1995.

## 2004-05 NBA Attendance

Official overall attendance in the NBA for the 2004-05 season was 21,296,497 for an average per game crowd of 17,314 over 1,230 games. Teams in each conference are ranked by attendance over 41 home games based on total tickets distributed. Rank column refers to rank in entire league. Numbers in parentheses indicate conference rank in 2003-04. Note that Charlotte was an expansion team in 2004-05 and that New Orleans played in the Eastern Conference in 2003-04.

### Western Conference

| | | Attendance | Rank | Average |
|---|---|---|---|---|
| 1 | Dallas (1) | 822,533 | 3 | 20,061 |
| 2 | LA Lakers (3) | 770,494 | 7 | 18,792 |
| 3 | Utah (2) | 769,014 | 8 | 18,756 |
| 4 | San Antonio (4) | 750,970 | 9 | 18,316 |
| 5 | Phoenix (9) | 726,066 | 11 | 17,708 |
| 6 | Denver (6) | 723,949 | 12 | 17,657 |
| 7 | Sacramento (7) | 709,997 | 13 | 17,317 |
| 8 | Minnesota (5) | 704,438 | 15 | 17,181 |
| 9 | LA Clippers (11) | 696,181 | 18 | 16,980 |
| 10 | Memphis (14) | 691,362 | 19 | 16,862 |
| 11 | Portland (8) | 680,374 | 20 | 16,594 |
| 12 | Seattle (13) | 675,490 | 21 | 16,475 |
| 13 | Golden St. (10) | 670,368 | 22 | 16,350 |
| 14 | Houston (12) | 663,444 | 23 | 16,181 |
| 15 | New Orleans (14) | 583,070 | 30 | 14,221 |
| | TOTAL | 10,637,750 | — | 17,297 |

### Eastern Conference

| | | Attendance | Rank | Average |
|---|---|---|---|---|
| 1 | Detroit (1) | 905,119 | 1 | 22,076 |
| 2 | Chicago (2) | 828,384 | 2 | 20,204 |
| 3 | Miami (11) | 815,143 | 4 | 19,881 |
| 4 | New York (4) | 800,144 | 5 | 19,515 |
| 5 | Cleveland (6) | 784,249 | 6 | 19,128 |
| 6 | Philadelphia (3) | 732,686 | 10 | 17,870 |
| 7 | Washington (10) | 705,069 | 14 | 17,196 |
| 8 | Toronto (5) | 703,388 | 16 | 17,155 |
| 9 | Indiana (8) | 696,764 | 17 | 16,994 |
| 10 | Boston (9) | 656,081 | 24 | 16,001 |
| 11 | Milwaukee (7) | 637,009 | 25 | 15,536 |
| 12 | New Jersey (12) | 618,677 | 26 | 15,089 |
| 13 | Orlando (13) | 597,942 | 27 | 14,583 |
| 14 | Atlanta (15) | 592,729 | 28 | 14,456 |
| 15 | Charlotte | 591,701 | 29 | 14,431 |
| | TOTAL | 10,658,747 | — | 17,331 |

## Home Courts

Listed below are the principal home courts used through the years by current NBA teams. The largest capacity of each arena is noted in the right-hand column. ABA arenas (1967-76) are included for Denver, Indiana, New Jersey and San Antonio.

## Western Conference

### Dallas Mavericks

| | | |
|---|---|---|
| 1980–2000 | Reunion Arena | .18,187 |
| 2001– | American Airlines Center | .19,200 |

### Denver Nuggets

| | | |
|---|---|---|
| 1967–75 | Auditorium Arena | .6,841 |
| 1975–99 | McNichols Sports Arena | .17,171 |
| | (1975 capacity—16,700) | |
| 1999– | Pepsi Center | .19,099 |

### Golden State Warriors

| | | |
|---|---|---|
| 1946–52 | Philadelphia Arena | .7,777 |
| 1952–62 | Convention Hall (Philadelphia) | .9,200 |
| | & Philadelphia Arena | .7,777 |
| 1962–64 | Cow Palace (San Francisco) | .13,862 |
| 1964–66 | Civic Auditorium | .7,500 |
| | & (USF Memorial Gym) | .6,000 |
| 1966–67 | Cow Palace, Civic Auditorium | |
| | & Oakland Coliseum Arena | .15,000 |
| 1967–71 | Cow Palace | .14,500 |
| 1971–96 | Oakland Coliseum Arena | .15,025 |
| | (1971 capacity—12,905) | |
| 1996–97 | San Jose Arena | .18,500 |
| 1997– | The Arena in Oakland | .19,596 |

### Houston Rockets

| | | |
|---|---|---|
| 1967–71 | San Diego Sports Arena | .14,000 |
| 1971–72 | Hofheinz Pavilion (Houston) | .10,218 |
| 1972–73 | Hofheinz Pavilion | .10,218 |
| | & HemisFair Arena (San Antonio) | .10,446 |
| 1973–75 | Hofheinz Pavilion | .10,218 |
| 1975–2002 | Compaq Center | .16,285 |
| 2003– | Toyota Center | .18,300 |

### Los Angeles Clippers

| | | |
|---|---|---|
| 1970–78 | Memorial Auditorium (Buffalo) | .17,300 |
| 1978–84 | San Diego Sports Arena | .12,167 |
| 1985–94 | Los Angeles Sports Arena | .16,005 |
| 1994–99 | Los Angeles Sports Arena | .16,021 |
| | & Arrowhead Pond | .18,211 |
| 1999– | Staples Center | .18,694 |

### Los Angeles Lakers

| | | |
|---|---|---|
| 1948–60 | Minneapolis Auditorium | .10,000 |
| 1960–67 | Los Angeles Sports Arena | .14,781 |
| 1967–99 | Great Western Forum (Inglewood, CA) | .17,505 |
| | (1967 capacity—17,086) | |
| 1999– | Staples Center | .18,997 |

### Memphis Grizzlies

| | | |
|---|---|---|
| 1995–2001 | General Motors Place (Vancouver) | .19,193 |
| 2001–03 | The Pyramid (Memphis, TN) | .19,342 |
| 2004– | FedEx Forum | .18,400 |

### Minnesota Timberwolves

| | | |
|---|---|---|
| 1989–90 | Hubert H. Humphrey Metrodome | .23,000 |
| 1990– | Target Center | .19,006 |

### New Orleans Hornets

| | | |
|---|---|---|
| 1988–2002 | Charlotte Coliseum | .19,925 |
| | (1988 capacity—23,500) | |

### New Orleans (Cont.)

| | | |
|---|---|---|
| 2002–05 | New Orleans Arena | .18,500 |
| 2005-06 | Ford Center (Oklahoma City) | .19,675 |
| | & Maravich Center (Baton Rouge) | .14,164 |

### Phoenix Suns

| | | |
|---|---|---|
| 1968–92 | Arizona Veterans' Memorial Coliseum | 14,487 |
| 1992– | America West Arena | .19,023 |

### Portland Trail Blazers

| | | |
|---|---|---|
| 1970–95 | Memorial Coliseum | .12,888 |
| 1995– | Rose Garden | .19,980 |
| | (1995 capacity—21,538) | |

### Sacramento Kings

| | | |
|---|---|---|
| 1948–55 | Edgarton Park Arena (Rochester, NY) | .5,000 |
| 1955–58 | Rochester War Memorial | .10,000 |
| 1958–72 | Cincinnati Gardens | .11,438 |
| 1972–74 | Municipal Auditorium (Kansas City) | .9,929 |
| | & Omaha (NE) Civic Auditorium | .9,136 |
| 1974–78 | Kemper Arena (Kansas City) | .16,785 |
| | & Omaha Civic Auditorium | .9,136 |
| 1978–85 | Kemper Arena | .16,886 |
| 1985–88 | ARCO Arena I | .10,333 |
| 1988– | ARCO Arena II | .17,317 |
| | (1988 capacity—16,517) | |

### San Antonio Spurs

| | | |
|---|---|---|
| 1967–70 | Memorial Auditorium (Dallas) | .8,088 |
| | & Moody Coliseum (Dallas) | .8,500 |
| 1970–71 | Moody Coliseum | .8,500 |
| | Tarrant County | |
| | Convention Center (Ft. Worth) | .13,500 |
| | & Municipal Coliseum (Lubbock) | .10,400 |
| 1971–73 | Moody Coliseum | .9,500 |
| | & Memorial Auditorium | .8,088 |
| 1973–93 | HemisFair Arena (San Antonio) | .16,057 |
| 1993–2002 | The Alamodome | .20,557 |
| 2002– | SBC Center | .18,500 |

### Seattle SuperSonics

| | | |
|---|---|---|
| 1967–78 | Seattle Center Coliseum | .14,098 |
| 1978–85 | Kingdome | .40,192 |
| 1985–94 | Seattle Center Coliseum | .14,252 |
| 1994–95 | Tacoma Dome | .19,000 |
| 1995– | KeyArena at Seattle Center | .17,072 |

### Utah Jazz

| | | |
|---|---|---|
| 1974–75 | Municipal Auditorium (New Orleans) | .7,853 |
| | & Louisiana Superdome | .47,284 |
| 1975–79 | Superdome | .47,284 |
| 1979–83 | Salt Palace (Salt Lake City) | .12,519 |
| 1983–84 | Salt Palace | .12,519 |
| | & Thomas & Mack Center (Las Vegas) | .18,500 |
| 1984–91 | Salt Palace | .12,616 |
| 1991– | Delta Center | .19,911 |

**Note:** The Sacramento (then Kansas City) Kings played 30 home games at Kansas City Municipal Auditorium during the 1979-80 season after the Kemper Auditorium roof collapsed during a severe rain and wind storm on June 4, 1979.

## Eastern Conference

### Atlanta Hawks

| | | |
|---|---|---|
| 1949–51 | Wharton Field House (Moline, IL) | .6,000 |
| 1951–55 | Milwaukee Arena | .11,000 |
| 1955–68 | Kiel Auditorium (St. Louis) | .10,000 |
| 1968–72 | Alexander Mem. Coliseum (Atlanta) | .7,166 |
| 1972–96 | The Omni | .16,378 |
| 1997–99 | Georgia Dome | .21,570 |
| | & Alexander Mem. Coliseum | .9,300 |
| 1999– | Philips Arena | .19,445 |

### Boston Celtics

| | | |
|---|---|---|
| 1946–95 | Boston Garden | .14,890 |
| 1995– | TD Banknorth Garden | .18,624 |

**Note:** From 1975-95 the Celtics played some regular season games at the Hartford Civic Center (15,418).

### Charlotte Bobcats

| | | |
|---|---|---|
| 2004-05 | Charlotte Coliseum | .19,925 |
| 2005– | Charlotte Arena | .18,500 |

### Chicago Bulls

| | | |
|---|---|---|
| 1966–67 | Chicago Amphitheater | .11,002 |
| 1967–94 | Chicago Stadium | .18,676 |
| 1994– | United Center | .21,711 |

### Cleveland Cavaliers

| | | |
|---|---|---|
| 1970–74 | Cleveland Arena | .11,000 |
| 1974–94 | The Coliseum (Richfield, OH) | .20,273 |
| 1994– | The Quicken Loans Arena | .20,562 |

### Detroit Pistons

| | | |
|---|---|---|
| 1948–52 | North Side H.S. Gym (Ft. Wayne, IN) | 3,800 |
| 1952–57 | Memorial Coliseum (Ft. Wayne) | 9,306 |
| 1957–61 | Olympia Stadium (Detroit) | 14,000 |
| 1961–78 | Cobo Arena | 11,147 |
| 1978–88 | Silverdome (Pontiac, MI) | 22,366 |
| 1988– | The Palace of Auburn Hills | 22,076 |

### Indiana Pacers

| | | |
|---|---|---|
| 1967–74 | State Fairgrounds (Indianapolis) | 9,479 |
| 1974–99 | Market Square Arena | 16,530 |
| | (1974 capacity—17,287) | |
| 1999– | Conseco Fieldhouse | 18,345 |

### Miami Heat

| | | |
|---|---|---|
| 1988–99 | Miami Arena | 15,200 |
| 2000– | AmericanAirlines Arena | 16,500 |

### Milwaukee Bucks

| | | |
|---|---|---|
| 1968–88 | Milwaukee Arena (The Mecca) | 11,052 |
| 1988– | Bradley Center | 18,717 |

### New Jersey Nets

| | | |
|---|---|---|
| 1967–68 | Teaneck (NJ) Armory | 3,500 |
| 1968–69 | Long Island Arena (Commack, NY) | 6,500 |
| 1969–71 | Island Garden (W. Hempstead, NY) | 5,200 |
| 1971–77 | Nassau Coliseum (Uniondale, NY) | 15,500 |
| 1977–81 | Rutgers Ath. Center (Piscataway, NJ) | 9,050 |
| 1981– | Continental Airlines Arena (E. Ruth., NJ) | 20,049 |

### New York Knicks

| | | |
|---|---|---|
| 1946–68 | Madison Sq. Garden III (50th St.) | 18,49 |
| 1968– | Madison Sq. Garden III (33rd St.) | 19,76 |
| | (1968 capacity—19,694) | |

### Orlando Magic

| | | |
|---|---|---|
| 1989– | TD Waterhouse Centre | 17,24 |

### Philadelphia 76ers

| | | |
|---|---|---|
| 1949–51 | State Fair Coliseum (Syracuse, NY) | 7,500 |
| 1951–63 | Onondaga County (NY) War Memorial | 8,000 |
| 1963–67 | Convention Hall (Philadelphia) | 12,000 |
| | & Philadelphia Arena | 7,77 |
| 1967–96 | CoreStates Spectrum | 18,13 |
| 1996– | Wachovia Center | 20,44 |

### Toronto Raptors

| | | |
|---|---|---|
| 1995–99 | SkyDome | 20,12 |
| 1999– | Air Canada Centre | 19,80 |

### Washington Wizards

| | | |
|---|---|---|
| 1961–62 | Chicago Amphitheater | 11,00 |
| 1962–63 | Chicago Coliseum | 7,10 |
| 1963–73 | Baltimore Civic Center | 12,28 |
| 1973–97 | USAir Arena (Landover, MD) | 18,75 |
| 1997– | MCI Center | 20,67 |

**Note:** From 1988-96 the Wizards (then Bullets) played fou regular season games at Baltimore Arena (12,756).

**Building Name Changes:** BOSTON—**TD Banknorth Garden** originally FleetCenter (1995-2005); CLEVELAND—**Th Quicken Loans Arena** originally Gund Arena (1994-2005); HOUSTON—**Compaq Center** originally The Summit (1975 97); NEW JERSEY—**Continental Airlines Arena** originally Byrne Meadowlands Arena (1981-96); ORLANDO—**T Waterhouse Centre** originally Orlando Arena (1989-99); PHILADELPHIA—**Wachovia Center** originally the CoreState Center (1996-98), then the First Union Center (1998-2003) and **CoreStates Spectrum** originally The Spectrum (1967-94 WASHINGTON—**USAir Arena** originally Capital Centre (1973-93).

## NATIONAL FOOTBALL LEAGUE

### American Football Conference

| | | Location | Built | Capacity | Fiel |
|---|---|---|---|---|---|
| Baltimore Ravens | **M&T Bank Stadium** | Baltimore, Md. | 1998 | **69,084** | Gras |
| Buffalo Bills | **Ralph Wilson Stadium** | Orchard Park, N.Y. | 1973 | **73,967** | Tur |
| Cincinnati Bengals | **Paul Brown Stadium** | Cincinnati, Ohio | 2000 | **65,352** | Gras |
| Cleveland Browns | **Cleveland Browns Stadium** | Cleveland, Ohio | 1999 | **73,200** | Gras |
| Denver Broncos | **INVESCO Field at Mile High** | Denver, Colo. | 2001 | **76,125** | Gras |
| Houston Texans | **Reliant Stadium** | Houston, Tex. | 2002 | **69,500** | Gras |
| Indianapolis Colts | **RCA Dome** | Indianapolis, Ind. | 1984 | **56,127** | Tur |
| Jacksonville Jaguars | **ALLTEL Stadium** | Jacksonville, Fla. | 1995 | **73,000** | Gras |
| Kansas City Chiefs | **Arrowhead Stadium** | Kansas City, Mo. | 1972 | **79,451** | Gras |
| Miami Dolphins | **Dolphins Stadium** | Miami, Fla. | 1987 | **75,540** | Gras |
| New England Patriots | **Gillette Stadium** | Foxboro, Mass. | 2002 | **68,000** | Gras |
| New York Jets | **Giants Stadium** | E. Rutherford, N.J. | 1976 | **80,062** | Gras |
| Oakland Raiders | **McAfee Coliseum** | Oakland, Calif. | 1966 | **63,132** | Gras |
| Pittsburgh Steelers | **Heinz Field** | Pittsburgh, Pa. | 2001 | **64,450** | Gras |
| San Diego Chargers | **Qualcomm Stadium** | San Diego, Calif. | 1967 | **71,000** | Gras |
| Tennessee Titans | **The Coliseum** | Nashville, Tenn. | 1999 | **68,798** | Gras |

### National Football Conference

| | | Location | Built | Capacity | Fiel |
|---|---|---|---|---|---|
| Arizona Cardinals | **Sun Devil Stadium** | Tempe, Ariz. | 1958 | **73,273** | Gras |
| Atlanta Falcons | **Georgia Dome** | Atlanta, Ga. | 1992 | **71,228** | Tur |
| Carolina Panthers | **Bank of America Stadium** | Charlotte, N.C. | 1996 | **73,500** | Gras |
| Chicago Bears | **Soldier Field** | Chicago, Ill. | 1924 | **63,000** | Gras |
| Dallas Cowboys | **Texas Stadium** | Irving, Texas | 1971 | **65,639** | Tur |
| Detroit Lions | **Ford Field** | Detroit, Mich. | 2002 | **65,000** | Tur |
| Green Bay Packers | **Lambeau Field** | Green Bay, Wis. | 1957 | **72,515** | Gras |
| Minnesota Vikings | **Hubert H. Humphrey Metrodome** | Minneapolis, Minn. | 1982 | **64,121** | Tur |
| New Orleans Saints* | **Tiger Stadium** | Baton Rouge, La. | 1924 | **91,644** | Gras |
| | **& Alamodome** | San Antonio, Tex. | 1993 | **65,000** | Tur |
| New York Giants | **Giants Stadium** | E. Rutherford, N.J. | 1976 | **80,062** | Gras |
| Philadelphia Eagles | **Lincoln Financial Field** | Philadelphia, Pa. | 2003 | **68,532** | Gras |
| St. Louis Rams | **Edward Jones Dome** | St. Louis, Mo. | 1995 | **66,000** | Tur |
| San Francisco 49ers | **Monster Park** | San Francisco, Calif. | 1960 | **69,400** | Gras |
| Seattle Seahawks | **Qwest Field** | Seattle, Wash. | 2002 | **67,000** | Gras |
| Tampa Bay Buccaneers | **Raymond James Stadium** | Tampa, Fla. | 1998 | **65,657** | Gras |
| Washington Redskins | **FedEx Field** | Raljon, Md. | 1997 | **86,484** | Gras |

*Due to damage caused by Hurricane Katrina the New Orleans Saints (capacity: 68,395) were forced out of the Louisian Superdome and arranged to play four regular-season games at LSU's Tiger Stadium and three at San Antonio's Alamodome

## National Football League (Cont.)

### Rank by Capacity

| AFC | | NFC | |
|---|---|---|---|
| NY Jets | 80,062 | Washington | 86,484 |
| Kansas City | 79,451 | NY Giants | 80,062 |
| Denver | 76,125 | Arizona | 73,273 |
| Miami | 75,540 | Carolina | 73,500 |
| Buffalo | 73,967 | Green Bay | 72,515 |
| Cleveland | 73,200 | Atlanta | 71,228 |
| Jacksonville | 73,000 | San Francisco | 69,400 |
| San Diego | 71,000 | Philadelphia | 68,532 |
| Houston | 69,500 | New Orleans | 68,395 |
| Baltimore | 69,084 | Seattle | 67,000 |
| Tennessee | 68,798 | St. Louis | 66,000 |
| New England | 68,000 | Tampa Bay | 65,657 |
| Cincinnati | 65,352 | Dallas | 65,639 |
| Pittsburgh | 64,450 | Detroit | 65,000 |
| Oakland | 63,132 | Minnesota | 64,121 |
| Indianapolis | 56,127 | Chicago | 63,000 |

### Rank by Age

| AFC | | NFC | |
|---|---|---|---|
| Oakland | 1966 | Chicago | 1924 |
| San Diego | 1967 | Green Bay | 1957 |
| Kansas City | 1972 | Arizona | 1958 |
| Buffalo | 1973 | San Francisco | 1960 |
| NY Jets | 1976 | Dallas | 1971 |
| Indianapolis | 1984 | New Orleans | 1975 |
| Miami | 1987 | NY Giants | 1976 |
| Jacksonville | 1995 | Minnesota | 1982 |
| Baltimore | 1998 | Atlanta | 1992 |
| Cleveland | 1999 | St. Louis | 1995 |
| Tennessee | 1999 | Carolina | 1996 |
| Cincinnati | 2000 | Washington | 1997 |
| Denver | 2001 | Tampa Bay | 1998 |
| Pittsburgh | 2001 | Seattle | 2002 |
| New England | 2002 | Detroit | 2002 |
| Houston | 2002 | Philadelphia | 2003 |

**Notes:** Chicago's Soldier Field was rebuilt and Green Bay's Lambeau Field was renovated in 2003.

## 2004 NFL Attendance

Overall paid attendance in the NFL for the 2004 season was 17,270,056 for an average per game crowd of 67,461 over 256 games. Teams in each conference are ranked by attendance over eight home games. Rank column indicates rank in entire league. Numbers in parentheses indicate conference rank in 2003.

### AFC

| | | Attendance | Rank | Average |
|---|---|---|---|---|
| 1 | N.Y. Jets (2) | 623,181 | 3 | 77,897 |
| 2 | Kansas City (1) | 623,010 | 4 | 77,876 |
| 3 | Denver (3) | 601,031 | 5 | 75,128 |
| 4 | Cleveland (5) | 584,840 | 7 | 73,105 |
| 5 | Miami (4) | 580,808 | 8 | 72,601 |
| 6 | Buffalo (6) | 574,399 | 9 | 71,799 |
| 7 | Houston (7) | 565,192 | 10 | 70,649 |
| 8 | Baltimore (8) | 558,594 | 13 | 69,824 |
| 9 | Jacksonville (16) | 555,464 | 14 | 69,433 |
| 10 | Tennessee (9) | 551,210 | 15 | 68,901 |
| 11 | New England (10) | 550,048 | 16 | 68,756 |
| 12 | Cincinnati (12) | 524,248 | 20 | 65,531 |
| 13 | Pittsburgh (13) | 507,385 | 26 | 63,423 |
| 14 | San Diego (11) | 485,462 | 29 | 60,682 |
| 15 | Indianapolis (14) | 456,791 | 30 | 57,098 |
| 16 | Oakland (15) | 405,936 | 31 | 50,742 |
| | TOTAL | 8,747,599 | — | 68,341 |

### NFC

| | | Attendance | Rank | Average |
|---|---|---|---|---|
| 1 | Washington (1) | 702,670 | 1 | 87,833 |
| 2 | NY Giants (2) | 629,874 | 2 | 78,734 |
| 3 | Carolina (3) | 586,259 | 6 | 73,282 |
| 4 | Atlanta (4) | 564,829 | 11 | 70,603 |
| 5 | Green Bay (5) | 564,400 | 12 | 70,550 |
| 6 | Philadelphia (7) | 540,870 | 17 | 67,608 |
| 7 | Seattle (12) | 533,436 | 18 | 66,679 |
| 8 | St. Louis (9) | 527,384 | 19 | 65,923 |
| 9 | Tampa Bay (10) | 522,720 | 21 | 65,340 |
| 10 | San Francisco (8) | 518,271 | 22 | 64,783 |
| 11 | New Orleans (6) | 513,178 | 23 | 64,147 |
| 12 | Minnesota (11) | 512,969 | 24 | 64,121 |
| 13 | Dallas (13) | 510,892 | 25 | 63,861 |
| 14 | Detroit (15) | 499,162 | 27 | 62,395 |
| 15 | Chicago (14) | 495,706 | 28 | 61,963 |
| 16 | Arizona (16) | 300,267 | 32 | 37,533 |
| | TOTAL | 8,522,887 | — | 66,585 |

## Home Fields

Listed below are the principal home fields used through the years by current NFL teams. The largest capacity of each stadium is noted in the right-hand column. All-America Football Conference stadiums (1946-49) are included for Cleveland and San Francisco.

### AFC

#### Baltimore Ravens

| | | |
|---|---|---|
| 1996–97 | Memorial Stadium | 65,000 |
| 1998– | M&T Bank Stadium | 69,084 |

#### Buffalo Bills

| | | |
|---|---|---|
| 1960–72 | War Memorial Stadium | 45,748 |
| 1973– | Ralph Wilson Stadium (Orchard Park, NY) | 73,967 |
| | (1973 capacity—80,020) | |

#### Cincinnati Bengals

| | | |
|---|---|---|
| 1968–69 | Nippert Stadium (Univ. of Cincinnati) | 26,500 |
| 1970–99 | Cinergy Field | 60,389 |
| | (1970 capacity—56,200) | |
| 2000– | Paul Brown Stadium | 65,352 |

#### Cleveland Browns

| | | |
|---|---|---|
| 1946–95 | Cleveland Stadium | 78,512 |
| | (1946 capacity—85,703) | |
| 1999– | Cleveland Browns Stadium | 73,200 |

#### Denver Broncos

| | | |
|---|---|---|
| 1960–2000 | Mile High Stadium | 76,123 |
| | (1960 capacity—34,000) | |
| 2001– | INVESCO Field at Mile High | 76,125 |

#### Houston Texans

| | | |
|---|---|---|
| 2002– | Reliant Stadium | 69,500 |

#### Indianapolis Colts

| | | |
|---|---|---|
| 1953–83 | Memorial Stadium (Baltimore) | 60,020 |
| 1984– | RCA Dome (Indianapolis) | 56,127 |
| | (1984 capacity—60,127) | |

#### Jacksonville Jaguars

| | | |
|---|---|---|
| 1995– | ALLTEL Stadium | 73,000 |

#### Kansas City Chiefs

| | | |
|---|---|---|
| 1960–62 | Cotton Bowl (Dallas) | 72,000 |
| 1963–71 | Municipal Stadium (Kansas City) | 47,000 |
| 1972– | Arrowhead Stadium | 79,451 |
| | (1972 capacity—78,097) | |

## Miami Dolphins

| | | |
|---|---|---|
| 1966–86 | Orange Bowl | .75,206 |
| 1987– | Dolphins Stadium | .75,540 |

## New England Patriots

| | | |
|---|---|---|
| 1960–62 | Nickerson Field (Boston Univ.) | .17,369 |
| 1963–68 | Fenway Park | .33,379 |
| 1969 | Alumni Stadium (Boston College) | .26,000 |
| 1970 | Harvard Stadium | .37,300 |
| 1971-2001 | Foxboro Stadium | .60,292 |
| | (1971 capacity—61,114) | |
| 2002– | Gillette Stadium (Foxboro, Mass.) | ..68,000 |

## New York Jets

| | | |
|---|---|---|
| 1960–63 | Polo Grounds | .55,987 |
| 1964–83 | Shea Stadium | .60,372 |
| 1984– | Giants Stadium (E. Rutherford, NJ) | ..80,062 |

## Oakland Raiders

| | | |
|---|---|---|
| 1960 | Kesar Stadium (San Francisco) | ..59,636 |
| 1961 | Candlestick Park | .42,500 |
| 1962–65 | Frank Youell Field (Oakland) | .20,000 |
| 1966–81 | Oakland-Alameda County Coliseum | .54,587 |
| 1982–94 | Memorial Coliseum (Los Angeles) | .67,800 |
| 1995– | McAfee Coliseum | .63,132 |

## Pittsburgh Steelers

| | | |
|---|---|---|
| 1933–57 | Forbes Field | .35,000 |
| 1958–63 | Forbes Field | .35,000 |
| | & Pitt Stadium | .54,500 |
| 1964–69 | Pitt Stadium | .54,500 |
| 1970– | Three Rivers Stadium | .59,600 |
| 2000 | (1970 capacity—49,000) | |
| 2001– | Heinz Field | .64,450 |

## San Diego Chargers

| | | |
|---|---|---|
| 1960 | Memorial Coliseum (Los Angeles) | ..92,604 |
| 1961–66 | Balboa Stadium (San Diego) | .34,000 |
| 1967– | Qualcomm Stadium | .71,000 |
| | (1967 capacity—54,000) | |

## Tennessee Titans

| | | |
|---|---|---|
| 1960–64 | Jeppesen Stadium (Houston) | .23,500 |
| 1965–67 | Rice Stadium (Rice Univ.) | .70,000 |
| 1968–96 | Astrodome | .59,969 |
| 1997 | Liberty Bowl (Memphis) | .62,380 |
| 1998 | Vanderbilt Stadium (Nashville) | .41,600 |
| 1999– | The Coliseum (Nashville) | .68,798 |

**Stadium Name Changes:** BALTIMORE—**M&T Bank Stadium** was originally named Ravens Stadium (1998-99) then was renamed PSInet Stadium (1999-2002) and renamed Ravens Stadium (2002-03); BUFFALO—**Ralph Wilson Stadium** originally Rich Stadium (1973-99); CINCINNATI—Cinergy Field originally Riverfront Stadium (1970-96); CLEVELAND—Cleveland Stadium originally Municipal Stadium (1932-74); DENVER—**Mile High Stadium** originally Bears Stadium (1948-66); INDIANAPOLIS—**RCA Dome** originally Hoosier Dome (1984-94); JACKSONVILLE—**ALLTEL Stadium** originally Jacksonville Municipal Stadium (1995-97); MIAMI—**Dolphins Stadium** originally Joe Robbie Stadium (1987-96), then Pro Player Stadium (1996-2005); NEW ENGLAND—Foxboro Stadium originally Schaefer Stadium (1971-82), then Sullivan Stadium (1983-89); **Gillette Stadium** originally CMGI Field; OAKLAND—**McAfee Coliseum** originally Oakland Alameda Coliseum (1995-99), Network Associates Coliseum (1999-2004); SAN DIEGO—**Qualcomm Stadium** originally San Diego Stadium (1967-81) then San Diego/Jack Murphy Stadium (1981-96); TENNESSEE—**The Coliseum** originally Adelphia Coliseum (1999-2001).

# NFC

## Arizona Cardinals

| | | |
|---|---|---|
| 1920–21 | Normal Field (Chicago) | .7,500 |
| 1922–25 | Comiskey Park | .28,000 |
| 1926–28 | Normal Field | .7,500 |
| 1929–59 | Comiskey Park | .52,000 |
| 1960–65 | Busch Stadium (St. Louis) | .34,000 |
| 1966–87 | Busch Memorial Stadium | .54,392 |
| 1988– | Sun Devil Stadium (Tempe, AZ) | ..73,273 |

## Atlanta Falcons

| | | |
|---|---|---|
| 1966-91 | Atlanta-Fulton County Stadium | .59,643 |
| 1992– | Georgia Dome | .71,228 |

## Carolina Panthers

| | | |
|---|---|---|
| 1995 | Memorial Stadium (Clemson, SC) | ...81,473 |
| 1996– | Bank of America Stadium | .73,500 |

## Chicago Bears

| | | |
|---|---|---|
| 1920 | Staley Field (Decatur, IL) | — |
| 1921–70 | Wrigley Field (Chicago) | .37,741 |
| 1971–2001 | Soldier Field | .66,944 |
| | (1971 capacity—55,049) | |
| 2002 | Memorial Stadium (Champaign, IL) | .69,249 |
| 2003– | Soldier Field | .63,000 |

## Dallas Cowboys

| | | |
|---|---|---|
| 1960–70 | Cotton Bowl | .72,132 |
| 1971– | Texas Stadium (Irving, TX) | .65,639 |
| | (1971 capacity—65,101) | |

## Detroit Lions

| | | |
|---|---|---|
| 1930–33 | Spartan Stadium (Portsmouth, OH) | ...8,200 |
| 1934–37 | Univ. of Detroit Stadium | .25,000 |
| 1938–74 | Tiger Stadium | .54,468 |
| 1975-2001 | Pontiac Silverdome | .80,311 |
| | (1975 capacity—80,638) | |
| 2002– | Ford Field | .65,000 |

## Green Bay Packers

| | | |
|---|---|---|
| 1921–22 | Hagemeister Brewery Park | — |
| 1923–24 | Bellevue Park | — |
| 1925–56 | City Stadium I | .24,800 |
| 1957– | Lambeau Field | .72,515 |
| | (1957 capacity—32,150) | |
| | (2002 capacity—62,500) | |

**Note:** The Packers played games in Milwaukee from 1933-94: at Borchert Field, State Fair Park and Marquette Stadium (1933-52), and County Stadium (1953-94).

## Minnesota Vikings

| | | |
|---|---|---|
| 1961–81 | Metropolitan Stadium (Bloomington) | .48,446 |
| 1982– | HHH Metrodome (Minneapolis) | .64,121 |
| | (1982 capacity—62,220) | |

## New Orleans Saints

| | | |
|---|---|---|
| 1967–74 | Tulane Stadium | .80,997 |
| 1975–2004 | Louisiana Superdome | .68,395 |
| | (1975 capacity—74,472) | |
| 2005 | Tiger Stadium (Baton Rouge) | .91,644 |
| | & Alamodome (San Antonio) | .65,000 |

**Note:** The Saints were unable to play at the Louisiana Superdome in the wake of Hurricane Katrina and played four home games at LSU's Tiger Stadium and three at the Alamodome in San Antonio in 2005.

## New York Giants

| | | |
|---|---|---|
| 1925–55 | Polo Grounds II | .55,200 |
| 1956–73 | Yankee Stadium I | .63,800 |
| 1973–74 | Yale Bowl (New Haven, CT) | .70,896 |
| 1975 | Shea Stadium | .60,372 |
| 1976– | Giants Stadium (E. Rutherford, NJ) | ..80,062 |
| | (1976 capacity—76,800) | |

## National Football League (Cont.)

### Philadelphia Eagles

| | | |
|---|---|---|
| 1933–35 | Baker Bowl | 18,800 |
| 1936–39 | Municipal Stadium | 73,702 |
| 1940 | Shibe Park | 33,608 |
| 1941 | Municipal Stadium | 73,702 |
| 1942 | Shibe Park | 33,608 |
| 1943 | Forbes Field (Pittsburgh) | 34,528 |
| 1944–57 | Shibe Park | 33,608 |
| 1958–70 | Franklin Field (Univ. of Penn.) | 60,546 |
| 1971–2002 | Veterans Stadium | 65,352 |
| 2003– | Lincoln Financial Field | 68,532 |

### St. Louis Rams

| | | |
|---|---|---|
| 1937–42 | Municipal Stadium (Cleveland) | 85,703 |
| 1937 | League Park (Cleveland) | — |
| 1938 | Shaw Stadium (Cleveland) | — |
| 1937 | League Park | — |
| 1943 | Suspended operations for one year. | |
| 1944–45 | Municipal Stadium | 85,703 |
| 1946–79 | Memorial Coliseum (Los Angeles) | 92,604 |
| 1980–94 | Anaheim Stadium | 69,008 |
| 1995 | Busch Stadium | 60,000 |
| 1995– | Edward Jones Dome | 66,000 |

### San Francisco 49ers

| | | |
|---|---|---|
| 1946–70 | Kezar Stadium | 59,636 |
| 1971– | Monster Park | 69,400 |
| | (1971 capacity—61,246) | |

### Seattle Seahawks

| | | |
|---|---|---|
| 1976–94 | Kingdome | 66,000 |
| 1994 | Kingdome | 66,400 |
| | & Husky Stadium | 72,500 |
| 1995–99 | Kingdome | 66,400 |
| 2000-01 | Husky Stadium | 72,500 |
| 2002– | Qwest Field | 67,000 |

### Tampa Bay Buccaneers

| | | |
|---|---|---|
| 1976–97 | Houlihan's Stadium | 74,300 |
| 1998– | Raymond James Stadium | 65,657 |

### Washington Redskins

| | | |
|---|---|---|
| 1932 | Braves Field (Boston) | 40,000 |
| 1933–36 | Fenway Park | 27,000 |
| 1937–60 | Griffith Stadium (Washington, DC) | 35,000 |
| 1961–97 | RFK Stadium | 56,454 |
| 1997– | FedEx Field (Raljon, MD) | 86,484 |

**Stadium Name Changes:** ATLANTA—**Atlanta-Fulton County Stadium** originally Atlanta Stadium (1966-74); CAROLINA—**Bank of America Stadium** originally Ericsson Stadium (1996-2004); CHICAGO—**Wrigley Field** originally Cubs Park (1916-25); DETROIT—**Tiger Stadium** originally Navin Field (1912-37), then Briggs Stadium (1938-60), also, **Pontiac Silverdome** originally Pontiac Metropolitan Stadium (1975); GREEN BAY—**Lambeau Field** originally City Stadium II (1957-64); PHILADELPHIA—**Shibe Park** renamed Connie Mack Stadium in 1953; ST. LOUIS—**Busch Memorial Stadium** renamed Busch Stadium in 1983, **Edward Jones Dome** originally Trans World Dome (1995-99), then The Dome at America's Center (2000-01); SAN FRANCISCO—**Monster Park** originally Candlestick Park (1960-94), then 3Com Park (1995-2001) and again Candlestick Park (2001-04); SEATTLE—**Qwest Field** originally Seahawks Stadium (2002-04); TAMPA BAY—**Raymond James Stadium** originally Tampa Stadium (1976-96), then **Houlihan's Stadium** (1996-98); WASHINGTON—**RFK Stadium** originally D.C. Stadium (1961-68), also, **FedEx Field** originally Jack Kent Cooke Stadium (1997-99).

## NATIONAL HOCKEY LEAGUE

### Western Conference

| | | Location | Built | Capacity |
|---|---|---|---|---|
| Anaheim, Mighty Ducks of | **Arrowhead Pond** | Anaheim, Calif. | 1993 | **17,174** |
| Calgary Flames | **Pengrowth Saddledome** | Calgary, Alb. | 1983 | **17,135** |
| Chicago Blackhawks | **United Center** | Chicago, Ill. | 1994 | **20,500** |
| Colorado Avalanche | **Pepsi Center** | Denver, Colo. | 1999 | **18,007** |
| Columbus Blue Jackets | **Nationwide Arena** | Columbus, Ohio | 2000 | **18,136** |
| Dallas Stars | **American Airlines Center** | Dallas, Texas | 2001 | **18,532** |
| Detroit Red Wings | **Joe Louis Arena** | Detroit, Mich. | 1979 | **20,058** |
| Edmonton Oilers | **Rexall Place** | Edmonton, Alb. | 1974 | **16,839** |
| Los Angeles Kings | **Staples Center** | Los Angeles, Calif. | 1999 | **18,118** |
| Minnesota Wild | **Xcel Energy Center** | St. Paul, Minn. | 2000 | **18,064** |
| Nashville Predators | **Gaylord Entertainment Center** | Nashville, Tenn. | 1994 | **17,113** |
| Phoenix Coyotes | **Glendale Arena** | Glendale, Ariz. | 2003 | **17,500** |
| St. Louis Blues | **Savvis Center** | St. Louis, Mo. | 1994 | **19,022** |
| San Jose Sharks | **HP Pavilion at San Jose** | San Jose, Calif. | 1993 | **17,496** |
| Vancouver Canucks | **General Motors Place** | Vancouver, B.C. | 1995 | **18,422** |

### Eastern Conference

| | | Location | Built | Capacity |
|---|---|---|---|---|
| Atlanta Thrashers | **Philips Arena** | Atlanta, Ga. | 1999 | **18,545** |
| Boston Bruins | **TD Banknorth Garden** | Boston, Mass. | 1995 | **17,565** |
| Buffalo Sabres | **HSBC Arena** | Buffalo, N.Y. | 1996 | **18,690** |
| Carolina Hurricanes | **RBC Center** | Raleigh, N.C. | 1999 | **18,730** |
| Florida Panthers | **BankAtlantic Center** | Sunrise, Fla. | 1998 | **19,250** |
| Montreal Canadiens | **Bell Centre** | Montreal, Que. | 1996 | **21,273** |
| New Jersey Devils | **Continental Airlines Arena** | E. Rutherford, N.J. | 1981 | **19,040** |
| New York Islanders | **Nassau Veterans' Mem. Coliseum** | Uniondale, N.Y. | 1972 | **16,234** |
| New York Rangers | **Madison Square Garden** | New York, N.Y. | 1968 | **18,200** |
| Ottawa Senators | **Corel Centre** | Kanata, Ont. | 1996 | **18,500** |
| Philadelphia Flyers | **Wachovia Center** | Philadelphia, Penn. | 1996 | **18,523** |
| Pittsburgh Penguins | **Mellon Arena** | Pittsburgh, Penn. | 1961 | **16,958** |
| Tampa Bay Lightning | **St. Pete Times Forum** | Tampa Bay, Fla. | 1996 | **19,758** |
| Toronto Maple Leafs | **Air Canada Centre** | Toronto, Ont. | 1999 | **18,819** |
| Washington Capitals | **MCI Center** | Washington, D.C. | 1997 | **18,672** |

## Rank by Capacity

| Western | | Eastern | |
|---|---|---|---|
| Chicago | .20,500 | Montreal | .21,273 |
| Detroit | .20,058 | Tampa Bay | .19,758 |
| St. Louis | .19,022 | Florida | .19,250 |
| Dallas | .18,532 | New Jersey | .19,040 |
| Vancouver | .18,422 | Toronto | .18,819 |
| Columbus | .18,136 | Carolina | .18,730 |
| Los Angeles | .18,118 | Buffalo | .18,690 |
| Minnesota | .18,064 | Washington | .18,672 |
| Colorado | .18,007 | Atlanta | .18,545 |
| Phoenix | .17,500 | Philadelphia | .18,523 |
| San Jose | .17,496 | Ottawa | .18,500 |
| Anaheim | .17,174 | NY Rangers | .18,200 |
| Calgary | .17,135 | Boston | .17,565 |
| Nashville | .17,113 | Pittsburgh | .16,958 |
| Edmonton | .16,839 | NY Islanders | .16,234 |

## Rank by Age

| Western | | Eastern | |
|---|---|---|---|
| Edmonton | .1974 | Pittsburgh | .1961 |
| Detroit | .1979 | NY Rangers | .1968 |
| Calgary | .1983 | NY Islanders | .1972 |
| Anaheim | .1993 | New Jersey | .1981 |
| San Jose | .1993 | Boston | .1995 |
| Chicago | .1994 | Montreal | .1996 |
| St. Louis | .1994 | Ottawa | .1996 |
| Nashville | .1994 | Buffalo | .1996 |
| Vancouver | .1995 | Philadelphia | .1996 |
| Colorado | .1999 | Tampa Bay | .1996 |
| Los Angeles | .1999 | Washington | .1997 |
| Columbus | .2000 | Florida | .1998 |
| Minnesota | .2000 | Toronto | .1999 |
| Dallas | .2001 | Carolina | .1999 |
| Phoenix | .2003 | Atlanta | .1999 |

## 2003-04 NHL Attendance

Official overall paid attendance for the 2003-04 season according to the NHL accounting office was 20,336,817 (paid tickets) for an average per game crowd of 16,534 over 1,230 games. Teams in each conference are ranked by attendance over 41 home games. Rank column refers to rank in entire league. Numbers in parentheses indicate conference rank in 2002-03.

### Western Conference

| | | Attendance | Rank | Average |
|---|---|---|---|---|
| 1 | Detroit (1) | .822,646 | 2 | 20,065 |
| 2 | Vancouver (5) | .763,867 | 5 | 18,631 |
| 3 | St. Louis (2) | .760,976 | 6 | 18,560 |
| 4 | Minnesota (4) | .759,774 | 7 | 18,531 |
| 5 | Dallas (3) | .752,556 | 8 | 18,355 |
| 6 | Colorado (6) | .738,287 | 10 | 18,007 |
| 7 | Los Angeles (8) | .733,185 | 11 | 17,883 |
| 8 | Edmonton (10) | .724,780 | 14 | 17,678 |
| 9 | Columbus (7) | .712,145 | 15 | 17,369 |
| 10 | Calgary (11) | .679,767 | 16 | 16,580 |
| 11 | San Jose (9) | .649,261 | 18 | 15,836 |
| 12 | Phoenix (14) | .634,242 | 19 | 15,469 |
| 13 | Anaheim (13) | .614,504 | 24 | 14,988 |
| 14 | Chicago (12) | .543,374 | 27 | 13,253 |
| 15 | Nashville (15) | .539,900 | 28 | 13,168 |
| | TOTAL | .10,429,266 | — | 16,958 |

### Eastern Conference

| | | Attendance | Rank | Average |
|---|---|---|---|---|
| 1 | Montreal (1) | .842,767 | 1 | 20,555 |
| 2 | Toronto (3) | .794,439 | 3 | 19,377 |
| 3 | Philadelphia (2) | .794,388 | 4 | 19,375 |
| 4 | NY Rangers (4) | .741,302 | 9 | 18,081 |
| 5 | Tampa Bay (6) | .730,634 | 12 | 17,820 |
| 6 | Ottawa (5) | .728,101 | 13 | 17,759 |
| 7 | Florida (9) | .653,380 | 17 | 15,936 |
| 8 | Buffalo (15) | .626,903 | 20 | 15,290 |
| 9 | Boston (10) | .620,469 | 21 | 15,133 |
| 10 | Atlanta (14) | .619,965 | 22 | 15,121 |
| 11 | New Jersey (12) | .617,459 | 23 | 15,060 |
| 12 | Washington (7) | .603,528 | 25 | 14,720 |
| 13 | NY Islanders (11) | .551,711 | 26 | 13,456 |
| 14 | Carolina (8) | .495,544 | 29 | 12,086 |
| 15 | Pittsburgh (13) | .486,961 | 30 | 11,877 |
| | TOTAL | .9,907,551 | — | 16,110 |

**Note:** Due to the lockout, there was no 2004-05 NHL season.

## Home Ice

Listed below are the principal home buildings used through the years by current NHL teams. The largest capacity of each arena is noted in the right hand column. World Hockey Association arenas (1972-79) are included for Edmonton, Hartford (now Carolina), Quebec (now Colorado) and Winnipeg (now Phoenix).

### Western Conference

#### Anaheim, Mighty Ducks of

| | | |
|---|---|---|
| 1993– | Arrowhead Pond | .17,174 |

#### Calgary Flames

| | | |
|---|---|---|
| 1972–80 | The Omni (Atlanta) | .15,278 |
| 1980–83 | Calgary Corral | .7,424 |
| 1983– | Pengrowth Saddledome | .17,135 |
| | (1983 capacity—16,674) | |

#### Chicago Blackhawks

| | | |
|---|---|---|
| 1926–29 | Chicago Coliseum | .5,000 |
| 1929–94 | Chicago Stadium | .17,317 |
| 1994– | United Center | .20,500 |

#### Colorado Avalanche

| | | |
|---|---|---|
| 1972–95 | Le Colisee de Quebec | .15,399 |
| 1995–99 | McNichols Arena (Denver) | .16,061 |
| 1999– | Pepsi Center | .18,007 |

#### Columbus Blue Jackets

| | | |
|---|---|---|
| 2000– | Nationwide Arena | .18,136 |

#### Dallas Stars

| | | |
|---|---|---|
| 1967–93 | Met Center (Bloomington, MN) | .15,174 |
| 1993–2000 | Reunion Arena (Dallas) | .17,001 |
| 2001– | American Airlines Center | .18,532 |

#### Detroit Red Wings

| | | |
|---|---|---|
| 1926–27 | Border Cities Arena (Windsor, Ont.) | .3,200 |
| 1927–79 | Olympia Stadium (Detroit) | .16,700 |
| 1979– | Joe Louis Arena | .20,058 |

#### Edmonton Oilers

| | | |
|---|---|---|
| 1972–74 | Edmonton Gardens | .7,200 |
| 1974– | Rexall Place | .16,839 |
| | (1974 capacity—15,513) | |

#### Los Angeles Kings

| | | |
|---|---|---|
| 1967–99 | Great Western Forum (Inglewood) | .16,005 |
| | (1967 capacity—15,651) | |
| 1999– | Staples Center | .18,118 |

**Note:** The Kings played 17 games at Long Beach Sports Arena and LA Sports Arena at the start of the 1967-68 season.

## National Hockey League (Cont.)

### Minnesota Wild

| | | |
|---|---|---|
| 2000– | Xcel Energy Center (St. Paul) | 18,064 |

### Nashville Predators

| | | |
|---|---|---|
| 1998– | Gaylord Entertainment Center | 17,113 |

### Phoenix Coyotes

| | | |
|---|---|---|
| 1972–96 | Winnipeg Arena | 15,393 |
| | (1972 capacity–10,177) | |
| 1996–2002 | America West (Phoenix) | 16,210 |
| 2003– | Glendale Arena (Glendale, Ariz.) | 17,500 |

### St. Louis Blues

| | | |
|---|---|---|
| 1967–94 | St. Louis Arena | 17,188 |
| 1994– | Savvis Center | 19,022 |

### San Jose Sharks

| | | |
|---|---|---|
| 1991–93 | Cow Palace (Daly City, CA) | 11,100 |
| 1993– | HP Pavilion at San Jose | 17,496 |

### Vancouver Canucks

| | | |
|---|---|---|
| 1970–95 | Pacific Coliseum | 16,150 |
| 1995– | General Motors Place | 18,422 |

**Building Name Changes:** CALGARY—**Pengrowth Saddledome** formerly named Canadian Airlines Saddledome (1996-2000) which was originally Olympic Saddledome (1983-95); DALLAS—**Met Center** in Minneapolis originally Metropolitan Sports Center (1967-82); EDMONTON—**Rexall Place** was formerly named Skyreach Centre (1999-2004) which was formerly named Edmonton Coliseum (1995-99) which was originally Northlands Coliseum (1974-94); LOS ANGELES—**Great Western Forum** originally The Forum (1967-88); NASHVILLE—**Gaylord Entertainment Center** originally Nashville Arena (1994-99); ST. LOUIS—**Savvis Center** originally Kiel Center (1994-2000), **St. Louis Arena** renamed The Checkerdome in 1977, then St. Louis Arena again in 1982; SAN JOSE—**HP Pavilion at San Jose** originally San Jose Arena (1993-2000), then Compaq Center at San Jose (2000-03).

## Eastern Conference

### Atlanta Thrashers

| | | |
|---|---|---|
| 1999– | Philips Arena | 18,545 |

### Boston Bruins

| | | |
|---|---|---|
| 1924–28 | Boston Arena | 6,200 |
| 1928–95 | Boston Garden | 14,448 |
| 1995– | TD Banknorth Garden | 17,565 |

### Buffalo Sabres

| | | |
|---|---|---|
| 1970–96 | Memorial Auditorium (The Aud) | 16,284 |
| | (1970 capacity–10,429) | |
| 1996– | HSBC Arena | 18,690 |

### Carolina Hurricanes

| | | |
|---|---|---|
| 1972–73 | Boston Garden | 14,442 |
| 1973–74 | Boston Garden (regular season) | 14,442 |
| | West Springfield (MA) Big E (playoffs) | 5,513 |
| 1974–75 | West Springfield Big E | 5,513 |
| | & Hartford (CT) Civic Center | 10,507 |
| 1975–77 | Hartford Civic Center | 10,507 |
| 1977–78 | Hartford Civic Center | 10,507 |
| | & Springfield (MA) Civic Center | 7,725 |
| 1978–79 | Springfield Civic Center | 7,725 |
| 1979–80 | Springfield Civic Center | 7,725 |
| | & Hartford Civic Center II | 14,250 |
| 1980–97 | Hartford Civic Center II | 15,635 |
| 1997–99 | Greensboro Coliseum | 21,500 |
| 1999– | RBC Center | 18,730 |

**Note:** The Hartford Civic Center roof caved in January 1978, forcing the Whalers to move their home games to Springfield, MA for two years.

### Florida Panthers

| | | |
|---|---|---|
| 1993–98 | Miami Arena | 14,703 |
| 1998– | BankAtlantic Center | 19,250 |

### Montreal Canadiens

| | | |
|---|---|---|
| 1910–21 | Jubilee Arena | 3,200 |
| 1913–18 | Montreal Arena (Westmount) | 6,000 |
| 1918–26 | Mount Royal Arena | 6,750 |
| 1926–68 | Montreal Forum I | 15,500 |
| 1968–96 | Montreal Forum II | 17,959 |
| 1996– | Bell Centre | 21,273 |

### New Jersey Devils

| | | |
|---|---|---|
| 1974–76 | Kemper Arena (Kansas City) | 16,300 |
| 1976–82 | McNichols Arena (Denver) | 15,900 |
| 1982– | Continental Airlines Arena | 19,040 |
| | (1982 capacity–19,023) | |

### New York Islanders

| | | |
|---|---|---|
| 1972– | Nassau Veterans' Mem. Coliseum | 16,234 |
| | (1972 capacity–14,500) | |

### New York Rangers

| | | |
|---|---|---|
| 1925–68 | Madison Square Garden III | 15,925 |
| 1968– | Madison Square Garden IV | 18,200 |
| | (1968 capacity–17,250) | |

### Ottawa Senators

| | | |
|---|---|---|
| 1992–96 | Ottawa Civic Center | 10,755 |
| 1996– | Corel Centre (Kanata) | 18,500 |

### Philadelphia Flyers

| | | |
|---|---|---|
| 1967–96 | CoreStates Spectrum | 17,380 |
| | (1967 capacity–14,558) | |
| 1996– | Wachovia Center | 18,523 |

### Pittsburgh Penguins

| | | |
|---|---|---|
| 1967– | Mellon Arena | 16,958 |
| | (1967 capacity–12,508) | |

### Tampa Bay Lightning

| | | |
|---|---|---|
| 1992–93 | Expo Hall-(Tampa) | 10,500 |
| 1993–96 | ThunderDome (St. Petersburg) | 26,000 |
| 1996– | St. Pete Times Forum | 19,758 |

### Toronto Maple Leafs

| | | |
|---|---|---|
| 1917–31 | Mutual Street Arena | 8,000 |
| 1931–99 | Maple Leaf Gardens | 15,746 |
| | (1931 capacity–13,542) | |
| 1999– | Air Canada Centre | 18,819 |

### Washington Capitals

| | | |
|---|---|---|
| 1974–97 | USAir Arena (Landover, MD) | 18,130 |
| 1997– | MCI Center | 18,672 |

**Building Name Changes:** BOSTON—**TD Banknorth Garden** originally FleetCenter (1995-2005); BUFFALO—**HSBC Arena** originally Marine Midland Arena (1996-99); CALGARY—**Pengrowth Saddledome** originally Canadian Airlines Arena (1983-2000); CAROLINA—**RBC Center** originally Raleigh Entertainment and Sports Arena (1999-2002); DALLAS—**American Airlines Center** originally Reunion Arena (1993-2000); FLORIDA—**BankAtlantic Center** formerly named Office Depot Center (2002-05) and originally National Car Rental Center (1998-2002); MONTREAL—**Bell Centre** originally Molson Centre (1996-2002); NEW JERSEY—**Continental Airlines Arena** originally Meadowlands Arena (1982-96); PHILADELPHIA—**Wachovia Center** originally the CoreStates Center (1996-98), then First Union Center (1998-2003) and **CoreStates Spectrum** originally The Spectrum (1967-94); PITTSBURGH—**Mellon Arena** originally Civic Arena (1967-2000); TAMPA BAY—**St. Pete Times Forum** originally Ice Palace (1996-2002); WASHINGTON—**USAir Arena** originally Capital Centre (1974-93).

## AUTO RACING

Formula One, NASCAR Winston Cup, Champ Car and Indy Racing League (IRL) racing circuits. Qualifying records accurate as of Sept. 30, 2005. Capacity figures for NASCAR, Champ Car and IRL tracks are approximate and pertain to grandstand seating only. Standing room and hillside terrain seating featured at most road courses are not included.

### Champ Car World Series

| | Location | Miles | Qual.mph record | Set by | Seats |
|---|---|---|---|---|---|
| Ansan South Korea | Ansan, South Korea | 1.900** | TBD | first race in late 2005 | |
| Burke Lakefront Airport | Cleveland, Ohio | 2.106** | 134.385 | Jimmy Vasser (1998) | 36,000 |
| Concord Pacific Place | Vancouver, B.C. | 1.781** | 106.260 | Cristiano da Matta (2002) | 65,000 |
| EuroSpeedway | Lausitz, Germany | 2.023 | 153.553 | Kenny Brack (2001) | 120,000 |
| Exhibition Place | Toronto, Ont. | 1.755** | 110.565 | Gil de Ferran (1999) | 60,000 |
| Finning International Speedway | Emondton, Alb. | 1.973** | 121.150 | A.J. Allmendinger (2005) | 70,000 |
| Fundidora Park | Monterrey, Mexico | 2.104* | 102.474 | Sebastien Bourdais (2004) | 61,871 |
| Circuit Gilles Villeneuve | Montreal, Que. | 2.709* | 122.726 | Christiano da Matta (2002) | 100,000 |
| Grand Prix of Denver | Denver, Colo. | 1.657** | 100.370 | Paul Tracy (2005) | |
| Mazda Raceway at Laguna Seca | Monterey, Calif. | 2.238* | 118.969 | Helio Castroneves (2000) | 8,000 |
| Las Vegas Motor Speedway | Las Vegas, Nev. | 1.500 | 206.186 | Patrick Carpentier (2004) | 126,000 |
| Long Beach | Long Beach, Calif. | 1.968** | 104.969 | Gil de Ferran (2000) | 63,000 |
| Autódromo Hermanos Rodríguez | Mexico City, Mexico | 2.786* | 116.733 | Sebastien Bourdais (2004) | |
| The Milwaukee Mile | West Allis, Wisc. | 1.032 | 185.500 | Patrick Carpentier (1998) | 45,000 |
| Portland International Raceway | Portland, Ore. | 1.964* | 122.768 | Helio Castroneves (2000) | 50,000 |
| Road America | Elkhart Lake, Wisc. | 4.048* | 145.924 | Dario Franchitti (2000) | 10,000 |
| Taylor Woodrow Grand Prix | San Jose, Calif. | 1.448** | 96.101 | Sebastien Bourdais (2005) | |
| Gold Coast-Surfers Paradise | Queensland, Australia | 2.795** | 111.547 | Cristiano da Matta (2002) | 55,000 |

*Road courses (not ovals). **Temporary street circuits. .

### IndyCar Series

Founded by Indianapolis Motor Speedway president Tony George, the IndyCar Series competes with CART and fielded 16 races, anchored by the Indianapolis 500, in 2004. Note that the track records listed are for normally-aspirated IRL cars unless otherwise noted by an asterisk.

| | Location | Miles | Qual.mph Record | Set by | Seats |
|---|---|---|---|---|---|
| California Speedway | Fontana, Calif. | 2.0 | 241.428† | Gil de Ferran (2000)* | 92,109 |
| Chicagoland Speedway | Joliet, Ill. | 1.5 | 222.137 | Robbie Buhl (2001) | 75,000 |
| Homestead-Miami Speedway | Homestead, Fla. | 1.5 | 217.388 | Buddy Rice (2004) | 65,000 |
| Indianapolis Motor Speedway | Indianapolis, Ind. | 2.5 | 237.498 | Arie Luyendyk (1996)* | 250,000 |
| Infineon Raceway | Sonoma, Calif. | 2.26* | 108.248 | Ryan Briscoe (2005) | 102,000 |
| Kansas Speedway | Kansas City, Kan. | 1.5 | 218.085 | Scott Dixon (2003) | 75,000 |
| Kentucky Speedway | Sparta, Ky. | 1.5 | 219.191 | Scott Goodyear (2000) | 70,000 |
| Michigan Intl. Speedway | Brooklyn, Mich. | 2.0 | 222.458 | Tomas Scheckter (2003) | 136,373 |
| The Milwaukee Mile | West Allis, Wisc. | 1.032 | 170.296 | Sam Hornish Jr. (2005) | 45,000 |
| Nashville Superspeedway | Nashville, Tenn. | 1.33 | 206.211 | Scott Dixon (2003) | 50,000 |
| Phoenix International Raceway | Phoenix, Ariz. | 1.0 | 183.599 | Arie Luyendyk (1996)* | 78,450 |
| Pikes Peak Int'l. Raceway | Fountain, Colo. | 1.0 | 179.874 | Greg Ray (2000) | 42,787 |
| Richmond International Raceway | Richmond, Va. | 0.75 | 176.244 | Sam Hornish Jr. (2005) | 95,920 |
| Grand Prix of St. Petersburg | St. Petersburg, Fla. | 1.8** | 103.664 | Bryan Herta (2005) | |
| Texas Motor Speedway | Fort Worth, Texas | 1.5 | 225.979 | Billy Boat (1998) | 154,861 |
| Twin Ring Motegi | Motegi, Japan | 1.549 | 206.996 | Scott Dixon (2003) | 50,000 |
| Watkins Glen International | Watkins Glen, N.Y. | 3.4 | 133.806 | Helio Castroneves (2005) | 35,000 |

*Road course. **Temporary street circuit. †Indicates world closed-course record for auto racing.

### NEXTEL Cup

| | Location | Miles | Qual.mph Record | Set by | Seats |
|---|---|---|---|---|---|
| Atlanta Motor Speedway | Hampton, Ga. | 1.54 | 197.478 | Geoff Bodine (1997) | 124,000 |
| Bristol Motor Speedway | Bristol, Tenn. | 0.533 | 128.709 | Ryan Newman (2003) | 147,000 |
| California Speedway | Fontana, Calif. | 2.0 | 188.245 | Kyle Busch (2005) | 92,000 |
| Chicagoland Speedway | Joliet, Ill. | 1.5 | 188.147 | Jimmie Johnson (2005) | 75,000 |
| Darlington International Raceway | Darlington, S.C. | 1.366 | 173.797 | Ward Burton (1996) | 65,000 |
| Daytona International Speedway | Daytona Beach, Fla. | 2.5 | 210.364 | Bill Elliott (1987) | 168,000 |
| Dover International Speedway | Dover, Del. | 1.0 | 161.522 | Jeremy Mayfield (2004) | 140,000 |
| Homestead-Miami Speedway | Homestead, Fla. | 1.5 | 181.111 | Jamie McMurray (2003) | 72,000 |
| Indianapolis Motor Speedway | Indianapolis, Ind. | 2.5 | 186.293 | Casey Mears (2004) | 250,000+ |
| Infineon Raceway | Sonoma, Calif. | 1.99* | 94.325 | Jeff Gordon (2005) | 42,500 |
| Kansas Speedway | Kansas City, Kan. | 1.5 | 180.373 | Jimmie Johnson (2003) | 75,000 |
| Las Vegas Motor Speedway | Las Vegas, Nev. | 1.5 | 174.904 | Kasey Kahne (2004) | 126,000 |
| Lowe's Motor Speedway | Concord, N.C. | 1.5 | 192.988 | Ryan Newman (2005) | 167,000 |
| Martinsville Speedway | Martinsville, Va. | 0.526 | 97.043 | Ryan Newman (2004) | 91,000 |
| Michigan Speedway | Brooklyn, Mich. | 2.0 | 194.232 | Ryan Newman (2005) | 136,384 |
| New Hampshire Int'l Speedway | Loudon, N.H. | 1.058 | 133.357 | Ryan Newman (2003) | 91,000 |
| Phoenix International Raceway | Phoenix, Ariz. | 1.0 | 135.854 | Ryan Newman (2004) | 76,812 |

## Auto Racing (Cont.)

| | | Miles | Qual.mph Record | Set by | |
|---|---|---|---|---|---|
| Pocono Raceway | Long Pond, Penn. | 2.5 | 172.533 | Kasey Kahne (2004) | 77,000 |
| Richmond International Raceway | Richmond, Va. | 0.75 | 129.983 | Brian Vickers (2004) | 107,097 |
| Talladega Superspeedway | Talladega, Ala. | 2.66 | 212.809 | Bill Elliott (1987) | 143,000 |
| Texas Motor Speedway | Ft. Worth, Texas | 1.5 | 194.224 | Bill Elliott (2002) | 154,861 |
| Watkins Glen International | Watkins Glen, N.Y. | 2.45* | 181.068 | Ricky Rudd (2000) | 40,000 |

*Road courses (not ovals).

## Formula One

Race track capacity figures unavailable.

| Grand Prix | | Miles | Qual.mph Record | Set by |
|---|---|---|---|---|
| Australian | Albert Park (Melbourne) | 3.295 | 140.537 | Michael Schumacher (2004) |
| Bahrain | Bahrain International (Sakhir) | 3.366 | 134.432 | Michael Schumacher (2004) |
| Belgian | Spa-Francorchamps | 4.333 | 143.418 | Mika Hakkinen (1998) |
| Brazilian | Interlagos (Sao Paulo) | 2.684 | 193.747 | Rubens Barrichello (2003) |
| British | Silverstone (Towcester) | 3.194 | 148.043 | Nigel Mansell (1992) |
| Canadian | Circuit Gilles Villeneuve (Montreal) | 2.747 | 133.941 | Juan Montoya (2002) |
| China | Shanghai International | 3.387 | 129.867 | Rubens Barrichello (2004) |
| European | Nürburgring (Nürburg, Germany) | 2.822 | 135.959 | Michael Schumacher (2001) |
| French | Magny Cours (Nevers) | 2.641 | 159.757 | Juan Montoya (2002) |
| German | Hockenheim (Germany) | 2.796 | 204.450 | Michael Schumacher (2002) |
| Hungarian | Hungaroring (Budapest) | 2.468 | 122.410 | Michael Schumacher (2005) |
| Italian | Autodromo Nazionale di Monza (Milan) | 3.585 | 161.460 | Juan Pablo Montoya (2002) |
| Japanese | Suzuka (Nagoya) | 3.644 | 138.565 | Michael Schumacher (2004) |
| Malaysian | Sepang (Kuala Lumpur) | 3.444 | 133.220 | Michael Schumacher (2004) |
| Monaco | Monte Carlo (Monaco) | 2.082 | 141.595 | Rubens Barrichello (2002) |
| San Marino | Autodromo Enzo e Dino Ferrari (Imola, Italy) | 3.063 | 138.362 | Jenson Button (2004) |
| Spanish | Catalunya (Barcelona) | 2.937 | 140.935 | Michael Schumacher (2004) |
| Turkish | Otodrom (Istanbul) | 3.293 | 137.323 | Kimi Raikkonen (2005) |
| United States | Indianapolis Motor Speedway | 2.606 | 133.595 | Rubens Barrichello (2004) |

## SOCCER

## World's Premier Soccer Stadiums

(Listed alphabetically by city)

| Stadium | Location | Seats | Stadium | Location | Seats |
|---|---|---|---|---|---|
| New Olympic | Athens, Greece | 72,000 | Estadio Azteca | Mexico City, Mexico | 106,000 |
| Eden Park | Auckland, New Zealand | 50,000 | Meazza (San Siro) | Milan, Italy | 85,700 |
| Nou Camp | Barcelona, Spain | 98,000 | Centenario | Montevideo, Uruguay | 76,609 |
| Workers' | Beijing, China | 72,000 | Luzhniki Stadion | Moscow, Russia | 80,840 |
| Olympiastadion | Berlin, Germany | 76,243 | Olympiastadion | Munich, Germany | 63,000 |
| Népstadion | Budapest, Hungary | 65,000 | San Paolo | Naples, Italy | 78,210 |
| Antonio Liberti | Buenos Aires, Argentina | 76,689 | Stade de France | Paris, France | 80,000 |
| National | Cairo, Egypt | 90,000 | Rungnado (May Day) | Pyongyang, N. Korea | 150,000 |
| Salt Lake | Calcutta, India | 120,000 | Maracana | Rio de Janeiro, Brazil | 70,000 |
| Millennium | Cardiff, Wales | 72,500 | King Fahd II | Riyadh, Saudi Arabia | 79,000 |
| Westfalenstadion | Dortmund, Germany | 68,600 | Olimpico | Rome, Italy | 82,307 |
| Lansdowne Road | Dublin, Ireland | 48,000 | Nacional | Santiago, Chile | 77,000 |
| Celtic Park | Glasgow, Scotland | 60,506 | Morumbi | Sao Paulo, Brazil | 80,000 |
| Hampden Park | Glasgow, Scotland | 52,670 | Chasmil | Seoul, S. Korea | 100,000 |
| FNB Stadium | Johannesburg, S. Africa | 90,000 | Stadium Australia | Sydney, Australia | 80,000 |
| Olympic Stadium | Kiev, Ukraine | 83,160 | Azadi | Tehran, Iran | 100,000 |
| new Estadio da Luz | Lisbon, Portugal | 65,000 | Delle Alpi | Turin, Italy | 69,041 |
| Santiago Bernabeu | Madrid, Spain | 106,500 | Ernst Happel | Vienna, Austria | 47,500 |
| Old Trafford | Manchester, England | 67,650 | International | Yokohama, Japan | 70,574 |

## Major League Soccer

The 12-team MLS is the only U.S. Division I professional outdoor league sanctioned by FIFA and U.S. Soccer. Note that all capacity figures are approximate given the adjustments of football stadium seating to soccer.

### Western Conference

| | Stadium | Built | Seats | Field |
|---|---|---|---|---|
| CD Chivas USA | Home Depot Center | 2003 | 27,000 | Grass |
| Colorado Rapids | INVESCO Field | 2001 | 17,500 | Grass |
| FC Dallas | Pizza Hut Park | 2005 | 21,193 | Grass |
| L.A. Galaxy | Home Depot Center | 2003 | 27,000 | Grass |
| Real Salt Lake | Rice-Eccles Stadium | 1927 | 45,634 | Grass |
| San Jose Earthquakes | Spartan | 1933 | 26,525 | Grass |

### Eastern Conference

| | Stadium | Built | Seats | Field |
|---|---|---|---|---|
| Chicago Fire | Bridgeview | 2006 | 20,000 | Grass |
| Columbus Crew | Columbus Crew | 1999 | 22,555 | Grass |
| D.C. United | RFK | 1961 | 26,169 | Grass |
| Kansas City Wizards | Arrowhead | 1972 | 20,571 | Grass |
| Metro Stars (N.Y./N.J.) | Giants | 1976 | 25,576 | Grass |
| N.E. Revolution | Gillette | 2002 | 21,000 | Grass |

## Horse Racing
### Triple Crown race tracks

| Race | Racetrack | Seats | Infield |
|---|---|---|---|
| Kentucky Derby | Churchill Downs | 48,500 | 65,000 |
| Preakness Stakes | Pimlico Race Course | 13,047 | 60,000 |
| Belmont Stakes | Belmont Park | 32,941 | N/A |

**Record crowds:** Kentucky Derby—163,628 (1974);
Preakness—112,668 (2004); Belmont—120,139 (2004).
**Note:** Belmont Park does not open infield for Belmont Stakes.

## Tennis
### Grand Slam center courts

| Event | Main Stadium | Seats |
|---|---|---|
| Australian Open | Melbourne Park | 15,021 |
| French Open | Stade Roland Garros | 16,300 |
| Wimbledon | Centre Court | 13,813 |
| U.S. Open | Arthur Ashe Stadium | 22,547 |

## COLLEGE BASKETBALL
### The 50 Largest Arenas

The 50 largest arenas in Division I for the 2005-06 NCAA regular season. Note that (*) indicates part-time home court.

| | | Seats | Home Team | | | Seats | Home Team |
|---|---|---|---|---|---|---|---|
| 1 | Carrier Dome | 33,000 | Syracuse | 26 | Allen Fieldhouse | 16,300 | Kansas |
| 2 | Thompson-Boling Arena | 24,535 | Tennessee | 27 | Hartford Civic Center | 16,294 | UConn* |
| 3 | Rupp Arena | 23,500 | Kentucky | 28 | L.A. Sports Arena | 16,161 | USC |
| 4 | Marriott Center | 22,700 | BYU | 29 | Save Mart Center | 16,116 | Fresno St. |
| 5 | Dean Smith Center | 21,800 | N. Carolina | 30 | Carver-Hawkeye Arena | 15,500 | Iowa |
| 6 | MCI Center | 20,674 | Georgetown* | | Pepsi Arena | 15,500 | Siena |
| 7 | Continental Airlines Arena | 20,049 | Seton Hall | | Qwest Center Omaha | 15,500 | Creighton |
| 8 | Savvis Center | 20,000 | Saint Louis | 33 | Bryce Jordan Center | 15,261 | Penn St. |
| 9 | RBC Center | 19,722 | N.C. State | 34 | United Spirit Arena | 15,098 | Texas Tech |
| 10 | Value City Arena | 19,500 | Ohio St. | 35 | Mizzou Arena | 15,061 | Missouri |
| 11 | Bud Walton Arena | 19,200 | Arkansas | 36 | Coleman Coliseum | 15,043 | Alabama |
| 12 | Wachovia Center | 19,010 | Villanova* | 37 | Arena-Auditorium | 15,028 | Wyoming |
| 13 | Freedom Hall | 18,865 | Louisville | 38 | Huntsman Center | 15,000 | Utah |
| 14 | Bradley Center | 18,717 | Marquette | 39 | Breslin Events Center | 14,992 | Michigan St. |
| 15 | Thomas & Mack Center | 18,500 | UNLV | 40 | LJVM Coliseum | 14,665 | Wake Forest |
| 16 | Madison Square Garden | 18,470 | St. John's* | 41 | Williams Arena | 14,625 | Minnesota |
| 17 | FedEx Forum | 18,400 | Memphis | 42 | McKale Center | 14,545 | Arizona |
| 18 | University Arena (The Pit) | 18,018 | New Mexico | 43 | Maravich Assembly Ctr | 14,236 | LSU |
| 19 | Comcast Center | 17,950 | Maryland | 44 | Wells Fargo Arena | 14,198 | Arizona St. |
| 20 | Colonial Center | 17,600 | South Carolina | 45 | Memorial Gym | 14,168 | Vanderbilt |
| 21 | Allstate Arena | 17,500 | DePaul | 46 | Mackey Arena | 14,123 | Purdue |
| 22 | Assembly Hall | 17,456 | Indiana | 47 | James H. Hilton Coliseum | 14,092 | Iowa St. |
| 23 | Herb Kohl Center | 17,142 | Wisconsin | 48 | WVU Coliseum | 14,000 | West Virginia |
| 24 | Frank Erwin Center | 16,755 | Texas | 49 | Crisler Arena | 13,751 | Michigan |
| 25 | Assembly Hall | 16,450 | Illinois | 50 | Wolstein Center | 13,610 | Cleveland St. |

### Division I Conference Home Courts

NCAA Division I conferences for the 2005-06 season. Teams with home games in more than one arena are noted.

#### America East

| | Home Floor | Seats |
|---|---|---|
| Albany | Rec & Convocation Ctr. | 5,000 |
| Binghamton | Events Center | 5,142 |
| Boston University | Case Gym | 1,800 |
| | & Agganis Arena | 5,687 |
| Hartford | Reich Family Pavilion | 3,977 |
| Maine | Alfond Arena | 5,712 |
| MD-Balt. County | RAC Arena | 4,024 |
| New Hampshire | Lundholm Gym | 3,500 |
| Stony Brook | SB Sports Complex | 4,103 |
| Vermont | Patrick Gym | 3,266 |

#### Atlantic Sun

| | Home Floor | Seats |
|---|---|---|
| Belmont | Municipal Auditorium | 5,000 |
| Campbell | Carter Gym | 1,050 |
| East Tennessee St. | Memorial Center | 12,000 |
| Fla. Atlantic | FAU Gym | 5,000 |
| Gardner-Webb | Paul Porter Arena | 5,000 |
| Jacksonville | Swisher Gym | 1,500 |
| Kennesaw St. | KSU Convocation Center | 4,500 |
| Lipscomb | Lipscomb U. Arena | 5,028 |
| Mercer | University Center | 3,200 |
| North Florida | UNF Arena | 5,800 |
| Stetson | Edmunds Center | 5,000 |

#### Atlantic Coast

| | Home Floor | Seats |
|---|---|---|
| Boston College | Silvio O. Conte Forum | 8,606 |
| Clemson | Littlejohn Coliseum | 11,020 |
| Duke | Cameron Indoor Stadium | 9,314 |
| Florida St. | Donald L. Tucker Center | 12,200 |
| Georgia Tech | Alexander Memorial Coliseum | 9,191 |
| Maryland | Comcast Center | 17,950 |
| Miami-FL | Convocation Center | 7,000 |
| North Carolina | Dean Smith Center | 21,800 |
| N.C. State | RBC Center | 19,722 |
| Virginia | University Hall | 8,392 |
| Virginia Tech | Cassell Coliseum | 10,052 |
| Wake Forest | LJVM Coliseum | 14,665 |

#### Atlantic 10

| | Home Floor | Seats |
|---|---|---|
| Charlotte | Halton Arena | 9,105 |
| Dayton | U. of Dayton Arena | 13,266 |
| Duquesne | Palumbo Center | 6,200 |
| Fordham | Rose Hill Gym | 3,470 |
| George Washington | Smith Center | 5,000 |
| La Salle | Tom Gola Arena | 4,000 |
| Massachusetts | Mullins Center | 9,493 |
| Rhode Island | Ryan Center | 7,657 |
| Richmond | Robins Center | 9,071 |
| St. Bonaventure | Reilly Center | 6,000 |
| Saint Louis | Savvis Center | 20,000 |
| St. Joseph's | Alumni Mem. Fieldhouse | 3,200 |
| Temple | Liacouras Center | 10,206 |
| Xavier-OH | Cintas Center | 10,250 |

## College Basketball (Cont.)

### Big East

| | Home Floor | Seats |
|---|---|---|
| Cincinnati | Fifth Third Arena | 13,176 |
| Connecticut | Gampel Pavilion | 10,027 |
| | & Hartford Civic Center | 16,294 |
| DePaul | Allstate Arena | 17,500 |
| Georgetown | MCI Center | 20,674 |
| | & McDonough Arena | 2,500 |
| Louisville | Freedom Hall | 18,865 |
| Marquette | Bradley Center | 18,717 |
| Notre Dame | Joyce Center | 11,418 |
| Pittsburgh | Petersen Event Center | 12,500 |
| Providence | Dunkin Donuts Center | 12,993 |
| Rutgers | Louis Brown Athletic Center (The RAC) | 9,000 |
| St. John's | Carnesecca Arena | 6,008 |
| | & Madison Square Garden | 18,470 |
| Seton Hall | Continental Airlines Arena | 20,049 |
| South Florida | Sun Dome | 10,411 |
| Syracuse | Carrier Dome | 33,000 |
| Villanova | The Pavilion | 6,500 |
| | & Wachovia Center | 19,010 |
| West Virginia | WVU Coliseum | 14,000 |

### Big Sky

| | Home Floor | Seats |
|---|---|---|
| Eastern Wash | Reese Court | 6,000 |
| Idaho St. | Reed Gym | 3,040 |
| Montana | Dahlberg Arena | 7,321 |
| Montana St. | Worthington Arena | 7,250 |
| Northern Arizona | Walkup Skydome | 7,000 |
| Northern Colorado | Butler-Hancock Sports Pavilion | 4,500 |
| Portland St. | Stott Center | 1,500 |
| Sacramento St. | Hornets Nest | 1,200 |
| Weber St. | Dee Events Center | 12,000 |

### Big South

| | Home Floor | Seats |
|---|---|---|
| Birmingham-Southern | Bill Battle Coliseum | 2,000 |
| Charleston Southern | CSU Fieldhouse | 1,500 |
| Coastal Carolina | Kimbel Gymnasium | 1,037 |
| High Point | Millis Center | 2,565 |
| Liberty | Vines Center | 9,000 |
| NC-Asheville | Justice Center | 1,100 |
| | & Asheville Civic Center | 6,000 |
| Radford | Dedmon Center | 5,000 |
| VMI | Cameron Hall | 5,800 |
| Winthrop | Winthrop Coliseum | 6,100 |

### Big Ten

| | Home Floor | Seats |
|---|---|---|
| Illinois | Assembly Hall | 16,450 |
| Indiana | Assembly Hall | 17,456 |
| Iowa | Carver-Hawkeye Arena | 15,500 |
| Michigan | Crisler Arena | 13,751 |
| Michigan St. | Breslin Events Center | 14,759 |
| Minnesota | Williams Arena | 14,625 |
| Northwestern | Welsh-Ryan Arena | 8,117 |
| Ohio St. | Value City Arena at Schottenstein Center | 19,500 |
| Penn St. | Bryce Jordan Center | 15,261 |
| Purdue | Mackey Arena | 14,123 |
| Wisconsin | Kohl Center | 17,142 |

### Big 12

| | Home Floor | Seats |
|---|---|---|
| Baylor | Ferrell Center | 10,284 |
| Colorado | Coors Events Conference Ctr. | 11,064 |
| Iowa St. | Hilton Coliseum | 14,092 |
| Kansas | Allen Fieldhouse | 16,300 |
| Kansas St. | Bramlage Coliseum | 13,595 |
| Missouri | Mizzou Arena | 15,061 |
| Nebraska | Devaney Sports Center | 13,500 |
| Oklahoma | Lloyd Noble Center | 12,000 |
| Oklahoma St. | Gallagher-Iba Arena | 13,611 |
| Texas | Erwin Center | 16,755 |
| Texas A&M | Reed Arena | 12,500 |
| Texas Tech | United Spirit Arena | 15,098 |

### Big West

| | Home Floor | Seats |
|---|---|---|
| Cal Poly | Mott Gym | 3,032 |
| CS-Fullerton | Titan Gym | 4,000 |
| CS-Northridge | The Matadome | 1,600 |
| Long Beach St. | The Walter Pyramid | 5,000 |
| Pacific | Alex G. Spanos Center | 6,150 |
| UC-Davis | The Pavilion | 7,200 |
| UC-Irvine | Bren Events Center | 5,000 |
| UC-Riverside | Student Rec. Center | 3,168 |
| UC-Santa Barbara | The Thunderdome | 6,000 |

### Colonial Athletic Association

| | Home Floor | Seats |
|---|---|---|
| Delaware | Bob Carpenter Center | 5,000 |
| Drexel | Daskalis Athletic Center | 2,300 |
| George Mason | Patriot Center | 10,000 |
| Georgia St. | GSU Sports Arena | 4,500 |
| Hofstra | Hofstra Arena | 5,124 |
| James Madison | JMU Convocation Center | 7,156 |
| Northeastern | Solomon Court | 1,500 |
| | & Matthews Arena | 6,000 |
| NC-Wilmington | Trask Coliseum | 6,100 |
| Old Dominion | Ted Constant Convocation Ctr. | 8,650 |
| Towson | Towson Center | 5,000 |
| VCU | Siegel Center | 7,500 |
| William & Mary | William & Mary Hall | 8,600 |

### Conference USA

| | Home Floor | Seats |
|---|---|---|
| UAB | Bartow Arena | 8,500 |
| Central Fla. | UCF Arena | 5,100 |
| East Carolina | Williams Arena at Minges Coliseum | 8,000 |
| Houston | Hofheinz Pavilion | 8,479 |
| Marshall | Cam Henderson Center | 9,043 |
| Memphis | FedEx Forum | 18,400 |
| Rice | Autry Court | 5,000 |
| SMU | Moody Coliseum | 8,998 |
| Southern Miss | Reed Green Coliseum | 8,095 |
| Tulane | Fogelman Arena | 3,600 |
| Tulsa | Reynolds Center | 8,355 |
| UTEP | Haskins Center | 12,000 |

### Horizon League

| | Home Floor | Seats |
|---|---|---|
| Butler | Hinkle Fieldhouse | 11,043 |
| Cleveland St. | Wolstein Center | 13,610 |
| Detroit Mercy | Calihan Hall | 8,837 |
| IL-Chicago | UIC Pavilion | 8,000 |
| Loyola-IL | Gentile Center | 5,200 |
| WI-Green Bay | Resch Center | 10,400 |
| WI-Milwaukee | U.S. Cellular Arena | 10,783 |
| Wright St. | Nutter Center | 10,632 |
| Youngstown St. | Beeghly Center | 6,500 |

### Men's Basketball Attendance Leaders

Schools ranked by average attendance for 2004-05 season.

| | | Gm | Attendance | Average |
|---|---|---|---|---|
| 1 | Syracuse | 18 | 413,605 | 22,978 |
| 2 | Kentucky | 15 | 337,796 | 22,520 |
| 3 | North Carolina | 15 | 307,840 | 20,522 |
| 4 | Louisville | 17 | 318,688 | 18,746 |
| 5 | Wisconsin | 16 | 274,272 | 17,142 |

### Ivy League

| | Home Floor | Seats |
|---|---|---|
| Brown | Pizzitola Sports Center | 2,800 |
| Columbia | Levien Gymnasium | 3,408 |
| Cornell | Newman Arena | 4,473 |
| Dartmouth | Leede Arena | 2,100 |
| Harvard | Lavietes Pavilion | 2,195 |
| Penn | The Palestra | 8,700 |
| Princeton | Jadwin Gymnasium | 6,854 |
| Yale | Payne Whitney Gym | 3,100 |

### Metro Atlantic

| | Home Floor | Seats |
|---|---|---|
| Canisius | Koessler Athletic Center | 2,176 |
| Fairfield | Arena at Harbor Yard | 9,000 |
| Iona | Mulcahy Center | 3,200 |
| Loyola-MD | Reitz Arena | 3,000 |
| Manhattan | Draddy Gymnasium | 3,000 |
| Marist | McCann Center | 3,944 |
| Niagara | Gallagher Center | 2,400 |
| Rider | Alumni Gymnasium | 1,650 |
| St. Peter's | Yanitelli Center | 3,200 |
| Siena | Pepsi Arena | 15,500 |

### Mid-American

| | Home Floor | Seats |
|---|---|---|
| Akron | JAR Arena | 5,942 |
| Ball St. | John E. Worthen Arena | 11,500 |
| Bowling Green | Anderson Arena | 5,000 |
| Buffalo | Alumni Arena | 6,100 |
| Central Mich. | Rose Arena | 5,200 |
| Eastern Mich. | Convocation Center | 8,824 |
| Kent St. | MAC Center | 6,327 |
| Miami-OH | Millett Hall | 9,200 |
| Northern Illinois | Convocation Center | 9,100 |
| Ohio Univ. | Convocation Center | 13,000 |
| Toledo | Savage Hall | 9,000 |
| Western Mich. | University Arena | 5,421 |

### Mid-Continent

| | Home Floor | Seats |
|---|---|---|
| Centenary | Gold Dome | 3,000 |
| Chicago St. | Dickens Athletic Center | 2,500 |
| IUPUI | IUPUI Gym | 2,000 |
| Missouri-KC | Municipal Auditorium | 9,827 |
| | & Kemper Arena | 18,646 |
| Oakland | Athletics Center O'Rena | 4,000 |
| Oral Roberts | Mabee Center | 10,575 |
| Southern Utah | Centrum | 5,300 |
| Valparaiso | Athletics-Recreation Center | 5,000 |
| Western Ill. | Western Hall | 5,139 |

### Mid-Eastern Athletic

| | Home Floor | Seats |
|---|---|---|
| Bethune-Cookman | Moore Gym | 3,000 |
| Coppin St. | Coppin Center | 3,000 |
| Delaware St. | Memorial Hall | 3,000 |
| Florida A&M | Gaither Gym | 3,365 |
| Hampton | Hampton Convocation Center | 7,500 |
| Howard | Burr Gym | 2,200 |
| MD-East.Shore | W.P. Hytche Center | 5,500 |
| Morgan St. | Hill Fieldhouse | 4,500 |
| Norfolk St. | Echols Hall | 7,600 |
| N. Carolina A&T | Corbett Sports Center | 6,700 |
| South Carolina St. | SHM Center | 3,200 |

### Missouri Valley

| | Home Floor | Seats |
|---|---|---|
| Bradley | Carver Arena | 11,300 |
| Creighton | Qwest Center OMAHA | 15,500 |
| Drake | Knapp Center | 7,002 |
| Evansville | Roberts Stadium | 11,600 |
| Illinois St. | Redbird Arena | 10,200 |
| Indiana St. | Hulman Center | 10,200 |
| Missouri St. | Hammons Student Center | 8,846 |
| Northern Iowa | UNI-Dome | 10,000 |
| Southern Ill. | SIU Arena | 10,000 |
| Wichita St. | Charles Koch Arena | 10,400 |

### Mountain West

| | Home Floor | Seats |
|---|---|---|
| Air Force | Clune Arena | 6,002 |
| BYU | Marriott Center | 22,700 |
| Colorado St. | Moby Arena | 8,745 |
| UNLV | Thomas & Mack Center | 18,500 |
| New Mexico | The Pit | 18,018 |
| San Diego St. | Cox Arena at the Aztec Bowl | 12,414 |
| TCU | Daniel-Meyer Coliseum | 7,201 |
| Utah | Jon M. Huntsman Center | 15,000 |
| Wyoming | Arena-Auditorium | 15,028 |

### Northeast

| | Home Floor | Seats |
|---|---|---|
| Central Conn. St. | Detrick Gym | 3,200 |
| Farleigh Dickinson | Rothman Center | 5,000 |
| LIU-Brooklyn | ARW Center | 3,000 |
| Monmouth | Boylan Gym | 2,500 |
| Mt. St. Mary's | Knott Arena | 3,121 |
| Quinnipiac | Burt Kahn Court | 2,000 |
| Robert Morris | Sewall Center | 3,056 |
| Sacred Heart | Pitt Center | 2,100 |
| St. Francis-NY | Pope Center | 1,200 |
| St. Francis-PA | DeGol Arena | 3,500 |
| Wagner | Spiro Sports Center | 2,100 |

### Ohio Valley

| | Home Floor | Seats |
|---|---|---|
| Austin Peay | Dunn Center | 9,000 |
| Eastern Illinois | Lantz Gym | 5,300 |
| Eastern Ky. | McBrayer Arena | 6,500 |
| Jacksonville St. | Mathews Coliseum | 5,500 |
| Morehead St. | Johnson Arena | 6,500 |
| Murray St. | Regional Special Events Ctr. | 8,602 |
| Samford | Seibert Hall | 4,000 |
| SE Missouri St. | Show Me Center | 7,000 |
| Tennessee-Martin | Skyhawk Arena | 6,700 |
| Tennessee St. | Gentry Complex | 10,500 |
| Tennessee Tech | Eblen Center | 10,152 |

### Pacific-10

| | Home Floor | Seats |
|---|---|---|
| Arizona | McKale Center | 14,545 |
| Arizona St. | Wells Fargo Arena | 14,198 |
| California | Haas Pavilion | 11,877 |
| Oregon | McArthur Court | 9,087 |
| Oregon St. | Gill Coliseum | 10,400 |
| Stanford | Maples Pavilion | 7,391 |
| UCLA | Pauley Pavilion | 12,819 |
| USC | LA Sports Arena | 16,161 |
| Washington | Bank of America Arena | 10,000 |
| Washington St. | Friel Court | 11,566 |

### NBA and College Buildings

Six division I teams play at least a portion of their home games in an NBA building and thanks to Hurricane Katrina one NBA team, the New Orleans Hornets, will be playing a portion of their home games on a college court in 2005-06.

| Building | College | NBA Team | Building | College | NBA Team |
|---|---|---|---|---|---|
| MCI Center | Georgetown | Wizards | Madison Square Garden | St. John's | Knicks |
| Continental Airlines Arena | Seton Hall | Nets | FedEx Forum | Memphis | Grizzlies |
| Wachovia Center | Villanova | 76ers | Maravich Center | LSU | Hornets |
| Bradley Center | Marquette | Bucks | | | |

## College Basketball (Cont.)

### Patriot League

| | Home Floor | Seats |
|---|---|---|
| American | Bender Arena | 4,500 |
| Army | Christl Arena | 5,043 |
| Bucknell | Gary A. Sojka Pavilion | 4,000 |
| Colgate | Cotterell Court | 3,000 |
| Holy Cross | Hart Recreation Center | 3,600 |
| Lafayette | Kirby Sports Center | 3,500 |
| Lehigh | Stabler Arena | 5,600 |
| Navy | Alumni Hall | 5,710 |

### Southeastern

| Eastern | Home Floor | Seats |
|---|---|---|
| Florida | O'Connell Center | 12,000 |
| Georgia | Stegeman Coliseum | 10,523 |
| Kentucky | Rupp Arena | 23,500 |
| South Carolina | Colonial Center | 17,600 |
| Tennessee | Thompson-Boling Arena | 24,535 |
| Vanderbilt | Memorial Gymnasium | 14,168 |
| **Western** | **Home Floor** | **Seats** |
| Alabama | Coleman Coliseum | 15,043 |
| Arkansas | Bud Walton Arena | 19,200 |
| Auburn | Beard-Eaves-Memorial Coliseum | 10,500 |
| LSU | Maravich Assembly Center | 14,164 |
| Mississippi | Tad Smith Coliseum | 8,700 |
| Mississippi St. | Humphrey Coliseum | 10,500 |

### Southern

| | Home Floor | Seats |
|---|---|---|
| Appalachian St. | Seby Jones Arena | 8,300 |
| The Citadel | McAlister Field House | 6,200 |
| Coll. of Charleston | John Kresse Arena | 5,000 |
| Davidson | Belk Arena | 5,700 |
| Elon | Koury Center | 2,000 |
| Furman | Timmons Arena | 5,000 |
| Ga. Southern | Hanner Fieldhouse | 5,500 |
| NC-Greensboro | Fleming Gymnasium | 2,320 |
| Chattanooga | McKenzie Arena | 11,218 |
| W. Carolina | Ramsey Center | 7,286 |
| Wofford | Johnson Arena | 3,500 |

### Southland

| | Home Floor | Seats |
|---|---|---|
| Lamar | Montagne Center | 10,080 |
| Louisiana-Monroe | Fant-Ewing Coliseum | 8,000 |
| McNeese St. | Burton Coliseum | 8,000 |
| Nicholls St. | Stopher Gym | 3,800 |
| Northwestern St. | Prather Coliseum | 4,300 |
| Sam Houston St. | Johnson Coliseum | 6,172 |
| SE Louisiana | University Center | 7,500 |
| S.F. Austin St. | W.R. Johnson Coliseum | 7,200 |
| Texas A&M-Corpus Christi | Memorial Coliseum | 4,000 |
| TX-Arlington | Texas Hall | 4,200 |
| TX-San Antonio | Convocation Center | 5,100 |
| Texas St. | Strahan Coliseum | 7,200 |

### Southwestern Athletic

| | Home Floor | Seats |
|---|---|---|
| Alabama A&M | Elmore Healh/Science Building | 6,000 |
| Alabama St. | Joe Reed Acadome | 8,000 |
| Alcorn St. | Whitney Complex | 7,000 |
| Arkansas-Pine Bluff | HPER Complex | 4,500 |
| Grambling St. | Tiger Memorial Gym | 4,500 |
| Jackson St. | Williams Center | 8,000 |
| Miss.Valley St. | Harrison HPER Athletic Complex | 6,000 |
| Prairie View A&M | The Baby Dome | 6,600 |
| Southern-BR | Clark Activity Center | 7,500 |
| TX Southern | Health & P.E. Building | 8,100 |

### Sun Belt

| | Home Floor | Seats |
|---|---|---|
| Arkansas-Little Rock | Stephens Center | 5,600 |
| Arkansas St | Convocation Center | 10,563 |
| Denver | Magness Arena | 7,200 |
| Florida International | Pharmed Arena | 5,000 |
| LA-Lafayette | The Cajundome | 11,550 |
| Middle Tennessee | Murphy Center | 11,520 |
| New Orleans | Lakefront Arena | 8,933 |
| North Texas | The Super Pit | 10,032 |
| South Alabama | Mitchell Center | 10,000 |
| Troy | Trojan Arena | 4,000 |
| Western Ky. | E.A. Diddle Arena | 7,326 |

### West Coast

| | Home Floor | Seats |
|---|---|---|
| Gonzaga | McCarthey Athletic Center | 6,000 |
| Loyola Marymount | Gersten Pavilion | 4,156 |
| Pepperdine | Firestone Fieldhouse | 3,104 |
| Portland | Chiles Center | 5,000 |
| St. Mary's-CA | McKeon Pavilion | 3,500 |
| San Diego | Jenny Craig Pavilion | 5,100 |
| San Francisco | War Memorial Gym | 5,300 |
| Santa Clara | Leavy Center | 5,000 |

### Western Athletic

| | Home Floor | Seats |
|---|---|---|
| Boise St. | BSU Pavilion | 12,380 |
| Fresno St. | Save Mart Center | 16,116 |
| Hawaii | Stan Sheriff Center | 10,300 |
| Idaho | Cowan Spectrum | 7,000 |
| Louisiana Tech | Thomas Assembly Center | 8,000 |
| Nevada | Lawlor Events Center | 11,200 |
| New Mexico St. | Pan American Center | 13,071 |
| San Jose St. | The Event Center | 5,000 |
| Utah St. | Dee Glen Smith Spectrum | 10,270 |

### Independents

| | Home Floor | Seats |
|---|---|---|
| IPFW | Hilliard Gates Sports Center | 2,700 |
| Longwood | Henry I. Willet Jr. Hall | 2,522 |
| North Dakota St. | Bison Sports Arena | 7,500 |
| Savannah St. | Wiley Gym | 2,100 |
| South Dakota St. | Frost Arena | 8,500 |
| Texas-Pan Am | Health/PE Fieldhouse | 3,500 |
| Utah Valley St. | McKay Center | 8,000 |

## Future NCAA Final Four Sites

### Men

| Year | Arena | Seats | Location |
|---|---|---|---|
| 2006 | RCA Dome | 47,100 | Indianapolis |
| 2007 | Georgia Dome | 40,000 | Atlanta |
| 2008 | Alamodome | 20,557* | San Antonio |
| 2009 | Ford Field | TBA | Detroit |
| 2010 | RCA Dome | 47,100 | Indianapolis |
| 2011 | Reliant Stadium | TBA | Houston |

### Women

| Year | Arena | Seats | Location |
|---|---|---|---|
| 2006 | TD Banknorth Garden | 18,624 | Boston |
| 2007 | Quicken Loans Arena | 20,562 | Cleveland |
| 2008 | St. Pete Times Forum | 19,758 | Tampa |
| 2009 | Edward Jones Dome | TBA | St. Louis |
| 2010 | Alamodome | 20,557* | San Antonio |

*This was the listed capacity for Spurs games at the Alamodome before they moved to the SBC Center. It is likely that the seating will be reconfigured to fit more spectators for the Final Four.

## COLLEGE FOOTBALL

### The 40 Largest I-A Stadiums

The 40 largest stadiums in NCAA Division I-A college football heading into the 2005 season. Note that (*) indicates stadium not on campus.

| | | Location | Seats | Home Team | Conference | Built | Field |
|---|---|---|---|---|---|---|---|
| 1 | Michigan Stadium | Ann Arbor, Mich. | 107,501 | Michigan | Big Ten | 1927 | Turf |
| 2 | Beaver Stadium | University Park, Penn. | 107,282 | Penn St. | Big Ten | 1960 | Grass |
| 3 | Neyland Stadium | Knoxville, Tenn. | 104,079 | Tennessee | SEC-East | 1921 | Grass |
| 4 | Ohio Stadium | Columbus, Ohio | 101,568 | Ohio St. | Big Ten | 1922 | Grass |
| 5 | Sanford Stadium | Athens, Ga. | 92,746 | Georgia | SEC-East | 1929 | Grass |
| 6 | Tiger Stadium | Baton Rouge, La. | 92,300 | LSU | SEC-West | 1924 | Grass |
| 7 | LA Memorial Coliseum* | Los Angeles, Calif. | 92,000 | USC | Pac-10 | 1923 | Grass |
| 8 | Rose Bowl* | Pasadena, Calif. | 91,500 | UCLA | Pac-10 | 1922 | Grass |
| 9 | Ben Hill Griffin Stadium at Florida Field | Gainesville, Fla. | 88,548 | Florida | SEC-East | 1929 | Grass |
| 10 | Jordan-Hare Stadium | Auburn, Ala. | 86,063 | Auburn | SEC-West | 1939 | Grass |
| 11 | Stanford Stadium | Stanford, Calif. | 85,500 | Stanford | Pac-10 | 1921 | Grass |
| 12 | Bryant-Denny Stadium | Tuscaloosa, Ala. | 83,818 | Alabama | SEC-West | 1929 | Grass |
| 13 | Legion Field* | Birmingham, Ala. | 83,091 | UAB | USA | 1927 | Grass |
| 14 | Kyle Field | College Station, Texas | 82,600 | Texas A&M | Big 12-South | 1925 | Grass |
| 15 | Gaylord Family-Oklahoma Memorial Stadium | Norman, Okla. | 82,112 | Oklahoma | Big 12-South | 1924 | Grass |
| 16 | Doak Campbell Stadium | Tallahasse, Fla. | 82,000 | Florida St. | ACC | 1950 | Grass |
| 17 | Memorial Stadium | Clemson, S.C. | 81,474 | Clemson | ACC | 1942 | Grass |
| 18 | Camp Randall Stadium | Madison, Wis. | 81,318 | Wisconsin | Big Ten | 1917 | Turf |
| 19 | Notre Dame Stadium | Notre Dame, Ind. | 80,795 | Notre Dame | Independent | 1930 | Grass |
| 20 | Williams-Brice Stadium | Columbia, S.C. | 80,250 | South Carolina | SEC-East | 1934 | Grass |
| 21 | Darrell K. Royal-Texas Memorial Stadium | Austin, Texas | 80,082 | Texas | Big 12-South | 1924 | Grass |
| 22 | Donald W. Reynolds Razorback Stadium | Fayetteville, Ark. | 80,000 | Arkansas | SEC-West | 1938 | Grass |
| 23 | Memorial Stadium | Lincoln, Neb. | 73,918 | Nebraska | Big 12-North | 1923 | Turf |
| 24 | Sun Devil Stadium | Tempe, Ariz. | 73,379 | Arizona St. | Pac-10 | 1959 | Grass |
| 25 | Memorial Stadium | Berkeley, Calif. | 73,347 | California | Pac-10 | 1923 | Turf |
| 26 | Husky Stadium | Seattle, Wash. | 72,500 | Washington | Pac-10 | 1920 | Turf |
| 27 | Orange Bowl* | Miami, Fla. | 72,319 | Miami-FL | ACC | 1935 | Grass |
| 28 | Spartan Stadium | East Lansing, Mich. | 72,027 | Michigan St. | Big Ten | 1957 | Turf |
| 29 | Qualcomm Stadium | San Diego, Calif. | 70,561 | San Diego St. | Mountain West | 1967 | Grass |
| 30 | Kinnick Stadium | Iowa City, Iowa | 70,397 | Iowa | Big Ten | 1929 | Grass |
| 31 | Citrus Bowl* | Orlando, Fla. | 70,188 | Central Florida | USA | 1936 | Grass |
| 32 | Rice Stadium | Houston, Texas | 70,000 | Rice | USA | 1950 | Turf |
| 33 | Louisiana Superdome* | New Orleans, La. | 69,767 | Tulane | USA | 1975 | Turf |
| 34 | Memorial Stadium | Champaign, Ill. | 69,249 | Illinois | Big Ten | 1923 | Turf |
| 35 | Lincoln Financial Field* | Philadelphia, Penn. | 68,532 | Temple | Independent | 2003 | Grass |
| 36 | Memorial Stadium | Columbia, Mo. | 68,349 | Missouri | Big 12-North | 1926 | Turf |
| 37 | Commonwealth | Lexington, Ky. | 67,606 | Kentucky | SEC-East | 1973 | Grass |
| 38 | Lane Stadium | Blacksburg, Va. | 66,233 | Va. Tech | ACC | 1965 | Grass |
| 39 | Raymond James Stadium* | Tampa, Fla. | 65,657 | South Florida | Big East | 1998 | Grass |
| 40 | LaVell Edwards Stadium | Provo, Utah | 65,000 | BYU | Mountain West | 1964 | Grass |

**Note:** The capacities for several stadiums including the Rose Bowl, Louisiana Superdome and Sun Devil Stadium are often listed differently for other events, such as bowl games, which they host.

### 2005 Conference Home Fields

NCAA Division I-A conference by conference listing includes member teams heading into the 2005 season. Note that (*) indicates stadium is not on campus. For the purposes of this list anything other than natural grass is called turf.

#### Atlantic Coast

| Atlantic | Stadium | Built | Seats | Field |
|---|---|---|---|---|
| Boston College | Alumni | 1957 | 44,500 | Turf |
| Clemson | Memorial | 1942 | 81,474 | Grass |
| Florida St. | Doak Campbell | 1950 | 82,000 | Grass |
| Maryland | Byrd | 1950 | 51,500 | Grass |
| N.C. State | Carter-Finley | 1966 | 53,800 | Grass |
| Wake Forest | Groves | 1968 | 31,500 | Grass |
| **Coastal** | **Stadium** | **Built** | **Seats** | **Field** |
| Duke | Wallace Wade | 1929 | 33,941 | Grass |
| Georgia Tech | Bobby Dodd | 1913 | 55,000 | Grass |
| Miami-FL | Orange Bowl* | 1935 | 72,319 | Grass |
| No. Carolina | Kenan Memorial | 1927 | 60,000 | Grass |
| Virginia | Scott | 1931 | 61,500 | Grass |
| Virginia Tech | Lane | 1965 | 66,233 | Grass |

#### Big East

| | Stadium | Built | Seats | Field |
|---|---|---|---|---|
| Cincinnati | Nippert | 1924 | 35,000 | Grass |
| Connecticut | Rentschler Field* | 2003 | 40,000 | Grass |
| Louisville | Papa John's Cardinal | 1998 | 42,000 | Turf |
| Pittsburgh | Heinz Field* | 2001 | 64,450 | Grass |
| Rutgers | Rutgers | 1994 | 41,500 | Grass |
| South Florida | Raymond James* | 1988 | 65,657 | Grass |
| Syracuse | Carrier Dome | 1980 | 49,262 | Turf |
| West Virginia | Milan Puskar | 1980 | 63,500 | Turf |

## College Football (Cont.)

### Big Ten

| | Stadium | Built | Seats | Field |
|---|---|---|---|---|
| Illinois | Memorial | 1923 | 69,249 | Turf |
| Indiana | Memorial | 1960 | 52,354 | Turf |
| Iowa | Kinnick | 1929 | 70,397 | Grass |
| Michigan | Michigan | 1927 | 107,501 | Turf |
| Michigan St. | Spartan | 1957 | 72,027 | Grass |
| Minnesota | HHH Metrodome* | 1982 | 64,172 | Turf |
| Northwestern | Ryan Field | 1926 | 47,130 | Grass |
| Ohio St. | Ohio | 1922 | 101,568 | Grass |
| Penn St. | Beaver | 1960 | 107,282 | Grass |
| Purdue | Ross-Ade | 1924 | 62,500 | Grass |
| Wisconsin | Camp Randall | 1917 | 76,634 | Turf |

### Big 12

| North | Stadium | Built | Seats | Field |
|---|---|---|---|---|
| Colorado | Folsom Field | 1924 | 53,750 | Turf |
| Iowa St. | Jack Trice Field | 1975 | 45,814 | Grass |
| Kansas | Memorial | 1921 | 50,250 | Turf |
| Kansas St. | Wagner Field | 1968 | 50,000 | Turf |
| Missouri | Memorial | 1926 | 68,349 | Turf |
| Nebraska | Memorial | 1923 | 73,918 | Turf |
| **South** | **Stadium** | **Built** | **Seats** | **Field** |
| Baylor | Floyd Casey | 1950 | 50,000 | Grass |
| Oklahoma | Gaylord Family-Oklahoma Memorial | 1924 | 82,112 | Grass |
| Oklahoma St. | Boone Pickens | 1920 | 48,000 | Turf |
| Texas | Royal-Memorial | 1924 | 80,082 | Grass |
| Texas A&M | Kyle Field | 1925 | 82,600 | Grass |
| Texas Tech | Jones SBC | 1947 | 53,702 | Turf |

**Note:** The annual Oklahoma-Texas game has been played at the Cotton Bowl (capacity 68,252) in Dallas since 1937.

### Conference USA

| East | Stadium | Built | Seats | Field |
|---|---|---|---|---|
| UAB | Legion Field | 1927 | 83,091 | Grass |
| C. Florida | Citrus Bowl | 1936 | 70,188 | Grass |
| E. Carolina | Dowdy-Ficklen | 1963 | 43,000 | Grass |
| Marshall | Joan C. Edwards | 1991 | 38,019 | Turf |
| Memphis | Liberty Bowl* | 1965 | 62,380 | Grass |
| Southern Miss | M.M. Roberts | 1976 | 33,000 | Grass |
| **West** | **Stadium** | **Built** | **Seats** | **Field** |
| Houston | Robertson | 1942 | 32,000 | Grass |
| Rice | Rice | 1950 | 70,000 | Turf |
| SMU | Gerald J. Ford Stadium | 2000 | 32,000 | Grass |
| Tulane | Superdome* | 1975 | 69,767 | Turf |
| Tulsa | Skelly | 1930 | 40,385 | Turf |
| UTEP | Sun Bowl* | 1963 | 51,500 | Turf |

### Mid-American

| | Stadium | Built | Seats | Field |
|---|---|---|---|---|
| Akron | Rubber Bowl* | 1940 | 35,202 | Turf |
| Ball St. | Ball State | 1967 | 21,581 | Grass |
| Bowling Green | Doyt Perry | 1966 | 30,599 | Grass |
| Buffalo | UB | 1993 | 31,000 | Grass |
| Central Mich. | Kelly/Shorts | 1972 | 30,199 | Grass |
| Eastern Mich. | Rynearson | 1969 | 30,200 | Turf |
| Kent | Dix | 1969 | 30,520 | Turf |
| Miami-OH | Fred Yager | 1983 | 30,012 | Grass |
| Northern Ill. | Huskie | 1965 | 31,000 | Grass |
| Ohio Univ. | Peden | 1929 | 24,000 | Grass |
| Toledo | Glass Bowl | 1937 | 26,248 | Turf |
| Western Mich. | Waldo | 1939 | 30,200 | Grass |

### Mountain West

| | Stadium | Built | Seats | Field |
|---|---|---|---|---|
| Air Force | Falcon | 1962 | 52,480 | Grass |
| BYU | LaVell Edwards | 1964 | 65,000 | Grass |
| Colorado St. | Hughes | 1968 | 30,000 | Grass |
| New Mexico | University | 1960 | 37,370 | Grass |
| San Diego St. | Qualcomm* | 1967 | 70,561 | Grass |
| TCU | Amon G. Carter | 1929 | 44,008 | Grass |
| UNLV | Sam Boyd* | 1971 | 36,800 | Grass |
| Utah | Rice-Eccles | 1927 | 45,634 | Grass |
| Wyoming | War Memorial | 1950 | 33,500 | Grass |

### Pacific-10

| | Stadium | Built | Seats | Field |
|---|---|---|---|---|
| Arizona | Arizona | 1928 | 56,002 | Grass |
| Arizona St. | Sun Devil | 1958 | 73,379 | Grass |
| California | Memorial | 1923 | 73,347 | Turf |
| Oregon | Autzen | 1967 | 53,800 | Turf |
| Oregon St. | Reser | 1953 | 43,000 | Turf |
| Stanford | Stanford | 1921 | 85,500 | Grass |
| UCLA | Rose Bowl* | 1922 | 91,500 | Grass |
| USC | LA Memorial Coliseum* | 1923 | 92,000 | Grass |
| Washington | Husky | 1920 | 72,500 | Turf |
| Washington St. | Martin | 1972 | 35,117 | Turf |

### Southeastern

| East | Stadium | Built | Seats | Field |
|---|---|---|---|---|
| Florida | Florida Field | 1929 | 90,000 | Grass |
| Georgia | Sanford | 1929 | 92,746 | Grass |
| Kentucky | Commonwealth | 1973 | 67,530 | Grass |
| South Carolina | Williams-Brice | 1934 | 80,250 | Grass |
| Tennessee | Neyland | 1921 | 104,079 | Grass |
| Vanderbilt | Vanderbilt | 1981 | 39,790 | Grass |
| **West** | **Stadium** | **Built** | **Seats** | **Field** |
| Alabama | Bryant-Denny | 1929 | 83,818 | Grass |
| Arkansas | Donald W. Reynolds & War Memorial* | 1938 | 80,000 | Grass |
| Auburn | Jordan-Hare | 1939 | 86,063 | Grass |
| LSU | Tiger | 1924 | 92,300 | Grass |
| Mississippi | Vaught-Hemingway | 1915 | 60,580 | Grass |
| Miss. St. | Davis Wade | 1915 | 55,082 | Grass |

**Note:** EAST–Vanderbilt Stadium was rebuilt in 1981.

### Sun Belt

| | Stadium | Built | Seats | Field |
|---|---|---|---|---|
| Arkansas St. | Indian | 1974 | 33,410 | Grass |
| Florida Atlantic | Lockhart | 1959 | 20,450 | Grass |
| Florida International | FIU | 1995 | 17,000 | Turf |
| UL-Lafayette | Cajun Field | 1971 | 31,000 | Grass |
| UL-Monroe | Malone | 1978 | 30,427 | Grass |
| Mid. Tennnessee | Johnny Red Floyd | 1933 | 30,788 | Turf |
| North Texas | Fouts Field | 1952 | 30,500 | Turf |
| Troy | Movie Gallery Veterans | 1950 | 30,000 | Turf |

### Western Athletic

| | Stadium | Built | Seats | Field |
|---|---|---|---|---|
| Boise St. | Bronco | 1970 | 30,000 | Turf |
| Fresno St. | Bulldog | 1980 | 41,031 | Grass |
| Hawaii | Aloha* | 1975 | 50,000 | Turf |
| Idaho | Kibbie Dome | 1975 | 16,000 | Turf |
| Louisiana Tech | Joe Aillet | 1968 | 30,600 | Grass |
| Nevada | Mackay | 1967 | 31,900 | Grass |
| New Mexico St. | Aggie Memorial | 1978 | 30,343 | Grass |
| San Jose St. | Spartan | 1933 | 30,456 | Grass |
| Utah St. | Romney | 1968 | 30,257 | Grass |

### I-A Independents

| | Stadium | Built | Seats | Field |
|---|---|---|---|---|
| Army | Michie | 1924 | 39,929 | Turf |
| Navy | Navy-Marine Corps Memorial | 1959 | 30,000 | Grass |
| Notre Dame | Notre Dame | 1930 | 80,795 | Grass |
| Temple | Lincoln Financial Field* | 2003 | 68,532 | Grass |

# Business

After 35 years of ownership, **Bud Selig** sold the Brewers to investor **Mark Attanasio** in January 2005.

AP/Wide World Photos

## 2004-05 Top 50 TV Sports Events

Final 2004-05 network television ratings for the top nationally telecast sports events, according to Nielsen Media Research. Covers period from Sept. 1, 2004 through Aug. 31, 2005. Events are listed with ratings points and audience share; each ratings point represents 1,096,000 households and shares indicate percentage of TV sets in use.

**Multiple entries:** SPORTS—NFL Football (40); Major League Baseball (8); NCAA Football bowl games (2). NETWORKS—FOX (26); ABC (13); CBS (13).

| | | Date | Net | Rtg/Sh |
|---|---|---|---|---|
| 1 | **Super Bowl XXXIX** (Patriots vs Eagles) | 2/6/05 | FOX | 41.1/62 |
| 2 | **NFC Championship Game** (Falcons at Eagles) | 1/23/05 | FOX | 25.8/46 |
| | **AFC Championship Game** (Patriots at Steelers) | 1/23/05 | CBS | 25.8/38 |
| 4 | **AFC Div. Playoff Game** (Colts at Patriots) | 1/16/05 | CBS | 23.2/40 |
| 5 | **MLB ALCS—Game 7** (Red Sox at Yankees) | 10/20/04 | FOX | 19.4/30 |
| | **NFC Div. Playoff Game** (Vikings at Eagles) | 1/16/05 | FOX | 19.4/41 |
| 7 | **NFC Wild Card Game** (Vikings at Packers) | 1/9/05 | FOX | 18.4/33 |
| 8 | **MLB World Series—Game 4** (Red Sox at Cardinals) | 10/27/04 | FOX | 18.2/30 |
| | **AFC Div. Playoff Game** (Jets at Steelers) | 1/15/05 | CBS | 18.2/36 |
| 10 | **AFC Wild Card Game** (Broncos at Colts) | 1/9/05 | CBS | 16.3/35 |
| 11 | **AFC Wild Card Game** (Jets at Chargers) | 1/8/05 | ABC | 16.0/28 |
| 12 | **MLB World Series—Game 2** (Cardinals at Red Sox) | 10/24/04 | FOX | 15.9/24 |
| 13 | **MLB ALCS—Game 6** (Red Sox at Yankees) | 10/19/04 | FOX | 15.7/25 |
| | **MLB World Series—Game 3** (Red Sox at Cardinals) | 10/26/04 | FOX | 15.7/24 |
| 15 | **NCAA Men's Basketball Championship Game** (UNC vs Illinois) | 4/4/05 | CBS | 15.0/23 |
| 16 | **NFC Wild Card Game** (Rams at Seahawks) | 1/8/05 | ABC | 14.6/29 |
| 17 | **NFL Regular Season Late Game** (Various teams) | 11/14/04 | FOX | 14.0/25 |
| | **NFC Div. Playoff Game** (Rams at Falcons) | 1/15/05 | FOX | 14.0/24 |
| 19 | **NFL Regular Season Late Game** (Various teams) | 10/31/04 | CBS | 13.8/27 |
| 20 | **MLB World Series—Game 1** (Cardinals at Red Sox) | 10/23/04 | FOX | 13.7/25 |
| | **NFL Regular Season Late Game** (Various teams) | 12/29/04 | CBS | 13.7/26 |
| | **Orange Bowl** (USC vs Oklahoma) | 1/4/05 | ABC | 13.7/22 |
| 23 | **NFL Regular Season Late Game** (Various teams) | 9/12/04 | FOX | 13.5/28 |
| | **NFL Regular Season Late Game** (Various teams) | 10/24/04 | FOX | 13.5/25 |
| 25 | **NFL Regular Season Late Game** (Various teams) | 11/28/04 | CBS | 13.4/25 |
| 26 | **NFL Regular Season Late Game** (Various teams) | 9/26/04 | FOX | 13.3/26 |
| | **NFL Regular Season Late Game** (Various teams) | 12/5/04 | FOX | 13.3/25 |
| | **NFL Regular Season Late Game** (Various teams) | 12/12/04 | FOX | 13.3/25 |
| 29 | **NFL Regular Season Late Game** (Various teams) | 9/19/04 | CBS | 13.2/27 |
| 30 | **NFL Monday Night Football** (Cowboys at Redskins) | 9/27/04 | ABC | 13.0/22 |
| | **MLB NLCS—Game 7** (Astros at Cardinals) | 10/21/04 | FOX | 13.0/20 |
| | **NFL Regular Season Early Game** (Various teams) | 12/26/04 | CBS | 13.0/30 |
| 33 | **NFL Monday Night Football** (Vikings at Eagles) | 9/20/04 | ABC | 12.8/21 |
| | **NFL Regular Season Late Game** (Various teams) | 11/21/04 | FOX | 12.8/24 |
| | **NFL Regular Season Late Game** (Various teams) | 1/2/05 | CBS | 12.8/22 |
| 36 | **NFL Monday Night Football** (Packers at Panthers) | 9/13/04 | ABC | 12.5/21 |
| 37 | **Rose Bowl** (Texas vs Michigan) | 1/1/05 | ABC | 12.4/23 |
| 38 | **NFL Regular Season Late Game** (Various teams) | 10/17/04 | CBS | 12.3/25 |
| 39 | **NFL Regular Season Early Game** (Various teams) | 11/7/04 | FOX | 11.9/28 |
| | **NFL Regular Season Late Game** (Various teams) | 12/26/04 | FOX | 11.9/24 |
| | **NBA Finals—Game 7** (Pistons at Spurs) | 6/23/05 | ABC | 11.9/22 |
| 42 | **NFL Monday Night Football** (Vikings at Colts) | 11/8/04 | ABC | 11.6/19 |
| | **NFL Monday Night Football** (Eagles at Cowboys) | 11/15/04 | ABC | 11.6/19 |
| | **NFL Thanksgiving Day Early Game** (Colts at Lions) | 11/25/04 | CBS | 11.6/30 |
| 45 | **NFL Monday Night Football** (Rams at Packers) | 11/29/04 | ABC | 11.5/18 |
| 46 | **NFL Thursday Night—Season Opener** (Colts at Patriots) | 9/9/04 | ABC | 11.4/20 |
| | **NFL Regular Season Early Game** (Various teams) | 12/19/04 | FOX | 11.4/25 |
| 48 | **MLB ALCS—Game 5** (Yankees at Red Sox) | 10/18/04 | FOX | 11.3/19 |
| | **NFL Thanksgiving Day Late Game** (Bears at Cowboys) | 11/25/04 | FOX | 11.3/29 |
| 50 | **NFL Monday Night Football** (Chiefs at Ravens) | 10/4/04 | ABC | 11.2/19 |
| | **NFL Regular Season Early Game** (Various teams) | 11/28/04 | FOX | 11.2/25 |
| | **NFL Regular Season Early Game** (Various teams) | 1/2/05 | FOX | 11.2/24 |

### Other top non-NFL TV sports events

| | | Date | Net | Rtg/Sh |
|---|---|---|---|---|
| 58 | **NASCAR Daytona 500** (Jeff Gordon wins) | 2/20/05 | FOX | 10.9/23 |
| | **NCAA Men's Basketball Semifinal** (UNC vs Michigan St.) | 4/2/05 | CBS | 10.9/19 |
| 66 | **NCAA Men's Basketball Elite Eight** (Michigan St. vs Kentucky) | 3/27/05 | CBS | 10.4/22 |
| 68 | **MLB LCS Games** (Red Sox at Yankees: Gm 2) (Astros at Cards: Gm 1) | 10/13/04 | FOX | 10.1/16 |
| 70 | **MLB ALCS—Game 1** (Red Sox at Yankees) | 10/12/04 | FOX | 10.0/16 |
| | **NCAA Men's Basketball Semifinal** (Illinois vs Louisville) | 4/2/05 | CBS | 10.0/20 |
| 75 | **Masters Golf—Final Round** (Tiger wins) | 4/10/05 | CBS | 9.8/22 |
| 79 | **MLB ALCS—Game 4** (Yankees at Red Sox) | 10/17/04 | FOX | 9.5/17 |
| | **Sugar Bowl** (Auburn at Virginia Tech) | 1/3/05 | ABC | 9.5/15 |
| 84 | **Kentucky Derby** (Giacomo wins) | 5/7/05 | NBC | 9.0/22 |

## All-Time Top-Rated TV Programs

NFL Football dominates television's All-Time Top-Rated 50 Programs with 22 Super Bowls and the 1981 NFC Championship Game making the list. Rankings based on surveys taken from January 1961 through August 31, 2005; include only sponsored programs seen on individual networks; and programs under 30 minutes scheduled duration are excluded. Programs are listed with ratings points, audience share and number of households watching, according to Nielsen Media Research.

**Multiple entries:** The Super Bowl (22); "Roots" (7); "The Beverly Hillbillies" and "The Thorn Birds" (3); "The Bob Hope Christmas Show," "The Ed Sullivan Show," "Gone With The Wind" and 1994 Winter Olympics (2).

|   | Program | Episode/Game | Net | Date | Rating | Share | Households |
|---|---|---|---|---|---|---|---|
| 1 | M*A*S*H (series) | Final episode | CBS | 2/28/83 | **60.2** | 77 | 50,150,000 |
| 2 | Dallas (series) | "Who Shot J.R.?" | CBS | 11/21/80 | **53.3** | 76 | 41,470,000 |
| 3 | Roots (mini-series) | Part 8 | ABC | 1/30/77 | **51.1** | 71 | 36,380,000 |
| 4 | **Super Bowl XVI** | 49ers 26, Bengals 21 | CBS | 1/24/82 | **49.1** | 73 | 40,020,000 |
| 5 | **Super Bowl XVII** | Redskins 27, Dolphins 17 | NBC | 1/30/83 | **48.6** | 69 | 40,480,000 |
| 6 | **XVII Winter Olympics** | Women's Figure Skating | CBS | 2/23/94 | **48.5** | 64 | 45,690,000 |
| 7 | **Super Bowl XX** | Bears 46, Patriots 10 | NBC | 1/26/86 | **48.3** | 70 | 41,490,000 |
| 8 | Gone With the Wind (movie) | Part 1 | NBC | 11/7/76 | **47.7** | 65 | 33,960,000 |
| 9 | Gone With the Wind (movie) | Part 2 | NBC | 11/8/76 | **47.4** | 64 | 33,750,000 |
| 10 | **Super Bowl XII** | Cowboys 27, Broncos 10 | CBS | 1/15/78 | **47.2** | 67 | 34,410,000 |
| 11 | **Super Bowl XIII** | Steelers 35, Cowboys 31 | NBC | 1/21/79 | **47.1** | 74 | 35,090,000 |
| 12 | Bob Hope Special | Christmas Show | NBC | 1/15/70 | **46.6** | 64 | 27,260,000 |
| 13 | **Super Bowl XVIII** | Raiders 38, Redskins 9 | CBS | 1/22/84 | **46.4** | 71 | 38,800,000 |
|  | **Super Bowl XIX** | 49ers 38, Dolphins 16 | ABC | 1/20/85 | **46.4** | 63 | 39,390,000 |
| 15 | **Super Bowl XIV** | Steelers 31, Rams 19 | CBS | 1/20/80 | **46.3** | 67 | 35,330,000 |
| 16 | **Super Bowl XXX** | Cowboys 27, Steelers 17 | NBC | 1/28/96 | **46.0** | 68 | 44,114,400 |
|  | ABC Theater (special) | "The Day After" | ABC | 11/20/83 | **46.0** | 62 | 38,550,000 |
| 18 | Roots (mini-series) | Part 6 | ABC | 1/28/77 | **45.9** | 66 | 32,680,000 |
|  | The Fugitive (series) | Final episode | ABC | 8/29/67 | **45.9** | 72 | 25,700,000 |
| 20 | **Super Bowl XXI** | Giants 39, Broncos 20 | CBS | 1/25/87 | **45.8** | 66 | 40,030,000 |
| 21 | Roots (mini-series) | Part 5 | ABC | 1/27/77 | **45.7** | 71 | 32,540,000 |
| 22 | **Super Bowl XXVIII** | Cowboys 30, Bills 13 | NBC | 1/30/94 | **45.5** | 66 | 42,860,000 |
|  | Cheers (series) | Final episode | NBC | 5/20/93 | **45.5** | 64 | 42,360,500 |
| 24 | The Ed Sullivan Show | Beatles' 1st appearance | CBS | 2/9/64 | **45.3** | 60 | 23,240,000 |
| 25 | **Super Bowl XXVII** | Cowboys 52, Bills 17 | NBC | 1/31/93 | **45.1** | 66 | 41,988,100 |
| 26 | Bob Hope Special | Christmas Show | NBC | 1/14/71 | **45.0** | 61 | 27,050,000 |
| 27 | Roots (mini-series) | Part 3 | ABC | 1/25/77 | **44.8** | 68 | 31,900,000 |
| 28 | **Super Bowl XXXII** | Broncos 31, Packers 24 | NBC | 1/25/98 | **44.5** | 67 | 43,630,000 |
| 29 | **Super Bowl XI** | Raiders 32, Vikings 14 | NBC | 1/9/77 | **44.4** | 73 | 31,610,000 |
|  | **Super Bowl XV** | Raiders 27, Eagles 10 | NBC | 1/25/81 | **44.4** | 63 | 34,540,000 |
| 31 | **Super Bowl VI** | Cowboys 24, Dolphins 3 | CBS | 1/16/72 | **44.2** | 74 | 27,450,000 |
| 32 | **XVII Winter Olympics** | Women's Figure Skating | CBS | 2/25/94 | **44.1** | 64 | 41,540,000 |
|  | Roots (mini-series) | Part 2 | ABC | 1/24/77 | **44.1** | 62 | 31,400,000 |
| 34 | The Beverly Hillbillies (series) | Regular episode | CBS | 1/8/64 | **44.0** | 65 | 22,570,000 |
| 35 | Roots (mini-series) | Part 4 | ABC | 1/26/77 | **43.8** | 66 | 31,190,000 |
|  | The Ed Sullivan Show | Beatles' 2nd appearance | CBS | 2/16/64 | **43.8** | 60 | 22,445,000 |
| 37 | **Super Bowl XXIII** | 49ers 20, Bengals 16 | NBC | 1/22/89 | **43.5** | 68 | 39,320,000 |
| 38 | The Academy Awards | John Wayne wins Oscar | ABC | 4/7/70 | **43.4** | 78 | 25,390,000 |
| 39 | **Super Bowl XXXI** | Packers 35, Patriots 21 | FOX | 1/26/97 | **43.3** | 65 | 42,000,000 |
|  | **Super Bowl XXXIV** | Rams 23, Titans 16 | ABC | 1/30/00 | **43.3** | 63 | 43,618,000 |
| 41 | The Thorn Birds (mini-series) | Part 3 | ABC | 3/29/83 | **43.2** | 62 | 35,990,000 |
| 42 | The Thorn Birds (mini-series) | Part 4 | ABC | 3/30/83 | **43.1** | 62 | 35,900,000 |
| 43 | **NFC Championship Game** | 49ers 28, Cowboys 27 | CBS | 1/10/82 | **42.9** | 62 | 34,940,000 |
| 44 | The Beverly Hillbillies (series) | Regular episode | CBS | 1/15/64 | **42.8** | 62 | 21,960,000 |
| 45 | **Super Bowl VII** | Dolphins 14, Redskins 7 | NBC | 1/14/73 | **42.7** | 72 | 27,670,000 |
| 46 | The Thorn Birds (mini-series) | Part 2 | ABC | 3/28/83 | **42.5** | 59 | 35,400,000 |
| 47 | **Super Bowl IX** | Steelers 16, Vikings 6 | NBC | 1/12/75 | **42.4** | 72 | 29,040,000 |
|  | The Beverly Hillbillies (series) | Regular episode | CBS | 2/26/64 | **42.4** | 60 | 21,750,000 |
| 49 | **Super Bowl X** | Steelers 21, Cowboys 17 | CBS | 1/18/76 | **42.3** | 78 | 29,440,000 |
|  | ABC Sunday Night Movie | "Airport" | ABC | 11/11/73 | **42.3** | 63 | 28,000,000 |
|  | ABC Sunday Night Movie | "Love Story" | ABC | 10/1/72 | **42.3** | 62 | 27,410,000 |
|  | Cinderella | Musical special | CBS | 2/22/65 | **42.3** | 59 | 22,250,000 |
|  | Roots (mini-series) | Part 7 | ABC | 1/29/77 | **42.3** | 65 | 30,120,000 |

## All-Time Top-Rated Cable TV Sports Events

All-time cable television for sports events, according to ESPN, Turner Sports research and The Sports Business Daily. Covers period from Sept. 1, 1980 through Aug. 31, 2005.

### NFL Telecasts

|   |   | Date | Net | Rtg |
|---|---|---|---|---|
| 1 | Chicago at Minnesota | 12/6/87 | ESPN | 17.6 |
| 2 | Detroit at Miami | 12/25/94 | ESPN | 15.1 |
| 3 | Chicago at Minnesota | 12/3/89 | ESPN | 14.7 |
| 4 | Cleveland at San Fran | 11/29/87 | ESPN | 14.2 |
| 5 | Pittsburgh at Houston | 12/30/90 | ESPN | 13.8 |

### Non-NFL Telecasts

|   |   | Date | Net | Rtg |
|---|---|---|---|---|
| 1 | MLB: Chicago (NL)-St. Louis | 9/7/98 | ESPN | 9.5 |
| 2 | NBA: Detroit-Boston | 6/1/88 | TBS | 8.8 |
| 3 | NBA: Chicago-Detroit | 5/31/89 | TBS | 8.2 |
| 4 | NBA: Detroit-Boston | 5/26/88 | TBS | 8.1 |
| 5 | MLB: Giants-Chicago (NL) | 9/28/98 | ESPN | 8.0 |

# *ESPN The Magazine's* Ultimate Standings
## Fan Satisfaction Rankings

*ESPN The Magazine*, in conjunction with *SportsNation*, surveyed over 40,000 fans in order to rank the current 122 major men's professional sports franchises (MLB, NFL, NBA, NHL). The following eight criteria were used:

**Bang for the Buck**: Revenues directly from fans divided by wins in the past three years; **Fan Relations**: Ease of access to players, coaches and management; **Ownership**: Honesty; loyalty to players and city; **Affordability**: Price of tickets, parking and concessions; **Stadium Experience**: Friendliness of environment, quality of game-day promotions; **Players**: Effort on the field, likability off it; **Coach/Manager**: Strong on-field leadership; **Championships**: Titles already won or expected soon.

**Note**: In 2005, no NHL teams were ranked due to the lack of a 2004-05 season. NHL teams are placed at the end, ordered by their 2004 ranking. Also note that since the Charlotte Bobcats and Houston Texans have not been in existence for three years, they could not be ranked in the "Bang for the Buck" category and therefore were not included in the overall ranking.

| Team | League | 2003 | 2004 | 2005 | Team | League | 2003 | 2004 | 2005 |
|---|---|---|---|---|---|---|---|---|---|
| Detroit Pistons | NBA | 13 | 4 | 1 | Seattle Mariners | MLB | 36 | 67 | 61 |
| San Antonio Spurs | NBA | 3 | 1 | 2 | Washington Wizards | NBA | 91 | 105 | 62 |
| Indianapolis Colts | NFL | 50 | 40 | 3 | Boston Celtics | NBA | 42 | 61 | 63 |
| New England Patriots | NFL | 16 | 13 | 4 | Pittsburgh Pirates | MLB | 97 | 102 | 64 |
| LA Angels of Anaheim | MLB | 10 | 6 | 5 | Los Angeles Clippers | NBA | 105 | 86 | 65 |
| Philadelphia Eagles | NFL | 7 | 23 | 6 | St. Louis Rams | NFL | 41 | 34 | 66 |
| Atlanta Falcons | NFL | 23 | 70 | 7 | Toronto Blue Jays | MLB | 69 | 47 | 67 |
| Green Bay Packers | NFL | 1 | 3 | 8 | Washington Nationals | MLB | 77 | 97 | 68 |
| Pittsburgh Steelers | NFL | 15 | 16 | 9 | Chicago Bears | NFL | 95 | 103 | 69 |
| Indiana Pacers | NBA | 12 | 17 | 10 | Chicago White Sox | MLB | 85 | 99 | 70 |
| St. Louis Cardinals | MLB | 17 | 18 | 11 | New York Giants | NFL | 43 | 90 | 71 |
| Carolina Panthers | NFL | 99 | 42 | 12 | Detroit Lions | NFL | 115 | 107 | 72 |
| Dallas Mavericks | NBA | 5 | 2 | 13 | Tampa Bay Devil Rays | MLB | 114 | 77 | 73 |
| Minnesota Timberwolves | NBA | 29 | 29 | 14 | Chicago Bulls | NBA | 104 | 93 | 74 |
| Buffalo Bills | NFL | 47 | 96 | 15 | Toronto Raptors | NBA | 54 | 50 | 75 |
| Atlanta Braves | MLB | 39 | 33 | 16 | New Jersey Nets | NBA | 66 | 80 | 76 |
| New York Yankees | MLB | 27 | 28 | 17 | New York Knicks | NBA | 117 | 116 | 77 |
| Miami Heat | NBA | 60 | 79 | 18 | Philadelphia Phillies | MLB | 71 | 58 | 78 |
| Tennessee Titans | NFL | 25 | 7 | 19 | Portland Trail Blazers | NBA | 110 | 115 | 79 |
| Utah Jazz | NBA | 35 | 26 | 20 | Golden State Warriors | NBA | 103 | 94 | 80 |
| Phoenix Suns | NBA | 62 | 55 | 21 | Minnesota Vikings | NFL | 102 | 106 | 81 |
| Baltimore Ravens | NFL | 19 | 22 | 22 | Arizona Cardinals | NFL | 112 | 119 | 82 |
| Sacramento Kings | NBA | 4 | 14 | 23 | New Orleans Hornets | NBA | 34 | 30 | 83 |
| Kansas City Chiefs | NFL | 28 | 5 | 24 | Oakland Raiders | NFL | 33 | 104 | 84 |
| Florida Marlins | MLB | 100 | 24 | 25 | Colorado Rockies | MLB | 101 | 100 | 85 |
| Denver Broncos | NFL | 32 | 19 | 26 | New York Mets | MLB | 88 | 111 | 86 |
| Houston Astros | MLB | 72 | 71 | 27 | New Orleans Saints | NFL | 48 | 78 | 87 |
| Jacksonville Jaguars | NFL | 70 | 75 | 28 | Atlanta Hawks | NBA | 111 | 117 | 88 |
| Minnesota Twins | MLB | 38 | 51 | 29 | San Francisco 49ers | NFL | 31 | 72 | 89 |
| Memphis Grizzlies | NBA | 73 | 38 | 30 | Cleveland Browns | NFL | 64 | 110 | 90 |
| Texas Rangers | MLB | 96 | 76 | 31 | Edmonton Oilers | NHL | 9 | 8 | — |
| Arizona Diamondbacks | MLB | 2 | 9 | 32 | Ottawa Senators | NHL | 26 | 10 | — |
| Seattle SuperSonics | NBA | 55 | 60 | 33 | Minnesota Wild | NHL | — | 11 | — |
| Cleveland Cavaliers | NBA | 106 | 82 | 34 | Colorado Avalanche | NHL | 14 | 12 | — |
| San Francisco Giants | MLB | 51 | 39 | 35 | Detroit Red Wings | NHL | 8 | 15 | — |
| Tampa Bay Buccaneers | NFL | 20 | 32 | 36 | Vancouver Canucks | NHL | 30 | 20 | — |
| San Diego Chargers | NFL | 80 | 118 | 37 | St. Louis Blues | NHL | 21 | 21 | — |
| Oakland Athletics | MLB | 11 | 66 | 38 | Tampa Bay Lightning | NHL | 79 | 27 | — |
| Dallas Cowboys | NFL | 94 | 36 | 39 | Mighty Ducks of Anaheim | NHL | 75 | 37 | — |
| Philadelphia 76ers | NBA | 24 | 35 | 40 | Philadelphia Flyers | NHL | 67 | 41 | — |
| New York Jets | NFL | 52 | 81 | 41 | Dallas Stars | NHL | 22 | 43 | — |
| Cleveland Indians | MLB | 92 | 87 | 42 | New Jersey Devils | NHL | 40 | 44 | — |
| Cincinnati Bengals | NFL | 118 | 74 | 43 | Los Angeles Kings | NHL | 45 | 48 | — |
| Orlando Magic | NBA | 44 | 108 | 44 | Columbus Blue Jackets | NHL | — | 49 | — |
| Milwaukee Brewers | MLB | 107 | 112 | 45 | Calgary Flames | NHL | 76 | 52 | — |
| Boston Red Sox | MLB | 89 | 95 | 46 | Nashville Predators | NHL | 74 | 56 | — |
| San Diego Padres | MLB | 59 | 62 | 47 | Atlanta Thrashers | NHL | 113 | 59 | — |
| Denver Nuggets | NBA | 84 | 68 | 48 | Buffalo Sabres | NHL | 90 | 63 | — |
| Los Angeles Lakers | NBA | 37 | 31 | 49 | Carolina Hurricanes | NHL | 18 | 65 | — |
| Baltimore Orioles | MLB | 98 | 84 | 50 | Phoenix Coyotes | NHL | 63 | 69 | — |
| Milwaukee Bucks | NBA | 58 | 46 | 51 | Montreal Canadiens | NHL | 49 | 73 | — |
| Los Angeles Dodgers | MLB | 56 | 64 | 52 | San Jose Sharks | NHL | 46 | 83 | — |
| Detroit Tigers | MLB | 116 | 113 | 53 | New York Islanders | NHL | 57 | 85 | — |
| Cincinnati Reds | MLB | 93 | 101 | 54 | Toronto Maple Leafs | NHL | 65 | 88 | — |
| Miami Dolphins | NFL | 6 | 57 | 55 | Boston Bruins | NHL | 81 | 89 | — |
| Houston Rockets | NBA | 61 | 53 | 56 | Pittsburgh Penguins | NHL | 53 | 91 | — |
| Chicago Cubs | MLB | 82 | 45 | 57 | Florida Panthers | NHL | 86 | 98 | — |
| Kansas City Royals | MLB | 83 | 25 | 58 | Washington Capitals | NHL | 68 | 109 | — |
| Seattle Seahawks | NFL | 78 | 54 | 59 | New York Rangers | NHL | 109 | 114 | — |
| Washington Redskins | NFL | 87 | 92 | 60 | Chicago Blackhawks | NHL | 108 | 120 | — |

## Team Payrolls

Team payrolls for active players during the 2004-05 season for the NBA, the 2003-04 season for the NHL (pre-lockout), the 2004 season for the NFL and the 2005 season (as of opening day) for Major League Baseball. Figures are in millions of dollars. **Note:** The NFL and NBA use a salary cap to limit payrolls. The NFL's cap was $80.5 million in 2004 and the NBA's cap was $43.87 million in 2004-05, though teams can circumvent the cap via bonuses and other exceptions. Under the new NHL labor agreement, a $39 million cap will be used for the 2005-06 season. **Sources:** *USA Today*, NHLPA, NFLPA and AP.

| # | NBA | # | MLB | # | NHL | # | NFL |
|---|-----|---|-----|---|-----|---|-----|
| 1 | New York ....$101.4 | 1 | NY Yankees ...$205.9 | 1 | Detroit .......$77.9 | 1 | Washington ..$118.0 |
| 2 | Dallas .......90.2 | 2 | Boston ......121.3 | 2 | NY Rangers ...76.5 | 2 | Philadelphia ..105.0 |
| 3 | Portland ......84.5 | 3 | NY Mets ......104.8 | 3 | Dallas .......68.6 | 3 | Houston .....97.5 |
| 4 | Philadelphia ...71.8 | 4 | Philadelphia ...95.3 | 4 | Philadelphia ..68.2 | 4 | Detroit ......94.6 |
| 5 | Minnesota .....70.2 | 5 | LA Angels ....95.0 | 5 | Colorado .....63.4 | 5 | Seattle ......94.0 |
| 6 | Memphis ......67.1 | 6 | St. Louis .....93.3 | 6 | Toronto ......62.5 | 6 | Miami .......93.9 |
| 7 | Orlando ......66.5 | 7 | San Francisco ..89.5 | 7 | St. Louis .....61.7 | 7 | NY Jets ......93.9 |
| 8 | LA Lakers .....65.9 | 8 | Chicago Cubs ..87.2 | 8 | Los Angeles ...53.8 | 8 | Minnesota ....92.4 |
| 9 | Indiana ......64.6 | 9 | Seattle ......85.9 | 9 | Anaheim .....53.3 | 9 | Indianapolis ..92.2 |
| 10 | Boston .......64.4 | 10 | Atlanta ......85.1 | 10 | Washington ...50.9 | 10 | Chicago .....87.8 |
| 11 | Sacramento ....63.1 | 11 | LA Dodgers ...81.0 | 11 | New Jersey ...48.9 | 11 | Carolina .....87.8 |
| 12 | Toronto ......62.3 | 12 | Houston ......76.8 | 12 | Boston .......46.6 | 12 | Cleveland ....87.7 |
| 13 | Houston ......60.3 | 13 | Chi. White Sox ..75.2 | 13 | Vancouver ....42.1 | 13 | Baltimore ....86.5 |
| 14 | Miami .......59.3 | 14 | Baltimore .....74.6 | 14 | NY Islanders ..40.9 | 14 | Kansas City ...84.6 |
| 15 | Chicago ......57.5 | 15 | Detroit ......69.0 | 15 | Ottawa ......39.6 | 15 | Atlanta ......82.7 |
| 16 | New Orleans ...57.1 | 16 | Arizona ......63.0 | 16 | Phoenix ......39.2 | 16 | Tampa Bay ....82.0 |
| 17 | Milwaukee .....56.5 | 17 | San Diego ....62.9 | 17 | Montreal .....38.9 | 17 | NY Giants ....81.7 |
| 18 | Golden State ...55.0 | 18 | Florida ......60.4 | 18 | Calgary ......36.4 | 18 | Green Bay ....80.4 |
| 19 | Detroit .......54.6 | 19 | Cincinnati .....59.7 | 19 | Carolina ......35.9 | 19 | Buffalo .......80.2 |
| 20 | Seattle .......53.5 | 20 | Minnesota .....56.6 | 20 | San Jose .....34.5 | 20 | Tennessee ....79.0 |
| 21 | New Jersey ....53.5 | 21 | Oakland ......55.9 | 21 | Tampa Bay ....34.1 | 21 | Arizona ......79.0 |
| 22 | Washington ....49.8 | 22 | Texas .......55.3 | 22 | Columbus .....34.0 | 22 | Pittsburgh ....78.0 |
| 23 | Cleveland .....49.2 | 23 | Washington ....48.6 | 23 | Edmonton .....33.4 | 23 | Oakland ......77.4 |
| 24 | San Antonio ...47.1 | 24 | Colorado .....47.8 | 24 | Buffalo .......33.0 | 24 | New England ..77.0 |
| 25 | Denver .......46.1 | 25 | Toronto ......45.3 | 25 | Chicago ......30.9 | 25 | St. Louis .....76.4 |
| 26 | LA Clippers ....45.2 | 26 | Cleveland .....41.8 | 26 | Atlanta ......28.5 | 26 | San Diego ....76.3 |
| 27 | Phoenix ......44.8 | 27 | Milwaukee .....40.2 | 27 | Minnesota .....27.2 | 27 | New Orleans ..73.3 |
| 28 | Utah ........43.2 | 28 | Pittsburgh .....38.1 | 28 | Florida ......26.1 | 28 | Denver .......72.6 |
| 29 | Atlanta ......41.3 | 29 | Kansas City ...36.9 | 29 | Pittsburgh ....23.4 | 29 | Jacksonville ...72.1 |
| 30 | Charlotte .....22.2 | 30 | Tampa Bay ....29.9 | 30 | Nashville ......21.9 | 30 | Cincinnati ....68.8 |
| | | | | | | 31 | Dallas .......65.4 |
| | | | | | | 32 | San Francisco ..63.0 |

## Top 10 Salaries In Each Sport

The top 10 highest paid athletes in the NBA (2004-05 season), the NHL (2003-04 - pre-lockout), Major League Baseball (2005 - opening day) and the NFL (2004). Figures are in millions of dollars. Note that NFL figures include signing bonuses **Sources:** *USA Today, Street & Smith's SportsBusiness Journal*, NHLPA and AP.

### NFL

| # | | Position | Team | Salary |
|---|---|----------|------|--------|
| 1 | Peyton Manning ... | Quarterback | Indianapolis | $35.038 |
| 2 | Chad Pennington .. | Quarterback | NY Jets | 19.004 |
| 3 | Jevon Kearse ..... | Def. Lineman | Philadelphia | 16.537 |
| 4 | LaDainian Tomlinson | Running Back | San Diego | 16.000 |
| 5 | Grant Wistrom .... | Def. Lineman | Seattle | 15.503 |
| 6 | Clinton Portis ..... | Running Back | Washington | 13.380 |
| 7 | John Tait ....... | Off. Lineman | Chicago | 13.085 |
| 8 | Michael Vick ..... | Quarterback | Atlanta | 12.502 |
| 9 | Antoine Winfield .. | Def. Back | Minnesota | 12.500 |
| 10 | LaVar Arrington .. | Linebacker | Washington | 11.835 |
| | **League Avg** | | | 1.330 |

### MLB

| # | | Position | Team | Salary |
|---|---|----------|------|--------|
| 1 | Alex Rodriguez ... | Third Base | NY Yankees | $25.705 |
| 2 | Barry Bonds ..... | Left Field | San Fran. | 22.000 |
| 3 | Manny Ramirez ... | Left Field | Boston | 19.807 |
| 4 | Derek Jeter ..... | Shortstop | NY Yankees | 19.600 |
| 5 | Mike Mussina .... | Pitcher | NY Yankees | 19.000 |
| 6 | Jeff Bagwell ..... | First Base | Houston | 18.000 |
| | Roger Clemens ... | Pitcher | Houston | 18.000 |
| 8 | Sammy Sosa ..... | Right Field | Baltimore | 17.875 |
| 9 | Mike Piazza ..... | Catcher | NY Mets | 16.071 |
| 10 | Chipper Jones .... | Third Base | Atlanta | 16.009 |
| | **League Avg** | | | 2.633 |

### NBA

| # | | Position | Team | Salary |
|---|---|----------|------|--------|
| 1 | Shaquille O'Neal .. | Center | Miami | $27.696 |
| 2 | Allan Houston ... | Guard | New York | 17.531 |
| | Chris Webber ... | Forward | Sac.-Phi. | 17.531 |
| 4 | Kevin Garnett .... | Forward | Minnesota | 16.000 |
| 5 | Jason Kidd ...... | Guard | New Jersey | 14.796 |
| | Jermaine O'Neal .. | Forward | Indiana | 14.796 |
| 7 | Eight tied at $14,625,000. | | | |
| | **League Avg** | | | 3.864 |

### NHL

| # | | Position | Team | Salary |
|---|---|----------|------|--------|
| 1 | Peter Forsberg ... | Center | Colorado | $11.000 |
| | Jaromir Jagr .... | Right Wing | Wash.-NYR | 11.000 |
| | Pavel Bure ...... | Right Wing | NY Rangers | 11.000 |
| 4 | Sergei Fedorov ... | Center | Anaheim | 10.000 |
| | Nicklas Lidstrom .. | Defenseman | Detroit | 10.000 |
| | Keith Tkachuk ... | Left Wing | St. Louis | 10.000 |
| 7 | Joe Sakic ...... | Center | Colorado | 9.881 |
| 8 | Chris Pronger .... | Defenseman | St. Louis | 9.500 |
| 9 | Rob Blake ...... | Defenseman | Colorado | 9.327 |
| 10 | Three tied at $9,000,000. | | | |
| | **League Avg** | | | 1.830 |

## Highest and Lowest Ticket Prices

The most expensive and least expensive average ticket prices for NFL and MLB franchises for the 2005 season, and NBA franchises for the 2004-05 season and NHL franchises for the 2003-04 season. Note that average ticket prices for each league are as follows: **NFL** $54.75, **MLB** $21.17, **NBA** $45.28 and **NHL** $43.57. **Source:** *Team Marketing Report*

### NFL

| Highest | Venue | Avg. Price |
|---|---|---|
| 1 New England | Gillette Stadium | $75.33 |
| 2 Washington | FedExField | 68.12 |
| 3 Kansas City | Arrowhead Stadium | 67.26 |
| 4 NY Giants | Giants Stadium | 66.67 |
| 5 NY Jets | Giants Stadium | 66.39 |

| Lowest | Venue | Avg. Price |
|---|---|---|
| 1 Buffalo | Ralph Wilson Stadium | $37.13 |
| 2 Arizona | Sun Devil Stadium | 39.72 |
| 3 Jacksonville | ALLTEL Stadium | 40.80 |
| 4 New Orleans | Louisiana Superdome | 42.36 |
| 5 Seattle | Qwest Field | 42.80 |

### MLB

| Highest | Venue | Avg. Price |
|---|---|---|
| 1 Boston | Fenway Park | $44.56 |
| 2 Chicago Cubs | Wrigley Field | 32.00 |
| 3 NY Yankees | Yankee Stadium | 27.34 |
| 4 Philadelphia | Citizens Bank Park | 26.58 |
| 5 Chicago White Sox | U.S. Cellular Field | 25.89 |

| Lowest | Venue | Avg. Price |
|---|---|---|
| 1 Tampa Bay | Tropicana Field | $13.70 |
| 2 Kansas City | Kauffman Stadium | 13.71 |
| 3 Colorado | Coors Field | 14.92 |
| 4 Florida | Dolphins Stadium | 15.55 |
| 5 Minnesota | HHH Metrodome | 16.25 |

### NBA

| Highest | Venue | Avg. Price |
|---|---|---|
| 1 LA Lakers | Staples Center | $77.66 |
| 2 New York | Madison Sq. Garden | 70.51 |
| 3 Sacramento | ARCO Arena | 66.00 |
| 4 Boston | FleetCenter | 55.93 |
| 5 New Jersey | Continental Airlines Arena | 55.44 |

| Lowest | Venue | Avg. Price |
|---|---|---|
| 1 Golden St. | The Arena in Oakland | $27.69 |
| 2 New Orleans | New Orleans Arena | 31.00 |
| 3 Seattle | KeyArena | 34.01 |
| 4 Denver | Pepsi Center | 35.50 |
| 5 Charlotte | Charlotte Coliseum | 36.61 |

### NHL

| Highest | Venue | Avg. Price |
|---|---|---|
| 1 Detroit | Joe Louis Arena | $57.11 |
| 2 Philadelphia | Wachovia Center | 57.06 |
| 3 Toronto | Air Canada Centre | 56.90 |
| 4 New Jersey | Continental Airlines Arena | 54.67 |
| 5 Boston | FleetCenter | 54.10 |

| Lowest | Venue | Avg. Price |
|---|---|---|
| 1 Florida | Office Depot Center | $29.76 |
| 2 Phoenix | Glendale Arena | 31.32 |
| 3 Carolina | RBC Center | 31.77 |
| 4 Atlanta | Philips Arena | 34.87 |
| 5 Buffalo | HSBC Arena | 35.46 |

## The Rights Stuff

Major sports and their television deals as of Sept. 1, 2005.

| League | Network | Yrs (Ends) | Amount |
|---|---|---|---|
| NFL | ESPN (MNF) | 8 (2013) | $8.8 billion |
| | NBC (Sun. nights) | 6 (2011) | 3.6 billion |
| | FOX (Sundays) | 6 (2011) | 4.4 billion |
| | CBS (Sundays) | 6 (2011) | 3.7 billion |
| | DirecTV (Sundays) | 5 (2010) | 3.5 billion |
| NBA | ABC/ESPN | 6 (2008) | $2.4 billion |
| | TNT | 6 (2008) | 2.2 billion |
| MLB | FOX | 6 (2006) | $2.5 billion |
| | ESPN | 8 (2013) | 2.368 billion |

| League | Network | Yrs (Ends) | Amount |
|---|---|---|---|
| NHL | NBC | 2 (2006) | — † |
| | OLN | 2 (2007) | $135 million |
| NCAA Men's Hoops Tournament | CBS | 11 (2013) | $6 billion |
| NCAA Women's Hoops Tournament | ESPN | 11 (2013) | $200 million@ |
| NCAA Football BCS | ABC | 8 (2006) | $930 million% |
| NASCAR | NBC/Turner | 6 (2006) | $1.2 billion |
| | FOX | 8 (2008) | 1.6 billion |
| Olympics | NBC | 13 (2008) | $3.5 billion # |
| | NBC | 9 (2012) | 2.2 billion # |
| PGA Tour | ABC, CBS, NBC, ESPN, USA and The Golf Channel | 4 (2006) | $850 million |
| WNBA | ABC/ESPN | 6 (2008) | undisclosed |

### Super Bowl TV Rights

| | | |
|---|---|---|
| 2006 ABC | 2009 NBC | 2012 NBC |
| 2007 CBS | 2010 CBS | |
| 2008 FOX | 2011 FOX | |

† NBC and the NHL agreed to a two-year deal whereby the two entities share advertising revenues. NBC paid no rights fees and has an option to renew the deal for an additional two years.

@ Also included are all rights to the College World Series and various other NCAA championships.

% ABC and the Rose Bowl agreed to a new eight-year deal (2007-2014) worth approximately $300 million to include eight Rose Bowls and two other BCS title games. In November 2004, FOX and the BCS inked a deal worth an estimated $320 million which gives them rights to the Fiesta, Orange and Sugar bowls from 2007-10 and the BCS National Championship Game from 2007-09.

# NBC paid approximately $3.5 billion for exclusive rights to the 1996 Summer Games (Atlanta), the 2000 Summer Games (Sydney), the 2002 Winter Games (Salt Lake City), the 2004 Summer Games (Athens), the 2006 Winter Games (Turin) and the 2008 Summer Games (Beijing). In July 2003, NBC announced a deal worth $2.2 billion which also gave them rights to the 2010 Winter Games (Vancouver) and the 2012 Summer Games (London).

**Note:** The NFL and NBA also have their own league-owned channels. The NFL Network shows preseason games while NBA TV offered 96 NBA regular season games during the 2004-05 season. MLB plans to begin its own Baseball Channel before the start of the 2006 season.

# Teams Bought in 2005

Seven major league clubs acquired new majority owners from Sept. 26, 2004 through Oct. 6, 2005.

## Major League Baseball

**Milwaukee Brewers:** On Jan. 13 MLB owners unanimously approved the sale of the Brewers from a group headed by commissioner Bud Selig to 47-year-old Los Angeles investor Mark Attanasio. The $220 million price reportedly included $100 million in cash, $110 million of stadium debt and $10 million in various liabilities. Attanasio is a senior partner in the investment firm Trust Company of the West. Selig had owned a share of the Brewers since the team's move from Seattle in 1970.

**Oakland Athletics:** On March 30 MLB owners unanimously approved the sale of the A's from Steve Schott and Ken Hofmann to Los Angeles real estate developer Lewis Wolff and his investment group for approximately $180 million. John Fisher, son of Gap chairman and CEO Don Fisher, is a majority investor. Wolff had been the team's V.P. for venue development since 2003.

**Tampa Bay Devil Rays:** After eight years of futility, founding Devil Rays owner Vince Naimoli relinquished control to New York investor Stuart Sternberg on Oct. 6. A group headed by Sternberg purchased just under 50 percent of the club in 2004 with an agreement to take control in 2007, but the group reportedly paid Naimoli an undisclosed sum to step aside early.

## NBA Basketball

**Cleveland Cavaliers:** Quicken Loans founder Michael Gilbert purchased the Cavaliers and operational control of the Gund Arena on March 1 for $375 million from Gordon Gund. Gilbert, 42, heads an investment group that also includes R&B artist Usher. Gund, who purchased the team with his brother George in 1983 for $20 million, will retain a minority stake in the team.

**Also of note:** On August 19 Atlanta Hawks/Thrashers co-owner and governor Steve Belkin agreed to sell his 30 percent stake to the other members of Atlanta Spirit LLC for an undisclosed amount, amidst a dispute surrounding the trade for guard Joe Johnson. The deal was expected to be finalized by the end of 2005. Co-owner Michael Gearon Jr. will serve as the team's new governor.

## NHL Hockey

**Mighty Ducks of Anaheim:** On June 16 the NHL's Board of Governors unanimously approved the sale of the Mighty Ducks from The Walt Disney Company to Dr. Henry Samueli and his wife, Susan, for a reported $75 million. The deal also includes Disney Ice, a Ducks practice facility. Samueli is co-founder, chairman and chief technical officer of Broadcom Corp.

**Vancouver Canucks:** Orca Bay Sports & Entertainment chairman John McCaw sold 50 percent of the club and its arena, General Motors Place, to Vancouver-based real estate developer Francesco Aquilini. The League's Board approved the sale on March 10. While terms of the deal are undisclosed, *Forbes* magazine estimates the Canucks' worth at $148 million (U.S.).

## NFL Football

**Minnesota Vikings:** On May 25, NFL owners unanimously approved the sale of the Vikings from Red McCombs to New Jersey real estate developer Zygi Wilf and his investment group for $600 million. A deal was originally struck with Arizona businessman Reggie Fowler, but when he reportedly lacked the necessary cash to close the deal, he became a limited investor.

## AWARDS

# The Peabody Award

Presented annually since 1940 for outstanding achievement in radio and television broadcasting. Named after Georgia banker and philanthropist George Foster Peabody, the awards are administered by the Henry W. Grady College of Journalism and Mass Communication at the University of Georgia.

## Television

**Year**
1960 **CBS** for coverage of 1960 Winter and Summer Olympic Games
1966 ABC's **"Wide World of Sports"** (for Outstanding Achievement in Promotion of International Understanding).
1968 **ABC Sports** coverage of both the 1968 Winter and Summer Olympic Games.
1972 **ABC Sports** coverage of the 1972 Summer Olympics in Munich.
1973 **Joe Garagiola** of NBC Sports (for "The Baseball World of Joe Garagiola").
1976 **ABC Sports** coverage of both the 1976 Winter and Summer Olympic Games.
1984 **Roone Arledge**, president of ABC News & Sports (for significant contributions to news and sports programming).
1986 **WFAA-TV**, Dallas for its investigation of the Southern Methodist University football program.
1988 **Jim McKay** of ABC Sports (for pioneering efforts and career accomplishments in the world of TV sports).
1991 **CBS Sports** coverage of the 1991 Masters golf tournament
    & **HBO Sports** and **Black Canyon Productions** for the baseball special "When It Was A Game."
1995 **Kartemquin Educational Films** and **KTCA-TV** in St. Paul, MN, presented on PBS for "Hoop Dreams"
    & **Turner Original Productions** for the baseball special "Hank Aaron: Chasing the Dream."
1996 **HBO Sports** for its documentary "The Journey of the African-American Athlete"
    & **Bud Greenspan**, a personal award for excellence in chronicling the Olympic Games.
1997 **HBO Pictures** and **The Thomas Carter Company** for the original movie "Don King: Only in America."
1998 **KTVX-TV**, Salt Lake City for its investigation into the policies and practices of the IOC during the Olympic bribery scandal & **HBO Sports** for its ongoing series of sports documentaries.
1999 **WCPO-TV**, Cincinnati for its investigation of fraud and misrepresentation in the construction of new sports stadiums, **HBO Sports** for its documentary "Dare to Compete: The Struggle of Women in Sports," and its documentary "Fists of Freedom: The Story of the '68 Summer Games" & **ESPN** for its "SportsCentury" series.
2000 **HBO Sports** for its documentary "Ali-Frazier 1: One Nation...Divisible."
2001 **The Ciesla Foundation** and **Cinemax** for the documentary "The Life and Times of Hank Greenberg."
2002 **ESPN** for "The Complete Angler," its documentary celebrating nature, art and fly-fishing.

## Radio

**Year**
1974 **WSB** radio in Atlanta for "Henry Aaron: A Man with a Mission."
1991 **Red Barber** of National Public Radio (for his six decades as a broadcaster and his 10 years as a commentator on NPR's "Morning Edition").

## National Emmy Awards
## Sports Programming

Presented by the Academy of Television Arts and Sciences since 1948. Eligibility period covered the calendar year from 1948-57 and since 1988. Note that due to space constraints, not every award is listed below.

**Multiple major award winners:** ABC "Wide World of Sports" (20), NFL Films Football coverage (15); HBO "Real Sports with Bryant Gumbel," and NBC Olympics coverage (11); CBS NFL Football coverage and ESPN "SportsCenter" (10); ABC Olympics coverage and ABC "Monday Night Football" (9); ESPN "Outside the Lines" and FOX MLB coverage (8); CBS NCAA Basketball coverage, CBS "NFL Today" and ESPN "GameDay/Sunday NFL Countdown" (5); ABC "The American Sportsman," ABC Indianapolis 500 coverage, CBS Golf coverage, CBS Tour de France coverage, ESPN "SportsCentury" series, FOX "NFL Sunday" and NBC Ironman Triathlon coverage (3); ABC Kentucky Derby coverage, ABC "Sportsbeat," Bud Greenspan Olympic specials, CBS Olympics coverage, ESPN "Speedworld," ESPN Sunday Night Football, ESPN Wimbledon coverage, HBO "Inside the NFL", MTV Sports series, The NBA on NBC and NBC World Series coverage (2).

### 1949
Coverage—"Wrestling" (KTLA, Los Angeles)

### 1950
Program—"Rams Football" (KNBH-TV, Los Angeles)

### 1954
Program—"Gillette Cavalcade of Sports" (NBC)

### 1965-66
Programs—"Wide World of Sports" (ABC), "Shell's Wonderful World of Golf" (NBC) and "CBS Golf Classic" (CBS)

### 1966-67
Program—"Wide World of Sports" (ABC)

### 1967-68
Program—"Wide World of Sports" (ABC)

### 1968-69
Program—"1968 Summer Olympics" (ABC)

### 1969-70
Programs—"NFL Football" (CBS) and "Wide World of Sports" (ABC)

### 1970-71
Program—"Wide World of Sports" (ABC)

### 1971-72
Program—"Wide World of Sports" (ABC)

### 1972-73
News Special—"Coverage of Munich Olympic Tragedy" (ABC)
Sports Programs—"1972 Summer Olympics" (ABC) and "Wide World of Sports" (ABC)

### 1973-74
Program—"Wide World of Sports" (ABC)

### 1974-75
Non-Edited Program— "Jimmy Connors vs. Rod Laver Tennis Challenge" (CBS)
Edited Program— "Wide World of Sports" (ABC)

### 1975-76
Live Special—"1975 World Series: Cincinnati vs. Boston" (NBC)
Live Series—"NFL Monday Night Football" (ABC)
Edited Specials—"1976 Winter Olympics" (ABC) and "Triumph and Tragedy: The Olympic Experience" (ABC)
Edited Series—"Wide World of Sports" (ABC)

### 1976-77
Live Special—"1976 Summer Olympics" (ABC)
Live Series—"The NFL Today/NFL Football" (CBS)
Edited Special—"1976 Summer Olympics Preview" (ABC)
Edited Series—"The Olympiad" (PBS)

### 1977-78
Live Special—"Muhammad Ali vs. Leon Spinks Heavyweight Championship Fight" (CBS)
Live Series—"The NFL Today/NFL Football" (CBS)
Edited Special—"The Impossible Dream: Ballooning Across the Atlantic" (CBS)
Edited Series—"The Way It Was" (PBS)

### 1978-79
Live Special—"Super Bowl XIII: Pittsburgh vs Dallas" (NBC)
Live Series—"NFL Monday Night Football" (ABC)
Edited Special—"Spirit of '78: The Flight of Double Eagle II" (ABC)
Edited Series—"The American Sportsman" (ABC)

### 1979-80
Live Special—"1980 Winter Olympics" (ABC)
Live Series—"NCAA College Football" (ABC)
Edited Special—"Gossamer Albatross: Flight of Imagination" (CBS)
Edited Series—"NFL Game of the Week" (NFL Films)

### 1980-81
Live Special—"1981 Kentucky Derby" (ABC)
Live Series—"PGA Golf Tour" (CBS)
Edited Special—"Wide World of Sports 20th Anniversary Show" (ABC)
Edited Series—"The American Sportsman" (ABC)

### 1981-82
Live Special—"1982 NCAA Basketball Final: North Carolina vs Georgetown" (CBS)
Live Series—"NFL Football" (CBS)
Edited Special—"1982 Indianapolis 500" (ABC)
Edited Series—"Wide World of Sports" (ABC)

### 1982-83
Live Special—"1982 World Series: St. Louis vs Milwaukee" (NBC)
Live Series—"NFL Football" (CBS)
Edited Special—"Wimbledon '83" (NBC)
Edited Series—"Wide World of Sports" (ABC)
Journalism—"ABC Sportsbeat" (ABC)

### 1983-84
No awards given

### 1984-85

Live Special—"1984 Summer Olympics" (ABC)
Live Series—No award given
Edited Special—"Road to the Super Bowl '85" (NFL Films)
Edited Series—"The American Sportsman" (ABC)
Journalism—"ABC Sportsbeat" (ABC), "CBS Sports Sunday" (CBS), Dick Schaap features (ABC) and 1984 Summer Olympic features (ABC)

### 1985-86

No awards given

### 1986-87

Live Special—"1987 Daytona 500" (CBS)
Live Series—"NFL Football" (CBS)
Edited Special—"Wide World of Sports 25th Anniversary Special" (ABC)
Edited Series—"Wide World of Sports" (ABC)

### 1987-88

Live Special—"1987 Kentucky Derby" (ABC)
Live Series—"NFL Monday Night Football" (ABC)
Edited Special—"Paris-Roubaix Bike Race" (CBS)
Edited Series—"Wide World of Sports" (ABC)

### 1988

Live Special—"1988 Summer Olympics" (NBC)
Live Series—"1988 NCAA Basketball" (CBS)
Edited Special—"Road to the Super Bowl '88" (NFL Films)
Edited Series—"Wide World of Sports" (ABC)
Studio Show—"NFL GameDay" (ESPN)
Journalism—1988 Summer Olympic reporting (NBC)

### 1989

Live Special—"1989 Indianapolis 500" (ABC)
Live Series—"NFL Monday Night Football" (ABC)
Edited Special—"Trans-Antarctica! The International Expedition" (ABC)
Edited Series—"This is the NFL" (NFL Films)
Studio Show—"NFL Today" (CBS)
Journalism—1989 World Series Game 3 earthquake coverage (ABC)

### 1990

Live Special—"1990 Indianapolis 500" (ABC)
Live Series—"1990 NCAA Basketball Tournament" (CBS)
Edited Special—"Road to Super Bowl XXIV" (NFL Films)
Edited Series—"Wide World of Sports" (ABC)
Studio Show—"SportsCenter" (ESPN)
Journalism—"Outside the Lines: The Autograph Game" (ESPN)

### 1991

Live Special—"1991 NBA Finals: Chicago vs LA Lakers" (NBC)
Live Series—"1991 NCAA Basketball Tournament" (CBS)
Edited Special—"Wide World of Sports 30th Anniversary Special" (ABC)
Edited Series—"This is the NFL" (NFL Films)
Studio Show—"NFL GameDay" (ESPN) and "NFL Live" (NBC)
Journalism—"Outside the Lines: Steroids–Whatever It Takes" (ESPN)

### 1992

Live Special—"1992 Breeders' Cup" (NBC)
Live Series—"1992 NCAA Basketball Tournament" (CBS)
Edited Special—"1992 Summer Olympics" (NBC)
Edited Series—"MTV Sports" (MTV)
Studio Show—"The NFL Today" (CBS)
Journalism—"Outside the Lines: Portraits in Black and White" (ESPN)

### 1993

Live Special—"1993 World Series" (CBS)
Live Series—"Monday Night Football" (ABC)
Edited Special—"Road to the Super Bowl" (NFL Films)
Edited Series—"This is the NFL" (NFL Films)
Studio Show—"The NFL Today" (CBS)
Journalism (TIE)—"Outside the Lines: Mitch Ivey Feature" (ESPN) and "SportsCenter: University of Houston Football" (ESPN).
Feature—"Arthur Ashe: His Life, His Legacy" (NBC).

### 1994

Live Special—"NHL Stanley Cup Finals" (ESPN)
Live Series—"Monday Night Football" (ABC)
Edited Special—"Lillehammer '94: 16 Days of Glory" (Disney/Cappy Productions)
Edited Series—"MTV Sports" (MTV)
Studio Show—"NFL GameDay" (ESPN)
Journalism—"1994 Winter Olympic Games: Mossad feature" (CBS)
Feature (TIE)—"Heroes of Telemark" on Winter Olympic Games (CBS); and "SportsCenter: Vanderbilt running back Brad Gaines" (ESPN).

### 1995

Live Special—"Cal Ripken 2131" (ESPN)
Live Series—"ESPN Speedworld" (ESPN)
Edited Special (quick turn-around)—"Outside the Lines: Playball–Opening Day in America" (ESPN)
Edited Special (long turn-around)—"Lillehammer, an Olympic Diary" (CBS)
Edited Series—"NFL Films Presents" (NFL Films)
Studio Show (TIE)—"NFL GameDay" (ESPN) and "FOX NFL Sunday"(FOX)
Journalism—"Real Sports with Bryant Gumbel: Broken Promises" (HBO)
Feature (TIE)—"SportsCenter: Jerry Quarry" (ESPN) and "Real Sports with Bryant Gumbel: Coach" (HBO).

### 1996

Live Special—"1996 World Series" (FOX)
Live Series—"ESPN Speedworld" (ESPN)
Edited Special—"Football America" (TNT/NFL Films)
Edited Series—"NFL Films Presents" (NFL Films)
Live Event Turnaround—"The Centennial Olympic Games" (NBC)
Studio Show—"SportsCenter" (ESPN)
Journalism—"Outside the Lines: AIDS in Sports" (ESPN)
Feature—"Real Sports with Bryant Gumbel: 1966 Texas Western NCAA Champs" (HBO).

---

### "Baseball" Wins Prime Time Emmy

Ken Burns's miniseries "Baseball" won the 1994 Emmy Award for Outstanding Informational Series. The nine-part documentary aired from Sept. 18-28, 1994 and ran more than 18 hours, drawing the largest audience in PBS history.

## National Emmy Awards (Cont.)

### 1997

Live Special—"The NBA Finals" (NBC)
Live Series—"NFL Monday Night Football" (ABC)
Edited Special—"Ironman Triathlon World Championship" (NBC/World Triathlon Corporation)
Edited Series—"NFL Films Presents" (NFL Films)
Live Event Turnaround—"Outside The Lines: Inside The Kentucky Derby" (ESPN)
Studio Show—"FOX NFL Sunday" (FOX)
Journalism—"Real Sports with Bryant Gumbel: Pros and Cons" (HBO)
Feature—"NFL Films Presents: Eddie George" (NFL Films).

### 1998

Live Special—"McGwire's 62nd Home Run Game" (FOX)
Live Series—"NBC Golf Tour" (NBC)
Edited Special—"A Cinderella Season: The Lady Vols Fight Back" (HBO)
Edited Series—"Real Sports with Bryant Gumbel" (HBO)
Live Event Turnaround—"Wimbledon '98" (NBC)
Studio Show—"FOX NFL Sunday" (FOX)
Journalism (TIE)—"Real Sports with Bryant Gumbel: Winning At All Costs" (HBO) and "Real Sports with Bryant Gumbel: Diamond Bucks" (HBO)
Feature—"NFL Films Presents: Steve Mariucci" (ESPN2 and NFL Films).

### 1999

Live Special—"2000 MLB All-Star Game" (FOX)
Live Series—"MLB Regular Season" (FOX)
Edited Special—"Ironman Triathlon World Championship" (NBC)
Edited Series—"SportsCentury: 50 Greatest Athletes" (ESPN)
Live Event Turnaround—"The World Track & Field Championships" (NBC)
Studio Show—"MLB Pre-Game Show" (FOX)
Journalism—"Real Sports with Bryant Gumbel: Fake Golf Clubs" (HBO)
Feature—"NFL Films Presents: Lt. Kalsu" (ESPN2)

### 2000

Live Special—"2000 World Series" (FOX)
Live Series—"NFL Sunday Night Football" (ESPN)
Edited Special—"Hoops and Hoosiers: The Story of the Final Four 2000" (CBS)
Edited Series—"SportsCentury: The Top 50 & Beyond" (ESPN)
Live Event Turnaround—"The Games of the XXVII Olympiad" (NBC)
Studio Show—"FOX NFL Sunday" (FOX)
Journalism—"Real Sports with Bryant Gumbel: Dominican Free-For-All" (HBO)
Feature—"The Games of the XXVII Olympiad" (NBC)

### 2001

Live Special—"2001 World Series" (FOX)
Live Series—"NASCAR on FOX" (FOX)
Edited Special—"ABC's Wide World of Sports 40th Anniversary Special" (ABC)
Edited Series—"SportsCentury" (ESPN Classic)
Live Event Turnaround—"Tour de France" (CBS)
Studio Show—Weekly—"Sunday NFL Countdown" (ESPN)
Studio Show—Daily—"Inside the NBA" (TNT/TBS)
Journalism—"Real Sports with Bryant Gumbel: Amare Stoudemire" (HBO)
Feature—"NFL Films Presents: Gerry Faust—The Golden Dream" (ESPN2)
Documentary—"Do You Believe in Miracles? The Story of the 1980 U.S. Hockey Team" (HBO)

### 2002

Live Special—"XIX Olympic Winter Games" (NBC)
Live Series—"The NBA on NBC" (NBC)
Edited Special—"America's Heroes: The Bravest vs. The Finest" (NBC)
Edited Series—"Real Sports with Bryant Gumbel" (HBO)
Live Event Turnaround—"Tour de France" (CBS)
Studio Show—Weekly—"Inside the NFL" (HBO & NFL Films)
Studio Show—Daily—"Baseball Tonight" (ESPN)
Journalism—"Outside the Lines, Weekly: Eligibility for Sale" (ESPN) and "Outside the Lines, Weekly: Iraqi Atletes, Tales of Torture" (ESPN)
Long Feature—"SportsCenter: Flight 93" (ESPN)
Short Feature—"SportsCenter: Chris Paul" (ESPN), "XIX Olympic Winter Games: Bill Johnson" (NBC) and "XIX Olympic Winter Games: The Sheas" (NBC)
Documentary—"Our Greatest Hopes, Our Worst Fears: The Tragedy of the Munich Games" (ABC)

### 2003

Live Special— "MLB on FOX: Post Season" (FOX)
Live Series— "ESPN NFL Sunday Night Football" (ESPN)
Edited Special— "Ironman Triathlon World Championship" (NBC/World Triathlon Corporation)
Edited Series/Anthology—Legendary Nights" (HBO)
Live Event Turnaround—"Tour de France" (CBS)
Studio Show—Weekly—"Sunday NFL Countdown" (ESPN)
Studio Show—Daily—"SportsCenter" (ESPN)
Journalism—"Real Sports with Bryant Gumbel: Marcus Dixon" (HBO)
Editing—"Jim McKay — My World in My Words " (HBO)
The Dick Schaap Outstanding Writing Award—"Wimbledon — Where is Wimbledon" (ESPN)
Long Feature—"NFL Films Presents on The NFL Network: Big Charlie's" (NFL Network/NFL Films) and "Real Sports with Bryant Gumbel: Alex Zanardi" (HBO)
Short Feature—"SportsCenter: Picking Up Butch" (ESPN)
Documentary—"The Curse of the Bambino" (HBO/Black Canyon Productions/Clear Channel Entertainment Television)

### 2004

Live Special—"The Masters" (CBS)
Live Series—"ABC's NFL Monday Night Football" (ABC)
Edited Special—"Ironman Triathlon World Championship" (NBC/Ironman Productions)
Edited Series/Anthology—"Real Sports with Bryant Gumbel" (HBO)
Live Event Turnaround—"The Games of the XXVIII Olympiad" (NBC)
Studio Show—Weekly—"Inside the NFL" (HBO)
Studio Show—Daily—"SportsCenter" (ESPN)
Journalism—"Real Sports with Bryant Gumbel: Sport o Sheikhs" (HBO)
Editing (TIE)—"NFL Films Presents on NFL Network: Michael Zagaris" (NFL Network/NFL Films) and "Wimbledon on NBC: Patrick Stewart Tease and Closing Thoughts" (NBC)
The Dick Schaap Outstanding Writing Award—"Wimbledon on ESPN2—Wimbledon Reflections" (ESPN2)
Long Feature—"SportsCenter: Ben Comen" (ESPN)
Short Feature—"The Super Bowl Today: NFL Quarterbacks" (CBS)
Documentary—"The Games of the XXVIII Olympiad Stylianos Kryiakides, The Journey of a Warrior" (NBC)

## Sportscasters of the Year
### National Emmy Awards

An Emmy Award for Sportscasters was first introduced in 1968 and given for Outstanding Host/Commentator for the 1967-68 TV season. Two awards, one for Outstanding Host or Play-by-Play and the other for Outstanding Analyst, were first presented in 1981 for the 1980-81 season. Three awards, for Outstanding Studio Host, Play-by-Play and Studio Analyst, have been given since the 1993 season, and one more, Sports Event Analyst, was added in 1997.

**Multiple winners:** Bob Costas and John Madden (14); Jim McKay (9); Joe Buck and Cris Collinsworth (5); Dick Enberg and Al Michaels (4); Keith Jackson and Tim McCarver (3); Terry Bradshaw, James Brown and Joe Morgan (2). Note that Jim McKay has won a total of 12 Emmy awards: eight for Host/Commentator, one for Host/Play-by-Play, two for Sports Writing and one for News Commentary.

| Season | Host/Commentator | Season | Host/Play-by-Play | Season | Analyst |
|---|---|---|---|---|---|
| 1967-68 | Jim McKay, ABC | 1980-81 | Dick Enberg, NBC | 1980-81 | Dick Button, ABC |
| 1968-69 | No award | 1981-82 | Jim McKay, ABC | 1981-82 | John Madden, CBS |
| 1969-70 | No award | 1982-83 | Dick Enberg, NBC | 1982-83 | John Madden, CBS |
| 1970-71 | Jim McKay, ABC | 1983-84 | No award | 1983-84 | No award |
|  | & Don Meredith, ABC | 1984-85 | George Michael, NBC | 1984-85 | No award |
| 1971-72 | No award | 1985-86 | No award | 1985-86 | No award |
| 1972-73 | Jim McKay, ABC | 1986-87 | Al Michaels, ABC | 1986-87 | John Madden, CBS |
| 1973-74 | Jim McKay, ABC | 1987-88 | Bob Costas, NBC | 1987-88 | John Madden, CBS |
| 1974-75 | Jim McKay, ABC | 1988 | Bob Costas, NBC | 1988 | John Madden, CBS |
| 1975-76 | Jim McKay, ABC | 1989 | Al Michaels, ABC | 1989 | John Madden, CBS |
| 1976-77 | Frank Gifford, ABC | 1990 | Dick Enberg, NBC | 1990 | John Madden, CBS |
| 1977-78 | Jack Whitaker, CBS | 1991 | Bob Costas, NBC | 1991 | John Madden, CBS |
| 1978-79 | Jim McKay, ABC | 1992 | Bob Costas, NBC | 1992 | John Madden, CBS |
| 1979-80 | Jim McKay, ABC |  |  |  |  |

### Studio Host

| Year | | Year | | Year | |
|---|---|---|---|---|---|
| 1993 | Bob Costas, NBC | 1998 | James Brown, FOX | 2002 | Bob Costas, HBO/NBC |
| 1994 | Bob Costas, NBC | 1999 | James Brown, FOX | 2003 | Bob Costas, HBO/NBC |
| 1995 | Bob Costas, NBC | 2000 | Bob Costas, NBC | 2004 | Bob Costas, HBO/NBC |
| 1996 | Bob Costas, NBC | 2001 | Bob Costas, HBO & |  |  |
| 1997 | Dan Patrick, ESPN |  | Ernie Johnson, TNT/TBS |  |  |

### Play-by-Play

| Year | | Year | | Year | |
|---|---|---|---|---|---|
| 1993 | Dick Enberg, NBC | 1997 | Bob Costas, NBC | 2001 | Joe Buck, FOX |
| 1994 | Keith Jackson, ABC | 1998 | Keith Jackson, ABC | 2002 | Joe Buck, FOX |
| 1995 | Al Michaels, ABC | 1999 | Joe Buck, FOX | 2003 | Joe Buck, FOX |
| 1996 | Keith Jackson, ABC | 2000 | Al Michaels, ABC | 2004 | Joe Buck, FOX |

### Studio Analyst

| Year | | Year | | Year | |
|---|---|---|---|---|---|
| 1993 | Billy Packer, CBS | 1997 | Cris Collinsworth, HBO/NBC | 2001 | Terry Bradshaw, FOX |
| 1994 | John Madden, FOX | 1998 | Cris Collinsworth, HBO/FOX | 2002 | Cris Collinsworth, HBO |
| 1995 | John Madden, FOX | 1999 | Terry Bradshaw, FOX | 2003 | Cris Collinsworth, HBO |
| 1996 | Howie Long, FOX | 2000 | Steve Lyons, FOX | 2004 | Cris Collinsworth, HBO |

### Sports Events Analyst

| Year | | Year | | Year | |
|---|---|---|---|---|---|
| 1997 | Joe Morgan, ESPN | 2000 | Tim McCarver, FOX | 2003 | John Madden, ABC |
| 1998 | John Madden, FOX | 2001 | Tim McCarver, FOX | 2004 | Joe Morgan, ESPN |
| 1999 | John Madden, FOX | 2002 | Tim McCarver, FOX |  |  |

### Lifetime Achievement Emmy Award

| Year | | Year | | Year | | Year | |
|---|---|---|---|---|---|---|---|
| 1989 | Jim McKay | 1993 | Pat Summerall | 1997 | Jim Simpson | 2001 | Herb Granath |
| 1990 | Lindsey Nelson | 1994 | Howard Cosell | 1998 | Keith Jackson | 2002 | Roone Arledge* |
| 1991 | Curt Gowdy | 1995 | Vin Scully | 1999 | Jack Buck | 2003 | Ed and Steve Sabol |
| 1992 | Chris Schenkel | 1996 | Frank Gifford | 2000 | Dick Enberg | 2004 | Chet Simmons |

*Arledge is the only recipient of two Lifetime Achievement Emmy Awards. In addition to sports, he won the lifetime award for "News and Documentary" in 2002.

## National Sportscasters and Sportswriters Assn. Award

Sportscaster of the Year presented annually since 1959 by the National Sportcasters and Sportswriters Association, based in Salisbury, N.C. Voting is done by NSSA members and selected national media.

**Multiple winners:** Bob Costas (8); Chris Berman (6) Keith Jackson (5); Lindsey Nelson and Chris Schenkel.(4); Joe Buck, Dick Enberg, Al Michaels and Vin Scully (3); Curt Gowdy and Ray Scott (2).

| Year | | Year | | Year | | Year | |
|------|--|------|--|------|--|------|--|
| 1959 | Lindsey Nelson | 1971 | Ray Scott | 1982 | Vin Scully | 1994 | Chris Berman |
| 1960 | Lindsey Nelson | 1972 | Keith Jackson | 1983 | Al Michaels | 1995 | Bob Costas |
| 1961 | Lindsey Nelson | 1973 | Keith Jackson | 1984 | John Madden | 1996 | Chris Berman |
| 1962 | Lindsey Nelson | 1974 | Keith Jackson | 1985 | Bob Costas | 1997 | Bob Costas |
| 1963 | Chris Schenkel | 1975 | Keith Jackson | 1986 | Al Michaels | 1998 | Jim Nantz |
| 1964 | Chris Schenkel | 1976 | Keith Jackson | 1987 | Bob Costas | 1999 | Dan Patrick |
| 1965 | Vin Scully | 1977 | Pat Summerall | 1988 | Bob Costas | 2000 | Bob Costas |
| 1966 | Curt Gowdy | 1978 | Vin Scully | 1989 | Chris Berman | 2001 | Chris Berman |
| 1967 | Chris Schenkel | 1979 | Dick Enberg | 1990 | Chris Berman | 2002 | Joe Buck |
| 1968 | Ray Scott | 1980 | Dick Enberg | 1991 | Bob Costas | 2003 | Joe Buck |
| 1969 | Curt Gowdy | | & Al Michaels | 1992 | Bob Costas | 2004 | Joe Buck |
| 1970 | Chris Schenkel | 1981 | Dick Enberg | 1993 | Chris Berman | | |

## The Pulitzer Prize

The Pulitzer Prizes for journalism, letters, drama and music have been presented annually since 1917 in the name of Joseph Pulitzer (1847-1911), the publisher of the *New York World*. Prizes are awarded by the president of Columbia University on the recommendation of a board of review. Sixteen Pulitzers have been awarded for newspaper sports reporting, sports commentary and sports photography.

### News Coverage

1935 **Bill Taylor,** *NY Herald Tribune*, for his reporting on the 1934 America's Cup yacht races.

### Special Citation

1952 **Max Kase**, *NY Journal-American*, for his reporting on the 1951 college basketball point-shaving scandal.

### Meritorious Public Service

1954 *Newsday* (Garden City, N.Y.) for its expose of New York State's race track scandals and labor racketeering.

### General Reporting

1956 **Arthur Daley**, *NY Times*, for his 1955 columns.

### Investigative Reporting

1981 **Clark Hallas** & **Robert Lowe,** *(Tucson) Arizona Daily Star*, for their 1980 investigation of the University of Arizona athletic department.

1986 **Jeffrey Marx** & **Michael York,** Lexington (Ky.) *Herald-Leader*, for their 1985 investigation of the basketball program at the University of Kentucky and other major colleges.

### Specialized Reporting

1985 **Randall Savage** & **Jackie Crosby,** Macon (Ga.) *Telegraph and News*, for their 1984 investigation of athletics and academics at the University of Georgia and Georgia Tech.

### Beat Reporting

2000 **George Dohrmann**, St. Paul (Min.) *Pioneer Press*, for his investigation that revealed academic fraud in the men's basketball program at the University of Minnesota.

### Feature Writing

1997 **Lisa Pollak**, *Baltimore Sun*, for her story about baseball umpire John Hirschbeck dealing with the death of one son and the illness of another from the same disease.

### Commentary

1976 **Red Smith**, *NY Times*, for his 1975 columns.
1981 **Dave Anderson,** *NY Times*, for his 1980 columns.
1990 **Jim Murray**, *LA Times*, for his 1989 columns.

### Photography

1949 **Nat Fein**, *NY Herald Tribune*, for his photo, "Babe Ruth Bows Out."

1952 **John Robinson** & **Don Ultang**, *Des Moines* (Iowa) *Register and Tribune*, for their sequence of six pictures of the 1951 Drake-Oklahoma A&M football game, in which Drake's Johnny Bright had his jaw broken.

1985 **The Photography Staff** of the *Orange County* (Calif.) *Register*, for their coverage of the 1984 Summer Olympics in Los Angeles.

1993 **William Snyder** & **Ken Geiger,** *The Dallas Morning News*, for their coverage of the 1992 Summer Olympics in Barcelona, Spain.

## Red Smith Award

Presented annually by the Associated Press Sports Editors (APSE) to a person who has made "major contributions to sports journalism" and named in honor of the late newspaper columnist for the *New York Herald-Tribune* and *New York Times*.

| Year | | Year | | Year | |
|------|--|------|--|------|--|
| 1981 | Red Smith, *NY Times* | 1990 | Dave Smith, *Dallas Morning News* | 2000 | Jerry Izenberg, *Newark Star Ledger* |
| 1982 | Jim Murray, *LA Times* | 1991 | Dave Kindred, *Nat'l Sports Daily* | | |
| 1983 | Shirley Povich, *Washington Post* | 1992 | Ed Storin, *Miami Herald* | 2001 | John Steadman, *Baltimore Sun* |
| 1984 | Fred Russell, *Nashville Banner* | 1993 | Tom McEwen, *Tampa Tribune* | 2002 | Dick Schaap, *ESPN* |
| 1985 | Blackie Sherrod, *Dallas Morning News* | 1994 | Dave Anderson, *NY Times* | | "The Sports Reporters" |
| | | 1995 | Richard Sandler, *Newsday* | 2003 | George Solomon, *Washington Post* |
| 1986 | Si Burick, *Dayton Daily News* | 1996 | Bill Dwyre, *LA Times* | | |
| 1987 | Will Grimsley, *AP* | 1997 | Jerome Holtzman, *Chicago Tribune* | 2004 | Jimmy Cannon, *NYC columnist* |
| 1988 | Furman Bisher, *Atlanta Journal* | 1998 | Sam Lacy, *Baltimore Afro-American* | 2005 | Mary Garber, *Winston-Salem Journal* |
| 1989 | Edwin Pope, *Miami Herald* | 1999 | Bud Collins, *Boston Globe* | | |

## Sportswriter of the Year
### NSSA Award

Presented annually since 1959 by the National Sportscasters and Sportswriters Association, based in Salisbury, N.C. Voting is done by NSSA members and selected national media.

**Multiple winners:** Jim Murray (14); Rick Reilly (10); Frank Deford (6); Red Smith (5); Will Grimsley (4); Peter Gammons (3).

| Year | | Year | | Year | |
|------|--|------|--|------|--|
| 1959 | Red Smith, NY Herald-Tribune | 1976 | Jim Murray, LA Times | 1993 | Peter Gammons, Boston Globe |
| 1960 | Red Smith, NY Herald-Tribune | 1977 | Jim Murray, LA Times | 1994 | Rick Reilly, Sports Ill. |
| 1961 | Red Smith, NY Herald-Tribune | 1978 | Will Grimsley, AP | 1995 | Rick Reilly, Sports Ill. |
| 1962 | Red Smith, NY Herald-Tribune | 1979 | Jim Murray, LA Times | 1996 | Rick Reilly, Sports Ill. |
| 1963 | Arthur Daley, NY Times | 1980 | Will Grimsley, AP | 1997 | Dave Kindred, The Sporting News |
| 1964 | Jim Murray, LA Times | 1981 | Will Grimsley, AP | | |
| 1965 | Red Smith, NY Herald-Tribune | 1982 | Frank Deford, Sports Ill. | 1998 | Mitch Albom, Detroit Free Press |
| 1966 | Jim Murray, LA Times | 1983 | Will Grimsley, AP | 1999 | Rick Reilly, Sports Ill. |
| 1967 | Jim Murray, LA Times | 1984 | Frank Deford, Sports Ill. | 2000 | Bob Ryan, Boston Globe |
| 1968 | Jim Murray, LA Times | 1985 | Frank Deford, Sports Ill. | 2001 | Rick Reilly, Sports Ill. |
| 1969 | Jim Murray, LA Times | 1986 | Frank Deford, Sports Ill. | 2002 | Rick Reilly, Sports Ill. |
| 1970 | Jim Murray, LA Times | 1987 | Frank Deford, Sports Ill. | 2003 | Rick Reilly, Sports Ill. |
| 1971 | Jim Murray, LA Times | 1988 | Frank Deford, Sports Ill. | 2004 | Rick Reilly, Sports Ill. |
| 1972 | Jim Murray, LA Times | 1989 | Peter Gammons, Sports Ill. | | |
| 1973 | Jim Murray, LA Times | 1990 | Peter Gammons, Boston Globe | | |
| 1974 | Jim Murray, LA Times | 1991 | Rick Reilly, Sports Ill. | | |
| 1975 | Jim Murray, LA Times | 1992 | Rick Reilly, Sports Ill. | | |

## Best Newspaper Sports Sections of 2004

Winners of the annual Associated Press Sports Editors contest for best daily and Sunday sports sections. Awards are divided into different categories, based on circulation figures. Selections are made by a committee of APSE members.

### Circulation Over 250,000

| Top 10 Daily | | Top 10 Sunday | |
|---|---|---|---|
| Boston Globe | New York Times | Atlanta Journal-Constitution | Los Angeles Times |
| Chicago Tribune | Orlando Sentinel | Boston Globe | Miami Herald |
| Dallas Morning News | St. Petersburg Times | Dallas Morning News | Minneapolis Star Tribune |
| Houston Chronicle | USA Today | Fort Worth Star-Telegram | Newark Star-Ledger |
| Los Angeles Times | Washington Post | Kansas City Star | Newsday (NY) |

### Circulation 100,000-250,000

| Top 10 Daily | | Top 10 Sunday | |
|---|---|---|---|
| Charlotte Observer | San Antonio Express-News | Buffalo News | Pittsburgh Post-Gazette |
| Detroit News | Seattle Times | The State | Raleigh News & Observer |
| Hartford Courant | Tampa Tribune | (Columbia, SC) | St. Paul Pioneer Press |
| Louisville Courier-Journal | The Journal News | Hartford Courant | Seattle Times |
| Palm Beach Post | (White Plains, NY) | Lexington Herald-Leader | Tampa Tribune |
| St. Paul Pioneer Press | | Palm Beach Post | |

## Best Sportswriting of 2004

Winners of the annual Associated Press Sports Editors Contest for best sportswriting in 2004. Eventual winners were chosen from five finalists in each writing division. Selections are made by a committee of APSE members. Note the investigative writing division included all circulation categories.

### Circulation over 250,000

| | | | |
|---|---|---|---|
| **Column:** | Bill Plaschke, Los Angeles Times | **Explanatory:** | Steve Fainaru, Dave Sheinin, Julie Tate and Margot Williams, Washington Post |
| **Feature:** | Mark Zeigler, San Diego Union-Tribune | | |
| **Breaking News:** | Lynn Bartels, Jody Berger, Brian Crecente, Owen Good, Burt Hubbard, Berry Morson, Javier Erik Olvera and Kevin Vaughn, Rocky Mountain News | **Project:** | Randy Covitz, Blair Kerkhoff, Jason King, Sam Mellinger, Joe Posnanski, Howard Richman, Derek Samson and Wright Thompson, Kansas City Star |
| **Game story:** | Linda Robertson, Miami Herald | | |

### Circulation 100,000-250,000

| | | | |
|---|---|---|---|
| **Column:** | Martin Fennelly, Tampa Tribune | **Game story:** | Geoff Calkins, Memphis Commerical Appeal |
| **Feature:** | Chuck Finder, Pittsburgh Post-Gazette | **Explanatory:** | David White, Fresno Bee |
| **Breaking News:** | Jorge Milian, Palm Beach Post | **Project:** | Zack McMillin, Memphis Commerical Appeal |

### All Categories

**Investigative:** Mark Fainaru-Wada and Lance Williams, San Francisco Chronicle

# Directory of Organizations

Listing of the major sports organizations, teams and media addresses and officials as of Oct. 4, 2005.

## AUTO RACING

### Champ Car World Series
5350 Lakeview Pkwy South Drive
Indianapolis, IN 46268
(317) 715-4100     www.champcarworldseries.com
CEO/Chairman . . . . . . . . . . . . . . . .Richard P. Eidswick
President . . . . . . . . . . . . . . . . . . . . . .Steve Johnson
Director of Public Relations . . . . . . . . . . . .Steve Shunck

### IRL
**(Indy Racing League)**
4565 West 16th St., Indianapolis, IN 46222
(317) 492-6526     www.indyracing.com
Founder . . . . . . . . . . . . . . . . . . . . . . . .Tony George
President-COO . . . . . . . . . . . . . . . . . . .Brian Barnhart
Director of Public Relations . . . . . . . . . . . .Tom Savage

### FIA—Formula One
**(Federation Internationale de L'Automobile)**
8 Place de la Concorde, Paris 75008 France
TEL: 011-33-1-43-12-44-55     www.fia.com
President . . . . . . . . . . . . . . . . . . . . . .Max Mosley
Deputy President (Sport) . . . . . . . . . . . . .Marco Piccinini

### NASCAR
**(National Assn. for Stock Car Auto Racing)**
P.O. Box 2875, Daytona Beach, FL 32120
(386) 253-0611     www.nascar.com
Chairman-CEO . . . . . . . . . . . . . . . . . . . . .Brian France
President . . . . . . . . . . . . . . . . . . . . . . . .Michael Helton
V.P. of Corporate Comm./Regional Touring . . . Jim Hunter

### NHRA
**(National Hot Rod Association)**
2035 Financial Way, Glendora, CA 91741
(626) 914-4761     www.nhra.com
President . . . . . . . . . . . . . . . . . . . . . . . .Tom Compton
Sr. V.P. of Racing Operations . . . . . . . . . . . .Graham Light
V.P. of Communications . . . . . . . . . . . Jerry Archambeault

## MAJOR LEAGUE BASEBALL

### Office of the Commissioner
245 Park Ave., 31st Floor, New York, NY 10167
(212) 931-7800     www.mlb.com
Commissioner . . . . . . . . . . . . . . . . . . . . . . .Bud Selig
President-COO . . . . . . . . . . . . . . . . . . . . .Robert DuPuy
Exec. V.P. of Baseball Ops. . . . . . . . . Jimmie Lee Solomon
Sr. V.P./General Counsel . . . . . . . . . . . . .Thomas Ostertag
Sr. V.P. of Public Relations . . . . . . . . . . . . .Richard Levin
V.P. of Public Relations . . . . . . . . . . . . . .Patrick Courtney

### Player Relations Committee
245 Park Ave., New York, NY 10167
(212) 931-7800
Executive V.P. for Labor Relations . . . . . . . . .Rob Manfred
Chief Labor Negotiator . . . . . . . . . . . . . .Frank Coonelly

### Major League Baseball Players Association
12 East 49th St., 24th Floor
New York, NY 10017
(212) 826-0808     www.mlbplayers.com
Exec. Director & General Counsel . . . . . . . . .Donald Fehr
Chief Operating Officer . . . . . . . . . . . . . . .Gene Orza
Director of Communications . . . . . . . . . . . .Greg Bouris

## AL

### American League Office
245 Park Ave., 31st Floor, New York, NY 10167
(212) 931-7800

### Baltimore Orioles
333 West Camden St., Baltimore, MD 21201
(410) 547-6156     www.theorioles.com
Managing General Partner . . . . . . . . . . . .Peter Angelos
Vice Chairman & COO . . . . . . . . . . . . . . . .Joseph Foss
Exec. V.P. of Baseball Operations . . . . . . . . . . Jim Beattie
V.P. of Baseball Operations . . . . . . . . . . . .Mike Flanagan
Director of Media Relations . . . . . . . . . . . . . .Bill Stetko

### Boston Red Sox
Fenway Park, 4 Yawkey Way, Boston, MA 02215
(617) 226-6613     www.redsox.com
Principal Owner . . . . . . . . . . . . . . . . . . . .John Henry
President-CEO . . . . . . . . . . . . . . . . . . .Larry Lucchino
Senior V.P./General Manager . . . . . . . . . . .Theo Epstein
V.P. of Media Relations . . . . . . . . . . . . . .Glenn Geffner

### Chicago White Sox
U.S. Cellular Field, 333 W. 35th St., Chicago, IL 60616
(312) 674-1000     www.whitesox.com
Chairman . . . . . . . . . . . . . . . . . . .Jerry Reinsdorf
Vice Chairman . . . . . . . . . . . . . . . . . . .Eddie Einhorn
Senior V.P./General Manager . . . . . . . . . . .Ken Williams
V.P. of Communications . . . . . . . . . . . . . . .Scott Reifert

### Cleveland Indians
Jacobs Field, 2401 Ontario St., Cleveland, OH 44115
(216) 420-4380     www.indians.com
Owner/CEO . . . . . . . . . . . . . . . . . . . .Lawrence Dolan
President . . . . . . . . . . . . . . . . . . . . . . . .Paul Dolan
Exec. V.P./General Manager . . . . . . . . . .Mark Shapiro
Director, Media Relations . . . . . . . . . . . . . .Bart Swain

### Detroit Tigers
Comerica Park, 2100 Woodward Ave., Detroit, MI 48201
(313) 471-2000     www.detroittigers.com
Owner and Director . . . . . . . . . . . . . . . . . . .Mike Ilitch
President/CEO/GM . . . . . . . . . . . . .Dave Dombrowski
Manager, Baseball Media Relations . . . . . . . .Brian Britten

### Kansas City Royals
One Royal Way, Kansas City, MO 64129
(816) 921-8000     www.kcroyals.com
Owner/CEO . . . . . . . . . . . . . . . . . . . . . .David Glass
President . . . . . . . . . . . . . . . . . . . . . . . .Dan Glass
Senior V.P./General Manager . . . . . . . . . . .Allard Baird
V.P. of Communications & Marketing . . . . . . .David Witty

### Los Angeles Angels of Anaheim
2000 Gene Autry Way, Anaheim, CA 92806
(714) 940-2000     www.angelsbaseball.com
Owner . . . . . . . . . . . . . . . . . . .Arturo "Arte" Moreno
President . . . . . . . . . . . . . . . . . . . . . . .Dennis Kuhl
V.P. & General Manager . . . . . . . . . . . . .Bill Stoneman
V.P. of Communications . . . . . . . . . . . . . . . .Tim Mead

### Minnesota Twins
Hubert H. Humphrey Metrodome
34 Kirby Puckett Place, Minneapolis, MN 55415
(612) 375-1366     www.mntwins.com
Owner . . . . . . . . . . . . . . . . . . . . . . . .Carl Pohlad
President . . . . . . . . . . . . . . . . . . . . .Dave St. Peter
V.P./General Manager . . . . . . . . . . . . . . . .Terry Ryan
Manager of Baseball Communications . . . . . .Sean Harlin

## New York Yankees
Yankee Stadium, 161st St. and River Ave., Bronx, NY 10451
(718) 293-4300               www.yankees.com
Principal Owner . . . . . . . . . . . . . .George Steinbrenner
President . . . . . . . . . . . . . . . . . . . . . . .Randy Levine
Sr. V.P./General Manager . . . . . . . . . . .Brian Cashman
Sr. Dir. of Media Relations . . . . . . . . . . . .Rick Cerrone

## Oakland Athletics
7000 Coliseum Way, Oakland, CA 94621
(510) 638-4900           www.oaklandathletics.com
Co-Owner/Managing Partner . . . . . . . . . . .Lewis Wolff
President . . . . . . . . . . . . . . . . . . . . . . .Mike Crowley
V.P./General Manager . . . . . . . . . . . . . . . .Billy Beane
Baseball Information Manager . . . . . . . . . .Mike Selleck

## Seattle Mariners
Safeco Field, P.O. Box 4100 , Seattle, WA 98104
(206) 346-4000              www.mariners.org
Chairman-CEO . . . . . . . . . . . . . . . . .Howard Lincoln
President-COO . . . . . . . . . . . . . . . . .Chuck Armstrong
Executive V.P./General Manager . . . . . . . . .Bill Bavasi
Director of Baseball Information . . . . . . . . . .Tim Hevly

## Tampa Bay Devil Rays
Tropicana Field, One Tropicana Drive
St. Petersburg, FL 33705
(727) 825-3137            www.devilrays.com
Principal Owner . . . . . . . . . . . . . . . .Stuart Sternberg
General Manager . . . . . . . . . . . . . . . . . . . . . . . . . .TBA
V.P. of Public Relations . . . . . . . . . . . . . . .Rick Vaughn

## Texas Rangers
1000 Ballpark Way #400, Arlington, TX 76011
(817) 273-5222          www.texasrangers.com
Owner/Chairman/CEO . . . . . . . . . . . . .Thomas Hicks
President . . . . . . . . . . . . . . . . . . . . . . . . .Jeff Cogen
General Manager . . . . . . . . . . . . . . . . . .Jon Daniels
Senior Dir., Baseball Media Relations . . . . . .Gregg Elkin

## Toronto Blue Jays
Rogers Centre, One Blue Jays Way, Suite 3200
Toronto, Ontario M5V 1J1
(416) 341-1000             www.bluejays.com
Majority Owner . . . . . . . . . . . . .Rogers Communications
President & CEO . . . . . . . . . . . . . . . . . .Paul Godfrey
Sr. V.P. of Baseball Ops./GM . . . . . . . . . . .J.P. Ricciardi
Director of Communications . . . . . . . . . .Jay Stenhouse

# NL

## National League Office
245 Park Ave., 31st Floor, New York, NY 10167
(212) 931-7800

## Arizona Diamondbacks
401 E. Jefferson St., Phoenix, AZ 85004
(602) 462-6500       www.azdiamondbacks.com
General Partner . . . . . . . . . . . . . . . . . . . . .Jeff Moorad
President . . . . . . . . . . . . . . . . . . . . .Richard H. Dozer
Interim General Manager . . . . . . . . . . . . .Bob Gebhard
Director of Public Relations . . . . . . . . . . .Mike Swanson

## Atlanta Braves
755 Hank Aaron Drive, Atlanta, GA 30315
(404) 522-7630         www.atlantabraves.com
President/Chairman . . . . . . . . . . . . . . . .Terry McGuirk
Exec. V.P./General Manager . . . . . . . .John Schuerholz
Director of Media Relations . . . . . . . . . . . .Brad Hainje

## Chicago Cubs
1060 West Addison St., Chicago, IL 60613
(773) 404-2827               www.cubs.com
Owner . . . . . . . . . . . . . . . . . . .The Tribune Company
President/CEO . . . . . . . . . . . . . . . . . .Andy MacPhail
V.P./General Manager . . . . . . . . . . . . . . . .Jim Hendry
Director of Media Relations . . . . . . . . . .Sharon Pannozzo

## Cincinnati Reds
Great American Ballpark, 100 Main St., Cincinnati, OH 45202
(513) 765-7000         www.cincinnatireds.com
Majority Owner-CEO . . . . . . . . . . . . . .Carl H. Lindner
General Manager . . . . . . . . . . . . . . . . . .Dan O'Brien
Director of Media Relations . . . . . . . . . . . .Rob Butcher

## Colorado Rockies
Coors Field, 2001 Blake St., Denver, CO 80205
(303) 292-0200        www.coloradorockies.com
Chairman/CEO . . . . . . . . . . . . . . . .Charles Monfort
President . . . . . . . . . . . . . . . . . . . . .Keli McGregor
Executive V.P./General Manager . . . . . . . .Dan O'Dowd
V.P., Communications/Public Relations . . . . . . . .Jay Alves

## Florida Marlins
2267 Dan Marino Blvd., Miami, FL 33056
(305) 626-7400            www.flamarlins.com
Owner . . . . . . . . . . . . . . . . . . . . . . . . .Jeffrey Loria
President . . . . . . . . . . . . . . . . . . . . . .David Samson
Senior V.P./General Manager . . . . . . . .Larry Beinfest
Director of Media Relations . . . . . . .Matthew Roebuck

## Houston Astros
Minute Maid Park, P.O. Box 288, Houston, TX 77001
(713) 259-8900             www.astros.com
Chairman-CEO . . . . . . . . . . . . . . .Drayton McLane Jr.
President of Baseball Ops. . . . . . . . . . . . . . .Tal Smith
General Manager . . . . . . . . . . . . . . . . . .Tim Purpura
Senior V.P., Communications . . . . . . . . . . . .Jay Lucas

## Los Angeles Dodgers
1000 Elysian Park Ave., Los Angeles, CA 90012
(323) 224-1500             www.dodgers.com
Chairman . . . . . . . . . . . . . . . . . . . . .Frank McCourt
Vice Chairman/President . . . . . . . . . . . .Jamie McCourt
Executive V.P./General Manager . . . . . . .Paul DePodesta
V.P., Public Relations . . . . . . . . . . . . . . . .John Olguin

## Milwaukee Brewers
Miller Park, One Brewers Way, Milwaukee, WI 53214
(414) 902-4400       www.milwaukeebrewers.com
Principal Owner/Chairman . . . . . . . . . . .Mark Attanasio
Executive V.P./General Manager . . . . . . .Doug Melvin
Asst. Dir. of Media Relations . . . . . . . . . .Nicole Saunches

## New York Mets
123-01 Roosevelt Ave., Flushing, NY 11368
(718) 507-6387              www.mets.com
Chairman/CEO . . . . . . . . . . . . . . . . . . .Fred Wilpon
President . . . . . . . . . . . . . . . . . . . . . . . . . .Saul Katz
Exec. V.P./ General Manager . . . . . . . . . .Omar Minaya
V.P. of Media Relations . . . . . . . . . . . . . . .Jay Horwitz

## Philadelphia Phillies
One Citizens Bank Way, Philadelphia, PA 19148
(215) 463-6000             www.phillies.com
General Partner/Pres./CEO . . . . . . .David Montgomery
Chairman . . . . . . . . . . . . . . . . . . . . . . . . .Bill Giles
General Manager & V.P. . . . . . . . . . . . . . . . .Ed Wade
V.P. of Public Relations . . . . . . . . . . . . . . .Larry Shenk

## Pittsburgh Pirates
115 Federal St., Pittsburgh, PA 15212
(412) 323-5000            www.pirateball.com
CEO/Managing General Partner . . . . .Kevin McClatchy
Senior V.P. & General Manager . . . . . . . .Dave Littlefield
Director of Media Relations . . . . . . . . . . . .Jim Trdinich

## St. Louis Cardinals
250 Stadium Plaza, St. Louis, MO 63102
(314) 421-3060          www.stlcardinals.com
Chairman/General Partner . . . . . . .William O. DeWitt Jr.
President . . . . . . . . . . . . . . . . . . . . . .Mark Lamping
Senior V.P./General Manager . . . . . . . .Walt Jocketty
Director of Media Relations . . . . . . . . . . . .Brian Bartow

### San Diego Padres
100 Park Blvd., San Diego, CA 92101
(619) 795-5000                    www.padres.com
Chairman . . . . . . . . . . . . . . . . . . . . . . . . . . John Moores
CEO . . . . . . . . . . . . . . . . . . . . . . . . . . . Sandy Alderson
Executive V.P./General Manager . . . . . . . . Kevin Towers
Director of Media Relations . . . . . . . . . . . . . Luis Garcia

### San Francisco Giants
24 Willie Mays Plaza, San Francisco, CA 94107
(415) 972-2000                    www.sfgiants.com
President/Managing Gen. Partner . . . . . . Peter Magowan
Executive V.P./COO . . . . . . . . . . . . . . . . . . . . Larry Baer
Senior V.P./General Manager . . . . . . . . . . Brian Sabean
Director of Media Relations . . . . . . . . . . . . Blake Rhodes

### Washington Nationals
RFK Stadium, 2400 East Capitol St., SE
Washington DC 20003
(202) 675-5100                    www.nationals.com
President . . . . . . . . . . . . . . . . . . . . . . . . . . . Tony Tavares
V.P./General Manager . . . . . . . . . . . . . . . . . Jim Bowden
V.P., Communications . . . . . . . . . . . . . . . . Chartese Berry
Dir. Baseball Information . . . . . . . . . . . . . . . John Dever

## PRO BASKETBALL

## NBA

### League Office
Olympic Tower, 645 Fifth Ave., New York, NY 10022
(212) 407-8000                    www.nba.com
Commissioner . . . . . . . . . . . . . . . . . . . . . . . . David Stern
Senior V.P. of Basketball Ops. . . . . . . . . . . Stuart Jackson
Deputy Commissioner . . . . . . . . . . . . . . . Russell Granik
Sr. V.P. of Basketball Communications . . Brian McIntyre
Executive V.P. Global Media . . . . . . . . . Heidi Ueberroth

### NBA Players Association
Two Penn Plaza, Suite 2430, New York, NY 10121
(212) 655-0880                    www.nbpa.com
Executive Director . . . . . . . . . . . . . . . . . . . . . Billy Hunter
Associate General Counsel . . . . . . . . . . . . Ron Klempner
President . . . . . . . . . . . . . . . . . . . . . . . . . . Antonio Davis
Director of Communications . . . . . . . . . . Dan Wasserman

### Atlanta Hawks
Centennial Tower, 101 Marietta St. NW, Suite 1900
Atlanta, GA 30303
(404) 827-3800                    www.hawks.com
Owner . . . . . . . . . . . . . . . . . . . . . . . . Atlanta Spirit, LLC
President/CEO . . . . . . . . . . . . . . . . . . . . . . Bernie Mullin
Exec. V.P./General Manager . . . . . . . . . . . . Billy Knight
V.P. of Media Relations . . . . . . . . . . . . . . . . Arthur Triche

### Boston Celtics
222 Causeway Street, Fourth Floor, Boston, MA 02114
(617) 854-8000                    www.celtics.com
CEO/Managing Partner . . . . . . . . . . . . . Wyc Grousbeck
President . . . . . . . . . . . . . . . . . . . . . . . . . Red Auerbach
Exec. Director of Basketball Ops. . . . . . . . . Danny Ainge
Vice President of Media Services . . . . . . . . . . . Jeff Twiss

### Charlotte Bobcats
129 West Trade St., Suite 700, Charlotte, NC 28202
(704) 424-4120              www.bobcatsbasketball.com
Majority Owner . . . . . . . . . . . . . . . . . . . Robert L. Johnson
President/COO . . . . . . . . . . . . . . . . . . . . . . Ed Tapscott
General Manager/Head Coach . . . . . . . Bernie Bickerstaff
Public Relations Director . . . . . . . . . . . . . . Scott Leightman

### Chicago Bulls
United Center, 1901 West Madison St., Chicago, IL 60612
(312) 455-4000                    www.bulls.com
Chairman . . . . . . . . . . . . . . . . . . . . . . . . Jerry Reinsdorf
Exec V.P. of Basketball Operations . . . . . . . . John Paxson
Sr. Dir. of Public & Media Relations . . . . . . . . Tim Hallam

### Cleveland Cavaliers
One Center Court, Cleveland, OH 44115
(216) 420-2000                    www.cavs.com
Majority Owner . . . . . . . . . . . . . . . . . . . . . . . Dan Gilbert
President . . . . . . . . . . . . . . . . . . . . . . . . Len Komoroski
General Manager . . . . . . . . . . . . . . . . . . . . Danny Ferry
V.P., Communications . . . . . . . . . . . . . . . . . Tad Carper

### Dallas Mavericks
2909 Taylor St., Dallas, TX 75226
(214) 747-6287              www.dallasmavericks.com
Owner . . . . . . . . . . . . . . . . . . . . . . . . . . . . Mark Cuban
President/CEO . . . . . . . . . . . . . . . . . . . . Terdema Ussery
President, Basketball Operations . . . . . . . . . Donn Nelson
Dir., Basketball Communications . . . . . . . . Sarah Melton

### Denver Nuggets
1000 Chopper Cir., Denver, CO 80204
(303) 405-1100                    www.nuggets.com
Owner . . . . . . . . . . . . . . . . . . . . . . . . . . . Stan Kroenke
General Manager . . . . . . . . . . . . . . . Kiki Vandeweghe
Sr. Dir. of Communications . . . . . . . . . . Teri Washington

### Detroit Pistons
The Palace of Auburn Hills
Four Championship Dr., Auburn Hills, MI 48326
(248) 377-0100                    www.pistons.com
Managing Partner . . . . . . . . . . . . . . . . William Davidson
President/CEO . . . . . . . . . . . . . . . . . . . . . . Tom Wilson
President of Basketball Operations . . . . . . . . Joe Dumars
V.P. of Public Relations . . . . . . . . . . . . . . . . Matt Dobek

### Golden State Warriors
1011 Broadway, Oakland, CA 94607
(510) 986-2200                    www.warriors.com
Owner-CEO . . . . . . . . . . . . . . . . . . . . . . . Chris Cohan
President . . . . . . . . . . . . . . . . . . . . . . . . Robert Rowell
Exec. V.P. of Basketball Operations . . . . . . . Chris Mullin
General Manager . . . . . . . . . . . . . . . . . . . Rod Higgins
Exec. Director of Public Relations . . . . . . . Raymond Ridder

### Houston Rockets
Toyota Center, 1510 Polk Street, Houston, TX 77002
(713) 758-7200                    www.rockets.com
Owner . . . . . . . . . . . . . . . . . . . . . . . Leslie L. Alexander
President-CEO . . . . . . . . . . . . . . . . . . . George Postolos
General Manager . . . . . . . . . . . . . . . . . Carroll Dawson
Director of Media Relations . . . . . . . . . . . . . Nelson Luis

### Indiana Pacers
125 S. Pennsylvania Street, Indianapolis, IN 46204
(317) 917-2500                    www.pacers.com
Owners . . . . . . . . . . . . . . . Melvin Simon & Herb Simon
CEO/President . . . . . . . . . . . . . . . . . . . . . Donnie Walsh
President of Basketball Ops. . . . . . . . . . . . . . Larry Bird
Director of Public Information . . . . . . . . . . David Benner

### Los Angeles Clippers
Staples Center, 1111 S. Figueroa St., Suite 1100
Los Angeles, CA 90015
(213) 742-7500                    www.clippers.com
Owner-Chairman . . . . . . . . . . . . . . . . Donald T. Sterling
Executive V.P. . . . . . . . . . . . . . . . . . . . . . Andy Roeser
V.P., Basketball Operations . . . . . . . . . . . . Elgin Baylor
V.P. of Communications . . . . . . . . . . . . . . . . Joe Safety

### Los Angeles Lakers
555 N. Nash St., El Segundo, CA 90245
(310) 426-6000                    www.lakers.com
Owner . . . . . . . . . . . . . . . . . . . . . . . . . . . . Jerry Buss
General Manager . . . . . . . . . . . . . . . . . Mitch Kupchak
Director of Public Relations . . . . . . . . . . . . . John Black

## Memphis Grizzlies
191 Beale Street, Memphis, TN 38103
(901) 888-4667                    www.grizzlies.com
Owner .........................Michael Heisley
GM/President of Basketball Ops. .........Jerry West
Director, Basketball Media Relations .......Stacey Mitch

## Miami Heat
AmericanAirlines Arena, 601 Biscayne Blvd.
Miami, FL 33132
(786) 777-4328                    www.heat.com
Managing General Partner ............Micky Arison
President, Basketball Operations .........Pat Riley
General Manager .....................Randy Pfund
V.P. of Sports Media Relations ..........Tim Donovan

## Milwaukee Bucks
1001 N. Fourth St., Milwaukee, WI 53203
(414) 227-0500                    www.bucks.com
President ..............Sen. Herb Kohl (D., Wisc.)
General Manager ....................Larry Harris
Director of Public Relations ...........Cheri Hanson

## Minnesota Timberwolves
Target Center
600 First Ave. North, Minneapolis, MN 55403
(612) 673-1600                    www.timberwolves.com
Owner ............................Glen Taylor
President .........................Chris Wright
V.P., Basketball Operations ..........Kevin McHale
V.P. of Communications ..............Ted Johnson

## New Jersey Nets
390 Murray Hill Pkwy., East Rutherford, NJ 07073
(201) 935-8888                    www.njnets.com
Owner ..........................Bruce Ratner
President/CEO .......................Rod Thorn
General Manager ..................Ed Stefanski
Director of Public Relations ...........Gary Sussman

## New Orleans Hornets
1501 Girod St., New Orleans, LA 70113
(504) 301-4000                    www.hornets.com
Majority Owner ....................George Shinn
President ..........................Paul Mott
General Manager ....................Jeff Bower
Sports Public Relations Manager ...........Scott Hall
**Note:** Team is playing 35 games in Oklahoma City and six in Baton Rouge in 2005-06.

## New York Knickerbockers
Madison Square Garden, Two Penn Plaza, 14th Floor
New York, NY 10121
(212) 465-6471                    www.knicks.com
Owner ...................Cablevision Systems Inc.
President/CEO (Cablevision) ...........James Dolan
President of Basketball Ops. ............Isiah Thomas
V.P. of Public Relations ..............Joe Favorito

## Orlando Magic
2 Magic Place
8701 Maitland Summit Blvd., Orlando, FL 32810
(407) 916-2400                    www.orlandomagic.com
Owner ..........................Rich DeVos
President/CEO ................Bob Vander Weide
Senior Vice President ................Pat Williams
Director of Communications ............Joel Glass

## Philadelphia 76ers
Wachovia Center
3601 S. Broad St., Philadelphia, PA 19148
(215) 339-7600                    www.76ers.com
Owner .....................Comcast-Spectacor
Chairman .........................Ed Snider
President/General Manager .............Billy King
V.P. of Communications ............Karen Frascona

## Phoenix Suns
201 E Jefferson St., Phoenix, AZ 85004
(602) 379-7900                    www.suns.com
Controlling Owner/Vice Chairman .......Robert Sarver
Chairman-CEO ..................Jerry Colangelo
President/General Manager ..........Bryan Colangelo
President/COO .....................Rick Welts
V.P. of Basketball Communications ..........Julie Fie

## Portland Trail Blazers
One Center Court, Suite 200, Portland, OR 97227
(503) 234-9291                    www.blazers.com
Owner-Chairman ...................Paul Allen
President .......................Steve Patterson
General Manager ....................John Nash
Executive Dir. of Communications .........Mike Hanson

## Sacramento Kings
One Sports Parkway, Sacramento, CA 95834
(916) 928-0000                    www.kings.com
Owners .................Joe and Gavin Maloof
President, Basketball Operations .........Geoff Petrie
V.P., Basketball Operations ..........Wayne Cooper
V.P., Media Relations .................Troy Hanson

## San Antonio Spurs
One SBC Center
San Antonio, TX 78219
(210) 444-5000                    www.spurs.com
Chairman/CEO .....................Peter Holt
Exec. V.P. of Basketball Ops./Head Coach ..Gregg Popovich
Senior V.P./General Manager ..........R.C. Buford
Director of Media Services .............Tom James

## Seattle SuperSonics
351 Elliott Ave. West, Suite 500
Seattle, WA 98119
(206) 281-5800                    www.supersonics.com
Chairman .......................Howard Schultz
President & CEO ...................Wally Walker
General Manager ....................Rick Sund
Director of Media Relations ...........Marc Moquin

## Toronto Raptors
40 Bay St., Suite 400
Toronto, Ontario M5J 2X2
(416) 815-5600                    www.raptors.com
Chairman ......................Larry Tanenbaum
President/CEO ..................Richard Peddie
General Manager ...................Rob Babcock
Director of Media Relations ..........Jim LaBumbard

## Utah Jazz
301 West South Temple
Salt Lake City, UT 84101
(801) 325-2500                    www.utahjazz.com
Owner ..........................Larry Miller
President .......................Dennis Haslam
Sr. V.P. of Basketball Operations ......Kevin O'Connor
Vice President, Communications ........Caroline Shaw

## Washington Wizards
MCI Center, 601 F Street NW
Washington, D.C., 20004
(202) 661-5000                    www.washingtonwizards.com
Chairman ..........................Abe Pollin
President .......................Susan O'Malley
President of Basketball Ops. ..........Ernie Grunfeld
Director of Player Personnel ...........Milt Newton
Director, Public Relations .............Zack Bolno

# Other Men's Pro Leagues

## Continental Basketball Association
1412 W. Idaho St., Ste. 235
Boise, ID 83702
(208) 429-0101                www.cbahoopsonline.com
Commissioner . . . . . . . . . . . . . . . . . . . . . . . .Gary Hunter
Dir. of Public/Media Relations . . . . . . . . . .Kris Kamann
    **Member teams (8)**: Albany Patroons, Dakota Wizards, Gary Steelheads, Idaho Stampede, Michigan Mayhem, Rockford Lightning, Sioux Falls Skyforce and Yakima Sun Kings. Franchise in Broomfield, CO joining in 2006-07.

## United States Basketball League
46 Quirk Road, Milford, CT 06460
(203) 877-9508                www.usbl.com
Commissioner . . . . . . . . . . . . . .Daniel T. Meisenheimer III
Dir. of Public Relations . . . . . . . . . . . . . . .Jacob Gordon
    **Member teams (8)**: Brooklyn Kings, Dodge City Legend, Kansas Cagerz, Nebraska Cranes, New Jersey Flyers, Oklahoma Storm, Pennsylvania ValleyDawgs and Westchester (NY) Wildfire.

## National Basketball Development League
24 Vardry Street, Suite 201, Greenville, SC 29601
(864) 248-1100                www.nbdl.com
President . . . . . . . . . . . . . . . . . . . . . . . . . . .Philip Evans
V.P. of Communications . . . . . . . . . . . . . . .Kent Partridge
    **Member teams (8)**: Albuquerque Thunderbirds, Arkansas RimRockers, Austin Toros, Fayetteville (NC) Patriots, Florida Flame, Fort Worth Flyers, Roanoke (VA) Dazzle and Tulsa 66ers.

# WNBA

## League Office
645 5th Ave., New York, NY 10022
(212) 688-9622                www.wnba.com
President . . . . . . . . . . . . . . . . . . . . . . . .Donna Orender
Chief Operating Officer . . . . . . . . . . . . . . . .Ann Sarnoff
Sr. V.P. of Player Personnel . . . . . . . . . . . . .Renee Brown
Sr. Director of Communications . . . . . . . .Sharon Robustelli

## Charlotte Sting
129 W. Trade Street, Suite 700, Charlotte, NC 28202
(704) 357-0252                www.charlottesting.com
Owner/President . . . . . . . . . . . . . . . .Robert L. Johnson
General Manager . . . . . . . . . . . . . . . . . . . . .Trudi Lacey
V.P. of Public Relations . . . . . . . . . . . . . .Scott Leightman

## Connecticut Sun
One Mohegan Sun Blvd., Uncasville, CT 06382
(860) 862-4000                www.wnba.com/sun
CEO . . . . . . . . . . . . . . . . . . . . . . . . . . . .Mitchell Etess
General Manager . . . . . . . . . . . . . . .Christopher Sienko
Media Relations Manager . . . . . . . . . . . . . .Bill Tavares

## Detroit Shock
The Palace of Auburn Hills
Four Championship Dr., Auburn Hills, MI 48326
(248) 377-0100                www.detroitshock.com
President . . . . . . . . . . . . . . . . . . . . . .Thomas S. Wilson
Head Coach/Dir. of Player Personnel . . . . . .Bill Laimbeer
Director of Media Relations . . . . . . . . . . . . .Paul Hickey

## Houston Comets
1510 Polk Street
Houston, TX 77002
(713) 627-9622                www.houstoncomets.com
Owner . . . . . . . . . . . . . . . . . . . . . . .Leslie L. Alexander
General Manager/Head Coach . . . . . . . .Van Chancellor
Director of Media Relations . . . . . . . . . . . . .Nelson Luis

## Indiana Fever
125 S. Pennsylvania St., Indianapolis, IN 46204
(317) 917-2500                www.feverbasketball.com
CEO/President . . . . . . . . . . . . . . . . . . . . .Donnie Walsh
COO/General Manager . . . . . . . . . . . .Kelly Krauskopf
Director of Media Relations . . . . . . . . . .Kevin Messenger

## Los Angeles Sparks
2151 E. Grand Ave., Suite 100
El Segundo, CA 90245
(310) 341-1000                www.lasparks.com
President . . . . . . . . . . . . . . . . . . . . . . . . .Johnny Buss
General Manager . . . . . . . . . . . . . . . . .Penny Toler
Director of Communications . . . . . . . . . . . . . . . . .TBA

## Minnesota Lynx
Target Center
600 First Ave. N., Minneapolis, MN 55403
(612) 673-8400                www.wnba.com/lynx
Owner . . . . . . . . . . . . . . . . . . . . . . . . . . .Glen Taylor
Chief Operating Officer . . . . . . . . . . . . . . .Roger Grffith
Head Coach . . . . . . . . . . . . . . . .Suzie McConnell Serio

## New York Liberty
Madison Square Garden
Two Penn Plaza, New York, NY 10121
(212) 564-9622                www.nyliberty.com
Owner . . . . . . . . . . . . . . . . . . . .Cablevision Systems Inc.
Senior V.P/General Manager . . . . . . . .Carol Blazejowski
V.P., Marketing & Communications . . . . . . . .Amy Scheer

## Phoenix Mercury
201 E. Jefferson St., Phoenix, AZ 85004
(602) 514-8333                www.phoenixmercury.com
President . . . . . . . . . . . . . . . . . . . . . .Bryan Colangelo
V.P., General Manager . . . . . . . . . . . . . . . .Seth Sulka
Communications Manager . . . . . . . . . .Candice Crawford

## Sacramento Monarchs
ARCO Arena, One Sports Parkway
Sacramento, CA 95834
(916) 928-0000                www.sacramentomonarchs.com
President, Basketball Ops. . . . . . . . . . . . . .John Thomas
General Manager/Head Coach . . . . . . .John Whisenant
Manager of Media Relations . . . . . . . . .Rebecca Brutlag

## San Antonio Silver Stars
One SBC Center, San Antonio, TX 78219
(210) 444-5000                www.wnba.com/silverstars
Chairman/CEO . . . . . . . . . . . . . . . . . . . . . .Peter Holt
COO . . . . . . . . . . . . . . . . . . . .Clarissa Davis-Wrightsil
General Manager/Head Coach . . . . . . . . . . .Dan Hughes
Manager, Media Services . . . . . . . . . . . . . . .Kris Davis

## Seattle Storm
351 Elliott Ave. W., Suite 500
Seattle, WA 98119
(206) 281-5800                www.wnba.com/storm
President & CEO . . . . . . . . . . . . . . . . . .Wally Walker
Chief Operating Officer . . . . . . . . . . . . . . .Karen Bryant
Sr. Dir. of Public Relations . . . . . . . . . . . . .Valerie O'Neil

## Washington Mystics
401 9th Street, NW
Washington, D.C. 20004
(202) 266-2361                www.wnba.com/mystics
President/Managing Partner . . . . . . . . . . .Sheila Johnson
General Manager . . . . . . . . . . . . . . . . .Linda Hargrove
Dir. of Public Relations . . . . . . . . . . . . . . .Ketsia Colimon

**Note:** The Chicago Sky will become the league's 14th team in 2006.

## BOWLING

**BPAA**
**(Bowling Proprietors' Assn. of America)**
P.O. Box 5802, Arlington, TX 76011
(817) 649-5105 www.bpaa.com
President ............................... Jeff Boje
Executive Director ................. John F. Berglund
Director of Public Relations ............ Cary Richmond

**PBA**
**(Professional Bowlers Association)**
719 Second Ave., Suite 701
Seattle, WA 98104
(206) 332-9688 www.pba.com
Chairman ............................ Chris Peters
President/CEO ........................ Steve Miller
Commissioner .................... Fred Schreyer
Manager of Public Relations .............. Jason Carr

**USBC**
**(United States Bowling Congress)**
5301 South 76th St., Greendale, WI 53129
(414) 514-2695 www.bowl.com
President ...................... Michael Carroll
CEO ............................... Roger Dalkin
Vice President ...................... Sam Lantto
Chief Information Officer ................. Tim Payne
**Note:** On Jan. 1, 2005, ABC, WIBC, YABA (Young American Bowling Alliance) and USA Bowling merged into the United States Bowling Congress.

## BOXING

**IBF**
**(International Boxing Federation)**
516 Main Street, 2nd Floor, East Orange, NJ 07018
(973) 414-0300 www.ibf-usba-boxing.com
President ...................... Marian Muhammad
Treasurer-Ratings Chairman ............. Daryl Peoples

**WBA**
**(World Boxing Association)**
P.O. Box 377, Maracay 2101, Estado Aragua
Venezuela
TEL: 011-58-244-663-1584 www.wbaonline.com
President ...................... Gilberto Mendoza
Administrator ....................... David Herrera
Ratings Chairman ............... Jose Oliver Gomez
TEL: (507) 614-0333

**WBC**
**(World Boxing Council)**
Cuzco 872, Col. Lindavista
C.P. 07300, Mexico City, D.F.
TEL: 011 (52.55) 5119-52-74 www.wbcboxing.com
President ....................... Jose Sulaiman
Ratings Chairman ...................... Frank Quill

**WBO**
**(World Boxing Organization)**
1st Federal Bldg.
1056 Ave Munoz Rivera, Suite 711-714
San Juan, P.R. 00927
(787) 765-4444 www.wbo-int.com
President ............... Francisco "Paco" Valcarcel
Past Pres./Chairman Champ. Committee .. Luis Batista Salas
Ratings Chairman ....................... Luis Perez

**Don King Productions, Inc.**
501 Fairway Dr.
Deerfield Beach, FL 33441
(954) 418-5800 www.donking.com
President ............................ Don King
Sr. V.P. of Boxing Ops. ............... Dana Jamison
V.P., Boxing Ops./Public Relations ...... Bob Goodman

**Top Rank**
3980 Howard Hughes Pkwy. Ste. 580
Las Vegas, NV 89109
(702) 732-2717 www.toprank.com
Chairman ............................ Bob Arum
Director of Public Relations ............ Lee Samuels

## COLLEGE SPORTS

**NAIA**
**(National Assn. of Intercollegiate Athletics)**
23500 W. 105th Street, Olathe, KS 66051
(913) 791-0044 www.naia.org
President-CEO ....................... Steve Baker
Director of Sports Information .......... Dawn Harmon

**NCAA**
**(National Collegiate Athletic Association)**
700 W. Washington St.
P.O. Box 6222, Indianapolis, IN 46206
(317) 917-6222 www.ncaa.org
President ........................... Myles Brand
V.P. of Enforcement .................. David Price
Managing Dir. of Public/Media Relations ... Bob Williams

**WSF**
**(Women's Sports Foundation)**
Eisenhower Park, East Meadow, NY 11554
(516) 542-4700 www.womenssportsfoundation.org
Founder ......................... Billie Jean King
Executive Director .................. Donna Lopiano
President (beginning Jan. 2005) ...... Dominique Dawes
Public Relations Coordinator ......... Eloise Longobardi

## Major NCAA Conferences
See pages 433-441 for football coaches, basketball coaches, nicknames and colors of all Division I-A and I-AA football schools and Division I basketball schools.

**ATLANTIC COAST CONFERENCE**
P.O. Drawer ACC
Greensboro, NC 27417-6724
(336) 854-8787 www.theacc.com
Founded: 1953
Commissioner ..................... John Swofford
Asst. Commis. of Media Relations ...... Brian Morrison
**2005-06 members:** BASKETBALL & FOOTBALL (12)— Boston College, Clemson, Duke, Florida St., Georgia Tech, Maryland, Miami-FL, North Carolina, N.C. State, Virginia, Virginia Tech and Wake Forest.

**Boston College**
Chestnut Hill, MA 02467
SID: (617) 552-3004 www.bceagles.com
Founded: 1863 Enrollment: 14,500
President ................... Rev. William P. Leahy, S.J.
Athletic Director ................... Gene DeFilippo
Sports Information Director ........... Chris Cameron

**Clemson University**
Clemson, SC 29633
SID: (864) 656-2114 www.clemsontigers.com
Founded: 1889 Enrollment: 16,403
President ....................... James F. Barker
Athletic Director ................ Terry Don Phillips
Asst. AD, Sports Information ............. Tim Bourret

**Duke University**
Durham, NC 27708
SID: (919) 684-2633 www.goduke.com
Founded: 1838 Enrollment: 6,092
President . . . . . . . . . . . . . . . . .Richard H. Brodhead
Athletic Director . . . . . . . . . . . . . . . . .Joe Alleva
Sports Information Director . . . . . . . . . . . .Jon Jackson

**Florida State University**
Tallahassee, FL 32306
SID: (850) 644-1403 www.seminoles.com
Founded: 1851 Enrollment: 38,886
President . . . . . . . . . . . . . . . . .Dr. T.K. Wetherell
Athletic Director . . . . . . . . . . . . . . . . .Dave Hart Jr.
Sports Information Director . . . . . . . . . . . .Rob Wilson

**Georgia Tech**
Atlanta, GA 30332
SID: (404) 894-5445 www.ramblinwreck.com
Founded: 1885 Enrollment: 16,000
President . . . . . . . . . . . . . . . .Dr. G. Wayne Clough
Athletic Director . . . . . . . . . . . . . . . . .Dave Braine
Sports Information Director . . . . . . . . . . .Allison George

**University of Maryland**
College Park, MD 20742
SID: (301) 314-7064 www.umterps.com
Founded: 1807 Enrollment: 35,329
President . . . . . . . . . . . . . . . .Dr. Clayton D. Mote Jr.
Athletic Director . . . . . . . . . . . . . . . . .Deborah Yow
Assoc. AD, Media Relations . . . . . . . . . . . . .Doug Dull

**University of Miami**
Coral Gables, FL 33146
SID: (305) 284-3244 www.hurricanesports.com
Founded: 1926 Enrollment: 15,250
President . . . . . . . . . . . . . . . . .Dr. Donna E. Shalala
Athletic Director . . . . . . . . . . . . . . . . .Paul Dee
Asst. Athletic Director/Communications . . . . . .Mark Pray

**University of North Carolina**
Chapel Hill, NC 27514
SID: (919) 962-2123 www.tarheelblue.com
Founded: 1789 Enrollment: 26,878
Chancellor . . . . . . . . . . . . . . . . .James Moeser
Athletic Director . . . . . . . . . . . . . . . . .Dick Baddour
Sports Information Director . . . . . . . . . . .Steve Kirschner

**North Carolina State University**
Raleigh, NC 27695
SID: (919) 515-2102 www.gopack.com
Founded: 1887 Enrollment: 29,637
Chancellor . . . . . . . . . . . . . . . .James L. Oblinger
Athletic Director . . . . . . . . . . . . . . . . .Lee Fowler
Asst. AD for Media Relations . . . . . .Annabelle Vaughan

**University of Virginia**
Charlottesville, VA 22904
SID: (434) 982-5500 www.virginiasports.com
Founded: 1819 Enrollment: 20,018
President . . . . . . . . . . . . . . . . .John T. Casteen III
Athletic Director . . . . . . . . . . . . . . . .Craig Littlepage
Sports Information Director . . . . . . . . . . . .Rich Murray

**Virginia Tech**
Blacksburg, VA 24061
SID: (540) 231-6726 www.hokiesports.com
Founded: 1872 Enrollment: 28,000
President . . . . . . . . . . . . . . . . .Charles W. Steger
Athletic Director . . . . . . . . . . . . . . . . .Jim Weaver
Sports Information Director . . . . . . . . . . . .Dave Smith

**Wake Forest University**
Winston-Salem, NC 27109
SID: (336) 758-5640 www.wakeforestsports.com
Founded: 1834 Enrollment: 4,037
President . . . . . . . . . . . . . . . . .Dr. Nathan O. Hatch
Athletic Director . . . . . . . . . . . . . . . . .Ron Wellman
Asst. Athletic Director/Media Relations . . . . .Dean Buchan

\*     \*     \*

**BIG EAST CONFERENCE**
222 Richmond Street, Suite 110
Providence, RI 02903
(401) 272-9108 www.bigeast.org
Founded: 1979
Commissioner . . . . . . . . . . . . . . . . .Mike Tranghese
Assoc. Commissioner/Communications . . . John Paquette
   **2005-06 members**: BASKETBALL (16)—Cincinnati,
Connecticut, DePaul, Georgetown, Louisville, Marquette,
Notre Dame, Pittsburgh, Providence, Rutgers, St. John's,
Seton Hall, South Florida, Syracuse, Villanova and West
Virginia; FOOTBALL (8)—Cincinnati, Connecticut, Louisville,
Pittsburgh, Rutgers, South Florida, Syracuse and West
Virginia.

**University of Cincinnati**
Cincinnati, OH 45221
SID: (513) 556-5191 www.ucbearcats.com
Founded: 1819 Enrollment: 33,000
President . . . . . . . . . . . . . . . . .Dr. Nancy L. Zimpher
Athletic Director (resigning Jan. 1, 2006) . . . . .Bob Goin
Asst. AD for Athletic Communications . . . . .Tom Hathaway

**University of Connecticut**
Storrs, CT 06269
SID: (860) 486-3531 www.uconnhuskies.com
Founded:1881 Enrollment: 27,579
President . . . . . . . . . . . . . . . . .Philip Austin
Athletic Director . . . . . . . . . . . . . . . . .Jeffrey Hathaway
Sports Information Director . . . . . . . . . . .Michael Enright

**DePaul University**
Chicago, IL 60614
SID: (773) 325-7525 www.depaulbluedemons.com
Founded: 1898 Enrollment: 24,300
President . . . . . . . . .Rev. Dennis H. Holtschneider, C.M.
Athletic Director . . . . . . . . . . . . . . . .Jean Lenti Ponsetto
Sports Information Director . . . . . . . . . . . . .Scott Reed

**Georgetown University**
Washington, DC 20057
SID: (202) 687-2492 www.guhoyas.com
Founded: 1789 Enrollment: 6,164
President . . . . . . . . . . . . . . . John J. DeGioia, Ph. D.
Athletic Director . . . . . . . . . . . . . . . . .Bernard Muir
Sr. Sports Communication Director . . . . . . .Bill Shapland

**University of Louisville**
Louisville, KY 40292
SID: (502) 852-6581 www.uoflsports.com
Founded: 1798 Enrollment: 22,000
President . . . . . . . . . . . . . . . . .Dr. James Ramsey
Athletic Director . . . . . . . . . . . . . . . . .Tom Jurich
Sports Information Director . . . . . . . . . . . .Kenny Klein

**Marquette University**
Milwaukee, WI 53233
SID: (414) 288-7447 www.gomarquette.com
Founded: 1881 Enrollment: 11,000
President . . . . . . . . . . . . . . . .Rev. Robert A. Wild S.J.
Athletic Director . . . . . . . . . . . . . . . . .Bill Cords
Asst. AD for Media Relations . . . . . . . . . . .Mike Broeker

## University of Notre Dame
Notre Dame, IN 46556
SID: (574) 631-7516     www.und.com
Founded: 1842     Enrollment: 8,332
President . . . . . . . . . . . . . . . . . . . . . . .Rev. John I. Jenkins
Athletic Director . . . . . . . . . . . . . . . . . . .Kevin White
Sports Information Director . . . . . . . . . . . . .John Heisler

## University of Pittsburgh
Pittsburgh, PA 15260
SID: (412) 648-8240     www.pittsburghpanthers.com
Founded: 1787     Enrollment: 32,107
Chancellor . . . . . . . . . . . . . . . . . . .Mark A. Nordenberg
Athletic Director . . . . . . . . . . . . . . . . . . . . . . .Jeff Long
Sports Information Director . . . . . . . . . . . . .E.J. Borghetti

## Providence College
Providence, RI 02918
SID: (401) 865-2272     www.friars.com
Founded: 1917     Enrollment: 3,700
President . . . . . . . . . . . . . . . .Rev. Brian J. Shanley, O.P.
Athletic Director . . . . . . . . . . . . . . . . . . .Robert Driscoll
Sports Information Director . . . . . . . . . . . . .Arthur Parks

## Rutgers University
New Brunswick, NJ 08903
SID: (732) 445-4200     www.scarletknights.com
Founded: 1766     Enrollment: 33,500
President . . . . . . . . . . . . . . . .Richard L. McCormick
Athletic Director . . . . . . . . . . . . . .Robert E. Mulcahy III
Sports Information Director . . . . . . . . . . .John Wooding

## St. John's University
Jamaica, NY 11439
SID: (718) 990-1520     www.redstormsports.com
Founded: 1870     Enrollment: 19,813
President . . . . . . . . . . . .Rev. Donald J. Harrington, CM
Athletic Director . . . . . . . . . . . . . . . . . . .Chris Monasch
Director of Athletic Communications . . . . . . . .Mark Fratto

## Seton Hall University
South Orange, NJ 07079
SID: (973) 761-9493     www.shupirates.com
Founded: 1856     Enrollment: 9,700
President . . . . . . . . . . . .Monsignor Robert T. Sheeran
Athletic Director . . . . . . . . . . . . .Joseph A. Quinlan Jr.
Assistant AD/Communications . . . . . . . . . .Jeff Andriesse

## University of South Florida
Tampa, FL 33620
SID: (813) 974-4086     www.gousfbulls.com
Founded: 1956     Enrollment: 42,950
President . . . . . . . . . . . . . . . . . .Judy Genshaft, Ph.D.
Athletic Director . . . . . . . . . . . . . . . . . .Doug Woolard
Sports Information Director . . . . . . . . . . . .John Gerdes

## Syracuse University
Syracuse, NY 13244
SID: (315) 443-2608     www.suathletics.com
Founded: 1870     Enrollment: 11,000
Chancellor/President . . . . . . . . . . . . . . . .Nancy Cantor
Athletic Director . . . . . . . . . . . . . . . . . .Dr. Daryl Gross
Sports Information Director . . . . . . . . . . . . . .Sue Edson

## Villanova University
Villanova, PA 19085
SID: (610) 519-4120     www.villanova.com
Founded: 1842     Enrollment: 6,295
President (through 2005-06) . .Rev. Edmund J. Dobbin, OSA
Athletic Director . . . . . . . . . . . . . . . . . .Vince Nicastro
Sports Information Director . . . . . . . . . . . .Dean Kenefick

## West Virginia University
Morgantown, WV 26507
SID: (304) 293-2821     www.msnsportsnet.com
Founded: 1867     Enrollment: 26,000
President . . . . . . . . . . . . . . . . . . . . . . .David Hardesty
Athletic Director . . . . . . . . . . . . . . . . . . .Ed Pastilong
Sports Information Director . . . . . . . . . . . . . .Shelly Poe

\*     \*     \*

## BIG 12 CONFERENCE
2201 Stemmons Fwy., 28th Floor
Dallas, TX 75207
(214) 742-1212     www.big12sports.com
Founded: 1996
Commissioner . . . . . . . . . . . . . . . . . . . .Kevin Weiberg
Asst. Commiss. for Communications . . . . . . . .Bob Burda
   **2005-06 members**: BASKETBALL & FOOTBALL (12)—
Baylor, Colorado, Iowa St., Kansas, Kansas St., Missouri,
Nebraska, Oklahoma, Oklahoma St., Texas, Texas A&M
and Texas Tech.

## Baylor University
Waco, TX 76711
SID: (254) 710-2743     www.baylorbears.com
Founded: 1845     Enrollment: 13,799
Interim President . . . . . . . . . . . . .William D. Underwood
Athletic Director . . . . . . . . . . . . . . . . . . . .Ian McCaw
Assoc. AD for Media Relations . . . . . . . . . . . .Nick Joos

## University of Colorado
Boulder, CO 80309
SID: (303) 492-5626     www.cubuffs.com
Founded: 1876     Enrollment: 27,954
President . . . . . . . . . . . . . . . . . . . . . . . .Hank Brown
Athletic Director . . . . . . . . . . . . . . . . . . . .Mike Bohn
Sports Information Director . . . . . . . . . . . . . .Dave Plati

## Iowa State University
Ames, IA 50011
SID: (515) 294-3372     www.cyclones.com
Founded: 1858     Enrollment: 26,380
President . . . . . . . . . . . . .Dr. Gregory L. Geoffroy
Athletic Director . . . . . . . . . . . . . . . . . . .Jamie Pollard
Sports Information Director . . . . . . . . . . .Tom Kroeschell

## University of Kansas
Lawrence, KS 66045
SID: (785) 864-3417     www.kuathletics.com
Founded: 1866     Enrollment: 28,890
Chancellor . . . . . . . . . . . . . . . . . . . .Robert Hemenway
Athletic Director . . . . . . . . . . . . . . . . . . . .Lew Perkins
Asst. AD for Media Relations . . . . . . . . . . . .Chris Theisen

## Kansas State University
Manhattan, KS 66502
SID: (785) 532-6735     www.k-statesports.com
Founded: 1863     Enrollment: 23,191
President . . . . . . . . . . . . . . . . . . . . . . . .Dr. Jon Wefald
Athletic Director . . . . . . . . . . . . . . . . . . . .Tim Weiser
Sports Information Director . . . . . . . . . . . .Garry Bowman

## University of Missouri
Columbia, MO 65205
SID: (573) 882-0712     www.mutigers.com
Founded: 1839     Enrollment: 27,088
Chancellor . . . . . . . . . . . . . . . . . . . . . .Brady J. Deaton
Athletic Director . . . . . . . . . . . . . . . . . .Michael Alden
Media Relations Director . . . . . . . . . . . . . .Chad Moller

## University of Nebraska
Lincoln, NE 68588
SID: (402) 472-2263     www.huskers.com
Founded: 1869     Enrollment: 22,000
Chancellor . . . . . . . . . . . . . . . . . . . .Harvey Perlman
Athletic Director . . . . . . . . . . . . . . . . .Steve Pederson
Associate AD for Communications . . . . . . .Chris Anderson

## University of Oklahoma
Norman, OK 73019
SID: (405) 325-8231     www.soonersports.com
Founded: 1890     Enrollment: 31,400
President . . . . . . . . . . . . . . . . . . . . .David Boren
Athletic Director . . . . . . . . . . . . . . . . .Joe Castiglione
Asst. AD for Media Relations . . . . . . . . .Kenny Mossman

## Oklahoma State University
Stillwater, OK 74078
SID: (405) 744-7714     www.okstate.com
Founded: 1890     Enrollment: 31,000
President . . . . . . . . . . . . . . . . .Dr. David J. Schimdly
V.P. for Athletic Programs/AD . . . . . . . . . .Mike Holder
Assoc. AD, Media Relations . . . . . . . . . . .Steve Buzzard

## University of Texas
Austin, TX 78713
SID: (512) 471-7437     www.texassports.com
Founded: 1883     Enrollment: 37,397
President (leaving 3/1/06) . . . . . . . . .Dr. Larry Faulkner
Athletic Director . . . . . . . . . . . . . . . . .DeLoss Dodds
Asst. AD for Media Relations . . . . . . . . . . .John Bianco

## Texas A&M University
College Station, TX 77843
SID: (979) 845-5725     www.aggieathletics.com
Founded: 1876     Enrollment: 44,571
President . . . . . . . . . . . . . . . . . . .Dr. Robert Gates
Athletic Director . . . . . . . . . . . . . . . . . . .Bill Byrne
Asst. AD for Media Relations . . . . . . . . . . .Alan Cannon

## Texas Tech University
Lubbock, TX 79409
SID: (806) 742-2770     www.texastech.com
Founded: 1923     Enrollment: 28,588
President . . . . . . . . . . . . . . . . . . . .Dr. Jon Whitmore
Athletic Director . . . . . . . . . . . . . . . . .Gerald Myers
Asst. AD for Media Relations . . . . . . . . . . .Chris Cook

*     *     *

## BIG TEN CONFERENCE
1500 West Higgins Road
Park Ridge, IL 60068-6300
(847) 696-1010     www.bigten.org
Founded: 1896
Commissioner . . . . . . . . . . . . . . . . . .James E. Delany
Asst. Commissioner/Communications . . . . .Scott Chipman
  **2005-06 members**: BASKETBALL & FOOTBALL (11)—
Illinois, Indiana, Iowa, Michigan, Michigan St., Minnesota,
Northwestern, Ohio St., Penn St., Purdue and Wisconsin.

## University of Illinois
Champaign, IL 61820
SID: (217) 244-6533     www.fightingillini.com
Founded: 1867     Enrollment: 36,738
President . . . . . . . . . . . . . . . . . . . B. Joseph White
Athletic Director . . . . . . . . . . . . . . . . . .Ron Guenther
Director of Communications . . . . . . . . . . . . .Kent Brown

## Indiana University
Bloomington, IN 47408
SID: (812) 855-9399     www.iuhoosiers.com
Founded: 1820     Enrollment: 37,821
President . . . . . . . . . . . . . . . . .Dr. Adam W. Herbert
Athletic Director . . . . . . . . . . . . . . . . .Rick Greenspan
Assoc. Dir. of Media Relations . . . . . . . . . . .Pete Rhoda

## University of Iowa
Iowa City, IA 52242
SID: (319) 335-9411     www.hawkeyesports.com
Founded: 1847     Enrollment: 29,697
President . . . . . . . . . . . . . . . . . . . . .David Skorton
Athletic Director . . . . . . . . . . . . . . . . .Bob Bowlsby
Sports Information Director . . . . . . . . . . . . .Phil Haddy

## University of Michigan
Ann Arbor, MI 48109
SID: (734) 763-4423     www.mgoblue.com
Founded: 1817     Enrollment: 39,031
President . . . . . . . . . . . . . . . . . .Mary Sue Coleman
Athletic Director . . . . . . . . . . . . . . . . .William Martin
Athletic Media Relations Director . . . . . . . . .Bruce Madej

## Michigan State University
East Lansing, MI 48824
SID: (517) 355-2271     www.msuspartans.com
Founded: 1855     Enrollment: 43,836
President . . . . . . . . . . . . . .Dr. Lou Anna Kimsey Simon
Athletic Director . . . . . . . . . . . . . . . . . . .Ron Mason
Asst. AD for Media Relations . . . . . . . .John Lewandowski

## University of Minnesota
Minneapolis, MN 55455
SID: (612) 625-4090     www.gophersports.com
Founded: 1851     Enrollment: 45,361
President . . . . . . . . . . . . . . . . . .Robert Bruininks
Athletic Director . . . . . . . . . . . . . . . . . .Joel Maturi
Director of Media Relations . . . . . . . . . . . .Mike Lockrem

## Northwestern University
Evanston, IL 60208
SID: (847) 491-7503     www.nusports.com
Founded: 1851     Enrollment: 7,700
President . . . . . . . . . . . . . . . . . . .Henry S. Bienen
Athletic Director . . . . . . . . . . . . . . . . .Mark Murphy
Asst. Athletic Director/Media Services . . . . . . .Mike Wolf

## Ohio State University
Columbus, OH 43210
SID: (614) 292-6861     www.ohiostatebuckeyes.com
Founded: 1870     Enrollment: 55,043
President . . . . . . . . . . . . . . . . . .Karen A. Holbrook
Athletic Director . . . . . . . . . . . . . . . . . .Gene Smith
Assoc. AD, Athletic Communications . . . . . .Steve Snapp

## Penn State University
University Park, PA 16802
SID: (814) 865-1757     www.gopsusports.com
Founded: 1855     Enrollment: 40,571
President . . . . . . . . . . . . . . . . . . .Graham Spanier
Athletic Director . . . . . . . . . . . . . . . . . .Tim Curley
Assoc. AD, Communications . . . . . . . . . . . .Jeff Nelson

## Purdue University
West Lafayette, IN 47907
SID: (765) 494-3201     www.purduesports.com
Founded: 1869     Enrollment: 38,564
President . . . . . . . . . . . . . . . . . .Martin C. Jischke
Athletic Director . . . . . . . . . . . . . . . . .Morgan Burke
Sports Information Director . . . . . . . . . . . . .Tom Schott

## University of Wisconsin
Madison, WI 53711
SID: (608) 262-1811     www.uwbadgers.com
Founded: 1848     Enrollment: 41,595
Chancellor . . . . . . . . . . . . . . . . . . . . . . . .John Wiley
Athletic Director . . . . . . . . . . . . . . . . . . . .Barry Alvarez
Director of Athletic Communications . . . . . .Justin Doherty

*     *     *

## CONFERENCE USA
5201 North O'Connor, Suite 300, Irving, TX 75039
(214) 774-1300     www.conferenceusa.com
Founded: 1995
Commissioner . . . . . . . . . . . . . . . . . . . .Britton Banowsky
Asst. Comm. for Media Relations . . . . .Russell Anderson
  **2005-06 members**: BASKETBALL (12)—UAB, Central
Florida, East Carolina, Houston, Marshall, Memphis, Rice,
SMU, Southern Miss, Tulane, Tulsa and UTEP; FOOTBALL
(12)—UAB, Central Florida, East Carolina, Houston, Marshall, Memphis, Rice, SMU, Southern Miss, Tulane, Tulsa and
UTEP.

## University of Alabama at Birmingham
Birmingham, AL 35294
SID: (205) 934-0723     www.uabsports.com
Founded: 1969     Enrollment: 16,693
President . . . . . . . . . . . . . . . . . . . .Carol Z. Garrison
Athletic Director . . . . . . . . . . . . . . . . . . .Watson Brown
Associate AD for Media Relations . . . . . . . .Norm Reilly

## University of Central Florida
Orlando, FL 32816
SID: (407) 823-2729     www.ucfathletics.com
Founded: 1963     Enrollment: 44,000
President . . . . . . . . . . . . . . . . . . . .Dr. John C. Hitt
Athletic Director . . . . . . . . . . . . . . . . . . .Steve Orsini
Asst. AD for Media Relations . . . . . . . . . . .John Marini

## East Carolina University
Greenville, NC 27858
SID: (252) 328-4522     www.ecupirates.com
Founded: 1907     Enrollment: 21,797
Chancellor . . . . . . . . . . . . . . . . . . . .Dr. Steve Ballard
Athletic Director . . . . . . . . . . . . . . . . . . .Terry Holland
Director of Athletic Media Relations . . . . .Tom McClellan

## University of Houston
Houston, TX 77204
SID: (713) 743-9404     www.uhcougars.com
Founded: 1927     Enrollment: 35,400
President . . . . . . . . . . . . . . . . . . . .Dr. Jay Gogue
Athletic Director . . . . . . . . . . . . . . . . . . .Dave Maggard
Sports Information Director . . . . . . . . . . .Chris Burkhalter

## Marshall University
Huntington, WV 25715
SID: (304) 696-5275     www.herdzone.com
Founded: 1837     Enrollment: 16,551
President . . . . . . . . . . . . . . . . . . . .Dr. Stephen J. Kopp
Athletic Director . . . . . . . . . . . . . . . . . . .Bob Marcum
Asst. AD for Media Relations . . . . . . . . . .Randy Burnside

## University of Memphis
Memphis, TN 38152
SID: (901) 678-2337     www.gotigersgo.com
Founded: 1912     Enrollment: 20,668
President . . . . . . . . . . . . . . . . . . . .Dr. Shirley Raines
Athletic Director . . . . . . . . . . . . . . . . . . .R.C. Johnson
Director of Athletic Media Relations . . .Jennifer Rodrigues

## Rice University
Houston, TX 77005
SID: (713) 348-5775     www.riceowls.com
Founded: 1912     Enrollment: 4,785
President . . . . . . . . . . . . . . . . . . . .Dr. David W. Leebron
Athletic Director . . . . . . . . . . . . . . . . . . .Bobby May
Asst. AD/Sports Information Director . . . . . . . .Bill Cousins

## SMU—Southern Methodist University
Dallas, TX 75275
SID: (214) 768-2883     www.smumustangs.com
Founded: 1911     Enrollment: 10,038
President . . . . . . . . . . . . . . . . . . . .Dr. R. Gerald Turner
Athletic Director . . . . . . . . . . . . . . . . . . .Jim Copeland
Asst. AD/Media Relations . . . . . . . . . . . . . .Brad Sutton

## University of Southern Mississippi
Hattiesburg, MS 39406
SID: (601) 266-4503     www.southernmiss.com
Founded: 1910     Enrollment: 15,259
President . . . . . . . . . . . . . . . . . . . .Dr. Shelby Thames
Athletic Director . . . . . . . . . . . . . . . . . . .Rich Giannini
Asst. AD for Media Relations . . . . . . . . . . .Mike Montoro

## Tulane University
New Orleans, LA 70118
SID: (504) 865-5506     www.tulanegreenwave.com
Founded: 1834     Enrollment: 13,214
President . . . . . . . . . . . . . . . . . . . .Dr. Scott S. Cowen
Athletic Director . . . . . . . . . . . . . . . . . . .Rick Dickson
Asst. AD for Media Relations . . . . . . . . . . .Donna Turner

## University of Tulsa
Tulsa, OK 74104
SID: (918) 631-2395     www.tulsahurricane.com
Founded: 1894     Enrollment: 4,100
President . . . . . . . . . . . . . . . . . . . .Dr. Steadman Upham
Interim Athletic Director . . . . . . . . . . . . . . . .Kevan Buck
Asst. AD/Media Relations . . . . . . . . . . . . . .Don Tomkalski

## UTEP—University of Texas at El Paso
El Paso, TX 79902
SID: (915) 747-6653     www.utepathletics.com
Founded: 1914     Enrollment: 18,542
President . . . . . . . . . . . . . . . . . . . .Dr. Diana Natalicio
Athletic Director . . . . . . . . . . . . . . . . . . .Bob Stull
Assoc. AD/Media Relations . . . . . . . . . . . . .Jeff Darby

*     *     *

## MID-AMERICAN CONFERENCE
24 Public Square, 15th Floor, Cleveland, OH 44113
(216) 566-4622     www.mac-sports.com
Founded: 1946
Commissioner . . . . . . . . . . . . . . . . . . . .Rick Chryst
Asst. Commissioner for Media Relations . . . . .Gary Richter
  **2005-06 members**: FOOTBALL & BASKETBALL (12)—
Akron, Ball St., Bowling Green, Buffalo, Central Michigan,
Eastern Michigan, Kent St., Miami-OH, Northern Illinois,
Ohio University, Toledo and Western Michigan.

## University of Akron
Akron, OH 44325
SID: (330) 972-7468     www.gozips.com
Founded: 1870     Enrollment: 24,300
President . . . . . . . . . . . . . . . . . . . .Dr. Luis Proenza
Athletic Director . . . . . . . . . . . . . . . . . . .Michael J. Thomas
Asst. AD/Media Relations . . . . . . . . . . . . .Shawn Nestor

## Ball State University
Muncie, IN 47306
SID: (765) 285-8242     www.ballstatesports.com
Founded: 1918     Enrollment: 18,043
President . . . . . . . . . . . . . . . . . . . .Dr. Jo Ann M. Gora
Athletic Director . . . . . . . .Lawrence "Bubba" Cunningham
Assoc. AD for External Affairs . . . . . . . . .Joe Hernandez

**Bowling Green State University**
Bowling Green, OH 43403
SID: (419) 372-7075 www.bgsufalcons.com
Founded: 1910 Enrollment: 20,975
President ...........................Dr. Sidney Ribeau
Athletic Director .........................Paul Krebs
Asst. AD for Athletic Communications .....J.D. Campbell

**University of Buffalo**
Buffalo, NY 14260
SID: (716) 645-6311 www.buffalobulls.com
Founded: 1846 Enrollment: 27,276
President ...................John B. Simpson, Ph.D
Athletic Director .....................Warde Manuel
Asst. AD for Communications ...........Paul Vecchio

**Central Michigan University**
Mt. Pleasant, MI 48859
SID: (989) 774-3277 www.cmuchippewas.com
Founded: 1892 Enrollment: 27,936
President ...........................Michael Rao
Athletic Director (retiring 1/15/06) .....Herb Deromedi
Sports Information Director .............Don Helinski

**Eastern Michigan University**
Ypsilanti, MI 48197
SID: (734) 487-0317 www.emich.edu/goeagles
Founded: 1849 Enrollment: 24,500
President ....................Dr. John A. Fallon III
Interim Athletic Director ...............Bob England
Sports Information Director .............Jim Streeter

**Kent State University**
Kent, OH 44242
SID: (330) 672-2110 www.kentstatesports.cpm
Founded: 1910 Enrollment: 36,000
President .......................Carol Cartwright
Athletic Director ...................Laing Kennedy
Dir. of Athletic Communications .........Jeff Schaefer

**Miami University**
Oxford, OH 45056
SID: (513) 529-4327 www.muredhawks.com
Founded: 1809 Enrollment: 16,300
President ......................James C. Garland
Athletic Director .......................Brad Bates
Asst. AD for External Affairs .............Mike Harris

**Northern Illinois University**
DeKalb, IL 60115
SID: (815) 753-1706 www.niuhuskies.com
Founded: 1895 Enrollment: 24,820
President .......................John G. Peters
Athletic Director .......................Jim Phillips
Sports Information Director ...........Michael Korcek

**Ohio University**
Athens, OH 45701
SID: (740) 593-1298 www.ohiobobcats.com
Founded: 1804 Enrollment: 28,598
President ..................Dr. Roderick J. McDavis
Athletic Director ......................Kirby Hocutt
Asst. AD for External Affairs .............Derek Scott

**University of Toledo**
Toledo, OH 43606
SID: (419) 530-4920 www.utrockets.com
Founded: 1872 Enrollment: 18,900
President ......................Dr. Daniel Johnson
Athletic Director ....................Mike O'Brien
Asst. AD, Media Relations .............Paul Helgren

**Western Michigan University**
Kalamazoo, MI 49008
SID: (269) 387-4138 www.wmubroncos.com
Founded: 1903 Enrollment: 27,829
President .....................Dr. Judith I. Bailey
Athletic Director ................Kathy Beauregard
Sports Information Director ..........Dan Jankowski

\* \* \*

**MOUNTAIN WEST CONFERENCE**
15455 Gleneagle Drive, Suite 200
Colorado Springs, CO 80921
(719) 488-4040 www.themwc.com
Founded: 1999
Commissioner .....................Craig Thompson
Asst. Comm. for Communications ......Javan Hedlund
**2005-06 members**: BASKETBALL & FOOTBALL (9)—
Air Force, BYU, Colorado St., UNLV, New Mexico, San
Diego St., TCU, Utah and Wyoming.

**U.S. Air Force Academy**
US Academy, CO 80840
SID: (719) 333-9263 www.airforcesports.com
Founded: 1954 Enrollment: 4,000
Superintendent .............Lt. Gen. John W. Rosa Jr.
Athletic Director ...................Dr. Hans J. Mueh
Asst. AD for Media Relations ..........Troy Garnhart

**Brigham Young University**
Provo, UT 84602
SID: (801) 422-4910 www.byucougars.com
Founded: 1875 Enrollment: 33,278
President ....................Cecil O. Samuelson
Athletic Director ....................Tom Holmoe
Assoc. AD, Communications ..............Duff Tittle

**Colorado State University**
Fort Collins, CO 80523
SID: (970) 491-5067 www.csurams.com
Founded: 1870 Enrollment: 25,382
President .......................Dr. Larry Penley
Athletic Director ....................Mark Driscoll
Sr. Assoc. AD/Media Relations Director ....Gary Ozzello

**University of New Mexico**
Albuquerque, NM 87131
SID: (505) 925-5520 www.golobos.com
Founded: 1889 Enrollment: 26,500
President ......................Louis Caldera
Athletic Director ....................Rudy Davalos
Assoc. AD, Media Relations .........Greg Remington

**San Diego State University**
San Diego, CA 92182
SID: (619) 594-5547 www.goaztecs.com
Founded: 1897 Enrollment: 34,174
President ...................Dr. Stephen L. Weber
Athletic Director ...................Jeff Schemmel
Interim Media Relations Dir. ............Michael May

**TCU—Texas Christian University**
Fort Worth, TX 76129
SID: (817) 257-7969 www.gofrogs.com
Founded: 1873 Enrollment: 8,632
Chancellor ...................Dr. Victor Boschini
Athletic Director ...........Dr. Daniel B. Morrison Jr.
Director of Media Relations ............Mark Cohen

**UNLV—University of Nevada, Las Vegas**
Las Vegas, NV 89154
SID: (702) 895-3207 www.unlvrebels.com
Founded: 1957 Enrollment: 27,000
President ......................Dr. Carol Harter
Athletic Director ....................Mike Hamrick
Sports Information Director ..........Andy Grossman

## University of Utah
Salt Lake City, UT 84112
SID: (801) 581-3510
Founded: 1850
President .........................Michael K. Young
Athletic Director ......................Dr. Chris Hill
Asst. AD, Sports Information .................Liz Abel

www.utahutes.com
Enrollment: 28,933

## University of Wyoming
Laramie, WY 82071
SID: (307) 766-2256
Founded: 1886
President ........................Tom Buchanan
Athletic Director ......................Gary Barta
Assoc. AD/Sports Info. Director .......Kevin McKinney

www.wyomingathletics.com
Enrollment: 13,162

\* \* \*

## PACIFIC-10 CONFERENCE
800 South Broadway, Suite 400
Walnut Creek, CA 94596
(925) 932-4411
Founded: 1915
Commissioner ......................Thomas Hansen
Asst. Commissioner, Public Relations ......Jim Muldoon
**2005-06 members**: BASKETBALL & FOOTBALL (10)—
Arizona, Arizona St., California, Oregon, Oregon St.,
Stanford, UCLA, USC, Washington and Washington St.

www.pac-10.org

## University of Arizona
Tucson, AZ 85721
SID: (520) 621-4163
Founded: 1885
President .........................Dr. Peter Likins
Athletic Director ...................Jim Livengood
Sports Information Director .........Tom Duddleston Jr.

www.arizonaathletics.com
Enrollment: 37,000

## Arizona State University
Tempe, AZ 85287
SID: (480) 965-5799
Founded: 1885
President ......................Dr. Michael Crow
V.P. for University Athletics ................Lisa Love
Asst. AD/Sports Informatton Director ......Mark Brand

www.thesundevils.com
Enrollment: 45,693

## University of California
Berkeley, CA 94720
SID: (510) 642-5363
Founded: 1868
Chancellor ..................Dr. Robert J. Birgeneau
Athletic Director ...................Sandy Barbour
Asst. AD for Media Relations ........Herb Benenson

www.calbears.com
Enrollment: 33,000

## University of Oregon
Eugene, OR 97401
SID: (541) 346-5488
Founded: 1876
President .....................Dave Frohnmayer
Athletic Director ........................Bill Moos
Asst. AD/Sports Information Director .....Dave Williford

www.goducks.com
Enrollment: 20,033

## Oregon State University
Corvallis, OR 97331
SID: (541) 737-3720
Founded: 1868
President ......................Dr. Edward Ray
Athletic Director ...................Bob De Carolis
Sports Information Director .............Steve Fenk

www.osubeavers.com
Enrollment: 19,000

## Stanford University
Stanford, CA 94305
SID: (650) 723-4418
Founded: 1891
President .....................John L. Hennessy
Athletic Director (stepping down 1/1/05) .....Ted Leland
Sports Information Director .............Gary Migdol

www.gostanford.com
Enrollment: 6,556

## UCLA—Univ. of California, Los Angeles
Los Angeles, CA 90024
SID: (310) 206-6831
Founded: 1919
Chancellor .......................Albert Carnesale
Athletic Director ...................Dan Guerrero
Sports Information Director ............Marc Dellins

www.uclabruins.com
Enrollment: 36,890

## USC—Univ. of Southern California
Los Angeles, CA 90089
SID: (213) 740-8480
Founded: 1880
President ......................Steven Sample
Athletic Director ...................Mike Garrett
Sports Information Director ............Tim Tessalone

www.usctrojans.com
Enrollment: 32,000

## University of Washington
Seattle, WA 98195
SID: (206) 543-2230
Founded: 1861
President ...................Dr. Mark A. Emmert
Athletic Director ........................Todd Turner
Asst. AD for Media Relations ............Jim Daves

www.gohuskies.com
Enrollment: 42,000

## Washington State University
Pullman, WA 99164
SID: (509) 335-2684
Founded: 1890
President ....................V. Lane Rawlins
Athletic Director .......................Jim Sterk
Asst. AD/Dir. of Media Relations ........Rod Commons

www.wsucougars.com
Enrollment: 21,000

\* \* \*

## SOUTHEASTERN CONFERENCE
2201 Richard Arrington Blvd. North
Birmingham, AL 35203
(205) 458-3000
Founded: 1933
Commissioner .......................Mike Slive
Assoc. Commis. of Media Relations .......Charles Bloom
**2005-06 members**: BASKETBALL & FOOTBALL (12)—
Alabama, Arkansas, Auburn, Florida, Georgia, Kentucky,
LSU, Mississippi St., Ole Miss, South Carolina, Tennessee
and Vanderbilt.

www.secsports.com

## University of Alabama
Tuscaloosa, AL 35487
SID: (205) 348-6084
Founded: 1831
President .....................Dr. Robert Witt
Athletic Director ........................Mal Moore
Assoc. AD for Media Relations ...........Larry White

www.rolltide.com
Enrollment: 20,969

## University of Arkansas
Fayetteville, AR 72701
SID: (479) 575-2751
Founded: 1871
Chancellor ........................Dr. John White
Athletic Director ...................Frank Broyles
Women's Athletic Director ................Bev Lewis
Asst. AD, Sports Information ............Kevin Trainor

www.hogwired.com
www.ladybacks.com
Enrollment: 16,449

## Auburn University
Auburn, AL 36831
SID: (334) 844-9800
Founded: 1856
Interim President .................Dr. Ed Richardson
Athletic Director ........................Jay Jacobs
Asst. AD, Media Relations .............Kirk Sampson

www.auburntigers.com
Enrollment: 23,152

## University of Florida
Gainesville, FL 32604
SID: (352) 375-4683 ext. 6100          www.gatorzone.com
Founded: 1853                          Enrollment: 48,164
President . . . . . . . . . . . . . . . . . .Dr. J. Bernard Machen
Athletic Director . . . . . . . . . . . . . . . . . .Jeremy Foley
Asst. AD for Sports Information . . . . . . . .Steve McClain

## University of Georgia
Athens, GA 30603
SID: (706) 542-1621                    www.georgiadogs.com
Founded: 1785                          Enrollment: 33,878
President . . . . . . . . . . . . . . . . . .Dr. Michael F. Adams
Athletic Director . . . . . . . . . . . . . . . . . .Damon Evans
Assoc. AD for Sports Communications . . . . .Claude Felton

## University of Kentucky
Lexington, KY 40506
SID: (859) 257-3838                    www.ukathletics.com
Founded: 1865                          Enrollment: 26,900
President . . . . . . . . . . . . . . . . . . . . .Dr. Lee Todd
Athletic Director . . . . . . . . . . . . . . . . . .Mitch Barnhart
Asst. AD/Media Relations . . . . . . . . . . . . .Scott Stricklin

## LSU—Louisiana State University
Baton Rouge, LA 70894
SID: (225) 578-8226                    www.lsusports.net
Founded: 1860                          Enrollment: 31,582
Chancellor . . . . . . . . . . . . . . . . . . . .Sean O'Keefe
Athletic Director . . . . . . . . . . . . . . . . . .Skip Bertman
Asst. AD for Sports Information . . . . . . .Michael Bonnette

## Mississippi State University
Starkville, MS 39762
SID: (662) 325-2703                    www.mstateathletics.com
Founded: 1878                          Enrollment: 15,934
President . . . . . . . . . . . . . . . . . . . .Dr. J. Charles Lee
Athletic Director . . . . . . . . . . . . . . . . . .Larry Templeton
Assoc. AD, Media & Public Relations . . . . .Mike Nemeth

## Ole Miss—University of Mississippi
University, MS 38677
SID: (662) 915-7522                    www.olemisssports.com
Founded: 1848                          Enrollment: 16,498
Chancellor . . . . . . . . . . . . . . . . . .Dr. Robert C. Khayat
Athletic Director . . . . . . . . . . . . . . . . . .Pete Boone
Assoc. AD for Media Relations . . . . . . .Langston Rogers

## University of South Carolina
Columbia, SC 29208
SID: (803) 777-5204                    www.uscsports.com
Founded: 1801                          Enrollment: 26,000
President . . . . . . . . . . . . . . . . . .Dr. Andrew Sorensen
Athletic Director . . . . . . . . . . . . . . . . . .Eric Hyman
Sports Information Director . . . . . . . . . . . . . .Steve Fink

## University of Tennessee
Knoxville, TN 37996                    www.utsports.com
                                       www.utladyvols.com
SID: (865) 974-1212                    Enrollment: 25,058
Founded: 1794
President . . . . . . . . . . . . . . . . . .Dr. John D. Petersen
Athletic Director . . . . . . . . . . . . . . . . . .Mike Hamilton
Women's Athletic Director . . . . . . . . . . . . .Joan Cronan
Sports Information Director . . . . . . . . . . . . . .Bud Ford

## Vanderbilt University
Nashville, TN 37212
SID: (615) 322-4121                    www.vucommodores.com
Founded: 1873                          Enrollment: 6,272
Chancellor . . . . . . . . . . . . . . . . . . . .Gordon Gee
Vice Chancellor . . . . . . . . . . . . . . . .David Williams II
Assoc. AD, Communications . . . . . . . . . .Rod Williamson

        *        *        *

## SUN BELT CONFERENCE
601 Poydras Street, Suite 2355
New Orleans, LA 70130
(504) 299-9066                         www.sunbeltsports.org
Founded: 1976
Commissioner . . . . . . . . . . . . . . . . . .Wright Waters
Asst. Commissioner/Media Relations . . . . .Todd Stewart
    **2005-06 members:** BASKETBALL (11)—Arkansas-Little
Rock, Arkansas St., Denver, Florida International,
LA-Lafayette, Middle Tennessee, New Orleans, North Texas,
South Alabama, Troy and Western Kentucky; FOOTBALL
(8)—Arkansas St., Florida Atlantic, Florida International, LA-
Lafayette, LA-Monroe, Middle Tennessee, North Texas and
Troy.

## Arkansas-Little Rock
Little Rock, AR 72204
SID: (501) 569-3449                    www.ualrtrojans.com
Founded: 1927                          Enrollment: 11,798
Chancellor . . . . . . . . . . . . . . . . . .Dr. Joel E. Anderson
Athletic Director . . . . . . . . . . . . . . . . . .Chris Peterson
Sports Information Director . . . . . . . . . . . . .Joe Angolia

## Arkansas State
Jonesboro, AR 72467
SID: (870) 972-2541                    www.asuindians.com
Founded: 1909                          Enrollment: 10,528
President . . . . . . . . . . . . . . . . . .Dr. J. Leslie Wyatt
Athletic Director . . . . . . . . . . . . . . . . . .Dr. Dean Lee
Asst. AD/Media Relations . . . . . . . . . . . . .Gina Bowman

## University of Denver
Denver, CO 80208
SID: (303) 871-4990                    www.denverpioneers.com
Founded: 1864                          Enrollment: 9,808
Chancellor . . . . . . . . . . . . . . . . . .Robert D. Coombe
Athletic Director . . . . . . . . . . . . . . .Peg Bradley-Doppes
Director of Media Relations . . . . . . . . . . . .Erich Bacher

## Florida Atlantic University
Boca Raton, FL 33431
SID: (561) 297-3163                    www.fausports.com
Founded: 1961                          Enrollment: 26,000
President . . . . . . . . . . . . . . . . . . . .Frank T. Bogan
Athletic Director . . . . . . . . . . . . . . . . . .Craig Angelos
Asst. AD/Media Relations . . . . . . . .Katrina McCormack

## Florida International University
Miami, FL 33199
SID: (305) 348-3164                    www.fiusports.com
Founded: 1972                          Enrollment: 34,000
President . . . . . . . . . . . . . . . . . .Modesto A. Maidique
Athletic Director . . . . . . . . . . . . . . . . . .Rick Mello
Asst. AD/Media Relations . . . . . . . . . . . . .Rich Kelch

## University of Louisiana at Lafayette
Lafayette, LA 70506
SID: (337) 851-2255                    www.ragincajuns.com
Founded: 1900                          Enrollment: 16,561
President . . . . . . . . . . . . . . . . . .Dr. Ray P. Authement
Interim Athletic Director . . . . . . . . . . . . .David Walker
Sports Information Director . . . . . . . . . . . .Daryl Cetnar

## University of Louisiana at Monroe
Monroe, LA 71209
SID: (318) 342-5442                    www.ulmathletics.com
Founded: 1931                          Enrollment: 8,563
President . . . . . . . . . . . . . . . . . .Dr. James E. Cofer
Athletic Director . . . . . . . . . . . . . . . . . .Bobby Staub
Media Relations Director . . . . . . . . . . . . . .Judy Wilson

## Middle Tennessee
Murfreesboro, TN 37132
SID: (615) 898-2450      www.goblueraiders.com
Founded: 1911      Enrollment: 22,322
President . . . . . . . . . . . . . . . . . . . .Dr. Sidney A. McPhee
Athletic Director . . . . . . . . . . . . . . . . . .Chris Massaro
Asst. AD/Media Relations Director . . . . . . .Mark Owens

## University of New Orleans
New Orleans, LA 70148
SID: (504) 280-6284      www.unoprivateers.com
Founded: 1958      Enrollment: 17,360
Chancellor . . . . . . . . . . . . . . . . . . . .Dr. Timothy P. Ryan
Athletic Director . . . . . . . . . . . . . . . . . . . . . Jim Miller
Sports Information Director . . . . . . . . . . . . .Jack Duggan

## University of North Texas
Denton, TX 76203
SID: (940) 565-2476      www.meangreensports.com
Founded: 1890      Enrollment: 31,112
President . . . . . . . . . . . . . . . . . . .Dr. Norval F. Pohl
Athletic Director . . . . . . . . . . . . . . . . .Rick Villarreal
Assoc. AD/Media Relations . . . . . . . . . . . . .Eric Capper

## University of South Alabama
Mobile, AL 36688
SID: (251) 460-7035      www.usajaguars.com
Founded: 1963      Enrollment: 13,538
President . . . . . . . . . . . . . . . . . . . . .V. Gordon Moulton
Athletic Director . . . . . . . . . . . . . . . . . . . .Joe Gottfried
Director of Athletic Media Relations . . . . . . . . . .Kit Strief

## Troy University
Troy, AL 36082
SID: (334) 670-3229      www.troytrojans.com
Founded: 1887      Enrollment: 27,117
Chancellor . . . . . . . . . . . . . . . . . .Dr. Jack Hawkins Jr.
Athletic Director . . . . . . . . . . . . . . . . . . . .Steve Dennis
Athletics Media Relations Dir. . . . . . . . . . . . .Ricky Hazel

## Western Kentucky University
Bowling Green, KY 42101
SID: (270) 745-4298      www.wkusports.com
Founded: 1906      Enrollment: 18,391
President . . . . . . . . . . . . . . . . . . .Dr. Gary Ransdell
Athletic Director . . . . . . . . . . . . .Dr. Camden Wood Selig
Dir. of Athletic Media Relations . . . . . . . .Brian Fremund

\*      \*      \*

## WESTERN ATHLETIC CONFERENCE
9250 East Costilla Ave., Suite 300
Englewood, CO 80112
(303) 799-9221      www.wacsports.com
Founded: 1962
Commissioner . . . . . . . . . . . . . . . . . . . . . .Karl Benson
Asst. Commiss./Media Relations . . . . . . . .Dave Chaffin
   **2005-06 members**: BASKETBALL & FOOTBALL (9)—
Boise St., Fresno St., Hawaii, Idaho, Louisiana Tech, Neva-
da, New Mexico St., San Jose St. and Utah St.

## Boise State
Boise, ID 83725
SID: (208) 426-1515      www.broncosports.com
Founded: 1932      Enrollment: 18,456
President . . . . . . . . . . . . . . . . . . . . . .Dr. Robert Kustra
Athletic Director . . . . . . . . . . . . . . . . . .Gene Bleymaier
Asst. AD/Media Relations . . . . . . . . . . . . . . .Max Corbet

## Fresno State University
Fresno, CA 93740
SID: (559) 278-2509      www.gobulldogs.com
Founded: 1911      Enrollment: 19,781
President . . . . . . . . . . . . . . . . . . .Dr. John D. Welty
Athletic Director . . . . . . . . . . . . . . . . . . . . .Thomas Boeh
Asst. AD/Communications . . . . . . . . . . . .Steve Weakland

## University of Hawaii
Honolulu, HI 96822
SID: (808) 956-7523      www.hawaiiathletics.com
Founded: 1907      Enrollment: 20,463
Interim President . . . . . . . . . . . . . . . . .David McClain
Athletic Director . . . . . . . . . . . . . . . . . .Herman Frazier
Media Relations Director . . . . . . . . . . . . . . .Lois Manin

## University of Idaho
Moscow, ID 83844
SID: (208) 885-0245      www.uiathletics.com
Founded: 1889      Enrollment: 12,824
President . . . . . . . . . . . . . . . . . . . . . . .Dr. Tim White
Athletic Director . . . . . . . . . . . . . . . . . . .Dr. Rob Spear
Asst. AD/Media Relations . . . . . . . . . . . . . .Becky Paull

## Louisiana Tech University
Ruston, LA 71272
SID: (318) 257-3144      www.latechsports.com
Founded: 1894      Enrollment: 11,975
President . . . . . . . . . . . . . . . . . . . . . . . .Dan Reneau
Athletic Director . . . . . . . . . . . . . . . . . . . . .Jim Oakes
Sports Information Director . . . . . . . . . . .Malcolm Butler

## University of Nevada
Reno, NV 89557
SID: (775) 784-6900      www.nevadawolfpack.com
Founded: 1874      Enrollment: 16,300
President . . . . . . . . . . . . . . . . . . . . . . . .Dr. John Lilley
Athletic Director . . . . . . . . . . . . . . . . . . . .Cary Groth
Director of Media Services . . . . . . . . . . . .Jamie Klund

## New Mexico State
Las Cruces, NM 88003
SID: (505) 646-3929      www.nmstatesports.com
Founded: 1888      Enrollment: 16,428
President . . . . . . . . . . . . . . . . . . .Michael V. Martin
Athletic Director . . . . . . . . . . . . . . . . . .McKinley Boston
Media Relations Coordinator . . . . . . . . . . . .Tyler Dunkel

## San Jose State University
San Jose, CA 95192
SID: (408) 924-1217      www.sjsuspartans.com
Founded: 1857      Enrollment: 30,068
President . . . . . . . . . . . . . . . . . . . . . . . .Don Kassing
Athletic Director . . . . . . . . . . . . . . . . . . .Tom Bowen
Sports Information Director . . . . . . . . . . . .Lawrence Fan

## Utah State University
Logan, UT 84322
SID: (435) 797-1361      www.utahstateaggies.com
Founded: 1888      Enrollment: 21,490
President . . . . . . . . . . . . . . . . . . . . . . . .Stan Albrecht
Athletic Director . . . . . . . . . . . . . . . . . .Randy Spetman
Asst. AD for Media Relations . . . . . . . . . . .Mike Strauss

\*      \*      \*

## Major Independents

Division I-A football independents in 2005.

### Army—U.S. Military Academy
West Point, NY 10996
SID: (845) 938-3303      www.goarmysports.com
Founded: 1802      Enrollment: 4,000
Superintendent . . . . . . . . .Lt. Gen. William J. Lennox, Jr.
Athletic Director . . . . . . . . . . . . . . . . . .Kevin Anderson
Sr. Assoc. AD for Media Relations . . . . . . . .Bob Beretta

### Navy—U.S. Naval Academy
Annapolis, MD 21402
SID: (410) 293-8775      www.navysports.com
Founded: 1845      Enrollment: 4,000
Superintendent . . . . . . .Vice Adm. Rodney P. Rempt, USN
Athletic Director . . . . . . . . . . . . . . . . . .Chet Gladchuk
Asst. AD/Sports Information Director . . . .Scott Strasemeier

### University of Notre Dame
Notre Dame, IN 46556
SID: (574) 631-7516      www.und.com
Founded: 1842      Enrollment: 8,332
President . . . . . . . . . . . . . . . . . . . . . .Rev. John I. Jenkins
Athletic Director . . . . . . . . . . . . . . . . . . . .Kevin White
Sports Information Director . . . . . . . . . . . . .John Heisler

### Temple University
Philadelphia, PA 19122
SID: (215) 204-7445      www.owlsports.com
Founded: 1884      Enrollment: 33,000
President . . . . . . . . . . . . . . . . . . . . . .Dr. David Adamany
Athletic Director . . . . . . . . . . . . . . . . . . . .Bill Bradshaw
Asst. AD/Sports Media Relations . . . . . . .Larry Dougherty

\*　　　\*　　　\*

## Other Major Division I Conferences
Conferences that play either Division I basketball or Division I-AA football, or both.

### America East
10 High St., Suite 860, Boston, MA 02110
(617) 695-6369      www.americaeast.com
Founded: 1979
Commissioner . . . . . . . . . . . . . . . . . . . . . .Patrick Nero
Dir. of Communications . . . . . . . . . . . . . . .K.J. Cardinal
    **2005-06 members**: BASKETBALL (9)—Albany, Binghamton, Boston University, Hartford, Maine, Maryland-Baltimore County, New Hampshire, Stony Brook and Vermont.

### Atlantic Sun Conference
3370 Vineville Ave., Suite 108-B
Macon, GA 31204
(478) 474-3394      www.atlanticsun.com
Founded: 1978
Commissioner . . . . . . . . . . . . . . . . . . . . . . . .Bill Bibb
Director of Media Relations . . . . . . . . .LaKesha Whitaker
    **2005-06 members**: BASKETBALL (11)—Belmont, Campbell, East Tennessee St., Florida Atlantic, Gardner-Webb, Jacksonville, Kennesaw St., Lipscomb, Mercer, North Florida and Stetson.

### Atlantic 10 Conference
230 S. Broad St., Suite 1700
Philadelphia, PA 19102
(215) 545-6678      www.atlantic10.org
Founded: 1976      A-10 Football founded: 1997
Commissioner . . . . . . . . . . . . . . . . . . . . . .Linda Bruno
Asst. Commissioner/P.R. . . . . . . . . . . . . . . .Ray Cella
    **2005-06 members**: BASKETBALL (14)—Charlotte, Dayton, Duquesne, Fordham, George Washington, La Salle, Massachusetts, Rhode Island, Richmond, St. Bonaventure, St. Joseph's, Saint Louis, Temple and Xavier-OH. FOOTBALL (12)—Delaware, Hofstra, James Madison, Maine, Massachusetts, New Hampshire, Northeastern, Rhode Island, Richmond, Towson, Villanova and William & Mary.

### Big Sky Conference
2491 Washington Blvd. Suite 201
Ogden, UT 84401
(801) 392-1978      www.bigskyconf.com
Founded: 1963
Commissioner . . . . . . . . . . . . . . . . . .Douglas Fullerton
Asst. Commissioner, Media Relations . . . . . . .Jon Kasper
    **2005-06 members**: BASKETBALL & FOOTBALL (8)—Eastern Washington, Idaho St., Montana, Montana St., Northern Arizona, Portland St., Sacramento St. and Weber St.

### Big South Conference
7233 Pineville-Matthews Rd., Suite 100
Charlotte, NC 28226
(704) 341-7990      www.bigsouthsports.com
Founded: 1983
Commissioner . . . . . . . . . . . . . . . . . .Kyle B. Kallander
Director of Public Relations . . . . . . . . . . .Mark Simpson
    **2005-06 members**: BASKETBALL (9)—Birmingham Southern, Charleston Southern, Coastal Carolina, High Point, Liberty, NC-Asheville, Radford, VMI and Winthrop. FOOTBALL (5)—Charleston Southern, Coastal Carolina, Gardner-Webb, Liberty and VMI.

### Big West Conference
Two Corporate Park, Suite 206
Irvine, CA 92606
(949) 261-2525      www.bigwest.org
Founded: 1969
Commissioner . . . . . . . . . . . . . . . . . . . . .Dennis Farrell
Information Director . . . . . . . . . . . . . . . .Mike Villamor
    **2005-06 members**: BASKETBALL (8)—CS-Fullerton, CS-Northridge, Cal Poly, Long Beach St., Pacific, UC-Irvine, UC-Riverside and UC-Santa Barbara.

### Colonial Athletic Association
8625 Patterson Ave.,
Richmond, VA 23229
(804) 754-1616      www.caasports.com
Founded: 1985
Commissioner . . . . . . . . . . . . . . . . . . .Thomas E. Yeager
Asst. Commissioner/Commun. . . . . . . . . . .Rob Washburn
    **2005-06 members**: BASKETBALL (12)—Delaware, Drexel, George Mason, Georgia St., Hofstra, James Madison, NC-Wilmington, Northeastern, Old Dominion, Towson, Virginia Commonwealth and William & Mary.

### Gateway Football Conference
1818 Chouteau Ave.
St. Louis, MO 63103
(314) 421-2268      www.gatewayfootball.org
Founded: 1985
Commissioner . . . . . . . . . . . . . . . . . . . . .Patty Viverito
Asst. Commissioner . . . . . . . . . . . . . . . . . . .Mike Kern
    **2005 members**: FOOTBALL (8)—Illinois St., Indiana St., Missouri St., Northern Iowa, Southern Illinois, Western Illinois, Western Kentucky and Youngstown St.

**Great West Football Conference**
Harris Center, 351 W. Center
Cedar City, UT 84720
(435) 865-8354                 www.greatwestfootball.com
Founded: 2004
Executive Committee Chair . . . . . . . . . . . . .Tom Douple
External Relations Chair . . . . . . . . . . . .Jay S. Hinrichs
   **2005 members**: FOOTBALL (6)—Cal Poly, North
Dakota St., Northern Colorado, South Dakota St., Southern
Utah and UC Davis.


**Horizon League**
·201 South Capitol Ave., Suite 500
Indianapolis, IN 46225
(317) 237-5622                 www.horizonleague.org
Founded: 1979
Commissioner . . . . . . . . . . . . . . . . . . . . . Jon LeCrone
Asst. Commiss. for Communications . . . . . . .Will Roleson
   **2005-06 members**: BASKETBALL (9)—Butler,
Cleveland St., Detroit Mercy, Illinois-Chicago, Loyola-
Chicago, Wisconsin-Green Bay, Wisconsin-Milwaukee,
Wright St. and Youngstown St.


**Ivy League**
228 Alexander Street
Princeton, NJ 08544
(609) 258-6426                 www.ivyleaguesports.com
Founded: 1954
Executive Director . . . . . . . . . . . . . . . . .Jeffrey Orleans
Assistant Director . . . . . . . . . . . . . . . . . . . .Brett Hoover
   **2005-06 members**: BASKETBALL & FOOTBALL (8)—
Brown, Columbia, Cornell, Dartmouth, Harvard,
Pennsylvania, Princeton and Yale.


**Metro Atlantic Athletic Conference**
712 Amboy Avenue
Edison, NJ 08837
(732) 738-5455                 www.maacsports.com
Founded: 1980
Commissioner . . . . . . . . . . . . . . . . . . . .Richard Ensor
Director of Media Relations . . . . . . . . . . .Jill Skotarczak
   **2005-06 members**: BASKETBALL (10)—Canisius,
Fairfield, Iona, Loyola-MD, Manhattan, Marist, Niagara, Rider,
Saint Peter's and Siena. FOOTBALL (5)—Duquesne, Iona, La
Salle, Marist and Saint Peter's.


**Mid-Continent Conference**
340 West Butterfield Rd., Ste 3D
Elmhurst, IL 60126
(630) 516-0661                 www.mid-con.com
Founded: 1982
Interim Commissioner . . . . . . . . . . . . . . . . . Jack Mehl
Director of Media Relations . . . . . . . . . . Kristina Petersen
   **2005-06 members**: BASKETBALL (9)—Centenary,
Chicago St., IUPUI, UMKC, Oakland, Oral Roberts, Southern
Utah, Valparaiso and Western Illinois.


**Mid-Eastern Athletic Conference**
222 Central Park Avenue, Suite 1150
Virginia Beach, VA 23462
(757) 416-7100                 www.meacsports.com
Founded: 1970
Commissioner . . . . . . . . . . . . . . . . . .Dr. Dennis Thomas
Director of Media Relations . . . . . . . . . . . .Michelle Jinks
   **2005-06 members**: BASKETBALL (11)—Bethune-
Cookman, Coppin St., Delaware St., Florida A&M,
Hampton, Howard, MD-Eastern Shore, Morgan St., Norfolk
St., North Carolina A&T and South Carolina St.; FOOTBALL
(9)—all but Coppin St. and MD-Eastern Shore.


**Missouri Valley Conference**
1818 Chouteau Ave.
St. Louis, MO 63103
(314) 421-0339                 www.mvc-sports.com
Founded: 1907
Commissioner . . . . . . . . . . . . . . . . . . . . . .Doug Elgin
Assoc. Commissioner, Communications . . . . . .Mike Kern
   **2005-06 members**: BASKETBALL (10)—Bradley,
Creighton, Drake, Evansville, Illinois St., Indiana St., Missouri
St., Northern Iowa, Southern Illinois and Wichita St.


**Northeast Conference**
200 Cottontail Lane, Vantage Court North
Somerset, NJ 08873
(732) 469-0440                 www.northeastconference.org
Founded: 1981
Commissioner . . . . . . . . . . . . . . . . . . . . John Iamarino
Associate Commissioner . . . . . . . . . . . . . . . .Ron Ratner
   **2005-06 members**: BASKETBALL (11)—Cent. Conn.
St., Fairleigh Dickinson, Long Island, Monmouth, Mount St.
Mary's, Quinnipiac, Robert Morris, Sacred Heart, St. Francis-
NY, St. Francis-PA and Wagner. FOOTBALL (8)—Albany,
Cent. Conn. St., Monmouth, Robert Morris, Sacred Heart, St.
Francis-PA, Stony Brook and Wagner.


**Ohio Valley Conference**
215 Centerview Drive, Suite 115
Brentwood, TN 37027
(615) 371-1698  .              www.ovcsports.com
Founded: 1948
Commissioner . . . . . . . . . . . . . .Dr. Jon A. Steinbrecher
Asst. Commissioner for Media Relations . . . . .Kim Melcher
   **2005-06 members**: BASKETBALL (11)—Austin Peay
St., Eastern Illinois, Eastern Kentucky, Jacksonville St.,
Morehead St., Murray St., Samford, SE Missouri St.,
Tennessee-Martin, Tennessee St. and Tennessee Tech; FOOT-
BALL (9)—all but Austin Peay St. and Morehead St.


**Patriot League**
3773 Corporate Pkwy, Suite 190
Center Valley, PA 18034
(610) 289-1950                 www.patriotleague.com
Founded: 1984
Executive Director . . . . . . . . . . .Carolyn Schlie Femovich
Asst. Exec. Dir. for External Relations . .Richard Wanninger
   **2005-06 members**: BASKETBALL (8)—American,
Army, Bucknell, Colgate, Holy Cross, Lafayette, Lehigh and
Navy; FOOTBALL (7)—Bucknell, Colgate, Fordham,
Georgetown, Holy Cross, Lafayette and Lehigh.


**Pioneer Football League**
1818 Chouteau Ave.
St. Louis, MO 63103
(314) 421-2268                 www.pioneer-football.org
Founded: 1993
Commissioner . . . . . . . . . . . . . . . . . . . . .Patty Viverito
Sports Information Director . . . . . . . . . . . . . .Cody Bush
   **2005 members**: FOOTBALL (9): Austin Peay St., Butler,
Davidson, Dayton, Drake, Jacksonville, Morehead St., San
Diego and Valparaiso.


**Southern Conference**
905 East Main St.
Spartanburg, SC 29302
(864) 591-5100                 www.soconsports.com
Founded: 1921
Interim Commissioner . . . . . . . . . . . . . . . . .Geoff Cabe
Assoc. Commissioner for Public Affairs . . .Bryan McGowan
   **2005-06 members**: BASKETBALL (11)—Appalachian
St., Chattanooga, The Citadel, College of Charleston,
Davidson, Elon, Furman, Georgia Southern, NC-Greensboro,
Western Carolina and Wofford; FOOTBALL (8)—all except
College of Charleston, Davidson and NC-Greensboro.

## Southland Conference

1700 Alma Drive, Suite 550
Plano, TX 75075
(972) 422-9500                    www.southland.org
Founded: 1963
Commissioner . . . . . . . . . . . . . . . . . . . . . .Tom Burnett
Assoc. Commissioner for Communications . . .Bruce Ludlow
   **2005-06 members**: BASKETBALL (11)—Lamar,
LA-Monroe, McNeese St., Nicholls St., Northwestern St.,
Sam Houston St., Southeastern Louisiana, Stephen F. Austin
St., Texas-Arlington, Texas-San Antonio and Texas St.; FOOT-
BALL (7)—McNeese St., Nicholls St., Northwestern St., Sam
Houston St., Southeastern Louisiana, Stephen F. Austin St.
and Texas St.

## Southwestern Athletic Conference

1527 Fifth Ave. North
Birmingham, AL 35204
(205) 251-7573                    www.swac.org
Founded: 1920
Commissioner . . . . . . . . . . . . . . . . . .Robert C. Vowels Jr.
Asst. Comm. for Media Relations . . . . . . .Wallace Dooley Jr.
   **2005-06 members**: BASKETBALL & FOOTBALL (10)—
Alabama A&M, Alabama St., Alcorn St., Arkansas-Pine Bluff,
Grambling St., Jackson St., Mississippi Valley St., Prairie View
A&M, Southern-Baton Rouge and Texas Southern.

## West Coast Conference

1200 Bayhill Dr., Suite 101
San Bruno, CA 94066
(650) 873-8622                    www.wccsports.com
Founded: 1952
Commissioner . . . . . . . . . . . . . . . . . . .Michael Gilleran
Director of Communications . . . . . . . . . . . . . .Jae Wilson
   **2005-06 members**: BASKETBALL (8)—Gonzaga,
Loyola Marymount, Pepperdine, Portland, Saint Mary's-CA,
San Diego, San Francisco and Santa Clara.

## PRO FOOTBALL

# National Football League

## League Office

280 Park Ave., New York, NY 10017
(212) 450-2000                    www.nfl.com
Commissioner . . . . . . . . . . . . . . . . . . . .Paul Tagliabue
Exec. Vice President/League Counsel . . . . . . . .Jeff Pash
Exec. V.P. for Labor Relations . . . . . . .Harold Henderson
Exec. V.P., Communications, Public Affairs . . .Joe Browne
V.P., Public Relations . . . . . . . . . . . . . . . . . . .Greg Aiello
AFC Info. Coordinator . . . . . . . . . . . . . . . . . .Steve Alic
NFC Info. Coordinator . . . . . . . . . . . . . . . .Mike Signora

## NFL Players Association

2021 L Street NW, Suite 600
Washington, DC 20036
(202) 463-2200                    www.nflpa.org
Executive Director . . . . . . . . . . . . . . . . . .Gene Upshaw
Asst. Exec. Director . . . . . . . . . . . . . . . . . . .Doug Allen
General Counsel . . . . . . . . . . . . . . .Richard Berthelsen
Director of Communications . . . . . . . . . . . .Carl Francis

## AFC

### Baltimore Ravens

11001 Winning Drive
Owings Mills, MD 21117
(410) 701-4000                    www.baltimoreravens.com
Owner . . . . . . . . . . . . . . . . . . . . . . .Stephen J. Bisciotti
President . . . . . . . . . . . . . . . . . . . . . .Richard W. Cass
General Manager/Executive V.P. . . . . . . .Ozzie Newsome
Sr. V.P. of Public & Community Relations . . . . .Kevin Byrne

### Buffalo Bills

One Bills Drive, Orchard Park, NY 14127
(716) 648-1800                    www.buffalobills.com
Chairman & Owner . . . . . . . . . . . . . . .Ralph C. Wilson Jr.
President & GM . . . . . . . . . . . . . . . . . . .Tom Donahoe
V.P. of Communications . . . . . . . . . . . . .Scott Berchtold

### Cincinnati Bengals

One Paul Brown Stadium, Cincinnati, OH 45202
(513) 621-3550                    www.bengals.com
President . . . . . . . . . . . . . . . . . . . . . . . . .Mike Brown
Sr. Vice President . . . . . . . . . . . . . . . . . . . .Pete Brown
Public Relations Director . . . . . . . . . . . . .Jack Brennan

### Cleveland Browns

76 Lou Groza Blvd., Berea, OH 44017
(440) 891-5000                    www.clevelandbrowns.com
Owner/Chairman . . . . . . . . . . . . . . . .Randolph Lerner
President/CEO . . . . . . . . . . . . . . . . . . . .John Collins
Sr. V.P./General Manager . . . . . . . . . . . . .Phil Savage
Vice President, Communications . . . . . . .Bill Bonsiewicz

### Denver Broncos

13655 Broncos Parkway, Englewood, CO 80112
(303) 649-9000                    www.denverbroncos.com
Owner-President-CEO . . . . . . . . . . . . . . . . .Pat Bowlen
Exec. V.P. of Football Ops./Head Coach . . .Mike Shanahan
General Manager . . . . . . . . . . . . . . . . . .Ted Sundquist
V.P. of Public Relations . . . . . . . . . . . . .Jim Saccomano

### Houston Texans

Two Reliant Park, Houston, TX 77054
(832) 667-2000                    www.houstontexans.com
Chairman & CEO . . . . . . . . . . . . . . . .Robert C. McNair
Sr. V.P. & GM of Football Ops. . . . . . . .Charley Casserly
V.P. of Communications . . . . . . . . . . . . . . .Tony Wyllie

### Indianapolis Colts

PO Box 535000, Indianapolis, IN 46253
(317) 297-2658                    www.colts.com
Owner-CEO . . . . . . . . . . . . . . . . . . . . . . . .Jim Irsay
President . . . . . . . . . . . . . . . . . . . . . . . . .Bill Polian
V.P. of Football Operations . . . . . . . . . . . .Chris Polian
V.P. of Public Relations . . . . . . . . . . . . . . .Craig Kelley

### Jacksonville Jaguars

One ALLTEL Stadium Place
Jacksonville, FL 32202
(904) 633-6000                    www.jaguars.com
Chairman & CEO . . . . . . . . . . . . . . . . .Wayne Weaver
Sr. V.P., Football Operations . . . . . . . . . . . .Paul Vance
V.P. of Communications & Media . . . . . . . .Dan Edwards

### Kansas City Chiefs

One Arrowhead Drive, Kansas City, MO 64129
(816) 920-9300                    www.kcchiefs.com
Owner-Founder . . . . . . . . . . . . . . . . . . .Lamar Hunt
Chairman . . . . . . . . . . . . . . . . . . . . . . . .Clark Hunt
President-CEO-General Manager . . . . . . . .Carl Peterson
Director of Public Relations . . . . . . . . . . . .Bob Moore

### Miami Dolphins

7500 SW 30th St., Davie, FL 33314
(954) 452-7000                    www.miamidolphins.com
Owner-Chairman . . . . . . . . . . . . . .H. Wayne Huizenga
CEO . . . . . . . . . . . . . . . . . . . . . . . . . . .Joe Bailey
General Manager . . . . . . . . . . . . . . . . .Randy Mueller
Sr. V.P. of Media Relations . . . . . . . . . . .Harvey Greene

### New England Patriots

One.Patriot Place, Foxboro, MA 02035
(508) 543-8200                    www.patriots.com
Owner-Chairman-CEO . . . . . . . . . . . . . . . . .Bob Kraft
Vice Chairman/President . . . . . . . . . . . . .Jonathan Kraft
V.P. of Player Personnel . . . . . . . . . . . . . . .Scott Pioli
Exec. Director of Media Relations . . . . . . . .Stacey James

## New York Jets
1000 Fulton Ave., Hempstead, NY 11550
(516) 560-8100 www.newyorkjets.com
Owner & Chairman .........Robert Wood Johnson IV
President ......................Jay Cross
Exec. V.P./General Manager ..........Terry Bradway
V.P. of Public Relations .............Ron Colangelo

## Oakland Raiders
1220 Harbor Bay Parkway, Alameda, CA 94502
(510) 864-5000 www.raiders.com
Owner — Manager of General Partners ......Al Davis
CEO ........................Amy Trask
Director of Player Personnel ..........Mike Lombardi
Director of Public Relations ...........Mike Taylor

## Pittsburgh Steelers
3400 South Water Street, Pittsburgh, PA 15203
(412) 432-7800 www.steelers.com
Chairman ......................Dan Rooney
President ......................Art Rooney II
Director of Football Operations ........Kevin Colbert
Communications Coordinator ..........Dave Lockett

## San Diego Chargers
4020 Murphy Canyon Rd.
San Diego, CA 92123
(858) 874-4500 www.chargers.com
Owner-Chairman ...................Alex Spanos
President-CEO ...................Dean Spanos
Exec. V.P./General Manager ............A.J. Smith
Director of Public Relations ...........Bill Johnston

## Tennessee Titans
460 Great Circle Road, Nashville, TN 37228
(615) 565-4000 www.titansonline.com
Owner/Chairman/President/CEO ..K.S. (Bud) Adams Jr.
Exec. V.P./General Manager ..........Floyd Reese
Exec. V.P./Head Coach ...............Jeff Fisher
Director of Media Services ...........Robbie Bohren

# NFC

## Arizona Cardinals
8701 S. Hardy Drive, Tempe, AZ 85284
(602) 379-0101 www.azcardinals.com
Owner-President ...................Bill Bidwill Sr.
V.P. of Football Operations .............Rod Graves
Director of Public Relations ...........Mark Dalton

## Atlanta Falcons
4400 Falcon Pkwy
Flowery Branch, GA 30542
(770) 965-3115 www.atlantafalcons.com
Owner-CEO ......................Arthur Blank
President/GM ...................Rich McKay
V.P. of Football Communications .......Reggie Roberts

## Carolina Panthers
800 South Mint St., Charlotte, NC 28202-1502
(704) 358-7000 www.panthers.com
Founder-Owner ................Jerry Richardson
President ....................Mark Richardson
General Manager ...................Marty Hurney
Director of Communications ..........Charlie Dayton

## Chicago Bears
1000 Football Drive, Lake Forest, IL 60045
(847) 295-6600 www.chicagobears.com
Chairman .................Michael McCaskey
President-CEO ....................Ted Phillips
General Manager ...................Jerry Angelo
Sr. Dir. of Corp. Communications ........Scott Hagel

## Dallas Cowboys
Cowboys Center, One Cowboys Parkway
Irving, TX 75063
(972) 556-9900 www.dallascowboys.com
Owner/GM ......................Jerry Jones
Exec. V.P./Dir. of Player Personnel/COO ..Stephen Jones
Public Relations Director .............Rich Dalrymple

## Detroit Lions
222 Republic Drive, Allen Park, MI 48101
(313) 216-4000 www.detroitlions.com
Owner & Chairman ............William Clay Ford
President & CEO ...................Matt Millen
Dir. of Pro Personnel ..............Sheldon White
Director of Media Relations ...........Matt Barnhart

## Green Bay Packers
1265 Lombardi Ave., Green Bay, WI 54304
(920) 496-5700 www.packers.com
President & CEO ...................Bob Harlan
Exec. V.P., GM, Dir. of Football Ops. ......Ted Thompson
Exec. V.P. & Head Coach ...........Mike Sherman
Director of Public Relations ...........Jeff Blumb

## Minnesota Vikings
9520 Viking Drive, Eden Prairie, MN 55344
(952) 828-6500 www.vikings.com
Owner/Chairman ...................Zygi Wilf
Owner/President ...................Mark Wilf
V.P. of Football Operations ...........Rob Brzezinski
Director of Public Relations ...........Bob Hagan

## New Orleans Saints (address/phone for 2005 season)
100 Montana St., Meeting Room N, San Antonio, TX 78203
(210) 704-6011 www.neworleanssaints.com
Owner ......................Tom Benson
Exec. V.P./General Manager ..........Mickey Loomis
Dir. of Player Personnel .............Rick Mueller
Director of Media/Public Relations ........Greg Bensel

## New York Giants
Giants Stadium, East Rutherford, NJ 07073
(201) 935-8111 www.giants.com
President/co-CEO ..............Wellington Mara
Chairman/co-CEO ..........Preston Robert Tisch
Senior V.P. & General Manager .........Ernie Accorsi
V.P. of Communications ..............Pat Hanlon

## Philadelphia Eagles
NovaCare Complex
One NovaCare Way
Philadelphia, PA 19145
(215) 463-2500 www.philadelphiaeagles.com
Owner-Chairman-CEO ...............Jeffrey Lurie
President/COO ....................Joe Banner
Head Coach/Exec. V.P. of Football Ops. .....Andy Reid
Dir. of Football Media Services ...........Derek Boyko

## St. Louis Rams
One Rams Way, St. Louis, MO 63045
(314) 982-7267 www.stlouisrams.com
Owner-Chairman ................Georgia Frontiere
Owner-Vice Chairman ...............Stan Kroenke
President ......................John Shaw
Pres. of Football Operations ...........Jay Zygmunt
Director of Football Media .............Duane Lewis

## San Francisco 49ers
4949 Centennial Blvd., Santa Clara, CA 95054
(408) 562-4949 www.sf49ers.com
Owner ..................Denise DeBartolo-York
Owner ......................John York
V.P. of Player Personnel ............Scot McCloughan
Director of Public Relations ...........Aaron Salkin

### Seattle Seahawks
11220 NE 53rd Street
Kirkland, WA 98033
(425) 827-9777     www.seahawks.com
Owner ................................. Paul Allen
CEO ................................. Tod Leiweke
President of Football Operations ........... Tim Ruskell
Director of Communications ......... Dave Pearson

### Tampa Bay Buccaneers
One Buccaneer Place
Tampa, FL 33607
(813) 870-2700     www.buccaneers.com
Owner-President .................... Malcolm Glazer
Exec. V.P.'s ... Bryan Glazer, Joel Glazer, Edward Glazer
General Manager ....................... Bruce Allen
Director of Public Relations ............. Jeff Kamis

### Washington Redskins
21300 Redskin Park Drive
Ashburn, VA 20147
(703) 726-7000     www.redskins.com
Owner ....................... Daniel M. Snyder
V.P. of Football Operations ............. Vinny Cerrato
Director of Public Relations ........... Patrick Wixted

## Canadian Football League

### League Office
50 Wellington St. East, 3rd Floor
Toronto, Ontario M5E 1C8
(416) 322-9650     www.cfl.ca
Commissioner ........................ Tom Wright
Sr. V.P. of Football Operations .......... Ed Chalupka
Dir. of Marketing & Communications ..... Alexis Redmond
   **Member teams** (9): West Division—British Columbia Lions, Calgary Stampeders, Edmonton Eskimos, Saskatchewan Roughriders and Winnipeg Blue Bombers. East Division—Hamilton Tiger-Cats, Montreal Alouettes, Ottawa Renegades and Toronto Argonauts.

## NFL Europe

### New York Office
280 Park Avenue
New York, NY 10017
(212) 450-2000     www.nfleurope.com
Sr. Vice President of Football Ops. ........... Art Shell
Managing Director .................... Jim Connelly
Director of Public Relations ........... David Tossell
Manager of Public Relations ........... Neil Reynolds
   **Member teams** (6): Amsterdam Admirals, Berlin Thunder, Cologne Centurions, Frankfurt Galaxy, Hamburg Sea Devils and Rhein Fire (Dusseldorf).

## Arena Football League
8700 West Bryn Mawr Avenue, Suite 120 S
Chicago, IL 60631
(773) 444-1000     www.arenafootball.com
(212) 252-8100 (N.Y. office)
Commissioner ..................... C. David Baker
V.P. of Football Operations ............. Jerry Trice
Senior V.P. of Communications ....... Chris McCloskey
   **Member teams** (18): American Conference—Arizona Rattlers, Chicago Rush, Colorado Crush, Columbus Destroyers, Grand Rapids Rampage, Las Vegas Gladiators, Los Angeles Avengers and San Jose SaberCats. National Conference—Austin Wranglers, Dallas Desperados, Georgia Force, Nashville Kats, New Orleans Voodoo, New York Dragons, Orlando Predators, Philadelphia Soul and Tampa Bay Storm. Joining in 2006: Utah Blaze.
   **Note:** New Orleans will not play in 2006 due to damgage to the New Orleans Arena from Hurricane Katrina.

## GOLF

### LPGA Tour
### (Ladies' Professional Golf Association)
100 International Golf Drive
Daytona Beach, FL 32124
(386) 274-6200     www.lpga.com
Commissioner .............. Carolyn Vesper Bivens
Director of Media Relations ........... Connie Wilson

### PGA of America
100 Avenue of the Champions
Palm Beach Gardens, FL 33410
(561) 624-8400     www.pga.com
President ....................... Roger Warren
CEO (retiring in 2006) ............... Jim Awtrey
Director of Public/Media Relations ...... Julius Mason

### PGA European Tour
Wentworth Drive, Virginia Water
Surrey, England GU25 4LX
TEL: 011-44-1344-840400     www.europeantour.com
Executive Director ............... George O'Grady
Director of Communications ........ Gordon Simpson

### PGA Tour
112 PGA Tour Blvd.
Ponte Vedra, FL 32082
(904) 285-3700     www.pgatour.com
Commissioner ...................... Tim Finchem
Senior V.P./Chief of Operations ......... Henry Hughes
Senior V.P. of Communications .......... Bob Combs

### USGA
### (United States Golf Association)
P.O. Box 708, Liberty Corner Road
Far Hills, NJ 07931
(908) 234-2300     www.usga.org
President ......................... Fred S. Ridley
President (beginning Feb. 4, 2006) ... Walter W. Driver Jr.
Executive Director .................... David Fay
Sr. Director of Communications ........ Marty Parkes

## PRO HOCKEY

## NHL
## National Hockey League
Commissioner ...................... Gary Bettman
Pres., NHL Enterprises ................. Ed Horne
Exec. V.P., Dir. of Hockey Ops. ........ Colin Campbell
Exec. V.P., Chief Legal Officer ............. Bill Daly
V.P. of Media Relations ................ Frank Brown

### League Offices

**Montreal**
1800 McGill College Ave., Suite 2600
Montreal, Quebec H3A 3J6
(514) 841-9220

**New York**
1251 Avenue of the Americas, 47th Floor
New York, NY 10020
(212) 789-2000

**Toronto**
50 Bay St., 11th Floor
Toronto, Ontario M5J 2X8
(416) 981-2777     www.nhl.com

## NHL Players' Association
777 Bay St., Suite 2400
P.O. Box 121
Toronto, Ontario M5G 2C8
(416) 313-2316 www.nhlpa.com
Executive Director . . . . . . . . . . . . . . . . . . . . . . .Ted Saskin
President . . . . . . . . . . . . . . . . . . . . . . . . . . . . .Trevor Linden
Media Relations . . . . . . . . . . . . . . . .Jonathan Weatherdon

## Anaheim, Mighty Ducks of
Arrowhead Pond of Anaheim
2695 Katella Ave.
Anaheim, CA 92806
(714) 940-2900 www.mightyducks.com
Owners . . . . . . . . . . . . . . . . . . . . .Henry & Susan Samueli
Exec. V.P/General Manager . . . . . . . . . . . .Brian Burke
Sr. V.P., Hockey Operations . . . . . . . . . . . . .Bob Murray
Director, Comm. and Team Services . . . . . . .Alex Gilchrist

## Atlanta Thrashers
Centennial Tower
101 Marietta Street NW, Suite 1900
Atlanta, GA 30303
(404) 878-3300 www.atlantathrashers.com
Owner . . . . . . . . . . . . . . . . . . . . . . . .Atlanta Spirit, LLC
President/CEO . . . . . . . . . . . . . . . . . . . . .Bernie Mullin
Exec. V.P./General Manager . . . . . . . . . . . .Don Waddell
Sr. V.P. of Communications . . . . . . . . . . . . . .Tom Hughes

## Boston Bruins
100 Legends Way
Boston, MA 02114
(617) 624-1900 www.bostonbruins.com
Owner, Chairman and CEO . . . . . . . . . . .Jeremy Jacobs
President . . . . . . . . . . . . . . . . . . . . . . . .Harry Sinden
V.P. & General Manager . . . . . . . . . . . . .Mike O'Connell
Director of Media Relations . . . . . . . . . . . .Heidi Holland

## Buffalo Sabres
HSBC Arena, One Seymour H. Knox III Plaza
Buffalo, NY 14203-3096
(716) 855-4100 www.sabres.com
Owner . . . . . . . . . . . . . . . . . . . . . . . .B. Thomas Golisano
General Manager . . . . . . . . . . . . . . . . . . . .Darcy Regier
Director of Public Relations . . . . . . . . . . . .Michael Gilbert

## Calgary Flames
P.O. Box 1540, Station M
Calgary, Alberta T2P 3B9
(403) 777-2177 www.calgaryflames.com
Owners . . . . . . . . . .Harley Hotchkiss, Murray Edwards,
Alvin G. Libin, Allan P. Markin, J.R. McCaig,
Clay Riddell, Byron and Daryl Seamen
President & CEO . . . . . . . . . . . . . . . . . . . . . . . .Ken King
General Manager/Head Coach . . . . . . . . . .Darryl Sutter
V.P. of Communications . . . . . . . . . . . . . . . .Peter Hanlon

## Carolina Hurricanes
RBC Center
1400 Edwards Mill Rd., Raleigh, NC 27607
(919) 467-7825 www.caneshockey.com
CEO/Owner/Governer . . . . . . . . . . . .Peter Karmanos Jr.
President & General Manager . . . . . . . . .Jim Rutherford
Dir., Media Relations . . . . . . . . . . . . . . . .Mike Sundheim

## Chicago Blackhawks
United Center, 1901 West Madison St.
Chicago, IL 60612
(312) 455-7000 www.chicagoblackhawks.com
Owner-President . . . . . . . . . . . . . . . . . . . .William Wirtz
Senior Vice President . . . . . . . . . . . . . . . . . .Bob Pulford
General Manager . . . . . . . . . . . . . . . . . . . . .Dale Tallon
Executive Director of Communications . . . . . Jim DeMaria

## Colorado Avalanche
1000 Chopper Cir., Denver, CO 80204
(303) 405-1100 www.coloradoavalanche.com
Owner & Governor . . . . . . . . . . . . . . . . . .Stan Kroenke
President/General Manager . . . . . . . . . . .Pierre Lacroix
Sr. V.P. of Comm. & Team Services . . . . .Jean Martineau

## Columbus Blue Jackets
200 W. Nationwide Boulevard
Columbus, OH 43215
(614) 246-4625 www.bluejackets.com
Majority Owner . . . . . . . . . . . . . . . .John H. McConnell
President/General Manager . . . . . . . . . .Doug MacLean
Exec. Director of Communications . . . . . . . .Todd Sharrock

## Dallas Stars
2601 Avenue of the Stars, Frisco, TX 75034
(214) 387-5600 www.dallasstars.com
Owner/Chairman . . . . . . . . . . . . . . . .Thomas O. Hicks
President . . . . . . . . . . . . . . . . . . . . . . . . . . . .Jim Lites
General Manager . . . . . . . . . . . . . . . .Doug Armstrong
Sr. Director of Hockey Comm. . . . . . . . . . . .Rob Scichili

## Detroit Red Wings
Joe Louis Arena, 600 Civic Center Drive
Detroit, MI 48226
(313) 396-7544 www.detroitredwings.com
Owner/Governor . . . . . . . . . . . . . . . . . . . .Mike Ilitch
Owner/Secretary-Treasurer . . . . . . . . . . . . .Marian Ilitch
General Manager . . . . . . . . . . . . . . . . . . .Ken Holland
Sr. Director of Communications . . . . . . . . . . .John Hahn

## Edmonton Oilers
11230 110th St., Edmonton, Alberta, T5G 3H7
(780) 414-4000 www.edmontonoilers.com
Owners . . . . . . . . . . . . . . .Edmonton Investors Group, Ltd.
President & CEO . . . . . . . . . . . . . . . . . . .Patrick LaForge
Exec. V.P./General Manager . . . . . . . . . . . .Kevin Lowe
V.P., Communications & Broadcasting . . . . . . . .Allan Watt

## Florida Panthers
BankAtlantic Center
One Panther Parkway, Sunrise, FL 33323
(954) 835-7000 www.flpanthers.com
Chairman/CEO . . . . . . . . . . . . . . . . . . . . .Alan Cohen
President . . . . . . . . . . . . . . . . . . . . . .Jordan Zimmerman
General Manager . . . . . . . . . . . . . . . . . . .Mike Keenan
Director of Media Relations . . . . . . . . . .Randy Sieminski

## Los Angeles Kings
1111 S. Figueroa, Los Angeles, CA 90015
(213) 742-7100 www.lakings.com
Majority Owners . . . . . . . .Philip Anschutz and Ed Roski
President/Governor . . . . . . . . . . . . . . . . .Tim Leiweke
Sr. V.P. & General Manager . . . . . . . . . . . .Dave Taylor
V.P. of Comm. & Broadcasting . . . . . . . . . . .Mike Altieri

## Minnesota Wild
317 Washington Street, St. Paul, MN 55102
(651) 602-6000 www.wild.com
Chairman . . . . . . . . . . . . . . . . . . . . . .Bob Naegele Jr.
CEO . . . . . . . . . . . . . . . . . . . . . . . . . .Jac Sperling
President/General Manager . . . . . . . . .Doug Risebrough
V.P. of Comm. & Broadcasting . . . . . . . . . .Bill Robertson

## Montreal Canadiens
Bell Centre, 1260 Gauchetiere St. West
Montreal, Quebec H3B 5E8
(514) 989-2829 www.canadiens.com
Owner . . . . . . . . . . . . . . . . . . . . .George N. Gillett Jr.
President . . . . . . . . . . . . . . . . . . . . . . . .Pierre Boivin
Exec. V.P./General Manager . . . . . . . . . . . .Bob Gainey
V.P. of Communications . . . . . . . . . . .Donald Beauchamp

## Nashville Predators
501 Broadway, Nashville, TN 37203
(615) 770-2300                www.nashvillepredators.com
Owner/Chairman/Governor . . . . . . . . . . .Craig Leipold
Exec. V.P. & General Manager . . . . . . . . . . .David Poile
Sr. V.P., Communications & Development . . . .Gerry Helper

## New Jersey Devils
Continental Airlines Arena, P.O. Box 504
East Rutherford, NJ 07073
(201) 935-6050                www.newjerseydevils.com
Chairman . . . . . . . . . . . . . . . . . . . . . . .Jeff Vanderbeek
President/CEO/General Manager . . . . . .Lou Lamoriello
Director of Public Relations . . . . . . . . . . . .Jeff Altstadter

## New York Islanders
1535 Old Country Road, Plainview, NY 11083
(516) 501-6700                www.newyorkislanders.com
Owner . . . . . . . . . . . . .Charles Wang & Sanjay Kumar
General Manager . . . . . . . . . . . . . . . . . . .Mike Milbury
V.P. of Communications . . . . . . . . . . . . . . . .Chris Botta

## New York Rangers
2 Pennsylvania Plaza, New York, NY 10121
(212) 465-6486                www.newyorkrangers.com
Owner . . . . . . . . . . . . . . . . . .Cablevision Systems Inc.
President (MSG) . . . . . . . . . . . . . . . . . . . .James Dolan
President/General Manager . . . . . . . . . . .Glen Sather
V.P. of Public Relations . . . . . . . . . . . . . . .John Rosasco

## Ottawa Senators
1000 Palladium Dr., Kanata, Ontario, K2V 1A5
(613) 599-0250                www.ottawasenators.com
Owner/Chairman/Governor . . . . . . . . . .Eugene Melnyk
President & CEO . . . . . . . . . . . . . . . . . . . .Roy Mlakar
General Manager . . . . . . . . . . . . . . . . . .John Muckler
Director of Communications . . . . . . . . . . . .Steve Keogh

## Philadelphia Flyers
3601 S. Broad St., Philadelphia, PA 19148
(215) 465-4500                www.philadelphiaflyers.com
Chairman . . . . . . . . . . . . . . . . . . . . . . . . . . .Ed Snider
President . . . . . . . . . . . . . . . . . . . . . . . . . . .Ron Ryan
General Manager . . . . . . . . . . . . . . . . . . . .Bob Clarke
Sr. Director of Communications . . . . . . . . . . . .Zack Hill

## Phoenix Coyotes
5800 W. Glenn Drive, Suite 350, Glendale, AZ 85301
(623) 463-8800                www.phoenixcoyotes.com
Chairman/Governor . . . . . . . . . . . . . . . .Steve Ellman
Managing Partner/Head Coach . . . . . .Wayne Gretzky
President/COO/Alt. Governor . . . . . . . . . .Douglas Moss
General Manager/Alt. Governor . . . . . . .Michael Barnett
V.P. of Communications . . . . . . . . . . . . . .Richard Nairn

## Pittsburgh Penguins
Mellon Arena, 66 Mario Lemieux Place
Pittsburgh, PA 15219
(412) 642-1800                www.pittsburghpenguins.com
Owner/Chairman/CEO . . . . . . . . . . . . .Mario Lemieux
President/Governor . . . . . . . . . . . . . . . . .Ken Sawyer
Exec. V.P. & General Manager . . . . . . . . . .Craig Patrick
V.P. of Communications . . . . . . . . . . . . . .Tom McMillan

## St. Louis Blues
Savvis Center, 1401 Clark Ave.
St. Louis, MO 63103
(314) 622-2500                www.stlouisblues.com
Owner/Chairman . . . . . . . . . . . . . . . . . . . . .Bill Laurie
President/CEO . . . . . . . . . . . . . . . . . . . . .Mark Sauer
Senior V.P./General Manager . . . . . . . . . . .Larry Pleau
Director of Communications . . . . . . . . . . .Chuck Menke

## San Jose Sharks
525 West Santa Clara St., San Jose, CA 95113
(408) 287-7070                www.sjsharks.com
Owner . . . .San Jose Sports and Entertainment Enterprises
President-CEO . . . . . . . . . . . . . . . . . . . .Greg Jamison
Exec. V.P. & General Manager . . . . . . . . . .Doug Wilson
Sr. Dir. of Communications . . . . . . . . . . . . . .Ken Arnold

## Tampa Bay Lightning
401 Channelside Drive, Tampa, FL 33602
(813) 301-6600                www.tampabaylightning.com
Owner . . . . . . . . . . . . . . . . . . . .Palace Sports & Ent.
CEO & Governor . . . . . . . . . . . . . . . . . . . .Tom Wilson
Exec. V.P. & General Manager . . . . . . . . . . .Jay Feaster
Director of Public Relations . . . . . . . . . . . . . .Jay Preble

## Toronto Maple Leafs
Air Canada Centre
40 Bay Street, Ste. 400, Toronto, Ontario M5J 2X2
(416) 815-5500                www.mapleleafs.com
Owner . . . . . . . . .Maple Leaf Sports & Entertainment, Ltd
Chairman . . . . . . . . . . . . . . . . . . . .Larry Tanenbaum
President/CEO . . . . . . . . . . . . . . . . . . .Richard Peddie
General Manager . . . . . . . . . . . . . . . . . .John Ferguson
Director of Media Relations . . . . . . . . . . . . . . .Pat Park

## Vancouver Canucks
General Motors Place, 800 Griffiths Way
Vancouver, B.C. V6B 6G1
(604) 899-4600                www.canucks.com
Chairman . . . . . . . . . . . . . . . . . . . . .John E. McCaw Jr.
Co-Owner . . . . . . . . . . . . . . . . . . .Francesco Aquilini
Sr. V.P. & General Manager . . . . . . . . . . . .Dave Nonis
Manager of Media Relations . . . . . . . . . .Chris Brumwell

## Washington Capitals
MCI Center, 401 Ninth St., Suite 750
Washington, D.C. 20004
(202) 266-2200                www.washingtoncaps.com
Majority Owner/Chairman . . . . . . . . . . . . . .Ted Leonsis
Owner/President . . . . . . . . . . . . . . . . . . . .Dick Patrick
V.P./General Manager . . . . . . . . . . . .George McPhee
Sr. Dir. of Communications . . . . . . . . . . . . . .Kurt Kehl

# Other Leagues/Organizations

## American Hockey League
One Monarch Place, Springfield, MA 01144
(413) 781-2030                www.theahl.com
President/CEO . . . . . . . . . . . . . . . . . .David Andrews
V.P. of Hockey Operations . . . . . . . . . . . . . . .Jim Mill
V.P. of Communications . . . . . . . . . .Jason Chaimovitch
    **Member teams (27):** Eastern Conference—Albany
River Rats, Binghamton Senators, Bridgeport Sound Tigers,
Hartford Wolf Pack, Hershey Bears, Lowell Lock Monsters,
Manchester Monarchs, Norfolk Admirals, Philadelphia Phan-
toms, Portland Pirates, Providence Bruins, Springfield Falcons
and Wilkes-Barre/Scranton Penguins.
    Western Conference—Chicago Wolves, Cleveland
Barons, Grand Rapids Griffins, Hamilton Bulldogs, Houston
Aeros, Iowa Stars, Manitoba Moose, Milwaukee Admirals,
Omaha Ak-Sar-Ben Knights, Peoria Rivermen, Rochester
Americans, San Antonio Rampage, Syracuse Crunch and
Toronto Marlies.

## International Ice Hockey Federation
Brandschenkestrasse 50, Postfach
CH-8039 Zurich, Switzerland
TEL: 011-411-562-2200                www.iihf.com
President . . . . . . . . . . . . . . . . . . . . . . . . .Rene Fasel
General Secretary . . . . . . . . . . . . . . .Jan-Ake Edvinsson
Director of P.R./Marketing . . . . . . . . . . .Kimmo Leinonen

## HORSE RACING

**NTRA**
**(National Thoroughbred Racing Association)**
Commissioner . . . . . . . . . . . . . . . . . . . .D.G. Van Clief Jr.
Executive Vice President . . . . . . . . . . . . . . . .Greg Avioli
V.P. of Marketing & Industry Relations . . . . .Keith Chamblin
Sr. Director of Media Relations . . . . . . . . . . . .Eric Wing

**New York Office**

800 Third Ave., Suite 901
New York, NY 10022
(212) 230-9500                    www.ntra.com

**Kentucky Office**

2525 Harrodsburg Rd.
Lexington, KY 40504
(859) 223-5444

**TRA**
**(Thoroughbred Racing Associations of N. America, Inc.)**
420 Fair Hill Drive, Suite 1
Elkton, MD 21921
(410) 392-9200                    www.tra-online.com
President . . . . . . . . . . . . . . . . . . . . . . . . . Joe Harper
Executive Vice President . . . . . . . . . .Christopher N. Scherf
Director of Services . . . . . . . . . . . . . . . . . .Tony DeMarco

**USTA**
**(United States Trotting Association)**
750 Michigan Ave.
Columbus, OH 43215
(614) 224-4575                    www.ustrotting.com
President . . . . . . . . . . . . . . . . . . . . . .F. Phillip Langley
Executive V.P. . . . . . . . . . . . . . . . . . .Eric M. Sharbaugh
Director of Public Relations . . . . . . . . . . . . .John Pawlak

## MEDIA

## PERIODICALS

**ESPN, The Magazine**
19 E 34th St., New York, NY 10016
(888) 267-3684                    www.espnmag.com
Editor in Chief . . . . . . . . . . . . . . . . . . . . .Gary Hoenig
Executive Editors . . .Gary Belsky, Neil Fine and Steve Wulf
Sr. Vice President/GM . . . . . . . . . . . . . . . . .Geoff Reiss
Sr. Vice President/Editorial Director . . . . . . John Papanek
Bristol Bureau Chief . . . . . . . . . . . . . . . . . .John Hassan

**Sports Illustrated**
135 West 50th St., New York, NY 10020
(212) 522-9797                    www.si.com
President . . . . . . . . . . . . . . . . . . . . . . John Squires
Managing Editor . . . . . . . . . . . . . . . . . .Terry McDonell
Executive Editors . . . . . . . . .Michael Bevans, Rob Fleder
                                      and Charlie Leerhsen

**The Sporting News**
10176 Corporate Square Dr., Suite 200
St. Louis, MO 63132
(314) 997-7111                    www.sportingnews.com
Senior V.P./Editorial Director . . . . . . . .John D. Rawlings
President/CEO . . . . . . . . . . . . . . . . . . . . . .Rick Allen

**The Sports Business Daily**
120 West Morehead St., Ste. 220
Charlotte, NC 28202
(704) 973-1500                    www.sportsbizdaily.com
Executive Editor . . . . . . . . . . . . . . . . . .Abe Madkour
Editor-at-Large . . . . . . . . . . . . . . . . . . . . .Terry Lefton
Media Relations Manager . . . . . . . . . . . . .Bill Magrath

**USA Today**
7950 Jones Branch Drive, McLean, VA 22108
(703) 854-3400                    www.usatoday.com
Owner . . . . . . . . . . . . . . . . . . . . . . . .Gannett Co.
President/Publisher . . . . . . . . . . . . . . . . . .Craig Moon
Editor . . . . . . . . . . . . . . . . . . . . . . . . . .Ken Paulson
Managing Editor/Sports . . . . . . . . . . . . . .Monte Lorell

## WIRE SERVICES

**Associated Press**
450 West 33rd Street, New York, NY 10001
(212) 621-1500                    www.ap.org
President/CEO . . . . . . . . . . . . . . . . . . . .Tom Curley
Sports Editor . . . . . . . . . . . . . . . . . . . .Terry Taylor
Deputy Sports Editor . . . . . . . . . . . . . . . . .Ben Walker

**United Press International**
1510 H Street NW
Washington, DC 20005
(202) 898-8000                    www.upi.com
Managing Editor, Sports . . . . . . . . . . . . . .Ron Colbert

**The Sports Network**
2200 Byberry Rd., Suite 200
Hatboro, PA 19040
(215) 441-8444                    www.sportsnetwork.com
CEO/President . . . . . . . . . . . . . . . . . .Mickey Charles
Director of Operations . . . . . . . . . . . . . . . .Phil Sokol
Press Secretary . . . . . . . . . .Maureen McGillian-Galeone

**Sportsticker**
ESPN Plaza, Building B, 4th Floor
Bristol, CT 06010
(860) 766-1899                    www.sportsticker.com
Mgr., Customer Marketing & Communication . .Lou Monaco
                                      (212) 515-1163

## TV NETWORKS

**ABC Sports**
47 West 66th St., 13th Floor, New York, NY 10023
(212) 456-4867                    www.abcsports.com
President . . . . . . . . . . . . . . . . . .George Bodenheimer
Senior V.P., Executive Producer . . . . . . . . . . .Mike Pearl
V.P. of Media Relations . . . . . . . . . . . . . .Mark Mandel

**CBS Sports**
51 West 52nd St., 25th Floor
New York, NY 10019
(212) 975-5230                    www.cbs.sportsline.com
President . . . . . . . . . . . . . . . . . . . . . .Sean McManus
Executive Producer . . . . . . . . . . . . . . . . .Tony Petitti
Sr. V.P., Programming . . . . .Rob Correa and Mike Aresco
V.P., Communications . . . . . . . . . . . .Leslie Anne Wade

**ESPN**
ESPN Plaza, Bristol, CT 06010
(860) 766-2000                    www.espn.com
President . . . . . . . . . . . . . . . . . .George Bodenheimer
Executive V.P. & Executive Editor . . . . . . . . .John Walsh
Vice President/Director of News . . . . . . . . . .Vince Doria
Senior V.P. of Consumer Communications . . . .Chris LaPlaca
V.P. of Communications . . . . . . . . . . . . . . .Mike Soltys

**FOX Sports**
10201 W. Pico Blvd., Los Angeles, CA 90035
(310) 369-6000                    www.foxsports.com
Chairman-CEO . . . . . . . . . . . . . . . . . . . .David Hill
President . . . . . . . . . . . . . . . . . . . . . . . . .Ed Goren
Sr. V.P. of Communications (NYC) . . . . . . . .Lou D'Ermilio
                                      (212) 556-2573

**The Golf Channel**
7580 Commerce Center Drive
Orlando, FL 32819
(407) 363-4653 www.thegolfchannel.com
Co-founder & Chairman . . . . . . . . . . . . .Arnold Palmer
President-CEO . . . . . . . . . . . . . . . . . .David Manougian
V.P. of Production/Executive Producer . . . . . .Tony Tortorici
Managing Dir. of Public Relations . . . . . . . .Dan Higgins

**HBO Sports**
1100 Ave. of the Americas
New York, NY 10036
(212) 512-1987 www.hbo.com/sports
President-CEO . . . . . . . . . . . . . . . . . .Ross Greenburg
Sr. V.P./Exec. Producer . . . . . . . . . . . . . .Rick Bernstein
Sr. V.P., Programming . . . . . . . . . . . . . . . .Kery Davis
Director of Publicity . . . . . . . . . . . . . . . .Ray Stallone

**NBC Sports**
30 Rockefeller Plaza, New York, NY 10112
(212) 664-2160 www.nbcsports.com
Chairman . . . . . . . . . . . . . . . . . . . . . . .Dick Ebersol
President . . . . . . . . . . . . . . . . . . . . . . .Ken Schanzer
Executive Producer . . . . . . . . . . . . . . . . .David Neal
V.P. of Communications . . . . . . . . . . . . .Mike McCarley

**NFL Network**
280 Park Ave.
New York, NY 10017
(212) 450-2000 www.nfl.com/nflnetwork
President/CEO . . . . . . . . . . . . . . . . . .Steve Bornstein
V.P. of Programming . . . . . . . . . . . . . . . .Charles Coplin
Director of Media Services . . . . . . . . . . . . .Seth Palansky

**TSN—The Sports Network**
9 Channel Nine Court
Scarborough, Ontario, M1S 4B5
(416) 332-7660 www.tsn.ca
President . . . . . . . . . . . . . . . . . . . . . . . .Phil King
Communications Manager . . . . . . . . . . .Andrea Goldstein

**Turner Sports**
One CNN Center
13th Floor, Atlanta, GA 30303
(404) 827-1735 www.si.com/turnersports
President . . . . . . . . . . . . . . . . . . . . . .David R. Levy
Senior V.P./Coordinating Producer . . . . . . . .Jeff Behnke
Senior V.P. of Public Relations . . . . . . . . . .Greg Hughes

**USA Network**
1230 Ave. of the Americas
New York, NY 10020
(212) 413-5000 www.usanetwork.com
Sr. V.P., Exec. Producer . . . . . . . . . . . . . .Gordon Beck

## OLYMPICS

**IOC**
**(International Olympic Committee)**
Chateau de Vidy
CH-1007 Lausanne, Switzerland
TEL: 011-41-21-621-6111 www.olympic.org
President . . . . . . . . . . . . . . . . . . . . . .Jacques Rogge
Director General . . . . . . . . . . . . . . . . . . .Urs Lacotte
Director of Communications . . . . . . . . . . . .Giselle Davies

**COC**
**(Canadian Olympic Committee)**
21 St. Clair Avenue E., Suite 900
Toronto, Ontario M4T 1L9
(416) 962-0262 www.olympic.ca
CEO . . . . . . . . . . . . . . . . . . . . . . . . .Chris Rudge
President . . . . . . . . . . . . . . . . . . . .Michael Chambers
IOC members . Richard Pound, James Worrall (Honourary)
Director of Communications . . . . . . . . . .Jackie DeSouza

**USOC**
**(United States Olympic Committee)**
One Olympic Plaza
Colorado Springs, CO 80909
(719) 632-5551 www.usolympicteam.com
Chairman . . . . . . . . . . . . . . . . . . . .Peter Ueberroth
CEO . . . . . . . . . . . . . . . . . . . . . . . . .Jim Scherr
IOC members . . .Anita DeFrantz, James Easton & Bob Ctvrlik
Chief Communications Officer . . . . . . . . . . .Darryl Seibel

## 2006 WINTER GAMES

**Turin Olympic Organizing Committee**
Corso Novara 96
10152 Turin, Italy
TEL: 011-39-011-11-2006 www.torino2006.org
President . . . . . . . . . . . . . . . . . . . .Valentino Castellani
CEO . . . . . . . . . . . . . . . . . . . . . . . .Cesare Vaciago
Chairman of Coord. Commission . . . . . .Jean Claude-Killy
Media Relations Manager . . . . . . . . . .Giuseppe Gattino
(XXth Olympic Winter Games, Feb. 10-26)

## 2008 SUMMER GAMES

**Beijing Olympic Organizing Committee**
24 Dongsi Shitiao St.
Beijing, China 100007
TEL: 86-10-64-00-9185 www.beijing-2008.org
President . . . . . . . . . . . . . . . . . . . . . . . .Liu Qi
Executive President . . . . . . . . . . . . . . . . . .Liu Peng
Executive President . . . . . . . . . . . . . . . .Wang Qishan
Executive President . . . . . . . . . . . . . . . .Deng Pufang
Exec. V.P./Secretary General . . . . . . . . . . . .Wang Wei
(XXIXth Olympic Summer Games, Aug. 8-24)

## 2010 WINTER GAMES

**Vancouver Olympic Organizing Committee**
Suite 400 — 1095 West Pender Street
Vancouver, B.C. Canada V6E 2M6
TEL: (778) 328-2010 www.vancouver2010.com
Chairman . . . . . . . . . . . . . . . . . . . . . . .Jack Poole
CEO . . . . . . . . . . . . . . . . . . . . . . . . .John Furlong
Sr. Vice President, Sport . . . . . . . .Cathy Priestner Allinger
Sr. V.P., Revenue, Mktg., Communications . . . .Dave Cobb
Communications Director . . . .Sam Corea (604-806-1019)
(XXIth Olympic Winter Games, Feb. 12-28)

## 2012 SUMMER GAMES

**London Olympic Organizing Committee**
1 Canada Square - 50th Floor, Canary Wharf
London E14 5LT
TEL: 011-020-7093-5000 www.london2012.org
Chairman . . . . . . . . . . . . . . . . . . . . . .Sebastian Coe
Chairman of IOC Coord. Commission . . . . .Denis Oswald
(XXXth Olympic Summer Games, July 27-Aug. 12)

## U.S. OLYMPICS TRAINING CENTERS

**Colorado Springs Training Center**
One Olympic Plaza, Colorado Springs, CO 80909
(719) 866-4500
Director . . . . . . . . . . . . . . . . . . . . . . . . .Mike English

**Lake Placid Training Center**
196 Old Military Road, Lake Placid, NY 12946
(518) 523-2600
Director . . . . . . . . . . . . . . . . . . . . . . . . . Jack Favro

**Chula Vista Training Center**
2800 Olympic Parkway, Chula Vista, CA 91915
(619) 656-1500
Director . . . . . . . . . . . . . . . . . . . . . . .Patrice Milkovich

## U.S. OLYMPIC ORGANIZATIONS

**National Archery Association**
711 North Tejon, Colorado Springs, CO 80909
(719) 866-4576                www.usarchery.org
President . . . . . . . . . . . . . . . . . . . . . . .Darrell Pace
Executive Director . . . . . . . . . . . . . . . . . .Brad Camp
Comm./Media Relations Mgr. . . . . . . .Mary Beth Vorwerk

**U.S. Badminton Association**
One Olympic Plaza, Colorado Springs, CO 80909
(719) 866-4808            www.usabadminton.org
President . . . . . . . . . . . . . . . . . . . . . . . . .Cliff Peters
Executive Director . . . . . . . . . . . . . . . . . .Dan Cloppas
Member & Financial Services . . . . . . . . . .Peggy Savosik

**USA Baseball**
PO Box 1131, Durham, NC 27701
(919) 474-8721            www.usabaseball.com
President . . . . . . . . . . . . . . . . . . . . . . . . .Mike Gaski
Executive Director & CEO . . . . . . . . . . . . .Paul Seiler
Dir. of Communications . . . . . . . . . . . .David Fannucchi

**USA Basketball**
5465 Mark Dabling Blvd.
Colorado Springs, CO 80918
(719) 590-4800            www.usabasketball.com
President . . . . . . . . . . . . . . . . . . . . . . .Tom Jernstedt
Executive Director . . . . . . . . . . . . . . . . . James Tooley
Asst. Exec. Director, Communications . . . . . .Craig Miller

**U.S. Biathlon Association**
29 Ethan Allen Ave.
Colchester, VT 05446
(802) 654-7833            www.usbiathlon.org
President . . . . . . . . . . . . . . . . . . . . . . . . . .Bill Lilly
Exec. Director . . . . . . . . . . . . . . . . . . . .Stephen Sands
Program Director . . . . . . . . . . . . . . . . . . .Max Cobb
Media Coordinator . . . . . . . . . . . . . . . . . Jerry Kokesh

**U.S. Bobsled and Skeleton Federation**
196 Old Military Road
Lake Placid, NY 12946
(518) 523-1842            www.usbsf.com
President . . . . . . . . . . . . . . . . . . . . . . . Jim Shea Sr.
Interim Executive Director . . . . . . . . . . . . .Robie Vaughn
Media/P.R. Manager . . . . . . . . . . . . . . . . .Tom LaDue

**USA Boxing**
One Olympic Plaza
Colorado Springs, CO 80909
(719) 866-4506            www.usaboxing.org
President . . . . . . . . . . . . . . . .Sandy Martinez-Pino
Executive Director . . . . . . . . . . . . . . . . . .Lamont Jones
Director of Media/Public Relations . . . . . Julie Goldsticker

**U.S. Canoe and Kayak Team**
301 South Tyron St., Suite 1750, Charlotte, NC 28202
(704) 348-4330            www.usack.org
Chair . . . . . . . . . . . . . . . . . . . . . . . . . .Mike Sloan
Executive Director . . . . . . . . . . . . . . .David Yarborough
Media Contact . . . . . . . . . . . . . . . . . . . . .Luke Dieker

**USA Curling**
1100 CenterPoint Drive, PO Box 866
Stevens Point, WI 54481
(715) 344-1199            www.usacurl.org
President . . . . . . . . . . . . . . . . . . . . .Mark Swandby
Executive Director . . . . . . . . . . . . . . . . .David Garber
Communications Director . . . . . . . . . . . . .Rick Patzke

**USA Cycling**
One Olympic Plaza, Colorado Springs, CO 80909
(719) 866-4581            www.usacycling.org
President . . . . . . . . . . . . . . . . . . . . .Jim Ochowicz
Executive Director/CEO . . . . . . . . .Gerard Bisceglia
Communications Director . . . . . . . . . . . . . .Andy Lee
Communications Coordinator . . . . . . . . . . . .Keri Fagan

**United States Diving, Inc.**
201 South Capitol Avenue, Suite 430
Indianapolis, IN 46225
(317) 237-5252            www.usadiving.org
President . . . . . . . . . . . . . . . . . . . . . . .Dave Burgering
Executive Director . . . . . . . . . . . . . . . . . . .Todd Smith
Director of Communications . . . . . . . . . .Kelli Servizzi

**U.S. Equestrian Federation**
4047 Iron Works Pkwy., Lexington, KY 40511
(859) 258-2472            www.usef.org
CEO . . . . . . . . . . . . . . . . . . . . . . . . John Long
President . . . . . . . . . . . . . . . . . . .David O'Connor
Public Relations Manager . . . . . . . . . . . . . .Sarah Lane

**U.S. Fencing Association**
711 North Tejon, Colorado Springs, CO 80903
(719) 866-4511            www.usfencing.org
President . . . . . . . . . . . . . . . . . . . . .Nancy Anderson
Executive Director . . . . . . . . . . . . . . . .Michael Massik
Media Relations Contact . . . . . . . . . . .Cindy Bent Findlay

**U.S. Field Hockey Association**
711 North Tejon, Colorado Springs, CO 80903
(719) 866-4567            www.usfieldhockey.com
President . . . . . . . . . . . . . . . . . . . . . . .Sharon Taylor
Executive Director . . . . . . . . . . . . . . . . .Sheila Walker
Director of Sport/Public Info. . . . . . . . . . .Howard Thomas

**U.S. Figure Skating Association**
20 First Street, Colorado Springs, CO 80906
(719) 635-5200            www.usfsa.org
President . . . . . . . . . . . . . . . . . . . . . .Ron Hershberger
Executive Director . . . . . . . . . . . . . . . . .David Raith
Asst. Exec. Dir., Corporate Relations/Mktg . .Ramsey Baker
Director of Media Services . . . . . . . . . . .Lindsay DeWall

**USA Gymnastics (Artistic, Rhythmic, Trampoline)**
201 South Capitol Avenue, Indianapolis, IN 46225
(317) 237-5050            www.usa-gymnastics.org
Chairman . . . . . . . . . . . . . . . . . . . . . .Ron Froehlich
President-CEO . . . . . . . . . . . . . . . . . . . .Steve Penny
Sr. Director, Communications . . . . . . . . . . . .Leslie King

**USA Hockey, Inc.**
1775 Bob Johnson Dr., Colorado Springs, CO 80906
(719) 576-8724            www.usahockey.com
President . . . . . . . . . . . . . . . . . . . . .Ron DeGregorio
Executive Director . . . . . . . . . . . . . . . . .Dave Ogrean
Dir. of Public and Media Relations . . . . . . .Dave Fischer

## United States Judo, Inc.
One Olympic Plaza, Suite 505
Colorado Springs, CO 80909
(719) 866-4730 www.usjudo.org
President . . . . . . . . . . . . . . . . . . . . . . . Dr. Ron Tripp
Executive Director . . . . . . . . . . . . . . . Jose Rodriguez
Media Contact . . . . . . . . . . . . . . . . . . Nicole Jomantas

## U.S. Luge Association
35 Church Street, Lake Placid, NY 12946
(518) 523-2071 www.usaluge.org
President . . . . . . . . . . . . . . . . . . . . . . Doug Bateman
Executive Director . . . . . . . . . . . . . . . . . . Ron Rossi
Public/Media Relations Manager . . . . . . . . . Jon Lundin

## U.S. Modern Pentathlon
5415 Bandera Rd., Suite 512
San Antonio, TX 78238
(210) 229-2004 www.usapentathlon.org
President . . . . . . . . . . . . . . . . . . . . . . Steve Richards
Executive Director . . . . . . . . . . . . . . . . Robert Marbut
Secretary/Treasurer . . . . . . . . . . . . . . Donna Normandin

## USRowing
201 South Capitol Avenue, Suite 400
Indianapolis, IN 46225
(317) 237-5656 www.usrowing.org
President . . . . . . . . . . . . . . . . . . . . . . Don Langford
Executive Director . . . . . . . . . . . . . . . . . Glenn Merry
Director of Communications . . . . . . . . . . . Brett Johnson

## U.S. Sailing Association
P.O. Box 1260, 15 Maritime Drive, Portsmouth, RI 02871
(401) 683-0800 www.ussailing.org
President . . . . . . . . . . . . . . . . . . . . . . Janet C. Baxter
Executive Director . . . . . . . . . . . . . . . Charlie Leighton
Communications Manager . . . . . . Marlieke de Lange Eaton

## USA Shooting
One Olympic Plaza, Colorado Springs, CO 80909
(719) 866-4670 www.usashooting.com
President . . . . . . . . . . . . . . . . . . . . . . . Dr. James Lally
Executive Director . . . . . . . . . . . . . . . . Robert Mitchell
Media Director . . . . . . . . . . . . . . . . . . . Sara Greenlee

## U.S. Ski & Snowboard Association
P.O. Box 100, 1500 Kearns Blvd.
Park City, UT 84060
(435) 649-9090 www.ussa.org
Chairman . . . . . . . . . . . . . . . . . . . . . . Chuck Ferries
CEO/President . . . . . . . . . . . . . . . . . . . . Bill Marolt
Public Relations Manager . . . . . . . . . . . . . Juliann Fritz

## U.S. Soccer Federation
1801 South Prairie Ave.
Chicago, IL 60616
(312) 808-1300 www.ussoccer.com
President (until 2006) . . . . . . . . Dr. S. Robert Contiguglia
Exec. Director/Secretary General . . . . . . . . . . Dan Flynn
Director of Communications . . . . . . . . . . . Jim Moorhouse

## Amateur Softball Association
2801 N.E. 50th Street
Oklahoma City, OK 73111
(405) 424-5266 www.softball.org
President . . . . . . . . . . . . . . . . . . . . . . . E.T. Colvin
Executive Director . . . . . . . . . . . . . . . . Ron Radigonda
Director of Communications . . . . . . . . . . . Brian McCall

## U.S. Speed Skating
P.O. Box 450639, Westlake, OH 44145
(440) 899-0128 www.usspeedskating.org
President . . . . . . . . . . . . . . . . . . . . . . . Andy Gabel
Executive Director . . . . . . . . . . . . . . . . Katie Marquard
Media/Public Relations Director . . . . . . . . . Melissa Scott

## USA Swimming
One Olympic Plaza, Colorado Springs, CO 80909
(719) 866-4578 www.usaswimming.org
President . . . . . . . . . . . . . . . . . . . . . . Ron Van Pool
Executive Director . . . . . . . . . . . . . . . . Chuck Wielgus
Coordinator, Media Services . . . . . . . . Sara Hunninghake

## U.S. Synchronized Swimming, Inc.
201 South Capitol Avenue, Suite 901
Indianapolis, IN 46225
(317) 237-5700 www.usasynchro.org
President . . . . . . . . . . . . . . . . . . . Virginia Jasontek
Executive Director . . . . . . . . . . . . . . . . . Terry Harper
Media Relations Director . . . . . . . . . . . . Mandy Haskett

## USA Table Tennis
One Olympic Plaza, Colorado Springs, CO 80909
(719) 866-4583 www.usatt.org
President . . . . . . . . . . . . . . . . Sheri Soderberg Pittman
Executive Director . . . . . . . . . . . . . . . Doru Gheorghe
Program and Marketing Coord. . . . . . . . . Tommy Perkins

## U.S. Taekwondo Union
One Olympic Plaza, Suite 104-C
Colorado Springs, CO 80909
(719) 866-4632 www.ustu.org
CEO/Secretary General . . . . . . . . . . Bob Gambardella
Director of Communications . . . . . . . . . . . Bill Kellick

## USA Team Handball
One Olympic Plaza, Colorado Springs, CO 80909
(719) 866-4036 www.usateamhandball.org
President . . . . . . . . . . . . . . . . . . . . . . . Mike Hurdle
Executive Director . . . . . . . . . . . . . . . Mike Cavanaugh
Program Director . . . . . . . . . . . . . . . . . . Kim Kedra

## U.S. Tennis Association
70 West Red Oak Lane
White Plains, NY 10604
(914) 696-7000 www.usta.com
Chairman/President . . . . . . . . . . . . Franklin R. Johnson
Executive Director/COO . . . . . . . . . . . D. Lee Hamilton
Man. Dir., Mktg. & Communications . . . . David Newman

## USA Track and Field
One RCA Dome, Suite 140
Indianapolis, IN 46225
(317) 261-0500 www.usatf.org
President . . . . . . . . . . . . . . . . . . . . . . . . Bill Roe
CEO . . . . . . . . . . . . . . . . . . . . . . . Craig Masback
Director of Communications . . . . . . . . . . . . Jill Geer

## USA Triathlon
1365 Garden of the Gods Road
Colorado Springs, CO 80907
(719) 597-9090 www.usatriathlon.org
President . . . . . . . . . . . . . . . . . . . . . . Brad Davison
Executive Director . . . . . . . . . . . . . . . . . Skip Gilbert
Communications Director . . . . . . . . . B.J. Hoeptner-Evans

## USA Volleyball
715 South Circle Drive
Colorado Springs, CO 80910
(719) 228-6800 www.usavolleyball.org
President . . . . . . . . . . . . . . . . . . . . . Albert Monaco
CEO . . . . . . . . . . . . . . . . . . . . . . . . . Doug Beal
Manager P.R./Publications . . . . . . . . . . . Paul Soriano

## United States Water Polo
1631 Mesa Ave., Ste. A-1, Colorado Springs, CO 80906
(719) 634-0699 www.usawaterpolo.com
President . . . . . . . . . . . . . . . . . . . . . . . Rich Foster
Executive Director . . . . . . . . . . . . . . . . . . Tom Seitz
Dir. of Media Relations . . . . . . . . . . . . . . Kelly Foster

## USA Weightlifting
One Olympic Plaza, Colorado Springs, CO 80909
(719) 866-4508 www.usaweightlifting.org
President .........................Dennis Snethen
Exec. Director ......................Wes Barnett
Membership Services ................Beth Connolly

## USA Wrestling
6155 Lehman Drive, Colorado Springs, CO 80918
(719) 598-8181 www.themat.com
President .........................Stan Dziedzic
Executive Director .....................Rich Bender
Dir. of Communications/Special Projects ....Gary Abbott

---

## SOCCER

### FIFA
**(Federation Internationale de Football Assn.)**
P.O. Box 85, 8030 Zurich, Switzerland
TEL: 011-41-43-222-7777 www.fifa.com
President ......................Joseph S. Blatter
General Secretary ...................Dr. Urs Linsi
Director of Communications ..........Markus Siegler

### MLS

**Major League Soccer**
110 E. 42nd Street, 10th Floor
New York, NY 10017
(212) 450-1200 www.mlsnet.com
Founder ......................Alan I. Rothenberg
Commissioner .......................Don Garber
Dir. of Media Relations .................Simon Borg

**Chicago Fire**
980 N. Michigan Ave., Suite 1998
Chicago, IL 60611
(312) 705-7200 www.chicago-fire.com
Investor/Operator ..........Philip F. Anschutz (AEG)
President ...........................John Guppy
Director of Communications ............Diana Lopez

**Club Deporto Chivas USA**
18400 Avalon Blvd., Suite 500
Carson, CA 90746
(310) 630-4550 www.cdchivasusa.com
Co-Owner ........................Jorge Vergara
Investor/Operator ...................Antonio Cue
General Manager/S.V.P. ..............Whit Haskell

**Colorado Rapids**
1000 Chopper Circle, Denver, CO 80204
(303) 405-1100 www.coloradorapids.com
Investor/Operator .........Kroenke Sports Enterprises
COO/General Manager ...........Charles R. Wright
Director of Media Relations ..........Jurgen Mainka

**Columbus Crew**
Columbus Crew Stadium
One Black & Gold Blvd., Columbus, OH 43211
(614) 447-2739 www.thecrew.com
Investor/Operator .................Hunt Sports Group
General Manager ..................Mark McCullers
Director of Public Relations .............Jeff Wuerth

**D.C. United**
2400 East Capitol St. SE
Washington, D.C. 20003
(202) 587-5000 www.dcunited.com
Investor/Operator ..........Philip F. Anschutz (AEG)
President/CEO ......................Kevin Payne
V.P., Communications ..................Doug Hicks

**FC Dallas**
14800 Quorum Drive, Suite 300
Dallas, TX 75254
(214) 979-0303 fc.dallas.mlsnet.com/mls/fcd
Investor/Operator ...............Hunt Sports Group
Interim President/GM ..................John Alper
V.P., Marketing & Communications ........Jeff Busch

**Kansas City Wizards**
2 Arrowhead Drive
Kansas City, MO 64129
(816) 920-9300 www.kcwizards.com
Investor/Operator ...............Hunt Sports Group
General Manager ...................Curt Johnson
Manager of Public Relations ..........Justin Gorman

**Los Angeles Galaxy**
18400 Avalon Blvd., Ste. 200
Carson, CA 90746
(310) 630-2200 www.lagalaxy.com
Investor/Operator .........Philip F. Anschutz (AEG)
President/General Manager ..........Doug Hamilton
Manager of Communications ..........Patrick Donnelly

**MetroStars**
One Harmon Plaza, 3rd Floor
Secaucus, NJ 07094
(201) 583-7000 www.metrostars.com
Investor/Operator .........Philip F. Anschutz (AEG)
President/GM ......................Alexei Lalas
Director of Public Relations ..........Matthew Chmura

**New England Revolution**
Gillette Stadium, One Patriot Place
Foxboro, MA 02035
(508) 543-5001 www.revolutionsoccer.net
Investor/Operator .........Robert Kraft/Jonathan Kraft
President, Kraft Soccer .................Sunil Gulati
General Manager ..................Craig Tornberg

**Real Salt Lake**
515 South 700 East, Suite 2R
Salt Lake City, UT 84102
(801) 924-8585 www.realsaltlake.com
Investor/Owner ...................Dave Checketts
General Manager ..................Steve Pastorino
Public Relations Manager .............Jamie Barton

**San Jose Earthquakes**
100 North Almaden Ave.
San Jose, CA 95110
(408) 288-2600 www.sjearthquakes.com
Investor/Operator .........Philip F. Anschutz (AEG)
Interim President/General Manager .....Kate McAllister
Sr. Director of Media Relations ...........Jed Mettee

### Other Soccer

**CONCACAF**
**(Confederation of North, Central American &**
**Caribbean Association Football)**
725 Fifth Ave., 17th Floor, New York, NY 10022
(212) 308-0044 www.concacaf.com
President ......................Jack Austin Warner
General Secretary ...................Chuck Blazer
Press Officer .......................Steven Torres

**U.S. Soccer**
**(United States Soccer Federation)**
1801 South Prairie Ave., Chicago, IL 60616
(312) 808-1300 www.ussoccer.com
President (until 2006) ........Dr. S. Robert Contiguglia
Exec. Director/Secretary General ..........Dan Flynn
Director of Communications ..........Jim Moorhouse

**MISL**
**(Major Indoor Soccer League)**
1175 Post Road East, Westport, CT 06880
(203) 222-4900                                                        www.misl.net
Commissioner . . . . . . . . . . . . . . . . . . . . . . . .Steve Ryan
Deputy Commissioner, Soccer Ops. . . . . . .David Grimaldi
V.P., Marketing & Communications . . . . . . . . Jaye Cavallo
   **Member teams** (8): Baltimore Blast, California Cougars, Chicago Storm, Cleveland Force, Kansas City Comets, Milwaukee Wave, Philadelphia Kixx and St. Louis Steamers. Future expansion: Detroit, MI in 2006-07, Newark, NJ in 2007-08.

## SWIMMING

**FINA**
**(Federation Internationale de Natation Amateur)**
4 ave de l'Avante Poste
1005 Lausanne, Switzerland
TEL: 011-4121-310-4710                                       www.fina.org
President . . . . . . . . . . . . . . . . . . . .Mustapha Larfaoui
Executive Director . . . . . . . . . . . . . . .Cornel Marculescu
Honorary Secretary . . . . . . . . . . . . . . .Bartolo Consolo

**USA Swimming**
One Olympic Plaza, Colorado Springs, CO 80909
(719) 866-4578                                    www.usaswimming.org
President . . . . . . . . . . . . . . . . . . . . . . .Ron Van Pool
Executive Director . . . . . . . . . . . . . . . .Chuck Wielgus
Coordinator, Media Services . . . . . . . .Sara Hunninghake

## TENNIS

**ATP Tour**
**(Association of Tennis Professionals)**
201 ATP Boulevard
Ponte Vedra Beach, FL 32082
(904) 285-8000                                          www.atptennis.com
Chairman . . . . . . . . . . . . . . . . . . . .Etienne de Villiers
Chief Executive Officer . . . . . . . . . . . . . . . . . . . .TBA
Senior V.P., Communications . . . . . . . . . . .David Higdon
V.P of Media Relations . . . . . . . . . . . . . . .Graeme Agars

**ITF**
**(International Tennis Federation)**
Bank Lane, Roehampton
London, England SW15 5XZ
TEL: 011-44-208-878-6464                              www.itftennis.com
President . . . . . . . . . . . . . . . . . .Francesco Ricci Bitti
Executive V.P. . . . . . . . . . . . . . . . . . . .Juan Margets
Head of Communications . . . . . . . . . .Barbara Travers

**World TeamTennis**
1776 Broadway, Suite 600, New York, NY 10019
(212) 586-3444                                                www.wtt.com
Director/Co-Founder . . . . . . . . . . . . . . .Billie Jean King
Commissioner & CEO . . . . . . . . . . . . . . . .Ilana Kloss
Public Relations . . . . . . . .Troy Ergenbright & Rosie Crews
                                —GEM Group (303-237-0616)
   **Member teams** (12): Boston Lobsters, Delaware Smash, Hartford FoxForce, Houston Wranglers, Kansas City Explorers, New York Buzz, New York Sportimes, Newport Beach Breakers, Philadelphia Freedoms, Sacramento Capitals, Springfield (Mo.) Lasers and St. Louis Aces.

**U.S. Tennis Association**
70 West Red Oak Lane
White Plains, NY 10604
(914) 696-7000                                                www.usta.com
Chairman/President . . . . . . . . . . . . . .Franklin R. Johnson
Executive Director/COO . . . . . . . . . . . .D. Lee Hamilton
Man. Dir., Mktg. & Communications . . . . .David Newman

**WTA Tour**
**(Women's Tennis Association)**
One Progress Plaza, Suite 1500
St. Petersburg, FL 33701
(727) 895-5000                                             www.wtatour.com
Chairman/CEO . . . . . . . . . . . . . . . . . . .Larry Scott
President (eff. Jan. 1, 2006) . . . . . . . . . . .Stacey Allaster
Dir. of Corporate Communications . . . . . . . . .Darrell Fry

## TRACK & FIELD

**IAAF**
**(International Association of Athletics Federations)**
17 rue Princesse Florestine, BP 359
MC 98007 Monaco
TEL: 011-377-93-10-8888                                     www.iaaf.org
President . . . . . . . . . . . . . . . . . . . . . .Lamine Diack
Senior V.P. . . . . . . . . . . . . . . . . . . . .Dr. Arne Ljungqvist
General Secretary . . . . . . . . . . . . . . . . . .Istvan Gyulai

**USA Track & Field**
One RCA Dome, Suite 140
Indianapolis, IN 46225
(317) 261-0500                                                www.usatf.org
President . . . . . . . . . . . . . . . . . . . . . . . .Bill Roe
CEO . . . . . . . . . . . . . . . . . . . . . . .Craig Masback
Director of Communications . . . . . . . . . . . . . .Jill Geer

## MISCELLANEOUS

**AAU**
**(Amateur Athletic Union)**
P.O. Box 22409, Lake Buena Vista, FL 32830
(407) 934-7200                                            www.aausports.org
President/CEO . . . . . . . . . . . . . . . . . .Bobby Dodd
Director of Sponsorships . . . . . . . . . . . . . .John Hodges

**All-American Soap Box Derby**
P.O. Box 7225, Akron, OH 44306
(330) 733-8723                                                www.aasbd.org
Executive Director . . . . . . . . . . . . . . . . .Tony DeLuca
General Manager . . . . . . . . . . . . . . . . . . . .Jeff Iula
Public Relations Director . . . . . . . . . . . . . . .Bob Troyer

**BASS, Inc.**
**(Bass Anglers Sportsmen Society)**
Celebration, FL 34747
(407) 566-2208                                          www.bassmaster.com
Owner . . . . . . . . . . . . . . . . . . . . . . . . . . .ESPN
V.P., General Manager . . . . . . . . . . . . . . .Don Rucks
Tournament Director . . . . . . . . . . . . . . . . .Trip Weldon
Director of Communications . . . . . . . . . .George McNeilly

**Iditarod Trail Committee**
P.O. Box 870800, Wasilla, AK 99687
(907) 376-5155                                                www.iditarod.com
Executive Director . . . . . . . . . . . . . . . . .Stan Hooley
Race Director . . . . . . . . . . . . . . . . . . . .Joanne Potts
Director of Public Relations . . . . . . . . . . .Chas St. George

**Little League Baseball, Incorporated**
P.O. Box 3485, Williamsport, PA 17701
(570) 326-1921                                             www.littleleague.org
CEO-President . . . . . . . . . . . . . . . . . . .Stephen Keener
Sr. Communications Executive . . . . . . . .Lance Van Auken

**Special Olympics**
1133 19th St., NW, Washington, DC 20036
(202) 628-3630                                        www.specialolympics.org
Founder/Honorary Chairman . . . .Eunice Kennedy Shriver
Chairman Emeritus . . . . . . . . . . . . . . . .Sargent Shriver
Chairman . . . . . . . . . . . . . . . . . . . .Timothy P. Shriver
President/CEO . . . . . . . . . . . . . . . . .Bruce Pasternack

# *International Sports*

American skier **Bode Miller** had a monster year on the slopes in 2005.

# Seven's the key number

*Lance Armstrong adds to his already considerable legend by winning an astounding seventh Tour de France.*

**Gerry Brown** *is co-editor of the ESPN Sports Almanac.*

Lance Armstrong's retirement is not unlike being back at the center of the peloton. Things ahead of him and behind him. The cancer, the ridiculously long hours on the bike, the constant aches and pains, are on his rear wheel and fading.

Coming up quick is more time for his three kids, his cause, his life. Retired at 33. Millions in the bank. Not a bad spot to be for sure. Pretty much the far end of the rainbow from a sick bed with a death sentence on his medical chart.

And he certainly left on his terms. He climbed the mountain, literally and figuratively, and chose not to coast home like plenty of living legends before him. There will be no Washington Wizards jersey to muddy the vivid memories of the famous yellow jersey.

Lance pulled The Barry and left the game before it could leave him behind. Retired running back Barry Sanders was a guy who got hit hard a time or two, but left on top. While cycling is (usually) a non-contact sport, there is no shortness of suffering.

That suffering is behind Armstrong now. And not only is he ready to put his own pain behind him, he's committed to fighting to end the pain of others as well.

"Lance Armstrong! You've won your seventh-straight Tour de France. What are you going to do now?"

Cure cancer?

He just might. Thanks to his global profile, the Lance Armstrong Foundation and his sponsor Nike have sold 55 million (and counting) of those ubiquitous yellow rubber bands to raise money and awareness about cancer research. In the process they sparked a fashion trend.

He announced that 2005 would be his final Tour but heading into the race some observers were not convinced that Armstrong would be leaving the game on top. His relatively poor performance in a tune-up race raised some eyebrows and questions about whether the perpetually young and hungry Armstrong might have suddenly got old or full.

AP/Wide World Photos

*Lance Armstrong* powered his way to a seventh Tour de France title in 2005.

Those eyebrows were lowered and furrowed soon enough and it was quickly apparent that any doubts had been nothing but wishful thinking.

In the Tour-opening individual time trial, Armstrong effectively ended the race for one of his biggest threats. It didn't matter much at all that Armstrong's time was actually second best on the day, thanks to fellow American David Zabriskie's near-record pace in the 19-kilometer stage. It was the fact that Armstrong, despite starting a full minute later, emotionally buried longtime chief rival Jan Ullrich by catching and passing the big German toward the end of the staggered-start ride.

"I gave it everything I could, but of course I didn't expect to be caught by Lance. This has never happened to me before and it's not great for my morale," said Ullrich after getting shemped by Armstrong for the umpteenth time.

After that it was business as usual for Armstrong and his team: stay near the front, make the contenders suffer, grab the yellow jersey and guard it like a prison dinner.

He won just one individual stage in his final tour but kept the yellow jersey for 17 days, the most in his remarkable career.

It wasn't the most impressive or dramatic of his wins but that is more a product of his now ho-hum heroics. When you always win, you don't always win.

That's been Armstrong's biggest

AP/Wide World Photos

*Jamaica's **Asafa Powell** became the world's fastest man in 2005, breaking Tim Montgomery's three-year-old world record in the 100 meters at Olympic Stadium in Athens.*

problem lately. The story is so good, some people will say it's too good.

They have even tried to revise the record books and take away his first Tour victory. In August 2005 French newspaper *L'Equipe* alleged that endurance-boosting EPO had recently been detected in some 1999-vintage Armstrong urine. The science involved is cloudy and the rules for testing old samples as-of-yet unwritten. The truth may never be known. But Armstrong denied the charges like he does everything else—with gusto—and has widely maintained his spotless reputation.

Armstrong's foes have never been able to answer this question: How do you beat a guy you can't break?

Anything he's going to endure in a bike race is weak Kool-Aid compared to the punch of pain he drank while battling cancer. Combine that with his disciplined, dedicated and well-organized Discovery Channel team and it equalled an historic seventh Armstrong win.

But with Armstrong's retirement, the rest of the world will once again have a shot to win cycling's biggest race.

But the American cooler is not exactly kicked. Armstrong's top lieutenant George Hincapie, who won a Tour stage in impressive fashion in 2005, and young David Zabriskie, who wore the yellow jersey for three days, both have bright futures. Levi Leipheimer finished sixth overall in 2005 and both he and former Armstrong teammate Floyd Landis could contend in the future.

# The Ten Biggest Stories
# of the Year in International Sports

**10** The U.S. men sweep the relays at the 2005 FINA World Championships, a feat it hadn't accomplished since 1982. The Americans enjoy their best medal haul since 1978, leading all countries with 39, including 17 golds.

**9** Kenyan Catherine "the Great" Ndereba outruns Elfenesh Alemu for the second consecutive year to win her unprecedented fourth Boston Marathon women's title. Ethiopian Hailu Negussie wins the men's race in 2:11:45.

**8** Russian Yelena Isinbayeva is at it again in 2005, breaking the women's pole vault record four times during the indoor season and five more times outdoors. Her final mark of 16-5¼ at the World Championships in Helsinki cinches her second consecutive IAAF Female Athlete of the Year award.

**7** In the most hotly contested vote in years, the International Olympic Committee awards the 2012 Summer Olympic Games to London, England. After four rounds of balloting, the British bid barely beats out the front-runner Paris by just four votes, 54-50. New York is eliminated in the second round, thanks largely to well-documented troubles with its stadium proposal.

**6** Michelle Kwan joins Maribel Vinson (1928-37) as the only two women to win the United States Figure Skating singles title nine times. Nine times. Johnny Weir takes the men's title for the second consecutive year. Both finish fourth at the World Championships in Moscow behind women's titlist Irina Slutskaya (Russia) and men's winner Stephane Lambiel (Switzerland).

**5** Australian Grant Hackett wins three gold medals (400-meter, 800-meter, 1500-meter freestyle) at the World Swimming Championships in Montreal giving him 10 all-time, second only to countryman Ian Thorpe's 11. Hackett swims a 7:38.65 in the 800 to break the world record set by Thorpe in 2001. It is just one of seven world records and ten additional meet records broken at the bi-annual championships.

**4** American speedster Justin Gatlin becomes just the second man (Maurice Greene, 1999) to win 100-meter and 200-meter gold at the same IAAF World Championships. The former University of Tennessee star and 2004 100-meter Olympic gold medalist also wins the 100 and 200 at the USA Outdoor Championships in June.

**3** Asafa Powell of Jamaica earns the unofficial title of "World's Fastest Man" after running a 9.77 in the 100-meter dash at Athens' Olympic Stadium in June to eclipse Tim Montgomery's three-year-old record. A groin pull forces him out of the World Championships two months later.

**2** New Hampshire native Bode Miller becomes the first American to win the World Cup alpine skiing overall title since Phil Mahre and Tamara McKinney accomplished the feat in 1983. He also edges Austrian hero Hermann Maier to take the Super G title and places second in the Downhill and Giant Slalom. He adds to his resume by taking the Downhill and Super G titles at the 2005 World Alpine Championships in Bormio, Italy.

**1** What's left to say? The world's greatest bike rider, Lance Armstrong, does it yet again, claiming a seventh-straight victory in the Tour de France. Armstrong, with the rock solid support of his Discovery Channel teammates, defeats good friend and runner-up Ivan Basso of Italy by four minutes, forty seconds and retires from racing with two more Tour titles than any other rider in history.

## Seventh Heaven

Lance Armstrong won a seventh-straight Tour de France in 2005. Here's a look at the rare individual "sept-peats" in sports history.

| | Consecutive Titles |
|---|---|
| Sonja Henie, Fig. Skating world titles | 10 |
| John Stockton, NBA assists title | 9 |
| Ingemar Stenmark, World Cup Slalom | 8 |
| Bob Cousy, NBA assists title | 8 |
| Wilt Chamberlain, NBA scoring titles | 7 |
| Michael Jordan, NBA scoring titles | 7 |
| Rickey Henderson, AL stolen bases | 7 |
| Dennis Rodman, NBA rebounding titles | 7 |
| Wayne Gretzky, NHL scoring titles | 7 |
| Bill Shoemaker, jockey money leader | 7 |

## Fastest Men Alive

Asafa Powell added his name to the list of 100-meter dash world record holders in 2005. Here's a look at the progression of that record since 1968 and the advent of automatic timing.

| Sprinter | Time |
|---|---|
| Jim Hines, USA, 1968 | 9.99 |
| Jim Hines, USA, 1968 | 9.95 |
| Calvin Smith, USA, 1983 | 9.93 |
| Carl Lewis, USA, 1988 | 9.92 |
| Leroy Burrell, USA, 1991 | 9.90 |
| Carl Lewis, USA, 1991 | 9.86 |
| Leroy Burrell, USA, 1994 | 9.85 |
| Donovan Bailey, Canada, 1996 | 9.84 |
| Maurice Greene, USA, 1999 | 9.79 |
| Tim Montgomery, USA, 2002 | 9.78 |
| Asafa Powell, Jamaica, 2005 | 9.77 |

# 2004-2005
# *Season in Review*

SPORTS ALMANAC

## TRACK & FIELD

### 2005 IAAF World Championships

The 10th IAAF World Championships in Athletics held in Helsinki, Finland, Aug. 6-14, 2005. Note that (WR) indicates world record and (CR) indicates championship meet record.

#### Final Medal Leaders

| | G | S | B | Total | | | G | S | B | Total |
|---|---|---|---|---|---|---|---|---|---|---|
| 1 United States | 14 | 8 | 3 | 25 | 5 France | | 2 | 1 | 4 | 7 |
| 2 Russia | 7 | 8 | 5 | 20 | Kenya | | 1 | 2 | 4 | 7 |
| 3 Ethiopia | 3 | 4 | 2 | 9 | 7 Cuba | | 2 | 4 | 0 | 6 |
| 4 Jamaica | 1 | 5 | 2 | 8 | 8 Belarus and Germany tied with 5 medals each. | | | | | |

#### MEN

| Event | | Time |
|---|---|---|
| 100 meters | Justin Gatlin, USA | 9.88 |
| 200 meters | Justin Gatlin, USA | 20.04 |
| 400 meters | Jeremy Wariner, USA | 43.93 |
| 800 meters | Rashid Ramzi, BRN | 1:44.24 |
| 1500 meters | Rashid Ramzi, BRN | 3:37.88 |
| 5000 meters | Benjamin Limo, KEN | 13:32.55 |
| 10,000 meters | Kenenisa Bekele, ETH | 27:08.33 |
| Marathon | Jaouad Gharib, MOR | 2:10:10 |
| 4x100m relay | France (Doucoure, Pognon, De Lepine, Dovy) | 38.08 |
| 4x400m relay | USA (Rock, Brew, Williamson, Wariner) | 2:56.91 |
| 110m hurdles | Ladji Doucoure, FRA | 13.07 |
| 400m hurdles | Bershawn Jackson, USA | 47.30 |
| 3000m steeple | Saif Saaeed Shaheen, QAT | 8:13.31 |
| 20k walk | Jefferson Perez, ECU | 1:18:35 |
| 50k walk | Sergey Kirdyapkin, RUS | 3:38:08 |

| Event | | Hgt/Dist |
|---|---|---|
| High Jump | Yuriy Krymarekno, UKR | 7-7¼ |
| Pole Vault | Rens Blom, NED | 19-0½ |
| Long Jump | Dwight Phillips, USA | 28-2¾ |
| Triple Jump | Walter Davis, USA | 57-7¾ |
| Shot Put | Adam Nelson, USA | 71-3½ |
| Discus | Virgilijus Alekna, LIT | 230-2 CR |
| Hammer | Ivan Tikhon, BLR | 275-2 CR |
| Javelin | Andrus Varnik, EST | 286-0 |
| Decathlon | Bryan Clay, USA | 8732 pts |

#### WOMEN

| Event | | Time |
|---|---|---|
| 100 meters | Lauryn Williams, USA | 10.93 |
| 200 meters | Allyson Felix, USA | 22.16 |
| 400 meters | Tonique Williams-Darling, BAH | 49.55 |
| 800 meters | Zulia Calatayud, CUB | 1:58.82 |
| 1500 meters | Tatyana Tomashova, RUS | 4:00.35 |
| 5000 meters | Tirunesh Dibaba, ETH | 14:38.59 CR |
| 10,000 meters | Tirunesh Dibaba, ETH | 30:24.02 |
| Marathon | Paula Radcliffe, GBR | 2:20.57 CR |
| 4x100m relay | USA (Daigle, Lee, Barber, Williams) | 41.78 |
| 4x400m relay | Russia (Pechonkina, Krasnomovets, Antyukh, Pospelova) | 3:20.95 |
| 100m hurdles | Michelle Perry, USA | 12.66 |
| 400m hurdles | Yuliya Pechonkina, RUS | 52.90 |
| 3000m steeple | Docus Inzikuru, UGA | 9:18.24 |
| 20k walk | Olimpiada Ivanova, RUS | 1:25:41 WR |

| Event | | Hgt/Dist |
|---|---|---|
| High Jump | Kajsa Bergqvist, SWE | 6-7½ |
| Pole Vault | Yelena Isinbayeva, RUS | 16-5¼ WR |
| Long Jump | Tianna Madison, USA | 22-7¼ |
| Triple Jump | Trecia Smith, JAM | 49-7 |
| Shot Put | Nadezhda Ostapchuk, BLR | 67-3½ |
| Discus | Franka Dietzsch, GER | 218-4 |
| Hammer | Olga Kuzenkova, RUS | 246-5 |
| Javelin | Osleidys Menendez, CUB | 235-3 WR |
| Heptathlon | Carolina Kluft, SWE | 6887 pts |

### World Outdoor Records Set in 2005

World outdoor records set or equaled between Sept. 29, 2005 and Sept. 28, 2005; (p) indicates record is pending ratification by the IAAF; (†) indicates the IAAF does not officially recognize world records in that event.

#### MEN

| Event | Name | Record | Old Mark | Former Holder |
|---|---|---|---|---|
| 100 meters | **Asafa Powell**, JAM | 9.77 | 9.78 | Tim Montgomery, USA (2002) |
| 10,000 meters | **Kenenisa Bekele**, ETH | 26:17.53p | 26:20.31 | Kenenisa Bekele, ETH (2004) |

#### WOMEN

| Event | Name | Record | Old Mark | Former Holder |
|---|---|---|---|---|
| 20km racewalk | **Olimpiada Ivanova**, RUS | 1:25:41p | 1:26:22 | Wang Yan, CHN (2001) & Yelena Nikolayeva, RUS (2003) |
| Pole Vault | **Yelena Isinbayeva**, RUS | 16-5¼ p | 16-4¾ | Yelena Isinbayeva, RUS (2005)* |
| Javelin | **Osleidys Menendez**, CUB | 235-3 p | 234-8 | Osleidys Menendez, CUB (2001) |
| Hammer | **Tatyana Lysenko**, RUS | 252-10 p | 249-7 | Mihaela Melinte, ROM (1999) |

* Isinbayeva held the women's pole vault record (16-1¾) heading into 2005 and broke her own record five times during the year. She jumped 16-2 on July 5 in Lausanne, then increased the mark to 16-2¾ on July 16 in Madrid, 16-3¼ and 16-4¾ on July 22 in London, and finally 16-5¼ at the World Championships in Helsinki on Aug. 12.

## World, Olympic and American Records
As of Sept. 28, 2005

World outdoor records officially recognized by the International Amateur Athletics Federation (IAAF); (p) indicates record is pending ratification. Note that marathon records are not officially recognized by the IAAF.

### MEN
### Running

| Event | | Time | | Date Set | Location |
|---|---|---|---|---|---|
| 100 meters: | World | 9.77 | **Asafa Powell**, Jamaica | June 14, 2005 | Athens |
| | Olympic | 9.84 | Donovan Bailey, Canada | July 27, 1996 | Atlanta |
| | American | 9.78 | Tim Montgomery | Sept. 14, 2002 | Paris |
| 200 meters: | World | 19.32 | **Michael Johnson**, USA | Aug. 1, 1996 | Atlanta |
| | Olympic | 19.32 | Johnson (same as World) | — | — |
| | American | 19.32 | Johnson (same as World) | — | — |
| 400 meters: | World | 43.18 | **Michael Johnson**, USA | Aug. 26, 1999 | Seville |
| | Olympic | 43.49 | Michael Johnson, USA | July 29, 1996 | Atlanta |
| | American | 43.18 | Johnson (same as World) | — | — |
| 800 meters: | World | 1:41.11 | **Wilson Kipketer**, Denmark | Aug. 24, 1997 | Cologne |
| | Olympic | 1:42.58 | Vebjoern Rodal, Norway | July 31, 1996 | Atlanta |
| | American | 1:42.60 | Johnny Gray | Aug. 28, 1985 | Koblenz, W. Ger. |
| 1000 meters: | World | 2:11.96 | **Noah Ngeny**, Kenya | Sept. 5, 1999 | Rieti, ITA |
| | Olympic | | Not an event | — | — |
| | American | 2:13.9 | Rick Wohlhuter | July 30, 1974 | Oslo |
| 1500 meters: | World | 3:26.00 | **Hicham El Guerrouj**, Morocco | July 14, 1998 | Rome |
| | Olympic | 3:32.07 | Noah Ngeny, Kenya | Sept. 29, 2000 | Sydney |
| | American | 3:29.30 | Bernard Lagat | Aug. 28, 2005 | Rieti, ITA |
| Mile: | World | 3:43.13 | **Hicham El Guerrouj**, Morocco | July 7, 1999 | Rome |
| | Olympic | | Not an event | — | — |
| | American | 3:47.69 | Steve Scott | July 7, 1982 | Oslo |
| 2000 meters: | World | 4:44.79 | **Hicham El Guerrouj**, Morocco | Sept. 7, 1999 | Berlin |
| | Olympic | | Not an event | — | — |
| | American | 4:52.44 | Jim Spivey | Sept. 15, 1987 | Lausanne, SWI |
| 3000 meters: | World | 7:20.67 | **Daniel Komen**, Kenya | Sept. 1, 1996 | Rieti, ITA |
| | Olympic | | Not an event | — | — |
| | American | 7:30.84 | Bob Kennedy | Aug. 8, 1998 | Monte Carlo |
| 5000 meters: | World | 12:37.35 | **Kenenisa Bekele**, Ethiopia | May 31, 2004 | Hengelo, NED |
| | Olympic | 13:05.59 | Said Aouita, Morocco | Aug. 11, 1984 | Los Angeles |
| | American | 12:58.21 | Bob Kennedy | Aug. 14, 1996 | Zurich |
| 10,000 meters: | World | 26:17.53p | **Kenenisa Bekele**, Ethiopia | Aug. 26, 2005 | Brussels |
| | Olympic | 27:05.10 | Kenenisa Bekele, Ethiopia | Aug. 20, 2004 | Athens |
| | American | 27:13.98 | Meb Keflezighi | May 4, 2001 | Stanford, Calif. |
| 20,000 meters: | World | 56:55.6 | **Arturo Barrios**, Mexico | Mar. 30, 1991 | La Fleche, FRA |
| | Olympic | | Not an event | — | — |
| | American | 58:15.0 | Bill Rodgers | Aug. 9, 1977 | Boston |
| Marathon: | World | 2:04:55 | **Paul Tergat**, KEN | Sept. 28, 2003 | Berlin |
| | Olympic | 2:09:21 | Carlos Lopes, Portugal | Aug. 12, 1984 | Los Angeles |
| | American | 2:05:38 | Khalid Khannouchi | Apr. 14, 2002 | London |

### Relays

| Event | | Time | | Date Set | Location |
|---|---|---|---|---|---|
| 4 x 100m: | World | 37.40 | **USA** (Marsh, Burrell, Mitchell, C. Lewis) | Aug. 8, 1992 | Barcelona |
| | | 37.40 | **USA** (Drummond, Cason, Mitchell, Burrell) | Aug. 21, 1993 | Stuttgart |
| | Olympic | 37.40 | USA (same as World - 1992) | — | — |
| | American | 37.40 | USA (same as World) | — | — |
| 4 x 200m: | World | 1:18.68 | **USA** (Marsh, Burrell, Heard, C. Lewis) | Apr. 17, 1994 | Walnut, Calif. |
| | Olympic | | Not an event | — | — |
| | American | 1:18.68 | USA (same as World) | — | — |
| 4 x 400m: | World | 2:54.20 | **USA** (Young, Pettigrew, Washington, Johnson) | July 22, 1998 | Uniondale, N.Y. |
| | Olympic | 2:55.74 | USA (Valmon, Watts, Johnson, S. Lewis) | Aug. 8, 1992 | Barcelona |
| | American | 2:54.20 | USA (same as World) | — | — |
| 4 x 800m: | World | 7:03.89 | **Great Britain** (Elliott, Cook, Cram, Coe) | Aug. 30, 1982 | London |
| | Olympic | | Not an event | — | — |
| | American | 7:06.5 | Santa Monica TC (J. Robinson, Mack, E. Jones, Gray) | Apr. 26, 1986 | Walnut, Calif. |
| 4 x 1500m: | World | 14:38.8 | **West Germany** (Wessinghage, Hudak, Lederer, Fleschen) | Aug. 17, 1977 | Cologne |
| | Olympic | | Not an event | — | — |
| | American | 14:46.3 | USA (Aldredge, Clifford, Harbour, Duits) | June 24, 1979 | Bourges, FRA |

### Steeplechase

| Event | | Time | | Date Set | Location |
|---|---|---|---|---|---|
| 3000 meters: | World | 7:53.63 | **Saif Saaeed Shaheen**, Qatar | Sept. 3, 2004 | Brussels |
| | Olympic | 8:05.51 | Julius Kariuki, Kenya | Sept. 30, 1988 | Seoul |
| | American | 8:09.17 | Henry Marsh | Aug. 28, 1985 | Koblenz, W. Ger |

**Note:** A men's steeplechase course consists of 28 hurdles (3 feet high) and seven water jumps (12 feet long).

## Hurdles

| Event | | Time | | Date Set | Location |
|---|---|---|---|---|---|
| 110 meters: | World | 12.91 | **Colin Jackson**, Great Britain | Aug. 20, 1993 | Stuttgart |
| | | 12.91 | **Xiang Liu**, China | Aug. 27, 2004 | Athens |
| | Olympic | 12.91 | Liu (same as World) | — | — |
| | American | 12.92 | Roger Kingdom | Aug. 16, 1989 | Zurich |
| | | 12.92 | Allen Johnson | June 23, 1996 | Atlanta |
| | | 12.92 | Allen Johnson | Aug. 23, 1996 | Brussels |
| 400 meters: | World | 46.78 | **Kevin Young**, USA | Aug. 6, 1992 | Barcelona |
| | Olympic | 46.78 | Young (same as World) | — | — |
| | American | 46.78 | Young (same as World) | — | — |

**Note:** The 10 hurdles at 110 meters are 3 feet, 6 inches high and those at 400 meters are 3 feet.

## Walking

| Event | | Time | | Date Set | Location |
|---|---|---|---|---|---|
| 20 km: | World | 1:17:21 | **Jefferson Perez**, Ecuador | Aug. 23, 2003 | Paris |
| | Olympic | 1:18:59 | Robert Korzeniowski, Poland | Sept. 22, 2000 | Sydney |
| | American | 1:22:02 | Tim Seaman | May 22, 2004 | Copenhagen, DEN |
| 50 km: | World | 3:35:29p | **Denis Nizhegorodov**, Russia | June 13, 2004 | Cheboksary, RUS |
| | Olympic | 3:38:29 | Vyacheslav Ivanenko, USSR | Sept. 30, 1988 | Seoul |
| | American | 3:48:04 | Curt Clausen | May 2, 1999 | Deauville, FRA |

## Field Events

| Event | | Mark | | Date Set | Location |
|---|---|---|---|---|---|
| High Jump: | World | 8-0½ | **Javier Sotomayor**, Cuba | July 27, 1993 | Salamanca, SPA |
| | Olympic | 7-10 | Charles Austin, USA | July 28, 1996 | Atlanta |
| | American | 7-10½ | Charles Austin | Aug. 7, 1991 | Zurich |
| Pole Vault: | World | 20-1¾ | **Sergey Bubka**, Ukraine | July 31, 1994 | Sestriere, ITA |
| | Olympic | 19-6¼ | Tim Mack, USA | Aug. 27, 2004 | Athens |
| | American | 19-9¼ | Jeff Hartwig | June 14, 2000 | Jonesboro, Ark. |
| Long Jump: | World | 29-4½ | **Mike Powell**, USA | Aug. 30, 1991 | Tokyo |
| | Olympic | 29-2½ | Bob Beamon, USA | Oct. 18, 1968 | Mexico City |
| | American | 29-4½ | Powell (same as World) | — | — |
| Triple Jump: | World | 60- 0¼ | **Jonathan Edwards**, GBR | Aug. 7, 1995 | Göteborg, SWE |
| | Olympic | 59-4¼ | Kenny Harrison, USA | July 27, 1996 | Atlanta |
| | American | 59-4¼ | Kenny Harrison (same as Olympic) | — | — |
| Shot Put: | World | 75-10¼ | **Randy Barnes**, USA | May 20, 1990 | Los Angeles |
| | Olympic | 73- 8¾ | Ulf Timmermann, East Germany | Sept. 23, 1988 | Seoul |
| | American | 75-10¼ | Barnes (same as World) | — | — |
| Discus: | World | 243-0 | **Jurgen Schult**, East Germany | June 6, 1986 | Neubrandenburg |
| | Olympic | 229-3½ | Virgilijus Alekna, Lithuania | Aug. 23, 2004 | Athens |
| | American | 237-4 | Ben Plucknett | July 7, 1981 | Stockholm |
| Javelin: | World | 323-1 | **Jan Zelezny**, Czech Republic | May 25, 1996 | Jena, GER |
| | Olympic | 295-10 | Jan Zelezny, Czech Republic | Sept. 23, 2000 | Sydney |
| | American | 287-8 | Breaux Greer | Sept 19, 2004 | Monaco |
| Hammer: | World | 284-7 | **Yuriy Sedykh**, USSR | Aug. 30, 1986 | Stuttgart |
| | Olympic | 278-2 | Sergey Litvinov, USSR | Sept. 26, 1988 | Seoul |
| | American | 270-9 | Lance Deal | Sept. 7, 1996 | Milan |

**Note:** The international weights for men—**Shot** (16 lbs); **Discus** (4 lbs/6.55 oz); **Javelin** (minimum 1 lb/12¼ oz.); **Hammer** (16 lbs).

## Decathlon

| Event | | Points | | Date Set | Location |
|---|---|---|---|---|---|
| Ten Events: | World | 9026 | **Roman Sebrle**, Czech Republic | May 26-27, 2001 | Gotzis, AUT |
| | Olympic | 8893 | Roman Sebrle, Czech Republic | Aug. 23-24, 2004 | Athens |
| | American | 8891 | Dan O'Brien | Sept. 4-5, 1992 | Talence, FRA |

**Note:** Sebrle's WR times and distances, in order over two days—**100m** (10.64); **LJ** (26-7¼); **Shot** (50-3½); **HJ** (6-11½); **400m** (47.79); **110m H** (13.92); **Discus** (157-3); **PV** (15-9); **Jav** (230-2); **1500m** (4:21.98).

## WOMEN
## Running

| Event | | Time | | Date Set | Location |
|---|---|---|---|---|---|
| 100 meters: | World | 10.49 | **Florence Griffith Joyner**, USA | July 16, 1988 | Indianapolis |
| | Olympic | 10.62 | Florence Griffith Joyner, USA | Sept. 24, 1988 | Seoul |
| | American | 10.49 | Griffith Joyner (same as World) | — | — |
| 200 meters: | World | 21.34 | **Florence Griffith Joyner**, USA | Sept. 29, 1988 | Seoul |
| | Olympic | 21.34 | Griffith Joyner (same as World) | — | — |
| | American | 21.34 | Griffith Joyner (same as World) | — | — |
| 400 meters: | World | 47.60 | **Marita Koch**, East Germany | Oct. 6, 1985 | Canberra, AUS |
| | Olympic | 48.25 | Marie-Jose Perec, France | July 29, 1996 | Atlanta |
| | American | 48.83 | Valerie Brisco | Aug. 6, 1984 | Los Angeles |
| 800 meters: | World | 1:53.28 | **Jarmila Kratochvilova**, Czech. | July 26, 1983 | Munich |
| | Olympic | 1:53.42 | Nadezhda Olizarenko, USSR | July 27, 1980 | Moscow |
| | American | 1:56.40 | Jearl Miles-Clark | Aug. 11, 1999 | Zurich |

## World, Olympic and American Outdoor Records (Cont.)

| Event | Time | | Date Set | Location |
|---|---|---|---|---|
| 1000 meters: | **World** . . . . 2:28.98 | **Svetlana Masterkova**, Russia | Aug. 23, 1996 | Brussels |
| | Olympic . . . . . . . . . | Not an event | — | |
| | American . . . 2:31.80 | Regina Jacobs | July 3, 1999 | Brunswick, Me. |
| 1500 meters: | **World** . . . . . 3:50.46 | **Qu Yunxia**, China | Sept. 11, 1993 | Beijing |
| | Olympic . . . 3:53.96 | Paula Ivan, Romania | Oct. 1, 1988 | Seoul |
| | American . . 3:57.12 | Mary Slaney | July 26, 1983 | Stockholm |
| Mile: | **World** . . . . . 4:12.56 | **Svetlana Masterkova**, Russia | Aug. 14, 1996 | Zurich |
| | Olympic . . . . . . . . | Not an event | — | |
| | American . . 4:16.71 | Mary Slaney | Aug. 21, 1985 | Zurich |
| 2000 meters: | **World** . . . . . 5:25.36 | **Sonia O'Sullivan**, Ireland | July 8, 1994 | Edinburgh |
| | Olympic . . . . . . . . | Not an event | — | |
| | American . . 5:32.7 | Mary Slaney | Aug. 3, 1984 | Eugene, Ore. |
| 3000 meters: | **World** . . . . . 8:06.11 | **Wang Junxia**, China | Sept. 13, 1993 | Beijing |
| | Olympic . . 8:26.53 | Tatyana Samolenko, USSR | Sept. 25, 1988 | Seoul |
| | American . . 8:25.83 | Mary Slaney | Sept. 7, 1985 | Rome |
| 5000 meters: | **World** . . . . 14:24.68 | **Elvan Abeylegesse**, Turkey | June 11, 2004 | Bergen, NOR |
| | Olympic . . 14:40.79 | Gabriela Szabo, Romania | Sept. 25, 2000 | Sydney |
| | American . . 14:45.35 | Regina Jacobs | July 27, 2000 | Sacramento |
| 10,000 meters: | **World** . . . 29:31.78 | **Wang Junxia**, China | Sept. 8, 1993 | Beijing |
| | Olympic . . 30:17.49 | Derartu Tulu, Ethiopia | Sept. 30, 2000 | Sydney |
| | American . . . 30:50.32p | Deena Drossin | May 3, 2002 | Stanford, Calif. |
| Marathon: | **World** . . . . . . 2:15:25† | **Paula Radcliffe**, Great Britain | Apr. 13, 2003 | London |
| | Olympic . . 2:23:14 | Naoko Takahashi, Japan | Sept. 24, 2000 | Sydney |
| | American . . 2:21:16 | Deena Drossin | Apr. 13, 2003 | London |

### Relays

| Event | Time | | Date Set | Location |
|---|---|---|---|---|
| 4 x 100m: | **World** . . . . . 41.37 | **East Germany** (Gladisch, Rieger, Auerswald, Gohr) | Oct. 6, 1985 | Canberra, AUS |
| | Olympic . . . . 41.60 | East Germany (Muller, Wockel, Auerswald, Gohr) | Aug. 1, 1980 | Moscow |
| | American . . . . 41.47 | USA (Gaines, Jones, Miller, Devers) | Aug. 9, 1997 | Athens |
| 4 x 200m: | **World** . . . 1:27.46 | **USA** (Jenkins, Colander-Richardson, Perry, Jones) | Apr. 29, 2000 | Philadelphia |
| | Olympic . . . . . . . . | Not an event | — | — |
| | American . . 1:27.46 | USA (same as World) | — | — |
| 4 x 400m: | **World** . . . 3:15.17 | **USSR** (Ledovskaya, Nazarova, Pinigina, Bryzgina) | Oct. 1, 1988 | Seoul |
| | Olympic . . . 3:15.17 | USSR (same as World) | Oct. 1, 1988 | Seoul |
| | American . . 3:15.51 | USA (Howard, Dixon, Brisco, Griffith Joyner) | Oct. 1, 1988 | Seoul |
| 4 x 800m: | **World** . . . 7:50.17 | **USSR** (Olizarenko, Gurina, Borisova, Podyalovskaya) | Aug. 5, 1984 | Moscow |
| | Olympic . . . . . . . . | Not an event | — | — |
| | American . . 8:17.09 | Athletics West (Addison, Arbogast, Decker Slaney, Mullen) | Apr. 24, 1983 | Walnut, Calif. |

### Hurdles

| Event | Time | | Date Set | Location |
|---|---|---|---|---|
| 100 meters: | **World** . . . . . . 12.21 | **Yordanka Donkova**, Bulgaria | Aug. 20, 1988 | Stara Zagora, BUL |
| | Olympic . . . . . . 12.37 | Joanna Hayes, USA | Aug. 24, 2004 | Athens |
| | American . . . . . 12.33 | Gail Devers | July 23, 2000 | Sacramento |
| 400 meters: | **World** . . . . . . 52.34 | **Yuliya Pechonkina**, Russia | Aug. 8, 2003 | Tula, RUS |
| | Olympic . . . . . 52.77 | Fani Halkia, Greece | Aug. 22, 2004 | Athens |
| | American . . 52.61 | Kim Batten | Aug. 11, 1995 | Göteborg, SWE |

**Note:** The 10 hurdles at 110 meters are 3 feet, 6 inches high and those at 400 meters are 3 feet.

### Walking

| Event | Time | | Date Set | Location |
|---|---|---|---|---|
| 20 km: | **World** . . . . . . 1:25:41p | **Olimpiada Ivanova**, Russia | Aug. 7, 2005 | Helsinki |
| | Olympic . . . . . 1:29:05 | Wang Liping, China | Sept. 28, 2000 | Sydney |
| | American . . . . 1:31:51 | Michelle Rohl | May 13, 2000 | Kenosha, Wis. |

### Steeplechase

| Event | Time | | Date Set | Location |
|---|---|---|---|---|
| 3000 meters: | **World** . . . . . . 9:01.59 | **Gulnara Samitova**, Russia | July 4, 2004 | Heraklion, GRE |
| | Olympic . . . . . . . . . | Not an event | — | |
| | American . . 9:29.32 | Briana Shook | July 31, 2004 | Heusden-Zolder, BEL |

**Note:** A women's steeplechase course consists of 28 hurdles (30 inches high) and seven water jumps (10 feet long).

## Field Events

| Event | | Mark | | Date Set | Location |
|---|---|---|---|---|---|
| High Jump: | **World** | 6-10¼ | **Stefka Kostadinova**, Bulgaria | Aug. 30, 1987 | Rome |
| | Olympic | 6-9 | Yelena Slesarenko, Russia | Aug. 28, 2004 | Athens |
| | American | 6-8 | Louise Ritter | July 8, 1988 | Austin, Texas |
| | | 6-8 | Louise Ritter | Sept. 30, 1988 | Seoul |
| Pole Vault: | **World** | 16-5¼p | **Yelena Isinbayeva**, Russia | Aug. 12, 2005 | Helsinki |
| | Olympic | 16-1¼ | Yelena Isinbayeva, Russia | Aug. 24, 2004 | Athens |
| | American | 15-10 | Stacy Dragila | June 8, 2004 | Ostrava, CZR |
| Long Jump: | **World** | 24-8¼ | **Galina Chistyakova**, USSR | June 11, 1988 | Leningrad |
| | Olympic | 24-3¼ | Jackie Joyner-Kersee, USA | Sept. 29, 1988 | Seoul |
| | American | 24-7 | Jackie Joyner-Kersee | May 22, 1994 | New York |
| Triple Jump: | **World** | 50-10¼ | **Inessa Kravets**, Ukraine | Aug. 10, 1995 | Göteborg, SWE |
| | Olympic | 50-3½ | Inessa Kravets, Ukraine | July 31, 1996 | Atlanta |
| | American | 47-5 | Tiombe Hurd | July 11, 2004 | Sacramento, Calif. |
| Shot Put: | **World** | 74-3 | **Natalya Lisovskaya**, USSR | June 7, 1987 | Moscow |
| | Olympic | 73-6¼ | Ilona Slupianek, E. Germany | July 24, 1980 | Moscow |
| | American | 66-2½ | Ramona Pagel | June 25, 1988 | San Diego |
| Discus: | **World** | 252-0 | **Gabriele Reinsch**, E. Germany | July 9, 1988 | Neubrandenburg |
| | Olympic | 237-2½ | Martina Hellmann, E. Germany | Sept. 29, 1988 | Seoul |
| | American | 227-10 | Suzy Powell | Apr. 27, 2002 | La Jolla, Calif. |
| Javelin: | **World** | 235-3 | **Osleidys Menendez**, Cuba | Aug. 14, 2005 | Helsinki |
| | Olympic | 234-8 | Osleidys Menendez, Cuba | Aug. 27, 2004 | Athens |
| | American | 199-8 | Kim Kreiner | Aug. 7, 2003 | Santo Domingo |
| Hammer: | **World** | 252-10 | **Tatyana Lysenko**, Russia | July 15, 2005 | Moscow |
| | Olympic | 246-1 | Olga Kuzenkova, Russia | Aug. 25, 2004 | Athens |
| | American | 242-4 | Erin Gilreath | June 25, 2005 | Carson, Calif. |

**Note:** The international weights for women—**Shot** (8 lbs/13 oz); **Discus** (2 lbs/3.27 oz); **Javelin** (minimum 1 lb/5.16 oz); **Hammer** (8 lbs/13 oz).

## Heptathlon

| | | Points | | Date Set | Location |
|---|---|---|---|---|---|
| Seven Events: | **World** | 7291 | **Jackie Joyner-Kersee**, USA | Sept. 23-24, 1988 | Seoul |
| | Olympic | 7291 | Joyner-Kersee (same as World) | — | — |
| | American | 7291 | Joyner-Kersee (same as World) | — | — |

**Note:** Joyner-Kersee's WR times and distances, in order over two days—**100m H** (12.69); **HJ** (61¼); **Shot** (51-10); **200m** (22.56); **LJ** (2310¼); **Jav** (149-10); **800m** (2:08.51).

# World and American Indoor Records

As of Sept. 28, 2005

World indoor records officially recognized by the International Amateur Athletics Federation (IAAF); (p) indicates record is pending ratification by the IAAF; (a) indicates record was set at an altitude over 1000 meters.

## MEN
### Running

| Event | | Time | | Date Set | Location |
|---|---|---|---|---|---|
| 50 meters: | **World** | 5.56a | **Donovan Bailey**, Canada | Feb. 9, 1996 | Reno, Nev. |
| | | 5.56 | **Maurice Greene**, USA | Feb. 13, 1999 | Los Angeles |
| | American | 5.56 | Greene (same as World) | Feb. 13, 1999 | Los Angeles |
| 60 meters: | **World** | 6.39 | **Maurice Greene**, USA | Feb. 3, 1998 | Madrid |
| | | 6.39 | **Maurice Greene**, USA | Mar. 3, 2001 | Atlanta |
| | American | 6.39 | Greene (same as World) | — | — |
| 200 meters: | **World** | 19.92 | **Frankie Fredericks**, Namibia | Feb. 18, 1996 | Lievin, FRA |
| | American | 20.10 | Wallace Spearmon | Mar. 11, 2005 | Fayetteville, Ark. |
| 400 meters: | **World** | 44.57 | **Kerron Clement**, USA | Mar. 12, 2005 | Fayetteville, Ark. |
| | American | 44.57 | Clement (same as World) | — | — |

## World Indoor Records Set in 2005

World indoor records set or equaled between Sept. 29, 2004 and Sept. 29, 2005.

### MEN

| Event | Name | Record | Old Mark | Former Holder |
|---|---|---|---|---|
| 400 meters | **Kerron Clement**, USA | 44.57 | 44.63 | Michael Johnson, USA (1995) |

### WOMEN

| Event | Name | Record | Old Mark | Former Holder |
|---|---|---|---|---|
| 5000 meters | **Tirunesh Dibaba**, ETH | 14:32.93 | 14:39.29 | Berhane Adere, ETH (2004) |
| 4 x 200m relay | **Russia** | 1:32.41 | 1:32.55 | West Germany (1988) & Germany (1999) |
| Pole Vault | **Yelena Isinbayeva**, RUS | 16-0¾ | 16-0½ | Yelena Isinbayeva, RUS (2005)* |

* Isinbayeva held the women's pole vault record (15-11¼) heading into 2005 and broke her own record four times during the year. She jumped 15-11¾ on Feb. 12 in Donetsk, Ukraine, then increased the mark to 16-0 on Feb. 18 in Birmingham, U.K., 16-0½ on Feb. 26 in Lievin, France and finally 16-0¾ on March 6 in Madrid.

## World and American Indoor Records (Cont.)

| | | | | |
|---|---|---|---|---|
| 800 meters: | **World** . . . . 1:42.67 | **Wilson Kipketer**, Denmark | Mar. 9, 1997 | Paris |
| | American . . . 1:45.00 | Johnny Gray | Mar. 8, 1992 | Sindelfingen, GER |
| 1000 meters: | **World** . . . . 2:14.96 | **Wilson Kipketer**, Denmark | Feb. 20, 2000 | Birmingham, ENG |
| | American . . 2:17.86 | David Krummenacker | Jan. 27, 2002 | Boston |
| 1500 meters: | **World** . . . 3:31.18 | **Hicham El Guerrouj**, Morocco | Feb. 2, 1997 | Stuttgart |
| | American . . 3:38.12 | Jeff Atkinson | Mar. 5, 1989 | Budapest |
| Mile: | **World** . . . 3:48.45 | **Hicham El Guerrouj**, Morocco | Feb. 12, 1997 | Ghent, BEL |
| | American . . . 3:51.8 | Steve Scott | Feb. 20, 1981 | San Diego |
| 3000 meters: | **World** . . . 7:24.90 | **Daniel Komen**, Kenya | Feb. 6, 1998 | Budapest |
| | American . . 7:39.23 | Tim Broe | Jan. 27, 2002 | Boston |
| 5000 meters: | **World** . . . 12:49.60 | **Kenenisa Bekele**, Ethiopia | Feb. 20, 2004 | Birmingham, ENG |
| | American . . 13:20.55 | Doug Padilla | Feb. 12, 1982 | New York |

**Note:** The Mile run is 1,609.344 meters.

### Hurdles

| Event | Time | | Date Set | Location |
|---|---|---|---|---|
| 50 meters: | **World** . . . . . . 6.25 | **Mark McKoy**, Canada | Mar. 5, 1986 | Kobe, JPN |
| | American . . . . . 6.35 | Greg Foster | Jan. 27, 1985 | Rosemont, Ill. |
| | 6.35 | Greg Foster | Jan. 31, 1987 | Ottawa |
| 60 meters: | **World** . . . . . . 7.30 | **Colin Jackson**, Great Britain | Mar. 6, 1994 | Sindelfingen, GER |
| | American . . . . 7.36 | Greg Foster | Jan. 16, 1987 | Los Angeles |
| | 7.36 | Allen Johnson | March 6, 2004 | Budapest |

**Note:** The hurdles for both distances are 3 feet, 6 inches high. There are four hurdles in the 50 meters and five in the 60.

### Walking

| Event | Time | | Date Set | Location |
|---|---|---|---|---|
| 5000 meters: | **World** . . 18:07.08 | **Mikhail Shchennikov**, Russia | Feb. 14, 1995 | Moscow |
| | American . 19:18.40 | Tim Lewis | Mar. 7, 1987 | Indianapolis |

### Relays

| Event | Time | | Date Set | Location |
|---|---|---|---|---|
| 4 x 200 meters: | **World** . . . . 1:22.11 | **Great Britain** | Mar. 3, 1991 | Glasgow |
| | American . . 1:22.71 | National Team | Mar. 3, 1991 | Glasgow |
| 4 x 400 meters: | **World** . . . . 3:02.83 | **United States** | Mar. 7, 1999 | Maebashi, JPN |
| | American . . 3:02.83 | National Team (same as World) | Mar. 7, 1999 | Maebashi, JPN |
| 4 x 800 meters: | **World** . . . . 7:13.94 | **United States** | Feb. 6, 2000 | Boston |
| | American . . . 7:13.94 | Global Athletics (same as World) | Feb. 6, 2000 | Boston |

### Field Events

| Event | Mark | | Date Set | Location |
|---|---|---|---|---|
| High Jump: | **World** . . . . . . 7-11½ | **Javier Sotomayor**, Cuba | Mar. 4, 1989 | Budapest |
| | American . . . . 7-10½ | Hollis Conway | Mar. 10, 1991 | Seville |
| Pole Vault: | **World** . . . . . . 20-2 | **Sergey Bubka**, Ukraine | Feb. 21, 1993 | Donyetsk, UKR |
| | American . . . . 19-9 | Jeff Hartwig | Mar. 10, 2002 | Sindelfingen, GER |
| Long Jump: | **World** . . . . 28-10¼ | **Carl Lewis**, USA | Jan. 27, 1984 | New York |
| | American . . . . 28-10¼ | Lewis (same as World) | — | |
| Triple Jump: | **World** . . . . . . 58-6 | **Aliecer Urrutia**, Cuba | Mar. 1, 1997 | Sindelfingen, GER |
| | 58-6 | **Christian Olsson**, Sweden | Mar. 7, 2004 | Budapest |
| | American . . . . . 58-3¼ | Mike Conley | Feb. 27, 1987 | New York |
| Shot Put: | **World** . . . . . . 74-4¼ | **Randy Barnes**, USA | Jan. 20, 1989 | Los Angeles |
| | American . . . . 74-4¼ | Barnes (same as World) | — | |

**Note:** The international shot put weight for men is 16 lbs.

### Heptathlon

| Event | Points | | Date Set | Location |
|---|---|---|---|---|
| Seven Events: | **World** . . . . . . 6476 | **Dan O'Brien**, USA | Mar. 13-14, 1993 | Toronto |
| | American . . . . 6476 | O'Brien (same as World) | — | |

**Note:** O'Brien's WR times and distances, in order over two days—**60m** (6.67); **LJ** (25-8¾); **SP** (52-6¾); **HJ** (6-11¾); **60m H** (7.85); **PV** (17-0¾); **1000m** (2:57.96).

### WOMEN
### Running

| Event | Time | | Date Set | Location |
|---|---|---|---|---|
| 50 meters: | **World** . . . . . . 5.96 | **Irina Privalova**, Russia | Feb. 9, 1995 | Madrid |
| | American . . . . 6.02 | Gail Devers | Feb. 21, 1999 | Lievin, FRA |
| 60 meters: | **World** . . . . . . 6.92 | **Irina Privalova**, Russia | Feb. 11, 1993 | Madrid |
| | 6.92 | **Irina Privalova**, Russia | Feb. 9, 1995 | Madrid |
| | American . . . . 6.95 | Gail Devers | Mar. 12, 1993 | Toronto |
| | 6.95 | Marion Jones | Mar. 7, 1998 | Maebashi, JPN |
| 200 meters: | **World** . . . . . . 21.87 | **Merlene Ottey**, Jamaica | Feb. 13, 1993 | Lievin, FRA |
| | American . . . . 22.18 | Michelle Collins | Mar. 15, 2003 | Birmingham, ENG |

| 400 meters: | **World** . . . . .49.59 | **Jarmila Kratochvilova**, Czech. | Mar. 7, 1982 | Milan |
| | American . . . .50.64 | Diane Dixon | Mar. 10, 1991 | Seville |
| 800 meters: | **World** . . . .1:55.82 | **Jolanda Ceplak**, Slovenia | Mar. 3, 2002 | Vienna |
| | American . .1:58.71 | Nicole Teter | Mar. 2, 2002 | New York |
| 1000 meters: | **World** . . .2:30.94 | **Maria Mutola**, Mozambique | Feb. 25, 1999 | Stockholm |
| | American . .2:34.19 | Jennifer Toomey | Feb. 20, 2004 | Birmingham, ENG |
| 1500 meters: | **World** . . .3:59.98 | **Regina Jacobs**, USA | Feb. 1, 2003 | Boston |
| | American . .3:59.98 | Jacobs (same as World) | — | — |
| Mile: | **World** . . . .4:17.14 | **Doina Melinte**, Romania | Feb. 9, 1990 | E. Rutherford, N.J. |
| | American . . .4:20.5 | Mary Slaney | Feb. 19, 1982 | San Diego |
| 3000 meters: | **World** . . . .8:29.15 | **Berhane Adere**, Ethiopia | Feb. 3, 2002 | Stuttgart |
| | American . .8:39.14 | Regina Jacobs | Mar. 7, 1999 | Maebashi, JPN |
| 5000 meters: | **World** . . .14:32.93 | **Tirunesh Dibaba**, Ethiopia | Jan. 29, 2005 | Boston |
| | American . .15:07.33 | Marla Runyan | Feb. 18, 2001 | New York City |

**Note:** The Mile run is 1,609.344 meters.

## Hurdles

| Event | Time | | Date Set | Location |
|---|---|---|---|---|
| 50 meters: | **World** . . . . . . .6.58 | **Cornelia Oschkenat**, E. Ger. | Feb. 20, 1988 | East Berlin |
| | American . . . .6.67a | Jackie Joyner-Kersee | Feb. 10, 1995 | Reno, Nev. |
| 60 meters: | **World** . . . . . . .7.69 | **Ludmila Engquist**, USSR | Feb. 4, 1990 | Chelyabinsk, USSR |
| | American . . . .7.74 | Gail Devers | Mar. 1, 2003 | Boston |

**Note:** The hurdles for both distances are 2 feet, 9 inches high. There are four hurdles in the 50 meters and five in the 60.

## Walking

| Event | Time | | Date Set | Location |
|---|---|---|---|---|
| 3000 meters: | **World** . . .11:35.34p | **Gillian O'Sullivan**, IRL | Feb. 15, 2003 | Belfast |
| | American . .12:20.79 | Debbi Lawrence | Mar. 12, 1993 | Toronto |

## Relays

| Event | Time | | Date Set | Location |
|---|---|---|---|---|
| 4 x 200 meters: | **World** . . . . 1:32.41 | **Russia** | Jan. 29, 2005 | Glasgow |
| | American 1:33.24 | National Team | Feb. 12, 1994 | Glasgow |
| 4 x 400 meters: | **World** . . . 3:23.88 | **Russia** | Mar. 7, 2004 | Budapest |
| | American . . 3:27.59 | National Team | Mar. 7, 1999 | Maebashi, JPN |
| 4 x 800 meters: | **World** . . .8:18.71 | **Russia** | Feb. 4, 1994 | Moscow |
| | American . . . 8:25.5 | Villanova | Feb. 7, 1987 | Gainesville, Fla. |

## Field Events

| Event | Mark | | Date Set | Location |
|---|---|---|---|---|
| High Jump: | **World** . . . . . . .6-9½ | **Heike Henkel**, Germany | Feb. 9, 1992 | Karlsruhe, GER |
| | American . . . . . .6-7 | Tisha Waller | Feb. 28, 1998 | Atlanta |
| Pole Vault: | **World** . . . . . .16-0¾ | **Yelena Isinbayeva**, Russia | Mar. 6, 2005 | Madrid |
| | American . . 15-9¼ | Stacy Dragila, USA | Mar. 6, 2004 | Budapest |
| Long Jump: | **World** . . . . . .24-2¼ | **Heike Drechsler**, E. Germany | Feb. 13, 1988 | Vienna |
| | American . . 23-4¾ | Jackie Joyner-Kersee | Mar. 5, 1994 | Atlanta |
| Triple Jump: | **World** . . . . . .50-4¾ | **Tatyana Lebedeva**, Russia | Mar. 6, 2004 | Budapest |
| | American . . 46-8¼ | Sheila Hudson | Mar. 4, 1995 | Atlanta |
| Shot Put: | **World** . . . . .73-10 | **Helena Fibingerova**, Czech. | Feb. 19, 1977 | Jablonec, CZE |
| | American . . 65-0¾ | Ramona Pagel | Feb. 20, 1987 | Inglewood, Calif. |

**Note:** The international shotput weight for women is 8 lbs. and 13 oz.

## Pentathlon

| | Points | | Date Set | Location |
|---|---|---|---|---|
| Five Events: | **World** . . . . . . 4991 | **Irina Byelova**, Russia | Feb. 14-15, 1992 | Berlin |
| | American . . . . 4753 | DeDee Nathan | Mar. 4-5, 1999 | Maebashi, JPN |

**Note:** Byelova's WR times and distances, in order over two days—**60m H** (8.22); **HJ** (6-4); **SP** (43-5¾); **LJ** (21-1¾); **800m** (2:10.26).

---

## 2005 IAAF World Cross Country Championships

The 33rd IAAF World Cross Country Championships held in St. Etienne/St. Galmier, France (March 19-20).

| MEN | | | | WOMEN | | |
|---|---|---|---|---|---|---|
| 12 km . . . . . . . . . .1. | Kenenisa Bekele, Ethiopia | 35:06 | 8 km . . . . . . . . . .1. | Tirunesh Dibaba, Ethiopia | 26:34 |
| (7.45 mi) | 2. Zersenay Tadesse, Eritrea | 35:20 | (4.97 mi) | 2. Alice Timbilili, Kenya | 26:37 |
| | 3. Abdullah Ahmad Hassan, Qatar | 35:34 | | 3. Werknesh Kidane, Ethiopia | 26:37 |
| | *Best USA*—Matt Withrow, 60th | 38:41 | | *Best USA*—Colleen De Reuck, 13th | 27:51 |

## SWIMMING

# 2005 FINA World Championships

The 11th FINA World Championships in swimming, diving, synchronized swimming and water polo held in Montreal, Canada, July 17-31, 2005. Note that (WR) indicates world record and (CR) indicates championship meet record.

## Final Medal Leaders — Swimming Top 10

| | | G | S | B | Total | | | G | S | B | Total |
|---|---|---|---|---|---|---|---|---|---|---|---|
| 1 | United States | 17 | 15 | 7 | 39 | 6 Russia | 5 | 3 | 2 | 10 |
| 2 | Australia | 13 | 8 | 4 | 25 | Canada | 3 | 4 | 3 | 10 |
| 3 | China | 5 | 5 | 7 | 17 | 8 Italy | 1 | 3 | 3 | 7 |
| 4 | Germany | 2 | 7 | 4 | 13 | 9 Four countries tied with 5 medals each. | | | | |
| 5 | Japan | 0 | 5 | 7 | 12 | | | | | |

### MEN

| Event | | Time | |
|---|---|---|---|
| 50m free | Roland Schoeman, RSA | 21.69 | CR |
| 100m free | Filippo Magnini, ITA | 48.12 | CR |
| 200m free | Michael Phelps, USA | 1:45.20 | |
| 400m free | Grant Hackett, AUS | 3:42.91 | |
| 800m free | Grant Hackett, AUS | 7:38.65 | WR |
| 1500m free | Grant Hackett, AUS | 14:42.58 | |
| 50m back | Aristeidis Grigoriadis, GRE | 24.95 | |
| 100m back | Aaron Peirsol, USA | 53.62 | |
| 200m back | Aaron Peirsol, USA | 1:54.66 | WR |
| 50m breast | Mark Warnecke, GER | 27.63 | |
| 100m breast | Brendan Hahsen, USA | 59.37 | CR |
| 200m breast | Brendan Hansen, USA | 2:09.85 | |
| 50m fly | Roland Schoeman, RSA | 22.96 | WR |
| 100m fly | Ian Crocker, USA | 50.40 | WR |
| 200m fly | Pawel Korzeniowksi, POL | 1:55.02 | |
| 200m I.M. | Michael Phelps, USA | 1:56.68 | |
| 400m I.M. | Laszlo Cseh, HUN | 4:09.63 | |

### WOMEN

| Event | | Time | |
|---|---|---|---|
| 50m free | Lisbeth Lenton, AUS | 24.59 | |
| 100m free | Jodie Henry, AUS | 54.18 | |
| 200m free | Solenne Figues, FRA | 1:58.60 | |
| 400m free | Laure Manaudou, FRA | 4:06.44 | |
| 800m free | Kate Ziegler, USA | 8:25.31 | |
| 1500m free | Kate Ziegler, USA | 16:00.41 | |
| 50m back | Giaan Rooney, AUS | 28.63 | |
| 100m back | Kirsty Coventry, ZIM | 1:00.24 | |
| 200m back | Kirsty Coventry, ZIM | 2:08.52 | |
| 50m breast | Jade Edmistone, AUS | 30.45 | WR |
| 100m breast | Leisel Jones, AUS | 1:06.25 | |
| 200m breast | Leisel Jones, AUS | 2:21.72 | WR |
| 50m fly | Danni Miatke, AUS | 26.11 | |
| 100m fly | Jessicah Schipper, AUS | 57.23 | CR |
| 200m fly | Otylia Jedrzejczak, POL | 2:05.61 | WR |
| 200m I.M. | Katie Hoff, USA | 2:10.41 | CR |
| 400m I.M. | Katie Hoff, USA | 4:36.07 | CR |

### Men's Relays

| Event | | Time | |
|---|---|---|---|
| 4x100m free | USA (Phelps, Walker, Dusing, Lezak) | 3:13.77 | CR |
| 4x200m free | USA (Phelps, Lochte, Vanderkaay, Keller) | 7:06.58 | |
| 4x100m medley | USA (Peirsol, Hansen, Crocker, Lezak) | 3:31.85 | |

### Women's Relays

| Event | | Time | |
|---|---|---|---|
| 4x100m free | Australia (Henry, Mills, Reese, Lenton) | 3:37.32 | CR |
| 4x200m free | USA (Coughlin, Hoff, Myers, Sandeno) | 7:53.70 | CR |
| 4x100m medley | Australia (Edington, Jones, Schipper, Lenton) | 3:57.47 | CR |

### Men's Open Water

| Event | | Time |
|---|---|---|
| 5km | Thomas Lurz, GER | 51:17.2 |
| 10km | Chip Peterson, USA | 1:46:38.1 |
| 25km | David Meca, ESP | 5:00:21.4 |

### Women's Open Water

| Event | | Time |
|---|---|---|
| 5km | Larisa Ilchenko, RUS | 55:40.1 |
| 10km | Edith Van Dijk, NED | 1:56:00.5 |
| 25km | Edith Van Dijk, NED | 5:25:06.6 |

## Diving

### MEN

| Event | | Points |
|---|---|---|
| 1m springboard | Alexandre Despatie, CAN | 489.69 |
| 3m springboard | Alexandre Despatie, CAN | 813.60 |
| 10m platform | Hu Jia, CHN | 698.01 |
| 3m springboard (synchronized) | Wang Feng & He Chong, CHN | 384.42 |
| 10m platform (synchronized) | Dmitry Dobrosok & Glen Galperin, RUS | 392.88 |

### WOMEN

| Event | | Points |
|---|---|---|
| 1m springboard | Blythe Hartley, CAN | 325.65 |
| 3m springboard | Guo Jingjing, CHN | 645.54 |
| 10m platform | Laura Wilkinson, USA | 564.87 |
| 3m springboard (synchronized) | Li Ting & Guo Jingjing, CHN | 349.80 |
| 10m platform (synchronized) | Jia Tong & Yuan Pei Lin, CHN | 351.60 |

## Synchronized Swimming

| Event | | Points |
|---|---|---|
| Solo | Virginie Dedieu, FRA | 99.001 |
| Duet | Anastasia Davydova & Anastasia Ermakova, RUS | 99.667 |
| Team | Russia | 99.667 |
| Free | Russia | 99.333 |

## Water Polo

### Men's Final

| | | | | | | | |
|---|---|---|---|---|---|---|---|
| Serbia & Montenegro | 1 | 2 | 2 | 3 | — | 8 |
| Hungary | 1 | 2 | 2 | 2 | — | 7 |

### Women's Final

| | | | | | | | |
|---|---|---|---|---|---|---|---|
| Hungary | 2 | 5 | 0 | 0 | 3 | — | 10 |
| USA | 2 | 1 | 1 | 3 | 0 | — | 7 |

## World, Olympic and American Records
### As of September 28, 2005

World long course records officially recognized by the Federation Internationale de Natation Amateur (FINA). Note that (p) indicates preliminary heat; (r) relay lead-off split; and (s) indicates split time. Note that (*) denotes that a record is awaiting ratification.

## MEN

### Freestyle

| Distance | | Time | | Date Set | Location |
|---|---|---|---|---|---|
| 50 meters: | World | 21.64 | Aleksandr Popov, Russia | June 16, 2000 | Moscow |
| | Olympic | 21.91 | Aleksandr Popov, Unified Team | July 30, 1992 | Barcelona |
| | American | 21.76 | Gary Hall Jr. | Aug. 15, 2000 | Indianapolis |
| 100 meters: | World | 47.84p | P. van den Hoogenband, NED | Sept. 19, 2000 | Sydney |
| | Olympic | 47.84p | P. van den Hoogenband, NED | — | — |
| | American | 48.17p | (same as World) Jason Lezak | July 10, 2004 | Long Beach, Calif. |
| 200 meters: | World | 1:44.06 | Ian Thorpe, Australia | July 25, 2001 | Fukuoka, JPN |
| | Olympic | 1:44.71 | Ian Thorpe, Australia | Aug. 16, 2004 | Athens |
| | American | 1:45.20 | Michael Phelps | July 26, 2005 | Montreal |
| 400 meters: | World | 3:40.08 | Ian Thorpe, Australia | July 30, 2002 | Manchester, GBR |
| | Olympic | 3:40.59 | Ian Thorpe, Australia | Sept. 16, 2000 | Sydney |
| | American | 3:44.11 | Klete Keller | Aug. 14, 2004 | Athens |
| 800 meters: | World | 7:38.65 | Grant Hackett, Australia | July 27, 2005 | Montreal |
| | Olympic | | Not an event | | |
| | American | 7:45.63 | Larsen Jensen | July 27, 2005 | Montreal |
| 1500 meters: | World | 14:34.56 | Grant Hackett, Australia | July 29, 2001 | Fukuoka, JPN |
| | Olympic | 14:43.40 | Grant Hackett, Australia | Aug. 21, 2004 | Athens |
| | American | 14:45.29 | Larsen Jensen | Aug. 21, 2004 | Athens |

### Backstroke

| Distance | | Time | | Date Set | Location |
|---|---|---|---|---|---|
| 50 meters: | World | 24.80 | Thomas Rupprath, Germany | July 27, 2003 | Barcelona |
| | Olympic | | Not an event | | |
| | American | 24.99 | Lenny Krayzelburg | Aug. 28, 1999 | Sydney |
| 100 meters: | World | 53.17 | Aaron Peirsol, USA | April 2, 2005 | Indianapolis |
| | Olympic | 53.45r | Aaron Peirsol, USA | Aug. 21, 2004 | Athens |
| | American | 53.17 | Peirsol (same as World) | — | — |
| 200 meters: | World | 1:54.66 | Aaron Peirsol, USA | July 29, 2005 | Montreal |
| | Olympic | 1:54.95 | Aaron Peirsol, USA | Aug. 19, 2004 | Athens |
| | American | 1:54.66 | Peirsol (same as World) | | |

### Breaststroke

| Distance | | Time | | Date Set | Location |
|---|---|---|---|---|---|
| 50 meters: | World | 27.18 | Oleg Lisogor, Ukraine | Aug. 1, 2002 | Berlin |
| | Olympic | | Not an event | — | |
| | American | 27.39 | Ed Moses | Mar. 31, 2001 | Austin, Texas |
| 100 meters: | World | 59.30 | Brendan Hansen, USA | July 8, 2004 | Long Beach, Calif. |
| | Olympic | 1:00.01p | Brendan Hansen, USA | Aug. 14, 2004 | Athens |
| | American | 59.30 | Hansen (same as Olympic) | — | — |
| 200 meters: | World | 2:09.04 | Brendan Hansen, USA | July 11, 2004 | Long Beach, Calif. |
| | Olympic | 2:09.44 | Kosuke Kitajima, Japan | Aug. 18, 2004 | Athens |
| | American | 2:09.04 | Hansen (same as Olympic) | | |

### Butterfly

| Distance | | Time | | Date Set | Location |
|---|---|---|---|---|---|
| 50 meters: | World | 22.96 | Roland Schoeman, South Africa | July 25, 2005 | Montreal |
| | Olympic | | Not an event | — | |
| | American | 23.12 | Ian Crocker | July 25, 2005 | Montreal |
| 100 meters: | World | 50.40 | Ian Crocker, USA | July 30, 2005 | Montreal |
| | Olympic | 51.25 | Michael Phelps, USA | Aug. 20, 2004 | Athens |
| | American | 50.40 | Crocker (same as World) | — | — |
| 200 meters: | World | 1:53.93p | Michael Phelps, USA | July 22, 2003 | Barcelona |
| | Olympic | 1:54.04 | Michael Phleps, USA | Aug. 17, 2004 | Athens |
| | American | 1:53.93p | Phelps (same as World) | — | — |

### Individual Medley

| Distance | | Time | | Date Set | Location |
|---|---|---|---|---|---|
| 200 meters: | World | 1:55.94 | Michael Phelps, USA | Aug. 9, 2003 | College Park, Md. |
| | Olympic | 1:57.14 | Michael Phelps, USA | Aug. 19, 2004 | Athens |
| | American | 1:55.94 | Phelps (same as World) | | |
| 400 meters: | World | 4:08.26 | Michael Phelps, USA | Aug. 14, 2004 | Athens |
| | Olympic | 4:08.26 | Phelps (same as World) | — | — |
| | American | 4:08.26 | Phelps (same as World) | — | — |

## Swimming (Cont.)

### Relays

| Distance | | Time | | Date Set | Location |
|---|---|---|---|---|---|
| 4x100m free: | World | 3:13.17 | **South Africa** (Schoeman, Ferns, Townsend, Neethling) | Aug. 15, 2004 | Athens |
| | Olympic | 3:13.17 | South Africa (same as world) | — | |
| | American | 3:13.77 | USA (Phelps, Walker, Dusing, Lezak) | July 24, 2005 | Montreal |
| 4x200m free: | World | 7:04.66 | **Australia** (Hackett, Klim, Kirby, Thorpe) | July 27, 2001 | Fukuoka, JPN |
| | Olympic | 7:07.05 | Australia (Thorpe, Klim, Pearson, Kirby) | Sept. 19, 2000 | Sydney |
| | American | 7:06.58 | USA (Phelps, Lochte, Vanderkaay, Keller) | July 29, 2005 | Montreal |
| 4x100m medley: | World | 3:30.68 | **USA** (Peirsol, Hansen, Crocker, Lezak) | Aug. 21, 2004 | Athens |
| | Olympic | 3:30.68 | USA (same as World) | — | — |
| | American | 3:30.68 | USA (same as World) | — | — |

## WOMEN

### Freestyle

| Distance | | Time | | Date Set | Location |
|---|---|---|---|---|---|
| 50 meters: | World | 24.13p | **Inge de Bruijn**, Netherlands | Sept. 22, 2000 | Sydney |
| | Olympic | 24.13p | de Bruijn (same as World) | | |
| | American | 24.63 | Dara Torres | Sept. 23, 2000 | Sydney |
| 100 meters: | World | 53.52p | **Jodie Henry**, Australia | Aug. 18, 2004 | Athens |
| | Olympic | 53.52p | Henty (same as World) | | |
| | American | 53.99 | Natalie Coughlin | Aug. 29, 2002 | Yokohama, JPN |
| 200 meters: | World | 1:56.64 | **Franziska van Almsick**, Ger. | Aug. 3, 2002 | Berlin |
| | Olympic | 1:57.65 | Heike Friedrich, E. Germany | Sept. 21, 1988 | Seoul |
| | American | 1:57.41r | Lindsay Benko | July 24, 2003 | Barcelona |
| 400 meters: | World | 4:03.85 | **Janet Evans**, USA | Sept. 22, 1988 | Seoul |
| | Olympic | 4:03.85 | Evans (same as World) | — | — |
| | American | 4:03.85 | Evans (same as World) | — | — |
| 800 meters: | World | 8:16.22 | **Janet Evans**, USA | Aug. 20, 1989 | Tokyo |
| | Olympic | 8:19.67 | Brooke Bennett, USA | Sept. 22, 2000 | Sydney |
| | American | 8:16.22 | Evans (same as World) | — | — |
| 1500 meters: | World | 15:52.10 | **Janet Evans**, USA | Mar. 26, 1988 | Orlando |
| | Olympic | | Not an event | — | — |
| | American | 15:52.10 | Evans (same as World) | — | — |

### Backstroke

| Distance | | Time | | Date Set | Location |
|---|---|---|---|---|---|
| 50 meters: | World | 28.19 | **Janine Pietsch**, Germany | May 25, 2005 | Berlin |
| | Olympic | | Not an event | — | — |
| | American | 28.49p | Natalie Coughlin | July 23, 2001 | Fukuoka, JPN |
| 100 meters: | World | 59.58 | **Natalie Coughlin**, USA | Aug. 13, 2002 | Ft. Lauderdale, Fla. |
| | Olympic | 59.68r | Natalie Coughlin, USA | Aug. 21, 2004 | Athens |
| | American | 59.58 | Coughlin (same as World) | — | — |
| 200 meters: | World | 2:06.62 | **Krisztina Egerszegi**, Hungary | Aug. 25, 1991 | Athens |
| | Olympic | 2:07.06 | Krisztina Egerszegi, Hungary | July 31, 1992 | Barcelona |
| | American | 2:08.53 | Natalie Coughlin | Aug. 16, 2002 | Ft. Lauderdale, Fla. |

### Breaststroke

| Distance | | Time | | Date Set | Location |
|---|---|---|---|---|---|
| 50 meters: | World | 30.45 | **Jade Edmistone**, Australia | July 31, 2005 | Montreal |
| | Olympic | | Not an event | — | — |
| | American | 30.85 | Jessica Hardy | July 31, 2005 | Montreal |
| 100 meters: | World | 1:06.20 | **Jessica Hardy**, USA | July 26, 2005 | Montreal |
| | Olympic | 1:06.64 | Luo Xuejuan, China | Aug. 16, 2004 | Athens |
| | American | 1:06.20 | Hardy (same as World) | — | — |
| 200 meters: | World | 2:21.72 | **Leisel Jones**, AUS | July 29, 2005 | Montreal |
| | Olympic | 2:23.37 | Amanda Beard, USA | Aug. 19, 2004 | Athens |
| | American | 2:22.44 | Amanda Beard | July 12, 2004 | Long Beach, Calif. |

## World Swimming Records Set in 2005

World long course records set or equaled between Sept. 29, 2004 and Sept. 28, 2005; (*) indicates record is awaiting ratification. (r) indicates relay leadoff split.

### MEN

| Event | Name | Record | Old Mark | Former Holder |
|---|---|---|---|---|
| 800m freestyle | **Grant Hackett,** AUS | 7:38.65 | 7:39.16 | Ian Thorpe, AUS (2001) |
| 100m backstroke | **Aaron Peirsol,** USA | 53.17 | 53.45r | Aaron Peirsol, USA (2004) |
| 200m backstroke | **Aaron Peirsol,** USA | 1:54.66 | 1:54.74 | Aaron Peirsol, USA (2004) |
| 50m butterfly (1) | **Roland Schoeman,** RSA | 23.01 | 23.30 | Ian Crocker, USA (2004) |
| 50m butterfly (2) | **Roland Schoeman,** RSA | 22.96 | 23.01 | Roland Schoeman (RSA 2005) |
| 100m butterfly | **Ian Crocker,** USA | 50.40 | 50.76 | Ian Crocker, USA (2004) |

### WOMEN

| Event | Name | Record | Old Mark | Former Holder |
|---|---|---|---|---|
| 50m backstroke | **Janine Pietsch,** GER | 28.19 | 28.25 | Sandra Volker, GER (2000) |
| 50m breaststroke | **Jade Edmistone,** AUS | 30.45 | 30.57 | Zoe Baker, GBR (2002) |
| 100m breaststroke | **Jessica Hardy,** USA | 1:06.20 | 1:06.37 | Leisel Jones, AUS (2003) |
| 200m breaststroke | **Leisel Jones,** AUS | 2:21.72 | 2:22.44 | Amanda Beard, USA (2004) |
| 200m butterfly | **Otylia Jedrzejczak,** POL | 2:05.61 | 2:05.78 | Otylia Jedrzejczak, POL (2002) |

### Butterfly

| Distance | | Time | | Date Set | Location |
|---|---|---|---|---|---|
| 50 meters: | World | 25.57 | **Anna-Karin Kammerling,** SWE | July 30, 2002 | Berlin |
| | Olympic | | Not an event | — | — |
| | American | 26.00 | Jenny Thompson | July 26, 2003 | Barcelona |
| 100 meters: | World | 56.61 | **Inge de Bruijn,** Netherlands | Sept. 17, 2000 | Sydney |
| | Olympic | 56.61 | de Bruijn (same as World) | — | — |
| | American | 57.58p | Dara Torres | Aug. 9, 2000 | Indianapolis |
| 200 meters: | World | 2:05.61 | **Otylia Jedrejczak,** Poland | July 28, 2005 | Montreal |
| | Olympic | 2:05.88 | Misty Hyman, USA | Sept. 20, 2000 | Sydney |
| | American | 2:05.88 | Hyman (same as Olympic) | — | — |

### Individual Medley

| Distance | | Time | | Date Set | Location |
|---|---|---|---|---|---|
| 200 meters: | World | 2:09.72 | **Wu Yanyan,** China | Oct. 17, 1997 | Shanghai |
| | Olympic | 2:10.68 | Yana Klochkova, Ukraine | Sept. 19, 2000 | Sydney |
| | American | 2:10.41 | Katie Hoff | July 25, 2005 | Montreal |
| 400 meters: | World | 4:33.59 | **Yana Klochkova,** Ukraine | Sept. 16, 2000 | Sydney |
| | Olympic | 4:33.59 | Klochkova, UKR (same as World) | — | — |
| | American | 4:34.95 | Kaitlin Sandeno | Aug. 14, 2004 | Athens |

### Relays

| Distance | | Time | | Date Set | Location |
|---|---|---|---|---|---|
| 4x100m free: | World | 3:35.94 | **Australia** (Mills, Lenton, Thomas, Henry) | Aug. 14, 2004 | Athens |
| | Olympic | 3:35.94 | Australia (same as World) | — | — |
| | American | 3:36.39 | USA (Joyce, Coughlin, Weir, Thompson) | Aug. 14, 2004 | Athens |
| 4x200m free: | World | 7:53.42 | **USA** (Coughlin, Piper, Vollmer, Sandeno) | Aug. 18, 2004 | Athens |
| | Olympic | 7:53.42 | USA (same as World) | — | — |
| | American | 7:53.42 | USA (same as World) | — | — |
| 4x100m medley: | World | 3:57.32 | **Australia** (Rooney, Jones, Thomas, Henry) | Aug. 21, 2004 | Athens |
| | Olympic | 3:57.32 | Australia (same as World) | — | — |
| | American | 3:58.30 | USA (Bedford, Quann, Thompson, Torres) | Sept. 23, 2000 | Sydney |

## Alpine Skiing
### World Cup Champions
#### Top Five Standings

##### MEN

**Overall** 1. Bode Miller, USA (1648 pts); 2. Benjamin Raich, AUT (1454); 3. Hermann Maier, AUT (1295); 4. Michael Walchhofer, AUT (1012); 5. Daron Rahlves, USA (984).

**Downhill** 1. Michael Walchhofer, AUT (681 pts); 2. Bode Miller, USA (618); 3. Hermann Maier, AUT (451); 4. Daron Rahlves, USA (444); 5. Hans Grugger, AUT (418).

**Slalom** 1. Benjamin Raich, AUT (552 pts); 2. Rainer Schoenfelder, AUT (408); 3. Manfred Pranger, AUT (396); 4. Giorgio Rocca, ITA (390); 5. Alois Vogl, GER (310).

**Giant Slalom** 1. Benjamin Raich, AUT (423 pts); 2. Bode Miller, USA (420); 3. Thomas Grandi, CAN (366); 4. Hermann Maier, AUT (362); 5. Massimiliano Blardone, ITA (345).

**Super G** 1. Bode Miller, USA (470 pts); 2. Hermann Maier, AUT (453); 3. Daron Rahlves, USA (362); 4. Didier Defago, SWI (286); 5. Michael Walchhofer, AUT (265).

**Combined** 1. Benjamin Raich, AUT (100 pts); 2. Lasse Kjus, NOR (80); 3. Didier Defago, SWI (60); 4. Daniel Albrecht, SWI (50); 5. Kjetil Andre Aamodt, NOR (45).

**Nation's Cup Champion**: Austria

##### WOMEN

**Overall** 1. Anja Paerson, SWE (1359 pts); 2. Janica Kostelic, CRO (1356); 3. Renate Goetschl, AUT (1164); 4. Michaela Dorfmeister, AUT (1122); 5. Tanja Poutiainen, FIN (1039). *Best USA*—Lindsey Kildow (6th, 914 pts).

**Downhill** 1. Renate Goetschl, AUT (567 pts); 2. Hilde Gerg, GER (495); 3. Michaela Dorfmeister, AUT (432); 4. Janica Kostelic, CRO (387); 5. Lindsey Kildow, USA (384).

**Slalom** 1. Tanja Poutiainen, FIN (570 pts); 2. Janica Kostelic, CRO (400); 3. Marlies Schild, AUT (376); 4. Kristina Koznick, USA (355); 5. Sarah Schleper, USA (337).

**Giant Slalom** 1. Tanja Poutiainen, FIN (461 pts); 2. Anja Paerson, SWE (410); 3. Maria Jose Rienda Contreras, ESP (384); 4. Tina Maze, SLO (366); 5. Genevieve Simard, CAN (241). *Best USA*—Julia Mancuso (t-7th, 230 pts).

**Super G** 1. Michaela Dorfmeister, AUT (493 pts); 2. Renate Goetschl, AUT (416); 3. Lindsey Kildow, USA (396); 4. Anja Paerson, SWE (359); 5. Hilde Gerg, GER (296).

**Combined** 1. Janica Kostelic, CRO (100 pts); 2. Anja Paerson, SWE (80); 3. Emily Brydon, CAN (60); 4. Nicole Hosp, AUT (50); 5. Lindsey Kildow, USA (45).

**Nation's Cup Champion**: Austria

## 2005 Alpine World Championships
at Bormio, Italy (Jan. 29-Feb. 13)

##### MEN

| | |
|---|---|
| Downhill | Bode Miller, United States |
| Slalom | Benjamin Raich, Austria |
| Giant Slalom | Hermann Maier, Austria |
| Super G | Bode Miller, United States |
| Combined | Benjamin Raich, Austria |

##### WOMEN

| | |
|---|---|
| Downhill | Janica Kostelic, Croatia |
| Slalom | Janica Kostelic, Croatia |
| Giant Slalom | Anja Paerson, Sweden |
| Super G | Anja Paerson, Sweden |
| Combined | Janica Kostelic, Croatia |
| Nations | Germany |

(men & women combined)

## Freestyle Skiing
### World Cup Champions

##### MEN

| | |
|---|---|
| Overall | Jeremy Bloom, United States |
| Aerials | Jeret Peterson, United States |
| Moguls | Jeremy Bloom, United States |
| Ski Cross | Tomas Kraus, Czech Republic |

##### WOMEN

| | |
|---|---|
| Overall | Nina Li, China |
| Aerials | Nina Li, China |
| Moguls | Jennifer Heil, Canada |
| Ski Cross | Ophelie David, France |

## 2005 Freestyle World Championships
at Ruka, Finland (March 17-20)

##### MEN

| | |
|---|---|
| Aerials | Steve Omischl, Canada |
| Moguls | Nathan Roberts, United States |
| Dual Moguls | Toby Dawson, United States |
| Halfpipe | Mathias Wecxsteen, France |
| Ski Cross | Tomas Kraus, Czech Republic |

##### WOMEN

| | |
|---|---|
| Aerials | Nina Li, China |
| Moguls | Hannah Kearney, United States |
| Dual Moguls | Jennifer Heil, Canada |
| Halfpipe | Sarah Burke, Canada |
| Ski Cross | Karin Huttary, Austria |

## Snowboarding
### World Cup Champions

##### MEN

| | |
|---|---|
| Halfpipe | Mathieu Crepel, France |
| Parallel Slalom | Philipp Schoch, Switzerland |
| Snowboardcross | Xavier Delerue, France |
| Big Air | Jukka Eratuli, Finland |

##### WOMEN

| | |
|---|---|
| Halfpipe | Melo Imai, Japan |
| Parallel Slalom | Daniela Meuli, Switzerland |
| Snowboardcross | Doresia Krings, Austria |
| Big Air | Daniela Meuli, Switzerland |

## 2005 World Snowboarding Championships
at Whistler, British Columbia (Jan. 15-23)

##### MEN

| | |
|---|---|
| Halfpipe | Antti Autti, Finland |
| Parallel Slalom | Jasey Jay Anderson, Canada |
| Parallel Giant Slalom | Jasey Jay Anderson, Canada |
| Snowboardcross | Seth Wescott, United States |
| Big Air | Antti Autti, Finland |

##### WOMEN

| | |
|---|---|
| Halfpipe | Doriane Vidal, France |
| Parallel Slalom | Daniela Meuli, Switzerland |
| Parallel Giant Slalom | Manuela Riegler, Austria |
| Snowboardcross | Lindsey Jacobellis, United States |

## Nordic Skiing

### World Cup Champions

#### MEN

Cross Country - Overall . . . . . .Axel Teichmann, Germany
Cross Country - Distance . . . . .Axel Teichmann, Germany
Cross Country - Sprint . . . . . . .Tor Arne Hetland, Norway
Nordic Combined - Overall . . .Hannu Manninen, Finland
Nordic Combined - Sprint . . . .Hannu Manninen, Finland

Ski Jumping - Overall . . . . . . . . . .Janne Ahonen, Finland
Ski Jumping - Four Hills . . . . . . . . .Janne Ahonen, Finland
Ski Jumping - Nordic Tournament .Matti Hautamaeki, Finland

#### WOMEN

Cross Country - Overall . . . . . . .Marit Bjoergen, Norway
Cross Country - Distance . . . . . .Marit Bjoergen, Norway
Cross Country - Sprint . . . . . . . .Marit Bjoergen, Norway

### 2005 Nordic World Championships

at Oberstdorf, Germany (Feb. 16-27)

#### MEN

Sprint . . . . . . . . . . . . . . . . . . . .Vassilli Rotchev, Russia
15-k Freestyle . . . . . . . . . . . . . .Pietro Piller Cottrer, Italy
50-k Classic . . . . . . . . . . . . . . . . . . .Frode Estil, Norway
Pursuit (15-kClassic+15k Free) . . . . .Vincent Vittoz, France
4x10-k Relay . . . . . . . . . . . . . . . . . . . . . . . . . .Norway
Team Sprint . . . . . . . . . . . . . . . . . . . . . . . . . . .Norway

Nordic Combined - Indiv. . . . .Ronny Ackermann, Germany
Nordic Combined - Sprint . . .Ronny Ackermann, Germany
Nordic Combined - Team . . . . . . . . . . . . . . . . .Norway

Ski Jumping - K90m . . . . . . . . . . .Rok Benkovic, Slovenia
Ski Jumping - K90m Team . . . . . . . . . . . . . . . . .Austria
Ski Jumping - K120m . . . . . . . .Janne Ahonen, Finland
Ski Jumping - K120m Team . . . . . . . . . . . . . . . .Austria

#### WOMEN

Sprint . . . . . . . . . . . . . . . . . . . .Emelie Oehrstig, Sweden
10-k Freestyle . . . .Katerina Neumannova, Czech Republic
30-k Classic . . . . . . . . . . . . . . .Marit Bjoergen, Norway
Pursuit (7.5-k Classic+7.5k Free) . Julija Tchepalova, Russia
4x5-k Relay . . . . . . . . . . . . . . . . . . . . . . . . . . .Norway
Team Sprint . . . . . . . . . . . . . . . . . . . . . . . . . . .Norway

## Speed Skating

### World Cup Champions

#### MEN

100 meters . . . . . . . . . . . . . . . . .Yu Fengtong, China
500 meters . . . . . . . . . . . Jeremy Wotherspoon, Canada
1000 meters . . . . . . . . .Erben Wennemars, Netherlands
1500 meters . . . . . . . . . . . .Mark Tuitert, Netherlands
5000/10,000 meters . . . . . . . .Oystein Grodum, Norway

#### WOMEN

100 meters . . . . . . . . . . . . . . . . .Sayuri Osuga, Japan
500 meters . . . . . . . . . . . . . . . . . .Wang Manli, China
1000 meters . . . . . . . . . . . . .Chiara Simionato, Italy
1500 meters . . . . . . . . . . . . . .Cindy Klassen, Canada
3000/5000 meters . . . . . . . .Claudia Pechstein, Germany

### 2005 World Allround Championships

at Moscow, Russia (Feb. 5-6)

#### MEN

500 meters . . . . . . . . . . . . . .Takahiro Ushiyama, Japan
1500 meters . . . . . . . . . . . .Shani Davis, United States
5000 meters . . . . . . . . . . . .Oystein Grodum, Norway
10,000 meters . . . . . . . . . . .Oystein Grodum, Norway
All-Around . . . . . . . . . . . . . .Shani Davis, United States

#### WOMEN

500 meters . . . . . . . . . . . . . . .Anni Friesinger, Germany
1500 meters . . . . . . . . . . . . . .Anni Friesinger, Germany
3000 meters . . . . . . . . . . . . . .Anni Friesinger, Germany
5000 meters . . . . . . . . . . . . . .Anni Friesinger, Germany
All-Around . . . . . . . . . . . . . . .Anni Friesinger, Germany

### 2005 World Short Track Championships

at Beijing, China (March 11-13)

#### MEN

500 meters . . . . . . . . . . .Francois-Luis Tremblay, Canada
1000 meters . . . . . . . . .Apolo Anton Ohno, United States
1500 meters . . . . . . . . . . . . . .Ahn Hyun-Soo, S. Korea
3000 meters . . . . . . . . .Apolo Anton Ohno, United States
5000 meter relay . . . . . . . . . . . . . . . . . . . . . . .Canada
All-Around . . . . . . . . . . . . . . . .Ahn Hyun-Soo, S. Korea

#### WOMEN

500 meters . . . . . . . . . . . . . . . . .Yang Yang A, China
1000 meters . . . . . . . . . . .Choi Eun-Kyung, S. Korea
1500 meters . . . . . . . . . . . . . . . .Jin Sun-Yu, S. Korea
3000 meters . . . . . . . . . . . . . .Kang Yun-Mi, S. Korea
3000 meter relay . . . . . . . . . . . . . . . . . . . . . . .Canada
All-Around . . . . . . . . . . . . . . . . .Jin Sun-Yu, S. Korea

## Figure Skating

### World Championships

at Moscow, Russia (March 14-20)

**Men's** —1. Stephane Lambiel, Switzerland; 2. Jeffrey Buttle, USA; 3. Evan Lyacek, USA; 4. Johnny Weir, USA; 5. Li Chengjiang, China.

**Women's** —1. Irina Slutskaya, Russia; 2. Sasha Cohen, USA; 3. Carolina Kostner, Italy; 4. Michelle Kwan, USA; 5. Fumie Suguri, Japan.

**Pairs** —1. Tatiana Totmianina & Maxim Marinin, Russia; 2. Maria Petrova & Alexei Tikhonov, Russia; 3. Zhang Dan & Zhang Hao, China; 4. Pang Qing & Tong Jian, China; 5. Julia Obertas & Sergei Slavnov, Russia.

**Ice Dance** —1. Tatiana Navka & Roman Kostomarov, Russia; 2. Tanith Belbin & Benjamin Agosto, USA; 3. Elena Grushina & Ruslan Goncharov, Ukraine; 4. Isabelle Delobel & Olivier Schoenfelder, France; 5. Albena Denkova & Maxim Staviski, Bulgaria.

### U.S. Championships

at Portland, Ore (Jan. 9-16)

**Men's** . . . . . . . . . . . . . . . . . . . . . . . .Johnny Weir
**Women's** . . . . . . . . . . . . . . . . . . . . .Michelle Kwan
**Pairs** . . . . . . . . . . . . . . . . . . . . . .Kathryn Orscher
    & Garrett Lucash
**Ice Dance** . . . . . . . . . . . . . . . . . . . . .Tanith Belbin
    & Benjamin Agosto

### European Championships

at Turin, Italy (Jan. 25-30)

**Men's** . . . . . . . . . . . . . . . . . . .Evgeni Plushenko, Russia
**Women's** . . . . . . . . . . . . . . . . . . .Irina Slutskaya, Russia
**Pairs** . . . . . . . . . . . . . . . . . . .Tatiana Totmianina
    & Maxim Marinin, Russia
**Ice Dance** . . . . . . . . . . . . . . . . . . . .Tatiana Navka
    & Roman Kostomarov, Russia

## SUMMER SPORTS

# Cycling
## 2005 Tour de France

The 92nd Tour de France (July 2-24) ran 21 stages, covering 3,608 kilometers (2,242 miles) starting in Fromentine, winding through the French countryside, passing through the Alps and Pyrenees and finishing in Paris on the Avenue des Champs-Elysees. Thirty three-year-old Texan Lance Armstrong, riding for the Discovery Channel team, won his unprecedented seventh consecutive Tour, completing the grueling event in 86 hours, 15 minutes and two seconds. He defeated his closest rival, Ivan Basso of Italy, by four minutes and 40 seconds. Unless he changes his mind, this was the last Tour for Armstrong, who goes out on top as the greatest rider in the history of the race. "Vive le Tour! Forever," he said after his final win.

| | Team | Behind | | | Team | Behind |
|---|---|---|---|---|---|---|
| 1 Lance Armstrong, USA | Discovery | — | 6 Levi Leipheimer, USA | | Gerolsteiner | 11:21 |
| 2 Ivan Basso, ITA | CSC | 4:40 | 7 Mickael Rasmussen, DEN | | Rabobank | 11:33 |
| 3 Jan Ullrich, GER | T-Mobile | 6:21 | 8 Cadel Evans, AUS | | Davitamon-Lotto | 11:55 |
| 4 Francisco Mancebo, ESP | Illes Balears | 9:59 | 9 Floyd Landis, USA | | Phonak Hearing | 12:44 |
| 5 Alexandre Vinokourov, KAZ | T-Mobile | 11:01 | 10 Oscar Pereiro Sio, ESP | | Phonak Hearing | 16:04 |

## Other Worldwide Champions

2005 Major UCI (Union Cycliste Internationale) Road results through Sept. 26. Note that in some instances, the date shown below is the final day of that particular race.

### MEN

| Race | Winner | Race | Winner |
|---|---|---|---|
| Jan. 23: Tour Down Under (AUS) | Luis Sanchez, ESP | Apr. 3: Tour de Flanders (BEL) | Tom Boonen, BEL |
| Feb. 6: Tour de Langwaki (MAS) | Ryan Cox, RSA | Apr. 6: Gent-Wevelgem (BEL) | Nico Mattan, BEL |
| Feb. 13: Mediterranean Tour (FRA) | Jens Voigt, GER | Apr. 10: Paris-Roubaix (FRA) | Tom Boonen, BEL |
| Feb. 17: Ruta del Sol (ESP) | Francisco Cabello, ESP | Apr. 17: Amstel Gold Race (NED) | Danilo Di Luca, ITA |
| Feb. 26: Tour of Valencia (ESP) | Alessandro Petacchi, ITA | Apr. 20: Fleche Wallonne (BEL) | Danilo Di Luca, ITA |
| Feb. 26: Omloop Het Volk (BEL) | Nick Nuyens, BEL | May 1: Tour de Romandie (SWI) | Santiago Botero, COL |
| Mar. 13: Paris-Nice (FRA) | Bobby Julich, USA | May 8: Four Days of Dunkirk (FRA) | Pierrick Fedrigo, FRA |
| Mar. 15: Tirreno-Adriatico (ITA) | Oscar Freire, ESP | May 29: Giro d'Italia (ITA) | Paolo Savoldelli, ITA |
| Mar. 19: Milan-San Remo (ITA) | Alessandro Petacchi, ITA | June 12: Dauphine Libere (FRA) | Inigo Landaluze, ESP |
| Mar. 25: Setmana Catalana (ESP) | Alberto Contador, ESP | June 19: Tour of Switzerland (SWI) | Aitor Gonzalez, ESP |
| Mar. 27: Criterium Int'l (FRA) | Bobby Julich, USA | Sept. 18: Tour of Spain (ESP) | Roberto Heras, ESP |

### WOMEN

| Race | Winner | Race | Winner |
|---|---|---|---|
| Feb. 24: Geelong Women's Tour (AUS) | Oenone Wood, AUS | May 28: Montreal World Cup (CAN) | G. Jeanson, CAN |
| Mar. 19: Primavera Rosa (ITA) | Trixi Worrack, GER | June 5: Wachovia Liberty Classic (USA) | Ina Teutenberg, GER |
| Apr. 3: Tour de Flanders (BEL) | M. Melchers-Van Poppel, NED | July 10: Giro d'Italia Femminile (ITA) | Nicole Brandli, SWI |
| Apr. 20: Fleche Wallonne (BEL) | Nicole Cooke, GBR | Aug. 20: GP of Wales | Judith Arndt, GER |
| May 8: GP Feminas Castilla y Leon (ESP) | Susanne Ljungskog, SWE | Sept. 4: Rotterdam Tour (NED) | Ina Teutenberg, GER |
| May 22: Tour de L'Aude (FRA) | Amber Neben, USA | Sept. 11: Tour of Nuremberg (GER) | Giorgia Bronzini, ITA |

# Gymnastics
## 2005 U.S. Championships
at Indianapolis, Ind. (August 10-13)

| MEN | | WOMEN | |
|---|---|---|---|
| All-Around | Todd Thornton | All-Around | Nastia Liukin |
| High Bar | Justin Spring | Vault | Alicia Sacramone |
| Parallel Bars | DJ Bucher | Uneven Bars | Nastia Liukin |
| Vault | Sean Golden | Balance Beam | Nastia Liukin |
| Pommel Horse | Yewki Tomita | Floor Exercise | Alicia Sacramone |
| Rings | Sean Golden | Rhythmic: All-Around | Olga Karmansky |
| Floor Exercise | Guillermo Alvarez | Rhythmic: Clubs | Lisa Wang |
| | | Rhythmic: Rope | Olga Karmansky |
| | | Rhythmic: Ball | (tie) Olga Karmansky & Lisa Wang |
| | | Rhythmic: Ribbon | Olga Karmansky |

**Note:** The 38th Artistic Gymnastics World Championships were scheduled for Nov. 21-27, 2005 at Rod Laver Arena in Melbourne, Australia.

## Marathons
## 2005 Boston Marathon

The 109th edition of the Boston Marathon was held Monday, April 18, 2005 and run, as always, from Hopkinton through Ashland, Framingham, Natick, Wellesley, Newton and Brookline to Boston, Mass. Ethiopia's Hailu Negussie battled unseasonably warm temperatures in the seventies to break the tape in 2:11:45. It was just the second time in the last 15 years that the winner of the world's oldest annual marathon was not from Kenya. Colorado's Alan Culpepper (fourth) gave the U.S. its highest finish since 1987. The Kenyans, led by runner-up Wilson Onsare, grabbed five of the top seven spots.

In the women's division, 32-year-old Kenyan Catherine Ndereba successfully defended her title, winning an unprecedented fourth time (2:25:13). For the second straight year, Ethiopian Elfenesh Alemu placed second. Trailing the leaders by 80 seconds at the halfway point, "Catherine the Great" made her move, took the lead at the 20-mile mark and widened the gap in Newton's notorious hills. Each race winner earned $100,000. **Distance:** 26.2 miles.

### MEN

| | | Time |
|---|---|---|
| 1 | Hailu Negussie, Ethiopia | 2:11:45 |
| 2 | Wilson Onsare, Kenya | 2:12:21 |
| 3 | Benson Cherono, Kenya | 2:12:48 |
| 4 | Alan Culpepper, United States | 2:13:39 |
| 5 | Robert Kipkoech Cheruiyot, Kenya | 2:14:30 |

### WOMEN

| | | Time |
|---|---|---|
| 1 | Catherine Ndereba, Kenya | 2:25:13 |
| 2 | Elfenesh Alemu, Ethiopia | 2:27:03 |
| 3 | Bruna Genovese, Italy | 2:29:51 |
| 4 | Svetlana Zakharova, Russia | 2:31:34 |
| 5 | Madina Biktagirova, Russia | 2:32:41 |

**Best USA:** 12th—Emily Levan, Maine, 2:43:14

### WHEELCHAIR

| | | Time |
|---|---|---|
| 1 | Ernst Van Dyk, South Africa | 1:24:11 |
| 2 | Krige Schabort, South Africa | 1:30:03 |
| 3 | Franz Nietlispach, Switzerland | 1:30:34 |

### WHEELCHAIR

| | | Time |
|---|---|---|
| 1 | Cheri Blauwet, United States | 1:47:45 |
| 2 | Diane Roy, Canada | 1:50:53 |
| 3 | Sandra Graf, Switzerland | 1:51:46 |

## Other 2005 Winners

### Tokyo

| | | | |
|---|---|---|---|
| Feb. 13 | Men | Toshinari Takaoka, JPN | 2:07:41 |
| | (No women's division) | | |

### Paris

| | | | |
|---|---|---|---|
| Apr. 10 | Men | Salim Kipsang, KEN | 2:08:04 |
| | Women | Lydiya Grigoryeva, RUS | 2:27:03 |

### Los Angeles

| | | | |
|---|---|---|---|
| Mar. 6 | Men | Mark Saina, KEN | 2:09:35 |
| | Women | Lyubov Denisova, RUS | 2:26:11 |

### Rotterdam

| | | | |
|---|---|---|---|
| Apr. 10 | Men | Jimmy Muindi, KEN | 2:07:50 |
| | Women | Lornah Kiplagat, NED | 2:27:36 |

### Rome

| | | | |
|---|---|---|---|
| Mar. 13 | Men | Alberico Di Cecco, ITA | 2:08:02 |
| | Women | Silviya Skvortsova, RUS | 2:28:01 |

### London

| | | | |
|---|---|---|---|
| Apr. 17 | Men | Martin Lel, KEN | 2:07:26 |
| | Women | Paula Radcliffe, GBR | 2:17:42 |

## Late 2004

### Chicago

| | | | |
|---|---|---|---|
| Oct. 10 | Men | Evans Rutto, KEN | 2:06:16 |
| | Women | C. Tomescu-Dita, ROM | 2:23:45 |

### Tokyo Women's

| | | | |
|---|---|---|---|
| Nov. 21 | Women | Bruna Genovese, ITA | 2:26:34 |

### New York City

| | | | |
|---|---|---|---|
| Nov. 7 | Men | Hendrik Ramaala, RSA | 2:09:28 |
| | Women | Paula Radcliffe, GBR | 2:23:10 |

### Fukuoka

| | | | |
|---|---|---|---|
| Dec. 5 | Men | Tsuyoshi Ogata, JPN | 2:09:10 |
| | (No women's division) | | |

## Rowing
## 2005 World Championships
at Gifu, Japan (August 29-Sept. 4)

### MEN

| | |
|---|---|
| Eights | United States, 5:22.75 |
| Coxed Pairs | Australia, 7:16.61 |
| Coxed Fours | France, 6:02.42 |
| Coxless Pairs | New Zealand, 6:52.51 |
| Coxless Fours | Great Britain, 6:11.59 |
| Single Sculls | Mahe Drysdale, New Zealand, 7:16.42 |
| Double Sculls | Slovenia, 6:37.61 |
| Quad Sculls | Poland, 5:34.96 |

### WOMEN

| | |
|---|---|
| Eights | Australia, 5:58.10 |
| Coxless Pairs | New Zealand, 7:43.83 |
| Coxless Fours | Australia, 6:55.56 |
| Single Sculls | Ekaterina Karsten, Belarus, 7:48.35 |
| Double Sculls | New Zealand, 7:08.03 |
| Quad Sculls | Great Britain, 6:09.59 |

# 1882-2005
# Through the Years

SPORTS ALMANAC

---

## TRACK & FIELD

### IAAF World Championships

While the Summer Olympics have served as the unofficial world outdoor championships for track and field throughout the centuries, a separate World Championship meet was started in 1983 by the International Amateur Athletic Federation (IAAF). The meet was held every four years from 1983-91, but began an every-other-year cycle in 1993. World Championship sites include Helsinki (1983, 2005), Rome (1987), Tokyo (1991), Stuttgart (1993), Göteborg, Sweden (1995), Athens (1997), Seville, Spain (1999), Edmonton (2001) and Paris (2003). Looking forward, the Championships will be held in O'saka, Japan (2007) and Berlin (2009). Note that (WR) indicates world record and (CR) indicates championship meet record.

### MEN

**Multiple gold medals** (including relays): Michael Johnson (9); Carl Lewis (8); Sergey Bubka (6); Maurice Greene and Lars Riedel (5); Hicham El Guerrouj, Haile Gebrselassie, Allen Johnson, Ivan Pedroso, Antonio Pettigrew and Calvin Smith (4); Donovan Bailey, Tomas Dvorak, Greg Foster, John Godina, Werner Gunthor, Wilson Kipketer, Moses Kiptanui, Robert Korzeniowski, Dennis Mitchell, Noureddine Morceli, Dan O'Brien, Butch Reynolds and Jan Zelezny (3); Andrey Abduvaliyev, Virgilijus Alekena, Abel Anton, Kenenisa Bekele, Derrick Brew, Leroy Burrell, John Capel, Andre Cason, Stephane Diagana, Maurizio Damilano, Ladji Doucoure, Jon Drummond, Jonathan Edwards, Justin Gatlin, Jaouad Gharib, Colin Jackson, Ismael Kirui, Billy Konchellah, Sergey Litvinov, Tim Montgomery, Edwin Moses, Dwight Phillips, Mike Powell, Rashid Ramzi, Felix Sanchez, Saif Saaeed Shaheen, Javier Sotomayor, Angelo Taylor, Ivan Tikhon, Jeremy Wariner, Bernard Williams and Jerome Young (2).

#### 100 Meters

| Year | | Time | |
|---|---|---|---|
| 1983 | Carl Lewis, USA | 10.07 | |
| 1987 | Carl Lewis, USA | 9.93 | |
| 1991 | Carl Lewis, USA | 9.86 | **WR** |
| 1993 | Linford Christie, GBR | 9.87 | |
| 1995 | Donovan Bailey, CAN | 9.97 | |
| 1997 | Maurice Greene, USA | 9.86 | |
| 1999 | Maurice Greene, USA | 9.80 | **CR** |
| 2001 | Maurice Greene, USA | 9.82 | |
| 2003 | Kim Collins, SKN | 10.07 | |
| 2005 | Justin Gatlin, USA | 9.88 | |

**Note:** Ben Johnson was the original winner in 1987, but was stripped of his title and world record time (9.83) following his 1989 admission of drug taking.

#### 200 Meters

| Year | | Time | |
|---|---|---|---|
| 1983 | Calvin Smith, USA | 20.14 | |
| 1987 | Calvin Smith, USA | 20.16 | |
| 1991 | Michael Johnson, USA | 20.01 | |
| 1993 | Frank Fredericks, NAM | 19.85 | |
| 1995 | Michael Johnson, USA | 19.79 | **CR** |
| 1997 | Ato Boldon, USA | 20.04 | |
| 1999 | Maurice Greene, USA | 19.90 | |
| 2001 | Konstantinos Kenteris, GRE | 20.04 | |
| 2003 | John Capel, USA | 20.30 | |
| 2005 | Justin Gatlin, USA | 20.04 | |

#### 400 Meters

| Year | | Time | |
|---|---|---|---|
| 1983 | Bert Cameron, JAM | 45.05 | |
| 1987 | Thomas Schonlebe, E. Ger | 44.33 | |
| 1991 | Antonio Pettigrew, USA | 44.57 | |
| 1993 | Michael Johnson, USA | 43.65 | |
| 1995 | Michael Johnson, USA | 43.39 | |
| 1997 | Michael Johnson, USA | 44.12 | |
| 1999 | Michael Johnson, USA | 43.18 | **WR** |
| 2001 | Avard Moncur, BAH | 44.64 | |
| 2003 | Jerome Young, USA | 44.50 | |
| 2005 | Jeremy Wariner, USA | 43.93 | |

#### 800 Meters

| Year | | Time | |
|---|---|---|---|
| 1983 | Willi Wülbeck, W. Ger | 1:43.65 | |
| 1987 | Billy Konchellah, KEN | 1:43.06 | **CR** |
| 1991 | Billy Konchellah, KEN | 1:43.99 | |
| 1993 | Paul Ruto, KEN | 1:44.71 | |
| 1995 | Wilson Kipketer, DEN | 1:45.08 | |
| 1997 | Wilson Kipketer, DEN | 1:43.38 | |
| 1999 | Wilson Kipketer, DEN | 1:43.30 | |
| 2001 | Andre Bucher, SWI | 1:43.70 | |
| 2003 | Djabir Said-Guerni, ALG | 1:44.81 | |
| 2005 | Rashid Ramzi, BRN | 1:44.24 | |

#### 1500 Meters

| Year | | Time | |
|---|---|---|---|
| 1983 | Steve Cram, GBR | 3:41.59 | |
| 1987 | Abdi Bile, SOM | 3:36.80 | |
| 1991 | Noureddine Morceli, ALG | 3:32.84 | |
| 1993 | Noureddine Morceli, ALG | 3:34.24 | |
| 1995 | Noureddine Morceli, ALG | 3:33.73 | |
| 1997 | Hicham El Guerrouj, MOR | 3:35.83 | |
| 1999 | Hicham El Guerrouj, MOR | 3:27.65 | **CR** |
| 2001 | Hicham El Guerrouj, MOR | 3:30.68 | |
| 2003 | Hicham El Guerrouj, MOR | 3:31.77 | |
| 2005 | Rashid Ramzi, BRN | 3:37.88 | |

#### 5000 Meters

| Year | | Time | |
|---|---|---|---|
| 1983 | Eammon Coghlan, IRL | 13:28.53 | |
| 1987 | Said Aouita, MOR | 13:26.44 | |
| 1991 | Yobes Ondieki, KEN | 13:14.45 | |
| 1993 | Ismael Kirui, KEN | 13:02.75 | |
| 1995 | Ismael Kirui, KEN | 13:16.77 | |
| 1997 | Daniel Komen, KEN | 13:07.38 | |
| 1999 | Salah Hissou, MOR | 12:58.13 | |
| 2001 | Richard Limo, KEN | 13:00.77 | |
| 2003 | Eliud Kipchoge, KEN | 12:52.79 | **CR** |
| 2005 | Benjamin Limo, KEN | 13:32.55 | |

## 10,000 Meters

| Year | | Time | |
|------|------|------|------|
| 1983 | Alberto Cova, ITA | 28:01.04 | |
| 1987 | Paul Kipkoech, KEN | 27:38.63 | |
| 1991 | Moses Tanui, KEN | 27:38.74 | |
| 1993 | Haile Gebrselassie, ETH | 27:46.02 | |
| 1995 | Haile Gebrselassie, ETH | 27:12.95 | |
| 1997 | Haile Gebrselassie, ETH | 27:24.58 | |
| 1999 | Haile Gebrselassie, ETH | 27:57.27 | |
| 2001 | Charles Kamathi, KEN | 27:53.25 | |
| 2003 | Kenenisa Bekele, ETH. | 26:49.57 | CR |
| 2005 | Kenenisa Bekele, ETH. | 27:08.33 | |

## Marathon

| Year | | Time | |
|------|------|------|------|
| 1983 | Rob de Castella, AUS | 2:10:03 | |
| 1987 | Douglas Wakiihuri, KEN | 2:11:48 | |
| 1991 | Hiromi Taniguchi, JPN | 2:14:57 | |
| 1993 | Mark Plaatjes, USA | 2:13:57 | |
| 1995 | Martin Fiz, SPA | 2:11:41 | |
| 1997 | Abel Anton, SPA | 2:13:16 | |
| 1999 | Abel Anton, SPA | 2:13:36 | |
| 2001 | Gezahegne Abera, ETH | 2:12:42 | |
| 2003 | Jaouad Gharib, MOR | 2:08:31 | CR |
| 2005 | Jaouad Gharib, MOR | 2:10:10 | |

## 110-Meter Hurdles

| Year | | Time | |
|------|------|------|------|
| 1983 | Greg Foster, USA | 13.42 | |
| 1987 | Greg Foster, USA | 13.21 | |
| 1991 | Greg Foster, USA | 13.06 | |
| 1993 | Colin Jackson, GBR | 12.91 | WR |
| 1995 | Allen Johnson, USA | 13.00 | |
| 1997 | Allen Johnson, USA | 12.93 | |
| 1999 | Colin Jackson, GBR | 13.04 | |
| 2001 | Allen Johnson, USA | 13.04 | |
| 2003 | Allen Johnson, USA | 13.12 | |
| 2005 | Ladji Doucoure, FRA | 13.07 | |

## 400-Meter Hurdles

| Year | | Time | |
|------|------|------|------|
| 1983 | Edwin Moses, USA | 47.50 | |
| 1987 | Edwin Moses, USA | 47.46 | |
| 1991 | Samuel Matete, ZAM | 47.64 | |
| 1993 | Kevin Young, USA | 47.18 | CR |
| 1995 | Derrick Adkins, USA | 47.98 | |
| 1997 | Stephane Diagana, FRA | 47.70 | |
| 1999 | Fabrizio Mori, ITA | 47.72 | |
| 2001 | Felix Sanchez, DOM | 47.49 | |
| 2003 | Felix Sanchez, DOM | 47.25 | |
| 2005 | Bershawn Jackson, USA | 47.30 | |

## 3000-Meter Steeplechase

| Year | | Time | |
|------|------|------|------|
| 1983 | Patriz Ilg, W. Ger | 8:15.06 | |
| 1987 | Francesco Panetta, ITA | 8:08.57 | |
| 1991 | Moses Kiptanui, KEN | 8:12.59 | |
| 1993 | Moses Kiptanui, KEN | 8:06.36 | |
| 1995 | Moses Kiptanui, KEN | 8:04.16 | CR |
| 1997 | Wilson B. Kipketer, KEN | 8:05.84 | |
| 1999 | Christopher Koskei, KEN | 8:11.76 | |
| 2001 | Reuben Kosgei, KEN | 8:15.16 | |
| 2003 | Saif Saaeed Shaheen, QAT | 8:04.39 | |
| 2005 | Saif Saaeed Shaheen, QAT | 8:13.31 | |

## 4 x 100-Meter Relay

| Year | | Time | |
|------|------|------|------|
| 1983 | United States | 37.86 | WR |
| 1987 | United States | 37.90 | |
| 1991 | United States | 37.50 | WR |
| 1993 | United States | 37.48 | CR |
| 1995 | Canada | 38.31 | |
| 1997 | Canada | 37.86 | |
| 1999 | United States | 37.59 | |
| 2001 | United States | 37.96 | |
| 2003 | United States | 38.06 | |
| 2005 | France | 38.08 | |

## 4 x 400-Meter Relay

| Year | | Time | |
|------|------|------|------|
| 1983 | Soviet Union | 3:00.79 | |
| 1987 | United States | 2:57.29 | |
| 1991 | Great Britain | 2:57.53 | |
| 1993 | United States | 2:54.29 | WR |
| 1995 | United States | 2:57.32 | |
| 1997 | United States | 2:56.47 | |
| 1999 | United States | 2:56.45 | |
| 2001 | United States | 2:57.54 | |
| 2003 | France | 2:58.88* | |
| 2005 | United States | 2:56.91 | |

*The United States was stripped of its 2003 gold after lead runner Calvin Harrison's second doping violation. As a result, Tyree Washington, Derrick Brew and Jerome Young also lost their gold.

## 20-Kilometer Walk

| Year | | Time | |
|------|------|------|------|
| 1983 | Ernesto Canto, MEX | 1:20.49 | |
| 1987 | Maurizio Damilano, ITA | 1:20.45 | |
| 1991 | Maurizio Damilano, ITA | 1:19.37 | |
| 1993 | Valentin Massana, SPA | 1:22.31 | |
| 1995 | Michele Didoni, ITA | 1:19.59 | |
| 1997 | Daniel Garcia, MEX | 1:21:43 | |
| 1999 | Ilya Markov, RUS | 1:23:34 | |
| 2001 | Roman Rasskazov, RUS | 1:20:31 | |
| 2003 | Jefferson Perez, ECU | 1:17:21 | WR |
| 2005 | Jefferson Perez, ECU | 1:18:35 | |

## 50-Kilometer Walk

| Year | | Time | |
|------|------|------|------|
| 1983 | Ronald Weigel, E. Ger | 3:43:08 | |
| 1987 | Hartwig Gauder, E. Ger | 3:40:53 | |
| 1991 | Aleksandr Potashov, USSR | 3:53:09 | |
| 1993 | Jesus Angel Garcia, SPA | 3:41:41 | |
| 1995 | Valentin Kononen, FIN | 3:43:42 | |
| 1997 | Robert Korzeniowski, POL | 3:44:46 | |
| 1999 | Ivano Brugnetti, ITA | 3:47:54* | |
| 2001 | Robert Korzeniowski, POL | 3:42:08 | |
| 2003 | Robert Korzeniowski, POL | 3:36:03 | WR |
| 2005 | Sergey Kirdyapkin, RUS | 3:38:08 | |

* Original winner German Skurygin, RUS, was stripped of his 1999 title after testing positive for a banned substance.

## High Jump

| Year | | Height | |
|------|------|------|------|
| 1983 | Gennedy Avdeyenko, USSR | 7-7¼ | |
| 1987 | Patrik Sjoberg, SWE | 7-9¾ | |
| 1991 | Charles Austin, USA | 7-9¾ | |
| 1993 | Javier Sotomayor, CUB | 7-10½ | CR |
| 1995 | Troy Kemp, BAH | 7-9¼ | |
| 1997 | Javier Sotomayor, CUB | 7-9¼ | |
| 1999 | Vyacheslav Voronin, RUS | 7-9¼ | |
| 2001 | Martin Buss, GER | 7-8¾ | |
| 2003 | Jacques Freitag, RSA | 7-8½ | |
| 2005 | Yuriy Krymarenko, UKR | 7-7¼ | |

# Track & Field (Cont.)

## Pole Vault

| Year | | Height | |
|------|------|--------|---|
| 1983 | Sergey Bubka, USSR | 18- 8¼ | |
| 1987 | Sergey Bubka, USSR | 19- 2¼ | |
| 1991 | Sergey Bubka, USSR | 19- 6¼ | |
| 1993 | Sergey Bubka, UKR | 19- 8¼ | |
| 1995 | Sergey Bubka, UKR | 19- 5 | |
| 1997 | Sergey Bubka, UKR | 19- 8½ | |
| 1999 | Maksim Tarasov, RUS | 19- 9 | |
| 2001 | Dmitri Markov, AUS | 19-10¼ | **CR** |
| 2003 | Giuseppe Gibilisco, ITA | 19- 4¼ | |
| 2005 | Rens Blom, NED | 19- 0½ | |

## Long Jump

| Year | | Distance | |
|------|------|----------|---|
| 1983 | Carl Lewis, USA | 28- 0¾ | |
| 1987 | Carl Lewis, USA | 28- 0¼ | |
| 1991 | Mike Powell, USA | 29- 4½ | **WR** |
| 1993 | Mike Powell, USA | 28- 2¼ | |
| 1995 | Ivan Pedroso, CUB | 28- 6½ | |
| 1997 | Ivan Pedroso, CUB | 27- 7½ | |
| 1999 | Ivan Pedroso, CUB | 28- 1 | |
| 2001 | Ivan Pedroso, CUB | 27- 6¾ | |
| 2003 | Dwight Phillips, USA | 27- 3¾ | |
| 2005 | Dwight Phillips, USA | 28- 2¾ | |

## Triple Jump

| Year | | Distance | |
|------|------|----------|---|
| 1983 | Zdzislaw Hoffmann, POL | 57- 2 | |
| 1987 | Khristo Markov, BUL | 58- 9 | |
| 1991 | Kenny Harrison, USA | 58- 4 | |
| 1993 | Mike Conley, USA | 58- 7¼ | |
| 1995 | Jonathan Edwards, GBR | 60- 0¼ | **WR** |
| 1997 | Yoelvis Quesada, CUB | 58- 6¾ | |
| 1999 | Charles Michael Friedek, GER | 57- 8½ | |
| 2001 | Jonathan Edwards, GBR | 58- 9½ | |
| 2003 | Christian Olsson, SWE | 58- 1¾ | |
| 2005 | Walter Davis, USA | 57- 7¾ | |

## Shot Put

| Year | | Distance | |
|------|------|----------|---|
| 1983 | Edward Sarul, POL | 70- 2¼ | |
| 1987 | Werner Günthör, SWI | 72-11¼ | **CR** |
| 1991 | Werner Günthör, SWI | 71- 1¼ | |
| 1993 | Werner Günthör, SWI | 72- 1 | |
| 1995 | John Godina, USA | 70- 5¼ | |
| 1997 | John Godina, USA | 70- 4¼ | |
| 1999 | C.J. Hunter, USA | 71- 6 | |
| 2001 | John Godina, USA | 71- 9 | |
| 2003 | Andrei Mikhnevich, BLR | 71- 2 | |
| 2005 | Adam Nelson, USA | 71- 3½ | |

## Discus

| Year | | Distance | |
|------|------|----------|---|
| 1983 | Imrich Bugar, CZE | 222- 2 | |
| 1987 | Jurgen Schult, E. Ger | 225- 6 | |
| 1991 | Lars Riedel, GER | 217- 2 | |
| 1993 | Lars Riedel, GER | 222- 2 | |
| 1995 | Lars Riedel, GER | 225- 7 | |
| 1997 | Lars Riedel, GER | 224-10 | |
| 1999 | Anthony Washington, USA | 226- 7 | |
| 2001 | Lars Riedel, GER | 228- 9 | |
| 2003 | Virgilijus Alekna, LIT | 228- 7 | |
| 2005 | Virgilijus Alekna, LIT | 230- 2 | **CR** |

## Hammer Throw

| Year | | Distance | |
|------|------|----------|---|
| 1983 | Sergey Litvinov, USSR | 271- 3 | |
| 1987 | Sergey Litvinov, USSR | 272- 6 | |
| 1991 | Yuri Sedykh, USSR | 268- 0 | |
| 1993 | Andrey Abduvaliyev, TAJ | 267-10 | |
| 1995 | Andrey Abduvaliyev, TAJ | 267- 7 | |
| 1997 | Heinz Weis, GER | 268- 4 | |
| 1999 | Karsten Kobs, GER | 263- 3 | |
| 2001 | Szymon Ziolkowski, POL | 273- 7 | |
| 2003 | Ivan Tikhon, BLR | 272- 5 | |
| 2005 | Ivan Tikhon, BLR | 275- 2 | **CR** |

## Javelin

| Year | | Distance | |
|------|------|----------|---|
| 1983 | Detlef Michel, E. Ger | 293-7 | |
| 1987 | Seppo Raty, FIN | 274-1 | |
| 1991 | Kimmo Kinnunen, FIN | 297-11 | |
| 1993 | Jan Zelezny, CZR | 282-1 | |
| 1995 | Jan Zelezny, CZR | 293-11 | |
| 1997 | Marius Corbett, S. Afr. | 290-0 | |
| 1999 | Aki Parviainen, FIN | 293-8 | |
| 2001 | Jan Zelezny, CZR | 304- 5 | **CR** |
| 2003 | Sergey Makarov, RUS | 280- 3 | |
| 2005 | Andrus Varnik, EST | 286- 0 | |

## Decathlon

| Year | | Points | |
|------|------|--------|---|
| 1983 | Daley Thompson, GBR | 8714 | |
| 1987 | Torsten Voss, E. Ger | 8680 | |
| 1991 | Dan O'Brien, USA | 8812 | |
| 1993 | Dan O'Brien, USA | 8817 | |
| 1995 | Dan O'Brien, USA | 8695 | |
| 1997 | Tomas Dvorak, CZR | 8837 | |
| 1999 | Tomas Dvorak, CZR | 8744 | |
| 2001 | Tomas Dvorak, CZR | 8902 | **CR** |
| 2003 | Tom Pappas, USA | 8750 | |
| 2005 | Bryan Clay, USA | 8732 | |

## WOMEN

**Multiple gold medals** (including relays): Gail Devers (5), Jearl Miles Clark, Jackie Joyner-Kersee and Marion Jones (4); Tirunesh Dibaba, Tatyana Samolenko Dorovskikh, Silke Gladisch, Marita Koch, Astrid Kumbernuss, Maria Mutola, Merlene Ottey, Gabriela Szabo and Gwen Torrence (3); Me'Lisa Barber, Hassiba Boulmerka, Sabine Braun, Olga Bryzgina, Hestrie Cloete, Mary Decker, Franka Dietzsch, Stacy Dragila, Heike Daute Drechsler, Lyudmila Narozhilenko Enquist, Cathy Freeman, Chryste Gaines, Trine Hattestad, Martina Optiz Hellmann, Olimpiada Ivanova, Stefka Kostadinova, Katrin Krabbe, Jarmila Kratochvilova, Tatyana Lebedeva, Mirela Manjani, Fiona May, Osleidys Menendez, Inger Miller, Yipsi Moreno, Marie-José Pérec, Yuliya Pechonkina, Zhanna Pintusevich-Block, Ana Quirot, Tatyana Tomashova and Huang Zhihong (2).

## 100 Meters

| Year | | Time | |
|------|------|------|---|
| 1983 | Marlies Gohr, E. Ger | 10.97 | |
| 1987 | Silke Gladisch, E. Ger | 10.90 | |
| 1991 | Katrin Krabbe, GER | 10.99 | |
| 1993 | Gail Devers, USA | 10.81 | |
| 1995 | Gwen Torrence, USA | 10.85 | |
| 1997 | Marion Jones, USA | 10.83 | |
| 1999 | Marion Jones, USA | 10.70 | **CR** |
| 2001 | Zhanna Pintusevich-Block, UKR | 10.82 | |
| 2003 | Torri Edwards, USA | 10.93* | |
| 2005 | Lauryn Williams, USA | 10.93 | |

*Original winner Kelli White, USA, was stripped of her medal.

## 200 Meters

| Year | | Time | |
|------|------|------|---|
| 1983 | Marita Koch, E. Ger | 22.13 | |
| 1987 | Silke Gladisch, E. Ger | 21.74 | **CR** |
| 1991 | Katrin Krabbe, GER | 22.09 | |
| 1993 | Merlene Ottey, JAM | 21.98 | |
| 1995 | Merlene Ottey, JAM | 22.12 | |
| 1997 | Zhanna Pintusevich, UKR | 22.32 | |
| 1999 | Inger Miller, USA | 21.77 | |
| 2001 | Marion Jones, USA | 22.39 | |
| 2003 | Anastasiya Kapachinskaya, RUS | 22.38* | |
| 2005 | Allyson Felix, USA | 22.16 | |

*Original winner Kelli White, USA, was stripped of her medal.

## 400 Meters

| Year | | Time | |
|------|---|------|---|
| 1983 | Jarmila Kratochvilova, CZE | .47.99 | WR |
| 1987 | Olga Bryzgina, USSR | .49.38 | |
| 1991 | Marie-José Pérec, FRA | .49.13 | |
| 1993 | Jearl Miles, USA | .49.82 | |
| 1995 | Marie-José Pérec, FRA | .49.28 | |
| 1997 | Cathy Freeman, AUS | .49.77 | |
| 1999 | Cathy Freeman, AUS | .49.67 | |
| 2001 | Amy Mbacke Thiam, SEN | .49.86 | |
| 2003 | Ana Guevara, MEX | .48.89 | |
| 2005 | Tonique Williams-Darling, BAH | .49.55 | |

## 800 Meters

| Year | | Time | |
|------|---|------|---|
| 1983 | Jarmila Kratochvilova, CZE | 1:54.68 | CR |
| 1987 | Sigrun Wodars, E. Ger | 1:55.26 | |
| 1991 | Lilia Nurutdinova, USSR | 1:57.50 | |
| 1993 | Maria Mutola, MOZ | 1:55.43 | |
| 1995 | Ana Quirot, CUB | 1:56.11 | |
| 1997 | Ana Quirot, CUB | 1:57.14 | |
| 1999 | Ludmila Formanova, CZR | 1:56.68 | |
| 2001 | Maria Mutola, MOZ | 1:57.17 | |
| 2003 | Maria Mutola, MOZ | 1:59.89 | |
| 2005 | Zulia Calatayud, CUB | 1:58.82 | |

## 1500 Meters

| Year | | Time | |
|------|---|------|---|
| 1983 | Mary Decker, USA | 4:00.90 | |
| 1987 | Tatiana Samolenko, USSR | 3:58.56 | |
| 1991 | Hassiba Boulmerka, ALG | 4:02.21 | |
| 1993 | Liu Dong, CHN | 4:00.50 | |
| 1995 | Hassiba Boulmerka, ALG | 4:02.42 | |
| 1997 | Carla Sacramento, POR | 4:04.24 | |
| 1999 | Svetlana Masterkova, RUS | 3:59.53 | |
| 2001 | Gabriela Szabo, ROM | 4:00.57 | |
| 2003 | Tatyana Tomashova, RUS | 3:58.52 | CR |
| 2005 | Tatyana Tomashova, RUS | 4:00.35 | |

## 5000 Meters

Held as 3000-meter race from 1983-93

| Year | | Time | |
|------|---|------|---|
| 1983 | Mary Decker, USA | 8:34.62 | |
| 1987 | Tatyana Samolenko, USSR | 8:38.73 | |
| 1991 | T. Samolenko Dorovskikh, USSR | 8:35.82 | |
| 1993 | Qu Yunxia, CHN | 8:28.71 | |
| 1995 | Sonia O'Sullivan, IRL | 14:46.47 | |
| 1997 | Gabriela Szabo, ROM | 14:57.68 | |
| 1999 | Gabriela Szabo, ROM | 14:41.82 | |
| 2001 | Olga Yegorova, RUS | 15:03.39 | |
| 2003 | Tirunesh Dibaba, ETH | 14:51.72 | |
| 2005 | Tirunesh Dibaba, ETH | 14:38.59 | CR |

## 10,000 Meters

| Year | | Time | |
|------|---|------|---|
| 1983 | Not held | | |
| 1987 | Ingrid Kristiansen, NOR | 31:05.85 | |
| 1991 | Liz McColgan, GBR | 31:14.31 | |
| 1993 | Wang Junxia, CHN | 30:49.30 | |
| 1995 | Fernanda Ribeiro, POR | 31:04.99 | |
| 1997 | Sally Barsosio, KEN | 31:32.92 | |
| 1999 | Gete Wami, ETH | 30:24.56 | |
| 2001 | Derartu Tulu, ETH | 31:48.81 | |
| 2003 | Berhane Adere, ETH | 30:04.18 | CR |
| 2005 | Tirunesh Dibaba, ETH | 30:24.02 | |

## 3000-Meter Steeplechase

| Year | | Time |
|------|---|------|
| 2005 | Docus Inzikuru, UGA | 9:18.24 |

## Marathon

| Year | | Time | |
|------|---|------|---|
| 1983 | Grete Waitz, NOR | 2:28:09 | |
| 1987 | Rose Mota, POR | 2:25:17 | |
| 1991 | Wanda Panfil, POL | 2:29:53 | |
| 1993 | Junko Asari, JPN | 2:30:03 | |
| 1995 | Manuela Machado, POR | 2:25:39 | |
| 1997 | Hiromi Suzuki, JPN | 2:29:48 | |
| 1999 | Jong Song-Ok, N. Kor | 2:26:59 | |
| 2001 | Lidia Simon, ROM | 2:26:01 | |
| 2003 | Catherine Ndereba, KEN | 2:23:55 | |
| 2005 | Paula Radcliffe, GBR | 2:20:57 | CR |

## 100-Meter Hurdles

| Year | | Time | |
|------|---|------|---|
| 1983 | Bettine Jahn, E. Ger | 12.35W | |
| 1987 | Ginka Zagorcheva, BUL | 12.34 | CR |
| 1991 | Lyudmila Narozhilenko, USSR | 12.59 | |
| 1993 | Gail Devers, USA | 12.46 | |
| 1995 | Gail Devers, USA | 12.68 | |
| 1997 | Ludmila Enquist, SWE | 12.50 | |
| 1999 | Gail Devers, USA | 12.37 | |
| 2001 | Anjanette Kirkland, USA | 12.42 | |
| 2003 | Perdita Felicien, CAN | 12.53 | |
| 2005 | Michelle Perry, USA | 12.66 | |

W indicates wind-aided.

## 400-Meter Hurdles

| Year | | Time | |
|------|---|------|---|
| 1983 | Yekaterina Fesenko, USSR | .54.14 | |
| 1987 | Sabine Busch, E. Ger | .53.62 | |
| 1991 | Tatiana Ledovskaya, USSR | .53.11 | |
| 1993 | Sally Gunnell, GBR | .52.74 | WR |
| 1995 | Kim Batten, USA | .52.61 | WR |
| 1997 | Nezha Bidouane, MOR | .52.97 | |
| 1999 | Daima Pernia, CUB | .52.89 | |
| 2001 | Nezha Bidouane, MOR | .53.34 | |
| 2003 | Jana Pittman, AUS | .53.22 | |
| 2005 | Yuliya Pechonkina, RUS | .52.90 | |

## 4 x 100-Meter Relay

| Year | | Time | |
|------|---|------|---|
| 1983 | East Germany | .41.76 | |
| 1987 | United States | .41.58 | |
| 1991 | Jamaica | .41.94 | |
| 1993 | Russia | .41.49 | |
| 1995 | United States | .42.12 | |
| 1997 | United States | .41.47 | CR |
| 1999 | Bahamas | .41.92 | |
| 2001 | Germany | .42.32* | |
| 2003 | France | .41.78 | |
| 2005 | United States | .41.78 | |

*The United States was stripped of its 2001 gold after lead runner Kelli White tested positive for a stimulant. As a result, Chryste Gaines, Inger Miller and Marion Jones also lost their gold.

## 4 x 400-Meter Relay

| Year | | Time | |
|------|---|------|---|
| 1983 | East Germany | 3:19.73 | |
| 1987 | East Germany | 3:18.63 | |
| 1991 | Soviet Union | 3:18.43 | |
| 1993 | United States | 3:16.71 | CR |
| 1995 | United States | 3:22.39 | |
| 1997 | Germany | 3:20.92 | |
| 1999 | Russia | 3:21.98 | |
| 2001 | Jamaica | 3:20.65 | |
| 2003 | United States | 3:22.63 | |
| 2005 | Russia | 3:20.95 | |

## Track & Field (Cont.)

### 20-Kilometer Walk

Held as 10-Kilometer race from 1987-97

| Year | | Time |
|------|------|------|
| 1983 | Not held | |
| 1987 | Irina Strakhova, USSR | .44:12 |
| 1991 | Alina Ivanova, USSR | .42:57 |
| 1993 | Sari Essayah, FIN | .42:59 |
| 1995 | Irina Stankina, RUS | .42:13 |
| 1997 | Anna Sidoti, ITA | .42:55 |
| 1999 | Hongyu Liu, CHN | 1:30:50 |
| 2001 | Olimpiada Ivanova, RUS | 1:27:48 |
| 2003 | Yelena Nikolayeva, RUS | 1:26:52 |
| 2005 | Olimpiada Ivanova, RUS | 1:25:41 **WR** |

### High Jump

| Year | | Height |
|------|------|------|
| 1983 | Tamara Bykova, USSR | .6- 7 |
| 1987 | Stefka Kostadinova, BUL | .6-10¼ **WR** |
| 1991 | Heike Henkel, GER | .6- 8¾ |
| 1993 | Ioamnet Quintero, CUB | .6- 6¼ |
| 1995 | Stefka Kostadinova, BUL | .6- 7 |
| 1997 | Hanne Haugland, NOR | .6- 6¼ |
| 1999 | Inga Babakova, UKR | .6- 6¼ |
| 2001 | Hestrie Cloete, RSA | .6- 6¾ |
| 2003 | Hestrie Cloete, RSA | .6- 9 |
| 2005 | Kajsa Bergqvist, SWE | .6- 7½ |

### Pole Vault

| Year | | Height |
|------|------|------|
| 1999 | Stacy Dragila, USA | .15- 1 |
| 2001 | Stacy Dragila, USA | .15- 7 |
| 2003 | Svetlana Feofanova, RUS | .15- 7 |
| 2005 | Yelena Isinbayeva, RUS | .16-5¼ **WR** |

### Long Jump

| Year | | Distance |
|------|------|------|
| 1983 | Heike Daute, E. Ger | .23-10¼W |
| 1987 | Jackie Joyner-Kersee, USA | .24- 1¾ **CR** |
| 1991 | Jackie Joyner-Kersee, USA | .24- 0¼ |
| 1993 | Heike Drechsler, GER | .23- 4 |
| 1995 | Fiona May, ITA | .22-10¾W |
| 1997 | Lyudmila Galkina, RUS | .23- 1¾ |
| 1999 | Niurka Montalvo, SPA | .23- 2 |
| 2001 | Fiona May, ITA | .23- 0½ |
| 2003 | Eunice Barber, FRA | .22-11¼ |
| 2005 | Tianna Madison, USA | .22- 7¼ |

W indicates wind-aided.

### Triple Jump

| Year | | Distance |
|------|------|------|
| 1993 | Ana Biryukova, RUS | .46- 6¼ |
| 1995 | Inessa Kravets, UKR | .50- 10¾ **WR** |
| 1997 | Sarka Kasparkova, CZR | .49- 10½ |
| 1999 | Paraskevi Tsiamita, GRE | .48- 10 |
| 2001 | Tatyana Lebedeva, RUS | .50- 0½ |
| 2003 | Tatyana Lebedeva, RUS | .49- 9¾ |
| 2005 | Trecia Smith, JAM | .49- 7 |

### Shot Put

| Year | | Distance | |
|------|------|------|------|
| 1983 | Helena Fibingerova, CZE | .69- 0 | |
| 1987 | Natalia Lisovskaya, USSR | .69- 8 | **CR** |
| 1991 | Huang Zhihong, CHN | .68- 4 | |
| 1993 | Huang Zhihong, CHN | .67- 6 | |
| 1995 | Astrid Kumbernuss, GER | .69- 7½ | |
| 1997 | Astrid Kumbernuss, GER | .67- 11½ | |
| 1999 | Astrid Kumbernuss, GER | .65- 1½ | |
| 2001 | Yanina Korolchik, BLR | .67- 7½ | |
| 2003 | Svetlana Krivelyova, RUS | .67- 8¼ | |
| 2005 | Nadezhda Ostapchuk, BLR | .67- 3½ | |

### Discus

| Year | | Distance | |
|------|------|------|------|
| 1983 | Martina Opitz, E. Ger | .226- 2 | |
| 1987 | Martina Opitz Hellmann, E. Ger | .235- 0 | **CR** |
| 1991 | Tsvetanka Khristova, BUL | .233- 0 | |
| 1993 | Olga Burova, RUS | .221- 1 | |
| 1995 | Ellina Zvereva, BLR | .225- 2 | |
| 1997 | Beatrice Faumuina, NZE | .219- 3 | |
| 1999 | Franka Dietzsch, GER | .223- 6 | |
| 2001 | Natalya Sadova, RUS | .224-11 | |
| 2003 | Irina Yatchenko, BLR | .220-10 | |
| 2005 | Franka Dietzsch, GER | .218- 4 | |

### Hammer Throw

| Year | | Distance | |
|------|------|------|------|
| 1999 | Mihaela Melinte, ROM | .246-8¾ | **CR** |
| 2001 | Yipsi Moreno, CUB | .231- 9 | |
| 2003 | Yipsi Moreno, CUB | .240- 7 | |
| 2005 | Olga Kuzenkova, RUS | .246- 5 | |

### Javelin

| Year | | Distance | |
|------|------|------|------|
| 1983 | Tiina Lillak, FIN | .232- 4 | |
| 1987 | Fatima Whitbread, GBR | .251- 5 | **CR** |
| 1991 | Xu Demei, CHN | .225- 8 | |
| 1993 | Trine Hattestad, NOR | .227- 0 | |
| 1995 | Natalya Shikolenko, BLR | .221- 8 | |
| 1997 | Trine Hattestad, NOR | .225- 8 | |
| 1999 | Mirela Manjani-Tzelili, GRE | .220- 1 | |
| 2001 | Osleidys Menendez, CUB | .228- 1 | |
| 2003 | Mirela Manjani, GRE | .218- 3 | |
| 2005 | Osleidys Menendez, CUB | .235- 3 | **WR** |

### Heptathlon

| Year | | Points | |
|------|------|------|------|
| 1983 | Ramona Neubert, E. Ger | 6770 | |
| 1987 | Jackie Joyner-Kersee, USA | 7128 | **CR** |
| 1991 | Sabine Braun, GER | 6672 | |
| 1993 | Jackie Joyner-Kersee, USA | 6837 | |
| 1995 | Ghada Shouaa, SYR | 6651 | |
| 1997 | Sabine Braun, GER | 6739 | |
| 1999 | Eunice Barber, FRA | 6861 | |
| 2001 | Yelena Prokhorova, RUS | 6694 | |
| 2003 | Carolina Kluft, SWE | 7001 | |
| 2005 | Carolina Kluft, SWE | 6887 | |

## World Cross Country Championships

### MEN

**Multiple winners**: John Ngugi and Paul Tergat (5); Kenenisa Bekele (4); Carlos Lopes (3); Mohammed Mourhit, Khalid Skah, William Sigei, John Treacy and Craig Virgin (2).

| Year | | Year | | Year | |
|------|------|------|------|------|------|
| 1973 | Pekka Paivarinta, Finland | 1980 | Craig Virgin, USA | 1987 | John Ngugi, Kenya |
| 1974 | Eric DeBeck, Belgium | 1981 | Craig Virgin, USA | 1988 | John Ngugi, Kenya |
| 1975 | Ian Stewart, Scotland | 1982 | Mohammed Kedir, Ethiopia | 1989 | John Ngugi, Kenya |
| 1976 | Carlos Lopes, Portugal | 1983 | Bekele Debele, Ethiopia | 1990 | Khalid Skah, Morocco |
| 1977 | Leon Schots, Belgium | 1984 | Carlos Lopes, Portugal | 1991 | Khalid Skah, Morocco |
| 1978 | John Treacy, Ireland | 1985 | Carlos Lopes, Portugal | 1992 | John Ngugi, Kenya |
| 1979 | John Treacy, Ireland | 1986 | John Ngugi, Kenya | 1993 | William Sigei, Kenya |

| Year | | Year | | Year | |
|---|---|---|---|---|---|
| 1994 | William Sigei, Kenya | 1998 | Paul Tergat, Kenya | 2002 | Kenenisa Bekele, Ethiopia |
| 1995 | Paul Tergat, Kenya | 1999 | Paul Tergat, Kenya | 2003 | Kenenisa Bekele, Ethiopia |
| 1996 | Paul Tergat, Kenya | 2000 | Mohammed Mourhit, Belgium | 2004 | Kenenisa Bekele, Ethiopia |
| 1997 | Paul Tergat, Kenya | 2001 | Mohammed Mourhit, Belgium | 2005 | Kenenisa Bekele, Ethiopia |

## WOMEN

**Multiple winners**: Grete Waitz (5); Lynn Jennings and Derartu Tulu (3); Zola Budd, Paola Cacchi, Maricica Puica, Paula Radcliffe, Annette Sergent, Carmen Valero and Gete Wami (2).

| Year | | Year | | Year | |
|---|---|---|---|---|---|
| 1973 | Paola Cacchi, Italy | 1984 | Maricica Puica, Romania | 1995 | Derartu Tulu, Ethiopia |
| 1974 | Paola Cacchi, Italy | 1985 | Zola Budd, England | 1996 | Gete Wami, Ethiopia |
| 1975 | Julie Brown, USA | 1986 | Zola Budd, England | 1997 | Derartu Tulu, Ethiopia |
| 1976 | Carmen Valero, Spain | 1987 | Annette Sergent, France | 1998 | Sonia O'Sullivan, Ireland |
| 1977 | Carmen Valero, Spain | 1988 | Ingrid Kristiansen, Norway | 1999 | Gete Wami, Ethiopia |
| 1978 | Grete Waitz, Norway | 1989 | Annette Sergent, France | 2000 | Derartu Tulu, Ethiopia |
| 1979 | Grete Waitz, Norway | 1990 | Lynn Jennings, USA | 2001 | Paula Radcliffe, Gr. Britain |
| 1980 | Grete Waitz, Norway | 1991 | Lynn Jennings, USA | 2002 | Paula Radcliffe, Gr. Britain |
| 1981 | Grete Waitz, Norway | 1992 | Lynn Jennings, USA | 2003 | Werknesh Kidane, Ethiopia |
| 1982 | Maricica Puica, Romania | 1993 | Albertina Dias, Portugal | 2004 | Benita Johnson, Australia |
| 1983 | Grete Waitz, Norway | 1994 | Helen Chepngeno, Kenya | 2005 | Tirunesh Dibaba, Ethiopia |

## Marathons
### Boston

America's oldest regularly contested foot race, the Boston Marathon is held on Patriots' Day every April. It has been run at four different distances: 24 miles, 1232 yards (1897-1923); 26 miles, 209 yards (1924-26); 26 miles, 385 yards (1927-52, since 1957); 25 miles, 958 yards (1953-56).

### MEN

**Multiple winners:** Clarence DeMar (7); Gerard Cote and Bill Rodgers (4); Ibrahim Hussein, Cosmas Ndeti, Eino Oksanen and Leslie Pawson (3); Tarzan Brown, Jim Caffrey, John A. Kelley, John Miles, Toshihiko Seko, Geoff Smith, Moses Tanui and Aurele Vandendriessche (2).

| Year | | Time | Year | | Time |
|---|---|---|---|---|---|
| 1897 | John McDermott, New York | 2:55:10 | 1934 | Dave Komonen, Canada | 2:32:53 |
| 1898 | Ronald McDonald, Massachusetts | 2:42:00 | 1935 | John A. Kelley, Massachusetts | 2:32:07 |
| 1899 | Lawrence Brignolia, Massachusetts | 2:54:38 | 1936 | Ellison (Tarzan) Brown, Rhode Island | 2:33:40 |
| | | | 1937 | Walter Young, Canada | 2:33:20 |
| 1900 | Jim Caffrey, Canada | 2:39:44 | 1938 | Leslie Pawson, Rhode Island | 2:35:34 |
| 1901 | Jim Caffrey, Canada | 2:29:23 | 1939 | Ellison (Tarzan) Brown, Rhode Island | 2:28:51 |
| 1902 | Sam Mellor, New York | 2:43:12 | | | |
| 1903 | J.C. Lorden, Massachusetts | 2:41:29 | 1940 | Gerard Cote, Canada | 2:28:28 |
| 1904 | Mike Spring, New York | 2:38:04 | 1941 | Leslie Pawson, Rhode Island | 2:30:38 |
| 1905 | Fred Lorz, New York | 2:38:25 | 1942 | Joe Smith, Massachusetts | 2:26:51 |
| 1906 | Tim Ford, Massachusetts | 2:45:45 | 1943 | Gerard Cote, Canada | 2:28:25 |
| 1907 | Tom Longboat, Canada | 2:24:24 | 1944 | Gerard Cote, Canada | 2:31:50 |
| 1908 | Tom Morrissey, New York | 2:25:43 | 1945 | John A. Kelley, Massachusetts | 2:30:40 |
| 1909 | Henri Renaud, New Hampshire | 2:53:36 | 1946 | Stylianos Kyriakides, Greece | 2:29:27 |
| | | | 1947 | Yun Bok Suh, Korea | 2:25:39 |
| 1910 | Fred Cameron, Nova Scotia | 2:28:52 | 1948 | Gerard Cote, Canada | 2:31:02 |
| 1911 | Clarence DeMar, Massachusetts | 2:21:39 | 1949 | Karle Leandersson, Sweden | 2:31:50 |
| 1912 | Mike Ryan, Illinois | 2:21:18 | | | |
| 1913 | Fritz Carlson, Minnesota | 2:25:14 | 1950 | Kee Yonh Ham, Korea | 2:32:39 |
| 1914 | James Duffy, Canada | 2:25:01 | 1951 | Shigeki Tanaka, Japan | 2:27:45 |
| 1915 | Edouard Fabre, Canada | 2:31:41 | 1952 | Doroteo Flores, Guatemala | 2:31:53 |
| 1916 | Arthur Roth, Massachusetts | 2:27:16 | 1953 | Keizo Yamada, Japan | 2:18:51 |
| 1917 | Bill Kennedy, New York | 2:28:37 | 1954 | Veiko Karvonen, Finland | 2:20:39 |
| 1918 | World War relay race | | 1955 | Hideo Hamamura, Japan | 2:18:22 |
| 1919 | Carl Linder, Massachusetts | 2:29:13 | 1956 | Antti Viskari, Finland | 2:14:14 |
| | | | 1957 | John J. Kelley, Connecticut | 2:20:05 |
| 1920 | Peter Trivoulidas, New York | 2:29:31 | 1958 | Franjo Mihalic, Yugoslavia | 2:25:54 |
| 1921 | Frank Zuna, New Jersey | 2:18:57 | 1959 | Eino Oksanen, Finland | 2:22:42 |
| 1922 | Clarence DeMar, Massachusetts | 2:18:10 | | | |
| 1923 | Clarence DeMar, Massachusetts | 2:23:37 | 1960 | Paavo Kotila, Finland | 2:20:54 |
| 1924 | Clarence DeMar, Massachusetts | 2:29:40 | 1961 | Eino Oksanen, Finland | 2:23:39 |
| 1925 | Charles Mellor, Illinois | 2:33:00 | 1962 | Eino Oksanen, Finland | 2:23:48 |
| 1926 | John Miles, Nova Scotia | 2:25:40 | 1963 | Aurele Vandendriessche, Belgium | 2:18:58 |
| 1927 | Clarence DeMar, Massachusetts | 2:40:22 | 1964 | Aurele Vandendriessche, Belgium | 2:19:59 |
| 1928 | Clarence DeMar, Massachusetts | 2:37:07 | 1965 | Morio Shigematsu, Japan | 2:16:33 |
| 1929 | John Miles, Nova Scotia | 2:33:08 | 1966 | Kenji Kimihara, Japan | 2:17:11 |
| | | | 1967 | David McKenzie, New Zealand | 2:15:45 |
| 1930 | Clarence DeMar, Massachusetts | 2:34:48 | 1968 | Amby Burfoot, Connecticut | 2:22:17 |
| 1931 | James Henigan, Massachusetts | 2:46:45 | 1969 | Yoshiaki Unetani, Japan | 2:13:49 |
| 1932 | Paul deBruyn, Germany | 2:33:36 | | | |
| 1933 | Leslie Pawson, Rhode Island | 2:31:01 | 1970 | Ron Hill, England | 2:10:30 |

## Boston Marathon (Cont.)

| Year | Time | Year | Time |
|---|---|---|---|
| 1971 Alvaro Mejia, Colombia | 2:18:45 | 1990 Gelindo Bordin, Italy | 2:08:19 |
| 1972 Olavi Suomalainen, Finland | 2:15:39 | 1991 Ibrahim Hussein, Kenya | 2:11:06 |
| 1973 Jon Anderson, Oregon | 2:16:03 | 1992 Ibrahim Hussein, Kenya | 2:08:14 |
| 1974 Neil Cusack, Ireland | 2:13:39 | 1993 Cosmas Ndeti, Kenya | 2:09:33 |
| 1975 Bill Rodgers, Massachusetts | 2:09:55 | 1994 Cosmas Ndeti, Kenya | 2:07:15* |
| 1976 Jack Fultz, Pennsylvania | 2:20:19 | 1995 Cosmas Ndeti, Kenya | 2:09:22 |
| 1977 Jerome Drayton, Canada | 2:14:46 | 1996 Moses Tanui, Kenya | 2:09:16 |
| 1978 Bill Rodgers, Massachusetts | 2:10:13 | 1997 Lameck Aguta, Kenya | 2:10:34 |
| 1979 Bill Rodgers, Massachusetts | 2:09:27 | 1998 Moses Tanui, Kenya | 2:07:34 |
| | | 1999 Joseph Chebet, Kenya | 2:09:52 |
| 1980 Bill Rodgers, Massachusetts | 2:12:11 | | |
| 1981 Toshihiko Seko, Japan | 2:09:26 | 2000 Elijah Lagat, Kenya | 2:09:47 |
| 1982 Alberto Salazar, Oregon | 2:08:52 | 2001 Lee Bong-Ju, South Korea | 2:09:43 |
| 1983 Greg Meyer, New Jersey | 2:09:00 | 2002 Rodgers Rop, Kenya | 2:09:02 |
| 1984 Geoff Smith, England | 2:10:34 | 2003 Robert Kipoech Cheruiyot, Kenya | 2:10:11 |
| 1985 Geoff Smith, England | 2:14:05 | 2004 Timothy Cherigat, Kenya | 2:10:37 |
| 1986 Rob de Castella, Australia | 2:07:51 | 2005 Hailu Negussie, Ethiopia | 2:11:45 |
| 1987 Toshihiko Seko, Japan | 2:11:50 | *Course record. | |
| 1988 Ibrahim Hussein, Kenya | 2:08:43 | | |
| 1989 Abebe Mekonnen, Ethiopia | 2:09:06 | | |

### WOMEN

**Multiple winners:** Catherine Ndereba (4); Rosa Mota, Uta Pippig and Fatuma Roba (3); Joan Benoit, Miki Gorman, Ingrid Kristiansen and Olga Markova (2).

| Year | Time | Year | Time |
|---|---|---|---|
| 1972 Nina Kuscsik, New York | 3:08:58 | 1990 Rosa Mota, Portugal | 2:25:23 |
| 1973 Jacqueline Hansen, California | 3:05:59 | 1991 Wanda Panfil, Poland | 2:24:18 |
| 1974 Miki Gorman, California | 2:47:11 | 1992 Olga Markova, CIS | 2:23:43 |
| 1975 Liane Winter, West Germany | 2:42:24 | 1993 Olga Markova, Russia | 2:25:27 |
| 1976 Kim Merritt, Wisconsin | 2:47:10 | 1994 Uta Pippig, Germany | 2:21:45 |
| 1977 Miki Gorman, California | 2:48:33 | 1995 Uta Pippig, Germany | 2:25:11 |
| 1978 Gayle Barron, Georgia | 2:44:52 | 1996 Uta Pippig, Germany | 2:27:12 |
| 1979 Joan Benoit, Maine | 2:35:15 | 1997 Fatuma Roba, Ethiopia | 2:26:23 |
| | | 1998 Fatuma Roba, Ethiopia | 2:23:21 |
| 1980 Jacqueline Gareau, Canada | 2:34:28 | 1999 Fatuma Roba, Ethiopia | 2:23:25 |
| 1981 Allison Roe, New Zealand | 2:26:46 | | |
| 1982 Charlotte Teske, West Germany | 2:29:33 | 2000 Catherine Ndereba, Kenya | 2:26:11 |
| 1983 Joan Benoit, Maine | 2:22:43 | 2001 Catherine Ndereba, Kenya | 2:23:53 |
| 1984 Lorraine Moller, New Zealand | 2:29:28 | 2002 Margaret Okayo, Kenya | 2:20:43* |
| 1985 Lisa Larsen Weidenbach, Mass | 2:34:06 | 2003 Svetlana Zakharova, Russia | 2:25:20 |
| 1986 Ingrid Kristiansen, Norway | 2:24:55 | 2004 Catherine Ndereba, Kenya | 2:24:27 |
| 1987 Rosa Mota, Portugal | 2:25:21 | 2005 Catherine Ndereba, Kenya | 2:25:13 |
| 1988 Rosa Mota, Portugal | 2:24:30 | *Course record. | |
| 1989 Ingrid Kristiansen, Norway | 2:24:33 | | |

## New York City

Started in 1970, the New York City Marathon is run in the fall, usually on the first Sunday in November. The route winds through all of the city's five boroughs and finishes in Central Park.

### MEN

**Multiple winners:** Bill Rodgers (4); Alberto Salazar (3); Tom Fleming, John Kagwe, Orlando Pizzolato and German Silva (2).

| Year | Time | Year | Time | Year | Time |
|---|---|---|---|---|---|
| 1970 Gary Muhrcke, USA | 2:31:38 | 1983 Rod Dixon, NZE | 2:08:59 | 1996 Giacomo Leone, ITA | 2:09:54 |
| 1971 Norman Higgins, USA | 2:22:54 | 1984 Orlando Pizzolato, ITA | 2:14:53 | 1997 John Kagwe, KEN | 2:08:12 |
| 1972 Sheldon Karlin, USA | 2:27:52 | 1985 Orlando Pizzolato, ITA | 2:11:34 | 1998 John Kagwe, KEN | 2:08:45 |
| 1973 Tom Fleming, USA | 2:21:54 | 1986 Gianni Poli, ITA | 2:11:06 | 1999 Joseph Chebet, KEN | 2:09:14 |
| 1974 Norbert Sander, USA | 2:26:30 | 1987 Ibrahim Hussein, KEN | 2:11:01 | | |
| 1975 Tom Fleming, USA | 2:19:27 | 1988 Steve Jones, WAL | 2:08:20 | 2000 Abdelkhader El Mouaziz, MOR | 2:10:08 |
| 1976 Bill Rodgers, USA | 2:10:09 | 1989 Juma Ikangaa, TAN | 2:08:01 | 2001 Tesfaye Jifar, ETH | 2:07:43* |
| 1977 Bill Rodgers, USA | 2:11:28 | | | 2002 Rodgers Rop, KEN | 2:08:07 |
| 1978 Bill Rodgers, USA | 2:12:12 | 1990 Douglas Wakiihuri, KEN | 2:12:39 | 2003 Martin Lel, KEN | 2:10:30 |
| 1979 Bill Rodgers, USA | 2:11:42 | 1991 Salvador Garcia, MEX | 2:09:28 | 2004 Hendrik Ramaala, RSA | 2:09:28 |
| | | 1992 Willie Mtolo, S. Afr. | 2:09:29 | | |
| 1980 Alberto Salazar, USA | 2:09:41 | 1993 Andres Espinosa, MEX | 2:10:04 | *Course record. | |
| 1981 Alberto Salazar, USA | 2:08:13 | 1994 German Silva, MEX | 2:11:21 | | |
| 1982 Alberto Salazar, USA | 2:09:29 | 1995 German Silva, MEX | 2:11:00 | | |

## WOMEN

**Multiple winners:** Grete Waitz (9); Miki Gorman, Nina Kuscsik, Margaret Okayo and Tegla Loroupe (2).

| Year | Time | Year | Time | Year | Time |
|---|---|---|---|---|---|
| 1970 No Finisher | | 1982 Grete Waitz, NOR | 2:27:14 | 1994 Tegla Loroupe, KEN | 2:27:37 |
| 1971 Beth Bonner, USA | 2:55:22 | 1983 Grete Waitz, NOR | 2:27:00 | 1995 Tegla Loroupe, KEN | 2:28:06 |
| 1972 Nina Kuscsik, USA | 3:08:41 | 1984 Grete Waitz, NOR | 2:29:30 | 1996 Anuta Catuna, ROM | 2:28:18 |
| 1973 Nina Kuscsik, USA | 2:57:07 | 1985 Grete Waitz, NOR | 2:28:34 | 1997 F. Rochat-Moser, SWI | 2:28:43 |
| 1974 Katherine Switzer, USA | 3:07:29 | 1986 Grete Waitz, NOR | 2:28:06 | 1998 Franca Fiacconi, ITA | 2:25:17 |
| 1975 Kim Merritt, USA | 2:46:14 | 1987 Priscilla Welch, GBR | 2:30:17 | 1999 Adriana Fernandez, MEX | 2:25:06 |
| 1976 Miki Gorman, USA | 2:39:11 | 1988 Grete Waitz, NOR | 2:28:07 | 2000 Ludmila Petrova, RUS | 2:25:45 |
| 1977 Miki Gorman, USA | 2:43:10 | 1989 Ingrid Kristiansen, NOR | 2:25:30 | 2001 Margaret Okayo, KEN | 2:24:21 |
| 1978 Grete Waitz, NOR | 2:32:30 | 1990 Wanda Panfil, POL | 2:30:45 | 2002 Joyce Chepchumba, KEN | 2:25:56 |
| 1979 Grete Waitz, NOR | 2:27:33 | 1991 Liz McColgan, GBR | 2:27:23 | 2003 Margaret Okayo, KEN | 2:22:31* |
| 1980 Grete Waitz, NOR | 2:25:41 | 1992 Lisa Ondieki, AUS | 2:24:40 | 2004 Paula Radcliffe, GBR | 2:23:10 |
| 1981 Allison Roe, NZE | 2:25:29 | 1993 Uta Pippig, GER | 2:26:24 | *Course record. | |

# Annual Awards

## Track & Field News Athletes of the Year

Voted on by an international panel of track and field experts and presented since 1959 for men and 1974 for women.

### MEN

**Multiple winners:** Hicham El Guerrouj and Carl Lewis (3); Sergey Bubka, Sebastian Coe, Haile Gebrselassie, Michael Johnson, Alberto Juantorena, Noureddine Morceli, Jim Ryun and Peter Snell (2).

| Year | Event | Year | Event |
|---|---|---|---|
| 1959 Martin Lauer, W. Germany | 110H/Decathlon | 1982 Carl Lewis, USA | 100/200/Long Jump |
| 1960 Rafer Johnson, USA | Decathlon | 1983 Carl Lewis, USA | 100/200/Long Jump |
| 1961 Ralph Boston, USA | Long Jump/110 Hurdles | 1984 Carl Lewis, USA | 100/200/Long Jump |
| 1962 Peter Snell, New Zealand | 800/1500 | 1985 Said Aouita, Morocco | 1500/5000 |
| 1963 C.K. Yang, Taiwan | Decathlon/Pole Vault | 1986 Yuri Sedykh, USSR | Hammer Throw |
| 1964 Peter Snell, New Zealand | 800/1500 | 1987 Ben Johnson, Canada | 100 |
| 1965 Ron Clarke, Australia | 5000/10,000 | 1988 Sergey Bubka, USSR | Pole Vault |
| 1966 Jim Ryun, USA | 800/1500 | 1989 Roger Kingdom, USA | 110 Hurdles |
| 1967 Jim Ryun, USA | 1500 | 1990 Michael Johnson, USA | 200/400 |
| 1968 Bob Beamon, USA | Long Jump | 1991 Sergey Bubka, USSR | Pole Vault |
| 1969 Bill Toomey, USA | Decathlon | 1992 Kevin Young, USA | 400 Hurdles |
| 1970 Randy Matson, USA | Shot Put | 1993 Noureddine Morceli, Algeria | Mile/1500/3000 |
| 1971 Rod Milburn, USA | 110 Hurdles | 1994 Noureddine Morceli, Algeria | Mile/1500/3000 |
| 1972 Lasse Viren, Finland | 5000/10,000 | 1995 Haile Gebrselassie, Ethiopia | 5000/10,000 |
| 1973 Ben Jipcho, Kenya | 1500/5000/Steeplechase | 1996 Michael Johnson, USA | 200/400 |
| 1974 Rick Wohlhuter, USA | 800/1500 | 1997 Wilson Kipketer, Denmark | 800 |
| 1975 John Walker, New Zealand | 800/1500 | 1998 Haile Gebrselassie, Ethiopia | 3000/5000/10,000 |
| 1976 Alberto Juantorena, Cuba | 400/800 | 1999 Hicham El Guerrouj, Morocco | Mile/1500 |
| 1977 Alberto Juantorena, Cuba | 400/800 | 2000 Virgilijus Alekna, Lithuania | Discus |
| 1978 Henry Rono, Kenya | 5000/10,000/Steeplechase | 2001 Hicham El Guerrouj, Morocco | Mile/1500 |
| 1979 Sebastian Coe, Great Britain | 800/1500 | 2002 Hicham El Guerrouj, Morocco | Mile/1500 |
| 1980 Edwin Moses, USA | 400 Hurdles | 2003 Felix Sanchez, Dominican Republic | 400 Hurdles |
| 1981 Sebastian Coe, Great Britain | 800/1500 | 2004 Kenenisa Bekele, Ethiopia | 5000/10,000 |

### WOMEN

**Multiple winners:** Marita Koch (4); Marion Jones and Jackie Joyner-Kersee (3); Evelyn Ashford (2).

| Year | Event | Year | Event |
|---|---|---|---|
| 1974 Irena Szewinska, Poland | 100/200/400 | 1990 Merlene Ottey, Jamaica | 100/200 |
| 1975 Faina Melnik, USSR | Shot Put/Discus | 1991 Heike Henkel, Germany | High Jump |
| 1976 Tatiana Kazankina, USSR | 800/1500 | 1992 Heike Drechsler, Germany | Long Jump |
| 1977 Rosemarie Ackermann, E. Germany | High Jump | 1993 Wang Junxia, China | 1500/3000/10,000 |
| 1978 Marita Koch, E. Germany | 100/200/400 | 1994 Jackie Joyner-Kersee, USA | 100H/Heptathlon/LJ |
| 1979 Marita Koch, E. Germany | 100/200/400 | 1995 Sonia O'Sullivan, Ireland | 1500/3000/5000 |
| 1980 Ilona Briesenick, E. Germany | Shot Put | 1996 Svetlana Masterkova, Russia | 800/1500 |
| 1981 Evelyn Ashford, USA | 100/200 | 1997 Marion Jones, USA | 100/200 |
| 1982 Marita Koch, E. Germany | 100/200/400 | 1998 Marion Jones, USA | 100/200/LJ |
| 1983 Jarmila Kratochvilova, Czech | 200/400/800 | 1999 Gabriela Szabo, Romania | 3000/5000 |
| 1984 Evelyn Ashford, USA | 100 | 2000 Marion Jones, USA | 100/200/LJ |
| 1985 Marita Koch, E. Germany | 100/200/400 | 2001 Stacy Dragila, USA | Pole Vault |
| 1986 Jackie Joyner-Kersee, USA | Heptathlon/Long Jump | 2002 Paula Radcliffe, Gr. Britain | 3000/5000/10k/Mar |
| 1987 Jackie Joyner-Kersee, USA | 100H/Heptathlon/LJ | 2003 Maria Mutola, Mozambique | 800 |
| 1988 Florence Griffith Joyner, USA | 100/200 | 2004 Yelena Isinbayeva, Russia | Pole Vault |
| 1989 Ana Quirot, Cuba | 400/800 | | |

## SWIMMING & DIVING

# FINA World Championships

While the Summer Olympics have served as the unofficial world championships for swimming and diving throughout the centuries, a separate World Championship meet was started in 1973 by the Federation Internationale de Natation Amateur (FINA). The meet has varied between being held every two years, every three years or every four years. Currently it is held every two years. Sites have been Belgrade (1973); Cali, COL (1975); West Berlin (1978); Guayaquil, ECU (1982); Madrid (1986); Perth (1991 & 98), Rome (1994), Fukuoka, JPN (2001), Barcelona (2003) and Montreal (2005). Looking forward, the Championships will be held in Melbourne (2007) and Rome (2009).

## MEN

**Most gold medals** (including relays): Ian Thorpe (11); Grant Hackett (10); Michael Phelps (8); Jim Montgomery and Aaron Peirsol (7); Matt Biondi, Michael Klim and Aleksandr Popov (6); Rowdy Gaines and Brendan Hansen (5); Joe Bottom, Ian Crocker, Tamas Darnyi, Michael Gross, Tom Jager, David McCagg, Vladimir Salnikov, Tim Shaw and Matt Welsh (4); Billy Forrester, Andras Hargitay, Jason Lezak, Roland Matthes, John Murphy, Jeff Rouse, Norbert Rozsa and David Wilkie (3).

### 50-Meter Freestyle

| Year | | Time | |
|---|---|---|---|
| 1973-82 Not held | | | |
| 1986 | Tom Jager, USA | .22.49 | |
| 1991 | Tom Jager, USA | .22.16 | |
| 1994 | Aleksandr Popov, RUS | .22.17 | |
| 1998 | Bill Pilczuk, USA | .22.29 | |
| 2001 | Anthony Ervin, USA | .22.09 | |
| 2003 | Aleksandr Popov, RUS | .21.92 | |
| 2005 | Roland Schoeman, RSA | .21.69 | CR |

### 100-Meter Freestyle

| Year | | Time | |
|---|---|---|---|
| 1973 | Jim Montgomery, USA | .51.70 | |
| 1975 | Tim Shaw, USA | .51.25 | |
| 1978 | David McCagg, USA | .50.24 | |
| 1982 | Jorg Woithe, E. Ger | .50.18 | |
| 1986 | Matt Biondi, USA | .48.94 | |
| 1991 | Matt Biondi, USA | .49.18 | |
| 1994 | Aleksandr Popov, RUS | .49.12 | |
| 1998 | Aleksandr Popov, RUS | .48.93 | |
| 2001 | Anthony Ervin, USA | .48.33 | |
| 2003 | Aleksandr Popov, RUS | .48.42 | |
| 2005 | Filippo Magnini, ITA | .48.12 | CR |

### 200-Meter Freestyle

| Year | | Time | |
|---|---|---|---|
| 1973 | Jim Montgomery, USA | 1:53.02 | |
| 1975 | Tim Shaw, USA | 1:52.04 | |
| 1978 | Billy Forrester, USA | 1:51.02 | |
| 1982 | Michael Gross, W. Ger | 1:49.84 | |
| 1986 | Michael Gross, W. Ger | 1:47.92 | |
| 1991 | Giorgio Lamberti, ITA | 1:47.27 | |
| 1994 | Antti Kasvio, FIN | 1:47.32 | |
| 1998 | Michael Klim, AUS | 1:47.41 | |
| 2001 | Ian Thorpe, AUS | 1:44.06 | WR |
| 2003 | Ian Thorpe, AUS | 1:45.14 | |
| 2005 | Michael Phelps, USA | 1:45.20 | |

### 400-Meter Freestyle

| Year | | Time | |
|---|---|---|---|
| 1973 | Rick DeMont, USA | 3:58.18 | |
| 1975 | Tim Shaw, USA | 3:54.88 | |
| 1978 | Vladimir Salnikov, USSR | 3:51.94 | |
| 1982 | Vladimir Salnikov, USSR | 3:51.30 | |
| 1986 | Rainer Henkel, W. Ger | 3:50.05 | |
| 1991 | Jorg Hoffman, GER | 3:48.04 | |
| 1994 | Kieren Perkins, AUS | 3:43.80 | |
| 1998 | Ian Thorpe, AUS | 3:46.29 | |
| 2001 | Ian Thorpe, AUS | 3:40.17 | WR |
| 2003 | Ian Thorpe, AUS | 3:42.58 | |
| 2005 | Grant Hackett, AUS | 3:42.91 | |

### 800-Meter Freestyle

| Year | | Time | |
|---|---|---|---|
| 1973-98 Not held | | | |
| 2001 | Ian Thorpe, AUS | 7:39.16 | |
| 2003 | Grant Hackett, AUS | 7:43.82 | |
| 2005 | Grant Hackett, AUS | 7:38.65 | WR |

### 1500-Meter Freestyle

| Year | | Time | |
|---|---|---|---|
| 1973 | Stephen Holland, AUS | 15:31.85 | |
| 1975 | Tim Shaw, USA | 15:28.92 | |
| 1978 | Vladimir Salnikov, USSR | 15:03.99 | |
| 1982 | Vladimir Salnikov, USSR | 15:01.77 | |
| 1986 | Rainer Henkel, W. Ger | 15:05.31 | |
| 1991 | Jorg Hoffman, GER | 14:50.36 | |
| 1994 | Kieren Perkins, AUS | 14:50.52 | |
| 1998 | Grant Hackett, AUS | 14:51.70 | |
| 2001 | Grant Hackett, AUS | 14:34.56 | WR |
| 2003 | Grant Hackett, AUS | 14:43.14 | |
| 2005 | Grant Hackett, AUS | 14:42.58 | |

### 50-Meter Backstroke

| Year | | Time | |
|---|---|---|---|
| 1973-98 Not held | | | |
| 2001 | Randall Bal, USA | 25.34 | |
| 2003 | Thomas Rupprath, GER | 24.80 | WR |
| 2005 | Aristeidis Grigoriadis, GRE | 24.95 | |

### 100-Meter Backstroke

| Year | | Time | |
|---|---|---|---|
| 1973 | Roland Matthes, E. Ger | .57.47 | |
| 1975 | Roland Matthes, E. Ger | .58.15 | |
| 1978 | Bob Jackson, USA | .56.36 | |
| 1982 | Dirk Richter, E. Ger | .55.95 | |
| 1986 | Igor Polianski, USSR | .55.58 | |
| 1991 | Jeff Rouse, USA | .55.23 | |
| 1994 | Martin Lopez-Zubero, SPA | .55.17 | |
| 1998 | Lenny Krayzelburg, USA | .55.00 | |
| 2001 | Matt Welsh, AUS | .54.31 | |
| 2003 | Aaron Peirsol, USA | .53.61 | CR |
| 2005 | Aaron Peirsol, USA | .53.62 | |

### 200-Meter Backstroke

| Year | | Time | |
|---|---|---|---|
| 1973 | Roland Matthes, E. Ger | 2:01.87 | |
| 1975 | Zoltan Varraszto, HUN | 2:05.05 | |
| 1978 | Jesse Vassallo, USA | 2:02.16 | |
| 1982 | Rick Carey, USA | 2:00.82 | |
| 1986 | Igor Polianski, USSR | 1:58.78 | |
| 1991 | Martin Zubero, SPA | 1:59.52 | |
| 1994 | Vladimir Selkov, RUS | 1:57.42 | |
| 1998 | Lenny Krayzelburg, USA | 1:58.84 | |
| 2001 | Aaron Peirsol, USA | 1:57.13 | |
| 2003 | Aaron Peirsol, USA | 1:55.92 | |
| 2005 | Aaron Peirsol, USA | 1:54.66 | WR |

## 50-Meter Breaststroke

| Year | | Time |
|------|------|------|
| 1973-98 | Not held | |
| 2001 | Oleg Lisogor, UKR | .27.52 |
| 2003 | James Gibson, GBR | .27.56 |
| 2005 | Mark Warnecke, GER | .27.63 |

## 100-Meter Breaststroke

| Year | | Time | |
|------|------|------|------|
| 1973 | John Hencken, USA | 1:04.02 | |
| 1975 | David Wilkie, GBR | 1:04.26 | |
| 1978 | Walter Kusch, W. Ger | 1:03.56 | |
| 1982 | Steve Lundquist, USA | 1:02.75 | |
| 1986 | Victor Davis, CAN | 1:02.71 | |
| 1991 | Norbert Rozsa, HUN | 1:01.45 | |
| 1994 | Norbert Rozsa, HUN | 1:01.24 | |
| 1998 | Frederik deBurghgraeve, BEL | 1:01.34 | |
| 2001 | Roman Sloudnov, RUS | 1:00.16 | |
| 2003 | Kosuke Kitajima, JPN | .59.78 | |
| 2005 | Brendan Hansen, USA | .59.37 | CR |

## 200-Meter Breaststroke

| Year | | Time | |
|------|------|------|------|
| 1973 | David Wilkie, GBR | 2:19.28 | |
| 1975 | David Wilkie, GBR | 2:18.23 | |
| 1978 | Nick Nevid, USA | 2:18.37 | |
| 1982 | Victor Davis, CAN | 2:14.77 | |
| 1986 | Jozsef Szabo, HUN | 2:14.27 | |
| 1991 | Mike Barrowman, USA | 2:11.23 | |
| 1994 | Norbert Rozsa, HUN | 2:12.81 | |
| 1998 | Kurt Grote, USA | 2:13.40 | |
| 2001 | Brendan Hansen, USA | 2:10.69 | |
| 2003 | Kosuke Kitajima, JPN | 2:09.42 | WR |
| 2005 | Brendan Hansen, USA | 2:09.85 | |

## 50-Meter Butterfly

| Year | | Time | |
|------|------|------|------|
| 1973-98 | Not held | | |
| 2001 | Geoff Huegill, AUS | .23.50 | |
| 2003 | Matt Welsh, AUS | .23.43 | |
| 2005 | Roland Schoeman, RSA | .22.96 | WR |

## 100-Meter Butterfly

| Year | | Time | |
|------|------|------|------|
| 1973 | Bruce Robertson, CAN | .55.69 | |
| 1975 | Greg Jagenburg, USA | .55.63 | |
| 1978 | Joe Bottom, USA | .54.30 | |
| 1982 | Matt Gribble, USA | .53.88 | |
| 1986 | Pablo Morales, USA | .53.54 | |
| 1991 | Anthony Nesty, SUR | .53.29 | |
| 1994 | Rafal Szukala, POL | .53.51 | |
| 1998 | Michael Klim, AUS | .52.25 | |
| 2001 | Lars Frolander, SWE | .52.10 | |
| 2003 | Ian Crocker, USA | .50.98 | |
| 2005 | Ian Crocker, USA | .50.40 | WR |

## 200-Meter Butterfly

| Year | | Time | |
|------|------|------|------|
| 1973 | Robin Backhaus, USA | 2:03.32 | |
| 1975 | Billy Forrester, USA | 2:01.95 | |
| 1978 | Mike Bruner, USA | 1:59.38 | |
| 1982 | Michael Gross, W. Ger | 1:58.85 | |
| 1986 | Michael Gross, W. Ger | 1:56.53 | |
| 1991 | Melvin Stewart, USA | 1:55.69 | WR |
| 1994 | Denis Pankratov, RUS | 1:56.54 | |
| 1998 | Denys Sylantyev, UKR | 1:56.61 | |
| 2001 | Michael Phelps, USA | 1:54.58 | WR |
| 2003 | Michael Phelps, USA | 1:54.35 | |
| 2005 | Pawel Korzeniowski, POL | 1:55.02 | |

## 200-Meter Individual Medley

| Year | | Time | |
|------|------|------|------|
| 1973 | Gunnar Larsson, SWE | 2:08.36 | |
| 1975 | Andras Hargitay, HUN | 2:07.72 | |
| 1978 | Graham Smith, CAN | 2:03.65 | |
| 1982 | Alexander Sidorenko, USSR | 2:03.30 | |
| 1986 | Tamás Darnyi, HUN | 2:01.57 | |
| 1991 | Tamás Darnyi, HUN | 1:59.36 | |
| 1994 | Janis Sievinen, FIN | 1:58.16 | |
| 1998 | Marcel Wouda, NET | 2:01.18 | |
| 2001 | Massimiliano Rosolino, ITA | 1:59.71 | |
| 2003 | Michael Phelps, USA | 1:56.04 | WR |
| 2005 | Michael Phelps, USA | 1:56.68 | |

## 400-Meter Individual Medley

| Year | | Time | |
|------|------|------|------|
| 1973 | Andras Hargitay, HUN | 4:31.11 | |
| 1975 | Andras Hargitay, HUN | 4:32.57 | |
| 1978 | Jesse Vassallo, USA | 4:20.05 | |
| 1982 | Ricardo Prado, BRA | 4:19.78 | |
| 1986 | Tamás Darnyi, HUN | 4:18.98 | |
| 1991 | Tamás Darnyi, HUN | 4:12.36 | |
| 1994 | Tom Dolan, USA | 4:12.30 | |
| 1998 | Tom Dolan, USA | 4:14.95 | |
| 2001 | Alessio Boggiatto, ITA | 4:13.15 | |
| 2003 | Michael Phelps, USA | 4:09.09 | WR |
| 2005 | Laszlo Cseh, HUN | 4:09.63 | |

## 4 x 100-Meter Freestyle Relay

| Year | | Time | |
|------|------|------|------|
| 1973 | United States | 3:27.18 | |
| 1975 | United States | 3:24.85 | |
| 1978 | United States | 3:19.74 | |
| 1982 | United States | 3:19.26 | |
| 1986 | United States | 3:19.98 | |
| 1991 | United States | 3:17.15 | |
| 1994 | United States | 3:16.90 | |
| 1998 | United States | 3:16.69 | |
| 2001 | Australia | 3:14.10 | |
| 2003 | Russia | 3:14.06 | |
| 2005 | United States | 3:13.77 | CR |

## 4 x 200-Meter Freestyle Relay

| Year | | Time | |
|------|------|------|------|
| 1973 | United States | 7:33.22 | |
| 1975 | West Germany | 7:39.44 | |
| 1978 | United States | 7:20.82 | |
| 1982 | United States | 7:21.09 | |
| 1986 | East Germany | 7:15.91 | |
| 1991 | Germany | 7:13.50 | |
| 1994 | Sweden | 7:17.34 | |
| 1998 | Australia | 7:12.48 | |
| 2001 | Australia | 7:04.66 | WR |
| 2003 | Australia | 7:08.58 | |
| 2005 | United States | 7:06.58 | |

## 4 x 100-Meter Medley Relay

| Year | | Time | |
|------|------|------|------|
| 1973 | United States | 3:49.49 | |
| 1975 | United States | 3:49.00 | |
| 1978 | United States | 3:44.63 | |
| 1982 | United States | 3:40.84 | |
| 1986 | United States | 3:41.25 | |
| 1991 | United States | 3:39.66 | |
| 1994 | United States | 3:37.74 | |
| 1998 | Australia | 3:37.98 | |
| 2001 | Australia | 3:35.35 | |
| 2003 | United States | 3:31.54 | WR |
| 2005 | United States | 3:31.85 | |

## Swimming & Diving (Cont.)

## WOMEN

**Most gold medals** (including relays): Kornelia Ender (8); Kristin Otto (7); Jenny Thompson (6); Inge De Bruijn, Hannah Stockbauer and Luo Xuejuan (5); Tracy Caulkins, Heike Friedrich, Le Jingyi, Leisel Jones, Jana Klochkova, Rosemarie Kother and Ulrike Richter (4); Hannalore Anke, Lu Bin, He Cihong, Natalie Coughlin, Janet Evans, Nicole Haislett, Katie Hoff, Lisbeth Lenton, Lui Limin, Birgit Meineke, Joan Pennington, Manuela Stellmach, Petria Thomas, Amy Van Dyken, Renate Vogel and Cynthia Woodhead (3).

### 50-Meter Freestyle

| Year | | Time |
|---|---|---|
| 1973-82 Not held | | |
| 1986 | Tamara Costache, ROM | .25.28 |
| 1991 | Zhuang Yong, CHN | .25.47 |
| 1994 | Le Jingyi, CHN | .24.51 | **WR** |
| 1998 | Amy Van Dyken, USA | .25.15 |
| 2001 | Inge de Bruijn, NED | .24.47 |
| 2003 | Inge de Bruijn, NED | .24.47 |
| 2005 | Lisbeth Lenton, AUS | .24.59 |

### 100-Meter Freestyle

| Year | | Time |
|---|---|---|
| 1973 | Kornelia Ender, E. Ger | .57.54 |
| 1975 | Kornelia Ender, E. Ger | .56.50 |
| 1978 | Barbara Krause, E. Ger | .55.68 |
| 1982 | Birgit Meineke, E. Ger | .55.79 |
| 1986 | Kristin Otto, E. Ger | .55.05 |
| 1991 | Nicole Haislett, USA | .55.17 |
| 1994 | Le Jingyi, CHN | .54.01 | **WR** |
| 1998 | Jenny Thompson, USA | .54.95 |
| 2001 | Inge de Bruijn, NED | .54.18 |
| 2003 | Hanna-Maria Seppala, FIN | .54.37 |
| 2005 | Jodie Henry, AUS | .54.18 |

### 200-Meter Freestyle

| Year | | Time |
|---|---|---|
| 1973 | Keena Rothhammer, USA | 2:04.99 |
| 1975 | Shirley Babashoff, USA | 2:02.50 |
| 1978 | Cynthia Woodhead, USA | 1:58.53 |
| 1982 | Annemarie Verstappen, NED | 1:59.53 |
| 1986 | Heike Friedrich, E. Ger | 1:58.26 |
| 1991 | Hayley Lewis, AUS | 2:00.48 |
| 1994 | Franziska Van Almsick, GER | 1:56.78 | **WR** |
| 1998 | Claudia Poll, CRC | 1:58.90 |
| 2001 | Giaan Rooney, AUS | 1:58.57 |
| 2003 | Alena Popchenko, BLR | 1:58.32 |
| 2005 | Solenne Figues, FRA | 1:58.60 |

### 400-Meter Freestyle

| Year | | Time |
|---|---|---|
| 1973 | Heather Greenwood, USA | 4:20.28 |
| 1975 | Shirley Babashoff, USA | 4:22.70 |
| 1978 | Tracey Wickham, AUS | 4:06.28 | **WR** |
| 1982 | Carmela Schmidt. E. Ger | 4:08.98 |
| 1986 | Heike Friedrich, E. Ger | 4:07.45 |
| 1991 | Janet Evans, USA | 4:08.63 |
| 1994 | Yang Aihua, CHN | 4:09.64 |
| 1998 | Yan Chen, CHN | 4:06.72 |
| 2001 | Yana Klochkova, UKR | 4:07.30 |
| 2003 | Hannah Stockbauer, GER | 4:06.75 |
| 2005 | Laure Manaudou. FRA | 4:06.44 |

### 800-Meter Freestyle

| Year | | Time |
|---|---|---|
| 1973 | Novella Calligaris, ITA | 8:52.97 |
| 1975 | Jenny Turrall, AUS | 8:44.75 |
| 1978 | Tracey Wickham, AUS | 8:25.94 |
| 1982 | Kim Linehan, USA | 8:27.48 |
| 1986 | Astrid Strauss, E. Ger | 8:28.24 |
| 1991 | Janet Evans, USA | 8:24.05 |
| 1994 | Janet Evans, USA | 8:29.85 |
| 1998 | Brooke Bennett, USA | 8:28.71 |
| 2001 | Hannah Stockbauer, GER | 8:24.66 |
| 2003 | Hannah Stockbauer, GER | 8:23.66 | **CR** |
| 2005 | Kate Ziegler, USA | 8:25.31 |

### 1500-Meter Freestyle

| Year | | Time |
|---|---|---|
| 1973-98 Not held | | |
| 2001 | Hannah Stockbauer, GER | 16:01.02 |
| 2003 | Hannah Stockbauer, GER | 16:00.18 | **CR** |
| 2005 | Kate Ziegler, USA | 16:00.41 |

### 50-Meter Backstroke

| Year | | Time |
|---|---|---|
| 1973-98 Not held | | |
| 2001 | Haley Cope, USA | .28.51 |
| 2003 | Nina Zhivanevskaya, ESP | .28.48 | **CR** |
| 2005 | Giaan Rooney, AUS | .28.63 |

### 100-Meter Backstroke

| Year | | Time |
|---|---|---|
| 1973 | Ulrike Richter, E. Ger | 1:05.42 |
| 1975 | Ulrike Richter, E. Ger | 1:03.30 |
| 1978 | Linda Jezek, USA | 1:02.55 |
| 1982 | Kristin Otto, E. Ger | 1:01.30 |
| 1986 | Betsy Mitchell, USA | 1:01.74 |
| 1991 | Krisztina Egerszegi, HUN | 1:01.78 |
| 1994 | He Cihong, CHN | 1:00.57 |
| 1998 | Lea Maurer, USA | 1:01.16 |
| 2001 | Natalie Coughlin, USA | 1:00.37 |
| 2003 | Antje Buschschulte, GER | 1:00.50 |
| 2005 | Kirsty Coventry, ZIM | 1:00.24 |

### 200-Meter Backstroke

| Year | | Time |
|---|---|---|
| 1973 | Melissa Belote, USA | 2:20.52 |
| 1975 | Birgit Treiber, E. Ger | 2:15.46 |
| 1978 | Linda Jezek, USA | 2:11.93 |
| 1982 | Cornelia Sirch, E. Ger | 2:09.91 |
| 1986 | Cornelia Sirch, E. Ger | 2:11.37 |
| 1991 | Krisztina Egerszegi, HUN | 2:09.15 |
| 1994 | He Cihong, CHN | 2:07.40 | **CR** |
| 1998 | Roxanna Maracineanu, FRA | 2:11.26 |
| 2001 | Diana Iuliana Mocanu, ROM | 2:09.94 |
| 2003 | Katy Sexton, GBR | 2:08.74 |
| 2005 | Kirsty Coventry, ZIM | 2:08.52 |

### 50-Meter Breaststroke

| Year | | Time |
|---|---|---|
| 1973-82 Not held | | |
| 2001 | Luo Xuejuan, CHN | .30.84 |
| 2003 | Luo Xuejuan, CHN | .30.67 |
| 2005 | Jade Edmistone, AUS | .30.45 | **WR** |

### 100-Meter Breaststroke

| Year | | Time |
|---|---|---|
| 1973 | Renate Vogel, E. Ger | 1:13.74 |
| 1975 | Hannalore Anke, E. Ger | 1:12.72 |
| 1978 | Julia Bogdanova, USSR | 1:10.31 |
| 1982 | Ute Geweniger, E. Ger | 1:09.14 |
| 1986 | Sylvia Gerasch, E. Ger | 1:08.11 |
| 1991 | Linley Frame, AUS | 1:08.81 |
| 1994 | Samantha Riley, AUS | 1:07.69 |
| 1998 | Kristy Kowal, USA | 1:08.42 |
| 2001 | Luo Xuejuan, CHN | 1:07.18 |
| 2003 | Luo Xuejuan, CHN | 1:06.80 |
| 2005 | Leisel Jones, AUS | 1:06.25 |

## 200-Meter Breaststroke

| Year | | Time |
|---|---|---|
| 1973 | Renate Vogel, E. Ger | 2:40.01 |
| 1975 | Hannalore Anke, E. Ger | 2:37.25 |
| 1978 | Lina Kachushite, USSR | 2:31.42 |
| 1982 | Svetlana Varganova, USSR | 2:28.82 |
| 1986 | Silke Hoerner, E. Ger | 2:27.40 |
| 1991 | Elena Volkova, USSR | 2:29.53 |
| 1994 | Samantha Riley, AUS | 2:26.87 |
| 1998 | Agnes Kovacs, HUN | 2:25.45 |
| 2001 | Agnes Kovacs, HUN | 2:24.90 |
| 2003 | Amanda Beard, USA | 2:22.99 |
| 2005 | Leisel Jones, AUS | 2:21.72 **WR** |

## 50-Meter Butterfly

| Year | | Time |
|---|---|---|
| 1973-98 | Not held | |
| 2001 | Inge de Bruijn, NED | 25.90 |
| 2003 | Inge de Bruijn, NED | 25.84 **CR** |
| 2005 | Danni Miatke, AUS | 26.11 |

## 100-Meter Butterfly

| Year | | Time |
|---|---|---|
| 1973 | Kornelia Ender, E. Ger | 1:02.53 |
| 1975 | Kornelia Ender, E. Ger | 1:01.24 |
| 1978 | Joan Pennington, USA | 1:00.20 |
| 1982 | Mary T. Meagher, USA | 59.41 |
| 1986 | Kornelia Gressler, E. Ger | 59.51 |
| 1991 | Qian Hong, CHN | 59.68 |
| 1994 | Liu Limin, CHN | 58.98 |
| 1998 | Jenny Thompson, USA | 58.46 |
| 2001 | Petria Thomas, AUS | 58.27 |
| 2003 | Jenny Thompson, USA | 57.96 |
| 2005 | Jessicah Schipper, AUS | 57.23 **CR** |

## 200-Meter Butterfly

| Year | | Time |
|---|---|---|
| 1973 | Rosemarie Kother, E. Ger | 2:13.76 |
| 1975 | Rosemarie Kother, E. Ger | 2:15.92 |
| 1978 | Tracy Caulkins, USA | 2:09.78 |
| 1982 | Ines Geissler, E. Ger | 2:08.66 |
| 1986 | Mary T. Meagher, USA | 2:08.41 |
| 1991 | Summer Sanders, USA | 2:09.24 |
| 1994 | Liu Limin, CHN | 2:07.25 |
| 1998 | Susie O'Neill, AUS | 2:07.93 |
| 2001 | Petria Thomas, AUS | 2:06.73 |
| 2003 | Otylia Jedrzejczak, POL | 2:07.56 |
| 2005 | Otylia Jedrzejczak, POL | 2:05.61 **WR** |

## 200-Meter Individual Medley

| Year | | Time |
|---|---|---|
| 1973 | Andre Huebner, E. Ger | 2:20.51 |
| 1975 | Kathy Heddy, USA | 2:19.80 |
| 1978 | Tracy Caulkins, USA | 2:19.80 |
| 1982 | Petra Schneider, E. Ger | 2:11.79 |
| 1986 | Kristin Otto, E. Ger | 2:15.56 |
| 1991 | Lin Li, CHN | 2:13.40 |
| 1994 | Lu Bin, CHN | 2:12.34 |
| 1998 | Yanyan Wu, CHN | 2:10.88 |
| 2001 | Maggie Bowen, USA | 2:11.93 |
| 2003 | Yana Klochkova, UKR | 2:10.75 |
| 2005 | Katie Hoff, USA | 2:10.41 **WR** |

## 400-Meter Individual Medley

| Year | | Time |
|---|---|---|
| 1973 | Gudrun Wegner, E. Ger | 4:57.71 |
| 1975 | Ulrike Tauber, E. Ger | 4:52.76 |
| 1978 | Tracy Caulkins, USA | 4:40.83 |
| 1982 | Petra Schneider, E. Ger | 4:36.10 |
| 1986 | Kathleen Nord, E. Ger | 4:43.75 |
| 1991 | Lin Li, CHN | 4:41.45 |
| 1994 | Dai Guohong, CHN | 4:39.14 |
| 1998 | Yan Chen, CHN | 4:36.66 |
| 2001 | Yana Klochkova, UKR | 4:36.98 |
| 2003 | Yana Klochkova, UKR | 4:36.74 |
| 2005 | Katie Hoff, USA | 4:36.07 **CR** |

## 4 x 100-Meter Freestyle Relay

| Year | | Time |
|---|---|---|
| 1973 | East Germany | 3:52.45 |
| 1975 | East Germany | 3:49.37 |
| 1978 | United States | 3:43.43 |
| 1982 | East Germany | 3:43.97 |
| 1986 | East Germany | 3:40.57 |
| 1991 | United States | 3:43.26 |
| 1994 | China | 3:37.91 |
| 1998 | United States | 3:42.11 |
| 2001 | Germany | 3:39.58 |
| 2003 | United States | 3:38.09 |
| 2005 | Australia | 3:37.32 **CR** |

## 4 x 200-Meter Freestyle Relay

| Year | | Time |
|---|---|---|
| 1973-82 | Not held | |
| 1986 | East Germany | 7:59.33 |
| 1991 | Germany | 8:02.56 |
| 1994 | China | 7:57.96 |
| 1998 | Germany | 8:01.46 |
| 2001 | Great Britain | 7:58.69 |
| 2003 | United States | 7:55.70 |
| 2005 | United States | 7:53.70 **CR** |

## 4 x 100-Meter Medley Relay

| Year | | Time |
|---|---|---|
| 1973 | East Germany | 4:16.84 |
| 1975 | East Germany | 4:14.74 |
| 1978 | United States | 4:08.21 |
| 1982 | East Germany | 4:05.80 |
| 1986 | East Germany | 4:04.82 |
| 1991 | United States | 4:06.51 |
| 1994 | China | 4:01.67 |
| 1998 | United States | 4:01.93 |
| 2001 | Australia | 4:01.50 |
| 2003 | China | 3:59.89 |
| 2005 | Australia | 3:57.47 **CR** |

# Diving

**Multiple Gold Medals:** MEN–Greg Louganis and Dmitri Sautin (5); Phil Boggs and Alexandre Despatie (3); Klaus Dibiasi, Wang Feng, Hu Jia, Tian Liang and Yu Zhuocheng (2). WOMEN–Guo Jingjing (6); Irina Kalinina and Gao Min (3); Blythe Hartley, Irina Lashko, Fu Mingxia, Wu Mingxia and Li Ting (2).

## MEN

### 1-Meter Springboard

| Year | | Pts |
|---|---|---|
| 1973-86 | Not Held | |
| 1991 | Edwin Jongejans, NED | 588.51 |
| 1994 | Evan Stewart, ZIM | 382.14 |
| 1998 | Yu Zhuocheng, CHN | 417.54 |
| 2001 | Wang Feng, CHN | 444.03 |
| 2003 | Xu Xiang, CHN | 431.94 |
| 2005 | Alexandre Despatie, CAN | 489.69 |

### 3-Meter Springboard

| Year | | Pts |
|---|---|---|
| 1973 | Phil Boggs, USA | 618.57 |
| 1975 | Phil Boggs, USA | 597.12 |
| 1978 | Phil Boggs, USA | 913.95 |
| 1982 | Greg Louganis, USA | 752.67 |
| 1986 | Greg Louganis, USA | 750.06 |
| 1991 | Kent Ferguson, USA | 650.25 |
| 1994 | Yu Zhuocheng, CHN | 655.44 |
| 1998 | Dmitri Sautin, RUS | 746.79 |
| 2001 | Dmitri Sautin, RUS | 725.82 |
| 2003 | Alexander Dobroskok, RUS | 788.37 |
| 2005 | Alexandre Despatie, CAN | 813.60 |

## Swimming & Diving (Cont.)

### Platform

| Year | | Pts |
|---|---|---|
| 1973 | Klaus Dibiasi, ITA | 559.53 |
| 1975 | Klaus Dibiasi, ITA | 547.98 |
| 1978 | Greg Louganis, USA | 844.11 |
| 1982 | Greg Louganis, USA | 634.26 |
| 1986 | Greg Louganis, USA | 668.58 |
| 1991 | Sun Shuwei, CHN | 626.79 |
| 1994 | Dmitri Sautin, RUS | 634.71 |
| 1998 | Dmitri Sautin, RUS | 750.99 |
| 2001 | Tian Liang, CHN | 688.77 |
| 2003 | Alexandre Despatie, CAN | 716.91 |
| 2005 | Hu Jia, CHN | 698.01 |

### 3-Meter Synchronized

| Year | | Pts |
|---|---|---|
| 1973-98 | Not held | |
| 2001 | Peng Bo & Wang Kenan, CHN | 342.63 |
| 2003 | Alexander Dobroskok & Dmitri Sautin, RUS | 369.18 |
| 2005 | He Chong & Wang Feng, CHN | 384.42 |

### 10-Meter Synchronized

| Year | | Pts |
|---|---|---|
| 1973-98 | Not held | |
| 2001 | Tian Liang & Hu Jia, CHN | 361.41 |
| 2003 | Mathew Helm & Robert Newbery, AUS | 384.60 |
| 2005 | Dmitry Dobrosok & Glen Galperin, RUS | 392.88 |

### WOMEN
#### 1-Meter Springboard

| Year | | Pts |
|---|---|---|
| 1973-86 | Not held | |
| 1991 | Gao Min, CHN | 478.26 |
| 1994 | Chen Lixia, CHN | 279.30 |
| 1998 | Irina Lashko, RUS | 296.07 |
| 2001 | Blythe Hartley, CAN | 300.81 |
| 2003 | Irina Lashko, AUS | 299.97 |
| 2005 | Blythe Hartley, CAN | 325.65 |

### 3-Meter Springboard

| Year | | Pts |
|---|---|---|
| 1973 | Christa Koehler, E. Ger | 442.17 |
| 1975 | Irina Kalinina, USSR | 489.81 |
| 1978 | Irina Kalinina, USSR | 691.43 |
| 1982 | Megan Neyer, USA | 501.03 |
| 1986 | Gao Min, CHN | 582.90 |
| 1991 | Gao Min, CHN | 539.01 |
| 1994 | Tan Shuping, CHN | 548.49 |
| 1998 | Yulia Pakhalina, RUS | 544.52 |
| 2001 | Guo Jingjing, CHN | 596.67 |
| 2003 | Guo Jingjing, CHN | 617.94 |
| 2005 | Guo Jingjing, CHN | 645.54 |

### Platform

| Year | | Pts |
|---|---|---|
| 1973 | Ulrike Knape, SWE | 406.77 |
| 1975 | Janet Ely, USA | 403.89 |
| 1978 | Irina Kalinina, USSR | 412.71 |
| 1982 | Wendy Wyland, USA | 438.79 |
| 1986 | Chen Lin, CHN | 449.67 |
| 1991 | Fu Mingxia, CHN | 426.51 |
| 1994 | Fu Mingxia, CHN | 434.04 |
| 1998 | Olena Zhupyna | 550.41 |
| 2001 | Xu Mian, CHN | 532.65 |
| 2003 | Emilie Heymans, CAN | 597.45 |
| 2005 | Laura Wilkinson, USA | 564.87 |

### 3-Meter Synchronized

| Year | | Pts |
|---|---|---|
| 1973-98 | Not held | |
| 2001 | Wu Minxia & Guo Jingjing, CHN | 347.31 |
| 2003 | Wu Minxia & Guo Jingjing, CHN | 357.30 |
| 2005 | Li Ting & Guo Jingjing, CHN | 351.60 |

### 10-Meter Synchronized

| Year | | Pts |
|---|---|---|
| 1973-98 | Not held | |
| 2001 | Duan Qing & Sang Xue, CHN | 329.94 |
| 2003 | Lao Lishi & Li Ting, CHN | 344.58 |
| 2005 | Jia Tong & Yuan Pei Lin, CHN | 344.58 |

---

### ALPINE SKIING

## World Cup Overall Champions

World Cup Overall Champions (downhill and slalom events combined) since the tour was organized in 1967.

### MEN

**Multiple winners:** Marc Girardelli (5); Hermann Maier, Gustavo Thoeni and Pirmin Zurbriggen (4); Phil Mahre and Ingemar Stenmark (3); Stephan Eberharter, Jean-Claude Killy, Lasse Kjus and Karl Schranz (2).

| Year | | Year | | Year | |
|---|---|---|---|---|---|
| 1967 | Jean-Claude Killy, France | 1980 | Andreas Wenzel, Liechtenstein | 1993 | Marc Girardelli, Luxembourg |
| 1968 | Jean-Claude Killy, France | 1981 | Phil Mahre, USA | 1994 | Kjetil Andre Aamodt, Norway |
| 1969 | Karl Schranz, Austria | 1982 | Phil Mahre, USA | 1995 | Alberto Tomba, Italy |
| 1970 | Karl Schranz, Austria | 1983 | Phil Mahre, USA | 1996 | Lasse Kjus, Norway |
| 1971 | Gustavo Thoeni, Italy | 1984 | Pirmin Zurbriggen, Switzerland | 1997 | Luc Alphand, France |
| 1972 | Gustavo Thoeni, Italy | 1985 | Marc Girardelli, Luxembourg | 1998 | Hermann Maier, Austria |
| 1973 | Gustavo Thoeni, Italy | 1986 | Marc Girardelli, Luxembourg | 1999 | Lasse Kjus, Norway |
| 1974 | Piero Gros, Italy | 1987 | Pirmin Zurbriggen, Switzerland | 2000 | Hermann Maier, Austria |
| 1975 | Gustavo Thoeni, Italy | 1988 | Pirmin Zurbriggen, Switzerland | 2001 | Hermann Maier, Austria |
| 1976 | Ingemar Stenmark, Sweden | 1989 | Marc Girardelli, Luxembourg | 2002 | Stephan Eberharter, Austria |
| 1977 | Ingemar Stenmark, Sweden | 1990 | Pirmin Zurbriggen, Switzerland | 2003 | Stephan Eberharter, Austria |
| 1978 | Ingemar Stenmark, Sweden | 1991 | Marc Girardelli, Luxembourg | 2004 | Hermann Maier, Austria |
| 1979 | Peter Luescher, Switzerland | 1992 | Paul Accola, Switzerland | 2005 | Bode Miller, USA |

## WOMEN

**Multiple winners:** Annemarie Moser-Proell (6); Petra Kronberger and Vreni Schneider (3); Janica Kostelic, Michela Figini, Nancy Greene, Erika Hess, Anja Paerson, Katja Seizinger, Maria Walliser and Hanni Wenzel (2).

| Year | | Year | | Year | |
|------|--|------|--|------|--|
| 1967 | Nancy Greene, Canada | 1980 | Hanni Wenzel, Liechtenstein | 1993 | Anita Wachter, Austria |
| 1968 | Nancy Greene, Canada | 1981 | Marie-Therese Nadig, SWI | 1994 | Vreni Schneider, Switzerland |
| 1969 | Gertrud Gabi, Austria | 1982 | Erika Hess, Switzerland | 1995 | Vreni Schneider, Switzerland |
| 1970 | Michele Jacot, France | 1983 | Tamara McKinney, USA | 1996 | Katja Seizinger, Germany |
| 1971 | Annemarie Pröll, Austria | 1984 | Erika Hess, Switzerland | 1997 | Pernilla Wiberg, Sweden |
| 1972 | Annemarie Pröll, Austria | 1985 | Michela Figini, Switzerland | 1998 | Katja Seizinger, Germany |
| 1973 | Annemarie Pröll, Austria | 1986 | Maria Walliser, Switzerland | 1999 | Alexandra Meissnitzer, Austria |
| 1974 | Annemarie Pröll, Austria | 1987 | Maria Walliser, Switzerland | 2000 | Renate Goetschl, Austria |
| 1975 | Annemarie Moser-Pröll, Austria | 1988 | Michela Figini, Switzerland | 2001 | Janica Kostelic, Croatia |
| 1976 | Rosi Mittermaier, W. Germany | 1989 | Vreni Schneider, Switzerland | 2002 | Michaela Dorfmeister, Austria |
| 1977 | Lise-Marie Morerod, Switzerland | 1990 | Petra Kronberger, Austria | 2003 | Janica Kostelic, Croatia |
| 1978 | Hanni Wenzel, Liechtenstein | 1991 | Petra Kronberger, Austria | 2004 | Anja Paerson, Sweden |
| 1979 | Annemarie Moser-Pröll, Austria | 1992 | Petra Kronberger, Austria | 2005 | Anja Paerson, Sweden |

## World Cup Event Champions

World Cup Champions in each individual event since the tour was organized in 1967.

## MEN

### Downhill

**Multiple winners:** Franz Klammer (5); Luc Alphand, Stephan Eberharter, Franz Heinzer and Peter Muller (3); Roland Collumbin, Marc Girardelli, Helmut Hoflehner, Hermann Maier, Bernard Russi, Karl Schranz and Pirmin Zurbriggen (2).

| Year | | Year | | Year | |
|------|--|------|--|------|--|
| 1967 | Jean-Claude Killy, France | 1980 | Peter Muller, Switzerland | 1993 | Franz Heinzer, Switzerland |
| 1968 | Gerhard Nenning, Austria | 1981 | Harti Weirather, Austria | 1994 | Marc Girardelli, Luxembourg |
| 1969 | Karl Schranz, Austria | 1982 | Steve Podborski, Canada | 1995 | Luc Alphand, France |
| 1970 | Karl Schranz, Austria | | Peter Muller, Switzerland | 1996 | Luc Alphand, France |
| | Karl Cordin, Austria | 1983 | Franz Klammer, Austria | 1997 | Luc Alphand, France |
| 1971 | Bernard Russi, Switzerland | 1984 | Urs Raber, Switzerland | 1998 | Andreas Schifferer, Austria |
| 1972 | Bernard Russi, Switzerland | 1985 | Helmut Hoflehner, Austria | 1999 | Lasse Kjus, Norway |
| 1973 | Roland Collumbin, Switzerland | 1986 | Peter Wirnsberger, Austria | 2000 | Hermann Maier, Austria |
| 1974 | Roland Collumbin, Switzerland | 1987 | Pirmin Zurbriggen, Switzerland | 2001 | Hermann Maier, Austria |
| 1975 | Franz Klammer, Austria | 1988 | Pirmin Zurbriggen, Switzerland | 2002 | Stephan Eberharter, Austria |
| 1976 | Franz Klammer, Austria | 1989 | Marc Girardelli, Luxembourg | 2003 | Stephan Eberharter, Austria |
| 1977 | Franz Klammer, Austria | 1990 | Helmut Hoflehner, Austria | 2004 | Stephan Eberharter, Austria |
| 1978 | Franz Klammer, Austria | 1991 | Franz Heinzer, Switzerland | 2005 | Michael Walchhofer, Austria |
| 1979 | Peter Muller, Switzerland | 1992 | Franz Heinzer, Switzerland | | |

### Slalom

**Multiple winners:** Ingemar Stenmark (8); Alberto Tomba (4); Jean-Noel Augert and Marc Girardelli (3); Armin Bittner, Benjamin Raich, Thomas Sykora and Gustavo Thoeni (2).

| Year | | Year | | Year | |
|------|--|------|--|------|--|
| 1967 | Jean-Claude Killy, France | 1980 | Ingemar Stenmark, Sweden | 1994 | Alberto Tomba, Italy |
| 1968 | Domeng Giovanoli, Switzerland | 1981 | Ingemar Stenmark, Sweden | 1995 | Alberto Tomba, Italy |
| 1969 | Jean-Noel Augert, France | 1982 | Phil Mahre, USA | 1996 | Sebastien Amiez, France |
| 1970 | Patrick Russel, France | 1983 | Ingemar Stenmark, Sweden | 1997 | Thomas Sykora, Austria |
| | Alain Penz, France | 1984 | Marc Girardelli, Luxembourg | 1998 | Thomas Sykora, Austria |
| 1971 | Jean-Noel Augert, France | 1985 | Marc Girardelli, Luxembourg | 1999 | Thomas Stangassinger, Austria |
| 1972 | Jean-Noel Augert, France | 1986 | Rok Petrovic, Yugoslavia | 2000 | Kjetil Andre Aamodt, Norway |
| 1973 | Gustavo Thoeni, Italy | 1987 | Bojan Krizaj, Yugoslavia | 2001 | Benjamin Raich, Austria |
| 1974 | Gustavo Thoeni, Italy | 1988 | Alberto Tomba, Italy | 2002 | Ivica Kostelic, Croatia |
| 1975 | Ingemar Stenmark, Sweden | 1989 | Armin Bittner, West Germany | 2003 | Kalle Palander, Finland |
| 1976 | Ingemar Stenmark, Sweden | 1990 | Armin Bittner, West Germany | 2004 | Rainer Schoenfelder, Austria |
| 1977 | Ingemar Stenmark, Sweden | 1991 | Marc Girardelli, Luxembourg | 2005 | Benjamin Raich, Austria |
| 1978 | Ingemar Stenmark, Sweden | 1992 | Alberto Tomba, Italy | | |
| 1979 | Ingemar Stenmark, Sweden | 1993 | Tomas Fogdof, Sweden | | |

### Giant Slalom

**Multiple winners:** Ingemar Stenmark (8); Michael von Gruenigen and Alberto Tomba (4); Hermann Maier and Pirmin Zurbriggen (8); Joel Gaspoz, Jean-Claude Killy, Phil Mahre and Gustavo Thoeni (2).

| Year | | Year | | Year | |
|------|--|------|--|------|--|
| 1967 | Jean-Claude Killy, France | 1976 | Ingemar Stenmark, Sweden | 1984 | Ingemar Stenmark, Sweden |
| 1968 | Jean-Claude Killy, France | 1977 | Heini Hemmi, Switzerland | | Pirmin Zurbriggen, Switzerland |
| 1969 | Karl Schranz, Austria | | Ingemar Stenmark, Sweden | 1985 | Marc Girardelli, Luxembourg |
| 1970 | Gustavo Thoeni, Italy | 1978 | Ingemar Stenmark, Sweden | 1986 | Joel Gaspoz, Switzerland |
| 1971 | Patrick Russel, France | 1979 | Ingemar Stenmark, Sweden | 1987 | Joel Gaspoz, Switzerland |
| 1972 | Gustavo Thoeni, Italy | 1980 | Ingemar Stenmark, Sweden | | Pirmin Zurbriggen, Switzerland |
| 1973 | Hans Hinterseer, Austria | 1981 | Ingemar Stenmark, Sweden | 1988 | Alberto Tomba, Italy |
| 1974 | Piero Gros, Italy | 1982 | Phil Mahre, USA | 1989 | Pirmin Zurbriggen, Switzerland |
| 1975 | Ingemar Stenmark, Sweden | 1983 | Phil Mahre, USA | | |

## Alpine Skiing (Cont.)

| Year | Year | Year |
|---|---|---|
| 1990 Ole-Cristian Furuseth, Norway | 1995 Alberto Tomba, Italy | 2001 Hermann Maier, Austria |
|      Gunther Mader, Austria | 1996 Michael von Gruenigen, SWI | 2002 Frederic Covili, France |
| 1991 Alberto Tomba, Italy | 1997 Michael von Gruenigen, SWI | 2003 Michael von Gruenigen, SWI |
| 1992 Alberto Tomba, Italy | 1998 Hermann Maier, Austria | 2004 Bode Miller, USA |
| 1993 Kjetil Andre Aamodt, Norway | 1999 Michael von Gruenigen, SWI | 2005 Benjamin Raich, Austria |
| 1994 Christian Mayer, Austria | 2000 Hermann Maier, Austria | |

### Super G

**Multiple winners:** Hermann Maier (5); Pirmin Zurbriggen (4); Stephan Eberharter (2).

| Year | Year | Year |
|---|---|---|
| 1986 Markus Wasmeier, W. Ger. | 1993 Kjetil Andre Aamodt, Norway | 2000 Hermann Maier, Austria |
| 1987 Pirmin Zurbriggen, Switzerland | 1994 Jan Einar Thorsen, Norway | 2001 Hermann Maier, Austria |
| 1988 Pirmin Zurbriggen, Switzerland | 1995 Peter Runggaldier, Italy | 2002 Stephan Eberharter, Austria |
| 1989 Pirmin Zurbriggen, Switzerland | 1996 Atle Skaardal, Norway | 2003 Stephan Eberharter, Austria |
| 1990 Pirmin Zurbriggen, Switzerland | 1997 Luc Alphand, France | 2004 Hermann Maier, Austria |
| 1991 Franz Heinzer, Switzerland | 1998 Hermann Maier, Austria | 2005 Bode Miller, USA |
| 1992 Paul Accola, Switzerland | 1999 Hermann Maier, Austria | |

### Combined

**Multiple winners:** Marc Girardelli and Andreas Wenzel (4); Kjetil Andre Aamodt and Phil Mahre (3); Bode Miller and Pirmin Zurbriggen (2).

| Year | Year | Year |
|---|---|---|
| 1979 Andreas Wenzel, Liechtenstein | 1988 Hubert Strolz, Austria | 1997-99 Not awarded |
| 1980 Andreas Wenzel, Liechtenstein | 1989 Marc Girardelli, Luxembourg | 2000 Kjetil Andre Aamodt, Norway |
| 1981 Phil Mahre, USA | 1990 Pirmin Zurbriggen, Switzerland | 2001 Lasse Kjus, Norway |
| 1982 Phil Mahre, USA | 1991 Marc Girardelli, Luxembourg | 2002 Kjetil Andre Aamodt, Norway |
| 1983 Phil Mahre, USA | 1992 Paul Accola, Switzerland | 2003 Bode Miller, USA |
| 1984 Andreas Wenzel, Liechtenstein | 1993 Marc Girardelli, Luxembourg | 2004 Bode Miller, USA |
| 1985 Andreas Wenzel, Liechtenstein | 1994 Kjetil Andre Aamodt, Norway | 2005 Benjamin Raich, Austria |
| 1986 Markus Wasmeier, W. Ger | 1995 Marc Girardelli, Luxembourg | |
| 1987 Pirmin Zurbriggen, Switzerland | 1996 Gunther Mader, Austria | |

## WOMEN
### Downhill

**Multiple winners:** Annemarie Moser-Pröll (7), Michela Figini, Renate Goetschl and Katja Seizinger (4); Isolde Kostner, Isabelle Mir, Marie-Therese Nadig, Picabo Street, Bridgitte Totschnig-Habersatter and Maria Walliser (2).

| Year | Year | Year |
|---|---|---|
| 1967 Marielle Goitschel, France | 1980 Marie-Therese Nadig, SWI | 1994 Katja Seizinger, Germany |
| 1968 Isabelle Mir, France | 1981 Marie-Therese Nadig, SWI | 1995 Picabo Street, USA |
|      Olga Pall, Austria | 1982 Marie-Cecile Gros-Gaudenier, FRA | 1996 Picabo Street, USA |
| 1969 Wiltrud Drexel, Austria | 1983 Doris De Agostini, Switzerland | 1997 Renate Goetschl, Austria |
| 1970 Isabelle Mir, France | 1984 Maria Walliser, Switzerland | 1998 Katja Seizinger, Germany |
| 1971 Annemarie Pröll, Austria | 1985 Michela Figini, Switzerland | 1999 Renate Goetschl, Austria |
| 1972 Annemarie Pröll, Austria | 1986 Maria Walliser, Switzerland | 2000 Regina Haeusl, Germany |
| 1973 Annemarie Pröll, Austria | 1987 Michela Figini, Switzerland | 2001 Isolde Kostner, Italy |
| 1974 Annemarie Pröll, Austria | 1988 Michela Figini, Switzerland | 2002 Isolde Kostner, Italy |
| 1975 Annemarie Moser-Pröll, Austria | 1989 Michela Figini, Switzerland | 2003 Michaela Dorfmeister, Austria |
| 1976 Bridgitte Totschnig-Habersatter, AUT | 1990 Katrin Gutensohn-Knopf, GER | 2004 Renate Goetschl, Austria |
| 1977 Bridgitte Totschnig-Habersatter, AUT | 1991 Chantal Bournissen, SWI | 2005 Renate Goetschl, Austria |
| 1978 Annemarie Moser-Pröll, Austria | 1992 Katja Seizinger, Germany | |
| 1979 Annemarie Moser-Pröll, Austria | 1993 Katja Seizinger, Germany | |

### Slalom

**Multiple winners:** Vreni Schneider (6); Erika Hess (5); Janica Kostelic, Marielle Goitschel, Britt Lafforgue, Lisa-Marie Morerod and Roswitha Steiner (2).

| Year | Year | Year |
|---|---|---|
| 1967 Marielle Goitschel, France | 1981 Erika Hess, Switzerland | 1993 Vreni Schneider, Switzerland |
| 1968 Marielle Goitschel, France | 1982 Erika Hess, Switzerland | 1994 Vreni Schneider, Switzerland |
| 1969 Gertrud Gabl, Austria | 1983 Erika Hess, Switzerland | 1995 Vreni Schneider, Switzerland |
| 1970 Ingrid Lafforgue, France | 1984 Tamara McKinney, USA | 1996 Elfi Eder, Austria |
| 1971 Britt Lafforgue, France | 1985 Erika Hess, Switzerland | 1997 Pernilla Wiberg, Sweden |
| 1972 Britt Lafforgue, France | 1986 Roswitha Steiner, Austria | 1998 Ylva Nowen, Sweden |
| 1973 Patricia Emonet, France |      Erika Hess, Switzerland | 1999 Sabine Egger, Austria |
| 1974 Christa Zechmeister, W. Germany | 1987 Corrine Schmidhauser, | 2000 Spela Pretnar, Slovenia |
| 1975 Lisa-Marie Morerod, Switzerland |      Switzerland | 2001 Janica Kostelic, Croatia |
| 1976 Rosi Mittermaier, W. Germany | 1988 Roswitha Steiner, Austria | 2002 Laure Pequegnot, France |
| 1977 Lisa-Marie Morerod, Switzerland | 1989 Vreni Schneider, Switzerland | 2003 Janica Kostelic, Croatia |
| 1978 Hanni Wenzel, Liechtenstein | 1990 Vreni Schneider, Switzerland | 2004 Anja Paerson, Sweden |
| 1979 Regina Sackl, Austria | 1991 Petra Kronberger, Austria | 2005 Tanja Poutiainen, Finland |
| 1980 Perrine Pelene, France | 1992 Vreni Schneider, Switzerland | |

### Giant Slalom

**Multiple winners:** Vreni Schneider (5); Lisa-Marie Morerod and Annemarie Moser-Pröll (3); Martina Ertl, Nancy Greene, Carole Merle, Sonja Nef, Anja Paerson, Anita Wachter and Hanni Wenzel (2).

| Year | Year | Year |
|---|---|---|
| 1967 Nancy Greene, Canada | 1980 Hanni Wenzel, Liechtenstein | 1992 Carole Merle, France |
| 1968 Nancy Greene, Canada | 1981 Marie-Therese Nadig, SWI | 1993 Carole Merle, France |
| 1969 Marilyn Cochran, USA | 1982 Irene Epple, West Germany | 1994 Anita Wachter, Austria |
| 1970 Michele Jacot, France | 1983 Tamara McKinney, USA | 1995 Vreni Schneider, Switzerland |
| Francoise Macchi, France | 1984 Erika Hess, Switzerland | 1996 Martina Ertl, Germany |
| 1971 Annemarie Pröll, Austria | 1985 Maria Keihl, West Germany | 1997 Deborah Compagnoni, Italy |
| 1972 Annemarie Pröll, Austria | Michela Figini, Switzerland | 1998 Martina Ertl, Germany |
| 1973 Monika Kaserer, Austria | 1986 Vreni Schneider, Switzerland | 1999 Alexandra Meissnitzer, Austria |
| 1974 Hanni Wenzel, Liechtenstein | 1987 Vreni Schneider, Switzerland | 2000 Michaela Dorfmeister, Austria |
| 1975 Annemarie Moser-Pröll, Austria | Maria Walliser, Switzerland | 2001 Sonja Nef, Switzerland |
| 1976 Lisa-Marie Morerod, SWI | 1988 Mateja Svet, Yugoslavia | 2002 Sonja Nef, Switzerland |
| 1977 Lisa-Marie Morerod, SWI | 1989 Vreni Schneider, Switzerland | 2003 Anja Paerson, Sweden |
| 1978 Lisa-Marie Morerod, SWI | 1990 Anita Wachter, Austria | 2004 Anja Paerson, Sweden |
| 1979 Christa Kinshofer, W. Ger. | 1991 Vreni Schneider, Switzerland | 2005 Tanja Poutiainen, Finland |

### Super G

**Multiple winners:** Katja Seizinger (5); Carole Merle (4); Hilde Gerg and Renate Goetschl (2).

| Year | Year | Year |
|---|---|---|
| 1986 Maria Kiehl, West Germany | 1993 Katja Seizinger, Germany | 2000 Renate Goetschl, Austria |
| 1987 Maria Walliser, Switzerland | 1994 Katja Seizinger, Germany | 2001 Regine Cavagnoud, France |
| 1988 Michela Figini, Switzerland | 1995 Katja Seizinger, Germany | 2002 Hilde Gerg, Germany |
| 1989 Carole Merle, France | 1996 Katja Seizinger, Germany | 2003 Carole Montillet, France |
| 1990 Carole Merle, France | 1997 Hilde Gerg, Germany | 2004 Renate Goetschl, Austria |
| 1991 Carole Merle, France | 1998 Katja Seizinger, Germany | 2005 Michaela Dorfmeister, Austria |
| 1992 Carole Merle, France | 1999 Alexandra Meissnitzer, Austria | |

### Combined

**Multiple winners:** Brigitte Oertli (5); Janica Kostelic, Anita Wachter and Hanni Wenzel (3); Sabine Ginther, Renate Goetschl and Pernilla Wiberg (2).

| Year | Year | Year |
|---|---|---|
| 1979 Annemarie Moser-Pröll, Austria | 1987 Brigitte Oertli, Switzerland | 1996 Anita Wachter, Austria |
| Hanni Wenzel, Liechtenstein | 1988 Brigitte Oertli, Switzerland | 1997–99 Not Awarded |
| 1980 Hanni Wenzel, Liechtenstein | 1989 Brigitte Oertli, Switzerland | 2000 Renate Goetschl, Austria |
| 1981 Maria-Therese Nadig, | 1989 Brigitte Oertli, Switzerland | 2001 Janica Kostelic, Croatia |
| Switzerland | 1990 Anita Wachter, Austria | 2002 Renate Goetschl, Austria |
| 1982 Irene Epple, West Germany | 1991 Sabine Ginther, Austria | 2003 Janica Kostelic, Croatia |
| 1983 Hanni Wenzel, Liechtenstein | 1992 Sabine Ginther, Austria | 2004 Not Awarded |
| 1984 Erika Hess, Switzerland | 1993 Anita Wachter, Austria | 2005 Janica Kostelic, Croatia |
| 1985 Brigitte Oertli, Switzerland | 1994 Pernilla Wiberg, Sweden | |
| 1986 Maria Walliser, Switzerland | 1995 Pernilla Wiberg, Sweden | |

---

## FIGURE SKATING

## World Champions

Skaters who won World and Olympic championships in the same year are listed in **bold** type.

### MEN

**Multiple winners:** Ulrich Salchow (10); Karl Schafer (7); Dick Button (5); Willy Bockl, Kurt Browning, Scott Hamilton and Hayes Jenkins and Alexei Yagudin (4); Emmerich Danzer, Gillis Grafstrom, Gustav Hugel, David Jenkins, Fritz Kachler, Ondrej Nepela, Evgeni Plushenko and Elvis Stojko (3); Brian Boitano, Gilbert Fuchs, Jan Hoffmann, Felix Kaspar, Vladimir Kovalev and Tim Wood (2).

| Year | Year | Year |
|---|---|---|
| 1896 Gilbert Fuchs, Germany | 1908 **Ulrich Salchow**, Sweden | 1926 Willy Bockl, Austria |
| 1897 Gustav Hugel, Austria | 1909 Ulrich Salchow, Sweden | 1927 Willy Bockl, Austria |
| 1898 Henning Grenander, Sweden | 1910 Ulrich Salchow, Sweden | 1928 Willy Bockl, Austria |
| 1899 Gustav Hugel, Austria | 1911 Ulrich Salchow, Sweden | 1929 Gillis Grafstrom, Sweden |
| 1900 Gustav Hugel, Austria | 1912 Fritz Kachler, Austria | 1930 Karl Schafer, Austria |
| 1901 Ulrich Salchow, Sweden | 1913 Fritz Kachler, Austria | 1931 Karl Schafer, Austria |
| 1902 Ulrich Salchow, Sweden | 1914 Gosta Sandhal, Sweden | 1932 **Karl Schafer**, Austria |
| 1903 Ulrich Salchow, Sweden | 1915-21 Not held | 1933 Karl Schafer, Austria |
| 1904 Ulrich Salchow, Sweden | 1922 Gillis Grafstrom, Sweden | 1934 Karl Schafer, Austria |
| 1905 Ulrich Salchow, Sweden | 1923 Fritz Kachler, Austria | 1935 Karl Schafer, Austria |
| 1906 Gilbert Fuchs, Germany | 1924 **Gillis Grafstrom,** Sweden | 1936 **Karl Schafer**, Austria |
| 1907 Ulrich Salchow, Sweden | 1925 Willy Bockl, Austria | 1937 Felix Kaspar, Austria |

## Figure Skating (Cont.)

| Year | | Year | | Year | |
|------|------|------|------|------|------|
| 1938 | Felix Kaspar, Austria | 1968 | Emmerich Danzer, Austria | 1993 | Kurt Browning, Canada |
| 1939 | Graham Sharp, Britain | 1969 | Tim Wood, USA | 1994 | Elvis Stojko, Canada |
| 1940-46 | Not held | 1970 | Tim Wood, USA | 1995 | Elvis Stojko, Canada |
| 1947 | Hans Gerschwiler, Switzerland | 1971 | Ondrej Nepela, Czechoslovakia | 1996 | Todd Eldredge, USA |
| 1948 | **Dick Button**, USA | 1972 | **Ondrej Nepela**, Czechoslovakia | 1997 | Elvis Stojko, Canada |
| 1949 | Dick Button, USA | 1973 | Ondrej Nepela, Czechoslovakia | 1998 | Alexei Yagudin, Russia |
| | | 1974 | Jan Hoffmann, E. Germany | 1999 | Alexei Yagudin, Russia |
| 1950 | Dick Button, USA | 1975 | Sergie Volkov, USSR | | |
| 1951 | Dick Button, USA | 1976 | **John Curry**, Britain | 2000 | Alexei Yagudin, Russia |
| 1952 | **Dick Button**, USA | 1977 | Vladimir Kovalev, USSR | 2001 | Evgeni Plushenko, Russia |
| 1953 | Hayes Jenkins, USA | 1978 | Charles Tickner, USA | 2002 | **Alexei Yagudin**, Russia |
| 1954 | Hayes Jenkins, USA | 1979 | Vladimir Kovalev, USSR | 2003 | Evgeni Plushenko, Russia |
| 1955 | Hayes Jenkins, USA | | | 2004 | Evgeni Plushenko, Russia |
| 1956 | **Hayes Jenkins**, USA | 1980 | Jan Hoffmann, E. Germany | 2005 | Stephane Lambiel, Switzerland |
| 1957 | David Jenkins, USA | 1981 | Scott Hamilton, USA | | |
| 1958 | David Jenkins, USA | 1982 | Scott Hamilton, USA | | |
| 1959 | David Jenkins, USA | 1983 | Scott Hamilton, USA | | |
| | | 1984 | **Scott Hamilton**, USA | | |
| 1960 | Alan Giletti, France | 1985 | Alexander Fadeev, USSR | | |
| 1961 | Not held | 1986 | Brian Boitano, USA | | |
| 1962 | Donald Jackson, Canada | 1987 | Brian Orser, Canada | | |
| 1963 | Donald McPherson, Canada | 1988 | **Brian Boitano**, USA | | |
| 1964 | **Manfred Schnelldorfer**, W. Germany | 1989 | Kurt Browning, Canada | | |
| 1965 | Alain Calmat, France | 1990 | Kurt Browning, Canada | | |
| 1966 | Emmerich Danzer, Austria | 1991 | Kurt Browning, Canada | | |
| 1967 | Emmerich Danzer, Austria | 1992 | **Viktor Petrenko**, CIS | | |

## WOMEN

**Multiple winners:** Sonja Henie (10); Carol Heiss, Michelle Kwan and Herma Planck Szabo (5); Lily Kronberger and Katarina Witt (4); Sjoukje Dijkstra, Peggy Fleming and Meray Horvath (3); Tenley Albright, Linda Fratianne, Anett Poetzsch, Beatrix Schuba, Barbara Ann Scott, Gabriele Seyfert, Irina Slutskaya, Megan Taylor, Alena Vrzanova and Kristi Yamaguchi (2).

| Year | | Year | | Year | |
|------|------|------|------|------|------|
| 1906 | Madge Syers, Britain | 1949 | Alena Vrzanova, Czechoslovakia | 1980 | **Anett Poetzsch**, E. Germany |
| 1907 | Madge Syers, Britain | 1950 | Alena Vrzanova, Czechoslovakia | 1981 | Denise Biellmann, Switzerland |
| 1908 | Lily Kronberger, Hungary | 1951 | Jeannette Altwegg, Britain | 1982 | Elaine Zayak, USA |
| 1909 | Lily Kronberger, Hungary | 1952 | Jacqueline Du Bief, France | 1983 | Rosalyn Sumners, USA |
| 1910 | Lily Kronberger, Hungary | 1953 | Tenley Albright, USA | 1984 | **Katarina Witt**, E. Germany |
| 1911 | Lily Kronberger, Hungary | 1954 | Gundi Busch, W. Germany | 1985 | Katarina Witt, E. Germany |
| 1912 | Meray Horvath, Hungary | 1955 | Tenley Albright, USA | 1986 | Debi Thomas, USA |
| 1913 | Meray Horvath, Hungary | 1956 | Carol Heiss, USA | 1987 | Katarina Witt, E. Germany |
| 1914 | Meray Horvath, Hungary | 1957 | Carol Heiss, USA | 1988 | **Katarina Witt**, E. Germany |
| 1915-21 | Not held | 1958 | Carol Heiss, USA | 1989 | Midori Ito, Japan |
| 1922 | Herma Planck-Szabo, Austria | 1959 | Carol Heiss, USA | 1990 | Jill Trenary, USA |
| 1923 | Herma Planck-Szabo, Austria | 1960 | **Carol Heiss**, USA | 1991 | Kristi Yamaguchi, USA |
| 1924 | **Herma Planck-Szabo**, AUT | 1961 | Not held | 1992 | **Kristi Yamaguchi**, USA |
| 1925 | Herma Planck-Szabo, Austria | 1962 | Sjoukje Dijkstra, Netherlands | 1993 | Oksana Baiul, Ukraine |
| 1926 | Herma Planck-Szabo, Austria | 1963 | Sjoukje Dijkstra, Netherlands | 1994 | Yuka Sato, Japan |
| 1927 | Sonja Henie, Norway | 1964 | **Sjoukje Dijkstra**, Netherlands | 1995 | Lu Chen, China |
| 1928 | **Sonja Henie**, Norway | 1965 | Petra Burka, Canada | 1996 | Michelle Kwan, USA |
| 1929 | Sonja Henie, Norway | 1966 | Peggy Fleming, USA | 1997 | Tara Lipinski, USA |
| 1930 | Sonja Henie, Norway | 1967 | Peggy Fleming, USA | 1998 | Michelle Kwan, USA |
| 1931 | Sonja Henie, Norway | 1968 | **Peggy Fleming**, USA | 1999 | Maria Butyrskaya, Russia |
| 1932 | **Sonja Henie**, Norway | 1969 | Gabriele Seyfert, E. Germany | 2000 | Michelle Kwan, USA |
| 1933 | Sonja Henie, Norway | 1970 | Gabriele Seyfert, E. Germany | 2001 | Michelle Kwan, USA |
| 1934 | Sonja Henie, Norway | 1971 | Beatrix Schuba, Austria | 2002 | Irina Slutskaya, Russia |
| 1935 | Sonja Henie, Norway | 1972 | **Beatrix Schuba**, Austria | 2003 | Michelle Kwan, USA |
| 1936 | **Sonja Henie**, Norway | 1973 | Karen Magnussen, Canada | 2004 | Shizuka Arakawa, Japan |
| 1937 | Cecilia Colledge, Britain | 1974 | Christine Errath, E. Germany | 2005 | Irina Slutskaya, Russia |
| 1938 | Megan Taylor, Britain | 1975 | Dianne DeLeeuw, Netherlands | | |
| 1939 | Megan Taylor, Britain | 1976 | **Dorothy Hamill**, USA | | |
| 1940-46 | Not held | 1977 | Linda Fratianne, USA | | |
| 1947 | Barbara Ann Scott, Canada | 1978 | Anett Poetzsch, E. Germany | | |
| 1948 | **Barbara Ann Scott**, Canada | 1979 | Linda Fratianne, USA | | |

## U.S. Champions

Skaters who won U.S., World and Olympic championships in same year are in **bold** type.

### MEN

**Multiple winners:** Dick Button and Roger Turner (7); Todd Eldredge (6); Sherwin Badger and Robin Lee (5); Brian Boitano, Scott Hamilton, David Jenkins, Hayes Jenkins and Charles Tickner (4); Gordon McKellen, Nathaniel Niles, Michael Weiss and Tim Wood (3); Scott Allen, Christopher Bowman, Scott Davis, Eugene Turner, Gary Visconti and Johnny Weir (2).

| Year | | Year | | Year | | Year | |
|---|---|---|---|---|---|---|---|
| 1914 | Norman Scott | 1940 | Eugene Turner | 1965 | Gary Visconti | 1989 | Christopher Bowman |
| 1915-17 | Not held | 1941 | Eugene Turner | 1966 | Scott Allen | 1990 | Todd Eldredge |
| 1918 | Nathaniel Niles | 1942 | Robert Specht | 1967 | Gary Visconti | 1991 | Todd Eldredge |
| 1919 | Not held | 1943 | Arthur Vaughn | 1968 | Tim Wood | 1992 | Christopher Bowman |
| 1920 | Sherwin Badger | 1944-45 | Not held | 1969 | Tim Wood | 1993 | Scott Davis |
| 1921 | Sherwin Badger | 1946 | Dick Button | 1970 | Tim Wood | 1994 | Scott Davis |
| 1922 | Sherwin Badger | 1947 | Dick Button | 1971 | John (Misha) Petkevich | 1995 | Todd Eldredge |
| 1923 | Sherwin Badger | 1948 | **Dick Button** | 1972 | Ken Shelley | 1996 | Rudy Galindo |
| 1924 | Sherwin Badger | 1949 | Dick Button | 1973 | Gordon McKellen | 1997 | Todd Eldredge |
| 1925 | Nathaniel Niles | 1950 | Dick Button | 1974 | Gordon McKellen | 1998 | Todd Eldredge |
| 1926 | Chris Christenson | 1951 | Dick Button | 1975 | Gordon McKellen | 1999 | Michael Weiss |
| 1927 | Nathaniel Niles | 1952 | **Dick Button** | 1976 | Terry Kubicka | 2000 | Michael Weiss |
| 1928 | Roger Turner | 1953 | Hayes Jenkins | 1977 | Charles Tickner | 2001 | Tim Goebel |
| 1929 | Roger Turner | 1954 | Hayes Jenkins | 1978 | Charles Tickner | 2002 | Todd Eldredge |
| 1930 | Roger Turner | 1955 | Hayes Jenkins | 1979 | Charles Tickner | 2003 | Michael Weiss |
| 1931 | Roger Turner | 1956 | **Hayes Jenkins** | 1980 | Charles Tickner | 2004 | Johnny Weir |
| 1932 | Roger Turner | 1957 | David Jenkins | 1981 | Scott Hamilton | 2005 | Johnny Weir |
| 1933 | Roger Turner | 1958 | David Jenkins | 1982 | Scott Hamilton | | |
| 1934 | Roger Turner | 1959 | David Jenkins | 1983 | Scott Hamilton | | |
| 1935 | Robin Lee | 1960 | David Jenkins | 1984 | **Scott Hamilton** | | |
| 1936 | Robin Lee | 1961 | Bradley Lord | 1985 | Brian Boitano | | |
| 1937 | Robin Lee | 1962 | Monty Hoyt | 1986 | Brian Boitano | | |
| 1938 | Robin Lee | 1963 | Thomas Litz | 1987 | Brian Boitano | | |
| 1939 | Robin Lee | 1964 | Scott Allen | 1988 | **Brian Boitano** | | |

### WOMEN

**Multiple winners:** Michelle Kwan and Maribel Vinson (9); Theresa Weld Blanchard and Gretchen Merrill (6); Tenley Albright, Peggy Fleming and Janet Lynn (5); Linda Fratianne and Carol Heiss (4); Dorothy Hamill, Beatrix Loughran, Rosalyn Summers, Joan Tozzer and Jill Trenary (3); Yvonne Sherman and Debi Thomas (2).

| Year | | Year | | Year | | Year | |
|---|---|---|---|---|---|---|---|
| 1914 | Theresa Weld | 1940 | Joan Tozzer | 1964 | Peggy Fleming | 1988 | Debi Thomas |
| 1915-17 | Not held | 1941 | Jane Vaughn | 1965 | Peggy Fleming | 1989 | Jill Trenary |
| 1918 | Rosemary Beresford | 1942 | Jane Sullivan | 1966 | Peggy Fleming | 1990 | Jill Trenary |
| 1919 | Not held | 1943 | Gretchen Merrill | 1967 | Peggy Fleming | 1991 | Tonya Harding |
| 1920 | Theresa Weld | 1944 | Gretchen Merrill | 1968 | **Peggy Fleming** | 1992 | **Kristi Yamaguchi** |
| 1921 | Theresa Blanchard | 1945 | Gretchen Merrill | 1969 | Janet Lynn | 1993 | Nancy Kerrigan |
| 1922 | Theresa Blanchard | 1946 | Gretchen Merrill | 1970 | Janet Lynn | 1994 | vacated* |
| 1923 | Theresa Blanchard | 1947 | Gretchen Merrill | 1971 | Janet Lynn | 1995 | Nicole Bobek |
| 1924 | Theresa Blanchard | 1948 | Gretchen Merrill | 1972 | Janet Lynn | 1996 | Michelle Kwan |
| 1925 | Beatrix Loughran | 1949 | Yvonne Sherman | 1973 | Janet Lynn | 1997 | Tara Lipinski |
| 1926 | Beatrix Loughran | 1950 | Yvonne Sherman | 1974 | Dorothy Hamill | 1998 | Michelle Kwan |
| 1927 | Beatrix Loughran | 1951 | Sonya Klopfer | 1975 | Dorothy Hamill | 1999 | Michelle Kwan |
| 1928 | Maribel Vinson | 1952 | Tenley Albright | 1976 | **Dorothy Hamill** | 2000 | Michelle Kwan |
| 1929 | Maribel Vinson | 1953 | Tenley Albright | 1977 | Linda Fratianne | 2001 | Michelle Kwan |
| 1930 | Maribel Vinson | 1954 | Tenley Albright | 1978 | Linda Fratianne | 2002 | Michelle Kwan |
| 1931 | Maribel Vinson | 1955 | Tenley Albright | 1979 | Linda Fratianne | 2003 | Michelle Kwan |
| 1932 | Maribel Vinson | 1956 | Tenley Albright | 1980 | Linda Fratianne | 2004 | Michelle Kwan |
| 1933 | Maribel Vinson | 1957 | Carol Heiss | 1981 | Elaine Zayak | 2005 | Michelle Kwan |
| 1934 | Suzanne Davis | 1958 | Carol Heiss | 1982 | Rosalyn Sumners | | |
| 1935 | Maribel Vinson | 1959 | Carol Heiss | 1983 | Rosalyn Sumners | | |
| 1936 | Maribel Vinson | 1960 | **Carol Heiss** | 1984 | Rosalyn Sumners | | |
| 1937 | Maribel Vinson | 1961 | Laurence Owen | 1985 | Tiffany Chin | | |
| 1938 | Joan Tozzer | 1962 | Barbara Pursley | 1986 | Debi Thomas | | |
| 1939 | Joan Tozzer | 1963 | Lorraine Hanlon | 1987 | Jill Trenary | | |

* Tonya Harding was stripped of the 1994 women's title and banned from membership in the U.S. Figure Skating Assn. for life on June 30, 1994 for violating the USFSA Code of Ethics after she pleaded guilty to a charge of conspiracy to hinder the prosecution related to the Jan. 6, 1994 attack on Nancy Kerrigan.

## TOUR DE FRANCE

The world's premier cycling event, the Tour de France is staged throughout the country (sometimes passing through neighboring countries) over four weeks. The 1946 Tour, however, the first after World War II, was only a five-day race.

**Multiple winners:** Lance Armstrong (7); Jacques Anquetil, Bernard Hinault, Miguel Induráin and Eddy Merckx (5); Louison Bobet, Greg LeMond and Philippe Thys (3); Gino Bartali Ottavio Bottecchia, Fausto Coppi, Laurent Fignon, Nicholas Frantz, Firmin Lambot, André Leducq, Sylvere Maes, Antonin Magne, Lucien Petit-Breton and Bernard Thevenet (2).

| Year | | Time (hrs:min:sec) | Year | | Time (hrs:min:sec) |
|---|---|---|---|---|---|
| 1903 | Maurice Garin, France | 94:33:14 | 1959 | Federico Bahamontes, Spain | 113:50:54 |
| 1904 | Henri Cornet, France | 96:05:55 | 1960 | Gastone Nencini, Italy | 112:08:42 |
| 1905 | Louis Trousselier, France | 112:18:09 | 1961 | Jacques Anquetil, France | 122:01:33 |
| 1906 | René Pottier, France | 185:47:26 | 1962 | Jacques Anquetil, France | 114:31:54 |
| 1907 | Lucien Petit-Breton, France | 156:22:30 | 1963 | Jacques Anquetil, France | 113:30:05 |
| 1908 | Lucien Petit-Breton, France | 156:09:31 | 1964 | Jacques Anquetil, France | 127:09:44 |
| 1909 | Francois Faber, Luxembourg | 156:55:10 | 1965 | Felice Gimondi, Italy | 116:42:06 |
| 1910 | Octave Lapize, France | 163:52:38 | 1966 | Lucien Aimar, France | 117:34:21 |
| 1911 | Gustave Garrigou, France | 195:35:25 | 1967 | Roger Pingeon, France | 136:53:50 |
| 1912 | Odile Defraye, Belgium | 184:50:00 | 1968 | Jan Janssen, Netherlands | 133:49:42 |
| 1913 | Philippe Thys, Belgium | 197:54:00 | 1969 | Eddy Merckx, Belgium | 116:16:02 |
| 1914 | Philippe Thys, Belgium | 200:28:49 | 1970 | Eddy Merckx, Belgium | 119:31:48 |
| 1915-18 Not held | | | 1971 | Eddy Merckx, Belgium | 96:45:14 |
| 1919 | Firmin Lambot, Belgium | 231:07:15 | 1972 | Eddy Merckx, Belgium | 108:17:18 |
| 1920 | Philippe Thys, Belgium | 228:36:13 | 1973 | Luis Ocana, Spain | 122:25:34 |
| 1921 | Léon Scieur, Belgium | 221:50:00 | 1974 | Eddy Merckx, Belgium | 116:16:58 |
| 1922 | Firmin Lambot, Belgium | 222:08:06 | 1975 | Bernard Thevenet, France | 114:35:31 |
| 1923 | Henri Pelissier, France | 222:15:30 | 1976 | Lucien van Impe, Belgium | 116:22:23 |
| 1924 | Ottavio Bottecchia, Italy | 226:18:21 | 1977 | Bernard Thevenet, France | 115:38:30 |
| 1925 | Ottavio Bottecchia, Italy | 219:10:13 | 1978 | Bernard Hinault, France | 108:18:00 |
| 1926 | Lucien Buysse, Belgium | 238:44:25 | 1979 | Bernard Hinault, France | 103:06:50 |
| 1927 | Nicholas Frantz, Luxembourg | 198:16:42 | 1980 | Joop Zoetemelk, Netherlands | 109:19:14 |
| 1928 | Nicholas Frantz, Luxembourg | 192:48:58 | 1981 | Bernard Hinault, France | 96:19:38 |
| 1929 | Maurice Dewaele, Belgium | 186:39:16 | 1982 | Bernard Hinault, France | 92:08:46 |
| 1930 | André Leducq, France | 172:12:10 | 1983 | Laurent Fignon, France | 105:07:52 |
| 1931 | Antonin Magne, France | 177:10:03 | 1984 | Laurent Fignon, France | 112:03:40 |
| 1932 | André Leducq, France | 154:11:49 | 1985 | Bernard Hinault, France | 113:24:23 |
| 1933 | Georges Speicher, France | 147:51:37 | 1986 | Greg LeMond, USA | 110:35:19 |
| 1934 | Antonin Magne, France | 147:03:58 | 1987 | Stephen Roche, Ireland | 115:27:42 |
| 1935 | Romain Maes, Belgium | 141:32:00 | 1988 | Pedro Delgado, Spain | 84:27:53 |
| 1936 | Sylvere Maes, Belgium | 142:47:32 | 1989 | Greg LeMond, USA | 87:38:35 |
| 1937 | Roger Lapebie, France | 138:58:31 | 1990 | Greg LeMond, USA | 90:43:20 |
| 1938 | Gino Bartali, Italy | 148:29:12 | 1991 | Miguel Induráin, Spain | 101:01:20 |
| 1939 | Sylvere Maes, Belgium | 132:03:17 | 1992 | Miguel Induráin, Spain | 100:49:30 |
| 1940-45 Not held | | | 1993 | Miguel Induráin, Spain | 95:57:09 |
| 1946 | Jean Lazarides, France | 44:31:42 | 1994 | Miguel Induráin, Spain | 103:38:38 |
| 1947 | Jean Robic, France | 148:11:25 | 1995 | Miguel Induráin, Spain | 92:44:59 |
| 1948 | Gino Bartali, Italy | 147:10:36 | 1996 | Bjarne Riis, Denmark | 95:57:16 |
| 1949 | Fausto Coppi, Italy | 149:40:49 | 1997 | Jan Ullrich, Germany | 100:30:35 |
| 1950 | Ferdinand Kubler, Switzerland | 145:36:56 | 1998 | Marco Pantani, Italy | 92:49:46 |
| 1951 | Hugo Koblet, Switzerland | 142:20:14 | 1999 | Lance Armstrong, USA | 91:32:16 |
| 1952 | Fausto Coppi, Italy | 151:57:20 | 2000 | Lance Armstrong, USA | 92:33:08 |
| 1953 | Louison Bobet, France | 129:23:25 | 2001 | Lance Armstrong, USA | 86:17:28 |
| 1954 | Louison Bobet, France | 140:06:50 | 2002 | Lance Armstrong, USA | 82:05:12 |
| 1955 | Louison Bobet, France | 130:29:26 | 2003 | Lance Armstrong, USA | 83:41:12 |
| 1956 | Roger Walkowiak, France | 124:01:16 | 2004 | Lance Armstrong, USA | 83:36:02 |
| 1957 | Jacques Anquetil, France | 135:44:42 | 2005 | Lance Armstrong, USA | 86:15:02 |
| 1958 | Charly Gaul, Luxembourg | 116:59:05 | | | |

## RUGBY

### World Cup

The inaugural Rugby World Cup was held in 1987. Like soccer's World Cup, it is held every four years. Sixteen national teams were assembled for the first three tournaments but beginning in 1999, 20 teams played for the William Webb Ellis Cup, named for the game's inventor. The Rugby World Cup is now billed as the world's third largest athletic event, behind the Olympics and the soccer World Cup.

| Year | Winner | Score | Runner up | Host Country |
|---|---|---|---|---|
| 1987 | New Zealand | 29-9 | France | Australia & New Zealand |
| 1991 | Australia | 12-6 | England | United Kingdom & France |
| 1995 | South Africa | 15-12 | New Zealand | South Africa |
| 1999 | Australia | 35-12 | France | Wales |
| 2003 | England | 20-17 | Australia | Australia |

# Olympics

**London** celebrated in 2005 as it was awarded
the 2012 Summer Games by the IOC.

AP/Wide World Photos

# 1924-2002
# Through the Years

SPORTS ALMANAC

## The Winter Olympics

The move toward a winter version of the Olympics began in 1908 when figure skating made an appearance at the Summer Games in London. Ten-time world champion Ulrich Salchow of Sweden, who originated the backwards, one revolution jump that bears his name, and Madge Syers of Britain were the first singles champions. Germans Anna Hubler and Heinrich Berger won the pairs competition.

Organizers of the 1916 Summer Games in Berlin planned to introduce a "Skiing Olympia," featuring nordic events in the Black Forest, but the Games were cancelled after the outbreak of World War I in 1914.

The Games resumed in 1920 at Antwerp, Belgium, where figure skating returned and ice hockey was added as a medal event. Sweden's Gillis Grafstrom and Magda Julin took individual honors, while Ludovika and Walter Jakobsson were the top pair. In hockey, Canada won the gold medal with the United States second and Czechoslovakia third.

Despite the objections of Modern Olympics' founder Baron Pierre de Coubertin and the resistance of the Scandinavian countries, which had staged their own Nordic championships every four or five years from 1901-26 in Sweden, the International Olympic Committee sanctioned an "International Winter Sports Week" at Chamonix, France, in 1924. The 11-day event, which included nordic skiing, speed skating, figure skating, ice hockey and bobsledding, was a huge success and was retroactively called the first Olympic Winter Games.

Seventy years after those first cold weather Games, the 17th edition of the Winter Olympics took place in Lillehammer, Norway, in 1994. The event ended the four-year Olympic cycle of staging both Winter and Summer Games in the same year and began a new schedule that calls for the two Games to alternate every two years.

| Year | No | Location | Dates | Nations | Most medals | USA medals |
|------|-----|----------|-------|---------|-------------|------------|
| 1924 | I | Chamonix, FRA . . . . . . . . . . | Jan. 25-Feb. 4 | 16 | Norway (4-7-6–17) | 1-2-1–4 (3rd) |
| 1928 | II | St. Moritz, SWI . . . . . . . . . | Feb. 11-19 | 25 | Norway (6-4-5–15) | 2-2-2– 6 (2nd) |
| 1932 | III | Lake Placid, USA . . . . . . . . . | Feb. 4-15 | 17 | USA (6-4-2–12) | 6-4-2–12 (1st) |
| 1936-a | IV | Garmisch-Partenkirchen, GER . . | Feb. 6-16 | 28 | Norway (7-5-3–15) | 1-0-3– 4 (T-5th) |
| 1940-a | – | Sapporo, JPN . . . . . . . . . . . | Cancelled (WWII) | | | |
| 1944 | – | Cortina d'Ampezzo, ITA . . . . . | Cancelled (WWII) | | | |
| 1948 | V | St. Moritz, SWI . . . . . . . . . . | Jan. 30-Feb. 8 | 28 | Norway (4-3-3–10), Sweden (4-3-3–10) & Switzerland (3-4-3–10) | 3-4-2– 9 (4th) |
| 1952-b | VI | Oslo, NOR . . . . . . . . . . . . | Feb. 14-25 | 30 | Norway (7-3-6–16) | 4-6-1–11 (2nd) |
| 1956-c | VII | Cortina d'Ampezzo, ITA . . . . . | Jan. 26-Feb. 5 | 32 | USSR (7-3-6–16) | 2-3-2– 7 (T-4th) |
| 1960 | VIII | Squaw Valley, USA . . . . . . . | Feb. 18-28 | 30 | USSR (7-5-9–21) | 3-4-3–10 (2nd) |
| 1964 | IX | Innsbruck, AUT . . . . . . . . . | Jan. 29-Feb. 9 | 36 | USSR (11-8-6–25) | 1-2-3– 6 (7th) |
| 1968-d | X | Grenoble, FRA . . . . . . . . . . | Feb. 6-18 | 37 | Norway (6-6-2–14) | 1-5-1– 7 (T-7th) |
| 1972 | XI | Sapporo, JPN . . . . . . . . . . | Feb. 3-13 | 35 | USSR (8-5-3–16) | 3-2-3– 8 (6th) |
| 1976-e | XII | Innsbruck, AUT . . . . . . . . . | Feb. 4-15 | 37 | USSR (13-6-8–27) | 3-3-4–10 (T-3rd) |
| 1980 | XIII | Lake Placid, USA . . . . . . . . . | Feb. 14-23 | 37 | E. Germany (9-7-7–23) | 6-4-2–12 (3rd) |
| 1984 | XIV | Sarajevo, YUG . . . . . . . . . . | Feb. 7-19 | 49 | USSR (6-10-9–25) | 4-4-0– 8 (T-5th) |
| 1988 | XV | Calgary, CAN . . . . . . . . . . | Feb. 13-28 | 57 | USSR (11-9-9–29) | 2-1-3– 6 (T-8th) |
| 1992-f | XVI | Albertville, FRA . . . . . . . . . | Feb. 8-23 | 63 | Germany (10-10-6–26) | 5-4-2–11 (6th) |
| 1994-g | XVII | Lillehammer, NOR . . . . . . . . | Feb. 12-27 | 67 | Norway (10-11-5–26) | 6-5-2–13 (T-5th) |
| 1998 | XVIII | Nagano, JPN . . . . . . . . . . . | Feb. 7-22 | 72 | Germany (12-9-8–29) | 6-3-4–13 (5th) |
| 2002 | XIX | Salt Lake City, USA . . . . . . . | Feb. 8-24 | 78 | Germany (12-16-7–35) | 10-13-11–34 (2nd) |
| 2006 | XX | Turin, ITA . . . . . . . . . . . . | Feb. 10-26 | | | |
| 2010 | XXI | Vancouver, CAN . . . . . . . . . | Feb. 12-28 | | | |

**a**–The 1940 Winter Games are originally scheduled for Sapporo, but Japan resigns as host in 1937 when the Sino-Japanese war breaks out. St. Moritz is the next choice, but the Swiss feel that ski instructors should not be considered professionals and the IOC withdraws its offer. Finally, Garmisch-Partenkirchen is asked to serve again as host, but the Germans invade Poland in 1939 and the Games are eventually cancelled.

**b**–Germany and Japan are allowed to rejoin the Olympic community for the first time since World War II. Though a divided country, the Germans send a joint East-West team through 1964.

**c**–The Soviet Union (USSR) participates in its first Winter Olympics and takes home the most medals, including the gold medal in ice hockey.

**d**–East Germany and West Germany officially send separate teams for the first time and will continue to do so through 1988.

**e**–The IOC grants the 1976 Winter Games to Denver in May 1970, but in 1972 Colorado voters reject a $5 million bond issue to finance the undertaking. Denver immediately withdraws as host and the IOC selects Innsbruck, the site of the 1964 Games, to take over.

**f**–Germany sends a single team after East and West German reunification in 1990 and the USSR competes as the Unified Team after the breakup of the Soviet Union in 1991.

**g**–The IOC moves the Winter Games' four-year cycle ahead two years in order to separate them from the Summer Games and alternate Olympics every two years.

# 1924
### Chamonix

The first Winter Olympic Games were actually called "The International Winter Sports Week" and went on for 11 days in the French Alps, 60 miles northeast of Grenoble.

As expected, the Scandinavians dominated the 16–nation field. Norway and Finland won 27 of the 43 medals available, including all four Nordic events and four of the five speed skating races. Speed skater Clas Thunberg of Finland and Norwegian Nordic skier and jumper Thorleif Haug each won three gold medals.

American speed skater Charles Jewtraw won the first event of the Games with an upset in the 500 meters. But the most remarkable U.S. medal was the bronze won by Anders Haugen in the ski jump. Due to a scoring error at the time he didn't receive it until 1974 – when he was 83 years old.

In its first four hockey games, Canada beat Switzerland 33–0, Czechoslovakia 30–0, Sweden 22–0 and Great Britain 19–2, before winning the tournament with a 6–1 victory over the U.S. in the final.

## Top 5 Standings

National medal standings are not recognized by the IOC. The unofficial point totals are based on 3 points for a gold medal, 2 for a silver and 1 for a bronze. Total medals are in parentheses.

| | Gold | Silver | Bronze | Points |
|---|---|---|---|---|
| 1 Norway (17) | 4 | 7 | 6 | 32 |
| 2 Finland (10) | 4 | 3 | 3 | 21 |
| 3 Austria (3) | 2 | 1 | 0 | 8 |
| USA (4) | 1 | 2 | 1 | 8 |
| 5 Switzerland (2) | 1 | 0 | 1 | 4 |
| Great Britain (3) | 0 | 1 | 2 | 4 |

## Leading Medal Winners

Number of individual medals won on the left; gold, silver and bronze breakdown to the right.

| No | | Sport | G-S-B |
|---|---|---|---|
| 5 | Clas Thunberg, FIN | Sp. Skate | 3-1-1 |
| 5 | Roald Larsen, NOR | Sp. Skate | 0-2-3 |
| 3 | Thorleif Haug, NOR | X-country & Nordic Combined | 3-0-0 |
| 3 | Julius Skutnabb, FIN | Sp. Skate | 1-1-1 |
| 3 | Johan Gröttumsbråten, NOR | X-country & Nordic Combined | 0-1-2 |
| 2 | Thoralf Strömstad, NOR | X-country & Nordic Combined | 0-2-0 |

## Bobsled

| Event | | Time |
|---|---|---|
| 4-Man | SWI (Eduard Scherrer, Alfred Neveu, Alfred Schläppi, Heinrich Schläppi) | 5:45.54 |

## Figure Skating

| Event | | Points |
|---|---|---|
| Men | Gillis Grafström, SWE | 367.89 |
| Women | Herma Planck-Szabó, AUT | 299.17 |
| Pairs | Helene Engelmann & Albert Berger, AUT | 10.64 |

## Ice Hockey
### Championship Round

Records include games played in two 4–team preliminary pools. Canada and Sweden qualified from one pool, the U.S. and Britain from the other.

| | | Gm | W-L-T | GF | GA |
|---|---|---|---|---|---|
| 1 | Canada | 5 | 5-0-0 | 110 | 3 |
| 2 | USA | 5 | 4-1-0 | 73 | 6 |
| 3 | Great Britain | 5 | 3-2-0 | 40 | 38 |
| 4 | Sweden | 5 | 2-3-0 | 21 | 49 |

**Semifinals:** Canada over Britain, 19–2; USA over Sweden, 20–0. **Third place:** Britain over Sweden, 4–3 (also decided European title). **Final:** Canada over USA, 6–1.

## Nordic Skiing
### Cross Country

| Event | | Time |
|---|---|---|
| 18km | Thorleif Haug, NOR | 1:14:31 |
| 50km | Thorleif Haug, NOR | 3:44:32 |

### Ski Jumping

| Event | | Points |
|---|---|---|
| 90m | Jacob Thams, NOR | 18.906 |

### Nordic Combined

| Event | | Points |
|---|---|---|
| 18km/Jump | Thorleif Haug, NOR | 18.906 |

## Speed Skating

| Event | | Time |
|---|---|---|
| 500m | Charles Jewtraw, USA | 44.0 |
| 1500m | Clas Thunberg, FIN | 2:20.8 |
| 5000m | Clas Thunberg, FIN | 8:39.0 |
| 10,000m | Julius Skutnabb, FIN | 18:04.8 |
| Combined | Clas Thunberg, FIN | 5.5 pts |

# 1928
### St. Moritz

Sonja Henie of Norway was only 11 years old in 1924 when she participated in her first Olympics and finished last in women's figure skating. Three years later, she won the world championship at age 14 and the year after that was Olympic champion at 15.

Henie would go on to win two more gold medals, a record that her coach, men's champion Gillis Grafstrom of Sweden, set in 1928 with his third straight victory in the Winter Games.

Otherwise, St. Moritz was plagued with warm weather that slowed bobsled and cross-country runs and cancelled the 10,000–meter speed skating race. Speed skater Bernt Evensen of Norway led the Games with three medals, sharing the 500–meter title with Finland's Clas Thunberg. Norway also got two gold medals from Johan Gröttumsbråten in cross-country and the Nordic Combined and led the 25 nations competing with six gold and 15 overall medals. The U.S. edged Sweden for second place.

## Top 5 Standings

National medal standings are not recognized by the IOC. The unofficial point totals are based on 3 points for a gold medal, 2 for a silver and 1 for a bronze. Total medals are in parentheses.

| | Gold | Silver | Bronze | Points |
|---|---|---|---|---|
| 1 Norway (15) | 6 | 4 | 5 | 31 |
| 2 USA (6) | 2 | 2 | 2 | 12 |
| 3 Sweden (5) | 2 | 2 | 1 | 11 |
| 4 Finland (4) | 2 | 1 | 1 | 9 |
| 5 Austria (4) | 0 | 3 | 1 | 7 |

## Leading Medal Winners

Number of individual medals won on the left; gold, silver and bronze breakdown to the right.

| No | | Sport | G-S-B |
|---|---|---|---|
| 3 | Bernt Evensen, NOR | Sp. Skate | 1-1-1 |
| 2 | Johan Gröttumsbråten, NOR | X-country | 2-0-0 |
| 2 | Clas Thunberg, FIN | Sp. Skate | 2-0-0 |
| 2 | Jennison Heaton, USA | Bobsled & Cresta | 1-1-0 |
| 2 | Ivar Ballangrud, NOR | Sp. Skate | 1-0-1 |

**Note:** Evensen also placed second in the 10,000—meter speed skating race that was later disallowed due to thawing ice conditions.

## Bobsled

| Event | | Time |
|---|---|---|
| 5-Man | USA (Billy Fiske, Nion Tucker, Geoff Mason, Clifford Gray, Richard Parke) | 3:20.5 |

## Cresta (Toboggan)

| Event | | Time |
|---|---|---|
| 1-Man | Jennison Heaton, USA | 3:01.8 |

## Figure Skating

| Event | | Points |
|---|---|---|
| Men | Gillis Grafström, SWE | 1630.75 |
| Women | Sonja Henie, NOR | 2452.25 |
| Pairs | Andrée Joly & Pierre Brunet, FRA | 100.50 |

## Ice Hockey

### Championship Round

(Overall record in parentheses)

| | Gm | W-L-T | Pts | GF | GA |
|---|---|---|---|---|---|
| 1 Canada (3-0-0) | 3 | 3-0-0 | 6 | 38 | 0 |
| 2 Sweden (3-1-1) | 3 | 2-1-0 | 4 | 7 | 12 |
| 3 Switzerland (2-2-1) | 3 | 1-2-0 | 2 | 4 | 17 |
| 4 Britain (2-4-0) | 3 | 0-3-0 | 0 | 1 | 21 |

**Note:** Canada received a bye to the 4—team championship round robin. The 10 other competing countries—not including the USA which did not send a team—were divided into three pools with the winners advancing to the final round. The Canadians routed Sweden, 11–0; Britain 14–0 and the Swiss, 13–0.

## Nordic Skiing

### Cross Country

| Event | | Time |
|---|---|---|
| 18km | Johan Gröttumsbråten, NOR | 1:37:01 |
| 50km | Per Erik Hedlund, SWE | 4:52:03 |

### Ski Jumping

| Event | | Points |
|---|---|---|
| 90m | Alf Andersen, NOR | 19.208 |

### Nordic Combined

| Event | | Points |
|---|---|---|
| 18km/Jump | Johan Gröttumsbråten, NOR | 17.833 |

## Speed Skating

| Event | | Time |
|---|---|---|
| 500m | Bernt Evensen, NOR & Clas Thunberg, FIN | 43.4 **OR** |
| 1500m | Clas Thunberg, FIN | 2:21.1 |
| 5000m | Ivar Ballangrud, NOR | 8:50.5 |
| 10,000m | No decision (thawing of ice) | |

**Note:** Irving Jaffee of USA had the fastest time in the 10,000 meters (18:36.5) before the race was cancelled.

III Olympic Winter Games

Lake Placid, USA
February 4-13, 1932

# 1932

**Lake Placid**

Back in 1928, American Irving Jaffee had the fastest time in the 10,000—meter speed skating race at St. Moritz only to lose his gold medal when thawing ice made it necessary to call the event off with no official winner.

Four years later, Jaffee won the 10,000 and the 5,000—meter races and local hero Jack Shea won at 500 and 1,500 meters as the U.S. swept all four speed skating events—which were run as actual races (not timed heats) for the first time in Olympic history.

Billy Fiske, who had driven the 5—man U.S. bobsled to a gold medal at St. Moritz when he was only 16, steered the 4—man sled to victory in 1932. On board was Eddie Eagan, the 1920 Olympic light heavyweight champion, who remains the only athlete ever to win gold medals in both the Winter and Summer Games.

Canada won its fourth consecutive hockey gold medal, but 38-year-old Gillis Grafstrom of Sweden missed in his bid for a fourth straight men's figure skating title, placing second to 22-year-old Austrian Karl Schafer.

## Top 5 Standings

National medal standings are not recognized by the IOC. The unofficial point totals are based on 3 points for a gold medal, 2 for a silver and 1 for a bronze. Total medals are in parentheses.

| | Gold | Silver | Bronze | Points |
|---|---|---|---|---|
| 1 USA (12) | 6 | 4 | 2 | 28 |
| 2 Norway (10) | 3 | 4 | 3 | 20 |
| 3 Canada (7) | 1 | 1 | 5 | 10 |
| 4 Sweden (3) | 1 | 2 | 0 | 7 |
| 5 Finland (3) | 1 | 1 | 1 | 6 |

## Leading Medal Winners

Number of individual medals won on the left; gold, silver and bronze breakdown to the right.

| No | | Sport | G-S-B |
|---|---|---|---|
| 2 | Irving Jaffee, USA | Sp. Skate | 2-0-0 |
| 2 | Jack Shea, USA | Sp. Skate | 2-0-0 |
| 2 | Veli Saarinen, FIN | X-country | 1-0-1 |
| 2 | Alex Hurd, CAN | Sp. Skate | 0-1-1 |
| 2 | William Logan, CAN | Sp. Skate | 0-0-2 |

## Bobsled

| Event | | Time |
|---|---|---|
| 2-Man | USA (J.Hubert Stevens & Curtis Stevens) | .8:14.74 |
| 4-Man | USA (Billy Fiske, Eddie Eagan, Clifford Gray, Jay O'Brien) | 7:53.68 |

## Figure Skating

| Event | | Points |
|---|---|---|
| Men | Karl Schäfer, AUT | 2602.0 |
| Women | Sonja Henie, NOR | 2302.5 |
| Pairs | Andrée Joly Brunet & Pierre Brunet, FRA | .76.7 |

## Ice Hockey

| | | Gm | W-L-T | Pts | GF | GA |
|---|---|---|---|---|---|---|
| 1 | Canada | 6 | 5-0-1 | 11 | 32 | 4 |
| 2 | USA | 6 | 4-1-1 | 9 | 27 | 5 |
| 3 | Germany | 6 | 2-4-0 | 4 | 7 | 26 |
| 4 | Poland | 6 | 0-6-0 | 0 | 3 | 34 |

**Note:** Due to the worldwide Depression, only four teams competed. Each side played the other teams twice. Canada beat the U.S., 2–1, in their first game and tied the Americans, 2–2, in triple overtime in the second. A win by the U.S. in Game 2 would have resulted in a third contest to decide the gold medal.

## Nordic Skiing

### Cross Country

| Event | | Time |
|---|---|---|
| 18km | Sven Utterström, SWE | .1:23.07 |
| 50km | Veli Saarinen, FIN | .4:28.00 |

### Ski Jumping

| Event | | Points |
|---|---|---|
| 90m | Birger Rudd, NOR | .228.1 |

### Nordic Combined

| Event | | Points |
|---|---|---|
| 18km/Jump | Johan Gröttumsbråten, NOR | .446.00 |

### Speed Skating

| Event | | Time | |
|---|---|---|---|
| 500m | Jack Shea, USA | .43.4 | **OR** |
| 1500m | Jack Shea, USA | 2:57.5 | |
| 5000m | Irving Jaffee, USA | 9:40.8 | |
| 10,000m | Irving Jaffee, USA | 19:13.6 | |

**Note:** For the only time in the history of the Winter Games, all events were staged as races rather than two-man heats against the clock.

# 1936

### Garmisch-Partenkirchen

The fourth Winter Olympic Games were held in the neighboring villages of Garmisch and Partenkirchen in Germany's Bavarian Alps and included Alpine skiing for the first time.

Also featured in these Games were Norwegians Ivar Ballangrud and Sonja Henie, and Rudi Ball—the Jewish star of the German hockey team.

Ballangrud won three individual gold medals and narrowly missed a fourth in speed skating, but his heroics paled compared to the attention lavished on Henie, who won her third straight gold medal. A week later, she won the world championship for the 10th year in a row, then turned pro. Moving to the U.S., she toured in her own skating show, starred in nine Hollywood movies and was worth more than $45 million when she died in 1969 at age 57.

Ball, who had been the best player on Germany's bronze medal-winning hockey team in 1932, was invited back from voluntary exile in France to lead the 1936 German squad. He was the only Jew on the German Winter Olympic team and his presence was a token gesture by the government of Adolf Hitler to mollify anxious IOC officials who objected to the Nazis' fervent anti-Semitism.

The story of the hockey tournament, however, wasn't one German Jew, but 11 British Canadians, who led Britain to the gold medal and stopped Canada's undefeated Olympic winning streak at 20. The best of the imported Brits was goaltender Jimmy Foster, who allowed just three goals in eight games.

After winning six gold medals in 1932, the U.S. had to settle for one this time, in the two-man bobsled driven by Ivan Brown.

## Top 10 Standings

National medal standings are not recognized by the IOC. The unofficial point totals are based on 3 points for a gold medal, 2 for a silver and 1 for a bronze. Total medals are in parentheses.

| | | Gold | Silver | Bronze | Pts |
|---|---|---|---|---|---|
| 1 | Norway (15) | 7 | 5 | 3 | 34 |
| 2 | Germany (6) | 3 | 3 | 0 | 15 |
| 3 | Sweden (7) | 2 | 2 | 3 | 13 |
| 4 | Finland (6) | 1 | 2 | 3 | 10 |
| 5 | Switzerland (3) | 1 | 2 | 0 | 7 |
| 6 | Austria (4) | 1 | 1 | 2 | 7 |
| 7 | Great Britain (3) | 1 | 1 | 1 | 6 |
| 8 | USA (4) | 1 | 0 | 3 | 6 |
| 9 | Canada (1) | 0 | 1 | 0 | 2 |
| 10 | France (1) | 0 | 0 | 1 | 1 |
| | Hungary (1) | 0 | 0 | 1 | 1 |

## Leading Medal Winners

Number of individual medals won on the left; gold, silver and bronze breakdown to the right.

| No | | Sport | G-S-B |
|---|---|---|---|
| 4 | Ivar Ballangrud, NOR | Sp. Skate | 3-1-0 |
| 3 | Oddbjörn Hagen, NOR | X-country & Nordic Combined | 1-2-0 |
| 3 | Birger Vasenius, FIN | Sp. Skate | 0-2-1 |
| 2 | Ernst Baier, GER | Fig. Skate | 1-1-0 |
| 2 | Joseph Beerli, SWI | Bobsled | 1-1-0 |
| 2 | Erik Larsson, SWE | X-country | 1-0-1 |
| 2 | Fritz Feierabend, SWI | Bobsled | 0-2-0 |
| 2 | Olaf Hoffsbakken, NOR | X-country | 0-2-0 |
| 2 | Sverre Brodahl, NOR | X-country | 0-1-1 |

## Alpine Skiing

### MEN

| Event | | Pts |
|---|---|---|
| Combined | Franz Pfnür, GER | .99.25 |

### WOMEN

| Event | | Pts |
|---|---|---|
| Combined | Christl Cranz, GER | .97.06 |

## Bobsled

| Event | | Time |
|---|---|---|
| 2-Man | USA (Ivan Brown & Alan Washbond) | ...5:29.29 |
| 4-Man | SWI (Pierre Musy, Arnold Gartmann, Charles Bouvier, Joseph Beerli) | .......5:19.85 |

## Figure Skating

| Event | | Points |
|---|---|---|
| Men | Karl Schäfer, AUT | ...........2959.0 |
| Women | Sonja Henie, NOR | ...................425.5 |
| Pairs | Maxi Herber & Ernst Baier, GER | .........11.5 |

## Ice Hockey

### Championship Round

(Overall records in parentheses)

| | | Gm | W-L-T | Pts | GF | GA |
|---|---|---|---|---|---|---|
| 1 | Great Britain (5-0-2) | 3 | 2-0-1 | 5 | 7 | 1 |
| 2 | Canada (7-1-0) | 3 | 2-1-0 | 4 | 9 | 2 |
| 3 | USA (5-2-1) | 3 | 1-1-1 | 3 | 2 | 1 |
| 4 | Czechoslovakia (5-3-0) | 3 | 0-3-0 | 0 | 0 | 14 |

**Scores:** Britain beat Canada, 2–1; Czech., 5–0; and tied the U.S., 0–0 (OT). Canada beat Czech., 7–0, and the U.S., 1–0. The U.S. beat Czech., 2–0.

## Nordic Skiing

### Cross Country

| Event | | Time |
|---|---|---|
| 18km | Erik-August Larsson, SWE | ...........1:14:38 |
| 50km | Elis Wiklund, SWE | ................3:30:11 |
| 4x10km | FIN (Sulo Nurmela, Klaes Karppinen, Matti Lähde, Kalle Jalkanen) | ........2:41:33 |

### Ski Jumping

| Event | | Points |
|---|---|---|
| 90m | Birger Rudd, NOR | ...................232.0 |

### Nordic Combined

| Event | | Points |
|---|---|---|
| 18km/Jump | Oddbjörn Hagen, NOR | ...........430.3 |

## Speed Skating

| Event | | Time | |
|---|---|---|---|
| 500m | Ivar Ballangrud, NOR | .........43.4 | =OR |
| 1500m | Charles Mathisen, NOR | .......2:19.2 | OR |
| 5000m | Ivar Ballangrud, NOR | ........8:19.6 | OR |
| 10,000m | Ivar Ballangrud, NOR | .......17:24.3 | OR |

# 1948
## St. Moritz

The Winter Games originally scheduled for Sapporo, Japan (1940) and Cortina d'Ampezzo, Italy (1944) were cancelled because of World War II. Untouched by the war, the Swiss resort town of St. Moritz was picked to host the 1948 Games and 28 countries sent 706 athletes to compete.

The United States sent two hockey teams, one sanctioned by the American Olympic Committee and one by the American Hockey Association. The IOC ruled that the AOC team could march in the opening parade and the AHA team could play in the tournament, but neither would be eligible for a medal. Canada and Czechoslovakia each finished with 7–0–1 records, but the Canadians won the gold medal by goal differential, 64–62. Czech team member Jaroslav Drobny later distinguished himself as a tennis player, winning the men's singles title at Wimbledon in 1954.

Dick Button of Englewood, N.J., became the first American to win a figure skating gold medal, an achievement that also earned him the Sullivan Award as U.S. amateur athlete of the year.

Alpine skier Gretchen Fraser won a gold medal in the slalom and a silver in the combined for the Americans. French Alpine skier Henri Oreiller was the men's top individual performer with two golds and a bronze.

## Top 10 Standings

National medal standings are not recognized by the IOC. The unofficial point totals are based on 3 points for a gold medal, 2 for a silver and 1 for a bronze. Total medals are in parentheses.

| | | Gold | Silver | Bronze | Pts |
|---|---|---|---|---|---|
| 1 | Norway (10) | 4 | 3 | 3 | 21 |
| | Sweden (10) | 4 | 3 | 3 | 21 |
| 3 | Switzerland (10) | 3 | 4 | 3 | 20 |
| 4 | USA (9) | 3 | 4 | 2 | 19 |
| 5 | Austria (8) | 1 | 3 | 4 | 13 |
| 6 | Finland (6) | 1 | 3 | 2 | 11 |
| 7 | France (5) | 2 | 1 | 2 | 10 |
| 8 | Canada (3) | 2 | 0 | 1 | 7 |
| 9 | Belgium (2) | 1 | 1 | 0 | 5 |
| 10 | Italy (1) | 1 | 0 | 0 | 3 |

## Leading Medal Winners

Number of individual medals won on the left; gold, silver and bronze breakdown to the right.

### MEN

| No | | Sport | G-S-B |
|---|---|---|---|
| 3 | Henri Oreiller, FRA | Alpine | 2-0-1 |
| 2 | Martin Lundström, SWE | X-country | 2-0-0 |
| 2 | Nils Östensson, SWE | X-country | 1-1-0 |
| 2 | Ake Seyffarth, SWE | Sp. Skate | 1-1-0 |
| 2 | Gunnar Eriksson, SWE | X-country | 1-0-1 |
| 2 | Karl Molitor, SWI | Alpine | 1-0-1 |
| 2 | James Couttet, FRA | Alpine | 0-1-1 |
| 2 | Odd Lundberg, NOR | Sp. Skate | 0-1-1 |

### WOMEN

| No | | Sport | G-S-B |
|---|---|---|---|
| 2 | Trude Beiser, AUT | Alpine | 1-1-0 |
| 2 | Gretche n Fraser, USA | Alpine | 1-1-0 |
| 2 | Erika Mahringer, AUT | Alpine | 0-0-2 |

## Alpine Skiing

### MEN

| Event | | Time |
|---|---|---|
| Downhill | Henri Oreiller, FRA | .........2:55.0 |
| Slalom | Edi Reinalter, SWI | ...............2:10.3 |
| Combined | Henri Oreiller, FRA | ..........3.27 pts |

### WOMEN

| Event | | Time |
|---|---|---|
| Downhill | Hedy Schlunegger, SWI | ...........2:28.3 |
| Slalom | Gretchen Fraser, USA | ...............1:57.2 |
| Combined | Trude Beiser, AUT | ..............6.58 pts |

## Bobsled

| Event | | Time |
|---|---|---|
| 2-Man | SWI (Felix Endrich & Friedrich Waller) | 5:29.2 |
| 4-Man | USA (Francis Tyler, Patrick Martin, Edward Rimkus, William D'Amico) | 5:20.1 |

## Cresta (Toboggan)

| Event | | Time |
|---|---|---|
| 1-Man | Nino Bibbia, ITA | 5:23.2 |

## Figure Skating

| Event | | Points |
|---|---|---|
| Men | Dick Button, USA | 191.177 |
| Women | Barbara Ann Scott, CAN | 163.077 |
| Pairs | Micheline Lannoy & Pierre Baugniet, BEL | 11.227 |

## Ice Hockey

| | | Gm | W-L-T | Pts | GF | GA |
|---|---|---|---|---|---|---|
| 1 | Canada | 8 | 7-0-1 | 15 | 69 | 5 |
| 2 | Czechoslovakia | 8 | 7-0-1 | 15 | 80 | 18 |
| 3 | Switzerland | 8 | 6-2-0 | 12 | 67 | 21 |
| 4 | USA (AHA) | 8 | 5-3-0 | 10 | 86 | 33 |
| 5 | Sweden | 8 | 4-4-0 | 8 | 55 | 28 |
| 6 | Great Britain | 8 | 3-5-0 | 6 | 39 | 47 |
| 7 | Poland | 8 | 2-6-0 | 4 | 20 | 97 |
| 8 | Austria | 8 | 1-7-0 | 2 | 33 | 77 |
| 9 | Italy | 8 | 0-8-0 | 0 | 24 | 156 |

**Note:** Canada won championship on goal differential, 64–62.

## Nordic Skiing
### Cross Country

| Event | | Time |
|---|---|---|
| 18km | Martin Lundstrom, SWE | 1:13:50.0 |
| 50km | Nils Karlsson, SWE | 3:47:48.0 |
| 4x10km | SWE (Nils Östensson, Nils Täpp, Gunnar Eriksson, Martin Lundström) | 2:32:08.0 |

### Ski Jumping

| Event | | Points |
|---|---|---|
| 90m | Peter Hugsted, NOR | 228.1 |

### Nordic Combined

| Event | | Points |
|---|---|---|
| 18km/Jump | Heikki Hasu, FIN | 448.80 |

## Speed Skating

| Event | | Time | |
|---|---|---|---|
| 500m | Finn Helgesen, NOR | 43.1 | OR |
| 1500m | Sverre Farstad, NOR | 2:17.6 | OR |
| 5000m | Reidar Liaklev, NOR | 8:29.4 | |
| 10,000m | Ake Seyffarth, SWE | 17:26.3 | |

# 1952
## Oslo

Dick Button, who had revolutionized figure skating with his athletic jumps and spins at St. Moritz in 1948, repeated his gold medal performance in '52. The 22-year-old Harvard senior also won the world championship for the fifth straight year, then turned pro.

Andrea Mead Lawrence, a 19-year-old whose parents built the Pico Peak ski resort in Vermont became the first U.S. skier to win two Olympic gold medals, taking both the slalom and giant slalom.

The star of the Games, however, was 28-year-old Norwegian truck driver Hjalmar Andersen who, urged on by his cheering countrymen, won three speed skating gold medals in three days and set Olympic records in two of the races.

The U.S. finished second to Norway in the overall medal count and was runner-up to Canada in hockey. The gold medal was the Canadians' seventh in eight Olympics and, as it turned out, their last.

## Top 10 Standings

National medal standings are not recognized by the IOC. The unofficial point totals are based on 3 points for a gold medal, 2 for a silver and 1 for a bronze. Total medals are in parentheses.

| | | Gold | Silver | Bronze | Pts |
|---|---|---|---|---|---|
| 1 | Norway (16) | 7 | 3 | 6 | 33 |
| 2 | USA (11) | 4 | 6 | 1 | 25 |
| 3 | Finland (9) | 3 | 4 | 2 | 19 |
| 4 | Austria (8) | 2 | 4 | 2 | 16 |
| 5 | Germany (7) | 3 | 2 | 2 | 15 |
| 6 | Holland (3) | 0 | 3 | 0 | 6 |
| 7 | Canada (2) | 1 | 0 | 1 | 4 |
| | Italy (2) | 1 | 0 | 1 | 4 |
| | Sweden (4) | 0 | 0 | 4 | 4 |
| 10 | Great Britain (1) | 1 | 0 | 0 | 3 |

## Leading Medal Winners

Number of individual medals won on the left; gold, silver and bronze breakdown to the right.

### MEN

| No | | Sport | G-S-B |
|---|---|---|---|
| 3 | Hjalmar Andersen, NOR | Sp. Skate | 3-0-0 |
| 2 | Andreas Ostler, GER | Bobsled | 2-0-0 |
| 2 | Lorenz Nieberl, GER | Bobsled | 2-0-0 |
| 2 | Hallgeir Brenden, NOR | X-country | 1-1-0 |
| 2 | Stein Eriksen, NOR | Alpine | 1-1-0 |
| 2 | Heikki Hasu, FIN | X-country & Nordic Combined | 1-1-0 |
| 2 | Tapio Mäkelä, FIN | X-country | 1-1-0 |
| 2 | Othmar Schneider, AUT | Alpine | 1-1-0 |
| 2 | Paavo Lonkila, FIN | X-country | 1-0-1 |
| 2 | Stan Benham, USA | Bobsled | 0-2-0 |
| 2 | Kees Broekman, NED | Sp. Skate | 0-2-0 |
| 2 | Patrick Martin, USA | Bobsled | 0-2-0 |
| 2 | Magnar Estenstad, NOR | X-country | 0-1-1 |
| 2 | Christian Pravda, AUT | Alpine | 0-1-1 |
| 2 | Fritz Feierabend, SWI | Bobsled | 0-0-2 |
| 2 | Stephan Waser, SWI | Bobsled | 0-0-2 |

### WOMEN

| No | | Sport | G-S-B |
|---|---|---|---|
| 3 | Annemarie Buchner, GER | Alpine | 0-1-2 |
| 2 | Andrea Mead Lawrence, USA | Alpine | 2-0-0 |

## Alpine Skiing
### MEN

| Event | | Time |
|---|---|---|
| Downhill | Zeno Colò, ITA | 2:30.8 |
| Slalom | Othmar Schneider, AUT | 2:00.0 |
| G.Slalom | Stein Eriksen, NOR | 2:25.0 |

### WOMEN

| Event | | Time |
|---|---|---|
| Downhill | Trude Jochum-Beiser, AUT | 1:47.1 |
| Slalom | Andrea Mead Lawrence, USA | 2:10.6 |
| G.Slalom | Andrea Mead Lawrence, USA | 2:06.8 |

## Bobsled

| Event | | Time |
|---|---|---|
| 2-Man | GER (Andreas Ostler & Lorenz Nieberl) | 5:24.54 |
| 4-Man | GER (Andreas Ostler, Friedrich Kuhn, Lorenz Nieberl, Franz Kemser) | 5:07.84 |

## Figure Skating

| Event | | Points |
|---|---|---|
| Men | Dick Button, USA | 1730.3 |
| Women | Jeanette Altwegg, GBR | 1455.8 |
| Pairs | Ria Falk & Paul Falk, GER | 102.6 |

## Ice Hockey

| | | Gm | W-L-T | Pts | GF | GA |
|---|---|---|---|---|---|---|
| 1 | Canada | 8 | 7-0-1 | 15 | 71 | 14 |
| 2 | USA | 8 | 6-1-1 | 13 | 43 | 21 |
| 3 | Sweden | 8 | 6-2-0 | 12 | 48 | 19 |
| 4 | Czechoslovakia | 8 | 6-2-0 | 12 | 47 | 18 |
| 5 | Switzerland | 8 | 4-4-0 | 8 | 40 | 40 |
| 6 | Poland | 8 | 2-5-1 | 5 | 21 | 56 |
| 7 | Finland | 8 | 2-6-0 | 4 | 21 | 60 |
| 8 | Germany | 8 | 1-6-1 | 3 | 21 | 53 |
| 9 | Norway | 8 | 0-8-0 | 0 | 15 | 46 |

**Note:** Sweden defeated Czechoslovakia 5–3, in a playoff game to decide third place and the 1952 European championship.

## Nordic Skiing
### MEN
#### Cross Country

| Event | | Time |
|---|---|---|
| 18km | Hallgeir Brenden, NOR | 1:01:34.0 |
| 50km | Veikko Hakulinen, FIN | 3:33:33.0 |
| 4x10km | FIN (Heikki Hasu, Paavo Lonkila, Urpo Korhonen, Tapio Mäkelä) | 2:20:16.0 |

#### Ski Jumping

| Event | | Points |
|---|---|---|
| 90m | Arnfinn Bergman, NOR | 226.0 |

#### Nordic Combined

| Event | | Points |
|---|---|---|
| 18km/Jump | Simon Slåttvik, NOR | 51.621 |

### WOMEN
#### Cross Country

| Event | | Time |
|---|---|---|
| 10km | Lydia Widerman, FIN | 41:40.0 |

## Speed Skating
### MEN

| Event | | Time | |
|---|---|---|---|
| 500m | Ken Henry, USA | 43.2 | |
| 1500m | Hjalmar Andersen, NOR | 2:20.4 | |
| 5000m | Hjalmar Andersen, NOR | 8:10.6 | OR |
| 10,000m | Hjalmar Andersen, NOR | 16:45.8 | OR |

# 1956
### Cortina d'Ampezzo

The Soviet Union emerged from the shadows of the Cold War in 1952 to make its Olympic debut at the Summer Games in Helsinki. Finishing a close second to the United States in overall medal count (74–71), the Russians served notice that they were an athletic superpower to be reckoned with.

In 1956, the USSR made its first appearance in the Winter Games and not only outmedaled the 32–nation field, but dethroned Canada as hockey champion. Four of the USSR's seven gold medals came in speed skating, where Yevgeny Grishin led the way with gold medals in the 500 and 1,500 meters.

Despite a shortage of snow in northern Italy, the outstanding performance of the VIIth Winter Games belonged to a skier named Sailer. By winning the downhill, slalom and giant slalom, Toni Sailer of Austria became the first skier to sweep all three Alpine events and only the fifth winter athlete to win three gold medals at one Olympics.

Swedish cross-country skier Sixten Jernberg, who would eventually participate in three Winter Games and win a total of nine medals, led all contestants in Cortina with four, including a gold at 50 kilometers.

The women's and men's figure skating titles were won by Americans Tenley Albright and Hayes Jenkins, who were both reigning world champions. Albright had won a silver medal in 1952, while Jenkins had finished fourth.

## Top 10 Standings

National medal standings are not recognized by the IOC. The unofficial point totals are based on 3 points for a gold medal, 2 for a silver and 1 for a bronze. Total medals are in parentheses.

| | | Gold | Silver | Bronze | Pts |
|---|---|---|---|---|---|
| 1 | USSR (16) | 7 | 3 | 6 | 33 |
| 2 | Austria (11) | 4 | 3 | 4 | 22 |
| 3 | Sweden (10) | 2 | 4 | 4 | 18 |
| 4 | Finland (7) | 3 | 3 | 1 | 16 |
| 5 | Switzerland (6) | 3 | 2 | 1 | 14 |
| | USA (7) | 2 | 3 | 2 | 14 |
| 7 | Norway (4) | 2 | 1 | 1 | 9 |
| 8 | Italy (3) | 1 | 2 | 0 | 7 |
| 9 | Germany (2) | 1 | 0 | 1 | 4 |
| | Canada (3) | 0 | 1 | 2 | 4 |

## Leading Medal Winners

Number of individual medals won on the left; gold, silver and bronze breakdown to the right.

### MEN

| No | | Sport | G-S-B |
|---|---|---|---|
| 4 | Sixten Jernberg, SWE | X-country | 1-2-1 |
| 3 | Toni Sailer, AUT | Alpine | 3-0-0 |
| 3 | Veikko Hakulinen, FIN | X-country | 1-2-0 |
| 3 | Pavel Kolchin, USSR | X-country | 1-0-2 |
| 2 | Yevgeny Grishin, USSR | Sp. Skate | 2-0-0 |
| 2 | Sigvard Ericsson, SWE | Sp. Skate | 1-1-0 |
| 2 | Fedor Terentyev, USSR | X-country | 1-0-1 |
| 2 | Renzo Alvera, ITA | Bobsled | 0-2-0 |
| 2 | Eugenio Monti, ITA | Bobsled | 0-2-0 |
| 2 | Andreas Molterer, AUT | Alpine | 0-1-1 |
| 2 | Oleg Goncharenko, USSR | Sp. Skate | 0-0-2 |

### WOMEN

| No | | Sport | G-S-B |
|---|---|---|---|
| 2 | Lyubov Kozyreva, USSR | X-country | 1-1-0 |
| 2 | Radya Eroshina, USSR | X-country | 0-2-0 |
| 2 | Sonja Edstrom, SWE | X-country | 0-0-2 |

## Alpine Skiing

### MEN

| Event | | Time |
|---|---|---|
| Downhill | Toni Sailer, AUT | 2:52.2 |
| Slalom | Toni Sailer, AUT | 3:14.7 |
| G.Slalom | Toni Sailer, AUT | 3:00.1 |

### WOMEN

| Event | | Time |
|---|---|---|
| Downhill | Madeleine Berthod, SWI | 1:40.7 |
| Slalom | Renée Colliard, SWI | 1:52.3 |
| G.Slalom | Ossi Reichert, GER | 1:56.5 |

## Bobsled

| Event | | Time |
|---|---|---|
| 2-Man | ITA (Lamberto Dalla Costa & Giacomo Conti) | 5:30.14 |
| 4-Man | SWI (Franz Kapus, Gottfried Diener, Robert Alt, Heinrich Angst) | 5:10.44 |

## Figure Skating

| Event | | Points |
|---|---|---|
| Men | Hayes Jenkins, USA | 166.43 |
| Women | Tenley Albright, USA | 169.67 |
| Pairs | Elisabeth Schwartz & Kurt Oppelt, AUT | 11.31 |

## Ice Hockey

(Overall records in parentheses)

| | | Gm | W-L-T | Pts | GF | GA |
|---|---|---|---|---|---|---|
| 1 | USSR (7-0-0) | 5 | 5-0-0 | 10 | 25 | 5 |
| 2 | USA (5-2-0) | 5 | 4-1-0 | 8 | 26 | 12 |
| 3 | Canada (6-2-0) | 5 | 3-2-0 | 6 | 23 | 11 |
| 4 | Sweden (2-4-1) | 5 | 1-3-1 | 3 | 10 | 22 |
| 5 | Czechoslovakia (3-4-0) | 5 | 1-4-0 | 2 | 20 | 30 |
| 6 | Germany (1-5-2) | 5 | 0-4-1 | 1 | 6 | 35 |

**Note:** The USSR beat the U.S., 4–0, and Canada, 2–0. The U.S. beat Canada, 4–1.

## Nordic Skiing

### MEN

#### Cross Country

| Event | | Time |
|---|---|---|
| 15km | Hallgeir Brenden, NOR | 49:39.0 |
| 30km | Veikko Hakulinen, FIN | 1:44:06.0 |
| 50km | Sixten Jernberg, SWE | 2:50:27.0 |
| 4x10km | USSR (Fedor Terentyev, Pavel Kolchin, Nikolai Anikin, Vladimir Kuzin) | 2:15:30.0 |

#### Ski Jumping

| Event | | Points |
|---|---|---|
| 90m | Antti Hyvärinen, FIN | 227.0 |

#### Nordic Combined

| Event | | Points |
|---|---|---|
| 15km/Jump | Sverre Stenersen, NOR | 455.000 |

### WOMEN

#### Cross Country

| Event | | Time |
|---|---|---|
| 10km | Lyubov Kosyreva, USSR | 38:11.0 |
| 3x5km | FIN (Sirkka Polkunen, Mirja Hietamies, Siira Rantanen) | 1:09:01.0 |

## Speed Skating

### MEN

| Event | | Time | |
|---|---|---|---|
| 500m | Yevgeny Grishin, USSR | 40.2 | **WR** |
| 1500m | Yevgeny Grishin, USSR & Yuri Mikhailov, USSR | 2:08.6 | **WR** |
| 5000m | Boris Shilkov, USSR | 7:48.7 | **OR** |
| 10,000m | Sigvard Ericsson, SWE | 16:35.9 | **OR** |

# 1960
## Squaw Valley

The first Winter Olympics in the U.S. since 1932 was held at an obscure California ski resort near Lake Tahoe that had no bobsled run and in the days leading up to the opening ceremony, no snow. Luckily, an 11th hour drop in temperature changed a drenching rain into a much-needed blizzard and the Games got off to a wintry start.

The most exciting venue, however, was indoors at Blyth Arena where the underdog U.S. hockey team upset the Russians and Canadians to win the gold medal for the first time ever. Led by forwards Billy Cleary and Roger Christian and goaltender Jack McCartan, the Americans beat Canada 2–1, USSR 3–2, and the Czechs 9–4, in their last three games to clinch the title.

Blyth was also where Carol Heiss and David Jenkins won the women's and men's figure skating gold medals. Heiss had won a silver and Jenkins a bronze in 1956. Shortly after the Games, Heiss married Jenkins' older brother Hayes, the men's gold medalist in '56.

Outside, speed skater Yevgeny Grishin of the USSR won at 500 and 1,500 meters for the second Olympics in a row. In fact, Grishin's victory in the 1,500 was his second straight tie at that distance—sharing gold medals with teammate Yuri Mikhailov in 1956 and Norway's Roald Aas in '60. This was also the first year women could compete in speed skating and the Soviets' Lydia Skoblikova won twice, at 1,500 and 3,000 meters. She would go on to win four gold medals at Innsbruck in 1964.

At 35, three-time Olympic cross-country skier Veikko Hakulinen of Finland was the only athlete at Squaw Valley to claim three medals (for a career total of seven). He came from 20 seconds back on the anchor leg to win gold in the 40–kilometer relay.

Sweden's Klas Lestander won the first Olympic biathlon competition. A popular Scandinavian sport that combines cross-country skiing and shooting, Lestander recorded the 15th best time over the 20-kilometer course but was perfect on each of his 20 rifle shots.

Nineteen-year-old Alpine skier Penny Pitou was America's top medalist, placing second in both the downhill and slalom events. She was later married for a few years to 1964 men's downhill champion Egon Zimmermann of Austria.

## Top 10 Standings

National medal standings are not recognized by the IOC. The unofficial point totals are based on 3 points for a gold medal, 2 for a silver and 1 for a bronze. Total medals are in parentheses.

| | | Gold | Silver | Bronze | Pts |
|---|---|---|---|---|---|
| 1 | USSR (21) | 7 | 5 | 9 | 40 |
| 2 | USA (10) | 3 | 4 | 3 | 20 |
| 3 | Germany (8) | 4 | 3 | 1 | 19 |
| 4 | Norway (6) | 3 | 3 | 0 | 15 |
| | Sweden (7) | 3 | 2 | 2 | 15 |
| | Finland (8) | 2 | 3 | 3 | 15 |
| 7 | Austria (6) | 1 | 2 | 3 | 10 |
| 8 | Canada (4) | 2 | 1 | 1 | 9 |
| 9 | Switzerland (2) | 2 | 0 | 0 | 6 |
| 10 | France (3) | 1 | 0 | 2 | 5 |

## Leading Medal Winners

Number of individual medals won on the left; gold, silver and bronze breakdown to the right.

### MEN

| No | | Sport | G-S-B |
|---|---|---|---|
| 3 | Veikko Hakulinen, FIN | X-country | 1-1-1 |
| 2 | Yevgeny Grishin, USSR | Sp. Skate | 2-0-0 |
| 2 | Håkon Brusveen, NOR | X-country | 1-1-0 |
| 2 | Knut Johannesen, NOR | Sp. Skate | 1-1-0 |
| 2 | Sixten Jernberg, SWE | X-country | 1-1-0 |
| 2 | Viktor Kosichkin, USSR | Sp. Skate | 1-1-0 |
| 2 | Ernst Hinterseer, AUT | Alpine | 1-0-1 |
| 2 | Rolf Rämgård, SWE | X-country | 0-1-1 |
| 2 | Nikolai Anikin, USSR | X-country | 0-0-2 |

### WOMEN

| No | | Sport | G-S-B |
|---|---|---|---|
| 2 | Lydia Skoblikova, USSR | Sp. Skate | 2-0-0 |
| 2 | Maria Gusakova, USSR | X-country | 1-1-0 |
| 2 | Helga Haase, GER | Sp. Skate | 1-1-0 |
| 2 | Penny Pitou, USA | Alpine | 0-2-0 |
| 2 | Lyubov Baranova, USSR | X-country | 0-2-0 |
| 2 | Radya Eroshina, USSR | X-country | 0-1-1 |

## Alpine Skiing

### MEN

| Event | | Time |
|---|---|---|
| Downhill | Jean Vuarnet, FRA | 2:06.0 |
| Slalom | Ernst Hinterseer, AUT | 2:08.9 |
| G.Slalom | Roger Staub, SWI | 1:48.3 |

### WOMEN

| Event | | Time |
|---|---|---|
| Downhill | Heidi Biebl, GER | 1:37.6 |
| Slalom | Anne Heggtveit, CAN | 1:49.6 |
| G.Slalom | Avonne Rüegg, SWI | 1:39.9 |

## Biathlon

| Event | | MT | Adj.Time |
|---|---|---|---|
| 20 km | Klas Lestander, SWE | 0 | 1:33:21.6 |

## Figure Skating

| Event | | Points |
|---|---|---|
| Men | David Jenkins, USA | 1440.2 |
| Women | Carol Heiss, USA | 1490.1 |
| Pairs | Barbara Wagner & Robert Paul, CAN | 80.4 |

## Ice Hockey

### Championship Round

(Overall records in parentheses)

| | | Gm | W-L-T | Pts | GF | GA |
|---|---|---|---|---|---|---|
| 1 | USA (7-0-0) | 5 | 5-0-0 | 10 | 29 | 11 |
| 2 | Canada (6-1-0) | 5 | 4-1-0 | 8 | 31 | 12 |
| 3 | USSR (4-2-1) | 5 | 2-2-1 | 5 | 24 | 19 |
| 4 | Czechoslovakia (3-4-0) | 5 | 2-3-0 | 4 | 21 | 23 |
| 5 | Sweden (2-4-1) | 5 | 1-3-1 | 3 | 19 | 19 |
| 6 | Germany (1-6-0) | 5 | 0-5-0 | 0 | 5 | 45 |

**Note:** The U.S. beat Canada, 2–1, the USSR, 3–2, and Czech., 9–4, in its last three games. Canada beat the USSR, 8–5, and Sweden tied the Russians, 2–2.

## Nordic Skiing

### MEN

#### Cross Country

| Event | | Time |
|---|---|---|
| 15km | Håkon Brusveen, NOR | 51:55.5 |
| 30km | Sixten Jernberg, SWE | 1:51:03.9 |
| 50km | Kalevi Hämäläinen, FIN | 2:59:06.3 |
| 4x10km | FIN (Toimi Alatalo, Eero Mäntyranta, Väinö Huhtala, Veikko Hakulinen) | 2:18:45.6 |

### Ski Jumping

| Event | | Points |
|---|---|---|
| 80m | Helmut Recknagel, GER | 227.2 |

### Nordic Combined

| Event | | Points |
|---|---|---|
| 15km/Jump | Georg Thoma, GER | 457.952 |

### WOMEN

#### Cross Country

| Event | | Time |
|---|---|---|
| 10km | Marija Gusakova, USSR | 39:46.6 |
| 3x5km | SWE (Irma Johansson, Britt Strandberg, Sonja Ruthström) | 1:04:21.4 |

## Speed Skating

### MEN

| Event | | Time | |
|---|---|---|---|
| 500m | Yevgeny Grishin, USSR | 40.2 | =WR |
| 1500m | Roald Aas, NOR | 2:10.4 | WR |
| | & Yevgeny Grishin, USSR | 2:10.4 | WR |
| 5000m | Viktor Kosichkin, USSR | 7:51.3 | |
| 10,000m | Knut Johannesen, NOR | 15:46.6 | |

### WOMEN

| Event | | Time | |
|---|---|---|---|
| 500m | Helga Haase, GER | 45.9 | |
| 1000m | Klara Guseva, USSR | 1:34.1 | |
| 1500m | Lydia Skoblikova, USSR | 2:25.2 | WR |
| 3000m | Lydia Skoblikova, USSR | 5:14.3 | |

# 1964
## Innsbruck

Death and unseasonably mild weather hung over the ninth Winter Games in the Tyrolean Alps.

Two athletes, 50–year-old British luger Kazimierz Kay-Skyszpeski and 19–year-old Australian downhill skier Ross Milne, were killed taking practice runs less than a week before the Games began. And three years before, on Feb. 15, 1961, a plane crash in Belgium had killed 18 members of the U.S. figure skating team—including America's top female skater, 16-year-old Laurence Owen.

Springlike temperatures plagued Innsbruck both before and during the Games, forcing the Austrian military to carry in over 50,000 cubic meters of snow from higher elevations.

The USSR won 11 gold medals—a combined seven by speed skater Lydia Skoblikova (4) and cross-country skier Claudia Boyarskikh (3). Other stars included the skiing Goitschel sisters, Christine and Marielle, of France; and cross-country skiers Eero Mäntyranta of Finland and 34-year-old Sixten Jernberg of Sweden.

The lone U.S. gold medal was won by 23-year-old barber Terry McDermott in speed skating.

## Top 10 Standings

National medal standings are not recognized by the IOC. The unofficial point totals are based on 3 points for a gold medal, 2 for a silver and 1 for a bronze. Total medals are in parentheses.

| | Gold | Silver | Bronze | Pts |
|---|---|---|---|---|
| 1 USSR (25) | 11 | 8 | 6 | 55 |
| 2 Norway (15) | 3 | 6 | 6 | 27 |
| 3 Austria (12) | 4 | 5 | 3 | 25 |
| 4 Finland (10) | 3 | 4 | 3 | 20 |
| 5 France (7) | 3 | 4 | 0 | 17 |
| 6 Sweden (7) | 3 | 3 | 1 | 16 |
| Germany (8) | 3 | 2 | 3 | 16 |
| 8 USA (6) | 1 | 2 | 3 | 10 |
| 9 Holland (2) | 1 | 1 | 0 | 5 |
| Canada (3) | 1 | 0 | 2 | 5 |
| Italy (4) | 0 | 1 | 3 | 5 |

## Leading Medal Winners

Number of individual medals won on the left; gold, silver and bronze breakdown to the right.

### MEN

| No | | Sport | G-S-B |
|---|---|---|---|
| 3 | Eero Mäntyranta, FIN | X-country | 2-1-0 |
| 3 | Sixten Jernberg, SWE | X-country | 2-0-1 |
| 2 | Toralf Engan, NOR | Ski Jump | 1-1-0 |
| 2 | Veikko Kankkonen, FIN | Ski Jump | 1-1-0 |
| 2 | Assar Rönnlund, SWE | X-country | 1-1-0 |
| 2 | Knut Johannesen, NOR | Sp. Skate | 1-0-1 |
| 2 | Pepi Stiegler, AUT | Alpine | 1-0-1 |
| 2 | Harald Grönningen, NOR | X-country | 0-2-0 |
| 2 | Fred Maier, NOR | Sp. Skate | 0-1-1 |
| 2 | Arto Tiainen, FIN | X-country | 0-1-1 |
| 2 | Torgeir Brandtzaeg, NOR | Ski Jump | 0-0-2 |
| 2 | Eugenio Monti, ITA | Bobsled | 0-0-2 |
| 2 | Sergio Siorpaes, ITA | Bobsled | 0-0-2 |
| 2 | Igor Voronchikin, USSR | X-country | 0-0-2 |

### WOMEN

| No | | Sport | G-S-B |
|---|---|---|---|
| 4 | Lydia Skoblikova, USSR | Sp. Skate | 4-0-0 |
| 3 | Claudia Boyarskikh, USSR | X-country | 3-0-0 |
| 2 | Christine Goitschel, FRA | Alpine | 1-1-0 |
| 2 | Marielle Goitschel, FRA | Alpine | 1-1-0 |
| 2 | Eudokia Mekshilo, USSR | X-country | 1-1-0 |
| 2 | Alevtina Kolchina, USSR | X-country | 1-0-1 |
| 2 | Mirja Lehtonen, FIN | X-country | 0-1-1 |
| 2 | Kaija Mustonen, FIN | Sp. Skate | 0-1-1 |
| 2 | Jean Saubert, USA | Alpine | 0-1-1 |
| 2 | Irina Yegorova, USSR | Sp. Skate | 0-2-0 |

## Alpine Skiing
### MEN

| Event | | Time |
|---|---|---|
| Downhill | Egon Zimmermann, AUT | 2:18.16 |
| Slalom | Pepi Stiegler, AUT | 2:11.13 |
| G.Slalom | Francois Bonlieu, FRA | 1:46.71 |

**Note:** In the Slalom, Billy Kidd (2nd) and Jimmy Heuga (3rd) won the first U.S. men's Alpine medals ever.

### WOMEN

| Event | | Time |
|---|---|---|
| Downhill | Christl Haas, AUT | 1:55.39 |
| Slalom | Christine Goitschel, FRA | 1:29.86 |
| G.Slalom | Marielle Goitschel, FRA | 1:52.24 |

## Biathlon

| Event | | MT | Adj.Time |
|---|---|---|---|
| 20 km | Vladimir Melanin, USSR | 0 | 1:20:26.8 |

## Bobsled

| Event | | Time |
|---|---|---|
| 2-Man | GBR (Tony Nash & Robin Dixon) | 4:21.90 |
| 4-Man | CAN (Victor Emery, Peter Kirby, Doug Anakin, John Emery) | 4:14.46 |

## Figure Skating

| Event | | Points |
|---|---|---|
| Men | Manfred Schnelldorfer, GER | 1916.9 |
| Women | Sjoukje Dijkstra, NED | 2018.5 |
| Pairs | Lyudmila Belousova & Oleg Protopopov, USSR | 104.4 |

## Ice Hockey
### Championship Round

(Overall records in parentheses)

| | | Gm | W-L-T | Pts | GF | GA |
|---|---|---|---|---|---|---|
| 1 | USSR (8-0-0) | 7 | 7-0-0 | 14 | 54 | 10 |
| 2 | Sweden (6-2-0) | 7 | 5-2-0 | 10 | 47 | 16 |
| 3 | Czechoslovakia (6-2-0) | 7 | 5-2-0 | 10 | 38 | 19 |
| 4 | Canada (6-2-0) | 7 | 5-2-0 | 10 | 32 | 17 |
| 5 | USA (3-5-0) | 7 | 2-5-0 | 4 | 29 | 33 |
| 6 | Finland (3-5-0) | 7 | 2-5-0 | 4 | 10 | 31 |
| 7 | Germany (3-5-0) | 7 | 2-5-0 | 4 | 13 | 49 |
| 8 | Switzerland (1-7-0) | 7 | 0-7-0 | 0 | 9 | 57 |

## Luge
### MEN

| Event | | Time |
|---|---|---|
| 1-Seat | Thomas Köhler, GER | 3:26.77 |
| 2-Seat | Josef Feistmantl & Manfred Stengl, AUT | 1:41.62 |

### WOMEN

| Event | | Time |
|---|---|---|
| 1-Seat | Ortrun Enderlein, GER | 3:24.67 |

## Nordic Skiing
### MEN
### Cross Country

| Event | | Time |
|---|---|---|
| 15km | Eero Mäntyranta, FIN | 50:54.1 |
| 30km | Eero Mäntyranta, FIN | 1:30:50.7 |
| 50km | Sixten Jernberg, SWE | 2:43:52.6 |
| 4x10km | SWE (Karl-Åke Asph, Sixten Jernberg, Janne Stefansson, Assar Rönnlund) | 2:18:34.6 |

### Ski Jumping

| Event | | Points |
|---|---|---|
| 70m | Veikko Kankkonen, FIN | .229.9 |
| 80m | Toralf Engan, NOR | .230.7 |

### Nordic Combined

| Event | | Points |
|---|---|---|
| 15km/Jump | Tormod Knutsen, NOR | .469.28 |

## WOMEN
### Cross Country

| Event | | Time |
|---|---|---|
| 5km | Claudia Boyarskikh, USSR | .17:50.5 |
| 10km | Claudia Boyarskikh, USSR | .40:24.3 |
| 3x5km | USSR (Alevtina Kolchina, Eudokia Mekshilo, Claudia Boyarskikh) | .59:20.2 |

## Speed Skating
### MEN

| Event | | Time | |
|---|---|---|---|
| 500m | Terry McDermott, USA | .40.1 | OR |
| 1500m | Ants Antson, USSR | .2:10.3 | |
| 5000m | Knut Johannesen, NOR | .7:38.4 | OR |
| 10,000m | Jonny Nilsson, SWE | .15:50.1 | |

### WOMEN

| Event | | Time | |
|---|---|---|---|
| 500m | Lydia Skoblikova, USSR | .45.0 | OR |
| 1000m | Lydia Skoblikova, USSR | .1:33.2 | OR |
| 1500m | Lydia Skoblikova, USSR | .2:22.6 | OR |
| 3000m | Lydia Skoblikova, USSR | .5:14.9 | |

# 1968
### Grenoble

For the first time since they began attending the Winter Games in 1956, the Russians did not win the most medals—Norway did.

This was also the first year that the IOC permitted East and West Germany to participate as separate countries.

The host French team finished fourth in the overall standings—their best showing ever—thanks mainly to 24-year-old Jean-Claude Killy, who became the first skier to sweep all three Alpine events since Toni Sailer in 1956.

Killy was awarded his third gold medal in the slalom only after original winner Karl Schranz of Austria was disqualified for missing two gates on his second run in the two-heat race. Schranz had been allowed to retake his second heat run when a spectator interrupted his initial attempt, but officials ruled the missed gates came before the interruption.

Once again, the U.S. won only one gold medal—19-year-old Peggy Fleming in women's figure skating. Three of the five silver medals won by the U.S. came in one event—the women's 500-meter speed skating race, where Jenny Fish, Dianne Holum and Mary Myers tied for second place with a time of 46.3 seconds.

## Top 10 Standings

National medal standings are not recognized by the IOC. The unofficial point totals are based on 3 points for a gold medal, 2 for a silver and 1 for a bronze. Total medals are in parentheses.

| | | Gold | Silver | Bronze | Pts |
|---|---|---|---|---|---|
| 1 | Norway (14) | 6 | 6 | 2 | 32 |
| 2 | USSR (13) | 5 | 5 | 3 | 28 |
| 3 | Austria (11) | 3 | 4 | 4 | 21 |
| 4 | France (9) | 4 | 3 | 2 | 20 |
| 5 | Holland (9) | 3 | 3 | 3 | 18 |
| 6 | Sweden (8) | 3 | 2 | 3 | 16 |
| 7 | USA (7) | 1 | 5 | 1 | 14 |
| 8 | West Germany (7) | 2 | 2 | 3 | 13 |
| 9 | Italy (4) | 4 | 0 | 0 | 12 |
| 10 | East Germany (5) | 1 | 2 | 2 | 9 |
| . | Finland (5) | 1 | 2 | 2 | 9 |

## Leading Medal Winners

Number of individual medals won on the left; gold, silver and bronze breakdown to the right.

### MEN

| No | | Sport | G-S-B |
|---|---|---|---|
| 3 | Jean-Claude Killy, FRA | Alpine | 3-0-0 |
| 3 | Eero Mäntyranta, FIN | X-country | 0-1-2 |
| 2 | Eugenio Monti, ITA | Bobsled | 2-0-0 |
| 2 | Luciano De Paolis, ITA | Bobsled | 2-0-0 |
| 2 | Ole Ellefsaeter, NOR | X-country | 2-0-0 |
| 2 | Harald Grönningen, NOR | X-country | 2-0-0 |
| 2 | Thomas Köhler, E.Ger. | Luge | 1-1-0 |
| 2 | Fred Maier, NOR | Sp. Skate | 1-1-0 |
| 2 | Odd Martinsen, NOR | X-country | 1-1-0 |
| 2 | Jiri Raska, CZE | Ski Jump | 1-1-0 |
| 2 | Manfred Schmid, AUT | Luge | 1-1-0 |
| 2 | Magnar Solberg, NOR | Biathlon | 1-1-0 |
| 2 | Aleksandr Tikhonov, USSR | Biathlon | 1-1-0 |
| 2 | Kees Verkerk, NED | Sp. Skate | 1-1-0 |
| 2 | Klaus Bonsack, E. Ger. | Luge | 1-0-1 |
| 2 | Vladimir Goundartsev, USSR | Biathlon | 1-0-1 |
| 2 | Gunnar Larsson, SWE | X-country | 0-1-1 |

### WOMEN

| No | | Sport | G-S-B |
|---|---|---|---|
| 3 | Toini Gustafsson, SWE | X-country | 2-1-0 |
| 2 | Carolina Geijssen, NED | Sp. Skate | 1-1-0 |
| 2 | Nancy Greene, CAN | Alpine | 1-1-0 |
| 2 | Berit Mördre, NOR | X-country | 1-1-0 |
| 2 | Kaija Mustonen, FIN | Sp. Skate | 1-1-0 |
| 2 | Lyudmila Titova, USSR | Sp. Skate | 1-1-0 |
| 2 | Inger Aufles, NOR | X-country | 1-0-1 |
| 2 | Annie Famose, FRA | Alpine | 0-1-1 |
| 2 | Dianne Holum, USA | Sp. Skate | 0-1-1 |
| 2 | Galina Kulakova, USSR | X-country | 0-1-1 |
| 2 | Christina Kaiser, NED | Sp. Skate | 0-0-2 |
| 2 | Alevtina Kolchina, USSR | X-country | 0-0-2 |

## Alpine Skiing
### MEN

| Event | | Time |
|---|---|---|
| Downhill | Jean-Claude Killy, FRA | .1:59.85 |
| Slalom | Jean-Claude Killy, FRA | .1:39.73 |
| G.Slalom | Jean-Claude Killy, FRA | .3:29.28 |

### WOMEN

| Event | | Time |
|---|---|---|
| Downhill | Olga Pall, AUT | .1:40.87 |
| Slalom | Marielle Goitschel, FRA | .1:25.86 |
| G.Slalom | Nancy Greene, CAN | .1:51.97 |

## Biathlon

| Event | | MT | Adj.Time |
|---|---|---|---|
| 20 km | Magnar Solberg, NOR . . . . . . . .0 | | 1:13:45.9 |
| 4x7.5km | USSR (Tikonov, Pousanov, Mamatov, Goundartsev) . . . . . . .2 | | 2:13:02.4 |

## Bobsled

| Event | | Time |
|---|---|---|
| 2-Man | ITA (Eugenio Monti & Luciano De Paolis) . .4:41.54 | |
| 4-Man | ITA (Eugenio Monti, Luciano De Paolis, Roberto Zandonella, Mario Armano) . . . .2:17.39 | |

## Figure Skating

| Event | | Points |
|---|---|---|
| Men | Wolfgang Schwarz, AUT . . . . . . . . . . . . .1904.1 | |
| Women | Peggy Fleming, USA . . . . . . . . . . . . . . . .1970.5 | |
| Pairs | Lyudmila Belousova & Oleg Protopopov, USSR . . . . . . . . . . . .315.2 | |

## Ice Hockey
### Group A
(Overall records in parentheses)

| | | Gm | W-L-T | Pts | GF | GA |
|---|---|---|---|---|---|---|
| 1 | USSR . . . . . . . . . . . . . . . .7 | | 6-1-0 | 12 | 48 | 10 |
| 2 | Czechoslovakia . . . . . . . .7 | | 5-1-1 | 11 | 33 | 17 |
| 3 | Canada . . . . . . . . . . . . .7 | | 5-2-0 | 10 | 28 | 15 |
| 4 | Sweden . . . . . . . . . . . . .7 | | 4-2-1 | 9 | 23 | 18 |
| 5 | Finland (4-3-1) . . . . . . . .7 | | 3-3-1 | 9 | 17 | 23 |
| 6 | USA . . . . . . . . . . . . . . .7 | | 2-4-1 | 5 | 23 | 28 |
| 7 | West Germany (2-6-0) . . . .7 | | 1-6-0 | 2 | 13 | 39 |
| 8 | East Germany (1-7-0) . . . . .7 | | 0-7-0 | 0 | 13 | 48 |

**Note:** Finland and the two Germanys had to win an elimination round game to qualify for Group A.

## Luge
### MEN

| Event | | Time |
|---|---|---|
| 1-Seat | Manfred Schmid, AUT . . . . . . . . . . . . . .2:52.48 | |
| 2-Seat | Klaus Bonsack & Thomas Köhler, E. Ger . .1:35.85 | |

### WOMEN

| Event | | Time |
|---|---|---|
| 1-Seat | Erica Lechner, ITA . . . . . . . . . . . . . . . . .2:28.66 | |

**Note:** Defending champion Ortrun Enderlein and teammate Anna Maria Müller of East Germany finished 1–2, but were disqualified for heating the blades of their toboggans.

## Nordic Skiing
### MEN
#### Cross Country

| Event | | Time |
|---|---|---|
| 15km | Harold Grönningen, NOR . . . . . . . . . .47:54.2 | |
| 30km | Franco Nones, ITA . . . . . . . . . . . . . .1:35:39.2 | |
| 50km | Ole Ellefsaeter, NOR . . . . . . . . . . . . .2:28:45.8 | |
| 4x10km | NOR (Martinsen, Tyldum, Grönningen, Ellefsaeter) . . . . . . . . . . . . . . . . . . .2:08:33.5 | |

#### Ski Jumping

| Event | | Points |
|---|---|---|
| 70m | Jiri Raska, CZE . . . . . . . . . . . . . . . . . .216.5 | |
| 90m | Vladimir Beloussov, USSR . . . . . . . . . . . .231.3 | |

#### Nordic Combined

| Event | | Points |
|---|---|---|
| 15km/Jump | Franz Keller, W. Ger. . . . . . . . . . . .449.04 | |

### WOMEN
#### Cross Country

| Event | | Time |
|---|---|---|
| 5km | Toini Gustafsson, SWE . . . . . . . . . . . . .16:45.2 | |
| 10km | Toini Gustafsson, SWE . . . . . . . . . . . . .36:46.5 | |
| 3x5km | NOR (Aufles, Damon-Enger, Mördre) . . . .57:30.0 | |

## Speed Skating
### MEN

| Event | | Time | |
|---|---|---|---|
| 500m | Erhard Keller, W. Ger. . . . . . . . . . .40.3 | | |
| 1500m | Kees Verkerk, NED . . . . . . . . . . .2:03.4 | | OR |
| 5000m | Fred Maier, NOR . . . . . . . . . . . .7:22.4 | | WR |
| 10,000m | Johnny Höglin, SWE . . . . . . . .15:23.6 | | OR |

### WOMEN

| Event | | Time | |
|---|---|---|---|
| 500m | Lyudmila Titova, USSR . . . . . . . . . .46.1 | | |
| 1000m | Carolina Geijssen, NED . . . . . . . .1:32.6 | | OR |
| 1500m | Kaija Mustonen, FIN . . . . . . . . .2:22.4 | | OR |
| 3000m | Johanna Schut, NED . . . . . . . . .4:56.2 | | OR |

# 1972
## Sapporo

The biggest controversy in the 48–year history of the Winter Games erupted just three days before the opening ceremonies were scheduled to get underway in northern Japan. That's when retiring IOC president Avery Brundage threatened to disqualify 40 Alpine skiers for professionalism.

At Grenoble in 1968, Brundage had demanded that all trademarks be removed from competitors' skis, but settled for having the offensive skis taken away from medal winners before they could be photographed. Now, the 84–year-old guardian of the Olympic flame wanted all the pros thrown out.

A compromise was reached when the IOC executive committee voted 28–14 to make an example of skiing's most commercialized star, 33-year-old Austrian World Cup champion Karl Schranz, who reportedly earned over $50,000 a year "testing" ski equipment.

All other offenders were allowed to participate.

Said Schranz after being banished: "This thing of amateur purity is something that dates back to the 19th century when amateur sportsmen were regarded as gentlemen and everyone else was an outcast. The Olympics should be a competition of skill and strength and speed—and no more."

Schranz retired after the Games, having never won an Olympic gold medal.

The amateurism question caused controversy in the ice hockey event as well. Canada refused to send a team to Sapporo, having withdrawn from international amateur competition in 1969 to protest use of "professional amateurs" by Russia and other eastern bloc countries.

## Top 10 Standings

National medal standings are not recognized by the IOC. The unofficial point totals are based on 3 points for a gold medal, 2 for a silver and 1 for a bronze. Total medals are in parentheses.

| | | Gold | Silver | Bronze | Pts |
|---|---|---|---|---|---|
| 1 | USSR (16) | 8 | 5 | 3 | 37 |
| 2 | East Germany (14) | 4 | 3 | 7 | 25 |
| 3 | Switzerland (10) | 4 | 3 | 3 | 21 |
| | Norway (12) | 2 | 5 | 5 | 21 |
| 5 | Holland (9) | 4 | 3 | 2 | 20 |
| 6 | USA (8) | 3 | 2 | 3 | 16 |
| 7 | West Germany (5) | 3 | 1 | 1 | 12 |
| 8 | Italy (5) | 2 | 2 | 1 | 11 |
| 9 | Austria (5) | 1 | 2 | 2 | 9 |
| | Finland (5) | 0 | 4 | 1 | 9 |

## Leading Medal Winners

Number of individual medals won on the left; gold, silver and bronze breakdown to the right.

### MEN

| No | | Sport | G-S-B |
|---|---|---|---|
| 3 | Ard Schenk, NED | Sp. Skate | 3-0-0 |
| 3 | Vyacheslav Vedenine, USSR | X-country | 2-0-1 |
| 3 | Pål Tyldum, NOR | X-country | 1-2-0 |
| 2 | Fedor Simashov, USSR | X-country | 1-1-0 |
| 2 | Gustav Thöni, ITA | Alpine | 1-1-0 |
| 2 | Wolfgang Zimmerer, W. Ger. | Bobsled | 1-0-1 |
| 2 | Peter Utzschneider, W. Ger. | Bobsled | 1-0-1 |
| 2 | Jean Wicki, SWI | Bobsled | 1-0-1 |
| 2 | Edy Hubacher, SWI | Bobsled | 1-0-1 |
| 2 | Roar Grönvold, NOR | Sp. Skate | 0-2-0 |
| 2 | Ivar Formo, NOR | X-country | 0-1-1 |
| 2 | Johs Harviken, NOR | X-country | 0-1-1 |
| 2 | Hansjorg Knauthe, E. Ger. | Biathlon | 0-1-1 |
| 2 | Wolfram Fiedler, E. Ger. | Luge | 0-0-2 |
| 2 | Sten Stensen, NOR | Sp. Skate | 0-0-2 |

### WOMEN

| No | | Sport | G-S-B |
|---|---|---|---|
| 3 | Galina Kulakova, USSR | X-country | 3-0-0 |
| 3 | Marjatta Kajosmaa, FIN | X-country | 0-2-1 |
| 2 | Marie-Theres Nadig, SWI | Alpine | 2-0-0 |
| 2 | Dianne Holum, USA | Sp. Skate | 1-1-0 |
| 2 | Christina Baas-Kaiser, NED | Sp. Skate | 1-1-0 |
| 2 | Alevtina Olunina, USSR | X-country | 1-1-0 |
| 2 | Anne Henning, USA | Sp. Skate | 1-0-1 |
| 2 | Annemarie Pröll, FRA | Alpine | 0-2-0 |
| 2 | Atje Keulen-Deelstra, NED | Sp. Skate | 0-1-1 |

## Alpine Skiing

### MEN

| Event | | Time |
|---|---|---|
| Downhill | Bernhard Russi, SWI | 1:51.43 |
| Slalom | Francisco Ochoa, SPA | 1:49.27 |
| G.Slalom | Gustav Thöni, ITA | 3:09.62 |

### WOMEN

| Event | | Time |
|---|---|---|
| Downhil | lMarie-Theres Nadig, SWI | 1:36.68 |
| Slalom | Barbara Cochran, USA | 1:31.24 |
| G.Slalom | Marie-Theres Nadig, SWI | 1:29.90 |

## Biathlon

| Event | | MT | Adj.Time |
|---|---|---|---|
| 20 km | Magnar Solberg, NOR | 2 | 1:15:55.50 |
| 4x7.5km | USSR (Tikonov, Safine, Biakov, Mamatov) | 3 | 1:51:44.92 |

## Bobsled

| Event | | Time |
|---|---|---|
| 2-Man | W. Ger. (Wolfgang Zimmerer & Peter Utzschneider) | 4:57.07 |
| 4-Man | SWI (Jean Wicki, Edy Hubacher, Hans Leutenegger, Werner Camichel) | 4:43.07 |

## Figure Skating

| Event | | Points |
|---|---|---|
| Men | Ondrej Nepela, CZE | 2739.1 |
| Women | Trixi Schuba, AUT | 2751.5 |
| Pairs | Irina Rodnina & Aleksei Ulanov, USSR | 420.4 |

## Ice Hockey

### Group A

(Overall records in parentheses)

| | | Gm | W-L-T | Pts | GF | GA |
|---|---|---|---|---|---|---|
| 1 | USSR (4-0-1) | 5 | 4-0-1 | 9 | 33 | 13 |
| 2 | USA (3-2-0) | 5 | 3-2-0 | 6 | 18 | 15 |
| 3 | Czechoslovakia (4-2-0) | 5 | 3-2-0 | 6 | 26 | 13 |
| 4 | Sweden (3-2-1) | 5 | 2-2-1 | 5 | 17 | 13 |
| 5 | Finland (3-3-0) | 5 | 2-3-0 | 4 | 14 | 24 |
| 6 | Poland (1-5-0) | 5 | 0-5-0 | 0 | 9 | 39 |

**Note:** Pivotal game—USSR over Czech., 5–2, in final contest for both teams. The 5–1 U.S. victory over the Czechs gave the Americans second place. Also, the USSR received a bye to Group A while the other seven teams had to win a one-game elimination round to qualify.

## Luge

### MEN

| Event | | Time |
|---|---|---|
| 1-Seat | Wolfgang Scheidel, E. Ger. | 3:27.58 |
| 2-Seat | (TIE) Horst Hörnlein & Reinhard Bredow, E. Ger. | 1:28.35 |
| | Paul Hildgartner & Walter Plaikner, ITA | 1:28.35 |

### WOMEN

| Event | | Time |
|---|---|---|
| 1-Seat | Anna-Maria Müller, E. Ger. | 2:59.18 |

## Nordic Skiing

### MEN

#### Cross Country

| Event | | Time |
|---|---|---|
| 15km | Sven-Ake Lundbäck, SWE | 45:28.24 |
| 30km | Vyacheslav Vedenine, USSR | 1:36:31.15 |
| 50km | Pål Tyldum, NOR | 2:43:14.75 |
| 4x10km | USSR (Voronkov, Skobov, Simachev, Vedenine) | 2:04:47.94 |

#### Ski Jumping

| Event | | Points |
|---|---|---|
| 70m | Yukio Kasaya, JPN | 244.2 |
| 90m | Wojciech Fortuna, POL | 219.9 |

#### Nordic Combined

| Event | | Points |
|---|---|---|
| 15km/Jump | Ulrich Wehling, E. Ger. | 413.340 |

### WOMEN

#### Cross Country

| Event | | Time |
|---|---|---|
| 5km | Galina Kulakova, USSR | 17:00.50 |
| 10km | Galina Kulakova, USSR | 34:17.82 |
| 3x5km | USSR (Moukhatcheva, Olunina, Kulakova) | 48:46.15 |

## Speed Skating
### MEN

| Event | | Time | |
|---|---|---|---|
| 500m | Erhard Keller, W. Ger. | 39.44 | OR |
| 1500m | Ard Schenk, NED | 2:02.96 | OR |
| 5000m | Ard Schenk, NED | 7:23.61 | |
| 10,000m | Ard Schenk, NED | 15:01.35 | OR |

### WOMEN

| Event | | Time | |
|---|---|---|---|
| 500m | Anne Henning, USA | 43.33 | OR |
| 1000m | Monika Pflug, W. Ger. | 1:31.40 | OR |
| 1500m | Dianne Holum, USA | 2:20.85 | OR |
| 3000m | Christina Baas-Kaiser, NED | 4:52.14 | OR |

# 1976
## Innsbruck

The IOC originally gave the 1976 Winter Games to Denver, but in 1972 Colorado voters rejected a $5 million bond issue to finance the undertaking. Denver immediately withdrew as host and the IOC called on Innsbruck, site of the 1964 Games.

For the second straight Winter Carnival the USSR and East Germany finished 1–2 in overall medals. In 1972, Dutch speed skater Ard Schenk and Soviet cross-country skier Galina Kulakova each won three gold medals. In '76, nobody won three, but 25-year-old West German skier Rosi Mittermaier almost did—winning two golds and a silver in the women's Alpine events.

The Russian hockey team, which had won the gold medal in 1972 and then battled the NHL's Team Canada to a virtual standoff six months later, returned with most of the same players and won its fourth straight Olympic title.

In figure skating, 19-year-old Dorothy Hamill of the U.S. and John Curry of Britain won gold medals. Both were coached by Carlo Fassi, who also coached Peggy Fleming in 1968.

Also, Bill Koch became the first U.S. skier to ever win an Olympic cross-country medal when he placed second in the 30-kilometer race.

## Top 10 Standings

National medal standings are not recognized by the IOC. The unofficial point totals are based on 3 points for a gold medal, 2 for a silver and 1 for a bronze. Total medals are in parentheses.

| | | Gold | Silver | Bronze | Pts |
|---|---|---|---|---|---|
| 1 | USSR (27) | 13 | 6 | 8 | 59 |
| 2 | East Germany (19) | 7 | 5 | 7 | 38 |
| 3 | USA (10) | 3 | 3 | 4 | 19 |
| | West Germany (10) | 2 | 5 | 3 | 19 |
| 5 | Norway (7) | 3 | 3 | 1 | 16 |
| 6 | Finland (7) | 2 | 4 | 1 | 15 |
| 7 | Austria (6) | 2 | 2 | 2 | 12 |
| 8 | Switzerland (5) | 1 | 3 | 1 | 10 |
| | Holland (6) | 1 | 2 | 3 | 10 |
| 10 | Italy (4) | 1 | 2 | 1 | 8 |

## Leading Medal Winners

Number of individual medals won on the left; gold, silver and bronze breakdown to the right.

### MEN

| No | | Sport | G-S-B |
|---|---|---|---|
| 3 | Hans van Helden, NED | Sp. Skate | 0-0-3 |
| 2 | Bernhard Germeshausen, E. Ger. | Bobsled | 2-0-0 |
| 2 | Nikolai Kruglov, USSR | Biathlon | 2-0-0 |
| 2 | Meinhard Nehmer, E. Ger. | Bobsled | 2-0-0 |
| 2 | Ivar Formo, NOR | X-country | 1-1-0 |
| 2 | Piet Kleine, NED | Sp. Skate | 1-1-0 |
| 2 | Nikolai Bazhuko, USSR | X-country | 1-0-1 |
| 2 | Aleksandr Elizarov, USSR | Biathlon | 1-0-1 |
| 2 | Arto Koivisto, FIN | X-country | 1-0-1 |
| 2 | Hans Rinn, E. Ger. | Luge | 1-0-1 |
| 2 | Sergei Saveliev, USSR | X-country | 1-0-1 |
| 2 | Karl Schnabl, AUT | Ski Jump | 1-0-1 |
| 2 | Sten Stensen, NOR | Sp. Skate | 1-1-0 |
| 2 | Neikki Ikola, FIN | Biathlon | 0-2-0 |
| 2 | Yevgeny Beliaev, USSR | X-country | 0-1-1 |
| 2 | Josef Benz, SWI | Bobsled | 0-1-1 |
| 2 | Valery Muratov, USSR | Sp. Skate | 0-1-1 |
| 2 | Erich Scharer, SWI | Bobsled | 0-1-1 |
| 2 | Manfred Schumann, W. Ger. | Bobsled | 0-1-1 |
| 2 | Wolfgang Zimmerer, W. Ger. | Bobsled | 0-1-1 |
| 2 | Ivan Garanin, USSR | X-country | 0-0-2 |

### WOMEN

| No | | Sport | G-S-B |
|---|---|---|---|
| 4 | Tatiana Averina, USSR | Sp. Skate | 2-0-2 |
| 3 | Rosi Mittermaier, W. Ger. | Alpine | 2-1-0 |
| 3 | Raisa Smetanina, USSR | X-country | 2-1-0 |
| 3 | Helena Takalo, FIN | X-country | 1-2-0 |
| 3 | Sheila Young, USA | Sp. Skate | 1-1-1 |
| 2 | Galina Kulakova, USSR | X-country | 1-0-1 |

## Alpine Skiing
### MEN

| Event | | Time |
|---|---|---|
| Downhill | Franz Klammer, AUT | 1:45.73 |
| Slalom | Piero Gros, ITA | 2:03.29 |
| G.Slalom | Heini Hemmi, SWI | 3:26.97 |

### WOMEN

| Event | | Time |
|---|---|---|
| Downhill | Rosi Mittermaier, W. Ger. | 1:46.16 |
| Slalom | Rosi Mittermaier, W. Ger. | 1:30.54 |
| G.Slalom | Kathy Kreiner, CAN | 1:29.13 |

**Note:** Mittermaier finished second in the GS, missing the first women's alpine sweep by an eighth of a second.

## Biathlon

| Event | | MT | Adj.Time |
|---|---|---|---|
| 20 km | Nikolai Kruglov, USSR | 2 | 1:14:12.26 |
| 4x7.5km | USSR (Elizarov, Biakov, Kruglov, Tikonov) | 0 | 1:57:55.64 |

## Bobsled

| Event | | Time |
|---|---|---|
| 2-Man | E. Ger. (Meinhard Nehmer & Bernhard Germeshausen) | 3:44.42 |
| 4-Man | E. Ger. (Meinhard Nehmer, Jochen Babock, Bernhard Germeshausen, Bernhard Lehmann) | 3:40.43 |

## Figure Skating

| Event | | Points |
|---|---|---|
| Men | John Curry, GBR | 192.74 |
| Women | Dorothy Hamill, USA | 193.80 |
| Pairs | Irina Rodnina & Aleksandr Zaitsev, USSR | 140.54 |
| Dance | Lyudmila Pakhomova & Aleksandr Gorshkov, USSR | 209.92 |

## Ice Hockey
### Group A
(Overall records in parentheses)

| | Gm | W-L-T | Pts | GF | GA |
|---|---|---|---|---|---|
| 1   USSR (6-0-0) . . . . . . . . . . . | 5 | 5-0-0 | 10 | 40 | 11 |
| 2   Czechoslovakia (3-2-0) . . . . | 4 | 2-2-0 | 6 | 17 | 10 |
| 3   West Germany (3-3-0) . . . . | 5 | 2-3-0 | 4 | 21 | 24 |
| 4   Finland (3-3-0) . . . . . . . . . . | 5 | 2-3-0 | 4 | 19 | 18 |
| 5   USA (3-3-0) . . . . . . . . . . . | 5 | 2-3-0 | 4 | 15 | 21 |
| 6   Poland (1-4-0) . . . . . . . . . . | 5 | 0-4-0 | 0 | 9 | 37 |

**Note:** Czechoslovakia's 7–1 win over Poland was disallowed when a Czech player flunked a random postgame drug test. The Czechs were given a loss and their goals vs. Poland were deleted from the records. The U.S. missed a bronze medal in its final game with a 4–1 loss to West Germany.

## Luge
### MEN

| Event | | Time |
|---|---|---|
| 1-Seat | Dettlef Günther, E. Ger. . . . . . . . . . . . | 3:27.688 |
| 2-Seat | Hans Rinn & Norbert Hahn, E. Ger. . . . | 1:25.604 |

### WOMEN

| Event | | Time |
|---|---|---|
| 1-Seat | Margit Schumann, E. Ger. . . . . . . . . . | 2:50.621 |

## Nordic Skiing
### MEN
#### Cross Country

| Event | | Time |
|---|---|---|
| 15km | Nikolai Bazhukov, USSR . . . . . . . . . . | .43:58.47 |
| 30km | Sergei Saveliev, USSR . . . . . . . . . . . . | 1:30:29.38 |
| 50km | Ivar Formo, NOR . . . . . . . . . . . . . . . | 2:37:30.05 |
| 4x10km | FIN (Pitkänen, Mieto, Teurajärvi, Koivisto) . . . . . . . . . . . . | 2:07:59.72 |

#### Ski Jumping

| Event | | Points |
|---|---|---|
| 70m | Hans-Goerg Aschenbach, E. Ger. . . . . . . | 252.0 |
| 90m | Karl Schnabl, AUT . . . . . . . . . . . . . . . . | 234.8 |

#### Nordic Combined

| Event | | Points |
|---|---|---|
| 15km/Jump | Ulrich Wehling, E. Ger. . . . . . . . . . | 423.39 |

### WOMEN
#### Cross Country

| Event | | Time |
|---|---|---|
| 5km | Helena Takalo, FIN . . . . . . . . . . . . | 15:48.69 |
| 10km | Raisa Smetanina, USSR . . . . . . . . . . . . | 30:13.41 |
| 4x5km | USSR (Baldycheva, Amosova, Smetanina, Kulakova) . . . . . . . . . . . . . . . . . . . . | 1:07:49.75 |

## Speed Skating
### MEN

| Event | | Time | |
|---|---|---|---|
| 500m | Yevgeny Kulikov, USSR . . . . . . . . . | .39.17 | OR |
| 1000m | Peter Mueller, USA . . . . . . . . . . | 1:19.32 | |
| 1500m | Jan Egil Storholt, NOR . . . . . . . | 1:59.38 | OR |
| 5000m | Sten Stensen, NOR . . . . . . . . . . | .7:24.48 | OR |
| 10,000m | Piet Kleine, NED . . . . . . . . . . | 14:50.59 | OR |

### WOMEN

| Event | | Time | |
|---|---|---|---|
| 500m | Sheila Young, USA . . . . . . . . . . | .42.76 | OR |
| 1000m | Tatiana Averina, USSR . . . . . . . . | 1:28.43 | OR |
| 1500m | Galina Stepanskaya, USSR . . . . | 2:16.58 | OR |
| 3000m | Tatiana Averina, USSR . . . . . . | .4:45.19 | OR |

# 1980
## Lake Placid

XIII OLYMPIC WINTER GAMES LAKE PLACID 1980

Eric and the Miracles.

Over 1,100 athletes from 37 countries participated in the 1980 Winter Games, but the only ones most people will ever remember are 21-year-old American speed skater Eric Heiden, who won five individual gold medals, and the U.S. hockey team—a bunch of college kids (average age 22) who beat the unbeatable Russians.

No one before or since Heiden has won five individual gold medals in a single Olympic Games (three of swimmer Mark Spitz's seven gold medals were for relay races). And Heiden's sweep of the men's speed skating events has never been duplicated.

The hockey team, on the other hand, was a decided underdog. Seeded seventh out of 12 teams in the first round, they had also been routed, 10–3, by the Soviet Union in an exhibition game only a week before the Olympics.

Nevertheless, the Americans reached the final round with a 4–0–1 record. Playing in front of a boisterous, flag-waving home crowd, the U.S. upset the Soviets, 4–3 (captain Mike Eruzione scored the winning goal midway through the third period and goalie Jim Craig made 39 saves), then beat Finland, 4–2, to win the gold medal. "Do you believe in miracles?" asked ABC-TV announcer Al Michaels as the final seconds ticked off against the Russians. "Yes-s-s!"

That game was played on Feb. 22—five days short of exactly 20 years after the 1960 U.S. team beat the USSR, 3–2, on their way to the gold medal at Squaw Valley. Other links to the past included right wing Dave Christian, whose father Billy and uncle Roger were linemates on the 1960 team, and coach Herb Brooks, who had been the last player cut from the 1960 squad.

Swedish Alpine skier Ingemar Stenmark, who would retire in 1989 with 86 World Cup victories, won the slalom and GS for his only two Olympic wins.

## Top 10 Standings

National medal standings are not recognized by the IOC. The unofficial point totals are based on 3 points for a gold medal, 2 for a silver and 1 for a bronze. Total medals are in parentheses.

| | Gold | Silver | Bronze | Pts |
|---|---|---|---|---|
| 1   USSR (22) . . . . . . . . . . . | 10 | 6 | 6 | 48 |
|     East Germany (23) . . . . . | 9 | 7 | 7 | 48 |
| 3   USA (12) . . . . . . . . . . . . | 6 | 4 | 2 | 28 |
| 4   Finland (9) . . . . . . . . . . . | 1 | 5 | 3 | 16 |
| 5   Austria (7) . . . . . . . . . . . | 3 | 2 | 2 | 15 |
|     Norway (10) . . . . . . . . . | 1 | 3 | 6 | 15 |
| 7   Sweden (4) . . . . . . . . . . | 3 | 0 | 1 | 10 |
|     Liechtenstein (4) . . . . . . | 2 | 2 | 0 | 10 |
| 9   Holland (4) . . . . . . . . . . | 1 | 2 | 1 | 8 |
|     Switzerland (5) . . . . . . . | 1 | 1 | 3 | 8 |

AP/Wide World Photos

*The **U.S. men's hockey team** celebrates its 4-3 upset of the Soviet Union in the semifinals at the 1980 Olympic Winter Games in Lake Placid, N.Y. The team beat Finland (4-2) in the finals to win the gold medal.*

## Leading Medal Winners

Number of individual medals won on the left; gold, silver and bronze breakdown to the right.

### MEN

| No | | Sport | G-S-B |
|----|---|-------|-------|
| 5 | Eric Heiden, USA | Sp. Skating | 5-0-0 |
| 3 | Nikolai Zimatov, USSR | X-country | 3-0-0 |
| 3 | Anatoly Alyabiev, USSR | Biathlon | 2-0-1 |
| 3 | Frank Ullrich, E. Ger. | Biathlon | 1-2-0 |
| 3 | Juha Mieto, FIN | X-country | 0-2-1 |
| 2 | Ingemar Stenmark, SWE | Alpine | 2-0-0 |
| 2 | Vladimir Alikin, USSR | Biathlon | 1-1-0 |
| 2 | Josef Benz, SWI | Bobsled | 1-1-0 |
| 2 | Hans Jurgen Gerhardt, E. Ger. | Bobsled | 1-1-0 |
| 2 | Bernhard Germeshausen, E. Ger. | Bobsled | 1-1-0 |
| 2 | Vasili Rochev, USSR | X-country | 1-1-0 |
| 2 | Erich Schärer, SWI | Bobsled | 1-1-0 |
| 2 | Bogdan Musiol, E. Ger. | Bobsled | 1-0-1 |
| 2 | Meinhard Nehmer, E. Ger. | Bobsled | 1-0-1 |
| 2 | Kai Arne Stenshjemmet, NOR | Sp. Skating | 0-2-0 |
| 2 | Ove Aunli, NOR | X-country | 0-1-1 |
| 2 | Eberhard Rosch, E. Ger. | Biathlon | 0-1-1 |
| 2 | Tom Erik Oxholm, NOR | Sp. Skate | 0-0-2 |

### WOMEN

| No | | Sport | G-S-B |
|----|---|-------|-------|
| 3 | Hanni Wenzel, LIE | Alpine | 2-1-0 |
| 2 | Barbara Petzold, E. Ger. | X-country | 2-0-0 |
| 2 | Raisa Smetanina, USSR | X-country | 1-1-0 |
| 2 | Natalia Petruseva, USSR | Sp. Skate | 1-0-1 |
| 2 | Leah Mueller, USA | Sp. Skate | 0-2-0 |
| 2 | Hilkka Riihivuori, FIN | X-country | 0-2-0 |
| 2 | Sabine Becker, E. Ger. | Sp. Skate | 0-1-1 |

## Alpine Skiing

### MEN

| Event | | Time |
|-------|---|------|
| Downhill | Leonhard Stock, AUT | 1:45.50 |
| Slalom | Ingemar Stenmark, SWE | 1:44.26 |
| G.Slalom | Ingemar Stenmark, SWE | 2:40.74 |

### WOMEN

| Event | | Time |
|-------|---|------|
| Downhill | Annemarie Moser-Pröll, AUT | 1:37.52 |
| Slalom | Hanni Wenzel, LIE | 1:25.09 |
| G.Slalom | Hanni Wenzel, LIE | 2:41.66 |

## Biathlon

| Event | | MT | Adj.Time |
|-------|---|----|----------|
| 10km | Frank Ullrich, E. Ger. | 2 | 32:10.69 |
| 20km | Anatoly Alyabiev, USSR | 0 | 1:08:16.31 |
| 4x7.5km | USSR (Alikin, Tikonov, Barnashov, Alyabiev) | 0 | 1:34:03.27 |

## Bobsled

| Event | | Time |
|-------|---|------|
| 2-Man | SWI (Erich Schärer & Josef Benz) | 4:09.36 |
| 4-Man | E. Ger (Meinhard Nehmer, Bogdan Musiol, Bernhard Germeshausen, Hans-Jürgen Gerhardt) | 3:59.92 |

## Figure Skating

| Event | | Points |
|-------|---|--------|
| Men | Robin Cousins, GBR | 189.48 |
| Women | Anett Pötzsch, E. Ger. | 189,00 |
| Pairs | Irina Rodnina & Aleksandr Zaitsev, USSR | 147.26 |
| Dance | Natalia Linichuk & Gennady Karponosov, USSR | 205.48 |

## Ice Hockey
### Medal Round

(Overall records in parentheses)

| | | Gm | W-L-T | Pts | GF | GA |
|---|---|---|---|---|---|---|
| 1 | USA (6-0-1) | 3 | 2-0-1 | 5 | 10 | 7 |
| 2 | USSR (6-1-0) | 3 | 2-1-0 | 4 | 16 | 8 |
| 3 | Sweden (4-1-2) | 3 | 0-1-2 | 2 | 7 | 14 |
| 4 | Finland (3-3-1) | 3 | 0-2-1 | 1 | 7 | 11 |

**Note:** Games against common opponents carried over from the preliminary round. FIRST ROUND—USA tied Sweden, 2–2, and USSR over Finland, 4–2. MEDAL ROUND—USA over USSR, 4–3, and Finland, 4–2; USSR over Sweden, 9–2; and Sweden tied Finland, 3–3.

## Luge
### MEN

| Event | | Time |
|---|---|---|
| 1-Seat | Bernhard Glass, E. Ger. | 2:54.796 |
| 2-Seat | Hans Rinn & Norbert Hahn, E. Ger. | 1:19.331 |

### WOMEN

| Event | | Time |
|---|---|---|
| 1-Seat | Vera Zozulia, USSR | 2:36.537 |

## Nordic Skiing
### MEN
#### Cross Country

| Event | | Time |
|---|---|---|
| 15km | Thomas Wassberg, SWE | 41:57.63 |
| 30km | Nikolai Zimyatov, USSR | 1:27:02.80 |
| 50km | Nikolai Zimyatov, USSR | 2:27:24.60 |
| 4x10km | USSR (Rochev, Bazhukov, Beliaev, Zimyatov) | 1:57:03.46 |

#### Ski Jumping

| Event | | Points |
|---|---|---|
| 70m | Anton Innauer, AUT | 266.3 |
| 90m | Jouko Törmänen, FIN | 271.0 |

#### Nordic Combined

| Event | | Points |
|---|---|---|
| 15km/Jump | Ulrich Wehling, E. Ger. | 432.200 |

### WOMEN
#### Cross Country

| Event | | Time |
|---|---|---|
| 5km | Raisa Smetanina, USSR | 15:06.92 |
| 10km | Barbara Petzold, E. Ger. | 30:31.54 |
| 4x5km | E. Ger. (Rostock, Anding, Hesse, Petzold) | 1:02:11.10 |

## Speed Skating
### MEN

| Event | | Time | |
|---|---|---|---|
| 500m | Eric Heiden, USA | 38.03 | OR |
| 1000m | Eric Heiden, USA | 1:15.18 | OR |
| 1500m | Eric Heiden, USA | 1:55.44 | OR |
| 5000m | Eric Heiden, USA | 7:02.29 | OR |
| 10,000m | Eric Heiden, USA | 14:28.13 | WR |

### WOMEN

| Event | | Time | |
|---|---|---|---|
| 500m | Karin Enke, E. Ger. | 41.78 | OR |
| 1000m | Natalia Petruseva, USSR | 1:24.10 | OR |
| 1500m | Annie Borckink, NED | 2:10.95 | OR |
| 3000m | Bjoerg Eva Jensen, NOR | 4:32.13 | OR |

# 1984
### Sarajevo

In 1980, the Soviet Union and East Germany finished the Winter Games in a virtual tie for the unofficial team championship. The USSR won more gold medals (10-9), but the GDR won more overall medals (23-22).

In 1984, the East Germans edged into the lead in the battle of state-controlled athletic programs, winning three more golds (9-6), while the Soviets won one more overall medal (25-24).

Karin Enke was the top East German performer, taking two gold medals and two silvers in the four women's speed skating events. Teammate Andrea Schöne won a gold and two silvers. Cross-country skier Marja-Liisa Hämäläinen of Finland was the only athlete to win three events and one of only three—Enke and Swedish cross-country skier Gunde Svan were the others—to win four overall medals.

The U.S. hockey team failed to qualify for the medal round, but the men's Alpine ski team, which had never won an event before, won twice. Bill Johnson took the downhill and the Mahre brothers, Phil and Steve, finished 1-2 in the slalom.

## Top 10 Standings

National medal standings are not recognized by the IOC. The unofficial point totals are based on 3 points for a gold medal, 2 for a silver and 1 for a bronze. Total medals are in parentheses.

| | | Gold | Silver | Bronze | Pts |
|---|---|---|---|---|---|
| 1 | East Germany (24) | 9 | 9 | 6 | 51 |
| 2 | USSR (25) | 6 | 10 | 9 | 47 |
| 3 | Finland (13) | 4 | 3 | 6 | 24 |
| 4 | USA (8) | 4 | 4 | 0 | 20 |
| 5 | Sweden (8) | 4 | 2 | 2 | 18 |
| 6 | Norway (9) | 3 | 2 | 4 | 17 |
| 7 | Switzerland (5) | 2 | 2 | 1 | 11 |
| 8 | Canada (4) | 2 | 1 | 1 | 9 |
| | West Germany (4) | 2 | 1 | 1 | 9 |
| 10 | Czechoslovakia (6) | 0 | 2 | 4 | 8 |

## Leading Medal Winners

Number of individual medals won on the left; gold, silver and bronze breakdown to the right.

### MEN

| No | | Sport | G-S-B |
|---|---|---|---|
| 4 | Gunde Svan, SWE | X-country | 2-1-1 |
| 3 | Gaétan Boucher, CAN | Sp. Skating | 2-0-1 |
| 3 | Peter Angerer, W. Ger. | Biathlon | 1-1-1 |
| 3 | Eirik Kvalfoss, NOR | Biathlon | 1-1-1 |
| 3 | Aki Karvonen, FIN | X-country | 0-1-2 |
| 2 | Wolfgang Hoppe, E. Ger. | Bobsled | 2-0-0 |
| 2 | Dietmar Schauerhammer, E. Ger. | Bobsled | 2-0-0 |
| 2 | Thomas Wassberg, SWE | X-country | 2-0-0 |
| 2 | Tomas Gustafson, SWE | Sp. Skate | 2-0-0 |
| 2 | Igor Malkov, USSR | Sp. Skate | 1-1-0 |
| 2 | Matti Nykänen, FIN | Ski Jump | 1-1-0 |
| 2 | Jens Weissflog, E. Ger. | Ski Jump | 1-1-0 |
| 2 | Nikolai Zimyatov, USSR | X-country | 1-1-0 |
| 2 | Sergei Khlebnikov, USSR | Sp. Skate | 0-2-0 |

| No | | Sport | G-S-B |
|----|--|-------|-------|
| 2 | Bernhard Lehmann, E. Ger. . . . . . .Bobsled | | 0-2-0 |
| 2 | Bogdan Musiol, E. Ger. . . . . . . . .Bobsled | | 0-2-0 |
| 2 | Aleksandr Zavialov, USSR | X-country | 0-2-0 |
| 2 | Harri Kirvesniemi, FIN . . . . . . . .X-country | | 0-0-2 |
| 2 | Rene Schofisch, E. Ger. . . . . . . .Sp. Skate | | 0-0-2 |

## WOMEN

| No | | Sport | G-S-B |
|----|--|-------|-------|
| 4 | Marja-Liisa Hämäläinen, FIN . . . .X-country | | 3-0-1 |
| 4 | Karin Enke, E. Ger. . . . . . . . . .Sp. Skating | | 2-2-0 |
| 3 | Andrea Schöne, E. Ger. . . . . . .Sp. Skating | | 1-2-0 |
| 2 | Berit Aunli, NOR . . . . . . . . . . .X-country | | 1-1-0 |
| 2 | Anne Jahren, NOR . . . . . . . . . .X-country | | 1-0-1 |
| 2 | Brit Pettersen, NOR . . . . . . . . .X-country | | 1-0-1 |
| 2 | Kvetoslava Jeriova, CZE . . . . . .X-country | | 0-1-1 |
| 2 | Perrine Pelen, FRA . . . . . . . . . . . .Alpine | | 0-1-1 |
| 2 | Natalia Petruseva, USSR . . . . . . .Sp. Skate | | 0-0-2 |

## Alpine Skiing
### MEN

| Event | | Time |
|-------|--|------|
| Downhill | Bill Johnson, USA . . . . . . . . . . . . .1:45.59 | |
| Slalom | Phil Mahre, USA . . . . . . . . . . . . . .1:39.41 | |
| G.Slalom | Max Julen, SWI . . . . . . . . . . . . . . .2:41.18 | |

### WOMEN

| Event | | Time |
|-------|--|------|
| Downhill | Michela Figini, SWI . . . . . . . . . . . . .1:13.36 | |
| Slalom | Paoletta Magoni, ITA . . . . . . . . . . . .1:36.47 | |
| G.Slalom | Debbie Armstrong, USA . . . . . . . . . . .2:20.98 | |

## Biathlon

| Event | | MT | Adj.Time |
|-------|--|----|----------|
| 10km | Erik Kvalfoss, NOR . . . . . . . . . . | 2 | 30:53.8 |
| 20km | Peter Angerer, W. Ger. . . . . . . . | 2 | 1:11:52.7 |
| 4x7.5km | USSR (Vasiliev, Kachkarov, | | |
| | Algimantas, Buligin) . . . . . . . . . | 2 | 1:38:51.7 |

## Bobsled

| Event | | Time |
|-------|--|------|
| 2-Man | E. Ger. (Wolfgang Hoppe | |
| | & Dietmar Schauerhammer) . . . . . . . . .3:25.56 | |
| 4-Man | E. Ger. (Wolfgang Hoppe, | |
| | Roland Wetzig, Dietmar Schauerhammer, | |
| | Andreas Kirchner) . . . . . . . . . . . . . . .3:20.22 | |

## Figure Skating

| Event | | Points |
|-------|--|--------|
| Men | Scott Hamilton, USA . . . . . . . . . . . . . . . . .3.4 | |
| Women | Katarina Witt, E. Ger. . . . . . . . . . . . . . . . .3.2 | |
| Pairs | Elena Valova & Oleg Vasiliev, USSR . . . . . . . .1.4 | |
| Dance | Jayne Torvill & Christopher Dean, GBR . . . . . .2.0 | |

## Ice Hockey
### Medal Round

(Overall records in parentheses)

| | | Gm | W-L-T | Pts | GF | GA |
|--|--|----|-------|-----|----|----|
| 1 | USSR (7-0-0) . . . . . . . . . .3 | | 3-0-0 | 6 | 16 | 1 |
| 2 | Czechoslovakia (6-1-0) . . . .3 | | 2-1-0 | 4 | 6 | 3 |
| 3 | Sweden (4-2-1) . . . . . . . . .3 | | 1-2-0 | 2 | 3 | 12 |
| 4 | Canada (4-3-0) . . . . . . . . .3 | | 0-3-0 | 0 | 0 | 10 |

**Note:** Games against common opponents carried over from the preliminary round. MEDAL ROUND—the USSR beat Sweden, 10–1, Canada, 4–0, and the Czechs, 2–0, the Czechs beat Canada, 4–0, and Sweden, 2–0; and Sweden beat Canada, 2–0.

**Also:** The U.S., featuring future NHL stars Chris Chelios and Pat LaFontaine, failed to qualify for the Medal Round, finishing 7th overall with a record of 2–2–2.

## Luge
### MEN

| Event | | Time |
|-------|--|------|
| 1-Seat | Paul Hildgartner, ITA . . . . . . . . . . . . .3:04.258 | |
| 2-Seat | Hans Stanggassinger | |
| | & Franz Wembacher, W. Ger. . . . . . .1:23.620 | |

### WOMEN

| Event | | Time |
|-------|--|------|
| 1-Seat | Steffi Martin, E. Ger. . . . . . . . . . . . . .2:46.570 | |

## Nordic Skiing
### MEN
#### Cross Country

| Event | | Time |
|-------|--|------|
| 15km | Gunde Svan, SWE . . . . . . . . . . . . . .41:25.6 | |
| 30km | Nikolai Zimyatov, USSR . . . . . . . . .1:28:56.3 | |
| 50km | Thomas Wassberg, SWE . . . . . . . . .2:15:55.8 | |
| 4x10km | SWE (Wassberg, Kohlberg, | |
| | Ottoson, Svan) . . . . . . . . . . . . . . . .1:55:06.3 | |

#### Ski Jumping

| Event | | Points |
|-------|--|--------|
| 70m | Jens Weissflog, E. Ger. . . . . . . . . . . . . .215.2 | |
| 90m | Matti Nykänen, FIN . . . . . . . . . . . . . . .231.2 | |

#### Nordic Combined

| Event | | Points |
|-------|--|--------|
| 15km/Jump | Tom Sandberg, NOR . . . . . . . . . .422.595 | |

### WOMEN
#### Cross Country

| Event | | Time |
|-------|--|------|
| 5km | Marja-Liisa Hämäläinen, FIN . . . . . . . . .17:04.0 | |
| 10km | Marja-Liisa Hämäläinen, FIN . . . . . . . .31:44.2 | |
| 20km | Marja-Liisa Hämäläinen, FIN . . . . . . .1:01:45.0 | |
| 4x5km | NOR (Nybråten, Jahren, | |
| | Pettersen, Aunli) . . . . . . . . . . . . . . . .1:06:49.7 | |

## Speed Skating
### MEN

| Event | | Time |
|-------|--|------|
| 500m | Sergei Fokichev, USSR . . . . . . . . . . . . .38.19 | |
| 1000m | Gaétan Boucher, CAN . . . . . . . . . .1:15.80 | |
| 1500m | Gaétan Boucher, CAN . . . . . . . . . . . .1:58.36 | |
| 5000m | Tomas Gustafson, SWE . . . . . . . . . .7:12.28 | |
| 10,000m | Igor Malkov, USSR . . . . . . . . . . . .14:39.90 | |

### WOMEN

| Event | | Time | |
|-------|--|------|--|
| 500m | Christa Rothenburger, E. Ger. . . . .41.02 | | OR |
| 1000m | Karin Enke, E. Ger. . . . . . . . . . .1:21.61 | | OR |
| 1500m | Karin Enke, E. Ger. . . . . . . . . . .2:03.42 | | WR |
| 3000m | Andrea Schöne, E. Ger. . . . . . .4:24.79 | | OR |

# 1988
## Calgary

A record 1,750 athletes from 57 nations came to western Canada for the first Olympics north of the U.S. border. The Games featured an indoor speed skating oval and sporadic chinook winds that sent temperatures into the unwintry 70s. Matti Nykänen of Finland became the first pure ski jumper to capture three titles, winning gold medals at 70 and 90 meters and adding a third in the new team jumping competition.

Nykänen may have been the most decorated jumper in Calgary, but he wasn't the most celebrated. That honor belonged to Michael (Eddie the Eagle) Edwards, the accident-prone flying plasterer from Britain. Edwards finished 58th and last in the 70–meter jump and 55th and last in the 90–meter and was welcomed home after the Games by hundreds of fans at London's Heathrow Airport.

Back on the serious side, Dutch speed skater Yvonne van Gennip won three gold medals; East German figure skater Katarina Witt won her second straight women's title; and the USSR beat East Germany in both gold and overall medals in the last winterized confrontation of Communist superpowers.

## Top 10 Standings

National medal standings are not recognized by the IOC. The unofficial point totals are based on 3 points for a gold medal, 2 for a silver and 1 for a bronze. Total medals are in parentheses.

|  |  | Gold | Silver | Bronze | Pts |
|---|---|---|---|---|---|
| 1 | USSR (29) | 11 | 9 | 9 | 60 |
| 2 | East Germany (25) | 9 | 10 | 6 | 53 |
| 3 | Switzerland (15) | 5 | 5 | 5 | 30 |
| 4 | Austria (10) | 3 | 5 | 2 | 21 |
| 5 | Finland (7) | 4 | 1 | 2 | 16 |
|  | West Germany (8) | 2 | 4 | 2 | 16 |
| 7 | Netherlands (7) | 3 | 2 | 2 | 15 |
| 8 | Sweden (6) | 4 | 0 | 2 | 14 |
| 9 | USA (6) | 2 | 1 | 3 | 11 |
| 10 | Italy (5) | 2 | 1 | 2 | 10 |

## Leading Medal Winners

Number of individual medals won on the left; gold, silver and bronze breakdown to the right.

### MEN

| No |  | Sport | G-S-B |
|---|---|---|---|
| 3 | Matti Nykänen, FIN | Ski Jump | 3-0-0 |
| 3 | Valery Medvedtsev, USSR | Biathlon | 1-2-0 |
| 3 | Vladimir Smirnov, USSR | X-country | 0-2-1 |
| 2 | Alberto Tomba, ITA | Alpine | 2-0-0 |
| 2 | Frank-Peter Rötsch, E. Ger. | Biathlon | 2-0-0 |
| 2 | Gunde Svan, SWE | X-country | 2-0-0 |
| 2 | Tomas Gustafson, SWE | Sp. Skate | 2-0-0 |
| 2 | Hubert Strolz, AUT | Alpine | 1-1-0 |
| 2 | Mikhail Deviatiarov, USSR | X-country | 1-1-0 |
| 2 | Hippolyt Kempf, SWI | Nordic Comb. | 1-1-0 |
| 2 | Jens-Uwe Mey, E. Ger. | Sp. Skate | 1-1-0 |
| 2 | Alexei Prokurorov, USSR | X-country | 1-1-0 |
| 2 | Sergei Chepikov, USSR | Biathlon | 1-0-1 |
| 2 | Ianis Kipours, USSR | Bobsled | 1-0-1 |
| 2 | Vladimir Kozlov, USSR | Bobsled | 1-0-1 |
| 2 | Franck Piccard, FRA | Alpine | 1-0-1 |
| 2 | Pirmin Zurbriggen, SWI | Alpine | 1-0-1 |
| 2 | Wolfgang Hoppe, E. Ger. | Bobsled | 0-2-0 |
| 2 | Bogdan Musiol, E. Ger. | Bobsled | 0-2-0 |
| 2 | Matjaz Debelak, YUG | Ski Jump | 0-1-1 |
| 2 | Michael Hadschieff, AUT | Sp. Skate | 0-1-1 |
| 2 | Erik Johnsen, NOR | Ski Jump | 0-1-1 |
| 2 | Klaus Sulzenbacher, AUT | Nordic Comb. | 0-1-1 |
| 2 | Leo Visser, NED | Sp. Skate | 0-1-1 |
| 2 | Johann Passler, ITA | Biathlon | 0-0-2 |

### WOMEN

| No |  | Sport | G-S-B |
|---|---|---|---|
| 3 | Yvonne van Gennip, NED | Sp. Skating | 3-0-0 |
| 3 | Tamara Tikhonova, USSR | X-country | 2-1-0 |
| 3 | Marjo Matikänen, FIN | X-country | 1-0-2 |
| 3 | Andrea Ehrig, E. Ger. | Sp. Skating | 0-2-1 |
| 2 | Karin Kania, E. Ger. | Sp. Skating | 0-2-1 |
| 2 | Vreni Schneider, SWI | Alpine | 2-0-0 |
| 2 | Anfissa Reztsova, USSR | X-country | 1-1-0 |
| 2 | Christa Rothenburger, E. Ger. | Sp. Skate | 1-1-0 |
| 2 | Bonnie Blair, USA | Sp. Skate | 1-0-1 |
| 2 | Vida Ventsene, USSR | X-country | 1-0-1 |
| 2 | Brigitte Oertli, SWI | Alpine | 0-2-0 |
| 2 | Christa Kinshofer, W. Ger. | Alpine | 0-1-1 |
| 2 | Raisa Smetanina, USSR | X-country | 0-1-1 |
| 2 | Karen Percy, CAN | Alpine | 0-0-2 |
| 2 | Maria Walliser, SWI | Alpine | 0-0-2 |
| 2 | Gabi Zange, E. Ger. | Sp. Skate | 0-0-2 |

## Alpine Skiing
### MEN

| Event |  | Time |
|---|---|---|
| Downhill | Pirmin Zurbriggen, SWI | 1:59.63 |
| Slalom | Alberto Tomba, ITA | 1:39.47 |
| G.Slalom | Alberto Tomba, ITA | 2:06.37 |
| Super GS | Franck Piccard, FRA | 1:39.66 |
| Combined | Hubert Strolz, AUT | 36.55 pts |

### WOMEN

| Event |  | Time |
|---|---|---|
| Downhill | Marina Kiehl, W. Ger. | 1:25.86 |
| Slalom | Vreni Schneider, SWI | 1:36.69 |
| G.Slalom | Vreni Schneider, SWI | 2:06.49 |
| Super GS | Sigrid Wolf, AUT | 1:19.03 |
| Combined | Anita Wachter, AUT | 29.25 pts |

## Biathlon

| Event |  | MT | Adj.Time |
|---|---|---|---|
| 10km | Frank-Peter Rötsch, E. Ger. | 1 | 25:08.1 |
| 20km | Frank-Peter Rötsch, E. Ger. | 3 | 56:33.3 |
| 4x7.5km | USSR (Vasiliev, Chepikov, Popov, Medvedtsev) | 0 | 1:22:30.0 |

## Bobsled

| Event |  | Time |
|---|---|---|
| 2-Man | USSR (Janis Kipours & Vladimir Kozlov) | 3:53.48 |
| 4-Man | SWI (Ekkehard Fasser, Kurt Meier, Marcel Fässler, Werner Stocker) | 3:47.51 |

## Figure Skating

| Event |  | Points |
|---|---|---|
| Men | Brian Boitano, USA | 3.0 |
| Women | Katarina Witt, E. Ger. | 4.2 |
| Pairs | Ekaterina Gordeeva & Sergei Grinkov, USSR | 1.4 |
| Dance | Natalya Bestemianova & Andrei Bukin, USSR | 2.0 |

## Ice Hockey
### Medal Round

(Overall records in parentheses)

| | | Gm | W-L-T | Pts | GF | GA |
|---|---|---|---|---|---|---|
| 1 | USSR (7-1-0) | .5 | 4-1-0 | 8 | 25 | 7 |
| 2 | Finland (5-2-1) | .5 | 3-1-1 | 7 | 18 | 10 |
| 3 | Sweden (4-1-3) | .5 | 2-1-2 | 6 | 15 | 16 |
| 4 | Canada (5-2-1) | .5 | 5-2-1 | 5 | 17 | 14 |
| 5 | West Germany (4-4-0) | .5 | 1-4-0 | 2 | 8 | 26 |
| 6 | Czecholsovakia (4-4-0) | .5 | 1-4-0 | 2 | 12 | 22 |

**Note:** Games against common opponents carried over from the preliminary round. The USSR lost its final game to Finland, 2–1, after clinching the gold medal.

**Also:** The U.S. finished 4th in its preliminary pool with a 2–3 record. The top three teams in each of two 6–team pools qualified for the medal round.

## Luge
### MEN

| Event | | Time |
|---|---|---|
| 1-Seat | Jens Müller, E. Ger. | 3:05.548 |
| 2-Seat | Joerg Hoffmann | |
| | & Jochen Pietzsch, E. Ger. | 1:31.940 |

### WOMEN

| Event | | Time |
|---|---|---|
| 1-Seat | Steffi Martin Walter, E. Ger. | 3:03.973 |

## Nordic Skiing
### MEN
#### Cross Country

| Event | | Time |
|---|---|---|
| 15 km | Mikhail Deviatiarov, USSR | 41:18.9 |
| 30 km | Alexei Prokurorov, USSR | 1:24:26.3 |
| 50 km | Gunde Svan, SWE | 2:04:30.9 |
| 4x10 km | SWE (Ottosson, Wassberg, | |
| | Svan, Mogren) | 1:43:58.6 |

### Ski Jumping

| Event | | Points |
|---|---|---|
| 70m | Matti Nykänen, FIN | 229.1 |
| 90m | Matti Nykänen, FIN | 224.0 |
| Team | FIN (Nikkola, Nykänen, | |
| | Ylipulli, Puikkonen) | 634.4 |

### Nordic Combined

| Event | | Points |
|---|---|---|
| Indiv. | Hippolyt Kempf, SWI | 432.23 |
| Team | W. Ger. (Pohl, Schwarz, Müller) | 792.08 |

### WOMEN
#### Cross Country

| Event | | Time |
|---|---|---|
| 5km | Marjo Matikänen, FIN | 15:04.0 |
| 10km | Vida Ventsene, USSR | 30:08.3 |
| 20km | Tamara Tikhonova, USSR | 55:53.6 |
| 4x5km | USSR (Nagueikina, Gavriliuk, | |
| | Tikhonova, Reztsova) | 59:51.1 |

## Speed Skating
### MEN

| Event | | Time | |
|---|---|---|---|
| 500m | Jens-Uwe Mey, E. Ger. | 36.45 | WR |
| 1000m | Nikolai Gouliaev, USSR | 1:13.03 | OR |
| 1500m | André Hoffmann, E. Ger. | 1:52.06 | WR |
| 5000m | Tomas Gustafson, SWE | 6:44.63 | WR |
| 10,000m | Tomas Gustafson, SWE | 13:48.20 | WR |

### WOMEN

| Event | | Time | |
|---|---|---|---|
| 500m | Bonnie Blair, USA | 39.10 | WR |
| 1000m | Christa Rothenburger, E. Ger. | 1:17.65 | WR |
| 1500m | Yvonne van Gennip, NED | 2:00.68 | OR |
| 3000m | Yvonne van Gennip, NED | 4:11.94 | WR |
| 5000m | Yvonne van Gennip, NED | 7:14.13 | WR |

# 1992
## Albertville

The first Olympics since the reunification of Germany in 1990 and the breakup of the Soviet Union in 1991 resulted in a record 2,174 athletes from 65 countries as the Winter Games were staged in the French Alps for the third time. Despite all the political turmoil at home, Germany's combined East-West squad and the Unified Team of ex-Soviet athletes were again the biggest winners with the Germans edging the Unifieds in total medals, 26-23.

The female stars of the UT cross-country contingent made the most medal news as Lyubov Egorova (3 gold and 2 silver) and Elena Valbe (1 gold and 4 bronze), each won five and 39–year-old Raisa Smetanina set a Winter Games record with her 10th career medal as a member of the victorious 20–kilometer relay team.

Norway won as many gold medals (9) as the Unified Team, thanks mainly to cross-country skiers Bjorn Dählie and Vegard Ulvang, who each carried off three golds and a silver. Norwegians also won gold in alpine skiing for the first time in 40 years as Finn Christian Jagge (slalom) and Kjetil Andre Aamodt (Super G) made like Stein Eriksen in 1952.

Led by Bonnie Blair's victories at 500 and 1,000 meters in speed skating, women won all five gold medals collected by the U.S. Blair was joined by figure skater Kristi Yamaguchi, freestyle skier Donna Weinbrecht and short track speed skater Cathy Turner.

## Top 10 Standings

National medal standings are not recognized by the IOC. The unofficial point totals are based on 3 points for a gold medal, 2 for a silver and 1 for a bronze. Total medals are in parentheses.

| | | Gold | Silver | Bronze | Points |
|---|---|---|---|---|---|
| 1 | Germany (26) | 10 | 10 | 6 | 56 |
| 2 | Unified Team (23) | 9 | 6 | 8 | 47 |
| 3 | Norway (20) | 9 | 6 | 5 | 44 |
| 4 | Austria (21) | 6 | 7 | 8 | 40 |
| 5 | Italy (14) | 4 | 6 | 4 | 28 |
| 6 | United States (11) | 5 | 4 | 2 | 25 |
| 7 | France (9) | 3 | 5 | 1 | 20 |
| 8 | Finland (7) | 3 | 1 | 3 | 14 |
| | Canada (7) | 2 | 3 | 2 | 14 |
| 10 | Japan (7) | 1 | 2 | 4 | 11 |

## Leading Medal Winners

Number of individual medals won on the left; gold, silver and bronze breakdown to the right.

### MEN

| No | | Sport | G-S-B |
|----|------|-------|-------|
| 4 | Bjorn Dählie, NOR . . . . . . . . . .X-country | | 3-1-0 |
| 4 | Vegard Ulvang, NOR . . . . . . . .X-country | | 3-1-0 |
| 3 | Mark Kirchner, GER . . . . . . . . .Biathlon | | 2-1-0 |
| 3 | Toni Nieminen, FIN . . . . . . . . . .Ski Jump | | 2-0-1 |
| 3 | Martin Hollwarth, AUT . . . . . . .Ski Jump | | 0-3-0 |
| 3 | Giorgio Vanzetta, ITA . . . . . . .X-country | | 0-1-2 |
| 2 | Kim Ki Hoon, S.Kor . . . . . . . .ST Sp. Skate | | 2-0-0 |
| 2 | Ricco Gross, GER . . . . . . . . . . .Biathlon | | 1-1-0 |
| 2 | Johann Koss, NOR . . . . . . . . . .Sp. Skate | | 1-1-0 |
| 2 | Alberto Tomba, ITA . . . . . . . . . . .Alpine | | 1-1-0 |
| 2 | Ernst Vettori, AUT . . . . . . . . . .Ski Jump | | 1-1-0 |
| 2 | Kjetil Andre Aamodt, NOR . . . . . . .Alpine | | 1-0-1 |
| 2 | Donat Acklin, SWI . . . . . . . . . . .Bobsled | | 1-0-1 |
| 2 | Geir Karlstad, NOR . . . . . . . . . .Sp. Skate | | 1-0-1 |
| 2 | Terje Langli, NOR . . . . . . . . . .X-country | | 1-0-1 |
| 2 | Gustav Weder, SWI . . . . . . . . . .Bobsled | | 1-0-1 |
| 2 | Lee Joon Ho, S.Kor . . . . . .ST Sp. Skate | | 1-0-1 |
| 2 | Marco Albarello, ITA . . . . . . . .X-country | | 0-2-0 |
| 2 | Frederic Blackburn, CAN . . . .ST Sp. Skate | | 0-2-0 |
| 2 | Marc Girardelli, LUX . . . . . . . . . .Alpine | | 0-2-0 |
| 2 | Heinz Kuttin, AUT . . . . . . . . . .Ski Jump | | 0-1-1 |
| 2 | Mikael Lofren, SWE . . . . . . . . . .Biathlon | | 0-0-2 |
| 2 | Klaus Sulzenbacher, AUT . . .Nordic Comb. | | 0-0-2 |
| 2 | Leo Visser, NED . . . . . . . . . . . .Sp. Skate | | 0-0-2 |

### WOMEN

| No | | Sport | G-S-B |
|----|------|-------|-------|
| 5 | Lyubov Egorova, UT . . . . . . . . .X-country | | 3-2-0 |
| 5 | Elena Valbe, UT . . . . . . . . . . .X-country | | 1-0-4 |
| 3 | Gunda Niemann, GER . . . . . . .Sp. Skate | | 2-1-0 |
| 3 | Antje Misersky, GER . . . . . . . . .Biathlon | | 1-2-0 |
| 3 | Stefania Belmondo, ITA . . . . . .X-country | | 1-1-1 |
| 2 | Bonnie Blair, USA . . . . . . . . . . .Sp.Skate | | 2-0-0 |
| 2 | Petra Kronberger, AUT . . . . . . . . .Alpine | | 2-0-0 |
| 2 | Marjut Lukkarinen, FIN . . . . . . .X-country | | 1-1-0 |
| 2 | Cathy Turner, USA . . . . . . . .ST Sp. Skate | | 1-1-0 |
| 2 | Anfisa Reztsova, UT . . . . . . . . .Biathlon | | 1-0-1 |
| 2 | Ye Qiaobo, CHN . . . . . . . . . . .Sp. Skate | | 0-2-0 |
| 2 | Anita Wachter, AUT . . . . . . . . . . .Alpine | | 0-2-0 |
| 2 | Heike Warnicke, GER . . . . . . . .Sp. Skate | | 0-2-0 |
| 2 | Elena Belova, UT . . . . . . . . . . . .Biathlon | | 0-0-2 |

## Alpine Skiing

### MEN

| Event | | Time |
|-------|------|------|
| Downhill | Patrick Ortlieb, AUT . . . . . . . . . . . . | 1:50.37 |
| Slalom | Finn Christian Jagge, NOR . . . . . . | 1:44.39 |
| Giant Slalom | Alberto Tomba, ITA . . . . . . . . . . . | 2:06.98 |
| Super G | Kjetil Andre Aamodt, NOR . . . . . . | 1:13.04 |
| Combined | Josef Polig, ITA . . . . . . . . . . . . . | 14.58 pts |

### WOMEN

| Event | | Time |
|-------|------|------|
| Downhill | Kerrin Lee-Gartner, CAN . . . . . . . | 1:52.55 |
| Slalom | Petra Krenberger, AUT . . . . . . . . . | 1:32.68 |
| Giant Slalom | Pernilla Wiberg, SWE . . . . . . . . | 2:12.74 |
| Super G | Deborah Compagnoni, ITA . . . . . | 1:21.22 |
| Combined | Petra Kronberger, AUT . . . . . . . . . | 2.55 pts |

## Biathlon

### MEN

| Event | | MT | Time |
|-------|------|----|------|
| 10km | Mark Kircher, GER . . . . . . .0 | | 26:02.3 |
| 20km | Yevgeny Redkine, UT . . . . . .0 | | 57:34.4 |
| 4x7.5km relay | Germany (Gross, Steinigen, Kirchner, Fischer) . . . .0 | | 1:24:43.5 |

### WOMEN

| Event | | MT | Time |
|-------|------|----|------|
| 7.5km | Anfisa Reztsova, UT . . . . . . . .3 | | 24:29.2 |
| 15km | Antje Misersky, GER . . . . . .1 | | 51:47.2 |
| 3x7.5km relay | France (Niogret, Claudel, Briand) . . . . . . . . . . . . . . .0 | | 1:15:55.6 |

## Bobsled

| Event | | Time |
|-------|------|------|
| 2-Man | SWI (Gustav Weder & Donat Acklin) . . . . | 4:03.26 |
| 4-Man | AUT (Ingo Appelt, Harald Winkler, Gerhard Haidacher, Thomas Schroll) . . . . . . . . . | 3:53.90 |

## Figure Skating

| Event | | FP |
|-------|------|----|
| Men | Viktor Petrenko, UT . . . . . . . . . . . . . . . . . . . | 1.5 |
| Women | Kristi Yamaguchi, USA . . . . . . . . . . . . . . . . . | 1.5 |
| Pairs | Natalya Mishkutienok & Artur Dmitriev, UT | 1.5 |
| Dance | Marina Klimova & Sergei Ponomarenko, UT | 2.0 |

## Freestyle Skiing

| Event | | Pts |
|-------|------|-----|
| Men's Moguls | Edgar Grospiron, FRA . . . . . . . . | 25.81 |
| Women's Moguls | Donna Weinbrecht, USA . . . . . . . | 23.69 |

## Ice Hockey

### Round Robin Standings

First four teams in each group advanced to medal round.

| Group A | Gm | W-L-T | Pts | GF | GA |
|---------|----|-------|-----|----|----|
| United States . . . . . . . . . . . . . .5 | | 4-0-1 | 9 | 18 | 7 |
| Sweden . . . . . . . . . . . . . . . . . .5 | | 3-0-2 | 8 | 22 | 11 |
| Finland . . . . . . . . . . . . . . . . . .5 | | 3-1-1 | 7 | 22 | 11 |
| Germany . . . . . . . . . . . . . . . . .5 | | 2-3-0 | 4 | 11 | 12 |
| Italy . . . . . . . . . . . . . . . . . . . .5 | | 1-4-0 | 2 | 18 | 24 |
| Poland . . . . . . . . . . . . . . . . . .5 | | 0-5-0 | 0 | 4 | 30 |

| Group B | Gm | W-L-T | Pts | GF | GA |
|---------|----|-------|-----|----|----|
| Canada . . . . . . . . . . . . . . . . . .5 | | 4-1-0 | 8 | 28 | 9 |
| Unified Team . . . . . . . . . . . . . .5 | | 4-1-0 | 8 | 32 | 10 |
| Czechoslovakia . . . . . . . . . . . .5 | | 4-1-0 | 8 | 25 | 15 |
| France . . . . . . . . . . . . . . . . . .5 | | 2-3-0 | 4 | 14 | 22 |
| Switzerland . . . . . . . . . . . . . . .5 | | 1-4-0 | 2 | 13 | 25 |
| Norway . . . . . . . . . . . . . . . . . .5 | | 0-5-0 | 0 | 7 | 38 |

**Note:** First place tie broken by goal differential in common games.

### Quarterfinals

Canada 3 . . . . . . . . . . . . . . . . . . . . . . . . . . .Germany 3
(Canada wins shootout, 3-2)
Czechoslovakia 3 . . . . . . . . . . . . . . . . . . . . . .Sweden 1
United States 4 . . . . . . . . . . . . . . . . . . . . . . . . .France 1
Unified Team 6 . . . . . . . . . . . . . . . . . . . . . . . .Finland 1

### Semifinals

Canada 4 . . . . . . . . . . . . . . . . . . . . . .Czechoslovakia 2
Unified Team 5 . . . . . . . . . . . . . . . . . . . .United States 2

### Bronze Medal

Czechoslovakia 6 . . . . . . . . . . . . . . . . . . . .United States 2

### Gold Medal

Unified Team 3 . . . . . . . . . . . . . . . . . . . . . . .Canada 1

## Luge
### MEN

| Event | | Time |
|---|---|---|
| Singles | Georg Hackl, GER | 3:02.363 |
| Doubles | Stefan Krausse & Jan Behrendt, GER | 1:32.053 |

### WOMEN

| Event | | Time |
|---|---|---|
| Singles | Doris Neuner, AUT | 3:06.696 |

## Nordic Skiing
### MEN
#### Cross Country

| Event | | Time |
|---|---|---|
| 10km | Vegard Ulvang, NOR | 27:36.0 |
| 15km | Bjorn Dählie, NOR | 38:01.9 |
| 30km | Vegard Ulvang, NOR | 1:22:27.8 |
| 50km | Bjorn Dählie, NOR | 2:03:41.5 |
| 4x10km | NOR (Langli, Ulvang, Skjedal, Dahlie) | 1:39:26.0 |

#### Ski Jumping

| Event | | Pts |
|---|---|---|
| 90m | Ernst Vettori, AUT | 222.8 |
| 120m | Toni Nieminen, FIN | 239.5 |
| Team (120m) | FIN (Nikkola, Laitinen, Laakkonen, Nieminen) | 644.4 |

#### Nordic Combined

| Event | | Pts |
|---|---|---|
| Indiv. | Fabrice Guy, FRA | 426.47 |
| Team | JPN (Mikata, Kono, Ogiwara) | 1247.18 |

### WOMEN
#### Cross Country

| Event | | Time |
|---|---|---|
| 5km | Marjut Lukkarinen, FIN | 14:13.8 |
| 10km | Lyubov Egorova, RUS | 25:53.7 |
| 15km | Lyubov Egorova, RUS | 42:20.8 |
| 30km | Stefania Belmondo, ITA | 1:22:30.1 |
| 4x5km | UT (Valbe, Smetanina, Lasutina, Egorova) | 59:34.8 |

## Speed Skating
### MEN
#### Long Track

| Event | | Time |
|---|---|---|
| 500m | Uwe-Jens Mey, GER | 37.14 |
| 1000m | Olaf Zinke, GER | 1:14.85 |
| 1500m | Johann Olav Koss, NOR | 1:54.81 |
| 5000m | Geir Karlstad, NOR | 6:59.97 |
| 10,000m | Bart Veldkamp, NED | 14:12.12 |

#### Short Track

| Event | | Time | |
|---|---|---|---|
| 1000m | Ki-Hoon Kim, S. Kor | 1:30.76 | WR |
| 4x1250m | S.Kor (Kim, Lee, Jmo, Song) | 7:14.02 | WR |

### WOMEN
#### Long Track

| Event | | Time |
|---|---|---|
| 500m | Bonnie Blair, USA | 40.33 |
| 1000m | Bonnie Blair, USA | 1:21.90 |
| 1500m | Jacqueline Borner, GER | 2:05.87 |
| 3000m | Gunda Niemann, GER | 4:19.90 |
| 5000m | Gunda Niemann, GER | 7:31.57 |

#### Short Track

| Event | | Time |
|---|---|---|
| 500m | Cathy Turner, USA | 47.04 |
| 4x750m | CAN (Cutrone, Daigle, Lambert, Perreault) | 4:36.62 |

# 1994
## Lillehammer

For better or worse, the Lillehammer games may be best evoked in most people's memories by two names. Tonya and Nancy. It was an ugly attack before the U.S. Figure Skating Championships on skater Nancy Kerrigan by cohorts of teammate and rival Tonya Harding that set up the most anticipated moment of the Games. Harding's goons were arrested following the Kerrigan clubbing and charged in a plot to improve Harding's chances of medaling by removing Kerrigan from competition. The plan failed and Kerrigan did compete, finishing with the silver medal. She actually tied 16-year-old Ukrainian orphan Oksana Baiul but missed the gold on the artistic merit tiebreaker. Harding, who had to threaten a lawsuit to avoid being barred from the Games by the USOC, ended up in eighth. The broadcast of the women's skating final was the sixth highest-rated program of any sort in U.S. television history.

There are so many more names symbolic of these games, however. Norway's Johann Olav Koss set three world records and won three golds in the men's 1500-, 5000- and 10,000-meter speed skating events. American speed skaters had success as well. Dan Jansen finally caught that elusive medal, winning the 1000-meter gold with a world record in his final event. Bonnie Blair won two golds in the women's 500- and 1000-meter races. And those were just the speed skaters.

The games were the most environmentally friendly Olympics in history as well. Norway's recycling and energy-saving techniques were so successful that the IOC revised its procedure for choosing host cities as a result.

## Top 10 Standings

National medal standings are not recognized by the IOC. The unofficial point totals are based on 3 points for a gold medal, 2 for a silver and 1 for a bronze. Total medals are in parentheses.

| | | Gold | Silver | Bronze | Points |
|---|---|---|---|---|---|
| 1 | Norway (26) | 10 | 11 | 5 | 57 |
| 2 | Russia (23) | 11 | 8 | 4 | 53 |
| 3 | Germany (24) | 9 | 7 | 8 | 49 |
| 4 | Italy (20) | 7 | 5 | 8 | 39 |
| 5 | United States (13) | 6 | 5 | 2 | 30 |
| 6 | Canada (13) | 3 | 6 | 4 | 25 |
| 7 | Switzerland (9) | 3 | 4 | 2 | 19 |
| 8 | Austria (9) | 2 | 3 | 4 | 16 |
| 9 | South Korea (6) | 4 | 1 | 1 | 15 |
| 10 | Japan (5) | 1 | 2 | 2 | 9 |

## Leading Medal Winners

Number of individual medals won on the left; gold, silver and bronze breakdown to the right.

### MEN

| No | | Sport | G-S-B |
|----|---|-------|-------|
| 4 | Bjorn Dählie, NOR | X-country | 2-2-0 |
| 3 | Johann Olav Koss, NOR | Sp. Skating | 3-0-0 |
| 3 | Vladimir Smirnov, KAZ | X-country | 1-2-0 |
| 3 | Sergei Tarasov, RUS | Biathlon | 1-1-1 |
| 3 | Kjetil Andre Aamodt, NOR | Alpine | 0-2-1 |
| 3 | Mika Myllyla, FIN | X-country | 0-1-2 |
| 2 | Markus Wasmeier, GER | Alpine | 2-0-0 |
| 2 | Jens Weissflog, GER | Ski Jumping | 2-0-0 |
| 2 | Donat Acklin, SWI | Bobsled | 1-1-0 |
| 2 | Thomas Alsgaard, NOR | X-country | 1-1-0 |
| 2 | Espen Bredesen, NOR | Ski Jumping | 1-1-0 |
| 2 | Ji-Hoon Chae, S.Kor | ST Sp. Skating | 1-1-0 |
| 2 | Ricco Gross, GER | Biathlon | 1-1-0 |
| 2 | Takanori Kono, JPN | Nordic Comb. | 1-1-0 |
| 2 | Frank Luck,. GER | Biathlon | 1-1-0 |
| 2 | Fred Borre Lundberg, NOR | Nordic Comb. | 1-1-0 |
| 2 | Tommy Moe, USA | Alpine | 1-1-0 |
| 2 | Sergei Chepikov, RUS | Biathlon | 1-1-0 |
| 2 | Mirko Vuillermin, ITA | ST. Sp. Skating | 1-1-0 |
| 2 | Gustav Weder, SWI | Bobsled | 1-1-0 |
| 2 | Marco Albarello, ITA | X-Country | 1-0-1 |
| 2 | Silvio Fauner, ITA | X-Country | 1-0-1 |
| 2 | Sven Fischer, GER | Biathlon | 1-0-1 |
| 2 | Dieter Thoma, GER | Ski Jumping | 1-0-1 |
| 2 | Kjell Storelid, NOR | Sp. Skating | 0-2-0 |
| 2 | Sergei Klevchenya, RUS | Sp. Skating | 0-1-1 |
| 2 | Rintje Ritsma, NED | Sp. Skating | 0-1-1 |
| 2 | Sture Sivertsen, NOR | X-Country | 0-1-1 |
| 2 | Bjarte Engen Vik, NOR | Nordic Comb. | 0-1-1 |
| 2 | Andreas Goldberger, AUT | Ski Jumping | 0-0-2 |

### WOMEN

| No | | Sport | G-S-B |
|----|---|-------|-------|
| 5 | Manuela Di Centa, ITA | X-Country | 2-2-1 |
| 4 | Lyubov Egorova, RUS | X-Country | 3-1-0 |
| 3 | Vreni Schneider, SWI | Alpine | 1-1-1 |
| 2 | Myriam Bedard, CAN | Biathlon | 2-0-0 |
| 2 | Bonnie Blair, USA | Sp. Skating | 2-0-0 |
| 2 | Lee-Kyung Chun, S. Kor | ST Sp. Skating | 2-0-0 |
| 2 | Emese Hunyady, AUT | Sp. Skating | 1-1-0 |
| 2 | Nina Gavriluk, RUS | X-Country | 1-0-1 |
| 2 | So-Hee Kim, S. Kor | ST Sp. Skating | 1-0-1 |
| 2 | Claudia Pechstein, GER | Sp. Skating | 1-0-1 |
| 2 | Cathy Turner, USA | ST Sp. Skating | 1-0-1 |
| 2 | Ann Briand, FRA | Biathlon | 0-1-1 |
| 2 | Ursula Disl, GER | Biathlon | 0-1-1 |
| 2 | Gunda Niemann, GER | Sp. Skating | 0-1-1 |
| 2 | Stefania Belmondo, ITA | X-Country | 0-0-2 |
| 2 | M.L. Kirvesniemi, FIN | X-Country | 0-0-2 |
| 2 | Isolde Kostner, ITA | Alpine | 0-0-2 |
| 2 | Amy Peterson, USA | ST Sp. Skating | 0-0-2 |

## Alpine Skiing

### MEN

| Event | | Time |
|-------|---|------|
| Downhill | Tommy Moe, USA | 1:45.75 |
| Slalom | Thomas Stangassinger, AUT | 2:02.02 |
| Giant Slalom | Markus Wasmeier, GER | 2:52.46 |
| Super G | Markus Wasmeier, GER | 1:32.53 |
| Combined | Lasse Kjus, NOR | 3:17.53 |

### WOMEN

| Event | | Time |
|-------|---|------|
| Downhill | Katja Seizinger, GER | 1:35.93 |
| Slalom | Vreni Schneider, SWI | 1:56.01 |
| Giant Slalom | Deborah Compagnoni, ITA | 2:30.97 |
| Super G | Diann Roffe-Steinrotter, USA | 1:22.15 |
| Combined | Pernilla Wiberg, SWE | 3:05.16 |

## Biathlon

### MEN

| Event | | MT | Time |
|-------|---|----|------|
| 10km | Sergei Chepikov, RUS | 0 | 28:07.0 |
| 20km | Sergei Tarasov, RUS | 3 | 57:25.3 |
| 4x7.5km relay | Germany | 0 | 1:30:22.1 |

### WOMEN

| Event | | MT | Time |
|-------|---|----|------|
| 7.5km | Myriam Bedard, CAN | 2 | 26:08.8 |
| 15km | Myriam Bedard, CAN | 2 | 52:06.6 |
| 4x7.5km relay | Russia | 0 | 1:47:19.5 |

## Bobsled

| Event | | Time |
|-------|---|------|
| 2-Man | SWI (Gustav Weder & Donat Acklin) | 3:30.81 |
| 4-Man | GER (Harald Czudaj, Karsten Brannasch, Olaf Hampel, Alexander Szelig) | 3:27.78 |

## Freestyle Skiing

### MEN

| Event | | Pts |
|-------|---|-----|
| Aerials | Andreas Schoenbaechler, SWI | 234.67 |
| Moguls | Jean-Luc Brassard, CAN | 27.24 |

### WOMEN

| Event | | Pts |
|-------|---|-----|
| Aerials | Lina Cherjazova, UZB | 166.84 |
| Moguls | Stine Lise Hattestad, NOR | 25.97 |

## Figure Skating

| Event | | FP |
|-------|---|----|
| Men | Alexei Urmanov, RUS | 1.5 |
| Women | Oksana Baiul, UKR | 2.0 |
| Pairs | Ekaterina Gordeeva & Sergei Grinkov, RUS | 1.5 |
| Dance | Oksana Gritschuk & Yevgeny Platov, RUS | 3.0 |

## Ice Hockey

### Round Robin Standings

First four teams in each group advanced to medal round.

| Group A | Gm | W-L-T | Pts | GF | GA |
|---------|----|-------|-----|----|----|
| Finland | 5 | 5-0-0 | 10 | 25 | 4 |
| Germany | 5 | 3-2-0 | 6 | 11 | 14 |
| Czech Republic | 5 | 3-2-0 | 6 | 16 | 11 |
| Russia | 5 | 3-2-0 | 6 | 20 | 14 |
| Austria | 5 | 1-4-0 | 2 | 13 | 28 |
| Norway | 5 | 0-5-0 | 0 | 5 | 19 |

**Note:** Second place tie broken by goal differential in common games.

| Group B | Gm | W-L-T | Pts | GF | GA |
|---------|----|-------|-----|----|----|
| Slovakia | 5 | 3-0-2 | 8 | 26 | 14 |
| Canada | 5 | 3-1-1 | 7 | 17 | 11 |
| Sweden | 5 | 3-1-1 | 7 | 23 | 13 |
| United States | 5 | 1-1-3 | 5 | 21 | 17 |
| Italy | 5 | 1-4-0 | 2 | 15 | 31 |
| France | 5 | 0-4-1 | 1 | 11 | 27 |

**Note:** Second place tie broken by goal differential in common games.

### Quarterfinals

| | | |
|---|---|---|
| Sweden 3 | | Germany 0 |
| Canada 3 | OT | Czech Republic 2 |
| Finland 6 | | United States 1 |
| Russia 3 | OT | Slovakia 2 |

### Semifinals

| | |
|---|---|
| Sweden 4 | Russia 3 |
| Canada 5 | Finland 3 |

### Bronze Medal

| | |
|---|---|
| Finland 4 | Russia 0 |

### Gold Medal

Sweden 2 . . . . . . . . . . . . . . OT . . . . . . . . Canada 2

(Sweden wins shootout, 3-2)

## Luge
### MEN

| Event | | Time |
|---|---|---|
| Singles | Georg Hackl, GER . . . . . . . . . . . . . . | .3:21.571 |
| Doubles | Kurt Brugger & Wilfried Huber, ITA . . . . | 1:36.720 |

### WOMEN

| Event | | Time |
|---|---|---|
| Singles | Gerda Weissensteiner, ITA . . . . . . . . . | .3:15.517 |

## Nordic Skiing
### MEN
#### Cross Country

| Event | | Time |
|---|---|---|
| 10km | Bjorn Dåhlie, NOR . . . . . . . . . . . . . . | .24:20.1 |
| 15km | Bjorn Dåhlie, NOR . . . . . . . . . . . . . . | 1:00:08.8 |
| 30km | Thomas Alsgaard, NOR . . . . . . . . . . . . | 1:12:26.4 |
| 50km | Vladimir Smirnov, KAZ . . . . . . . . . . . | 2:07:20.3 |
| 4x10km | ITA (De Zolt, Albarello, Vanzetta, Fauner) . . . . . . . . . . . . . . . . . . . . | 1:41:15.0 |

#### Ski Jumping

| Event | | Pts |
|---|---|---|
| 90m | Espen Bredesen, NOR . . . . . . . . . . | .282.0 |
| 120m | Jens Weissflog, GER . . . . . . . . . . . . | .274.5 |
| Team (120m) | GER (Jaekle, Duffner, Thoma, Weissflog) . . . . . . . . . . . . . . | .970.1 |

#### Nordic Combined

| Event | | Pts |
|---|---|---|
| Indiv. | Fred Borre Lundberg, NOR . . . . . . . . . | .457.970 |
| Team | JPN (Kono, Abe, Ogiwara) . . . . . . . . | 1368.860 |

### WOMEN
#### Cross Country

| Event | | Time |
|---|---|---|
| 5km | Lyubov Egorova, RUS . . . . . . . . . . . . . | .14:08.8 |
| 10km | Lyubov Egorova, RUS . . . . . . . . . . . . . | .41:38.1 |
| 15km | Manuela Di Centa, ITA . . . . . . . . . . . . | .39:44.5 |
| 30km | Manuela Di Centa, ITA . . . . . . . . . . . . | 1:25:41.6 |
| 4x5km | RUS (Valbe, Lazutina, Gavriluk, Egorova) . . . . . . . . . . . . . . . . . . . . | .57:12.5 |

## Speed Skating
### MEN
#### Long Track

| Event | | Time | |
|---|---|---|---|
| 500m | Aleksandr Golubev, RUS . . . . . . . | .36.33 | OR |
| 1000m | Dan Jansen, USA . . . . . . . . . . . | 1:12.43 | WR |
| 1500m | Johann Olav Koss, NOR . . . . . . | 1:51.29 | WR |
| 5000m | Johann Olav Koss, NOR . . . . . . | 6:34.96 | WR |
| 10,000m | Johann Olav Koss, NOR . . . . . . | 13:30.55 | WR |

#### Short Track

| Event | | Time | |
|---|---|---|---|
| 500m | Ji-Hoon Chae, S. Kor . . . . . . . | .43.45 | |
| 1000m | Ki-Hoon Kim, S. Kor . . . . . . . . | 1:34.57 | |
| 5000m relay | Italy . . . . . . . . . . . . . . . . | .7:11.74 | OR |

### WOMEN
#### Long Track

| Event | | Time |
|---|---|---|
| 500m | Bonnie Blair, USA . . . . . . . . . . . . . . . | .39.25 |
| 1000m | Bonnie Blair, USA . . . . . . . . . . . . . . | 1:18.74 |
| 1500m | Emese Hunyady, AUT . . . . . . . . . . . | 2:02.19 |
| 3000m | Svetlana Bazhanova, RUS . . . . . . . . . | .4:17.43 |
| 5000m | Claudia Pechstein, GER . . . . . . . . . . | .7:14.37 |

#### Short Track

| Event | | Time | |
|---|---|---|---|
| 500m | Cathy Turner, USA . . . . . . | .45.98 | OR |
| 1000m | Lee-Kyung Chun, S. Kor . | 1:36.87 | |
| 3000m Relay | South Korea . . . . . . . . . | .4:26.64 | WR |

# 1998
## Nagano

The 18th Winter Games included a record 2,177 athletes from 72 countries and marked the Olympics first trip to Asia in 26 years.

Nagano was pummeled by snow, sleet, rain and even a minor earthquake during the Games. The weather caused countless delays and rescheduling got so bad that organizers had to cram the men's super G, women's downhill, and women's combined downhill into one day—the first tripleheader in Olympic Alpine history.

Germany won the most medals (29) for the second time in its third Winter Games as a unified team. The team from host Japan surpassed expectations, winning more gold medals (five) and total medals (10) than any previous Japanese team. And the United States tied its previous best (1994), by winning 13 medals.

Austria's Hermann Maier provided the Games' most enduring image. A horrifying spill during the men's downhill spun him airborne like a rag-doll and sent him crashing through two retaining fences. Amazingly, he recovered to win two gold medals within the next six days.

American Picabo Street won gold in the women's Super G by 0.01 seconds, the closest Alpine race in Olympic history—and she did it wearing longer downhill skis.

For the third straight Winter Games a woman won the most medals. Russia's Larissa Lazutina medaled in all five cross-country events, earning three golds, a silver and a bronze. Cross-country veteran Bjorn Dåhlie, of Norway, won four medals, thus becoming the winningest Winter Games athlete ever with eight career gold medals and 12 overall.

U.S. figure skater Tara Lipinski, 15, became the youngest woman in history to win a gold medal at the Winter Games, and turned pro two months later. The U.S. won the first women's hockey gold medal, while the U.S. men's team—which included pros for the first time—drew ire for its disappointing sixth-place finish and room-trashing antics. The Czech Republic, which (as Czechoslovakia) had won seven Olympic hockey medals, but no golds, was a surprise winner, upsetting Russia 1-0 in the men's hockey final behind the dominating net play of goaltender Dominik Hasek.

Curling and snowboarding also made their Olympic debuts in Nagano.

## Top 10 Standings

National medal standings are not recognized by the IOC. The unofficial point totals are based on 3 points for a gold medal, 2 for a silver and 1 for a bronze. Total medals are in parentheses.

| | Gold | Silver | Bronze | Points |
|---|---|---|---|---|
| 1 Germany (29) ......12 | | 9 | 8 | 62 |
| 2 Norway (25) .......10 | | 10 | 5 | 55 |
| 3 Russia (18) .........9 | | 6 | 3 | 42 |
| 4 Canada (15) ........6 | | 5 | 4 | 32 |
| 5 Austria (17) ........3 | | 5 | 9 | 28 |
| United States (13) ....6 | | 3 | 4 | 28 |
| 7 Netherlands (11) .....5 | | 4 | 2 | 25 |
| 8 Japan (10) .........5 | | 1 | 4 | 21 |
| 9 Finland (12) ........2 | | 4 | 6 | 20 |
| Italy (10) .........2 | | 6 | 2 | 20 |

## Leading Medal Winners

Number of individual medals won on the left; gold, silver and bronze breakdown to the right.

### MEN

| No | | Sport | G-S-B |
|---|---|---|---|
| 4 | Bjorn Dählie, NOR ..........X-country | | 3-1-0 |
| 3 | Kazuyoshi Funaki, JPN ....Ski Jumping | | 2-1-0 |
| 3 | Rintje Ritsma, NED ..........Sp. Skating | | 0-1-2 |
| 3 | Mika Myllylae, FIN ..........X-country | | 1-0-2 |
| 2 | Gianni Romme, NED ........Sp. Skating | | 2-0-0 |
| 2 | Thomas Alsgaard, NOR ......X-country | | 2-0-0 |
| 2 | Hermann Maier, AUT ...........Alpine | | 2-0-0 |
| 2 | Bjarte Engen Vik, NOR ....Nordic Comb. | | 2-0-0 |
| 2 | Ids Postma, NED ..........Sp. Skating | | 1-1-0 |
| 2 | Jani Soininen, FIN ..........Ski Jumping | | 1-1-0 |
| 2 | Erling Jevne, NOR ...........X-country | | 1-1-0 |
| 2 | Ole Bjoerndalen, NOR ........Biathlon | | 1-1-0 |
| 2 | Halvard Hanevold, NOR .......Biathlon | | 1-1-0 |
| 2 | Kim Dong Sung, KOR .....ST Sp. Skating | | 1-1-0 |
| 2 | Christoph Langen, GER ........Bobsled | | 1-0-1 |
| 2 | Markus Zimmerman, GER .......Bobsled | | 1-0-1 |
| 2 | Eric Bedard, CAN ........ST Sp. Skating | | 1-0-1 |
| 2 | Masahiko Harada, JPN ....Ski Jumping | | 1-0-1 |
| 2 | Hiroyasu Shimizu, JPN .......Sp. Skating | | 1-0-1 |
| 2 | Lasse Kjus, NOR ...............Alpine | | 0-2-0 |
| 2 | Samppa Lajunen, FIN .....Nordic Comb. | | 0-2-0 |
| 2 | Silvio Fauner, ITA ............X-country | | 0-1-1 |
| 2 | Li Jiajun, CHN ..........ST Sp. Skating | | 0-1-1 |
| 2 | An Yulong, CHN ........ST Sp. Skating | | 0-1-1 |
| 2 | Andreas Widhoelzl, AUT .....Ski Jumping | | 0-0-2 |

### WOMEN

| No | | Sport | G-S-B |
|---|---|---|---|
| 5 | Larissa Lazutina, RUS .........X-country | | 3-1-1 |
| 3 | Olga Danilova, RUS ..........X-country | | 2-1-0 |
| 3 | Katja Seizinger, GER ..........Alpine | | 2-0-1 |
| 3 | Lee-Kyung Chun, KOR .....ST Sp. Skating | | 2-0-1 |
| 3 | G. Niemann-Stirnemann, GER ..Sp. Skating | | 1-2-0 |
| 3 | Ursula Disl, GER .............Biathlon | | 1-1-1 |
| 3 | Yang S. Yang, CHN .....ST Sp. Skating | | 0-3-0 |
| 2 | Marianne Timmer, NED ......Sp. Skating | | 2-0-0 |
| 2 | Galina Kukleva, RUS ...........Biathlon | | 1-1-0 |
| 2 | Deborah Compagnoni, ITA .......Alpine | | 1-1-0 |
| 2 | Claudia Pechstein, GER ......Sp. Skating | | 1-1-0 |
| 2 | Hilde Gerg, GER .............Alpine | | 1-0-1 |
| 2 | Catriona LeMay Doan, CAN ..Sp. Skating | | 1-0-1 |
| 2 | Katrin Apel, GER .............Biathlon | | 1-0-1 |
| 2 | Annie Perreault, CAN ....ST Sp. Skating | | 1-0-1 |
| 2 | Katerina Neumannova, CZR ....X-country | | 0-1-1 |
| 2 | Bente Martinsen, NOR ........X-country | | 0-1-1 |
| 2 | Anita Moen-Guidon, NOR .....X-country | | 0-1-1 |
| 2 | Chris Witty, USA ...........Sp. Skating | | 0-1-1 |
| 2 | Stefania Belmondo, ITA .......X-country | | 0-1-1 |
| 2 | Alexandra Meissnitzer, AUT .......Alpine | | 0-1-1 |

## Alpine Skiing

### MEN

| Event | | Time |
|---|---|---|
| Downhill | Jean-Luc Cretier, FRA ...........1:50.11 | |
| Slalom | Hans-Petter Buraas, NOR ........1:49.31 | |
| Giant Slalom | Hermann Maier, AUT ..........2:38.51 | |
| Super G | Hermann Maier, AUT ...........1:34.82 | |
| Combined | Mario Reiter, AUT .............3:08.06 | |

### WOMEN

| Event | | Time |
|---|---|---|
| Downhill | Katja Seizinger, GER ..........1:28.89 | |
| Slalom | Hilde Gerg, GER ............1:32.40 | |
| Giant Slalom | Deborah Compagnoni, ITA .......2:50.59 | |
| Super G | Picabo Street, USA ...........1:18.02 | |
| Combined | Katja Seizinger, GER ..........2:40.74 | |

## Biathlon

### MEN

| Event | | MT | Time |
|---|---|---|---|
| 10km | Ole Einar Bjoerndalen, NOR ..0 | | 27:16.2 |
| 20km | Halvard Hanevold, NOR ....1 | | 56:16.4 |
| 4x7.5km relay | Germany .............6 | | 1:21:36.2 |

### WOMEN

| Event | | MT | Time |
|---|---|---|---|
| 7.5km | Galina Koukleva, RUS .....1 | | 23:08.0 |
| 15km | Ekaterina Dafovska, BUL ....1 | | 54:52.0 |
| 4x7.5km relay | Germany ...........11 | | 1:40:13.6 |

## Bobsled

| Event | | Time |
|---|---|---|
| 2-Man | Italy I (Günther Huber & Antonio Tartaglia) ................3:37.24 | |
| | Canada I (Pierre Leuders & Dave McEachern) .................3:37.24 | |
| 4-Man | GER II (Christoph Langen, Markus Zimmermann, Marco Jakobs, Olaf Hampel) ........2:39.41 | |

## Curling

### MEN

#### Round Robin Standings

(Overall records in parentheses)

| | Gm | W-L-T | PF | PA |
|---|---|---|---|---|
| Canada ................7 | | 6-1-0 | 57 | 32 |
| Switzerland ................7 | | 5-2-0 | 44 | 28 |
| Norway ................7 | | 5-2-0 | 42 | 35 |
| United States ................7 | | 3-4-0 | 34 | 46 |

**Note:** Japan (3-4-0), Sweden (3-4-0), Britain (2-5-0), and Germany (1-6-0) were eliminated.

#### Semifinals

| | |
|---|---|
| Canada 7 ..........................United States 1 | |
| Switzerland 8 ........................Norway 7 | |

#### Bronze Medal

Norway 9 ........................United States 4

#### Gold Medal

Switzerland 9 ........................Canada 3

## WOMEN
### Round Robin Standings

|  | Gm | W-L-T | PF | PA |
|---|---|---|---|---|
| Canada | .7 | 6-1-0 | 51 | 34 |
| Sweden | .7 | 6-1-0 | 54 | 32 |
| Denmark | .7 | 5-2-0 | 46 | 34 |
| Britain | .7 | 4-3-0 | 38 | 44 |

**Note:** Japan (2-5-0), Norway (2-5-0), United States (2-5-0), and Germany (1-6-0) were eliminated.

### Semifinals

Canada 6 . . . . . . . . . . . . . . . . . . . . . . . . . .Britain 5
Denmark 7 . . . . . . . . . . . . . . . . . . . . . . . .Sweden 5

### Bronze Medal

Sweden 10 . . . . . . . . . . . . . . . . . . . . . . . . .Britain 6

### Gold Medal

Canada 7 . . . . . . . . . . . . . . . . . . . . . . . .Denmark 5

## Figure Skating

| Event |  | FP |
|---|---|---|
| Men | Ilia Kulik, RUS | .1.5 |
| Women | Tara Lipinski, USA | .2.0 |
| Pairs | Oksana Kazakova & Artur Dmitriev, RUS | .1.5 |
| Dance | Pasha Grishuk & Yevgeny Platov, RUS | .2.0 |

## Freestyle Skiing
### MEN

| Event |  | Pts |
|---|---|---|
| Aerials | Eric Bergoust, USA | .255.64 |
| Moguls | Jonny Moseley, USA | .26.93 |

### WOMEN

| Event |  | Pts |
|---|---|---|
| Aerials | Nikki Stone, USA | .193.00 |
| Moguls | Tae Satoya, JPN | .25.06 |

## Ice Hockey
### MEN
#### Final Round Standings
(Overall records in parentheses)

| Group C | Gm | W-L-T | Pts | GF | GA |
|---|---|---|---|---|---|
| Russia | .3 | 3-0-0 | 6 | 15 | 6 |
| Czech Republic | .3 | 2-1-0 | 4 | 12 | 4 |
| Finland | .3 | 1-2-0 | 2 | 11 | 9 |
| Kazakhstan (2-4-0) | .3 | 0-3-0 | 0 | 6 | 25 |

| Group D | Gm | W-L-T | Pts | GF | GA |
|---|---|---|---|---|---|
| Canada | .3 | 3-0-0 | 6 | 12 | 3 |
| Sweden | .3 | 2-1-0 | 4 | 11 | 7 |
| United States | .3 | 1-2-0 | 2 | 8 | 10 |
| Belarus (2-3-1) | .3 | 0-3-0 | 0 | 4 | 15 |

**Note:** Kazakhstan and Belarus reached the final round by winning preliminary Group A and Group B, respectively.

#### Quarterfinals

Czech Republic 4 . . . . . . . . . . . . . . .United States 1
Russia 4 . . . . . . . . . . . . . . . . . . . . . . . . . .Belarus 1
Canada 4 . . . . . . . . . . . . . . . . . . . .Kazakhstan 1
Finland 2 . . . . . . . . . . . . . . . . . . . . . . . . . .Sweden 1

#### Semifinals

Czech Republic 2 . . . . . . . . . . . . . . . . . . .Canada 1
(Czech Republic wins shootout, 1-0)
Russia 7 . . . . . . . . . . . . . . . . . . . . . . . . . . .Finland 4

#### Bronze Medal

Finland 3 . . . . . . . . . . . . . . . . . . . . . . . . . .Canada 2

#### Gold Medal

Czech Republic 1 . . . . . . . . . . . . . . . . . . . .Russia 0

## WOMEN
### Final Round Standings

|  | Gm | W-L-T | Pts | GF | GA |
|---|---|---|---|---|---|
| United States | .6 | 6-0-0 | 12 | 36 | 8 |
| Canada | .6 | 4-2-0 | 8 | 29 | 15 |
| Finland | .6 | 4-2-0 | 8 | 31 | 11 |
| China | .6 | 2-4-0 | 4 | 11 | 19 |
| Sweden | .5 | 1-4-0 | 2 | 10 | 21 |
| Japan | .5 | 0-5-0 | 0 | 2 | 45 |

### Bronze Medal

Finland 4 . . . . . . . . . . . . . . . . . . . . . . . . . . .China 1

### Gold Medal

United States 3 . . . . . . . . . . . . . . . . . . . .Canada 1

## Luge
### MEN

| Event |  | Time |
|---|---|---|
| Singles | Georg Hackl, GER | .3:18.436 |
| Doubles | Stefan Krausse & Jan Behrendt, GER | .1:41.105 |

### WOMEN

| Event |  | Time |
|---|---|---|
| Singles | Silke Kraushaar, GER | .3:23.779 |

## Nordic Skiing
### MEN
#### Cross Country

| Event |  | Time |
|---|---|---|
| 10km | Bjorn Dählie, NOR | .27:24.5 |
| 15km | Thomas Alsgaard, NOR | .1:07/01.7 |
| 30km | Mika Myllylae, FIN | .1:33:55.8 |
| 50km | Bjorn Dählie, NOR | .2:05:08.2 |
| 4x10km | NOR (Sivertsen, Jevne, Dählie, Alsgaard) | .1:40:55.7 |

#### Ski Jumping

| Event |  | Pts |
|---|---|---|
| 90m | Jani Soininen, FIN | .234.5 |
| 120m | Kazuyoshi Funaki, JPN | .272.3 |
| Team (120m) | JPN (Takanobu, Hiroya, Masahiko, Kazuyoshi) | .933.0 |

#### Nordic Combined

| Event |  | Pts |
|---|---|---|
| Indiv. | Bjarte Engen Vik, NOR | .41:21.1 |
| Team | NOR (Skard, Braaten, Vik, Lundberg) | .54:11.5 |

### WOMEN
#### Cross Country

| Event |  | Time |
|---|---|---|
| 5km | Larissa Lazutina, RUS | .17:37.9 |
| 10km | Larissa Lazutina, RUS | .46:06.9 |
| 15km | Olga Danilova, RUS | .46:55.4 |
| 30km | Julija Tchepalova, RUS | .1:22:01.5 |
| 4x5km | RUS (Gavryliouk, Danilova, Valbe, Lazutina) | .55:13.5 |

## Speed Skating
### MEN
#### Long Track

| Event |  | Time |  |
|---|---|---|---|
| 500m | Hiroyasu Shimizu, JPN | .71.35 |  |
| 1000m | Ids Postma, NED | .1:10.64 | OR |
| 1500m | Aadne Sondral, NOR | .1:47.87 | WR |
| 5000m | Gianni Romme, NED | .6:22.20 | WR |
| 10,000m | Gianni Romme, NED | .13:15.33 | WR |

### Short Track

| Event | | Time |
|---|---|---|
| 500m | Takafumi Nishitani, JPN | .....42.862 |
| 1000m | Dong-Sung Kim, KOR | ....1:32.375 |
| 5000m relay | Canada | .......7:06.075 |

### WOMEN

### Long Track

| Event | | Time | |
|---|---|---|---|
| 500m | Catriona Lemay-Doan, CAN | ....76.60 | |
| 1000m | Marianne Timmer, NED | .......1:16.51 | **OR** |
| 1500m | Marianne Timmer, NED | ....1:57.58 | **WR** |
| 3000m | Gunda Niemann-Stirnemann, GER | ....4:07.29 | **OR** |
| 5000m | Claudia Pechstein, GER | .....6:59.61 | **WR** |

### Short Track

| Event | | Time | |
|---|---|---|---|
| 500m | Annie Perreault, CAN | ...46.568 | |
| 1000m | Lee-Kyung Chun, KOR | ....1:42.776 | |
| 3000m Relay | South Korea | ........4:16.260 | **WR** |

## Snowboarding

### MEN

| Event | | Time |
|---|---|---|
| Giant Slalom | Ross Rebagliati, CAN | .........2:03.96 |
| Halfpipe | Gian Simmen, SWI | ...........85.2 pts |

### WOMEN

| Event | | Time |
|---|---|---|
| Giant Slalom | Karine Ruby, FRA | .............2:17.34 |
| Halfpipe | Nicola Thost, GER | ............74.6 pts |

# 2002
## Salt Lake City

SALT LAKE 2002

For Salt Lake City it appeared that the fourth time was the charm. After three failed previous bids, the 19th Winter Games were awarded to the Utah capital but it wasn't long before it was learned that the happy ending may have been too good to be true. In December 1998 a member of the IOC's executive board turned whistle-blower and a massive bid-rigging scandal captured global headlines. The fall-out that ensued and ensnared other Olympic cities like Atlanta, Sydney and Nagano led to an overhaul to the IOC's entire bid process. The lavish gifts offered by members of the Salt Lake Organizing Committee allegedly included cash, college scholarships, medical treatment, and trips to the Super Bowl, Disneyland, and Las Vegas. Still, the Games must go on and many observers surely thought that once they finally arrived all the attention would be rightly given to the tremendous athletes in competition. Not so fast. Controversy struck again in one of the Winter Olympics showcase events. Canadian pairs figure skaters Jamie Sale and David Pelletier skated, what seemed to nearly every person in the world, the best program but were awarded the silver medal behind the gold-winning Russians Elena Berezhnaya and Anton Sikharulidze. The resulting clamor led to an investigation that quickly unearthed collusion amongst the judges. The French judge at the center of the scandal was Marie-Reine Le Gougne admitted to comprimising her scores as part of a back-room deal with the Russians to make sure the French Ice Dancing team would later win gold. After the Games more dominoes fell and the scandal widened to include the President of the International Skating Union

Making headlines for the right reasons was Croatian skier Janica Kostelic, who won a record-tying three Alpine golds and added a silver to secure her own spot in Olympic history. Salt Lake City also hosted the arrivals of American slalom star Bode Miller and Swiss ski jumper Simon Ammann, a surprising gold medal performance from figure skater Sarah Hughes, and third-generation Olympian Jim Shea Jr.'s inspirational gold-medal win in skeleton's return to the Games.

## Top 10 Standings

National medal standings are not recognized by the IOC. The unofficial point totals are based on 3 points for a gold medal, 2 for a silver and 1 for a bronze. Total medals in parentheses.

| | | Gold | Silver | Bronze | Points |
|---|---|---|---|---|---|
| 1 | Germany (35) | 12 | 16 | 7 | 75 |
| 2 | United States (34) | 10 | 13 | 11 | 67 |
| 3 | Norway (24) | 11 | 7 | 6 | 53 |
| 4 | Russia (16) | 6 | 6 | 4 | 34 |
| 5 | Canada (17) | 6 | 3 | 8 | 32 |
| 6 | Austria (17) | 2 | 4 | 11 | 25 |
| 7 | Italy (12) | 4 | 4 | 4 | 24 |
| | France (11) | 4 | 5 | 2 | 24 |
| 9 | Switzerland (11) | 3 | 2 | 6 | 19 |
| | Netherlands (8) | 3 | 5 | 0 | 19 |

## Leading Medal Winners

Number of individual medals won on the left; gold, silver and bronze breakdown to the right.

### MEN

| No | | Sport | G-S-B |
|---|---|---|---|
| 4 | Ole Einar Bjoerndalen, NOR | ....Biathlon | 4-0-0 |
| 3 | Samppa Lajunen, FIN | .....Nordic Comb. | 3-0-0 |
| 3 | Jochem Uytdehaage, NED | ....Sp. Skating | 2-1-0 |
| 3 | Marc Gagnon, CAN | ....ST Sp. Skating | 2-0-1 |
| 3 | Frode Estil, NOR | .....Cross Country | 1-2-0 |
| 3 | Stephan Eberharter, AUT | ........Alpine | 1-1-1 |
| 3 | Felix Gottwald, AUT | .....Nordic Comb. | 0-0-3 |
| 2 | Simon Ammann, SWI | ......Ski Jumping | 2-0-0 |
| 2 | Kjetil Andre Aamodt, NOR | ......Alpine | 2-0-0 |
| 2 | Johann Muehlegg, SPA | ....Cross Country | 2-0-0 |
| 2 | Jaakko Tallus, FIN | .....Nordic Comb. | 1-1-0 |
| 2 | Sven Hannawald, GER | ......Ski Jumping | 1-1-0 |
| 2 | Derek Parra, USA | ........Sp. Skating | 1-1-0 |
| 2 | Apolo Anton Ohno, USA | ....ST Sp. Skating | 1-1-0 |
| 2 | Thomas Alsgaard, NOR | ....Cross Country | 1-1-0 |
| 2 | Jonathan Guilmette, CAN | ....ST Sp. Skating | 1-1-0 |
| 2 | Andrus Veerpalu, EST | ....Cross Country | 1-1-0 |
| 2 | Mathieu Turcotte, CAN | ....ST Sp. Skating | 1-0-1 |
| 2 | Sven Fischer, GER | ...........Biathlon | 0-2-0 |
| 2 | Frank Luck, GER | ...........Biathlon | 0-2-0 |
| 2 | Ronny Ackermann, GER | ...Nordic Comb. | 0-2-0 |
| 2 | Bode Miller, USA | .............Alpine | 0-2-0 |
| 2 | Adam Malysz, POL | ......Ski Jumping | 0-1-1 |
| 2 | Matti Hautamaeki, FIN | ......Ski Jumping | 0-1-1 |
| 2 | Cristian Zorzi, ITA | ......Cross Country | 0-1-1 |

AP/Wide World Photos

*Canadian pairs skaters **Jamie Sale** and **David Pelletier**, left, had their silver medals upgraded to gold in a special ceremony after a judging scandal erupted following their second-place finish at the 2002 Winter Games in Salt Lake City.*

| No | | Sport | G-S-B |
|----|----|----|----|
| 2 | Raphael Poiree, FRA | Biathlon | 0-1-1 |
| 2 | Ricco Gross, GER | Biathlon | 0-1-1 |
| 2 | Lasse Kjus, NOR | Alpine | 0-1-1 |
| 2 | Li Jiajun, CHN | ST Sp. Skating | 0-1-1 |
| 2 | Benjamin Raich, AUT | Alpine | 0-0-2 |

### WOMEN

| No | | Sport | G-S-B |
|----|----|----|----|
| 4 | Janica Kostelic, CRO | Alpine | 3-1-0 |
| 3 | Kati Wilhelm, GER | Biathlon | 2-1-0 |
| 3 | Yang Yang (A), CHN | ST Sp. Skating | 2-1-0 |
| 3 | Bente Skari, NOR | Cross Country | 1-1-1 |
| 3 | Sabine Voelker, GER | Sp. Skating | 0-2-1 |
| 2 | Andrea Henkel, GER | Biathlon | 2-0-0 |
| 2 | Claudia Pechstein, GER | Sp. Skating | 2-0-0 |
| 2 | Olga Danilova, RUS | Cross Country | 1-1-0 |
| 2 | Uschi Disl, GER | Biathlon | 1-1-0 |
| 2 | Choi Eun-Kyung, S. Kor. | ST Sp. Skating | 1-1-0 |
| 2 | Evi Sachenbacher, GER | Cross Country | 1-1-0 |
| 2 | Ko Gi-Hyun, S. Kor. | ST Sp. Skating | 1-1-0 |
| 2 | Stefania Belmondo, ITA | Cross Country | 1-1-0 |
| 2 | Olga Pyleva, RUS | Biathlon | 1-0-1 |
| 2 | Julija Tchepalova, RUS | Cross Country | 1-0-1 |
| 2 | Liv Grete Poiree, NOR | Biathlon | 0-2-0 |
| 2 | Larissa Lazutina, RUS | Cross Country | 0-2-0 |
| 2 | Renate Goetschl, AUT | Alpine | 0-1-1 |
| 2 | Wang Chunlu, CHN | ST Sp. Skating | 0-1-1 |
| 2 | Anita Moen, NOR | Cross Country | 0-1-1 |
| 2 | Anja Paerson, SWE | Alpine | 0-1-1 |
| 2 | Evgenia Radanova, BUL | ST Sp. Skating | 0-1-1 |
| 2 | Yang Yang (S), CHN | ST Sp. Skating | 0-1-1 |
| 2 | Magdalena Forsberg, SWE | Biathlon | 0-0-2 |
| 2 | Jennifer Rodriguez , USA | Sp. Skating | 0-0-2 |

## Alpine Skiing

### MEN

| Event | | Time |
|----|----|----|
| Downhill | Fritz Strobl, AUT | 1:39.13 |
| Slalom | Jean-Pierre, FRA | 1:41.06 |
| Giant Slalom | Stephan Eberharter, AUT | 2:23.28 |
| Super G | Kjetil Andre Aamodt, NOR | 1:21.58 |
| Combined | Kjetil Andre Aamodt, NOR | 3:17.56 |

### WOMEN

| Event | | Time |
|----|----|----|
| Downhill | Carole Montillet, FRA | 1:39.56 |
| Slalom | Janica Kostelic, CRO | 1:46.10 |
| Giant Slalom | Janica Kostelic, CRO | 2:30.01 |
| Super G | Daniela Ceccarelli, ITA | 1:13.59 |
| Combined | Janica Kostelic, CRO | 2:43.28 |

## Biathlon

### MEN

| Event | | MT | Time |
|----|----|----|----|
| 10km | Ole Einar Bjoerndalen, NOR | .0 | 24:51.3 |
| 12.5km | Ole Einar Bjoerndalen, NOR | .2 | 32:34.6 |
| 20km | Ole Einar Bjoerndalen, NOR | .2 | 51:03.3 |
| 4x7.5km relay | Norway | .0 | 1:23:42.3 |

### WOMEN

| Event | | MT | Time |
|----|----|----|----|
| 7.5km | Kati Wilhelm, GER | .0 | 20:41.4 |
| 10km | Olga Pyleva, RUS | .1 | 31:07.7 |
| 15km | Andrea Henkel, GER | .1 | 47:29.1 |
| 4x7.5km relay | Germany | .1 | 1:27:55.0 |

## Bobsled

### MEN

| Event | | Time |
|---|---|---|
| 2-Man | Germany I (Christoph Langen & Markus Zimmermann) | 3:37.24 |
| 4-Man | Germany II (Andre Lange, Enrico Kuehn, Kevin Kuske, Carsten Embach) | 3:07.51 |

### WOMEN

| Event | | Time |
|---|---|---|
| 2-Woman | United States II (Jill Bakken & Vonetta Flowers) | 1:37.76 |

## Curling

### MEN

#### Round Robin Standings

| | W-L | | W-L |
|---|---|---|---|
| Canada | 8-1 | Germany | 4-5 |
| Norway | 7-2 | United States | 3-6 |
| Sweden | 6-3 | Denmark | 3-6 |
| Switzerland | 6-3 | Great Britain | 3-6 |
| Finland | 5-4 | France | 0-9 |

#### Semifinals

Canada 6 .......................................Sweden 4
Norway 7 .....................................Switzerland 6

#### Bronze Medal

Switzerland 7 ..................................Sweden 6

#### Gold Medal

Norway 6 .....................................Canada 5

### WOMEN

#### Round Robin Standings

| | W-L | | W-L |
|---|---|---|---|
| Canada | 8-1 | Sweden | 5-4 |
| Switzerland | 7-2 | Norway | 4-5 |
| United States | 6-3 | Denmark | 2-7 |
| Great Britain | 5-4 | Russia | 2-7 |
| Germany | 5-4 | Japan | 1-8 |

#### Semifinals

Switzerland 9 ..............................United States 4
Great Britain 6 ...............................Canada 5

#### Bronze Medal

Canada 9 .................................United States 5

#### Gold Medal

Great Britain 4 ..............................Switzerland 3

## Figure Skating

| Event | | FP |
|---|---|---|
| Men | Alexei Yagudin, RUS | 1.5 |
| Women | Sarah Hughes, USA | 3.0 |
| Pairs* | Elena Berezhnaya & Anton Sikharulidze, RUS | 1.5 |
| | Jamie Sale & David Pelletier, CAN | 3.0 |
| Dance | Marina Anissina & Gwendal Peizerat, FRA | 2.0 |

*Canada's Sale & Pelletier placed second to Berezhnaya & Sikharulidze in the free skate, according to five of the event's nine judges, but were later awarded gold medals after French judge Marie-Reine Le Gougne admitted to officials that she had been pressured to put the Russians first.

## Freestyle Skiing

### MEN

| Event | | Pts |
|---|---|---|
| Aerials | Ales Valenta, CZR | 257.02 |
| Moguls | Janne Lahtela, FIN | 27.97 |

### WOMEN

| Event | | Pts |
|---|---|---|
| Aerials | Alisa Camplin, AUS | 193.47 |
| Moguls | Kari Traa, NOR | 25.94 |

## Ice Hockey

### MEN

#### Final Round Standings

| Group C | Gm | W-L-T | Pts | GF | GA |
|---|---|---|---|---|---|
| Sweden | 3 | 3-0-0 | 6 | 14 | 4 |
| Czech Republic | 3 | 1-1-1 | 3 | 12 | 7 |
| Canada | 3 | 1-1-1 | 3 | 8 | 10 |
| Germany | 3 | 0-3-0 | 0 | 5 | 18 |
| Group D | Gm | W-L-T | Pts | GF | GA |
| Belarus | 3 | 2-1-0 | 4 | 5 | 3 |
| Ukraine | 3 | 2-1-0 | 4 | 9 | 5 |
| Switzerland | 3 | 1-1-1 | 3 | 7 | 9 |
| France | 3 | 0-2-1 | 1 | 6 | 10 |

#### Quarterfinals

Belarus 4 ....................................Sweden 3
Russia 1 ................................Czech Republic 0
United States 5 ...............................Germany 0
Canada 2 ....................................Finland 1

#### Semifinals

Canada 7 ....................................Belarus 1
United States 3 ...............................Russia 2

#### Bronze Medal

Russia 7 ....................................Belarus 2

#### Gold Medal

Canada 5 ................................United States 2

### WOMEN

#### Preliminary Round Standings

| Group A | Gm | W-L-T | Pts | GF | GA |
|---|---|---|---|---|---|
| Canada | 3 | 3-0-0 | 6 | 25 | 0 |
| Sweden | 3 | 2-1-0 | 4 | 10 | 13 |
| Russia | 3 | 1-2-0 | 2 | 6 | 11 |
| Kazakhstan | 3 | 0-3-0 | 0 | 1 | 18 |
| Group B | Gm | W-L-T | Pts | GF | GA |
| United States | 3 | 3-0-0 | 6 | 27 | 1 |
| Finland | 3 | 2-1-0 | 4 | 7 | 6 |
| Germany | 3 | 0-2-1 | 1 | 6 | 18 |
| China | 3 | 0-2-1 | 1 | 6 | 21 |

#### Semifinals

Canada 7 ....................................Finland 3
United States 4 ...............................Sweden 2

#### Bronze Medal

Sweden 2 ....................................Finland 1

#### Gold Medal

Canada 3 ................................United States 2

## Luge
### MEN

| Event | | Time |
|---|---|---|
| Singles | Armin Zoeggeler, ITA | 2:57.941 |
| Doubles | Patric-Fritz Leitner & Alexander Resch, GER | 1:26.082 |

### WOMEN

| Event | | Time |
|---|---|---|
| Singles | Sylke Otto, GER | 2:52.464 |

## Nordic Skiing

### MEN
#### Cross Country

| Event | | Time |
|---|---|---|
| 1.5km | Tor Arne Hetland, NOR | 27:24.5 |
| 15km | Andrus Veerpalu, EST | 37:07.4 |
| Pursuit | Johann Muehlegg, SPA | 49:20.4 |
| 30km | Johann Muehlegg, SPA | 1:09:28.9 |
| 50km | Mikhail Ivanov, RUS* | 2:06:20.8 |
| 4x10km | NOR (Anders Aukland, Frode Estil, Kristen Skjeldal, Thomas Alsgaard ) | 1:32:45.5 |

*Ivanov finished second to Spain's Johann Muehlegg, who was stripped of his gold medal after test results revealed he failed a pre-race drug test. He was ordered to leave the Games but allowed to keep the two gold medals he won earlier.

#### Ski Jumping

| Event | | Pts |
|---|---|---|
| 90m | Simon Ammann, SWI | 269.0 |
| 120m | Simon Ammann, SWI | 281.4 |
| Team (120m) | GER (Sven Hannawald, Stephan Hocke, Michael Uhrmann, Martin Schmitt) | 974.1 |

#### Nordic Combined

| Event | | Time |
|---|---|---|
| Indiv. | Samppa Lajunen, FIN | 39:11.7 |
| Sprint | Samppa Lajunen, FIN | 16:40.1 |
| Team | FIN (Jari Mantila, Hannu Manninen, Jaakko Tallus, Samppa Lajunen ) | 48:42.2 |

### WOMEN
#### Cross Country

| Event | | Time |
|---|---|---|
| 1.5km | Julija Tchepalova, RUS | 3:10.6 |
| 10km | Bente Skari, NOR | 28:05.6 |
| Pursuit | Olga Danilova, RUS | 24:52.1 |
| 15km | Stefania Belmondo, ITA | 39:54.4 |
| 30km | Gabriella Paruzzi, ITA* | 1:30:57.1 |
| 4x5km | GER (Manuela Henkel, Viola Bauer, Claudia Kuenzel, Evi Sachenbacher ) | 49:30.6 |

*Paruzzi finished second to Russia's Larissa Lazutina, who was stripped of her gold medal and ordered to leave the Games after failing a subsequent drug test. She was allowed to keep the two silver medals she won earlier but was barred from participating in the 20-km team relay.

## Skeleton
### MEN

| Event | | Time |
|---|---|---|
| Singles | Jim Shea Jr., USA | 1:41.96 |

### WOMEN

| Event | | Pts |
|---|---|---|
| Singles | Tristan Gale, USA | 1:45.11 |

## Snowboarding
### MEN

| Event | | Pts |
|---|---|---|
| Halfpipe | Ross Powers, USA | 46.1 |
| Giant Slalom | Philipp Schoch, SWI | |

### WOMEN

| Event | | Pts |
|---|---|---|
| Halfpipe | Kelly Clark, USA | 47.9 |
| Giant Slalom | Isabelle Blanc, FRA | |

## Speed Skating
### MEN
#### Long Track

| Event | | Time | |
|---|---|---|---|
| 500m | Casey FitzRandolph, USA | 69.23 | OR |
| 1000m | Gerard van Velde, NED | 1:07.18 | WR |
| 1500m | Derek Parra, USA | 1:43.95 | WR |
| 5000m | Jochem Uytdehaage, NED | 6:14.66 | WR |
| 10,000m | Jochem Uytdehaage, NED | 12:58.92 | WR |

#### Short Track

| Event | | Time | |
|---|---|---|---|
| 500m | Marc Gagnon, CAN | 41.802 | OR |
| 1000m | Steven Bradbury, AUS | 1:29.109 | |
| 1500m | Apolo Anton Ohno*, USA | 2:18.541 | |
| 5000m relay | Canada | 6:51.579 | |

*Ohno finished second to Kim Dong-Sung, of South Korea, in the final, but was awarded the gold medal by chief referee James Hewish, who adjudged that Kim was guilty of cross-tracking, or interfering, with Ohno's path.

### WOMEN
#### Long Track

| Event | | Time | |
|---|---|---|---|
| 500m | Catriona Lemay-Doan, CAN | 74.75 | OR |
| 1000m | Chris Witty, USA | 1:13.83 | WR |
| 1500m | Anni Friesinger, GER | 1:54.02 | WR |
| 3000m | Claudia Pechstein, GER | 3:57.70 | WR |
| 5000m | Claudia Pechstein, GER | 6:46.91 | WR |

#### Short Track

| Event | | Time | |
|---|---|---|---|
| 500m | Yang Yang (A), CHN | 44.187 | |
| 1000m | Yang Yang (A), CHN | 1:36.391 | |
| 1500m | Ko Gi-Hyun, S.Kor | 2:31.581 | |
| 3000m Relay | South Korea | 4:12.793 | WR |

---

### Youngest and Oldest Gold Medalists in an Individual Event at Winter Olympics

#### Youngest

MEN—Toni Nieminen, FIN (16 years, 261 days) Large Hill Ski Jumping, 1992.
WOMEN—Tara Lipinski, USA (15 years, 256 days) Figure Skating, 1998.

#### Oldest

MEN—Magnar Solberg, NOR (35 years, 4 days) 20k Biathlon, 1972.
WOMEN—Christina Baas-Kaiser, NED (33 years, 268 days) 3000m Speed Skating, 1972.

## Turin 2006 and beyond...

The next Winter Games are set for Feb. 10-26, 2006 in Turin, located in the heart of the Italian Alps. **Turin** was selected according to a new procedure adopted in the aftermath of the bid-rigging scandals involving previous Olympic votes that were exposed prior to the 2002 Salt Lake City Winter Games. The new bid process prohibits visits by IOC members to the candidate cities. Following the presentations of the six cities on June 19, 1999 at the 109th IOC Session in Seoul, South Korea, a selection college was elected and appointed in order to choose two finalist cities. **Sion**, Switzerland and Turin, Italy were chosen. The full IOC session then elected the host city from the two finalist cities. Turin was elected by a vote of 53-36. It will be the second time Italy hosts the Winter Games, after Cortina d'Ampezzo hosted in 1956.

In a 2003 vote, the **2010 Winter Olympics** were awarded to Vancouver, Canada who narrowly edged PyeongChang, South Korea and third place Salzburg, Austria. The site of the **2014 Winter Games** will be announced in July 2007 at the IOC meeting in Guatemala City. The list of bid cities that will compete for the Games is: Almaty (Kazakhstan), Borjomi (Georgia), Jaca (Spain), PyeongChang (South Korea), Salzburg (Austria), Sofia (Bulgaria) and Sochi (Russia).

On the slate for future editions of the Summer Olympics is **Beijing** who was awarded the 2008 Games in 2001, beating out Toronto, Paris, Istanbul and Osaka. More recently, on July 6, 2005,

**London** was named the host city for the **2012 Summer Olympics**, outpolling Paris, New York, Moscow and Madrid. Tragically, just two days after the city received the great news, bombs erupted on the London mass transit system, killing 52 and injuring dozens.

**Athens**, the host city of the 2004 Summer Games, is dealing with **budget hangovers**. The total cost of hosting the Games, including improvements to public transportation, came to a grand total of $15 billion, triple the original estimates. Meanwhile, city officials are still uncertain about how to make future use of many of the Olympic venues that were built to last after choosing to go against the recent trend of building temporary structures. The main Olympic stadium has no shortage of future tenants but the separate stadiums built for sports that have no real following in Greece, like baseball, softball and field hockey, have no prospects. But the bills for the basic upkeep of the facilities, at more than $100 million a year, keep coming. The budget trouble Athens is currently facing should offer a hard-earned lesson for future host cities to avoid similar pitfalls. Still, the Greeks, after serious questions about whether they would be able to get their acts together after serious construction delays, managed to meet the deadline and host a successful Games.

From the Italian Ministry of Superfluous Information...Cartoon characters named **Neve** and **Gliz** (above), representing a ball of snow and a block of ice, are the official mascots for the 2006 Turin Olympics. What happened to the Alberto Tomba bobbleheads?

## Turin: W2W4

First off, don't expect the U.S. to win 34 medals like they did in 2002. The Games are not on our property in 2006 and we've never won more than 13 Winter medals away from home.

That being said, New Hampshire's **Bode Miller** (at right) already has reservations for a *Wheaties* Box in 2006. Miller dominated the World Cup circuit in 2005 and expects to add some color to the two silvers he won in Salt Lake City. A threat to win any Alpine event, Miller has a chance to earn the title of greatest American skier of all-time. Don't overlook his teammate **Daron Rahlves** in the speed events. On the women's team, look for young Minnesota transplant **Linsdey Kildow** to challenge for medals in the downhill and super G.

Veteran figure skater **Michelle Kwan**, winner of nine U.S. championships and five world championships but zero Olympic gold medals, will go for the ultimate prize one more time in Turin. Can the crafty 20-something put it all together on the world's biggest stage and hold off any 2006 versions of teenage gold medal winners Tara Lipinski and Sarah Hughes? She will have a **new scoring system**, tested at the 2005 World Championships, to help make things interesting and, hopefully, fair. Under the new rules, to help head off any residual controversies,12 judges will be used, but the final score will be the sum of nine randomly chosen judge's scores with the high and low dropped. Critics of the **New Judging System** (NJS) point out that the judges marks will be anonymous and that the system has no paper trail and an overall lack of transparency.

Short track speedskater **Apolo Anton Ohno** won gold (by disqualification) and silver at Salt Lake City four years ago and will be looking for indisputable glory in Turin. His 1500-meter gold medal in 2002 came after a South Korean rival was DQ'd for bumping Ohno. He continues to rank among the best short-trackers in the world but Ohno could be outshone by his friend **Shani Davis** (below), a speed skater attempting two firsts in

2006: to become the first African-American to make the U.S. long track team and to be the first skater to compete in both long track and short track at the same Games. Davis holds the world record in the long-track 1,500 meters and was an alternate on the U.S. short-track team in 2002. But to make the short-track team again in 2006 he will confront reminders of the allegations that his spot on the 2002 team was undeserved. In the final race of the Olympic Trials with Ohno and Rusty Smith already guaranteed a spot on the team, Davis needed nothing short of a long-shot victory in the race to make the team. Davis pulled off the big upset but questions quickly arose about whether Ohno and Smith laid back to help a buddy at the expense of another skater. If Davis can make both teams in 2006 and win an Olympic medal then he might be able to put those nasty rumors on ice permanently.

–Gerry Brown

## Event-by-Event

Gold medal winners from 1924-2002 in the following events: Alpine Skiing, Biathlon, Bobsled, Cross Country Skiing, Curling, Figure Skating, Freestyle Skiing, Ice Hockey, Luge, Nordic Combined, Skeleton, Ski Jumping, Snowboarding and Speed Skating.

### ALPINE SKIING

### MEN

**Multiple gold medals**: Kjetil Andre Aamodt, Jean-Claude Killy, Toni Sailer and Alberto Tomba (3); Hermann Maier, Henri Oreiller, Ingemar Stenmark and Markus Wasmeier (2).

#### Downhill

| Year | | Time | Year | | Time |
|------|---|------|------|---|------|
| 1948 | Henri Oreiller, FRA | 2:55.0 | 1980 | Leonhard Stock, AUS | 1:45.50 |
| 1952 | Zeno Colò, ITA | 2:30.8 | 1984 | Bill Johnson, USA | 1:45.59 |
| 1956 | Toni Sailer, AUT | 2:52.2 | 1988 | Pirmin Zurbriggen, SWI | 1:59.63 |
| 1960 | Jean Vuarnet, FRA | 2:06.0 | 1992 | Patrick Ortlieb, AUT | 1:50.37 |
| 1964 | Egon Zimmermann, AUT | 2:18.16 | 1994 | Tommy Moe, USA | 1:45.75 |
| 1968 | Jean-Claude Killy, FRA | 1:59.85 | 1998 | Jean-Luc Cretier, FRA | 1:50.11 |
| 1972 | Bernhard Russi, SWI | 1:51.43 | 2002 | Fritz Strobl, AUT | 1:39.13 |
| 1976 | Franz Klammer AUT | 1:45.73 | | | |

#### Slalom

| Year | | Time | Year | | Time |
|------|---|------|------|---|------|
| 1948 | Edi Reinalter, SWI | 2:10.3 | 1980 | Ingemar Stenmark, SWE | 1:44.26 |
| 1952 | Othmar Schneider, AUT | 2:00.0 | 1984 | Phil Mahre, USA | 1:39.41 |
| 1956 | Toni Sailer, AUT | 3:14.7 | 1988 | Alberto Tomba, ITA | 1:39.47 |
| 1960 | Ernst Hinterseer, AUT | 2:08.9 | 1992 | Finn Christian Jagge, NOR | 1:44.39 |
| 1964 | Pepi Stiegler, AUT | 2:11.13 | 1994 | Thomas Stangassinger, AUT | 2:02.02 |
| 1968 | Jean-Claude Killy, FRA | 1:39.73 | 1998 | Hans-Petter Buraas, NOR | 1:49.31 |
| 1972 | Francisco Ochoa, SPA | 1:49.27 | 2002 | Jean-Pierre Vidal, FRA | 1:41.06 |
| 1976 | Piero Gros, ITA | 2:03.29 | | | |

#### Giant Slalom

| Year | | Time | Year | | Time |
|------|---|------|------|---|------|
| 1952 | Stein Eriksen, NOR | 2:25.0 | 1980 | Ingemar Stenmark, SWE | 2:40.74 |
| 1956 | Toni Sailer, AUS | 3:00.1 | 1984 | Max Julen, SWI | 2:41.18 |
| 1960 | Roger Staub, SWI | 1:48.3 | 1988 | Alberto Tomba, ITA | 2:06.37 |
| 1964 | Francois Bonlieu, FRA | 1:46.71 | 1992 | Alberto Tomba, ITA | 2:06.98 |
| 1968 | Jean-Claude Killy, FRA | 3:29.28 | 1994 | Markus Wasmeier, GER | 2:52.46 |
| 1972 | Gustav Thöni, ITA | 3:09.62 | 1998 | Hermann Maier, AUT | 2:38.51 |
| 1976 | Heini Hemmi, SWI | 3:26.97 | 2002 | Stephan Eberharter, AUT | 2:23.28 |

#### Super G

| Year | | Time | Year | | Time |
|------|---|------|------|---|------|
| 1988 | Frank Piccard, FRA | 1:39.66 | 1998 | Hermann Maier, AUT | 1:34.82 |
| 1992 | Kjetil Andre Aamodt, NOR | 1:13.04 | 2002 | Kjetil Andre Aamodt, NOR | 1:21.58 |
| 1994 | Markus Wasmeier, GER | 1:32.53 | | | |

#### Alpine Combined

| Year | | Points | Year | | Time |
|------|---|--------|------|---|------|
| 1936 | Franz Pfnür, GER | 99.25 | 1994 | Lasse Kjus, NOR | 3:17.53 |
| 1948 | Henri Oreiller, FRA | 3.27 | 1998 | Mario Reiter, AUT | 3:08.06 |
| 1952-84 Not held | | | 2002 | Kjetil Andre Aamodt, NOR | 3:17.56 |
| 1988 | Hubert Strolz, AUT | 36.55 | | | |
| 1992 | Josef Polig, ITA | 14.58 | | | |

### WOMEN

**Multiple gold medals**: Deborah Compagnoni, Janica Kostelic, Vreni Schneider and Katja Seizinger (3); Marielle Goitschel, Trude Jochum-Beiser, Petra Kronberger, Andrea Mead Lawrence, Rosi Mittermaier, Marie-Theres Nadig, Hanni Wenzel and Pernilla Wiberg (2).

#### Downhill

| Year | | Time | Year | | Time |
|------|---|------|------|---|------|
| 1948 | Hedy Schlunegger, SWI | 2:28.3 | 1980 | Annemarie Moser-Pröll, AUT | 1:37.52 |
| 1952 | Trude Jochum-Beiser, AUT | 1:47.1 | 1984 | Michela Figini, SWI | 1:13.36 |
| 1956 | Madeleine Berthod, SWI | 1:40.7 | 1988 | Marina Kiehl, W. Ger | 1:25.86 |
| 1960 | Heidi Biebl, GER | 1:37.6 | 1992 | Kerrin Lee-Gartner, CAN | 1:52.55 |
| 1964 | Christl Haas, AUT | 1:55.39 | 1994 | Katja Seizinger, GER | 1:35.93 |
| 1968 | Olga Pall, AUT | 1:40.87 | 1998 | Katja Seizinger, GER | 1:28.89 |
| 1972 | Marie-Theres Nadig, SWI | 1:36.68 | 2002 | Carole Montillet, FRA | 1:39.56 |
| 1976 | Rosi Mittermaier, W. Ger | 1:46.16 | | | |

## Slalom

| Year | | Time | Year | | Time |
|---|---|---|---|---|---|
| 1948 | Gretchen Fraser, USA | 1:57.2 | 1980 | Hanni Wenzel, LIE | 1:25.09 |
| 1952 | Andrea Mead Lawrence, USA | 2:10.6 | 1984 | Paoletta Magoni, ITA | 1:36.47 |
| 1956 | Renée Colliard, SWI | 1:52.3 | 1988 | Vreni Schneider, SWI | 1:36.69 |
| 1960 | Anne Heggtveit, CAN | 1:49.6 | 1992 | Petra Kronberger, AUT | 1:32.68 |
| 1964 | Christine Goitschel, FRA | 1:29.86 | 1994 | Vreni Schneider, SWI | 1:56.01 |
| 1968 | Marielle Goitschel, FRA | 1:25.86 | 1998 | Hilde Gerg, GER | 1:32.40 |
| 1972 | Barbara Cochran, USA | 1:31.24 | 2002 | Janica Kostelic, CRO | 1:46.10 |
| 1976 | Rosi Mittermaier, W. Ger | 1:30.54 | | | |

## Giant Slalom

| Year | | Time | Year | | Time |
|---|---|---|---|---|---|
| 1952 | Andrea Mead Lawrence, USA | 2:06.8 | 1980 | Hanni Wenzel, LIE | 2:41.66 |
| 1956 | Ossi Reichert, GER | 1:56.5 | 1984 | Debbie Armstrong, USA | 2:20.98 |
| 1960 | Yvonne Rügg, SWI | 1:39.9 | 1988 | Vreni Schneider, SWI | 2:06.49 |
| 1964 | Marielle Goitschel, FRA | 1:52.24 | 1992 | Pernilla Wiberg, SWE | 2:12.74 |
| 1968 | Nancy Greene, CAN | 1:51.97 | 1994 | Deborah Compagnoni, ITA | 2:30.97 |
| 1972 | Marie-Theres Nadig, SWI | 1:29.90 | 1998 | Deborah Compagnoni, ITA | 2:50.59 |
| 1976 | Kathy Kreiner, CAN | 1:29.13 | 2002 | Janica Kostelic, CRO | 2:30.01 |

## Super G

| Year | | Time | Year | | Time |
|---|---|---|---|---|---|
| 1988 | Sigrid Wolf, AUT | 1:19.03 | 1998 | Picabo Street, USA | 1:18.02 |
| 1992 | Deborah Compagnoni, ITA | 1:21.22 | 2002 | Daniela Ceccarelli, ITA | 1:13.59 |
| 1994 | Diann Roffe-Steinrotter, USA | 1:22.15 | | | |

## Alpine Combined

| Year | | Points | Year | | Time |
|---|---|---|---|---|---|
| 1936 | Christl Cranz, GER | .97.06 | 1994 | Pernilla Wiberg, SWE | 3:05.16 |
| 1948 | Trude Beiser, AUT | .6.58 | 1998 | Katja Seizinger, GER | 2:40.74 |
| 1952-84 | Not held | | 2002 | Janica Kostelic, CRO | 2:43.28 |
| 1988 | Anita Wachter, AUT | .29.25 | | | |
| 1992 | Petra Kronberger, AUT | .2.55 | | | |

## BIATHLON

### MEN

**Multiple gold medals** (including relays): Ole Einar Bjoerndalen (5); Aleksandr Tikhonov (4); Mark Kirchner and Ricco Gross (3); Anatoly Alyabyev, Ivan Biakov, Sergei Chepikov, Sven Fischer, Halvard Hanevold, Frank Luck, Viktor Mamatov, Frank-Peter Roetsch, Magnar Solberg and Dmitri Vasilyev (2).

### 10 kilometers

| Year | | Time | Year | | Time |
|---|---|---|---|---|---|
| 1980 | Frank Ulrich, E. Ger | 32:10.69 | 1994 | Sergei Chepikov, RUS | 28:07.0 |
| 1984 | Erik Kvalfoss, NOR | 30:53.8 | 1998 | Ole Einar Bjoerndalen, NOR | 27:16.2 |
| 1988 | Frank-Peter Roetsch, E. Ger | 25:08.1 | 2002 | Ole Einar Bjoerndalen, NOR | 24:51.3 |
| 1992 | Mark Kirchner, GER | 26:02.3 | | | |

### 12.5 kilometers

| Year | | Time |
|---|---|---|
| 2002 | Ole Einar Bjoerndalen, NOR | 32:34.6 |

### 20 kilometers

| Year | | Time | Year | | Time |
|---|---|---|---|---|---|
| 1960 | Klas Lestander, SWE | 1:33:21.6 | 1984 | Peter Angerer, W. Ger | 1:11:52.7 |
| 1964 | Vladimir Melanin, USSR | 1:20:26.8 | 1988 | Frank-Peter Roetsch, E. Ger | 56:33.3 |
| 1968 | Magnar Solberg, NOR | 1:13:45.9 | 1992 | Yevgeny Redkine, UT | 57:34.4 |
| 1972 | Magnar Solberg, NOR | 1:15:55.50 | 1994 | Sergei Tarasov, RUS | 57:25.3 |
| 1976 | Nikolai Kruglov, USSR | 1:14:12.26 | 1998 | Halvard Hanevold, NOR | 56:16.4 |
| 1980 | Anatoly Alyabyev, USSR | 1:08:16.31 | 2002 | Ole Einar Bjoerndalen, NOR | 51:03.3 |

### 4x7.5-kilometer Relay

| Year | | Time | Year | | Time | Year | | Time |
|---|---|---|---|---|---|---|---|---|
| 1968 | Soviet Union | 2:13:02.4 | 1984 | Soviet Union | 1:38:51.7 | 1998 | Germany | 1:21:36.2 |
| 1972 | Soviet Union | 1:51:44.92 | 1988 | Soviet Union | 1:22:30.0 | 2002 | Norway | 1:23:42.3 |
| 1976 | Soviet Union | 1:57:55.64 | 1992 | Germany | 1:24:43.5 | | | |
| 1980 | Soviet Union | 1:34:03.27 | 1994 | Germany | 1:30:22.1 | | | |

## BIATHLON (Cont.)
### WOMEN

**Multiple gold medals** (including relays): Myriam Bedard, Andrea Henkel, Anfisa Reztsova and Kati Wilhelm (2). Note that Reztsova won a third gold medal in 1988 in the cross country 4x5-kilometer relay.

#### 7.5 kilometers

| Year | | Time | Year | | Time |
|------|--|------|------|--|------|
| 1992 | Anfisa Reztsova, UT | 24:29.2 | 1998 | Galina Koukleva, RUS | 23:08.0 |
| 1994 | Myriam Bedard, CAN | 26:08.8 | 2002 | Kati Wilhelm, GER | 20:41.4 |

#### 10 kilometers

| Year | | Time |
|------|--|------|
| 2002 | Olga Pyleva, RUS | 31:07.7 |

#### 15 kilometers

| Year | | Time | Year | | Time |
|------|--|------|------|--|------|
| 1992 | Antje Misersky, GER | 51:47.2 | 1998 | Ekaterina Dafovska, BUL | 54:52.0 |
| 1994 | Myriam Bedard, CAN | 52:06.6 | 2002 | Andrea Henkel, GER | 47:29.1 |

#### 4x7.5-kilometer Relay

| Year | | Time | Year | | Time |
|------|--|------|------|--|------|
| 1992 | France | 1:15:55.6 | 1998 | Germany | 1:40:13.6 |
| 1994 | Russia | 1:47:19.5 | 2002 | Germany | 1:27:55.0 |

**Note:** Event featured three skiers per team in 1992.

## BOBSLED

A two-woman bobsled event was added in 2002. Only drivers are listed in parentheses.

**Multiple gold medals**: DRIVERS—Meinhard Nehmer (3); Billy Fiske, Wolfgang Hoppe, Christoph Langen, Eugenio Monti, Andreas Ostler and Gustav Weder (2). CREW—Bernard Germeshausen (3); Donat Acklin, Luciano De Paolis, Cliff Gray, Lorenz Nieberl and Dietmar Schauerhammer (2).

### Two-Man

| Year | | Time | Year | | Time |
|------|--|------|------|--|------|
| 1932 | United States (Hubert Stevens) | 8:14.74 | 1976 | East Germany (Meinhard Nehmer) | 3:44.42 |
| 1936 | United States (Ivan Brown) | 5:29.29 | 1980 | Switzerland (Erich Schärer) | 4:09.36 |
| 1948 | Switzerland (Felix Endrich) | 5:29.2 | 1984 | East Germany (Wolfgang Hoppe) | 3:25.56 |
| 1952 | Germany (Andreas Ostler) | 5:24.54 | 1988 | Soviet Union (Janis Kipurs) | 3:54.19 |
| 1956 | Italy (Lamberto Dalla Costa) | 5:30.14 | 1992 | Switzerland I (Gustav Weder) | 4:03.26 |
| 1960 | Not held | | 1994 | Switzerland I (Gustav Weder) | 3:30.81 |
| 1964 | Great Britain (Anthony Nash) | 4:21.90 | 1998 | (TIE) Italy I (Guenther Huber) | 3:37.24 |
| 1968 | Italy (Eugenio Monti) | 4:41.54 | | & Canada I (Pierre Lueders) | 3:37.24 |
| 1972 | West Germany (Wolfgang Zimmerer) | 4:57.07 | 2002 | Germany I (Christoph Langen) | 3:10.11 |

### Two-Woman

| Year | | Time |
|------|--|------|
| 2002 | United States II (Jill Bakken) | 1:37.76 |

### Four-Man

| Year | | Time | Year | | Time |
|------|--|------|------|--|------|
| 1924 | Switzerland (Eduard Scherrer) | 5:45.54 | 1972 | Switzerland (Jean Wicki) | 4:43.07 |
| 1928 | United States (Billy Fiske) | 3:20.5 | 1976 | East Germany (Meinhard Nehmer) | 3:40.43 |
| 1932 | United States (Billy Fiske) | 7:53.68 | 1980 | East Germany (Meinhard Nehmer) | 3:59.92 |
| 1936 | Switzerland (Pierre Musy) | 5:19.85 | 1984 | East Germany (Wolfgang Hoppe) | 3:20.22 |
| 1948 | United States (Francis Tyler) | 5:20.1 | 1988 | Switzerland (Ekkehard Fasser) | 3:47.51 |
| 1952 | Germany (Andreas Ostler) | 5:07.84 | 1992 | Austria I (Ingo Appelt) | 3:53.90 |
| 1956 | Switzerland (Franz Kapus) | 5:10.44 | 1994 | Germany II (Harald Czudaj) | 3:27.78 |
| 1960 | Not held | | 1998 | Germany II (Christoph Langen) | 2:39.41 |
| 1964 | Canada (Vic Emery) | 4:14.46 | 2002 | Germany II (Andre Lange) | 3:07.51 |
| 1968 | Italy (Eugenio Monti) | 2:17.39 | | | |

**Note:** Five-man sleds were used in 1928.

## CROSS COUNTRY SKIING

Starting with the 1988 Winter Games in Calgary, the classical and freestyle (i.e., skating) techniques were designated for specific events. The Pursuit race was introduced in 1992 and revamped after the 1998 Nagano Games. The Sprint was added in 2002.

### MEN

**Multiple gold medals** (including relays): Bjorn Dählie (8); Thomas Alsgaard, Sixten Jernberg, Gunde Svan, Thomas Wassberg and Nikolai Zimyatov (4); Veikko Hakulinen, Eero Mäntyranta and Vegard Ulvang (3); Hallgeir Brenden, Harald Grönningen, Thorleif Haug, Johann Muehlegg, Jan Ottoson, Kristen Skjeldal, Päl Tyldum and Vyacheslav Vedenine (2).

**Multiple gold medals** (including Nordic Combined): Johan Gröttumsbråten and Thorleif Haug (3).

### 1.5-kilometer Sprint
New event in 2002.

| Year | | Time |
|------|---|------|
| 2002 | Tor Arne Hetland, NOR | 2:56.9 |

### 10 kilometers
Held as a classical event.

| Year | | Time | Year | | Time |
|------|---|------|------|---|------|
| 1992 | Vegard Ulvang, NOR | 27:36.0 | 1998 | Bjorn Dählie, NOR | 27:24.5 |
| 1994 | Bjorn Dählie, NOR | 24:20.1 | 2002 | Not held | |

### Combined Pursuit (10km)
From 1992-98 the pursuit included a 10-km classical race and a 15-km freestyle race contested on separate days. Beginning in 2002, the pursuit was shortened to two 5-kilometer races held on the same day.

| Year | | Time | Year | | Time |
|------|---|------|------|---|------|
| 1992 | Bjorn Dählie, NOR | 1:05:37.9 | 1998 | Thomas Alsgaard, NOR | 1:07:01.7 |
| 1994 | Bjorn Dählie, NOR | 1:00:08.8 | 2002 | Johann Muehlegg, SPA | 49:20.4 |

### 15 kilometers
Held over 18 kilometers from 1924-52. Held as a classical event from 1956-88, and since 2002. Replaced by the 15-km combined pursuit (1992-98).

| Year | | Time | Year | | Time |
|------|---|------|------|---|------|
| 1924 | Thorleif Haug, NOR | 1:14:31.0 | 1968 | Harald Grönningen, NOR | 47:54.2 |
| 1928 | Johan Gröttumsbräten, NOR | 1:37:01.0 | 1972 | Sven-Ake Lundback, SWE | 45:28.24 |
| 1932 | Sven Utterström, SWE | 1:23:07.0 | 1976 | Nikolai Bazhukov, USSR | 43:58.47 |
| 1936 | Erik-August Larsson, SWE | 1:14:38.0 | 1980 | Thomas Wassberg, SWE | 41:57.63 |
| 1948 | Martin Lundström, SWE | 1:13:50.0 | 1984 | Gunde Svan, SWE | 41:25.6 |
| 1952 | Hallgeir Brenden, NOR | 1:01:34.0 | 1988 | Mikhail Devyatyarov, USSR | 41:18.9 |
| 1956 | Hallgeir Brenden, NOR | 49:39.0 | 1992-98 | Not held | |
| 1960 | Hakon Brusveen, NOR | 51:55.5 | 2002 | Andrus Veerpalu, EST | 37:07.4 |
| 1964 | Eero Mäntyranta, FIN | 50:54.1 | | | |

### 30 kilometers
Held as a freestyle event from 1956-94, and since 2002. Held as a classical event in 1998.

| Year | | Time | Year | | Time |
|------|---|------|------|---|------|
| 1956 | Veikko Hakulinen, FIN | 1:44:06.0 | 1984 | Nikolai Zimyatov, USSR | 1:28:56.3 |
| 1960 | Sixten Jernberg, SWE | 1:51:03.9 | 1988 | Alexei Prokurorov, USSR | 1:24:26.3 |
| 1964 | Eero Mäntyranta, FIN | 1:30:50.7 | 1992 | Vegard Ulvang, NOR | 1:22:27.8 |
| 1968 | Franco Nones, ITA | 1:35:39.2 | 1994 | Thomas Alsgaard, NOR | 1:12:26.4 |
| 1972 | Vyacheslav Vedenine, USSR | 1:36:31.15 | 1998 | Mika Myllylae, FIN | 1:33:55.8 |
| 1976 | Sergei Saveliev, USSR | 1:30:29.38 | 2002 | Johann Muehlegg, SPA | 1:09:28.9 |
| 1980 | Nikolai Zimyatov, USSR | 1:27:02.80 | | | |

### 50 kilometers
Held as a classical event from 1924-94, and since 2002. Held as a freestyle event in 1998.

| Year | | Time | Year | | Time |
|------|---|------|------|---|------|
| 1924 | Thorleif Haug, NOR | 3:44:32.0 | 1972 | Pål Tyldum, NOR | 2:43:14.75 |
| 1928 | Per Erik Hedlund, SWE | 4:52:03.0 | 1976 | Ivar Formo, NOR | 2:37:30.05 |
| 1932 | Veli Saarinen, FIN | 4:28:00.0 | 1980 | Nikolai Zimyatov, USSR | 2:27:24.60 |
| 1936 | Elis Wiklund, SWE | 3:30:11.0 | 1984 | Thomas Wassberg, SWE | 2:15:55.8 |
| 1948 | Nils Karlsson, SWE | 3:47:48.0 | 1988 | Gunde Svan, SWE | 2:04:30.9 |
| 1952 | Veikko Hakulinen, FIN | 3:33:33.0 | 1992 | Bjorn Dählie, NOR | 2:03:41.5 |
| 1956 | Sixten Jernberg, SWE | 2:50:27.0 | 1994 | Vladimir Smirnov, KAZ | 2:07:20.3 |
| 1960 | Kalevi Hämäläinen, FIN | 2:59:06.3 | 1998 | Bjorn Dählie, NOR | 2:05:08.2 |
| 1964 | Sixten Jernberg, SWE | 2:43:52.6 | 2002 | Mikhail Ivanov, RUS* | 2:06:20.8 |
| 1968 | Ole Ellefsaeter, NOR | 2:28:45.8 | | | |

*Ivanov finished second to Johann Muehlegg of Spain, who was disqualified for failing a drug test.

### 4x10-kilometer Mixed Relay
Two classical and two freestyle legs.

| Year | | Time | Year | | Time | Year | | Time |
|------|---|------|------|---|------|------|---|------|
| 1936 | Finland | 2:41:33.0 | 1968 | Norway | 2:08:33.5 | 1992 | Norway | 1:39:26.0 |
| 1948 | Sweden | 2:32:08.0 | 1972 | Soviet Union | 2:04:47.94 | 1994 | Italy | 1:41:15.0 |
| 1952 | Finland | 2:20:16.0 | 1976 | Finland | 2:07:59.72 | 1998 | Norway | 1:40:55.7 |
| 1956 | Soviet Union | 2:15:30.0 | 1980 | Soviet Union | 1:57:03.46 | 2002 | Norway | 1:32:45.5 |
| 1960 | Finland | 2:18:45.6 | 1984 | Sweden | 1:55:06.3 | | | |
| 1964 | Sweden | 2:18:34.6 | 1988 | Sweden | 1:43:58.6 | | | |

## CROSS COUNTRY SKIING (Cont.)
### WOMEN

**Multiple gold medals** (including relays): Lyubov Egorova (6); Larissa Lazutina (5); Galina Kulakova and Raisa Smetanina (4); Claudia Boyarskikh, Olga Danilova and Marja-Liisa Hämäläinen and Elena Valbe (3); Stefania Belmondo, Manuela Di Centa, Nina Gavriluk, Toini Gustafsson, Barbara Petzold and Julija Tchepalova (2).

**Multiple gold medals** (including relays and Biathlon): Anfisa Reztsova (2).

### 1.5-kilometer Sprint
New event in 2002.

| Year | | Time |
|------|------|------|
| 2002 | Julija Tchepalova, RUS | 3:10.6 |

### 5 kilometers
Held as a classical event from 1964-98. From 1992-98 it was half of the combined pursuit event. Discontinued after 1998.

| Year | | Time | Year | | Time |
|------|------|------|------|------|------|
| 1964 | Claudia Boyarskikh, USSR | 17:50.5 | 1984 | Marja-Liisa Hämäläinen, FIN | 17:04.0 |
| 1968 | Toini Gustafsson, SWE | 16:45.2 | 1988 | Marjo Matikainen, FIN | 15:04.0 |
| 1972 | Galina Kulakova, USSR | 17:00.50 | 1992 | Marjut Lukkarinen, FIN | 14:13.8 |
| 1976 | Helena Takalo, FIN | 15:48.69 | 1994 | Lyubov Egorova, RUS | 14:08.8 |
| 1980 | Raisa Smetanina, USSR | 15:06.92 | 1998 | Larissa Lazutina, RUS | 17:37.9 |

### Combined Pursuit (10km)
From 1992-98 the pursuit consisted of a 10-km freestyle race in which the starting order was determined by order of finish in the 5-km classical race contested on separate days. Beginning in 2002, the pursuit was shortened to a 5-km classical race followed by a 5-km freestyle race contested on the same day. The 5-km classical is no longer a separate medal event.

| Year | | Time | Year | | Time |
|------|------|------|------|------|------|
| 1992 | Lyubov Egorova, UT | 40:07.7 | 1998 | Larissa Lazutina, RUS | 46:06.9 |
| 1994 | Lyubov Egorova, RUS | 41:38.1 | 2002 | Olga Danilova, RUS | 24:52.1 |

### 10 kilometers
Held as a classical event from 1952-88, and since 2002. Replaced by 10-km combined pursuit from 1992-98.

| Year | | Time | Year | | Time |
|------|------|------|------|------|------|
| 1952 | Lydia Wideman, FIN | 41:40.0 | 1976 | Raisa Smetanina, USSR | 30:13.41 |
| 1956 | Lyubov Kosyreva, USSR | 38:11.0 | 1980 | Barbara Petzold, E. Ger | 30:31.54 |
| 1960 | Maria Gusakova, USSR | 39:46.6 | 1984 | Marja-Liisa Hämäläinen, FIN | 31:44.2 |
| 1964 | Claudia Boyarskikh, USSR | 40:24.3 | 1988 | Vida Venciene, USSR | 30:08.3 |
| 1968 | Toini Gustafsson, SWE | 36:46.5 | 1992 | Not held | |
| 1972 | Galina Kulakova, USSR | 34:17.82 | 2002 | Bente Skari, NOR | 28:05.6 |

### 15 kilometers
Held as a freestyle event from 1992-94, and since 2002. Held as a classical event in 1998.

| Year | | Time | Year | | Time |
|------|------|------|------|------|------|
| 1992 | Lyubov Egorova, UT | 42:20.8 | 1998 | Olga Danilova, RUS | 46:55.4 |
| 1994 | Manuela Di Centa, ITA | 39:44.5 | 2002 | Stefania Belmondo, ITA | 39:54.4 |

### 20 kilometers
Held as a classical event from 1984-88. Discontinued in 1992 and replaced by the 30-kilometer freestyle.

| Year | | Time | Year | | Time |
|------|------|------|------|------|------|
| 1984 | Marja-Liisa Hämäläinen, FIN | 1:01:45.0 | 1988 | Tamara Tikhonova, USSR | 55:53.6 |

### 30 kilometers
Replaced 20-km classical event in 1992. Held as a freestyle event 1992-98. Held as a classical event since 2002.

| Year | | Time | Year | | Time |
|------|------|------|------|------|------|
| 1992 | Stefania Belmondo, ITA | 1:22:30.1 | 1998 | Julija Tchepalova, RUS | 1:22:01.5 |
| 1994 | Manuela Di Centa, ITA | 1:25:41.6 | 2002 | Gabriella Paruzzi, ITA* | 1:30:57.1 |

*Paruzzi finished second to Larissa Lazutina of Russia, who was disqualified after failing a drug test.

### 4x5-kilometer Relay
Two classical and two freestyle legs since 1992. Event featured three skiers per team from 1956-72.

| Year | | Time | Year | | Time | Year | | Time |
|------|------|------|------|------|------|------|------|------|
| 1956 | Finland | 1:09:01.0 | 1976 | Soviet Union | 1:07:49.75 | 1994 | Russia | 57:12.5 |
| 1960 | Sweden | 1:04:21.4 | 1980 | East Germany | 1:02:11.10 | 1998 | Russia | 55:13.5 |
| 1964 | Soviet Union | 59:20.2 | 1984 | Norway | 1:06:49.7 | 2002 | Germany | 49:30.6 |
| 1968 | Norway | 57:30.0 | 1988 | Soviet Union | 59:51.1 | | | |
| 1972 | Soviet Union | 48:46.15 | 1992 | Unified Team | 59:34.8 | | | |

## CURLING

| MEN | WOMEN |
|---|---|
| **Year** | **Year** |
| 1998 **Switzerland**, Canada, Norway | 1998 **Canada**, Denmark, Sweden |
| 2002 **Norway**, Canada, Switzerland | 2002 **Great Britain**, Switzerland, Canada |

## FIGURE SKATING

### MEN

**Multiple gold medals**: Gillis Grafström (3); Dick Button and Karl Schäfer (2).

| Year | | Year | | Year | |
|---|---|---|---|---|---|
| 1908 | Ulrich Salchow ........SWE | 1952 | Dick Button .............USA | 1984 | Scott Hamilton ..........USA |
| 1912 | Not held | 1956 | Hayes Alan Jenkins ......USA | 1988 | Brian Boitano ...........USA |
| 1920 | Gillis Grafström .......SWE | 1960 | David Jenkins ...........USA | 1992 | Victor Petrenko ..........UT |
| 1924 | Gillis Grafström .......SWE | 1964 | Manfred Schnelldorfer ....GER | 1994 | Alexei Urmanov .........RUS |
| 1928 | Gillis Grafström .......SWE | 1968 | Wolfgang Schwarz .......AUT | 1998 | Ilia Kulik .............RUS |
| 1932 | Karl Schäfer ..........AUT | 1972 | Ondrej Nepela ..........CZE | 2002 | Alexei Yagudin .........RUS |
| 1936 | Karl Schäfer ..........AUT | 1976 | John Curry ............GBR | | |
| 1948 | Dick Button ...........USA | 1980 | Robin Cousins ..........GBR | | |

### WOMEN

**Multiple gold medals**: Sonja Henie (3); Katarina Witt (2).

| Year | | Year | | Year | |
|---|---|---|---|---|---|
| 1908 | Madge Syers ..........GBR | 1952 | Jeanette Altwegg ........GBR | 1984 | Katarina Witt .........E. Ger |
| 1912 | Not held | 1956 | Tenley Albright .........USA | 1988 | Katarina Witt .........E. Ger |
| 1920 | Magda Julin-Mauroy .....SWE | 1960 | Carol Heiss ............USA | 1992 | Kristi Yamaguchi ........USA |
| 1924 | Herma Planck-Szabö ....AUT | 1964 | Sjoukje Dijkstra .........NED | 1994 | Oksana Baiul ..........UKR |
| 1928 | Sonja Henie ..........NOR | 1968 | Peggy Fleming ..........USA | 1998 | Tara Lipinski ...........USA |
| 1932 | Sonja Henie ..........NOR | 1972 | Beatrix Schuba ..........AUT | 2002 | Sarah Hughes ..........USA |
| 1936 | Sonja Henie ..........NOR | 1976 | Dorothy Hamill .........USA | | |
| 1948 | Barbara Ann Scott ......CAN | 1980 | Anett Poetzsch ........E. Ger | | |

### Pairs

**Multiple gold medals**: MEN–Pierre Brunet, Artur Dmitriev, Sergei Grinkov, Oleg Protopopov and Aleksandr Zaitsev (2). WOMEN–Irina Rodnina (3); Ludmila Belousova, Ekaterina Gordeeva and Andree Joly Brunet (2).

| Year | | Year | |
|---|---|---|---|
| 1908 | Anna Hübler & Heinrich Burger        Germany | 1968 | Ludmila Belousova & Oleg Protopopov ......USSR |
| 1912 | Not held | 1972 | Irina Rodnina & Aleksei Ulanov ..........USSR |
| 1920 | Ludovika & Walter Jakobsson ..........Finland | 1976 | Irina Rodnina & Aleksandr Zaitsev .........USSR |
| 1924 | Helene Engelmann & Alfred Berger .......Austria | 1980 | Irina Rodnina & Aleksandr Zaitsev .........USSR |
| 1928 | Andrée Joly & Pierre Brunet ............France | 1984 | Elena Valova & Oleg Vasiliev ...........USSR |
| 1932 | Andrée & Pierre Brunet ...............France | 1988 | Ekaterina Gordeeva & Sergei Grinkov ......USSR |
| 1936 | Maxi Herber & Ernst Baier ...........Germany | 1992 | Natalia Mishkutienok & Arthur Dmitriev .......UT |
| 1948 | Micheline Lannoy & Pierre Baugniet .....Belgium | 1994 | Ekaterina Gordeeva & Sergei Grinkov ......RUS |
| 1952 | Ria & Paul Falk ...........·.....Germany | 1998 | Oksana Kazakova & Artur Dmitriev .........RUS |
| 1956 | Elisabeth Schwartz & Kurt Oppelt .......Austria | 2002 | Elena Berezhnaya & Anton Sikharulidze .....RUS |
| 1960 | Barbara Wagner & Robert Paul .........Canada | | Jamie Sale & David Pelletier* .............CAN |
| 1964 | Ludmila Belousova & Oleg Protopopov ....USSR | | |

*Originally awarded silver medals, Sale & Pelletier later had them upgraded to gold after an investigation by the International Olympic Committee and the International Skating Union concluded that a judge was guilty of misconduct.

### Ice Dancing

**Multiple gold medals**: Oksana Grishuk & Yevgeny Platov (2).

| Year | | Year | |
|---|---|---|---|
| 1976 | Lyudmila Pakhomova & Aleksandr Gorshkov ..USSR | 1992 | Marina Klimova & Sergei Ponomarenko .......UT |
| 1980 | Natalia Linichuk & Gennady Karponosov ....USSR | 1994 | Oksana Grishuk & Yevgeny Platov .........RUS |
| 1984 | Jayne Torvill & Christopher Dean .....Great Britain | 1998 | Oksana Grishuk & Yevgeny Platov .........RUS |
| 1988 | Natalia Bestemianova & Andrei Bukin ......USSR | 2002 | Marina Anissina & Gwendal Peizerat ........FRA |

## FREESTYLE SKIING

### MEN
#### Aerials

| Year | | Points |
|---|---|---|
| 1994 | Andreas Schoebaechler, SWI ..........234.67 |
| 1998 | Eric Bergoust, USA .................255.64 |
| 2002 | Ales Valenta, CZR .................257.02 |

### WOMEN
#### Aerials

| Year | | Points |
|---|---|---|
| 1994 | Lina Cherjazova, UZB ...............166.84 |
| 1998 | Nikki Stone, USA ..................193.00 |
| 2002 | Alisa Camplin, AUS ................193.47 |

#### Moguls

| Year | | Points |
|---|---|---|
| 1994 | Jean-Luc Brassard, CAN .............27.24 |
| 1998 | Jonny Moseley, USA ................26.93 |
| 2002 | Janne Lahtela, FIN .................27.97 |

#### Moguls

| Year | | Points |
|---|---|---|
| 1994 | Stine Lise Hattestad, NOR .............25.97 |
| 1998 | Tae Satoya, JPN ...................25.06 |
| 2002 | Kari Traa, NOR ...................25.94 |

## ICE HOCKEY

### MEN

**Multiple gold medals:** Soviet Union/Unified Team (8); Canada (7); United States (2).

| Year | | | Year | | |
|---|---|---|---|---|---|
| 1920 | **Canada**, United States Czechoslovakia | | 1980 | **United States**, Soviet Union, Sweden | |
| 1924 | **Canada**, United States, Great Britain | | 1984 | **Soviet Union**, Czechoslovakia, Sweden | |
| 1928 | **Canada**, Sweden, Switzerland | | 1988 | **Soviet Union**, Finland, Sweden | |
| 1932 | **Canada**, United States, Germany | | 1992 | **Unified Team**, Canada, Czechoslovakia | |
| 1936 | **Great Britain**, Canada, United States | | 1994 | **Sweden**, Canada, Finland | |
| 1948 | **Canada**, Czechoslovakia, Switzerland | | 1998 | **Czech Republic**, Russia, Finland | |
| 1952 | **Canada**, United States, Sweden | | 2002 | **Canada**, United States, Russia | |
| 1956 | **Soviet Union**, United States, Canada | | | | |
| 1960 | **United States**, Canada, Soviet Union | | | **WOMEN** | |
| 1964 | **Soviet Union**, Sweden, Czechoslovakia | | Year | | |
| 1968 | **Soviet Union**, Czechoslovakia, Canada | | 1998 | **United States**, Canada, Finland | |
| 1972 | **Soviet Union**, United States, Czechoslovakia | | 2002 | **Canada**, United States, Sweden | |
| 1976 | **Soviet Union**, Czechoslovakia, West Germany | | | | |

### U.S. Gold Medal Hockey Teams

#### 1960

**Forwards:** Billy Christian, Roger Christian, Billy Cleary, Gene Grazia, Paul Johnson, Bob McVey, Dick Meredith, Weldy Olson, Dick Rodenheiser and Tom Williams. **Defensemen:** Bob Cleary, Jack Kirrane (captain), John Mayasich, Bob Owen and Rod Paavola. **Goaltenders:** Jack McCartan and Larry Palmer. **Coach:** Jack Riley.

#### 1980

**Forwards:** Neal Broten, Steve Christoff, Mike Eruzione (captain), John Harrington, Mark Johnson, Rob McClanahan, Mark Pavelich, Buzz Schneider, Dave Silk, Eric Strobel, Phil Verchota and Mark Wells. **Defensemen:** Bill Baker, Dave Christian, Ken Morrow, Jack O'Callahan, Mike Ramsey and Bob Suter. **Goaltenders:** Jim Craig and Steve Janaszak. **Coach:** Herb Brooks.

#### 1998

**Forwards:** Laurie Baker, Alana Blahoski, Lisa Brown-Miller, Karen Bye, Tricia Dunn, Cammi Granato, Katie King, Shelley Looney, A.J. Mleczko, Jenny Schmidgall, Gretchen Ulion, Sandra Whyte. **Defensemen:** Chris Bailey, Colleen Coyne, Sue Mertz, Tara Mounsey, Vicki Movessian, Angela Ruggiero. **Goaltenders:** Sarah DeCosta and Sarah Tueting. **Coach:** Ben Smith.

## LUGE

### MEN

**Multiple gold medals:** (including doubles): Georg Hackl (3); Jan Behrendt, Norbert Hahn, Paul Hildgartner, Thomas Köhler, Stefan Krausse and Hans Rinn (2).

#### Singles

| Year | | Time | Year | | Time |
|---|---|---|---|---|---|
| 1964 | Thomas Köhler, GER | 3:26.77 | 1988 | Jens Müller, E. Ger | 3:05.548 |
| 1968 | Manfred Schmid, AUT | 2:52.48 | 1992 | Georg Hackl, GER | 3:02.363 |
| 1972 | Wolfgang Scheidel, E. Ger | 3:27.58 | 1994 | Georg Hackl, GER | 3:21.571 |
| 1976 | Dettlef Günther, E. Ger | 3:27.688 | 1998 | Georg Hackl, GER | 3:18.436 |
| 1980 | Bernhard Glass, E. Ger | 2:54.796 | 2002 | Armin Zoeggeler, ITA | 2:57.941 |
| 1984 | Paul Hildgartner, ITA | 3:04.258 | | | |

#### Doubles

| Year | | Time | Year | | Time |
|---|---|---|---|---|---|
| 1964 | Josef Feistmantl & Manfred Stengl, AUT | 1:41.62 | 1988 | Joerg Hoffmann & Jochen Pietzsch, E. Ger. | 1:31.940 |
| 1968 | Klaus Bonsack & Thomas Köhler, E. Ger. | 1:35.85 | 1992 | Jan Behrendt & Stefan Krausse, GER | 1:32.053 |
| 1972 | (TIE) Paul Hildgartner/Walter Plaikner, ITA | 1:28.35 | 1994 | Kurt Brugger & Wilfred Huber, ITA | 1:36.720 |
| | & Richard Bredow/Horst Hornlein, E. Ger. | 1:28.35 | 1998 | Jan Behrendt & Stefan Krausse, GER | 1:41.105 |
| 1976 | Norbert Hahn & Hans Rinn, E. Ger. | 1:25.604 | 2002 | Patric-Fritz Leitner & Alexander Resch, GER | 1:26.082 |
| 1980 | Norbert Hahn & Hans Rinn, E. Ger. | 1:19.331 | | | |
| 1984 | Hans Stangassinger & Franz Wembacher, W. Ger. | 1:23.620 | | | |

### WOMEN

**Multiple gold medals:** Steffi Martin Walter (2).

#### Singles

| Year | | Time | Year | | Time |
|---|---|---|---|---|---|
| 1964 | Ortrun Enderlein, GER | 3:24.67 | 1988 | Steffi Martin Walter, E. Ger | 3:03.973 |
| 1968 | Erica Lechner, ITA | 2:28.66 | 1992 | Doris Neuner, AUT | 3:06.696 |
| 1972 | Anna-Maria Müller, E. Ger | 2:59.18 | 1994 | Gerda Weissensteiner, ITA | 3:15.517 |
| 1976 | Margit Schumann, E. Ger | 2:50.621 | 1998 | Silke Kraushaar, GER | 3:23.779 |
| 1980 | Vera Zozulya, USSR | 2:36.537 | 2002 | Sylke Otto, GER | 2:52.464 |
| 1984 | Steffi Martin, E. Ger | 2:46.570 | | | |

## NORDIC COMBINED

Ski jumping followed by a cross country race. Judges stopped converting cross country times into points after the 1994 Games. The times listed are final cross country times adjusted to include the competitors' staggered start time. The staggered start is determined by the Gundersen Method, which is a table that converts final ski jumping point differentials into time intervals.

**Multiple gold medals:** Samppa Lajunen and Ulrich Wehling (3); Bjarte Engen Vik, Johan Gröttumsbråten, Fred Boerre Lundberg, Takanori Kono and Kenji Ogiwara (2).

### Individual

| Year | | Points | Year | | Points |
|------|------|------|------|------|------|
| 1924 | Thorleif Haug, NOR | 18.906 | 1972 | Ulrich Wehling, E. Ger | 413.340 |
| 1928 | Johan Gröttumsbråten, NOR | 17.833 | 1976 | Ulrich Wehling, E. Ger | 423.39 |
| 1932 | Johan Gröttumsbråten, NOR | 446.00 | 1980 | Ulrich Wehling, E. Ger | 432.200 |
| 1936 | Oddbjörn Hagen, NOR | 430.3 | 1984 | Tom Sandberg, NOR | 422.595 |
| 1948 | Heikki Hasu, FIN | 448.80 | 1988 | Hippolyt Kempf, SWI | 432.230 |
| 1952 | Simon Slattvik, NOR | 451.621 | 1992 | Fabrice Guy, FRA | 426.470 |
| 1956 | Sverre Stenersen, NOR | 455.000 | 1994 | Fred Boerre Lundberg, NOR | 457.970 |
| 1960 | Georg Thoma, GER | 457.952 | | | Time |
| 1964 | Tormod Knutsen, NOR | 469.28 | 1998 | Bjarte Engen Vik, NOR | 41:21.1 |
| 1968 | Franz Keller, W. Ger | 449.04 | 2002 | Samppa Lajunen, FIN | 39:11.7 |

### Sprint

New event in 2002.

| Year | | Time |
|------|------|------|
| 2002 | Samppa Lajunen, FIN | 16:40.1 |

### Team

| Year | | Points | Year | | Time |
|------|------|------|------|------|------|
| 1988 | West Germany | 792.08 | 1998 | Norway | 54:11.5 |
| 1992 | Japan | 1247.180 | 2002 | Finland | 48:42.2 |
| 1994 | Japan | 1368.860 | | | |

## SKELETON

| MEN | | | WOMEN | | |
|------|------|------|------|------|------|
| **Singles** | | | **Singles** | | |
| Year | | Time | Year | | Time |
| 1928 | Jennison Heaton, USA | 3:01.8 | 2002 | Tristan Gale, USA | 1:45.11 |
| 1932-36 | Not held | | | | |
| 1948 | Nino Bibbia, ITA | 5:23.2 | | | |
| 1952-98 | Not held | | | | |
| 2002 | Jim Shea, USA | 1:41.96 | | | |

**Note:** This event was called Cresta when it was held in 1928 and 1948.

## SKI JUMPING

**Multiple gold medals** (including team jumping): Matti Nykänen (4); Jens Weissflog (3); Simon Ammann, Birger Ruud and Toni Nieminen (2).

### Normal Hill–90 Meters

| Year | | Points | Year | | Points |
|------|------|------|------|------|------|
| 1924-60 | Not held | | 1984 | Jens Weissflog, E. Ger | 215.2 |
| 1964 | Veikko Kankkonen, FIN | 229.9 | 1988 | Matti Nykänen, FIN | 229.1 |
| 1968 | Jiri Raska, CZE | 216.5 | 1992 | Ernst Vettori, AUT | 222.8 |
| 1972 | Yukio Kasaya, JPN | 244.2 | 1994 | Espen Bredesen, NOR | 282.0 |
| 1976 | Hans-Georg Aschenbach, E. Ger | 252.0 | 1998 | Jani Soininen, FIN | 234.5 |
| 1980 | Anton Innauer, AUT | 266.3 | 2002 | Simon Ammann, SWI | 269.0 |

**Note:** Jump held at 70 meters from 1964-92.

### Large Hill–120 Meters

| Year | | Points | Year | | Points |
|------|------|------|------|------|------|
| 1924 | Jacob Tullin Thams, NOR | 18.960 | 1972 | Wojciech Fortuna, POL | 219.9 |
| 1928 | Alf Andersen, NOR | 19.208 | 1976 | Karl Schäabl, AUT | 234.8 |
| 1932 | Birger Ruud, NOR | 228.1 | 1980 | Jouko Törmänen, FIN | 271.0 |
| 1936 | Birger Ruud, NOR | 232.0 | 1984 | Matti Nykänen, FIN | 231.2 |
| 1948 | Petter Hugsted, NOR | 228.1 | 1988 | Matti Nykänen, FIN | 224.0 |
| 1952 | Arnfinn Bergmann, NOR | 226.0 | 1992 | Toni Nieminen, FIN | 239.5 |
| 1956 | Antti Hyvärinen, FIN | 227.0 | 1994 | Jens Weissflog, GER | 274.5 |
| 1960 | Helmut Recknagel, GER | 227.2 | 1998 | Kazuyoshi Funaki, JPN | 272.3 |
| 1964 | Toralf Engan, NOR | 230.7 | 2002 | Simon Ammann, SWI | 281.4 |
| 1968 | Vladimir Beloussov, USSR | 231.3 | | | |

**Note:** Jump held at various lengths from 1924-56; at 80 meters from 1960-64; and at 90 meters from 1968-88.

## SKI JUMPING (Cont.)
### Team Large Hill

| Year | | Points | Year | | Points |
|---|---|---|---|---|---|
| 1988 | Finland | 634.4 | 1998 | Japan | 933.0 |
| 1992 | Finland | 644.4 | 2002 | Germany | 974.1 |
| 1994 | Germany | 970.1 | | | |

## SNOWBOARDING

### MEN
### Halfpipe

| Year | | Points | Year | | Points |
|---|---|---|---|---|---|
| 1998 | Gian Simmen, SWI | 85.2 | | | |
| 2002 | Ross Powers, USA | 46.1 | | | |

### Giant Slalom (Discont.)

Discontinued after 1998, replaced by Parallel Giant Slalom.

| Year | | Time |
|---|---|---|
| 1998 | Ross Rebagliati, CAN | 2:03.96 |

### Parallel Giant Slalom

| Year | | |
|---|---|---|
| 2002 | Philipp Schoch | SWI |

### WOMEN
### Halfpipe

| Year | | Points |
|---|---|---|
| 1998 | Nicola Thost, GER | 74.6 |
| 2002 | Kelly Clark, USA | 47.9 |

### Giant Slalom (Discont.)

Discontinued after 1998, replaced by Parallel Giant Slalom.

| Year | | Time |
|---|---|---|
| 1998 | Karine Ruby, FRA | 2:17.34 |

### Parallel Giant Slalom

| Year | | |
|---|---|---|
| 2002 | Isabelle Blanc | FRA |

## SPEED SKATING
### MEN

**Multiple gold medals:** Eric Heiden and Clas Thunberg (5); Ivar Ballangrud, Yevgeny Grishin and Johann Olav Koss (4); Hjalmar Andersen, Tomas Gustafson, Irving Jaffee and Ard Schenk (3); Gaétan Boucher, Knut Johannesen, Erhard Keller, Uwe-Jens Mey, Gianni Romme, Jack Shea and Jochem Uytdehaage (2). Note that Thunberg's total includes the All-Around, which was contested for the only time in 1924.

### 500 meters

| Year | | Time | | Year | | Time | |
|---|---|---|---|---|---|---|---|
| 1924 | Charles Jewtraw, USA | 44.0 | | 1968 | Erhard Keller, W. Ger | 40.3 | |
| 1928 | (TIE) Bernt Evensen, NOR | 43.4 | OR | 1972 | Erhard Keller, W. Ger | 39.44 | OR |
| | & Clas Thunberg, FIN | 43.4 | OR | 1976 | Yevgeny Kulikov, USSR | 39.17 | OR |
| 1932 | Jack Shea, USA | 43.4 | =OR | 1980 | Eric Heiden, USA | 38.03 | OR |
| 1936 | Ivar Ballangrud, NOR | 43.4 | OR | 1984 | Sergei Fokichev, USSR | 38.19 | |
| 1948 | Finn Helgesen, NOR | 43.1 | OR | 1988 | Uwe-Jens Mey, E. Ger | 36.45 | WR |
| 1952 | Ken Henry, USA | 43.2 | | 1992 | Uwe-Jens Mey, GER | 37.14 | |
| 1956 | Yevgeny Grishin, USSR | 40.2 | =WR | 1994 | Aleksandr Golubev, RUS | 36.33 | OR |
| 1960 | Yevgeny Grishin, USSR | 40.2 | =WR | 1998 | Hiroyashu Shimizu, JPN | 71.35* | OR |
| 1964 | Terry McDermott, USA | 40.1 | OR | 2002 | Casey FitzRandolph, USA | 69.23 | OR |

*The two-race final was introduced; skater with the lowest combined time wins gold.

### 1000 meters

| Year | | Time | | Year | | Time | |
|---|---|---|---|---|---|---|---|
| 1924-72 Not held | | | | 1992 | Olaf Zinke, GER | 1:14.85 | |
| 1976 | Peter Mueller, USA | 1:19.32 | | 1994 | Dan Jansen, USA | 1:12.43 | WR |
| 1980 | Eric Heiden, USA | 1:15.18 | OR | 1998 | Ids Postma, NED | 1:10.64 | OR |
| 1984 | Gaétan Boucher, CAN | 1:15.80 | | 2002 | Gerard van Velde, NED | 1:07.18 | WR |
| 1988 | Nikolai Gulyaev, USSR | 1:13.03 | OR | | | | |

### 1500 meters

| Year | | Time | | Year | | Time | |
|---|---|---|---|---|---|---|---|
| 1924 | Clas Thunberg, FIN | 2:20.8 | | 1968 | Kees Verkerk, NED | 2:03.4 | OR |
| 1928 | Clas Thunberg, FIN | 2:21.1 | | 1972 | Ard Schenk, NED | 2:02.96 | OR |
| 1932 | Jack Shea, USA | 2:57.5 | | 1976 | Jan Egil Storholt, NOR | 1:59.38 | OR |
| 1936 | Charles Mathisen, NOR | 2:19.2 | OR | 1980 | Eric Heiden, USA | 1:55.44 | OR |
| 1948 | Sverre Farstad, NOR | 2:17.6 | OR | 1984 | Gaétan Boucher, CAN | 1:58.36 | |
| 1952 | Hjalmar Andersen, NOR | 2:20.4 | | 1988 | Andre Hoffman, E. Ger | 1:52.06 | WR |
| 1956 | (TIE) Yevgeny Grishin, USSR | 2:08.6 | WR | 1992 | Johann Olav Koss, NOR | 1:54.81 | |
| | & Yuri Mikhailov, USSR | 2:08.6 | WR | 1994 | Johann Olav Koss, NOR | 1:51.29 | WR |
| 1960 | (TIE) Roald Aas, NOR | 2:10.4 | | 1998 | Aadne Sondral, NOR | 1:47.87 | WR |
| | & Yevgeny Grishin, USSR | 2:10.4 | | 2002 | Derek Parra, USA | 1:43.95 | WR |
| 1964 | Ants Antson, USSR | 2:10.3 | | | | | |

### 5000 meters

| Year | | Time | | Year | | Time | |
|---|---|---|---|---|---|---|---|
| 1924 | Clas Thunberg, FIN | 8:39.0 | | 1932 | Irving Jaffee, USA | 9:40.8 | |
| 1928 | Ivar Ballangrud, NOR | 8:50.5 | | 1936 | Ivar Ballangrud, NOR | 8:19.6 | OR |

| Year | | Time | |
|------|--|------|--|
| 1948 | Reidar Liaklev, NOR | 8:29.4 | |
| 1952 | Hjalmar Andersen, NOR | 8:10.6 | OR |
| 1956 | Boris Shilkov, USSR | 7:48.7 | OR |
| 1960 | Viktor Kosichkin, USSR | 7:51.3 | |
| 1964 | Knut Johannesen, NOR | 7:38.4 | OR |
| 1968 | Fred Anton Maier, NOR | 7:22.4 | WR |
| 1972 | Ard Schenk, NED | 7:23.61 | |
| 1976 | Sten Stensen, NOR | 7:24.48 | |

| Year | | Time | |
|------|--|------|--|
| 1980 | Eric Heiden, USA | 7:02.29 | OR |
| 1984 | Tomas Gustafson, SWE | 7:12.28 | |
| 1988 | Tomas Gustafson, SWE | 6:44.63 | WR |
| 1992 | Geir Karlstad, NOR | 6:59.97 | |
| 1994 | Johann Olav Koss, NOR | 6:34.96 | WR |
| 1998 | Gianni Romme, NED | 6:22.20 | WR |
| 2002 | Jochem Uytdehaage, NED | 6:14.66 | WR |

## 10,000 meters

| Year | | Time | |
|------|--|------|--|
| 1924 | Julius Skutnabb, FIN | 18:04.8 | |
| 1928 | Irving Jaffee, USA* | 18:36.5 | |
| 1932 | Irving Jaffee, USA | 19:13.6 | |
| 1936 | Ivar Ballangrud, NOR | 17:24.3 | OR |
| 1948 | Ake Seyffarth, SWE | 17:26.3 | |
| 1952 | Hjalmar Andersen, NOR | 16:45.8 | OR |
| 1956 | Sigvard Ericsson, SWE | 16:35.9 | OR |
| 1960 | Knut Johannesen, NOR | 15:46.6 | WR |
| 1964 | Jonny Nilsson, SWE | 15:50.1 | |
| 1968 | Johnny Höglin, SWE | 15:23.6 | OR |

| Year | | Time | |
|------|--|------|--|
| 1972 | Ard Schenk, NED | 15:01.35 | OR |
| 1976 | Piet Kleine, NED | 14:50.59 | OR |
| 1980 | Eric Heiden, USA | 14:28.13 | WR |
| 1984 | Igor Malkov, USSR | 14:39.90 | |
| 1988 | Tomas Gustafson, SWE | 13:48.20 | WR |
| 1992 | Bart Veldkamp, NED | 14:12.12 | |
| 1994 | Johann Olav Koss, NOR | 13:30.55 | WR |
| 1998 | Gianni Romme, NED | 13:15.33 | WR |
| 2002 | Jochem Uytdehaage, NED | 12:58.92 | WR |

*Unofficial, according to the IOC. Jaffee recorded the fastest time, but the event was called off in progress due to thawing ice.

## WOMEN

**Multiple gold medals:** Lydia Skoblikova (6); Bonnie Blair (5); Claudia Pechstein (4); Karin Enke, Gunda Niemann-Stirnemann and Yvonne van Gennip (3); Tatiana Averina, Catriona Lemay-Doan, Christa Rothenburger and Marianne Timmer (2).

## 500 meters

| Year | | Time | |
|------|--|------|--|
| 1960 | Helga Haase, GER | 45.9 | |
| 1964 | Lydia Skoblikova, USSR | 45.0 | OR |
| 1968 | Lyudmila Titova, USSR | 46.1 | |
| 1972 | Anne Henning, USA | 43.33 | OR |
| 1976 | Sheila Young, USA | 42.76 | OR |
| 1980 | Karin Enke, E. Ger | 41.78 | OR |

| Year | | Time | |
|------|--|------|--|
| 1984 | Christa Rothenburger, E. Ger | 41.02 | OR |
| 1988 | Bonnie Blair, USA | 39.10 | WR |
| 1992 | Bonnie Blair, USA | 40.33 | |
| 1994 | Bonnie Blair, USA | 39.25 | |
| 1998 | Catriona Lemay-Doan, CAN | 76.60* | OR |
| 2002 | Catriona Lemay-Doan, CAN | 74.75 | OR |

*The two-race final was introduced; skater with the lowest combined time wins gold.

## 1000 meters

| Year | | Time | |
|------|--|------|--|
| 1960 | Klara Guseva, USSR | 1:34.1 | |
| 1964 | Lydia Skoblikova, USSR | 1:33.2 | OR |
| 1968 | Carolina Geijssen, NED | 1:32.6 | OR |
| 1972 | Monika Pflug, W. Ger | 1:31.40 | OR |
| 1976 | Tatiana Averina, USSR | 1:28.43 | OR |
| 1980 | Natalia Petruseva, USSR | 1:24.10 | OR |

| Year | | Time | |
|------|--|------|--|
| 1984 | Karin Enke, E. Ger | 1:21.61 | OR |
| 1988 | Christa Rothenburger, E. Ger | 1:17.65 | WR |
| 1992 | Bonnie Blair, USA | 1:21.90 | |
| 1994 | Bonnie Blair, USA | 1:18.74 | |
| 1998 | Marianne Timmer, NED | 1:16.51 | OR |
| 2002 | Chris Witty, USA | 1:13.83 | WR |

## 1500 meters

| Year | | Time | |
|------|--|------|--|
| 1960 | Lydia Skoblikova, USSR | 2:25.2 | WR |
| 1964 | Lydia Skoblikova, USSR | 2:22.6 | OR |
| 1968 | Kaija Mustonen, FIN | 2:22.4 | OR |
| 1972 | Dianne Holum, USA | 2:20.85 | OR |
| 1976 | Galina Stepanskaya, USSR | 2:16.58 | OR |
| 1980 | Annie Borckink, NED | 2:10.95 | OR |

| Year | | Time | |
|------|--|------|--|
| 1984 | Karin Enke, E. Ger | 2:03.42 | WR |
| 1988 | Yvonne van Gennip, NED | 2:00.68 | OR |
| 1992 | Jacqueline Börner, GER | 2:05.87 | |
| 1994 | Emese Hunyady, AUT | 2:02.19 | |
| 1998 | Marianne Timmer, NED | 1:57.58 | WR |
| 2002 | Anni Friesinger, GER | 1:54.02 | WR |

## 3000 meters

| Year | | Time | |
|------|--|------|--|
| 1960 | Lydia Skoblikova, USSR | 5:14.3 | |
| 1964 | Lydia Skoblikova, USSR | 5:14.9 | |
| 1968 | Johanna Schut, NED | 4:56.2 | OR |
| 1972 | Christina Baas-Kaiser, NED | 4:52.14 | OR |
| 1976 | Tatiana Averina, USSR | 4:45.19 | OR |
| 1980 | Bjorg Eva Jensen, NOR | 4:32.13 | OR |

| Year | | Time | |
|------|--|------|--|
| 1984 | Andrea Schöne, E. Ger | 4:24.79 | OR |
| 1988 | Yvonne van Gennip, NED | 4:11.94 | WR |
| 1992 | Gunda Niemann, GER | 4:19.90 | |
| 1994 | Svetlana Bazhanova, RUS | 4:17.43 | |
| 1998 | Gunda Niemann-Stirnemann, GER | 4:07.29 | OR |
| 2002 | Claudia Pechstein, GER | 3:57.70 | WR |

## 5000 meters

| Year | | Time | |
|------|--|------|--|
| 1960-84 | Not held | | |
| 1988 | Yvonne van Gennip, NED | 7:14.13 | WR |
| 1992 | Gunda Niemann, GER | 7:31.57 | |

| Year | | Time | |
|------|--|------|--|
| 1994 | Claudia Pechstein, GER | 7:14.37 | |
| 1998 | Claudia Pechstein, GER | 6:59.61 | WR |
| 2002 | Claudia Pechstein, GER | 6:46.91 | WR |

## SHORT TRACK SPEED SKATING

### MEN

**Multiple gold medals** (including relays): Marc Gagnon and Kim Ki-Hoon (3).

#### 500 meters

| Year | | Time | |
|------|--|------|--|
| 1994 | Chae Ji-Hoon, S. Kor. | .43.45 | |
| 1998 | Takafumi Nishitani, JPN | .42.862 | |
| 2002 | Marc Gagnon, CAN | .41.802 | **OR** |

#### 1000 meters

| Year | | Time | |
|------|--|------|--|
| 1992 | Kim Ki-Hoon, S. Kor. | 1:30.76 | **WR** |
| 1994 | Kim Ki-Hoon, S. Kor. | 1:34.57 | |
| 1998 | Kim Dong-Sung, S. Kor. | 1:32.375 | |
| 2002 | Steven Bradbury, AUS | 1:29.109 | |

#### 1500 meters

| Year | | Time |
|------|--|------|
| 2002 | Apolo Anton Ohno, USA* | 2:18.541 |

*Ohno finished second to South Korea's Kim Dong-Sung, who was disqualifed for cross-tracking.

#### 5000–m Relay

| Year | | Time | |
|------|--|------|--|
| 1992 | South Korea | .7:14.02 | **WR** |
| 1994 | Italy | .7:11.74 | **OR** |
| 1998 | Canada | .7:06.075 | |
| 2002 | Canada | .6:51.579 | |

### WOMEN

**Multiple gold medals** (including relays): Chun Lee-Kyung (4); Kim Yun-Mi, Annie Perrault, Cathy Turner, Won Hye-Kyung and Yang Yang (A) (2)

#### 500 meters

| Year | | Time | |
|------|--|------|--|
| 1992 | Cathy Turner, USA | .47.04 | |
| 1994 | Cathy Turner, USA | .45.98 | **OR** |
| 1998 | Annie Perrault, CAN | .46.568 | |
| 2002 | Yang Yang (A), CHN | .44.187 | |

#### 1000 meters

| Year | | Time |
|------|--|------|
| 1994 | Chun Lee-Kyung, S. Kor. | 1:36.87 |
| 1998 | Chun Lee-Kyung, S. Kor. | 1:42.776 |
| 2002 | Yang Yang (A), CHN | 1:36.391 |

#### 1500 meters

| Year | | Time |
|------|--|------|
| 2002 | Ko Gi-Hyun, S. Kor. | 2:31.581 |

#### 3000–m Relay

| Year | | Time | |
|------|--|------|--|
| 1992 | Canada | 4:36.62 | |
| 1994 | South Korea | 4:26.64 | **WR** |
| 1998 | South Korea | 4:16.260 | **WR** |
| 2002 | South Korea | 4:12.793 | **WR** |

## Athletes with Winter and Summer Medals

Only three athletes have won medals in both the Winter and Summer Olympics:

**Eddie Eagan**, USA–Light Heavyweight Boxing gold (1920) and Four-man Bobsled gold (1932).

**Jacob Tullin Thams**, Norway–Ski Jumping gold (1924) and 8-meter Yachting silver (1936).

**Christa Luding-Rothenburger**, East Germany–Speed Skating gold at 500 meters (1984) and 1,000m (1988), silver at 500m (1988) and bronze at 500m (1992) and Match Sprint Cycling silver (1988). Luding-Rothenburger is the only athlete to ever win medals in both Winter and Summer Games in the same year.

## All-Time Leading Medal Winners
### MEN

| No | | Sport | G-S-B | No | | Sport | G-S-B |
|----|--|-------|-------|----|--|-------|-------|
| 12 | Bjorn Dählie, NOR | Cross Country | 8-4-0 | 5 | **Eric Heiden, USA** | Speed Skating | 5-0-0 |
| 9 | Sixten Jernberg, SWE | Cross Country | 4-3-2 | 5 | Yevgeny Grishin, USSR | Speed Skating | 4-1-0 |
| 7 | Clas Thunberg, FIN | Speed Skating | 5-1-1 | 5 | Johann Olav Koss, NOR | Speed Skating | 4-1-0 |
| 7 | Ivar Ballangrud, NOR | Speed Skating | 4-2-1 | 5 | Matti Nykänen, FIN | Ski Jumping | 4-1-0 |
| 7 | Ricco Gross, GER | Biathlon | 3-3-1 | 5 | Aleksandr Tikhonov, USSR | Biathlon | 4-1-0 |
| 7 | Veikko Hakulinen, FIN | Cross Country | 3-3-1 | 5 | Nikolai Zimyatov, USSR | Cross Country | 4-1-0 |
| 7 | Kjetil Andre Aamodt, NOR | Alpine | 3-2-2 | 5 | Georg Hackl, GER | Luge | 3-2-0 |
| 7 | Eero Mäntyranta, FIN | Cross Country | 3-2-2 | 5 | Samppa Lajunen, FIN | Cross Country | 3-2-0 |
| 7 | Bogdan Musiol, E. Ger/GER | Bobsled | 1-5-1 | 5 | Alberto Tomba, ITA | Alpine | 3-2-0 |
| 6 | Ole Einar Bjoerndalen, NOR | Biathlon | 5-1-0 | 5 | Marc Gagnon, CAN | ST Sp. Skating | 3-0-2 |
| 6 | Thomas Alsgaard, NOR | Cross Country | 4-2-0 | 5 | Harald Grönningen, NOR | Cross Country | 2-3-0 |
| 6 | Gunde Svan, SWE | Cross Country | 4-1-1 | 5 | Frank Luck, GER | Biathlon | 2-3-0 |
| 6 | Vegard Ulvang, NOR | Cross Country | 3-2-1 | 5 | Päl Tyldum, NOR | Cross Country | 2-3-0 |
| 6 | Johan Gröttumsbråten, NOR | Nordic | 3-1-2 | 5 | Sven Fischer, GER | Biathlon | 2-2-1 |
| 6 | Wolfgang Hoppe. E. Ger/GER | Bobsled | 2-3-1 | 5 | Knut Johannesen, NOR | Speed Skating | 2-2-1 |
| 6 | Eugenio Monti, ITA | Bobsled | 2-2-2 | 5 | Lasse Kjus, NOR | Alpine | 1-3-1 |
| 6 | Vladimir Smirnov, USSR/UT/KAZ | X-country | 1-4-1 | 5 | Peter Angerer, W. Ger/GER | Biathlon | 1-2-2 |
| 6 | Mika Myllylae, FIN | Cross Country | 1-1-4 | 5 | Juha Mieto, FIN | Cross Country | 1-2-2 |
| 6 | Roald Larsen, NOR | Speed Skating | 0-2-4 | 5 | Fritz Feierabend, SWI | Bobsled | 0-3-2 |
| 6 | Harri Kirvesniemi, FIN | Cross Country | 0-0-6 | 5 | Rintje Ritsma, NED | Speed Skating | 0-2-3 |

### WOMEN

| No | | Sport | G-S-B | No | | Sport | G-S-B |
|----|--|-------|-------|----|--|-------|-------|
| 10 | Raisa Smetanina, USSR/UT | Cross Country | 4-5-1 | 8 | Gunda Neimann-Stirnemann, GER | Speed Skating | 3-4-1 |
| 9 | Lyubov Egorova, UT/RUS | Cross Country | 6-3-0 | 8 | Ursula Disl, GER | Biathlon | 2-4-2 |
| 9 | Larissa Lazutina, UT/RUS | Cross Country | 5-3-1 | 7 | Claudia Pechstein, GER | Speed Skating | 4-1-2 |
| 9 | Stefania Belmondo, ITA | Cross Country | 2-3-4 | 7 | Marja-Liisa (Hämäläinen) Kirvesniemi, FIN | Cross Country | 3-0-4 |
| 8 | Galina Kulakova, USSR | Cross Country | 4-2-2 | | | | |
| 8 | Karin (Enke) Kania, E. Ger | Speed Skating | 3-4-1 | | | | |

| No | | Sport | G-S-B |
|---|---|---|---|
| 7 | Elena Valbe, UT/RUS | Cross Country | 3-0-4 |
| 7 | Andrea (Mitscherlich, Schöne) Ehrig, E. Ger | Speed Skating | 1-5-1 |
| 6 | Lydia Skoblikova, USSR | Speed Skating | 6-0-0 |
| 6 | **Bonnie Blair, USA** | Speed Skating | 5-0-1 |
| 6 | Manuela Di Centa, ITA | Cross Country | 2-2-2 |
| 5 | Lee-Kyung Chun, S. Kor | ST Sp. Skating | 4-0-1 |
| 5 | Olga Danilova, RUS | Cross Country | 3-2-0 |

| No | | Sport | G-S-B |
|---|---|---|---|
| 5 | Anfisa Reztsova, USSR/UT | CC/Biathlon | 3-1-1 |
| 5 | Vreni Schneider, SWI | Alpine | 3-1-1 |
| 5 | Katja Seizinger, GER | Alpine | 3-0-2 |
| 5 | Helena Takalo, FIN | Cross Country | 1-3-1 |
| 5 | Bente (Martinsen) Skari, NOR | Cross Country | 1-2-2 |
| 5 | Alevtina Kolchina, USSR | Cross Country | 1-1-3 |
| 5 | Yang Yang (S), CHN | ST Sp. Skating | 0-4-1 |
| 5 | Anita Moen, NOR | Cross Country | 0-3-2 |

## Games Medaled In

MEN–**Aamodt** (1992,94,2002); **Alsgaard** (1994,98,2002); **Angerer** (1980,84,88); **Ballangrud** (1928,32,36); **Bjoerndalen** (1998,2002); **Dählie** (1992,94,98); **Feierabend** (1936,48,52); **Fischer** (1994,98,2002); **Gagnon** (1994,98,2002); **Grishin** (1956,60,64); **Gross** (1992,94,98,2002); **Gröttumsbråten** (1924,28,32); **Grönningen** (1960,64,68); **Hackl** (1988,92,94,98,2002); **Hakulinen** (1952,56,60); **Heiden** (1980); **Hoppe** (1984,88,92,94); **Jernberg** (1956,60,64); **Johannesen** (1956,60,64); **Kirvesniemi** (1980,84,92,94,98); **Kjus** (1994,98,2002); **Koss** (1992,94); **Lajunen** (1998,2002);**Larsen** (1924,28); **Luck** (1994,98,2002); **Mäntyranta** (1960,64,68); **Mieto** (1976,80,84); **Monti** (1956,60,64,68); **Musiol** (1980,84,88,92); **Myllylae** (1994,98); **Nykänen** (1984,88); **Ritsma** (1994,98); **Smirnov** (1988,92,94,98); **Svan** (1984,88); **Thunberg** (1924,28); **Tikhonov** (1968,72,76,80); **Tomba** (1988,92,94); **Tyldum** (1968,72,76); **Ulvang** (1988,92,94); **Zimyatov** (1980,84).

WOMEN–**Belmondo** (1992,94,98,2002); **Blair** (1988,92,94); **Chun** (1994,98,2002); **Danilova** (1998,2002); **Di Centa** (1992,94); **Disl** (1992,94,98,2002); **Egorova** (1992,94); **Ehrig** (1976,80,84,88); **Kania** (1980,84,88); **Kirvesniemi** (1984,88,94); **Kolchina** (1956,64,68); **Kulakova** (1968,72,76,80); **Lazutina** (1992,94,98,2002); **Moen** (1994,98,2002); **Niemann-Stirnemann** (1992,94,98); **Pechstein** (1992,94,98,2002); **Reztsova** (1988,92,94); **Schneider** (1988,92,94); **Seizinger** (1992,94,98); **Skari** (1998,2002); **Skoblikova** (1960,64); **Smetanina** (1976,80,84,88,92); **Takalo** (1972,76,80); **Valbe** (1992,94,98); **Yang** (1998,2002).

---

## Most Gold Medals
### MEN

| No | | Sport | G-S-B |
|---|---|---|---|
| 8 | Bjorn Dählie, NOR | Cross Country | 8-4-0 |
| 5 | Clas Thunberg, FIN | Speed Skating | 5-1-1 |
| 5 | Ole Einar Bjoerndalen, NOR | Biathlon | 5-1-0 |
| 5 | **Eric Heiden, USA** | Speed Skating | 5-0-0 |
| 4 | Sixten Jernberg, SWE | Cross Country | 4-3-2 |
| 4 | Ivar Ballangrud, NOR | Speed Skating | 4-2-1 |
| 4 | Thomas Alsgaard, NOR | Cross Country | 4-2-0 |
| 4 | Gunde Svan, SWE | Cross Country | 4-1-1 |
| 4 | Yevgeny Grishin, USSR | Speed Skating | 4-1-0 |
| 4 | Johann Olav Koss, NOR | Speed Skating | 4-1-0 |
| 4 | Matti Nykänen, FIN | Ski Jumping | 4-1-0 |
| 4 | Aleksandr Tikhonov, USSR | Biathlon | 4-1-0 |
| 4 | Nikolai Zimyatov, USSR | Cross Country | 4-1-0 |

| No | | Sport | G-S-B |
|---|---|---|---|
| 4 | Thomas Wassberg, SWE | Cross Country | 4-0-0 |

### WOMEN

| No | | Sport | G-S-B |
|---|---|---|---|
| 6 | Lyubov Egorova, UT/RUS | Cross Country | 6-3-0 |
| 6 | Lydia Skoblikova, USSR | Speed Skating | 6-0-0 |
| 5 | Larissa Lanina, USSR/UT | Cross Country | 4-5-1 |
| 4 | Galina Kulakova, USSR | Cross Country | 4-2-2 |
| 4 | Claudia Pechstein, GER | ST Sp. Skating | 4-1-2 |
| 4 | Lee-Kyung Chun, S. Kor | ST Sp. Skating | 4-0-1 |

---

## All-Time Leading USA Medalists
### MEN

| No | | Sport | G-S-B |
|---|---|---|---|
| 5 | Eric Heiden | Speed Skating | 5-0-0 |
| 3* | Irving Jaffee | Speed Skating | 3-0-0 |
| 3 | Pat Martin | Bobsled | 1-2-0 |
| 3 | John Heaton | Bobsled/Skeleton | 0-2-1 |
| 2 | Dick Button | Figure Skating | 2-0-0 |
| 2† | Eddie Eagan | Boxing/Bobsled | 2-0-0 |
| 2 | Billy Fiske | Bobsled | 2-0-0 |
| 2 | Cliff Gray | Bobsled | 2-0-0 |
| 2 | Jack Shea | Speed Skating | 2-0-0 |
| 2 | Apolo Anton Ohno | ST Sp. Skating | 1-1-0 |
| 2 | Billy Cleary | Ice Hockey | 1-1-0 |
| 2 | Jennison Heaton | Bobsled/Skeleton | 1-1-0 |
| 2 | David Jenkins | Figure Skating | 1-1-0 |
| 2 | John Mayasich | Ice Hockey | 1-1-0 |

| No | | Sport | G-S-B |
|---|---|---|---|
| 2 | Terry McDermott | Speed Skating | 1-1-0 |
| 2 | Dick Meredith | Ice Hockey | 1-1-0 |
| 2 | Tommy Moe | Alpine | 1-1-0 |
| 2 | Weldy Olson | Ice Hockey | 1-1-0 |
| 2 | Derek Parra | Speed Skating | 1-1-0 |
| 2 | Dick Rodenheiser | Ice Hockey | 1-1-0 |
| 2 | Ross Powers | Snowboarding | 1-0-1 |
| 2 | Stan Benham | Bobsled | 0-2-0 |
| 2 | Herb Drury | Ice Hockey | 0-2-0 |
| 2 | Eric Flaim | Sp. Skate/ST Sp. Skate | 0-2-0 |
| 2 | Bode Miller | Alpine | 0-2-0 |
| 2 | Frank Synott | Ice Hockey | 0-2-0 |
| 2 | John Garrison | Ice Hockey | 0-1-1 |

*Jaffee is generally given credit for a third gold medal in the 10,000-meter Speed Skating race of 1928. He had the fastest time before the race was cancelled due to thawing ice. The IOC considers the race unofficial.
†Eagan won the light heavyweight boxing title at the 1920 Summer Games in Antwerp and the four-man Bobsled at the 1932 Winter Games in Lake Placid. He is the only athlete ever to win gold medals in both the Winter and Summer Olympics.

## WOMEN

| No | | Sport | G-S-B | No | | Sport | G-S-B |
|----|---|-------|-------|----|---|-------|-------|
| 6 | Bonnie Blair | Speed Skating | 5-0-1 | 2 | Carol Heiss | Figure Skating | 1-1-0 |
| 4 | Cathy Turner | ST Sp. Skating | 2-1-1 | 2 | Katie King | Ice Hockey | 1-1-0 |
| 4 | Dianne Holum | Speed Skating | 1-2-1 | 2 | Shelley Looney | Ice Hockey | 1-1-0 |
| 3 | Chris Witty | Speed Skating | 1-1-1 | 2 | Sue Merz | Ice Hockey | 1-1-0 |
| 3 | Sheila Young | Speed Skating | 1-1-1 | 2 | A.J. Mleczko | Ice Hockey | 1-1-0 |
| 3 | Leah Poulos Mueller | Speed Skating | 0-3-0 | 2 | Tara Mounsey | Ice Hockey | 1-1-0 |
| 3 | Beatrix Loughran | Figure Skating | 0-2-1 | 2 | Diann Roffe-Steinrotter | Alpine | 1-1-0 |
| 3 | Amy Peterson | ST Sp. Skating | 0-2-1 | 2 | Angela Ruggiero | Ice Hockey | 1-1-0 |
| 2 | Andrea Mead Lawrence | Alpine | 2-0-0 | 2 | Picabo Street | Alpine | 1-1-0 |
| 2 | Tenley Albright | Figure Skating | 1-1-0 | 2 | Sarah Teuting | Ice Hockey | 1-1-0 |
| 2 | Chris Bailey | Ice Hockey | 1-1-0 | 2 | Anne Henning | Speed Skating | 1-0-1 |
| 2 | Laurie Baker | Ice Hockey | 1-1-0 | 2 | Penny Pitou | Alpine | 0-2-0 |
| 2 | Karyn Bye | Ice Hockey | 1-1-0 | 2 | Nancy Kerrigan | Figure Skating | 0-1-1 |
| 2 | Sara DeCosta | Ice Hockey | 1-1-0 | 2 | Michelle Kwan | Figure Skating | 0-1-1 |
| 2 | Tricia Dunn | Ice Hockey | 1-1-0 | 2 | Jean Saubert | Alpine | 0-1-1 |
| 2 | Gretchen Fraser | Alpine | 1-1-0 | 2 | Nikki Ziegelmeyer | ST Sp. Skating | 0-1-1 |
| 2 | Cammi Granato | Ice Hockey | 1-1-0 | 2 | Jennifer Rodriguez | Speed Skating | 0-0-2 |

**Note:** The term ST Sp. Skating refers to Short Track (or pack) Speed Skating.

## All-Time Medal Standings, 1924-2002

All-time Winter Games medal standings, according to *The Golden Book of the Olympic Games*. Medal counts include figure skating medals (1908 and '20) and hockey medals (1920) awarded at the Summer Games. National medal standings for the Winter and Summer Games are not recognized by the IOC.

| | | G | S | B | Total | | | G | S | B | Total |
|---|---|---|---|---|-------|---|---|---|---|---|-------|
| 1 | Norway | 94 | 94 | 75 | 263 | 25 | Czech Republic (1998–) | 2 | 1 | 2 | 5 |
| 2 | Soviet Union (1956-88) | 78 | 57 | 59 | 194 | | Kazakhstan (1994–) | 1 | 2 | 2 | 5 |
| 3 | **United States** | 69 | 72 | 52 | 193 | | Belgium | 1 | 1 | 3 | 5 |
| 4 | Austria | 41 | 57 | 64 | 162 | | Bulgaria | 1 | 1 | 3 | 5 |
| 5 | Finland | 42 | 51 | 49 | 142 | | Belarus (1994–) | 0 | 2 | 3 | 5 |
| 6 | Germany (1928-36, 52-64, 92–) | 47 | 46 | 32 | 125 | 30 | Croatia | 3 | 1 | 0 | 4 |
| 7 | East Germany (1968-88) | 43 | 39 | 36 | 118 | | Spain | 3 | 0 | 1 | 4 |
| 8 | Sweden | 39 | 30 | 39 | 108 | | Australia | 2 | 0 | 2 | 4 |
| 9 | Switzerland | 32 | 33 | 38 | 103 | | Yugoslavia (1924-88) | 0 | 3 | 1 | 4 |
| 10 | Canada | 31 | 28 | 37 | 96 | | Slovenia | 0 | 0 | 4 | 4 |
| 11 | Italy | 31 | 31 | 27 | 89 | 35 | Estonia | 1 | 1 | 1 | 3 |
| 12 | France | 22 | 22 | 28 | 72 | | Ukraine (1994–) | 1 | 1 | 1 | 3 |
| 13 | Netherlands | 22 | 28 | 19 | 69 | | Slovenia (1992–) | 0 | 0 | 3 | 3 |
| 14 | Russia (1994–) | 27 | 20 | 11 | 58 | 38 | Luxembourg | 0 | 2 | 0 | 2 |
| 15 | West Germany (1968-88) | 18 | 20 | 19 | 57 | | North Korea | 0 | 1 | 1 | 2 |
| 16 | Japan | 8 | 10 | 13 | 31 | 40 | Uzbekistan (1994–) | 1 | 0 | 0 | 1 |
| 17 | Great Britain | 8 | 4 | 14 | 26 | | Denmark | 0 | 1 | 0 | 1 |
| | Czechoslovakia (1924-92) | 2 | 8 | 16 | 26 | | New Zealand | 0 | 1 | 0 | 1 |
| 19 | Unified Team (1992) | 9 | 6 | 8 | 23 | | Romania | 0 | 0 | 1 | 1 |

| | | G | S | B | Total |
|---|---|---|---|---|-------|
| 20 | China | 2 | 12 | 8 | 22 |
| 21 | South Korea | 11 | 5 | 4 | 20 |
| 22 | Liechtenstein | 2 | 2 | 5 | 9 |
| 23 | Poland | 1 | 2 | 3 | 6 |
| | Hungary | 0 | 2 | 4 | 6 |

| **Combined totals** | G | S | B | Total |
|---------------------|---|---|---|-------|
| Germany/E. Ger/W. Ger | 108 | 105 | 87 | 300 |
| USSR/UT/Russia | 114 | 83 | 78 | 275 |

**Notes:** Athletes from the USSR participated in the Winter Games from 1956-88, returned as the Unified Team in 1992 after the breakup of the Soviet Union (in 1991) and then competed for the independent republics of Belarus, Kazakhstan, Russia, Ukraine, Uzbekistan and three others in 1994. Yugoslavia divided into Croatia and Bosnia-Herzegovina in 1992, while Czechoslovakia split into Slovakia and the Czech Republic in 1993.

Germany was barred from the Olympics in 1924 and 1948 as an aggressor nation in both World Wars I and II. Divided into East and West Germany after WWII, both countries competed under one flag from 1952-64, then as separate teams from 1968-88. Germany was reunified in 1990.

# 1896-2004
# Through the Years

SPORTS ALMANAC

## Modern Olympic Games

The original Olympic Games were celebrated as a religious festival from 776 B.C. until 393 A.D., when Roman emperor Theodosius I banned all pagan festivals (the Olympics celebrated the Greek god Zeus). On June 23, 1894, French educator Baron Pierre de Coubertin, speaking at the Sorbonne in Paris to a gathering of international sports leaders, proposed that the ancient games be revived on an international scale. The idea was enthusiastically received and the Modern Olympics were born. The first Olympics were held two years later in Athens, where 245 athletes from 14 nations competed in the ancient Panathenaic stadium to large and ardent crowds. Americans captured nine out of 12 track and field events, but Greece won the most medals with 47.

## The Summer Olympics

| Year | No | Location | Dates | Nations | Most medals | USA medals | |
|---|---|---|---|---|---|---|---|
| 1896 | I | Athens, GRE . . . . . | Apr. 6-15 | 14 | Greece (10-19-18—47) | 11- 6- 2— 19 | (2nd) |
| 1900 | II | Paris, FRA . . . . . . | May 20-Oct. 28 | 26 | France (26-37-32—95) | 18-14-15— 47 | (2nd) |
| 1904 | III | St. Louis, USA. . . . | July 1-Nov. 23 | 13 | USA (78-84-82—244) | 78-84-82—244 | (1st) |
| 1906-a | — | Athens, GRE . . . . | Apr. 22-May 2 | 20 | France (15-9-16—40) | 12-6- 6— 24 | (3rd) |
| 1908 | IV | London, GBR . . . . | Apr. 27-Oct. 31 | 22 | Britain (54-46-38—138) | 23-12-12— 47 | (2nd) |
| 1912 | V | Stockholm, SWE | May 5-July 22 | 28 | Sweden (23-24-17—64) | 25-18-20— 63 | (2nd) |
| 1916 | VI | Berlin, GER . . . . . | Cancelled (WWI) | | | | |
| 1920 | VII | Antwerp, BEL . . . . | Apr. 20-Sept. 12 | 29 | USA (41-27-27—95) | 41-27-27— 95 | (1st) |
| 1924 | VIII | Paris, FRA . . . . . . | May 4-July 27 | 44 | USA (45-27-27—99) | 45-27-27— 99 | (1st) |
| 1928 | IX | Amsterdam, NED . | May 17-Aug. 12 | 46 | USA (22-18-16—56) | 22-18-16— 56 | (1st) |
| 1932 | X | Los Angeles, USA. | July 30-Aug. 14 | 37 | USA (41-32-30—103) | 41-32-30—103 | (1st) |
| 1936 | XI | Berlin, GER . . . . . | Aug. 1-16 | 49 | Germany (33-26-30—89) | 24-20-12— 56 | (2nd) |
| 1940-b | XII | Tokyo, JPN . . . . . . | Cancelled (WWII) | | | | |
| 1944 | XIII | London, GBR . . . . | Cancelled (WWII) | | | | |
| 1948 | XIV | London, GBR . . . . | July 29-Aug. 14 | 59 | USA (38-27-19—84) | 38-27-19— 84 | (1st) |
| 1952-cd | XV | Helsinki, FIN . . . . . | July 19-Aug. 3 | 69 | USA (40-19-17—76) | 40-19-17— 76 | (1st) |
| 1956-e | XVI | Melbourne, AUS . . | Nov. 22-Dec. 8 | 72 | USSR (37-29-32—98) | 32-25-17— 74 | (2nd) |
| 1960 | XVII | Rome, ITA . . . . . . | Aug. 25-Sept. 11 | 83 | USSR (43-29-31—103) | 34-21-16— 71 | (2nd) |
| 1964 | XVIII | Tokyo, JPN . . . . . | Oct. 10-24 | 93 | USSR (30-31-35—96) | 36-26-28— 90 | (2nd) |
| 1968-f | XIX | Mexico City, MEX | Oct. 12-27 | 112 | USA (45-28-34—107) | 45-28-34—107 | (1st) |
| 1972 | XX | Munich, W. GER . . | Aug. 26-Sept. 10 | 121 | USSR (50-27-22—99) | 33-31-30— 94 | (2nd) |
| 1976-g | XXI | Montreal, CAN . . . | July 17-Aug. 1 | 92 | USSR (49-41-35—125) | 34-35-25— 94 | (3rd) |
| 1980-h | XXII | Moscow, USSR . . . | July 19-Aug. 3 | 80 | USSR (80-69-46—195) | Boycotted games | |
| 1984-i | XXIII | Los Angeles, USA . | July 28-Aug. 12 | 140 | USA (83-61-30—174) | 83-61-30—174 | (1st) |
| 1988 | XXIV | Seoul, S. KOR . . . . | Sept. 17-Oct. 2 | 159 | USSR (55-31-46—132) | 36-31-27— 94 | (3rd) |
| 1992-j | XXV | Barcelona, SPA . . . | July 25-Aug. 9 | 169 | UT (45-38-29—112) | 37-34-37—108 | (2nd) |
| 1996 | XXVI | Atlanta, USA . . . . . | July 20-Aug. 4 | 197 | USA (44-32-25—101) | 44-32-25—101 | (1st) |
| 2000 | XXVII | Sydney, AUS . . . . | Sept. 15-Oct. 1 | 199 | USA (40-24-33—97) | 40-24-33—97 | (1st) |
| 2004 | XXVIII | Athens, GRE . . . . . | Aug. 13-29 | 202 | USA (35-39-29—103) | 35-39-29—103 | (1st) |
| 2008 | XXIX | Beijing, CHN . . . . | Aug. 8-24 | | | | |
| 2012 | XXX | London, ENG . . . . | July 27-Aug. 12 | | | | |

**a**—The 1906 Intercalated Games in Athens are considered unofficial by the IOC because they did not take place in the four-year cycle established in 1896. However, most record books include these interim games with the others.

**b**—The 1940 Summer Games are originally scheduled for Tokyo, but Japan resigns as host after the outbreak of the Sino-Japanese War in 1937. Helsinki is the next choice, but the IOC cancels the Games after Soviet troops invade Finland in 1939.

**c**—Germany and Japan are allowed to rejoin the Olympic community for the first Summer Games since 1936. Though a divided country, the Germans send a joint East-West team until 1964.

**d**—The Soviet Union (USSR) participates in its first Olympics, Winter or Summer, since the Russian revolution in 1917 and takes home the second most medals (22-30-19—71).

**e**—Due to Australian quarantine laws, the equestrian events for the 1956 Games are held in Stockholm, June 10-17.

**f**—East Germany and West Germany send separate teams for the first time and will continue to do so through 1988.

**g**—The 1976 Games are boycotted by 32 nations, most of them from black Africa, because the IOC will not ban New Zealand. Earlier that year, a rugby team from New Zealand had toured racially segregated South Africa.

**h**—The 1980 Games are boycotted by 64 nations, led by the USA, to protest the Soviet invasion of Afghanistan on Dec. 27, 1979.

**i**—The 1984 Games are boycotted by 14 Eastern Bloc nations, led by the USSR, to protest America's overcommercialization of the Games, inadequate security and an anti-Soviet attitude by the U.S. government. Most believe, however, the communist walkout is simply revenge for 1980.

**j**—Germany sends a single team after East and West German reunification in 1990 and the USSR competes as the Unified Team after the breakup of the Soviet Union in 1991.

## Event-by-Event

Gold medal winners from 1896-2004 in the following events: Baseball, Basketball, Boxing, Diving, Field Hockey, Gymnastics, Soccer, Softball, Swimming, Tennis and Track & Field.

## BASEBALL

**Multiple gold medals:** Cuba (3).

| Year | | Year | |
|------|--|------|--|
| 1992 | **Cuba**, Taiwan, Japan | 2000 | **United States**, Cuba, South Korea |
| 1996 | **Cuba**, Japan, United States | 2004 | **Cuba**, Australia, Japan |

### U.S. Medal-Winning Baseball Teams

**1996** (bronze medal): P–Kris Benson, R.A. Dickey, Seth Greisinger, Billy Koch, Braden Looper, Jim Parque and Jeff Weaver; C–A.J. Hinch, Matt LeCroy and Brian Lloyd; INF–Troy Glaus, Kip Harkrider, Travis Lee, Warren Morris, Augie Ojeda and Jason Williams; OF–Chad Allen, Chad Green, Jacque Jones and Mark Kotsay; Manager–Skip Bertman. Final: Cuba over Japan, 13-9.

**2000** (gold medal): P–Kurt Ainsworth, Ryan Franklin, Chris George, Shane Heams, Rick Krivda, Roy Oswalt, Jon Rauch, Bobby Seay, Ben Sheets, Todd Williams and Tim Young; C–Pat Borders, Marcus Jensen and Mike Kinkade; INF–Brent Abernathy, Sean Burroughs, John Cotton, Gookie Dawkins, Adam Everett and Doug Mientkiewicz; OF–Mike Neill, Anthony Sanders, Brad Wilkerson and Ernie Young; Manager–Tommy Lasorda. Final: USA over Cuba, 4-0.

## BASKETBALL

### MEN

**Multiple gold medals:** USA (12), USSR (2).

| Year | | Year | |
|------|--|------|--|
| 1936 | **United States**, Canada, Mexico | 1976 | **United States**, Yugoslavia, Soviet Union |
| 1948 | **United States**, France, Brazil | 1980 | **Yugoslavia**, Italy, Soviet Union |
| 1952 | **United States**, Soviet Union, Uruguay | 1984 | **United States**, Spain, Yugoslavia |
| 1956 | **United States**, Soviet Union, Uruguay | 1988 | **Soviet Union**, Yugoslavia, United States |
| 1960 | **United States**, Soviet Union, Brazil | 1992 | **United States**, Croatia, Lithuania |
| 1964 | **United States**, Soviet Union, Brazil | 1996 | **United States**, Yugoslavia, Lithuania |
| 1968 | **United States**, Yugoslavia, Soviet Union | 2000 | **United States**, France, Lithuania |
| 1972 | **Soviet Union**, United States, Cuba | 2004 | **Argentina**, Italy, United States |

### U.S. Medal-Winning Men's Basketball Teams

**1936** (gold medal): Sam Balter, Ralph Bishop, Joe Fortenberry, Tex Gibbons, Francis Johnson, Carl Knowles, Frank Lubin, Art Mollner, Don Piper, Jack Ragland, Carl Shy, Willard Schmidt, Duane Swanson and William Wheatley. Coach–Jim Needles; Assistant–Gene Johnson. Final: USA over Canada, 19-8.

**1948** (gold medal): Cliff Barker, Don Barksdale, Ralph Beard, Louis Beck, Vince Boryla, Gordon Carpenter, Alex Groza, Wallace Jones, Bob Kurland, Ray Lumpp, R.C. Pitts, Jesse Renick, Robert (Jackie) Robinson and Ken Rollins. Coach–Omar Browning; Assistant–Adolph Rupp. Final: USA over France, 65-21.

**1952** (gold medal): Ron Bontemps, Mark Freiberger, Wayne Glasgow, Charlie Hoag, Bill Hougland, John Keller, Dean Kelley, Bob Kenney, Bob Kurland, Bill Lienhard, Clyde Lovellette, Frank McCabe, Dan Pippin and Howie Williams. Coach–Warren Womble; Assistant–Forrest (Phog) Allen. Final: USA over USSR, 36-25.

**1956** (gold medal): Dick Boushka, Carl Cain, Chuck Darling, Bill Evans, Gib Ford, Burdy Haldorson, Bill Hougland, Bob Jeangerard, K.C. Jones, Bill Russell, Ron Tomsic and Jim Walsh. Coach–Gerald Tucker; Assistant–Bruce Drake. Final: USA over USSR, 89-55.

**1960** (gold medal): Jay Arnette, Walt Bellamy, Bob Boozer, Terry Dischinger, Jerry Lucas, Oscar Robertson, Adrian Smith, Burdy Haldorson, Darrall Imhoff, Allen Kelley, Lester Lane and Jerry West. Coach–Pete Newell; Assistant–Warren Womble. Final round: USA defeated USSR (81-57), Italy (112-81) and Brazil (90-63) in round robin.

**1964** (gold medal): Jim (Bad News) Barnes, Bill Bradley, Larry Brown, Joe Caldwell, Mel Counts, Dick Davies, Walt Hazzard, Lucious Jackson, Pete McCaffrey, Jeff Mullins, Jerry Shipp and George Wilson. Coach–Hank Iba; Assistant–Henry Vaughn. Final: USA over USSR, 73-59.

**1968** (gold medal): Mike Barrett, John Clawson, Don Dee, Cal Fowler, Spencer Haywood, Bill Hosket, Jim King, Glynn Saulters, Charlie Scott, Mike Silliman, Ken Spain, and Jo Jo White. Coach–Hank Iba; Assistant–Henry Vaughn. Final: USA over Yugoslavia, 65-50.

**1972** (silver medal refused): Mike Bantom, Jim Brewer, Tom Burleson, Doug Collins, Kenny Davis, Jim Forbes, Tom Henderson, Bobby Jones, Dwight Jones, Kevin Joyce, Tom McMillen and Ed Ratleff. Coach–Hank Iba; Assistants– John Bach and Don Haskins. Final: USSR over USA, 51-50.

**1976** (gold medal): Tate Armstrong, Quinn Buckner, Kenny Carr, Adrian Dantley, Walter Davis, Phil Ford, Ernie Grunfeld, Phil Hubbard, Mitch Kupchak, Tommy LaGarde, Scott May and Steve Sheppard. Coach–Dean Smith; Assistants–Bill Guthridge and John Thompson. Final: USA over Yugoslavia, 95-74.

**1980** (no medal): USA boycotted Moscow Games. Final: Yugoslavia over Italy, 86-77.

**1984** (gold medal): Steve Alford, Patrick Ewing, Vern Fleming, Michael Jordan, Joe Kleine, Jon Koncak, Chris Mullin, Sam Perkins, Alvin Robertson, Wayman Tisdale, Jeff Turner and Leon Wood. Coach–Bobby Knight; Assistants– Don Donoher and George Raveling. Final: USA over Spain, 96-65.

**1988** (bronze medal): Stacey Augmon, Willie Anderson, Bimbo Coles, Jeff Grayer, Hersey Hawkins, Dan Majerle, Danny Manning, Mitch Richmond, J.R. Reid, David Robinson, Charles D. Smith and Charles E. Smith. Coach–John Thompson; Assistants–George Raveling and Mary Fenlon. Final: USSR over Yugoslavia, 76-63.

**1992** (gold medal): Charles Barkley, Larry Bird, Clyde Drexler, Patrick Ewing, Magic Johnson, Michael Jordan, Christian Laettner, Karl Malone, Chris Mullin, Scottie Pippen, David Robinson and John Stockton. Coach–Chuck Daly; Assistants–Lenny Wilkens, Mike Krzyzewski and P.J. Carlesimo. Final: USA over Croatia, 117-85.

**1996** (gold medal): Charles Barkley, Anfernee Hardaway, Grant Hill, Karl Malone, Reggie Miller, Hakeem Olajuwon, Shaquille O'Neal, Gary Payton, Scottie Pippen, David Robinson and John Stockton. Coach–Lenny Wilkens; Assistants–Bobby Cremins, Clem Haskins and Jerry Sloan. Final: USA over Yugoslavia, 95-69.

**2000** (gold medal): Shareef Abdur-Rahim, Ray Allen, Vin Baker, Vince Carter, Kevin Garnett, Tim Hardaway, Allan Houston, Jason Kidd, Antonio McDyess, Alonzo Mourning, Gary Payton and Steve Smith. Coach–Rudy Tomjanovich; Assistants–Larry Brown, Gene Keady and Tubby Smith. Final: USA over France, 85-75.

**2004** (bronze medal): Carmelo Anthony, Carlos Boozer, Tim Duncan, Allen Iverson, LeBron James, Richard Jefferson, Stephon Marbury, Shawn Marion, Lamar Odom, Emeka Okafor, Amare Stoudemire, Dwyane Wade. Coach—Larry Brown; Assistants—Gregg Popovich, Roy Williams, Oliver Purnell, Dr. Sheldon Burns. Final—USA over Lithuania, 104-96.

## WOMEN

**Multiple gold medals:** USA (4), USSR/UT (3).

| Year | | Year | |
|---|---|---|---|
| 1976 | **Soviet Union**, United States, Bulgaria | 1992 | **Unified Team**, China, United States |
| 1980 | **Soviet Union**, Bulgaria, Yugoslavia | 1996 | **United States**, Brazil, Australia |
| 1984 | **United States**, South Korea, China | 2000 | **United States**, Australia, Brazil |
| 1988 | **United States**, Yugoslavia, Soviet Union | 2004 | **United States**, Australia, Russia |

### U.S. Gold Medal-Winning Women's Basketball Teams

**1984** (gold medal): Cathy Boswell, Denise Curry, Anne Donovan, Teresa Edwards, Lea Henry, Janice Lawrence, Pamela McGee, Carol Menken-Schaudt, Cheryl Miller, Kim Mulkey, Cindy Noble and Lynette Woodard. Coach–Pat Summitt; Assistant–Kay Yow. Final: USA over South Korea, 85-55.

**1988** (gold medal): Cindy Brown, Vicky Bullett, Cynthia Cooper, Anne Donovan, Teresa Edwards, Kamie Ethridge, Jennifer Gillom, Bridgette Gordon, Andrea Lloyd, Katrina McClain, Suzie McConnell and Teresa Weatherspoon. Coach–Kay Yow; Assistants–Sylvia Hatchell and Susan Yow. Final: USA over Yugoslavia, 77-70.

**1996** (gold medal): Jennifer Azzi, Ruthie Bolton, Teresa Edwards, Venus Lacy, Lisa Leslie, Rebecca Lobo, Katrina McClain, Nikki McCray, Carla McGee, Dawn Staley, Katy Steding and Sheryl Swoopes. Coach–Tara VanDerveer; Assistants–Ceal Barry, Nancy Darsch and Marian Washington. Final: USA over Brazil, 111-87.

**2000** (gold medal): Ruthie Bolton-Holyfield, Teresa Edwards, Yolanda Griffith, Chamique Holdsclaw, Lisa Leslie, Nikki McCray, DeLisha Milton, Katie Smith, Dawn Staley, Sheryl Swoopes, Natalie Williams and Kara Wolters. Coach—Nell Fortner; Assistants–Geno Auriemma and Peggie Gillom. Final: USA over Australia, 76-54.

**2004** (gold medal): Sue Bird, Swin Cash, Tamika Catchings, Yolanda Griffith, Shannon Johnson, Lisa Leslie, Ruth Riley, Katie Smith, Dawn Staley, Sheryl Swoopes, Diana Taurasi, Tina Thompson. Coach—Van Chancellor; Assistants—Anne Donovan, Gail Goestenkors, C. Vivian Stringer. Final: USA over Australia, 74-63.

## BOXING

**Multiple gold medals:** László Papp, Felix Savon and Teófilo Stevenson (3); Ariel Hernandez, Angel Herrera, Mario Kindelan, Oliver Kirk, Jerzy Kulej, Boris Lagutin, Harry Mallin, Guillermo Rigondeaux, Oleg Saitov and Hector Vinent (2). All fighters won titles in consecutive Olympics, except Kirk, who won both the bantamweight and featherweight titles in 1904 (he only had to fight once in each division).

### Light Flyweight (106 lbs)

| Year | | Final Match | Year | | Final Match |
|---|---|---|---|---|---|
| 1968 | Francisco Rodriguez, VEN | Decision, 3-2 | 1988 | Ivailo Hristov, BUL | Decision, 5-0 |
| 1972 | György Gedó, HUN | Decision, 5-0 | 1992 | Rogelio Marcelo, CUB | Decision, 24-10 |
| 1976 | Jorge Hernandez, CUB | Decision, 4-1 | 1996 | Daniel Petrov Bojilov, BUL | Decision, 19-6 |
| 1980 | Shamil Sabyrov, USSR | Decision, 3-2 | 2000 | Brahim Asloum, FRA | Decision, 23-10 |
| 1984 | Paul Gonzales, USA | Default | 2004 | Yan Bhartelemy, CUB | Decision, 21-16 |

### Flyweight (112 lbs)

| Year | | Final Match | Year | | Final Match |
|---|---|---|---|---|---|
| 1904 | George Finnegan, USA | Stopped, 1st | 1968 | Ricardo Delgado, MEX | Decision, 5-0 |
| 1920 | Frank Di Gennara, USA | Decision | 1972 | Georgi Kostadinov, BUL | Decision, 5-0 |
| 1924 | Fidel LaBarba, USA | Decision | 1976 | Leo Randolph, USA | Decision, 3-2 |
| 1928 | Antal Kocsis, HUN | Decision | 1980 | Peter Lessov, BUL | Stopped, 2nd |
| 1932 | István Énekes, HUN | Decision | 1984 | Steve McCrory, USA | Decision, 4-1 |
| 1936 | Willi Kaiser, GER | Decision | 1988 | Kim Kwang-Sun, S. Kor | Decision, 4-1 |
| 1948 | Pascual Perez, ARG | Decision | 1992 | Su Choi-Chol, N. Kor | Decision, 12-2 |
| 1952 | Nate Brooks, USA | Decision, 3-0 | 1996 | Maikro Romero, CUB | Decision, 12-11 |
| 1956 | Terence Spinks, GBR | Decision | 2000 | Wijan Ponlid, THA | Decision, 19-12 |
| 1960 | Gyula Török, HUN | Decision, 3-2 | 2004 | Yuriorkis Gamboa, CUB | Decision, 38-23 |
| 1964 | Fernando Atzori, ITA | Decision, 4-1 | | | |

### Bantamweight (119 lbs)

| Year | | Final Match | Year | | Final Match |
|---|---|---|---|---|---|
| 1904 | Oliver Kirk, USA | Stopped, 3rd | 1964 | Takao Sakurai, JPN | Stopped, 2nd |
| 1908 | Henry Thomas, GBR | Decision | 1968 | Valery Sokolov, USSR | Stopped, 2nd |
| 1920 | Clarence Walker, RSA | Decision | 1972 | Orlando Martinez, CUB | Decision, 5-0 |
| 1924 | William Smith, RSA | Decision | 1976 | Gu Yong-Ju, N. Kor | Decision, 5-0 |
| 1928 | Vittorio Tamagnini, ITA | Decision | 1980 | Juan Hernandez, CUB | Decision, 5-0 |
| 1932 | Horace Gwynne, CAN | Decision | 1984 | Maurizio Stecca, ITA | Decision, 4-1 |
| 1936 | Ulderico Sergo, ITA | Decision | 1988 | Kennedy McKinney, USA | Decision, 5-0 |
| 1948 | Tibor Csik, HUN | Decision | 1992 | Joel Casamayor, CUB | Decision, 14-8 |
| 1952 | Pentti Hämäläinen, FIN | Decision, 2-1 | 1996 | Istvan Kovacs, HUN | Decision, 14-7 |
| 1956 | Wolfgang Behrendt, GER | Decision | 2000 | Guillermo Rigondeaux, CUB | Decision, 18-12 |
| 1960 | Oleg Grigoryev, USSR | Decision | 2004 | Guillermo Rigondeaux, CUB | Decision, 22-13 |

## Boxing (Cont.)

### Featherweight (125 lbs)

| Year | | Final Match | Year | | Final Match |
|------|--|-------------|------|--|-------------|
| 1904 | Oliver Kirk, USA | Decision | 1964 | Stanislav Stepashkin, USSR | Decision, 3-2 |
| 1908 | Richard Gunn, GBR | Decision | 1968 | Antonio Roldan, MEX | Won on Disq. |
| 1920 | Paul Fritsch, FRA | Decision | 1972 | Boris Kousnetsov, USSR | Decision, 3-2 |
| 1924 | John Fields, USA | Decision | 1976 | Angel Herrera, CUB | KO, 2nd |
| 1928 | Lambertus van Klaveren, NED | Decision | 1980 | Rudi Fink, E. Ger | Decision, 4-1 |
| 1932 | Carmelo Robledo, ARG | Decision | 1984 | Meldrick Taylor, USA | Decision, 5-0 |
| 1936 | Oscar Casanovas, ARG | Decision | 1988 | Giovanni Parisi, ITA | Stopped, 1st |
| 1948 | Ernesto Formenti, ITA | Decision | 1992 | Andreas Tews, GER | Decision, 16-7 |
| 1952 | Jan Zachara, CZE | Decision, 2-1 | 1996 | Somluck Kamsing, THA | Decision, 8-5 |
| 1956 | Vladimir Safronov, USSR | Decision | 2000 | Bekzat Sattarkhanov, KAZ | Decision, 22-14 |
| 1960 | Francesco Musso, ITA | Decision, 4-1 | 2004 | Alexei Tichtchenko, RUS | Decision, 39-17 |

### Lightweight (132 lbs)

| Year | | Final Match | Year | | Final Match |
|------|--|-------------|------|--|-------------|
| 1904 | Harry Spanger, USA | Decision | 1964 | Józef Grudzien, POL | Decision |
| 1908 | Frederick Grace, GBR | Decision | 1968 | Ronnie Harris, USA | Decision, 5-0 |
| 1920 | Samuel Mosberg, USA | Decision | 1972 | Jan Szczepanski, POL | Decision, 5-0 |
| 1924 | Hans Nielsen, DEN | Decision | 1976 | Howard Davis, USA | Decision, 5-0 |
| 1928 | Carlo Orlandi, ITA | Decision | 1980 | Angel Herrera, CUB | Stopped, 3rd |
| 1932 | Lawrence Stevens, S. Afr | Decision | 1984 | Pernell Whitaker, USA | Foe quit, 2nd |
| 1936 | Imre Harangi, HUN | Decision | 1988 | Andreas Zuelow, E. Ger | Decision, 5-0 |
| 1948 | Gerald Dreyer, S. Afr | Decision | 1992 | Oscar De La Hoya, USA | Decision, 7-2 |
| 1952 | Aureliano Bolognesi, ITA | Decision, 2-1 | 1996 | Hocine Soltani, ALG | Tiebreak, 3-3 |
| 1956 | Richard McTaggart, GBR | Decision, 4-1 | 2000 | Mario Kindelan, CUB | Decision, 14-4 |
| 1960 | Kazimierz Pazdzior, POL | Decision, 4-1 | 2004 | Mario Kindelan, CUB | Decision, 30-22 |

### Light Welterweight (141 lbs)

| Year | | Final Match | Year | | Final Match |
|------|--|-------------|------|--|-------------|
| 1952 | Charles Adkins, USA | Decision, 2-1 | 1980 | Patrizio Oliva, ITA | Decision, 4-1 |
| 1956 | Vladimir Yengibaryan, USSR | Decision | 1984 | Jerry Page, USA | Decision, 5-0 |
| 1960 | Bohumil Nemecek, CZE | Decision, 5-0 | 1988 | Vyacheslav Yanovsky, USSR | Decision, 5-0 |
| 1964 | Jerzy Kulej, POL | Decision, 5-0 | 1992 | Hector Vinent, CUB | Decision, 11-1 |
| 1968 | Jerzy Kulej, POL | Decision, 3-2 | 1996 | Hector Vinent, CUB | Decision, 20-13 |
| 1972 | Ray Seales, USA | Decision, 3-2 | 2000 | Mahamadkadyz Abdullaev, UZB | Decision, 27-20 |
| 1976 | Ray Leonard, USA | Decision, 5-0 | 2004 | Manus Boonjumnong, THA | Decision, 17-11 |

### Welterweight (152 lbs)

| Year | | Final Match | Year | | Final Match |
|------|--|-------------|------|--|-------------|
| 1904 | Albert Young, USA | Decision | 1968 | Manfred Wolke, E. Ger | Decision, 4-1 |
| 1920 | Bert Schneider, CAN | Decision | 1972 | Emilio Correa, CUB | Decision, 5-0 |
| 1924 | Jean Delarge, BEL | Decision | 1976 | Jochen Bachfeld, E. Ger | Decision, 3-2 |
| 1928 | Edward Morgan, NZE | Decision | 1980 | Andrés Aldama, CUB | Decision, 4-1 |
| 1932 | Edward Flynn, USA | Decision | 1984 | Mark Breland, USA | Decision, 5-0 |
| 1936 | Sten Suvio, FIN | Decision | 1988 | Robert Wangila, KEN | KO, 2nd |
| 1948 | Julius Torma, CZE | Decision | 1992 | Michael Carruth, IRE | Decision, 13-10 |
| 1952 | Zygmunt Chychla, POL | Decision, 3-0 | 1996 | Oleg Saitov, RUS | Decision, 14-9 |
| 1956 | Nicolae Linca, ROM | Decision, 3-2 | 2000 | Oleg Saitov, RUS | Decision, 24-16 |
| 1960 | Nino Benvenuti, ITA | Decision, 4-1 | 2004 | Bakhtiyar Artayev, KAZ | Decision, 36-26 |
| 1964 | Marian Kasprzyk, POL | Decision, 4-1 | | | |

### Light Middleweight (156 lbs)

| Year | | Final Match | Year | | Final Match |
|------|--|-------------|------|--|-------------|
| 1952 | László Papp, HUN | Decision, 3-0 | 1980 | Armando Martinez, CUB | Decision, 4-1 |
| 1956 | László Papp, HUN | Decision | 1984 | Frank Tate, USA | Decision, 5-0 |
| 1960 | Skeeter McClure, USA | Decision, 4-1 | 1988 | Park Si-Hun, S. Kor | Decision, 3-2 |
| 1964 | Boris Lagutin, USSR | Decision, 4-1 | 1992 | Juan Lemus, CUB | Decision, 6-1 |
| 1968 | Boris Lagutin, USSR | Decision, 5-0 | 1996 | David Reid, USA | KO, 3rd |
| 1972 | Dieter Kottysch, W. Ger | Decision, 3-2 | 2000 | Yermakhan Ibraimov, KAZ | Decision, 25-23 |
| 1976 | Jerzy Rybicki, POL | Decision, 5-0 | 2004 | weight class eliminated. | |

### Middleweight (165 lbs)

| Year | | Final Match | Year | | Final Match |
|------|--|-------------|------|--|-------------|
| 1904 | Charles Mayer, USA | Stopped, 3rd | 1964 | Valery Popenchenko, USSR | Stopped, 1st |
| 1908 | John Douglas, GBR | Decision | 1968 | Christopher Finnegan, GBR | Decision, 3-2 |
| 1920 | Harry Mallin, GBR | Decision | 1972 | Vyacheslav Lemechev, USSR | KO, 1st |
| 1924 | Harry Mallin, GBR | Decision | 1976 | Michael Spinks, USA | Stopped, 3rd |
| 1928 | Piero Toscani, ITA | Decision | 1980 | José Gomez, CUB | Decision, 4-1 |
| 1932 | Carmen Barth, USA | Decision | 1984 | Shin Joon-Sup, S. Kor | Decision, 3-2 |
| 1936 | Jean Despeaux, FRA | Decision | 1988 | Henry Maske, E. Ger | Decision, 5-0 |
| 1948 | László Papp, HUN | Decision | 1992 | Ariel Hernandez, CUB | Decision, 12-7 |
| 1952 | Floyd Patterson, USA | KO, 1st | 1996 | Ariel Hernandez, CUB | Decision, 11-3 |
| 1956 | Gennady Schatkov, USSR | KO, 1st | 2000 | Jorge Gutierrez, CUB | Decision, 17-15 |
| 1960 | Eddie Crook, USA | Decision, 3-2 | 2004 | Gaydarbek Gaydarbekov, RUS | Decision, 28-18 |

### Light Heavyweight (178 lbs)

| Year | | Final Match | Year | | Final Match |
|---|---|---|---|---|---|
| 1920 | Eddie Eagan, USA | Decision | 1968 | Dan Poznjak, USSR | Default |
| 1924 | Harry Mitchell, GBR | Decision | 1972 | Mate Parlov, YUG | Stopped, 2nd |
| 1928 | Victor Avendaño, ARG | Decision | 1976 | Leon Spinks, USA | Stopped, 3rd |
| 1932 | David Carstens, S. Afr | Decision | 1980 | Slobodan Kacar, YUG | Decision, 4-1 |
| 1936 | Roger Michelot, FRA | Decision | 1984 | Anton Josipovic, YUG | Default |
| 1948 | George Hunter, S. Afr | Decision | 1988 | Andrew Maynard, USA | Decision, 5-0 |
| 1952 | Norvel Lee, USA | Decision, 3-0 | 1992 | Torsten May, GER | Decision, 8-3 |
| 1956 | Jim Boyd, USA | Decision | 1996 | Vasilii Jirov, KAZ | Decision, 17-4 |
| 1960 | Cassius Clay, USA | Decision, 5-0 | 2000 | Alexander Lebziak, RUS | Decision, 20-6 |
| 1964 | Cosimo Pinto, ITA | Decision, 3-2 | 2004 | Andre Ward, USA | Decision, 20-13 |

**Note:** Cassius Clay changed his name to Muhammad Ali after winning the world heavyweight championship in 1964.

### Heavyweight (201 lbs)

| Year | | Final Match | Year | | Final Match |
|---|---|---|---|---|---|
| 1984 | Henry Tillman, USA | Decision, 5-0 | 1996 | Felix Savon, CUB | Decision, 20-2 |
| 1988 | Ray Mercer, USA | KO, 1st | 2000 | Felix Savon, CUB | Decision, 21-13 |
| 1992 | Felix Savon, CUB | Decision, 14-1 | 2004 | Odlanier Solis, CUB | Decision, 22-13 |

### Super Heavyweight (Unlimited)

| Year | | Final Match | Year | | Final Match |
|---|---|---|---|---|---|
| 1904 | Samuel Berger, USA | Decision | 1964 | Joe Frazier, USA | Decision, 3-2 |
| 1908 | Albert Oldham, GBR | KO, 1st | 1968 | George Foreman, USA | Stopped, 2nd |
| 1920 | Ronald Rawson, GBR | Decision | 1972 | Teófilo Stevenson, CUB | Default |
| 1924 | Otto von Porat, NOR | Decision | 1976 | Teófilo Stevenson, CUB | KO, 3rd |
| 1928 | Arturo Rodriguez Jurado, ARG | Stopped, 1st | 1980 | Teófilo Stevenson, CUB | Decision, 4-1 |
| 1932 | Santiago Lovell, ARG | Decision | 1984 | Tyrell Biggs, USA | Decision, 4-1 |
| 1936 | Herbert Runge, GER | Decision | 1988 | Lennox Lewis, CAN | Stopped, 2nd |
| 1948 | Rafael Iglesias, ARG | KO, 2nd | 1992 | Roberto Balado, CUB | Decision, 13-2 |
| 1952 | Ed Sanders, USA | Won on Disq.* | 1996 | Vladimir Klichko, UKR | Decision, 7-3 |
| 1956 | Pete Rademacher, USA | Stopped, 1st | 2000 | Audley Harrison, GBR | Decision, 30-16 |
| 1960 | Franco De Piccoli, ITA | KO, 1st | 2004 | Alexander Povetkin, RUS | walkover† |

*Sanders' opponent, Ingemar Johansson, was disqualified in 2nd round for not trying.
†Povetkin was awarded the gold when his opponet Mohamed Aly failed a pre-fight physical due to a shoulder injury.
**Note:** Super Heavyweight was called heavyweight through 1980.

## DIVING

### MEN

**Multiple gold medals**: Greg Louganis (4); Klaus Dibiasi and Xiong Ni (3); Pete Desjardins, Sammy Lee, Tian Liang, Bob Webster and Albert White (2).

### Springboard

| Year | | Points | Year | | Points |
|---|---|---|---|---|---|
| 1908 | Albert Zürner, GER | 85.5 | 1964 | Ken Sitzberger, USA | 159.90 |
| 1912 | Paul Günther, GER | 79.23 | 1968 | Bernie Wrightson, USA | 170.15 |
| 1920 | Louis Kuehn, USA | 675.4 | 1972 | Vladimir Vasin, USSR | 594.09 |
| 1924 | Albert White, USA | 696.4 | 1976 | Phil Boggs, USA | 619.05 |
| 1928 | Pete Desjardins, USA | 185.04 | 1980 | Aleksandr Portnov, USSR | 905.03 |
| 1932 | Michael Galitzen, USA | 161.38 | 1984 | Greg Louganis, USA | 754.41 |
| 1936 | Richard Degener, USA | 163.57 | 1988 | Greg Louganis, USA | 730.80 |
| 1948 | Bruce Harlan, USA | 163.64 | 1992 | Mark Lenzi, USA | 676.53 |
| 1952 | David Browning, USA | 205.29 | 1996 | Xiong Ni, CHN | 701.46 |
| 1956 | Bob Clotworthy, USA | 159.56 | 2000 | Xiong Ni, CHN | 708.72 |
| 1960 | Gary Tobian, USA | 170.00 | 2004 | Peng Bo, CHN | 787.38 |

### Platform

| Year | | Points | Year | | Points |
|---|---|---|---|---|---|
| 1904 | George Sheldon, USA | 12.66 | 1960 | Bob Webster, USA | 165.56 |
| 1906 | Gottlob Walz, GER | 156.0 | 1964 | Bob Webster, USA | 148.58 |
| 1908 | Hjalmar Johansson, SWE | 83.75 | 1968 | Klaus Dibiasi, ITA | 164.18 |
| 1912 | Erik Adlerz, SWE | 73.94 | 1972 | Klaus Dibiasi, ITA | 504.12 |
| 1920 | Clarence Pinkston, USA | 100.67 | 1976 | Klaus Dibiasi, ITA | 600.51 |
| 1924 | Albert White, USA | 97.46 | 1980 | Falk Hoffmann, E. Ger | 835.65 |
| 1928 | Pete Desjardins, USA | 98.74 | 1984 | Greg Louganis, USA | 710.91 |
| 1932 | Harold Smith, USA | 124.80 | 1988 | Greg Louganis, USA | 638.61 |
| 1936 | Marshall Wayne, USA | 113.58 | 1992 | Sun Shuwei, CHN | 677.31 |
| 1948 | Sammy Lee, USA | 130.05 | 1996 | Dmitri Sautin, RUS | 692.34 |
| 1952 | Sammy Lee, USA | 156.28 | 2000 | Tian Liang, CHN | 724.53 |
| 1956 | Joaquin Capilla, MEX | 152.44 | 2004 | Hu Jia, CHN | 748.08 |

## Diving (Cont.)

### Synchronized Platform

| Year | | Points | Year | | Points |
|---|---|---|---|---|---|
| 2000 | Igor Louckachine & Dmitri Sautin, RUS | 365.04 | 2004 | Tian Liang & Yang Jinghui, CHN | 383.88 |

### Synchronized Springboard

| Year | | Points | Year | | Points |
|---|---|---|---|---|---|
| 2000 | Xiao Hailiang & Xiong Ni, CHN | 365.58 | 2004 | Nikolaos Siranidis & Thomas Bimis, GRE | 353.34 |

### WOMEN

**Multiple gold medals**: Pat McCormick and Fu Mingxia (4); Ingrid Engel-Krämer (3); Vicki Draves, Dorothy Poynton Hill, Guo Jingjing and Gao Min (2).

### Springboard

| Year | | Points | Year | | Points |
|---|---|---|---|---|---|
| 1920 | Aileen Riggin, USA | 539.9 | 1968 | Sue Gossick, USA | 150.77 |
| 1924 | Elizabeth Becker, USA | 474.5 | 1972 | Micki King, USA | 450.03 |
| 1928 | Helen Meany, USA | 78.62 | 1976 | Jennifer Chandler, USA | 506.19 |
| 1932 | Georgia Coleman, USA | 87.52 | 1980 | Irina Kalinina, USSR | 725.91 |
| 1936 | Marjorie Gestring, USA | 89.27 | 1984 | Sylvie Bernier, CAN | 530.70 |
| 1948 | Vicki Draves, USA | 108.74 | 1988 | Gao Min, CHN | 580.23 |
| 1952 | Pat McCormick, USA | 147.30 | 1992 | Gao Min, CHN | 572.40 |
| 1956 | Pat McCormick, USA | 142.36 | 1996 | Fu Mingxia, CHN | 547.68 |
| 1960 | Ingrid Krämer, GER | 155.81 | 2000 | Fu Mingxia, CHN | 609.42 |
| 1964 | Ingrid Engel-Krämer, GER | 145.00 | 2004 | Guo Jingjing, CHN | 633.15 |

### Platform

| Year | | Points | Year | | Points |
|---|---|---|---|---|---|
| 1912 | Greta Johansson, SWE | 39.9 | 1968 | Milena Duchková, CZE | 109.59 |
| 1920 | Stefani Fryland-Clausen, DEN | 34.6 | 1972 | Ulrika Knape, SWE | 390.00 |
| 1924 | Caroline Smith, USA | 33.2 | 1976 | Elena Vaytsekhovskaya, USSR | 406.59 |
| 1928 | Elizabeth Becker Pinkston, USA | 31.6 | 1980 | Martina Jäschke, E. Ger | 596.25 |
| 1932 | Dorothy Poynton, USA | 40.26 | 1984 | Zhou Jihong, CHN | 435.51 |
| 1936 | Dorothy Poynton Hill, USA | 33.93 | 1988 | Xu Yanmei, CHN | 445.20 |
| 1948 | Vicki Draves, USA | 68.87 | 1992 | Fu Mingxia, CHN | 461.43 |
| 1952 | Pat McCormick, USA | 79.37 | 1996 | Fu Mingxia, CHN | 521.58 |
| 1956 | Pat McCormick, USA | 84.85 | 2000 | Laura Wilkinson, USA | 543.75 |
| 1960 | Ingrid Krämer, GER | 91.28 | 2004 | Chantelle Newberry, AUS | 590.31 |
| 1964 | Lesley Bush, USA | 99.80 | | | |

### Synchronized Platform

| Year | | Points | Year | | Points |
|---|---|---|---|---|---|
| 2000 | Li Na & Sang Xue, CHN | 345.12 | 2004 | Lao Lishi & Li Ting, CHN | 53.40 |

### Synchronized Springboard

| Year | | Points | Year | | Points |
|---|---|---|---|---|---|
| 2000 | Vera Ilyina & Yulia Pakhalina, RUS | 332.64 | 2004 | Wu Minxia & Guo Jingjing, CHN | 336.90 |

## FIELD HOCKEY

### MEN

**Multiple gold medals**: India (8); Great Britain and Pakistan (3); West Germany/Germany and Netherlands (2).

| Year | | Year | |
|---|---|---|---|
| 1908 | **Great Britain**, Ireland, Scotland | 1968 | **Pakistan**, Australia, India |
| 1920 | **Great Britain**, Denmark, Belgium | 1972 | **West Germany**, Pakistan, India |
| 1928 | **India**, Netherlands, Germany | 1976 | **New Zealand**, Australia, Pakistan |
| 1932 | **India**, Japan, United States | 1980 | **India**, Spain, Soviet Union |
| 1936 | **India**, Germany, Netherlands | 1984 | **Pakistan**, West Germany, Great Britain |
| 1948 | **India**, Great Britain, Netherlands | 1988 | **Great Britain**, West Germany, Netherlands |
| 1952 | **India**, Netherlands, Great Britain | 1992 | **Germany**, Australia, Pakistan |
| 1956 | **India**, Pakistan, Germany | 1996 | **Netherlands**, Spain, Australia |
| 1960 | **Pakistan**, India, Spain | 2000 | **Netherlands**, South Korea, Australia |
| 1964 | **India**, Pakistan, Australia | 2004 | **Australia**, Netherlands, Germany |

### WOMEN

**Multiple gold medals**: Australia (3).

| Year | | Year | |
|---|---|---|---|
| 1980 | **Zimbabwe**, Czechoslovakia, Soviet Union | 1996 | **Australia**, South Korea, Netherlands |
| 1984 | **Netherlands**, West Germany, United States | 2000 | **Australia**, Argentina, Netherlands |
| 1988 | **Australia**, South Korea, Netherlands | 2004 | **Germany**, Netherlands, Argentina |
| 1992 | **Spain**, Germany, Great Britain | | |

## GYMNASTICS

### MEN

**At least 4 gold medals** (including team events): Sawao Kato (8); Nikolai Andrianov, Viktor Chukarin and Boris Shakhlin (7); Akinori Nakayama and Vitaly Scherbo (6); Yukio Endo, Anton Heida, Mitsuo Tsukahara and Takashi Ono (5); Vladimir Artemov, Georges Miez, Valentin Muratov and Alexei Nemov (4).

### All-Around

| Year | | Points | Year | | Points |
|------|---|--------|------|---|--------|
| 1900 | Gustave Sandras, FRA | 302 | 1960 | Boris Shakhlin, USSR | 115.95 |
| 1904 | Julius Lenhart, AUT | 69.80 | 1964 | Yukio Endo, JPN | 115.95 |
| 1906 | Pierre Payssé, FRA | 97.0 | 1968 | Sawao Kato, JPN | 115.9 |
| 1908 | Alberto Braglia, ITA | 317.0 | 1972 | Sawao Kato, JPN | 114.650 |
| 1912 | Alberto Braglia, ITA | 135.0 | 1976 | Nikolai Andrianov, USSR | 116.65 |
| 1920 | Giorgio Zampori, ITA | 88.35 | 1980 | Aleksandr Dityatin, USSR | 118.65 |
| 1924 | Leon Stukelj, YUG | 110.340 | 1984 | Koji Gushiken, JPN | 118.7 |
| 1928 | Georges Miez, SWI | 247.500 | 1988 | Vladimir Artemov, USSR | 119.125 |
| 1932 | Romeo Neri, ITA | 140.625 | 1992 | Vitaly Scherbo, UT | 59.025 |
| 1936 | Alfred Schwarzmann, GER | 113.100 | 1996 | Li Xiaoshuang, CHN | 58.423 |
| 1948 | Veikko Huhtanen, FIN | 229.7 | 2000 | Alexei Nemov, RUS | 58.474 |
| 1952 | Viktor Chukarin, USSR | 115.7 | 2004 | Paul Hamm, USA | 57.823 |
| 1956 | Viktor Chukarin, USSR | 114.25 | | | |

### High Bar

| Year | | Points | Year | | Points |
|------|---|--------|------|---|--------|
| 1896 | Hermann Weingärtner, GER | – | 1968 | (TIE) Akinori Nakayama, JPN | 19.55 |
| 1904 | (TIE) Anton Heida, USA | 40 | | & Mikhail Voronin, USSR | 19.55 |
| | & Edward Hennig, USA | 40 | 1972 | Mitsuo Tsukahara, JPN | 19.725 |
| 1924 | Leon Stukelj, YUG | 19.73 | 1976 | Mitsuo Tsukahara, JPN | 19.675 |
| 1928 | Georges Miez, SWI | 19.17 | 1980 | Stoyan Deltchev, BUL | 19.825 |
| 1932 | Dallas Bixler, USA | 18.33 | 1984 | Shinji Morisue, JPN | 20.00 |
| 1936 | Aleksanteri Saarvala, FIN | 19.367 | 1988 | (TIE) Vladimir Artemov, USSR | 19.900 |
| 1948 | Josef Stalder, SWI | 19.85 | | & Valeri Lyukin, USSR | 19.900 |
| 1952 | Jack Günthard, SWI | 19.55 | 1992 | Trent Dimas, USA | 9.875 |
| 1956 | Takashi Ono, JPN | 19.60 | 1996 | Andreas Wecker, GER | 9.850 |
| 1960 | Takashi Ono, JPN | 19.60 | 2000 | Alexei Nemov, RUS | 9.787 |
| 1964 | Boris Shakhlin, USSR | 19.625 | 2004 | Igor Cassina, ITA | 9.812 |

### Parallel Bars

| Year | | Points | Year | | Points |
|------|---|--------|------|---|--------|
| 1896 | Alfred Flatow, GER | – | 1968 | Akinori Nakayama, JPN | 19.475 |
| 1904 | George Eyser, USA | 44 | 1972 | Sawao Kato, JPN | 19.475 |
| 1924 | August Güttinger, SWI | 21.63 | 1976 | Sawao Kato, JPN | 19.675 |
| 1928 | Ladislav Vácha, CZE | 18.83 | 1980 | Aleksandr Tkachyov, USSR | 19.775 |
| 1932 | Romeo Neri, ITA | 18.97 | 1984 | Bart Conner, USA | 19.95 |
| 1936 | Konrad Frey, GER | 19.067 | 1988 | Vladimir Artemov, USSR | 19.925 |
| 1948 | Michael Reusch, SWI | 19.75 | 1992 | Vitaly Scherbo, UT | 9.900 |
| 1952 | Hans Eugster, SWI | 19.65 | 1996 | Rustam Sharipov, UKR | 9.837 |
| 1956 | Viktor Chukarin, USSR | 19.20 | 2000 | Li Xiaopeng, CHN | 9.825 |
| 1960 | Boris Shakhlin, USSR | 19.40 | 2004 | Valeri Goncharov, UKR | 9.787 |
| 1964 | Yukio Endo, JPN | 19.675 | | | |

### Vault

| Year | | Points | Year | | Points |
|------|---|--------|------|---|--------|
| 1896 | Karl Schumann, GER | – | 1964 | Haruhiro Yamashita, JPN | 19.60 |
| 1904 | (TIE) George Eyser, USA | 36 | 1968 | Mikhail Voronin, USSR | 19.00 |
| | & Anton Heida, USA | 36 | 1972 | Klaus Köste, E. Ger | 18.85 |
| 1924 | Frank Kriz, USA | 9.98 | 1976 | Nikolai Andrianov, USSR | 19.45 |
| 1928 | Eugen Mack, SWI | 9.58 | 1980 | Nikolai Andrianov, USSR | 19.825 |
| 1932 | Savino Guglielmetti, ITA | 18.03 | 1984 | Lou Yun, CHN | 19.95 |
| 1936 | Alfred Schwarzmann, GER | 19.20 | 1988 | Lou Yun, CHN | 19.875 |
| 1948 | Paavo Aaltonen, FIN | 19.55 | 1992 | Vitaly Scherbo, UT | 9.856 |
| 1952 | Viktor Chukarin, USSR | 19.20 | 1996 | Alexei Nemov, RUS | 9.787 |
| 1956 | (TIE) Helmut Bantz, GER | 18.85 | 2000 | Gervasio Deferr, SPA | 9.712 |
| | & Valentin Muratov, USSR | 18.85 | 2004 | Gervasio Deferr, SPA | 9.737 |
| 1960 | (TIE) Takashi Ono, JPN | 19.35 | | | |
| | & Boris Shakhlin, USSR | 19.35 | | | |

## Gymnastics (Cont.)

### Pommel Horse

| Year | | Points | Year | | Points |
|------|--|--------|------|--|--------|
| 1896 | Louis Zutter, SWI | .– | 1968 | Miroslav Cerar, YUG | 19.325 |
| 1904 | Anton Heida, USA | .42 | 1972 | Viktor Klimenko, SOV | 19.125 |
| 1924 | Josef Wilhelm, SWI | 21.23 | 1976 | Zoltán Magyar, HUN | 19.70 |
| 1928 | Hermann Hänggi, SWI | 19.75 | 1980 | Zoltán Magyar, HUN | 19.925 |
| 1932 | Istvän Pelle, HUN | 19.07 | 1984 | (TIE) Li Ning, CHN | 19.95 |
| 1936 | Konrad Frey, GER | 19.333 | | & Peter Vidmar, USA | 19.95 |
| 1948 | (TIE) Paavo Aaltonen, FIN | 19.35 | 1988 | (TIE) Dmitri Bilozerchev, USSR, | 19.95 |
| | Veikko Huhtanen, FIN | 19.35 | | Zsolt Borkai, HUN | 19.95 |
| | & Heikki Savolainen, FIN | 19.35 | | & Lyubomir Geraskov, BUL | 19.95 |
| 1952 | Viktor Chukarin, USSR | 19.50 | 1992 | (TIE) Pae Gil-Su, N. Kor | 9.925 |
| 1956 | Boris Shakhlin, USSR | 19.25 | | & Vitaly Scherbo, UT | 9.925 |
| 1960 | (TIE) Eugen Ekman, FIN | 19.375 | 1996 | Li Donghua, SWI | 9.875 |
| | & Boris Shakhlin, USSR | 19.375 | 2000 | Marius Urzica, ROM | 9.862 |
| 1964 | Miroslav Cerar, YUG | 19.525 | 2004 | Teng Haibin, CHN | 9.837 |

### Rings

| Year | | Points | Year | | Points |
|------|--|--------|------|--|--------|
| 1896 | Ioannis Mitropoulos, GRE | .– | 1972 | Akinori Nakayama, JPN | 19.35 |
| 1904 | Hermann Glass, USA | .45 | 1976 | Nikolai Andrianov, USSR | 19.65 |
| 1924 | Francesco Martino, ITA | 21.553 | 1980 | Aleksandr Dityatin, USSR | 19.875 |
| 1928 | Leon Stukelj, YUG | 19.25 | 1984 | (TIE) Koji Gushiken, JPN | 19.85 |
| 1932 | George Gulack, USA | 18.97 | | & Li Ning, CHN | 19.85 |
| 1936 | Alois Hudec, CZE | 19.433 | 1988 | (TIE) Holger Behrendt, E. Ger | 19.925 |
| 1948 | Karl Frei, SWI | 19.80 | | & Dmitri Bilozerchev, USSR | 19.925 |
| 1952 | Grant Shaginyan, USSR | 19.75 | 1992 | Vitaly Scherbo, UT | 9.937 |
| 1956 | Albert Azaryan, USSR | 19.35 | 1996 | Yuri Chechi, ITA | 9.887 |
| 1960 | Albert Azaryan, USSR | 19.725 | 2000 | Szilveszter Csollany, HUN | 9.850 |
| 1964 | Takuji Haytta, JPN | 19.475 | 2004 | Dimonsthenis Tampakos, GRE | 9.862 |
| 1968 | Akinori Nakayama, JPN | 19.45 | | | |

### Floor Exercise

| Year | | Points | Year | | Points |
|------|--|--------|------|--|--------|
| 1932 | Istvan Pelle, HUN | 9.60 | 1976 | Nikolai Andrianov, USSR | 19.45 |
| 1936 | Georges Miez, SWI | 18.666 | 1980 | Roland Brückner, E. Ger | 19.75 |
| 1948 | Ferenc Pataki, HUN | 19.35 | 1984 | Li Ning, CHN | 19.925 |
| 1952 | William Thoresson, SWE | 19.25 | 1988 | Sergei Kharkov, USSR | 19.925 |
| 1956 | Valentin Muratov, USSR | 19.20 | 1992 | Li Xiaosahuang, CHN | 9.925 |
| 1960 | Nobuyuki Aihara, JPN | 19.45 | 1996 | Ioannis Melissanidis, GRE | 9.850 |
| 1964 | Franco Menichelli, ITA | 19.45 | 2000 | Igors Vihrovs, LAT | 9.812 |
| 1968 | Sawao Kato, JPN | 19.475 | 2004 | Kyle Shewfelt, CAN | 9.787 |
| 1972 | Nikolai Andrianov, USSR | 19.175 | | | |

### Team Combined Exercises

| Year | | Points | Year | | Points |
|------|--|--------|------|--|--------|
| 1904 | United States | 374.43 | 1960 | Japan | 575.20 |
| 1906 | Norway | 19.00 | 1964 | Japan | 577.95 |
| 1908 | Sweden | .438 | 1968 | Japan | 575.90 |
| 1912 | Italy | 265.75 | 1972 | Japan | 571.25 |
| 1920 | Italy | 359.855 | 1976 | Japan | 576.85 |
| 1924 | Italy | 839.058 | 1980 | Soviet Union | 598.60 |
| 1928 | Switzerland | 1718.625 | 1984 | United States | 591.40 |
| 1932 | Italy | 541.850 | 1988 | Soviet Union | 593.35 |
| 1936 | Germany | 657.430 | 1992 | Unified Team | 585.45 |
| 1948 | Finland | 1358.30 | 1996 | Russia | 576.778 |
| 1952 | Soviet Union | 574.40 | 2000 | China | 231.919 |
| 1956 | Soviet Union | 568.25 | 2004 | Japan | 173.821 |

## WOMEN

**At least 4 gold medals** (including team events): Larissa Latynina (9); Vera Cáslavská (7); Polina Astakhova, Nadia Comaneci, Agnes Keleti and Nelli Kim (5); Olga Korbut, Ecaterina Szabó and Lyudmila Tourischeva (4).

### All-Around

| Year | | Points | Year | | Points |
|------|------|--------|------|------|--------|
| 1952 | Maria Gorokhovskaya, USSR | 76.78 | 1980 | Yelena Davydova, USSR | 79.15 |
| 1956 | Larissa Latynina, USSR | 74.933 | 1984 | Mary Lou Retton, USA | 79.175 |
| 1960 | Larissa Latynina, USSR | 77.031 | 1988 | Yelena Shushunova, USSR | 79.662 |
| 1964 | Vera Cáslavská, CZE | 77.564 | 1992 | Tatiana Gutsu, UT | 39.737 |
| 1968 | Vera Cáslavská, CZE | 78.25 | 1996 | Lilia Podkopayeva, UKR | 39.255 |
| 1972 | Lyudmila Tourischeva, USSR | 77.025 | 2000 | Simona Amanar, ROM* | 38.642 |
| 1976 | Nadia Comaneci, ROM | 79.275 | 2004 | Carly Patterson, USA | 38.387 |

*Amanar finished second to **Andreea Raducan**, Romania, who was disqualified for testing positive for pseudo-ephedrine, a drug banned by the IOC and found in Nurofen—an over-the-counter medicine she purportedly took to treat a cold.

### Vault

| Year | | Points | Year | | Points |
|------|------|--------|------|------|--------|
| 1952 | Yekaterina Kalinchuk, USSR | 19.20 | 1984 | Ecaterina Szabó, ROM | 19.875 |
| 1956 | Larissa Latynina, USSR | 18.833 | 1988 | Svetlana Boginskaya, USSR | 19.905 |
| 1960 | Margarita Nikolayeva, USSR | 19.316 | 1992 | (TIE) Henrietta Onodi, HUN | 9.925 |
| 1964 | Vera Cáslavská, CZE | 19.483 | | & Lavinia Milosovici, ROM | 9.925 |
| 1968 | Vera Cáslavská, CZE | 19.775 | 1996 | Simona Amanar, ROM | 9.775 |
| 1972 | Karin Janz, E. Ger | 19.525 | 2000 | Elena Zamolodtchikova, RUS | 9.731 |
| 1976 | Nelli Kim, USSR | 19.80 | 2004 | Monica Rosu, ROM | 9.656 |
| 1980 | Natalia Shaposhnikova, USSR | 19.725 | | | |

### Uneven Bars

| Year | | Points | Year | | Points |
|------|------|--------|------|------|--------|
| 1952 | Margit Korondi, HUN | 19.40 | 1984 | (TIE) Julianne McNamora, USA | 19.95 |
| 1956 | Agnes Keleti, HUN | 18.966 | | & Ma Yanhong, CHN | 19.95 |
| 1960 | Polina Astakhova, USSR | 19.616 | 1988 | Daniela Silivas, ROM | 20.00 |
| 1964 | Polina Astakhova, USSR | 19.332 | 1992 | Lu Li, CHN | 10.00 |
| 1968 | Vera Cáslavská, CZE | 19.65 | 1996 | Svetlana Khorkina, RUS | 9.850 |
| 1972 | Karin Janz, E. Ger | 19.675 | 2000 | Svetlana Khorkina, RUS | 9.862 |
| 1976 | Nadia Comaneci, ROM | 20.00 | 2004 | Emilie Lepennec, FRA | 9.687 |
| 1980 | Maxi Gnauck, E. Ger | 19.875 | | | |

### Balance Beam

| Year | | Points | Year | | Points |
|------|------|--------|------|------|--------|
| 1952 | Nina Bocharova, USSR | 19.22 | 1984 | (TIE) Simona Pauca, ROM | 19.80 |
| 1956 | Agnes Keleti, HUN | 18.80 | | & Ecaterina Szabó, ROM | 19.80 |
| 1960 | Eva Bosakova, CZE | 19.283 | 1988 | Daniela Silivas, ROM | 19.924 |
| 1964 | Vera Cáslavská, CZE | 19.449 | 1992 | Tatiana Lyssenko, UT | 9.975 |
| 1968 | Natalya Kuchinskaya, USSR | 19.65 | 1996 | Shannon Miller, USA | 9.862 |
| 1972 | Olga Korbut, USSR | 19.40 | 2000 | Liu Xuan, CHN | 9.825 |
| 1976 | Nadia Comaneci, ROM | 19.95 | 2004 | Catalina Ponor, ROM | 9.787 |
| 1980 | Nadia Comaneci, ROM | 19.80 | | | |

### Floor Exercise

| Year | | Points | Year | | Points |
|------|------|--------|------|------|--------|
| 1952 | Agnes Keleti, HUN | 19.36 | 1980 | (TIE) Nadia Comaneci, ROM | 19.875 |
| 1956 | (TIE) Agnes Keleti, HUN | 18.733 | | & Nelli Kim, USSR | 19.875 |
| | & Larissa Latynina, USSR | 18.733 | 1984 | Ecaterina Szabó, ROM | 19.975 |
| 1960 | Larissa Latynina, USSR | 19.583 | 1988 | Daniela Silivas, ROM | 19.937 |
| 1964 | Larissa Latynina, USSR | 19.599 | 1992 | Lavinia Milosovici, ROM | 10.000 |
| 1968 | (TIE) Vera Cáslavská, CZE | 19.675 | 1996 | Lilia Podkopayeva, UKR | 9.887 |
| | & Larissa Petrik, USSR | 19.675 | 2000 | Elena Zamolodtchikova, RUS | 9.850 |
| 1972 | Olga Korbut, USSR | 19.575 | 2004 | Catalina Ponor, ROM | 9.750 |
| 1976 | Nelli Kim, USSR | 19.85 | | | |

### Team Combined Exercises

| Year | | Points | Year | | Points |
|------|------|--------|------|------|--------|
| 1928 | Netherlands | 316.75 | 1976 | Soviet Union | 466.00 |
| 1936 | Germany | 506.50 | 1980 | Soviet Union | 394.90 |
| 1948 | Czechoslovakia | 445.45 | 1984 | Romania | 392.02 |
| 1952 | Soviet Union | 527.03 | 1988 | Soviet Union | 395.475 |
| 1956 | Soviet Union | 444.800 | 1992 | Unified Team | 395.666 |
| 1960 | Soviet Union | 382.320 | 1996 | United States | 389.225 |
| 1964 | Soviet Union | 280.890 | 2000 | Romania | 154.608 |
| 1968 | Soviet Union | 382.85 | 2004 | Romania | 114.283 |
| 1972 | Soviet Union | 380.50 | | | |

## SOCCER

### MEN

**Multiple gold medals**: Great Britain and Hungary (3); Uruguay and USSR (2).

| Year | | Year | |
|---|---|---|---|
| 1900 | **Great Britain**, France, Belgium | 1960 | **Yugoslavia**, Denmark, Hungary |
| 1904 | **Canada**, USA I, USA II | 1964 | **Hungary**, Czechoslovakia, Germany |
| 1906 | **Denmark**, Smyrna (Int'l entry), Greece | 1968 | **Hungary**, Bulgaria, Japan |
| 1908 | **Great Britain**, Denmark, Netherlands | 1972 | **Poland**, Hungary, East Germany & Soviet Union |
| 1912 | **Great Britain**, Denmark, Netherlands | 1976 | **East Germany**, Poland, Soviet Union |
| 1920 | **Belgium**, Spain, Netherlands | 1980 | **Czechoslovakia**, East Germany, Soviet Union |
| 1924 | **Uruguay**, Switzerland, Sweden | 1984 | **France**, Brazil, Yugoslavia |
| 1928 | **Uruguay**, Argentina, Italy | 1988 | **Soviet Union**, Brazil, West Germany |
| 1936 | **Italy**, Austria, Norway | 1992 | **Spain**, Poland, Ghana |
| 1948 | **Sweden**, Yugoslavia, Denmark | 1996 | **Nigeria**, Argentina, Brazil |
| 1952 | **Hungary**, Yugoslavia, Sweden | 2000 | **Cameroon**, Spain, Chile |
| 1956 | **Soviet Union**, Yugoslavia, Bulgaria | 2004 | **Argentina**, Paraguay, Italy |

### WOMEN

**Multiple gold medals**: United States (2).

| Year | | Year | |
|---|---|---|---|
| 1996 | **United States**, China, Norway | 2004 | **United States**, Brazil, Germany |
| 2000 | **Norway**, United States, Germany | | |

## SOFTBALL

**Multiple gold medals:** United States (3).

| Year | | Year | |
|---|---|---|---|
| 1996 | **United States**, China, Australia | 2004 | **United States**, Australia, Japan |
| 2000 | **United States**, Japan, Australia | | |

### U.S. Medal-Winning Softball Teams

**1996** (gold medal): P–Lisa Fernandez, Michele Granger, Lori Harrigan and Michele Smith; C–Gillian Boxx and Shelly Stokes; INF–Sheila Cornell, Kim Maher, Leah O'Brien, Dot Richardson, Julie Smith and Dani Tyler; OF–Laura Berg, Dionna Harris; Manager–Ralph Raymond. Final: USA over China, 3-1.

**2000** (gold medal): P–Lisa Fernandez, Lori Harrigan, Danielle Henderson, Michele Smith and Christa Williams; C–Stacey Nuveman and Michelle Venturella; INF–Jennifer Brundage, Crystl Bustos, Sheila Douty, Jennifer McFalls and Dot Richardson; OF–Christie Ambrosi, Laura Berg, Leah O'Brien-Amico; Manager–Ralph Raymond. Final: USA over Japan, 2-1.

**2004** (gold medal): P–Lisa Fernandez, Jennie Finch, Lori Harrigan and Catherine Osterman; C–Stacey Nuveman and Jenny Topping; INF–Crystl Bustos, Jaime Clark, Lovieanne Jung and Natasha Watley; OF–Laura Berg, Nicole Giordano, Kelly Kretschman, Jessica Mendoza and Leah O'Brien-Amico; UT–Tairia Flowers, Amanda Freed and Lauren Lappin ; Manager–Mike Candrea. Final: USA over Australia, 5-1.

## SWIMMING

World and Olympic records below that appear to be broken or equaled by winning times in subsequent years, but are not so indicated, were all broken in preliminary heats leading up to the finals. Some events were not held at every Olympics.

### MEN

**At least 4 gold medals** (including relays): Mark Spitz (9); Matt Biondi (8); Gary Hall Jr. and Michael Phelps (6); Charles Daniels, Tom Jager, Don Schollander, Ian Thorpe and Johnny Weissmuller (5); Tamás Darnyi, Roland Matthes, John Naber, Aleksandr Popov, Murray Rose, Vladimir Salnikov and Henry Taylor (4).

#### 50-meter Freestyle

| Year | | Time | | Year | | Time | |
|---|---|---|---|---|---|---|---|
| 1904 | Zoltán Halmay, HUN (50 yds) | 28.0 | | 1996 | Aleksandr Popov, RUS | 22.13 | |
| 1906-84 | Not held | | | 2000 | (TIE) Anthony Ervin, USA | 21.98 | |
| 1988 | Matt Biondi, USA | 22.14 | **WR** | | & Gary Hall Jr., USA | 21.98 | |
| 1992 | Aleksandr Popov, UT | 21.91 | **OR** | 2004 | Gary Hall Jr., USA | 21.93 | |

#### 100-meter Freestyle

| Year | | Time | | Year | | Time | |
|---|---|---|---|---|---|---|---|
| 1896 | Alfréd Hajós, HUN | 1:22.2 | **OR** | 1936 | Ferenc Csik, HUN | 57.6 | |
| 1904 | Zoltán Halmay, HUN (100 yds) | 1:02.8 | | 1948 | Wally Ris, USA | 57.3 | **OR** |
| 1906 | Charles Daniels, USA | 1:13.4 | | 1952 | Clarke Scholes, USA | 57.4 | |
| 1908 | Charles Daniels, USA | 1:05.6 | **WR** | 1956 | Jon Henricks, AUS | 55.4 | **OR** |
| 1912 | Duke Kahanamoku, USA | 1:03.4 | | 1960 | John Devitt, AUS | 55.2 | **OR** |
| 1920 | Duke Kahanamoku, USA | 1:00.4 | **WR** | 1964 | Don Schollander, USA | 53.4 | **OR** |
| 1924 | Johnny Weissmuller, USA | 59.0 | **OR** | 1968 | Michael Wenden, AUS | 52.2 | **WR** |
| 1928 | Johnny Weissmuller, USA | 58.6 | **OR** | 1972 | Mark Spitz, USA | 51.22 | **WR** |
| 1932 | Yasuji Miyazaki, JPN | 58.2 | | 1976 | Jim Montgomery, USA | 49.99 | **WR** |

| Year | | Time | | Year | | Time | |
|---|---|---|---|---|---|---|---|
| 1980 | Jorg Woithe, E. Ger | .50.40 | | 1996 | Aleksandr Popov, RUS | .48.74 | |
| 1984 | Rowdy Gaines, USA | .49.80 | OR | 2000 | Pieter van den Hoogenband, NED | .48.30 | |
| 1988 | Matt Biondi, USA | .48.63 | OR | 2004 | Pieter van den Hoogenband, NED | .48.17 | |
| 1992 | Aleksandr Popov, UT | .49.02 | | | | | |

## 200-meter Freestyle

| Year | | Time | | Year | | Time | |
|---|---|---|---|---|---|---|---|
| 1900 | Frederick Lane, AUS (220 yds) | .2:25.2 | OR | 1984 | Michael Gross, W. Ger | .1:47.44 | WR |
| 1904 | Charles Daniels, USA (220 yds) | .2:44.2 | | 1988 | Duncan Armstrong, AUS | .1:47.25 | WR |
| 1968 | Michael Wenden, AUS | .1:55.2 | OR | 1992 | Yevgeny Sadovyi, UT | .1:46.70 | WR |
| 1972 | Mark Spitz, USA | .1:52.78 | WR | 1996 | Danyon Loader, NZE | .1:47.63 | |
| 1976 | Bruce Furniss, USA | .1:50.29 | WR | 2000 | Pieter van den Hoogenband, NED | .1:45.35 | WR |
| 1980 | Sergei Kopliakov, USSR | .1:49.81 | OR | 2004 | Ian Thorpe, AUS | .1:44.71 | OR |

## 400-meter Freestyle

| Year | | Time | | Year | | Time | |
|---|---|---|---|---|---|---|---|
| 1896 | Paul Neumann, AUT (550m) | .8:12.6 | | 1960 | Murray Rose, AUS | .4:18.3 | OR |
| 1904 | Charles Daniels, USA (440 yds) | .6:16.2 | | 1964 | Don Schollander, USA | .4:12.2 | OR |
| 1906 | Otto Scheff, AUT | .6:23.8 | | 1968 | Mike Burton, USA | .4:09.0 | OR |
| 1908 | Henry Taylor, GBR | .5:36.8 | | 1972 | Bradford Cooper, AUS* | .4:00.27 | OR |
| 1912 | George Hodgson, CAN | .5:24.4 | | 1976 | Brian Goodell, USA | .3:51.93 | WR |
| 1920 | Norman Ross, USA | .5:26.8 | | 1980 | Vladimir Salnikov, USSR | .3:51.31 | |
| 1924 | Johnny Weissmuller, USA | .5:04.2 | OR | 1984 | George DiCarlo, USA | .3:51.23 | |
| 1928 | Alberto Zorilla, ARG | .5:01.6 | OR | 1988 | Uwe Dassler, E. Ger | .3:46.95 | WR |
| 1932 | Buster Crabbe, USA | .4:48.4 | OR | 1992 | Yevgeny Sadovyi, UT | .3:45.00 | WR |
| 1936 | Jack Medica, USA | .4:44.5 | OR | 1996 | Danyon Loader, NZE | .3:47.97 | |
| 1948 | Bill Smith, USA | .4:41.0 | OR | 2000 | Ian Thorpe, AUS | .3:40.59 | WR |
| 1952 | Jean Boiteux, FRA | .4:30.7 | OR | 2004 | Ian Thorpe, AUS | .3:43.10 | |
| 1956 | Murray Rose, AUS | .4:27.3 | OR | | | | |

*Cooper finished second to Rick DeMont of the U.S., who was disqualified when he flunked the post-race drug test (his asthma medication was on the IOC's banned list).

## 1500-meter Freestyle

| Year | | Time | | Year | | Time | |
|---|---|---|---|---|---|---|---|
| 1896 | Alfréd Hajós, HUN (1200m) | .18:22.2 | OR | 1956 | Murray Rose, AUS | .17:58.9 | |
| 1900 | John Arthur Jarvis, GBR (1000m) | .13:40.2 | | 1960 | Jon Konrads, AUS | .17:19.6 | OR |
| 1904 | Emil Rausch, GER (1 mile) | .27:18.2 | | 1964 | Robert Windle, AUS | .17:01.7 | OR |
| 1906 | Henry Taylor, GBR (1 mile) | .28:28.0 | | 1968 | Mike Burton, USA | .16:38.9 | OR |
| 1908 | Henry Taylor, GBR | .22:48.4 | WR | 1972 | Mike Burton, USA | .15:52.58 | WR |
| 1912 | George Hodgson, CAN | .22:00.0 | WR | 1976 | Brian Goodell, USA | .15:02.40 | WR |
| 1920 | Norman Ross, USA | .22:23.2 | | 1980 | Vladimir Salnikov, USSR | .14:58.27 | WR |
| 1924 | Andrew (Boy) Charlton, AUS | .20:06.6 | WR | 1984 | Mike O'Brien, USA | .15:05.20 | |
| 1928 | Arne Borge, SWE | .19:51.8 | OR | 1988 | Vladimir Salnikov, USSR | .15:00.40 | |
| 1932 | Kusuo Kitamura, JPN | .19:12.4 | | 1992 | Kieren Perkins, AUS | .14:43.48 | WR |
| 1936 | Noboru Terada, JPN | .19:13.7 | | 1996 | Kieren Perkins, AUS | .14:56.40 | |
| 1948 | James McLane, USA | .19:18.5 | | 2000 | Grant Hackett, AUS | .14:48.33 | |
| 1952 | Ford Konno, USA | .18:30.3 | OR | 2004 | Grant Hackett, AUS | .14:43.40 | OR |

## 100-meter Backstroke

| Year | | Time | | Year | | Time | |
|---|---|---|---|---|---|---|---|
| 1904 | Walter Brack, GER (100 yds) | .1:16.8 | | 1960 | David Theile, AUS | .1:01.9 | OR |
| 1908 | Arno Bieberstein, GER | .1:24.6 | WR | 1968 | Roland Matthes, E. Ger | .58.7 | OR |
| 1912 | Harry Hebner, USA | .1:21.2 | | 1972 | Roland Matthes, E. Ger | .56.58 | OR |
| 1920 | Warren Kealoha, USA | .1:15.2 | | 1976 | John Naber, USA | .55.49 | WR |
| 1924 | Warren Kealoha, USA | .1:13.2 | OR | 1980 | Bengt Baron, SWE | .56.33 | |
| 1928 | George Kojac, USA | .1:08.2 | WR | 1984 | Rick Carey, USA | .55.79 | |
| 1932 | Masaji Kiyokawa, JPN | .1:08.6 | | 1988 | Daichi Suzuki, JPN | .55.05 | |
| 1936 | Adolf Kiefer, USA | .1:05.9 | OR | 1992 | Mark Tewksbury, CAN | .53.98 | OR |
| 1948 | Allen Stack, USA | .1:06.4 | | 1996 | Jeff Rouse, USA | .54.10 | |
| 1952 | Yoshinobu Oyakawa, USA | .1:05.4 | OR | 2000 | Lenny Krayzelburg, USA | .53.72 | OR |
| 1956 | David Theile, AUS | .1:02.2 | OR | 2004 | Aaron Peirsol, USA | .54.06 | |

## 200-meter Backstroke

| Year | | Time | | Year | | Time | |
|---|---|---|---|---|---|---|---|
| 1900 | Ernst Hoppenberg, GER | .2:47.0 | | 1984 | Rick Carey, USA | .2:00.23 | |
| 1964 | Jed Graef, USA | .2:10.3 | WR | 1988 | Igor Poliansky, USSR | .1:59.37 | |
| 1968 | Roland Matthes, E. Ger | .2:09.6 | OR | 1992 | Martin Lopez-Zubero, SPA | .1:58.47 | OR |
| 1972 | Roland Matthes, E. Ger | .2:02.82 | =WR | 1996 | Brad Bridgewater, USA | .1:58.54 | |
| 1976 | John Naber, USA | .1:59.19 | WR | 2000 | Lenny Krayzelburg, USA | .1:56.76 | OR |
| 1980 | Sándor Wládar, HUN | .2:01.93 | | 2004 | Aaron Peirsol, USA | .1:54.95 | OR |

## 100-meter Breaststroke

| Year | | Time | | Year | | Time | |
|------|------|------|------|------|------|------|------|
| 1968 | Don McKenzie, USA | 1:07.7 | OR | 1988 | Adrian Moorhouse, GBR | 1:02.04 | |
| 1972 | Nobutaka Taguchi, JPN | 1:04.94 | WR | 1992 | Nelson Diebel, USA | 1:01.50 | OR |
| 1976 | John Hencken, USA | 1:03.11 | WR | 1996 | Fred deBurghgraeve, BEL | 1:00.60 | |
| 1980 | Duncan Goodhew, GBR | 1:03.44 | | 2000 | Domenico Fioravanti, ITA | 1:00.46 | OR |
| 1984 | Steve Lundquist, USA | 1:01.65 | WR | 2004 | Kosuke Kitajima, JPN | 1:00.08 | |

## 200-meter Breaststroke

| Year | | Time | | Year | | Time | |
|------|------|------|------|------|------|------|------|
| 1908 | Frederick Holman, GBR | 3:09.2 | WR | 1964 | Ian O'Brien, AUS | 2:27.8 | WR |
| 1912 | Walter Bathe, GER | 3:01.8 | OR | 1968 | Felipe Muñoz, MEX | 2:28.7 | |
| 1920 | Hakan Malmroth, SWE | 3:04.4 | | 1972 | John Hencken, USA | 2:21.55 | WR |
| 1924 | Robert Skelton, USA | 2:56.6 | | 1976 | David Wilkie, GBR | 2:15.11 | WR |
| 1928 | Yoshiyuki Tsuruta, JPN | 2:48.8 | OR | 1980 | Robertas Zhulpa, USSR | 2:15.85 | |
| 1932 | Yoshiyuki Tsuruta, JPN | 2:45.4 | | 1984 | Victor Davis, CAN | 2:13.34 | WR |
| 1936 | Tetsuo Hamuro, JPN | 2:41.5 | OR | 1988 | József Szabó, HUN | 2:13.52 | |
| 1948 | Joseph Verdeur, USA | 2:39.3 | OR | 1992 | Mike Barrowman, USA | 2:10.16 | WR |
| 1952 | John Davies, AUS | 2:34.4 | OR | 1996 | Norbert Rozsa, HUN | 2:12.57 | |
| 1956 | Masaru Furukawa, JPN | 2:34.7* | OR | 2000 | Domenico Fioravanti, ITA | 2:10.87 | |
| 1960 | Bill Mulliken, USA | 2:37.4 | | 2004 | Kosuke Kitajima, JPN | 2:09.44 | OR |

*In 1956, the butterfly stroke and breaststroke were separated into two different events.

## 100-meter Butterfly

| Year | | Time | | Year | | Time | |
|------|------|------|------|------|------|------|------|
| 1968 | Doug Russell, USA | 55.9 | OR | 1988 | Anthony Nesty, SUR | 53.0 | OR |
| 1972 | Mark Spitz, USA | 54.27 | WR | 1992 | Pablo Morales, USA | 53.32 | |
| 1976 | Matt Vogel, USA | 54.35 | | 1996 | Dennis Pankratov, RUS | 52.27 | |
| 1980 | Pär Arvidsson, SWE | 54.92 | | 2000 | Lars Frolander, SWE | 52.00 | |
| 1984 | Michael Gross, W. Ger | 53.08 | WR | 2004 | Michael Phelps, USA | 51.25 | OR |

## 200-meter Butterfly

| Year | | Time | | Year | | Time | |
|------|------|------|------|------|------|------|------|
| 1956 | Bill Yorzyk, USA | 2:19.3 | OR | 1980 | Sergei Fesenko, USSR | 1:59.76 | |
| 1960 | Mike Troy, USA | 2:12.8 | WR | 1984 | Jon Sieben, AUS | 1:57.04 | WR |
| 1964 | Kevin Berry, AUS | 2:06.6 | WR | 1988 | Michael Gross, W. Ger | 1:56.94 | OR |
| 1968 | Carl Robie, USA | 2:08.7 | | 1992 | Melvin Stewart, USA | 1:56.26 | OR |
| 1972 | Mark Spitz, USA | 2:00.70 | WR | 1996 | Dennis Pankratov, RUS | 1:56.51 | |
| 1976 | Mike Bruner, USA | 1:59.23 | WR | 2000 | Tom Malchow, USA | 1:55.35 | OR |
| | | | | 2004 | Michael Phelps, USA | 1:54.04 | OR |

## 200-meter Individual Medley

| Year | | Time | | Year | | Time | |
|------|------|------|------|------|------|------|------|
| 1968 | Charles Hickcox, USA | 2:12.0 | OR | 1992 | Tamás Darnyi, HUN | 2:00.76 | |
| 1972 | Gunnar Larsson, SWE | 2:07.17 | WR | 1996 | Attila Czene, HUN | 1:59.91 | |
| 1984 | Alex Baumann, CAN | 2:01.42 | WR | 2000 | Massimiliano Rosolino, ITA | 1:58.98 | OR |
| 1988 | Tamás Darnyi, HUN | 2:00.17 | WR | 2004 | Michael Phelps, USA | 1:57.14 | OR |

## 400-meter Individual Medley

| Year | | Time | | Year | | Time | |
|------|------|------|------|------|------|------|------|
| 1964 | Richard Roth, USA | 4:45.4 | WR | 1988 | Tamás Darnyi, HUN | 4:14.75 | WR |
| 1968 | Charles Hickcox, USA | 4:48.4 | | 1992 | Tamás Darnyi, HUN | 4:14.23 | OR |
| 1972 | Gunnar Larsson, SWE | 4:31.98 | OR | 1996 | Tom Dolan, USA | 4:14.90 | |
| 1976 | Rod Strachan, USA | 4:23.68 | WR | 2000 | Tom Dolan, USA | 4:11.76 | WR |
| 1980 | Aleksandr Sidorenko, USSR | 4:22.89 | OR | 2004 | Michael Phelps, USA | 4:08.26 | WR |
| 1984 | Alex Baumann, CAN | 4:17.41 | WR | | | | |

## 4x100-meter Freestyle Relay

| Year | | Time | | Year | | Time | |
|------|------|------|------|------|------|------|------|
| 1964 | United States | 3:32.2 | WR | 1988 | United States | 3:16.53 | WR |
| 1968 | United States | 3:31.7 | WR | 1992 | United States | 3:16.74 | |
| 1972 | United States | 3:26.42 | WR | 1996 | United States | 3:15.41 | |
| 1976-80 | Not held | | | 2000 | Australia | 3:13.67 | WR |
| 1984 | United States | 3:19.03 | WR | 2004 | South Africa | 3:13.17 | WR |

## 4x200-meter Freestyle Relay

| Year | | Time | | Year | | Time | |
|------|------|------|------|------|------|------|------|
| 1906 | Hungary (x250m) | 16:52.4 | | 1948 | United States | 8:46.0 | WR |
| 1908 | Great Britain | 10:55.6 | WR | 1952 | United States | 8:31.1 | OR |
| 1912 | Australia/New Zealand | 10:11.6 | WR | 1956 | Australia | 8:23.6 | WR |
| 1920 | United States | 10:04.4 | WR | 1960 | United States | 8:10.2 | WR |
| 1924 | United States | 9:53.4 | WR | 1964 | United States | 7:52.1 | WR |
| 1928 | United States | 9:36.2 | WR | 1968 | United States | 7:52.33 | |
| 1932 | Japan | 8:58.4 | WR | 1972 | United States | 7:35.78 | WR |
| 1936 | Japan | 8:51.5 | | 1976 | United States | 7:23.22 | WR |

| Year | | Time | | Year | | Time | |
|------|--|------|--|------|--|------|--|
| 1980 | Soviet Union | 7:23.50 | | 1996 | United States | 7:14.84 | |
| 1984 | United States | 7:15.69 | WR | 2000 | Australia | 7:07.05 | WR |
| 1988 | United States | 7:12.51 | WR | 2004 | United States | 7:07.33 | |
| 1992 | Unified Team | 7:11.95 | WR | | | | |

### 4x100-meter Medley Relay

| Year | | Time | | Year | | Time | |
|------|--|------|--|------|--|------|--|
| 1960 | United States | 4:05.4 | WR | 1984 | United States | 3:39.30 | WR |
| 1964 | United States | 3:58.4 | WR | 1988 | United States | 3:36.93 | WR |
| 1968 | United States | 3:54.9 | WR | 1992 | United States | 3:36.93 | =WR |
| 1972 | United States | 3:48.16 | WR | 1996 | United States | 3:34.84 | |
| 1976 | United States | 3:42.22 | WR | 2000 | United States | 3:33.73 | WR |
| 1980 | Australia | 3:45.70 | | 2004 | United States | 3:30.68 | WR |

## WOMEN

**At least 4 gold medals** (including relays): Jenny Thompson (8); Kristin Otto and Amy Van Dyken (6); Krisztina Egerszegi (5), Kornelia Ender, Janet Evans, Dawn Fraser and Dara Torres (4).

### 50-meter Freestyle

| Year | | Time | | Year | | Time |
|------|--|------|--|------|--|------|
| 1988 | Kristin Otto, E. Ger | 25.49 | OR | 2000 | Inge de Bruijn, NED | 24.32 |
| 1992 | Yang Wenyi, CHN | 24.79 | WR | 2004 | Inge de Bruijn, NED | 24.58 |
| 1996 | Amy Van Dyken, USA | 24.87 | | | | |

### 100-meter Freestyle

| Year | | Time | | Year | | Time | |
|------|--|------|--|------|--|------|--|
| 1912 | Fanny Durack, AUS | 1:22.2 | | 1968 | Jan Henne, USA | 1:00.0 | |
| 1920 | Ethelda Bleibtrey, USA | 1:13.6 | WR | 1972 | Sandra Neilson, USA | 58.59 | OR |
| 1924 | Ethel Lackie, USA | 1:12.4 | | 1976 | Kornelia Ender, E. Ger | 55.65 | WR |
| 1928 | Albina Osipowich, USA | 1:11.0 | OR | 1980 | Barbara Krause, E. Ger | 54.79 | WR |
| 1932 | Helene Madison, USA | 1:06.8 | OR | 1984 | (TIE) Nancy Hogshead, USA | 55.92 | |
| 1936 | Rie Mastenbroek, NED | 1:05.9 | OR | | & Carrie Steinseifer, USA | 55.92 | |
| 1948 | Greta Andersen, DEN | 1:06.3 | | 1988 | Kristin Otto, E. Ger | 54.93 | |
| 1952 | Katalin Szöke, HUN | 1:06.8 | | 1992 | Zhuang Yong, CHN | 54.65 | OR |
| 1956 | Dawn Fraser, AUS | 1:02.0 | WR | 1996 | Le Jingyi, CHN | 54.50 | |
| 1960 | Dawn Fraser, AUS | 1:01.2 | OR | 2000 | Inge de Bruijn, NED | 53.83 | |
| 1964 | Dawn Fraser, AUS | 59.5 | OR | 2004 | Jodie Henry, AUS | 53.84 | |

### 200-meter Freestyle

| Year | | Time | | Year | | Time | |
|------|--|------|--|------|--|------|--|
| 1968 | Debbie Meyer, USA | 2:10.5 | OR | 1988 | Heike Friedrich, E. Ger | 1:57.65 | OR |
| 1972 | Shane Gould, AUS | 2:03.56 | WR | 1992 | Nicole Haislett, USA | 1:57.90 | |
| 1976 | Kornelia Ender, E. Ger | 1:59.26 | WR | 1996 | Claudia Poll, CRC | 1:58.16 | |
| 1980 | Barbara Krause, E. Ger | 1:58.33 | WR | 2000 | Susie O'Neill, AUS | 1:58.24 | |
| 1984 | Mary Wayte, USA | 1:59.23 | | 2004 | Camelia Potec, ROM | 1:58.03 | |

### 400-meter Freestyle

| Year | | Time | | Year | | Time | |
|------|--|------|--|------|--|------|--|
| 1920 | Ethelda Bleibtrey, USA (300m) | 4:34.0 | WR | 1968 | Debbie Meyer, USA | 4:31.8 | OR |
| 1924 | Martha Norelius, USA | 6:02.2 | OR | 1972 | Shane Gould, AUS | 4:19.44 | WR |
| 1928 | Martha Norelius, USA | 5:42.8 | WR | 1976 | Petra Thümer, E. Ger | 4:09.89 | WR |
| 1932 | Helene Madison, USA | 5:28.5 | WR | 1980 | Ines Diers, E. Ger | 4:08.76 | OR |
| 1936 | Rie Mastenbroek, NED | 5:26.4 | OR | 1984 | Tiffany Cohen, USA | 4:07.10 | OR |
| 1948 | Ann Curtis, USA | 5:17.8 | OR | 1988 | Janet Evans, USA | 4:03.85 | WR |
| 1952 | Valéria Gyenge, HUN | 5:12.1 | OR | 1992 | Dagmar Hase, GER | 4:07.18 | |
| 1956 | Lorraine Crapp, AUS | 4:54.6 | OR | 1996 | Michelle Smith, IRE | 4:07.25 | |
| 1960 | Chris von Saltza, USA | 4:50.6 | OR | 2000 | Brooke Bennett, USA | 4:05.80 | |
| 1964 | Ginny Duenkel, USA | 4:43.3 | OR | 2004 | Laure Manaudou, FRA | 4:05.34 | |

### 800-meter Freestyle

| Year | | Time | | Year | | Time | |
|------|--|------|--|------|--|------|--|
| 1968 | Debbie Meyer, USA | 9:24.0 | OR | 1988 | Janet Evans, USA | 8:20.20 | OR |
| 1972 | Keena Rothhammer, USA | 8:53.68 | WR | 1992 | Janet Evans, USA | 8:25.52 | |
| 1976 | Petra Thümer, E. Ger | 8:37.14 | WR | 1996 | Brooke Bennett, USA | 8:27.89 | |
| 1980 | Michelle Ford, AUS | 8:28.90 | OR | 2000 | Brooke Bennett, USA | 8:19.67 | OR |
| 1984 | Tiffany Cohen, USA | 8:24.95 | OR | 2004 | Ai Shibata, JPN | 8:24.54 | |

### 100-meter Backstroke

| Year | | Time | | Year | | Time | |
|------|--|------|--|------|--|------|--|
| 1924 | Sybil Bauer, USA | 1:23.2 | OR | 1972 | Melissa Belote, USA | 1:05.78 | OR |
| 1928 | Maria Braun, NED | 1:22.0 | | 1976 | Ulrike Richter, E. Ger | 1:01.83 | OR |
| 1932 | Eleanor Holm, USA | 1:19.4 | | 1980 | Rica Reinisch, E. Ger | 1:00.86 | WR |
| 1936 | Dina Senff, NED | 1:18.9 | | 1984 | Theresa Andrews, USA | 1:02.55 | |
| 1948 | Karen-Margrete Harup, DEN | 1:14.4 | OR | 1988 | Kristin Otto, E. Ger | 1:00.89 | |
| 1952 | Joan Harrison, S. Afr. | 1:14.3 | | 1992 | Krisztina Egerszegi, HUN | 1:00.68 | OR |
| 1956 | Judy Grinham, GBR | 1:12.9 | OR | 1996 | Beth Botsford, USA | 1:01.19 | |
| 1960 | Lynn Burke, USA | 1:09.3 | OR | 2000 | Diana Mocanu, ROM | 1:00.21 | OR |
| 1964 | Cathy Ferguson, USA | 1:07.7 | WR | 2004 | Natalie Coughlin, USA | 1:03.37 | |
| 1968 | Kaye Hall, USA | 1:06.2 | WR | | | | |

### 200-meter Backstroke

| Year | | Time | | Year | | Time | |
|------|--|------|--|------|--|------|--|
| 1968 | Pokey Watson, USA | 2:24.8 | OR | 1988 | Krisztina Egerszegi, HUN | 2:09.29 | OR |
| 1972 | Melissa Belote, USA | 2:19.19 | WR | 1992 | Krisztina Egerszegi, HUN | 2:07.06 | OR |
| 1976 | Ulrike Richter, E. Ger | 2:13.43 | OR | 1996 | Krisztina Egerszegi, HUN | 2:07.83 | |
| 1980 | Rica Reinisch, E. Ger | 2:11.77 | WR | 2000 | Diana Mocanu, ROM | 2:08.16 | |
| 1984 | Jolanda de Rover, NED | 2:12.38 | | 2004 | Kirsty Coventry, ZIM | 2:09.19 | |

### 100-meter Breaststroke

| Year | | Time | | Year | | Time | |
|------|--|------|--|------|--|------|--|
| 1968 | Djurdjica Bjedov, YUG | 1:15.8 | OR | 1988 | Tania Dangalakova, BUL | 1:07.95 | OR |
| 1972 | Cathy Carr, USA | 1:13.58 | WR | 1992 | Yelena Rudkovskaya, UT | 1:08.00 | |
| 1976 | Hannelore Anke, E. Ger | 1:11.16 | | 1996 | Penny Heyns, RSA | 1:07.73 | |
| 1980 | Ute Geweniger, E. Ger | 1:10.22 | | 2000 | Megan Quann, USA | 1:07.05 | |
| 1984 | Petra van Staveren, NED | 1:09.88 | OR | 2004 | Luo Xuejuan, CHN | 1:06.64 | OR |

### 200-meter Breaststroke

| Year | | Time | | Year | | Time | |
|------|--|------|--|------|--|------|--|
| 1924 | Lucy Morton, GBR | 3:33.2 | OR | 1972 | Beverley Whitfield, AUS | 2:41.71 | OR |
| 1928 | Hilde Schrader, GER | 3:12.6 | | 1976 | Marina Koshevaya, USSR | 2:33.35 | WR |
| 1932 | Clare Dennis, AUS | 3:06.3 | OR | 1980 | Lina Kaciusyte, USSR | 2:29.54 | OR |
| 1936 | Hideko Maehata, JPN | 3:03.6 | | 1984 | Anne Ottenbrite, CAN | 2:30.38 | |
| 1948 | Petronella van Vliet, NED | 2:57.2 | | 1988 | Silke Hörner, E. Ger | 2:26.71 | WR |
| 1952 | éva Székely, HUN | 2:51.7 | OR | 1992 | Kyoko Iwasaki, JPN | 2:26.65 | OR |
| 1956 | Ursula Happe, GER | 2:53.1 | | 1996 | Penny Heyns, RSA | 2:25.41 | |
| 1960 | Anita Lonsbrough, GBR | 2:49.5 | WR | 2000 | Agnes Kovacs, HUN | 2:24.35 | |
| 1964 | Galina Prozumenshikova, USSR | 2:46.4 | OR | 2004 | Amanda Beard, USA | 2:23.37 | OR |
| 1968 | Sharon Wichman, USA | 2:44.4 | OR | | | | |

### 100-meter Butterfly

| Year | | Time | | Year | | Time | |
|------|--|------|--|------|--|------|--|
| 1956 | Shelley Mann, USA | 1:11.0 | OR | 1984 | Mary T. Meagher, USA | .59.26 | |
| 1960 | Carolyn Schuler, USA | 1:09.5 | OR | 1988 | Kristin Otto, E. Ger | .59.00 | OR |
| 1964 | Sharon Stouder, USA | 1:04.7 | WR | 1992 | Qian Hong, CHN | .58.62 | OR |
| 1968 | Lynn McClements, AUS | 1:05.5 | | 1996 | Amy Van Dyken, USA | .59.13 | |
| 1972 | Mayumi Aoki, JPN | 1:03.34 | WR | 2000 | Inge de Bruijn, NED | .56.61 | WR |
| 1976 | Kornelia Ender, E. Ger | 1:00.13 | =WR | 2004 | Petria Thomas, AUS | .57.72 | |
| 1980 | Caren Metschuck, E. Ger | 1:00.42 | | | | | |

### 200-meter Butterfly

| Year | | Time | | Year | | Time | |
|------|--|------|--|------|--|------|--|
| 1968 | Ada Kok, NED | 2:24.7 | OR | 1988 | Kathleen Nord, E. Ger | 2:09.51 | |
| 1972 | Karen Moe, USA | 2:15.57 | WR | 1992 | Summer Sanders, USA | 2:08.67 | |
| 1976 | Andrea Pollack, E. Ger | 2:11.41 | OR | 1996 | Susie O'Neill, AUS | 2:07.76 | |
| 1980 | Ines Geissler, E. Ger | 2:10.44 | OR | 2000 | Misty Hyman, USA | 2:05.88 | OR |
| 1984 | Mary T. Meagher, USA | 2:06.90 | OR | 2004 | Otylia Jedrzejczak, POL | 2:06.05 | |

### 200-meter Individual Medley

| Year | | Time | | Year | | Time | |
|------|--|------|--|------|--|------|--|
| 1968 | Claudia Kolb, USA | 2:24.7 | OR | 1992 | Lin Li, CHN | 2:11.65 | WR |
| 1972 | Shane Gould, AUS | 2:23.07 | WR | 1996 | Michelle Smith, IRE | 2:13.93 | |
| 1984 | Tracy Caulkins, USA | 2:12.64 | OR | 2000 | Yana Klochkova, UKR | 2:10.68 | OR |
| 1988 | Daniela Hunger, E. Ger | 2:12.59 | OR | 2004 | Yana Klochkova, UKR | 2:11.14 | |

### 400-meter Individual Medley

| Year | | Time | | Year | | Time | |
|------|--|------|--|------|--|------|--|
| 1964 | Donna de Varona, USA | 5:18.7 | OR | 1988 | Janet Evans, USA | 4:37.76 | |
| 1968 | Claudia Kolb, USA | 5:08.5 | OR | 1992 | Krisztina Egerszegi, HUN | 4:36.54 | |
| 1972 | Gail Neall, AUS | 5:02.97 | WR | 1996 | Michelle Smith, IRE | 4:39.18 | |
| 1976 | Ulrike Tauber, E. Ger | 4:42.77 | WR | 2000 | Yana Klochkova, UKR | 4:33.59 | WR |
| 1980 | Petra Schneider, E. Ger | 4:36.29 | WR | 2004 | Yana Klochkova, UKR | 4:34.83 | |
| 1984 | Tracy Caulkins, USA | 4:39.24 | | | | | |

### 4x100-meter Freestyle Relay

| Year | | Time | | Year | | Time | |
|------|--|------|--|------|--|------|--|
| 1912 | Great Britain | 5:52.8 | WR | 1968 | United States | 4:02.5 | OR |
| 1920 | United States | 5:11.6 | WR | 1972 | United States | 3:55.19 | WR |
| 1924 | United States | 4:58.8 | WR | 1976 | United States | 3:44.82 | WR |
| 1928 | United States | 4:47.6 | WR | 1980 | East Germany | 3:42.71 | WR |
| 1932 | United States | 4:38.0 | WR | 1984 | United States | 3:43.43 | |
| 1936 | Netherlands | 4:36.0 | WR | 1988 | East Germany | 3:40.63 | OR |
| 1948 | United States | 4:29.2 | WR | 1992 | United States | 3:39.46 | WR |
| 1952 | Hungary | 4:24.4 | WR | 1996 | United States | 3:39.29 | |
| 1956 | Australia | 4:17.1 | WR | 2000 | United States | 3:36.61 | WR |
| 1960 | United States | 4:08.9 | WR | 2004 | Australia | 3:35.94 | WR |
| 1964 | United States | 4:03.8 | WR | | | | |

## 4x200-meter Freestyle Relay

| Year | | Time | | Year | | Time | |
|------|--|------|--|------|--|------|--|
| 1996 | United States | 7:59.87 | | 2004 | United States | 7:53.42 | **WR** |
| 2000 | United States | 7:57.80 | **OR** | | | | |

## 4x100-meter Medley Relay

| Year | | Time | | Year | | Time | |
|------|--|------|--|------|--|------|--|
| 1960 | United States | 4:41.1 | **WR** | 1984 | United States | 4:08.34 | |
| 1964 | United States | 4:33.9 | **WR** | 1988 | East Germany | 4:03.74 | **OR** |
| 1968 | United States | 4:28.3 | **OR** | 1992 | United States | 4:02.54 | **WR** |
| 1972 | United States | 4:20.75 | **WR** | 1996 | United States | 4:02.88 | |
| 1976 | East Germany | 4:07.95 | **WR** | 2000 | United States | 3:58.30 | **WR** |
| 1980 | East Germany | 4:06.67 | **WR** | 2004 | Australia | 3:57.32 | **WR** |

## TENNIS

### MEN

**Multiple gold medals** (including men's doubles): John Boland, Max Decugis, Laurie Doherty, Reggie Doherty, Arthur Gore, Andre Grobert, Nicolas Massu, Vincent Richards, Charles Winslow and Beals Wright (2).

### Singles

| Year | | | Year | | |
|------|--|--|------|--|--|
| 1896 | John Boland | Great Britain/Ireland | 1920 | Louis Raymond | South Africa |
| 1900 | Laurie Doherty, | Great Britain | 1924 | Vincent Richards | United States |
| 1904 | Beals Wright | United States | 1928-84 | Not held | |
| 1906 | Max Decugis | France | 1988 | Miloslav Mecir | Czechoslovakia |
| 1908 | Josiah Ritchie | Great Britain | 1992 | Marc Rosset | Switzerland |
| | (Indoor) Arthur Gore | Great Britain | 1996 | Andre Agassi | United States |
| 1912 | Charles Winslow | South Africa | 2000 | Yevgeny Kafelnikov | Russia |
| | (Indoor) André Gobert | France | 2004 | Nicolas Massu | Chile |

### Doubles

| Year | | Year | |
|------|--|------|--|
| 1896 | John Boland, IRE & Fritz Traun, GER | 1920 | Noel Turnbull & Max Woosnam, GBR |
| 1900 | Laurie and Reggie Doherty, GBR | 1924 | Vincent Richards & Frank Hunter, USA |
| 1904 | Edgar Leonard & Beals Wright, USA | 1928-84 | Not held |
| 1906 | Max Decugis & Maurice Germot, FRA | 1988 | Ken Flach & Robert Seguso, USA |
| 1908 | George Hillyard & Reggie Doherty, GBR | 1992 | Boris Becker & Michael Stich, GER |
| | (Indoor) Arthur Gore & Herbert Barrett, GBR | 1996 | Todd Woodbridge & Mark Woodforde, AUS |
| 1912 | Charles Winslow & Harold Kitson, S. Afr. | 2000 | Sebastien Lareau & Daniel Nestor, CAN |
| | (Indoor) Andre Gobert & Maurice Germot, FRA | 2004 | Fernando Gonzalez & Nicolas Massu, CHI |

### WOMEN

**Multiple gold medals** (including women's doubles): Helen Wills, Gigi Fernandez, Mary Joe Fernandez and Venus Williams (2).

### Singles

| Year | | | Year | | |
|------|--|--|------|--|--|
| 1900 | Charlotte Cooper | Great Britain | 1924 | Helen Wills | United States |
| 1906 | Esmee Simiriotou | Greece | 1928-84 | Not held | |
| 1908 | Dorothea Chambers | Great Britain | 1988 | Steffi Graf | West Germany |
| | (Indoor) Gwen Eastlake-Smith | Great Britain | 1992 | Jennifer Capriati | United States |
| 1912 | Marguerite Broquedis | France | 1996 | Lindsay Davenport | United States |
| | (Indoor) Edith Hannam | Great Britain | 2000 | Venus Williams | United States |
| 1920 | Suzanne Lenglen | France | 2004 | Justine Henin-Hardenne | Belgium |

### Doubles

| Year | | Year | |
|------|--|------|--|
| 1920 | Winifred McNair & Kitty McKane, GBR | 1992 | Gigi Fernandez & Mary Joe Fernandez, USA |
| 1924 | Hazel Wightman & Helen Wills, USA | 1996 | Gigi Fernandez & Mary Joe Fernandez, USA |
| 1928-84 | Not held | 2000 | Serena Williams & Venus Williams, USA |
| 1988 | Pam Shriver & Zina Garrison, USA | 2004 | Li Ting & Sun Tian Tian, CHN |

## TRACK & FIELD

World and Olympic records below that appear to be broken or equaled by winning times, heights and distances in subsequent years, but are not so indicated, were all broken in preliminary races and field events leading up to the finals.

### MEN

**At least 4 gold medals** (including relays and discontinued events): Ray Ewry (10); Carl Lewis and Paavo Nurmi (9); Ville Ritola and Martin Sheridan (5); Harrison Dillard, Archie Hahn, Michael Johnson, Hannes Kolehmainen, Alvin Kraenzlein, Eric Lemming, Jim Lightbody, Al Oerter, Jesse Owens, Meyer Prinstein, Mel Sheppard, Lasse Viren and Emil Zátopek (4). Note that all of Ewry's gold medals came before 1912, in the Standing High Jump, Standing Long Jump and Standing Triple Jump.

### 100 meters

| Year | | Time | | Year | | Time | |
|---|---|---|---|---|---|---|---|
| 1896 | Tom Burke, USA | 12.0 | | 1960 | Armin Hary, GER | 10.2 | **OR** |
| 1900 | Frank Jarvis, USA | 11.0 | | 1964 | Bob Hayes, USA | 10.0 | **=WR** |
| 1904 | Archie Hahn, USA | 11.0 | | 1968 | Jim Hines, USA | 9.95 | **WR** |
| 1906 | Archie Hahn, USA | 11.2 | | 1972 | Valery Borzov, USSR | 10.14 | |
| 1908 | Reggie Walker, S. Afr. | 10.8 | **=OR** | 1976 | Hasely Crawford, TRI | 10.06 | |
| 1912 | Ralph Craig, USA | 10.8 | | 1980 | Allan Wells, GBR | 10.25 | |
| 1920 | Charley Paddock, USA | 10.8 | | 1984 | Carl Lewis, USA | 9.99 | |
| 1924 | Harold Abrahams, GBR | 10.6 | **=OR** | 1988 | Carl Lewis, USA* | 9.92 | **WR** |
| 1928 | Percy Williams, CAN | 10.8 | | 1992 | Linford Christie, GBR | 9.96 | |
| 1932 | Eddie Tolan, USA | 10.3 | **OR** | 1996 | Donovan Bailey, CAN | 9.84 | **WR** |
| 1936 | Jesse Owens, USA | 10.3w | | 2000 | Maurice Greene, USA | 9.87 | |
| 1948 | Harrison Dillard, USA | 10.3 | **=OR** | 2004 | Justin Gatlin, USA | 9.85 | |
| 1952 | Lindy Remigino, USA | 10.4 | | | | | |
| 1956 | Bobby Morrow, USA | 10.5 | | | | | |

windicates wind-aided.

*Lewis finished second to Ben Johnson of Canada, who set a world record of 9.79 seconds. Two days later, Johnson was stripped of his gold medal and his record when he tested positive for steroid use in a post-race drug test.

### 200 meters

| Year | | Time | | Year | | Time | |
|---|---|---|---|---|---|---|---|
| 1900 | Walter Tewksbury, USA | 22.2 | | 1960 | Livio Berruti, ITA | 20.5 | **=WR** |
| 1904 | Archie Hahn, USA | 21.6 | **OR** | 1964 | Henry Carr, USA | 20.3 | **OR** |
| 1908 | Bobby Kerr, CAN | 22.6 | | 1968 | Tommie Smith, USA | 19.83 | **WR** |
| 1912 | Ralph Craig, USA | 21.7 | | 1972 | Valery Borzov, USSR | 20.00 | |
| 1920 | Allen Woodring, USA | 22.0 | | 1976 | Donald Quarrie, JAM | 20.23 | |
| 1924 | Jackson Scholz, USA | 21.6 | | 1980 | Pietro Mennea, ITA | 20.19 | |
| 1928 | Percy Williams, CAN | 21.8 | | 1984 | Carl Lewis, USA | 19.80 | **OR** |
| 1932 | Eddie Tolan, USA | 21.2 | **OR** | 1988 | Joe DeLoach, USA | 19.75 | **OR** |
| 1936 | Jesse Owens, USA | 20.7 | **OR** | 1992 | Mike Marsh, USA | 20.01 | |
| 1948 | Mel Patton, USA | 21.1 | | 1996 | Michael Johnson, USA | 19.32 | **WR** |
| 1952 | Andy Stanfield, USA | 20.7 | | 2000 | Konstantinos Kenteris, GRE | 20.09 | |
| 1956 | Bobby Morrow, USA | 20.6 | **OR** | 2004 | Shawn Crawford, USA | 19.79 | |

### 400 meters

| Year | | Time | | Year | | Time | |
|---|---|---|---|---|---|---|---|
| 1896 | Tom Burke, USA | 54.2 | | 1956 | Charley Jenkins, USA | 46.7 | |
| 1900 | Maxey Long, USA | 49.4 | **OR** | 1960 | Otis Davis, USA | 44.9 | **WR** |
| 1904 | Harry Hillman, USA | 49.2 | **OR** | 1964 | Mike Larrabee, USA | 45.1 | |
| 1906 | Paul Pilgrim, USA | 53.2 | | 1968 | Lee Evans, USA | 43.86 | **WR** |
| 1908 | Wyndham Halswelle, GBR | 50.0 | | 1972 | Vince Matthews, USA | 44.66 | |
| 1912 | Charlie Reidpath, USA | 48.2 | **OR** | 1976 | Alberto Juantorena, CUB | 44.26 | |
| 1920 | Bevil Rudd, S. Afr. | 49.6 | | 1980 | Viktor Markin, USSR | 44.60 | |
| 1924 | Eric Liddell, GBR | 47.6 | **OR** | 1984 | Alonzo Babers, USA | 44.27 | |
| 1928 | Ray Barbuti, USA | 47.8 | | 1988 | Steve Lewis, USA | 43.87 | |
| 1932 | Bill Carr, USA | 46.2 | **WR** | 1992 | Quincy Watts, USA | 43.50 | **OR** |
| 1936 | Archie Williams, USA | 46.5 | | 1996 | Michael Johnson, USA | 43.49 | **OR** |
| 1948 | Arthur Wint, JAM | 46.2 | | 2000 | Michael Johnson, USA | 43.84 | |
| 1952 | George Rhoden, JAM | 45.9 | **OR** | 2004 | Jeremy Wariner, USA | 44.00 | |

### 800 meters

| Year | | Time | | Year | | Time | |
|---|---|---|---|---|---|---|---|
| 1896 | Teddy Flack, AUS | 2:11.0 | | 1956 | Tom Courtney, USA | 1:47.7 | **OR** |
| 1900 | Alfred Tysoe, GBR | 2:01.2 | | 1960 | Peter Snell, NZE | 1:46.3 | **OR** |
| 1904 | Jim Lightbody, USA | 1:56.0 | **OR** | 1964 | Peter Snell, NZE | 1:45.1 | **OR** |
| 1906 | Paul Pilgrim, USA | 2:01.5 | | 1968 | Ralph Doubell, AUS | 1:44.3 | **=WR** |
| 1908 | Mel Sheppard, USA | 1:52.8 | **WR** | 1972 | Dave Wottle, USA | 1:45.9 | |
| 1912 | Ted Meredith, USA | 1:51.9 | **WR** | 1976 | Alberto Juantorena, CUB | 1:43.50 | **WR** |
| 1920 | Albert Hill, GBR | 1:53.4 | | 1980 | Steve Ovett, GBR | 1:45.4 | |
| 1924 | Douglas Lowe, GBR | 1:52.4 | | 1984 | Joaquim Cruz, BRA | 1:43.00 | **OR** |
| 1928 | Douglas Lowe, GBR | 1:51.8 | **OR** | 1988 | Paul Ereng, KEN | 1:43.45 | |
| 1932 | Tommy Hampson, GBR | 1:49.7 | **WR** | 1992 | William Tanui, KEN | 1:43.66 | |
| 1936 | John Woodruff, USA | 1:52.9 | | 1996 | Vebjoern Rodal, NOR | 1:42.58 | **OR** |
| 1948 | Mal Whitfield, USA | 1:49.2 | **OR** | 2000 | Nils Schumann, GER | 1:45.08 | |
| 1952 | Mal Whitfield, USA | 1:49.2 | **=OR** | 2004 | Yuriy Borzakovskiy, RUS | 1:44.45 | |

## 1500 meters

| Year | Time | | Year | Time | |
|------|------|---|------|------|---|
| 1896 Teddy Flack, AUS | 4:33.2 | | 1956 Ron Delany, IRE | 3:41.2 | OR |
| 1900 Charles Bennett, GBR | 4:06.2 | WR | 1960 Herb Elliott, AUS | 3:35.6 | WR |
| 1904 Jim Lightbody, USA | 4:05.4 | WR | 1964 Peter Snell, NZE | 3:38.1 | |
| 1906 Jim Lightbody, USA | 4:12.0 | | 1968 Kip Keino, KEN | 3:34.9 | OR |
| 1908 Mel Sheppard, USA | 4:03.4 | OR | 1972 Pekka Vasala, FIN | 3:36.3 | |
| 1912 Arnold Jackson, GBR | 3:56.8 | OR | 1976 John Walker, NZE | 3:39.17 | |
| 1920 Albert Hill, GBR | 4:01.8 | | 1980 Sebastian Coe, GBR | 3:38.4 | |
| 1924 Paavo Nurmi, FIN | 3:53.6 | OR | 1984 Sebastian Coe, GBR | 3:32.53 | OR |
| 1928 Harry Larva, FIN | 3:53.2 | OR | 1988 Peter Rono, KEN | 3:35.96 | |
| 1932 Luigi Beccali, ITA | 3:51.2 | OR | 1992 Fermin Cacho, SPA | 3:40.12 | |
| 1936 John Lovelock, NZE | 3:47.8 | WR | 1996 Noureddine Morceli, ALG | 3:35.78 | |
| 1948 Henry Eriksson, SWE | 3:49.8 | | 2000 Noah Ngeny, KEN | 3:32.07 | OR |
| 1952 Josy Barthel, LUX | 3:45.1 | OR | 2004 Hicham El Guerrouj, MOR | 3:34.18 | |

## 5000 meters

| Year | Time | | Year | Time | |
|------|------|---|------|------|---|
| 1912 Hannes Kolehmainen, FIN | 14:36.6 | WR | 1968 Mohamed Gammoudi, TUN | 14:05.0 | |
| 1920 Joseph Guillemot, FRA | 14:55.6 | | 1972 Lasse Viren, FIN | 13:26.4 | OR |
| 1924 Paavo Nurmi, FIN | 14:31.2 | OR | 1976 Lasse Viren, FIN | 13:24.76 | |
| 1928 Ville Ritola, FIN | 14:38.0 | | 1980 Miruts Yifter, ETH | 13:21.0 | |
| 1932 Lauri Lehtinen, FIN | 14:30.0 | OR | 1984 Said Aouita, MOR | 13:05.59 | OR |
| 1936 Gunnar Höckert, FIN | 14:22.2 | OR | 1988 John Ngugi, KEN | 13:11.70 | |
| 1948 Gaston Reiff, BEL | 14:17.6 | OR | 1992 Dieter Baumann, GER | 13:12.52 | |
| 1952 Emil Zátopek, CZE | 14:06.6 | OR | 1996 Venuste Niyongabo, BUR | 13:07.96 | |
| 1956 Vladimir Kuts, USSR | 13:39.6 | OR | 2000 Millon Wolde, ETH | 13:35.49 | |
| 1960 Murray Halberg, NZE | 13:43.4 | | 2004 Hicham El Guerrouj, MOR | 13:14.39 | |
| 1964 Bob Schul, USA | 13:48.8 | | | | |

## 10,000 meters

| Year | Time | | Year | Time | |
|------|------|---|------|------|---|
| 1912 Hannes Kolehmainen, FIN | 31:20.8 | | 1968 Naftali Temu, KEN | 29:27.4 | |
| 1920 Paavo Nurmi, FIN | 31:45.8 | | 1972 Lasse Viren, FIN | 27:38.4 | WR |
| 1924 Ville Ritola, FIN | 30:23.2 | WR | 1976 Lasse Viren, FIN | 27:40.38 | |
| 1928 Paavo Nurmi, FIN | 30:18.8 | OR | 1980 Miruts Yifter, ETH | 27:42.7 | |
| 1932 Janusz Kusocinski, POL | 30:11.4 | OR | 1984 Alberto Cova, ITA | 27:47.54 | |
| 1936 Ilmari Salminen, FIN | 30:15.4 | | 1988 Brahim Boutaib, MOR | 27:21.46 | OR |
| 1948 Emil Zátopek, CZE | 29:59.6 | OR | 1992 Khalid Skah, MOR | 27:46.70 | |
| 1952 Emil Zátopek, CZE | 29:17.0 | OR | 1996 Haile Gebrselassie, ETH | 27:07.34 | OR |
| 1956 Vladimir Kuts, USSR | 28:45.6 | OR | 2000 Haile Gebrselassie, ETH | 27:18.20 | |
| 1960 Pyotr Bolotnikov, USSR | 28:32.2 | OR | 2004 Kenenisa Bekele, ETH | 27:05.10 | OR |
| 1964 Billy Mills, USA | 28:24.4 | OR | | | |

## Marathon

| Year | Time | | Year | Time | |
|------|------|---|------|------|---|
| 1896 Spiridon Louis, GRE | 2:58:50 | | 1956 Alain Mimoun, FRA | 2:25:00.0 | |
| 1900 Michel Théato, FRA | 2:59:45 | | 1960 Abebe Bikila, ETH | 2:15:16.2 | WB |
| 1904 Thomas Hicks, USA | 3:28:53 | | 1964 Abebe Bikila, ETH | 2:12:11.2 | WB |
| 1906 Billy Sherring, CAN | 2:51:23.6 | | 1968 Mamo Wolde, ETH | 2:20:26.4 | |
| 1908 Johnny Hayes, USA* | 2:55:18.4 | OR | 1972 Frank Shorter, USA | 2:12:19.8 | |
| 1912 Kenneth McArthur, S. Afr. | 2:36:54.8 | | 1976 Waldemar Cierpinski, E. Ger | 2:09:55.0 | OR |
| 1920 Hannes Kolehmainen, FIN | 2:32:35.8 | WB | 1980 Waldemar Cierpinski, E. Ger | 2:11:03.0 | |
| 1924 Albin Stenroos, FIN | 2:41:22.6 | | 1984 Carlos Lopes, POR | 2:09:21.0 | OR |
| 1928 Boughéra El Ouafi, FRA | 2:32:57.0 | | 1988 Gelindo Bordin, ITA | 2:10:32 | |
| 1932 Juan Carlos Zabala, ARG | 2:31:36.0 | OR | 1992 Hwang Young-Cho, S. Kor | 2:13:23 | |
| 1936 Sohn Kee-Chung, JPN† | 2:29:19.2 | OR | 1996 Josia Thugwane, RSA | 2:12:36 | |
| 1948 Delfo Cabrera, ARG | 2:34:51.6 | | 2000 Gezahenge Abera, ETH | 2:10:11 | |
| 1952 Emil Zátopek, CZE | 2:23:03.2 | OR | 2004 Stefano Baldini, ITA | 2:10:55 | |

*Dorando Pietri of Italy placed first, but was disqualified for being helped across the finish line.
†Sohn was a Korean, but he was forced to compete under the name Kitei Son by Japan, which occupied Korea at the time.
**Note:** Marathon distances—40,000 meters (1896,1904); 40,260 meters (1900); 41,860 meters (1906); 42,195 meters (1908 and since 1924); 40,200 meters (1912); 42,750 meters (1920). Current distance of 42,195 meters measures 26 miles, 385 yards.

## 110-meter Hurdles

| Year | Time | | Year | Time | |
|------|------|---|------|------|---|
| 1896 Tom Curtis, USA | 17.6 | | 1956 Lee Calhoun, USA | 13.5 | OR |
| 1900 Alvin Kraenzlein, USA | 15.4 | OR | 1960 Lee Calhoun, USA | 13.8 | |
| 1904 Frederick Schule, USA | 16.0 | | 1964 Hayes Jones, USA | 13.6 | |
| 1906 Robert Leavitt, USA | 16.2 | | 1968 Willie Davenport, USA | 13.3 | OR |
| 1908 Forrest Smithson, USA | 15.0 | WR | 1972 Rod Milburn, USA | 13.24 | =WR |
| 1912 Frederick Kelly, USA | 15.1 | | 1976 Guy Drut, FRA | 13.30 | |
| 1920 Earl Thomson, CAN | 14.8 | WR | 1980 Thomas Munkelt, E. Ger | 13.39 | |
| 1924 Daniel Kinsey, USA | 15.0 | | 1984 Roger Kingdom, USA | 13.20 | OR |
| 1928 Syd Atkinson, S. Afr. | 14.8 | | 1988 Roger Kingdom, USA | 12.98 | OR |
| 1932 George Saling, USA | 14.6 | | 1992 Mark McKoy, CAN | 13.12 | |
| 1936 Forrest (Spec) Towns, USA | 14.2 | | 1996 Allen Johnson, USA | 12.95 | OR |
| 1948 William Porter, USA | 13.9 | OR | 2000 Anier Garcia, CUB | 13.00 | |
| 1952 Harrison Dillard, USA | 13.7 | OR | 2004 Liu Xiang, CHN | 12.91 | OR |

## 400-meter Hurdles

| Year | | Time | | Year | | Time | |
|---|---|---|---|---|---|---|---|
| 1900 | Walter Tewksbury, USA | .57.6 | | 1964 | Rex Cawley, USA | .49.6 | |
| 1904 | Harry Hillman, USA | .53.0 | | 1968 | David Hemery, GBR | .48.12 | **WR** |
| 1908 | Charley Bacon, USA | .55.0 | **WR** | 1972 | John Akii-Bua, UGA | .47.82 | **WR** |
| 1920 | Frank Loomis, USA | .54.0 | **WR** | 1976 | Edwin Moses, USA | .47.64 | **WR** |
| 1924 | Morgan Taylor, USA | .52.6 | | 1980 | Volker Beck, E. Ger | .48.70 | |
| 1928 | David Burghley, GBR | .53.4 | **OR** | 1984 | Edwin Moses, USA | .47.75 | |
| 1932 | Bob Tisdall, IRE | .51.7 | | 1988 | Andre Phillips, USA | .47.19 | **OR** |
| 1936 | Glenn Hardin, USA | .52.4 | | 1992 | Kevin Young, USA | .46.78 | **WR** |
| 1948 | Roy Cochran, USA | .51.1 | **OR** | 1996 | Derrick Adkins, USA | .47.54 | |
| 1952 | Charley Moore, USA | .50.8 | **OR** | 2000 | Angelo Taylor, USA | .47.50 | |
| 1956 | Glenn Davis, USA | .50.1 | **=OR** | 2004 | Felix Sanchez, DOM | .47.63 | |
| 1960 | Glenn Davis, USA | .49.3 | **OR** | | | | |

## 3000-meter Steeplechase

| Year | | Time | | Year | | Time | |
|---|---|---|---|---|---|---|---|
| 1900 | George Orton, CAN | 7:34.4 | | 1964 | Gaston Roelants, BEL | .8:30.8 | **OR** |
| 1904 | Jim Lightbody, USA | 7:39.6 | | 1968 | Amos Biwott, KEN | .8:51.0 | |
| 1908 | Arthur Russell, GBR | 10:47.8 | | 1972 | Kip Keino, KEN | .8:23.6 | **OR** |
| 1920 | Percy Hodge, GBR | 10:00.4 | **OR** | 1976 | Anders Gärderud, SWE | .8:08.2 | **WR** |
| 1924 | Ville Ritola, FIN | 9:33.6 | **OR** | 1980 | Bronislaw Malinowski, POL | .8:09.7 | |
| 1928 | Toivo Loukola, FIN | 9:21.8 | **WR** | 1984 | Julius Korir, KEN | .8:11.80 | |
| 1932 | Volmari Iso-Hollo, FIN | 10:33.4* | | 1988 | Julius Kariuki, KEN | .8:05.51 | **OR** |
| 1936 | Volmari Iso-Hollo, FIN | 9:03.8 | **WR** | 1992 | Matthew Birir, KEN | .8:08.84 | |
| 1948 | Thore Sjöstrand, SWE | 9:04.6 | | 1996 | Joseph Keter, KEN | .8:07.12 | |
| 1952 | Horace Ashenfelter, USA | 8:45.4 | **WR** | 2000 | Reuben Kosgei, KEN | .8:21.43 | |
| 1956 | Chris Brasher, GBR | 8:41.2 | **OR** | 2004 | Ezekiel Kemboi, KEN | .8:05.81 | |
| 1960 | Zdzislaw Krzyszkowiak, POL | 8:34.2 | **OR** | | | | |

*Iso-Hollo ran one extra lap due to lap counter's mistake.

**Note:** Other steeplechase distances– 2500 meters (1900); 2590 meters (1904); 3200 meters (1908) and 3460 meters (1932).

## 4x100-meter Relay

| Year | | Time | | Year | | Time | |
|---|---|---|---|---|---|---|---|
| 1912 | Great Britain | .42.4 | | 1968 | United States | .38.23 | **WR** |
| 1920 | United States | .42.2 | **WR** | 1972 | United States | .38.19 | **WR** |
| 1924 | United States | .41.0 | **=WR** | 1976 | United States | .38.33 | |
| 1928 | United States | .41.0 | **=WR** | 1980 | Soviet Union | .38.26 | |
| 1932 | United States | .40.0 | **WR** | 1984 | United States | .37.83 | **WR** |
| 1936 | United States | .39.8 | **WR** | 1988 | Soviet Union | .38.19 | |
| 1948 | United States | .40.6 | | 1992 | United States | .37.40 | **WR** |
| 1952 | United States | .40.1 | | 1996 | Canada | .37.69 | |
| 1956 | United States | .39.5 | **WR** | 2000 | United States | .37.61 | |
| 1960 | Germany | .39.5 | **=WR** | 2004 | Great Britain | .38.07 | |
| 1964 | United States | .39.0 | | | | | |

## 4x400-meter Relay

| Year | | Time | | Year | | Time | |
|---|---|---|---|---|---|---|---|
| 1908 | United States | 3:29.4 | | 1964 | United States | 3:00.7 | **WR** |
| 1912 | United States | 3:16.6 | **WR** | 1968 | United States | 2:56.16 | **WR** |
| 1920 | Great Britain | 3:22.2 | | 1972 | Kenya | 2:59.8 | |
| 1924 | United States | 3:16.0 | **WR** | 1976 | United States | 2:58.65 | |
| 1928 | United States | 3:14.2 | **WR** | 1980 | Soviet Union | 3:01.1 | |
| 1932 | United States | 3:08.2 | **WR** | 1984 | United States | 2:57.91 | |
| 1936 | Great Britain | 3:09.0 | | 1988 | United States | 2:56.16 | **=WR** |
| 1948 | United States | 3:10.4 | | 1992 | United States | 2:55.74 | **WR** |
| 1952 | Jamaica | 3:03.9 | **WR** | 1996 | United States | 2:55.99 | |
| 1956 | United States | 3:04.8 | | 2000 | United States | 2:56.35 | |
| 1960 | United States | 3:02.2 | **WR** | 2004 | United States | 2:55.91 | |

## 20-kilometer Walk

| Year | | Time | | Year | | Time | |
|---|---|---|---|---|---|---|---|
| 1956 | Leonid Spirin, USSR | 1:31:27.4 | | 1984 | Ernesto Canto, MEX | 1:23:13 | **OR** |
| 1960 | Vladimir Golubnichiy, USSR | 1:34:07.2 | | 1988 | Jozef Pribilinec, CZE | 1:19:57 | **OR** |
| 1964 | Ken Matthews, GBR | 1:29:34.0 | **OR** | 1992 | Daniel Plaza Montero, SPA | 1:21:45 | |
| 1968 | Vladimir Golubnichiy, USSR | 1:33:58.4 | | 1996 | Jefferson Perez, ECU | 1:20:07 | |
| 1972 | Peter Frenkel, E. Ger | 1:26:42.4 | **OR** | 2000 | Robert Korzeniowski, POL | 1:18:59 | **OR** |
| 1976 | Daniel Bautista, MEX | 1:24:40.6 | **OR** | 2004 | Ivano Brugnetti, ITA | 1:19:40 | |
| 1980 | Maurizio Damilano, ITA | 1:23:35.5 | **OR** | | | | |

## 50-kilometer Walk

| Year | | Time | | Year | | Time | |
|---|---|---|---|---|---|---|---|
| 1932 | Thomas Green, GBR | 4:50:10 | | 1976 | Not held | | |
| 1936 | Harold Whitlock, GBR | 4:30:41.4 | OR | 1980 | Hartwig Gauder, E. Ger | 3:49:24.0 | OR |
| 1948 | John Ljunggren, SWE | 4:41:52 | | 1984 | Raul Gonzalez, MEX | 3:47:26 | OR |
| 1952 | Giuseppe Dordoni, ITA | 4:28:07.8 | OR | 1988 | Vyacheslav Ivanenko, USSR | 3:38:29 | OR |
| 1956 | Norman Read, NZE | 4:30:42.8 | | 1992 | Andrei Perlov, UT | 3:50:13 | |
| 1960 | Don Thompson, GBR | 4:25:30.0 | OR | 1996 | Robert Korzeniowski, POL | 3:43:30 | |
| 1964 | Abdon Pamich, ITA | 4:11:12.4 | OR | 2000 | Robert Korzeniowski, POL | 3:42:22 | |
| 1968 | Christoph Höhne, E. Ger | 4:20:13.6 | | 2004 | Robert Korzeniowski, POL | 3:38:46 | |
| 1972 | Bernd Kannenberg, W. Ger | 3:56:11.6 | OR | | | | |

## High Jump

| Year | | Height | | Year | | Height | |
|---|---|---|---|---|---|---|---|
| 1896 | Ellery Clark, USA | 5-11¼ | | 1956 | Charley Dumas, USA | 6-11½ | OR |
| 1900 | Irving Baxter, USA | 6- 2¾ | OR | 1960 | Robert Shavlakadze, USSR | 7- 1 | OR |
| 1904 | Sam Jones, USA | 5-11 | | 1964 | Valery Brumel, USSR | 7- 1¾ | OR |
| 1906 | Cornelius Leahy, GBR/IRE | 5-10 | | 1968 | Dick Fosbury, USA | 7- 4¼ | OR |
| 1908 | Harry Porter, USA | 6- 3 | OR | 1972 | Yuri Tarmak, USSR | 7- 3¾ | |
| 1912 | Alma Richards, USA | 6- 4 | OR | 1976 | Jacek Wszola, POL | 7- 4½ | OR |
| 1920 | Richmond Landon, USA | 6- 4 | =OR | 1980 | Gerd Wessig, E. Ger | 7- 8¾ | WR |
| 1924 | Harold Osborn, USA | 6- 6 | OR | 1984 | Dietmar Mögenburg, W. Ger | 7- 8½ | |
| 1928 | Bob King, USA | 6- 4½ | | 1988 | Gennady Avdeyenko, USSR | 7- 9¾ | OR |
| 1932 | Duncan McNaughton, CAN | 6- 5½ | | 1992 | Javier Sotomayor, CUB | 7- 8 | |
| 1936 | Cornelius Johnson, USA | 6- 8 | OR | 1996 | Charles Austin, USA | 7-10 | OR |
| 1948 | John Winter, AUS | 6- 6 | | 2000 | Sergey Klugin, RUS | 7- 8½ | |
| 1952 | Walt Davis, USA | 6- 8½ | OR | 2004 | Stefan Holm, SWE | 7- 8¾ | |

## Pole Vault

| Year | | Height | | Year | | Height | |
|---|---|---|---|---|---|---|---|
| 1896 | William Hoyt, USA | 10-10 | | 1956 | Bob Richards, USA | 14-11½ | OR |
| 1900 | Irving Baxter, USA | 10-10 | | 1960 | Don Bragg, USA | 15- 5 | OR |
| 1904 | Charles Dvorak, USA | 11- 5¾ | | 1964 | Fred Hansen, USA | 16- 8¾ | OR |
| 1906 | Fernand Gonder, FRA | 11- 5¾ | | 1968 | Bob Seagren, USA | 17-8½ | OR |
| 1908 | (TIE) Edward Cooke, USA | 12- 2 | | 1972 | Wolfgang Nordwig, E. Ger | 18- 0½ | OR |
| | & Alfred Gilbert, USA | 12- 2 | OR | 1976 | Tadeusz Slusarski, POL | 18- 0½ | =OR |
| 1912 | Harry Babcock, USA | 12-11½ | | 1980 | Wladyslaw Kozakiewicz, POL | 18-11½ | WR |
| 1920 | Frank Foss, USA | 13- 5 | WR | 1984 | Pierre Quinon, FRA | 18-10¼ | |
| 1924 | Lee Barnes, USA | 12-11½ | | 1988 | Sergey Bubka, USSR | 19- 4¼ | OR |
| 1928 | Sabin Carr, USA | 13- 9¼ | | 1992 | Maksim Tarasov, UT | 19-0¼ | |
| 1932 | Bill Miller, USA | 14-1¾ | OR | 1996 | Jean Galfione, FRA | 19- 5¼ | OR |
| 1936 | Earle Meadows, USA | 14- 3¼ | OR | 2000 | Nick Hysong, USA | 19-4¼ | |
| 1948 | Guinn Smith, USA | 14-1¼ | | 2004 | Timothy Mack, USA | 19-6¼ | |
| 1952 | Bob Richards, USA | 14-11 | OR | | | | |

## Long Jump

| Year | | Distance | | Year | | Distance | |
|---|---|---|---|---|---|---|---|
| 1896 | Ellery Clark, USA | 20-10 | | 1956 | Greg Bell, USA | 25- 8¼ | |
| 1900 | Alvin Kraenzlein, USA | 23- 6¾ | OR | 1960 | Ralph Boston, USA | 26-7¾ | OR |
| 1904 | Meyer Prinstein, USA | 24- 1 | OR | 1964 | Lynn Davies, GBR | 26- 5¾ | |
| 1906 | Meyer Prinstein, USA | 23- 7½ | | 1968 | Bob Beamon, USA | 29- 2½ | WR |
| 1908 | Frank Irons, USA | 24- 6½ | OR | 1972 | Randy Williams, USA | 27-0½ | |
| 1912 | Albert Gutterson, USA | 24-11¼ | OR | 1976 | Arnie Robinson, USA | 27- 4¾ | |
| 1920 | William Petersson, SWE | 23-5½ | | 1980 | Lutz Dombrowski, E. Ger | 28- 0¼ | |
| 1924 | De Hart Hubbard, USA | 24- 5 | | 1984 | Carl Lewis, USA | 28-0¼ | |
| 1928 | Ed Hamm, USA | 25- 4½ | OR | 1988 | Carl Lewis, USA | 28- 7¼ | |
| 1932 | Ed Gordon, USA | 25- 0¾ | | 1992 | Carl Lewis, USA | 28- 5½ | |
| 1936 | Jesse Owens, USA | 26-5½ | OR | 1996 | Carl Lewis, USA | 27-10¾ | |
| 1948 | Willie Steele, USA | 25- 8 | | 2000 | Ivan Pedroso, CUB | 28- 0¾ | |
| 1952 | Jerome Biffle, USA | 24-10 | | 2004 | Dwight Phillips, USA | 28- 2¼ | |

## Triple Jump

| Year | Athlete | Distance | |
|---|---|---|---|
| 1896 | James Connolly, USA | 44-11¾ | |
| 1900 | Meyer Prinstein, USA | 47-5¾ | OR |
| 1904 | Meyer Prinstein, USA | 47-1 | |
| 1906 | Peter O'Connor, GBR/IRE | 46-2¼ | |
| 1908 | Timothy Ahearne, GBR/IRE | 48-11¼ | OR |
| 1912 | Gustaf Lindblom, SWE | 48-5¼ | |
| 1920 | Vilho Tuulos, FIN | 47-7 | |
| 1924 | Nick Winter, AUS | 50-11¼ | WR |
| 1928 | Mikio Oda, JPN | 49-11 | |
| 1932 | Chuhei Nambu, JPN | 51-7 | WR |
| 1936 | Naoto Tajima, JPN | 52-6 | WR |
| 1948 | Arne Ahman, SWE | 50-6¼ | |
| 1952 | Adhemar da Silva, BRA | 53-2¾ | WR |
| 1956 | Adhemar da Silva, BRA | 53-7¾ | OR |
| 1960 | Józef Schmidt, POL | 55-2 | |
| 1964 | Józef Schmidt, POL | 55-3½ | OR |
| 1968 | Viktor Saneyev, USSR | 57-0¾ | WR |
| 1972 | Viktor Saneyev, USSR | 56-11¼ | |
| 1976 | Viktor Saneyev, USSR | 56-8¾ | |
| 1980 | Jack Uudmäe, USSR | 56-11¼ | |
| 1984 | Al Joyner, USA | 56-7½ | |
| 1988 | Khristo Markov, BUL | 57-9¼ | OR |
| 1992 | Mike Conley, USA | 59-7½W | OR |
| 1996 | Kenny Harrison, USA | 59-4¼ | OR |
| 2000 | Jonathan Edwards, GBR | 58-1¼ | |
| 2004 | Christian Olsson, SWE | 58-4½ | |

Windicates wind-aided.

## Shot Put

| Year | Athlete | Distance | |
|---|---|---|---|
| 1896 | Bob Garrett, USA | 36-9¾ | |
| 1900 | Richard Sheldon, USA | 46-3¼ | OR |
| 1904 | Ralph Rose, USA | 48-7 | WR |
| 1906 | Martin Sheridan, USA | 40-5¼ | |
| 1908 | Ralph Rose, USA | 46-7½ | |
| 1912 | Patrick McDonald, USA | 50-4 | OR |
| 1920 | Ville Pörhölä, FIN | 48-7¼ | |
| 1924 | Bud Houser, USA | 49-2¼ | |
| 1928 | John Kuck, USA | 52-0¾ | WR |
| 1932 | Leo Sexton, USA | 52-6 | OR |
| 1936 | Hans Woellke, GER | 53-1¾ | OR |
| 1948 | Wilbur Thompson, USA | 56-2 | OR |
| 1952 | Parry O'Brien, USA | 57-1½ | OR |
| 1956 | Parry O'Brien, USA | 60-11¼ | OR |
| 1960 | Bill Nieder, USA | 64-6¾ | OR |
| 1964 | Dallas Long, USA | 66-8½ | OR |
| 1968 | Randy Matson, USA | 67-4¾ | |
| 1972 | Wladyslaw Komar, POL | 69-6 | OR |
| 1976 | Udo Beyer, E. Ger | 69-0¾ | OR |
| 1980 | Vladimir Kiselyov, USSR | 70-0½ | OR |
| 1984 | Alessandro Andrei, ITA | 69-9 | |
| 1988 | Ulf Timmermann, E. Ger | 73-8¾ | OR |
| 1992 | Mike Stulce, USA | 71-2½ | |
| 1996 | Randy Barnes, USA | 70-11¼ | |
| 2000 | Arsi Harju, FIN | 69-10¼ | |
| 2004 | Yuriy Bilonog, UKR | 69-5¼ | |

## Discus Throw

| Year | Athlete | Distance | |
|---|---|---|---|
| 1896 | Bob Garrett, USA | 95-7½ | |
| 1900 | Rudolf Bauer, HUN | 118-3 | OR |
| 1904 | Martin Sheridan, USA | 128-10½ | OR |
| 1906 | Martin Sheridan, USA | 136-0 | |
| 1908 | Martin Sheridan, USA | 134-2 | OR |
| 1912 | Armas Taipale, FIN | 148-3 | OR |
| 1920 | Elmer Niklander, FIN | 146-7 | |
| 1924 | Bud Houser, USA | 151-4 | OR |
| 1928 | Bud Houser, USA | 155-3 | OR |
| 1932 | John Anderson, USA | 162-4 | OR |
| 1936 | Ken Carpenter, USA | 165-7 | OR |
| 1948 | Adolfo Consolini, ITA | 173-2 | OR |
| 1952 | Sim Iness, USA | 180-6 | OR |
| 1956 | Al Oerter, USA | 184-11 | OR |
| 1960 | Al Oerter, USA | 194-2 | OR |
| 1964 | Al Oerter, USA | 200-1 | OR |
| 1968 | Al Oerter, USA | 212-6 | OR |
| 1972 | Ludvik Danek, CZE | 211-3 | |
| 1976 | Mac Wilkins, USA | 221-5 | |
| 1980 | Viktor Rashchupkin, USSR | 218-8 | |
| 1984 | Rolf Danneberg, W. Ger | 218-6 | |
| 1988 | Jürgen Schult, E. Ger | 225-9 | OR |
| 1992 | Romas Ubartas, LIT | 213-8 | |
| 1996 | Lars Riedel, GER | 227-8 | |
| 2000 | Virgilijus Alekna, LIT | 227-4 | |
| 2004 | Virgilijus Alekna, LIT* | 229-3 | OR |

*Hungary's **Robert Fazekas** had a throw of 232 feet, 8 inches, and was initially declared the winner, but he was disqualified for failing to submit to a drug test following the competition.

## Hammer Throw

| Year | Athlete | Distance | |
|---|---|---|---|
| 1900 | John Flanagan, USA | 163-1 | |
| 1904 | John Flanagan, USA | 168-1 | OR |
| 1908 | John Flanagan, USA | 170-4 | OR |
| 1912 | Matt McGrath, USA | 179-7 | OR |
| 1920 | Pat Ryan, USA | 173-5 | |
| 1924 | Fred Tootell, USA | 174-10 | |
| 1928 | Pat O'Callaghan, IRE | 168-7 | |
| 1932 | Pat O'Callaghan, IRE | 176-11 | |
| 1936 | Karl Hein, GER | 185-4 | OR |
| 1948 | Imre Németh, HUN | 183-11 | |
| 1952 | József Csérmák, HUN | 197-11 | WR |
| 1956 | Harold Connolly, USA | 207-3 | OR |
| 1960 | Vasily Rudenkov, USSR | 220-2 | OR |
| 1964 | Romuald Klim, USSR | 228-10 | OR |
| 1968 | Gyula Zsivótzky, HUN | 240-8 | OR |
| 1972 | Anatoly Bondarchuk, USSR | 247-8 | OR |
| 1976 | Yuri Sedykh, USSR | 254-4 | OR |
| 1980 | Yuri Sedykh, USSR | 268-4 | WR |
| 1984 | Juha Tiainen, FIN | 256-2 | |
| 1988 | Sergey Litvinov, USSR | 278-2 | OR |
| 1992 | Andrei Abduvaliyev, UT | 270-9 | |
| 1996 | Balazs Kiss, HUN | 266-6 | |
| 2000 | Szymon Ziolkowski, POL | 262-6 | |
| 2004 | Koji Murofushi, JPN* | 272-0 | |

Hungary's **Adrian Annus** was initially awarded the gold medal for his throw of 272-11, but after questions were raised about the legitimacy of his post-competition drug test, and he failed to submit to a follow-up test, he was disqualified and stripped of the gold.

### Javelin Throw

| Year | | Distance | | Year | | Distance | |
|---|---|---|---|---|---|---|---|
| 1908 | Eric Lemming, SWE | 179-10 | WR | 1964 | Pauli Nevala, FIN | 271- 2 | |
| 1912 | Eric Lemming, SWE | 198-11 | WR | 1968 | Jänis Lüsis, USSR | 295- 7 | OR |
| 1920 | Jonni Myyrä, FIN | 215-10 | OR | 1972 | Klaus Wolfermann, W. Ger | 296-10 | OR |
| 1924 | Jonni Myyrä, FIN | 206- 7 | | 1976 | Miklos Németh, HUN | 310- 4 | WR |
| 1928 | Erik Lundkvist, SWE | 218- 6 | OR | 1980 | Dainis Kula, USSR | 299- 2 | |
| 1932 | Matti Järvinen, FIN | 238- 6 | OR | 1984 | Arto Härkönen, FIN | 284- 8 | |
| 1936 | Gerhard Stöck, GER | *235- 8 | | 1988 | Tapio Korjus, FIN | 276- 6 | |
| 1948 | Kai Tapio Rautavaara, FIN | 228-10 | | 1992 | Jan Zelezny, CZE | 294- 2* | OR |
| 1952 | Cy Young, USA | 242- 1 | OR | 1996 | Jan Zelezny, CZR | 289- 3 | |
| 1956 | Egil Danielson, NOR | 281- 2 | WR | 2000 | Jan Zelezny, CZR | 295- 10 | OR |
| 1960 | Viktor Tsibulenko, USSR | 277- 8 | | 2004 | Andreas Thorkildsen, NOR | 283- 9 | |

*In 1986 the balance point of the javelin was modified and new records have been kept since.

### Decathlon

| Year | | Points | | Year | | Points | |
|---|---|---|---|---|---|---|---|
| 1904 | Thomas Kiely, IRE | 6036 | | 1964 | Willi Holdorf, GER | 7887 | |
| 1906-08 | Not held | | | 1968 | Bill Toomey, USA | 8193 | OR |
| 1912 | Jim Thorpe, USA | 8412 | WR | 1972 | Nikolai Avilov, USSR | 8454 | WR |
| 1920 | Helge Lövland, NOR | 6803 | | 1976 | Bruce Jenner, USA | 8617 | WR |
| 1924 | Harold Osborn, USA | 7711 | WR | 1980 | Daley Thompson, GBR | 8495 | |
| 1928 | Paavo Yrjölä, FIN | 8053 | WR | 1984 | Daley Thompson, GBR | 8798 | =WR |
| 1932 | Jim Bausch, USA | 8462 | WR | 1988 | Christian Schenk, E. Ger | 8488 | |
| 1936 | Glenn Morris, USA | 7900 | WR | 1992 | Robert Zmelik, CZE | 8611 | |
| 1948 | Bob Mathias, USA | 7139 | | 1996 | Dan O'Brien, USA | 8824 | |
| 1952 | Bob Mathias, USA | 7887 | WR | 2000 | Erki Nool, EST | 8641 | |
| 1956 | Milt Campbell, USA | 7937 | OR | 2004 | Roman Sebrle, CZE | 8893 | OR |
| 1960 | Rafer Johnson, USA | 8392 | OR | | | | |

### WOMEN

**At least 4 gold medals** (including relays): Evelyn Ashford, Fanny Blankers-Koen, Betty Cuthbert and Bärbel Eckert Wöckel (4).

### 100 meters

| Year | | Time | | Year | | Time | |
|---|---|---|---|---|---|---|---|
| 1928 | Betty Robinson, USA | 12.2 | =WR | 1972 | Renate Stecher, E. Ger | 11.07 | |
| 1932 | Stella Walsh, POL* | 11.9 | =WR | 1976 | Annegret Richter, W. Ger | 11.08 | |
| 1936 | Helen Stephens, USA | 11.5W | | 1980 | Lyudmila Kondratyeva, USSR | 11.06 | |
| 1948 | Fanny Blankers-Koen, NED | 11.9 | | 1984 | Evelyn Ashford, USA | 10.97 | OR |
| 1952 | Marjorie Jackson, AUS | 11.5 | =WR | 1988 | Florence Griffith Joyner, USA | 10.54W | |
| 1956 | Betty Cuthbert, AUS | 11.5 | | 1992 | Gail Devers, USA | 10.82 | OR |
| 1960 | Wilma Rudolph, USA | 11.0W | | 1996 | Gail Devers, USA | 10.94 | |
| 1964 | Wyomia Tyus, USA | 11.4 | | 2000 | Marion Jones, USA | 10.75 | |
| 1968 | Wyomia Tyus, USA | 11.08 | WR | 2004 | Yuliya Nesterenko, BLR | 10.93 | |

*An autopsy performed after Walsh's death in 1980 revealed that she was a man.
Windicates wind-aided.

### 200 meters

| Year | | Time | | Year | | Time | |
|---|---|---|---|---|---|---|---|
| 1948 | Fanny Blankers-Koen, NED | 24.4 | | 1980 | Bärbel Eckert Wockel, E. Ger | 22.03 | OR |
| 1952 | Marjorie Jackson, AUS | 23.7 | OR | 1984 | Valerie Brisco-Hooks, USA | 21.81 | OR |
| 1956 | Betty Cuthbert, AUS | 23.4 | =OR | 1988 | Florence Griffith Joyner, USA | 21.34 | WR |
| 1960 | Wilma Rudolph, USA | 24.0 | | 1992 | Gwen Torrence, USA | 21.81 | |
| 1964 | Edith McGuire, USA | 23.0 | OR | 1996 | Marie-Jose Perec, FRA | 22.12 | |
| 1968 | Irena Szewinska, POL | 22.5 | WR | 2000 | Marion Jones, USA | 21.84 | |
| 1972 | Renate Stecher, E. Ger | 22.40 | =WR | 2004 | Veronica Campbell, JAM | 22.05 | |
| 1976 | Bärbel Eckert, E. Ger | 22.37 | OR | | | | |

### 400 meters

| Year | | Time | | Year | | Time | |
|---|---|---|---|---|---|---|---|
| 1964 | Betty Cuthbert, AUS | 52.0 | | 1988 | Olga Bryzgina, USSR | 48.65 | OR |
| 1968 | Colette Besson, FRA | 52.03 | =OR | 1992 | Marie-Jose Perec, FRA | 48.83 | |
| 1972 | Monika Zehrt, E. Ger | 51.08 | OR | 1996 | Marie-Jose Perec, FRA | 48.25 | OR |
| 1976 | Irena Szewinska, POL | 49.29 | WR | 2000 | Cathy Freeman, AUS | 49.11 | |
| 1980 | Marita Koch, E. Ger | 48.88 | OR | 2004 | Tonique Williams-Darling, BAH | 49.41 | |
| 1984 | Valerie Brisco-Hooks, USA | 48.83 | OR | | | | |

### 800 meters

| Year | | Time | | Year | | Time | |
|---|---|---|---|---|---|---|---|
| 1928 | Lina Radke, GER | 2:16.8 | WR | 1980 | Nadezhda Olizarenko, USSR | 1:53.42 | WR |
| 1932-56 | Not held | | | 1984 | Doina Melinte, ROM | 1:57.60 | |
| 1960 | Lyudmila Shevtsova, USSR | 2:04.3 | =WR | 1988 | Sigrun Wodars, E. Ger | 1:56.10 | |
| 1964 | Ann Packer, GBR | 2:01.1 | OR | 1992 | Ellen van Langen, NED | 1:55.54 | |
| 1968 | Madeline Manning, USA | 2:00.9 | OR | 1996 | Svetlana Masterkova, RUS | 1:57.73 | |
| 1972 | Hildegard Falck, W. Ger | 1:58.55 | OR | 2000 | Maria Mutola, MOZ | 1:56.15 | |
| 1976 | Tatyana Kazankina, USSR | 1:54.94 | WR | 2004 | Kelly Holmes, GBR | 1:56.38 | |

## 1500 meters

| Year | | Time | | Year | | Time | |
|------|------|------|------|------|------|------|------|
| 1972 | Lyudmila Bragina, USSR | 4:01.4 | **WR** | 1992 | Hassiba Boulmerka, ALG | 3:55.30 | |
| 1976 | Tatyana Kazankina, USSR | 4:05.48 | | 1996 | Svetlana Masterkova, RUS | 4:00.83 | |
| 1980 | Tatyana Kazankina, USSR | 3:56.6 | **OR** | 2000 | Nouria Merah-Benida, ALG | 4:05.10 | |
| 1984 | Gabriella Dorio, ITA | 4:03.25 | | 2004 | Kelly Holmes, GBR | 3:57.90 | |
| 1988 | Paula Ivan, ROM | 3:53.96 | **OR** | | | | |

## 5000 meters

| Year | | Time | | Year | | Time | |
|------|------|------|------|------|------|------|------|
| 1984 | Maricica Puica, ROM | 8:35.96 | | 1996 | Wang Junxia, CHN | 14:59.88 | |
| 1988 | Tatyana Samolenko, USSR | 8:26.53 | **OR** | 2000 | Gabriela Szabo, ROM | 14:40.79 | **OR** |
| 1992 | Elena Romanova, UT | 8:46.04 | | 2004 | Meseret Defar, ETH | 14:45.65 | |

**Note:** Event held over 3000 meters from 1984-92.

## 10,000 meters

| Year | | Time | | Year | | Time | |
|------|------|------|------|------|------|------|------|
| 1988 | Olga Bondarenko, USSR | 31:05.21 | **OR** | 2000 | Derartu Tulu, ETH | 30:17.49 | **OR** |
| 1992 | Derartu Tulu, ETH | 31:06.02 | | 2004 | Xing Huina, CHN | 30:24.36 | |
| 1996 | Fernanda Ribeiro, POR | 31:01.63 | **OR** | | | | |

## Marathon

| Year | | Time | Year | | Time |
|------|------|------|------|------|------|
| 1984 | Joan Benoit, USA | 2:24:52 | 1996 | Fatuma Roba, ETH | 2:26:05 |
| 1988 | Rosa Mota, POR | 2:25:40 | 2000 | Naoko Takahashi, JPN | 2:23:14 |
| 1992 | Valentina Yegorova, UT | 2:32:41 | 2004 | Mizuki Noguchi, JPN | 2:26:20 |

## 100-meter Hurdles

| Year | | Time | | Year | | Time | |
|------|------|------|------|------|------|------|------|
| 1932 | Babe Didrikson, USA | 11.7 | **WR** | 1980 | Vera Komisova, USSR | 12.56 | **OR** |
| 1936 | Trebisonda Valla, ITA | 11.7 | | 1984 | Benita Fitzgerald-Brown, USA | 12.84 | |
| 1948 | Fanny Blankers-Koen, NED | 11.2 | **OR** | 1988 | Yordanka Donkova, BUL | 12.38 | **OR** |
| 1952 | Shirley Strickland, AUS | 10.9 | **WR** | 1992 | Paraskevi Patoulidou, GRE | 12.64 | |
| 1956 | Shirley Strickland, AUS | 10.7 | **OR** | 1996 | Ludmila Enquist, SWE | 12.58 | |
| 1960 | Irina Press, USSR | 10.8 | | 2000 | Olga Shishigina, KAZ | 12.65 | |
| 1964 | Karin Balzer, GER | 10.5ʷ | | 2004 | Joanna Hayes, USA | 12.37 | **OR** |
| 1968 | Maureen Caird, AUS | 10.3 | **OR** | | | | |
| 1972 | Annelie Ehrhardt, E. Ger | 12.59 | **WR** | | | | |
| 1976 | Johanna Schaller, E. Ger | 12.77 | | | | | |

ʷindicates wind-aided.

**Note:** Event held over 80 meters from 1932-68.

## 400-meter Hurdles

| Year | | Time | | Year | | Time | |
|------|------|------|------|------|------|------|------|
| 1984 | Nawal El Moutawakel, MOR | 54.61 | **OR** | 1996 | Deon Hemmings, JAM | 52.82 | **OR** |
| 1988 | Debra Flintoff-King, AUS | 53.17 | **OR** | 2000 | Irina Privalova, RUS | 53.02 | |
| 1992 | Sally Gunnell, GBR | 53.23 | | 2004 | Fani Halkia, GRE | 52.82 | |

## 4x100-meter Relay

| Year | | Time | | Year | | Time | |
|------|------|------|------|------|------|------|------|
| 1928 | Canada | 48.4 | **WR** | 1972 | West Germany | 42.81 | **WR** |
| 1932 | United States | 46.9 | **WR** | 1976 | East Germany | 42.55 | **OR** |
| 1936 | United States | 46.9 | | 1980 | East Germany | 41.60 | **OR** |
| 1948 | Holland | 47.5 | | 1984 | United States | 41.65 | |
| 1952 | United States | 45.9 | **WR** | 1988 | United States | 41.98 | |
| 1956 | Australia | 44.5 | **WR** | 1992 | United States | 42.11 | |
| 1960 | United States | 44.5 | | 1996 | United States | 41.95 | |
| 1964 | Poland | 43.6 | | 2000 | Bahamas | 42.20 | |
| 1968 | United States | 42.87 | **WR** | 2004 | Jamaica | 41.73 | |

## 4x400-meter Relay

| Year | | Time | | Year | | Time |
|------|------|------|------|------|------|------|
| 1972 | East Germany | 3:23.0 | **WR** | 1992 | Unified Team | 3:20.20 |
| 1976 | East Germany | 3:19.23 | **WR** | 1996 | United States | 3:20.91 |
| 1980 | Soviet Union | 3:20.2 | | 2000 | United States | 3:22.62 |
| 1984 | United States | 3:18.29 | **OR** | 2004 | United States | 3:19.01 |
| 1988 | Soviet Union | 3:15.18 | **WR** | | | |

## 20-kilometer Walk

| Year | | Time | Year | | Time |
|------|------|------|------|------|------|
| 1992 | Chen Yueling, CHN | 44:32 | 2000 | Wang Liping, CHN | 1:29:05 |
| 1996 | Yelena Ninikolayeva, RUS | 41:49 | 2004 | Athanasia Tsoumeleka, GRE | 1:29:12 |

**Note:** Event was held over 10 kilometers from 1992-96.

## Pole Vault

| Year | | Height | | Year | | Height | |
|------|------|------|------|------|------|------|------|
| 2000 | Stacy Dragila, USA | 15-1 | **OR** | 2004 | Yelena Isinbayeva, RUS | 16-1¼ | **WR** |

## High Jump

| Year | | Height | | Year | | Height | |
|------|---|--------|---|------|---|--------|---|
| 1928 | Ethel Catherwood, CAN | 5- 2½ | | 1972 | Ulrike Meyfarth, W. Ger | 6- 3½ | =WR |
| 1932 | Jean Shiley, USA | 5- 5¼ | WR | 1976 | Rosemarie Ackermann, E. Ger | 6-4 | OR |
| 1936 | Ibolya Csák, HUN | 5- 3 | | 1980 | Sara Simeoni, ITA | 6- 5½ | OR |
| 1948 | Alice Coachman, USA | 5- 6 | OR | 1984 | Ulrike Meyfarth, W. Ger | 6-7½ | OR |
| 1952 | Esther Brand, RSA | 5- 5¾ | | 1988 | Louise Ritter, USA | 6- 8 | OR |
| 1956 | Mildred McDaniel, USA | 5- 9¼ | OR | 1992 | Heike Henkel, GER | 6-7½ | |
| 1960 | Iolanda Balas, ROM | 6-0¾ | OR | 1996 | Stefka Kostadinova, BUL | 6- 8¾ | OR |
| 1964 | Iolanda Balas, ROM | 6- 2¾ | OR | 2000 | Yelena Yelesina, RUS | 6- 7 | |
| 1968 | Miloslava Rezkova, CZE | 5-11½ | | 2004 | Yelena Slesarenko, RUS | 6- 9 | OR |

## Long Jump

| Year | | Distance | | Year | | Distance | |
|------|---|----------|---|------|---|----------|---|
| 1948 | Olga Gyarmati, HUN | 18- 8¼ | | 1980 | Tatyana Kolpakova, USSR | 23-2 | OR |
| 1952 | Yvette Williams, NZE | 20- 5¾ | OR | 1984 | Anisoara Cusmir-Stanciu, ROM | 22-10 | |
| 1956 | Elzbieta Krzesinska, POL | 20-10 | =WR | 1988 | Jackie Joyner-Kersee, USA | 24-3¼ | OR |
| 1960 | Vyera Krepkina, USSR | 20-10¾ | OR | 1992 | Heike Drechsler, GER | 23-5¼ | |
| 1964 | Mary Rand, GBR | 22- 2¼ | WR | 1996 | Chioma Ajunwa, NGR | 23-4½ | |
| 1968 | Viorica Viscopoleanu, ROM | 22- 4½ | WR | 2000 | Heike Drechsler, GER | 22-11¼ | |
| 1972 | Heidemarie Rosendahl, W. Ger | 22- 3 | | 2004 | Tatyana Lebedeva, RUS | 23-2½ | |
| 1976 | Angela Voigt, E. Ger | 22-0¾ | | | | | |

## Triple Jump

| Year | | Distance | | Year | | Distance | |
|------|---|----------|---|------|---|----------|---|
| 1996 | Inessa Kravets, UKR | 50-3½ | | 2004 | Francoise Mbango Etone, CMR | 50-2½ | |
| 2000 | Tereza Marinova, BUL | 49-10½ | | | | | |

## Shot Put

| Year | | Distance | | Year | | Distance | |
|------|---|----------|---|------|---|----------|---|
| 1948 | Micheline Ostermeyer, FRA | 45- 1½ | | 1980 | Ilona Slupianek, E. Ger | 73- 6¼ | OR |
| 1952 | Galina Zybina, USSR | 50- 1¾ | WR | 1984 | Claudia Losch, W. Ger | 67-2¼ | |
| 1956 | Tamara Tyshkevich, USSR | 54- 5 | OR | 1988 | Natalia Lisovskaya, USSR | 72- 11¾ | |
| 1960 | Tamara Press, USSR | 56- 10 | OR | 1992 | Svetlana Krivaleva, UT | 69- 1¼ | |
| 1964 | Tamara Press, USSR | 59- 6¼ | OR | 1996 | Astrid Kumbernuss, GER | 67-5½ | |
| 1968 | Margitta Gummel, E. Ger | 64- 4 | WR | 2000 | Yanina Korolchik, BLR | 67- 5½ | |
| 1972 | Nadezhda Chizhova, USSR | 69-0 | WR | 2004 | Yumileidi Cumba, CUB* | 64-3¼ | |
| 1976 | Ivanka Hristova, BUL | 69-5¼ | OR | | | | |

*Russia's Irina Korzhanenko (69- 1¼) was stripped of the gold for failing a post-competition drug test.

## Discus Throw

| Year | | Distance | | Year | | Distance | |
|------|---|----------|---|------|---|----------|---|
| 1928 | Halina Konopacka, POL | 129-11¾ | WR | 1972 | Faina Melnik, USSR | 218- 7 | OR |
| 1932 | Lillian Copeland, USA | 133- 2 | OR | 1976 | Evelin Schlaak, E. Ger | 226- 4 | OR |
| 1936 | Gisela Mauermayer, GER | 156- 3 | OR | 1980 | Evelin Schlaak Jahl, E. Ger | 229- 6 | OR |
| 1948 | Micheline Ostermeyer, FRA | 137-6 | | 1984 | Ria Stalman, NED | 214- 5 | |
| 1952 | Nina Romaschkova, USSR | 168- 8 | OR | 1988 | Martina Hellmann, E. Ger | 237- 2½ | OR |
| 1956 | Olga Fikotová, CZE | 176- 1 | OR | 1992 | Maritza Marten, CUB | 229-10 | |
| 1960 | Nina Ponomaryeva, USSR | 180- 9 | OR | 1996 | Ilke Wyludda, GER | 228-6 | |
| 1964 | Tamara Press, USSR | 187-10 | OR | 2000 | Ellina Zvereva, BLR | 224-5 | |
| 1968 | Lia Manoliu, ROM | 191- 2 | OR | 2004 | Natalya Sadova, RUS | 219-10 | |

## Hammer Throw

| Year | | Distance | | Year | | Distance | |
|------|---|----------|---|------|---|----------|---|
| 2000 | Kamila Skolimowska, POL | 233- 5¾ | OR | 2004 | Olga Kuzenkova, RUS | 246-1 | OR |

## Javelin Throw

| Year | | Distance | | Year | | Distance | |
|------|---|----------|---|------|---|----------|---|
| 1932 | Babe Didrikson, USA | 143- 4 | | 1976 | Ruth Fuchs, E. Ger | 216- 4 | OR |
| 1936 | Tilly Fleischer, GER | 148- 3 | OR | 1980 | Maria Colon Rueñes, CUB | 224- 5 | OR |
| 1948 | Herma Bauma, AUT | 149- 6 | OR | 1984 | Tessa Sanderson, GBR | 228- 2 | OR |
| 1952 | Dana Zátopková, CZE | 165- 7 | OR | 1988 | Petra Felke, E. Ger | 245- 0 | OR |
| 1956 | Ineze Jaunzeme, USSR | 176- 8 | OR | 1992 | Silke Renk, GER | 224-2 | |
| 1960 | Elvira Ozolina, USSR | 183- 8 | OR | 1996 | Heli Rantanen, FIN | 222-11 | |
| 1964 | Mihaela Penes, ROM | 198- 7 | OR | 2000 | Trine Hattestad, NOR | 226-1 | OR |
| 1968 | Angéla Németh, HUN | 198- 0 | | 2004 | Osleidys Menendez, CUB | 234-8 | OR |
| 1972 | Ruth Fuchs, E. Ger | 209- 7 | OR | | | | |

## Heptathlon

| Year | | Points | | Year | | Points | |
|------|---|--------|---|------|---|--------|---|
| 1964 | Irina Press, USSR | 5246 | WR | 1988 | Jackie Joyner-Kersee, USA | 7291 | WR |
| 1968 | Ingrid Becker, W. Ger | 5098 | | 1992 | Jackie Joyner-Kersee, USA | 7044 | |
| 1972 | Mary Peters, GBR | 4801 | WR | 1996 | Ghada Shouaa, SYR | 6780 | |
| 1976 | Siegrun Siegl, E. Ger | 4745 | | 2000 | Denise Lewis, GBR | 6584 | |
| 1980 | Nadezhda Tkachenko, USSR | 5083 | WR | 2004 | Carolina Kluft, SWE | 6952 | |
| 1984 | Glynis Nunn, AUS | 6390 | OR | | | | |

Note: Seven-event Heptathlon replaced five-event Pentathlon in 1984.

## All-Time Leading Medal Winners – Single Games

Athletes who have won the most medals in a single Summer Olympics. Totals include individual, relay and team medals. U.S. athletes are in **bold** type.

### MEN

| No | | Sport | G-S-B | No | | Sport | G-S-B |
|----|---|-------|-------|----|---|-------|-------|
| 8† | **Michael Phelps**, USA (2004) | Swim | 6-0-2 | 6 | Takashi Ono, JPN (1960) | Gym | 3-1-2 |
| 8 | Aleksandr Dityatin, USSR (1980) | Gym | 3-4-1 | 6 | Viktor Chukarin, USSR (1956) | Gym | 4-2-0 |
| 7 | **Mark Spitz**, USA (1972) | Swim | 7-0-0 | 6 | Konrad Frey, GER (1936) | Gym | 3-1-2 |
| 7 | **Willis Lee**, USA (1920) | Shoot | 5-1-1 | 6 | Ville Ritola, FIN (1924) | Track | 4-2-0 |
| 7 | **Matt Biondi**, USA (1988) | Swim* | 5-1-1 | 6 | Hubert Van Innis, BEL (1920) | Arch | 4-2-0 |
| 7 | Boris Shakhlin, USSR (1960) | Gym | 4-2-1 | 6 | **Carl Osburn**, USA (1920) | Shoot | 4-1-1 |
| 7 | **Lloyd Spooner**, USA (1920) | Shoot | 4-1-2 | 6 | Louis Richardet, SWI (1906) | Shoot | 3-3-0 |
| 7 | Mikhail Voronin, USSR (1968) | Gym | 2-4-1 | 6 | **Anton Heida**, USA (1904) | Gym | 5-1-0 |
| 7 | Nikolai Andrianov, USSR (1976) | Gym | 2-4-1 | 6 | **George Eyser**, USA (1904) | Gym | 3-2-1 |
| 6 | Vitaly Scherbo, UT (1992) | Gym | 6-0-0 | 6 | **Burton Downing**, USA (1904) | Cycle | 2-3-1 |
| 6 | Li Ning, CHN (1984) | Gym | 3-2-1 | 6 | Alexei Nemov, RUS (1996) | Gym | 2-1-3 |
| 6 | Akinori Nakayama, JPN (1968) | Gym | 4-1-1 | 6 | Alexei Nemov, RUS (2000) | Gym | 2-1-3 |

†Includes gold medal as preliminary member of 1st-place relay team.

### WOMEN

| No | | Sport | G-S-B | No | | Sport | G-S-B |
|----|---|-------|-------|----|---|-------|-------|
| 7 | Maria Gorokhovskaya, USSR (1952) | Gym | 2-5-0 | 5 | Shane Gould, AUS (1972) | Swim | 3-1-1 |
| 6 | Kristin Otto, E. Ger (1988) | Swim | 6-0-0 | 5 | Nadia Comaneci, ROM (1976) | Gym | 3-1-1 |
| 6 | Agnes Keleti, HUN (1956) | Gym | 4-2-0 | 5 | Karin Janz, E. Ger (1972) | Gym | 2-2-1 |
| 6 | Vera Cáslavská, CZE (1968) | Gym | 4-2-0 | 5 | Ines Diers, E. Ger-(1980) | Swim | 2-2-1 |
| 6 | Larisa Latynina, USSR (1956) | Gym | 4-1-1 | 5 | **Shirley Babashoff**, USA (1976) | Swim | 1-4-0 |
| 6 | Larisa Latynina, USSR (1960) | Gym | 3-2-1 | 5 | **Mary Lou Retton**, USA (1984) | Gym | 1-2-2 |
| 6 | Daniela Silivas, ROM (1988) | Gym | 3-2-1 | 5 | **Shannon Miller**, USA (1992) | Gym | 0-2-3 |
| 6 | Larisa Latynina, USSR (1964) | Gym | 2-2-2 | 5 | **Marion Jones**, USA (2000) | Track | 3-0-2 |
| 6 | Margit Korondi, HUN (1956) | Gym | 1-1-4 | 5 | **Dara Torres**, USA (2000) | Swim | 2-0-3 |
| 6 | Kornelia Ender, E. Ger (1976) | Gym | 4-1-0 | 5 | **Natalie Coughlin**, USA (2004) | Swim | 2-2-1 |
| 5 | Ecaterina Szabó, ROM (1984) | Gym | 4-1-0 | | | | |

## All-Time Leading Medal Winners – Career

### MEN

| No | | Sport | G-S-B | No | | Sport | G-S-B |
|----|---|-------|-------|----|---|-------|-------|
| 15 | Nikolai Andrianov, USSR | Gymnastics | 7-5-3 | 10 | **Carl Lewis**, USA | Track/Field | 9-1-0 |
| 13 | Boris Shakhlin, USSR | Gymnastics | 7-4-2 | 10 | Aladár Gerevich, HUN | Fencing | 7-1-2 |
| 13 | Edoardo Mangiarotti, ITA | Fencing | 6-5-2 | 10 | Akinori Nakayama, JPN | Gymnastics | 6-2-2 |
| 13 | Takashi Ono, JPN | Gymnastics | 5-4-4 | 10 | Aleksandr Dityatin, USSR | Gymnastics | 3-6-1 |
| 12 | Paavo Nurmi, FIN | Track/Field | 9-3-0 | 9 | Vitaly Scherbo, BLR | Gymnastics | 6-0-3 |
| 12 | Sawao Kato, JPN | Gymnastics | 8-3-1 | 9 | **Gary Hall Jr.**, USA | Swimming | 5-3-1 |
| 12 | Alexei Nemov, RUS | Gymnastics | 4-2-6 | 9* | **Martin Sheridan**, USA | Track/Field | 5-3-1 |
| 11 | **Mark Spitz**, USA | Swimming | 9-1-1 | 9* | Zoltán Halmay, HUN | Swimming | 3-5-1 |
| 11† | **Matt Biondi**, USA | Swimming | 8-2-1 | 9 | Giulio Gaudini, ITA | Fencing | 3-4-2 |
| 11 | Viktor Chukarin, USSR | Gymnastics | 7-3-1 | 9 | Mikhail Voronin, USSR | Gymnastics | 2-6-1 |
| 11 | **Carl Osburn**, USA | Shooting | 5-4-2 | 9 | Heikki Savolainen, FIN | Gymnastics | 2-1-6 |
| 10* | **Ray Ewry**, USA | Track/Field | 10-0-0 | 9 | Yuri Titov, USSR | Gymnastics | 1-5-3 |

†Includes gold medal as preliminary member of 1st-place relay team.
*Medals won by Ewry (2-0-0), Sheridan (2-3-0) and Halmay (1-1-0) at the 1906 Intercalated games are not officially recognized by the IOC.

### Games Participated In

**Andrianov** (1972,76,80); **Biondi** (1984,88,92); **Chukarin** (1952,56); **Dityatin** (1976,80); **Ewry** (1900,04,06,08); **Gerevich** (1932,36,48,52,56,60); **Gaudini** (1928,32,36); **Hall Jr.** (1996,2000,04); **Halmay** (1900,04,06,08); **Kato** (1968,72,76); **Lewis** (1984,88,92,96); **Mangiarotti** (1936,48,52,56,60); **Nakayama** (1968,72); **Nemov** (1996,2000) **Nurmi** (1920,24,28); **Ono** (1952,56,60,64); **Osburn** (1912,20, 24); **Savolainen** (1928,32,36,48,52); **Scherbo** (1992,96); **Shakhlin** (1956,60,64); **Sheridan** (1904,06,08); **Spitz** (1968,72); **Titov** (1956,60,64); **Voronin** (1968,72).

### Most Individual Medals

Not including team competition.

| | | Sport | G-S-B |
|---|---|-------|-------|
| **Men:** | 12-Nikolai Andrianov, USSR | Gym | 6-3-3 |
| **Women:** | 15-Larissa Latynina, USSR | Gym | 7-5-3 |

## WOMEN

| No | | Sport | G-S-B | No | | Sport | G-S-B |
|----|----|-------|-------|----|----|-------|-------|
| 18 | Larissa Latynina, USSR | Gymnastics | 9-5-4 | 8 | **Shirley Babashoff**, USA | Swimming | 2-6-0 |
| 12 | **Jenny Thompson**, USA | Swimming | 8-3-1 | 8 | Sofia Muratova, USSR | Gymnastics | 2-2-4 |
| 11 | Vera Cáslavská, CZE | Gymnastics | 7-4-0 | 8 | Inge de Bruijn, NED | Swimming | 4-2-2 |
| 10 | Birgit Fischer, GER | Canoe/Kayak | 7-3-0 | 8 | Krisztina Egerszegi, HUN | Swimming | 5-1-1 |
| 10 | Agnes Keleti, HUN | Gymnastics | 5-3-2 | 7 | Irena Kirszenstein Szewinska, POL | Track/Field | 3-2-2 |
| 10 | Polina Astakhova, USSR | Gymnastics | 5-2-3 | 7 | Shirley Strickland, AUS | Track/Field | 3-1-3 |
| 9 | Nadia Comaneci, ROM | Gymnastics | 5-3-1 | 7 | Maria Gorokhovskaya, USSR | Gymnastics | 2-5-0 |
| 9 | Lyudmila Tourischeva, USSR | Gymnastics | 4-3-2 | 7 | Ildiko Sagine-Ujlaki-Rejto, HUN | Fencing | 2-3-2 |
| 9 | **Dara Torres**, USA | Swimming | 4-1-4 | 7 | **Shannon Miller**, USA | Gymnastics | 2-2-3 |
| 8 | Kornelia Ender, E. Ger | Swimming | 4-4-0 | 7 | Susie O'Neill, AUS | Swimming | 2-4-1 |
| 8 | Dawn Fraser, AUS | Swimming | 4-4-0 | 7 | Merlene Ottey, JAM | Track/Field | 0-2-5 |

### Games Participated In

**Astakhova** (1956,60,64); **Babashoff** (1972,76); **Cáslavská** (1960,64,68); **Comaneci** (1976,80); **de Bruijn** (2000,04); **Egerszegi** (1988,92,96); **Ender** (1972,76); **Fischer** (1980,92,96,2000); **Fraser** (1956,60,64); **Gorokhovskaya** (1952); **Keleti** (1952,56); **Latynina** (1956,60,64); **Miller** (1992,96); **Muratova** (1956,60); **O'Neill** (1996,2000) **Ottey** (1980,84,88,92,96) **Sagine-Ujlaki-Rejto** (1960,64,68,72,76); **Strickland** (1948,52,56); **Szewinska** (1964,68,72,76,80); **Thompson** (1992,96,2000,04); **Torres** (1984,88,92,2000) **Tourischeva** (1968, 72,76).

## Most Gold Medals

### MEN

| No | | Sport | G-S-B | No | | Sport | G-S-B |
|----|----|-------|-------|----|----|-------|-------|
| 10* | **Ray Ewry**, USA | Track/Field | 10-0-0 | 7 | Boris Shakhlin, USSR | Gymnastics | 7-4-2 |
| 9 | Paavo Nurmi, FIN | Track/Field | 9-3-0 | 7 | Viktor Chukarin, USSR | Gymnastics | 7-3-1 |
| 9 | **Mark Spitz**, USA | Swimming | 9-1-1 | 7 | Aladar Gerevich, HUN | Fencing | 7-1-2 |
| 9 | **Carl Lewis**, USA | Track/Field | 9-1-0 | | | | |
| 8 | Sawao Kato, JPN | Gymnastics | 8-3-1 | | | | |
| 8† | **Matt Biondi**, USA | Swimming | 8-2-1 | | | | |
| 7 | Nikolai Andrianov, USSR | Gymnastics | 7-5-3 | | | | |

*Medals won by Ewry (2-0-0) at the 1906 Intercalated games are not officially recognized by the IOC.

†Includes gold medal as preliminary member of 1st-place relay team.

### WOMEN

| No | | Sport | G-S-B | No | | Sport | G-S-B |
|----|----|-------|-------|----|----|-------|-------|
| 9 | Larissa Latynina, USSR | Gymnastics | 9-5-4 | 4 | Lyudmila Tourischeva, USSR | Gymnastics | 4-3-2 |
| 8 | **Jenny Thompson**, USA | Swimming | 8-3-1 | 4 | **Dara Torres**, USA | Swimming | 4-1-4 |
| 7 | Vera Cáslavská, CZE | Gymnastics | 7-4-0 | 4 | **Evelyn Ashford**, USA | Track/Field | 4-1-0 |
| 7 | Birgit Fischer, GER | Canoe/Kayak | 7-3-0 | 4 | **Janet Evans**, USA | Swimming | 4-1-0 |
| 6† | Kristin Otto, E. Ger | Swimming | 6-0-0 | 4 | Fu Mingxia, CHN | Diving | 4-1-0 |
| 6† | **Amy Van Dyken**, USA | Swimming | 6-0-0 | 4 | Fanny Blankers-Koen, NED | Track/Field | 4-0-0 |
| 5 | Agnes Keleti, HUN | Gymnastics | 5-3-2 | 4 | Betty Cuthbert, AUS | Track/Field | 4-0-0 |
| 5 | Nadia Comaneci, ROM | Gymnastics | 5-3-1 | 4 | **Pat McCormick**, USA | Diving | 4-0-0 |
| 5 | Polina Astakhova, USSR | Gymnastics | 5-2-3 | 4 | Bärbel Eckert Wäckel, E. Ger. | Track/Field | 4-0-0 |
| 5 | Krisztina Egerszegi, HUN | Swimming | 5-1-1 | 4 | Inge de Bruijn, NED | Swimming | 4-2-2 |
| 4 | Kornelia Ender, E. Ger | Swimming | 4-4-0 | | | | |
| 4 | Dawn Fraser, AUS | Swimming | 4-4-0 | | | | |

†Includes gold medal as preliminary member of 1st-place relay team.

## All-Time Leading Medal Winners – Career (Cont.)
### Most Silver Medals

| MEN | | | | WOMEN | | | |
|---|---|---|---|---|---|---|---|
| No | | Sport | G-S-B | No | | Sport | G-S-B |
| 6 | Alexandr Dityatin, USSR | Gymnastics | 3-6-1 | 6 | **Shirley Babashoff**, USA | Swimming | 2-6-0 |
| 6 | Mikhail Voronin, USSR | Gymnastics | 2-6-1 | 5 | Larissa Latynina, USSR | Gymnastics | 9-5-4 |
| 5 | Nikolai Andrianov, USSR | Gymnastics | 7-5-3 | 5 | Maria Gorokhovskaya, USSR | Gymnastics | 2-5-0 |
| 5 | Edoardo Mangiarotti, ITA | Fencing | 6-5-2 | 4 | Vera Cáslavská, CZE | Gymnastics | 7-4-0 |
| 5 | Zoltán Halmay, HUN | Swimming | 3-5-1 | 4 | Kornelia Ender, E. Ger | Swimming | 4-4-0 |
| 5 | Gustavo Marzi, ITA | Fencing | 2-5-0 | 4 | Dawn Fraser, AUS | Swimming | 4-4-0 |
| 5 | Yuri Titov, USSR | Gymnastics | 1-5-3 | 4 | Erica Zuchold, E. Ger | Gymnastics | 0-4-1 |
| 5 | Viktor Lisitsky, USSR | Gymnastics | 0-5-0 | | | | |

### Most Bronze Medals

| MEN | | | | WOMEN | | | |
|---|---|---|---|---|---|---|---|
| No | | Sport | G-S-B | No | | Sport | G-S-B |
| 6 | Alexei Nemov, RUS | Gymnastics | 4-2-6 | 5 | Merlene Ottey, JAM | Track/Field | 0-2-5 |
| 6 | Heikki Savolainen, FIN | Gymnastics | 2-1-6 | 4 | Larissa Latynina, USSR | Gymnastics | 9-5-4 |
| 5 | Daniel Revenu, FRA | Fencing | 1-0-5 | 4 | **Dara Torres**, USA | Swimming | 4-1-4 |
| 5 | Philip Edwards, CAN | Track/Field | 0-0-5 | 4 | Sofia Muratova, USSR | Gymnastics | 2-2-4 |
| 5 | Adrianus Jong, NED | Fencing | 0-0-5 | | | | |

## All-Time Leading USA Medal Winners
### Most Overall Medals
#### MEN

| No | | Sport | G-S-B | No | | Sport | G-S-B |
|---|---|---|---|---|---|---|---|
| 11 | Mark Spitz | Swimming | 9-1-1 | 6 | Anton Heida | Gymnastics | 5-1-0 |
| 11† | Matt Biondi | Swimming | 8-2-1 | 6 | Don Schollander | Swimming | 5-1-0 |
| 11 | Carl Osburn | Shooting | 5-4-2 | 6 | Johnny Weissmuller | Swim/Water Polo | 5-0-1 |
| 10* | Ray Ewry | Track/Field | 10-0-0 | 6 | Alfred Lane | Shooting | 5-0-1 |
| 10 | Carl Lewis | Track/Field | 9-1-0 | 6 | Jim Lightbody | Track/Field | 4-2-0 |
| 9 | Gary Hall Jr. | Swimming | 5-3-1 | 6 | George Eyser | Gymnastics | 3-2-1 |
| 9* | Martin Sheridan | Track/Field | 5-3-1 | 6 | Ralph Rose | Track/Field | 3-2-1 |
| 8† | Michael Phelps | Swimming | 6-0-2 | 6 | Michael Plumb | Equestrian | 2-4-0 |
| 8 | Charles Daniels | Swimming | 5-1-2 | 6 | Burton Downing | Cycling | 2-3-1 |
| 7‡ | Tom Jager | Swimming | 5-1-1 | 6 | Bob Garrett | Track/Field | 2-2-2 |
| 7 | Willis Lee | Shooting | 5-1-1 | | | | |
| 7 | Lloyd Spooner | Shooting | 4-1-2 | | | | |

†Includes gold medal as prelim. member of 1st-place relay team.
*Medals won by Ewry (2-0-0) and Sheridan (2-3-0) at the 1906 Intercalated games are not officially recognized by the IOC:
‡Includes 3 gold medals as prelim. member of 1st-place relay teams.

### Games Participated In
**Biondi** (1984,88,92); **Daniels** (1904,06,08); **Downing** (1904); **Ewry** (1900,04,06,08); **Eyser** (1904); **Garrett** (1896,1900); **Hall Jr.** (1996,2000,04) **Heida** (1904); **Jager** (1984,88,92); **Lane** (1912,20); **Lee** (1920); **Lewis** (1984,88,92,96); **Lightbody** (1904,06); **Osburn** (1912,20,24); **Phelps** (2004), **Plumb** (1960, 64,68,72,76,84); **Rose** (1904,08,12); **Schollander** (1964, 68); **Sheridan** (1904,06,08); **Spitz** (1968,72); **Spooner** (1920); **Weissmuller** (1924,28).

#### WOMEN

| No | | Sport | G-S-B | No | | Sport | G-S-B |
|---|---|---|---|---|---|---|---|
| 12 | Jenny Thompson | Swimming | 8-3-1 | 5 | Evelyn Ashford | Track/Field | 4-1-0 |
| 9 | Dara Torres | Swimming | 4-1-4 | 5 | Janet Evans | Swimming | 4-1-0 |
| 8 | Shirley Babashoff | Swimming | 2-6-0 | 5 | Florence Griffith Joyner | Track/Field | 3-2-0 |
| 7 | Shannon Miller | Gymnastics | 2-2-3 | 5† | Mary T. Meagher | Swimming | 3-1-1 |
| 7 | Amanda Beard | Swimming | 2-4-1 | 5 | Gwen Torrence | Track/Field | 3-2-0 |
| 6† | Amy Van Dyken | Swimming | 6-0-0 | 5 | Marion Jones | Track/Field | 3-0-2 |
| 6 | Jackie Joyner-Kersee | Track/Field | 3-1-2 | 5 | Mary Lou Retton | Gymnastics | 1-2-2 |
| 6 | Angel Martino | Swimming | 3-0-3 | 5 | Natalie Coughlin | Swimming | 2-2-1 |

†Includes gold medal as prelim. member of 1st-place relay team.

### Games Participated In
**Ashford** (1976,84,88,92); **Babashoff** (1972,76); **Beard** (1996,2000,04); **Coughlin** (2004), **Evans** (1988,92,96); **Griffith Joyner** (1984,88); **Jones** (2000); **Joyner-Kersee** (1984,88,92,96); **Martino** (1992,96); **McCormick** (1952,56); **Meagher** (1984,88); **Miller** (1992, 96); **Retton** (1984); **Thompson** (1988,92,96,2000,04); **Torrence** (1988,92,96); **Torres** (1984,88,92,2000); **Van Dyken** (1996,2000).

## Most Gold Medals

### MEN

| No | | Sport | G-S-B |
|---|---|---|---|
| 10* | Raymond Ewry | Track/Field | 10-0-0 |
| 9 | Mark Spitz | Swimming | 9-1-1 |
| 9 | Carl Lewis | Track/Field | 9-1-0 |
| 8† | Matt Biondi | Swimming | 8-2-1 |
| 6† | Michael Phelps | Swimming | 6-0-2 |
| 5 | Carl Osburn | Shooting | 5-4-2 |
| 5* | Martin Sheridan | Track/Field | 5-3-1 |
| 5 | Charles Daniels | Swimming | 5-1-2 |
| 5‡ | Tom Jager | Swimming | 5-1-1 |
| 5 | Willis Lee | Shooting | 5-1-1 |
| 5 | Anton Heida | Gymnastics | 5-1-0 |
| 5 | Don Schollander | Swimming | 5-1-0 |
| 5 | Johnny Weissmuller | Swim/Water Polo | 5-0-1 |
| 5 | Alfred Lane | Shooting | 5-0-1 |
| 5 | Morris Fisher | Shooting | 5-0-0 |
| 5 | Gary Hall Jr. | Swimming | 5-3-1 |
| 4 | Jim Lightbody | Track/Field | 4-2-0 |
| 4 | Lloyd Spooner | Shooting | 4-1-2 |
| 4 | Greg Louganis | Diving | 4-1-0 |
| 4 | John Naber | Swimming | 4-1-0 |
| 4 | Meyer Prinstein | Track/Field | 4-1-0 |
| 4 | Mel Sheppard | Track/Field | 4-1-0 |
| 4 | Marcus Hurley | Cycling | 4-0-1 |
| 4† | Jon Olsen | Swimming | 4-0-1 |
| 4 | Archie Hahn | Track/Field | 4-0-0 |
| 4 | Alvin Kraenzlein | Track/Field | 4-0-0 |
| 4 | Al Oerter | Track/Field | 4-0-0 |
| 4 | Jesse Owens | Track/Field | 4-0-0 |

*Medals won by Ewry (2-0-0) and Sheridan (2-3-0) at the 1906 Intercalated games are not officially recognized by the IOC.
†Includes gold medal as preliminary member of 1st-place relay team.
‡Includes 3 gold medals as preliminary member of 1st-place relay teams.

### WOMEN

| No | | Sport | G-S-B |
|---|---|---|---|
| 8 | Jenny Thompson | Swimming | 8-3-1 |
| 6† | Amy Van Dyken | Swimming | 6-0-0 |
| 4 | Dara Torres | Swimming | 4-1-4 |
| 4 | Evelyn Ashford | Track/Field | 4-1-0 |
| 4 | Janet Evans | Swimming | 4-1-0 |
| 4 | Pat McCormick | Diving | 4-0-0 |
| 3 | Florence Griffith Joyner | Track/Field | 3-2-0 |
| 3 | Jackie Joyner-Kersee | Track/Field | 3-1-2 |
| 3† | Mary T. Meagher | Swimming | 3-1-1 |
| 3 | Gwen Torrence | Track/Field | 3-1-1 |
| 3 | Valerie Brisco-Hooks | Track/Field | 3-1-0 |
| 3 | Nancy Hogshead | Swimming | 3-1-0 |
| 3 | Sharon Stouder | Swimming | 3-1-0 |
| 3 | Wyomia Tyus | Track/Field | 3-1-0 |
| 3 | Chris von Saltza | Swimming | 3-1-0 |
| 3 | Wilma Rudolph | Track/Field | 3-0-1 |
| 3 | Melissa Belote | Swimming | 3-0-0 |
| 3 | Ethelda Bleibtrey | Swimming | 3-0-0 |
| 3 | Tracy Caulkins | Swimming | 3-0-0 |
| 3† | Nicole Haislett | Swimming | 3-0-0 |
| 3 | Helen Madison | Swimming | 3-0-0 |
| 3 | Debbie Meyer | Swimming | 3-0-0 |
| 3 | Sandra Neilson | Swimming | 3-0-0 |
| 3 | Martha Norelius | Swimming | 3-0-0 |
| 3† | Carrie Steinseifer | Swimming | 3-0-0 |
| 3‡ | Ashley Tappin | Swimming | 3-0-0 |

†Includes gold medal as preliminary member of 1st-place relay team.
‡Includes 3 gold medals as preliminary member of 1st-place relay teams

## Most Silver Medals

### MEN

| No | | Sport | G-S-B |
|---|---|---|---|
| 4 | Carl Osburn | Shooting | 5-4-2 |
| 4 | Michael Plumb | Equestrian | 2-4-0 |
| 3 | Martin Sheridan | Track/Field | 5-3-1 |
| 3 | Burton Downing | Cycling | 2-3-1 |
| 3 | Irving Baxter | Track/Field | 2-3-0 |

| No | | Sport | G-S-B |
|---|---|---|---|
| 3 | Earl Thomson | Equestrian | 2-3-0 |
| 3 | Alexander McKee | Swimming | 0-3-0 |

### WOMEN

| No | | Sport | G-S-B |
|---|---|---|---|
| 6 | Shirley Babashoff | Swimming | 2-6-0 |

## All-Time Medal Standings, 1896-2004

All-time Summer Games medal standings, based on *The Golden Book of the Olympic Games*. Medal counts include the 1906 Intercalated Games, which are not recognized by the IOC.

| | | G | S | B | Total |
|---|---|---|---|---|---|
| 1 | **United States** | 907 | 697 | 615 | 2219 |
| 2 | USSR (1952-88) | 395 | 319 | 296 | 1010 |
| 3 | Great Britain | 189 | 242 | 237 | 668 |
| 4 | France | 199 | 202 | 230 | 631 |
| 5 | Italy | 189 | 154 | 168 | 511 |
| 6 | Germany (1896-64,92–) | 151 | 154 | 178 | 483 |
| 7 | Sweden | 140 | 157 | 179 | 476 |
| 8 | Hungary | 158 | 141 | 161 | 460 |
| 9 | East Germany (1968-88) | 159 | 150 | 136 | 445 |
| 10 | Australia | 119 | 126 | 154 | 399 |
| 11 | Japan | 113 | 106 | 114 | 333 |
| 12 | West Germany (1968-88) | 77 | 104 | 120 | 301 |
| 13 | Finland | 101 | 83 | 114 | 298 |
| 14 | China | 112 | 96 | 78 | 286 |
| 15 | Romania | 82 | 88 | 114 | 284 |
| 16 | Poland | 59 | 74 | 118 | 251 |
| 17 | Russia (1896-1912, 96–) | 85 | 79 | 84 | 248 |
| 18 | Canada | 54 | 87 | 101 | 242 |
| 19 | Netherlands | 65 | 76 | 94 | 234 |
| 20 | Bulgaria | 50 | 83 | 74 | 207 |
| 21 | Switzerland | 48 | 76 | 64 | 188 |
| 22 | South Korea | 55 | 64 | 65 | 184 |
| 23 | Denmark | 42 | 63 | 64 | 169 |
| 24 | Cuba | 64 | 51 | 49 | 164 |
| 25 | Belgium | 38 | 51 | 54 | 143 |
| 26 | Czechoslovakia (1924-92) | 49 | 49 | 44 | 142 |
| | Greece | 38 | 54 | 50 | 142 |
| 28 | Norway | 54 | 44 | 42 | 140 |
| 29 | Unified Team (1992) | 45 | 38 | 29 | 112 |
| 30 | Spain | 28 | 39 | 27 | 94 |
| 31 | Yugoslavia (1924-88,96-2000) | 28 | 32 | 33 | 93 |
| | Austria | 22 | 36 | 35 | 93 |
| 33 | New Zealand | 33 | 14 | 32 | 79 |
| 34 | Brazil | 16 | 22 | 38 | 76 |
| 35 | Turkey | 36 | 19 | 19 | 74 |
| 36 | Rep. of S. Africa (1904-60, 92–) | 20 | 23 | 26 | 69 |

## All-Time Medal Standings, 1896-2004 (Cont.)

| | | G | S | B | Total | | | G | S | B | Total |
|---|---|---|---|---|---|---|---|---|---|---|---|
| 37 | Kenya | 17 | 24 | 20 | 61 | 95 | Hong Kong | 1 | 1 | 0 | 2 |
| 38 | Argentina | 15 | 23 | 22 | 60 | | Dominican Republic | 1 | 0 | 1 | 2 |
| 39 | Mexico | 10 | 18 | 23 | 51 | | Japan/Korea | 1 | 0 | 1 | 2 |
| 40 | Iran | 10 | 15 | 21 | 46 | | Mozambique | 1 | 0 | 1 | 2 |
| | Ukraine | 12 | 15 | 19 | 46 | | Surinam | 1 | 0 | 1 | 2 |
| 42 | Jamaica | 7 | 21 | 14 | 42 | | Serbia & Montenegro | 0 | 2 | 0 | 2 |
| 43 | North Korea | 8 | 11 | 16 | 35 | | Tanzania | 0 | 2 | 0 | 2 |
| 44 | Belarus | 5 | 9 | 18 | 32 | | Great Britain/USA | 0 | 1 | 1 | 2 |
| 45 | Ethiopia | 14 | 5 | 12 | 31 | | Haiti | 0 | 1 | 1 | 2 |
| 46 | Estonia | 8 | 7 | 14 | 29 | | Russia/Estonia | 0 | 1 | 1 | 2 |
| 47 | Czech Republic | 7 | 9 | 11 | 27 | | Saudi Arabia | 0 | 1 | 1 | 2 |
| 48 | Ireland | 9 | 6 | 6 | 21 | | United Arab Republic | 0 | 1 | 1 | 2 |
| | Egypt | 7 | 6 | 8 | 21 | | Zambia | 0 | 1 | 1 | 2 |
| 50 | Great Britain/Ireland | 6 | 11 | 3 | 20 | | The Antilles | 0 | 0 | 2 | 2 |
| | Portugal | 3 | 6 | 11 | 20 | | Panama | 0 | 0 | 2 | 2 |
| | Indonesia | 5 | 8 | 7 | 20 | | Qatar | 0 | 0 | 2 | 2 |
| 53 | Nigeria | 2 | 8 | 9 | 19 | 111 | Australia/New Zealand | 1 | 0 | 0 | 1 |
| | Morocco | 6 | 4 | 9 | 19 | | Burkina Faso | 1 | 0 | 0 | 1 |
| 55 | India | 8 | 4 | 5 | 17 | | Cuba/USA | 1 | 0 | 0 | 1 |
| | Thailand | 5 | 2 | 10 | 17 | | Denmark/Sweden | 1 | 0 | 0 | 1 |
| 57 | Mongolia | 0 | 5 | 10 | 15 | | Ecuador | 1 | 0 | 0 | 1 |
| | Chinese Taipei | 2 | 6 | 7 | 15 | | Gr. Britain/Ireland/Germany | 1 | 0 | 0 | 1 |
| | Kazakhstan | 4 | 8 | 3 | 15 | | Gr. Britain/Ireland/USA | 1 | 0 | 0 | 1 |
| 60 | Latvia | 1 | 10 | 3 | 14 | | Ireland/USA | 1 | 0 | 0 | 1 |
| | Slovakia | 4 | 6 | 4 | 14 | | United Arab Emirates | 1 | 0 | 0 | 1 |
| 62 | Algeria | 4 | 1 | 7 | 12 | | Belgium/Greece | 0 | 1 | 0 | 1 |
| | Trinidad & Tobago | 1 | 3 | 8 | 12 | | Ceylon | 0 | 1 | 0 | 1 |
| | Lithuania | 4 | 2 | 6 | 12 | | France/USA | 0 | 1 | 0 | 1 |
| | Chile | 2 | 6 | 4 | 12 | | France/Gr. Britain/Ireland | 0 | 1 | 0 | 1 |
| | Georgia | 2 | 2 | 8 | 12 | | Ivory Coast | 0 | 1 | 0 | 1 |
| | Croatia | 3 | 4 | 5 | 12 | | Netherlands Antilles | 0 | 1 | 0 | 1 |
| 68 | Uzbekistan | 3 | 3 | 5 | 11 | | Paraguay | 0 | 1 | 0 | 1 |
| 69 | Pakistan | 3 | 3 | 4 | 10 | | Senegal | 0 | 1 | 0 | 1 |
| | Uruguay | 2 | 2 | 6 | 10 | | Singapore | 0 | 1 | 0 | 1 |
| | Venezuela | 1 | 2 | 7 | 10 | | Smyrna | 0 | 1 | 0 | 1 |
| | Slovenia | 2 | 3 | 5 | 10 | | Tonga | 0 | 1 | 0 | 1 |
| 73 | Azerbaijan | 3 | 1 | 5 | 9 | | Vietnam | 0 | 1 | 0 | 1 |
| | Philippines | 0 | 2 | 7 | 9 | | Virgin Islands | 0 | 1 | 0 | 1 |
| 75 | Bahamas | 3 | 2 | 3 | 8 | | Australia/Great Britain | 0 | 0 | 1 | 1 |
| | Colombia | 1 | 2 | 5 | 8 | | Barbados | 0 | 0 | 1 | 1 |
| 77 | Uganda | 1 | 3 | 2 | 6 | | Bermuda | 0 | 0 | 1 | 1 |
| | Tunisia | 1 | 2 | 3 | 6 | | Bohemia/Great Britain | 0 | 0 | 1 | 1 |
| | Bohemia | 0 | 1 | 5 | 6 | | Djibouti | 0 | 0 | 1 | 1 |
| | Puerto Rico | 0 | 1 | 5 | 6 | | Eritrea | 0 | 0 | 1 | 1 |
| | Israel | 1 | 1 | 4 | 6 | | France/Great Britain | 0 | 0 | 1 | 1 |
| 82 | Cameroon | 2 | 1 | 1 | 4 | | Guyana | 0 | 0 | 1 | 1 |
| | Zimbabwe | 2 | 1 | 1 | 4 | | Iraq | 0 | 0 | 1 | 1 |
| | Peru | 1 | 3 | 0 | 4 | | Kuwait | 0 | 0 | 1 | 1 |
| | Costa Rica | 1 | 1 | 2 | 4 | | Kyrgyzstan | 0 | 0 | 1 | 1 |
| | Namibia | 0 | 4 | 0 | 4 | | Macedonia | 0 | 0 | 1 | 1 |
| | Lebanon | 0 | 2 | 2 | 4 | | Mexico/Spain | 0 | 0 | 1 | 1 |
| | Moldova | 0 | 2 | 2 | 4 | | Niger | 0 | 0 | 1 | 1 |
| | Ghana | 0 | 1 | 3 | 4 | | Scotland | 0 | 0 | 1 | 1 |
| 90 | Luxembourg | 2 | 1 | 0 | 3 | | Sri Lanka | 0 | 0 | 1 | 1 |
| | Armenia | 1 | 1 | 1 | 3 | | Thessalonika | 0 | 0 | 1 | 1 |
| | Iceland | 0 | 1 | 2 | 3 | | Wales | 0 | 0 | 1 | 1 |
| | Malaysia | 0 | 1 | 2 | 3 | | | | | | |
| | Syria | 1 | 1 | 1 | 3 | | | | | | |

| **Combined totals:** | G | S | B | Total |
|---|---|---|---|---|
| USSR/UT/Russia | 525 | 436 | 409 | 1370 |
| Germany/E. Ger/W. Ger | 388 | 408 | 434 | 1230 |

**Notes:** Athletes from the USSR participated in the Summer Games from 1952-88, returned as the Unified Team in 1992 after the breakup of the Soviet Union (in 1991) and have competed as independent republics since the 1994 Winter Games. Germany was barred from the Olympics in 1924 and 1948 following World Wars I and II. Divided into East and West Germany after WWII, both countries competed together from 1952-64, then separately from 1968-88. Germany was reunified in 1990. Czechoslovakia split into Slovakia and the Czech Republic in 1993. Croatia and Bosnia-Herzegovina gained independence from Yugoslavia in 1991. Yugoslavia was not invited to the 1992 games (though Serbian and Montenegrin athletes were allowed to compete as independent athletes) but returned in 1996 and competed under the name Serbia & Montenegro starting in 2004. South Africa was banned from 1964-88 for using the apartheid policy in the selection of its teams. It returned in 1992 as the Republic of South Africa (RSA).

# Soccer

*Liverpool captain* **Steven Gerrard** *raises the trophy after the Reds' 2005 win over AC Milan in the UEFA Champions League Final.*

AP/Wide World Photos

# Can the USA Go All the Way?

*With an impressive qualifying run in the books, Team USA looks to make a run at the best in the world at next summer's World Cup in Germany.*

**Gerry Brown**
is co-editor of the ESPN Sports Almanac

The United States is a threat to win the 2006 World Cup.

Are they one of the favorites in Germany? Certainly not, but the fact that a realistic case can be made that they have a shot—albeit an outside one—would have been hard to believe not long ago.

So has the USA finished their well laid out plan to threaten for a World Cup by 2010 with four years to spare? Time will tell.

Project 2010 was organized by U.S. Soccer (and heavily promoted by Nike) in 1998 with the stated goal of building the U.S. men's national team into a legitimate World Cup contender by 2010.

The team performed exceptionally in the final stage of World Cup qualifying in 2005, where they finished atop the CONCACAF standings for the first time since the final phase expanded to six teams in 1994. They finished the season with a record of 13-3-3, their only losses

coming at Mexico, in a friendly against England and at Costa Rica, after they had already qualified for Germany.

In July 2005, the United States reached sixth place in FIFA's World Rankings, ahead of traditional European soccer powers like France, England, Germany and Italy, winners of a combined eight World Cups.

That newly earned international respect should help them in the all-important tournament draw. If the United States can avoid being placed in a group with big boys like Brazil and Argentina then their shot of advancing out of group play is substantially better.

Once the tournament moves to a single-elimination format beginning in the second round and if things break right with the bracket, the referee's whistle and any funny bounces, the Americans could find themselves in the hunt.

AP/Wide World Photos

*Head coach **Bruce Arena** led the United States Men's National Team through a successful World Cup Qualifying run and is looking to make some noise next summer in Germany.*

At the last World Cup in 2002, the United States advanced to the quarterfinals before losing a tight 1-0 game against eventual runners-up Germany to fall just short of the final four.

That was U.S. National Team head coach Bruce Arena's first World Cup in charge. Hired in October 1998, just after the USA's last-place finish at the World Cup in France that year, Arena is now the longest-tenured national team coach in the world.

With four more years to evaluate talent and four more MLS seasons to sharpen the skills of many American players, Arena's job should be a little bit easier. He has the unquestioned respect of his players as the winningest U.S. national team coach in history.

Major League Soccer has gone a long way toward improving the U.S. national team. The recent emergence of young intuitive scorers like the New England Revolution's Taylor Twellman bode well for the future of the national team. Twellman has led the MLS in scoring two out of the last three seasons and scored his first goal for the national team against Panama in October 2005.

But the top scoring threats for 2006 will probably be proven international scorers like Eddie Johnson

*The **Brazilian National Team** is the best in the world. They reaffirmed this fact with a win a the Confederations Cup in 2005 and are the favorites at the 2006 World Cup in Germany.*

and Landon Donovan. Johnson has performed well for FC Dallas in the MLS, scored a hat trick in a 2004 World Cup qualifier against Panama and has eight international goals in eight games. Donovan has been the poster boy of American soccer for years now and already has World Cup results, scoring twice in 2002.

Goalkeeping has been a strength of recent American teams and next year should be no different. Keeper Brad Friedel set a high bar with his superb play in 2002. With Friedel's retirement veteran Kasey Keller is now the undisputed starter and has the talent and experience to come up big in Germany.

Keller could get some help keeping the ball out of the net with the development of big young defender Oguchi Onyewu. "Gooch" has played in the Belgian first division recently and has been pursued by many of Europe's top clubs, including Manchester United. The six-foot-four, 210-pound center back was born and raised in Maryland to Nigerian parents and starred at Clemson.

His impressive size and ability should translate into a spot on the roster for 2006 but his propensity for collecting red cards could keep him off the field.

America is ready. Is the world?

# The Ten Biggest Stories of the Year in Soccer

**10** **Major League Soccer continues to grow**, announcing plans for expansion to Toronto (and potentially another city) for the 2007 season. The league builds more soccer-dedicated stadiums as well including: Pizza Hut Park in Texas, Chicago's new Bridgeview Stadium, the recently announced new stadiums for Real Salt Lake to be built in Sandy, Utah and the MetroStars in Harrison, N.J. Other cities that the MLS is considering for expansion reportedly include Houston, Philadelphia, Cleveland, Milwaukee and St. Louis.

**9** **A European team wins the final edition of the annual Toyota Cup** when Portugal's FC Porto beats Colombia's Once Caldas, 8-7, in a thrilling penalty kick shootout following a 0-0 draw in regulation. The Toyota Cup, also called the European/South American Cup, pit the club champions of Europe and South America against each other every year. It served as the de facto world championship of professional soccer since 1960 but will be replaced going forward by...

**8** **The FIFA Club World Championship merges** with the Toyota Cup beginning in December 2005, and in recognition of club soccer's global reach, it will now be open to teams from around the world rather that only Europe and South America. FIFA tried to replace the Toyota Cup for the first time five years ago and held a club world championship tournament in 2000 but it failed to hold another until 2005 due to a variety of factors, including the bankruptcy of its marketing partners ISL.

**7** **Notre Dame wins the NCAA women's College Cup** in a penalty kick shootout, 4-3, against UCLA following a 1-1 draw and two overtimes. Irish goalkeeper Erika Bohn stonewalls the Bruins and turns aside a penalty kick late in regulation to preserve the tie and send the game into overtime, where she helps deliver the victory, saving two more in the shootout.

**6** Under first-year head coach Mike Freitag **Indiana University wins the NCAA men's College Cup**, 3-2, in a penalty kick shootout over the Gauchos of UC Santa Barbara. It's the first time that both the men's and women's NCAA title games go to a shootout in the same season.

**5** **Greece stunningly fails to qualify** for the 2006 World Cup just one year after winning the 2004 European Championships in Portugal and staking their claim as the best team on the Continent.

**4 Brazil wins the FIFA Confederations Cup**, beating their South American rivals Argentina, 4-1, in the final held in Germany. With the convincing win, Brazil cements their place as the best team in the world and the favorites to repeat as World Cup champions when they return to Germany next year.

**3 The U.S. Women's National Team continues to excel** despite the recent retirement of several of their stars, including Mia Hamm. This transitional squad, led by players like Abby Wambach, Aly Wagner and Shannon Boxx goes undefeated and *unscored* upon in 2005.

**2 Liverpool wins** the 2005 UEFA Champions League in an epic final against AC Milan. The Reds pull off one of soccer's all-time comebacks, climbing out of a 3-0 halftime hole in a six minute span in the second half to force overtime. The game goes to a shootout where Liverpool prevails, 3-2.

**1 The U.S. Men's National Team qualifies** for the 2006 World Cup with room to spare. Finishing atop the CONCACAF standings and delivering some convincing wins along the way, Bruce Arena's team looks like it could surpass its surprising run to the quarterfinals in the last World Cup in 2002.

## Big Money Clubs

*Forbes Magazine* recently ranked the values of the world's richest soccer clubs. The world's most valuable club, Manchester United, is worth nearly $1.2 billion, more than America's top-valued sports franchise (the Washington Redskins at $952 million). Two of the top 10 battled in the 2005 UEFA Champions League final.

| | Team (Country) | Value ($ mil) |
|---|---|---|
| 1 | Manchester United (England) | $1.186 |
| 2 | Juventus (Italy) | 828 |
| 3 | AC Milan (Italy) | 759 |
| 4 | Real Madrid (Spain) | 751 |
| 5 | Bayern Munich (Germany) | 617 |
| 6 | Internazionale (Italy) | 558 |
| 7 | Arsenal (England) | 482 |
| 8 | Liverpool (England) | 447 |
| 9 | Newcastle United (England) | 398 |
| 10 | Borussia Dortmund (Germany) | 355 |

## 2007 World Cup

While the Men's World Cup takes center stage in 2006, the world's women's national teams will be getting ready to begin qualifying for the 2007 Women's World Cup to be held in China. Here's a listing of the 16 berths to be awarded by confederation:

| | Berths |
|---|---|
| Host (China) | 1 |
| Asia | 2½ |
| Africa | 2 |
| South America | 2 |
| North/Central America | 2½ |
| Oceania | 1 |
| Europe | 5 |

**Note:** The third-place teams from Asia and North/Central America will meet in a playoff to decide the 16th spot in the 2007 Women's World Cup.

# 2004-2005
# *Season in Review*

**SPORTS ALMANAC**

## 2005 FIFA Confederations Cup

The FIFA Confederations Cup is contested by the continental champions of Africa, Asia, Europe, North America, Oceania and South America (plus host Germany and reigning World Cup champions Brazil). Played in Germany June 15-29, 2005 for the seventh time since its inception in 1992.

### First Round

Round robin; each team played the other three teams in its group once. Note that three points were awarded for a win and one point for a tie. (*) indicates team advanced to second round.

| Group A | W | L | T | Pts | GF | GA |
|---|---|---|---|---|---|---|
| *Germany | 2 | 0 | 1 | 7 | 9 | 5 |
| *Argentina | 2 | 0 | 1 | 7 | 8 | 5 |
| Tunisia | 1 | 2 | 0 | 3 | 3 | 5 |
| Australia | 0 | 3 | 0 | 0 | 5 | 10 |

| Group B | W | L | T | Pts | GF | GA |
|---|---|---|---|---|---|---|
| *Mexico | 2 | 0 | 1 | 7 | 3 | 1 |
| *Brazil | 1 | 1 | 1 | 4 | 5 | 3 |
| Japan | 1 | 1 | 1 | 4 | 4 | 4 |
| Greece | 0 | 2 | 1 | 1 | 0 | 4 |

#### Results

| Date | Site | Result |
|---|---|---|
| June 15 | Cologne | Argentina 2, Tunisia 1 |
| June 15 | Frankfurt | Germany 4, Australia 3 |
| June 18 | Cologne | Germany 3, Tunisia 0 |
| June 18 | Nuremberg | Argentina 4, Australia 2 |
| June 21 | Leipzig | Tunisia 2, Australia 0 |
| June 21 | Nuremberg | Argentina 2, Germany 2 |

#### Results

| Date | Site | Result |
|---|---|---|
| June 16 | Hanover | Mexico 2, Japan 1 |
| June 16 | Leipzig | Brazil 3, Greece 0 |
| June 19 | Hanover | Mexico 1, Brazil 0 |
| June 19 | Frankfurt | Japan 1, Greece 0 |
| June 22 | Frankfurt | Greece 0, Mexico 0 |
| June 22 | Cologne | Japan 2, Brazil 2 |

### Semifinals

| Date | Site | Result |
|---|---|---|
| June 25 | Nuremberg | Brazil 3, Germany 2 |
| June 26 | Hanover | Mexico 1, Argentina 1 |

Argentina advanced on penalty kicks, 6-5

### Third-place

| Date | Site | Result |
|---|---|---|
| June 29 | Leipzig | Germany 4, Mexico 3 OT |

### Final

| Date | Site | Result |
|---|---|---|
| June 29 | Frankfurt | Brazil 4, Argentina 1 |

**Goal:** Brazil—Adriano (11th), Kaka (16th), Ronaldinho (47th), Adriano (63th); Argentina—Pablo Aimar (65th).

### Top Scorers
#### Goals Scored

| | Goals |
|---|---|
| Adriano, Brazil | 5 |
| John Aloisi, Australia | 4 |
| Michael Ballack, Germany | 4 |
| Luciano Figueroa, Argentina | 4 |
| Four players tied at 3 each. | |

#### Assists

| | Assists |
|---|---|
| Robinho, Brazil | 3 |
| Cicinho, Brazil | 3 |
| Six players tied with 2 each. | |

### Most Valuable Player

Adriano, Brazil, F

---

## Countdown to Germany 2006

| Dec. 9, 2005 | The final tournament draw held in Leipzig, Germany |
| June 9, 2006 | Opening match of 2006 World Cup in Munich |
| July 9, 2006 | Championship match in Berlin. |

### 27 teams qualified for World Cup Finals (32 totals slots)
(as of Oct. 15, 2005)

**FIFA WORLD CUP**
**GERMANY**
**2006**

**Africa** (5 slots)

| | |
|---|---|
| Angola | Ivory Coast |
| Togo | Ghana |
| Tunisia | |

**Europe** (14 slots)

| | | |
|---|---|---|
| England | France | Germany |
| Ukraine | Netherlands | Poland |
| Croatia | Italy | Portugal |
| Serbia & Montenegro | Sweden | |

**Asia** (4.5 slots)

| | |
|---|---|
| Japan | Iran |
| South Korea | Saudi Arabia |

**South America** (4.5 slots)

| | |
|---|---|
| Argentina | Brazil |
| Ecuador | Paraguay |

**North/Central America** (3.5 slots)

| | | |
|---|---|---|
| USA | Mexico | Costa Rica |

**Note:** Two-leg, total-goal playoffs were scheduled for Nov. 12 & 16, 2005 to determine the final five spots for Germany. The match-ups: Oceania champs **Australia** vs. 5th-place S. American team **Uruguay**. Fourth-place North/Central American team **Trinidad & Tobago** vs. 5th-place Asian team **Bahrain**. In Europe, the six lowest group runners-up battled for three spots. **Slovakia** vs. **Spain**; **Switzerland** vs. **Turkey**; **Czech Republic** vs. **Norway**.

# FIFA Top 50 World Rankings

FIFA announced a new monthly world ranking system on Aug. 13, 1993 designed to "provide a constant international comparison of national team performances." The rankings are based on a mathematical formula that weighs strength of schedule, importance of matches and goals scored for and against. Games considered include World Cup qualifying and final rounds, Continental championship qualifying and final rounds, and friendly matches.

The formula was altered slightly in January 1999. Now the rankings annually take into account a team's seven best matches of the last eight years, thereby favoring some teams that have been consistent over a long period of time but that may have stumbled just recently. At the end of the year, FIFA designates a Team of the Year. Teams of the Year so far have been Germany (1993), Brazil (1994-2000, 2002-04) and France (2001). The USA reached their highest-ever ranking (6th) in July 2005.

## 2004

| # | Team | Points | 2003 Rank | # | Team | Points | 2003 Rank | # | Team | Points | 2003 Rank |
|---|------|--------|-----------|---|------|--------|-----------|---|------|--------|-----------|
| 1 | Brazil | 843 | 1 | 18 | Greece | 706 | 30 | 35 | Norway | 633 | 42 |
| 2 | France | 792 | 2 | 19 | Germany | 705 | 12 | | Tunisia | 633 | 45 |
| 3 | Argentina | 785 | 5 | 20 | Iran | 697 | 28 | 37 | Bulgaria | 623 | 34 |
| 4 | Czech Republic | 777 | 6 | 21 | Nigeria | 690 | 35 | 38 | South Africa | 619 | 36 |
| 5 | Spain | 765 | 3 | 22 | South Korea | 688 | 22 | 39 | Ecuador | 616 | 37 |
| 6 | Netherlands | 758 | 4 | 23 | Cameroon | 677 | 14 | 40 | Cote d'Ivoire | 611 | 70 |
| 7 | Mexico | 753 | 7 | | Croatia | 677 | 20 | | Jordan | 611 | 47 |
| 8 | England | 752 | 8 | 25 | Poland | 672 | 25 | 42 | Slovenia | 608 | 31 |
| 9 | Portugal | 747 | 17 | 26 | Colombia | 669 | 39 | 43 | Finland | 607 | 40 |
| 10 | Italy | 738 | 10 | 27 | Costa Rica | 668 | 17 | 44 | Iraq | 603 | 43 |
| 11 | USA | 726 | 11 | 28 | Saudi Arabia | 665 | 38 | 45 | Belgium | 600 | 16 |
| 12 | Ireland | 716 | 14 | 29 | Romania | 664 | 24 | 46 | Serbia & Montenegro | 599 | 41 |
| 13 | Sweden | 715 | 19 | 30 | Paraguay | 661 | 22 | 47 | Uzbekistan | 598 | 81 |
| 14 | Denmark | 711 | 13 | 31 | Senegal | 657 | 33 | 48 | Israel | 595 | 51 |
| | Turkey | 711 | 8 | 32 | Russia | 652 | 24 | 49 | Bahrain | 594 | 64 |
| 16 | Uruguay | 708 | 21 | 33 | Morocco | 646 | 38 | | Jamaica | 594 | 46 |
| 17 | Japan | 707 | 29 | 34 | Egypt | 644 | 32 | | | | |

## 2005 (as of Sept. 14)

| # | Team | Points | 2004 Rank | # | Team | Points | 2004 Rank | # | Team | Points | 2004 Rank |
|---|------|--------|-----------|---|------|--------|-----------|---|------|--------|-----------|
| 1 | Brazil | 839 | 1 | 18 | Iran | 702 | 20 | 35 | Senegal | 652 | 31 |
| 2 | Netherlands | 785 | 6 | 19 | Costa Rica | 700 | 27 | 36 | Morocco | 649 | 33 |
| 3 | Argentina | 778 | 3 | 20 | Greece | 699 | 18 | 37 | Norway | 647 | 35 |
| 4 | Czech Republic | 777 | 6 | 21 | Ireland | 694 | 12 | 38 | Switzerland | 643 | 51 |
| 5 | Mexico | 771 | 7 | 22 | Cameroon | 688 | 23 | 39 | Ukraine | 636 | 57 |
| 6 | France | 770 | 2 | 23 | Tunisia | 687 | 35 | 40 | Finland | 629 | 43 |
| 7 | USA | 768 | 11 | 24 | Croatia | 686 | 23 | 41 | Jamaica | 623 | 49 |
| 8 | Spain | 750 | 5 | 25 | Uruguay | 680 | 16 | 42 | South Africa | 622 | 38 |
| 9 | Portugal | 743 | 9 | 26 | Colombia | 677 | 26 | 43 | Honduras | 620 | 59 |
| 10 | Sweden | 740 | 13 | | South Korea | 677 | 22 | 44 | Israel | 616 | 48 |
| 11 | England | 738 | 8 | 28 | Saudi Arabia | 675 | 28 | 45 | Bulgaria | 613 | 37 |
| 12 | Turkey | 731 | 14 | 29 | Nigeria | 672 | 21 | | Slovakia | 613 | 53 |
| 13 | Italy | 725 | 10 | 30 | Russia | 669 | 32 | 47 | Belgium | 608 | 45 |
| 14 | Denmark | 721 | 14 | 31 | Egypt | 662 | 34 | 48 | Serbia & Montenegro | 601 | 46 |
| 15 | Germany | 718 | 19 | 32 | Romania | 660 | 29 | 49 | Zimbabwe | 598 | 60 |
| 16 | Japan | 716 | 17 | 33 | Ecuador | 658 | 39 | 50 | Australia | 593 | 58 |
| 17 | Poland | 705 | 25 | 34 | Paraguay | 656 | 30 | | Cote d'Ivoire | 593 | 40 |

# FIFA Women's World Rankings

As part of its growing recognition of women's soccer FIFA began ranking the women's national teams in 2002 following the inaugural FIFA Women's U19 World Championship in Canada. The rankings are currently released four times a year and are calculated in a similar manner to the men's rankings. The first women's international was held on April 17, 1971 (France vs. the Netherlands). The Top 30 teams are listed below.

## 2005 (as of Sept. 16)

| # | Team | Points | 2004 Rank | # | Team | Points | 2004 Rank | # | Team | Points | 2004 Rank |
|---|------|--------|-----------|---|------|--------|-----------|---|------|--------|-----------|
| 1 | Germany | 2233 | 1 | 11 | Japan | 1908 | 13 | 21 | New Zealand | 1751 | 21 |
| 2 | USA | 2191 | 2 | 12 | Canada | 1904 | 11 | 22 | South Korea | 1748 | 26 |
| 3 | Norway | 2094 | 3 | 13 | Russia | 1893 | 12 | 23 | Czech Republic | 1745 | 22 |
| 4 | Brazil | 2053 | 4 | 14 | England | 1872 | 14 | 24 | Chinese Taipei | 1741 | 23 |
| 5 | France | 2029 | 9 | | Finland | 1872 | 16 | 25 | Nigeria | 1739 | 24 |
| 6 | Sweden | 2005 | 5 | 16 | Australia | 1852 | 15 | 26 | Mexico | 1733 | 25 |
| 7 | North Korea | 1999 | 8 | 17 | Iceland | 1818 | 18 | 27 | Switzerland | 1687 | 30 |
| 8 | Denmark | 1981 | 7 | 18 | Netherlands | 1799 | 17 | 28 | Serbia & Montenegro | 1681 | 31 |
| 9 | China | 1957 | 6 | 19 | Ukraine | 1783 | 19 | 29 | Scotland | 1675 | 29 |
| 10 | Italy | 1931 | 10 | 20 | Spain | 1754 | 20 | 30 | Belgium | 1674 | 27 |

## U.S. Men's National Team
## 2005 Schedule and Results

Through Oct. 12, 2005. Games in **bold** type are 2006 World Cup qualifying matches.

| Date | | Result | USA Goals | Site |
|------|------|--------|-----------|------|
| Feb. 9 | **Trinidad & Tobago** | W, 2-1 | Johnson, Lewis | Port-of-Spain, Trinidad |
| Mar. 9 | Colombia | W, 3-0 | Noonan, Marshall, Mathis | Fullerton, Calif. |
| Mar. 19 | Honduras | W, 1-0 | Johnson | Albuquerque, N.M. |
| Mar. 27 | **Mexico** | L, 1-2 | Lewis | Mexico City |
| Mar. 30 | **Guatemala** | W, 2-0 | Johnson, Ralston | Birmingham, Ala. |
| May 28 | England | L, 1-2 | Dempsey | Chicago, Ill. |
| June 4 | **Costa Rica** | W, 3-0 | Donovan (2), McBride | Salt Lake City, Utah |
| June 8 | **Panama** | W, 3-0 | Bocanegra, Donovan, McBride | Panama City |
| July 7 | Cuba | W, 4-1 | Dempsey, Donovan (2), Beasley | Seattle, Wash. |
| July 9 | Canada | W, 2-0 | own goal, Donovan | Seattle, Wash. |
| July 12 | Costa Rica | T, 0-0 | — | Foxboro, Mass. |
| July 16 | Jamaica | W, 3-1 | Wolff, Beasley (2) | Foxboro, Mass. |
| July 21 | Honduras | W, 2-1 | O'Brien, Onyewu | E. Rutherford, N.J. |
| July 24 | Panama | T, 0-0 (3-1 pks) | — | E. Rutherford, N.J. |
| Aug. 17 | **Trinidad & Tobago** | W, 1-0 | McBride | E. Hartford, Conn. |
| Sept. 3 | **Mexico** | W, 2-0 | Ralston, Beasley | Columbus, Ohio |
| Sept. 7 | **Guatemala** | T, 0-0 | — | Guatemala City |
| Oct. 8 | **Costa Rica** | L, 0-3 | — | San Jose, Costa Rica |
| Oct. 12 | **Panama** | W, 2-0 | Martino, Twellman | Foxboro, Mass. |

**Overall record:** 13-3-3. **Team scoring:** Goals For–30; Goals Against–11.

## 2005 U.S. Men's National Team Statistics

Individual statistics through Oct. 7, 2005. Note that the column labeled "Career C/G" refers to career caps and goals.

| Forwards | GP | GS | Mins | G | A | Pts | Career C/G |
|----------|----|----|------|---|---|-----|------------|
| Conor Casey | 2 | 1 | 75 | 0 | 0 | 0 | 8/0 |
| Jeff Cunningham | 2 | 1 | 57 | 0 | 0 | 0 | 10/0 |
| Landon Donovan | 15 | 12 | 1169 | 6 | 6 | 18 | 73/25 |
| Eddie Johnson | 6 | 5 | 460 | 3 | 1 | 7 | 9/8 |
| Brian McBride | 7 | 6 | 529 | 3 | 1 | 7 | 90/29 |
| Taylor Twellman | 3 | 1 | 106 | 0 | 0 | 0 | 11/0 |
| Josh Wolff | 9 | 7 | 485 | 1 | 0 | 2 | 37/8 |

| Defenders | GP | GS | Mins | G | A | Pts | Career C/G |
|-----------|----|----|------|---|---|-----|------------|
| Chris Albright | 5 | 4 | 369 | 0 | 0 | 0 | 16/1 |
| Gregg Berhalter | 5 | 3 | 279 | 0 | 0 | 0 | 41/0 |
| Carlos Bocanegra | 6 | 5 | 452 | 1 | 1 | 3 | 36/6 |
| Nat Borchers | 2 | 1 | 95 | 0 | 0 | 0 | 36/6 |
| Steve Cherundolo | 9 | 9 | 736 | 0 | 1 | 1 | 30/0 |
| Jimmy Conrad | 7 | 6 | 615 | 0 | 0 | 0 | 7/0 |
| Bobby Convey | 6 | 3 | 306 | 0 | 1 | 1 | 33/1 |
| Cory Gibbs | 3 | 3 | 270 | 0 | 0 | 0 | 16/0 |
| Frankie Hejduk | 7 | 5 | 573 | 0 | 0 | 0 | 68/5 |
| Ritchie Kotschau | 1 | 1 | 90 | 0 | 0 | 0 | 1/0 |
| Chad Marshall | 3 | 3 | 270 | 1 | 0 | 2 | 3/1 |
| Brian Mullan | 1 | 1 | 90 | 0 | 0 | 0 | 2/0 |
| Oguchi Onyewu | 8 | 8 | 750 | 1 | 1 | 3 | 1/0 |
| Eddie Pope | 6 | 6 | 396 | 0 | 0 | 0 | 72/6 |
| Tony Sanneh | 2 | 2 | 180 | 0 | 0 | 0 | 1/0 |
| Greg Vanney | 5 | 5 | 480 | 0 | 0 | 0 | 37/1 |

| Midfielders | GP | GS | Mins | G | A | Pts | Career C/G |
|-------------|----|----|------|---|---|-----|------------|
| Chris Armas | 8 | 5 | 546 | 0 | 1 | 1 | 66/2 |
| DaMarcus Beasley | 11 | 9 | 857 | 4 | 4 | 12 | 52/12 |
| Brad Davis | 2 | 1 | 112 | 0 | 0 | 0 | 2/0 |
| Clint Dempsey | 12 | 7 | 699 | 2 | 1 | 5 | 13/2 |
| Eddie Gaven | 1 | 0 | 15 | 0 | 0 | 0 | 2/0 |
| Eddie Lewis | 5 | 5 | 434 | 2 | 0 | 4 | 66/8 |
| Kyle Martino | 2 | 0 | 36 | 0 | 0 | 0 | 5/0 |
| Pablo Mastroeni | 10 | 9 | 737 | 0 | 0 | 0 | 42/0 |
| Clint Mathis | 2 | 2 | 129 | 1 | 1 | 3 | 46/12 |
| Pat Noonan | 9 | 5 | 447 | 1 | 0 | 2 | 46/12 |
| John O'Brien | 7 | 6 | 483 | 1 | 0 | 2 | 28/3 |
| Ben Olsen | 4 | 2 | 205 | 0 | 0 | 0 | 26/4 |
| Santino Quaranta | 4 | 2 | 248 | 0 | 1 | 1 | 6/0 |
| Steve Ralston | 14 | 12 | 1034 | 2 | 3 | 7 | 31/7 |
| Claudio Reyna | 3 | 3 | 270 | 0 | 1 | 1 | 108/8 |
| Clyde Simms | 1 | 0 | 0 | 0 | 0 | 0 | 1/0 |
| Kerry Zavagnin | 4 | 3 | 276 | 0 | 0 | 0 | 14/0 |

| Goalkeepers | GP | GS | Mins | W-L-T | SO | GAA | Career Caps |
|-------------|----|----|------|-------|----|----|-------------|
| Jon Busch | 1 | 1 | 90 | 1-0-0 | 1 | 0.00 | 1 |
| Joe Cannon | 1 | 1 | 45 | 1-0-0 | 0 | 0.00 | 2 |
| Marcus Hahnemann | 2 | 2 | 180 | 1-0-1 | 1 | 0.50 | 6 |
| Kevin Hartman | 1 | 0 | 45 | 0-0-0 | 0 | 0.00 | 3 |
| Kasey Keller | 13 | 13 | 1200 | 9-2-2 | 8 | 0.53 | 88 |

### CONCACAF WorldCup Qualifying Final Standings

Top three teams qualify automatically; **Trinidad & Tobago**, the fourth-place team, will have a two-game, home-and-home playoff against **Bahrain**, the fifth-place Asian team, for a spot at the 2006 World Cup in Germany. (*) denotes World Cup qualifier.

| Team | GP | W | L | T | GF | GA | GD | Pts |
|------|----|----|----|----|----|----|----|-----|
| *United States | 10 | 7 | 2 | 1 | 16 | 6 | +10 | 22 |
| *Mexico | 10 | 7 | 2 | 1 | 22 | 9 | +11 | 22 |
| *Costa Rica | 10 | 5 | 4 | 1 | 15 | 14 | +1 | 16 |
| Trinidad & Tobago | 10 | 4 | 5 | 1 | 10 | 15 | -5 | 13 |
| Guatemala | 10 | 3 | 5 | 2 | 16 | 18 | -2 | 11 |
| Panama | 10 | 0 | 8 | 2 | 4 | 21 | -17 | 2 |

**Note:** The United States was awarded first place for its 3-2 goal differential over Mexico in head-to-head competition.

## U.S. Women's National Team
### 2005 Schedule and Results

| Date | | Result | USA Goals | Site |
|------|------|--------|-----------|------|
| Mar. 9 | France | W, 1-0 | Welsh | Ferreiras, Portugal |
| Mar. 11 | Finland | W, 3-0 | Welsh (2), Wambach | Guia, Portugal |
| Mar. 13 | Denmark | W, 4-0 | Wambach, Welsh, Lilly (2) | San Antonio, Portugal |
| Mar. 15 | Germany | W, 1-0 | Welsh | Faro, Portugal |
| June 26 | Canada | W, 2-0 | Chalupny, Welsh | Virginia Beach, Va. |
| July 10 | Ukraine | W, 7-0 | Welsh, Lilly, Wagner, Fotopoulos (2), Milbrett, O'Reilly | Portland, Ore. |
| July 24 | Iceland | W, 3-0 | Boxx, Fotopoulous (2) | Carson, Calif. |
| Oct. 16 | Australia | T, 0-0 | — | Fullerton, Calif. |
| Oct. 23 | Mexico | | | |

**Overall record:** 7-0-1. **Team Scoring:** Goals for–21; Goals against–0.

---

## FIFA Under-17 Men's World Cup

Officially the FIFA U-17 World Championship, contested for the 11th time since its inception in 1985. Held Sept. 16-Oct. 2, 2005 in Peru.

### Quarterfinals

| Date | Site | Result |
|------|------|--------|
| Sept. 25 | Piura | Mexico 3, Costa Rica 1 OT |
| Sept. 25 | Iquitos | Turkey 5, China 1 |
| Sept. 26 | Trujillo | Netherlands 2, **USA** 0 |
| Sept. 26 | Iquitos | Brazil 3, North Korea 1 OT |

### Semifinals

| Date | Site | Result |
|------|------|--------|
| Sept. 29 | Chiclayo | Mexico 4, Netherlands 0 |
| Sept. 29 | Trujillo | Brazil 4, Turkey 3 |

### Final

| Date | Site | Result |
|------|------|--------|
| Oct. 2 | Lima | Mexico 3, Brazil 0 |

---

## FIFA Under-20 Men's World Cup

Officially the FIFA World Youth Championship, contested for the 15th time since its inception in 1977. Held June 10-July 2, 2005 in the Netherlands.

### First Round

Round robin; each team played the other three teams in its group once. Note that three points were awarded for a win and one point for a tie. (*) indicates team advanced to second round.

| Group A | W | L | T | Pts | GF | GA |
|---------|---|---|---|-----|----|----|
| *Netherlands | 3 | 0 | 0 | 9 | 6 | 1 |
| *Japan | 0 | 1 | 2 | 2 | 3 | 4 |
| Benin | 0 | 1 | 2 | 2 | 2 | 3 |
| Australia | 0 | 1 | 2 | 2 | 2 | 5 |

| Group B | W | L | T | Pts | GF | GA |
|---------|---|---|---|-----|----|----|
| *China | 3 | 0 | 0 | 9 | 9 | 4 |
| *Ukraine | 1 | 1 | 1 | 4 | 6 | 1 |
| *Turkey | 1 | 1 | 1 | 4 | 4 | 4 |
| Panama | 0 | 3 | 0 | 0 | 2 | 8 |

| Group C | W | L | T | Pts | GF | GA |
|---------|---|---|---|-----|----|----|
| *Spain | 3 | 0 | 0 | 9 | 13 | 1 |
| *Morocco | 2 | 1 | 0 | 6 | 7 | 3 |
| *Chile | 1 | 2 | 0 | 6 | 7 | 3 |
| Honduras | 0 | 3 | 0 | 0 | 0 | 15 |

| Group D | W | L | T | Pts | GF | GA |
|---------|---|---|---|-----|----|----|
| *USA | 2 | 0 | 1 | 7 | 2 | 0 |
| *Argentina | 2 | 1 | 0 | 6 | 3 | 1 |
| *Germany | 1 | 1 | 1 | 4 | 2 | 1 |
| Egypt | 0 | 3 | 0 | 0 | 0 | 5 |

| Group E | W | L | T | Pts | GF | GA |
|---------|---|---|---|-----|----|----|
| *Colombia | 3 | 0 | 0 | 9 | 6 | 0 |
| *Syria | 1 | 1 | 1 | 4 | 3 | 4 |
| *Italy | 1 | 2 | 0 | 3 | 5 | 5 |
| Canada | 0 | 2 | 1 | 1 | 2 | 7 |

| Group F | W | L | T | Pts | GF | GA |
|---------|---|---|---|-----|----|----|
| *Brazil | 2 | 0 | 1 | 7 | 3 | 0 |
| *Nigeria | 1 | 1 | 1 | 4 | 4 | 2 |
| South Korea | 1 | 2 | 0 | 3 | 3 | 5 |
| Switzerland | 1 | 2 | 0 | 3 | 2 | 5 |

### Round of 16

| Date | Site | Result |
|------|------|--------|
| June 21 | Enschede | Italy 3, USA 1 |
| June 21 | Enschede | Morocco 1, Japan 0 |
| June 21 | Tilburg | Brazil 1, Syria 0 |
| June 21 | Tilburg | Germany 3, China 2 |
| June 22 | Doetinchem | Nigeria 1, Ukraine 0 |
| June 22 | Doetinchem | Netherlands 3, Chile 0 |
| June 22 | Emmen | Argentina 2, Colombia 1 |
| June 22 | Emmen | Spain 2, Turkey 0 |

### Quarterfinals

| Date | Site | Result |
|------|------|--------|
| June 24 | Utrecht | Morocco 2, Italy 2 |
| | | Morrocco advances on shoot-out, 4-2 |
| June 24 | Tilburg | Brazil 2, Germany 1 OT |
| June 25 | Kerkrade | Nigeria 1, Netherlands 1 |
| | | Nigeria advances on shoot-out, 10-9 |
| June 25 | Enshede | Argentina 3, Spain 1 |

### Semifinals

| Date | Site | Result |
|------|------|--------|
| June 28 | Utrecht | Argentina 2, Brazil 1 |
| June 28 | Kerkrade | Nigeria 3, Morocco 0 |

### Third Place

| Date | Site | Result |
|------|------|--------|
| July 2 | Utrecht | Brazil 2, Morocco 0 |

### Final

| Date | Site | Result |
|------|------|--------|
| July 2 | Utrecht | Argentina 2, Nigeria 1 |

### Goal Scoring Leaders

| | Goals |
|------|-------|
| Lionel Messi, Argentina | 6 |
| Oleksandr Aliev, Ukraine | 5 |
| Llorente, Spain | 5 |
| Graziano Pelle, Italy | 4 |
| Silva, Spain | 4 |

## Club Team Competition

### 2004 Toyota Cup

Also known as the European/South American Cup and, formerly known as the Intercontinental Cup; a year-end match for the Club World Championship between the UEFA Champions League (formerly the European Cup) and Copa Libertadores winners. Its winner was generally recognized as the Club World Champion but with the recent advent of FIFA's Club World Championship it will no longer be a South America vs. Europe affair (see shaded box below). In the 2004 (and final) edition of the European/South American Cup Portugal's FC Porto beat Once Caldas of Colombia. The event was held 43 times and South America won the all-time Interncontinental/Toyota Cup series with Europe, 22-21.

### Final

Dec. 12 at International Stadium, Yokohama, Japan.

FC Porto (Portugal) 0 . . . .Once Caldas (Colombia) 0

**FC Porto wins, 8-7, on penalty kicks**

## FIFA Club World Championship

The FIFA Club World Championship (now officially the FIFA Club World Championship TOYOTA Cup Japan) merged with the Toyota Cup (a.k.a European/South American Cup) in 2005 and is now open to the champions from the African, Asian, Oceanic and North/Central American soccer federations as well as Europe and South America. The four newcomers will play-off for the right to face the seeded European and South American sides in the semi-finals. Like the Toyota Cup, the new six-team knockout tournament will still be held each December in Japan. The previous edition of the FIFA Club World Championship was played once (held in 2000 and won by Brazil's Corinthians) but it fell apart while the Toyota Cup continued uninterrupted. The 2005 FIFA Club World Championship TOYOTA Cup was scheduled for December 11-18. Liverpool (Europe), Deportivo Saprissa (North/Central America), Sao Paulo (South America) and Sydney FC (Oceania) have already qualified and just the Asian and African teams were yet to be determined as of press time. As the European and South American teams, respectively, Liverpool and Sao Paulo will receive byes into the semis.

### Tournament Format

#### Quarterfinals

| # | Date | Match | Site |
|---|------|-------|------|
| 1 | Dec. 11, 2005 | Asia Champions vs. Africa Champions | Tokyo |
| 2 | Dec. 12, 2005 | Sydney FC vs. Deportivo Saprissa | Toyota |

#### Semifinals

| 3 | Dec. 14, 2005 | W1 vs. Sao Paulo FC | Tokyo |
| 4 | Dec. 15, 2005 | W2 vs. Liverpool FC | Yokohama |

#### Match for 5th place

| 5 | Dec. 16, 2005 | L1 vs. L2 | Tokyo |

#### Match for 3rd place

| 6 | Dec. 18, 2005 | L3 vs. L4 | Yokohama |

#### Finals

| 7 | Dec. 18, 2005 | W3 vs. W4 | Yokohama |

## SOUTH AMERICA

### 2005 Libertadores Cup

Contested by the league champions of South America's football union. Two-leg Semifinals and two-leg Final; home teams listed first. Winners São Paulo of Brazil qualified for the 2005 FIFA Club World Championship in Japan in December. See the shaded box above.

**Final Four:** Atletico Paranaense (Brazil), Chivas de Guadalajara (Mexico), River Plate (Argentina) and São Paulo (Brazil).

### Semifinals

#### Atletico Paranaense vs. Guadalajara

Atletico Paranaense 3 . . . . . . . . . . . . . . . .Guadalajara 0
Guadalajara 2 . . . . . . . . . . . . . . . .Atletico Paranaense 2
Atletico Paranaense won 5-2 on penalty kicks

#### São Paulo vs. River Plate

São Paulo 2 . . . . . . . . . . . . . . . . . . . . . . . . .River Plate 0
River Plate 2 . . . . . . . . . . . . . . . . . . . . . . . .São Paulo 3
São Paulo won 5-2 on aggregate

### Final

Matches played July 6 in Porto Alegre, Brazil and July 14 in São Paulo, Brazil.

Atletico Paranaense 1 . . . . . . . . . . . . . . . . . .São Paulo 1
São Paulo 4 . . . . . . . . . . . . . . . . . .Atletico Paranaense 0
São Paulo won 5-1 on aggregate

## EUROPE

There are two major European club competitions sanctioned by the Union of European Football Associations (UEFA). The constantly evolving **Champions League** is currently a 74-team tournament made up from UEFA member countries. The teams are ranked 1-74 depending on how they finish in their own domestic leagues. UEFA ranks the quality of the 52 European national football associations (from number one Spain to number 52 San Marino) and assigns each association a number weighted by their respective ranking (UEFA calls this number a coefficient). Each team's domestic league finish is then multiplied by the coefficient and finally ranked (countries can enter a maximum of four teams).

The defending champions and the other 15 highest-ranked teams form Group 1 and are given a direct entry into the League but the remaining 16 teams are determined by dividing teams 17-74 into three groups–Group 2 (teams 17-34), Group 3 (35-50) and Group 4 (51-74). The 24 teams in the lowest Group (Group 4) play two-leg, total goal elimination series. The 12 survivors advance to the Second Qualifying Phase and join the 16 teams from Group 3 to play 14 two-leg, total goal elimination series. The 14 clubs that survive this phase join the 18 teams from Group 2 to play in the Third Qualifying Phase. The winning clubs from the 16 two-leg, total goal elimination series advance to the Champions League for the right to play against the top-ranked 16 teams in Europe.

The 32 teams are separated into eight groups of four and play a round-robin series of home-and-home matches. Starting for the 2003-04 Champions League, the eight group winners and eight group runners-up advance to the next round where they are paired and play two home-and-home matches. The home-and-home series are played through the semifinals until ultimately ah single championship match for the European club championship is held.

The updated **UEFA Cup**, which is basically a combination of the what was known as the Cup Winners' Cup (played between national cup champions) and the old UEFA Cup (sort of a "best of the rest" tournament), is single-elimination throughout and features 121 additional teams plus teams that have been already eliminated from the Champions League.

## 2004-05 Champions League

Following the first three qualifying phases, the first group phase starts with six-game double round-robin format in eight four-team groups (Sept. 13-Nov. 13); top two teams in each group advance to second group phase (Nov. 26-Mar. 19) where four, four-team groups compete in the same format. Group winners and runners-up advance to the quarterfinals. While the third-place team from each of the eight groups moves to the third round of the UEFA Cup tournament. (*) indicates team advanced to the next round (of the Champions League). Note that in results listing under each table the home team is listed first.

### Group Phase

| Group A | W | L | T | GF | GA | Pts |
|---|---|---|---|---|---|---|
| *Monaco (France) | 4 | 2 | 0 | 10 | 4 | 12 |
| *Liverpool (England) | 3 | 2 | 1 | 6 | 3 | 10 |
| Olympiacos (Greece) | 3 | 2 | 1 | 5 | 5 | 10 |
| Deportivo La Coruna (Spain) | 0 | 4 | 2 | 0 | 9 | 2 |

| Group B | W | L | T | GF | GA | Pts |
|---|---|---|---|---|---|---|
| *Leverkusen (Germany) | 3 | 1 | 2 | 13 | 7 | 11 |
| *Real Madrid (Spain) | 3 | 1 | 2 | 11 | 8 | 11 |
| Dynamo Kyiv (Ukraine) | 3 | 2 | 1 | 11 | 8 | 10 |
| Roma (Italy) | 0 | 5 | 1 | 4 | 16 | 1 |

| Group C | W | L | T | GF | GA | Pts |
|---|---|---|---|---|---|---|
| *Juventus (Italy) | 5 | 0 | 1 | 6 | 1 | 16 |
| *Bayern (Germany) | 3 | 2 | 1 | 12 | 5 | 10 |
| Ajax (Netherlands) | 1 | 4 | 1 | 6 | 10 | 4 |
| M. Tel-Aviv (Israel) | 1 | 4 | 1 | 4 | 12 | 4 |

| Group D | W | L | T | GF | GA | Pts |
|---|---|---|---|---|---|---|
| *Lyon (France) | 4 | 1 | 1 | 17 | 8 | 13 |
| *Manchester United (England) | 3 | 1 | 2 | 14 | 9 | 11 |
| Fenerbahce (Turkey) | 3 | 3 | 0 | 10 | 13 | 9 |
| Sparta (Czech Republic) | 0 | 5 | 1 | 2 | 13 | 1 |

| Group E | W | L | T | GF | GA | Pts |
|---|---|---|---|---|---|---|
| *Arsenal (England) | 2 | 0 | 4 | 11 | 6 | 10 |
| *PSV (Germany) | 3 | 2 | 1 | 6 | 7 | 10 |
| Panathinaikos (Greece) | 2 | 1 | 3 | 11 | 8 | 9 |
| Rosenborg (Norway) | 0 | 4 | 2 | 6 | 13 | 2 |

| Group F | W | L | T | GF | GA | Pts |
|---|---|---|---|---|---|---|
| *AC Milan (Italy) | 4 | 1 | 1 | 10 | 3 | 13 |
| *Barcelona (Spain) | 3 | 2 | 1 | 9 | 6 | 10 |
| FC Shakhtar (Ukraine) | 2 | 4 | 0 | 5 | 9 | 6 |
| Celtic (Scotland) | 1 | 3 | 2 | 4 | 10 | 5 |

| Group G | W | L | T | GF | GA | Pts |
|---|---|---|---|---|---|---|
| *Internazionale (Italy) | 4 | 0 | 2 | 14 | 3 | 14 |
| *Bremen (Germany) | 4 | 1 | 1 | 12 | 6 | 13 |
| Valencia (Spain) | 2 | 3 | 1 | 6 | 10 | 7 |
| Anderlecht (Belgium) | 0 | 6 | 0 | 4 | 17 | 0 |

| Group H | W | L | T | GF | GA | Pts |
|---|---|---|---|---|---|---|
| *Chelsea (England) | 4 | 1 | 1 | 10 | 3 | 13 |
| *FC Porto (Portugal) | 2 | 2 | 2 | 4 | 6 | 8 |
| CSKA Moscow (Russia) | 2 | 3 | 1 | 5 | 5 | 7 |
| PSG (France) | 1 | 3 | 2 | 3 | 8 | 5 |

### Round of 16
Two legs, total goals; home team listed first.

#### Real Madrid vs. Juventus
Feb. 22   Real Madrid 1 . . . . . . . . . . . . . . . Juventus 0
Mar 9   Juventus 2 . . . . . . . . . . . . . . Real Madrid 0
Juventus wins 2-1 on aggregate

#### Liverpool vs. Leverkusen
Feb. 22   Liverpool 3 . . . . . . . . . . . . . . . Leverkusen 1
Mar. 9   Leverkusen 1 . . . . . . . . . . . . . . . Liverpool 3
Liverpool wins 6-2 on aggregate

#### Bayern vs. Arsenal
Feb. 22   Bayern 3 . . . . . . . . . . . . . . . . . Arsenal 1
Mar. 9   Arsenal 1 . . . . . . . . . . . . . . . . . Bayern 0
Bayern wins 3-2 on aggregate

#### PSV vs. Monaco
Feb. 22   PSV 1 . . . . . . . . . . . . . . . . . . Monaco 0
Mar. 9   Monaco 0 . . . . . . . . . . . . . . . . . PSV 2
PSV wins 3-0 on aggregate

#### Barcelona vs. Chelsea
Feb. 23   Barcelona 2 . . . . . . . . . . . . . . . Chelsea 1
Mar. 8   Chelsea 4 . . . . . . . . . . . . . . . Barcelona 2
Chelsea wins 5-4 on aggregate

#### Bremen vs. Lyon
Feb. 23   Bremen 0 . . . . . . . . . . . . . . . . . . Lyon 3
Mar. 8   Lyon 7 . . . . . . . . . . . . . . . . . . . Bremen 2
Lyon wins 10-2 on aggregate

#### Manchester United vs. AC Milan
Feb. 23   Manchester United 0 . . . . . . . . . . AC Milan 1
Mar. 8   AC Milan 1 . . . . . . . . . . Manchester United 0
AC Milan wins 2-0 on aggregate

#### FC Porto vs. Internazionale
Feb. 23   FC Porto 1 . . . . . . . . . . . . . Internazionale 1
Mar. 15   Internazionale 3 . . . . . . . . . . . . . FC Porto 1
Internazionale wins 4-2 on aggregate

### Quarterfinals
Two legs, total goals; home team listed first.

#### AC Milan vs. Internazionale
Apr. 6   AC Milan 2 . . . . . . . . . . . . . .Internazionale 0
Apr. 12   Internazionale 0 . . . . . . . . . . . . . .AC Milan 3
AC Milan wins 5-0 on aggregate

#### Lyon vs. PSV Eindhoven
Apr. 5   Lyon 1 . . . . . . . . . . . . . . . . . .PSV Eindhoven 1
Apr. 13   PSV Eindhoven 1 . . . . . . . . . . . . . . . .Lyon 1
Aggregate tied 2-2, PSV advances 4-2 on penalty kicks

#### Liverpool vs. Juventus
Apr. 5   Liverpool 2 . . . . . . . . . . . . . . . .Juventus 1
Apr. 13   Juventus 0 . . . . . . . . . . . . . . . . . .Liverpool 0
Liverpool wins 2-1 on aggregate

#### Chelsea vs. Bayern Munich
Apr. 6   Chelsea 4 . . . . . . . . . . . . . .Bayern Munich 2
Apr. 12   Bayern Munich 3 . . . . . . . . . . . . . .Chelsea 2
Chelsea wins 6-5 on aggregate

### Semifinals
Two legs, total goals; home team listed first.

#### AC Milan vs. PSV Eindhoven
Apr. 26   AC Milan 2 . . . . . . . . . . . . .PSV Eindhoven 0
May 4   PSV Eindhoven 3 . . . . . . . . . . . . .AC Milan 1
Aggregate tied 3-3, AC Milan advances on away goals.

#### Liverpool vs. Chelsea
Apr. 27   Chelsea 0 . . . . . . . . . . . . . . . . . .Liverpool 0
May 3   Liverpool 1 . . . . . . . . . . . . . . . . . .Chelsea 0
Liverpool wins 1-0 on aggregate

### Final
#### Liverpool vs. AC Milan
May 25, 2005 at Ataturk Stadium in Istanbul, Turkey.
**Attendance:** 65,000

Liverpool 3 . . . . . . . . . . . . . . . . . . . . . . . . . .AC Milan 3
**Liverpool wins, 3-2, on penalty kicks**

## 2005 UEFA Cup
Two-leg Quarterfinals and Semifinals, one-game Final; home team listed first.

**Final Eight:** FK Austria (Austria), Auxerre (France), Alkmaar (Netherlands), CSKA Moscow (Russia), Newcastle (England), Sporting Lisbon (Portugal), Parma (Italy), Villarreal (Spain).

### Quarterfinals

#### CSKA Moscow vs. Auxerre
Apr. 7   CSKA Moscow 2 . . . . . . . . . . . . . .Auxerre 0
Apr. 14   Auxerre 2 . . . . . . . . . . . .CSKA Moscow 0
CSKA Moscow wins 4-2 on aggregate

#### Newcastle vs. Sporting Lisbon
Apr. 7   Newcastle 1 . . . . . . . . . . . . . . . .Sporting 0
Apr. 14   Sporting 4 . . . . . . . . . . . . . . .Newcastle 1
Sporting wins 4-2 on aggregate

#### FK Austria vs. Parma
Apr. 7   FK Austria 1 . . . . . . . . . . . . . . . . . .Parma 0
Apr. 14   Parma 0 . . . . . . . . . . . . . . . . . .FK Austria 0
Aggregate tied 1-1, Parma advances on away goals.

#### Villarreal vs. Alkmaar
Apr. 7   Villarreal 1 . . . . . . . . . . . . . . . . . .Alkmaar 0
Apr. 14   Alkmaar 1 . . . . . . . . . . . . . . . . . .Villarreal 1
Alkmaar wins 3-2 on aggregate

### Semifinals

#### CSKA Moscow vs. Parma
Apr 28   Parma 0   . . . . . . . . . . . . . .CSKA Moscow 0
May 5   CSKA Moscow 3 . . . . . . . . . . . . . . .Parma 0
CSKA Moscow wins 3-0 on aggregate

#### Sporting Lisbon vs. Alkmaar
Apr. 28   Sporting 2 . . . . . . . . . . . . . . . . . . . . .Alkmaar 1
May 5   Alkmaar 3 . . . . . . . . . . . . . . . . . . . . .Sporting 2
Aggregate tied 4-4, Sporting advance on away goals

### Final
#### CSKA Moscow vs. Sporting Lisbon
May 18 in Lisbon, Portugal. **Attendance:** 46,500

Sporting Lisbon 1 . . . . . . . . . . . . . . . . . .CSKA Moscow 3

## 2005 Lamar Hunt U.S. Open Cup
Dating back to 1914, the U.S. Open Cup is the oldest soccer competition in the United States and is among the oldest in the world. The U.S. Open Cup is a single-elimination tournament open to all amateur and professional teams in the United States. Forty-two teams competed in the 2005 Lamar Hunt U.S. Open Cup. The tournament was renamed for the U.S. Soccer pioneer and MLS Team owner in 1999. Teams listed below are in the MLS, unless otherwise noted.

### Quarterfinals
Los Angeles Galaxy def. San Jose Earthquakes, 2-1
Minnesota Thunder (USL 1) def. Kansas City Wizards, 3-1
Chicago Fire def. Rochester Raging Rhinos (USL 1), on PKs
FC Dallas def. D.C. United, on PKs

### Semifinals
Los Angeles Galaxy def. Minnesota Thunder, 5-2
FC Dallas def. Chicago Fire, 1-0

**Final** (Sept. 28, 2005)
Los Angeles Galaxy def. FC Dallas, 1-0

## Major League Soccer
## 2005 Final Regular Season Standings

Conference champions (*) and playoff qualifiers (†) are noted. Teams receive three points for a win and one for a tie. The GF and GA columns refer to Goals For and Goals Against in regulation play. Number of seasons listed after each head coach refers to current tenure with club through the 2005 season.

### Eastern Conference

| Team | W | L | T | Pts | GF | GA |
|------|---|---|---|-----|----|----|
| *N.E. Revolution | 17 | 7 | 8 | **59** | 55 | 37 |
| †D.C. United | 16 | 10 | 6 | **54** | 58 | 37 |
| †Chicago Fire | 15 | 13 | 4 | **49** | 49 | 50 |
| †MetroStars | 12 | 9 | 11 | **47** | 53 | 49 |
| Kansas City Wizards | 11 | 9 | 12 | **45** | 52 | 44 |
| Columbus Crew | 11 | 16 | 5 | **38** | 34 | 45 |

**Head Coaches: NE**—Steve Nicol (5th season); **DC**—Peter Nowak (2nd); **Chi**—Dave Sarachan (3rd); **Met**—Bob Bradley (3rd, 10-9-10) was fired on Oct. 4, 2005 and replaced on an interim basis by assistant Mo Johnston (2-0-1); **KC**—Bob Gansler (7th); **Clb**—Greg Andrulis (5th, 4-10-2) was fired on July 12, 2005 and replaced on an interim basis by assistant Robert Warzycha (7-6-3).

### Western Conference

| Team | W | L | T | Pts | GF | GA |
|------|---|---|---|-----|----|----|
| *San Jose Earthquakes | 18 | 4 | 10 | **64** | 53 | 31 |
| †FC Dallas | 13 | 10 | 9 | **48** | 52 | 44 |
| †Colorado Rapids | 13 | 13 | 6 | **45** | 40 | 37 |
| †Los Angeles Galaxy | 13 | 13 | 6 | **45** | 44 | 45 |
| Real Salt Lake | 5 | 22 | 5 | **20** | 30 | 65 |
| Chivas USA | 4 | 22 | 6 | **18** | 31 | 67 |

**Head Coaches: SJ**—Dominic Kinnear (2nd); **Dal**—Colin Clarke (3rd); **Colo**—Fernando Clavijo (1st); **LA**—Steve Sampson (2nd); **RSL**—John Ellinger (1st); **Chv**—Thomas Rongen (1st, 1-8-1) was fired on May 30, 2005 and replaced on an interim basis by assistant Javier "Zully" Ledesma (0-0-1) then by Hans Westerhof (3-14-4).

## Leading Scorers

### Points

| | Gm | G | A | Pts |
|---|---|---|---|---|
| Taylor Twellman, NE | 25 | 17 | 7 | 41 |
| Jaime Moreno, DC | 29 | 16 | 7 | 39 |
| Landon Donovan, LA | 22 | 12 | 10 | 34 |
| Amado Guevara, Met | 26 | 11 | 11 | 33 |
| Christian Gomez, DC | 31 | 11 | 9 | 31 |
| Dwayne De Rosario, SJ | 28 | 9 | 13 | 31 |
| Josh Wolff, KC | 22 | 10 | 10 | 30 |
| Clint Dempsey, NE | 26 | 10 | 9 | 29 |
| Jeff Cunningham, Col | 26 | 12 | 3 | 27 |
| Youri Djorkaeff, Met | 24 | 10 | 7 | 27 |

### Goals

| | Gm | No |
|---|---|---|
| Taylor Twellman, NE | 25 | 17 |
| Jaime Moreno, DC | 29 | 16 |
| Jeff Cunningham, Col | 26 | 12 |
| Landon Donovan, LA | 22 | 12 |
| Christian Gomez, DC | 31 | 11 |
| Herculez Gomez, LA | 22 | 11 |
| Amado Guevara, Met | 26 | 11 |
| Carlos Ruiz, Dal | 19 | 11 |
| Clint Dempsey, NE | 26 | 10 |
| Youri Djorkaeff, Met | 24 | 10 |
| Josh Wolff, KC | 22 | 10 |

### Assists

| | Gm | No |
|---|---|---|
| Dwayne De Rosario, SJ | 28 | 13 |
| Ronnie O'Brien, Dal | 28 | 12 |
| Simon Elliott, Clb | 32 | 11 |
| Amado Guevara, Met | 26 | 11 |
| Landon Donovan, LA | 22 | 10 |
| Josh Wolff, KC | 22 | 10 |
| Ronald Cerritos, SJ | 30 | 9 |
| Clint Dempsey, NE | 26 | 9 |
| Christian Gomez, DC | 31 | 9 |
| Chris Klein, KC | 31 | 9 |

### Shots

| | Gm | No |
|---|---|---|
| Chris Klein, KC | 31 | 84 |
| Ronnie O'Brien, Dal | 28 | 83 |
| Taylor Twellman, NE | 25 | 82 |
| Jaime Moreno, DC | 29 | 77 |
| Youri Djorkaeff, Met | 24 | 76 |
| Edson Buddle, Clb | 23 | 70 |
| Dwayne De Rosario, SJ | 28 | 70 |
| Amado Guevara, Met | 26 | 67 |
| Jason Kreis, RSL | 24 | 65 |
| Davy Arnaud, KC | 31 | 64 |
| Christian Gomez, DC | 31 | 64 |

### Shots on Goal

| | Gm | No |
|---|---|---|
| Taylor Twellman, NE | 25 | 51 |
| Jaime Moreno, DC | 29 | 46 |
| Christian Gomez, DC | 31 | 37 |
| Ronnie O'Brien, Dal | 28 | 37 |
| Dwayne De Rosario, SJ | 28 | 34 |
| Chris Klein, KC | 31 | 34 |
| Youri Djorkaeff, Met | 24 | 33 |
| Landon Donovan, LA | 22 | 32 |
| Chris Rolfe, Chi | 29 | 32 |
| Jeff Cunningham, Col | 26 | 31 |
| Amado Guevara, Met | 26 | 31 |
| Jason Kreis, RSL | 24 | 31 |

### Game-Winning Goals

| | Gm | GWG |
|---|---|---|
| Landon Donovan, LA | 22 | 7 |
| Taylor Twellman, NE | 25 | 6 |
| Jeff Cunningham, Col | 26 | 5 |
| Clint Dempsey, NE | 26 | 5 |
| Dwayne De Rosario, SJ | 28 | 5 |
| Youri Djorkaeff, Met | 24 | 5 |

## MLS All-Star Game

### MLS 4, Fulham FC 1

Played Saturday, July 30, 2005 at Columbus Crew Stadium between a team of MLS All-Stars and English Premier League team Fulham FC.

**Attendance:** 23,309; **MVP:** Taylor Twellman, MLS (New England Revolution).

| | 1 | 2 | Final |
|---|---|---|---|
| Fulham FC | 1 | 0 | —1 |
| MLS All-Stars | 1 | 3 | —4 |

### Scoring

**1st Half:** MLS—Taylor Twellman (Landon Donovan) 23rd; FFC—Claus Jensen (penalty kick) 36th.
**2nd Half:** MLS—Ronnie O'Brien (Clint Dempsey) 56th. MLS—Jeff Cunningham (Christian Gomez) 85th. MLS—Jeff Cunningham (Shalrie Joseph) 89th.

### Fouls Committed

| | Gm | No |
|---|---|---|
| Simo Valakari, Dal | 28 | 78 |
| Eddie Robinson, SJ | 29 | 68 |
| Shalrie Joseph, NE | 31 | 65 |
| Kyle Beckerman, Col | 30 | 60 |
| Ricardo Clark, SJ | 30 | 58 |
| Ronnie O'Brien, Dal | 28 | 58 |
| Ben Olsen, DC | 23 | 58 |
| Davy Arnaud, KC | 31 | 53 |
| Jean Philippe Peguero, Col | 26 | 52 |
| Joshua Gros, DC | 30 | 51 |

### Fouls Suffered

| | Gm | No |
|---|---|---|
| Alejandro Moreno, SJ | 31 | 102 |
| Davy Arnaud, KC | 31 | 85 |
| Brian Mullan, SJ | 25 | 79 |
| Andy Williams, RSL | 26 | 79 |
| Kyle Martino, Clb | 27 | 77 |
| Clint Dempsey, NE | 26 | 71 |
| Eddie Gaven, Met | 28 | 67 |
| Justin Mapp, Chi | 29 | 62 |
| Jose Cancela, NE | 25 | 59 |
| Dwayne De Rosario, SJ | 28 | 58 |

### Offsides

| | Gm | Offs |
|---|---|---|
| Ronald Cerritos, SJ | 30 | 41 |
| Carlos Ruiz, Dal | 19 | 36 |
| Taylor Twellman, NE | 25 | 33 |
| Davy Arnaud, KC | 31 | 30 |
| Ante Razov, Met | 25 | 30 |
| Sergio Galvan Rey, Met | 27 | 28 |
| Jean Philippe Peguero, Col | 26 | 27 |
| Jeff Cunningham, Col | 26 | 26 |
| Jason Kreis, RSL | 24 | 23 |
| Alejandro Moreno, SJ | 31 | 23 |

### Cautions

| | Gm | No |
|---|---|---|
| Michael Bradley, Met | 30 | 9 |
| Jose Burciaga Jr., KC | 31 | 9 |
| Clarence Goodson, Dal | 29 | 9 |
| Amado Guevara, Met | 26 | 9 |
| Alain Nkong, Col | 28 | 9 |
| Five tied with 8 each. | | |

### Corner Kicks

| | Gm | CKs |
|---|---|---|
| Christian Gomez, DC | 31 | 88 |
| Jose Cancela, NE | 25 | 87 |
| Landon Donovan, LA | 22 | 83 |
| Thiago, Chi | 27 | 75 |
| Andy Williams, RSL | 26 | 73 |
| Amado Guevara, Met | 26 | 71 |
| Justin Mapp, Chi | 29 | 71 |
| Simon Elliott, Clb | 32 | 66 |
| Ramon Ramirez, Chv | 31 | 60 |
| Chris Klein, KC | 31 | 56 |

### Minutes Played

| | Mins |
|---|---|
| Todd Dunivant, LA | 2880 |
| Simon Elliott, Clb | 2880 |
| Pat Onstad, SJ | 2880 |
| Bo Oshoniyi, KC | 2880 |
| Michael Parkhurst, NE | 2880 |
| Kevin Hartman, LA | 2790 |
| Jay Heaps, NE | 2790 |
| Shalrie Joseph, NE | 2788 |
| Matt Reis, NE | 2784 |
| Chris Klein, KC | 2765 |

### 2005 MLS Attendance

Number in parentheses indicates last year's rank.

| | Gm | Total | Avg |
|---|---|---|---|
| Los Angeles (1) | 16 | 387,256 | 24,204 |
| Real Salt Lake | 16 | 288,586 | 18,037 |
| Chicago (4) | 16 | 275,811 | 17,238 |
| CD Chivas USA | 16 | 273,284 | 17,080 |
| D.C. United (2) | 16 | 266,617 | 16,664 |
| MetroStars (3) | 16 | 241,230 | 15,077 |
| Colorado (7) | 16 | 218,206 | 13,638 |
| San José (8) | 16 | 208,594 | 13,037 |
| Columbus (5) | 16 | 206,654 | 12,916 |
| New England (9) | 16 | 200,397 | 12,525 |
| Dallas (10) | 16 | 179,021 | 11,189 |
| Kansas City (6) | 16 | 155,060 | 9,691 |
| TOTAL | 192 | 2,900,716 | 15,108 |

## Leading Goaltenders

### Goals Against Average

| | Gm | Min | Shts | Svs | GAA | W-L-T |
|---|---|---|---|---|---|---|
| Pat Onstad, SJ | 32 | 2880 | 136 | 105 | **0.97** | 18-4-10 |
| Jonny Walker, Clb | 16 | 1440 | 84 | 66 | **1.13** | 6-8-2 |
| Matt Reis, NE | 31 | 2784 | 150 | 115 | **1.13** | 16-7-8 |
| Nick Rimando, DC | 30 | 2700 | 127 | 92 | **1.17** | 15-9-6 |
| Joe Cannon, Col | 27 | 2399 | 132 | 100 | **1.20** | 10-12-4 |
| Zach Wells, Met | 17 | 1530 | 90 | 69 | **1.24** | 6-4-7 |
| Scott Garlick, Dal | 28 | 2457 | 135 | 98 | **1.36** | 13-8-7 |
| Bo Oshoniyi, KC | 32 | 2880 | 156 | 112 | **1.38** | 11-9-12 |
| Kevin Hartman, LA | 31 | 2790 | 137 | 94 | **1.39** | 13-13-5 |
| Zach Thornton, Chi | 27 | 2310 | 124 | 82 | **1.64** | 12-10-2 |
| Tony Meola, Met | 15 | 1350 | 111 | 83 | **1.87** | 6-5-4 |
| Brad Guzan, Chv | 24 | 2079 | 150 | 104 | **1.99** | 3-16-4 |

### Save Percentage

| | Svs | SOG | SV Pct |
|---|---|---|---|
| Pat Onstad, SJ | 105 | 136 | 77.2 |
| Jonny Walker, Clb | 66 | 87 | 75.9 |
| Zach Wells, Met | 69 | 95 | 72.6 |
| Scott Garlick, Dal | 98 | 135 | 72.6 |
| Joe Cannon, Col | 100 | 139 | 71.9 |
| Nick Rimando, DC | 92 | 128 | 71.9 |
| Matt Reis, NE | 155 | 162 | 71.0 |

### Saves

| | Gm | No |
|---|---|---|
| Matt Reis, NE | 31 | 115 |
| D.J. Countess, RSL | 27 | 112 |
| Bo Oshoniyi, KC | 32 | 112 |
| Pat Onstad, SJ | 32 | 105 |
| Brad Guzan, Chv | 24 | 104 |

### Shutouts

| | Gm | No |
|---|---|---|
| Pat Onstad, SJ | 32 | 12 |
| Nick Rimando, DC | 30 | 11 |
| Matt Reis, NE | 31 | 10 |
| Joe Cannon, Col | 27 | 8 |
| Bo Oshoniyi, KC | 32 | 7 |

### Wins

| | Gm | No |
|---|---|---|
| Pat Onstad, SJ | 32 | 18 |
| Matt Reis, NE | 31 | 16 |
| Nick Rimando, DC | 30 | 15 |
| Scott Garlick, Dal | 28 | 13 |
| Kevin Hartman, LA | 31 | 13 |
| Zach Thornton, Chi | 27 | 12 |
| Bo Oshoniyi, KC | 32 | 11 |

## Major League Soccer (Cont.)
### Team-by-Team Statistics
Players who played with more than one club during the season are listed with final team.
### Eastern Conference

#### Chicago Fire

| (min. 10 Gms) | Pos | Gm | Min | G | A | Pts |
|---|---|---|---|---|---|---|
| Chris Rolfe | F | 29 | 1942 | 8 | 5 | 21 |
| Nate Jaqua | F | 18 | 1361 | 7 | 3 | 17 |
| Thiago | M | 27 | 2220 | 6 | 7 | 19 |
| Jesse Marsch | M | 28 | 1947 | 5 | 2 | 12 |
| Justin Mapp | M/F | 29 | 2356 | 3 | 8 | 14 |
| Lubos Reiter | F | 14 | 772 | 3 | 2 | 8 |
| Gonzalo Segares | D | 21 | 1864 | 3 | 2 | 8 |
| Chris Armas | M | 22 | 1879 | 2 | 2 | 6 |
| Ivan Guerrero | M/D | 26 | 2314 | 2 | 5 | 9 |
| Andy Herron | F | 20 | 983 | 2 | 2 | 6 |
| Chad Barrett | F | 20 | 597 | 1 | 4 | 6 |
| Samuel Caballero | D | 17 | 1440 | 1 | 1 | 3 |
| Jim Curtin | D | 27 | 2144 | 1 | 3 | 5 |
| C.J. Brown | D | 20 | 1658 | 0 | 2 | 2 |
| Logan Pause | D/M | 27 | 2094 | 0 | 2 | 2 |
| Tony Sanneh | D/M | 12 | 989 | 0 | 1 | 1 |

| Top Goalkeepers | Gm | Min | W-L-T | Shts | Svs | GAA |
|---|---|---|---|---|---|---|
| Zach Thornton | 26 | 2310 | 12-10-2 | 126 | 82 | 1.64 |

#### Columbus Crew

| (min. 9 Gms) | Pos | Gm | Min | G | A | Pts |
|---|---|---|---|---|---|---|
| Edson Buddle | F | 23 | 1762 | 9 | 2 | 20 |
| Knox Cameron | F | 20 | 804 | 4 | 1 | 9 |
| Cornell Glen | F | 22 | 1241 | 4 | 4 | 12 |
| Frankie Hejduk | D/M | 18 | 1396 | 3 | 0 | 6 |
| John Wolyniec | F | 17 | 890 | 3 | 1 | 7 |
| Chris Henderson | M | 21 | 1767 | 2 | 3 | 7 |
| Eric Vasquez | M | 11 | 703 | 2 | 0 | 4 |
| Simon Elliott | M | 32 | 2880 | 1 | 11 | 13 |
| Chad Marshall | D | 30 | 2655 | 1 | 3 | 5 |
| Domenic Mediate | M/F | 11 | 478 | 1 | 0 | 2 |
| Mario Rodriguez | M | 19 | 1310 | 1 | 0 | 2 |
| David Testo | M/F | 17 | 1031 | 1 | 3 | 5 |
| Robin Fraser | D | 29 | 2607 | 0 | 0 | 0 |
| Kyle Martino | M | 27 | 2248 | 0 | 8 | 8 |
| Mark Schulte | D | 19 | 1540 | 0 | 1 | 1 |
| Marcus Storey | F | 12 | 382 | 0 | 1 | 1 |
| Danny Szetela | M | 16 | 1117 | 0 | 1 | 1 |
| Chris Wingert | D/M | 27 | 1896 | 0 | 0 | 0 |

| Top Goalkeepers | Gm | Min | W-L-T | Shts | Svs | GAA |
|---|---|---|---|---|---|---|
| Jonny Walker | 16 | 1440 | 6-8-2 | 87 | 66 | 1.12 |
| Jon Busch | 9 | 765 | 3-5-1 | 50 | 34 | 1.65 |

#### D.C. United

| | Pos | Gm | Min | G | A | Pts |
|---|---|---|---|---|---|---|
| Jaime Moreno | F | 29 | 2445 | 16 | 7 | 39 |
| Christian Gomez | M | 31 | 2419 | 11 | 9 | 31 |
| Santino Quaranta | F | 18 | 1185 | 5 | 5 | 15 |
| Freddy Adu | F/M | 25 | 1487 | 4 | 6 | 14 |
| Joshua Gros | M | 30 | 2563 | 4 | 4 | 12 |
| Dema Kovalenko | M | 26 | 2057 | 4 | 4 | 12 |
| Bobby Boswell | D | 27 | 2344 | 3 | 1 | 7 |
| Ben Olsen | M | 23 | 1874 | 2 | 4 | 8 |
| Jamil Walker | F | 22 | 732 | 2 | 7 | 11 |
| Brian Carroll | M | 32 | 2567 | 1 | 3 | 5 |
| Bryan Namoff | D | 17 | 1348 | 1 | 1 | 3 |
| Alecko Eskandarian | F | 12 | 661 | 0 | 1 | 1 |
| Brandon Prideaux | D | 29 | 2455 | 0 | 0 | 0 |
| Clyde Simms | M | 26 | 1263 | 0 | 1 | 1 |
| David Stokes | D | 10 | 390 | 0 | 1 | 1 |
| John Wilson | D | 17 | 1099 | 0 | 2 | 2 |

| Top Goalkeepers | Gm | Min | W-L-T | Shts | Svs | GAA |
|---|---|---|---|---|---|---|
| Nick Rimando | 30 | 2700 | 15-9-6 | 128 | 92 | 1.17 |

#### Kansas City Wizards

| (min. 9 Gms) | Pos | Gm | Min | G | A | Pts |
|---|---|---|---|---|---|---|
| Josh Wolff | F | 22 | 1910 | 10 | 10 | 30 |
| Scott Sealy | F | 28 | 1669 | 9 | 2 | 20 |
| Chris Klein | M | 31 | 2765 | 7 | 9 | 23 |
| Sasha Victorine | M | 30 | 2658 | 7 | 4 | 18 |
| Davy Arnaud | F/M | 31 | 2527 | 5 | 4 | 14 |
| Jack Jewsbury | M/F | 29 | 1001 | 4 | 0 | 8 |
| Jose Burciaga Jr. | D | 31 | 2667 | 2 | 4 | 8 |
| Jimmy Conrad | D | 25 | 2241 | 2 | 2 | 6 |
| Preki | M | 16 | 478 | 2 | 2 | 6 |
| Alex Zotinca | M/D | 16 | 1061 | 1 | 1 | 3 |
| Nick Garcia | D | 30 | 2678 | 0 | 0 | 0 |
| Diego Gutierrez | M | 21 | 1701 | 0 | 2 | 2 |
| Brian Roberts | D | 11 | 338 | 0 | 1 | 1 |
| Shavar Thomas | D | 25 | 2012 | 0 | 0 | 0 |
| Kerry Zavagnin | M | 28 | 2421 | 0 | 4 | 4 |

| Goalkeeper | Gm | Min | W-L-T | Shts | Svs | GAA |
|---|---|---|---|---|---|---|
| Bo Oshoniyi | 32 | 2880 | 11-9-12 | 163 | 112 | 1.38 |

#### MetroStars

| (min. 10 Gms) | Pos | Gm | Min | G | A | Pts |
|---|---|---|---|---|---|---|
| Amado Guevara | M | 26 | 2284 | 11 | 11 | 33 |
| Youri Djorkaeff | F/M | 24 | 1986 | 10 | 7 | 27 |
| Eddie Gaven | M | 28 | 2257 | 8 | 4 | 20 |
| Sergio Galvan Rey | F | 27 | 1598 | 7 | 0 | 14 |
| Ante Razov | F | 18 | 1431 | 6 | 5 | 17 |
| Mike Magee | M/F | 29 | 1835 | 5 | 5 | 15 |
| Abbe Ibrahim | F | 16 | 577 | 2 | 3 | 7 |
| Michael Bradley | M | 30 | 2628 | 1 | 4 | 6 |
| Jeff Agoos | D | 25 | 2150 | 0 | 0 | 0 |
| Chris Leitch | D | 28 | 2344 | 0 | 1 | 1 |
| Mark Lisi | M | 28 | 1971 | 0 | 5 | 5 |
| Carlos Mendes | D | 24 | 1916 | 0 | 0 | 0 |
| Jeff Parke | D | 21 | 1632 | 0 | 1 | 1 |
| Tim Regan | D/M | 20 | 1643 | 0 | 0 | 0 |
| Seth Stammler | D | 10 | 361 | 0 | 1 | 1 |
| Tim Ward | D | 13 | 1034 | 0 | 3 | 3 |

| Goalkeepers | Gm | Min | W-L-T | Shts | Svs | GAA |
|---|---|---|---|---|---|---|
| Zach Wells | 17 | 1530 | 6-4-7 | 95 | 69 | 1.24 |
| Tony Meola | 15 | 1350 | 6-5-4 | 117 | 83 | 1.87 |

#### New England Revolution

| (min. 9 Gms) | Pos | Gm | Min | G | A | Pts |
|---|---|---|---|---|---|---|
| Taylor Twellman | F | 25 | 2226 | 17 | 7 | 41 |
| Clint Dempsey | M | 26 | 2319 | 10 | 9 | 29 |
| Pat Noonan | F | 21 | 1843 | 8 | 7 | 23 |
| Shalrie Joseph | M | 31 | 2788 | 6 | 5 | 17 |
| Khano Smith | F | 23 | 928 | 3 | 2 | 8 |
| Jose Cancela | M | 25 | 1643 | 2 | 5 | 9 |
| Andy Doman | M | 30 | 1960 | 2 | 5 | 9 |
| Jay Heaps | D | 31 | 2790 | 1 | 5 | 7 |
| Marshall Leonard | M/D | 27 | 1923 | 1 | 1 | 3 |
| Steve Ralston | M/D | 21 | 1857 | 1 | 6 | 8 |
| James Riley | M/D | 23 | 1294 | 1 | 3 | 5 |
| Joe Franchino | D | 24 | 2011 | 0 | 3 | 3 |
| Avery John | D | 14 | 1167 | 0 | 1 | 1 |
| Michael Parkhurst | D | 32 | 2880 | 0 | 0 | 0 |
| Connally Edozien | F/M | 9 | 220 | 0 | 0 | 0 |

| Goalkeepers | Gm | Min | W-L-T | Shts | Svs | GAA |
|---|---|---|---|---|---|---|
| Matt Reis | 31 | 2784 | 16-7-8 | 162 | 115 | 1.13 |

## Western Conference

### Club Deportivo Chivas USA

| (min. 9 Gms) | Pos | Gm | Min | G | A | Pts |
|---|---|---|---|---|---|---|
| Hector Cuadros | M | 26 | 1694 | 4 | 4 | 12 |
| Ezra Hendrickson | D | 31 | 2745 | 3 | 1 | 7 |
| Thiago Martins | F | 22 | 1779 | 3 | 1 | 7 |
| Juan Francisco Palencia | F | 9 | 810 | 3 | 1 | 7 |
| Isacc Romo | F | 25 | 1190 | 3 | 1 | 7 |
| Antonio Martinez | F/M | 25 | 1602 | 2 | 3 | 7 |
| Ramon Ramirez | M | 31 | 2573 | 2 | 6 | 10 |
| Douglas Sequeira | D | 23 | 2070 | 2 | 1 | 5 |
| Matt Taylor | F | 21 | 1304 | 2 | 2 | 6 |
| Arturo Torres | F | 23 | 1367 | 2 | 2 | 6 |
| Esteban Arias | M/D | 15 | 1141 | 1 | 0 | 2 |
| Juan Pablo Garcia | M | 9 | 771 | 1 | 0 | 2 |
| Ryan Suarez | D | 15 | 1168 | 1 | 0 | 2 |
| Armando Begines | F | 22 | 1659 | 0 | 0 | 0 |
| Francisco Gomez | D/M | 12 | 648 | 0 | 1 | 1 |
| Alfonso Loera | D | 12 | 877 | 0 | 0 | 0 |
| Francisco Mendoza | M | 24 | 1878 | 0 | 2 | 2 |
| Jesus Ochoa | M | 16 | 1030 | 0 | 0 | 0 |
| Orlando Perez | D | 27 | 2070 | 0 | 3 | 3 |

| Goalkeepers | Gm | Min | W-L-T | Shts | Svs | GAA |
|---|---|---|---|---|---|---|
| Brad Guzan | 24 | 2079 | 3-16-4 | 156 | 104 | 1.99 |

### Colorado Rapids

| (min. 9 Gms) | Pos | Gm | Min | G | A | Pts |
|---|---|---|---|---|---|---|
| Jeff Cunningham | F | 26 | 1670 | 12 | 3 | 27 |
| Jean Philippe Peguero | F | 26 | 1842 | 7 | 6 | 20 |
| Alain Nkong | M | 28 | 1732 | 5 | 4 | 14 |
| Terry Cooke | M | 20 | 1492 | 2 | 2 | 6 |
| Luchi Gonzalez | F | 20 | 1449 | 2 | 2 | 6 |
| Kyle Beckerman | M | 30 | 2343 | 1 | 4 | 6 |
| Eric Denton | D | 31 | 2693 | 1 | 5 | 7 |
| Wolde Harris | F | 10 | 505 | 1 | 0 | 2 |
| Pablo Mastroeni | M/D | 14 | 943 | 1 | 0 | 2 |
| Nat Borchers | D | 31 | 2721 | 0 | 1 | 1 |
| Leo Cullen | M | 15 | 750 | 0 | 1 | 1 |
| Hunter Freeman | D/M | 20 | 1217 | 0 | 1 | 1 |
| Dan Gargan | M | 12 | 512 | 0 | 2 | 2 |
| Ritchie Kotschau | D | 28 | 2272 | 0 | 2 | 2 |
| Ricky Lewis | D | 16 | 1298 | 0 | 0 | 0 |
| Guy Melamed | M/D | 14 | 911 | 0 | 1 | 1 |
| Mike Petke | D | 19 | 1623 | 0 | 0 | 0 |

| Goalkeepers | Gm | Min | W-L-T | Shts | Svs | GAA |
|---|---|---|---|---|---|---|
| Joe Cannon | 27 | 2399 | 10-12-4 | 139 | 100 | 1.20 |

### FC Dallas

| (min. 9 Gms) | Pos | Gm | Min | G | A | Pts |
|---|---|---|---|---|---|---|
| Carlos Ruiz | F | 19 | 1549 | 11 | 2 | 24 |
| Roberto Mina | F | 21 | 1270 | 7 | 4 | 18 |
| Ronnie O'Brien | M | 28 | 2512 | 6 | 12 | 24 |
| Eddie Johnson | F | 15 | 1180 | 5 | 2 | 12 |
| Ramon Nunez | M | 21 | 1141 | 5 | 3 | 13 |
| Abe Thompson | F | 18 | 674 | 4 | 0 | 8 |
| Aaron Pitchkolan | M | 20 | 1442 | 3 | 1 | 7 |
| Arturo Alvarez | M/F | 24 | 1285 | 2 | 4 | 8 |
| Clarence Goodson | D | 29 | 2488 | 2 | 1 | 5 |
| Bobby Rhine | D | 28 | 2438 | 2 | 8 | 12 |
| Chris Gbandi | D | 17 | 1519 | 1 | 1 | 3 |
| Oscar Pareja | M | 18 | 646 | 1 | 1 | 3 |
| Steve Jolley | D | 13 | 1057 | 0 | 0 | 0 |
| Drew Moor | D | 20 | 936 | 0 | 0 | 0 |
| Carey Talley | M | 20 | 1092 | 0 | 3 | 3 |
| Simo Valakari | M | 28 | 2471 | 0 | 1 | 1 |
| Greg Vanney | D | 25 | 2210 | 0 | 1 | 1 |
| David Wagenfuhr | D | 19 | 1369 | 0 | 2 | 2 |

| Goalkeepers | Gm | Min | W-L-T | Shts | Svs | GAA |
|---|---|---|---|---|---|---|
| Scott Garlick | 28 | 2457 | 13-8-7 | 135 | 98 | 1.36 |

### Los Angeles Galaxy

| | Pos | Gm | Min | G | A | Pts |
|---|---|---|---|---|---|---|
| Landon Donovan | F | 22 | 1887 | 12 | 10 | 34 |
| Herculez Gomez | F | 22 | 1508 | 11 | 2 | 24 |
| Peter Vagenas | M | 29 | 2478 | 5 | 4 | 14 |
| Jovan Kirovski | F | 24 | 1704 | 4 | 4 | 12 |
| Cobi Jones | F | 31 | 2397 | 3 | 6 | 12 |
| Chris Albright | D | 22 | 1773 | 1 | 2 | 4 |
| Pablo Chinchilla | D | 19 | 1400 | 1 | 0 | 2 |
| Ednaldo da Conceicao | F | 19 | 951 | 1 | 3 | 5 |
| Tyrone Marshall | D | 25 | 2085 | 1 | 2 | 4 |
| Guillermo Ramirez | M | 24 | 1593 | 1 | 1 | 3 |
| Mubarike Chisoni | M | 11 | 308 | 0 | 0 | 0 |
| Todd Dunivant | D | 32 | 2880 | 0 | 2 | 2 |
| Ned Grabavoy | M | 12 | 656 | 0 | 3 | 3 |
| Ugo Ihemelu | D | 25 | 2031 | 0 | 1 | 1 |
| Paulo Nagamura | M | 25 | 2028 | 0 | 2 | 2 |
| Joseph Ngwenya | F | 16 | 620 | 0 | 0 | 0 |
| Troy Roberts | D | 14 | 822 | 0 | 0 | 0 |
| Michael Umana | D | 15 | 756 | 0 | 0 | 0 |

| Goalkeepers | Gm | Min | W-L-T | Shts | Svs | GAA |
|---|---|---|---|---|---|---|
| Kevin Hartman | 31 | 2790 | 13-13-5 | 138 | 94 | 1.39 |

### Real Salt Lake

| (min. 9 Gms) | Pos | Gm | Min | G | A | Pts |
|---|---|---|---|---|---|---|
| Jason Kreis | F | 24 | 2160 | 9 | 4 | 22 |
| Andy Williams | M | 26 | 2102 | 5 | 3 | 13 |
| Jordan Cila | F/M | 12 | 646 | 3 | 1 | 7 |
| Clint Mathis | M/F | 27 | 2123 | 3 | 4 | 10 |
| Brian Dunseth | D | 24 | 2011 | 2 | 0 | 4 |
| Seth Trembly | M/D | 22 | 1176 | 2 | 0 | 4 |
| Jamie Watson | F | 19 | 818 | 2 | 1 | 5 |
| Chris Brown | M/F | 29 | 2125 | 1 | 1 | 3 |
| Eddie Pope | D | 20 | 1756 | 1 | 0 | 2 |
| Melvin Tarley | F | 9 | 729 | 1 | 1 | 3 |
| Nelson Akwari | D | 23 | 1887 | 0 | 0 | 0 |
| Paul Broome | M | 11 | 917 | 0 | 0 | 0 |
| Kenny Cutler | M | 19 | 1699 | 0 | 0 | 0 |
| Leslie Fitzpatrick | M | 18 | 716 | 0 | 2 | 2 |
| Brian Kamler | M | 28 | 2028 | 0 | 0 | 0 |
| Rusty Pierce | D | 15 | 1200 | 0 | 1 | 1 |
| Robert Scarlett | M/D | 9 | 720 | 0 | 2 | 2 |

| Top Goalkeepers | Gm | Min | W-L-T | Shts | Svs | GAA |
|---|---|---|---|---|---|---|
| D.J. Countess | 27 | 2422 | 4-19-4 | 170 | 112 | 2.01 |

### San Jose Earthquakes

| (min. 9 Gms) | Pos | Gm | Min | G | A | Pts |
|---|---|---|---|---|---|---|
| Dwayne De Rosario | M/F | 28 | 2375 | 9 | 13 | 31 |
| Alejandro Moreno | F | 31 | 2167 | 8 | 4 | 20 |
| Brian Ching | F | 16 | 990 | 7 | 5 | 19 |
| Ronald Cerritos | F | 30 | 2308 | 6 | 9 | 21 |
| Mark Chung | M | 30 | 2487 | 7 | 7 | 21 |
| Ricardo Clark | M/D | 30 | 2492 | 3 | 2 | 8 |
| Brian Mullan | M/F | 25 | 1996 | 3 | 6 | 12 |
| Danny Califf | D | 20 | 1742 | 2 | 0 | 4 |
| Brad Davis | M | 18 | 1408 | 2 | 8 | 12 |
| Wade Barrett | D | 30 | 2664 | 1 | 2 | 4 |
| Kelly Gray | M/D | 20 | 1773 | 1 | 2 | 4 |
| Julian Nash | F | 10 | 233 | 1 | 1 | 3 |
| Eddie Robinson | D | 29 | 2450 | 1 | 1 | 3 |
| Ryan Cochrane | D | 14 | 776 | 0 | 0 | 0 |
| Danny O'Rourke | M | 13 | 1050 | 0 | 0 | 0 |
| Ian Russell | M | 13 | 235 | 0 | 0 | 0 |

| Goalkeepers | Gm | Min | W-L-T | Shts | Svs | GAA |
|---|---|---|---|---|---|---|
| Pat Onstad | 32 | 2880 | 18-4-10 | 136 | 105 | 0.97 |

# United Soccer Leagues
## First Division

In November of 2004, as part of the newly reformed United Soccer Leagues, the A-League was renamed the USL First Division. The USL First Division is the second level of soccer (behind only Major League Soccer) in the United States and Division I in Canada. Playoff qualifiers (*) are noted. Top two teams receive a bye into the semifinals.

## 2005 Final Standings

| Team | W | L | T | GF | GA | Pts |
|---|---|---|---|---|---|---|
| *Montreal Impact | 18 | 3 | 7 | 37 | 15 | 61 |
| *Rochester Raging Rhinos | 15 | 7 | 6 | 45 | 27 | 51 |
| *Vancouver Whitecaps | 12 | 7 | 9 | 37 | 21 | 45 |
| *Seattle Sounders | 11 | 6 | 11 | 33 | 25 | 44 |
| *Portland Timbers | 10 | 9 | 9 | 40 | 42 | 39 |
| *Richmond Kickers | 10 | 9 | 9 | 28 | 30 | 39 |
| Puerto Rico Islanders | 10 | 10 | 8 | 46 | 43 | 38 |
| Atlanta Silverbacks | 10 | 15 | 3 | 40 | 52 | 33 |
| Charleston Battery | 7 | 11 | 10 | 27 | 36 | 31 |
| Minnesota Thunder | 7 | 11 | 10 | 37 | 42 | 31 |
| Virginia Beach Mariners | 7 | 14 | 7 | 26 | 39 | 28 |
| Toronto Lynx | 3 | 17 | 8 | 26 | 50 | 17 |

## Leaders
### Goals

| | Gms | Goals |
|---|---|---|
| Jason Jordan, Vancouver | 27 | 17 |
| Fabian Dawkins, Atlanta | 26 | 15 |
| Mauricio Salles-De Alencar, Puerto Rico | 26 | 14 |
| Dan Antoniuk, Portland | 24 | 13 |
| Kirk Wilson, Rochester | 22 | 9 |
| Byron Alvarez, Portland | 26 | 9 |
| Corey Woolfolk, Puerto Rico | 26 | 9 |
| Mauro Biello, Montreal | 28 | 9 |
| Matthew Delicate, Richmond | 27 | 8 |
| Johnny Menyongar, Minnesota | 27 | 8 |

### Points

| | Gms | Pts |
|---|---|---|
| Jason Jordan, Vancouver | 27 | 37 |
| Fabian Dawkins, Atlanta | 26 | 34 |
| Mauricio Salles-De Alencar, Puerto Rico | 26 | 29 |
| Dan Antoniuk, Portland | 24 | 28 |
| Kirk Wilson, Rochester | 22 | 23 |
| Corey Woolfolk, Puerto Rico | 26 | 23 |

## Playoffs
### First Round (Total Goals)

#### Vancouver vs. Richmond

Sept. 16    Richmond 0, Vancouver 0    at Richmond
Sept. 18    Vancouver 0, Richmond 0    at Vancouver
Aggregate tied 0-0, Richmond advances 5-4 on PKs

#### Seattle vs. Portland

Sept. 16    Portland 0, Seattle 1    at Portland
Sept. 18    Seattle 2, Portland 0    at Seattle
Seattle wins 2-1 on aggregate

### Semifinals (Total Goals)
#### Montreal vs. Seattle

Sept. 23    Montreal 2, Seattle 2    at Seattle
Sept. 25    Seattle 2, Montreal 1    at Montreal
Seattle wins 2-1 on aggregate

#### Rochester vs. Richmond

Sept. 23    Richmond 3, Rochester 1    at Richmond
Sept. 25    Rochester 1, Richmond 1    at Rochester
Richmond wins 4-2 on aggregate

### Final

Oct. 1 at Qwest Field, Seattle, Wash. **Attendance:** 8,011

Seattle 1 . . . . . . . . . . . . . . . . . . Richmond 1
**Seattle wins, 4-3, on penalty kicks**

**Scoring**
**1st Half:** RICH—Sascha Gorres (unassisted), 24th.
**2nd Half:** SEA—Maykel Galindo (Ryan Edwards), 73rd.

**Game MVP:** Preston Burpo, Seattle, GK

# Awards
## 2004 FIFA World Players of the Year

As determined by a global vote of 302 national team coaches and captains from 157 FIFA member associations. First-place votes listed and total points. Players receive five points for 1st place votes, three points for 2nd place votes and one point for third place votes. Top 10 vote-getters listed below. USA national team players in **bold** type.

### MEN

| | | 1st | Pts |
|---|---|---|---|
| 1 | Ronaldinho, Brazil | 89 | 620 |
| 2 | Thierry Henry, France | 79 | 552 |
| 3 | Andriy Shevchenko, Ukraine | 34 | 253 |
| 4 | Pavel Nedved, Czech Rep. | 12 | 178 |
| 5 | Zinedine Zidane, France | 17 | 150 |
| 6 | Adriano, Brazil | 8 | 98 |
| 7 | Deco, Portugal | 6 | 96 |
| | Ronaldo, Brazil | 6 | 96 |
| 9 | Ruud van Nistelrooy, Netherlands | 5 | 67 |
| 10 | Kaka, Brazil | 4 | 64 |
| | Wayne Rooney, England | 2 | 64 |

### WOMEN

| | | 1st | Pts |
|---|---|---|---|
| 1 | Birgit Prinz, Germany | 46 | 376 |
| 2 | **Mia Hamm**, USA | 40 | 286 |
| 3 | Marta, Brazil | 39 | 281 |
| 4 | **Abby Wambach**, USA | 16 | 126 |
| 5 | **Kristine Lilly**, USA | 10 | 109 |
| | Hanna Ljungberg, Sweden | 8 | 109 |
| 7 | **Shannon Boxx**, USA | 14 | 102 |
| 8 | Victoria Svensson, Sweden | 6 | 89 |
| | Renate Lingor, Germany | 11 | 89 |
| 10 | Cristiane, Brazil | 9 | 80 |

## Colleges
### MEN
### 2004 Final *Soccer America* Top 25

Final 2004 regular season poll including games through Nov. 14. Conducted by the national weekly *Soccer America* and released on Nov. 15. Listing includes records through conference playoffs as well as NCAA tournament record and team lost to. Teams in **bold** type went on to reach College Cup. All tournament games decided by penalty kicks are considered ties.

| | Nov. 14 Record | NCAA Recap | | Nov. 14 Record | NCAA Recap |
|---|---|---|---|---|---|
| 1 New Mexico | 16-1-1 | 1-1 (Virginia) | 14 Memphis | 16-3-1 | 0-1 (Ohio St.) |
| 2 SMU | 15-3-1 | 1-1 (Tulsa) | 15 Washington | 11-6-2 | 0-1 (Portland) |
| 3 UCLA | 13-3-2 | 1-1 (St. John's) | 16 Creighton | 13-4-1 | 1-1 (Maryland) |
| 4 Virginia | 16-4-0 | 2-1 (Duke) | 17 **Duke** | 14-4-0 | 4-1 (UCSB) |
| 5 **UC Santa Barbara** | 17-2-1 | 4-1 (Indiana) | 18 James Madison | 15-3-1 | did not play |
| 6 California | 12-3-3 | 1-1 (SMU) | 19 San Francisco | 14-4-1 | 0-1 (WI-Milwaukee) |
| 7 UNC-Greensboro | 18-2-1 | 1-1 (UCSB) | 20 Santa Clara | 15-5-0 | 0-1 (California) |
| 8 **Maryland** | 15-5-1 | 3-1 (Indiana) | 21 Boston College | 12-4-2 | 1-1 (Indiana) |
| 9 Michigan St. | 12-6-1 | 0-1 (Tulsa) | 22 South Carolina | 12-6-1 | 0-1 (Charleston) |
| 10 **Indiana** | 14-4-1 | 5-0 | 23 Florida International | 11-6-0 | 0-1 (C. Florida) |
| 11 Connecticut | 11-7-3 | 1-1 (Boston College) | 24 Virginia Commonwealth | 11-5-2 | 2-1 (UCSB) |
| 12 Notre Dame | 13-2-3 | 0-1 (Ohio St.) | 25 College of Charleston | 16-5-1 | 1-1 (NC-Greensboro) |
| 13 Wake Forest | 13-5-1 | 1-1 (VCU) | | | |

## NCAA Division I Tournament

### First Round (Nov. 19 or 20)

at Central Florida 1 . . . . . . . . . .at Florida International 0
George Washington 1 . . . . . . . . . . .at North Carolina 0
WI-Milwaukee 3 . . . . . . . . . . . . . .at San Francisco 1
College of Charleston 3 . . . . . . . . .at South Carolina 2
at Ohio St. 1 . . . . . . . . . . . . . . . . . . . . .Memphis 0
at Duke 3 . . . . . . . . . . . . . . . . . .Coastal Carolina 1
Portland 5 . . . . . . . . . . . . . . . .at Washington 3
at American 3 . . . . . . . . . . . . . . . .Long Island 0
Hofstra 2 . . . . . . . . . . . . . . . . . . .at Seton Hall 1
at Northwestern 4 . . . . . . . . . . .Western Illinois 1
at Boston University 2 . . . . . . . . . . . .Dartmouth 2
*Boston University advanced on PKs*
at Loyola Marymount 1 . . . . . . . . . .at CS-Northridge 0
at California 2 . . . . . . . . .OT . . . . . .Santa Clara 1
at Tulsa 3 . . . . . . . . . . . . . . . . . .Michigan St. 1
at Connecticut 2 . . . . . . . . .OT . . . . . . . . .Marist 1
at Michigan 2 . . . . . . . . . . . . . . . . . . . . .Akron 1

### Second Round (Nov. 23)

at Wake Forest 5 . . . . . . . . . . . .Central Florida 0
at Virginia Commonwealth 2 . . . . .George Washington 0
at UC Santa Barbara 2 . . . .2 OT . . . . .WI-Milwaukee 1
at NC-Greensboro 2 . . . . . . . . . .College of Charleston 1
Ohio St. 2 . . . . . . . . . . . . . . . .at Notre Dame 1
Duke 2 . . . . . . . . . . . . . .OT . . . . .at Old Dominion 1
at New Mexico 4 . . . . . . . . . . . . . . . . .Portland 1
at Virginia 2 . . . . . . . . . . . . . . . . . .American 1
at Maryland 4 . . . . . . . . . . . . . . . . . . .Hofstra 0
at Creighton 3 . . . . . . . . . . . . . . . .Northwestern 1
at St. John's 3 . . . . . . . . . . . . . .Boston University 1
at UCLA 3 . . . . . . . . . . . . . . . .Loyola Marymount 0
at Southern Methodist 1 . . . . . . . . . . . . . .California 0
Tulsa 1 . . . . . . . . . . . . .2 OT . . . . . . .at Penn St. 1
*Tulsa advanced on PKs*
at Boston College 1 . . . . . . . . . . . . . . .Connecticut 0
at Indiana 1 . . . . . . . . . . . . . . . . . . . . .Michigan 0

### Third Round (Nov. 27 or 28)

Virginia Commonwealth 2 2OT . . . . . .at Wake Forest 2
*Virginia Commonwealth advanced on PKs*
UC Santa Barbara 1 . . . .OT . . . . .at NC-Greensboro 0
at Duke 3 . . . . . . . . . . . . . . . . . . . . . .Ohio St. 0
at Virginia 1 . . . . . . . . .2 OT . . . . . .New Mexico 1
*Virginia advanced on PKs*
at Maryland 0 . . . . . . . . .2 OT . . . . . . . .Creighton 0
*Maryland advanced on PKs*
St. John's 2 . . . . . . . . . . . . . . . . . . . .at UCLA 1
Tulsa 2 . . . . . . . . . . . . .2 OT .at Southern Methodist 1
at Indiana 1 . . . . . . . . . . . . . . . . .Boston College 0

### Quarterfinals (Dec. 3, 4 or 5)

at UC Santa Barbara 4 . . . . . .Virginia Commonwealth 1
Duke 3 . . . . . . . . . . . . . . . . . . . . . .at Virginia 0
at Maryland 1 . . . . . . . . . . . . . . . . .St. John's 0
at Indiana 4 . . . . . . . . . . . . . . . . . . . . . .Tulsa 0

---

### 2004 College Cup
at Carson, California (Dec. 10 & 12)

#### Semifinals

UC Santa Barbara 5 . . . . . . . . . . . . . . . . .Duke 0
Indiana 3 . . . . . . . . . .2 OT . . . . . . .Maryland 2

#### Championship

Indiana 1 . . . . . . . . . .2 OT . . .UC Santa Barbara 1

#### Scoring
**1st Half:** IND—Jacob Peterson (Jed Zayner), 26:23
**2nd Half:** UCSB—Drew McAthy (unassisted), 81:01
#### Indiana won, 3-2, on penalty kicks

**Final records:** Indiana (19-4-1); UCSB (21-3-1).
**Offensive MVP:** Drew McAthy, UC Santa Barbara, F
**Defensive MVP:** Jay Nolly, Indiana, GK

# WOMEN
## 2004 Final *Soccer America* Top 25

Final 2004 regular season poll including games through Nov. 7. Conducted by the national weekly *Soccer America* and released on Nov. 8. Listing includes records through conference playoffs as well as NCAA tournament record and team lost to. Teams in **bold** type went on to reach College Cup. All tournament games decided by penalty kicks are considered ties.

| | Nov. 7 Record | NCAA Recap | | Nov. 7 Record | NCAA Recap |
|---|---|---|---|---|---|
| 1 North Carolina | 18-0-2 | 2-1 (Santa Clara) | 14 Tennessee | 15-4-2 | 1-1 (Ohio St.) |
| 2 Virginia | 14-2-1 | 1-1 (Duke) | 15 Washington | 14-4-1 | 3-1 (Princeton) |
| 3 **Notre Dame** | 19-1-1 | 5-0-1 | 16 Texas | 13-6-2 | 1-1 (Portland) |
| 4 **Santa Clara** | 14-4-2 | 4-1 (Notre Dame0 | 17 Kansas | 17-4-0 | 1-1 (Nebraska) |
| 5 Portland | 17-3-0 | 3-1 (Notre Dame | 18 California | 11-5-3 | 0-1 (Santa Clara) |
| 6 Ohio State | 17-3-3 | 3-1 (UCLA) | 19 Stanford | 12-5-3 | 1-1 (Santa Clara) |
| 7 Penn St. | 18-2-1 | 1-1 (Maryland) | 20 Duke | 13-7-0 | 2-1 (UCLA) |
| 8 Florida | 16-3-3 | 0-1 (C. Florida) | 21 Dayton | 20-1-0 | 0-1 (Wisconsin) |
| 9 Connecticut | 16-6-1 | 2-1 (Notre Dame) | 22 Auburn | 14-3-2 | 1-1 (Washington) |
| 10 **UCLA** | 13-6-0 | 5-0-1 (Notre Dame) | 23 SMU | 15-3-3 | 0-1 (W. Virginia) |
| 11 **Princeton** | 15-2-0 | 4-1 (UCLA) | 24 Florida St. | 12-5-2 | 0-0-1 (Boston Coll.) |
| 12 Texas A&M | 17-5-0 | 1-1 (Illinois) | 25 Clemson | 10-7-2 | 0-1 (Auburn) |
| 13 Arizona | 15-5-0 | 0-1 (Colgate) | | | |

## NCAA Division I Tournament

### First Round (Nov. 12)

| | | |
|---|---|---|
| at North Carolina 6 | Campbell | 0 |
| William & Mary 2 | Virginia Tech | 1 |
| Stanford 2 | Cal Poly | 0 |
| at Santa Clara 2 | California | 1 |
| at Texas A&M 10 | Texas St. | 0 |
| Illinois 2 | Rice | 0 |
| Nebraska 3 | Oral Roberts | 0 |
| at Kansas 3 | Creighton | 1 |
| at Portland 3 | Weber St. | 0 |
| Colorado 3 | Utah | 0 |
| West Virginia 2 | SMU | 1 |
| at Texas 3 | North Texas | 0 |
| Colgate 1 | Arizona | 0 |
| at Connecticut 2 | Harvard | 1 |
| Wisconsin 2 | OT | Dayton 1 |
| at Notre Dame 4 | Eastern Illinois | 0 |
| at Virginia 6 | James Madison | 0 |
| Duke 2 | Virginia Commonwealth | 1 |
| San Diego 1 | 2 OT | UNLV 0 |
| at UCLA 1 | Pepperdine | 0 |
| at Tennessee 2 | Furman | 0 |
| UAB 3 | Wake Forest | 0 |
| Detroit 3 | Michigan | 2 |
| at Ohio St. 2 | Bowling Green | 0 |
| at Princeton 5 | Central Conn. St. | 0 |
| Villanova 2 | Yale | 1 |
| Boston College 0 | Florida St. | 0 |

Boston College advanced on PKs

| | | |
|---|---|---|
| Central Florida 3 | at Florida | 2 |
| Washington 5 | Birmingham-Southern | 0 |
| at Auburn 2 | Clemson | 0 |
| Maryland 3 | Loyola | 0 |
| at Penn St. 6 | Binghamton | 1 |

### Second Round (Nov. 14)

| | | |
|---|---|---|
| at North Carolina 6 | William & Mary | 0 |
| Santa Clara 1 | 2 OT | Stanford 0 |
| at Illinois 2 | Texas A&M | 1 |
| Nebraska 2 | 2 OT | Kansas 0 |
| Portland 3 | Colorado | 0 |
| Texas 2 | West Virginia | 1 |
| Connecticut 4 | Colgate | 0 |
| Notre Dame 1 | Wisconsin | 0 |
| Duke 3 | Virginia | 0 |
| at UCLA 3 | San Diego | 0 |
| Tennessee 1 | UAB | 0 |

| | | |
|---|---|---|
| Ohio St. 3 | Detroit | 2 |
| Princeton 1 | 2 OT | Villanova 0 |
| Boston College 2 | Central Florida | 1 |
| Washington 1 | Auburn | 0 |
| Maryland 1 | Penn St. | 0 |

### Third Round (Nov. 19-21)

| | | |
|---|---|---|
| Santa Clara 1 | OT | North Carolina 0 |
| at Illinois 2 | Nebraska | 1 |
| at Portland 2 | Texas | 0 |
| at Notre Dame 2 | Connecticut | 0 |
| at UCLA 2 | Duke | 0 |
| at Ohio St. 1 | Tennessee | 0 |
| at Princeton 2 | Boston College | 0 |
| at Washington 1 | Maryland | 0 |

### Quarterfinals (Nov. 26-28)

| | | |
|---|---|---|
| at Santa Clara 2 | Illinois | 0 |
| at Notre Dame 3 | Portland | 1 |
| UCLA 1 | at Ohio St. | 0 |
| at Princeton 3 | Washington | 1 |

---

## 2004 College Cup
at Cary, N.C. (Dec. 3 & 5)

### Semifinals

| | | |
|---|---|---|
| Notre Dame 1 | Santa Clara | 0 |
| UCLA 2 | Princeton | 0 |

### Championship

| | | |
|---|---|---|
| Notre Dame 1 | 2 OT | UCLA 1 |

### Scoring

**2nd Half:** UCLA—own goal (59:30); ND—Katie Thorlakson (penalty) (73:10).

**Notre Dame won, 4-3, on penalty kicks**

**Attendance:** 7,644
**Final records:** Notre Dame (24-1-2), UCLA (18-6-1).
**Offensive MVP:** Katie Thorlakson, Notre Dame, F
**Defensive MVP:** Erika Bohn, Notre Dame, GK

## 2004 Annual Awards

### Men's Players of the Year

MAC/Hermann Trophy . . . . .Danny O'Rourke, Indiana, M
*Soccer America* . . . . . . . . . . . . . . .Ryan Pore, Tulsa, F
NCAA Div. II . . . . . . . . . . . . . . Bobby McAlister, Seattle
NCAA Div. III . . . . . . .Patrick McGinnis, Colorado College
JuCo Div. I . . . . . . . . . . . .Dane Richards, San Jacinto JC
JuCo Div. III . . . . . . . . . . . .Ismael Ibarra,Hartnell College

### Women's Players of the Year

MAC/Hermann Trophy . . . . .Christine Sinclair, Portland, F
*Soccer America* . . . . . .Katie Thorlakson, North Dame, F
NCAA Div. II . . . . . . . . . . . . . .Ymara Guante, Metro St.
NCAA Div. III . . . . . . . . . . . . Jessica Elsen, Wheaton (Ill.)
JuCo Div. I . . . . . . . . . .Melissa Hornfeck, Monroe CC
JuCo Div. III . . . .Kristin Childers, Long Beach City College

### NSCAA Coaches of the Year

Women's Div. I . . . . . . . . . . . .Julie Shackford, Princeton
Men's Div. I . . . . . . . . .Tim Vom Steeg, UC Santa Barbara
Women's Div. II . . . . . . . . . .Danny Sanchez, Metro St.
Men's Div. II . . . . . . . . . . . . . . . .Peter Fewing, Seattle
Women's Div. III . . . . . . . . . . . .Peter Felske, Wheaton (Ill.)
Men's Div. III . . . . . . . . . . . . . . . .David Brandt, Messiah
Women's NAIA . . . . . . . .Drew Burwash, Lindsey Wilson
Men's NAIA . . . . . . . . . . . . . .Carl Hutter, Lindenwood U.
Men's Juco Div. I . . . . . .Marc Zagara, Georgia Perimeter
Men's JuCo Div. III . . . . . . . Jose Vasquez, Santa Ana CC
Women's JuCo Div. I . . . . . . . .Tracey Britton, Monroe CC.
Women's JuCo Div. III . . . . . . .Michael Murphy, Richland

## Division I All-America Teams

### MEN

The 2004 first team All-America selections of the National Soccer Coaches Association of America (NSCAA). Holdover from the 2003 NSCAA All-America first team are in **bold** type.

GOALKEEPER—Christopher Sawyer, Notre Dame.

DEFENDERS—Ugochukwu Ihemelu, SMU; Drew Moor, Indiana; Gonzalo Segares, VCU.

MIDFIELDERS—**C.J. Klaas**, Washington; Mike Enfield, UCLA; Sacha Kljestan, Seton Hall; Danny O'Rourke, Indiana.

FORWARDS—Justin Moose, Wake Forest; Randi Patterson, NC-Greensboro; Ryan Pore, Tulsa; Jeff Rowland, New Mexico.

### WOMEN

The 2004 first team All-America selections of the National Soccer Coaches Association of America (NSCAA). Holdovers from the 2003 NSCAA All-America first team are in **bold** type.

GOALKEEPER—Nicole Barnhart, Stanford.

DEFENDERS—**Keeley Dowling**, Tennessee; Holly Gault, Kansas; Natalie Jacobs, Penn St.

MIDFIELDERS—Lori Chalupny, North Carolina; Lindsey Huie, Portland; Diana Matheson, Princeton; Leslie Osborne, Santa Clara.

FORWARDS—**Tiffany Weimer**, Penn St.; Esmeralda Negron, Princeton; Heather O'Reilly, North Carolina; Christine Sinclair, Portland.

## Small College Final Fours

### MEN

#### NCAA Division II
at Wichita Falls, Texas. (Dec. 3-5)

**Semifinals:** Southern Illinois-Edwardsville def. NC-Pembroke, 4-1; Seattle def. Dowling, 2-1.
**Championship:** Seattle def. Southern Illinois-Edwardsville, 2-1. Final records: Seattle (22-0-1), Southern Illinois-Edwardsville (19-3-2).

#### NCAA Division III
at Greensboro, N.C. (Nov. 26-27)

**Semifinals:** UC Santa Cruz def. Geneseo St., 3-1; Messiah def. Salisbury, 1-0.
**Championship:** Messiah def. UC Santa Cruz, 4-0; Final records: Messiah (23-2-0), UC Santa Cruz (22-2-1).

#### NAIA
at Olathe, Kan.

**Semifinals:** Lindenwood (Mo.) def. Berry (Ga.), 1-0; Auburn Montgomery (Ala.) def. Lindsey Wilson (Ky.), 1-0.
**Championship:** Lindenwood (Mo.) def. Auburn Montgomery (Ala.), 1-0).

### WOMEN

#### NCAA Division II
at Wichita Falls, Texas. (Dec. 2-4)

**Semifinals:** Adelphi def. Carson-Newman, 2-1; Metro St. def. Nebraska-Omaha, 2-0.
**Championship:** Metro St. def. Adelphi, 3-2. Final records: Metro St. (25-1), Adelphi (19-4-1).

#### NCAA Division III
at Greensboro, N.C. (Nov. 26-27)

**Semifinals:** Wheaton (Ill.) def. Wheaton (Mass.), 3-1; Pugent Sound def. Messiah, 3-0.
**Championship:** Wheaton (Ill.) def. Puget Sound, 1-1 (5-4 on PKs). Final records: Wheaton (35-1-1), Puget Sound (22-1-1).

#### NAIA
at Santa Barbara, Calif. (Nov. 22-23)

**Semifinals:** Lindsey Wilson (Ky.) def. Concordia (Ore.), 2-0; Westmont (Calif.) def. William Jewell (Mo.), 5-1.
**Championship:** Lindsey Wilson (Ky.) def. Concordia (Ore.), 2-0.

# 1900-2005
# *Through the Years*

SPORTS ALMANAC

## The World Cup

The Federation Internationale de Football Association (FIFA) began the World Cup championship tournament in 1930 with a 13-team field in Uruguay. Sixty-four years later, 138 countries competed in qualifying rounds to fill 24 berths in the 1994 World Cup finals. FIFA increased the World Cup '98 tournament field from 24 to 32 teams, and it remained at 32 in 2002 including automatic berths for defending champion France and co-hosts Japan and South Korea. The other 29 slots were allotted by region: Europe (13), Africa (5), South America (4), CONCACAF (3), Asia (2), the two remaining positions were determined via two home-and-away playoff series. One was between the #14 European team (Ireland) and the #3 Asian team (Iran) and the other was between the #5 South American team (Uruguay) and the champion of Oceania (Australia).

Tournaments have been played once in Asia (Japan/South Korea), three times in North America (Mexico 2 and U.S.), four times in South America (Argentina, Chile, Brazil and Uruguay) and nine times in Europe (France 2, Italy 2, England, Spain, Sweden, Switzerland and West Germany). Following an outcry when Germany was awarded the 2006 World Cup over South Africa, FIFA announced that, starting in 2010, the World Cup will be rotated among six continents.

Brazil retired the first World Cup (called the Jules Rimet Trophy after FIFA's first president) in 1970 after winning it for the third time. The new trophy, first presented in 1974, is known as simply the World Cup.

**Multiple winners:** Brazil (5); Italy and West Germany (3); Argentina and Uruguay (2).

| Year | Champion | Manager | Score | Runner-up | Host Country | Third Place |
|------|----------|---------|-------|-----------|--------------|-------------|
| 1930 | Uruguay | Alberto Suppici | 4-2 | Argentina | Uruguay | No game |
| 1934 | Italy | Vittório Pozzo | 2-1* | Czechoslovakia | Italy | Germany 3, Austria 2 |
| 1938 | Italy | Vittório Pozzo | 4-2 | Hungary | France | Brazil 4, Sweden 2 |
| 1942-46 | Not held | | | | | |
| 1950 | Uruguay | Juan Lopez | 2-1 | Brazil | Brazil | No game |
| 1954 | West Germany | Sepp Herberger | 3-2 | Hungary | Switzerland | Austria 3, Uruguay 1 |
| 1958 | Brazil | Vicente Feola | 5-2 | Sweden | Sweden | France 6, W. Ger. 3 |
| 1962 | Brazil | Aimoré Moreira | 3-1 | Czechoslovakia | Chile | Chile 1, Yugoslavia 0 |
| 1966 | England | Alf Ramsey | 4-2* | W. Germany | England | Portugal 2, USSR 1 |
| 1970 | Brazil | Mario Zagalo | 4-1 | Italy | Mexico | W. Ger. 1, Uruguay 0 |
| 1974 | West Germany | Helmut Schoen | 2-1 | Netherlands | W. Germany | Poland 1, Brazil 0 |
| 1978 | Argentina | Cesar Menotti | 3-1* | Netherlands | Argentina | Brazil 2, Italy 1 |
| 1982 | Italy | Enzo Bearzot | 3-1 | W. Germany | Spain | Poland 3, France 2 |
| 1986 | Argentina | Carlos Bilardo | 3-2 | W. Germany | Mexico | France 4, Belgium 2* |
| 1990 | West Germany | Franz Beckenbauer | 1-0 | Argentina | Italy | Italy 2, England 1 |
| 1994 | Brazil | Carlos Parreira | 0-0† | Italy | USA | Sweden 4, Bulgaria 0 |
| 1998 | France | Aimé Jacquet | 3-0 | Brazil | France | Croatia 2, Netherlands 1 |
| 2002 | Brazil | Luiz Felipe Scolari | 2-0 | Germany | Japan/S. Korea | Turkey 3, S. Korea 2 |
| 2006 | at Germany (June 9-July 9) | | | | | |
| 2010 | at South Africa (TBD) | | | | | |

*Winning goals scored in overtime (no sudden death); †Brazil defeated Italy in shootout (3-2) after scoreless overtime period.

## All-Time World Cup Leaders

### Career Goals

World Cup scoring leaders through 2002. Years listed are years played in World Cup.

| | No |
|---|---|
| Gerd Müller, West Germany (1970, 74) | 14 |
| Just Fontaine, France (1958) | 13 |
| Pelé, Brazil (1958, 62, 66, 70) | 12 |
| Ronaldo, Brazil (1994, 98, 2002) | 12 |
| Sandor Kocsis, Hungary (1954) | 11 |
| Juergen Klinsmann, Germany (1990, 94, 98) | 11 |
| Helmut Rahn, West Germany (1954, 58) | 10 |
| Teofilo Cubillas, Peru (1970, 78) | 10 |
| Gregorz Lato, Poland (1974, 78, 82) | 10 |
| Gary Lineker, England (1986, 90) | 10 |

### Most Valuable Player

Officially, the Golden Ball Award, the Most Valuable Player of the World Cup tournament has been selected since 1982 by a panel of international soccer journalists.

| Year | | Year | |
|------|---|------|---|
| 1982 | Paolo Rossi, Italy | 1994 | Romario, Brazil |
| 1986 | Diego Maradona, Arg. | 1998 | Ronaldo, Brazil |
| 1990 | Toto Schillaci, Italy | 2002 | Oliver Kahn, Germany |

### Single Tournament Goals

World Cup tournament scoring leaders through 2002.

| Year | | Gm | No |
|------|---|----|----|
| 1930 | Guillermo Stabile, Argentina | 4 | 8 |
| 1934 | Angelo Schiavio, Italy | 3 | 4 |
| | Oldrich Nejedly, Czechoslovakia | 4 | 4 |
| | Edmund Conen, Germany | 4 | 4 |
| 1938 | Leônidas, Brazil | 3 | 8 |
| 1950 | Ademir, Brazil | 6 | 7 |
| 1954 | Sandor Kocsis, Hungary | 5 | 11 |
| 1958 | Just Fontaine, France | 6 | 13 |
| 1962 | Drazen Jerkovic, Yugoslavia | 6 | 5 |
| 1966 | Eusébio, Portugal | 6 | 9 |
| 1970 | Gerd Müller, West Germany | 6 | 10 |
| 1974 | Grzegorz Lato, Poland | 7 | 7 |
| 1978 | Mario Kempes, Argentina | 7 | 6 |
| 1982 | Paolo Rossi, Italy | 7 | 6 |
| 1986 | Gary Lineker, England | 5 | 6 |
| 1990 | Toto Schillaci, Italy | 7 | 6 |
| 1994 | Oleg Salenko, Russia | 3 | 6 |
| | Hristo Stoitchkov, Bulgaria | 7 | 6 |
| 1998 | Davor Suker, Croatia | 7 | 6 |
| 2002 | Ronaldo, Brazil | 7 | 8 |

## All-Time World Cup Ranking Table

Since the first World Cup in 1930, Brazil is the only country to play in all 17 final tournaments. The FIFA all-time table below ranks all nations that have ever qualified for a World Cup final tournament by points earned through 2002. Victories, which earned two points from 1930-90, were awarded three points starting in 1994. Note that Germany's appearances include 10 made by West Germany from 1954-90. Participants in the 2002 World Cup final are in **bold** type.

| | | App | Gm | W | L | T | Pts | GF | GA |
|---|---|---|---|---|---|---|---|---|---|
| 1 | Brazil | 17 | 87 | 60 | 13 | 14 | 141 | 191 | 82 |
| 2 | Germany | 15 | 85 | 50 | 17 | 18 | 123 | 176 | 106 |
| 3 | Italy | 15 | 70 | 39 | 14 | 17 | 96 | 110 | 67 |
| 4 | Argentina | 13 | 60 | 30 | 19 | 11 | 72 | 102 | 71 |
| 5 | England | 11 | 50 | 26 | 13 | 15 | 61 | 68 | 45 |
| 6 | Spain | 11 | 45 | 20 | 15 | 10 | 54 | 71 | 53 |
| 7 | France | 11 | 44 | 21 | 16 | 7 | 49 | 86 | 61 |
| 8 | Sweden | 10 | 42 | 15 | 16 | 10 | 42 | 71 | 65 |
| 9 | Russia | 9 | 37 | 17 | 14 | 6 | 41 | 64 | 44 |
| 10 | Yugoslavia | 9 | 37 | 16 | 13 | 8 | 40 | 60 | 46 |
| | Uruguay | 10 | 40 | 15 | 15 | 10 | 40 | 65 | 57 |
| 12 | Netherlands | 7 | 31 | 14 | 9 | 9 | 37 | 56 | 36 |
| 13 | Poland | 6 | 28 | 14 | 9 | 5 | 34 | 42 | 36 |
| 14 | Hungary | 9 | 32 | 15 | 14 | 3 | 33 | 87 | 57 |
| | Mexico | 12 | 41 | 10 | 20 | 11 | 33 | 43 | 80 |
| 16 | Belgium | 11 | 36 | 10 | 17 | 9 | 30 | 46 | 63 |
| 17 | Austria | 7 | 29 | 12 | 13 | 4 | 28 | 43 | 47 |
| 18 | Czech Republic | 8 | 30 | 11 | 14 | 5 | 27 | 44 | 45 |
| 19 | Romania | 7 | 21 | 8 | 8 | 5 | 21 | 30 | 32 |
| 20 | Chile | 7 | 25 | 7 | 12 | 6 | 20 | 31 | 40 |
| 21 | Paraguay | 6 | 19 | 5 | 8 | 6 | 18 | 25 | 34 |
| | Denmark | 3 | 13 | 7 | 4 | 2 | 18 | 24 | 18 |
| 23 | South Korea | 6 | 21 | 4 | 12 | 5 | 17 | 19 | 49 |
| 24 | Cameroon | 5 | 17 | 4 | 6 | 7 | 16 | 15 | 29 |
| | USA | 7 | 22 | 6 | 14 | 2 | 16 | 25 | 45 |
| 26 | Portugal | 3 | 12 | 7 | 5 | 0 | 15 | 25 | 16 |
| | Scotland | 8 | 23 | 4 | 12 | 7 | 15 | 25 | 41 |
| | Switzerland | 7 | 22 | 6 | 13 | 3 | 15 | 33 | 51 |
| | Turkey | 2 | 10 | 4 | 4 | 1 | 15 | 20 | 17 |
| 30 | Bulgaria | 7 | 26 | 3 | 15 | 8 | 14 | 22 | 53 |
| 31 | Croatia | 2 | 10 | 6 | 4 | 0 | 13 | 13 | 8 |
| 32 | Ireland | 3 | 13 | 2 | 4 | 7 | 12 | 10 | 10 |
| 33 | Peru | 4 | 15 | 4 | 8 | 3 | 11 | 19 | 31 |
| | No. Ireland | 3 | 13 | 3 | 5 | 5 | 11 | 13 | 23 |
| 35 | Nigeria | 3 | 11 | 4 | 6 | 1 | 9 | 14 | 16 |
| 36 | Morocco | 4 | 13 | 2 | 7 | 4 | 8 | 12 | 18 |
| | Colombia | 4 | 13 | 3 | 8 | 2 | 8 | 14 | 23 |
| | Costa Rica | 2 | 7 | 3 | 3 | 1 | 8 | 9 | 12 |
| | Senegal | 1 | 5 | 2 | 1 | 2 | 8 | 7 | 6 |
| 40 | Norway | 2 | 8 | 2 | 3 | 3 | 7 | 7 | 8 |
| | Japan | 2 | 7 | 2 | 4 | 1 | 7 | 6 | 7 |
| 42 | East Germany | 1 | 6 | 2 | 2 | 2 | 6 | 5 | 5 |
| | South Africa | 2 | 6 | 1 | 2 | 3 | 6 | 8 | 11 |
| 44 | Saudi Arabia | 3 | 10 | 2 | 7 | 1 | 5 | 7 | 25 |
| | Algeria | 2 | 6 | 2 | 3 | 1 | 5 | 6 | 10 |
| | Wales | 1 | 5 | 1 | 1 | 3 | 5 | 4 | 4 |
| | Tunisia | 3 | 9 | 1 | 5 | 3 | 5 | 5 | 11 |
| 48 | Iran | 2 | 6 | 1 | 4 | 1 | 3 | 4 | 12 |
| | North Korea | 1 | 4 | 1 | 2 | 1 | 3 | 5 | 9 |
| | Cuba | 1 | 3 | 1 | 1 | 1 | 3 | 5 | 12 |
| | Jamaica | 1 | 3 | 1 | 2 | 0 | 3 | 3 | 9 |
| 52 | Ecuador | 1 | 3 | 1 | 2 | 0 | 2 | 2 | 4 |
| | Egypt | 2 | 4 | 0 | 2 | 2 | 2 | 3 | 6 |
| | Honduras | 1 | 3 | 0 | 1 | 2 | 2 | 2 | 3 |
| | Israel | 1 | 3 | 0 | 1 | 2 | 2 | 1 | 3 |
| 56 | Bolivia | 3 | 6 | 0 | 5 | 1 | 1 | 1 | 20 |
| | Australia | 1 | 3 | 0 | 2 | 1 | 1 | 0 | 5 |
| | Kuwait | 1 | 3 | 0 | 2 | 1 | 1 | 2 | 6 |
| 59 | El Salvador | 2 | 6 | 0 | 6 | 0 | 0 | 1 | 22 |
| | Canada | 1 | 3 | 0 | 3 | 0 | 0 | 0 | 5 |
| | East Indies | 1 | 1 | 0 | 1 | 0 | 0 | 0 | 6 |
| | Greece | 1 | 3 | 0 | 3 | 0 | 0 | 0 | 10 |
| | Haiti | 1 | 3 | 0 | 3 | 0 | 0 | 2 | 14 |
| | Iraq | 1 | 3 | 0 | 3 | 0 | 0 | 1 | 4 |
| | Slovenia | 1 | 3 | 0 | 2 | 1 | 0 | 2 | 7 |
| | New Zealand | 1 | 3 | 0 | 3 | 0 | 0 | 2 | 12 |
| | UAE | 1 | 3 | 0 | 3 | 0 | 0 | 2 | 11 |
| | China | 1 | 3 | 0 | 3 | 0 | 0 | 0 | 9 |
| | Zaire | 1 | 3 | 0 | 3 | 0 | 0 | 0 | 14 |

## The United States in the World Cup

While the United States has fielded a national team every year of the World Cup, only seven of those teams have been able to make it past the preliminary competition and qualify for the final World Cup tournament. The 1994 national team automatically qualified because the U.S. served as host of the event for the first time. The U.S. played in three of the first four World Cups (1930, '34 and '50) and each of the last four (1990, '94, '98 and 2002). The Americans have a record of 6-14-2 in 22 World Cup matches.

### 1930

#### 1st Round Matches

United States 3 . . . . . . . . . . . . . . . . . . . . . . . . . . . . . . Belgium 0
United States 3 . . . . . . . . . . . . . . . . . . . . . . . . . . . . Paraguay 0

#### Semifinals

Argentina 6 . . . . . . . . . . . . . . . . . . . . . . . United States 1

**U.S. Scoring**—Bert Patenaude (3), Bart McGhee (2), James Brown and Thomas Florie.

### 1934

#### 1st Round Match

Italy 7 . . . . . . . . . . . . . . . . . . . . . . . . . . . . . . United States 1

**U.S. Scoring**—Buff Donelli (who later became a noted college and NFL football coach).

### 1950

#### 1st Round Matches

Spain 3 . . . . . . . . . . . . . . . . . . . . . . . . . . . . United States 1
United States 1 . . . . . . . . . . . . . . . . . . . . . . . . . England 0
Chile 5 . . . . . . . . . . . . . . . . . . . . . . . . . . . . United States 2

**U.S. Scoring**—Joe Gaetjens, Joe Maca, John Souza and Frank Wallace.

### 1990

#### 1st Round Matches

Czechoslovakia 5 . . . . . . . . . . . . . . . . . . . . United States 1
Italy 1 . . . . . . . . . . . . . . . . . . . . . . . . . . . . . United States 0
Austria 2 . . . . . . . . . . . . . . . . . . . . . . . . . United States 1

**U.S. Scoring**—Paul Caligiuri and Bruce Murray.

### 1994

#### 1st Round Matches

United States 1 . . . . . . . . . . . . . . . . . . . . . . Switzerland 1
United States 2 . . . . . . . . . . . . . . . . . . . . . . . . Colombia 1
Romania 1 . . . . . . . . . . . . . . . . . . . . . . . . United States 0

#### Round of 16

Brazil 1 . . . . . . . . . . . . . . . . . . . . . . . . . . United States 0

**U.S. Scoring**—Eric Wynalda, Earnie Stewart and own goal (Colombia defender Andres Escobar).

## 1998
### 1st Round Matches

Germany 2 . . . . . . . . . . . . . . . . . . . . . . .United States 0
Iran 2 . . . . . . . . . . . . . . . . . . . . . . . . .United States 1
Yugoslavia 1 . . . . . . . . . . . . . . . . . . . . .United States 0

**U.S. Scoring**–Brian McBride.

## 2002
### 1st Round Matches

United States 3 . . . . . . . . . . . . . . . . . . . . .Portugal 2
United States 1 . . . . . . . . . . . . . . . . . . . . .So. Korea 1
Poland 3 . . . . . . . . . . . . . . . . . . . . . .United States 1

### Round of 16
United States 2 . . . . . . . . . . . . . . . . . . . . . .Mexico 0

### Round of 8
Germany 1 . . . . . . . . . . . . . . . . . . . . . .United States 0

**U.S. Scoring**– Landon Donovan (2), Brian McBride (2), John O'Brien, own goal (Portugal defender Jorge Costa) and Clint Mathis.

# World Cup Finals

Brazil and Germany (formerly West Germany) have played in the most Cup finals with seven but faced each other for the first time in a final in 2002. Note that a four-team round robin determined the 1950 championship–the deciding game turned out to be the last one of the tournament between Uruguay and Brazil.

## 1930
### Uruguay 4, Argentina 2
(at Montevideo, Uruguay)

|  |  | 1 | 2–T |
|---|---|---|---|
| **July 30** | Uruguay (4-0) . . . . . . . . . . . . . . . | 1 | 3–4 |
|  | Argentina (4-1) . . . . . . . . . . . . . . | 2 | 0–2 |

**Goals:** Uruguay–Pablo Dorado (12th minute), Pedro Cea (54th), Santos Iriarte (68th), Castro (89th); Argentina–Carlos Peucelle (20th), Guillermo Stabile (37th).

**Uruguay**–Ballesteros, Nasazzi, Mascheroni, Andrade, Fernandez, Gestido, Dorado, Scarone, Castro, Cea, Iriarte.

**Argentina**–Botasso, Della Torre, Paternoster, J. Evaristo, Monti, Suarez, Peucelle, Varallo, Stabile, Ferreira, M. Evaristo.

**Attendance:** 90,000. **Referee:** Langenus (Belgium).

## 1934
### Italy 2, Czechoslovakia 1 (OT)
(at Rome)

|  |  | 1 | 2 | OT–T |
|---|---|---|---|---|
| **June 10** | Italy (4-0-1) . . . . . . . . . . . . . . . | 0 | 1 | 1–2 |
|  | Czechoslovakia (3-1) . . . . . . . . . | 0 | 1 | 0–1 |

**Goals:** Italy–Raimondo Orsi (80th minute), Angelo Schiavio (95th); Czechoslovakia–Puc (70th).

**Italy**–Combi, Monzeglio, Allemandi, Ferraris IV, Monti, Bertolini, Guaita, Meazza, Schiavio, Ferrari, Orsi.

**Czechoslovakia**–Planicka, Zenisek, Ctyroky, Kostalek, Cambal, Krcil, Junek, Svoboda, Sobotka, Nejedly, Puc.

**Attendance:** 55,000. **Referee:** Eklind (Sweden).

## 1938
### Italy 4, Hungary 2
(at Paris)

|  |  | 1 | 2–T |
|---|---|---|---|
| **June 19** | Italy (4-0) . . . . . . . . . . . . . . . . . | 3 | 1–4 |
|  | Hungary (3-1) . . . . . . . . . . . . . . | 1 | 1–2 |

**Goals:** Italy–Gino Colaussi (5th minute), Silvio Piola (16th), Colaussi (35th), Piola (82nd); Hungary–Titkos (7th), Georges Sarosi (70th).

**Italy**–Olivieri, Foni, Rava, Serantoni, Andreolo, Locatelli, Biavati, Meazza, Piola, Ferrari, Colaussi.

**Hungary**–Szabo, Polgar, Biro, Szalay, Szucs, Lazar, Sas, Vincze, G. Sarosi, Szengeller, Titkos.

**Attendance:** 65,000. **Referee:** Capdeville (France).

## 1950
### Uruguay 2, Brazil 1
(at Rio de Janeiro)

|  |  | 1 | 2–T |
|---|---|---|---|
| **July 16** | Uruguay (3-0-1) . . . . . . . . . . . . . | 0 | 2–2 |
|  | Brazil (4-1-1) . . . . . . . . . . . . . . | 0 | 1–1 |

**Goals:** Uruguay–Juan Schiaffino (66th minute), Chico Ghiggia (79th); Brazil–Friaca (47th).

**Uruguay**–Maspoli, M. Gonzales, Tejera, Gambetta, Varela, Andrade, Ghiggia, Perez, Miguez, Schiaffino, Moran.

**Brazil**–Barbosa, Augusto, Juvenal, Bauer, Danilo, Bigode, Friaca, Zizinho, Ademir, Jair, Chico.

**Attendance:** 199,854. **Referee:** Reader (England).

## 1954
### West Germany 3, Hungary 2
(at Berne, Switzerland)

|  |  | 1 | 2–T |
|---|---|---|---|
| **July 4** | West Germany (4-1) . . . . . . . . . . . | 2 | 1–3 |
|  | Hungary (4-1) . . . . . . . . . . . . . . | 2 | 0–2 |

**Goals:** West Germany–Max Morlock (10th minute), Helmut Rahn (18th), Rahn (84th); Hungary–Ferenc Puskas (4th), Zoltan Czibor (9th).

**West Germany**–Turek, Posipal, Liebrich, Kohlmeyer, Eckel, Mai, Rahn, Morlock, O. Walter, F. Walter, Schaefer.

**Hungary**–Grosics, Buzansky, Lorant, Lantos, Bozsik, Zakarias, Czibor, Kocsis, Hidegkuti, Puskas, J. Toth.

**Attendance:** 60,000. **Referee:** Ling (England).

## 1958
### Brazil 5, Sweden 2
(at Stockholm)

|  |  | 1 | 2–T |
|---|---|---|---|
| **June 29** | Brazil (5-0-1) . . . . . . . . . . . . . . . | 2 | 3–5 |
|  | Sweden (4-1-1) . . . . . . . . . . . . . | 1 | 1–2 |

**Goals:** Brazil–Vava (9th minute), Vava (32nd), Pelé (55th), Mario Zagalo (68th), Pelé (90th); Sweden–Nils Liedholm (3rd), Agne Simonsson (80th).

**Brazil**–Gilmar, D. Santos, N. Santos, Zito, Bellini, Orlando, Garrincha, Didi, Vava, Pelé, Zagalo.

**Sweden**–Svensson, Bergmark, Axbom, Boerjesson, Gustavsson, Parling, Hamrin, Gren, Simonsson, Liedholm, Skoglund.

**Attendance:** 49,737. **Referee:** Guigue (France).

## World Cup Finals (Cont.)

### 1962

#### Brazil 3, Czechoslovakia 1

(at Santiago, Chile)

|  | 1 | 2–T |
|---|---|---|
| **June 17** Brazil (5-0-1) | 1 | 2–3 |
| Czechoslovakia (3-2-1) | 1 | 0–1 |

**Goals:** Brazil—Amarildo (17th minute), Zito (68th), Vava (77th); Czechoslovakia—Josef Masopust (15th).
**Brazil**—Gilmar, D. Santos, N. Santos, Zito, Mauro, Zozimo, Garrincha, Didi, Vava, Amarildo, Zagalo.
**Czechoslovakia**—Schroiff, Tichy, Novak, Pluskal, Popluhar, Masopust, Pospichal, Scherer, Kvasniak, Kadraba, Jelinek.
**Attendance:** 68,679. **Referee:** Latishev (USSR).

### 1966

#### England 4, West Germany 2 (OT)

(at London)

|  | 1 | 2 | OT–T |
|---|---|---|---|
| **July 30** England (5-0-1) | 1 | 1 | 2–4 |
| West Germany (4-1-1) | 1 | 1 | 0–2 |

**Goals:** England—Geoff Hurst (18th minute), Martin Peters (78th), Hurst (101st), Hurst (120th); West Germany—Helmut Haller (12th), Wolfgang Weber (90th).
**England**—Banks, Cohen, Wilson, Stiles, J. Charlton, Moore, Ball, Hurst, B. Charlton, Hunt, Peters.
**West Germany**—Tilkowski, Hottges, Schnellinger, Beckenbauer, Schulz, Weber, Haller, Seeler, Held, Overath, Emmerich.
**Attendance:** 93,802. **Referee:** Dienst (Switzerland).

### 1970

#### Brazil 4, Italy 1

(at Mexico City)

|  | 1 | 2–T |
|---|---|---|
| **June 21** Brazil (6-0) | 1 | 3–4 |
| Italy (3-1-2) | 1 | 0–1 |

**Goals:** Brazil—Pelé (18th minute), Gerson (65th), Jairzinho (70th), Carlos Alberto (86th); Italy—Roberto Boninsegna (37th).
**Brazil**—Felix, C. Alberto, Everaldo, Clodoaldo, Brito, Piazza, Jairzinho, Gerson, Tostão, Pelé, Rivelino.
**Italy**—Albertosi, Burgnich, Facchetti, Bertini (Juliano, 73rd), Rosato, Cera, Domenghini, Mazzola, Boninsegna (Rivera, 84th), De Sisti, Riva.
**Attendance:** 107,412. **Referee:** Glockner (E. Germany).

### 1974

#### West Germany 2, Netherlands 1

(at Munich)

|  | 1 | 2–T |
|---|---|---|
| **July 7** West Germany (6-1) | 2 | 0–2 |
| Netherlands (5-1-1) | 1 | 0–1 |

**Goals:** West Germany—Paul Breitner (25th minute, penalty kick), Gerd Müller (43rd); Netherlands—Johan Neeskens (1st, penalty kick).
**West Germany**—Maier, Beckenbauer, Vogts, Breitner, Schwarzenbeck, Overath, Bonhof, Hoeness, Grabowski, Muller, Holzenbein.
**Netherlands**—Jongbloed, Suurbier, Rijsbergen (De Jong, 58th), Krol, Haan, Jansen, Van Hanegem, Neeskens, Rep, Cruyff, Rensenbrink (R. Van de Kerkhof, 46th).
**Attendance:** 77,833. **Referee:** Taylor (England).

### 1978

#### Argentina 3, Netherlands 1 (OT)

(at Buenos Aires)

|  | 1 | 2 | OT–T |
|---|---|---|---|
| **June 25** Argentina (5-1-1) | 1 | 0 | 2–3 |
| Netherlands (3-2-2) | 0 | 1 | 0–1 |

**Goals:** Argentina—Mario Kempes (37th minute), Kempes (104th), Daniel Bertoni (114th); Netherlands—Dirk Nanninga (81st).
**Argentina**—Fillol, Olguin, L. Galvan, Passarella, Tarantini, Ardiles (Larrosa, 65th), Gallego, Kempes, Luque, Bertoni, Ortiz (Houseman, 77th).
**Netherlands**—Jongbloed, Jansen (Suurbier, 72nd), Brandts, Krol, Poortvliet, Haan, Neeskens, W. Van de Kerkhof, R. Van de Kerkhof, Rep (Nanninga, 58th), Rensenbrink.
**Attendance:** 77,260. **Referee:** Gonella (Italy).

### 1982

#### Italy 3, West Germany 1

(at Madrid)

|  | 1 | 2–T |
|---|---|---|
| **July 11** Italy (4-0-3) | 0 | 3–3 |
| West Germany (4-2-1) | 0 | 1–1 |

**Goals:** Italy—Paolo Rossi (57th minute), Marco Tardelli (68th), Alessandro Altobelli (81st); West Germany—Paul Breitner (83rd).
**Italy**—Zoff, Scirea, Gentile, Cabrini, Collovati, Bergomi, Tardelli, Oriali, Conti, Rossi, Graziani (Altobelli, 8th, and Causio, 89th).
**West Germany**—Schumacher, Stielike, Kaltz, Briegel, K.H. Forster, B. Forster, Breitner, Dremmler (Hrubesch, 61st), Littbarski, Fischer, Rummenigge (Muller, 69th).
**Attendance:** 90,080. **Referee:** Coelho (Brazil).

### 1986

#### Argentina 3, West Germany 2

(at Mexico City)

|  | 1 | 2–T |
|---|---|---|
| **June 29** Argentina (6-0-1) | 1 | 2–3 |
| West Germany (4-2-1) | 0 | 2–2 |

**Goals:** Argentina—Jose Brown (22nd minute), Jorge Valdano (55th), Jorge Burruchaga (83rd); West Germany—Karl-Heinz Rummenigge (73rd), Rudi Voller (81st).
**Argentina**—Pumpido, Cuciuffo, Olarticoechea, Ruggeri, Brown, Batista, Burruchaga (Trobbiani, 89th), Giusti, Enrique, Maradona, Valdano.
**West Germany**—Schumacher, Jakobs, B. Forster, Berthold, Briegel, Eder, Brehme, Matthaus, Rummenigge, Magath (Hoeness, 61st), Allofs (Voller, 46th).
**Attendance:** 114,590. **Referee:** Filho (Brazil).

### 1990

#### West Germany 1, Argentina 0

(at Rome)

|  | 1 | 2–T |
|---|---|---|
| **July 8** West Germany (6-0-1) | 0 | 1–1 |
| Argentina (4-2-1) | 0 | 0–0 |

**Goals:** West Germany—Andreas Brehme (85th minute, penalty kick).
**West Germany**—Illgner, Berthold (Reuter, 73th), Kohler, Augenthaler, Buchwald, Brehme, Haessler, Matthaus, Littbarski, Klinsmann, Voller.
**Argentina:** Goycoechea, Ruggeri (Monzon, 46th), Simon, Serrizuela, Lorenzo, Basualdo, Troglio, Burruchaga (Calderon, 53rd), Sensini, Dezotti, Maradona.
**Attendance:** 73,603. **Referee:** Codesal (Mexico).

## 1994
### Brazil 0, Italy 0 (Shootout)
(at Pasadena, Calif.)

| | 1 | 2 | OT– | T |
|---|---|---|---|---|
| July 17   Brazil (6-0-1) .............. | 0 | 0 | 0– | 0* |
| Italy (4-2-1) .............. | 0 | 0 | 0– | 0 |

*Brazil wins shootout, 3-2.

**Shootout** (five shots each, alternating): ITA–Baresi (miss, 0-0); BRA–Santos (blocked, 0-0); ITA– Albertini (goal, 1-0); BRA–Romario (goal, 1-1); ITA–Evani (goal, 2-1); BRA–Branco (goal, 2-2); ITA–Massaro (blocked, 2-2); BRA–Dunga (goal, 2-3); ITA–R. Baggio (miss, 2-3).

**Brazil**–Taffarel, Jorginho (Cafu, 21st minute), Branco, Aldair, Santos, Mazinho, Silva, Dunga, Zinho (Viola, 106th), Bebeto, Romario.

**Italy**–Pagliuca, Mussi (Apolloni, 35th minute), Baresi, Benarrivo, Maldini, Albertini, D. Baggio (Evani, 95th), Berti, Donadoni, R. Baggio, Massaro.

**Attendance:** 94,194. **Referee:** Puhl (Hungary).

## 1998
### France 3, Brazil 0
(at Paris)

| | 1 | 2– | T |
|---|---|---|---|
| July 12   Brazil (6-1) ................. | 0 | 0– | 0 |
| France (7-0) ................. | 2 | 1– | 3 |

**Goals:** France–Zinedine Zidane (27th and 46th minutes), Petit (92).

**Brazil**–Taffarel, Cafu, Aldair, Baiano, Carlos, Sampaio (Edmundo, 74th minute), Dunga, Rivaldo, Leonardo (Denilson, 46th minute), Bebeto, Ronaldo.

**France**–Barthez, Lizarazu, Desailly, Thuram, Leboeuf, Djorkaeff (Viera, 75th minute), Deschamps, Zidane, Petit, Karembeu (Boghossian, 57th minute), Guivarc'h, Dugarry.

**Attendance:** 75,000. **Referee:** Belqola (Morocco).

## 2002
### Brazil 2, Germany 0
(at Yokohama, Japan)

| | 1 | 2– | T |
|---|---|---|---|
| June 30   Germany (5-2) .............. | 0 | 0– | 0 |
| Brazil (7-0) ................. | 0 | 2– | 2 |

**Goals:** Brazil–Ronaldo (67th and 79th minutes).

**Germany**–Kahn, Linke, Ramelow, Neuville, Hamann, Klose (Bierhoff, 74th minute), Jeremies (Asamoah, 77th minute), Bode (Ziege, 84th minute), Schneider, Metzelder, Frings.

**Brazil**–Marcos, Cafu, Lucio, Junior, Edmilson, Carlos, Silva, Ronaldo (Denilson, 90th minute), Rivaldo, Ronaldinho (Paulista, 85th minute), Kleberson.

**Attendance:** 69,029. **Referee:** Collina (Italy).

## Year-by-Year Comparisons

How the 17 World Cup tournaments have compared in nations qualifying, matches played, players participating, goals scored, average goals per game, overall attendance and attendance per game.

| Year | Host | Continent | Nations | Matches | Players | Goals Scored | Per Game | Attendance Overall | Per Game |
|---|---|---|---|---|---|---|---|---|---|
| 1930 | Uruguay | So. America | 13 | 18 | 189 | 70 | 3.8 | 589,300 | 32,739 |
| 1934 | Italy | Europe | 16 | 17 | 208 | 70 | 4.1 | 361,000 | 21,235 |
| 1938 | France | Europe | 15 | 18 | 210 | 84 | 4.7 | 376,000 | 20,889 |
| 1942-46 | Not held | | | | | | | | |
| 1950 | Brazil | So. America | 13 | 22 | 192 | 88 | 4.0 | 1,044,763 | 47,489 |
| 1954 | Switzerland | Europe | 16 | 26 | 233 | 140 | 5.3 | 872,000 | 33,538 |
| 1958 | Sweden | Europe | 16 | 35 | 241 | 126 | 3.6 | 819,402 | 23,411 |
| 1962 | Chile | So. America | 16 | 32 | 252 | 89 | 2.8 | 892,812 | 27,900 |
| 1966 | England | Europe | 16 | 32 | 254 | 89 | 2.8 | 1,464,944 | 45,780 |
| 1970 | Mexico | No. America | 16 | 32 | 270 | 95 | 3.0 | 1,690,890 | 52,840 |
| 1974 | West Germany | Europe | 16 | 38 | 264 | 97 | 2.6 | 1,809,953 | 47,630 |
| 1978 | Argentina | So. America | 16 | 38 | 277 | 102 | 2.7 | 1,685,602 | 44,358 |
| 1982 | Spain | Europe | 24 | 52 | 396 | 146 | 2.8 | 2,108,723 | 40,552 |
| 1986 | Mexico | No. America | 24 | 52 | 414 | 132 | 2.5 | 2,393,031 | 46,020 |
| 1990 | Italy | Europe | 24 | 52 | 413 | 115 | 2.2 | 2,516,354 | 48,391 |
| 1994 | United States | No. America | 24 | 52 | 437 | 140 | 2.7 | 3,587,088 | 68,982 |
| 1998 | France | Europe | 32 | 64 | 704 | 171 | 2.7 | 2,775,400 | 43,366 |
| 2002 | Japan/So. Korea | Asia | 32 | 64 | 736 | 161 | 2.5 | 2,705,197 | 42,269 |

## World Cup Shootouts
Introduced in 1982; winning sides in **bold** type.

| Year | Round | | Final | SO |
|---|---|---|---|---|
| 1982 | Semi | **W. Germany** vs. France | 3-3 | (5-4) |
| 1986 | Quarter | **Belgium** vs. Spain | 1-1 | (5-4) |
| | Quarter | **France** vs. Brazil | 1-1 | (4-3) |
| | Quarter | **W. Germany** vs. Mexico | 0-0 | (4-1) |
| 1990 | Second | **Ireland** vs. Romania | 0-0 | (5-4) |
| | Quarter | **Argentina** vs. Yugoslavia | 0-0 | (3-2) |
| | Semi | **Argentina** vs. Italy | 1-1 | (4-3) |
| | Semi | **W. Germany** vs. England | 1-1 | (4-3) |

| Year | Round | | Final | SO |
|---|---|---|---|---|
| 1994 | Second | **Bulgaria** vs. Mexico | 1-1 | (3-1) |
| | Quarter | **Sweden** vs. Romania | 2-2 | (5-4) |
| | Final | **Brazil** vs. Italy | 0-0 | (3-2) |
| 1998 | Second | **Argentina** vs. England | 2-2 | (4-3) |
| | Quarter | **France** vs. Italy | 0-0 | (4-3) |
| 2002 | Second | **Spain** vs. Ireland | 1-1 | (3-2) |
| | Quarter | **So. Korea** vs. Spain | 0-0 | (5-3) |

## World Team of the 20th Century

The team, comprised of the century's best players, was voted on by a panel that included 250 international soccer journalists and released on June 10, 1998 in conjunction with the opening of the 1998 World Cup. The panel first selected the European and South American Teams of the Century and then chose the World Team from those two lists.

### World Team

| Pos | | Pos | |
|-----|-----|-----|-----|
| GK | Lev Yashin, Soviet Union | MF | Johan Cruyff, Netherlands |
| D | Carlos Alberto, Brazil | MF | Alfredo Di Stefano, Argentina |
| D | Franz Beckenbauer, West Germany | MF | Michel Platini, France |
| D | Bobby Moore, England | F | Pele, Brazil |
| D | Nilton Santos, Brazil | F | Garrincha, Brazil |
| | | F | Diego Maradona, Argentina |

### European Team

| Pos | |
|-----|-----|
| GK | Lev Yashin, Soviet Union |
| D | Paolo Maldini, Italy |
| D | Franz Beckenbauer, West Germany |
| D | Bobby Moore, England |
| D | Franco Baresi, Italy |
| MF | Johan Cruyff, Netherlands |
| MF | Eusebio, Portugal |
| MF | Michel Platini, France |
| F | Ferenc Puskas, Hungary |
| F | Bobby Charlton, England |
| F | Marco Van Basten, Netherlands |

### South American Team

| Pos | |
|-----|-----|
| GK | Ubaldo Fillol, Argentina |
| D | Carlos Alberto, Brazil |
| D | Elias Figueroa, Chile |
| D | Daniel Passarella, Argentina |
| D | Nilton Santos, Brazil |
| MF | Didi, Brazil |
| MF | Alfredo Di Stefano, Argentina |
| MF | Rivelino, Brazil |
| F | Pele, Brazil |
| F | Garrincha, Brazil |
| F | Diego Maradona, Argentina |

## OTHER WORLDWIDE COMPETITION

## The Olympic Games

Held every four years since 1896, except during World War I (1916) and World War II (1940-44). Soccer was not a medal sport in 1896 at Athens or in 1932 at Los Angeles. By agreement between FIFA and the IOC, Olympic soccer competition is currently limited to players 23 years old and under with a few exceptions.

**Multiple winners:** England and Hungary (3); Soviet Union and Uruguay (2).

### MEN

| Year | | Year | |
|------|-----|------|-----|
| 1900 | **England**, France, Belgium | 1964 | **Hungary**, Czechoslovakia, Germany |
| 1904 | **Canada**, USA I, USA II | 1968 | **Hungary**, Bulgaria, Japan |
| 1906 | **Denmark**, Smyrna (Int'l entry), Greece | 1972 | **Poland**, Hungary, East Germany & Soviet Union |
| 1908 | **England**, Denmark, Netherlands | 1976 | **East Germany**, Poland, Soviet Union |
| 1912 | **England**, Denmark, Netherlands | 1980 | **Czechoslovakia**, East Germany, Soviet Union |
| 1920 | **Belgium**, Spain, Netherlands | 1984 | **France**, Brazil, Yugoslavia |
| 1924 | **Uruguay**, Switzerland, Sweden | 1988 | **Soviet Union**, Brazil, West Germany |
| 1928 | **Uruguay**, Argentina, Italy | 1992 | **Spain**, Poland, Ghana |
| 1936 | **Italy**, Austria, Norway | 1996 | **Nigeria**, Argentina, Brazil |
| 1948 | **Sweden**, Yugoslavia, Denmark | 2000 | **Cameroon**, Spain, Chile |
| 1952 | **Hungary**, Yugoslavia, Sweden | 2004 | **Argentina**, Paraguay, Italy |
| 1956 | **Soviet Union**, Yugoslavia, Bulgaria | 2008 | (at Beijing, China) |
| 1960 | **Yugoslavia**, Denmark, Hungary | | |

### WOMEN

**Multiple winners:** United States (2).

| Year | | Year | |
|------|-----|------|-----|
| 1996 | **USA**, China, Norway | 2004 | **USA**, Brazil, Germany |
| 2000 | **Norway**, USA, Germany | 2008 | (at Beijing, China) |

## The Under-20 World Cup

Held every two years since 1977. Officially, the FIFA World Youth Championship.

**Multiple winners:** Argentina (5); Brazil (3); Portugal (2).

| Year | | Year | | Year | |
|------|-----|------|-----|------|-----|
| 1977 | Soviet Union | 1987 | Yugoslavia | 1997 | Argentina |
| 1979 | Argentina | 1989 | Portugal | 1999 | Spain |
| 1981 | West Germany | 1991 | Portugal | 2001 | Argentina |
| 1983 | Brazil | 1993 | Brazil | 2003 | Brazil |
| 1985 | Brazil | 1995 | Argentina | 2005 | Argentina |

## The Under-17 World Cup

Held every two years since 1985. Officially, the FIFA U-17 World Championship.

**Multiple winners:** Brazil (3); Ghana and Nigeria (2).

| Year | | Year | |
|---|---|---|---|
| 1985 | Nigeria | 1997 | Brazil |
| 1987 | Soviet Union | 1999 | Brazil |
| 1989 | Saudi Arabia | 2001 | France |
| 1991 | Ghana | 2003 | Brazil |
| 1993 | Nigeria | 2005 | Mexico |
| 1995 | Ghana | | |

## Indoor World Championship

First held in 1989. Officially, the FIFA Futsal World Championship.

**Multiple winners:** Brazil (3), Spain (2).

| Year | | Year | |
|---|---|---|---|
| 1989 | Brazil | 2000 | Spain |
| 1992 | Brazil | 2004 | Spain |
| 1996 | Brazil | | |

## Women's World Cup

First held in 1991. Officially, the FIFA Women's World Championship.

**Multiple winner:** United States (2).

| Year | | Year | |
|---|---|---|---|
| 1991 | United States | 2003 | Germany |
| 1995 | Norway | 2007 | (at China) |
| 1999 | United States | | |

## Confederations Cup

First held in 1992. Contested by the Continental champions of Africa, Asia, Europe, North America and South America and originally called the Intercontinental Championship for the King Fahd Cup until it was redubbed the FIFA/Confederations Cup for the King Fahd Trophy in 1997.

**Multiple winners:** Brazil and France (2).

| Year | | Year | |
|---|---|---|---|
| 1992 | Argentina | 2001 | France |
| 1995 | Denmark | 2003 | France |
| 1997 | Brazil | 2005 | Brazil |
| 1999 | Mexico | | |

## CONTINENTAL COMPETITION

### European Championship

Held every four years since 1960. Officially, the European Football Championship. Winners receive the Henri Delaunay trophy, named for the Frenchman who first proposed the idea of a European Soccer Championship in 1927. The first one would not be played until five years after his death in 1955.

**Multiple winners:** Germany/West Germany (3); France (2).

| Year | | Year | | Year | | Year | |
|---|---|---|---|---|---|---|---|
| 1960 | Soviet Union | 1972 | West Germany | 1984 | France | 1996 | Germany |
| 1964 | Spain | 1976 | Czechoslovakia | 1988 | Netherlands | 2000 | France |
| 1968 | Italy | 1980 | West Germany | 1992 | Denmark | 2004 | Greece |

### Copa America

Held irregularly since 1916. Unofficially, the Championship of South America.

**Multiple winners:** Argentina and Uruguay (14); Brazil (6); Paraguay and Peru (2).

| Year | | Year | | Year | | Year | | Year | |
|---|---|---|---|---|---|---|---|---|---|
| 1916 | Uruguay | 1926 | Uruguay | 1946 | Argentina | 1963 | Bolivia | 1995 | Uruguay |
| 1917 | Uruguay | 1927 | Argentina | 1947 | Argentina | 1967 | Uruguay | 1997 | Brazil |
| 1919 | Brazil | 1929 | Argentina | 1949 | Brazil | 1975 | Peru | 1999 | Brazil |
| 1920 | Uruguay | 1935 | Uruguay | 1953 | Paraguay | 1979 | Paraguay | 2001 | Colombia |
| 1921 | Argentina | 1937 | Argentina | 1955 | Argentina | 1983 | Uruguay | 2004 | Brazil |
| 1922 | Brazil | 1939 | Peru | 1956 | Uruguay | 1987 | Uruguay | | |
| 1923 | Uruguay | 1941 | Argentina | 1957 | Argentina | 1989 | Brazil | | |
| 1924 | Uruguay | 1942 | Uruguay | 1958 | Argentina | 1991 | Argentina | | |
| 1925 | Argentina | 1945 | Argentina | 1959 | Uruguay | 1993 | Argentina | | |

### African Nations Cup

Contested since 1957 and held every two years since 1968.

**Multiple winners:** Cameroon, Egypt and Ghana (4); Congo/Zaire (3); Nigeria (2).

| Year | | Year | | Year | | Year | | Year | |
|---|---|---|---|---|---|---|---|---|---|
| 1957 | Egypt | 1968 | Zaire | 1978 | Ghana | 1988 | Cameroon | 1998 | Egypt |
| 1959 | Egypt | 1970 | Sudan | 1980 | Nigeria | 1990 | Algeria | 2000 | Cameroon |
| 1962 | Ethiopia | 1972 | Congo | 1982 | Ghana | 1992 | Ivory Coast | 2002 | Cameroon |
| 1963 | Ghana | 1974 | Zaire | 1984 | Cameroon | 1994 | Nigeria | 2004 | Tunisia |
| 1965 | Ghana | 1976 | Morocco | 1986 | Egypt | 1996 | South Africa | | |

### CONCACAF Gold Cup

The Confederation of North, Central American and Caribbean Football Championship. Contested irregularly from 1963-81 and revived as CONCACAF Gold Cup in 1991.

**Multiple winners:** Mexico (7); Costa Rica and United States (2).

| Year | | Year | | Year | | Year | | Year | |
|---|---|---|---|---|---|---|---|---|---|
| 1963 | Costa Rica | 1969 | Costa Rica | 1977 | Mexico | 1993 | Mexico | 2000 | Canada |
| 1965 | Mexico | 1971 | Mexico | 1981 | Honduras | 1996 | Mexico | 2003 | Mexico |
| 1967 | Guatemala | 1973 | Haiti | 1991 | United States | 1998 | Mexico | 2005 | United States |

## CLUB COMPETITION

## FIFA Club World Championship

The FIFA Club World Championship merged with the Toyota Cup, previously the unofficial world club championship, beginning in December 2005 in Tokyo. FIFA previously held an eight-team world club championship tournament in 2000—won by Brazil's **Corinthians**—but the tournament was not held again until late 2005 when it replaced the Toyota Cup.

### Toyota Cup

Also known as the **European/South American Cup** and Intercontinental Cup. Until 2005, it was contested annually in December between the winners of the European Champions League (formerly European Cup) and South America's Copa Libertadores for the unofficial World Club Championship. Four European Cup winners refused to participate in the championship match in the 1970s and were replaced each time by the European Cup runner-up: Panathinaikos (Greece) for Ajax Amsterdam (Netherlands) in 1971; Juventus (Italy) for Ajax in 1973; Atlético Madrid (Spain) for Bayern Munich (West Germany) in 1974; and Malmo (Sweden) for Nottingham Forest (England) in 1979. Another European Cup winner, Marseille of France, was prohibited by the Union of European Football Associations (UEFA) from playing for the 1993 Toyota Cup because of its involvement in a match-rigging scandal. Best-of-three game format from 1960-68, then a two-game/total goals format from 1969-79. Toyota became Cup sponsor in 1980, changed the format to a one-game championship and moved it to Toyko.

   **Multiple winners:** AC Milan, Boca Juniors, Nacional, Penarol and Real Madrid (3); Ajax Amsterdam, Bayern Munich, FC Porto, Independiente, Inter Milan, Juventus, Santos and Sao Paulo (2).

| Year | | Year | | Year | |
|---|---|---|---|---|---|
| 1960 | Real Madrid (Spain) | 1975 | Not held | 1990 | AC Milan (Italy) |
| 1961 | Penarol (Uruguay) | 1976 | Bayern Munich (W. Germany) | 1991 | Red Star (Yugoslavia) |
| 1962 | Santos (Brazil) | 1977 | Boca Juniors (Argentina) | 1992 | Sao Paulo (Brazil) |
| 1963 | Santos (Brazil) | 1978 | Not held | 1993 | Sao Paulo (Brazil) |
| 1964 | Inter Milan (Italy) | 1979 | Olimpia (Paraguay) | 1994 | Velez Sarsfield (Argentina) |
| 1965 | Inter Milan (Italy) | 1980 | Nacional (Uruguay) | 1995 | Ajax Amsterdam (Netherlands) |
| 1966 | Penarol (Uruguay) | 1981 | Flamengo (Brazil) | 1996 | Juventus (Italy) |
| 1967 | Racing Club (Argentina) | 1982 | Penarol (Uruguay) | 1997 | Borussia Dortmund (Germany) |
| 1968 | Estudiantes (Argentina) | 1983 | Gremio (Brazil) | 1998 | Real Madrid (Spain) |
| 1969 | AC Milan (Italy) | 1984 | Independiente (Argentina) | 1999 | Manchester United (England) |
| 1970 | Feyenoord (Netherlands) | 1985 | Juventus (Italy) | 2000 | Boca Juniors (Argentina) |
| 1971 | Nacional (Uruguay) | 1986 | River Plate (Argentina) | 2001 | Bayern Munich (Germany) |
| 1972 | Ajax Amsterdam (Netherlands) | 1987 | FC Porto (Portugal) | 2002 | Real Madrid (Spain) |
| 1973 | Independiente (Argentina) | 1988 | Nacional (Uruguay) | 2003 | Boca Juniors (Argentina) |
| 1974 | Atlético Madrid (Spain) | 1989 | AC Milan (Italy) | 2004 | FC Porto (Portugal) |

## European Cup/UEFA Champions League

Contested annually since the 1955-56 season by the league champions of the member countries of the Union of European Football Associations (UEFA). In 1999, UEFA announced the formation of a new competition called the UEFA Champions League to take the place of the Cup competition.

   **Multiple winners:** Real Madrid (9); AC Milan (6); Ajax Amsterdam, Bayern Munich and Liverpool (4); Benfica, FC Porto, Inter Milan, Juventus and Nottingham Forest (2).

| Year | | Year | | Year | |
|---|---|---|---|---|---|
| 1956 | Real Madrid (Spain) | 1973 | Ajax Amsterdam (Netherlands) | 1990 | AC Milan (Italy) |
| 1957 | Real Madrid (Spain) | 1974 | Bayern Munich (W. Germany) | 1991 | Red Star Belgrade (Yugo.) |
| 1958 | Real Madrid (Spain) | 1975 | Bayern Munich (W. Germany) | 1992 | Barcelona (Spain) |
| 1959 | Real Madrid (Spain) | 1976 | Bayern Munich (W. Germany) | 1993 | Marseille (France)* |
| 1960 | Real Madrid (Spain) | 1977 | Liverpool (England) | 1994 | AC Milan (Italy) |
| 1961 | Benfica (Portugal) | 1978 | Liverpool (England) | 1995 | Ajax Amsterdam (Netherlands) |
| 1962 | Benfica (Portugal) | 1979 | Nottingham Forest (England) | 1996 | Juventus (Italy) |
| 1963 | AC Milan (Italy) | 1980 | Nottingham Forest (England) | 1997 | Borussia Dortmund (Germany) |
| 1964 | Inter Milan (Italy) | 1981 | Liverpool (England) | 1998 | Real Madrid (Spain) |
| 1965 | Inter Milan (Italy) | 1982 | Aston Villa (England) | 1999 | Manchester United (England) |
| 1966 | Real Madrid (Spain) | 1983 | SV Hamburg (W. Germany) | 2000 | Real Madrid (Spain) |
| 1967 | Glasgow Celtic (Scotland) | 1984 | Liverpool (England) | 2001 | Bayern Munich (Germany) |
| 1968 | Manchester United (England) | 1985 | Juventus (Italy) | 2002 | Real Madrid (Spain) |
| 1969 | AC Milan (Italy) | 1986 | Steaua Bucharest (Romania) | 2003 | AC Milan (Italy) |
| 1970 | Feyenoord (Netherlands) | 1987 | FC Porto (Portugal) | 2004 | FC Porto (Portugal) |
| 1971 | Ajax Amsterdam (Netherlands) | 1988 | PSV Eindhoven (Netherlands) | 2005 | Liverpool (England) |
| 1972 | Ajax Amsterdam (Netherlands) | 1989 | AC Milan (Italy) | | *title vacated |

## European Cup Winner's Cup

Contested annually from the 1960-61 season through the 1999-2000 season by the cup winners of the member countries of the Union of European Football Associations (UEFA). The Cup Winner's Cup was absorbed by the UEFA Cup in 2000.

   **Multiple winners:** Barcelona (4); AC Milan, RSC Anderlecht, Chelsea and Dinamo Kiev (2).

| Year | | Year | | Year | |
|---|---|---|---|---|---|
| 1961 | Fiorentina (Italy) | 1966 | Borussia Dortmund (W.Germany) | 1971 | Chelsea (England) |
| 1962 | Atletico Madrid (Spain) | 1967 | Bayern Munich (W. Germany) | 1972 | Glasgow Rangers (Scotland) |
| 1963 | Tottenham Hotspur (England) | 1968 | AC Milan (Italy) | 1973 | AC Milan (Italy) |
| 1964 | Sporting Lisbon (Portugal) | 1969 | Slovan Bratislava (Czech.) | 1974 | FC Magdeburg (E. Germany) |
| 1965 | West Ham United (England) | 1970 | Manchester City (England) | 1975 | Dinamo Kiev (USSR) |

| Year | | Year | | Year | |
|------|---|------|---|------|---|
| 1976 | RSC Anderlecht (Belgium) | 1984 | Juventus (Italy) | 1992 | Werder Bremen (Germany) |
| 1977 | SV Hamburg (W. Germany) | 1985 | Everton (England) | 1993 | Parma (Italy) |
| 1978 | RSC Anderlecht (Belgium) | 1986 | Dinamo Kiev (USSR) | 1994 | Arsenal (England) |
| 1979 | Barcelona (Spain) | 1987 | Ajax Amsterdam (Netherlands) | 1995 | Real Zaragoza (Spain) |
| 1980 | Valencia (Spain) | 1988 | Mechelen (Belgium) | 1996 | Paris St. Germain (France) |
| 1981 | Dinamo Tbilisi (USSR) | 1989 | Barcelona (Spain) | 1997 | Barcelona (Spain) |
| 1982 | Barcelona (Spain) | 1990 | Sampdoria (Italy) | 1998 | Chelsea (England) |
| 1983 | Aberdeen (Scotland) | 1991 | Manchester United (England) | 1999 | Lazio (Italy) |

## UEFA Cup

Contested annually since the 1957-58 season by teams other than league champions and cup winners of the Union of European Football Associations (UEFA). Teams selected by UEFA based on each country's previous performance in the tournament. Teams from England were banned from UEFA Cup play from 1985-90 for the criminal behavior of their supporters. In 1999, with the formation of the new Champions League, UEFA announced that the UEFA Cup would be expanded and include any teams that would have normally played in the Cup Winner's Cup.

**Multiple winners:** Barcelona, Inter Milan, Juventus, Liverpool and Valencia (3); Borussia Mönchengladbach, Feyenoord, IFK Göteborg, Leeds United, Parma, Real Madrid and Tottenham Hotspur (2).

| Year | | Year | | Year | |
|------|---|------|---|------|---|
| 1958 | Barcelona (Spain) | 1975 | Borussia Mönchengladbach (W. Germany) | 1990 | Juventus (Italy) |
| 1959 | Not held | | | 1991 | Inter Milan (Italy) |
| 1960 | Barcelona (Spain) | 1976 | Liverpool (England) | 1992 | Ajax Amsterdam (Netherlands) |
| 1961 | AS Roma (Italy) | 1977 | Juventus (Italy) | 1993 | Juventus (Italy) |
| 1962 | Valencia (Spain) | 1978 | PSV Eindhoven (Netherlands) | 1994 | Inter Milan (Italy) |
| 1963 | Valencia (Spain) | 1979 | Borussia Mönchengladbach (W. Germany) | 1995 | Parma (Italy) |
| 1964 | Real Zaragoza (Spain) | | | 1996 | Bayern Munich (Germany) |
| 1965 | Ferencvaros (Hungary) | 1980 | Eintracht Frankfurt (W. Germany) | 1997 | Schalke 04 (Germany) |
| 1966 | Barcelona (Spain) | 1981 | Ipswich Town (England) | 1998 | Inter Milan (Italy) |
| 1967 | Dinamo Zagreb (Yugoslavia) | 1982 | IFK Göteborg (Sweden) | 1999 | Parma (Italy) |
| 1968 | Leeds United (England) | 1983 | RSC Anderlecht (Belgium) | 2000 | Galatasaray (Turkey) |
| 1969 | Newcastle United (England) | 1984 | Tottenham Hotspur (England) | 2001 | Liverpool (England) |
| 1970 | Arsenal (England) | 1985 | Real Madrid (Spain) | 2002 | Feyenoord (Netherlands) |
| 1971 | Leeds United (England) | 1986 | Real Madrid (Spain) | 2003 | FC Porto (Portugal) |
| 1972 | Tottenham Hotspur (England) | 1987 | IFK Göteborg (Sweden) | 2004 | Valencia (Spain) |
| 1973 | Liverpool (England) | 1988 | Bayer Leverkusen (W. Germany) | 2005 | CSKA Moscow (Russia) |
| 1974 | Feyenoord (Netherlands) | 1989 | Napoli (Italy) | | |

## Copa Libertadores

Contested annually since the 1955-56 season by the league champions of South America's football union.

**Multiple winners:** Independiente (7); Boca Juniors and Peñarol (5); Estudiantes, Nacional-Uruguay, Olimpia and São Paulo (3); Cruzeiro, Gremio, River Plate and Santos (2).

| Year | | Year | | Year | |
|------|---|------|---|------|---|
| 1960 | Peñarol (Uruguay) | 1976 | Cruzeiro (Brazil) | 1992 | São Paulo (Brazil) |
| 1961 | Peñarol (Uruguay) | 1977 | Boca Juniors (Argentina) | 1993 | São Paulo (Brazil) |
| 1962 | Santos (Brazil) | 1978 | Boca Juniors (Argentina) | 1994 | Velez Sarsfield (Argentina) |
| 1963 | Santos (Brazil) | 1979 | Olimpia (Paraguay) | 1995 | Gremio (Brazil) |
| 1964 | Independiente (Argentina) | 1980 | Nacional (Uruguay) | 1996 | River Plate (Argentina) |
| 1965 | Independiente (Argentina) | 1981 | Flamengo (Brazil) | 1997 | Cruzeiro (Brazil) |
| 1966 | Peñarol (Uruguay) | 1982 | Peñarol (Uruguay) | 1998 | Vasco da Gama (Brazil) |
| 1967 | Racing Club (Argentina) | 1983 | Gremio (Brazil) | 1999 | Palmeiras (Brazil) |
| 1968 | Estudiantes de la Plata (Argentina) | 1984 | Independiente (Argentina) | 2000 | Boca Juniors (Argentina) |
| 1969 | Estudiantes de la Plata (Argentina) | 1985 | Argentinos Jrs. (Argentina) | 2001 | Boca Juniors (Argentina) |
| 1970 | Estudiantes de la Plata (Argentina) | 1986 | River Plate (Argentina) | 2002 | Olimpia (Paraguay) |
| 1971 | Nacional (Uruguay) | 1987 | Peñarol (Uruguay) | 2003 | Boca Juniors (Argentina) |
| 1972 | Independiente (Argentina) | 1988 | Nacional (Uruguay) | 2004 | Once Caldas (Colombia) |
| 1973 | Independiente (Argentina) | 1989 | Nacional Medellin (Colombia) | 2005 | São Paulo (Brazil) |
| 1974 | Independiente (Argentina) | 1990 | Olimpia (Paraguay) | | |
| 1975 | Independiente (Argentina) | 1991 | Colo Colo (Chile) | | |

## Annual Awards
### World Player of the Year

Presented by FIFA, the European Sports Magazine Association (ESM) and Adidas, the sports equipment manufacturer, since 1991. Winners are selected by national team coaches and captains from around the world.

**Multiple winners:** Ronaldo and Zinedine Zidane (3).

| Year | | Nat'l Team | Year | | Nat'l Team |
|------|---|-----------|------|---|-----------|
| 1991 | Lothar Matthäus, Inter Milan | Germany | 1998 | Zinedine Zidane, Juventus | France |
| 1992 | Marco Van Basten, AC Milan | Netherlands | 1999 | Rivaldo, Barcelona | Brazil |
| 1993 | Roberto Baggio, Juventus | Italy | 2000 | Zinedine Zidane, Juventus | France |
| 1994 | Romario, Barcelona | Brazil | 2001 | Luis Figo, Real Madrid | Portugal |
| 1995 | George Weah, AC Milan | Liberia | 2002 | Ronaldo, Real Madrid | Brazil |
| 1996 | Ronaldo, Barcelona | Brazil | 2003 | Zinedine Zidane, Real Madrid | France |
| 1997 | Ronaldo, Inter Milan | Brazil | 2004 | Ronaldinho, Barcelona | Brazil |

## Women's World Player of the Year

Presented by FIFA since 2001. Winners are selected by national team coaches from around the world.

**Multiple winner:** Mia Hamm and Birgit Prinz (2).

| Year | | Nat'l Team | Year | | Nat'l Team |
|------|--|-----------|------|--|-----------|
| 2001 | Mia Hamm, Washington Freedom | USA | 2003 | Birgit Prinz, FFC Frankfurt | Germany |
| 2002 | Mia Hamm, Washington Freedom | USA | 2004 | Birgit Prinz, FFC Frankfurt | Germany |

## European Player of the Year

Officially, the "Ballon d'Or," or "Golden Ball," and presented by *France Football* magazine since 1956. Candidates are limited to European players in European leagues and winners are selected by a poll of European soccer journalists.

**Multiple winners:** Johan Cruyff, Michel Platini and Marco Van Basten (3); Franz Beckenbauer, Alfredo di Stéfano, Kevin Keegan, Ronaldo and Karl-Heinz Rummenigge (2).

| Year | | Nat'l Team | Year | | Nat'l Team |
|------|--|-----------|------|--|-----------|
| 1956 | Stanley Matthews, Blackpool | England | 1981 | K.H. Rummenigge, Bayern Munich | W. Ger. |
| 1957 | Alfredo di Stéfano, Real Madrid | Arg./Spain | 1982 | Paolo Rossi, Juventus | Italy |
| 1958 | Raymond Kopa, Real Madrid | France | 1983 | Michel Platini, Juventus | France |
| 1959 | Alfredo di Stéfano, Real Madrid | Arg./Spain | 1984 | Michel Platini, Juventus | France |
| 1960 | Luis Suarez, Barcelona | Spain | 1985 | Michel Platini, Juventus | France |
| 1961 | Enrique Sivori, Juventus | Arg./Italy | 1986 | Igor Belanov, Dinamo Kiev | Soviet Union |
| 1962 | Josef Masopust, Dukla Prague | Czech. | 1987 | Ruud Gullit, AC Milan | Netherlands |
| 1963 | Lev Yashin, Dinamo Moscow | Soviet Union | 1988 | Marco Van Basten, AC Milan | Netherlands |
| 1964 | Denis Law, Manchester United | Scotland | 1989 | Marco Van Basten, AC Milan | Netherlands |
| 1965 | Eusébio, Benfica | Portugal | 1990 | Lothar Matthäus, Inter Milan | W. Ger. |
| 1966 | Bobby Charlton, Manchester United | England | 1991 | Jean-Pierre Papin, Marseille | France |
| 1967 | Florian Albert, Ferencvaros | Hungary | 1992 | Marco Van Basten, AC Milan | Netherlands |
| 1968 | George Best, Manchester United | No. Ireland | 1993 | Roberto Baggio, Juventus | Italy |
| 1969 | Gianni Rivera, AC Milan | Italy | 1994 | Hristo Stoitchkov, Barcelona | Bulgaria |
| 1970 | Gerd Müller, Bayern Munich | W. Ger. | 1995 | George Weah, AC Milan | Liberia |
| 1971 | Johan Cruyff, Ajax Amsterdam | Netherlands | 1996 | Matthias Sammer, Bor. Dortmund | Germany |
| 1972 | Franz Beckenbauer, Bayern Munich | W. Ger. | 1997 | Ronaldo, Inter Milan | Brazil |
| 1973 | Johan Cruyff, Barcelona | Netherlands | 1998 | Zinedine Zidane, Juventus | France |
| 1974 | Johan Cruyff, Barcelona | Netherlands | 1999 | Rivaldo, Barcelona | Brazil |
| 1975 | Oleg Blokhin, Dinamo Kiev | Soviet Union | 2000 | Luis Figo, Real Madrid | Portugal |
| 1976 | Franz Beckenbauer, Bayern Munich | W. Ger. | 2001 | Michael Owen, Liverpool | England |
| 1977 | Allan Simonsen, B. Mönchengladbach | Denmark | 2002 | Ronaldo, Real Madrid | Brazil |
| 1978 | Kevin Keegan, SV Hamburg | England | 2003 | Pavel Nedved, Juventus | Czech Republic |
| 1979 | Kevin Keegan, SV Hamburg | England | 2004 | Andriy Schevchenko, AC Milan | Ukraine |
| 1980 | K.H. Rummenigge, Bayern Munich | W. Ger. | | | |

## South American Player of the Year

Presented by *El Mundo* of Venezuela from 1971-1985 and *El Pais* of Uruguay since 1986. Candidates are limited to South American players in South American leagues and winners are selected by a poll of South American sports editors.

**Multiple winners:** Elias Figueroa and Zico (3); Enzo Francescoli, Diego Maradona, Carlos Tevez and Carlos Valderrama (2).

| Year | | Nat'l Team | Year | | Nat'l Team |
|------|--|-----------|------|--|-----------|
| 1971 | Tostao, Cruzeiro | Brazil | 1988 | Ruben Paz, Racing Buenos Aires | Uruguay |
| 1972 | Teofilo Cubillas, Alianza Lima | Peru | 1989 | Bebeto, Vasco da Gama | Brazil |
| 1973 | Pelé, Santos | Brazil | 1990 | Raul Amarilla, Olimpia | Paraguay |
| 1974 | Elias Figueroa, Internacional | Chile | 1991 | Oscar Ruggeri, Velez Sarsfield | Argentina |
| 1975 | Elias Figueroa, Internacional | Chile | 1992 | Rai, Sao Paulo | Brazil |
| 1976 | Elias Figueroa, Internacional | Chile | 1993 | Carlos Valderrama, Atl. Junior | Colombia |
| 1977 | Zico, Flamengo | Brazil | 1994 | Cafu, Sao Paulo | Brazil |
| 1978 | Mario Kempes, Valencia | Argentina | 1995 | Enzo Francescoli, River Plate | Uruguay |
| 1979 | Diego Maradona, Argentinos Juniors | Argentina | 1996 | Jose Luis Chilavert, Velez Sarsfield | Paraguay |
| 1980 | Diego Maradona, Boca Juniors | Argentina | 1997 | Marcelo Salas, River Plate | Chile |
| 1981 | Zico, Flamengo | Brazil | 1998 | Martin Palermo, Boca Juniors | Argentina |
| 1982 | Zico, Flamengo | Brazil | 1999 | Javier Saviola, River Plate | Argentina |
| 1983 | Socrates, Corinthians | Brazil | 2000 | Romario, Vasco da Gama | Brazil |
| 1984 | Enzo Francescoli, River Plate | Uruguay | 2001 | Juan Roman Riquelme, Boca Juniors | Argentina |
| 1985 | Julio Cesar Romero, Fluminense | Paraguay | 2002 | Jose Cardozo, Toluca | Paraguay |
| 1986 | Antonio Alzamendi, River Plate | Uruguay | 2003 | Carlos Tevez, Boca Juniors | Argentina |
| 1987 | Carlos Valderrama, Deportivo Cali | Colombia | 2004 | Carlos Tevez, Boca Juniors | Argentina |

## Asian Player of the Year

Presented by the Asian Football Confederation since 1994. Prior to 1994 it was awarded unoffically.

**Multiple winners:** Kim Joo-Sung (3); Hidetoshi Nakata (2).

| Year | | Year | | Year | |
|------|--|------|--|------|--|
| 1988 | Ahmed Radhi, Iraq | 1991 | Kim Joo-Sung, South Korea | 1994 | Saeed Al-Owairan, S. Arabia |
| 1989 | Kim Joo-Sung, South Korea | 1992 | no award | 1995 | Masami Ihara, Japan |
| 1990 | Kim Joo-Sung, South Korea | 1993 | Kazuyoshi Miura, Japan | 1996 | Khodadad Azizi, Iran |

| Year | | Year | | Year | |
|------|--|------|--|------|--|
| 1997 | Hidetoshi Nakata, Japan | 2000 | Nawaf Al-Temyat, S. Arabia | 2003 | Mehdi Mahdavikia, Iran |
| 1998 | Hidetoshi Nakata, Japan | 2001 | Fan Zhiyi, China | 2004 | Ali Karimi, Iran |
| 1999 | Ali Daei, Iran | 2002 | Shinji Ono, Japan | | |

## African Player of the Year

Officially, the African "Ballon d'Or" and presented by *France Football* magazine from 1970-96. The Arican Player of the Year award has been presented by the CAF (African Football Confederation) since 1997. All African players are eligible for the award.

**Multiple winners:** George Weah and Abedi Pelé (3); El Hadji Diouf, Nwankwo Kanu, Roger Milla and Thomas N'Kono (2).

| Year | | Year | | Year | |
|------|--|------|--|------|--|
| 1970 | Salif Keita, Mali | 1982 | Thomas N'Kono, Cameroon | 1994 | George Weah, Liberia |
| 1971 | Ibrahim Sunday, Ghana | 1983 | Mahmoud Al-Khatib, Egypt | 1995 | George Weah, Liberia |
| 1972 | Cherif Souleymane, Guinea | 1984 | Theophile Abega, Cameroon | 1996 | Nwankwo Kanu, Nigeria |
| 1973 | Tshimimu Bwanga, Zaire | 1985 | Mohamed Timoumi, Morocco | 1997 | Victor Ikpeba, Nigeria |
| 1974 | Paul Moukila, Congo | 1986 | Badou Zaki, Morocco | 1998 | Mustapha Hadji, Morocco |
| 1975 | Ahmed Faras, Morocco | 1987 | Rabah Madjer, Algeria | 1999 | Nwankwo Kanu, Nigeria |
| 1976 | Roger Milla, Cameroon | 1988 | Kalusha Bwalya, Zambia | 2000 | Patrick Mboma, Cameroon |
| 1977 | Dhiab Tarak, Tunisia | 1989 | George Weah, Liberia | 2001 | El Hadji Diouf, Senegal |
| 1978 | Abdul Razak, Ghana | 1990 | Roger Milla, Cameroon | 2002 | El Hadji Diouf, Senegal |
| 1979 | Thomas N'Kono, Cameroon | 1991 | Abedi Pelé, Ghana | 2003 | Samuel Eto'o Fils, Cameroon |
| 1980 | Jean Manga Onguene, Cameroon | 1992 | Abedi Pelé, Ghana | 2004 | Samuel Eto'o Fils, Cameroon |
| 1981 | Lakhdar Belloumi, Algeria | 1993 | Abedi Pelé, Ghana | | |

## U.S. Player of the Year

Presented by Honda and the Spanish-speaking radio show "Futbol de Primera" since 1991. Candidates are limited to American players who have played with the U.S. National Team and winners are selected by a panel of U.S. soccer journalists.

**Multiple winners:** Landon Donovan (3); Eric Wynalda (2).

| Year | | Year | | Year | | Year | |
|------|--|------|--|------|--|------|--|
| 1991 | Hugo Perez | 1995 | Alexi Lalas | 1999 | Kasey Keller | 2003 | Landon Donovan |
| 1992 | Eric Wynalda | 1996 | Eric Wynalda | 2000 | Claudio Reyna | 2004 | Landon Donovan |
| 1993 | Thomas Dooley | 1997 | Eddie Pope | 2001 | Earnie Stewart | | |
| 1994 | Marcelo Balboa | 1998 | Cobi Jones | 2002 | Landon Donovan | | |

## U.S. PRO LEAGUES

## OUTDOOR
## Major League Soccer

Sanctioned by U.S. Soccer and FIFA, the international soccer federation. MLS was founded on the heels of the successful 1994 World Cup tournament hosted by the United States and it remains the only FIFA-sanctioned division I outdoor league in the United States. The annual MLS title game is known as the MLS Cup.

**Multiple winners:** D.C. United (4); San Jose (2).

### MLS Cup

| Year | Winner | Head Coach | Score | Loser | Head Coach | Site |
|------|--------|------------|-------|-------|------------|------|
| 1996 | D.C. United | Bruce Arena | 3-2 OT | Los Angeles Galaxy | Lothar Osiander | Foxboro, Mass. |
| 1997 | D.C. United | Bruce Arena | 2-1 | Colorado Rapids | Glen Myernick | Washington, D.C. |
| 1998 | Chicago Fire | Bob Bradley | 2-0 | D.C. United | Bruce Arena | Pasadena, Calif. |
| 1999 | D.C. United | Thomas Rongen | 2-0 | Los Angeles Galaxy | Sigi Schmid | Foxboro, Mass. |
| 2000 | K.C. Wizards | Bob Gansler | 1-0 | Chicago Fire | Bob Bradley | Washington, D.C. |
| 2001 | San Jose Earthquakes | Frank Yallop | 2-1 OT | Los Angeles Galaxy | Sigi Schmid | Columbus, Ohio |
| 2002 | Los Angeles Galaxy | Sigi Schmid | 1-0 2OT | N.E. Revolution | Steve Nicol | Foxboro, Mass. |
| 2003 | San Jose Earthquakes | Frank Yallop | 4-2 | Chicago Fire | Dave Sarachan | Carson, Calif. |
| 2004 | D.C. United | Peter Nowak | 3-2 | K.C. Wizards | Bob Gansler | Carson, Calif. |

### MLS Cup '96
**D.C. United, 3-2 (OT)**
Oct. 20 at Foxboro Stadium, Foxboro, Mass.
Attendance: 34,643

| | 1 | 2 | OT | |
|--|---|---|----|--|
| Los Angeles Galaxy | 1 | 1 | 0 | —2 |
| D.C. United | 0 | 2 | 1 | —3 |

**First Half:** LA–Eduardo Hurtado (Mauricio Cienfuegos), 5th minute.
**Second Half:** LA–Chris Armas (unassisted), 56th; DC–Tony Sanneh (Marco Etcheverry), 73rd; DC–Shawn Medved (unassisted), 82nd.
**Overtime:** DC–Eddie Pope (Etcheverry), 94th.
**MVP:** Marco Etcheverry, D.C. United, Midfielder

### MLS Cup '97
**D.C. United, 2-1**
Oct. 26 at RFK Stadium, Washington, D.C.
Attendance: 57,431

| | 1 | 2 | |
|--|---|---|--|
| Colorado Rapids | 0 | 1 | —1 |
| D.C. United | 1 | 1 | —2 |

**First Half:** DC–Jaime Moreno (Tony Sanneh, David Vaudreuil), 37th minute.
**Second Half:** DC–Sanneh (John Harkes, Richie Williams), 68th; COL–Adrian Paz (David Patino, Matt Kmosko), 75th.
**MVP:** Jaime Moreno, D.C. United, Forward

## MLS Cup '98
### Chicago Fire, 2-0
Oct. 25 at the Rose Bowl, Pasadena, Calif.
Attendance: 51,350

|  | 1 | 2 |  |
|---|---|---|---|
| D.C. United | 0 | 0 | —0 |
| Chicago | 2 | 0 | —2 |

**First Half:** CHI–Jerzy Podbrozny (Peter Nowak, Ante Razov), 29th minute; CHI–Diego Gutierrez (Nowak), 45th.
**MVP:** Nowak, Chicago, Midfielder

## MLS Cup '99
### D.C. United, 2-0
Nov. 21 at Foxboro Stadium, Foxboro, Mass.
Attendance: 44,910

|  | 1 | 2 |  |
|---|---|---|---|
| D.C. United | 2 | 0 | —2 |
| Los Angeles | 0 | 0 | —0 |

**First Half:** DC–Jaime Moreno (Roy Lassiter), 19th minute; DC–Ben Olsen (unassisted), 48th
**MVP:** Olsen, D.C. United, Midfielder

## MLS Cup 2000
### Kansas City Wizards, 1-0
Oct. 15 at RFK Stadium, Washington, D.C.
Attendance: 39,159

|  | 1 | 2 |  |
|---|---|---|---|
| Chicago | 0 | 0 | —0 |
| Kansas City | 1 | 0 | —1 |

**First Half:** DC– Miklos Molnar (Chris Klein), 11th minute.
**MVP:** Tony Meola, Kansas City, Goalkeeper

## MLS Cup 2001
### San Jose Earthquakes, 2-1 (OT)
Oct. 21 at Crew Stadium, Columbus, Ohio
Attendance: 21,626

|  | 1 | 2 | OT |  |
|---|---|---|---|---|
| San Jose | 1 | 0 | 1 | —2 |
| Los Angeles | 1 | 0 | 0 | —1 |

**First Half:** LA–Luis Hernandez (Greg Vanney, Kevin Hartman), 21st minute; SJ–Landon Donovan (Ian Russell, Richard Mulrooney), 43rd. **Overtime:** SJ–Dwayne DeRosario (Ronnie Ekelund, Zak Ibsen), 96th.

**MVP:** Dwayne DeRosario, San Jose, Forward

## MLS Cup 2002
### Los Angeles Galaxy, 1-0 (2 OT)
Oct. 20 at Gillette Stadium, Foxboro, Mass.
Attendance: 61,316

|  | 1 | 2 | 1OT | 2OT |  |
|---|---|---|---|---|---|
| Los Angeles | 0 | 0 | 0 | 1 | —1 |
| New England | 0 | 0 | 0 | 0 | —0 |

**2nd OT:** LA–Carlos Ruiz, (Tyrone Marshall, Chris Albright), 113th minute.
**MVP:** Carlos Ruiz, Los Angeles, F

## MLS Cup 2003
### San Jose Earthquakes, 4-2
Nov. 23 at Home Depot Center, Carson, Calif.
Attendance: 27,000

|  | 1 | 2 |  |
|---|---|---|---|
| San Jose | 2 | 2 | —4 |
| Chicago | 0 | 2 | —2 |

**First Half:** SJ– Ronnie Ekelund (unassisted), 5th minute; SJ–Landon Donovan (Jamil Walker), 38th.

**Second Half:** CHI–DaMarcus Beasley (Andy Williams), 49th; SJ–Richard Mulrooney (Craig Waibel), 50th; CHI–own goal (Chris Roner), 54th; SJ–Donovan (Dwayne De Rosario, Brian Mullan), 71st.
**MVP:** Landon Donovan, San Jose, F

## MLS Cup 2004
### D.C. United, 3-2
Nov. 14 at Home Depot Center, Carson, Calif.
Attendance: 25,797

|  | 1 | 2 |  |
|---|---|---|---|
| D.C. United | 3 | 0 | —3 |
| Kansas City | 1 | 1 | —2 |

**First Half:** KC– Jose Burciaga Jr. (unassisted), 6th minute; DC–Alecko Eskandarian (Brian Carroll), 19th. DC–Alecko Eskandarian (unassisted), 23rd. DC–own goal (Alex Zotinca), 26th.

**Second Half:** KC–Josh Wolff (penalty kick), 58th.
**MVP:** Alecko Eskandarian, D.C. United, F

## MLS Cup 2005
The 2005 MLS Cup was scheduled for Nov. 13, 2005 at Pizza Hut Park in Frisco, Texas.

# Regular Season

## Most Valuable Player
**Multiple winner:** Preki (2).
1996 Carlos Valderrama, Tampa Bay
1997 Preki, Kansas City
1998 Marco Etcheverry, D.C.
1999 Jason Kreis, Dallas
2000 Tony Meola, Kansas City
2001 Alex Pineda Chacón, Miami
2002 Carlos Ruiz, LA
2003 Preki, Kansas City
2004 Amado Guevara, MetroStars

## Rookie of the Year
1996 Steve Ralston, Tampa Bay
1997 Mike Duhaney, Tampa Bay
1998 Ben Olsen, D.C.
1999 Jay Heaps, Miami
2000 Carlos Bocanegra, Chicago
2001 Rodrigo Faria, MetroStars
2002 Kyle Martino, Columbus
2003 Damani Ralph, Chicago
2004 Clint Dempsey, New England

## Leading Scorer
**Multiple winner:** Preki and Taylor Twellman (2).

|  |  | G | A | Pts |
|---|---|---|---|---|
| 1996 | Roy Lassiter, Tampa Bay | 27 | 4 | 58 |
| 1997 | Preki, Kansas City | 12 | 17 | 41 |
| 1998 | Stern John, Columbus | 26 | 5 | 57 |
| 1999 | Jason Kreis, Dallas | 18 | 15 | 51 |
| 2000 | Mamadou Diallo, Tampa Bay | 26 | 4 | 56 |
| 2001 | Alex Pineda Chacón, Miami | 19 | 9 | 47 |
| 2002 | Taylor Twellman, New England | 23 | 6 | 52 |
| 2003 | Preki, Kansas City | 12 | 17 | 41 |
| 2004 | Pat Noonan, New England | 11 | 8 | 30 |
|  | & Amado Guevara, MetroStars | 10 | 10 | 30 |
| 2005 | Taylor Twellman, New England | 17 | 7 | 41 |

## Other U.S. Pro Leagues (Cont.)
## National Professional Soccer League (1967)

Not sanctioned by FIFA, the international soccer federation. The NPSL recruited individual players to fill the rosters of its 10 teams. The league lasted only one season.

| | Playoff Final | | | Regular Season | | | |
|---|---|---|---|---|---|---|---|
| Year | Winner | Scores | Loser | Leading Scorer | G | A | Pts |
| 1967 | Oakland Clippers | 0-1, 4-1 | Baltimore Bays | Yanko Daucik, Toronto . . . . . . . . . . . . . .20 | 8 | 48 | |

## United Soccer Association (1967)

Sanctioned by FIFA. Originally called the North American Soccer League, it became the USA to avoid being confused with the National Professional Soccer League (see above). Instead of recruiting individual players, the USA imported 12 entire teams from Europe to represent its 12 franchises. It, too, only lasted a season. The league champion Los Angeles Wolves were actually Wolverhampton of England and the runner-up Washington Whips were Aberdeen of Scotland.

| | Playoff Final | | | Regular Season | | | |
|---|---|---|---|---|---|---|---|
| Year | Winner | Score | Loser | Leading Scorer | G | A | Pts |
| 1967 | Los Angeles Wolves | 6-5 (OT) | Washington Whips | Roberto Boninsegna, Chicago . . . . . . . . . .10 | 1 | 21 | |

## North American Soccer League (1968-84)

The NPSL and USA merged to form the NASL in 1968 and the new league lasted through 1984. The NASL championship was known as the Soccer Bowl from 1975-84. One game decided the NASL title every year but five. There were no playoffs in 1969; a two-game/aggregate goals format was used in 1968 and '70; and a best-of-three games format was used in 1971 and '84; (*) indicates overtime and (†) indicates game decided by shootout.

**Multiple winners:** NY Cosmos (5); Chicago (2).

| | Playoff Final | | | Regular Season | | | |
|---|---|---|---|---|---|---|---|
| Year | Winner | Score(s) | Loser | Leading Scorer | G | A | Pts |
| 1968 | Atlanta Chiefs | 0-0,3-0 | San Diego Toros | John Kowalik, Chicago . . . . . . . . . . .30 | 9 | 69 | |
| 1969 | Kansas City Spurs | No game | Atlanta Chiefs | Kaiser Motaung, Atlanta . . . . . . . . . .16 | 4 | 36 | |
| 1970 | Rochester Lancers | 3-0,1-3 | Washington Darts | Kirk Apostolidis, Dallas . . . . . . . .16 | 3 | 35 | |
| 1971 | Dallas Tornado | 1-2*,4-1,2-0 | Atlanta Chiefs | Carlos Metidieri, Rochester . . . . . . .19 | 8 | 46 | |
| 1972 | New York Cosmos | 2-1 | St. Louis Stars | Randy Horton, New York . . . . . . . . .9 | 4 | 22 | |
| 1973 | Philadelphia Atoms | 2-0 | Dallas Tornado | Kyle Rote Jr., Dallas . . . . . . . . . . .10 | 10 | 30 | |
| 1974 | Los Angeles Aztecs | 3-3† | Miami Toros | Paul Child, San Jose . . . . . . . . . . . .15 | 6 | 36 | |
| 1975 | Tampa Bay Rowdies | 2-0 | Portland Timbers | Steve David, Miami . . . . . . . . . . . .23 | 6 | 52 | |
| 1976 | Toronto Metros | 3-0 | Minnesota Kicks | Giorgio Chinaglia, New York . . . . . .19 | 11 | 49 | |
| 1977 | New York Cosmos | 2-1 | Seattle Sounders | Steve David, Los Angeles . . . . . . . .26 | 6 | 58 | |
| 1978 | New York Cosmos | 3-1 | Tampa Bay Rowdies | Giorgio Chinaglia, New York . . . . . .34 | 11 | 79 | |
| 1979 | Vancouver Whitecaps | 2-1 | Tampa Bay Rowdies | Oscar Fabbiani, Tampa Bay . . . . . . .25 | 8 | 58 | |
| 1980 | New York Cosmos | 3-0 | Ft. Laud. Strikers | Giorgio Chinaglia, New York . . . . . .32 | 13 | 77 | |
| 1981 | Chicago Sting | 0-0† | New York Cosmos | Giorgio Chinaglia, New York . . . . . .29 | 16 | 74 | |
| 1982 | New York Cosmos | 1-0 | Seattle Sounders | Giorgio Chinaglia, New York . . . . . .20 | 15 | 55 | |
| 1983 | Tulsa Roughnecks | 2-0 | Toronto Blizzard | Roberto Cabanas, New York . . . . . . .25 | 16 | 66 | |
| 1984 | Chicago Sting | 2-1,3-2 | Toronto Blizzard | Steve Zungul, Golden Bay . . . . . . . .20 | 10 | 50 | |

**Note:** In 1969, Kansas City won the NASL regular season championship with 110 points to 109 for Atlanta. There were no playoffs.

### Regular Season MVP
Regular season Most Valuable Player as designated by the NASL.

**Multiple winner:** Carlos Metidieri (2).

| Year | | Year | | Year | |
|---|---|---|---|---|---|
| 1967 | Rueben Navarro, Phila (NPSL) | 1973 | Warren Archibald, Miami | 1979 | Johan Cruyff, Los Angeles |
| 1968 | John Kowalik, Chicago | 1974 | Peter Silvester, Baltimore | 1980 | Roger Davies, Seattle |
| 1969 | Cirilio Fernandez, KC | 1975 | Steve David, Miami | 1981 | Giorgio Chinaglia, New York |
| 1970 | Carlos Metidieri, Rochester | 1976 | Pelé, New York | 1982 | Peter Ward, Seattle |
| 1971 | Carlos Metidieri, Rochester | 1977 | Franz Beckenbauer, New York | 1983 | Roberto Cabanas, New York |
| 1972 | Randy Horton, New York | 1978 | Mike Flanagan, New England | 1984 | Steve Zungul, Golden Bay |

## USL First Division/A-League

The American Professional Soccer League was formed in 1990 with the merger of the Western Soccer League and the New American Soccer League. The APSL was officially sanctioned as an outdoor pro league in 1992 and changed its name to the A-League in 1995. The league was reorganized under the umbrella of the United Soccer Leagues and renamed the USL First Division in 2005.

**Multiple winners:** Rochester and Seattle (3); Colorado, Milwaukee and Montreal (2).

| Year | | Year | | Year | |
|---|---|---|---|---|---|
| 1990 | Maryland Bays | 1996 | Seattle Sounders | 2002 | Milwaukee Rampage |
| 1991 | SF Bay Blackhawks | 1997 | Milwaukee Rampage | 2003 | Charleston Battery |
| 1992 | Colorado Foxes | 1998 | Rochester Rhinos | 2004 | Montreal Impact |
| 1993 | Colorado Foxes | 1999 | Minnesota Thunder | 2005 | Seattle Sounders |
| 1994 | Montreal Impact | 2000 | Rochester Rhinos | | |
| 1995 | Seattle Sounders | 2001 | Rochester Rhinos | | |

## Women's United Soccer Association (2001-03)

The eight-team WUSA was formed in 2000 as the top women's outdoor professional league and play began in 2001. The league championship game is known as the Founders Cup. The league folded following the 2003 season.

### Founders Cup

| Year | Winner | Score | Loser | Site |
|------|--------|-------|-------|------|
| 2001 | Bay Area CyberRays | 3-3* | Atlanta Beat | Foxboro, Mass. |
| 2002 | Carolina Courage | 3-2 | Washington Freedom | Atlanta, Ga. |
| 2003 | Washington Freedom | 2-1 OT | Atlanta Beat | San Diego, Calif. |

*Bay Area won shoot-out, 4-2.

### Regular Season

#### WUSA Most Valuable Player

2001 Tiffeny Milbrett, New York
2002 Marinette Pichon, Philadelphia
2003 Maren Meinert, Boston

#### WUSA Leading Scorer

| | | G | A | Pts |
|---|---|---|---|-----|
| 2001 | Tiffeny Milbrett, New York | 16 | 3 | 35 |
| 2002 | Katia, San Jose | 15 | 5 | 35 |
| 2003 | Mia Hamm, Washington | 11 | 11 | 33 |
| | & Abby Wambach, Washington | 13 | 7 | 33 |

## INDOOR

## Major Soccer League (1978-92)

Originally the Major Indoor Soccer League from 1978-79 season through 1989-90. The MISL championship was decided by one game in 1980 and 1981; a best-of-three games series in 1979, best-of-five games in 1982 and 1983; and best-of-seven games since 1984. The MSL folded after the 1991-92 season.

**Multiple winners:** San Diego (8); New York (4).

### Playoff Final | Regular Season

| Year | Winner | Series | Loser | Leading Scorer | G | A | Pts |
|------|--------|--------|-------|----------------|---|---|-----|
| 1979 | New York Arrows | 2-0 | Philadelphia | Fred Grgurev, Philadelphia | 46 | 28 | 74 |
| 1980 | New York Arrows | 7-4 (1 game) | Houston | Steve Zungul, New York | 90 | 46 | 136 |
| 1981 | New York Arrows | 6-5 (1 game) | St. Louis | Steve Zungul, New York | 108 | 44 | 152 |
| 1982 | New York Arrows | 3-2 (LWWLW) | St. Louis | Steve Zungul, New York | 103 | 60 | 163 |
| 1983 | San Diego Sockers | 3-2 (WWLLW) | Baltimore | Steve Zungul, NY/Golden Bay | 75 | 47 | 122 |
| 1984 | Baltimore Blast | 4-1 (LWWWW) | St. Louis | Stan Stamenkovic, Baltimore | 34 | 63 | 97 |
| 1985 | San Diego Sockers | 4-1 (WWLWW) | Baltimore | Steve Zungul, San Diego | 68 | 68 | 136 |
| 1986 | San Diego Sockers | 4-3 (WLLLWWW) | Minnesota | Steve Zungul, Tacoma | 55 | 60 | 115 |
| 1987 | Dallas Sidekicks | 4-3 (LLWWLWW) | Tacoma | Tatu, Dallas | 73 | 38 | 111 |
| 1988 | San Diego Sockers | 4-0 | Cleveland | Eric Rasmussen, Wichita | 55 | 57 | 112 |
| 1989 | San Diego Sockers | 4-3 (LWWWLLW) | Baltimore | Preki, Tacoma | 51 | 53 | 104 |
| 1990 | San Diego Sockers | 4-2 (LWWWLW) | Baltimore | Tatu, Dallas | 64 | 49 | 113 |
| 1991 | San Diego Sockers | 4-2 (WLWLWW) | Cleveland | Tatu, Dallas | 78 | 66 | 144 |
| 1992 | San Diego Sockers | 4-2 (WWWLLW) | Dallas | Zoran Karic, Cleveland | 39 | 63 | 102 |

### Playoff MVPs | Regular Season MVPs

MSL playoff Most Valuable Players, selected by a panel of soccer media covering the playoffs.

**Multiple winners:** Steve Zungul (4); Brian Quinn (2).

| Year | | Year | |
|------|---|------|---|
| 1979 | Shep Messing, NY | 1986 | Brian Quinn, SD |
| 1980 | Steve Zungul, NY | 1987 | Tatu, Dallas |
| 1981 | Steve Zungul, NY | 1988 | Hugo Perez, SD |
| 1982 | Steve Zungul, NY | 1989 | Victor Nogueira, SD |
| 1983 | Juli Veee, SD | 1990 | Brian Quinn, SD |
| 1984 | Scott Manning, Bal. | 1991 | Ben Collins, SD |
| 1985 | Steve Zungul, SD | 1992 | Thompson Usiyan, SD |

MSL regular season Most Valuable Players, selected by a panel of soccer media from every city in the league.

**Multiple winners:** Steve Zungul (6); Victor Nogueira and Tatu (2).

| Year | | Year | |
|------|---|------|---|
| 1979 | Steve Zungul, NY | 1986 | Steve Zungul, SD/Tac. |
| 1980 | Steve Zungul, NY | 1987 | Tatu, Dallas |
| 1981 | Steve Zungul, NY | 1988 | Erik Rasmussen, Wich. |
| 1982 | Steve Zungul, NY | 1989 | Preki, Tacoma |
| | & Stan Terlecki, Pit. | 1990 | Tatu, Dallas |
| 1983 | Alan Mayer, SD | 1991 | Victor Nogueira, SD |
| 1984 | Stan Stamenkovic, Bal. | 1992 | Victor Nogueira, SD |
| 1985 | Steve Zungul, SD | | |

## NASL Indoor Champions (1980-84)

The North American Soccer League started an indoor league in the fall of 1979. The indoor NASL, which featured many of the same teams and players who played in the outdoor NASL, crowned champions from 1980-82 before suspending play. It was revived for the 1983-84 indoor season but folded for good in 1984. The NASL held indoor tournaments in 1975 (San Jose Earthquakes won) and 1976 (Tampa Bay Rowdies won) before the indoor league was started.

**Multiple winner:** San Diego (2).

| Year | | Year | | Year | | Year | |
|------|---|------|---|------|---|------|---|
| 1980 | Tampa Bay Rowdies | 1982 | San Diego Sockers | 1983 | Play suspended | 1984 | San Diego Sockers |
| 1981 | Edmonton Drillers | | | | | | |

## Major Indoor Soccer League

The winter indoor MISL began as the American Indoor Soccer Association in 1984-85, then changed its name to the National Professional Soccer League in 1989-90 and was known as the NPSL until 2001 when the name was changed again and the league was relaunched as the MISL.

**Multiple winners:** Canton (5); Milwaukee (4); Cleveland (3); Baltimore and Kansas City (2).

| Year | | Year | | Year | | Year | |
|------|--|------|--|------|--|------|--|
| 1985 | Canton (OH) Invaders | 1991 | Chicago Power | 1997 | Kansas City Attack | 2003 | Baltimore Blast |
| 1986 | Canton Invaders | 1992 | Detroit Rockers | 1998 | Milwaukee Wave | 2004 | Baltimore Blast |
| 1987 | Louisville Thunder | 1993 | Kansas City Attack | 1999 | Cleveland Crunch | 2005 | Milwaukee Wave |
| 1988 | Canton Invaders | 1994 | Cleveland Crunch | 2000 | Milwaukee Wave | | |
| 1989 | Canton Invaders | 1995 | St. Louis Ambush | 2001 | Milwaukee Wave | | |
| 1990 | Canton Invaders | 1996 | Cleveland Crunch | 2002 | Philadelphia Kixx | | |

## Continental Indoor Soccer League (1993-97)

The summer indoor CISL played its first season in 1993 and folded following the 1997 season.

**Multiple winner:** Monterrey (2).

| Year | | Year | | Year | |
|------|--|------|--|------|--|
| 1993 | Dallas Sidekicks | 1995 | Monterrey La Raza | 1997 | Seattle Seadogs |
| 1994 | Las Vegas Dustdevils | 1996 | Monterrey La Raza | | |

## U.S. COLLEGES

## NCAA Men's Division I Champions

NCAA Division I champions since the first title was contested in 1959. The championship has been shared three times—in 1967, 1968 and 1989. There was a playoff for third place from 1974-81.

**Multiple winners:** Saint Louis (10); Indiana (7); San Francisco and Virginia (5); UCLA (4); Clemson, Connecticut, Howard and Michigan St. (2).

| Year | Winner | Head Coach | Score | Runner-up | Host/Site | Semifinalists |
|------|--------|-----------|-------|-----------|-----------|---------------|
| 1959 | Saint Louis | Bob Guelker | 5-2 | Bridgeport | Connecticut | West Chester, CCNY |
| 1960 | Saint Louis | Bob Guelker | 3-2 | Maryland | Brooklyn | West Chester, Connecticut |
| 1961 | West Chester | Mel Lorback | 2-0 | Saint Louis | Saint Louis | Bridgeport, Connecticut |
| 1962 | Saint Louis | Bob Guelker | 4-3 | Maryland | Saint Louis | Mich. St., Springfield |
| 1963 | Saint Louis | Bob Guelker | 3-0 | Navy | Rutgers | Army, Maryland |
| 1964 | Navy | F.H. Warner | 1-0 | Michigan St. | Brown | Army, Saint Louis |
| 1965 | Saint Louis | Bob Guelker | 1-0 | Michigan St. | Saint Louis | Army, Navy |
| 1966 | San Francisco | Steve Negoesco | 5-2 | LIU-Brooklyn | California | Army, Mich. St. |
| 1967-a | Michigan St. & Saint Louis | Gene Kenney Harry Keough | 0-0 | – | Saint Louis | LIU-Bklyn, Navy |
| 1968-b | Michigan St. & Maryland | Gene Kenney Doyle Royal | 2-2 (2 OT) | – | Ga. Tech | Brown, San Jose St. |
| 1969 | Saint Louis | Harry Keough | 4-0 | San Francisco | San Jose St. | Harvard, Maryland |
| 1970 | Saint Louis | Harry Keough | 1-0 | UCLA | SIU-Ed'sville | Hartwick, Howard |
| 1971-c | Howard | Lincoln Phillips | 3-2 | Saint Louis | Miami | Harvard, San Fran. |
| 1972 | Saint Louis | Harry Keough | 4-2 | UCLA | Miami | Cornell, Howard |
| 1973 | Saint Louis | Harry Keough | 2-1 (OT) | UCLA | Miami | Brown, Clemson |

| Year | Winner | Head Coach | Score | Runner-up | Host/Site | Third Place |
|------|--------|-----------|-------|-----------|-----------|-------------|
| 1974 | Howard | Lincoln Phillips | 2-1 (4OT) | Saint Louis | Saint Louis | Hartwick 3, UCLA 1 |
| 1975 | San Francisco | Steve Negoesco | 4-0 | SIU-Ed'sville | SIU-Ed'sville | Brown 2, Howard 0 |
| 1976 | San Francisco | Steve Negoesco | 1-0 | Indiana | Penn | Hartwick 4, Clemson 3 |
| 1977 | Hartwick | Jim Lennox | 2-1 | San Francisco | California | SIU-Ed'sville 3, Brown 2 |
| 1978-d | San Francisco | Steve Negoesco | 4-3 (OT) | Indiana | Tampa | Clemson 6, Phi. Textile 2 |
| 1979 | SIU-Ed'sville | Bob Guelker | 3-2 | Clemson | Tampa | Penn St. 2, Columbia 1 |
| 1980 | San Francisco | Steve Negoesco | 4-3 (OT) | Indiana | Tampa | Ala. A&M 2, Hartwick 0 |
| 1981 | Connecticut | Joe Morrone | 2-1 (OT) | Alabama A&M | Stanford | East. Ill. 4, Phi. Textile 2 |

| Year | Winner | Head Coach | Score | Runner-up | Host/Site | Semifinalists |
|------|--------|-----------|-------|-----------|-----------|---------------|
| 1982 | Indiana | Jerry Yeagley | 2-1 (8 OT) | Duke | Ft. Lauderdale | Connecticut, SIU-Ed'sville |
| 1983 | Indiana | Jerry Yeagley | 1-0 (2 OT) | Columbia | Ft. Lauderdale | Connecticut, Virginia |
| 1984 | Clemson | I.M. Ibrahim | 2-1 | Indiana | Seattle | Hartwick, UCLA |
| 1985 | UCLA | Sigi Schmid | 1-0 (8 OT) | American | Seattle | Evansville, Hartwick |
| 1986 | Duke | John Rennie | 1-0 | Akron | Tacoma | Fresno St., Harvard |
| 1987 | Clemson | I.M. Ibrahim | 2-0 | San Diego St. | Clemson | Harvard, N. Carolina |
| 1988 | Indiana | Jerry Yeagley | 1-0 | Howard | Indiana | Portland, S. Carolina |
| 1989-e | Santa Clara & Virginia | Steve Sampson Bruce Arena | 1-1 (2 OT) | – | Rutgers | Indiana, Rutgers |

| Year | Winner | Head Coach | Score | Runner-up | Host/Site | Semifinalists |
|------|--------|-----------|-------|-----------|-----------|---------------|
| 1990-f | UCLA | Sigi Schmid | 0-0 (PKs) | Rutgers | South Fla. | Evansville, N.C. State |
| 1991-g | Virginia | Bruce Arena | 0-0 (PKs) | Santa Clara | Tampa | Indiana, Saint Louis |
| 1992 | Virginia | Bruce Arena | 2-0 | San Diego | Davidson | Davidson, Duke |
| 1993 | Virginia | Bruce Arena | 2-0 | South Carolina | Davidson | CS-Fullerton, Princeton |
| 1994 | Virginia | Bruce Arena | 1-0 | Indiana | Davidson | Rutgers, UCLA |
| 1995 | Wisconsin | Jim Launder | 2-0 | Duke | Richmond | Portland, Virginia |
| 1996 | St. John's | Dave Masur | 4-1 | Fla. International | Richmond | Creighton, NC-Charlotte |
| 1997 | UCLA | Sigi Schmid | 2-0 | Virginia | Richmond | Indiana, Saint Louis |
| 1998 | Indiana | Jerry Yeagley | 3-1 | Stanford | Richmond | Maryland, Santa Clara |
| 1999 | Indiana | Jerry Yeagley | 1-0 | Santa Clara | Charlotte | Connecticut, UCLA |
| 2000 | Connecticut | Ray Reid | 2-0 | Creighton | Charlotte | Indiana, Southern Methodist |
| 2001 | North Carolina | Elmar Bolowich | 2-0 | Indiana | Columbus | St. John's, Stanford |
| 2002 | UCLA | Tom Fitzgerald | 1-0 | Stanford | Dallas | Creighton, Maryland |
| 2003 | Indiana | Jerry Yeagley | 2-1 | St. John's | Columbus | Maryland, Santa Clara |
| 2004-h | Indiana | Mike Freitag | 1-1 (PKs) | UCSB | Carson, Calif. | Duke, Maryland |

**a**–game declared a draw due to inclement weather after regulation time; **b**–game declared a draw after two overtimes; **c**–Howard vacated title for using ineligible player; **d**–San Francisco vacated title for using ineligible player; **e**–game declared a draw due to inclement weather after two overtimes; **f**–UCLA wins on penalty kicks (4-3) after four overtimes; **g**–Virginia wins on penalty kicks (3-1) after four overtimes; **h**–Indiana wins on penalty kicks (3-2) after two overtimes.

## Women's NCAA Division I Champions

NCAA Division I women's champions since the first tournament was contested in 1982.

**Multiple winner:** North Carolina (17).

| Year | Winner | Coach | Score | Runner-up | Host/Site |
|------|--------|-------|-------|-----------|-----------|
| 1982 | North Carolina | Anson Dorrance | 2-0 | Central Florida | Central Florida |
| 1983 | North Carolina | Anson Dorrance | 4-0 | George Mason | Central Florida |
| 1984 | North Carolina | Anson Dorrance | 2-0 | Connecticut | North Carolina |
| 1985 | George Mason | Hank Leung | 2-0 | North Carolina | George Mason |
| 1986 | North Carolina | Anson Dorrance | 2-0 | Colorado College | George Mason |
| 1987 | North Carolina | Anson Dorrance | 1-0 | Massachusetts | Massachusetts |
| 1988 | North Carolina | Anson Dorrance | 4-1 | N.C. State | North Carolina |
| 1989 | North Carolina | Anson Dorrance | 2-0 | Colorado College | N.C. State |
| 1990 | North Carolina | Anson Dorrance | 6-0 | Connecticut | North Carolina |
| 1991 | North Carolina | Anson Dorrance | 3-1 | Wisconsin | North Carolina |
| 1992 | North Carolina | Anson Dorrance | 9-1 | Duke | North Carolina |
| 1993 | North Carolina | Anson Dorrance | 6-0 | George Mason | North Carolina |
| 1994 | North Carolina | Anson Dorrance | 5-0 | Notre Dame | Portland |
| 1995 | Notre Dame | Chris Petrucelli | 1-0 (3OT) | Portland | North Carolina |
| 1996 | North Carolina | Anson Dorrance | 1-0 (2OT) | Notre Dame | Santa Clara |
| 1997 | North Carolina | Anson Dorrance | 2-0 | Connecticut | NC-Greensboro |
| 1998 | Florida | Becky Burleigh | 1-0 | North Carolina | NC-Greensboro |
| 1999 | North Carolina | Anson Dorrance | 2-0 | Notre Dame | San Jose, Calif. |
| 2000 | North Carolina | Anson Dorrance | 2-1 | UCLA | San Jose, Calif. |
| 2001 | Santa Clara | Jerry Smith | 1-0 | North Carolina | Dallas |
| 2002 | Portland | Clive Charles | 2-1 (2OT) | Santa Clara | Austin |
| 2003 | North Carolina | Anson Dorrance | 6-0 | Connecticut | Cary, N.C. |
| 2004-a | Notre Dame | Randy Waldrum | 1-1 (PKs) | UCLA | Cary, N.C. |

**a**–Notre Dame wins on penalty kicks (4-3) after two overtimes.

## Annual Awards
### MEN
### Hermann Trophy

College Player of the Year. Voted on by Division I college coaches and selected sportswriters and first presented in 1967 in the name of Robert Hermann, one of the founders of the North American Soccer League.

**Multiple winners:** Mike Fisher, Mike Seerey, Ken Snow and Al Trost (2).

| Year | | Year | | Year | |
|------|--|------|--|------|--|
| 1967 | Dov Markus, LIU | 1980 | Joe Morrone, Jr. Connecticut | 1993 | Claudio Reyna, Virginia |
| 1968 | Manuel Hernandez, San Jose St. | 1981 | Armando Betancourt, Indiana | 1994 | Brian Maisonneuve, Indiana |
| 1969 | Al Trost, Saint Louis | 1982 | Joe Ulrich, Duke | 1995 | Mike Fisher, Virginia |
| 1970 | Al Trost, Saint Louis | 1983 | Mike Jeffries, Duke | 1996 | Mike Fisher, Virginia |
| 1971 | Mike Seerey, Saint Louis | 1984 | Amr Aly, Columbia | 1997 | Johnny Torres, Creighton |
| 1972 | Mike Seerey, Saint Louis | 1985 | Tom Kain, Duke | 1998 | Wojtek Krakowiak, Clemson |
| 1973 | Dan Counce, Saint Louis | 1986 | John Kerr, Duke | 1999 | Ali Curtis, Duke |
| 1974 | Farrukh Quraishi, Oneonta St. | 1987 | Bruce Murray, Clemson | 2000 | Chris Gbandi, Connecticut |
| 1975 | Steve Ralbovsky, Brown | 1988 | Ken Snow, Indiana | 2001 | Luchi Gonzalez, SMU |
| 1976 | Glenn Myernick, Hartwick | 1989 | Tony Meola, Virginia | 2002 | Alecko Eskandarian, Virginia |
| 1977 | Billy Gazonas, Hartwick | 1990 | Ken Snow, Indiana | 2003 | Chris Wingert, St. John's |
| 1978 | Angelo DiBernardo, Indiana | 1991 | Alexi Lalas, Rutgers | 2004 | Danny O'Rourke, Indiana |
| 1979 | Jim Stamatis, Penn St. | 1992 | Brad Friedel, UCLA | | |

## Missouri Athletic Club Award

College Player of the Year. Voted on by men's team coaches around the country from Division I to junior college level and first presented in 1986 by the Missouri Athletic Club of St. Louis.

**Multiple winners:** Claudio Reyna and Ken Snow (2).

| Year | | Year | | Year | |
|------|--|------|--|------|--|
| 1986 | John Kerr, Duke | 1992 | Claudio Reyna, Virginia | 1998 | Jay Heaps, Duke |
| 1987 | John Harkes, Virginia | 1993 | Claudio Reyna, Virginia | 1999 | Sasha Victorine, UCLA |
| 1988 | Ken Snow, Indiana | 1994 | Todd Yeagley, Indiana | 2000 | Ali Curtis, Duke |
| 1989 | Tony Meola, Virginia | 1995 | Matt McKeon, St. Louis | 2001 | Luchi Gonzalez, SMU |
| 1990 | Ken Snow, Indiana | 1996 | Mike Fisher, Virginia | 2002 | merged with Hermann Trophy. |
| 1991 | Alexi Lalas, Rutgers | 1997 | Johnny Torres, Creighton | | |

## Coach of the Year

Men's Coach of the Year. Voted on by the National Soccer Coaches Association of America. From 1973-81 all Senior College coaches were eligible. In 1982, the award was split into several divisions. The Division I Coach of the Year is listed since 1982.

**Multiple winner:** Jerry Yeagley (6).

| Year | | Year | | Year | |
|------|--|------|--|------|--|
| 1973 | Robert Guelker, SIU-Edwardsville | 1984 | James Lennox, Hartwick | 1995 | Jim Launder, Wisconsin |
| 1974 | Jack MacKenzie, Quincy College | 1985 | Peter Mehleft, American | 1996 | Dave Masur, St. John's |
| 1975 | Paul Reinhardt, Vermont | 1986 | Steve Parker, Akron | 1997 | Sigi Schmid, UCLA |
| 1976 | Jerry Yeagley, Indiana | 1987 | Anson Dorrance, N. Carolina | 1998 | Jerry Yeagley, Indiana |
| 1977 | Klass Deboer, Cleveland St. | 1988 | Keith Tucker, Howard | 1999 | Jerry Yeagley, Indiana |
| 1978 | Cliff McCrath, Seattle Pacific | 1989 | Steve Sampson, Santa Clara | 2000 | Ray Reid, Connecticut |
| 1979 | Walter Bahr, Penn St. | 1990 | Bob Reasso, Rutgers | 2001 | Elmar Bolowich, North Carolina |
| 1980 | Jerry Yeagley, Indiana | 1991 | Mitch Murray, Santa Clara | 2002 | Tom Fitzgerald, UCLA |
| 1981 | Schellas Hyndman, E. Illinois | 1992 | Charles Slagle, Davidson | 2003 | Jerry Yeagley, Indiana |
| 1982 | John Rennie, Duke | 1993 | Bob Bradley, Princeton | 2004 | Tim Vom Steeg, UCSB |
| 1983 | Dieter Ficken, Columbia | 1994 | Jerry Yeagley, Indiana | | |

# WOMEN
## Hermann Trophy

Women's College Player of the year. Voted on by Division I college coaches and selected sportswriters and first presented in 1988 in the name of Robert Hermann, one of the founders of the North American Soccer League.

**Multiple winners:** Mia Hamm and Cindy Parlow (2).

| Year | | Year | | Year | |
|------|--|------|--|------|--|
| 1988 | Michelle Akers, Central Fla. | 1994 | Tisha Venturini, N. Carolina | 2000 | Anne Makinen, Notre Dame |
| 1989 | Shannon Higgins, N. Carolina | 1995 | Shannon McMillan, Portland | 2001 | Christie Welsh, Penn St. |
| 1990 | April Kater, Massachusetts | 1996 | Cindy Daws, Notre Dame | 2002 | Aly Wagner, Santa Clara |
| 1991 | Kristine Lilly, N. Carolina | 1997 | Cindy Parlow, N. Carolina | 2003 | Catherine Reddick, N. Carolina |
| 1992 | Mia Hamm, N. Carolina | 1998 | Cindy Parlow, N. Carolina | 2004 | Christine Sinclair, Portland |
| 1993 | Mia Hamm, N. Carolina | 1999 | Mandy Clemens, Santa Clara | | |

## Missouri Athletic Club Award

Women's College Player of the Year. Voted on by women's team coaches around the country from Division I to junior college level and first presented in 1991 by the Missouri Athletic Club of St. Louis.

**Multiple winners:** Mia Hamm and Cindy Parlow (2).

| Year | | Year | | Year | |
|------|--|------|--|------|--|
| 1991 | Kristine Lilly, N. Carolina | 1995 | Shannon McMillan, Portland | 1999 | Mandy Clemens, Santa Clara |
| 1992 | Mia Hamm, N. Carolina | 1996 | Cindy Daws, Notre Dame | 2000 | Anne Makinen, Notre Dame |
| 1993 | Mia Hamm, N. Carolina | 1997 | Cindy Parlow, N. Carolina | 2001 | Christie Welsh, Penn St. |
| 1994 | Tisha Venturini, N. Carolina | 1998 | Cindy Parlow, N. Carolina | 2002 | merged with Hermann Trophy. |

## Coach of the Year

Women's Coach of the Year. Voted on by the National Soccer Coaches Association of America. From 1982-87 all Senior College coaches were eligible. In 1988, the award was split into several divisions. The Division I Coach of the Year is listed since 1988.

**Multiple winners:** Anson Dorrance (3); Kalenkeni M. Banda and Chris Petrucelli (2).

| Year | | Year | | Year | |
|------|--|------|--|------|--|
| 1982 | Anson Dorrance, N. Carolina | 1990 | Lauren Gregg, Virginia | 1998 | Becky Burleigh, Florida |
| 1983 | David Lombardo, Keene St. | 1991 | Greg Ryan, Wisc-Madison | 1999 | Patrick Farmer, Penn St. |
| 1984 | Phillip Picince, Brown | 1992 | Bell Hempen, Duke | 2000 | Jillian Ellis, UCLA |
| 1985 | Kalenkeni M. Banda, UMass | 1993 | Jac Cicala, George Mason | 2001 | Jerry Smith, Santa Clara |
| 1986 | Anson Dorrance, N. Carolina | 1994 | Chris Petrucelli, Norte Dame | 2002 | Clive Charles, Portland |
| 1987 | Kalenkeni M. Banda, UMass | 1995 | Chris Petrucelli, Norte Dame | 2003 | Anson Dorrance, N. Carolina |
| 1988 | Larry Gross, N.C. State | 1996 | John Walker, Nebraska | 2004 | Julie Shackford, Princeton |
| 1989 | Austin Daniels, Hartford | 1997 | Len Tsantiris, Connecticut | | |

# Bowling

**Liz Johnson** *made history in 2005, advancing to the finals of the Banquet Open in March.*

PBA Tour

# Patrick's Day

*Patrick Allen breaks out in 2004-05,
winning his first major among his
three Tour victories.*

**Michael Morrison**
*is co-editor of the ESPN Sports Almanac.*

During his first five seasons on the PBA Tour, Patrick Allen's name appeared on the season-ending money list just once (eighth in 2004). He had shown plenty of potential and the ability to perform under pressure with his 2001 win at the Greater Detroit Open, his first Tour victory in his first television appearance. But while he steadily climbed the money list each year since, it just hadn't registered in the win column, as he recorded just one other win since Detroit.

And then came the 2004-05 season. The lefty from Tarrytown, N.Y. enjoyed a career season, winning three tournaments, his first major at the PBA Denny's World Championship in April and earned $350,740, far and away the tops on the season money list.

His earnings for the year were the second-highest in PBA Tour history, behind only Walter Ray Williams Jr. in 2003 ($419,700), and more than doubled his combined earnings during his first five seasons on the Tour.

Allen also proved he had a knack for bowling well in the season's biggest tournaments, finishing in the top five in each of the four majors. He was runner-up in the first two major events of the season, losing to Danny Wiseman, 268-183, in the finals of the Miller High Life Masters in October 2004, then losing the championship match of the U.S. Open by a single pin to Chris Barnes, 213-212.

At the World Championship in Michigan, he finally broke through. After defeating Jason Couch in the round of eight, Allen struck 11 times to soundly defeat Mike Scroggins, 279-198, in the semis, setting up a championship match with 24-year-old Chris Loschetter. With six consecutive strikes in frames three through eight, Allen gave himself a 23-pin cushion heading into the final frame. It was simply too much for Loschetter to overcome and Allen came away with the 235-210 victory, in the process becoming the first lefty to win the World

PBA Tour

***Tommy Jones***, *left, and **Patrick Allen**, right, rose to the top of the PBA Tour in 2004-05 with a combined seven wins and almost $575,000 in earnings.*

Championship since Eric Forkel in 1992. It also earned him a coveted four-year exemption, assuring him a spot on the PBA Tour through 2008-09.

Allen's other two victories in 2005 came in Dallas and Birmingham in consecutive weeks in January as he became the first bowler since Williams Jr. in 2000 (and first lefty since Parker Bohn III) to win back-to-back titles.

His three wins made him the frontrunner for the PBA Player of the Year Award, named for Chris Schenkel, ABC's voice of the PBA Tour from 1962-97, who died in September 2005 at 82.

Allen was hardly a shoo-in however.

In fact, South Carolina's Tommy Jones did Allen one better, winning four tournaments, to make him the Tour's first four-time winner since Bohn in 2001-02. They were the first four wins of his five-year PBA Tour career.

Jones won early and often in 2004-05, opening the year with a victory at the Japan Cup. He made it to four championship rounds and won them all. He followed his win in Japan with a December win in Denver, a February win at the Cambridge Credit Classic and finally at the Banquet Open in March over runner-up Liz Johnson, who made plenty of headlines of her own in 2004-05.

PBA Tour

**PBA Tour trucks** made their way throughout the country in 2005, carrying bowlers' equipment from Tour stop to Tour stop.

Earlier in the season at the Uniroyal Tire Classic, Johnson became the first woman to qualify for a PBA event. At the Banquet Open, she essentially made that record obsolete, defeating Barnes, Mike DeVaney, Richard Wolfe and Wes Malott to advance to the Finals.

Ultimately she lost to Jones, 219-192, but served notice that although the PWBA may have disbanded in 2003, women can most certainly compete with men at bowling's highest level.

Jones went 8-0 in televised rounds in 2004-05 and earned $224,130 (behind only Allen). Like Allen, he earned more in one season than he had over the rest of his career.

With both Allen and Jones enjoying breakout years and perennial stars Barnes and Steve Jaros each winning their first major — Jaros' coming at the season-ending Tournament of Champions — award voters had their work cut out for them.

In the end, however, they chose Allen's three wins *with* a major over Jones' four wins *without* one. Surely his gaudy earnings for the year didn't hurt.

"I take a lot of pride in this award because there are a lot of great players that have never won it," said Allen.

"Bowling on Tour is a lot more difficult than I ever imagined...but hard work can pay off."

And then some.

# The Ten Biggest Stories of the Year in Bowling

**10** An annual report by the National Federation of State High School Associations (NFSH) shows bowling as the fastest growing high school sport in the country. Boys participation grew 16.3 percent from 2004 to 2005 while the number of high school girls bowling increased 15.6 percent.

**9** *A League of Ordinary Gentlemen*, billed as "The Definitive Documentary on Professional Bowling," opens in the Fall of 2005 to excellent reviews. The film discusses bowling's changing (and not always positive) reputation throughout the years and follows bowlers Walter Ray Williams Jr., Pete Weber, Chris Barnes and Wayne Webb and then-President & CEO Steve Miller during the 2003 season.

**8** The inaugural Motel 6 Roll to Riches takes place in Fort Worth, Texas in April and offers a winner-take-all $200,000 first prize, highest in league history. Only the Tour's four major winners, plus two players selected by fan vote, are allowed to compete. Chris Barnes defeats Tommy Jones in the finals, boosting his season-long money haul to $394,300. Since it's an unofficial PBA event, however, the cash doesn't count towards his official earnings.

**7** Former PWBA star and two-time BWAA women's bowler of the year Carolyn Dorin-Ballard throws back-to-back 300 games at a PBA Regional Tour event in August, becoming the first woman with consecutive perfect games in PBA history.

**6** Hall of Famers end their streaks. On January 16, Parker Bohn III won the El Paso Classic, ending his 51-event winless streak. It is his first title since 2002 and the 30th of his career. Not to be outdone, one month later Amleto Monacelli ends a seven-year, 125-event winless streak with his title at the Jackson Hewitt Tax Service Open.

**5** It's a pretty quiet year for Walter Ray Williams Jr. — by *his* standards. His only win of the season (at the Uniroyal Tire Classic) gives him 40 for his career, one behind all-time leader Earl Anthony. Williams' 227.07 average is the second best season-long average in Tour history. The two-sport star also places second at the World Horseshoe Pitching tournament in July — throwing *lefty*. The six-time World Horseshoe champ was trying to become the first person to win the title with his right hand and his left hand.

**4**     The PBA and Denny's agree to an historic three-year, multi-million dollar sponsorship deal in early October, marking the first time the PBA will have a title sponsor. Among other things, the Tour will be promoted in 1,600 Denny's restaurants while Denny's will continue to serve as the "official restaurant" of the PBA.

**3**     The bowling community suffers two major losses in 2005. Dick Weber, winner of 26 PBA titles and six more on the Senior Tour, dies on February 13. And Chris Schenkel, voice of the PBA on ABC for over 30 years and the namesake of the Tour's Player of the Year award, dies on September 11. Both are members of the PBA Hall of Fame.

**2**     In November 2004, Liz Johnson of Cheektowaga, N.Y. becomes the first woman to qualify for a PBA event by finishing fourth in the qualifying round of the Uniroyal Tire Classic. She loses in the Round of 64, but four months later at the Banquet Open, she advances all the way to the Finals before losing to Tommy Jones.

**1**     Patrick Allen wins consecutive tournaments in Dallas and Birmingham, then defeats Chris Loschetter in the finals of the PBA Denny's World Championship for his first major title. He earns a Tour-leading $350,740 for the year and wins the Chris Schenkel Award as the 2004-05 PBA Player of the Year.

## INSIDE the numbers

### A Long Time Comin'

Well it's about time! The four major tournament winners in 2004-05 all recorded the first major titles of their careers. They combined for 25 regular PBA titles before their major wins.

**Stats prior to first Major win**

|  | Seasons | Events | Wins |
| --- | --- | --- | --- |
| Danny Wiseman | 16 | 378 | 10 |
| Chris Barnes | 6 | 155 | 5 |
| Patrick Allen | 5 | 105 | 4 |
| Steve Jaros | 20 | 378 | 6 |
| TOTAL | 47 | 1,016 | 25 |

**Source:** Professional Bowlers Association

*Chris Barnes defeated Patrick Allen by a single pin, 213-212, in the Finals of the U.S. Open on February 20.* **Did you know**, *the largest margin of victory on the PBA Tour is 172 pins — when Larry Laub beat Mark Estes, 299-118, in 1975.*

# 2004-2005
# *Season in Review*

SPORTS ALMANAC

## Tournament Results

Winners of stepladder finals in all PBA and Senior PBA tournaments from Sept. 15, 2004 through Sept. 28, 2005; major tournaments in **bold** type.

## PBA
### 2004-05 Season

| Final | Event | Winner | Earnings | Score | Runner-up |
|---|---|---|---|---|---|
| Sept. 20 | Dydo Drinco Japan Cup | Tommy Jones | $50,000 | 195-169 | Minoru Sendan |
| Oct. 31 | **Miller High Life Masters** | Danny Wiseman | 100,000 | 268-183 | Patrick Allen |
| | presented by the American Bowling Congress | | | | |
| Nov. 7 | Chicago Open | Brian Himmler | 40,000 | 277-217 | Brian Voss |
| Nov. 14 | Uniroyal Tire Classic | Walter Ray Williams Jr. | 40,000 | 268-248 | Doug Kent |
| Nov. 21 | BowlersParadise.com Open | Rick Lawrence | 40,000 | 233-198 | Brad Angelo |
| Nov. 28 | Pepsi Open | Jason Hurd | 40,000 | 226-190 | Mike Edwards |
| Dec. 5 | Denver Open | Tommy Jones | 40,000 | 224-179 | Brian Voss |
| Dec. 12 | Earl Anthony Medford Classic | Mike Wolfe | 40,000 | 214-212 | Norm Duke |
| Dec. 19 | Orange County Classic | Brian Voss | 40,000 | 226-181 | Michael Machuga |
| Jan. 9 | Geico Open | Mika Koivuniemi | 40,000 | 200-196 | Parker Bohn III |
| Jan. 16 | El Paso Classic | Parker Bohn III | 40,000 | 288-235 | Robert Smith |
| Jan. 23 | Dallas Open | Patrick Allen | 40,000 | 267-183 | Brad Angelo |
| Jan. 30 | Birmingham Open | Patrick Allen | 40,000 | 218-216 | Mike DeVaney |
| Feb. 6 | Atlanta Classic | Norm Duke | 40,000 | 246-226 | Ryan Shafer |
| Feb. 13 | Jackson Hewitt Tax Service Open | Amleto Monacelli | 40,000 | 215-195 | David Traber |
| Feb. 20 | **U.S. Open** | Chris Barnes | 100,000 | 213-212 | Patrick Allen |
| | presented by Odor-Eaters | | | | |
| Feb. 27 | Cambridge Credit Classic | Tommy Jones | 40,000 | 266-217 | Tony Reyes |
| Mar. 6 | Baby Ruth Real Deal Classic | Mika Koivuniemi | 40,000 | 267-226 | Jim Pratt |
| Mar. 20 | Banquet Open | Tommy Jones | 40,000 | 219-192 | Liz Johnson |
| Apr. 3 | **PBA Denny's World Championship** | Patrick Allen | 120,000 | 235-210 | Christopher Loschetter |
| Apr. 10 | **Dexter Tournament of Champions** | Steve Jaros | 100,000 | 248-242 | Norm Duke |
| Apr. 14 | Motel 6 Roll to Riches | Chris Barnes | 200,000 | —* | Tommy Jones |

*The Motel 6 Roll to Riches is not an official PBA Tour event. It is a winner-take-all showdown between the season's four major winners, along with two players selected by fan vote (Norm Duke and Tommy Jones). In the final match, the first bowler with six strikes wins.

## 2005-06 PBA Tour Schedule

Major tournaments are in **bold** type. See Updates chapter for results through late-October.

**September—**Dydo Drinco Japan Cup, Yokohama, JPN (Sept. 14-17).

**October—**Tulsa Championship, Owasso, Okla. (Oct. 26-30).

**November—**Mile High Classic, Lakewood, Colo (Nov. 2-6); Greater Omaha Classic, Council Bluffs, Iowa (Nov. 9-13); **Miller High Life USBC Masters**, Milwaukee, Wis. (Nov. 14-20); Chicago Classic, Vernon Hills, Ill. (Nov. 23-27).

**December—**BowlersParadise.com Classic, Hammond, Ind. (Nov. 30-Dec. 4); Keystone State Championship, Mechanicsburg, Penn. (Dec. 7-11); Empire State Classic, Clifton Park, N.Y. (Dec. 14-18).

**January 2005—**Earl Anthony Medford Classic, Medford, Ore. (Jan. 4-8); Dick Weber Open, Fountain Valley, Calif. (Jan. 10-15); Phoenix Classic, Phoenix, Ariz. (Jan. 18-22); Southern Classic, Trussville, Ala. (Jan. 25-29).

**February—**Atlanta Classic, Norcross, Ga. (Feb. 1-5); West Virginia Championship, Parkersburg, W.V. (Feb. 8-12); **U.S. Open**, North Brunswick, N.J. (Feb. 12-19); Northeast Championship, Cheektowaga, N.Y. (Feb. 22-26).

**March—**Pepsi Championship, Fairlawn, Ohio (Mar. 1-5); Motor City Classic, Taylor, Mich. (Mar. 15-19); **PBA Denny's World Championship**, Indianapolis, Ind. (Mar. 20-26).

**April—**Great Lakes Classic, Grand Rapids, Mich. (Mar. 29-Apr. 2); **Dexter Tournament of Champions**, Uncasville, Conn. (Apr. 5-9).

## Tournament Results (Cont.)

## PBA Majors

### Miller High Life Masters presented by the American Bowling Congress

**Edition:** 55th  **Dates:** Oct. 24-31, 2004
**Site:** Miller Park in Milwaukee, Wis. (finals)
**Prize Fund:** $350,000

#### Championship Round

| | | Total pins | Earnings |
|---|---|---|---|
| 1 | Danny Wiseman | 268 (1 game) | $100,000 |
| 2 | Patrick Allen | 669 (3 games) | 50,000 |
| 3 | Patrick Healey Jr. | 219 (1 game) | 25,000 |
| 4 | Brian Boghosian | 183 (1 game) | 15,000 |

**Playoff Results:** Allen def. Boghosian, 238-153; Allen def. Healey Jr., 248-219; and in the championship game, Wiseman def. Allen, 268-183.

### PBA Denny's World Championship

**Edition:** 46th  **Dates:** Mar. 26-Apr. 3, 2005
**Site:** Taylor Lanes in Taylor, Mich.
**Prize Fund:** $438,000

#### Championship Round

| | | Total pins | Earnings |
|---|---|---|---|
| 1 | Patrick Allen | 514 (2 games) | $120,000 |
| 2 | Chris Loschetter | 441 (2 games) | 50,000 |
| 3 | Brian Voss | 165 (1 game) | 20,000 |
| | Mike Scroggins | 198 (1 game) | 20,000 |

**Playoff Results:** Loschetter def. Voss, 231-165; Allen def. Scroggins, 279-198; and in the championship game, Allen def. Loschetter, 235-210.

### U.S. Open presented by Odor-Eaters

**Edition:** 62nd  **Dates:** Feb. 13-20, 2005
**Site:** Brunswick Zone Carolier in North Brunswick, N.J.
**Prize Fund:** $350,000

#### Championship Round

| | | Total pins | Earnings |
|---|---|---|---|
| 1 | Chris Barnes | 213 (1 game) | $100,000 |
| 2 | Patrick Allen | 406 (2 games) | 50,000 |
| 3 | Mika Koivuniemi | 194 (1 game) | 25,000 |
| 4 | Walter Ray Williams Jr. | 179 (1 game) | 15,000 |

**Playoff Results:** Koivuniemi def. Williams Jr., 212-179; Allen def. Koivuniemi, 194-194 (18-17 in sudden death roll-off), and in the championship game, Barnes def. Allen, 213-212.

### Dexter Tournament of Champions

**Edition:** 39th  **Dates:** Apr. 6-10, 2005
**Site:** Mohegan Sun in Uncasville, Conn.
**Prize Fund:** $230,000

#### Championship Round

| | | Total pins | Earnings |
|---|---|---|---|
| 1 | Steve Jaros | 495 (2 games) | $100,000 |
| 2 | Norm Duke | 498 (2 games) | 30,000 |
| 3 | Randy Pedersen | 255 (1 game) | 10,000 |
| | Bryan Goebel | 186 (1 game) | 10,000 |

**Playoff Results:** Jaros def. Goebel, 247-186; Duke def. Pedersen, 256-255; and in the championship game, Jaros def. Duke, 248-242.

## Senior PBA

### 2005 Spring/Summer Tour

| Final | Event | Winner | Earnings | Score | Runner-up |
|---|---|---|---|---|---|
| Apr. 20 | Empire State Open | Henry Gonzalez | $8,000 | 2 games to 1 | Vince Mazzanti Jr. |
| Apr. 27 | Clarksville Open | Dale Eagle | 8,000 | 2 games to 0 | Tom Baker |
| May 4 | Chillicothe Open | Bob Glass | 8,000 | 2 games to 1 | Gene Stus |
| May 20 | **Senior U.S. Open** | Tom Baker | 20,000 | 234-214 | Dennis Psaropoulos |
| June 10 | Tuscon Open | Matt Surina | 8,000 | 2 games to 1 | Tom Baker |
| June 16 | **ABC Senior Masters** | Vince Mazzanti Jr. | 20,000 | 697-627 | Robert Glass |
| June 23 | Northern California Classic | Ross Packard | 8,000 | 2 games to 1 | Vince Mazzanti Jr. |
| June 30 | Epicenter Classic | Dale Eagle | 8,000 | 2 games to 0 | Robert Glass |
| Aug. 3 | Manassas Open | Ray Johnson | 8,000 | 2 games to 1 | Guppy Troup |
| Aug. 11 | Lake County Open presented by Storm | Gene Vincent | 8,000 | 2 games to 1 | Roger LeClair |
| Aug. 17 | Jackson Open | Charlie Tapp | 8,000 | 2 games to 1 | Vince Mazzanti Jr. |

**Note:** In 2005, all tournaments on the Senior PBA Tour followed a best-of-three match-play final-round format with the exception of the Senior U.S. Open, which used a traditional step-ladder single-match final round. The ABC Senior Masters used a best-of-three match format, however each match was comprised of three games.

---

### PBA Tour goes exempt in 2004-05

Beginning with the 2004-05 season, the PBA Tour is now structured as an all-exempt field. Each of the 17 standard tournaments (majors not included) are limited to 64 bowlers, 58 of whom have exempt status for the entire Tour season.

Of the 58 who have exemption for the entire season, 47 come directly as a result of their performance during the prior season (17 standard event champions, four major champions and the remaining 26 from season points lists). The remaining 11 season-long qualifiers come from the PBA Tour Trials (in 2005, these were held May 31-June 5 in Merrillville, Ind.).

The other six bowlers (bringing the weekly total to 64) change from week to week. Five come from a "Weekly Qualifier" held on the Wednesday morning of each tournament. The final participant is chosen by the PBA Tour commissioner in what is known as the "Weekly Commissioner Exemption."

## Tour Leaders

Official standings for 2004-05. Note that (TB) indicates Tournaments Bowled; (CR) Championship Rounds as Stepladder or Match-play Finalist; and (1st) Titles Won.

### PBA
### 2004-05

#### Top 10 Money Winners

|   |   | TB | CR | 1st | Earnings |
|---|---|----|----|-----|----------|
| 1 | Patrick Allen | 21 | 5 | 3 | $350,740 |
| 2 | Tommy Jones | 21 | 4 | 4 | 224,130 |
| 3 | Chris Barnes | 21 | 5 | 1 | 194,300 |
| 4 | Danny Wiseman | 21 | 3 | 1 | 186,050 |
| 5 | Mika Koivuniemi | 21 | 4 | 2 | 163,800 |
| 6 | Steve Jaros | 21 | 3 | 1 | 158,000 |
| 7 | Brian Voss | 21 | 5 | 1 | 147,120 |
| 8 | Norm Duke | 20 | 5 | 1 | 142,770 |
| 9 | Walter Ray Williams Jr. | 21 | 5 | 1 | 131,250 |
| 10 | Parker Bohn III | 20 | 2 | 1 | 109,900 |

#### Top 10 Averages

|   |   | TB | Avg |
|---|---|----|-----|
| 1 | Walter Ray Williams Jr. | 21 | 227.07 |
| 2 | Chris Barnes | 21 | 226.69 |
| 3 | Robert Smith | 21 | 224.26 |
| 4 | Jason Couch | 21 | 224.03 |
| 5 | Mika Koivuniemi | 21 | 223.73 |
| 6 | Patrick Allen | 21 | 223.50 |
| 7 | Tommy Jones | 21 | 222.99 |
| 8 | Brad Angelo | 20 | 222.61 |
| 9 | Danny Wiseman | 21 | 221.79 |
| 10 | Tom Baker | 20 | 221.59 |

**Note:** Statistics do not include the Motel 6 Roll to Riches, which is not an official PBA Tour event.

### Senior PBA
### 2005

#### Top 10 Money Winners

|   |   | TB | CR | 1st | Earnings |
|---|---|----|----|-----|----------|
| 1 | Tom Baker | 10 | 3 | 1 | $40,050 |
| 2 | Robert Glass | 11 | 5 | 1 | 38,500 |
| 3 | Vince Mazzanti Jr. | 11 | 4 | 1 | 36,600 |
| 4 | Dale Eagle | 11 | 2 | 2 | 28,800 |
| 5 | Don Sylvia | 11 | 3 | 0 | 19,550 |
| 6 | Henry Gonzalez | 10 | 1 | 1 | 18,270 |
| 7 | Roger Bowker | 9 | 1 | 0 | 15,900 |
| 8 | Roger LeClair | 11 | 2 | 0 | 15,450 |
| 9 | Ron Winger | 11 | 1 | 0 | 14,340 |
| 10 | Roger Kossert | 8 | 1 | 0 | 12,800 |

#### Top 10 Averages

|   |   | TB | Avg |
|---|---|----|-----|
| 1 | Tom Baker | 10 | 226.97 |
| 2 | Robert Glass | 11 | 222.45 |
| 3 | Roger Bowker | 9 | 220.47 |
| 4 | Dale Eagle | 11 | 219.37 |
| 5 | Henry Gonzalez | 10 | 218.84 |
| 6 | Don Sylvia | 11 | 218.06 |
| 7 | John Bennett | 7 | 217.69 |
| 8 | Guppy Troup | 6 | 216.71 |
| 9 | James Brenner | 7 | 216.57 |
| 10 | Ron Winger | 11 | 216.33 |

**Note:** Earnings include ABC Senior Masters.

## Women's Bowling

**Note:** The Professional Women's Bowling Association (PWBA) national tour was cancelled in the fall of 2003 due to a lack of operating funds. There was no national tour in 2005.

## Majors

### WIBC Queens

**Edition:** 45th
**Site:** Riverlanes in Tulsa, Okla.
**Prize Fund:** $167,775
**Dates:** May 14-18, 2005

#### Championship Round

|   |   | Total pins | Earnings |
|---|---|-----------|----------|
| 1 | Tennelle Milligan | 407 (2 games) | $25,000 |
| 2 | Anne Marie Duggan | 622 (3 games) | 20,000 |
| 3 | Jennifer Swanson | 655 (3 games) | 14,500 |
| 4 | Michelle Feldman | 201 (1 game) | 10,500 |
| 5 | Karen Morris | 172 (1 game) | 8,000 |

**Playoff Results:** Swanson def. Morris, 239-172; Swanson def. Feldman, 225-201; Duggan def. Swanson, 266-191; and in the two championship games, Duggan def. Milligan, 219-205, then Milligan def. Duggan, 202-177.

(Since Milligan hadn't lost yet in the double-elimination match play, a second championship game was needed after Duggan def. Milligan in the first.)

**Note:** Beginning in 2006, the WIBC Queens Tournament will be called the USBC Queens Tournament. In 2006 it will be held at the National Bowling Stadium in Reno, Nev., June 17-21, 2006.

## NCAA Women's Bowling Championship

It was like deja vu all over again as Nebraska successfully defended its title at the second annual NCAA Women's Bowling Championship at Wekiva Lanes in Orlando. Like they did in 2004, the Huskers fell behind, two games to one, in the best-of-seven finals against rival Central Missouri State before winning three straight to claim the title, four games to two. Sophomore Amanda Burgoyne averaged 251 through qualifying and was named the tournament's first MVP. Nebraska rolled through the double-elimination tournament with a 4-0 record and finished out the season at 69-8, while Central Missouri State fell to 89-21. Fairleigh Dickinson placed third. (*Orlando, FL; April 14-16, 2005.*)

# 1942-2005
# *Through the Years*

SPORTS ALMANAC

## Major Championships
### MEN
### U.S. Open

Started in 1941 by the Bowling Proprietors' Association of America, 18 years before the founding of the Professional Bowlers Association. Originally the BPAA All-Star Tournament, it became the U.S. Open in 1971.

**Multiple winners:** Don Carter and Dick Weber (4); Dave Husted and Pete Weber (3); Del Ballard Jr., Marshall Holman, Junie McMahon, Connie Schwoegler, Andy Varipapa and Walter Ray Williams Jr. (2).

| Year | | Year | | Year | | Year | |
|---|---|---|---|---|---|---|---|
| 1942 | John Crimmins | 1958 | Don Carter | 1974 | Larry Laub | 1990 | Ron Palombi Jr. |
| 1943 | Connie Schwoegler | 1959 | Billy Welu | 1975 | Steve Neff | 1991 | Pete Weber |
| 1944 | Ned Day | 1960 | Harry Smith | 1976 | Paul Moser | 1992 | Robert Lawrence |
| 1945 | Buddy Bomar | 1961 | Bill Tucker | 1977 | Johnny Petraglia | 1993 | Del Ballard Jr. |
| 1946 | Joe Wilman | 1962 | Dick Weber | 1978 | Nelson Burton Jr. | 1994 | Justin Hromek |
| 1947 | Andy Varipapa | 1963 | Dick Weber | 1979 | Joe Berardi | 1995 | Dave Husted |
| 1948 | Andy Varipapa | 1964 | Bob Strampe | 1980 | Steve Martin | 1996 | Dave Husted |
| 1949 | Connie Schwoegler | 1965 | Dick Weber | 1981 | Marshall Holman | 1997 | Not held |
| 1950 | Junie McMahon | 1966 | Dick Weber | 1982 | Dave Husted | 1998 | Walter Ray Williams Jr. |
| 1951 | Dick Hoover | 1967 | Les Schissler | 1983 | Gary Dickinson | 1999 | Bob Learn Jr. |
| 1952 | Junie McMahon | 1968 | Jim Stefanich | 1984 | Mark Roth | 2000 | Robert Smith |
| 1953 | Don Carter | 1969 | Harry Hardwick | 1985 | Marshall Holman | 2001 | Miko Koivuniemi |
| 1954 | Don Carter | 1970 | Bobby Cooper | 1986 | Steve Cook | 2003 | Walter Ray Williams Jr. |
| 1955 | Steve Nagy | 1971 | Mike Limongello | 1987 | Del Ballard Jr. | 2004 | Pete Weber |
| 1956 | Bill Lillard | 1972 | Don Johnson | 1988 | Pete Weber | 2005 | Chris Barnes |
| 1957 | Don Carter | 1973 | Mike McGrath | 1989 | Mike Aulby | | |

## PBA World Championship

The Professional Bowlers Association was formed in 1958 and its first national championship tournament was held in Memphis in 1960. Formerly known as the PBA National Championship, the name was changed in 2002. The tournament was held in various locations (1960-80), Toledo, Ohio (1981-2002) and Taylor, Mich. (2003–).

**Multiple winners:** Earl Anthony (6); Mike Aulby, Dave Davis, Mike McGrath, Pete Weber, Walter Ray Williams Jr. and Wayne Zahn (2).

| Year | | Year | | Year | | Year | |
|---|---|---|---|---|---|---|---|
| 1960 | Don Carter | 1972 | Johnny Guenther | 1984 | Bob Chamberlain | 1996 | Butch Soper |
| 1961 | Dave Soutar | 1973 | Earl Anthony | 1985 | Mike Aulby | 1997 | Rick Steelsmith |
| 1962 | Carmen Salvino | 1974 | Earl Anthony | 1986 | Tom Crites | 1998 | Pete Weber |
| 1963 | Billy Hardwick | 1975 | Earl Anthony | 1987 | Randy Pedersen | 1999 | Tim Criss |
| 1964 | Bob Strampe | 1976 | Paul Colwell | 1988 | Brian Voss | 2000 | Norm Duke |
| 1965 | Dave Davis | 1977 | Tommy Hudson | 1989 | Pete Weber | 2001 | Walter Ray Williams Jr. |
| 1966 | Wayne Zahn | 1978 | Warren Nelson | 1990 | Jim Pencak | 2002 | Doug Kent |
| 1967 | Dave Davis | 1979 | Mike Aulby | 1991 | Mike Miller | 2003 | Walter Ray Williams Jr. |
| 1968 | Wayne Zahn | 1980 | Johnny Petraglia | 1992 | Eric Forkel | 2004 | Tom Baker |
| 1969 | Mike McGrath | 1981 | Earl Anthony | 1993 | Ron Palombi Jr. | 2005 | Patrick Allen |
| 1970 | Mike McGrath | 1982 | Earl Anthony | 1994 | David Traber | | |
| 1971 | Mike Limongello | 1983 | Earl Anthony | 1995 | Scott Alexander | | |

## Tournament of Champions

Originally the Firestone Tournament of Champions (1965-93), the tournament has also been sponsored by General Tire (1994), Brunswick Corp. (1995-2000) and Dexter (2002–). Held in Akron, Ohio in 1965, then Fairlawn, Ohio (1966-94), Lake Zurich, Ill. (1995-96, 2000), Reno, N.V. (1997), Overland Park, Kan. (1998-99) and Uncasville, Conn. (2002–).

**Multiple winners:** Jason Couch and Mike Durbin (3); Earl Anthony, Dave Davis, Jim Godman, Marshall Holman and Mark Williams (2).

| Year | | Year | | Year | | Year | |
|---|---|---|---|---|---|---|---|
| 1965 | Billy Hardwick | 1975 | Dave Davis | 1985 | Mark Williams | 1995 | Mike Aulby |
| 1966 | Wayne Zahn | 1976 | Marshall Holman | 1986 | Marshall Holman | 1996 | Dave D'Entremont |
| 1967 | Jim Stefanich | 1977 | Mike Berlin | 1987 | Pete Weber | 1997 | John Gant |
| 1968 | Dave Davis | 1978 | Earl Anthony | 1988 | Mark Williams | 1998 | Bryan Goebel |
| 1969 | Jim Godman | 1979 | George Pappas | 1989 | Del Ballard Jr. | 1999 | Jason Couch |
| 1970 | Don Johnson | 1980 | Wayne Webb | 1990 | Dave Ferraro | 2000 | Jason Couch |
| 1971 | Johnny Petraglia | 1981 | Steve Cook | 1991 | David Ozio | 2001 | Not held |
| 1972 | Mike Durbin | 1982 | Mike Durbin | 1992 | Marc McDowell | 2002 | Jason Couch |
| 1973 | Jim Godman | 1983 | Joe Berardi | 1993 | George Branham III | 2003 | Patrick Healey Jr. |
| 1974 | Earl Anthony | 1984 | Mike Durbin | 1994 | Norm Duke | 2005 | Steve Jaros |

## ABC Masters Tournament

Sponsored by the American Bowling Congress, the Masters became an official PBA Tour title event in 1998. It is open to qualified pros and amateurs. **Note:** Beginning in 2006, the tournament will be known as the Miller High Life USBC Masters.

**Multiple winners:** Mike Aulby (3); Earl Anthony, Billy Golembiewski, Dick Hoover and Billy Welu (2).

| Year | | Year | | Year | | Year | |
|------|--|------|--|------|--|------|--|
| 1951 | Lee Jouglard | 1965 | Billy Welu | 1979 | Doug Myers | 1993 | Norm Duke |
| 1952 | Willard Taylor | 1966 | Bob Strampe | 1980 | Neil Burton | 1994 | Steve Fehr |
| 1953 | Rudy Habetler | 1967 | Lou Scalia | 1981 | Randy Lightfoot | 1995 | Mike Aulby |
| 1954 | Red Elkins | 1968 | Pete Tountas | 1982 | Joe Berardi | 1996 | Ernie Schlegel |
| 1955 | Buzz Fazio | 1969 | Jim Chestney | 1983 | Mike Lastowski | 1997 | Jason Queen |
| 1956 | Dick Hoover | 1970 | Don Glover | 1984 | Earl Anthony | 1998 | Mike Aulby |
| 1957 | Dick Hoover | 1971 | Jim Godman | 1985 | Steve Wunderlich | 1999 | Brian Boghosian |
| 1958 | Tom Hennessey | 1972 | Bill Beach | 1986 | Mark Fahy | 2000 | Mika Koivuniemi |
| 1959 | Ray Bluth | 1973 | Dave Soutar | 1987 | Rick Steelsmith | 2001 | Parker Bohn III |
| 1960 | Billy Golembiewski | 1974 | Paul Colwell | 1988 | Del Ballard Jr. | 2002 | Brett Wolfe |
| 1961 | Don Carter | 1975 | Eddie Ressler Jr. | 1989 | Mike Aulby | 2003 | Bryon Smith |
| 1962 | Billy Golembiewski | 1976 | Nelson Burton Jr. | 1990 | Chris Warren | 2004*| Walter Ray Williams Jr. |
| 1963 | Harry Smith | 1977 | Earl Anthony | 1991 | Doug Kent | 2004*| Danny Wiseman |
| 1964 | Billy Welu | 1978 | Frank Ellenburg | 1992 | Ken Johnson | *held Jan. and Oct., 2004 | |

## WOMEN
## U.S. Open

Started by the Bowling Proprietors' Association of America in 1949. Originally the BPAA Women's All-Star Tournament (1949-70); and U.S. Open from 1971-2003. There were two BPAA All-Star tournaments in 1955, in January and December.

**Multiple winners:** Marion Ladewig (8); Donna Adamek, Paula Sperber Carter, Pat Costello, Dotty Fothergill, Dana Miller-Mackie, Aleta Sill and Sylvia Wene (2).

| Year | | Year | | Year | | Year | |
|------|--|------|--|------|--|------|--|
| 1949 | Marion Ladewig | 1963 | Marion Ladewig | 1978 | Donna Adamek | 1993 | Dede Davidson |
| 1950 | Marion Ladewig | 1964 | LaVerne Carter | 1979 | Diana Silva | 1994 | Aleta Sill |
| 1951 | Marion Ladewig | 1965 | Ann Slattery | 1980 | Patty Costello | 1995 | Cheryl Daniels |
| 1952 | Marion Ladewig | 1966 | Joy Abel | 1981 | Donna Adamek | 1996 | Liz Johnson |
| 1953 | Not held | 1967 | Gloria Simon | 1982 | Shinobu Saitoh | 1997 | Not held |
| 1954 | Marion Ladewig | 1968 | Dotty Fothergill | 1983 | Dana Miller | 1998 | Aleta Sill |
| 1955 | Sylvia Wene | 1969 | Dotty Fothergill | 1984 | Karen Ellingsworth | 1999 | Kim Adler |
| 1955 | Anita Cantaline | 1970 | Mary Baker | 1985 | Pat Mercatanti | 2000 | Tennelle Grijalva |
| 1956 | Marion Ladewig | 1971 | Paula Sperber | 1986 | Wendy Macpherson | 2001 | Kim Terrell |
| 1957 | Not held | 1972 | Lorrie Koch | 1987 | Carol Norman | 2002 | Not held |
| 1958 | Merle Matthews | 1973 | Millie Martorella | 1988 | Lisa Wagner | 2003 | Kelly Kulick |
| 1959 | Marion Ladewig | 1974 | Patty Costello | 1989 | Robin Romeo | 2004 | discontinued |
| 1960 | Sylvia Wene | 1975 | Paula Sperber Carter | 1990 | Dana Miller-Mackie | | |
| 1961 | Phyllis Notaro | 1976 | Patty Costello | 1991 | Anne Marie Duggan | | |
| 1962 | Shirley Garms | 1977 | Betty Morris | 1992 | Tish Johnson | | |

## WIBC Queens

Sponsored by the Women's International Bowling Congress, the Queens is open to qualified pros and amateurs. **Note:** Beginning in 2006, the tournament will be known as the USBC Queens, sponsored by the United States Bowling Congress.

**Multiple winners:** Wendy Macpherson and Millie Martorella (3); Donna Adamek, Dotty Fothergill, Aleta Sill and Katsuko Sugimoto (2).

| Year | | Year | | Year | | Year | |
|------|--|------|--|------|--|------|--|
| 1961 | Janet Harman | 1973 | Dotty Fothergill | 1985 | Aleta Sill | 1997 | Sandra Jo Odom |
| 1962 | Dorothy Wilkinson | 1974 | Judy Soutar | 1986 | Cora Fiebig | 1998 | Lynda Norry |
| 1963 | Irene Monterosso | 1975 | Cindy Powell | 1987 | Cathy Almeida | 1999 | Leanne Barrette |
| 1964 | D.D. Jacobson | 1976 | Pam Rutherford | 1988 | Wendy Macpherson | 2000 | Wendy Macpherson |
| 1965 | Betty Kuczynski | 1977 | Dana Stewart | 1989 | Carol Gianotti | 2001 | Carolyn Dorin-Ballard |
| 1966 | Judy Lee | 1978 | Loa Boxberger | 1990 | Patty Ann | 2002 | Kim Terrell |
| 1967 | Millie Martorella | 1979 | Donna Adamek | 1991 | Dede Davidson | 2003 | Wendy Macpherson |
| 1968 | Phyllis Massey | 1980 | Donna Adamek | 1992 | Cindy Coburn-Carroll | 2004 | Marianne DiRupo |
| 1969 | Ann Feigel | 1981 | Katsuko Sugimoto | 1993 | Jan Schmidt | 2005 | Tennelle Milligan |
| 1970 | Millie Martorella | 1982 | Katsuko Sugimoto | 1994 | Anne Marie Duggan | | |
| 1971 | Millie Martorella | 1983 | Aleta Sill | 1995 | Sandra Postma | | |
| 1972 | Dotty Fothergill | 1984 | Kazue Inahashi | 1996 | Lisa Wagner | | |

## WPBA National Championship (1960-1980)

The Women's Professional Bowling Association National Championship tournament was discontinued when the WPBA broke up in 1981. The WPBA changed its name from the Professional Women Bowlers Association (PWBA) in 1978.

**Multiple winners:** Patty Costello (3); Dotty Fothergill (2).

| Year | | Year | | Year | | Year | |
|------|--|------|--|------|--|------|--|
| 1960 | Marion Ladewig | 1966 | Judy Lee | 1972 | Patty Costello | 1978 | Toni Gillard |
| 1961 | Shirley Garms | 1967 | Betty Mivelaz | 1973 | Betty Morris | 1979 | Cindy Coburn |
| 1962 | Stephanie Balogh | 1968 | Dotty Fothergill | 1974 | Pat Costello | 1980 | Donna Adamek |
| 1963 | Janet Harman | 1969 | Dotty Fothergill | 1975 | Pam Buckner | | |
| 1964 | Betty Kuczynski | 1970 | Bobbe North | 1976 | Patty Costello | | |
| 1965 | Helen Duval | 1971 | Patty Costello | 1977 | Vesma Grinfelds | | |

## Annual Leaders
### Average
#### PBA Tour

The George Young Memorial Award, named after the late ABC Hall of Fame bowler. Based on at least 16 national PBA tournaments from 1959-78, and at least 400 games of tour competition since 1979.

**Multiple winners:** Mark Roth and Walter Ray Williams Jr. (6); Earl Anthony (5); Marshall Holman (3); Parker Bohn III, Norm Duke, Billy Hardwick, Don Johnson and Wayne Zahn (2).

| Year | Avg | Year | Avg | Year | Avg |
|---|---|---|---|---|---|
| 1962 Don Carter | 212.84 | 1977 Mark Roth | 218.17 | 1992 Dave Ferraro | 219.70 |
| 1963 Billy Hardwick | 210.35 | 1978 Mark Roth | 219.83 | 1993 Walter Ray Williams Jr. | 222.98 |
| 1964 Ray Bluth | 210.51 | 1979 Mark Roth | 221.66 | 1994 Norm Duke | 222.83 |
| 1965 Dick Weber | 211.90 | 1980 Earl Anthony | 218.54 | 1995 Mike Aulby | 225.49 |
| 1966 Wayne Zahn | 208.63 | 1981 Mark Roth | 216.70 | 1996 Walter Ray Williams Jr. | 225.37 |
| 1967 Wayne Zahn | 212.14 | 1982 Marshall Holman | 216.15 | 1997 Walter Ray Williams Jr. | 222.00 |
| 1968 Jim Stefanich | 211.90 | 1983 Earl Anthony | 216.65 | 1998 Walter Ray Williams Jr. | 226.13 |
| 1969 Billy Hardwick | 212.96 | 1984 Marshall Holman | 213.91 | 1999 Parker Bohn III | 228.04 |
| 1970 Nelson Burton Jr. | 214.91 | 1985 Mark Baker | 213.72 | 2000 Chris Barnes | 220.93 |
| 1971 Don Johnson | 213.98 | 1986 John Gant | 214.38 | 2002 Parker Bohn III | 221.54 |
| 1972 Don Johnson | 215.29 | 1987 Marshall Holman | 216.80 | 2003 Walter Ray Williams Jr. | 224.94 |
| 1973 Earl Anthony | 215.80 | 1988 Mark Roth | 218.04 | 2004 Mika Koivuniemi | 222.73 |
| 1974 Earl Anthony | 219.34 | 1989 Pete Weber | 215.43 | 2005 Walter Ray Williams Jr. | 227.07 |
| 1975 Earl Anthony | 219.06 | 1990 Amleto Monacelli | 218.16 | | |
| 1976 Mark Roth | 215.97 | 1991 Norm Duke | 218.21 | | |

**Note:** After its first nine events of 2001, the PBA instituted a new September-to-March schedule with the statistics for those first nine tournaments rolled over into players' final 2001-02 statistics.

#### PWBA Tour

The Professional Women's Bowling Association (PWBA) went by the name Ladies Professional Bowling Tour (LPBT) from 1981-97 and the Women's Professional Bowling Association prior to that. This table is based on at least 282 games of tour competition, with the expection of 2003 when the minimum was 122 games. In 2003 the fall season was unexpectedly cancelled, shortening the year to eight tournaments. There was no PWBA Tour in 2004 or 2005.

**Multiple winners:** Leanne Barrette (4); Nikki Gianulias, Wendy Macpherson and Lisa Rathgeber Wagner (3); Carolyn Dorin-Ballard, Anne Marie Duggan and Aleta Sill (2).

| Year | Avg | Year | Avg | Year | Avg |
|---|---|---|---|---|---|
| 1981 Nikki Gianulias | 213.71 | 1989 Lisa Wagner | 211.87 | 1997 Wendy Macpherson | 214.68 |
| 1982 Nikki Gianulias | 210.63 | 1990 Leanne Barrette | 211.53 | 1998 Dede Davidson | 217.25 |
| 1983 Lisa Rathgeber | 208.50 | 1991 Leanne Barrette | 211.48 | 1999 Wendy Macpherson | 218.85 |
| 1984 Aleta Sill | 210.68 | 1992 Leanne Barrette | 211.36 | 2000 Cara Honeychurch | 215.18 |
| 1985 Aleta Sill | 211.10 | 1993 Tish Johnson | 215.39 | 2001 Carolyn Dorin-Ballard | 214.73 |
| 1986 Nikki Gianulias | 213.89 | 1994 Anne Marie Duggan | 213.47 | 2002 Leanne Barrette | 216.45 |
| 1987 Wendy Macpherson | 211.11 | 1995 Anne Marie Duggan | 215.79 | 2003 Carolyn Dorin-Ballard | 215.22 |
| 1988 Lisa Wagner | 213.02 | 1996 Tammy Turner | 215.23 | | |

## Money Won
### PBA Tour

**Multiple winners:** Earl Anthony and Walter Ray Williams Jr. (6); Mark Roth and Dick Weber (4); Mike Aulby (3); Parker Bohn III, Don Carter and Norm Duke (2).

| Year | Earnings | Year | Earnings | Year | Earnings |
|---|---|---|---|---|---|
| 1959 Dick Weber | $7,672 | 1975 Earl Anthony | $107,585 | 1991 David Ozio | $225,585 |
| 1960 Don Carter | 22,525 | 1976 Earl Anthony | 110,833 | 1992 Marc McDowell | 176,215 |
| 1961 Dick Weber | 26,280 | 1977 Mark Roth | 105,583 | 1993 Walter Ray Williams Jr. | 296,370 |
| 1962 Don Carter | 49,972 | 1978 Mark Roth | 134,500 | 1994 Norm Duke | 273,752 |
| 1963 Dick Weber | 46,333 | 1979 Mark Roth | 124,517 | 1995 Mike Aulby | 219,792 |
| 1964 Bob Strampe | 33,592 | 1980 Wayne Webb | 116,700 | 1996 Walter Ray Williams Jr. | 244,630 |
| 1965 Dick Weber | 47,675 | 1981 Earl Anthony | 164,735 | 1997 Walter Ray Williams Jr. | 240,544 |
| 1966 Wayne Zahn | 54,720 | 1982 Earl Anthony | 134,760 | 1998 Walter Ray Williams Jr. | 238,225 |
| 1967 Dave Davis | 54,165 | 1983 Earl Anthony | 135,605 | 1999 Parker Bohn III | 232,595 |
| 1968 Jim Stefanich | 67,375 | 1984 Mark Roth | 158,712 | 2000 Norm Duke | 136,900 |
| 1969 Billy Hardwick | 64,160 | 1985 Mike Aulby | 201,200 | 2002 Parker Bohn III | 245,200 |
| 1970 Mike McGrath | 52,049 | 1986 Walter Ray Williams Jr. | 145,550 | 2003 Walter Ray Williams Jr. | 419,700 |
| 1971 Johnny Petraglia | 85,065 | 1987 Pete Weber | 179,516 | 2004 Mika Koivuniemi | 238,590 |
| 1972 Don Johnson | 56,648 | 1988 Brian Voss | 225,485 | 2005 Patrick Allen | 350,740 |
| 1973 Don McCune | 69,000 | 1989 Mike Aulby | 298,237 | | |
| 1974 Earl Anthony | 99,585 | 1990 Amleto Monacelli | 204,775 | | |

**Note:** After its first nine events of 2001, the PBA instituted a new September-to-March schedule with the statistics for those first nine tournaments rolled over into players' final 2001-02 statistics.

## WPBA and PWBA Tours

WPBA leaders through 1980; PWBA leaders since 1981. Totals include the WIBC Queens, but do not include TV incentives. In 2003 the fall season was unexpectedly cancelled, shortening the year to eight tournaments. There was no PWBA Tour in 2004 or 2005.

**Multiple winners:** Aleta Sill (6); Donna Adamek and Wendy Macpherson (4); Patty Costello, Tish Johnson and Betty Morris (3); Carolyn Dorin-Ballard and Dotty Fothergill (2).

| Year | Earnings | Year | Earnings | Year | Earnings |
|---|---|---|---|---|---|
| 1965 Betty Kuczynski | $ 3,792 | 1978 Donna Adamek | $31,000 | 1991 Leanne Barrette | $87,618 |
| 1966 Joy Abel | 5,795 | 1979 Donna Adamek | 26,280 | 1992 Tish Johnson | 96,872 |
| 1967 Shirley Garms | 4,920 | 1980 Donna Adamek | 31,907 | 1993 Aleta Sill | 57,995 |
| 1968 Dotty Fothergill | 16,170 | 1981 Donna Adamek | 41,270 | 1994 Aleta Sill | 126,325 |
| 1969 Dotty Fothergill | 9,220 | 1982 Nikki Gianulias | 45,875 | 1995 Tish Johnson | 123,440 |
| 1970 Patty Costello | 9,317 | 1983 Aleta Sill | 42,525 | 1996 Wendy Macpherson | 107,230 |
| 1971 Vesma Grinfelds | 4,925 | 1984 Aleta Sill | 81,452 | 1997 Wendy Macpherson | 165,425 |
| 1972 Patty Costello | 11,350 | 1985 Aleta Sill | 52,655 | 1998 Carol Gianotti-Block | 150,350 |
| 1973 Judy Cook | 11,200 | 1986 Aleta Sill | 36,212 | 1999 Wendy Macpherson | 86,265 |
| 1974 Betty Morris | 30,037 | 1987 Betty Morris | 55,095 | 2000 Wendy Macpherson | 108,525 |
| 1975 Judy Soutar | 20,395 | 1988 Lisa Wagner | 105,500 | 2001 Carolyn Dorin-Ballard | 135,045 |
| 1976 Patty Costello | 39,585 | 1989 Robin Romeo | 113,750 | 2002 Michelle Feldman | 80,905 |
| 1977 Betty Morris | 23,802 | 1990 Tish Johnson | 94,420 | 2003 Carolyn Dorin-Ballard | 53,750 |

## All-Time Leaders

All-time leading money winners on the PBA and PWBA tours, through Sept. 22, 2005. PBA figures date back to 1959, while PWBA figures include Women's Pro Bowlers Association (WPBA) earnings through 1980. National tour titles are also listed.

## Money Won

### PBA Top 20

| | | Titles | Earnings |
|---|---|---|---|
| 1 | Walter Ray Williams Jr. | 40 | $3,369,632 |
| 2 | Pete Weber | 31 | 2,628,518 |
| 3 | Parker Bohn III | 30 | 2,311,864 |
| 4 | Brian Voss | 23 | 2,202,197 |
| 5 | Mike Aulby | 27 | 2,094,060 |
| 6 | Norm Duke | 22 | 2,025,811 |
| 7 | Amleto Monacelli | 19 | 2,011,543 |
| 8 | Marshall Holman | 22 | 1,699,390 |
| 9 | Dave Husted | 14 | 1,612,723 |
| 10 | Mark Roth | 34 | 1,611,886 |
| 11 | Earl Anthony | 41 | 1,441,061 |
| 12 | Wayne Webb | 20 | 1,399,341 |
| 13 | David Ozio | 11 | 1,387,266 |
| 14 | Tom Baker | 10 | 1,315,752 |
| 15 | Gary Dickinson | 8 | 1,284,806 |
| 16 | Jason Couch | 11 | 1,253,723 |
| 17 | Danny Wiseman | 11 | 1,191,628 |
| 18 | Del Ballard Jr. | 12 | 1,170,232 |
| 19 | Mark Williams | 7 | 1,169,527 |
| 20 | Dave Soutar | 17 | 1,114,537 |

### WPBA-PWBA Top 10

| | | Titles | Earnings |
|---|---|---|---|
| 1 | Wendy Macpherson | 20 | $1,238,960 |
| 2 | Tish Johnson | 25 | 1,098,563 |
| 3 | Aleta Sill | 31 | 1,071,194 |
| 4 | Leanne Barrette | 26 | 1,028,994 |
| 5 | Anne Marie Duggan | 15 | 955,809 |
| 6 | Carol Gianotti-Block | 16 | 918,777 |
| 7 | Carolyn Dorin-Ballard | 20 | 916,477 |
| 8 | Lisa (Rathgeber) Wagner | 32 | 853,796 |
| 9 | Kim Adler | 15 | 827,493 |
| 10 | Cheryl Daniels | 10 | 754,545 |

### Senior PBA Top 5

| | | Titles | Earnings |
|---|---|---|---|
| 1 | Dave Soutar | 7 | $475,415 |
| 2 | Gene Stus | 11 | 471,630 |
| 3 | Gary Dickinson | 11 | 452,346 |
| 4 | John Handegard | 14 | 444,593 |
| 5 | Teata Semiz | 8 | 405,213 |

## Annual Awards
### MEN
### BWAA Bowler of the Year

Winners selected by Bowling Writers Association of America.

**Multiple winners:** Walter Ray Williams Jr. (8); Earl Anthony and Don Carter (6); Mark Roth (4); Mike Aulby and Dick Weber (3); Parker Bohn III, Buddy Bomar, Ned Day, Norm Duke, Billy Hardwick, Don Johnson and Steve Nagy (2).

| Year | | Year | | Year | | Year | |
|---|---|---|---|---|---|---|---|
| 1942 | John Crimmins | 1958 | Don Carter | 1974 | Earl Anthony | 1990 | Amleto Monacelli |
| 1943 | Ned Day | 1959 | Ed Lubanski | 1975 | Earl Anthony | 1991 | David Ozio |
| 1944 | Ned Day | 1960 | Don Carter | 1976 | Earl Anthony | 1992 | Marc McDowell |
| 1945 | Buddy Bomar | 1961 | Dick Weber | 1977 | Mark Roth | 1993 | Walter Ray Williams Jr. |
| 1946 | Joe Wilman | 1962 | Don Carter | 1978 | Mark Roth | 1994 | Norm Duke |
| 1947 | Buddy Bomar | 1963 | Dick Weber | 1979 | Mark Roth | 1995 | Mike Aulby |
| 1948 | Andy Varipapa | 1964 | Billy Hardwick | 1980 | Wayne Webb | 1996 | Walter Ray Williams Jr. |
| 1949 | Connie Schwoegler | 1965 | Dick Weber | 1981 | Earl Anthony | 1997 | Walter Ray Williams Jr. |
| 1950 | Junie McMahon | 1966 | Wayne Zahn | 1982 | Earl Anthony | 1998 | Walter Ray Williams Jr. |
| 1951 | Lee Jouglard | 1967 | Dave Davis | 1983 | Earl Anthony | 1999 | Parker Bohn III |
| 1952 | Steve Nagy | 1968 | Jim Stefanich | 1984 | Mark Roth | 2000 | Norm Duke |
| 1953 | Don Carter | 1969 | Billy Hardwick | 1985 | Mike Aulby | 2001 | Parker Bohn III |
| 1954 | Don Carter | 1970 | Nelson Burton Jr. | 1986 | Walter Ray Williams Jr. | 2002 | Walter Ray Williams Jr. |
| 1955 | Steve Nagy | 1971 | Don Johnson | 1987 | Marshall Holman | 2003 | Walter Ray Williams Jr. |
| 1956 | Bill Lillard | 1972 | Don Johnson | 1988 | Brian Voss | 2004 | Walter Ray Williams Jr. |
| 1957 | Don Carter | 1973 | Don McCune | 1989 | Mike Aulby | | |

## Annual Awards (Cont.)
### PBA Player of the Year

Named after longtime broadcaster Chris Schenkel, winners are selected by members of Professional Bowlers Association. The PBA Player of the Year has differed from the BWAA Bowler of the Year four times–in 1963, '64, '89 and '92.

**Multiple winners:** Earl Anthony and Walter Ray Williams Jr. (6); Mark Roth (4); Mike Aulby, Parker Bohn III, Norm Duke, Billy Hardwick, Don Johnson and Amleto Monacelli (2).

| Year | | Year | | Year | | Year | |
|------|--|------|--|------|--|------|--|
| 1963 | Billy Hardwick | 1974 | Earl Anthony | 1985 | Mike Aulby | 1996 | Walter Ray Williams Jr. |
| 1964 | Bob Strampe | 1975 | Earl Anthony | 1986 | Walter Ray Williams Jr. | 1997 | Walter Ray Williams Jr. |
| 1965 | Dick Weber | 1976 | Earl Anthony | 1987 | Marshall Holman | 1998 | Walter Ray Williams Jr. |
| 1966 | Wayne Zahn | 1977 | Mark Roth | 1988 | Brian Voss | 1999 | Parker Bohn III |
| 1967 | Dave Davis | 1978 | Mark Roth | 1989 | Amleto Monacelli | 2000 | Norm Duke |
| 1968 | Jim Stefanich | 1979 | Mark Roth | 1990 | Amleto Monacelli | 2002 | Parker Bohn III |
| 1969 | Billy Hardwick | 1980 | Wayne Webb | 1991 | David Ozio | 2003 | Walter Ray Williams Jr. |
| 1970 | Nelson Burton Jr. | 1981 | Earl Anthony | 1992 | Dave Ferraro | 2004 | Mika Koivuniemi |
| 1971 | Don Johnson | 1982 | Earl Anthony | 1993 | Walter Ray Williams Jr. | 2005 | Patrick Allen |
| 1972 | Don Johnson | 1983 | Earl Anthony | 1994 | Norm Duke | | |
| 1973 | Don McCune | 1984 | Mark Roth | 1995 | Mike Aulby | | |

**Note:** After its first nine events of 2001, the PBA instituted a new September-to-March schedule with the statistics for those first nine tournaments rolled over into players' final 2001-02 statistics. Individual awards were handed out in 2002.

### PBA Rookie of the Year

Named after PBA Hall of Famer Harry Golden, who was the PBA's national tournament director for 30 years. Winner selected by members of Professional Bowlers Association.

| Year | | Year | | Year | | Year | |
|------|--|------|--|------|--|------|--|
| 1964 | Jerry McCoy | 1975 | Guy Rowbury | 1986 | Marc McDowell | 1997 | Anthony Lombardo |
| 1965 | Jim Godman | 1976 | Mike Berlin | 1987 | Ryan Shafer | 1998 | Chris Barnes |
| 1966 | Bobby Cooper | 1977 | Steve Martin | 1988 | Rick Steelsmith | 1999 | Paul Fleming |
| 1967 | Mike Durbin | 1978 | Joseph Groskind | 1989 | Steve Hoskins | 2000 | Joe Ciccone |
| 1968 | Bob McGregor | 1979 | Mike Aulby | 1990 | Brad Kiszewski | 2002 | Tommy Jones |
| 1969 | Larry Lichstein | 1980 | Pete Weber | 1991 | Ricky Ward | 2003 | Brad Angelo |
| 1970 | Denny Krick | 1981 | Mark Fahy | 1992 | Jason Couch | 2004 | Chris Johnson |
| 1971 | Tye Critchlow | 1982 | Mike Steinbach | 1993 | Mark Scroggins | 2005 | No bowler qualified |
| 1972 | Tommy Hudson | 1983 | Toby Contreras | 1994 | Tony Ament | | |
| 1973 | Steve Neff | 1984 | John Gant | 1995 | Billy Myers Jr. | | |
| 1974 | Cliff McNealy | 1985 | Tom Crites | 1996 | C.K. Moore | | |

## WOMEN
### BWAA Bowler of the Year

Winners selected by Bowling Writers Association of America. **Multiple winners:** Marion Ladewig (9); Donna Adamek, Lisa Rathgeber Wagner and Wendy Macpherson (4); Tish Johnson and Betty Morris (3); Leanne Barrette, Patty Costello, Carolyn Dorin-Ballard, Dotty Fothergill, Shirley Garms, Val Mikiel, Aleta Sill, Judy Soutar and Sylvia Wene (2).

| Year | | Year | | Year | | Year | |
|------|--|------|--|------|--|------|--|
| 1948 | Val Mikiel | 1963 | Marion Ladewig | 1978 | Donna Adamek | 1993 | Lisa Wagner |
| 1949 | Val Mikiel | 1964 | LaVerne Carter | 1979 | Donna Adamek | 1994 | Anne Marie Duggan |
| 1950 | Marion Ladewig | 1965 | Betty Kuczynski | 1980 | Donna Adamek | 1995 | Tish Johnson |
| 1951 | Marion Ladewig | 1966 | Joy Abel | 1981 | Donna Adamek | 1996 | Wendy Macpherson |
| 1952 | Marion Ladewig | 1967 | Millie Martorella | 1982 | Nikki Gianulias | 1997 | Wendy Macpherson |
| 1953 | Marion Ladewig | 1968 | Dotty Fothergill | 1983 | Lisa Rathgeber | 1998 | Carol Gianotti-Block |
| 1954 | Marion Ladewig | 1969 | Dotty Fothergill | 1984 | Aleta Sill | 1999 | Wendy Macpherson |
| 1955 | Sylvia Wene | 1970 | Mary Baker | 1985 | Aleta Sill | 2000 | Wendy Macpherson |
| 1956 | Anita Cantaline | 1971 | Paula Sperber | 1986 | Lisa Wagner | 2001 | Carolyn Dorin-Ballard |
| 1957 | Marion Ladewig | 1972 | Patty Costello | 1987 | Betty Morris | 2002 | Leanne Barrette |
| 1958 | Marion Ladewig | 1973 | Judy Soutar | 1988 | Lisa Wagner | 2003 | Carolyn Dorin-Ballard |
| 1959 | Marion Ladewig | 1974 | Betty Morris | 1989 | Robin Romeo | 2004 | Shannon Pluhowsky |
| 1960 | Sylvia Wene | 1975 | Judy Soutar | 1990 | Tish Johnson | | |
| 1961 | Shirley Garms | 1976 | Patty Costello | 1991 | Leanne Barrette | | |
| 1962 | Shirley Garms | 1977 | Betty Morris | 1992 | Tish Johnson | | |

### PWBA Player of the Year

Winners selected by members of Professional Women's Bowling Association. The PWBA Player of the Year has differed from the BWAA Bowler of the Year four times–in 1985, '86, '90 and 2002. This award was known as the LPBT Player of the Year Award from 1983-97. In 2003, PWBA suspended operations due to a lack of operating funds.

**Multiple winners:** Wendy Macpherson (4); Lisa Rathgeber Wagner (3); Leanne Barrette and Tish Johnson (2).

| Year | | Year | | Year | | Year | |
|------|--|------|--|------|--|------|--|
| 1983 | Lisa Rathgeber | 1988 | Lisa Wagner | 1993 | Lisa Wagner | 1998 | Carol Gianotti-Block |
| 1984 | Aleta Sill | 1989 | Robin Romeo | 1994 | Anne Marie Duggan | 1999 | Wendy Macpherson |
| 1985 | Patty Costello | 1990 | Leanne Barrette | 1995 | Tish Johnson | 2000 | Wendy Macpherson |
| 1986 | Jeanne Maiden | 1991 | Leanne Barrette | 1996 | Wendy Macpherson | 2001 | Carolyn Dorin-Ballard |
| 1987 | Betty Morris | 1992 | Tish Johnson | 1997 | Wendy Macpherson | 2002 | Michelle Feldman |

# Horse Racing

***Giacomo***, with Mike Smith aboard, won the
2005 Kentucky Derby at 50-1 odds.

AP/Wide World Photos

# Close Call

*Afleet Alex and jockey Jeremy Rose recover from a near fall to win the thrilling 2005 Preakness.*

**Michael Morrison**
*is co-editor of the ESPN Sports Almanac.*

It was one of those sports moments you just hate to see – the kind that immediately make you gasp, like a fiery auto crash or a batter getting plunked in the helmet with a 95-mph fastball. They rarely happen in horse racing, and when they do, there's almost never a happy ending.

At the 130th Preakness Stakes in May, race favorite Afleet Alex passed the three-quarter pole in seventh place as jockey Jeremy Rose began to make his move. By the final turn, Rose had guided his horse past Closing Argument and Greeley's Galaxy and set his sights on race leader Scrappy T, now just a length ahead as they entered the stretch.

And then it happened. Without warning, Scrappy T swerved to the right and directly into the charging Afleet Alex's path. It was unintentional, but in the heat of the moment, that doesn't matter. Afleet Alex's front heels clipped the back heels of Scrappy T and it appeared as though

we were all about to witness something horrendous. Afleet Alex's legs buckled and his knees appeared to touch the dirt. Rose, now out of his saddle and nearly thrown over his horse's neck, hung on for dear life.

"I hang on well when I'm scared," Rose said. "I planned on hitting the ground, I really did. I had a spot picked out. I figured, we're going to get run over; hopefully a couple of [horses] will miss us."

Miraculously, and spectacularly, Afleet Alex didn't go down. Somehow he managed to get his legs back underneath him and regain his stride — not such an easy task for a 1,200-pound, top-heavy thoroughbred moving at 30 miles per hour. Not only did he find his composure, he surged down the stretch at the behest of Rose and crossed the finish line $4\frac{3}{4}$ lengths ahead of runner-up Scrappy T.

"I've seen horses take bad steps and still win," said Alex's trainer Tim Ritchey,

AP/Wide World Photos

*Afleet Alex*, no. 12 in the middle, nearly falls to his knees after knocking heels with Scrappy T, right, at the Preakness in May. He hung on, and so did jockey Jeremy Rose, to win by 4¾ lengths.

"but I haven't seen them stumble that bad, gather themselves in a Grade I race and still win."

Ritchey, a 30-year journeyman from the suburbs of Pittsburgh added, "The Steelers had the Immaculate Reception. What do you call this? The Immaculate Recovery?"

Placing third, five lengths behind Scrappy T, was Giacomo, a gray colt ridden by Mike Smith and trained by John Shirreffs. Just two weeks prior, Giacomo shocked the experts and practically all 156,435 in attendance by winning the Kentucky Derby as a 50-1 longshot, despite winning just once in his seven previous races.

Giacomo found himself in 18th place at the three-quarter mark of the Derby but Smith adeptly angled and weaved his horse through traffic into sixth place at the stretch. With five strides to go, Giacomo took the lead and hung on for a half-length win.

Score one for the little guys! Shirreffs had never entered a horse in the Derby, while Smith recorded his first Derby win in 11 starts. High-profile trainers Nick Zito, Todd Pletcher, Bob Baffert and D. Wayne Lukas entered a combined ten horses in the field of 20 and were completely shut out of the top five. Zito saddled a record-tying five horses, including pre-race favorite Bellamy Road — owned

AP/Wide World Photos

*It's safe to say Afleet Alex's seven-length win at the **Belmont Stakes** was just a bit easier than his breathtaking win three weeks earlier at the Preakness.*

by New York Yankees owner George Steinbrenner – who finished a disappointing seventh.

Closing Argument, himself a 71-1 longshot, placed second, while Afleet Alex took third.

The Belmont Stakes had seen a Triple Crown possibility the last three years and in six of the last eight. But Giacomo's win at the Derby and Afleet Alex's win in the Preakness meant racing fans would have to wait at least another year for the first Triple Crown winner since Affirmed in 1978.

The lack of any Triple Crown drama at the 137th Belmont hurt television ratings and lowered attendance to 62,274, just over half of its 2004 total. Those who did watch, however, saw favorite Afleet Alex cruise to a resounding seven-length win, and in the process, lay claim to the title of the world's best 3-year-old.

Andromeda's Hero, trained by Zito, placed second. Giacomo briefly held the lead at the quarter pole but faded down the stretch to finish in seventh.

Afleet Alex became the 11th horse to win the Triple Crown's final two legs after not winning the Kentucky Derby. Rose took the blame for his horse's third-place performance at Churchill Downs.

continued on page 774

# The Ten Biggest Stories of the Year in Horse Racing

**10** Thoroughbred trainer Todd Pletcher, fresh off his Eclipse Award season in 2004, picks up right where he left off, earning almost $13 million through late September 2005 thanks to such powerhouses as Ashado, Power Alley and English Channel.

**9** Vivid Photo wins the 80th running of the $1.5 million Hambletonian, harness racing's most prestigious event. Driven and trained by the "King of the County Fairs," Roger Hammer, the 3-year-old gelding came from well off the pace to finish the mile in 1:52³/₅ for the victory.

**8** Three-year-old colt Lost in the Fog, under jockey Russell Baze, is a perfect eight-for-eight in 2005 (through early October) and 10-for-10 dating back to 2004. His average margin of victory in those wins is 6½ lengths.

**7** Hall of famer Pat Day, the winningest jockey of all time with close to $300 million in earnings, retires in August. He leaves the sport with four Eclipse Awards and 8,803 wins—including nine in Triple Crown races—in 33 years of racing.

**6** Russell Baze, 46, rides Queen of the Hunt to victory on June 2 at Golden Gate Fields for the 9,000th win of his career. He joins Laffit Pincay Jr. (9,530) as the only two jockeys in the 9,000-win club.

**5** Hall of Fame harness racing trainer-driver Stanley Dancer dies at the age of 78. He trained five Hambletonian winners (and drove four of them) and won the Triple Crown twice – with Nevele Pride (1968) and Super Bowl (1972).

**4** Saint Liam wins the Donn and Stephen Foster Handicaps early in the year, then adds to his resume with a win at the Woodward Stakes in September under Jerry Bailey. His one loss (through early October) comes to Rock Hard Ten at the Santa Anita Handicap but he gets his chance for revenge at the Breeders' Cup Classic (see *Updates* chapter).

**3** Afleet Alex, trained by Tim Ritchey and owned by Cash is King LLC, proves he is 2005's top 3-year-old with an impressive seven-length win at the Belmont Stakes.

**2** After clipping heels with leader Scrappy T and coming dangerously close to crashing to the dirt, Afleet Alex not only finishes the race with jockey Jeremy Rose aboard, but surges to a thrilling 4³/₄-length victory at the 130th Preakness.

**1** Giacomo, a 50-1 longshot, muscles his way past the favorites, grabs the lead down the stretch and powers to an improbable win at the Kentucky Derby. He edges 71-1 Closing Argument by a half-length.

"I messed up," he said. "Obviously he's the best 3-year-old in the country. He should have won."

But Ritchey certainly wasn't looking for someone to blame. Neither was breeder John Silvertand, who looked to his horse for inspiration to help him through his ongoing battle with cancer. And neither

were the five owners, high school friends who formed Cash is King LLC and pooled their money to purchase Afleet Alex for $75,000 in May 2004.

Said Ritchey, "If someone told me back in March we would win two legs of the Triple Crown, we would have been pretty ecstatic."

## Where did everyone go?

The absence of a Triple Crown bid put a serious damper on the attendance totals at the 2005 Belmont Stakes. Listed are attendance figures since 1997 and the horses bidding for the Triple Crown.

| Year | Horse | Attendance |
|------|-------|-----------|
| 1997 | Silver Charm | 70,682 |
| 1998 | Real Quiet | 80,162 |
| 1999 | Charismatic | 85,818 |
| 2000 | NONE | 67,810 |
| 2001 | NONE | 73,857 |
| 2002 | War Emblem | 103,222 |
| 2003 | Funny Cide | 101,864 |
| 2004 | Smarty Jones | 120,139* |
| 2005 | NONE | 62,274 |

* New York racing record

## Color-coded

Of the 137 horses that have won the Belmont Stakes since its inaugural race in 1867, 52 of them were bay-colored, including 2005 winner Afleet Alex. Listed are the colors of every winner:

| Color | No. of winners |
|-------|---------------|
| Bay | 52 |
| Chestnut | 50 |
| Brown | 29 |
| Black | 3 |
| Gray | 2 |
| Roan | 1 |

**Sources**:
belmontstakes.nyra.com & *USA Today*

Kentucky Derby winner Giacomo, who went off at 50-1 odds, paid the second highest $2 win wager in Derby history with $102.80, behind only Donerail's $184.90 in 1913. **Did you know** that if you put down a buck and hit the Superfecta (top four horses in order), you would have walked away with $864,253.50. Seven people did.

# 2004-2005
# *Season in Review*

SPORTS ALMANAC

## Thoroughbred Racing
### Major Stakes Races

Winners of major stakes races from Nov. 28, 2004 through Sept. 25, 2005; (T) indicates turf race course; F indicates furlongs.

### Late 2004

| Date | Race | Track | Miles | Winner | Jockey | Purse |
|------|------|-------|-------|--------|--------|-------|
| Nov. 28 | Citation Handicap | Hollywood Park | 1 1/16 | Leroidesanimaux | Jon Court | $400,000 |
| Nov. 28 | Japan Cup* | Nakayama | 1 1/2 (T) | Zenno Rob Roy (JPN) | Olivier Peslier | 3,966,666 |
| Nov. 28 | Matriarch Stakes | Hollywood Park | 1 1/8 (T) | Intercontinental | Jerry Bailey | 500,000 |
| Nov. 30 | Hollywood Derby | Hollywood Park | 1 1/8 (T) | Good Reward | Jerry Bailey | 500,000 |
| Dec. 12 | Hong Kong Cup* | Sha Tin | 1 1/4 (T) | Alexander Goldrun | Kevin Manning | 2,314,800 |

### 2005 (through Sept. 25)

| Date | Race | Track | Miles | Winner | Jockey | Purse |
|------|------|-------|-------|--------|--------|-------|
| Jan. 29 | Sunshine Millions Classic | Santa Anita | 1 1/8 | Musique Toujours | Jorge Chavez | $1,000,000 |
| Feb. 5 | Charles H. Strub Stakes | Santa Anita | 1 1/8 | Rock Hard Ten | Gary Stevens | 300,000 |
| Feb. 5 | Donn Handicap | Gulfstream | 1 1/8 | Saint Liam | Edgar Prado | 500,000 |
| Feb. 5 | Hutcheson Stakes | Gulfstream | 7 1/2 F | Proud Accolade | John Velazquez | 150,000 |
| Feb. 13 | San Vicente Stakes | Santa Anita | 7 F | Fusaichi Rock Star | David Flores | 150,000 |
| Feb. 13 | Santa Maria Handicap | Santa Anita | 1 1/16 | Miss Loren (ARG) | Jose Valdivia Jr. | 250,000 |
| Mar. 5 | Fountain of Youth Stakes | Gulfstream | 1 1/8 | High Fly | Jerry Bailey | 300,000 |
| Mar. 5 | Santa Anita Handicap | Santa Anita | 1 1/4 | Rock Hard Ten | Gary Stevens | 1,000,000 |
| Mar. 5 | Swale Stakes | Gulfstream | 7 F | Lost in the Fog | Russell Baze | 150,000 |
| Mar. 12 | Louisiana Derby | Fair Grounds | 1 1/16 | High Limit | Ramon Dominguez | 600,000 |
| Mar. 12 | El Camino Real Derby | Bay Meadows | 1 1/16 | Uncle Denny | Russell Baze | 200,000 |
| Mar. 12 | New Orleans Handicap | Fair Grounds | 1 1/8 | Badge of Silver | Jerry Bailey | 500,000 |
| Mar. 12 | Santa Margarita Handicap | Santa Anita | 1 1/8 | Tarlow | Patrick Valenzuela | 300,000 |
| Mar. 13 | Santa Anita Oaks | Santa Anita | 1 1/16 | Sweet Catomine | Corey Nakatani | 300,000 |
| Mar. 19 | San Felipe Stakes | Santa Anita | 1 1/16 | Consolidator | Rafael Bejarano | 250,000 |
| Mar. 19 | Rebel Stakes | Oaklawn | 1 1/16 | Greater Good | John McKee | 250,000 |
| Mar. 19 | Tampa Bay Derby | Tampa Bay | 1 1/16 | Sun King | Edgar Prado | 250,000 |
| Mar. 26 | Lane's End Stakes | Turfway | 1 1/8 | Flower Alley | Jorge Chavez | 500,000 |
| Mar. 26 | UAE Derby | Nad al-Sheba | 1 1/8 | Blues and Royals | Kerrin McEvoy | 2,000,000 |
| Mar. 26 | Dubai World Cup | Nad al-Sheba | 1 1/4 | Roses in May | John Velazquez | 6,000,000 |
| Apr. 2 | Florida Derby | Gulfstream | 1 1/8 | High Fly | Jerry Bailey | 1,000,000 |
| Apr. 2 | WinStar Derby | Sunland | 1 1/8 | Thor's Echo | Corey Nakatani | 500,000 |
| Apr. 9 | Santa Anita Derby | Santa Anita | 1 1/8 | Buzzards Bay | Mark Guidry | 750,000 |
| Apr. 9 | Ashland Stakes | Keeneland | 1 1/16 | Sis City | Edgar Prado | 500,000 |
| Apr. 9 | Oaklawn Handicap | Oaklawn | 1 1/8 | Grand Reward | John McKee | 500,000 |
| Apr. 9 | Apple Blossom Handicap | Oaklawn | 1 1/16 | Dream of Summer | Patrick Valenzuela | 500,000 |
| Apr. 9 | Illinois Derby | Hawthorne | 1 1/8 | Greeley's Galaxy | Kent Desormeaux | 500,000 |
| Apr. 9 | Wood Memorial | Aqueduct | 1 1/8 | Bellamy Road | Javier Castellano | 750,000 |
| Apr. 16 | Blue Grass Stakes | Keeneland | 1 1/8 | Bandini | John Velazquez | 750,000 |
| Apr. 16 | Arkansas Derby | Oaklawn | 1 1/8 | Afleet Alex | Jeremy Rose | 1,000,000 |
| Apr. 22 | Queen Elizabeth II Cup* | Sha Tin | 1 1/4 (T) | Vengeance of Rain | Anthony Delpech | 1,796,200 |
| Apr. 23 | Coolmore Lexington Stakes | Keeneland | 1 1/16 | Coin Silver | Javier Castellano | 325,000 |
| May 6 | Kentucky Oaks | Churchill Downs | 1 1/8 | Summerly | Jerry Bailey | 554,400 |
| May 7 | **Kentucky Derby** | Churchill Downs | 1 1/4 | Giacomo | Mike Smith | 2,399,600 |
| May 7 | Woodford Reserve Classic | Churchill Downs | 1 1/8 (T) | America Alive | Robby Albarado | 470,400 |
| May 14 | Pimlico Special | Pimlico | 1 3/16 | Eddington | Eibar Coa | 500,000 |
| May 15 | Singapore Airlines Cup* | Singapore | 1 1/4 (T) | Mummify | Danny Nikolic | 1,773,813 |
| May 20 | Black-Eyed Susan Stakes | Pimlico | 1 1/8 | Spun Sugar | John Velazquez | 200,000 |
| May 21 | **Preakness Stakes** | Pimlico | 1 3/16 | Afleet Alex | Jeremy Rose | 1,000,000 |
| May 28 | Peter Pan Stakes | Belmont | 1 1/8 | Oratory | Jerry Bailey | 200,000 |
| May 30 | Gamely BC Handicap | Hollywood Park | 1 1/8 (T) | Mea Domina | Tyler Baze | 441,500 |
| May 30 | Shoemaker BC Mile | Hollywood Park | 1 (T) | Castledale | Rene Douglas | 369,000 |
| May 30 | Metropolitan Handicap | Belmont | 1 | Ghostzapper | Javier Castellano | 750,000 |
| June 4 | Acorn Stakes | Belmont | 1 | Round Pond | Stewart Elliott | 250,000 |
| June 4 | English Derby | Epsom Downs | 1 1/2 (T) | Motivator | Johnny Murtagh | 2,266,250 |
| June 11 | **Belmont Stakes** | Belmont | 1 1/2 | Afleet Alex | Jeremy Rose | 1,000,000 |
| June 11 | Manhattan Handicap | Belmont | 1 1/4 (T) | Good Reward | Jerry Bailey | 400,000 |

## Major Stakes Races (Cont.)

| Date | Race | Track | Miles | Winner | Jockey | Purse |
|------|------|-------|-------|--------|--------|-------|
| June 11 | Charles Whittingham H | Hollywood Park | 1¼ (T) | Sweet Return | Alex Solis | $350,000 |
| June 18 | Stephen Foster Handicap | Churchill Downs | 1⅛ | Saint Liam | Edgar Prado | 828,000 |
| June 18 | Ogden Phipps Handicap | Belmont | 1¹⁄₁₆ | Ashado | John Velazquez | 300,000 |
| June 25 | Colonial Turf Cup Stakes | Colonial Downs | 1³⁄₁₆ (T) | English Channel | John Velazquez | 500,000 |
| June 25 | Mother Goose Stakes | Belmont | 1⅛ | Smuggler | Edgar Prado | 300,000 |
| June 26 | Queen's Plate | Woodbine | 1¼ | Wild Desert | Patrick Valenzuela | 812,698 |
| June 26 | Irish Derby | Curragh | 1½ (T) | Hurricane Run | Kieren Fallon | 1,515,417 |
| July 2 | Suburban Handicap | Belmont | 1¼ | Offlee Wild | Edgar Prado | 500,000 |
| July 2 | United Nations Stakes | Monmouth Park | 1⅜ (T) | Better Talk Now | Ramon Dominguez | 750,000 |
| July 3 | American Oaks | Hollywood Park | 1¼ (T) | Cesario (JPN) | Yuichi Fukunaga | 750,000 |
| July 9 | Hollywood Gold Cup | Hollywood Park | 1¼ | Lava Man | Patrick Valenzuela | 750,000 |
| July 9 | Swaps BC Stakes | Hollywood Park | 1⅛ | Surf Cat | Alex Solis | 361,000 |
| July 10 | Princess Rooney Handicap | Calder | 6 F | Madcap Escapade | Jerry Bailey | 500,000 |
| July 10 | Smile Sprint Handicap | Calder | 6 F | Woke Up Dreamin | Mike Smith | 500,000 |
| July 16 | Virginia Derby | Colonial Downs | 1¼ (T) | English Channel | John Velazquez | 750,000 |
| July 16 | Delaware Oaks | Delaware | 1¹⁄₁₆ | R Lady Joy | Jose Lezcano | 500,300 |
| July 17 | Delaware Handicap | Delaware | 1¼ | Island Sun | Jerry Bailey | 1,001,800 |
| July 23 | Coaching Club Am. Oaks | Belmont | 1¼ | Smuggler | Edgar Prado | 500,000 |
| July 23 | K. George VI and Q. Elizabeth Diamond Stakes* | Newbury | 1½ (T) | Azamour (IRE) | Michael Kinane | 1,222,613 |
| July 23 | John C. Mabee Handicap | Del Mar | 1⅛ (T) | Amorama (FRA) | Martin Pedroza | 400,000 |
| July 24 | Eddie Read Handicap | Del Mar | 1⅛ (T) | Sweet Return | Alex Solis | 400,000 |
| July 30 | Diana Handicap | Saratoga | 1⅛ (T) | Sand Springs | John Velazquez | 500,000 |
| July 30 | Jim Dandy Stakes | Saratoga | 1⅛ | Flower Alley | John Velazquez | 490,000 |
| July 31 | Go for Wand Handicap | Saratoga | 1⅛ | Ashado | John Velazquez | 250,000 |
| Aug. 6 | Test Stakes | Saratoga | 7 F | Leave Me Alone | Kent Desormeaux | 250,000 |
| Aug. 6 | Whitney Handicap | Saratoga | 1⅛ | Commentator | Gary Stevens | 750,000 |
| Aug. 7 | Haskell Invitational | Monmouth | 1⅛ | Roman Ruler | Jerry Bailey | 1,015,000 |
| Aug. 13 | Sword Dancer Invitational | Saratoga | 1½ (T) | King's Drama (IRE) | Jorge Chavez | 500,000 |
| Aug. 13 | Arlington Million* | Arlington | 1¼ (T) | Powerscourt (GB) | Kieren Fallon | 1,000,000 |
| Aug. 13 | Beverly D. Stakes | Arlington | 1³⁄₁₆ (T) | Angara (GB) | Gary Stevens | 750,000 |
| Aug. 13 | Secretariat Stakes | Arlington | 1¼ (T) | Gun Salute | Cornelio Velasquez | 400,000 |
| Aug. 14 | West Virginia Derby | Mountaineer Park | 1⅛ | Real Dandy | Mark Guidry | 750,000 |
| Aug. 20 | Alabama Stakes | Saratoga | 1¼ | Sweet Symphony | Jerry Bailey | 750,000 |
| Aug. 21 | Pacific Classic | Del Mar | 1¼ | Borrego | Garrett Gomez | 1,000,000 |
| Aug. 26 | Personal Ensign Handicap | Saratoga | 1¼ | Shadow Cast | Robby Albarado | 400,000 |
| Aug. 27 | Travers Stakes | Saratoga | 1¼ | Flower Alley | John Velazquez | 1,000,000 |
| Sept. 4 | Grosser Preis von Baden* | Baden-Baden | 1½ (T) | Warrsan | Kerrin McEvoy | 1,047,384 |
| Sept. 5 | Pennsylvania Derby | Philadelphia | 1⅛ | Sun King | Rafael Bejarano | 750,000 |
| Sept. 10 | Man o' War Stakes | Belmont | 1⅜ (T) | Better Talk Now | Ramon Dominguez | 500,000 |
| Sept. 10 | The Woodward Stakes | Belmont | 1⅛ | Saint Liam | Jerry Bailey | 500,000 |
| Sept. 10 | Irish Champion Stakes* | Leopardstown | 1¼ (T) | Oratorio (IRE) | Kieren Fallon | 1,109,812 |
| Sept. 11 | Ruffian Handicap | Belmont | 1¹⁄₁₆ | Stellar Jayne | Jerry Bailey | 300,000 |
| Sept. 17 | Futurity Stakes | Belmont | 7 F | Private Vow | Jerry Bailey | 300,000 |
| Sept. 17 | Kentucky Cup Classic | Turfway | 1⅛ | Shaniko | Rafael Bejarano | 350,000 |
| Sept. 17 | Matron Stakes | Belmont | 1 | Folklore | Edgar Prado | 300,000 |
| Sept. 18 | Atto Mile | Woodbine | 1 (T) | Leroidesanimaux | John Velazquez | 849,757 |
| Sept. 24 | Hawthorne Gold Cup | Hawthorne | 1¼ | Super Frolic | Victor Espinoza | 750,000 |

*World Series Racing Championship series race.

# NTRA National Thoroughbred Poll

The NTRA Thoroughbred Poll conducted by National Thoroughbred Racing Association, covering races through Sept. 25, 2005. Rankings are based on the votes of horse racing media representatives on a 10-9-8-7-6-5-4-3-2-1 basis. First place votes are in parentheses.

| | | Pts | Age | Sex | '05 Record Sts—1-2-3 | Owner | Trainer |
|---|---|-----|-----|-----|----------------------|-------|---------|
| 1 | Saint Liam (8) | 138 | 5 | Horse | 5—3-1-0 | Mr. & Mrs. William K. Warren Jr. | Richard Dutrow Jr. |
| 2 | Lost In The Fog (3) | 117 | 3 | Colt | 7—7-0-0 | Harry J. Aleo | Greg Gilchrist |
| 3 | Leroidesanimaux (1) | 101 | 5 | Horse | 3—3-0-0 | TNT Stud | Bobby Frankel |
| 4 | Afleet Alex (3) | 93 | 3 | Colt | 6—4-0-1 | Cash is King, LLC | Tim Ritchey |
| 5 | Flower Alley | 72 | 3 | Colt | 7—4-2-0 | Melnyk Racing Stables, Inc. | Todd Pletcher |
| 6 | Better Talk Now | 41 | 6 | Gelding | 5—3-0-0 | Bushwood Stables | Graham Motion |
| 7 | Commentator | 37 | 4 | Gelding | 4—2-0-1 | Tracy & Carol Farmer | Nick Zito |
| 8 | Kitten's Joy | 36 | 4 | Colt | 3—2-1-0 | Ken & Sarah Ramsey | Dale Romans |
| 9 | Rock Hard Ten | 35 | 4 | Colt | 2—2-0-0 | Mercedes Stables & M. Paulson | Richard Mandella |
| 10 | Powerscourt | 27 | 5 | Horse | 4—1-1-0 | Mrs. John Magnier | Aidan O'Brien |

**Others receiving votes: 11.** Megahertz (20 points); **12.** Stella Jayne (12); **13.** Ghostzapper, Sweet Symphony and Ashado (11); **16.** Roses In May and First Samurai (10); **18.** Giacomo (9); **19.** Borrego (7); **20.** Lava Man (6); **21.** High Fly (5); **22.** English Channel and Private Vow (3); **24.** Bellamy Road, Folklore, Sorcerer's Stone and Sun King (2); **28.** Cesario, Shakespeare and Suave (1).

## The 2005 Triple Crown

### 131ST KENTUCKY DERBY

Grade I for three-year-olds; 10th race at Churchill Downs in Louisville. **Date**—May 7, 2005; **Distance**—1¼ miles; **Stakes Purse**—$2,399,600 ($1,639,600 to winner; $400,000 for 2nd; $200,000 for 3rd; $100,000 for 4th; $60,000 for 5th); **Track**—Fast; **Off**—6:11 p.m. EDT; **Favorite**—Bellamy Road (5-2 odds). **Winner**—Giacomo; **Field**—20 horses; **Time**—2:02.75; **Start**—Good; **Won**—Driving; **Sire**—Holy Bull (Great Above); **Dam**—Set Them Free (Stop the Music); **Record** (going into race)—7 starts, 1 win, 2 seconds, 2 thirds; **Last start**—4th in Santa Anita Derby (Apr. 9); **Breeder**—Mr. & Mrs. Jerome S. Moss (Ky.).

| Order of Finish | Jockey | PP | 1/4 | 1/2 | 3/4 | Mile | Stretch | Finish | To $1 |
|---|---|---|---|---|---|---|---|---|---|
| Giacomo | Mike Smith | 10 | 18-½ | 18-2½ | 18-1½ | 11-hd | 6-½ | 1-½ | 50.30 |
| Closing Argument | Cornelio Velasquez | 18 | 5-hd | 6-½ | 6-hd | 4-hd | 1-½ | 2-½ | 71.60 |
| Afleet Alex | Jeremy Rose | 12 | 11-hd | 11-½ | 9-½ | 6-1½ | 2-1 | 3-2½ | 4.60 |
| Don't Get Mad | Tyler Baze | 17 | 19-6 | 19-3½ | 19-3½ | 10-hd | 7-½ | 4-2¾ | 29.20 |
| Buzzards Bay | Mark Guidry | 20 | 10-½ | 10-hd | 7-½ | 5-½ | 5-hd | 5-½ | 46.30 |
| Wilko | Corey Nakatani | 14 | 13-½ | 14-hd | 16-2½ | 13-1½ | 10-½ | 6-no | 21.70 |
| Bellamy Road | Javier Castellano | 16 | 3-½ | 5-2 | 5-2 | 2-hd | 3-hd | 7-¾ | 2.60 |
| Andromeda's Hero | Rafael Bejarano | 2 | 16-hd | 15-2 | 13-hd | 16-2 | 14-1½ | 8-no | 57.30 |
| Flower Alley | Jorge Chavez | 7 | 4-hd | 3-hd | 2-hd | 7-1½ | 8-1 | 9-hd | 41.30 |
| High Fly | Jerry Bailey | 11 | 6-1 | 4-1 | 3-hd | 1-hd | 4-1 | 10-nk | 7.10 |
| Greeley's Galaxy | Kent Desormeaux | 9 | 17-1 | 16-½ | 14-hd | 8-hd | 12-2½ | 11-2¼ | 21.00 |
| Coin Silver | Patrick Valenzuela | 5 | 14-½ | 12-hd | 12-1½ | 9-2 | 11-1 | 12-1¼ | 38.60 |
| Greater Good | John McKee | 8 | 20 | 20 | 20 | 17-½ | 15-½ | 13-¾ | 58.40 |
| Noble Causeway | Gary Stevens | 4 | 12-hd | 13-2½ | 15-hd | 12-hd | 13-½ | 14-2½ | 12.30 |
| Sun King | Edgar Prado | 3 | 9-½ | 9-hd | 8-hd | 15-1½ | 16-4 | 15-4 | 15.70 |
| Spanish Chestnut | Joe Bravo | 13 | 1-½ | 1-1½ | 1-1½ | 3-hd | 9-hd | 16-7 | 71.00 |
| Sort It Out | Brice Blanc | 1 | 15-½ | 17-hd | 17-hd | 18-4 | 17-2½ | 17-3¼ | 61.90 |
| Going Wild | Jose Valdivia Jr. | 19 | 2-1 | 2-1 | 4-½ | 14-hd | 18-5½ | 18-3½ | 59.50 |
| Bandini | John Velazquez | 15 | 7-hd | 8-2 | 11-1½ | 20 | 19-3 | 19-12 | 6.80 |
| High Limit | Ramon Dominguez | 6 | 8-2 | 7-hd | 10-3½ | 19-hd | 20 | 20 | 22.50 |

**Times**—22.28; 45.38; 1:09.59; 1:35.88; 2:02.75.

**$2 Mutuel Prices**—#10 Giacomo ($102.60, $45.80, $19.80); #18 Closing Argument ($70.00, $24.80); #12 Afleet Alex ($4.60). **Exacta**—(10-18) for $9,814.80; **Trifecta**—(10-18-12) for $133,134.80; **$1 Superfecta**—(10-18-12-17) for $864,253.50; **Scratched**—none; **Overweights**—none. **Attendance**—156,435; **TV Rating**—9.0/22 share (NBC).

**Trainers & Owners** (by finish): **1**—John Shirreffs & Mr. and Mrs. Jerome Moss; **2**—Kiaran McLaughlin & Philip and Marcia Cohen; **3**—Tim Ritchey & Cash is King LLC; **4**—Ronald Ellis & B Wayne Hughes; **5**—Jeff Mullins & Fog City Stable; **6**—Craig Dollase & J. Paul Reddam and Susan Roy; **7**—Nick Zito & Kinsman Stable; **8**—Nick Zito & Robert LaPenta; **9**—Todd Pletcher & Melnyk Racing Stables, Inc.; **10**—Nick Zito & Live Oak Plantation; **11**—Warren Stute & B. Wayne Hughes; **12**—Todd Pletcher & Peachtree Stable; **13**—Robert Holthus & Lewis G. Lakin; **14**—Nick Zito & My Meadowview Farm; **15**—Nick Zito & Tracy Farmer; **16**—Patrick Biartcone & Derrick Smith/Michael Tabor; **17**—Bob Baffert & Stonerside Stable/Preferred Pals Stable; **18**—D. Wayne Lukas & Robert and Beverly Lewis; **19**—Todd Pletcher & Derrick Smith/Michael Tabor; **20**—Robert Frankel & Gary and Mary West.

### 130TH PREAKNESS STAKES

Grade I for three-year-olds; 12th race at Pimlico in Baltimore. **Date**—May 21, 2005; **Distance**—1³⁄₁₆ miles; **Stakes Purse**—$1,000,000 ($650,000 to winner; $200,000 for 2nd; $100,000 for 3rd; $50,000 for 4th); **Track**—Fast; **Off**—6:21 p.m. EDT; **Favorite**—Afleet Alex (5-2 odds). **Winner**—Afleet Alex; **Field**—14 horses; **Time**—1:55.04; **Start**—Good; **Won**—Driving; **Sire**—Northern Afleet (Afleet); **Dam**—Maggy Hawk (Hawkster); **Record** (going into race)—10 starts, 6 wins, 2 seconds, 1 third; **Last start**—3rd in Kentucky Derby (May 7); **Breeder**—John Martin Silverland (Fla.).

| Order of Finish | Jockey | PP | 1/4 | 1/2 | 3/4 | Stretch | Finish | To $1 |
|---|---|---|---|---|---|---|---|---|
| Afleet Alex | Jeremy Rose | 12 | 10-2 | 10-1 | 7-½ | 1-hd | 1-4¾ | 3.30 |
| Scrappy T | Ramon Dominguez | 5 | 3-2 | 3-hd | 2-1 | 2-4 | 2-5 | 13.30 |
| Giacomo | Mike Smith | 13 | 11-hd | 11-3½ | 10-hd | 5-2 | 3-1 | 6.00 |
| Sun King | Rafael Bejarano | 10 | 8-½ | 9-1½ | 9-2 | 4-hd | 4-1 | 21.10 |
| High Limit | Edgar Prado | 11 | 1-½ | 1-hd | 1-½ | 3-3 | 5-6¾ | 18.70 |
| Noble Causeway | Gary Stevens | 3 | 14 | 13-1 | 13-3 | 7-½ | 6-1¼ | 11.30 |
| Greeley's Galaxy | David Flores | 4 | 9-1 | 8-½ | 5-½ | 6-2½ | 7-1 | 9.40 |
| Malibu Moonshine | Steve Hamilton | 1 | 13-2½ | 12-½ | 12-hd | 8-3 | 8-6 | 24.00 |
| Closing Argument | Cornelio Velasquez | 7 | 5-2½ | 5-½ | 6-1 | 9-1 | 9-2¼ | 7.20 |
| High Fly | Jerry Bailey | 2 | 6-hd | 6-1 | 8-½ | 10-3 | 10-5¼ | 5.10 |
| Hal's Image | Jose Santos | 6 | 12-2 | 14 | 14 | 13-4 | 11-¾ | 23.50 |
| Wilko | Corey Nakatani | 9 | 7-1½ | 7-hd | 11-2½ | 12-1½ | 12-1 | 13.30 |
| Galloping Grocer | Joe Bravo | 8 | 4-hd | 4-2 | 4-½ | 11-1 | 13-6 | 27.00 |
| Going Wild | Robby Albarado | 14 | 2-1 | 2-1½ | 3-½ | 14 | 14 | 26.50 |

**Times**—23.17; 46.07; 1:10.72; 1:36.04; 1:55.04.

**$2 Mutuel Prices**—#12 Afleet Alex ($8.60, $5.00, $3.20); #5 Scrappy T ($11.20, $5.80); #13 Giacomo ($4.80). **Exacta**—(12-5) for $152.60; **Trifecta**—(12-5-13) for $872.00; **$1 Superfecta**—(12-5-13-10) for $10,362.30; **Scratched**—none; **Overweights**—none. **Attendance**—115,318; **TV Rating**—5.1/13 share (NBC).

**Trainers & Owners** (by finish): **1**—Tim Ritchey & Cash is King LLC; **2**—Rob Bailes & Marshall Dowell; **3**—John Shirreffs & Mr. and Mrs. Jerome Moss; **4**—Nick Zito & Tracy Farmer; **5**—Robert Frankel & Gary and Mary West; **6**—Nick Zito & My Meadowview Farm; **7**—Warren Stute & B. Wayne Hughes; **8**—King Leatherbury & Woodrow Marriott; **9**—Kiaran McLaughlin & Philip and Marcia Cohen; **10**—Nick Zito & Live Oak Plantation; **11**—Barry Rose & Rose Family Stable; **12**—Craig Dollase & J. Paul Reddam and Susan Roy; **13**—Dominick Schettino & Robert Rosenthal and Bernice Waldbaum; **14**—D. Wayne Lukas & Robert and Beverly Lewis.

## The 2005 Triple Crown (Cont.)

### 137TH BELMONT STAKES

Grade I for three-year-olds; 11th race at Belmont Park in Elmont, N.Y. **Date**—June 11, 2005; **Distance**—1½ miles; **Stakes Purse**—$1,000,000 ($600,000 to winner; $200,000 for 2nd; $110,000 for 3rd; $60,000 for 4th; $30,000 for 5th); **Track**—Fast; **Off**—6:34 p.m. EDT; **Favorite**—Afleet Alex (6-5 odds). **Winner**—Afleet Alex; **Field**—11 horses; **Time**—2:28.75; **Start**—Good for all but Reverberate; **Won**—Driving; **Sire**—Northern Afleet (Afleet); **Dam**—Maggy Hawk (Hawkster); **Record** (going into race)—11 starts, 7 wins, 2 seconds, 1 third; **Last Start**—1st in Preakness (May 21); **Breeder**—John Martin Silvertand (Fla.).

| Order of Finish | Jockey | PP | 1/4 | 1/2 | Mile | 1-1/4 | Stretch | Finish | To $1 |
|---|---|---|---|---|---|---|---|---|---|
| Afleet Alex | Jeremy Rose | 9 | 9-hd | 8-hd | 8-hd | 2-½ | 1-6 | 1-7 | 1.15 |
| Andromeda's Hero | Rafael Bejarano | 7 | 10-8 | 10-7 | 9-3 | 4-hd | 2-2½ | 2-6¾ | 11.90 |
| Nolan's Cat | Norberto Arroyo Jr. | 1 | 11 | 11 | 11 | 7-½ | 5-2 | 3-2¼ | 20.50 |
| Indy Storm | Edgar Prado | 10 | 7-½ | 6-hd | 6-1½ | 6-hd | 8-½ | 4-1 | 17.10 |
| A.P. Arrow | Jerry Bailey | 3 | 2-½ | 2-hd | 2-hd | 5-½ | 7-hd | 5-nk | 16.40 |
| Chekhov | Gary Stevens | 11 | 4-½ | 4-1½ | 7-hd | 9-6 | 6-hd | 6-½ | 15.10 |
| Giacomo | Mike Smith | 5 | 5-½ | 5-½ | 4-½ | 1-hd | 4-½ | 7-hd | 5.10 |
| Southern Africa | Jon Court | 4 | 3-½ | 3-½ | 3-½ | 3-2½ | 3-½ | 8-4¼ | 15.40 |
| Watchmon | Javier Castellano | 6 | 6-hd | 7-2½ | 5-hd | 8-1½ | 9-12 | 9-12 | 20.60 |
| Reverberate | Jose Santos | 8 | 8-hd | 9-½ | 10-2½ | 10-½ | 10-hd | 10-¾ | 11.80 |
| Pinpoint | John Velazquez | 2 | 1-1 | 1-½ | 1-hd | 11 | 11 | 11 | 15.60 |

**Times**—24.47; 48.62; 1:12.92; 1:38.05; 2:04.25; 2:28.75.

**$2 Mutuel Prices**—#9 Afleet Alex ($4.30, $3.60, $3.00); #7 Andromeda's Hero ($8.20, $5.80); #1 Nolan's Cat ($7.20). **Exacta**—(9-7) for $44.00; **Trifecta**—(9-7-1) for $1,249.00; **Superfecta**—(9-7-1-10) for $14,219.00; **Scratched**—none; **Overweights**—none; **Attendance**—62,274; **TV Rating**—5.0/11 share (NBC).

**Trainers & Owners** (by finish): **1**—Tim Ritchey & Cash is King LLC; **2**—Nick Zito & Robert LaPenta; **3**—Dale Romans & Ken and Sarah Ramsey; **4**—Nick Zito & Tracy Farmer; **5**—D. Wayne Lukas & Allen E. Paulson Living Trust; **6**—Patrick Biancone & Michael Tabor and Derrick Smith; **7**—John Shirreffs & Mr. and Mrs. Jerome S. Moss; **8**—Michael Puhich & Al and Saundra Kirkwood; **9**—Patrick Reynolds & Paul Pompa Jr.; **10**—Sal Russo & Centennial Farms; **11**—Nick Zito & Arthur B. Hancock III.

## 2004-05 Money Leaders

Official Top 10 standings for 2004 and unofficial Top 10 standings for 2005, through Sept. 25. Results are based on North American races, plus all World Series Racing Championship series races. Source: *Equibase Company*.

### FINAL 2004

| HORSES | Age | Sts | 1-2-3 | Earnings |
|---|---|---|---|---|
| Smarty Jones | 3 | 7 | 6-1-0 | $7,563,535 |
| Pleasantly Perfect | 6 | 5 | 3-1-1 | 4,840,000 |
| Ghostzapper | 4 | 4 | 4-0-0 | 2,590,000 |
| Zenno Rob Roy (JPN) | 4 | 1 | 1-0-0 | 2,469,753 |
| Ashado | 3 | 8 | 5-2-1 | 2,259,640 |
| Roses in May | 4 | 6 | 5-1-0 | 1,723,277 |
| Kitten's Joy | 3 | 8 | 6-2-0 | 1,625,796 |
| Southern Image | 4 | 4 | 3-1-0 | 1,612,150 |
| Medaglia d'Oro | 5 | 2 | 1-1-0 | 1,500,000 |
| Savabeel (AUS) | 3 | 1 | 1-0-0 | 1,493,790 |

| JOCKEYS | Mts | 1st | Earnings |
|---|---|---|---|
| John Velazquez | 1327 | 335 | $22,248,661 |
| Edgar Prado | 1445 | 281 | 18,342,106 |
| Victor Espinoza | 1336 | 240 | 15,933,757 |
| Jerry Bailey | 642 | 148 | 15,703,844 |
| Stewart Elliott | 1363 | 262 | 14,533,061 |
| Javier Castellano | 1283 | 212 | 13,038,943 |
| Corey Nakatani | 1080 | 220 | 12,466,557 |
| Rafael Bejarano | 1922 | 445 | 12,210,087 |
| Alex Solis | 556 | 120 | 11,554,851 |
| Ramon Dominguez | 1353 | 383 | 11,507,889 |

| TRAINERS | Sts | 1st | Earnings |
|---|---|---|---|
| Todd Pletcher | 948 | 240 | $17,511,923 |
| Bobby Frankel | 492 | 135 | 16,805,911 |
| Steve Asmussen | 2293 | 555 | 14,003,202 |
| John Servis | 284 | 68 | 8,922,686 |
| Bob Baffert | 562 | 105 | 7,627,913 |
| Richard Dutrow Jr. | 603 | 166 | 7,576,986 |
| Scott Lake | 1688 | 374 | 7,420,036 |
| Dale Romans | 580 | 109 | 7,081,653 |
| Doug O'Neill | 939 | 170 | 7,004,827 |
| Nick Zito | 452 | 86 | 6,967,792 |

### 2005 (Through Sept. 25)

| HORSES | Age | Sts | 1-2-3 | Earnings |
|---|---|---|---|---|
| Roses In May | 5 | 2 | 1-1-0 | $3,695,000 |
| Afleet Alex | 3 | 6 | 4-0-1 | 2,085,000 |
| Giacomo | 3 | 6 | 1-1-2 | 1,846,876 |
| Flower Alley | 3 | 7 | 4-2-0 | 1,449,200 |
| Saint Liam | 5 | 5 | 3-1-0 | 1,263,360 |
| Dynever | 5 | 2 | 0-2-0 | 1,220,000 |
| Sun King | 3 | 8 | 4-1-0 | 1,034,800 |
| Borrego | 4 | 6 | 2-1-2 | 936,600 |
| English Channel | 3 | 6 | 4-1-0 | 925,091 |
| High Fly | 3 | 7 | 3-1-1 | 901,500 |

| JOCKEYS | Mts | 1st | Earnings |
|---|---|---|---|
| John Velazquez | 919 | 193 | $17,787,870 |
| Edgar Prado | 1193 | 239 | 13,230,215 |
| Jerry Bailey | 558 | 148 | 12,910,386 |
| Rafael Bejarano | 980 | 189 | 9,834,421 |
| Victor Espinoza | 860 | 154 | 9,614,097 |
| Javier Castellano | 926 | 168 | 9,561,687 |
| Pat Valenzuela | 732 | 146 | 9,071,806 |
| Garrett Gomez | 984 | 172 | 8,325,093 |
| Cornelio Velasquez | 1099 | 154 | 8,184,647 |
| Ramon Dominguez | 943 | 211 | 7,990,506 |

| TRAINERS | Sts | 1st | Earnings |
|---|---|---|---|
| Todd Pletcher | 728 | 171 | $12,955,847 |
| Bobby Frankel | 451 | 100 | 10,981,052 |
| Steve Asmussen | 1676 | 353 | 10,005,168 |
| Doug O'Neill | 708 | 134 | 7,505,066 |
| Bill Mott | 473 | 114 | 7,162,142 |
| Nick Zito | 341 | 59 | 7,036,803 |
| Scott Lake | 1276 | 306 | 6,688,944 |
| Dale Romans | 339 | 65 | 6,570,835 |
| Richard Dutrow Jr. | 399 | 108 | 5,070,804 |
| Jeff Mullins | 350 | 83 | 4,632,598 |

## Harness Racing
## 2004-05 Major Stakes Races

Winners of major stakes races from Oct. 19, 2004 through Sept. 25, 2005; all paces and trots cover one mile; (BC) indicates year-end Breeders' Crown series.

### Late 2004

| Date | Race | Raceway | Winner | Time | Driver | Purse |
|------|------|---------|--------|------|--------|-------|
| Oct. 23 | BC 3-Yr-Old Colt Pace | Woodbine | Western Terror | 1:50²/₅ | Brian Sears | $555,000 |
| Oct. 23 | BC 3-Yr-Old Filly Pace | Woodbine | Rainbow Blue | 1:51 | Ron Pierce | 610,000 |
| Oct. 23 | BC 3-Yr-Old Colt Trot | Woodbine | Yankee Slide | 1:54⁴/₅ | Brian Sears | 500,000 |
| Oct. 23 | BC 3-Yr-Old Filly Trot | Woodbine | Housethatruthbuilt | 1:53³/₅ | Brian Sears | 500,000 |
| Oct. 23 | BC 2-Yr-Old Colt Pace | Woodbine | Village Jolt | 1:51¹/₅ | Ron Pierce | 663,200 |
| Oct. 23 | BC 2-Yr-Old Filly Pace | Woodbine | Restive Hanover | 1:52⁴/₅ | Andy Miller | 576,800 |
| Oct. 23 | BC 2-Yr-Old Colt Trot | Woodbine | Ken Warkentin | 1:57¹/₅ | David Miller | 525,900 |
| Oct. 23 | BC 2-Yr-Old Filly Trot | Woodbine | Flirtin Miss | 1:56¹/₅ | John Campbell | 558,900 |

### 2005 (through Sept. 25)

| Date | Race | Raceway | Winner | Time | Driver | Purse |
|------|------|---------|--------|------|--------|-------|
| May 28 | New Jersey Classic | Meadowlands | Rocknroll Hanover | 1:51 | Brian Sears | $500,000 |
| June 18 | North American Cup | Woodbine | Rocknroll Hanover | 1:49⁴/₅ | Brian Sears | 1,215,000 |
| June 25 | Canadian Pacing Derby | Mohawk | Ponder | 1:49²/₅ | Jack Moiseyev | 673,110 |
| June 25 | Hoosier Cup | Hoosier Park | Dawn ofa New Day | 1:50³/₅ | David Miller | 500,000 |
| July 9 | William Haughton Open Pace | Meadowlands | Dr. No | 1:50¹/₅ | Cat Manzi | 700,000 |
| July 15 | Stanley Dancer Trot | Meadowlands | Classic Photo | 1:53⁴/₅ | Ron Pierce | 350,000 |
| July 16 | Meadowlands Pace | Meadowlands | Rocknroll Hanover | 1:48³/₅ | Brian Sears | 1,000,000 |
| Aug. 4 | Peter Haughton Memorial | Meadowlands | Keystone Savage | 1:58 | Brian Sears | 460,000 |
| Aug. 4 | Merrie Annabelle Final | Meadowlands | Miss Wisconsin | 1:56³/₅ | Mike Lachance | 390,000 |
| Aug. 5 | Sweetheart Pace | Meadowlands | Lonesome Day | 1:53¹/₅ | David Miller | 330,000 |
| Aug. 5 | Woodrow Wilson Pace | Meadowlands | Western Ace | 1:51²/₅ | Ron Pierce | 375,000 |
| Aug. 6 | **Hambletonian** | Meadowlands | Vivid Photo | 1:52³/₅ | Roger Hammer | 1,500,000 |
| Aug. 6 | Hambletonian Oaks | Meadowlands | Jalopy | 1:53⁴/₅ | Jeff Gregory | 750,000 |
| Aug. 6 | Mistletoe Shalee | Meadowlands | Chotat Milk | 1:51 | David Miller | 357,160 |
| Aug. 6 | Nat Ray | Meadowlands | Hellava Rush | 1:51 | Cat Manzi | 300,000 |
| Aug. 6 | U.S. Pacing Championship | Meadowlands | Boulder Creek | 1:48⁴/₅ | Brian Sears | 375,000 |
| Aug. 13 | Coors Del Miller Adios | The Meadows | Village Jolt | 1:52¹/₅ | Ron Pierce | 321,800 |
| Aug. 20 | **Yonkers Trot** | Freehold | Strong Yankee | 1:56¹/₅ | Brian Sears | 297,816 |
| Aug. 27 | Fan Hanover Pace | Mohawk | Cabrini Hanover | 1:52¹/₅ | Brian Sears | 571,284 |
| Sept. 3 | BC Open Pace | Mohawk | Boulder Creek | 1:52 | Brian Sears | 500,000 |
| Sept. 3 | BC Mare Trot | Mohawk | Peaceful Way | 1:53¹/₅ | Trevor Ritchie | 250,000 |
| Sept. 3 | BC Open Trot | Mohawk | Mr. Muscleman | 1:52 | Ron Pierce | 800,000 |
| Sept. 3 | BC Mare Pace | Mohawk | Loyal Opposition | 1:51 | George Brennan | 331,500 |
| Sept. 3 | World Trotting Derby | DuQuoin | Vivid Photo | 1:51²/₅ | Roger Hammer | 525,000 |
| Sept. 5 | **Cane Pace** | Freehold | Royal Flush Shark | 1:52⁴/₅ | Eric Ledford | 346,000 |
| Sept. 17 | Metro Pace | Mohawk | Jereme's Jet | 1:50⁴/₅ | Paul MacDonell | 840,000 |
| Sept. 17 | Maple Leaf Trot | Mohawk | Mr. Muscleman | 1:52¹/₅ | Ron Pierce | 771,540 |
| Sept. 17 | Canadian Trotting Classic | Mohawk | Classic Photo | 1:52³/₅ | Ron Pierce | 850,000 |
| Sept. 22 | **Little Brown Jug** | Delaware | P-Forty-Seven | 1:52¹/₅ | Dave Palone | 569,032 |

## 2004-05 Money Leaders

Official Top 10 standings for 2004 and unofficial Top 10 standings for 2005 through Sept. 25.

### FINAL 2004     2005 (through Sept. 25)

| HORSES | Age | Sts | 1-2-3 | Earnings | HORSES | Age | Sts | 1-2-3 | Earnings |
|--------|-----|-----|-------|----------|--------|-----|-----|-------|----------|
| Windsong's Legacy | 3tc | 12 | 9-2-1 | $1,713,806 | Rocknroll Hanover | 3ph | 12 | 8-3-1 | $1,644,552 |
| Rainbow Blue | 3pf | 21 | 20-0-0 | 1,195,010 | Classic Photo | 3th | 16 | 10-3-3 | 1,376,829 |
| Timesarechanging | 3pg | 22 | 10-6-3 | 1,175,574 | Mr. Muscleman | 5tg | 14 | 12-1-0 | 1,364,220 |
| Holborn Hanover | 3pg | 26 | 7-5-4 | 1,125,876 | Vivid Photo | 3tg | 19 | 14-3-0 | 1,255,844 |
| Western Terror | 3pc | 24 | 8-4-5 | 1,112,739 | Boulder Creek | 5pg | 21 | 5-6-2 | 937,645 |
| Cantab Hall | 3tc | 13 | 4-5-2 | 980,966 | Ponder | 4ph | 25 | 8-11-3 | 794,652 |
| Village Jolt | 2pc | 10 | 6-2-0 | 918,577 | Strong Yankee | 3th | 14 | 4-5-1 | 767,943 |
| Metropolitan | 3pc | 20 | 4-5-2 | 852,597 | Burning Point | 5pm | 27 | 8-7-3 | 687,142 |
| Royal Mattjesty | 5ph | 29 | 8-8-5 | 850,186 | Cabrini Hanover | 3pm | 12 | 7-3-2 | 677,225 |
| Housethatruthbuilt | 3tf | 15 | 11-3-1 | 848,109 | American Ideal | 3ph | 18 | 9-4-1 | 623,979 |

| DRIVERS | Mts | 1st | Earnings | DRIVERS | Mts | 1st | Earnings |
|---------|-----|-----|----------|---------|-----|-----|----------|
| Ron Pierce | 2213 | 395 | $12,327,863 | Brian Sears | 1899 | 339 | $11,917,184 |
| Brian Sears | 1995 | 353 | 10,028,306 | Ron Pierce | 2011 | 336 | 10,633,065 |
| David Miller | 2417 | 353 | 8,493,176 | David Miller | 2218 | 348 | 8,607,586 |
| Cat Manzi | 3294 | 651 | 7,693,362 | Cat Manzi | 2760 | 528 | 7,032,274 |
| George Brennan | 2118 | 322 | 7,521,453 | George Brennan | 1867 | 289 | 6,505,114 |
| John Campbell | 962 | 151 | 7,240,312 | Mark MacDonald | 3182 | 497 | 5,124,915 |
| Luc Ouellette | 2191 | 370 | 7,185,998 | Paul MacDonell | 1430 | 208 | 4,973,334 |
| Mike Lachance | 1620 | 180 | 6,696,056 | Luc Ouellette | 1667 | 241 | 4,888,893 |
| Chris Christoforou | 2358 | 398 | 6,022,677 | Jack Moiseyev | 1283 | 174 | 4,336,802 |
| Paul MacDonell | 1839 | 230 | 5,865,450 | Eric Ledford | 1048 | 166 | 4,167,934 |

# 1867-2005
# *Through the Years*

SPORTS ALMANAC

## Thoroughbred Racing

### The Triple Crown

The term "Triple Crown" was coined by sportswriter Charles Hatton while covering the 1930 victories of Gallant Fox in the Kentucky Derby, Preakness Stakes and Belmont Stakes. Before then, only Sir Barton (1919) had won all three races in the same year. Since then, nine horses have won the Triple Crown. Two trainers, James (Sunny Jim) Fitzsimmons and Ben A. Jones, have saddled two Triple Crown champions, while Eddie Arcaro is the only jockey to ride two champions.

| Year | | Jockey | Trainer | Owner | Sire/Dam |
|------|---|--------|---------|-------|----------|
| 1919 | **Sir Barton** | Johnny Loftus | H. Guy Bedwell | J.K.L. Ross | Star Shoot/Lady Sterling |
| 1930 | **Gallant Fox** | Earl Sande | J.E. Fitzsimmons | Belair Stud | Sir Gallahad III/Marguerite |
| 1935 | **Omaha** | Willie Saunders | J.E. Fitzsimmons | Belair Stud | Gallant Fox/Flambino |
| 1937 | **War Admiral** | Charley Kurtsinger | George Conway | Samuel Riddle | Man o' War/Brushup |
| 1941 | **Whirlaway** | Eddie Arcaro | Ben A. Jones | Calumet Farm | Blenheim II/Dustwhirl |
| 1943 | **Count Fleet** | Johnny Longden | Don Cameron | Mrs. J.D. Hertz | Reigh Count/Quickly |
| 1946 | **Assault** | Warren Mehrtens | Max Hirsch | King Ranch | Bold Venture/Igual |
| 1948 | **Citation** | Eddie Arcaro | Ben A. Jones | Calumet Farm | Bull Lea/Hydroplane II |
| 1973 | **Secretariat** | Ron Turcotte | Lucien Laurin | Meadow Stable | Bold Ruler/Somethingroyal |
| 1977 | **Seattle Slew** | Jean Cruguet | Billy Turner | Karen Taylor | Bold Reasoning/My Charmer |
| 1978 | **Affirmed** | Steve Cauthen | Laz Barrera | Harbor View Farm | Exclusive Native/Won't Tell You |

**Note:** Gallant Fox (1930) is the only Triple Crown winner to sire another Triple Crown winner, Omaha (1935). Wm. Woodward Sr., owner of Belair Stud, was breeder-owner of both horses and both were trained by Sunny Jim Fitzsimmons.

### Triple Crown Near Misses

Forty-nine horses have won two legs of the Triple Crown. Of those, eighteen won the Kentucky Derby (KD) and Preakness Stakes (PS) only to be beaten in the Belmont Stakes (BS). Two others, Burgoo King (1932) and Bold Venture (1936), won the Derby and Preakness, but were forced out of the Belmont with the same injury—a bowed tendon—that effectively ended their racing careers. In 1978, Alydar finished second to Affirmed in all three races, the only time that has happened. Note that the Preakness preceded the Kentucky Derby in 1922, '23 and '31; (*) indicates won on disqualification.

| Year | | KD | PS | BS |
|------|---|-----|-----|-----|
| 1877 | **Cloverbrook** | DNS | won | won |
| 1878 | **Duke of Magenta** | DNS | won | won |
| 1880 | **Grenada** | DNS | won | won |
| 1881 | **Saunterer** | DNS | won | won |
| 1895 | **Belmar** | DNS | won | won |
| 1920 | **Man o' War** | DNS | won | won |
| 1922 | **Pillory** | DNS | won | won |
| 1923 | **Zev** | won | 12th | won |
| 1931 | **Twenty Grand** | won | 2nd | won |
| 1932 | **Burgoo King** | won | won | DNS |
| 1936 | **Bold Venture** | won | won | DNS |
| 1939 | **Johnstown** | won | 5th | won |
| 1940 | **Bimelech** | 2nd | won | won |
| 1942 | **Shut Out** | won | 5th | won |
| 1944 | **Pensive** | won | won | 2nd |
| 1949 | **Capot** | 2nd | won | won |
| 1950 | **Middleground** | won | 2nd | won |
| 1953 | **Native Dancer** | 2nd | won | won |
| 1955 | **Nashua** | 2nd | won | won |
| 1956 | **Needles** | won | 2nd | won |
| 1958 | **Tim Tam** | won | won | 2nd |
| 1961 | **Carry Back** | won | won | 7th |
| 1963 | **Chateaugay** | won | 2nd | won |
| 1964 | **Northern Dancer** | won | won | 3rd |

| Year | | KD | PS | BS |
|------|---|-----|-----|-----|
| 1966 | **Kauai King** | won | won | 4th |
| 1967 | **Damascus** | 3rd | won | won |
| 1968 | **Forward Pass** | won* | won | 2nd |
| 1969 | **Majestic Prince** | won | won | 2nd |
| 1971 | **Canonero II** | won | won | 4th |
| 1972 | **Riva Ridge** | won | 4th | won |
| 1974 | **Little Current** | 5th | won | won |
| 1976 | **Bold Forbes** | won | 3rd | won |
| 1979 | **Spectacular Bid** | won | won | 3rd |
| 1981 | **Pleasant Colony** | won | won | 3rd |
| 1984 | **Swale** | won | 7th | won |
| 1987 | **Alysheba** | won | won | 4th |
| 1988 | **Risen Star** | 3rd | won | won |
| 1989 | **Sunday Silence** | won | won | 2nd |
| 1991 | **Hansel** | 10th | won | won |
| 1994 | **Tabasco Cat** | 6th | won | won |
| 1995 | **Thunder Gulch** | won | 3rd | won |
| 1997 | **Silver Charm** | won | won | 2nd |
| 1998 | **Real Quiet** | won | won | 2nd |
| 1999 | **Charismatic** | won | won | 3rd |
| 2001 | **Point Given** | 5th | won | won |
| 2002 | **War Emblem** | won | won | 8th |
| 2003 | **Funny Cide** | won | won | 3rd |
| 2004 | **Smarty Jones** | won | won | 2nd |
| 2005 | **Afleet Alex** | 3rd | won | won |

## The Triple Crown Challenge (1987-93)

Seeking to make the Triple Crown more than just a media event and to insure that owners would not be attracted to more lucrative races, officials at Churchill Downs, the Maryland Jockey Club and the New York Racing Association created Triple Crown Productions in 1985 and announced that a $1 million bonus would be given to the horse that performs best in the Kentucky Derby, Preakness Stakes and Belmont Stakes. Furthermore, a bonus of $5 million would be presented to any horse winning all three races.

Revised in 1991, the rules stated that the winning horse must: 1. finish all three races; 2. earn points by finishing first, second, third or fourth in at least one of the three races; and 3. earn the highest number of points based on the following system–10 points to win, five to place, three to show and one to finish fourth. In the event of a tie, the $1 million is distributed equally among the top point-getters. From 1987-90, the system was five points to win, three to place and one to show. The Triple Crown Challenge was discontinued in 1994.

| Year | | KD | PS | BS | Pts |
|---|---|---|---|---|---|
| 1987 | 1 **Bet Twice** | 2nd | 2nd | 1st– | 11 |
| | 2 Alysheba | 1st | 1st | 4th– | 10 |
| | 3 Cryptoclearance | 4th | 3rd | 2nd– | 4 |
| 1988 | 1 **Risen Star** | 3rd | 1st | 1st– | 11 |
| | 2 Winning Colors | 1st | 3rd | 6th– | 6 |
| | 3 Brian's Time | 6th | 2nd | 3rd– | 4 |
| 1989 | 1 **Sunday Silence** | 1st | 1st | 2nd– | 13 |
| | 2 Easy Goer | 2nd | 2nd | 1st– | 11 |
| | 3 Hawkster | 5th | 5th | 5th– | 0 |
| 1990 | 1 **Unbridled** | 1st | 2nd | 4th– | 8 |
| | 2 Summer Squall | 2nd | 1st | DNR– | 8 |
| | 3 Go and Go | DNR | DNR | 1st– | 5 |
| | (Unbridled was only horse to run all three races.) | | | | |

| Year | | KD | PS | BS | Pts |
|---|---|---|---|---|---|
| 1991 | 1 **Hansel** | 10th | 1st | 1st– | 20 |
| | 2 Strike the Gold | 1st | 6th | 2nd– | 15 |
| | 3 Mane Minister | 3rd | 3rd | 3rd– | 9 |
| 1992 | 1 **Pine Bluff** | 5th | 1st | 3rd– | 13 |
| | 2 Casual Lies | 2nd | 3rd | 5th– | 8 |
| | (No other horses ran all three races.) | | | | |
| 1993 | 1 **Sea Hero** | 1st | 5th | 7th– | 10 |
| | 2 Wild Gale | 3rd | 8th | 3rd– | 6 |
| | (No other horses ran all three races.) | | | | |

## Kentucky Derby

For three-year-olds. Held the first Saturday in May at Churchill Downs in Louisville, Ky. Inaugurated in 1875. Originally run at 1½ miles (1875-95), shortened to present 1¼ miles in 1896.

**Trainers with most wins:** Ben Jones (6); D. Wayne Lukas and Dick Thompson (4); Bob Baffert, Sunny Jim Fitzsimmons and Max Hirsch (3).

**Jockeys with most wins:** Eddie Arcaro and Bill Hartack (5); Bill Shoemaker (4); Angel Cordero Jr., Issac Murphy, Earl Sande and Gary Stevens (3).

**Winning fillies:** Regret (1915), Genuine Risk (1980) and Winning Colors (1988).

| Year | Winner (Margin) | Time | Jockey | Trainer | 2nd place | 3rd place |
|---|---|---|---|---|---|---|
| 1875 | **Aristides** (1) | 2:37¾ | Oliver Lewis | Ansel Anderson | Volcano | Verdigris |
| 1876 | **Vagrant** (2) | 2:38¼ | Bobby Swim | James Williams | Creedmore | Harry Hill |
| 1877 | **Baden-Baden** (2) | 2:38 | Billy Walker | Ed Brown | Leonard | King William |
| 1878 | **Day Star** (2) | 2:37¼ | Jimmy Carter | Lee Paul | Himyar | Leveler |
| 1879 | **Lord Murphy** (1) | 2:37 | Charlie Shauer | George Rice | Falsetto | Strathmore |
| 1880 | **Fonso** (1) | 2:37½ | George Lewis | Tice Hutsell | Kimball | Bancroft |
| 1881 | **Hindoo** (4) | 2:40 | Jim McLaughlin | James Rowe Sr. | Lelex | Alfambra |
| 1882 | **Apollo** (½) | 2:40¼ | Babe Hurd | Green Morris | Runnymede | Bengal |
| 1883 | **Leonatus** (3) | 2:43 | Billy Donohue | John McGinty | Drake Carter | Lord Raglan |
| 1884 | **Buchanan** (2) | 2:40¼ | Isaac Murphy | William Bird | Loftin | Audrain |
| 1885 | **Joe Cotton** (nk) | 2:37¼ | Babe Henderson | Alex Perry | Bersan | Ten Booker |
| 1886 | **Ben Ali** (½) | 2:36½ | Paul Duffy | Jim Murphy | Blue Wing | Free Knight |
| 1887 | **Montrose** (2) | 2:39¼ | Isaac Lewis | John McGinty | Jim Gore | Jacobin |
| 1888 | **MacBeth II** (1) | 2:38¼ | George Covington | John Campbell | Gallifet | White |
| 1889 | **Spokane** (ns) | 2:34½ | Thomas Kiley | John Rodegap | Proctor Knott | Once Again |
| 1890 | **Riley** (2) | 2:45 | Isaac Murphy | Edward Corrigan | Bill Letcher | Robespierre |
| 1891 | **Kingman** (1) | 2:52¼ | Isaac Murphy | Dud Allen | Balgowan | High Tariff |
| 1892 | **Azra** (ns) | 2:41½ | Lonnie Clayton | John Morris | Huron | Phil Dwyer |
| 1893 | **Lookout** (5) | 2:39¼ | Eddie Kunze | Wm. McDaniel | Plutus | Boundless |
| 1894 | **Chant** (2) | 2:41 | Frank Goodale | Eugene Leigh | Pearl Song | Sigurd |
| 1895 | **Halma** (3) | 2:37½ | Soup Perkins | Byron McClelland | Basso | Laureate |
| 1896 | **Ben Brush** (ns) | 2:07¾ | Willie Simms | Hardy Campbell | Ben Eder | Semper Ego |
| 1897 | **Typhoon II** (hd) | 2:12½ | Buttons Garner | J.C. Cahn | Ornament | Dr. Catlett |
| 1898 | **Plaudit** (nk) | 2:09 | Willie Simms | John E. Madden | Lieber Karl | Isabey |
| 1899 | **Manuel** (2) | 2:12 | Fred Taral | Robert Walden | Corsini | Mazo |
| 1900 | **Lieut. Gibson** (4) | 2:06¼ | Jimmy Boland | Charles Hughes | Florizar | Thrive |
| 1901 | **His Eminence** (2) | 2:07¾ | Jimmy Winkfield | F.B. Van Meter | Sannazarro | Driscoll |
| 1902 | **Alan-a-Dale** (ns) | 2:08¾ | Jimmy Winkfield | T.C. McDowell | Inventor | The Rival |
| 1903 | **Judge Himes** (¾) | 2:09 | Hal Booker | J.P. Mayberry | Early | Bourbon |
| 1904 | **Elwood** (½) | 2:08½ | Shorty Prior | C.E. Durnell | Ed Tierney | Brancas |
| 1905 | **Agile** (3) | 2:10¾ | Jack Martin | Robert Tucker | Ram's Horn | Layson |
| 1906 | **Sir Huon** (2) | 2:08⅘ | Roscoe Troxler | Pete Coyne | Lady Navarre | James Reddick |
| 1907 | **Pink Star** (2) | 2:12⅗ | Andy Minder | W.H. Fizer | Zal | Ovelando |
| 1908 | **Stone Street** (1) | 2:15⅕ | Arthur Pickens | J.W. Hall | Sir Cleges | Dunvegan |
| 1909 | **Wintergreen** (4) | 2:08⅕ | Vincent Powers | Charles Mack | Miami | Dr. Barkley |

## Kentucky Derby (Cont.)

| Year | Winner (Margin) | Time | Jockey | Trainer | 2nd place | 3rd place |
|---|---|---|---|---|---|---|
| 1910 | **Donau** (½) | 2:06⅖ | Fred Herbert | George Ham | Joe Morris | Fighting Bob |
| 1911 | **Meridian** (¾) | 2:05 | George Archibald | Albert Ewing | Governor Gray | Colston |
| 1912 | **Worth** (nk) | 2:09⅖ | C.H. Shilling | Frank Taylor | Duval | Flamma |
| 1913 | **Donerail** (½) | 2:04⅘ | Roscoe Goose | Thomas Hayes | Ten Point | Gowell |
| 1914 | **Old Rosebud** (8) | 2:03⅖ | John McCabe | F.D. Weir | Hodge | Bronzewing |
| 1915 | **Regret** (2) | 2:05⅖ | Joe Notter | James Rowe Sr. | Pebbles | Sharpshooter |
| 1916 | **George Smith** (nk) | 2:04 | Johnny Loftus | Hollie Hughes | Star Hawk | Franklin |
| 1917 | **Omar Khayyam** (2) | 2:04⅗ | Charles Borel | C.T. Patterson | Ticket | Midway |
| 1918 | **Exterminator** (1) | 2:10⅘ | William Knapp | Henry McDaniel | Escoba | Viva America |
| 1919 | **SIR BARTON** (5) | 2:09⅘ | Johnny Loftus | H. Guy Bedwell | Billy Kelly | Under Fire |
| 1920 | **Paul Jones** (hd) | 2:09 | Ted Rice | Billy Garth | Upset | On Watch |
| 1921 | **Behave Yourself** (hd) | 2:04⅕ | Charles Thompson | Dick Thompson | Black Servant | Prudery |
| 1922 | **Morvich** (1½) | 2:04⅗ | Albert Johnson | Fred Burlew | Bet Mosie | John Finn |
| 1923 | **Zev** (1½) | 2:05⅖ | Earl Sande | David Leary | Martingale | Vigil |
| 1924 | **Black Gold** (½) | 2:05⅕ | John Mooney | Hanly Webb | Chilhowee | Beau Butler |
| 1925 | **Flying Ebony** (1½) | 2:07⅗ | Earl Sande | William Duke | Captain Hal | Son of John |
| 1926 | **Bubbling Over** (5) | 2:03⅘ | Albert Johnson | Dick Thompson | Bagenbaggage | Rock Man |
| 1927 | **Whiskery** (hd) | 2:06 | Linus McAtee | Fred Hopkins | Osmand | Jock |
| 1928 | **Reigh Count** (3) | 2:10⅖ | Chick Lang | Bert Michell | Misstep | Toro |
| 1929 | **Clyde Van Dusen** (2) | 2:10⅘ | Linus McAtee | Clyde Van Dusen | Naishapur | Panchio |
| 1930 | **GALLANT FOX** (2) | 2:07⅗ | Earl Sande | Jim Fitzsimmons | Gallant Knight | Ned O. |
| 1931 | **Twenty Grand** (4) | 2:01⅘ | Charley Kurtsinger | James Rowe Jr. | Sweep All | Mate |
| 1932 | **Burgoo King** (5) | 2:05⅕ | Eugene James | Dick Thompson | Economic | Stepenfetchit |
| 1933 | **Brokers Tip** (ns) | 2:06⅘ | Don Meade | Dick Thompson | Head Play | Charley O. |
| 1934 | **Cavalcade** (2½) | 2:04 | Mack Garner | Bob Smith | Discovery | Agrarian |
| 1935 | **OMAHA** (1½) | 2:05 | Willie Saunders | Jim Fitzsimmons | Roman Soldier | Whiskolo |
| 1936 | **Bold Venture** (hd) | 2:03⅗ | Ira Hanford | Max Hirsch | Brevity | Indian Broom |
| 1937 | **WAR ADMIRAL** (1¾) | 2:03⅕ | Charley Kurtsinger | George Conway | Pompoon | Reaping Reward |
| 1938 | **Lawrin** (1) | 2:04⅘ | Eddie Arcaro | Ben Jones | Dauber | Can't Wait |
| 1939 | **Johnstown** (8) | 2:03⅖ | James Stout | Jim Fitzsimmons | Challedon | Heather Broom |
| 1940 | **Gallahadion** (1½) | 2:05 | Carroll Bierman | Roy Waldron | Bimelech | Dit |
| 1941 | **WHIRLAWAY** (8) | 2:01⅖ | Eddie Arcaro | Ben Jones | Staretor | Market Wise |
| 1942 | **Shut Out** (2½) | 2:04⅖ | Wayne Wright | John Gaver | Alsab | Valdina Orphan |
| 1943 | **COUNT FLEET** (3) | 2:04 | Johnny Longden | Don Cameron | Blue Swords | Slide Rule |
| 1944 | **Pensive** (4½) | 2:04⅕ | Conn McCreary | Ben Jones | Broadcloth | Stir Up |
| 1945 | **Hoop Jr** (6) | 2:07 | Eddie Arcaro | Ivan Parke | Pot O'Luck | Darby Dieppe |
| 1946 | **ASSAULT** (8) | 2:06⅗ | Warren Mehrtens | Max Hirsch | Spy Song | Hampden |
| 1947 | **Jet Pilot** (hd) | 2:06⅘ | Eric Guerin | Tom Smith | Phalanx | Faultless |
| 1948 | **CITATION** (3½) | 2:05⅖ | Eddie Arcaro | Ben Jones | Coaltown | My Request |
| 1949 | **Ponder** (3) | 2:04⅕ | Steve Brooks | Ben Jones | Capot | Palestinian |
| 1950 | **Middleground** (1¼) | 2:01⅗ | William Boland | Max Hirsch | Hill Prince | Mr. Trouble |
| 1951 | **Count Turf** (4) | 2:02⅗ | Conn McCreary | Sol Rutchick | Royal Mustang | Ruhe |
| 1952 | **Hill Gail** (2) | 2:01⅗ | Eddie Arcaro | Ben Jones | Sub Fleet | Blue Man |
| 1953 | **Dark Star** (hd) | 2:02 | Hank Moreno | Eddie Hayward | Native Dancer | Invigorator |
| 1954 | **Determine** (1½) | 2:03 | Raymond York | Willie Molter | Hasty Road | Hasseyampa |
| 1955 | **Swaps** (1½) | 2:01⅘ | Bill Shoemaker | Mesh Tenney | Nashua | Summer Tan |
| 1956 | **Needles** (¾) | 2:03⅖ | David Erb | Hugh Fontaine | Fabius | Come On Red |
| 1957 | **Iron Liege** (ns) | 2:02⅕ | Bill Hartack | Jimmy Jones | Gallant Man | Round Table |
| 1958 | **Tim Tam** (½) | 2:05 | Ismael Valenzuela | Jimmy Jones | Lincoln Road | Noureddin |
| 1959 | **Tomy Lee** (ns) | 2:02⅕ | Bill Shoemaker | Frank Childs | Sword Dancer | First Landing |
| 1960 | **Venetian Way** (3½) | 2:02⅖ | Bill Hartack | Victor Sovinski | Bally Ache | Victoria Park |
| 1961 | **Carry Back** (¾) | 2:04 | John Sellers | Jack Price | Crozier | Bass Clef |
| 1962 | **Decidedly** (2¼) | 2:00⅖ | Bill Hartack | Horatio Luro | Roman Line | Ridan |
| 1963 | **Chateaugay** (1¼) | 2:01⅘ | Braulio Baeza | James Conway | Never Bend | Candy Spots |
| 1964 | **Northern Dancer** (nk) | 2:00 | Bill Hartack | Horatio Luro | Hill Rise | The Scoundrel |
| 1965 | **Lucky Debonair** (nk) | 2:01⅕ | Bill Shoemaker | Frank Catrone | Dapper Dan | Tom Rolfe |
| 1966 | **Kauai King** (½) | 2:02 | Don Brumfield | Henry Forrest | Advocator | Blue Skyer |
| 1967 | **Proud Clarion** (1) | 2:00⅗ | Bobby Ussery | Loyd Gentry | Barbs Delight | Damascus |
| 1968 | **Forward Pass*** (nk) | — | Ismael Valenzuela | Henry Forrest | Francie's Hat | T.V. Commercial |
| 1969 | **Majestic Prince** (nk) | 2:01⅘ | Bill Hartack | Johnny Longden | Arts and Letters | Dike |
| 1970 | **Dust Commander** (5) | 2:03⅖ | Mike Manganello | Don Combs | My Dad George | High Echelon |
| 1971 | **Canonero II** (3¼) | 2:03⅕ | Gustavo Avila | Juan Arias | Jim French | Bold Reason |
| 1972 | **Riva Ridge** (3¼) | 2:01⅘ | Ron Turcotte | Lucien Laurin | No Le Hace | Hold Your Peace |
| 1973 | **SECRETARIAT** (2½) | 1:59⅖ | Ron Turcotte | Lucien Laurin | Sham | Our Native |
| 1974 | **Cannonade** (2¼) | 2:04 | Angel Cordero Jr. | Woody Stephens | Hudson County | Agitate |
| 1975 | **Foolish Pleasure** (1¾) | 2:02 | Jacinto Vasquez | LeRoy Jolley | Avatar | Diabolo |
| 1976 | **Bold Forbes** (1) | 2:01⅗ | Angel Cordero Jr. | Laz Barrera | Honest Pleasure | Elocutionist |
| 1977 | **SEATTLE SLEW** (1¾) | 2:02⅕ | Jean Cruguet | Billy Turner | Run Dusty Run | Sanhedrin |
| 1978 | **AFFIRMED** (1½) | 2:01⅕ | Steve Cauthen | Laz Barrera | Alydar | Believe It |

| Year | Winner (Margin) | Time | Jockey | Trainer | 2nd place | 3rd place |
|---|---|---|---|---|---|---|
| 1979 | **Spectacular Bid** (2¾) | 2:02⅖ | Ron Franklin | Bud Delp | General Assembly | Golden Act |
| 1980 | **Genuine Risk** (1) | 2:02 | Jacinto Vasquez | LeRoy Jolley | Rumbo | Jaklin Klugman |
| 1981 | **Pleasant Colony** (¾) | 2:02 | Jorge Velasquez | John Campo | Woodchopper | Partez |
| 1982 | **Gato Del Sol** (2½) | 2:02⅖ | E. Delahoussaye | Eddie Gregson | Laser Light | Reinvested |
| 1983 | **Sunny's Halo** (2) | 2:02⅕ | E. Delahoussaye | David Cross Jr. | Desert Wine | Caveat |
| 1984 | **Swale** (3¼) | 2:02⅖ | Laffit Pincay Jr. | Woody Stephens | Coax Me Chad | At The Threshold |
| 1985 | **Spend A Buck** (5¼) | 2:00⅕ | Angel Cordero Jr. | Cam Gambolati | Stephan's Odyssey | Chief's Crown |
| 1986 | **Ferdinand** (2¼) | 2:02⅘ | Bill Shoemaker | Chas. Whittingham | Bold Arrangement | Broad Brush |
| 1987 | **Alysheba** (¾) | 2:03⅖ | Chris McCarron | Jack Van Berg | Bet Twice | Avies Copy |
| 1988 | **Winning Colors** (nk) | 2:02⅕ | Gary Stevens | D. Wayne Lukas | Forty Niner | Risen Star |
| 1989 | **Sunday Silence** (2½) | 2:05 | Pat Valenzuela | Chas. Whittingham | Easy Goer | Awe Inspiring |
| 1990 | **Unbridled** (3½) | 2:02 | Craig Perret | Carl Nafzger | Summer Squall | Pleasant Tap |
| 1991 | **Strike the Gold** (1¾) | 2:03 | Chris Antley | Nick Zito | Best Pal | Mane Minister |
| 1992 | **Lil E. Tee** (1) | 2:03 | Pat Day | Lynn Whiting | Casual Lies | Dance Floor |
| 1993 | **Sea Hero** (2½) | 2:02⅖ | Jerry Bailey | Mack Miller | Prairie Bayou | Wild Gale |
| 1994 | **Go For Gin** (2) | 2:03⅗ | Chris McCarron | Nick Zito | Strodes Creek | Blumin Affair |
| 1995 | **Thunder Gulch** (2¼) | 2:01⅕ | Gary Stevens | D. Wayne Lukas | Tejano Run | Timber Country |
| 1996 | **Grindstone** (ns) | 2:01 | Jerry Bailey | D. Wayne Lukas | Cavonnier | Prince of Thieves |
| 1997 | **Silver Charm** (hd) | 2:02⅖ | Gary Stevens | Bob Baffert | Captain Bodgit | Free House |
| 1998 | **Real Quiet** (½) | 2:02⅕ | Kent Desormeaux | Bob Baffert | Victory Gallop | Indian Charlie |
| 1999 | **Charismatic** (nk) | 2:03⅕ | Chris Antley | D. Wayne Lukas | Menifee | Cat Thief |
| 2000 | **Fusaichi Pegasus** (1½) | 2:01⅕ | Kent Desormeaux | Neil Drysdale | Aptitude | Impeachment |
| 2001 | **Monarchos** (4¾) | 1:59⅘ | Jorge Chavez | John Ward Jr. | Invisible Ink | Congaree |
| 2002 | **War Emblem** (4) | 2:01 | Victor Espinoza | Bob Baffert | Proud Citizen | Perfect Drift |
| 2003 | **Funny Cide** (1¾) | 2:01 | Jose Santos | Barclay Tagg | Empire Maker | Peace Rules |
| 2004 | **Smarty Jones** (2¾) | 2:04 | Stewart Elliott | John Servis | Lion Heart | Imperialism |
| 2005 | **Giacomo** (½) | 2:02¾ | Mike Smith | John Shirreffs | Closing Argument | Afleet Alex |

*Dancer's Image finished first (in 2:02½), but was disqualified after traces of prohibited medication were found in his system.

## Preakness Stakes

For three-year-olds. Held two weeks after the Kentucky Derby at Pimlico Race Course in Baltimore. Inaugurated 1873. Note that the 1918 race was held over two divisions. Originally run at 1½ miles (1873-88), then at 1¼ miles (1889), 1½ miles (1890), 1¹⁄₁₆ miles (1894-1900), 1 mile & 70 yards (1901-07), 1¹⁄₁₆ miles (1908), 1 mile (1909-1910), 1⅛ miles (1911-24), and the present 1³⁄₁₆ miles since 1925.

**Trainers with most wins:** Robert W. Walden (7); T.J. Healey and D. Wayne Lukas (5); Bob Baffert, Sunny Jim Fitzsimmons and Jimmy Jones (4); J. Whalen (3).

**Jockeys with most wins:** Eddie Arcaro (6); Pat Day (5); G. Barbee, Bill Hartack and Lloyd Hughes (3).

**Winning fillies:** Flocarline (1903), Whimsical (1906), Rhine Maiden (1915) and Nellie Morse (1924).

| Year | Winner (Margin) | Time | Jockey | Trainer | 2nd place | 3rd place |
|---|---|---|---|---|---|---|
| 1873 | **Survivor** (10) | 2:43 | G. Barbee | A.D. Pryor | John Boulger | Artist |
| 1874 | **Culpepper** (¾) | 2:56½ | W. Donohue | H. Gaffney | King Amadeus | Scratch |
| 1875 | **Tom Ochiltree** (2) | 2:43½ | L. Hughes | R.W. Walden | Viator | Bay Final |
| 1876 | **Shirley** (4) | 2:44¾ | G. Barbee | W. Brown | Rappahannock | Compliment |
| 1877 | **Cloverbrook** (2) | 2:45½ | C. Holloway | J. Walden | Bombast | Lucifer |
| 1878 | **Duke of Magenta** (2) | 2:41¾ | C. Holloway | R.W. Walden | Bayard | Albert |
| 1879 | **Harold** (1) | 2:40½ | L. Hughes | R.W. Walden | Jericho | Rochester |
| 1880 | **Grenada** (¾) | 2:40½ | L. Hughes | R.W. Walden | Oden | Emily F. |
| 1881 | **Saunterer** (½) | 2:40½ | T. Costello | R.W. Walden | Compensation | Baltic |
| 1882 | **Vanguard** (nk) | 2:44½ | T. Costello | R.W. Walden | Heck | Col. Watson |
| 1883 | **Jacobus** (4) | 2:42½ | G. Barbee | R. Dwyer | Parnell | (2-horse race) |
| 1884 | **Knight of Ellerslie** (2) | 2:39½ | S. Fisher | T.B. Doswell | Welcher | (2-horse race) |
| 1885 | **Tecumseh** (2) | 2:49 | Jim McLaughlin | C. Littlefield | Wickham | John C. |
| 1886 | **The Bard** (3) | 2:45 | S. Fisher | J. Huggins | Eurus | Elkwood |
| 1887 | **Dunboyne** (1) | 2:39½ | W. Donohue | W. Jennings | Mahoney | Raymond |
| 1888 | **Refund** (3) | 2:49 | F. Littlefield | R.W. Walden | Bertha B.* | Glendale |
| 1889 | **Buddhist** (8) | 2:17½ | W. Anderson | J. Rogers | Japhet | (2-horse race) |
| 1890 | **Montague** (3) | 2:36¾ | W. Martin | E. Feakes | Philosophy | Barrister |
| 1891-93 | Not held | | | | | |
| 1894 | **Assignee** (3) | 1:49¼ | F. Taral | W. Lakeland | Potentate | Ed Kearney |
| 1895 | **Belmar** (1) | 1:50½ | F. Taral | E. Feakes | April Fool | Sue Kittie |
| 1896 | **Margrave** (1) | 1:51 | H. Griffin | Byron McClelland | Hamilton II | Intermission |
| 1897 | **Paul Kauvar** (1½) | 1:51¼ | T. Thorpe | T.P. Hayes | Elkins | On Deck |
| 1898 | **Sly Fox** (2) | 1:49¾ | W. Simms | H. Campbell | The Huguenot | Nuto |
| 1899 | **Half Time** (1) | 1:47 | R. Clawson | F. McCabe | Filigrane | Lackland |
| 1900 | **Hindus** (hd) | 1:48⅖ | H. Spencer | J.H. Morris | Sarmatian | Ten Candles |
| 1901 | **The Parader** (2) | 1:47⅕ | F. Landry | T.J. Healey | Sadie S. | Dr. Barlow |
| 1902 | **Old England** (ns) | 1:45⅘ | L. Jackson | G.B. Morris | Maj. Daingerfield | Namtor |
| 1903 | **Flocarline** (½) | 1:44⅘ | W. Gannon | H.C. Riddle | Mackey Dwyer | Rightful |
| 1904 | **Bryn Mawr** (1) | 1:44⅕ | E. Hildebrand | W.F. Presgrave | Wotan | Dolly Spanker |
| 1905 | **Cairngorm** (hd) | 1:45⅘ | W. Davis | A.J. Joyner | Kiamesha | Coy Maid |

## Preakness Stakes (Cont.)

| Year | Winner (Margin) | Time | Jockey | Trainer | 2nd place | 3rd place |
|---|---|---|---|---|---|---|
| 1906 | **Whimsical** (4) | 1:45 | Walter Miller | T.J. Gaynor | Content | Larabie |
| 1907 | **Don Enrique** (1) | 1:45⅖ | G. Mountain | J. Whalen | Ethon | Zambesi |
| 1908 | **Royal Tourist** (4) | 1:46⅖ | Eddie Dugan | A.J. Joyner | Live Wire | Robert Cooper |
| 1909 | **Effendi** (1) | 1:39⅘ | Willie Doyle | F.C. Frisbie | Fashion Plate | Hill Top |
| 1910 | **Layminster** (½) | 1:40⅗ | R. Estep | J.S. Healy | Dalhousie | Sager |
| 1911 | **Watervale** (1) | 1:51 | Eddie Dugan | J. Whalen | Zeus | The Nigger |
| 1912 | **Colonel Holloway** (5) | 1:56⅗ | C. Turner | D. Woodford | Bwana Tumbo | Tipsand |
| 1913 | **Buskin** (nk) | 1:53⅖ | James Butwell | J. Whalen | Kleburne | Barnegat |
| 1914 | **Holiday** (¾) | 1:53⅘ | A. Schuttinger | J.S. Healy | Brave Cunarder | Defendum |
| 1915 | **Rhine Maiden** (1½) | 1:58 | Douglas Hoffman | F. Devers | Half Rock | Runes |
| 1916 | **Damrosch** (1½) | 1:54⅘ | Linus McAtee | A.G. Weston | Greenwood | Achievement |
| 1917 | **Kalitan** (2) | 1:54⅖ | E. Haynes | Bill Hurley | Al M. Dick | Kentucky Boy |
| 1918 | **War Cloud** (¾) | 1:53⅗ | Johnny Loftus | W.B. Jennings | Sunny Slope | Lanius |
| 1918 | **Jack Hare Jr** (2) | 1:53⅖ | Charles Peak | F.D. Weir | The Porter | Kate Bright |
| 1919 | **SIR BARTON** (4) | 1:53 | Johnny Loftus | H. Guy Bedwell | Eternal | Sweep On |
| 1920 | **Man o' War** (1½) | 1:51⅗ | Clarence Kummer | L. Feustel | Upset | Wildair |
| 1921 | **Broomspun** (¾) | 1:54⅕ | F. Coltiletti | James Rowe Sr. | Polly Ann | Jeg |
| 1922 | **Pillory** (hd) | 1:51⅗ | L. Morris | Thomas Healey | Hea | June Grass |
| 1923 | **Vigil** (1¼) | 1:53⅗ | B. Marinelli | Thomas Healey | General Thatcher | Rialto |
| 1924 | **Nellie Morse** (1½) | 1:57⅕ | John Merimee | A.B. Gordon | Transmute | Mad Play |
| 1925 | **Coventry** (4) | 1:59 | Clarence Kummer | William Duke | Backbone | Almadel |
| 1926 | **Display** (hd) | 1:59⅘ | John Maiben | Thomas Healey | Blondin | Mars |
| 1927 | **Bostonian** (½) | 2:01⅗ | Whitey Abel | Fred Hopkins | Sir Harry | Whiskery |
| 1928 | **Victorian** (ns) | 2:00⅕ | Sonny Workman | James Rowe Jr. | Toro | Solace |
| 1929 | **Dr. Freeland** (1) | 2:01⅗ | Louis Schaefer | Thomas Healey | Minotaur | African |
| 1930 | **GALLANT FOX** (¾) | 2:00⅗ | Earl Sande | Jim Fitzsimmons | Crack Brigade | Snowflake |
| 1931 | **Mate** (1½) | 1:59 | George Ellis | J.W. Healy | Twenty Grand | Ladder |
| 1932 | **Burgoo King** (hd) | 1:59⅘ | Eugene James | Dick Thompson | Tick On | Boatswain |
| 1933 | **Head Play** (4) | 2:02 | Charley Kurtsinger | Thomas Hayes | Ladysman | Utopian |
| 1934 | **High Quest** (ns) | 1:58⅕ | Robert Jones | Bob Smith | Cavalcade | Discovery |
| 1935 | **OMAHA** (6) | 1:58⅖ | Willie Saunders | Jim Fitzsimmons | Firethorn | Psychic Bid |
| 1936 | **Bold Venture** (ns) | 1:59 | George Woolf | Max Hirsch | Granville | Jean Bart |
| 1937 | **WAR ADMIRAL** (hd) | 1:58⅖ | Charley Kurtsinger | George Conway | Pompoon | Flying Scot |
| 1938 | **Dauber** (7) | 1:59⅘ | Maurice Peters | Dick Handlen | Cravat | Menow |
| 1939 | **Challedon** (1¼) | 1:59⅘ | George Seabo | Louis Schaefer | Gilded Knight | Volitant |
| 1940 | **Bimelech** (3) | 1:58⅗ | F.A. Smith | Bill Hurley | Mioland | Gallahadion |
| 1941 | **WHIRLAWAY** (5½) | 1:58⅘ | Eddie Arcaro | Ben Jones | King Cole | Our Boots |
| 1942 | **Alsab** (1) | 1:57 | Basil James | Sarge Swenke | Requested & Sun Again (dead heat) | |
| 1943 | **COUNT FLEET** (8) | 1:57⅖ | Johnny Longden | Don Cameron | Blue Swords | Vincentive |
| 1944 | **Pensive** (¾) | 1:59⅕ | Conn McCreary | Ben Jones | Platter | Stir Up |
| 1945 | **Polynesian** (2½) | 1:58⅘ | W.D. Wright | Morris Dixon | Hoop Jr. | Darby Dieppe |
| 1946 | **ASSAULT** (nk) | 2:01⅖ | Warren Mehrtens | Max Hirsch | Lord Boswell | Hampden |
| 1947 | **Faultless** (1¼) | 1:59 | Doug Dodson | Jimmy Jones | On Trust | Phalanx |
| 1948 | **CITATION** (5½) | 2:02⅖ | Eddie Arcaro | Jimmy Jones | Vulcan's Forge | Bovard |
| 1949 | **Capot** (hd) | 1:56 | Ted Atkinson | J.M. Gaver | Palestinian | Noble Impulse |
| 1950 | **Hill Prince** (5) | 1:59⅕ | Eddie Arcaro | Casey Hayes | Middleground | Dooly |
| 1951 | **Bold** (7) | 1:56⅖ | Eddie Arcaro | Preston Burch | Counterpoint | Alerted |
| 1952 | **Blue Man** (3½) | 1:57⅖ | Conn McCreary | Woody Stephens | Jampol | One Count |
| 1953 | **Native Dancer** (nk) | 1:57⅘ | Eric Guerin | Bill Winfrey | Jamie K. | Royal Bay Gem |
| 1954 | **Hasty Road** (nk) | 1:57⅖ | Johnny Adams | Harry Trotsek | Correlation | Hasseyampa |
| 1955 | **Nashua** (1) | 1:54⅗ | Eddie Arcaro | Jim Fitzsimmons | Saratoga | Traffic Judge |
| 1956 | **Fabius** (¾) | 1:58⅖ | Bill Hartack | Jimmy Jones | Needles | No Regrets |
| 1957 | **Bold Ruler** (2) | 1:56⅕ | Eddie Arcaro | Jim Fitzsimmons | Iron Liege | Inside Tract |
| 1958 | **Tim Tam** (1½) | 1:57⅕ | Ismael Valenzuela | Jimmy Jones | Lincoln Road | Gone Fishin' |
| 1959 | **Royal Orbit** (4) | 1:57 | William Harmatz | R. Cornell | Sword Dancer | Dunce |
| 1960 | **Bally Ache** (4) | 1:57⅗ | Bobby Ussery | Jimmy Pitt | Victoria Park | Celtic Ash |
| 1961 | **Carry Back** (¾) | 1:57⅗ | Johnny Sellers | Jack Price | Globemaster | Crozier |
| 1962 | **Greek Money** (ns) | 1:56⅕ | John Rotz | V.W. Raines | Ridan | Roman Line |
| 1963 | **Candy Spots** (3½) | 1:56⅕ | Bill Shoemaker | Mesh Tenney | Chateaugay | Never Bend |
| 1964 | **Northern Dancer** (2¼) | 1:56⅘ | Bill Hartack | Horatio Luro | The Scoundrel | Hill Rise |
| 1965 | **Tom Rolfe** (nk) | 1:56⅕ | Ron Turcotte | Frank Whiteley | Dapper Dan | Hail To All |
| 1966 | **Kauai King** (1¾) | 1:55⅖ | Don Brumfield | Henry Forrest | Stupendous | Amberoid |
| 1967 | **Damascus** (2¼) | 1:55⅕ | Bill Shoemaker | Frank Whiteley | In Reality | Proud Clarion |
| 1968 | **Forward Pass** (6) | 1:56⅘ | Ismael Valenzuela | Henry Forrest | Out Of the Way | Nodouble |
| 1969 | **Majestic Prince** (hd) | 1:55⅗ | Bill Hartack | Johnny Longden | Arts and Letters | Jay Ray |
| 1970 | **Personality** (nk) | 1:56⅕ | Eddie Belmonte | John Jacobs | My Dad George | Silent Screen |
| 1971 | **Canonero II** (1½) | 1:54 | Gustavo Avila | Juan Arias | Eastern Fleet | Jim French |
| 1972 | **Bee Bee Bee** (1¼) | 1:55⅗ | Eldon Nelson | Red Carroll | No Le Hace | Key To The Mint |
| 1973 | **SECRETARIAT** (2½) | 1:54⅖ | Ron Turcotte | Lucien Laurin | Sham | Our Native |

| Year | Winner (Margin) | Time | Jockey | Trainer | 2nd place | 3rd place |
|---|---|---|---|---|---|---|
| 1974 | **Little Current** (7) | 1:54⅗ | Miguel Rivera | Lou Rondinello | Neapolitan Way | Cannonade |
| 1975 | **Master Derby** (1) | 1:56⅖ | Darrel McHargue | Smiley Adams | Foolish Pleasure | Diabolo |
| 1976 | **Elocutionist** (3½) | 1:55 | John Lively | Paul Adwell | Play The Red | Bold Forbes |
| 1977 | **SEATTLE SLEW** (1½) | 1:54⅖ | Jean Cruguet | Billy Turner | Iron Constitution | Run Dusty Run |
| 1978 | **AFFIRMED** (nk) | 1:54⅖ | Steve Cauthen | Laz Barrera | Alydar | Believe It |
| 1979 | **Spectacular Bid** (3½) | 1:54⅕ | Ron Franklin | Bud Delp | Golden Act | Screen King |
| 1980 | **Codex** (4¾) | 1:54⅕ | Angel Cordero Jr. | D. Wayne Lukas | Genuine Risk | Colonel Moran |
| 1981 | **Pleasant Colony** (1) | 1:54⅗ | Jorge Velasquez | John Campo | Bold Ego | Paristo |
| 1982 | **Aloma's Ruler** (½) | 1:55⅖ | Jack Kaenel | John Lenzini Jr. | Linkage | Cut Away |
| 1983 | **Deputed Testamony** (2¾) | 1:55⅖ | Donald Miller Jr. | Bill Boniface | Desert Wine | High Honors |
| 1984 | **Gate Dancer** (1½) | 1:53⅗ | Angel Cordero Jr. | Jack Van Berg | Play On | Fight Over |
| 1985 | **Tank's Prospect** (hd) | 1:53⅖ | Pat Day | D. Wayne Lukas | Chief's Crown | Eternal Prince |
| 1986 | **Snow Chief** (4) | 1:54⅘ | Alex Solis | Melvin Stute | Ferdinand | Broad Brush |
| 1987 | **Alysheba** (½) | 1:55⅘ | Chris McCarron | Jack Van Berg | Bet Twice | Cryptoclearance |
| 1988 | **Risen Star** (1¼) | 1:56⅕ | E. Delahoussaye | Louie Roussel III | Brian's Time | Winning Colors |
| 1989 | **Sunday Silence** (ns) | 1:53⅘ | Pat Valenzuela | Chas. Whittingham | Easy Goer | Rock Point |
| 1990 | **Summer Squall** (2¼) | 1:53⅗ | Pat Day | Neil Howard | Unbridled | Mister Frisky |
| 1991 | **Hansel** (7) | 1:54 | Jerry Bailey | Frank Brothers | Corporate Report | Mane Minister |
| 1992 | **Pine Bluff** (¾) | 1:55⅗ | Chris McCarron | Tom Bohannan | Alydeed | Casual Lies |
| 1993 | **Prairie Bayou** (½) | 1:56⅗ | Mike Smith | Tom Bohannan | Cherokee Run | El Bakan |
| 1994 | **Tabasco Cat** (¾) | 1:56⅖ | Pat Day | D. Wayne Lukas | Go For Gin | Concern |
| 1995 | **Timber Country** (½) | 1:54⅖ | Pat Day | D. Wayne Lukas | Oliver's Twist | Thunder Gulch |
| 1996 | **Louis Quatorze** (3¼) | 1:53⅖ | Pat Day | Nick Zito | Skip Away | Editor's Note |
| 1997 | **Silver Charm** (hd) | 1:54⅖ | Gary Stevens | Bob Baffert | Free House | Captain Bodgit |
| 1998 | **Real Quiet** (2¼) | 1:54⅘ | Kent Desormeaux | Bob Baffert | Victory Gallop | Classic Cat |
| 1999 | **Charismatic** (1½) | 1:55⅕ | Chris Antley | D. Wayne Lukas | Menifee | Badge |
| 2000 | **Red Bullet** (3¾) | 1:56 | Jerry Bailey | Joe Orseno | Fusaichi Pegasus | Impeachment |
| 2001 | **Point Given** (2¼) | 1:55⅖ | Gary Stevens | Bob Baffert | A P Valentine | Congaree |
| 2002 | **War Emblem** (¾) | 1:56⅕ | Victor Espinoza | Bob Baffert | Magic Weisner | Proud Citizen |
| 2003 | **Funny Cide** (9¾) | 1:55⅗ | Jose Santos | Barclay Tagg | Midway Road | Scrimshaw |
| 2004 | **Smarty Jones** (11½) | 1:55⅖ | Stewart Elliott | John Servis | Rock Hard Ten | Eddington |
| 2005 | **Afleet Alex** (4¾) | 1:55 | Jeremy Rose | Tim Ritchey | Scrappy T | Giacomo |

* Later named Judge Murray.

AP/Wide World Photos

*Jockey Eddie Arcaro waves from atop* ***Citation*** *after his 5½-length victory in the Preakness on May 15, 1948. From left are owner Warren Wright, trainer Jimmy Jones and an unidentified groom.*

## Belmont Stakes

For three-year-olds. Held three weeks after Preakness Stakes at Belmont Park in Elmont, N.Y. Inaugurated in 1867 at Jerome Park, moved to Morris Park in 1890 and then to Belmont Park in 1905.

Originally run at 1 mile and 5 furlongs (1867-89), then 1¼ miles (1890-1905), 1⅜ miles (1906-25), and the present 1½ miles since 1926.

**Trainers with most wins:** James Rowe Sr. (8); Sam Hildreth (7); Sunny Jim Fitzsimmons (6); Woody Stephens (5); Max Hirsch, D. Wayne Lukas and Robert W. Walden (4); Elliott Burch, Lucien Laurin, F. McCabe and D. McDaniel (3).

**Jockeys with most wins:** Eddie Arcaro and Jim McLaughlin (6); Earl Sande and Bill Shoemaker (5); Braulio Baeza, Pat Day, Laffit Pincay Jr., Gary Stevens and James Stout (3).

**Winning fillies:** Ruthless (1867) and Tanya (1905).

| Year | Winner (Margin) | Time | Jockey | Trainer | 2nd place | 3rd place |
|---|---|---|---|---|---|---|
| 1867 | **Ruthless** (½) | 3:05 | J. Gilpatrick | A.J. Minor | DeCourcey | Rivoli |
| 1868 | **General Duke** (2) | 3:02 | Bobby Swim | A. Thompson | Northumberland | Fanny Ludlow |
| 1869 | **Fenian** (6) | 3:04¼ | C. Miller | J. Pincus | Glenelg | Invercauld |
| 1870 | **Kingfisher** (nk) | 2:59½ | W. Dick | R. Colston | Foster | Midday |
| 1871 | **Harry Bassett** (3) | 2:56 | W. Miller | D. McDaniel | Stockwood | By the Sea |
| 1872 | **Joe Daniels** (¾) | 2:58¼ | James Roe | D. McDaniel | Meteor | Shylock |
| 1873 | **Springbok** (¾) | 3:01¾ | James Roe | D. McDaniel | Count d'Orsay | Strachino |
| 1874 | **Saxon** (nk) | 2:39½ | G. Barbee | W. Prior | Grinstead | Aaron Pennington |
| 1875 | **Calvin** (2) | 2:42¼ | Bobby Swim | A. Williams | Aristides | Milner |
| 1876 | **Algerine** (½) | 2:40½ | Billy Donohue | Major Doswell | Fiddlesticks | Barricade |
| 1877 | **Cloverbrook** (1) | 2:46 | C. Holloway | J. Walden | Loiterer | Baden-Baden |
| 1878 | **Duke of Magenta** (2) | 2:43½ | L. Hughes | R.W. Walden | Bramble | Sparta |
| 1879 | **Spendthrift** (6) | 2:42¾ | George Evans | T. Puryear | Monitor | Jericho |
| 1880 | **Grenada** (nk) | 2:47 | L. Hughes | R.W. Walden | Ferncliffe | Turenne |
| 1881 | **Saunterer** (nk) | 2:47 | T. Costello | R.W. Walden | Eole | Baltic |
| 1882 | **Forester** (5) | 2:43 | Jim McLaughlin | L. Stuart | Babcock | Wyoming |
| 1883 | **George Kinney** (3) | 2:42½ | Jim McLaughlin | James Rowe Sr. | Trombone | Renegade |
| 1884 | **Panique** (nk) | 2:42 | Jim McLaughlin | James Rowe Sr. | Knight of Ellerslie | Himalaya |
| 1885 | **Tyrant** (3) | 2:43 | Paul Duffy | W. Claypool | St. Augustine | Tecumseh |
| 1886 | **Inspector B** (1) | 2:41 | Jim McLaughlin | F. McCabe | The Bard | Linden |
| 1887 | **Hanover** (15) | 2:43½ | Jim McLaughlin | F. McCabe | Oneko | (2-horse race) |
| 1888 | **Sir Dixon** (15) | 2:40¼ | Jim McLaughlin | F. McCabe | Prince Royal | (2-horse race) |
| 1889 | **Eric** (½) | 2:47¼ | W. Hayward | J. Huggins | Diablo | Zephyrus |
| 1890 | **Burlington** (2) | 2:07¾ | Pike Barnes | A. Cooper | Devotee | Padishah |
| 1891 | **Foxford** (nk) | 2:08¾ | Ed Garrison | M. Donavan | Montana | Laurestan |
| 1892 | **Patron** (6) | 2:12 | W. Hayward | L. Stuart | Shellbark | (2-horse race) |
| 1893 | **Commanche** (hd) | 1:53¼ | Willie Simms | G. Hannon | Dr. Rice | Rainbow |
| 1894 | **Henry of Navarre** (1½) | 1:56½ | Willie Simms | B. McClelland | Prig | Assignee |
| 1895 | **Belmar** (hd) | 2:11½ | Fred Taral | E. Feakes | Counter Tenor | Nanki Poo |
| 1896 | **Hastings** (hd) | 2:24½ | H. Griffin | J.J. Hyland | Handspring | Hamilton II |
| 1897 | **Scottish Chieftain** (1) | 2:23¼ | J. Scherrer | M. Byrnes | On Deck | Octagon |
| 1898 | **Bowling Brook** (6) | 2:32 | F. Littlefield | R.W. Walden | Previous | Hamburg |
| 1899 | **Jean Beraud** (hd) | 2:23 | R. Clawson | Sam Hildreth | Half Time | Glengar |
| 1900 | **Ildrim** (ns) | 2:21¼ | Nash Turner | H.E. Leigh | Petruchio | Missionary |
| 1901 | **Commando** (2) | 2:21 | H. Spencer | James Rowe Sr. | The Parader | All Green |
| 1902 | **Masterman** (2) | 2:22⅗ | John Bullman | J.J. Hyland | Renald | King Hanover |
| 1903 | **Africander** (2) | 2:21¾ | John Bullman | R. Miller | Whorler | Red Knight |
| 1904 | **Delhi** (4) | 2:06⅗ | George Odom | James Rowe Sr. | Graziallo | Rapid Water |
| 1905 | **Tanya** (½) | 2:08 | E. Hildebrand | J.W. Rogers | Blandy | Hot Shot |
| 1906 | **Burgomaster** (4) | 2:20 | Lucien Lyne | J.W. Rogers | The Quail | Accountant |
| 1907 | **Peter Pan** (1) | N/A | G. Mountain | James Rowe Sr. | Superman | Frank Gill |
| 1908 | **Colin** (hd) | N/A | Joe Notter | James Rowe Sr. | Fair Play | King James |
| 1909 | **Joe Madden** (8) | 2:21⅗ | E. Dugan | Sam Hildreth | Wise Mason | Donald MacDonald |
| 1910 | **Sweep** (6) | 2:22 | James Butwell | James Rowe Sr. | Duke of Ormonde | (2-horse race) |
| 1911-12 | Not held | | | | | |
| 1913 | **Prince Eugene** (½) | 2:18 | Roscoe Troxler | James Rowe Sr. | Rock View | Flying Fairy |
| 1914 | **Luke McLuke** (8) | 2:20 | Merritt Buxton | J.F. Schorr | Gainer | Charlestonian |
| 1915 | **The Finn** (4) | 2:18⅖ | George Byrne | E.W. Heffner | Half Rock | Pebbles |
| 1916 | **Friar Rock** (3) | 2:22 | E. Haynes | Sam Hildreth | Spur | Churchill |
| 1917 | **Hourless** (10) | 2:17⅘ | James Butwell | Sam Hildreth | Skeptic | Wonderful |
| 1918 | **Johren** (2) | 2:20⅖ | Frank Robinson | A. Simons | War Cloud | Cum Sah |
| 1919 | **SIR BARTON** (5) | 2:17⅖ | John Loftus | H. Guy Bedwell | Sweep On | Natural Bridge |
| 1920 | **Man o' War** (20) | 2:14⅕ | Clarence Kummer | L. Feustel | Donnacona | (2-horse race) |
| 1921 | **Grey Lag** (3) | 2:16⅘ | Earl Sande | Sam Hildreth | Sporting Blood | Leonardo II |
| 1922 | **Pillory** (2) | 2:18⅘ | C.H. Miller | T.J. Healey | Snob II | Hea |
| 1923 | **Zev** (1½) | 2:19 | Earl Sande | Sam Hildreth | Chickvale | Rialto |
| 1924 | **Mad Play** (2) | 2:18⅘ | Earl Sande | Sam Hildreth | Mr. Mutt | Modest |
| 1925 | **American Flag** (8) | 2:16⅘ | Albert Johnson | G.R. Tompkins | Dangerous | Swope |
| 1926 | **Crusader** (1) | 2:32⅕ | Albert Johnson | George Conway | Espino | Haste |

| Year | Winner (Margin) | Time | Jockey | Trainer | 2nd place | 3rd place |
|---|---|---|---|---|---|---|
| 1927 | **Chance Shot** (1½) | 2:32⅖ | Earl Sande | Pete Coyne | Bois de Rose | Flambino |
| 1928 | **Vito** (3) | 2:33⅕ | Clarence Kummer | Max Hirsch | Genie | Diavolo |
| 1929 | **Blue Larkspur** (¾) | 2:32⅘ | Mack Garner | C. Hastings | African | Jack High |
| 1930 | **GALLANT FOX** (3) | 2:31⅗ | Earl Sande | Jim Fitzsimmons | Whichone | Questionnaire |
| 1931 | **Twenty Grand** (10) | 2:29⅗ | Charley Kurtsinger | James Rowe Jr. | Sun Meadow | Jamestown |
| 1932 | **Faireno** (1½) | 2:32⅘ | Tom Malley | Jim Fitzsimmons | Osculator | Flag Pole |
| 1933 | **Hurryoff** (1½) | 2:32⅗ | Mack Garner | H. McDaniel | Nimbus | Union |
| 1934 | **Peace Chance** (6) | 2:29⅕ | W.D. Wright | Pete Coyne | High Quest | Good Goods |
| 1935 | **OMAHA** (1½) | 2:30⅗ | Willie Saunders | Jim Fitzsimmons | Firethorn | Rosemont |
| 1936 | **Granville** (ns) | 2:30 | James Stout | Jim Fitzsimmons | Mr. Bones | Hollyrood |
| 1937 | **WAR ADMIRAL** (3) | 2:28⅗ | Charley Kurtsinger | George Conway | Sceneshifter | Vamoose |
| 1938 | **Pasteurized** (nk) | 2:29⅖ | James Stout | George Odom | Dauber | Cravat |
| 1939 | **Johnstown** (5) | 2:29⅗ | James Stout | Jim Fitzsimmons | Belay | Gilded Knight |
| 1940 | **Bimelech** (¾) | 2:29⅗ | Fred Smith | Bill Hurley | Your Chance | Andy K. |
| 1941 | **WHIRLAWAY** (2½) | 2:31 | Eddie Arcaro | Ben Jones | Robert Morris | Yankee Chance |
| 1942 | **Shut Out** (2) | 2:29⅕ | Eddie Arcaro | John Gaver | Alsab | Lochinvar |
| 1943 | **COUNT FLEET** (25) | 2:28⅕ | Johnny Longden | Don Cameron | Fairy Manhurst | Deseronto |
| 1944 | **Bounding Home** (½) | 2:32⅕ | G.L. Smith | Matt Brady | Pensive | Bull Dandy |
| 1945 | **Pavot** (5) | 2:30⅕ | Eddie Arcaro | Oscar White | Wildlife | Jeep |
| 1946 | **ASSAULT** (3) | 2:30⅘ | Warren Mehrtens | Max Hirsch | Natchez | Cable |
| 1947 | **Phalanx** (5) | 2:29⅖ | R. Donoso | Syl Veitch | Tide Rips | Tailspin |
| 1948 | **CITATION** (8) | 2:28⅕ | Eddie Arcaro | Jimmy Jones | Better Self | Escadru |
| 1949 | **Capot** (½) | 2:30⅕ | Ted Atkinson | John Gaver | Ponder | Palestinian |
| 1950 | **Middleground** (1) | 2:28⅗ | William Boland | Max Hirsch | Lights Up | Mr. Trouble |
| 1951 | **Counterpoint** (4) | 2:29 | David Gorman | Syl Veitch | Battlefield | Battle Morn |
| 1952 | **One Count** (2½) | 2:30⅕ | Eddie Arcaro | Oscar White | Blue Man | Armageddon |
| 1953 | **Native Dancer** (nk) | 2:28⅗ | Eric Guerin | Bill Winfrey | Jamie K. | Royal Bay Gem |
| 1954 | **High Gun** (nk) | 2:30⅘ | Eric Guerin | Max Hirsch | Fisherman | Limelight |
| 1955 | **Nashua** (9) | 2:29 | Eddie Arcaro | Jim Fitzsimmons | Blazing Count | Portersville |
| 1956 | **Needles** (nk) | 2:29⅘ | David Erb | Hugh Fontaine | Career Boy | Fabius |
| 1957 | **Gallant Man** (8) | 2:26⅗ | Bill Shoemaker | John Nerud | Inside Tract | Bold Ruler |
| 1958 | **Cavan** (6) | 2:30⅕ | Pete Anderson | Tom Barry | Tim Tam | Flamingo |
| 1959 | **Sword Dancer** (¾) | 2:28⅖ | Bill Shoemaker | Elliott Burch | Bagdad | Royal Orbit |
| 1960 | **Celtic Ash** (5½) | 2:29⅕ | Bill Hartack | Tom Barry | Venetian Way | Disperse |
| 1961 | **Sherluck** (2¼) | 2:29⅕ | Braulio Baeza | Harold Young | Globemaster | Guadalcanal |
| 1962 | **Jaipur** (ns) | 2:28⅘ | Bill Shoemaker | B. Mulholland | Admiral's Voyage | Crimson Satan |
| 1963 | **Chateaugay** (2½) | 2:30⅕ | Braulio Baeza | James Conway | Candy Spots | Choker |
| 1964 | **Quadrangle** (2) | 2:28⅖ | Manuel Ycaza | Elliott Burch | Roman Brother | Northern Dancer |
| 1965 | **Hail to All** (nk) | 2:28⅖ | John Sellers | Eddie Yowell | Tom Rolfe | First Family |
| 1966 | **Amberoid** (2½) | 2:29⅗ | William Boland | Lucien Laurin | Buffle | Advocator |
| 1967 | **Damascus** (2½) | 2:28⅘ | Bill Shoemaker | F.Y. Whiteley Jr. | Cool Reception | Gentleman James |
| 1968 | **Stage Door Johnny** (1¼) | 2:27⅕ | Gus Gustines | John Gaver | Forward Pass | Call Me Prince |
| 1969 | **Arts and Letters** (5½) | 2:28⅘ | Braulio Baeza | Elliott Burch | Majestic Prince | Dike |
| 1970 | **High Echelon** (¾) | 2:34 | John Rotz | John Jacobs | Needles N Pens | Naskra |
| 1971 | **Pass Catcher** (¾) | 2:30⅖ | Walter Blum | Eddie Yowell | Jim French | Bold Reason |
| 1972 | **Riva Ridge** (7) | 2:28 | Ron Turcotte | Lucien Laurin | Ruritania | Cloudy Dawn |
| 1973 | **SECRETARIAT** (31) | 2:24 | Ron Turcotte | Lucien Laurin | Twice A Prince | My Gallant |
| 1974 | **Little Current** (7) | 2:29⅕ | Miguel Rivera | Lou Rondinello | Jolly Johu | Cannonade |
| 1975 | **Avatar** (nk) | 2:28⅕ | Bill Shoemaker | Tommy Doyle | Foolish Pleasure | Master Derby |
| 1976 | **Bold Forbes** (nk) | 2:29 | Angel Cordero Jr. | Laz Barrera | McKenzie Bridge | Great Contractor |
| 1977 | **SEATTLE SLEW** (4) | 2:29⅗ | Jean Cruguet | Billy Turner | Run Dusty Run | Sanhedrin |
| 1978 | **AFFIRMED** (hd) | 2:26⅘ | Steve Cauthen | Laz Barrera | Alydar | Darby Creek Road |
| 1979 | **Coastal** (3¼) | 2:28⅗ | Ruben Hernandez | David Whiteley | Golden Act | Spectacular Bid |
| 1980 | **Temperence Hill** (2) | 2:29⅘ | Eddie Maple | Joseph Cantey | Genuine Risk | Rockhill Native |
| 1981 | **Summing** (nk) | 2:29 | George Martens | Luis Barerra | Highland Blade | Pleasant Colony |
| 1982 | **Conquistador Cielo** (14) | 2:28⅕ | Laffit Pincay Jr. | Woody Stephens | Gato Del Sol | Illuminate |
| 1983 | **Caveat** (3½) | 2:27⅘ | Laffit Pincay Jr. | Woody Stephens | Slew o' Gold | Barberstown |
| 1984 | **Swale** (4) | 2:27⅕ | Laffit Pincay Jr. | Woody Stephens | Pine Circle | Morning Bob |
| 1985 | **Creme Fraiche** (½) | 2:27 | Eddie Maple | Woody Stephens | Stephan's Odyssey | Chief's Crown |
| 1986 | **Danzig Connection** (1¼) | 2:29⅘ | Chris McCarron | Woody Stephens | Johns Treasure | Ferdinand |
| 1987 | **Bet Twice** (14) | 2:28⅕ | Craig Perret | Jimmy Croll | Cryptoclearance | Gulch |
| 1988 | **Risen Star** (14¾) | 2:26⅖ | E. Delahoussaye | Louie Roussel III | Kingpost | Brian's Time |
| 1989 | **Easy Goer** (8) | 2:26 | Pat Day | Shug McGaughey | Sunday Silence | Le Voyageur |
| 1990 | **Go And Go** (8¼) | 2:27⅕ | Michael Kinane | Dermot Weld | Thirty Six Red | Baron de Vaux |
| 1991 | **Hansel** (hd) | 2:28 | Jerry Bailey | Frank Brothers | Strike the Gold | Mane Minister |
| 1992 | **A.P. Indy** (¾) | 2:26 | E. Delahoussaye | Neil Drysdale | My Memoirs | Pine Bluff |
| 1993 | **Colonial Affair** (2) | 2:29⅘ | Julie Krone | Scotty Schulhofer | Kissin Kris | Wild Gale |
| 1994 | **Tabasco Cat** (2) | 2:26⅘ | Pat Day | D. Wayne Lukas | Go For Gin | Strodes Creek |
| 1995 | **Thunder Gulch** (2) | 2:32 | Gary Stevens | D. Wayne Lukas | Star Standard | Citadeed |
| 1996 | **Editor's Note** (1) | 2:28⅘ | Rene Douglas | D. Wayne Lukas | Skip Away | My Flag |

## Belmont Stakes (Cont.)

| Year | Winner (Margin) | Time | Jockey | Trainer | 2nd place | 3rd place |
|---|---|---|---|---|---|---|
| 1997 | **Touch Gold** (¾) | 2:28⅘ | Chris McCarron | David Hofmans | Silver Charm | Free House |
| 1998 | **Victory Gallop** (ns) | 2:29 | Gary Stevens | Elliott Walden | Real Quiet | Thomas Jo |
| 1999 | **Lemon Drop Kid** (hd) | 2:27⅘ | Jose Santos | Scotty Schulhofer | Vision and Verse | Charismatic |
| 2000 | **Commendable** (1½) | 2:31⅕ | Pat Day | D. Wayne Lukas | Aptitude | Unshaded |
| 2001 | **Point Given** (12¼) | 2:26⅖ | Gary Stevens | Bob Baffert | A P Valentine | Monarchos |
| 2002 | **Sarava** (½) | 2:29⅗ | Edgar Prado | Ken McPeek | Medaglia d'Oro | Sunday Break |
| 2003 | **Empire Maker** (¾) | 2:28⅕ | Jerry Bailey | Bobby Frankel | Ten Most Wanted | Funny Cide |
| 2004 | **Birdstone** (1) | 2:27⅖ | Edgar Prado | Nick Zito | Smarty Jones | Royal Assault |
| 2005 | **Afleet Alex** (7) | 2:28⅗ | Jeremy Rose | Tim Ritchey | Andromeda's Hero | Nolan's Cat |

## Breeders' Cup Championship

Inaugurated on Nov. 10, 1984, the Breeders' Cup World Thoroughbred Championships consists of eight races on one track on one day late in the year to determine thoroughbred racing's principle champions.

The Breeders' Cup has been (will be) held at the following tracks (in alphabetical order): Aqueduct Racetrack (N.Y.) in 1985; Arlington Park (Ill.) in 2002; Belmont Park (N.Y.) in 1990, '95, 2001 and '05; Churchill Downs (Ky.) in 1988, '91, '94, '98, 2000 and '06; Gulfstream Park (Fla.) in 1989, '92 and '99; Hollywood Park (Calif.) in 1984, '87 and '97; Lone Star Park (Texas) in 2004; Monmouth Park (N.J.) in 2007; Santa Anita Park (Calif.) in 1986, '93 and 2003 and Woodbine (Toronto) in 1996.

**Horses with most wins:** Bayakoa, Da Hoss, High Chaparral, Lure, Miesque and Tiznow (2).

**Trainers with most wins:** D. Wayne Lukas (17); Shug McGaughey (8); Neil Drysdale and Richard Mandella (6); Bill Mott (5); Ron McAnally (4); Bob Baffert, Pascal Bary, Francois Boutin, Patrick Byrne, Julio Canani, Andre Fabre, Bobby Frankel, Aidan O'Brien and Sir Michael Stoute (3).

**Jockeys with most wins:** Jerry Bailey (14); Pat Day (12); Mike Smith (10); Chris McCarron (9); Gary Stevens (8); Eddie Delahoussaye, Laffit Pincay Jr., Jose Santos and Pat Valenzuela (7); Corey Nakatani and John Velazquez (6); Angel Cordero Jr., Frankie Dettori and Craig Perret (4); David Flores, Michael Kinane, Randy Romero and Alex Solis (3).

### Juvenile

Distances: one mile (1984-85, 87); 1 1/16 miles (1986, 1988-2001, 2003–), 1⅛ miles (2002).

| Year | Winner (Margin) | Time | Jockey | Trainer | 2nd place | 3rd place |
|---|---|---|---|---|---|---|
| 1984 | **Chief's Crown** (¾) | 1:36⅕ | Don MacBeth | Roger Laurin | Tank's Prospect | Spend A Buck |
| 1985 | **Tasso** (ns) | 1:36⅕ | Laffit Pincay Jr. | Neil Drysdale | Storm Cat | Scat Dancer |
| 1986 | **Capote** (1¼) | 1:43⅘ | Laffit Pincay Jr. | D. Wayne Lukas | Qualify | Alysheba |
| 1987 | **Success Express** (1¾) | 1:35⅕ | Jose Santos | D. Wayne Lukas | Regal Classic | Tejano |
| 1988 | **Is It True** (1¼) | 1:46⅗ | Laffit Pincay Jr. | D. Wayne Lukas | Easy Goer | Tagel |
| 1989 | **Rhythm** (2) | 1:43⅗ | Craig Perret | Shug McGaughey | Grand Canyon | Slavic |
| 1990 | **Fly So Free** (3) | 1:43⅖ | Jose Santos | Scotty Schulhofer | Take Me Out | Lost Mountain |
| 1991 | **Arazi** (4¾) | 1:44⅗ | Pat Valenzuela | Francois Boutin | Bertrando | Snappy Landing |
| 1992 | **Gilded Time** (¾) | 1:43⅖ | Chris McCarron | Darrell Vienna | It'sali'lknownfact | River Special |
| 1993 | **Brocco** (5) | 1:42⅘ | Gary Stevens | Randy Winick | Blumin Affair | Tabasco Cat |
| 1994 | **Timber Country** (½) | 1:44⅖ | Pat Day | D. Wayne Lukas | Eltish | Tejano Run |
| 1995 | **Unbridled's Song** (nk) | 1:41⅗ | Mike Smith | James Ryerson | Hennessy | Editor's Note |
| 1996 | **Boston Harbor** (nk) | 1:43⅖ | Jerry Bailey | D. Wayne Lukas | Acceptable | Ordway |
| 1997 | **Favorite Trick** (5½) | 1:41⅖ | Pat Day | Patrick Byrne | Dawson's Legacy | Nationalore |
| 1998 | **Answer Lively** (hd) | 1:44 | Jerry Bailey | Bobby Barnett | Aly's Alley | Cat Thief |
| 1999 | **Anees** (2½) | 1:42⅕ | Gary Stevens | Alex Hassinger Jr. | Chief Seattle | High Yield |
| 2000 | **Macho Uno** (ns) | 1:42 | Jerry Bailey | Joe Orseno | Point Given | Street Cry |
| 2001 | **Johannesburg** (2¼) | 1:42⅕ | Michael Kinane | Aidan O'Brien | Repent | Siphonic |
| 2002 | **Vindication** (2¾) | 1:49⅗ | Mike Smith | Bob Baffert | Kafwain | Hold That Tiger |
| 2003 | **Action This Day** (2¼) | 1:43⅗ | David Flores | Richard Mandella | Minister Eric | Chapel Royal |
| 2004 | **Wilko** (¾) | 1:42 | Frankie Dettori | Jeremy Noseda | Afleet Alex | Sun King |

## Breeders' Cup Leaders

The all-time money-winning horses and jockeys in the history of the Breeders' Cup through 2004.

### Top 10 Horses

| | | Sts | 1-2-3 | Earnings |
|---|---|---|---|---|
| 1 | Tiznow | 2 | 2-0-0 | $4,560,400 |
| 2 | Awesome Again | 1 | 1-0-0 | 2,662,400 |
| 3 | Pleasantly Perfect | 2 | 1-0-1 | 2,520,000 |
| 4 | Skip Away | 2 | 1-0-0 | 2,288,000 |
| 5 | Cat Thief | 3 | 1-0-1 | 2,200,000 |
| 6 | Alysheba | 3 | 1-1-1 | 2,133,000 |
| 7 | Alphabet Soup | 1 | 1-0-0 | 2,080,000 |
| | Volponi | 2 | 1-0-0 | 2,080,000 |
| | Ghostzapper | 1 | 1-0-0 | 2,080,000 |
| 10 | Cigar | 2 | 1-0-1 | 2,040,000 |

### Top 10 Jockeys

| | | Sts | 1-2-3 | Earnings |
|---|---|---|---|---|
| 1 | Pat Day | 117 | 12-17-11 | $23,033,360 |
| 2 | Jerry Bailey | 95 | 14-11-12 | 19,069,340 |
| 3 | Chris McCarron | 101 | 9-12-7 | 17,669,600 |
| 4 | Gary Stevens | 93 | 8-15-10 | 13,441,160 |
| 5 | Mike Smith | 52 | 10-6-3 | 10,505,760 |
| 6 | Jose Santos | 59 | 7-2-4 | 8,008,800 |
| 7 | Corey Nakatani | 56 | 6-7-7 | 7,905,280 |
| 8 | Eddie Delahoussaye | 68 | 7-3-6 | 7,775,000 |
| 9 | Alex Solis | 47 | 3-7-4 | 6,827,660 |
| 10 | Laffit Pincay Jr. | 61 | 7-4-9 | 6,811,000 |

## Juvenile Fillies

Distances: one mile (1984-85, 87); 1 1/16 miles (1986, 1988-2001, 2003–); 1⅛ miles (2002).

| Year | Winner (Margin) | Time | Jockey | Trainer | 2nd place | 3rd place |
|---|---|---|---|---|---|---|
| 1984 | **Outstandingly*** | 1:37⅘ | Walter Guerra | Pancho Martin | Dusty Heart | Fine Spirit |
| 1985 | **Twilight Ridge** (1) | 1:35⅘ | Jorge Velasquez | D. Wayne Lukas | Family Style | Steal A Kiss |
| 1986 | **Brave Raj** (5½) | 1:43⅕ | Pat Valenzuela | Melvin Stute | Tappiano | Saros Brig |
| 1987 | **Epitome** (ns) | 1:36⅖ | Pat Day | Phil Hauswald | Jeanne Jones | Dream Team |
| 1988 | **Open Mind** (1¾) | 1:46⅗ | Angel Cordero Jr. | D. Wayne Lukas | Darby Shuffle | Lea Lucinda |
| 1989 | **Go for Wand** (2¾) | 1:44⅕ | Randy Romero | Wm. Badgett Jr. | Sweet Roberta | Stella Madrid |
| 1990 | **Meadow Star** (5) | 1:44 | Jose Santos | LeRoy Jolley | Private Treasure | Dance Smartly |
| 1991 | **Pleasant Stage** (nk) | 1:46⅖ | E. Delahoussaye | Chris Speckert | La Spia | Cadillac Women |
| 1992 | **Eliza** (nk) | 1:42⅘ | Pat Valenzuela | Alex Hassinger | Educated Risk | Boots 'n Jackie |
| 1993 | **Phone Chatter** (hd) | 1:43 | Laffit Pincay Jr. | Richard Mandella | Sardula | Heavenly Prize |
| 1994 | **Flanders** (hd) | 1:45⅕ | Pat Day | D. Wayne Lukas | Serena's Song | Stormy Blues |
| 1995 | **My Flag** (½) | 1:42⅖ | Jerry Bailey | Shug McGaughey | Cara Rafaela | Golden Attraction |
| 1996 | **Storm Song** (4½) | 1:43⅗ | Craig Perret | Nick Zito | Love That Jazz | Critical Factor |
| 1997 | **Countess Diana** (8½) | 1:42⅕ | Shane Sellers | Patrick Byrne | Career Collection | Primaly |
| 1998 | **Silverbulletday** (½) | 1:43⅗ | Gary Stevens | Bob Baffert | Excellent Meeting | Three Ring |
| 1999 | **Cash Run** (1¼) | 1:43⅕ | Jerry Bailey | D. Wayne Lukas | Chilukki | Surfside |
| 2000 | **Caressing** (½) | 1:42⅗ | John Velazquez | David Vance | Platinum Tiara | She's a Devil Due |
| 2001 | **Tempera** (1½) | 1:41⅖ | David Flores | Eoin Harty | Imperial Gesture | Bella Bellucci |
| 2002 | **Storm Flag Flying** (½) | 1:49⅗ | John Velazquez | Shug McGaughey | Composure | Santa Catarina |
| 2003 | **Halfbridled** (2½) | 1:42⅗ | Julie Krone | Richard Mandella | Ashado | Victory U.S.A. |
| 2004 | **Sweet Catomine** (3¾) | 1:41⅗ | Corey Nakatani | Julio Canani | Balletto | Runway Model |

*In 1984, winner Fran's Valentine was disqualified for interference in the stretch and placed 10th.

## Sprint

Distance: six furlongs (since 1984).

| Year | Winner (Margin) | Time | Jockey | Trainer | 2nd place | 3rd place |
|---|---|---|---|---|---|---|
| 1984 | **Eillo** (ns) | 1:10⅕ | Craig Perret | Budd Lepman | Commemorate | Fighting Fit |
| 1985 | **Precisionist** (¾) | 1:08⅖ | Chris McCarron | L.R. Fenstermaker | Smile | Mt. Livermore |
| 1986 | **Smile** (1¼) | 1:08⅖ | Jacinto Vasquez | Scotty Schulhofer | Pine Tree Lane | Bedside Promise |
| 1987 | **Very Subtle** (4) | 1:08⅘ | Pat Valenzuela | Melvin Stute | Groovy | Exclusive Enough |
| 1988 | **Gulch** (¾) | 1:10⅖ | Angel Cordero Jr. | D. Wayne Lukas | Play The King | Afleet |
| 1989 | **Dancing Spree** (nk) | 1:09 | Angel Cordero Jr. | Shug McGaughey | Safely Kept | Dispersal |
| 1990 | **Safely Kept** (nk) | 1:09⅗ | Craig Perret | Alan Goldberg | Dayjur | Black Tie Affair |
| 1991 | **Sheikh Albadou** (nk) | 1:09⅕ | Pat Eddery | Alexander Scott | Pleasant Tap | Robyn Dancer |
| 1992 | **Thirty Slews** (nk) | 1:08⅕ | Eddie Delahoussaye | Bob Baffert | Meafara | Rubiano |
| 1993 | **Cardmania** (nk) | 1:08⅗ | Eddie Delahoussaye | Derek Meredith | Meafara | Gilded Time |
| 1994 | **Cherokee Run** (nk) | 1:09⅖ | Mike Smith | Frank Alexander | Soviet Problem | Cardmania |
| 1995 | **Desert Stormer** (nk) | 1:09 | Kent Desormeaux | Frank Lyons | Mr. Greeley | Lit de Justice |
| 1996 | **Lit de Justice** (1¼) | 1:08⅗ | Corey Nakatani | Jenine Sahadi | Paying Dues | Honour and Glory |
| 1997 | **Elmhurst** ½) | 1:08⅕ | Corey Nakatani | Jenine Sahadi | Hesabull | Bet On Sunshine |
| 1998 | **Reraise** (2) | 1:09 | Corey Nakatani | Craig Dollase | Grand Slam | Kona Gold |
| 1999 | **Artax** (½) | 1:07⅘ | Jorge Chavez | Louis Albertrani | Kona Gold | Big Jag |
| 2000 | **Kona Gold** (½) | 1:07⅗ | Alex Solis | Bruce Headley | Honest Lady | Bet On Sunshine |
| 2001 | **Squirtle Squirt** (½) | 1:08⅖ | Jerry Bailey | Bobby Frankel | Xtra Heat | Caller One |
| 2002 | **Orientate** (½) | 1:08⅘ | Jerry Bailey | D. Wayne Lukas | Thunderello | Crafty C.T. |
| 2003 | **Cajun Beat** (2¼) | 1:07⅗ | Cornelio Velasquez | Stephen Margolis | Bluesthestandard | Shake You Down |
| 2004 | **Speightstown** (1¼) | 1:08 | John Velazquez | Todd Pletcher | Kela | My Cousin Matt |

## Mile

| Year | Winner (Margin) | Time | Jockey | Trainer | 2nd place | 3rd place |
|---|---|---|---|---|---|---|
| 1984 | **Royal Heroine** (1½) | 1:32⅗ | Fernando Toro | John Gosden | Star Choice | Cozzene |
| 1985 | **Cozzene** (2¼) | 1:35 | Walter Guerra | Jan Nerud | Al Mamoon* | Shadeed |
| 1986 | **Last Tycoon** (hd) | 1:35⅕ | Yves St.-Martin | Robert Collet | Palace Music | Fred Astaire |
| 1987 | **Miesque** (3½) | 1:32⅘ | Freddie Head | Francois Boutin | Show Dancer | Sonic Lady |
| 1988 | **Miesque** (4) | 1:38⅗ | Freddie Head | Francois Boutin | Steinlen | Simply Majestic |
| 1989 | **Steinlen** (¾) | 1:37⅕ | Jose Santos | D. Wayne Lukas | Sabona | Most Welcome |
| 1990 | **Royal Academy** (nk) | 1:35⅕ | Lester Piggott | M.V. O'Brien | Itsallgreektome | Priolo |
| 1991 | **Opening Verse** (2¼) | 1:37⅖ | Pat Valenzuela | Dick Lundy | Val des Bois | Star of Cozzene |
| 1992 | **Lure** (3) | 1:32⅘ | Mike Smith | Shug McGaughey | Paradise Creek | Brief Truce |

**DID YOU KNOW?**

*Only 35 horses have entered a Breeders' Cup race with odds of 100-1 or higher (through 2004). **Did you know**, just one of those horses finished in the money? Arcangues, under jockey Jerry Bailey, won the $3 million Classic in 1993 with odds of 133-1.*

## Breeders' Cup Championship (Cont.)

### Mile (Cont.)

| Year | Winner (Margin) | Time | Jockey | Trainer | 2nd place | 3rd place |
|---|---|---|---|---|---|---|
| 1993 | **Lure** (2¼) | 1:33⅖ | Mike Smith | Shug McGaughey | Ski Paradise | Fourstars Allstar |
| 1994 | **Barathea** (hd) | 1:34⅖ | Frankie Dettori | Luca Cumani | Johann Quatz | Unfinished Symph |
| 1995 | **Ridgewood Pearl** (2) | 1:43⅗ | John Murtagh | John Oxx | Fastness | Sayyedati |
| 1996 | **Da Hoss** (1½) | 1:35⅘ | Gary Stevens | Michael Dickinson | Spinning World | Same Old Wish |
| 1997 | **Spinning World** (2) | 1:32⅗ | Cash Asmussen | Jonathan Pease | Geri | Decorated Hero |
| 1998 | **Da Hoss** (hd) | 1:35⅕ | John Velazquez | Michael Dickinson | Hawksley Hill | Labeeb |
| 1999 | **Silic** (nk) | 1:34⅕ | Corey Nakatani | Julio Canani | Tuzla | Docksider |
| 2000 | **War Chant** (nk) | 1:34⅗ | Gary Stevens | Neil Drysdale | North East Bound | Dansili |
| 2001 | **Val Royal** (1¾) | 1:32 | Jose Valdivia | Julio Canani | Forbidden Apple | Bach |
| 2002 | **Domedriver** (¾) | 1:36⅘ | Thierry Thulliez | Pascal Bary | Rock of Gibraltar | Good Journey |
| 2003 | **Six Perfections** (¾) | 1:33⅘ | Jerry Bailey | Pascal Bary | Touch of the Blues | Century City |
| 2004 | **Singletary** (½) | 1:36⅘ | David Flores | Donald Chatlos Jr. | Antonius Pius | Six Perfections |

*In 1985, 2nd place finisher Palace Music was disqualified for interference and placed 9th.

### Distaff

Distances: 1¼ miles (1984-87); 1⅛ miles (since 1988).

| Year | Winner (Margin) | Time | Jockey | Trainer | 2nd place | 3rd place |
|---|---|---|---|---|---|---|
| 1984 | **Princess Rooney** (7) | 2:02⅖ | Eddie Delahoussaye | Neil Drysdale | Life's Magic | Adored |
| 1985 | **Life's Magic** (6¼) | 2:02 | Angel Cordero Jr. | D. Wayne Lukas | Lady's Secret | DontstopThemusic |
| 1986 | **Lady's Secret** (2½) | 2:01⅕ | Pat Day | D. Wayne Lukas | Fran's Valentine | Outstandingly |
| 1987 | **Sacahuista** (2¼) | 2:02⅘ | Randy Romero | D. Wayne Lukas | Clabber Girl | Oueee Bebe |
| 1988 | **Personal Ensign** (ns) | 1:52 | Randy Romero | Shug McGaughey | Winning Colors | Goodbye Halo |
| 1989 | **Bayakoa** (1½) | 1:47⅖ | Laffit Pincay Jr. | Ron McAnally | Gorgeous | Open Mind |
| 1990 | **Bayakoa** (6¾) | 1:49⅕ | Laffit Pincay Jr. | Ron McAnally | Colonial Waters | Valay Maid |
| 1991 | **Dance Smartly** (½) | 1:50⅘ | Pat Day | Jim Day | Versailles Treaty | Brought to Mind |
| 1992 | **Paseana** (4) | 1:48 | Chris McCarron | Ron McAnally | Versailles Treaty | Magical Maiden |
| 1993 | **Hollywood Wildcat** (ns) | 1:48⅕ | Eddie Delahoussaye | Neil Drysdale | Paseana | Re Toss |
| 1994 | **One Dreamer** (nk) | 1:50⅗ | Gary Stevens | Thomas Proctor | Heavenly Prize | Miss Dominique |
| 1995 | **Inside Information** (13½) | 1:46 | Mike Smith | Shug McGaughey | Heavenly Prize | Lakeway |
| 1996 | **Jewel Princess** (1½) | 1:48⅕ | Corey Nakatani | Wallace Dollase | Serena's Song | Different |
| 1997 | **Ajina** (2) | 1:47⅕ | Mike Smith | Bill Mott | Sharp Cat | Escena |
| 1998 | **Escena** (ns) | 1:49⅘ | Gary Stevens | Bill Mott | Banshee Breeze | Keeper Hill |
| 1999 | **Beautiful Pleasure** (¾) | 1:47⅖ | Jorge Chavez | John Ward Jr. | Banshee Breeze | Heritage of Gold |
| 2000 | **Spain** (1½) | 1:47⅗ | Victor Espinoza | D. Wayne Lukas | Surfside | Heritage of Gold |
| 2001 | **Unbridled Elaine** (hd) | 1:49⅕ | Pat Day | Dallas Stewart | Spain | Two Item Limit |
| 2002 | **Azeri** (5) | 1:48⅗ | Mike Smith | Laura de Seroux | Farda Amiga | Imperial Gesture |
| 2003 | **Adoration** (4½) | 1:49⅕ | Pat Valenzuela | David Hofmans | Elloluv | Got Koko |
| 2004 | **Ashado** (1¼) | 1:48⅕ | John Velazquez | Todd Pletcher | Storm Flag Flying | Stellar Jayne |

### Turf

Distance: 1½ miles (since 1984).

| Year | Winner (Margin) | Time | Jockey | Trainer | 2nd place | 3rd place |
|---|---|---|---|---|---|---|
| 1984 | **Lashkari** (nk) | 2:25⅕ | Yves St.-Martin | de Royer-Dupre | All Along | Raami |
| 1985 | **Pebbles** (nk) | 2:27 | Pat Eddery | Clive Brittain | StrawberryRoad II | Mourjane |
| 1986 | **Manila** (nk) | 2:25⅖ | Jose Santos | Leroy Jolley | Theatrical | Estrapade |
| 1987 | **Theatrical** (½) | 2:24⅖ | Pat Day | Bill Mott | Trempolino | Village Star II |
| 1988 | **Gt. Communicator** (½) | 2:35⅕ | Ray Sibille | Thad Ackel | Sunshine Forever | Indian Skimmer |
| 1989 | **Prized** (hd) | 2:28 | Eddie Delahoussaye | Neil Drysdale | Sierra Roberta | Star Lift |
| 1990 | **In The Wings** (½) | 2:29⅗ | Gary Stevens | Andre Fabre | With Approval | El Senor |
| 1991 | **Miss Alleged** (2) | 2:30⅘ | Eric Legrix | Pascal Bary | Itsallgreektome | Quest for Fame |
| 1992 | **Fraise** (ns) | 2:24 | Pat Valenzuela | Bill Mott | Sky Classic | Quest for Fame |
| 1993 | **Kotashaan** (½) | 2:25 | Kent Desormeaux | Richard Mandella | Bien Bien | Luazur |
| 1994 | **Tikkanen** (1½) | 2:26⅖ | Mike Smith | Jonathan Pease | Hatoof | Paradise Creek |
| 1995 | **Northern Spur** (nk) | 2:42 | Chris McCarron | Ron McAnally | Freedom Cry | Carnegie |
| 1996 | **Pilsudski** (1¼) | 2:30⅕ | Walter Swinburn | Sir Michael Stoute | Singspiel | Swain |
| 1997 | **Chief Bearhart** (¾) | 2:24 | Jose Santos | Mark Frostad | Borgia | Flag Down |
| 1998 | **Buck's Boy** (1¼) | 2:28⅗ | Shane Sellers | Noel Hickey | Yagli | Dushyantor |
| 1999 | **Daylami** (2½) | 2:24⅗ | Frankie Dettori | Saeed bin Suroor | Royal Anthem | Buck's Boy |
| 2000 | **Kalanisi** (½) | 2:26⅘ | John Murtagh | Sir Michael Stoute | Quiet Resolve | John's Call |
| 2001 | **Fantastic Light** (¾) | 2:24⅕ | Frankie Dettori | Saeed bin Suroor | Milan | Timboroa |
| 2002 | **High Chaparral** (1¼) | 2:30⅕ | Michael Kinane | Aidan O'Brien | With Anticipation | Falcon Flight |
| 2003 | **High Chaparral*** | 2:24⅕ | Michael Kinane | Aidan O'Brien | — | Falbrav |
| | & **Johar*** | 2:24⅕ | Alex Solis | Richard Mandella | | |
| 2004 | **Better Talk Now** (1¾) | 2:29⅗ | Ramon Dominguez | H. Graham Motion | Kitten's Joy | Powerscourt |

*in 2003, High Chaparral and Johar finished in a dead heat, the first in Breeders' Cup history.

## Filly & Mare Turf

Distance: 1⅜ miles (1999-2000, 2004); 1¼ miles (2001-03).

| Year | Winner (Margin) | Time | Jockey | Trainer | 2nd place | 3rd place |
|---|---|---|---|---|---|---|
| 1999 | **Soaring Softly** (¾) | 2:13⅘ | Jerry Bailey | James J. Toner | Coretta | Zomarradah |
| 2000 | **Perfect Sting** (¾) | 2:13 | Jerry Bailey | Joe Orseno | Tout Charmant | Catella |
| 2001 | **Banks Hill** (5½) | 2:00⅕ | Olivier Peslier | Andre Fabre | Spook Express | Spring Oak |
| 2002 | **Starine** (1½) | 2:03⅗ | John Velazquez | Bobby Frankel | Banks Hill | Islington |
| 2003 | **Islington** (nk) | 1:59 | Kieren Fallon | Sir Michael Stoute | L'Ancresse | Yesterday |
| 2004 | **Ouija Board** (1½) | 2:18⅕ | Kieren Fallon | Edward Dunlop | Film Maker | Wonder Again |

## Classic

Distance: 1¼ miles (since 1984).

| Year | Winner (Margin) | Time | Jockey | Trainer | 2nd place | 3rd place |
|---|---|---|---|---|---|---|
| 1984 | **Wild Again** (hd) | 2:03⅖ | Pat Day | Vincent Timphony | Slew o' Gold | Gate Dancer* |
| 1985 | **Proud Truth** (hd) | 2:00⅘ | Jorge Velasquez | John Veitch | Gate Dancer | Turkoman |
| 1986 | **Skywalker** (1¼) | 2:00⅖ | Laffit Pincay Jr. | M. Whittingham | Turkoman | Precisionist |
| 1987 | **Ferdinand** (ns) | 2:01⅖ | Bill Shoemaker | C. Whittingham | Alysheba | Judge Angelucci |
| 1988 | **Alysheba** (ns) | 2:04⅘ | Chris McCarron | Jack Van Berg | Seeking the Gold | Waquoit |
| 1989 | **Sunday Silence** (½) | 2:00⅕ | Chris McCarron | C. Whittingham | Easy Goer | Blushing John |
| 1990 | **Unbridled** (1) | 2:02⅕ | Pat Day | Carl Nafzger | Ibn Bey | Thirty Six Red |
| 1991 | **Black Tie Affair** (1¼) | 2:02⅘ | Jerry Bailey | Ernie Poulos | Twilight Agenda | Unbridled |
| 1992 | **A.P. Indy** (2) | 2:00⅕ | Eddie Delahoussaye | Neil Drysdale | Pleasant Tap | Jolypha |
| 1993 | **Arcangues** (2) | 2:00⅘ | Jerry Bailey | Andre Fabre | Bertrando | Kissin Kris |
| 1994 | **Concern** (nk) | 2:02⅖ | Jerry Bailey | Richard Small | Tabasco Cat | Dramatic Gold |
| 1995 | **Cigar** (2½) | 1:59⅖ | Jerry Bailey | Bill Mott | L'Carriere | Unaccounted For |
| 1996 | **Alphabet Soup** (ns) | 2:01 | Chris McCarron | David Hofmans | Louis Quatorze | Cigar |
| 1997 | **Skip Away** (6) | 1:59⅕ | Mike Smith | Hubert Hine | Deputy Commander | Dowty |
| 1998 | **Awesome Again** (¾) | 2:02 | Pat Day | Patrick Byrne | Silver Charm | Swain |
| 1999 | **Cat Thief** (1¼) | 1:59⅖ | Pat Day | D. Wayne Lukas | Budroyale | Golden Missile |
| 2000 | **Tiznow** (nk) | 2:00⅗ | Chris McCarron | Jay Robbins | Giant's Causeway | Captain Steve |
| 2001 | **Tiznow** (ns) | 2:00⅗ | Chris McCarron | Jay Robbins | Sakhee | Albert the Great |
| 2002 | **Volponi** (6½) | 2:01⅖ | Jose Santos | Philip Johnson | Medaglia d'Oro | Milwaukee Brew |
| 2003 | **Pleasantly Perfect** (1½) | 1:59⅘ | Alex Solis | Richard Mandella | Medaglia d'Oro | Dynever |
| 2004 | **Ghostzapper** (3) | 1:59 | Javier Castellano | Bobby Frankel | Roses in May | Pleasantly Perfect |

*In 1984, 2nd place finisher Gate Dancer was disqualified for interference and placed 3rd.

# Annual Money Leaders

## Horses

Annual money-leading horses since 1910, according to *The American Racing Manual.*

**Multiple leaders:** Round Table, Buckpasser, Alysheba and Cigar (2).

| Year | | Age | Sts | 1-2-3 | Earnings |
|---|---|---|---|---|---|
| 1910 | Novelty | 2 | 16 | 11— | $72,630 |
| 1911 | Worth | 2 | 13 | 10— | 16,645 |
| 1912 | Star Charter | 4 | 17 | 6— | 14,655 |
| 1913 | Old Rosebud | 2 | 14 | 12— | 19,057 |
| 1914 | Roamer | 3 | 16 | 12— | 29,105 |
| 1915 | Borrow | 7 | 9 | 4— | 20,195 |
| 1916 | Campfire | 2 | 9 | 6— | 49,735 |
| 1917 | Sun Briar | 2 | 9 | 5— | 59,505 |
| 1918 | Eternal | 2 | 8 | 6— | 56,173 |
| 1919 | Sir Barton | 3 | 13 | 8-3-2 | 88,250 |
| 1920 | Man o' War | 3 | 11 | 11-0-0 | 166,140 |
| 1921 | Morvich | 2 | 11 | 11-0-0 | 115,234 |
| 1922 | Pillory | 3 | 7 | 4-1-1 | 95,654 |
| 1923 | Zev | 3 | 14 | 12-1-0 | 272,008 |
| 1924 | Sarzen | 3 | 12 | 8-1-1 | 95,640 |
| 1925 | Pompey | 2 | 10 | 7-2-0 | 121,630 |
| 1926 | Crusader | 3 | 15 | 9-4-0 | 166,033 |
| 1927 | Anita Peabody | 2 | 7 | 6-0-1 | 111,905 |
| 1928 | High Strung | 2 | 6 | 5-0-0 | 153,590 |
| 1929 | Blue Larkspur | 3 | 6 | 4-1-0 | 153,450 |
| 1930 | Gallant Fox | 3 | 10 | 9-1-0 | 308,275 |
| 1931 | Gallant Flight | 2 | 7 | 7-0-0 | 219,000 |
| 1932 | Gusto | 3 | 16 | 4-3-2 | 145,940 |
| 1933 | Singing Wood | 2 | 9 | 3-2-2 | 88,050 |
| 1934 | Cavalcade | 3 | 7 | 6-1-0 | 111,235 |
| 1935 | Omaha | 3 | 9 | 6-1-2 | 142,255 |
| 1936 | Granville | 3 | 11 | 7-3-0 | 110,295 |
| 1937 | Seabiscuit | 4 | 15 | 11-2-2 | 168,580 |
| 1938 | Stagehand | 3 | 15 | 8-2-3 | $189,710 |
| 1939 | Challedon | 3 | 15 | 9-2-3 | 184,535 |
| 1940 | Bimelech | 3 | 7 | 4-2-1 | 110,005 |
| 1941 | Whirlaway | 3 | 20 | 13-5-2 | 272,386 |
| 1942 | Shut Out | 3 | 12 | 8-2-0 | 238,872 |
| 1943 | Count Fleet | 3 | 6 | 6-0-0 | 174,055 |
| 1944 | Pavot | 2 | 8 | 8-0-0 | 179,040 |
| 1945 | Busher | 3 | 13 | 10-2-1 | 273,735 |
| 1946 | Assault | 3 | 15 | 8-2-3 | 424,195 |
| 1947 | Armed | 6 | 17 | 11-4-1 | 376,325 |
| 1948 | Citation | 3 | 20 | 19-1-0 | 709,470 |
| 1949 | Ponder | 3 | 21 | 9-5-2 | 321,825 |
| 1950 | Noor | 5 | 12 | 7-4-1 | 346,940 |
| 1951 | Counterpoint | 3 | 15 | 7-2-1 | 250,525 |
| 1952 | Crafty Admiral | 4 | 16 | 9-4-1 | 277,225 |
| 1953 | Native Dancer | 3 | 10 | 9-1-0 | 513,425 |
| 1954 | Determine | 3 | 15 | 10-3-2 | 328,700 |
| 1955 | Nashua | 3 | 12 | 10-1-1 | 752,550 |
| 1956 | Needles | 3 | 8 | 4-2-0 | 440,850 |
| 1957 | Round Table | 3 | 22 | 15-1-3 | 600,383 |
| 1958 | Round Table | 4 | 20 | 14-4-0 | 662,780 |
| 1959 | Sword Dancer | 3 | 13 | 8-4-0 | 537,004 |
| 1960 | Bally Ache | 3 | 15 | 10-3-1 | 445,045 |
| 1961 | Carry Back | 3 | 16 | 9-1-3 | 565,349 |
| 1962 | Never Bend | 2 | 10 | 7-1-2 | 402,969 |
| 1963 | Candy Spots | 3 | 12 | 7-2-1 | 604,481 |
| 1964 | Gun Bow | 4 | 16 | 8-4-2 | 580,100 |
| 1965 | Buckpasser | 2 | 11 | 9-1-0 | 568,096 |

## Annual Money Leaders (Cont.)

### Horses (Cont.)

| Year | | Age | Sts | 1-2-3 | Earnings | Year | | Age | Sts | 1-2-3 | Earnings |
|---|---|---|---|---|---|---|---|---|---|---|---|
| 1966 | Buckpasser | 3 | 14 | 13-1-0 | $669,078 | 1986 | Snow Chief | 3 | 9 | 6-1-1 | $1,875,200 |
| 1967 | Damascus | 3 | 16 | 12-3-1 | 817,941 | 1987 | Alysheba | 3 | 10 | 3-3-1 | 2,511,156 |
| 1968 | Forward Pass | 3 | 13 | 7-2-0 | 546,674 | 1988 | Alysheba | 4 | 9 | 7-1-0 | 3,808,600 |
| 1969 | Arts and Letters | 3 | 14 | 8-5-1 | 555,604 | 1989 | Sunday Silence | 3 | 9 | 7-2-0 | 4,578,454 |
| 1970 | Personality | 3 | 18 | 8-2-1 | 444,049 | 1990 | Unbridled | 3 | 11 | 4-3-2 | 3,718,149 |
| 1971 | Riva Ridge | 2 | 9 | 7-0-0 | 503,263 | 1991 | Dance Smartly | 3 | 8 | 8-0-0 | 2,876,821 |
| 1972 | Droll Role | 4 | 19 | 7-3-4 | 471,633 | 1992 | A.P. Indy | 3 | 7 | 5-0-1 | 2,622,560 |
| 1973 | Secretariat | 3 | 12 | 9-2-1 | 860,404 | 1993 | Kotashaan (FRA) | 5 | 10 | 6-3-0 | 2,619,014 |
| 1974 | Chris Evert | 3 | 8 | 5-1-2 | 551,063 | 1994 | Paradise Creek | 5 | 11 | 8-2-1 | 2,610,187 |
| 1975 | Foolish Pleasure | 3 | 11 | 5-4-1 | 716,278 | 1995 | Cigar | 5 | 10 | 10-0-0 | 4,819,800 |
| 1976 | Forego | 6 | 8 | 6-1-1 | 401,701 | 1996 | Cigar | 6 | 8 | 5-2-1 | 4,910,000 |
| 1977 | Seattle Slew | 3 | 7 | 6-1-1 | 641,370 | 1997 | Skip Away | 4 | 11 | 4-5-2 | 4,089,000 |
| 1978 | Affirmed | 3 | 11 | 8-2-0 | 901,541 | 1998 | Silver Charm | 4 | 9 | 6-2-0 | 4,696,506 |
| 1979 | Spectacular Bid | 3 | 12 | 10-1-1 | 1,279,334 | 1999 | Almutawakel | 4 | 4 | 1-1-1 | 3,290,000 |
| 1980 | Temperence Hill | 3 | 17 | 8-3-1 | 1,130,452 | 2000 | Dubai Millennium (GBR) | 4 | 1 | 1-0-0 | 3,600,000 |
| 1981 | John Henry | 6 | 10 | 8-0-0 | 1,798,030 | 2001 | Captain Steve | 4 | 6 | 2-1-1 | 4,201,200 |
| 1982 | Perrault (GBR) | 5 | 8 | 4-1-2 | 1,197,400 | 2002 | Street Cry (IRE) | 4 | 3 | 2-1-0 | 4,266,615 |
| 1983 | All Along (FRA) | 4 | 7 | 4-1-1 | 2,138,963 | 2003 | Moon Ballad (IRE) | 4 | 3 | 1-0-0 | 3,651,101 |
| 1984 | Slew o' Gold | 4 | 6 | 5-1-0 | 2,627,944 | 2004 | Smarty Jones | 3 | 7 | 6-1-0 | 7,563,535 |
| 1985 | Spend A Buck | 3 | 7 | 5-1-1 | 3,552,704 | | | | | | |

## Jockeys

Annual money-leading jockeys since 1910, according to *The American Racing Manual*.

**Multiple leaders:** Bill Shoemaker (10); Laffit Pincay Jr. (7); Eddie Arcaro and Jerry Bailey (6); Braulio Baeza (5); Chris McCarron and Jose Santos (4); Angel Cordero Jr. and Earl Sande (3); Ted Atkinson, Pat Day, Laverne Fator, Mack Garner, Bill Hartack, Charley Kurtsinger, Johnny Longden, Mike Smith, Gary Stevens, Sonny Workman and Wayne Wright (2).

| Year | | Mts | Wins | Earnings | Year | | Mts | Wins | Earnings |
|---|---|---|---|---|---|---|---|---|---|
| 1910 | Carroll Shilling | 506 | 172 | $176,030 | 1948 | Eddie Arcaro | 726 | 188 | $1,686,230 |
| 1911 | Ted Koerner | 813 | 162 | 88,308 | 1949 | Steve Brooks | 906 | 209 | 1,316,817 |
| 1912 | Jimmy Butwell | 684 | 144 | 79,843 | 1950 | Eddie Arcaro | 888 | 195 | 1,410,160 |
| 1913 | Merritt Buxton | 887 | 146 | 82,552 | 1951 | Bill Shoemaker | 1161 | 257 | 1,329,890 |
| 1914 | J. McCahey | 824 | 155 | 121,845 | 1952 | Eddie Arcaro | 807 | 188 | 1,859,591 |
| 1915 | Mack Garner | 775 | 151 | 96,628 | 1953 | Bill Shoemaker | 1683 | 485 | 1,784,187 |
| 1916 | John McTaggart | 832 | 150 | 155,055 | 1954 | Bill Shoemaker | 1251 | 380 | 1,876,760 |
| 1917 | Frank Robinson | 731 | 147 | 148,057 | 1955 | Eddie Arcaro | 820 | 158 | 1,864,796 |
| 1918 | Lucien Luke | 756 | 178 | 201,864 | 1956 | Bill Hartack | 1387 | 347 | 2,343,955 |
| 1919 | John Loftus | 177 | 65 | 252,707 | 1957 | Bill Hartack | 1238 | 341 | 3,060,501 |
| 1920 | Clarence Kummer | 353 | 87 | 292,376 | 1958 | Bill Shoemaker | 1133 | 300 | 2,961,693 |
| 1921 | Earl Sande | 340 | 112 | 263,043 | 1959 | Bill Shoemaker | 1285 | 347 | 2,843,133 |
| 1922 | Albert Johnson | 297 | 43 | 345,054 | 1960 | Bill Shoemaker | 1227 | 274 | 2,123,961 |
| 1923 | Earl Sande | 430 | 122 | 569,394 | 1961 | Bill Shoemaker | 1256 | 304 | 2,690,819 |
| 1924 | Ivan Parke | 844 | 205 | 290,395 | 1962 | Bill Shoemaker | 1126 | 311 | 2,916,844 |
| 1925 | Laverne Fator | 315 | 81 | 305,775 | 1963 | Bill Shoemaker | 1203 | 271 | 2,526,925 |
| 1926 | Laverne Fator | 511 | 143 | 361,435 | 1964 | Bill Shoemaker | 1056 | 246 | 2,649,553 |
| 1927 | Earl Sande | 179 | 49 | 277,877 | 1965 | Braulio Baeza | 1245 | 270 | 2,582,702 |
| 1928 | Linus McAtee | 235 | 55 | 301,295 | 1966 | Braulio Baeza | 1341 | 298 | 2,951,022 |
| 1929 | Mack Garner | 274 | 57 | 314,975 | 1967 | Braulio Baeza | 1064 | 256 | 3,088,888 |
| 1930 | Sonny Workman | 571 | 152 | 420,438 | 1968 | Braulio Baeza | 1089 | 201 | 2,835,108 |
| 1931 | Charley Kurtsinger | 519 | 93 | 392,095 | 1969 | Jorge Velasquez | 1442 | 258 | 2,542,315 |
| 1932 | Sonny Workman | 378 | 87 | 385,070 | 1970 | Laffit Pincay Jr. | 1328 | 269 | 2,626,526 |
| 1933 | Robert Jones | 471 | 63 | 226,285 | 1971 | Laffit Pincay Jr. | 1627 | 380 | 3,784,377 |
| 1934 | Wayne Wright | 919 | 174 | 287,185 | 1972 | Laffit Pincay Jr. | 1388 | 289 | 3,225,827 |
| 1935 | Silvio Coucci | 749 | 141 | 319,760 | 1973 | Laffit Pincay Jr. | 1444 | 350 | 4,093,492 |
| 1936 | Wayne Wright | 670 | 100 | 264,000 | 1974 | Laffit Pincay Jr. | 1278 | 341 | 4,251,060 |
| 1937 | Charley Kurtsinger | 765 | 120 | 384,202 | 1975 | Laffit Pincay Jr. | 1190 | 196 | 3,674,398 |
| 1938 | Nick Wall | 658 | 97 | 385,161 | 1976 | Angel Cordero Jr. | 1534 | 274 | 4,709,500 |
| 1939 | Basil James | 904 | 191 | 353,333 | 1977 | Steve Cauthen | 2075 | 487 | 6,151,750 |
| 1940 | Eddie Arcaro | 783 | 132 | 343,661 | 1978 | Darrel McHargue | 1762 | 375 | 6,188,353 |
| 1941 | Don Meade | 1164 | 210 | 398,627 | 1979 | Laffit Pincay Jr. | 1708 | 420 | 8,183,535 |
| 1942 | Eddie Arcaro | 687 | 123 | 481,949 | 1980 | Chris McCarron | 1964 | 405 | 7,666,100 |
| 1943 | Johnny Longden | 871 | 173 | 573,276 | 1981 | Chris McCarron | 1494 | 326 | 8,397,604 |
| 1944 | Ted Atkinson | 1539 | 287 | 899,101 | 1982 | Angel Cordero Jr. | 1838 | 397 | 9,702,520 |
| 1945 | Johnny Longden | 778 | 180 | 981,977 | 1983 | Angel Cordero Jr. | 1792 | 362 | 10,116,807 |
| 1946 | Ted Atkinson | 1377 | 233 | 1,036,825 | 1984 | Chris McCarron | 1565 | 356 | 12,038,213 |
| 1947 | Douglas Dodson | 646 | 141 | 1,429,949 | 1985 | Laffit Pincay Jr. | 1409 | 289 | 13,415,049 |

| Year | | Mts | Wins | Earnings |
|------|--|-----|------|----------|
| 1986 | Jose Santos | 1636 | 329 | $11,329,297 |
| 1987 | Jose Santos | 1639 | 305 | 12,407,355 |
| 1988 | Jose Santos | 1867 | 370 | 14,877,298 |
| 1989 | Jose Santos | 1459 | 285 | 13,847,003 |
| 1990 | Gary Stevens | 1504 | 283 | 13,881,198 |
| 1991 | Chris McCarron | 1440 | 265 | 14,456,073 |
| 1992 | Kent Desormeaux | 1568 | 361 | 14,193,006 |
| 1993 | Mike Smith | 1510 | 343 | 14,024,815 |
| 1994 | Mike Smith | 1484 | 317 | 15,979,820 |
| 1995 | Jerry Bailey | 1367 | 287 | 16,311,876 |

| Year | | Mts | Wins | Earnings |
|------|--|-----|------|----------|
| 1996 | Jerry Bailey | 1187 | 298 | $19,465,376 |
| 1997 | Jerry Bailey | 1136 | 269 | 18,206,013 |
| 1998 | Gary Stevens | 869 | 178 | 19,358,840 |
| 1999 | Pat Day | 1265 | 254 | 18,092,845 |
| 2000 | Pat Day | 1219 | 267 | 17,479,838 |
| 2001 | Jerry Bailey | 912 | 227 | 22,597,720 |
| 2002 | Jerry Bailey | 833 | 214 | 22,871,814 |
| 2003 | Jerry Bailey | 776 | 206 | 23,354,960 |
| 2004 | John Velazquez | 1327 | 335 | 22,248,661 |

## Trainers

Annual money-leading trainers since 1908, according to *The American Racing Manual.*

**Multiple Leaders:** D. Wayne Lukas (14); Sam Hildreth (9); Charlie Whittingham (7); Sunny Jim Fitzsimmons and Jimmy Jones (5); Bob Baffert, Laz Barrera, Ben Jones and Willie Molter (4); Hirsch Jacobs, Eddie Neloy and James Rowe Sr. (3); H. Guy Bedwell, Bobby Frankel, Jack Gaver, John Schorr, Humming Bob Smith, Silent Tom Smith and Mesh Tenney (2).

| Year | | Wins | Earnings |
|------|--|------|----------|
| 1908 | James Rowe Sr. | 50 | $284,335 |
| 1909 | Sam Hildreth | 73 | 123,942 |
| 1910 | Sam Hildreth | 84 | 148,010 |
| 1911 | Sam Hildreth | 67 | 49,418 |
| 1912 | John Schorr | 63 | 58,110 |
| 1913 | James Rowe Sr. | 18 | 45,936 |
| 1914 | R.C. Benson | 45 | 59,315 |
| 1915 | James Rowe Sr. | 19 | 75,596 |
| 1916 | Sam Hildreth | 39 | 70,950 |
| 1917 | Sam Hildreth | 23 | 61,698 |
| 1918 | H. Guy Bedwell | 53 | 80,296 |
| 1919 | H. Guy Bedwell | 63 | 208,728 |
| 1920 | Louis Feustel | 22 | 186,087 |
| 1921 | Sam Hildreth | 85 | 262,768 |
| 1922 | Sam Hildreth | 74 | 247,014 |
| 1923 | Sam Hildreth | 75 | 392,124 |
| 1924 | Sam Hildreth | 77 | 255,608 |
| 1925 | G.R. Tompkins | 30 | 199,245 |
| 1926 | Scott Harlan | 21 | 205,681 |
| 1927 | W.H. Bringloe | 63 | 216,563 |
| 1928 | John Schorr | 65 | 258,425 |
| 1929 | James Rowe Jr. | 25 | 314,881 |
| 1930 | Sunny Jim Fitzsimmons | 47 | 397,355 |
| 1931 | Big Jim Healy | 33 | 297,300 |
| 1932 | Sunny Jim Fitzsimmons | 68 | 266,650 |
| 1933 | Humming Bob Smith | 53 | 135,720 |
| 1934 | Humming Bob Smith | 43 | 249,938 |
| 1935 | Bud Stotler | 87 | 303,005 |
| 1936 | Sunny Jim Fitzsimmons | 42 | 193,415 |
| 1937 | Robert McGarvey | 46 | 209,925 |
| 1938 | Earl Sande | 15 | 226,495 |
| 1939 | Sunny Jim Fitzsimmons | 45 | 266,205 |
| 1940 | Silent Tom Smith | 14 | 269,200 |
| 1941 | Ben Jones | 70 | 475,318 |
| 1942 | Jack Gaver | 48 | 406,547 |
| 1943 | Ben Jones | 73 | 267,915 |
| 1944 | Ben Jones | 60 | 601,660 |
| 1945 | Silent Tom Smith | 52 | 510,655 |
| 1946 | Hirsch Jacobs | 99 | 560,077 |
| 1947 | Jimmy Jones | 85 | 1,334,805 |
| 1948 | Jimmy Jones | 81 | 1,118,670 |
| 1949 | Jimmy Jones | 76 | 978,587 |
| 1950 | Preston Burch | 96 | 637,754 |
| 1951 | Jack Gaver | 42 | 616,392 |
| 1952 | Ben Jones | 29 | 662,137 |
| 1953 | Harry Trotsek | 54 | 1,028,873 |
| 1954 | Willie Molter | 136 | 1,107,860 |
| 1955 | Sunny Jim Fitzsimmons | 66 | 1,270,055 |
| 1956 | Willie Molter | 142 | 1,227,402 |
| 1957 | Jimmy Jones | 70 | 1,150,910 |

| Year | | | Wins | Earnings |
|------|--|--|------|----------|
| 1958 | Willie Molter | | 69 | $1,116,544 |
| 1959 | Willie Molter | | 71 | 847,290 |
| 1960 | Hirsch Jacobs | | 97 | 748,349 |
| 1961 | Jimmy Jones | | 62 | 759,856 |
| 1962 | Mesh Tenney | | 58 | 1,099,474 |

| Year | | Sts | Wins | Earnings |
|------|--|-----|------|----------|
| 1963 | Mesh Tenney | 192 | 40 | $860,703 |
| 1964 | Bill Winfrey | 287 | 61 | 1,350,534 |
| 1965 | Hirsch Jacobs | 610 | 91 | 1,331,628 |
| 1966 | Eddie Neloy | 282 | 93 | 2,456,250 |
| 1967 | Eddie Neloy | 262 | 72 | 1,776,089 |
| 1968 | Eddie Neloy | 212 | 52 | 1,233,101 |
| 1969 | Elliott Burch | 156 | 26 | 1,067,936 |
| 1970 | Charlie Whittingham | 551 | 82 | 1,302,354 |
| 1971 | Charlie Whittingham | 393 | 77 | 1,737,115 |
| 1972 | Charlie Whittingham | 429 | 79 | 1,734,020 |
| 1973 | Charlie Whittingham | 423 | 85 | 1,865,385 |
| 1974 | Pancho Martin | 846 | 166 | 2,408,419 |
| 1975 | Charlie Whittingham | 487 | 3 | 2,437,244 |
| 1976 | Jack Van Berg | 2362 | 496 | 2,976,196 |
| 1977 | Laz Barrera | 781 | 127 | 2,715,848 |
| 1978 | Laz Barrera | 592 | 100 | 3,307,164 |
| 1979 | Laz Barrera | 492 | 98 | 3,608,517 |
| 1980 | Laz Barrera | 559 | 99 | 2,969,151 |
| 1981 | Charlie Whittingham | 376 | 74 | 3,993,302 |
| 1982 | Charlie Whittingham | 410 | 63 | 4,587,457 |
| 1983 | D. Wayne Lukas | 595 | 78 | 4,267,261 |
| 1984 | D. Wayne Lukas | 805 | 131 | 5,835,921 |
| 1985 | D. Wayne Lukas | 1140 | 218 | 11,155,188 |
| 1986 | D. Wayne Lukas | 1510 | 259 | 12,345,180 |
| 1987 | D. Wayne Lukas | 1735 | 343 | 17,502,110 |
| 1988 | D. Wayne Lukas | 1500 | 318 | 17,842,358 |
| 1989 | D. Wayne Lukas | 1398 | 305 | 16,103,998 |
| 1990 | D. Wayne Lukas | 1396 | 267 | 14,508,871 |
| 1991 | D. Wayne Lukas | 1497 | 289 | 15,942,223 |
| 1992 | D. Wayne Lukas | 1349 | 230 | 9,806,436 |
| 1993 | Bobby Frankel | 345 | 79 | 8,933,252 |
| 1994 | D. Wayne Lukas | 693 | 147 | 9,247,457 |
| 1995 | D. Wayne Lukas | 837 | 194 | 12,834,483 |
| 1996 | D. Wayne Lukas | 1006 | 192 | 15,966,344 |
| 1997 | D. Wayne Lukas | 824 | 169 | 9,993,569 |
| 1998 | Bob Baffert | 538 | 139 | 15,000,870 |
| 1999 | Bob Baffert | 735 | 169 | 16,934,607 |
| 2000 | Bob Baffert | 678 | 146 | 11,831,605 |
| 2001 | Bob Baffert | 660 | 138 | 16,354,996 |
| 2002 | Bobby Frankel | 480 | 117 | 17,748,340 |
| 2003 | Bobby Frankel | 413 | 114 | 19,143,289 |
| 2004 | Todd Pletcher | 948 | 240 | 17,511,923 |

## All-Time Leaders

The all-time leading horses, trainers and jockeys of North America. Records are courtesy of the *Equibase Company* and include all available earnings from races in foreign countries. Horses must have had at least one start in the United States or Canada. Note that horses, jockeys and trainers who were active in 2005 are in **bold** type.

Records are through Oct. 8, 2005.

### Top 20 Horses—Earnings

| | | Sts | 1st | 2nd | 3rd | Earnings | | | | Sts | 1st | 2nd | 3rd | Earnings |
|---|---|---|---|---|---|---|---|---|---|---|---|---|---|---|
| 1 | Cigar | 33 | 19 | 4 | 5 | $9,999,815 | 11 | Singspiel (IRE) | 20 | 9 | 8 | 0 | $5,952,825 |
| 2 | Skip Away | 38 | 18 | 10 | 6 | 9,616,360 | 12 | Falbrav (IRE) | 26 | 13 | 5 | 5 | 5,825,517 |
| 3 | Fantastic Light | 25 | 12 | 5 | 3 | 8,486,957 | 13 | Medaglia d'Oro | 17 | 8 | 7 | 0 | 5,754,720 |
| 4 | Pleasantly Perfect | 18 | 9 | 3 | 2 | 7,789,880 | 14 | Best Pal | 47 | 18 | 11 | 4 | 5,668,245 |
| 5 | Smarty Jones | 9 | 8 | 1 | 0 | 7,613,155 | 15 | Taiki Blizzard | 23 | 6 | 8 | 2 | 5,523,549 |
| 6 | Silver Charm | 24 | 12 | 7 | 2 | 6,944,369 | 16 | Roses in May | 13 | 8 | 4 | 0 | 5,490,187 |
| 7 | Captain Steve | 25 | 9 | 3 | 7 | 6,828,356 | 17 | High Chaparral (IRE) | 13 | 10 | 1 | 2 | 5,331,231 |
| 8 | Alysheba | 26 | 11 | 8 | 2 | 6,679,242 | 18 | Sulamani (IRE) | 17 | 9 | 3 | 1 | 5,252,368 |
| 9 | John Henry | 83 | 39 | 15 | 9 | 6,591,860 | 19 | Street Cry (IRE) | 12 | 5 | 6 | 1 | 5,150,837 |
| 10 | Tiznow | 15 | 8 | 4 | 2 | 6,427,830 | 20 | Preeminence (JPN) | 50 | 13 | 9 | 7 | 5,042,956 |

### Top 10 Jockeys—Races Won

| | | Yrs | Wins | Earnings |
|---|---|---|---|---|
| 1 | Laffit Pincay Jr. | 37 | 9530 | $237,120,625 |
| 2 | **Russell Baze** | 32 | 9108 | 136,728,571 |
| 3 | Bill Shoemaker | 42 | 8833 | 123,375,524 |
| 4 | **Pat Day** | 33 | 8803 | 297,912,019 |
| 5 | David Gall | 43 | 7396 | 24,972,821 |
| 6 | Chris McCarron | 29 | 7141 | 263,985,505 |
| 7 | **Angel Cordero Jr.** | 35 | 7057 | 164,570,227 |
| 8 | Jorge Velasquez | 33 | 6795 | 125,544,379 |
| 9 | Sandy Hawley | 31 | 6449 | 88,681,292 |
| 10 | Larry Snyder | 35 | 6388 | 47,207,289 |

### Top 10 Jockeys—Earnings

| | | Yrs | Wins | Earnings |
|---|---|---|---|---|
| 1 | **Pat Day** | 33 | 8803 | $297,912,019 |
| 2 | Jerry Bailey | 31 | 5871 | 291,381,061 |
| 3 | Chris McCarron | 29 | 7141 | 263,985,505 |
| 4 | Laffit Pincay Jr. | 37 | 9530 | 237,120,625 |
| 5 | **Gary Stevens** | 27 | 4878 | 220,256,621 |
| 6 | Eddie Delahoussaye | 36 | 6384 | 195,884,940 |
| 7 | **Alex Solis** | 25 | 4285 | 187,097,278 |
| 8 | **Jose Santos** | 22 | 3962 | 179,543,549 |
| 9 | **Kent Desormeaux** | 20 | 4533 | 178,402,073 |
| 10 | **Mike Smith** | 24 | 4513 | 174,769,028 |

### Top 10 Trainers—Races Won

| | | Wins | Earnings |
|---|---|---|---|
| 1 | **Dale Baird** | 9143 | $31,057,789 |
| 2 | **Jack Van Berg** | 6353 | 80,730,596 |
| 3 | **King Leatherbury** | 6102 | 53,421,304 |
| 4 | **Richard Hazelton** | 4618 | 37,392,592 |
| 5 | **Jerry Hollendorfer** | 4451 | 79,155,209 |
| 6 | **D. Wayne Lukas** | 4359 | 243,796,576 |
| 7 | Frank Merrill Jr. | 3974 | 16,980,632 |
| 8 | Richard Dutrow Sr. | 3665 | 36,189,085 |
| 9 | **Grover Delp** | 3646 | 40,267,008 |
| 10 | **H. Allen Jerkens** | 3622 | 89,691,127 |

### Top 10 Trainers—Earnings

| | | Wins | Earnings |
|---|---|---|---|
| 1 | **D. Wayne Lukas** | 4359 | $243,796,576 |
| 2 | **Bobby Frankel** | 3234 | 185,147,477 |
| 3 | **Bill Mott** | 3403 | 142,597,950 |
| 4 | **Ron McAnally** | 2453 | 115,332,280 |
| 5 | **Bob Baffert** | 1518 | 111,219,274 |
| 6 | Charles Whittingham | 2534 | 109,215,527 |
| 7 | **Richard Mandella** | 1687 | 101,651,802 |
| 8 | **H. Allen Jerkens** | 3622 | 89,691,127 |
| 9 | **Claude McGaughey III** | 1442 | 89,404,049 |
| 10 | **Todd Pletcher** | 1333 | 81,817,630 |

## Horse of the Year (1936-70)

In 1971, the *Daily Racing Form*, the Thoroughbred Racing Associations, and the National Turf Writers Assn. joined forces to create the Eclipse Awards. Before then, however, the *Racing Form* (1936-70) and the TRA (1950-70) issued separate selections for Horse of the Year. Their picks differed only four times from 1950-70 and are so noted. Horses listed in CAPITAL letters are Triple Crown winners; (f) indicates female.

**Multiple winners:** Kelso (5); Challedon, Native Dancer and Whirlaway (2).

| Year | | Year | | Year | | Year | |
|---|---|---|---|---|---|---|---|
| 1936 | Granville | 1946 | ASSAULT | 1955 | Nashua | 1964 | Kelso |
| 1937 | WAR ADMIRAL | 1947 | Armed | 1956 | Swaps | 1965 | Roman Brother (DRF) |
| 1938 | Seabiscuit | 1948 | CITATION | 1957 | Bold Ruler (DRF) | | Moccasin (TRA) |
| 1939 | Challedon | 1949 | Capot | | Dedicate (TRA) | 1966 | Buckpasser |
| 1940 | Challedon | 1950 | Hill Prince | 1958 | Round Table | 1967 | Damascus |
| 1941 | WHIRLAWAY | 1951 | Counterpoint | 1959 | Sword Dancer | 1968 | Dr. Fager |
| 1942 | Whirlaway | 1952 | One Count (DRF) | 1960 | Kelso | 1969 | Arts and Letters |
| 1943 | COUNT FLEET | | Native Dancer (TRA) | 1961 | Kelso | 1970 | Fort Marcy (DRF) |
| 1944 | Twilight Tear (f) | 1953 | Tom Fool | 1962 | Kelso | | Personality (TRA) |
| 1945 | Busher (f) | 1954 | Native Dancer | 1963 | Kelso | | |

# Eclipse Awards

The Eclipse Awards, honoring the Horse of the Year and other champions of the sport, are sponsored by the National Thoroughbred Racing Association (NTRA), *Daily Racing Form* and the National Turf Writers Assn. In 1998, the NTRA replaced the Thoroughbred Racing Associations of North America as co-sponsor.

The awards are named after the 18th century racehorse and sire, Eclipse, who began racing at age five and was unbeaten in 18 starts (eight wins were walkovers). As a stallion, Eclipse sired winners of 344 races, including three Epsom Derby champions.

Horses listed in CAPITAL letters won the Triple Crown that year. Age of horse in parentheses where necessary.

**Multiple winners:** (horses): Forego (8); John Henry (7); Affirmed, Lonesome Glory and Secretariat (5); Azeri, Cigar, Flatterer, Seattle Slew, Skip Away and Spectacular Bid (4); Ack Ack, Susan's Girl, Tiznow and Zaccio (3); All Along, Alysheba, Bayakoa, Black Tie Affair, Cafe Prince, Charismatic, Conquistador Cielo, Desert Vixen, Favorite Trick, Ferdinand, Flawlessly, Flat Top, Ghostzapper, Go for Wand, High Chaparral, Holy Bull, Housebuster, Kotashaan, Lady's Secret, Life's Magic, Miesque, Mineshaft, Morley Street, Open Mind, Paseana, Point Given, Riva Ridge, Silverbulletday, Slew o' Gold and Spend A Buck (2).

**Multiple winners:** (people): Jerry Bailey (7); Juddmonte Farms and Laffit Pincay Jr. (6); Bobby Frankel (5); Laz Barrera, Pat Day, John Franks, D. Wayne Lukas, Allen Paulson, Ogden Phipps and Frank Stronach (4); Bob Baffert, Steve Cauthen, Harbor View Farm, Fred W. Hooper, Nelson Bunker Hunt, Mr. & Mrs. Gene Klein, Dan Lasater, John & Betty Mabee, Paul Mellon, Bill Shoemaker, Edward Taylor and Charlie Whittingham (3); Braulio Baeza, C.T. Chenery, Claiborne Farm, Angel Cordero Jr., Kent Desormeaux, Richard Englander, William S. Farish, John W. Galbreath, Chris McCarron, Bill Mott and Mike Smith (2).

## Horse of the Year

| Year | | Year | | Year | | Year | |
|---|---|---|---|---|---|---|---|
| 1971 | Ack Ack (5) | 1980 | Spectacular Bid (4) | 1989 | Sunday Silence (3) | 1998 | Skip Away (5) |
| 1972 | Secretariat (2) | 1981 | John Henry (6) | 1990 | Criminal Type (5) | 1999 | Charismatic (3) |
| 1973 | SECRETARIAT (3) | 1982 | Conquistador Cielo (3) | 1991 | Black Tie Affair (5) | 2000 | Tiznow (3) |
| 1974 | Forego (4) | 1983 | All Along (4) | 1992 | A.P. Indy (3) | 2001 | Point Given (3) |
| 1975 | Forego (5) | 1984 | John Henry (9) | 1993 | Kotashaan (5) | 2002 | Azeri (4) |
| 1976 | Forego (6) | 1985 | Spend A Buck (3) | 1994 | Holy Bull (3) | 2003 | Mineshaft (4) |
| 1977 | SEATTLE SLEW (3) | 1986 | Lady's Secret (4) | 1995 | Cigar (5) | 2004 | Ghostzapper (4) |
| 1978 | AFFIRMED (3) | 1987 | Ferdinand (4) | 1996 | Cigar (6) | | |
| 1979 | Affirmed (4) | 1988 | Alysheba (4) | 1997 | Favorite Trick (2) | | |

## Older Male

| Year | | Year | | Year | | Year | |
|---|---|---|---|---|---|---|---|
| 1971 | Ack Ack (5) | 1980 | Spectacular Bid (4) | 1989 | Blushing John (4) | 1998 | Skip Away (5) |
| 1972 | Autobiography (4) | 1981 | John Henry (6) | 1990 | Criminal Type (5) | 1999 | Victory Gallop (4) |
| 1973 | Riva Ridge (4) | 1982 | Lemhi Gold (4) | 1991 | Black Tie Affair (5) | 2000 | Lemon Drop Kid (4) |
| 1974 | Forego (4) | 1983 | Bates Motel (4) | 1992 | Pleasant Tap (5) | 2001 | Tiznow (4) |
| 1975 | Forego (5) | 1984 | Slew o' Gold (4) | 1993 | Bertrando (4) | 2002 | Left Bank (5) |
| 1976 | Forego (6) | 1985 | Vanlandingham (4) | 1994 | The Wicked North (4) | 2003 | Mineshaft (4) |
| 1977 | Forego (7) | 1986 | Turkoman (4) | 1995 | Cigar (5) | 2004 | Ghostzapper (4) |
| 1978 | Seattle Slew (4) | 1987 | Ferdinand (4) | 1996 | Cigar (6) | | |
| 1979 | Affirmed (4) | 1988 | Alysheba (4) | 1997 | Skip Away (4) | | |

## Older Female

| Year | | Year | | Year | | Year | |
|---|---|---|---|---|---|---|---|
| 1971 | Shuvee (5) | 1980 | Glorious Song (4) | 1989 | Bayakoa (5) | 1998 | Escena (5) |
| 1972 | Typecast (6) | 1981 | Relaxing (5) | 1990 | Bayakoa (6) | 1999 | Beautiful Pleasure (4) |
| 1973 | Susan's Girl (4) | 1982 | Track Robbery (6) | 1991 | Queena (5) | 2000 | Riboletta (5) |
| 1974 | Desert Vixen (4) | 1983 | Amb. of Luck (4) | 1992 | Paseana (5) | 2001 | Gourmet Girl (6) |
| 1975 | Susan's Girl (6) | 1984 | Princess Rooney (4) | 1993 | Paseana (6) | 2002 | Azeri (4) |
| 1976 | Proud Delta (4) | 1985 | Life's Magic (4) | 1994 | Sky Beauty (4) | 2003 | Azeri (5) |
| 1977 | Cascapedia (4) | 1986 | Lady's Secret (4) | 1995 | Inside Information (4) | 2004 | Azeri (6) |
| 1978 | Late Bloomer (4) | 1987 | North Sider (5) | 1996 | Jewel Princess (4) | | |
| 1979 | Waya (5) | 1988 | Personal Ensign (4) | 1997 | Hidden Lake (4) | | |

## 3-Year-Old Male

| Year | | Year | | Year | | Year | |
|---|---|---|---|---|---|---|---|
| 1971 | Canonero II | 1980 | Temperence Hill | 1989 | Sunday Silence | 1998 | Real Quiet |
| 1972 | Key to the Mint | 1981 | Pleasant Colony | 1990 | Unbridled | 1999 | Charismatic |
| 1973 | SECRETARIAT | 1982 | Conquistador Cielo | 1991 | Hansel | 2000 | Tiznow |
| 1974 | Little Current | 1983 | Slew o' Gold | 1992 | A.P. Indy | 2001 | Point Given |
| 1975 | Wajima | 1984 | Swale | 1993 | Prairie Bayou | 2002 | War Emblem |
| 1976 | Bold Forbes | 1985 | Spend A Buck | 1994 | Holy Bull | 2003 | Funny Cide |
| 1977 | SEATTLE SLEW | 1986 | Snow Chief | 1995 | Thunder Gulch | 2004 | Smarty Jones |
| 1978 | AFFIRMED | 1987 | Alysheba | 1996 | Skip Away | | |
| 1979 | Spectacular Bid | 1988 | Risen Star | 1997 | Silver Charm | | |

## Eclipse Awards (Cont.)

### 3-Year-Old Filly

| Year | | Year | | Year | | Year | |
|------|--|------|--|------|--|------|--|
| 1971 | Turkish Trousers | 1980 | Genuine Risk | 1989 | Open Mind | 1998 | Banshee Breeze |
| 1972 | Susan's Girl | 1981 | Wayward Lass | 1990 | Go for Wand | 1999 | Silverbulletday |
| 1973 | Desert Vixen | 1982 | Christmas Past | 1991 | Dance Smartly | 2000 | Surfside |
| 1974 | Chris Evert | 1983 | Heartlight No. One | 1992 | Saratoga Dew | 2001 | Xtra Heat |
| 1975 | Ruffian | 1984 | Life's Magic | 1993 | Hollywood Wildcat | 2002 | Farda Amiga |
| 1976 | Revidere | 1985 | Mom's Command | 1994 | Heavenly Prize | 2003 | Bird Town |
| 1977 | Our Mims | 1986 | Tiffany Lass | 1995 | Serena's Song | 2004 | Ashado |
| 1978 | Tempest Queen | 1987 | Sacahuista | 1996 | Yanks Music | | |
| 1979 | Davona Dale | 1988 | Winning Colors | 1997 | Ajina | | |

### 2-Year-Old Male

| Year | | Year | | Year | | Year | |
|------|--|------|--|------|--|------|--|
| 1971 | Riva Ridge | 1980 | Lord Avie | 1989 | Rhythm | 1998 | Answer Lively |
| 1972 | Secretariat | 1981 | Deputy Minister | 1990 | Fly So Free | 1999 | Anees |
| 1973 | Protagonist | 1982 | Roving Boy | 1991 | Arazi | 2000 | Macho Uno |
| 1974 | Foolish Pleasure | 1983 | Devil's Bag | 1992 | Gilded Time | 2001 | Johannesburg |
| 1975 | Honest Pleasure | 1984 | Chief's Crown | 1993 | Dehere | 2002 | Vindication |
| 1976 | Seattle Slew | 1985 | Tasso | 1994 | Timber Country | 2003 | Action This Day |
| 1977 | Affirmed | 1986 | Capote | 1995 | Maria's Mon | 2004 | Declan's Moon |
| 1978 | Spectacular Bid | 1987 | Forty Niner | 1996 | Boston Harbor | | |
| 1979 | Rockhill Native | 1988 | Easy Goer | 1997 | Favorite Trick | | |

### 2-Year-Old Filly

| Year | | Year | | Year | | Year | |
|------|--|------|--|------|--|------|--|
| 1971 | Numbered Account | 1979 | Smart Angle | 1988 | Open Mind | 1997 | Countess Diana |
| 1972 | La Prevoyante | 1980 | Heavenly Cause | 1989 | Go for Wand | 1998 | Silverbulletday |
| 1973 | Talking Picture | 1981 | Before Dawn | 1990 | Meadow Star | 1999 | Chilukki |
| 1974 | Ruffian | 1982 | Landaluce | 1991 | Pleasant Stage | 2000 | Caressing |
| 1975 | Dearly Precious | 1983 | Althea | 1992 | Eliza | 2001 | Tempera |
| 1976 | Sensational | 1984 | Outstandingly | 1993 | Phone Chatter | 2002 | Storm Flag Flying |
| 1977 | Lakeville Miss | 1985 | Family Style | 1994 | Flanders | 2003 | Halfbridled |
| 1978 | (TIE) Candy Eclair | 1986 | Brave Raj | 1995 | Golden Attraction | 2004 | Sweet Catomine |
| | & It's in the Air | 1987 | Epitome | 1996 | Storm Song | | |

### Champion Turf Horse

| Year | | Year | | Year | | Year | |
|------|--|------|--|------|--|------|--|
| 1971 | Run the Gantlet (3) | 1973 | SECRETARIAT (3) | 1975 | Snow Knight (4) | 1977 | Johnny D (3) |
| 1972 | Cougar II (6) | 1974 | Dahlia (4) | 1976 | Youth (3) | 1978 | Mac Diarmida (3) |

### Champion Male Turf Horse

| Year | | Year | | Year | | Year | |
|------|--|------|--|------|--|------|--|
| 1979 | Bowl Game (5) | 1986 | Manila (3) | 1993 | Kotashaan (5) | 2000 | Kalanisi (4) |
| 1980 | John Henry (5) | 1987 | Theatrical (5) | 1994 | Paradise Creek (5) | 2001 | Fantastic Light (5) |
| 1981 | John Henry (6) | 1988 | Sunshine Forever (3) | 1995 | Northern Spur (4) | 2002 | High Chaparral (3) |
| 1982 | Perrault (5) | 1989 | Steinlen (6) | 1996 | Singspiel (4) | 2003 | High Chaparral (4) |
| 1983 | John Henry (8) | 1990 | Itsallgreektome (3) | 1997 | Chief Bearhart (4) | 2004 | Kitten's Joy (3) |
| 1984 | John Henry (9) | 1991 | Tight Spot (4) | 1998 | Buck's Boy (5) | | |
| 1985 | Cozzene (4) | 1992 | Sky Classic (5) | 1999 | Daylami (5) | | |

### Champion Female Turf Horse

| Year | | Year | | Year | | Year | |
|------|--|------|--|------|--|------|--|
| 1979 | Trillion (5) | 1986 | Estrapade (6) | 1993 | Flawlessly (5) | 2000 | Perfect Sting (4) |
| 1980 | Just A Game II (4) | 1987 | Miesque (3) | 1994 | Hatoof (5) | 2001 | Banks Hill (3) |
| 1981 | De La Rose (3) | 1988 | Miesque (4) | 1995 | Possibly Perfect (5) | 2002 | Golden Apples (4) |
| 1982 | April Run (4) | 1989 | Brown Bess (7) | 1996 | Wandesta (5) | 2003 | Islington (4) |
| 1983 | All Along (4) | 1990 | Laugh and Be Merry (5) | 1997 | Ryafan (3) | 2004 | Ouija Board (3) |
| 1984 | Royal Heroine (4) | 1991 | Miss Alleged (4) | 1998 | Fiji (4) | | |
| 1985 | Pebbles (4) | 1992 | Flawlessly (4) | 1999 | Soaring Softly (4) | | |

## Sprinter

| Year | | Year | | Year | | Year | |
|------|--|------|--|------|--|------|--|
| 1971 | Ack Ack (5) | 1979 | Star de Naskra (4) | 1988 | Gulch (4) | 1997 | Smoke Glacken (3) |
| 1972 | Chou Croute (4) | 1980 | Plugged Nickle (3) | 1989 | Safely Kept (3) | 1998 | Reraise (3) |
| 1973 | Shecky Greene (3) | 1981 | Guilty Conscience (5) | 1990 | Housebuster (3) | 1999 | Artax (4) |
| 1974 | Forego (4) | 1982 | Gold Beauty (3) | 1991 | Housebuster (4) | 2000 | Kona Gold (6) |
| 1975 | Gallant Bob (3) | 1983 | Chinook Pass (4) | 1992 | Rubiano (5) | 2001 | Squirtle Squirt (3) |
| 1976 | My Juliet (4) | 1984 | Eillo (4) | 1993 | Cardmania (7) | 2002 | Orientate (4) |
| 1977 | What a Summer (4) | 1985 | Precisionist (4) | 1994 | Cherokee Run (4) | 2003 | Aldebaran (5) |
| 1978 | (TIE ) Dr. Patches (4) | 1986 | Smile (4) | 1995 | Not Surprising (4) | 2004 | Speightstown (6) |
|  | & J.O. Tobin (4) | 1987 | Groovy (4) | 1996 | Lit de Justice (6) |  |  |

## Steeplechase or Hurdle Horse

| Year | | Year | | Year | | Year | |
|------|--|------|--|------|--|------|--|
| 1971 | Shadow Brook (7) | 1980 | Zaccio (4) | 1989 | Highland Bud (4) | 1998 | Flat Top (5) |
| 1972 | Soothsayer (5) | 1981 | Zaccio (5) | 1990 | Morley Street (6) | 1999 | Lonesome Glory (11) |
| 1973 | Athenian Idol (5) | 1982 | Zaccio (6) | 1991 | Morley Street (7) | 2000 | All Gong (6) |
| 1974 | Gran Kan (8) | 1983 | Flatterer (4) | 1992 | Lonesome Glory (4) | 2001 | Pompeyo (8) |
| 1975 | Life's Illusion (4) | 1984 | Flatterer (5) | 1993 | Lonesome Glory (5) | 2002 | Flat Top (9) |
| 1976 | Straight and True (6) | 1985 | Flatterer (6) | 1994 | Warm Spell (6) | 2003 | McDynamo (6) |
| 1977 | Cafe Prince (7) | 1986 | Flatterer (7) | 1995 | Lonesome Glory (7) | 2004 | Hirapour (8) |
| 1978 | Cafe Prince (8) | 1987 | Inlander (6) | 1996 | Correggio (5) |  |  |
| 1979 | Martie's Anger (4) | 1988 | Jimmy Lorenzo (6) | 1997 | Lonesome Glory (9) |  |  |

## Outstanding Jockey

| Year | | Year | | Year | | Year | |
|------|--|------|--|------|--|------|--|
| 1971 | Laffit Pincay Jr. | 1980 | Chris McCarron | 1989 | Kent Desormeaux | 1998 | Gary Stevens |
| 1972 | Braulio Baeza | 1981 | Bill Shoemaker | 1990 | Craig Perret | 1999 | Jorge Chavez |
| 1973 | Laffit Pincay Jr. | 1982 | Angel Cordero Jr. | 1991 | Pat Day | 2000 | Jerry Bailey |
| 1974 | Laffit Pincay Jr. | 1983 | Angel Cordero Jr. | 1992 | Kent Desormeaux | 2001 | Jerry Bailey |
| 1975 | Braulio Baeza | 1984 | Pat Day | 1993 | Mike Smith | 2002 | Jerry Bailey |
| 1976 | Sandy Hawley | 1985 | Laffit Pincay Jr. | 1994 | Mike Smith | 2003 | Jerry Bailey |
| 1977 | Steve Cauthen | 1986 | Pat Day | 1995 | Jerry Bailey | 2004 | John Velazquez |
| 1978 | Darrel McHargue | 1987 | Pat Day | 1996 | Jerry Bailey |  |  |
| 1979 | Laffit Pincay Jr. | 1988 | Jose Santos | 1997 | Jerry Bailey |  |  |

## Outstanding Apprentice Jockey

| Year | | Year | | Year | | Year | |
|------|--|------|--|------|--|------|--|
| 1971 | Gene St. Leon | 1981 | Richard Migliore | 1991 | Mickey Walls | 2000 | Tyler Baze |
| 1972 | Thomas Wallis | 1982 | Alberto Delgado | 1992 | Rosemary Homeister | 2001 | Jeremy Rose |
| 1973 | Steve Valdez | 1983 | Declan Murphy | 1993 | Juan Umana | 2002 | Ryan Fogelsonger |
| 1974 | Chris McCarron | 1984 | Wesley Ward | 1994 | Dale Beckner | 2003 | Eddie Castro |
| 1975 | Jimmy Edwards | 1985 | Art Madrid Jr. | 1995 | Ramon B. Perez | 2004 | Brian Hernandez Jr. |
| 1976 | George Martens | 1986 | Allen Stacy | 1996 | Neil Poznansky |  |  |
| 1977 | Steve Cauthen | 1987 | Kent Desormeaux | 1997 | Roberto Rosado |  |  |
| 1978 | Ron Franklin | 1988 | Steve Capanas |  | & Philip Teator |  |  |
| 1979 | Cash Asmussen | 1989 | Michael Luzzi | 1998 | Shaun Bridgmohan |  |  |
| 1980 | Frank Lovato Jr. | 1990 | Mark Johnston | 1999 | Ariel Smith |  |  |

## Outstanding Trainer

| Year | | Year | | Year | | Year | |
|------|--|------|--|------|--|------|--|
| 1971 | Charlie Whittingham | 1980 | Bud Delp | 1989 | Charlie Whittingham | 1998 | Bob Baffert |
| 1972 | Lucien Laurin | 1981 | Ron McAnally | 1990 | Carl Nafzger | 1999 | Bob Baffert |
| 1973 | H. Allen Jerkens | 1982 | Charlie Whittingham | 1991 | Ron McAnally | 2000 | Bobby Frankel |
| 1974 | Sherill Ward | 1983 | Woody Stephens | 1992 | Ron McAnally | 2001 | Bobby Frankel |
| 1975 | Steve DiMauro | 1984 | Jack Van Berg | 1993 | Bobby Frankel | 2002 | Bobby Frankel |
| 1976 | Laz Barrera | 1985 | D. Wayne Lukas | 1994 | D. Wayne Lukas | 2003 | Bobby Frankel |
| 1977 | Laz Barrera | 1986 | D. Wayne Lukas | 1995 | Bill Mott | 2004 | Todd Pletcher |
| 1978 | Laz Barrera | 1987 | D. Wayne Lukas | 1996 | Bill Mott |  |  |
| 1979 | Laz Barrera | 1988 | Shug McGaughey | 1997 | Bob Baffert |  |  |

## Outstanding Owner

| Year | | Year | | Year | | Year | |
|------|--|------|--|------|--|------|--|
| 1971 | Mr. & Mrs. E.E. Fogleson | 1980 | Mr. & Mrs. Bertram Firestone | 1988 | Ogden Phipps | 1997 | Carolyn Hine |
| 1972-73 | No award | 1981 | Dotsam Stable | 1989 | Ogden Phipps | 1998 | Frank Stronach |
| 1974 | Dan Lasater | 1982 | Viola Sommer | 1990 | Frances Genter | 1999 | Frank Stronach |
| 1975 | Dan Lasater | 1983 | John Franks | 1991 | Sam-Son Farms | 2000 | Frank Stronach |
| 1976 | Dan Lasater | 1984 | John Franks | 1992 | Juddmonte Farms | 2001 | Richard Englander |
| 1977 | Maxwell Gluck | 1985 | Mr. & Mrs. Gene Klein | 1993 | John Franks | 2002 | Richard Englander |
| 1978 | Harbor View Farm | 1986 | Mr. & Mrs. Gene Klein | 1994 | John Franks | 2003 | Juddmonte Farms |
| 1979 | Harbor View Farm | 1987 | Mr. & Mrs. Gene Klein | 1995 | Allen Paulson | 2004 | Ken & Sarah Ramsey |
|  |  |  |  | 1996 | Allen Paulson |  |  |

## Eclipse Awards (Cont.)

### Outstanding Breeder

| Year | | Year | | Year | | Year | |
|------|--|------|--|------|--|------|--|
| 1971 | Paul Mellon | 1980 | Mrs. Henry Paxson | 1989 | North Ridge Farm | 1998 | John & Betty Mabee |
| 1972 | C.T. Chenery | 1981 | Golden Chance Farm | 1990 | Calumet Farm | 1999 | William S. Farish |
| 1973 | C.T. Chenery | 1982 | Fred W. Hooper | 1991 | John & Betty Mabee | 2000 | Frank Stronach |
| 1974 | John W. Galbreath | 1983 | Edward P. Taylor | 1992 | William S. Farish | 2001 | Juddmonte Farms |
| 1975 | Fred W. Hooper | 1984 | Claiborne Farm | 1993 | Allan Paulson | 2002 | Juddmonte Farms |
| 1976 | Nelson Bunker Hunt | 1985 | Nelson Bunker Hunt | 1994 | William T. Young | 2003 | Juddmonte Farms |
| 1977 | Edward P. Taylor | 1986 | Paul Mellon | 1995 | Juddmonte Farms | 2004 | Adena Springs |
| 1978 | Harbor View Farm | 1987 | Nelson Bunker Hunt | 1996 | Farnsworth Farms | | |
| 1979 | Claiborne Farm | 1988 | Ogden Phipps | 1997 | John & Betty Mabee | | |

### Award of Merit

| Year | | Year | | Year | | Year | |
|------|--|------|--|------|--|------|--|
| 1976 | Jack J. Dreyfus | 1986 | Herman Cohen | 1993 | Paul Mellon | 2001 | Pete Pederson |
| 1977 | Steve Cauthen | 1987 | J.B. Faulconer | 1994 | Alfred G. Vanderbilt | | & Harry T. Mangurian |
| 1978 | Dinny Phipps | 1988 | John Forsythe | 1995 | Ted Bassett III | 2002 | Ogden Phipps |
| 1979 | Jimmy Kilroe | 1989 | Michael Sandler | 1996 | Allen Paulson | | & Howard Battle |
| 1980 | John D. Shapiro | 1990 | Warner L. Jones | 1997 | Bob & Beverly Lewis | 2003 | Richard Duchossois |
| 1981 | Bill Shoemaker | 1991 | Fred W. Hooper | 1998 | D.G. Van Clief Jr. | 2004 | Oaklawn Park & |
| 1984 | John Gaines | 1992 | Joe Hirsch | 2000 | Jim McKay | | the Cella family |
| 1985 | Keene Daingerfield | | & Robert P. Strub | | | | |

### Special Award

| Year | | Year | | Year | | Year | |
|------|--|------|--|------|--|------|--|
| 1971 | Robert J. Kleberg | 1985 | Arlington Park | 1995 | Russell Baze | 2001 | Sheikh Mohammed |
| 1974 | Charles Hatton | 1987 | Anheuser-Busch | 1998 | Oak Tree Racing | | al-Maktoum |
| 1976 | Bill Shoemaker | 1988 | Edward J. DeBartolo Sr. | | Assoc. | 2002 | Keeneland Library |
| 1980 | John T. Landry | 1989 | Richard Duchossois | 1999 | Laffit Pincay Jr. | 2004 | Dale Baird |
| | & Pierre E. Bellocq | 1994 | Eddie Arcaro | 2000 | John Hettinger | | |
| 1984 | C.V. Whitney | | & John Longden | | | | |

---

## HARNESS RACING

### Triple Crown Winners

#### PACERS

Ten three-year-olds have won the Cane Pace, Little Brown Jug and Messenger Stakes in the same year since the Pacing Triple Crown was established in 1956. No trainer or driver has won it more than once.

| Year | | Driver | Trainer | Owner |
|------|--|--------|---------|-------|
| 1959 | **Adios Butler** | Clint Hodgins | Paige West | Paige West & Angelo Pellillo |
| 1965 | **Bret Hanover** | Frank Ervin | Frank Ervin | Richard Downing |
| 1966 | **Romeo Hanover** | Bill Myer & George Sholty* | Jerry Silverman | Lucky Star Stables & Morton Finder |
| 1968 | **Rum Customer** | Billy Haughton | Billy Haughton | Kennilworth Farms & L.C. Mancuso |
| 1970 | **Most Happy Fella** | Stanley Dancer | Stanley Dancer | Egyptian Acres Stable |
| 1980 | **Niatross** | Clint Galbraith | Clint Galbraith | Niagara Acres, Niatross Stables & Clint Galbraith |
| 1983 | **Ralph Hanover** | Ron Waples | Stew Firlotte | Waples Stable, Pointsetta Stable, Grant's Direct Stable & P.J. Baugh |
| 1997 | **Western Dreamer** | Mike Lachance | Bill Robinson Stable | Matthew, Daniel and Patrick Daly |
| 1999 | **Blissful Hall** | Ron Pierce | Benn Wallace | Daniel Plouffe |
| 2003 | **No Pan Intended** | David Miller | Ivan Sugg | Bob Glazer |

*Myer drove Romeo Hanover in the Cane, Sholty in the other two races.

#### TROTTERS

Seven three-year-olds have won the Yonkers Trot, Hambletonian and Kentucky Futurity in the same year since the Trotting Triple Crown was established in 1955. Stanley Dancer is the only driver/trainer to win it twice.

| Year | | Driver/Trainer | Owner |
|------|--|----------------|-------|
| 1955 | **Scott Frost** | Joe O'Brien | S.A. Camp Farms |
| 1963 | **Speedy Scot** | Ralph Baldwin | Castleton Farms |
| 1964 | **Ayres** | John Simpson Sr. | Charlotte Sheppard |
| 1968 | **Nevele Pride** | Stanley Dancer | Nevele Acres & Lou Resnick |
| 1969 | **Lindy's Pride** | Howard Beissinger | Lindy Farms |
| 1972 | **Super Bowl** | Stanley Dancer | Rachel Dancer & Rose Hild Breeding Farm |
| 2004 | **Windsong's Legacy** | Trond Smedshammer | Fredrick Lindegaard |

## Triple Crown Near Misses

### PACERS

Nine horses have won the first two legs of the Triple Crown, but not the third. The Cane Pace (CP), Little Brown Jug (LBJ), and Messenger Stakes (MS) have not always been run in the same order so numbers after races won indicate sequence for that year.

| Year | CP | LBJ | MS | Year | CP | LBJ | MS |
|------|-----|------|------|------|-----|------|------|
| 1957 **Torpid** | won, 1 | won, 2 | DNF* | 1990 **Jake and Elwood** | won, 1 | NE | won, 2 |
| 1960 **Countess Adios** | won, 2 | NE | won, 1 | 1992 **Western Hanover** | won, 1 | 2nd* | won, 2 |
| 1971 **Albatross** | won, 2 | 2nd* | won, 1 | 1993 **Rijadh** | won, 1 | 2nd* | won, 2 |
| 1976 **Keystone Ore** | won, 1 | won, 2 | 2nd* | 1998 **Shady Character** | won, 1 | won, 2 | 6th* |
| 1986 **Barberry Spur** | won, 1 | won, 2 | 2nd* | | | | |

**\*Winning horses:** Meadow Lands (1957), Nansemond (1971), Windshield Wiper (1976), Amity Chef (1986), Fake Left (1992), Life Sign (1993), Fit for Life (1998).

**Note:** Torpid (1957) scratched before the final heat; Countess Adios (1960) and Jake and Elwood (1990) not eligible for Little Brown Jug.

### TROTTERS

Eight horses have won the first two legs of the Triple Crown– the Yonkers Trot (YT) and the Hambletonian (Ham)–but not the third. The winner of the Kentucky Futurity (KF) is listed.

| Year | YT | Ham | KF | Year | YT | Ham | KF |
|------|-----|------|------|------|-----|------|------|
| 1962 **A.C.'s Viking** | won | won | Safe Mission | 1987 **Mack Lobell** | won | won | Napoletano |
| 1976 **Steve Lobell** | won | won | Quick Pay | 1993 **American Winner** | won | won | Pine Chip |
| 1977 **Green Speed** | won | won | Texas | 1996 **Continentalvictory** | won | won | Running Sea |
| 1978 **Speedy Somolli** | won | won | Doublemint | 1998 **Muscles Yankee** | won | won | Trade Balance |

**Note:** Green Speed (1977) was not eligible for the Kentucky Futurity; Continentalvictory (1996) was withdrawn from the Kentucky Futurity due to a leg injury.

## The Hambletonian

For three-year-old trotters. Inaugurated in 1926 and has been held in Syracuse, N.Y.; Lexington, Ky.; Goshen, N.Y.; Yonkers, N.Y.; Du Quoin, Ill.; and since 1981 at The Meadowlands in East Rutherford, N.J.

Run at one mile since 1947. Winning horse must win two heats.

**Drivers with most wins:** John Campbell (5); Stanley Dancer, Billy Haughton, Mike Lachance and Ben White (4); Howard Beissinger, Del Cameron and Henry Thomas (3).

| Year | Driver | Fastest Heat | Year | Driver | Fastest Heat |
|------|--------|--------------|------|--------|--------------|
| 1926 **Guy McKinney** | Nat Ray | 2:04¾ | 1959 **Diller Hanover** | Frank Ervin | 2:01⅕ |
| 1927 **Iosola's Worthy** | Marvin Childs | 2:03¾ | 1960 **Blaze Hanover** | Joe O'Brien | 1:59⅗ |
| 1928 **Spencer** | W.H. Lessee | 2:02½ | 1961 **Harlan Dean** | James Arthur | 1:58⅖ |
| 1929 **Walter Dear** | Walter Cox | 2:02¾ | 1962 **A.C.'s Viking** | Sanders Russell | 1:59⅗ |
| 1930 **Hanover's Bertha** | Tom Berry | 2:03 | 1963 **Speedy Scot** | Ralph Baldwin | 1:57⅗ |
| 1931 **Calumet Butler** | R.D. McMahon | 2:03¼ | 1964 **Ayres** | John Simpson Sr. | 1:56⅘ |
| 1932 **The Marchioness** | Will Caton | 2:01¼ | 1965 **Egyptian Candor** | Del Cameron | 2:03⅘ |
| 1933 **Mary Reynolds** | Ben White | 2:03¾ | 1966 **Kerry Way** | Frank Ervin | 1:58⅘ |
| 1934 **Lord Jim** | Doc Parshall | 2:02¾ | 1967 **Speedy Streak** | Del Cameron | 2:00 |
| 1935 **Greyhound** | Sep Palin | 2:02¼ | 1968 **Nevele Pride** | Stanley Dancer | 1:59⅖ |
| 1936 **Rosalind** | Ben White | 2:01¾ | 1969 **Lindy's Pride** | Howard Beissinger | 1:57⅗ |
| 1937 **Shirley Hanover** | Henry Thomas | 2:01½ | 1970 **Timothy T** | John Simpson Jr. | 1:58⅖ |
| 1938 **McLin Hanover** | Henry Tomas | 2:01¼ | 1971 **Speedy Crown** | Howard Beissinger | 1:57⅗ |
| 1939 **Peter Astra** | Doc Parshall | 2:04¼ | 1972 **Super Bowl** | Stanley Dancer | 1:56⅖ |
| 1940 **Spencer Scott** | Fred Egan | 2:02 | 1973 **Flirth** | Ralph Baldwin | 1:57⅕ |
| 1941 **Bill Gallon** | Lee Smith | 2:05 | 1974 **Christopher T** | Billy Haughton | 1:58⅗ |
| 1942 **The Ambassador** | Ben White | 2:04 | 1975 **Bonefish** | Stanley Dancer | 1:59 |
| 1943 **Volo Song** | Ben White | 2:02½ | 1976 **Steve Lobell** | Billy Haughton | 1:56⅖ |
| 1944 **Yankee Maid** | Henry Thomas | 2:04 | 1977 **Green Speed** | Billy Haughton | 1:55⅗ |
| 1945 **Titan Hanover** | Harry Pownall Sr. | 2:04 | 1978 **Speedy Somolli** | Howard Beissinger | 1:55 |
| 1946 **Chestertown** | Thomas Berry | 2:02½ | 1979 **Legend Hanover** | George Sholty | 1:56⅕ |
| 1947 **Hoot Mon** | Sep Palin | 2:00 | 1980 **Burgomeister** | Billy Haughton | 1:56⅗ |
| 1948 **Demon Hanover** | Harrison Hoyt | 2:02 | 1981 **Shiaway St. Pat** | Ray Remmen | 2:01⅕ |
| 1949 **Miss Tilly** | Fred Egan | 2:01⅖ | 1982 **Speed Bowl** | Tommy Haughton | 1:56⅘ |
| 1950 **Lusty Song** | Del Miller | 2:02 | 1983 **Duenna** | Stanley Dancer | 1:57⅖ |
| 1951 **Mainliner** | Guy Crippen | 2:02⅗ | 1984 **Historic Freight** | Ben Webster | 1:56⅖ |
| 1952 **Sharp Note** | Bion Shively | 2:02⅗ | 1985 **Prakas** | Bill O'Donnell | 1:54⅘ |
| 1953 **Helicopter** | Harry Harvey | 2:01⅗ | 1986 **Nuclear Kosmos** | Ulf Thoresen | 1:55⅖ |
| 1954 **Newport Dream** | Del Cameron | 2:02⅘ | 1987 **Mack Lobell** | John Campbell | 1:53⅗ |
| 1955 **Scott Frost** | Joe O'Brien | 2:00⅗ | 1988 **Armbro Goal** | John Campbell | 1:54⅗ |
| 1956 **The Intruder** | Ned Bower | 2:01⅖ | 1989 **Park Avenue Joe** | Ron Waples | 1:54⅗ |
| 1957 **Hickory Smoke** | John Simpson Sr. | 2:00⅕ | & **Probe** * | Bill Fahy | |
| 1958 **Emily's Pride** | Flave Nipe | 1:59⅘ | | | |

*In 1989, Park Avenue Joe and Probe finished in a dead heat in the race-off. They were later declared co-winners, but Park Avenue Joe was awarded 1st place money because his three-race summary (2-1-1) was better than Probe's (1-9-1).

## Harness Racing (Cont.)

### The Hambletonian (Cont.)

| Year | | Driver | Fastest Heat | Year | | Driver | Fastest Heat |
|------|---|--------|--------------|------|---|--------|--------------|
| 1990 | **Harmonious** | John Campbell | 1:54⅕ | 1998 | **Muscles Yankee** | John Campbell | 1:52⅖ |
| 1991 | **Giant Victory** | Jack Moiseyev | 1:54⅘ | 1999 | **Self Possessed** | Mike Lachance | 1:51¾ |
| 1992 | **Alf Palema** | Mickey McNichol | 1:56⅖ | 2000 | **Yankee Paco** | Trevor Ritchie | 1:53⅖ |
| 1993 | **American Winner** | Ron Pierce | 1:53⅕ | 2001 | **Scarlet Knight** | Stefan Melander | 1:53⅘ |
| 1994 | **Victory Dream** | Mike Lachance | 1:54⅕ | 2002 | **Chip Chip Hooray** | Eric Ledford | 1:53⅗ |
| 1995 | **Tagliabue** | John Campbell | 1:54⅘ | 2003 | **Amigo Hall** | Mike Lachance | 1:54 |
| 1996 | **Continentalvictory** | Mike Lachance | 1:52⅘ | 2004 | **Windsong's Legacy** | T. Smedshammer | 1:54½ |
| 1997 | **Malabar Man** | Mal Burroughs | 1:55 | 2005 | **Vivid Photo** | Roger Hammer | 1:52⅗ |

## All-Time Leaders

The all-time winning trotters, pacers and drivers through 2004, according to *The Trotting and Pacing Guide*. Purses for horses include races in foreign countries. Earnings and wins for drivers include only races held in North America.

### Top 10 Horses—Earnings

| | | T/P | Yrs | Earnings |
|---|---|-----|-----|----------|
| 1 | Varenne | T | 1998-2002 | $5,636,255 |
| 2 | Moni Maker | T | 1995-2000 | 5,589,256 |
| 3 | Gallo Blue Chip | P | 1999-2004 | 4,260,959 |
| 4 | Peace Corps | T | 1988-93 | 4,137,737 |
| 5 | Ourasi | T | 1988-90 | 4,010,105 |
| 6 | Mack Lobell | T | 1986-91 | 3,917,594 |
| 7 | Victory Tilly | T | 1997-2003 | 3,745,896 |
| 8 | Magician | T | 1997-2004 | 3,614,801 |
| 9 | Reve d'Udon | T | 1985-92 | 3,611,351 |
| 10 | Zoogin | T | 1992-99 | 3,513,324 |

### Top 10 Drivers—Races Won

| | | Yrs | 1st | Earnings |
|---|---|-----|-----|----------|
| 1 | Herve Filion | 38 | 15,086 | $87,388,081 |
| 2 | Walter Case Jr. | 26 | 11,027 | 43,680,566 |
| 3 | Cat Manzi | 37 | 10,717 | 101,846,729 |
| 4 | Dave Palone | 23 | 10,054 | 45,688,318 |
| 5 | Dave Magee | 32 | 9,847 | 79,099,555 |
| 6 | Mike Lachance | 37 | 9,655 | 162,508,747 |
| 7 | John Campbell | 33 | 9,416 | 227,052,881 |
| 8 | Tony Morgan | 31 | 9,160 | 59,920,033 |
| 9 | Bill (Zeke) Parker Jr. | 34 | 8,711 | 21,578,875 |
| 10 | Jack Moiseyev | 29 | 8,611 | 95,986,006 |

## Annual Awards

### Harness Horse of the Year

Selected since 1947 by U.S. Trotting Association and the U.S. Harness Writers Association; age of winning horse is noted; (t) indicates trotter and (p) indicates pacer.

**Multiple winners:** Bret Hanover and Nevele Pride (3); Adios Butler, Albatross, Cam Fella, Good Time, Mack Lobell, Moni Maker, Niatross and Scott Frost (2).

| Year | | Year | | Year | | Year | |
|------|---|------|---|------|---|------|---|
| 1947 | Victory Song (4t) | 1962 | Su Mac Lad (8t) | 1977 | Green Speed (3t) | 1992 | Artsplace (4p) |
| 1948 | Rodney (4t) | 1963 | Speedy Scot (3t) | 1978 | Abercrombie (3p) | 1993 | Staying Together (4p) |
| 1949 | Good Time (3p) | 1964 | Bret Hanover (2p) | 1979 | Niatross (2p) | 1994 | Cam's Card Shark (3p) |
| 1950 | Proximity (8t) | 1965 | Bret Hanover (3p) | 1980 | Niatross (3p) | 1995 | CR Kay Suzie (3t) |
| 1951 | Pronto Don (6t) | 1966 | Bret Hanover (4p) | 1981 | Fan Hanover (3p) | 1996 | Continentalvictory (3t) |
| 1952 | Good Time (6p) | 1967 | Nevele Pride (2t) | 1982 | Cam Fella (3p) | 1997 | Malabar Man (3t) |
| 1953 | Hi Lo's Forbes (5p) | 1968 | Nevele Pride (3t) | 1983 | Cam Fella (4p) | 1998 | Moni Maker (5t) |
| 1954 | Stenographer (3t) | 1969 | Nevele Pride (4t) | 1984 | Fancy Crown (3t) | 1999 | Moni Maker (6t) |
| 1955 | Scott Frost (3t) | 1970 | Fresh Yankee (7t) | 1985 | Nihilator (3p) | 2000 | Gallo Blue Chip (3p) |
| 1956 | Scott Frost (4t) | 1971 | Albatross (3p) | 1986 | Forrest Skipper (4p) | 2001 | Bunny Lake (3p) |
| 1957 | Torpid (3p) | 1972 | Albatross (4p) | 1987 | Mack Lobell (3t) | 2002 | Real Desire (4p) |
| 1958 | Emily's Pride (3t) | 1973 | Sir Dalrae (4p) | 1988 | Mack Lobell (4t) | 2003 | No Pan Intended (3p) |
| 1959 | Bye Bye Byrd (4p) | 1974 | Delmonica Hanover (5t) | 1989 | Matt's Scooter (4p) | 2004 | Rainbow Blue (3p) |
| 1960 | Adios Butler (4p) | 1975 | Savoir (7t) | 1990 | Beach Towel (3p) | | |
| 1961 | Adios Butler (5p) | 1976 | Keystone Ore (3p) | 1991 | Precious Bunny (3p) | | |

### Driver of the Year

Determined by Universal Driving Rating System (UDR) and presented by the Harness Tracks of America since 1968. Eligible drivers must have at least 1,000 starts for the season.

**Multiple winners:** Herve Filion (10); Dave Palone (4); John Campbell, Walter Case Jr. and Mike Lachance (3); Tony Morgan, Bill O'Donnell, Luc Ouellette and Ron Waples (2).

| Year | | Year | | Year | | Year | |
|------|---|------|---|------|---|------|---|
| 1968 | Stanley Dancer | 1978 | Carmine Abbatiello & Herve Filion | 1987 | Mike Lachance | 1996 | Tony Morgan & Luc Ouellette |
| 1969 | Herve Filion | | | 1988 | John Campbell | | |
| 1970 | Herve Filion | 1979 | Ron Waples | 1989 | Herve Filion | 1997 | Tony Morgan |
| 1971 | Herve Filion | 1980 | Ron Waples | 1990 | John Campbell | 1998 | Walter Case Jr. |
| 1972 | Herve Filion | 1981 | Herve Filion | 1991 | Walter Case Jr. | 1999 | Dave Palone |
| 1973 | Herve Filion | 1982 | Bill O'Donnell | 1992 | Walter Case Jr. | 2000 | Dave Palone |
| 1974 | Herve Filion | 1983 | John Campbell | 1993 | Jack Moiseyev | 2001 | Stephane Bouchard |
| 1975 | Joe O'Brien | 1984 | Bill O'Donnell | 1994 | Dave Magee | 2002 | Tony Morgan |
| 1976 | Herve Filion | 1985 | Mike Lachance | 1995 | Luc Ouellette | 2003 | Dave Palone |
| 1977 | Donald Dancer | 1986 | Mike Lachance | | | 2004 | Dave Palone |

# *Tennis*

Apparently Spain's **Rafael Nadal** was hungry for a French Open title in 2005.

AP/Wide World Photos

# Roger More Than Andre Can Handle

*Roger Federer is the best player in the game but Agassi's run at the U.S. Open made it a year to remember.*

**Gerry Brown**
*is co-editor of the ESPN Sports Almanac.*

When Andre Agassi was Roger Federer's age he was beating old guys too. And for a two-week period in late summer, Agassi was beating the young guys again.

At the 2005 U.S. Open, and at 35 years old and past his prime, Agassi was trying to turn back the clock and the relentless shots of Roger Federer, the young world No. 1 and the long term future—not to mention present—of tennis.

And Agassi, recognized as the greatest returner in tennis history, seemed to be returning himself to the form that won him eight Grand Slam singles titles in a Hall of Fame career. He was beating the younger guys for two weeks at Flushing Meadows and the crowd was loving every bit of it.

Of course, the fans and media were reminded of an even older guy's legendary power grab 10 years back. At 39 years old Jimmy Connors electrified an entire city but fell short in his attempt to seize the throne as king of Queens in 1995, losing in the semifinals.

The credits appeared about to roll on Agassi's feel-good movie in the quarterfinals, when he faced the fellow resurgent American James Blake. Blake was in the process of writing a fairytale script of his own, getting into the tournament on a wildcard entry, then playing like a top seed.

In the last year Blake had been climbing out of the hole created when he broke his neck while training and was dug deeper just weeks later with the death of his father.

Not that it was all pain and sorrow for Blake, a Harvard graduate. He had a boisterous fan club (the J-Block), a girlfriend with movie star looks, and—for a while—it looked like he had Agassi beaten.

He steamrolled the aging and seemingly failing former champ in the first two sets of their match, 6-3, 6-3, and was poised to end the drama when Agassi flicked a switch and transposed the scores in the third and fourth sets to force a decisive fifth set.

Again it looked like Blake had the

AP/Wide World Photos

***Andre Agassi*** *(left) won the crowd but* ***Roger Federer*** *won the match when the living legend faced the growing legend in the men's singles final at the 2005 U.S. Open.*

upper hand when he served for the match at 5-4 in the fifth in the wee hours of the morning. But Andre held fast, got to the tie break and pulled off one of the most impressive wins of his career, blowing kisses to the delirious crowd that hung around past 1 a.m. to see some history in the making.

The semifinals provided another five-set fanfest and Agassi rode the wave past Robby Ginepri to become the oldest Grand Slam finalist since 39-year-old Ken Rosewall lost to Connors in both the U.S. Open and Wimbledon finals in 1974.

Unfortunately for Andre, the giant was waiting for him at the top of the beanstalk. The giant was Federer, far and away the best player in the world.

And unlike Agassi, the giant is in his prime.

For a while Agassi looked like he might have enough magic to slay the beast, splitting the first two sets and forcing a third-set tie break, but in end Federer was just too young and too much. A primetime Andre might not have fared much better.

"He's the best I've ever played against. There's nowhere to go," said Agassi, who defined his career with his long rivalry with Pete Sampras, winner of more Grand Slams titles (14) than any man in history...so far. Since Sampras retired tennis observers have questioned if we'd ever see another player like him.

Federer, who finished 2005 with

AP/Wide World Photos

*Venus Williams* had reason to shout after winning her third Wimbledon title in 2005.

six career Grand Slam titles, is only 24 years old and, as of press time, had won an incredible 24 consecutive finals, twice the previous open-era record. Maybe the question should be, who will stop the giant?

On the women's tour, American Venus Williams returned to glory when she won the third Wimbledon singles title of her career but her first Grand Slam title of any kind in four years with her marathon victory over top seed and world No. 1 Lindsay Davenport. Despite her two previous Wimbledon titles and long track record, Williams had struggled somewhat in recent seasons, winning just one tournament in more than a year and, as a result, she was seeded 14th at the All England Club.

The onetime world No. 1 had fallen to No. 2—in her family. Little sister Serena had eclipsed Venus' early success and looked to be the Williams family standard bearer for years to come.

But in 2005 Venus showed she was far from ready to concede the sibling rivalry. She became the lowest seeded Wimbledon champ in history and, along the way, dethroned defending champion and current tennis "it girl" Maria Sharapova in the semis.

After not losing a set for the entire tournament, Williams dropped the first one in the finals but came back to beat Davenport in the longest Wimbledon final in history. In the process she became the first woman in 70 years to win at Wimbledon after facing a match point in the final.

# The Ten Biggest Stories of the Year in Tennis

**10** **Tennis goes high-tech.** The International Tennis Federation announces that its new electronic instant replay system, created by British entrepreneur Paul Hawkins, is technically sound and ready for use. The system uses video and computer analysis to prepare a photo of a given shot's exact landing point in under five seconds. Officials from the ATP and WTA Tours meet with the ITF in October to decide where the system will be first implemented.

**9** **A doping scandal**, usually reserved for baseball, football and cycling circles, takes aim at tennis in the fall when French newspaper L'Equipe reports that Argentine Mariano Puerta tested positive for a banned stimulant following his loss to Rafael Nadal in the French Open. Puerta, who had already been suspended for a postive test in 2003, could face a lifetime ban.

**8** **Serena Williams grabs** her seventh Grand Slam singles title, and 15th overall, with her win over Lindsay Davenport in the finals of the Australian Open. It is her only victory of the year, however, as a balky left knee limits her to just nine more tournaments the rest of the way and prematurely shuts down her season in late September.

**7** **American James Blake**, whose 2004 was marred by a life-threatening injury and the death of his father, returns with a bang in 2005, breaking into the top 25 on the ATP Tour and advancing to the quarterfinals of the U.S. Open. Blake had suffered a broken vertebra after crashing into a net post before the 2004 Italian Open, then endured a viral infection that partially paralyzed the left side of his face for weeks.

**6** **Kim Clijsters wins** eight titles through late October and finally breaks through with her first Grand Slam victory after being thwarted in four previous Grand Slam finals. The 22-year-old Belgian defeats Mary Pierce in straight sets, 6-3, 6-1, at the U.S. Open. Pierce also reaches the French Open finals but falls to Justine Henin-Hardenne in straight sets.

**5** With three Tour victories through late October, 18-year-old Russian **Maria Sharapova takes the No. 1** WTA ranking from Lindsay Davenport in late summer.

Davenport, however, wins five tournaments and becomes the ninth woman in WTA history to win 50 career singles titles (see list on page 826) with her win over Amelie Mauresmo at the Porsche Tennis Grand Prix on October 9.

**4 Rafael Nadal wows** the crowd in Roland Garros with a four-set victory over Mariano Puerta in the finals of the French Open. The 19-year-old Spaniard in capri pants becomes the youngest male Grand Slam winner since 17-year-old Michael Chang won the French in 1989. He vaults from a No. 46 ranking in 2004 to second in the world in 2005.

**3 Venus Williams**, who had fallen from the WTA top 10 in 2005, fights back from championship point to defeat Lindsay Davenport, 4-6, 7-6, 9-7, in the Wimbledon finals. It is Williams' fifth Grand Slam title and first in four years. At two hours and 45 minutes, the match is the longest women's Wimbledon final on record.

**2 Fan-favorite Andre Agassi**, 35, steals the show at the 2005 U.S. Open with three consecutive five-set victories to become the oldest Grand Slam finalist in 31 years. He ultimately loses to Roger Federer in four sets, ending his bid for a ninth Grand Slam title.

**1 Top-ranked Roger Federer** continues the dominance he showed in 2004 with 11 more victories and Grand Slam titles at Wimbledon and the U.S. Open. The Wimbledon victory is his third straight, making him just the fourth player in the last 90 years to accomplish that feat. By late October he had already clinched the Indesit ATP Champions race and won a record 24th consecutive finals match.

## INSIDE the numbers

### Aged to Perfection

Jonas Bjorkman's win at the Vietnam Open on October 2 made him the fifth player over 30 to win an ATP tournament in 2005.

| | Tournament | Age |
|---|---|---|
| Andre Agassi | Mercedes-Benz Cup | 35 |
| Wayne Arthurs | Tennis Channel Open | 33 |
| Jonas Bjorkman | Vietnam Open | 33 |
| Kenneth Carlsen | Regions Morgan Keegan Championships | 31 |
| Greg Rusedski | Hall of Fame Champ's | 31 |

### Roger That

Through late October, Roger Federer had won 31 consecutive matches, tied for seventh on the ATP all-time list (during the Open Era). The top six are listed below.

| | Years | Wins |
|---|---|---|
| Guillermo Villas | 1977 | 46 |
| Ivan Lendl | 1981-82 | 44 |
| John McEnroe | 1984 | 42 |
| Bjorn Borg | 1979-80 | 38 |
| Bjorn Borg | 1978 | 35 |
| Thomas Muster | 1995 | 35 |

**Source:** ATP Tennis Weekly

# 2004-2005
# *Season in Review*

SPORTS ALMANAC

## Tournament Results

Winners of men's and women's pro singles championships from Nov. 7, 2004 through Oct. 9, 2005.

### Men's ATP Tour

#### Late 2004

| Finals | Tournament | Winner | Earnings | Runner-Up | Score |
|---|---|---|---|---|---|
| Nov. 7 | TMS—Paris | Marat Safin | $583,877 | R. Stepanek | 63 76 63 |
| Nov. 14 | Tennis Masters Cup (Houston) | Roger Federer | 1,520,000 | L. Hewitt | 63 62 (rain) |
| Dec. 5 | Davis Cup Final (Seville) | Spain | — | United States | 3-2 |

#### 2005

| Finals | Tournament | Winner | Earnings | Runner-Up | Score |
|---|---|---|---|---|---|
| Jan. 9 | Qatar ExxonMobil Open (Doha) | Roger Federer | $142,000 | I. Ljubicic | 63 61 |
| Jan. 9 | Next Generation Hardcourts (Adelaide) | Joachim Johansson | 52,000 | T. Dent | 75 63 |
| Jan. 9 | Chennai Open | Carlos Moya | 52,000 | P. Srichaphan | 36 64 76 |
| Jan. 15 | Medibank International (Sydney) | Lleyton Hewitt | 48,600 | I. Minar | 75 60 |
| Jan. 15 | Heineken Open (Auckland) | Fernando Gonzalez | 48,600 | O. Rochus | 64 62 |
| Jan. 30 | **Australian Open** (Melbourne) | Marat Safin | 917,000 | L. Hewitt | 16 63 64 64 |
| Feb. 6 | Milan Indoors | Robin Soderling | 66,000 | R. Stepanek | 63 67 76 |
| Feb. 6 | Millennium Int'l Champs (Delray Beach) | Xavier Malisse | 52,000 | J. Novak | 76 62 |
| Feb. 6 | BellSouth Open (Vina Del Mar) | Gaston Gaudio | 45,000 | F. Gonzalez | 63 64 |
| Feb. 13 | SAP Open (San Jose) | Andy Roddick | 52,000 | C. Saulnier | 60 64 |
| Feb. 13 | ATP Buenos Aires | Gaston Gaudio | 52,000 | M. Puerta | 64 64 |
| Feb. 13 | Open 13 (Marseille) | Joachim Johansson | 92,506 | I. Ljubicic | 75 64 |
| Feb. 20 | Regions Morgan Keegan Champs (Memphis) | Kenneth Carlsen | 128,000 | M. Mirnyi | 75 75 |
| Feb. 20 | ABN/AMRO World Tennis Tournament (Rotterdam) | Roger Federer | 192,000 | I. Ljubicic | 57 75 76 |
| Feb. 20 | Brasil Open (Costa Do Sauipe) | Rafael Nadal | 52,000 | A. Martin | 60 67 61 |
| Feb. 27 | Mexican Open (Acapulco) | Rafael Nadal | 128,000 | A. Montanes | 61 60 |
| Feb. 27 | Dubai Tennis Championships | Roger Federer | 187,500 | I. Ljubicic | 61 67 63 |
| Feb. 27 | Tennis Channel Open (Scottsdale) | Wayne Arthurs | 52,000 | M. Ancic | 75 63 |
| Mar. 20 | TMS—Pacific Life Open (Indian Wells) | Roger Federer | 421,000 | L. Hewitt | 62 64 64 |
| Apr. 3 | TMS—Nasdaq 100 Open (Miami) | Roger Federer | 533,350 | R. Nadal | 26 67 76 63 61 |
| Apr. 10 | Valencia Open | Igor Andreev | 60,290 | D. Ferrer | 63 57 63 |
| Apr. 10 | Grand Prix Hassan II (Casablanca) | Mariano Puerta | 56,930 | J. Monaco | 64 61 |
| Apr. 17 | TMS—Monte Carlo Open | Rafael Nadal | 512,000 | G. Coria | 63 61 06 75 |
| Apr. 24 | U.S. Clay Court Championships (Houston) | Andy Roddick | 52,000 | S. Grosjean | 62 62 |
| Apr. 24 | Open Seat Godo (Barcelona) | Rafael Nadal | 196,027 | J.C. Ferrero | 61 76 63 |
| May 1 | Estoril Open | Gaston Gaudio | 96,000 | T. Robredo | 61 26 61 |
| May 1 | BMW Open by Credit Suisse (Munich) | David Nalbandian | 57,000 | A. Pavel | 64 61 |
| May 8 | TMS—Telecom Italia Masters (Rome) | Rafael Nadal | 435,750 | G. Coria | 64 36 63 46 76 |
| May 15 | TMS—Hamburg | Roger Federer | 429,080 | G. Coria | 46 64 62 63 |
| May 21 | Int'l Raiffeisen Grand Prix (St. Poelten) | Nikolay Davydenko | 55,352 | J. Melzer | 63 26 64 |
| May 21 | ATP World Team Championship (Dusseldorf) | Germany | 413,000 | Argentina | 2-1 |
| June 5 | **French Open** (Roland Garros) | Rafael Nadal | 1,075,978 | M. Puerta | 67 63 61 75 |
| June 12 | Gerry Weber Open (Halle) | Roger Federer | 116,342 | M. Safin | 64 67 64 |
| June 12 | Stella Artois Championships (London) | Andy Roddick | 97,575 | I. Karlovic | 76 76 |
| June 19 | 10tele.com Open (Nottingham) | Richard Gasquet | 44,100 | M. Mirnyi | 62 63 |
| June 19 | Ordina Open ('s-Hertogenbosch) | Mario Ancic | 44,100 | M. Llodra | 75 64 |
| July 3 | **Wimbledon** (London) | Roger Federer | 751,371 | A. Roddick | 62 76 64 |
| July 10 | Allianz Swiss Open (Gstaad) | Gaston Gaudio | 70,278 | S. Wawrinka | 64 64 |
| July 10 | Hall of Fame Championships (Newport) | Greg Rusedski | 52,000 | V. Spadea | 76 26 64 |
| July 10 | Synsam Swedish Open (Bastad) | Rafael Nadal | 52,758 | T. Berdych | 26 62 64 |
| July 24 | Priority Telecom Open (Amersfoort) | Fernando Gonzalez | 53,231 | A. Calleri | 75 63 |
| July 24 | Mercedes Cup (Stuttgart) | Rafael Nadal | 126,016 | G. Gaudio | 63 63 64 |
| July 24 | RCA Championships (Indianapolis) | Robby Ginepri | 74,250 | T. Dent | 46 60 30 (ret.) |
| July 31 | Mercedes-Benz Cup (Los Angeles) | Andre Agassi | 52,000 | G. Muller | 64 75 |
| July 31 | Croatia Open (Umag) | Guillermo Coria | 56,630 | C. Moya | 62 46 62 |
| July 31 | Generali Open (Kitzbuhel) | Gaston Gaudio | $134,075 | F. Verdasco | 26 62 64 64 |

## Tournament Results (Cont.)

| Finals | Tournament | Winner | Earnings | Runner-Up | Score |
|--------|-----------|--------|----------|-----------|-------|
| Aug. 7 | Idea Prokom Open (Sopot) . . . . . . . . . . . . | Gael Monfils | $72,970 | F. Mayer | 76 46 75 |
| Aug. 7 | Legg Mason Classic (Washington D.C.) . . . | Andy Roddick | 74,250 | J. Blake | 75 63 |
| Aug. 14 | TMS—Rogers Masters (Montreal) . . . . . . . | Rafael Nadal | 400,000 | A. Agassi | 63 46 62 |
| Aug. 21 | TMS—Western & Southern Financial Group Masters (Cincinnati) . . . . . . . . . . . | Roger Federer | 400,000 | A. Roddick | 63 75 |
| Aug. 28 | Pilot Pen (New Haven) . . . . . . . . . . . . . . . | James Blake | 84,000 | F. Lopez | 36 75 61 |
| Sept. 11 | **U.S. Open** (Flushing) . . . . . . . . . . . . . . | Roger Federer | 1,100,000 | A. Agassi | 63 26 76 61 |
| Sept. 18 | China Open (Beijing) . . . . . . . . . . . . . . . . | Rafael Nadal | 69,200 | G. Coria | 57 61 61 |
| Sept. 18 | Romanian Open (Bucharest) . . . . . . . . . . | Florent Serra | 53,000 | I. Andreev | 63 64 |
| Oct. 2 | Campionati Internationali di Sicilia (Palermo) | Igor Andreev | 53,000 | F. Volandri | 06 61 63 |
| Oct. 2 | Vietnam Open (Ho Chi Minh City) . . . . . . | Jonas Bjorkman | 52,000 | R. Stepanek | 63 76 |
| Oct. 2 | Thailand Open (Bangkok) . . . . . . . . . . . . | Roger Federer | 76,500 | A. Murray | 63 75 |
| Oct. 9 | Open de Moselle (Metz) . . . . . . . . . . . . . | Ivan Ljubicic | 53,500 | G. Monfils | 76 60 |
| Oct. 9 | AIG Japan Open (Tokyo) . . . . . . . . . . . . . | Wesley Moodie | 118,000 | M. Ancic | 16 76 64 |

**Note**: TMS indicates tournament is part of the ATP Tennis Masters Series.

## Women's WTA Tour

### Late 2004

| Finals | Tournament | Winner | Earnings | Runner-Up | Score |
|--------|-----------|--------|----------|-----------|-------|
| Nov. 7 | Advanta Championships (Philadelphia) . . . | Amelie Mauresmo | $93,000 | V. Zvonareva | 36 62 62 |
| Nov. 7 | Bell Challenge (Quebec) . . . . . . . . . . . . . | Martina Sucha | 27,000 | A. Spears | 75 36 62 |
| Nov. 15 | WTA Championships (Los Angeles) . . . . . . | Maria Sharapova | 1,000,000 | S. Williams | 46 62 64 |
| Nov. 28 | 2004 Fed Cup Final (Moscow) . . . . . . . . . | Russia | — | France | 3-2 |

### 2005

| Finals | Tournament | Winner | Earnings | Runner-Up | Score |
|--------|-----------|--------|----------|-----------|-------|
| Jan. 8 | Uncle Toby's Hardcourts (Gold Coast) . . . . | Patty Schnyder | $27,000 | S. Stosur | 16 63 75 |
| Jan. 8 | ASB Bank Classic (Auckland) . . . . . . . . . . | Katarina Srebotnik | 22,000 | S. Asagoe | 57 75 64 |
| Jan. 14 | Moorilla International (Hobart) . . . . . . . . . | Zheng Jie | 16,000 | G. Dulko | 62 60 |
| Jan. 15 | Canberra Women's Classic . . . . . . . . . . . . | Ana Ivanovic | 16,000 | M. Czink | 75 61 |
| Jan. 15 | Medibank International (Sydney) . . . . . . . . | Alicia Molik | 93,000 | S. Stosur | 67 64 75 |
| Jan. 30 | **Australian Open** (Melbourne) . . . . . . . . . | Serena Williams | 821,904 · | L. Davenport | 26 63 60 |
| Feb. 6 | Toray Pan Pacific Open (Tokyo) . . . . . . . . | Maria Sharapova | 189,000 | L. Davenport | 61 36 76 |
| Feb. 6 | Volvo Women's Open (Pattaya City) . . . . . | Conchita Martinez | 25,650 | A. Groenefeld | 63 36 63 |
| Feb. 12 | Open Gaz de France (Paris) . . . . . . . . . . . | Dinara Safina | 93,000 | A. Mauresmo | 64 26 63 |
| Feb. 12 | Hyderabad Open . . . . . . . . . . . . . . . . . . | Sania Mirza | 22,000 | A. Bondarenko | 64 57 63 |
| Feb. 19 | Regions Morgan Keegan Championships and Cellular South Cup (Memphis) . . . . . | Vera Zvonareva | 27,000 | M. Shaughnessy | 76 62 |
| Feb. 20 | Proximus Diamond Games (Antwerp) . . . . . | Amelie Mauresmo | 93,000 | V. Williams | 46 75 64 |
| Feb. 20 | Copa Colsanitas (Bogota) . . . . . . . . . . . . | Flavia Pennetta | 27,000 | L. Dominguez Lino | 76 64 |
| Feb. 26 | Qatar Total Open (Doha) . . . . . . . . . . . . | Maria Sharapova | 94,000 | A. Molik | 46 61 64 |
| Feb. 27 | Abierto Mexicano de Tenis (Acapulco) . . . . | Flavia Pennetta | 27,500 | L. Cervanova | 36 75 63 |
| Mar. 5 | Dubai Duty Free Women's Open . . . . . . . . | Lindsay Davenport | 159,000 | J. Jankovic | 64 36 64 |
| Mar. 19 | Pacific Life Open (Indian Wells) . . . . . . . . | Kim Clijsters | 332,000 | L. Davenport | 64 46 62 |
| Apr. 3 | Nasdaq 100 Open (Miami) . . . . . . . . . . . | Kim Clijsters | 400,000 | M. Sharapova | 63 75 |
| Apr. 10 | Bausch & Lomb Championships (Amelia Island) . . . . . . . . . . . . . . . . . . | Lindsay Davenport | 93,000 | S. Farina Elia | 75 75 |
| Apr. 17 | Family Circle Cup (Charleston) . . . . . . . . . | Justine Henin-Hardenne | 189,000 | E. Dementieva | 75 64 |
| May 1 | J&S Cup (Warsaw) . . . . . . . . . . . . . . . . . | Justine Henin-Hardenne | 93,000 | S. Kuznetsova | 36 62 75 |
| May 1 | Estoril Open . . . . . . . . . . . . . . . . . . . . . . | Lucie Safarova | 22,000 | Na Li | 67 64 63 |
| May 8 | Qatar Total German Open (Berlin) . . . . . . . | Justine Henin-Hardenne | 189,000 | N. Petrova | 63 46 63 |
| May 8 | Grand Prix De S.A.R. (Rabat) . . . . . . . . . . | Nuria Llagostera Vives | 22,000 | Zheng Jie | 64 62 |
| May 15 | Telecom Italian Masters (Rome) . . . . . . . . | Amelie Mauresmo | 189,000 | P. Schnyder | 26 63 64 |
| May 15 | ECM Prague Open . . . . . . . . . . . . . . . . . | Dinara Safina | 22,000 | Z. Ondraskova | 76 63 |
| May 21 | Strasbourg International . . . . . . . . . . . . . . | A. Medina Garrigues | 27,000 | M. Domachowska | 64 63 |
| May 21 | Istanbul Cup . . . . . . . . . . . . . . . . . . . . . | Venus Williams | 30,500 | N. Vaidisova | 63 62 |
| June 5 | **French Open** (Roland Garros) . . . . . . . . | J. Henin-Hardenne | 1,060,343 | M. Pierce | 61 61 |
| June 12 | DFS Classic (Birmingham) . . . . . . . . . . . . | Maria Sharapova | 31,000 | J. Jankovic | 62 46 61 |
| June 18 | Ordina Open ('s-Hertogenbosch) . . . . . . . | Klara Koukalova | 27,000 | L. Safarovaq | 36 62 62 |
| June 18 | Hastings Direct Int'l Champs (Eastbourne) . . . | Kim Clijsters | 93,000 | V. Douchevina | 75 60 |
| July 2 | **Wimbledon** (London) . . . . . . . . . . . . . . | Venus Williams | 715,576 | L. Davenport | 46 76 97 |
| July 17 | Modena International . . . . . . . . . . . . . . . . | Anna Smashnova | 22,000 | T. Garbin | 66 (3-0, ret.) |
| July 24 | Palermo International . . . . . . . . . . . . . . . . | A. Medina Garrigues | 22,000 | K. Koukalova | 64 60 |
| July 24 | Western & Southern Open (Cincinnati) . . . · | Patty Schnyder | 27,000 | A. Morigami | 64 60 |
| July 31 | Bank of the West Classic (Stanford) . . . . . . | Kim Clijsters | 93,000 | V. Williams | 75 62 |
| July 31 | Tippmix Budapest Grand Prix . . . . . . . . . . | Anna Smashnova | 22,000 | C. Castano | 62 62 |

| Finals | Tournament | Winner | Earnings | Runner-Up | Score |
|--------|-----------|--------|----------|-----------|-------|
| Aug. 7 | Acura Classic (San Diego) | Mary Pierce | $189,000 | A. Sugiyama | 60 63 |
| Aug. 14 | Nordea Nordic Light Open (Stockholm) | Katarina Srebotnik | 22,000 | A. Myskina | 75 62 |
| Aug. 14 | JP Morgan Chase Open (Los Angeles) | Kim Clijsters | 93,000 | D. Hantuchova | 64 61 |
| Aug. 21 | Rogers Cup (Toronto) | Kim Clijsters | 189,000 | J. Henin-Hardenne | 75 61 |
| Aug. 27 | Pilot Pen Tennis (New Haven) | Lindsay Davenport | 95,000 | A. Mauresmo | 64 64 |
| Aug. 27 | Forest Hills Women's Tennis Classic | Lucie Safarova | 22,000 | S. Mirza | 36 75 64 |
| Sept. 10 | **U.S. Open** (Flushing) | Kim Clijsters | 1,100,000 | M. Pierce | 63 61 |
| Sept. 18 | 2005 Fed Cup Final (Paris) | Russia | — | France | 3-2 |
| Sept. 18 | Wismilak International (Bali) | Lindsay Davenport | 35,000 | F. Schiavone | 62 64 |
| Sept. 25 | Banka Koper Slovenia Open (Portoroz) | Klara Koukalova | 22,000 | K. Srebotnik | 62 46 63 |
| Sept. 25 | Sunfeast Open (Kolkata) | Anastasia Myskina | 27,000 | K. Sprem | 62 62 |
| Sept. 25 | China Open (Beijing) | Maria Kirilenko | 93,000 | A. Groenefeld | 63 64 |
| Oct. 2 | Fortis Championships (Luxembourg) | Kim Clijsters | 93,000 | A. Groenefeld | 62 64 |
| Oct. 2 | Guangzhou International | Yan Zi | 27,000 | N. Llagostera Vives | 64 40 (ret.) |
| Oct. 2 | Hansol Korea Open | Nicole Vaidisova | 22,000 | J. Jankovic | 75 63 |
| Oct. 9 | Porsche Grand Prix (Filderstadt) | Lindsay Davenport | 98,500 | A. Mauresmo | 62 64 |
| Oct. 9 | AIG Japan Open (Tokyo) | Nicole Vaidisova | 27,000 | T. Golovin | 76 32 (ret.) |
| Oct. 9 | Tashkent Open | Michaella Krajicek | 22,000 | A. Amanmuradova | 60 46 63 |

## 2005 Grand Slam Tournaments
## Australian Open

### MEN'S SINGLES

FINAL EIGHT—# 1 Roger Federer; #2 Andy Roddick; #3 Lleyton Hewitt; #4 Marat Safin; #8 Andre Agassi; #9 David Nalbandian; # 20 Dominik Hrbaty; #26 Nikolay Davydenko.

#### Quarterfinals

Federer def. Agassi . . . . . . . . . . . . . . . . .63 64 64
Safin def. Hrbaty . . . . . . . . . . . . . . . . .62 64 62
Hewitt def. Nalbandian . . . . . . . . . . . .63 62 16 36 10-8
Roddick def. Davydenko . . . . . . . . . . .63 75 41 (ret.)

#### Semifinals

Safin def. Federer . . . . . . . . . .57 64 57 76(6) 97
Hewitt def. Roddick . . . . . . . . . . . . . .36 76(3) 76(4) 61

#### Final

Safin def. Hewitt . . . . . . . . . . . . . . . . . .16 63 64 64

### WOMEN'S SINGLES

FINAL EIGHT—#1 Lindsay Davenport; #2 Amelie Mauresmo; #4 Maria Sharapova; #5 Svetlana Kuznetsova; #7 Serena Williams; #10 Alicia Molik; #12 Patty Schnyder; #19 Nathalie Dechy.

#### Quarterfinals

Williams def. Mauresmo . . . . . . . . . . . . . . . .62 62
Sharapova def. Kuznetsova . . . . . . . . . . . .46 62 62
Davenport def. Molik . . . . . . . . . . . . . .64 46 97
Dechy def. Schnyder . . . . . . . . . . . . . . . . . .57 61 75

#### Semifinals

Williams def. Sharapova . . . . . . . . . . . . . . .26 75 86
Davenport def. Dechy . . . . . . . . . . . . . .26 76(5) 64

#### Final

Williams def. Davenport . . . . . . . . . . . . . . .26 63 60

### DOUBLES FINALS

**Men**—#5 Wayne Black & Kevin Ullyett def. #2 Bob Bryan & Mike Bryan, 6-4, 6-4.

**Women**—#6 Svetlana Kuznetsova & Alicia Molik def. #15 Lindsay Davenport & Corina Morariu, 6-3, 6-4.

**Mixed**—Samantha Stosur & Scott Draper def. #4 Liezel Huber & Kevin Ullyett, 6-2, 2-6, 7-6 (10-6).

## French Open

### MEN'S SINGLES

FINAL EIGHT—#1 Roger Federer; #4 Rafael Nadal; #9 Guillermo Canas; #12 Nikolay Davydenko; #15 Tommy Robredo; #20 David Ferrer; plus unseeded Mariano Puerta and Victor Hanescu.

#### Quarterfinals

Federer def. Hanescu . . . . . . . . . . . . . . . .62 76(3) 63
Nadal def. Ferrer . . . . . . . . . . . . . . . . . . . . .75 62 60
Puerta def. Canas . . . . . . . . . . . . . . .62 36 16 63 64
Davydenko def. Robredo . . . . . . . . . . . .36 61 62 46 64

#### Semifinals

Nadal def. Federer . . . . . . . . . . . . . . . .63 46 64 63
Puerta def. Davydenko . . . . . . . . . . . .63 57 26 64 64

#### Final

Nadal def. Puerta . . . . . . . . . . . . . . . . . .67(6) 63 61 75

### WOMEN'S SINGLES

FINAL EIGHT—#1 Lindsay Davenport; #2 Maria Sharapova; #7 Nadia Petrova; #10 Justine Henin-Hardenne; #16 Elena Likhovtseva; #21 Mary Pierce; #29 Ana Ivanovic; plus unseeded Sesil Karatantcheva.

#### Quarterfinals

Pierce def. Davenport . . . . . . . . . . . . . . . . .63 62
Henin-Hardenne def. Sharapova . . . . . . . . . . .64 62
Petrova def. Ivanovic . . . . . . . . . . . . . . . . . .62 62
Likhovtseva def. Karatantcheva . . . . . . . . . . .26 64 64

#### Semifinals

Henin-Hardenne def. Petrova . . . . . . . . . . . . .62 63
Pierce def. Likhovtseva . . . . . . . . . . . . . . . . .61 61

#### Final

Henin-Hardenne def. Pierce . . . . . . . . . . . . . .61 61

### DOUBLES FINALS

**Men**—#2 Jonas Bjorkman & Max Mirnyi def. #3 Bob Bryan & Mike Bryan, 2-6, 6-1, 6-4.

**Women**—#1 Virginia Ruano Pascual & Paola Suarez def. #2 Cara Black & Liezel Huber, 4-6, 6-3, 6-3.

**Mixed**—Daniela Hantuchova & Fabrice Santoro def. #6 Martina Navratilova & Leander Paes, 3-6, 6-3, 6-2.

# Wimbledon

## MEN'S SINGLES

FINAL EIGHT—#1 Roger Federer; #2 Andy Roddick; #3 Lleyton Hewitt; #9 Sebastien Grosjean; #12 Thomas Johansson; #18 David Nalbandian; #21 Fernando Gonzalez; #26 Feliciano Lopez.

### Quarterfinals

Roddick def. Grosjean . . . . . . . . . . . . .36 62 61 36 63
Johansson def. Nalbandian . . . . . . . . . . . .76(5) 62 62
Federer def. Gonzalez . . . . . . . . . . . . . . .75 62 76(2)
Hewitt def. Lopez . . . . . . . . . . . . . . . . . .75 64 76(2)

### Semifinals

Roddick def. Johansson . . . . . . . . .67(6) 62 76(10) 76(5)
Federer def. Hewitt . . . . . . . . . . . . . . .63 64 76(4)

### Final

Federer def. Roddick . . . . . . . . . . . . . . . .62 76(2) 64

## WOMEN'S SINGLES

FINAL EIGHT—#1 Lindsay Davenport; #2 Maria Sharapova; #3 Amelie Mauresmo; #5 Svetlana Kuznetsova; #8 Nadia Petrova; #9 Anastasia Myskina; #12 Mary Pierce; #14 Venus Williams.

### Quarterfinals

Davenport def. Kuznetsova . . . . . . . . . . . . . .76(1) 63
Williams def. Pierce . . . . . . . . . . . . . . . .60 76(10)
Sharapova def. Petrova . . . . . . . . . . . . . . .76(6) 63
Mauresmo def. Myskina . . . . . . . . . . . . . . . .63 64

### Semifinals

Davenport def. Mauresmo . . . . . . . . . . . .67(5) 76(4) 64
Williams def. Sharapova . . . . . . . . . . . . . .76(2) 61

### Final

Williams def. Davenport . . . . . . . . . . .46 76(4) 97

## DOUBLES FINALS

**Men**—Stephen Huss & Wesley Moodie def. #2 Bob Bryan & Mike Bryan, 7-6 (7-4), 6-3, 6-7 (2-7), 6-3.

**Women**—#2 Cara Black & Liezel Huber def. Svetlana Kutzetsova & Amelie Mauresmo, 6-2, 6-1.

**Mixed**—Mary Pierce & Mahesh Bhupathi def. Tatiana Perebiynis & Paul Hanley, 6-4, 6-2.

# U.S. Open

## MEN'S SINGLES

FINAL EIGHT—#1 Roger Federer; #3 Lleyton Hewitt; #7 Andre Agassi; #8 Guillermo Coria; #11 David Nalbandian; plus unseeded James Blake, Robby Ginepri and Jarkko Nieminen.

### Quarterfinals

Federer def. Nalbandian . . . . . . . . . . . . . . . .62 64 61
Hewitt def. Nieminen . . . . . . . . . . .26 61 36 63 61
Agassi def. Blake . . . . . . . . . . . . . .36 36 63 63 76(6)
Ginepri def. Coria . . . . . . . . . . . . .46 61 75 36 75

### Semifinals

Federer def. Hewitt . . . . . . . . . . . .63 76(0) 46 63
Agassi def. Ginepri . . . . . . . . . . . . .64 57 63 46 63

### Final

Federer def. Agassi . . . . . . . . . . . . .63 26 76(1) 61

## WOMEN'S SINGLES

FINAL EIGHT—#1 Maria Sharapova; #2 Lindsay Davenport; #3 Amelie Mauresmo; #4 Kim Clijsters; #6 Elena Dementieva; #9 Nadia Petrova; #10 Venus Williams; #12 Mary Pierce.

### Quarterfinals

Dementieva def. Davenport . . . . . . . . . . . .61 36 76(6)
Pierce def. Mauresmo . . . . . . . . . . . . . . . . . .64 61
Clijsters def. Williams . . . . . . . . . . . . . . . . . .46 75 61
Sharapova def. Petrova . . . . . . . . . . . . . . .75 46 64

### Semifinals

Clijsters def. Sharapova . . . . . . . . . . . .62 67(4) 63
Pierce def. Dementieva . . . . . . . . . . . . . . .36 62 62

### Final

Clijsters def. Pierce . . . . . . . . . . . . . . . . . .63 61

## DOUBLES FINALS

**Men**—#2 Bob Bryan & Mike Bryan def. #1 Jonas Bjorkman & Max Mirnyi, 6-1, 6-4.

**Women**—#6 Lisa Raymond & Samantha Stosur def. #14 Elena Dementieva & Flavia Pennetta, 6-2, 5-7, 6-3.

**Mixed**—Daniela Hantuchova & Mahesh Bhupathi def. Katarina Srebotnik & Nenad Zimonjic, 6-4, 6-2.

# Fed Cup

Originally the Federation Cup and started in 1963 by the International Tennis Federation as the Davis Cup of women's tennis.

## 2004

### Quarterfinals (July 10-11)

| Winner | Loser |
| --- | --- |
| at Austria 4 | United States 1 |
| Russia 4 | at Argentina 1 |
| France 3 | at Italy 2 |
| at Spain 3 | Belgium 2 |

### Semifinals (in Moscow, Nov. 24-25)

| Winner | Loser |
| --- | --- |
| Russia 5 | Austria 0 |
| France 5 | Spain 0 |

### Finals (in Moscow, Nov. 27-28)
### Russia 3, France 2

**Singles**—Nathalie Dechy (FRA) def. Svetlana Kuznetsova (RUS) 3-6, 7-6(4), 8-6; Anastasia Myskina (RUS) def. Tatiana Golovin (FRA) 6-4, 7-6(5); Myskina (RUS) def. Dechy 6-3, 6-4; Golovin (FRA) def. Kuznetsova 6-4, 6-1.

**Doubles**—Vera Zvonareva & Myskina (RUS) def. Marion Bartoli & Emilie Loit (FRA) 7-6(5), 7-5.

## 2005

### Quarterfinals (April 23-24)

| Winner | Loser |
| --- | --- |
| at United States 5 | Belgium 0 |
| Russia 4 | at Italy 1 |
| at Spain 3 | Argentina 2 |
| France 4 | at Austria 1 |

### Semifinals (July 9-10)

| Winner | Loser |
| --- | --- |
| at Russia 4 | United States 1 |
| at France 3 | Spain 1 |

### Finals (in Paris, Sept. 17-18)
### Russia 3, France 2

**Singles**—Elena Dementieva (RUS) def. Mary Pierce (FRA) 7-6(1), 2-6, 6-1; Amelie Mauresmo (FRA) def. Anastasia Myskina (RUS) 6-4, 6-2; Dementieva (RUS) def. Mauresmo (FRA) 6-4, 4-6, 6-2; Pierce (FRA) def. Myskina (RUS) 4-6, 6-4, 6-2.

**Doubles**—Dinara Safina & Dementieva (RUS) def. Mauresmo & Pierce (FRA) 6-4, 1-6, 6-3.

## Singles Leaders

Official Top 20 rankings and money leaders of men's and women's tours for 2004 and unofficial rankings for 2005 (through Oct. 9), as compiled by the ATP Tour (Association of Tennis Professionals) and WTA (Women's Tennis Association). Note that money lists include doubles earnings.

## Final 2004 Rankings and Money Won

Listed are events won and times a finalist and semifinalist (Finish, 1-2-SF), match record (W-L), and earnings for the year.

### MEN

| | | Finish 1-2-SF | W-L | Earnings |
|---|---|---|---|---|
| 1 | Roger Federer | 11-0-0 | 74-6 | $6,357,547 |
| 2 | Andy Roddick | 4-4-3 | 74-16 | 2,604,590 |
| 3 | Lleyton Hewitt | 4-4-3 | 68-18 | 2,766,051 |
| 4 | Marat Safin | 3-2-4 | 52-23 | 2,273,283 |
| 5 | Carlos Moya | 3-2-2 | 57-19 | 1,448,209 |
| 6 | Tim Henman | 0-1-4 | 44-22 | 1,508,177 |
| 7 | Guillermo Coria | 2-4-0 | 39-14 | 1,697,155 |
| 8 | Andre Agassi | 1-1-5 | 37-13 | 1,177,254 |
| 9 | David Nalbandian | 0-3-1 | 34-14 | 1,045,985 |
| 10 | Gaston Gaudio | 1-4-0 | 37-24 | 1,639,171 |
| 11 | Guillermo Canas | 3-1-2 | 40-22 | 780,701 |
| 12 | Joachim Johansson | 1-0-1 | 35-22 | 828,744 |
| 13 | Tommy Robredo | 1-0-3 | 43-25 | 861,357 |
| 14 | Dominik Hrbaty | 3-1-1 | 42-26 | 808,944 |
| 15 | Sebastien Grosjean | 0-1-1 | 28-15 | 755,795 |
| 16 | Mikhail Youzhny | 1-1-2 | 42-27 | 725,948 |
| 17 | Tommy Haas | 2-0-2 | 37-22 | 610,793 |
| 18 | Andrei Pavel | 0-0-1 | 34-24 | 656,141 |
| 19 | Nicolas Massu | 2-0-2 | 42-28 | 854,533 |
| 20 | Vincent Spadea | 1-1-2 | 40-29 | 704,105 |

### WOMEN

| | | Finish 1-2-SF | W-L | Earnings |
|---|---|---|---|---|
| 1 | Lindsay Davenport | 7-2-4 | 63-9 | $2,220,005 |
| 2 | Amelie Mauresmo | 5-4-3 | 63-11 | 1,964,070 |
| 3 | Anastasia Myskina | 3-1-6 | 55-18 | 2,115,847 |
| 4 | Maria Sharapova | 5-1-3 | 55-15 | 2,506,263 |
| 5 | Svetlana Kuznetsova | 3-4-1 | 60-23 | 2,060,590 |
| 6 | Elena Dementieva | 1-4-4 | 39-23 | 1,825,688 |
| 7 | Serena Williams | 2-3-1 | 39-9 | 2,251,798 |
| 8 | Justine Henin-Hardenne | 5-0-2 | 35-4 | 1,570,656 |
| 9 | Venus Williams | 2-2-1 | 44-12 | 1,474,128 |
| 10 | Jennifer Capriati | 0-2-3 | 29-12 | 1,290,061 |
| 11 | Vera Zvonareva | 1-2-6 | 54-27 | 988,017 |
| 12 | Nadia Petrova | 0-1-5 | 40-25 | 965,969 |
| 13 | Alicia Molik | 3-1-1 | 46-20 | 651,235 |
| 14 | Patty Schnyder | 0-0-4 | 34-22 | 632,194 |
| 15 | Elena Bovina | 1-2-1 | 37-17 | 508,449 |
| 16 | Paola Suarez | 1-0-2 | 39-18 | 1,271,189 |
| 17 | Ai Sugiyama | 1-0-1 | 33-25 | 736,354 |
| 18 | Karolina Sprem | 0-0-3 | 35-24 | 395,118 |
| 19 | Francesca Schiavone | 0-0-2 | 38-26 | 458,796 |
| 20 | Silvia Farina Elia | 0-2-3 | 44-25 | 446,251 |

## 2005 Tour Rankings (through Oct. 9)

Listed are tournaments won and times a finalist and semifinalist (Finish, 1-2-SF), match record (W-L), and points earned (Pts). The **Indesit ATP Race** replaced the men's pro tennis tour's 27-year-old computer ranking system in 2000. Under the new system players start from zero on Jan. 1 and accumulate points during the calendar year with the player accumulating the most points becoming the World No. 1. Points are awarded in 18 tournaments: nine Tennis Masters Series events, four Grand Slams and five other International Series events. The Tennis Master Cup will count as a 19th tournament for those that qualify.

### MEN

Final ATP Tour singles rankings will be based on points earned from 18 tournaments played in 2005. Tournaments, titles and match won-lost records are for 2005 only.

| Rank 05 | (04) | | Finish 1-2-SF | W-L | Pts |
|---|---|---|---|---|---|
| 1 | 1 | Roger Federer | 11-0-2 | 77-3 | 1245 |
| 2 | 46 | Rafael Nadal | 10-1-0 | 74-10 | 853 |
| 3 | 2 | Andy Roddick | 4-2-3 | 51-12 | 548 |
| 4 | 3 | Lleyton Hewitt | 1-2-3 | 37-9 | 498 |
| 5 | 8 | Andre Agassi | 1-2-3 | 38-11 | 455 |
| 6 | 7 | Guillermo Coria | 1-3-1 | 53-21 | 422 |
| 7 | 28 | Nikolay Davydenko | 1-0-6 | 48-25 | 378 |
| 8 | 4 | Marat Safin | 1-1-0 | 27-11 | 346 |
| 9 | 10 | Gaston Gaudio | 5-1-0 | 50-15 | 344 |
| 10 | — | Mariano Puerta | 1-3-2 | 36-20 | 324 |
| 11 | 94 | Richard Gasquet | 1-1-1 | 31-11 | 274 |
| | 43 | David Ferrer | 0-1-4 | 39-25 | 274 |
| 13 | 29 | Mario Ancic | 1-2-2 | 40-22 | 270 |
| 14 | 9 | David Nalbandian | 1-0-0 | 32-14 | 266 |
| 15 | 21 | Fernando Gonzalez | 2-1-0 | 39-19 | 263 |
| 16 | 30 | Thomas Johansson | 0-0-5 | 39-22 | 257 |
| | 31 | Juan Carlos Ferrero | 0-1-2 | 40-23 | 257 |
| 18 | 21 | Ivan Ljubicic | 1-4-1 | 42-18 | 254 |
| 19 | 58 | Robby Ginepri | 1-0-2 | 33-20 | 244 |
| | 13 | Tommy Robredo | 0-1-2 | 37-20 | 244 |

### WOMEN

WTA Tour singles ranking system based on total Round and Quality Points for each tournament played during the last 12 months (capped at 17 tournaments). Tournaments, titles and match won-lost records, however, are for 2005 only.

| Rank 05 | (04) | | Finish 1-2-SF | W-L | Pts |
|---|---|---|---|---|---|
| 1 | 4 | Maria Sharapova | 3-1-6 | 50-9 | 4631 |
| 2 | 1 | Lindsay Davenport | 5-4-0 | 54-8 | 4562 |
| 3 | 22 | Kim Clijsters | 8-0-1 | 61-7 | 4467 |
| 4 | 2 | Amelie Mauresmo | 2-3-4 | 48-14 | 3936 |
| 5 | 8 | Justine Henin-Hardenne | 4-1-0 | 34-5 | 2936 |
| 6 | 9 | Venus Williams | 2-2-1 | 37-10 | 2883 |
| 7 | 29 | Mary Pierce | 1-2-0 | 35-12 | 2844 |
| 8 | 6 | Elena Dementieva | 0-1-5 | 40-15 | 2820 |
| 9 | 12 | Nadia Petrova | 0-1-3 | 43-18 | 2535 |
| 10 | 14 | Patty Schnyder | 2-1-5 | 49-20 | 2458 |
| 11 | 7 | Serena Williams | 1-0-1 | 21-7 | 2383 |
| 12 | 3 | Anastasia Myskina | 1-1-2 | 31-T8 | 2209 |
| 13 | 13 | Alicia Molik | 1-1-1 | 17-12 | 1736 |
| 14 | 21 | Nathalie Dechy | 0-0-3 | 35-23 | 1705 |
| 15 | 5 | Svetlana Kuznetsova | 0-1-2 | 27-15 | 1621 |
| 16 | 24 | Elena Likhovtseva | 0-0-2 | 28-19 | 1482 |
| 17 | 31 | Daniela Hantuchova | 0-1-3 | 34-23 | 1439 |
| 18 | 75 | Nicole Vaidisova | 2-1-1 | 40-14 | 1411 |
| 19 | 28 | Jelena Jankovic | 0-3-1 | 35-25 | 1407 |
| 20 | 101 | Ana Ivanovic | 1-0-1 | 34-12 | 1402 |

## 2005 Money Winners

Amounts include singles and doubles earnings through Oct. 9, 2005.

### MEN

| | | Earnings | | | Earnings | | | Earnings |
|---|---|---|---|---|---|---|---|---|
| 1 | Roger Federer | .$5,317,018 | 11 | Mariano Puerta | .$922,773 | 21 | Richard Gasquet | .$653,373 |
| 2 | Rafael Nadal | .3,424,751 | 12 | Jonas Bjorkman | .905,551 | 22 | Mario Ancic | .574,170 |
| 3 | Andre Agassi | .1,584,596 | 13 | David Ferrer | .811,922 | 23 | Bob Bryan | .627,747 |
| 4 | Andy Roddick | .1,556,385 | 14 | Thomas Johansson | .770,031 | | Mike Bryan | .627,747 |
| 5 | Lleyton Hewitt | .1,459,437 | 15 | Fernando Gonzalez | .733,465 | 25 | Juan Carlos Ferrero | .607,243 |
| 6 | Marat Safin | .1,288,115 | 16 | Ivan Ljubicic | .695,524 | 26 | Radek Stepanek | .591,360 |
| 7 | Guillermo Coria | .1,134,296 | 17 | David Nalbandian | .669,536 | 27 | Feliciano Lopez | .578,554 |
| 8 | Nikolay Davydenko | .1,036,719 | 18 | Tommy Robredo | .669,018 | 28 | Sebastien Grosjean | .550,609 |
| 9 | Max Mirnyi | .999,481 | 19 | Dominik Hrbaty | .668,731 | 29 | Nicolas Kiefer | .545,098 |
| 10 | Gaston Gaudio | .933,524 | 20 | Robby Ginepri | .661,996 | 30 | Igor Andreev | .520,845 |

### WOMEN

| | | Earnings | | | Earnings | | | Earnings |
|---|---|---|---|---|---|---|---|---|
| 1 | Kim Clijsters | .$3,631,706 | 11 | Svetlana Kuznetsova | .$915,968 | 21 | V. Ruano Pascual | .$492,492 |
| 2 | Lindsay Davenport | .2,055,490 | 12 | Patty Schnyder | .777,693 | 22 | Cara Black | .468,190 |
| 3 | Mary Pierce | .1,794,403 | 13 | Elena Likhovtseva | .714,371 | 23 | Conchita Martinez | .449,903 |
| 4 | J. Henin-Hardenne | .1,705,173 | 14 | Daniela Hantuchova | .639,662 | 24 | Flavia Pennetta | .433,532 |
| 5 | Maria Sharapova | .1,542,283 | 15 | Alicia Molik | .616,033 | 25 | Jelena Jankovic | .413,291 |
| 6 | Venus Williams | .1,509,065 | 16 | Nathalie Dechy | .599,106 | 26 | Ai Sugiyama | .410,667 |
| 7 | Amelie Mauresmo | .1,294,508 | 17 | Samantha Stosur | .581,687 | 27 | Dinara Safina | .404,267 |
| 8 | Serena Williams | .1,076,226 | 18 | Anastasia Myskina | .558,749 | 28 | Liezel Huber | .392,202 |
| 9 | Nadia Petrova | .961,950 | 19 | Anna-Lena Groenefeld | .527,561 | 29 | Ana Ivanovic | .391,747 |
| 10 | Elena Dementieva | .939,661 | 20 | Lisa Raymond | .495,591 | 30 | Vera Zvonareva | .376,864 |

## Davis Cup

Carlos Moya defeated Andy Roddick on the clay courts of Olympic Stadium in Seville to clinch Spain's second Davis Cup in five years. Moya and teen sensation Rafael Nadal led the Spaniards, who played in front of over 27,000 boisterous fans. The United States has 31 Davis Cup titles but hasn't won since 1995.

### 2004 FINAL
#### Spain 3, United States 2
at Seville, Spain (Dec. 3-5)

**Day One**—Carlos Moya (ESP) def. Mardy Fish (USA) 6-4, 6-2, 6-3; Rafael Nadal (ESP) def. Andy Roddick (USA) 6-7 (6-8], 6-2, 7-6 (8-6], 6-2.

**Day Two**—Bob Bryan & Mike Bryan (USA) def. Juan Carlos Ferrero & Tommy Robredo (ESP) 6-0, 6-3, 6-2.

**Day Three**—Moya (ESP) def. Roddick (USA) 6-2, 7-6 (7-1], 7-6 (7-5]; Fish (USA) def. Robredo (ESP) 7-6 (10-8], 6-2.

### 2005 Early Rounds
#### FIRST ROUND
(March 4-6)

| Winner | Loser |
|---|---|
| Croatia 3 | at United States 2 |
| at Australia 5 | Austria 0 |
| at Russia 4 | Chile 1 |
| at Romania 3 | Belarus 2 |
| Netherlands 3 | at Switzerland 2 |
| at France 3 | Sweden 2 |
| at Slovakia 3 | Spain 1 |
| at Argentina 5 | Czech Republic 0 |

#### QUARTERFINALS
(July 15-17)

| Winner | Loser |
|---|---|
| at Slovakia 4 | Netherlands 1 |
| Argentina 4 | at Australia 1 |
| at Russia 3 | France 2 |
| at Croatia 4 | Romania 1 |

### SEMIFINALS
#### Slovakia 4, Argentina 1
at Bratislava, Slovakia (Sept. 23-25)

**Day One**—Karol Beck (SVK) def. Guillermo Coria (ARG) 7-5, 6-4, 6-4; David Nalbandian (ARG) def. Dominik Hrbaty (SVK) 3-6, 7-5, 7-5, 6-3.

**Day Two**—Beck & Michal Mertinak (SVK) def. Nalbandian & Mariano Puerta (ARG) 7-6 (7-5], 7-5, 7-6 (7-5].

**Day Three**—Hrbaty (SVK) def. Coria (ARG) 7-6 (7-2], 6-2, 6-3; Karol Kucera (SVK) def. Mariano Puerta (ARG) 4-6, 6-3, 2-1 (ret.].

#### Croatia 3, Russia 2
at Split, Croatia (Sept. 23-25)

**Day One**—Nikolay Davydenko (RUS) def. Mario Ancic (CRO) 7-5, 6-4, 5-7, 6-4; Ivan Ljubicic (CRO) def. Mikhail Youzhny (RUS) 3-6, 6-3, 6-4, 4-6, 6-4.

**Day Two**—Ancic & Ljubicic (CRO) def. Igor Andreev & Dmitry Tursunov (RUS) 6-2, 4-6, 7-6 (7-5], 3-6, 6-4.

**Day Three**—Ljubicic (CRO) def. Davydenko (RUS) 6-3, 7-6 (8-6], 6-4; Tursunov (RUS) def. Ivo Karlovic (RUS) 6-4, 6-4.

### 2005 FINAL

The 2005 Davis Cup final between Slovakia and Croatia was to be held from Dec. 2-4 in Slovakia. It is the first time either country has advanced to the Davis Cup final.

# 1877-2005
# Through the Years

ESPN SPORTS ALMANAC

## Grand Slam Championships
### Australian Open
#### MEN

Became an Open Championship in 1969. Two tournaments were held in 1977; the first in January, the second in December. Tournament moved back to January in 1987, so no championship was decided in 1986. **Surface:** Synpave Rebound Ace (hardcourt surface composed of polyurethane and synthetic rubber).

**Multiple winners:** Roy Emerson (6); Andre Agassi, Jack Crawford and Ken Rosewall (4); James Anderson, Rod Laver, Adrian Quist, Mats Wilander and Pat Wood (3); Boris Becker, Jack Bromwich, Ashley Cooper, Jim Courier, Stefan Edberg, Rodney Heath, Johan Kriek, Ivan Lendl, John Newcombe, Pete Sampras, Frank Sedgman, Guillermo Vilas and Tony Wilding (2).

| Year | Winner | Loser | Score | Year | Winner | Loser | Score |
|------|--------|-------|-------|------|--------|-------|-------|
| 1905 | Rodney Heath | A. Curtis | 46 63 64 64 | 1959 | Alex Olmedo | N. Fraser | 61 62 36 63 |
| 1906 | Tony Wilding | H. Parker | 60 64 64 | 1960 | Rod Laver | N. Fraser | 57 36 63 86 86 |
| 1907 | Horace Rice | H. Parker | 63 64 64 | 1961 | Roy Emerson | R. Laver | 16 63 75 64 |
| 1908 | Fred Alexander | A. Dunlop | 36 36 60 62 63 | 1962 | Rod Laver | R. Emerson | 86 06 64 64 |
| 1909 | Tony Wilding | E. Parker | 61 75 62 | 1963 | Roy Emerson | K. Fletcher | 63 63 61 |
| 1910 | Rodney Heath | H. Rice | 64 63 62 | 1964 | Roy Emerson | F. Stolle | 63 64 62 |
| 1911 | Norman Brookes | H. Rice | 61 62 63 | 1965 | Roy Emerson | F. Stolle | 79 26 64 75 61 |
| 1912 | J. Cecil Parke | A. Beamish | 36 63 16 61 75 | 1966 | Roy Emerson | A. Ashe | 64 68 62 63 |
| 1913 | Ernie Parker | H. Parker | 26 61 62 63 | 1967 | Roy Emerson | A. Ashe | 64 61 61 |
| 1914 | Pat Wood | G. Patterson | 64 63 57 61 | 1968 | Bill Bowrey | J. Gisbert | 75 26 97 64 |
| 1915 | Gordon Lowe | H. Rice | 46 61 61 64 | 1969 | Rod Laver | A. Gimeno | 63 64 75 |
| 1916-18 | Not held World War I | | | 1970 | Arthur Ashe | D. Crealy | 64 97 62 |
| 1919 | A.R.F. Kingscote | E. Pockley | 64 60 63 | 1971 | Ken Rosewall | A. Ashe | 61 75 63 |
| 1920 | Pat Wood | R. Thomas | 63 46 68 61 63 | 1972 | Ken Rosewall | M. Anderson | 76 63 75 |
| 1921 | Rhys Gemmell | A. Hedeman | 75 61 64 | 1973 | John Newcombe | O. Parun | 63 67 75 61 |
| 1922 | James Anderson | G. Patterson | 60 36 36 63 62 | 1974 | Jimmy Connors | P. Dent | 76 64 46 63 |
| 1923 | Pat Wood | C.B. St. John | 61 61 63 | 1975 | John Newcombe | J. Connors | 75 36 64 75 |
| 1924 | James Anderson | R. Schlesinger | 63 64 36 57 63 | 1976 | Mark Edmondson | J. Newcombe | 67 63 76 61 |
| 1925 | James Anderson | G. Patterson | 11-9 26 62 63 | 1977 | Roscoe Tanner | G. Vilas | 63 63 63 |
| 1926 | John Hawkes | J. Willard | 61 63 61 | | Vitas Gerulaitis | J. Lloyd | 63 76 57 36 62 |
| 1927 | Gerald Patterson | J. Hawkes | 36 64 36 18-16 63 | 1978 | Guillermo Vilas | J. Marks | 64 64 36 63 |
| 1928 | Jean Borotra | R.O. Cummings | 64 61 46 57 63 | 1979 | Guillermo Vilas | J. Sadri | 76 63 62 |
| 1929 | John Gregory | R. Schlesinger | 62 62 57 75 | 1980 | Brian Teacher | K. Warwick | 75 76 63 |
| 1930 | Gar Moon | H. Hopman | 63 61 63 | 1981 | Johan Kriek | S. Denton | 62 76 67 64 |
| 1931 | Jack Crawford | H. Hopman | 64 62 26 61 | 1982 | Johan Kriek | S. Denton | 63 63 62 |
| 1932 | Jack Crawford | H. Hopman | 46 63 36 63 61 | 1983 | Mats Wilander | I. Lendl | 61 64 64 |
| 1933 | Jack Crawford | K. Gledhill | 26 75 63 62 | 1984 | Mats Wilander | K. Curren | 67 64 76 62 |
| 1934 | Fred Perry | J. Crawford | 63 75 61 | 1985 | Stefan Edberg | M. Wilander | 64 63 63 |
| 1935 | Jack Crawford | F. Perry | 26 64 64 64 | 1986 | Not held | | |
| 1936 | Adrian Quist | J. Crawford | 62 63 46 36 97 | 1987 | Stefan Edberg | P. Cash | 63 64 36 57 63 |
| 1937 | Viv McGrath | J. Bromwich | 63 16 60 26 61 | 1988 | Mats Wilander | P. Cash | 63 67 36 61 86 |
| 1938 | Don Budge | J. Bromwich | 64 62 61 | 1989 | Ivan Lendl | M. Mecir | 62 62 62 |
| 1939 | Jack Bromwich | A. Quist | 64 61 63 | 1990 | Ivan Lendl | S. Edberg | 46 76 52 (ret.) |
| 1940 | Adrian Quist | J. Crawford | 63 61 62 | 1991 | Boris Becker | I. Lendl | 16 64 64 64 |
| 1941-45 | Not held World War II | | | 1992 | Jim Courier | S. Edberg | 63 36 64 62 |
| 1946 | Jack Bromwich | D. Pails | 57 63 75 36 62 | 1993 | Jim Courier | S. Edberg | 62 61 26 75 |
| 1947 | Dinny Pails | J. Bromwich | 46 64 36 75 86 | 1994 | Pete Sampras | T. Martin | 76 64 64 |
| 1948 | Adrian Quist | J. Bromwich | 64 36 63 26 63 | 1995 | Andre Agassi | P. Sampras | 46 61 76 64 |
| 1949 | Frank Sedgman | J. Bromwich | 63 63 62 | 1996 | Boris Becker | M. Chang | 62 64 26 62 |
| 1950 | Frank Sedgman | K. McGregor | 63 64 46 61 | 1997 | Pete Sampras | C. Moya | 62 63 63 |
| 1951 | Dick Savitt | K. McGregor | 63 26 63 61 | 1998 | Petr Korda | M. Rios | 62 62 62 |
| 1952 | Ken McGregor | F. Sedgman | 75 12-10 26 62 | 1999 | Yevgeny Kafelnikov | T. Enqvist | 46 60 63 76 |
| 1953 | Ken Rosewall | M. Rose | 60 63 64 | 2000 | Andre Agassi | Y. Kafelnikov | 36 63 62 64 |
| 1954 | Mervyn Rose | R. Hartwig | 62 06 64 62 | 2001 | Andre Agassi | A. Clement | 64 62 62 |
| 1955 | Ken Rosewall | L. Hoad | 97 64 64 | 2002 | Thomas Johansson | M. Safin | 36 64 64 76 |
| 1956 | Lew Hoad | K. Rosewall | 64 36 64 75 | 2003 | Andre Agassi | R. Schuettler | 62 62 61 |
| 1957 | Ashley Cooper | N. Fraser | 63 9-11 64 62 | 2004 | Roger Federer | M. Safin | 76 64 62 |
| 1958 | Ashley Cooper | M. Anderson | 75 63 64 | 2005 | Marat Safin | L. Hewitt | 16 63 64 64 |

## WOMEN

Became an Open Championship in 1969. Two tournaments were held in 1977, the first in January, the second in December. Tournament moved back to January in 1987, so no championship was decided in 1986.

**Multiple winners:** Margaret Smith Court (11); Nancye Wynne Bolton (6); Daphne Akhurst (5); Evonne Goolagong Cawley, Steffi Graf and Monica Seles (4); Joan Hartigan, Martina Hingis and Martina Navratilova (3); Coral Buttsworth, Jennifer Capriati, Chris Evert Lloyd, Thelma Long, Hana Mandlikova, Mall Molesworth, Mary Carter Reitano and Serena Williams (2).

| Year | Winner | Loser | Score |
|---|---|---|---|
| 1922 | Mall Molesworth | E. Boyd | 63 10-8 |
| 1923 | Mall Molesworth | E. Boyd | 61 75 |
| 1924 | Sylvia Lance | E. Boyd | 63 36 64 |
| 1925 | Daphne Akhurst | E. Boyd | 16 86 64 |
| 1926 | Daphne Akhurst | E. Boyd | 61 63 |
| 1927 | Esna Boyd | S. Harper | 57 61 62 |
| 1928 | Daphne Akhurst | E. Boyd | 75 62 |
| 1929 | Daphne Akhurst | L. Bickerton | 61 57 62 |
| 1930 | Daphne Akhurst | S. Harper | 10-8 26 75 |
| 1931 | Coral Buttsworth | M. Crawford | 16 63 64 |
| 1932 | Coral Buttsworth | K. Le Messurier | 97 64 |
| 1933 | Joan Hartigan | C. Buttsworth | 64 63 |
| 1934 | Joan Hartigan | M. Molesworth | 61 64 |
| 1935 | Dorothy Round | N. Lyle | 16 61 63 |
| 1936 | Joan Hartigan | N. Wynne | 64 64 |
| 1937 | Nancye Wynne | E. Westacott | 63 57 64 |
| 1938 | Dorothy Bundy | D. Stevenson | 63 62 |
| 1939 | Emily Westacott | N. Hopman | 61 62 |
| 1940 | Nancye Wynne | T. Coyne | 57 64 60 |
| 1941-45 | Not held World War II | | |
| 1946 | Nancye Bolton | J. Fitch | 64 64 |
| 1947 | Nancye Bolton | N. Hopman | 63 62 |
| 1948 | Nancye Bolton | M. Toomey | 63 61 |
| 1949 | Doris Hart | N. Bolton | 63 64 |
| 1950 | Louise Brough | D. Hart | 64 36 64 |
| 1951 | Nancye Bolton | T. Long | 61 75 |
| 1952 | Thelma Long | H. Angwin | 62 63 |
| 1953 | Maureen Connolly | J. Sampson | 63 62 |
| 1954 | Thelma Long | J. Staley | 63 64 |
| 1955 | Beryl Penrose | T. Long | 64 63 |
| 1956 | Mary Carter | T. Long | 36 62 97 |
| 1957 | Shirley Fry | A. Gibson | 63 64 |
| 1958 | Angela Mortimer | L. Coghlan | 63 64 |
| 1959 | Mary Reitano | R. Schuurman | 62 63 |
| 1960 | Margaret Smith | J. Lehane | 75 62 |
| 1961 | Margaret Smith | J. Lehane | 61 64 |
| 1962 | Margaret Smith | J. Lehane | 60 62 |
| 1963 | Margaret Smith | J. Lehane | 62 62 |
| 1964 | Margaret Smith | L. Turner | 63 62 |
| 1965 | Margaret Smith | M. Bueno | 57 64 52 (ret) |
| 1966 | Margaret Smith | N. Richey | walkover |
| 1967 | Nancy Richey | L. Turner | 61 64 |
| 1968 | Billie Jean King | M. Smith | 61 62 |
| 1969 | Margaret Court | B.J. King | 64 61 |
| 1970 | Margaret Court | K. Melville | 61 63 |
| 1971 | Margaret Court | E. Goolagong | 26 76 75 |
| 1972 | Virginia Wade | E. Goolagong | 64 64 |
| 1973 | Margaret Court | E. Goolagong | 64 75 |
| 1974 | Evonne Goolagong | C. Evert | 76 46 60 |
| 1975 | Evonne Goolagong | M. Navratilova | 63 62 |
| 1976 | Evonne Cawley | R. Tomanova | 62 62 |
| 1977 | Kerry Reid | D. Balestrat | 75 62 |
|  | Evonne Cawley | H. Gourlay | 63 60 |
| 1978 | Chris O'Neil | B. Nagelsen | 63 76 |
| 1979 | Barbara Jordan | S. Walsh | 63 63 |
| 1980 | Hana Mandlikova | W. Turnbull | 60 75 |
| 1981 | Martina Navratilova | C. Evert Lloyd | 67 64 75 |
| 1982 | Chris Evert Lloyd | M. Navratilova | 63 26 63 |
| 1983 | Martina Navratilova | K. Jordan | 62 76 |
| 1984 | Chris Evert Lloyd | H. Sukova | 67 61 63 |
| 1985 | Martina Navratilova | C. Evert Lloyd | 62 46 62 |
| 1986 | Not held | | |
| 1987 | Hana Mandlikova | M. Navratilova | 75 76 |
| 1988 | Steffi Graf | C. Evert | 61 76 |
| 1989 | Steffi Graf | H. Sukova | 64 64 |
| 1990 | Steffi Graf | M.J. Fernandez | 63 64 |
| 1991 | Monica Seles | J. Novotna | 57 63 61 |
| 1992 | Monica Seles | M.J. Fernandez | 62 63 |
| 1993 | Monica Seles | S. Graf | 46 63 62 |
| 1994 | Steffi Graf | A.S. Vicario | 60 62 |
| 1995 | Mary Pierce | A.S. Vicario | 63 62 |
| 1996 | Monica Seles | A. Huber | 64 61 |
| 1997 | Martina Hingis | M. Pierce | 62 62 |
| 1998 | Martina Hingis | C. Martinez | 63 63 |
| 1999 | Martina Hingis | A. Mauresmo | 62 63 |
| 2000 | Lindsay Davenport | M. Hingis | 61 75 |
| 2001 | Jennifer Capriati | M. Hingis | 64 63 |
| 2002 | Jennifer Capriati | M. Hingis | 46 76 62 |
| 2003 | Serena Williams | V. Williams | 76 36 64 |
| 2004 | J. Henin-Hardenne | K. Clijsters | 63 46 63 |
| 2005 | Serena Williams | L. Davenport | 26 63 60 |

## French Open
### MEN

From 1891 to 1925, entry was restricted to members of French clubs. Became an Open Championship in 1968, but closed to contract pros in 1972. Note that Max Decugis won eight tournaments before 1925 (1903-04, 1907-09, 1912-14) to lead all men. **Surface:** Red clay.

**Multiple winners** (since 1925): Bjorn Borg (6); Henri Cochet (4); Gustavo Kuerten, Rene Lacoste, Ivan Lendl and Mats Wilander (3); Sergi Bruguera, Jim Courier, Jaroslav Drobny, Roy Emerson, Jan Kodes, Rod Laver, Frank Parker, Nicola Pietrangeli, Ken Rosewall, Manuel Santana, Tony Trabert and Gottfried von Cramm (2).

| Year | Winner | Loser | Score |
|---|---|---|---|
| 1925 | Rene Lacoste | J. Borotra | 75 61 64 |
| 1926 | Henri Cochet | R. Lacoste | 62 64 63 |
| 1927 | Rene Lacoste | B. Tilden | 64 46 57 63 11-9 |
| 1928 | Henri Cochet | R. Lacoste | 57 63 61 63 |
| 1929 | Rene Lacoste | B. Borotra | 63 26 60 26 86 |
| 1930 | Henri Cochet | B. Tilden | 36 86 63 61 |
| 1931 | Jean Borotra | C. Boussus | 26 64 75 64 |
| 1932 | Henri Cochet | G. de Stefani | 60 64 46 63 |
| 1933 | Jack Crawford | H. Cochet | 86 61 63 |
| 1934 | Gottfried von Cramm | J. Crawford | 64 79 36 75 63 |
| 1935 | Fred Perry | G. von Cramm | 32 61 63 |
| 1936 | Gottfried von Cramm | F. Perry | 60 26 62 26 60 |
| 1937 | Henner Henkel | H. Austin | 61 64 63 |
| 1938 | Don Budge | R. Menzel | 63 62 64 |
| 1939 | Don McNeill | B. Riggs | 75 60 63 |
| 1940-45 | Not held World War II | | |
| 1946 | Marcel Bernard | J. Drobny | 36 26 61 64 63 |
| 1947 | Joseph Asboth | E. Sturgess | 86 75 64 |
| 1948 | Frank Parker | J. Drobny | 64 75 57 86 |
| 1949 | Frank Parker | B. Patty | 63 16 61 64 |
| 1950 | Budge Patty | J. Drobny | 61 62 36 57 75 |
| 1951 | Jaroslav Drobny | E. Sturgess | 63 6416 62 |
| 1952 | Jaroslav Drobny | F. Sedgman | 62 60 36 64 |
| 1953 | Ken Rosewall | V. Seixas | 63 6416 62 |
| 1954 | Tony Trabert | A. Larsen | 64 75 61 |
| 1955 | Tony Trabert | S. Davidson | 26 61 64 62 |

| Year | Winner | Loser | Score | Year | Winner | Loser | Score |
|------|--------|-------|-------|------|--------|-------|-------|
| 1956 | Lew Hoad | S. Davidson | 64 86 63 | 1981 | Bjorn Borg | I. Lendl | 61 46 62 36 61 |
| 1957 | Sven Davidson | H. Flam | 63 64 64 | 1982 | Mats Wilander | G. Vilas | 16 76 60 64 |
| 1958 | Mervyn Rose | L. Ayala | 63 64 64 | 1983 | Yannick Noah | M. Wilander | 62 75 76 |
| 1959 | Nicola Pietrangeli | I. Vermaak | 36 63 64 61 | 1984 | Ivan Lendl | J. McEnroe | 36 26 64 75 75 |
| 1960 | Nicola Pietrangeli | L. Ayala | 36 63 64 46 63 | 1985 | Mats Wilander | I. Lendl | 36 64 62 62 |
| 1961 | Manuel Santana | N. Pietrangeli | 46 61 36 60 62 | 1986 | Ivan Lendl | M. Pernfors | 63 62 64 |
| 1962 | Rod Laver | R. Emerson | 36 26 63 97 62 | 1987 | Ivan Lendl | M. Wilander | 75 62 36 76 |
| 1963 | Roy Emerson | P. Darmon | 36 61 64 64 | 1988 | Mats Wilander | H. Leconte | 75 62 61 |
| 1964 | Manuel Santana | N. Pietrangeli | 63 61 46 75 | 1989 | Michael Chang | S. Edberg | 61 36 46 64 62 |
| 1965 | Fred Stolle | T. Roche | 36 60 62 63 | 1990 | Andres Gomez | A. Agassi | 63 26 64 64 |
| 1966 | Tony Roche | I. Gulyas | 61 64 75 | 1991 | Jim Courier | A. Agassi | 36 64 26 61 64 |
| 1967 | Roy Emerson | T. Roche | 61 64 26 62 | 1992 | Jim Courier | P. Korda | 75 62 61 |
| 1968 | Ken Rosewall | R. Laver | 63 61 26 62 | 1993 | Sergi Bruguera | J. Courier | 64 26 62 36 63 |
| 1969 | Rod Laver | K. Rosewall | 64 63 64 | 1994 | Sergi Bruguera | A. Berasategui | 63 75 26 61 |
| 1970 | Jan Kodes | Z. Franulovic | 62 64 60 | 1995 | Thomas Muster | M. Chang | 75 62 64 |
| 1971 | Jan Kodes | I. Nastase | 86 62 26 75 | 1996 | Yevgeny Kafelnikov | M. Stich | 76 75 76 |
| 1972 | Andres Gimeno | P. Proisy | 46 63 61 61 | 1997 | Gustavo Kuerten | S. Bruguera | 63 64 62 |
| 1973 | Ilie Nastase | N. Pilic | 63 63 60 | 1998 | Carlos Moya | A. Corretja | 63 75 63 |
| 1974 | Bjorn Borg | M. Orantes | 26 67 60 61 61 | 1999 | Andre Agassi | A. Medvedev | 16 26 64 63 64 |
| 1975 | Bjorn Borg | G. Vilas | 62 63 64 | 2000 | Gustavo Kuerten | M. Norman | 62 63 26 76 |
| 1976 | Adriano Panatta | H. Solomon | 61 64 46 76 | 2001 | Gustavo Kuerten | A. Corretja | 67 75 62 60 |
| 1977 | Guillermo Vilas | B. Gottfried | 60 63 60 | 2002 | Albert Costa | J. C. Ferrero | 61 60 46 63 |
| 1978 | Bjorn Borg | G. Vilas | 61 61 63 | 2003 | Juan Carlos Ferrero | M. Verkerk | 61 63 62 |
| 1979 | Bjorn Borg | V. Pecci | 63 61 67 64 | 2004 | Gaston Gaudio | G. Coria | 06 36 64 61 86 |
| 1980 | Bjorn Borg | V. Gerulaitis | 64 61 62 | 2005 | Rafael Nadal | M. Puerta | 67 63 61 75 |

## WOMEN

From 1897 to 1925, entry was restricted to members of French clubs. Became an Open Championship in 1968, but closed to contract pros in 1972. Note that Suzanne Lenglen won two titles prior to 1925, giving her six total.

**Multiple winners** (since 1925): Chris Evert Lloyd (7); Steffi Graf (6); Margaret Smith Court (5); Helen Wills Moody (4); Arantxa Sanchez Vicario, Monica Seles and Hilde Sperling (3); Maureen Connolly, Margaret Osborne du Pont, Doris Hart, Justine Henin-Hardenne, Ann Haydon Jones, Suzanne Lenglen, Simone Mathieu, Margaret Scriven, Martina Navratilova and Lesley Turner (2).

| Year | Winner | Loser | Score | Year | Winner | Loser | Score |
|------|--------|-------|-------|------|--------|-------|-------|
| 1925 | Suzanne Lenglen | K. McKane | 61 62 | 1968 | Nancy Richey | A. Jones | 57 64 61 |
| 1926 | Suzanne Lenglen | M. Browne | 61 60 | 1969 | Margaret Court | A. Jones | 61 46 63 |
| 1927 | Kea Bouman | I. Peacock | 62 64 | 1970 | Margaret Court | H. Niessen | 62 64 |
| 1928 | Helen Wills | E. Bennett | 61 62 | 1971 | Evonne Goolagong | H. Gourlay | 63 75 |
| 1929 | Helen Wills | S. Mathieu | 63 64 | 1972 | Billie Jean King | E. Goolagong | 63 63 |
| 1930 | Helen Moody | H. Jacobs | 62 61 | 1973 | Margaret Court | C. Evert | 67 76 64 |
| 1931 | Cilly Aussem | B. Nuthall | 86 61 | 1974 | Chris Evert | O. Morozova | 61 62 |
| 1932 | Helen Moody | S. Mathieu | 75 61 | 1975 | Chris Evert | M. Navratilova | 26 62 61 |
| 1933 | Margaret Scriven | S. Mathieu | 62 46 64 | 1976 | Sue Barker | R. Tomanova | 62 06 62 |
| 1934 | Margaret Scriven | H. Jacobs | 75 46 61 | 1977 | Mima Jausovec | F. Mihai | 62 67 61 |
| 1935 | Hilde Sperling | S. Mathieu | 62 61 | 1978 | Virginia Ruzici | M. Jausovec | 62 62 |
| 1936 | Hilde Sperling | S. Mathieu | 63 64 | 1979 | Chris Evert Lloyd | W. Turnbull | 62 60 |
| 1937 | Hilde Sperling | S. Mathieu | 62 64 | 1980 | Chris Evert Lloyd | V. Ruzici | 60 63 |
| 1938 | Simone Mathieu | N. Landry | 60 63 | 1981 | Hana Mandlikova | S. Hanika | 62 64 |
| 1939 | Simone Mathieu | J. Jedrzejowska | 63 86 | 1982 | Martina Navratilova | A. Jaeger | 76 61 |
| 1940-45 | Not held World War II | | | 1983 | Chris Evert Lloyd | M. Jausovec | 61 62 |
| 1946 | Margaret Osborne | P. Betz | 16 86 75 | 1984 | Martina Navratilova | C. Evert Lloyd | 63 61 |
| 1947 | Patricia Todd | D. Hart | 63 36 64 | 1985 | Chris Evert Lloyd | M. Navratilova | 63 67 75 |
| 1948 | Nelly Landry | S. Fry | 62 06 60 | 1986 | Chris Evert Lloyd | M. Navratilova | 26 63 63 |
| 1949 | Margaret du Pont | N. Adamson | 75 62 | 1987 | Steffi Graf | M. Navratilova | 64 46 86 |
| 1950 | Doris Hart | P. Todd | 64 46 62 | 1988 | Steffi Graf | N. Zvereva | 60 60 |
| 1951 | Shirley Fry | D. Hart | 63 36 63 | 1989 | A. Sanchez Vicario | S. Graf | 76 36 75 |
| 1952 | Doris Hart | S. Fry | 64 64 | 1990 | Monica Seles | S. Graf | 76 64 |
| 1953 | Maureen Connolly | D. Hart | 62 64 | 1991 | Monica Seles | A.S. Vicario | 63 64 |
| 1954 | Maureen Connolly | G. Bucaille | 64 61 | 1992 | Monica Seles | S. Graf | 62 36 10-8 |
| 1955 | Angela Mortimer | D. Knode | 26 75 10-8 | 1993 | Steffi Graf | M.J. Fernandez | 46 62 64 |
| 1956 | Althea Gibson | A. Mortimer | 60 12-10 | 1994 | A. Sanchez Vicario | M. Pierce | 64 64 |
| 1957 | Shirley Bloomer | D. Knode | 61 63 | 1995 | Steffi Graf | A.S. Vicario | 76 46 60 |
| 1958 | Suzi Kormoczi | S. Bloomer | 64 16 62 | 1996 | Steffi Graf | A.S. Vicario | 63 67 10-8 |
| 1959 | Christine Truman | S. Kormoczi | 64 75 | 1997 | Iva Majoli | M. Hingis | 64 62 |
| 1960 | Darlene Hard | Y. Ramirez | 63 64 | 1998 | A. Sanchez Vicario | M. Seles | 76 06 62 |
| 1961 | Ann Haydon | Y. Ramirez | 62 61 | 1999 | Steffi Graf | M. Hingis | 46 75 62 |
| 1962 | Margaret Smith | L. Turner | 63 36 75 | 2000 | Mary Pierce | C. Martinez | 62 75 |
| 1963 | Lesley Turner | A. Jones | 26 63 75 | 2001 | Jennifer Capriati | K. Clijsters | 16 64 1210 |
| 1964 | Margaret Smith | M. Bueno | 57 61 62 | 2002 | Serena Williams | V. Williams | 75 63 |
| 1965 | Lesley Turner | M. Smith | 63 64 | 2003 | J. Henin-Hardenne | K. Clijsters | 60 64 |
| 1966 | Ann Jones | N. Richey | 63 61 | 2004 | Anastasia Myskina | E. Dementieva | 61 62 |
| 1967 | Francoise Durr | L. Turner | 46 63 64 | 2005 | J. Henin-Hardenne | M. Pierce | 61 61 |

## Wimbledon
### MEN

Officially called "The Lawn Tennis Championships" at the All England Club, Wimbledon. Challenge round system (defending champion qualified for following year's final) used from 1877-1921. Became an Open Championship in 1968, but closed to contract pros in 1972. **Surface:** Grass.

**Multiple winners:** Willie Renshaw and Pete Sampras (7); Bjorn Borg and Laurie Doherty (5); Reggie Doherty, Rod Laver and Tony Wilding (4); Wilfred Baddeley, Boris Becker, Roger Federer, Arthur Gore, John McEnroe, John Newcombe, Fred Perry and Bill Tilden (3); Jean Borotra, Norman Brookes, Don Budge, Henri Cochet, Jimmy Connors, Stefan Edberg, Roy Emerson, John Hartley, Lew Hoad, Rene Lacoste, Gerald Patterson and Joshua Pim (2).

| Year | Winner | Loser | Score | Year | Winner | Loser | Score |
|---|---|---|---|---|---|---|---|
| 1877 | Spencer Gore | W. Marshall | 61 62 64 | 1946 | Yvon Petra | G. Brown | 62 64 79 57 64 |
| 1878 | Frank Hadow | S. Gore | 75 61 97 | 1947 | Jack Kramer | T. Brown | 61 63 62 |
| 1879 | John Hartley | V. St. L. Goold | 62 64 62 | 1948 | Bob Falkenburg | J. Bromwich | 75 06 62 36 75 |
| 1880 | John Hartley | H. Lawford | 60 62 26 63 | 1949 | Ted Schroeder | J. Drobny | 36 60 63 46 64 |
| 1881 | Willie Renshaw | J. Hartley | 60 61 61 | 1950 | Budge Patty | F. Sedgman | 61 8-10 62 63 |
| 1882 | Willie Renshaw | E. Renshaw | 61 26 46 62 62 | 1951 | Dick Savitt | K. McGregor | 64 64 64 |
| 1883 | Willie Renshaw | E. Renshaw | 26 63 63 46 63 | 1952 | Frank Sedgman | J. Drobny | 46 62 63 62 |
| 1884 | Willie Renshaw | H. Lawford | 60 64 97 | 1953 | Vic Seixas | K. Nielsen | 97 63 64 |
| 1885 | Willie Renshaw | H. Lawford | 75 62 46 75 | 1954 | Jaroslav Drobny | K. Rosewall | 13-11 46 62 97 |
| 1886 | Willie Renshaw | H. Lawford | 60 57 63 64 | 1955 | Tony Trabert | K. Nielsen | 63 75 61 |
| 1887 | Herbert Lawford | E. Renshaw | 16 63 36 64 64 | 1956 | Lew Hoad | K. Rosewall | 62 46 75 64 |
| 1888 | Ernest Renshaw | H. Lawford | 63 75 60 | 1957 | Lew Hoad | A. Cooper | 62 61 62 |
| 1889 | Willie Renshaw | E. Renshaw | 64 61 36 60 | 1958 | Ashley Cooper | N. Fraser | 36 63 64 13-11 |
| 1890 | Willoughby Hamilton | W. Renshaw | 68 62 36 61 61 | 1959 | Alex Olmedo | R. Laver | 64 63 64 |
| 1891 | Wilfred Baddeley | J. Pim | 64 16 75 60 | 1960 | Neale Fraser | R. Laver | 64 36 97 75 |
| 1892 | Wilfred Baddeley | J. Pim | 46 63 63 62 | 1961 | Rod Laver | C. McKinley | 63 61 64 |
| 1893 | Joshua Pim | W. Baddeley | 36 61 63 62 | 1962 | Rod Laver | M. Mulligan | 62 62 61 |
| 1894 | Joshua Pim | W. Baddeley | 10-8 62 86 | 1963 | Chuck McKinley | F. Stolle | 97 61 64 |
| 1895 | Wilfred Baddeley | W. Eaves | 46 26 86 62 63 | 1964 | Roy Emerson | F. Stolle | 64 12-10 46 63 |
| 1896 | Harold Mahony | W. Baddeley | 62 68 57 86 63 | 1965 | Roy Emerson | F. Stolle | 62 64 64 |
| 1897 | Reggie Doherty | H. Mahony | 64 64 63 | 1966 | Manuel Santana | D. Ralston | 64 11-9 64 |
| 1898 | Reggie Doherty | L. Doherty | 63 63 26 57 61 | 1967 | John Newcombe | W. Bungert | 63 61 61 |
| 1899 | Reggie Doherty | A. Gore | 16 46 62 63 63 | 1968 | Rod Laver | T. Roche | 63 64 62 |
| 1900 | Reggie Doherty | S. Smith | 68 63 61 62 | 1969 | Rod Laver | J. Newcombe | 64 57 64 64 |
| 1901 | Arthur Gore | R. Doherty | 46 75 64 64 | 1970 | John Newcombe | K. Rosewall | 57 63 62 36 61 |
| 1902 | Laurie Doherty | A. Gore | 64 63 36 60 | 1971 | John Newcombe | S. Smith | 63 57 26 64 64 |
| 1903 | Laurie Doherty | F. Riseley | 75 63 60 | 1972 | Stan Smith | I. Nastase | 46 63 63 46 75 |
| 1904 | Laurie Doherty | F. Riseley | 61 75 86 | 1973 | Jan Kodes | A. Metreveli | 61 98 63 |
| 1905 | Laurie Doherty | N. Brookes | 86 62 64 | 1974 | Jimmy Connors | K. Rosewall | 61 61 64 |
| 1906 | Laurie Doherty | F. Riseley | 64 46 62 63 | 1975 | Arthur Ashe | J. Connors | 61 61 57 64 |
| 1907 | Norman Brookes | A. Gore | 64 62 62 | 1976 | Bjorn Borg | I. Nastase | 64 62 97 |
| 1908 | Arthur Gore | R. Barrett | 63 62 46 36 64 | 1977 | Bjorn Borg | J. Connors | 36 62 61 57 64 |
| 1909 | Arthur Gore | M. Ritchie | 68 16 62 62 62 | 1978 | Bjorn Borg | J. Connors | 62 62 63 |
| 1910 | Tony Wilding | A. Gore | 64 75 46 62 | 1979 | Bjorn Borg | R. Tanner | 67 61 36 63 64 |
| 1911 | Tony Wilding | R. Barrett | 64 46 26 62 (ret) | 1980 | Bjorn Borg | J. McEnroe | 16 75 63 67 86 |
| 1912 | Tony Wilding | A. Gore | 64 64 46 64 | 1981 | John McEnroe | B. Borg | 46 76 76 64 |
| 1913 | Tony Wilding | M. McLoughlin | 86 63 10-8 | 1982 | Jimmy Connors | J. McEnroe | 36 63 67 76 64 |
| 1914 | Norman Brookes | T. Wilding | 64 64 75 | 1983 | John McEnroe | C. Lewis | 62 62 62 |
| 1915-18 Not held World War I | | | | 1984 | John McEnroe | J. Connors | 61 61 62 |
| 1919 | Gerald Patterson | N. Brookes | 63 75 62 | 1985 | Boris Becker | K. Curren | 63 67 76 64 |
| 1920 | Bill Tilden | G. Patterson | 26 63 62 64 | 1986 | Boris Becker | I. Lendl | 64 63 75 |
| 1921 | Bill Tilden | B. Norton | 46 26 61 60 75 | 1987 | Pat Cash | I. Lendl | 76 62 75 |
| 1922 | Gerald Patterson | R. Lycett | 63 64 62 | 1988 | Stefan Edberg | B. Becker | 46 76 64 62 |
| 1923 | Bill Johnston | F. Hunter | 60 63 61 | 1989 | Boris Becker | S. Edberg | 60 76 64 |
| 1924 | Jean Borotra | R. Lacoste | 61 36 61 36 64 | 1990 | Stefan Edberg | B. Becker | 62 62 36 36 64 |
| 1925 | Rene Lacoste | J. Borotra | 63 63 46 86 | 1991 | Michael Stich | B. Becker | 64 76 64 |
| 1926 | Jean Borotra | H. Kinsey | 86 61 63 | 1992 | Andre Agassi | G. Ivanisevic | 67 64 64 16 64 |
| 1927 | Henri Cochet | J. Borotra | 46 46 63 64 75 | 1993 | Pete Sampras | J. Courier | 76 76 36 63 |
| 1928 | Rene Lacoste | H. Cochet | 61 46 64 62 | 1994 | Pete Sampras | G. Ivanisevic | 76 76 60 |
| 1929 | Henri Cochet | J. Borotra | 64 63 64 | 1995 | Pete Sampras | B. Becker | 67 62 64 62 |
| 1930 | Bill Tilden | W. Allison | 63 97 64 | 1996 | Richard Krajicek | M. Washington | 63 64 63 |
| 1931 | Sidney Wood | F. Shields | walkover | 1997 | Pete Sampras | C. Pioline | 64 62 64 |
| 1932 | Ellsworth Vines | H. Austin | 64 62 60 | 1998 | Pete Sampras | G. Ivanisevic | 67 76 64 36 62 |
| 1933 | Jack Crawford | E. Vines | 46 11-9 62 26 64 | 1999 | Pete Sampras | A. Agassi | 63 64 75 |
| 1934 | Fred Perry | J. Crawford | 63 60 75 | 2000 | Pete Sampras | P. Rafter | 67 76 64 62 |
| 1935 | Fred Perry | G. von Cramm | 62 64 64 | 2001 | Goran Ivanisevic | P. Rafter | 63 36 63 26 97 |
| 1936 | Fred Perry | G. von Cramm | 61 61 60 | 2002 | Lleyton Hewitt | D. Nalbandian | 61 63 62 |
| 1937 | Don Budge | G. von Cramm | 63 64 62 | 2003 | Roger Federer | M. Philippoussis | 76 62 76 |
| 1938 | Don Budge | H. Austin | 61 60 63 | 2004 | Roger Federer | A. Roddick | 46 75 76 64 |
| 1939 | Bobby Riggs | E. Cooke | 26 86 36 63 62 | 2005 | Roger Federer | A. Roddick | 62 76 64 |
| 1940-45 Not held World War II | | | | | | | |

## WOMEN

Officially called "The Lawn Tennis Championships" at the All England Club, Wimbledon. Challenge round system (defending champion qualified for following year's final) used from 1877-1921. Became an Open Championship in 1968, but closed to contract pros in 1972.

**Multiple winners:** Martina Navratilova (9); Helen Wills Moody (8); Dorothea Douglass Chambers and Steffi Graf (7); Blanche Bingley Hillyard, Billie Jean King and Suzanne Lenglen (6); Lottie Dod and Charlotte Cooper Sterry (5); Louise Brough (4); Maria Bueno, Maureen Connolly, Margaret Smith Court, Chris Evert Lloyd and Venus Williams (3); Evonne Goolagong Cawley, Althea Gibson, Kitty McKane Godfree, Dorothy Round, May Sutton, Maud Watson and Serena Williams (2).

| Year | Winner | Loser | Score |
|------|--------|-------|-------|
| 1884 | Maud Watson | L. Watson | 68 63 63 |
| 1885 | Maud Watson | B. Bingley | 61 75 |
| 1886 | Blanche Bingley | M. Watson | 63 63 |
| 1887 | Lottie Dod | B. Bingley | 62 60 |
| 1888 | Lottie Dod | B. Hillyard | 63 63 |
| 1889 | Blanche Hillyard | L. Rice | 46 86 64 |
| 1890 | Lena Rice | M. Jacks | 64 61 |
| 1891 | Lottie Dod | B. Hillyard | 62 61 |
| 1892 | Lottie Dod | B. Hillyard | 61 61 |
| 1893 | Lottie Dod | B. Hillyard | 68 61 64 |
| 1894 | Blanche Hillyard | E. Austin | 61 61 |
| 1895 | Charlotte Cooper | H. Jackson | 75 86 |
| 1896 | Charlotte Cooper | A. Pickering | 62 63 |
| 1897 | Blanche Hillyard | C. Cooper | 57 75 62 |
| 1898 | Charlotte Cooper | L. Martin | 64 64 |
| 1899 | Blanche Hillyard | C. Cooper | 62 63 |
| 1900 | Blanche Hillyard | C. Cooper | 46 64 64 |
| 1901 | Charlotte Sterry | B. Hillyard | 62 62 |
| 1902 | Muriel Robb | C. Sterry | 75 61 |
| 1903 | Dorothea Douglass | E. Thomson | 46 64 62 |
| 1904 | Dorothea Douglass | C. Sterry | 60 63 |
| 1905 | May Sutton | D. Douglass | 63 64 |
| 1906 | Dorothea Douglass | M. Sutton | 63 97 |
| 1907 | May Sutton | D. Chambers | 61 64 |
| 1908 | Charlotte Sterry | A. Morton | 64 64 |
| 1909 | Dora Boothby | A. Morton | 64 46 86 |
| 1910 | Dorothea Chambers | D. Boothby | 62 62 |
| 1911 | Dorothea Chambers | D. Boothby | 60 60 |
| 1912 | Ethel Larcombe | C. Sterry | 63 61 |
| 1913 | Dorothea Chambers | R. McNair | 60 64 |
| 1914 | Dorothea Chambers | E. Larcombe | 75 64 |
| 1915-18 | Not held World War I | | |
| 1919 | Suzanne Lenglen | D. Chambers | 10-8 46 97 |
| 1920 | Suzanne Lenglen | D. Chambers | 63 60 |
| 1921 | Suzanne Lenglen | E. Ryan | 62 60 |
| 1922 | Suzanne Lenglen | M. Mallory | 62 60 |
| 1923 | Suzanne Lenglen | K. McKane | 62 62 |
| 1924 | Kitty McKane | H. Wills | 46 64 64 |
| 1925 | Suzanne Lenglen | J. Fry | 62 60 |
| 1926 | Kitty Godfree | L. de Alvarez | 62 46 63 |
| 1927 | Helen Wills | L. de Alvarez | 62 64 |
| 1928 | Helen Wills | L. de Alvarez | 62 63 |
| 1929 | Helen Wills | H. Jacobs | 61 62 |
| 1930 | Helen Moody | E. Ryan | 62 62 |
| 1931 | Cilly Aussem | H. Krahwinkel | 62 75 |
| 1932 | Helen Moody | H. Jacobs | 63 61 |
| 1933 | Helen Moody | D. Round | 64 68 63 |
| 1934 | Dorothy Round | H. Jacobs | 62 57 63 |
| 1935 | Helen Moody | H. Jacobs | 63 36 75 |
| 1936 | Helen Jacobs | H.K. Sperling | 62 46 75 |
| 1937 | Dorothy Round | J. Jedrzejowska | 62 26 75 |
| 1938 | Helen Moody | H. Jacobs | 64 60 |
| 1939 | Alice Marble | K. Stammers | 62 60 |
| 1940-45 | Not held World War II | | |
| 1946 | Pauline Betz | L. Brough | 62 64 |
| 1947 | Margaret Osborne | D. Hart | 62 64 |
| 1948 | Louise Brough | D. Hart | 63 86 |
| 1949 | Louise Brough | M. du Pont | 10-8 16 10-8 |

| Year | Winner | Loser | Score |
|------|--------|-------|-------|
| 1950 | Louise Brough | M. du Pont | 61 36 61 |
| 1951 | Doris Hart | S. Fry | 61 60 |
| 1952 | Maureen Connolly | L. Brough | 75 63 |
| 1953 | Maureen Connolly | D. Hart | 86 75 |
| 1954 | Maureen Connolly | L. Brough | 62 75 |
| 1955 | Louise Brough | B. Fleitz | 75 86 |
| 1956 | Shirley Fry | A. Buxton | 63 61 |
| 1957 | Althea Gibson | D. Hard | 63 62 |
| 1958 | Althea Gibson | A. Mortimer | 86 62 |
| 1959 | Maria Bueno | D. Hard | 64 63 |
| 1960 | Maria Bueno | S. Reynolds | 86 60 |
| 1961 | Angela Mortimer | C. Truman | 46 64 75 |
| 1962 | Karen Susman | V. Sukova | 64 64 |
| 1963 | Margaret Smith | B.J. Moffitt | 63 64 |
| 1964 | Maria Bueno | M. Smith | 64 79 63 |
| 1965 | Margaret Smith | M. Bueno | 64 75 |
| 1966 | Billie Jean King | M. Bueno | 63 36 61 |
| 1967 | Billie Jean King | A. Jones | 63 64 |
| 1968 | Billie Jean King | J. Tegart | 97 75 |
| 1969 | Ann Jones | B.J. King | 36 63 62 |
| 1970 | Margaret Court | B.J. King | 14-12 11-9 |
| 1971 | Evonne Goolagong | M. Court | 64 61 |
| 1972 | Billie Jean King | E. Goolagong | 63 63 |
| 1973 | Billie Jean King | C. Evert | 60 75 |
| 1974 | Chris Evert | O. Morozova | 60 64 |
| 1975 | Billie Jean King | E. Cawley | 60 61 |
| 1976 | Chris Evert | E. Cawley | 63 46 86 |
| 1977 | Virginia Wade | B. Stove | 46 63 61 |
| 1978 | Martina Navratilova | C. Evert | 26 64 75 |
| 1979 | Martina Navratilova | C. Evert Lloyd | 64 64 |
| 1980 | Evonne Cawley | C. Evert Lloyd | 61 76 |
| 1981 | Chris Evert Lloyd | H. Mandlikova | 62 62 |
| 1982 | Martina Navratilova | C. Evert Lloyd | 61 36 62 |
| 1983 | Martina Navratilova | A. Jaeger | 60 63 |
| 1984 | Martina Navratilova | C. Evert Lloyd | 76 62 |
| 1985 | Martina Navratilova | C. Evert Lloyd | 46 63 62 |
| 1986 | Martina Navratilova | H. Mandlikova | 76 63 |
| 1987 | Martina Navratilova | S. Graf | 75 63 |
| 1988 | Steffi Graf | M. Navratilova | 57 62 61 |
| 1989 | Steffi Graf | M. Navratilova | 62 67 61 |
| 1990 | Martina Navratilova | Z. Garrison | 64 61 |
| 1991 | Steffi Graf | G. Sabatini | 64 36 86 |
| 1992 | Steffi Graf | M. Seles | 62 61 |
| 1993 | Steffi Graf | J. Novotna | 76 16 64 |
| 1994 | Conchita Martinez | M. Navratilova | 64 36 63 |
| 1995 | Steffi Graf | A.S. Vicario | 46 61 75 |
| 1996 | Steffi Graf | A.S. Vicario | 63 75 |
| 1997 | Martina Hingis | J. Novotna | 26 63 63 |
| 1998 | Jana Novotna | N. Tauziat | 64 76 |
| 1999 | Lindsay Davenport | S. Graf | 64 75 |
| 2000 | Venus Williams | L. Davenport | 63 76 |
| 2001 | Venus Williams | J. Henin | 61 36 60 |
| 2002 | Serena Williams | V. Williams | 76 63 |
| 2003 | Serena Williams | V. Williams | 46 64 62 |
| 2004 | Maria Sharapova | S. Williams | 61 64 |
| 2005 | Venus Williams | L. Davenport | 46 76 97 |

## U.S. Open
### MEN

Challenge round system (defending champion qualified for following year's final) used from 1884 to 1911. Known as the Patriotic Tournament in 1917 during World War I. Amateur and Open Championships held in 1968 and '69. Became an exclusively Open Championship in 1970. **Surface:** Decoturf II (acrylic cement).

**Multiple winners:** Bill Larned, Richard Sears and Bill Tilden (7); Jimmy Connors and Pete Sampras (5); John McEnroe and Robert Wrenn (4); Oliver Campbell, Ivan Lendl, Fred Perry and Malcolm Whitman (3); Andre Agassi, Don Budge, Stefan Edberg, Roy Emerson, Roger Federer, Neale Fraser, Pancho Gonzales, Bill Johnston, Jack Kramer, Rene Lacoste, Rod Laver, Maurice McLoughlin, Lindley Murray, John Newcombe, Frank Parker, Patrick Rafter, Bobby Riggs, Ken Rosewall, Frank Sedgman, Henry Slocum Jr., Tony Trabert, Ellsworth Vines and Dick Williams (2).

| Year | Winner | Loser | Score | Year | Winner | Loser | Score |
|---|---|---|---|---|---|---|---|
| 1881 | Richard Sears | W. Glyn | 60 63 62 | 1945 | Frank Parker | B. Talbert | 14-12 61 62 |
| 1882 | Richard Sears | C. Clark | 61 63 60 | 1946 | Jack Kramer | T. Brown, Jr. | 97 63 60 |
| 1883 | Richard Sears | J. Dwight | 62 60 97 | 1947 | Jack Kramer | F. Parker | 46 26 61 60 63 |
| 1884 | Richard Sears | H. Taylor | 60 16 60 62 | 1948 | Pancho Gonzales | E. Sturgess | 62 63 14-12 |
| 1885 | Richard Sears | G. Brinley | 63 46 60 63 | 1949 | Pancho Gonzales | F. Schroeder | 16-18 26 61 62 64 |
| 1886 | Richard Sears | R. Beeckman | 46 61 63 64 | 1950 | Arthur Larsen | H. Flam | 63 46 57 64 63 |
| 1887 | Richard Sears | H. Slocum Jr. | 61 63 62 | 1951 | Frank Sedgman | V. Seixas | 64 61 61 |
| 1888 | Henry Slocum Jr. | H. Taylor | 64 61 60 | 1952 | Frank Sedgman | G. Mulloy | 61 62 63 |
| 1889 | Henry Slocum Jr. | Q. Shaw | 63 61 46 62 | 1953 | Tony Trabert | V. Seixas | 63 62 63 |
| 1890 | Oliver Campbell | H. Slocum Jr. | 62 46 63 61 | 1954 | Vic Seixas | R. Hartwig | 36 62 64 64 |
| 1891 | Oliver Campbell | C. Hobart | 26 75 79 61 62 | 1955 | Tony Trabert | K. Rosewall | 97 63 63 |
| 1892 | Oliver Campbell | F. Hovey | 75 36 63 75 | 1956 | Ken Rosewall | L. Hoad | 46 62 63 63 |
| 1893 | Robert Wrenn | F. Hovey | 64 36 64 64 | 1957 | Mal Anderson | A. Cooper | 10-8 75 64 |
| 1894 | Robert Wrenn | M. Goodbody | 68 61 64 64 | 1958 | Ashley Cooper | M. Anderson | 62 36 46 10-8 86 |
| 1895 | Fred Hovey | R. Wrenn | 63 62 64 | 1959 | Neale Fraser | A. Olmedo | 63 57 62 64 |
| 1896 | Robert Wrenn | F. Hovey | 75 36 60 16 61 | 1960 | Neale Fraser | R. Laver | 64 64 97 |
| 1897 | Robert Wrenn | W. Eaves | 46 86 63 26 62 | 1961 | Roy Emerson | R. Laver | 75 63 62 |
| 1898 | Malcolm Whitman | D. Davis | 36 62 62 61 | 1962 | Rod Laver | R. Emerson | 62 64 57 64 |
| 1899 | Malcolm Whitman | P. Paret | 61 62 36 75 | 1963 | Rafael Osuna | F. Froehling | 75 64 62 |
| 1900 | Malcolm Whitman | B. Larned | 64 16 62 62 | 1964 | Roy Emerson | F. Stolle | 64 62 64 |
| 1901 | Bill Larned | B. Wright | 62 68 64 64 | 1965 | Manuel Santana | C. Drysdale | 62 79 75 61 |
| 1902 | Bill Larned | R. Doherty | 46 62 64 86 | 1966 | Fred Stolle | J. Newcombe | 46 12-10 63 64 |
| 1903 | Laurie Doherty | B. Larned | 60 63 10-8 | 1967 | John Newcombe | C. Graebner | 64 64 86 |
| 1904 | Holcombe Ward | B. Clothier | 10-8 64 97 | 1968 | Am-Arthur Ashe | B. Lutz | 46 63 8-10 60 64 |
| 1905 | Beals Wright | H. Ward | 62 61 11-9 |  | Op-Arthur Ashe | T. Okker | 14-12 57 63 36 63 |
| 1906 | Bill Clothier | B. Wright | 63 60 64 | 1969 | Am-Stan Smith | B. Lutz | 97 63 61 |
| 1907 | Bill Larned | R. LeRoy | 62 62 64 |  | Op-Rod Laver | T. Roche | 79 61 63 62 |
| 1908 | Bill Larned | B. Wright | 61 62 86 | 1970 | Ken Rosewall | T. Roche | 26 64 76 63 |
| 1909 | Bill Larned | B. Clothier | 61 62 57 16 61 | 1971 | Stan Smith | J. Kodes | 36 63 62 76 |
| 1910 | Bill Larned | T. Bundy | 61 57 60 68 61 | 1972 | Ilie Nastase | A. Ashe | 36 63 67 64 63 |
| 1911 | Bill Larned | M. McLoughlin | 64 64 62 | 1973 | John Newcombe | J. Kodes | 64 16 46 62 63 |
| 1912 | Maurice McLoughlin | W.F. Johnson | 36 26 62 64 62 | 1974 | Jimmy Connors | K. Rosewall | 61 60 61 |
| 1913 | Maurice McLoughlin | R. Williams | 64 57 63 61 | 1975 | Manuel Orantes | J. Connors | 64 63 63 |
| 1914 | Dick Williams | M. McLoughlin | 63 86 10-8 | 1976 | Jimmy Connors | B. Borg | 64 36 76 64 |
| 1915 | Bill Johnston | M. McLoughlin | 16 60 75 10-8 | 1977 | Guillermo Vilas | J. Connors | 26 63 76 60 |
| 1916 | Dick Williams | B. Johnston | 46 64 06 62 64 | 1978 | Jimmy Connors | B. Borg | 64 62 62 |
| 1917 | Lindley Murray | N. Niles | 57 86 63 63 | 1979 | John McEnroe | V. Gerulaitis | 75 63 63 |
| 1918 | Lindley Murray | B. Tilden | 63 61 75 | 1980 | John McEnroe | B. Borg | 76 61 67 57 64 |
| 1919 | Bill Johnston | B. Tilden | 64 64 63 | 1981 | John McEnroe | B. Borg | 46 62 64 63 |
| 1920 | Bill Tilden | B. Johnston | 61 16 75 57 63 | 1982 | Jimmy Connors | I. Lendl | 63 62 46 64 |
| 1921 | Bill Tilden | W. Johnson | 61 63 61 | 1983 | Jimmy Connors | I. Lendl | 63 67 75 60 |
| 1922 | Bill Tilden | B. Johnston | 46 36 62 63 64 | 1984 | John McEnroe | I. Lendl | 63 64 61 |
| 1923 | Bill Tilden | B. Johnston | 64 61 64 | 1985 | Ivan Lendl | J. McEnroe | 76 63 64 |
| 1924 | Bill Tilden | B. Johnston | 61 97 62 | 1986 | Ivan Lendl | M. Mecir | 64 62 60 |
| 1925 | Bill Tilden | B. Johnston | 46 11-9 63 46 63 | 1987 | Ivan Lendl | M. Wilander | 67 60 76 64 |
| 1926 | Rene Lacoste | J. Borotra | 64 60 64 | 1988 | Mats Wilander | I. Lendl | 64 46 63 57 64 |
| 1927 | Rene Lacoste | B. Tilden | 11-9 63 11-9 | 1989 | Boris Becker | I. Lendl | 76 16 63 76 |
| 1928 | Henri Cochet | F. Hunter | 46 64 36 75 63 | 1990 | Pete Sampras | A. Agassi | 64 63 62 |
| 1929 | Bill Tilden | F. Hunter | 36 63 46 62 64 | 1991 | Stefan Edberg | J. Courier | 62 64 60 |
| 1930 | John Doeg | F. Shields | 10-8 16 64 16-14 | 1992 | Stefan Edberg | P. Sampras | 36 64 76 62 |
| 1931 | Ellsworth Vines | G. Lott Jr. | 79 63 97 75 | 1993 | Pete Sampras | C. Pioline | 64 64 63 |
| 1932 | Ellsworth Vines | H. Cochet | 64 64 64 | 1994 | Andre Agassi | M. Stich | 61 76 75 |
| 1933 | Fred Perry | J. Crawford | 63 11-13 46 60 61 | 1995 | Pete Sampras | A. Agassi | 64 63 46 75 |
| 1934 | Fred Perry | W. Allison | 64 63 16 86 | 1996 | Pete Sampras | M. Chang | 61 64 76 |
| 1935 | Wilmer Allison | S. Wood | 62 62 63 | 1997 | Patrick Rafter | G. Rusedski | 63 62 46 75 |
| 1936 | Fred Perry | D. Budge | 26 62 86 16 10-8 | 1998 | Patrick Rafter | M. Philippoussis | 63 36 62 60 |
| 1937 | Don Budge | G. von Cramm | 61 79 61 36 61 | 1999 | Andre Agassi | T. Martin | 64 67 67 63 62 |
| 1938 | Don Budge | G. Mako | 63 68 62 61 | 2000 | Marat Safin | P. Sampras | 64 63 63 |
| 1939 | Bobby Riggs | S.W. van Horn | 64 62 64 | 2001 | Lleyton Hewitt | P. Sampras | 76 61 61 |
| 1940 | Don McNeill | B. Riggs | 46 68 63 63 75 | 2002 | Pete Sampras | A. Agassi | 63 64 57 64 |
| 1941 | Bobby Riggs | F. Kovacs | 57 61 63 63 | 2003 | Andy Roddick | J.C. Ferrero | 63 76 63 |
| 1942 | Fred Schroeder | F. Parker | 86 75 36 46 62 | 2004 | Roger Federer | L. Hewitt | 60 76 60 |
| 1943 | Joe Hunt | J. Kramer | 63 68 10-8 60 | 2005 | Roger Federer | A. Agassi | 63 26 76 61 |
| 1944 | Frank Parker | B. Talbert | 64 36 63 63 |  |  |  |  |

## WOMEN

Challenge round system used from 1887-1918. Five set final played from 1887 to 1901. Amateur and Open Championships held in 1968 and '69. Became an exclusively Open Championship in 1970.

**Multiple winners:** Molla Bjurstedt Mallory (8); Helen Wills Moody (7); Chris Evert Lloyd (6); Margaret Smith Court and Steffi Graf (5); Pauline Betz, Maria Bueno, Helen Jacobs, Billie Jean King, Alice Marble, Elisabeth Moore, Martina Navratilova and Hazel Hotchkiss Wightman (4); Juliette Atkinson, Mary Browne, Maureen Connolly and Margaret Osborne du Pont (3); Tracy Austin, Mabel Cahill, Sarah Palfrey Cooke, Althea Gibson, Darlene Hard, Doris Hart, Marion Jones, Monica Seles, Bertha Townsend, Serena Williams and Venus Williams (2).

| Year | Winner | Loser | Score | Year | Winner | Loser | Score |
|------|--------|-------|-------|------|--------|-------|-------|
| 1887 | Ellen Hansell | L. Knight | 61 60 | 1948 | Margaret du Pont | L. Brough | 46 64 15-13 |
| 1888 | Bertha Townsend | E. Hansell | 63 65 | 1949 | Margaret du Pont | D. Hart | 64 61 |
| 1889 | Bertha Townsend | L. Voorhes | 75 62 | 1950 | Margaret du Pont | D. Hart | 64 63 |
| 1890 | Ellen Roosevelt | B. Townsend | 62 62 | 1951 | Maureen Connolly | S. Fry | 63 16 64 |
| 1891 | Mabel Cahill | E. Roosevelt | 64 61 46 63 | 1952 | Maureen Connolly | D. Hart | 63 75 |
| 1892 | Mabel Cahill | E. Moore | 57 63 64 46 62 | 1953 | Maureen Connolly | D. Hart | 62 64 |
| 1893 | Aline Terry | A. Schultz | 61 63 | 1954 | Doris Hart | L. Brough | 68 61 86 |
| 1894 | Helen Hellwig | A. Terry | 75 36 60 36 63 | 1955 | Doris Hart | P. Ward | 64 62 |
| 1895 | Juliette Atkinson | H. Hellwig | 64 62 61 | 1956 | Shirley Fry | A. Gibson | 63 64 |
| 1896 | Elisabeth Moore | J. Atkinson | 64 46 62 62 | 1957 | Althea Gibson | L. Brough | 63 62 |
| 1897 | Juliette Atkinson | E. Moore | 63 63 46 36 63 | 1958 | Althea Gibson | D. Hard | 36 61 62 |
| 1898 | Juliette Atkinson | M. Jones | 63 57 64 26 75 | 1959 | Maria Bueno | C. Truman | 61 64 |
| 1899 | Marion Jones | M. Banks | 61 61 75 | 1960 | Darlene Hard | M. Bueno | 64 10-12 64 |
| 1900 | Myrtle McAteer | E. Parker | 62 62 60 | 1961 | Darlene Hard | A. Haydon | 63 64 |
| 1901 | Elisabeth Moore | M. McAteer | 64 36 75 26 62 | 1962 | Margaret Smith | D. Hard | 97 64 |
| 1902 | Marion Jones | E. Moore | 61 10(ret) | 1963 | Maria Bueno | M. Smith | 75 64 |
| 1903 | Elisabeth Moore | M. Jones | 75 86 | 1964 | Maria Bueno | C. Graebner | 61 60 |
| 1904 | May Sutton | E. Moore | 61 62 | 1965 | Margaret Smith | B.J. Moffitt | 86 75 |
| 1905 | Elisabeth Moore | H. Homans | 64 57 61 | 1966 | Maria Bueno | N. Richey | 63 61 |
| 1906 | Helen Homans | M. Barger-Wallach | 64 63 | 1967 | Billie Jean King | A. Jones | 11-9 64 |
| 1907 | Evelyn Sears | C. Neely | 63 62 | 1968 | Am-Margaret Court | M. Bueno | 62 62 |
| 1908 | Maud B. Wallach | Ev. Sears | 63 16 63 | | Op-Virginia Wade | B.J. King | 64 62 |
| 1909 | Hazel Hotchkiss | M. Barger-Wallach | 60 61 | 1969 | Am-Margaret Court | V. Wade | 46 63 60 |
| 1910 | Hazel Hotchkiss | L. Hammond | 64 62 | | Op-Margaret Court | N. Richey | 62 62 |
| 1911 | Hazel Hotchkiss | F. Sutton | 8-10 61 97 | 1970 | Margaret Court | R. Casals | 62 26 61 |
| 1912 | Mary Browne | E. Sears | 64 62 | 1971 | Billie Jean King | R. Casals | 64 76 |
| 1913 | Mary Browne | D. Green | 62 75 | 1972 | Billie Jean King | K. Melville | 63 75 |
| 1914 | Mary Browne | M. Wagner | 62 16 61 | 1973 | Margaret Court | E. Goolagong | 76 57 62 |
| 1915 | Molla Bjurstedt | H. Wightman | 46 62 60 | 1974 | Billie Jean King | E. Goolagong | 36 63 75 |
| 1916 | Molla Bjurstedt | L. Raymond | 60 61 | 1975 | Chris Evert | E. Cawley | 57 64 62 |
| 1917 | Molla Bjurstedt | M. Vanderhoef | 46 60 62 | 1976 | Chris Evert | E. Cawley | 63 60 |
| 1918 | Molla Bjurstedt | E. Goss | 64 63 | 1977 | Chris Evert | W. Turnbull | 76 62 |
| 1919 | Hazel Wightman | M. Zinderstein | 61 62 | 1978 | Chris Evert | P. Shriver | 75 64 |
| 1920 | Molla Mallory | M. Zinderstein | 63 61 | 1979 | Tracy Austin | C. Evert Lloyd | 64 63 |
| 1921 | Molla Mallory | M. Browne | 46 64 62 | 1980 | Chris Evert Lloyd | H. Mandlikova | 57 61 61 |
| 1922 | Molla Mallory | H. Wills | 63 61 | 1981 | Tracy Austin | M. Navratilova | 16 76 76 |
| 1923 | Helen Wills | M. Mallory | 62 61 | 1982 | Chris Evert Lloyd | H. Mandlikova | 63 61 |
| 1924 | Helen Wills | M. Mallory | 61 63 | 1983 | Martina Navratilova | C. Evert Lloyd | 61 63 |
| 1925 | Helen Wills | K. McKane | 36 60 62 | 1984 | Martina Navratilova | C. Evert Lloyd | 46 64 64 |
| 1926 | Molla Mallory | E. Ryan | 46 64 97 | 1985 | Hana Mandlikova | M. Navratilova | 76 16 76 |
| 1927 | Helen Wills | B. Nuthall | 61 64 | 1986 | Martina Navratilova | H. Sukova | 63 62 |
| 1928 | Helen Wills | H. Jacobs | 62 61 | 1987 | Martina Navratilova | S. Graf | 76 61 |
| 1929 | Helen Wills | P. Watson | 64 62 | 1988 | Steffi Graf | G. Sabatini | 63 36 61 |
| 1930 | Betty Nuthall | A. Harper | 61 64 | 1989 | Steffi Graf | M. Navratilova | 36 75 61 |
| 1931 | Helen Moody | E. Whittingstall | 64 61 | 1990 | Gabriela Sabatini | S. Graf | 62 76 |
| 1932 | Helen Jacobs | C. Babcock | 62 62 | 1991 | Monica Seles | M. Navratilova | 76 61 |
| 1933 | Helen Jacobs | H. Moody | 86 36 30(ret) | 1992 | Monica Seles | A.S. Vicario | 63 63 |
| 1934 | Helen Jacobs | S. Palfrey | 61 64 | 1993 | Steffi Graf | H. Sukova | 63 63 |
| 1935 | Helen Jacobs | S. Fabyan | 62 64 | 1994 | A. Sanchez Vicario | S. Graf | 16 76 64 |
| 1936 | Alice Marble | H. Jacobs | 46 63 62 | 1995 | Steffi Graf | M. Seles | 76 06 63 |
| 1937 | Anita Lizana | J. Jedrzejowska | 64 62 | 1996 | Steffi Graf | M. Seles | 75 64 |
| 1938 | Alice Marble | N. Wynne | 60 63 | 1997 | Martina Hingis | V. Williams | 60 64 |
| 1939 | Alice Marble | H. Jacobs | 60 8-10 64 | 1998 | Lindsay Davenport | M. Hingis | 63 75 |
| 1940 | Alice Marble | H. Jacobs | 62 63 | 1999 | Serena Williams | M. Hingis | 63 76 |
| 1941 | Sarah Cooke | P. Betz | 75 62 | 2000 | Venus Williams | L. Davenport | 64 75 |
| 1942 | Pauline Betz | L. Brough | 46 61 64 | 2001 | Venus Williams | S. Williams | 62 64 |
| 1943 | Pauline Betz | L. Brough | 63 57 63 | 2002 | Serena Williams | V. Williams | 64 63 |
| 1944 | Pauline Betz | M. Osborne | 63 86 | 2003 | J. Henin-Hardenne | K. Clijsters | 75 61 |
| 1945 | Sarah Cooke | P. Betz | 36 86 64 | 2004 | Svetlana Kuznetsova | E. Dementieva | 63 75 |
| 1946 | Pauline Betz | P. Canning | 11-9 63 | 2005 | Kim Clijsters | M. Pierce | 63 61 |
| 1947 | Louise Brough | M. Osborne | 86 46 61 | | | | |

# TENNIS

## Grand Slam Summary

Singles winners of the four Grand Slam tournaments—Australian, French, Wimbledon and United States—since the French was opened to all comers in 1925. Note that there were two Australian Opens in 1977 and none in 1986.

### MEN

**Three wins in one year:** Jack Crawford (1933); Fred Perry (1934); Tony Trabert (1955); Lew Hoad (1956); Ashley Cooper (1958); Roy Emerson (1964); Jimmy Connors (1974); Mats Wilander (1988); Roger Federer (2004).

**Two wins in one year:** Roy Emerson and Pete Sampras (4 times); Bjorn Borg (3 times); Rene Lacoste, Ivan Lendl, John Newcombe and Fred Perry (twice); Andre Agassi, Boris Becker, Don Budge, Henri Cochet, Jimmy Connors, Jim Courier, Roger Federer, Neale Fraser, Jack Kramer, John McEnroe, Alex Olmedo, Budge Patty, Bobby Riggs, Ken Rosewall, Dick Savitt, Frank Sedgman and Guillermo Vilas (once).

| Year | Australian | French | Wimbledon | U.S. | Year | Australian | French | Wimbledon | U.S. |
|---|---|---|---|---|---|---|---|---|---|
| 1925 | Anderson | Lacoste | Lacoste | Tilden | 1966 | Emerson | Roche | Santana | Stolle |
| 1926 | Hawkes | Cochet | Borotra | Lacoste | 1967 | Emerson | Emerson | Newcombe | Newcombe |
| 1927 | Patterson | Lacoste | Cochet | Lacoste | 1968 | Bowrey | Rosewall | Laver | Ashe |
| 1928 | Borotra | Cochet | Lacoste | Cochet | 1969 | **Laver** | **Laver** | **Laver** | **Laver** |
| 1929 | Gregory | Lacoste | Cochet | Tilden | 1970 | Ashe | Kodes | Newcombe | Rosewall |
| 1930 | Moon | Cochet | Tilden | Doeg | 1971 | Rosewall | Kodes | Newcombe | Smith |
| 1931 | Crawford | Borotra | Wood | Vines | 1972 | Rosewall | Gimeno | Smith | Nastase |
| 1932 | Crawford | Cochet | Vines | Vines | 1973 | Newcombe | Nastase | Kodes | Newcombe |
| 1933 | Crawford | Crawford | Crawford | Perry | 1974 | Connors | Borg | Connors | Connors |
| 1934 | Perry | von Cramm | Perry | Perry | 1975 | Newcombe | Borg | Ashe | Orantes |
| 1935 | Crawford | Perry | Perry | Allison | 1976 | Edmondson | Panatta | Borg | Connors |
| 1936 | Quist | von Cramm | Perry | Perry | 1977 | Tanner | Vilas | Borg | Vilas |
| 1937 | McGrath | Henkel | Budge | Budge | | & Gerulaitis | | | |
| 1938 | **Budge** | **Budge** | **Budge** | **Budge** | 1978 | Vilas | Borg | Borg | Connors |
| 1939 | Bromwich | McNeill | Riggs | Riggs | 1979 | Vilas | Borg | Borg | McEnroe |
| 1940 | Quist | — | — | McNeill | 1980 | Teacher | Borg | Borg | McEnroe |
| 1941 | — | — | — | Riggs | 1981 | Kriek | Borg | McEnroe | McEnroe |
| 1942 | — | — | — | Schroeder | 1982 | Kriek | Wilander | Connors | Connors |
| 1943 | — | — | — | Hunt | 1983 | Wilander | Noah | McEnroe | Connors |
| 1944 | — | — | — | Parker | 1984 | Wilander | Lendl | McEnroe | McEnroe |
| 1945 | — | — | — | Parker | 1985 | Edberg | Wilander | Becker | Lendl |
| 1946 | Bromwich | Bernard | Petra | Kramer | 1986 | — | Lendl | Becker | Lendl |
| 1947 | Pails | Asboth | Kramer | Kramer | 1987 | Edberg | Lendl | Cash | Lendl |
| 1948 | Quist | Parker | Falkenburg | Gonzales | 1988 | Wilander | Wilander | Edberg | Wilander |
| 1949 | Sedgman | Parker | Schroeder | Gonzales | 1989 | Lendl | Chang | Becker | Becker |
| 1950 | Sedgman | Patty | Patty | Larsen | 1990 | Lendl | Gomez | Edberg | Sampras |
| 1951 | Savitt | Drobny | Savitt | Sedgman | 1991 | Becker | Courier | Stich | Edberg |
| 1952 | McGregor | Drobny | Sedgman | Sedgman | 1992 | Courier | Courier | Agassi | Edberg |
| 1953 | Rosewall | Rosewall | Seixas | Trabert | 1993 | Courier | Bruguera | Sampras | Sampras |
| 1954 | Rose | Trabert | Drobny | Seixas | 1994 | Sampras | Bruguera | Sampras | Agassi |
| 1955 | Rosewall | Trabert | Trabert | Trabert | 1995 | Agassi | Muster | Sampras | Sampras |
| 1956 | Hoad | Hoad | Hoad | Rosewall | 1996 | Becker | Kafelnikov | Krajicek | Sampras |
| 1957 | Cooper | Davidson | Hoad | Anderson | 1997 | Sampras | Kuerten | Sampras | Rafter |
| 1958 | Cooper | Rose | Cooper | Cooper | 1998 | Korda | Moya | Sampras | Rafter |
| 1959 | Olmedo | Pietrangeli | Olmedo | Fraser | 1999 | Kafelnikov | Agassi | Sampras | Agassi |
| 1960 | Laver | Pietrangeli | Fraser | Fraser | 2000 | Agassi | Kuerten | Sampras | Safin |
| 1961 | Emerson | Santana | Laver | Emerson | 2001 | Agassi | Kuerten | Ivanisevic | Hewitt |
| 1962 | **Laver** | **Laver** | **Laver** | **Laver** | 2002 | Johansson | Costa | Hewitt | Sampras |
| 1963 | Emerson | Emerson | McKinley | Osuna | 2003 | Agassi | Ferrero | Federer | Roddick |
| 1964 | Emerson | Santana | Emerson | Emerson | 2004 | Federer | Gaudio | Federer | Federer |
| 1965 | Emerson | Stolle | Emerson | Santana | 2005 | Safin | Nadal | Federer | Federer |

## Men's, Women's & Mixed Doubles Grand Slam

The tennis Grand Slam has only been accomplished in doubles competition six times in the same calendar year. Here are the doubles teams to accomplish the feat. The two men and three women to win the singles Grand Slam are noted in the Grand Slam Summary tables.

### Men's Doubles

1951 . . . . . . . . . . . . . . . .Frank Sedgman, Australia
& Ken McGregor, Australia

### Mixed Doubles

1963 . . . . . . . . . . . . . . . .Ken Fletcher, Australia
& Margaret Smith, Australia

1967 . . . . . . . . . . .Owen Davidson and two partners*

*Davidson's partners: AUS–Lesley Turner; FR, WIM, U.S.–
Billie Jean King.

### Women's Doubles

1960 . . . . . . . . . .Maria Bueno, Brazil & two partners†

1984 . . . . . . . . . . . . . .Martina Navratilova, USA
& Pam Shriver, USA

1998 . . . .Martina Hingis, Switzerland & two partners#

†Bueno's partners: AUS–Christine Truman; FR, WIM,
U.S.–Darlene Hard.

#Hingis' partners: AUS–Mirjana Lucic; FR, WIM, U.S.–
Jana Novotna.

## WOMEN

**Three in one year:** Helen Wills Moody (1928 and '29); Margaret Smith Court (1962, '65, '69 and '73); Billie Jean King (1972); Martina Navratilova (1983 and '84); Steffi Graf (1989, '93, '95 and '96); Monica Seles (1991 and '92); Martina Hingis (1997) and Serena Williams (2002).

**Two in one year:** Chris Evert Lloyd (5 times); Helen Wills Moody and Martina Navratilova (3 times); Maria Bueno, Maureen Connolly, Margaret Smith Court, Althea Gibson, Billie Jean King and Venus Williams (twice); Cilly Aussem, Pauline Betz, Louise Brough, Jennifer Capriati, Evonne Goolagong Cawley, Margaret Osborne du Pont, Shirley Fry, Darlene Hard, Justine Henin-Hardenne, Suzanne Lenglen, Alice Marble, Arantxa Sanchez Vicario and Serena Williams (once).

| Year | Australian | French | Wimbledon | U.S. |
|---|---|---|---|---|
| 1925 | Akhurst | Lenglen | Lenglen | Wills |
| 1926 | Akhurst | Lenglen | Godfree | Mallory |
| 1927 | Boyd | Bouman | Wills | Wills |
| 1928 | Akhurst | Wills | Wills | Wills |
| 1929 | Akhurst | Wills | Wills | Wills |
| 1930 | Akhurst | Moody | Moody | Nuthall |
| 1931 | Buttsworth | Aussem | Aussem | Moody |
| 1932 | Buttsworth | Moody | Moody | Jacobs |
| 1933 | Hartigan | Scriven | Moody | Jacobs |
| 1934 | Hartigan | Scriven | Round | Jacobs |
| 1935 | Round | Sperling | Moody | Jacobs |
| 1936 | Hartigan | Sperling | Jacobs | Marble |
| 1937 | Wynne | Sperling | Round | Lizana |
| 1938 | Bundy | Mathieu | Moody | Marble |
| 1939 | Westacott | Mathieu | Marble | Marble |
| 1940 | Wynne | — | — | Marble |
| 1941 | — | — | — | Cooke |
| 1942 | — | — | — | Betz |
| 1943 | — | — | — | Betz |
| 1944 | — | — | — | Betz |
| 1945 | — | — | — | Cooke |
| 1946 | Bolton | Osborne | Betz | Betz |
| 1947 | Bolton | Todd | Osborne | Brough |
| 1948 | Bolton | Landry | Brough | du Pont |
| 1949 | Hart | du Pont | Brough | du Pont |
| 1950 | Brough | Hart | Brough | du Pont |
| 1951 | Bolton | Fry | Hart | Connolly |
| 1952 | Long | Hart | Connolly | Connolly |
| 1953 | **Connolly** | **Connolly** | **Connolly** | **Connolly** |
| 1954 | Long | Connolly | Connolly | Hart |
| 1955 | Penrose | Mortimer | Brough | Hart |
| 1956 | Carter | Gibson | Fry | Fry |
| 1957 | Fry | Bloomer | Gibson | Gibson |
| 1958 | Mortimer | Kormoczi | Gibson | Gibson |
| 1959 | Reitano | Truman | Bueno | Bueno |
| 1960 | Smith | Hard | Bueno | Hard |
| 1961 | Smith | Haydon | Mortimer | Hard |
| 1962 | Smith | Smith | Susman | Smith |
| 1963 | Smith | Turner | Smith | Bueno |
| 1964 | Smith | Smith | Bueno | Bueno |
| 1965 | Smith | Turner | Smith | Smith |

| Year | Australian | French | Wimbledon | U.S. |
|---|---|---|---|---|
| 1966 | Smith | Jones | King | Bueno |
| 1967 | Richey | Durr | King | King |
| 1968 | King | Richey | King | Wade |
| 1969 | Court | Court | Jones | Court |
| 1970 | **Court** | **Court** | **Court** | **Court** |
| 1971 | Court | Goolagong | Goolagong | King |
| 1972 | Wade | King | King | King |
| 1973 | Court | Court | King | Court |
| 1974 | Goolagong | Evert | Evert | King |
| 1975 | Goolagong | Evert | King | Evert |
| 1976 | Cawley | Barker | Evert | Evert |
| 1977 | Reid & Cawley | Jausovec | Wade | Evert |
| 1978 | O'Neil | Ruzici | Navratilova | Evert |
| 1979 | Jordan | Evert Lloyd | Navratilova | Austin |
| 1980 | Mandlikova | Evert Lloyd | Cawley | Evert Lloyd |
| 1981 | Navratilova | Mandlikova | Evert Lloyd | Austin |
| 1982 | Evert Lloyd | Navratilova | Navratilova | Evert Lloyd |
| 1983 | Navratilova | Evert Lloyd | Navratilova | Navratilova |
| 1984 | Evert Lloyd | Navratilova | Navratilova | Navratilova |
| 1985 | Navratilova | Evert Lloyd | Navratilova | Mandlikova |
| 1986 | — | Evert Lloyd | Navratilova | Navratilova |
| 1987 | Mandlikova | Graf | Navratilova | Navratilova |
| 1988 | **Graf** | **Graf** | **Graf** | **Graf** |
| 1989 | Graf | Vicario | Graf | Graf |
| 1990 | Graf | Seles | Navratilova | Sabatini |
| 1991 | Seles | Seles | Graf | Seles |
| 1992 | Seles | Seles | Graf | Seles |
| 1993 | Seles | Graf | Graf | Graf |
| 1994 | Graf | Vicario | Martinez | Vicario |
| 1995 | Pierce | Graf | Graf | Graf |
| 1996 | Seles | Graf | Graf | Graf |
| 1997 | Hingis | Majoli | Hingis | Hingis |
| 1998 | Hingis | Vicario | Novotna | Davenport |
| 1999 | Hingis | Graf | Davenport | S. Williams |
| 2000 | Davenport | Pierce | V. Williams | V. Williams |
| 2001 | Capriati | Capriati | V. Williams | V. Williams |
| 2002 | Capriati | S. Williams | S. Williams | S. Williams |
| 2003 | S. Williams | H-Hardenne | S. Williams | H-Hardenne |
| 2004 | H-Hardenne | Myskina | Sharapova | Kuznetsova |
| 2005 | S. Williams | H-Hardenne | V. Williams | Clijsters |

## Overall Leaders

All-Time Grand Slam titleists including all singles and doubles championships at the four major tournaments. Titles listed under each heading are singles, doubles and mixed doubles. Players active in 2005 are in **bold** type.

| | | **MEN** | | | | | | Total |
|---|---|---|---|---|---|---|---|---|
| | | Career | Australian | French | Wimbledon | U.S. | S-D-M | Titles |
| 1 | Roy Emerson . . . . . . . . . . . . . . . | 1959-71 | 6-3-0 | 2-6-0 | 2-3-0 | 2-4-0 | 12-16-0 | 28 |
| 2 | John Newcombe . . . . . . . . . . . . | 1965-76 | 2-5-0 | 0-3-0 | 3-6-0 | 2-3-1 | 7-17-1 | 25 |
| 3 | Frank Sedgman . . . . . . . . . . . . . | 1949-52 | 2-2-2 | 0-2-2 | 1-3-2 | 2-2-2 | 5-9-8 | 22 |
| | **Todd Woodbridge** . . . . . . . . . . | 1988— | 0-3-1 | 0-1-1 | 0-9-1 | 0-3-3 | 0-16-6 | 22 |
| 5 | Bill Tilden . . . . . . . . . . . . . . . . | 1913-30 | * | 0-0-1 | 3-1-0 | 7-5-4 | 10-6-5 | 21 |
| 6 | Rod Laver . . . . . . . . . . . . . . . . | 1959-71 | 3-4-0 | 2-1-1 | 4-1-2 | 2-0-0 | 11-6-3 | 20 |
| 7 | Jack Bromwich . . . . . . . . . . . . . | 1938-50 | 2-8-1 | 0-0-0 | 0-2-2 | 0-3-1 | 2-13-4 | 19 |
| | Neale Fraser . . . . . . . . . . . . . . | 1957-62 | 0-3-1 | 0-3-0 | 1-2-1 | 2-3-3 | 3-11-5 | 19 |
| 9 | Ken Rosewall . . . . . . . . . . . . . . | 1953-72 | 4-3-0 | 2-2-0 | 0-2-0 | 2-2-1 | 8-9-1 | 18 |
| | Jean Borotra . . . . . . . . . . . . . . | 1925-36 | 1-1-1 | 1-5-2 | 2-3-1 | 0-0-1 | 4-9-5 | 18 |
| | Fred Stolle . . . . . . . . . . . . . . . | 1962-69 | 0-3-1 | 1-2-0 | 0-2-3 | 1-3-2 | 2-10-6 | 18 |
| 12 | John McEnroe . . . . . . . . . . . . . | 1977-93 | 0-0-0 | 0-0-1 | 3-5-0 | 4-4-0 | 7-9-1 | 17 |
| | Jack Crawford . . . . . . . . . . . . . | 1929-35 | 4-4-3 | 1-1-1 | 1-1-1 | 0-0-0 | 6-6-5 | 17 |
| | Mark Woodforde . . . . . . . . . . . . | 1985-2000 | 0-2-2 | 0-1-1 | 0-6-1 | 0-3-1 | 0-12-5 | 17 |
| | Adrian Quist . . . . . . . . . . . . . . | 1936-50 | 3-10-0 | 0-1-0 | 0-2-0 | 0-1-0 | 3-14-0 | 17 |

## Grand Slam Overall Leaders (Cont.)
### WOMEN

| | | Career | Australian | French | Wimbledon | U.S. | S-D-M | Total Titles |
|---|---|---|---|---|---|---|---|---|
| 1 | Margaret Smith Court | 1960-75 | 11-8-2 | 5-4-4 | 3-2-5 | 5-5-8 | 24-19-19 | 62 |
| 2 | **Martina Navratilova** | 1974-95, 2000— | 3-8-1 | 2-7-2 | 9-7-4 | 4-9-2 | 18-31-9 | 58 |
| 3 | Billie Jean King | 1961-81 | 1-0-1 | 1-1-2 | 6-10-4 | 4-5-4 | 12-16-11 | 39 |
| 4 | Margaret du Pont | 1941-62 | * | 2-3-0 | 1-5-1 | 3-13-9 | 6-21-10 | 37 |
| 5 | Louise Brough | 1942-57 | 1-1-0 | 0-3-0 | 4-5-4 | 1-12-4 | 6-21-8 | 35 |
| | Doris Hart | 1948-55 | 1-1-2 | 2-5-3 | 1-4-5 | 2-4-5 | 6-14-15 | 35 |
| 7 | Helen Wills Moody | 1923-38 | * | 4-2-0 | 8-3-1 | 7-4-2 | 19-9-3 | 31 |
| 8 | Elizabeth Ryan | 1914-34 | * | 0-4-0 | 0-12-7 | 0-1-2 | 0-17-9 | 26 |
| 9 | Suzanne Lenglen | 1919-26 | * | 6-2-2 | 6-6-3 | 0-0-0 | 12-8-5 | 25 |
| 10 | Steffi Graf | 1982-99 | 4-0-0 | 6-0-0 | 7-1-0 | 5-0-0 | 22-1-0 | 23 |
| 11 | Pam Shriver | 1981-97 | 0-7-0 | 0-4-1 | 0-5-0 | 0-5-0 | 0-21-1 | 22 |
| 12 | Chris Evert | 1974-89 | 2-0-0 | 7-2-0 | 3-1-0 | 6-0-0 | 18-3-0 | 21 |
| | Darlene Hard | 1958-69 | * | 1-3-2 | 0-4-3 | 2-6-0 | 3-13-5 | 21 |
| 14 | Natasha Zvereva | 1989-2002 | 0-3-2 | 0-6-0 | 0-5-0 | 0-4-0 | 0-18-2 | 20 |
| | Nancye Wynne Bolton | 1935-52 | 6-10-4 | 0-0-0 | 0-0-0 | 0-0-0 | 6-10-4 | 20 |
| | Maria Bueno | 1958-68 | 0-1-0 | 0-1-1 | 3-5-0 | 4-5-0 | 7-12-1 | 20 |

## All-Time Grand Slam Singles Titles

Men and women with the most singles championships in the Australian, French, Wimbledon and U.S. championships, through 2005. Note that (*) indicates player never played in that particular Grand Slam event; and players active in singles play in 2005 are in **bold** type.

### Top 10 Men

| | | Aus | Fre | Wim | US | Total |
|---|---|---|---|---|---|---|
| 1 | Pete Sampras | 2 | 0 | 7 | 5 | 14 |
| 2 | Roy Emerson | 6 | 2 | 2 | 2 | 12 |
| 3 | Bjorn Borg | 0 | 6 | 5 | 0 | 11 |
| | Rod Laver | 3 | 2 | 4 | 2 | 11 |
| 5 | Bill Tilden | * | 0 | 3 | 7 | 10 |
| 6 | **Andre Agassi** | 4 | 1 | 1 | 2 | 8 |
| | Jimmy Connors | 1 | 0 | 2 | 5 | 8 |
| | Ivan Lendl | 2 | 3 | 0 | 3 | 8 |
| | Fred Perry | 1 | 1 | 3 | 3 | 8 |
| | Ken Rosewall | 4 | 2 | 0 | 2 | 8 |

### Top 10 Women

| | | Aus | Fre | Wim | US | Total |
|---|---|---|---|---|---|---|
| 1 | Margaret Smith Court | 11 | 5 | 3 | 5 | 24 |
| 2 | Steffi Graf | 4 | 6 | 7 | 5 | 22 |
| 3 | Helen Wills Moody | * | 4 | 8 | 7 | 19 |
| 4 | Chris Evert | 2 | 7 | 3 | 6 | 18 |
| | **Martina Navratilova** | 3 | 2 | 9 | 4 | 18 |
| 6 | Billie Jean King | 1 | 1 | 6 | 4 | 12 |
| | Suzanne Lenglen | * | 6 | 6 | 0 | 12 |
| 8 | Maureen Connolly | 1 | 2 | 3 | 3 | 9 |
| | Monica Seles | 4 | 3 | 0 | 2 | 9 |
| 10 | Molla Bjurstedt Mallory | * | * | 0 | 8 | 8 |

## Annual Number One Players

Unofficial world rankings for men and women determined by the *London Daily Telegraph* from 1914-72. Since then, official world rankings computed by men's and women's tours. Rankings included only amateur players from 1914 until the arrival of open (professional) tennis in 1968. No rankings were released during World Wars I and II.

### MEN

**Multiple winners:** Pete Sampras and Bill Tilden (6); Jimmy Connors (5); Henri Cochet, Rod Laver, Ivan Lendl and John McEnroe (4); John Newcombe and Fred Perry (3); Bjorn Borg, Don Budge, Ashley Cooper, Stefan Edberg, Roy Emerson, Neale Fraser, Lleyton Hewitt, Jack Kramer, Rene Lacoste, Ilie Nastase, Frank Sedgman and Tony Trabert (2).

| Year | | Year | | Year | | Year | |
|---|---|---|---|---|---|---|---|
| 1914 | Maurice McLoughlin | 1938 | Don Budge | 1964 | Roy Emerson | 1985 | Ivan Lendl |
| 1915-18 | No rankings | 1939 | Bobby Riggs | 1965 | Roy Emerson | 1986 | Ivan Lendl |
| 1919 | Gerald Patterson | 1940-45 | No rankings | 1966 | Manuel Santana | 1987 | Ivan Lendl |
| 1920 | Bill Tilden | 1946 | Jack Kramer | 1967 | John Newcombe | 1988 | Mats Wilander |
| 1921 | Bill Tilden | 1947 | Jack Kramer | 1968 | Rod Laver | 1989 | Ivan Lendl |
| 1922 | Bill Tilden | 1948 | Frank Parker | 1969 | Rod Laver | | |
| 1923 | Bill Tilden | 1949 | Pancho Gonzales | 1970 | John Newcombe | 1990 | Stefan Edberg |
| 1924 | Bill Tilden | 1950 | Budge Patty | 1971 | John Newcombe | 1991 | Stefan Edberg |
| 1925 | Bill Tilden | 1951 | Frank Sedgman | 1972 | Ilie Nastase | 1992 | Jim Courier |
| 1926 | Rene Lacoste | 1952 | Frank Sedgman | 1973 | Ilie Nastase | 1993 | Pete Sampras |
| 1927 | Rene Lacoste | 1953 | Tony Trabert | 1974 | Jimmy Connors | 1994 | Pete Sampras |
| 1928 | Henri Cochet | 1954 | Jaroslav Drobny | 1975 | Jimmy Connors | 1995 | Pete Sampras |
| 1929 | Henri Cochet | 1955 | Tony Trabert | 1976 | Jimmy Connors | 1996 | Pete Sampras |
| 1930 | Henri Cochet | 1956 | Lew Hoad | 1977 | Jimmy Connors | 1997 | Pete Sampras |
| 1931 | Henri Cochet | 1957 | Ashley Cooper | 1978 | Jimmy Connors | 1998 | Pete Sampras |
| 1932 | Ellsworth Vines | 1958 | Ashley Cooper | 1979 | Bjorn Borg | 1999 | Andre Agassi |
| 1933 | Jack Crawford | 1959 | Neale Fraser | | | | |
| 1934 | Fred Perry | 1960 | Neale Fraser | 1980 | Bjorn Borg | 2000 | Gustavo Kuerten |
| 1935 | Fred Perry | 1961 | Rod Laver | 1981 | John McEnroe | 2001 | Lleyton Hewitt |
| 1936 | Fred Perry | 1962 | Rod Laver | 1982 | John McEnroe | 2002 | Lleyton Hewitt |
| 1937 | Don Budge | 1963 | Rafael Osuna | 1983 | John McEnroe | 2003 | Andy Roddick |
| | | | | 1984 | John McEnroe | 2004 | Roger Federer |

## WOMEN

**Multiple winners:** Helen Wills Moody (9); Steffi Graf (8); Margaret Smith Court and Martina Navratilova (7); Chris Evert Lloyd and Billie Jean King (5); Margaret Osborne du Pont (4); Maureen Connolly, Lindsay Davenport, Martina Hingis and Monica Seles (3); Maria Bueno, Althea Gibson and Suzanne Lenglen (2).

| Year | | Year | | Year | | Year | |
|------|---|------|---|------|---|------|---|
| 1925 | Suzanne Lenglen | 1949 | Margaret du Pont | 1968 | Billie Jean King | 1987 | Steffi Graf |
| 1926 | Suzanne Lenglen | | | 1969 | Margaret Court | 1988 | Steffi Graf |
| 1927 | Helen Wills | 1950 | Margaret du Pont | | | 1989 | Steffi Graf |
| 1928 | Helen Wills | 1951 | Doris Hart | 1970 | Margaret Court | | |
| 1929 | Helen Wills Moody | 1952 | Maureen Connolly | 1971 | Evonne Goolagong | 1990 | Steffi Graf |
| | | 1953 | Maureen Connolly | 1972 | Billie Jean King | 1991 | Monica Seles |
| 1930 | Helen Wills Moody | 1954 | Maureen Connolly | 1973 | Margaret Court | 1992 | Monica Seles |
| 1931 | Helen Wills Moody | 1955 | Louise Brough | 1974 | Billie Jean King | 1993 | Steffi Graf |
| 1932 | Helen Wills Moody | 1956 | Shirley Fry | 1975 | Chris Evert | 1994 | Steffi Graf |
| 1933 | Helen Wills Moody | 1957 | Althea Gibson | 1976 | Chris Evert | 1995 | Steffi Graf |
| 1934 | Dorothy Round | 1958 | Althea Gibson | 1977 | Chris Evert | | & Monica Seles* |
| 1935 | Helen Wills Moody | 1959 | Maria Bueno | 1978 | Martina Navratilova | | |
| 1936 | Helen Jacobs | | | 1979 | Martina Navratilova | 1996 | Steffi Graf |
| 1937 | Anita Lizana | 1960 | Maria Bueno | | | 1997 | Martina Hingis |
| 1938 | Helen Wills Moody | 1961 | Angela Mortimer | 1980 | Chris Evert Lloyd | 1998 | Lindsay Davenport |
| 1939 | Alice Marble | 1962 | Margaret Smith | 1981 | Chris Evert Lloyd | 1999 | Martina Hingis |
| | | 1963 | Margaret Smith | 1982 | Martina Navratilova | | |
| 1940-45 | No rankings | 1964 | Margaret Smith | 1983 | Martina Navratilova | 2000 | Martina Hingis |
| 1946 | Pauline Betz | 1965 | Margaret Smith | 1984 | Martina Navratilova | 2001 | Lindsay Davenport |
| 1947 | Margaret Osborne | 1966 | Billie Jean King | 1985 | Martina Navratilova | 2002 | Serena Williams |
| 1948 | Margaret du Pont | 1967 | Billie Jean King | 1986 | Martina Navratilova | 2003 | Justine Henin-Hardenne |
| | | | | | | 2004 | Lindsay Davenport |

*Upon her return to the WTA Tour on Aug. 15, 1995, Seles retained her #1 ranking and was co-ranked at #1 through her first six tournaments (August '95–May '96). Seles was on leave since April 1993 when she was stabbed by a fan during a match.

## Annual Top 10 World Rankings (since 1968)

Year by year Top 10 world computer rankings for men (ATP Tour) and women (WTA Tour) since the arrival of open tennis in 1968. Rankings from 1968-72 made by Lance Tingay of the *London Daily Telegraph*. Since 1973 the WTA Tour and ATP tour had compiled its own computer rankings. Since 2000, the men's rankings reflect the final standings of the ATP Champions Race.

## MEN

| | 1968 | | 1971 | | 1974 | | 1977 | | 1980 |
|---|------|---|------|---|------|---|------|---|------|
| 1 | Rod Laver | 1 | John Newcombe | 1 | Jimmy Connors | 1 | Jimmy Connors | 1 | Bjorn Borg |
| 2 | Arthur Ashe | 2 | Stan Smith | 2 | John Newcombe | 2 | Guillermo Vilas | 2 | John McEnroe |
| 3 | Ken Rosewall | 3 | Rod Laver | 3 | Bjorn Borg | 3 | Bjorn Borg | 3 | Jimmy Connors |
| 4 | Tom Okker | 4 | Ken Rosewall | 4 | Rod Laver | 4 | Vitas Gerulaitis | 4 | Gene Mayer |
| 5 | Tony Roche | 5 | Jan Kodes | 5 | Guillermo Vilas | 5 | Brian Gottfried | 5 | Guillermo Vilas |
| 6 | John Newcombe | 6 | Arthur Ashe | 6 | Tom Okker | 6 | Eddie Dibbs | 6 | Ivan Lendl |
| 7 | Clark Graebner | 7 | Tom Okker | 7 | Arthur Ashe | 7 | Manuel Orantes | 7 | Harold Solomon |
| 8 | Dennis Ralston | 8 | Marty Riessen | 8 | Ken Rosewall | 8 | Raul Ramirez | 8 | Jose-Luis Clerc |
| 9 | Cliff Drysdale | 9 | Cliff Drysdale | 9 | Stan Smith | 9 | Ilie Nastase | 9 | Vitas Gerulaitis |
| 10 | Pancho Gonzales | 10 | Ilie Nastase | 10 | Ilie Nastase | 10 | Dick Stockton | 10 | Eliot Teltscher |

| | 1969 | | 1972 | | 1975 | | 1978 | | 1981 |
|---|------|---|------|---|------|---|------|---|------|
| 1 | Rod Laver | 1 | Stan Smith | 1 | Jimmy Connors | 1 | Jimmy Connors | 1 | John McEnroe |
| 2 | Tony Roche | 2 | Ken Rosewall | 2 | Guillermo Vilas | 2 | Bjorn Borg | 2 | Ivan Lendl |
| 3 | John Newcombe | 3 | Ilie Nastase | 3 | Bjorn Borg | 3 | Guillermo Vilas | 3 | Jimmy Connors |
| 4 | Tom Okker | 4 | Rod Laver | 4 | Arthur Ashe | 4 | John McEnroe | 4 | Bjorn Borg |
| 5 | Ken Rosewall | 5 | Arthur Ashe | 5 | Manuel Orantes | 5 | Vitas Gerulaitis | 5 | Jose-Luis Clerc |
| 6 | Arthur Ashe | 6 | John Newcombe | 6 | Ken Rosewall | 6 | Eddie Dibbs | 6 | Guillermo Vilas |
| 7 | Cliff Drysdale | 7 | Bob Lutz | 7 | Ilie Nastase | 7 | Brian Gottfried | 7 | Gene Mayer |
| 8 | Pancho Gonzales | 8 | Tom Okker | 8 | John Alexander | 8 | Raul Ramirez | 8 | Eliot Teltscher |
| 9 | Andres Gimeno | 9 | Marty Riessen | 9 | Roscoe Tanner | 9 | Harold Solomon | 9 | Vitas Gerulaitis |
| 10 | Fred Stolle | 10 | Andres Gimeno | 10 | Rod Laver | 10 | Corrado Barazzutti | 10 | Peter McNamara |

| | 1970 | | 1973 | | 1976 | | 1979 | | 1982 |
|---|------|---|------|---|------|---|------|---|------|
| 1 | John Newcombe | 1 | Ilie Nastase | 1 | Jimmy Connors | 1 | Bjorn Borg | 1 | John McEnroe |
| 2 | Ken Rosewall | 2 | John Newcombe | 2 | Bjorn Borg | 2 | Jimmy Connors | 2 | Jimmy Connors |
| 3 | Tony Roche | 3 | Jimmy Connors | 3 | Ilie Nastase | 3 | John McEnroe | 3 | Ivan Lendl |
| 4 | Rod Laver | 4 | Tom Okker | 4 | Manuel Orantes | 4 | Vitas Gerulaitis | 4 | Guillermo Vilas |
| 5 | Arthur Ashe | 5 | Stan Smith | 5 | Raul Ramirez | 5 | Roscoe Tanner | 5 | Vitas Gerulaitis |
| 6 | Ilie Nastase | 6 | Ken Rosewall | 6 | Guillermo Vilas | 6 | Guillermo Vilas | 6 | Jose-Luis Clerc |
| 7 | Tom Okker | 7 | Manuel Orantes | 7 | Adriano Panatta | 7 | Arthur Ashe | 7 | Mats Wilander |
| 8 | Roger Taylor | 8 | Rod Laver | 8 | Harold Solomon | 8 | Harold Solomon | 8 | Gene Mayer |
| 9 | Jan Kodes | 9 | Jan Kodes | 9 | Eddie Dibbs | 9 | Jose Higueras | 9 | Yannick Noah |
| 10 | Cliff Richey | 10 | Arthur Ashe | 10 | Brian Gottfried | 10 | Eddie Dibbs | 10 | Peter McNamara |

# Annual Top 10 World Rankings (since 1968) (Cont.)

## MEN

### 1983
1 John McEnroe
2 Ivan Lendl
3 Jimmy Connors
4 Mats Wilander
5 Yannick Noah
6 Jimmy Arias
7 Jose Higueras
8 Jose-Luis Clerc
9 Kevin Curren
10 Gene Mayer

### 1984
1 John McEnroe
2 Jimmy Connors
3 Ivan Lendl
4 Mats Wilander
5 Andres Gomez
6 Anders Jarryd
7 Henrik Sundstrom
8 Pat Cash
9 Eliot Teltscher
10 Yannick Noah

### 1985
1 Ivan Lendl
2 John McEnroe
3 Mats Wilander
4 Jimmy Connors
5 Stefan Edberg
6 Boris Becker
7 Yannick Noah
8 Anders Jarryd
9 Miloslav Mecir
10 Kevin Curren

### 1986
1 Ivan Lendl
2 Boris Becker
3 Mats Wilander
4 Yannick Noah
5 Stefan Edberg
6 Henri Leconte
7 Joakim Nystrom
8 Jimmy Connors
9 Miloslav Mecir
10 Andres Gomez

### 1987
1 Ivan Lendl
2 Stefan Edberg
3 Mats Wilander
4 Jimmy Connors
5 Boris Becker
6 Miloslav Mecir
7 Pat Cash
8 Yannick Noah
9 Tim Mayotte
10 John McEnroe

### 1988
1 Mats Wilander
2 Ivan Lendl
3 Andre Agassi
4 Boris Becker
5 Stefan Edberg
6 Kent Carlsson
7 Jimmy Connors
8 Jakob Hlasek
9 Henri Leconte
10 Tim Mayotte

### 1989
1 Ivan Lendl
2 Boris Becker
3 Stefan Edberg
4 John McEnroe
5 Michael Chang
6 Brad Gilbert
7 Andre Agassi
8 Aaron Krickstein
9 Alberto Mancini
10 Jay Berger

### 1990
1 Stefan Edberg
2 Boris Becker
3 Ivan Lendl
4 Andre Agassi
5 Pete Sampras
6 Andres Gomez
7 Thomas Muster
8 Emilio Sanchez
9 Goran Ivanisevic
10 Brad Gilbert

### 1991
1 Stefan Edberg
2 Jim Courier
3 Boris Becker
4 Michael Stich
5 Ivan Lendl
6 Pete Sampras
7 Guy Forget
8 Karel Novacek
9 Petr Korda
10 Andre Agassi

### 1992
1 Jim Courier
2 Stefan Edberg
3 Pete Sampras
4 Goran Ivanisevic
5 Boris Becker
6 Michael Chang
7 Petr Korda
8 Ivan Lendl
9 Andre Agassi
10 Richard Krajicek

### 1993
1 Pete Sampras
2 Michael Stich
3 Jim Courier
4 Sergi Bruguera
5 Stefan Edberg
6 Andrei Medvedev
7 Goran Ivanisevic
8 Michael Chang
9 Thomas Muster
10 Cedric Pioline

### 1994
1 Pete Sampras
2 Andre Agassi
3 Boris Becker
4 Sergi Bruguera
5 Goran Ivanisevic
6 Michael Chang
7 Stefan Edberg
8 Alberto Berasategui
9 Michael Stich
10 Todd Martin

### 1995
1 Pete Sampras
2 Andre Agassi
3 Thomas Muster
4 Boris Becker
5 Michael Chang
6 Yevgeny Kafelnikov
7 Thomas Enqvist
8 Jim Courier
9 Wayne Ferreira
10 Goran Ivanisevic

### 1996
1 Pete Sampras
2 Michael Chang
3 Yevgeny Kafelnikov
4 Goran Ivanisevic
5 Thomas Muster
6 Boris Becker
7 Richard Krajicek
8 Andre Agassi
9 Thomas Enqvist
10 Wayne Ferreira

### 1997
1 Pete Sampras
2 Patrick Rafter
3 Michael Chang
4 Jonas Bjorkman
5 Yevgeny Kafelnikov
6 Greg Rusedski
7 Carlos Moya
8 Sergi Bruguera
9 Thomas Muster
10 Marcelo Rios

### 1998
1 Pete Sampras
2 Marcelo Rios
3 Alex Corretja
4 Patrick Rafter
5 Carlos Moya
6 Andre Agassi
7 Tim Henman
8 Karol Kucera
9 Greg Rusedski
10 Richard Krajicek

### 1999
1 Andre Agassi
2 Yevgeny Kafelnikov
3 Pete Sampras
4 Thomas Enqvist
5 Gustavo Kuerten
6 Nicolas Kiefer
7 Todd Martin
8 Nicolas Lapentti
9 Marcelo Rios
10 Richard Krajicek

### 2000
1 Gustavo Kuerten
2 Marat Safin
3 Pete Sampras
4 Magnus Norman
5 Yevgeny Kafelnikov
6 Andre Agassi
7 Lleyton Hewitt
8 Alex Corretja
9 Thomas Enqvist
10 Tim Henman

### 2001
1 Lleyton Hewitt
2 Gustavo Kuerten
3 Andre Agassi
4 Yevgeny Kafelnikov
5 Juan Carlos Ferrero
6 Sebastien Grosjean
7 Patrick Rafter
8 Tommy Haas
9 Tim Henman
10 Pete Sampras

### 2002
1 Lleyton Hewitt
2 Andre Agassi
3 Marat Safin
4 Juan Carlos Ferrero
5 Carlos Moya
6 Roger Federer
7 Jiri Novak
8 Tim Henman
9 Albert Costa
10 Andy Roddick

### 2003
1 Andy Roddick
2 Roger Federer
3 Juan Carlos Ferrero
4 Andre Agassi
5 Guillermo Coria
6 Rainer Schuettler
7 Carlos Moya
8 David Nalbandian
9 Mark Philippoussis
10 Sebastien Grosjean

### 2004
1 Roger Federer
2 Andy Roddick
3 Lleyton Hewitt
4 Marat Safin
5 Carlos Moya
6 Tim Henman
7 Guillermo Coria
8 Andre Agassi
9 David Nalbandian
10 Gaston Gaudio

## WOMEN

### 1968
1 Billie Jean King
2 Virginia Wade
3 Nancy Richey
4 Maria Bueno
5 Margaret Court
6 Ann Jones
7 Judy Tegart
8 Annette du Plooy
9 Leslie Bowrey
10 Rosie Casals

### 1969
1 Margaret Court
2 Ann Jones
3 Billie Jean King
4 Nancy Richey
5 Julie Heldman
6 Rosie Casals
7 Kerry Melville
8 Peaches Bartkowicz
9 Virginia Wade
10 Leslie Bowrey

### 1970
1 Margaret Court
2 Billie Jean King
3 Rosie Casals
4 Virginia Wade
5 Helga Niessen
6 Kerry Melville
7 Julie Heldman
8 Karen Krantzcke
9 Francoise Durr
10 Nancy R. Gunter

### 1971
1 Evonne Goolagong
2 Billie Jean King
3 Margaret Court
4 Rosie Casals
5 Kerry Melville
6 Virginia Wade
7 Judy Tegart
8 Francoise Durr
9 Helga N. Masthoff
10 Chris Evert

### 1972
1 Billie Jean King
2 Evonne Goolagong
3 Chris Evert
4 Margaret Court
5 Kerry Melville
6 Virginia Wade
7 Rosie Casals
8 Nancy R. Gunter
9 Francoise Durr
10 Linda Tuero

### 1973
1 Margaret S. Court
2 Billie Jean King
3 Evonne G. Cawley
4 Chris Evert
5 Rosie Casals
6 Virginia Wade
7 Kerry Reid
8 Nancy Richey
9 Julie Heldman
10 Helga Masthoff

### 1974
1 Billie Jean King
2 Evonne G. Cawley
3 Chris Evert
4 Virginia Wade
5 Julie Heldman
6 Rosie Casals
7 Kerry Reid
8 Olga Morozova
9 Lesley Hunt
10 Francoise Durr

### 1975
1 Chris Evert
2 Billie Jean King
3 Evonne G. Cawley
4 Martina Navratilova
5 Virginia Wade
6 Margaret S. Court
7 Olga Morozova
8 Nancy Richey
9 Francoise Durr
10 Rosie Casals

### 1976
1 Chris Evert
2 Evonne G. Cawley
3 Virginia Wade
4 Martina Navratilova
5 Sue Barker
6 Betty Stove
7 Dianne Balestrat
8 Mima Jausovec
9 Rosie Casals
10 Francoise Durr

### 1977
1 Chris Evert
2 Billie Jean King
3 Martina Navratilova
4 Virginia Wade
5 Sue Barker
6 Rosie Casals
7 Betty Stove
8 Dianne Balestrat
9 Wendy Turnbull
10 Kerry Reid

### 1978
1 Martina Navratilova
2 Chris Evert Lloyd
3 Evonne G. Cawley
4 Virginia Wade
5 Billie Jean King
6 Tracy Austin
7 Wendy Turnbull
8 Kerry Reid
9 Betty Stove
10 Dianne Balestrat

### 1979
1 Martina Navratilova
2 Chris Evert Lloyd
3 Tracy Austin
4 Evonne G. Cawley
5 Billie Jean King
6 Dianne Balestrat
7 Wendy Turnbull
8 Virginia Wade
9 Kerry Reid
10 Sue Barker

### 1980
1 Chris Evert Lloyd
2 Tracy Austin
3 Martina Navratilova
4 Hana Mandlikova
5 Evonne G. Cawley
6 Billie Jean King
7 Andrea Jaeger
8 Wendy Turnbull
9 Pam Shriver
10 Greer Stevens

### 1981
1 Chris Evert Lloyd
2 Tracy Austin
3 Martina Navratilova
4 Andrea Jaeger
5 Hana Mandlikova
6 Sylvia Hanika
7 Pam Shriver
8 Wendy Turnbull
9 Bettina Bunge
10 Barbara Potter

### 1982
1 Martina Navratilova
2 Chris Evert Lloyd
3 Andrea Jaeger
4 Tracy Austin
5 Wendy Turnbull
6 Pam Shriver
7 Hana Mandlikova
8 Barbara Potter
9 Bettina Bunge
10 Sylvia Hanika

### 1983
1 Martina Navratilova
2 Chris Evert Lloyd
3 Andrea Jaeger
4 Pam Shriver
5 Sylvia Hanika
6 Jo Durie
7 Bettina Bunge
8 Wendy Turnbull
9 Tracy Austin
10 Zina Garrison

### 1984
1 Martina Navratilova
2 Chris Evert Lloyd
3 Hana Mandlikova
4 Pam Shriver
5 Wendy Turnbull
6 Manuela Maleeva
7 Helena Sukova
8 Claudia Kohde-Kilsch
9 Zina Garrison
10 Kathy Jordan

### 1985
1 Martina Navratilova
2 Chris Evert Lloyd
3 Hana Mandlikova
4 Pam Shriver
5 Claudia Kohde-Kilsch
6 Steffi Graf
7 Manuela Maleeva
8 Zina Garrison
9 Helena Sukova
10 Bonnie Gadusek

### 1986
1 Martina Navratilova
2 Chris Evert Lloyd
3 Steffi Graf
4 Hana Mandlikova
5 Helena Sukova
6 Pam Shriver
7 Claudia Kohde-Kilsch
8 M. Maleeva-Fragniere
9 Zina Garrison
10 Gabriela Sabatini

### 1987
1 Steffi Graf
2 Martina Navratilova
3 Chris Evert
4 Pam Shriver
5 Hana Mandlikova
6 Gabriela Sabatini
7 Helena Sukova
8 M. Maleeva-Fragniere
9 Zina Garrison
10 Claudia Kohde-Kilsch

### 1988
1 Steffi Graf
2 Martina Navratilova
3 Chris Evert
4 Gabriela Sabatini
5 Pam Shriver
6 M. Maleeva-Fragniere
7 Natalia Zvereva
8 Helena Sukova
9 Zina Garrison
10 Barbara Potter

### 1989
1 Steffi Graf
2 Martina Navratilova
3 Gabriela Sabatini
4 Z. Garrison-Jackson
5 A. Sanchez Vicario
6 Monica Seles
7 Conchita Martinez
8 Helena Sukova
9 M. Maleeva-Fragniere
10 Chris Evert

### 1990
1 Steffi Graf
2 Monica Seles
3 Martina Navratilova
4 Mary Joe Fernandez
5 Gabriela Sabatini
6 Katerina Maleeva
7 A. Sanchez Vicario
8 Jennifer Capriati
9 M. Maleeva-Fragniere
10 Z. Garrison-Jackson

### 1991
1 Monica Seles
2 Steffi Graf
3 Gabriela Sabatini
4 Martina Navratilova
5 A. Sanchez Vicario
6 Jennifer Capriati
7 Jana Novotna
8 Mary Joe Fernandez
9 Conchita Martinez
10 M. Maleeva-Fragniere

### 1992
1 Monica Seles
2 Steffi Graf
3 Gabriela Sabatini
4 A. Sanchez Vicario
5 Martina Navratilova
6 Mary Joe Fernandez
7 Jennifer Capriati
8 Conchita Martinez
9 M. Maleeva-Fragniere
10 Jana Novotna

### 1993
1 Steffi Graf
2 A. Sanchez Vicario
3 Martina Navratilova
4 Conchita Martinez
5 Gabriela Sabatini
6 Jana Novotna
7 Mary Joe Fernandez
8 Monica Seles
9 Jennifer Capriati
10 Anke Huber

### 1994
1 Steffi Graf
2 A. Sanchez Vicario
3 Conchita Martinez
4 Jana Novotna
5 Mary Pierce
6 Lindsay Davenport
7 Gabriela Sabatini
8 Martina Navratilova
9 Kimiko Date
10 Natasha Zvereva

### 1995
1 Steffi Graf
  Monica Seles*
3 Conchita Martinez
4 A. Sanchez Vicario
5 Kimiko Date
6 Mary Pierce
7 Magdalena Maleeva
8 Gabriela Sabatini
9 Mary Joe Fernandez
10 Iva Majoli
  Anke Huber

### 1996
1 Steffi Graf
2 Monica Seles†
  A. Sanchez Vicario
3 Jana Novotna
4 Martina Hingis
5 Conchita Martinez
6 Anke Huber
7 Iva Majoli
8 Kimiko Date
9 Lindsay Davenport
10 Barbara Paulus

## Annual Top 10 World Rankings (since 1968) (Cont.)

### WOMEN

| **1997** | **1999** | **2001** | **2003** |
|---|---|---|---|
| 1 Martina Hingis | 1 Martina Hingis | 1 Lindsay Davenport | 1 Justine Henin-Hardenne |
| 2 Jana Novotna | 2 Lindsay Davenport | 2 Jennifer Capriati | 2 Kim Clijsters |
| 3 Lindsay Davenport | 3 Venus Williams | 3 Venus Williams | 3 Serena Williams |
| 4 Amanda Coetzer | 4 Serena Williams | 4 Martina Hingis | 4 Amelie Mauresmo |
| 5 Monica Seles | 5 Mary Pierce | 5 Kim Clijsters | 5 Lindsay Davenport |
| 6 Iva Majoli | 6 Monica Seles | 6 Serena Williams | 6 Jennifer Capriati |
| 7 Mary Pierce | 7 Nathalie Tauziat | 7 Justine Henin | 7 Anastasia Myskina |
| 8 Irina Spirlea | 8 Barbara Schett. | 8 Jelena Dokic | 8 Elena Dementieva |
| 9 A. Sanchez Vicario | 9 Julie Halard-Decugis | 9 Amelie Mauresmo | 9 Chanda Rubin |
| 10 Mary Joe Fernandez | 10 Amelie Mauresmo | 10 Monica Seles | 10 Ai Sugiyama |

| **1998** | **2000** | **2002** | **2004** |
|---|---|---|---|
| 1 Lindsay Davenport | 1 Martina Hingis | 1 Serena Williams | 1 Lindsay Davenport |
| 2 Martina Hingis | 2 Lindsay Davenport | 2 Venus Williams | 2 Amelie Mauresmo |
| 3 Jana Novotna | 3 Venus Williams | 3 Jennifer Capriati | 3 Anastasia Myskina |
| 4 A. Sanchez Vicario | 4 Monica Seles | 4 Kim Clijsters | 4 Maria Sharapova |
| 5 Venus Williams | 5 Conchita Martinez | 5 Justine Henin-Hardenne | 5 Svetlana Kuznetsova |
| 6 Monica Seles | 6 Serena Williams | 6 Amelie Mauresmo | 6 Elena Dementieva |
| 7 Mary Pierce | 7 Mary Pierce | 7 Monica Seles | 7 Serena Williams |
| 8 Conchita Martinez | 8 Anna Kournikova | 8 Daniela Hantuchova | 8 Justine Henin-Hardenne |
| 9 Steffi Graf | 9 A. Sanchez Vicario | 9 Jelena Dokic | 9 Venus Williams |
| 10 Nathalie Tauziat | 10 Nathalie Tauziat | 10 Martina Hingis | 10 Jennifer Capriati |

*Returning to the WTA Tour on Aug. 15, 1995, Seles was co-ranked #1 for her first six tournaments. Seles had been absent from the Tour since April 1993 when she was stabbed by a fan during a match. She was ranked #1 at the time of the stabbing.
†Seles' ranking was revised in May 1996. The revision stipulated that her new modified ranking would be calculated using a divisor of the actual number of tournaments she had played (13), and she would be co-ranked with the player whose average is immediately below her average (Sanchez Vicario).

## All-Time Leaders

### Tournaments Won (singles)

All-time tournament wins from the arrival of open tennis in 1968 through 2005 (through Oct. 9). Men's totals include ATP Tour, Grand Prix and WCT tournaments. Players active in singles play in 2005 are in **bold** type.

#### MEN

| | | Total | | | Total | | | Total |
|---|---|---|---|---|---|---|---|---|
| 1 | Jimmy Connors | 109 | 12 | Stefan Edberg | 41 | 23 | Yevgeny Kafelnikov | 26 |
| 2 | Ivan Lendl | 94 | 13 | Stan Smith | 39 | 24 | Jose-Luis Clerc | 25 |
| 3 | John McEnroe | 77 | 14 | Michael Chang | 34 | | Brian Gottfried | 25 |
| 4 | Pete Sampras | 64 | 15 | Arthur Ashe | 33 | 26 | **Lleyton Hewitt** | 24 |
| 5 | Bjorn Borg | 62 | | **Roger Federer** | 33 | 27 | Jim Courier | 23 |
| | Guillermo Vilas | 62 | | Mats Wilander | 33 | | Yannick Noah | 23 |
| 7 | **Andre Agassi** | 60 | 18 | John Newcombe | 32 | 29 | Eddie Dibbs | 22 |
| 8 | Ilie Nastase | 57 | | Manuel Orantes | 32 | | Goran Ivanisevic | 22 |
| 9 | Boris Becker | 49 | | Ken Rosewall | 32 | | Harold Solomon | 22 |
| 10 | Rod Laver | 47 | 21 | Tom Okker | 31 | | | |
| 11 | Thomas Muster | 44 | 22 | Vitas Gerulaitis | 27 | | | |

#### WOMEN

| | | Total | | | Total | | | Total |
|---|---|---|---|---|---|---|---|---|
| 1 | **Martina Navratilova** | 167 | 11 | **Conchita Martinez** | 33 | 21 | Jana Novotna | 24 |
| 2 | Chris Evert | 154 | | **Venus Williams** | 33 | 22 | **J. Henin-Hardenne** | 23 |
| 3 | Steffi Graf | 107 | 13 | Olga Morozova | 31 | 23 | Kerry Melville Reid | 22 |
| 4 | Margaret Smith Court | 92 | 14 | Tracy Austin | 30 | 24 | Pam Shriver | 21 |
| 5 | E. Goolagong Cawley | 68 | 15 | **Kim Clijsters** | 29 | 25 | Julie Heldman | 20 |
| 6 | Billie Jean King | 67 | | Arantxa Sanchez-Vicario | 29 | 26 | M. Maleeva-Fragniere | 19 |
| 7 | Virginia Wade | 55 | 17 | Hana Mandlikova | 27 | | Nancy Richey | 19 |
| 8 | Monica Seles | 53 | | Gabriela Sabatini | 27 | 28 | Virginia Ruzici | 17 |
| 9 | **Lindsay Davenport** | 50 | 19 | **Serena Williams** | 26 | | Regina Marsikova | 17 |
| 10 | **Martina Hingis** | 40 | 20 | Nancy Richey | 25 | | **Mary Pierce** | 17 |
| | | | | | | | **Amelie Mauresmo** | 17 |

## Money Won

All-time money winners from the arrival of open tennis in 1968 through 2005 (through Oct. 9). Totals include doubles earnings.

### MEN

| | | Earnings | | | | Earnings | | | | Earnings |
|---|---|---|---|---|---|---|---|---|---|---|
| 1 | Pete Sampras | $43,280,489 | 10 | Lleyton Hewitt | $15,962,457 | | 19 | Carlos Moya | $11,571,979 |
| 2 | Andre Agassi | 30,951,275 | 11 | Gustavo Kuerten | 14,699,343 | | 20 | Patrick Rafter | 11,127,058 |
| 3 | Boris Becker | 25,080,956 | 12 | Jim Courier | 14,034,132 | | 21 | Tim Henman | 11,016,812 |
| 4 | Yevgeny Kafelnikov | 23,883,797 | 13 | Michael Stich | 12,592,483 | | 22 | Petr Korda | 10,448,450 |
| 5 | Ivan Lendl | 21,262,417 | 14 | John McEnroe | 12,539,622 | | 23 | Thomas Enqvist | 10,428,491 |
| 6 | Stefan Edberg | 20,630,941 | 15 | Thomas Muster | 12,224,410 | | 24 | Alex Corretja | 10,411,354 |
| 7 | Goran Ivanisevic | 19,876,579 | 16 | Marat Safin | 12,206,048 | | 25 | Juan Carlos Ferrero | 10,119,228 |
| 8 | Roger Federer | 19,412,573 | 17 | Jonas Bjorkman | 12,028,534 | | | | |
| 9 | Michael Chang | 19,145,632 | 18 | Sergi Bruguera | 11,632,199 | | | | |

### WOMEN

| | | Earnings | | | | Earnings | | | | Earnings |
|---|---|---|---|---|---|---|---|---|---|---|
| 1 | Steffi Graf | $21,895,277 | 10 | Conchita Martinez | $11,459,442 | | 19 | Nathalie Tauziat | $6,649,907 |
| 2 | Mart. Navratilova | 21,400,871 | 11 | Jana Novotna | 11,249,284 | | 20 | Helena Sukova | 6,391,245 |
| 3 | Lindsay Davenport | 20,750,465 | 12 | Jennifer Capriati | 10,206,639 | | 21 | Lisa Raymond | 6,043,049 |
| 4 | Martina Hingis | 18,345,825 | 13 | J. Henin-Hardenne | 9,368,509 | | 22 | Elena Dementieva | 5,798,916 |
| 5 | A. Sanchez-Vicario | 16,942,640 | 14 | Mary Pierce | 8,898,891 | | 23 | Amanda Coetzer | 5,594,821 |
| 6 | Venus Williams | 16,012,656 | 15 | Chris Evert | 8,896,195 | | 24 | Ai Sugiyama | 5,521,467 |
| 7 | Serena Williams | 15,874,887 | 16 | Gabriela Sabatini | 8,785,850 | | 25 | Pam Shriver | 5,460,566 |
| 8 | Monica Seles | 14,891,762 | 17 | Amelie Mauresmo | 7,983,555 | | | | |
| 9 | Kim Clijsters | 12,534,697 | 18 | Natasha Zvereva | 7,792,503 | | | | |

## Year-end Tournaments

### MEN

### Tennis Masters Cup

The year-end championship featuring the top eight players in the Tennis Masters Series rankings. Two groups of four players square off in a round-robin tournament followed by a single-elimination semifinals and finals. Originally called the Masters in 1970, the tournament followed a round-robin format, but was revised in 1972 to include a round-robin to decide the four semi-finalists then a single elimination format after that. Replaced by ATP Tour World Championship from 1990 through 1999.

**Multiple Winners:** Ivan Lendl and Pete Sampras (5); Ilie Nastase (4); Boris Becker and John McEnroe (3); Bjorn Borg, Roger Federer and Lleyton Hewitt (2).

| Year | Winner | Runner-Up |
|---|---|---|
| 1970 | Stan Smith (4-1) * | Rod Laver (4-1) |
| 1971 | Ilie Nastase (6-0) | Stan Smith (4-2) |

| Year | Winner | Loser | Score |
|---|---|---|---|
| 1972 | Ilie Nastase | S. Smith | 63 62 36 26 63 |
| 1973 | Ilie Nastase | T. Okker | 63 75 46 63 |
| 1974 | Guillermo Vilas | I. Nastase | 76 62 36 36 64 |
| 1975 | Ilie Nastase | B. Borg | 62 62 61 |
| 1976 | Manuel Orantes | W. Fibak | 57 62 06 76 61 |
| 1978 | Jimmy Connors | B. Borg | 64 16 64 |
| 1979 | John McEnroe | A. Ashe | 67 63 75 |
| 1980 | Bjorn Borg | V. Gerulaitis | 62 62 |
| 1981 | Bjorn Borg | I. Lendl | 64 62 62 |
| 1982 | Ivan Lendl | V. Gerulaitis | 67 26 76 62 64 |
| 1983 | Ivan Lendl | J. McEnroe | 64 64 62 |
| 1984 | John McEnroe | I. Lendl | 63 64 64 |
| 1985 | John McEnroe | I. Lendl | 75 60 64 |
| 1986 | Ivan Lendl | B. Becker | 62 76 63 |
| 1986 | Ivan Lendl | B. Becker | 64 64 64 |

| Year | Winner | Loser | Score |
|---|---|---|---|
| 1987 | Ivan Lendl | M. Wilander | 62 62 63 |
| 1988 | Boris Becker | I. Lendl | 57 76 36 62 76 |
| 1989 | Stefan Edberg | B. Becker | 46 76 63 61 |
| 1990 | Andre Agassi | S. Edberg | 57 76 75 62 |
| 1991 | Pete Sampras | J. Courier | 36 76 63 64 |
| 1992 | Boris Becker | J. Courier | 64 63 75 |
| 1993 | Michael Stich | P. Sampras | 76 26 76 62 |
| 1994 | Pete Sampras | B. Becker | 46 63 75 64 |
| 1995 | Boris Becker | M. Chang | 76 60 76 |
| 1996 | Pete Sampras | B. Becker | 36 76 76 67 64 |
| 1997 | Pete Sampras | Y. Kafelnikov | 63 62 62 |
| 1998 | Alex Corretja | C. Moya | 36 36 75 63 75 |
| 1999 | Pete Sampras | A. Agassi | 61 75 64 |
| 2000 | Gustavo Kuerten | A. Agassi | 64 64 64 |
| 2001 | Lleyton Hewitt | S. Grosjean | 63 63 64 |
| 2002 | Lleyton Hewitt | J.C. Ferrero | 75 75 26 26 64 |
| 2003 | Roger Federer | A. Agassi | 63 60 64 |
| 2004 | Roger Federer | L. Hewitt | 63 62 (rain) |

*Smith was declared the winner because he beat Laver in their round-robin match (4-6, 6-3, 6-4).
**Note:** The tournament switched from December to January in 1977-78, then back to December in 1986.

### Playing Sites

**1970**—Tokyo; **1971**—Paris; **1972**—Barcelona; **1973**—Boston; **1974**—Melbourne; **1975**—Stockholm; **1976, 2003-04**—Houston; **1977-89**—New York City; **1990-95**—Frankfurt, GER; **1996-99**—Hannover, GER; **2000**—Lisbon, POR; **2001**—Sydney, AUS; **2002, 2005-07**—Shanghai, CHN.

### WCT Championship (1971-89)

World Championship Tennis was established in 1967 to promote professional tennis and led the way into the open era. Its major singles and doubles championships were held every May among the top eight regular season finishers on the circuit from 1971 until the WCT folded in 1989.

**Multiple winners:** John McEnroe (5), Jimmy Connors, Ivan Lendl and Ken Rosewall (2).

| Year | Winner | Loser | Score | Year | Winner | Loser | Score |
|---|---|---|---|---|---|---|---|
| 1971 | Ken Rosewall | R. Laver | 64 16 76 76 | 1973 | Stan Smith | A. Ashe | 63 63 46 64 |
| 1972 | Ken Rosewall | R. Laver | 46 60 63 67 76 | 1974 | John Newcombe | B. Borg | 46 63 63 62 |

## Year-end Tournaments (Cont.)

| Year | Winner | Loser | Score | Year | Winner | Loser | Score |
|------|--------|-------|-------|------|--------|-------|-------|
| 1975 | Arthur Ashe | B. Borg | 36 64 64 60 | 1983 | John McEnroe | I. Lendl | 62 46 63 67 76 |
| 1976 | Bjorn Borg | G. Vilas | 16 61 75 61 | 1984 | John McEnroe | J. Connors | 61 62 63 |
| 1977 | Jimmy Connors | D. Stockton | 67 61 64 63 | 1985 | Ivan Lendl | T. Mayotte | 76 64 61 |
| 1978 | Vitas Gerulaitis | E. Dibbs | 63 62 61 | 1986 | Anders Jarryd | B. Becker | 67 61 61 64 |
| 1979 | John McEnroe | B. Borg | 75 46 62 76 | 1987 | Miloslav Mecir | J. McEnroe | 60 36 62 62 |
| 1980 | Jimmy Connors | J. McEnroe | 26 76 61 62 | 1988 | Boris Becker | S. Edberg | 64 16 75 62 |
| 1981 | John McEnroe | J. Kriek | 61 62 64 | 1989 | John McEnroe | B. Gilbert | 63 63 76 |
| 1982 | Ivan Lendl | J. McEnroe | 62 36 63 63 | | | | |

## WOMEN

### WTA Championships

The WTA Tour's year-end tournament took place in March from 1972 until 1986 when the WTA decided to adopt a January-to-November playing season. Given the changeover, two championships were held in 1986. Held in Boca Raton (1972-73), Los Angeles (1974-76, 2002-05), New York (1977, 1979-2000), Oakland (1978), Munich (2001), Madrid (2006).

**Multiple winners:** Martina Navratilova (8); Steffi Graf (5); Chris Evert (4); Monica Seles (3); Kim Clijsters, Evonne Goolagong, Martina Hingis and Gabriela Sabatini (2).

| Year | Winner | Loser | Score | Year | Winner | Loser | Score |
|------|--------|-------|-------|------|--------|-------|-------|
| 1972 | Chris Evert | K. Reid | 75 64 | 1988 | Gabriela Sabatini | P. Shriver | 75 62 62 |
| 1973 | Chris Evert | N. Richey | 63 63 | 1989 | Steffi Graf | M. Navratilova | 64 75 26 62 |
| 1974 | Evonne Goolagong | C. Evert | 63 64 | 1990 | Monica Seles | G. Sabatini | 64 57 36 64 62 |
| 1975 | Chris Evert | M. Navratilova | 64 62 | 1991 | Monica Seles | M. Navratilova | 64 36 75 60 |
| 1976 | Evonne Goolagong | C. Evert | 63 57 63 | 1992 | Monica Seles | M. Navratilova | 75 63 61 |
| 1977 | Chris Evert | S. Barker | 26 61 61 | 1993 | Steffi Graf | A. S. Vicario | 61 64 36 61 |
| 1978 | M. Navratilova | E. Goolagong | 76 64 | 1994 | Gabriela Sabatini | L. Davenport | 63 62 64 |
| 1979 | M. Navratilova | T. Austin | 63 36 62 | 1995 | Steffi Graf | A. Huber | 61 26 61 46 63 |
| 1980 | Tracy Austin | M. Navratilova | 62 26 62 | 1996 | Steffi Graf | M. Hingis | 63 46 60 46 60 |
| 1981 | M. Navratilova | A. Jaeger | 63 76 | 1997 | Jana Novotna | M. Pierce | 76 62 63 |
| 1982 | Sylvia Hanika | M. Navratilova | 16 63 64 | 1998 | Martina Hingis | L. Davenport | 75 64 46 62 |
| 1983 | M. Navratilova | C. Evert | 62 60 | 1999 | Lindsay Davenport | M. Hingis | 64 62 |
| 1984 | M. Navratilova | C. Evert | 63 75 61 | 2000 | Martina Hingis | M. Seles | 67 64 64 |
| 1985 | M. Navratilova | H. Sukova | 63 75 64 | 2001 | Serena Williams | L. Davenport | walkover |
| 1986 | M. Navratilova | H. Mandlikova | 62 60 36 61 | 2002 | Kim Clijsters | S. Williams | 75 63 |
| 1986 | M. Navratilova | S. Graf | 76 63 62 | 2003 | Kim Clijsters | A. Mauresmo | 62 60 |
| 1987 | Steffi Graf | G. Sabatini | 46 64 60 64 | 2004 | Maria Sharapova | S. Williams | 46 62 64 |

**Note:** The final was best-of-five sets from 1984-98 and best-of-three sets from 1972-83 and since 1999.

## Davis Cup

Established in 1900 as an annual international tournament by American player Dwight Davis. Originally called the International Lawn Tennis Challenge Trophy. Challenge round system until 1972. Since 1981, the top 16 nations in the world have played a straight knockout tournament over the course of a year. The format is a best-of-five match of two singles, one doubles and two singles over three days. Note that from 1900-24 Australia and New Zealand competed together as Australasia.

**Multiple winners:** USA (31); Australia (22); France (9); Sweden (7); Australasia (6); British Isles (5); Britain (4); Germany (3); Spain (2).

### Challenge Rounds

| Year | Winner | Loser | Score | Site | Year | Winner | Loser | Score | Site |
|------|--------|-------|-------|------|------|--------|-------|-------|------|
| 1900 | USA | British Isles | 3-0 | Boston | 1927 | France | USA | 3-2 | Philadelphia |
| 1901 | Not held | | | | 1928 | France | USA | 4-1 | Paris |
| 1902 | USA | British Isles | 3-2 | New York | 1929 | France | USA | 3-2 | Paris |
| 1903 | British Isles | USA | 4-1 | Boston | 1930 | France | USA | 4-1 | Paris |
| 1904 | British Isles | Belgium | 5-0 | Wimbledon | 1931 | France | Britain | 3-2 | Paris |
| 1905 | British Isles | USA | 5-0 | Wimbledon | 1932 | France | USA | 3-2 | Paris |
| 1906 | British Isles | USA | 5-0 | Wimbledon | 1933 | Britain | France | 3-2 | Paris |
| 1907 | Australasia | British Isles | 3-2 | Wimbledon | 1934 | Britain | USA | 4-1 | Wimbledon |
| 1908 | Australasia | USA | 3-2 | Melbourne | 1935 | Britain | USA | 5-0 | Wimbledon |
| 1909 | Australasia | USA | 5-0 | Sydney | 1936 | Britain | Australia | 3-2 | Wimbledon |
| 1910 | Not held | | | | 1937 | USA | Britain | 4-1 | Wimbledon |
| 1911 | Australasia | USA | 5-0 | Christchurch, NZ | 1938 | USA | Australia | 3-2 | Philadelphia |
| 1912 | British Isles | Australasia | 3-2 | Melbourne | 1939 | Australia | USA | 3-2 | Philadelphia |
| 1913 | USA | British Isles | 3-2 | Wimbledon | 1940-45 | Not held World War II | | | |
| 1914 | Australasia | USA | 3-2 | New York | 1946 | USA | Australia | 5-0 | Melbourne |
| 1915-18 | Not held World War I | | | | 1947 | USA | Australia | 4-1 | New York |
| 1919 | Australasia | British Isles | 4-1 | Sydney | 1948 | USA | Australia | 5-0 | New York |
| 1920 | USA | Australasia | 5-0 | Auckland, NZ | 1949 | USA | Australia | 4-1 | New York |
| 1921 | USA | Japan | 5-0 | New York | 1950 | Australia | USA | 4-1 | New York |
| 1922 | USA | Australasia | 4-1 | New York | 1951 | Australia | USA | 3-2 | Sydney |
| 1923 | USA | Australasia | 4-1 | New York | 1952 | Australia | USA | 4-1 | Adelaide |
| 1924 | USA | Australia | 5-0 | Philadelphia | 1953 | Australia | USA | 3-2 | Melbourne |
| 1925 | USA | France | 5-0 | Philadelphia | 1954 | USA | Australia | 3-2 | Sydney |
| 1926 | USA | France | 4-1 | Philadelphia | 1955 | Australia | USA | 5-0 | New York |

| Year | Winner | Loser | Score | Site | Year | Winner | Loser | Score | Site |
|------|--------|-------|-------|------|------|--------|-------|-------|------|
| 1956 | Australia | USA | 5-0 | Adelaide | 1962 | Australia | Mexico | 5-0 | Brisbane |
| 1957 | Australia | USA | 3-2 | Melbourne | 1963 | USA | Australia | 3-2 | Adelaide |
| 1958 | USA | Australia | 3-2 | Brisbane | 1964 | Australia | USA | 3-2 | Cleveland |
| 1959 | Australia | USA | 3-2 | New York | 1965 | Australia | Spain | 4-1 | Sydney |
| 1960 | Australia | Italy | 4-1 | Sydney | 1966 | Australia | India | 4-1 | Melbourne |
| 1961 | Australia | Italy | 5-0 | Melbourne | 1967 | Australia | Spain | 4-1 | Brisbane |

## Final Rounds

| Year | Winner | Loser | Score | Site | Year | Winner | Loser | Score | Site |
|------|--------|-------|-------|------|------|--------|-------|-------|------|
| 1968 | USA | Australia | 4-1 | Adelaide | 1987 | Sweden | India | 5-0 | Göteborg |
| 1969 | USA | Romania | 5-0 | Cleveland | 1988 | W. Germany | Sweden | 4-1 | Göteborg |
| 1970 | USA | W. Germany | 5-0 | Cleveland | 1989 | W. Germany | Sweden | 3-2 | Stuttgart |
| 1971 | USA | Romania | 3-2 | Charlotte | 1990 | USA | Australia | 3-2 | St. Petersburg |
| 1972 | USA | Romania | 3-2 | Bucharest | 1991 | France | USA | 3-1 | Lyon |
| 1973 | Australia | USA | 5-0 | Cleveland | 1992 | USA | Switzerland | 3-1 | Ft. Worth |
| 1974 | So. Africa | India | walkover | Not held | 1993 | Germany | Australia | 4-1 | Dusseldorf |
| 1975 | Sweden | Czech. | 3-2 | Stockholm | 1994 | Sweden | Russia | 4-1 | Moscow |
| 1976 | Italy | Chile | 4-1 | Santiago | 1995 | USA | Russia | 3-2 | Moscow |
| 1977 | Australia | Italy | 3-1 | Sydney | 1996 | France | Sweden | 3-2 | Malmo |
| 1978 | USA | Britain | 4-1 | Palm Springs | 1997 | Sweden | USA | 5-0 | Göteborg |
| 1979 | USA | Italy | 5-0 | San Francisco | 1998 | Sweden | Italy | 4-1 | Milan |
| 1980 | Czech. | Italy | 4-1 | Prague | 1999 | Australia | France | 3-2 | Nice |
| 1981 | USA | Argentina | 3-1 | Cincinnati | 2000 | Spain | Australia | 3-1 | Barcelona |
| 1982 | USA | France | 4-1 | Grenoble | 2001 | France | Australia | 3-2 | Melbourne |
| 1983 | Australia | Sweden | 3-2 | Melbourne | 2002 | Russia | France | 3-2 | Paris |
| 1984 | Sweden | USA | 4-1 | Göteborg | 2003 | Australia | Spain | 3-1 | Melbourne |
| 1985 | Sweden | W. Germany | 3-2 | Munich | 2004 | Spain | USA | 3-2 | Seville |
| 1986 | Australia | Sweden | 3-2 | Melbourne | | | | | |

**Note:** In 1974, India refused to play the final as a protest against the South African government's policies of apartheid.

## Fed Cup

Originally the Federation Cup started by the International Tennis Federation as the Davis Cup of women's tennis. Played by 32 teams over one week at one site from 1963-94. Tournament changed to Davis Cup-style format of four rounds and home site in 1995. Currently 16 teams compete in a knockout format, with winners advancing to the quarterfinals, semifinals and finals.

**Multiple winners:** USA (17); Australia (7); Czechoslovakia and Spain (5); France, Germany and Russia (2).

| Year | Winner | Loser | Score | Site | Year | Winner | Loser | Score | Site |
|------|--------|-------|-------|------|------|--------|-------|-------|------|
| 1963 | USA | Australia | 2-1 | London | 1985 | Czech. | USA | 2-1 | Japan |
| 1964 | Australia | USA | 2-1 | Philadelphia | 1986 | USA | Czech. | 3-0 | Prague |
| 1965 | Australia | USA | 2-1 | Melbourne | 1987 | W. Germany | USA | 2-1 | Vancouver |
| 1966 | USA | W. Germany | 3-0 | Italy | 1988 | Czech. | USSR | 2-1 | Melbourne |
| 1967 | USA | Britain | 2-0 | W. Germany | 1989 | USA | Spain | 3-0 | Tokyo |
| 1968 | Australia | Holland | 3-0 | Paris | 1990 | USA | USSR | 2-1 | Atlanta |
| 1969 | USA | Australia | 2-1 | Athens | 1991 | Spain | USA | 2-1 | Nottingham |
| 1970 | Australia | Britain | 3-0 | W. Germany | 1992 | Germany | Spain | 2-1 | Frankfurt |
| 1971 | Australia | Britain | 3-0 | Perth | 1993 | Spain | Australia | 3-0 | Frankfurt |
| 1972 | So. Africa | Britain | 2-1 | So. Africa | 1994 | Spain | USA | 3-0 | Frankfurt |
| 1973 | Australia | So. Africa | 3-0 | W. Germany | 1995 | Spain | USA | 3-2 | Valencia |
| 1974 | Australia | USA | 2-1 | Italy | 1996 | USA | Spain | 5-0 | Atlantic City |
| 1975 | Czech. | Australia | 3-0 | France | 1997 | France | Netherlands | 4-1 | Netherlands |
| 1976 | USA | Australia | 2-1 | Philadelphia | 1998 | Spain | Switzerland | 3-2 | Geneva |
| 1977 | USA | Australia | 2-1 | Eastbourne | 1999 | USA | Russia | 4-1 | Palo Alto |
| 1978 | USA | Australia | 2-1 | Melbourne | 2000 | USA | Spain | 5-0 | Las Vegas |
| 1979 | USA | Australia | 3-0 | Spain | 2001 | Belgium | Russia | 2-1 | Madrid |
| 1980 | USA | Australia | 3-0 | W. Germany | 2002 | Slovakia | Spain | 3-1 | Canary Islands |
| 1981 | USA | Britain | 3-0 | Tokyo | 2003 | France | USA | 4-1 | Moscow |
| 1982 | USA | W. Germany | 3-0 | Santa Clara | 2004 | Russia | France | 3-2 | Moscow |
| 1983 | Czech. | W. Germany | 2-1 | Zurich | 2005 | Russia | France | 3-2 | Paris |
| 1984 | Czech. | Australia | 2-1 | Brazil | | | | | |

## COLLEGES

NCAA team titles were not sanctioned until 1946. NCAA women's individual and team championships started in 1982.

## Men's NCAA Individual Champions (1883-1945)

**Multiple winners:** Malcolm Chace and Pancho Segura (3); Edward Chandler, George Church, E.B. Dewhurst, Fred Hovey, Frank Guernsey, W.P. Knapp, Robert LeRoy, P.S. Sears, Cliff Sutter, Ernest Sutter and Richard Williams (2).

| Year | | Year | | Year | |
|------|--|------|--|------|--|
| 1883 | J. Clark, Harvard (spring) | 1887 | P.S. Sears, Harvard | 1891 | Fred Hovey, Harvard |
| | H. Taylor, Harvard (fall) | 1888 | P.S. Sears, Harvard | 1892 | William Larned, Cornell |
| 1884 | W.P. Knapp, Yale | 1889 | R.P. Huntington Jr., Yale | 1893 | Malcolm Chace, Brown |
| 1885 | W.P. Knapp, Yale | 1890 | Fred Hovey, Harvard | 1894 | Malcolm Chace, Yale |
| 1886 | G.M. Brinley, Trinity, CT | 1891 | Fred Hovey, Harvard | 1895 | Malcolm Chace, Yale |

## Colleges (Cont.)

| Year | | Year | | Year | |
|---|---|---|---|---|---|
| 1896 | Malcolm Whitman, Harvard | 1912 | George Church, Princeton | 1930 | Cliff Sutter, Tulane |
| 1897 | S.G. Thompson, Princeton | 1913 | Richard Williams, Harv. | 1931 | Keith Gledhill, Stanford |
| 1898 | Leo Ware, Harvard | 1914 | George Church, Princeton | 1932 | Cliff Sutter, Tulane |
| 1899 | Dwight Davis, Harvard | 1915 | Richard Williams, Harv. | 1933 | Jack Tidball, UCLA |
| 1900 | Ray Little, Princeton | 1916 | G.C. Caner, Harvard | 1934 | Gene Mako, USC |
| 1901 | Fred Alexander, Princeton | 1917-1918 | Not held | 1935 | Wilbur Hess, Rice |
| 1902 | William Clothier, Harvard | 1919 | Charles Garland, Yale | 1936 | Ernest Sutter, Tulane |
| 1903 | E.B. Dewhurst, Penn | 1920 | Lascelles Banks, Yale | 1937 | Ernest Sutter, Tulane |
| 1904 | Robert LeRoy, Columbia | 1921 | Philip Neer, Stanford | 1938 | Frank Guernsey, Rice |
| 1905 | E.B. Dewhurst, Penn | 1922 | Lucien Williams, Yale | 1939 | Frank Guernsey, Rice |
| 1906 | Robert LeRoy, Columbia | 1923 | Carl Fischer, Phi. Osteo. | 1940 | Don McNeill, Kenyon |
| 1907 | G.P. Gardner Jr., Harvard | 1924 | Wallace Scott, Wash. | 1941 | Joseph Hunt, Navy |
| 1908 | Nat Niles, Harvard | 1925 | Edward Chandler, Calif. | 1942 | Ted Schroeder, Stanford |
| 1909 | Wallace Johnson, Penn | 1926 | Edward Chandler, Calif. | 1943 | Pancho Segura, Miami-FL |
| 1910 | R.A. Holden Jr., Yale | 1927 | Wilmer Allison, Texas | 1944 | Pancho Segura, Miami-FL |
| 1911 | E.H. Whitney, Harvard | 1928 | Julius Seligson, Lehigh | 1945 | Pancho Segura, Miami-FL |
| | | 1929 | Berkeley Bell, Texas | | |

### NCAA Men's Division I Champions

**Multiple winners** (Teams): Stanford (17); UCLA and USC (16); Georgia (4); William & Mary (2). (Players): Matias Boeker, Alex Olmedo, Mikael Pernfors, Dennis Ralston and Ham Richardson (2).

| Year | Team winner | Individual Champion | Year | Team winner | Individual Champion |
|---|---|---|---|---|---|
| 1946 | USC | Bob Falkenburg, USC | 1976 | USC & UCLA | Bill Scanlon, Trinity-TX |
| 1947 | Wm. & Mary | Gardner Larned, Wm.& Mary | 1977 | Stanford | Matt Mitchell, Stanford |
| 1948 | Wm. & Mary | Harry Likas, San Francisco | 1978 | Stanford | John McEnroe, Stanford |
| 1949 | San Francisco | Jack Tuero, Tulane | 1979 | UCLA | Kevin Curren, Texas |
| 1950 | UCLA | Herbert Flam, UCLA | 1980 | Stanford | Robert Van't Hof, USC |
| 1951 | USC | Tony Trabert, Cincinnati | 1981 | Stanford | Tim Mayotte, Stanford |
| 1952 | UCLA | Hugh Stewart, USC | 1982 | UCLA | Mike Leach, Michigan |
| 1953 | UCLA | Ham Richardson, Tulane | 1983 | Stanford | Greg Holmes, Utah |
| 1954 | UCLA | Ham Richardson, Tulane | 1984 | UCLA | Mikael Pernfors, Georgia |
| 1955 | USC | Jose Aguero, Tulane | 1985 | Georgia | Mikael Pernfors, Georgia |
| 1956 | UCLA | Alex Olmedo, USC | 1986 | Stanford | Dan Goldie, Stanford |
| 1957 | Michigan | Barry MacKay, Michigan | 1987 | Georgia | Andrew Burrow, Miami-FL |
| 1958 | USC | Alex Olmedo, USC | 1988 | Stanford | Robby Weiss, Pepperdine |
| 1959 | Tulane & Notre Dame | Whitney Reed, San Jose St. | 1989 | Stanford | Donni Leaycraft, LSU |
| 1960 | UCLA | Larry Nagler, UCLA | 1990 | Stanford | Steve Bryan, Texas |
| 1961 | UCLA | Allen Fox, UCLA | 1991 | USC | Jared Palmer, Stanford |
| 1962 | USC | Rafael Osuna, USC | 1992 | Stanford | Alex O'Brien Stanford |
| 1963 | USC | Dennis Ralston, USC | 1993 | USC | Chris Woodruff, Tennessee |
| 1964 | USC | Dennis Ralston, USC | 1994 | USC | Mark Merklein, Florida |
| 1965 | UCLA | Arthur Ashe, UCLA | 1995 | Stanford | Sargis Sargsian, Ariz. St. |
| 1966 | USC | Charlie Pasarell, UCLA | 1996 | Stanford | Cecil Mamiit, USC |
| 1967 | USC | Bob Lutz, USC | 1997 | Stanford | Luke Smith, UNLV |
| 1968 | USC | Stan Smith, USC | 1998 | Stanford | Bob Bryan, Stanford |
| 1969 | USC | Joaquin Loyo-Mayo, USC | 1999 | Georgia | Jeff Morrison, Florida |
| 1970 | UCLA | Jeff Borowiak, UCLA | 2000 | Stanford | Alex Kim, Stanford |
| 1971 | UCLA | Jimmy Connors, UCLA | 2001 | Georgia | Matias Boeker, Georgia |
| 1972 | Trinity-TX | Dick Stockton, Trinity-TX | 2002 | USC | Matias Boeker, Georgia |
| 1973 | Stanford | Alex Mayer, Stanford | 2003 | Illinois | Amer Delic, Illinois |
| 1974 | Stanford | John Whitlinger, Stanford | 2004 | Baylor | Benjamin Becker, Baylor |
| 1975 | UCLA | Bill Martin, UCLA | 2005 | UCLA | Benedikt Dorsch, Baylor |

### NCAA Women's Division I Champions

**Multiple winners** (Teams): Stanford (14); Florida (4); Georgia, Texas and USC (2). (Players): Sandra Birch, Patty Fendick, Laura Granville, Amber Liu and Lisa Raymond (2).

| Year | Team winner | Individual Champion | Year | Team winner | Individual Champion |
|---|---|---|---|---|---|
| 1982 | Stanford | Alycia Moulton, Stanford | 1994 | Georgia | Angela Lettiere, Georgia |
| 1983 | USC | Beth Herr, USC | 1995 | Texas | Keri Phoebus, UCLA |
| 1984 | Stanford | Lisa Spain, Georgia | 1996 | Florida | Jill Craybas, Florida |
| 1985 | USC | Linda Gates, Stanford | 1997 | Stanford | Lilia Osterloh, Stanford |
| 1986 | Stanford | Patty Fendick, Stanford | 1998 | Florida | Vanessa Webb, Duke |
| 1987 | Stanford | Patty Fendick, Stanford | 1999 | Stanford | Zuzana Lesenarova, S. Diego |
| 1988 | Stanford | Shaun Stafford, Florida | 2000 | Georgia | Laura Granville, Stanford |
| 1989 | Stanford | Sandra Birch, Stanford | 2001 | Stanford | Laura Granville, Stanford |
| 1990 | Stanford | Debbie Graham, Stanford | 2002 | Stanford | Bea Bielik, Wake Forest |
| 1991 | Stanford | Sandra Birch, Stanford | 2003 | Florida | Amber Liu, Stanford |
| 1992 | Florida | Lisa Raymond, Florida | 2004 | Stanford | Amber Liu, Stanford |
| 1993 | Texas | Lisa Raymond, Florida | 2005 | Stanford | Zuzana Zemenova, Baylor |

# *Golf*

*After 45 Masters that included six green jackets,* **Jack Nicklaus** *said goodbye to Augusta in 2005.*

# Master Stroke

*Tiger produces a shot for the ages on the 16th hole of the Masters, then holds on for a playoff win.*

**Michael Morrison**
*is co-editor of the ESPN Sports Almanac.*

Tiger Woods and caddie Steve Williams carefully examined the terrain at the par-3 16th at Augusta National. He had just hit his tee shot long and left, and his ball now rested 30 feet from the hole and right up against the fringe of the second cut of rough.

His 2005 Masters had been a rollercoaster ride to that point...and the real ride was just beginning.

After an opening-round 74 that left him seven strokes back of leader Chris DiMarco, Tiger found both his swing and his swagger and over the next two rounds, played some of the most inspired golf of his career. An astonishing 13-under-par 66-65 over the next two rounds, a run that included a Masters record-tying seven consecutive birdies, left him with a three-shot lead over second-place DiMarco heading into the final 18 holes.

As the lead increased to four shots early on Sunday, fans, pundits and the Masters tailor were already sizing him up for his fourth green jacket. DiMarco, however, wasn't ready to cave in, and by the 14th hole had closed the deficit to one stroke.

After the pair recorded matching pars on 15, DiMarco drilled his tee shot to the center of the green, about 15 feet below the cup, leaving himself a very makeable birdie putt. With Tiger in his precarious spot off the green, it appeared as though the tournament was about to be evened up. And then came the shot.

Tiger had seen Davis Love III make a similar shot in 1999, though without the unfavorable lie, and knew that if he got his ball to the right spot on the green, at the right speed, the slope would funnel the ball right to the hole.

AP/Wide World Photos

***Tiger Woods*** *strikes a familiar pose as he celebrates his tournament-winning birdie putt on the first sudden-death hole of the Masters on April 10.*

Simply put...he hit the spot. Woods chipped a low runner onto the green, and sure enough, the ball took a sharp right turn, rumbled down the slope and made a beeline straight for the cup. It then lost its speed and stopped on the lip for what seemed like an eternity. While Tiger's stomach fluttered, Nike execs around the world rejoiced as the familiar Swoosh on the side of the ball posed perfectly for the cameras.

Somehow, either gravity took over or Carl Spackler was hunting gophers somewhere on the course, but the ball took one more rota-tion...and dropped into the hole. The gallery roared, Tiger and Williams pumped fists and high-fived. And DiMarco stood in disbelief.

"I was just trying to throw the ball up there on the hill and let it feed down there and hopefully have a makeable putt," Woods said. "All of a sudden, it looked pretty good, and all of a sudden it looked like really good, and it looked like how could it not go in, and how did it not go in, and all of a sudden it went in."

DiMarco held strong. While he missed his birdie putt on 16, he parred 17 and 18, and watched

***Michelle Wie*** *had plenty of reason to smile in 2005, even though her first LPGA tournament as a professional turned out to be a learning experience, rather than a money-making one. Her fourth-place finish was wiped out when she was DQ'd over an illegal drop.*

Woods lose any momentum he may have gained on 16 by bogeying the final two holes.

We were all square and headed to the first hole of sudden death...which is all Tiger would need.

Both players hit good-looking drives off the tee, but while Tiger landed his second shot 15 feet from the pin, DiMarco came up short of the green. After a chip and a putt for par, all he could do was watch as Tiger calmly sank his 15-foot putt for the birdie and the victory.

It was Tiger's ninth major championship (he would add No. 10 three months later at the British Open) and he improved to 7-1 in playoffs, including 2-0 in majors.

DiMarco suffered his second playoff loss in a major in the last eight months, as he also lost to Vijay Singh in the 2004 PGA Championship. Still, he looked Tiger in the eye in a major and didn't blink, which is more than most Tour players can say.

"Any time you can make Tiger hiccup a little bit, you know you're doing something right," DiMarco said. "I was throwing up on myself all day, but it was as much fun as I've ever had."

# The Ten Biggest Stories
# of the Year in Golf

**10** The crafty U.S. squad reclaims the Solheim Cup with an impressive display on the final day, winning 7½ of the 12 available points. For the first time in 11 years, the match is all square heading into Sunday's singles matches. Rookie Paula Creamer, 19, sets the tone for the Americans, thrashing veteran Laura Davies, 7&5 and Meg Mallon clinches the Cup with a 3&1 win over Karen Stupples.

**9** Casey Martin calls it a career after failing to advance out of the first round at a PGA qualifying event in late October. Martin suffers from a circulatory disease known as Klippel-Trenaunay-Webber Syndrome, which makes it difficult to walk for long stretches. He made headlines in the late 90's for suing the PGA Tour for the right to use a cart in competition.

**8** Chris DiMarco rolls in a dramatic 15-foot birdie putt on the final hole of his match against Stuart Appleby to give the United States a 18½-15½ win over the International Team and sole possession of the Presidents' Cup.

**7** Phil Mickelson grabs major win number two with a one-stroke victory over Steve Elkington and Thomas Bjorn at the PGA Championship at Baltusrol. He is the first player since Tiger Woods in 2000 to lead the PGA Championship wire-to-wire.

**6** New Zealander Michael Campbell becomes a national hero in his native country as he fends off a late challenge from Tiger Woods to win the 105th U.S. Open at Pinehurst, the first major title of his career. Woods finishes second, two strokes back. Third-round leader and two-time U.S. Open champ Retief Goosen opens the door for Campbell, carding a shocking final-round 81.

**5** Ho-hum, just another run-of-the-mill year for LPGA star Annika Sorenstam. The dominant Swede adds two more major titles to her collection, winning the Kraft Nabisco Championship by eight strokes over Rosie Jones and following that up with her third LPGA Championship in early June. She has eight Tour victories through late October, matching her gaudy total from 2004.

**4** After a runner-up finish at the LPGA Championship and a third-place showing at the Women's British Open, 16-year-old big-hitter Michelle Wie decides it's time to start making a little money. Endorsements aside, she has to wait a little longer than expected for her first payday when she is disqualified from her first tournament as a pro in mid-October. Wie takes a bad drop out of the bushes in the third round, wiping out a fourth-place finish and the accompanying $53,126 check.

**3** Apparently his swing *did* need some adjusting after all. Tiger Woods tames St. Andrews, shooting a 66-67 in the opening two rounds and turning in the first wire-to-wire victory at the British Open in 32 years.

**2** After 45 tournament appearances at Augusta and a closet full of green jackets (six, to be exact), 65-year-old legend Jack Nicklaus plays in his final Masters. He misses the cut but still manages to thrill the crowd with his emotional farewell.

**1** Tiger Woods shoots a Masters record-tying seven consecutive birdies en route to a third-round 65, and holds on to win his fourth green jacket in the first sudden-death hole of a playoff with Chris DiMarco. The shot of the tournament—and perhaps the year—comes on the 16th hole as Woods chips onto the slope of the green and watches his ball roll slowly down the hill, hang on the lip for two seconds (Nike swoosh in perfect view of the TV cameras), then finally fall into the cup. Fist pumps ensue.

## In the Cut

Tiger Woods missed the cut at the Byron Nelson Championship in May—coincidentally at the tournament of the man whose record he broke in 2003—ending his record streak of cuts made at 142. Here's a look at the PGA Tour record for consecutive money finishes.

| Player | Cuts | Years |
|---|---|---|
| Tiger Woods | 142 | 1998-2005 |
| Byron Nelson | 113 | 1941-48 |
| Jack Nicklaus | 105 | 1970-76 |
| Hale Irwin | 86 | 1975-79 |
| Dow Firnsterwald | 72 | 1955-58 |
| Tom Kite | 53 | 1980-82 |
| Vijay Singh | 53 | 1995-98 |

## Second Fiddle

It's well documented that Jack Nicklaus, who played his final competitive tournament at the British Open in 2005, won a record 18 majors in his career. But he also finished second 19 times (7 British Opens, 4 Masters, 4 U.S. Opens, 4 PGA Championships). Here's a look at the all-time also-rans in majors.

| Player | Seconds |
|---|---|
| Jack Nicklaus | 19 |
| Arnold Palmer | 10 |
| Sam Snead | 8 |
| Greg Norman | 8 |
| Tom Watson | 7 |
| Ben Hogan | 6 |
| Byron Nelson | 6 |
| Gary Player | 6 |
| Harry Vardon | 6 |

# 2004-2005
# *Season In Review*

SPORTS ALMANAC

## Tournament Results

Schedules and results of PGA, European PGA, Champions and LPGA tournaments from Nov. 7, 2004 through Oct. 9, 2005.

### PGA Tour
### Late 2004

| Last Rd | Tournament | Winner | Earnings | Runner-Up |
|---|---|---|---|---|
| Nov. 7 | The Tour Championship . . . . . . . . . . . | Retief Goosen (269) | $1,080,000 | T. Woods (273) |
| Nov. 14@ | Franklin Templeton Shootout . . . . . . . | Hank Kuehne/ | 300,000 | S. Flesch/ |
| | | Jeff Sluman (187) | (each) | J. Leonard (189) |
| Nov. 21@ | WGC: World Cup . . . . . . . . . . . . . | England—Paul Casey/ | 700,000 | Spain—S. Garcia/ |
| | | Luke Donald (257) | (each) | M.A. Jimenez (258) |
| Nov. 28@ | Merrill Lynch Skins Game . . . . . . . . . | Fred Couples (8 skins) | 640,000 | T. Woods (5 skins) |
| Nov. 28@ | Shinhan Korea Golf Championship . . . | Arron Oberholser (284) | 1,000,000 | M.A. Jimenez & K. Na (286) |
| Dec. 12@ | Target World Challenge . . . . . . . . . . | Tiger Woods (268) | 1,250,000 | P. Harrington (270) |
| Jan. 1@ | Tommy Bahama Challenge† . . . . . . . | American stars* | 400,000 | International stars |

*Playoffs: Tommy Bahama—Americans won on 1st hole.

@ Unofficial PGA Tour money event.

† Inaugural tournament; pits four young American stars (under 30) in stroke play vs. four young international stars.

### 2005 (through Oct. 9)

| Last Rd | Tournament | Winner | Earnings | Runner-Up |
|---|---|---|---|---|
| Jan. 9 | Mercedes Championships . . . . . . . . . | Stuart Appleby (271) | $1,060,000 | J. Kaye (272) |
| Jan. 16 | Sony Open in Hawaii . . . . . . . . . . . | Vijay Singh (269) | 864,000 | E. Els (270) |
| Jan. 23 | Buick Invitational . . . . . . . . . . . . . | Tiger Woods (272) | 864,000 | 3-way tie (275)# |
| Jan 30 | Bob Hope Chrysler Classic . . . . . . . | Justin Leonard (332)+ | 846,000 | T. Clark & J. Ogilvie (335) |
| Feb. 6 | FBR Open . . . . . . . . . . . . . . . . . | Phil Mickelson (267) | 936,000 | S. McCarron & K. Na (272) |
| Feb. 13 | AT&T Pebble Beach Pro-Am . . . . . . . | Phil Mickelson (269) | 954,000 | M. Weir (273) |
| Feb. 20 | Nissan Open . . . . . . . . . . . . . . . . | Adam Scott (133)*% | 864,000 | C. Campbell (133) |
| Feb. 27 | WGC: Accenture Match Play | | | |
| | Championship . . . . . . . . . . . . . . | David Toms (6&5) | 1,300,000 | C. DiMarco |
| Feb. 27 | Chrysler Classic of Tucson . . . . . . . | Geoff Ogilvy (269)* | 540,000 | M. Calcavecchia & K. Na (269) |
| Mar. 6 | Ford Championship at Doral . . . . . . . | Tiger Woods (264) | 990,000 | P. Mickelson (265) |
| Mar. 13 | Honda Classic . . . . . . . . . . . . . . . | Padraig Harrington (274)* | 990,000 | J. Ogilvy & V. Singh (274) |
| Mar. 20 | Bay Hill Invitational . . . . . . . . . . . | Kenny Perry (276) | 900,000 | G. McDowell & V. Singh (278) |
| Mar. 27 | The Players Championship . . . . . . . . | Fred Funk (279) | 1,440,000 | 3-way tie (280)# |
| Apr. 3 | BellSouth Classic . . . . . . . . . . . . . | Phil Mickelson (208)*% | 900,000 | 4-way tie (208)# |
| Apr. 10 | **The Masters** (Augusta, Ga.) . . . . . . | Tiger Woods (276)* | 1,260,000 | C. DiMarco (276) |
| Apr. 17 | MCI Heritage . . . . . . . . . . . . . . . | Peter Lonard (277) | 936,000 | 4-way tie (279)# |
| Apr. 24 | Shell Houston Open . . . . . . . . . . . | Vijay Singh (275)* | 900,000 | J. Daly (275) |
| May 1 | Zurich Classic of New Orleans . . . . . | Tim Petrovic (275)* | 990,000 | J. Driscoll (275) |
| May 8 | Wachovia Championship . . . . . . . . . | Vijay Singh (276)* | 1,080,000 | J. Furyk & S. Garcia (276) |
| May 15 | EDS Byron Nelson Championship . . . | Ted Purdy (265) | 1,116,000 | S. O'Hair (266) |
| May 22 | Bank of America Colonial . . . . . . . . | Kenny Perry (261) | 1,008,000 | B. Mayfair (268) |
| May 29 | FedEx St. Jude Classic . . . . . . . . . . | Justin Leonard (266) | 882,000 | D. Toms (267) |
| June 5 | The Memorial Tournament . . . . . . . . | Bart Bryant (272) | 990,000 | F. Couples (273) |
| June 12 | Booz Allen Classic . . . . . . . . . . . . | Sergio Garcia (270) | 900,000 | 3-way tie (272)# |
| June 19 | **U.S. Open** (Pinehurst, N.C.) . . . . . . | Michael Campbell (280) | 1,170,000 | T. Woods (282) |
| June 26 | Barclays Classic . . . . . . . . . . . . . . | Padraig Harrington (274) | 1,035,000 | J. Furyk (275) |
| July 3 | Cialis Western Open . . . . . . . . . . . | Jim Furyk (270) | 900,000 | T. Woods (272) |
| July 10 | John Deere Classic . . . . . . . . . . . . | Sean O'Hair (268) | 720,000 | R. Damron & H. Kuehne (269) |
| July 17 | B.C. Open . . . . . . . . . . . . . . . . . | Jason Bohn (264) | 540,000 | 4-way tie (265)# |
| July 17 | **British Open** (St. Andrews) . . . . . . . | Tiger Woods (274) | 1,261,584 | C. Montgomerie (279) |
| July 24 | U.S. Bank Championship . . . . . . . . . | Ben Crane (260) | 684,000 | S. Verplank (264) |
| July 31 | Buick Open . . . . . . . . . . . . . . . . . | Vijay Singh (264) | 828,000 | Z. Johnson & T. Woods (268) |
| Aug. 7 | The International† . . . . . . . . . . . . . | Retief Goosen (+32) | 900,000 | B. Jobe (+31) |
| Aug. 15 | **PGA Championship** (Baltusrol, N.J.) | Phil Mickelson (276) | 1,170,000 | S. Elkington & T. Bjorn (277) |
| Aug. 21 | WGC: NEC Invitational . . . . . . . . . . | Tiger Woods (274) | 1,300,000 | C. DiMarco (275) |
| Aug. 21 | Reno-Tahoe Open . . . . . . . . . . . . . | Vaughn Taylor (267) | 540,000 | J. Kaye (270) |
| Aug. 28 | Buick Championship . . . . . . . . . . . | Brad Faxon (266)* | 774,000 | T. van der Walt (266) |

## PGA Tour Results (Cont.)

| Last Rd | Tournament | Winner | Earnings | Runner-Up |
|---|---|---|---|---|
| Sept. 5 | Deutsche Bank Championship | Olin Browne (270) | $990,000 | J. Bohn (271) |
| Sept. 11 | Bell Canadian Open | Mark Calcavecchia (275) | 900,000 | B. Crane & R. Moore (276) |
| Sept. 18 | 84 Lumber Classic of Pennsylvania | Jason Gore (274) | 792,000 | C. Franco (275) |
| Sept. 25 | The Presidents Cup | United States (18½) | — | International (15½) |
| Sept. 25 | Valero Texas Open | Robert Gamez (262) | 630,000 | O. Browne (265) |
| Oct. 2 | Chrysler Classic of Greensboro | K.J. Choi (266) | 900,000 | S. Maruyama (268) |
| Oct. 9 | WGC: American Express Championship | Tiger Woods (270) | 1,300,000 | J. Daly (270) |

% Weather-shortened.

+ Bob Hope Chrysler Classic is a five-round, 90-hole event played over five days.

† The scoring for The International is based on a modified Stableford system (8 points for a double eagle, 5 for an eagle, 2 for a birdie, 0 for a par, −1 for a bogey, −3 for double bogey or worse).

**\*Playoffs: Nissan**—Scott won on 1st hole; **Chrysler**—Ogilvy won on 2nd hole; **Honda**—Harrington won on 2nd hole; **BellSouth**—Mickelson won on 4th hole; **Masters**—Woods won on 1st hole; **Shell**—Singh won on 1st hole; **Zurich**—Petrovic won on 1st hole; **Wachovia**—Singh won on 4th hole; **Buick Champ.**—Faxon won on 1st hole; **WGC-AmEx**—Woods won on 2nd hole.

**#Second place ties** (3 players or more): 4-WAY—**BellSouth** (A. Atwal, R. Beem, B. Jobe, J.M. Olazabal); **MCI Heritage** (B. Andrade, D. Clarke, J. Furyk, D. Love III); **B.C. Open** (J.P. Hayes, B. Jones, R. Palmer, J. Rollins). 3-WAY—**Buick Invit.** (L. Donald, C. Howell III, T. Lehman); **TPC** (T. Lehman, S. Verplank, L. Donald); **Booz Allen** (D. Love III, B. Crane, A. Scott).

## PGA Majors

### The Masters

**Edition:** 69th | **Dates:** April 7–10
**Site:** Augusta National GC, Augusta, Ga.
**Par:** 36-36—72 (7290 yards) | **Purse:** $7,000,000

| | | 1 2 3 4 | Tot | Earnings |
|---|---|---|---|---|
| 1 | Tiger Woods* | 74-66-65-71— | 276 | $1,260,000 |
| 2 | Chris DiMarco* | 67-67-74-68— | 276 | 756,000 |
| 3 | Retief Goosen | 71-75-70-67— | 283 | 406,000 |
| | Luke Donald | 68-77-69-69— | 283 | 406,000 |
| 5 | Vijay Singh | 68-73-71-72— | 284 | 237,300 |
| | Mike Weir | 74-71-68-71— | 284 | 237,300 |
| | Mark Hensby | 69-73-70-72— | 284 | 237,300 |
| | Rod Pampling | 73-71-70-70— | 284 | 237,300 |
| | Trevor Immelman | 73-73-65-73— | 284 | 237,300 |
| 10 | Phil Mickelson | 70-72-69-74— | 285 | 189,000 |

**Early round leaders:** 1st—DiMarco (67); 2nd—DiMarco (134); 3rd—Woods (205).

**Top amateur:** Ryan Moore (288, tied for 13th).

\* Woods (3) defeated DiMarco (4) on the 1st hole of a sudden-death playoff.

### U.S. Open

**Edition:** 105th | **Dates:** June 16–19
**Site:** Pinehurst No. 2, Pinehurst, N.C.
**Par:** 35-35—70 (7214 yards) | **Purse:** $6,250,000

| | | 1 2 3 4 | Tot | Earnings |
|---|---|---|---|---|
| 1 | Michael Campbell | 71-69-71-69— | 280 | $1,170,000 |
| 2 | Tiger Woods | 70-71-72-69— | 282 | 700,000 |
| 3 | Sergio Garcia | 71-69-75-70— | 285 | 320,039 |
| | Tim Clark | 76-69-70-70— | 285 | 320,039 |
| | Mark Hensby | 71-68-72-74— | 285 | 320,039 |
| 6 | Davis Love III | 77-70-70-69— | 286 | 187,813 |
| | Rocco Mediate | 67-74-74-71— | 286 | 187,813 |
| | Vijay Singh | 70-70-74-72— | 286 | 187,813 |
| 9 | Nick Price | 72-71-72-72— | 287 | 150,834 |
| | Arron Oberholser | 76-67-71-73— | 287 | 150,834 |

**Early round leaders:** 1st—Mediate & Olin Browne (67); 2nd—Browne, Retief Goosen & Jason Gore (138); 3rd—Goosen (207).

**Top amateur:** Matt Every (291, tied for 28th).

### British Open

**Edition:** 134th | **Dates:** July 14–17
**Site:** St. Andrews, Fife, Scotland
**Par:** 36-36—72 (7279 yards) | **Purse:** $7,500,000

| | | 1 2 3 4 | Tot | Earnings |
|---|---|---|---|---|
| 1 | Tiger Woods | 66-67-71-70— | 274 | $1,261,584 |
| 2 | Colin Montgomerie | 71-66-70-72— | 279 | 753,446 |
| 3 | Fred Couples | 68-71-73-68— | 280 | 424,909 |
| | Jose Maria Olazabal | 68-70-68-74— | 280 | 424,909 |
| 5 | Geoff Ogilvy | 71-74-67-69— | 281 | 214,060 |
| | Bernhard Langer | 71-69-70-71— | 281 | 214,060 |
| | Michael Campbell | 69-72-68-72— | 281 | 214,060 |
| | Vijay Singh | 69-69-71-72— | 281 | 214,060 |
| | Sergio Garcia | 70-69-69-73— | 281 | 214,060 |
| | Retief Goosen | 68-73-66-74— | 281 | 214,060 |

**Early round leaders:** 1st—Woods (66); 2nd—Woods (133); 3rd—Woods (204).

**Top amateur:** Lloyd Saltman (283, tied for 15th).

### PGA Championship

**Edition:** 87th | **Dates:** Aug. 11–15
**Site:** Baltusrol Golf Club, Springfield, N.J.
**Par:** 34-36—70 (7392 yards) | **Purse:** $6,250,000

| | | 1 2 3 4 | Tot | Earnings |
|---|---|---|---|---|
| 1 | Phil Mickelson | 67-65-72-72— | 276 | $1,170,000 |
| 2 | Steve Elkington | 68-70-68-71— | 277 | 572,000 |
| | Thomas Bjorn | 71-71-63-72— | 277 | 572,000 |
| 4 | Tiger Woods | 75-69-66-68— | 278 | 286,000 |
| | Davis Love III | 68-68-68-74— | 278 | 286,000 |
| 6 | Geoff Ogilvy | 69-69-72-69— | 279 | 201,500 |
| | Michael Campbell | 73-68-69-69— | 279 | 201,500 |
| | Retief Goosen | 68-70-69-72— | 279 | 201,500 |
| | Pat Perez | 68-71-67-73— | 279 | 201,500 |
| 10 | Ted Purdy | 69-75-70-66— | 280 | 131,800 |
| | David Toms | 71-72-69-68— | 280 | 131,800 |
| | Steve Flesch | 70-71-69-70— | 280 | 131,800 |
| | Dudley Hart | 70-73-66-71— | 280 | 131,800 |
| | Vijay Singh | 70-67-69-74— | 280 | 131,800 |

**Early round leaders:** 1st—Mickelson, Ben Curtis, Stuart Appleby, Rory Sabbatini, Stephen Ames & Trevor Immelman (67); 2nd—Mickelson (132); 3rd—Mickelson & Love III (204).

**Top amateur:** none.

## European PGA Tour

Official money won on the European Tour is presented in euros (E).

### Late 2004

| Last Rd | Tournament | Winner | Earnings | Runner-Up |
|---|---|---|---|---|
| Nov. 21 | WGC: World Cup | England—Paul Casey/ Luke Donald (257) | E539,583 (each) | Spain—S. Garcia/ M.A. Jimenez (258) |
| Nov. 28 | Volvo China Open | Stephen Dodd (269) | 127,621 | T. Bjorn (279) |
| Dec. 5 | Omega Hong Kong Open | Miguel Angel Jimenez (266) | 100,338 | P. Harrington & J. Kingston (267) |
| Dec. 12 | dunhill Championship | Charl Schwartzel (281)* | 114,311 | N. Cheetham (281) |

**\*Playoffs: dunhill Championship**—Schwartzel won on 1st hole.

### 2005 (through Oct. 9)

| Last Rd | Tournament | Winner | Earnings | Runner-Up |
|---|---|---|---|---|
| Jan. 23 | South African Airways Open | Tim Clark (273) | E112,689 | C. Schwartzel & G. Havret (279) |
| Jan. 30 | Caltex Singapore Masters | Nick Dougherty (270) | 127,718 | M. Lafeber & C. Montgomerie (275) |
| Feb. 6 | Heineken Classic | Craig Parry (270)* | 225,368 | N. O'Hern (270) |
| Feb. 13 | Holden New Zealand Open | Niclas Fasth (266)* | 156,671 | M. Tunnicliff (266) |
| Feb. 20 | Carlsberg Malaysian Open | Thongchai Jaidee (267) | 156,763 | J. Randhawa (270) |
| Feb. 27 | WGC: Accenture Match Play Championship | David Toms (6&5) | 994,261 | C. DiMarco |
| Mar. 6 | Dubai Desert Classic | Ernie Els (269) | 277,878 | S. Dodd & M.A. Jimenez (270) |
| Mar. 13 | Qatar Masters | Ernie Els (276) | 188,765 | H. Stenson (277) |
| Mar. 20 | TCL Classic | Paul Casey (266)* | 123,773 | P. McGinley (266) |
| Mar. 27 | Indonesia Open | Thaworn Wiratchant (255) | 125,205 | R. Jacquelin (260) |
| Apr. 3 | Portugal Open | Paul Broadhurst (271) | 208,330 | P. Lawrie (272) |
| Apr. 10 | Madeira Island Open | Robert-Jan Derksen (275) | 100,000 | G. Orr & A. McLardy (277) |
| Apr. 10 | The Masters Tournament | Tiger Woods (276)* | 977,045 | C. DiMarco (276) |
| Apr. 17 | Spanish Open | Peter Hanson (280)* | 275,000 | P. Gustafsson (280) |
| Apr. 24 | Johnnie Walker Classic | Adam Scott (270) | 305,049 | R. Goosen (273) |
| May 1 | BMW Asian Open | Ernie Els (262) | 191,307 | S. Wakefield (275) |
| May 8 | Telecom Italia Open | Steve Webster (270) | 216,660 | 3-way tie (273)# |
| May 15 | Daily Telegraph Dunlop Masters | Thomas Bjorn (282)* | 417,753 | B. Davis & D. Howell (282) |
| May 22 | Nissan Irish Open | Stephen Dodd (279)* | 333,330 | D. Howell (279) |
| May 29 | BMW Championship | Angel Cabrera (273) | 666,660 | P. McGinley (275) |
| June 5 | Celtic Manor Wales Open | Miguel Angel Jimenez (262) | 362,567 | M. Erlandsson & J.M. Lara (266) |
| June 12 | KLM Open | G. Fernandez-Castano (269) | 250,000 | G. Emerson (271) |
| June 19 | U.S. Open | Michael Campbell (280) | 964,792 | T. Woods (282) |
| June 19 | Aa St. Omer Open | Joakim Backstrom (280)* | 66,660 | P. Dwyer (280) |
| June 26 | French Open | Jean-Francois Remesy (273)* | 583,330 | J. Van de Velde (273) |
| July 3 | Smurfit European Open | Kenneth Ferrie (285) | 577,816 | G. Storm & C. Montgomerie (287) |
| July 10 | The Barclays Scottish Open | Tim Clark (265) | 592,388 | D. Clarke & M. Lafeber (267) |
| July 17 | British Open (St. Andrews) | Tiger Woods (274) | 1,047,362 | C. Montgomerie (279) |
| July 24 | Deutsche Bank TPC | Niclas Fasth (274)* | 550,000 | A. Cabrera (274) |
| July 31 | Scandinavian Masters | Mark Hensby (262)* | 266,660 | H. Stenson (262) |
| Aug. 7 | Johnnie Walker Championship | Emanuele Canonica (281) | 338,443 | 4-way tie (273)# |
| Aug. 14 | PGA Championship | Phil Mickelson (276) | 949,138 | S. Elkington & T. Bjorn (277) |
| Aug. 14 | Cadillac Russian Open | Mikael Lundberg (273)* | 67,600 | A. Butterfield (273) |
| Aug. 21 | WGC: NEC Invitational | Tiger Woods (274) | 1,046,024 | C. DiMarco (275) |
| Aug. 28 | BMW International Open | David Howell (265) | 333,330 | J. Daly & B. Rumford (266) |
| Sept. 4 | Omega European Masters | Sergio Garcia (270) | 283,330 | P. Gustafsson (271) |
| Sept. 11 | Linde German Masters | Retief Goosen (268) | 500,000 | 4-way tie (269)# |
| Sept. 18 | HSBC World Match Play | Michael Campbell (2&1) | 601,828 | P. McGinley |

## The Official World Golf Ranking

Begun in 1986, the Official World Golf Ranking (formerly the Sony World Ranking) combines the best golfers on the world's six leading professional tours (U.S. PGA Tour, European Tour, Japan Golf Tour, South African PGA Tour, Asian PGA Tour and the PGA Tour of Australasia) in conjunction with the Canadian, Nationwide and Challenge Tours. Rankings are based on a rolling two-year period and weighted in favor of more recent results. Points are awarded after each worldwide tournament according to finish. Final points-per-tournament averages are determined by dividing a player's total points by the number of tournaments played over that two-year period (through Oct. 9, 2005).

| | | Avg | | | Avg | | | Avg |
|---|---|---|---|---|---|---|---|---|
| 1 | Tiger Woods, USA | 18.18 | 6 | Sergio Garcia, ESP | 7.61 | 11 | Angel Cabrera, ARG | 5.04 |
| 2 | Vijay Singh, FIJ | 11.94 | 7 | Adam Scott, AUS | 5.50 | 12 | Kenny Perry, USA | 5.01 |
| 3 | Phil Mickelson, USA | 9.64 | 8 | Chris DiMarco, USA | 5.38 | 13 | Padraig Harrington, IRE | 4.78 |
| 4 | Ernie Els, RSA | 8.87 | 9 | Jim Furyk, USA | 5.14 | 14 | Colin Montgomerie, SCO | 4.71 |
| 5 | Retief Goosen, RSA | 8.80 | 10 | David Toms, USA | 5.10 | 15 | Michael Campbell, NZ | 4.68 |

## European PGA Tour Results (Cont.)

| Last Rd | Tournament | Winner | Earnings | Runner-Up |
|---|---|---|---|---|
| Sept. 25 | The Seve Trophy | Gr. Britain & Ireland (16½) | — | Continental Europe (11½) |
| Oct. 2 | dunhill Links Championship | Colin Montgomerie (279) | £662,415 | K. Ferrie (280) |
| Oct. 9 | WGC: American Express Championship | Tiger Woods (270)* | 1,078,120 | J. Daly (270) |
| Oct. 9 | Abama Canarias Open | John Bickerton (274) | 75,000 | S. Little & M. Kirk (279) |

@ European Tour approved special event.

**\*Playoffs: Heineken Classic**—Parry won on 4th hole; **New Zealand**—Fasth won on 2nd hole; **TCL Classic**—Casey won on 2nd hole; **Masters**—Woods won on 1st hole; **Spanish**—Hanson won on 1st hole; **Dunlop Masters**—Bjorn won on 2nd hole; **Irish**—Dodd won on 1st hole; **Aa St Omer**—Backstrom won on 1st hole; **French**—Remesy won on 1st hole; **Deutsche Bank TPC**—Fasth won on 3rd hole; **Scandinavian**—Hensby won on 2nd hole; **Russian**—Lundberg won on 4th hole; **WGC-AmEx**—Woods won on 2nd hole.

**#Second place ties** (3 players or more): 4-WAY—**Johnnie Walker Champ** (B. Dredge, D. Lynn, N. Colsaerts, B. Lane); **Linde German** (J.M. Olazabal, H. Stenson, D. Lynn, N. Dougherty). 3-WAY—**Telecom Italia** (A. Hansen, B. Dredge, R. Finch).

## Champions Tour
(formerly Senior PGA Tour)

### Late 2004

| Last Rd | Tournament | Winner | Earnings | Runner-Up |
|---|---|---|---|---|
| Nov. 22@ | UBS Cup | United States (14) | $150,000 (each) | Rest of the World (10) |
| Dec. 5@ | Office Depot Father/Son Challenge | Larry/Drew Nelson (119) | $100,000 (each) | Bob/David Charles (122) |

### 2005 (through Oct. 9)

| Last Rd | Tournament | Winner | Earnings | Runner-Up |
|---|---|---|---|---|
| Jan. 23 | MasterCard Championship | Dana Quigley (198)* | $272,000 | T. Watson (198) |
| Jan. 30 | Turtle Bay Championship | Hale Irwin (200) | 225,000 | D. Quigley (205) |
| Feb. 6@ | Wendy's Champions Skins Game | Jack Nicklaus (11 skins) | 340,000 | C. Stadler (5 skins) |
| Feb. 20 | ACE Group Classic | Mark James (203) | 240,000 | H. Irwin & T. Wargo (205) |
| Feb. 27 | Outback Steakhouse Pro-Am | Hale Irwin (134)% | 240,000 | M. Hatalsky & M. McNulty (135) |
| Mar. 13 | SBC Classic | Des Smyth (211) | 232,500 | M. McNulty & D.A. Weibring (212) |
| Mar. 20 | Toshiba Senior Classic | Mark Johnson (200) | 247,500 | K. Fergus & W. Levi (204) |
| Apr. 24 | Liberty Mutual Legends of Golf | Des Smyth (208) | 382,000 | T. Jenkins (210) |
| May 1 | FedEx Kinko's Classic | Jim Thorpe (206) | 247,500 | D. Quigley (210) |
| May 15 | Blue Angels Classic | Jim Thorpe (194)* | 225,000 | M. Hatalsky (194) |
| May 22 | Bruno's Memorial Classic | D.A. Weibring (201) | 225,000 | T. Jenkins & T. Kite (203) |
| May 29 | **Senior PGA Championship** (Ligonier, Penn.) | Mike Reid (280)* | 360,000 | D. Quigley & J. Pate (280) |
| June 5 | Allianz Championship | Tom Jenkins (204)* | 225,000 | D.A. Weibring (204) |
| June 12 | Bayer Advantage Classic | Dana Quigley (133)*% | 248,000 | T. Watson & G. Morgan (133) |
| June 26 | Bank of America Championship | Mark McNulty (204)* | 232,500 | D. Pooley & T. Purtzer (204) |
| July 3 | Commerce Bank Championship | Ron Streck (197) | 225,000 | J. Ahern (200) |
| July 10 | **Ford Senior Players Championship** (Dearborn, Mich.) | Peter Jacobsen (273) | 375,000 | H. Irwin (274) |
| July 24 | **Senior British Open** (Aberdeen, Scotland) | Tom Watson (280)* | 274,099 | D. Smyth (280) |
| July 31 | **U.S. Senior Open** (Kettering, Ohio) | Allen Doyle (274) | 470,000 | D.A. Weibring & L. Roberts (275) |
| Aug. 7 | 3M Championship | Tom Purtzer (201) | 262,500 | L. Nielsen & C. Stadler (202) |
| Aug. 21 | Boeing Greater Seattle Classic | David Eger (199) | 240,000 | T. Kite (202) |
| Aug. 28 | **JELD-WEN Tradition** (Aloha, Ore.) | Loren Roberts (273)* | 375,000 | D. Quigley (273) |
| Sept. 4 | Wal-Mart First Tee Open | Hale Irwin (203) | 300,000 | 3-way tie (204)# |
| Sept. 18 | Constellation Energy Classic | Bob Gilder (198) | 255,000 | M. Hatalsky (202) |
| Sept. 23 | Georgia-Pacific Grand Champions | Mike McCullough (133) | 85,000 | B. Summerhays (135) |
| Oct. 2 | SAS Championship | Hale Irwin (203) | 285,000 | B. Gilder & T. Jenkins (205) |
| Oct. 9 | Greater Hickory Classic | Jay Haas (200) | 240,000 | D. Quigley (202) |

%Weather-shortened.

@Unofficial Champions Tour money event.

**\*Playoffs: MasterCard**—Quigley won on 3rd hole; **Blue Angels**—Thorpe won on 3rd hole; **Sr. PGA Champ**—Reid won on 1st hole; **Allianz**—Jenkins won on 2nd hole; **Bayer Advantage**—Quigley won on 1st hole; **Bank of America**—McNulty won on 2nd hole; **Sr. British**—Watson won on 3rd hole; **JELD-WEN**—Roberts won on 2nd hole.

**#Second place tie** (3 players or more): 3-WAY—**Wal-Mart First Tee Open** (M. Hatalsky, C. Stadler, G. Morgan).

## Champions Tour Majors

### Senior PGA Championship

**Edition:** 66th     **Dates:** May 26-29
**Site:** Laurel Valley Golf Club, Ligonier, Penn.
**Par:** 36-36—72 (7107 yards)     **Purse:** $2,000,000

| | | 1 2 3 4 | Tot | Earnings |
|---|---|---|---|---|
| 1 | Mike Reid* | 70-70-70-70— | 280 | $360,000 |
| 2 | Dana Quigley* | 71-71-66-72— | 280 | 176,000 |
| | Jerry Pate* | 70-68-72-70— | 280 | 176,000 |
| 4 | Morris Hatalsky | 74-70-70-70— | 284 | 96,000 |
| 5 | Tom Jenkins | 74-70-72-71— | 287 | 76,000 |
| 6 | Allen Doyle | 72-73-71-72— | 288 | 60,000 |
| | Peter Jacobsen | 71-71-71-75— | 288 | 60,000 |
| | Des Smyth | 74-76-70-68— | 288 | 60,000 |
| | Mark McNulty | 74-66-76-72— | 288 | 60,000 |
| 10 | Tom Kite | 71-73-74-71— | 289 | 44,250 |
| | Mark James | 73-71-75-70— | 289 | 44,250 |
| | Dave Barr | 69-72-71-77— | 289 | 44,250 |
| | R.W. Eaks | 69-70-73-77— | 289 | 44,250 |

**Early round leaders:** 1st—Graham Marsh (68); 2nd—Pate (138); 3rd—Quigley (208).

**Top amateur:** none.

*Reid (4) defeated Quigley (DNF) and Pate (DNF) on the 1st hole of a sudden-death playoff.

### Ford Sr. Players Championship

**Edition:** 23rd     **Dates:** July 7-10
**Site:** TPC of Michigan, Dearborn, Mich.
**Par:** 36-36—72 (7069 yards)     **Purse:** $2,500,000

| | | 1 2 3 4 | Tot | Earnings |
|---|---|---|---|---|
| 1 | Peter Jacobsen | 70-66-71-66— | 273 | $375,000 |
| 2 | Hale Irwin | 68-68-68-70— | 274 | 220,000 |
| 3 | Tom McKnight | 68-67-70-71— | 276 | 165,000 |
| | Tom Watson | 66-72-70-68— | 276 | 165,000 |
| 5 | Allen Doyle | 74-67-69-68— | 278 | 87,500 |
| | Gary McCord | 68-71-69-70— | 278 | 87,500 |
| | Gil Morgan | 72-66-67-73— | 278 | 87,500 |
| | Larry Nelson | 68-74-67-69— | 278 | 87,500 |
| | Dana Quigley | 67-66-72-73— | 278 | 87,500 |
| | D.A. Weibring | 70-70-73-65— | 278 | 87,500 |

**Early round leaders:** 1st—Graham Marsh (64); 2nd—Quigley (133); 3rd—Irwin (204).

**Top amateur:** none.

### Senior British Open

**Edition:** 19th (3rd as major)     **Dates:** July 21-24
**Site:** Royal Aberdeen Golf Club, Aberdeen, Scotland
**Par:** 36-35—71 (6836 yards)     **Purse:** $1,738,201

| | | 1 2 3 4 | Tot | Earnings |
|---|---|---|---|---|
| 1 | Tom Watson* | 75-71-64-70— | 280 | $274,099 |
| 2 | Des Smyth | 73-72-66-68— | 280 | 182,819 |
| 3 | Greg Norman | 76-67-70-68— | 281 | 102,917 |
| 4 | Craig Stadler | 73-68-70-72— | 283 | 82,247 |
| 5 | Loren Roberts | 72-74-71-67— | 284 | 69,688 |
| 6 | Derrick Cooper | 73-70-64-70— | 287 | 53,447 |
| | David Eger | 80-70-72-65— | 287 | 53,447 |
| 8 | Mark McNulty | 76-72-72-68— | 288 | 41,080 |
| 9 | Martin Gray | 77-73-71-69— | 290 | 33,321 |
| | Eduardo Romero | 75-71-75-69— | 290 | 33,321 |
| | Ray Stewart | 73-77-75-65— | 290 | 33,321 |

**Early round leaders:** 1st—Roberts (72); 2nd—Stadler (141); 3rd—Watson (210).

**Top amateur:** Adrian Morrow (301, tied for 46th).

*Watson (4-4-3) defeated Smyth (4-4-4) on the 3rd hole of a sudden-death playoff.

### U.S. Senior Open

**Edition:** 26th     **Dates:** July 28-31
**Site:** NCR Country Club, Kettering, Ohio
**Par:** 36-35—71 (7000 yards)     **Purse:** $2,600,000

| | | 1 2 3 4 | Tot | Earnings |
|---|---|---|---|---|
| 1 | Allen Doyle | 71-67-73-63— | 274 | $470,000 |
| 2 | D.A. Weibring | 70-67-68-70— | 275 | 227,457 |
| | Loren Roberts | 66-67-69-73— | 275 | 227,457 |
| 4 | Greg Norman | 68-70-69-69— | 276 | 121,887 |
| 5 | Wayne Levi | 68-67-74-68— | 277 | 93,100 |
| | Tom Watson | 68-65-73-71— | 277 | 93,100 |
| 7 | Mark McNulty | 70-67-74-67— | 278 | 75,720 |
| | Craig Stadler | 64-69-69-76— | 278 | 75,720 |
| 9 | Dana Quigley | 73-71-66-69— | 279 | 61,846 |
| | Rodger Davis | 69-72-67-71— | 279 | 61,846 |
| | Des Smyth | 70-66-70-73— | 279 | 61,846 |

**Early round leaders:** 1st—Stadler (64); 2nd—Roberts, Watson & Stadler (133); 3rd—Roberts & Stadler (202).

**Top amateur:** George Zahringer & Greg Reynolds (288, tied for 31st).

### JELD-WEN Tradition

**Edition:** 17th     **Dates:** Aug. 25-28
**Site:** The Reserve Vineyards & Golf Club, Aloha, Ore.
**Par:** 35-37—72 (7212 yards)     **Purse:** $2,500,000

| | | 1 2 3 4 | Tot | Earnings |
|---|---|---|---|---|
| 1 | Loren Roberts* | 67-69-70-67— | 273 | $375,000 |
| 2 | Dana Quigley* | 73-72-68-67— | 273 | 220,000 |
| 3 | Gil Morgan | 69-64-70-71— | 274 | 180,000 |
| 4 | Mark James | 71-66-70-68— | 275 | 150,000 |
| 5 | James Mason | 71-70-68-67— | 276 | 103,333 |
| | Tom Jenkins | 69-66-69-72— | 276 | 103,333 |
| | Doug Tewell | 70-67-66-73— | 276 | 103,333 |
| 8 | Mark McNulty | 71-65-70-71— | 277 | $80,000 |
| 9 | R.W. Eaks | 68-74-70-69— | 281 | 62,500 |
| | Mike Reid | 72-71-70-68— | 281 | 62,500 |
| | Tom Watson | 74-71-70-66— | 281 | 62,500 |
| | D.A. Weibring | 67-70-70-74— | 281 | 62,500 |

**Early round leaders:** 1st—Roberts, Quigley, Weibring & John Harris (67); 2nd—Morgan (133); 3rd—Morgan & Tewell (203).

**Top amateur:** none.

*Roberts (4-5) defeated Quigley (4-DNF) on the 2nd hole of a sudden-death playoff.

# LPGA Tour

## Late 2004

| Last Rd | Tournament | Winner | Earnings | Runner-Up |
|---|---|---|---|---|
| Nov. 7 | Mizuno Classic | Annika Sorenstam (194) | $150,000 | 3-way tie (203)# |
| Nov. 14 | The Mitchell Company TOC | Heather Daly-Donofrio (269) | 130,000 | L. Diaz (273) |
| Nov. 21 | ADT Tour Championship | Annika Sorenstam (275)* | 215,000 | C. Kerr (275) |

**\*Playoffs: Mobile ADT Tour Championship**—Sorenstam won on 1st hole.

**#Second place ties** (3 players or more): 3-WAY—**Mizuno** (A. Miyazato, M. Ohba, Gr. Park).

## 2005 (through Oct. 9)

| Last Rd | Tournament | Winner | Earnings | Runner-Up |
|---|---|---|---|---|
| Feb. 13 | Women's World Cup of Golf | Japan (289) | $200,000 | The Philippines & Korea (291) |
| Feb. 26 | SBS Open at Turtle Bay | Jennifer Rosales (208) | 150,000 | C. Kerr & M. Wie (210) |
| Mar. 6 | MasterCard Classic | Annika Sorenstam (209) | 180,000 | K. Webb (212) |
| Mar. 20 | Safeway International | Annika Sorenstam (277)* | 210,000 | L. Ochoa (277) |
| Mar. 27 | **Kraft Nabisco Championship** (Rancho Mirage, Calif.) | Annika Sorenstam (273) | 270,000 | R. Jones (281) |
| Apr. 16 | Takefuji Classic | Wendy Ward (200) | 165,000 | L. Ochoa (202) |
| Apr. 24 | Corona Morelia Championship | Carin Koch (279) | 150,000 | K. Icher (285) |
| May 1 | Franklin American Mortgage Champ. | Stacy Prammanasudh (274) | 150,000 | L. Ochoa (277) |
| May 8 | Michelob Ultra Open | Cristie Kerr (276) | 330,000 | J. McGill (281) |
| May 15 | Chick-fil-A Charity Championship | Annika Sorenstam (265) | 240,000 | C. Kung (275) |
| May 22 | Sybase Classic | Paula Creamer (278) | 187,500 | J. Jang & Gl. Park (279) |
| May 29 | Corning Classic | Jimin Kang (273) | 165,000 | A. Sorenstam & M. Lee (275) |
| June 5 | ShopRite Classic | Annika Sorenstam (196) | 210,000 | J. Inkster (200) |
| June 12 | **McDonald's LPGA Championship** (Havre de Grace, Md.) | Annika Sorenstam (277) | 270,000 | M. Wie (280) |
| June 19 | Wegmans Rochester | Lorena Ochoa (273) | 225,000 | P. Creamer (277) |
| June 26 | **U.S. Women's Open** (Cherry Hills Village, Colo.) | Birdie Kim (287) | 560,000 | M. Pressel & B. Lang (289) |
| July 3 | HSBC Women's World Match Play | Marisa Baena (1-up) | 500,000 | M.Lee |
| July 10 | Jamie Farr Owens Corning Classic | Heather Bowie (274)* | 180,000 | Gl. Park (274) |
| July 17 | BMO Canadian Women's Open | Meena Lee (279) | 195,000 | K. Hull (280) |
| July 23 | Evian Masters | Paula Creamer (273) | 375,000 | L. Ochoa & M. Wie (281) |
| July 31 | **Weetabix Women's British Open** (Merseyside, England) | Jeong Jang (272) | 280,208 | S. Gustafson (276) |
| Aug. 21 | Safeway Classic | Soo-Yun Kang (201) | 210,000 | J. Jang (205) |
| Aug. 28 | Wendy's Championship for Children | Cristie Kerr (270) | 165,000 | A. Sorenstam & P. Creamer (271) |
| Sept. 4 | State Farm Classic | Pat Hurst (271) | 195,000 | C. Kerr (274) |
| Sept. 11 | The Solheim Cup | USA (15½) | — | Europe (12½) |
| Sept. 18 | John Q. Hammons Hotel Classic | Annika Sorenstam (208) | 150,000 | P. Creamer (209) |
| Oct. 2 | Office Depot Championship | Hee-Won Han (201) | 195,000 | S-Y Kang (203) |
| Oct. 9 | Longs Drugs Challenge | Nicole Perrot (270) | 150,000 | H-W Han (271) |

**\*Playoffs: Safeway**—Sorenstam won on 1st hole; **Jamie Farr**—Bowie won on 3rd hole.

# LPGA Majors

## Kraft Nabisco Championship

**Edition:** 34th       **Dates:** March 24-27
**Site:** Mission Hills CC, Rancho Mirage, Calif.
**Par:** 36-36—72 (6535 yards)      **Purse:** $1,800,000

| | 1 2 3 4 | Tot | Earnings |
|---|---|---|---|
| 1 Annika Sorenstam | 70-69-66-68 | 273 | $270,000 |
| 2 Rosie Jones | 69-70-71-71 | 281 | 166,003 |
| 3 Laura Diaz | 75-69-71-68 | 283 | 106,791 |
|    Cristie Kerr | 72-70-70-71 | 283 | 106,791 |
| 5 Grace Park | 73-68-76-67 | 284 | 68,165 |
|    Mi Hyun Kim | 69-71-72-72 | 284 | 68,165 |
| 7 Juli Inkster | 70-74-72-69 | 285 | 51,350 |
| 8 Lorie Kane | 71-76-69-70 | 286 | 44,988 |
| 9 Candie Kung | 72-73-71-71 | 287 | 34,591 |
|    Wendy Doolan | 74-69-73-71 | 287 | 34,591 |
|    Dorothy Delasin | 71-72-73-71 | 287 | 34,591 |
|    Beth Daniel | 74-72-69-72 | 287 | 34,591 |
|    Reilley Rankin | 73-68-74-72 | 287 | 34,591 |

**Early round leaders:** 1st—Jones, Kim & Karen Stupples (69); 2nd—Sorenstam & Jones (139); 3rd—Sorenstam (205).
**Top amateur:** Michelle Wie (288, tied for 14th).

## McDonald's LPGA Championship

**Edition:** 51st       **Dates:** June 9-12
**Site:** Bulle Rock Golf Course, Havre de Grace, Md.
**Par:** 36-36—72 (6488 yards)      **Purse:** $1,800,000

| | 1 2 3 4 | Tot | Earnings |
|---|---|---|---|
| 1 Annika Sorenstam | 68-67-69-73 | 277 | $270,000 |
| 2 a-Michelle Wie | 69-71-71-69 | 280 | amateur |
| 3 Paula Creamer | 68-73-74-67 | 282 | 140,517 |
|    Laura Davies | 67-70-74-71 | 282 | 140,517 |
| 5 Lorena Ochoa | 72-72-68-72 | 284 | 82,486 |
|    Natalie Gulbis | 67-71-73-73 | 284 | 82,486 |
| 7 Mi Hyun Kim | 69-75-74-67 | 285 | 43,993 |
|    Pat Hurst | 72-73-71-69 | 285 | 43,993 |
|    Gloria Park | 71-71-72-71 | 285 | 43,993 |
|    Carin Koch | 74-70-69-72 | 285 | 43,993 |
|    Moira Dunn | 71-68-72-74 | 285 | 43,993 |
|    Young Kim | 73-68-68-76 | 285 | 43,993 |

**Early round leaders:** 1st—Davies, Gulbis & Laura Diaz (67); 2nd—Sorenstam (135); 3rd—Sorenstam (204).

## U.S. Women's Open

**Edition:** 60th      **Dates:** June 23-26
**Site:** Cherry Hills CC, Cherry Hills Village, Colo.
**Par:** 35-36–71 (6749 yds)      **Purse:** $3,100,000

| | 1 2 3 4 | Tot | Earnings |
|---|---|---|---|
| 1 Birdie Kim | 74-72-69-72 | 287 | $560,000 |
| 2 a-Brittany Lang | 69-77-72-71 | 289 | amateur |
|   a-Morgan Pressel | 71-73-70-75 | 289 | amateur |
| 4 Lorie Kane | 74-71-76-69 | 290 | 272,723 |
|   Natalie Gulbis | 70-75-74-71 | 290 | 272,723 |
| 6 Lorena Ochoa | 74-68-77-72 | 291 | 116,310 |
|   Karine Icher | 69-75-75-72 | 291 | 116,310 |
|   Candie Kung | 73-73-71-74 | 291 | 116,310 |
|   Young Jo | 74-71-70-76 | 291 | 116,310 |
| 10 Cristie Kerr | 74-71-72-75 | 292 | 80,523 |
|   Angela Stanford | 69-74-73-76 | 292 | 80,523 |
|   Karen Stupples | 75-70-69-78 | 292 | 80,523 |

**Early round leaders:** 1st—Lang, Icher, Stanford & Michelle Wie (69); 2nd—Nicole Perrot (140); 3rd—Pressel, Stupples & Wie (214).

## Weetabix Women's British Open

**Edition:** 12th      **Dates:** July 28-31
**Site:** Royal Birkdale GC, Merseyside, England
**Par:** 35-37–72 (6463 yards)      **Purse:** $1,800,000

| | 1 2 3 4 | Tot | Earnings |
|---|---|---|---|
| 1 Jeong Jang | 68-66-69-69 | 272 | $280,208 |
| 2 Sophie Gustafson | 69-73-67-67 | 276 | 175,130 |
| 3 a-Michelle Wie | 75-67-67-69 | 278 | amateur |
|   Young Kim | 74-68-67-69 | 278 | 122,591 |
| 5 Liselotte Neumann | 71-70-68-70 | 279 | 81,144 |
|   Annika Sorenstam | 73-69-66-71 | 279 | 81,144 |
|   Cristie Kerr | 73-66-69-71 | 279 | 81,144 |
| 8 Natalie Gulbis | 76-70-68-66 | 280 | 58,669 |
|   Grace Park | 77-68-67-68 | 280 | 58,669 |
|   a-Louise Stahle | 73-65-73-69 | 280 | amateur |

**Early round leaders:** 1st—Jang (68); 2nd—Jang (134); 3rd—Jang (203).

# National Team Competition
## 2005 Solheim Cup

The 9th Solheim Cup tournament, Sept. 9-11, at Crooked Stick Golf Club, Carmel, Ind.

### Rosters

The 2005 U.S. Team was chosen on the basis of points awarded for wins and top 20 finishes at official LPGA events over a two-year qualifying period. The top 10 finishers on the points list automatically qualified for the 12-member team, and U.S. Captain Nancy Lopez selected the final two players.

The 2005 European Team players were chosen on the basis of points awarded weekly to the top 10 finishers at official Ladies European Tour (LET) events. The top seven players in the LET points standings automatically qualify for the 12-member team. European Team captain Catrin Nilsmark selected the final five players.

**United States:** Qualifiers—Cristie Kerr, Meg Mallon, Juli Inkster, Rosie Jones, Pat Hurst, Natalie Gulbis, Christina Kim, Paula Creamer, Michele Redman and Laura Diaz; Captain's selections—Beth Daniel and Wendy Ward.

**Europe:** Qualifiers—Annika Sorenstam (Sweden), Laura Davies (England), Ludivine Kreutz (France), Maria Hjorth (Sweden), Iben Tinning (Denmark), Trish Johnson (England) and Gwladys Nocera (France); Captain's selections—Carin Koch (Sweden), Sophie Gustafson (Sweden), Suzann Pettersen (Norway), Karen Stupples (England) and Catriona Matthew (Scotland).

### First Day

#### Foursome Match Results

| Winner | Score | Loser |
|---|---|---|
| Koch/Matthew | halved | Daniel/Creamer |
| Davies/Hjorth | 2&1 | Kerr/Gulbis |
| Gustafson/Johnson | halved | Kim/Hurst |
| Sorenstam/Pettersen | 1-up | Redman/Diaz |

Europe wins morning, 3-1

#### Four-Ball Match Results

| Winner | Score | Loser |
|---|---|---|
| Jones/Mallon | 3&2 | Hjorth/Tinning |
| Kerr/Gulbis | 2&1 | Gustafson/Stupples |
| Sorenstam/Matthiew | 2&1 | Hurst/Ward |
| Davies/Petterson | 4&3 | Creamer/Inkster |

Teams split afternoon, 2-2; (Europe leads, 5-3)

### Second Day

#### Foursome Match Results

| Winner | Score | Loser |
|---|---|---|
| Kim/Gulbis | 4&2 | Nocera/Kreutz |
| Creamer/Inkster | 3&2 | Davies/Hjorth |
| Gustafson/Koch | 5&3 | Diaz/Ward |
| Redman/Hurst | 2-up | Sorenstam/Matthew |

USA wins morning, 3-1; (Match tied, 6-6)

#### Four-Ball Match Results

| Winner | Score | Loser |
|---|---|---|
| Tinning/Johnson | halved | Daniel/Inkster |
| Gustafson/Pettersen | halved | Jones/Mallon |
| Kerr/Creamer | 1-up | Koch/Matthew |
| Davies/Sorenstam | 4&2 | Hurst/Kim |

Teams split afternoon, 2-2; (Match tied, 8-8)

### Third Day
#### Singles Match Results

| Winner | Score | Loser |
|---|---|---|
| Inkster | 2&1 | Gustafson |
| Creamer | 7&5 | Davies |
| Hurst | 2&1 | Johnson |
| Diaz | 6&5 | Tinning |
| Kim | 5&4 | Kreutz |
| Sorenstam | 4&3 | Daniel |

| Winner | Score | Loser |
|---|---|---|
| Gulbis | 2&1 | Hjorth |
| Matthew | 3&2 | Ward |
| Koch | 2&1 | Redman |
| Nocera | 2&1 | Kerr |
| Mallon | 3&1 | Stupples |
| Pettersen | halved | Jones |

USA wins day, 7½-4½

**United States wins Solheim Cup, 15½-12½**

## National Team Competition (Cont.)
## 2005 Presidents Cup

The 6th Presidents Cup tournament, Sept. 20-25, at Robert Trent Jones Golf Club, Prince William County, Va. The Presidents Cup is a biennial event played in non-Ryder Cup years that matches the United States against the world's best non-European players.

### Rosters

The 2005 U.S. Team was chosen on the basis of official earnings (top 10) from the beginning of the 2004 season through the 2005 PGA Championship, plus two captain's selections. The International Team is chosen on the basis of the Official World Golf Ranking (top 10 non American/Europeans) plus two captain's selections.

**United States:** Captain—Jack Nicklaus; Qualifiers—Tiger Woods, Phil Mickelson, David Toms, Kenny Perry, Chris DiMarco, Jim Furyk, Fred Funk, Stewart Cink, Davis Love III, Scott Verplank; Captain's selections—Justin Leonard, Fred Couples.

**International:** Captain—Gary Player; Qualifiers—Vijay Singh (Fiji), Retief Goosen (South Africa), Adam Scott (Australia), Angel Cabrera (Argentina), Tim Clark (South Africa), Michael Campbell (New Zealand), Stuart Appleby (Australia), Mike Weir (Canada), Nick O'Hern (Australia), Mark Hensby (Australia); Captain's selections—Peter Lonard (Australia), Trevor Immelman (South Africa). Note that Ernie Els was ranked second in the International Presidents Cup team standings but was unable to play due to injury.

### First Day
### Alternate-Shot Match Results

| Winner | Score | Loser |
|---|---|---|
| Scott/Goosen | .4&3 | Woods/Couples |
| Funk/Furyk | halved | Singh/Hensby |
| Mickelson/DiMarco | 1-up | O'Hern/Clark |
| Leonard/Verplank | .4&2 | Lonard/Appleby |
| Campbell/Cabrera | .2&1 | Love III/Perry |
| Immelman/Weir | .6&5 | Toms/Cink |

International wins day, 3½-2½

### Second Day
### Four-Ball Match Results

| Winner | Score | Loser |
|---|---|---|
| Mickelson/DiMarco | halved | Cabrera/Campbell |
| Scott/Goosen | .3&1 | Couples/Toms |
| Leonard/Verplank | .2&1 | Immelman/Weir |
| Funk/Cink | halved | Singh/Hensby |
| Lonard/O'Hern | .3&2 | Love III/Perry |
| Woods/Furyk | .3&2 | Appleby/Hensby |

Teams split day, 3-3; (Int'l leads, 6½-5½)

### Third Day

### Four-Ball Match Results

| Winner | Score | Loser |
|---|---|---|
| Goosen/Scott | .5&4 | Leonard/Verplank |
| Mickelson/DiMarco | .6&5 | Lonard/O'Hern |
| Love III/Couples | halved | Campbell/Cabrera |
| Hensby/Clark | .5&3 | Perry/Cink |
| Woods/Furyk | .2-up | Singh/Appleby |

Teams split, 2½-2½; (Int'l leads, 9-8)

### Alternate-Shot Match Results

| Winner | Score | Loser |
|---|---|---|
| Leonard/Verplank | halved | Goosen/Scott |
| Mickelson/DiMarco | .5&3 | Cabrera/Campbell |
| Woods/Furyk | halved | Singh/Appleby |
| Clark/O'Hern | .2&1 | Funk/Toms |
| Love III/Cink | .1-up | Immelman/Weir |

USA wins, 3-2; (Match tied, 11-11)

### Fourth Day

### Singles Match Results

| Winner | Score | Loser | Winner | Score | Loser |
|---|---|---|---|---|---|
| Leonard | .4&3 | Clark | Furyk | .3&2 | Scott |
| Toms | .2&1 | Immelman | Lonard | .3&2 | Cink |
| Goosen | .2&1 | Woods | Campbell | .3&2 | Funk |
| Perry | .4&3 | Hensby | Love III | .4&3 | O'Hern |
| Couples | .1-up | Singh | Mickelson | halved | Cabrera |
| Weir | .3&2 | Verplank | DiMarco | .1-up | Appleby |

USA wins day, 7½-4½

**United States wins Presidents Cup, 18½-15½**

### Overall Records

One point is awarded for a win. One-half point is awarded for a half.

| United States | W | L | H | Pts |
|---|---|---|---|---|
| Chris DiMarco | 4 | 0 | 1 | 4.5 |
| Jim Furyk | 3 | 0 | 2 | 4.0 |
| Phil Mickelson | 3 | 0 | 2 | 4.0 |
| Justin Leonard | 3 | 1 | 1 | 3.5 |
| Tiger Woods | 2 | 2 | 1 | 3.0 |
| Scott Verplank | 2 | 2 | 1 | 2.5 |
| Davis Love III | 2 | 2 | 1 | 2.5 |
| Fred Couples | 1 | 2 | 1 | 1.5 |
| Stewart Cink | 1 | 3 | 1 | 1.5 |
| Kenny Perry | 1 | 3 | 0 | 1.0 |
| David Toms | 1 | 3 | 0 | 1.0 |
| Fred Funk | 0 | 2 | 2 | 1.0 |

| International | W | L | H | Pts |
|---|---|---|---|---|
| Retief Goosen | 4 | 0 | 1 | 4.5 |
| Adam Scott | 3 | 1 | 1 | 3.5 |
| Michael Campbell | 2 | 1 | 2 | 3.0 |
| Tim Clark | 2 | 2 | 1 | 2.5 |
| Angel Cabrera | 1 | 1 | 3 | 2.5 |
| Peter Lonard | 2 | 2 | 0 | 2.0 |
| Mike Weir | 2 | 2 | 0 | 2.0 |
| Nick O'Hern | 2 | 3 | 0 | 2.0 |
| Mark Hensby | 1 | 2 | 1 | 1.5 |
| Vijay Singh | 0 | 2 | 3 | 1.5 |
| Trevor Immelman | 1 | 3 | 0 | 1.0 |
| Stuart Appleby | 0 | 4 | 1 | 0.5 |

## Money Leaders

Official money leaders of PGA, European PGA, Champions and LPGA tours for 2004 and unofficial money leaders for 2005, through Oct. 9, as compiled by the PGA, European PGA and LPGA. All European amounts are in euros (E).

### PGA

Arnold Palmer Award standings: listed are tournaments played (TP); cuts made (CM); 1st, 2nd and 3rd place finishes; and earnings for the year.

| | FINAL 2004 | TP | CM | Finish 1-2-3 | Earnings | | 2005 (through Oct. 9) | TP | CM | Finish 1-2-3 | Earnings |
|---|---|---|---|---|---|---|---|---|---|---|---|
| 1 | Vijay Singh | 29 | 28 | 9-2-1 | $10,905,166 | 1 | Tiger Woods | 19 | 18 | 6-3-2 | $9,913,024 |
| 2 | Ernie Els | 16 | 15 | 3-2-1 | 5,787,225 | 2 | Vijay Singh | 27 | 25 | 4-2-3 | 7,733,503 |
| 3 | Phil Mickelson | 22 | 19 | 2-2-3 | 5,784,823 | 3 | Phil Mickelson | 20 | 20 | 4-1-0 | 5,699,605 |
| 4 | Tiger Woods | 19 | 19 | 1-3-3 | 5,365,472 | 4 | David Toms | 23 | 18 | 1-1-1 | 3,843,713 |
| 5 | Stewart Cink | 28 | 24 | 2-1-0 | 4,450,270 | 5 | Jim Furyk | 24 | 21 | 1-3-0 | 3,664,769 |
| 6 | Retief Goosen | 16 | 13 | 2-0-1 | 3,385,573 | 6 | Kenny Perry | 22 | 18 | 2-0-1 | 3,483,655 |
| 7 | Adam Scott | 16 | 12 | 2-1-1 | 3,724,984 | 7 | Chris DiMarco | 22 | 16 | 0-3-1 | 3,432,548 |
| 8 | Stephen Ames | 27 | 21 | 1-0-1 | 3,303,205 | 8 | Retief Goosen | 15 | 14 | 1-0-2 | 3,185,275 |
| 9 | Sergio Garcia | 18 | 16 | 2-0-0 | 3,239,215 | 9 | Sergio Garcia | 19 | 16 | 1-1-2 | 3,089,875 |
| 10 | Davis Love III | 24 | 18 | 0-2-1 | 3,075,092 | 10 | Fred Funk | 27 | 20 | 1-0-1 | 2,668,874 |

### European PGA

Order of Merit standings: listed are tournaments played (TP); cuts made (CM); 1st, 2nd and 3rd place finishes; and earnings for the year.

| | FINAL 2004 | TP | CM | Finish 1-2-3 | Earnings | | 2005 (through Oct. 9) | TP | CM | Finish 1-2-3 | Earnings |
|---|---|---|---|---|---|---|---|---|---|---|---|
| 1 | Ernie Els | 15 | 15 | 3-2-2 | E4,061,905 | 1 | Colin Montgomerie | 23 | 19 | 1-3-1 | E2,565,089 |
| 2 | Retief Goosen | 13 | 13 | 2-0-0 | 2,325,202 | 2 | Michael Campbell | 21 | 15 | 2-0-1 | 2,434,069 |
| 3 | Padraig Harrington | 20 | 18 | 2-2-2 | 1,910,394 | 3 | Retief Goosen | 13 | 12 | 1-1-2 | 2,261,211 |
| 4 | Miguel Angel Jimenez | 27 | 23 | 4-2-1 | 1,886,237 | 4 | Angel Cabrera | 16 | 14 | 1-1-2 | 1,834,027 |
| 5 | Thomas Levet | 28 | 22 | 1-2-2 | 1,727,945 | 5 | David Howell | 18 | 16 | 1-2-0 | 1,769,208 |
| 6 | Graeme McDowell | 31 | 24 | 1-2-2 | 1,648,862 | 6 | Paul McGinley | 22 | 20 | 0-3-1 | 1,629,763 |
| 7 | Lee Westwood | 21 | 17 | 0-2-0 | 1,592,766 | 7 | Thomas Bjorn | 23 | 20 | 1-1-2 | 1,561,190 |
| 8 | Darren Clarke | 19 | 15 | 0-0-3 | 1,563,803 | 8 | Henrik Stenson | 23 | 20 | 0-3-4 | 1,535,750 |
| 9 | Ian Poulter | 25 | 19 | 1-0-1 | 1,533,158 | 9 | Kenneth Ferrie | 27 | 17 | 1-1-0 | 1,338,537 |
| 10 | David Howell | 26 | 23 | 0-0-3 | 1,501,502 | 10 | Sergio Garcia | 9 | 8 | 1-0-2 | 1,272,251 |

### Champions Tour

| | FINAL 2004 | TP | CM | Finish 1-2-3 | Earnings | | 2005 (through Oct. 9) | TP | CM | Finish 1-2-3 | Earnings |
|---|---|---|---|---|---|---|---|---|---|---|---|
| 1 | Craig Stadler | 21 | 21 | 5-1-2 | $2,306,066 | 1 | Dana Quigley | 24 | 24 | 2-5-0 | $1,953,098 |
| 2 | Hale Irwin | 23 | 23 | 2-3-1 | 2,035,397 | 2 | Hale Irwin | 19 | 19 | 4-2-1 | 1,794,767 |
| 3 | Tom Kite | 27 | 27 | 1-3-2 | 1,831,211 | 3 | D.A. Weibring | 22 | 22 | 1-3-0 | 1,476,256 |
| 4 | Gil Morgan | 26 | 26 | 1-2-3 | 1,606,453 | 4 | Tom Jenkins | 24 | 24 | 1-3-1 | 1,399,334 |
| 5 | Bruce Fleisher | 28 | 27 | 2-1-1 | 1,537,571 | 5 | Mark McNulty | 20 | 20 | 1-2-0 | 1,341,352 |
| 6 | Larry Nelson | 25 | 24 | 2-2-1 | 1,428,224 | 6 | Morris Hatalsky | 22 | 22 | 0-4-0 | 1,223,356 |
| 7 | Mark McNulty | 20 | 20 | 3-0-0 | 1,423,048 | 7 | Craig Stadler | 19 | 18 | 0-2-1 | 1,170,698 |
| 8 | D.A. Weibring | 25 | 25 | 1-2-0 | 1,413,795 | 8 | Des Smyth | 19 | 19 | 2-1-0 | 1,167,473 |
| 9 | Jim Thorpe | 26 | 25 | 2-1-0 | 1,378,343 | 9 | Tom Watson | 12 | 12 | 1-2-2 | 1,092,482 |
| 10 | Allen Doyle | 27 | 27 | 1-1-1 | 1,298,555 | 10 | Gil Morgan | 22 | 22 | 0-2-2 | 1,091,570 |

### LPGA

| | FINAL 2004 | TP | CM | Finish 1-2-3 | Earnings | | 2005 (through Oct. 9) | TP | CM | Finish 1-2-3 | Earnings |
|---|---|---|---|---|---|---|---|---|---|---|---|
| 1 | Annika Sorenstam | 18 | 18 | 8-4-0 | $2,544,707 | 1 | Annika Sorenstam | 16 | 16 | 7-2-0 | $1,992,604 |
| 2 | Grace Park | 24 | 22 | 2-7-3 | 1,525,471 | 2 | Paula Creamer | 21 | 19 | 2-3-2 | 1,332,254 |
| 3 | Lorena Ochoa | 27 | 27 | 2-1-5 | 1,450,824 | 3 | Cristie Kerr | 20 | 18 | 2-2-4 | 1,301,524 |
| 4 | Meg Mallon | 21 | 19 | 3-1-0 | 1,358,623 | 4 | Lorena Ochoa | 20 | 17 | 1-4-0 | 1,165,932 |
| 5 | Cristie Kerr | 24 | 20 | 3-2-0 | 1,189,990 | 5 | Jeong Jang | 22 | 21 | 1-2-0 | 990,821 |
| 6 | Karen Stupples | 25 | 23 | 2-1-1 | 968,852 | 6 | Natalie Gulbis | 23 | 22 | 0-0-2 | 937,761 |
| 7 | Mi Hyun Kim | 28 | 24 | 0-1-1 | 931,693 | 7 | Hee-Won Han | 23 | 21 | 1-1-2 | 781,364 |
| 8 | Hee-Won Han | 28 | 24 | 1-1-1 | 840,605 | 8 | Meena Lee | 23 | 14 | 1-2-0 | 761,416 |
| 9 | Karrie Webb | 22 | 21 | 1-1-2 | 748,316 | 9 | Candie Kung | 21 | 21 | 0-1-0 | 708,417 |
| 10 | Jennifer Rosales | 21 | 20 | 1-0-0 | 693,625 | 10 | Gloria Park | 23 | 21 | 0-2-1 | 699,462 |

# 1860-2005
# *Through the Years*

SPORTS ALMANAC

## Major Golf Championships
## MEN
## The Masters

The Masters has been played every year (except during World War II) since 1934 at the Augusta National Golf Club in Augusta, Ga. Both the course and the tournament were created by Bobby Jones; (*) indicates playoff winner.

**Multiple winners:** Jack Nicklaus (6); Arnold Palmer and Tiger Woods (4); Jimmy Demaret, Nick Faldo, Gary Player and Sam Snead (3); Seve Ballesteros, Ben Crenshaw, Ben Hogan, Bernhard Langer, Byron Nelson, Jose Maria Olazabal, Horton Smith and Tom Watson (2).

| Year | Winner | Score | Runner-up |
|---|---|---|---|
| 1934 | Horton Smith | .284 | Craig Wood (285) |
| 1935 | Gene Sarazen* | .282 | Craig Wood (282) |
| 1936 | Horton Smith | .285 | Harry Cooper (286) |
| 1937 | Byron Nelson | .283 | Ralph Guldahl (285) |
| 1938 | Henry Picard | .285 | Ralph Guldahl & Harry Cooper (287) |
| 1939 | Ralph Guldahl | .279 | Sam Snead (280) |
| 1940 | Jimmy Demaret | .280 | Lloyd Mangrum (284) |
| 1941 | Craig Wood | .280 | Byron Nelson (283) |
| 1942 | Byron Nelson* | .280 | Ben Hogan (280) |
| 1943-45 | Not held | | World War II |
| 1946 | Herman Keiser | .282 | Ben Hogan (283) |
| 1947 | Jimmy Demaret | .281 | Frank Stranahan & Byron Nelson (283) |
| 1948 | Claude Harmon | .279 | Cary Middlecoff (284) |
| 1949 | Sam Snead | .282 | Lloyd Mangrum & Johnny Bulla (285) |
| 1950 | Jimmy Demaret | .283 | Jim Ferrier (285) |
| 1951 | Ben Hogan | .280 | Skee Riegel (282) |
| 1952 | Sam Snead | .286 | Jack Burke Jr. (290) |
| 1953 | Ben Hogan | .274 | Porky Oliver (279) |
| 1954 | Sam Snead* | .289 | Ben Hogan (289) |
| 1955 | Cary Middlecoff | .279 | Ben Hogan (286) |
| 1956 | Jack Burke Jr. | .289 | Ken Venturi (290) |
| 1957 | Doug Ford | .283 | Sam Snead (286) |
| 1958 | Arnold Palmer | .284 | Doug Ford & Fred Hawkins (285) |
| 1959 | Art Wall Jr. | .284 | Cary Middlecoff (285) |
| 1960 | Arnold Palmer | .282 | Ken Venturi (283) |
| 1961 | Gary Player | .280 | Arnold Palmer & Charles R. Coe (281) |
| 1962 | Arnold Palmer* | .280 | Dow Finsterwald & Gary Player (280) |
| 1963 | Jack Nicklaus | .286 | Tony Lema (287) |
| 1964 | Arnold Palmer | .276 | Jack Nicklaus & Dave Marr (282) |
| 1965 | Jack Nicklaus | .271 | Arnold Palmer & Gary Player (280) |
| 1966 | Jack Nicklaus* | .288 | Gay Brewer Jr. & Tommy Jacobs (288) |
| 1967 | Gay Brewer Jr. | .280 | Bobby Nichols (281) |
| 1968 | Bob Goalby | .277 | Roberto DeVicenzo (278) |
| 1969 | George Archer | .281 | Billy Casper, George Knudson & Tom Weiskopf (282) |
| 1970 | Billy Casper* | .279 | Gene Littler (279) |
| 1971 | Charles Coody | .279 | Jack Nicklaus & Johnny Miller (281) |

| Year | Winner | Score | Runner-up |
|---|---|---|---|
| 1972 | Jack Nicklaus | .286 | Bruce Crampton, Bobby Mitchell & Tom Weiskopf (289) |
| 1973 | Tommy Aaron | .283 | J.C. Snead (284) |
| 1974 | Gary Player | .278 | Tom Weiskopf, & Dave Stockton (280) |
| 1975 | Jack Nicklaus | .276 | Johnny Miller & Tom Weiskopf (277) |
| 1976 | Ray Floyd | .271 | Ben Crenshaw (279) |
| 1977 | Tom Watson | .276 | Jack Nicklaus (278) |
| 1978 | Gary Player | .277 | Hubert Green, Rod Funseth & Tom Watson (278) |
| 1979 | Fuzzy Zoeller* | .280 | Ed Sneed & Tom Watson (280) |
| 1980 | Seve Ballesteros | .275 | Gibby Gilbert & Jack Newton (279) |
| 1981 | Tom Watson | .280 | Jack Nicklaus & Johnny Miller (282) |
| 1982 | Craig Stadler* | .284 | Dan Pohl (284) |
| 1983 | Seve Ballesteros | .280 | Ben Crenshaw & Tom Kite (284) |
| 1984 | Ben Crenshaw | .277 | Tom Watson (279) |
| 1985 | Bernhard Langer | .282 | Curtis Strange, Seve Ballesteros & Ray Floyd (284) |
| 1986 | Jack Nicklaus | .279 | Greg Norman & Tom Kite (280) |
| 1987 | Larry Mize* | .285 | Seve Ballesteros & Greg Norman (285) |
| 1988 | Sandy Lyle | .281 | Mark Calcavecchia (282) |
| 1989 | Nick Faldo* | .283 | Scott Hoch (283) |
| 1990 | Nick Faldo* | .278 | Ray Floyd (278) |
| 1991 | Ian Woosnam | .277 | J.M. Olazabal (278) |
| 1992 | Fred Couples | .275 | Ray Floyd (277) |
| 1993 | Bernhard Langer | .277 | Chip Beck (281) |
| 1994 | J.M. Olazabal | .279 | Tom Lehman (281) |
| 1995 | Ben Crenshaw | .274 | Davis Love III (275) |
| 1996 | Nick Faldo | .276 | Greg Norman (281) |
| 1997 | Tiger Woods | .270 | Tom Kite (282) |
| 1998 | Mark O'Meara | .279 | Fred Couples & David Duval (280) |
| 1999 | J.M. Olazabal | .280 | Davis Love III (282) |
| 2000 | Vijay Singh | .278 | Ernie Els (281) |
| 2001 | Tiger Woods | .272 | David Duval (274) |
| 2002 | Tiger Woods | .276 | Retief Goosen (279) |
| 2003 | Mike Weir* | .281 | Len Mattiace (281) |
| 2004 | Phil Mickelson | .279 | Ernie Els (280) |
| 2005 | Tiger Woods* | .276 | Chris DiMarco (276) |

**\*PLAYOFFS:**

**1935:** Gene Sarazen (144) def. Craig Wood (149) in 36 holes. **1942:** Byron Nelson (69) def. Ben Hogan (70) in 18 holes. **1954:** Sam Snead (70) def. Ben Hogan (71) in 18 holes. **1962:** Arnold Palmer (68) def. Gary Player (71) and Dow Finsterwald (77) in 18 holes. **1966:** Jack Nicklaus (70) def. Tommy Jacobs (72) and Gay Brewer Jr. (78) in 18 holes. **1970:** Billy Casper (69) def. Gene Littler (74) in 18 holes. **1979:** Fuzzy Zoeller (4-3) def. Ed Sneed (4-4) and Tom Watson (4-4) on 2nd hole of sudden death. **1982:** Craig Stadler (4) def. Dan Pohl (5) on 1st hole of sudden death. **1987:** Larry Mize (4-3) def. Greg Norman (4-4) and Seve Ballesteros (5) on 2nd hole of sudden death. **1989:** Nick Faldo (5-3) def. Scott Hoch (5-4) on 2nd hole of sudden death. **1990:** Nick Faldo (4-4) def. Raymond Floyd (4) on 2nd hole of sudden death. **2003:** Mike Weir (5) def. Len Mattiace (6) on 1st hole of sudden death. **2005:** Tiger Woods (3) def. Chris DiMarco (4) on 1st hole of sudden death.

## U.S. Open

Played at a different course each year, the U.S. Open was launched by the new U.S. Golf Association in 1895. The Open was a 36-hole event from 1895-97 and has been 72 holes since then. It switched from a 3-day, 36-hole Saturday finish to 4 days of play in 1965. Note that (*) indicates playoff winner and (a) indicates amateur.

**Multiple winners:** Willie Anderson, Ben Hogan, Bobby Jones and Jack Nicklaus (4); Hale Irwin (3); Julius Boros, Billy Casper, Ernie Els, Retief Goosen, Ralph Guldahl, Walter Hagen, Lee Janzen, John McDermott, Cary Middlecoff, Andy North, Gene Sarazen, Alex Smith, Payne Stewart, Curtis Strange, Lee Trevino and Tiger Woods (2).

| Year | Winner | Score | Runner-up | Course | Location |
|---|---|---|---|---|---|
| 1895 | Horace Rawlins | 173 | Willie Dunn (175) | Newport GC | Newport, R.I. |
| 1896 | James Foulis | 152 | Horace Rawlins (155) | Shinnecock Hills GC | Southampton, N.Y. |
| 1897 | Joe Lloyd | 162 | Willie Anderson (163) | Chicago GC | Wheaton, Ill. |
| 1898 | Fred Herd | 328 | Alex Smith (335) | Myopia Hunt Club | Hamilton, Mass. |
| 1899 | Willie Smith | 315 | George Low, W.H. Way & Val Fitzjohn (326) | Baltimore CC | Baltimore |
| 1900 | Harry Vardon | 313 | J.H. Taylor (315) | Chicago GC | Wheaton, Ill. |
| 1901 | Willie Anderson* | 331 | Alex Smith (331) | Myopia Hunt Club | Hamilton, Mass. |
| 1902 | Laurie Auchterlonie | 307 | Stewart Gardner (313) | Garden City GC | Garden City, N.Y. |
| 1903 | Willie Anderson* | 307 | David Brown (307) | Baltusrol GC | Springfield, N.J. |
| 1904 | Willie Anderson | 303 | Gil Nicholls (308) | Glen View Club | Golf, Ill. |
| 1905 | Willie Anderson | 314 | Alex Smith (316) | Myopia Hunt Club | Hamilton, Mass. |
| 1906 | Alex Smith | 295 | Willie Smith (302) | Onwentsia Club | Lake Forest, Ill. |
| 1907 | Alec Ross | 302 | Gil Nicholls (304) | Phila. Cricket Club | Chestnut Hill, Pa. |
| 1908 | Fred McLeod* | 322 | Willie Smith (322) | Myopia Hunt Club | Hamilton, Mass. |
| 1909 | George Sargent | 290 | Tom McNamara (294) | Englewood GC | Englewood, N.J. |
| 1910 | Alex Smith* | 298 | Macdonald Smith & John McDermott (298) | Phila. Cricket Club | Chestnut Hill, Pa. |
| 1911 | John McDermott* | 307 | George Simpson & Mike Brady (307) | Chicago GC | Wheaton, Ill. |
| 1912 | John McDermott | 294 | Tom McNamara (296) | CC of Buffalo | Buffalo |
| 1913 | a-Francis Ouimet* | 304 | Harry Vardon & Ted Ray (304) | The Country Club | Brookline, Mass. |
| 1914 | Walter Hagen | 290 | a-Chick Evans (291) | Midlothian CC | Blue Island, Ill. |
| 1915 | a-John Travers | 297 | Tom McNamara (298) | Baltusrol GC | Springfield, N.J. |
| 1916 | a-Chick Evans | 286 | Jock Hutchinson (288) | Minikahda Club | Minneapolis |
| 1917-18 | Not held | | World War I | | |
| 1919 | Walter Hagen* | 301 | Mike Brady (301) | Brae Burn CC | West Newton, Mass. |
| 1920 | Ted Ray | 295 | Jock Hutchison, Jack Burke, Leo Diegel & Harry Vardon (296) | Inverness Club | Toledo, Ohio |
| 1921 | Jim Barnes | 289 | Walter Hagen & Fred McLeod (298) | Columbia CC | Chevy Chase, Md. |
| 1922 | Gene Sarazen | 288 | a-Bobby Jones & John Black (289) | Skokie CC | Glencoe, Ill. |
| 1923 | a-Bobby Jones* | 296 | Bobby Cruickshank (296) | Inwood CC | Inwood, N.Y. |
| 1924 | Cyril Walker | 297 | a-Bobby Jones (300) | Oakland Hills CC | Birmingham, Mich. |
| 1925 | Willie Macfarlane* | 291 | a-Bobby Jones (291) | Worcester CC | Worcester, Mass. |
| 1926 | a-Bobby Jones | 293 | Joe Turnesa (294) | Scioto CC | Columbus, Ohio |
| 1927 | Tommy Armour* | 301 | Harry Cooper (301) | Oakmont CC | Oakmont, Pa. |
| 1928 | Johnny Farrell* | 294 | a-Bobby Jones (294) | Olympia Fields CC | Matteson, Ill. |
| 1929 | a-Bobby Jones* | 294 | Al Espinosa (294) | Winged Foot CC | Mamaroneck, N.Y. |
| 1930 | a-Bobby Jones | 287 | Macdonald Smith (289) | Interlachen CC | Hopkins, Minn. |
| 1931 | Billy Burke* | 292 | George Von Elm (292) | Inverness Club | Toledo, Ohio |
| 1932 | Gene Sarazen | 286 | Bobby Cruickshank & Phil Perkins (289) | Fresh Meadow CC | Flushing, N.Y. |
| 1933 | a-Johnny Goodman | 287 | Ralph Guldahl (288) | North Shore GC | Glenview, Ill. |
| 1934 | Olin Dutra | 293 | Gene Sarazen (294) | Merion Cricket Club | Ardmore, Pa. |
| 1935 | Sam Parks Jr. | 299 | Jimmy Thomson (301) | Oakmont CC | Oakmont, Pa. |
| 1936 | Tony Manero | 282 | Harry E. Cooper (284) | Baltusrol GC | Springfield, N.J. |
| 1937 | Ralph Guldahl | 281 | Sam Snead (283) | Oakland Hills CC | Birmingham, Mich. |
| 1938 | Ralph Guldahl | 284 | Dick Metz (290) | Cherry Hills CC | Denver |

## U.S. Open (Cont.)

| Year | Winner | Score | Runner-up | Course | Location |
|------|--------|-------|-----------|--------|----------|
| 1939 | Byron Nelson* | .284 | Craig Wood<br>& Denny Shute (284) | Philadelphia CC | Philadelphia |
| 1940 | Lawson Little* | .287 | Gene Sarazen (287) | Canterbury GC | Cleveland |
| 1941 | Craig Wood | .284 | Denny Shute (287) | Colonial Club | Ft. Worth |
| 1942-45 | Not held | | World War II | | |
| 1946 | Lloyd Mangrum* | .284 | Byron Nelson<br>& Vic Ghezzi (284) | Canterbury GC | Cleveland |
| 1947 | Lew Worsham* | .282 | Sam Snead (282) | St. Louis CC | Clayton, Mo. |
| 1948 | Ben Hogan | .276 | Jimmy Demaret (278) | Riviera CC | Los Angeles |
| 1949 | Cary Middlecoff | .286 | Clayton Heafner<br>& Sam Snead (287) | Medinah CC | Medinah, Ill. |
| 1950 | Ben Hogan* | .287 | Lloyd Mangrum<br>& George Fazio (287) | Merion Golf Club | Ardmore, Pa. |
| 1951 | Ben Hogan | .287 | Clayton Heafner (289) | Oakland Hills CC | Birmingham, Mich. |
| 1952 | Julius Boros | .281 | Porky Oliver (285) | Northwood Club | Dallas |
| 1953 | Ben Hogan | .283 | Sam Snead (289) | Oakmont CC | Oakmont, Pa. |
| 1954 | Ed Furgol | .284 | Gene Littler (285) | Baltusrol GC | Springfield, N.J. |
| 1955 | Jack Fleck* | .287 | Ben Hogan (287) | Olympic CC | San Francisco |
| 1956 | Cary Middlecoff | .281 | Ben Hogan<br>& Julius Boros (282) | Oak Hill CC | Rochester, N.Y. |
| 1957 | Dick Mayer* | .282 | Cary Middlecoff (282) | Inverness Club | Toledo, Ohio |
| 1958 | Tommy Bolt | .283 | Gary Player (287) | Southern Hills CC | Tulsa |
| 1959 | Billy Casper | .282 | Bob Rosburg (283) | Winged Foot GC | Mamaroneck, N.Y. |
| 1960 | Arnold Palmer | .280 | Jack Nicklaus (282) | Cherry Hills CC | Denver |
| 1961 | Gene Littler | .281 | Doug Sanders<br>& Bob Goalby (282) | Oakland Hills CC | Birmingham, Mich. |
| 1962 | Jack Nicklaus* | .283 | Arnold Palmer (283) | Oakmont CC | Oakmont, Pa. |
| 1963 | Julius Boros* | .293 | Arnold Palmer<br>& Jacky Cupit (293) | The Country Club | Brookline, Mass. |
| 1964 | Ken Venturi | .278 | Tommy Jacobs (282) | Congressional CC | Bethesda, Md. |
| 1965 | Gary Player* | .282 | Kel Nagle (282) | Bellerive CC | St. Louis |
| 1966 | Billy Casper* | .278 | Arnold Palmer (278) | Olympic CC | San Francisco |
| 1967 | Jack Nicklaus | .275 | Arnold Palmer (279) | Baltusrol GC | Springfield, N.J. |
| 1968 | Lee Trevino | .275 | Jack Nicklaus (279) | Oak Hill CC | Rochester, N.Y. |
| 1969 | Orville Moody | .281 | Al Geiberger, Deane Beman<br>& Bob Rosburg (282) | Champions GC | Houston |
| 1970 | Tony Jacklin | .281 | Dave Hill (288) | Hazeltine National GC | Chaska, Minn. |
| 1971 | Lee Trevino* | .280 | Jack Nicklaus (280) | Merion GC | Ardmore, Pa. |
| 1972 | Jack Nicklaus | .290 | Bruce Crampton (293) | Pebble Beach GL | Pebble Beach, Calif. |
| 1973 | Johnny Miller | .279 | John Schlee (280) | Oakmont CC | Oakmont, Pa. |
| 1974 | Hale Irwin | .287 | Forest Fezler (289) | Winged Foot GC | Mamaroneck, N.Y. |
| 1975 | Lou Graham* | .287 | John Mahaffey (287) | Medinah CC | Medinah, Ill. |
| 1976 | Jerry Pate | .277 | Al Geiberger<br>& Tom Weiskopf (279) | Atlanta AC | Duluth, Ga. |
| 1977 | Hubert Green | .278 | Lou Graham (279) | Southern Hills CC | Tulsa |
| 1978 | Andy North | .285 | Dave Stockton<br>& J.C. Snead (286) | Cherry Hills CC | Denver |
| 1979 | Hale Irwin | .284 | Gary Player<br>& Jerry Pate (286) | Inverness Club | Toledo, Ohio |
| 1980 | Jack Nicklaus | .272 | Isao Aoki (274) | Baltusrol GC | Springfield, N.J. |
| 1981 | David Graham | .273 | George Burns<br>& Bill Rogers (276) | Merion GC | Ardmore, Pa. |
| 1982 | Tom Watson | .282 | Jack Nicklaus (284) | Pebble Beach GL | Pebble Beach, Calif. |
| 1983 | Larry Nelson | .280 | Tom Watson (281) | Oakmont CC | Oakmont, Pa. |
| 1984 | Fuzzy Zoeller* | .276 | Greg Norman (276) | Winged Foot GC | Mamaroneck, N.Y. |
| 1985 | Andy North | .279 | Dave Barr, T.C. Chen<br>& Denis Watson (280) | Oakland Hills CC | Birmingham, Mich. |
| 1986 | Ray Floyd | .279 | Lanny Wadkins<br>& Chip Beck (281) | Shinnecock Hills GC | Southampton, N.Y. |
| 1987 | Scott Simpson | .277 | Tom Watson (278) | Olympic Club | San Francisco |
| 1988 | Curtis Strange* | .278 | Nick Faldo (278) | The Country Club | Brookline, Mass. |
| 1989 | Curtis Strange | .278 | Chip Beck, Ian Woosnam<br>& Mark McCumber (279) | Oak Hill CC | Rochester, N.Y. |
| 1990 | Hale Irwin* | .280 | Mike Donald (280) | Medinah CC | Medinah, Ill. |
| 1991 | Payne Stewart* | .282 | Scott Simpson (282) | Hazeltine National GC | Chaska, Minn. |
| 1992 | Tom Kite | .285 | Jeff Sluman (287) | Pebble Beach GL | Pebble Beach, Calif. |
| 1993 | Lee Janzen | .272 | Payne Stewart (274) | Baltusrol GC | Springfield, N.J. |

| Year | Winner | Score | Runner-up | Course | Location |
|------|--------|-------|-----------|--------|----------|
| 1994 | Ernie Els* | .279 | Colin Montgomerie (279) & Loren Roberts (279) | Oakmont CC | Oakmont, Pa. |
| 1995 | Corey Pavin | .280 | Greg Norman (282) | Shinnecock Hills GC | Southampton, N.Y. |
| 1996 | Steve Jones | .278 | Davis Love III & Tom Lehman (279) | Oakland Hills CC | Bloomfield Hills, Mich. |
| 1997 | Ernie Els | .276 | Colin Montgomerie (277) | Congressional CC | Bethesda, Md. |
| 1998 | Lee Janzen | .280 | Payne Stewart (281) | Olympic Club | San Francisco |
| 1999 | Payne Stewart | .279 | Phil Mickelson (280) | Pinehurst CC | Pinehurst, N.C. |
| 2000 | Tiger Woods | .272 | Miguel Angel Jimenez & Ernie Els (287) | Pebble Beach GL | Pebble Beach, Calif. |
| 2001 | Retief Goosen* | .276 | Mark Brooks (276) | Southern Hills CC | Tulsa |
| 2002 | Tiger Woods | .277 | Phil Mickelson (280) | Bethpage Black | Farmingdale, N.Y. |
| 2003 | Jim Furyk | .272 | Stephen Leaney (275) | Olympia Fields CC | Olympia Fields, Ill. |
| 2004 | Retief Goosen | .276 | Phil Mickelson (278) | Shinnecock Hills GC | Southampton, N.Y. |
| 2005 | Michael Campbell | .280 | Tiger Woods (282) | Pinehurst CC | Pinehurst, N.C. |

## *PLAYOFFS:

**1901:** Willie Anderson (85) def. Alex Smith (86) in 18 holes. **1903:** Willie Anderson (82) def. David Brown (84) in 18 holes. **1908:** Fred McLeod (77) def. Willie Smith (83) in 18 holes. **1910:** Alex Smith (71) def. John McDermott (75) & Macdonald Smith (77) in 18 holes. **1911:** John McDermott (80) def. Mike Brady (82) & George Simpson (85) in 18 holes. **1913:** Francis Ouimet (72) def. Harry Vardon (77) & Edward Ray (78) in 18 holes. **1919:** Walter Hagen (77) def. Mike Brady (78) in 18 holes. **1923:** Bobby Jones (76) def. Bobby Cruickshank (78) in 18 holes. **1925:** Willie Macfarlane (75-72—147) def. Bobby Jones (75-73—148) in 36 holes. **1927:** Tommy Armour (76) def. Harry Cooper (79) in 18 holes.**1928:** Johnny Farrell (70-73—143) def. Bobby Jones (73-71—144) in 36 holes. **1929:** Bobby Jones (141) def. Al Espinosa (164) in 36 holes. **1931:** Billy Burke (149-148) def. George Von Elm (149-149) in 72 holes. **1939:** Byron Nelson (68-70) def. Craig Wood (68-73) and Denny Shute (76) in 36 holes. **1940:** Lawson Little (70) def. Gene Sarazen (73) in 18 holes. **1946:** Lloyd Mangrum (72-72—144) def. Byron Nelson (72-73—145) and Vic Ghezzi (72-73—145) in 36 holes. **1947:** Lew Worsham (69) def. Sam Snead (70) in 18 holes.

**1950:** Ben Hogan (69) def. Lloyd Mangrum (73) & George Fazio (75) in 18 holes. **1955:** Jack Fleck (69) def. Ben Hogan (72) in 18 holes. **1957:** Dick Mayer (72) def. Cary Middlecoff (79) in 18 holes. **1962:** Jack Nicklaus (71) def. Arnold Palmer (74) in 18 holes. **1963:** Julius Boros (70) def. Jacky Cupit (73) & Arnold Palmer (76) in 18 holes. **1965:** Gary Player (71) def. Kel Nagle (74) in 18 holes. **1966:** Billy Casper (69) def. Arnold Palmer (73) in 18 holes. **1971:** Lee Trevino (68) def. Jack Nicklaus (71) in 18 holes. **1975:** Lou Graham (71) def. John Mahaffey (73) in 18 holes. **1984:** Fuzzy Zoeller (67) def. Greg Norman (75) in 18 holes. **1988:** Curtis Strange (71) def. Nick Faldo (75) in 18 holes. **1990:** Hale Irwin (74-3) def. Mike Donald (74-4) on 1st hole of sudden death after 18 holes. **1991:** Payne Stewart (75) def. Scott Simpson (77) in 18 holes. **1994:** Ernie Els (74-4-4) def. Loren Roberts (74-4-5) and Colin Montgomerie (78) on 2nd hole of sudden death after 18 holes; **2001:** Goosen (70) def. Brooks (72) in 18 holes.

---

## Vardon Trophy

Awarded since 1937 by the PGA of America to the PGA Tour regular with the lowest adjusted scoring average, based on a minimum of 60 rounds. The award is named after Harry Vardon, the six-time British Open champion who also won the U.S. Open in 1900. A point system was used from 1937-41.

**Multiple winners:** Billy Casper, Lee Trevino and Tiger Woods (5); Arnold Palmer and Sam Snead (4); Ben Hogan, Greg Norman and Tom Watson (3); Fred Couples, Bruce Crampton, Tom Kite, Lloyd Mangrum and Nick Price (2).

| Year | | Pts | Year | | Avg | Year | | Avg |
|------|--|-----|------|--|-----|------|--|-----|
| 1937 | Harry Cooper | .500 | 1962 | Arnold Palmer | .70.27 | 1984 | Calvin Peete | .70.56 |
| 1938 | Sam Snead | .520 | 1963 | Billy Casper | .70.58 | 1985 | Don Pooley | .70.36 |
| 1939 | Byron Nelson | .473 | 1964 | Arnold Palmer | .70.01 | 1986 | Scott Hoch | .70.08 |
| 1940 | Ben Hogan | .423 | 1965 | Billy Casper | .70.85 | 1987 | Dan Pohl | .70.25 |
| 1941 | Ben Hogan | .494 | 1966 | Billy Casper | .70.27 | 1988 | Chip Beck | .69.46 |
| 1942-46 | No award | | 1967 | Arnold Palmer | .70.18 | 1989 | Greg Norman | .69.49 |
| **Year** | | **Avg** | 1968 | Billy Casper | .69.82 | 1990 | Greg Norman | .69.10 |
| 1947 | Jimmy Demaret | .69.90 | 1969 | Dave Hill | .70.34 | 1991 | Fred Couples | .69.59 |
| 1948 | Ben Hogan | .69.30 | 1970 | Lee Trevino | .70.64 | 1992 | Fred Couples | .69.38 |
| 1949 | Sam Snead | .69.37 | 1971 | Lee Trevino | .70.27 | 1993 | Nick Price | .69.11 |
| 1950 | Sam Snead | .69.23 | 1972 | Lee Trevino | .70.89 | 1994 | Greg Norman | .68.81 |
| 1951 | Lloyd Mangrum | .70.05 | 1973 | Bruce Crampton | .70.57 | 1995 | Steve Elkington | .69.62 |
| 1952 | Jack Burke | .70.54 | 1974 | Lee Trevino | .70.53 | 1996 | Tom Lehman | .69.32 |
| 1953 | Lloyd Mangrum | .70.22 | 1975 | Bruce Crampton | .70.51 | 1997 | Nick Price | .68.98 |
| 1954 | E.J. Harrison | .70.41 | 1976 | Don January | .70.56 | 1998 | David Duval | .69.13 |
| 1955 | Sam Snead | .69.86 | 1977 | Tom Watson | .70.32 | 1999 | Tiger Woods | .68.43 |
| 1956 | Cary Middlecoff | .70.35 | 1978 | Tom Watson | .70.16 | 2000 | Tiger Woods | .67.79 |
| 1957 | Dow Finsterwald | .70.30 | 1979 | Tom Watson | .70.27 | 2001 | Tiger Woods | .68.81 |
| 1958 | Bob Rosburg | .70.11 | 1980 | Lee Trevino | .69.73 | 2002 | Tiger Woods | .68.56 |
| 1959 | Art Wall | .70.35 | 1981 | Tom Kite | .69.80 | 2003 | Tiger Woods | .68.41 |
| 1960 | Billy Casper | .69.95 | 1982 | Tom Kite | .70.21 | 2004 | Vijay Singh | .68.84 |
| 1961 | Arnold Palmer | .69.85 | 1983 | Ray Floyd | .70.61 | | | |

## British Open

The oldest of the Majors, the Open began in 1860 to determine "the champion golfer of the world." While only professional golfers participated in the first year of the tournament, amateurs have been invited ever since. Competition was extended from 36 to 72 holes in 1892. Conducted by the Royal and Ancient Golf Club of St. Andrews, the Open is rotated among select golf courses in England and Scotland. Note that (*) indicates playoff winner and (a) indicates amateur winner.

**Multiple winners:** Harry Vardon (6); James Braid, J.H. Taylor, Peter Thomson and Tom Watson (5); Walter Hagen, Bobby Locke, Tom Morris Sr., Tom Morris Jr. and Willie Park (4); Jamie Anderson, Seve Ballesteros, Henry Cotton, Nick Faldo, Bob Ferguson, Bobby Jones, Jack Nicklaus and Gary Player (3); Harold Hilton, Bob Martin, Greg Norman, Arnold Palmer, Willie Park Jr., Lee Trevino and Tiger Woods (2).

| Year | Winner | Score | Runner-up | Course | Location |
|------|--------|-------|-----------|--------|----------|
| 1860 | Willie Park | 174 | Tom Morris Sr. (176) | Prestwick Club | Ayrshire, Scotland |
| 1861 | Tom Morris Sr. | 163 | Willie Park (167) | Prestwick Club | Ayrshire, Scotland |
| 1862 | Tom Morris Sr. | 163 | Willie Park (176) | Prestwick Club | Ayrshire, Scotland |
| 1863 | Willie Park | 168 | Tom Morris Sr. (170) | Prestwick Club | Ayrshire, Scotland |
| 1864 | Tom Morris Sr. | 167 | Andrew Strath (169) | Prestwick Club | Ayrshire, Scotland |
| 1865 | Andrew Strath | 162 | Willie Park (164) | Prestwick Club | Ayrshire, Scotland |
| 1866 | Willie Park | 169 | David Park (171) | Prestwick Club | Ayrshire, Scotland |
| 1867 | Tom Morris Sr. | 170 | Willie Park (172) | Prestwick Club | Ayrshire, Scotland |
| 1868 | Tom Morris Jr. | 157 | Robert Andrew (159) | Prestwick Club | Ayrshire, Scotland |
| 1869 | Tom Morris Jr. | 154 | Tom Morris Sr. (157) | Prestwick Club | Ayrshire, Scotland |
| 1870 | Tom Morris Jr. | 149 | Bob Kirk (161) | Prestwick Club | Ayrshire, Scotland |
| 1871 | Not held | | | | |
| 1872 | Tom Morris Jr. | 166 | David Strath (169) | Prestwick Club | Ayrshire, Scotland |
| 1873 | Tom Kidd | 179 | Jamie Anderson (180) | St. Andrews | St. Andrews, Scotland |
| 1874 | Mungo Park | 159 | Tom Morris Jr. (161) | Musselburgh | Musselburgh, Scotland |
| 1875 | Willie Park | 166 | Bob Martin (168) | Prestwick Club | Ayrshire, Scotland |
| 1876 | Bob Martin* | 176 | David Strath (176) | St. Andrews | St. Andrews, Scotland |
| 1877 | Jamie Anderson | 160 | Bob Pringle (162) | Musselburgh | Musselburgh, Scotland |
| 1878 | Jamie Anderson | 157 | Bob Kirk (159) | Prestwick Club | Ayrshire, Scotland |
| 1879 | Jamie Anderson | 169 | Andrew Kirkaldy & James Allan (172) | St. Andrews | St. Andrews, Scotland |
| 1880 | Bob Ferguson | 162 | Peter Paxton (167) | Musselburgh | Musselburgh, Scotland |
| 1881 | Bob Ferguson | 170 | Jamie Anderson (173) | Prestwick Club | Ayrshire, Scotland |
| 1882 | Bob Ferguson | 171 | Willie Fernie (174) | St. Andrews | St. Andrews, Scotland |
| 1883 | Willie Fernie* | 159 | Bob Ferguson (159) | Musselburgh | Musselburgh, Scotland |
| 1884 | Jack Simpson | 160 | Douglas Rolland & Willie Fernie (164) | Prestwick Club | Ayrshire, Scotland |
| 1885 | Bob Martin | 171 | Archie Simpson (172) | St. Andrews | St. Andrews, Scotland |
| 1886 | David Brown | 157 | Willie Campbell (159) | Musselburgh | Musselburgh, Scotland |
| 1887 | Willie Park Jr. | 161 | Bob Martin (162) | Prestwick Club | Ayrshire, Scotland |
| 1888 | Jack Burns | 171 | David Anderson & Ben Sayers (172) | St. Andrews | St. Andrews, Scotland |
| 1889 | Willie Park Jr.* | 155 | Andrew Kirkaldy (155) | Musselburgh | Musselburgh, Scotland |
| 1890 | a-John Ball | 164 | Willie Fernie (167) & A. Simpson (167) | Prestwick Club | Ayrshire, Scotland |
| 1891 | Hugh Kirkaldy | 166 | Andrew Kirkaldy & Willie Fernie (168) | St. Andrews | St. Andrews, Scotland |
| 1892 | a-Harold Hilton | 305 | John Ball, Sandy Herd & Hugh Kirkaldy (308) | Muirfield | Gullane, Scotland |
| 1893 | Willie Auchterlonie | 322 | Johnny Laidley (324) | Prestwick Club | Ayrshire, Scotland |
| 1894 | J.H. Taylor | 326 | Douglas Rolland (331) | Royal St. George's | Sandwich, England |
| 1895 | J.H. Taylor | 322 | Sandy Herd (326) | St. Andrews | St. Andrews, Scotland |
| 1896 | Harry Vardon* | 316 | J.H. Taylor (316) | Muirfield | Gullane, Scotland |
| 1897 | a-Harold Hilton | 314 | James Braid (315) | Hoylake | Hoylake, England |
| 1898 | Harry Vardon | 307 | Willie Park Jr. (308) | Prestwick Club | Ayrshire, Scotland |
| 1899 | Harry Vardon | 310 | Jack White (315) | Royal St. George's | Sandwich, England |
| 1900 | J.H. Taylor | 309 | Harry Vardon (317) | St. Andrews | St. Andrews, Scotland |
| 1901 | James Braid | 309 | Harry Vardon (312) | Muirfield | Gullane, Scotland |
| 1902 | Sandy Herd | 307 | Harry Vardon (308) | Hoylake | Hoylake, England |
| 1903 | Harry Vardon | 300 | Tom Vardon (306) | Prestwick Club | Ayrshire, Scotland |
| 1904 | Jack White | 296 | James Braid (297) | Royal St. George's | Sandwich, England |
| 1905 | James Braid | 318 | J.H. Taylor (323) & Rowland Jones (323) | St. Andrews | St. Andrews, Scotland |
| 1906 | James Braid | 300 | J.H. Taylor (304) | Muirfield | Gullane, Scotland |
| 1907 | Arnaud Massy | 312 | J.H. Taylor (314) | Hoylake | Hoylake, England |
| 1908 | James Braid | 291 | Tom Ball (299) | Prestwick Club | Ayrshire, Scotland |
| 1909 | J.H. Taylor | 295 | James Braid (299) | Deal | Deal, England |
| 1910 | James Braid | 299 | Sandy Herd (303) | St. Andrews | St. Andrews, Scotland |
| 1911 | Harry Vardon* | 303 | Arnaud Massy (303) | Royal St. George's | Sandwich, England |
| 1912 | Ted Ray | 295 | Harry Vardon (299) | Muirfield | Gullane, Scotland |

| Year | Winner | Score | Runner-up | Course | Location |
|---|---|---|---|---|---|
| 1913 | J.H. Taylor | 304 | Ted Ray (312) | Hoylake | Hoylake, England |
| 1914 | Harry Vardon | 306 | J.H. Taylor (309) | Prestwick Club | Ayrshire, Scotland |
| 1915-19 | Not held | | World War I | | |
| 1920 | George Duncan | 303 | Sandy Herd (305) | Deal | Deal, England |
| 1921 | Jock Hutchison* | 296 | Roger Wethered (296) | St. Andrews | St. Andrews, Scotland |
| 1922 | Walter Hagen | 300 | George Duncan & Jim Barnes (301) | Royal St. George's | Sandwich, England |
| 1923 | Arthur Havers | 295 | Walter Hagen (296) | Royal Troon | Troon, Scotland |
| 1924 | Walter Hagen | 301 | Ernest Whitcombe (302) | Hoylake | Hoylake, England |
| 1925 | Jim Barnes | 300 | Archie Compston & Ted Ray (301) | Prestwick Club | Ayrshire, Scotland |
| 1926 | a-Bobby Jones | 291 | Al Watrous (293) | Royal Lytham | Lytham, England |
| 1927 | a-Bobby Jones | 285 | Aubrey Boomer (291) | St. Andrews | St. Andrews, Scotland |
| 1928 | Walter Hagen | 292 | Gene Sarazen (294) | Royal St. George's | Sandwich, England |
| 1929 | Walter Hagen | 292 | Johnny Farrell (298) | Muirfield | Gullane, Scotland |
| 1930 | a-Bobby Jones | 291 | Macdonald Smith & Leo Diegel (293) | Hoylake | Hoylake, England |
| 1931 | Tommy Armour | 296 | Jose Jurado (297) | Carnoustie | Carnoustie, Scotland |
| 1932 | Gene Sarazen | 283 | Macdonald Smith (288) | Prince's | Prince's, England |
| 1933 | Denny Shute* | 292 | Craig Wood (292) | St. Andrews | St. Andrews, Scotland |
| 1934 | Henry Cotton | 283 | Sid Brews (288) | Royal St. George's | Sandwich, England |
| 1935 | Alf Perry | 283 | Alf Padgham (287) | Muirfield | Gullane, Scotland |
| 1936 | Alf Padgham | 287 | Jimmy Adams (288) | Hoylake | Hoylake, England |
| 1937 | Henry Cotton | 290 | Reg Whitcombe (292) | Carnoustie | Carnoustie, Scotland |
| 1938 | Reg Whitcombe | 295 | Jimmy Adams (297) | Royal St. George's | Sandwich, England |
| 1939 | Dick Burton | 290 | Johnny Bulla (292) | St. Andrews | St. Andrews, Scotland |
| 1940-45 | Not held | | World War II | | |
| 1946 | Sam Snead | 290 | Bobby Locke (294) & Johnny Bulla (294) | St. Andrews | St. Andrews, Scotland |
| 1947 | Fred Daly | 293 | Frank Stranahan & Reg Horne (294) | Hoylake | Hoylake, England |
| 1948 | Henry Cotton | 284 | Fred Daly (289) | Muirfield | Gullane, Scotland |
| 1949 | Bobby Locke* | 283 | Harry Bradshaw (283) | Royal St. George's | Sandwich, England |
| 1950 | Bobby Locke | 279 | Roberto de Vicenzo (281) | Royal Troon | Troon, Scotland |
| 1951 | Max Faulkner | 285 | Tony Cerda (287) | Royal Portrush | Portrush, Ireland |
| 1952 | Bobby Locke | 287 | Peter Thomson (288) | Royal Lytham | Lytham, England |
| 1953 | Ben Hogan | 282 | Frank Stranahan, Dai Rees, Tony Cerda & Peter Thomson (286) | Carnoustie | Carnoustie, Scotland |
| 1954 | Peter Thomson | 283 | Sid Scott, Dai Rees & Bobby Locke (284) | Royal Birkdale | Southport, England |
| 1955 | Peter Thomson | 281 | Johny Fallon (283) | St. Andrews | St. Andrews, Scotland |
| 1956 | Peter Thomson | 286 | Flory Van Donck (289) | Hoylake | Hoylake, England |
| 1957 | Bobby Locke | 279 | Peter Thomson (282) | St. Andrews | St. Andrews, Scotland |
| 1958 | Peter Thomson* | 278 | Dave Thomas (278) | Royal Lytham | Lytham, England |
| 1959 | Gary Player | 284 | Flory Van Donck & Fred Bullock (286) | Muirfield | Gullane, Scotland |
| 1960 | Kel Nagle | 278 | Arnold Palmer (279) | St. Andrews | St. Andrews, Scotland |
| 1961 | Arnold Palmer | 284 | Dai Rees (285) | Royal Birkdale | Southport, England |
| 1962 | Arnold Palmer | 276 | Kel Nagle (282) | Royal Troon | Troon, Scotland |
| 1963 | Bob Charles* | 277 | Phil Rodgers (277) | Royal Lytham | Lytham, England |
| 1964 | Tony Lema | 279 | Jack Nicklaus (284) | St. Andrews | St. Andrews, Scotland |
| 1965 | Peter Thomson | 285 | Christy O'Connor & Brian Huggett (287) | Royal Birkdale | Southport, England |
| 1966 | Jack Nicklaus | 282 | Doug Sanders & Dave Thomas (283) | Muirfield | Gullane, Scotland |
| 1967 | Roberto de Vicenzo | 278 | Jack Nicklaus (280) | Hoylake | Hoylake, England |
| 1968 | Gary Player | 289 | Jack Nicklaus & Bob Charles (291) | Carnoustie | Carnoustie, Scotland |
| 1969 | Tony Jacklin | 280 | Bob Charles (282) | Royal Lytham | Lytham, England |
| 1970 | Jack Nicklaus* | 283 | Doug Sanders (283) | St. Andrews | St. Andrews, Scotland |
| 1971 | Lee Trevino | 278 | Lu Liang Huan (279) | Royal Birkdale | Southport, England |
| 1972 | Lee Trevino | 278 | Jack Nicklaus (279) | Muirfield | Gullane, Scotland |
| 1973 | Tom Weiskopf | 276 | Johnny Miller & Neil Coles (279) | Royal Troon | Troon, Scotland |
| 1974 | Gary Player | 282 | Peter Oosterhuis (286) | Royal Lytham | Lytham, England |
| 1975 | Tom Watson* | 279 | Jack Newton (279) | Carnoustie | Carnoustie, Scotland |
| 1976 | Johnny Miller | 279 | Seve Ballesteros & Jack Nicklaus (285) | Royal Birkdale | Southport, England |
| 1977 | Tom Watson | 268 | Jack Nicklaus (269) | Turnberry | Turnberry, Scotland |

## British Open (Cont.)

| Year | Winner | Score | Runner-up | Course | Location |
|------|--------|-------|-----------|--------|----------|
| 1978 | Jack Nicklaus | 281 | Tom Kite, Ray Floyd, Ben Crenshaw & Simon Owen (283) | St. Andrews | St. Andrews, Scotland |
| 1979 | Seve Ballesteros | 283 | Jack Nicklaus & Ben Crenshaw (286) | Royal Lytham | Lytham, England |
| 1980 | Tom Watson | 271 | Lee Trevino (275) | Muirfield | Gullane, Scotland |
| 1981 | Bill Rogers | 276 | Bernhard Langer (280) | Royal St. George's | Sandwich, England |
| 1982 | Tom Watson | 284 | Peter Oosterhuis & Nick Price (285) | Royal Troon | Troon, Scotland |
| 1983 | Tom Watson | 275 | Hale Irwin & Andy Bean (276) | Royal Birkdale | Southport, England |
| 1984 | Seve Ballesteros | 276 | Bernhard Langer & Tom Watson (278) | St. Andrews | St. Andrews, Scotland |
| 1985 | Sandy Lyle | 282 | Payne Stewart (283) | Royal St. George's | Sandwich, England |
| 1986 | Greg Norman | 280 | Gordon J. Brand (285) | Turnberry | Turnberry, Scotland |
| 1987 | Nick Faldo | 279 | Paul Azinger & Rodger Davis (280) | Muirfield | Gullane, Scotland |
| 1988 | Seve Ballesteros | 273 | Nick Price (275) | Royal Lytham | Lytham, England |
| 1989 | Mark Calcavecchia* | 275 | Greg Norman & Wayne Grady (275) | Royal Troon | Troon, Scotland |
| 1990 | Nick Faldo | 270 | Payne Stewart & Mark McNulty (275) | St. Andrews | St. Andrews, Scotland |
| 1991 | Ian Baker-Finch | 272 | Mike Harwood (274) | Royal Birkdale | Southport, England |
| 1992 | Nick Faldo | 272 | John Cook (273) | Muirfield | Gullane, Scotland |
| 1993 | Greg Norman | 267 | Nick Faldo (269) | Royal St. George's | Sandwich, England |
| 1994 | Nick Price | 268 | Jesper Parnevik (269) | Turnberry | Turnberry, Scotland |
| 1995 | John Daly* | 282 | Costantino Rocca (282) | St. Andrews | St. Andrews, Scotland |
| 1996 | Tom Lehman | 271 | Mark McCumber & Ernie Els (273) | Royal Lytham | Lytham, England |
| 1997 | Justin Leonard | 272 | Jesper Parnevik & Darren Clarke (275) | Royal Troon | Troon, Scotland |
| 1998 | Mark O'Meara* | 280 | Brian Watts (280) | Royal Birkdale | Southport, England |
| 1999 | Paul Lawrie* | 290 | Justin Leonard & Jean Van de Velde (290) | Carnoustie | Carnoustie, Scotland |
| 2000 | Tiger Woods | 269 | Thomas Bjorn & Ernie Els (277) | St. Andrews | St. Andrews, Scotland |
| 2001 | David Duval | 274 | Niclas Fasth (277) | Royal Lytham | Lytham, England |
| 2002 | Ernie Els* | 278 | Thomas Levet, Stuart Appleby & Steve Elkington (278) | Muirfield | Gullane, Scotland |
| 2003 | Ben Curtis | 283 | Vijay Singh & Thomas Bjorn (284) | Royal St. George's | Sandwich, England |
| 2004 | Todd Hamilton* | 274 | Ernie Els (274) | Royal Troon | Troon, Scotland |
| 2005 | Tiger Woods | 274 | Colin Montgomerie (279) | St. Andrews | St. Andrews, Scotland |

**\*PLAYOFFS:**

**1876:** Bob Martin awarded title when David Strath refused playoff. **1883:** Willie Fernie (158) def. Robert Ferguson (159) in 36 holes. **1889:** Willie Park Jr. (158) def. Andrew Kirkaldy (163) in 36 holes. **1896:** Harry Vardon (157) def. John H. Taylor (161) in 36 holes. **1911:** Harry Vardon won when Arnaud Massy conceded at 35th hole. **1921:** Jock Hutchison (150) def. Roger Wethered (159) in 36 holes. **1933:** Denny Shute (149) def. Craig Wood (154) in 36 holes. **1949:** Bobby Locke (135) def. Harry Bradshaw (147) in 36 holes. **1958:** Peter Thomson (139) def. Dave Thomas (143) in 36 holes. **1963:** Bob Charles (140) def. Phil Rodgers (148) in 36 holes. **1970:** Jack Nicklaus (72) def. Doug Sanders (73) in 18 holes. **1975:** Tom Watson (71) def. Jack Newton (72) in 18 holes. **1989:** Mark Calcavecchia (4-3-3-3—13) def. Wayne Grady (4-4-4-4—16) and Greg Norman (3-3-4) in 4 holes. **1995:** John Daly (3-4-4-4—15) def. Costantino Rocca (4-5-7-3—19) in 4 holes. **1998:** Mark O'Meara (4-4-5-4—17) def. Brian Watts (5-4-5-5—19) in 4 holes. **1999:** Paul Lawrie (5-4-3-3—15) def. Justin Leonard (5-4-4-5—18) and Jean Van de Velde (6-4-3-5—18) in 4 holes. **2002:** Els (4-3-5-4—16) and Levet (4-2-5-5—16) remained tied after a four-hole playoff that also included Appleby (4-4-4-5—17) and Elkington (5-3-4-5—17). The pair moved on to sudden death, where Els (4) def. Levet (5) on the 1st hole. **2004:** Todd Hamilton (4-4-3-4—15) def. Ernie Els (4-4-4-4—16) in 4 holes.

## PGA Championship

The PGA Championship began in 1916 as a professional golfers match play tournament, but switched to stroke play in 1958. Conducted by the PGA of America, the tournament is played on a different course each year.

**Multiple winners:** Walter Hagen and Jack Nicklaus (5); Gene Sarazen and Sam Snead (3); Jim Barnes, Leo Diegel, Ray Floyd, Ben Hogan, Byron Nelson, Larry Nelson, Gary Player, Nick Price, Paul Runyan, Denny Shute, Vijay Singh, Dave Stockton, Lee Trevino and Tiger Woods (2).

| Year | Winner | Score | Runner-up | Course | Location |
|------|--------|-------|-----------|--------|----------|
| 1916 | Jim Barnes | 1-up | Jock Hutchison | Siwanoy CC | Bronxville, N.Y. |
| 1917-18 | Not held | | World War I | | |
| 1919 | Jim Barnes | 6 & 5 | Fred McLeod | Engineers CC | Roslyn, N.Y. |
| 1920 | Jock Hutchison | 1-up | J. Douglas Edgar | Flossmoor CC | Flossmoor, Ill. |

| Year | Winner | Score | Runner-up | Course | Location |
|------|--------|-------|-----------|--------|----------|
| 1921 | Walter Hagen | 3 & 2 | Jim Barnes | Inwood CC | Inwood, N.Y. |
| 1922 | Gene Sarazen | 4 & 3 | Emmet French | Oakmont CC | Oakmont, Pa. |
| 1923 | Gene Sarazen* | 1-up/38 | Walter Hagen | Pelham CC | Pelham, N.Y. |
| 1924 | Walter Hagen | 2-up | Jim Barnes | French Lick CC | French Lick, Ind. |
| 1925 | Walter Hagen | 6 & 5 | Bill Mehlhorn | Olympia Fields CC | Matteson, Ill. |
| 1926 | Walter Hagen | 5 & 3 | Leo Diegel | Salisbury GC | Westbury, N.Y. |
| 1927 | Walter Hagen | 1-up | Joe Turnesa | Cedar Crest CC | Dallas |
| 1928 | Leo Diegel | 6 & 5 | Al Espinosa | Five Farms CC | Baltimore |
| 1929 | Leo Diegel | 6 & 4 | John Farrell | Hillcrest CC | Los Angeles |
| 1930 | Tommy Armour | 1-up | Gene Sarazen | Fresh Meadow CC | Flushing, N.Y. |
| 1931 | Tom Creavy | 2 & 1 | Denny Shute | Wannamoisett CC | Rumford, R.I. |
| 1932 | Olin Dutra | 4 & 3 | Frank Walsh | Keller GC | St. Paul, Minn. |
| 1933 | Gene Sarazen | 5 & 4 | Willie Goggin | Blue Mound CC | Milwaukee |
| 1934 | Paul Runyan* | 1-up/38 | Craig Wood | Park CC | Williamsville, N.Y. |
| 1935 | Johnny Revolta | 5 & 4 | Tommy Armour | Twin Hills CC | Oklahoma City |
| 1936 | Denny Shute | 3 & 2 | Jimmy Thomson | Pinehurst CC | Pinehurst, N.C. |
| 1937 | Denny Shute* | 1-up/37 | Harold McSpaden | Pittsburgh FC | Aspinwall, Pa. |
| 1938 | Paul Runyan | 8 & 7 | Sam Snead | Shawnee CC | Shawnee-on-Del, Pa. |
| 1939 | Henry Picard* | 1-up/37 | Byron Nelson | Pomonok CC | Flushing, N.Y. |
| 1940 | Byron Nelson | 1-up | Sam Snead | Hershey CC | Hershey, Pa. |
| 1941 | Vic Ghezzi* | 1-up/38 | Byron Nelson | Cherry Hills CC | Denver |
| 1942 | Sam Snead | 2 & 1 | Jim Turnesa | Seaview CC | Atlantic City, N.J. |
| 1943 | Not held | | World War II | | |
| 1944 | Bob Hamilton | 1-up | Byron Nelson | Manito G & CC | Spokane, Wash. |
| 1945 | Byron Nelson | 4 & 3 | Sam Byrd | Morraine CC | Dayton, Ohio |
| 1946 | Ben Hogan | 6 & 4 | Porky Oliver | Portland GC | Portland, Ore. |
| 1947 | Jim Ferrier | 2 & 1 | Chick Harbert | Plum Hollow CC | Detroit |
| 1948 | Ben Hogan | 7 & 6 | Mike Turnesa | Norwood Hills CC | St. Louis |
| 1949 | Sam Snead | 3 & 2 | John Palmer | Hermitage CC | Richmond, Va. |
| 1950 | Chandler Harper | 4 & 3 | Henry Williams Jr. | Scioto CC | Columbus, Ohio |
| 1951 | Sam Snead | 7 & 6 | Walter Burkemo | Oakmont CC | Oakmont, Pa. |
| 1952 | Jim Turnesa | 1-up | Chick Harbert | Big Spring CC | Louisville |
| 1953 | Walter Burkemo | 2 & 1 | Felice Torza | Birmingham CC | Birmingham, Mich. |
| 1954 | Chick Harbert | 4 & 3 | Walter Burkemo | Keller GC | St. Paul, Minn. |
| 1955 | Doug Ford | 4 & 3 | Cary Middlecoff | Meadowbrook CC | Detroit |
| 1956 | Jack Burke | 3 & 2 | Ted Kroll | Blue Hill CC | Boston |
| 1957 | Lionel Hebert | 2 & 1 | Dow Finsterwald | Miami Valley GC | Dayton, Ohio |
| 1958 | Dow Finsterwald | 276 | Billy Casper (278) | Llanerch CC | Havertown, Pa. |
| 1959 | Bob Rosburg | 277 | Jerry Barber & Doug Sanders (278) | Minneapolis CC | St. Louis Park, Minn. |
| 1960 | Jay Hebert | 281 | Jim Ferrier (282) | Firestone CC | Akron, Ohio |
| 1961 | Jerry Barber** | 277 | Don January (277) | Olympia Fields CC | Matteson, Ill. |
| 1962 | Gary Player | 278 | Bob Goalby (279) | Aronimink GC | Newtown Square, Pa. |
| 1963 | Jack Nicklaus | 279 | Dave Ragan (281) | Dallas AC | Dallas |
| 1964 | Bobby Nichols | 271 | Jack Nicklaus & Arnold Palmer (274) | Columbus CC | Columbus, Ohio |
| 1965 | Dave Marr | 280 | Jack Nicklaus & Billy Casper (282) | Laurel Valley GC | Ligonier, Pa. |
| 1966 | Al Geiberger | 280 | Dudley Wysong (284) | Firestone CC | Akron, Ohio |
| 1967 | Don January** | 281 | Don Massengale (281) | Columbine CC | Littleton, Colo. |
| 1968 | Julius Boros | 281 | Arnold Palmer & Bob Charles (282) | Pecan Valley CC | San Antonio |
| 1969 | Ray Floyd | 276 | Gary Player (277) | NCR GC | Dayton, Ohio |
| 1970 | Dave Stockton | 279 | Arnold Palmer & Bob Murphy (281) | Southern Hills CC | Tulsa |
| 1971 | Jack Nicklaus | 281 | Billy Casper (283) | PGA National GC | Palm Beach Gardens, Fla. |
| 1972 | Gary Player | 281 | Jim Jamieson & Tommy Aaron (283) | Oakland Hills GC | Birmingham, Mich. |
| 1973 | Jack Nicklaus | 277 | Bruce Crampton (281) | Canterbury GC | Cleveland |
| 1974 | Lee Trevino | 276 | Jack Nicklaus (277) | Tanglewood GC | Winston-Salem, N.C. |
| 1975 | Jack Nicklaus | 276 | Bruce Crampton (278) | Firestone CC | Akron, Ohio |
| 1976 | Dave Stockton | 281 | Don January & Ray Floyd (282) | Congressional CC | Bethesda, Md. |
| 1977 | Lanny Wadkins** | 282 | Gene Littler (282) | Pebble Beach GL | Pebble Beach, Calif. |
| 1978 | John Mahaffey** | 276 | Jerry Pate & Tom Watson (276) | Oakmont CC | Oakmont, Pa. |
| 1979 | David Graham** | 272 | Ben Crenshaw (272) | Oakland Hills GC | Birmingham, Mich. |
| 1980 | Jack Nicklaus | 274 | Andy Bean (281) | Oak Hill CC | Rochester, N.Y. |
| 1981 | Larry Nelson | 273 | Fuzzy Zoeller (277) | Atlanta AC | Duluth, Ga. |
| 1982 | Ray Floyd | 272 | Lanny Wadkins (275) | Southern Hills CC | Tulsa |
| 1983 | Hal Sutton | 274 | Jack Nicklaus (275) | Riviera CC | Los Angeles |

## PGA Championship (Cont.)

| Year | Winner | Score | Runner-up | Course | Location |
|------|--------|-------|-----------|--------|----------|
| 1984 | Lee Trevino | 273 | Lanny Wadkins & Gary Player (277) | Shoal Creek | Birmingham, Ala. |
| 1985 | Hubert Green | 278 | Lee Trevino (280) | Cherry Hills CC | Denver |
| 1986 | Bob Tway | 276 | Greg Norman (278) | Inverness Club | Toledo, Ohio |
| 1987 | Larry Nelson** | 287 | Lanny Wadkins (287) | PGA National | Palm Beach Gardens, Fla. |
| 1988 | Jeff Sluman | 272 | Paul Azinger 275) | Oak Tree GC | Edmond, Okla. |
| 1989 | Payne Stewart | 276 | Andy Bean, Mike Reid & Curtis Strange (277) | Kemper Lakes GC | Hawthorn Woods, Ill. |
| 1990 | Wayne Grady | 282 | Fred Couples (285) | Shoal Creek | Birmingham, Ala. |
| 1991 | John Daly | 276 | Bruce Lietzke (279) | Crooked Stick GC | Carmel, Ind. |
| 1992 | Nick Price | 278 | Nick Faldo, John Cook, Jim Gallagher & Gene Sauers (281) | Bellerive CC | St. Louis |
| 1993 | Paul Azinger** | 272 | Greg Norman (272) | Inverness Club | Toledo, Ohio |
| 1994 | Nick Price | 269 | Corey Pavin (275) | Southern Hills CC | Tulsa |
| 1995 | Steve Elkington** | 267 | Colin Montgomerie (267) | Riviera CC | Pacific Palisades, Calif. |
| 1996 | Mark Brooks** | 277 | Kenny Perry (277) | Valhalla GC | Louisville, Ky. |
| 1997 | Davis Love III | 269 | Justin Leonard (274) | Winged Foot GC | Mamaroneck, N.Y. |
| 1998 | Vijay Singh | 271 | Steve Stricker (273) | Sahalee CC | Redmond, Wash. |
| 1999 | Tiger Woods | 277 | Sergio Garcia (278) | Medinah CC | Medinah, Ill. |
| 2000 | Tiger Woods** | 270 | Bob May (270) | Valhalla GC | Louisville, Ky. |
| 2001 | David Toms | 265 | Phil Mickelson (266) | Atlanta AC | Duluth, Ga. |
| 2002 | Rich Beem | 278 | Tiger Woods (279) | Hazeltine National GC | Chaska, Minn. |
| 2003 | Shaun Micheel | 276 | Chad Campbell (278) | Oak Hill CC | Rochester, N.Y. |
| 2004 | Vijay Singh** | 280 | Chris DiMarco & Justin Leonard (280) | Whistling Straits | Kohler, Wis. |
| 2005 | Phil Mickelson | 276 | Steve Elkington & Thomas Bjorn (277) | Baltusrol GC | Springfield, N.J. |

*While the PGA Championship was a match play tournament from 1916-57, the two finalists played 36 holes for the title. In the five years that a playoff was necessary, the match was decided on the 37th or 38th hole.

**PLAYOFFS:**

**1961:** Jerry Barber (67) def. Don January (68) in 18 holes. **1967:** Don January (69) def. Don Massengale (71) in 18 holes. **1977:** Lanny Wadkins (4-4-4) def. Gene Littler (4-4-5) on 3rd hole of sudden death. **1978:** John Mahaffey (4-3) def. Jerry Pate (4-4) and Tom Watson (4-5) on 2nd hole of sudden death. **1979:** David Graham (4-4-2) def. Ben Crenshaw (4-4-4) on 3rd hole of sudden death. **1987:** Larry Nelson (4) def. Lanny Wadkins (5) on 1st hole of sudden death. **1993:** Paul Azinger (4-4) def. Greg Norman (4-5) on 2nd hole of sudden death. **1995:** Steve Elkington (3) def. Colin Montgomerie (4) on 1st hole of sudden death. **1996:** Mark Brooks (4) def. Kenny Perry (5) on 1st hole of sudden death. **2000:** Tiger Woods (3-4-5—12) won a three-hole playoff over Bob May (4-4-5—13). **2004:** Vijay Singh (3-3-4—10) won a three-hole playoff over Chris DiMarco (4-3-DNF) and Justin Leonard (4-3-DNF).

## Grand Slam Summary

The only golfer ever to win a recognized Grand Slam—four major championships in a single season—was Bobby Jones in 1930. That year, Jones won the U.S. and British Opens as well as the U.S. and British Amateurs.

The men's professional Grand Slam—the Masters, U.S. Open, British Open and PGA Championship—did not gain acceptance until 30 years later when Arnold Palmer won the 1960 Masters and U.S. Open. The media wrote that the popular Palmer was chasing the "new" Grand Slam and would have to win the British Open and the PGA to claim it. He did not, but then nobody has before or since.

**Three wins in one year** (2): Ben Hogan (1953) and Tiger Woods (2000). **Two wins in one year** (21): Jack Nicklaus (5 times); Tiger Woods (3 times); Ben Hogan, Arnold Palmer and Tom Watson (twice); Nick Faldo, Mark O'Meara, Gary Player, Nick Price, Sam Snead, Lee Trevino and Craig Wood (once).

| Year | Masters | US Open | Brit. Open | PGA | Year | Masters | US Open | Brit. Open | PGA |
|------|---------|---------|------------|-----|------|---------|---------|------------|-----|
| 1934 | H. Smith | Dutra | Cotton | Runyan | 1952 | Snead | Boros | Locke | Turnesa |
| 1935 | Sarazen | Parks | Perry | Revolta | 1953 | Hogan | Hogan | Hogan | Burkemo |
| 1936 | H. Smith | Manero | Padgham | Shute | 1954 | Snead | Furgol | Thomson | Harbert |
| 1937 | B. Nelson | Guldahl | Cotton | Shute | 1955 | Middlecoff | Fleck | Thomson | Ford |
| 1938 | Picard | Guldahl | Whitcombe | Runyan | 1956 | Burke | Middlecoff | Thomson | Burke |
| 1939 | Guldahl | B. Nelson | Burton | Picard | 1957 | Ford | Mayer | Locke | L. Hebert |
| 1940 | Demaret | Little | — | B. Nelson | 1958 | Palmer | Bolt | Thomson | Finsterwald |
| 1941 | Wood | Wood | — | Ghezzi | 1959 | Wall | Casper | Player | Rosburg |
| 1942 | B. Nelson | — | — | Snead | 1960 | Palmer | Palmer | Nagle | J. Hebert |
| 1943 | — | — | — | — | 1961 | Player | Littler | Palmer | J. Barber |
| 1944 | — | — | — | Hamilton | 1962 | Palmer | Nicklaus | Palmer | Player |
| 1945 | — | — | — | B. Nelson | 1963 | Nicklaus | Boros | Charles | Nicklaus |
| 1946 | Keiser | Mangrum | Snead | Hogan | 1964 | Palmer | Venturi | Lema | Nichols |
| 1947 | Demaret | Worsham | F. Daly | Ferrier | 1965 | Nicklaus | Player | Thomson | Marr |
| 1948 | Harmon | Hogan | Cotton | Hogan | 1966 | Nicklaus | Casper | Nicklaus | Geiberger |
| 1949 | Snead | Middlecoff | Locke | Snead | 1967 | Brewer Jr. | Nicklaus | De Vicenzo | January |
| 1950 | Demaret | Hogan | Locke | Harper | 1968 | Goalby | Trevino | Player | Boros |
| 1951 | Hogan | Hogan | Faulkner | Snead | 1969 | Archer | Moody | Jacklin | Floyd |

| Year | Masters | US Open | Brit. Open | PGA | Year | Masters | US Open | Brit. Open | PGA |
|------|---------|---------|------------|-----|------|---------|---------|------------|-----|
| 1970 | Casper | Jacklin | Nicklaus | Stockton | 1988 | Lyle | Strange | Ballesteros | Sluman |
| 1971 | Coody | Trevino | Trevino | Nicklaus | 1989 | Faldo | Strange | Calcavecchia | Stewart |
| 1972 | Nicklaus | Nicklaus | Trevino | Player | 1990 | Faldo | Irwin | Faldo | Grady |
| 1973 | Aaron | J. Miller | Weiskopf | Nicklaus | 1991 | Woosnam | Stewart | Baker-Finch | J. Daly |
| 1974 | Player | Irwin | Player | Trevino | 1992 | Couples | Kite | Faldo | Price |
| 1975 | Nicklaus | L. Graham | T. Watson | Nicklaus | 1993 | Langer | Janzen | Norman | Azinger |
| 1976 | Floyd | J. Pate | Miller | Stockton | 1994 | Olazabal | Els | Price | Price |
| 1977 | T. Watson | H. Green | T. Watson | L. Wadkins | 1995 | Crenshaw | Pavin | Daly | Elkington |
| 1978 | Player | North | Nicklaus | Mahaffey | 1996 | Faldo | S. Jones | Lehman | Brooks |
| 1979 | Zoeller | Irwin | Ballesteros | D. Graham | 1997 | Woods | Els | Leonard | Love |
| 1980 | Ballesteros | Nicklaus | T. Watson | Nicklaus | 1998 | O'Meara | Janzen | O'Meara | Singh |
| 1981 | T. Watson | D. Graham | Rogers | L. Nelson | 1999 | Olazabal | Stewart | Lawrie | Woods |
| 1982 | Stadler | T. Watson | T. Watson | Floyd | 2000 | Singh | Woods | Woods | Woods |
| 1983 | Ballesteros | L. Nelson | T. Watson | Sutton | 2001 | Woods | Goosen | Duval | Toms |
| 1984 | Crenshaw | Zoeller | Ballesteros | Trevino | 2002 | Woods | Woods | Els | Beem |
| 1985 | Langer | North | Lyle | H. Green | 2003 | Weir | Furyk | Curtis | Micheel |
| 1986 | Nicklaus | Floyd | Norman | Tway | 2004 | Mickelson | Goosen | Hamilton | Singh |
| 1987 | Mize | S. Simpson | Faldo | L. Nelson | 2005 | Woods | Campbell | Woods | Mickelson |

## U.S. Amateur

Match play from 1895-64, stroke play from 1965-72, match play 1973-79, 36-hole stroke-play qualifying before match play since 1979.

**Multiple winners:** Bobby Jones (5); Jerry Travers (4); Walter Travis and Tiger Woods (3); Deane Beman, Charles Coe, Gary Cowan, H. Chandler Egan, Chick Evans, Lawson Little, Jack Nicklaus, Francis Ouimet, Jay Sigel, William Turnesa, Bud Ward, Harvie Ward, and H.J. Whigham (2).

| Year | | Year | | Year | | Year | |
|------|--|------|--|------|--|------|--|
| 1895 | Charles Macdonald | 1923 | Max Marston | 1953 | Gene Littler | 1980 | Hal Sutton |
| 1896 | H.J. Whigham | 1924 | Bobby Jones | 1954 | Arnold Palmer | 1981 | Nathaniel Crosby |
| 1897 | H.J. Whigham | 1925 | Bobby Jones | 1955 | Harvie Ward | 1982 | Jay Sigel |
| 1898 | Findlay Douglas | 1926 | George Von Elm | 1956 | Harvie Ward | 1983 | Jay Sigel |
| 1899 | H.M. Harriman | 1927 | Bobby Jones | 1957 | Hillman Robbins | 1984 | Scott Verplank |
| 1900 | Walter Travis | 1928 | Bobby Jones | 1958 | Charles Coe | 1985 | Sam Randolph |
| 1901 | Walter Travis | 1929 | Harrison Johnston | 1959 | Jack Nicklaus | 1986 | Buddy Alexander |
| 1902 | Louis James | 1930 | Bobby Jones | 1960 | Deane Beman | 1987 | Billy Mayfair |
| 1903 | Walter Travis | 1931 | Francis Ouimet | 1961 | Jack Nicklaus | 1988 | Eric Meeks |
| 1904 | H. Chandler Egan | 1932 | Ross Somerville | 1962 | Labron Harris | 1989 | Chris Patton |
| 1905 | H. Chandler Egan | 1933 | George Dunlap | 1963 | Deane Beman | 1990 | Phil Mickelson |
| 1906 | Eben Byers | 1934 | Lawson Little | 1964 | Bill Campbell | 1991 | Mitch Voges |
| 1907 | Jerry Travers | 1935 | Lawson Little | 1965 | Bob Murphy | 1992 | Justin Leonard |
| 1908 | Jerry Travers | 1936 | John Fischer | 1966 | Gary Cowan | 1993 | John Harris |
| 1909 | Robert Gardner | 1937 | John Goodman | 1967 | Bob Dickson | 1994 | Tiger Woods |
| 1910 | W.C. Fownes Jr. | 1938 | William Turnesa | 1968 | Bruce Fleisher | 1995 | Tiger Woods |
| 1911 | Harold Hilton | 1939 | Bud Ward | 1969 | Steve Melnyk | 1996 | Tiger Woods |
| 1912 | Jerry Travers | 1940 | Richard Chapman | 1970 | Lanny Wadkins | 1997 | Matt Kuchar |
| 1913 | Jerry Travers | 1941 | Bud Ward | 1971 | Gary Cowan | 1998 | Hank Kuehne |
| 1914 | Francis Ouimet | 1942-45 | Not held | 1972 | Vinny Giles | 1999 | David Gossett |
| 1915 | Robert Gardner | 1946 | Ted Bishop | 1973 | Craig Stadler | 2000 | Jeff Quinney |
| 1916 | Chick Evans | 1947 | Skee Riegel | 1974 | Jerry Pate | 2001 | Bubba Dickerson |
| 1917-18 | Not held | 1948 | William Turnesa | 1975 | Fred Ridley | 2002 | Ricky Barnes |
| 1919 | Davidson Herron | 1949 | Charles Coe | 1976 | Bill Sander | 2003 | Nick Flanagan |
| 1920 | Chick Evans | 1950 | Sam Urzetta | 1977 | John Fought | 2004 | Ryan Moore |
| 1921 | Jesse Guilford | 1951 | Billy Maxwell | 1978 | John Cook | 2005 | Edoardo Molinari |
| 1922 | Jess Sweetser | 1952 | Jack Westland | 1979 | Mark O'Meara | | |

## Major Championship Leaders

Through 2005; active PGA players in **bold** type.

| | US Open | British Open | PGA | Masters | US Am | British Am | Total |
|--|---------|--------------|-----|---------|-------|------------|-------|
| **Jack Nicklaus** | 4 | 3 | 5 | 6 | 2 | 0 | **20** |
| Bobby Jones | 4 | 3 | 0 | 0 | 5 | 1 | **13** |
| **Tiger Woods** | 2 | 2 | 2 | 4 | 3 | 0 | **13** |
| Walter Hagen | 2 | 4 | 5 | 0 | 0 | 0 | **11** |
| Ben Hogan | 4 | 1 | 2 | 2 | 0 | 0 | **9** |
| **Gary Player** | 1 | 3 | 2 | 3 | 0 | 0 | **9** |
| John Ball | 0 | 1 | 0 | 0 | 0 | 8 | **9** |
| Arnold Palmer | 1 | 2 | 0 | 4 | 1 | 0 | **8** |
| **Tom Watson** | 1 | 5 | 2 | 2 | 0 | 0 | **8** |
| Harold Hilton | 0 | 2 | 0 | 0 | 1 | 4 | **7** |
| Gene Sarazen | 2 | 1 | 3 | 1 | 0 | 0 | **7** |
| Sam Snead | 0 | 1 | 3 | 3 | 0 | 0 | **7** |
| Harry Vardon | 1 | 6 | 0 | 0 | 0 | 0 | **7** |

## British Amateur

Match play since 1885. **Multiple winners:** John Ball (8); Michael Bonnallack (5); Harold Hilton (4); Joe Carr (3); Horace Hutchinson, Ernest Holderness, Trevor Homer, Johnny Laidley, Lawson Little, Peter McEvoy, Dick Siderowf, Frank Stranahan, Freddie Tait, Cyril Tolley and Gary Wolstenholme (2).

| Year | | Year | | Year | | Year | |
|------|--|------|--|------|--|------|--|
| 1885 | Allen MacFie | 1913 | Harold Hilton | 1950 | Frank Stranahan | 1978 | Peter McEvoy |
| 1886 | Horace Hutchinson | 1914 | J.L.C. Jenkins | 1951 | Richard Chapman | 1979 | Jay Sigel |
| 1887 | Horace Hutchinson | 1915-19 | Not held | 1952 | Harvie Ward | 1980 | Duncan Evans |
| 1888 | John Ball | 1920 | Cyril Tolley | 1953 | Joe Carr | 1981 | Phillipe Ploujoux |
| 1889 | Johnny Laidley | 1921 | William Hunter | 1954 | Douglas Bachli | 1982 | Martin Thompson |
| 1890 | John Ball | 1922 | Ernest Holderness | 1955 | Joe Conrad | 1983 | Philip Parkin |
| 1891 | Johnny Laidley | 1923 | Roger Wethered | 1956 | John Beharrell | 1984 | Jose-Maria Olazabal |
| 1892 | John Ball | 1924 | Ernest Holderness | 1957 | Reid Jack | 1985 | Garth McGimpsey |
| 1893 | Peter Anderson | 1925 | Robert Harris | 1958 | Joe Carr | 1986 | David Curry |
| 1894 | John Ball | 1926 | Jess Sweetser | 1959 | Deane Beman | 1987 | Paul Mayo |
| 1895 | Leslie Balfour-Melville | 1927 | William Tweddell | 1960 | Joe Carr | 1988 | Christian Hardin |
| 1896 | Freddie Tait | 1928 | Thomas Perkins | 1961 | Michael Bonallack | 1989 | Stephen Dodd |
| 1897 | Jack Allan | 1929 | Cyril Tolley | 1962 | Richard Davies | 1990 | Rolf Muntz |
| 1898 | Freddie Tait | 1930 | Bobby Jones | 1963 | Michael Lunt | 1991 | Gary Wolstenholme |
| 1899 | John Ball | 1931 | Eric Smith | 1964 | Gordon Clark | 1992 | Stephen Dundas |
| 1900 | Harold Hilton | 1932 | John deForest | 1965 | Michael Bonallack | 1993 | Ian Pyman |
| 1901 | Harold Hilton | 1933 | Michael Scott | 1966 | Bobby Cole | 1994 | Lee James |
| 1902 | Charles Hutchings | 1934 | Lawson Little | 1967 | Bob Dickson | 1995 | Gordon Sherry |
| 1903 | Robert Maxwell | 1935 | Lawson Little | 1968 | Michael Bonallack | 1996 | Warren Bledon |
| 1904 | Walter Travis | 1936 | Hector Thomson | 1969 | Michael Bonallack | 1997 | Craig Watson |
| 1905 | Arthur Barry | 1937 | Robert Sweeny Jr. | 1970 | Michael Bonallack | 1998 | Sergio Garcia |
| 1906 | James Robb | 1938 | Charles Yates | 1971 | Steve Melnyk | 1999 | Graeme Storm |
| 1907 | John Ball | 1939 | Alexander Kyle | 1972 | Trevor Homer | 2000 | Mikko Ilonen |
| 1908 | E.A. Lassen | 1940-45 | Not held | 1973 | Dick Siderowf | 2001 | Michael Hoey |
| 1909 | Robert Maxwell | 1946 | James Bruen | 1974 | Trevor Homer | 2002 | Alejandro Larrazabal |
| 1910 | John Ball | 1947 | William Turnesa | 1975 | Vinny Giles | 2003 | Gary Wolstenholme |
| 1911 | Harold Hilton | 1948 | Frank Stranahan | 1976 | Dick Siderowf | 2004 | Stuart Wilson |
| 1912 | John Ball | 1949 | Samuel McCready | 1977 | Peter McEvoy | 2005 | Brian McElhinney |

# WOMEN
## Kraft Nabisco Championship

Formerly known as the Colgate Dinah Shore (1972-81) and the Nabisco Dinah Shore (1982-99), the tournament became the LPGA's fourth designated major championship in 1983. Shore's name, which was dropped from the tournament in 2000, is preserved with the Nabisco Dinah Shore Trophy, which is awarded to the winner. The tourney has been played at Mission Hills CC in Rancho Mirage, Calif., since it began; (*) indicates playoff winner.

**Multiple winners:** (as a major): Amy Alcott, Betsy King and Annika Sorenstam (3); Juli Inkster and Dottie Pepper (2).

| Year | Winner | Score | Runner-up | Year | Winner | Score | Runner-up |
|------|--------|-------|-----------|------|--------|-------|-----------|
| 1972 | Jane Blalock | 213 | Carol Mann & Judy Rankin (216) | 1990 | Betsy King | 283 | Kathy Postlewait & Shirley Furlong (285) |
| 1973 | Mickey Wright | 284 | Joyce Kazmierski (286) | 1991 | Amy Alcott | 273 | Dottie Pepper (281) |
| 1974 | Jo Anne Prentice* | 289 | Jane Blalock & Sandra Haynie (289) | 1992 | Dottie Pepper* | 279 | Juli Inkster (279) |
| 1975 | Sandra Palmer | 283 | Kathy McMullen (284) | 1993 | Helen Alfredsson | 284 | Amy Benz & Tina Barrett (286) |
| 1976 | Judy Rankin | 285 | Betty Burfeindt (288) | 1994 | Donna Andrews | 276 | Laura Davies (277) |
| 1977 | Kathy Whitworth | 289 | JoAnne Carner & Sally Little (290) | 1995 | Nanci Bowen | 285 | Susie Redman (286) |
| 1978 | Sandra Post* | 283 | Penny Pulz (283) | 1996 | Patty Sheehan | 281 | Kelly Robbins, Meg Mallon & Annika Sorenstam (276) |
| 1979 | Sandra Post | 276 | Nancy Lopez (277) | | | | |
| 1980 | Donna Caponi | 275 | Amy Alcott (277) | | | | |
| 1981 | Nancy Lopez | 277 | Carolyn Hill (279) | 1997 | Betsy King | 276 | Kris Tschetter (278) |
| 1982 | Sally Little | 278 | Hollis Stacy & Sandra Haynie (281) | 1998 | Pat Hurst | 281 | Helen Dobson (282) |
| | | | | 1999 | Dottie Pepper | 269 | Meg Mallon (275) |
| 1983 | Amy Alcott | 282 | Beth Daniel & Kathy Whitworth (284) | 2000 | Karrie Webb | 274 | Dottie Pepper (284) |
| 1984 | Juli Inkster* | 280 | Pat Bradley (280) | 2001 | Annika Sorenstam | 281 | Akiko Fukushima, Janice Moodie, Dottie Pepper, Rachel Teske & Karrie Webb (284) |
| 1985 | Alice Miller | 275 | Jan Stephenson (278) | | | | |
| 1986 | Pat Bradley | 280 | Val Skinner (282) | | | | |
| 1987 | Betsy King* | 283 | Patty Sheehan (283) | 2002 | Annika Sorenstam | 280 | Liselotte Neumann (281) |
| 1988 | Amy Alcott | 274 | Colleen Walker (276) | 2003 | P. Meunier-Lebouc | 281 | Annika Sorenstam (282) |
| 1989 | Juli Inkster | 279 | Tammie Green & JoAnne Carner (284) | 2004 | Grace Park | 277 | Aree Song (278) |
| | | | | 2005 | Annika Sorenstam | 273 | Rosie Jones (281) |

### *PLAYOFFS:

**1974:** Jo Ann Prentice def. Jane Blalock in sudden death. **1978:** Sandra Post def. Penny Pulz in sudden death. **1984:** Juli Inkster def. Pat Bradley in sudden death. **1987:** Betsy King def. Patty Sheehan in sudden death. **1992:** Dottie Pepper def. Juli Inkster in sudden death.

## U.S. Women's Open

The U.S. Women's Open began under the direction of the defunct Women's Professional Golfers Assn. in 1946, passed to the LPGA in 1949 and to the USGA in 1953. The tournament used a match play format its first year then switched to stroke play; (*) indicates playoff winner and (a) indicates amateur.

**Multiple winners:** Betsy Rawls and Mickey Wright (4); Susie Maxwell Berning, Hollis Stacy and Babe Zaharias (3); JoAnne Carner, Donna Caponi, Juli Inkster, Betsy King, Meg Mallon, Patty Sheehan, Annika Sorenstam, Louise Suggs and Karrie Webb (2).

| Year | Winner | Score | Runner-up | Course | Location |
|------|--------|-------|-----------|--------|----------|
| 1946 | Patty Berg | 5&4 | Betsy Jameson | Spokane CC | Spokane, Wash. |
| 1947 | Betty Jameson | 295 | a-Sally Sessions & a-Polly Riley (301) | Starmount Forest CC | Greensboro, N.C. |
| 1948 | Babe Zaharias | 300 | Betty Hicks (308) | Atlantic City CC | Northfield, N.J. |
| 1949 | Louise Suggs | 291 | Babe Zaharias (305) | Prince Georges CC | Landover, Md. |
| 1950 | Babe Zaharias | 291 | a-Betsy Rawls (300) | Rolling Hills CC | Wichita, Kan. |
| 1951 | Betsy Rawls | 293 | Louise Suggs (298) | Druid Hills GC | Atlanta, Ga. |
| 1952 | Louise Suggs | 284 | Marlene Hagge (291) | Bala GC | Philadelphia, Penn. |
| 1953 | Betsy Rawls* | 302 | Jackie Pung (302) | CC of Rochester | Rochester, N.Y. |
| 1954 | Babe Zaharias | 291 | Betty Hicks (303) | Salem CC | Peabody, Mass. |
| 1955 | Fay Crocker | 299 | Mary Lena Faulk (303) | Wichita CC | Wichita, Kan. |
| 1956 | Kathy Cornelius* | 302 | Barbara McIntire (302) | Northland CC | Duluth, Minn. |
| 1957 | Betsy Rawls | 299 | Patty Berg (305) | Winged Foot GC | Mamaroneck, N.Y. |
| 1958 | Mickey Wright | 290 | Louise Suggs (295) | Forest Lake CC | Detroit, Mich. |
| 1959 | Mickey Wright | 287 | Louise Suggs (289) | Churchill Valley CC | Pittsburgh, Penn. |
| 1960 | Betsy Rawls | 292 | Joyce Ziske (293) | Worcester CC | Worcester, Mass. |
| 1961 | Mickey Wright | 293 | Betsy Rawls (299) | Baltusrol GC | Springfield, N.J. |
| 1962 | Murle Breer | 301 | Jo Anne Prentice & Ruth Jessen (303) | Dunes GC | Myrtle Beach, S.C. |
| 1963 | Mary Mills | 289 | Sandra Haynie & Louise Suggs (292) | Kenwood CC | Cincinnati, Ohio |
| 1964 | Mickey Wright* | 290 | Ruth Jessen (290) | San Diego CC | Chula Vista, Calif. |
| 1965 | Carol Mann | 290 | Kathy Cornelius (292) | Atlantic City CC | Northfield, N.J. |
| 1966 | Sandra Spuzich | 297 | Carol Mann (298) | Hazeltine National GC | Chaska, Minn. |
| 1967 | a-Catherine LaCoste | 294 | Susie Berning & Beth Stone (296) | Hot Springs GC | Hot Springs, Va. |
| 1968 | Susie Berning | 289 | Mickey Wright (292) | Moselem Springs GC | Fleetwood, Penn. |
| 1969 | Donna Caponi | 294 | Peggy Wilson (295) | Scenic Hills CC | Pensacola, Fla. |
| 1970 | Donna Caponi | 287 | Sandra Haynie (288) | Muskogee CC | Muskogee, Okla. |
| 1971 | JoAnne Carner | 288 | Kathy Whitworth (295) | Kahkwa CC | Erie, Penn. |
| 1972 | Susie Berning | 299 | Kathy Ahern, Pam Barnett & Judy Rankin (300) | Winged Foot GC | Mamaroneck, N.Y. |
| 1973 | Susie Berning | 290 | Gloria Ehret (295) | CC of Rochester | Rochester, N.Y. |
| 1974 | Sandra Haynie | 295 | Carol Mann & Beth Stone (296) | La Grange CC | La Grange, Ill. |
| 1975 | Sandra Palmer | 295 | JoAnne Carner, a-Nancy Lopez & Sandra Post (299) | Atlantic City CC | Northfield, N.J. |
| 1976 | JoAnne Carner* | 292 | Sandra Palmer (292) | Rolling Green CC | Springfield, Penn. |
| 1977 | Hollis Stacy | 292 | Nancy Lopez (294) | Hazeltine National GC | Chaska, Minn. |
| 1978 | Hollis Stacy | 289 | JoAnne Carner & Sally Little (290) | CC of Indianapolis | Indianapolis, Ind. |
| 1979 | Jerilyn Britz | 284 | Debbie Massey & Sandra Palmer (286) | Brooklawn CC | Fairfield, Conn. |
| 1980 | Amy Alcott | 280 | Hollis Stacy (289) | Richland CC | Nashville, Tenn. |
| 1981 | Pat Bradley | 279 | Beth Daniel (280) | La Grange CC | La Grange, Ill. |
| 1982 | Janet Anderson | 283 | Beth Daniel, Sandra Haynie & Donna White (289) | Del Paso CC | Sacramento, Calif. |
| 1983 | Jan Stephenson | 290 | JoAnne Carner (291) | Cedar Ridge CC | Tulsa, Okla. |
| 1984 | Hollis Stacy | 290 | Rosie Jones (291) | Salem CC | Peabody, Mass. |
| 1985 | Kathy Baker | 280 | Judy Dickenson (283) | Baltusrol GC | Springfield, N.J. |
| 1986 | Jane Geddes* | 287 | Sally Little (287) | NCR GC | Dayton, Ohio |
| 1987 | Laura Davies* | 285 | Ayako Okamoto & JoAnne Carner (285) | Plainfield CC | Plainfield, N.J. |
| 1988 | Liselotte Neumann | 277 | Patty Sheehan (280) | Baltimore CC | Baltimore, Md. |
| 1989 | Betsy King | 278 | Nancy Lopez (282) | Indianwood GC | Lake Orion, Mich. |
| 1990 | Betsy King | 284 | Patty Sheehan (285) | Atlanta Athletic Club | Duluth, Ga. |
| 1991 | Meg Mallon | 283 | Pat Bradley (285) | Colonial CC | Ft. Worth, Texas |
| 1992 | Patty Sheehan* | 280 | Juli Inkster (280) | Oakmont CC | Oakmont, Penn. |
| 1993 | Lauri Merten | 280 | Donna Andrews & Helen Alfredsson (281) | Crooked Stick GC | Carmel, Ind. |
| 1994 | Patty Sheehan | 277 | Tammie Green (278) | Indianwood CC | Lake Orion, Mich. |
| 1995 | Annika Sorenstam | 278 | Meg Mallon (279) | The Broadmoor | Colorado Springs, Colo. |
| 1996 | Annika Sorenstam | 272 | Kris Tschetter (278) | Pine Needles Lodge & GC | Southern Pines, N.C. |
| 1997 | Alison Nicholas | 274 | Nancy Lopez (275) | Pumpkin Ridge GC | Cornelius, Ore. |

## U.S. Women's Open (Cont.)

| Year | Winner | Score | Runner-up | Course | Location |
|---|---|---|---|---|---|
| 1998 | Se Ri Pak* | 290 | a-Jenny Chuasiriporn (290) | Blackwolf Run GC | Kohler, Wis. |
| 1999 | Juli Inkster | 272 | Sherri Turner (277) | Old Waverly GC | West Point, Miss. |
| 2000 | Karrie Webb | 282 | Cristie Kerr & Meg Mallon (287) | Merit Club | Libertyville, Ill. |
| 2001 | Karrie Webb | 273 | Se Ri Pak (281) | Pine Needles Lodge & GC | Southern Pines, N.C. |
| 2002 | Juli Inkster | 276 | Annika Sorenstam (278) | Prairie Dunes CC | Hutchinson, Kan. |
| 2003 | Hilary Lunke* | 283 | Angela Stanford & Kelly Robbins (283) | Pumpkin Ridge GC | North Plains, Ore. |
| 2004 | Meg Mallon | 274 | Annika Sorenstam (276) | Orchards GC | South Hadley, Mass. |
| 2005 | Birdie Kim | 287 | a-Brittany Lang & a-Morgan Pressel (289) | Cherry Hills CC | Cherry Hills Vill., Colo. |

### *PLAYOFFS:

**1953:** Betsy Rawls (70) def. Jackie Pung (77) in 18 holes. **1956:** Kathy Cornelius (75) def. Barbara McIntire (82) in 18 holes. **1964:** Mickey Wright (70) def. Ruth Jessen (72) in 18 holes. **1976:** JoAnne Carner (76) def. Sandra Palmer (78) in 18 holes. **1986:** Jane Geddes (71) def. Sally Little (73) in 18 holes. **1987:** Laura Davies (71) def. Ayako Okamoto (73) and JoAnne Carner (74) in 18 holes. **1992:** Patty Sheehan (72) def. Juli Inkster (74) in 18 holes. **1998:** Se Ri Pak def. Jenny Chuasiriporn on the second sudden death hole after both players were tied after an 18-hole playoff. **2003:** Hilary Lunke (70) def. Angela Stanford (71) and Kelly Robbins (73) in 18 holes.

## LPGA Championship

Officially the McDonald's LPGA Championship since 1994 (Mazda was the title sponsor from 1987-93), the tournament began in 1955 and has had extended stays at the Stardust CC in Las Vegas (1961-66), Pleasant Valley CC in Sutton, Mass. (1967-68, 70-74), the Jack Nicklaus Sports Center at Kings Island, Ohio (1978-89), Bethesda CC in Maryland (1990-93), DuPont CC in Wilmington, Del. (1994-2004) and Bulle Rock GC in Havre de Grace, Md. (2005–); (*) indicates playoff winner, (a) amateur and (#) weather-shortened.

**Multiple winners:** Mickey Wright (4); Nancy Lopez, Patty Sheehan, Annika Sorenstam and Kathy Whitworth (3); Donna Caponi, Laura Davies, Sandra Haynie, Juli Inkster, Mary Mills, Se Ri Pak and Betsy Rawls (2).

| Year | Winner | Score | Runner-up | Year | Winner | Score | Runner-up |
|---|---|---|---|---|---|---|---|
| 1955 | Beverly Hanson | 220 | Louise Suggs (223) | 1982 | Jan Stephenson | 279 | JoAnne Carner (281) |
| 1956 | Marlene Hagge* | 291 | Patty Berg (291) | 1983 | Patty Sheehan | 279 | Sandra Haynie (281) |
| 1957 | Louise Suggs | 285 | Wiffi Smith (288) | 1984 | Patty Sheehan | 272 | Beth Daniel & Pat Bradley (282) |
| 1958 | Mickey Wright | 288 | Fay Crocker (294) | | | | |
| 1959 | Betsy Rawls | 288 | Patty Berg (289) | 1985 | Nancy Lopez | 273 | Alice Miller (281) |
| 1960 | Mickey Wright | 292 | Louise Suggs (295) | 1986 | Pat Bradley | 277 | Patty Sheehan (278) |
| 1961 | Mickey Wright | 287 | Louise Suggs (296) | 1987 | Jane Geddes | 275 | Betsy King (275) |
| 1962 | Judy Kimball | 282 | Shirley Spork (286) | 1988 | Sherri Turner | 281 | Amy Alcott (282) |
| 1963 | Mickey Wright | 294 | Mary Lena Faulk & Mary Mills (296) | 1989 | Nancy Lopez | 274 | Ayako Okamoto (277) |
| 1964 | Mary Mills | 278 | Mickey Wright (280) | 1990 | Beth Daniel | 280 | Rosie Jones (281) |
| 1965 | Sandra Haynie | 279 | Clifford A. Creed (280) | 1991 | Meg Mallon | 274 | Pat Bradley & Ayako Okamoto (275) |
| 1966 | Gloria Ehret | 282 | Mickey Wright (285) | | | | |
| 1967 | Kathy Whitworth | 284 | Shirley Englehorn (285) | 1992 | Betsy King | 267 | JoAnne Carner, Karen Noble & Liselotte Neumann (278) |
| 1968 | Sandra Post | 294 | Kathy Whitworth (294) | | | | |
| 1969 | Betsy Rawls | 293 | Susie Berning & Carol Mann (297) | 1993 | Patty Sheehan | 275 | Lauri Merten (276) |
| 1970 | Shirley Englehorn | 285 | Kathy Whitworth (285) | 1994 | Laura Davies | 279 | Alice Ritzman (280) |
| 1971 | Kathy Whitworth | 288 | Kathy Ahern (292) | 1995 | Kelly Robbins | 274 | Laura Davies (275) |
| 1972 | Kathy Ahern | 293 | Jane Blalock (299) | 1996 | Laura Davies# | 213 | Julie Piers (214) |
| 1973 | Mary Mills | 288 | Betty Burfeindt (289) | 1997 | Chris Johnson* | 281 | Leta Lindley (281) |
| 1974 | Sandra Haynie | 288 | JoAnne Carner (290) | 1998 | Se Ri Pak | 273 | Donna Andrews & Lisa Hackney (276) |
| 1975 | Kathy Whitworth | 288 | Sandra Haynie (289) | | | | |
| 1976 | Betty Burfeindt | 287 | Judy Rankin (288) | 1999 | Juli Inkster | 268 | Liselotte Neumann (272) |
| 1977 | Chako Higuchi | 279 | Pat Bradley, Sandra Post & Judy Rankin (282) | 2000 | Juli Inkster* | 281 | Stefania Croce (281) |
| | | | | 2001 | Karrie Webb | 270 | Laura Diaz (272) |
| 1978 | Nancy Lopez | 275 | Amy Alcott (281) | 2002 | Se Ri Pak | 279 | Beth Daniel (282) |
| 1979 | Donna Caponi | 279 | Jerilyn Britz (282) | 2003 | Annika Sorenstam* | 278 | Grace Park (278) |
| 1980 | Sally Little | 285 | Jane Blalock (288) | 2004 | Annika Sorenstam | 271 | Shi Hyun Ahn (274) |
| 1981 | Donna Caponi | 280 | Jerilyn Britz & Pat Meyers (281) | 2005 | Annika Sorenstam | 277 | a-Michelle Wie (280) |

### *PLAYOFFS:

**1956:** Marlene Hagge def. Patti Berg in sudden death. **1968:** Sandra Post (68) def. Kathy Whitworth (75) in 18 holes. **1970:** Shirley Englehorn def. Kathy Whitworth in sudden death. **1997:** Chris Johnson def. Leta Lindley in sudden death. **2000:** Juli Inkster def. Stefania Croce in sudden death. **2003:** Annika Sorenstam def. Grace Park in sudden death.

## Women's British Open

Sponsored by Weetabix, this has been an official stop on the LPGA Tour since 1994, and it became the fourth designated major championship in 2001 when it replaced the du Maurier Classic.

**Multiple winners** Karrie Webb (3); and Sherri Steinhauer (2); (as a major): none.

| Year | Winner | Score | Runner-up | Course | Location |
|---|---|---|---|---|---|
| 1994 | Liselotte Neumann | 280 | Dottie Mochrie & Annika Sorenstam (283) | Woburn G&CC | Milton Keynes, England |
| 1995 | Karrie Webb | 278 | Annika Sorenstam & Jill McGill (284) | Woburn G&CC | Milton Keynes, England |
| 1996 | Emilee Klein | 277 | Penny Hammel & Amy Alcott (284) | Woburn G&CC | Milton Keynes, England |
| 1997 | Karrie Webb | 269 | Rosie Jones (277) | Sunningdale GC | Berkshire, England |
| 1998 | Sherri Steinhauer | 292 | Sophie Gustafson & Brandie Burton (293) | Royal Lytham | Lytham, England |
| 1999 | Sherri Steinhauer | 283 | Annika Sorenstam (284) | Woburn G&CC | Milton Keynes, England |
| 2000 | Sophie Gustafson | 282 | Kirsty Taylor, Liselotte Neumann, Becky Iverson & Meg Mallon (284) | Royal Birkdale | Southport, England |
| 2001 | Se Ri Pak | 277 | Mi Hyun Kim (279) | Sunningdale GC | Berkshire, England |
| 2002 | Karrie Webb | 273 | Michelle Ellis & Paula Marti (275) | Turnberry GC | Turnberry, Scotland |
| 2003 | Annika Sorenstam | 278 | Se Ri Pak (279) | Royal Lytham | Lytham, England |
| 2004 | Karen Stupples | 269 | Rachel Teske (274) | Sunningdale GC | Berkshire, England |
| 2005 | Jeong Jang | 272 | Sophie Gustafson (276) | Royal Birkdale GC | Merseyside, England |

## du Maurier Classic (1979-2000)

The du Maurier Classic was considered a major title on the women's tour from 1979 until it was discontinued in 2000; (*) indicates playoff winner.

**Multiple winners** (as a major): Pat Bradley (3); Brandie Burton (2).

| Year | | Year | | Year | | Year | |
|---|---|---|---|---|---|---|---|
| 1973 | Jocelyne Bourassa | 1980 | Pat Bradley | 1987 | Jody Rosenthal | 1994 | Martha Nause |
| 1974 | Carole Jo Skala | 1981 | Jan Stephenson | 1988 | Sally Little | 1995 | Jenny Lidback |
| 1975 | JoAnne Carner | 1982 | Sandra Haynie | 1989 | Tammie Green | 1996 | Laura Davies |
| 1976 | Donna Caponi | 1983 | Hollis Stacy | 1990 | Cathy Johnston | 1997 | Colleen Walker |
| 1977 | Judy Rankin | 1984 | Juli Inkster | 1991 | Nancy Scranton | 1998 | Brandie Burton |
| 1978 | JoAnne Carner | 1985 | Pat Bradley | 1992 | Sherri Steinhauer | 1999 | Karrie Webb |
| 1979 | Amy Alcott | 1986 | Pat Bradley* | 1993 | Brandie Burton* | 2000 | Meg Mallon |

## Titleholders Championship (1937-72)

The Titleholders was considered a major title on the women's tour until it was discontinued after the 1972 tournament.

**Multiple winners:** Patty Berg (7); Louise Suggs (4); Babe Zaharias (3); Dorothy Kirby, Marilynn Smith, Kathy Whitworth and Mickey Wright (2).

| Year | | Year | | Year | | Year | |
|---|---|---|---|---|---|---|---|
| 1937 | Patty Berg | 1947 | Babe Zaharias | 1955 | Patty Berg | 1963 | Marilynn Smith |
| 1938 | Patty Berg | 1948 | Patty Berg | 1956 | Louise Suggs | 1964 | Marilynn Smith |
| 1939 | Patty Berg | 1949 | Peggy Kirk | 1957 | Patty Berg | 1965 | Kathy Whitworth |
| 1940 | Betty Hicks | 1950 | Babe Zaharias | 1958 | Beverly Hanson | 1966 | Kathy Whitworth |
| 1941 | Dorothy Kirby | 1951 | Pat O'Sullivan | 1959 | Louise Suggs | 1967-71 | Not held |
| 1942 | Dorothy Kirby | 1952 | Babe Zaharias | 1960 | Fay Crocker | 1972 | Sandra Palmer |
| 1943-45 | Not held | 1953 | Patty Berg | 1961 | Mickey Wright | | |
| 1946 | Louise Suggs | 1954 | Louise Suggs | 1962 | Mickey Wright | | |

## Western Open (1930-67)

The Western Open was considered a major title on the women's tour until it was discontinued after the 1967 tournament.

**Multiple winners:** Patty Berg (7); Louise Suggs and Babe Zaharias (4); Mickey Wright (3); June Beebe, Opal Hill, Betty Jameson and Betsy Rawls (2).

| Year | | Year | | Year | | Year | |
|---|---|---|---|---|---|---|---|
| 1930 | Mrs. Lee Mida | 1940 | Babe Zaharias | 1950 | Babe Zaharias | 1960 | Joyce Ziske |
| 1931 | June Beebe | 1941 | Patty Berg | 1951 | Patty Berg | 1961 | Mary Lena Faulk |
| 1932 | Jane Weiller | 1942 | Betty Jameson | 1952 | Betsy Rawls | 1962 | Mickey Wright |
| 1933 | June Beebe | 1943 | Patty Berg | 1953 | Louise Suggs | 1963 | Mickey Wright |
| 1934 | Marian McDougall | 1944 | Babe Zaharias | 1954 | Betty Jameson | 1964 | Carol Mann |
| 1935 | Opal Hill | 1945 | Babe Zaharias | 1955 | Patty Berg | 1965 | Susie Maxwell |
| 1936 | Opal Hill | 1946 | Louise Suggs | 1956 | Beverly Hanson | 1966 | Mickey Wright |
| 1937 | Betty Hicks | 1947 | Louise Suggs | 1957 | Patty Berg | 1967 | Kathy Whitworth |
| 1938 | Bea Barrett | 1948 | Patty Berg | 1958 | Patty Berg | | |
| 1939 | Helen Dettweiler | 1949 | Louise Suggs | 1959 | Betsy Rawls | | |

## Grand Slam Summary

From 1955-66, the U.S. Open, LPGA Championship, Western Open and Titleholders tournaments served as the Women's Grand Slam. From 1983-2000 the U.S. Open, LPGA, du Maurier Classic and Nabisco Championship were the major events. In 2001, the Weetabix Women's British Open replaced the du Maurier Classic as the tour's fourth major. No one has won a four-event Grand Slam on the women's tour.

**Three wins in one year** (3): Babe Zaharias (1950), Mickey Wright (1961) and Pat Bradley (1986).

**Two wins in one year** (19): Patty Berg and Mickey Wright (3 times); Juli Inkster, Annika Sorenstam, Louise Suggs and Karrie Webb (twice); Laura Davies, Sandra Haynie, Betsy King, Meg Mallon, Se Ri Pak, Betsy Rawls and Kathy Whitworth (once).

| Year | LPGA | US Open | T'holders | Western | Year | LPGA | US Open | T'holders | Western |
|------|------|---------|-----------|---------|------|------|---------|-----------|---------|
| 1937 | — | — | Berg | Hicks | 1974 | Haynie | Haynie | — | — |
| 1938 | — | — | Berg | Barrett | 1975 | Whitworth | Palmer | — | — |
| 1939 | — | — | Berg | Dettweiler | 1976 | Burfeindt | Carner | — | — |
| 1940 | — | — | Hicks | Zaharias | 1977 | Higuchi | Stacy | — | — |
| 1941 | — | — | Kirby | Berg | 1978 | Lopez | Stacy | — | — |
| 1942 | — | — | Kirby | Jameson | **Year** | **LPGA** | **US Open** | **duMaurier** | **Nabisco** |
| 1943 | — | — | — | Berg | 1979 | Caponi | Britz | Alcott | — |
| 1944 | — | — | — | Zaharias | 1980 | Little | Alcott | Bradley | — |
| 1945 | — | — | — | Zaharias | 1981 | Caponi | Bradley | Stephenson | — |
| 1946 | — | Berg | Suggs | Suggs | 1982 | Stephenson | Anderson | Haynie | — |
| 1947 | — | Jameson | Zaharias | Suggs | 1983 | Sheehan | Stephenson | Stacy | Alcott |
| 1948 | — | Zaharias | Berg | Berg | 1984 | Sheehan | Stacy | Inkster | Inkster |
| 1949 | — | Suggs | Kirk | Suggs | 1985 | Lopez | Baker | Bradley | Miller |
| 1950 | — | Zaharias | Zaharias | Zaharias | 1986 | Bradley | Geddes | Bradley | Bradley |
| 1951 | — | Rawls | O'Sullivan | Berg | 1987 | Geddes | Davies | Rosenthal | King |
| 1952 | — | Suggs | Zaharias | Rawls | 1988 | Turner | Neumann | Little | Alcott |
| 1953 | — | Rawls | Berg | Suggs | 1989 | Lopez | King | Green | Inkster |
| 1954 | — | Zaharias | Suggs | Jameson | 1990 | Daniel | King | Johnston | King |
| 1955 | Hanson | Crocker | Berg | Berg | 1991 | Mallon | Mallon | Scranton | Alcott |
| 1956 | Hagge | Cornelius | Suggs | Hanson | 1992 | King | Sheehan | Steinhauer | Pepper |
| 1957 | Suggs | Rawls | Berg | Berg | 1993 | Sheehan | Merten | Burton | Alfredsson |
| 1958 | Wright | Wright | Hanson | Berg | 1994 | Davies | Sheehan | Nause | Andrews |
| 1959 | Rawls | Wright | Suggs | Rawls | 1995 | Robbins | Sorenstam | Lidback | Bowen |
| 1960 | Wright | Rawls | Crocker | Ziske | 1996 | Davies | Sorenstam | Davies | Sheehan |
| 1961 | Wright | Wright | Wright | Faulk | 1997 | Johnson | Nicholas | Walker | King |
| 1962 | Kimball | Lindstrom | Wright | Wright | 1998 | Pak | Pak | Burton | Hurst |
| 1963 | Wright | Mills | M. Smith | Wright | 1999 | Inkster | Inkster | Webb | Pepper |
| 1964 | Mills | Wright | M. Smith | Mann | 2000 | Inkster | Webb | Mallon | Webb |
| 1965 | Haynie | Mann | Whitworth | Maxwell | **Year** | **LPGA** | **US Open** | **Brit. Open** | **Nabisco** |
| 1966 | Ehret | Spuzich | Whitworth | Wright | 2001 | Webb | Webb | Pak | Sorenstam |
| 1967 | Whitworth | a-LaCoste | — | Whitworth | 2002 | Pak | Inkster | Webb | Sorenstam |
| 1968 | Post | Berning | — | — | 2003 | Sorenstam | Lunke | Sorenstam | Meunier-Lebouc |
| 1969 | Rawls | Caponi | — | — | | | | | |
| 1970 | Englehorn | Caponi | — | — | 2004 | Sorenstam | Mallon | Stupples | Park |
| 1971 | Whitworth | Carner | — | — | 2005 | Sorenstam | Kim | Jang | Sorenstam |
| 1972 | Ahern | Berning | Palmer | — | | | | | |
| 1973 | Mills | Berning | — | — | | | | | |

## Major Championship Leaders

Through 2005; active LPGA players in **bold** type.

| | US Open | LPGA | Nabisco | British Open | duM | Title | Western | US Am | Brit Am | Total |
|---|---------|------|---------|--------------|-----|-------|---------|-------|---------|-------|
| Patty Berg | 1 | 0 | 0 | 0 | 0 | 7 | 7 | 1 | 0 | **16** |
| Mickey Wright | 4 | 4 | 0 | 0 | 0 | 2 | 3 | 0 | 0 | **13** |
| Louise Suggs | 2 | 1 | 0 | 0 | 0 | 4 | 4 | 1 | 1 | **13** |
| Babe Didrikson Zaharias | 3 | 0 | 0 | 0 | 0 | 3 | 4 | 1 | 1 | **12** |
| **Juli Inkster** | 2 | 2 | 2 | 0 | 1 | 0 | 0 | 3 | 0 | **10** |
| **Annika Sorenstam** | 2 | 3 | 3 | 1 | 0 | 0 | 0 | 0 | 0 | **9** |
| Betsy Rawls | 4 | 2 | 0 | 0 | 0 | 0 | 2 | 0 | 0 | **8** |
| **JoAnne Carner** | 2 | 0 | 0 | 0 | 0 | 0 | 0 | 5 | 0 | **7** |
| Kathy Whitworth | 0 | 3 | 0 | 0 | 0 | 2 | 1 | 0 | 0 | **6** |
| **Pat Bradley** | 1 | 1 | 1 | 0 | 3 | 0 | 0 | 0 | 0 | **6** |
| **Betsy King** | 2 | 1 | 3 | 0 | 0 | 0 | 0 | 0 | 0 | **6** |
| **Patty Sheehan** | 2 | 3 | 1 | 0 | 0 | 0 | 0 | 0 | 0 | **6** |
| Glenna C. Vare | 0 | 0 | 0 | 0 | 0 | 0 | 0 | 6 | 0 | **6** |
| **Karrie Webb** | 2 | 1 | 1 | 1 | 1 | 0 | 0 | 0 | 0 | **6** |

**Tournaments:** U.S. Open, LPGA Championship, Nabisco Championship, British Open, du Maurier Classic (1979-2000), Titleholders (1930-72), Western Open (1937-67), U.S. Amateur and British Amateur.

## U.S. Women's Amateur
Stroke play in 1895, match play since 1896.

**Multiple winners:** Glenna Collett Vare (6); JoAnne Gunderson Carner (5); Margaret Curtis, Beatrix Hoyt, Dorothy Campbell Hurd, Juli Inkster, Alexa Stirling, Virginia Van Wie, Anne Quast Decker Welts (3); Kay Cockerill, Beth Daniel, Vicki Goetze, Katherine Harley, Genevieve Hecker, Betty Jameson, Kelli Kuehne and Barbara McIntire (2).

| Year | | Year | | Year | | Year | |
|---|---|---|---|---|---|---|---|
| 1895 | Mrs. C.S. Brown | 1924 | Dorothy C. Hurd | 1955 | Patricia Lesser | 1983 | Joanne Pacillo |
| 1896 | Beatrix Hoyt | 1925 | Glenna Collett | 1956 | Marlene Stewart | 1984 | Deb Richard |
| 1897 | Beatrix Hoyt | 1926 | Helen Stetson | 1957 | JoAnne Gunderson | 1985 | Michiko Hattori |
| 1898 | Beatrix Hoyt | 1927 | Miriam Burns Horn | 1958 | Anne Quast | 1986 | Kay Cockerill |
| 1899 | Ruth Underhill | 1928 | Glenna Collett | 1959 | Barbara McIntire | 1987 | Kay Cockerill |
| 1900 | Frances Griscom | 1929 | Glenna Collett | 1960 | JoAnne Gunderson | 1988 | Pearl Sinn |
| 1901 | Genevieve Hecker | 1930 | Glenna Collett | 1961 | Anne Quast Decker | 1989 | Vicki Goetze |
| 1902 | Genevieve Hecker | 1931 | Helen Hicks | 1962 | JoAnne Gunderson | 1990 | Pat Hurst |
| 1903 | Bessie Anthony | 1932 | Virginia Van Wie | 1963 | Anne Quast Welts | 1991 | Amy Fruhwirth |
| 1904 | Georgianna Bishop | 1933 | Virginia Van Wie | 1964 | Barbara McIntire | 1992 | Vicki Goetze |
| 1905 | Pauline Mackay | 1934 | Virginia Van Wie | 1965 | Jean Ashley | 1993 | Jill McGill |
| 1906 | Harriot Curtis | 1935 | Glenna Collett Vare | 1966 | JoAnne G. Carner | 1994 | Wendy Ward |
| 1907 | Margaret Curtis | 1936 | Pamela Barton | 1967 | Mary Lou Dill | 1995 | Kelli Kuehne |
| 1908 | Katherine Harley | 1937 | Estelle Lawson | 1968 | JoAnne G. Carner | 1996 | Kelli Kuehne |
| 1909 | Dorothy Campbell | 1938 | Patty Berg | 1969 | Catherine Lacoste | 1997 | Silvia Cavalleri |
| 1910 | Dorothy Campbell | 1939 | Betty Jameson | 1970 | Martha Wilkinson | 1998 | Grace Park |
| 1911 | Margaret Curtis | 1940 | Betty Jameson | 1971 | Laura Baugh | 1999 | Dorothy Delasin |
| 1912 | Margaret Curtis | 1941 | Elizabeth Hicks | 1972 | Mary Budke | 2000 | Marcy Newton |
| 1913 | Gladys Ravenscroft | 1942-45 | Not held | 1973 | Carol Semple | 2001 | Meredith Duncan |
| 1914 | Katherine Harley | 1946 | Babe D. Zaharias | 1974 | Cynthia Hill | 2002 | Becky Lucidi |
| 1915 | Florence Vanderbeck | 1947 | Louise Suggs | 1975 | Beth Daniel | 2003 | V. Nirapathpongporn |
| 1916 | Alexa Stirling | 1948 | Grace Lenczyk | 1976 | Donna Horton | 2004 | Jane Park |
| 1917-18 | Not held | 1949 | Dorothy Porter | 1977 | Beth Daniel | 2005 | Morgan Pressel |
| 1919 | Alexa Stirling | 1950 | Beverly Hanson | 1978 | Cathy Sherk | | |
| 1920 | Alexa Stirling | 1951 | Dorothy Kirby | 1979 | Carolyn Hill | | |
| 1921 | Marion Hollins | 1952 | Jacqueline Pung | 1980 | Juli Inkster | | |
| 1922 | Glenna Collett | 1953 | Mary Lena Faulk | 1981 | Juli Inkster | | |
| 1923 | Edith Cummings | 1954 | Barbara Romack | 1982 | Juli Inkster | | |

## British Women's Amateur
Match play since 1893.

**Multiple winners:** Cecil Leitch and Joyce Wethered (4); May Hezlet, Lady Margaret Scott, Jessie Anderson Valentine, Brigitte Varangot and Enid Wilson (3); Rhona Adair, Pam Barton, Dorothy Campbell, Elizabeth Chadwick, Helen Holm, Rebecca Hudson, Marley Spearman, Louise Stahle, Frances Stephens and Michelle Walker (2).

| Year | | Year | | Year | | Year | |
|---|---|---|---|---|---|---|---|
| 1893 | Lady Margaret Scott | 1923 | Doris Chambers | 1954 | Frances Stephens | 1980 | Anne Quast Sander |
| 1894 | Lady Margaret Scott | 1924 | Joyce Wethered | 1955 | Jessie Valentine | 1981 | Belle Robertson |
| 1895 | Lady Margaret Scott | 1925 | Joyce Wethered | 1956 | Wiffi Smith | 1982 | Kitrina Douglas |
| 1896 | Amy Pascoe | 1926 | Cecil Leitch | 1957 | Philomena Garvey | 1983 | Jill Thornhill |
| 1897 | Edith Orr | 1927 | Simone de la Chaume | 1958 | Jessie Valentine | 1984 | Jody Rosenthal |
| 1898 | Lena Thomson | 1928 | Nanette le Blan | 1959 | Elizabeth Price | 1985 | Lillian Behan |
| 1899 | May Hezlet | 1929 | Joyce Wethered | 1960 | Barbara McIntire | 1986 | Marnie McGuire |
| 1900 | Rhona Adair | 1930 | Diana Fishwick | 1961 | Marley Spearman | 1987 | Janet Collingham |
| 1901 | Mary Graham | 1931 | Enid Wilson | 1962 | Marley Spearman | 1988 | Joanne Furby |
| 1902 | May Hezlet | 1932 | Enid Wilson | 1963 | Brigitte Varangot | 1989 | Helen Dobson |
| 1903 | Rhona Adair | 1933 | Enid Wilson | 1964 | Carol Sorenson | 1990 | Julie Wade Hall |
| 1904 | Lottie Dod | 1934 | Helen Holm | 1965 | Brigitte Varangot | 1991 | Valerie Michaud |
| 1905 | Bertha Thompson | 1935 | Wanda Morgan | 1966 | Elizabeth Chadwick | 1992 | Bernille Pedersen |
| 1906 | Mrs. W. Kennion | 1936 | Pam Barton | 1967 | Elizabeth Chadwick | 1993 | Catriona Lambert |
| 1907 | May Hezlet | 1937 | Jessie Anderson | 1968 | Brigitte Varangot | 1994 | Emma Duggleby |
| 1908 | Maud Titterton | 1938 | Helen Holm | 1969 | Catherine Lacoste | 1995 | Julie Wade Hall |
| 1909 | Dorothy Campbell | 1939 | Pam Barton | 1970 | Dinah Oxley | 1996 | Kelli Kuehne |
| 1910 | Elsie Grant-Suttie | 1940-45 | Not held | 1971 | Michelle Walker | 1997 | Alison Rose |
| 1911 | Dorothy Campbell | 1946 | Jean Hetherington | 1972 | Michelle Walker | 1998 | Kim Rostron |
| 1912 | Gladys Ravenscroft | 1947 | Babe Zaharias | 1973 | Ann Irvin | 1999 | Marine Monnet |
| 1913 | Muriel Dodd | 1948 | Louise Suggs | 1974 | Carol Semple | 2000 | Rebecca Hudson |
| 1914 | Cecil Leitch | 1949 | Frances Stephens | 1975 | Nancy Roth Syms | 2001 | Marta Prieto |
| 1915-19 | Not held | 1950 | Lally de St. Sauveur | 1976 | Cathy Panton | 2002 | Rebecca Hudson |
| 1920 | Cecil Leitch | 1951 | Catherine MacCann | 1977 | Angela Uzielli | 2003 | Elisa Serramia |
| 1921 | Cecil Leitch | 1952 | Moira Paterson | 1978 | Edwina Kennedy | 2004 | Louise Stahle |
| 1922 | Joyce Wethered | 1953 | Marlene Stewart | 1979 | Maureen Madill | 2005 | Louise Stahle |

## Vare Trophy

The Vare Trophy for best scoring average by a player on the LPGA Tour has been awarded since 1953 by the LPGA. The award is named after Glenna Collett Vare, winner of six U.S. women's amateur titles from 1922-35.

**Multiple winners:** Kathy Whitworth (7); JoAnne Carner, Annika Sorenstam and Mickey Wright (5); Patty Berg, Beth Daniel, Nancy Lopez, Judy Rankin and Karrie Webb (3); Pat Bradley and Betsy King (2).

| Year | | Avg | Year | | Avg | Year | | Avg |
|---|---|---|---|---|---|---|---|---|
| 1953 | Patty Berg | .75.00 | 1971 | Kathy Whitworth | .72.88 | 1989 | Beth Daniel | .70.38 |
| 1954 | Babe Zaharias | .75.48 | 1972 | Kathy Whitworth | .72.38 | 1990 | Beth Daniel | .70.54 |
| 1955 | Patty Berg | .74.47 | 1973 | Judy Rankin | .73.08 | 1991 | Pat Bradley | .70.66 |
| 1956 | Patty Berg | .74.57 | 1974 | JoAnne Carner | .72.87 | 1992 | Dottie Pepper | .70.80 |
| 1957 | Louise Suggs | .74.64 | 1975 | JoAnne Carner | .72.40 | 1993 | Betsy King | .70.85 |
| 1958 | Beverly Hanson | .74.92 | 1976 | Judy Rankin | .72.25 | 1994 | Beth Daniel | .70.90 |
| 1959 | Betsy Rawls | .74.03 | 1977 | Judy Rankin | .72.16 | 1995 | Annika Sorenstam | .71.00 |
| 1960 | Mickey Wright | .73.25 | 1978 | Nancy Lopez | .71.76 | 1996 | Annika Sorenstam | .70.47 |
| 1961 | Mickey Wright | .73.55 | 1979 | Nancy Lopez | .71.20 | 1997 | Karrie Webb | .70.00 |
| 1962 | Mickey Wright | .73.67 | 1980 | Amy Alcott | .71.51 | 1998 | Annika Sorenstam | .69.99 |
| 1963 | Mickey Wright | .72.81 | 1981 | JoAnne Carner | .71.75 | 1999 | Karrie Webb | .69.43 |
| 1964 | Mickey Wright | .72.46 | 1982 | JoAnne Carner | .71.49 | 2000 | Karrie Webb | .70.05 |
| 1965 | Kathy Whitworth | .72.61 | 1983 | JoAnne Carner | .71.41 | 2001 | Annika Sorenstam | .69.42 |
| 1966 | Kathy Whitworth | .72.60 | 1984 | Patty Sheehan | .71.40 | 2002 | Annika Sorenstam | .68.70 |
| 1967 | Kathy Whitworth | .72.74 | 1985 | Nancy Lopez | .70.73 | 2003 | Se Ri Pak | .70.03 |
| 1968 | Carol Mann | .72.04 | 1986 | Pat Bradley | .71.10 | 2004 | Grace Park | .69.99 |
| 1969 | Kathy Whitworth | .72.38 | 1987 | Betsy King | .71.14 | | | |
| 1970 | Kathy Whitworth | .72.26 | 1988 | Colleen Walker | .71.26 | | | |

## Champions Tour
(formerly Senior PGA Tour)

### Senior PGA Championship

First played in 1937. Two championships played in 1979 and 1984.

**Multiple winners:** Sam Snead (6); Hale Irwin (4); Gary Player, Al Watrous and Eddie Williams (3); Julius Boros, Jock Hutchison, Don January, Arnold Palmer, Paul Runyan, Gene Sarazen and Lee Trevino (2).

| Year | | Year | | Year | | Year | |
|---|---|---|---|---|---|---|---|
| 1937 | Jock Hutchison | 1956 | Pete Burke | 1974 | Roberto De Vicenzo | 1990 | Gary Player |
| 1938 | Fred McLeod* | 1957 | Al Watrous | 1975 | Charlie Sifford* | 1991 | Jack Nicklaus |
| 1939 | Not held | 1958 | Gene Sarazen | 1976 | Pete Cooper | 1992 | Lee Trevino |
| 1940 | Otto Hackbarth* | 1959 | Willie Goggin | 1977 | Julius Boros | 1993 | Tom Wargo* |
| 1941 | Jack Burke | 1960 | Dick Metz | 1978 | Joe Jiminez* | 1994 | Lee Trevino |
| 1942 | Eddie Williams | 1961 | Paul Runyan | 1979 | Jack Fleck* | 1995 | Ray Floyd |
| 1943-44 | Not held | 1962 | Paul Runyan | 1979 | Don January | 1996 | Hale Irwin |
| 1945 | Eddie Williams | 1963 | Herman Barron | 1980 | Arnold Palmer* | 1997 | Hale Irwin |
| 1946 | Eddie Williams* | 1964 | Sam Snead | 1981 | Miller Barber | 1998 | Hale Irwin |
| 1947 | Jock Hutchison | 1965 | Sam Snead | 1982 | Don January | 1999 | Allen Doyle |
| 1948 | Charles McKenna | 1966 | Fred Haas | 1983 | Not held | 2000 | Doug Tewell |
| 1949 | Marshall Crichton | 1967 | Sam Snead | 1984 | Arnold Palmer | 2001 | Tom Watson |
| 1950 | Al Watrous | 1968 | Chandler Harper | 1984 | Peter Thomson | 2002 | Fuzzy Zoeller |
| 1951 | Al Watrous* | 1969 | Tommy Bolt | 1985 | Not held | 2003 | John Jacobs |
| 1952 | Ernest Newnham | 1970 | Sam Snead | 1986 | Gary Player | 2004 | Hale Irwin |
| 1953 | Harry Schwab | 1971 | Julius Boros | 1987 | Chi Chi Rodriguez | 2005 | Mike Reid* |
| 1954 | Gene Sarazen | 1972 | Sam Snead | 1988 | Gary Player | | |
| 1955 | Mortie Dutra | 1973 | Sam Snead | 1989 | Larry Mowry | | |

**\*PLAYOFFS:**

**1938:** Fred McLeod def. Otto Hackbarth in 18 holes. **1940:** Otto Hackbarth def. Jock Hutchison in 36 holes. **1946:** Eddie Williams def. Jock Hutchison in 18 holes. **1951:** Al Watrous def. Jock Hutchison in 18 holes. **1975:** Charlie Sifford def. Fred Wampler on 1st extra hole **1978:** Joe Jiminez def. Paul Harney on 1st extra hole. **1979:** Jack Fleck def. Bill Johnston on 1st extra hole. **1980:** Arnold Palmer def. Paul Harney on 1st extra hole. **1993:** Tom Wargo def. Bruce Crampton on 2nd extra hole. **2005:** Mike Reid def. Dana Quigley and Jerry Pate on 1st extra hole.

## Major Senior Championship Leaders

Through 2005. All players are still active. **Note:** The Senior British Open became the Champions Tour's fifth major in 2003.

| | | Sr. PGA | US Open | Sr. Play | Trad | Br. Open | Tot | | | Sr. PGA | US Open | Sr. Play | Trad | Br. Open | Tot |
|---|---|---|---|---|---|---|---|---|---|---|---|---|---|---|---|
| 1 | Jack Nicklaus | .1 | 2 | 1 | 4 | 0 | 8 | 4 | Ray Floyd | .1 | 0 | 2 | 1 | 0 | 4 |
| 2 | Hale Irwin | .4 | 2 | 1 | 0 | 0 | 7 | | Lee Trevino | .2 | 1 | 0 | 1 | 0 | 4 |
| 3 | Gary Player | .3 | 2 | 1 | 0 | 0 | 6 | | Tom Watson | .1 | 0 | 0 | 1 | 2 | 4 |

## U.S. Senior Open

Established in 1980 for senior players 55 years old and over, the minimum age was dropped to 50 (the Champions Tour entry age) in 1981. Arnold Palmer, Billy Casper, Hale Irwin, Orville Moody, Jack Nicklaus and Lee Trevino are the only golfers who have won both the U.S. Open and U.S. Senior Open.

**Multiple winners:** Miller Barber (3); Hale Irwin, Jack Nicklaus and Gary Player (2).

| Year | | Year | | Year | | Year | |
|------|--|------|--|------|--|------|--|
| 1980 | Roberto De Vicenzo | 1987 | Gary Player | 1994 | Simon Hobday | 2001 | Bruce Fleisher |
| 1981 | Arnold Palmer* | 1988 | Gary Player* | 1995 | Tom Weiskopf | 2002 | Don Pooley* |
| 1982 | Miller Barber | 1989 | Orville Moody | 1996 | Dave Stockton | 2003 | Bruce Lietzke |
| 1983 | Bill Casper* | 1990 | Lee Trevino | 1997 | Graham Marsh | 2004 | Peter Jacobsen |
| 1984 | Miller Barber | 1991 | Jack Nicklaus* | 1998 | Hale Irwin | 2005 | Allen Doyle |
| 1985 | Miller Barber | 1992 | Larry Laoretti | 1999 | Dave Eichelberger | | |
| 1986 | Dale Douglass | 1993 | Jack Nicklaus | 2000 | Hale Irwin | | |

### *PLAYOFFS:

**1981:** Arnold Palmer (70) def. Bob Stone (74) and Billy Casper (77) in 18 holes. **1983:** Tied at 75 after 18-hole playoff, Casper def. Rod Funseth with a birdie on the 1st extra hole. **1988:** Gary Player (68) def. Bob Charles (70) in 18 holes. **1991:** Jack Nicklaus (65) def. Chi Chi Rodriguez (69) in 18 holes. **2002:** Don Pooley and Tom Watson remained tied after a three hole playoff and Pooley won on the second hole of sudden death.

## Senior Players Championship

Sponsored by Ford since 1993. First played in 1983 and contested in Cleveland (1983-86), Ponte Vedra, Fla. (1987-89) and Dearborn, Mich. (since 1990).

**Multiple winners:** Ray Floyd, Arnold Palmer and Dave Stockton (2).

| Year | | Year | | Year | | Year | |
|------|--|------|--|------|--|------|--|
| 1983 | Miller Barber | 1989 | Orville Moody | 1995 | J.C. Snead* | 2001 | Allen Doyle* |
| 1984 | Arnold Palmer | 1990 | Jack Nicklaus | 1996 | Ray Floyd | 2002 | Stewart Ginn |
| 1985 | Arnold Palmer | 1991 | Jim Albus | 1997 | Larry Gilbert | 2003 | Craig Stadler |
| 1986 | Chi Chi Rodriguez | 1992 | Dave Stockton | 1998 | Gil Morgan | 2004 | Mark James |
| 1987 | Gary Player | 1993 | Jim Colbert | 1999 | Hale Irwin | 2005 | Peter Jacobsen |
| 1988 | Billy Casper | 1994 | Dave Stockton | 2000 | Ray Floyd | | |

### *PLAYOFFS:

**1995:** J.C. Snead def. Jack Nicklaus on 1st extra hole. **2001:** Allen Doyle def. Doug Tewell on 1st extra hole.

## The Tradition

Sponsored by window and door manufacturer JELD-WEN since 2003, it was formerly called The Tradition at Desert Mountain (1989-91), The Tradition (1992-99) and The Countrywide Tradition (2000-02). Held at GC at Desert Mountain in Scottsdale, Ariz. (1989-2001), Superstition Mountain (Ariz.) G & CC (2002) and The Reserve Vineyards & GC in Aloha, Ore. (2003—).

**Multiple winners:** Jack Nicklaus (4); Gil Morgan (2).

| Year | | Year | | Year | | Year | |
|------|--|------|--|------|--|------|--|
| 1989 | Don Bies | 1994 | Ray Floyd* | 1999 | Graham Marsh | 2004 | Craig Stadler |
| 1990 | Jack Nicklaus | 1995 | Jack Nicklaus* | 2000 | Tom Kite | 2005 | Loren Roberts* |
| 1991 | Jack Nicklaus | 1996 | Jack Nicklaus | 2001 | Doug Tewell | | |
| 1992 | Lee Trevino | 1997 | Gil Morgan | 2002 | Jim Thorpe* | | |
| 1993 | Tom Shaw | 1998 | Gil Morgan | 2003 | Tom Watson | | |

### *PLAYOFFS:

**1994:** Ray Floyd def. Dale Douglass on 1st extra hole. **1995:** Jack Nicklaus def. Isao Aoki on 3rd extra hole. **2002:** Jim Thorpe def. John Jacobs on 1st extra hole. **2005:** Loren Roberts def. Dana Quigley on 2nd extra hole.

## Senior British Open

First played in 1987 and contested in Turnberry, Scotland (1987-90, 2003), Lytham, England (1991-94), Portrush, Ireland (1995-99, 2004), Newcastle, Ireland (2000-02) and Royal Aberdeen, Scotland (2005). In 2003 it became the fifth designated major championship on the Champions Tour.

**Multiple winners:** Gary Player (3); Brian Barnes, Bob Charles, Christy O'Connor Jr. and Tom Watson (2). (as a major): Watson (2).

| Year | | Year | | Year | | Year | |
|------|--|------|--|------|--|------|--|
| 1987 | Neil Coles | 1992 | John Fourie | 1997 | Gary Player | 2002 | Noboru Sugai |
| 1988 | Gary Player | 1993 | Bob Charles | 1998 | Brian Huggett | 2003 | Tom Watson* |
| 1989 | Bob Charles | 1994 | Tom Wargo | 1999 | Christy O'Connor Jr. | 2004 | Pete Oakley |
| 1990 | Gary Player | 1995 | Brian Barnes | 2000 | Christy O'Connor Jr. | 2005 | Tom Watson* |
| 1991 | Bobby Verwey | 1996 | Brian Barnes | 2001 | Ian Stanley | | |

### *PLAYOFFS (as a Major):

**2003:** Tom Watson def. Carl Mason on 2nd extra hole. **2005:** Tom Watson def. Des Smyth on 3rd extra hole.

## Champions Tour (Cont.)
### Grand Slam Summary

The Senior Grand Slam had officially consisted of The Tradition, the Senior PGA Championship, the Senior Players Championship and the U.S. Senior Open from 1990-2002. In 2003, the Senior British Open was added. Jack Nicklaus won three of the four events in 1991, but no one has won all four (or now five) in one season.

**Three wins in one year:** Jack Nicklaus (1991). **Two wins in one year** (8): Gary Player (twice); Hale Irwin, Gil Morgan, Orville Moody, Jack Nicklaus, Arnold Palmer, Lee Trevino and Tom Watson (once).

| Year | Tradition | Sr. PGA | Players | US Open | Year | Tradition | Sr. PGA | Players | US Open |
|------|-----------|---------|---------|---------|------|-----------|---------|---------|---------|
| 1983 | — | — | M. Barber | Casper | 1993 | Shaw | Wargo | Colbert | Nicklaus |
| 1984 | — | Palmer | Palmer | M. Barber | 1994 | Floyd | Trevino | Stockton | Hobday |
| 1985 | — | Thomson | Palmer | M. Barber | 1995 | Nicklaus | Floyd | Snead | Weiskopf |
| 1986 | — | Player | Rodriguez | Douglass | 1996 | Nicklaus | Irwin | Floyd | Stockton |
| 1987 | — | Rodriguez | Player | Player | 1997 | Morgan | Irwin | Gilbert | Marsh |
| 1988 | — | Player | Casper | Player | 1998 | Morgan | Irwin | Morgan | Irwin |
| 1989 | Bies | Mowry | Moody | Moody | 1999 | Marsh | Doyle | Irwin | Eichelberger |
| 1990 | Nicklaus | Player | Nicklaus | Trevino | 2000 | Kite | Tewell | Floyd | Irwin |
| 1991 | Nicklaus | Nicklaus | Albus | Nicklaus | 2001 | Tewell | Watson | Doyle | Fleisher |
| 1992 | Trevino | Trevino | Stockton | Laoretti | 2002 | Thorpe | Zoeller | Ginn | Pooley |

| Year | Tradition | Sr. PGA | Players | US Open | Sr. Brit. Open |
|------|-----------|---------|---------|---------|----------------|
| 2003 | Watson | Jacobs | Stadler | Lietzke | Watson |
| 2004 | Stadler | Irwin | James | Jacobsen | Oakley |
| 2005 | Roberts | Reid | Jacobsen | Doyle | Watson |

## Annual Money Leaders

Official annual money leaders on the PGA, European PGA, Champions and LPGA tours.

### PGA

**Multiple leaders:** Jack Nicklaus (8); Ben Hogan, Tom Watson and Tiger Woods (5); Arnold Palmer (4); Greg Norman, Sam Snead and Curtis Strange (3); Julius Boros, Billy Casper, Tom Kite, Byron Nelson, Nick Price and Vijay Singh (2).

| Year | | Earnings | Year | | Earnings | Year | | Earnings |
|------|--|----------|------|--|----------|------|--|----------|
| 1934 | Paul Runyan | $6,767 | 1958 | Arnold Palmer | $42,608 | 1982 | Craig Stadler | $446,462 |
| 1935 | Johnny Revolta | 9,543 | 1959 | Art Wall | 53,168 | 1983 | Hal Sutton | 426,668 |
| 1936 | Horton Smith | 7,682 | 1960 | Arnold Palmer | 75,263 | 1984 | Tom Watson | 476,260 |
| 1937 | Harry Cooper | 14,139 | 1961 | Gary Player | 64,540 | 1985 | Curtis Strange | 542,321 |
| 1938 | Sam Snead | 19,534 | 1962 | Arnold Palmer | 81,448 | 1986 | Greg Norman | 653,296 |
| 1939 | Henry Picard | 10,303 | 1963 | Arnold Palmer | 128,230 | 1987 | Curtis Strange | 925,941 |
| 1940 | Ben Hogan | 10,655 | 1964 | Jack Nicklaus | 113,285 | 1988 | Curtis Strange | 1,147,644 |
| 1941 | Ben Hogan | 18,358 | 1965 | Jack Nicklaus | 140,752 | 1989 | Tom Kite | 1,395,278 |
| 1942 | Ben Hogan | 13,143 | 1966 | Billy Casper | 121,945 | 1990 | Greg Norman | 1,165,477 |
| 1943 | No records kept | | 1967 | Jack Nicklaus | 188,998 | 1991 | Corey Pavin | 979,430 |
| 1944 | Byron Nelson | 37,968 | 1968 | Billy Casper | 205,169 | 1992 | Fred Couples | 1,344,188 |
| 1945 | Byron Nelson | 63,336 | 1969 | Frank Beard | 164,707 | 1993 | Nick Price | 1,478,557 |
| 1946 | Ben Hogan | 42,556 | 1970 | Lee Trevino | 157,037 | 1994 | Nick Price | 1,499,927 |
| 1947 | Jimmy Demaret | 27,937 | 1971 | Jack Nicklaus | 244,491 | 1995 | Greg Norman | 1,654,959 |
| 1948 | Ben Hogan | 32,112 | 1972 | Jack Nicklaus | 320,542 | 1996 | Tom Lehman | 1,780,159 |
| 1949 | Sam Snead | 31,594 | 1973 | Jack Nicklaus | 308,362 | 1997 | Tiger Woods | 2,066,833 |
| 1950 | Sam Snead | 35,759 | 1974 | Johnny Miller | 353,022 | 1998 | David Duval | 2,591,031 |
| 1951 | Lloyd Mangrum | 26,089 | 1975 | Jack Nicklaus | 298,149 | 1999 | Tiger Woods | 6,616,585 |
| 1952 | Julius Boros | 37,033 | 1976 | Jack Nicklaus | 266,439 | 2000 | Tiger Woods | 9,188,321 |
| 1953 | Lew Worsham | 34,002 | 1977 | Tom Watson | 310,653 | 2001 | Tiger Woods | 5,687,777 |
| 1954 | Bob Toski | 65,820 | 1978 | Tom Watson | 362,429 | 2002 | Tiger Woods | 6,912,625 |
| 1955 | Julius Boros | 63,122 | 1979 | Tom Watson | 462,636 | 2003 | Vijay Singh | 7,573,907 |
| 1956 | Ted Kroll | 72,836 | 1980 | Tom Watson | 530,808 | 2004 | Vijay Singh | 10,905,166 |
| 1957 | Dick Mayer | 65,835 | 1981 | Tom Kite | 375,699 | | | |

**Note:** In 1944-45, Nelson's winnings were in War Bonds.

### Champions Tour

**Multiple leaders:** Hale Irwin and Don January (3); Miller Barber, Bob Charles, Jim Colbert, Dave Stockton and Lee Trevino (2).

| Year | | Earnings | Year | | Earnings | Year | | Earnings |
|------|--|----------|------|--|----------|------|--|----------|
| 1980 | Don January | $44,100 | 1989 | Bob Charles | $725,887 | 1998 | Hale Irwin | $2,861,945 |
| 1981 | Miller Barber | 83,136 | 1990 | Lee Trevino | 1,190,518 | 1999 | Bruce Fleisher | 2,515,705 |
| 1982 | Miller Barber | 106,890 | 1991 | Mike Hill | 1,065,657 | 2000 | Larry Nelson | 2,708,005 |
| 1983 | Don January | 237,571 | 1992 | Lee Trevino | 1,027,002 | 2001 | Allen Doyle | 2,553,582 |
| 1984 | Don January | 328,597 | 1993 | Dave Stockton | 1,175,944 | 2002 | Hale Irwin | 3,028,304 |
| 1985 | Peter Thomson | 386,724 | 1994 | Dave Stockton | 1,402,519 | 2003 | Tom Watson | 1,853,108 |
| 1986 | Bruce Crampton | 454,299 | 1995 | Jim Colbert | 1,444,386 | 2004 | Craig Stadler | 2,306,066 |
| 1987 | Chi Chi Rodriguez | 509,145 | 1996 | Jim Colbert | 1,627,890 | | | |
| 1988 | Bob Charles | 533,929 | 1997 | Hale Irwin | 2,343,364 | | | |

## European PGA

Official money in the Volvo Order of Merit was awarded in British pounds from 1961-98 and euros (E) since 1999.

**Multiple leaders:** Colin Montgomerie (7); Seve Ballesteros (6); Sandy Lyle (3); Gay Brewer Jr., Ernie Els, Nick Faldo, Retief Goosen, Bernard Hunt, Bernhard Langer, Peter Thomson and Ian Woosnam (2).

| Year | | Earnings | Year | | Earnings | Year | | Earnings |
|---|---|---|---|---|---|---|---|---|
| 1961 | Bernard Hunt | £4,492 | 1976 | Seve Ballesteros | £39,504 | 1991 | Seve Ballesteros | £790,811 |
| 1962 | Peter Thomson | 5,764 | 1977 | Seve Ballesteros | 46,436 | 1992 | Nick Faldo | 1,220,540 |
| 1963 | Bernard Hunt | 7,209 | 1978 | Seve Ballesteros | 54,348 | 1993 | Colin Montgomerie | 798,145 |
| 1964 | Neil Coles | 7,890 | 1979 | Sandy Lyle | 49,233 | 1994 | Colin Montgomerie | 920,647 |
| 1965 | Peter Thomson | 7,011 | 1980 | Greg Norman | 74,829 | 1995 | Colin Montgomerie | 1,038,718 |
| 1966 | Bruce Devlin | 13,205 | 1981 | Bernhard Langer | 95,991 | 1996 | Colin Montgomerie | 1,034,752 |
| 1967 | Gay Brewer Jr. | 20,235 | 1982 | Sandy Lyle | 86,141 | 1997 | Colin Montgomerie | 1,583,904 |
| 1968 | Gay Brewer Jr. | 23,107 | 1983 | Nick Faldo | 140,761 | 1998 | Colin Montgomerie | 1,082,833 |
| 1969 | Billy Casper | 23,483 | 1984 | Bernhard Langer | 160,883 | 1999 | C. Montgomerie | E2,066,885 |
| 1970 | Christy O'Connor | 31,532 | 1985 | Sandy Lyle | 254,711 | 2000 | Lee Westwood | 3,125,147 |
| 1971 | Gary Player | 11,281 | 1986 | Seve Ballesteros | 259,275 | 2001 | Retief Goosen | 2,862,806 |
| 1972 | Bob Charles | 18,538 | 1987 | Ian Woosnam | 439,075 | 2002 | Retief Goosen | 2,360,128 |
| 1973 | Tony Jacklin | 24,839 | 1988 | Seve Ballesteros | 502,000 | 2003 | Ernie Els | 2,975,374 |
| 1974 | Peter Oosterhuis | 32,127 | 1989 | Ronan Rafferty | 465,981 | 2004 | Ernie Els | 4,061,905 |
| 1975 | Dale Hayes | 20,507 | 1990 | Ian Woosnam | 737,977 | | | |

## LPGA

**Multiple leaders:** Kathy Whitworth (8); Annika Sorenstam (7); Mickey Wright (4); Patty Berg, JoAnne Carner, Beth Daniel, Betsy King, Nancy Lopez and Karrie Webb (3); Pat Bradley, Judy Rankin, Betsy Rawls, Louise Suggs and Babe Zaharias (2).

| Year | | Earnings | Year | | Earnings | Year | | Earnings |
|---|---|---|---|---|---|---|---|---|
| 1950 | Babe Zaharias | $14,800 | 1969 | Carol Mann | $49,152 | 1988 | Sherri Turner | $350,851 |
| 1951 | Babe Zaharias | 15,087 | 1970 | Kathy Whitworth | 30,235 | 1989 | Betsy King | 654,132 |
| 1952 | Betsy Rawls | 14,505 | 1971 | Kathy Whitworth | 41,181 | 1990 | Beth Daniel | 863,578 |
| 1953 | Louise Suggs | 19,816 | 1972 | Kathy Whitworth | 65,063 | 1991 | Pat Bradley | 763,118 |
| 1954 | Patty Berg | 16,011 | 1973 | Kathy Whitworth | 82,864 | 1992 | Dottie Pepper | 693,335 |
| 1955 | Patty Berg | 16,492 | 1974 | JoAnne Carner | 87,094 | 1993 | Betsy King | 595,992 |
| 1956 | Marlene Hagge | 20,235 | 1975 | Sandra Palmer | 76,374 | 1994 | Laura Davies | 687,201 |
| 1957 | Patty Berg | 16,272 | 1976 | Judy Rankin | 150,734 | 1995 | Annika Sorenstam | 666,533 |
| 1958 | Beverly Hanson | 12,639 | 1977 | Judy Rankin | 122,890 | 1996 | Karrie Webb | 1,002,000 |
| 1959 | Betsy Rawls | 26,774 | 1978 | Nancy Lopez | 189,814 | 1997 | Annika Sorenstam | 1,236,789 |
| 1960 | Louise Suggs | 16,892 | 1979 | Nancy Lopez | 197,489 | 1998 | Annika Sorenstam | 1,092,748 |
| 1961 | Mickey Wright | 22,236 | 1980 | Beth Daniel | 231,000 | 1999 | Karrie Webb | 1,591,959 |
| 1962 | Mickey Wright | 21,641 | 1981 | Beth Daniel | 206,998 | 2000 | Karrie Webb | 1,876,853 |
| 1963 | Mickey Wright | 31,269 | 1982 | JoAnne Carner | 310,400 | 2001 | Annika Sorenstam | 2,105,868 |
| 1964 | Mickey Wright | 29,800 | 1983 | JoAnne Carner | 291,404 | 2002 | Annika Sorenstam | 2,863,904 |
| 1965 | Kathy Whitworth | 28,658 | 1984 | Betsy King | 266,771 | 2003 | Annika Sorenstam | 2,029,506 |
| 1966 | Kathy Whitworth | 33,517 | 1985 | Nancy Lopez | 416,472 | 2004 | Annika Sorenstam | 2,544,707 |
| 1967 | Kathy Whitworth | 32,937 | 1986 | Pat Bradley | 492,021 | | | |
| 1968 | Kathy Whitworth | 48,379 | 1987 | Ayako Okamoto | 466,034 | | | |

## All-Time Leaders

PGA, Champions Tour and LPGA leaders through Oct. 9, 2005.

### Tournaments Won

| | PGA | No | | Champions | No | | LPGA | No |
|---|---|---|---|---|---|---|---|---|
| 1 | Sam Snead | 82 | 1 | Hale Irwin | 44 | 1 | Kathy Whitworth | 88 |
| 2 | Jack Nicklaus | 73 | 2 | Lee Trevino | 29 | 2 | Mickey Wright | 82 |
| 3 | Ben Hogan | 64 | 3 | Miller Barber | 24 | 3 | Annika Sorenstam | 63 |
| 4 | Arnold Palmer | 62 | 4 | Bob Charles | 23 | 4 | Patty Berg | 60 |
| 5 | Byron Nelson | 52 | | Gil Morgan | 23 | 5 | Louise Suggs | 58 |
| 6 | Billy Casper | 51 | 6 | Don January | 22 | 6 | Betsy Rawls | 55 |
| 7 | Tiger Woods | 46 | | Chi Chi Rodriguez | 22 | 7 | Nancy Lopez | 48 |
| 8 | Walter Hagen | 44 | 8 | Bruce Crampton | 20 | 8 | JoAnne Carner | 43 |
| 9 | Cary Middlecoff | 40 | | Jim Colbert | 20 | 9 | Sandra Haynie | 42 |
| 10 | Gene Sarazen | 39 | 10 | George Archer | 19 | 10 | Babe Zaharias | 41 |
| | Tom Watson | 39 | | Larry Nelson | 19 | 11 | Carol Mann | 38 |
| 12 | Lloyd Mangrum | 36 | | Gary Player | 19 | 12 | Patty Sheehan | 35 |
| 13 | Horton Smith | 32 | 13 | Mike Hill | 18 | 13 | Betsy King | 34 |
| 14 | Harry Cooper | 31 | | Bruce Fleisher | 18 | 14 | Beth Daniel | 33 |
| | Jimmy Demaret | 31 | 15 | Dave Stockton | 14 | 15 | Pat Bradley | 31 |
| 16 | Leo Diegel | 30 | | Raymond Floyd | 14 | 16 | Juli Inkster | 30 |
| 17 | Gene Littler | 29 | 17 | Jim Dent | 12 | | Karrie Webb | 30 |
| | Paul Runyan | 29 | 18 | Five tied with 11 wins. | | 18 | Amy Alcott | 29 |
| | Lee Trevino | 29 | | | | 19 | Jane Blalock | 27 |
| 20 | Vijay Singh | 28 | | | | 20 | Judy Rankin | 26 |
| | | | | | | | Marlene Hagge | 26 |

## All-Time Leaders (Cont.)
### Money Won
All-time earnings through Oct. 9, 2005.

### PGA

| | | Earnings | | | Earnings | | | Earnings |
|---|---|---|---|---|---|---|---|---|
| 1 | Tiger Woods | $55,055,760 | 10 | Kenny Perry | $19,392,833 | 19 | Jeff Sluman | $16,489,445 |
| 2 | Vijay Singh | 44,493,591 | 11 | Scott Hoch | 18,487,114 | 20 | David Duval | 16,363,979 |
| 3 | Phil Mickelson | 35,257,533 | 12 | Fred Couples | 18,328,603 | 21 | Scott Verplank | 15,695,464 |
| 4 | Davis Love III | 31,419,634 | 13 | Mark Calcavecchia | 18,288,972 | 22 | Stewart Cink | 15,598,641 |
| 5 | Ernie Els | 26,094,175 | 14 | Fred Funk | 17,688,180 | 23 | Hal Sutton | 15,267,685 |
| 6 | Jim Furyk | 23,396,151 | 15 | Chris DiMarco | 17,041,925 | 24 | Stuart Appleby | 15,159,638 |
| 7 | David Toms | 22,786,628 | 16 | Brad Faxon | 17,028,228 | 25 | Loren Roberts | 14,692,278 |
| 8 | Nick Price | 20,317,580 | 17 | Tom Lehman | 16,987,859 | | | |
| 9 | Justin Leonard | 20,190,273 | 18 | Mike Weir | 16,970,211 | | | |

### European PGA
Official earnings in Euros (E) for European Tour members only.

| | | Earnings | | | Earnings | | | Earnings |
|---|---|---|---|---|---|---|---|---|
| 1 | C. Montgomerie | E19,575,101 | 10 | J. Maria Olazabal | E9,960,975 | 19 | David Howell | E6,769,474 |
| 2 | Ernie Els | 16,911,676 | 11 | M. Angel Jimenez | 9,955,206 | 20 | Barry Lane | 5,975,879 |
| 3 | Darren Clarke | 14,716,886 | 12 | Michael Campbell | 9,517,177 | 21 | Ian Poulter | 5,958,016 |
| 4 | Retief Goosen | 14,494,773 | 13 | Ian Woosnam | 9,386,971 | 22 | Paul Lawrie | 5,919,216 |
| 5 | Bernhard Langer | 12,111,921 | 14 | Angel Cabrera | 8,179,615 | 23 | Sam Torrance | 5,461,157 |
| 6 | Padraig Harrington | 11,931,265 | 15 | Nick Faldo | 7,980,977 | 24 | Mark McNulty | 5,366,794 |
| 7 | Lee Westwood | 11,538,420 | 16 | Paul McGinley | 7,734,016 | 25 | Seve Ballesteros | 5,328,216 |
| 8 | Thomas Bjorn | 10,383,486 | 17 | Eduardo Romero | 7,403,414 | | | |
| 9 | Vijay Singh | 10,279,103 | 18 | Sergio Garcia | 7,225,976 | | | |

### Champions Tour

| | | Earnings | | | Earnings | | | Earnings |
|---|---|---|---|---|---|---|---|---|
| 1 | Hale Irwin | $28,353,763 | 10 | Raymond Floyd | $14,301,534 | 19 | George Archer | $10,211,507 |
| 2 | Gil Morgan | 20,669,986 | 11 | Greg Norman | 14,188,469 | 20 | Doug Tewell | 10,173,865 |
| 3 | Tom Kite | 19,253,210 | 12 | Lee Trevino | 13,255,220 | 21 | Bob Gilder | 10,136,507 |
| 4 | Tom Watson | 17,202,748 | 13 | Jim Colbert | 13,061,109 | 22 | Isao Aoki | 10,005,743 |
| 5 | Larry Nelson | 16,186,905 | 14 | Dana Quigley | 12,208,629 | 23 | Tom Jenkins | 9,721,779 |
| 6 | Loren Roberts | 15,523,660 | 15 | Bruce Lietzke | 12,127,254 | 24 | Bob Charles | 9,539,438 |
| 7 | Jay Haas | 15,260,591 | 16 | Jim Thorpe | 12,020,647 | 25 | J.C. Snead | 9,449,441 |
| 8 | Craig Stadler | 14,656,120 | 17 | Dave Stockton | 12,012,427 | | | |
| 9 | Bruce Fleisher | 14,414,156 | 18 | Allen Doyle | 11,301,930 | | | |

### LPGA

| | | Earnings | | | Earnings | | | Earnings |
|---|---|---|---|---|---|---|---|---|
| 1 | Annika Sorenstam | $17,737,128 | 10 | Dottie Pepper | $6,827,284 | 19 | Grace Park | $4,983,119 |
| 2 | Karrie Webb | 10,704,287 | 11 | Lorie Kane | 6,127,601 | 20 | Rachel Hetherington | 4,559,879 |
| 3 | Juli Inkster | 9,871,082 | 12 | Pat Bradley | 5,750,965 | 21 | Sherri Steinhauer | 4,523,891 |
| 4 | Meg Mallon | 8,762,007 | 13 | Kelly Robbins | 5,716,765 | 22 | Michele Redman | 4,436,034 |
| 5 | Beth Daniel | 8,495,545 | 14 | Patty Sheehan | 5,513,409 | 23 | Pat Hurst | 4,330,866 |
| 6 | Rosie Jones | 8,262,817 | 15 | Liselotte Neumann | 5,347,250 | 24 | Catriona Matthew | 4,265,110 |
| 7 | Se Ri Pak | 8,081,987 | 16 | Nancy Lopez | 5,320,877 | 25 | Brandie Burton | 4,114,564 |
| 8 | Betsy King | 7,637,621 | 17 | Mu Hyun Kim | 5,106,146 | | | |
| 9 | Laura Davies | 7,342,982 | 18 | Cristie Kerr | 5,093,351 | | | |

## Official World Golf Ranking

Begun in 1986, the Official World Golf Ranking (formerly the Sony World Ranking) combines the best golfers on the six pro men's tours which make up the International Federation of PGA Tours. Rankings are based on a rolling two-year period and weighed in favor of more recent results. While annual winners are not announced, certain players reaching No. 1 have dominated each year.

**Multiple winners** (at year's end): Tiger Woods (7); Greg Norman (6); Nick Faldo (3); Seve Ballesteros (2).

| Year | | Year | | Year | | Year | |
|---|---|---|---|---|---|---|---|
| 1986 | Seve Ballesteros | 1990 | Nick Faldo | 1994 | Nick Price | 2000 | Tiger Woods |
| 1987 | Greg Norman | | & Greg Norman | 1995 | Greg Norman | 2001 | Tiger Woods |
| 1988 | Greg Norman | 1991 | Ian Woosnam | 1996 | Greg Norman | 2002 | Tiger Woods |
| 1989 | Seve Ballesteros | 1992 | Fred Couples | 1997 | Tiger Woods | 2003 | Tiger Woods |
| | & Greg Norman | | & Nick Faldo | 1998 | Tiger Woods | 2004 | Vijay Singh |
| | | 1993 | Nick Faldo | 1999 | Tiger Woods | | |

## Annual Awards

### PGA of America Player of the Year

Awarded by the PGA of America; based on points scale that weighs performance in major tournaments, regular events, money earned and scoring average. **Note:** As of Oct. 9, Tiger Woods had already clinched the award for 2005.

**Multiple winners:** Tiger Woods (7); Tom Watson (6); Jack Nicklaus (5); Ben Hogan (4); Julius Boros, Billy Casper, Arnold Palmer and Nick Price.

| Year | | Year | | Year | | Year | |
|------|------|------|------|------|------|------|------|
| 1948 | Ben Hogan | 1963 | Julius Boros | 1978 | Tom Watson | 1993 | Nick Price |
| 1949 | Sam Snead | 1964 | Ken Venturi | 1979 | Tom Watson | 1994 | Nick Price |
| 1950 | Ben Hogan | 1965 | Dave Marr | 1980 | Tom Watson | 1995 | Greg Norman |
| 1951 | Ben Hogan | 1966 | Billy Casper | 1981 | Bill Rogers | 1996 | Tom Lehman |
| 1952 | Julius Boros | 1967 | Jack Nicklaus | 1982 | Tom Watson | 1997 | Tiger Woods |
| 1953 | Ben Hogan | 1968 | No award | 1983 | Hal Sutton | 1998 | Mark O'Meara |
| 1954 | Ed Furgol | 1969 | Orville Moody | 1984 | Tom Watson | 1999 | Tiger Woods |
| 1955 | Doug Ford | 1970 | Billy Casper | 1985 | Lanny Wadkins | 2000 | Tiger Woods |
| 1956 | Jack Burke | 1971 | Lee Trevino | 1986 | Bob Tway | 2001 | Tiger Woods |
| 1957 | Dick Mayer | 1972 | Jack Nicklaus | 1987 | Paul Azinger | 2002 | Tiger Woods |
| 1958 | Dow Finsterwald | 1973 | Jack Nicklaus | 1988 | Curtis Strange | 2003 | Tiger Woods |
| 1959 | Art Wall Jr. | 1974 | Johnny Miller | 1989 | Tom Kite | 2004 | Vijay Singh |
| 1960 | Arnold Palmer | 1975 | Jack Nicklaus | 1990 | Nick Faldo | 2005 | Tiger Woods |
| 1961 | Jerry Barber | 1976 | Jack Nicklaus | 1991 | Corey Pavin | | |
| 1962 | Arnold Palmer | 1977 | Tom Watson | 1992 | Fred Couples | | |

### PGA Tour Player of the Year

Award by the PGA Tour starting in 1990. Winner voted on by tour members from list of nominees. Winner receives the Jack Nicklaus Trophy, which originated in 1997.

**Multiple winners:** Tiger Woods (6); Fred Couples and Nick Price (2).

| Year | | Year | | Year | | Year | |
|------|------|------|------|------|------|------|------|
| 1990 | Wayne Levi | 1994 | Nick Price | 1998 | Mark O'Meara | 2002 | Tiger Woods |
| 1991 | Fred Couples | 1995 | Greg Norman | 1999 | Tiger Woods | 2003 | Tiger Woods |
| 1992 | Fred Couples | 1996 | Tom Lehman | 2000 | Tiger Woods | 2004 | Vijay Singh |
| 1993 | Nick Price | 1997 | Tiger Woods | 2001 | Tiger Woods | | |

### PGA Tour Rookie of the Year

Awarded by the PGA Tour in 1990. Winner voted on by tour members from list of first-year nominees.

| Year | | Year | | Year | | Year | |
|------|------|------|------|------|------|------|------|
| 1990 | Robert Gamez | 1994 | Ernie Els | 1998 | Steve Flesch | 2002 | Jonathan Byrd |
| 1991 | John Daly | 1995 | Woody Austin | 1999 | Carlos Franco | 2003 | Ben Curtis |
| 1992 | Mark Carnevale | 1996 | Tiger Woods | 2000 | Michael Clark II | 2004 | Todd Hamilton |
| 1993 | Vijay Singh | 1997 | Stewart Cink | 2001 | Charles Howell III | | |

### Champions Tour Player of the Year

Awarded by the Champions Tour starting in 1990. Winner voted on by tour members from list of nominees.

**Multiple winner:** Hale Irwin and Lee Trevino (3); Jim Colbert (2).

| Year | | Year | | Year | | Year | |
|------|------|------|------|------|------|------|------|
| 1990 | Lee Trevino | 1993 | Dave Stockton | 1997 | Hale Irwin | 2001 | Allen Doyle |
| 1991 | George Archer | 1994 | Lee Trevino | 1998 | Hale Irwin | 2002 | Hale Irwin |
| | & Mike Hill | 1995 | Jim Colbert | 1999 | Bruce Fleisher | 2003 | Tom Watson |
| 1992 | Lee Trevino | 1996 | Jim Colbert | 2000 | Larry Nelson | 2004 | Craig Stadler |

### European Golfer of the Year

Formerly the Ritz Club Trophy (1985-92), Johnnie Walker Trophy (1993-97) and Asprey Golfer of the Year (1998-2004); voting done by panel of European golf writers and tour members.

**Multiple winners:** Colin Montgomerie (4); Seve Ballesteros, Ernie Els, and Nick Faldo (3); Bernhard Langer and Lee Westwood (2).

| Year | | Year | | Year | | Year | |
|------|------|------|------|------|------|------|------|
| 1985 | Bernhard Langer | 1990 | Nick Faldo | 1995 | Colin Montgomerie | 2000 | Lee Westwood |
| 1986 | Seve Ballesteros | 1991 | Seve Ballesteros | 1996 | Colin Montgomerie | 2001 | Retief Goosen |
| 1987 | Ian Woosnam | 1992 | Nick Faldo | 1997 | Colin Montgomerie | 2002 | Ernie Els |
| 1988 | Seve Ballesteros | 1993 | Bernhard Langer | 1998 | Lee Westwood | 2003 | Ernie Els |
| 1989 | Nick Faldo | 1994 | Ernie Els | 1999 | Colin Montgomerie | 2004 | Vijay Singh |

## Annual Awards (Cont.)
### LPGA Player of the Year

Sponsored by Rolex and awarded by the LPGA; based on performance points accumulated during the year.

**Multiple winners:** Annika Sorenstam and Kathy Whitworth (7); Nancy Lopez (4); JoAnne Carner, Beth Daniel and Betsy King (3); Pat Bradley, Judy Rankin and Karrie Webb (2).

| Year | | Year | | Year | | Year | |
|---|---|---|---|---|---|---|---|
| 1966 | Kathy Whitworth | 1976 | Judy Rankin | 1986 | Pat Bradley | 1996 | Laura Davies |
| 1967 | Kathy Whitworth | 1977 | Judy Rankin | 1987 | Ayako Okamoto | 1997 | Annika Sorenstam |
| 1968 | Kathy Whitworth | 1978 | Nancy Lopez | 1988 | Nancy Lopez | 1998 | Annika Sorenstam |
| 1969 | Kathy Whitworth | 1979 | Nancy Lopez | 1989 | Betsy King | 1999 | Karrie Webb |
| 1970 | Sandra Haynie | 1980 | Beth Daniel | 1990 | Beth Daniel | 2000 | Karrie Webb |
| 1971 | Kathy Whitworth | 1981 | JoAnne Carner | 1991 | Pat Bradley | 2001 | Annika Sorenstam |
| 1972 | Kathy Whitworth | 1982 | JoAnne Carner | 1992 | Dottie Mochrie | 2002 | Annika Sorenstam |
| 1973 | Kathy Whitworth | 1983 | Patty Sheehan | 1993 | Betsy King | 2003 | Annika Sorenstam |
| 1974 | JoAnne Carner | 1984 | Betsy King | 1994 | Beth Daniel | 2004 | Annika Sorenstam |
| 1975 | Sandra Palmer | 1985 | Nancy Lopez | 1995 | Annika Sorenstam | | |

### LPGA Rookie of the Year

Sponsored by Rolex and awarded by the LPGA; based on performance points accumulated during the year. Winner receives Louise Suggs Trophy, which originated in 2000. Officially the Louise Suggs Rolex Rookie of the Year.

| Year | | Year | | Year | | Year | |
|---|---|---|---|---|---|---|---|
| 1962 | Mary Mills | 1973 | Laura Baugh | 1984 | Juli Inkster | 1995 | Pat Hurst |
| 1963 | Clifford Ann Creed | 1974 | Jan Stephenson | 1985 | Penny Hammel | 1996 | Karrie Webb |
| 1964 | Susie Berning | 1975 | Amy Alcott | 1986 | Jody Rosenthal | 1997 | Lisa Hackney |
| 1965 | Margie Masters | 1976 | Bonnie Lauer | 1987 | Tammie Green | 1998 | Se Ri Pak |
| 1966 | Jan Ferraris | 1977 | Debbie Massey | 1988 | Liselotte Neumann | 1999 | Mi Hyun Kim |
| 1967 | Sharron Moran | 1978 | Nancy Lopez | 1989 | Pamela Wright | 2000 | Dorothy Delasin |
| 1968 | Sandra Post | 1979 | Beth Daniel | 1990 | Hiromi Kobayashi | 2001 | Hee-Won Han |
| 1969 | Jane Blalock | 1980 | Myra Van Hoose | 1991 | Brandie Burton | 2002 | Beth Bauer |
| 1970 | JoAnne Carner | 1981 | Patty Sheehan | 1992 | Helen Alfredsson | 2003 | Lorena Ochoa |
| 1971 | Sally Little | 1982 | Patti Rizzo | 1993 | Suzanne Strudwick | 2004 | Shi Hyun Ahn |
| 1972 | Jocelyne Bourassa | 1983 | Stephanie Farwig | 1994 | Annika Sorenstam | | |

# National Team Competition
## MEN
### Ryder Cup

The Ryder Cup was presented by British seed merchant and businessman Samuel Ryder in 1927 for competition between professional golfers from Great Britain and the United States. The British team was expanded to include Irish players in 1973 and the rest of Europe in 1979. The 2001 event was postponed due to the attacks on America, causing the event to switch from an odd- to even-year schedule. The United States leads the series 24-9-2 after 35 matches.

| Year | | Year | | Year | | Year | |
|---|---|---|---|---|---|---|---|
| 1927 | USA, 9½-2½ | 1951 | USA, 9½-2½ | 1969 | Draw, 16-16 | 1987 | Europe, 15-13 |
| 1929 | Britain-Ireland, 7-5 | 1953 | USA, 6½-5½ | 1971 | USA, 18½-13½ | 1989 | Draw, 14-14 |
| 1931 | USA, 9-3 | 1955 | USA, 8-4 | 1973 | USA, 19-13 | 1991 | USA, 14½-13½ |
| 1933 | Great Britain, 6½-5½ | 1957 | Britain-Ireland, 7½-4½ | 1975 | USA, 21-11 | 1993 | USA, 15-13 |
| 1935 | USA, 9-3 | 1959 | USA, 8½-3½ | 1977 | USA, 12½-13½ | 1995 | Europe, 14½-13½ |
| 1937 | USA, 8-4 | 1961 | USA, 14½-9½ | 1979 | USA, 17-11 | 1997 | Europe, 14½-13½ |
| 1939-45 | Not held | 1963 | USA, 23-9 | 1981 | USA, 18½-9½ | 1999 | USA, 14½-13½ |
| 1947 | USA, 11-1 | 1965 | USA, 19½-12½ | 1983 | USA, 14½-13½ | 2002 | Europe, 15½-12½ |
| 1949 | USA, 7-5 | 1967 | USA, 23½-8½ | 1985 | Europe, 16½-11½ | 2004 | Europe, 18½-9½ |

### Playing Sites

**1927**—Worcester CC (Mass.); **1929**—Moortown, England; **1931**—Scioto CC (Ohio); **1933**—Southport & Ainsdale, England; **1935**—Ridgewood CC (N.J.); **1937**—Southport & Ainsdale, England; **1939-45**—Not held. **1947**—Portland CC (Ore.); **1949**—Ganton GC, England; **1951**—Pinehurst CC (N.C.); **1953**—Wentworth, England; **1955**—Thunderbird Ranch & CC (Calif.); **1957**—Lindrick GC, England; **1959**—Eldorado CC (Calif.); **1961**—Royal Lytham & St. Annes, England; **1963**—East Lake CC (Ga.); **1965**—Royal Birkdale, England; **1967**—Champions GC (Tex.); **1969**—Royal Birkdale, England; **1971**—Old Warson CC (Mo.); **1973**—Muirfield, Scotland; **1975**—Laurel Valley GC (Pa.); **1977**—Royal Lytham & St. Annes, England; **1979**—The Greenbrier (W.Va.); **1981**—Walton Heath GC, England; **1983**—PGA National GC (Fla.); **1985**—The Belfry, England; **1987**—Muirfield Village GC (Ohio); **1989**—The Belfry, England; **1991**—Ocean Course (S.C.); **1993**—The Belfry, England; **1995**—Oak Hill CC (N.Y.); **1997**—Valderrama, Costa del Sol, Spain; **1999**—The Country Club (Mass.); **2002**—The Belfry, England; **2004**—Oakland Hills CC (Mich.); **2006**—Kildare Hotel & CC, Ireland; **2008**—Valhalla GC (Ky.); **2010**—Celtic Manor, Wales; **2012**—Medinah CC (Ill.); **2014**—Gleneagles, Scotland; **2016**—Hazeltine National GC (Minn); **2018**—TBA (Europe); **2020**—Whistling Straits (Wisc.).

### Presidents Cup

The Presidents Cup is a biennial event played in non-Ryder Cup years in which the world's best non-European players compete against players from the United States. The U.S. leads the series, 4-1-1. In 2003 the match was called off due to darkness after three sudden-death playoff holes. It was deemed a tie with both teams sharing the Cup until 2005.

| Year | | Year | | Year | |
|---|---|---|---|---|---|
| 1994 | USA, 20-12 | 1998 | International, 20½-11½ | 2003 | Tie, 17-17 |
| 1996 | USA, 16½-15½ | 2000 | USA, 21½-10½ | 2005 | USA, 18½-15½ |

## Walker Cup

The Walker Cup was presented by American businessman George Herbert Walker in 1922 for competition between amateur golfers from Great Britain, Ireland and the United States. The U.S. leads the series against the combined Great Britain-Ireland team, 32-7-1, after 40 matches.

| Year | Year | Year | Year |
|---|---|---|---|
| 1922 USA, 8-4 | 1949 USA, 10-2 | 1973 USA, 14-10 | 1995 Britain-Ireland, 14-10 |
| 1923 USA, 6½-5½ | 1951 USA, 7½-4½ | 1975 USA, 15½-8½ | 1997 USA, 18-6 |
| 1924 USA, 9-3 | 1953 USA, 9-3 | 1977 USA, 16-8 | 1999 Britain-Ireland, 15-9 |
| 1926 USA, 6½-5½ | 1955 USA, 10-2 | 1979 USA, 15½-8½ | 2001 Britain-Ireland, 15-9 |
| 1928 USA, 11-1 | 1957 USA, 8½-3½ | 1981 USA, 15-9 | 2003 Britain-Ireland, |
| 1930 USA, 10-2 | 1959 USA, 9-3 | 1983 USA, 13½-10½ | 12½-11½ |
| 1932 USA, 9½-2½ | 1961 USA, 11-1 | 1985 USA, 13-11 | 2005 USA, 12½-11½ |
| 1934 USA, 9½-2½ | 1963 USA, 14-10 | 1987 USA, 16½-7½ | |
| 1936 USA, 10½-1½ | 1965 Draw, 12-12 | 1989 Britain-Ireland, | |
| 1938 Britain-Ireland, 7½-4½ | 1967 USA, 15-9 | 12½-11½ | |
| 1940-46 Not held | 1969 USA, 13-11 | 1991 USA, 14-10 | |
| 1947 USA, 8-4 | 1971 Britain-Ireland, 13-11 | 1993 USA, 19-5 | |

# WOMEN

## Solheim Cup

The Solheim Cup was presented by the Karsten Manufacturing Co. in 1990 for competition between women professional golfers from Europe and the United States. The event was switched from even- to odd-numbered years after 2002 so it would not conflict with the men's Ryder Cup event. The U.S. leads the series, 6-3.

| Year | Year | Year |
|---|---|---|
| 1990 USA, 11½-4½ | 1996 USA, 17-11 | 2002 USA, 15½-12½ |
| 1992 Europe, 11½-6½ | 1998 USA, 16-12 | 2003 Europe, 17½-10½ |
| 1994 USA, 13-7 | 2000 Europe, 14½-11½ | 2005 USA, 15½-12½ |

### Playing Sites

**1990**—Lake Nona CC (Fla.); **1992**—Dalmahoy CC, Scotland; **1994**—The Greenbrier (W. Va.); **1996**—Marriott St. Pierre Hotel G&CC, Wales; **1998**—Muirfield Village GC (Ohio); **2000**—Loch Lomond GC, Scotland; **2002**—Interlachen CC (Minn.); **2003**—Barseback G&CC, Sweden; **2005**—Crooked Stick GC (Ind.); **2007**—Halmstad GC (Sweden); **2009**—Rich Harvest Farms (Ill.).

## Curtis Cup

Named after British golfing sisters Harriot and Margaret Curtis, the Curtis Cup was first contested in 1932 between teams of women amateurs from the United States and the British Isles.

Competed for every other year since 1932 (except during WWII). The U.S. leads the series, 24-6-3, after 33 matches.

| Year | Year | Year | Year |
|---|---|---|---|
| 1932 USA, 5½-3½ | 1956 British Isles, 5-4 | 1974 USA, 13-5 | 1992 British Isles, 10-8 |
| 1934 USA, 6½-2½ | 1958 Draw, 4½-4½ | 1976 USA, 11½-6½ | 1994 Draw, 9-9 |
| 1936 Draw, 4½-4½ | 1960 USA, 6½-2½ | 1978 USA, 12-6 | 1996 British Isles, 11½-6½ |
| 1938 USA, 5½-3½ | 1962 USA, 8-1 | 1980 USA, 13-5 | 1998 USA, 10-8 |
| 1940-46 Not held | 1964 USA, 10½-7½ | 1982 USA, 14½-3½ | 2000 USA, 10-8 |
| 1948 USA, 6½-2½ | 1966 USA, 13-5 | 1984 USA, 9½-8½ | 2002 USA, 11-7 |
| 1950 USA, 7½-1½ | 1968 USA, 10½-7½ | 1986 British Isles, 13-5 | 2004 USA, 10-8 |
| 1952 British Isles, 5-4 | 1970 USA, 11½-6½ | 1988 British Isles, 11-7 | |
| 1954 USA, 6-3 | 1972 USA, 10-8 | 1990 USA, 14-4 | |

## COLLEGES

## Men's NCAA Division I Champions

College championships decided by match play from 1897-1964 and stroke play since 1965.

**Multiple winners** (Teams): Yale (21); Houston (16); Oklahoma St. (9); Stanford (7); Harvard (6); Florida, LSU and North Texas (4); Wake Forest (3); Arizona St., Georgia, Michigan, Ohio St. and Texas (2).

**Multiple winners** (Individuals): Ben Crenshaw and Phil Mickelson (3); Dick Crawford, Dexter Cummings, G.T. Dunlop, Fred Lamprecht and Scott Simpson (2).

| Year | Team winner | Individual champion | Year | Team winner | Individual champion |
|---|---|---|---|---|---|
| 1897 | Yale | Louis Bayard, Princeton | 1905 | Yale | Robert Abbott, Yale |
| 1898 | Harvard (spring) | John Reid, Yale | 1906 | Yale | W.E. Clow Jr., Yale |
| 1898 | Yale (fall) | James Curtis, Harvard | 1907 | Yale | Ellis Knowles, Yale |
| 1899 | Harvard | Percy Pyne, Princeton | 1908 | Yale | H.H. Wilder, Harvard |
| | | | 1909 | Yale | Albert Seckel, Princeton |
| 1900 | Not held | | 1910 | Yale | Robert Hunter, Yale |
| 1901 | Harvard | H. Lindsley, Harvard | 1911 | Yale | George Stanley, Yale |
| 1902 | Yale (spring) | Chas. Hitchcock Jr., Yale | 1912 | Yale | F.C. Davison, Harvard |
| 1902 | Harvard (fall) | Chandler Egan, Harvard | 1913 | Yale | Nathaniel Wheeler, Yale |
| 1903 | Harvard | F.O. Reinhart, Princeton | 1914 | Princeton | Edward Allis, Harvard |
| 1904 | Harvard | A.L. White, Harvard | | | |

## Colleges (Cont.)

| Year | Team winner | Individual champion | Year | Team winner | Individual champion |
|------|-------------|--------------------|------|-------------|--------------------|
| 1915 | Yale | Francis Blossom, Yale | 1962 | Houston | Kermit Zarley, Houston |
| 1916 | Princeton | J.W. Hubbell, Harvard | 1963 | Oklahoma St. | R.H. Sikes, Arkansas |
| 1917-18 | Not held | | 1964 | Houston | Terry Small, San Jose St. |
| 1919 | Princeton | A.L. Walker Jr., Columbia | 1965 | Houston | Marty Fleckman, Houston |
| | | | 1966 | Houston | Bob Murphy, Florida |
| 1920 | Princeton | Jess Sweetser, Yale | 1967 | Houston | Hale Irwin, Colorado |
| 1921 | Dartmouth | Simpson Dean, Princeton | 1968 | Florida | Grier Jones, Oklahoma St. |
| 1922 | Princeton | Pollack Boyd, Dartmouth | 1969 | Houston | Bob Clark, Cal St.-LA |
| 1923 | Princeton | Dexter Cummings, Yale | | | |
| 1924 | Yale | Dexter Cummings, Yale | 1970 | Houston | John Mahaffey, Houston |
| 1925 | Yale | Fred Lamprecht, Tulane | 1971 | Texas | Ben Crenshaw, Texas |
| 1926 | Yale | Fred Lamprecht, Tulane | 1972 | Texas | Ben Crenshaw, Texas |
| 1927 | Princeton | Watts Gunn, Georgia Tech | | | & Tom Kite, Texas |
| 1928 | Princeton | Maurice McCarthy, G'town | 1973 | Florida | Ben Crenshaw, Texas |
| 1929 | Princeton | Tom Aycock, Yale | 1974 | Wake Forest | Curtis Strange, W.Forest |
| | | | 1975 | Wake Forest | Jay Haas, Wake Forest |
| 1930 | Princeton | G.T. Dunlap Jr., Princeton | 1976 | Oklahoma St. | Scott Simpson, USC |
| 1931 | Yale | G.T. Dunlap Jr., Princeton | 1977 | Houston | Scott Simpson, USC |
| 1932 | Yale | J.W. Fischer, Michigan | 1978 | Oklahoma St. | David Edwards, Okla. St. |
| 1933 | Yale | Walter Emery, Oklahoma | 1979 | Ohio St. | Gary Hallberg, Wake Forest |
| 1934 | Michigan | Charles Yates, Ga.Tech | | | |
| 1935 | Michigan | Ed White, Texas | 1980 | Oklahoma St. | Jay Don Blake, Utah St. |
| 1936 | Yale | Charles Kocsis, Michigan | 1981 | Brigham Young | Ron Commans, USC |
| 1937 | Princeton | Fred Haas Jr., LSU | 1982 | Houston | Billy Ray Brown, Houston |
| 1938 | Stanford | John Burke, Georgetown | 1983 | Oklahoma St. | Jim Carter, Arizona St. |
| 1939 | Stanford | Vincent D'Antoni, Tulane | 1984 | Houston | John Inman, N.Carolina |
| | | | 1985 | Houston | Clark Burroughs, Ohio St. |
| 1940 | Princeton & LSU | Dixon Brooke, Virginia | 1986 | Wake Forest | Scott Verplank, Okla. St. |
| 1941 | Stanford | Earl Stewart, LSU | 1987 | Oklahoma St. | Brian Watts, Oklahoma St. |
| 1942 | LSU & Stanford | Frank Tatum Jr., Stanford | 1988 | UCLA | E.J. Pfister, Oklahoma St. |
| 1943 | Yale | Wallace Ulrich, Carleton | 1989 | Oklahoma | Phil Mickelson, Ariz. St. |
| 1944 | Notre Dame | Louis Lick, Minnesota | | | |
| 1945 | Ohio State | John Lorms, Ohio St. | 1990 | Arizona St. | Phil Mickelson, Ariz. St. |
| 1946 | Stanford | George Hamer, Georgia | 1991 | Oklahoma St. | Warren Schuette, UNLV |
| 1947 | LSU | Dave Barclay, Michigan | 1992 | Arizona | Phil Mickelson, Ariz. St. |
| 1948 | San Jose St. | Bob Harris, San Jose St. | 1993 | Florida | Todd Demsey, Ariz. St. |
| 1949 | North Texas | Harvie Ward, N.Carolina | 1994 | Stanford | Justin Leonard, Texas |
| | | | 1995 | Oklahoma St. | Chip Spratlin, Auburn |
| 1950 | North Texas | Fred Wampler, Purdue | 1996 | Arizona St. | Tiger Woods, Stanford |
| 1951 | North Texas | Tom Nieporte, Ohio St. | 1997 | Pepperdine | Charles Warren, Clemson |
| 1952 | North Texas | Jim Vickers, Oklahoma | 1998 | UNLV | James McLean, Minnesota |
| 1953 | Stanford | Earl Moeller, Oklahoma St. | 1999 | Georgia | Luke Donald, Northwestern |
| 1954 | SMU | Hillman Robbins, Memphis St. | | | |
| 1955 | LSU | Joe Campbell, Purdue | 2000 | Oklahoma St. | Charles Howell, Oklahoma St. |
| 1956 | Houston | Rick Jones, Ohio St. | 2001 | Florida | Nick Gilliam, Florida |
| 1957 | Houston | Rex Baxter Jr., Houston | 2002 | Minnesota | Troy Matteson, Georgia Tech |
| 1958 | Houston | Phil Rodgers, Houston | 2003 | Clemson | Alejandro Canizares, Ariz. St. |
| 1959 | Houston | Dick Crawford, Houston | 2004 | California | Ryan Moore, UNLV |
| 1960 | Houston | Dick Crawford, Houston | 2005 | Georgia | James Lepp, Washington |
| 1961 | Purdue | Jack Nicklaus, Ohio St. | | | |

## Women's NCAA Division I Champions
College championships decided by stroke play since 1982.

**Multiple winners** (teams): Arizona St. (6); Duke (3); Arizona, Florida, San Jose St., Tulsa and UCLA (2).

| Year | Team winner | Individual champion | Year | Team winner | Individual champion |
|------|-------------|--------------------|------|-------------|--------------------|
| 1982 | Tulsa | Kathy Baker, Tulsa | 1994 | Arizona St. | Emilee Klein, Ariz. St. |
| 1983 | TCU | Penny Hammel, Miami | 1995 | Arizona St. | K. Mourgue d'Algue, Ariz. St. |
| 1984 | Miami-FL | Cindy Schreyer, Georgia | 1996 | Arizona | Marisa Baena, Arizona |
| 1985 | Florida | Danielle Ammaccapane, Ariz.St. | 1997 | Arizona St. | Heather Bowie, Texas |
| 1986 | Florida | Page Dunlap, Florida | 1998 | Arizona St. | Jennifer Rosales, USC |
| 1987 | San Jose St. | Caroline Keggi, New Mexico | 1999 | Duke | Grace Park, Arizona St. |
| 1988 | Tulsa | Melissa McNamara, Tulsa | | | |
| 1989 | San Jose St. | Pat Hurst, San Jose St. | 2000 | Arizona | Jenna Daniels, Arizona |
| | | | 2001 | Georgia | Candy Hannemann, Duke |
| 1990 | Arizona St. | Susan Slaughter, Arizona | 2002 | Duke | Virada Nirapathpongporn, Duke |
| 1991 | UCLA | Annika Sorenstam, Arizona | 2003 | USC | Mikaela Parmlid, USC |
| 1992 | San Jose St. | Vicki Goetze, Georgia | 2004 | UCLA | Sarah Huarte, California |
| 1993 | Arizona St. | Charlotta Sorenstam, Ariz. St. | 2005 | Duke | Anna Grzebien, Duke |

# Auto Racing

***Danica Patrick*** *tuned out her detractors and proved
she had talent to go along with her looks, winning three
poles in 2005 and placing fourth in the Indy 500.*

AP/Wide World Photos

# Men Behaving Badly

*Dented fenders and choice words are the order of the day in 2005...and on one occasion, the nastiness isn't reserved just for men.*

**Michael Morrison**
*is co-editor of the ESPN Sports Almanac.*

We've all been there. Anyone who's driven 65 mph on their local highway and witnessed the madness going on outside their car has felt pangs of road rage in one form or another.

"Wow, look at that guy...he's all over the road!"

"Hey that person just cut me off!"

For some people, the anger is inevitable...and out of their control. What they do have control of, however, is the way they act on that anger. In the 2005 auto racing seasons, drivers acted...and then some.

When cars millimeters apart from each other are moving at speeds close to 200 mph, there's not a whole lot of room for error. Swapping paint is nothing new to the auto racing world. Heck in some races, it's actually considered strategy. Still, there are rules to be followed — many of the unwritten variety, and when it comes to those unwritten rules, drivers have always been able to police themselves. More and more, however, it seems as though the talented new generation of drivers are taking too many liberties with these rules and putting others in jeopardy.

And that's all veteran Dale Jarrett was getting at when he put 27-year-old Ryan Newman into the wall on lap 317 of the California Speedway in early September.

As Jarrett's teammate Elliott Sadler explained, "Dale just decided he had enough. He was getting tired of getting run over by these young guys. He just wanted to set an example that he wasn't going to take it anymore...I mean, some guys will run over you each and every week, then get there on TV with a little smile and say they're sorry like everything's OK."

Alright so maybe Jarrett didn't need to be so blatant about it, but regardless, his actions seemed to work as four

AP/Wide World Photos

**Robby Gordon** *hurls his helmet at Michael Waltrip's car under caution, after the two collided, knocking Gordon out of the race on September 18 in Loudon, N.H.*

weeks later he ended his 98-race drought with a win at Talladega.

Jarrett and Newman certainly weren't the only combatants in 2005. Tony Stewart, who was relatively calm all year, had his share of dustups with Jimmie Johnson and Jeff Gordon.

NASCAR rookie Kyle Busch, brother of 2004 Nextel Cup champion Kurt (who previously had his own little war with Jimmy Spencer), was put on probation in August for slamming into Anthony Lazzaro at Watkins Glen.

"The punk crashed into me on the cool-down lap," said a befuddled Lazarro. "It shows me this guy never built or worked on a car."

The bad blood truly became a spectacle at the Sylvania 300 in New Hampshire in mid-September when three ugly incidents overshadowed an impressive victory by Newman. When Chase contender Kurt Busch was taken out by also-ran Scott Riggs, Busch took exception, storming down pit row on foot to teach Riggs' crew chief about the art of payback.

The younger Busch also tussled in Loudon, this time with usually mild-mannered Kasey Kahne. After being hit by Busch, Kahne waited for him to come around the track — while the race was still under caution, no less, and slam into him.

*Budding NASCAR star **Carl Edwards**, doing his trademark post-win flip, had three wins through October and was one of five Roush racers in the Chase for the Nextel Cup.*

The most memorable image from the day, however, was a fired-up Robby Gordon standing in traffic and whipping his helmet at Michael Waltrip's car minutes after Waltrip wrecked him.

The fisticuffs in 2005 weren't reserved for just the NASCAR circuit — or for that matter, for men! In mid-October, Indy Racing League rookie Danica Patrick was unhappy with fellow driver Jacque Lazier after the two crashed and spun into the wall in Fontana — and she let him know it.

Lazier initially claimed that Patrick punched him in the head while the two drivers were in the rescue vehicle. Patrick disagreed, saying she merely poked him in the head with two fingers and yelled, "you've got to use this."

Lazier later changed his story to match Patrick's, but also added, "My [4-year-old] son hits harder than she does."

NASCAR spokesman Jim Hunter acknowledged that all the animosity is good for ratings, but also realized things are starting to get out of hand,

"I guess there's a fine line there. Someone has to maintain control of the events."

# The Ten Biggest Stories
# of the Year in Auto Racing

**10**   **A bit of NASCAR tradition in the rear-view mirror.** Jimmie Johnson wins the final Southern 500 in late 2004. First held in 1950, the longtime Darlington Labor Day weekend tradition was NASCAR's oldest superspeedway race. It has been permanently renamed and rescheduled and is now run under the lights in November as the Dodge Charger 500.

**9**   **Kurt Busch leaves Roush Racing** and signs a multi-year contract with Penske. Busch will be taking over for retiring legend Rusty Wallace in the No. 2 car but is technically still under contract with Roush through 2006. So unless he's released from his contract early (unknown at press time) he'll have to wait until 2007 to make the switch. It will depend upon whether Ganassi releases Penske's early-signee Jamie McMurray from his 2006 deal to start tipping the dominoes.

**8**   **Gentlemen, change your tires.** Formula One's U.S. Grand Prix in Indianapolis turns into a joke when Michelin's tires prove unsafe for racing and only six cars run. The problems are not discovered until the practice sessions begin at the Brickyard, too late to make a change. The teams with Bridgestone tires (Ferrari, Jordan and Minardi) are the only ones to take part in the race. Michael Schumacher gets the hollow victory and the fans get their money back.

**7**   **The king is dead?** Fernando Alonso and Kimi Raikkonen dominate the Formula One schedule, winning seven races apiece. Michael Schumacher, who's held the Formula One circuit in his glove compartment in recent years, wins just one race (see #8) and take three second-place finishes.

**6**   **Dan's the Man.** Despite the disparity in ink, magazine covers and air time, it's Englishman Dan Wheldon that dominates the Indy Racing League, not Danica. Wheldon wins six races in 2005, including the Indianapolis 500.

**5**   **Danica's the Woman.** Rookie driver Danica Patrick takes the sports world over and goes a long way toward justifying all the attention with an impressive fourth place showing at the Indianapolis 500. Patrick also finishes fourth at the Japan 300 and takes three poles.

**4**   **Sebastien Bourdais wins six** Champ Car races (through Oct. 31) and five poles in 2005, locking up his second straight series points title. Entering the season-ending Gran Premio de Mexico, the Newman/Haas driver has won 13 of the last 26 Champ Car races run. Bourdais will attempt to become the first three-time consecutive champion since Ted Horn, who did it from 1946-1948.

**3**     **Kyle Busch wins** the Sony HD 500 at the California Speedway in September and becomes, at age 20, the youngest driver in history to win a Nextel Cup race. The rookie wins from the 25th position and just beats the long-standing record set by Donald Thomas, who was four days older when he won at Atlanta in November 1952.

**2**     **Jeff Gordon wins his third Daytona 500** and three other races but narrowly misses out on the Chase for the Nextel Cup and loses crew chief Robbie Loomis, who returns to Petty Enterprises in 2006.

**1**     **All five Roush Racing cars qualify for the Chase** for the Nextel Cup and, shortly thereafter, NASCAR chairman Brian France announces that he is studying plans to place limits on the number of teams a single owner can field in the Series. As of press time (Oct. 31), Jack Roush's drivers Greg Biffle, Carl Edwards, Matt Kenseth, Mark Martin and Kurt Busch all trailed Chase leader Tony Stewart with three races remaining. Martin, who got his 35th win in 2005, announced he will postpone retirement for one more year and return with Roush in 2006.

## INSIDE the numbers

### Wipeout!

While his aggressive style of driving earned him over $4 million in 2004, Robby Gordon also led the Nextel Cup series in accidents and spinouts.

| | Accidents & Spins | Races | Rate |
|---|---|---|---|
| Robby Gordon | 17 | 36 | 47% |
| Brendan Gaughan | 15 | 36 | 42% |
| Kasey Kahne | 15 | 36 | 42% |
| Ryan Newman | 13 | 36 | 36% |
| Jimmy Spencer | 9 | 26 | 35% |
| Brian Vickers | 12 | 36 | 33% |
| Ricky Rudd | 12 | 36 | 33% |
| Scott Riggs | 11 | 35 | 31% |
| Scott Wimmer | 11 | 35 | 31% |
| Ricky Craven | 8 | 26 | 31% |

### Something Old, Something New

Within the span of a month in the fall of 2005, Kyle Busch became the youngest driver to win a Nextel Cup race and Dale Jarrett bcame the fifth-oldest to win. The top five in each category are below.

| Oldest | Age | Year |
|---|---|---|
| Harry Gant | 52 yrs, 7 mos, 6 days | 1992 |
| Morgan Sheppard | 51–4–27 | 1993 |
| Bobby Allison | 50–2–11 | 1988 |
| Dale Earnhardt | 49–5–16 | 2000 |
| Dale Jarrett | 48–10–6 | 2005 |

| Youngest | Age | Year |
|---|---|---|
| Kyle Busch | 20 yrs, 4 mos, 2 days | 2005 |
| Donald Thomas | 20–4–6 | 1952 |
| Fireball Roberts | 21–6–24 | 1950 |
| Bobby Hillin Jr. | 22–1–22 | 1986 |
| Richard Petty | 22–7–26 | 1960 |

**Source:** NASCAR and USA Today

# 2004-2005 Season in Review

SPORTS ALMANAC

## NASCAR RESULTS

### Nextel Cup Series

Results of NASCAR Nextel Cup races from Nov. 7, 2004 through Oct. 15, 2005. **Note**: Earnings include bonus money. See *Updates* chapter (pages 953-956) for later results.

#### Late 2004

| Date | Event | Location | Winner (Pos.) | Avg.mph | Earnings | Pole | Qual.mph |
|---|---|---|---|---|---|---|---|
| Nov. 7 | Checker Auto Parts 500 | Phoenix | Dale Earnhardt Jr. (14) | 94.848 | $274,503 | R. Newman | 134.854 |
| Nov. 14 | Mountain Dew Southern 500 | Darlington | Jimmie Johnson (4) | 125.044 | 269,675 | K. Busch | —** |
| Nov. 21 | Ford 400 | Homestead | Greg Biffle (2) | 105.623 | 374,850 | K. Busch | 179.319 |

**Winning cars** (entire 2004 season): CHEVROLET (22)—Johnson 8, Earnhardt Jr. 6, J. Gordon 5, Stewart 2, Nemechek; FORD (10)—Busch 3, Kenseth 2, Biffle and Sadler 2, Martin; DODGE (4)—Newman 2, Mayfield, Wallace.

**Qualifying was cancelled due to weather and the pole was awarded to the current Nextel Cup points leader.

#### 2005 Season (through Oct. 15)

| Date | Event | Location | Winner (Pos.) | Avg.mph | Earnings | Pole | Qual.mph |
|---|---|---|---|---|---|---|---|
| Feb. 20 | **Daytona 500** | Daytona | Jeff Gordon (15) | 135.173 | $1,497,150 | D. Jarrett | 188.312 |
| Feb. 27 | Auto Club 500 | Fontana | Greg Biffle (5) | 139.697 | 288,650 | Ky. Busch | 188.245 |
| Mar. 13 | UAW-DaimlerChrysler 400 | Las Vegas | Jimmie Johnson (9) | 121.038 | 428,066 | R. Newman | 173.745 |
| Mar. 20 | Golden Corral 500 | Atlanta | Carl Edwards (4) | 143.478 | 165,450 | R. Newman | 194.690 |
| Apr. 3 | Food City 500 | Bristol | Kevin Harvick (13) | 77.496 | 189,001 | E. Sadler | 127.733 |
| Apr. 10 | Advance Auto Parts 500 | Martinsville | Jeff Gordon (16) | 72.099 | 186,051 | S. Riggs | 96.671 |
| Apr. 17 | Samsung/Radio Shack 500 | Ft. Worth | Greg Biffle (5) | 130.055 | 540,250 | R. Newman | 192.582 |
| Apr. 23 | Subway Fresh 500 | Phoenix | Kurt Busch (2) | 102.707 | 269,000 | J. Gordon | 133.675 |
| May 1 | Aaron's 499 | Talladega | Jeff Gordon (2) | 146.904 | 365,116 | K. Harvick | 189.804 |
| May 7 | Dodge Charger 500 | Darlington | Greg Biffle (3) | 123.031 | 300,575 | K. Kahne | 170.024 |
| May 14 | Chevy Amer. Revolution 400 | Richmond | Kasey Kahne (1) | 100.316 | 257,325 | K. Kahne | 129.964 |
| May 28@ | Nextel All-Star Challenge | Charlotte | Mark Martin (2) | 113.951 | 1,101,325 | R. Newman | 132.306 |
| May 29 | **Coca-Cola 600** | Charlotte | Jimmie Johnson (5) | 114.698 | 470,091 | R. Newman | 192.988 |
| June 5 | MBNA RacePoints 400 | Dover | Greg Biffle (2) | 122.626 | 282,800 | J. Johnson | —** |
| June 12 | Pocono 500 | Pocono | Carl Edwards (29) | 129.177 | 196,150 | M. Waltrip | 169.052 |
| June 19 | Batman Begins 400 | Michigan | Greg Biffle (25) | 150.596 | 171,075 | R. Newman | 194.232 |
| June 26 | Dodge/Save Mart 350 | Sonoma | Tony Stewart (7) | 72.845 | 348,761 | J. Gordon | 94.325 |
| July 2 | Pepsi 400 | Daytona | Tony Stewart (1) | 131.016 | 368,261 | T. Stewart | 185.582 |
| July 10 | USG Sheetrock 400 | Joliet | Dale Earnhardt Jr. (25) | 127.638 | 325,033 | J. Johnson | 188.147 |
| July 17 | New England 300 | Loudon | Tony Stewart (13) | 102.608 | 283,986 | B. Vickers | 130.327 |
| July 24 | Pennsylvania 500 | Pocono | Kurt Busch (2) | 125.283 | 261,275 | J. McMurray | 168.760 |
| Aug. 7 | **Allstate 400/Brickyard** | Indianapolis | Tony Stewart (22) | 118.782 | 554,661 | E. Sadler | 184.117 |
| Aug. 14 | Sirius at The Glen | Watkins Glen | Tony Stewart (1) | 86.804 | 269,006 | T. Stewart | —** |
| Aug. 21 | GFS Marketplace 400 | Michigan | Jeremy Mayfield (11) | 141.551 | 181,550 | J. Nemechek | 191.530 |
| Aug. 27 | Sharpie 500 | Bristol | Matt Kenseth (1) | 84.678 | 360,536 | M. Kenseth | 127.300 |
| Sept. 4 | Sony HD 500 | Fontana | Kyle Busch (25) | 136.356 | 241,065 | C. Edwards | 185.061 |
| Sept. 10 | Chevy Rock & Roll 400 | Richmond | Kurt Busch (5) | 98.567 | 242,900 | K. Harvick | 128.425 |

#### — Chase for the Nextel Cup —

| Date | Event | Location | Winner (Pos.) | Avg.mph | Earnings | Pole | Qual.mph |
|---|---|---|---|---|---|---|---|
| Sept. 18 | Sylvania 300 | Loudon | Ryan Newman (13) | 95.891 | 248,866 | T. Stewart | 131.143 |
| Sept. 25 | MBNA RacePoints 400 | Dover | Jimmie Johnson (5) | 115.054 | 296,641 | R. Newman | 158.103 |
| Oct. 2 | **UAW-Ford 500** | Talladega | Dale Jarrett (2) | 143.818 | 239,833 | E. Sadler | 189.260 |
| Oct. 9 | Banquet 400 | Kansas City | Mark Martin (19) | 137.774 | 339,725 | M. Kenseth | 180.856 |
| Oct. 15 | UAW-GM Quality 500 | Charlotte | Jimmie Johnson (3) | 120.334 | 264,991 | E. Sadler | 193.216 |

@ A non-points exhibition event, formerly known as The Winston.

**Qualifying was cancelled due to weather and the pole was awarded to the current Nextel Cup points leader.

**Winning Cars:** CHEVROLET (15)—Stewart 5, Johnson 4, Gordon 3, Ky. Busch, Earnhardt Jr. and Harvick; FORD (13)—Biffle 5, Ku. Busch, Edwards 2, Kenseth, Jarrett and Martin; DODGE (3)—Kahne, Mayfield and Newman.

**Remaining Races** (5): Subway 500 in Martinsville (Oct. 23); Bass Pro Shops MBNA 500 in Atlanta (Oct. 30); Dickies 500 in Fort Worth (Nov. 6); Checker Auto Parts 500 in Phoenix (Nov. 13); Ford 400 in Homestead (Nov. 21). See *Updates* for later results.

## 2005 Daytona 500

**Date**—Sunday, Feb. 20, 2005, at Daytona International Speedway. **Distance**—500 miles; **Course**—2.5 miles; **Field**—43 cars; **Average speed**—135.173 mph; **Margin of victory**—0.158 seconds; **Time of race**—3 hours, 45 minutes, 16 seconds; **Caution flags**—11 for 45 laps; **Lead changes**—22 among 12 drivers; **Lap leaders**—Stewart (107), Waltrip (42), Gordon (29), Wimmer (8), Burton (6), Johnson (3), Earnhardt Jr. and Nemechek (2), Petty, Newman, Mayfield and Harvick (1). **Pole sitter**—Dale Jarrett at 188.312 mph.

**Attendance**—200,000 (estimated). **Rating**—10.9/23 share (FOX). (r) indicates rookie driver.

| | Driver | Start | Sponsor | Car | Laps | Ended | Earnings |
|---|---|---|---|---|---|---|---|
| 1 | Jeff Gordon | 15 | DuPont | Chevrolet | 203 | Running | $1,497,150 |
| 2 | Kurt Busch | 13 | Sharpie/IRWIN Industrial Tools | Ford | 203 | Running | 1,106,130 |
| 3 | Dale Earnhardt Jr. | 5 | Budweiser | Chevrolet | 203 | Running | 828,796 |
| 4 | Scott Riggs | 12 | Valvoline | Chevrolet | 203 | Running | 643,896 |
| 5 | Jimmie Johnson | 2 | Lowe's | Chevrolet | 203 | Running | 533,579 |
| 6 | Mark Martin | 32 | Viagra | Ford | 203 | Running | 395,313 |
| 7 | Tony Stewart | 4 | The Home Depot | Chevrolet | 203 | Running | 442,610 |
| 8 | Sterling Marlin | 18 | Coors Light | Dodge | 203 | Running | 341,341 |
| 9 | Kevin Lepage | 8 | Patron Tequila | Dodge | 203 | Running | 307,108 |
| 10 | Rusty Wallace | 36 | Miller Lite | Dodge | 203 | Running | 317,646 |
| 11 | Elliott Sadler | 39 | M&M's | Ford | 203 | Running | 318,604 |
| 12 | Carl Edwards | 27 | Office Depot | Ford | 203 | Running | 278,963 |
| 13 | Joe Nemechek | 34 | U.S. Army | Chevrolet | 203 | Running | 290,671 |
| 14 | Dave Blaney | 38 | Jack Daniel's | Chevrolet | 203 | Running | 270,363 |
| 15 | Dale Jarrett | 1 | UPS | Ford | 203 | Running | 307,596 |
| 16 | Jeff Green | 26 | Cheerios | Dodge | 203 | Running | 289,499 |
| 17 | Kyle Petty | 33 | Georgia-Pacific/Brawny | Dodge | 203 | Running | 273,321 |
| 18 | Mike Bliss | 35 | NetZero/Best Buy | Chevrolet | 203 | Running | 258,538 |
| 19 | r-Travis Kvapil | 25 | Kodak/Jasper Engines | Dodge | 203 | Running | 267,788 |
| 20 | Ryan Newman | 9 | ALLTEL | Dodge | 203 | Running | 306,479 |
| 21 | Brian Vickers | 28 | GMAC/ditech.com | Chevrolet | 203 | Running | 266,738 |
| 22 | Kasey Kahne | 37 | Dodge Dealers/UAW | Dodge | 203 | Running | 288,388 |
| 23 | Jeremy Mayfield | 24 | Dodge Dealers/UAW | Dodge | 203 | Running | 283,158 |
| 24 | Ricky Rudd | 11 | Motorcraft Quality Parts | Ford | 202 | Running | 287,002 |
| 25 | Greg Biffle | 23 | National Guard | Ford | 201 | Running | 269,613 |
| 26 | Casey Mears | 29 | Target | Dodge | 199 | Running | 273,321 |
| 27 | Boris Said | 41 | CENTRIX Financial | Chevrolet | 198 | Running | 249,838 |
| 28 | Kevin Harvick | 30 | GM Goodwrench | Chevrolet | 198 | Running | 288,799 |
| 29 | Jeff Burton | 6 | Cingular Wireless | Chevrolet | 194 | Running | 294,608 |
| 30 | Mike Skinner | 7 | Argent Mortgage | Dodge | 187 | Accident | 260,113 |
| 31 | John Andretti | 42 | VB/APlus at Sunoco | Ford | 187 | Accident | 247,538 |
| 32 | Jamie McMurray | 17 | Texaco/Havoline | Dodge | 184 | Accident | 257,613 |
| 33 | Scott Wimmer | 16 | Caterpillar | Dodge | 182 | Accident | 265,110 |
| 34 | Martin Truex Jr. | 10 | Bass Pro Shops | Chevrolet | 178 | Engine | 252,593 |
| 35 | Bobby Hamilton Jr. | 22 | Tide Coldwater | Chevrolet | 173 | Running | 245,468 |
| 36 | Jason Leffler | 40 | FedEx Express | Chevrolet | 168 | Accident | 244,988 |
| 37 | Michael Waltrip | 3 | NAPA Auto Parts | Chevrolet | 161 | Engine | 304,563 |
| 38 | r-Kyle Busch | 19 | Kellogg's | Chevrolet | 148 | Running | 252,063 |
| 39 | Ken Schrader | 31 | Schwan's Home Service | Dodge | 120 | Engine | 243,288 |
| 40 | Kenny Wallace | 21 | Aaron's | Chevrolet | 39 | Engine | 243,038 |
| 41 | Mike Wallace | 43 | Lucas Oil Products | Chevrolet | 35 | Overheating | 242,388 |
| 42 | Matt Kenseth | 14 | DeWalt Power Tools | Ford | 34 | Engine | 292,124 |
| 43 | Bobby Labonte | 20 | Interstate Batteries | Chevrolet | 14 | Engine | 276,444 |

## Top 5 Finishing Order + Pole

### 2005 NEXTEL CUP SEASON (through Oct. 15)

| No. | Event | Winner | 2nd | 3rd | 4th | 5th | Pole |
|---|---|---|---|---|---|---|---|
| 1 | Daytona 500 | J. Gordon | Ku. Busch | D. Earnhardt Jr. | S. Riggs | J. Johnson | D. Jarrett |
| 2 | Auto Club 500 | G. Biffle | J. Johnson | Ku. Busch | J. McMurray | C. Edwards | Ky. Busch |
| 3 | UAW-DaimerChrysler 400 | J. Johnson | Ky. Busch | M. Kahne | J. Gordon | K. Harvick | R. Newman |
| 4 | Golden Corral 500 | C. Edwards | J. Johnson | G. Biffle | M. Martin | K. Kahne | R. Newman |
| 5 | Food City 500 | K. Harvick | E. Sadler | T. Stewart | D. Earnhardt Jr. | D. Jarrett | E. Sadler |
| 6 | Advance Auto Parts 500 | J. Gordon | K. Kahne | M. Martin | R. Newman | R. Wallace | S. Riggs |
| 7 | Samsung/RadioShack 500 | G. Biffle | J. McMurray | J. Johnson | C. Mears | S. Marlin | R. Newman |
| 8 | Subway Fresh 500 | Ku. Busch | M. Waltrip | J. Burton | D. Earnhardt Jr. | B. Vickers | J. Gordon |
| 9 | Aaron's 499 | J. Gordon | T. Stewart | M. Waltrip | J. Mayfield | J. McMurray | K. Harvick |
| 10 | Dodge Charger 500 | G. Biffle | J. Gordon | K. Kahne | M. Martin | R. Newman | K. Kahne |
| 11 | Chevy Amer. Revol. 400 | K. Kahne | T. Stewart | R. Newman | Ky. Busch | K. Harvick | K. Kahne |
| 12 | Coca-Cola 600 | J. Gordon | B. Labonte | C. Edwards | J. Mayfield | R. Newman | R. Newman |
| 13 | MBNA RacePoints 400 | G. Biffle | Ky. Busch | M. Martin | J. Johnson | R. Wallace | J. Johnson |
| 14 | Pocono 500 | C. Edwards | B. Vickers | J. Nemechek | Ky. Busch | M. Waltrip | M. Waltrip |
| 15 | Batman Begins 400 | G. Biffle | T. Stewart | M. Martin | M. Kenseth | C. Edwards | R. Newman |

| No. | Event | Winner | 2nd | 3rd | 4th | 5th | Pole |
|---|---|---|---|---|---|---|---|
| 16 | Dodge/Save Mart 350 | T. Stewart | R. Rudd | Ku. Busch | R. Wallace | D. Jarrett | J. Gordon |
| 17 | Pepsi 400 | T. Stewart | J. McMurray | D. Earnhardt Jr. | R. Wallace | D. Jarrett | T. Stewart |
| 18 | USG Sheetrock 400 | D. Earnhardt Jr. | M. Kenseth | J. Johnson | B. Vickers | T. Stewart | J. Johnson |
| 19 | New England 300 | T. Stewart | Ku. Busch | B. Labonte | Ky. Busch | G. Biffle | B. Vickers |
| 20 | Pennsylvania 500 | Ku. Busch | R. Wallace | M. Martin | C. Edwards | R. Newman | J. McMurray |
| 21 | Allstate 400 @ Brickyard | T. Stewart | K. Kahne | B. Vickers | J. Mayfield | M. Kenseth | E. Sadler |
| 22 | Sirius at The Glen | T. Stewart | R. Gordon | B. Said | S. Pruett | J. Johnson | T. Stewart |
| 23 | GFS Marketplace 400 | J. Mayfield | S. Riggs | M. Kenseth | C. Edwards | T. Stewart | J. Nemechek |
| 24 | Sharpie 500 | M. Kenseth | J. Burton | G. Biffle | R. Rudd | R. Wallace | M. Kenseth |
| 25 | Sony HD 500 | Ky. Busch | G. Biffle | B. Vickers | C. Edwards | T. Stewart | C. Edwards |
| 26 | Chevy Rock & Roll 400 | Ku. Busch | M. Kenseth | G. Biffle | Ky. Busch | R. Wallace | K. Harvick |
| | — Chase for the Nextel Cup — | | | | | | |
| 27 | Sylvania 300 | R. Newman | T. Stewart | M. Kenseth | G. Biffle | D. Earnhardt Jr. | T. Stewart |
| 28 | MBNA RacePoints 400 | J. Johnson | Ky. Busch | R. Wallace | M. Martin | R. Newman | R. Newman |
| 29 | UAW-Ford 500 | D. Jarrett | T. Stewart | M. Kenseth | R. Newman | C. Edwards | E. Sadler |
| 30 | Banquet 400 | M. Martin | G. Biffle | C. Edwards | T. Stewart | M. Kenseth | M. Kenseth |
| 31 | UAW-GM 500 | J. Johnson | Ku. Busch | G. Biffle | J. Nemechek | M. Martin | E. Sadler |

## Chase for the Nextel Cup Standings

Official Top 10 NASCAR Nextel Cup point leaders for 2004 and unofficial leaders for 2005 as of Oct. 15. Points are awarded for all qualifying drivers (winner received 180) and lap leaders. Earnings include in-season bonuses. Listed are starts (Sts), top-5 finishes (1-2-3-4-5), poles won (PW) and points (Pts).

NASCAR conducted its first playoff system in 2004, known as the "Chase for the Nextel Cup." After the first 26 official races, the top 10 drivers in the point standings (plus anyone within 400 pts. of the leader) are eligible for the "chase" over the final ten races of the season. All drivers in the "chase" have their point totals adjusted, with the first-place driver beginning with 5,050 points, the second with 5,045 and so on in five-point increments. Drivers not in the top 10 still participate in the final ten races, but are not eligible for the championship.

### FINAL 2004

| | | Finishes | | | | | Finishes | | |
|---|---|---|---|---|---|---|---|---|---|
| | Sts | 1-2-3-4-5 | PW | Pts | | Sts | 1-2-3-4-5 | PW | Pts |
| 1 Kurt Busch | 36 | 3-0-0-2-5 | 1 | 6506 | 6 Tony Stewart | 36 | 2-2-1-2-3 | 0 | 6326 |
| 2 Jimmie Johnson | 36 | 8-5-1-4-2 | 1* | 6498 | 7 Ryan Newman | 36 | 2-2-4-0-3 | 9 | 6180 |
| 3 Jeff Gordon | 36 | 5-2-6-2-1 | 6* | 6490 | 8 Matt Kenseth | 36 | 2-1-1-2-2 | 0 | 6069 |
| 4 Mark Martin | 36 | 1-5-2-0-2 | 0 | 6399 | 9 Elliott Sadler | 36 | 2-0-1-1-4 | 0 | 6024 |
| 5 Dale Earnhardt Jr. | 36 | 6-2-5-1-2 | 0 | 6368 | 10 Jeremy Mayfield | 36 | 1-2-0-0-2 | 2 | 6000 |

*Does not include poles awarded for being points leader when qualification was cancelled.

### 2005

| "Chase" Qualifiers | | | | | | "Chase" Standings | | | | |
|---|---|---|---|---|---|---|---|---|---|---|
| (through Sept. 10, Race 26) | | | | | | (through Oct. 15) | | | | |
| | | Finishes | | Old | New | | | Finishes | | |
| | Sts | 1-2-3-4-5 | PW | Pts | Pts | | Sts | 1-2-3-4-5 | PW | Pts |
| 1 Tony Stewart | 26 | 5-3-1-0-3 | 1* | 3716 | 5050 | 1 Tony Stewart | 31 | 5-5-1-1-3 | 2* | 5777 |
| 2 Greg Biffle | 26 | 5-1-3-0-1 | 0 | 3531 | 5045 | Jimmie Johnson | 31 | 4-2-2-1-2 | 1* | 5777 |
| 3 Rusty Wallace | 26 | 0-1-0-2-4 | 0 | 3412 | 5040 | 3 Greg Biffle | 31 | 5-2-4-1-1 | 0 | 5766 |
| 4 Jimmie Johnson | 26 | 2-2-2-1-2 | 1* | 3400 | 5035 | 4 Ryan Newman | 31 | 1-0-1-2-4 | 6 | 5760 |
| 5 Kurt Busch | 26 | 3-2-3-0-0 | 0 | 3304 | 5030 | 5 Mark Martin | 31 | 1-0-4-3-1 | 0 | 5726 |
| 6 Mark Martin | 26 | 0-0-4-2-0 | 0 | 3273 | 5025 | 6 Carl Edwards | 31 | 2-0-2-3-3 | 1 | 5723 |
| 7 Jeremy Mayfield | 26 | 1-0-0-3-0 | 0 | 3228 | 5020 | 7 Rusty Wallace | 31 | 0-1-1-2-4 | 0 | 5685 |
| 8 Matt Kenseth | 26 | 1-2-1-1-1 | 1 | 3114 | 5015 | 8 Jeremy Mayfield | 31 | 1-0-0-3-0 | 0 | 5662 |
| Carl Edwards | 26 | 2-0-1-3-2 | 1 | 3114 | 5015 | 9 Matt Kenseth | 31 | 1-2-3-1-2 | 2 | 5653 |
| 10 Ryan Newman | 26 | 0-0-1-1-3 | 5 | 3055 | 5005 | 10 Kurt Busch | 31 | 3-3-3-0-0 | 0 | 5365 |

**Drivers 11-15** (after Race 26): **11.** E. Sadler; **12.** J. Gordon; **13.** J. McMurray; **14.** K. Harvick; **15.** J. Nemechek.

*Does not include poles awarded for being points leader when qualification was cancelled.

## Money Leaders

### FINAL 2004

| | Earnings |
|---|---|
| 1 Dale Earnhardt Jr. | $7,201,380 |
| 2 Jeff Gordon | 6,437,660 |
| 3 Matt Kenseth | 6,223,890 |
| 4 Tony Stewart | 6,221,710 |
| 5 Jimmie Johnson | 5,692,620 |
| 6 Elliott Sadler | 5,158,360 |
| 7 Ryan Newman | 5,152,670 |
| 8 Kasey Kahne | 4,759,020 |
| 9 Kevin Harvick | 4,739,010 |
| 10 Bobby Labonte | 4,570,540 |

### 2005 (through Oct. 15)

| | Earnings |
|---|---|
| 1 Tony Stewart | $6,207,330 |
| 2 Kurt Busch | 6,099,720 |
| 3 Jimmie Johnson | 6,089,410 |
| 4 Jeff Gordon | 5,995,200 |
| 5 Mark Martin | 5,084,250 |
| 6 Dale Earnhardt Jr. | 5,049,420 |
| 7 Ryan Newman | 4,924,630 |
| 8 Greg Biffle | 4,923,230 |
| 9 Matt Kenseth | 4,913,990 |
| 10 Elliott Sadler | 4,394,840 |

## CHAMP CAR RESULTS

Schedule and results of Champ Car World Series races from Nov. 7, 2004 through Sept. 24, 2005. Officially the "Bridgestone Presents The Champ Car World Series Powered By Ford" as of the 2003 season. Note that Champ Car does not release per-race winnings. See *Updates* chapter for later results.

### Champ Car World Series

#### Late 2004

| Date | Event | Location | Winner (Pos.) | Time | Avg.mph | Pole | Qual.mph |
|------|-------|----------|---------------|------|---------|------|----------|
| Nov. 7 | Gran Premio Telmex-Tecate | Mexico City | Sebastien Bourdais (1) | 1:39:02.662 | 106.327 | S. Bourdais | 116.733 |

**Winning cars** (entire 2004 season): FORD-COSWORTH/LOLA (14)—Bourdais 7, Junqueira and Tracy 2, Carpentier, Hunter-Reay and Tagliani.

#### 2005 Season

| Date | Event | Location | Winner (Pos.) | Time | Avg.mph | Pole | Qual.mph |
|------|-------|----------|---------------|------|---------|------|----------|
| Apr. 10 | Toyota GP | Long Beach | Sebastien Bourdais (4) | 1:46:29.768 | 89.811 | P. Tracy | 104.983 |
| May 22 | Tecate Telmex Monterrey GP | Monterrey | Bruno Junqueira (5) | 2:03:38.021 | 77.602 | S. Bourdais | 102.875 |
| June 4 | Time Warner 225 pres. by U.S. Bank | Milwaukee | Paul Tracy (5) | 1:45:01.259 | 130.301 | J. Vasser | 176.235 |
| June 19 | GP of Portland | Portland | Cristiano da Matta (10) | 1:51:51.404 | 110.616 | J. Wilson | 122.308 |
| June 26 | GP of Cleveland pres. by U.S. Bank | Cleveland | Paul Tracy (1) | 1:45:43.856 | 108.755 | P. Tracy | 132.040 |
| July 10 | Molson Indy | Toronto | Justin Wilson (3) | 1:46:10.177 | 85.296 | S. Bourdais | 107.904 |
| July 17 | West Edmonton Mall GP | Edmonton | Sebastien Bourdais (10) | 1:38:55.730 | 105.302 | A. Allmendinger | 116.306 |
| July 31 | Taylor Woodrow GP | San Jose | Sebastien Bourdais (1) | 1:45:42.889 | 76.431 | S. Bourdais | 96.101 |
| Aug. 14 | Centrix Financial GP of Denver | Denver | Sebastien Bourdais (2) | 1:49:45.135 | 87.868 | P. Tracy | 100.370 |
| Aug. 28 | Molson Indy | Montreal | Oriol Servia (2) | 1:59:10.516 | 107.746 | S. Bourdais | 121.305 |
| Sept. 24 | Hurricane Relief 400 | Las Vegas | Sebastien Bourdais (1) | 1:26:22.636 | 172.962 | S. Bourdais | 204.693 |

**Winning cars (Engine/Chassis):** FORD-COSWORTH/LOLA (11)—Bourdais 5, Tracy 2, da Matta, Junqueira, Servia and Wilson.

**Remaining Races** (2): Lexmark Indy 300 in Queensland (Oct. 23); Grand Premio de Mexico in Mexico City (Nov. 6).

### Top 5 Finishing Order + Pole

#### 2005 SEASON (through Sept. 24)

| No. | Event | Winner | 2nd | 3rd | 4th | 5th | Pole |
|-----|-------|--------|-----|-----|-----|-----|------|
| 1 | GP of Long Beach | S. Bourdais | P. Tracy | B. Junqueira | J. Wilson | M. Dominguez | P. Tracy |
| 2 | Monterrey GP | B. Junqueira | A. Ranger | A. Tagliani | J. Wilson | S. Bourdais | S. Bourdais |
| 3 | Time Warner 225 | P. Tracy | A. Allmendinger | O. Servia | J. Wilson | J. Vasser | J. Vasser |
| 4 | GP of Portland | C. da Matta | S. Bourdais | P. Tracy | M. Dominguez | A. Allmendinger | J. Wilson |
| 5 | GP of Cleveland | P. Tracy | A. Allmendinger | O. Servia | A. Tagliani | S. Bourdais | P. Tracy |
| 6 | Molson Indy Toronto | J. Wilson | O. Servia | A. Tagliani | J. Vasser | S. Bourdais | S. Bourdais |
| 7 | GP of Edmonton | S. Bourdais | O. Servia | P. Tracy | J. Wilson | M. Dominguez | A. Allmendinger |
| 8 | Taylor Woodrow GP | S. Bourdais | P. Tracy | O. Servia | J. Wilson | M. Dominguez | S. Bourdais |
| 9 | GP of Denver | S. Bourdais | M. Dominguez | A. Allmendinger | O. Servia | R. Lavin | P. Tracy |
| 10 | Molson Indy Montreal | O. Servia | T. Glock | J. Wilson | S. Bourdais | A. Tagliani | S. Bourdais |
| 11 | Hurricane Relief 400 | S. Bourdais | O. Servia | J. Vasser | M. Dominguez | R. Lavin | S. Bourdais |

The Champ Car World Series has redesigned its cars for the 2007 season, making them smaller, safer and less expensive to operate.

**Did you know** that currently teams spend $450,000 for every rolling chassis they use, approximately $500,000 for spare parts during the year and another $200,000 on wheels and tires? And that doesn't even include the engine, which is leased each year.

## Champ Car Point Standings

Official Top 10 Champ Car World Series point leaders for 2004 and unofficial leaders for 2005 (through Sept. 24). Points are awarded for places 1 to 20, for the pole winner at oval events, fastest driver on each day of qualifying at road/street events, lap leaders and most positions gained. Listed are starts (Sts), top-5 finishes, poles won (PW) and points (Pts). (r) indicates rookie driver.

### FINAL 2004

| | | Sts | Finishes 1-2-3-4-5 | PW | Pts |
|---|---|---|---|---|---|
| 1 | Sebastien Bourdais | 14 | 7-1-2-0-1 | 8 | 369 |
| 2 | Bruno Junqueira | 14 | 2-7-1-1-0 | 1 | 341 |
| 3 | Patrick Carpentier | 14 | 1-2-2-3-0 | 1 | 266 |
| 4 | Paul Tracy | 14 | 2-1-1-2-1 | 3 | 254 |
| 5 | Mario Dominguez | 14 | 0-0-3-1-2 | 0 | 244 |
| 6 | r-A.J. Allmendinger | 14 | 0-0-2-0-3 | 0 | 229 |
| 7 | Alex Tagliani | 14 | 1-0-1-0-1 | 0 | 218 |
| 8 | Jimmy Vasser | 14 | 0-1-0-1-3 | 0 | 201 |
| 9 | Ryan Hunter-Reay | 14 | 1-0-0-1-2 | 1 | 199 |
| | Oriol Servia | 14 | 0-0-1-1-0 | 0 | 199 |

### 2005 (through Sept. 24)

| | | Sts | Finishes 1-2-3-4-5 | PW | Pts |
|---|---|---|---|---|---|
| 1 | Sebastien Bourdais | 11 | 5-1-0-1-3 | 5 | 310 |
| 2 | Oriol Servia | 11 | 1-3-3-1-0 | 0 | 243 |
| 3 | Paul Tracy | 11 | 2-2-2-0-0 | 3 | 216 |
| 4 | Justin Wilson | 11 | 1-0-1-5-0 | 1 | 214 |
| 5 | Mario Dominguez | 11 | 0-1-0-2-3 | 0 | 186 |
| 6 | Jimmy Vasser | 11 | 0-0-1-1-1 | 1 | 173 |
| 7 | A.J. Allmendinger | 11 | 0-2-1-0-1 | 1 | 172 |
| 8 | Alex Tagliani | 11 | 0-0-2-1-1 | 0 | 169 |
| 9 | r-Timo Glock | 11 | 0-1-0-0-0 | 0 | 162 |
| 10 | Cristiano da Matta | 11 | 1-0-0-0-0 | 0 | 130 |

## Money Leaders

### FINAL 2004

| | | Earnings |
|---|---|---|
| 1 | Sebastien Bourdais | $843,500 |
| 2 | Bruno Junqueira | 738,500 |
| 3 | Patrick Carpentier | 577,500 |
| 4 | Paul Tracy | 571,000 |
| 5 | Mario Dominguez | 488,000 |
| 6 | Alex Tagliani | 477,500 |
| 7 | r-A.J. Allmendinger | 469,000 |
| 8 | Ryan Hunter-Reay | 459,000 |
| 9 | Jimmy Vasser | 448,500 |
| 10 | Michel Jourdain Jr. | 432,500 |

### 2005 (through Sept. 24)

| | | Earnings |
|---|---|---|
| 1 | Sebastien Bourdais | $577,500 |
| 2 | Oriol Servia | 435,000 |
| 3 | Paul Tracy | 417,500 |
| 4 | Justin Wilson | 366,000 |
| 5 | Mario Dominguez | 306,000 |
| 6 | A.J. Allmendinger | 300,500 |
| 7 | Alex Tagliani | 283,000 |
| 8 | Jimmy Vasser | 277,000 |
| 9 | Cristiano da Matta | 268,000 |
| 10 | r-Timo Glock | 265,500 |

## INDY RACING LEAGUE RESULTS

### IndyCar Series

Schedule and results of IndyCar Series events during the 2005 season.

### 2005 Season

| Date | Event | Location | Winner (Pos.) | Time | Avg.mph | Pole | Qual.mph |
|---|---|---|---|---|---|---|---|
| Mar. 6 | Toyota 300 | Homestead | Dan Wheldon (11) | 2:05:27.8062 | 142.033 | T. Scheckter | 215.115 |
| Mar. 19 | XM Satellite Radio 200 | Phoenix | Sam Hornish Jr. (6) | 1:30:23.6019 | 137.753 | B. Herta | 176.612 |
| Apr. 3 | Honda GP | St. Petersburg | Dan Wheldon (9) | 2:09:54.1074 | 83.140 | B. Herta | 103.664 |
| Apr. 30 | Japan 300 | Motegi | Dan Wheldon (5) | 2:16:46.0711 | 133.365 | S. Hornish Jr. | 204.740 |
| May 29 | **Indianapolis 500**† | Indianapolis | Dan Wheldon (16) | 3:10:21.0769 | 157.603 | T. Kanaan | 227.566 |
| June 11 | Bombardier 500 | Ft. Worth | Tomas Scheckter (1) | 1:45:47.2701 | 165.047 | T. Scheckter | 213.847 |
| June 25 | SunTrust Challenge | Richmond | Helio Castroneves (2) | 1:38:33.1105 | 114.153 | S. Hornish Jr. | 176.244 |
| July 3 | Argent Mortgage 300 | Kansas City | Tony Kanaan (8) | 1:41:03.0136 | 180.504 | D. Patrick | 214.668 |
| July 16 | Firestone 200 | Nashville | Dario Franchitti (4) | 1:57:12.9129 | 133.089 | T. Scheckter | —** |
| July 24 | A.J. Foyt 225 | Milwaukee | Sam Hornish Jr. (1) | 1:51:38.6759 | 122.733 | S. Hornish Jr. | 170.296 |
| July 31 | Firestone 400 | Michigan | Bryan Herta (1) | 2:23:32.5979 | 167.197 | B. Herta | 219.141 |
| Aug. 14 | Amber Alert Portal 300 | Kentucky | Scott Sharp (7) | 1:40:55.1889 | 175.981 | D. Patrick | —** |
| Aug. 21 | Honda 225 | Pikes Peak | Dan Wheldon (11) | 1:27:46.9201 | 153.790 | H. Castroneves | 175.423 |
| Aug. 28 | Argent Mortgage GP | Infineon | Tony Kanaan (3) | 2:01:15.9187 | 91.040 | R. Briscoe | 219.141 |
| Sept. 11 | Peak Antifreeze 300 | Joliet | Dan Wheldon (5) | 1:47:49.6126 | 169.160 | D. Patrick | 215.970 |
| Sept. 25 | Watkins Glen GP | Watkins Glen | Scott Dixon (4) | 1:45:42.3804 | 114.771 | H. Castroneves | 133.806 |
| Oct. 16 | Toyota 400 | Fontana | Dario Franchitti (1) | 2:22:22.6114 | 168.567 | D. Franchitti | 219.398 |

**Qualifying was canceled due to inclement weather and the pole was awarded based on practice times.

**Winning cars (Chassis/Engine):** DALLARA/HONDA (11)—Wheldon 6, Franchitti and Kanaan 2, Herta; DALLARA/TOYOTA (3)—Hornish Jr. 2 and Castroneves; PANOZ G FORCE/HONDA (1)—Sharp; PANOZ G FORCE/TOYOTA (1)—Dixon; DALLARA/CHEVROLET (1)—Scheckter.

## Indy Racing League Results (Cont.)

### 89th Indianapolis 500

**Date**—Sunday, May 29, 2005, at Indianapolis Motor Speedway. **Distance**—500 miles; **Course**—2.5 mile oval; **Field**—33 cars; **Winner's average speed**—157.603 mph; **Margin of victory**—under caution; **Time of race**—3 hours, 10 minutes, 21.0769 seconds; **Caution flags**—8 for 46 laps; **Lead changes**—27 by 7 drivers; **Lap leaders**—Hornish Jr. (77), Kanaan (54), Wheldon (30), Patrick (19), Franchitti (15), Meira (3), Junqueira (2); **Pole Sitter**—Tony Kanaan at 227.566 mph; **Attendance**—400,000 (est.); **TV Rating**—6.6/17 (ABC). Note that (r) indicates rookie driver.

| | Driver | Start | Country | Car | Laps | Ended | Earnings |
|---|---|---|---|---|---|---|---|
| 1 | Dan Wheldon | 16 | England | D/H/F | 200 | Running | $1,537,805 |
| 2 | Vitor Meira | 7 | Brazil | P/H/F | 200 | Running | 656,955 |
| 3 | Bryan Herta | 18 | United States | D/H/F | 200 | Running | 457,505 |
| 4 | r-Danica Patrick | 4 | United States | P/H/F | 200 | Running | 378,855 |
| 5 | Buddy Lazier | 9 | United States | D/C/F | 200 | Running | 288,805 |
| 6 | Dario Franchitti | 6 | Scotland | D/H/F | 200 | Running | 309,055 |
| 7 | Scott Sharp | 3 | United States | P/H/F | 200 | Running | 295,305 |
| 8 | Tony Kanaan | 1 | Brazil | D/H/F | 200 | Running | 467,105 |
| 9 | Helio Castroneves | 5 | Brazil | D/T/F | 200 | Running | 277,805 |
| 10 | r-Ryan Briscoe | 24 | Australia | P/T/F | 199 | Running | 273,555 |
| 11 | Ed Carpenter | 26 | United States | D/T/F | 199 | Running | 258,305 |
| 12 | r-Sebastien Bourdais | 15 | France | P/H/F | 198 | Accident | 234,555 |
| 13 | Alex Barron | 22 | United States | D/T/F | 197 | Running | 254,805 |
| 14 | Adrian Fernandez | 14 | Mexico | P/H/F | 197 | Running | 226,305 |
| 15 | Felipe Giaffone | 33 | Brazil | P/T/F | 194 | Running | 247,305 |
| 16 | Jaques Lazier | 27 | United States | P/T/F | 189 | Running | 219,305 |
| 17 | Kosuke Matsuura | 8 | Japan | P/F/H | 186 | Accident | 236,305 |
| 18 | Roger Yasukawa | 17 | United States | D/H/F | 167 | Mechanical | 233,305 |
| 19 | r-Tomas Enge | 10 | Czech Republic | D/C/F | 155 | Accident | 232,055 |
| 20 | Tomas Scheckter | 11 | South Africa | D/C/F | 154 | Accident | 257,305 |
| 21 | r-Patrick Carpentier | 25 | Canada | D/T/F | 153 | Mechanical | 231,055 |
| 22 | r-Jeff Bucknum | 21 | United States | D/H/F | 150 | Accident | 222,555 |
| 23 | Sam Hornish Jr. | 2 | United States | D/T/F | 146 | Accident | 391,455 |
| 24 | Scott Dixon | 13 | New Zealand | P/T/F | 113 | Accident | 225,805 |
| 25 | Richie Hearn | 20 | United States | P/C/F | 112 | Accident | 202,305 |
| 26 | Kenny Brack | 23 | Sweden | P/H/F | 92 | Mechanical | 275,805 |
| 27 | Jeff Ward | 31 | Scotland | D/T/F | 92 | Handling | 194,805 |
| 28 | A.J. Foyt IV | 28 | United States | D/T/F | 84 | Handling | 218,805 |
| 29 | Darren Manning | 19 | England | P/T/F | 82 | Mechanical | 212,805 |
| 30 | Bruno Junqueira | 12 | Brazil | P/H/F | 76 | Accident | 192,205 |
| 31 | Marty Roth | 29 | Canada | D/C/F | 47 | Handling | 195,305 |
| 32 | Jimmy Kite | 32 | United States | D/T/F | 47 | Handling | 210,305 |
| 33 | Larry Foyt | 30 | United States | D/T/F | 14 | Accident | 189,305 |

**Car Legend:** Chassis/Engine/Tires. D—Dallara, P—Panoz G Force (chassis); C—Chevrolet, H—Honda, T—Toyota (engine); F—Firestone (tires).

## Top 5 Finishing Order + Pole

### 2005 Season

| No. | Event | Winner | 2nd | 3rd | 4th | 5th | Pole |
|---|---|---|---|---|---|---|---|
| 1 | Toyota 300 | D. Wheldon | S. Hornish Jr. | T. Kanaan | V. Meira | H. Castroneves | T. Scheckter |
| 2 | XM Satellite Radio 200 | S. Hornish Jr. | H. Castroneves | T. Kanaan | D. Franchitti | S. Sharp | B. Herta |
| 3 | Honda GP of St. Pete | D. Wheldon | T. Kanaan | D. Franchitti | B. Herta | V. Meira | B. Herta |
| 4 | Japan 300 | D. Wheldon | S. Sharp | B. Rice | D. Patrick | B. Herta | S. Hornish Jr. |
| 5 | Indy 500 | D. Wheldon | V. Meira | B. Herta | D. Patrick | B. Lazier | T. Kanaan |
| 6 | Bombardier 500 | T. Scheckter | S. Hornish Jr. | T. Kanaan | S. Sharp | H. Castroneves | T. Scheckter |
| 7 | SunTrust Challenge | H. Castroneves | D. Franchitti | P. Carpentier | T. Scheckter | D. Wheldon | S. Hornish Jr. |
| 8 | Argent Mortgage 300 | T. Kanaan | D. Wheldon | V. Meira | D. Franchitti | T. Scheckter | D. Patrick |
| 9 | Firestone 200 | D. Franchitti | S. Hornish Jr. | P. Carpentier | S. Sharp | H. Castroneves | T. Scheckter |
| 10 | AJ Foyt 225 | S. Hornish Jr. | D. Franchitti | T. Scheckter | T. Kanaan | D. Wheldon | S. Hornish Jr. |
| 11 | Fireston 400 | B. Herta | D. Wheldon | T. Scheckter | T. Kanaan | S. Hornish Jr. | B. Herta |
| 12 | Amber Alert Portal 300 | S. Sharp | V. Meira | D. Wheldon | A. Barron | H. Castroneves | D. Patrick |
| 13 | Honda 225 | D. Wheldon | S. Hornish Jr. | T. Kanaan | H. Castroneves | V. Meira | H. Castroneves |
| 14 | Argent Mortgage GP | T. Kanaan | B. Rice | A. Barron | P. Carpenter | T. Enge | R. Briscoe |
| 15 | Peak Antifreeze 300 | D. Wheldon | H. Castroneves | S. Hornish Jr. | T. Scheckter | T. Kanaan | D. Patrick |
| 16 | Watkins Glen GP | S. Dixon | T. Kanaan | D. Franchitti | G. Pantano | D. Wheldon | H. Castroneves |
| 17 | Toyota 400 | D. Franchitti | T. Kanaan | V. Meira | S. Sharp | S. Hornish Jr. | D. Franchitti |

## 2005 Indy Racing League Point Standings & Money Leaders

Final top-10 Indy Racing League driver points leaders and money leaders for 2005. Points are awarded for places 1 to 33 (winner receives 50) and overall lap leader. Listed are starts (Sts), top-5 finishes, poles won (PW) and points (Pts).

### Points

| | | Sts | Finishes 1-2-3-4-5 | PW | Pts |
|---|---|---|---|---|---|
| 1 | Dan Wheldon | 17 | 6-2-1-0-3 | 0 | 628 |
| 2 | Tony Kanaan | 17 | 2-3-4-2-1 | 1 | 518 |
| 3 | Sam Hornish Jr. | 17 | 2-4-1-0-2 | 3 | 512 |
| 4 | Dario Franchitti | 17 | 2-2-2-2-0 | 1 | 498 |
| 5 | Scott Sharp | 17 | 1-1-0-3-1 | 0 | 444 |
| 6 | Helio Castroneves | 17 | 1-2-0-1-4 | 2 | 440 |
| 7 | Vitor Meira | 17 | 0-2-2-1-2 | 0 | 422 |
| 8 | Bryan Herta | 17 | 1-0-1-1-1 | 3 | 397 |
| 9 | Tomas Scheckter | 17 | 1-0-2-2-1 | 3 | 390 |
| 10 | Patrick Carpentier | 17 | 0-0-2-1-0 | 0 | 376 |

### Earnings

| | | Earnings |
|---|---|---|
| 1 | Dan Wheldon | $2,711,005 |
| 2 | Tony Kanaan | 1,554,105 |
| 3 | Vitor Meira | 1,453,454 |
| 4 | Sam Hornish Jr. | 1,424,505 |
| 5 | Dario Franchitti | 1,299,555 |
| 6 | Bryan Herta | 1,251,805 |
| 7 | Scott Sharp | 1,160,055 |
| 8 | Helio Castroneves | 1,150,805 |
| 9 | Tomas Scheckter | 1,082,805 |
| 10 | r-Danica Patrick | 1,037,655 |

## FORMULA ONE RESULTS

Results of Formula One Grand Prix races in 2005

### 2005 Season

| Date | Grand Prix | Location | Winner (Pos.) | Time | Avg.mph | Pole |
|---|---|---|---|---|---|---|
| Mar. 6 | Australian | Melbourne | Giancarlo Fisichella (1) | 1:24:17.336 | 133.699 | G. Fisichella |
| Mar. 20 | Malaysian | Kuala Lumpur | Fernando Alonso (1) | 1:31:33.736 | 126.391 | F. Alsonso |
| Apr. 3 | Bahrain | Bahrain | Fernando Alonso (1) | 1:29:18.351 | 128.390 | F. Alonso |
| Apr. 24 | San Marino | Imola | Fernando Alonso (2) | 1:27:41.921 | 129.925 | K. Raikkonen |
| May 8 | Spanish | Catalunya | Kimi Raikkonen (1) | 1:27:16.830 | 138.418 | K. Raikkonen |
| May 22 | Monaco | Monaco | Kimi Raikkonen (1) | 1:45:15.556 | 92.293 | K. Raikkonen |
| May 29 | European | Nurburgring | Fernando Alonso (6) | 1:31:46.648 | 123.399 | N. Heidfeld |
| June 12 | Canadian | Montreal | Kimi Raikkonen (7) | 1:32:09.290 | 123.426 | J. Button |
| June 19 | U.S. | Indianapolis | Michael Schumacher (5) | 1:29:43.181 | 127.168 | J. Trulli |
| July 3 | French | Magny-Cours | Fernando Alonso (1) | 1:31:22.233 | 125.940 | F. Alonso |
| July 10 | British | Silverstone | Juan Pablo Montoya (3) | 1:24:29.588 | 136.089 | F. Alonso |
| July 24 | German | Hockenheim | Fernando Alonso (3) | 1:26:28.599 | 132.130 | K. Raikkonen |
| July 31 | Hungarian | Budapest | Kimi Raikkonen (4) | 1:37:25.552 | 117.376 | M. Schumacher |
| Aug. 21 | Turkish | Istanbul | Kimi Raikkonen (1) | 1:24:34.454 | 136.417 | K. Raikkonen |
| Sept. 4 | Italian | Monza | Juan Pablo Montoya (1) | 1:14:28.659 | 153.538 | J. Montoya |
| Sept. 11 | Belgian | Spa Francorchamps | Kimi Raikkonen (2) | 1:30:01.295 | 127.037 | J. Montoya |
| Sept. 25 | Brazilian | Sao Paolo | Juan Pablo Montoya (2) | 1:29:20.574 | 127.681 | F. Alonso |
| Oct. 9 | Japanese | Suzuka | Kimi Raikkonen (17) | 1:29:02.212 | 128.816 | R. Schumacher |
| Oct. 16 | Chinese | Shanghai | Fernando Alonso (1) | 1:39:53.618 | 114.502 | F. Alonso |

**Winning Constructors:** McLAREN-MERCEDES (10)—Raikkonen 7, Montoya 3; RENAULT (8)—Alonso 7, Fisichella; FERRARI (1)—M. Schumacher.

## Top 5 Finishing Order + Pole

### 2005 Season

| No. | Event | Winner | 2nd | 3rd | 4th | 5th | Pole |
|---|---|---|---|---|---|---|---|
| 1 | Australian | G. Fisichella | R. Barrichello | F. Alonso | D. Coulthard | M. Webber | G. Fisichella |
| 2 | Malaysian | F. Alonso | J. Trulli | N. Heidfeld | J. Montoya | R. Schumacher | F. Alonso |
| 3 | Bahrain | F. Alonso | J. Trulli | K. Raikkonen | R. Schumacher | P. de la Rosa | F. Alonso |
| 4 | San Marino | F. Alonso | M. Schumacher | J. Button | A. Wurz | T. Sato | K. Raikkonen |
| 5 | Spanish | K. Raikkonen | F. Alonso | J. Trulli | R. Schumacher | G. Fisichella | K. Raikkonen |
| 6 | Monaco | K. Raikkonen | N. Heidfeld | M. Webber | F. Alonso | J. Montoya | K. Raikkonen |
| 7 | European | F. Alonso | N. Heidfeld | R. Barrichello | D. Coulthard | M. Schumacher | N. Heidfeld |
| 8 | Canadian | K. Raikkonen | M. Schumacher | R. Barrichello | F. Massa | M. Webber | J. Button |
| 9 | U.S. | M. Schumacher | R. Barrichello | T. Monteiro | N. Karthikeyan | C. Albers | J. Trulli |
| 10 | French | F. Alonso | K. Raikkonen | M. Schumacher | J. Button | J. Trulli | F. Alonso |
| 11 | British | J. Montoya | F. Alonso | K. Raikkonen | G. Fisichella | J. Button | F. Alonso |
| 12 | German | F. Alonso | J. Montoya | J. Button | G. Fisichella | M. Schumacher | K. Raikkonen |
| 13 | Hungarian | K. Raikkonen | M. Schumacher | R. Schumacher | J. Trulli | J. Button | M. Schumacher |
| 14 | Turkish | K. Raikkonen | F. Alonso | J. Montoya | G. Fisichella | J. Button | K. Raikkonen |
| 15 | Italian | J. Montoya | F. Alonso | G. Fisichella | K. Raikkonen | J. Trulli | J. Montoya |
| 16 | Belgian | K. Raikkonen | F. Alonso | J. Button | M. Webber | R. Barrichello | J. Montoya |
| 17 | Brazilian | J. Montoya | K. Raikkonen | F. Alõnson | M. Schumacher | G. Fisichella | F. Alonso |
| 18 | Japanese | K. Raikkonen | G. Fisichella | F. Alonso | M. Webber | J. Button | R. Schumacher |
| 19 | Chinese | F. Alonso | K. Raikkonen | R. Schumacher | G. Fisichella | C. Klien | F. Alonso |

## Formula One Results (Cont.)

### 2005 Formula One Point Standings

Final top-10 Formula One World Drivers and Constructors Championship point leaders for 2005. Points are awarded for places 1 through 8 only (i.e., 10-8-6-5-4-3-2-1). Listed are starts (Sts), top-8 finishes, poles won (PW) and points (Pts). **Note:** Formula One does not keep money leader standings.

#### Drivers

| | | Sts | Finishes 1-2-3-4-5-6-7-8 | PW | Pts |
|---|---|---|---|---|---|
| 1 | Fernando Alonso | 19 | 7-5-3-1-0-0-0-0 | 6 | 133 |
| 2 | Kimi Raikkonen | 19 | 7-3-2-1-0-0-0-1 | 5 | 112 |
| 3 | Michael Schumacher | 19 | 1-3-1-1-2-1-3-0 | 1 | 62 |
| 4 | Juan Pablo Montoya | 17 | 3-1-1-1-1-1-2-0 | 2 | 60 |
| 5 | Giancarlo Fisichella | 19 | 1-1-1-4-2-2-0-0 | 1 | 58 |
| 6 | Ralf Schumacher | 18 | 0-0-2-2-1-4-2-3 | 1 | 45 |
| 7 | Jarno Trulli | 19 | 0-2-1-1-3-1-0-1 | 1 | 43 |
| 8 | Rubens Barrichello | 19 | 0-2-2-0-1-1-1-1 | 0 | 38 |
| 9 | Jenson Button | 17 | 0-0-2-1-4-0-1-2 | 1 | 37 |
| 10 | Mark Webber | 19 | 0-0-1-2-2-2-3-0 | 0 | 36 |

#### Constructors

| | | Pts |
|---|---|---|
| 1 | Renault | 191 |
| 2 | McLaren-Mercedes | 182 |
| 3 | Ferrari | 100 |
| 4 | Toyota | 88 |
| 5 | Williams-BMW | 66 |
| 6 | BAR-Honda | 38 |
| 7 | Red Bull | 34 |
| 8 | Sauber-Petronas | 20 |
| 9 | Jordan-Toyota | 12 |
| 10 | Minardi-Cosworth | 7 |

## NHRA RESULTS

Winners of National Hot Rod Association's POWERade Drag Racing events in the Top Fuel, Funny Car and Pro Stock divisions through Oct. 9, 2005. All times are based on two cars racing head-to-head from a standing start over a straight line, quarter-mile course. Differences in reaction time account for apparently faster losing times.

### 2005 Season (through Oct. 9)

| Date | Event | Event | Winner | Time | MPH | 2nd Place | Time | MPH |
|---|---|---|---|---|---|---|---|---|
| Feb. 13 | Carquest Winternationals | Top Fuel | Scott Kalitta | 4.487 | 328.46 | D. Herbert | 5.371 | 181.84 |
| | | Funny Car | Tommy Johnson Jr. | 4.741 | 327.59 | P. Burkart | 7.069 | 123.34 |
| | | Pro Stock | Dave Connolly | 6.711 | 204.98 | W. Johnson | 6.802 | 203.31 |
| Feb. 27 | Kragen Nationals | Top Fuel | Tony Schumacher | 4.485 | 329.50 | M. Lucas | 4.967 | 207.53 |
| | | Funny Car | John Force | 4.802 | 324.12 | R. Capps | 4.856 | 321.27 |
| | | Pro Stock | Allen Johnson | 6.801 | 202.36 | R. Krisher | 6.887 | 190.65 |
| Mar. 20 | Mac Tools Gatornationals | Top Fuel | Doug Kalitta | 5.182 | 296.24 | L. Dixon | 5.925 | 169.81 |
| | | Funny Car | Whit Bazemore | 4.987 | 315.67 | B. Gilbertson | 5.362 | 194.30 |
| | | Pro Stock | Jason Line | 6.716 | 205.90 | D. Connolly | 6.749 | 205.66 |
| Apr. 10 | O'Reilly Spring Nationals | Top Fuel | Tony Schumacher | 4.505 | 335.32 | C. McClenathan | 4.511 | 327.74 |
| | | Funny Car | Robert Hight | 4.786 | 326.16 | C. Pedregon | 4.818 | 321.12 |
| | | Pro Stock | Warren Johnson | 6.714 | 205.01 | J. Line | 6.735 | 204.29 |

## Major 2005 Endurance Races

### 24 Hours of Daytona

Feb. 5-6, at Daytona Beach, Fla.

Officially the Rolex 24 at Daytona and first held in 1962 (as a 3-hour race). An IMSA Camel GT race for exotic prototype sports cars and contested over a 3.56-mile road course at Daytona International Speedway. Listed are qualifying position, drivers, chassis and laps completed.

**1** (2) Wayne Taylor, Max Angelelli and Emmanuel Collard; PONTIAC RILEY; 710 laps (2,527.6 miles) at 105.204 mph; margin of victory—11 laps.

**2** (8) Butch Leitzinger, Elliott Forbes-Robinson and Jimmie Johnson; PONTIAC CRAWFORD, 699 laps.

**3** (6) Andy Wallace, Jan Lammers and Tony Stewart; PONTIAC CRAWFORD, 699 laps.

**4** (4) Stefan Johansson, Jamie McMurray and Cort Wagner; LEXUS RILEY, 698 laps.

**5** (10) Fabrizio Gollin, Mateo Bobbi and Didier Theys; LEXUS DORAN, 697 laps.

**Top qualifier:** Scott Pruett, LEXUS RILEY, 119.856 mph.

### 24 Hours of Le Mans

June 18-19, at Le Mans, France

Officially the Le Mans Grand Prix d'Endurance and first held in 1923. Contested over the 8.48-mile Circuit de la Sarthe in Le Mans, France. Listed are qualifying position, drivers, car, and laps completed.

**1** (8) JJ Lehto, Marco Werner and Tom Kristensen; AUDI R8; 370 laps (3,137.6 miles) at 130.733 mph.

**2** (1) Jean-Christophe Bouillion, Emmanuel Collard and Erik Comas; PESCAROLO-JUDD; 368 laps.

**3** (3) Emmanuele Pirro, Frank Biela and Allan McNish; AUDI R8; 364 laps.

**4** (12) Jean-Marc Gounon, Stephane Ortelli and Franck Montagny; AUDI R8; 362 laps.

**5** (5) Oliver Gavin, Olivier Beretta and Jan Magnussen; CORVETTE C6-R; 349 laps.

**Top qualifier:** Bouillion, Collard and Comas, PESCAROLO-JUDD, 3:34.715 (142.171 mph).

| Date | Event | Event | Winner | Time | MPH | 2nd Place | Time | MPH |
|---|---|---|---|---|---|---|---|---|
| Apr. 17 | SummitRacing.com Nationals | Top Fuel | Larry Dixon | 4.591 | 326.40 | D. Kalitta | 4.648 | 319.52 |
| | | Funny Car | Whit Bazemore | 4.976 | 315.12 | T. Bartone | 4.983 | 303.23 |
| | | Pro Stock | Dave Connolly | 6.879 | 201.46 | G. Anderson | 6.955 | 200.77 |
| May 1 | Thunder Valley Nationals | Top Fuel | Doug Kalitta | 4.593 | 322.50 | R. Fuller | 4.588 | 327.35 |
| | | Funny Car | Gary Scelzi | 4.815 | 329.26 | J. Arend | 4.971 | 282.42 |
| | | Pro Stock | Warren Johnson | 6.756 | 203.89 | R. Stevens | 6.777 | 203.22 |
| May 15 | Southern Nationals | Top Fuel | Doug Kalitta | 4.567 | 325.69 | D. Baca | 4.851 | 232.39 |
| | | Funny Car | John Force | 4.772 | 325.61 | R. Hight | 4.796 | 323.04 |
| | | Pro Stock | Greg Anderson | 6.781 | 202.61 | J. Line | 6.781 | 203.83 |
| May 22 | Pontiac Performance Nationals | Top Fuel | Tony Schumacher | 4.489 | 336.15 | D. Kalitta | 4.513 | 324.90 |
| | | Funny Car | John Force | 4.776 | 324.51 | G. Scelzi | 4.764 | 326.79 |
| | | Pro Stock | Greg Anderson | 6.737 | 204.35 | K. Johnson | 6.787 | 204.20 |
| May 29 | O'Reilly Summer Nationals | Top Fuel | David Grubnic | 4.600 | 320.28 | L. Dixon | 10.051 | 101.08 |
| | | Funny Car | John Force | 4.809 | 320.97 | T. Johnson Jr. | 8.167 | 107.62 |
| | | Pro Stock | Greg Anderson | 6.768 | 203.65 | D. Connolly | 6.907 | 203.68 |
| June 12 | Carquest Auto Parts Nationals | Top Fuel | Scott Kalitta | 4.518 | 330.15 | R. Fuller | 4.602 | 323.58 |
| | | Funny Car | Gary Scelzi | 4.740 | 330.80 | E. Medlen | 4.805 | 321.73 |
| | | Pro Stock | Jason Line | 6.783 | 203.09 | J. Coughlin | 6.800 | 202.68 |
| June 19 | K&N Filters SuperNationals | Top Fuel | Larry Dixon | 4.533 | 329.91 | D. Grubnic | 6.798 | 135.44 |
| | | Funny Car | Del Worsham | 4.866 | 321.19 | R. Capps | 4.911 | 315.49 |
| | | Pro Stock | Jason Line | 6.692 | 205.98 | W. Johnson | 6.714 | 207.50 |
| June 26 | Sears Craftsman Nationals | Top Fuel | Brandon Bernstein | 4.553 | 324.59 | M. Lucas | 4.793 | 314.31 |
| | | Funny Car | Ron Capps | 4.862 | 321.04 | T. Wilkerson | 7.808 | 112.65 |
| | | Pro Stock | Kurt Johnson | 6.729 | 205.19 | G. Anderson | 6.735 | 204.32 |
| July 17 | Mopar Mile-High Nationals | Top Fuel | Tony Schumacher | 4.617 | 331.45 | M. Lucas | 4.778 | 309.91 |
| | | Funny Car | Robert Hight | 4.897 | 316.60 | P. Burkart | 5.650 | 187.57 |
| | | Pro Stock | Warren Johnson | 7.131 | 193.16 | D. Connolly | 7.928 | 130.78 |
| July 24 | Carquest Auto Parts Nationals | Top Fuel | Brandon Bernstein | 4.527 | 329.99 | T. Schumacher | 6.021 | 154.35 |
| | | Funny Car | Eric Medlen | 4.887 | 310.48 | R. Hight | 4.933 | 305.63 |
| | | Pro Stock | Kurt Johnson | 16.32 | 75.14 | R. Krisher | — | —# |
| July 31 | Fram-Autolite Nationals | Top Fuel | Doug Kalitta | 4.665 | 319.90 | D. Herbert | 4.603 | 319.98 |
| | | Funny Car | Gary Scelzi | 4.984 | 295.21 | R. Capps | 5.079 | 293.60 |
| | | Pro Stock | Greg Anderson | 6.732 | 205.63 | K. Johnson | 6.760 | 204.23 |
| Aug. 14 | Lucas Oil Nationals | Top Fuel | Doug Kalitta | 4.593 | 325.92 | L. Dixon | 6.799 | 119.62 |
| | | Funny Car | Eric Medlen | 4.826 | 315.42 | J. Force | 4.787 | 321.12 |
| | | Pro Stock | Kurt Johnson | 6.726 | 204.57 | G. Stanfield | 6.778 | 203.71 |
| Aug. 21 | O'Reilly Mid-South Nationals | Top Fuel | Rod Fuller | 4.612 | 313.07 | T. Schumacher | 5.747 | 172.41 |
| | | Funny Car | Eric Medlen | 4.911 | 300.13 | R. Capps | 4.985 | 302.35 |
| | | Pro Stock | Greg Anderson | 6.801 | 201.49 | K. Johnson | 6.834 | 201.88 |
| Sept. 5 | Mac Tools U.S. Nationals | Top Fuel | Larry Dixon | 4.521 | 326.71 | T. Schumacher | 8.143 | 107.27 |
| | | Funny Car | Del Worsham | 4.874 | 320.05 | F. Pedregon | 4.904 | 313.07 |
| | | Pro Stock | Greg Anderson | 6.718 | 205.26 | R. Stevens | 6.779 | 203.98 |
| Sept. 18 | Toyo Tires Nationals | Top Fuel | Tony Schumacher | 4.498 | 323.74 | L. Dixon | 4.575 | 322.11 |
| | | Funny Car | Tony Pedregon | 6.349 | 191.02 | J. Force | 8.339 | 125.82 |
| | | Pro Stock | Greg Anderson | 6.721 | 205.19 | J. Yates | 6.771 | 204.57 |
| Oct. 2 | Ameriquest Mortgage Nationals | Top Fuel | Tony Schumacher | 4.535 | 328.94 | D. Herbert | 9.877 | 82.52 |
| | | Funny Car | Ron Capps | 4.760 | 327.82 | T. Pedregon | 7.369 | 138.50 |
| | | Pro Stock | Jason Line | 6.719 | 205.88 | E. Enders | 6.772 | 203.77 |
| Oct. 9 | O'Reilly Fall Nationals | Top Fuel | Tony Schumacher | 4.523 | 331.77 | D. Herbert | 4.629 | 320.05 |
| | | Funny Car | John Force | 4.797 | 324.05 | F. Pedregon | — | —@ |
| | | Pro Stock | Greg Anderson | 6.690 | 206.61 | J. Line | 6.713 | 206.48 |

\# Krisher crashed in the semifinals and did not participate in the finals.
@ Pedregon's car died in the staging area and could not compete.

**Remaining Races** (2): ACDelco Las Vegas Nationals (Oct. 23); Automobile Club of Southern California Finals in Pomona (Nov. 6).

## NHRA POWERade Point Standings (through Oct. 9)

### Top Fuel

| | | Points |
|---|---|---|
| 1 | Tony Schumacher | 1746 |
| 2 | Larry Dixon | 1478 |
| 3 | Doug Kalitta | 1475 |
| 4 | David Grubnic | 1263 |
| 5 | Doug Herbert | 1247 |
| 6 | Morgan Lucas | 1246 |
| 7 | Brandon Bernstein | 1216 |
| 8 | Scott Kalitta | 1039 |
| 9 | Cory McClenathan | 1031 |
| 10 | Rod Fuller | 733 |

### Funny Car

| | | Points |
|---|---|---|
| 1 | John Force | 1396 |
| 2 | Gary Scelzi | 1360 |
| 3 | Ron Capps | 1339 |
| 4 | Robert Hight | 1292 |
| 5 | Eric Medlen | 1263 |
| 6 | Tommy Johnson | 1167 |
| 7 | Whit Bazemore | 1129 |
| 8 | Del Worsham | 1103 |
| 9 | Tony Pedregon | 1089 |
| 10 | Cruz Pedregon | 941 |

### Pro Stock

| | | Points |
|---|---|---|
| 1 | Greg Anderson | 1751 |
| 2 | Kurt Johnson | 1507 |
| 3 | Jason Line | 1466 |
| 4 | Warren Johnson | 1425 |
| 5 | Dave Connolly | 1230 |
| 6 | Ron Krisher | 994 |
| | Greg Stanfield | 994 |
| 8 | Jeg Coughlin | 976 |
| 9 | Richie Stevens | 974 |
| 10 | Jim Yates | 910 |

# 1909-2005
# *Through the Years*

SPORTS ALMANAC

## NASCAR CIRCUIT

### The Crown Jewels
### Daytona 500

Held over 200 laps on 2.5-mile oval at Daytona International Speedway in Daytona Beach, Fla. First race in 1959, although stock car racing at Daytona dates back to 1936. Winners who started from pole position are in **bold** type.

**Multiple winners:** Richard Petty (7); Cale Yarborough (4); Bobby Allison, Jeff Gordon and Dale Jarrett (3); Bill Elliott, Sterling Marlin and Michael Waltrip (2). **Multiple poles:** Buddy Baker and Cale Yarborough (4); Bill Elliott, Dale Jarrett, Fireball Roberts and Ken Schrader (3); Donnie Allison (2).

| Year | Winner | Car | Owner | MPH | Pole Sitter | MPH |
|------|--------|-----|-------|-----|-------------|-----|
| 1959 | Lee Petty | Oldsmobile | Petty Enterprises | 135.521 | Bob Welborn | 140.121 |
| 1960 | Junior Johnson | Chevrolet | Ray Fox | 124.740 | Cotton Owens | 149.892 |
| 1961 | Marvin Panch | Pontiac | Smokey Yunick | 149.601 | Fireball Roberts | 155.709 |
| 1962 | **Fireball Roberts** | Pontiac | Smokey Yunick | 152.529 | Fireball Roberts | 156.999 |
| 1963 | Tiny Lund | Ford | Wood Brothers | 151.566 | Fireball Roberts | 160.943 |
| 1964 | Richard Petty | Plymouth | Petty Enterprises | 154.334 | Paul Goldsmith | 174.910 |
| 1965-a | Fred Lorenzen | Ford | Holman-Moody | 141.539 | Darel Dieringer | 171.151 |
| 1966-b | **Richard Petty** | Plymouth | Petty Enterprises | 160.627 | Richard Petty | 175.165 |
| 1967 | Mario Andretti | Ford | Holman-Moody | 149.926 | Curtis Turner | 180.831 |
| 1968 | **Cale Yarborough** | Mercury | Wood Brothers | 143.251 | Cale Yarborough | 189.222 |
| 1969 | Lee Roy Yarbrough | Ford | Junior Johnson | 157.950 | Buddy Baker | 188.901 |
| 1970 | Pete Hamilton | Plymouth | Petty Enterprises | 149.601 | Cale Yarborough | 194.015 |
| 1971 | Richard Petty | Plymouth | Petty Enterprises | 144.462 | A.J. Foyt | 182.744 |
| 1972 | A.J. Foyt | Mercury | Wood Brothers | 161.550 | Bobby Isaac | 186.632 |
| 1973 | Richard Petty | Dodge | Petty Enterprises | 157.205 | Buddy Baker | 185.662 |
| 1974-c | Richard Petty | Dodge | Petty Enterprises | 140.894 | David Pearson | 185.017 |
| 1975 | Benny Parsons | Chevrolet | L.G. DeWitt | 153.649 | Donnie Allison | 185.827 |
| 1976 | David Pearson | Mercury | Wood Brothers | 152.181 | Ramo Stott | 183.456 |
| 1977 | Cale Yarborough | Chevrolet | Junior Johnson | 153.218 | Donnie Allison | 188.048 |
| 1978 | Bobby Allison | Ford | Bud Moore | 159.730 | Cale Yarborough | 187.536 |
| 1979 | Richard Petty | Oldsmobile | Petty Enterprises | 143.977 | Buddy Baker | 196.049 |
| 1980 | **Buddy Baker** | Oldsmobile | Ranier Racing | 177.602* | Buddy Baker | 194.099 |
| 1981 | Richard Petty | Buick | Petty Enterprises | 169.651 | Bobby Allison | 194.624 |
| 1982 | Bobby Allison | Buick | DiGard Racing | 153.991 | Benny Parsons | 196.317 |
| 1983 | Cale Yarborough | Pontiac | Ranier Racing | 155.979 | Ricky Rudd | 198.864 |
| 1984 | **Cale Yarborough** | Chevrolet | Ranier Racing | 150.994 | Cale Yarborough | 201.848 |
| 1985 | **Bill Elliott** | Ford | Melling Racing | 172.265 | Bill Elliott | 205.114 |
| 1986 | Geoff Bodine | Chevrolet | Hendrick Motorsports | 148.124 | Bill Elliott | 205.039 |
| 1987 | **Bill Elliott** | Ford | Melling Racing | 176.263 | Bill Elliott | 210.364† |
| 1988 | Bobby Allison | Buick | Stavola Brothers | 137.531 | Ken Schrader | 198.823 |
| 1989 | Darrell Waltrip | Chevrolet | Hendrick Motorsports | 148.466 | Ken Schrader | 196.996 |
| 1990 | Derrike Cope | Chevrolet | Bob Whitcomb | 165.761 | Ken Schrader | 196.515 |
| 1991 | Ernie Irvan | Chevrolet | Morgan-McClure | 148.148 | Davey Allison | 195.955 |
| 1992 | Davey Allison | Ford | Robert Yates | 160.256 | Sterling Martin | 192.213 |
| 1993 | Dale Jarrett | Chevrolet | Joe Gibbs Racing | 154.972 | Kyle Petty | 189.426 |
| 1994 | Sterling Marlin | Chevrolet | Morgan-McClure | 156.931 | Loy Allen | 190.158 |
| 1995 | Sterling Marlin | Chevrolet | Morgan-McClure | 141.710 | Dale Jarrett | 193.498 |
| 1996 | Dale Jarrett | Ford | Robert Yates | 154.308 | Dale Earnhardt | 189.510 |
| 1997 | Jeff Gordon | Chevrolet | Rick Hendrick | 148.295 | Mike Skinner | 189.813 |
| 1998 | Dale Earnhardt | Chevrolet | Richard Childress | 172.712 | Bobby Labonte | 192.415 |
| 1999 | **Jeff Gordon** | Chevrolet | Rick Hendrick | 161.551 | Jeff Gordon | 195.067 |
| 2000 | **Dale Jarrett** | Ford | Robert Yates | 155.669 | Dale Jarrett | 191.091 |
| 2001 | Michael Waltrip | Chevrolet | Dale Earnhardt, Inc. | 161.783 | Bill Elliott | 183.565 |
| 2002 | Ward Burton | Dodge | Bill Davis | 142.971 | Jimmie Johnson | 185.831 |
| 2003-d | Michael Waltrip | Chevrolet | Dale Earnhardt, Inc. | 133.870 | Jeff Green | 186.606 |
| 2004 | Dale Earnhardt Jr. | Chevrolet | Dale Earnhardt, Inc. | 156.345 | Greg Biffle | 188.387 |
| 2005 | Jeff Gordon | Chevrolet | Rick Hendrick | 135.173 | Dale Jarrett | 188.312 |

*Track and race record for winning speed. †Track and race record for qualifying speed.

**Notes: a**—rain shortened 1965 race to 332.5 miles; **b**—rain shortened 1966 race to 495 miles; **c**—in 1974, race shortened 50 miles due to energy crisis; **d**—rain shortened 2003 race to 272.5 miles. **Also:** Pole sitters determined by pole qualifying race (1959-65); by two-lap average (1966-68); by fastest single lap (since 1969).

## UAW-Ford 500

Held over 188 laps on 2.66-mile tri-oval at Talladega Superspeedway in Talladega, Ala.

Previously known as Winston 500 (1970-93, 1997-2000), Winston Select 500 (1994-96) and EA Sports 500 (2001-04). It became the UAW-Ford 500 in 2005. Winners who started from pole position are in **bold** type.

**Multiple winners:** Dale Earnhardt (4); Bobby Allison, Davey Allison, Buddy Baker, Dale Earnhardt Jr. and David Pearson (3); Dale Jarrett, Mark Martin, Darrell Waltrip and Cale Yarborough (2).

| Year | | Year | | Year | | Year | |
|------|--|------|--|------|--|------|--|
| 1970 | Pete Hamilton | 1979 | Bobby Allison | 1988 | Phil Parsons | 1997 | Mark Martin |
| 1971 | **Donnie Allison** | 1980 | Buddy Baker | 1989 | Davey Allison | 1998 | Dale Jarrett |
| 1972 | David Pearson | 1981 | **Bobby Allison** | 1990 | **Dale Earnhardt** | 1999 | Dale Earnhardt |
| 1973 | David Pearson | 1982 | Darrell Waltrip | 1991 | Harry Gant | 2000 | Dale Earnhardt |
| 1974 | **David Pearson** | 1983 | Richard Petty | 1992 | Davey Allison | 2001 | Dale Earnhardt Jr. |
| 1975 | **Buddy Baker** | 1984 | **Cale Yarborough** | 1993 | Ernie Irvan | 2002 | Dale Earnhardt Jr. |
| 1976 | Buddy Baker | 1985 | **Bill Elliott** | 1994 | Dale Earnhardt | 2003 | Michael Waltrip |
| 1977 | Darrell Waltrip | 1986 | Bobby Allison | 1995 | **Mark Martin** | 2004 | Dale Earnhardt Jr. |
| 1978 | **Cale Yarborough** | 1987 | Davey Allison | 1996 | Sterling Marlin | 2005 | Dale Jarrett |

## Coca-Cola 600

Held over 400 laps on 1.5-mile oval at Lowe's Motor Speedway in Concord, N.C.

Previously known as World 600 (1960-85). It has been Coca-Cola 600 since 1986 (in 2002, sponsors announced a one-time-only name change to The Coca-Cola Racing Family 600). Winners who started from pole position are in **bold** type.

**Multiple winners:** Darrell Waltrip (5); Bobby Allison, Buddy Baker, Dale Earnhardt, Jeff Gordon, Jimmie Johnson and David Pearson (3); Neil Bonnett, Jeff Burton, Fred Lorenzen, Jim Paschal and Richard Petty (2).

| Year | | Year | | Year | | Year | |
|------|--|------|--|------|--|------|--|
| 1960 | Joe Lee Johnson | 1972 | Buddy Baker | 1984 | Bobby Allison | 1996 | Dale Jarrett |
| 1961 | David Pearson | 1973 | **Buddy Baker** | 1985 | Darrell Waltrip | 1997 | **Jeff Gordon**\* |
| 1962 | Nelson Stacy | 1974 | **David Pearson** | 1986 | Dale Earnhardt | 1998 | **Jeff Gordon** |
| 1963 | Fred Lorenzen | 1975 | Richard Petty | 1987 | Kyle Petty | 1999 | Jeff Burton |
| 1964 | Jim Paschal | 1976 | **David Pearson** | 1988 | Darrell Waltrip | 2000 | Matt Kenseth |
| 1965 | **Fred Lorenzen** | 1977 | Richard Petty | 1989 | Darrell Waltrip | 2001 | Jeff Burton |
| 1966 | Marvin Panch | 1978 | Darrell Waltrip | 1990 | Rusty Wallace | 2002 | Mark Martin |
| 1967 | Jim Paschal | 1979 | Darrell Waltrip | 1991 | Davey Allison | 2003 | Jimmie Johnson\* |
| 1968 | Buddy Baker\* | 1980 | Benny Parsons | 1992 | Dale Earnhardt | 2004 | **Jimmie Johnson** |
| 1969 | Lee Roy Yarbrough | 1981 | Bobby Allison | 1993 | Dale Earnhardt | 2005 | Jimmie Johnson |
| 1970 | Donnie Allison | 1982 | Neil Bonnett | 1994 | **Jeff Gordon** | | |
| 1971 | Bobby Allison | 1983 | Neil Bonnett | 1995 | Bobby Labonte | | |

\* rain-shortened.

## Allstate 400 at the Brickyard

Held over 160 laps at 2.5-mile Indianapolis Motor Speedway in Indianapolis, Ind.

Previously known as Brickyard 400 (1994-2004). Winners who started from pole position are in **bold** type.

**Multiple winners:** Jeff Gordon (4); Dale Jarrett (2).

| Year | | Year | | Year | | Year | | Year | |
|------|--|------|--|------|--|------|--|------|--|
| 1994 | Jeff Gordon | 1997 | Ricky Rudd | 2000 | Bobby Labonte | 2002 | Bill Elliott | 2004 | Jeff Gordon |
| 1995 | Dale Earnhardt | 1998 | Jeff Gordon | 2001 | Jeff Gordon | 2003 | **Kevin Harvick** | 2005 | Tony Stewart |
| 1996 | Dale Jarrett | 1999 | Dale Jarrett | | | | | | |

## Mountain Dew Southern 500

Final race held in 2004. Held over 367 laps on 1.366-mile oval at Darlington International Raceway in Darlington, S.C.

Previously known as Southern 500 (1950-88); Heinz 500 (1989-91); and Pepsi Southern 500 (1998-2000). It was the Mountain Dew Southern 500 from 1992-97, and 2001-04. Winners who started from pole position are in **bold** type.

**Multiple winners:** Jeff Gordon and Cale Yarborough (5); Bobby Allison (4); Buck Baker, Dale Earnhardt, Bill Elliott, David Pearson and Herb Thomas (3); Harry Gant and Fireball Roberts (2).

| Year | | Year | | Year | | Year | |
|------|--|------|--|------|--|------|--|
| 1950 | Johnny Mantz | 1964 | Buck Baker | 1978 | Cale Yarborough | 1992 | Darrell Waltrip\* |
| 1951 | Herb Thomas | 1965 | Ned Jarrett | 1979 | David Pearson | 1993 | Mark Martin\* |
| 1952 | **Fonty Flock** | 1966 | Darel Dieringer | 1980 | Terry Labonte | 1994 | Bill Elliott |
| 1953 | Buck Baker | 1967 | **Richard Petty** | 1981 | Neil Bonnett | 1995 | Jeff Gordon |
| 1954 | Herb Thomas | 1968 | Cale Yarborough | 1982 | Cale Yarborough | 1996 | Jeff Gordon |
| 1955 | Herb Thomas | 1969 | Lee Roy Yarbrough\* | 1983 | Bobby Allison | 1997 | Jeff Gordon\* |
| 1956 | Curtis Turner | 1970 | Buddy Baker | 1984 | **Harry Gant** | 1998 | Jeff Gordon |
| 1957 | Speedy Thompson | 1971 | **Bobby Allison** | 1985 | **Bill Elliott** | 1999 | Jeff Burton\* |
| 1958 | Fireball Roberts | 1972 | **Bobby Allison** | 1986 | **Tim Richmond** | 2000 | Bobby Labonte\* |
| 1959 | Jim Reed | 1973 | Cale Yarborough | 1987 | Dale Earnhardt\* | 2001 | Ward Burton |
| 1960 | Buck Baker | 1974 | Cale Yarborough | 1988 | **Bill Elliott** | 2002 | Jeff Gordon |
| 1961 | Nelson Stacy | 1975 | Bobby Allison | 1989 | Dale Earnhardt | 2003 | Terry Labonte |
| 1962 | Larry Frank | 1976 | **David Pearson** | 1990 | **Dale Earnhardt** | 2004 | Jimmie Johnson |
| 1963 | Fireball Roberts | 1977 | David Pearson | 1991 | Harry Gant | | \* rain-shortened. |

## NASCAR Circuit (Cont.)

### Nextel Cup Series Champions

Originally the Grand National Championship, 1949-70, then the Winston Cup Series Championship, 1971-2003, and based on official NASCAR records. Note that earnings totals include bonus awards.

**Multiple winners:** (drivers) Dale Earnhardt and Richard Petty (7); Jeff Gordon (4); David Pearson, Lee Petty, Darrell Waltrip and Cale Yarborough (3); Buck Baker, Tim Flock, Ned Jarrett, Terry Labonte, Herb Thomas and Joe Weatherly (2).

**Multiple winners:** (cars) Chevrolet (22); Ford (7); Plymouth (5); Dodge, Oldsmobile and Pontiac (4); Buick and Hudson (3); and Chrysler (2).

| Year | Car # | Driver | Car | Owner | Sts | Wins | Poles | Earnings |
|------|-------|--------|-----|-------|-----|------|-------|----------|
| 1949 | 22 | Red Byron | Oldsmobile | Raymond Parks | 5 | 2 | | $5,800 |
| 1950 | 60 | Bill Rexford | Oldsmobile | Julian Buesink | 17 | 1 | 0 | 6,175 |
| 1951 | 92 | Herb Thomas | Hudson | Herb Thomas | 34 | 7 | 4 | 18,200 |
| 1952 | 91 | Tim Flock | Hudson | Ted Chester | 33 | 8 | 4 | 20,210 |
| 1953 | 92 | Herb Thomas | Hudson | Herb Thomas | 37 | 11 | 10 | 27,300 |
| 1954 | 42 | Lee Petty | Chrysler | Herb Thomas | 34 | 7 | 3 | 26,706 |
| 1955 | 300 | Tim Flock | Chrysler | Carl Kiekhaefer | 38 | 18 | 19 | 33,750 |
| 1956 | 300B | Buck Baker | Chevrolet | Carl Kiekhaefer | 48 | 14 | 12 | 29,790 |
| 1957 | 87 | Buck Baker | Chevrolet | Buck Baker | 40 | 10 | 5 | 24,712 |
| 1958 | 42 | Lee Petty | Oldsmobile | Petty Enterprises | 49 | 7 | 4 | 20,600 |
| 1959 | 42 | Lee Petty | Plymouth | Petty Enterprises | 42 | 10 | 2 | 45,570 |
| 1960 | 4 | Rex White | Chevrolet | White-Clements | 40 | 6 | 3 | 45,260 |
| 1961 | 11 | Ned Jarrett | Chevrolet | W.G. Holloway Jr. | 46 | 1 | 4 | 27,285 |
| 1962 | 8 | Joe Weatherly | Pontiac | Bud Moore | 52 | 9 | 6 | 56,110 |
| 1963 | 8 | Joe Weatherly | Mercury | Wood Brothers | 53 | 3 | 6 | 58,110 |
| 1964 | 43 | Richard Petty | Plymouth | Petty Enterprises | 61 | 9 | 8 | 98,810 |
| 1965 | 11 | Ned Jarrett | Ford | Bondy Long | 54 | 13 | 9 | 77,960 |
| 1966 | 6 | David Pearson | Dodge | Cotton Owens | 42 | 14 | 7 | 59,205 |
| 1967 | 43 | Richard Petty | Plymouth | Petty Enterprises | 48 | 27 | 18 | 130,275 |
| 1968 | 17 | David Pearson | Ford | Holman-Moody | 48 | 16 | 12 | 118,842 |
| 1969 | 17 | David Pearson | Ford | Holman-Moody | 51 | 11 | 14 | 183,700 |
| 1970 | 71 | Bobby Isaac | Dodge | Nord Krauskopf | 47 | 11 | 13 | 121,470 |
| 1971 | 43 | Richard Petty | Plymouth | Petty Enterprises | 46 | 21 | 9 | 309,225 |
| 1972 | 43 | Richard Petty | Plymouth | Petty Enterprises | 31 | 8 | 3 | 227,015 |
| 1973 | 72 | Benny Parsons | Chevrolet | L.G. DeWitt | 28 | 1 | 0 | 114,345 |
| 1974 | 43 | Richard Petty | Dodge | Petty Enterprises | 30 | 10 | 7 | 299,175 |
| 1975 | 43 | Richard Petty | Dodge | Petty Enterprises | 30 | 13 | 3 | 378,865 |
| 1976 | 11 | Cale Yarborough | Chevrolet | Junior Johnson | 30 | 9 | 2 | 387,173 |
| 1977 | 11 | Cale Yarborough | Chevrolet | Junior Johnson | 30 | 9 | 3 | 477,499 |
| 1978 | 11 | Cale Yarborough | Oldsmobile | Junior Johnson | 30 | 10 | 8 | 530,751 |
| 1979 | 43 | Richard Petty | Chevrolet | Petty Enterprises | 31 | 5 | 1 | 531,292 |
| 1980 | 2 | Dale Earnhardt | Chevrolet | Rod Osterlund | 31 | 5 | 0 | 588,926 |
| 1981 | 11 | Darrell Waltrip | Buick | Junior Johnson | 31 | 12 | 11 | 693,342 |
| 1982 | 11 | Darrell Waltrip | Buick | Junior Johnson | 30 | 12 | 7 | 873,118 |
| 1983 | 22 | Bobby Allison | Buick | Bill Gardner | 30 | 6 | 0 | 828,355 |
| 1984 | 44 | Terry Labonte | Chevrolet | Billy Hagan | 30 | 2 | 2 | 713,010 |
| 1985 | 11 | Darrell Waltrip | Chevrolet | Junior Johnson | 28 | 3 | 4 | 1,318,735 |
| 1986 | 3 | Dale Earnhardt | Chevrolet | Richard Childress | 29 | 5 | 1 | 1,783,880 |
| 1987 | 3 | Dale Earnhardt | Chevrolet | Richard Childress | 29 | 11 | 1 | 2,099,243 |
| 1988 | 9 | Bill Elliott | Ford | Harry Meling | 29 | 6 | 6 | 1,574,639 |
| 1989 | 27 | Rusty Wallace | Pontiac | Raymond Beadle | 29 | 6 | 4 | 2,247,950 |
| 1990 | 3 | Dale Earnhardt | Chevrolet | Richard Childress | 29 | 9 | 4 | 3,083,056 |
| 1991 | 3 | Dale Earnhardt | Chevrolet | Richard Childress | 29 | 4 | 0 | 2,396,685 |
| 1992 | 7 | Alan Kulwicki | Ford | Alan Kulwicki | 29 | 2 | 6 | 2,322,561 |
| 1993 | 3 | Dale Earnhardt | Chevrolet | Richard Childress | 30 | 6 | 2 | 3,353,789 |
| 1994 | 3 | Dale Earnhardt | Chevrolet | Richard Childress | 31 | 4 | 2 | 3,400,733 |
| 1995 | 24 | Jeff Gordon | Chevrolet | Rick Hendrick | 31 | 7 | 8 | 4,347,343 |
| 1996 | 5 | Terry Labonte | Chevrolet | Rick Hendrick | 31 | 2 | 4 | 4,030,648 |
| 1997 | 24 | Jeff Gordon | Chevrolet | Rick Hendrick | 32 | 10 | 1 | 6,375,658 |
| 1998 | 24 | Jeff Gordon | Chevrolet | Rick Hendrick | 33 | 13 | 7 | 9,306,584 |
| 1999 | 88 | Dale Jarrett | Ford | Robert Yates | 34 | 4 | 0 | 6,649,596 |
| 2000 | 18 | Bobby Labonte | Pontiac | Joe Gibbs | 34 | 4 | 2 | 7,361,387 |
| 2001 | 24 | Jeff Gordon | Chevrolet | Rick Hendrick | 36 | 6 | 6 | 10,879,757 |
| 2002 | 20 | Tony Stewart | Pontiac | Joe Gibbs | 36 | 3 | 2 | 9,163,761 |
| 2003 | 17 | Matt Kenseth | Ford | Mark Martin | 36 | 1 | 0 | 4,038,120 |
| 2004 | 97 | Kurt Busch | Ford | Roush Racing | 36 | 3 | 1 | 4,200,330 |

## NASCAR Rookie of the Year

Sponsored by Raybestos, the official brake of NASCAR, and presented to rookie driver who accumulates the most Nextel Cup Series Raybestos Rookie of the Year points based on their best 17 finishes.

| Year | | Year | | Year | | Year | |
|------|--|------|--|------|--|------|--|
| 1958 | Shorty Rollins | 1960 | David Pearson | 1962 | Tom Cox | 1964 | Doug Cooper |
| 1959 | Richard Petty | 1961 | Woodie Wilson | 1963 | Billy Wade | 1965 | Sam McQuagg |

| Year | | Year | | Year | | Year | |
|---|---|---|---|---|---|---|---|
| 1966 | James Hylton | 1976 | Skip Manning | 1986 | Alan Kulwicki | 1996 | Johnny Benson |
| 1967 | Donnie Allison | 1977 | Ricky Rudd | 1987 | Davey Allison | 1997 | Mike Skinner |
| 1968 | Pete Hamilton | 1978 | Ronnie Thomas | 1988 | Ken Bouchard | 1998 | Kenny Irwin |
| 1969 | Dick Brooks | 1979 | Dale Earnhardt | 1989 | Dick Trickle | 1999 | Tony Stewart |
| 1970 | Bill Dennis | 1980 | Jody Ridley | 1990 | Rob Moroso | 2000 | Matt Kenseth |
| 1971 | Walter Ballard | 1981 | Ron Bouchard | 1991 | Bobby Hamilton | 2001 | Kevin Harvick |
| 1972 | Larry Smith | 1982 | Geoff Bodine | 1992 | Jimmy Hensley | 2002 | Ryan Newman |
| 1973 | Lennie Pond | 1983 | Sterling Marlin | 1993 | Jeff Gordon | 2003 | Jamie McMurray |
| 1974 | Earl Ross | 1984 | Rusty Wallace | 1994 | Jeff Burton | 2004 | Kasey Kahne |
| 1975 | Bruce Hill | 1985 | Ken Schrader | 1995 | Ricky Craven | | |

## All-Time Leaders

NASCAR's all-time Top 20 drivers in victories, pole positions and earnings based on records through Oct. 16, 2005. Drivers active in 2005 are in **bold** type.

### Victories

| | | | | | | | |
|---|---|---|---|---|---|---|---|
| 1 Richard Petty | 200 | 7 Jeff Gordon | 72 | 13 Buck Baker | 46 | **Dale Jarrett** | 32 |
| 2 David Pearson | 105 | 8 Lee Petty | 55 | 14 **Bill Elliott** | 44 | 20 Fred Lorenzen | 26 |
| 3 Bobby Allison | 84 | **Rusty Wallace** | 55 | 15 Tim Flock | 40 | Rex White | 26 |
| Darrell Waltrip | 84 | 10 Ned Jarrett | 50 | 16 Bobby Isaac | 37 | | |
| 5 Cale Yarborough | 83 | Junior Johnson | 50 | 17 **Mark Martin** | 35 | | |
| 6 Dale Earnhardt | 76 | 12 Herb Thomas | 48 | 18 Fireball Roberts | 32 | | |

### Pole Positions

| | | | | | | | |
|---|---|---|---|---|---|---|---|
| 1 Richard Petty | 126 | 6 **Bill Elliott** | 55 | 11 **Mark Martin** | 41 | 16 **Rusty Wallace** | 36 |
| 2 David Pearson | 113 | 7 **Jeff Gordon** | 54 | 12 Buddy Baker | 40 | 17 Ned Jarrett | 35 |
| 3 Cale Yarborough | 70 | 8 Bobby Isaac | 51 | 13 Tim Flock | 39 | Fireball Roberts | 35 |
| 4 Darrell Waltrip | 59 | 9 Junior Johnson | 47 | Herb Thomas | 39 | Rex White | 35 |
| 5 Bobby Allison | 57 | 10 Buck Baker | 44 | 15 **Geoff Bodine** | 37 | 20 Fonty Flock | 34 |

### Earnings (unofficial)

| | | | | | | |
|---|---|---|---|---|---|---|
| 1 **Jeff Gordon** | $69,443,675 | 8 **Tony Stewart** | $38,594,261 | 15 **Ken Schrader** | $27,922,711 |
| 2 **Dale Jarrett** | 50,421,073 | 9 **Jeff Burton** | 38,458,245 | 16 **Jeremy Mayfield** | 25,141,546 |
| 3 **Mark Martin** | 49,251,815 | 10 **Terry Labonte** | 38,283,402 | 17 **Matt Kenseth** | 24,849,821 |
| 4 **Rusty Wallace** | 46,986,703 | 11 **Bill Elliott** | 37,028,201 | 18 Ward Burton | 23,655,764 |
| 5 **Bobby Labonte** | 43,470,789 | 12 **Sterling Marlin** | 35,774,158 | 19 **Kyle Petty** | 23,608,741 |
| 6 Dale Earnhardt | 41,742,384 | 13 **Dale Earnhardt Jr.** | 30,935,852 | 20 **Elliott Sadler** | 22,602,491 |
| 7 **Ricky Rudd** | 39,567,437 | 14 **Michael Waltrip** | 30,587,745 | | |

## CHAMP CAR CIRCUIT

## Champ Car Series Champions

Officially the "Bridgestone Presents The Champ Car World Series Powered by Ford" since 2003. Formerly, AAA (American Automobile Assn., 1909-55), USAC (U.S. Auto Club, 1956-78), CART (Championship Auto Racing Teams, 1979-91). CART was renamed IndyCar in 1992 and then lost use of the name in 1997. It was known as the FedEx Championship Series from 1998-2002.

**Multiple titles:** A.J. Foyt (7); Mario Andretti (4); Jimmy Bryan, Earl Cooper, Ted Horn, Rick Mears, Louie Meyer, Bobby Rahal, Al Unser (3); Tony Bettenhausen, Gil de Ferran, Ralph DePalma, Peter DePaolo, Joe Leonard, Rex Mays, Tommy Milton, Ralph Mulford, Jimmy Murphy, Wilbur Shaw, Al Unser Jr., Bobby Unser, Rodger Ward and Alex Zanardi (2).

### AAA

| Year | | Year | | Year | | Year | |
|---|---|---|---|---|---|---|---|
| 1909 | George Robertson | 1920 | Tommy Milton | 1931 | Louis Schneider | 1942-45 | No racing |
| 1910 | Ray Harroun | 1921 | Tommy Milton | 1932 | Bob Carey | 1946 | Ted Horn |
| 1911 | Ralph Mulford | 1922 | Jimmy Murphy | 1933 | Louie Meyer | 1947 | Ted Horn |
| 1912 | Ralph DePalma | 1923 | Eddie Hearne | 1934 | Bill Cummings | 1948 | Ted Horn |
| 1913 | Earl Cooper | 1924 | Jimmy Murphy | 1935 | Kelly Petillo | 1949 | Johnnie Parsons |
| 1914 | Ralph DePalma | 1925 | Peter DePaolo | 1936 | Mauri Rose | 1950 | Henry Banks |
| 1915 | Earl Cooper | 1926 | Harry Hartz | 1937 | Wilbur Shaw | 1951 | Tony Bettenhausen |
| 1916 | Dario Resta | 1927 | Peter DePaolo | 1938 | Floyd Roberts | 1952 | Chuck Stevenson |
| 1917 | Earl Cooper | 1928 | Louie Meyer | 1939 | Wilbur Shaw | 1953 | Sam Hanks |
| 1918 | Ralph Mulford | 1929 | Louie Meyer | 1940 | Rex Mays | 1954 | Jimmy Bryan |
| 1919 | Howard Wilcox | 1930 | Billy Arnold | 1941 | Rex Mays | 1955 | Bob Sweikert |

### USAC

| Year | | Year | | Year | | Year | |
|---|---|---|---|---|---|---|---|
| 1956 | Jimmy Bryan | 1962 | Rodger Ward | 1968 | Bobby Unser | 1974 | Bobby Unser |
| 1957 | Jimmy Bryan | 1963 | A.J. Foyt | 1969 | Mario Andretti | 1975 | A.J. Foyt |
| 1958 | Tony Bettenhausen | 1964 | A.J. Foyt | 1970 | Al Unser | 1976 | Gordon Johncock |
| 1959 | Rodger Ward | 1965 | Mario Andretti | 1971 | Joe Leonard | 1977 | Tom Sneva |
| 1960 | A.J. Foyt | 1966 | Mario Andretti | 1972 | Joe Leonard | 1978 | A.J. Foyt |
| 1961 | A.J. Foyt | 1967 | A.J. Foyt | 1973 | Roger McCluskey | | |

## CHAMP CAR Circuit (Cont.)
### Champ Car World Series (formerly CART)

| Year | Driver | Car | Team | Sts | Wins | Poles | Earnings |
|------|--------|-----|------|-----|------|-------|----------|
| 1979 | **Rick Mears** | Penske Ford | Penske | 14 | 3 | 2 | $408,078 |
| 1980 | **Johnny Rutherford** | Chaparral Ford | Chaparral | 12 | 5 | 3 | 503,595 |
| 1981 | **Rick Mears** | Penske Ford | Penske | 11 | 6 | 2 | 323,670 |
| 1982 | **Rick Mears** | Penske Ford | Penske | 11 | 4 | 8 | 306,454 |
| 1983 | **Al Unser** | Penske Ford | Penske | 13 | 1 | 0 | 500,109 |
| 1984 | **Mario Andretti** | Lola Ford | Newman/Haas | 16 | 6 | 8 | 931,929 |
| 1985 | **Al Unser** | March Ford | Penske | 14 | 1 | 1 | 843,885 |
| 1986 | **Bobby Rahal** | March Ford | TrueSports | 17 | 6 | 2 | 1,488,049 |
| 1987 | **Bobby Rahal** | Lola Ford | TrueSports | 15 | 3 | 1 | 1,261,098 |
| 1988 | **Danny Sullivan** | Penske Chevrolet | Penske | 15 | 4 | 9 | 1,222,791 |
| 1989 | **Emerson Fittipaldi** | Penske Chevrolet | Patrick | 15 | 5 | 4 | 2,166,078 |
| 1990 | **Al Unser Jr.** | Lola Chevrolet | Galles-Kraco | 16 | 6 | 1 | 1,946,833 |
| 1991 | **Michael Andretti** | Lola Chevrolet | Newman/Haas | 17 | 8 | 8 | 2,461,734 |
| 1992 | **Bobby Rahal** | Lola Chevrolet | Rahal-Hogan | 16 | 4 | 3 | 2,235,298 |
| 1993 | **Nigel Mansell** | Lola Ford | Newman/Haas | 15 | 5 | 7 | 2,526,953 |
| 1994 | **Al Unser Jr.** | Penske Ilmor | Marlboro Team Penske | 16 | 8 | 4 | 3,535,813 |
| 1995 | **Jacques Villeneuve** | Reynard Ford | Team Green | 17 | 4 | 6 | 2,996,269 |
| 1996 | **Jimmy Vasser** | Reynard Honda | Target Chip Ganassi | 16 | 4 | 4 | 3,071,500 |
| 1997 | **Alex Zanardi** | Reynard Honda | Target Chip Ganassi | 16 | 5 | 4 | 2,096,250 |
| 1998 | **Alex Zanardi** | Reynard Honda | Target Chip Ganassi | 19 | 7 | 0 | 2,229,250 |
| 1999 | **Juan Montoya** | Reynard Honda | Target Chip Ganassi | 20 | 7 | 7 | 1,973,000 |
| 2000 | **Gil de Ferran** | Reynard Honda | Marlboro Team Penske | 20 | 2 | 5 | 1,677,000 |
| 2001 | **Gil de Ferran** | Reynard Honda | Marlboro Team Penske | 20 | 2 | 5 | 1,761,500 |
| 2002 | **Cristiano da Matta** | Lola Toyota | Newman/Haas | 19 | 7 | 7 | 2,053,000 |
| 2003 | **Paul Tracy** | Lola Ford-Cosworth | Player's/Forsythe | 18 | 7 | 6 | 1,007,000 |
| 2004 | **Sebastien Bourdais** | Lola Ford-Cosworth | Newman/Haas | 14 | 7 | 8 | 843,500 |

### Champ Car Rookie of the Year

Officially, Jim Trueman Rookie of the Year Award. Named after the late founder of the two-time champion TrueSports Racing Team, it's presented to the rookie who accumulates the most Champ Car Series points among first year drivers.

| Year | | Year | | Year | | Year | |
|------|--|------|--|------|--|------|--|
| 1979 | Bill Alsup | 1986 | Dominic Dobson | 1993 | Nigel Mansell | 2000 | Kenny Brack |
| 1980 | Dennis Firestone | 1987 | Fabrizio Barbazza | 1994 | Jacques Villeneuve | 2001 | Scott Dixon |
| 1981 | Bob Lazier | 1988 | John Jones | 1995 | Gil de Ferran | 2002 | Mario Dominguez |
| 1982 | Bobby Rahal | 1989 | Bernard Jourdain | 1996 | Alex Zanardi | 2003 | Sebastien Bourdais |
| 1983 | Teo Fabi | 1990 | Eddie Cheever | 1997 | Patrick Carpentier | 2004 | A.J. Allmendinger |
| 1984 | Roberto Guerrero | 1991 | Jeff Andretti | 1998 | Tony Kanaan | | |
| 1985 | Arie Luyendyk | 1992 | Stefan Johansson | 1999 | Juan Montoya | | |

## All-Time Champ Car Leaders

Champ Car's all-time Top 20 drivers in victories, pole positions and earnings, based on records through Sept. 24, 2005. Drivers active in 2005 are in **bold** type. Totals include victories, poles and earnings before Champ Car (then CART) was established in 1979. Earnings totals include year-end performance awards. (*) Denotes driver is active, but in Indy Racing League; (†) denotes driver is active, but in Formula One; (**) denotes driver is active, but in NASCAR.

### Victories

| | | | | | |
|--|--|--|--|--|--|
| 1 A.J. Foyt .........67 | 7 **Paul Tracy** ........30 | 12 Ralph DePalma ....24 | 17 Earl Cooper ......20 |
| 2 Mario Andretti ....52 | 8 Rick Mears .......29 | Bobby Rahal .....24 | 18 Jimmy Bryan ......19 |
| 3 Michael Andretti ...42 | 9 Johnny Rutherford ..27 | 14 Tommy Milton .....23 | Jimmy Murphy ....19 |
| 4 Al Unser .........39 | 10 Rodger Ward ......26 | 15 Tony Bettenhausen ..22 | 20 Ralph Mulford ....17 |
| 5 Bobby Unser ......35 | 11 Gordon Johncock ..25 | Emerson Fittipaldi ..22 | Danny Sullivan ....17 |
| 6 Al Unser Jr. ......31 | | | |

### Pole Positions

| | | | | | |
|--|--|--|--|--|--|
| 1 Mario Andretti ....67 | 7 **Paul Tracy** ........25 | 12 Bobby Rahal ......18 | 16 Tony Bettenhausen ..14 |
| 2 A.J. Foyt .........53 | 8 Johnny Rutherford ..23 | **Sebastien** | Don Branson .....14 |
| 3 Bobby Unser ......49 | 9 Gordon Johncock ..20 | **Bourdais** ......18 | Tom Sneva .......14 |
| 4 Rick Mears .......40 | 10 Rex Mays .........19 | 14 Emerson Fittipaldi ..17 | Juan Montoya† .....14 |
| 5 Michael Andretti ...32 | Danny Sullivan ....19 | 15 Gil de Ferran .....16 | 20 Parnelli Jones .....12 |
| 6 Al Unser .........27 | | | |

### Earnings

| | | |
|--|--|--|
| 1 Al Unser Jr. .....$18,828,406 | 8 **Paul Tracy** .....$10,820,770 | 15 Alex Zanardi ......$5,893,750 |
| 2 Michael Andretti ...18,228,119 | 9 Danny Sullivan ......8,884,126 | 19 Christian Fittipaldi ...5,526,166 |
| 3 Bobby Rahal .......16,344,008 | 10 Arie Luyendyk ......7,732,188 | 16 Scott Pruett** .....5,440,144 |
| 4 Emerson Fittipaldi ..14,293,625 | 11 Gil de Ferran ......7,390,703 | 17 A.J. Foyt .........5,357,589 |
| 5 **Jimmy Vasser** ....11,709,249 | 12 Adrian Fernandez** .7,083,015 | 18 Teo Fabi .........5,045,881 |
| 6 Mario Andretti .....11,552,154 | 13 Raul Boesel .......6,971,887 | 20 Dario Franchitti* ....4,935,000 |
| 7 Rick Mears ........11,050,807 | 14 Al Unser ..........6,740,843 | |

## INDY RACING LEAGUE CIRCUIT
### Indianapolis 500

Held every Memorial Day weekend; 200 laps around a 2.5-mile oval at Indianapolis Motor Speedway. First race was held in 1911. The Indy Racing League began in 1996 and made the Indianapolis 500 its cornerstone event. Winning drivers are listed with starting positions. Winners who started from pole position are in **bold** type.

**Multiple wins:** A.J. Foyt, Rick Mears and Al Unser (4); Louis Meyer, Mauri Rose, Johnny Rutherford, Wilbur Shaw and Bobby Unser (3); Helio Castroneves, Emerson Fittipaldi, Gordon Johncock, Arie Luyendyk, Tommy Milton, Al Unser Jr., Bill Vukovich and Rodger Ward (2).

**Multiple poles:** Rick Mears (6); A.J. Foyt and Rex Mays (4); Mario Andretti, Arie Luyendyk, Johnny Rutherford and Tom Sneva (3); Scott Brayton, Bill Cummings, Ralph DePalma, Leon Duray, Parnelli Jones, Jimmy Murphy, Duke Nalon, Eddie Sachs and Bobby Unser (2).

| Year | Winner (Pos.) | Car | MPH | Pole Sitter | MPH |
|---|---|---|---|---|---|
| 1911 | Ray Harroun (28) | Marmon Wasp | 74.602 | Lewis Strang | – |
| 1912 | Joe Dawson (7) | National | 78.719 | Gil Anderson | – |
| 1913 | Jules Goux (7) | Peugeot | 75.933 | Caleb Bragg | – |
| 1914 | Rene Thomas (15) | Delage | 82.474 | Jean Chassagne | – |
| 1915 | Ralph DePalma (2) | Mercedes | 89.840 | Howard Wilcox | 98.90 |
| 1916-a | Dario Resta (4) | Peugeot | 84.001 | John Aitken | 96.69 |
| 1917-18 | Not held | World War I | | | |
| 1919 | Howdy Wilcox (2) | Peugeot | 88.050 | Rene Thomas | 104.78 |
| 1920 | Gaston Chevrolet (6) | Monroe | 88.618 | Ralph DePalma | 99.15 |
| 1921 | Tommy Milton (20) | Frontenac | 89.621 | Ralph DePalma | 100.75 |
| 1922 | **Jimmy Murphy** (1) | Murphy Special | 94.484 | Jimmy Murphy | 100.50 |
| 1923 | **Tommy Milton** (1) | H.C.S. Special | 90.954 | Tommy Milton | 108.17 |
| 1924 | L.L. Corum | | | | |
| | & Joe Boyer (21) | Duesenberg Special | 98.234 | Jimmy Murphy | 108.037 |
| 1925 | Peter DePaolo (2) | Duesenberg Special | 101.127 | Leon Duray | 113.196 |
| 1926-b | Frank Lockhart (20) | Miller Special | 95.904 | Earl Cooper | 111.735 |
| 1927 | George Souders (22) | Duesenberg | 97.545 | Frank Lockhart | 120.100 |
| 1928 | Louie Meyer (13) | Miller Special | 99.482 | Leon Duray | 122.391 |
| 1929 | Ray Keech (6) | Simplex Piston Ring Special | 97.585 | Cliff Woodbury | 120.599 |
| 1930 | **Billy Arnold** (1) | Miller-Hartz Special | 100.448 | Billy Arnold | 113.268 |
| 1931 | Louis Schneider (13) | Bowes Seal Fast Special | 96.629 | Russ Snowberger | 112.796 |
| 1932 | Fred Frame (27) | Miller-Hartz Special | 104.144 | Lou Moore | 117.363 |
| 1933 | Louie Meyer (6) | Tydol Special | 104.162 | Bill Cummings | 118.530 |
| 1934 | Bill Cummings (10) | Boyle Products Special | 104.863 | Kelly Petillo | 119.329 |
| 1935 | Kelly Petillo (22) | Gilmore Speedway Special | 106.240 | Rex Mays | 120.736 |
| 1936 | Louie Meyer (28) | Ring Free Special | 109.069 | Rex Mays | 119.644 |
| 1937 | Wilbur Shaw (2) | Shaw-Gilmore Special | 113.580 | Bill Cummings | 123.343 |
| 1938 | **Floyd Roberts** (1) | Burd Piston Ring Special | 117.200 | Floyd Roberts | 125.681 |
| 1939 | Wilbur Shaw (3) | Boyle Special | 115.035 | Jimmy Snyder | 130.138 |
| 1940 | Wilbur Shaw (2) | Boyle Special | 114.277 | Rex Mays | 127.850 |
| 1941 | Floyd Davis | | | | |
| | & Mauri Rose (17) | Noc-Out Hose Clamp Special | 115.117 | Mauri Rose | 128.691 |
| 1942-45 | Not held | World War II | | | |
| 1946 | George Robson (15) | Thorne Engineering Special | 114.820 | Cliff Bergere | 126.471 |
| 1947 | Mauri Rose (3) | Blue Crown Spark Plug Special | 116.338 | Ted Horn | 126.564 |
| 1948 | Mauri Rose (3) | Blue Crown Spark Plug Special | 119.814 | Rex Mays | 130.577 |
| 1949 | Bill Holland (4) | Blue Crown Spark Plug Special | 121.327 | Duke Nalon | 132.939 |
| 1950-c | Johnnie Parsons (5) | Wynn's Friction Proofing | 124.002 | Walt Faulkner | 134.343 |
| 1951 | Lee Wallard (2) | Belanger Special | 126.244 | Duke Nalon | 136.498 |
| 1952 | Troy Ruttman (7) | Agajanian Special | 128.922 | Fred Agabashian | 138.010 |
| 1953 | **Bill Vukovich** (1) | Fuel Injection Special | 128.740 | Bill Vukovich | 138.392 |
| 1954 | Bill Vukovich (19) | Fuel Injection Special | 130.840 | Jack McGrath | 141.033 |
| 1955 | Bob Sweikert (14) | John Zink Special | 128.213 | Jerry Hoyt | 140.045 |
| 1956 | **Pat Flaherty** (1) | John Zink Special | 128.490 | Pat Flaherty | 145.596 |
| 1957 | Sam Hanks (13) | Belond Exhaust Special | 135.601 | Pat O'Connor | 143.948 |
| 1958 | Jimmy Bryan (7) | Belond AP Parts Special | 133.791 | Dick Rathmann | 145.974 |
| 1959 | Rodger Ward (6) | Leader Card 500 Roadster | 135.857 | Johnny Thomson | 145.908 |
| 1960 | Jim Rathmann (2) | Ken-Paul Special | 138.767 | Eddie Sachs | 146.592 |
| 1961 | A.J. Foyt (7) | Bowes Seal Fast Special | 139.130 | Eddie Sachs | 147.481 |
| 1962 | Rodger Ward (2) | Leader Card 500 Roadster | 140.293 | Parnelli Jones | 150.370 |
| 1963 | **Parnelli Jones** (1) | Agajanian-Willard Special | 143.137 | Parnelli Jones | 151.153 |
| 1964 | A.J. Foyt (5) | Sheraton-Thompson Special | 147.350 | Jim Clark | 158.828 |
| 1965 | Jim Clark (2) | Lotus Ford | 150.686 | A.J. Foyt | 161.233 |
| 1966 | Graham Hill (15) | American Red Ball Special | 144.317 | Mario Andretti | 165.899 |
| 1967-d | A.J. Foyt (4) | Sheraton-Thompson Special | 151.207 | Mario Andretti | 168.982 |
| 1968 | Bobby Unser (3) | Rislone Special | 152.882 | Joe Leonard | 171.559 |
| 1969 | Mario Andretti (2) | STP Oil Treatment Special | 156.867 | A.J. Foyt | 170.568 |
| 1970 | **Al Unser** (1) | Johnny Lightning Special | 155.749 | Al Unser | 170.221 |

## Indy Racing League Circuit (Cont.)

| Year | Winner (Pos.) | Car | MPH | Pole Sitter | MPH |
|------|---------------|-----|-----|-------------|-----|
| 1971 | Al Unser (5) | Johnny Lightning Special | 157.735 | Peter Revson | 178.696 |
| 1972 | Mark Donohue (3) | Sunoco McLaren | 162.962 | Bobby Unser | 195.940 |
| 1973-e | Gordon Johncock (11) | STP Double Oil Filters | 159.036 | Johnny Rutherford | 198.413 |
| 1974 | Johnny Rutherford (25) | McLaren | 158.589 | A.J. Foyt | 191.632 |
| 1975-f | Bobby Unser (3) | Jorgensen Eagle | 149.213 | A.J. Foyt | 193.976 |
| 1976-g | **Johnny Rutherford** (1) | Hy-Gain McLaren/Goodyear | 148.725 | Johnny Rutherford | 188.957 |
| 1977 | A.J. Foyt (4) | Gilmore Racing Team | 161.331 | Tom Sneva | 198.884 |
| 1978 | Al Unser (5) | FNCTC Chaparral Lola | 161.363 | Tom Sneva | 202.156 |
| 1979 | **Rick Mears** (1) | The Gould Charge | 158.899 | Rick Mears | 193.736 |
| 1980 | **Johnny Rutherford** (1) | Pennzoil Chaparral | 142.862 | Johnny Rutherford | 192.256 |
| 1981-h | **Bobby Unser** (1) | Norton Spirit Penske PC-9B | 139.084 | Bobby Unser | 200.546 |
| 1982 | Gordon Johncock (5) | STP Oil Treatment | 162.029 | Rick Mears | 207.004 |
| 1983 | Tom Sneva (4) | Texaco Star | 162.117 | Teo Fabi | 207.395 |
| 1984 | Rick Mears (3) | Pennzoil Z-7 | 163.612 | Tom Sneva | 210.029 |
| 1985 | Danny Sullivan (8) | Miller American Special | 152.982 | Pancho Carter | 212.583 |
| 1986 | Bobby Rahal (4) | Budweiser/Truesports/March | 170.722 | Rick Mears | 216.828 |
| 1987 | Al Unser (20) | Cummins Holset Turbo | 162.175 | Mario Andretti | 215.390 |
| 1988 | **Rick Mears** (1) | Pennzoil Z-7/Penske Chevy V-8 | 144.809 | Rick Mears | 219.198 |
| 1989 | Emerson Fittipaldi (3) | Marlboro/Penske Chevy V-8 | 167.581 | Rick Mears | 223.885 |
| 1990 | Arie Luyendyk (3) | Domino's Pizza Chevrolet | 185.981* | Emerson Fittipaldi | 225.301 |
| 1991 | **Rick Mears** (1) | Marlboro Penske Chevy | 176.457 | Rick Mears | 224.113 |
| 1992 | Al Unser Jr. (12) | Valvoline Galmer '92 | 134.477 | Roberto Guerrero | 232.482 |
| 1993 | Emerson Fittipaldi (9) | Marlboro Penske Chevy | 157.207 | Arie Luyendyk | 223.967 |
| 1994 | **Al Unser Jr.** (1) | Marlboro Penske Mercedes | 160.872 | Al Unser Jr. | 228.011 |
| 1995 | Jacques Villeneuve (5) | Player's Ltd. Reynard Ford | 153.616 | Scott Brayton | 231.604 |
| 1996 | Buddy Lazier (5) | Reynard Ford | 147.956 | Tony Stewart | 233.100& |
| 1997 | **Arie Luyendyk** (1) | G-Force Olds Aurora | 145.827 | Arie Luyendyk | 218.263 |
| 1998 | Eddie Cheever Jr. (17) | Dallara Olds Aurora | 145.155 | Billy Boat | 223.503 |
| 1999 | Kenny Brack (8) | Dallara Olds Aurora | 153.176 | Arie Luyendyk | 225.179 |
| 2000 | Juan Montoya (2) | G-Force Olds Aurora | 167.607 | Greg Ray | 223.471 |
| 2001 | Helio Castroneves (11) | Dallara Olds Aurora | 153.601 | Scott Sharp | 226.037 |
| 2002-i | Helio Castroneves (13) | Dallara Chevrolet | 166.499 | Bruno Junqueira | 231.342 |
| 2003 | Gil de Ferran (10) | G-Force Toyota | 156.291 | Helio Castroneves | 231.725 |
| 2004-j | **Buddy Rice** (1) | G-Force Honda | 138.518 | Buddy Rice | 222.024 |
| 2005 | Dan Wheldon (16) | Dallara Honda | 157.603 | Tony Kanaan | 227.566 |

*Track record for winning time.

& Scott Brayton won the pole position with an avg. mph of 233.718 but was killed in a practice run. Stewart was awarded pole position with the next fastest speed.

**Notes: a**—1916 race scheduled for 300 miles; **b**—rain shortened 1926 race to 400 miles; **c**—rain shortened 1950 race to 345 miles; **d**—1967 race postponed due to rain after 18 laps (May 30), resumed next day (May 31); **e**—rain shortened 1973 race to 332.5 miles; **f**—rain shortened 1975 race to 435 miles; **g**—rain shortened 1976 race to 255 miles; **h**—in 1981, runner-up Mario Andretti was awarded 1st place when winner Bobby Unser was penalized a lap after the race was completed for passing cars illegally under the caution flag. Unser and car-owner Roger Penske appealed the race stewards' decision to the U.S. Auto Club. Four months later, USAC overturned the ruling, saying that the penalty was too harsh and Unser should be fined $40,000 rather than stripped of his championship; **i**—Team Green, runner-up Paul Tracy's team, appealed Castroneves' victory, citing video evidence and driver testimonials that proved Tracy passed Castroneves moments before the caution flag on lap 199. The IRL denied the appeal the following day; **j**—rain shortened 2004 race to 450 miles.

## Indy 500 Rookie of the Year

Officially the JP Morgan Chase Rookie of the Year Award and voted on by a panel of auto racing media. Award does not necessarily go to highest-finishing first-year driver. Graham Hill won the race on his first try in 1966, but the rookie award went to Jackie Stewart, who led with 10 laps to go only to lose oil pressure and finish 6th.

**Father and son winners:** Mario and Michael Andretti (1965 and 1984); Bill and Billy Vukovich III (1968 and 1988).

| Year | | Year | | Year | | Year | |
|------|--|------|--|------|--|------|--|
| 1952 | Art Cross | 1966 | Jackie Stewart | 1980 | Tim Richmond | 1993 | Nigel Mansell |
| 1953 | Jimmy Daywalt | 1967 | Denis Hulme | 1981 | Josele Garza | 1994 | Jacques Villeneuve |
| 1954 | Larry Crockett | 1968 | Bill Vukovich | 1982 | Jim Hickman | 1995 | Christian Fittipaldi |
| 1955 | Al Herman | 1969 | Mark Donohue | 1983 | Teo Fabi | 1996 | Tony Stewart |
| 1956 | Bob Veith | 1970 | Donnie Allison | 1984 | Michael Andretti | 1997 | Jeff Ward |
| 1957 | Don Edmunds | 1971 | Denny Zimmerman | | & Roberto Guerrero | 1998 | Steve Knapp |
| 1958 | George Amick | 1972 | Mike Hiss | 1985 | Arie Luyendyk | 1999 | Robby McGehee |
| 1959 | Bobby Grim | 1973 | Graham McRae | 1986 | Randy Lanier | 2000 | Juan Montoya |
| 1960 | Jim Hurtubise | 1974 | Pancho Carter | 1987 | Fabrizio Barbazza | 2001 | Helio Castroneves |
| 1961 | Parnelli Jones | 1975 | Bill Puterbaugh | 1988 | Billy Vukovich III | 2002 | Alex Barron |
| | & Bobby Marshman | 1976 | Vern Schuppan | 1989 | Bernard Jourdain | | & Tomas Scheckter |
| 1962 | Jimmy McElreath | 1977 | Jerry Sneva | | & Scott Pruett | 2003 | Tora Takagi |
| 1963 | Jim Clark | 1978 | Rick Mears | 1990 | Eddie Cheever | 2004 | Kosuke Matsuura |
| 1964 | Johnny White | | & Larry Rice | 1991 | Jeff Andretti | 2005 | Danica Patrick |
| 1965 | Mario Andretti | 1979 | Howdy Holmes | 1992 | Lyn St. James | | |

## IRL IndyCar Series Champions

The Indy Racing League (IRL) split from the open-wheel CART series in 1994. Led by Indianapolis Motor Speedway President Tony George, the league's inaugural three-race series began in January 1996 and ended with the league's keystone event—the Indianapolis 500. Past series' sponsors include Pep Boys (1998-99) and Northern Light Technology, Inc., an Internet search engine (2000-01). **Multiple winner:** Sam Hornish Jr. (2).

| Year | Driver | Car | Team | Sts | Wins | Poles | Earnings |
|------|--------|-----|------|-----|------|-------|----------|
| 1996 | **Buzz Calkins** | Reynard Ford | A.J. Foyt Enterprises | 3 | 1 | 0 | $345,553 |
|      | **Scott Sharp** | Lola Ford | A.J. Foyt Enterprises | 3 | 0 | 0 | 330,303 |
| 1997 | **Tony Stewart** | Dallara Oldsmobile | Team Menard | 10 | 1 | 4 | 1,142,450 |
| 1998 | **Kenny Brack** | Dallara Oldsmobile | A.J. Foyt Enterprises | 11 | 3 | 0 | 2,106,700 |
| 1999 | **Greg Ray** | Dallara Oldsmobile | Team Menard | 10 | 3 | 4 | 2,061,800 |
| 2000 | **Buddy Lazier** | Dallara Oldsmobile | Hemelgarn Racing | 9 | 2 | 1 | 2,176,200 |
| 2001 | **Sam Hornish Jr.** | Dallara Oldsmobile | Panther Racing | 13 | 3 | 0 | 2,477,025 |
| 2002 | **Sam Hornish Jr.** | Dallara Oldsmobile | Panther Racing | 15 | 5 | 2 | 2,470,615 |
| 2003 | **Scott Dixon** | G-Force Toyota | Target Chip Ganassi | 16 | 3 | 5 | 1,481,265 |
| 2004 | **Tony Kanaan** | Dallara Honda | Andretti Green Racing | 16 | 3 | 2 | 1,912,990 |
| 2005 | **Dan Wheldon** | Dallara Honda | Andretti Green Racing | 17 | 6 | 0 | 2,711,005 |

**Note:** In 1996, Calkins and Sharp were named co-champions after finishing the series tied in drivers' points (246).

## IRL Rookie of the Year

Officially the Bombardier Rookie of the Year Award, presented to rookie driver who accumulates the most points in the IRL standings.

| Year | | Year | | Year | | Year | |
|------|--|------|--|------|--|------|--|
| 1996 | None | 1999 | Scott Harrington | 2002 | Laurent Redon | 2004 | Kosuke Matsuura |
| 1997 | Jim Guthrie | 2000 | Airton Dare | 2003 | Dan Wheldon | 2005 | Danica Patrick |
| 1998 | Robby Unser | 2001 | Felipe Giaffone | | | | |

## All-Time IRL Leaders

IRL IndyCar Series all-time Top 10 drivers in victories, pole positions and earnings, based on records through Oct. 3, 2004. Earnings totals include season-ending contingency awards. Drivers active in 2004 are in **bold** type. (*) Denotes driver is active, but in NASCAR Nextel Cup Series.

### Victories

1  **Sam Hornish Jr.** . . . . . . .14
2  **Scott Sharp** . . . . . . . . . .9
   **Dan Wheldon** . . . . . . . . .9
4  **Buddy Lazier** . . . . . . . . . .8
5  **Helio Castroneves** . . . . .7
6  **Tony Kanaan** . . . . . . . . .6
7  Eddie Cheever Jr. . . . . . . .5
   Greg Ray . . . . . . . . . . . .5
   Gil de Ferran . . . . . . . . . .5
10 Four tied with 4 wins each.

### Pole Positions

1  Greg Ray . . . . . . . . . . . . .13
2  **Helio Castroneves** . . . . . .11
3  Billy Boat . . . . . . . . . . . . .9
4  **Tomas Scheckter** . . . . . . .8
   **Sam Hornish Jr.** . . . . . . . .8
5  Tony Stewart* . . . . . . . . . .7
6  **Tony Kanaan** . . . . . . . . . .6
7  **Scott Sharp** . . . . . . . . . . .5
   Gil de Ferran . . . . . . . . . . .5
   **Scott Dixon** . . . . . . . . . . .5
   **Buddy Rice** . . . . . . . . . . .5

### Earnings

1  **Buddy Lazier** . . . .$9,624,804
2  **Sam Hornish Jr.** . .9,267,100
3  **Scott Sharp** . . . . . .8,181,853
4  **Helio Castroneves** .8,048,050
5  Eddie Cheever Jr. . . .6,265,893
6  Greg Ray . . . . . . . . .6,250,690
7  **Kenny Brack** . . . . .5,983,575
8  **Tony Kanaan** . . . . .5,235,525
9  **Dan Wheldon** . . . .5,204,410
10 Robbie Buhl . . . . . . .5,095,158

## FORMULA ONE CIRCUIT

### United States Grand Prix

Federation Internationale Sportive Automobile (FISA) sanctioned two annual U.S. Grand Prix–USA/East and USA/West–from 1976-80 and 1983-84. Phoenix was the site of the U.S. Grand Prix from 1989-91. Indianapolis Motor Speedway has hosted the U.S. Grand Prix since 2000.

### Indianapolis 500

Officially sanctioned as Grand Prix race from 1950-60 only. See page 895 for details.

### U.S. Grand Prix—East

Held from 1959-80 and 1981-88 at the following locations: Sebring, Fla. (1959); Riverside, Calif. (1960); Watkins Glen, N.Y. (1961-80); and Detroit (1982-88). There was no race in 1981. Race discontinued in 1989.

**Multiple winners:** Jim Clark, Graham Hill and Ayrton Senna (3); James Hunt, Carlos Reutemann and Jackie Stewart (2).

| Year | | Car | Year | | Car |
|------|--|-----|------|--|-----|
| 1959 | Bruce McLaren, NZE | Cooper Climax | 1974 | Carlos Reutemann, ARG | Brabham Ford |
| 1960 | Stirling Moss, GBR | Lotus Climax | 1975 | Niki Lauda, AUT | Ferrari |
| 1961 | Innes Ireland, GBR | Lotus Climax | 1976 | James Hunt, GBR | McLaren Ford |
| 1962 | Jim Clark, GBR | Lotus Climax | 1977 | James Hunt, GBR | McLaren Ford |
| 1963 | Graham Hill, GBR | BRM | 1978 | Carlos Reutemann, ARG | Ferrari |
| 1964 | Graham Hill, GBR | BRM | 1979 | Gilles Villeneuve, CAN | Ferrari |
| 1965 | Graham Hill, GBR | BRM | 1980 | Alan Jones, AUS | Williams Ford |
| 1966 | Jim Clark, GBR | Lotus BRM | 1981 | Not held | |
| 1967 | Jim Clark, GBR | Lotus Ford | 1982 | John Watson, GBR | McLaren Ford |
| 1968 | Jackie Stewart, GBR | Matra Ford | 1983 | Michele Alboreto, ITA | Tyrrell Ford |
| 1969 | Jochen Rindt, AUT | Lotus Ford | 1984 | Nelson Piquet, BRA | Brabham BMW Turbo |
| 1970 | Emerson Fittipaldi, BRA | Lotus Ford | 1985 | Keke Rosberg, FIN | Williams Honda Turbo |
| 1971 | Francois Cevert, FRA | Tyrrell Ford | 1986 | Ayrton Senna, BRA | Lotus Renault Turbo |
| 1972 | Jackie Stewart, GBR | Tyrrell Ford | 1987 | Ayrton Senna, BRA | Lotus Honda Turbo |
| 1973 | Ronnie Peterson, SWE | Lotus Ford | 1988 | Ayrton Senna, BRA | McLaren Honda Turbo |

## Formula One Circuit (Cont.)
### U.S. Grand Prix—West

Held from 1976-83 at Long Beach, Calif. Races also held in Las Vegas (1981-82), Dallas (1984) and Phoenix (1989-91). Race discontinued in 1992.

**Multiple winners:** Alan Jones and Ayrton Senna (2).

| Year | | Car | Year | | Car |
|------|--|-----|------|--|-----|
| 1976 | Clay Regazzoni, SWI | Ferrari | 1983 | John Watson, GBR | McLaren Ford |
| 1977 | Mario Andretti, USA | Lotus Ford | 1984 | Keke Rosberg, FIN | Williams Honda Turbo |
| 1978 | Carlos Reutemann, ARG | Ferrari | 1985-88 Not held | | |
| 1979 | Gilles Villeneuve, CAN | Ferrari | 1989 | Alain Prost, FRA | McLaren Honda |
| 1980 | Nelson Piquet, BRA | Brabham Ford | 1990 | Ayrton Senna, BRA | McLaren Honda |
| 1981 | Alan Jones, AUS | Williams Ford | 1991 | Ayrton Senna, BRA | McLaren Honda |
| 1982 | Niki Lauda, AUT | McLaren Ford | | | |

### U.S. Grand Prix
Held since 2000 at Indianapolis Motor Speedway.

**Multiple winner:** Michael Schumacher (4).

| Year | | Car | Year | | Car |
|------|--|-----|------|--|-----|
| 2000 | Michael Schumacher, GER | Ferrari | 2003 | Michael Schumacher, GER | Ferrari |
| 2001 | Mika Hakkinen, FIN | McLaren Mercedes | 2004 | Michael Schumacher, GER | Ferrari |
| 2002 | Rubens Barrichello, BRA | Ferrari | 2005 | Michael Schumacher, GER | Ferrari |

## World Champions

Officially called the World Championship of Drivers and based on Formula One (Grand Prix) records through the 2005 season.

**Multiple winners:** Michael Schumacher (7); Juan-Manuel Fangio (5); Alain Prost (4); Jack Brabham, Niki Lauda, Nelson Piquet, Ayrton Senna and Jackie Stewart (3); Alberto Ascari, Jim Clark, Emerson Fittipaldi, Mika Hakkinen and Graham Hill (2).

| Year | Driver | Country | Car | Sts | Wins | Poles | Runner(s)-up |
|------|--------|---------|-----|-----|------|-------|--------------|
| 1950 | **Guiseppe Farina** | Italy | Alfa Romeo | 7 | 3 | 2 | J.M. Fangio, ARG |
| 1951 | **Juan-Manuel Fangio** | Argentina | Alfa Romeo | 8 | 3 | 4 | A. Ascari, ITA |
| 1952 | **Alberto Ascari** | Italy | Ferrari | 8 | 6 | 5 | G. Farina, ITA |
| 1953 | **Alberto Ascari** | Italy | Ferrari | 9 | 5 | 6 | J.M. Fangio, ARG |
| 1954 | **Juan-Manuel Fangio** | Argentina | Maserati/Mercedes | 9 | 6 | 5 | F. Gonzalez, ARG |
| 1955 | **Juan-Manuel Fangio** | Argentina | Mercedes | 7 | 4 | 5 | S. Moss, GBR |
| 1956 | **Juan-Manuel Fangio** | Argentina | Lancia/Ferrari | 8 | 3 | 5 | S. Moss, GBR |
| 1957 | **Juan-Manuel Fangio** | Argentina | Maserati | 8 | 4 | 4 | S. Moss, GBR |
| 1958 | **Mike Hawthorn** | Great Britain | Ferrari | 11 | 1 | 4 | S. Moss, GBR |
| 1959 | **Jack Brabham** | Australia | Cooper Climax | 9 | 2 | 1 | T. Brooks, GBR |
| 1960 | **Jack Brabham** | Australia | Cooper Climax | 10 | 5 | 3 | B. McLaren, NZE |
| 1961 | **Phil Hill** | United States | Ferrari | 8 | 2 | 5 | W. von Trips, GER |
| 1962 | **Graham Hill** | Great Britain | BRM | 9 | 4 | 1 | J. Clark, GBR |
| 1963 | **Jim Clark** | Great Britain | Lotus Climax | 10 | 7 | 7 | G. Hill, GBR & R. Ginther, USA |
| 1964 | **John Surtees** | Great Britain | Ferrari | 10 | 2 | 2 | G. Hill, GBR |
| 1965 | **Jim Clark** | Great Britain | Lotus Climax | 10 | 6 | 6 | G. Hill, GBR |
| 1966 | **Jack Brabham** | Australia | Brabham Repco | 9 | 4 | 3 | J. Surtees, GBR |
| 1967 | **Denis Hulme** | New Zealand | Brabham Repco | 11 | 2 | 0 | J. Brabham, AUS |
| 1968 | **Graham Hill** | Great Britain | Lotus Ford | 12 | 3 | 2 | J. Stewart, GBR |
| 1969 | **Jackie Stewart** | Great Britain | Matra Ford | 11 | 6 | 2 | J. Ickx, BEL |
| 1970 | **Jochen Rindt** | Austria | Lotus Ford | 13 | 5 | 3 | J. Ickx, BEL |
| 1971 | **Jackie Stewart** | Great Britain | Tyrrell Ford | 11 | 6 | 6 | R. Peterson, SWE |
| 1972 | **Emerson Fittipaldi** | Brazil | Lotus Ford | 12 | 5 | 3 | J. Stewart, GBR |
| 1973 | **Jackie Stewart** | Great Britain | Tyrrell Ford | 15 | 5 | 3 | E. Fittipaldi, BRA |
| 1974 | **Emerson Fittipaldi** | Brazil | McLaren Ford | 15 | 3 | 2 | C. Regazzoni, SWI |
| 1975 | **Niki Lauda** | Austria | Ferrari | 14 | 5 | 9 | E. Fittipaldi, BRA |
| 1976 | **James Hunt** | Great Britain | McLaren Ford | 16 | 6 | 8 | N. Lauda, AUT |
| 1977 | **Niki Lauda** | Austria | Ferrari | 17 | 3 | 2 | J. Scheckter, RSA |
| 1978 | **Mario Andretti** | United States | Lotus Ford | 16 | 6 | 8 | R. Peterson, SWE |
| 1979 | **Jody Scheckter** | South Africa | Ferrari | 15 | 3 | 1 | G. Villeneuve, CAN |
| 1980 | **Alan Jones** | Australia | Williams Ford | 14 | 5 | 3 | N. Piquet, BRA |
| 1981 | **Nelson Piquet** | Brazil | Brabham Ford | 15 | 3 | 4 | C. Reutemann, ARG |
| 1982 | **Keke Rosberg** | Finland | Williams Ford | 16 | 1 | 1 | D. Pironi, FRA & J. Watson, GBR |
| 1983 | **Nelson Piquet** | Brazil | Brabham BMW Turbo | 15 | 3 | 1 | A. Prost, FRA |
| 1984 | **Niki Lauda** | Austria | McL. TAG Turbo | 16 | 5 | 0 | A. Prost, FRA |
| 1985 | **Alain Prost** | France | McL. TAG Turbo | 16 | 5 | 2 | M. Alboreto, ITA |
| 1986 | **Alain Prost** | France | McL. TAG Turbo | 16 | 4 | 1 | N. Mansell, GBR |
| 1987 | **Nelson Piquet** | Brazil | Williams Honda Turbo | 16 | 3 | 4 | N. Mansell, GBR |
| 1988 | **Ayrton Senna** | Brazil | McLaren Honda Turbo | 16 | 8 | 13 | A. Prost, FRA |

| Year | Driver | Country | Car | Sts | Wins | Poles | Runner(s)-up |
|------|--------|---------|-----|-----|------|-------|--------------|
| 1989 | **Alain Prost** | France | McLaren Honda | 16 | 4 | 2 | A. Senna, BRA |
| 1990 | **Ayrton Senna** | Brazil | McLaren Honda | 16 | 6 | 10 | A. Prost, FRA |
| 1991 | **Ayrton Senna** | Brazil | McLaren Honda | 16 | 7 | 8 | N. Mansell, GBR |
| 1992 | **Nigel Mansell** | Great Britain | Williams Renault | 16 | 9 | 14 | R. Patrese, ITA |
| 1993 | **Alain Prost** | France | Williams Renault | 16 | 7 | 13 | A. Senna, BRA |
| 1994 | **Michael Schumacher** | Germany | Benetton Ford | 14 | 8 | 6 | D. Hill, GBR |
| 1995 | **Michael Schumacher** | Germany | Benetton Renault | 17 | 9 | 4 | D. Hill, GBR |
| 1996 | **Damon Hill** | Great Britain | Williams Renault | 16 | 8 | 9 | J. Villeneuve, CAN |
| 1997 | **Jacques Villeneuve** | Canada | Williams Renault | 17 | 7 | 10 | H.H. Frentzen, GER |
| 1998 | **Mika Hakkinen** | Finland | McLaren Mercedes | 16 | 8 | 9 | M. Schumacher, GER |
| 1999 | **Mika Hakkinen** | Finland | McLaren Mercedes | 16 | 5 | 11 | E. Irvine, GBR |
| 2000 | **Michael Schumacher** | Germany | Ferrari | 17 | 9 | 9 | M. Hakkinen, FIN |
| 2001 | **Michael Schumacher** | Germany | Ferrari | 17 | 9 | 11 | D. Coulthard, GBR |
| 2002 | **Michael Schumacher** | Germany | Ferrari | 17 | 11 | 7 | R. Barrichello, BRA |
| 2003 | **Michael Schumacher** | Germany | Ferrari | 16 | 6 | 5 | K. Raikkonen, FIN |
| 2004 | **Michael Schumacher** | Germany | Ferrari | 18 | 13 | 8 | R. Barrichello, BRA |
| 2005 | **Fernando Alonso** | Spain | Renault | 19 | 7 | 6 | K. Raikkonen, FIN |

## All-Time Leaders

The all-time Top 15 Grand Prix winning drivers, based on records through 2005. Listed are starts (Sts), poles won (Pole), wins (1st), second place finishes (2nd), and third (3rd). Drivers active in 2005 and career victories in **bold** type.

| | | Sts | Pole | 1st | 2nd | 3rd | | | Sts | Pole | 1st | 2nd | 3rd |
|--|--|-----|------|-----|-----|-----|--|--|-----|------|-----|-----|-----|
| 1 | **M. Schumacher** | 231 | 64 | **84** | 35 | 20 | 9 | Nelson Piquet | 207 | 24 | **23** | 20 | 17 |
| 2 | Alain Prost | 199 | 33 | **51** | 35 | 20 | 10 | Damon Hill | 99 | 20 | **22** | 15 | 5 |
| 3 | Ayrton Senna | 161 | 65 | **41** | 23 | 16 | 11 | Mika Hakkinen | 163 | 27 | **20** | 14 | 17 |
| 4 | Nigel Mansell | 187 | 32 | **31** | 17 | 11 | 12 | Stirling Moss | 66 | 16 | **16** | 5 | 3 |
| 5 | Jackie Stewart | 99 | 17 | **27** | 11 | 5 | 13 | Jack Brabham | 126 | 13 | **14** | 10 | 7 |
| 6 | Jim Clark | 72 | 33 | **25** | 1 | 6 | | Emerson Fittipaldi | 144 | 6 | **14** | 13 | 8 |
| | Niki Lauda | 171 | 24 | **25** | 20 | 9 | | Graham Hill | 176 | 13 | **14** | 15 | 7 |
| 8 | Juan-Manuel Fangio | 51 | 28 | **24** | 10 | 1 | | | | | | | |

## ENDURANCE RACES

### The 24 Hours of Le Mans

Officially, the Le Mans Grand Prix. First run May 22-23, 1923. All subsequent races have been held in June, except in 1956 (July) and 1968 (September). Originally contested on a 10.73-mile track, the circuit was shortened to 8.383 miles in 1932 and has fluxuated around 8.5 miles ever since.

**Multiple winners:** Tom Kristensen (7); Jacky Ickx (6); Derek Bell (5); Yannick Dalmas, Oliver Gendebien and Henri Pescarolo (4); Woolf Barnato, Frank Biela, Luigi Chinetti, Hurley Haywood, Phil Hill, Al Holbert, Klaus Ludwig and Emanuele Pirro (3); Sir Henry Birkin, Ivoe Bueb, Rinaldo Capello, Ron Flockhart, Jean-Pierre Jaussaud, Gerard Larrousse, JJ Lehto, Andre Rossignol, Raymond Sommer, Hans Stuck, Gijs van Lennep, Marco Werner and Jean-Pierre Wimille (2).

| Year | Drivers | Car | MPH |
|------|---------|-----|-----|
| 1923 | Andre Lagache & Rene Leonard | Chenard & Walcker | 57.21 |
| 1924 | John Duff & Francis Clement | Bentley | 53.78 |
| 1925 | Gerard de Courcelles & Andre Rossignol | La Lorraine | 57.84 |
| 1926 | Robert Bloch & Andre Rossignol | La Lorraine | 66.08 |
| 1927 | J.D. Benjafield & Sammy Davis | Bentley | 61.35 |
| 1928 | Woolf Barnato & Bernard Rubin | Bentley | 69.11 |
| 1929 | Woolf Barnato & Sir Henry Birkin | Bentley Speed 6 | 73.63 |
| 1930 | Woolf Barnato & Glen Kidston | Bentley Speed 6 | 75.88 |
| 1931 | Earl Howe & Sir Henry Birkin | Alfa Romeo | 78.13 |
| 1932 | Raymond Sommer & Luigi Chinetti | Alfa Romeo | 76.48 |
| 1933 | Raymond Sommer & Tazio Nuvolari | Alfa Romeo | 81.40 |
| 1934 | Luigi Chinetti & Philippe Etancelin | Alfa Romeo | 74.74 |
| 1935 | John Hindmarsh & Louis Fontes | Lagonda | 77.85 |
| 1936 | Not held | | |
| 1937 | Jean-Pierre Wimille & Robert Benoist | Bugatti 57G | 85.13 |
| 1938 | Eugene Chaboud & Jean Tremoulet | Delahaye | 82.36 |
| 1939 | Jean-Pierre Wimille & Pierre Veyron | Bugatti 57G | 86.86 |
| 1940-48 | Not held | | |
| 1949 | Luigi Chinetti & Lord Selsdon | Ferrari | 82.28 |
| 1950 | Louis Rosier & Jean-Louis Rosier | Talbot-Lago | 89.71 |
| 1951 | Peter Walker & Peter Whitehead | Jaguar C | 93.50 |
| 1952 | Hermann Lang & Fritz Reiss | Mercedes-Benz | 96.67 |
| 1953 | Tony Rolt & Duncan Hamilton | Jaguar C | 98.65 |
| 1954 | Froilan Gonzalez & Maurice Trintignant | Ferrari 375 | 105.13 |
| 1955 | Mike Hawthorn & Ivor Bueb | Jaguar D | 107.05 |

## ENDURANCE RACES (Cont.)

| Year | Drivers | Car | MPH |
|------|---------|-----|-----|
| 1956 | Ron Flockhart & Ninian Sanderson . Jaguar D | | 104.47 |
| 1957 | Ron Flockhart & Ivor Bueb ....... Jaguar D | | 113.83 |
| 1958 | Oliver Gendebien & Phil Hill ......... Ferrari 250 | | 106.18 |
| 1959 | Roy Salvadori & Carroll Shelby .... Aston Martin | | 112.55 |
| 1960 | Oliver Gendebien & Paul Fräre ....... Ferrari 250 | | 109.17 |
| 1961 | Oliver Gendebien & Phil Hill ......... Ferrari 250 | | 115.88 |
| 1962 | Oliver Gendebien & Phil Hill ......... Ferrari 250 | | 115.22 |
| 1963 | Lodovico Scarfiotti & Lorenzo Bandini .... Ferrari 250 | | 118.08 |
| 1964 | Jean Guichel & Nino Vaccarella .... Ferrari 275 | | 121.54 |
| 1965 | Masten Gregory & Jochen Rindt ..... Ferrari 250 | | 121.07 |
| 1966 | Bruce McLaren & Chris Amon ...... Ford Mk. II | | 125.37 |
| 1967 | A.J. Foyt & Dan Gurney ..... Ford Mk. IV | | 135.46 |
| 1968 | Pedro Rodriguez & Lucien Bianchi .... Ford GT40 | | 115.27 |
| 1969 | Jacky Ickx & Jackie Oliver ...... Ford GT40 | | 129.38 |
| 1970 | Hans Herrmann & Richard Attwood .. Porsche 917 | | 119.28 |
| 1971 | Gijs van Lennep & Helmut Marko .... Porsche 917 | | 138.13 |
| 1972 | Graham Hill & Henri Pescarolo .... Matra-Simca | | 121.45 |
| 1973 | Henri Pescarolo & Gerard Larrousse .. Matra-Simca | | 125.67 |
| 1974 | Henri Pescarolo & Gerard Larrousse .. Matra-Simca | | 119.27 |
| 1975 | Derek Bell & Jacky Ickx ....... Mirage-Ford | | 118.98 |
| 1976 | Jacky Ickx & Gijs van Lennep .. Porsche 936 | | 123.49 |
| 1977 | Jacky Ickx, Jurgen Barth & Hurley Haywood .. Porsche 936 | | 120.95 |
| 1978 | Jean-Pierre Jaussaud & Didier Pironi ...... Renault-Alpine | | 130.60 |
| 1979 | Klaus Ludwig, Bill Wittington & Don Whittington ... Porsche 935 | | 108.10 |
| 1980 | Jean-Pierre Jaussaud & Jean Rondeau .... Rondeau-Cosworth | | 119.23 |
| 1981 | Jacky Ickx & Derek Bell ....... Porsche 936 | | 124.94 |
| 1982 | Jacky Ickx & Derek Bell ....... Porsche 956 | | 126.85 |
| 1983 | Vern Schuppan, Hurley Haywood & Al Holbert ....... Porsche 956 | | 130.70 |
| 1984 | Klaus Ludwig & Henri Pescarolo ... Porsche 956 | | 126.88 |
| 1985 | Klaus Ludwig, Paolo Barilla & John Winter ..... Porsche 956 | | 131.75 |
| 1986 | Derek Bell, Hans Stuck & Al Holbert ........ Porsche 962 | | 128.75 |
| 1987 | Derek Bell, Hans Stuck & Al Holbert ........ Porsche 962 | | 124.06 |
| 1988 | Jan Lammers, Johnny Dumfries & Andy Wallace .... Jaguar XJR | | 137.75 |
| 1989 | Jochen Mass, Manuel Reuter & Stanley Dickens .... Sauber-Mercedes | | 136.39 |
| 1990 | John Nielsen, Price Cobb & Martin Brundle ... Jaguar XJR-12 | | 126.71 |
| 1991 | Volker Weider, Johnny Herbert & Bertrand Gachof ... Mazda 787B | | 127.31 |
| 1992 | Derek Warwick, Yannick Dalmas & Mark Blundell ..... Peugeot 905B | | 123.89 |
| 1993 | Geoff Brabham, Christophe Bouchut & Eric Helary ...... Peugeot 905 | | 132.58 |
| 1994 | Yannick Dalmas, Hurley Haywood & Mauro Baldi ...... Porsche 962LM | | 129.82 |
| 1995 | Yannick Dalmas, JJ Lehto & Masanori Sekiya ... McLaren BMW | | 105.00 |
| 1996 | Davy Jones, Manuel Reuter & Alexander Wurz ... TWR Porsche | | 124.65 |
| 1997 | Michele Alberto, Stefan Johansson & Tom Kristensen ..... TWR Porsche | | 126.88 |
| 1998 | Laurent Aiello, Stephane Ortelli & Allan McNish .. Porsche 911 GT1 | | 123.86 |
| 1999 | Yannick Dalmas, Joachim Winkelhock & Pierluigi Martini .... BMW V-12 LMR | | 129.38 |
| 2000 | Frank Biela, Tom Kristensen & Emanuele Pirro ... Audi R8 | | 128.34 |
| 2001 | Frank Biela, Tom Kristensen & Emanuele Pirro ... Audi R8 | | 129.66 |
| 2002 | Frank Biela, Tom Kristensen & Emanuele Pirro ... Audi R8 | | 131.89 |
| 2003 | Tom Kristensen, Rinaldo Capello & Guy Smith ....... Bentley Speed 8 | | 143.43 |
| 2004 | Tom Kristensen, Rinaldo Capello & Seiji Ara ......... Audi R8 | | 133.86 |
| 2005 | Tom Kristensen, JJ Lehto & Marco Werner ..... Audi R8 | | 130.73 |

The original start to the 24 Hours of Le Mans had drivers sprinting across the track to their unstarted cars. This practice was unsafe, however, as drivers would commonly take off without fastening their safety harnesses.

In 1969, Jacky Ickx took a stand by calmly walking to his car and fastening his harness belt before starting his engine. He went on to win the race...and he made his point. The "Le Mans start" was discontinued in 1970.

## The 24 Hours of Daytona

Officially, the Rolex 24 at Daytona. First run in 1962 as a three-hour race and won by Dan Gurney in a Lotus 19 Ford. Contested over a 3.56-mile course at Daytona (Fla.) International Speedway. There have been several distance changes since 1962: the event was a three-hour race (1962-63); a 2,000-kilometer race (1964-65); a 24-hour race (1966-71); a six-hour race (1972) and a 24-hour race again since 1973. The race was canceled in 1974 due to a national energy crisis.

**Multiple winners:** Hurley Haywood (5); Peter Gregg, Pedro Rodriguez and Bob Wollek (4); Derek Bell, Butch Leitzinger, Rolf Stommelen and Andy Wallace (3); Mauro Baldi, A.J. Foyt, Al Holbert, Ken Miles, John Paul Jr., Brian Redman, Elliott Forbes-Robinson, Lloyd Ruby, Wayne Taylor, Didier Theys and Al Unser Jr. (2).

| Year | Drivers | Car | MPH |
|---|---|---|---|
| 1962 | Dan Gurney | Lotus 19 Ford | 104.101 |
| 1963 | Pedro Rodriguez | Ferrari GTO | 102.074 |
| 1964 | Pedro Rodriguez & Phil Hill | Ferrari GTO | 98.230 |
| 1965 | Ken Miles & Lloyd Ruby | Ford GT | 99.944 |
| 1966 | Ken Miles & Lloyd Ruby | Ford Mk. II | 108.020 |
| 1967 | Lorenzo Bandini & Chris Amon | Ferrari 330 | 105.688 |
| 1968 | Vic Elford & Jochen Neerpasch | Porsche 907 | 106.697 |
| 1969 | Mark Donohue & Chuck Parsons | Lola Chevrolet | 99.268 |
| 1970 | Pedro Rodriguez & Leo Kinnunen | Porsche 917 | 114.866 |
| 1971 | Pedro Rodriguez & Jackie Oliver | Porsche 917K | 109.203 |
| 1972 | Mario Andretti & Jacky Ickx | Ferrari 312P | 122.573 |
| 1973 | Peter Gregg & Hurley Haywood | Porsche Carrera | 106.225 |
| 1974 | Not held | | |
| 1975 | Peter Gregg & Hurley Haywood | Porsche Carrera | 108.531 |
| 1976 | Peter Gregg, Brian Redman & John Fitzpatrick | BMW CSL | 104.040 |
| 1977 | Hurley Haywood, John Graves & Dave Helmick | Porsche Carrera | 108.801 |
| 1978 | Peter Gregg, Rolf Stommelen & Antoine Hezemans | Porsche Turbo | 108.743 |
| 1979 | Hurley Haywood, Ted Field & Danny Ongais | Porsche Turbo | 109.249 |
| 1980 | Rolf Stommelen, Volkert Merl & Reinhold Joest | Porsche Turbo | 114.303 |
| 1981 | Bobby Rahal, Brian Redman & Bob Garretson | Porsche Turbo | 113.153 |
| 1982 | John Paul Sr., John Paul Jr. & Rolf Stommelen | Porsche Turbo | 114.794 |
| 1983 | A.J. Foyt, Preston Henn, Bob Wollek & Claude Ballot-Lena | Porsche Turbo | 98.781 |
| 1984 | Sarel van der Merwe, Tony Martin & Graham Duxbury | March Porsche | 103.119 |
| 1985 | A.J. Foyt, Bob Wollek, Al Unser Sr. & Thierry Boutsen | Porsche 962 | 104.162 |
| 1986 | Al Holbert, Derek Bell & Al Unser Jr | Porsche 962 | 105.484 |
| 1987 | Al Holbert, Derek Bell, Chip Robinson & Al Unser Jr | Porsche 962 | 111.599 |
| 1988 | Raul Boesel, Martin Brundle & John Nielsen | Jaguar XJR-9 | 107.943 |
| 1989 | John Andretti, Derek Bell & Bob Wollek | Porsche 962 | 92.009 |
| 1990 | Davy Jones, Jan Lammers & Andy Wallace | Jaguar XJR-12 | 112.857 |
| 1991 | Hurley Haywood, John Winter, Frank Jelinski, Henri Pescarolo & Bob Wollek | Porsche 962-C | 106.633 |
| 1992 | Masahiro Hasemi, Kazuyoshi Hoshino & Toshio Suzuki | Nissan R-91 | 112.897 |
| 1993 | P.J. Jones, Mark Dismore & Rocky Moran | Toyota Eagle | 103.537 |
| 1994 | Paul Gentilozzi, Scott Pruett, Butch Leitzinger & Steve Millen | Nissan 300 ZXT | 104.80 |
| 1995 | Jurgen Lassig, Christophe Bouchut, Giovanni Lavaggi & Marco Werner | Porsche Spyder | 102.280 |
| 1996 | Wayne Taylor, Scott Sharp & Jim Pace | Oldsmobile Arness MK-III | 103.32 |
| 1997 | Rob Dyson, James Weaver, Butch Leitzinger, Andy Wallace, John Paul Jr., Eliot Forbes-Robinson & John Schneider | Ford R&S MK-III | 102.29 |
| 1998 | Mauro Baldi, Arie Luyendyk, Gianpiero Moretti & Didier Theys | Ferrari 333 | 105.40 |
| 1999 | Elliot Forbes-Robinson, Butch Leitzinger & Andy Wallace | Riley & Scott Ford | 104.957 |
| 2000 | Olivier Beretta, Dominique Dupuy & Karl Wendlinger | Dodge Viper | 107.207 |
| 2001 | Ron Fellows, Franck Freon, Chris Kneifel & Johnny O'Connell | Chevy Corvette | 97.293 |
| 2002 | Mauro Baldi, Fredy Lienhard, Max Papis & Didier Theys | Dallara LMP900 | 106.143 |
| 2003 | Kevin Buckler, Michael Schrom, Timo Bernhard & Jorg Bergmeister | Porsche GT3 RS | 115.969 |
| 2004 | Terry Borcheller, Forest Barber, Andy Pilgrim & Christian Fittipaldi | Pontiac Doran | 77.927 |
| 2005 | Wayne Taylor, Max Angelelli & Emmanuel Collard | Pontiac Riley | 105.204 |

## NHRA DRAG RACING

# NHRA Champions

Based on points earned during the NHRA POWERade Drag Racing series. The series, originally sponsored by the R.J. Reynolds Tobacco Company's Winston brand, began for Top Fuel, Funny Car and Pro Stock in 1975. The Coca-Cola Company's POWERade brand soft drink began a five-year sponsorship deal with the series in 2002.

## Top Fuel

**Multiple winners:** Joe Amato (5); Don Garlits, Shirley Muldowney and Gary Scelzi (3); Kenny Bernstein, Larry Dixon, Scott Kalitta and Tony Schumacher (2).

| Year | | Year | | Year | | Year | |
|------|------|------|------|------|------|------|------|
| 1975 | Don Garlits | 1983 | Gary Beck | 1991 | Joe Amato | 1999 | Tony Schumacher |
| 1976 | Richard Tharp | 1984 | Joe Amato | 1992 | Joe Amato | 2000 | Gary Scelzi |
| 1977 | Shirley Muldowney | 1985 | Don Garlits | 1993 | Eddie Hill | 2001 | Kenny Bernstein |
| 1978 | Kelly Brown | 1986 | Don Garlits | 1994 | Scott Kalitta | 2002 | Larry Dixon |
| 1979 | Rob Bruins | 1987 | Dick LaHaie | 1995 | Scott Kalitta | 2003 | Larry Dixon |
| 1980 | Shirley Muldowney | 1988 | Joe Amato | 1996 | Kenny Bernstein | 2004 | Tony Schumacher |
| 1981 | Jeb Allen | 1989 | Gary Ormsby | 1997 | Gary Scelzi | | |
| 1982 | Shirley Muldowney | 1990 | Joe Amato | 1998 | Gary Scelzi | | |

## Funny Car

**Multiple winners:** John Force (13); Don Prudhomme, Kenny Bernstein (4); Raymond Beadle (3); Frank Hawley (2).

| Year | | Year | | Year | | Year | |
|------|------|------|------|------|------|------|------|
| 1975 | Don Prudhomme | 1983 | Frank Hawley | 1991 | John Force | 1999 | John Force |
| 1976 | Don Prudhomme | 1984 | Mark Oswald | 1992 | Cruz Pedregon | 2000 | John Force |
| 1977 | Don Prudhomme | 1985 | Kenny Bernstein | 1993 | John Force | 2001 | John Force |
| 1978 | Don Prudhomme | 1986 | Kenny Bernstein | 1994 | John Force | 2002 | John Force |
| 1979 | Raymond Beadle | 1987 | Kenny Bernstein | 1995 | John Force | 2003 | Tony Pedregon |
| 1980 | Raymond Beadle | 1988 | Kenny Bernstein | 1996 | John Force | 2004 | John Force |
| 1981 | Raymond Beadle | 1989 | Bruce Larson | 1997 | John Force | | |
| 1982 | Frank Hawley | 1990 | John Force | 1998 | John Force | | |

## Pro Stock

**Multiple winners:** Bob Glidden (9); Warren Johnson (6); Lee Shepherd (4); Darrell Alderman, Greg Anderson, Jeg Coughlin Jr. and Jim Yates (2).

| Year | | Year | | Year | | Year | |
|------|------|------|------|------|------|------|------|
| 1975 | Bob Glidden | 1983 | Lee Shepherd | 1991 | Darrell Alderman | 1999 | Warren Johnson |
| 1976 | Larry Lombardo | 1984 | Lee Shepherd | 1992 | Warren Johnson | 2000 | Jeg Coughlin Jr. |
| 1977 | Don Nicholson | 1985 | Bob Glidden | 1993 | Warren Johnson | 2001 | Warren Johnson |
| 1978 | Bob Glidden | 1986 | Bob Glidden | 1994 | Darrell Alderman | 2002 | Jeg Coughlin Jr. |
| 1979 | Bob Glidden | 1987 | Bob Glidden | 1995 | Warren Johnson | 2003 | Greg Anderson |
| 1980 | Bob Glidden | 1988 | Bob Glidden | 1996 | Jim Yates | 2004 | Greg Anderson |
| 1981 | Lee Shepherd | 1989 | Bob Glidden | 1997 | Jim Yates | | |
| 1982 | Lee Shepherd | 1990 | John Myers | 1998 | Warren Johnson | | |

# All-Time Leaders
## Career Victories

All-time leaders through Oct. 9, 2005. Drivers active in 2005 are in **bold**.

| Top Fuel | | Funny Car | | Pro Stock | |
|----------|----|-----------|-----|-----------|----|
| 1 Joe Amato | 52 | 1 **John Force** | 119 | 1 **Warren Johnson** | 94 |
| 2 Kenny Bernstein | 39 | 2 Don Prudhomme | 35 | 2 Bob Glidden | 85 |
| 3 **Larry Dixon** | 38 | 3 Kenny Bernstein | 30 | 3 **Greg Anderson** | 39 |
| 4 Don Garlits | 35 | 4 **Tony Pedregon** | 28 | 4 **Jeg Coughlin** | 33 |
| 5 **Cory McClenathan** | 29 | 5 **Cruz Pedregon** | 23 | 5 **Kurt Johnson** | 31 |

# Fastest Mile-Per-Hour Speeds

Fastest performances in NHRA major event history through Oct. 9, 2005.

| Top Fuel | Funny Car | Pro Stock |
|----------|-----------|-----------|
| **MPH** | **MPH** | **MPH** |
| 337.58 .Tony Schumacher, 8/13/2005 | 333.58 .... John Force, 10/3/2004 | 208.23 ..Greg Anderson, 3/19/2005 |
| 336.15 .Tony Schumacher, 5/22/2005 | 333.25 .Whit Bazemore, 5/23/2004 | 208.17 . . . . Jason Line, 10/2/2005 |
| 335.57 .....Doug Kalitta, 4/3/2004 | 332.75 .... John Force, 10/2/2004 | 207.75 ..Greg Anderson, 10/2/2004 |
| 335.32 Tony Schumacher, 4/10/2005 | 331.53 ....Gary Scelzi, 2/13/2005 | 207.51 ..Dave Connolly, 3/19/2005 |
| 333.95 ...Scott Kalitta, 10/12/2003 | 331.45 .Tommy Johnson Jr., 9/30/2005 | 207.50 .Warren Johnson, 6/19/2005 |

# Boxing

*Jermain Taylor* is dripping in sweat and belts after beating undisputed middleweight champ Bernard Hopkins in 2005.

AP/Wide World Photos

# Deadly Consequences

*A fight for the ages and the deaths of two fighters reminded us of boxing's terrible risks and great rewards*

**Gerry Brown**
*is co-editor of the ESPN Sports Almanac.*

The fight was over. Then all of a sudden it wasn't. Then it was.

The staccato beat and a stunning reversal of fortune gave lightweight Diego Corrales a win in the most exciting fight in recent memory and Jose Luis Castillo a dizzy head full of questions. First and foremost of which was, what the %$@*#! just happened?

Just moments ago, wasn't he getting ready to enjoy a hard fought victory? His opponent was on the ground for the second time that round and had to be done for the day. Now, all of sudden, some guy was hugging him. That guy turned out to be referee Tony Weeks.

Weeks moved in for the man-hug when the impossible happened as it sometimes does in sports. Diego Corrales shook off the shots that put him on the mat and came back firing full blast, catching Castillo with some big punches and leaving him dazed and glazed.

It had to be the glazed look in Castillo's eyes that earned him the hug from Weeks. That or the useless gloves on his lifeless hands. Whatever it was, it signalled the close of a ferocious battle that left fight fans in awe and the combatants both bloodied and beaten up.

In the mega-hyped world of big-time boxing, designed to rack up ratings and those all-important pay-per-view buys, rarely is something better than advertised. But the Corrales-Castillo collision was an exceptional exception. Still in a sport that is based on doing harm to your opponent there can be a razor-thin line between glory and tragedy.

Boxing fans that cheer the naked aggression, magnificent courage and terrible grace that are displayed in the ring in the sport's best moments must also reconcile that with the potentially deadly consequences of such competition. Presumably the boxers have done so long ago.

A brutal reminder of the inherent danger of boxing took center stage when lightweight Leavander Johnson collapsed and later died following his title fight loss to Jesus Chavez.

AP/Wide World Photos

*Diego Corrales* (right) won his first meeting with lightweight champion *Jose Luis Castillo* in spectacular fashion, coming back from the brink to win their lightweight title bout.

Weeks, the man that saved Castillo from further injury and potentially permanent harm, was the referee in the Sept. 17 fateful fight between Johnson and Chavez. While the fight was, by definition, violent it was not in the same class of savagery that characterized the Corrales-Castillo bout five months previous.

Might it be possible that the very violence that brought fans to their feet on May 7 may have subconsciously desensitized Weeks just enough to delay his stoppage of the Johnson fight by a split-second. Especially, in light of the fact that Weeks was criticized in some circles for calling Castillo out too early despite his obviously dire circumstances (see photo above).

Not that it is even possible to know what effect that fight or any other may have had on Weeks or whether a second would have made a difference for Johnson that night. And it's important to note that no fight referee wants to become the next Ruby Goldstein, the hall of fame referee that became most famous not for the 39 world title fights he arbited but for ultimately acting too slow in the fatal 1962 Benny Paret-Emile Griffith title fight.

A rematch between Corrales and Castillo was a foregone conclusion and although the fight was exciting, it understandably failed to match the incredible drama of their first meeting.

Corrales could not weather Hurricane Jose Luis this time, getting knocked out in the fourth round of their rematch but he did not need to relin-

AP/Wide World Photos

*Despite appearances it was **Roy Jones** that needed assistance in his third meeting with light heavyweight rival **Antonio Tarver** in 2005. Tarver won by unanimous decision.*

quish his hard-fought WBC title when Castillo failed to make the lightweight limit of 135 pounds.

After repeated attempts, where Castillo actually came in heavier each time, he could not/would not sweat off the required weight and a corner man even brazenly attempted to fix the scales with his big toe. But with the momentum of all the money at stake, a deal was worked out and the fight went on as a non-title bout.

Despite the convincing win for Castillo, a third meeting appears inevitable. Sometimes rubber matches can be the most violent of all (e.g. Ali-Frazier III). For the sake of the long term health of Corrales and Castillo let's hope that it will not be like the dramatic but damaging "Thrilla in Manila" or the infamous rubber match that cost Benny Paret his life.

In the build up to the September rematch, Corrales claimed "I will die in that ring before I give up what I have taken."

He may have very well meant it, even after the deaths of Johnson and Mexican fighter Martin Sanchez in 2005, but for the sake of his own pregnant wife and the lives of today's and tomorrow's prize fighters it's a good thing that Weeks and referees like him are there to give a hug to a guy when necessary.

Even if, and often especially when, the fighter doesn't think he needs one.

# The Ten Biggest Stories of the Year in Boxing

**10** **Floyd Mayweather Jr. calls** 140-pound champ Arturo Gatti a "C-plus fighter" then adds injury to insult, totally dominating the slower man by consistently beating him to the punch. Mayweather stays unbeaten and takes Gatti's WBC junior welterweight title by technical knockout when Gatti's trainer Buddy McGirt stops the bout following the sixth round of their championship fight in Atlantic City.

**9** **Mike Tyson quits** on his stool against journeyman Kevin McBride and says he's done fighting for good, bringing a roller coaster fighting career to an apparent end. The debt-ridden former heavyweight champ and "baddest man on the planet" just looked bad, head-butting and attempting to break McBride's arm before calling it a night and a career.

**8** **James Toney wins** a world title in his fourth weight division with a unanimous decision over John Ruiz but loses the belt 12 days later when it is revealed that he failed a post-fight steroid test. Despite the end result, the 37-year-old former middleweight champion, and current portly banger, continues the resurrection of a career and looks to be in the heavyweight title mix for the next few years.

**7** **Fellow Mexicans and bitter rivals** Marco Antonio Barrera and Erik Morales meet for the third, and perhaps final, time in November 2004. In an exciting conclusion to a classically ferocious trilogy, Barrera pounds out a majority decision over his long-time adversary to capture the WBC super featherweight belt.

**6** **Undefeated but suspect** British junior welterweight Ricky Hatton stuns long-standing 140-pound division king Kostya Tszyu, beating down the 35-year-old and making him quit on his stool before the 12th round of their IBF title fight, sending the partisan sell-out crowd of 22,000 in Manchester, England into hysterics.

**5** **Zab Judah evens the score** in his rematch with undisputed 147-pound champion Cory Spinks taking his welterweight belts with a 9th-round stoppage of the son of fomer heavyweight champion Leon Spinks.

**4** **In the undisputed fight of the year**, lightweight slugger Diego Corrales gets up off the canvas, twice, to shock WBC champion Jose Luis Castillo, and the rest of the planet, by TKO in the 10th round of their dramatic toe-to-toe battle in Las Vegas. Castillo exacts revenge in their October rematch, knocking out Corrales in four rounds and setting the table for a highly anticipated third meeting.

**3** **Antonio Tarver ends** the speculation with a decisive 12-round victory over long-time rival Roy Jones Jr. in their third meeting. It's the third straight loss for the former pound-for-pound and four-division champ and may signal the end of his brilliant career. Tarver wins their final two meetings and can now move forward with his career.

**2** **Leavander Johnson** and **Martin Sanchez** both die as a result of injuries they sustained in the boxing ring.

**1** **Bernard Hopkins starts slow**, finishes strong but falls just short against Jermain Taylor ending his division-record 20 consecutive successful middleweight title defenses with a split decision loss. Hopkins blames the judges and readies himself for a December rematch that could be the final fight of his illustrious and long career.

## INSIDE the numbers

### Biggest fight in history

In December 2004, WBC Heavyweight champion Vitali Klitschko and Tyson-beater Danny Williams fought in the biggest heavyweight title fight in history. Actually, heaviest may be a better way to describe it. Klitschko weighed 250 pounds, while Williams crushed the scales at 270 pounds. Here's a look at the heaviest title fights in history, listed by total weight.

| Winner | Lbs | Loser | Lbs | Total Lbs |
|--------|-----|-------|-----|-----------|
| V. Klitschko | 250 | D. Williams | 270 | **520** |
| L. Lewis | 257 | V. Klitschko | 248 | **505** |
| L. Lewis | 247 | M. Grant | 250 | **497** |
| L. Lewis | 249 | D. Tua | 245 | **494** |
| P. Carnera | 259½ | P. Uzcudun | 229¼ | **488¾** |
| L. Lewis | 244 | A. Golota | 244 | **488** |

**Dates:** Klitschko-Williams (12/11/2004), Lewis-Klitschko (6/21/2003), Lewis-Grant (4/29/2000), Lewis-Tua (11/11/2000), Carnera-Uzcudun (10/22/1933), Lewis-Golota (10/4/1997).

### Long Journeyman Fighter

Indianapolis-area pugilist Reggie Strickland has won 66 pro fights, an impressive number by any measure. But the other half of his ring record is even more eye-opening. Strickland has lost 276 times in 363 career bouts through October 2005. The still-active Strickland ranks second on the all-time list of fighters with the most professional bouts.

#### Total Bouts

| | Division | Career | No |
|--|----------|--------|-----|
| Len Wickwar | Lt. Heavy | 1928–47 | 463 |
| Reggie Strickland | various | 1987– | 363 |
| Jack Britton | Welter | 1905–30 | 350 |
| Johnny Dundee | Feather | 1910–32 | 333 |
| Billy Bird | Welter | 1920–48 | 318 |
| George Marsden | n/a | 1928–46 | 311 |
| Maxie Rosenbloom | Lt. Heavy | 1923–39 | 299 |
| Harry Greb | Middle | 1913–26 | 298 |
| Young Stribling | Lt. Heavy | 1921–33 | 286 |
| Battling Levinsky | Lt. Heavy | 1910–29 | 282 |

# 2004-2005
# Season in Review

SPORTS ALMANAC

## Current Champions
## WBA, WBC and IBF Titleholders (through Oct. 26, 2005)

The champions of professional boxing's 17 principal weight divisions, as recognized by the Word Boxing Association (WBA), World Boxing Council (WBC) and International Boxing Federation (IBF). Where applicable, records listed below fighters' names indicate wins-losses-draws-no contest.

| | Weight Limit | WBA Champion | WBC Champion | IBF Champion |
|---|---|---|---|---|
| Heavyweight | — | John Ruiz<br>41-5-1, 28 KOs | Vitali Klitschko<br>35-2-0, 34 KOs | Chris Byrd<br>39-2-1, 2Q KOs |
| Cruiserweight | 190 lbs | Jean-Marc Mormeck<br>31-2-0, 21 KOs | Jean-Marc Mormeck<br>31-2-0, 21 KOs | O'Neil Bell<br>25-1-0, 23 KOs |
| Light Heavyweight | 175 lbs | Fabrice Tiozzo<br>47-2-0, 31 KOs | Tomasz Adamek<br>30-0-0, 21 KOs | Clinton Woods<br>38-3-1, 23 KOs |
| Super Middleweight | 168 lbs | Mikkel Kessler<br>35-0-0, 27 KOs | Markus Beyer<br>33-2-0, 12 KOs | Jeff Lacy<br>20-0-0, 16 KOs |
| Middleweight | 160 lbs | Jermain Taylor*<br>24-0-0, 17 KOs | Jermain Taylor<br>24-0-0, 17 KOs | Jermain Taylor<br>24-0-0, 17 KOs |
| Jr. Middleweight | 154 lbs | Alejandro Garcia<br>25-1-0, 24 KOs | Ricardo Mayorga<br>28-5-1, 22 KOs | Roman Karmazin<br>34-1-1, 21 KOs |
| Welterweight | 147 lbs | Zab Judah<br>34-2-0, 25 KOs | Zab Judah<br>34-2-0, 25 KOs | Zab Judah<br>34-2-0, 25 KOs |
| Jr. Welterweight | 140 lbs | Carlos Maussa<br>18-2-0, 16 KOs | Floyd Mayweather<br>34-0-0, 23 KOs | Ricky Hatton<br>39-0-0, 29 KOs |
| Lightweight | 135 lbs | Juan Diaz<br>28-0-0, 14 KOs | Diego Corrales<br>40-3-0, 33 KOs | Jesus Chavez<br>42-3-0, 29 KOs |
| Jr. Lightweight | 130 lbs | Vicente Mosquera<br>21-1-1, 10 KOs | Marco Antonio Barrera<br>61-4-0, 42 KOs | Marco Antonio Barrera<br>61-4-0, 42 KOs |
| Featherweight | 126 lbs | Juan Manuel Marquez*<br>44-2-1, 33 KOs | Chi In-jin<br>30-2-1, 18 KOs | Juan Manuel Marquez<br>44-2-1, 33 KOs |
| Jr. Featherweight | 122 lbs. | Mahyar Monshipour<br>28-2-2, 19 KOs | Oscar Larios<br>56-3-1, 36 KOs | Israel Vazquez<br>38-3-0, 27 KOs |
| Bantamweight | 118 lbs | Wladimir Sidorenko<br>17-0-0, 6 KOs | Hozumi Hasegawa<br>19-2-0, 6 KOs | Rafael Marquez<br>34-3-0, 30 KOs |
| Jr. Bantamweight | 115 lbs | Martin Castillo<br>29-1-0, 16 KOs | Masamori Tokuyama<br>31-3-1, 8 KOs | Luis Perez<br>23-1-0, 15 KOs |
| Flyweight | 112 lbs | Lorenzo Parra<br>26-0-0, 17 KOs | Pongsaklek Wonjongkam<br>58-2-0, 31 KOs | Vic Darchinyan<br>24-0-0, 19 KOs |
| Jr. Flyweight | 108 lbs | Roberto Vasquez<br>20-1-0, 17 KOs | Brian Viloria<br>18-0-0, 12 KOs | Will Grigsby<br>19-2-1, 7 KOs |
| Minimumweight | 105 lbs | Yutaka Niida<br>19-1-3, 8 KOs | Eagle Kyowa<br>14-1-0, 5 KOs | Muhammad Rachman<br>49-7-4, 21 KOs |

*Jermain Taylor is the WBA middleweight "super world champion;" Zab Judah is the WBA welterweight "super world champion;" Juan Manuel Marquez is the WBA featherweight "super world champion."

**Note:** The following weight divisions are also known by these names—**Cruiserweight** as Jr. Heavyweight; **Jr. Middleweight** as Super Welterweight; **Jr. Welterweight** as Super Lightweight; **Jr. Lightweight** as Super Featherweight; **Jr. Featherweight** as Super Bantamweight; **Jr. Bantamweight** as Super Flyweight; **Jr. Flyweight** as Light Flyweight; and **Minimumweight** as Strawweight or Mini-Flyweights.

## Major Bouts, 2004-05

Division by division, from Nov. 1, 2004 through Oct. 31, 2005.

WBA, WBC and IBF champions are listed in **bold** type. Note the following Result column abbreviations (in alphabetical order): **Disq.** (won by disqualification); **KO** (knockout); **MDraw** (majority draw); **NC** (no contest); **SDraw** (split draw); **TDraw** (technical draw); **TKO** (technical knockout); **TWm** (won by technical majority decision); **TWs** (won by technical split decision); **TWu** (won by technical unanimous decision); **Wm** (won by majority decision); **Ws** (won by split decision) and **Wu** (won by unanimous decision).

### Heavyweights

| Date | Winner | Loser | Result | Title | Site |
|---|---|---|---|---|---|
| Nov. 13 | **John Ruiz** | Andrew Golota | Wu 12 | **WBA** | New York City |
| Nov. 13 | **Chris Byrd** | Jameel McCline | Wu 12 | **IBF** | New York City |
| Nov. 13 | Larry Donald | Evander Holyfield | Wu 12 | — | New York City |
| Nov. 13 | Hasim Rahman | Kali Meehan | TKO 4 | — | New York City |
| Dec. 9 | Michael Moorer | Vassiliy Jirov | TKO 9 | — | Temecula, Calif. |
| Dec. 11 | **Vitali Klitschko** | Danny Williams | TKO 8 | **WBC** | Las Vegas |
| Apr. 23 | Wladimir Klitschko | Eliceo Castillo | KO 4 | — | Dortmund, Germany |
| Apr. 30 | James Toney | **John Ruiz** | Wu 12 | **WBA\*** | New York City |
| May 21 | Lamon Brewster | Andrew Golota | KO 1 | — | Chicago |
| June 11 | Kevin McBride | Mike Tyson | TKO 6† | — | Washington, D.C. |
| Aug. 13 | Hasim Rahman | Monte Barrett | Wu 12 | WBC‡ | Chicago |
| Sept. 24 | Wladimir Klitschko | Samuel Peter | Wu 12 | — | Atlantic City |
| Oct. 1 | **Chris Byrd** | DaVarryl Williamson | Wu 12 | **IBF** | Reno, Nev. |
| Oct. 1 | James Toney | Dominick Guinn | Wu 12 | — | Reno, Nev. |
| Oct. 21 | David Tua | Cisse Salif | Wu 10 | — | Hollywood, Fla. |
| Oct. 21 | Zuri Lawrence | Jameel McCline | Wu1- | — | Hollywood, Fla. |

*Toney won the WBA belt but on May 12 the fight was ruled a No Contest and was stripped of the title after testing positive for steroids following the bout.
†Tyson quit on his stool prior to the seventh round.
‡Rahman won the interim WBC belt.

### Cruiserweights (190 lbs)

#### (Jr. Heavyweights)

| Date | Winner | Loser | Result | Title | Site |
|---|---|---|---|---|---|
| Apr. 2 | **Jean-Marc Mormeck** | **Wayne Braithwaite** | Wu 12 | **WBA/WBC** | Worcester, Mass. |
| May 20 | O'Neil Bell | Dale Brown | Wu 12 | **IBF\*** | Hollywood, Fla. |
| Aug. 26 | **O'Neil Bell** | Sebastian Rothman | KO 11 | **IBF** | Hollywood, Fla. |
| Sept. 3 | Guillermo Jones | Wayne Braithwaite | TKO 4 | — | Cleveland, Ohio |

*Bell won the vacant title that was stripped from Kelvin Davis for not fighting the top-ranked contender within the allotted time frame.

### Light Heavyweights (175 lbs)

| Date | Winner | Loser | Result | Title | Site |
|---|---|---|---|---|---|
| Dec. 18 | Glen Johnson | Antonio Tarver | Ws 12* | — | Los Angeles |
| Dec. 18 | Julio Cesar Gonzalez | David Telesco | TKO 8 | — | Los Angeles |
| Feb. 26 | **Fabrice Tiozzo** | Dariusz Michalczewski | TKO 6 | **WBA** | Hamburg, Germany |
| Mar. 4 | Clinton Woods | Rico Hoye | TKO 5 | **IBF†** | Rotherham, England |
| May 21 | Tomasz Adamek | Paul Briggs | Wm 12 | **WBC‡** | Chicago |
| Sept. 9 | **Clinton Woods** | Julio Gonzalez | Wu 12 | **IBF** | Sheffield, England |
| Oct. 1 | Antonio Tarver | Roy Jones Jr. | Wu 12 | — | Tampa, Fla. |
| Oct. 15 | **Tomasz Adamek** | Thomas Ulrich | TKO 6 | **WBC** | Dusseldorf, Germany |

*Johnson (IBF) and Tarver (WBC) each gave up their title belts so that they could face each other to determine the unofficial light heavyweight champion in a more lucrative fight.
†Woods won the vacant IBF belt that Glen Johnson gave up to fight Antonio Tarver.
‡Adamek won the vacant WBC belt that Antonio Tarver gave up to fight Glen Johnson.

### Major Bouts Scheduled for Fall 2005

| Date | Division | Match-up | Title | Location |
|---|---|---|---|---|
| Nov. 5 | super middleweight | Jeff Lacy vs. Scott Pemberton | IBF | Stateline, Nev. |
| | bantamweight | Rafael Marquez vs. Silence Mabuza | IBF | Stateline, Nev. |
| Nov. 12 | heavyweight | Vital Klitschko vs. Hasim Rahman | WBC | Las Vegas |
| | welterweight | Antonio Margarito vs. Manuel Gomez | — | Las Vegas |
| Nov. 19 | super lightweight | Floyd Mayweather vs. Sharmba Mitchell | WBC | Portland, Ore. |
| | junior flyweight | Roberto Vasquez vs. Nerys Espinoza | WBA | Panama City, Panama |
| Nov. 25 | flyweight | Vic Darchinyan vs. Damaen Kelly | IBF | New South Wales, Australia |
| Nov. 26 | junior welterweight | Ricky Hatton vs. Carlos Maussa | IBF/WBA | South Yorkshire, England |
| Dec. 3 | middleweight | Jermain Taylor vs. Bernard Hopkins | WBA/WBC* | Las Vegas |
| | junior featherweight | Oscar Larios vs. Israel Vazquez | — | Las Vegas |
| Dec. 10 | middleweight | Winky Wright vs. Sam Soliman | — | Uncasville, Conn. |
| Dec. 17 | heavyweight | John Ruiz vs. Nicolay Valuev | WBA | Berlin, Germany |

*Taylor vacated the IBF title he won when he beat Hopkins, so that he could give Hopkins a rematch.

## Super Middleweights (168 lbs)

| Date | Winner | Loser | Result | Title | Site |
|------|--------|-------|--------|-------|------|
| Nov. 12 | Mikkel Kessler | Manuel Siaca | TKO 7 | **WBA\*** | Copenhagen, Denmark |
| Dec. 4 | **Jeff Lacy** | Omar Sheika | Wu 12 | **IBF** | Las Vegas |
| Dec. 18 | **Markus Beyer** | Yoshinori Nishizawa | Wu 12 | **WBC** | Bayreuth, Germany |
| Mar. 5 | **Jeff Lacy** | Rubin Williams | TKO 7 | **IBF** | Las Vegas |
| Mar. 12 | **Markus Beyer** | Danny Green | Wm 12 | **WBC** | Zwickau, Germany |
| June 8 | **Mikkel Kessler** | Anthony Mundine | Wu 12 | **WBA** | Sydney, Australia |
| Aug. 6 | **Jeff Lacy** | Robin Reid | TKO 7 | **IBF** | Tampa, Fla. |
| Sept. 3 | **Markus Beyer** | Omar Sheika | Wu 12 | **WBC** | Berlin |

\*Kessler won the WBA belt that was left vacant when former champ Sven Ottke retired.

## Middleweights (160 lbs)

| Date | Winner | Loser | Result | Title | Site |
|------|--------|-------|--------|-------|------|
| Dec. 4 | Jermain Taylor | William Joppy | Wu 12 | — | Little Rock, Arkansas |
| Feb. 19 | **Bernard Hopkins** | Howard Eastman | Wu 12 | **IBF/WBA/WBC** | Los Angeles |
| Feb. 19 | Jermain Taylor | Daniel Edouard | TKO 3 | — | Los Angeles |
| Mar. 26 | Fernando Vargas | Raymond Joval | Wu 10 | — | Corpus Chrisit, Tex. |
| May 14 | Winky Wright | Felix Trinidad | Wu 12 | — | Las Vegas |
| July 16 | Jermain Taylor | **Bernard Hopkins** | Ws 12 | **IBF/WBA/WBC** | Las Vegas |

\*Maseo won the vacant WBA title but note that Bernard Hopkins is the WBA middleweight "super world champion."

## Junior Middleweights (154 lbs)
### (Super Welterweights)

| Date | Winner | Loser | Result | Title | Site |
|------|--------|-------|--------|-------|------|
| Nov. 20 | **Winky Wright** | Shane Mosley | Wm 12 | **WBA/WBC** | Las Vegas |
| Jan. 29 | **Kassim Ouma** | Koffi Juntah | Wu 12 | **IBF** | Atlantic City |
| July 14 | Roman Karmazin | **Kassim Ouma** | Wu 12 | **IBF** | Las Vegas |
| Aug. 13 | Alejandro Garcia | Luca Messi | Wu 12 | **WBA\*** | Chicago |
| Aug. 13 | Ricardo Mayorga | Michele Piccirillo | Wu 12 | **WBC†** | Chicago |
| Aug. 20 | Fernando Vargas | Javier Castillejo | Wu 10 | — | Rosemont, Ill. |
| Oct. 22 | Vernon Forrest | Elco Garcia | TKO 10 | — | Temecula, Calif. |

\*Garcia won the title that was left vacant by Winky Wright when he moved up to middleweight.

†Mayorga won the title that was left vacant by when Javier Castillejo was stripped of the belt on May 31 for signing to fight Fernando Vargas rather than the No. 1 contender Ricardo Mayorga. Castillejo was originally the interim champ and was awarded the full-fledged WBC belt when Winky Wright moved up to middleweight.

## Welterweights (147 lbs)

| Date | Winner | Loser | Result | Title | Site |
|------|--------|-------|--------|-------|------|
| Feb. 5 | Zab Judah | **Cory Spinks** | TKO 9 | **IBF/WBA/WBC** | St. Louis |
| Apr. 2 | Luis Collazo | Jose Antonio Rivera | Ws 12 | **WBA\*** | Worcester, Mass. |
| May 14 | **Zab Judah** | Cosme Rivera | TKO 3 | **IBF/WBA/WBC** | Las Vegas |
| Aug. 13 | Luis Collazo | Miguel Angel Gonzalez | TKO 8 | **WBA** | Chicago |
| Sept. 17 | Shane Mosley | Jose Luis Cruz | Wu 10 | — | Las Vegas |

\*Collazo won the WBA belt but note that Zab Judah is the WBA welterweight "super world champion."

## Junior Welterweights (140 lbs)
### (Super Lightweights)

| Date | Winner | Loser | Result | Title | Site |
|------|--------|-------|--------|-------|------|
| Nov. 6 | **Kostya Tszyu** | Sharmba Mitchell | TKO 3 | **IBF\*** | Phoenix, Arizona |
| Dec. 11 | Ricky Hatton | Ray Oliveira | KO 10 | — | London |
| Dec. 11 | Miguel Cotto | Randall Bailey | TKO 6 | — | Las Vegas |
| Jan. 22 | Floyd Mayweather Jr. | Henry Bruseles | TKO 8 | — | Miami, Fla. |
| Jan. 29 | **Arturo Gatti** | James Leija | KO 5 | **WBC** | Atlantic City |
| Feb. 26 | Miguel Cotto | DeMarcus Corley | TKO 5 | — | Bayamon, Puerto Rico |
| June 4 | Ricky Hatton | **Kostya Tszyu** | TKO 11† | **IBF** | Manchester, England |
| June 11 | Miguel Cotto | Mohamad Abdulaev | TKO 9 | — | New York City |
| June 25 | Carlos Maussa | **Vivian Harris** | TKO 7 | **WBA** | Atlantic City |
| June 25 | Floyd Mayweather Jr. | **Arturo Gatti** | TKO 6 | **WBC** | Atlantic City |
| Sept. 24 | Miguel Cotto | Ricardo Torres | KO 7 | — | Atlantic City |

\*Kostya Tszyu, the IBF junior welterweight champion faced, and beat, the interim IBF super lightweight champ Sharmba Mitchell.

†Tszyu quit on his stool following the 11th round.

## Major Bouts, 2003-04 (Cont.)

### Lightweights (135 lbs)

| Date | Winner | Loser | Result | Title | Site |
|------|--------|-------|--------|-------|------|
| Nov. 4 | **Juan Diaz** | Julien Lorcy | Wu 12 | **WBA** | San Antonio, Texas |
| Dec. 4 | **Jose Luis Castillo** | Joel Casamayor | Ws 12 | **WBC** | Las Vegas |
| Dec. 11 | Acelino Freitas | Fernando Saucedo | Wu 10 | — | Sao Paulo, Brazil |
| Jan. 21 | **Juan Diaz** | Billy Irwin | TKO 9 | **WBA** | Houston, Texas |
| Mar. 5 | **Jose Luis Castillo** | Julio Diaz | TKO 10 | **WBC*** | Las Vegas |
| May 7 | Diego Corrales | **Jose Luis Castillo** | TKO 10 | **WBC** | Las Vegas |
| June 17 | Leavander Johnson | Stefano Zoff | TKO 7 | **IBF†** | Milan, Italy |
| June 18 | Ike Quartey | Verno Phillips | Wu 12 | — | Memphis, Tenn. |
| Sept. 3 | Zahir Raheem | Erik Morales | Wu 12 | — | Los Angeles |
| Sept. 17 | Jesus Chavez | **Leavander Johnson** | TKO 11 | **IBF** | Las Vegas |
| Oct. 8 | Jose Luis Castillo | **Diego Corrales** | KO 4 | — | Las Vegas |

*Julio Diaz vacated the IBF lightweight title he won in 2004 in order to face WBC champ Jose Luis Castillo.
†Johnson won the IBF title that was left vacant by Julio Diaz.

### Junior Lightweights (130 lbs)
#### (Super Featherweights)

| Date | Winner | Loser | Result | Title | Site |
|------|--------|-------|--------|-------|------|
| Nov. 27 | Marco Antonio Barrera | **Erik Morales** | Wm 12 | **WBC** | Las Vegas |
| Dec. 11 | Carlos Hernandez | Juan Carlos Ramirez | Ws 10 | — | Las Vegas |
| Dec. 11 | Carlos Navarro | Agapito Sanchez | TKO 11 | — | Las Vegas |
| Feb. 23 | Robbie Peden | Nate Campbell | TKO 8 | **IBF*** | Melbourne, Australia |
| Mar. 18 | Erik Morales | Manny Pacquiao | Wu 12 | — | Las Vegas |
| Apr. 9 | **Marco Antonio Barrera** | Mzonke Fana | TKO 2 | **WBC** | El Paso, Texas |
| Apr. 30 | Vicente Mosquera | **Yodsanan Nanthachai** | Wu 12 | **WBA** | New York City |
| Sept. 10 | Manny Pacquiao | Hector Velasquez | TKO 6 | — | Los Angeles |
| Sept. 17 | **Marco Antonio Barrera** | **Robbie Peden** | Wu 12 | **WBC/IBF** | Las Vegas |

*Peden won the vacant IBF title, that Erik Morales was stripped of for signing to fight Marco Antonio Barrera instead of the mandatory challenger.

### Featherweights (126 lbs)

| Date | Winner | Loser | Result | Title | Site |
|------|--------|-------|--------|-------|------|
| Dec. 3 | Ricardo Juarez | Guty Espadas Jr. | KO 2 | — | Atlantic City |
| Dec. 3 | Chris John | Jose Rojas | TDraw 4* | **WBA** | Tenggarong, Indonesia |
| Dec. 11 | Manny Pacquiao | Fahsan Por Thawatchai | TKO 4 | — | Manila, Philippines |
| Jan. 30 | **Chi In-Jin** | Tommy Browne | Wu 12 | **WBC** | Seoul, South Korea |
| Apr. 22 | Chris John | Derrick Gainer | Wu 12 | **WBA*** | Jakarta, Indonesia |
| May 7 | **Juan Manuel Marquez** | Victor Polo | Wu 12 | **WBA/IBF** | Las Vegas |
| Aug. 7 | Chris John | Tommy Browne | TKO 9 | **WBA** | Penrith, Australia |
| Aug. 20 | Humberto Soto | Rocky Juarez | Wu 12 | **WBC†** | Rosemont, Ill. |

*John retained the WBA title when the fight was ruled a technical draw following an accidental clash of heads the caused cuts to both men. Note that Juan Manuel Marquez is the WBA "super world champion."
†Soto won the interim WBC belt.

### Junior Featherweights (122 lbs)
#### (Super Bantamweights)

| Date | Winner | Loser | Result | Title | Site |
|------|--------|-------|--------|-------|------|
| Nov. 8 | **Mayhar Monshipour** | Yoddamrong Sithyodthong | TKO 6 | **WBA** | Paris-Bercy, France |
| Nov. 27 | **Oscar Larios** | Nedal Hussein | Wu 12 | **WBC** | Las Vegas |
| Dec. 28 | **Israel Vasquez** | Art Simonyan | TKO 5 | **IBF** | El Cajon, California |
| Feb. 10 | **Oscar Larios** | Wayne McCullough | Wu 12 | **WBC** | Lemoore, California |
| Apr. 29 | **Mahyar Monshipour** | Shigeru Nakazato | TKO 6 | **WBA** | Marseilles, France |
| May 31 | **Israel Vasquez** | Armando Guerrero | Wu 12 | **IBF** | Lynwood, Ill. |
| June 25 | **Mahyar Monshipour** | Julio Zarate | TKO 9 | **WBA** | Poitiers, France |
| July 16 | **Oscar Larios** | Wayne McCullough | TKO 10 | **WBC** | Las Vegas |
| Oct. 15 | Celestino Caballero | Yober Ortega | Wu 12 | **WBA*** | Panama City, Panama |

*Caballero won the interim WBA belt.

## Bantamweights (118 lbs)

| Date | Winner | Loser | Result | Title | Site |
|------|--------|-------|--------|-------|------|
| Nov. 27 | **Rafael Marquez** . . . . . Mauricio Pastrana | TKO 8 | **IBF** | Las Vegas |
| Feb. 26 | Wladimir Sidorenko . . . . Julio Zarate | Wu 12 | **WBA\*** | Hamburg, Germany |
| Apr. 16 | Hozumi Hasegawa . . . . . . **Veeraphol Sahaprom** · | Wu 12 | **WBC** | Tokyo |
| Aug. 31 | Poonsawat Kratingdaenggym . . . . . Ricardo Cordoba | Ws 12 | WBA† | Bangkok, Thailand |
| Sept. 25 | **Hozumi Hasegawa** . . . Gerardo Martinez | TKO 7 | **WBC** | Tokyo |

\*Sidorenko captured the WBA belt left vacant with the retirement of Johnny Bredahl.
†interim WBA title.

## Junior Bantamweights (115 lbs)
### (Super Flyweights)

| Date | Winner | Loser | Result | Title | Site |
|------|--------|-------|--------|-------|------|
| Dec. 3 | Martin Castillo . . . . . . . . **Alexander Munoz** | Wu 12 | **WBA** | Laredo, Texas |
| Jan. 3 | **Katsushige Kawashima** Jose Navarro | Ws 12 | **WBC** | Tokyo |
| Mar. 19 | **Martin Castillo** . . . . . . Eric Morel | Wu 12 | **WBA** | Las Vegas |
| Apr. 30 | **Luis Perez** . . . . . . . . . . Luis Bolano | KO 6 | **IBF** | New York City |
| June 26 | **Martin Castillo** . . . . . . Hideyasu Ishihara | Wu 12 | **WBA** | Nagoya, Japan |
| July 18 | Masmori Tokuyama . . . . . **Katsushige Kawashima** | Wu 12 | WBC | Tokyo |

## Flyweights (112 lbs)

| Date | Winner | Loser | Result | Title | Site |
|------|--------|-------|--------|-------|------|
| Dec. 16 | Vic Darchinyan . . . . . . . . **Irene Pacheco** | TKO 11 | **IBF** | Hollywood, Florida |
| Jan. 3 | **Lorenzo Parra** . . . . . . Trash Nakanuma | Wu 12 | **WBA** | Tokyo |
| Jan. 29 | **Pongsaklek Wonjongkam** . . . . . Noriyuki Komatsu | TKO 5 | **WBC** | Osaka, Japan |
| Mar. 27 | **Vic Darchinyan** . . . . . . Mzukisi Sikali | TKO 8 | **IBF** | Sydney, Australia |
| July 30 | Jorge Arce . . . . . . . . . . . Angel Priolo | KO 3 | WBC\* | La Paz, Mexico |
| Aug. 24 | **Vic Darchinyan** . . . . . . Jair Jimenez | TKO 5 | **IBF** | Sydney, Australia |
| Sept. 19 | **Lorenzo Parra** . . . . . . Takefumi Sakata | Wm 12 | **WBA** | Tokyo |
| Oct. 8 | Jorge Arce . . . . . . . . . . . Hussein Hussein | TKO 2 | WBC | Las Vegas |
| Oct. 10 | **Pongsaklek Wonjongkam** . . . . . Daisuke Naito | TWu 7† | **WBC** | Tokyo |

\*Arce won the interim WBC flyweight title but note that Pongsaklek Wonjongkam is the WBC flyweight champion.
†Wonjongkam won by technical decision when the fight was stopped after his opponent suffered a cut just over his right eye from a punch.

## Junior Flyweights (108 lbs)
### (Light Flyweights)

| Date | Winner | Loser | Result | Title | Site |
|------|--------|-------|--------|-------|------|
| Mar. 11 | Eric Ortiz . . . . . . . . . . . Jose Antonio Aguirre | TKO 7 | **WBC\*** | Mexico City |
| Apr. 29 | Roberto Vasquez . . . . . . . **Beibis Mendoza** | KO 10 | **WBA** | Panama City |
| May 15 | Will Grigsby . . . . . . . . . **Victor Burgos** | Wu 12 | **IBF** | Las Vegas |
| Sept. 10 | Brian Viloria . . . . . . . . . . **Eric Ortiz** | TKO 1 | **WBC** | Los Angeles |

\*Ortiz won the WBC belt that was left vacant when former champ Jorge Arce moved up in weight.

## Minimumweights (105 lbs)
### (Strawweights or Mini-Flyweights)

| Date | Winner | Loser | Result | Title | Site |
|------|--------|-------|--------|-------|------|
| Nov. 27 | Ivan Calderon . . . . . . . . Carlos Fajardo | Wu 12 | — | Las Vegas |
| Dec. 18 | Isaac Bustos . . . . . . . . . . **Eagle Kyowa**† | TKO 4 | **WBC** | Tokyo |
| Apr. 4 | Katsunari Takayama . . . . **Isaac Bustos** | Wu 12 | **WBC** | Osaka, Japan |
| Apr. 5 | **Muhammad Rachman** .Fahlan Sakreerin | TDraw 3\* | **IBF** | Merauke City, Indonesia |
| Apr. 16 | **Yutaka Niida** . . . . . . . Jae Won Kim | Wu 12 | **WBA** | Tokyo |
| Aug. 6 | Eagle Kyowa . . . . . . . . . **Katsunari Takayama** | Wu 12 | **WBC** | Tokyo |
| Sept. 25 | **Yutaka Niida** . . . . . . . Eriberto G ejon | Ws 12 | **WBA** | Tokyo |

†Eagle Kyowa was formerly known as Eagle Akakura.
\*Rachman retained his IBF belt when the fight was stopped in round three following an unintentional head butt.

# 1892-2005
# Through the Years

SPORTS ALMANAC

## World Heavyweight Championship Fights

Widely accepted world champions in **bold** type. Note following result abbreviations: KO (knockout), TKO (technical knockout), Wu (unanimous decision), Wm (majority decision), Ws (split decision), Ref (referee's decision), ND (no decision), Disq. (won on disqualification).

| Year | Date | Winner | Age | Wgt | Loser | Wgt | Result | Location |
|------|------|--------|-----|-----|-------|-----|--------|----------|
| 1892 | Sept. 7 | James J. Corbett | 26 | 178 | John L. Sullivan | 212 | KO 21 | New Orleans |
| 1894 | Jan. 25 | **James J. Corbett** | 27 | 184 | Charley Mitchell | 158 | KO 3 | Jacksonville, Fla. |
| 1897 | Mar. 17 | Bob Fitzsimmons | 34 | 167 | **James J. Corbett** | 183 | KO 14 | Carson City, Nev. |
| 1899 | June 9 | James J. Jeffries | 24 | 206 | **Bob Fitzsimmons** | 167 | KO 11 | Coney Island, N.Y. |
| 1899 | Nov. 3 | **James J. Jeffries** | 24 | 215 | Tom Sharkey | 183 | Ref 25 | Coney Island, N.Y. |
| 1900 | Apr. 6 | **James J. Jeffries** | 24 | NA | Jack Finnegan | NA | KO 1 | Detroit |
| 1900 | May 11 | **James J. Jeffries** | 25 | 218 | James J. Corbett | 188 | KO 23 | Coney Island, N.Y. |
| 1901 | Nov. 15 | **James J. Jeffries** | 26 | 211 | Gus Ruhlin | 194 | TKO 6 | San Francisco |
| 1902 | July 25 | **James J. Jeffries** | 27 | 219 | Bob Fitzsimmons | 172 | KO 8 | San Francisco |
| 1903 | Aug. 14 | **James J. Jeffries** | 28 | 220 | James J. Corbett | 190 | KO 10 | San Francisco |
| 1904 | Aug. 25 | **James J. Jeffries*** | 29 | 219 | Jack Munroe | 186 | TKO 2 | San Francisco |
| 1905 | July 3 | Marvin Hart | 28 | 190 | Jack Root | 171 | KO 12 | Reno, Nev. |
| 1906 | Feb. 23 | Tommy Burns | 24 | 180 | **Marvin Hart** | 188 | Ref 20 | Los Angeles |
| 1906 | Oct. 2 | **Tommy Burns** | 25 | NA | Jim Flynn | NA | KO 15 | Los Angeles |
| 1906 | Nov. 28 | **Tommy Burns** | 25 | 172 | Phila. Jack O'Brien | 163½ | Draw 20 | Los Angeles |
| 1907 | May 8 | **Tommy Burns** | 25 | 180 | Phila. Jack O'Brien | 167 | Ref 20 | Los Angeles |
| 1907 | July 4 | **Tommy Burns** | 26 | 181 | Bill Squires | 180 | KO 1 | Colma, Calif. |
| 1907 | Dec. 2 | **Tommy Burns** | 26 | 177 | Gunner Moir | 204 | KO 10 | London |
| 1908 | Feb. 10 | **Tommy Burns** | 26 | NA | Jack Palmer | NA | KO 4 | London |
| 1908 | Mar. 17 | **Tommy Burns** | 26 | NA | Jem Roche | NA | KO 1 | Dublin |
| 1908 | Apr. 18 | **Tommy Burns** | 26 | NA | Jewey Smith | NA | KO 5 | Paris |
| 1908 | June 13 | **Tommy Burns** | 26 | 184 | Bill Squires | 183 | KO 8 | Paris |
| 1908 | Aug. 24 | **Tommy Burns** | 27 | 181 | Bill Squires | 184 | KO 13 | Sydney |
| 1908 | Sept. 2 | **Tommy Burns** | 27 | 183 | Bill Lang | 187 | KO 6 | Melbourne |
| 1908 | Dec. 26 | Jack Johnson | 30 | 192 | **Tommy Burns** | 168 | TKO 14 | Sydney |
| 1909 | Mar. 10 | **Jack Johnson** | 30 | NA | Victor McLaglen | NA | ND 6 | Vancouver |
| 1909 | May 19 | **Jack Johnson** | 31 | 205 | Phila. Jack O'Brien | 161 | ND 6 | Philadelphia |
| 1909 | June 30 | **Jack Johnson** | 31 | 207 | Tony Ross | 214 | ND 6 | Pittsburgh |
| 1909 | Sept. 9 | **Jack Johnson** | 31 | 209 | Al Kaufman | 191 | ND 10 | San Francisco |
| 1909 | Oct. 16 | **Jack Johnson** | 31 | 205½ | Stanley Ketchel | 170¼ | KO 12 | Colma, Calif. |
| 1910 | July 4 | **Jack Johnson** | 32 | 208 | James J. Jeffries | 227 | KO 15 | Reno, Nev. |
| 1912 | July 4 | **Jack Johnson** | 34 | 195½ | Jim Flynn | 175 | TKO 9 | Las Vegas, Nev. |
| 1913 | Dec. 19 | **Jack Johnson** | 35 | NA | Jim Johnson | NA | Draw 10 | Paris |
| 1914 | June 27 | **Jack Johnson** | 36 | 221 | Frank Moran | 203 | Ref 20 | Paris |
| 1915 | Apr. 5 | Jess Willard | 33 | 230 | **Jack Johnson** | 205½ | KO 26 | Havana |
| 1916 | Mar. 25 | **Jess Willard** | 34 | 225 | Frank Moran | 203 | ND 10 | NYC (Mad.Sq. Garden) |
| 1919 | July 4 | Jack Dempsey | 24 | 187 | **Jess Willard** | 245 | TKO 4 | Toledo, Ohio |
| 1920 | Sept. 6 | **Jack Dempsey** | 25 | 185 | Billy Miske | 187 | KO 3 | Benton Harbor, Mich. |
| 1920 | Dec. 14 | **Jack Dempsey** | 25 | 188¼ | Bill Brennan | 197 | KO 12 | NYC (Mad. Sq. Garden) |
| 1921 | July 2 | **Jack Dempsey** | 26 | 188 | Georges Carpentier | 172 | KO 4 | Jersey City, N.J. |
| 1923 | July 4 | **Jack Dempsey** | 28 | 188 | Tommy Gibbons | 175½ | Ref 15 | Shelby, Mont. |
| 1923 | Sept. 14 | **Jack Dempsey** | 28 | 192½ | Luis Firpo | 216½ | KO 2 | NYC (Polo Grounds) |
| 1926 | Sept. 23 | Gene Tunney | 29 | 189½ | **Jack Dempsey** | 190 | Wu 10 | Philadelphia |
| 1927 | Sept. 22 | **Gene Tunney** | 30 | 189½ | Jack Dempsey | 192½ | Wu 10 | Chicago |
| 1928 | July 26 | **Gene Tunney**** | 31 | 192 | Tom Heeney | 203 | TKO 11 | NYC (Yankee Stadium) |
| 1930 | June 12 | Max Schmeling | 24 | 188 | Jack Sharkey | 197 | Disq. 4 | NYC (Yankee Stadium) |
| 1931 | July 3 | **Max Schmeling** | 25 | 189 | Young Stribling | 186½ | TKO 15 | Cleveland |

*James J. Jeffries retired as champion on May 13, 1905, then came out of retirement to fight Jack Johnson for the title in 1910.
**Gene Tunney retired as champion in 1928.

| Year | Date | Winner | Age | Wgt | Loser | Wgt | Result | Location |
|------|------|--------|-----|-----|-------|-----|--------|----------|
| 1932 | June 21 | Jack Sharkey | 29 | 205 | **Max Schmeling** | 188 | Ws 15 | Long Island City, N.Y. |
| 1933 | June 29 | Primo Carnera | 26 | 260½ | **Jack Sharkey** | 201 | KO 6 | Long Island City, N.Y. |
| 1933 | Oct. 22 | **Primo Carnera** | 26 | 259½ | Paulino Uzcudun | 229¼ | Wu 15 | Rome |
| 1934 | Mar. 1 | **Primo Carnera** | 27 | 270 | Tommy Loughran | 184 | Wu 15 | Miami |
| 1934 | June 14 | Max Baer | 25 | 209½ | **Primo Carnera** | 263¼ | TKO 11 | Long Island City, N.Y. |
| 1935 | June 13 | James J. Braddock | 29 | 193¾ | **Max Baer** | 209 | Wu 15 | Long Island City, N.Y. |
| 1937 | June 22 | Joe Louis | 23 | 197¼ | **James J. Braddock** | 197 | KO 8 | Chicago |
| 1937 | Aug. 30 | **Joe Louis** | 23 | 197 | Tommy Farr | 204¼ | Wu 15 | NYC (Yankee Stadium) |
| 1938 | Feb. 23 | **Joe Louis** | 23 | 200 | Nathan Mann | 193½ | KO 3 | NYC (Mad. Sq. Garden) |
| 1938 | Apr. 1 | **Joe Louis** | 23 | 202½ | Harry Thomas | 196 | KO 5 | Chicago |
| 1938 | June 22 | **Joe Louis** | 24 | 198¾ | Max Schmeling | 193 | KO 1 | NYC (Yankee Stadium) |
| 1939 | Jan. 25 | **Joe Louis** | 24 | 200¼ | John Henry Lewis | 180¾ | KO 1 | NYC (Mad. Sq. Garden) |
| 1939 | Apr. 17 | **Joe Louis** | 24 | 201¼ | Jack Roper | 204¾ | KO 1 | Los Angeles |
| 1939 | June 28 | **Joe Louis** | 25 | 200¾ | Tony Galento | 233¾ | TKO 4 | NYC (Yankee Stadium) |
| 1939 | Sept. 20 | **Joe Louis** | 25 | 200 | Bob Pastor | 183 | KO 11 | Detroit |
| 1940 | Feb. 9 | **Joe Louis** | 25 | 203 | Arturo Godoy | 202 | Ws 15 | NYC (Mad. Sq. Garden) |
| 1940 | Mar. 29 | **Joe Louis** | 25 | 201½ | Johnny Paychek | 187½ | KO 2 | NYC (Mad. Sq. Garden) |
| 1940 | June 20 | **Joe Louis** | 26 | 199 | Arturo Godoy | 201¼ | TKO 8 | NYC (Yankee Stadium) |
| 1940 | Dec. 16 | **Joe Louis** | 26 | 202¼ | Al McCoy | 180¾ | TKO 6 | Boston |
| 1941 | Jan. 31 | **Joe Louis** | 26 | 202½ | Red Burman | 188 | KO 5 | NYC (Mad. Sq. Garden) |
| 1941 | Feb. 17 | **Joe Louis** | 26 | 203½ | Gus Dorazio | 193½ | KO 2 | Philadelphia |
| 1941 | Mar. 21 | **Joe Louis** | 26 | 202 | Abe Simon | 254½ | TKO 13 | Detroit |
| 1941 | Apr. 8 | **Joe Louis** | 26 | 203½ | Tony Musto | 199½ | TKO 9 | St. Louis |
| 1941 | May 23 | **Joe Louis** | 27 | 201½ | Buddy Baer | 237½ | Disq. 7 | Washington, D.C. |
| 1941 | June 18 | **Joe Louis** | 27 | 199½ | Billy Conn | 174 | KO 13 | NYC (Polo Grounds) |
| 1941 | Sept. 29 | **Joe Louis** | 27 | 202¼ | Lou Nova | 202½ | TKO 6 | NYC (Polo Grounds) |
| 1942 | Jan. 9 | **Joe Louis** | 27 | 206¾ | Buddy Baer | 250 | KO 1 | NYC (Mad. Sq. Garden) |
| 1942 | Mar. 27 | **Joe Louis** | 27 | 207½ | Abe Simon | 255½ | KO 6 | NYC (Mad. Sq. Garden) |
| 1942-45 World War II | | | | | | | | |
| 1946 | June 9 | **Joe Louis** | 32 | 207 | Billy Conn | 187 | KO 8 | NYC (Yankee Stadium) |
| 1946 | Sept. 18 | **Joe Louis** | 32 | 211 | Tami Mauriello | 198½ | KO 1 | NYC (Yankee Stadium) |
| 1947 | Dec. 5 | **Joe Louis** | 33 | 211½ | Jersey Joe Walcott | 194½ | Ws 15 | NYC (Mad. Sq. Garden) |
| 1948 | June 25 | Joe Louis* | 34 | 213½ | Jersey Joe Walcott | 194¾ | KO 11 | NYC (Yankee Stadium) |
| 1949 | June 22 | **Ezzard Charles** | 27 | 181¾ | Jersey Joe Walcott | 195½ | Wu 15 | Chicago |
| 1949 | Aug. 10 | **Ezzard Charles** | 28 | 180 | Gus Lesnevich | 182 | TKO 8 | NYC (Yankee Stadium) |
| 1949 | Oct. 14 | **Ezzard Charles** | 28 | 182 | Pat Valentino | 188½ | KO 8 | San Francisco |
| 1950 | Aug. 15 | **Ezzard Charles** | 29 | 183¼ | Freddie Beshore | 184½ | TKO 14 | Buffalo |
| 1950 | Sept. 27 | **Ezzard Charles** | 29 | 184½ | Joe Louis | 218 | Wu 15 | NYC (Yankee Stadium) |
| 1950 | Dec. 5 | **Ezzard Charles** | 29 | 185 | Nick Barone | 178½ | KO 11 | Cincinnati |
| 1951 | Jan. 12 | **Ezzard Charles** | 29 | 185 | Lee Oma | 193 | TKO 10 | NYC (Mad. Sq. Garden) |
| 1951 | Mar. 7 | **Ezzard Charles** | 29 | 186 | Jersey Joe Walcott | 193 | Wu 15 | Detroit |
| 1951 | May 30 | **Ezzard Charles** | 29 | 182 | Joey Maxim | 181½ | Wu 15 | Chicago |
| 1951 | July 18 | Jersey Joe Walcott | 37 | 194 | **Ezzard Charles** | 182 | KO 7 | Pittsburgh |
| 1952 | June 5 | **Jersey Joe Walcott** | 38 | 196 | Ezzard Charles | 191½ | Wu 15 | Philadelphia |
| 1952 | Sept. 23 | Rocky Marciano | 29 | 184 | **Jersey Joe Walcott** | 196 | KO 13 | Philadelphia |
| 1953 | May 15 | **Rocky Marciano** | 29 | 184½ | Jersey Joe Walcott | 197¾ | KO 1 | Chicago |
| 1953 | Sept. 24 | **Rocky Marciano** | 30 | 185 | Roland LaStarza | 184¾ | TKO 11 | NYC (Polo Grounds) |
| 1954 | June 17 | **Rocky Marciano** | 30 | 187½ | Ezzard Charles | 185½ | Wu 15 | NYC (Yankee Stadium) |
| 1954 | Sept. 17 | **Rocky Marciano** | 31 | 187 | Ezzard Charles | 192½ | KO 8 | NYC (Yankee Stadium) |
| 1955 | May 16 | **Rocky Marciano** | 31 | 189 | Don Cockell | 205 | TKO 9 | San Francisco |
| 1955 | Sept. 21 | **Rocky Marciano**** | 32 | 188¼ | Archie Moore | 188 | KO 9 | NYC (Yankee Stadium) |
| 1956 | Nov. 30 | Floyd Patterson | 21 | 182¼ | Archie Moore | 187¾ | KO 5 | Chicago |
| 1957 | July 29 | **Floyd Patterson** | 22 | 184 | Tommy Jackson | 192½ | TKO 10 | NYC (Polo Grounds) |
| 1957 | Aug. 22 | **Floyd Patterson** | 22 | 187¼ | Pete Rademacher | 202 | KO 6 | Seattle |
| 1958 | Aug. 18 | **Floyd Patterson** | 23 | 184½ | Roy Harris | 194 | TKO 13 | Los Angeles |
| 1959 | May 1 | **Floyd Patterson** | 24 | 182½ | Brian London | 206 | KO 11 | Indianapolis |
| 1959 | June 26 | Ingemar Johansson | 26 | 196 | **Floyd Patterson** | 182 | TKO 3 | NYC (Yankee Stadium) |
| 1960 | June 20 | Floyd Patterson | 25 | 190 | **Ingemar Johansson** | 194¾ | KO 5 | NYC (Polo Grounds) |
| 1961 | Mar. 13 | **Floyd Patterson** | 26 | 194¾ | Ingemar Johansson | 206½ | KO 6 | Miami Beach |
| 1961 | Dec. 4 | **Floyd Patterson** | 26 | 188½ | Tom McNeeley | 197 | KO 4 | Toronto |
| 1962 | Sept. 25 | Sonny Liston | 30 | 214 | **Floyd Patterson** | 189 | KO 1 | Chicago |
| 1963 | July 22 | **Sonny Liston** | 31 | 215 | Floyd Patterson | 194½ | KO 1 | Las Vegas |
| 1964 | Feb. 25 | Cassius Clay** | 22 | 210½ | Sonny Liston | 218 | TKO 7 | Miami Beach |

*Joe Louis retired as champion on Mar. 1, 1949, then came out of retirement to fight Ezzard Charles for the title in 1950.
**Rocky Marciano retired as undefeated champion on Apr. 27, 1956.

## World Heavyweight Championship Fights (Cont.)

| Year | Date | Winner | Age | Wgt | Loser | Wgt | Result | Location |
|---|---|---|---|---|---|---|---|---|
| 1965 | Mar. 5 | Ernie Terrell WBA | 25 | 199 | Eddie Machen | 192 | Wu 15 | Chicago |
| 1965 | May 25 | **Muhammad Ali** | 23 | 206 | Sonny Liston | 215¼ | KO 1 | Lewiston, Maine |
| 1965 | Nov. 1 | Ernie Terrell WBA | 26 | 206 | George Chuvalo | 209 | Wu 15 | Toronto |
| 1965 | Nov. 22 | **Muhammad Ali** | 23 | 210 | Floyd Patterson | 196¾ | TKO 12 | Las Vegas |
| 1966 | Mar. 29 | **Muhammad Ali** | 24 | 214½ | George Chuvalo | 216 | Wu 15 | Toronto |
| 1966 | May 21 | **Muhammad Ali** | 24 | 201½ | Henry Cooper | 188 | TKO 6 | London |
| 1966 | June 28 | Ernie Terrell WBA | 27 | 209½ | Doug Jones | 187½ | Wu 15 | Houston |
| 1966 | Aug. 6 | **Muhammad Ali** | 24 | 209½ | Brian London | 201½ | KO 3 | London |
| 1966 | Sept. 10 | **Muhammad Ali** | 24 | 203½ | Karl Mildenberger | 194¼ | TKO 12 | Frankfurt, W. Ger. |
| 1966 | Nov. 14 | **Muhammad Ali** | 24 | 212¾ | Cleveland Williams | 210½ | TKO 3 | Houston |
| 1967 | Feb. 6 | **Muhammad Ali** | 25 | 212¼ | Ernie Terrell WBA | 212¼ | Wu 15 | Houston |
| 1967 | Mar. 22 | **Muhammad Ali** | 25 | 211½ | Zora Folley | 202½ | KO 7 | NYC (Mad. Sq. Garden) |
| 1968 | Mar. 4 | Joe Frazier | 24 | 204½ | Buster Mathis | 243½ | TKO 11 | NYC (Mad. Sq. Garden) |
| 1968 | Apr. 27 | Jimmy Ellis | 28 | 197 | Jerry Quarry | 195 | Wm 15 | Oakland |
| 1968 | June 24 | Joe Frazier NY | 24 | 203½ | Manuel Ramos | 208 | TKO 2 | NYC (Mad. Sq. Garden) |
| 1968 | Aug. 14 | Jimmy Ellis WBA | 28 | 198 | Floyd Patterson | 188 | Ref 15 | Stockholm |
| 1968 | Dec. 10 | Joe Frazier NY | 24 | 203 | Oscar Bonavena | 207 | Wu 15 | Philadelphia |
| 1969 | Apr. 22 | Joe Frazier NY | 25 | 204½ | Dave Zyglewicz | 190½ | KO 1 | Houston |
| 1969 | June 23 | Joe Frazier NY | 25 | 203½ | Jerry Quarry | 198½ | TKO 8 | NYC (Mad. Sq. Garden) |
| 1970 | Feb. 16 | Joe Frazier NY | 26 | 205 | Jimmy Ellis WBA | 201 | TKO 5 | NYC (Mad. Sq. Garden) |
| 1970 | Nov. 18 | **Joe Frazier** | 26 | 209 | Bob Foster | 188 | KO 2 | Detroit |
| 1971 | Mar. 8 | **Joe Frazier** | 27 | 205½ | Muhammad Ali | 215 | Wu 15 | NYC (Mad. Sq. Garden) |
| 1972 | Jan. 15 | **Joe Frazier** | 28 | 215½ | Terry Daniels | 195 | TKO 4 | New Orleans |
| 1972 | May 26 | **Joe Frazier** | 28 | 217½ | Ron Stander | 218 | TKO 5 | Omaha, Neb. |
| 1973 | Jan. 22 | George Foreman | 24 | 217½ | **Joe Frazier** | 214 | TKO 2 | Kingston, Jamaica |
| 1973 | Sept. 1 | **George Foreman** | 24 | 219½ | Jose (King) Roman | 196½ | KO 1 | Tokyo |
| 1974 | Mar. 26 | **George Foreman** | 25 | 224¾ | Ken Norton | 212¾ | TKO 2 | Caracas, Venezuela |
| 1974 | Oct. 30 | Muhammad Ali | 32 | 216½ | **George Foreman** | 220 | KO 8 | Kinshasa, Zaire |
| 1975 | Mar. 24 | **Muhammad Ali** | 33 | 223½ | Chuck Wepner | 225 | TKO 15 | Cleveland |
| 1975 | May 16 | **Muhammad Ali** | 33 | 224½ | Ron Lyle | 219 | TKO 11 | Las Vegas |
| 1975 | June 30 | **Muhammad Ali** | 33 | 224½ | Joe Bugner | 230 | Wu 15 | Kuala Lumpur, Malaysia |
| 1975 | Oct. 1 | **Muhammad Ali** | 33 | 224½ | Joe Frazier | 215 | TKO 14 | Manila, Philippines |
| 1976 | Feb. 20 | **Muhammad Ali** | 34 | 226 | Jean Pierre Coopman | 206 | KO 5 | San Juan, P.R. |
| 1976 | Apr. 30 | **Muhammad Ali** | 34 | 230 | Jimmy Young | 209 | Wu 15 | Landover, Md. |
| 1976 | May 24 | **Muhammad Ali** | 34 | 220 | Richard Dunn | 206½ | TKO 5 | Munich, W. Ger. |
| 1976 | Sept. 28 | **Muhammad Ali** | 34 | 221 | Ken Norton | 217½ | Wu 15 | NYC (Yankee Stadium) |
| 1977 | May 16 | **Muhammad Ali** | 35 | 221¼ | Alfredo Evangelista | 209¼ | Wu 15 | Landover, Md. |
| 1977 | Sept. 29 | **Muhammad Ali** | 35 | 225 | Earnie Shavers | 211¼ | Wu 15 | NYC (Mad. Sq. Garden) |
| 1978 | Feb. 15 | Leon Spinks | 24 | 197¼ | **Muhammad Ali** | 224¼ | Ws 15 | Las Vegas |
| 1978 | June 9 | Larry Holmes | 28 | 209 | Ken Norton WBC†† | 220 | Ws 15 | Las Vegas |
| 1978 | Sept. 15 | Muhammad Ali† | 36 | 221 | **Leon Spinks** | 201 | Wu 15 | New Orleans |
| 1978 | Nov. 10 | Larry Holmes WBC | 29 | 214 | Alfredo Evangelista | 208¼ | KO 7 | Las Vegas |
| 1979 | Mar. 23 | Larry Holmes WBC | 29 | 214 | Osvaldo Ocasio | 207 | TKO 7 | Las Vegas |
| 1979 | June 22 | Larry Holmes WBC | 29 | 215 | Mike Weaver | 202 | TKO 12 | NYC (Mad. Sq. Garden) |
| 1979 | Sept. 28 | Larry Holmes WBC | 29 | 210 | Earnie Shavers | 211 | TKO 11 | Las Vegas |
| 1979 | Oct. 20 | John Tate | 24 | 240 | Gerrie Coetzee | 222 | Wu 15 | Pretoria, S. Africa |
| 1980 | Feb. 3 | Larry Holmes WBC | 30 | 213½ | Lorenzo Zanon | 215 | TKO 6 | Las Vegas |
| 1980 | Mar. 31 | Mike Weaver | 27 | 232 | John Tate WBA | 232 | KO 15 | Knoxville, Tenn. |
| 1980 | Mar. 31 | Larry Holmes WBC | 30 | 211 | Leroy Jones | 254½ | TKO 8 | Las Vegas |
| 1980 | July 7 | Larry Holmes WBC | 30 | 214¼ | Scott LeDoux | 226 | TKO 7 | Minneapolis |
| 1980 | Oct. 2 | Larry Holmes WBC | 30 | 211½ | Muhammad Ali | 217½ | TKO 11 | Las Vegas |
| 1980 | Oct. 25 | Mike Weaver WBA | 28 | 210 | Gerrie Coetzee | 226½ | KO 13 | Sun City, S. Africa |
| 1981 | Apr. 11 | **Larry Holmes** | 31 | 215 | Trevor Berbick | 215½ | Wu 15 | Las Vegas |
| 1981 | June 12 | **Larry Holmes** | 31 | 212½ | Leon Spinks | 200¼ | TKO 3 | Detroit |
| 1981 | Oct. 3 | Mike Weaver WBA | 29 | 215 | James (Quick) Tillis | 209 | Wu 15 | Rosemont, Ill. |
| 1981 | Nov. 6 | **Larry Holmes** | 32 | 213¼ | Renaldo Snipes | 215¾ | TKO 11 | Pittsburgh |
| 1982 | June 11 | **Larry Holmes** | 32 | 212½ | Gerry Cooney | 225½ | TKO 13 | Las Vegas |
| 1982 | Nov. 26 | **Larry Holmes** | 33 | 217½ | Randall (Tex) Cobb | 234¼ | Wu 15 | Houston |
| 1982 | Dec. 10 | Michael Dokes | 24 | 216 | Mike Weaver WBA | 209¾ | TKO 1 | Las Vegas |

**After defeating Liston, Cassius Clay announced that he had changed his name to Muhammad Ali. He was later stripped of his title by the WBA and most state boxing commissions after refusing induction into the U.S. Army on Apr. 28, 1967.

† Muhammad Ali retired as champion on June 27, 1979, then came out of retirement to fight Larry Holmes for the title in 1980.

†† WBC recognized Ken Norton as world champion when Leon Spinks refused to meet Norton before Spinks' rematch with Muhammad Ali. Norton had scored a 15-round split decision over Jimmy Young on Nov. 5, 1977 in Las Vegas.

| Year | Date | Winner | Age | Wgt | Loser | Wgt | Result | Location |
|---|---|---|---|---|---|---|---|---|
| 1983 | Mar. 27 | **Larry Holmes** | 33 | 221 | Lucien Rodriguez | 209 | Wu 12 | Scranton, Pa. |
| 1983 | May 20 | Michael Dokes WBA | 24 | 223 | Mike Weaver | 218½ | Draw 15 | Las Vegas |
| 1983 | May 20 | **Larry Holmes** | 33 | 213 | Tim Witherspoon | 219½ | Ws 12 | Las Vegas |
| 1983 | Sept. 10 | **Larry Holmes** | 33 | 223 | Scott Frank | 211¼ | TKO 5 | Atlantic City |
| 1983 | Sept. 23 | Gerrie Coetzee | 28 | 215 | Michael Dokes WBA | 217 | KO 10 | Richfield, Ohio |
| 1983 | Nov. 25 | **Larry Holmes** | 34 | 219 | Marvis Frazier | 200 | TKO 1 | Las Vegas |
| 1984 | Mar. 9 | Tim Witherspoon* | 26 | 220¼ | Greg Page | 239½ | Wm 12 | Las Vegas |
| 1984 | Aug. 31 | Pinklon Thomas | 26 | 216 | Tim Witherspoon | 217 | Wm 12 | Las Vegas |
| 1984 | Nov. 9 | **Larry Holmes** IBF | 35 | 221½ | Bonecrusher Smith | 227 | TKO 12 | Las Vegas |
| 1984 | Dec. 1 | Greg Page | 26 | 236½ | Gerrie Coetzee WBA | 218 | KO 8 | Sun City, S. Africa |
| 1985 | Mar. 15 | **Larry Holmes** IBF | 35 | 223½ | David Bey | 233¼ | TKO 10 | Las Vegas |
| 1985 | Apr. 29 | Tony Tubbs | 26 | 229 | Greg Page WBA | 239½ | Wu 15 | Buffalo |
| 1985 | May 20 | **Larry Holmes** IBF | 35 | 224¼ | Carl Williams | 215 | Wu 15 | Las Vegas |
| 1985 | June 15 | Pinklon Thomas WBC | 27 | 220¼ | Mike Weaver | 221¼ | KO 8 | Las Vegas |
| 1985 | Sept. 21 | Michael Spinks | 29 | 200 | **Larry Holmes** IBF | 221½ | Wu 15 | Las Vegas |
| 1986 | Jan. 17 | Tim Witherspoon | 28 | 227 | Tony Tubbs WBA | 229 | Wm 15 | Atlanta |
| 1986 | Mar. 22 | Trevor Berbick | 33 | 218½ | Pinklon Thomas | 223¾ | Wu 15 | Las Vegas |
| 1986 | Apr. 19 | **Michael Spinks** IBF | 29 | 205 | Larry Holmes | 223 | Ws 15 | Las Vegas |
| 1986 | July 19 | Tim Witherspoon WBA | 28 | 234¾ | Frank Bruno | 228 | TKO 11 | Wembley, England |
| 1986 | Sept. 6 | **Michael Spinks** IBF | 30 | 201 | Steffen Tangstad | 214¾ | TKO 4 | Las Vegas |
| 1986 | Nov. 22 | Mike Tyson | 20 | 221¼ | Trevor Berbick WBC | 218½ | TKO 2 | Las Vegas |
| 1986 | Dec. 12 | Bonecrusher Smith | 33 | 228½ | Tim Witherspoon WBA | 233½ | TKO 1 | NYC (Mad. Sq. Garden) |
| 1987 | Mar. 7 | Mike Tyson WBC | 20 | 219 | Bonecrusher Smith WBA | 233 | Wu 12 | Las Vegas |
| 1987 | May 30 | Mike Tyson | 20 | 218¾ | Pinklon Thomas | 217¾ | TKO 6 | Las Vegas |
| 1987 | May 30 | Tony Tucker** | 28 | 222¼ | Buster Douglas | 227¼ | TKO 10 | Las Vegas |
| 1987 | June 15 | **Michael Spinks†** | 30 | 208¾ | Gerry Cooney | 238 | TKO 5 | Atlantic City |
| 1987 | Aug. 1 | Mike Tyson | 21 | 221 | Tony Tucker IBF | 221 | Wu 12 | Las Vegas |
| 1987 | Oct. 16 | Mike Tyson | 21 | 216 | Tyrell Biggs | 228¾ | TKO 7 | Atlantic City |
| 1988 | Jan. 22 | Mike Tyson | 21 | 215¾ | Larry Holmes | 225¾ | TKO 4 | Atlantic City |
| 1988 | Mar. 20 | Mike Tyson | 21 | 216¼ | Tony Tubbs | 238¼ | KO 2 | Tokyo |
| 1988 | June 27 | Mike Tyson | 21 | 218¼ | **Michael Spinks** | 212¼ | KO 1 | Atlantic City |
| 1989 | Feb. 25 | **Mike Tyson** | 22 | 218 | Frank Bruno | 228 | TKO 5 | Las Vegas |
| 1989 | July 21 | **Mike Tyson** | 23 | 219¼ | Carl Williams | 218 | TKO 1 | Atlantic City |
| 1990 | Feb. 10 | Buster Douglas | 29 | 231½ | **Mike Tyson** | 220½ | KO 10 | Tokyo |
| 1990 | Oct. 25 | Evander Holyfield | 28 | 208 | **Buster Douglas** | 246 | KO 3 | Las Vegas |
| 1991 | Apr. 19 | **Evander Holyfield** | 28 | 208 | George Foreman | 257 | Wu 12 | Atlantic City |
| 1991 | Nov. 23 | **Evander Holyfield** | 29 | 210 | Bert Cooper | 215 | TKO 7 | Atlanta |
| 1992 | June 19 | **Evander Holyfield** | 29 | 210 | Larry Holmes | 233 | Wu 12 | Las Vegas |
| 1992 | Nov. 13 | Riddick Bowe | 25 | 235 | **Evander Holyfield** | 205 | Wu 12 | Las Vegas |
| 1993 | Feb. 6 | **Riddick Bowe** | 25 | 243 | Michael Dokes | 244 | TKO 1 | NYC (Mad. Sq. Garden) |
| 1993 | May 8 | Lennox Lewis WBC‡ | 27 | 235 | Tony Tucker | 235 | Wu 12 | Las Vegas |
| 1993 | May 22 | **Riddick Bowe** | 25 | 244 | Jesse Ferguson | 224 | TKO 2 | Washington, D.C. |
| 1993 | Oct. 1 | Lennox Lewis WBC | 28 | 233 | Frank Bruno | 238 | TKO 7 | Cardiff, Wales |
| 1993 | Nov. 6 | Evander Holyfield | 31 | 217 | **Riddick Bowe** WBA/IBF | 246 | Wm 12 | Las Vegas |
| 1994 | Apr. 22 | Michael Moorer | 26 | 214 | **Evander Holyfield** | 214 | Wm 12 | Las Vegas |
| 1994 | May 6 | Lennox Lewis WBC | 28 | 235 | Phil Jackson | 218 | TKO 8 | Atlantic City |
| 1994 | Sept. 25 | Oliver McCall | 29 | 231¼ | **Lennox Lewis** WBC | 238 | TKO 2 | London |
| 1994 | Nov. 5 | George Foreman! | 45 | 250 | **Michael Moorer** | 222 | KO 10 | Las Vegas |
| 1995 | Apr. 8 | Oliver McCall WBC | 29 | 231 | Larry Holmes | 236 | Wu 12 | Las Vegas |
| 1995 | Apr. 8 | Bruce Seldon! | 28 | 236 | Tony Tucker | 240 | TKO 7 | Las Vegas |
| 1995 | Apr. 22 | **George Foreman**! | 46 | 256 | Axel Schulz | 221 | Ws 12 | Las Vegas |
| 1995 | Aug. 19 | Bruce Seldon WBA | 28 | 234 | Joe Hipp | 223 | TKO 10 | Las Vegas |
| 1995 | Sept. 2 | Frank Bruno | 33 | 248 | Oliver McCall WBC | 235 | Wu 12 | London |
| 1995 | Dec. 9 | Frans Botha* | 27 | 237 | Axel Schulz | 222 | Wu 12 | Stuttgart, GER |
| 1996 | Mar. 16 | Mike Tyson | 29 | 220 | Frank Bruno WBC | 247 | TKO 3 | Las Vegas |

*WBC recognized winner of Mar. 9, 1984 fight between Tim Witherspoon and Greg Page as world champion after Larry Holmes relinquished title in dispute. IBF then recognized Holmes.

**IBF recognized winner of May 30, 1987 fight between Tony Tucker and James (Buster) Douglas as world champion after Michael Spinks relinquished title in dispute.

†The July 15, 1987 Spinks-Cooney fight was not an official championship bout because it was not sanctioned by any boxing associations, councils or federations.

‡WBC recognized Lennox Lewis as world champion when Riddick Bowe gave up that portion of his title on Dec. 14, 1992, rather than fight Lewis, the WBC's mandatory challenger.

!George Foreman won WBA and IBF championships when he beat Michael Moorer on Nov. 5, 1994. He was stripped of WBA title on Mar. 4, 1995, when he refused to fight No. 1 contender Tony Tucker, and he relinquished IBF title on June 29, 1995, rather than give Axel Schulz a rematch. Tucker lost to Bruce Seldon in their April 8, 2001 fight for vacant WBA title.

## World Heavyweight Championship Fights (Cont.)

| Year | Date | Winner | Age | Wgt | Loser | Wgt | Result | Location |
|---|---|---|---|---|---|---|---|---|
| 1996 | June 22 | Michael Moorer* | 28 | 222 | Axel Schulz | 223 | Ws 12 | Dortmund, GER |
| 1996 | Sept. 7 | Mike Tyson WBC† | 30 | 219 | Bruce Seldon WBA | 229 | TKO 1 | Las Vegas |
| 1996 | Nov. 9 | Evander Holyfield | 34 | 215 | **Mike Tyson** WBA | 222 | TKO 11 | Las Vegas |
| 1997 | Feb. 7 | Lennox Lewis† | 31 | 251 | Oliver McCall | 237 | TKO 5 | Las Vegas |
| 1997 | Mar. 29 | Michael Moorer IBF | 29 | 212 | Vaughn Bean | 212 | Wm 12 | Las Vegas |
| 1997 | June 28 | **Evander Holyfield** WBA‡ | 34 | 218 | Mike Tyson | 218 | Disq. 3 | Las Vegas |
| 1997 | July 12 | Lennox Lewis WBC | 31 | 242 | Henry Akinwande | 237½ | Disq. 5 | Stateline, Nev. |
| 1997 | Oct. 4 | Lennox Lewis WBC | 32 | 244 | Andrew Golota | 244 | TKO 1 | Atlantic City |
| 1997 | Nov. 8 | Evander Holyfield WBA | 35 | 214 | Michael Moorer IBF | 223 | TKO 8 | Las Vegas |
| 1998 | Mar. 28 | Lennox Lewis WBC | 32 | 243 | Shannon Briggs | 228 | TKO 5 | Atlantic City |
| 1998 | Sept. 19 | **Evander Holyfield** WBA/IBF | 35 | 217 | Vaughn Bean | 231 | Wu 12 | Atlanta |
| 1998 | Sept. 26 | Lennox Lewis WBC | 33 | 250 | Zeljko Mavrovic | 220 | Wu 12 | Uncasville, Conn. |
| 1999 | Mar. 13 | Lennox Lewis WBC | 33 | 246 | **Evander Holyfield** WBA/IBF | 215 | Draw 12 | NYC (Mad. Sq. Garden) |
| 1999 | Nov. 13 | Lennox Lewis WBC | 34 | 240 | **Evander Holyfield** WBA/IBF | 218 | Wu 12 | Las Vegas |
| 2000 | Apr. 29 | **Lennox Lewis** WBC/IBF! | 34 | 247 | Michael Grant | 250 | KO 2 | NYC (Mad. Sq. Garden) |
| 2000 | July 15 | **Lennox Lewis** WBC/IBF | 34 | 250 | Frans Botha | 237 | TKO 2 | London |
| 2000 | Aug. 12 | Evander Holyfield | 37 | 221 | John Ruiz | 224 | Wu 12 | Las Vegas |
| 2000 | Nov. 11 | **Lennox Lewis** WBC/IBF | 35 | 249 | David Tua | 245 | Wu 12 | Las Vegas |
| 2001 | Mar. 3 | John Ruiz | 29 | 227 | Evander Holyfield | 217 | Wu 12 | Las Vegas |
| 2001 | Apr. 22 | Hasim Rahman | 28 | 237 | **Lennox Lewis** WBC/IBF | 253 | KO 5 | Johannesburg, S. Africa |
| 2001 | Nov. 17 | Lennox Lewis | 36 | 247 | **Hasim Rahman** WBC/IBF | 236 | KO 4 | Las Vegas |
| 2001 | Dec. 15 | **John Ruiz** WBA | 29 | 232 | Evander Holyfield | 219 | Draw 12 | Mashantucket, Conn. |
| 2002 | June 8 | **Lennox Lewis** WBC/IBF@ | 36 | 249 | Mike Tyson | 235 | KO 8 | Memphis, Tenn. |
| 2002 | July 27 | **John Ruiz** WBA | 30 | 233 | Kirk Johnson | 238 | Disq. 10 | Las Vegas |
| 2002 | Dec. 14 | Chris Byrd | 32 | 214 | Evander Holyfield | 220 | Wu 12 | Atlantic City |
| 2003 | Mar. 1 | Roy Jones Jr. | 34 | 193 | **John Ruiz** WBA | 226 | Wu 12 | Las Vegas |
| 2003 | June 21 | **Lennox Lewis** WBC | 37 | 257 | Vitali Klitschko | 248 | TKO 6 | Los Angeles |
| 2003 | Sept. 20 | **Chris Byrd** IBF | 33 | 212 | Fres Oquendo | 224 | Wu 12 | Uncasville, Conn. |
| 2003 | Dec. 13 | John Ruiz WBA% | 31 | 241 | Hasim Rahman | 246 | Wu 12 | Atlantic City |
| 2004 | Apr. 17 | **John Ruiz** WBA | 32 | 240 | Fres Oquendo | 222 | TKO 11 | NYC (Mad. Sq. Garden) |
| 2004 | Apr. 17 | **Chris Byrd** IBF | 33 | 210 | Andrew Golota | 237 | Draw 12 | NYC (Mad. Sq. Garden) |
| 2004 | Apr. 24 | Vitali Klitschko WBC^ | 32 | 245 | Corrie Sanders | 236 | TKO 8 | Los Angeles |
| 2004 | Nov. 13 | **John Ruiz** WBA | 32 | 226 | Andrew Golota | 240 | Wu 12 | NYC (Mad. Sq. Garden) |
| 2004 | Nov. 13 | **Chris Byrd** IBF | 34 | 214 | Jameel McCline | 270 | Wu 12 | NYC (Mad. Sq. Garden) |
| 2004 | Dec. 11 | **Vitali Klitschko** WBC | 33 | 250 | Danny Williams | 270 | TKO 8 | Las Vegas |
| 2005 | Apr. 30 | James Toney$ | 36 | 233 | **John Ruiz** WBA | 241 | NC | NYC (Mad. Sq. Garden) |
| 2005 | Oct. 1 | **Chris Byrd** IBF | 35 | 213 | DaVarryl Williamson | 225 | Wu 12 | Reno, Nev. |

*Frans Botha won the vacant IBF title with a controversial 12-round decision over Axel Schulz on Dec. 9, 1995, but after legal sparring, was eventually stripped of the IBF belt for using anabolic steroids. Moorer then claimed the revacated title with his June 22, 1996 win over Schulz.

†Mike Tyson won the WBC belt from Frank Bruno on Mar. 16, 1996 and still held it at the time of his Sept. 7, 1996 win over Bruce Seldon (although it was not at risk for that fight) but was forced to relinquish the title after the bout for not fighting mandatory challenge Lennox Lewis. Tyson also paid Lewis $4 million to step aside and allow the Tyson-Seldon bout to take place. Lewis then fought Oliver McCall for the vacant WBC belt. The fight was stopped 55 seconds into round 5 because, inexplicably, McCall was visibly distraught and stopped throwing punches.

‡Holyfield won the bout by disqualification and retained the WBA belt after Tyson spit out his mouthpiece and bit off a piece of Holyfield's ear. Tyson had received a two-point deduction from referee Mills Lane and after a stern warning and a short delay the fight was allowed to continue. Later in round 3, he bit Holyfield's other ear and Tyson was disqualified.

!Lewis was stripped of the WBA title for choosing to fight Michael Grant instead of John Ruiz, the WBA's #1 challenger. The WBA sanctioned the Evander Holyfield-John Ruiz August 12 bout for its vacant heavyweight belt.

@Lewis effectively sold his IBF title to promoter Don King for $1 million and a Range Rover in September 2002. Lewis stepped aside (in exchange for the car and substantial fee), relinquishing his IBF belt by declining to fight Chris Byrd the mandatory challenger. The IBF sanctioned the Dec. 14, 2002 fight between Byrd and Holyfield for its vacant heavyweight belt.

%Ruiz won the interim WBA title after Roy Jones Jr. declined to defend the title he won from Ruiz on Mar. 1, 2003. The interim tag was later dropped when Jones returned to the light heavyweight division.

^Klitschko won the WBC title vacated by the retirement of Lennox Lewis.

$Toney won a uaninmous 12-round decision but tested positive for steroids in a post-fight drug test.

## Muhammad Ali's Career Pro Record

Born Cassius Marcellus Clay, Jr. on Jan. 17, 1942, in Louisville; Amateur record of 100-5; won light-heavyweight gold medal at 1960 Olympic Games; Pro record of 56-5 with 37 KOs in 61 fights.

### 1960

| Date | Opponent (location) | Result |
|---|---|---|
| Oct. 29 | Tunney Hunsaker, Louisville | Wu 6 |
| Dec. 27 | Herb Siler, Miami Beach | TKO 4 |

### 1961

| Date | Opponent (location) | Result |
|---|---|---|
| Jan. 17 | Tony Esperti, Miami Beach | TKO 3 |
| Feb. 7 | Jim Robinson, Miami Beach | TKO 1 |
| Feb. 21 | Donnie Fleeman, Miami Beach | TKO 7 |
| Apr. 19 | Lamar Clark, Louisville | KO 2 |
| June 26 | Duke Sabedong, Las Vegas | Wu 10 |
| July 22 | Alonzo Johnson, Louisville | Wu 10 |
| Oct. 7 | Alex Miteff, Louisville | TKO 6 |
| Nov. 29 | Willi Besmanoff, Louisville | TKO 7 |

### 1962

| Date | Opponent (location) | Result |
|---|---|---|
| Feb. 10 | Sonny Banks, New York | TKO 4 |
| Feb. 28 | Don Warner, Miami Beach | TKO 4 |
| Apr. 23 | George Logan, Los Angeles | TKO 4 |
| May 19 | Billy Daniels, Los Angeles | TKO 7 |
| July 20 | Alejandro Lavorante, Los Angeles | KO 5 |
| Nov. 15 | Archie Moore, Los Angeles | KO 4 |

### 1963

| Date | Opponent (location) | Result |
|---|---|---|
| Jan. 24 | Charlie Powell, Pittsburgh | KO 3 |
| Mar. 13 | Doug Jones, New York | Wu 10 |
| June 18 | Henry Cooper, London | TKO 5 |

### 1964

| Date | Opponent (location) | Result |
|---|---|---|
| Feb. 25 | Sonny Liston, Miami Beach | TKO 7 |
| | (won World Heavyweight title) | |

After the fight, Clay announces he is a member of the Black Muslim religious sect and has changed his name to Muhammad Ali.

### 1965

| Date | Opponent (location) | Result |
|---|---|---|
| May 25 | Sonny Liston, Lewiston, Me | KO 1 |
| Nov. 22 | Floyd Patterson, Las Vegas | TKO 12 |

### 1966

| Date | Opponent (location) | Result |
|---|---|---|
| Mar. 29 | George Chuvalo, Toronto | Wu 15 |
| May 21 | Henry Cooper, London | TKO 6 |
| Aug. 6 | Brian London, London | KO 3 |
| Sept. 10 | Karl Mildenberger, Frankfurt | TKO 12 |
| Nov. 14 | Cleveland Williams, Houston | TKO 3 |

### 1967

| Date | Opponent (location) | Result |
|---|---|---|
| Feb. 6 | Ernie Terrell, Houston | Wu 15 |
| Mar. 22 | Zora Folley, New York | KO 7 |
| Apr. 28 | Refuses induction into U.S. Army and is stripped of world title by WBA and most state commissions the next day. | |
| June 20 | Found guilty of draft evasion in Houston; fined $10,000 and sentenced to 5 years; remains free pending appeals, but is barred from the ring. | |

### 1968-69 (Inactive)

### 1970

| Date | Opponent (location) | Result |
|---|---|---|
| Feb. 3 | Announces retirement. | |
| Oct. 26 | Jerry Quarry, Atlanta | TKO 3 |
| Dec. 7 | Oscar Bonavena, New York | TKO 15 |

### 1971

| Date | Opponent (location) | Result |
|---|---|---|
| Mar. 8 | Joe Frazier, New York | Lu 15 |
| | (for World Heavyweight title) | |
| June 28 | U.S. Supreme Court reverses Ali's 1967 conviction saying he had been drafted improperly. | |
| July 26 | Jimmy Ellis, Houston | TKO 12 |
| | (won vacant NABF Heavyweight title) | |
| Nov. 17 | Buster Mathis, Houston | Wu 12 |
| Dec. 26 | Jurgen Blin, Zurich | KO 7 |

### 1972

| Date | Opponent (location) | Result |
|---|---|---|
| Apr. 1 | Mac Foster, Tokyo | Wu 15 |
| May 1 | George Chuvalo, Vancouver | Wu 12 |
| June 27 | Jerry Quarry, Las Vegas | TKO 7 |
| July 19 | Al (Blue) Lewis, Dublin, Ire | TKO 11 |
| Sept. 20 | Floyd Patterson, New York | TKO 7 |
| Nov. 21 | Bob Foster, Stateline, Nev | TKO 8 |

### 1973

| Date | Opponent (location) | Result |
|---|---|---|
| Feb. 14 | Joe Bugner, Las Vegas | Wu 12 |
| Mar. 31 | Ken Norton, San Diego | Ls 12 |
| | (lost NABF Heavyweight title) | |
| Sept. 10 | Ken Norton, Inglewood, Calif | Ws 12 |
| | (regained NABF Heavyweight title) | |
| Oct. 20 | Rudi Lubbers, Jakarta, Indonesia | Wu 12 |

### 1974

| Date | Opponent (location) | Result |
|---|---|---|
| Jan. 28 | Joe Frazier, New York | Wu 12 |
| Oct. 30 | George Foreman, Kinshasa, Zaire | KO 8 |
| | (regained World Heavyweight title) | |

### 1975

| Date | Opponent (location) | Result |
|---|---|---|
| Mar. 24 | Chuck Wepner, Cleveland | TKO 15 |
| May 16 | Ron Lyle, Las Vegas | TKO 11 |
| June 30 | Joe Bugner, Kuala Lumpur, Malaysia | Wu 15 |
| Oct. 1 | Joe Frazier, Manila, Philippines | TKO 14 |

### 1976

| Date | Opponent (location) | Result |
|---|---|---|
| Feb. 20 | Jean Pierre Coopman, San Juan | KO 5 |
| Apr. 30 | Jimmy Young, Landover, Md | Wu 15 |
| May 24 | Richard Dunn, Munich | TKO 5 |
| Sept. 28 | Ken Norton, New York | Wu 15 |

### 1977

| Date | Opponent (location) | Result |
|---|---|---|
| May 16 | Alfredo Evangelista, Landover | Wu 15 |
| Sept. 29 | Earnie Shavers, New York | Wu 15 |

### 1978

| Date | Opponent (location) | Result |
|---|---|---|
| Feb. 15 | Leon Spinks, Las Vegas | Ls 15 |
| | (lost World Heavyweight title) | |
| Sept. 15 | Leon Spinks, New Orleans | Wu 15 |
| | (regained World Heavyweight title) | |

### 1979

| Date | | |
|---|---|---|
| June 27 | Announces retirement. | |

### 1980

| Date | Opponent (location) | Result |
|---|---|---|
| Oct. 2 | Larry Holmes, Las Vegas | TKO by 11 |

### 1981

| Date | Opponent (location) | Result |
|---|---|---|
| Dec. 11 | Trevor Berbick, Nassau | Lu 10 |
| | (retires after fight) | |

## Major Titleholders

Note the following sanctioning body abbreviations: NBA (National Boxing Association), WBA (World Boxing Association), WBC (World Boxing Council), GBR (Great Britain), IBF (International Boxing Federation), plus other national and state commissions. Fighters who retired as champion are indicated by (*) and champions who abandoned or relinquished their titles are indicated by (†).

### Heavyweights

Widely accepted champions in CAPITAL letters. Current champions in **bold** type (as of Oct. 31, 2005).

**Note:** Muhammad Ali was stripped of his world title in 1967 after refusing induction into the Army (see Muhammad Ali's Career Pro Record). George Foreman was stripped of his WBA and IBF titles in 1995, but remained active as linear champion.

| Champion | Held Title |
| --- | --- |
| JOHN L. SULLIVAN | 1885–92 |
| JAMES J. CORBETT | 1892–97 |
| BOB FITZSIMMONS | 1897–99 |
| JAMES J. JEFFRIES | 1899–1905* |
| MARVIN HART | 1905–06 |
| TOMMY BURNS | 1906–08 |
| JACK JOHNSON | 1908–15 |
| JESS WILLARD | 1915–19 |
| JACK DEMPSEY | 1919–26 |
| GENE TUNNEY | 1926–28* |
| MAX SCHMELING | 1930–32 |
| JACK SHARKEY | 1932–33 |
| PRIMO CARNERA | 1933–34 |
| MAX BAER | 1934–35 |
| JAMES J. BRADDOCK | 1935–37 |
| JOE LOUIS | 1937–49* |
| EZZARD CHARLES | 1949–51 |
| JERSEY JOE WALCOTT | 1951–52 |
| ROCKY MARCIANO | 1952–56* |
| FLOYD PATTERSON | 1956–59 |
| INGEMAR JOHANSSON | 1959–60 |
| FLOYD PATTERSON | 1960–62 |
| SONNY LISTON | 1962–64 |
| CASSIUS CLAY (MUHAMMAD ALI) | 1964–67 |
| Ernie Terrell (WBA) | 1965–67 |
| Joe Frazier (NY) | 1968–70 |
| Jimmy Ellis (WBA) | 1968–70 |
| JOE FRAZIER | 1970–73 |
| GEORGE FOREMAN | 1973–74 |
| MUHAMMAD ALI | 1974–78 |
| LEON SPINKS | 1978 |
| Ken Norton (WBC) | 1978 |
| Larry Holmes (WBC) | 1978–80 |
| MUHAMMAD ALI | 1978–79* |
| John Tate (WBA) | 1979–80 |
| Mike Weaver (WBA) | 1980–82 |
| LARRY HOLMES | 1980–85 |
| Michael Dokes (WBA) | 1982–83 |
| Gerrie Coetzee (WBA) | 1983–84 |

| Champion | Held Title |
| --- | --- |
| Tim Witherspoon (WBC) | 1984 |
| Pinklon Thomas (WBC) | 1984–86 |
| Greg Page (WBA) | 1984–85 |
| MICHAEL SPINKS | 1985–87 |
| Tim Witherspoon (WBA) | 1986 |
| Trevor Berbick (WBC) | 1986 |
| Mike Tyson (WBC) | 1986–87 |
| James (Bonecrusher) Smith (WBA) | 1986–87 |
| Tony Tucker (IBF) | 1987 |
| MIKE TYSON (WBC, WBA, IBF) | 1987–90 |
| BUSTER DOUGLAS (WBC, WBA, IBF) | 1990 |
| EVANDER HOLYFIELD (WBC, WBA, IBF) | 1990–92 |
| RIDDICK BOWE (WBA, IBF) | 1992–93 |
| Lennox Lewis (WBC) | 1992–94 |
| EVANDER HOLYFIELD (WBA, IBF) | 1993–94 |
| MICHAEL MOORER (WBA, IBF) | 1994 |
| Oliver McCall (WBC) | 1994–95 |
| GEORGE FOREMAN (WBA, IBF) | 1994–95 |
| Bruce Seldon (WBA) | 1995–96 |
| GEORGE FOREMAN | 1995–96 |
| Frank Bruno (WBC) | 1995–96 |
| Mike Tyson (WBC) | 1996† |
| Mike Tyson (WBA) | 1996 |
| Michael Moorer (IBF) | 1996–1997 |
| Evander Holyfield (WBA, IBF) | 1996–2000 |
| Lennox Lewis (WBC) | 1997–2000 |
| LENNOX LEWIS (WBA, WBC, IBF) | 2000 |
| Evander Holyfield (WBA) | 2000–01 |
| LENNOX LEWIS (WBC, IBF) | 2000–01 |
| John Ruiz (WBA) | 2001-03 |
| Hasim Rahman (WBC, IBF) | 2001 |
| LENNOX LEWIS (WBC, IBF) | 2001–02† |
| LENNOX LEWIS (WBC) | 2001–04* |
| Roy Jones Jr. (WBA) | 2003–04 |
| **Chris Byrd** (IBF) | 2003– |
| **John Ruiz** (WBA) | 2004– |
| **Vitali Klitschko** (WBC) | 2004– |

**Note:** John L. Sullivan held the Bare Knuckle championship from 1882-85.

### Cruiserweights

Current champions in **bold** type.

| Champion | Held Title |
| --- | --- |
| Marvin Camel (WBC) | 1980 |
| Carlos De Leon (WBC) | 1980–82 |
| Ossie Ocasio (WBA) | 1982–84 |
| S.T. Gordon (WBC) | 1982–83 |
| Carlos De Leon (WBC) | 1983–85 |
| Marvin Camel (IBF) | 1983–84 |
| Lee Roy Murphy (IBF) | 1984–86 |
| Piet Crous (WBA) | 1984–85 |
| Alfonso Ratliff (WBC) | 1985 |
| Dwight Braxton (WBA) | 1985–86 |
| Bernard Benton (WBC) | 1985–86 |
| Carlos De Leon (WBC) | 1986–88 |
| Evander Holyfield (WBA) | 1986–88 |
| Ricky Parkey (IBF) | 1986–87 |
| Evander Holyfield (WBA/IBF) | 1987–88 |
| Evander Holyfield | 1988† |
| Toufik Belbouli (WBA) | 1989 |
| Robert Daniels (WBA) | 1989–91 |
| Carlos De Leon (WBC) | 1989–90 |
| Glenn McCrory (IBF) | 1989–90 |
| Jeff Lampkin (IBF) | 1990 |
| Massimiliano Duran (WBC) | 1990–91 |

| Champion | Held Title |
| --- | --- |
| Bobby Czyz (WBA) | 1991–92† |
| Anaclet Wamba (WBC) | 1991–95 |
| James Pritchard (IBF) | 1991 |
| James Warring (IBF) | 1991–92 |
| Alfred Cole (IBF) | 1992–96 |
| Orlin Norris (WBA) | 1993–95 |
| Nate Miller (WBA) | 1995–97 |
| Marcelo Dominguez (WBC) | 1996–98 |
| Adolpho Washington (IBF) | 1996–97 |
| Uriah Grant (IBF) | 1997 |
| Imamu Mayfield (IBF) | 1997–98 |
| Arthur Williams (IBF) | 1998–99 |
| Fabrice Tiozzo (WBA) | 1997–2000 |
| Juan Carlos Gomez (WBC) | 1998–2002† |
| Vassiliy Jirov (IBF) | 1999–2003 |
| Virgil Hill (WBA) | 2000–02 |
| **Jean-Marc Mormeck** (WBA) | 2002– |
| Wayne Braithwaite (WBC) | 2002–05 |
| James Toney (IBF) | 2003† |
| Kelvin Davis (IBF) | 2004–05 |
| **Jean-Marc Mormeck** (WBA/WBC) | 2005– |
| **O'Neil Bell** (IBF) | 2005– |

## Light Heavyweights

Widely accepted champions in CAPITAL letters. Current champions in **bold** type.

| Champion | Held Title | Champion | Held Title |
|---|---|---|---|
| JACK ROOT | 1903 | Marvin Johnson (WBA) | 1979–80 |
| GEORGE GARDNER | 1903 | Eddie (Gregory) Mustapha Muhammad (WBA) | 1980–81 |
| BOB FITZSIMMONS | 1903–05 | Michael Spinks (WBA) | 1981–83 |
| PHILADELPHIA JACK O'BRIEN | 1905–12* | Dwight (Braxton) Muhammad Qawi (WBC) | 1981–83 |
| JACK DILLON | 1914–16 | MICHAEL SPINKS | 1983–85† |
| BATTLING LEVINSKY | 1916–20 | J.B. Williamson (WBC) | 1985–86 |
| GEORGES CARPENTIER | 1920–22 | Slobodan Kacar (IBF) | 1985–86 |
| BATTLING SIKI | 1922–23 | Marvin Johnson (WBA) | 1986–87 |
| MIKE McTIGUE | 1923–25 | Dennis Andries (WBC) | 1986–87 |
| PAUL BERLENBACH | 1925–26 | Bobby Czyz (IBF) | 1986–87 |
| JACK DELANEY | 1926–27† | Leslie Stewart (WBA) | 1987 |
| Jimmy Slattery (NBA) | 1927 | Virgil Hill (WBA) | 1987–91 |
| TOMMY LOUGHRAN | 1927–29 | Prince Charles Williams (IBF) | 1987–93 |
| JIMMY SLATTERY | 1930 | Thomas Hearns (WBC) | 1987 |
| MAXIE ROSENBLOOM | 1930–34 | Donny Lalonde (WBC) | 1987–88 |
| George Nichols (NBA) | 1932 | Sugar Ray Leonard (WBC) | 1988 |
| Bob Godwin (NBA) | 1933 | Dennis Andries (WBC) | 1989 |
| BOB OLIN | 1934–35 | Jeff Harding (WBC) | 1989–90 |
| JOHN HENRY LEWIS | 1935–38 | Dennis Andries (WBC) | 1990–91 |
| MELIO BETTINA (NY) | 1939 | Jeff Harding (WBC) | 1991–94 |
| Len Harvey (GBR) | 1939–42 | Thomas Hearns (WBA) | 1991–92 |
| BILLY CONN | 1939–40† | Iran Barkley (WBA) | 1992† |
| ANTON CHRISTOFORIDIS (NBA) | 1941 | Virgil Hill (WBA) | 1992–97 |
| GUS LESNEVICH | 1941–48 | Henry Maske (IBF) | 1993–96 |
| Freddie Mills (GBR) | 1942–46 | Virgil Hill (WBA/IBF) | 1996–97 |
| FREDDIE MILLS | 1948–50 | Mike McCallum (WBC) | 1994–95 |
| JOEY MAXIM | 1950–52 | Fabrice Tiozzo (WBC) | 1995–96 |
| ARCHIE MOORE | 1952–62 | Roy Jones Jr. (WBC) | 1996 |
| Harold Johnson (NBA) | 1961 | Montell Griffin (WBC) | 1996 |
| HAROLD JOHNSON | 1962–63 | D. Michaelczewski (WBA/IBF) | 1997† |
| WILLIE PASTRANO | 1963–65 | William Guthrie (IBF) | 1997–98 |
| Eddie Cotton (Mich.) | 1963–64 | Lou Del Valle (WBA) | 1997–98 |
| JOSE TORRES | 1965–66 | ROY JONES JR. (WBA/WBC) | 1997–2003† |
| DICK TIGER | 1966–68 | Reggie Johnson (IBF) | 1998–99 |
| BOB FOSTER | 1968–74* | ROY JONES JR. (WBA/WBC/IBF) | 1999–2003† |
| Vicente Rondon (WBA) | 1971–72 | Antonio Tarver (WBC/IBF) | 2003 |
| John Conteh (WBC) | 1974–77 | Mehdi Sahnoune (WBA) | 2003 |
| Victor Galindez (WBA) | 1974–78 | ROY JONES JR. (WBC) | 2003–04 |
| Miguel A. Cuello (WBC) | 1977–78 | Silvio Branco (WBA) | 2003–04 |
| Mate Parlov (WBC) | 1978 | Antonio Tarver (WBC) | 2003–04† |
| Mike Rossman (WBA) | 1978–79 | Glen Johnson (IBF) | 2004† |
| Marvin Johnson (WBC) | 1978–79 | **Fabrice Tiozzo** (WBA) | 2004– |
| Matthew (Franklin) Saad Muhammad (WBC) | 1979–81 | **ANTONIO TARVER** | 2005– |

## Super Middleweights

Current champions in **bold** type.

| Champion | Held Title | Champion | Held Title |
|---|---|---|---|
| Murray Sutherland (IBF) | 1984 | Robin Reid (WBC) | 1996–97 |
| Chong-Pal Park (IBF) | 1984–87 | Charles Brewer (IBF) | 1997–98 |
| Chong-Pal Park (IBF) | 1987–88 | Sven Ottke (IBF) | 1998–2004* |
| Graziano Rocchigiani (IBF) | 1988–89 | Thulane Malinga (WBC) | 1997–98 |
| Fugencio Obelmejias (WBA) | 1988–89 | Richie Woodhall (WBC) | 1998–99 |
| Ray Leonard (WBC) | 1988–90† | Byron Mitchell (WBA) | 1999–2000 |
| In-Chut Baek (WBA) | 1989–90 | Markus Beyer (WBC) | 1999–2000 |
| Lindell Holmes (IBF) | 1990–91 | Glenn Gatley (WBC) | 2000 |
| Christophe Tiozzo (WBA) | 1990–91 | Dingaan Thobela (WBC) | 2000 |
| Mauro Galvano (WBC) | 1990–92 | Bruno Girard (WBA) | 2000–01† |
| Victor Cordova (WBA) | 1991 | Dave Hilton (WBC) | 2000† |
| Darrin Van Horn (IBF) | 1991–92 | Byron Mitchell (WBA) | 2001–03 |
| Iran Barkley (WBA) | 1992 | Eric Lucas (WBC) | 2001–03 |
| Nigel Benn (WBC) | 1992–96 | Sven Ottke (IBF/WBA) | 2003–04* |
| James Toney (IBF) | 1992–94 | Markus Beyer (WBC) | 2003–04 |
| Michael Nunn (WBA) | 1992–94 | Anthony Mundine (WBA) | 2004 |
| Steve Little (WBA) | 1994 | Manny Siaca (WBA) | 2004 |
| Frank Liles (WBA) | 1994–99 | Cristian Sanavia (WBC) | 2004 |
| Roy Jones (IBF) | 1994–96 | **Jeff Lacy** (IBF) | 2004– |
| Thulane Malinga (WBC) | 1996 | **Markus Beyer** (WBC) | 2004– |
| Vincenzo Nardiello (WBC) | 1996 | **Mikkel Kessler** (WBA) | 2004– |

## Major Titleholders (Cont.)
### Middleweights

Widely accepted champions in CAPITAL letters. Current champions in **bold** type.

| Champion | Held Title | Champion | Held Title |
|---|---|---|---|
| JACK (NONPAREIL) DEMPSEY | 1884–91 | SUGAR RAY ROBINSON | 1957 |
| BOB FITZSIMMONS | 1891–97 | CARMEN BASILIO | 1957–58 |
| CHARLES (KID) McCOY | 1897–98 | SUGAR RAY ROBINSON | 1958–60 |
| TOMMY RYAN | 1898–1907 | Gene Fullmer (NBA) | 1959–62 |
| STANLEY KETCHEL | 1908 | PAUL PENDER | 1960–61 |
| BILLY PAPKE | 1908 | TERRY DOWNES | 1961–62 |
| STANLEY KETCHEL | 1908–10 | PAUL PENDER | 1962–63 |
| FRANK KLAUS | 1913 | Dick Tiger (WBA) | 1962–63 |
| GEORGE CHIP | 1913–14 | DICK TIGER | 1963 |
| AL McCOY | 1914–17 | JOEY GIARDELLO | 1963–65 |
| Jeff Smith (AUS) | 1914 | DICK TIGER | 1965–66 |
| Mick King (AUS) | 1914 | EMILE GRIFFITH | 1966–67 |
| Jeff Smith (AUS) | 1914–15 | NINO BENVENUTI | 1967 |
| Lee Darcy (AUS) | 1915–17 | EMILE GRIFFITH | 1967–68 |
| MIKE O'DOWD | 1917–20 | NINO BENVENUTI | 1968–70 |
| JOHNNY WILSON | 1920–23 | CARLOS MONZON | 1970–77* |
| Wm. Bryan Downey (Ohio) | 1921–22 | Rodrigo Valdez (WBC) | 1974–76 |
| Dave Rosenberg (NY) | 1922 | RODRIGO VALDEZ | 1977–78 |
| Jock Malone (Ohio) | 1922–23 | HUGO CORRO | 1978–79 |
| Mike O'Dowd (NY) | 1922 | VITO ANTUOFERMO | 1979–80 |
| Lou Bogash (NY) | 1923 | ALAN MINTER | 1980 |
| HARRY GREB | 1923–26 | MARVELOUS MARVIN HAGLER | 1980–87 |
| TIGER FLOWERS | 1926 | SUGAR RAY LEONARD | 1987 |
| MICKEY WALKER | 1926–31† | Frank Tate (IBF) | 1987–88 |
| GORILLA JONES | 1931–32 | Sumbu Kalambay (WBA) | 1987–89 |
| MARCEL THIL | 1932–37 | Thomas Hearns (WBC) | 1987–88 |
| Ben Jeby (NY) | 1932–33 | Iran Barkley (WBC) | 1988–89 |
| Lou Brouillard (NBA, NY) | 1933 | Michael Nunn (IBF) | 1988–91 |
| Vince Dundee (NBA, NY) | 1933–34 | Roberto Duran (WBC) | 1989–90* |
| Teddy Yarosz (NBA, NY) | 1934–35 | Mike McCallum (WBA) | 1989–91 |
| Babe Risko (NBA, NY) | 1935–36 | Julian Jackson (WBC) | 1990–93 |
| Freddie Steele (NBA, NY) | 1936–38 | James Toney (IBF) | 1991–93† |
| FRED APOSTOLI | 1937–39 | Reggie Johnson (WBA) | 1992–93 |
| Al Hostak (NBA) | 1938 | Roy Jones Jr. (IBF) | 1993–94† |
| Solly Krieger (NBA) | 1938–39 | Gerald McClellan (WBC) | 1993–95† |
| Al Hostak (NBA) | 1939–40 | John David Jackson (WBA) | 1993–94 |
| CEFERINO GARCIA | 1939–40 | Jorge Castro (WBA) | 1994–97 |
| KEN OVERLIN | 1940–41 | Julian Jackson (WBC) | 1995 |
| Tony Zale (NBA) | 1940–41 | Bernard Hopkins (IBF) | 1995– |
| BILLY SOOSE | 1941 | Quincy Taylor (WBC) | 1995–96 |
| TONY ZALE | 1941–47 | Shinji Takehara (WBA) | 1995–96 |
| ROCKY GRAZIANO | 1947–48 | William Joppy (WBA) | 1996–97 |
| TONY ZALE | 1948 | Keith Holmes (WBC) | 1996–98 |
| MARCEL CERDAN | 1948–49 | Julio Cesar Green (WBA) | 1997–98 |
| JAKE La MOTTA | 1949–51 | William Joppy (WBA) | 1998–2001 |
| SUGAR RAY ROBINSON | 1951 | Hassine Cherifi (WBC) | 1998–99 |
| RANDY TURPIN | 1951 | Keith Holmes (WBC) | 1999–2001 |
| SUGAR RAY ROBINSON | 1951–52* | Bernard Hopkins (IBF/WBC) | 2001– |
| CARL (BOBO) OLSON | 1953–55 | Felix Trinidad (WBA) | 2001 |
| SUGAR RAY ROBINSON | 1955–57 | BERNARD HOPKINS (IBF/WBA/WBC) | 2001–05 |
| GENE FULLMER | 1957 | **JERMAIN TAYLOR** (IBF/WBA/WBC) | 2005– |

### Junior Middleweights

Widely accepted champions in CAPITAL letters. Current champions in **bold** type.

| Champion | Held Title | Champion | Held Title |
|---|---|---|---|
| ERNILE GRIFFITH (EBU) | 1962–63 | KOICHI WAJIMA | 1976 |
| DENNIS MOYER | 1962–63 | JOSE DURAN | 1976 |
| RALPH DUPAS | 1963 | Eckhard Dagge (WBC) | 1976–77 |
| SANDRO MAZZINGHI | 1963–65 | MIGUEL ANGEL CASTELLINI | 1976–77 |
| NINO BENVENUTI | 1965–66 | EDDIE GAZO | 1977–78 |
| KI-SOO KIM | 1966–68 | Rocky Mattioli (WBC) | 1977–79 |
| SANDRO MAZZINGHI | 1968 | MASASHI KUDO | 1978–79 |
| FREDDLIE LITTLE | 1969–70 | Maurice Hope (WBC) | 1979–81 |
| CARMELO BOSSI | 1970–71 | AYUB KALULE | 1979–81 |
| KOICHI WAJIMA | 1971–74 | Wilfred Benitez (WBC) | 1981–82 |
| OSCAR ALBARADO | 1974–75 | SUGAR RAY LEONARD | 1981–82 |
| KOICHI WAJIMA | 1975 | Tadashi Mihara (WBA) | 1981–82 |
| Miguel de Oliveira (WBC) | 1975–76 | Davey Moore (WBA) | 1982–83 |
| JAE-DO YUH | 1975–76 | Thomas Hearns (WBC) | 1982–84 |
| Elisha Obed (WBC) | 1975–76 | Roberto Duran (WBA) | 1983–84 |

| Champion | Held Title |
|---|---|
| Mark Medal (IBF) | 1984 |
| THOMAS HEARNS | 1984–86 |
| Mike McCallum (WBA) | 1984–87 |
| Carlos Santos (IBF) | 1984–86 |
| Buster Drayton (IBF) | 1986–87 |
| Duane Thomas (WBC) | 1986–87 |
| Matthew Hilton (IBF) | 1987–88 |
| Lupe Aquino (IBF) | 1987 |
| Gianfranco Rosi (WBC) | 1987–88 |
| Julian Jackson (WBA) | 1987–90 |
| Donald Curry (WBC) | 1988–89 |
| Robert Hines (IBF) | 1988–89 |
| Darrin Van Horn (IBF) | 1989 |
| Rene Jacquote (WBC) | 1989 |
| John Mugabi (WBC) | 1989–90 |
| Gianfranco Rosi (IBF) | 1989–94 |
| Terry Norris (WBC) | 1990–94 |
| Gilbert Dele (WBA)† | 1991 |
| Vinny Pazienza (WBA) | 1991–92 |
| Julio Cesar Vasquez (WBA) | 1992–95 |
| Simon Brown (WBC) | 1994 |
| Terry Norris (WBC) | 1994– |
| Vincent Pettway (IBF) | 1994–95 |
| Paul Vaden (IBF) | 1995 |

| Champion | Held Title |
|---|---|
| Carl Daniels (WBA) | 1995 |
| Terry Norris (WBC) | 1995–97 |
| Terry Norris (IBF) | 1995–96 |
| Laurent Boudouani (WBA) | 1996–99 |
| Raul Marquez (IBF) | 1997 |
| Keith Mullings (WBC) | 1997–99 |
| Yori Boy Campas (IBF) | 1997–98 |
| Fernando Vargas (IBF) | 1998–2000 |
| Javier Castillejo (WBC) | 1999–2001 |
| David Reid (WBA) | 1999–00 |
| Felix Trinidad (WBA/IBF) | 2000–01† |
| Oscar De La Hoya (WBC) | 2001–03 |
| Fernando Vargas (WBA) | 2001–02 |
| Winky Wright (IBF) | 2001– |
| Oscar De La Hoya (WBA/WBC) | 2002-03 |
| Shane Mosley (WBA/WBC) | 2003–04 |
| WINKY WRIGHT (IBF/WBA/WBC) | 2004 |
| WINKY WRIGHT (WBA/WBC) | 2004–05† |
| Kassim Ouma (IBF) | 2004–05 |
| Javier Castillejo (WBC) | 2005 |
| **Roman Karmazin** (IBF) | 2005– |
| **Alejandro Garcia** (WBA) | 2005– |
| **Ricardo Mayorga** (WBC) | 2005– |

## Welterweights

Widely accepted champions in CAPITAL letters. Current champions in **bold** type.

| Champion | Held Title |
|---|---|
| PADDY DUFFY | 1888–90 |
| MYSTERIOUS BILLY SMITH | 1892–94 |
| TOMMY RYAN | 1894–98 |
| MYSTERIOUS BILLY SMITH | 1898–1900 |
| MATTY MATHEWS | 1900 |
| EDDIE CONNOLLY | 1900 |
| JAMES (RUBE) FERNS | 1900 |
| MATTY MATHEWS | 1900–01 |
| JAMES (RUBE) FERNS | 1901 |
| JOE WALCOTT | 1901–04 |
| THE DIXIE KID | 1904–05 |
| HONEY MELLODY | 1906–07 |
| Mike (Twin) Sullivan | 1907–08† |
| Harry Lewis | 1908–11 |
| Jimmy Gardner | 1908 |
| Jimmy Clabby | 1910–11 |
| WALDEMAR HOLBERG | 1914 |
| TOM McCORMICK | 1914 |
| MATT WELLS | 1914–15 |
| MIKE GLOVER | 1915 |
| JACK BRITTON | 1915 |
| TED (KID) LEWIS | 1915–16 |
| JACK BRITTON | 1916–17 |
| TED (KID) LEWIS | 1917–19 |
| JACK BRITTON | 1919–22 |
| MICKEY WALKER | 1922–26 |
| PETE LATZO | 1926–27 |
| JOE DUNDEE | 1927–29 |
| JACKIE FIELDS | 1929–30 |
| YOUNG JACK THOMPSON | 1930 |
| TOMMY FREEMAN | 1930–31 |
| YOUNG JACK THOMPSON | 1931 |
| LOU BROUILLARD | 1931–32 |
| JACKIE FIELDS | 1932–33 |
| YOUNG CORBETT III | 1933 |
| JIMMY McLARNIN | 1933–34 |
| BARNEY ROSS | 1934 |
| JIMMY McLARNIN | 1934–35 |
| BARNEY ROSS | 1935–38 |
| HENRY ARMSTRONG | 1938–40 |
| FRITZIE ZIVIC | 1940–41 |
| Izzy Jannazzo (Md.) | 1940–41 |
| Freddie (Red) Cochrane | 1941–46 |
| MARTY SERVO | 1946* |
| SUGAR RAY ROBINSON | 1946–51† |

| Champion | Held Title |
|---|---|
| Johnny Bratton | 1951 |
| KID GAVILAN | 1951–54 |
| JOHNNY SAXTON | 1954–55 |
| TONY DeMARCO | 1955 |
| CARMEN BASILIO | 1955–56 |
| JOHNNY SAXTON | 1956 |
| CARMEN BASILIO | 1956–57† |
| VIRGIL AKINS | 1958 |
| DON JORDAN | 1958–60 |
| BENNY (KID) PARET | 1960–61 |
| EMILE GRIFFITH | 1961 |
| BENNY (KID) PARET | 1961–62 |
| EMILE GRIFFITH | 1962–63 |
| LUIS RODRIGUEZ | 1963 |
| EMILE GRIFFITH | 1963–66† |
| Charlie Shipes (Calif.) | 1966–67 |
| CURTIS COKES | 1966–69 |
| JOSE NAPOLES | 1969–70 |
| BILLY BACKUS | 1970–71 |
| JOSE NAPOLES | 1971–75 |
| Hedgemon Lewis (NY) | 1972–73 |
| Angel Espada (WBA) | 1975–76 |
| JOHN H. STRACEY | 1975–76 |
| CARLOS PALOMINO | 1976–79 |
| Pipino Cuevas (WBA) | 1976–80 |
| WILFREDO BENITEZ | 1979 |
| SUGAR RAY LEONARD | 1979–80 |
| ROBERTO DURAN | 1980 |
| Thomas Hearns (WBA) | 1980–81 |
| SUGAR RAY LEONARD | 1980–82 |
| Donald Curry (WBA) | 1983–85 |
| Milton McCrory (WBC) | 1983–85 |
| DONALD CURRY | 1985–86 |
| LLOYD HONEYGHAN | 1986–87 |
| JORGE VACA (WBC) | 1987–88 |
| LLOYD HONEYGHAN (WBC) | 1988–89 |
| Mark Breland (WBA) | 1987 |
| Marlon Starling (WBA) | 1987–88 |
| Tomas Molinares (WBA) | 1988–89 |
| Simon Brown (IBF) | 1988–91 |
| Mark Breland (WBA) | 1989–90 |
| MARLON STARLING (WBC) | 1989–90 |
| Aaron Davis (WBA) | 1990–91 |
| Maurice Blocker (WBC) | 1990–91 |
| Meldrick Taylor (WBA) | 1991–92 |

## Major Titleholders (Cont.)
### Welterweights (Cont.)

| Champion | Held Title |
|---|---|
| Simon Brown (WBC) | 1991 |
| Maurice Blocker (IBF) | 1991–93 |
| Buddy McGirt (WBC) | 1991–93 |
| Crisanto Espana (WBA) | 1992–94 |
| Pernell Whitaker (WBC) | 1993–97 |
| Felix Trinidad (IBF) | 1993–99 |
| Ike Quartey (WBA) | 1994–98† |
| James Page (WBA) | 1998–2000† |
| Oscar De La Hoya (WBC) | 1997–99 |
| Felix Trinidad (WBC/IBF) | 1999–2000† |
| Oscar De La Hoya (WBC) | 2000 |

| Champion | Held Title |
|---|---|
| Shane Mosley (WBC) | 2000–00 |
| Andrew Lewis (WBA) | 2001–02 |
| Vernon Forrest (IBF) | 2001–02† |
| Champion | Held Title |
| Vernon Forrest (WBC) | 2002–03 |
| Richard Mayorga (WBA) | 2002–03 |
| Michele Piccirillo (IBF) | 2002–03 |
| Richard Mayorga (WBA/WBC) | 2003 |
| Cory Spinks (IBF) | 2003–05 |
| CORY SPINKS (IBF/WBA/WBC) | 2003–05 |
| **ZAB JUDAH** (IBF/WBA/WBC) | 2005– |

### Junior Welterweights
Widely accepted champions in CAPITAL letters. Current champions in **bold** type.

| Champion | Held Title | Champion | Held Title |
|---|---|---|---|
| PINKEY MITCHELL | 1922–25 | Gary Hinton (IBF) | 1986 |
| RED HERRING | 1925 | Rene Arredondo (WBC) | 1986 |
| MUSHY CALLAHAN | 1926–30 | Tsuyoshi Hamada (WBC) | 1986–87 |
| JACK (KID) BERG | 1930–31 | Joe Louis Manley (IBF) | 1986–87 |
| TONY CANZONERI | 1931–32 | Terry Marsh (IBF) | 1987 |
| JOHNNY JADICK | 1932–33 | Juan Coggi (WBA) | 1987–90 |
| Sammy Fuller | 1932–33 | Rene Arredondo (WBC) | 1987 |
| BATTLING SHAW | 1933 | Roger Mayweather (WBC) | 1987–89 |
| TONY CANZONERI | 1933 | James McGirt (IBF) | 1988 |
| BARNEY ROSS | 1933–35 | Meldrick Taylor (IBF) | 1988–90 |
| TIPPY LARKIN | 1946 | Julio Cesar Chavez (WBC) | 1989–94 |
| CARLOS ORTIZ | 1959–60 | Julio Cesar Chavez (IBF) | 1990–91 |
| DUILIO LOI | 1960–62 | Loreto Garza (WBA) | 1990–91 |
| EDDIE PERKINS | 1962 | Juan Coggi (WBA) | 1991 |
| DUILIO LOI | 1962–63 | Edwin Rosario (WBA) | 1991–92 |
| Roberto Cruz | 1963 | Rafael Pineda (IBF) | 1991–92 |
| EDDIE PERKINS | 1963–65 | Akinobu Hiranaka (WBA) | 1992 |
| CARLOS HERNANDEZ | 1965–66 | Pernell Whitaker (IBF) | 1992–93† |
| SANDRO LOPOPOLO | 1966–67 | Charles Murray (IBF) | 1993–94 |
| PAUL FUJII | 1967–68 | Jake Rodriguez (IBF) | 1994–95 |
| NICOLINO LOCHE | 1968–72 | Juan Coggi (WBA) | 1993–94 |
| Pedro Adigue (WBC) | 1968–70 | Frankie Randall (WBC) | 1994 |
| Bruno Arcari (WBC) | 1970–74 | Frankie Randall (WBA) | 1994–96 |
| ALFONSO FRAZER | 1972 | Juan Coggi (WBA) | 1996 |
| ANTONIO CERVANTES | 1972–76 | Julio Cesar Chavez (WBC) | 1994–96 |
| Perico Fernandez (WBC) | 1974–75 | Kostya Tszyu (IBF) | 1995–97 |
| Saensak Muangsurin (WBC) | 1975–76 | Frankie Randall (WBA) | 1996–97 |
| WILFRED BENITEZ | 1976–79 | Oscar De La Hoya (WBC) | 1996–97† |
| Miguel Velasquez (WBC) | 1976 | Khalid Rahilou (WBA) | 1997–98 |
| Saensak Muangsurin (WBC) | 1976–78 | Sharmba Mitchell (WBA) | 1998–2001 |
| Antonio Cervantes (WBA) | 1977–80 | Vincent Phillips (IBF) | 1997–99 |
| Sang-Hyun Kim (WBC) | 1978–80 | Terronn Millet (IBF) | 1999–00† |
| Saoul Mamby (WBC) | 1980–82 | Kostya Tszyu (WBC) | 1999–2005 |
| Aaron Pryor (WBA) | 1980–83 | Zab Judah (IBF) | 2000–01 |
| Leroy Haley (WBC) | 1982–83 | Kostya Tszyu (WBA/WBC) | 2001–04† |
| Aaron Pryor (IBF) | 1983–85 | KOSTYA TSZYU (IBF/WBA/WBC) | 2001–04† |
| Bruce Curry (WBC) | 1983–84 | KOSTYA TSZYU (IBF/WBC) | 2004–05 |
| Johnny Bumphus (WBA) | 1984 | Vivian Harris (WBA) | 2004–05 |
| Bill Costello (WBC) | 1984–85 | Arturo Gatti (WBA) | 2005 |
| Gene Hatcher (WBA) | 1984–85 | **Ricky Hatton** (IBF) | 2005– |
| Ubaldo Sacco (WBA) | 1985–86 | **Carlos Maussa** (WBA) | 2005– |
| Lonnie Smith (WBC) | 1985–86 | **Floyd Mayweather** (WBC) | 2005– |
| Patrizio Oliva (WBA) | 1986–87 | | |

### Lightweights
Widely accepted champions in CAPITAL letters. Current champions in **bold** type.

| Champion | Held Title | Champion | Held Title |
|---|---|---|---|
| JACK McAULIFFE | 1886–94 | AD WOLGAST | 1910–12 |
| GEORGE (KID) LAVIGNE | 1896–99 | WILLIE RITCHIE | 1912–14 |
| FRANK ERNE | 1899–02 | FREDDIE WELSH | 1915–17 |
| JOE GANS | 1902–04 | BENNY LEONARD | 1917–25* |
| JIMMY BRITT | 1904–05 | JIMMY GOODRICH | 1925 |
| BATTLING NELSON | 1905–06 | ROCKY KANSAS | 1925–26 |
| JOE GANS | 1906–08 | SAMMY MANDELL | 1926–30 |
| BATTLING NELSON | 1908–10 | AL SINGER | 1930 |

| Champion | Held Title |
|---|---|
| TONY CANZONERI | 1930–33 |
| BARNEY ROSS | 1933–35† |
| TONY CANZONERI | 1935–36 |
| LOU AMBERS | 1936–38 |
| HENRY ARMSTRONG | 1938–39 |
| LOU AMBERS | 1939–40 |
| Sammy Angott (NBA) | 1940–41 |
| LEW JENKINS | 1940–41 |
| SAMMY ANGOTT | 1941–42 |
| Beau Jack (NY) | 1942–43 |
| Slugger White (Md.) | 1943 |
| Bob Montgomery (NY) | 1943 |
| Sammy Angott (NBA) | 1943–44 |
| Beau Jack (NY) | 1943–44 |
| Bob Montgomery (NY) | 1944–47 |
| Juan Zurita (NBA) | 1944–45 |
| IKE WILLIAMS | 1947–51 |
| JAMES CARTER | 1951–52 |
| LAURO SALAS | 1952 |
| JAMES CARTER | 1952–54 |
| PADDY DeMARCO | 1954 |
| JAMES CARTER | 1954–55 |
| WALLACE (BUD) SMITH | 1955–56 |
| JOE BROWN | 1956–62 |
| CARLOS ORTIZ | 1962–65 |
| Kenny Lane (Mich.) | 1963–64 |
| ISMAEL LAGUNA | 1965 |
| CARLOS ORTIZ | 1965–68 |
| CARLOS TEO CRUZ | 1968–69 |
| MANDO RAMOS | 1969–70 |
| ISMAEL LAGUNA | 1970 |
| KEN BUCHANAN | 1970–72 |
| Pedro Carrasco (WBC) | 1971–72 |
| Mando Ramos (WBC) | 1972 |
| ROBERTO DURAN | 1972–79† |
| Chango Carmona (WBC) | 1972 |
| Rodolfo Gonzalez (WBC) | 1972–74 |
| Ishimatsu Suzuki (WBC) | 1974–76 |
| Esteban De Jesus (WBC) | 1976–78 |
| Jim Watt (WBC) | 1979–81 |
| Ernesto Espana (WBA) | 1979–80 |
| Hilmer Kenty (WBA) | 1980–81 |
| Sean O'Grady (WBA,WAA) | 1981 |
| Alexis Arguello (WBC) | 1981–82 |
| Claude Noel (WBA) | 1981 |
| Andrew Ganigan (WAA) | 1981–82 |
| Arturo Frias (WBA) | 1981–82 |
| Ray Mancini (WBA) | 1982–84 |
| ALEXIS ARGUELLO | 1982–83 |
| Edwin Rosario (WBC) | 1983–84 |
| Choo Choo Brown (IBF) | 1984 |

| Champion | Held Title |
|---|---|
| Livingstone Bramble (WBA) | 1984–86 |
| Harry Arroyo (IBF) | 1984–85 |
| Jose Luis Ramirez (WBC) | 1984–85 |
| Jimmy Paul (IBF) | 1985–86 |
| Hector Camacho (WBC) | 1985–86 |
| Edwin Rosario (WBA) | 1986–87 |
| Greg Haugen (IBF) | 1986–87 |
| Julio Cesar Chavez (WBA) | 1987–88 |
| Jose Luis Ramirez (WBC) | 1987–88 |
| JULIO CESAR CHAVEZ (WBC,WBA) | 1988–89 |
| Vinny Pazienza (IBF) | 1987–88 |
| Greg Haugen (IBF) | 1988–89 |
| Pernell Whitaker (IBF,WBC) | 1989–90 |
| Edwin Rosario (WBA) | 1989–90 |
| Juan Nazario (WBA) | 1990 |
| PERNELL WHITAKER (IBF, WBC, WBA) | 1990–92† |
| Joey Gamache (WBA) | 1992 |
| Miguel A. Gonzalez (WBC) | 1992–96 |
| Tony Lopez (WBA) | 1992–93 |
| Dingaan Thobela (WBA) | 1993 |
| Fred Pendleton (IBF) | 1993–94 |
| Orzubek Nazarov (WBA) | 1993–98 |
| Rafael Ruelas (IBF) | 1994–95 |
| Oscar De La Hoya (IBF) | 1995† |
| Phillip Holiday (IBF) | 1995–97 |
| Jean-Baptiste Mendy (WBC) | 1996–97 |
| Stevie Johnston (WBC) | 1997–98 |
| Shane Mosley (IBF) | 1997–99† |
| Cesar Bazan (WBC) | 1998–99 |
| Jean-Baptiste Mendy (WBA) | 1998–99 |
| Julien Lorcy (WBA) | 1999 |
| Stevie Johnston (WBC) | 1999–00 |
| Stefano Zoff (WBA) | 1999 |
| Israel Cardona (IBF) | 1999 |
| Paul Spadafora (IBF) | 1999–2004† |
| Gilberto Serrano (WBA) | 1999–00 |
| Takanori Hatakeyama (WBA) | 2000–01 |
| Jose Luis Castillo (WBC) | 2000–02 |
| Julien Lorcy (WBA) | 2001 |
| Raul Balbi (WBA) | 2001–02 |
| Leonard Dorin (WBA) | 2002–03 |
| Floyd Mayweather (WBC) | 2002–04† |
| Javier Jauregui (IBF) | 2003-04 |
| Lakva Sim (WBA) | 2004 |
| **Juan Diaz** (WBA) | 2004– |
| Jose Luis Castillo (WBC) | 2004–05 |
| Julio Diaz (IBF) | 2004–05 |
| **Diego Corrales** (WBC) | 2005– |
| Leavander Johnson (IBF) | 2005 |
| **Jesus Chavez** (IBF) | 2005– |

## Junior Lightweights

Widely accepted champions in CAPITAL letters. Current champions in **bold** type.

| Champion | Held Title |
|---|---|
| JOHNNY DUNDEE | 1921–23 |
| JACK BERNSTEIN | 1923 |
| JOHNNY DUNDEE | 1923–24 |
| STEVE (KID) SULLIVAN | 1924–25 |
| MIKE BALLERINO | 1925 |
| TOD MORGAN | 1925–29 |
| BENNY BASS | 1929–31 |
| KID CHOCOLATE | 1931–33 |
| FRANKIE KLICK | 1933–34 |
| SANDY SADDLER | 1949–50 |
| HAROLD GOMES | 1959–60 |
| GABRIEL (FLASH) ELORDE | 1960–67 |
| YOSHIAKI NUMATA | 1967 |
| HIROSHI KOBAYASHI | 1967–71 |
| Rene Barrientos (WBC) | 1969–70 |
| Yoshiaki Numata (WBC) | 1970–71 |
| ALFREDO MARCANO | 1971–72 |
| Ricardo Arredondo (WBC) | 1971–74 |
| BEN VILLAFLOR | 1972–73 |

| Champion | Held Title |
|---|---|
| KUNIAKI SHIBATA | 1973 |
| BEN VILLAFLOR | 1973–76 |
| Kuniaki Shibata (WBC) | 1974–75 |
| Alfredo Escalera (WBC) | 1975–78 |
| SAMUEL SERRANO | 1976–80 |
| Alexis Arguello (WBC) | 1978–80 |
| YASUTSUNE UEHARA | 1980–81 |
| Rafael Limon (WBC) | 1980–81 |
| Cornelius Boza-Edwards (WBC) | 1981 |
| SAMUEL SERRANO | 1981–83 |
| Rolando Navarrete (WBC) | 1981–82 |
| Rafael Limon (WBC) | 1982 |
| Bobby Chacon (WBC) | 1982–83 |
| ROGER MAYWEATHER | 1983–84 |
| Hector Camacho (WBC) | 1983–84 |
| ROCKY LOCKRIDGE | 1984–85 |
| Hwan-Kil Yuh (IBF) | 1984–85 |
| Julio Cesar Chavez (WBC) | 1984–87 |
| Lester Ellis (IBF) | 1985 |

## Major Titleholders (Cont.)
## Junior Lightweights (Cont.)

| Champion | Held Title | Champion | Held Title |
|---|---|---|---|
| WILFREDO GOMEZ | 1985–86 | Genaro Hernandez (WBC) | 1997–98 |
| Barry Michael (IBF) | 1985–87 | Floyd Mayweather Jr. (WBC) | 1998–2002† |
| ALFREDO LAYNE | 1986 | Takanori Hatakeyama (WBA) | 1998–99 |
| BRIAN MITCHELL | 1986–91 | Roberto Garcia (IBF) | 1998–99 |
| Rocky Lockridge (IBF) | 1987–88 | Lavka Sim (WBA) | 1999 |
| Azumah Nelson (WBC) | 1988–94 | Diego Corrales (IBF) | 1999–2001 |
| Tony Lopez (IBF) | 1988–89 | Baek Jong-Kwon (WBA) | 1999–2000 |
| Juan Molina (IBF) | 1989–90 | Joel Casamayor (WBA) | 2000–02 |
| Tony Lopez (IBF) | 1990–91 | Steve Forbes (IBF) | 2001–02† |
| Joey Gamache (WBA) | 1991 | Acelino Freitas (WBA) | 2002–04† |
| Brian Mitchell (IBF) | 1991 | Sirimongkol Singmanassak (WBC) | 2002–03 |
| Genaro Hernandez (WBA) | 1991–95 | Jesus Chavez (WBC) | 2003–04 |
| James Leija (WBC) | 1994 | Carlos Hernandez (IBF) | 2003–04 |
| Juan Molina (IBF) | 1991–95 | Erik Morales (WBC) | 2004 |
| Gabriel Ruelas (WBC) | 1994–95 | Erik Morales (IBF/WBC) | 2004 |
| Eddie Hopson (IBF) | 1995 | **Marco Antonio Barrera** (WBC) | 2004– |
| Tracy Patterson (IBF) | 1995 | **Marco Antonio Barrera** (IBF/WBC) | 2005– |
| Azumah Nelson (WBC) | 1995–97 | **Vicente Mosquera** (WBA) | 2005– |
| Choi Yong-Soo (WBA) | 1995–98 | | |
| Arturo Gatti (IBF) | 1995–98† | | |

## Featherweights

Widely accepted champions in CAPITAL letters. Current champions in **bold** type.

| Champion | Held Title | Champion | Held Title |
|---|---|---|---|
| TORPEDO BILLY MURPHY | 1890 | WILLIE PEP | 1949–50 |
| YOUNG GRIFFO | 1890–92 | SANDY SADDLER | 1950–57* |
| GEORGE DIXON | 1892–97 | HOGAN (KID) BASSEY | 1957–59 |
| SOLLY SMITH | 1897–98 | DAVEY MOORE | 1959–63 |
| Ben Jordan (GBR) | 1898–99 | ULTIMINIO (SUGAR) RAMOS | 1963–64 |
| Eddie Santry (GBR) | 1899–1900 | VICENTE SALDIVAR | 1964–67* |
| DAVE SULLIVAN | 1898 | Howard Winstone (GBR) | 1968 |
| GEORGE DIXON | 1898–1900 | Raul Rojas (WBA) | 1968 |
| TERRY McGOVERN | 1900–01 | Jose Legra (WBC) | 1968–69 |
| YOUNG CORBETT II | 1901–04 | Shozo Saijyo (WBA) | 1968–71 |
| JIMMY BRITT | 1904 | JOHNNY FAMECHON (WBC) | 1969–70 |
| ABE ATTELL | 1904 | VICENTE SALDIVAR (WBC) | 1970 |
| BROOKLYN TOMMY SULLIVAN | 1904–05 | KUNIAKI SHIBATA (WBC) | 1970–72 |
| ABE ATTELL | 1906–12 | Antonio Gomez (WBA) | 1971–72 |
| JOHNNY KILBANE | 1912–23 | CLEMENTE SANCHEZ (WBC) | 1972 |
| Jem Driscoll (GBR) | 1912–13 | Ernesto Marcel (WBA) | 1972–74 |
| EUGENE CRIQUI | 1923 | JOSE LEGRA (WBC) | 1972–73 |
| JOHNNY DUNDEE | 1923–24† | EDER JOFRE (WBC) | 1973–74 |
| LOUIS (KID) KAPLAN | 1925–26† | Ruben Olivares (WBA) | 1974 |
| Dick Finnegan (Mass.) | 1926–27 | Bobby Chacon (WBC) | 1974–75 |
| BENNY BASS | 1927–28 | ALEXIS ARGUELLO (WBA) | 1974–76† |
| TONY CANZONERI | 1928 | Ruben Olivares (WBA) | 1975 |
| ANDRE ROUTIS | 1928–29 | David (Poison) Kotey (WBC) | 1975–76 |
| BATTLING BATTALINO | 1929–32† | DANNY (LITTLE RED) LOPEZ (WBC) | 1976–80 |
| Tommy Paul (NBA) | 1932–33 | Rafael Ortega (WBA) | 1977 |
| Kid Chocolate (NY) | 1932–33 | Cecilio Lastra (WBA) | 1977–78 |
| Freddie Miller (NBA) | 1933–36 | Eusebio Pedroza (WBA) | 1978–85 |
| Baby Arizmendi (MEX) | 1935–36 | SALVADOR SANCHEZ (WBC) | 1980–82 |
| Mike Belloise (NY) | 1936–37 | Juan LaPorte (WBC) | 1982–84 |
| Petey Sarron (NBA) | 1936–37 | Wilfredo Gomez (WBC) | 1984 |
| HENRY ARMSTRONG | 1937–38† | Min-Keun Oh (IBF) | 1984–85 |
| Joey Archibald (NY) | 1938–39 | Azumah Nelson (WBC) | 1984–88 |
| Leo Rodak (NBA) | 1938–39 | Barry McGuigan (WBA) | 1985–86 |
| JOEY ARCHIBALD | 1939–40 | Ki-Young Chung (IBF) | 1985–86 |
| Petey Scalzo (NBA) | 1940–41 | Steve Cruz (WBA) | 1986–87 |
| Jimmy Perrin (La.) | 1940–41 | Antonio Rivera (IBF) | 1986–88 |
| HARRY JEFFRA | 1940–41 | Antonio Esparragoza (WBA) | 1987–91 |
| JOEY ARCHIBALD | 1941 | Calvin Grove (IBF) | 1988 |
| Richie Lemos (NBA) | 1941 | Jorge Paez (IBF) | 1988–91† |
| CHALKY WRIGHT | 1941–42 | Jeff Fenech (WBC) | 1988–90† |
| Jackie Wilson (NBA) | 1941–43 | Marcos Villasana (WBC) | 1990–91 |
| WILLIE PEP | 1942–48 | Yung-Kyun Park (WBA) | 1991–93 |
| Jackie Callura (NBA) | 1943 | Troy Dorsey (IBF) | 1991 |
| Phil Terranova (NBA) | 1943–44 | Manuel Medina (IBF) | 1991–93 |
| Sal Bartolo (NBA) | 1944–46 | Paul Hodkinson (WBC) | 1991–93 |
| SANDY SADDLER | 1948–49 | Tom Johnson (IBF) | 1993–97 |

| Champion | Held Title |
|---|---|
| Goyo Vargas (WBC) | 1993 |
| Kevin Kelley (WBC) | 1993–95 |
| Eloy Rojas (WBA) | 1993–96 |
| Alejandro Gonzalez (WBC) | 1995 |
| Manuel Medina (WBC) | 1995–96 |
| Wilfredo Vasquez (WBA) | 1996–98† |
| Luisito Espinosa (WBC) | 1995–99 |
| Naseem Hamed (IBF) | 1997† |
| Hector Lizarraga (IBF) | 1997–98 |
| Freddie Norwood (WBA) | 1998 |
| Manuel Medina (IBF) | 1998–99 |
| Antonio Cermeno (WBA) | 1998–99 |
| Cesar Soto (WBC) | 1999–00 |
| Paul Ingle (IBF) | 1999–2000 |
| Mbuelo Botile (IBF) | 2000–01 |
| Guty Espadas (WBC) | 2000–01 |
| Freddie Norwood (WBA) | 1999–00 |
| Derrick Gainer (WBA) | 2000–03 |
| Erik Morales (WBC) | 2001–02 |
| Frankie Toledo (IBF) | 2001 |
| Manuel Medina (IBF) | 2001–02 |
| Johnny Tapia (IBF) | 2002† |
| Erik Morales (WBC) | 2002–03† |
| **Juan Manuel Marquez** (IBF) | 2003– |
| **Juan Manuel Marquez** (IBF/WBA) | 2003– |
| **Chi In-jin** (WBC) | 2004– |

## Junior Featherweights

Current champions in **bold** type.

| Champion | Held Title |
|---|---|
| Jack (Kid) Wolfe | 1922–23 |
| Carl Duane | 1923–24 |
| Rigoberto Riasco (WBC) | 1976 |
| Royal Kobayashi (WBC) | 1976 |
| Dong-Kyun Yum (WBC) | 1976–77 |
| Wilfredo Gomez (WBC) | 1977–83 |
| Soo-Hwan Hong (WBA) | 1977–78 |
| Ricardo Cardona (WBA) | 1978–80 |
| Leo Randolph (WBA) | 1980 |
| Sergio Palma (WBA) | 1980–82 |
| Leonardo Cruz (WBA) | 1982–84 |
| Jaime Garza (WBC) | 1983 |
| Bobby Berna (IBF) | 1983–84 |
| Loris Stecca (WBA) | 1984 |
| Seung-Il Suh (IBF) | 1984–85 |
| Victor Callejas (WBA) | 1984–85 |
| Juan (Kid) Meza (WBC) | 1984–85 |
| Ji-Woo Kim (IBF) | 1985–86 |
| Lupe Pintor (WBC) | 1985–86 |
| Samart Payakaroon (WBC) | 1986–87 |
| Seung-Hoon Lee (IBF) | 1987–88 |
| Louie Espinoza (WBA) | 1987 |
| Jeff French (WBC) | 1987 |
| Julio Gervacio (WBA) | 1987–88 |
| Daniel Zaragoza (WBC) | 1988–90 |
| Jose Sanabria (IBF) | 1988–90 |
| Bernardo Pinango (WBA) | 1988 |
| Juan Jose Estrada (WBA) | 1988–89 |
| Fabrice Benichou (IBF) | 1989–90 |
| Jesus Salud (WBA) | 1989–90 |
| Welcome Ncita (IBF) | 1990–92 |
| Paul Banke (WBC) | 1990 |
| Luis Mendoza (WBA) | 1990–91 |
| Raul Perez (WBA) | 1992 |
| Pedro Decima (WBC) | 1990–91 |
| Kiyoshi Hatanaka (WBC) | 1991 |
| Daniel Zaragoza (WBC) | 1991–92 |
| Tracy Patterson (WBC) | 1992–94 |
| Kennedy McKinney (IBF) | 1993–94 |
| Wilfredo Vasquez (WBA) | 1992–95 |
| Vuyani Bungu (IBF) | 1994–99† |
| Hector Acero Sanchez (WBC) | 1994–95 |
| Antonio Cermeno (WBA) | 1995–98† |
| Daniel Zaragoza (WBC) | 1995–97 |
| Erik Morales (WBC) | 1997–00† |
| Enrique Sanchez (WBA) | 1998 |
| Nestor Garza (WBA) | 1998–00 |
| Lehlohonolo Ledwaba (IBF) | 1999–2001 |
| Clarence Adams (WBA) | 2000–01† |
| Willie Jorrin (WBC) | 2000–02 |
| Manny Pacquiao (IBF) | 2001–04† |
| Yorber Ortega (WBA) | 2001–02 |
| Yoddamrong Sithyodthong (WBA) | 2002 |
| Osamu Sato (WBA) | 2002 |
| Salim Medjkoune (WBA) | 2002–03 |
| **Oscar Larios** (WBC) | 2002– |
| **Mahyar Monshipour** (WBA) | 2003– |
| **Israel Vazquez** (IBF) | 2004– |

## Bantamweights

Widely accepted champions in CAPITAL letters. Current champions in **bold** type.

| Champion | Held Title |
|---|---|
| TOMMY (SPIDER) KELLY | 1887 |
| HUGHEY BOYLE | 1887–88 |
| TOMMY (SPIDER) KELLY | 1889 |
| CHAPPIE MORAN | 1889–90 |
| Tommy (Spider) Kelly | 1890–92 |
| GEORGE DIXON | 1890–91 |
| Billy Plummer | 1892–95 |
| JIMMY BARRY | 1894–99 |
| Pedlar Palmer | 1895–99 |
| TERRY McGOVERN | 1899–1900 |
| HARRY HARRIS | 1901–02 |
| DANNY DOUGHERTY | 1900–01 |
| HARRY FORBES | 1901–03 |
| FRANKIE NEIL | 1903–04 |
| JOE BOWKER | 1904–05 |
| JIMMY WALSH | 1905–06† |
| OWEN MORAN | 1907–08 |
| MONTE ATTELL | 1909–10 |
| FRANKIE CONLEY | 1910–11 |
| JOHNNY COULON | 1911–14 |
| Digger Stanley (GBR) | 1910–12 |
| Charles Ledoux (GBR) | 1912–13 |
| Eddie Campi (GBR) | 1913–14 |
| KID WILLIAMS | 1914–17 |
| Johnny Ertle | 1915–18 |
| PETE HERMAN | 1917–20 |
| Memphis Pal Moore | 1918–19 |
| JOE LYNCH | 1920–21 |
| PETE HERMAN | 1921 |
| JOHNNY BUFF | 1921–22 |
| JOE LYNCH | 1922–24 |
| ABE GOLDSTEIN | 1924 |
| CANNONBALL EDDIE MARTIN | 1924–25 |
| PHIL ROSENBERG | 1925–27 |
| Teddy Baldock (GBR) | 1927 |
| BUD TAYLOR (NBA) | 1927–28† |
| Willie Smith (GBR) | 1927–28 |
| Bushy Graham (NY) | 1928–29 |
| PANAMA AL BROWN | 1929–35 |
| Sixto Escobar (NBA) | 1934–35 |
| BALTAZAR SANGCHILLI | 1935–36 |
| Lou Salica (NBA) | 1935 |
| Sixto Escobar (NBA) | 1935–36 |
| TONY MARINO | 1936 |

## Major Titleholders (Cont.)
### Bantamweights (Cont.)

| Champion | Held Title | Champion | Held Title |
|---|---|---|---|
| SIXTO ESCOBAR | 1936–37 | Miguel (Happy) Lora (WBC) | 1985–88 |
| HARRY JEFFRA | 1937–38 | GABY CANIZALES | 1986 |
| SIXTO ESCOBAR | 1938–39* | BERNARDO PINANGO | 1986–87 |
| Georgie Pace (NBA) | 1939–40 | Wilfredo Vasquez (WBA) | 1987–88 |
| LOU SALICA | 1940–42 | Kevin Seabrooks (IBF) | 1987–88 |
| MANUEL ORTIZ | 1942–47 | Kaokor Gglaxy (WBA) | 1988 |
| HAROLD DADE | 1947 | Moon Sung-Kil (WBA) | 1988–89 |
| MANUEL ORTIZ | 1947–50 | Kaokor Galaxy (WBA) | 1989 |
| VIC TOWEEL | 1950–52 | Raul Perez (WBC) | 1988–91 |
| JIMMY CARRUTHERS | 1952–54* | Orlando Canizales (IBF) | 1988–94† |
| ROBERT COHEN | 1954–56 | Luisito Espinosa (WBA) | 1989–91 |
| Raul Macias (NBA) | 1955–57 | Greg Richardson | 1991 |
| MARIO D'AGATA | 1956–57 | Joichiro Tatsuyoshi (WBC) | 1991–92 |
| ALPHONSE HALIMI | 1957–59 | Israel Contreras (WBA) | 1991–92 |
| JOE BECERRA | 1959–60* | Eddie Cook (WBA) | 1992 |
| Johnny Caldwell (EBU) | 1961–62 | Victor Rabanales (WBC) | 1992–93 |
| EDER JOFRE | 1961–65 | Jorge Julio (WBA) | 1992–93 |
| MASAHIKO FIGHTING HARADA | 1965–68 | Jung-Il Byun (WBC) | 1993 |
| LIONEL ROSE | 1968–69 | Junior Jones (WBA) | 1993–94 |
| RUBEN OLIVARES | 1969–70 | Yasuei Yakushiji (WBC) | 1993–95 |
| CHUCHO CASTILLO | 1970–71 | John M. Johnson (WBA) | 1994 |
| RUBEN OLIVARES | 1971–72 | Daorung Chuvatana (WBA) | 1994–95 |
| RAFAEL HERRERA | 1972 | Harold Mestre (IBF) | 1995 |
| ENRIQUE PINDER | 1972–73 | Mbuelo Botile (IBF) | 1995–97 |
| ROMEO ANAYA | 1973 | Wayne McCullough (WBC) | 1995–96 |
| Rafael Herrera (WBC) | 1973–74 | Veeraphol Sahaprom (WBA) | 1995–96 |
| ARNOLD TAYLOR | 1973–74 | Nana Yaw Konadu (WBA) | 1996 |
| SOO-HWAN HONG | 1974–75 | Daorung Chuvatana (WBA) | 1996–97 |
| Rodolfo Martinez (WBC) | 1974–76 | Nana Yaw Konadu (WBA) | 1997–98 |
| ALFONSO ZAMORA | 1975–77 | Sirimongkol Singmanassak (WBC) | 1996–97 |
| Carlos Zarate (WBC) | 1976–79 | Tim Austin (IBF) | 1997–2003 |
| JORGE LUJAN | 1977–80 | Joichiro Tatsuyoshi (WBC) | 1997–98 |
| Lupe Pintor (WBC) | 1979–83 | Johnny Tapia (WBA) | 1998–99 |
| JULIAN SOLIS | 1980 | Veerapol Sahaprom (WBC) | 1998–2005 |
| JEFF CHANDLER | 1980–84 | Paulie Ayala (WBA) | 1999–2001 |
| Albert Davila (WBC) | 1983–85 | Eidy Moya (WBA) | 2001–02 |
| RICHARD SANDOVAL | 1984–86 | Johnny Bredahl (WBA) | 2002–04† |
| Satoshi Shingaki (IBF) | 1984–85 | **Rafael Marquez** (IBF) | 2003– |
| Jeff Fenech (IBF) | 1985 | **Wladimir Sidorenko** (WBA) | 2005– |
| Daniel Zaragoza (WBC) | 1985 | **Hozumi Hasegawa** (WBC) | 2005– |

## Junior Bantamweights

Widely accepted champions in CAPITAL letters. Current champions in **bold** type.

| Champion | Held Title | Champion | Held Title |
|---|---|---|---|
| Rafael Orono (WBC) | 1980–81 | Lee Hyung-Chul (WBA) | 1994–95 |
| Chul-Ho Kim (WBC) | 1981–82 | Jose Luis Bueno (WBC) | 1993–94 |
| Gustavo Ballas (WBA) | 1981 | Hiroshi Kawashima (WBC) | 1994–97 |
| Rafael Pedroza (WBA) | 1981–82 | Harold Grey (IBF) | 1994–95 |
| Jiro Watanabe (WBA) | 1982–84 | Alimi Goitia (WBA) | 1995–96 |
| Rafael Orono (WBC) | 1982–83 | Yokthai Sith-Oar (WBA) | 1996–97 |
| Payao Poontarat (WBC) | 1983–84 | Carlos Salazar (IBF) | 1995–96 |
| Joo-Do Chun (IBF) | 1983–85 | Harold Grey (IBF) | 1996 |
| JIRO WATANABE | 1984–86 | Danny Romero (IBF) | 1996–97 |
| Kaosai Galaxy ( WBA) | 1984 | Gerry Penalosa (WBC) | 1997–98 |
| Ellyas Pical (IBF) | 1985–86 | Johnny Tapia (IBF) | 1997–98† |
| Cesar Polanco (IBF) | 1986 | Satoshi Iida (WBA) | 1997–98 |
| GILBERTO ROMAN | 1986–87 | Cho In-Joo (WBC) | 1998–00 |
| Ellyas Pical (IBF) | 1986 | Jesus Rojas (WBA) | 1998–99 |
| Santos Laciar (WBC) | 1987 | Mark Johnson (IBF) | 1999–00† |
| Tae-Il Chang (IBF) | 1987 | Hideki Todaka (WBA) | 1999–2000 |
| Sugar Rojas (WBC) | 1987–88 | Masanori Tokuyama (WBC) | 2000–04 |
| Ellyas Pical (IBF) | 1987–89 | Felix Machado (IBF) | 2000–03 |
| Gilberto Roman (WBC) | 1988–89 | Leo Gamez (WBA) | 2000–01 |
| Juan Polo Perez (IBF) | 1989–90 | Celes Kobayashi (WBA) | 2001–02 |
| Nana Konadu (WBC) | 1989–90 | Alexander Munoz (WBA) | 2002–04 |
| Sung-Kil Moon (WBC) | 1990–93 | **Luis Perez** (IBF) | 2003– |
| Robert Quiroga (IBF) | 1990–93 | Katsushige Kawashima (WBC) | 2004–05 |
| Julio Borboa (IBF) | 1993–94 | **Martin Castillo** (WBA) | 2004– |
| Katsuya Onizuka (WBA) | 1993–94 | **Masmori Tokuyama** (WBC) | 2005– |

## Flyweights

Widely accepted champions in CAPITAL letters. Current champions in **bold** type.

| Champion | Held Title |
|---|---|
| Sid Smith (GBR) | 1913 |
| Bill Ladbury (GBR) | 1913–14 |
| Percy Jones (GBR) | 1914 |
| Joe Symonds (GBR) | 1914–16 |
| JIMMY WILDE | 1916–23 |
| PANCHO VILLA | 1923–25 |
| FIDEL LaBARBA | 1925–27* |
| FRENCHY BELANGER (NBA,IBU) | 1927–28 |
| Izzy Schwartz (NY) | 1927–29 |
| Johnny McCoy (Calif.) | 1927–28 |
| Newsboy Brown (Calif.) | 1928 |
| FRANKIE GENARO (NBA,IBU) | 1928–29 |
| Johnny Hill (GBR) | 1928–29 |
| SPIDER PLADNER (NBA,IBU) | 1929 |
| FRANKIE GENARO (NBA,IBU) | 1929–31 |
| Willie LaMorte (NY) | 1929–30 |
| Midget Wolgast (NY) | 1930–35 |
| YOUNG PEREZ (NBA,IBU) | 1931–32 |
| JACKIE BROWN (NBA,IBU) | 1932–35 |
| BENNY LYNCH | 1935–38† |
| Small Montana (NY,Calif.) | 1935–37 |
| PETER KANE | 1938–43 |
| Little Dado (NBA,Calif.) | 1938–40 |
| JACKIE PATERSON | 1943–48 |
| RINTY MONAGHAN | 1948–50* |
| TERRY ALLEN | 1950 |
| SALVADOR (DADO) MARINO | 1950–52 |
| YOSHIO SHIRAI | 1953–54 |
| PASCUAL PEREZ | 1954–60 |
| PONE KINGPETCH | 1960–62 |
| MASAHIKO (FIGHTING) HARADA | 1962–63 |
| PONE KINGPETCH | 1963 |
| HIROYUKI EBIHARA | 1963–64 |
| PONE KINGPETCH | 1964–65 |
| SALVATORE BURRINI | 1965–66 |
| Horacio Accavallo (WBA) | 1966–68 |
| WALTER McGOWAN | 1966 |
| CHARTCHAI CHIONOI | 1966–69 |
| EFREN TORRES | 1969–70 |
| Hiroyuki Ebihara (WBA) | 1969 |
| Bernabe Villacampo (WBA) | 1969–70 |
| CHARTCHAI CHIONOI | 1970 |
| Berkrerk Chartvanchai (WBA) | 1970 |
| Masao Ohba (WBA) | 1970–73 |
| ERBITO SALAVARRIA | 1970–73 |
| Betulio Gonzalez (WBC) | 1972 |
| Venice Borkorsor (WBC) | 1972–73 |
| VENICE BORKORSOR | 1973 |
| Chartchai Chionoi (WBA) | 1973–74 |
| Betulio Gonzalez (WBA) | 1973–74 |
| Shoji Oguma (WBC) | 1974–75 |
| Susumu Hanagata (WBA) | 1974–75 |
| Miguel Canto (WBC) | 1975–79 |
| Erbito Salavarria (WBA) | 1975–76 |
| Alfonso Lopez (WBA) | 1976 |
| Guty Espadas (WBA) | 1976–78 |
| Betulio Gonzalez (WBA) | 1978–79 |
| Chan-Hee Park (WBC) | 1979–80 |
| Luis Ibarra (WBA) | 1979–80 |

| Champion | Held Title |
|---|---|
| Tae-Shik Kim (WBA) | 1980 |
| Shoji Oguma (WBC) | 1980–81 |
| Peter Mathebula (WBA) | 1980–81 |
| Santos Laciar (WBA) | 1981 |
| Antonio Avelar (WBC) | 1981–82 |
| Luis Ibarra (WBA) | 1981 |
| Juan Herrera (WBA) | 1981–82 |
| Prudencio Cardona (WBC) | 1982 |
| Santos Laciar (WBA) | 1982–85 |
| Freddie Castillo (WBC) | 1982 |
| Eleoncio Mercedes (WBC) | 1982–83 |
| Charlie Magri (WBC) | 1983 |
| Frank Cedeno (WBC) | 1983–84 |
| Soon-Chun Kwon (IBF) | 1983–85 |
| Koji Kobayashi (WBC) | 1984 |
| Gabriel Bernal (WBC) | 1984 |
| Sot Chitalada (WBC) | 1984–88 |
| Hilario Zapate (WBA) | 1985–87 |
| Chong-Kwan Chung (IBF) | 1985–86 |
| Bi-Won Chung (IBF) | 1986 |
| Hi-Sup Shin (IBF) | 1986–87 |
| Dodie Penalosa (IBF) | 1987 |
| Fidel Bassa (WBA) | 1987–89 |
| Choi Chang-Ho (IBF) | 1987–88 |
| Rolando Bohol (IBF) | 1988 |
| Yong-Kang Kim (WBC) | 1988–89 |
| Duke McKenzie (IBF) | 1988–89 |
| Dave McAuley (IBF) | 1989–92 |
| Sot Chitalada (WBC) | 1989–91 |
| Jesus Rojas (WBA) | 1989–90 |
| Yul-Woo Lee (WBA) | 1990 |
| Leopard Tamakuma (WBA) | 1990–91 |
| Muangchai Kittikasem (WBC) | 1991–92 |
| Yong-Kang Kim (WBA) | 1991–92 |
| Rodolfo Blanco (IBF) | 1992 |
| Yuri Arbachakov (WBC) | 1992–97 |
| Aquiles Guzman (WBA) | 1992 |
| Phichit Sithbangprachan (IBF) | 1992–94† |
| David Griman (WBA) | 1992–94 |
| Saen Sor Ploenchit (WBA) | 1994–96 |
| Francisco Tejedor (IBF) | 1995 |
| Danny Romero (IBF) | 1995–96 |
| Mark Johnson (IBF) | 1996–99† |
| Jose Bonilla (WBA) | 1996–97 |
| Chatchai Sasakul (WBC) | 1997–98 |
| Hugo Soto (WBA) | 1998–99 |
| Manny Pacquiao (WBC) | 1998–99 |
| Irene Pacheco (IBF) | 1999–2005 |
| Leo Gamez (WBA) | 1999 |
| Medgoen Lukchaopormasak (WBC) | 1999–00 |
| Sornpichai Kratindaenggym (WBA) | 1999–00 |
| Eric Morel (WBA) | 2000–03 |
| Malcolm Tunacao (WBC) | 2000–01 |
| **Pongsaklek Wonjongkam** (WBC) | 2001– |
| **Lorenzo Parra** (WBA) | 2003– |
| **Vic Darchinyan** (IBF) | 2004– |

## Junior Flyweights

Current champions in **bold** type.

| Champion | Held Title |
|---|---|
| Franco Udella (WBC) | 1975 |
| Jaime Rios (WBA) | 1975–76 |
| Luis Estaba (WBC) | 1975–78 |
| Juan Guzman (WBA) | 1976 |
| Yoko Gushiken (WBA) | 1976–81 |
| Freddy Castillo (WBC) | 1978 |
| Netrnoi Vorasingh (WBC) | 1978 |
| Sung-Jun Kim (WBC) | 1978–80 |

| Champion | Held Title |
|---|---|
| Shigeo Nakajima (WBC) | 1980 |
| Hilario Zapata (WBC) | 1980–82 |
| Pedro Flores (WBA) | 1981 |
| Hwan-Jin Kim (WBA) | 1981 |
| Katsuo Tokashiki (WBA) | 1981–83 |
| Amado Urzua (WBC) | 1982 |
| Tadashi Tomori (WBC) | 1982 |
| Hilario Zapata (WBC) | 1982–83 |

## Major Titleholders (Cont.)
### Junior Flyweights

| Champion | Held Title |
|---|---|
| Jung-Koo Chang (WBC) | 1983–88 |
| Lupe Madera (WBA) | 1983–84 |
| Dodie Penalosa (IBF) | 1983–86 |
| Francisco Quiroz (WBA) | 1984–85 |
| Joey Olivo (WBA) | 1985 |
| Myung-Woo Yuh (WBA) | 1985–91 |
| Jum-Hwan Choi (IBF) | 1986–88 |
| Tacy Macalos (IBF) | 1988–89 |
| German Torres (WBC) | 1988–89 |
| Yul-Woo Lee (WBC) | 1989 |
| Muangchai Kittikasem (IBF) | 1989–90 |
| Humberto Gonzalez (WBC) | 1989–90 |
| Michael Carbajal (IBF) | 1990–94 |
| Rolando Pascua (WBC) | 1990 |
| Melchor Cob Castro (WBC) | 1991 |
| Humberto Gonzalez (WBC) | 1991–93 |
| Hirokia Ioka (WBA) | 1991–92 |
| Michael Carbajal (WBC) | 1993–94 |
| Myung-Woo Yuh (WBA) | 1993 |
| Leo Gamez (WBA) | 1993–95 |
| Humberto Gonzalez (WBC/IBF) | 1994–95 |

| Champion | Held Title |
|---|---|
| Choi Hi-Yong (WBA) | 1995–96 |
| Saman Sor Jaturong (WBC/IBF) | 1995–96 |
| Carlos Murillo (WBA) | 1996 |
| Keiji Yamaguchi (WBA) | 1996 |
| Michael Carbajal (IBF) | 1996–97 |
| Saman Sor Jaturong (WBC) | 1995–99 |
| Phichit Chor Siriwat (WBA) | 1996–00† |
| Mauricio Pastrana (IBF) | 1997–98† |
| Will Grigsby (IBF) | 1999 |
| Choi Yo-Sam (WBC) | 1999–2002 |
| Ricardo Lopez (IBF) | 1999–2003* |
| Beibis Mendoza (WBA) | 2000–01 |
| Rosendo Alvarez (WBA) | 2001–04† |
| Jorge Arce (WBC) | 2002–05† |
| Jose Victor Burgos (IBF) | 2003–05 |
| Eric Ortiz (WBC) | 2005 |
| **Roberto Vasquez** (WBA) | 2005– |
| **Brian Viloria** (WBC) | 2005– |
| **Will Grigsby** (IBF) | 2005– |

### Strawweights

Current champions in **bold** type.

| Champion | Held Title |
|---|---|
| Franco Udella (WBC) | 1975 |
| Jaime Rios (WBA) | 1975–76 |
| Luis Estraba (WBC) | 1975–78 |
| Juan Guzman (WBA) | 1976 |
| Yoko Gushiken (WBA) | 1976–81 |
| Freddy Castillo (WBC) | 1978 |
| Netrnoi Vorasingh (WBC) | 1978 |
| Sung-Jun Kim (WBC) | 1978–80 |
| Shigeo Nakajima (WBC) | 1980 |
| Hilario Zapata (WBC) | 1980–82 |
| Pedro Flores (WBA) | 1981 |
| Hwan-Jin Kim (WBA) | 1981 |
| Katsuo Tokashiki (WBA) | 1981–83 |
| Amado Urzua (WBC) | 1982 |
| Tadashi Tomori (WBC) | 1982 |
| Hilario Zapata (WBC) | 1982–83 |
| Jung-Koo Chang (WBC) | 1983–88 |
| Lupe Madera (WBA) | 1983–84 |
| Dodie Penalosa (IBF) | 1983–86 |
| Francisco Quiroz (WBA) | 1984–85 |
| Joey Olivo (WBA) | 1985 |
| Myung-Woo Yuh (WBA) | 1985–93 |
| Jum-Hwan Choi (IBF) | 1986–88 |
| Tacy Macalos (IBF) | 1988–89 |
| German Torres (WBC) | 1988–89 |
| Yul-Woo Lee (WBC) | 1989 |
| Muangchai Kittikasem (IBF) | 1989–90 |
| Humberto Gonzalez (WBC) | 1989–90 |

| Champion | Held Title |
|---|---|
| Michael Carbajal (IBF) | 1990 |
| Rolando Pascua (WBC) | 1990 |
| Melchor Cob Castro (WBC) | 1991 |
| Ricardo Lopez (WBC) | 1990–98 |
| Ratanapol Voraphin (IBF) | 1992–97 |
| Chana Porpaoin (WBA) | 1993–95 |
| Rosendo Alvarez (WBA) | 1995–98 |
| Ricardo Lopez (WBA/WBC) | 1998–99† |
| Zolani Petelo (IBF) | 1997–2001† |
| Wandee Chor Chareon (WBC) | 1999–00 |
| Noel Arambulet (WBA) | 1999–00† |
| Joma Gamboa (WBA) | 2000 |
| Keitaro Hoshino (WBA) | 2000–01 |
| Jose Antonio Aguirre (WBC) | 2000–04 |
| Chana Porpaoin (WBA) | 2001 |
| Robert Leyva (IBF) | 2001–02 |
| Yutaka Niida (WBA) | 2001* |
| Keitaro Hoshino (WBA) | 2002 |
| Noel Arambulent (WBA) | 2002–04 |
| Miguel Barrera (IBF) | 2002–03 |
| Edgar Cardenas (IBF) | 2003 |
| Daniel Reyes (IBF) | 2003–04 |
| Eagle Kyowa (WBC) | 2004 |
| **Yutaka Niida** (WBA) | 2004– |
| **Muhammad Rachman** (IBF) | 2004– |
| Isaac Bustos (WBC) | 2004–05 |
| Katsunari Takayama (WBC) | 2005 |
| **Eagle Kyowa** (WBC) | 2005– |

## Annual Awards
### *Ring Magazine* Fight of the Year

First presented in 1945 by Nat Fleischer, who started *The Ring* magazine in 1922.

**Multiple matchups:** Muhammad Ali vs. Joe Frazier, Marco Antonio Barrera vs. Erik Morales; Carmen Basilio vs. Sugar Ray Robinson, Arturo Gatti vs. Micky Ward and Rocky Graziano vs. Tony Zale (2).

**Multiple fights:** Muhammad Ali (6); Carmen Basilio (5); George Foreman, Arturo Gatti and Joe Frazier (4); Rocky Graziano, Rocky Marciano, Micky Ward and Tony Zale (3); Marco Antonio Barrera, Nino Benvenuti, Bobby Chacon, Ezzard Charles, Marvin Hagler, Thomas Hearns, Evander Holyfield, Sugar Ray Leonard, Erik Morales, Floyd Patterson, Sugar Ray Robinson, Jersey Joe Walcott (2).

| Year | Winner | Loser | Result | Year | Winner | Loser | Result |
|---|---|---|---|---|---|---|---|
| 1945 | Rocky Graziano | Red Cochrane | KO 10 | 1949 | Willie Pep | Sandy Saddler | W 15 |
| 1946 | Tony Zale | Rocky Graziano | KO 6 | 1950 | Jake LaMotta | Laurent Dauthuille | KO 15 |
| 1947 | Rocky Graziano | Tony Zale | KO 6 | 1951 | Jersey Joe Walcott | Ezzard Charles | KO 7 |
| 1948 | Marcel Cerdan | Tony Zale | KO 12 | | | | |

| Year | Winner | Loser | Result | | Year | Winner | Loser | Result |
|------|--------|-------|--------|---|------|--------|-------|--------|
| 1952 | Rocky Marciano | Jersey Joe Walcott | KO 13 | | 1979 | Danny Lopez | Mike Ayala | KO 15 |
| 1953 | Rocky Marciano | Roland LaStarza | KO 11 | | 1980 | Saad Muhammad | Yaqui Lopez | KO 14 |
| 1954 | Rocky Marciano | Ezzard Charles | KO 8 | | 1981 | Sugar Ray Leonard | Thomas Hearns | KO 14 |
| 1955 | Carmen Basilio | Tony DeMarco | KO 12 | | 1982 | Bobby Chacon | Rafael Limon | W 15 |
| 1956 | Carmen Basilio | Johnny Saxton | KO 9 | | 1983 | Bobby Chacon | C. Boza-Edwards | W 12 |
| 1957 | Carmen Basilio | Sugar Ray Robinson | W 15 | | 1984 | Jose Luis Ramirez | Edwin Rosario | KO 4 |
| 1958 | Sugar Ray Robinson | Carmen Basilio | W 15 | | 1985 | Marvin Hagler | Thomas Hearns | KO 3 |
| 1959 | Gene Fullmer | Carmen Basilio | KO 14 | | 1986 | Stevie Cruz | Barry McGuigan | W 15 |
| 1960 | Floyd Patterson | Ingemar Johansson | KO 5 | | 1987 | Sugar Ray Leonard | Marvin Hagler | W 12 |
| 1961 | Joe Brown | Dave Charnley | W 15 | | 1988 | Tony Lopez | Rocky Lockridge | W 12 |
| 1962 | Joey Giardello | Henry Hank | W 10 | | 1989 | Roberto Duran | Iran Barkley | W 12 |
| 1963 | Cassius Clay | Doug Jones | W 10 | | 1990 | Julio Cesar Chavez | Meldrick Taylor | KO 12 |
| 1964 | Cassius Clay | Sonny Liston | KO 7 | | 1991 | Robert Quiroga | Akeem Anifowoshe | W 12 |
| 1965 | Floyd Patterson | George Chuvalo | W 12 | | 1992 | Riddick Bowe | Evander Holyfield | W 12 |
| 1966 | Jose Torres | Eddie Cotton | W 15 | | 1993 | Michael Carbajal | Humberto Gonzalez | KO 7 |
| 1967 | Nino Benvenuti | Emile Griffith | W 15 | | 1994 | Jorge Castro | John David Jackson | TKO 9 |
| 1968 | Dick Tiger | Frank DePaula | W 10 | | 1995 | Saman Sorjaturong | Chiquita Gonzalez | KO 7 |
| 1969 | Joe Frazier | Jerry Quarry | KO 7 | | 1996 | Evander Holyfield | Mike Tyson | TKO 11 |
| 1970 | Carlos Monzon | Nino Benvenuti | KO 12 | | 1997 | Arturo Gatti | Gabriel Ruelas | KO 5 |
| 1971 | Joe Frazier | Muhammad Ali | W 15 | | 1998 | Ivan Robinson | Arturo Gatti | W 10 |
| 1972 | Bob Foster | Chris Finnegan | KO 14 | | 1999 | Paulie Ayala | Johnny Tapia | W 12 |
| 1973 | George Foreman | Joe Frazier | KO 2 | | 2000 | Erik Morales | Marco Antonio Barrera | W 12 |
| 1974 | Muhammad Ali | George Foreman | KO 8 | | 2001 | Micky Ward | Emanuel Burton | W 10 |
| 1975 | Muhammad Ali | Joe Frazier | KO 14 | | 2002 | Micky Ward | Arturo Gatti | W 10 |
| 1976 | George Foreman | Ron Lyle | KO 4 | | 2003 | Arturo Gatti | Micky Ward | W 10 |
| 1977 | Jimmy Young | George Foreman | W 12 | | 2004 | Marco Antonio | | |
| 1978 | Leon Spinks | Muhammad Ali | W 15 | | | Barrera | Erik Morales | W 12 |

## *Ring Magazine* Fighter of the Year

First presented in 1928 by Nat Fleischer, who started *The Ring* magazine in 1922.

**Multiple winners:** Muhammad Ali (5); Joe Louis (4); Joe Frazier, Evander Holyfield and Rocky Marciano (3); Ezzard Charles, George Foreman, Marvin Hagler, Thomas Hearns, Ingemar Johansson, Sugar Ray Leonard, Tommy Loughran, Floyd Patterson, Sugar Ray Robinson, Barney Ross, Dick Tiger, James Toney and Mike Tyson (2).

| Year | | Year | | Year | |
|------|---|------|---|------|---|
| 1928 | Gene Tunney | 1954 | Rocky Marciano | 1980 | Thomas Hearns |
| 1929 | Tommy Loughran | 1955 | Rocky Marciano | 1981 | Sugar Ray Leonard |
| 1930 | Max Schmeling | 1956 | Floyd Patterson | | & Salvador Sanchez |
| 1931 | Tommy Loughran | 1957 | Carmen Basilio | 1982 | Larry Holmes |
| 1932 | Jack Sharkey | 1958 | Ingemar Johansson | 1983 | Marvin Hagler |
| 1933 | No award | 1959 | Ingemar Johansson | 1984 | Thomas Hearns |
| 1934 | Tony Canzoneri | 1960 | Floyd Patterson | 1985 | Donald Curry |
| | & Barney Ross | 1961 | Joe Brown | | & Marvin Hagler |
| 1935 | Barney Ross | 1962 | Dick Tiger | 1986 | Mike Tyson |
| 1936 | Joe Louis | 1963 | Cassius Clay | 1987 | Evander Holyfield |
| 1937 | Henry Armstrong | 1964 | Emile Griffith | 1988 | Mike Tyson |
| 1938 | Joe Louis | 1965 | Dick Tiger | 1989 | Pernell Whitaker |
| 1939 | Joe Louis | 1966 | No award | | |
| | | 1967 | Joe Frazier | 1990 | Julio Cesar Chavez |
| 1940 | Billy Conn | 1968 | Nino Benvenuti | 1991 | James Toney |
| 1941 | Joe Louis | 1969 | Jose Napoles | 1992 | Riddick Bowe |
| 1942 | Sugar Ray Robinson | | | 1993 | Michael Carbajal |
| 1943 | Fred Apostoli | 1970 | Joe Frazier | 1994 | Roy Jones Jr. |
| 1944 | Beau Jack | 1971 | Joe Frazier | 1995 | Oscar De La Hoya |
| 1945 | Willie Pep | 1972 | Muhammad Ali | 1996 | Evander Holyfield |
| 1946 | Tony Zale | | & Carlos Monzon | 1997 | Evander Holyfield |
| 1947 | Gus Lesnevich | 1973 | George Foreman | 1998 | Floyd Mayweather Jr. |
| 1948 | Ike Williams | 1974 | Muhammad Ali | 1999 | Paulie Ayala |
| 1949 | Ezzard Charles | 1975 | Muhammad Ali | | |
| | | 1976 | George Foreman | 2000 | Felix Trinidad |
| 1950 | Ezzard Charles | 1977 | Carlos Zarate | 2001 | Bernard Hopkins |
| 1951 | Sugar Ray Robinson | 1978 | Muhammad Ali | 2002 | Vernon Forrest |
| 1952 | Rocky Marciano | 1979 | Sugar Ray Leonard | 2003 | James Toney |
| 1953 | Carl (Bobo) Olson | | | 2004 | Glen Johnson |

**Note:** Cassius Clay changed his name to Muhammad Ali after winning the heavyweight title in 1964.

## Triple Champions

Fighters who have won widely-accepted world titles in more than two divisions. Henry Armstrong is the only fighter listed to hold three titles simultaneously. Note that (*) indicates title claimant.

**Sugar Ray Leonard** (5) WBC Welterweight (1979-80,80-82); WBA Jr. Middleweight (1981); WBC Middleweight (1987); WBC Super Middleweight (1988-90); WBC Light Heavyweight (1988).

**Roy Jones Jr.** (4) IBF Middleweight (1993-94); IBF Super Middleweight (1994-96); WBC Light Heavyweight (1996, 1997-2003); WBA Light Heavyweight (1998–); IBF Light Heavyweight (1999-2003); WBA Heavyweight (2003-04).

**Oscar De La Hoya** (4) IBF Lightweight (1995-96); WBC Super Lightweight (1996-97); WBC Welterweight (1997-99); WBC Jr. Middleweight (2001-03); WBA Jr. Middleweight (2002-03).

**Roberto Duran** (4) Lightweight (1972-79); WBC Welterweight (1980); WBA Jr. Middleweight (1983-84); WBC Middleweight (1989-90).

**Leo Gamez** (4) WBA Strawweight (1988-90); WBA Jr. Flyweight (1993-95); WBA Flyweight (1999); WBA Junior Bantamweight (2000-01).

**Thomas Hearns** (4) WBA Welterweight (1980-81); WBC Jr. Middleweight (1982-84); WBC Light Heavyweight (1987); WBC Middleweight (1987-88); WBA Light Heavyweight (1991).

**James Toney** (4) IBF Middleweight (1991-93); IBF Super Middlweight (1992-94); IBF Cruiserweight (2003); WBA Heavyweight† (2005).

**Pernell Whitaker** (4) IBF/WBC/WBA Lightweight (1989-92); IBF Jr. Welterweight (1992-93); WBC Welterweight (1993-97); WBC Jr. Middleweight (1995).

**Alexis Arguello** (3) WBA Featherweight (1974-77); WBC Jr. Lightweight (1978-80); WBC Lightweight (1981-83).

**Henry Armstrong** (3) Featherweight (1937-38); Welterweight (1938-40); Lightweight (1938-39).

**Iran Barkley** (3) WBC Middleweight (1988-89); IBF Super Middleweight (1992-93); WBA Light Heavyweight (1992).

**Wilfredo Benitez** (3) Jr. Welterweight (1976-79); Welterweight (1979); WBC Jr. Middleweight (1981-82).

**Tony Canzoneri** (3) Featherweight (1928); Lightweight (1930-33); Jr. Welterweight (1931-32,33).

**Julio Cesar Chavez** (3) WBC Jr. Lightweight (1984-87); WBA/WBC Lightweight (1987-89); WBC/IBF Jr. Welterweight (1989-91); WBC Jr. Welterweight (1991-94, 1994).

**Jeff Fenech** (3) IBF Bantamweight (1985); WBC Jr. Featherweight (1986-88); WBC Featherweight (1988-90).

**Bob Fitzsimmons** (3) Middleweight (1891-97); Light Heavyweight (1903-05); Heavyweight (1897-99).

**Wilfredo Gomez** (3) WBC Super Bantamweight (1977-83); WBC Featherweight (1984); WBA Jr. Lightweight (1985-86).

**Emile Griffith** (3) Welterweight (1961,62-63,63-66); Jr. Middleweight (1962-63); Middleweight (1966-67,67-68).

**Floyd Mayweather** (3) Jr. Lighweight (1998-2002); Lightweight (2002-04); Jr. Welterweight (2005–)

**Mike McCallum** (3) WBA Jr. Middleweight (1984-88); WBA Middleweight (1989-91); WBC Light Heavyweight (1994-95).

**Terry McGovern** (3) Bantamweight (1889-1900); Featherweight (1900-01); Lightweight* (1900-01).

**Erik Morales** (3) WBC Jr. Featherweight (1997-2000); WBC Featherweight (2001-02); IBF/WBC Jr. Lightweight (2004)

**Barney Ross** (3) Lightweight (1933-35); Jr. Welterweight (1933-35); Welterweight (1934, 35-38).

**Johnny Tapia** (3) IBF Jr. Bantamweight (1997-98); WBA Bantamweight (1998-99); IBF Featherweight (2002).

**Felix Trinidad** (3) IBF/WBC Welterweight (1993-2000); WBA/IBF Jr. Middleweight (2000-01); WBA Middleweight (2001).

**Wilfredo Vazquez** (3) WBA Bantamweight (1987-88); WBA Jr. Featherweight (1992-95); WBA Featherweight (1996-98).

†Toney won the WBA belt on Apr. 30, 2005 but on two weeks later the fight was ruled a No Contest and he was stripped of the title after testing positive for steroids following the bout.

## All-Time Heavyweight Upsets

Buster Douglas was a 42-1 underdog when he defeated previously unbeaten heavyweight champion Mike Tyson on Feb. 10, 1990. That 10th-round knockout ranks as the biggest upset in boxing history. By comparison, 45-year-old George Foreman was only a 3-1 underdog before he unexpectedly won the title from Michael Moorer on Nov. 5, 1994.

Here are the best-known upsets in the annals of the heavyweight division. All fights were for the world championship except the Max Schmeling-Joe Louis bout.

| Date | Winner | Loser | Result | KO Time | Location |
|---|---|---|---|---|---|
| 9/7/1892 | James J. Corbett | John L. Sullivan | KO 21 | 1:30 | Olympic Club, New Orleans |
| 4/5/1915 | Jess Willard | Jack Johnson | KO 26 | 1:26 | Mariano Race Track, Havana |
| 9/23/26 | Gene Tunney | Jack Dempsey | Wu 10 | – | Sesquicentennial Stadium, Phila. |
| 6/13/35 | James J. Braddock | Max Baer | Wu 15 | – | Mad. Sq.Garden Bowl, L.I. City |
| 6/19/36 | Max Schmeling | Joe Louis | KO 12 | 2:29 | Yankee Stadium, New York |
| 7/18/51 | Jersey Joe Walcott | Ezzard Charles | KO 7 | 0:55 | Forbes Field, Pittsburgh |
| 6/26/59 | Ingemar Johansson | Floyd Patterson | TKO 3 | 2:03 | Yankee Stadium, New York |
| 2/25/64 | Cassius Clay | Sonny Liston | TKO 7 | * | Convention Hall, Miami Beach |
| 10/30/74 | Muhammad Ali | George Foreman | KO 8 | 2:58 | 20th of May Stadium, Zaire |
| 2/15/78 | Leon Spinks | Muhammad Ali | Ws 15 | – | Hilton Pavilion, Las Vegas |
| 9/21/85 | Michael Spinks | Larry Holmes | Wu 15 | – | Riviera Hotel, Las Vegas |
| 2/10/90 | Buster Douglas | Mike Tyson | KO 10 | 1:23 | Tokyo Dome, Tokyo |
| 11/5/94 | George Foreman | Michael Moorer | KO 10 | 2:03 | MGM Grand, Las Vegas |
| 11/9/96 | Evander Holyfield | Mike Tyson | TKO 11 | 0:37 | MGM Grand, Las Vegas |
| 4/22/2001 | Hasim Rahman | Lennox Lewis | KO 5 | 2:32 | Johannesburg, South Africa |

# Miscellaneous Sports

The boys from **West Oahu, Hawaii** won the Little League World Series in 2005.

AP/Wide World Photos

## CHESS

### World Champions

Garry Kasparov became the youngest man to win the world chess championship when he beat fellow Russian Anatoly Karpov in 1985 at age 22. In 1993, Kasparov and then-#1 challenger Nigel Short of England broke away from the established International Chess Federation (FIDE) to form the Professional Chess Association (the PCA was disbanded in 1998). FIDE retaliated by stripping Kasparov of the world title and arranging a playoff that was won by Karpov, the former title-holder. Karpov successfully defended the FIDE title several times before failing to show up for the 1999 FIDE World Championship Tournament that was won by Alexander Khalifman. Indian Viswanathan Anand won the 2000 FIDE World Championship.

In his first title defense in five years, Kasparov faced world #2 Vladimir Kramnik for 16 matches in the unofficial (though more widely recognized) world championship from Oct. 8-Nov. 4, 2000 in London. The 25-year-old Kramnik defeated the longtime world champion 8½-6½ in a stunning result. Kasparov failed to win a single game, but despite the loss was still the top-ranked player in the world. Ruslan Ponomariov of Ukraine won the 2002 FIDE title and a plan, known as the Prague Agreement, to unify the world chess championship was hatched. FIDE hosted a knockout tournament in 2003 which was won by the 18-year-old Ponomariov. Ponomariov was supposed to then play World No. 1 Kasparov. But Ponomariov could not agree to the terms set for his match with Kasparov and was stripped of his title.

Uzbekistan's Rustam Kasimdzhanov won the FIDE title in 2004 (however many of the world's top players didn't compete) and was scheduled to play Kasparov in 2005. The winner of that match was supposed to play the winner of the Kramnik-Peter Leko match (Kramnik retained his title in a 7-7 draw) but Kasparov withdrew from the Kasimdzhanov match in a financial dispute before it could take place, effectively ending the Prague Agreement. In 2005, the FIDE championship was won by 30-year-old Bulgarian Veselin Topalov. The tournament included eight of the world's top players; each played two games against the others in a round-robin format. However, Kramnik, the linear world champion, did not compete. He has said he would be open to playing the winner to unify the title. Meanwhile, Kasparov stunned many when he announced his retirement from professional chess in March 2005 after winning the prestigious Linares tournament in Spain, claiming there are no real challenges on the horizon. Despite his retirement, he remains the top-ranked player in the world.

| Years | | Years | | Years | |
|---|---|---|---|---|---|
| 1866-94 | Wilhelm Steinitz, Austria | 1957-58 | Vassily Smyslov, USSR | 1975-85 | Anatoly Karpov, USSR |
| 1894-1921 | Emanuel Lasker, Germany | 1958-59 | Mikhail Botvinnik, USSR | 1985-2000 | Garry Kasparov, RUS |
| 1921-27 | Jose Capablanca, Cuba | 1960-61 | Mikhail Tal, USSR | 2000— | Vladimir Kramnik, RUS |
| 1927-35 | Alexander Alekhine, France | 1961-63 | Mikhail Botvinnik, USSR | 2002-03 | Ruslan Ponomariov, UKR |
| 1935-37 | Max Euwe, Holland | 1963-69 | Tigran Petrosian, USSR | 2004-05 | Rustam Kasimdzhanov, UZB |
| 1937-46 | Alexander Alekhine, France | 1969-72 | Boris Spassky, USSR | 2005— | Veselin Topalov, BUL |
| 1948-57 | Mikhail Botvinnik, USSR | 1972-75 | Bobby Fischer, USA* | | |

*Fischer defaulted the championship in 1975.

## DOGS

### Iditarod Trail Sled Dog Race

In the closest finish in years, Norwegian Robert Sorlie won the Iditarod for the second time, passing under the burled arch on Nome, Alaska's Front Street that serves as the finish line just 34 minutes ahead of runner-up Ed Iten of Kotzebue, Alaska. The 47-year-old firefighter, who finished the race with eight dogs (16 are required to start the race), took the lead early in the race and never relinquished it, winning just over $72,000 and a new pickup truck at the 33rd edition of the annual race in 2005. Sorlie's nephew Bjornar Andersen finished fourth, a record for rookie mushers.

In even-numbered years the trail follows the 1,151-mile Northern Route, while in odd-numbered years, it takes a slightly different 1,161-mile Southern Route. The Iditarod, the longest sled dog race in the world, commemorates a 674-mile relay race from Nenana to Nome in 1925 when mushers and dog teams successfully delivered serum to stave off an outbreak of diphtheria among children.

**Multiple winners:** Rick Swenson (5); Martin Buser, Susan Butcher and Doug Swingley (4); Jeff King (3); Robert Sorlie (2).

| Year | | Elapsed Time | Year | | Elapsed Time |
|---|---|---|---|---|---|
| 1973 | Dick Wilmarth | 20 days, 00:49:41 | 1990 | Susan Butcher | 11 days, 01:53:23 |
| 1974 | Carl Huntington | 20 days, 15:02:07 | 1991 | Rick Swenson | 12 days, 16:34:39 |
| 1975 | Emmitt Peters | 14 days, 14:43:45 | 1992 | Martin Buser | 10 days, 19:17:00 |
| 1976 | Gerald Riley | 18 days, 22:58:17 | 1993 | Jeff King | 10 days, 15:38:15 |
| 1977 | Rick Swenson | 16 days, 16:27:13 | 1994 | Martin Buser | 10 days, 13:02:39 |
| 1978 | Dick Mackey | 14 days, 18:52:24 | 1995 | Doug Swingley | 9 days, 02:42:19 |
| 1979 | Rick Swenson | 15 days, 10:37:47 | 1996 | Jeff King | 9 days, 05:43:13 |
| 1980 | Joe May | 14 days, 07:11:51 | 1997 | Martin Buser | 9 days, 08:31:45 |
| 1981 | Rick Swenson | 12 days, 08:45:02 | 1998 | Jeff King | 9 days, 05:52:26 |
| 1982 | Rick Swenson | 16 days, 04:40:10 | 1999 | Doug Swingley | 9 days, 14:31:07 |
| 1983 | Rick Mackey | 12 days, 14:10:44 | 2000 | Doug Swingley | 9 days, 00:58:06 |
| 1984 | Dean Osmar | 12 days, 15:07:33 | 2001 | Doug Swingley | 9 days, 19:55:50 |
| 1985 | Libby Riddles | 18 days, 00:20:17 | 2002 | Martin Buser | 8 days, 22:46:02* |
| 1986 | Susan Butcher | 11 days, 15:06:00 | 2003 | Robert Sorlie | 9 days, 15:47:36 |
| 1987 | Susan Butcher | 11 days, 02:05:13 | 2004 | Mitch Seavey | 9 days, 12:20:22 |
| 1988 | Susan Butcher | 11 days, 11:41:40 | 2005 | Robert Sorlie | 9 days, 18:39:31 |
| 1989 | Joe Runyan | 11 days, 05:24:34 | *Race record. | | |

## Westminster Kennel Club

### Best in Show

The Best in Show prize at the 129th annual All-Breed Dog Show of the Westminster Kennel Club, held Feb. 14-15, 2005 at Madison Square Garden, went to Ch. Kan-Point's VJK Autumn Roses , a German shorthaired pointer. The 5-year-old, speckled bitch, who answers to the name Carlee, was selected among 2,581 dogs in 165 breeds. Carlee was handled by Michelle Ostermiller, who also handled 2004 Best in Show winner Josh, and is a direct descendant of the only other German shorthair to win Westminster's Best in Show (Ch. Gretchenhof Columbia River in 1974). The runners-up included the popular Norfolk terrier Coco, who returned to competition after having three puppies this year. The Westminster show is the most prestigious dog show in the country, and one of America's oldest annual sporting events.

**Multiple winners:** Ch. Warren Remedy (3); Ch. Chinoe's Adamant James, Ch. Comejo Wycollar Boy, Ch. Flornell Spicy Piece of Halleston; Ch. Matford Vic, Ch. My Own Brucie, Ch. Pendley Calling of Blarney, Ch. Rancho Dobe's Storm (2).

| Year | | Breed | Year | | Breed |
|------|--|-------|------|--|-------|
| 1907 | Warren Remedy | Fox Terrier | 1960 | Chick T'Sun of Caversham | Pekingese |
| 1908 | Warren Remedy | Fox Terrier | 1961 | Cappoquin Little Sister | Toy Poodle |
| 1909 | Warren Remedy | Fox Terrier | 1962 | Elfinbrook Simon | W. Highland Terrier |
| 1910 | Sabine Rarebit | Fox Terrier | 1963 | Wakefield's Black Knight | English Springer Spaniel |
| 1911 | Tickle Em Jock | Scottish Terrier | 1964 | Courtenay Fleetfoot of Pennyworth | Whippet |
| 1912 | Kenmore Sorceress | Airedale | 1965 | Carmichaels Fanfare | Scottish Terrier |
| 1913 | Strathway Prince Albert | Bulldog | 1966 | Zeloy Mooremaides Magic | Fox Terrier |
| 1914 | Brentwood Hero | Old English Sheepdog | 1967 | Bardene Bingo | Scottish Terrier |
| 1915 | Matford Vic | Old English Sheepdog | 1968 | Stingray of Derryabah | Lakeland Terrier |
| 1916 | Matford Vic | Old English Sheepdog | 1969 | Glamoor Good News | Skye Terrier |
| 1917 | Comejo Wycollar Boy | Fox Terrier | 1970 | Arriba's Prima Donna | Boxer |
| 1918 | Haymarket Faultless | Bull Terrier | 1971 | Chinoe's Adamant James | E.S. Spaniel |
| 1919 | Briergate Bright Beauty | Airedale | 1972 | Chinoe's Adamant James | E.S. Spaniel |
| 1920 | Comejo Wycollar Boy | Fox Terrier | 1973 | Acadia Command Performance | Standard Poodle |
| 1921 | Midkiff Seductive | Cocker Spaniel | 1974 | Gretchenhof Columbia River | German SH Pointer |
| 1922 | Boxwood Barkentine | Airedale | 1975 | Sir Lancelot of Barvan | Old Eng. Sheepdog |
| 1923 | No best-in-show award | | 1976 | Jo Ni's Red Baron of Crofton | Lakeland Terrier |
| 1924 | Barberryhill Bootlegger | Sealyham | 1977 | Dersade Bobby's Girl | Sealyham |
| 1925 | Governor Moscow | Pointer | 1978 | Cede Higgens | Yorkshire Terrier |
| 1926 | Signal Circuit | Fox Terrier | 1979 | Oak Tree's Irishtocrat | Irish Water Spaniel |
| 1927 | Pinegrade Perfection | Sealyham | 1980 | Sierra Cinnar | Siberian Husky |
| 1928 | Talavera Margaret | Fox Terrier | 1981 | Dhandy Favorite Woodchuck | Pug |
| 1929 | Land Loyalty of Bellhaven | Collie | 1982 | St. Aubrey Dragonora of Elsdon | Pekingese |
| 1930 | Pendley Calling of Blarney | Fox Terrier | 1983 | Kabik's The Challenger | Afghan Hound |
| 1931 | Pendley Calling of Blarney | Fox Terrier | 1984 | Seaward's Blackbeard | Newfoundland |
| 1932 | Nancolleth Markable | Pointer | 1985 | Braeburn's Close Encounter | Scottish Terrier |
| 1933 | Warland Protector of Shelterock | Airedale | 1986 | Marjetta National Acclaim | Pointer |
| 1934 | Flornell Spicy Bit of Halleston | Fox Terrier | 1987 | Covy Tucker Hill's Manhattan | German Shepherd |
| 1935 | Nunsoe Duc de la Terrace of Blakeen | Stan. Poodle | 1988 | Great Elms Prince Charming II | Pomeranian |
| 1936 | St. Margaret Magnificent of Clairedale | Sealyham | 1989 | Royal Tudor's Wild As The Wind | Doberman |
| 1937 | Flornell Spicy Bit of Halleston | Fox Terrier | 1990 | Wendessa Crown Prince | Pekingese |
| 1938 | Daro of Maridor | English Setter | 1991 | Whisperwind on a Carousel | Stan. Poodle |
| 1939 | Ferry v.Rauhfelsen of Giralda | Doberman | 1992 | Lonesome Dove | Fox Terrier |
| 1940 | My Own Brucie | Cocker Spaniel | 1993 | Salilyn's Condor | E.S. Spaniel |
| 1941 | My Own Brucie | Cocker Spaniel | 1994 | Chidley Willum | Norwich Terrier |
| 1942 | Wolvey Pattern of Edgerstoune | W. Highland Terrier | 1995 | Gaelforce Post Script | Scottish Terrier |
| 1943 | Pitter Patter of Piperscroft | Miniature Poodle | 1996 | Clussex Country Sunrise | Clumber Spaniel |
| 1944 | Flornell Rarebit of Twin Ponds | Welsh Terrier | 1997 | Parsifal di Casa Netzer | Standard Schnauzer |
| 1945 | Shieling's Signature | Scottish Terrier | 1998 | Fairewood Frolic | Norwich Terrier |
| 1946 | Hetherington Model Rhythm | Fox Terrier | 1999 | Loteki's Supernatural Being | Papillon |
| 1947 | Warlord of Mazelaine | Boxer | 2000 | Salilyn 'N Erin's Shameless | E.S. Spaniel |
| 1948 | Rock Ridge Night Rocket | Bedling. Terrier | 2001 | Special Times Just Right | Bichon Frise |
| 1949 | Mazelaine's Zazarac Brandy | Boxer | 2002 | Surrey Spice Girl | Miniature Poodle |
| 1950 | Walsing Winning Trick of Edgerstoune | Scot. Terrier | 2003 | Torums Scarf Michael | Kerry Blue Terrier |
| 1951 | Bang Away of Sirrah Crest | Boxer | 2004 | Darbydale's All Rise Pouchcove | Newfoundland |
| 1952 | Rancho Dobe's Storm | Doberman | 2005 | Kan-Point's VJK Autumn Roses | German SH Pointer |
| 1953 | Rancho Dobe's Storm | Doberman | | | |
| 1954 | Carmor's Rise and Shine | Cocker Spaniel | | | |
| 1955 | Kippax Fearnought | Bulldog | | | |
| 1956 | Wilber White Swan | Toy Poodle | | | |
| 1957 | Shirkhan of Grandeur | Afghan Hound | | | |
| 1958 | Puttencove Promise | Standard Poodle | | | |
| 1959 | Fontclair Festoon | Miniature Poodle | | | |

## FISHING

### IGFA All-Tackle World Records

All-tackle records are maintained for the heaviest fish of any species caught on any line up to 130-lb (60 kg) class and certified by the International Game Fish Association. Records logged through Dec. 31, 2004. **Address:** 300 Gulf Stream Way, Dania Beach, Fla. 33004. **Telephone:** (954) 927-2628. **Web:** www.igfa.org

## FRESHWATER FISH

| Species | Lbs-Oz | Where Caught | Date | Angler |
|---|---|---|---|---|
| Barramundi | 83-7 | N. Queensland, Australia | Sept. 23, 1999 | David Powell |
| Bass, Guadalupe | 3-11 | Lake Travis, TX | Sept. 25, 1983 | Allen Christenson Jr. |
| Bass, largemouth | 22-4 | Montgomery Lake, GA | June 2, 1932 | George W. Perry |
| Bass, Roanoke | 1-5 | Nottoway River, VA | Nov. 11, 1991 | Tom Elkins |
| Bass, rock | 3-0 | York River, Ontario | Aug. 1, 1974 | Peter Gulgin |
| | 3-0 | Lake Erie, PA | June 18, 1998 | Herbert G. Ratner Jr. |
| Bass, shoal | 8-12 | Apalachicola River, FL | Jan. 28, 1995 | Carl W. Davis |
| Bass, smallmouth | 10-14 | Dale Hollow, TN | Apr. 24, 1969 | John T. Gorman |
| Bass, spotted | 10-4 | Pine Flat Lake, CA | Apr. 21, 2001 | Bryan Shishido |
| Bass, striped (landlocked) | 67-8 | O'Neill Forebay, San Luis, CA | May 7, 1992 | Hank Ferguson |
| Bass, Suwannee | 3-14 | Suwannee River, FL | Mar. 2, 1985 | Ronnie Everett |
| Bass, white | 6-13 | Lake Orange, VA | July 31, 1989 | Ronald L. Sprouse |
| Bass, whiterock | 27-5 | Greers Ferry Lake, AR | Apr. 24, 1997 | Jerald C. Shaum |
| Bass, yellow | 2-9 | Duck River, TN | Feb. 27, 1998 | John T. Chappell |
| Bass, yellow (hybrid) | 3-5 | Big Cypress Bayou, TX | Mar. 27, 1991 | Patrick Collin Myers |
| Bluegill | 4-12 | Ketona Lake, AL | Apr. 9, 1950 | T.S. Hudson |
| Bowfin | 21-8 | Florence, SC | Jan. 29, 1980 | Robert L. Harmon |
| Buffalo, bigmouth | 70-5 | Bussey Brake, Bastrop, LA | Apr. 21, 1980 | Delbert Sisk |
| Buffalo, black | 63-6 | Mississippi River, IA | Aug. 14, 1999 | Jim Winters |
| Buffalo, smallmouth | 82-3 | Athens Lake, AL | June 6, 1993 | Randy Collins |
| Bullhead, black | 7-7 | Mill Pond, NY | Aug. 25, 1993 | Kevin Kelly |
| Bullhead, brown | 6-1 | Waterford, NY | Apr. 26, 1998 | Bobby Triplett |
| Bullhead, yellow | 4-4 | Mormon Lake, AZ | May 11, 1984 | Emily Williams |
| Burbot | 18-11 | Angenmanelren, Sweden | Oct. 22, 1996 | Margit Agren |
| Carp, bighead | 61-15 | Old Hickory Lake, TN | Mar. 27, 2002 | Rick Richard |
| Carp, black | 40-12 | Chiba, Japan | Apr. 1, 2000 | Kenichi Hosoi |
| Carp, common | 75-11 | St. Cassien, France | May 21, 1987 | Leo van der Gugten |
| Carp, crucian | 5-1 | Kalterersee, Italy | July 16, 1997 | Jorg Marquand |
| Catfish, blue | 124-0 | Mississippi River, IL | May 21, 2005 | Tim Pruitt |
| Catfish, channel | 58-0 | Santee-Cooper Res., SC | July 7, 1964 | W.B. Whaley |
| Catfish, flathead | 123-0 | Elk City Reservoir, KS | Mar. 14, 1998 | Ken Paulie |
| Catfish, flatwhiskered | 16-15 | Xingu River, Brazil | Aug. 7, 2001 | Ian-Arthur de Sulocki |
| Catfish, gilded | 85-8 | Amazon River, Brazil | Nov. 15, 1986 | Gilberto Fernandes |
| Catfish, redtail | 97-7 | Amazon River, Brazil | July 16, 1988 | Gilberto Fernandes |
| Catfish, sharptoothed | 79-5 | Orange River, South Africa | Dec. 5, 1992 | Hennie Moller |
| Catfish, white | 21-8 | East Lyme, CT | Apr. 22, 2001 | Thomas Urquhart |
| Char, Arctic | 32-9 | Tree River, Canada | July 30, 1981 | Jeffery Ward |
| Crappie, black | 4-8 | Kerr Lake, VA | Mar. 1, 1981 | L. Carl Herring Jr. |
| Crappie, white | 5-3 | Enid Dam, MS | July 31, 1957 | Fred L. Bright |
| Dolly Varden | 20-14 | Wulik River, AK | July 7, 2001 | Raz Reid |
| Dorado | 51-5 | Corrientes, Argentina | Sept. 27, 1984 | Armando Giudice |
| Drum, freshwater | 54-8 | Nickajack Lake, TN | Apr. 20, 1972 | Benny E. Hull |
| Gar, alligator | 279-0 | Rio Grande, TX | Dec. 2, 1951 | Bill Valverde |
| Gar, Florida | 10-0 | The Everglades, FL | Jan. 28, 2002 | Herbert G. Ratner Jr. |
| Gar, longnose | 50-5 | Trinity River, TX | July 30, 1954 | Townsend Miller |
| Gar, shortnose | 5-12 | Rend Lake, IL | July 16, 1995 | Donna K. Willmart |
| Gar, spotted | 9-12 | Lake Mexia, TX | Apr. 7, 1994 | Rick Rivard |
| Goldfish | 6-10 | Lake Hodges, CA | Apr. 17, 1996 | Florentino M. Abena |
| Grayling, Arctic | 5-15 | Katseyedie River, N.W.T. | Aug. 16, 1967 | Jeanne P. Branson |
| Inconnu | 53-0 | Pah River, AK | Aug. 20, 1986 | Lawrence E. Hudnall |
| Kokanee | 9-6 | Okanagan Lake, Brit. Columbia | June 18, 1988 | Norm Kuhn |
| Muskellunge | 67-8 | Hayward, WI | July 24, 1949 | Cal Johnson |
| Muskellunge, tiger | 51-3 | Lac Vieux-Desert, WI-MI | July 16, 1919 | John A. Knobla |
| Peacock, butterfly | 12-9 | Chiguao River, Venezuela | Jan. 6, 2000 | Antonio Campa G. |
| Peacock, speckled | 27-0 | Rio Negro, Brazil | Dec. 4, 1994 | Gerald (Doc) Lawson |
| Perch, Nile | 230-0 | Lake Nasser, Egypt | Dec. 20, 2000 | William Toth |
| Perch, white | 3-1 | Forest Hill Park, NJ | May 6, 1989 | Edward Tango |
| Perch, yellow | 4-3 | Bordentown, NJ | May, 1865 | Dr. C.C. Abbot |
| Pickerel, chain | 9-6 | Homerville, GA | Feb. 17, 1961 | Baxley McQuaig Jr. |
| Pickerel, grass | 1-0 | Dewart Lake, IN | June 9, 1990 | Mike Berg |
| Pickerel, redfin | 2-4 | Gall Berry Swamp, NC | June 27, 1997 | Edward C. Davis |
| Pike, northern | 55-1 | Lake of Grefeern, Germany | Oct. 16, 1986 | Lothar Louis |
| Redhorse, greater | 9-3 | Salmon River, Pulaski, NY | May 11, 1985 | Jason Wilson |

| Species | Lbs-Oz | Where Caught | Date | Angler |
|---|---|---|---|---|
| Redhorse, silver | 11-7 | Plum Creek, WI | May 29, 1985 | Neal D.G. Long |
| Salmon, Atlantic | 79-2 | Tana River, Norway | 1928 | Henrik Henriksen |
| Salmon, chinook | 97-4 | Kenai River, AK | May 17, 1985 | Les Anderson |
| Salmon, chum | 35-0 | Edye Pass, Brit. Columbia | July 11, 1995 | Todd Johansson |
| Salmon, coho | 33-4 | Salmon River, Pulaski, NY | Sept. 27, 1989 | Jerry Lifton |
| Salmon, pink | 14-13 | Monroe, WA | Sept. 30, 2001 | Alexander Minerich |
| Salmon, sockeye | 15-3 | Kenai River, AK | Aug. 9, 1987 | Stan Roach |
| Sauger | 8-12 | Lake Sakakawea, ND | Oct. 6, 1971 | Mike Fischer |
| Shad, American | 11-4 | Conn. River, S. Hadley, MA | May 19, 1986 | Bob Thibodo |
| Shad, gizzard | 4-6 | Lake Michigan, IN | Mar. 2, 1996 | Mike Berg |
| Sturgeon, lake | 168-0 | Georgian Bay, Canada | May 29, 1982 | Edward Paszkowski |
| Sturgeon, white | 468-0 | Benicia, CA | July 9, 1983 | Joey Pallotta 3rd |
| Tigerfish, giant | 97-0 | Zaire River, Kinshasa, Zaire | July 9, 1988 | Raymond Houtmans |
| Tilapia, spotted | 3-0 | Pembroke Pines, FL | Mar. 20, 1999 | Jay Wright Jr. |
| Trout, Apache | 5-3 | White Mountain, AZ | May 29, 1991 | John Baldwin |
| Trout, brook | 14-8 | Nipigon River, Ontario | July, 1916 | Dr. W.J. Cook |
| Trout, brown | 40-4 | Little Red River, AR | May 9, 1992 | Rip Collins |
| Trout, bull | 32-0 | Lake Pend Orielle, ID | Oct. 27, 1949 | N.L. Higgins |
| Trout, cutthroat | 41-0 | Pyramid Lake, NV | Dec., 1925 | John Skimmerhorn |
| Trout, golden | 11-0 | Cooks Lake, WY | Aug. 5, 1948 | Charles S. Reed |
| Trout, lake | 72-0 | Great Bear Lake, N.W.T. | Aug. 19, 1995 | Lloyd E. Bull |
| Trout, rainbow | 42-2 | Bell Island, AK | June 22, 1970 | David Robert White |
| Trout, tiger | 20-13 | Lake Michigan, WI | Aug. 12, 1978 | Peter M. Friedland |
| Walleye | 25-0 | Old Hickory Lake, TN | Aug. 2, 1960 | Mabry Harper |
| Warmouth | 2-7 | Guess Lake, Holt, FL | Oct. 19, 1985 | Tony D. Dempsey |
| Whitefish, lake | 14-6 | Meaford, Ontario | May 21, 1984 | Dennis M. Laycock |
| Whitefish, mountain | 5-8 | Elbow River, Manitoba | Aug. 1, 1995 | Randy G. Woo |
| Whitefish, round | 6-0 | Putahow River, Manitoba | June 14, 1984 | Allan J. Ristori |
| Zander | 25-2 | Trosa, Sweden | June 12, 1986 | Harry Lee Tennison |

## SALTWATER FISH

| Species | Lbs-Oz | Where Caught | Date | Angler |
|---|---|---|---|---|
| Albacore | 88-2 | Gran Canaria, Canary Islands | Nov. 19, 1977 | Siegfried Dickemann |
| Amberjack, greater | 155-12 | Challenger Bank, Bermuda | Aug. 16, 1992 | Larry Trott |
| Angelfish, gray | 4-0 | S.Beach Jetty, Miami, FL | July 12, 1999 | Rene G. de Dios |
| Barracuda, great | 85-0 | Christmas Is., Rep. of Kiribati | Apr. 11, 1992 | John W. Helfrich |
| Barracuda, Mexican | 21-0 | Phantom Island, Costa Rica | Mar. 27, 1987 | E. Greg Kent |
| Barracuda, pickhandle | 25-5 | Scottburgh, South Africa | July 3, 1996 | Demetrios Stamatis |
| Bass, barred sand | 13-3 | Huntington Beach, CA | Aug. 29, 1988 | Robert Halal |
| Bass, black sea | 10-4 | Virginia Beach, VA | Jan. 1, 2000 | Allan P. Paschall |
| Bass, European | 20-14 | Cap d'Agde, France | Sept. 8, 1999 | Robert Mari |
| Bass, giant sea | 563-8 | Anacapa Island, CA | Aug. 20, 1968 | J.D. McAdam Jr. |
| Bass, striped | 78-8 | Atlantic City, NJ | Sept. 21, 1982 | Albert R. McReynolds |
| Bluefish | 31-12 | Hatteras, NC | Jan. 30, 1972 | James M. Hussey |
| Bonefish | 19-0 | Zululand, South Africa | May 26, 1962 | Brian W. Batchelor |
| Bonito, Atlantic | 18-4 | Faial Island, Azores | July 8, 1953 | D. Gama Higgs |
| Bonito, Pacific | 21-3 | Malibu, CA | July 30, 1978 | Gino M. Picciolo |
| Cabezon | 23-0 | Juan de Fuca Strait, WA | Aug. 4, 1990 | Wesley Hunter |
| Cobia | 135-9 | Shark Bay, W. Australia | July 9, 1985 | Peter W. Goulding |
| Cod, Atlantic | 98-12 | Isle of Shoals, NH | June 8, 1969 | Alphonse Bielevich |
| Cod, Pacific | 35-0 | Unalaska Bay, AK | June 16, 1999 | Jim Johnson |
| Conger | 133-4 | South Devon, England | June 5, 1995 | Vic Evans |
| Dolphinfish | 88-0 | Highbourne Cay, Bahamas | May 5, 1998 | Richard D. Evans |
| Drum, black | 113-1 | Lewes, DE | Sept. 15, 1975 | Gerald M. Townsend |
| Drum, red | 94-2 | Avon, NC | Nov. 7, 1984 | David G. Deuel |
| Eel, American | 9-4 | Cape May, NJ | Nov. 9, 1995 | Jeff Pennick |
| Eel, marbled | 36-1 | Durban, South Africa | June 10, 1984 | Ferdie van Nooten |
| Flounder, southern | 20-9 | Nassau Sound, FL | Dec. 23, 1983 | Larenza Mungin |
| Flounder, summer | 22-7 | Montauk, NY | Sept. 15, 1975 | Charles Nappi |
| Grouper, goliath | 680-0 | Fernandina Beach, FL | May 20, 1961 | Lynn Joyner |
| Grouper, Warsaw | 436-12 | Gulf of Mexico, Destin, FL | Dec. 22, 1985 | Steve Haeusler |
| Haddock | 14-15 | Saltraumen, Germany | Aug. 15, 1997 | Heike Neblinger |
| Halibut, Atlantic | 355-6 | Valevag, Norway | Oct. 20, 1997 | Odd Arve Gunderstad |
| Halibut, California | 58-9 | Santa Rosa Island, CA | June 26, 1999 | Roger W. Borrell |
| Halibut, Pacific | 459-0 | Dutch Harbor, AK | June 11, 1996 | Jack Tragis |
| Jack, almaco (Pacific) | 132-0 | La Paz, Baja Calif., Mexico | July 21, 1964 | Howard H. Hahn |
| Jack, crevalle | 58-6 | Barra do Kwanza, Angola | Dec. 10, 2000 | Nuno A.P. da Silva |
| Jack, horse-eye | 29-8 | Ascencion Island, South Atlantic | May 28, 1993 | Mike Hanson |
| Kawakawa | 29-0 | Clarion Island, Mexico | Dec. 17, 1986 | Ronald Nakamura |
| Lingcod | 76-9 | Gulf of Alaska | Aug. 11, 2001 | Antwan D. Tinsley |
| Mackerel, cero | 17-2 | Islamorada, FL | Apr. 5, 1986 | G. Michael Mills |

## FISHING (Cont.)

| Species | Lbs-Oz | Where Caught | Date | Angler |
|---|---|---|---|---|
| Mackerel, king | .93-0 | San Juan, Puerto Rico | Apr. 18, 1999 | Steve Perez Graulau |
| Mackerel, Spanish | .13-0 | Ocracoke Inlet, NC | Nov. 4, 1987 | Robert Cranton |
| Marlin, Atlantic blue | 1402-2 | Vitoria, Brazil | Feb. 29, 1992 | Paulo R.A. Amorim |
| Marlin, black | 1560-0 | Cabo Blanco, Peru | Aug. 4, 1953 | A.C. Glassell Jr. |
| Marlin, Pacific blue | 1376-0 | Kaaiwi Point, Kona, HI | May 31, 1982 | Jay W. deBeaubien |
| Marlin, striped | .494-0 | Tutakaka, New Zealand | Jan. 16, 1986 | Bill Boniface |
| Marlin, white | .181-14 | Vitoria, Brazil | Dec. 8, 1979 | Evandro Luiz Coser |
| Permit | .56-2 | Ft. Lauderdale, FL | June 30, 1997 | Thomas Sebestyen |
| Pollack, European | .27-6 | Salcombe, Devon, England | Jan. 16, 1986 | Robert S. Milkins |
| Pollock | .50-0 | Salstraumen, Norway | Nov. 30, 1996 | Thor-Magnus Lekang |
| Pompano, African | .50-8 | Daytona Beach, FL | Apr. 21, 1990 | Tom Sargent |
| Roosterfish | 114-0 | La Paz, Baja Calif., Mexico | June 1, 1960 | Abe Sackheim |
| Runner, blue | 1.1-2 | Dauphin Island, AL | June 28, 1997 | Stacey M. Moiren |
| Runner, rainbow | .37-9 | Clarion Island, Mexico | Nov. 21, 1991 | Tom Pfleger |
| Sailfish, Atlantic | 141-1 | Luanda, Angola | Feb. 19, 1994 | Alfredo de Sousa Neves |
| Sailfish, Pacific | .221-0 | Santa Cruz Is., Ecuador | Feb. 12, 1947 | C.W. Stewart |
| Seabass, white | .83-12 | San Felipe, Mexico | Mar. 31, 1953 | L.C. Baumgardner |
| Seatrout, spotted | .17-7 | Ft. Pierce, FL | May 11, 1995 | Craig F. Carson |
| Shark, blue | .528-0 | Montauk Point, NY | Aug. 9, 2001 | Joe Seidel |
| Shark, great white | 2664-0 | Ceduna, S. Australia | Apr. 21, 1959 | Alfred Dean |
| Shark, Greenland | 1708-9 | Trondheimsfjord, Norway | Oct. 18, 1987 | Terje Nordtvedt |
| Shark, hammerhead | .991-0 | Sarasota, FL | May 30, 1982 | Allen Ogle |
| Shark, shortfin mako | 1221-0 | Chatham, MA | July 21, 2001 | Luke Sweeney |
| Shark, porbeagle | .507-0 | Pentland Firth, Scotland | Mar. 9, 1993 | Christopher Bennet |
| Shark, bigeye thresher | .802-0 | Tutukaka, New Zealand | Feb. 8, 1981 | Dianne North |
| Shark, tiger | 1780-0 | Cherry Grove, SC | June 14, 1964 | Walter Maxwell |
| Snapper, cubera | .121-8 | Cameron, LA | July 5, 1982 | Mike Hebert |
| Snapper, red | .50-4 | Gulf of Mexico, LA | June 23, 1996 | Capt. Doc Kennedy |
| Snook, Pacific black | .57-12 | Rio Naranjo, Quepos, Costa Rica | Aug. 23, 1991 | George Beck |
| Spearfish, Mediterranean | .90-13 | Madeira Island, Portugal | June 2, 1980 | Joseph Larkin |
| Swordfish | 1182-0 | Iquique, Chile | May 7, 1953 | Louis Marron |
| Tarpon | .283-4 | Sherbro Is., Sierra Leone | Apr. 16, 1991 | Yvon Victor Sebag |
| Tautog | .25-0 | Ocean City, NJ | Jan. 20, 1998 | Anthony R. Monica |
| Tuna, Atlantic bigeye | .392-6 | Gran Canaria, Puerto Rico | July 25, 1996 | Dieter Vogel |
| Tuna, blackfin | .45-8 | Key West, FL | May 4, 1996 | Sam J. Burnett |
| Tuna, bluefin | 1496-0 | Aulds Cove, Nova Scotia | Oct. 26, 1979 | Ken Fraser |
| Tuna, longtail | .79-2 | Montague Is., NSW, Australia | Apr. 12, 1982 | Tim Simpson |
| Tuna, Pacific bigeye | .435-0 | Cabo Blanco, Peru | Apr. 17, 1957 | Dr. Russell Lee |
| Tuna, skipjack | .45-4 | Flathead Bank, Mexico | Nov. 16, 1996 | Brian Evans |
| Tuna, southern bluefin | .348-5 | Whakatane, New Zealand | Jan. 16, 1981 | Rex Wood |
| Tuna, yellowfin | .388-12 | San Benedicto Island, Mexico | Apr. 1, 1977 | Curt Wiesenhutter |
| Tunny, little | .35-2 | Cap de Garde, Algeria | Dec. 14, 1988 | Jean Yves Chatard |
| Wahoo | .158-8 | Loreto, Baja Calif., Mexico | June 10, 1996 | Keith Winter |
| Weakfish | .19-2 | Jones Beach, Long Island, NY | Oct. 11, 1984 | Dennis R. Rooney |
| | .19-2 | Delaware Bay, DE | May 20, 1989 | William E. Thomas |

## Bassmasters Classic

Kevin VanDam landed a three-day total of just 12 pounds, 15 ounces in bass but it was enough for him to win the 35th annual CITGO Bassmasters Classic at the confluence of the Allegheny, Monongahela and Ohio rivers in Pittsburgh, Penn. VanDam's limit—the lowest winning total in Classic history—was six ounces more than runner-up and reigning Angler of the Year Aaron Martens. It was the third time in four years that Martens had to settle for second-place in fishing's biggest tournament. It was VanDam's second Bassmasters Classic and he earned $200,000 for the victory.

After struggling on the first day, VanDam finally found some success on a 20-year-old lure he first started catching bass on during his teen-age years. It was a chrome-colored Smithwick Rogue jerkbait that he fished on Bass Pro Shops' fluorocarbon line and spinning tackle.

The CITGO Bassmasters Classic, hosted by B.A.S.S. (Bass Anglers Sportsman Society), is professional bass fishing's world championship. Qualifiers for the three-day event include the 40 top pros on the CITGO Bassmaster Tour and the five top-ranked anglers from each of three CITGO Bassmasters Open circuits. Anglers may weigh only five bass per day and each bass must be at least 12 inches long. Only artificial lures are permitted. The first Classic, held at Lake Mead, Nev. in 1971, was a $10,000 winner-take-all event.

**Multiple winners:** Rick Clunn (4); George Cochran, Bobby Murray, Hank Parker and Kevin VanDam (2).

| Year | | Weight | Year | | Weight |
|---|---|---|---|---|---|
| 1971 | Bobby Murray, Hot Springs, Ark | 43-11 | 1979 | Hank Parker, Clover, S.C | 31-0 |
| 1972 | Don Butler, Tulsa, Okla | 38-11 | 1980 | Bo Dowden, Natchitoches, La | 54-10 |
| 1973 | Rayo Breckenridge, Paragould, Ark | 52-8 | 1981 | Stanley Mitchell, Fitzgerald, Ga | 35-2 |
| 1974 | Tommy Martin, Hemphill, Tex | 33-7 | 1982 | Paul Elias, Laurel, Miss | 32-8 |
| 1975 | Jack Hains, Rayne, La | 45-4 | 1983 | Larry Nixon, Hemphill, Tex | 18-1 |
| 1976 | Rick Clunn, Montgomery, Tex | 59-15 | 1984 | Rick Clunn, Montgomery, Tex | 75-9 |
| 1977 | Rick Clunn, Montgomery, Tex | 27-7 | 1985 | Jack Chancellor, Phenix City, Ala | 45-0 |
| 1978 | Bobby Murray, Nashville, Tenn | 37-9 | 1986 | Charlie Reed, Broken Bow, Okla | 23-9 |

| Year | | Weight |
|------|---|--------|
| 1987 | George Cochran, N. Little Rock, Ark | .15-5 |
| 1988 | Guido Hibdon, Gravois Mills, Mo | .28-8 |
| 1989 | Hank Parker, Denver, N.C. | .31-6 |
| 1990 | Rick Clunn, Montgomery, Tex | .34-5 |
| 1991 | Ken Cook, Meers, Okla | .33-2 |
| 1992 | Robert Hamilton Jr., Brandon, Miss | .59-6 |
| 1993 | David Fritts, Lexington, N.C. | .48-6 |
| 1994 | Bryan Kerchal, Newtown, Conn | .36-7 |
| 1995 | Mark Davis, Mount Ida, Ark. | .47-14 |
| 1996 | George Cochran, Hot Springs, Ark. | .31-14 |

| Year | | Weight |
|------|---|--------|
| 1997 | Dion Hibdon, Stover, Mo. | .34-13 |
| 1998 | Denny Brauer, Camdenton, Mo. | .46-3 |
| 1999 | Davy Hite, Prosperity, S.C. | .55-10 |
| 2000 | Woo Daves, Spring Grove, Va. | .27-13 |
| 2001 | Kevin VanDam, Kalamazoo, Mich. | .32-5 |
| 2002 | Jay Yelas, Tyler, Texas | .45-13 |
| 2003 | Michael Iaconelli, Woodbury Heights, N.J. | .37-14 |
| 2004 | Takahiro Omori, Emory, Texas | .39-2 |
| 2005 | Kevin VanDam, Kalamazoo, Mich. | .12-15 |

## LITTLE LEAGUE BASEBALL

## World Series

West Oahu of Ewa Beach, Hawaii pulled off an improbable come-from-behind victory to become the first team from the Aloha State to win the Little League World Series. Trailing the defending champions Willemstad, Curacao by three runs in the bottom of the sixth (and final) inning, the boys from West Oahu scraped together three runs to tie the game, 6-6, and send the title game to extra innings for just the second time in LLWS history. With no outs and the bases empty in the bottom of the seventh inning, Hawaii's Michael Memea won the game with a line-drive home run over the center-field wall. It was the first walk-off homer in Little League championship game history.

In the third-place game, Rancho Buena Vista, Calif. beat Chiba City, Japan, 5-4.

Played annually in late August in Williamsport, Penn. at Original Field in Williamsport from 1947-1958 and at Howard J. Lamade Stadium since 1959 and also at newly constructed Volunteer Stadium starting in 2001.

In order to be invited to the World Series, teams must first win their regional tournaments. There are eight regions from the U.S. (Great Lakes, Midwest, Mid-Atlantic, New England, Northwest, Southeast, Southwest and West) and eight outside of the U.S. (Asia, Canada, Caribbean, European, Latin America, Mexico, Pacific and Trans-Atlantic). The eight U.S. regions then play each other and the the eight international regions play each other and the two winners from each meet in the championship game. This insures that a team from the U.S. will always participate in the final game.

**Multiple winners:** Taiwan (16); Japan (6); California (5); Connecticut, New Jersey and Pennsylvania (4); Mexico (3); New York, South Korea, Texas and Venezuela (2).

| Year | Winner | Score | Loser |
|------|--------|-------|-------|
| 1947 | Williamsport, PA | 16-7 | Lock Haven, PA |
| 1948 | Lock Haven, PA | 6-5 | St. Petersburg, FL |
| 1949 | Hammonton, NJ | 5-0 | Pensacola, FL |
| 1950 | Houston, TX | 2-1 | Bridgeport, CT |
| 1951 | Stamford, CT | 3-0 | Austin, TX |
| 1952 | Norwalk, CT | 4-3 | Monongahela, PA |
| 1953 | Birmingham, AL | 1-0 | Schenectady, NY |
| 1954 | Schenectady, NY | 7-5 | Colton, CA |
| 1955 | Morrisville, PA | 4-3 | Merchantville, NJ |
| 1956 | Roswell, NM | 3-1 | Merchantville, NJ |
| 1957 | Monterrey, Mexico | 4-0 | La Mesa, CA |
| 1958 | Monterrey, Mexico | 10-1 | Kankakee, IL |
| 1959 | Hamtramck, MI | 12-0 | Auburn, CA |
| 1960 | Levittown, PA | 5-0 | Ft. Worth, TX |
| 1961 | El Cajon, CA | 4-2 | El Campo, TX |
| 1962 | San Jose, CA | 3-0 | Kankakee, IL |
| 1963 | Granada Hills, CA | 2-1 | Stratford, CT |
| 1964 | Staten Island, NY | 4-0 | Monterrey, Mex. |
| 1965 | Windsor Locks, CT | 3-1 | Stoney Creek, Can. |
| 1966 | Houston, TX | 8-2 | W. New York, NJ |
| 1967 | West Tokyo, Japan | 4-1 | Chicago, IL |
| 1968 | Osaka, Japan | 1-0 | Richmond, VA |
| 1969 | Taipei, Taiwan | 5-0 | Santa Clara, CA |
| 1970 | Wayne, NJ | 2-0 | Campbell, CA |
| 1971 | Tainan, Taiwan | 12-3 | Gary, IN |
| 1972 | Taipei, Taiwan | 6-0 | Hammond, IN |
| 1973 | Tainan City, Taiwan | 12-0 | Tucson, AZ |
| 1974 | Kao Hsiung, Taiwan | 12-1 | Red Bluff, CA |
| 1975 | Lakewood, NJ | 4-3* | Tampa, FL |
| 1976 | Tokyo, Japan | 10-3 | Campbell, CA |
| 1977 | Li-Teh, Taiwan | 7-2 | El Cajon, CA |
| 1978 | Pin-Tung, Taiwan | 11-1 | Danville, CA |
| 1979 | Hsien, Taiwan | 2-1 | Campbell, CA |
| 1980 | Hua Lian, Taiwan | 4-3 | Tampa, FL |
| 1981 | Tai-Chung, Taiwan | 4-2 | Tampa, FL |
| 1982 | Kirkland, WA | 6-0 | Hsien, Taiwan |
| 1983 | Marietta, GA | 3-1 | Barahona, D. Rep. |
| 1984 | Seoul, S. Korea | 6-2 | Altamonte, FL |
| 1985 | Seoul, S. Korea | 7-1 | Mexicali, Mex. |
| 1986 | Tainan Park, Taiwan | 12-0 | Tucson, AZ |
| 1987 | Hua Lian, Taiwan | 21-1 | Irvine, CA |
| 1988 | Tai Ping, Taiwan | 10-0 | Pearl City, HI |
| 1989 | Trumbull, CT | 5-2 | Kaohsiung, Taiwan |
| 1990 | Taipei, Taiwan | 9-0 | Shippensburg, PA |
| 1991 | Taichung, Taiwan | 11-0 | Danville, CA |
| 1992 | Long Beach, CA | 6-0 | Zamboanga, Phil. |
| 1993 | Long Beach, CA | 3-2 | Panama |
| 1994 | Maracaibo, Venezuela | 4-3 | Northridge, CA |
| 1995 | Tainan, Taiwan | 17-3 | Spring, TX |
| 1996 | Taipei, Taiwan | 13-3 | Cranston, RI (called after 5th inn.) |
| 1997 | Guadalupe, Mexico | 5-4 | Mission Viejo, CA |
| 1998 | Toms River, NJ | 12-9 | Kashima, Japan |
| 1999 | Osaka, Japan | 5-0 | Phenix City, AL |
| 2000 | Maracaibo, Venezuela | 3-2 | Bellaire, TX |
| 2001 | Tokyo, Japan | 2-1 | Apopka, FL |
| 2002 | Louisville, KY | 1-0 | Sendai, Japan |
| 2003 | Tokyo, Japan | 10-1 | Boynton Beach, FL |
| 2004 | Willemstad, Curacao | 5-2 | Thousand Oaks, CA |
| 2005 | West Oahu, Hawaii | 7-6 | Willemstad, Curacao |

* Foreign teams were banned from the tournament in 1975, but allowed back in the following year.

**Note:** In 1992, Zamboanga City of the Philippines beat Long Beach, 15-4, but was stripped of the title a month later when it was discovered that the team had used several players from outside the city limits. Long Beach was then awarded the title by forfeit, 6-0 (one run for each inning of the game).

AP/Wide World Photos

*Aussie gambler **Joseph Hachem** won the prestigious No-Limit Texas Hold-'em champions bracelet—and a ridiculous amount of cash—at the 2005 World Series of Poker in Las Vegas.*

## POKER

### World Series of Poker

Created by Benny Binion in 1970, the World Series of Poker is held each year at Binion's Horseshoe Casino in Las Vegas, Nev. and brings together the world's greatest poker players. The marquee event is the no-limit Texas hold-'em tournament. The first World Series was a seven-player tournament in which the champion Johnny Moss was chosen by a vote of his peers.

The 2005 World Champion was 39-year-old Australian Joseph Hachem, who beat out 5,627 entrants over eight days and won a first prize of $7.5 million—a larger payday than the winner of the Kentucky Derby, Wimbledon, Indianapolis 500 and the Masters combined. Hachem was riding the short stack at the final table for more than 11 hours but hung back and hung on as his competition slowly fell apart. Six hands into the final two-player showdown, Hachem flopped a seven-high straight for the victory over runner-up Steven Dannenmann.

Anyone that's over 21 years old and can pay the $10,000 entry fee can compete.

### No-Limit Texas Hold-'em Champions

**Multiple winners:** Johnny Moss and Stu Ungar (3); Doyle Brunson and Johnny Chan (2).

| Year | Champion | Prize Money | Year | Champion | Prize Money |
|------|----------|-------------|------|----------|-------------|
| 1970 | Johnny Moss | n/a | 1988 | Johnny Chan | $ 700,000 |
| 1971 | Johnny Moss | $ 30,000 | 1989 | Phil Hellmuth Jr. | .755,000 |
| 1972 | "Amarillo Slim" Preston | .80,000 | 1990 | Mansour Matloubi | .895,000 |
| 1973 | Puggy Pearson | .130,000 | 1991 | Brad Daugherty | .1,000,000 |
| 1974 | Johnny Moss | .160,000 | 1992 | Hamid Datsmalchi | .1,000,000 |
| 1975 | Sailor Roberts | .210,000 | 1993 | Jim Bechtel | .1,000,000 |
| 1976 | Doyle Brunson | .220,000 | 1994 | Russ Hamilton | .1,000,000 |
| 1977 | Doyle Brunson | .340,000 | 1995 | Dan Harrington | .1,000,000 |
| 1978 | Bobby Baldwin | .210,000 | 1996 | Huck Seed | .1,000,000 |
| 1979 | Hal Fowler | .270,000 | 1997 | Stu Ungar | .1,000,000 |
| 1980 | Stu Ungar | .385,000 | 1998 | Scotty Nguyen | .1,000,000 |
| 1981 | Stu Ungar | .375,000 | 1999 | Noel Furlong | .1,000,000 |
| 1982 | Jack Strauss | .520,000 | 2000 | Chris Ferguson | .1,500,000 |
| 1983 | Tom McEvoy | .580,000 | 2001 | Carlos Mortensen | .1,500,000 |
| 1984 | Jack Keller | .660,000 | 2002 | Robert Varkyoni | .2,000,000 |
| 1985 | Bill Smith | .700,000 | 2003 | Chris Moneymaker | .2,500,000 |
| 1986 | Berry Johnston | .570,000 | 2004 | Greg Raymer | .5,000,000 |
| 1987 | Johnny Chan | .625,000 | 2005 | Joseph Hachem | .7,500,000 |

## POWER BOAT RACING

### APBA Gold Cup

The American Power Boat Association Challenge Cup for unlimited hydroplane racing is the oldest active motorsports trophy in North America. The first Gold Cup was competed for on the Hudson River in New York in June and September 1904. Since then several cities have hosted the race, led by Detroit (35 times) and Seattle (14). Note that (*) indicates driver was also owner of the winning boat.

**Drivers with multiple wins:** Chip Hanauer (11); Bill Muncey (8); Dave Villwock and Gar Wood (5); Dean Chenoweth (4); Caleb Bragg, Tom D'Eath, Lou Fageol, Ron Musson, George Reis and J.M. Wainwright (3); Danny Foster, George Henley, Vic Kliesrath, E.J. Schroeder, Bill Schumacher, Zalmon G. Simmons Jr., Joe Taggart, Mark Tate and George Townsend (2).

| Year | Boat | Driver | Avg. MPH | Year | Boat | Driver | Avg. MPH |
|------|------|--------|----------|------|------|--------|----------|
| 1904 | Standard (June) | Carl Riotte* | 23.160 | 1960 | Not held | | |
| 1904 | Vingt-Et-Un II (Sept.) | W. Sharpe Kilmer* | 24.900 | 1961 | Miss Century 21 | Bill Muncey | 99.678 |
| | | | | 1962 | Miss Century 21 | Bill Muncey | 100.710 |
| 1905 | Chip I | J.M. Wainwright* | 15.000 | 1963 | Miss Bardahl | Ron Musson | 105.124 |
| 1906 | Chip II | J.M. Wainwright* | 25.000 | 1964 | Miss Bardahl | Ron Musson | 103.433 |
| 1907 | Chip II | J.M. Wainwright* | 23.903 | 1965 | Miss Bardahl | Ron Musson | 103.132 |
| 1908 | Dixie II | E.J. Schroeder* | 29.938 | 1966 | Tahoe Miss | Mira Slovak | 93.019 |
| 1909 | Dixie II | E.J. Schroeder* | 29.590 | 1967 | Miss Bardahl | Bill Shumacher | 101.484 |
| 1910 | Dixie III | F.K. Burnham* | 32.473 | 1968 | Miss Bardahl | Bill Shumacher | 108.173 |
| 1911 | MIT II | J.H. Hayden* | 37.000 | 1969 | Miss Budweiser | Bill Sterett | 98.504 |
| 1912 | P.D.Q. II | A.G. Miles* | 39.462 | 1970 | Miss Budweiser | Dean Chenoweth | 99.562 |
| 1913 | Ankle Deep | C.S. Mankowski* | 42.779 | 1971 | Miss Madison | Jim McCormick | 98.043 |
| 1914 | Baby Speed Demon II | Jim Blackton & Bob Edgren | 48.458 | 1972 | Atlas Van Lines | Bill Muncey | 104.277 |
| | | | | 1973 | Miss Budweiser | Dean Chenoweth | 99.043 |
| 1915 | Miss Detroit | Johnny Milot & Jack Beebe | 37.656 | 1974 | Pay 'n Pak | George Henley | 104.428 |
| | | | | 1975 | Pay 'n Pak | George Henley | 108.921 |
| 1916 | Miss Minneapolis | Bernard Smith | 48.860 | 1976 | Miss U.S. | Tom D'Eath | 100.412 |
| 1917 | Miss Detroit II | Gar Wood* | 54.410 | 1977 | Atlas Van Lines | Bill Muncey* | 111.822 |
| 1918 | Miss Detroit II | Gar Wood | 51.619 | 1978 | Atlas Van Lines | Bill Muncey* | 100.412 |
| 1919 | Miss Detroit III | Gar Wood* | 42.748 | 1979 | Atlas Van Lines | Bill Muncey* | 100.765 |
| 1920 | Miss America I | Gar Wood* | 62.022 | 1980 | Miss Budweiser | Dean Chenoweth | 106.932 |
| 1921 | Miss America I | Gar Wood* | 52.825 | 1981 | Miss Budweiser | Dean Chenoweth | 116.387 |
| 1922 | Packard Chriscraft | J.G. Vincent* | 40.253 | 1982 | Atlas Van Lines | Chip Hanauer | 120.050 |
| 1923 | Packard Chriscraft | Caleb Bragg | 43.867 | 1983 | Atlas Van Lines | Chip Hanauer | 118.507 |
| 1924 | Baby Bootlegger | Caleb Bragg* | 45.302 | 1984 | Atlas Van Lines | Chip Hanauer | 130.175 |
| 1925 | Baby Bootlegger | Caleb Bragg* | 47.240 | 1985 | Miller American | Chip Hanauer | 120.643 |
| 1926 | Greenwich Folly | George Townsend* | 47.984 | 1986 | Miller American | Chip Hanauer | 116.523 |
| | | | | 1987 | Miller American | Chip Hanauer | 127.620 |
| 1927 | Greenwich Folly | George Townsend* | 47.662 | 1988 | Miss Circus Circus | Chip Hanauer & Jim Prevost | 123.756 |
| 1928 | Not held | | | 1989 | Miss Budweiser | Tom D'Eath | 131.209 |
| 1929 | Imp | Richard Hoyt* | 48.662 | 1990 | Miss Budweiser | Tom D'Eath | 143.176 |
| 1930 | Hotsy Totsy | Vic Kliesrath* | 52.673 | 1991 | Winston Eagle | Mark Tate | 137.771 |
| 1931 | Hotsy Totsy | Vic Kliesrath* | 53.602 | 1992 | Miss Budweiser | Chip Hanauer | 136.282 |
| 1932 | Delphine IV | Bill Horn | 57.775 | 1993 | Miss Budweiser | Chip Hanauer | 141.296 |
| 1933 | El Lagarto | George Reis* | 56.260 | 1994 | Smokin' Joe's | Mark Tate | 145.532 |
| 1934 | El Lagarto | George Reis* | 55.000 | 1995 | Miss Budweiser | Chip Hanauer* | 149.160 |
| 1935 | El Lagarto | George Reis* | 55.056 | 1996 | Pico/American Dream | Dave Villwock | 149.328 |
| 1936 | Impshi | Kaye Don | 45.735 | | | | |
| 1937 | Notre Dame | Clell Perry | 63.675 | 1997 | Miss Budweiser | Dave Villwock | 129.366 |
| 1938 | Alagi | Theo Rossi* | 64.340 | 1998 | Miss Budweiser | Dave Villwock | 140.704 |
| 1939 | My Sin | Z.G. Simmons Jr.* | 66.133 | 1999 | Miss Pico | Chip Hanauer | 152.591 |
| 1940 | Hotsy Totsy III | Sidney Allen* | 48.295 | 2000 | Miss Budweiser | Dave Villwock | 139.416 |
| 1941 | My Sin | Z.G. Simmons Jr.* | 52.509 | 2001 | Tubby's Subs | Mike Hanson | 140.519 |
| 1942-45 | Not held | | | 2002 | Miss Budweiser | Dave Villwock | 143.093 |
| 1946 | Tempo VI | Guy Lombardo* | 68.132 | 2003 | Miss Fox Hills Chrysler Jeep-Sun Coatings | Mitch Evans | 144.152 |
| 1947 | Miss Peps V | Danny Foster | 57.000 | | | | |
| 1948 | Miss Great Lakes | Danny Foster | 46.845 | 2004 | Miss Detroit Yacht Club | Nate Brown | 141.195 |
| 1949 | My Sweetie | Bill Cantrell | 73.612 | | | | |
| 1950 | Slo-Mo-Shun IV | Ted Jones | 78.216 | 2005 | Miss Al Deeby Dodge | Terry Troxell | 142.345 |
| 1951 | Slo-Mo-Shun V | Lou Fageol | 90.871 | | | | |
| 1952 | Slo-Mo-Shun IV | Stan Dollar | 79.923 | | | | |
| 1953 | Slo-Mo-Shun IV | Joe Taggart & Lou Fageol | 99.108 | | | | |
| 1954 | Slo-Mo-Shun V | Lou Fageol | 92.613 | | | | |
| 1955 | Gale V | Lee Schoenith | 99.552 | | | | |
| 1956 | Miss Thriftway | Bill Muncey | 96.552 | | | | |
| 1957 | Miss Thriftway | Bill Muncey | 101.787 | | | | |
| 1958 | Hawaii Kai III | Jack Regas | 103.000 | | | | |
| 1959 | Maverick | Bill Stead | 104.481 | | | | |

## PRO RODEO

### All-Around Champion Cowboy

Trevor Brazile of Decatur, Texas, won his third straight All-Around Champion Cowboy belt buckle at the 46th National Finals Rodeo held Dec. 3-12, 2004 at the Thomas & Mack Center in Las Vegas. Brazile finished second in steer roping standings as well. Team ropers Speed Williams and Rich Skelton won a PRCA-record eighth straight title.

The Professional Rodeo Cowboys Association (PRCA) title of all-around world champion cowboy goes to the rodeo athlete who wins the most prize money in a single year in two or more events, earning a minimum of $3,000 in each event. Only prize money earned in sanctioned PRCA rodeos is counted. From 1929-44, all-around champions were named by the Rodeo Association of America (earnings for those years are not available).

**Multiple winners:** Ty Murray (7); Tom Ferguson and Larry Mahan (6); Jim Shoulders (5); Joe Beaver, Trevor Brazile, Lewis Feild and Dean Oliver (3); Everett Bowman, Louis Brooks, Clay Carr, Bill Linderman, Phil Lyne, Gerald Roberts, Casey Tibbs and Harry Tompkins (2).

| Year | | Year | | Year | | Year | |
|------|--|------|--|------|--|------|--|
| 1929 | Earl Thode | 1934 | Leonard Ward | 1939 | Paul Carney | 1943 | Louis Brooks |
| 1930 | Clay Carr | 1935 | Everett Bowman | 1940 | Fritz Truan | 1944 | Louis Brooks |
| 1931 | John Schneider | 1936 | John Bowman | 1941 | Homer Pettigrew | 1945 | No award |
| 1932 | Donald Nesbit | 1937 | Everett Bowman | 1942 | Gerald Roberts | 1946 | No award |
| 1933 | Clay Carr | 1938 | Burel Mulkey | | | | |

| Year | | Earnings | Year | | Earnings | Year | | Earnings |
|------|--|----------|------|--|----------|------|--|----------|
| 1947 | Todd Whatley | $18,642 | 1967 | Larry Mahan | $51,996 | 1986 | Lewis Feild | $166,042 |
| 1948 | Gerald Roberts | 21,766 | 1968 | Larry Mahan | 49,129 | 1987 | Lewis Feild | 144,335 |
| 1949 | Jim Shoulders | 21,495 | 1969 | Larry Mahan | 57,726 | 1988 | Dave Appleton | 121,546 |
| 1950 | Bill Linderman | 30,715 | 1970 | Larry Mahan | 41,493 | 1989 | Ty Murray | 134,806 |
| 1951 | Casey Tibbs | 29,104 | 1971 | Phil Lyne | 49,245 | 1990 | Ty Murray | 213,772 |
| 1952 | Harry Tompkins | 30,934 | 1972 | Phil Lyne | 60,852 | 1991 | Ty Murray | 244,231 |
| 1953 | Bill Linderman | 33,674 | 1973 | Larry Mahan | 64,447 | 1992 | Ty Murray | 225,992 |
| 1954 | Buck Rutherford | 40,404 | 1974 | Tom Ferguson | 66,929 | 1993 | Ty Murray | 297,896 |
| 1955 | Casey Tibbs | 42,065 | 1975 | Tom Ferguson | 50,300 | 1994 | Ty Murray | 246,170 |
| 1956 | Jim Shoulders | 43,381 | 1976 | Tom Ferguson | 87,908 | 1995 | Joe Beaver | 141,753 |
| 1957 | Jim Shoulders | 33,299 | 1977 | Tom Ferguson | 65,981 | 1996 | Joe Beaver | 166,103 |
| 1958 | Jim Shoulders | 32,212 | 1978 | Tom Ferguson | 83,734 | 1997 | Dan Mortensen | 184,559 |
| 1959 | Jim Shoulders | 32,905 | 1979 | Tom Ferguson | 96,272 | 1998 | Ty Murray | 264,673 |
| 1960 | Harry Tompkins | 32,522 | 1980 | Paul Tierney | 105,568 | 1999 | Fred Whitfield | 217,819 |
| 1961 | Benny Reynolds | 31,309 | 1981 | Jimmie Cooper | 105,861 | 2000 | Joe Beaver | 225,396 |
| 1962 | Tom Nesmith | 32,611 | 1982 | Chris Lybbert | 123,709 | 2001 | Cody Ohl | 296,419 |
| 1963 | Dean Oliver | 31,329 | 1983 | Roy Cooper | 153,391 | 2002 | Trevor Brazile | 273,998 |
| 1964 | Dean Oliver | 31,150 | 1984 | Dee Pickett | 122,618 | 2003 | Trevor Brazile | 294,839 |
| 1965 | Dean Oliver | 33,163 | 1985 | Lewis Feild | 130,347 | 2004 | Trevor Brazile | 253,170 |
| 1966 | Larry Mahan | 40,358 | | | | | | |

## SOAP BOX DERBY

### All-American Soap Box Derby

The 68th annual All-American Soap Box Derby was held on July 31, 2005 in Akron, Ohio. A record 502 boys and girls competed.

The AASBD is a coasting race for small gravity-powered cars built by their drivers and assembled within strict guidelines on size, weight and cost. The Derby was started by Dayton, Ohio newsman Myron Scott after he witnessed several boys racing handmade cars down a hill while on a photographic assignment in 1933. Scott decided to start an organized race for kids and the first All-American Soap Box Derby was held in Dayton in 1934. The race got its name because early on most cars were built from wooden soap boxes. The following year, the race was moved to Akron because of its central location and hilly terrain. In 1936, town leaders saw the need for a permanent site for the growing event and with the help of the Works Progress Administration, Derby Downs was constructed.

Held every summer at Derby Downs in Akron, Ohio, the Soap Box Derby is open to all boys and girls from 8 to 17 years old who qualify. There are three competitive divisions: 1. Stock (ages 8-17)— made up of generic, prefab racers that come from Derby-approved kits, can be assembled in four hours and don't exceed 200 pounds when driver, car and wheels are weighed together; 2. Super Stock (ages 10-17)— the same as Stock only with a weight limit of 220 pounds; 3. Masters (ages 11-17)— made up of racers designed by the drivers, but constructed with Derby-approved hardware. The racing ramp at Derby Downs is 989 feet, four inches with an 11 percent grade.

One champion reigned at the All-American Soap Box Derby each year from 1934-75; Junior and Senior division champions from 1976-87; Kit and Masters champions from 1988-91; Stock, Kit and Masters champions from 1992-94; Stock, Super Stock and Masters champions starting in 1995.

| Year | | Hometown | Age | Year | | Hometown | Age |
|------|--|----------|-----|------|--|----------|-----|
| 1934 | Robert Turner | Muncie, IN | 11 | 1942-45 | Not held | | |
| 1935 | Maurice Bale Jr. | Anderson, IN | 13 | 1946 | Gilbert Klecan | San Diego | 14 |
| 1936 | Herbert Muench Jr. | St. Louis | 14 | 1947 | Kenneth Holmboe | Charleston, WV | 14 |
| 1937 | Robert Ballard | White Plains, NY | 12 | 1948 | Donald Strub | Akron, OH | 13 |
| 1938 | Robert Berger | Omaha, NE | 14 | 1949 | Fred Derks | Akron, OH | 15 |
| 1939 | Clifton Hardesty | White Plains, NY | 11 | 1950 | Harold Williamson | Charleston, WV | 15 |
| 1940 | Thomas Fisher | Detroit | 12 | 1951 | Darwin Cooper | Williamsport, PA | 15 |
| 1941 | Claude Smith | Akron, OH | 14 | 1952 | Joe Lunn | Columbus, GA | 11 |

| Year | Hometown | Age | Year | Hometown | Age |
|---|---|---|---|---|---|
| 1953 Fred Mohler | Muncie, IN | 14 | 1989 KIT: David Schiller | Dayton, OH | 12 |
| 1954 Richard Kemp | Los Angeles | 14 | MAS: Faith Chavarria | Ventura, CA | 12 |
| 1955 Richard Rohrer | Rochester, NY | 14 | 1990 MAS: Sami Jones | Salem, OR | 13 |
| 1956 Norman Westfall | Rochester, NY | 14 | KIT: Mark Mihal | Valparaiso, IN | 14 |
| 1957 Terry Townsend | Anderson, IN | 14 | 1991 MAS: Danny Garland | San Diego, CA | 14 |
| 1958 James Miley | Muncie, IN | 15 | KIT: Paul Greenwald | Saginaw, MI | 13 |
| 1959 Barney Townsend | Anderson, IN | 13 | 1992 MAS: Bonnie Thornton | Redding, CA | 12 |
| 1960 Fredric Lake | South Bend, IN | 11 | KIT: Carolyn Fox | Sublimity, OR | 11 |
| 1961 Dick Dawson | Wichita, KS | 13 | STK: Loren Hurst | Hudson, OH | 10 |
| 1962 David Mann | Gary, IN | 14 | 1993 MAS: Dean Lutton | Delta, OH | 12 |
| 1963 Harold Conrad | Duluth, MN | 12 | KIT: D.M. Del Ferraro | Stow, OH | 12 |
| 1964 Gregory Schumacher | Tacoma, WA | 14 | STK: Owen Yuda | Boiling Springs, PA | 10 |
| 1965 Robert Logan | Santa Ana, CA | 12 | 1994 MAS: D.M. Del Ferraro | Akron, OH | 14 |
| 1966 David Krussow | Tacoma, WA | 14 | KIT: Joel Endres | Akron, OH | 14 |
| 1967 Kenneth Cline | Lincoln, NE | 13 | STK: Kristina Damond | Jamestown, NY | 13 |
| 1968 Branch Lew | Muncie, IN | 11 | 1995 MAS: J. Fensterbush | Kingman, AZ | 11 |
| 1969 Steve Souter | Midland, TX | 12 | SS: Darcie Davisson | Kingman, AZ | 11 |
| 1970 Samuel Gupton | Durham, NC | 13 | STK: Karen Thomas | Jamestown, NY | 11 |
| 1971 Larry Blair | Oroville, CA | 13 | 1996 MAS: Tim Scrofano | Conneaut, OH | 12 |
| 1972 Robert Lange Jr. | Boulder, CO | 14 | SS: Jeremy Phillips | Charlestown, WV | 14 |
| 1973 Bret Yarborough | Elk Grove, CA | 11 | STK: Matt Perez | No. Canton, OH | 12 |
| 1974 Curt Yarborough | Elk Grove, CA | 11 | 1997 MAS: Wade Wallace | Elk Hart, IN | 11 |
| 1975 Karren Stead | Lower Bucks, PA | 11 | SS: Dolline Vance | Salem, OR | 13 |
| 1976 JR: Phil Raber | Sugarcreek, OH | 11 | STK: Mark Stephens | Waynesboro, VA | 13 |
| SR: Joan Ferdinand | Canton, OH | 14 | 1998 MAS: James Marsh | Cleveland, OH | 12 |
| 1977 JR: Mark Ferdinand | Canton, OH | 10 | SS: Stacy Sharp | Kingman, AZ | 14 |
| SR: Steve Washburn | Bristol, CT | 15 | STK: Hailey Simpson | Salem, OR | 10 |
| 1978 JR: Darren Hart | Salem, OR | 11 | 1999 MAS: Allan Endres | Barberton, OH | 14 |
| SR: Greg Cardinal | Flint, MI | 13 | SS: Alisha Ebner | Salem, OR | 15 |
| 1979 JR: Russell Yurk | Flint, MI | 10 | STK: Justin Pillow | Deland, FL | 12 |
| SR: Craig Kitchen | Akron, OH | 14 | 2000 MAS: Cody Butler | Anderson, IN | 12 |
| 1980 JR: Chris Fulton | Indianapolis | 11 | SS: Derek Etherington | Anderson, IN | 11 |
| SR: Dan Porul | Sherman Oaks, CA | 12 | STK: Rachel Curran | Medina, OH | 13 |
| 1981 JR: Howie Fraley | Portsmouth, OH | 11 | 2001 MAS: Michael Flynn | Harrison Township, MI | 12 |
| SR: Tonia Schlegel | Hamilton, OH | 13 | SS: James Rogers | Hilton, NY | 15 |
| 1982 JR: Carol A. Sullivan | Rochester, NH | 10 | STK: Chad Eyerly | Alta Loma, CA | 13 |
| SR: Matt Wolfgang | Lehigh Val., PA | 12 | 2002 MAS: Evan Griffin | Winter Park, FL | 15 |
| 1983 JR: Tony Carlini | Del Mar, CA | 10 | SS: Roger Youmans Jr. | Spencerport, NY | 13 |
| SR: Mike Burdgick | Flint, MI | 14 | STK: Cameron Vannatta | Anderson, IN | 12 |
| 1984 JR: Chris Hess | Hamilton, OH | 11 | 2003 MAS: Anthony Marulli | Rochester, NY | 14 |
| SR: Anita Jackson | St. Louis | 15 | SS: Corey Harkins | Chicago | 14 |
| 1985 JR: Michael Gallo | Danbury, CT | 12 | STK: Nicholas Sibeto | New Castle, PA | 12 |
| SR: Matt Sheffer | York, PA | 14 | 2004 MAS: Hilary Pearson | Kansas City, MO | 14 |
| 1986 JR: Marc Behan | Dover, NH | 9 | SS: RickiLea Murphy | Mantua, OH | 12 |
| SR: Tami Jo Sullivan | Lancaster, OH | 13 | STK: Perrin Norris | Tullahoma, TN | 10 |
| 1987 JR: Matt Margules | Danbury, CT | 11 | 2005 MAS: Stephanie Inglezakis | Stow, OH | 16 |
| SR: Brian Drinkwater | Bristol, CT | 14 | SS: Tyler Gallagher | Mantua, OH | 14 |
| 1988 KIT: Jason Lamb | Des Moines, IA | 10 | STK: Nick Hoffaman | Lancaster, OH | 9 |
| MAS: David Duffield | Kansas City | 13 | | | |

## SOFTBALL

Men's and women's national champions since 1933 in Major Fast Pitch, Major Slow Pitch and Super Slow Pitch (men only). Sanctioned by the Amateur Softball Association of America.

## MEN
### Major Fast Pitch

**Multiple winners:** Clearwater Bombers (10); Raybestos Cardinals (5); Sealmasters (4); Briggs Beautyware, Decatur Pride, Pay'n Pak and Zollner Pistons (3); Billard Barbell, Farm Tavern, Frontier Players Casino, Hammer Air Field, Kodak Park, Meierhoffer, National Health Care, Penn Corp, Peterbilt Western and Tampa Bay Smokers (2).

| Year | Year | Year |
|---|---|---|
| 1933 J.L. Gill Boosters, Chicago | 1943 Hammer Air Field, Fresno, CA | 1953 Briggs Beautyware |
| 1934 Ke-Nash-A, Kenosha, WI | 1944 Hammer Air Field | 1954 Clearwater Bombers |
| 1935 Crimson Coaches, Toledo, OH | 1945 Zollner Pistons, Ft. Wayne, IN | 1955 Raybestos Cardinals, |
| 1936 Kodak Park, Rochester, NY | 1946 Zollner Pistons | 1956 Clearwater Bombers |
| 1937 Briggs Body Team, Detroit | 1947 Zollner Pistons | 1957 Clearwater Bombers |
| 1938 The Pohlers, Cincinnati | 1948 Briggs Beautyware, Detroit | 1958 Raybestos Cardinals |
| 1939 Carr's Boosters, Covington, KY | 1949 Tip Top Tailors, Toronto | 1959 Sealmasters, Aurora, IL |
| 1940 Kodak Park | 1950 Clearwater (FL) Bombers | 1960 Clearwater Bombers |
| 1941 Bendix Brakes, South Bend, IN | 1951 Dow Chemical, Midland, MI | 1961 Sealmasters |
| 1942 Deep Rock Oilers, Tulsa, OK | 1952 Briggs Beautyware | 1962 Clearwater Bombers |

## Softball (Cont.)

**Year**
1963 Clearwater Bombers
1964 Burch Tool, Detroit
1965 Sealmasters
1966 Clearwater Bombers
1967 Sealmasters
1968 Clearwater Bombers
1969 Raybestos Cardinals

1970 Raybestos Cardinals
1971 Welty Way, Cedar Rapids, IA
1972 Raybestos Cardinals
1973 Clearwater Bombers
1974 Gianella Bros., Santa Rosa, CA
1975 Rising Sun Hotel, Reading, PA
1976 Raybestos Cardinals
1977 Billard Barbell, Reading, PA
1978 Billard Barbell
1979 McArdle Pontiac/Cadillac,
       Midland, MI

**Year**
1980 Peterbilt Western, Seattle
1981 Archer Daniels Midland,
       Decatur, IL
1982 Peterbilt Western
1983 Franklin Cardinals,
       Stratford, CA
1984 California Kings, Merced, CA
1985 Pay'n Pak, Seattle
1986 Pay'n Pak
1987 Pay'n Pak
1988 TransAire, Elkhart, IN
1989 Penn Corp, Sioux City, IA

1990 Penn Corp
1991 Gianella Bros., Rohnert Park, CA
1992 National Health Care,
       Sioux City, IA
1993 National Health Care

**Year**
1994 Decatur (IL) Pride
1995 Decatur Pride
1996 Green Bay All-Car,
       Green Bay, WI
1997 Tampa Bay Smokers,
       Tampa Bay, FL
1998 Meierhoffer-Fleeman,
       St. Joseph, MO
1999 Decatur Pride

2000 Meierhoffer
2001 Frontier Players Casino,
       St. Joseph, MO
2002 Frontier Players Casino
2003 Farm Tavern, Madison, WI
2004 Farm Tavern
2005 Tampa Bay Smokers,
       Tampa Bay, FL

## Super Slow Pitch

**Multiple winners:** Ritch's/Superior (4); Howard's/Western Steer and Steele's Sports (3); Lighthouse/Worth and Long Haul (2).

**Year**
1981 Howard's/Western Steer,
       Denver, NC
1982 Jerry's Catering, Miami
1983 Howard's/Western Steer
1984 Howard's/Western Steer
1985 Steele's Sports, Grafton, OH
1986 Steele's Sports
1987 Steele's Sports
1988 Starpath, Monticello, KY

**Year**
1989 Ritch's Salvage, Harrisburg, NC
1990 Steele's Silver Bullets
1991 Sun Belt/Worth, Atlanta
1992 Ritch's/Superior,
       Windsor Locks, CT
1993 Ritch's/Superior
1994 Bellcorp., Tampa
1995 Lighthouse/Worth, Stone Mt., GA

**Year**
1996 Ritch's/Superior
1997 Ritch's/Superior
1998 Lighthouse/Worth
1999 Team Easton, California
2000 Team TPS, Louisville, KY
2001 Long Haul, Albertville, MN
2002 Long Haul
2003 Resmondo/Hagae,
       Canal Winchester, OH

## Major Slow Pitch

**Multiple winners:** Gatliff Auto Sales, Riverside Paving and Skip Hogan A.C. (3); Campbell Carpets, Hamilton Tailoring, Howard's Furniture, Long Haul TPS and New Construction (2).

**Year**
1953 Shields Construction, Newport, KY
1954 Waldneck's Tavern, Cincinnati
1955 Lang Pet Shop, Covington, KY
1956 Gatliff Auto Sales, Newport, KY
1957 Gatliff Auto Sales
1958 East Side Sports, Detroit
1959 Yorkshire Restaurant, Newport, KY
1960 Hamilton Tailoring, Cincinnati
1961 Hamilton Tailoring
1962 Skip Hogan A.C., Pittsburgh
1963 Gatliff Auto Sales
1964 Skip Hogan A.C.
1965 Skip Hogan A.C.
1966 Michael's Lounge, Detroit
1967 Jim's Sport Shop, Pittsburgh
1968 County Sports, Levittown, NY
1969 Copper Hearth, Milwaukee
1970 Little Caesar's, Southgate, MI
1971 Pile Drivers, Va. Beach, VA
1972 Jiffy Club, Louisville, KY

**Year**
1973 Howard's Furniture, Denver, NC
1974 Howard's Furniture
1975 Pyramid Cafe, Lakewood, OH
1976 Warren Motors, J'ville, FL
1977 Nelson Painting, Okla. City
1978 Campbell Carpets, Concord, CA
1979 Nelco Mfg. Co., Okla. City
1980 Campbell Carpets
1981 Elite Coating, Gordon, CA
1982 Triangle Sports, Minneapolis
1983 No.1 Electric & Heating,
       Gastonia, NC
1984 Lilly Air Systems, Chicago
1985 Blanton's Fayetteville, NC
1986 Non-Ferrous Metals, Cleveland
1987 Stapath, Monticello, KY
1988 Bell Corp/FAF, Tampa, FL
1989 Ritch's Salvage, Harrisburg, NC
1990 New Construction, Shelbyville, IN
1991 Riverside Paving, Louisville

**Year**
1992 Vernon's, Jacksonville, FL
1993 Back Porch/Destin (FL) Roofing
1994 Riverside Paving, Louisville
1995 Riverside Paving
1996 Bell II, Orlando, FL
1997 Long Haul TPS, Albertville, MN
1998 Chase Mortgage/Easton,
       Wilmington, NC
1999 Gasoline Heaven/Worth,
       Commack, NY
2000 Long Haul TPS
2001 New Construction
2002 Twin States/Worth,
       Montgomery, AL
2003 New Construction/B&J/Snap-On,
       Metamora, IL
2004 U.S. Vinyl, Houston, TX
2005 AM/Las Vegas/Benfield,
       Bowling Green, KY

# WOMEN
## Major Fast Pitch

**Multiple winners:** Raybestos/Stratford Brakettes (24); Orange Lionettes (9); Jax Maids (5); California Commotion (4); Arizona Ramblers and Redding Rebels (3); Hi-Ho Brakettes, J.J. Krieg's, National Screw & Manufacturing and Phoenix Storm (2).

| Year | Year | Year |
|------|------|------|
| 1933 Great Northerns, Chicago | 1958 Raybestos Brakettes, Stratford, CT | 1982 Raybestos Brakettes |
| 1934 Hart Motors, Chicago | | 1983 Raybestos Brakettes |
| 1935 Bloomer Girls, Cleveland | 1959 Raybestos Brakettes | 1984 Los Angeles Diamonds |
| 1936 Nat'l Screw & Mfg., Cleveland | 1960 Raybestos Brakettes | 1985 Hi-Ho Brakettes, Stratford, CT |
| 1937 Nat'l Screw & Mfg. | 1961 Gold Sox, Whittier, CA | 1986 So. California Invasion |
| 1938 J.J. Krieg's, Alameda, CA | 1962 Orange Lionettes | 1987 Orange County Majestics, Anaheim, CA |
| 1939 J.J. Krieg's | 1963 Raybestos Brakettes | |
| 1940 Arizona Ramblers, Phoenix | 1964 Erv Lind Florists, Portland, OR | 1988 Hi-Ho Brakettes |
| 1941 Higgins Midgets, Tulsa, OK | 1965 Orange Lionettes | 1989 Whittier (CA) Raiders |
| 1942 Jax Maids, New Orleans | 1966 Raybestos Brakettes | 1990 Raybestos Brakettes |
| 1943 Jax Maids | 1967 Raybestos Brakettes | 1991 Raybestos Brakettes |
| 1944 Lind & Pomeroy, Portland, OR | 1968 Raybestos Brakettes | 1992 Raybestos Brakettes |
| 1945 Jax Maids | 1969 Orange Lionettes | 1993 Redding (CA) Rebels |
| 1946 Jax Maids | 1970 Orange Lionettes | 1994 Redding Rebels |
| 1947 Jax Maids | 1971 Raybestos Brakettes | 1995 Redding Rebels |
| 1948 Arizona Ramblers | 1972 Raybestos Brakettes | 1996 California Commotion, Woodland Hills |
| 1949 Arizona Ramblers | 1973 Raybestos Brakettes | |
| 1950 Orange (CA) Lionettes | 1974 Raybestos Brakettes | 1997 California Commotion |
| 1951 Orange Lionettes | 1975 Raybestos Brakettes | 1998 California Commotion |
| 1952 Orange Lionettes | 1976 Raybestos Brakettes | 1999 California Commotion |
| 1953 Betsy Ross Rockets, Fresno, CA | 1977 Raybestos Brakettes | 2000 Phoenix Storm, Phoenix, AZ |
| 1954 Leach Motor Rockets, Fresno, CA | 1978 Raybestos Brakettes | 2001 Phoenix Storm |
| 1955 Orange Lionettes | 1979 Sun City (AZ) Saints | 2002 Stratford Brakettes, Stratford, CT |
| 1956 Orange Lionettes | 1980 Raybestos Brakettes | 2003 Stratford Brakettes |
| 1957 Hacienda Rockets, Fresno, CA | 1981 Orlando (FL) Rebels | 2004 Stratford Brakettes |

## Major Slow Pitch

**Multiple winners:** Spooks (5); Dana Gardens (4); Universal Plastics (3); Cannan's Illusions, Bob Hoffman's Dots, Key Ford Mustangs and Marks Brothers Dots (2).

| Year | Year | Year |
|------|------|------|
| 1959 Pearl Laundry, Richmond, VA | 1975 Marks Brothers Dots | 1988 Spooks |
| | 1976 Sorrento's Pizza, Cincinnati | 1989 Cannan's Illusions, Houston |
| 1960 Carolina Rockets, High Pt., NC | 1977 Fox Valley Lassies, St. Charles, IL | |
| 1961 Dairy Cottage, Covington, KY | | 1990 Spooks |
| 1962 Dana Gardens, Cincinnati | 1978 Bob Hoffman's Dots, Miami | 1991 Cannan's Illusions, San Antonio |
| 1963 Dana Gardens | 1979 Bob Hoffman's Dots | 1992 Universal Plastics, Cookeville, TN |
| 1964 Dana Gardens | | 1993 Universal Plastics |
| 1965 Art's Acres, Omaha, NE | 1980 Howard's Rubi-Otts, Graham, NC | 1994 Universal Plastics |
| 1966 Dana Gardens | | 1995 Armed Forces, Sacramento |
| 1967 Ridge Maintenance, Cleveland | 1981 Tifton (GA) Tomboys | 1996 Spooks |
| 1968 Escue Pontiac, Cincinnati | 1982 Richmond (VA) Stompers | 1997 Taylor's, Glendale, MD |
| 1969 Converse Dots, Hialeah, FL | 1983 Spooks, Anoka, MN | 1998 Not held |
| | 1984 Spooks | 1999 Lakerettes, Conneaut Lake, PA |
| 1970 Rutenschruder Floral, Cincinnati | 1985 Key Ford Mustangs, Pensacola, FL | |
| 1971 Gators, Ft. Lauderdale, FL | | 2000 Premier Sports, Pittsboro, NC |
| 1972 Riverside Ford, Cincinnati | 1986 Sur-Way Tomboys, Tifton, GA | 2001 Shooters/Nike, Orlando, FL |
| 1973 Sweeney Chevrolet, Cincinnati | 1987 Key Ford Mustangs | 2002 Diamond Queens, Nashville, TN |
| 1974 Marks Brothers Dots, Miami | | 2003 Not held |

## TRIATHLON
### World Championship

Contested since 1989, the Triathlon World Championship consists of a 1.5-kilometer swim, a 40-kilometer bike ride and a 10-kilometer run. The 2005 championship was held Oct. 9 in Hanolulu, Hawaii

**Multiple winners:** MEN—Simon Lessing (4); Peter Robertson and Spencer Smith (2). WOMEN—Emma Carney, Michellie Jones and Karen Smyers (2).

### MEN

| Year | Time | Year | Time |
|------|------|------|------|
| 1989 Mark Allen, United States | 1:58:46 | 1998 Simon Lessing, Great Britain | 1:55:31 |
| 1990 Greg Welch, Australia | 1:51:37 | 1999 Dimitry Gaag, Kazahkstan | 1:45:25 |
| 1991 Miles Stewart, Australia | 1:48:20 | 2000 Oliver Marceau, France | 1:51:41 |
| 1992 Simon Lessing, Great Britain | 1:49:04 | 2001 Peter Robertson, Australia | 1:48:01 |
| 1993 Spencer Smith, Great Britain | 1:51:20 | 2002 Iván Raña, Spain | 1:50:41 |
| 1994 Spencer Smith, Great Britain | 1:51:04 | 2003 Peter Robertson, Australia | 1:54:13 |
| 1995 Simon Lessing, Great Britain | 1:48:29 | 2004 Bevan Docherty, New Zealand | 1:41:04 |
| 1996 Simon Lessing, Great Britain | 1:39:50 | 2005 Diogo Sclebin, Brazil | 1:55:38 |
| 1997 Chris McCormack, Australia | 1:48:29 | | |

## WOMEN

| Year | | Time | Year | | Time |
|------|--|------|------|--|------|
| 1989 | Erin Baker, New Zealand | 2:10:01 | 1998 | Joanne King, Australia | 2:07:25 |
| 1990 | Karen Smyers, United States | 2:03:33 | 1999 | Loretta Harrop, Australia | 1:55:28 |
| 1991 | Joanne Ritchie, Canada | 2:02:04 | 2000 | Nicole Hackett, Australia | 1:54:43 |
| 1992 | Michellie Jones, Australia | 2:02:08 | 2001 | Siri Lindley, United States | 1:58:51 |
| 1993 | Michellie Jones, Australia | 2:07:41 | 2002 | Leanda Cave, Wales | 2:01:31 |
| 1994 | Emma Carney, Australia | 2:03:19 | 2003 | Emma Snowsill, Australia | 2:06:40 |
| 1995 | Karen Smyers, USA | 2:04:58 | 2004 | Sheila Taormina, United States | 1:52:17 |
| 1996 | Jackie Gallagher, Australia | 1:50:52 | 2005 | Margie Shapiro, United States | 2:07:10 |
| 1997 | Emma Carney, Australia | 1:59:22 | | | |

## Ironman Championship

Contested in Hawaii since 1978, the Ironman Triathlon Championship consists of a 2.4-mile swim, a 112-mile bike ride and 26.2-mile run. The race begins at 7 A.M. and continues all day until the course is closed at midnight.

## MEN

**Multiple winners:** Mark Allen and Dave Scott (6); Peter Reid (3); Tim DeBoom, Luc Van Lierde and Scott Tinley (2).

| Year | Date | Winner | Time | Runner-up | Margin | Start | Finish | Location |
|------|------|--------|------|-----------|--------|-------|--------|----------|
| I | 2/18/78 | Gordon Haller | 11:46 | John Dunbar | 34:00 | 15 | 12 | Waikiki Beach |
| II | 1/14/79 | Tom Warren | 11:15:56 | John Dunbar | 48:00 | 15 | 12 | Waikiki Beach |
| III | 1/10/80 | Dave Scott | 9:24:33 | Chuck Neumann | 1:08 | 108 | 95 | Ala Moana Park |
| IV | 2/14/81 | John Howard | 9:38:29 | Tom Warren | 26:00 | 326 | 299 | Kailua-Kona |
| V | 2/6/82 | Scott Tinley | 9:19:41 | Dave Scott | 17:16 | 580 | 541 | Kailua-Kona |
| VI | 10/9/82 | Dave Scott | 9:08:23 | Scott Tinley | 20:05 | 850 | 775 | Kailua-Kona |
| VII | 10/22/83 | Dave Scott | 9:05:57 | Scott Tinley | 0:33 | 964 | 835 | Kailua-Kona |
| VIII | 10/6/84 | Dave Scott | 8:54:20 | Scott Tinley | 24:25 | 1036 | 903 | Kailua-Kona |
| IX | 10/25/85 | Scott Tinley | 8:50:54 | Chris Hinshaw | 25:46 | 1018 | 965 | Kailua-Kona |
| X | 10/18/86 | Dave Scott | 8:28:37 | Mark Allen | 9:47 | 1039 | 951 | Kailua-Kona |
| XI | 10/10/87 | Dave Scott | 8:34:13 | Mark Allen | 11:06 | 1380 | 1284 | Kailua-Kona |
| XII | 10/22/88 | Scott Molina | 8:31:00 | Mike Pigg | 2:11 | 1277 | 1189 | Kailua-Kona |
| XIII | 10/15/89 | Mark Allen | 8:09:15 | Dave Scott | 0:58 | 1285 | 1231 | Kailua-Kona |
| XIV | 10/6/90 | Mark Allen | 8:28:17 | Scott Tinley | 9:23 | 1386 | 1255 | Kailua-Kona |
| XV | 10/19/91 | Mark Allen | 8:18:32 | Greg Welch | 6:01 | 1386 | 1235 | Kailua-Kona |
| XVI | 10/10/92 | Mark Allen | 8:09:08 | Cristian Bustos | 7:21 | 1364 | 1298 | Kailua-Kona |
| XVII | 10/30/93 | Mark Allen | 8:07:45 | Paulli Kiuru | 6:37 | 1438 | 1353 | Kailua-Kona |
| XVIII | 10/15/94 | Greg Welch | 8:20:27 | Dave Scott | 4:05 | 1405 | 1290 | Kailua-Kona |
| XIX | 10/7/95 | Mark Allen | 8:20:34 | Thomas Hellriegel | 2:25 | 1487 | 1323 | Kailua-Kona |
| XX | 10/26/96 | Luc Van Lierde | 8:04:08 | Thomas Hellriegel | 1:59 | 1420 | 1288 | Kailua-Kona |
| XXI | 10/18/97 | Thomas Hellriegel | 8:33:01 | Jurgen Zack | 6:17 | 1534 | 1365 | Kailua-Kona |
| XXII | 10/3/98 | Peter Reid | 8:24:20 | Luc Van Lierde | 7:37 | 1487 | 1379 | Kailua-Kona |
| XXIII | 10/23/99 | Luc Van Lierde | 8:17:17 | Peter Reid | 5:37 | 1471 | 1419 | Kailua-Kona |
| XXIV | 10/14/00 | Peter Reid | 8:21:01 | Tim DeBoom | 2:09 | 1525 | 1426 | Kailua-Kona |
| XXV | 10/6/01 | Tim DeBoom | 8:31:18 | Cameron Brown | 14:52 | 1558 | 1364 | Kailua-Kona |
| XXVI | 10/19/02 | Tim DeBoom | 8:29:56 | Peter Reid | 3:10 | 1540 | 1457 | Kailua-Kona |
| XXVII | 10/18/03 | Peter Reid | 8:22:35 | Rutger Beke | 5:51 | 1647 | 1569 | Kailua-Kona |
| XXVIII | 10/16/04 | Normann Stadler | 8:33:29 | Peter Reid | 10:11 | 1728 | 1579 | Kailua-Kona |
| XXVIX | 10/15/05 | Faris Al-Sultan | 8:14:17 | Cameron Brown | 5:19 | 1743 | 1688 | Kailua-Kona |

## WOMEN

**Multiple winners:** Paula Newby-Fraser (8); Natascha Badmann (6); Erin Baker, Lori Bowden and Sylviane Puntous (2).

| Year | Winner | Time | Runner-up | Year | Winner | Time | Runner-up |
|------|--------|------|-----------|------|--------|------|-----------|
| 1978 | No finishers | | | 1992 | Paula Newby-Fraser | 8:55:28 | Julie Anne White |
| 1979 | Lyn Lemaire | 12:55.00 | None | 1993 | Paula Newby-Fraser | 8:58:23 | Erin Baker |
| 1980 | Robin Beck | 11:21:24 | Eve Anderson | 1994 | Paula Newby-Fraser | 9:20:14 | Karen Smyers |
| 1981 | Linda Sweeney | 12:00:32 | Sally Edwards | 1995 | Karen Smyers | 9:16:46 | Isabelle Mouthon |
| 1982 | Kathleen McCartney | 11:09:40 | Julie Moss | 1996 | Paula Newby-Fraser | 9:06:49 | Natascha Badmann |
| 1982 | Julie Leach | 10:54:08 | Joann Dahlkoetter | 1997 | Heather Fuhr | 9:31:43 | Lori Bowden |
| 1983 | Sylviane Puntous | 10:43:36 | Patricia Puntous | 1998 | Natascha Badmann | 9:24:16 | Lori Bowden |
| 1984 | Sylviane Puntous | 10:25:13 | Patricia Puntous | 1999 | Lori Bowden | 9:13:02 | Karen Smyers |
| 1985 | Joanne Ernst | 10:25:22 | Liz Bulman | 2000 | Natascha Badmann | 9:26:17 | Lori Bowden |
| 1986 | Paula Newby-Fraser | 9:49:14 | Sylviane Puntous | 2001 | Natascha Badmann | 9:28:37 | Lori Bowden |
| 1987 | Erin Baker | 9:35:25 | Sylviane Puntous | 2002 | Natascha Badmann | 9:07:54 | Nina Kraft |
| 1988 | Paula Newby-Fraser | 9:01:01 | Erin Baker | 2003 | Lori Bowden | 9:11:55 | Natascha Badmann |
| 1989 | Paula Newby-Fraser | 9:00:56 | Sylviane Puntous | 2004 | Natascha Badmann* | 9:50:04 | Heather Fuhr |
| 1990 | Erin Baker | 9:13:42 | P. Newby-Fraser | 2005 | Natascha Badmann | 9:09:30 | Michellie Jones |
| 1991 | Paula Newby-Fraser | 9:07:52 | Erin Baker | | | | |

*Nina Kraft of Germany was the first woman to cross the finish line in 2004 with her time of 9:33:25 but she was disqualified after failing a post-race drug test by testing positive for EPO. Badmann finished second but was awarded the title (and Canada's Heather Fuhr became runner-up) following the test.

### X GAMES

The ESPN Extreme Games, originally envisioned as a biannual showcase for "alternative" sports, were first held June 24-July 1, 1995 in Newport and Providence, R.I. and Mt. Snow, Vt. The success of the inaugural event prompted organizers to make it an annual competition. Newport would again serve as host for the redubbed X Games in 1996. The X Games has evolved rapidly since its inception and have been held in several cities since. New sports and events have been added while others have been dropped.

**Summer X Games sites:** 1995–Newport/Providence, R.I. (and Mt. Snow, Vt.); 1996–Newport/Providence, R.I.; 1997–San Diego; 1998–San Diego; 1999–San Francisco; 2000–San Francisco; 2001–Philadelphia; 2002–Philadelphia; 2003–Los Angeles; 2004–Los Angeles; 2005–Los Angeles. **Winter X Games sites:** 1997–Snow Summit Mountain Resort, Big Bear Lake, Calif.; 1998–Crested Butte, Colo.; 1999–Crested Butte, Colo.; 2000– Mt. Snow, Vt.; 2001–Mt. Snow, Vt.; 2002–Aspen, Colo.; 2003–Aspen, Colo.; 2004–Aspen, Colo.; 2005–Aspen, Colo.

## SUMMER X GAMES
### Bicycle Stunt

| Year | Vert | Year | Dirt | Year | Street/Stunt Park | Year | Flatland |
|------|------|------|------|------|-------------------|------|----------|
| 1995 | Matt Hoffman | 1995 | Jay Miron | 1996 | Dave Mirra | 1997 | Trevor Meyer |
| 1996 | Matt Hoffman | 1996 | Joey Garcia | 1997 | Dave Mirra | 1998 | Trevor Meyer |
| 1997 | Dave Mirra | 1997 | T.J. Lavin | 1998 | Dave Mirra | 1999 | Trevor Meyer |
| 1998 | Dave Mirra | 1998 | Brian Foster | 1999 | Dave Mirra | 2000 | Martti Kuoppa |
| 1999 | Dave Mirra | 1999 | T.J. Lavin | 2000 | Dave Mirra | 2001 | Martti Kuoppa |
| 2000 | Jamie Bestwick | 2000 | Ryan Nyquist | 2001 | Bruce Crisman | 2002 | Martti Kuoppa |
| 2001 | Dave Mirra | 2001 | Stephen Murray | 2002 | Ryan Nyquist | 2003 | Simon O'Brien |
| 2002 | Dave Mirra | 2002 | Allan Cooke | 2003 | Ryan Nyquist | **Year** | **Downhill** |
| 2003 | Jamie Bestwick | 2003 | Ryan Nyquist | 2004 | Dave Mirra | 2001 | Brandon Meadows |
| 2004 | Dave Mirra | 2004 | Corey Bohan | 2005 | Dave Mirra | 2002 | Robbie Miranda |
| 2005 | Jamie Bestwick | 2005 | Corey Bohan | | | 2003 | Brandon Meadows |
| **Year** | **Vert Best Trick** | | | | | | |
| 2005 | Jamie Bestwick | | | | | | |

### Skateboarding

| Year | Vert Singles | Year | Vert Doubles | Year | Street/Park | Year | Women's Park |
|------|--------------|------|--------------|------|-------------|------|--------------|
| 1995 | Tony Hawk | 1997 | Hawk/Macdonald | 1995 | Chris Senn | 2003 | Vanessa Torres |
| 1996 | Andy Macdonald | 1998 | Hawk/Macdonald | 1996 | Rodil de Araujo Jr. | **Year** | **Women's Street** |
| 1997 | Tony Hawk | 1999 | Hawk/Macdonald | 1997 | Chris Senn | 2004 | Elissa Steamer |
| 1998 | Andy Macdonald | 2000 | Hawk/Macdonald | 1998 | Rodil de Araujo Jr. | 2005 | Elissa Steamer |
| 1999 | Bucky Lasek | 2001 | Hawk/Macdonald | 1999 | Chris Senn | **Year** | **Street Best Trick** |
| 2000 | Bucky Lasek | 2002 | Hawk/Macdonald | 2000 | Eric Koston | 2001 | Kerry Getz |
| 2001 | Bob Burnquist | 2003 | Lasek/Burnquist | 2001 | Kerry Getz | 2002 | Rodil de Araujo Jr. |
| 2002 | Pierre-Luc Gagnon | **Year** | **Vert Best Trick** | 2002 | Rodil de Araujo Jr. | 2003 | Chad Muska |
| 2003 | Bucky Lasek | 2000 | Bob Burnquist | **Year** | **Street** | **Year** | **Big Air** |
| 2004 | Bucky Lasek | 2001 | Matt Dove | 2003 | Eric Koston | 2004 | Danny Way |
| 2005 | Pierre-Luc Gagnon | 2002 | Pierre-Luc Gagnon | 2004 | Paul Rodriguez | 2005 | Danny Way |
| **Year** | **Women's Vert** | 2003 | Tony Hawk | 2005 | Paul Rodriguez | | |
| 2004 | L. Adams Hawkins | 2004 | Sandro Dias | **Year** | **Park** | | |
| 2005 | Cara-Beth Burnside | 2005 | Bob Burnquist | 2003 | Ryan Sheckler | | |

### Moto X

| Year | Freestyle |
|------|-----------|
| 1999 | Travis Pastrana |
| 2000 | Travis Pastrana |
| 2001 | Travis Pastrana |
| 2002 | Mike Metzger |
| 2003 | Travis Pastrana |
| 2004 | Nate Adams |
| 2005 | Travis Pastrana |
| **Year** | **Step Up** |
| 2001 | Tommy Clowers |
| 2002 | Tommy Clowers |
| 2003 | Matt Buyten |
| 2004 | Jeremy McGrath |
| 2005 | Tommy Clowers |
| **Year** | **Big Air** |
| 2001 | Kenny Bartman |
| 2002 | Mike Metzger |
| 2003 | Brian Deegan |
| **Year** | **Super Moto** |
| 2004 | Ben Bostrom |
| 2005 | Doug Henry |
| **Year** | **Best Trick** |
| 2004 | Chuck Carothers |
| 2005 | Jeremy Stenberg |

### Big-Air Snowboarding

| Year | Men |
|------|-----|
| 1997 | Peter Line |
| 1998 | Kevin Jones |
| 1999 | Peter Line |
| **Year** | **Women** |
| 1997 | Tina Dixon |
| 1998 | Janet Matthews |
| 1999 | Barrett Christy |

### Skysurfing

| Year | |
|------|--|
| 1995 | Fradet/Zipser |
| 1996 | Furrer/Scmid |
| 1997 | Hartman/Pappadato |
| 1998 | Rozov/Burch |
| 1999 | Fradet/Iodice |
| 2000 | Klaus/Rogers |

### Surfing

| Year | |
|------|--|
| 2003 | East Coast |
| 2004 | East Coast |
| 2005 | East Coast |

**Note:** The X Games surfing event is contested by teams of surfers from the East Coast and the West Coast.

### Bungee Jumping

| Year | |
|------|--|
| 1995 | Doug Anderson |
| 1996 | Peter Bihun |

### Street Luge

| Year | Dual |
|------|------|
| 1995 | Bob Pereyra |
| 1996 | Shawn Goular |
| 1997 | Biker Sherlock |
| 1998 | Biker Sherlock |
| 1999 | Dennis Derammelaere |
| 2000 | Bob Ozman |
| **Year** | **Mass** |
| 1995 | Shawn Gilbert |
| 1996 | Biker Sherlock |
| 1997 | Biker Sherlock |
| 1998 | Rat Sult |
| **Year** | **Super Mass** |
| 1997 | Biker Sherlock |
| 1998 | Rat Sult |
| 1999 | David Rogers |
| 2000 | Bob Pereyra |
| 2001 | Brent DeKeyser |
| **Year** | **King of the Hill** |
| 2001 | Dennis Derammelaere |

## Sportclimbing

| Year | Men's Difficulty |
|------|------------------|
| 1995 | Ian Vickers |
| 1996 | Arnaud Petit |
| 1997 | Francois Legrand |
| 1998 | Christian Core |
| 1999 | Chris Sharma |

| Year | Women's Difficulty |
|------|--------------------|
| 1995 | Robyn Erbersfield |
| 1996 | Katie Brown |
| 1997 | Katie Brown |
| 1998 | Katie Brown |
| 1999 | Stephanie Bodet |

| Year | Men's Speed |
|------|-------------|
| 1995 | Hans Florine |
| 1996 | Hans Florine |
| 1997 | Hans Florine |
| 1998 | Vladimir Netsvetaev |
| 1999 | Aaron Shamy |
| 2000 | Vladimir Zakharov |
| 2001 | Maxim Stenkovoy |
| 2002 | Maxim Stenkovoy |

| Year | Women's Speed |
|------|---------------|
| 1995 | Elena Ovtchinnikova |
| 1996 | Cecile Le Flem |
| 1997 | Elena Ovtchinnikova |
| 1998 | Elena Ovtchinnikova |
| 1999 | Renata Piszczek |
| 2000 | Etti Hendrawati |
| 2001 | Elena Repko |
| 2002 | Tori Allen |

## In-Line Skating

| Year | Men's Vert |
|------|------------|
| 1995 | Tom Fry |
| 1996 | Rene Hulgreen |
| 1997 | Tim Ward |
| 1998 | Cesar Mora |
| 1999 | Eito Yasutoko |
| 2000 | Eito Yasutoko |
| 2001 | Taig Khris |

| Year | Women's Vert |
|------|--------------|
| 1995 | Tash Hodgeson |
| 1996 | Fabiola da Silva |
| 1997 | Fabiola da Silva |
| 1998 | Fabiola da Silva |
| 1999 | Ayumi Kawasaki |
| 2000 | Fabiola da Silva |
| 2001 | Fabiola da Silva |

| Year | Combined Vert |
|------|---------------|
| 2002 | Takeshi Yasutoko |
| 2003 | Eito Yasutoko |
| 2004 | Takeshi Yasutoko |

**Note:** In 2002 the men's and women's vert events were combined.

| Year | Men's Park |
|------|------------|
| 1995 | Matt Salerno |
| 1996 | Arlo Eisenberg |
| 1997 | Arron Feinberg |
| 1998 | Jonathan Bergeron |
| 1999 | Nicky Adams |
| 2000 | Sven Boekhorst |
| 2001 | Jaren Grob |
| 2002 | Jaren Grob |
| 2003 | Bruno Lowe |

| Year | Women's Park |
|------|--------------|
| 1997 | Sayaka Yabe |
| 1998 | Jenny Curry |
| 1999 | Sayaka Yabe |
| 2000 | Fabiola da Silva |
| 2001 | Martina Svobodova |
| 2002 | Martina Svobodova |
| 2003 | Fabiola da Silva |

| Year | Vert Triples |
|------|--------------|
| 1998 | Malina/Fogarty/Popa |
| 1999 | Khris/Bujanda/Boekhorst |

| Year | Men's Downhill |
|------|----------------|
| 1995 | Derek Downing |
| 1996 | Dante Muse |
| 1997 | Derek Downing |
| 1998 | Patrick Naylor |

| Year | Women's Downhill |
|------|------------------|
| 1995 | Julie Brandt |
| 1996 | Gypsy Tidwell |
| 1997 | Gypsy Tidwell |
| 1998 | Julie Brandt |

### X-Venture Race

| Year | |
|------|--|
| 1995 | Team Threadbo |
| 1996 | Team Kobeer |
| 1997 | Team Presidio |

## Watersports

| Year | Barefoot Waterski Jumping |
|------|---------------------------|
| 1995 | Justin Seers |
| 1996 | Ron Scarpa |
| 1997 | Peter Fleck |
| 1998 | Peter Fleck |

| Year | Men's Wakeboarding |
|------|--------------------|
| 1996 | Parks Bonifay |
| 1997 | Jeremy Kovak |
| 1998 | Darin Shapiro |
| 1999 | Parks Bonifay |
| 2000 | Darin Shapiro |
| 2001 | Danny Harf |
| 2002 | Danny Harf |
| 2003 | Danny Harf |
| 2004 | Phillip Soven |
| 2005 | Danny Harf |

| Year | Women's Wakeboarding |
|------|----------------------|
| 1997 | Tara Hamilton |
| 1998 | Andrea Gaytan |
| 1999 | Meaghan Major |
| 2000 | Tara Hamilton |
| 2001 | Dallas Friday |
| 2002 | Emily Copeland |
| 2003 | Dallas Friday |
| 2004 | Dallas Friday |
| 2005 | Dallas Friday |

# WINTER X GAMES

## Ice Climbing

| Year | Men's Difficulty |
|------|------------------|
| 1997 | Jaren Ogden |
| 1998 | Will Gadd |
| 1999 | Will Gadd |

| Year | Women's Difficulty |
|------|--------------------|
| 1997 | Bird Lew |
| 1998 | Kim Csizmazia |
| 1999 | Kim Csizmazia |

| Year | Men's Speed |
|------|-------------|
| 1997 | Jared Ogden |
| 1998 | Will Gadd |

| Year | Women's Speed |
|------|---------------|
| 1997 | Bird Lew |
| 1998 | Kim Csizmazia |

### Super-modified Shovel Racing

| Year | |
|------|--|
| 1997 | Don Adkins |

### CrossOver

| Year | |
|------|--|
| 1997 | Brian Patch |
| 1998 | Event discontinued |

### Snow Mountain Bike Racing

| Year | Men's Downhill |
|------|----------------|
| 1997 | Shaun Palmer |
| 1998 | Andrew Shandro |

### Skiboarding

| Year | |
|------|--|
| 1998 | Mike Nick |
| 1999 | Chris Hawks |
| 2000 | Neal Lyons |

## Skiing

| Year | Men's Big Air |
|------|---------------|
| 1999 | J.F. Cusson |
| 2000 | Candide Thovex |
| 2001 | Tanner Hall |

| Year | Men's Skier X |
|------|---------------|
| 1998 | Dennis Rey |
| 1999 | Enak Gavaggio |
| 2000 | Shaun Palmer |
| 2001 | Zach Crist |
| 2002 | Reggie Crist |
| 2003 | Lars Lewen |
| 2004 | Casey Puckett |
| 2005 | Reggie Crist |

| Year | Women's Skier X |
|------|-----------------|
| 1999 | Aleisha Cline |
| 2000 | Anik Demers |
| 2001 | Aleisha Cline |
| 2002 | Aleisha Cline |
| 2003 | Aleisha Cline |
| 2004 | Karin Huttary |
| 2005 | Sanna Tidstrand |

| Year | SuperPipe |
|------|-----------|
| 2002 | Jon Olsson |
| 2003 | Candide Thovex |

| Year | Men's SuperPipe |
|------|-----------------|
| 2005 | Simon Dumont |

| Year | Women's SuperPipe |
|------|-------------------|
| 2005 | Grete Eliassen |

| Year | Women's Downhill |
|------|------------------|
| 1997 | Missy Giove |
| 1998 | Marla Streb |

| Year | Men's Speed |
|------|-------------|
| 1997 | Phil Tintsman |
| 1998 | Jurgen Beneke |

| Year | Men's Slopestyle |
|------|------------------|
| 2002 | Tanner Hall |
| 2003 | Not held |
| 2004 | Simon Dumont |
| 2005 | Charles Gagnier |

| Year | Women's Speed |
|------|---------------|
| 1997 | Cheri Elliott |
| 1998 | Elke Brutsaert |

| Year | Men's Biker X |
|------|---------------|
| 1999 | Steve Peat |
| 2000 | Myles Rockwell |

| Year | Women's Biker X |
|------|-----------------|
| 1999 | Tara Llanes |
| 2000 | Katrina Miller |

### Moto X

| Year | Big Air |
|------|---------|
| 2001 | Mike Jones |
| 2002 | Brian Deegan |
| Year | Best Trick |
| 2004 | Caleb Wyatt |

### Ultracross

| Year | |
|------|--|
| 2000 | McLain/Lind |
| 2001 | Palmer/Takizawa |
| 2002 | Wescott/Lind |
| 2003 | Delerue/Zackrisson |
| 2004 | Holland/Crist |
| 2005 | Huser/Andersson |

## Snowboarding

| Year | Men's Big Air |
|------|---------------|
| 1997 | Jimmy Halopoff |
| 1998 | Jason Borgstede |
| 1999 | Kevin Sansalone |
| 2000 | Peter Line |
| 2001 | Jussi Oksanen |

| Year | Women's Big Air |
|------|-----------------|
| 1997 | Barrett Christy |
| 1998 | Tina Basich |
| 1999 | Barrett Christy |
| 2000 | Tara Dakides |
| 2001 | Tara Dakides |

| Year | Men's Boarder X |
|------|-----------------|
| 1997 | Shaun Palmer |
| 1998 | Shaun Palmer |
| 1999 | Shaun Palmer |
| 2000 | Drew Neilson |
| 2001 | Scott Gaffney |
| 2002 | Philippe Conte |
| 2003 | Ueli Kestenholz |
| 2004 | Ueli Kestenholz |
| 2005 | Xavier de le Rue |

| Year | Women's Boarder X |
|------|-------------------|
| 1997 | Jennie Waara |
| 1998 | Tina Dixon |
| 1999 | Maelle Ricker |
| 2000 | Leslee Olson |
| 2001 | Line Oestvold |
| 2002 | Ine Poetzl |
| 2003 | Lindsey Jacobellis |
| 2004 | Lindsey Jacobellis |
| 2005 | Lindsey Jacobellis |

| Year | Men's Slopestyle |
|------|------------------|
| 1997 | Daniel Franck |
| 1998 | Ross Powers |
| 1999 | Peter Line |
| 2000 | Kevin Jones |
| 2001 | Kevin Jones |
| 2002 | Travis Rice |
| 2003 | Shaun White |
| 2004 | Shaun White |
| 2005 | Shaun White |

| Year | Men's Halfpipe |
|------|----------------|
| 1997 | Todd Richards |
| 1998 | Ross Powers |
| 1999 | Jimi Scott |
| 2000 | Todd Richards |

| Year | Women's Halfpipe |
|------|------------------|
| 1997 | Shannon Dunn |
| 1998 | Cara-Beth Burnside |
| 1999 | Michele Taggart |
| 2000 | S. Brun Kjeldaas |

| Year | Women's Slopestyle |
|------|--------------------|
| 1997 | Barrett Christy |
| 1998 | Jennie Waara |
| 1999 | Tara Dakides |
| 2000 | Tara Dakides |
| 2001 | Jaime MacLeod |
| 2002 | Tara Dakide |
| 2003 | Janna Meyen |
| 2004 | Janna Meyen |
| 2005 | Janna Meyen |

| Year | Men's Superpipe |
|------|-----------------|
| 2001 | Dan Kass |
| 2002 | J.J. Thomas |
| 2003 | Shaun White |
| 2004 | Steve Fisher |
| 2005 | Antti Autti |

| Year | Women's Superpipe |
|------|-------------------|
| 2001 | Shannon Dunn |
| 2002 | Kelly Clark |
| 2003 | Gretchen Bleiler |
| 2004 | Hannah Teter |
| 2005 | Gretchen Bleiler |

## Snomobiling

| Year | Snocross |
|------|----------|
| 1998 | Toni Haikonen |
| 1999 | Chris Vincent |
| 2000 | Tucker Hibbert |
| 2001 | Blair Morgan |
| 2002 | Blair Morgan |
| 2003 | Not held |
| 2004 | Michael Island |
| 2005 | Blair Morgan |

| Year | Hillcross |
|------|-----------|
| 2001 | Carl Kuster |
| 2002 | Carl Kuster |
| 2003 | T.J. Kullas |
| 2003 | Mike Metzger |
| 2004 | Levi LaVallee |

## Great Outdoor Games

**Sites:** Lake Placid (2000-02); Reno-Tahoe, Nev. (2003); Madison, Wis. (2004); Orlando, Fla. (2005).

### Fishing

| Year | Flyfishing |
|------|------------|
| 2000 | Tom Rowland |
| 2001 | Chuck Farneth |
| 2002 | Peter Erickson |
| 2003 | Lance Egan |
| 2004 | Lance Egan |

| Year | Flycasting |
|------|------------|
| 2002 | Carter Andrews |
| 2003 | Mike McFarland |
| 2004 | John Wilson |

| Year | Bass Fishing |
|------|--------------|
| 2000 | Peter Thliveros |
| 2001 | Peter Thliveros |
| 2002 | Shaw Grigsby |
| 2003 | S. Grigsby & G. Klein |
| 2004 | M. Gofron & D. Brauer |

### Target Sports

| Year | Rifle |
|------|-------|
| 2000 | Bob Mastroianni |
| 2001 | Jerry Miculek |
| 2002 | Jerry Miculek |
| 2003 | Doug Koenig |
| 2004 | Mike Cumming |

| Year | Shotgun |
|------|---------|
| 2000 | Doug Fuller |
| 2001 | Dustin Long |
| 2002 | Robbie Purser |
| 2003 | Scott Robertson |
| 2004 | Travis Mears |

| Year | Archery |
|------|---------|
| 2000 | Jackie Caudle |
| 2001 | Randy Hendrix |
| 2002 | Randy Hendrix |
| 2003 | Darren Collins |
| 2004 | Randy Hendrix |
| 2005 | Keith Brown |

### ATV

| Year | Terracross |
|------|------------|
| 2005 | Marty Hart |

| Year | Four Wheel Frenzy |
|------|-------------------|
| 2005 | John Natalie |

### Sporting Dogs

| Year | Retriever Trials |
|------|------------------|
| 2000 | Barry Lyons & Skeet |
| 2001 | Jerry Day & Super Sue |
| 2002 | A. Washburn & Ticket |
| 2003 | Chris Akin & Boomer |
| 2004 | J.P. Jackson & Achilles |

| Year | Big Air |
|------|---------|
| 2000 | Beth Gutteridge & Heidi |
| 2001 | Mike Wallace & Jerry |
| 2002 | Mike Jackson & Little Morgan |
| 2003 | Terry Casey & Skeeter |
| 2004 | Mike Jackson & Little Morgan |
| 2005 | Chris Piacun & Beau |

| Year | Agility (large dogs) |
|------|----------------------|
| 2000 | D. Bommarito & Lacey |
| 2001 | Julie Daniels & Spring |
| 2002 | Olga Chaiko & Luz |
| 2003 | S. Kluever & Ransom |
| 2004 | Marcus Topps & Juice |
| 2005 | Marcus Topps & Juice |

| Year | Superweave (large) |
|------|--------------------|
| 2003 | Ken Fairchild & Echo |
| 2004 | S. Kluever & Ransom |
| 2005 | Marcus Topps & Juice |

| Year | Agility (small dogs) |
|------|----------------------|
| 2001 | Jean LaValley & Taz |
| 2002 | Erin Schaefer & Jag |
| 2003 | C. Frank & Kimie |
| 2004 | Renee King & Hamlet |
| 2005 | Susan Garrett & DeCaff |

| Year | Superweave (small) |
|------|--------------------|
| 2003 | Jean LaValley & Taz |
| 2004 | Not held |

| Year | Disc Drive |
|------|------------|
| 2004 | Tim Gelb & Lock-Eye Razzle |

| Year | Launch |
|------|--------|
| 2005 | Angela Jones & Nestle |

| Year | Hot Zone |
|------|----------|
| 2005 | Ron Watson & Split |

### Timber Events

| Year | Endurance (women) |
|------|-------------------|
| 2000 | Sheree Taylor |
| 2001 | Penny Halvorson |
| 2002 | Sheree Taylor |
| 2003 | Peg Engasser |
| 2004 | Sheree Taylor |
| 2005 | Sheree Taylor |

| Year | Endurance (men) |
|------|-----------------|
| 2000 | Jason Wynyard |
| 2001 | Jason Wynyard |
| 2002 | Matt Bush |
| 2003 | Jason Wynyard |
| 2004 | Jason Wynyard |
| 2005 | Dion Lane |

| Year | Hot Saw |
|------|---------|
| 2000 | Harry Burnsworth |
| 2001 | Mel Lentz |
| 2002 | Mike Sullivan |
| 2003 | Mike Sullivan |
| 2004 | Matt Bush |
| 2005 | Harry Burnsworth |

| Year | Springboard |
|------|-------------|
| 2000 | Mitch Hewitt |
| 2001 | Mitch Hewitt |
| 2002 | Mitch Hewitt |
| 2003 | Dave Bolstad |
| 2004 | Dale Ryan |

| Year | Boom Run (men) |
|------|----------------|
| 2000 | J.R. Salzman |
| 2001 | J.R. Salzman |
| 2002 | Jamie Fischer |
| 2003 | Jamie Fischer |
| 2004 | J.R. Salzman |
| 2005 | Jamie Fischer |

| Year | Boom Run (women) |
|------|------------------|
| 2000 | Tina Salzman |
| 2001 | Mandy Erdmann |
| 2002 | Mandy Erdmann |
| 2003 | Abby Hoschler |
| 2004 | Mandy Erdmann |
| 2005 | Mandy Erdmann |

| Year | Boom Run (mixed) |
|------|------------------|
| 2003 | Jamie Fischer & Tanya Fischer |
| 2004 | J.R. Salzman & Shana Martin |

| Year | Log Rolling (men) |
|------|-------------------|
| 2000 | J.R. Salzman |
| 2001 | J.R. Salzman |
| 2002 | Darren Hudson |
| 2003 | Jamie Fischer |
| 2004 | J.R. Salzman |
| 2005 | J.R. Salzman |

| Year | Log Rolling (women) |
|------|---------------------|
| 2000 | Tina Salzman |
| 2001 | Tina Salzman |
| 2002 | Tina Bosworth |
| 2003 | Tina Bosworth |
| 2004 | Tina Bosworth |
| 2005 | Lizzie Hoeschler |

| Year | Speed Climbing |
|------|----------------|
| 2000 | Wade Stewart |
| 2001 | Brian Bartow |
| 2002 | Brian Bartow |
| 2003 | Brian Bartow |
| 2004 | Wade Stewart |
| 2005 | Brian Bartow |

| Year | Tree Topping |
|------|--------------|
| 2000 | Mick Lee |
| 2001 | Gregg Hart |
| 2002 | Wade Stewart |
| 2003 | Greg Hart |
| 2004 | Brian Bartow |

| Year | Team Relay |
|------|------------|
| 2001 | Team Halvorson |
| 2002 | Team Clarke |
| 2003 | Team Wynard |
| 2004 | Team Zalewski |
| 2005 | Team USA East |

| Year | SuperJack |
|------|-----------|
| 2005 | Cassidy Scheer |

## YACHTING

### The America's Cup

International yacht racing was launched in 1851 when England's Royal Yacht Squadron staged a 60-mile regatta around the Isle of Wight and offered a silver trophy to the winner. The 101-foot schooner *America*, sent over by the New York Yacht Club, won the race and the prize. Originally called the Hundred-Guinea Cup, the trophy was renamed The America's Cup after the winning boat's owners deeded it to the NYYC with instructions to defend it whenever challenged.

From 1870-1980, the NYYC successfully defended the Cup 25 straight times; first in large schooners and J-class boats that measured up to 140 feet in overall length, then in 12-meter boats. A foreign yacht finally won the Cup in 1983 when *Australia II* beat defender *Liberty* in the seventh and deciding race off Newport, R.I. Four years later, the San Diego Yacht Club's *Stars & Stripes* won the Cup back, sweeping the four races of the final series off Fremantle, Australia.

Then in 1988, New Zealand's Mercury Bay Boating Club, unwilling to wait the usual three- to four-year period between Cup defenses, challenged the SDYC to a match race, citing the Cup's 102-year-old Deed of Gift, which clearly stated that every challenge had to be honored. Mercury Bay announced it would race a 133-foot monohull. San Diego countered with a 60-foot catamaran. The resulting best-of-three series (Sept. 7-8) was a mismatch as the SDYC's catamaran *Stars & Stripes* won two straight by margins of better than 18 and 21 minutes. Mercury Bay syndicate leader Michael Fay protested the outcome and took the SDYC to court in New York State (where the Deed of Gift was first filed) claiming San Diego had violated the spirit of the deed by racing a catamaran instead of a monohull. N.Y. State Supreme Court judge Carmen Ciparick agreed and on March 28, 1989, ordered the SDYC to hand the Cup over to Mercury Bay. The SDYC refused, but did consent to the court's appointment of the New York Yacht Club as custodian of the Cup until an appeal was ruled on.

On Sept. 19, 1989, the Appellate Division of the N.Y. Supreme Court overturned Ciparick's decision and awarded the Cup back to the SDYC. An appeal by Mercury Bay was denied by the N.Y. Court of Appeals on April 26, 1990, ending three years of legal wrangling. To avoid the chaos of 1988-90, a new class of boat—75-foot monohulls with 110-foot masts—has been used by all competing countries since 1992. Note that (*) indicates skipper was also owner of the boat.

The America's Cup moved to Europe for the first time when the Swiss Alinghi Team beat Team New Zealand, 5-0, in the best-of-nine series in February and March 2003. The dates and location of the next America's Cup races are to be determined.

### Schooners And J-Class Boats

| Year | Winner | Skipper | Series | Loser | Skipper |
|------|--------|---------|--------|-------|---------|
| 1851 | *America* | Richard Brown | — | — | — |
| 1870 | *Magic* | Andrew Comstock | 1-0 | *Cambria*, GBR | J. Tannock |
| 1871 | *Columbia* (2-1) | Nelson Comstock | 4-0 | *Livonia*, GBR | J.R. Woods |
| | & *Sappho* (2-0) | Sam Greenwood | | | |
| 1876 | *Madeleine* | Josephus Williams | 2-0 | *Countess of Dufferin*, CAN | J.E. Ellsworth |
| 1881 | *Mischief* | Nathanael Clock | 2-0 | *Atalanta*, CAN | Alexander Cuthbert* |
| 1885 | *Puritan* | Aubrey Crocker | 2-0 | *Genesta*, GBR | John Carter |
| 1886 | *Mayflower* | Martin Stone | 2-0 | *Galatea*, GBR | Dan Bradford |
| 1887 | *Volunteer* | Henry Haff | 2-0 | *Thistle*, GBR | John Barr |
| 1893 | *Vigilant* | William Hansen | 3-0 | *Valkyrie II*, GBR | Wm. Granfield |
| 1895 | *Defender* | Henry Haff | 3-0 | *Valkyrie III*, GBR | Wm. Granfield |
| 1899 | *Columbia* | Charles Barr | 3-0 | *Shamrock I*, GBR | Archie Hogarth |
| 1901 | *Columbia* | Charles Barr | 3-0 | *Shamrock II*, GBR | E.A. Sycamore |
| 1903 | *Reliance* | Charles Barr | 3-0 | *Shamrock III*, GBR | Bob Wringe |
| 1920 | *Resolute* | Charles F. Adams | 3-2 | *Shamrock IV*, GBR | William Burton |
| 1930 | *Enterprise* | Harold Vanderbilt* | 4-0 | *Shamrock V*, GBR | Ned Heard |
| 1934 | *Rainbow* | Harold Vanderbilt* | 4-2 | *Endeavour*, GBR | T.O.M. Sopwith |
| 1937 | *Ranger* | Harold Vanderbilt* | 4-0 | *Endeavour II*, GBR | T.O.M. Sopwith |

### 12-Meter Boats

| Year | Winner | Skipper | Series | Loser | Skipper |
|------|--------|---------|--------|-------|---------|
| 1958 | *Columbia* | Briggs Cunningham | 4-0 | *Sceptre*, GBR | Graham Mann |
| 1962 | *Weatherly* | Bus Mosbacher | 4-1 | *Gretel*, AUS | Jock Sturrock |
| 1964 | *Constellation* | Bob Bavier & Eric Ridder | 4-0 | *Sovereign*, AUS | Peter Scott |
| 1967 | *Intrepid* | Bus Mosbacher | 4-0 | *Dame Pattie*, AUS | Jock Sturrock |
| 1970 | *Intrepid* | Bill Ficker | 4-1 | *Gretel II*, AUS | Jim Hardy |
| 1974 | *Courageous* | Ted Hood | 4-0 | *Southern Cross*, AUS | John Cuneo |
| 1977 | *Courageous* | Ted Turner | 4-0 | *Australia* | Noel Robins |
| 1980 | *Freedom* | Dennis Conner | 4-1 | *Australia* | Jim Hardy |
| 1983 | *Australia II* | John Bertrand | 4-3 | *Liberty*, USA | Dennis Conner |
| 1987 | *Stars & Stripes* | Dennis Conner | 4-0 | *Kookaburra III*, AUS | Iain Murray |

### 60-ft Catamaran vs 133-ft Monohull

| Year | Winner | Skipper | Series | Loser | Skipper |
|------|--------|---------|--------|-------|---------|
| 1988 | *Stars & Stripes* | Dennis Conner | 2-0 | *New Zealand*, NZE | David Barnes |

### 75-ft International America's Cup Class

| Year | Winner | Skipper | Series | Loser | Skipper |
|------|--------|---------|--------|-------|---------|
| 1992 | *America* [3] | Bill Koch* & Buddy Melges | 4-1 | *Il Moro di Venezia*, ITA | Paul Cayard |
| 1995 | *Black Magic*, NZE | Russell Coutts | 5-0 | *Young America*, USA | Dennis Conner & Paul Cayard |
| 2000 | *Black Magic*, NZE | Russell Coutts & Dean Barker | 5-0 | *Luna Rossa*, ITA | Francesco de Angelis |
| 2003 | *Alinghi*, SWI | Russell Coutts | 5-0 | *New Zealand*, NZE | Dean Barker |

# Deaths

Former World Heavyweight Champ **Max Schmelling** died in 2005 at age 99.

AP/Wide World Photos

Notable deaths in the world of sports from Nov. 1, 2004-Oct. 30, 2005.

**Ted Abernathy, 71;** side-armed reliever who appeared in 681 games and earned 148 saves from 1955-72 with seven major league teams (Washington, Chicago, Cincinnati, Cleveland, Atlanta, St. Louis and Kansas City); twice led the NL in saves during the 1960s with 31 for the Cubs in 1965 and 28 saves with the Reds in 1967; in Gastonia, N.C.; Dec. 18.

**George Archer, 65;** won the 1969 Masters and 11 other PGA Tour titles with his steady putter; proved the golf adage that you "drive for show, but putt for dough," winning more than $10 million in a 40-year pro golf career, playing in nearly a thousand tournaments; won the green jacket, sinking big putts down the stretch to hold off Billy Casper and Tom Weiskopf; after a long battle with Burkitts Lymphoma; in Incline Village, Nev.; Sept. 25.

**Angelo Argea, 75;** longtime caddie for Jack Nicklaus, winning 40 tournaments with the Golden Bear, including the U.S. Open, British Open and PGA Championship from 1963-82; known for his distinctive head of silver hair; of liver cancer, in Canton, Ohio; Oct. 10.

**Doug Ault, 54;** first baseman/DH who hit two home runs in the expansion franchise Toronto Blue Jays very first game in 1977, including the first in club history; career batting average of .236 with 17 home runs in 256 games over a four-year big league career; hit .245 with 11 homers and 65 RBI in his rookie season (1977); of a self-inflicted gunshot wound; in Tarpon Spring, Fla.; Dec. 22, 2004.

**Joe Bauman, 83;** minor league slugger who hit 72 home runs in 1954 for the Roswell (N.M.) Rockets of the Class C Longhorn Leauge; in that famous season, the 6-foot-4, 235-pound Bauman also hit .400 and knocked in 224 runs; his 72 homer organized-baseball single season record stood until Barry Bonds broke it in 2001; never played in the big leagues but hit 337 homers in his nine-year minor league career; of pneumonia; in Roswell, N.M.; Sept. 20.

**Todd Bell, 46;** former Pro Bowl safety for the Chicago Bears; played seven season with the Bears but spent the team's Super Bowl-winning season in 1985 on the injured reserve list; also played for the Philadelphia Eagles moving with the Bears' defensive coordinator Buddy Ryan; prior to the NFL, Bell was a star at Ohio State and was named All-Big Ten in his junior and senior seasons; of a heart attack; in Columbus, Ohio; Mar. 16.

**Colette Besson, 59;** surprise Olympic gold medallist for France at the 1968 Summer Olympics in Mexico City, winning the women's 400-meter dash; coming from behind in the last 50 meters to edge the race favorite, Great Britain's Lillian Board, at the tape; of throat cancer; in La Rochelle, France; Aug. 9.

**Vince Cazzetta, 79;** former head basketball coach at Seattle University (1959-1963); won 96 games in five seasons; later went on to coach the Pittsburgh Pipers of the American Basketball Association, leading them to the ABA title in 1968, winning the ABA Coach of the Year award in the process; also scouted for two NBA teams (Minnesota and Toronto); in Hartford, Conn.; May 4.

**Donn Clendenon, 70;** big-hitting first baseman who helped lead the New York Mets to the 1969 World Series title, hitting three home runs in five games to upset the favored Baltimore Orioles; finished his 12-year big league career with 159 home runs, 1,273 hits and batting average of .274; of leukemia; in Sioux Falls, S.D.; Sept. 17.

**Jason Collier, 28;** 7-foot center for the Atlanta Hawks; drafted in the first round out of Georgia Tech in 2000; averaged 5.6 points and 2.9 rebounds in his five-year NBA career; of a heart attack; in Atlanta, Ga.; Oct. 15.

**Slade Cutter, 93;** All-America tackle at Navy playing three seasons of varsity football; became an instant legend when he kicked the winning field goal in 1934 against Army for a 3-0 victory before a crowd of 79,000 at Philadelphia's Franklin Field, it was Navy's first win against Army in 13 years; won a chest full of medals during World War II as Commanding Officer of the submarine USS Seahorse including four Navy Crosses, two Silver Star, a Bronze Star and a Presidential Unit Citation; inducted into the College Football Hall of Fame in 1967; of heart failure; June 9.

**John D'Amico, 67;** NHL linesman who worked 1,689 regular season games, 247 playoff games including 52 Stanley Cup Finals games; inducted into the Hockey Hall of Fame in 1993; of cancer; in Toronto; May 29.

**Stanley Dancer, 78;** Harness racing hall of fame trainer-driver who won the trotting Triple Crown twice—with Nevele Pride (1968) and Super Bowl (1972) as well as the pacing Triple Crown with Most Happy Fella (1970); following a long illness, in East Rutherford, N.J.; Sept. 8.

**Glenn Davis, 80;** elusive halfback who won the 1946 Heisman Trophy and helped lead Army to three national national titles in the 1940s; shared the Army backfield with fullback Felix "Doc" Blanchard, and became known as "Mr. Outside" to Blanchard's "Mr. Inside"; averaged an amazing 11.5 yards per carry in 1945, setting a record that still stands (and almost certainly always will); scored 59 touchdowns in his collegiate career; later won an NFL championship with the Los Angeles Rams in 1951 before suffering a knee injury in 1952 that prematurely curtailed his career; of prostate cancer; in La Quinta, Calif.; Mar. 9.

**Bernard Diliberto, 73;** New Orleans sports talk show host and commentator who was known for his malaprops, sharp criticism and most famously for originated the custom of Saints fans wearing paper bags on their heads; of a heart attack; in Metairie, La.; Jan. 7.

**Kwane Doster, 21;** Vanderbilt junior running back; three-year letter winner; named the Southeastern Conference's freshman of the year in 2002; in a drive-by shooting; in Tampa, Fla.; Dec. 26, 2004.

**Clarence "Big House" Gaines, 81;** legendary college basketball coach who retired in 1993 after a 47-year career at Div. II Winston-Salem State; amassed 828 wins (828-447) and ranks fifth on the NCAA all-time list behind only Dean Smith, Adolph Rupp, Bob Knight and Jim Phelan; coached future NBA star Earl "The Pearl" Monroe, ESPN's Stephen A. Smith, and, in track, Eugene Walcott (now known as National of Islam Minister Louis Farrakhan), had his best season in 1967 (with Monroe) finishing the year with a 31-1 record and an NCAA title; got his nickname as a 6-foot-5, 265-pound freshman basketball player at Morgan State, when a team manager reportedly told him,

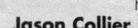

NBA Media

**Jason Collier**

Arena Football League

**Al Lucas**

AP/Wide World Photos

**Clarence "Big House" Gaines**

"the only thing I've seen as big as you is a house;" also was two-time All-American in football at Morgan State; inducted into the Basketball Hall of Fame in 1982; following a stroke; in Winston-Salem, N.C.; Apr. 18

**John R. Gaines, 76;** successful Kentucky thoroughbred and standardbred horse breeder who founded horse racing's Breeders' Cup series in 1984; never owned a Breeders' Cup winner but was part-owner a seven stallions that sired Cup winners; cause of death not reported; in Lexington, Ky.; Feb. 11.

**Prentice Gautt, 67;** running back who walked on at the University of Oklahoma, earning a spot and becoming the first black player in the school's history; later earned a scholarship and was twice named All-Big Eight; named Orange Bowl MVP in 1959; named to the academic All-America team as a senior and went on to earn master's and doctorate degrees in psychology; played in the NFL from 1961-67 with the Cleveland Browns and St. Louis Cardinals; in Lawrence, Kan.; after being hospitalized with flulike symptoms; Mar. 17.

**Alexander Gomelsky, 77;** gold-medal winning Soviet basketball coach whose team ended the 21-game win streak of the United States at the 1988 Summer Olympics; known as the father of Soviet basketball, he also coached the Soviet Olympic team in to a silver medal in 1964, and bronze medals in 1968 and 1980; inducted into the Basketball Hall of Fame in 1995; after a long illness; in Moscow, Russia; Aug. 16.

**Sue Gunter, 66;** longtime college basketball coach at LSU (1982-2004); served as the head coach of the 1980 U.S. Olympic women's basketball team, that never competed due to the Olympic boycott; at LSU, her teams made 14 NCAA appearances and won 442 games in 22 seasons to make her the winningest coach in school history; her career coaching record was 708-308 including stays at Middle Tennessee, Stephen F. Austin and LSU; she was inducted into the Basketball Hall of Fame in 2005; of emphysema; in Baton Rouge, La.; Aug. 4.

**Johnny Haynes, 71;** English soccer star; sharp-passing midfielder who played for England in the 1958 and 1962 World Cups and scored 18 goals in 56 international appearances; captained England's 1962 World Cup team; also played professional soccer with Fulham for 18 years, scoring 145 goals in 594 games; of injuries sustained in a car crash; in Edinburgh, Great Britain; Oct. 18.

**Thomas Herrion, 23;** offensive lineman for the San Francisco 49ers who collapsed in the lockerroom and died following a preseason game with the Denver Broncos; the 6-foot-3, 310-pound guard was a captain at University of Utah in 2003 and was signed as an undrafted free agent by Dallas in 2004 before joining the Niners in 2005; in Denver, Colo.; Aug. 21.

**Sidney "Sonny" Hertzberg, 82;** guard for several NBA teams including the New York Knickerbockers and the Boston Celtics; was a teammate of legendary Knicks coach Red Holzman at CCNY; scored a team-high 14 points for the Knicks for their 1946 home opener; also later served as a scout and assistant coach with New York; in Woodmere, N.Y.; July 26.

**Leavander Johnson, 35;** veteran lightweight boxer who died from injuries sustained in his title fight with Jesus Chavez; lost his title in a 11th round TKO loss to Chavez five days prior to his death; he left the ring under his own power but needed medical attention immediately after the bout and was rushed to the hospital where he underwent brain surgery; in Las Vegas, Nev.; Sept. 22.

**Bill King, 78;** longtime radio announcer for baseball's Oakland Athletics; also once served as play-by-play man for NBA's Golden State Warriors and NFL's Oakland Raiders; called "arguably the most recognizable voice in the history of Bay Arena broadcasting;" from complications following hip surgery; in San Leandro, Calif.; Oct. 18.

**Hal Lebovitz, 89;** hall of fame columnist for several newspapers in the Cleveland area including The News-Herald and The Morning Journal of Lorain; penned the "Ask Hal" column, answering readers' questions about sports; presented with the 1999 J.G. Taylor Spink Award by the Baseball Writers of America; of cancer; in Cleveland; Oct. 18.

**David Little, 46;** Pro Bowl linebacker for the Pittsburgh Steelers in 1990; played 179 games in 12 seasons for the Steelers after being drafted in the seventh round out of Florida in 1981; younger brother to Miami Dolphins All-Pro guard Larry Little; in a weightlifting accident at home; in Miami, Fla.; Mar 17.

**Al Lucas, 26;** Three hundred-pound defensive lineman for the Arena Football League's Los Angeles Avengers; died of an injury sustained in a game against the New York Dragons; during a first-quarter kickoff Lucas bent over to make a tackle and was apparently kicked in the head; he did not move after falling to the ground; also played 20 games in the NFL with the Carolina Panthers in 2000 and 2001; in Los Angeles, Apr. 10.

**Clifton "Coo Coo" Marlin, 73;** one of NASCAR's early stars and the father of Nextel Cup driver Sterling Marlin; of lung cancer; made 165 Winston Cup starts from 1966 to 1980 earning 51 top-10 finishes but no victories; in Columbia, Tenn.; Aug. 14.

**Frank Mangiapane, 79;** veteran college basketball referee in the New York area; was a teammate of Dolph Schayes at NYU that made the NCAA tournament twice; played six games with the original New York Knicks in 1946; of a ruptured abdominal aorta; in Long Beach, N.Y.; July 31.

**Wellington Mara, 89;** hall of fame longtime New York Giants owner, who, along with his brother Jack, in the 1960's, ushered in the NFL current climate of revenue sharing by agreeing to split television rights fees with the rest of the league despite their status as owners of the league's flagship franchise in the nation's largest media market; inducted into the Pro Football Hall of Fame in 1997; of cancer, in Rye, N.Y.; Oct. 25.

**Frank Mathers, 80;** All-Star defenseman with two teams in the AHL and with the NHL's Toronto Maple Leafs; one of two men to be inducted into the Hockey Hall of Fame primarily to his AHL performance where he scored 67 goals and tallied 340 assists in 799 games with the Pittsburgh Hornets and Hershey Bears; won two Calder Cups (1958-59) as a player-coach with Bears; won four more Calder Cups as a coach and team president; the cause of death not reported; in Hershey, Pa.; Feb. 9.

**Bobby Mattick, 89;** managed the Toronto Blue Jays in 1980 and 1981; stayed with the club in scouting and player development; also played 206 big league games from 1938-42; as an outfielder with the Chicago Cubs and Cincinnati Reds, batting .233 with no homers and 64 RBI; following a stroke; in Scottsdale, Ariz.; Dec. 17.

**Gene Mauch, 79;** former Major League manager with four teams (Angels, Phillies, Expos and Twins) over 26 seasons; won 1,901 games—good for 11th all-time; also sixth on all-time list of games managed with 3,938; highly regarded three-time National League Manager of the year who may be best known for his teams' noteworthy collapses; managed the 1986 California Angels to within one strike of the World Series before losing the ALCS to Boston; also managed the 1982 Angels who won the first two games of the then Best-of-Five ALCS, only to lose the final three to Milwaukee; of cancer; in Rancho Mirage, Calif.; Aug. 8.

**James "Banks" McFadden, 88;** All-American football and basketball player at Clemson in 1939 and was named the nation's most versatile athlete; he led the Tigers to a 9-1 record and a win over Boston College in the 1940 Cotton Bowl; he was the fourth overall pick in the 1940 NFL Draft, still the Clemson record for highest pick; played one season with pro football's Brooklyn Dodgers; of cancer; in Ormond Beach, Fla.; June 4.

**Jim McMillin, 91;** won rowing gold for the United States at the 1936 Summer Olympics in Berlin as part of the eight-oared crew from the University of Washington that competed for the USA; teammate of Bob Moch (see below); their boat came from last place to

beat the favored crews from Germany and Italy; cause of death not reported; in Bremerton, Wash.; Aug. 22.

**John McMullen, 87;** former U.S. Navy officer who became owner of the NHL New Jersey Devils and baseball's Houston Astros; bought the NHL Colorado franchise in 1982 and moved it to the Meadowlands where the Devils won two Stanley Cups before he sold the club in 2000 for $175 million; owned the Astros from 1979-92, selling to Drayton McLane Jr. for $115 million; cause of death not reported; in Montclair, N.J.; Sept. 16.

**George Mikan, 80;** hulking center who helped build today's NBA with his considerable talent and wide appeal during the early days of professional basketball; his size and ability enabled the 6-foot-10 Mikan to dominate games and led to numerous rule changes, including the institution of the goaltending rule and widening of the lane; the national college player of the year with DePaul in 1946 he went on to lead the NBA's Minneapolis Lakers to five titles in the franchise's first six years of existence; Mikan led the NBA in scoring three times (1949-52) in rebounding twice (1952-53); following a long battle with diabetes and kidney disease; in Scottsdale, Ariz.; June 2.

**Sam Mills, 45;** five-time Pro Bowl linebacker with New Orleans and Carolina; undersized but skilled player who spent 12 seasons in the NFL after going undrafted out of Montclair (N.J.) State; after failing to make the NFL or CFL initially, he caught on with the upstart USFL and parlayed that into a long pro career; later served as an assistant coach with Carolina; of intestinal cancer; in Charlotte, N.C.; Apr. 18.

**Skip Minisi, 78;** big-play halfback with Pennsylvania and Navy; rushed for a team-high 551 yards and scored eight touchdowns in his freshman year with Penn; made the All-America team in 1947; first round pick by the NFL's New York Giants in 1948, playing one season as a halfback and defensive back; inducted into the College Football Hall of Fame in 1985; in Paoli, Penn.; May 5.

**Bob Moch, 90;** coxswain who won rowing gold for the United States at the 1936 Summer Olympics in Berlin as part of the eight-oared crew from the University of Washington that competed for the USA; teammate of Jim McMillin (see above); their boat came from last place to beat the favored crews from Germany and Italy; after a stroke; in Seattle, Wash.; Jan. 18.

**Cliff Montgomery, 94;** captain and quarterback of Columbia's Rose Bowl-winning team in 1934, pulling off the huge upset to shutout 18-point favorites Stanford, 7-0; "Monty" won the Rose Bowl MVP award; his teams lost only three games in his three Ivy League seasons; played one season of professional football for the Brooklyn Dodgers; was awarded the Silver Star while serving in the Navy during World War II, for saving the lives of 400 sailors at Okinawa in 1945 by bringing his ship alongside a sinking and burning destroyer in heavy seas just before it exploded; elected to the College Footbal Hall of Fame in 1963; he later served as a football official for 30 years, including five Army-Navy games; in Mineola, N.Y.; Apr. 21.

**Johnny Oates, 58;** former big league manager (career record 797-746) and player; who managed the Texas Rangers to the club's first three postseason appearances (1996, 1998, 1999) and shared the manager of the year award with New York's Joe Torre

NFL Media

**Sam Mills**

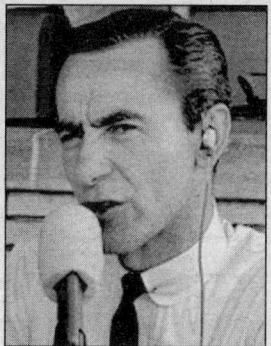

AP/Wide World Photos

**Chris Schenkel**

PBA Tour

**Dick Weber**

in 1996; also managed the Baltimore Orioles from 1991-94; played for five teams in his 11-year major league playing career as a lefthanded hitting catcher; of cancer; in Richmond, Va., Dec. 24, 2004.

**Mickey Owen, 89;** All-Star catcher for the Brooklyn Dodgers; remembered for his strong throwing arm and the game-extending passed ball he allowed in Game 4 of the 1941 World Series against the arch rival New York Yankees; leading 4-3 with no one on base and two outs in the ninth inning, the Yankees outfielder Tommy Henrich swung and missed at strike three from Brooklyn reliever Hugh Casey but Owen couldn't squeeze the ball and Henrich reached first to start a furious Yankees rally; the Dodgers would lose the game, the Series and four more World Series to the Yankees before finally beating them in the Fall Classic in 1955; finished his career with a .255 batting average; from the complications of Alzheimer's disease; in Mount Vernon, Mo.; July 13.

**Michael Park, 39;** European rally car co-driver who was killed during a race when the car he was riding in smashed into a tree; in a car crash; in Wales, Sept. 18.

**Jim Parker, 71;** hall of fame offensive lineman with the Baltimore Colts; first team NFL All-Pro eight times in 11 seasons blocking for Johnny Unitas and Lenny Moore; two-way star at Ohio State in the 1950s; played guard on the offensive line, blocking for legendary halfback Hopalong Cassady; played middle linebacker on defense; was a two-time consensus All-American at guard (1955-56); won the Outland Trophy in 1954 as nation's best interior lineman; inducted into the Pro Football Hall of Fame in 1973 and the College Football Hall of Fame in 1974; his coach at OSU Woody Hayes, called Parker "the best offensive lineman I have ever coached" and presented Parker at his induction into the Hall of Fame; of complications from diabetes; July 18.

**Shawntice Polk, 22;** three-time All-Pac 10 center on the University of Arizona's women's basketball team; the 6-foot-5 Polk led the Pac-10 in blocked shots in 2004-05 helping lead the Wildcats to a 20-12 record and the NCAA tournament; following a collapse at Arizona's McKale Center; in Tucson, Ariz.; Sept. 26.

**Barney Poole, 81;** three-time All-American end at two schools; due to the eligibility rules during World War II, Poole was able to play seven seasons of varsity football at three schools (Mississippi, North Carolina and Army); was named All-America at Army in 1944 and at Ole Miss in 1947 and 1948; known as a prolific receiver and clutch tackler; cause of death not reported; in Mississippi; Apr. 12.

**Dick Radatz, 67;** dominating relief pitcher for the Boston Red Sox in the 1960s; the 6-foot-5 righthander was nicknamed "The Monster" for his size and surly on-mound demeanor; he pitched seven seasons in the majors with five teams, most successfully in Boston; set the major league record for strikeouts in a season by a reliever with 181 in 1964; struck out Mickey Mantle 44 times in 63 meetings; finished his career with a record of 52-43, 122 saves and a 3.13 ERA; in a accidental fall down the stairs at his home; in Easton, Mass.; Mar. 17.

**Ted Radcliffe, 103;** former Negro League star pitcher and catcher, who at the time of his death was believed to be the oldest living professional ballplayer; nicknamed "Double Duty" by sportswriter Damon Runyon after catching Satchel Paige in the first game of a doubleheader and then pitching a shutout in the second game; six-time All-Star (three times as a pitcher and three times as a catcher); of cancer; in Chicago, Ill.; Aug. 11.

**Reggie Roby, 43;** three-time Pro Bowl punter with five NFL teams in a 16-year career; a sixth-round pick out of Iowa by the Miami Dolphins in 1983; became known for wearing a watch during games to time the hang time of his high, booming kicks; had perhaps his best season when he led the AFC with a punting average of 45.7 yards in 1991; in Nashville, Tenn.; Feb. 22.

**Lou Rossini, 84;** coached NYU to the 1960 Final Four and to the NCAA tournament three times overall in the early 1960s; compiled a 185-137 record at NYU and coached five future NBA players including Boston Celtics star Tom "Satch" Sanders; also coached the Puerto Rico at the 1964 Summer Olympics in Tokyo, Columbia and St. Francis (N.Y.) College from 1975-79, finishing his coaching career with a 357-256 record; suffered from Alzheimer's disease and died in his sleep; in Famington, Mich.; Oct. 21.

**Martin Sanchez, 26;** Mexican super lightweight boxer who died from injuries sustained in the ring; was knocked out in the ninth round by Russian Rustam Nugaev in an ESPN Deportes-televised bout but walked out of ring waving to the crowd; underwent emergency brain surgery to remove a subdural hematoma; in Las Vegas, Nev.; July 2.

**Chris Schenkel, 82;** hall of fame and Emmy-winning sportscaster who covered a wide variety of sports and events during his 60-year radio and television career; the smooth baritone's many assignments included the Masters, Indianapolis 500, several Summer Olympics, NFL football and he also had a longtime job as the voice of professional bowling; he called the 1958 NFL Championship game between the Baltimore Colts and New York Giants, considered one of the greatest games in leauge history; the Indiana native was inducted into 16 halls of fame, including the National Sportscaster and Sportswriters hall; after a long battle with emphysema; in Fort Wayne, Ind.; Sept. 11.

**Max Schmelling, 99;** German heavyweight champion who twice fought Joe Louis; as 10-1 underdog he upset the unbeaten Louis on June 19, 1936 knocking him out in the 12th round; his success against Louis in their first meeting was co-opted by the Nazi Party and became part of its Aryan supremacy propaganda; he refused to join the Nazi party and despite pressure he kept his Jewish manager and reportedly used his influence to save Jewish friends from concentration camps; lost his rematch with Louis, getting knocked out in the 1st round; he became the first European world heavyweight champ in 1930 when he beat American Jack Sharkey by disqualification (Sharkey was DQ'd for a low blow); built a long-lasting friendship with Louis after their fighting days; finished his career with a 56-10-4 record and 39 knockouts; when in Hollenstedt, Germany, Feb. 2.

**Doug Schmied, 21;** 6-foot-3, 285-pound senior offensive lineman at Illinois Wesleyan; he became ill at summer practice and later died of heatstroke; in Peoria, Ill.; Aug. 19.

**Jack Stephens, 81;** former chairman of the Masters Tournament and Augusta National Golf Club from 1991 to 1998; a patron of Navy football, the field at Navy Marine Corp Stadium in Annapolis bears his name; cause of death not reported; in Little Rock, Ark.; July 23.

**Hank Stram, 82;** Hall of Fame coach with the Kansas City Chiefs; led the Chiefs to two Super Bowls, winning Super Bowl IV, 23-7, over Minnesota; also coached the Chiefs to AFL titles in 1962, 1966 and 1969; became head coach of the expansion Dallas Texans in 1960 and moved to Kansas City when the team relocated there (and became the Chiefs) in 1963; compiled a 136-100-10 record in 17 seasons with the Chiefs and New Orleans Saints; from complications from diabetes; in Covington, La.; July 4.

**Paul Suzuki, 77;** volunteer official at the U.S. Track and Field Championships, who was killed after being struck in the head by a shot put during a practice session; in Carson, Calif.; June 22.

**Chuck Thompson, 83;** longtime Baltimore radio announcer who called play-by-play for baseball's Orioles and the NFL's Baltimore Colts for decades; known for his deep voice and popular call "Ain't the beer cold!" following a home run or touchdown; received the Baseball Hall of Fame's Ford Frick Award in 1993; macular degeneration took his sight in recent years, cutting short his baseball broadcasting career after 50 years; following a stroke; in Towson, Md.; Mar. 6.

**Dave Velzy, 77;** a surfing pioneer who became the world's largest maker of surfboards; legendary surfers Duke Kahanamoku, George Downing and Mickey Dora rode his boards; of lung cancer, in Mission Viejo, Calif.; May. 26.

**Bob Ward, 77;** two-time All-American lineman at Maryland (1950-51); dominated opponents despite his lack of size for the position, never weighing over 185 pounds; anchored the offensive line on the 1951 undefeated Terrapins that upset top-ranked Tennesse in the Sugar Bowl for Maryland's first national championship; cause of death not reported; in Annapolis, Md.; Apr. 29.

**Dick Weber, 75;** Hall of fame bowler who won 26 PBA Tour and six Senior Tour events; three-time national bowler of the year (1961, 1963, 1965); elected to the ABC Hall of Fame in 1970 and to the Professional Bowlers Association Hall of Fame in 1975; one of the legends of his sport, Weber had been an ambassador for bowling in recent years; father of current PBA star Pete; in his sleep; in suburban St. Louis, Mo.; Feb. 13.

**Reggie White, 43;** 13-time Pro Bowl NFL defensive end for three teams (Philadelphia, Green Bay and Carolina) in a 16-year NFL career; named the NFL's Defensive Player of the Year in 1987 and 1998; He retired from football after the 2000 season as the NFL's all-time leader in sacks with 198 (since passed by Bruce Smith); an All-American senior season at the University of Tennessee, White started his pro career in 1984 with the upstart USFL's Memphis Showboats. He would join the NFL's Philadelphia Eagles after the USFL folded in 1985; he signed as a free agent with Green Bay in 1993 and, along with quarterback Brett Favre, helped lead the Packers to two Super Bowls, including a win over New England in Super Bowl XXXI; retired after the 1998 season but returned for a final season in the NFL with the Carolina Panthers in 2000; also an ordained minister; his image was tarnished somewhat in 1998 when he gave a speech to the Wisconsin Legislature and denounced homosexuality and used ethnic stereotypeshe; he later apologized; from cardiac arrhythmia caused by sarcoidosis; in Huntersville, N.C.; Dec. 26, 2004.

**Al Widmar, 80;** former pitching coach for the Toronto Blue Jays (1979-89); players the he coached include Dave Steib, Doyle Alexander and Jimmy Key; also pitched in 114 major league games himself, posting a 13-30 record and 5.21 ERA; of colon cancer; in Tulsa, Okla.; Oct. 15.

**Charlie Williams, 61;** umpire who became first African-American to work home plate in a World Series game since 1993, calling balls and strikes for Game 4 at Philadelphia's Veterans Stadium; at 4 hours, 14 minutes, the game is the longest in World Series history; also umpired the 1985 and 1995 All-Star Games and the 1989 and 1997 NLCS; of complications from diabetes; in Oak Lawn, Ill.; Sept. 10.

**Sergei Zholtok, 31;** NHL center who played 588 games from 1992-2004 with six teams (Boston Bruins, Ottawa Senators, Montreal Canadiens, Edmonton Oilers, Minnesota Wild and Nashville Predators); scored 111 goals and added 147 assists in his career; played for Latvia's Riga 2000 during the NHL lockout where he left a game and collapsed and died on his way to the lockerroom; and of a heart ailment; in Latvia; Nov. 3, 2004.

# *Updates*

**Saint Liam** and jockey **Jerry Bailey** won
the $4 million Breeders' Cup Classic at Belmont.

AP/Wide World Photos

## AUTO RACING

## Late 2005 Results
### NASCAR
#### Chase for the Nextel Cup

| Date | Event | Location | Winner (Pos) | Avg.mph | Earnings | Pole | Qual.mph |
|------|-------|----------|--------------|---------|----------|------|----------|
| Oct. 23 | Subway 500 . . . . . . . | Martinsville | Jeff Gordon (15) | 69.695 | $194,926 | T. Stewart | 98.083 |
| Oct. 30 | Bass Pro Shops MBNA 500 | Atlanta | Carl Edwards (2) | 146.834 | 314,700 | R. Newman | 193.928 |

**Winning Cars:** CHEVROLET (1)—Gordon; FORD (1)—Edwards.
**Remaining Races** (3): Dickies 500 in Texas (Nov. 6); Checker Auto Parts 500 in Phoenix (Nov. 13); Ford 400 in Homestead-Miami (Nov. 20).

### Champ Car World Series

| Date | Event | Location | Winner | Time | Avg.mph | Pole | Qual.mph |
|------|-------|----------|--------|------|---------|------|----------|
| Oct. 23 | Lexmark Indy 300 . . . | Queensland | Sebastien Bourdais | 1:39:26.671 | 96.123 | O. Servia | 108.642 |

**Winning Cars:** FORD/LOLA (1)—Bourdais.
**Remaining Race:** Gran Premio de Mexico in Mexico City (Nov. 6).

### NHRA

| Date | | Event | Winner | Time | MPH | 2nd Place | Time | MPH |
|------|--|-------|--------|------|-----|-----------|------|-----|
| Oct. 23 | Las Vegas Nationals . . . | Top Fuel | Tony Schumacher | 4.486 | 327.19 | D. Grubnic | 4.587 | 324.28 |
| | | Funny Car | Ron Capps | 4.780 | 325.69 | G. Scelzi | 4.819 | 324.51 |
| | | Pro Stock | Kurt Johnson | 6.839 | 202.27 | G. Anderson | 6.821 | 202.27 |

**Remaining Event** (1): Automobile Club of Southern California NHRA Finals in Pomona, Cal. (Nov. 3-6).

## GOLF

## Late 2005 Tournament Results
### PGA Tour

| Last Rd | Tournament | Winner | Earnings | Runner-Up |
|---------|-----------|--------|----------|-----------|
| Oct. 16 | Michelin Championship at Las Vegas. . . | Wes Short Jr. (266)* | $720,000 | J. Furyk (266) |
| Oct. 23 | Funai Classic at Walt Disney World . . . | Lucas Glover (265) | 792,000 | T. Pernice Jr. (266) |
| Oct. 30 | Chrysler Championship . . . . . . . . . . . | Carl Pettersson (275) | 954,000 | C. Campbell (276) |

***Playoffs: Michelin**—Short won on the second hole.
**Remaining Events** (8): Southern Farm Bureau Classic (Nov. 3-6); The Tour Championship (Nov. 3-6); Franklin Templeton Shootout (Nov. 10-13); Tommy Bahama Challenge (Nov. 8); World Golf Championships: Algarve World Cup (Nov. 17-20); Merrill Lynch Skins Game (Nov. 26-27); Bard Capital Challenge (Nov. 28-Dec. 4); PGA Tour Qualifying Tournament (Nov. 29-Dec. 5); Target World Challenge (Dec. 8-11).
**Note:** The Tour Championship (Nov. 3-6) is the final official PGA Tour event of 2005.

### European PGA Tour

| Last Rd | Tournament | Winner | Earnings | Runner-Up |
|---------|-----------|--------|----------|-----------|
| Oct. 16 | Open de Madrid. . . . . . . . . . . . . . . . | Raphael Jacquelin (261) | E 166,660 | P. Lawrie (264) |
| Oct. 23 | Mallorca Classic . . . . . . . . . . . . . . . | Jose Maria Olazabal (270) | 250,000 | 3-way tie (275) |
| Oct. 30 | Volvo Masters Valderrama . . . . . . . . . . | Paul McGinley (274) | 666,660 | S. Garcia (276) |

**Second place ties** (three players or more): **Mallorca** (S. Garcia, J.M. Lara and P. Broadhurst).
**Remaining Event:** World Golf Championships: Algarve World Cup (Nov. 17-20).

### Champions Tour

| Last Rd | Tournament | Winner | Earnings | Runner-Up |
|---------|-----------|--------|----------|-----------|
| Oct. 16 | Administaff Small Business Classic. . . . . | Mark McNulty (200) | $240,000 | G. Morgan (201) |
| Oct. 23 | SBC Championship . . . . . . . . . . . . . . | Jay Haas (199) | 232,000 | T. Purtzer (201) |
| Oct. 30 | Charles Schwab Cup Championship . . . | Tom Watson (272 | 440,000 | J. Haas (273)) |

**Remaining Events** (3): UBS Cup (Nov. 14-20); Father-Son Challenge (Dec. 3-4); Wendy's Three-Tour Challenge (Dec. 17-18).

### LPGA Tour

| Last Rd | Tournament | Winner | Earnings | Runner-Up |
|---------|-----------|--------|----------|-----------|
| Oct. 16 | Samsung World Championship. . . . . . . | Annika Sorenstam (270) | $212,500 | P. Creamer (278) |
| Oct. 30 | CJ Nine Bridges Classic. . . . . . . . . . . . | Jee Youn Lee (211) | 202,500 | C. Koch & M-H Kim (214) |

**Remaining Events** (4): Mizuno Classic (Nov. 4-6); Mitchell Company Tournament of Champions (Nov. 10-13); ADT Championship (Nov. 17-20); Wendy's Three-Tour Challenge (Dec. 17-18).

## TENNIS

# Late 2005 Tournament Results
## Men's Tour

| Finals | Tournament | Winner | Earnings | Loser | Score |
|---|---|---|---|---|---|
| Oct. 16 | Kremlin Cup (Moscow) | Igor Andreev | $142,000 | N. Kiefer | 57 76 62 |
| Oct. 16 | BA-CA Tennis Trophy (Vienna) | Ivan Ljubicic | 108,600 | J.C. Ferrero | 62 64 76 |
| Oct. 16 | Stockholm Open | James Blake | 96,000 | P. Srichaphan | 61 76 |
| Oct. 24 | TMS—Madrid | Rafael Nadal | 450,000 | I. Ljubicic | 36 26 63 64 76 |
| Oct. 30 | St. Petersburg Open | Thomas Johansson | 142,000 | N. Kiefer | 64 62 |
| Oct. 30 | Swiss Indoors (Basel) | Fernando Gonzalez | 145,000 | M. Baghdatis | 67 63 75 64 |
| Oct. 30 | Grand Prix of Tennis (Lyon) | Andy Roddick | 115,000 | G. Monfils | 63 62 |

**Remaining Events** (3): BNP Paribas Paris Masters (Nov. 6); Tennis Masters Cup Shanghai (Nov. 20); Davis Cup Final (Dec. 4).

## Women's Tour

| Finals | Tournament | Winner | Earnings | Loser | Score |
|---|---|---|---|---|---|
| Oct. 16 | Kremlin Cup (Moscow) | Mary Pierce | $189,000 | F. Schiavone | 64 63 |
| Oct. 16 | Thailand Open (Bangkok) | Nicole Vaidisova | 30,500 | N. Petrova | 61 67 75 |
| Oct. 23 | Zurich Open | Lindsay Davenport | 189,000 | P. Schnyder | 76 63 |
| Oct. 30 | Gaz De France Stars (Hasselt, Belgium) | Kim Clijsters | 26,650 | F. Schiavone | 62 63 |
| Oct. 30 | Generali Open (Linz) | Nadia Petrova | 93,000 | P. Schnyder | 46 63 61 |

**Remaining Events** (3): Advanta Championships (Nov. 6); Bell Challenge (Nov. 6); WTA Tour Championships (Nov. 13).

## THOROUGHBRED RACING

# Late 2005 Major Stakes Races

| Date | Race | Location | Miles | Winner | Jockey | Purse |
|---|---|---|---|---|---|---|
| Oct. 1 | Vosburgh Stakes | Belmont | 6 F | Taste of Paradise | Garrett Gomez | $ 500,000 |
| Oct. 1 | Beldame Stakes | Belmont | 1 1/8 | Ashado | John Velazquez | 750,000 |
| Oct. 1 | Flower Bowl Invitational | Belmont | 1 1/4 (T) | Riskaverse | Jose Santos | 750,000 |
| Oct. 1 | Joe Hirsch Turf Classic Invit. | Belmont | 1 1/2 (T) | Shakespeare | Jerry Bailey | 750,000 |
| Oct. 1 | Jockey Club Gold Cup | Belmont | 1 1/4 | Borrego | Garrett Gomez | 1,000,000 |
| Oct. 1 | Yellow Ribbon Stakes | Santa Anita | 1 1/4 (T) | Megahertz | Alex Solis | 500,000 |
| Oct. 1 | Oak Leaf Stakes | Santa Anita | 1 1/16 | Diamond Omi | David Flores | 200,000 |
| Oct. 2 | Goodwood B.C. Handicap | Santa Anita | 1 1/8 | Rock Hard Ten | Gary Stevens | 484,000 |
| Oct. 2 | Lady's Secret BC Handicap | Santa Anita | 1 1/16 | Healthy Addiction | Garrett Gomez | 250,000 |
| Oct. 2 | Clement L. Hirsch Turf Championship Stakes | Santa Anita | 1 1/4 (T) | Fourty Niners Son | Corey Nakatami | 250,000 |
| Oct. 2 | Norfolk Stakes | Santa Anita | 1 1/16 | Brother Derek | Alex Solis | 200,000 |
| Oct. 2 | Prix de l'Arc de Triomphe* | Longchamp | 1 1/2 (T) | Hurricane Run (IRE) | K.F. Fallon | E 1,800,000 |
| Oct. 2 | Kelso Handicap | Belmont | 1 (T) | Artie Schiller | Edgar Prado | 350,000 |
| Oct. 7 | Darley Alcibiades Stakes | Keeneland | 1 1/16 | She Says It Best | Eddie Martin Jr. | 400,000 |
| Oct. 8 | Phoenix B.C. Stakes | Keeneland | 6 F | Elusive Jazz | Robby Albarado | 250,000 |
| Oct. 8 | Frizette Stakes | Belmont | 1 1/16 | Adieu | John Velazquez | 500,000 |
| Oct. 8 | Champagne Stakes | Belmont | 1 1/16 | First Samurai | Jerry Bailey | 500,000 |
| Oct. 8 | Oak Tree B.C. Mile | Santa Anita | 1 (T) | Singletary | David Flores | 249,000 |
| Oct. 8 | Ancient Title B.C. Handicap | Santa Anita | 6 F | Captain Squire | Alex Solis | 250,000 |
| Oct. 8 | Lane's End Futurity Stakes | Keeneland | 1 1/16 | Dawn of War | John Jacinto | 500,000 |
| Oct. 9 | Shadwell Turf Mile | Keeneland | 1 (T) | Host | Rafael Bejarano | 600,000 |
| Oct. 9 | WinStar Galaxy Stakes | Keeneland | 1 1/16 (T) | Intercontinental | Jerry Bailey | 400,000 |
| Oct. 9 | Juddmonte Spinster Stakes | Keeneland | 1 1/8 | Pampered Princess | Eddie Castro | 500,000 |
| Oct. 15 | Oak Tree Derby | Santa Anita | 1 1/8 | Aragorn | Patrick Valenzuela | 150,000 |
| Oct. 15 | QE II Challenge Cup | Keeneland | 1 1/8 (T) | Sweet Talker | Rafael Bejarano | 500,000 |
| Oct. 15 | My Dear Girl Stakes | Calder | 1 1/16 | Consider Thesource | Sebastian Madrid | 400,000 |
| Oct. 15 | In Reality Stakes | Calder | 1 1/16 | Blazing Rate | Cecilio Penalba | 400,000 |
| Oct. 22 | Empire Classic Handicap | Belmont | 1 1/8 | Spite the Devil | Javier Castellano | 250,000 |
| Oct. 23 | Nearctic Handicap | Woodbine | 6 F (T) | Steel Light | Corey Nakatani | 500,000 |
| Oct. 23 | E.P. Taylor Stakes | Woodbine | 1 1/4 (T) | Honey Ryder | John Velazquez | 1,000,000 |
| Oct. 23 | Canadian International* | Woodbine | 1 1/2 (T) | Relaxed Gesture (IRE) | Corey Nakatani | 2,000,000 |
| Oct. 29 | Breeders' Cup - Distaff | Belmont | 1 1/8 | Pleasant Home | Cornelio Velazquez | 2,000,000 |
| Oct. 29 | Breeders' Cup - Juv. Fillies | Belmont | 1 1/16 | Folklore | Edgar Prado | 1,060,000 |
| Oct. 29 | Breeders' Cup - Mile | Belmont | 1 (T) | Artie Schiller | Garrett Gomez | 1,856,925 |
| Oct. 29 | Breeders' Cup - Sprint | Belmont | 6 F | Silver Train | Edgar Prado | 1,000,000 |
| Oct. 29 | Breeders' Cup - F&M Turf | Belmont | 1 1/4 (T) | Intercontinental | Rafael Bejarano | 1,060,000 |
| Oct. 29 | Breeders' Cup - Juvenile | Belmont | 1 1/16 | Stevie Wonderboy | Garrett Gomez | 1,590,000 |
| Oct. 29 | Breeders' Cup - Turf* | Belmont | 1 1/2 (T) | Shirocco (FRA) | Christophe Soumillon | 2,090,760 |
| Oct. 29 | Breeders' Cup - Classic* | Belmont | 1 1/4 | Saint Liam | Jerry Bailey | 4,680,000 |

*World Series Racing Championship race.

## HARNESS RACING
### Late 2005 Major Stakes Races

| Date | Race | Raceway | Winner | Driver | Purse |
|------|------|---------|--------|--------|-------|
| Oct. 1 | **Kentucky Futurity** | Lexington | Strong Yankee | Brian Sears | $391,000 |

**Note:** Strong Yankee won the first heat in 1:50.6, and Vivid Photo won the second in 1:52.2 to force the race-off in harness racing's final Triple Crown race.

## BOWLING
### Late 2004 Results
#### PBA

| Final | Event | Winner | Earnings | Final | Runner-Up |
|-------|-------|--------|----------|-------|-----------|
| Sept. 20 | Japan Cup | Tommy Jones | $50,000 | 222-215 | Norm Duke |
| Oct. 30 | Tulsa Championship | Tommy Jones | 40,000 | 289-248 | Wes Malott |

**Remaining 2005 Events:** see the PBA Tour schedule on page 761.

## SOCCER

### Major League Soccer Playoffs

| **Eastern Conference** | **Western Conference** |
|---|---|
| **Semifinals** (Total Goals) | **Semifinals** (Total Goals) |

**New England Revolution vs. MetroStars**

| Oct. 22 | at MetroStars 1 | New England 0 |
|---|---|---|
| Oct. 29 | at New England 3 | MetroStars 1 |

Revolution advances on aggregate, 3-2

**D.C. United vs. Chicago Fire**

| Oct. 23 | D.C. United 0 | at Chicago 0 |
|---|---|---|
| Oct. 30 | Chicago 4 | at D.C. United 0 |

Chicago advances on aggregate, 4-0

**FC Dallas vs. Colorado Rapids**

| Oct. 22 | at Colorado 0 | Dallas 0 |
|---|---|---|
| Oct. 29 | at Dallas 2 | Colorado 2 |

Aggregate tied, 2-2. Colorado advances, 5-4, on PKs

**Los Angeles Galaxy vs. San Jose Earthquakes**

| Oct. 23 | at Los Angeles 3 | San Jose 1 |
|---|---|---|
| Oct. 29 | at San Jose 1 | Los Angeles 1 |

Los Angeles advances on aggregate, 4-2

**Finals** (Single Elimination)

Chicago Fire at New England

**Finals** (Single Elimination)

Colorado vs. Los Angeles

**MLS Cup 2005**
Nov. 13 at Pizza Hut Park
Frisco, Texas

## RESEARCH MATERIAL

Many sources were used in the gathering of information for this almanac. Day-to-day material was almost always found in copies of *USA Today*, *The Boston Globe*, and *The South Florida Sun-Sentinel* or online at various World Wide Web addresses (see below).

Several weekly and bi-weekly periodicals were also used in the past year's pursuit of facts and figures, among them— *Baseball America*, *ESPN the Magazine*, *The NCAA News*, *Soccer America*, *Sports Illustrated*, *The Sporting News*, *Street & Smith's Sports Business Journal*, *Track & Field News* and *USA Today Baseball Weekly*.

In addition, the following books provided background material for one or more chapters of the almanac.

### Arenas & Ballparks

**The Ballparks**, by Bill Shannon and George Kalinsky; Hawthorn Books, Inc. (1975); New York.

**Diamonds**, by Michael Gershman; Houghton Mifflin Co. (1993); Boston.

**Green Cathedrals** (Revised Edition), by Philip Lowry; Addison-Wesley Publishing Co. (1992); Reading, Mass.

**The NFL's Encyclopedic History of Professional Football**, Macmillan Publishing Co. (1977); New York.

**Take Me Out to the Ballpark**, by Lowell Reidenbaugh; The Sporting News Publishing Co. (1983); St. Louis.

**24 Seconds to Shoot** (An Informal History of the NBA), by Leonard Koppett; Macmillan Publishing Co. (1968); New York.

### Auto Racing

**Indy: 75 Years of Racing's Greatest Spectacle**, by Rich Taylor; St. Martin's Press (1991); New York.

**2003 CART FedEx Championship Series Media Guide**; Championship Auto Racing Teams; Troy, Mich.

**2003 Indy Racing League Media Guide**, by IMS Publications; Indianapolis.

**2003 NASCAR Winston Cup Series Media Guide**, compiled and edited by Sports Marketing Enterprises; NASCAR Winston Cup Series; Winston-Salem, N.C.

**Marlboro Grand Prix Guide**, 1950-1998 (1999 Edition), compiled by Jacques Deschenaux and Claude Michele Deschenaux; Charles Stewart & Company Ltd; Brentford, England.

NASCAR Online, produced by Turner Sports Interactive, http://www.nascar.com

CART Online, maintained by CART and VFX Digital Solutions, http://www.cart.com

Indy Racing Online, maintained by IRL, http://www.indyracingleague.com

NHRA Online, maintained by NHRA, http://www.nhra.com

### Baseball

**The All-Star Game** (A Pictorial History, 1933 to Present), by Donald Honig; The Sporting News Publishing Co. (1987); St. Louis.

**The Baseball Chronology**, edited by James Charlton; Macmillan Publishing Co. (1991); New York.

**The Baseball Encyclopedia** (Ninth Edition), editorial director, Rick Wolff; Macmillan Publishing Co. (1993); New York.

**The Complete 2002 Baseball Record Book**, edited by Craig Carter; The Sporting News Publishing Co.; St. Louis.

**The Scrapbook History of Baseball** by Jordan Deutsch, Richard Cohen, Roland Johnson and David Neft; Bobbs-Merrill Company, Inc. (1975); Indianapolis/New York.

**2002 Sporting News Official Baseball Guide**, edited by Craig Carter and Dave Sloan; The Sporting News Publishing Co.; St. Louis.

**2002 Sporting News Official Baseball Register**, edited by Jeff Paur, David Walton, John Duxbury; The Sporting News Publishing Co.; St. Louis.

**The Sports Encyclopedia: Baseball** (1996 Edition), edited by David Neft and Richard Cohen; St. Martin's Press; New York.

**Total Baseball** (Seventh Edition), edited by John Thorn, Pete Palmer and Michael Gershman; Total Sports Publishing (2001); Kingston, N.Y.

The Official Site of Major League Baseball, produced by Major League Baseball Properties, Inc., http://www.mlb.com

### College Basketball

**All the Moves** (A History of College Basketball), by Neil D. Issacs; J.B. Lippincott Company (1975); New York.

**College Basketball, U.S.A.** (Since 1892), by John D. McCallum; Stein and Day (1978); New York.

**Collegiate Basketball: Facts and Figures on the Cage Sport**, by Edwin C. Caudle; The Paragon Press (1960); Montgomery, Ala.

**The Encyclopedia of the NCAA Basketball Tournament**, written and compiled by Jim Savage; Dell Publishing (1990); New York.

**The Final Four** (Reliving America's Basketball Classic), compiled by Billy Reed; Host Communications, Inc. (1988); Lexington, Ky.

**2000 NCAA Final Four Records Book**, compiled by Gary Johnson; edited by Marty Benson; NCAA Books; Indianapolis.

**The Modern Encyclopedia of Basketball** (Second Revised Edition), edited by Zander Hollander; Dolphins Books (1979); Doubleday & Company, Inc.; Garden City, N.Y.

**2000 NCAA Men's Records Book**, compiled by Gary Johnson and Sean Straziscar; edited by Marty Benson; NCAA Books; Indianapolis.

**2000 NCAA Women's Records Book**, compiled by Richard M. Campbell and Jenifer L. Scheibler; edited by Vanessa L. Abell; NCAA Books; Indianapolis.

NCAA Online, produced by National Collegiate Athletic Association, http://www.ncaa.org

Plus many 2004-2005 NCAA Division I conference guides from America East to the WAC.

### Pro Basketball

**The Official NBA Basketball Encyclopedia** (Third Edition), edited by Jan Hubbard; Doubleday (2000); New York.

**2002-03 Sporting News Official NBA Guide**; edited by Craig Carter and Rob Reheuser; The Sporting News Publishing Co.; St. Louis.

**2002-03 Sporting News Official NBA Register**, edited by David Walton, John Gardella; The Sporting News Publishing Co.; St. Louis.

NBA Online, produced by NBA Media Ventures, LLC, ESPN Internet Ventures, http://www.nba.com

### Bowling

**1995 Bowlers Journal Annual & Almanac**; Luby Publishing; Chicago.

**2001 PWBA Guide**, Professional Women's Bowling Association; Rockford, Ill.

**2002-03 PBA Tour Media Guide**; Professional Bowlers Association; Seattle, Wash.

PBA Online, produced by the Pro Bowlers Association, http://www.pba.com

### Boxing

**The Boxing Record Book** (1996 Edition), edited by Phill Marder; Fight Fax Inc.; Sicklerville, N.J.

**The Ring 1985 Record Book & Boxing Encyclopedia**, edited by Herbert G. Goldman; The Ring Publishing Corp.; New York.

**The Ring: Boxing, The 20th Century**, Steven Farhood, editor-in-chief; BDD Illustrated Books (1993); New York.

## College Sports

**1994-95 National Collegiate Championships**, edited by Ted Breidenthal; NCAA Books; Overland Park, Kan.
**1999-2000 National Directory of College Athletics**, edited by Kevin Cleary; Collegiate Directories, Inc.; Cleveland.
NCAA Online, produced by National Collegiate Athletic Association, http://www.ncaa.org
NAIA.org, produced by National Association of Intercollegiate Athletics, http://www.naia.org

## College Football

**Football: A College History**, by Tom Perrin; McFarland & Company, Inc. (1987); Jefferson, N.C.
**Football: Facts & Figures**, by Dr. L.H. Baker; Farrar & Rinehart, Inc. (1945); New York.
**Great College Football Coaches of the Twenties and Thirties**, by Tim Cohane; Arlington House (1973); New Rochelle, N.Y.
**2000 NCAA College Football Records Book**, compiled by Richard M. Campbell, John Painter and Sean Straziscar; edited by Scott Deitch; NCAA Books; Indianapolis.
**Saturday Afternoon**, by Richard Whittirigham; Workman Publishing Co., Inc. (1985); New York.
**Saturday's America**, by Dan Jenkins; Sports Illustrated Books; Little, Brown & Company (1970); Boston.
**Tournament of Roses, The First 100 Years**, by Joe Hendrickson; Knapp Press (1989); Los Angeles.
NCAA Online, produced by National Collegiate Athletic Association, http://www.ncaa.org
Plus numerous college football team and conference guides, especially the 2001 guides compiled by the Atlantic Coast Conference, Big Ten, Big 12 and Southeastern Conference.

## Pro Football

**2002 Canadian Football League Guide**, compiled by the CFL Communications Dept.; Toronto.
**The Football Encyclopedia** (The Complete History of NFL Football from 1892 to the Present), compiled by David Neft and Richard Cohen; St. Martin's Press (1994); New York.
**The Official NFL Encyclopedia**, by Beau Riffenburgh; New American Library (1986); New York.
**Official NFL 1999 Record and Fact Book**, compiled by the NFL Communications Dept. and Seymour Siwoff, Elias Sports Bureau; edited by Chris McCloskey and Matt Marini; produced by NFL Properties, Inc.; Los Angeles.
**The Scrapbook History of Pro Football**, by Richard Cohen, Jordan Deutsch, Roland Johnson and David Neft; Bobbs-Merrill Company, Inc. (1976); Indianapolis/New York.
**2003 Sporting News Football Guide**, edited by Craig Carter, Terry Shea and Christen Sager; The Sporting News Publishing Co.; St. Louis.
**2003 Sporting News Football Register**, edited Brendan Roberts; The Sporting News Publishing Co.; St. Louis.
**1995 Sporting News Super Bowl Book**, edited by Tom Dienhart, Joe Hoppel and Dave Sloan; The Sporting News Publishing Co.; St. Louis.
**Total Football II**, edited by Bob Carroll, Michael Gershman, David Neft and John Thorn; HarperCollins; New York.
NFL Online, produced by NFL Enterprises http://www.nfl.com
CFL Online, produced by SLAM! Sports, http://www.cfl.ca

## Golf

**The Encyclopedia of Golf** (Revised Edition), compiled by Nevin H. Gibson; A.S. Barnes and Company (1964); New York.
**Guinness Golf Records: Facts and Champions**, by Donald Steel; Guinness Superlatives Ltd. (1987); Middlesex, England.
**The History of the PGA Tour**, by Al Barkow; Doubleday (1989); New York.
**The Illustrated History of Women's Golf**, by Rhonda Glenn, Taylor Publishing Co. (1991); Dallas.

**2003 LPGA Player Guide**, produced by LPGA Communications Dept.; Ladies Professional Golf Assn. Tour; Daytona Beach, Fla.
**2003 PGA Tour Guide**, written and edited by Chuck Adams, James Cramer, Nelson Luis and Lee Patterson; Professional Golfers Assn. Tour; Ponte Vedra, Fla.
**Official Guide of the PGA Championships**; Triumph Books (1994); Chicago.
**The PGA World Golf Hall of Fame Book**, by Gerald Astor, Prentice Hall Press (1991); New York.
**2003 Champions Tour Guide**, written and edited by Dave Senko, Phil Stambaugh and Joan Von Thron-Alexander; Professional Golfers Assn. Tour; Ponte Vedra, Fla.
**Pro-Golf 2003, PGA European Tour Media Guide**, Virginia Water, Surrey, England.
**The Random House International Encyclopedia of Golf**, by Malcolm Campbell; Random House (1991); New York.
**USGA Record Books** (1895-1959, 1960-80 and 1981-90); U.S. Golf Association; Far Hills, N.J.
LPGA Online, produced by the LPGA and Ignite Sports Media LLC., http://www.lpga.com
PGA Online, produced by the PGA of America, http://www.pgaonline.com
PGATour Online, produced by PGA Tour Inc., http://www.pgatour.com

## Hockey

**Canada Cup '87: The Official History**, No.1 Publications Ltd.; Toronto.
**The Complete Encyclopedia of Hockey**; edited by Zander Hollander; Visible Ink Press (1993); Detroit.
**The Hockey Encyclopedia**, by Stan Fischler and Shirley Walton Fischler; research editor, Bob Duff; Macmillan Publishing Co. (1983); New York.
**Hockey Hall of Fame** (The Official History of the Game and Its Greatest Stars), by Dan Diamond and Joseph Romain; Doubleday (1988); New York.
**The National Hockey League**, by Edward F. Dolan Jr.; W H Smith Publishers Inc. (1986); New York.
**The Official National Hockey League 75th Anniversary Commemorative Book**, edited by Dan Diamond; McClelland & Stewart, Inc. (1991); Toronto.
**2003 Official NHL Guide & Record Book**, compiled by the NHL Public Relations Dept.; New York/Montreal/Toronto.
**2003 Sporting News Hockey Guide**, edited by Craig Carter; The Sporting News Publishing Co.; St. Louis.
**2003 Sporting News Hockey Register**, edited by David Walton; The Sporting News Publishing Co.; St. Louis.
**The Stanley Cup**, by Joseph Romain and James Duplacey; Gallery Books (1989); New York.
**The Trail of the Stanley Cup** (Volumes I-III), by Charles L. Coleman; Progressive Publications Inc. (1969); Sherbrooke, Quebec.
**Total Hockey** (Second Edition), edited by Dan Diamond, et al.; Total Sports Publishing; Kingston, N.Y.
NHL Online, produced by the NHL Interactive Cyber Enterprises, http://www.nhl.com

## Horse Racing

**1999 NTRA Media Guide**, compiled by the National Thoroughbred Racing Association; New York.
**1997 American Racing Manual**, compiled by the Daily Racing Form; Hightstown, N.J.
**1997 Breeders' Cup Statistics**; Breeders' Cup Limited; Lexington, Ky.
**1996 Directory and Record Book**, Thoroughbred Racing Associations of North America Inc.; Elkton, Md.
**2001 Trotting and Pacing Guide**, compiled and edited by John Pawlak; United States Trotting Association; Columbus, Ohio.
USTA Online, produced by the USTA, http://www.ustrotting.com
NTRA Online, hosted by Equibase Company LLC, http://www.ntra.com
Equibase.com, hosted by Equibase Company LLC, http://www.equibase.com

## International Sports

**Athletics: A History of Modern Track and Field** (1860-1990, Men and Women), by Roberto Quercetani; Vallardi & Associati (1990); Milan, Italy.

**1999 International Track & Field Annual**, Association of Track & Field Statisticians; edited by Peter Matthews; SportsBooks Ltd.; Surrey, England.

**Track & Field News' Little Blue Book**; Metric conversion tables; From the editors of Track & Field News (1989); Los Altos, Calif.

US Ski Team Online, produced by US Ski Team and SportsLine USA, http://www.usskiteam.com

## Miscellaneous

**The America's Cup 1851-1987** (Sailing for Supremacy), by Gary Lester and Richard Sleeman; Lester-Townsend Publishing (1986); Sydney, Australia.

**The Encyclopedia of Sports** (Fifth Revised Edition), by Frank G. Menke; revisions by Suzanne Treat; A.S. Barnes and Co., Inc. (1975); Cranbury, N.J.

**ESPN SportsCentury**, edited by Michael MacCambridge; Hyperion (1999); New York.

**The Great American Sports Book**, by George Gipe; Doubleday & Company, Inc. (1978); Garden City, N.Y.

**1999 Official PRCA Media Guide**, edited by Steve Fleming; Professional Rodeo Cowboys Association; Colorado Springs.

**The Sail Magazine Book of Sailing**, by Peter Johnson; Alfred A. Knopf (1989); New York.

**Ten Years of the Ironman,** Triathlete magazine; October, 1988; Santa Monica, Calif.

**The Ultimate Book of Sports Lists**, by Mike Meserole; DK Publishing (1999); New York.

Iditarod Online, produced by the Iditarod Trail Committee and GCI, http://www.iditarod.com

PRCA Online, produced by the Pro Rodeo Cowboys Association, http://www.prorodeo.com

## Olympics

**All That Glitters Is Not Gold** (An Irreverent Look at the Olympic Games) by William O. Johnson, Jr.; G.P. Putnam's Sons (1972); New York.

**Barcelona/Albertville 1992**; edited by Lisa H. Albertson; for U.S. Olympic Committee by Commemorative Publications; Salt Lake City.

**Chamonix to Lillehammer** (The Glory of the Olympic Winter Games); edited by Lisa H. Albertson; for U.S. Olympic Committee by Commemorative Publication (1994); Salt Lake City.

**The Complete Book of the Olympics** (1992 Edition); by David Wallechinsky; Little, Brown and Co.; Boston.

**The Games Must Go On** (Avery Brundage and the Olympic Movement), by Allen Guttmann; Columbia University Press (1984); New York.

**The Golden Book of the Olympic Games**, edited by Erich Kamper and Bill Mallon; Vallardi & Associati (1992); Milan, Italy.

**Hitler's Games** (The 1936 Olympics), by Duff Hart-Davis; Harper & Row (1986); New York/London.

**An Illustrated History of the Olympics** (Third Edition); by Dick Schaap; Alfred A. Knopf (1975); New York.

**The Nazi Olympics**, by Richard D. Mandell; Souvenir Press (1972); London.

**The Official USOC Book of the 1984 Olympic Games** (1984), by Dick Schaap; Random House/ABC Sports; New York.

**The Olympics: A History of the Games**, by William Oscar Johnson; Oxmoor House (1992); Birmingham, Ala.

**Pursuit of Excellence** (The Olympic Story), by The Associated Press and Grolier; Grolier Enterprises Inc. (1979); Danbury, Conn.

**The Story of the Olympic Games** (776 B.C. to 1948 A.D.), by John Kieran and Arthur Daley; J.B. Lippincott Company (1948); Philadelphia/New York.

**United States Olympic Books** (Seven Editions): 1936 and 1948-88; U.S. Olympic Association; New York.

**The USA and the Olympic Movement**, produced by the USOC Information Dept.; edited by Gayle Plant; U.S. Olympic Committee (1988); Colorado Springs.

## Soccer

**The American Encyclopedia of Soccer**, edited by Zander Hollander; Everest House Publishers (1980); New York.

**The European Football Yearbook** (1994-95 Edition), edited by Mike Hammond; Sports Projects Ltd; West Midlands, England.

**The Guinness Book of Soccer Facts & Feats**, by Jack Rollin; Guinness Superlatives Ltd. (1978); Middlesex, England.

**History of Soccer's World Cup**, by Michael Archer; Chartwell Books, Inc. (1978); Secaucus, N.J.

**The Simplest Game**, by Paul Gardner; Collier Books (1994); New York.

**The Story of the World Cup**, by Brian Glanville; Faber and Faber Limited (1993); London/Boston.

**2001 MLS Official Media Guide**, edited by the MLS Communications staff; Los Angeles.

**1991-92 MSL Official Guide**, Major (Indoor) Soccer League; Overland Park, Kan.

FIFA Online, produced by FIFA, http://www.fifa.com

MLSnet, produced by Major League Soccer, http://mlsnet.com

## Tennis

**Bud Collins' Modern Encyclopedia of Tennis**, edited by Bud Collins and Zander Hollander; Visible Ink Press (1994); Detroit.

**The Illustrated Encyclopedia of World Tennis**, by John Haylett and Richard Evans; Exeter Books (1989); New York.

**Official Encyclopedia of Tennis**, edited by the staff of the U.S. Lawn Tennis Assn.; Harper & Row (1972); New York.

**2004 ATP Tour Player Guide**, edited by Greg Sharko; Association of Tennis Professionals Tour Publications; Ponte Vedra Beach, Fla.

**2004 WTA Tour Media Guide**, compiled by Sanex WTA Public Relations staff; St. Petersburg, Fla.

ATP TourOnline, produced by ATP Tour, Inc., http://www.atptour.com

WTA Tour Online, produced by the WTA Tour, http://www.wtatour.com

## Who's Who

**The Guinness International Who's Who of Sport**, edited by Peter Mathews, Ian Buchanan and Bill Mallon; Guinness Publishing (1993); Middlesex, England.

**101 Greatest Athletes of the Century**, by Will Grimsley and the Associated Press Sports Staff; Bonanza Books (1987); Crown Publishers, Inc.; New York.

**The New York Times Book of Sports Legends**, edited by Joseph Vecchione; Simon & Schuster (1991); New York.

**Superstars**, by Frank Litsky; Vineyard Books, Inc. (1975); Secaucus, N.J.

**A Who's Who of Sports Champions** (Their Stories and Records), by Ralph Hickok, Houghton Mifflin Co. (1995); Boston.

## Other Reference Books/Sites

**Facts & Dates of American Sports**, by Gorton Carruth & Eugene Ehrlich; Harper & Row, Publishers, Inc. (1988); New York.

**Sports Market Place 1997** (January Edition), edited by Kevin J. Myers; Franklin Quest Sports; Phoenix, Ariz.

**The World Book Encyclopedia** (1988 Edition); World Book, Inc.; Chicago.

**The World Book Yearbook** (Annual Supplements, 1954-95); World Book, Inc.; Chicago.

ESPN.com, produced by ESPN Internet Ventures., http://espn.com

CBS SportsLine, produced by CBS and SportsLine USA, http://cbs.sportsline.com